Funk & Wagnalls

STANDARD DICTIONARY

Funk & Wagnalls

STANDARD DICTIONARY

HarperPaperbacks

A Division of HarperCollins*Publishers*

HarperPaperbacks *A Division of* HarperCollins*Publishers*
10 East 53rd Street, New York, N.Y. 10022

First HarperPaperbacks printing: August 1991

Printed in the United States of America

10 9 8 7 6 5 4 3 2

CONTENTS

PREFACE

This dictionary is based on the Funk & Wagnalls Standard® Desk Dictionary and other dictionaries in the Funk & Wagnalls Standard® dictionary series, reference works familiar to and respected by generations of readers. Included in the more than 82,000 entries in this completely re-edited and reset version are hundreds of new words and new meanings of old words.

The general vocabularly words, which make up the major part of this dictionary, are grouped together in the main A–Z section. For the convenience of the dictionary user, geographical information has been gathered together in another section. Here are the names, including syllable division and pronunciation, and populations of the states of the United States, its capital cities and cities with populations over 100,000, countries of the world, world capitals and world cities, and Canadian provinces and their capitals. This geographic section also includes the names, syllable divisions, and pronunciations of major geographic features of the world, such as rivers, lakes, mountains, islands, seas. A comprehensive and completely revised abbreviation and acronym section follows the geographic section.

An added feature is the Basic Style Manual, a guide to word usage, capitalization, spelling, punctuation, confusing words, grammar, and forms of business correspondence. A section of weights and measures, including conversion factors that allow the interchanging of metric and customary U.S. units, supplements the vocabulary and grammar information offered.

Readers will be better able to use this dictionary if they first read the Guide to the Dictionary which follows this preface.

Staff: Supervisory editors, Patrick Barrett and Carol Cohen. Chief revising editor, Norman Hoss; associate revising editors, Martin Apter, Myrna Breskin, Robert Haycraft, Geoffrey Horn, Ruth Koenigsberg, Margaret Miner, and Eugene Shewmaker. Copyediting and proofreading: chief copyeditor, Janet Field (also principal editorial reader), William Betts, James Daly, Nancy Nightingale, John Samoylenko, Doris Sullivan, and Selma Yampolsky. Editorial assistants, Dennis Chin and Helen Moore.

General vocabulary words and phrases, prefixes and suffixes, and foreign terms are grouped together in the main A through Z section of this dictionary. Following the main vocabulary section are separate sections for geographical entries and abbreviations and acronyms, the Basic Style Manual, and tables of weights and measures, including conversion factors.

Main Entry

The main entry is a word, phrase, prefix, suffix, combining form, or foreign term that together with related entries make up an entry block in this dictionary. The main entry in the entry block is set so that it juts out into the margin of the column. These main entries are printed in an order based on letter-by-letter alphabetizing, a system in which phrases and hyphenated words are treated as if they were solid words. Therefore, **night school** follows **nightmare,** not **night,** and **go-go** follows **goggle.**

When several main entry words have the same spellings but differ in origin and meaning, each is made into a separate entry block, and the main terms are set off with superscripts. For example, **lark**¹ (bird) and **lark**² (a good time).

The main entry word is not repeated when a new part of speech is introduced within an entry block. Instead, a boldface dash is added before the new part of speech, and it stands for the main entry word. For example,

nov•el (nov′əl) *adj.* New, strange, or unusual. **—***n.* A fictional prose narrative of considerable length. . . .

The *n.pl.* designation following the pronunciation of some main entry nouns means that the main entry word is given in the plural. For example,

folk•ways (fōk′wāz′) *n.pl. Sociol.* The traditional habits, customs, and behavior of a group, tribe, or nation.

When no singular form of the noun is shown, the entry word is usually used only in the plural and it takes a plural verb. If the plural entry word takes a singular verb, the reader will find a note, which is: (*construed as sing.*). If the plural entry can take either a singular or plural verb, the note is: (*construed as sing. or pl.*).

Some plural nouns have been made entry titles even though they have singular forms, because the plural form is far more common than the singular. In such cases the singular form is shown in the entry as follows:

al•gae (al′jē) *n. pl. of* **al•ga** (al′gə)

Related Entries

Entries related to the main entry are printed in boldface within the main entry block. A common phrase, such as **to know the ropes,** which cannot be understood from the definitions of the separate words in the phrase, is one type of such an entry. Phrases such as these are placed in the entry block of the key word in the phrase, in this case, **rope.**

Within the definitions themselves, there may be boldface entries whose definitions are easily understood in context. For example,

> **dai·sy** (dā′zē) *n. pl.* **·sies** A plant of the composite family; esp., the **oxeye daisy** of the U.S., having a yellow disk and white rays, and the **English daisy,** having a small yellow disk and white or rose rays.

At the end of some entries there are forms of the main entry made by the addition of familiar suffixes. These derivative forms are not defined since their meaning is readily understood from the meanings of the main entry. Such entries begin with a dash and each ends with the part of speech label. An example of this type of run-on entry is:

—key′punch′er *n.*

which appears at the end of the entry for the noun **keypunch.** When two derivative forms of the same part of speech have the same sense, they are separated by commas. For example,

—cap′tain·cy, cap′tain·ship *n.*

Following some main entries, such as those for prefixes, there are lists of compound words or phrases formed with the main entry word. These self-explanatory words or phrases are undefined but are offered to give the dictionary reader guidance in hyphenation, spelling, spacing between elements, and capitalization. See, for example, the lists at **non-** and **self.**

Syllable Division

A centered dot divides the main entry into syllables. These syllable divisions are the points at which a hyphen may be used when the full word will not fit at the end of a line and must be broken. Words in phrases are divided into syllables only when the words are not found as main entries in the dictionary. For example, **senior citizen** is not divided into syllables because both **senior** and **citizen** are entries themselves, **senior** being entered and divided in the S's and **citizen** in the C's. However, **Achilles** in the **A•chil•les' heel** entry is divided into syllables because **Achilles** does not have a separate entry.

Prefixes, suffixes, and combining forms are not divided into syllables because their syllable breaks vary with the compound word formed by adding them.

Plurals of Nouns

Since the plurals of most nouns are formed by adding *-s*, the dictionary shows plurals only when they are formed in a different way or when the plurals are spelled in a way that might not be expected. Some examples:

ech·o (ek′ō) *n.* *pl.* **ech·oes**
ar·my (är′mē) *n.* *pl.* **·mies**
jock·ey (jok′ē) *n.* *pl.* **·eys**
wolf (wo͝olf) *n.* *pl.* **wolves** (wo͝olvz)
ap·pa·ra·tus (ap′ə·rat′əs, -rā′təs) *n.* *pl.* **·tus**
mon·goose (mong′go͞os, mung′-) *n.* *pl.* **·goos·es**

In most cases only the syllables that change in spelling are shown.

Comparison of Adjectives and Adverbs

Entries for adjectives and adverbs do not show the comparative and superlative forms when these forms are regular: that is, when they are made by adding *-er* or *-est* or, for adverbs, when they are made by supplying the words *more* or *most* (cold, colder, coldest; slowly, more slowly, most slowly). Frequently, only the affected syllables are shown. Some examples:

nut·ty (nut′ē) *adj.* **·ti·er, ·ti·est**
grim (grim) *adj.* **grim·mer, grim·mest**
bad (bad) *adj.* **worse, worst**
well (wel) *adv.* **bet·ter, best**

Past Tense, Past Participle, and Present Participle of Verbs

When an entry for a verb does not show the past tense or the participles, these forms of the verb are constructed regularly: that is, by adding *-ed* to form the past tense and the past participle and by adding *-ing* to form the present participle (jump, jumped, jumping). Parts of the verb not formed this way are shown. For example,

de·fy (di·fī′) *v.t.* **·fied, ·fy·ing**
in·clude (in·klo͞od′) *v.t.* **·clud·ed, ·clud·ing**
eat (ēt) *v.* **ate, eat·en, eat·ing**

Pronunciation

Pronunciations are shown in parentheses after each main entry and are added after other boldface entries within an entry block when the pronunciation of these related entries differs significantly from that of the main entry in sound or stress. Using the pronunciation key which appears on page 13a and on the inside covers, the reader will be able to produce a pronunciation acceptable to any educated American. However, educated speakers pronounce words in different ways, and this dictionary gives many, but not all, of these variant pronunciations. Preferences vary, and no significance should be attached to the order of these variants.

In many places, the first pronunciation is followed by a partial pronunciation, which is a pronunciation for the part that varies. Hyphens in these partial pronunciations stand for the parts not printed, parts pronounced the same as shown in the first full pronunciation. For example, in the pronunciation of

vi·va·cious (vi·vā′shəs, vī-) *adj.*

the first syllable changes, but the last two syllables remain the same.

This system is followed for any partial pronunciation within an entry block. For example, the pronunciation of the first syllable, **phle,** in **phlebitic** in the following entry

phle·bi·tis (fli·bī′tis) *n. Pathol.* Inflammation of the inner membrane of a vein. —**phle·bit·ic** (-bit′ik) *adj.*

is the same as the first syllable of the main entry.

The syllable breaks in the pronunciation may not match those in the boldface entry. The former are based on sound of speech and the latter are based on the parts or roots that make up the word.

Stress

There are two stress marks. The bold mark (kan′dəl) represents the primary stress, the strongest syllable in the word. A lighter mark indicates a syllable receiving a stress of lesser intensity (kan′dəl·līt′). When two syllables in a pronunciation are marked with bold stress marks, both receive equal stress (wel′dun′). Note that the stress mark follows the syllable to which it applies.

Parts of Speech

The abbreviations for part of speech, the grammatical description of the *use* of a word in a sentence, are printed in italic before the definition to which each applies or before other information that applies to that part of speech only. Part of speech labels follow undefined words found at the end of some entries. The abbreviations used in this dictionary for the parts of speech are:

n. noun
v. verb (which is further differentiated into *v.t.* for transitive verb and *v.i.* for intransitive verb)
adj. adjective
adv. adverb
prep. preposition
conj. conjunction
interj. interjection
pron. pronoun

Every part of speech for a word is defined within one entry block; none is made a separate main entry.

Definitions

The definitions within each part of speech are grouped so that their related meanings are together. There is, otherwise, no significance to their order; the first definition is not necessarily for the earliest use, nor is it the most frequently used.

Definitions never consist of a single synonym. One-word definitions are cross references to fully defined forms. (See CROSS REFERENCES, farther along in this Guide.)

Variations in Spelling

Acceptable spellings that vary from the spelling of the main entry are cited following the definition.

lar·gess (lär·jes′) *n.* Liberal giving; also, something liberally given. Also **lar·gesse′**.
e·on (ē′ən, ē′on) *n.* 1. An incalculable period of time. 2. *Geol.* A time interval including two or more eras. Also spelled *aeon.*

Variants are printed either in italic or boldface. The italic variant indicates that the entry referred to, *aeon* in the above example, may be found at its alphabetical position should the reader wish to check its syllabification or pronunciation. Boldface variants which have no pronunciation are pronounced the same as the main entry.

Since more than one spelling of the plural of nouns or the participles or past tense of verbs may be acceptable, variants are given in boldface immediately following the first form:

bus (bus) *n. pl.* **bus·es** or **bus·ses**
kid·nap (kid′nap) *v.t.* **·naped** or **·napped, ·nap·ing** or **·nap·ping**

Usage and Labels

Aids to usage, in several forms, have been offered to supplement bare-bones definitions that the editors felt might not be adequate to give the reader confidence in using a word or phrase. The aids easiest to spot are italic labels, but helpful information is often found just after the definition proper, and set off from it with a colon. Sometimes these are phrases or sentences directly illustrating the use of a term:

one-horse (wun′hôrs′) *adj. Informal* Small, unimportant: a *one-horse* town.
na·ture (nā′chər) *n.* 1. The essential character of something: the *nature* of democracy. 2. . . .

and sometimes there are notes about specific applications, cautions, etc., as:

:said of a disease
:used contemptuously
:considered vulgar
:distinguished from
:opposed to
:with *from* or *of*

Labels preceding definitions serve several functions. Style labels include *Informal, Dial.* (for dialectal), *Slang,* and *Illit.* (for illiterate). The label *Informal* indicates that the term is acceptable in the casual conversation of educated people but should be used only for special effect in a formal context such as a speech, a business report, a scholarly paper, etc. *Dial.* indicates a nonstandard term that is regularly used by people in specific regions, though it may be known to a wider audience. *Slang* labels a use that is intentionally outside standard English. Much slang is ephemeral, but some of it may become standard English and some standard English words have slang applications. *Slang* is not to be confused with the label *Illit.*, which designates a usage that is regarded as incorrect by those who are educated.

Rare, Archaic, and *Obs.* (for obsolete) are currency labels. *Rare* labels words that were never in frequent use but are included because of their significant occurrence in literature. *Archaic* labels very old words, once common, that are now used only in well-defined circumstances, such as a church service. *Obs.* labels words of the more recent past that would not be used in any current context because they sound old-fashioned. Words that refer to objects no longer in use or concepts or ideas not commonly heard today are not labeled archaic or obsolete. The definitions for these terms explain that the object or idea was popular in earlier times.

Field labels identify definitions that apply especially to specific areas of study or activity. However, some of the fields of learning overlap, such as physics and chemistry, and the labeled terms may be used in more than one discipline. Examples of field labels are *Math.* (for mathematics), *Printing, Econ.* (for economics), *Eccl.* (for ecclesiastical). Field labels are usually abbreviated, as listed on page 14a.

Foreign language labels are applied to words that despite familiarity in English retain a foreign pronunciation. A *Brit.* (for British) label or a *Canadian* label is applied to words or phrases that may be known to Americans but are used primarily in Great Britain or in Canada.

Collateral Adjectives

A feature unique to the Funk & Wagnalls dictionaries is the addition at some noun entries of adjectival forms of the noun so remote in spelling that they may not be brought to mind by the noun. For example: *canine* at the **dog** entry, *brachial* at the **arm** entry, and *thermal* at the **heat** entry. These collateral adjectives are marked by a diamond, ◆, in the noun entry.

Cross References

Cross references are directions to see another entry for additional information. The entry to look for is generally indicated in small capital letters, as

tsar . . . See CZAR.
feet . . . Plural of FOOT.
Old English . . . See under ENGLISH.

Some entries are defined by citing another form:

cou·gar (ko͞o′gər) *n.* The puma.

Here, complete information will be found under the word **puma.**

Cross references are also used to indicate where more information may be found, or when an important distinction might otherwise be missed, as

analog computer . . . :Compare DIGITAL COMPUTER.
petit mal . . . :distinguished from *grand mal.*
sycamore . . . :also called *buttonwood.*

Word Origins

The origin (etymology) of an entry word is given in square brackets following the definition. The only symbols used are <, meaning "derived from," +, meaning "added on" or "combined with," and a question mark, ?, meaning "perhaps." If only one word follows the symbol <, that word is the earliest form known to have contributed to the modern word. This earliest form is usually a Greek or Latin word. If a word is borrowed directly from a modern language, only the name of the language is given in the etymology. Language abbreviations are found on page 14a.

The abbreviation Cf. indicates that the word given in the etymology is not necessarily the origin of the entry but is a word from another language that descended from the same root. Nonlinguistic information appears in the etymology for words derived from names or coined for a special purpose. Words set in small capitals in etymologies are cross references. The origin of the entry word or phrase can be found in the etymology of the word or words referred to.

Many Americans, and even some Canadians, have some strangely unwarranted notions of what the English spoken in Canada is, or ought to be, like. Americans who went to school before World War II would have seen maps on which all the parts of the old British Empire were colored red. By far the biggest piece of red was the Dominion of Canada, hence the expectation that the English spoken in Canada would be "British."

Visitors to Canada from the northern states—New York and westward—are often surprised to find that the Canadians they meet sound very much like themselves—and southerners may find that Canadians sound like "Yankees." This is not surprising, since the basic English-speaking population of eastern Canada came from the northern states and established a pronunciation which strongly influenced other provinces through the westward migration of settlers from Ontario. The major movement from the United States into Canada came as a result of the American Revolution, when colonists who had remained loyal to the King were obliged to leave the new nation. There had been a smaller earlier migration from New England into Nova Scotia and New Brunswick, after the expulsion of the Acadians.

The English which came to Ontario was based on the speech of settlers from Pennsylvania and New York. The most prominent groups in this migration were Pennsylvanians originally from Northern Ireland, "York staters" who had moved into New York from New England, and Hudson Valley Dutch whose ancestors had spread up river from the New York City area where Dutch settlement had begun in the seventeenth century. Nova Scotia and New Brunswick, with settlements of "His Majesty's Yankees" already, received many more New Englanders, others from the New York City area, and possibly some from the southern colonies.

Ontario remained attractive to Americans, so that by 1830 an estimated 80 percent of the English-speaking population was of American origin. This laid a language base which no single group of later settlers could challenge. It is therefore not surprising that the speech of most Canadians is largely similar to that of a large number of Americans.

Pronunciation

After being with Canadians for a little while, the perceptive American will notice that the vowel sounds of 'write' and 'ride' do not match each other, nor do the vowels of the noun 'house' and the verb 'to house.' This is presumed to be the mark of a Canadian speaker, but is shared in parts of the United States, most notably eastern Virginia.

Regional accents are not particularly noticeable in Canada presumably because migration from the Ontario heartland set the pattern for much of the west, but Newfoundland, with its distinctive English and Irish settlement, Prince Edward Island where similar settlement had Scots as well, and Cape Breton Island and northern mainland Nova Scotia, which were solid Scottish settlements, show different accents. "Yankee" is also spoken along the St. Croix River in New Brunswick and in parts of southern Nova Scotia settled from New England. In the heartland where many non-North Americans settled, such as the Ottawa River valley where

Scots and Irish congregated, there is also relief from the monotonous general pattern. Ottawa Valley speech is hard to represent without phonetics, but a sample is the pronunciation of the town of Perth as *Parth.* The *r* in this region is especially "hard."

In many regions of the English-speaking world, the pronunciation of such words as *half, past, bath,* and *aunt* will be found to vary between the vowel of *father* and that of *cat.* In most of Canada the *cat* vowel predominates, but in the Maritime Provinces of the eastern seaboard the *father* vowel is preferred. There are also areas of mixed usage, such as southwestern Ontario. *Dance* is generally pronounced with the *cat* vowel in Canada, while *tomato* which American language-worriers argue about as either *tomayto* or *tomahto* has a third rival in Canada with the *cat* vowel.

Some other individual words vary between American and British preferences. Most Canadians long ago adopted the American preferred pronunciation of *schedule* but broadcast standards adopted about 1940 on the model of those of the British Broadcasting Corporation strengthened the use of *shedule.* Until a generation ago the office of clerk was pronounced as the name *Clark,* but this is disappearing even in official and church usage, as in *County Clerk* and *Clerk of Session.*

Patterns of stress in longer words generally parallel those used by Americans of the northern states. *Controversy* has its stress on the first syllable, rather than the second as is the British tendency, and the same pattern is followed in *laboratory.* The British tendency to lose unstressed syllables as in *medicine* ("medsin") and *secretary* ("secretry") is resisted and *secretary,* indeed, has a relatively strong stress on the last syllable.

Spelling

On the whole Canadians have resisted the spelling reforms of Noah Webster, retaining *-our* spellings as in *honour* and *flavour*; *-re* spellings in *centre* and *theatre*; the longer spellings of words like *programme*; and double consonants in *traveller* and *jeweller.* Schools are tending to be less prescriptive and dictionaries produced in Canada now list alternate spellings of the American and British conventions. In most matters Canadians have not followed British patterns. *Connection* is never spelled with an *x* and *civilization* has a *z* rather than an *s,* although the name of the letter is *zed,* not *zee.* Both the spellings *defense* and *defence* are in use in Canada as are the spellings *pajamas* and *pyjamas. Tyre* and *kerb* look like foreign words to Canadians and when they look them up in Canadian dictionaries they will find them labelled "Brit." *Gaol* is also labelled "Brit." although it had currency in Canadian newspapers well into the 1930's. It now appears only as preserved in stone over the doors of old county lockups.

Vocabulary

The differences between the Canadian vocabulary and that of the United States largely arise from a different national history rather than from a direct British inheritance. Visitors could be misled by the word *lift* on elevators in some old buildings. This word came with the equipment, of British manufacture. The word *pram,* popular a few years ago, had a special, restricted Canadian meaning—a large imported baby carriage with overlapping large wheels for mounting curbs (not "kerbs") —not just any baby carriage.

Dictionary editors make conflicting claims to many words as Canadianisms or

Americanisms. There are even rival claims to such elevating terms as *hootch* and *skid row*. But a few contributions seem peculiarly Canadian, such as *portage* from the language of French Voyageurs, and *woodchuck*, an Anglicization of the Algonkian Indian word for groundhog. *White-out* has been formed in recent times on the model of *black-out* to describe the blotting out of landscape features by intense light conditions or fine blowing snow in the Arctic (pronounced *Artic* by old Artic hands).

Special Canadian conditions have made possible such startling statements as "We went to Separate Schools together," since in some provinces religious groups have the right to tax support for their own (Separate) schools. In Ontario a *concession* may not have been conceded, but be only the name for a land-survey unit.

Canadians have exported the vocabulary of their peculiar sports hockey and lacrosse. *Hockey* is never modified when the game played on ice is referred to. To natives this is the base form. *Field hockey* is the game played on grass. *Lacrosse* is the product of French imagination because the stick used resembles a bishop's staff.

Canadian science and technology have been responsible for a few exports, although *variable pitch propeller* is hardly a startling vocabulary item, but *insulin* and *kerosene* are two authentic coinages.

Where British terms hold sway is in the realms of administration and defense. Although terminology is not identical, the historical British connection is reflected in *House of Commons* for the elected house of *Parliament* and the *Privy Council* which advises the Governor General. In the electoral system an old term *riding*, used for a subdivision of some English counties, has been adopted for what Americans would call an *electoral district*. Another ancient term, *reeve*, seems to survive only in Canada as the name for the elected head of a rural municipality. Some terms are misleading for Americans. A *sheriff* in Canada is not a law-enforcement officer, but an officer of the courts; a *Lieutenant-Governor* is the official and ceremonial head of a Provincial Government; and the *Senate* is an appointed body of the national government with limited powers.

British garrisons were maintained in Canada until early in the present century and troops raised in both Britain and Canada served together. Thus military terminology reflects British usage. This is most striking in the pronunciation of *lieutenant* as *leftenant*, and the peculiar Canadian pronunciation *karki*, an overcorrection of the British pronunciation of *khaki*, in which an *r*, presumed to have been dropped, was "replaced." Some rank designations may sound a bit exotic, as in *Lance Corporal* (private first class), *Bombardier* (artillery corporal)—the equivalent to American *bombardier* in the air force is *bomb aimer*. A *Sub-Lieutenant* in the Navy holds a rank overlapping with Ensign and Lieutenant j.g. and is not necessarily associated with submarines. One very sticky item among the military is the term *Guard of Honour*—never *Honor Guard*!

Although some cities once had *tramway companies* and *trams* the terms seem to have gone with the streetcars. Rails were once laid on *sleepers*, but now they are supported by *ties* and *sleepers* are flannelette pajamas with feet in them. These changes reflect the general adoption of American terminology in the field of transportation. Although Canada imports automobiles from all countries, most Canadians drive Detroit iron and use the accompanying terms.

One peculiarity of timetable terminology is the result of bilingualism. Canadian trains arrive, but they no longer leave. *Arr.* and *Dep.* are abbreviations clear to both French and English speakers. Air and rail timetables use the 24-hour clock. Canadian road signs will be intelligible to Americans, but speeds and distances are now in kilometres (Km/h) which bureaucrats decree shall be stressed on the first syllable (without complete success; the British pattern of stressing the second syllable is widely heard). And gas is now measured in litres. The spellings of official metrication follow the British pattern, except for weights, where *gram* and *kilogram* are officially preferred.

Echoing the earlier borrowings from native languages and French, Canadians have named two of their satellites *Anik*, from the Inuit (Eskimo) word for "brother" and *Alouette*, French "lark."

H. R. Wilson
University of Western Ontario
London, Canada

PRONUNCIATION KEY

a	add, map
ā	ace, rate
â(r)	care, air
ä	palm, father
b	bat, rub
ch	check, catch
d	dog, rod
e	end, pet
ē	even, tree
f	fit, half
g	go, log
h	hope, hate
i	it, give
ī	ice, write
j	joy, ledge
k	cool, take
l	look, rule
m	move, seem
n	nice, tin
ng	ring, song
o	odd, hot
ō	open, so
ô	order, jaw
oi	oil, boy
ou	out, now
o͞o	pool, food
o͝o	took, full
p	pit, stop
r	run, poor
s	see, pass
sh	sure, rush
t	talk, sit
th	thin, both
t͟h	this, bathe
u	up, done
û(r)	urn, term
yo͞o	use, few
v	vain, eve
w	win, away
y	yet, yearn
z	zest, muse
zh	vision, pleasure

ə the schwa, representing the vowel in unstressed syllables, varies widely from the sound of (u) in *up* to the sound of (i) in *it*. It represents the sound spelled

a in *above*
e in *sicken*
i in *clarity*
o in *melon*
u in *focus*

Foreign Sounds

ȧ This is a vowel midway in quality between (a) and (ä), as in French *ami, patte.*

œ Round the lips for (ō) and pronounce (ā), as in French *peu*, German *schön.*

ü Round the lips for (o͞o) and pronounce (ē), as in French *vue*, German *grün.*

kh Pronounce a guttural (h) with the tongue in position for (k), as in German *ach*, Scottish *loch.*

ṅ This symbol indicates that the preceding vowel is nasal.

ʼ This symbol indicates that a preceding letter is voiceless, as in French *fiacre* (fyȧ′krʼ); that a preceding (y) is pronounced in a separate syllable followed by a slight schwa sound, as in French *fille* (fē′yʼ); or that a consonant preceding a (y) is palatalized, as in Russian *oblast* (ô′blestyʼ).

The primary stress mark (′) is placed after the syllable having the heavier stress or accent; the secondary stress mark (ʹ) follows a syllable having a lighter stress, as in *com·men·da·tion* (komʹen·dā′shən).

The (r) in final position as in *star* (stär) and before a consonant as in *heart* (härt) is regularly given in pronunciations, but pronunciations without (r) are acceptable.

In a few words, such as *button* (but′n) and *sudden* (sud′n), no vowel appears in the unstressed syllable because the (n) constitutes the whole syllable.

ABBREVIATIONS USED IN THIS BOOK

A.D. year of our Lord
adj. adjective
adv. adverb
Aeron. Aeronautics
AF Anglo-French
Agric. Agriculture
Alg. Algebra
alter. alteration
Am.Ind. American Indian
Am.Sp. American Spanish
Anat. Anatomy
Anthropol. Anthropology
appar. apparently
Archeol. Archeology
Archit. Architecture
assoc. association
Astron. Astronomy
aug. augmentative
Austral. Australian
Bacteriol. Bacteriology
B.C. Before Christ
Biochem. Biochemistry
Biol. Biology
Bot. Botany
Brit. British
c. century
cap. capitalized
cf. compare
Chem. Chemistry
Chron. Chronicles
compar. comparative
conj. conjunction
contr. contraction
Crystall. Crystallography
Dan. Danish
def. definition
Dent. Dentistry
Deut. Deuteronomy
Dial. Dialect, Dialectal
dim. diminutive
Du. Dutch
E. English
Eccl. Ecclesiastical
Eccles. Ecclesiastes
Ecol. Ecology
Econ. Economics
Electr. Electricity
Engin. Engineering
Entomol. Entomology
esp. especially
est. estimate
Esth. Esther
Ex. Exodus
Ezek. Ezekiel
F, Fr. French
fem. feminine
freq. frequentative
G, Ger. German
Gen. Genesis
Geog. Geography
Geol. Geology
Geom. Geometry
Gk. Greek
Gmc. Germanic
Govt. Government
Gram. Grammar
HG High German
Hind. Hindustani
Hung. Hungarian
Icel. Icelandic
Illit. Illiterate
imit. imitative
infl. influence, influenced
intens. intensive
interj. interjection
Ital. Italian
Jap. Japanese
L, Lat. Latin
Lev. Leviticus
LG Low German
LGk. Late Greek
Ling. Linguistics
lit. literally
LL Late Latin
M Middle
masc. masculine
Math. Mathematics
MDu. Middle Dutch
ME Middle English
Mech. Mechanics
Med. Medicine, Medieval
Med.Gk. Medieval Greek
Med.L. Medieval Latin
Metall. Metallurgy
Meteorol. Meteorology
MF Middle French
MHG Middle High German
Mil. Military
Mineral. Mineralogy
MLG Middle Low German
n. noun
Nah. Nahum
N.Am.Ind. North American Indian
Naut. Nautical
NE Northeast
neut. neuter
NL New Latin
Norw. Norwegian
Num. Numbers
NW Northwest
O Old
Obs. Obsolete
ODan. Old Danish
OE Old English
OF Old French
OHG Old High German
OIrish Old Irish
ON Old Norse
orig. original, originally
Ornithol. Ornithology
OS Old Saxon
Paleontol. Paleontology
Pathol. Pathology
Pg. Portuguese
Phil. Philippians
Philos. Philosophy
Phonet. Phonetics
Photog. Photography
Physiol. Physiology
pl. plural
pop. population
pp. past participle, pages
ppr. present participle
prep. preposition
prob. probably
pron. pronoun
pronun. pronunciation
Prov. Proverbs
Ps. Psalms
Psychoanal. Psychoanalysis
Psychol. Psychology
pt. preterit
ref. reference
Rom. Romans
Russ. Russian
S.Am.Ind. South American Indian
Scand. Scandinavian
Scot. Scottish
SE Southeast
sing. singular
Skt. Sanskrit
Sociol. Sociology
S. of Sol. Song of Solomon
Sp. Spanish
Stat. Statistics
superl. superlative
Surg. Surgery
SW Southwest
Sw. Swedish
Telecom. Telecommunication
Theol. Theology
trans. translation
Trig. Trigonometry
ult. ultimately
U.S. United States
U.S.S.R. Union of Soviet Socialist Republics
usu. usually
v. verb
var. variant
Vet. Veterinary medicine
v.i. intransitive verb
v.t. transitive verb
WGmc. West Germanic
Zool. Zoology
< from
+ plus
? possibly

TABLE OF ENGLISH SPELLINGS

Following is a list of words exemplifying the possible spellings for the sounds of English. The sounds represented by these spellings are shown in the pronunciation symbols used in this dictionary, followed by their equivalents in the International Phonetic Alphabet.

Dictionary Key	IPA Symbol	Examples
a	æ	cat, pl*ai*d, c*al*f, l*au*gh
ā	eɪ,e	m*a*te, b*ai*t, g*ao*l, g*au*ge, p*ay*, st*ea*k, sk*ei*n, w*eigh*, pr*ey*
â(r)	ɛ,ɛr	d*a*re, f*ai*r, pr*ay*er, wh*e*re, b*ea*r, th*ei*r
ȧ	a	b*a*r, *a*sk, c*o*t (a vowel midway in quality between [æ] and [ɑ], used in some regional American speech)
ä	ɑ	d*a*rt, *ah*, s*e*rgeant, h*ea*rt
b	b	*b*oy, ru*bb*er
ch	tʃ	*ch*ip, ba*tch*, righ*te*ous, bas*ti*on, struc*tu*re
d	d	*d*ay, la*dd*er, call*ed*
e	ɛ	m*a*ny, *ae*sthete, s*ai*d, s*ay*s, b*e*t, st*ea*dy, h*ei*fer, l*eo*pard, fr*ie*nd, f*oe*tid
ē	i	C*ae*sar, qu*ay*, sc*e*ne, m*ea*t, s*ee*, s*ei*ze, p*eo*ple, k*ey*, rav*i*ne, gr*ie*f, ph*oe*b*e*, cit*y*
f	f	*f*ake, co*ff*in, cou*gh*, ha*lf*, *ph*ase
g	g	*g*ate, be*gg*ar, *gh*oul, *gu*ard, va*gue*
h	h	*h*ot, *wh*om
hw	hw, ʍ	*wh*ale
i	ɪ	pr*e*tty, b*ee*n, t*i*n, s*ie*ve, w*o*men, b*u*sy, g*ui*lt, l*y*nch
ī	aɪ	*ai*sle, *aye*, sl*eigh*t, *eye*, d*i*me, p*ie*, s*igh*, g*ui*le, b*uy*, tr*y*, l*ye*
j	dʒ	e*dge*, sol*di*er, mo*d*ulate, ra*ge*, exa*gg*erate, *j*oy
k	k	*c*an, a*cc*ost, sa*cch*arine, *ch*ord, ta*ck*, a*cq*uit, *k*ing, ta*lk*, li*qu*or
l	l	*l*et, ga*ll*
m	m	dra*chm*, phle*gm*, pa*lm*, *m*ake, li*mb*, gra*mm*ar, conde*mn*
n	n	*gn*ome, *kn*ow, *mn*emonic, *n*ote, ba*nn*er, *pn*eumatic
ng	ŋ	si*n*k, ri*ng*, meri*ngue*
o	ɑ,ɒ	w*a*tch, p*o*t
ō	oʊ,o	b*eau*, y*eo*man, s*ew*, *o*ver, s*oa*p, r*oe*, *oh*, br*oo*ch, s*ou*l, th*ough*, gr*ow*
ô	ɔ	b*a*ll, b*al*k, f*au*lt, d*aw*n, c*o*rd, br*oa*d, *ough*t
oi	ɔɪ	p*oi*son, t*oy*
ou	aʊ	*ou*t, b*ough*, c*ow*
o͞o	u	rh*eu*m, dr*ew*, m*o*ve, can*oe*, m*oo*d, gr*ou*p, thr*ough*, fl*u*ke, s*ue*, fr*ui*t
o͝o	ʊ	w*o*lf, f*oo*t, c*ou*ld, p*u*ll
p	p	ma*p*, ha*pp*en
r	r	*r*ose, *rh*ubarb, ma*rr*y, dia*rrh*ea, *wr*iggle
s	s	*c*ite, di*ce*, *ps*yche, *s*aw, *sc*ene, *sch*ism, ma*ss*
sh	ʃ	o*ce*an, *ch*ivalry, vi*ci*ous, *psh*aw, *s*ure, *sch*ist, pre*sc*ience, nau*se*ous, *sh*all, pen*si*on, ti*ss*ue, fi*ss*ion, po*ti*on
t	t	walk*ed*, thou*ght*, *phth*isic, *pt*armigan, *t*one, *Th*omas, bu*tt*er
th	θ	*th*ick
t͟h	ð	*th*is, ba*the*
u	ʌ	s*o*me, d*oe*s, bl*oo*d, y*ou*ng, s*u*n
yo͞o	ju,ɪu	b*eau*ty, *eu*logy, qu*eue*, p*ew*, *ewe*, adi*eu*, v*iew*, f*u*se, c*ue*, *you*th, *yu*le
û(r)	ər,ɝ	y*ea*rn, f*e*rn, *e*rr, g*i*rl, w*o*rm, j*ou*rnal, b*u*rn, g*ue*rdon, m*y*rtle
v	v	o*f*, Ste*ph*en, *v*ise, fli*vv*er
w	w	*ch*oir, q*u*ilt, *w*ill
y	j	o*n*i*on, hallelu*j*ah, *y*et
z	z	wa*s*, sci*ss*ors, *x*ylophone, *z*oo, mu*zz*le
zh	ʒ	rou*ge*, plea*s*ure, inci*si*on, sei*z*ure, gla*zi*er
ə	ə	*a*bove, fount*ai*n, dark*e*n, clar*i*ty, parl*ia*ment, cann*o*n, porp*oi*se, vici*ou*s, loc*u*s
ər	ər,ɚ	mort*ar*, broth*er*, elix*ir*, don*or*, glam*our*, aug*ur*, nat*ure*, zeph*yr*

A

a, A (ā) *n. pl.* **a's** or **as, A's** or **As, aes** (āz) 1. The first letter of the English alphabet. 2. Any sound represented by the letter *a*. —*symbol* 1. Primacy in class. 2. *Music* The sixth tone in the diatonic scale of C.

a[1] (ə, *stressed* ā) *indefinite article* or *adj.* In each; to each; for each: one dollar *a* bushel. [OE *on, an* in, on, at]

a[2] (ə, *stressed* ā) *indefinite article* or *adj.* One; any; some; each: expressing singleness, unity, etc., more or less indefinitely. It is used: 1. Before a noun expressing an individual object or idea: *a* bird; *a* hope. 2. Before an abstract noun used concretely: to show *a* kindness. 3. Before a collective noun: *a* crowd. 4. Before a proper noun denoting a type: He is *a* Hercules in strength. 5. Before plural nouns: with *few, great many,* or *good many*: *a* few books. 6. After *on, at,* or *of,* denoting oneness, sameness: birds of *a* feather. ◆Before vowel sounds the form becomes *an*. [Reduced form of AN used before consonant sounds]

a-[1] *prefix* In; on; at: *aboard, asleep, agog, agoing.* [OE *on, an* in, on, at]

a-[2] *prefix* Up; on; away: *arise, abide.* [OE *ā-* up, on, away]

a-[3] *prefix* Of; from: *athirst, akin, anew.* [OE *of* off, of]

a-[4] *prefix* 1. Without; not: *achromatic.* 2. Apart from; unconcerned with: *amoral.* [Reduced form of AN-]

aard·vark (ärd′värk′) *n.* A burrowing, ant-eating African mammal. [< Afrikaans < Du. *aarde* earth + *vark* pig]

aard·wolf (ärd′wo͞olf′) *n.* A hyenalike mammal of Africa. [< Afrikaans < Du. *aarde* earth + *wolf* wolf]

ab- *prefix* Off; from; away: *absolve, abduct, abrogate.* Also: **a-** before *m, p, v,* as in *avocation*; **abs-** before *c, t,* as in *abscess, abstract.* [< L *ab* from]

a·back (ə·bak′) *adv. Naut.* Back against the mast: said of sails so blown by the wind. —**taken aback** Disconcerted; surprised. [OE *on bæc* on or to the back]

ab·a·cus (ab′ə·kəs) *n. pl.* **·cus·es** or **·ci** (-sī) 1. A calculator with sliding counters. 2. *Archit.* A slab forming the top of a capital. [< Gk. *abax* counting table]

a·baft (ə·baft′) *Naut. adv.* Toward the stern; aft. —*prep.* Further aft than; astern of. [OE *on* on, at + *be* by + *æftan* behind, back]

ab·a·lo·ne (ab′ə·lō′nē) *n.* An edible mollusk having a shell lined with mother-of-pearl. [< Am. Sp.]

a·ban·don (ə·ban′dən) *v.t.* 1. To give up wholly; desert; forsake. 2. To surrender or give over: with *to.* 3. To yield (oneself) without restraint, as to an emotion. —*n.* Utter surrender to one's feelings or impulses. [< OF *abandoner* < *mettre a bandon* to put under another's control] —**a·ban′don·er** *n.* —**a·ban′don·ment** *n.*

a·ban·doned (ə·ban′dənd) *adj.* 1. Deserted; forsaken. 2. Unrestrained. 3. Profligate; shameless.

a·base (ə·bās′) *v.t.* **a·based, a·bas·ing** To lower in position, rank, prestige, or estimation; cast down; humble. [< LL *abassare* to lower] —**a·bas′ed·ly** *adv.* —**a·bas′ed·ness** *n.* —**a·base′ment** *n.* —**a·bas′er** *n.*

a·bash (ə·bash′) *v.t.* To deprive of self-possession; make ashamed. [< OF *esbaïr* to astonish] —**a·bash′ed·ly** *adv.* —**a·bash′·ment** *n.*

a·bate (ə·bāt′) *v.* **a·bat·ed, a·bat·ing** *v.t.* 1. To make less in quantity or intensity. 2. To end by legal action. —*v.i.* 3. To become less. 4. To become void. [< OF *abatre* to beat down] —**a·bat′a·ble** *adj.* —**a·bat′er** *n.* —**a·bate′ment** *n.*

ab·ba·cy (ab′ə·sē) *n. pl.* **·cies** The office of an abbot.

ab·bé (ab′ā, *Fr.* à·bā′) *n.* In France, a title of a priest or other cleric. [< F]

ab·bess (ab′is) *n.* The female superior of a community of nuns. [< OF *abbesse*]

ab·bey (ab′ē) *n. pl.* **·beys** 1. A monastery or convent under the rule of an abbot or abbess. 2. An abbey church. [< Aramaic *abbā* father]

ab·bot (ab′ət) *n.* The superior of a community of monks. [< Aramaic *abbā* father] —**ab′bot·cy, ab′bot·ship** *n.*

ab·bre·vi·ate (ə·brē′vē·āt) *v.t.* **·at·ed, ·at·ing** 1. To make briefer. 2. To shorten, as a word. [< L *ad-* to + *breviare* to shorten] —**ab·bre′vi·a′tor** *n.*

ab·bre·vi·a·tion (ə·brē′vē·ā′shən) *n.* 1. A shortened form of a word or phrase. 2. The act of abbreviating.

ABC (a′bē′sē′) *n. pl.* **ABC's** or **ABCs** 1. *Usu. pl.* The alphabet. 2. *Usu. pl.* The rudiments.

ab·di·cate (ab′də·kāt) *v.t. & v.i.* **·cat·ed, ·cat·ing** To give up formally, as a throne. [< L *abdicare* to renounce] —**ab·di·ca·ble** (ab′di·kə·bəl) *adj.* —**ab′di·ca′tion** *n.* —**ab′di·ca′tive** *adj.* —**ab′di·ca′tor** *n.*

ab·do·men (ab′də·mən, ab·dō′mən) *n.* 1. In mammals, the body cavity between the diaphragm and pelvis, containing the viscera. 2. In arthropods, the hindmost of the main body divisions. [< L] —**ab·dom·i·nal** (ab·dom′ə·nəl) *adj.* —**ab·dom′i·nal·ly** *adv.*

ab·duct (ab·dukt′) *v.t.* To carry away (a person) by force; kidnap. [< L *ab-* away + *ducere* to lead] —**ab·duc′tion** *n.* —**ab·duc′·tor** *n.*

a·beam (ə·bēm′) *adv. Naut.* At right angles to the keel of a vessel.

a·bed (ə·bed′) *adv.* In bed.

ab·er·ra·tion (ab′ə·rā′shən) *n.* Deviation from the normal or expected. [< L *ab-* from

+ *errare* to wander] **—ab·er·rance** (ab·er′əns), **ab·er·ran·cy** (ab·er′ən·sē) *n.* **—ab·er·rant** (ab·er′ənt, ab′ər·ənt) *adj.*

a·bet (ə·bet′) *v.t.* **a·bet·ted, a·bet·ting** To encourage and incite, esp. wrongdoing. [< OF *a-* to + *beter* to tease, bait] **—a·bet′·ment, a·bet′tal** *n.* **—a·bet′tor** or **a·bet′ter** *n.*

a·bey·ance (ə·bā′əns) *n.* Suspension or temporary inaction. Also **a·bey′an·cy.** [< OF *a-* to, at + *bair* to gape] **—a·bey′ant** *adj.*

ab·hor (ab·hôr′) *v.t.* **·horred, ·hor·ring** To regard with repugnance; loathe. [< L *ab-* from + *horrere* to shudder] **—ab·hor′rer** *n.*

ab·hor·rence (ab·hôr′əns, -hor′-) *n.* 1. A feeling of loathing. 2. Something repugnant.

ab·hor·rent (ab·hôr′ənt, -hor′-) *adj.* 1. Repugnant or detestable. 2. Opposed: with *to.* **—ab·hor′rent·ly** *adv.*

a·bide (ə·bīd′) *v.* **a·bode** or **a·bid·ed, a·bid·ing** *v.i.* 1. To remain in a place. *—v.t.* 2. To wait for. 3. To put up with. **—to abide by** To behave in accordance with. [OE *ābīdan*] **—a·bi′dance** *n.* **—a·bid′er** *n.* **—a·bid′ing·ly** *adv.*

a·bil·i·ty (ə·bil′ə·tē) *n. pl.* **·ties** 1. The state or quality of being able; capacity. 2. A talent or skill. [< L *habilis* suitable]

ab·ject (ab′jekt, ab·jekt′) *adj.* Sunk to a low condition; helpless or hopeless. [< L *ab-* away + *jacere* to throw] **—ab·jec′tive** *adj.* **—ab′ject·ly** *adv.* **—ab′ject·ness, ab·jec′tion** *n.*

ab·jure (ab·jŏŏr′) *v.t.* **·jured, ·jur·ing** 1. To renounce under oath. 2. To retract, as an opinion. [< L *ab-* away + *jurare* to swear] **—ab′ju·ra′tion** *n.* **—ab·jur′a·to·ry** *adj.* **—ab·jur′er** *n.*

ab·la·tive (ab′lə·tiv) *adj. Gram.* In some languages, as Latin, designating a case expressing separation, position, motion from, etc. [< L *ablatus* carried away] **—ab′la·tive** *n.*

a·blaze (ə·blāz′) *adv.* On fire. *—adj.* 1. Flaming. 2. Zealous.

a·ble (ā′bəl) *adj.* **a·bler, a·blest** 1. Having adequate power. 2. Having superior abilities. [< L *habilis* suitable, fit] **—a′bly** *adv.*

-able *suffix* 1. Likely to: *changeable.* 2. Capable of; worthy of: *eatable, salable.* Also spelled **-ble, -ible.** [< L *-abilis, -bilis, -ibilis*]

a·bloom (ə·blŏŏm′) *adj. & adv.* In blossom.

ab·lu·tion (ab·lŏŏ′shən) *n.* A cleansing of the body, esp. as a ceremony. [< L *ab-* away + *luere* to wash] **—ab·lu′tion·ar′y** *adj.*

-ably *suffix* In the manner of: *peaceably.*

ab·ne·gate (ab′nə·gāt) *v.t.* **·gat·ed, ·gat·ing** To deny; renounce. [< L *ab-* away + *negare* to deny] **—ab′ne·ga′tion** *n.* **—ab′ne·ga′tor** *n.*

ab·nor·mal (ab·nôr′məl) *adj.* Different from the normal. [< L *ab-* from + *norma* rule] **—ab·nor′mal·ly** *adv.*

ab·nor·mal·i·ty (ab′nôr·mal′ə·tē) *n. pl.* **·ties** 1. The state of being abnormal. 2. An abnormal thing.

a·board (ə·bôrd′) *adv.* 1. Into, in, or on a ship, train, etc. 2. Alongside. **—a·board′** *prep.*

a·bode (ə·bōd′) Past tense and past participle of ABIDE. *—n.* 1. A dwelling; home. 2. A time of abiding; sojourn. [OE *ābād*]

a·bol·ish (ə·bol′ish) *v.t.* To do away with. [< L *abolere* to destroy] **—a·bol′ish·a·ble** *adj.* **—a·bol′ish·er** *n.* **—a·bol′ish·ment** *n.*

ab·o·li·tion (ab′ə·lish′ən) *n.* 1. The act of abolishing. 2. *Sometimes cap.* The abolishing of slavery in the United States. **—ab′o·li′tion·al, ab′o·li′tion·ar′y** *adj.* **—ab′o·li′·tion·ism** *n.* **—ab′o·li′tion·ist** *n.*

A-bomb (ā′bom′) *n.* An atomic bomb.

a·bom·i·na·ble (ə·bom′in·ə·bəl) *adj.* 1. Detestable; loathsome. 2. Very disagreeable; bad. **—a·bom′i·na·bly** *adv.*

abominable snowman A legendary manlike animal said to inhabit the Himalayas: also called *yeti.* [< Tibetan *metkokhangmi*, lit., evil-smelling man of the snows]

a·bom·i·nate (ə·bom′ə·nāt) *v.t.* **·nat·ed, ·nat·ing** To regard with loathing; abhor. [< L *abominari* to abhor as an ill omen] **—a·bom′i·na′tion** *n.* **—a·bom′i·na′tor** *n.*

ab·o·rig·i·nal (ab′ə·rij′ə·nəl) *adj.* 1. Of or pertaining to aborigines. 2. Native; indigenous. **—ab′o·rig′i·nal·ly** *adv.*

ab·o·rig·i·ne (ab′ə·rij′ə·nē) *n.* One of the original inhabitants of an area. [< L *ab origine* from the beginning]

a·bort (ə·bôrt′) *v.t. & v.i.* 1. To undergo or cause the abortion of a fetus. 2. To fail or cause to fail of completion. [< L *aboriri* to miscarry] **—a·bor′tive** *adj.* **—a·bor′tive·ly** *adv.*

a·bor·tion (ə·bôr′shən) *n.* 1. The premature expulsion of a fetus; miscarriage. 2. Such expulsion produced artificially. 3. The defective result of a premature birth. 4. Partial or complete arrest of development. **—a·bor′tion·al** *adj.*

a·bor·tion·ist (ə·bôr′shən·ist) *n.* One who causes an abortion.

a·bound (ə·bound′) *v.i.* 1. To be plentiful. 2. To be full; teem. [< L *ab-* from + *undare* to flow in waves]

a·bout (ə·bout′) *adv.* 1. Approximately; nearly. 2. Nearby; in the vicinity. 3. To a reversed position. 4. Astir; active. 5. On every side; around. *—prep.* 1. On every side of. 2. Near; close to. 3. Concerning; in reference to. 4. Nearly ready: with *to.* [OE *onbūtan* around]

a·bout-face (*n.* ə·bout′fās′; *v.* ə·bout′fās′) *n.* 1. *Mil.* A turn to the rear when halted. 2. Any reversal, as of opinion. *—v.i.* **-faced, -fac·ing** To perform an about-face.

a·bove (ə·buv′) *adv.* 1. In or to a higher place. 2. Superior in rank or position. 3. In preceding text. 4. In heaven. *—adj.* Written or named before. *—n.* That which precedes in text. *—prep.* 1. Higher than; over. 2. More than; beyond. 3. Superior to; beyond the influence of. [ME *abofen* < OE *onbufan*]

Above as a combining form having the meaning earlier in order:

above-captioned	**above-mentioned**
above-cited	**above-named**
above-given	**above-written**

a·bove·board (ə·buv′bôrd′) *adj. & adv.* Without concealment or trickery.

ab·ra·ca·dab·ra (ab′rə·kə·dab′rə) *n.* 1. A spell; incantation. 2. Jargon; nonsensical words. [< L]

a·brade (ə·brād′) *v.t.* **a·brad·ed, a·brad·ing** To rub or wear off by friction. [< L *abradere* to scrape away] **—a·bra′dant** *adj. & n.* **—a·brad′er** *n.*

a·bra·sion (ə·brā′zhən) *n.* 1. A wearing or rubbing away. 2. An abraded area.

a·bra·sive (ə·brā′siv, -ziv) *adj.* 1. Wearing

away. 2. Emotionally irritating. —*n.* An abrading substance.

a·breast (ə·brest′) *adv.* & *adj.* Side by side. —**abreast of** (or **with**) 1. Side by side with. 2. Informed of recent developments.

a·bridge (ə·brij′) *v.t.* **a·bridged, a·bridg·ing** 1. To make shorter, as in words or time. 2. To curtail, as rights. [< OF *abregier* < L *abbreviare* to shorten] —**a·bridg′a·ble** or **a·bridge′a·ble** *adj.* —**a·bridg′er** *n.*

a·bridg·ment (ə·brij′mənt) *n.* 1. The act of abridging. 2. A condensation, as of a book. Also **a·bridge′ment.**

a·broad (ə·brôd′) *adv.* 1. Out of one's abode. 2. In or to foreign lands. 3. At large; in circulation. [ME]

ab·ro·gate (ab′rə·gāt) *v.t.* **·gat·ed, ·gat·ing** To annul by authority, as a law. [< L *ab-* away + *rogare* to propose a law] —**ab·ro·ga·ble** (ab′rə·gə·bəl) *adj.* —**ab′ro·ga′tion** *n.* —**ab′ro·ga′tive** *adj.* —**ab′ro·ga′tor** *n.*

a·brupt (ə·brupt′) *adj.* 1. Beginning, ending, or changing suddenly. 2. Cutting short amenities; brusque. 3. Steep, as a cliff. [< L *ab-* off + *rumpere* to break] —**a·brupt′ly** *adv.* —**a·brupt′ness** *n.*

ab·scess (ab′ses) *Pathol.* *n.* A collection of pus in inflamed tissue. —*v.i.* To form an abscess. [< L *ab-* away + *cedere* to go] —**ab′scessed** *adj.*

ab·scis·sa (ab·sis′ə) *n.* *pl.* **ab·scis·sas** or **ab·scis·sae** (-sis′ē) *Math.* The distance of any point from the vertical or Y-axis in a coordinate system, measured on a line parallel to the horizontal or X-axis. [< L *ab-* off + *scindere* to cut]

ab·scis·sion (ab·sizh′ən, -sish′ən) *n.* The act of cutting off or removing. [< L *ab-* off + *scindere* to cut]

ab·scond (ab·skond′) *v.i.* To depart suddenly and secretly, esp. to escape the law. [< L *ab-* away + *condere* to store away, conceal] —**ab·scond′er** *n.*

ab·sence (ab′səns) *n.* 1. The state of being absent. 2. The period of being away. 3. Lack.

ab·sent (*adj.* ab′sənt; *v.* ab·sent′) *adj.* 1. Not present; away. 2. Lacking; nonexistent. 3. Inattentive; absent-minded. —*v.t.* To take or keep (oneself) away. [< L *ab-* away + *esse* to be] —**ab′sent·ly** *adv.*

ab·sen·tee (ab′sən·tē′) *n.* One who is absent, as from a job. —*adj.* Temporarily absent. —**ab′sen·tee′ism** *n.*

ab·sent-mind·ed (ab′sənt·mīn′did) *adj.* Lost in thought and inattentive to one's surroundings or business; forgetful. —**ab′·sent-mind′ed·ly** *adv.* —**ab′sent-mind′ed·ness** *n.*

absent without leave *Mil.* Absent without authorization but not intending to desert. Abbr. *A.W.O.L.*

ab·sinthe (ab′sinth) *n.* 1. A green, bitter liqueur having the flavor of licorice and wormwood. 2. Wormwood. Also **ab′sinth.** [< F < L *absinthium* wormwood]

ab·so·lute (ab′sə·lo͞ot) *adj.* 1. Free from restriction; unlimited; unconditional. 2. Complete; perfect. 3. Unadulterated; pure. 4. Not relative to anything else; independent. 5. Positive; certain. 6. *Gram.* Not related to other words in the sentence. [< L *ab-* from + *solvere* to loosen] —**ab′so·lute** *n.* —**ab′so·lute′ly** *adv.*

absolute pitch *Music* The ability to produce or name the pitch of any note: also *perfect pitch.*

absolute zero The hypothetical temperature at which a body contains no heat, equal to about −273.16°C. or −459.7°F.

ab·so·lu·tion (ab′sə·lo͞o′shən) *n.* 1. The act of absolving, as from guilt. 2. *Eccl.* A remission of sin and its penalties pronounced by a priest. [< L *ab-* from + *solvere* to loosen]

ab·so·lut·ism (ab′sə·lo͞o·tiz′əm) *n.* In government, the doctrine or practice of unlimited authority and control; despotism. —**ab′so·lut′ist** *n.*

ab·solve (ab·solv′, -zolv′, əb-) *v.t.* **·solved, ·solv·ing** 1. To free from the penalties or consequences of an action. 2. To release, as from an obligation. 3. *Eccl.* To grant a remission of sin. [< L *ab-* from + *solvere* to loosen] —**ab·solv′a·ble** *adj.* —**ab·solv′er** *n.*

ab·sorb (ab·sôrb′, -zôrb′) *v.t.* 1. To drink in or suck up, as through or into pores. 2. To engross completely. 3. To take up or in by chemical or molecular action, as gases, heat, liquid, light, etc. 4. To take in and incorporate. 5. To receive the force or action of. [< L *ab-* from + *sorbere* to suck in] —**ab·sorb′a·bil′i·ty** *n.* —**ab·sorb′a·ble** *adj.* —**ab·sorb′er** *n.* —**ab·sorb′ing** *adj.*

ab·sor·bent (ab·sôr′bənt, -zôr′-) *adj.* Absorbing or tending to absorb: *absorbent* cotton. —*n.* A substance, duct, etc., that absorbs. —**ab·sor′ben·cy** *n.*

ab·sorp·tion (ab·sôrp′shən, -zôrp′-) *n.* 1. The act or process of absorbing or being absorbed. 2. Assimilation, as by digestion. 3. Preoccupation of the mind. —**ab·sorp′tive** *adj.*

ab·stain (ab·stān′) *v.i.* To keep oneself back; refrain voluntarily: with *from.* [< L *abstinere* to hold back] —**ab·stain′er** *n.*

ab·ste·mi·ous (ab·stē′mē·əs) *adj.* Eating and drinking sparingly; abstinent; temperate. [< L *ab-* from + *temetum* intoxicating drink] —**ab·ste′mi·ous·ly** *adv.* —**ab·ste′mi·ous·ness** *n.*

ab·sten·tion (ab·sten′shən) *n.* An abstaining. —**ab·sten′tious** *adj.*

ab·sti·nence (ab′stə·nəns) *n.* The act or practice of abstaining from some or all food, liquor, etc. [< L *abstinere* to hold back] —**ab′sti·nent** *adj.* —**ab′sti·nent·ly** *adv.*

ab·stract (*adj.* ab·strakt′, ab′strakt; *n.* ab′·strakt; *v. defs. 1 & 2* ab·strakt′; *v. def. 3* ab′strakt) *adj.* 1. Considered apart from matter or from specific examples; not concrete. 2. Theoretical; ideal, as opposed to practical. 3. Abstruse. 4. Considered or expressed without reference to particular example, as numbers, attributes, or qualities. 5. In art, generalized; nonrepresentational. —*n.* 1. A summary or epitome, as of a document. 2. The essence of some larger object or whole. 3. An abstract idea or term. —*v.t.* 1. To take away; remove. 2. To withdraw (the attention, interest, etc.). 3. To make an abstract of; summarize. [< L *ab-* away + *trahere* to draw] —**ab·stract′er** *n.* —**ab·stract′ly** *adv.* —**ab·stract′ness** *n.*

ab·stract·ed (ab·strak′tid) *adj.* 1. Lost in thought; absentminded. 2. Separated from all else; apart. —**ab·stract′ed·ly** *adv.* —**ab·stract′ed·ness** *n.*

ab·strac·tion (ab·strak′shən) *n.* 1. The process of abstracting. 2. A product of this process; concept. 3. Absence of mind; preoccupation. 4. An art form or work of art in which the qualities are abstract. —**ab·strac′tive** *adj.* —**ab·strac′tive·ly** *adv.* —**ab·strac′tive·ness** *n.*

ab·struse (ab·stro͞os′) *adj.* Hard to understand. [< L *ab-* away + *trudere* to thrust] —**ab·struse′ly** *adv.* —**ab·struse′ness** *n.*

ab·surd (ab·sûrd′, -zûrd′) *adj.* Irrational; ridiculous. [< L *ab-* completely + *surdus* deaf, dull] —**ab·surd′ly** *adv.* —**ab·surd′ness** *n.*

ab·surd·i·ty (ab·sûr′də·tē, -zûr′-) *n. pl.* **·ties** 1. The quality of being absurd. 2. Something absurd.

a·bun·dance (ə·bun′dəns) *n.* 1. A plentiful or overflowing supply. 2. Wealth; affluence.

a·bun·dant (ə·bun′dənt) *adj.* 1. Existing in plentiful supply; ample. 2. Abounding. [< L *abundare.* See ABOUND.] —**a·bun′dant·ly** *adv.*

a·buse (*v.* ə·byo͞oz′; *n.* ə·byo͞os′) *v.t.* **a·bused, a·bus·ing** 1. To use improperly or injuriously; misuse. 2. To hurt by treating wrongly; injure. 3. To speak in coarse or bad terms of or to; revile. —*n.* 1. Improper or injurious use; misuse. 2. Ill-treatment; injury. 3. Abusive language; slander. [< L *abusus,* pp. of *abuti* to misuse] —**a·bus′er** *n.*

a·bu·sive (ə·byo͞o′siv) *adj.* 1. Mistreating. 2. Insulting; vituperative. —**a·bu′sive·ly** *adv.* —**a·bu′sive·ness** *n.*

a·but (ə·but′) *v.t. & v.i.* **a·but·ted, a·but·ting** To touch, join, or adjoin; border. [< OF *a-* to + *bout* end] —**a·but′ter** *n.*

a·but·ment (ə·but′mənt) *n.* 1. The act of abutting. 2. A supporting or buttressing structure.

a·bys·mal (ə·biz′məl) *adj.* Unfathomable; immeasurable; extreme: an *abysmal* ignorance. —**a·bys′mal·ly** *adv.*

a·byss (ə·bis′) *n.* 1. A bottomless gulf; chasm. 2. Any profound depth or void. [< Gk. *a-* without + *byssos* bottom] —**a·bys′sal** *adj.*

Ab·ys·sin·i·an (ab′ə·sin′ē·ən) *adj & n.* Ethiopian.

-ac *suffix* 1. Having; affected by: *insomniac.* 2. Pertaining to; of: *cardiac.* [< Gk. *-akos* or L *-acus* or F *-aque*]

a·ca·cia (ə·kā′shə) *n.* Any of various flowering, leguminous trees and shrubs of the tropics and warm temperate regions. [< Gk. *akakia,* thorny tree < *akē* point]

ac·a·dem·ic (ak′ə·dem′ik) *adj.* 1. Pertaining to an academy, college, or university; scholarly. 2. Having to do with liberal arts rather than technical studies. 3. Theoretical, as opposed to practical. 4. Pedantic. Also **ac′a·dem′i·cal.** —*n.* A college student or faculty member. —**ac′a·dem′i·cal·ly** *adv.*

a·cad·e·mi·cian (ə·kad′ə·mish′ən, ak′ə·də-) *n.* A member of an academy of art, science, or literature.

ac·a·dem·i·cism (ak′ə·dem′ə·siz′əm) *n.* Pedantic formalism, as in art. Also **a·cad·e·mism** (ə·kad′ə·miz′əm).

a·cad·e·my (ə·kad′ə·mē) *n. pl.* **·mies** 1. A secondary school, usually a private one. 2. A school giving instruction in some science or art. 3. A learned society for the advancement of arts or sciences. [after Gk. *Akadēmeia* the grove where Plato taught]

A·ca·di·a (ə·kā′dē·ə) A former name for a region in eastern Canada, including Nova Scotia and New Brunswick.

A·ca·di·an (ə·kā′dē·ən) *adj.* Of or pertaining to Acadia or Nova Scotia. —*n.* One of the early French settlers of Acadia or their descendants. See CAJUN.

a·can·thus (ə·kan′thəs) *n. pl.* **·thus·es** or **·thi** (-thī) 1. A plant having large spiny leaves, common in the Mediterranean region. 2. *Archit.* A decorative representation of its leaf. [< Gk. *akanthos*]

a cap·pel·la (ä′ kə·pel′ə) *Music* Sung without accompaniment. [< Ital., in chapel style]

ac·cede (ak·sēd′) *v.i.* **·ced·ed, ·ced·ing** 1. To give one's consent; agree; assent: with *to.* 2. To come into or enter upon an office: with *to.* [< L *ad-* to + *cedere* to yield]

ac·cel·er·an·do (ak·sel′ə·ran′dō, *Ital.* ät·chā′lā·rän′dō) *Music adj. & adv.* With gradually quickening tempo. [< Ital.]

ac·cel·er·ant (ak·sel′ər·ənt) *n.* That which accelerates.

ac·cel·er·ate (ak·sel′ə·rāt) *v.* **·at·ed, ·at·ing** *v.t.* 1. To cause to act or move faster. 2. To hasten the natural or usual course of. 3. To cause to happen ahead of time. 4. To cause a change in rate of velocity. —*v.i.* 5. To move or become faster. [< L *ad-* to + *celerare* to hasten]

ac·cel·er·a·tion (ak·sel′ə·rā′shən) *n.* 1. The act of accelerating or being accelerated. 2. *Physics* The rate at which the velocity of a body changes per unit of time.

ac·cel·er·a·tor (ak·sel′ə·rā′tər) *n.* 1. One who or that which accelerates. 2. *Physics* Any of various devices for accelerating the velocity of atomic particles. 3. *Mech.* The foot throttle of an automobile.

ac·cent (*n.* ak′sent; *v.* ak′sent, ak·sent′) *n.* 1. The emphasis given in speech, poetry, music, etc., to a particular sound, syllable, or word. 2. A mark used to indicate the place of accent in a word. The **primary accent** notes the chief stress, and the **secondary accent** a weaker stress. 3. A mark used to show the quality of a vowel. In French, the accents are acute (´), grave (`), and circumflex (ˆ). 4. Mode of utterance; pronunciation: a Southern *accent.* —*v.t.* 1. To accent; stress. 2. To mark for accent. 3. To accentuate. [< L *ad-* to + *cantus* a singing] —**ac·cen·tu·al** (ak·sen′cho͞o·əl) *adj.* —**ac·cen′tu·al·ly** *adv.*

ac·cen·tu·ate (ak·sen′cho͞o·āt) *v.t.* **·at·ed, ·at·ing** To accent; emphasize. —**ac·cen′tu·a′tion** *n.*

ac·cept (ak·sept′) *v.t.* 1. To receive with favor, willingness, or consent. 2. To give an affirmative answer to. 3. To receive as satisfactory. 4. To resign oneself to; submit to. 5. To believe in. [< L *ad-* to + *capere* to take] —**ac·cept′er** *n.*

ac·cept·a·ble (ak·sep′tə·bəl) *adj.* Worthy of acceptance. —**ac·cept′a·ble·ness, ac·cept′a·bil′i·ty** *n.* —**ac·cept′a·bly** *adv.*

ac·cep·tance (ak·sep′təns) *n.* 1. The act of accepting. 2. The state of being accepted or acceptable. 3. Favorable reception. 4. Assent; belief. Also **ac·cep′tan·cy.** —**ac·cep′tant** *adj.*

ac·cep·ta·tion (ak′sep·tā′shən) *n.* The accepted meaning of a word or expression.

ac·cept·ed (ak·sep′tid) *adj.* Commonly recognized, believed, or approved; popular.
ac·cess (ak′ses) *n.* 1. The act of coming to or near. 2. A passage; path. 3. The state or quality of being approachable; accessibility. 4. An outburst of emotion, etc. [< L *accedere* to yield]
ac·ces·si·ble (ak·ses′ə·bəl) *adj.* 1. Easy of access; approachable. 2. Attainable; obtainable. 3. Open to the influence of. **—ac·ces′·si·bil′i·ty** *n.* **—ac·ces′si·bly** *adv.*
ac·ces·sion (ak·sesh′ən) *n.* 1. The act of attaining an office, dignity, or right. 2. An increase by addition; something added. 3. Assent; agreement. **—ac·ces′sion·al** *adj.*
ac·ces·so·ry (ak·ses′ər·ē) *n. pl.* **·ries** 1. Something added for convenience, display, etc., as to an automobile or to one's attire. 2. *Law* A person who, though absent, aids or encourages another to commit a crime. [< L *accedere* to yield] **—ac·ces′so·ry** *adj.*
ac·ci·dent (ak′sə·dənt) *n.* 1. An unintended happening. 2. A mishap involving injury, loss, or death. 3. Chance; fortune. [< L *ad-* upon + *cadere* to fall] **—ac·ci·den·tal** (ak′sə·den′təl) *adj.* **—ac′ci·den′tal·ly** *adv.*
ac·claim (ə·klām′) *v.t.* 1. To proclaim with applause; hail. 2. To shout approval of. **—***v.i.* 3. To applaud; shout approval. **—***n.* A shout of applause. [< L *ad-* to + *clamare* to shout] **—ac·claim′a·ble** *adj.* **—ac·claim′er** *n.*
ac·cla·ma·tion (ak′lə·mā′shən) *n.* 1. The act of acclaiming or of being acclaimed. 2. A shout of applause or welcome. 3. An oral vote of approval, as in a public assembly. **—ac·clam·a·to·ry** (ə·klam′ə·tôr′ē) *adj.*
ac·cli·mate (ak′lə·māt, ə·klī′mit) *v.t. & v.i.* **·mat·ed, ·mat·ing** To adapt to a new climate or environment. [< F *à-* to + *climat* climate] **—ac′cli·ma′tion** *n.*
ac·cli·ma·tize (ə·klī′mə·tīz) *v.t. & v.i.* **·tized, ·tiz·ing** To acclimate. **—ac·cli′ma·ti·za′tion** *n.*
ac·cliv·i·ty (ə·kliv′ə·tē) *n. pl.* **·ties** An upward slope. [< L *ad-* to + *clivus* hill]
ac·co·lade (ak′ə·lād′) *n.* 1. A conferring of praise; an honor. 2. The salutation (formerly an embrace, now a light tap with a sword) in conferring knighthood. [< F < Ital. *accollare* to embrace about the neck]
ac·com·mo·date (ə·kom′ə·dāt) *v.* **·dat·ed, ·dat·ing** *v.t.* 1. To do a favor for; oblige; help. 2. To provide for; give lodging to. 3. To be suitable for; contain comfortably. 4. To adapt or modify, as to new conditions. **—***v.i.* 5. To be or become adjusted. [< L *ad-* to + *commodare* to make fit, suit] **—ac·com′mo·da′tive** *adj.*
ac·com·mo·dat·ing (ə·kom′ə·dā′ting) *adj.* Obliging. **—ac·com′mo·dat′ing·ly** *adv.*
ac·com·mo·da·tion (ə·kom′ə·dā′shən) *n.* 1. The act of accommodating, or the state of being accommodated; adjustment; adaptation. 2. Reconciliation; compromise. 3. Anything that supplies a need; convenience. 4. *Usu. pl.* Lodging, board, etc.
ac·com·pa·ni·ment (ə·kum′pə·ni·mənt, ə·kump′ni-) *n.* 1. Anything that accompanies something. 2. *Music* A subordinate part supporting a leading voice, instrument, etc.
ac·com·pa·nist (ə·kum′pə·nist, ə·kump′·nist) *n.* One who plays or sings the accompaniment. Also **ac·com′pa·ny·ist.**
ac·com·pa·ny (ə·kum′pə·nē) *v.t.* **·nied, ·ny·ing** 1. To go with; attend; escort. 2. To be or coexist with. 3. To play a musical accompaniment to or for. [< F *à-* to + *compagne* companion]
ac·com·plice (ə·kom′plis) *n.* A partner in crime. [*a*, indefinite article + F *complice* accomplice]
ac·com·plish (ə·kom′plish, -kum′-) *v.t.* To bring to pass or to completion. [< L *ad-* to + *complere* to fill up, complete] **—ac·com′plish·a·ble** *adj.*
ac·com·plished (ə·kom′plisht, -kum′-) *adj.* 1. Completed; done. 2. Proficient; skilled.
ac·com·plish·ment (ə·kom′plish·mənt, -kum′-) *n.* 1. The act of accomplishing. 2. Something accomplished; achievement.
ac·cord (ə·kôrd′) *v.t.* 1. To render as due; grant. 2. To make harmonize or agree. **—***v.i.* 3. To agree; harmonize. **—***n.* 1. Harmony, as of sentiment, colors, sounds, etc.; agreement. 2. A settlement of any difference, as between governments. **—of one's own accord** By one's own choice. [< L *ad-* to + *cor* heart] **—ac·cord′ance** *n.* **—ac·cord′ant** *adj.* **—ac·cord′ant·ly** *adv.*
ac·cord·ing (ə·kôr′ding) *adj.* Being in accord or agreement; harmonizing. **—according to** 1. In accordance with. 2. As stated by; on the authority of.
ac·cord·ing·ly (ə·kôr′ding·lē) *adv.* 1. In accord; correspondingly. 2. Consequently; so.
ac·cor·di·on (ə·kôr′dē·ən) *n.* A portable musical wind instrument with metallic reeds, a keyboard, and bellows. [< Ital. *accordare* to harmonize] **—ac·cor′di·on·ist** *n.*
ac·cost (ə·kôst′, ə·kost′) *v.t.* To speak to first; address; greet. [< L *ad-* to + *costa* rib]
ac·count (ə·kount′) *v.t.* 1. To hold to be; consider; estimate. **—***v.i.* 2. To provide a reckoning, as of funds paid or received: with *to* or *with* (someone), *for* (something). 3. To give a rational explanation: with *for*. 4. To be responsible; answer: with *for*. **—***n.* 1. A record of events; narrative; description. 2. An explanation. 3. A record of monetary transactions: business *account*; charge *account*; bank *account*. 4. A company that is a client or customer. 5. Worth; importance. 6. Profit; advantage. **—on account of** Because of. **—on no account** Under no circumstances. [< L *ad-* to + *computare* to reckon together]
ac·count·a·ble (ə·koun′tə·bəl) *adj.* 1. Liable to be called to account; responsible. 2. Capable of being explained. **—ac·count′a·bil′i·ty** *n.* **—ac·count′a·bly** *adv.*
ac·count·ant (ə·koun′tənt) *n.* One skilled in accounting. **—ac·count′an·cy** *n.*
ac·count·ing (ə·koun′ting) *n.* The system of recording, classifying, and summarizing business and financial transactions.
ac·cou·ter (ə·ko͞o′tər) *v.t.* To furnish with dress or trappings; equip, as for military service. Also **ac·cou′tre.** [< F *accoutrer*]
ac·cou·ter·ment (ə·ko͞o′tər·mənt, -trə·mənt) *n.* 1. *pl.* Equipment; trappings; esp., the equipment of a soldier other than arms and dress. 2. The act of accoutering. Also **ac·cou′tre·ment.**
ac·cred·it (ə·kred′it) *v.t.* 1. To give credit to as the owner, author, or creator of; attribute to. 2. To accept as true; believe. 3. To certify

as fulfilling official requirements. [< L *ad-* to + *credere* to believe, trust]

ac·cred·i·ta·tion (ə·kred′ə·tā′shən) *n.* The granting of approved status to an academic institution.

ac·cre·tion (ə·krē′shən) *n.* 1. Growth by external additions or by adhesion or inclusion. 2. An external addition; something added.

ac·crue (ə·kro͞o′) *v.i.* **·crued, ·cru·ing** 1. To come as a natural result or increment, as by growth: with *to.* 2. To accumulate, as the interest on money. [< F *accrû* < L *ad-* to + *crescere* to grow] **—ac·cru′al, ac·crue′ment** *n.*

ac·cu·mu·late (ə·kyo͞om′yə·lāt) *v.* **·lat·ed, ·lat·ing** *v.t.* 1. To heap or pile up; amass; collect. *—v.i.* 2. To become greater in quantity or number; increase. [< L *ad-* to + *cumulare* to heap] **—ac·cu′mu·la′tor** *n.*

ac·cu·mu·la·tion (ə·kyo͞om′yə·lā′shən) *n.* 1. The act or process of accumulating. 2. That which is accumulated. 3. The addition of earnings or profits to capital. **—ac·cu′·mu·la′tive** *adj.*

ac·cu·rate (ak′yər·it) *adj.* Being without error; precise; exact. [< L *ad-* to + *cura* care] **—ac′cu·ra·cy, ac′cu·rate·ness** *n.* **—ac′cu·rate·ly** *adv.*

ac·curs·ed (ə·kûr′sid, ə·kûrst′) *adj.* 1. Lying under a curse; doomed. 2. Deserving a curse; detestable. Also **ac·curst′**. **—ac·curs′ed·ly** *adv.* **—ac·curs′ed·ness** *n.*

ac·cu·sa·tion (ak′yo͞o·zā′shən) *n.* 1. The act of accusing, or the state of being accused. 2. The crime or act charged. Also **ac·cu·sal** (ə·kyo͞o′zəl). **—ac·cu·sa·to·ry** (ə·kyo͞o′zə·tôr′ē) *adj.*

ac·cu·sa·tive (ə·kyo͞o′zə·tiv) *Gram. adj.* Denoting the case that signifies the direct object of a verb or preposition; objective. *—n.* The objective case in English or another language. [< L *accusativus*] **—ac·cu′sa·tive·ly** *adv.*

ac·cuse (ə·kyo͞oz′) *v.t.* **·cused, ·cus·ing** 1. To charge with fault or error; blame; censure. 2. To bring charges against, as of a crime. [< L *accusare* to call to account] **—ac·cus′er** *n.* **—ac·cus′ing·ly** *adv.*

ac·cused (ə·kyo͞ozd′) *n. Law* The defendant or defendants in a criminal case.

ac·cus·tom (ə·kus′təm) *v.t.* To familiarize by custom or use; habituate or inure.

ac·cus·tomed (ə·kus′təmd) *adj.* 1. Habitual; usual. 2. In the habit of: *accustomed* to hard work.

AC/DC (ā′sē·dē′sē) *adj. Slang* Sexually attracted to men and women. [ref. to appliances that operate on both forms of electrical current]

ace (ās) *n.* 1. A playing card, die, etc., having a single spot. 2. A very small amount or degree. 3. One who excells in a particular field. 4. In tennis and similar games, a point won by a single stroke, as upon the service. **—ace in the hole** *Slang* A hidden advantage. *—v.t.* **aced** (āst), **ac·ing** To score a point against in a single stroke, as in tennis. *—adj. Slang* Excellent; superlative. [< L *as* unity, unit]

-acea *suffix Zool.* Used in forming names of classes and orders of animals. [< L, neut. pl. of *-aceus*]

-aceae *suffix Bot.* Used in forming names of families of plants. [< L, fem. pl. of *-aceus*]

a·cen·tric (ā·sen′trik) *adj.* Without a center; off center.

-aceous *suffix* Of the nature of; belonging or pertaining to; like: used to form adjectives corresponding to nouns ending in *-acea, -aceae.* [< L *-aceus* of the nature of]

ac·er·bate (as′ər·bāt) *v.t.* **·bat·ed, ·bat·ing** 1. To make sour; embitter. 2. To exasperate. [< L *acerbus* sharp]

a·cer·bi·ty (ə·sûr′bə·tē) *n. pl.* **·ties** 1. Sourness or bitterness, as that of unripe fruit. 2. Severity, as of temper, etc.; harshness.

ac·e·tal (as′ə·tal) *n. Med.* A volatile, colorless liquid, used in hypnotics.

ac·e·tate (as′ə·tāt) *n.* 1. *Chem.* A salt or ester of acetic acid. 2. Cellulose acetate, or one of its products.

a·ce·tic (ə·sē′tik) *adj.* Pertaining to or like vinegar; sour. [< L *acetum* vinegar + -IC]

acetic acid *Chem.* A colorless, pungent liquid, occurring in a dilute form in vinegar.

a·cet·i·fy (ə·set′ə·fī) *v.t. & v.i.* **·fied, ·fy·ing** To change into acid or vinegar. **—a·cet′i·fi·ca′tion** *n.* **—a·cet′i·fi′er** *n.*

ac·e·tone (as′ə·tōn) *n. Chem.* A clear, flammable liquid, used as a solvent for fats, camphor, and resins.

a·cet·y·lene (ə·set′ə·lēn) *n. Chem.* A colorless hydrocarbon gas, used as an illuminant and for cutting metals.

ac·e·tyl·sal·i·cyl·ic acid (as′ə·til·sal′ə·sil′·ik) Aspirin.

A·chae·an (ə·kē′ən) *adj.* Pertaining to Achaea, its people, or their culture. *—n.* A member of one of the four major tribes of ancient Greece.

ache (āk) *v.i.* **ached** (ākt), **ach·ing** 1. To suffer dull, continued pain. 2. *Informal* To yearn; be eager. *—n.* A local, dull, and protracted pain. [OE *acan*] **—ach′ing·ly** *adv.*

a·chene (ā·kēn′) *n. Bot.* A small, dry, one-seeded seed case, as in the dandelion. [< Gk. *a-* not + *chainein* to gape]

a·chieve (ə·chēv′) *v.* **a·chieved, a·chiev·ing** *v.t.* 1. To accomplish; do successfully. 2. To win or attain, as by effort or skill. *—v.i.* 3. To accomplish something. [< OF *achever* to finish] **—a·chiev′a·ble** *adj.* **—a·chiev′er** *n.*

a·chieve·ment (ə·chēv′mənt) *n.* 1. Something accomplished. 2. The act of achieving.

A·chil·les′ heel (ə·kil′ēz) A vulnerable point. [after the Greek hero *Achilles*, who was vulnerable only in his right heel]

Achilles′ tendon *Anat.* The tendon connecting the calf muscles to the heel bone.

ach·ro·mat·ic (ak′rə·mat′ik) *adj.* Transmitting light without separating it into its constituent colors, as a lens. [< Gk. *a-* without + *chrōma* color] **—ach′ro·mat′i·cal·ly** *adv.* **—a·chro·ma·tism** (ā·krō′mə·tiz′əm) *n.* **—a·chro·ma·tize** (ā·krō′mə·tīz) *v.t.*

a·chro·mic (ā·krō′mik) *adj.* Colorless. Also **a·chro′mous.**

ac·id (as′id) *adj.* 1. Sharp to the taste, as vinegar; sour. 2. *Chem.* Pertaining to or like an acid. 3. Sharp-tempered; biting. *—n.* 1. Any sour substance. 2. *Chem.* A water-soluble compound, sour to the taste, that dissolves certain metals, reacts with bases to form salts, and reddens litmus. 3. *Slang* Lysergic acid diethylamide (*LSD*), a hallucinogenic drug. [< L *acidus*] **—ac′id·ly** *adv.* **—ac′id·ness** *n.*

a·cid·ic (ə·sid′ik) *adj.* 1. *Geol.* Containing a

high percentage of silica: said of rocks. 2. *Chem.* Acid. —**a·cid′i·ty** *n.*

a·cid·i·fy (ə·sid′ə·fī) *v.t. & v.i.* ·**fied,** ·**fy·ing** To make or become acid; change into an acid. —**a·cid′i·fi·ca′tion** *n.* —**a·cid′i·fi′er** *n.*

ac·i·do·sis (as′ə·dō′sis) *n. Pathol.* Acid intoxication due to faulty metabolism.

acid test A final, decisive test.

a·cid·u·late (ə·sij′o͞o·lāt) *v.t.* ·**lat·ed,** ·**lat·ing** To make somewhat acid or sour. —**a·cid′·u·la′tion** *n.*

a·cid·u·lous (ə·sij′o͞o·ləs) *adj.* 1. Slightly acid; sour. 2. Bitter or rancorous. [< L *acidulus* slightly sour]

-acious *suffix of adjectives* Abounding in; characterized by; given to: *efficacious, vivacious.* [< L *-ax, -acis* + -OUS]

-acity *suffix* Quality or state of: used to form abstract nouns corresponding to adjectives ending in *-acious.* [< L *-acitas*]

ack-ack (ak′ak′) *n.* Antiaircraft fire. [British radio operator's code for *A.A.* (antiaircraft)]

ac·knowl·edge (ak·nol′ij) *v.t.* ·**edged,** ·**edg·ing** 1. To admit the truth or fact of; confess. 2. To recognize as or avow to be. 3. To admit the validity of, as a claim or right. 4. To express thanks for. 5. To report receipt or arrival of. [Earlier *aknowledge* < ME *knowleche* to admit]

ac·knowl·edg·ment (ak·nol′ij·mənt) *n.* 1. The act of admitting or acknowledging. 2. Recognition of something done; expression of gratitude. 3. Something done or given in return. Also **ac·knowl′edge·ment.**

ac·me (ak′mē) *n.* The highest point. [< Gk. *akmē* point]

ac·ne (ak′nē) *n. Pathol.* A skin disease marked by pimples, chiefly on the face. [? Alter. of Gk. *akmē* point]

ac·o·lyte (ak′ə·līt) *n.* 1. An attendant or assistant. 2. An altar boy. 3. In the Roman Catholic Church, a member of the highest minor order. [< Gk. *akolouthos* follower, attendant]

ac·o·nite (ak′ə·nīt) *n.* 1. The monkshood, or any similar plant. 2. An extract of this plant, used as a sedative. [< Gk. *akoniton*]

a·corn (ā′kôrn, ā′kərn) *n.* The fruit of the oak, a one-seeded nut. [OE *æcern*]

a·cous·tic (ə·ko͞os′tik) *adj.* 1. Pertaining to hearing, heard sound, or the science of sound. 2. Adapted for conveying sound or aiding hearing. Also **a·cous′ti·cal.** [< Gk. *akouein* to hear] —**a·cous′ti·cal·ly** *adv.*

a·cous·tics (ə·ko͞os′tiks) *n.pl.* (*construed as sing. in def. 1*) 1. The branch of physics that treats of sound. 2. The sound-transmitting qualities of an auditorium, room, etc. —**ac·ous·ti·cian** (a′ko͞o·stish′ən) *n.*

ac·quaint (ə·kwānt′) *v.t.* 1. To make familiar or conversant. 2. To cause to know; inform. [< OF *acointer* < LL *adcognitare* to make known]

ac·quain·tance (ə·kwān′təns) *n.* 1. Knowledge of any person or thing. 2. A person or persons with whom one is acquainted. —**ac·quain′tance·ship** *n.*

ac·quaint·ed (ə·kwān′tid) *adj.* Having acquaintance; having personal knowledge: with *with.*

ac·qui·esce (ak′wē·es′) *v.i.* ·**esced** (-est′), ·**esc·ing** To consent or concur tacitly; assent; comply. [< L *ad-* to + *quiescere* to rest] —**ac′qui·esc′ing·ly** *adv.*

ac·qui·es·cence (ak′wē·es′əns) *n.* Quiet submission; passive consent. —**ac′qui·es′·cent** *adj.*

ac·quire (ə·kwīr′) *v.t.* ·**quired,** ·**quir·ing** 1. To obtain by one's own endeavor or action. 2. To come to possess; receive. [< L *ad-* to + *quaerere* to seek] —**ac·quir′a·ble** *adj.* —**ac·quir′er** *n.*

ac·quire·ment (ə·kwīr′mənt) *n.* 1. The act of acquiring. 2. Something acquired, as a skill; attainment.

ac·qui·si·tion (ak′wə·zish′ən) *n.* 1. The act of acquiring. 2. Anything gained or acquired.

ac·quis·i·tive (ə·kwiz′ə·tiv) *adj.* Able or inclined to acquire (money, property, etc.); grasping. —**ac·quis′i·tive·ly** *adv.* —**ac·quis′i·tive·ness** *n.*

ac·quit (ə·kwit′) *v.t.* ·**quit·ted,** ·**quit·ting** 1. To free or clear, as from an accusation. 2. To relieve, as of an obligation. 3. To conduct (oneself); behave. [< L *ad-* to + *quietare* to settle, quiet] —**ac·quit′tal** *n.* —**ac·quit′ter** *n.*

ac·quit·tance (ə·kwit′ns) *n.* 1. A release, as from a debt. 2. Satisfaction of indebtedness or obligation. 3. A receipt.

a·cre (ā′kər) *n.* 1. A measure of land, equal to 43,560 square feet or 4,047 square meters. 2. *pl.* Lands; estate. [OE *æcer* field]

a·cre·age (ā′kər·ij) *n.* Area in acres; acres collectively.

ac·rid (ak′rid) *adj.* 1. Cutting or burning to the taste or smell. 2. Sharp and satirical, as speech. [< L *acer, acris*] —**a·crid·i·ty** (ə·krid′ə·tē), **ac′rid·ness** *n.* —**ac′rid·ly** *adv.*

ac·ri·mo·ny (ak′rə·mō′nē) *n. pl.* ·**nies** Sharpness or bitterness of speech or temper; acridity. [< L *acer* sharp] —**ac′ri·mo′ni·ous** *adj.* —**ac′ri·mo′ni·ous·ly** *adv.* —**ac′ri·mo′·ni·ous·ness** *n.*

acro- *combining form* 1. At the tip or end of. 2. *Med.* Pertaining to the extremities. [< Gk. *akros* at the end]

ac·ro·bat (ak′rə·bat) *n.* One skilled in feats requiring muscular coordination, as in tumbling, trapeze performing, etc.; a gymnast. [< Gk. *akrobatos* walking on tiptoe] —**ac′ro·bat′ic** or ·**i·cal** *adj.* —**ac′ro·bat′i·cal·ly** *adv.*

ac·ro·bat·ics (ak′rə·bat′iks) *n.pl.* The skills or activities of an acrobat, as in gymnastics.

ac·ro·nym (ak′rə·nim) *n.* A word formed by combining initial letters (*NATO, laser*) or syllables and letters (*radar, sonar*) of a series of words or a compound term. [< ACRO- + *-nym* name]

a·crop·o·lis (ə·krop′ə·lis) *n.* The citadel of an ancient Greek city. —**the Acropolis** The citadel of Athens. [< Gk. *akros* at the top + *polis* city]

a·cross (ə·krôs′) *adv.* 1. From one side to the other. 2. On or at the other side. 3. Crosswise; crossed, as arms. —*prep.* 1. On, to, or from the other side of. 2. Through or over the surface of. [< A-[1] + CROSS]

a·cros·tic (ə·krôs′tik) *n.* A poem or other composition in which initial or other letters, taken in order, form a word or phrase. [< Gk. *akros* at the end + *stichos* line of verse] —**a·cros′tic** *adj.* —**a·cros′ti·cal·ly** *adv.*

a·cryl·ic (ə·kril′ik) *n.* 1. A thermoplastic resin used in castings, adhesives, and coatings. Also **acrylic resin.** 2. A paint (**acrylic paint**) made from acrylic resin. 3. An acrylic resin painting. 4. A synthetic fiber (acrylic fiber).

acrylic acid *Chem.* Any of a series of acids having a sharp, acrid odor, and used in plastics.

act (akt) *v.t.* 1. To play the part of; impersonate, as in a drama. 2. To perform as if on a stage; feign the character of. 3. To behave as suitable to. —*v.i.* 4. To behave or conduct oneself. 5. To carry out a purpose or function; perform. 6. To produce an effect. 7. To serve temporarily or as a substitute, as in some office or capacity. 8. To perform on the stage; be an actor. 9. To pretend; play a part so as to appear. —**to act up** *Informal* To behave mischievously; appear troublesome. —*n.* 1. The exertion of mental or physical power; a doing: taken in the very *act.* 2. A law; edict. 3. One of the main divisions of a play or opera. 4. A short theatrical performance. 5. *Informal* Something feigned; a pose. [< L *actum* a thing done]

act·a·ble (ak′tə·bəl) *adj.* That can be acted, as a role in a play. —**act′a·bil′i·ty** *n.*

ACTH *A*drenocortico*t*rophic *h*ormone, a pituitary hormone that stimulates the secretion of cortisone by the adrenal cortex.

act·ing (ak′ting) *adj.* 1. Operating or officiating, especially in place of another: *acting* secretary. 2. Functioning; working. —*n.* 1. The occupation of an actor. 2. Pretense or simulation.

ac·ti·nide series (ak′ti·nīd) *Chem.* A series of radioactive elements beginning with actinium and ending with lawrencium.

ac·tin·ism (ak′tin·iz′əm) *n.* 1. The property of radiant energy that effects chemical changes. 2. The production of such change. —**ac·tin′ic** or **·i·cal** *adj.* —**ac·tin′i·cal·ly** *adv.*

ac·tin·i·um (ak·tin′ē·əm) *n.* A radioactive element (symbol Ac), isolated from pitchblende, and having a half life of about 13 years. [< Gk. *aktis, aktinos* ray]

ac·ti·noid (ak′ti·noid) *adj.* Having the form of rays; radiate, as a starfish.

ac·tion (ak′shən) *n.* 1. The process of acting, doing, or working; operation. 2. The result of putting forth power; a deed; act. 3. *pl.* Habitual behavior; conduct. 4. Activity; energy. 5. The exertion of power; influence. 6. *Mech.* The mechanism by which a machine operates. 7. *Mil.* A battle; combat. 8. *Law* A lawsuit. 9. In literature, the series of connected events that form the plot in a story or play. 10. *Slang* Lively or exciting social activity; excitement: where the *action* is. [< L *agere* to do]

ac·tion·a·ble (ak′shən·ə·bəl) *adj.* Affording ground for prosecution, as a trespass or a libel. —**ac′tion·a·bly** *adv.*

ac·ti·vate (ak′tə·vāt) *v.t.* **·vat·ed, ·vat·ing** 1. To make active. 2. To organize (a military unit) for its assigned function. 3. *Physics* To make radioactive. 4. *Chem.* To promote or hasten a reaction in, as by heat. —**ac′ti·va′tion** *n.* —**ac′ti·va′tor** *n.*

ac·tive (ak′tiv) *adj.* 1. Abounding in or exhibiting action; busy. 2. Being in or pertaining to a state of action; not extinct or quiescent. 3. Agile; quick; nimble. 4. Characterized by much activity; brisk; lively. 5. Bearing interest: *active* investments. 6. In business, busy; productive: *active* accounts. 7. *Gram.* Designating a voice of the verb that indicates that the subject of the sentence is performing the action. —*n. Gram.* The active voice. [< L *activus* < *agere* to do] —**ac′tive·ly** *adv.* —**ac′tive·ness** *n.*

ac·tiv·i·ty (ak·tiv′ə·tē) *n. pl.* **·ties** 1. The state of being active; action. 2. Brisk or vigorous movement or action; liveliness; energy. 3. A particular action or sphere of action.

act of God *Law* An event caused by the operations of nature and not due to human action or negligence.

ac·tor (ak′tər) *n.* 1. A player on the stage, in motion pictures, etc. 2. One who does something.

ac·tress (ak′tris) *n.* A woman who acts, as on the stage.

Acts of the Apostles The fifth book of the New Testament. Also **Acts.**

ac·tu·al (ak′cho͞o·əl) *adj.* 1. Existing in fact; real. 2. Being in existence or action now; existent; present. [< L *actus* a doing] —**ac′tu·al·ness** *n.*

ac·tu·al·i·ty (ak′cho͞o·al′ə·tē) *n. pl.* **·ties** 1. The state or quality of being actual; reality; realism. 2. *pl.* Actual circumstances or conditions.

ac·tu·al·ize (ak′cho͞o·əl·īz′) *v.t.* **·ized, ·iz·ing** 1. To make real; realize in action. 2. To represent realistically. —**ac′tu·al·i·za′tion** *n.*

ac·tu·al·ly (ak′cho͞o·əl·ē) *adv.* As a matter of fact; really.

ac·tu·ar·y (ak′cho͞o·er′ē) *n. pl.* **·ar·ies** A statistician who calculates and states risks, premiums, etc., for insurance purposes. [< L *actuarius* clerk] —**ac·tu·ar·i·al** (ak′cho͞o·âr′ē·əl) *adj.* —**ac′tu·ar′i·al·ly** *adv.*

ac·tu·ate (ak′cho͞o·āt) *v.t.* **·at·ed, ·at·ing** 1. To set into action or motion, as a mechanism. 2. To incite or influence to action. [< L *actus* a doing] —**ac′tu·a′tion** *n.* —**ac′tu·a′tor** *n.*

acu- *combining form* Needle; point. [< L *acus*]

a·cu·i·ty (ə·kyo͞o′ə·tē) *n.* Acuteness; sharpness. [< L *acus* needle]

a·cu·men (ə·kyo͞o′mən, ak′yo͞o·mən) *n.* Quickness of insight or discernment. [< L *acuere* to sharpen]

a·cu·mi·nate (ə·kyo͞o′mə·nāt; *for adj., also* -nit) *v.t.* **·nat·ed, ·nat·ing** To sharpen; make pointed. —*adj.* Ending in a long, tapering point, as a leaf, feather, fin, etc.: also **a·cu′mi·nat′ed.** [< L *acuminatus*, pp. of *acuminare* to point, sharpen] —**a·cu′mi·na′tion** *n.*

ac·u·punc·ture (ak′yə·pungk′chər) *n.* The practice, orig. Chinese, of puncturing the body at certain points with fine needles as a medical treatment. [< ACU- + PUNCTURE]

a·cute (ə·kyo͞ot′) *adj.* 1. Coming to a crisis quickly; violent: said of a disease: opposed to *chronic.* 2. Of the greatest importance; crucial. 3. Affecting keenly; poignant; intense. 4. Keenly discerning or sensitive. [< L *acutus*, pp. of *acuere* to sharpen] —**a·cute′ly** *adv.* —**a·cute′ness** *n.*

acute accent See ACCENT (def. 3).

acute angle *Geom.* An angle of less than 90°.

-acy *suffix of nouns* Forming nouns of quality, state, or condition from adjectives ending in

-acious, and nouns and adjectives ending in *-ate*: *fallacy, celibacy.* [< L *-acia, -atia* < Gk. *-ateia*]

ad (ad) *n.* 1. *Informal* An advertisement. 2. In tennis, advantage.

ad- *prefix* To; toward; near: *adhere*: also spelled *a-, ab-, ac-, af-, ag-, al-, an-, ap-, ar-* before various consonants. [< L *ad* to]

-ad *suffix of nouns* Of or pertaining to; used to form: **a** Collective numerals: *triad.* **b** Names of poems: *Iliad.* [< Gk. *-as, -ados*]

ad·age (ad′ij) *n.* A maxim; proverb. [< L *ad-* to + root of *aio* I say]

a·da·gio (ə·dä′jō, -zhē·ō, -zhō) *Music adj. & adv.* In slow time. **—***n.* A composition in adagio time. [< Ital.]

ad·a·mant (ad′ə·mənt, -mant) *n.* A very hard mineral. **—***adj.* 1. Immovable; unyielding. 2. Very hard. [< Gk. *a-* not + *damaein* to conquer] **—ad·a·man·tine** (ad′ə·man′tin, -tēn) *adj.*

Adam's apple The prominence made by the thyroid cartilage at the front of the human throat, conspicuous in males.

a·dapt (ə·dapt′) *v.t.* 1. To fit for a new use; make suitable. 2. To adjust (oneself or itself) to a new situation or environment. **—***v.i.* 3. To become adjusted to a circumstance or environment. [< L *ad-* to + *aptare* to fit] **—a·dapt′a·bil′i·ty** *n.* **—a·dapt′a·ble** *adj.*

ad·ap·ta·tion (ad′əp·tā′shən) *n.* 1. The act of adapting or the state of being adapted. 2. Anything produced by adapting. **—ad′ap·ta′tion·al** *adj.*

a·dapt·er (ə·dap′tər) *n.* 1. A person or thing that adapts. 2. *Mech.* **a** A device that connects parts not designed to fit together. **b** A device that extends or alters the function of an apparatus. Also **a·dap′tor.**

a·dap·tive (ə·dap′tiv) *adj.* Capable of, fit for, or manifesting adaptation. **—a·dap′·tive·ly** *adv.*

add (ad) *v.t.* 1. To join or unite, so as to increase the importance, size, quantity, or scope: with *to.* 2. To find the sum of, as a column of figures. 3. To say or write further. **—***v.i.* 4. To make or be an addition: with *to.* 5. To perform arithmetical addition. **—to add up** 1. To accumulate to a total. 2. *Informal* To make sense. [< L *ad-* to + *dare* to give, put] **—add′a·ble** or **add′i·ble** *adj.*

ad·dend (ad′ənd, ə·dend′) *n.* A number that is to be added to another.

ad·den·dum (ə·den′dəm) *n. pl.* **·da** A thing added; a supplement, as to a book. [< L, neut. gerundive of *addere* to add]

ad·der (ad′ər) *n.* 1. A viper, esp. the common European viper. 2. Any of various other snakes, as the puff adder. [ME *a nadder* < OE *nædre*]

ad·dict (*v.* ə·dikt′; *n.* ad′ikt) *v.t.* To devote (one) habitually: with *to.* **—***n.* One who is given to some habit, esp. to the use of drugs. [< L *ad-* to + *dicere* to say] **—ad·dic′tion, ad·dict′ed·ness** *n.* **—ad·dic′tive** *adj.*

ad·di·tion (ə·dish′ən) *n.* 1. The act of adding. 2. That which is added. 3. The combining of quantities in one sum. **—ad·di′tion·al** *adj.* **—ad·di′tion·al·ly** *adv.*

ad·di·tive (ad′ə·tiv) *n.* Something added or to be added to a product or device. **—ad′di·tive** *adj.* **—ad′di·tive·ly** *adv.*

ad·dle (ad′l) *v.t. & v.i.* **·dled, ·dling** 1. To become or cause to become confused. 2. To spoil, as eggs. [OE *adela* liquid filth]

ad·dle·brained (ad′l·brānd′) *adj.* Confused; mixed up. Also **ad′dle·head′ed, ad′dle·pat′·ed, ad′dle·wit′ted.**

ad·dress (ə·dres′; *for n. def. 2, also* ad′res) *v.t.* **·dressed, ·dress·ing** 1. To speak to. 2. To devote (oneself): with *to*: to *address* oneself to a task. 3. To mark with a destination, as a letter. **—***n.* 1. A formal discourse. 2. One's residence or other place to receive communications, as mail. 3. The manner of a person. 4. Adroitness; tact. [< OF < L *ad-* to + *directus* straight] **—ad·dress′er** or **ad·dress′or** *n.*

ad·dress·ee (ad′res·ē′, ə·dres′ē′) *n.* One to whom mail, etc., is addressed.

ad·duce (ə·do͞os′, ə·dyo͞os′) *v.t.* **·duced, ·duc·ing** To present for proof or consideration. [< L *ad-* to + *ducere* to lead] **—ad·duce′a·ble** or **ad·duc′i·ble** *adj.*

-ade *suffix* 1. Act or action: *cannonade.* 2. A fruit drink: *lemonade.* [< F < L *-ata*, fem. pp. ending]

ad·e·nine (ad′ə·nēn) *n. Chem.* A base that is a genetic coding constituent of DNA and RNA.

ad·e·noid (ad′ə·noid) *adj.* Of or like a gland. Also **ad′e·noi′dal.** **—***n. Usu. pl. Pathol.* An enlarged lymphoid growth behind the pharynx. [< Gk. *adēn* gland + -OID]

a·dept (ə·dept′) *adj.* Highly skilled; proficient. [< L *ad-* to + *apisci* to get] **—a·dept** (ə·dept′, ad′ept) *n.* **—a·dept′ly** *adv.* **—a·dept′ness** *n.*

ad·e·quate (ad′ə·kwit) *adj.* 1. Equal to what is required; fully sufficient. 2. Barely sufficient. [< L *ad-* to + *aequus* equal] **—ad′e·qua·cy, ad′e·quate·ness** *n.* **—ad′e·quate·ly** *adv.*

ad·here (ad·hir′) *v.i.* **·hered, ·her·ing** 1. To stick fast or together. 2. To be devoted, as to a cause. 3. To follow closely or without deviation. [< L *ad-* to + *haerere* to stick] **—ad·her′ence** *n.* **—ad·her′ent** *n.* **—ad·her′er** *n.*

ad·he·sion (ad·hē′zhən) *n.* 1. The state of being joined. 2. Firm attachment, as to a cause. 3. *Physics* The binding force exerted by molecules of unlike substances in contact. 4. *Med.* Abnormal surface union of dissimilar tissues. [See ADHERE.]

ad·he·sive (ad·hē′siv) *adj.* Tending to adhere. **—ad·he′sive** *n.* **—ad·he′sive·ly** *adv.* **—ad·he′sive·ness** *n.*

ad hoc (ad hok′) *Latin* For this purpose.

ad·i·a·bat·ic (ad′ē·ə·bat′ik, ā′dē·ə-) *adj. Physics* Occurring without gain or loss of heat. [< Gk. *a-* not + *dia-* through + *bainein* to go + -IC]

a·dieu (ə·do͞o′, ə·dyo͞o′; *Fr.* å·dyœ′) *n. pl.* **a·dieus,** *Fr.* **a·dieux** (å·dyœ′) A farewell. **—***interj.* Good-by: lit., to God (I commend you). [< F]

ad in·fi·ni·tum (ad in′fə·nī′təm) *Latin* Endlessly; forever.

ad in·ter·im (ad in′tə·rim) *Latin* In the meantime.

a·di·os (ä′dē·ōs′, ad′ē·ōs′; *Sp.* ä·thyōs′) *interj.* Farewell: lit., to God (I commend you). [< Sp.]

ad·i·pose (ad′ə·pōs) *adj.* Of or pertaining to fat; fatty. Also **ad·i·pous** (ad′ə·pəs). **—***n.*

Fat. [< L *adeps, adipis* fat] **—ad′i·pose′·ness, ad·i·pos·i·ty** (ad′ə·pos′ə·tē) *n.*

ad·ja·cent (ə·jā′sənt) *adj.* Lying near or close at hand; adjoining; contiguous. [< L *ad-* near + *jacere* to lie] **—ad·ja′cen·cy** *n.* **—ad·ja′cent·ly** *adv.*

ad·jec·tive (aj′ik·tiv) *n. Gram.* Any of a class of words used to limit or qualify a noun. [< L *adjicere* to add to < *ad-* to + *jacere* to throw] **—ad·jec·ti·val** (aj′ik·tī′vəl) *adj.* **—ad′jec·ti′val·ly** *adv.*

ad·join (ə·join′) *v.t.* 1. To be next to; border upon. *—v.i.* 2. To lie close together. [< L < *ad-* to + *jungere* to join] **—ad·join′ing** *adj.*

ad·journ (ə·jûrn′) *v.t.* 1. To put off to another time. *—v.i.* 2. To come to a close. 3. *Informal* To move or go to another place. [< L *ad-* to + *diurnus* daily] **—ad·journ′·ment** *n.*

ad·judge (ə·juj′) *v.t.* **·judged, ·judg·ing** 1. To decide judicially, as a case. 2. To order by law. 3. To award by law, as damages. [< L *ad-* to + *judicare* to judge]

ad·ju·di·cate (ə·jo͞o′də·kāt) *v.t. & v.i.* **·cat·ed, ·cat·ing** To determine judicially. **—ad·ju′di·ca′tion** *n.* **—ad·ju′di·ca′tor** *n.*

ad·junct (aj′ungkt) *n.* Something joined in a subordinate position. [See ADJOIN.] **—ad′·junct, ad·junc·tive** (ə·jungk′tiv) *adj.* **—ad·junc′tive·ly** *adv.*

ad·jure (ə·jo͝or′) *v.t.* **·jured, ·jur·ing** To charge or entreat solemnly. [< L *ad-* to + *jurare* to swear] **—ad·ju·ra·tion** (aj′o͞o·rā′·shən) *n.* **—ad·jur′a·to′ry** *adj.* **—ad·jur′er** or **ad·ju′ror** *n.*

ad·just (ə·just′) *v.t.* 1. To arrange so as to fit or match. 2. To settle, as differences, claims, or figures. 3. To regulate or make accurate. *—v.i.* 4. To adapt oneself. [< L *ad-* to + *juxta* near; refashioned on F *juste* right < L *justus*] **—ad·just′a·ble** *adj.* **—ad·just′er** or **ad·jus′tor** *n.* **—ad·jus′tive** *adj.* **—ad·just′·ment** *n.*

ad·ju·tant (aj′o͞o·tənt) *n. Mil.* A staff officer who assists a commanding officer in administrative duties. [< L *adjutare* to assist] **—ad′ju·tan·cy, ad′ju·tant·ship** *n.*

ad-lib (ad′lib′) *Informal v.t. & v.i.* **-libbed, -lib·bing** To improvise in performance. [< AD LIBITUM] **—ad′-lib′** *n. & adj.* **—ad lib** *adv.*

ad lib·i·tum (ad lib′ə·təm) *Music* Freely; to be played as the performer wishes. [< L]

ad·min·is·ter (ad·min′is·tər) *v.t.* 1. To direct or manage. 2. To apply, as treatment. 3. To inflict; mete out. 4. To tender, as an oath. *—v.i.* 5. To help; minister: with *to.* Also **ad·min·is·trate** (ad·min′is·trāt). [< L *ad-* to + *ministrare* to serve] **—ad·min·is·te·ri·al** (ad·min′is·tir′ē·əl) *adj.* **—ad·min′·is·tra·ble** *adj.*

ad·min·is·tra·tion (ad·min′is·trā′shən) *n.* 1. The act of administering, or the state of being administered. 2. The executive personnel of a government, institution, etc.; also, their policies. **—ad·min′is·tra′tive** *adj.* **—ad·min′is·tra′tive·ly** *adv.*

ad·min·is·tra·tor (ad·min′is·trā′tər) *n.* 1. One who administers something; an executive. 2. *Law* One commissioned to administer the property of a deceased or incompetent person. [< L] **—ad·min′is·tra′tor·ship** *n.*

ad·mi·ra·ble (ad′mər·ə·bəl) *adj.* Worthy of admiration; excellent. **—ad′mi·ra·ble·ness, ad′mi·ra·bil′i·ty** *n.* **—ad′mi·ra·bly** *adv.*

ad·mi·ral (ad′mər·əl) *n.* 1. The supreme commander of a navy or fleet. 2. A naval rank above commodore. [< Arabic *amīr-al* commander of the]

Admiral of the Fleet The highest rank in the U.S. Navy, corresponding to General of the Army. Also *Fleet Admiral.*

ad·mi·ral·ty (ad′mər·əl·tē) *n. pl.* **·ties** 1. The office of an admiral. 2. *Law* Maritime law or courts. 3. *cap.* The British naval department.

ad·mire (ad·mīr′) *v.t.* **·mired, ·mir·ing** 1. To regard with wonder, pleasure, and approbation. 2. To have respect for. [< L *ad-* at + *mirari* to wonder] **—ad·mi·ra·tion** (ad′mə·rā′shən) *n.* **—ad·mir′er** *n.* **—ad·mir′ing** *adj.* **—ad·mir′ing·ly** *adv.*

ad·mis·si·ble (ad·mis′ə·bəl) *adj.* Worthy of being considered; allowable. **—ad·mis′si·bil′·i·ty, ad·mis′si·ble·ness** *n.* **—ad·mis′si·bly** *adv.*

ad·mis·sion (ad·mish′ən) *n.* 1. The act of admitting. 2. Authority to enter. 3. An entrance fee. 4. Anything conceded. **—ad·mis′sive** (-mis′iv), **ad·mis′so·ry** (-mis′ər·ē) *adj.*

ad·mit (ad·mit′) *v.* **·mit·ted, ·mit·ting** *v.t.* 1. To allow to enter. 2. To allow to join. 3. To have room or possibility for. 4. To concede or avow. *—v.i.* 5. To afford possibility or opportunity: This problem *admits* of several solutions. [< L *ad-* to + *mittere* to send] **—ad·mit′ted·ly** *adv.*

ad·mit·tance (ad·mit′ns) *n.* 1. The act of admitting, or the fact of being admitted; entrance. 2. Right or permission to enter.

ad·mix (ad·miks′) *v.t. & v.i.* **·mixed** or **·mixt, ·mix·ing** To mingle or mix with something else. [< L *ad-* to + *miscere* to mix]

ad·mix·ture (ad·miks′chər) *n.* 1. The state of being mixed. 2. Anything added in mixing.

ad·mon·ish (ad·mon′ish) *v.t.* 1. To administer mild reproof to. 2. To caution against. [< L *ad-* to + *monere* to warn **—ad·mon′ish·er** *n.* **—ad·mo·ni·tion** (ad′·mə·nish′ən) *n.* **—ad·mon′i·to′ry** *adj.*

ad nau·se·am (ad nô′zē·əm, -sē-, -zhē-, -shē-; äd) *Latin* To the point of nausea or disgust.

a·do (ə·do͞o′) *n.* Activity; bustle; fuss. [ME *at do* to do]

a·do·be (ə·dō′bē) *n.* 1. An unburnt, sun-dried brick. 2. The clay of which such bricks are made. 3. A structure made of such bricks. [< Sp.] **—a·do′be** *adj.*

ad·o·les·cence (ad′ə·les′əns) *n.* The period of growth from puberty to adulthood. Also **ad′o·les′cen·cy.** [< L *ad-* to + *alescere* to grow]

ad·o·les·cent (ad′ə·les′ənt) *adj.* 1. Approaching adulthood. 2. Characteristic of or pertaining to youth. *—n.* A person in the period of adolescence.

A·don·is (ə·don′is, ə·dō′nis) *n.* A man of rare beauty. [after Gk. *Adōnis* a youth loved by Aphrodite]

a·dopt (ə·dopt′) *v.t.* 1. To take into one's family or as one's child. 2. To follow as one's own, as a course of action. 3. To put into effect. [< L *ad-* to + *optare* to choose] **—a·dopt′a·ble** *adj.* **—a·dopt′er** *n.* **—a·dop′·tion** *n.* **—a·dop′tive** *adj.* **—a·dop′tive·ly** *adv.*

a·dor·a·ble (ə·dôr′ə·bəl) *adj.* 1. Worthy of

adoration. 2. *Informal* Delightful; lovable. **—a·dor′a·ble·ness, a·dor′a·bil′i·ty** *n.* **—a·dor′a·bly** *adv.*
a·dore (ə·dôr′) *v.t.* **·dored, ·dor·ing** 1. To render divine honors to; worship. 2. To love or honor with intense devotion. 3. *Informal* To like especially. [< L *ad-* to + *orare* to speak, pray] **—ad·o·ra·tion** (ad′ə·rā′shən) *n.* **—a·dor′er** *n.* **—a·dor′ing·ly** *adv.*
a·dorn (ə·dôrn′) *v.t.* To decorate with or as with ornaments. [< L *ad-* to + *ornare* to deck out] **—a·dorn′er** *n.* **—a·dorn′ment** *n.*
ad·re·nal (ə·drē′nəl) *Physiol.* *n.* An adrenal gland. **—*adj.*** Of or from the adrenal glands. [< L *ad-* near + RENAL]
adrenal gland One of a pair of ductless glands near the kidneys, secreting epinephrine and certain steroids. Also called *suprarenal gland.*
Ad·ren·a·lin (ə·dren′ə·lin) *n.* Proprietary name for a brand of epinephrine. Also **ad·ren′a·line** (-lin).
ad·re·no·cor·ti·co·tro·phic hormone (ə·drē′·nō·kôr′ti·kō·trō′fik) *Physiol.* ACTH.
a·drift (ə·drift′) *adv. & adj.* Without moorings; drifting.
a·droit (ə·droit′) *adj.* Skillful; expert. [< F *à* to + *droit* right] **—a·droit′ly** *adv.* **—a·droit′ness** *n.*
ad·sorb (ad·sôrb′, -zôrb′) *v.t.* *Chem.* To hold molecules on the surface of (a solid) by electrochemical attraction. [< L *ad-* to + *sorbere* to suck in] **—ad·sor′bent** *n. & adj.* **—ad·sorp·tion** (ad·sôrp′shən, -zôrp′-) *n.* **—ad·sorp·tive** (ad·sôrp′tiv, -zôrp′-) *adj.*
ad·u·late (aj′o͝o·lāt) *v.t.* **·lat·ed, ·lat·ing** To flatter or praise extravagantly. [< L *adulari* to fawn] **—ad′u·la′tion** *n.* **—ad′u·la′tor** *n.* **—ad·u·la·to·ry** (aj′o͝o·lə·tôr′ē) *adj.*
a·dult (ə·dult′, ad′ult) *n.* 1. A person who has attained the age of maturity or legal majority. 2. *Biol.* A fully developed animal or plant. [< L *ad-* to + *alescere* to grow] **—a·dult′** *adj.* **—a·dult′hood** *n.* **—a·dult′ness** *n.*
a·dul·ter·ant (ə·dul′tər·ənt) *n.* An adulterating substance. **—a·dul′ter·ant** *adj.*
a·dul·ter·ate (ə·dul′tə·rāt; *for adj., also* -tər·it) *v.t.* **·at·ed, ·at·ing** To make impure or inferior by admixture of other ingredients. **—*adj.*** Corrupted; debased. [< L *ad-* to + *alter* other, different] **—a·dul′ter·a′tion** *n.* **—a·dul′ter·a′tor** *n.*
a·dul·ter·y (ə·dul′tər·ē) *n. pl.* **·ter·ies** The voluntary sexual intercourse of a married person with someone not the spouse. [< L *adulterium*] **—a·dul′ter·er** *n.* **—a·dul′ter·ess** (-tər·is, -tris) *n. fem.* **—a·dul′ter·ous** *adj.* **—a·dul′ter·ous·ly** *adv.*
ad·um·brate (ad′um·brāt, ə·dum′-) *v.t.* **·brat·ed, ·brat·ing** 1. To outline sketchily. 2. To overshadow; darken. [< L *ad-* to + *umbrare* to shade] **—ad′um·bra′tion** *n.* **—ad·um·bra·tive** (ə·dum′brə·tiv) *adj.*
ad va·lo·rem (ad və·lôr′əm) *Latin* In proportion to the value.
ad·vance (ad·vans′) *v.* **·vanced, ·vanc·ing** *v.t.* 1. To move forward or upward. 2. To offer; propose. 3. To further; promote. 4. To make occur earlier. 5. To raise (a rate, price, etc.). 6. To pay, as money or interest, before legally due. 7. To lend, as money. **—*v.i.*** 8. To move or go forward. 9. To make progress. **—*adj.*** 1. Being before in time. 2. Being or going before. **—*n.*** 1. The act of going forward. 2. Improvement; promotion. 3. An increase or rise, as of prices. 4. *pl.* Personal approaches; overtures. 5. Goods or money supplied on credit. **—in advance** Before due; beforehand. [< OF *avancier* < L *ab-* away + *ante* before] **—ad·vanc′er** *n.* **—ad·vance′ment** *n.*
ad·vanced (ad·vanst′) *adj.* 1. In advance of others, as in progress or thought. 2. In front; moved forward. 3. At a late or forward stage, as of life, time, etc.
ad·van·tage (ad·van′tij) *n.* 1. Any circumstance favoring success. 2. Benefit or gain. 3. A better state or position; superiority. 4. In tennis, the first point scored after deuce. **—to take advantage of** 1. To avail oneself of. 2. To impose upon; use selfishly. [< OF *avant* before < L *ab ante* from before]
ad·van·ta·geous (ad′vən·tā′jəs) *adj.* Profitable; favorable; beneficial. **—ad′van·ta′geous·ly** *adv.* **—ad′van·ta′geous·ness** *n.*
ad·vent (ad′vent) *n.* A coming or arrival. [< L *ad-* to + *venire* to come]
Ad·vent (ad′vent) *n.* 1. The birth of Christ. 2. The Second Coming of Christ as promised in scripture. 3. The season prior to Christmas.
Ad·vent·ist (ad′ven·tist, ad·ven′-) *n.* A member of a denomination that believes the Second Coming of Christ is imminent. The largest U.S. Adventist bodies are the **Advent Christian Church** and the **Seventh-Day Adventists.**
ad·ven·ti·tious (ad′ven·tish′əs) *adj.* 1. Not inherent; accidentally acquired. 2. *Biol.* Occurring abnormally in development or habitat. [< L *adventicius* coming from abroad] **—ad′ven·ti′tious·ly** *adv.* **—ad′ven·ti′tious·ness** *n.*
ad·ven·ture (ad·ven′chər) *n.* 1. A hazardous or perilous undertaking. 2. A stirring or thrilling experience. 3. A commercial speculation. [< L *adventura* about to happen] **—ad·ven′ture** *v.i. & v.t.* **·tured, ·tur·ing**
ad·ven·tur·er (ad·ven′chər·ər) *n.* 1. One who seeks after or takes part in adventures. 2. A person who seeks advancement by questionable means. **—ad·ven′tur·ess** *n. fem.*
ad·ven·tur·ous (ad·ven′chər·əs) *adj.* 1. Disposed to seek adventures or take risks; venturesome. Also **ad·ven′ture·some** (-səm). 2. Attended with risk; hazardous. **—ad·ven′tur·ous·ly** *adv.* **—ad·ven′tur·ous·ness** *n.*
ad·verb (ad′vûrb) *n.* *Gram.* Any of a class of words used to modify the meaning of a verb, adjective, or other adverb. [< L *ad-* to + *verbum* verb] **—ad·ver′bi·al** *adj.* **—ad·ver′bi·al·ly** *adv.*
ad·ver·sar·y (ad′vər·ser′ē) *n. pl.* **·sar·ies** One actively opposed to another.
ad·ver·sa·tive (ad·vûr′sə·tiv) *adj.* Expressing opposition or antithesis. **—*n.*** An antithetic word or proposition. [< L *adversatus* opposite] **—ad·ver′sa·tive·ly** *adv.*
ad·verse (ad·vûrs′, ad′vûrs) *adj.* 1. Opposed; antagonistic. 2. Unpropitious; detrimental. 3. Opposite. [< L *ad-* to + *vertere* to turn] **—ad·verse′ly** *adv.* **—ad·verse′ness** *n.*
ad·ver·si·ty (ad·vûr′sə·tē) *n. pl.* **·ties** A condition of hardship or affliction.
ad·vert (ad·vûrt′) *v.i.* To call attention; refer: with *to.* [< L *ad-* to + *vertere* to turn]
ad·ver·tent (ad·vûr′tənt) *adj.* Giving attention; heedful. **—ad·ver′tence, ad·ver′ten·cy** *n.* **—ad·ver′tent·ly** *adv.*
ad·ver·tise (ad′vər·tīz, ad′vər·tīz′) *v.t.*

•tised, •tis•ing To make known by public notice, generally in order to sell. Also **ad′ver•tize.** [< L *advertere* to direct one's attention to] —**ad′ver•tis′er** *n.*

ad•ver•tise•ment (ad′vər•tīz′mənt, ad•vûr′•tis•mənt, -tiz-) *n.* A public notice, usually seeking to sell. Also **ad′ver•tize′ment.** Abbr. *ad., adv., advt.*

ad•ver•tis•ing (ad′vər•tī′zing) *n.* 1. Advertisements collectively. 2. The business of making advertisements. Also **ad′ver•tiz′ing.**

ad•vice (ad•vīs′) *n.* 1. Counsel given to encourage or dissuade. 2. *Often pl.* Information; notification. [< L *ad-* to + *videre* to see]

ad•vis•a•ble (ad•vī′zə•bəl) *adj.* Proper to be recommended. —**ad•vis′a•bil′i•ty, ad•vis′a•ble•ness** *n.* —**ad•vis′a•bly** *adv.*

ad•vise (ad•vīz′) *v.* •vised, •vis•ing *v.t.* 1. To give advice to; counsel. 2. To recommend. 3. To notify; inform: with *of.* —*v.i.* 4. To take counsel: with *with.* [< L *ad-* to + *videre* to see] —**ad•vis′er** or **ad•vis′or** *n.*

ad•vised (ad•vīzd′) *adj.* Planned; deliberate: chiefly in *ill-advised, well-advised.* —**ad•vis′ed•ly** *adv.*

ad•vise•ment (ad•vīz′mənt) *n.* Consultation; deliberation.

ad•vi•so•ry (ad•vī′zər•ē) *adj.* 1. Having power to advise. 2. Given as advice; not mandatory.

ad•vo•cate (*v.* ad′və•kāt; *for n., also* -kit) *v.t.* •cat•ed, •cat•ing To speak or write in favor of; defend; recommend. —*n.* One who pleads the cause of another; an intercessor. [< L *ad-* to + *vocare* to call] —**ad•vo•ca•cy** (ad′və•kə•sē) *n.* —**ad′vo•ca′tor** *n.* —**ad•voc•a•to•ry** (ad•vok′ə•tôr′ē) *adj.*

adz (adz) *n.* A hand cutting tool with its blade at right angles to its handle. Also **adze.** [OE *adesa*]

ae•gis (ē′jis) *n.* A protecting influence; sponsoring agency or power. Also spelled *egis.* [< Gk. *aigis* goatskin]

-aemia See -EMIA.

ae•o•li•an (ē•ō′lē•ən) *adj.* Pertaining to or caused by the winds. Also spelled *eolian.* [after L *Aeolus,* god of the winds]

ae•on (ē′ən, ē′on) See EON.

aer- Var. of AERO-.

aer•ate (âr′āt) *v.t.* •at•ed, •at•ing 1. To supply or charge with air or gas. 2. To purify by exposure to air. —**aer•a′tion** *n.* —**aer′a•tor** *n.*

aeri- Var. of AERO-.

aer•i•al (âr′ē•əl) *adj.* 1. Of or in the air. 2. Light as air; airy; intangible. 3. Of, by, or pertaining to aircraft. —*n.* An antenna, as in television. [< L *aer* air] —**aer′i•al•ly** *adv.*

aer•i•al•ist (âr′ē•əl•ist) *n.* One who performs on a tightrope, trapeze, etc.

aer•ie (âr′ē, ir′ē) *n.* A high nest, as of an eagle. Also spelled *aery, eyrie.* [< L *area* open space]

aer•i•fy (âr′ə•fī) *v.t.* •fied, •fy•ing 1. To aerate. 2. To change into a gaseous form. —**aer′i•fi•ca′tion** *n.*

aero- *combining form* 1. Air; of the air. 2. Of aircraft. 3. Gas; of gases. Also *aer-, aeri-.* [< Gk. *aēr* air]

aer•obe (âr′ōb) *n.* A microorganism that requires free oxygen. [< AERO- + Gk. *bios* life] —**aer•o′bic** *adj.*

aer•o•bics (âr•ō′biks) *n.pl.* (*construed as sing. or pl.*) Exercises emphasizing increased oxygen consumption without muscle strain. [< AERO- + Gk. *bios* life]

aer•o•drome (âr′ə•drōm) *n. Brit.* An airport.

aer•o•dy•nam•ics (âr′ō•dī•nam′iks) *n.pl.* (*construed as sing.*) The branch of physics that treats of the laws of motion of gases. —**aer′o•dy•nam′ic** *adj.* —**aer′o•dy•nam′i•cal•ly** *adv.*

aer•ol•o•gy (âr•ol′ə•jē) *n. pl.* •gies The scientific study of the atmosphere. —**aer•o•log•ic** (âr′ə•loj′ik) or •i•cal *adj.* —**aer•ol′o•gist** *n.*

aer•o•naut (âr′ə•nôt) *n.* One who pilots a balloon or dirigible. [< AERO- + Gk. *nautēs* sailor]

aer•o•nau•tics (âr′ə•nô′tiks) *n.pl.* (*construed as sing.*) 1. The science or art of navigating aircraft. 2. The design and performance of aircraft. —**aer′o•nau′tic** or •ti•cal *adj.*

aer•o•pause (âr′ə•pôz) *n. Meteorol.* The atmosphere near outer space.

aer•o•plane (âr′ə•plān) *n. Brit.* An airplane.

aer•o•sol (âr′ə•sōl, -sol) *n.* 1. A suspension of solid or liquid particles in a gas. 2. A gas-charged dispenser of aerosol: also **aerosol bomb.**

aer•o•space (âr′ō•spās) *n.* The earth's atmosphere and outer space. —*adj.* Designating the technology of aviation and space flight.

aer•y (âr′ē, ir′ē) See AERIE.

aes•thete (es′thēt) See ESTHETE.

aes•ti•val (es′tə•vəl, es•tī′-) See ESTIVAL.

ae•ther (ē′thər) See ETHER.

a•far (ə•fär′) *adv.* At, from, or to a distance; remotely.

af•fa•ble (af′ə•bəl) *adj.* Easy to approach; friendly. [< L *ad-* to + *fari* to speak] —**af′•fa•bil′i•ty, af′fa•ble•ness** *n.* —**af′fa•bly** *adv.*

af•fair (ə•fâr′) *n.* 1. Anything done or to be done. 2. *pl.* Matters of business or concern. 3. A party or entertainment. 4. A love affair. [< L *ad-* to + *facere* to do]

af•fect[1] (*v.* ə•fekt′; *n.* af′ekt) *v.t.* 1. To have an effect upon. 2. To move emotionally. —*n. Psychol.* Emotion; feeling. [< L *ad-* to + *facere* to do; noun < G *affekt*]

af•fect[2] (ə•fekt′) *v.t.* 1. To adopt as one's style. 2. To imitate. [< L *affectare* to aim at] —**af•fect′er** *n.*

af•fec•ta•tion (af′ek•tā′shən) *n.* A studied pretense; artificiality.

af•fect•ed (ə•fek′tid) *adj.* 1. Artificial; feigned. 2. Showing affectation. —**af•fect′ed•ly** *adv.* —**af•fect′ed•ness** *n.*

af•fect•ing (ə•fek′ting) *adj.* Stirring tender emotions. —**af•fect′ing•ly** *adv.*

af•fec•tion (ə•fek′shən) *n.* 1. Fond attachment or kind feeling. 2. A disease.

af•fec•tion•ate (ə•fek′shən•it) *adj.* Having affection; loving. —**af•fec′tion•ate•ly** *adv.* —**af•fec′tion•ate•ness** *n.*

af•fer•ent (af′ər•ənt) *adj. Physiol.* Conducting inward, or toward a center. [< L *ad-* to + *ferre* to bear]

af•fi•ance (ə•fī′əns) *v.t.* •anced, •anc•ing To promise in marriage; betroth. [< OF *afiance* trust, confidence] —**af•fi′an•cer** *n.*

af•fi•da•vit (af′ə•dā′vit) *n. Law* A sworn, written declaration. [< Med.L, he has stated on oath]

af•fil•i•ate (*v.* ə•fil′ē•āt; *n.* ə•fil′ē•it) *v.t. &*

v.i. **·at·ed, ·at·ing** To associate, as a member or branch: with *to* or *with.* —*n.* An affiliated person, company, etc. [< L *affiliare* to adopt < *ad-* to + *filius* son] —**af·fil′i·a′·tion** *n.*

af·fin·i·ty (ə·fin′ə·tē) *n. pl.* **·ties** 1. A natural attraction. 2. Any close relationship. 3. Relationship by marriage. [< L *affinis* adjacent, related < *ad-* to + *finis* end]

af·firm (ə·fûrm′) *v.t.* 1. To declare or state positively. 2. To confirm or ratify. —*v.i.* 3. *Law* To make a formal declaration, but not under oath. [< L *ad-* to + *firmare* to make firm] —**af·firm′a·ble** *adj.* —**af·firm′a·bly** *adv.* —**af·firm′ance** *n.* —**af·firm′ant** *adj. & n.* —**af·fir·ma·tion** (af′ər·mā′shən) *n.* —**af·firm′er** *n.*

af·firm·a·tive (ə·fûr′mə·tiv) *adj.* 1. Asserting that the fact is so. 2. Asserting positive ideas. Also **af·firm′a·to′ry.** —*n.* An expression of assent. —**af·firm′a·tive·ly** *adv.*

af·fix (*v.* ə·fiks′; *n.* af′iks) *v.t.* 1. To attach; fasten. 2. To assign, as blame. —*n. Gram.* A prefix, suffix, or infix to a word. [< L *affigere* < *ad-* to + *figere* to fasten]

af·fla·tus (ə·flā′təs) *n.* Any creative inspiration. [< L *ad-* to + *flare* to blow]

af·flict (ə·flikt′) *v.t.* To cause to suffer. [< L *ad-* to + *fligere* to dash, strike] —**af·flict′er** *n.* —**af·flic′tion** *n.* —**af·flic′tive** *adj.* —**af·flic′tive·ly** *adv.*

af·flu·ent (af′lo͞o·ənt) *adj.* 1. Abounding; abundant. 2. Wealthy; opulent. [< L *ad-* to + *fluere* to flow] —**af′flu·ence** *n.* —**af′flu·ent·ly** *adv.*

af·ford (ə·fôrd′) *v.t.* 1. To have sufficient means for. 2. To incur without detriment. 3. To provide or furnish. [OE *geforthian* to further, promote] —**af·ford′a·ble** *adj.*

af·fray (ə·frā′) *n.* A public brawl or fight. [< OF *effrei*]

af·front (ə·frunt′) *v.t.* 1. To insult openly. 2. To confront in defiance. —*n.* An insult. [< LL *affrontare* to strike against] —**af·front′er** *n.* —**af·fron′tive** *adj.*

af·ghan (af′gən, -gan) *n.* A wool coverlet, knitted or crocheted in colors.

Af·ghan (af′gan, -gən) *n.* A native of Afghanistan. —*adj.* Of or pertaining to Afghanistan, its inhabitants, etc.

a·fi·cio·na·do (ə·fish′ə·nä′dō, *Sp.* ä·fē·thyō·nä′thō, -fē·syō-) *n. pl.* **·dos** (-dōz, *Sp.* -thos) An avid follower; devotee. [< Sp.]

a·field (ə·fēld′) *adv.* 1. Off the track; astray. 2. In or to the field.

a·fire (ə·fīr′) *adv. & adj.* On fire.

a·flame (ə·flām′) *adv. & adj.* Flaming.

af·la·tox·in (af′lə·tok′sin) *n.* A toxin thought to be carcinogenic, produced by molds in corn and other meals.

a·float (ə·flōt′) *adv. & adj.* 1. Floating; not touching land. 2. Overflowed; flooded.

a·foot (ə·fo͝ot′) *adv.* 1. On foot. 2. In progress or motion; astir. [ME *on fot*]

afore- *combining form* Before or previously: **aforecited, aforegiven, aforementioned, aforesaid, aforetime, aforetold.** [OE *onforan,* blended with *æt-foran* before]

a·fore·thought (ə·fôr′thôt′) *adj.* Intended beforehand: malice *aforethought.*

a·foul (ə·foul′) *adv. & adj.* Entangled. —**to run afoul of** To get into difficulties with.

a·fraid (ə·frād′) *adj.* 1. Filled with fear. 2. Regretful to say: I'm *afraid* you are wrong. [Orig. pp. of verb *affray*]

A-frame (ā′frām′) *n.* A building shaped like the capital letter A in front and back.

a·fresh (ə·fresh′) *adv.* Once more; anew.

Af·ri·can (af′ri·kən) *adj.* Of or pertaining to Africa or its inhabitants. —*n.* 1. A native inhabitant of Africa. 2. A member of one of the African peoples.

Af·ri·kaans (af′ri·käns′, -känz′) *n.* The Dutch dialect spoken in South Africa.

Af·ri·ka·ner (af′ri·kä′nər) *n.* An Afrikaans-speaking South African of Dutch ancestry.

Af·ro (af′rō) *n. pl.* **Af·ros** A hair style in which tightly curled hair is allowed to assume a natural rounded mass. Also **af′ro.**

Af·ro-A·mer·i·can (af′rō·ə·mer′ə·kən) *adj.* Of or pertaining to Americans of black African descent. —**Af′ro-A·mer′i·can** *n.*

aft (aft) *adv. Naut.* At or toward the stern. [OE *æftan* behind]

af·ter (af′tər) *prep.* 1. Following in position or time: day *after* day. 2. In search or pursuit of: to strive *after* wisdom. 3. Concerning: to inquire *after* one's health. 4. In conformity with: a man *after* my own heart. 5. In honor of: named *after* him. —*adv.* Following in position or time. —*adj.* 1. Following in time or place: in *after* years. 2. *Naut.* Toward the stern. —*conj.* Following the time that: *After* I went home, I ate. [OE *æfter*]

af·ter·birth (af′tər·bûrth′) *n.* The placenta and fetal membranes expelled from the uterus after childbirth.

af·ter·burn·er (af′tər·bûr′nər) *n.* 1. A device for injecting fuel into the exhaust of a jet engine to increase thrust. 2. A device for breaking down unburned compounds in an automobile exhaust. —**af′ter·burn′ing** *n.*

af·ter·ef·fect (af′tər·ə·fekt′) *n.* An effect succeeding its cause after an interval.

af·ter·glow (af′tər·glō′) *n.* A glow after a light has disappeared.

af·ter·im·age (af′tər·im′ij) *n. Physiol.* The persistence of an image after stimulation.

af·ter·math (af′tər·math′) *n.* Result; consequence. [AFTER + OE *mæth* harvest]

af·ter·noon (af′tər·no͞on′) *n.* 1. The part of the day between noon and sunset. 2. The later part: *afternoon* of life. —**af′ter·noon′** *adj.*

af·ter·taste (af′tər·tāst′) *n.* A taste persisting after eating.

af·ter·thought (af′tər·thôt′) *n.* An idea that occurs to one after decision or action.

af·ter·ward (af′tər·wərd) *adv.* In time following. Also **af′ter·wards.** [OE *æfterweard*]

a·gain (ə·gen′, *esp. Brit.* ə·gān′) *adv.* 1. Once more; anew. 2. Once repeated. 3. To the same place; over the same course; back. 4. Further; moreover. 5. On the other hand. [OE *ongegn*]

a·gainst (ə·genst′, *esp. Brit.* ə·gānst′) *prep.* 1. In the opposite direction to. 2. In contact or collision with; upon. 3. In opposition to; contrary to. 4. In preparation for. 5. To the debit of. [OE *ongegn* again + *-es,* adv. suffix]

a·gape (ə·gāp′, ə·gap′) *adv. & adj.* Gaping.

a·gar-a·gar (ā′gär·ā′gär, ā′gər-, ā′gär-, ag′ər-) *n.* A gelatinous substance obtained from seaweeds, used as a thickener or as an emulsifier and in culture mediums. Also **a′gar.** [< Malay]

ag·ate (ag′it) *n.* 1. A quartz with usually banded colors. 2. A playing marble. [after Gk. *Achatēs*, a river in Sicily] —**ag′ate** *adj.*

a·ga·ve (ə·gä′vē) *n.* Any desert plant of the amaryllis family, as the century plant. [after Gk. *Agauē*, a proper name]

age (āj) *n.* 1. The period of existence of a person, thing, nation, etc. 2. The time of maturity, when full civil rights are attained. 3. The closing period of life. 4. Any notable period in history. 5. *Informal* A long time. —*v.t. & v.i.* **aged, ag·ing** or **age·ing** 1. To make or become old. 2. To undergo or subject to, as a food or beverage, so as to bring to a ripe or usable state. [< L *aetas* age, span of life]

-age *suffix of nouns* 1. Collection or aggregate of: *leafage.* 2. Condition, office, service, or other relation or connection of: *haulage.* [< OF < L *-aticum*, neut. adj. suffix]

a·ged (ā′jid *for defs. 1 & 2;* ājd *for defs. 3 & 4*) *adj.* 1. Advanced in years; old. 2. Characteristic of old age. 3. At the age of: a child *aged* six. 4. Treated by aging. —**a′ged·ness** *n.*

age·ism (āj′iz·əm) *n.* Social discrimination against the elderly. [by analogy with RACISM] —**age′ist** *n.*

age·less (āj′lis) *adj.* 1. Not seeming to grow old. 2. Having no limits of duration; eternal.

a·gen·cy (ā′jən·sē) *n. pl.* **·cies** 1. Means; instrumentality. 2. An establishment where business is done for others. 3. The office or function of an agent. [< L *agere* to do]

a·gen·da (ə·jen′də) *n.* A list of things to be done, esp. a program for a meeting. [< L, pl. of *agendum* < *agere* to do]

a·gent (ā′jənt) *n.* 1. One who or that which acts. 2. One who acts for another. 3. A means by which something is done. [< L *agens, agentis*, ppr. of *agere* to do] —**a·gen·tial** (ā·jen′shəl) *adj.*

a·gent pro·vo·ca·teur (å·zhäṅ′ prô·vô·kå·tœr′) *pl.* **a·gents pro·vo·ca·teurs** (å·zhäṅ′ prô·vô·kå·tœr′) *French* A secret agent employed to incite a person or group to actions that will incur punishment.

ag·gior·na·men·to (ə·jôr′nə·men′tō) *n.* Adaptation, as of old customs and principles, to contemporary mores; modernization. [< Ital. *aggionare* to bring up to date]

ag·glom·er·ate (ə·glom′ə·rāt; *for adj. & n., also* -ər·it) *v.t. & v.i.* **·at·ed, ·at·ing** To gather, form, or grow into a mass. —*adj.* Gathered into a mass. —*n.* A mass of varied things. [< L *ad-* to + *glomerare* to gather into a ball] —**ag·glom′er·a′tion** *n.* —**ag·glom′er·a′tive** *adj.*

ag·glu·ti·nate (ə·gloo͞′tə·nāt; *for adj., also* -nit) *v.t. & v.i.* **·nat·ed, ·nat·ing** 1. To join by adhesion. 2. *Physiol.* To mass together, as bacteria. —*adj.* Joined by adhesion. [< L *ad-* to + *glutinare* to glue] —**ag·glu′ti·na′·tion** *n.* —**ag·glu′ti·na′tive** *adj.*

ag·gran·dize (ə·gran′dīz, ag′rən·dīz) *v.t.* **·dized, ·diz·ing** 1. To make greater. 2. To make appear greater; exalt. [< L *ad-* to + *grandire* to make great] —**ag·gran·dize·ment** (ə·gran′diz·mənt) *n.* —**ag·gran′diz·er** *n.*

ag·gra·vate (ag′rə·vāt) *v.t.* **·vat·ed, ·vat·ing** 1. To make worse, as an illness. 2. *Informal* To exasperate. [< L *ad-* to + *gravare* to make heavy] —**ag′gra·vat′ing** *adj.* —**ag′gra·vat′ing·ly** *adv.* —**ag′gra·va′tion** *n.* —**ag′gra·va′tive** *adj.*

ag·gre·gate (*v.* ag′rə·gāt; *adj. & n.* -git) *v.t.* **·gat·ed, ·gat·ing** 1. To bring together, into a whole. 2. To form a whole. —*adj.* Collected into a whole. —*n.* The whole of anything. [< L *ad-* to + *gregare* to collect] —**ag′gre·ga′tion** *n.* —**ag′gre·ga′tive** *adj.* —**ag′gre·ga′tor** *n.*

ag·gres·sion (ə·gresh′ən) *n.* 1. An unprovoked attack. 2. Hostile behavior. [< L *ad-* to + *gradi* to go] —**ag·gres′sor** (-gres′ər) *n.*

ag·gres·sive (ə·gres′iv) *adj.* 1. Attacking. 2. Boldly assertive. —**ag·gres′sive·ly** *adv.* —**ag·gres′sive·ness** *n.*

ag·grieve (ə·grēv′) *v.t.* **·grieved, ·griev·ing** 1. To cause sorrow to. 2. To give cause for complaint. [< L *aggravare*]

a·ghast (ə·gast′) *adj.* Struck with horror. [OE *ā* + *gæstan* to terrify; infl. by *ghost*]

ag·ile (aj′əl, aj′īl) *adj.* Able to move quickly and easily. [< L *agere* to move] —**ag′ile·ly** *adv.* —**a·gil·i·ty** (ə·jil′ə·tē) *n.*

ag·ing (ā′jing) *n.* 1. The process or the effects of growing mature or old. 2. Any artificial process for producing the effects of age. Also *Brit.* **age′ing.**

ag·i·tate (aj′ə·tāt) *v.* **·tat·ed, ·tat·ing** *v.t.* 1. To shake or stir vigorously. 2. To excite or perturb. —*v.i.* 3. To excite, or endeavor to excite, public interest and action. [< L *agitare* to set in motion] —**ag′i·ta′tion** *n.* —**ag′i·ta′tor** *n.*

a·gleam (ə·glēm′) *adv. & adj.* Bright; gleaming.

a·glit·ter (ə·glit′ər) *adv. & adj.* Glittering.

a·glow (ə·glō′) *adv. & adj.* In a glow; glowing.

ag·nos·ti·cism (ag·nos′tə·siz′əm) *n.* The doctrine that man cannot know ultimate truth. [< Gk. *a-* not + *gignōskein* to know] —**ag·nos′tic** *adj. & n.*

a·go (ə·gō′) *adv.* In the past: long *ago.* —*adj.* Gone by: a year *ago.* [OE *āgān* past, gone away]

a·gog (ə·gog′) *adv. & adj.* In a state of eager curiosity. [< MF *en gogues* in a merry mood]

a-go-go (ä·gō′gō) *adj.* See GO-GO.

ag·o·nize (ag′ə·nīz) *v.i.* **·nized, ·niz·ing** 1. To suffer extreme anguish. 2. To make convulsive efforts. [< Gk. *agōnizesthai* to contend, strive] —**ag′o·niz′ing·ly** *adv.*

ag·o·ny (ag′ə·nē) *n. pl.* **·nies** 1. Intense suffering. 2. Any intense emotion. 3. Violent striving. [< Gk. *agōn* contest]

a·grar·i·an (ə·grâr′ē·ən) *adj.* 1. Pertaining to land or its use. 2. Concerning farming. —*n.* One who advocates equal distribution of farm land. [< L *ager* field] —**a·grar′i·an·ism** *n.*

a·gree (ə·grē′) *v.i.* **a·greed, a·gree·ing** 1. To give consent. 2. To be in harmony. 3. To be of one mind. 4. To be acceptable; suit. 5. To be consistent with. 6. *Gram.* To correspond in person, number, case, or gender. [< L *ad-* to + *gratus* pleasing]

a·gree·a·ble (ə·grē′ə·bəl) *adj.* 1. Pleasant to the senses. 2. Suitable. 3. Ready to consent. —**a·gree′a·bil′i·ty, a·gree′a·ble·ness** *n.* —**a·gree′a·bly** *adv.*

a·gree·ment (ə·grē′mənt) *n.* 1. The act of

coming into accord. 2. The state of being in accord; conformity. 3. A contract.

ag·ri·busi·ness (ag′rə·biz′nəs) *n.* Agriculture combined with related enterprises requiring large capitalization.

ag·ri·cul·ture (ag′rə·kul′chər) *n.* The cultivation of crops and raising of livestock. [< L *ager* field + *cultura* cultivation] **—ag′ri·cul′tur·al** *adj.* **—ag′ri·cul′tur·al·ly** *adv.* **—ag′ri·cul′tur·ist, ag′ri·cul′tur·al·ist** *n.*

a·gron·o·my (ə·gron′ə·mē) *n.* The application of scientific principles to the cultivation of land. [< Gk. *agros* field + *nemein* to distribute, manage] **—ag·ro·nom·ic** (ag′rə·nom′ik) or **·i·cal** *adj.* **—a·gron′o·mist** *n.*

a·ground (ə·ground′) *adv. & adj.* On the shore or bottom, as a vessel; stranded.

a·gue (ā′gyōō) *n. Pathol.* A periodic malarial fever marked by intermittent chills. [< L (*febris*) *acuta* acute (fever)] **—a′gu·ish** *adj.*

ah (ä) *interj.* An exclamation of surprise, satisfaction, contempt, etc. [ME]

a·ha (ä·hä′) *interj.* An exclamation expressing, triumph, mockery, etc. [ME]

a·head (ə·hed′) *adv.* 1. At the front. 2. In advance. 3. Onward; forward. **—ahead of** In advance of, as in time, rank, achievement, etc. **—to be ahead** *Informal* To be winning. **—to get ahead** To improve one's lot.

a·hoy (ə·hoi′) *interj. Naut.* Used in hailing a vessel.

aid (ād) *v.t. & v.i.* To render assistance (to); help. **—***n.* 1. Assistance; help. 2. One who or that which affords assistance. 3. An aide. [< OF < L *ad-* to + *juvare* to help] **—aid′er** *n.*

aide (ād) *n.* 1. An aide-de-camp. 2. An assistant. [< F]

aide-de-camp (ād′də·kamp′) *n. pl.* **aides-de-camp** A military officer serving a superior officer as confidential assistant: also *aide.* [< F *aide de camp,* lit., field assistant]

ai·grette (ā′gret, ā·gret′) *n.* A tuft of decorative feathers, esp. a showy plume on a hat. Also **ai′gret.** [< F, heron]

ai·ki·do (ī·kē′dō) *n.* A Japanese system of self-defense using an opponent's strength against him. [< Japanese *ai* together + *ki* spirit + *do* art]

ail (āl) *v.t.* 1. To cause uneasiness or pain to. **—***v.i.* 2. To be ill; feel pain. [OE *eglan*]

ai·lan·thus (ā·lan′thəs) *n.* A deciduous Asiatic tree having greenish flowers. [< Amboinese *ai lanto* tree of heaven]

ai·le·ron (ā′lə·ron) *n.* A movable surface of an airplane wing, used to bank an airplane. [< F]

ail·ment (āl′ment) *n.* A slight illness.

aim (ām) *v.t.* 1. To direct, as a weapon or act, toward some object or person. **—***v.i.* 2. To have a purpose; try: with *to.* **—***n.* 1. The direction of anything aimed. 2. Design; purpose. [< L *aestimare* to estimate]

aim·less (ām′lis) *adj.* Wanting in aim or purpose. **—aim′less·ly** *adv.* **—aim′less·ness** *n.*

ain't (ānt) *Illit. & Dial.* Am not: also used for *are not, is not, has not,* and *have not.* ◆*Ain't* is nonstandard, although users of standard English sometimes employ it casually.

air (âr) *n.* 1. The mixture of gases surrounding the earth. 2. A light wind; breeze. 3. Characteristic manner. 4. *pl.* Affectation: to put on *airs.* 5. A melody; tune. **—in the air** Prevalent; abroad, as gossip. **—on the air** Being broadcast, as by radio. **—***v.t.* 1. To expose to the air; ventilate. 2. To make public. [< Gk. *aēr* air, mist]

Air as a combining form has the meanings:

1. By means of air:

air-blasted	**air-driven**
air-blown	**air-filled**
air-cured	**air-heated**
air-dried	**air-insulated**

2. Conducting, confining, or regulating air:

air compressor	**air filter**
air duct	**air regulator**

3. Filled with air:

air chamber	**air mattress**
air jacket	**air sac**

4. Operated by compressed air:

air brake	**air gun**
air brush	**air hammer**
air drill	**air motor**

5. Done by or suitable for aircraft:

air attack	**air race**
air echelon	**air rescue**
air express	**air show**
air freight	**air strike**
air group	**air war**

air bag A plastic bag that inflates in automobile crashes to protect those in the front seat.

air base A base for operations by aircraft.

air·borne (âr′bôrn′) *adj.* Carried by or through the air.

air-con·di·tion (âr′kən·dish′ən) *v.t.* To equip with a system that controls temperature, humidity, and purity of indoor air. **—air′-con·di′tioned** *adj.* **—air conditioner —air conditioning**

air-cooled (âr′kōōld′) *adj.* Cooled, as an engine, directly by flow of air. **—air′cool′** *v.t.*

air·craft (âr′kraft′) *n. pl.* **·craft** Any form of craft designed for flight through the air.

aircraft carrier A ship on which aircraft may land and take off.

air·drome (âr′drōme′) *n. Brit.* An airport.

air·drop (âr′drop′) *n.* Delivery of supplies from an aircraft in flight. **—***v.t.* **·dropped, ·drop·ping** To drop (supplies, etc.) from an aircraft.

Aire·dale (âr′dāl) *n.* A large terrier with a wiry tan coat. [after *Airedale* (the Aire river valley), England]

air·field (âr′fēld′) *n.* An airport.

air·foil (âr′foil′) *n.* A surface, as an airplane wing, designed to respond to air movement.

air force The air arm of a country's defense forces.

air·ing (âr′ing) *n.* 1. An exposure to air, as for drying. 2. Public exposure or discussion. 3. Exercise out of doors.

air lane A route regularly used by airplanes.

air·lift (âr′lift′) *n.* An emergency supply line by aircraft. **—***v.t.* To move by airlift.

air·line (âr′līn′) *n.* An air transportation system. **—air′lin′er** *n.*

air lock An airtight chamber for maintaining air pressure.

air mail 1. Mail carried by airplane. 2. A system of carrying mail by airplane. Also **airmail** (âr′māl′). **—air′-mail′** or **air′mail′** *adj. & v.t.*

air·man (âr′mən) *n. pl.* **·men** (-mən) 1. An aviator; flyer. 2. An enlisted man or woman in the U.S. Air Force, ranking below a sergeant.

air mile See under MILE.

air·plane (âr′plān′) *n.* A heavier-than-air, powered flying craft having wings. Also, *Brit., aeroplane.*

air pocket A sinking mass of cooled air that causes an aircraft to make a sudden drop.

air·port (âr′pôrt′) *n.* A field laid out as a base for aircraft, including all appurtenances.

air raid An attack by military aircraft.

air·ship (âr′ship′) *n.* A lighter-than-air, powered flying craft.

air·sick·ness (âr′sik′nis) *n.* Motion sickness caused by air travel. **—air′sick′** *adj.*

air·space (âr′spās′) *n.* That portion of the atmosphere overlying a designated area.

air speed The speed of an airplane with relation to the air.

air·strip (âr′strip′) *n.* A flat surface used as an airfield.

air·tight (âr′tīt′) *adj.* 1. Not allowing air to pass. 2. Having no weak places: an *airtight* case.

air·way (âr′wā′) *n.* An air lane.

air·wor·thy (âr′wûr′thē) *adj.* Fit to fly: said of aircraft. **—air′wor′thi·ness** *n.*

air·y (âr′ē) *adj.* **air·i·er, air·i·est** 1. Of or pertaining to the air. 2. Thin or light as air; delicate. 3. Lively; gay. 4. Unsubstantial as air. 5. Open to the air; breezy. **—air′i·ly** *adv.* **—air′i·ness** *n.*

aisle (īl) *n.* 1. A passageway between rows of seats. 2. A division of a church at the side of a nave. [< MF < L *ala* wing]

a·jar (ə·jär′) *adv.* & *adj.* Partly open, as a door. [ME *a-* on + *char* < OE *cerr* turn]

a·kim·bo (ə·kim′bō) *adv.* & *adj.* With hands on hips. [ME *in keneboue* in a sharp bow]

a·kin (ə·kin′) *adj.* 1. Related by blood. 2. Of similar nature. [< A-[3] + KIN]

-al[1] *suffix of adjectives and nouns* Characterized by: *personal, musical.* [< L *-alis*]

-al[2] *suffix of nouns* Used in nouns formed from verbs: *betrayal, refusal.* [< L *-alis*]

à la (ä′lä, ä′lə; *Fr.* à là) In the style of. Also **a la.** [< F]

al·a·bas·ter (al′ə·bas′tər) *n.* 1. A white or tinted fine-grained gypsum. 2. A banded variety of calcite. **—***adj.* Made of or like alabaster; smooth and white: also **al′a·bas′·trine** (-trin). [< Gk. *alabast(r)os* alabaster box]

à la carte (ä′ lə kärt′) By the bill of fare; each item having a separate price. [< F]

a·lac·ri·ty (ə·lak′rə·tē) *n.* Cheerful promptitude. [< L *alacer* lively] **—a·lac′ri·tous** *adj.*

à la king (ä′ lə king′) Cooked in cream sauce.

à la mode (ä′ lə mōd′, al′ ə mōd′) 1. In style; fashionable. 2. In cookery: **a** Served with ice cream: said of pie. **b** Braised with vegetables. [< F]

a·lar (ā′lər) *adj.* 1. Of a wing. 2. Wing-shaped. [< L *ala* wing] **—a′late, a′lat·ed** *adj.*

a·larm (ə·lärm′) *n.* 1. Sudden fear or apprehension. 2. Any signal, as by an automatic device, intended to awaken or apprise of danger. **—***v.t.* 1. To strike with sudden fear. 2. To give warning to. [< Ital. *all' arme* to arms] **—a·larm′a·ble** *adj.*

a·larm·ing (ə·lär′ming) *adj.* Exciting alarm; causing apprehension. **—a·larm′ing·ly** *adv.*

a·larm·ist (ə·lär′mist) *n.* 1. One who needlessly excites or alarms. 2. One who is easily alarmed. **—a·larm′ist** *adj.*

a·las (ə·las′) *interj.* Expressing regret, sorrow, etc. [< OF *a* ah! + *las* wretched]

alb (alb) *n. Eccl.* A white linen eucharistic vestment reaching to the ankles. [OE < L *alba* (*vestis*) white (garment)]

al·ba·core (al′bə·kôr) *n.* Any of various tunas or large related fishes of the Atlantic. [< Arabic *al* the + *bukr* young camel]

Al·ba·ni·an (al·bā′nē·ən, -bān′yən) **—***n.* 1. A native or inhabitant of Albania. 2. The language of Albania. **—Al·ba′ni·an** *adj.*

al·ba·tross (al′bə·trôs, -tros) *n. pl.* **·tross·es** or **tross** A large, web-footed sea bird. [< Sp., Pg. *alcatraz* frigate bird]

al·be·it (ôl·bē′it) *conj.* Even though. [ME *al be it* although it be]

al·bi·no (al·bī′no) *n. pl.* **·nos** 1. A person lacking pigment in the skin, hair, and eyes. 2. Any plant or animal lacking normal pigmentation. [< L *albus* white] **—al·bin·ic** (al·bin′ik) *adj.* **—al·bin·ism** (al′bə·niz′əm) *n.* **—al·bi′no** *adj.*

al·bum (al′bəm) *n.* 1. A booklike container for stamps, pictures, phonograph records, etc. 2. A phonograph record or set of records. [< L, blank tablet]

al·bu·men (al·byōō′mən) *n.* 1. The white of an egg. 2. Albumin. [< L *albus* white]

al·bu·min (al·byōō′mən) *n. Biochem.* Any of a class of water-soluble proteins found in animal and vegetable tissues. [< ALBUMEN] **—al·bu′mi·nous** *adj.*

al·caz·ar (al′kə·zär, *Sp.* äl·kä′thär) *n.* A Moorish castle or fortress in Spain. [< Arabic *al-qasr* the castle]

al·che·my (al′kə·mē) *n.* 1. The chemistry of the Middle Ages, concerned primarily with the transmutation of base metals into gold. 2. Any process of transmutation. [< Med.L *alchimia* < Gk. *cheein* to pour] **—al·chem·ic** (al·kem′ik) *adj.* **—al·chem′i·cal·ly** *adv.* **—al′che·mist** *n.* **—al′che·mis′tic** or **·ti·cal** *adj.*

al·co·hol (al′kə·hôl, -hol) *n.* 1. Ethanol, a colorless, flammable, volatile liquid that is the intoxicating agent in liquors. 2. Drinks containing alcohol. 3. Methanol. 4. *Chem.* Any of a group of organic compounds containing a hydroxyl group and similar to ethanol in construction. [< Arabic *al-kohl* the fine powder (of antimony)]

al·co·hol·ic (al′kə·hôl′ik, -hol′-) *adj.* 1. Containing or using alcohol. 2. Suffering from alcoholism. **—***n.* One who suffers from alcoholism.

al·co·hol·ism (al′kə·hôl′iz·əm, -hol′-) *n.* 1. Alcoholic poisoning. 2. An abnormal craving for alcohol.

al·cove (al′kōv) *n.* 1. A recess at the side of a room. 2. Any secluded spot. [< Arabic *al-qobbah* the vaulted chamber]

al·de·hyde (al′də·hīd) *n. Chem.* Any of a group of compounds derived from the alcohols, and intermediate between the alcohols and the acids.

al·der (ôl′dər) *n.* A small tree of the birch family, bearing catkins. [OE *alor*]

al·der·man (ôl′dər·mən) *n. pl.* **·men** A member of a city governing body. [OE *eald* old, senior + *man*] **—al′der·man·ship′** *n.* **—al′der·man′ic** (-man′ik) *adj.*

ale (āl) *n.* A fermented malt flavored with hops, resembling beer. [OE *ealu*]

a·le·a·tor·y (ā′lē·ə·tôr′ē) *adj.* 1. Dependent on chance. 2. *Music* Consisting of or containing random elements. Also **a′le·a·to′ric.** [< L *aleator* gambler]

a·lee (ə·lē′) *adv.* *Naut.* At, on, or to the lee side. [< ON]

a·lem·bic (ə·lem′bik) *n.* 1. An apparatus formerly used in distilling. 2. Anything that tests, purifies, or transforms. [< Gk. *ambix* cup]

a·lert (ə·lûrt′) *adj.* 1. Keenly watchful. 2. Lively; nimble. 3. Intelligent; bright. —*n.* A warning against attack. —*v.t.* To warn, as of a threatened attack. [< Ital. *all'erta* on the watch] —**a·lert′ly** *adv.* —**a·lert′ness** *n.*

Al·e·ut (al′ē·ōōt) *n.* *pl.* **Al·e·uts** or **Al·e·ut** 1. A native of the Aleutian Islands. 2. The language of the Aleuts. —**A·leu·tian** (ə·lōō′shən), **A·leu′tic** *adj.*

ale·wife (āl′wīf′) *n.* *pl.* **·wives** A small North American herringlike fish. [Origin unknown]

Al·ex·an·dri·an (al′ig·zan′drē·ən) *adj.* 1. Of Alexandria in Egypt. 2. Of Alexander the Great. 3. In prosody, Alexandrine. —*n.* 1. An inhabitant of Alexandria. 2. An Alexandrine verse.

Al·ex·an·drine (al′ig·zan′drin, -drēn) *n.* In prosody, a line of six iambic feet. —**Al′ex·an′drine** *adj.*

al·fal·fa (al·fal′fə) *n.* A cloverlike plant of the bean family, used as forage. [< Arabic *al-fasfasah*, the best fodder]

al·fres·co (al·fres′kō) *adv. & adj.* Occurring outdoors, as a meal. Also **al fresco.** [< Ital., in the open air]

al·gae (al′jē) *n.pl. of* **al·ga** (al′gə) A group of primitive, chlorophyll-bearing plants widely distributed in fresh and salt water, including seaweeds and kelps. [< L, seaweed] —**al·gal** (al′gəl) *adj.*

al·ge·bra (al′jə·brə) *n.* The branch of mathematics that treats of quantity and relations of numbers in the abstract by means of letters and symbols. [< Arabic *al-jebr* the reunion of broken parts, bone-setting] —**al·ge·bra·ic** (al′jə·brā′ik) or **·i·cal** *adj.* —**al′ge·bra′i·cal·ly** *adv.* —**al′ge·bra′ist** *n.*

Al·ge·ri·an (al·je′ri·ən) *adj.* Of Algeria. —*n.* A citizen or inhabitant of Algeria.

Al·gon·qui·an (al·gong′kē·ən, -kwē·ən) *n.* *pl.* **·qui·an** or **·qui·ans** 1. A family of North American Indian languages. 2. A member of an Algonquian-speaking tribe. —**Al·gon′·qui·an** *adj.*

Al·gon·quin (al·gong′kin, -kwin) *n.* *pl.* **·quin** or **·quins** 1. A member of certain northeastern Algonquian tribes. 2. The Algonquian language: also **Algonkian.**

al·go·rithm (al′gə·rith′əm) *n.* A step-by-step problem-solving procedure, as with a computer. [after *al-Khwarizmi*, 9th c. Arabian mathematician] —**al′go·rith′mic** *adj.*

a·li·as (ā′lē·əs) *n.* *pl.* **·as·es** An assumed name. —*adv.* Called by an assumed name: Miller, *alias* Brown. [< L, at another time]

al·i·bi (al′ə·bī) *n.* *pl.* **·bis** 1. *Law* A defense that the suspect was elsewhere during the crime. 2. *Informal* An excuse. —*v.i.* **·bied, ·bi·ing** *Informal* To make excuses. [< L, elsewhere]

al·ien (āl′yən, ā′lē·ən) *adj.* 1. Of another country; foreign. 2. Not one's own; strange. 3. Not consistent with: with *to.* —*n.* 1. A foreign resident who is not a citizen. 2. A member of a foreign people. 3. One estranged or excluded. [< L *alius* another]

al·ien·a·ble (āl′yən·ə·bəl, ā′lē·ən-) *adj.* *Law* Capable of being transferred in ownership. —**al′ien·a·bil′i·ty** *n.*

al·ien·ate (āl′yən·āt, ā′lē·ən-) *v.t.* **·at·ed, ·at·ing** 1. To make indifferent or unfriendly; estrange. 2. To turn away: to *alienate* the affections. 3. *Law* To transfer, as property. [< L *alienare* to estrange] —**al′ien·a′tion** *n.* —**al′ien·a′tor** *n.*

al·ien·ee (āl′yən·ē′, ā′lē·ən·ē′) *n.* *Law* One to whom property is transferred.

al·ien·ist (āl′yən·ist, ā′lē·ən-) *n.* A doctor accepted by a court as an expert on mental competence. [< L *alienus* insane] —**al′ien·ism** *n.*

al·ien·or (āl′yən·ər, ā′lē·ən·ôr′) *n.* *Law* One who alienates property to another. Also **al′ien·er.** [< AF]

al·i·form (al′ə·fôrm, ā′lə·fôrm) *adj.* Wing-shaped. [< F *ala* wing + -FORM]

a·light[1] (ə·līt′) *v.i.* **a·light·ed** or **a·lit, a·light·ing** 1. To descend and come to rest. 2. To come by accidentally: with *on* or *upon.* [OE *ālihtan*]

a·light[2] (ə·līt′) *adj. & adv.* Lighted; burning.

a·lign (ə·līn′) *v.t.* 1. To bring into a straight line. 2. To put (oneself, one's party, etc.) on one side of an issue. —*v.i.* 3. To fall into line. Also spelled *aline.* [< F *aligner* to place in a line]

a·lign·ment (ə·līn′mənt) *n.* 1. Arrangement in a straight line. 2. The state of being on one side of an issue. Also spelled *alinement.*

a·like (ə·līk′) *adj.* Having precise or close resemblance. —*adv.* In the same or like manner. [Fusion of ON *ālīkr* and OE *gelīc, anlīc*] —**a·like′ness** *n.*

al·i·ment (al′ə·mənt) *n.* Food; nutriment. —*v.t.* To furnish with food. [< L *alere* to nourish] —**al·i·men·tal** (al′ə·men′təl) *adj.* —**al′i·men′tal·ly** *adv.*

al·i·men·ta·ry (al′ə·men′trē, -tə·rē) *adj.* 1. Supplying nourishment. 2. Relating to nourishment or nutrition.

alimentary canal The food canal between the mouth and the anus, including esophagus, stomach, and intestines. Also **alimentary tract.**

al·i·men·ta·tion (al′ə·men·tā′shən) *n.* 1. The act or process of supplying or receiving nourishment. 2. Maintenance; support. —**al·i·men·ta·tive** (al′ə·men′tə·tiv) *adj.*

al·i·mo·ny (al′ə·mō′nē) *n.* *Law* The allowance made from one spouse to the other after a divorce. [< L *alere* to nourish]

a·line (ə·līn′) See ALIGN.

a·lit (ə·lit′) Alternative past tense and past participle of ALIGHT[1].

a·live (ə·līv′) *adj.* 1. In a living or functioning state. 2. Continuing: to keep hope *alive.* 3. Animated: *alive* with enthusiasm. 4. Aware: with *to.* 5. Abounding. [OE *on līfe* in life]

a·liz·a·rin (ə·liz′ə·rin) *n.* An orange-red compound, used as a dye. Also **a·liz·a·rine** (ə·liz′ə·rin, -rēn). [< Arabic *al-asārah* the juice]

al·ka·li (al′kə·lī) *n.* *pl.* **·lis** or **·lies** *Chem.* 1. A hydroxide of a metal, capable of neutralizing acids and of turning red litmus paper blue; base. 2. Any of various basic salts found in soil and ground water. [< Arabic *al-qaliy* the ashes of saltwort] **—al·ka·line** (al′kə·lin, -līn) *adj.* **—al·ka·lin·i·ty** (al′kə·lin′ə·tē) *n.*

al·ka·lize (al′kə·līz) *v.t. & v.i.* **·lized, ·liz·ing** To make alkaline. **—al′ka·li·za′tion** *n.*

al·ka·loid (al′kə·loid) *n. Chem.* Any of a class of nitrogenous organic bases, esp. of plant origin, having a physiological effect on animals and man, as strychnine, morphine, caffeine, etc. **—al′ka·loi′dal** *adj.*

al·kyd (al′kid) *n.* A durable synthetic resin used in paints and adhesives.

all (ôl) *adj.* 1. The entire substance or extent of: *all* Europe. 2. The entire number of: known to *all* men. 3. The greatest possible: in *all* haste. 4. Any whatever: beyond *all* doubt. —*n.* Everything that one has: to give one's *all.* —*pron.* Every part or person: *All* failed. **—after all** Everything else being considered. **—all in all** Taken as a whole. **—all told** With everything included. **—at all** In any way or degree: no luck *at all.* **—for all** To the degree that: *For all* I care, you can go. **—in all** Including everything; all told: ten books *in all.* —*adv.* 1. Wholly; entirely: fallen *all* to bits. 2. For each; on each side: a score of three *all.* **—all but** Almost; on the verge of. **—all in** *Informal* Wearied. **—all out** Making every effort. **—all the (better, more,** etc.) So much the (better, more, etc.). [OE *eall*]

All as a combining form has the meanings:
1. Wholly or totally:

all-absorbing	**all-holy**
all-beautiful	**all-important**
all-colored	**all-inclusive**
all-compelling	**all-knowing**
all-covering	**all-pervasive**
all-encompassing	**all-powerful**
all-engrossing	**all-seeing**
all-foreseeing	**all-telling**
all-forgiving	**all-wood**

2. Representing the whole or the best of the whole:

all-American	**all-star**
all-city	**all-state**

Al·lah (al′ə, ä′lə) In Islam, the one supreme being; God. [< Arabic]

all-a·round (ôl′ə·round′) *adj.* All-round.

al·lay (ə·lā′) *v.t.* **·layed, ·lay·ing** 1. To reduce the intensity of. 2. To pacify; calm. [OE *a-* away + *lecgan* to lay] **—al·lay′er** *n.*

al·lege (ə·lej′) *v.t.* **·leged, ·leg·ing** 1. To assert to be true before proving. 2. To plead as an excuse, in support of a position. [< L *ex-* out + *litigare* to sue; infl. by *allegare* to send a message] **—al·lege′a·ble** *adj.* **—al·leged** (ə·lejd′, ə·lej′id) *adj.* **—al·leg′ed·ly** *adv.* **—al·leg′er** *n.*

al·le·giance (ə·lē′jəns) *n.* 1. An obligation of fidelity to a government or sovereign. 2. Fidelity, as to a principle. [ME *allegeaunce* < OF *liege* liege]

al·le·go·ry (al′ə·gôr′ē) *n. pl.* **·ries** A story or other artistic representation in which characters and events represent ideals or principles. [< Gk. *allos* other + *agoreuein* to speak publicly] **—al′le·gor′ic** or **·i·cal** *adj.* **—al′le·gor′ist** *n.*

al·le·gro (ə·lā′grō, ə·leg′rō; *Ital.* äl·lā′grō) *Music adj. & adv.* Lively. —*n. pl.* **·gros** A composition in such tempo. [< Ital.]

al·lele (ə·lēl′) *n. Genetics* 1. Either of a pair or one of a number of mutually exclusive hereditary characteristics. 2. The gene occurring at a given location on a chromosome. Also **al·le·lo·morph** (ə·lē′lə·môrf, ə·lel′ə-). [< Gk. *allēlōn* of one another + *morphē* form] **—al·le′lo·mor′phic** *adj.* **—al·le′lo·mor′phism** *n.*

al·le·lu·ia (al′ə·lo͞o′yə) *n. & interj.* Hallelujah. Also **al′le·lu′iah.**

al·ler·gen (al′ər·jən) *n.* Any substance capable of producing allergy. Also **al′ler·gin.** **—al′ler·gen′ic** (-jen′ik) *adj.*

al·ler·gist (al′ər·jist) *n.* A specialist in the treatment of allergies.

al·ler·gy (al′ər·jē) *n. pl.* **·gies** *Med.* A pathological condition of heightened sensitivity to a substance. [< Gk. *allos* other + *ergon* work] **—al·ler·gic** (ə·lûr′jik) *adj.*

al·le·vi·ate (ə·lē′vē·āt) *v.t.* **·at·ed, ·at·ing** To make easier to bear. [< L *ad-* to + *levis* light, not heavy] **—al·le′vi·a′tive, al·le′vi·a·to′ry** (-ə·tôr′ē) *adj.*

al·ley (al′ē) *n.* 1. A narrow street. 2. A bowling alley. [< OF *alee* a going, passage]

al·li·ance (ə·lī′əns) *n.* 1. Any union, coalition, or agreement between persons, sovereigns, nations, etc. 2. Relationship in characteristics. [< L *ad-* to + *ligare* to bind]

al·lied (ə·līd′, al′īd) *adj.* 1. United, confederated, or leagued. 2. Closely related: *allied* interests.

al·li·ga·tor (al′ə·gā′tər) *n.* 1. A large reptile of the southern U.S. and the Yangtze River, China, having a shorter, blunter snout than the crocodile. 2. Leather made from the skin of the alligator. [< Sp. *el lagarto* the lizard]

alligator pear An avocado.

al·lit·er·ate (ə·lit′ə·rāt) *v.* **·at·ed, ·at·ing** *v.i.* 1. To use alliteration. 2. To contain alliteration. —*v.t.* 3. To make alliterative. [< L *ad-* to + *littera* letter (of the alphabet)]

al·lit·er·a·tion (ə·lit′ə·rā′shən) *n.* The occurrence of two or more words having the same initial sound, as in "a fair field full of folk." **—al·lit·er·a·tive** (ə·lit′ə·rā′tiv, -ər·ə·tiv) *adj.* **—al·lit′er·a′tive·ly** *adv.* **—al·lit′er·a′tive·ness** *n.*

al·lo·cate (al′ə·kāt) *v.t.* **·cat·ed, ·cat·ing** To set apart or assign, as funds. [< L *ad-* to + *locare* to place] **—al·lo·ca·ble** (al′ə·kə·bəl) *adj.* **—al′lo·ca′tion** *n.*

al·lot (ə·lot′) *v.t.* **·lot·ted, ·lot·ting** To assign or apportion. [< OF *a-* to + *loter* to apportion] **—al·lot′ment** *n.*

al·lot·ro·py (ə·lot′rə·pē) *n. Chem.* Variation in properties and form of a substance without change of composition. Also **al·lot′ro·pism.** [< Gk. *allos* other + *tropos* turn, manner] **—al·lo·trope** (al′ə·trōp) *n.* **—al·lo·trop·ic** (al′ə·trop′ik) or **·i·cal** *adj.* **—al′lo·trop′i·cal·ly** *adv.*

all-out (ôl′out′) *adj.* Complete and entire.

all·o·ver (ôl′ō′vər) *adj.* Extending everywhere.

al·low (ə·lou′) *v.t. & v.i.* 1. To permit to occur or do. 2. To concede; admit. 3. To make provision for. 4. To make concession of: to *allow* a month to pay. 5. *Dial.* To say; declare. [< OF *alouer* to place, use, assign, ult. < L *ad-* to + *laudare* to praise] **—al·low′a·ble** *adj.* **—al·low′a·bly** *adv.*

al·low·ance (ə·lou′əns) *n.* 1. That which is

allowed. **2.** A sum of money given at regular intervals. **3.** A discount for a purchase. **4.** The act of allowing; toleration; sanction. **5.** Admission; acceptance. —*v.t.* **·anced, ·anc·ing** To put on an allowance.

al·loy (*n.* al′oi, ə·loi′; *v.* ə·loi′) *n.* **1.** *Metall.* A mixture formed by fusion of two or more metals or of a metal and a nonmetal. **2.** Anything that reduces purity. —*v.t.* **1.** To mix (metals) so as to form an alloy. **2.** To modify or debase, as by mixture. [< L *ad-* to + *ligare* to bind]

all-purpose (ôl′pûr′pəs) *adj.* Generally useful.

all right **1.** Satisfactory. **2.** Correct. **3.** Uninjured. **4.** Certainly. **5.** Yes. —**all-right** (ôl′rīt′) *adj.*

all-round (ôl′round′) *adj.* **1.** Of comprehensive range or scope. **2.** Excelling in all or many aspects. Also *all-around.*

All Saints' Day *Eccl.* November 1, in some Christian churches a festival commemorative of all saints. Also **All Saints.**

All Souls' Day *Eccl.* November 2, in some Christian churches a day of commemoration for the souls of all deceased. Also **All Souls.**

all·spice (ôl′spīs′) *n.* The dried berry of the pimento used as a spice.

al·lude (ə·lo͞od′) *v.i.* **·lud·ed, ·lud·ing** To make indirect or casual reference: with *to.* [< L *ad-* to + *ludere* to play] —**al·lu·sion** (ə·lo͞o′zhən) *n.* —**al·lu·sive** (ə·lo͞o′siv) *adj.* —**al·lu′sive·ly** *adv.* —**al·lu′sive·ness** *n.*

al·lure (ə·lo͝or′) *v.t. & v.i.* **·lured, ·lur·ing** To attract; entice. —*n.* That which allures. [< OF *a-* to + *leurre* lure] —**al·lure′ment** *n.* —**al·lur′er** *n.* —**al·lur′ing** *adj.* —**al·lur′ing·ly** *adv.*

al·lu·vi·um (ə·lo͞o′vē·əm) *n. pl.* **·vi·a** or **·vi·ums** A deposit, as of sand or mud, transported and laid down by flowing water. [< L] —**al·lu′vi·al** *adj. & n.*

al·ly (ə·lī′, al′ī) *v.t. & v.i.* **·lied, ·ly·ing** To unite by some relationship: with *to* or *with.* —*n. pl.* **·lies** **1.** A person, country, or organization associated with another. **2.** Any friendly helper. [< L *ad-* to + *ligare* to bind]

al·ma ma·ter (al′mə mä′tər, al′mə mā′tər, äl′mə mä′tər) The school that one has attended. Also **Al′ma Ma′ter.** [< L, fostering mother]

al·ma·nac (ôl′mə·nak) *n.* A publication giving information under headings dated for the year. [< Arabic *al-manākh*]

al·might·y (ôl·mīt′ē) *adj.* Able to do all things. —**the Almighty** God; the Supreme Being. [OE *eal* all + *mihtig* mighty] —**al·might′i·ly** *adv.* —**al·might′i·ness** *n.*

al·mond (ä′mənd, am′ənd) *n.* **1.** A small tree of the rose family, widely cultivated for its nuts. **2.** The kernel of the fruit of the almond tree. [< Gk. *amygdalē*]

al·most (ôl′mōst, ôl·mōst′) *adv.* Approximately; very nearly; all but. [OE *ealmǣst*]

alms (ämz) *n. sing. & pl.* A gift for the poor. ◆ Collateral adjective: *eleemosynary.* [< Gk. *eleēmosynē* alms < *eleos* pity]

alms·house (ämz′hous′) *n.* A poorhouse.

al·oe (al′ō) *n. pl.* **·oes** **1.** An Old World plant of the lily family. **2.** *pl.* (*construed as sing.*) A cathartic drug made from the juice of certain aloe species. [< Gk. *aloē*] —**al′o·et′ic** or **·i·cal** *adj.*

a·loft (ə·lôft′, ə·loft′) *adv.* **1.** In or to a high or higher place. **2.** *Naut.* On or to a ship's upper rigging. [< ON *ā lopt* in (the) air]

a·lo·ha (ə·lō′ə, ä·lō′hä) *n. & interj. Hawaiian* Love: used as a salutation and a farewell.

a·lone (ə·lōn′) *adv. & adj.* **1.** Without company; solitary. **2.** Excluding all others; only: He *alone* survived. [ME *al one*]

a·long (ə·lông′, ə·long′) *adv.* **1.** Progressively onward in a course: The years roll *along* quickly. **2.** In company; together. **3.** Advanced in its natural course. —**all along** From the outset; throughout. —*prep.* Throughout or over the length of. [OE *andlang* continuous]

a·long·shore (ə·lông′shôr′, ə·long′-) *adv.* Along the coast or shore.

a·long·side (ə·lông′sīd′, ə·long′-) *adv.* Close to the side. —*prep.* Side by side with.

a·loof (ə·lo͞of′) *adj.* Distant, esp. in manner; unsympathetic. —*adv.* Apart: to stand *aloof.* [< A-[1] + Du. *loef* windward] —**a·loof′ly** *adv.* —**a·loof′ness** *n.*

a·loud (ə·loud′) *adv.* Loudly or audibly.

alp (alp) *n.* A lofty mountain. [Back formation < *Alpes* the Alps]

al·pac·a (al·pak′ə) *n.* **1.** A domesticated ruminant of South America. **2.** Its wool, or cloth made of this wool. [< Sp. < Aymara *allpaca*]

al·pen·stock (al′pən·stok′) *n.* An iron-pointed staff used by mountain climbers. [< G]

al·pha (al′fə) *n.* **1.** The first letter in the Greek alphabet (A, α), corresponding to English *a.* **2.** The first of anything. [< Gk. < Hebrew letter *āleph*]

al·pha·bet (al′fə·bet) *n.* The letters that form a written language, in an order fixed by custom. [< Gk. *alpha* + *bēta*, the first two Greek letters]

al·pha·bet·i·cal (al′fə·bet′i·kəl) *adj.* **1.** Arranged in the order of the alphabet. **2.** Pertaining to or expressed by an alphabet. Also **al′pha·bet′ic.** —**al′pha·bet′i·cal·ly** *adv.*

al·pha·bet·ize (al′fə·bə·tīz′) *v.t.* **·ized, ·iz·ing** To put in alphabetical order. —**al·pha·bet·i·za·tion** (al′fə·bet′ə·zā′shən) *n.* —**al′pha·bet·iz′er** *n.*

al·pha·nu·mer·ic (al′fə·no͞o·mer′ik, -nyo͞o-) *adj.* Consisting of the letters of the alphabet and numerals, as a computer code. Also **al′pha·nu·mer′i·cal.**

alpha particle *Physics* The positively charged nucleus of the helium atom.

alpha ray *Physics* A stream of alpha particles.

alpha rhythm *Physiol.* A form of brain wave associated with awake relaxation: also **alpha wave.**

al·pine (al′pīn, -pin) *adj. Biol.* Inhabiting or growing in mountain regions.

Al·pine (al′pīn, -pin) *adj.* Pertaining to or characteristic of the Alps. [< L *Alpes* the Alps]

al·read·y (ôl·red′ē) *adv.* Before or by the time mentioned.

Al·sa·tian (al·sā′shən) *adj.* Of or pertaining to Alsace. —*n.* **1.** A native or inhabitant of Alsace. **2.** A German shepherd dog.

al·so (ôl′sō) *adv.* In addition; besides; likewise. [OE *alswā, ealswā* all (wholly) so]

al·so-ran (ôl′sō·ran′) *n. Informal* An unsuccessful competitor.

Al·ta·ic (al·tā′ik) *adj.* Of the Altai Mountains or the languages spoken there. Also **Al·tai·an** (al·tā′ən, -tī′-).

al·tar (ôl′tər) *n.* A raised place or structure regarded as the center of worship. [< L *altus* high]

altar boy An attendant at the altar; acolyte.

al·tar·piece (ôl′tər·pēs′) *n.* Work of art over and behind an altar.

al·ter (ôl′tər) *v.t.* 1. To cause to be different. 2. To castrate or spay. —*v.i.* 3. To change. [< L, other] —**al′ter·a·bil′i·ty, al′ter·a·ble·ness** *n.* —**al′ter·a·ble** *adj.* —**al′ter·a·bly** *adv.*

al·ter·a·tion (ôl′tə·rā′shən) *n.* 1. The act or process of altering. 2. Any change.

al·ter·cate (ôl′tər·kāt, al′-) *v.i.* **·cat·ed, ·cat·ing** To dispute vehemently. [< L *alter* other]

al·ter·ca·tion (ôl′tər·kā′shən, al′-) *n.* A heated dispute.

al·ter e·go (ôl′tər ē′gō, al′tər eg′ō) 1. Another self; a double. 2. An intimate friend. [< L, lit., other I]

al·ter·nate (*v.* ôl′tər·nāt, al′-; *adj.* & *n.* ôl′tər·nit, al′-) *v.t.* & *v.i.* **·nat·ed, ·nat·ing** To follow or make to follow by turns, as in place, condition, etc. —*adj.* 1. Occurring or following by turns. 2. Referring to every other of a series. 3. Alternative: *alternate* plans. —*n.* A substitute or second. [< L *alternus* every second one] —**al′ter·nate·ly** *adv.* —**al′ter·na′tion** *n.*

alternating current *Electr.* A current that reverses its direction of flow at regular intervals.

al·ter·na·tive (ôl·tûr′nə·tiv, al-) *n.* 1. A choice between two things. 2. One of two or more things to be chosen. [< Med.L *alternativus*] —**al·ter′na·tive** *adj.* —**al·ter′na·tive·ly** *adv.* —**al·ter′na·tive·ness** *n.*

al·ter·na·tor (ôl′tər·nā′tər, al′-) *n.* *Electr.* A generator giving an alternating current. Also **al′ter·nat′er.**

al·though (ôl·thō′) *conj.* Notwithstanding the fact that. Also **al·tho′.**

al·tim·e·ter (al·tim′ə·tər, al′tə·mē′tər) *n.* An instrument for determining altitude. —**al·tim′e·try** *n.*

al·ti·tude (al′tə·to͞od, -tyo͞od) *n.* 1. Elevation above any given point, esp. above mean sea level; height. 2. *Astron.* Angular elevation above the horizon. 3. *Geom.* The vertical distance from the base of a figure to its highest point. [< L *altus* high] —**al′ti·tu′di·nal** *adj.*

al·to (al′tō) *Music n. pl.* **·tos** 1. A musical part for the lower range of the female voice. 2. A voice or instrument that performs this part. [< L *altus* high] —**al′to** *adj.*

al·to·geth·er (ôl′tə·geth′ər, ôl′tə·geth′ər) *adv.* 1. Completely; wholly. 2. With everything included; without exception. —**in the altogether** *Informal* Nude.

al·tru·ism (al′tro͞o·iz′əm) *n.* Selfless devotion to the welfare of others. [< L *alter* other] —**al′tru·ist** *n.* —**al′tru·is′tic** *adj.* —**al′tru·is′ti·cal·ly** *adv.*

al·um (al′əm) *n.* *Chem.* An astringent, crystalline, double sulfate of aluminum and potassium. [< L *alumen*]

a·lu·mi·na (ə·lo͞o′mə·nə) *n.* *Chem.* Aluminum oxide, occurring in nature in bauxite and as corundum in the sapphire and ruby. Also **al·u·min** (al′yə·min), **al·u·mine** (al′yə·mēn, -min). [< L *alumen* alum]

a·lu·mi·num (ə·lo͞o′mə·nəm) *n.* A light, bluish white, malleable, ductile metallic element (symbol Al) found only in combination. Also *Brit.* **al·u·min·i·um** (al′yə·min′ē·əm). [< L *alumen* alum] —**a·lu′mi·nous** *adj.*

a·lum·na (ə·lum′nə) *n.* *pl.* **·nae** (-nē) A female graduate of a school. [< L]

a·lum·nus (ə·lum′nəs) *n.* *pl.* **·ni** (-nī) A male graduate of a school. [< L, foster son, pupil]

al·ways (ôl′wāz, -wiz) *adv.* 1. Perpetually; for all time. 2. At every time. [ME *alles weyes* < OE *aelne weg*]

am (am, *unstressed* əm) Present indicative, first person singular, of BE. [OE *eom, am*]

a·mah (ä′mə, am′ə) *n.* In India and the Orient, a female attendant for children; esp., a wet nurse. Also **a′ma.** [< Anglo-Indian < Pg. *ama* nurse]

a·mal·gam (ə·mal′gəm) *n.* 1. An alloy of mercury with another metal. 2. Any combination of two or more things. [< Gk. *malagma* an emollient]

a·mal·ga·mate (ə·mal′gə·māt) *v.t.* & *v.i.* **·mat·ed, ·mat·ing** 1. To form an amalgam. 2. To unite or combine. —**a·mal′ga·ma·ble** (-mə·bəl) *adj.* —**a·mal′ga·ma′tion** *n.* —**a·mal′ga·ma′tive** *adj.* —**a·mal′ga·mat′or** or **a·mal′ga·mat′er** *n.*

a·man·u·en·sis (ə·man′yo͞o·en′sis) *n.* *pl.* **·ses** (-sēz) One who copies manuscript or takes dictation; secretary. [< L (*servus*) *a manu* hand (servant), secretary]

am·a·ranth (am′ə·ranth) *n.* 1. Any of various related plants having showy flowers. 2. *Poetic* An imaginary nonfading flower. [< Gk. *a-* not + *marainein* to wither] —**am′a·ran′thine** (-ran′thin) *adj.*

am·a·ryl·lis (am′ə·ril′is) *n.* A bulbous plant, producing large, lilylike flowers. [< Gk. *Amaryllis*, fem. personal name]

a·mass (ə·mas′) *v.t.* To accumulate, as riches. [< OF *a-* to + *masser* to pile up] **a·mass′able** *adj.* —**a·mass′er** *n.* —**a·mass′ment** *n.*

am·a·teur (am′ə·cho͝or, -to͝or, -tyo͝or, am′ə·tûr′) *n.* 1. One who practices an art, sport, or science for pleasure, without pay. 2. One who is not expert. [< F < L *amare* to love] —**am′a·teur** *adj.* —**am′a·teur·ism** *n.*

am·a·teur·ish (am′ə·cho͝or′ish, -to͝or′-, -tyo͝or′-, -tûr′-) *adj.* Lacking the skill of an expert or professional. —**am′a·teur′ish·ly** *adv.* —**am′a·teur′ish·ness** *n.*

am·a·to·ry (am′ə·tôr′ē) *adj.* Pertaining to or exciting sexual love. [< L *amare* to love]

a·maze (ə·māz′) *v.t.* **a·mazed, a·maz·ing** To overwhelm, as by wonder; to astonish. [OE *āmasian*] —**a·maz′ed·ly** *adv.* —**a·maze′ment** *n.* —**a·maz′ing** *adj.* —**a·maz′ing·ly** *adv.*

Am·a·zon (am′ə·zon, -zən) *n.* 1. In Greek mythology, one of a race of female warriors. 2. Any physically strong and aggressive woman or girl: also **am′a·zon.** [< Gk. *a-* without + *mazōs* breast, from the fable that they cut off the right breast to facilitate use of the bow] —**Am′a·zo′ni·an** (-zō′ne·ən) *adj.*

am·bas·sa·dor (am·bas′ə·dər, -dôr) *n.* 1. A diplomat of the highest rank, representing one government to another. 2. A personal representative. [ME *ambassadour*, ult. < LL *ambactus* servant, goer about] —**am·bas′sa·**

do′ri·al (-dôr′ē·əl) *adj.* **—am·bas′sa·dor·ship** *n.*

am·ber (am′bər) *n.* 1. A brownish yellow fossilized vegetable resin, used in jewelry, etc. 2. The color of amber. [< Arabic *anbar* ambergris] **—am′ber** *adj.*

am·ber·gris (am′bər·grēs, -gris) *n.* A secretion of the sperm whale, used in perfumery. [< F *ambre gris* gray amber]

am·bi·dex·trous (am′bə·dek′strəs) *adj.* Able to use both hands equally well. [< L *ambi-* both + *dexter* right (hand)] **—am′bi·dex′trous·ly** *adv.* **—am′bi·dex·ter′i·ty** (-dek·ster′ə·tē), **am′bi·dex′trous·ness** *n.*

am·bi·ence (am′bē·əns, *Fr.* äṅ·byäns′) *n.* Surroundings, esp. the pervading atmosphere. Also **am′bi·ance.** [< F]

am·bi·ent (am′bē·ənt) *adj.* Surrounding; compassing. [< L *ambi-* around + *ire* to go]

am·big·u·ous (am·big′yo͞o·əs) *adj.* 1. Capable of being understood in more senses than one. 2. Doubtful or uncertain. [< L *ambi-* around + *agere* to go] **—am·bi·gu·i·ty** (am′bə·gyo͞o′ə·tē), **am·big′u·ous·ness** *n.* **—am·big′u·ous·ly** *adv.*

am·bi·tion (am·bish′ən) *n.* 1. Eager desire to succeed. 2. The object of aspiration. [< L *ambitio, -onis* a going about (to solicit votes)] **—am·bi′tion·less** *adj.*

am·bi·tious (am·bish′əs) *adj.* 1. Actuated or characterized by ambition. 2. Challenging: an *ambitious* project. **—am·bi′tious·ly** *adv.* **—am·bi′tious·ness** *n.*

am·biv·a·lent (am·biv′ə·lənt) *adj.* Experiencing or marked by contradictory emotions. [< L *ambo* both + *valens, -entis,* ppr. of *valere* to be strong, be worth] **—am·biv′a·lence** *n.*

am·ble (am′bəl) *v.i.* **·bled, ·bling** To walk or proceed leisurely. **—***n.* A certain easy gait, esp. of a horse. [< L *ambulare* to walk] **—am′bler** *n.* **—am′bling·ly** *adv.*

am·bro·sia (am·brō′zhə, -zhē·ə) *n.* 1. In classical mythology, the food of the gods. 2. Any delicious food or drink. [< Gk. *a-* not + *brotos* mortal] **—am·bro′sial, am·bro′sian** *adj.*

am·bu·lance (am′byə·ləns) *n.* A vehicle equipped for conveying the sick and wounded. [< F, field hospital < L *ambulare* to walk]

ambulance chaser *Slang* An unscrupulous lawyer who encourages accident victims to sue for damages. **—ambulance chasing**

am·bu·lant (am′byə·lənt) *adj.* Walking or moving about.

am·bu·la·to·ry (am′byə·lə·tôr′ē) *adj.* 1. Of or for walking. 2. Able to walk, as an invalid. **—***n. pl.* **·ries** A sheltered place for walking, as a cloister. [< L *ambulare* to walk]

am·bus·cade (am′bəs·kād′) *n.* An ambush. **—***v.t.* **·cad·ed, ·cad·ing** To ambush. [See AMBUSH.] **—am′bus·cad′er** *n.*

am·bush (am′bo͝osh) *n.* 1. An attack from hiding. 2. A position for surprise attack. Also **am′bush·ment.** **—***v.t.* To attack from hiding. [< L *in-* in + *boscus* a wood] **—am′bush·er** *n.*

a·me·ba (ə·mē′bə) *n. pl.* **·bas** or **·bae** (-bē) A unicellular protozoan found in soil and stagnant water, of indefinite and changing shape, and reproducing by division: also spelled *amoeba.* [< Gk. *amoibē* change] **—a·me′bic** or **a·moe′bic** *adj.*

a·me·boid (ə·mē′boid) *adj.* Resembling an ameba, as in its change of form: also spelled *amoeboid.*

a·mel·io·rate (ə·mēl′yə·rāt) *v.t.* & *v.i.* **·rat·ed, ·rat·ing** To make or become better. [< L *ad-* to + *meliorare* to better] **—a·mel′io·ra·ble** (-yər·ə·bəl) *adj.* **—a·mel′io·rant** (-rənt) *n.* **—a·mel′io·ra′tion** *n.* **—a·mel·io·ra·tive** (ə·mēl′yə·rā′tiv, -rə·tiv) *adj.* **—a·mel′io·ra′tor** *n.*

a·men (ā′men′, ä′-) *interj.* Expressing solemn affirmation, usu. at the end of a prayer. [< Hebrew *āmēn* verily]

a·me·na·ble (ə·mē′nə·bəl, ə·men′ə-) *adj.* 1. Capable of being persuaded. 2. Liable to be called to account. [< AF *a-* to + *mener* to lead < L *minare* to drive with threats] **—a·me′na·bil′i·ty, a·me′na·ble·ness** *n.* **—a·me′na·bly** *adv.*

a·mend (ə·mend′) *v.t.* 1. To change for the better; improve. 2. To change or alter by authority. [< L *emendare* to free from faults] **—a·mend′a·ble** *adj.* **—a·mend′a·ble·ness** *n.* **—a·mend′er** *n.*

a·mend·a·to·ry (ə·men′də·tôr′ē) *adj.* Tending to amend; corrective.

a·mend·ment (ə·mend′mənt) *n.* 1. A removal of faults; correction. 2. A changing, as of a law. 3. The statement of such a change.

a·mends (ə·mendz′) *n.pl.* Reparation: make *amends* for. [< L *mendum* fault]

a·men·i·ty (ə·men′ə·tē, ə·mē′nə·tē) *n. pl.* **·ties** 1. Agreeableness; pleasantness. 2. *Usu. pl.* An act or expression of courtesy; civility. 3. *pl.* Comforts; conveniences. [< L *amoenus* pleasant]

a·merce (ə·mûrs′) *v.t.* **a·merced, a·merc·ing** 1. To penalize by an assessment or arbitrary fine. 2. To punish. [< AF *a merci* at the mercy of] **—a·merce′a·ble** *adj.* **—a·merce′ment** *n.* **—a·merc′er** *n.*

A·mer·i·can (ə·mer′ə·kən) *adj.* 1. Pertaining to the United States of America. 2. Pertaining to North or South America. **—***n.* 1. A citizen of the United States. 2. An inhabitant of America.

A·mer·i·ca·na (ə·mer′ə·kä′nə, -kan′ə, -kā′nə) *n.pl.* American artifacts, literary papers, etc., esp. in a historical collection.

American English The English language as used in the United States.

A·mer·i·can·ism (ə·mer′ə·kən·iz′əm) *n.* 1. A trait, custom, or tradition especially characteristic of the United States. 2. A usage characteristic of American English.

A·mer·i·can·ize (ə·mer′ə·kən·īz′) *v.t.* & *v.i.* **·ized, ·iz·ing** To make or become American in spirit, methods, speech, etc. **—A·mer′i·can·i·za′tion** *n.*

American plan At a hotel, the system of paying for room and meals at a fixed, inclusive rate.

am·er·ic·i·um (am′ə·rish′ē·əm) *n.* An unstable radioactive element (symbol Am), resulting from the bombardment of uranium and plutonium by high-energy helium ions. [< NL, after *America*]

Am·er·in·di·an (am′ə·rin′dē·ən) *adj.* Of or pertaining to the American Indians or the Eskimos. Also **Am′er·in′dic.** **—Am′er·in′di·an** or **Am′er·ind** *n.*

am·e·thyst (am′ə·thist) *n.* A purple quartz or corundum used as a gem. [< Gk. *a-* not

+ *methystos* drunken (because wearing of the gem was believed to prevent drunkenness)]

a·mi·a·ble (ā′mē·ə·bəl) *adj.* 1. Pleasing in disposition; kindly. 2. Free from irritation; friendly: an *amiable* rivalry. [< L *amicus* friend] **—a′mi·a·bil′i·ty, a′mi·a·ble·ness** *n.* **—a′mi·a·bly** *adv.*

am·i·ca·ble (am′i·kə·bəl) *adj.* Friendly; peaceable. [< L *amicabilis* friendly] **—am′i·ca·bil′i·ty, am′i·ca·ble·ness** *n.* **—am′i·ca·bly** *adv.*

a·mid (ə·mid′) *prep.* In the midst of; among. Also *amidst, midst.* [OE *on middan* in the middle]

a·mid·ships (ə·mid′ships′) *adv. Naut.* Halfway between bow and stern; toward the middle of a ship. Also *midships.*

a·midst (ə·midst′) *prep.* Amid. [ME *amidde* + -s[3] + *t*]

a·mi·no acid (ə·mē′nō, am′ə·nō) *Biochem.* Any of a group of organic compounds containing the amino group (NH_2) combined with the carboxyl radical (COOH) and forming an essential part of the protein molecule.

Am·ish (am′ish, ä′mish) *n.pl.* A sect of Mennonites. [after the founder, Jacob *Ammann*, a 17th c. Mennonite]

a·miss (ə·mis′) *adj.* Out of order; improper: used predicatively: Something is *amiss.* *—adv.* In a defective way; erroneously. **—to take amiss** To take offense at. [ME < *a-* at + *mis* failure]

am·i·ty (am′ə·tē) *n.* Peaceful relations, as between nations. [< L *amicus* friend]

am·me·ter (am′mē′tər) *n. Electr.* An instrument for measuring amperage.

am·mo·nia (ə·mōn′yə, ə·mō′nē·ə) *n.* 1. A colorless, pungent, suffocating gas, obtained chiefly by synthesis from nitrogen and hydrogen. 2. Ammonium hydroxide. [< NL (*sal* salt) + *ammoniacus* < Gk. *ammōniakon* of *Ammōn*, an Egyptian god] **—am·mo·ni·ac** (ə·mō′nē·ak) *adj.*

am·mo·ni·um (ə·mō′nē·əm) *n. Chem* The univalent radical NH_4, that reacts with negative ions to form compounds such as ammonium hydroxide.

ammonium hydroxide *Chem.* A compound formed of ammonia in water, used as a cleaning solvent.

am·mu·ni·tion (am′yə·nish′ən) *n.* 1. Any of various articles used in the discharge of firearms and ordnance, as cartridges, shells, rockets, etc. 2. Any resources for attack or defense. [< L *munire* to fortify]

am·ne·sia (am·nē′zhə, -zhē·ə) *n.* Partial or total loss or impairment of memory. [< Gk. *a-* not + *mnasthai* to remember] **—am·ne′si·ac** (-zē·ak), **am·ne′sic** (-sik, -zik) *n. & adj.* **—am·nes·tic** (am·nes′tik) *adj.*

am·nes·ty (am′nəs·tē) *n. pl.* **·ties** A general pardon by which a government absolves offenders. [< Gk. *a-* not + *mnasthai* to remember] **—am′nes·ty** *v.t.* **·tied, ·ty·ing**

am·ni·o·cen·te·sis (am′nē·ō·sen·tē′sis) *n. pl.* **·ses** (-sēz) *Med.* The insertion of a hollow needle into the amnion and the withdrawal of fluid in order to diagnose disorders of the fetus or determine its sex. [< AMNION + Gk. *kentēsis* pricking]

am·ni·on (am′nē·on, -ən) *n. pl.* **·ni·ons** or **·ni·a** (-nē·ə) *Biol.* A membraneous sac, filled with a fluid (**amniotic fluid**), and enclosing the embryo or fetus of mammals, birds, and reptiles. [< Gk., caul] **—am′ni·ot′ic** *adj.*

a·moe·ba (ə·mē′bə) See AMEBA.

a·mok (ə·muk′, ə·mok′) See AMUCK.

a·mong (ə·mung′) *prep.* 1. In the midst of. 2. In or by the class, number, or group of: He was *among* the dead. 3. In portions for each of: Divide it *among* you. 4. Reciprocally between: disputes *among* friends. Also **a·mongst′.** [OE *on gemonge* in the crowd]

a·mon·til·la·do (ə·mon′tə·lä′dō, *Sp.* ä·mōn′·tē·lyä′thō) *n.* A pale dry sherry. [< Sp.]

a·mor·al (ā·môr′əl, ā·mor′əl) *adj.* Not subject to or concerned with moral or ethical values. **—a·mo·ral·i·ty** (ā′mə·ral′ə·tē) *n.* **—a·mor′al·ly** *adv.*

am·o·rous (am′ər·əs) *adj.* 1. Tending to fall in love; loving. 2. Of or related to sexual love. 3. In love; enamored; often with *of*: *amorous* of the truth. [< L *amor* love] **—am′o·rous·ly** *adv.* **—am′o·rous·ness** *n.*

a·mor·phous (ə·môr′fəs) *adj.* 1. Without definite form or character. 2. *Chem.* Uncrystallized. [< Gk. *a-* without + *morphē* form] **—a·mor′phism** *n.* **—a·mor′phous·ly** *adv.* **—a·mor′phous·ness** *n.*

am·or·tize (am′ər·tīz, ə·môr′tīz) *v.t.* **·tized, ·tiz·ing** To extinguish gradually, as a debt or liability, by installment payments or by a sinking fund. Also, *Brit.* **am′or·tise.** [< OF *amortir* to extinguish < L *ad-* to + *mors, mortis* death] **—am′or·tiz′a·ble** *adj.* **—am′·or·ti·za′tion, a·mor·tize·ment** (ə·môr′tiz·ment) *n.*

A·mos (ā′məs) *n.* A book of the Old Testament containing the prophecies of Amos, 8th c. B.C. Hebrew minor prophet.

a·mount (ə·mount′) *n.* 1. A sum total of two or more quantities. 2. The value of the principal with the interest upon it, as in a loan. 3. The entire significance, value, or effect. 4. Quantity: a considerable *amount* of discussion. *—v.i.* 1. To reach in number or quantity: with *to*: to *amount* to ten dollars. 2. To be equivalent in effect or importance: with *to*: It *amounts* to treason. [< L *ad-* to + *mons, montis* mountain]

a·mour (ə·mo͝or′) *n.* A love affair, esp. a secret or illicit one. [< F]

am·per·age (am′pər·ij, am·pir′ij) *n. Electr.* The strength of a current in amperes.

am·pere (am′pir, am·pir′) *n. Electr.* The practical unit of current strength, produced by an electromotive force of one volt across a resistance of one ohm. Abbr. *amp.* [after A. M. *Ampère*, 1775–1836, French physicist]

am·per·sand (am′pər·sand, am′pər·sand′) *n.* The character &, meaning *and.* [< *and per se and*, lit., & by itself = and]

am·phet·a·mine (am·fet′ə·mēn, -min) *n.* An acrid liquid compound, or one of its derivatives, used as a stimulant. [< A(LPHA)-M(ETHYL)-PH(ENYL)-ET(HYL)-AMINE]

amphi- *prefix* 1. On both or all sides; around: *amphitheater.* 2. Of both kinds; in two ways. [< Gk. *amphi* around]

am·phib·i·an (am·fib′ē·ən) *adj.* 1. *Zool.* Of or pertaining to a class of cold-blooded, chiefly egg-laying vertebrates adapted for life both on land and in water, as frogs. 2. Amphibious. *—n.* 1. An amphibian animal or plant. 2. An airplane capable of operating from land or water. 3. A vehicle capable of self-propulsion on land or water.

am·phib·i·ous (am·fib′ē·əs) *adj.* 1. Adapted to life on land or in water. 2. Capable of operating on or from land or water. [< Gk. *amphi-* of two kinds + *bios* life] —**am·phib′i·ous·ly** *adv.* —**am·phib′i·ous·ness** *n.*

am·phi·bole (am′fə·bōl) *n. Mineral.* Any of a class of minerals, consisting chiefly of calcium, magnesium, iron, aluminum, and sodium combined with silica. [< Gk. *amphi-* around + *ballein* to throw]

am·phi·the·a·ter (am′fə·thē′ə·tər) *n.* An oval or round structure having tiers of seats around an arena. Also *Brit.* **am′phi·the′a·tre.** [< Gk. *amphi-* around + *theatron* theater]

am·pho·ra (am′fə·rə) *n. pl.* **·rae** (-rē) In ancient Greece and Rome, a tall, two-handled earthenware jar, narrow at the neck and the base. [< Gk. *amphi-* on both sides + *phoreus* bearer] —**am′pho·ral** *adj.*

am·ple (am′pəl) *adj.* 1. Of great dimension, capacity, amount, degree, etc.; large. 2. More than enough; abundant. [< L *amplus* large, abundant] —**am′ple·ness** *n.* —**am′ply** *adv.*

am·pli·fy (am′plə·fī) *v.* **·fied, ·fy·ing** *v.t.* 1. To enlarge or increase in scope, significance, or power. 2. To add to so as to make more complete, as by illustrations. 3. To exaggerate; magnify. 4. *Electronics* To increase the strength or amplitude of, as electromagnetic impulses. —*v.i.* 5. To make additional remarks. [< L *amplus* large + *facere* to make] —**am′pli·fi·ca′tion** *n.* —**am′pli·fi′er** *n.*

am·pli·tude (am′plə·to͞od, -tyo͞od) *n.* 1. Greatness of extent; largeness; breadth. 2. Fullness; abundance. 3. *Physics* **a** The extent of the swing of a vibrating body on each side of the mean position. **b** The peak value attained by a wave or an alternating current during one complete cycle. [< L *amplus* large]

amplitude modulation *Telecom.* Radio transmission in which the carrier wave is modulated by varying the amplitude in accordance with the strength of the signal. Compare FREQUENCY MODULATION. Abbr. *a.m., A.M.*

am·pule (am′pyo͞ol) *n. Med.* A sealed vial used as a container for one dose of a hypodermic solution. Also **am·poule** (am′po͞ol), **am·pul** (am′pul, am′po͞ol). [< L *ampulla* flask]

am·pu·tate (am′pyo͞o·tāt) *v.t. & v.i.* **·tat·ed, ·tat·ing** To cut off (a limb, etc.) by surgery. [< L *ambi-* around + *putare* to trim] —**am′pu·ta′tion** *n.* —**am′pu·ta′tor** *n.*

am·pu·tee (am′pyo͞o·tē′) *n.* One who has had a limb or limbs amputated.

a·muck (ə·muk′) *adv.* In a murderous frenzy: only in the phrase **to run amuck.** Also *amok.* [< Malay *amoq* furious attack]

am·u·let (am′yə·lit) *n.* Anything worn as a charm against danger. [< L *amuletum*]

a·muse (ə·myo͞oz′) *v.t.* **a·mused, a·mus·ing** 1. To occupy pleasingly. 2. To cause to laugh or smile. [< MF *à* at + OF *muser* to stare] —**a·muse′ment** *n.*

amusement park A park having various devices for entertainment, as roller coasters, shooting galleries, etc.

a·mus·ing (ə·myo͞o′zing) *adj.* 1. Entertaining or diverting. 2. Arousing laughter or mirth. —**a·mus′ing·ly** *adv.*

am·y·lase (am′ə·lās) *n. Biochem.* An enzyme that promotes the conversion of starch and glycogen into maltose. [< Gk. *amylon* starch]

an (an, *unstressed* ən) *indefinite article* or *adj.* Equivalent to the article *a*, but used before words beginning with a vowel sound, as *an* eagle, and sometimes before words beginning with *h* in an unstressed syllable, as *an* historian. [OE *ān* one]

an- *prefix* Without; not: *anarchy.* Also, before consonants (except *h*), *a-*. [< Gk.]

-an *suffix* Used to form adjectives and nouns denoting: 1. Of, belonging to, or characteristic of: *Italian, Lutheran, Mozartean.* 2. Skilled in: *artisan, grammarian.* Also *-ean, -ian.* [< L *-anus*]

ana- *prefix* 1. Up; upward: *anadromous.* 2. Back; backward: *anapest.* 3. Anew: sometimes capable of being rendered *re-*, as *anabaptism*, rebaptism. 4. Thoroughly: *analysis.* Also, before vowels or *h*, **an-**. [< Gk. *ana* up, back]

-ana *suffix* Pertaining to: added to names of notable persons, places, etc., to indicate a collection, such as writings or anecdotes, about the subject: *Americana.* Also *-iana.* [< L, neut. pl. of *-anus*]

a·nab·o·lism (ə·nab′ə·liz′əm) *n. Biol.* The process by which food is converted into protoplasm: opposed to *catabolism.* [< Gk. *anabolē* a heaping up] —**an·a·bol·ic** (an′ə·bol′ik) *adj.*

a·nach·ro·nism (ə·nak′rə·niz′əm) *n.* 1. The assigning of an event, person, etc., to a wrong, esp. an earlier, date. 2. Something out of its proper time. [< Gk. *ana-* against + *chronos* time] —**a·nach′ro·nis′tic** or **·ti·cal, a·nach′ro·nous** *adj.*

an·a·con·da (an′ə·kon′də) *n.* 1. A large, nonvenomous tropical serpent that crushes its prey in its coils. 2. Any boa constrictor. [? < Singhalese]

an·aer·obe (an′ə·rōb) *n.* An anaerobic organism.

an·aer·o·bic (an′ə·rō′bik) *adj.* Living or functioning in the absence of free oxygen. [< AN- + AERO- + Gk. *bios* life] —**an′aer·o′bi·cal·ly** *adv.*

an·aes·the·sia (an′is·thē′zhə, -zhē·ə), **an·aes·thet·ic** (an′is·thet′ik), etc. See ANESTHESIA, etc.

an·a·gram (an′ə·gram) *n.* 1. A word or phrase formed by transposing the letters of another word or phrase. 2. *pl.* (*construed as sing.*) A game in which the players make words by transposing or adding letters. [< Gk. *ana-* backwards + *gramma* letter] —**an·a·gram·mat·ic** (an′ə·grə·mat′ik) or **·i·cal** *adj.* —**an′a·gram·mat′i·cal·ly** *adv.*

a·nal (ā′nəl) *adj. Anat.* Of, pertaining to, or situated in the region of the anus. [< L *anus* + -AL[1]]

an·a·lects (an′ə·lekts) *n.pl.* Selections from a literary work or group of works. Also **an′a·lec′ta.** [< Gk. *ana-* up + *legein* to gather]

an·al·ge·si·a (an′əl·jē′zē·ə, -sē·ə) *n. Pathol.* Inability to feel pain. Also **an·al·gi·a** (an·al′jē·ə) [< Gk. *an-* without + *algos* pain]

an·al·ge·sic (an′əl·jē′zik, -sik) *n.* A drug for the alleviation of pain. —**an′al·ge′sic** *adj.*

analog computer A computer that solves problems by substituting analogous quantities, as voltage, etc., for the variables of the problems. Compare DIGITAL COMPUTER.

a·nal·o·gous (ə·nal′ə·gəs) *adj.* 1. Resembling or comparable in certain respects. 2. *Biol.* Having a similar function but differing in origin and structure, as the wings of birds and insects: distinguished from *homologous.* **—a·nal′o·gous·ly** *adv.* **—a·nal′o·gous·ness** *n.*

an·a·logue (an′ə·lôg, -log) *n.* Anything analogous to something else. Also **an′a·log.**

a·nal·o·gy (ə·nal′ə·jē) *n. pl.* **·gies** 1. Agreement or resemblance in certain aspects. 2. *Biol.* A similarity in function and appearance, but not in structure or origin. 3. *Logic* Inference that items showing some resemblances will show others. [< Gk. *ana-* according to + *logos* proportion]

a·nal·y·sis (ə·nal′ə·sis) *n. pl.* **·ses** (-sēz) 1. The separation of a whole into its parts or elements: opposed to *synthesis.* 2. A statement of the results of this. 3. A method of determining or describing the nature of a thing by separating it into its parts. 4. *Chem.* The determination of the kind, quantity, and proportions of constituents forming a compound or substance. 5. Psychoanalysis. [< Gk. *ana-* throughout + *lyein* to loosen] **—an·a·lyt·ic** (an′ə·lit′ik) or **·i·cal** *adj.* **—an′a·lyt′i·cal·ly** *adv.*

an·a·lyst (an′ə·list) *n.* 1. One who analyzes or is skilled in analysis. 2. A psychoanalyst.

an·a·lyze (an′ə·līz) *v.t.* **·lyzed, ·lyz·ing** 1. To separate into constituent parts or elements, esp. to determine the nature, form, etc., of the whole. 2. To examine critically or minutely. 3. To psychoanalyze. Also *Brit.* **an′a·lyse.** [See ANALYSIS.] **—an′a·lyz′a·ble** *adj.* **—an′a·ly·za′tion** *n.* **—an′a·lyz′er** *n.*

an·a·pest (an′ə·pest) *n.* 1. In prosody, a metrical foot consisting of two short or unaccented syllables followed by one long or accented syllable (˘ ˘ ¯). 2. A line of verse made up of such feet. Also **an′a·paest.** [< Gk. *ana-* back + *paiein* to strike] **—an′a·pes′tic** *adj.*

an·ar·chism (an′ər·kiz′əm) *n.* 1. The theory that all forms of government are incompatible with individual and social liberty and should be abolished. 2. The methods of anarchists. **—an′ar·chis′tic** *adj.*

an·ar·chist (an′ər·kist) *n.* 1. One who believes in and advocates anarchism. 2. One who encourages anarchy. Also **an·arch** (an′ärk).

an·ar·chy (an′ər·kē) *n.* 1. Absence of government. 2. Lawless confusion and political disorder. 3. General disorder. [< Gk. *an-* without + *archos* leader] **—an·ar·chic** (an·är′kik) or **·chi·cal** *adj.* **—an·ar′·chi·cal·ly** *adv.*

a·nas·to·mo·sis (ə·nas′tə·mō′sis) *n. pl.* **·ses** (-sēz) Any union, interlacing, or running together, as of blood vessels, veins of a leaf, river channels, etc. [< Gk. *anastomōsis* opening] **—a·nas′to·mot′ic** (-mot′ik) *adj.*

a·nath·e·ma (ə·nath′ə·mə) *n. pl.* **·mas** or **·ma·ta** (-mə·tə) 1. A formal ban or curse, as excommunication. 2. One who or that which is cursed or shunned. [< Gk., a thing devoted (to evil)]

a·nath·e·ma·tize (ə·nath′ə·mə·tīz′) *v.t.* **·tized, ·tiz·ing** To pronounce an anathema against; curse.

a·nat·o·mist (ə·nat′ə·mist) *n.* One skilled in anatomy.

a·nat·o·mize (ə·nat′ə·mīz) *v.t.* **·mized, ·miz·ing** 1. To dissect (an animal or plant) to investigate its structure. 2. To examine minutely; analyze. **—a·nat′o·mi·za′tion** *n.*

a·nat·o·my (ə·nat′ə·mē) *n. pl.* **·mies** 1. The structure of a plant or animal, or of any of its parts. 2. The science of the structure of plants or animals. 3. The art or practice of anatomizing. [< Gk. *ana-* up + *temnein* to cut] **—an·a·tom·i·cal** (an′ə·tom′i·kəl) or **an′a·tom′ic** *adj.* **—an′a·tom′i·cal·ly** *adv.*

-ance *suffix of nouns* Used to form nouns of action, quality, state, or condition from adjectives ending in *-ant,* and also directly from verbs, as in *abundance, forbearance.* Compare -ANCY. [< F *-ance* < L *-antia, -entia*]

an·ces·tor (an′ses·tər) *n.* 1. One from whom a person or other organism is biologically descended. 2. Anything considered as a forerunner of a later thing. [< ANTE- + L *cedere* to go] **—an′ces·tress** (-tris) *n.fem.*

an·ces·try (an′ses·trē) *n. pl.* **·tries** A line or body of ancestors; ancestors collectively. **—an·ces′tral** *adj.* **—an·ces′tral·ly** *adv.*

an·chor (ang′kər) *n.* 1. A heavy implement, usu. of iron or steel, with hooks or flukes to grip the bottom, attached to a cable and dropped from a ship or boat to hold it in place. 2. Anything that makes stable or secure. **—at anchor** Anchored, as a ship. **—***v.t.* 1. To secure by an anchor. 2. To fix firmly. **—***v.i.* 3. To lie at anchor, as a ship. [< Gk. *ankyra*]

an·chor·age (ang′kər·ij) *n.* A place for anchoring.

an·cho·rite (ang′kə·rīt) *n.* One who has withdrawn from the world for religious reasons; hermit. Also **an′cho·ret** (-rit, -ret). [< Gk. *ana-* back + *chōreein* to withdraw] **—an′cho·rit′ic** (-rit′ik) *adj.*

an·chor·man (ang′kər·man′) *n. pl.* **·men** (-men′) 1. The final competitor on a relay team. 2. A broadcaster who coordinates and comments on reports by other broadcasters.

an·cho·vy (an′chō·vē, -chə·vē, an·chō′vē) *n. pl.* **·vies** or **·vy** 1. A very small, herringlike fish inhabiting warm seas, valued as a delicacy. 2. *U.S.* Smelt. [< Sp., Pg. *anchova*]

an·cien ré·gime (äṅ·syaṅ′ rā·zhēm′) *French* A former political and social system; esp., the system in France before the revolution of 1789. Also **Ancient Regime.**

an·cient (ān′shənt) *adj.* 1. Existing or occurring in times long past, esp. before the fall of the Western Roman Empire, in A.D. 476. 2. Very old. **—***n.* 1. One who lived in ancient times. 2. An aged or venerable person. [< OF *ancien* < L *ante* before] **—an′cient·ness** *n.* **—an′cient·ly** *adv.*

an·cil·lar·y (an′sə·ler′ē) *adj.* Subordinate; auxiliary. [< L *ancilla* maid]

-ancy *suffix of nouns* A modern variant of -ANCE: used to form new words expressing quality, state, or condition (*infancy, vacancy*), or to refashion older nouns of quality in *-ance* (*constancy*). [< L *-antia*]

and (and, *unstressed* ənd, ən, ′n) *conj.* 1. Also; added to; as well as: a particle denoting addition, emphasis, or union, used as a connective between words, phrases, clauses, and sentences. 2. As a result or consequence:

Make one move *and* you are dead! 3. To: with *come, go, try,* etc.: Try *and* stop me. [OE *ond, and*]

an·dan·te (an·dan′tē, *Ital.* än·dän′tā) *Music adj. & adv.* Moderately slow; slower than allegro but faster than largo. **—*n.*** An andante movement or passage. [< Ital., walking]

An·de·an (an·dē′ən, an′dē·ən) *adj.* Of the Andes.

and·i·ron (and′ī′ərn) *n.* One of two metal supports for holding wood in an open fireplace. [< OF *andier*; infl. by *iron*]

and/or Either *and* or *or*, according to the meaning intended.

andro- *combining form* 1. Man in general. 2. The male sex. 3. *Bot.* Stamen; anther. [< Gk. *anēr, andros* man]

an·dro·gen (an′drə·jən) *n. Biochem.* Any of various hormones that control the development of masculine characteristics. **—an′dro·gen′ic** (-jen′ik) *adj.*

an·drog·y·nous (an·droj′ə·nəs) *adj.* 1. Having the characteristics of both sexes; hermaphroditic. 2. *Bot.* Having the male and female flowers in the same cluster. Also **an·drog′y·nal, an·dro·gyn·ic** (an′drə·jin′ik). [< Gk. *anēr, andros* man + *gynē* woman] **—an·drog′y·ny** *n.*

an·droid (an′droid) *adj.* Having human shape. **—*n.*** An android robot. [< Gk. *andros* man + *-eides* like]

An·drom·e·da (an·drom′ə·də) *n.* A constellation of the northern hemisphere.

an·ec·dote (an′ik·dōt) *n.* A brief story of an interesting or entertaining nature. [< Gk. *an-* not + *ekdotos* published] **—an′ec·dot′al** *adj.*

an·ec·dot·ist (an′ik·dō′tist) *n.* One who collects, publishes, or is given to telling anecdotes.

a·ne·mi·a (ə·nē′mē·ə) *n. Pathol.* A deficiency in hemoglobin or the number of red corpuscles in the blood. [< Gk. *an-* without + *haima* blood] **—a·ne′mic** *adj.*

a·nem·o·graph (ə·nem′ə·graf) *n. Meteorol.* A recording anemometer. **—a·nem′o·graph′ic** *adj.*

an·e·mom·e·ter (an′ə·mom′ə·tər) *n. Meteorol.* An instrument for measuring the velocity and direction of the wind. **—an·e·mo·met·ric** (an′ə·mō·met′rik) or **·ri·cal** *adj.* **—an′e·mom′e·try** *n.*

a·nem·o·ne (ə·nem′ə·nē) *n.* 1. A plant having flowers with no petals but showy, multicolored sepals: also called *windflower.* 2. *Zool.* The sea anemone. [< Gk. *anemos* wind]

an·es·the·sia (an′is·thē′zhə, -zhē·ə) *n.* Partial or total loss of physical sensation, particularly of pain, due to disease or certain drugs: also spelled *anaesthesia.* Also **an·es·the·sis** (an′is·thē′sis). [< Gk. *an-* without + *aisthēsis* sensation]

an·es·the·si·ol·o·gy (an′əs·thē·zē·ol′ə·jē) *n. Med.* The science of using anesthetics: also spelled *anaesthesiology.* **—an′es·the·si·ol′o·gist** *n.*

an·es·thet·ic (an′is·thet′ik) *n.* A drug, gas, etc., that causes anesthesia. **—*adj.*** 1. Pertaining to or like anesthesia. 2. Producing anesthesia. Also spelled *anaesthetic.* **—an·es·the·tist** (ə·nes′thə·tist) *n.* **—an·es·the·tize** (ə·nes′thə·tīz) *v.t.* **·tized, ·tiz·ing**

an·eu·rysm (an′yə·riz′əm) *n. Pathol.* A swelling of the wall of an artery, forming a sac. Also **an′eu·rism.** [< Gk. *ana-* up + *eurys* wide] **—an′eu·rys′mal** or **an′eu·ris′mal** *adj.*

a·new (ə·nōō′, ə·nyōō′) *adv.* 1. Again. 2. Over again in a different way. [OE *of nīwe*]

an·gel (ān′jəl) *n.* 1. *Theol.* A spiritual being attendant upon the Deity; a heavenly messenger. 2. A person likened to an angel in qualities of goodness, beauty, etc. 3. *Informal* A financial backer, as of a play, etc. [< Gk. *angelos* messenger]

angel dust A crystalline, powdered form of PCP, that is inhaled or swallowed, or smoked with marijuana, mint, or parsley for its hallucinogenic and euphoric effects, and that may produce symptoms like those of schizophrenia.

an·gel·fish (ān′jəl·fish′) *n. pl.* **·fish** or **·fish·es** 1. A raylike shark having winglike pectoral fins. 2. A fish of warm seas having brilliant coloration, as the porgy.

an·gel·ic (an·jel′ik) *adj.* 1. Pertaining to, of, or consisting of angels; celestial. 2. Like an angel; pure; beautiful. Also **an·gel′i·cal.** **—an·gel′i·cal·ly** *adv.*

an·gel·i·ca (an·jel′i·kə) *n.* A fragrant plant of the parsley family, used in flavoring and medicines. [< Med.L *(herba) angelica* angelic (herb)]

an·ge·lus (an′jə·ləs) *n. Eccl.* 1. A prayer used to commemorate the Annunciation. 2. A bell rung at morning, noon, and night as a call to recite this prayer: also called **angelus bell.** Also **An′ge·lus.** [< L]

an·ger (ang′gər) *n.* A feeling of strong displeasure and antagonism directed against the cause of an assumed wrong or injury. **—*v.t. & v.i.*** To make or become angry or enraged. [< ON *angr* grief]

an·gi·na (an·jī′nə, an′jə·nə) *n. Pathol.* 1. Any disease characterized by spasmodic suffocation, as croup. 2. Angina pectoris. [< L, quinsy < *angere* to choke]

angina pec·to·ris (pek′tə·ris) *Pathol.* A defect of coronary circulation, characterized by paroxysmal pain below the breast bone. [< NL, angina of the chest]

an·gi·o·sperm (an′jē·ə·spûrm′) *n.* Any of a class of plants having the seeds in a closed seed vessel. [< Gk. *angeion* vessel + *sperma* seed]

an·gle[1] (ang′gəl) *v.i.* **·gled, ·gling** 1. To fish with a hook and line. 2. To try to get something slyly or artfully: with *for.* **—*n.*** 1. A selfish motive. 2. A devious method for achieving a purpose. [OE *angel* fishhook]

an·gle[2] (ang′gəl) *n.* 1. *Geom.* **a** The figure or space made by the meeting of two straight lines or of two plane surfaces. **b** The arc of rotation between these lines or surfaces, measured in degrees. 2. A projecting corner, as of a building. 3. The direction from which a thing is seen. **—*v.t. & v.i.*** **·gled, ·gling** To move or turn at an angle or by angles. [< L *angulus* corner, angle]

An·gle (ang′gel) *n.* A member of a Germanic tribe that migrated to Britain in the 5th c. [< L *Anglus*] **—An′gli·an** *adj. & n.*

angle iron An angled piece of iron or steel, used to join or strengthen beams, etc.

angle of incidence *Physics* The angle relative to the perpendicular drawn from the point at which an object, beam of light, etc., strikes a surface.

an·gler (ang′glər) *n.* 1. One who fishes with rod, hook, and line. 2. One who schemes to obtain something.

an·gle·worm (ang′gəl·wûrm′) *n.* An earthworm, commonly used as bait on fishhooks.

An·gli·can (ang′glə·kən) *adj.* Of the Church of England, or of the churches that agree with it in faith and order. —*n.* A member of an Anglican Church. [< Med.L *Anglicanus* < L *Angli* the Angles]

Anglican Church 1. The Church of England. 2. A body of churches mostly derived from the Church of England and in communion with it. —**An′gli·can·ism** *n.*

An·gli·cism (ang′glə·siz′əm) *n.* An idiom or turn of phrase peculiar to the English language.

An·gli·cize (ang′glə·sīz) *v.t.* **·cized, ·ciz·ing** To give an English form, style, or idiom to. Also *Brit.* **An′gli·cise.** —**An′gli·ci·za′tion** *n.*

An·gli·fy (ang′glə·fī) *v.t. & v.i.* **·fied, ·fy·ing** To Anglicize.

an·gling (ang′gling) *n.* The act or art of fishing with a hook, line, and rod.

An·glo (ang′glō) *n. pl.* **·glos** A non-Latin Caucasian resident of the U.S. [Shortened from *Anglo-American*]

Anglo- *combining form* English; English and: *Anglophile, Anglo-Norman.*

An·glo·phile (ang′glə·fīl, -fil) *n.* A lover of England or its people, customs, institutions, or manners. Also **An′glo·phil** (-fil). —**An′·glo·phil′ic** (-fil′ik) *adj.*

An·glo·pho·bi·a (ang′glə·fō′bē·ə) *n.* Hatred or dread of England or its customs, people, or institutions. —**An′glo·phobe** *n. & adj.* —**An′glo·pho′bic** (-fō′bik, -fob′ik) *adj.*

An·glo-Sax·on (ang′glō·sak′sən) *n.* 1. A member of one of the Germanic tribes (Angles, Saxons, and Jutes) that dominated England from the 5th to 12th c. 2. Their West Germanic language; Old English. See under ENGLISH. 3. A person of English nationality or descent. —**An′glo-Sax′on** *adj.*

An·go·ra (ang·gôr′ə) *n.* 1. A goat having long, silky hair. 2. Its wool, or yarn or cloth made of its wool: also **an·go′ra.** 3. A variety of cat (**Angora cat**) with long, silky hair.

an·gry (ang′grē) *adj.* **an·gri·er, an·gri·est** 1. Feeling or showing anger; wrathful. 2. Badly inflamed, as an infection. —**an·gri·ly** (ang′grə·lē) *adv.* —**an′gri·ness** *n.*

ang·strom (ang′strəm) *n.* A linear unit equal to 10^{-8} centimeter, used for minute measurements, as of wavelengths of light. Also **angstrom unit.** [after A. J. *Angström,* 1814–75, Swedish physicist]

an·guish (ang′gwish) *n.* Excruciating mental or bodily pain; agony. —*v.i.* To suffer anguish. [< OF *anguisse* < L *angustia* tightness, difficulty] —**an′guished** *adj.*

an·gu·lar (ang′gyə·lər) *adj.* 1. Having, forming, or constituting an angle; sharp-cornered. 2. Measured by an angle. 3. Pertaining to angles. 4. Bony; gaunt. [< L *angulus* corner, angle] —**an′gu·lar′i·ty** (-lar′ə·tē) *n.* —**an′gu·lar·ly** *adv.*

an·hy·dride (an·hī′drīd, -drid) *n. Chem.* A compound related to another compound, especially an acid or base, by the absence of water of crystallization.

an·hy·drous (an·hī′drəs) *adj.* Without water. [< Gk. *an-* without + *hydōr* water]

an·i·line (an′ə·lin, -līn) *n. Chem.* A colorless, oily, poisonous compound, the base of many coal-tar dyes, chiefly made from nitrobenzene. [< Arabic *an-nīl* the blue < Skt. *nīlī* indigo] —**an′i·line** *adj.*

an·i·mad·ver·sion (an′ə·mad·vûr′zhən, -shən) *n.* A censorious comment or reflection.

an·i·mad·vert (an′ə·mad·vûrt′) *v.i.* To comment critically, usu. in an adverse sense: with *on* or *upon.* [< L *animus* mind + *advertere* to turn to]

an·i·mal (an′ə·məl) *n.* 1. A sentient living organism typically capable of voluntary motion and sensation: distinguished from *plant.* 2. Any such creature as distinguished from man. 3. A bestial human being. —*adj.* 1. Of or resembling animals. 2. Carnal; sensual: *animal* appetites. [< L *anima* breath, soul, life]

an·i·mal·cule (an′ə·mal′kyōōl) *n.* An animal of microscopic smallness, as an ameba. Also **an′i·mal′cu·lum** (-kyə·ləm). [< L *animalculum*] —**an′i·mal′cu·lar** (-kyə·lər) *adj.*

an·i·mal·ism (an′ə·məl·iz′əm) *n.* 1. Bestial sensuality. 2. The doctrine that man is entirely animal, having no soul. —**an′i·mal·ist** *n.* —**an′i·mal·is′tic** *adj.*

animal kingdom Animal organisms collectively, as distinguished from plants.

animal magnetism Mesmerism.

an·i·mate (*v.* an′ə·māt; *adj.* an′ə·mit) *v.t.* **·mat·ed, ·mat·ing** 1. To impart life to; make alive. 2. To move to action. 3. To produce the illusion of motion in (a projected film) by a series of drawings. —*adj.* 1. Possessing animal life; living. 2. Full of life; vivacious; lively: also **an′i·mat′ed.** [< L *anima* breath, soul] —**an′i·mat′ed·ly** *adv.* —**an′i·ma′tor** or **an′i·ma′ter** *n.*

animated cartoon See CARTOON.

an·i·ma·tion (an′ə·mā′shən) *n.* 1. The act of imparting life, or the state of possessing life. 2. The quality of being lively or quick; vivacity. 3. The making of animated films.

an·i·mism (an′ə·miz′əm) *n.* The doctrine that natural objects and phenomena possess a soul. [< L *anima* soul] —**an′i·mist** *n.* —**an′i·mis′tic** *adj.*

an·i·mos·i·ty (an′ə·mos′ə·tē) *n. pl.* **·ties** Active and vehement enmity; hatred. [< L *animositas, -tatis* high spirit]

an·i·mus (an′ə·məs) *n.* Hostile feeling; animosity. [< L]

an·i·on (an′ī′ən) *n. Chem.* A negative ion: opposed to *cation.* [< Gk. *anienai* to go up] —**an′i·on′ic** (-on′ik) *adj.*

an·ise (an′is) *n.* A small South European and North African plant that furnishes a fragrant seed (**aniseed**) used for flavoring. [< Gk. *anison*]

an·i·sette (an′ə·zet′, -set′) *n.* A cordial made from or flavored with aniseed. [< F]

an·kle (ang′kəl) *n.* 1. The joint connecting the foot and the leg. 2. The part of the leg between the foot and the calf near the ankle joint. [ME *ankel* < OE *anclēow*]

an·kle·bone (ang′kəl·bōn′) *n.* The talus.

an·klet (ang′klit) *n.* 1. An ornament or fetter for the ankle. 2. A short sock reaching just above the ankle.

an·nals (an′əlz) *n.pl.* 1. A record of events in their chronological order, year by year. 2.

History or records. 3. A periodical publication of discoveries, transactions, etc. [< L *annus* year] **—an′nal·ist** *n.* **—an′nal·is′tic** *adj.*

an·neal (ə·nēl′) *v.t.* 1. To reduce the brittleness of, as glass and various metals, by heating and then slowly cooling. 2. To toughen, as the will. [OE *onælan* to burn]

an·ne·lid (an′ə·lid) *Zool. adj.* Belonging to a phylum of segmented worms, including the earthworm and leeches. [< L *annellus* ring] **—an′ne·lid** *n.*

an·nex (*v.* ə·neks′; *n.* an′eks) *v.t.* 1. To append, as an addition. 2. To incorporate (territory) into a larger political unit. **—***n.* An addition to a building. [< L *ad-* to + *nectere* to tie] **—an·nex′a·ble** *adj.* **—an′nex·a′tion** *n*

an·ni·hi·late (ə·nī′ə·lāt) *v.t.* **·lat·ed, ·lat·ing** To destroy utterly. [< L *ad-* to + *nihil* nothing] **—an·ni′hi·la′tion** *n.* **—an·ni′hi·la′tive** *adj.* **—an·ni′hi·la′tor** *n.*

an·ni·ver·sa·ry (an′ə·vûr′sər·ē) *n. pl.* **·ries** 1. A date on which an event occurred in some preceding year. 2. A celebration on such occasion. [< L *annus* year + *versus,* pp. of *vertere* to turn] **—an′ni·ver′sa·ry** *adj.*

an·no Dom·i·ni (an′ō dom′ə·nē, -nī) In the (designated) year of the Christian era. [< L, in the year of the Lord] Abbr. *A.D.*

an·no·tate (an′ō·tāt) *v.t. & v.i.* **·tat·ed, ·tat·ing** To provide (a text, etc.) with explanatory or critical notes. [< L *ad-* to + *notare* to note, mark] **—an′no·ta′tion** *n.* **—an′no·ta′tive** *adj.* **—an′no·ta′tor** *n.*

an·nounce (ə·nouns′) *v.t.* **·nounced, ·nounc·ing** 1. To make known publicly or officially; proclaim. 2. To give notice of the approach or arrival of. [< L *ad-* to + *nuntiare* to report] **—an·nounce′ment** *n.*

an·nounc·er (ə·noun′sər) *n.* 1. One who announces. 2. A person who identifies the station, introduces programs, etc., on radio or television.

an·noy (ə·noi′) *v.t.* To be troublesome to; bother; irritate. [< L *in odio* in hatred] **—an·noy′er** *n.*

an·noy·ance (ə·noi′əns) *n.* 1. One who or that which annoys. 2. The act of annoying or the state of being annoyed.

an·noy·ing (ə·noi′ing) *adj.* Irritating; irksome. **—an·noy′ing·ly** *adv.*

an·nu·al (an′yōō·əl) *adj.* 1. Returning, performed, or occurring every year. 2. Reckoned by the year. **—***n.* 1. A publication issued once a year. 2. A plant living for one year or season. [< L *annualis* yearly] **—an′nu·al·ly** *adv.*

an·nu·i·ty (ə·nōō′ə·tē, ə·nyōō′-) *n. pl.* **·ties** 1. An income other than salary, paid yearly. 2. An investment plan that provides yearly payments. [< Med.L *annuitas, -tatis*] **—an·nu′i·tant** *n.*

an·nul (ə·nul′) *v.t.* **·nulled, ·nul·ling** To put an end to; nullify, esp. a marriage. [< L *ad-* to + *nullus* none] **—an·nul′la·ble** *adj.* **—an·nul′ment** *n.*

an·nu·lar (an′yə·lər) *adj.* Ring-shaped. **—an′nu·lar·ly** *adv.*

annular eclipse *Astron.* A solar eclipse in which a narrow ring of the sun is visible beyond the dark mass of the moon.

an·nu·late (an′yə·lit, -lāt) *adj.* Furnished with rings; ringed. **—an′nu·la′tion** *n.*

an·nu·lus (an′yə·ləs) *n. pl.* **·li** (-lī) or **·lus·es** A ringlike body or space. [< L, ring]

an·nun·ci·ate (ə·nun′sē·āt) *v.t.* **·at·ed, ·at·ing** To announce. [< L *annuntiare* to report]

an·nun·ci·a·tion (ə·nun′sē·ā′shən) *n.* The act of announcing, or that which is announced; proclamation. **—the Annunciation** The announcement of the Incarnation to the Virgin Mary by an angel (*Luke* i 28–38); also, the festival (March 25) commemorating this event.

an·nun·ci·a·tor (ə·nun′sē·ā′tər) *n.* 1. An announcer. 2. An electrical indicator used in hotels, etc., that shows the source of calls.

an·ode (an′ōd) *n. Electr.* 1. The positive electrode in an electrolytic cell. 2. The plate of an electron tube toward which electrons are attracted. [< Gk. *anodos* a way up]

an·o·dyne (an′ə·dīn) *n. Med.* Anything that relieves pain or soothes. [< Gk. *an-* without + *odynē* pain] **—an′o·dyne** *adj.*

a·noint (ə·noint′) *v.t.* To apply oil or ointment to, esp. in a religious ceremony. [< L *in-* on + *ungere* to smear] **—a·noint′er** *n.* **—a·noint′ment** *n.*

a·nom·a·lous (ə·nom′ə·ləs) *adj.* Exceptional; abnormal. [< Gk. *an-* not + *homalos* even]

a·nom·a·ly (ə·nom′ə·lē) *n. pl.* **·lies** 1. Deviation from rule, type, or form; irregularity. 2. Anything anomalous. **—a·nom′a·lis′tic** *adj.*

a·non (ə·non′) *adv.* 1. In a little while; soon. 2. At another time; again. [OE *on ān* in one]

an·o·nym (an′ə·nim) *n.* 1. An anonymous person or writer. 2. A pseudonym.

a·non·y·mous (ə·non′ə·məs) *adj.* 1. Having or bearing no name. 2. Of unknown authorship. [< Gk. *an-* without + *onoma* name] **—an·o·nym·i·ty** (an′ə·nim′ə·tē), **a·non′y·mous·ness** *n.* **—a·non′y·mous·ly** *adv.*

a·noph·e·les (ə·nof′ə·lēz) *n.* A mosquito carrying the malaria parasite. [< Gk. *anōphelēs* harmful] **—a·noph′e·line** (-līn, -lin) *adj.*

an·o·rex·i·a (an′ə·rek′sē·ə) *n. Med.* Loss of appetite. [< Gk. *an-* without + *orexis* appetite]

an·oth·er (ə·nuth′ər) *adj. & pron.* 1. An additional; one more. 2. Not the same; a different one.

an·ox·i·a (an·ok′sē·ə) *n. Pathol.* An insufficient oxygen supply to the body tissues.

an·swer (an′sər) *v.i.* 1. To reply or respond. 2. To be responsible or accountable: with *for* or *to.* 3. To serve the purpose. 4. To correspond or match, as in appearance: with *to.* **—***v.t.* 5. To speak, write, or act in response or reply to. 6. To be sufficient for; fulfill. 7. To conform or correspond to; match. **—***n.* 1. A reply. 2. Any action in return or in kind; retaliation. 3. A solution to a problem. [OE *andswarian*] **—an′swer·er** *n.*

an·swer·a·ble (an′sər·ə·bəl) *adj.* 1. Accountable; responsible. 2. That may be answered. **—an′swer·a·bly** *adv.*

ant (ant) *n.* Any of a family of small, usu. wingless insects that live in colonies. [OE *æmete*]

-ant *suffix* 1. Forming adjectives that mean in the act or process of doing (what is denoted by the stem): *militant.* 2. One who or that which does (what is indicated by the stem): *servant.* [< L *-ans, -ens,* present participial suffixes]

ant·ac·id (ant·as′id) *n.* An alkaline remedy for stomach acidity.

an·tag·o·nism (an·tag′ə·niz′əm) *n.* Active opposition or resistance; hostility.

an·tag·o·nist (an·tag′ə·nist) *n.* 1. An adversary; opponent. 2. *Anat.* A muscle that acts counter to another muscle. **—an·tag′o·nis′tic** *adj.* **—an·tag′o·nis′ti·cal·ly** *adv.*

an·tag·o·nize (an·tag′ə·nīz) *v.t.* **·nized, ·niz·ing** 1. To make unfriendly; make an enemy of. 2. To struggle against; oppose. [< Gk. *anti-* against + *agōnizesthai* to struggle, strive]

Ant·arc·tic (ant·ärk′tik, -är′tik) *adj.* Of or relating to the South Pole, or the regions within the Antarctic Circle. [< Gk. *anti-* opposite + *arktos* the Bear (a northern constellation), the north]

ant bear An anteater of tropical America.

an·te (an′tē) *v.t. & v.i.* **·ted** or **·teed, ·te·ing** In poker, to put up (one's stake). **—***n.* In poker, the stake put up before receiving the hand. [< L, before]

ante- *prefix* Before in time, order, or position. [< L *ante* before] Some self-explanatory words beginning with *ante-*:

ante-Christian	**antenatal**
antehistoric	**antenumber**
antehuman	**anterevolutional**
antelocation	**anteroom**
antemarital	**ante-Victorian**

ant·eat·er (ant′ē′tər) *n.* Any of several mammals that feed on ants, as the aardvark.

an·te·bel·lum (an′tē·bel′əm) *adj.* Before the war; esp., before the Civil War in the United States. [< L]

an·te·ce·dent (an′tə·sēd′nt) *adj.* Prior; preceding. **—***n.* 1. One who or that which precedes. 2. *Gram.* The word, phrase, or clause to which a pronoun refers. 3. *pl.* One's past life, ancestry, etc. [< ANTE- + L *cedere* to go] **—an′te·cede′** *v.t. & v.i.* **—an′te·ce′·dence** *n.* **—an′te·ce′dent·ly** *adv.*

an·te·cham·ber (an′ti·chām′bər) *n.* A small room that leads to a larger or main room.

an·te·date (an′ti·dāt′) *v.t.* **·dat·ed, ·dat·ing** 1. To precede in time. 2. To assign to a date earlier than the actual one.

an·te·di·lu·vian (an′ti·di·lo͞o′vē·ən) *adj.* 1. Before the Biblical flood. 2. Antiquated; primitive. [< ANTE- + L *diluvium* deluge]

an·te·lope (an′tə·lōp) *n. pl.* **·lope** or **·lopes** 1. Any of various swift, hollow-horned animals, as the gazelle; also, leather made from its hide. 2. The pronghorn. [< LGk. *antholops*]

an·te me·rid·i·em (an′tē mə·rid′ē·em) *Latin* Before noon. Abbr. *a.m., A.M.*

an·ten·na (an·ten′ə) *n. pl.* **·ten·nae** (-ten′ē) *for def. 1,* **·ten·nas** *for def. 2* 1. *Entomol.* One of the paired sense organs on the head of an insect or other arthropod. 2. *Telecom.* A system of wires, etc., for transmitting or receiving electromagnetic waves. [< L, yard for a sail]

an·te·pe·nult (an′ti·pē′nult, -pi·nult′) *n.* The third syllable from the end of a word. [< L] **—an′te·pe·nul′ti·mate** (-pi·nul′tə·mit) *adj. & n.*

an·te·ri·or (an·tir′ē·ər) *adj.* 1. Earlier; prior. 2. Farther front or forward. [< L, compar. of *ante* before] **—an·te′ri·or·ly** *adv.*

an·them (an′thəm) *n.* 1. A song or hymn of gladness or praise. 2. A musical composition, usu. set to words from the Bible. [< Gk. *anti-* against + *phōnē* voice]

an·ther (an′thər) *n. Bot.* The pollen-bearing part of a stamen. [< Gk. *anthos* flower]

an·thol·o·gy (an·thol′ə·jē) *n. pl.* **·gies** A collection of literary pieces. [< Gk. *anthos* flower + *legein* to gather] **—an·tho·log·i·cal** (an′thə·loj′i·kəl) *adj.* **—an·thol′o·gist** *n.* **—an·thol′o·gize** *v.t. & v.i.* **·gized, ·giz·ing**

an·thra·cite (an′thrə·sīt) *n.* Coal that burns slowly and with great heat: also called *hard coal.* [< Gk. *anthrax* coal] **—an′thra·cit′ic** (-sit′ik) *adj.*

an·thrax (an′thraks) *n. Pathol.* An infectious disease of cattle and sheep, sometimes fatal to man. [< Gk., coal]

anthropo- *combining form* Man; human: *anthropology.* Also, before vowels, **anthrop-.** [< Gk. *anthrōpos* man]

an·thro·po·cen·tric (an′thrə·pō·sen′trik) *adj.* Interpreting the universe in terms of human values.

an·thro·pog·e·ny (an′thrə·poj′ə·nē) *n.* The branch of anthropology that treats of the origin and development of man. Also **an·thro·po·gen·e·sis** (an′thrə·pō·jen′ə·sis).

an·thro·poid (an′thrə·poid) *adj.* Like a human being in form or other characteristics, as the gorilla and chimpanzee. Also **an′thro·poi′dal.** **—***n.* An ape.

an·thro·pol·o·gy (an′thrə·pol′ə·jē) *n.* The science treating of the physical, social, material, and cultural development of man. **—an·thro·po·log·i·cal** (an′thrə·pə·loj′i·kəl) or **·log′ic** *adj.* **—an′thro·po·log′i·cal·ly** *adv.* **—an′thro·pol′o·gist** *n.*

an·thro·po·mor·phism (an′thrə·pō·môr′fiz·əm) *n.* The ascription of human form or characteristics to a deity, or to any being or thing not human. **—an′thro·po·mor′phic** *adj.* **—an′thro·po·mor′phist** *n.*

an·ti (an′tī, an′tē) *n. pl.* **·tis** *Informal* One opposed to some policy, group, etc.

anti- *prefix*

1. Against; opposed to:

anti-American	**antinoise**
antifeminism	**antipollution**
antigrowth	**antireligious**
anti-imperialist	**antisubmarine**
anti-intellectual	**antivivisection**
antilabor	**antiwar**

2. Opposite to; reverse:

anticlockwise	**antilogic**
anticyclic	**antipole**

3. Rivaling; spurious:

antiemperor	**anti-Messiah**
antiking	**antiprophet**

4. Counteracting; curative; neutralizing:

antibacterial	**anticolic**
anticlogging	**antimalarial**
anticoagulant	**antivirus**

Also, before vowels, **ant-.** [< Gk. *anti* against]

an·ti·air·craft (an′tē·âr′kraft′, an′tī-) *adj.* Used for defense against aircraft.

an·ti·bal·lis·tic missile (an′tē·bə·lis′tik, an′·tī-) A missile designed to intercept and destroy a ballistic missile in flight.

an·ti·bi·ot·ic (an′ti·bī·ot′ik, an′tī-, an′ti·bē·ot′ik) *n. Biochem.* Any of a large class of substances derived from molds and soil bacteria, having the power of destroying or arresting the growth of microorganisms. [< Gk. *anti-* against + *bios* life] **—an′ti·bi·ot′ic** *adj.*

an·ti·bod·y (an′ti·bod′ē) *n. pl.* **·bod·ies** *Biochem.* Any of a class of proteins serving to immunize the body against specific antigens.

an·tic (an′tik) *n.* 1. *Usually pl.* A prank; caper. 2. A clown; buffoon. *—adj.* Odd; fantastic; ludicrous. [< Ital. *antico* old, grotesque] **—an′tic·ly** *adv.*

an·ti·christ (an′ti·krīst′) *n. Often cap.* A denier or opponent of Christ or Christianity.

An·ti·christ (an′ti·krīst′) *n.* The blasphemous antagonist of Christ. I *John* ii 18.

an·tic·i·pate (an·tis′ə·pāt) *v.t.* **·pat·ed, ·pat·ing** 1. To experience or realize beforehand. 2. To look forward to. 3. To act or arrive sooner than, esp. to forestall. 4. To foresee and fulfill beforehand. [< ANTE- + L *capere* to take] **—an·tic′i·pa′tion** *n.* **—an·tic′i·pa·to′ry** (-pə·tôr′ē) *adj.*

an·ti·cler·i·cal (an′ti·kler′i·kəl) *adj.* Opposed to clerical influence in political and civic affairs. **—an′ti·cler′i·cal·ism** *n.*

an·ti·cli·max (an′ti·klī′maks) *n.* 1. In rhetoric, a ludicrous decrease in the importance or impressiveness of what is said. 2. Any similar descent or fall. **—an′ti·cli·mac′tic** *adj.*

an·ti·cline (an′ti·klīn) *n. Geol.* Downward-sloping, parallel folds in stratified rock. [< Gk. *anti-* opposite + *klinein* to slope] **—an′ti·cli′nal** *adj.*

an·ti·cy·clone (an′ti·sī′klōn) *n. Meteorol.* An atmospheric condition in which winds spiral outward from a center of high pressure. **—an′ti·cy·clon′ic** (-klon′ik) *adj.*

an·ti·dote (an′ti·dōt) *n.* 1. Anything that will counteract the effects of poison. 2. Anything that similarly counteracts (something). [< Gk. *anti-* against + *didonai* to give] **—an′ti·do′tal** *adj.* **—an′ti·do′tal·ly** *adv.*

an·ti·freeze (an′ti·frēz′) *n.* A liquid of low freezing point, used in combustion-engine radiators to prevent freezing.

an·ti·gen (an′tə·jən) *n. Biochem.* A toxin or other substance that causes the development of antibodies. **—an′ti·gen′ic** (-jen′ik) *adj.*

an·ti·his·ta·mine (an′ti·his′tə·mēn, -min) *n. Med.* A drug that neutralizes the action of histamine, used to treat hay fever, asthma, etc. **—an′ti·his′ta·min′ic** (-min′ik) *adj.*

an·ti·knock (an′ti·nok′) *n.* An agent for preventing premature combustion in an internal-combustion engine.

an·ti·log·a·rithm (an′ti·lôg′ə·rith′əm, -log′-) *n. Math.* The number corresponding to a given logarithm. Also **an′ti·log.**

an·ti·ma·cas·sar (an′ti·mə·kas′ər) *n.* A covering to protect the backs and arms of furniture.

an·ti·mat·ter (an′ti·mat′ər) *n. Physics* A hypothetical form of matter composed of antiparticles.

an·ti·mo·ny (an′tə·mō′nē) *n.* A silver-white, crystalline, metallic element (symbol Sb). [< Med.L *antimonium*]

an·ti·par·ti·cle (an′ti·pär′ti·kəl) *n. Physics* An atomic particle having mass equal to an electron, proton, neutron, etc., but with opposite charge and magnetic characteristics.

an·ti·pas·to (än′tē·päs′tō) *n. pl.* **·tos** A course served as an appetizer. [< Ital.]

an·tip·a·thy (an·tip′ə·thē) *n. pl.* **·thies** 1. An instinctive feeling of aversion or dislike. 2. The object of such a feeling. [< Gk. *anti-* against + *pathein* to feel, suffer] **—an·ti·pa·thet·ic** (an′ti·pə·thet′ik) *adj.* **—an′ti·pa·thet′i·cal·ly** *adv.*

an·ti·per·son·nel (an′ti·pûr′sə·nel′, an′tī-) *adj. Mil.* Designating weapons that are employed specifically against troops.

an·ti·per·spi·rant (an′ti·pûr′spə·rənt, an′tī-) *n.* A skin astringent that lessens perspiration.

an·ti·phon (an′tə·fon) *n.* A verse of a psalm or hymn said or chanted in response to another. [< Gk. *anti-* against + *phōnē* voice] **—an·tiph·o·nal** (an·tif′ə·nəl) *adj.* **—an·tiph′o·nal·ly** *adv.*

an·ti·pode (an′ti·pōd) *n.* An exact opposite.

an·tip·o·des (an·tip′ə·dēz) *n.* (*construed as sing. or pl.*) 1. A region on the opposite side of the earth, or its inhabitants. 2. An opposite or opposites. [< Gk. *anti-* opposite + *pous* foot] **—an·tip′o·dal** *adj.*

an·ti·py·ret·ic (an′ti·pī·ret′ik) *Med. adj.* Reducing fever. [< Gk. *anti-* curative + *pyretos* fever] **—an′ti·py·ret′ic** *n.*

an·ti·quar·i·an (an′ti·kwâr′ē·ən) *adj.* Pertaining to antiques or antiquaries. *—n.* An antiquary. **—an′ti·quar′i·an·ism** *n.*

an·ti·quar·y (an′ti·kwer′ē) *n. pl.* **·quar·ies** One who collects, deals in, or studies antiques or antiquities.

an·ti·quate (an′ti·kwāt) *v.t.* **·quat·ed, ·quat·ing** To make old or out-of-date. [< L *antiquare* to make old] **—an′ti·qua′tion** *n.*

an·ti·quat·ed (an′ti·kwā′tid) *adj.* 1. Out-of-date; old-fashioned; obsolete. 2. Ancient; very old.

an·tique (an·tēk′) *adj.* 1. Of or pertaining to ancient times. 2. Of an earlier period: an *antique* chair. 3. Old-fashioned; out-of-date. *—n.* Any old object, usu. one prized for its rarity, style or craft, etc. *—v.t.* **an·tiqued, an·ti·quing** To give the appearance of an antique to. [< L *antiquus* ancient] **—an·tique′ly** *adv.* **—an·tique′ness** *n.*

an·tiq·ui·ty (an·tik′wə·tē) *n. pl.* **·ties** 1. The quality of being ancient. 2. Ancient times, esp. before the Middle Ages. 3. *Usu. pl.* Ancient relics.

an·ti-Sem·i·tism (an′ti·sem′ə·tiz′əm, an′tī-) *n.* Discrimination against or intolerance of Jews, Jewish culture, etc. **—an′ti-Sem′ite** (-sem′īt) *n.* **—an′ti-Se·mit′ic** (-sə·mit′ik) *adj.*

an·ti·sep·tic (an′tə·sep′tik) *adj.* 1. Preventing or counteracting infection by destruction or inhibition of pathogenic microorganisms. 2. Free of pathogenic microorganisms; aseptic. Also **an′ti·sep′ti·cal.** *—n.* Any antiseptic substance. [< Gk. *anti-* counteracting + *sēpsis* putrefaction] **—an′ti·sep′ti·cal·ly** *adv.*

an·ti·se·rum (an′ti·sir′əm) *n.* A serum that provides immunity from specific diseases.

an·ti·slav·er·y (an′ti·slā′vər·ē, -slāv′rē, an′tī-) *adj.* Opposed to human slavery.

an·ti·so·cial (an′ti·sō′shəl, an′tī-) *adj.* 1. Unsociable. 2. Opposed to or disruptive of society.

an·ti·spas·mod·ic (an′ti·spaz·mod′ik) *adj. Med.* Relieving or checking spasms. **—an′ti·spas·mod′ic** *n.*

an·tith·e·sis (an·tith′ə·sis) *n. pl.* **·ses** (-sēz)

1. The balancing of two contrasted words, ideas, or phrases against each other. Example: *My prayers go up; my thoughts remain below.* 2. The direct opposite. [< Gk. *anti-* against + *tithenai* to place] **—an·ti·thet·i·cal** (an′tə·thet′i·kəl) *adj.* **—an′ti·thet′i·cal·ly** *adv.*

an·ti·tox·in (an′ti·tok′sin) *n. Biochem.* An antibody formed in living tissues that neutralizes a specific toxin; also, serum containing this. **—an′ti·tox′ic** *adj.*

an·ti·trust (an′ti·trust′) *adj.* Pertaining to the regulation of trusts, monopolies, etc.

an·ti·ven·in (an′ti·ven′ən) *n.* An antitoxin for a venom; also, serum containing this.

ant·ler (ant′lər) *n. Usu. pl.* Either of the branched horns on the head of members of the deer family. [< ANTE- + L *oculus* eye] **—ant′lered** *adj.*

ant lion An insect whose larva preys on ants and other insects.

an·to·nym (an′tə·nim) *n.* A word that is the opposite of another in meaning: opposed to *synonym.* [< Gk. *anti-* opposite + *onoma, onyma* name]

an·trum (an′trəm) *n. pl.* **·tra** *Anat.* A cavity, usu. in a bone, esp. a sinus in the upper jaw. [< Gk. *antron* cave]

a·nus (ā′nəs) *n. Anat.* The excretory opening at the lower extremity of the alimentary canal. [< L, orig., ring]

an·vil (an′vil, -vəl) *n.* 1. A heavy block of iron or steel on which metal may be forged. 2. *Anat.* The incus. [OE *anfilt*]

anx·i·e·ty (ang·zī′ə·tē) *n. pl.* **·ties** 1. Disturbance of mind regarding some event; worry. 2. *Psychiatry* A tense emotional state characterized by fear and apprehension without apparent cause.

anx·ious (angk′shəs, ang′-) *adj.* 1. Troubled in mind. 2. Causing anxiety; distressing. 3. Both eager and concerned: with *for* or *to.* [< L *angere* to choke, distress] **—anx′ious·ly** *adv.* **—anx′ious·ness** *n.*

an·y (en′ē) *adj.* 1. One, no matter which; a or an, or (plural) some: Have we *any* choice? 2. Some, however much or little: Did he eat *any* supper? 3. Every: *Any* fool knows that. *—pron.* One or more of a number: Have *any* of the guests arrived? *—adv.* At all; to any extent: Are they *any* nearer? [OE *ǣnig* < *ān* one]

an·y·bod·y (en′i·bod′ē, -bud′ē) *pron.* Any person whatever; anyone.

an·y·how (en′i·hou′) *adv.* 1. By whatever means. 2. Notwithstanding; whatever the case.

an·y·one (en′i·wun′, -wən) *pron.* Any person.

an·y·thing (en′i·thing′) *pron.* Any object, event, or matter whatever.

an·y·way (en′i·wā′) *adv.* 1. In any manner. 2. Nevertheless; anyhow.

an·y·where (en′i·hwâr′) *adv.* In, at, or to any place.

an·y·wise (en′i·wīz′) *adv.* In any manner.

A-OK (ā′ō·kā′) *adj. Informal* Satisfactory without question.

A-one (ā′wun′) *adj. Informal* Excellent. Also **A-1.**

a·or·ta (ā·ôr′tə) *n. pl.* **·tas** or **·tae** (-tē) *Anat.* The main artery that carries blood from the heart. [< Gk. *aeirein* to raise, heave] **—a·or′tal, a·or′tic** *adj.*

a·pace (ə·pās′) *adv.* Rapidly; quickly. [< A-¹ + PACE]

a·pache (ə·päsh′, ə·pash′; *Fr.* à·pàsh′) *n.* A ruffian or gangster of Paris. [< F < APACHE]

A·pach·e (ə·pach′ē) *n. pl.* **A·pach·es** or **A·pach·e** One of a group of Indians, inhabiting the southern and SW U.S.

a·part (ə·pärt′) *adv.* 1. Separated; not together. 2. One from another. 3. Separately for some use or purpose. 4. Aside; to one side. 5. In pieces or to pieces. *—adj.* Separate; distinct. [< MF *à* to + *part* the side]

a·part·heid (ə·pär′tāt) *n.* In the Republic of South Africa, the official policy of segregation enforced against nonwhites. [< Afrikaans, apartness]

a·part·ment (ə·pärt′mənt) *n.* A room or suite of rooms in a building, equipped for housekeeping. Abbr. *apt.* [< F *appartement* < Ital. *appartamento*]

apartment house A multiple-dwelling building divided into apartments.

ap·a·thy (ap′ə·thē) *n. pl.* **·thies** 1. Lack of emotion. 2. Indifference. [< Gk. *a-* without + *pathos* feeling] **—ap·a·thet·ic** (ap′ə·thet′ik) *adj.* **—ap′a·thet′i·cal·ly** *adv.*

ape (āp) *n.* 1. A large, tailless, Old World primate, as a gorilla or chimpanzee. 2. Loosely, any monkey. *—v.t.* **aped, ap·ing** To imitate; mimic. [OE *apa*]

ape-man (āp′man′) *n. pl.* **-men** An extinct primate, structurally intermediate between man and the higher apes.

a·per·çu (à·per·sü′) *n. pl.* **·çus** *French* 1. An insight; perception. 2. A digest or outline.

a·pé·ri·tif (à·pā·rē·tēf′) *n. French* A drink of liquor or wine taken as an appetizer.

ap·er·ture (ap′ər·chŏŏr, -chər) *n.* An opening; orifice. [< L *aperire* to open] **—ap′er·tur·al** *adj.* **—ap′er·tured** *adj.*

a·pex (ā′peks) *n. pl.* **a·pex·es** or **ap·i·ces** (ap′ə·sēz, ā′pə-) 1. The highest point; peak. 2. Climax. [< L]

a·pha·sia (ə·fā′zhə, -zhē·ə) *n.* Partial or total loss of the power of speech. [< Gk. *a-* not + *phanai* to speak] **—a·pha·sic** (ə·fā′zik, -sik), **a·pha·si·ac** (ə·fā′zē·ak) *adj. & n.*

a·phe·li·on (ə·fē′lē·ən) *n. pl.* **·li·a** *Astron.* The point in an orbit, as of a planet, farthest from the sun: opposed to *perihelion.* [< AP(O)- + Gk. *hēlios* sun] **—a·phe′li·an** *adj.*

a·phet·ic (ə·fet′ik) *adj.* Describing the loss of a short or unaccented vowel from the beginning of a word, as in *mend* for *amend.* [< Gk. *aphienai* to let go] **—aph·e·sis** (af′ə·sis) *n.*

a·phid (ā′fid, af′id) *n.* A small, juice-sucking insect, injurious to plants. **—a·phid·i·an** (ə·fid′ē·ən) *adj.*

aph·o·rism (af′ə·riz′əm) *n.* 1. A brief statement of a truth or principle. 2. A proverb; maxim. [< APO- + Gk. *horizein* to divide] **—aph′o·rist** *n.* **—aph′o·ris′tic** or **·i·cal** *adj.* **—aph′o·ris′ti·cal·ly** *adv.*

aph·ro·dis·i·ac (af′rə·diz′ē·ak) *adj.* Arousing or increasing sexual desire or potency. *—n.* A supposed aphrodisiac drug, food, etc. [< Gk. *aphrodisiakos* < *Aphroditē*, goddess of love]

a·pi·a·ry (ā′pē·er′ē) *n. pl.* **·ar·ies** A place where bees are kept; a set of hives with bees, etc. [< L *apiarium* < *apis* bee] —**a′pi·ar′i·an** *adj.* —**a·pi·ar·ist** (ā′pē·ə·rist) *n.*

ap·i·cal (ap′i·kəl, ā′pi-) *adj.* Of or situated at the apex or peak.

ap·i·ces (ap′ə·sēz, ā′pə-) Alternative plural of APEX.

a·pi·cul·ture (ā′pi·kul′chər) *n.* The raising and care of bees. [< L *apis* bee + CULTURE] —**a′pi·cul′tur·al** *adj.* —**a′pi·cul′tur·ist** *n.*

a·piece (ə·pēs′) *adv.* For or to each one; each.

ap·ish (ā′pish) *adj.* Like an ape; servilely imitative; foolish and tricky. —**ap′ish·ly** *adv.* —**ap′ish·ness** *n.*

a·plomb (ə·plom′, *Fr.* à·plôn′) *n.* Assurance; self-confidence. [< F *à* according to + *plomb* plumb bob]

apo- *prefix* Off; from; away: *apostasy.* Also **ap-** before vowels. [< Gk. *apo* from, off]

a·poc·a·lypse (ə·pok′ə·lips) *n.* 1. A prophecy or revelation. 2. *cap.* The book of Revelation, the last book of the New Testament. [< APO- + Gk. *kalyptein* to cover] —**a·poc′a·lyp′tic** or **·ti·cal** *adj.* —**a·poc′a·lyp′ti·cal·ly** *adv.*

A·poc·ry·pha (ə·pok′rə·fə) *n.pl.* (*often construed as sing.*) Those books of the Septuagint included in the Vulgate but rejected by Protestants and Hebrews as uncanonical. [< Gk. *apokryphos* hidden]

a·poc·ry·phal (ə·pok′rə·fəl) *adj.* Having little or no authenticity. —**a·poc′ry·phal·ly** *adv.* —**a·poc′ry·phal·ness** *n.*

ap·o·cyn·thi·on (ap·ə·sin′thē·ən) *n. Astron.* Apolune. [< APO- + L *Cynthia,* moon]

ap·o·gee (ap′ə·jē) *n.* 1. *Astron.* That point in the orbit of an object or celestial body which is farthest from the earth: opposed to *perigee.* 2. The highest point; climax. [< Gk. *apogaion* far from earth] —**ap′o·ge′al, ap′o·ge′an** *adj.*

A·pol·lo (ə·pol′ō) *n.* A handsome young man. [after *Apollōn* Apollo, Greek god of music, poetry, and sunlight]

a·pol·o·get·ic (ə·pol′ə·jet′ik) *adj.* 1. Of the nature of an apology; excusing. 2. Defending or explaining. Also **a·pol′o·get′i·cal.** [< Gk. *apologia* a speech in defense] —**a·pol′o·get′i·cal·ly** *adv.*

a·pol·o·get·ics (ə·pol′ə·jet′iks) *n.pl.* (*construed as sing.*) The branch of theology that defends Christianity.

ap·o·lo·gi·a (ap′ə·lō′jē·ə) *n.* A justification or defense. [< Gk.]

a·pol·o·gist (ə·pol′ə·jist) *n.* One who argues in defense of any person or cause.

a·pol·o·gize (ə·pol′ə·jīz) *v.i.* **·gized, ·giz·ing** To acknowledge, with regret, an offense. —**a·pol′o·giz′er** *n.*

a·pol·o·gy (ə·pol′ə·jē) *n. pl.* **·gies** A statement or explanation expressing regret for some error or offense. [< Gk. *apologia* a speech in defense]

ap·o·lune (ap′ə·lo͞on) *n. Astron.* That point in the lunar orbit of a body which is farthest from the moon. [< APO- + F *lune* moon]

ap·o·plex·y (ap′ə·plek′sē) *n. Pathol.* Sudden paralysis and loss of sensation caused by a blood clot or hemorrhage in the brain. [< APO- + Gk. *plēssein* to strike] —**ap′o·plec′tic** *adj.*

a·port (ə·pôrt′) *adj. Naut.* On or toward the port side.

a·pos·ta·sy (ə·pos′tə·sē) *n. pl.* **·sies** Desertion of one's faith, religion, party, or principles. Also **a·pos′ta·cy.** [< APO- + Gk. *stasis* a standing] —**a·pos′tate** (-tāt, -tit) *adj.* & *n.* —**a·pos′ta·tize** (-tīz) *v.i.* **·tized, ·tiz·ing**

a pos·te·ri·o·ri (ā′ pos·tir′ē·ôr′ī) 1. *Logic* Reasoning from facts to principles or from effect to cause. 2. Inductive; empirical. [< L, from the later]

a·pos·tle (ə·pos′əl) *n.* 1. One of the twelve disciples originally commissioned by Christ to preach the gospel (*Matt.* x 2–4). 2. One of a class of missionaries in the early church (I *Cor.* xii 28). 3. The earliest or foremost advocate of a cause. [OE *apostol* < L *apostolus* < Gk. *apostolos* one sent forth]

Apostles' Creed A traditional and still widely accepted Christian confession of faith.

ap·os·tol·ic (ap′ə·stol′ik) *adj.* 1. Of or pertaining to an apostle, the apostles, or their times. 2. According to the doctrine or practice of the apostles. 3. *Often cap.* Papal.

a·pos·tro·phe[1] (ə·pos′trə·fē) *n.* A symbol (') written above the line to mark the omission of a letter or letters from a word, to indicate the possessive case, or to denote certain plurals: Cross your *t's.* [< APO- + Gk. *strephein* to turn] —**a·pos′tro·phize** *v.t.* & *v.i.* **·phized, ·phiz·ing**

a·pos·tro·phe[2] (ə·pos′trə·fē) *n.* A digression from a discourse; esp., a turning aside to speak to an absent person. —**ap·os·troph·ic** (ap′ə·strof′ik) *adj.* —**a·pos′tro·phize** *v.t.* & *v.i.* **·phized, ·phiz·ing**

apothecaries' weight A system of weights used in pharmacy.

a·poth·e·car·y (ə·poth′ə·ker′ē) *n. pl.* **·car·ies** A druggist. [< APO- + Gk. *tithenai* to put]

ap·o·thegm (ap′ə·them) *n.* A terse, instructive, practical saying; maxim: also **ap′o·phthegm.** [< APO- + Gk. *pthengesthai* to utter] —**ap·o·theg·mat·ic** (ap′ə·theg·mat′·ik) or **·i·cal** *adj.*

a·poth·e·o·sis (ə·poth′ē·ō′sis, ap′ə·thē′ə·sis) *n. pl.* **·ses** (-sēz) Deification; supreme exaltation of any person, principle, etc. [< APO- + Gk. *theos* god]

a·poth·e·o·size (ə·poth′ē·ə·sīz′, ap′ə·thē′ə·sīz) *v.t.* **·sized, ·siz·ing** To deify; glorify; exalt.

ap·pall (ə·pôl′) *v.t.* To fill with dismay or horror; shock. Also *Brit.* **ap·pal′.** [< OF *apallir* to pale] —**ap·pal′ling** *adj.* —**ap·pal′·ling·ly** *adv.*

ap·pa·ra·tus (ap′ə·rat′əs, -rā′təs) *n. pl.* **·tus** or (rarely) **·tus·es** 1. A device, machine, or assembly of tools, instruments, materials, equipment, etc., for a particular purpose. 2. An organization of political activists. [< L *ad-* to + *parare* to prepare]

ap·par·el (ə·par′əl) *n.* Clothing; attire. —*v.t.* **·eled** or **·elled, ·el·ing** or **·el·ling** To clothe; dress. [< OF *apareiller* to prepare]

ap·par·ent (ə·par′ənt, ə·pâr′-) *adj.* 1. Readily perceived by the mind; obvious. 2. Easily seen; visible. 3. Seeming, in distinction from real or actual. [< L *apparere* to appear] —**ap·par′ent·ly** *adv.* —**ap·par′ent·ness** *n.*

ap·pa·ri·tion (ap′ə·rish′ən) *n.* 1. An appearance, esp. an eerie or unexpected one. 2. Phantom; ghost. [< L *apparitio, -onis* < *apparere* to appear] —**ap′pa·ri′tion·al** *adj.*

ap·peal (ə·pēl′) *n.* 1. An earnest entreaty for aid, sympathy, or the like. 2. The quality of being attractive. 3. *Law* **a** The carrying of a case to a higher tribunal for a rehearing. **b** A case so carried. —*v.t.* 1. *Law* To refer or remove, as a case, to a higher court. —*v.i.* 2. To make a plea or request, as for sympathy or aid. 3. To awaken a favorable response; be interesting. 4. *Law* To remove a case, or request that a case be moved, to a higher court. 5. To resort or have recourse: with *to*. [< L *appellare* to accost, call upon] —**ap·peal′a·ble** *adj.* —**ap·peal′er** *n.* —**ap·peal′ing** *adj.* —**ap·peal′ing·ly** *adv.*

ap·pear (ə·pir′) *v.i.* 1. To come into view. 2. To seem. 3. To be clear to the mind; be obvious. 4. To come before the public. 5. *Law* To come formally into court. [< L *ad-* to + *parere* to come forth, appear]

ap·pear·ance (ə·pir′əns) *n.* 1. The act of appearing or coming into view. 2. External or physical aspect; presence: a commanding *appearance*. 3. *pl.* Circumstances or indications: *Appearances* are against him. 4. Outward show; pretense.

ap·pease (ə·pēz′) *v.t.* **·peased, ·peas·ing** 1. To placate by making concessions or yielding to demands. 2. To satisfy or allay. [< OF *apaisier* < L *pax* peace] —**ap·peas′a·ble** *adj.* —**ap·peas′a·bly** *adv.* —**ap·pease′ment** *n.* —**ap·peas′er** *n.* —**ap·peas′ing·ly** *adv.*

ap·pel·lant (ə·pel′ənt) *adj.* *Law* Of or pertaining to an appeal. —*n.* One who appeals, in any sense.

ap·pel·late (ə·pel′it) *adj.* *Law* Pertaining to or having jurisdiction of appeals: an *appellate* court.

ap·pel·la·tion (ap′ə·lā′shən) *n.* 1. A name or title. 2. The act of naming. [< L *appellare* to name]

ap·pend (ə·pend′) *v.t.* 1. To add, as something subordinate or supplemental. 2. To hang or attach. [< L *ad-* to + *pendere* to hang] —**ap·pen′dant** or **ap·pen′dent** *adj. & n.*

ap·pend·age (ə·pen′dij) *n.* 1. Anything appended. 2. *Zool.* Any part joined to or diverging from the axial trunk, as a limb.

ap·pen·dec·to·my (ap′ən·dek′tə·mē) *n. pl.* **·mies** *Surg.* The removal of the vermiform appendix.

ap·pen·di·ces (ə·pen′də·sēz) Alternative plural of APPENDIX.

ap·pen·di·ci·tis (ə·pen′də·sī′tis) *n.* *Pathol.* Inflammation of the vermiform appendix.

ap·pen·dix (ə·pen′diks) *n. pl.* **·dix·es** or **·di·ces** (-də·sēz) 1. An addition or appendage, as of supplementary matter at the end of a book. 2. The vermiform appendix. [< L, an appendage]

ap·per·cep·tion (ap′ər·sep′shən) *n.* Conscious perception. [< F *apercevoir* to see, recognize] —**ap′per·cep′tive** *adj.*

ap·per·tain (ap′ər·tān′) *v.i.* To pertain or belong as by right or fitness; relate: with *to*. [< L *ad-* to + *pertinere* to reach to]

ap·pe·tite (ap′ə·tīt) *n.* 1. A desire for food or drink. 2. Any physical craving or natural desire. 3. A strong liking. [< L *ad-* to + *petere* to seek] —**ap′pe·ti′tive** *adj.*

ap·pe·tiz·er (ap′ə·tī′zər) *n.* Anything that excites appetite, esp. food or drink served before a meal. Also *Brit.* **ap′pe·tis′er.**

ap·pe·tiz·ing (ap′ə·tī′zing) *adj.* Stimulating to the appetite. Also *Brit.* **ap′pe·tis′ing.** —**ap′pe·tiz′ing·ly** *adv.*

ap·plaud (ə·plôd′) *v.t. & v.i.* 1. To express approval (of) by clapping the hands. 2. To commend; praise. [< L *ad-* to + *plaudere* to clap hands, strike] —**ap·plaud′er** *n.* —**ap·plaud′ing·ly** *adv.*

ap·plause (ə·plôz′) *n.* Approval, esp. as shown by clapping the hands, shouting, etc.

ap·ple (ap′əl) *n.* 1. The fleshy, edible, usu. roundish fruit of a widely distributed tree of the rose family. 2. The similar fruit of several allied species, as the crab apple. [OE *æppel*]

ap·ple·jack (ap′əl·jak′) *n.* Brandy made from cider.

ap·ple·sauce (ap′əl·sôs′) *n.* 1. Apples stewed to a pulp. 2. *Slang* Nonsense; bunk.

ap·pli·ance (ə·plī′əns) *n.* A device or instrument; esp., an electrically powered device for household work.

ap·pli·ca·ble (ap′li·kə·bəl, ə·plik′ə-) *adj.* Capable of application; relevant; fitting. [< L *applicare* to apply + -ABLE] —**ap′pli·ca·bil′i·ty, ap′pli·ca·ble·ness** *n.* —**ap′pli·ca·bly** *adv.*

ap·pli·cant (ap′li·kənt) *n.* One who applies, as for a job.

ap·pli·ca·tion (ap′li·kā′shən) *n.* 1. The act of applying. 2. That which is applied. 3. A use for a special purpose. 4. Capacity of being used; relevance. 5. Close attention. 6. A formal, written request, esp. for employment.

ap·pli·ca·tive (ap′li·kā′tiv) *adj.* Applicatory.

ap·pli·ca·tor (ap′li·kā′tər) *n.* An instrument or utensil for applying medication, etc.

ap·pli·ca·to·ry (ap′li·kə·tôr′ē) *adj.* Fit for application; practical.

ap·plied (ə·plīd′) *adj.* Put in practice; utilized: said of sciences, fields of study, etc.

ap·pli·qué (ap′li·kā′) *adj.* Applied: said of ornaments, as in needlework, sewn to the surface of cloth. —*n.* Decoration so applied. —*v.t.* **·quéd, ·qué·ing** (-kā′ing) To decorate by appliqué work. [< F]

ap·ply (ə·plī′) *v.* **·plied, ·ply·ing** *v.t.* 1. To bring into contact with something; put on or to. 2. To devote or put to a particular use. 3. To connect, as an epithet, with a particular person or thing. 4. To give (oneself) wholly to; devote. —*v.i.* 5. To make a request or petition; ask: with *for*. 6. To be relevant. [< L *ad-* to + *plicare* to fold]

ap·point (ə·point′) *v.t.* 1. To name or select, as a person, a time and place, etc. 2. To ordain, as by decree; command. 3. To fit out; equip: used chiefly in combination in the past participle: a *well-appointed* yacht.

ap·point·ee (ə·poin′tē′) *n.* One appointed to an office.

ap·poin·tive (ə·poin′tiv) *adj.* Filled by appointment.

ap·point·ment (ə·point′mənt) *n.* 1. The act of appointing or placing in office. 2. A position held by someone appointed. 3. An agreement to meet or to be somewhere; engagement. 4. *Usually pl.* Furnishings.

ap·por·tion (ə·pôr′shən) *v.t.* To divide and assign proportionally; allot. [< OF *a-* to + *portionner* to divide] —**ap·por′tion·ment** *n.*

ap·pose (ə·pōz′) *v.t.* **·posed, ·pos·ing** To arrange side by side. [< OF *a-* to + *poser* to put]

ap·po·site (ap′ə·zit) *adj.* Fit for or appropriate. [< L *apponere* to put near to] —**ap′po·site·ly** *adv.* —**ap′po·site·ness** *n.*

ap·po·si·tion (ap′ə·zish′ən) *n.* 1. The placing

of one noun or noun phrase next to another so that the second explains the first, as *Joan, president* of the class. 2. The act of opposing or the state of being opposed. —**ap′po·si′tion·al** *adj.* —**ap′po·si′tion·al·ly** *adv.*

ap·pos·i·tive (ə·poz′ə·tiv) *adj.* Of or in apposition. —*n.* A word or phrase in apposition. —**ap·pos′i·tive·ly** *adv.*

ap·praise (ə·prāz′) *v.t.* **·praised, ·prais·ing** 1. To make an official valuation of; set a price or value on. 2. To estimate the amount, quality, or worth of; judge. —**ap·prais′a·ble** *adj.* —**ap·prais′al** *n.* —**ap·prais′er** *n.*

ap·pre·ci·a·ble (ə·prē′shē·ə·bəl, -shə·bəl) *adj.* Capable of being valued or estimated. —**ap·pre′ci·a·bly** *adv.*

ap·pre·ci·ate (ə·prē′shē·āt) *v.* **·at·ed, ·at·ing** *v.t.* 1. To be aware of the value, importance, or magnitude of. 2. To esteem adequately or highly. 3. To show gratitude for. 4. To increase the price or value of. —*v.i.* 5. To rise in value. [< LL *appretiare* to set a value on] —**ap·pre′ci·a′tion** *n.* —**ap·pre′ci·a′tor** *n.*

ap·pre·ci·a·tive (ə·prē′shē·ā′tiv, -shə·tiv) *adj.* Showing appreciation. —**ap·pre′ci·a′·tive·ly** *adv.* —**ap·pre′ci·a′tive·ness** *n.*

ap·pre·ci·a·to·ry (ə·prē′shē·ə·tôr′ē, -shə-) *adj.* Appreciative. —**ap·pre′ci·a·to′ri·ly** *adv.*

ap·pre·hend (ap′rə·hend′) *v.t.* 1. To lay hold of or grasp mentally; understand. 2. To expect with anxious foreboding; dread. 3. To arrest; take into custody. —*v.i.* 4. To understand. [< L *ad-* to + *prehendere* to seize] —**ap′pre·hen′sion** (-hen′shən) *n.*

ap·pre·hen·si·ble (ap′rə·hen′sə·bəl) *adj.* Capable of being apprehended. —**ap′pre·hen′si·bil′i·ty** *n.*

ap·pre·hen·sive (ap′rə·hen′siv) *adj.* Fearful; anxious. —**ap′pre·hen′sive·ly** *adv.* —**ap′pre·hen′sive·ness** *n.*

ap·pren·tice (ə·pren′tis) *n.* 1. One who is bound by a legal agreement to serve another for a fixed period of time in order to learn a trade or business. 2. Any learner or beginner. —*v.t.* **·ticed, ·tic·ing** To bind or take as an apprentice. [< OF *aprendre* to learn] —**ap·pren′tice·ship** *n.*

ap·prise (ə·prīz′) *v.t.* **·prised, ·pris·ing** To notify; inform. Also **ap·prize′**. [< F *apprendre* to cause to learn]

ap·prize (ə·prīz′) *v.t.* **·prized, ·priz·ing** To appraise. Also **ap·prise′**. [Prob. < OF *a-* on, to + *prisier* to value]

ap·proach (ə·prōch′) *v.i.* 1. To come near or nearer in time or space. —*v.t.* 2. To come near or nearer to. 3. To come close to; approximate. 4. To make advances to; offer a proposal or bribe to. 5. To start to deal with: to *approach* a problem. —*n.* 1. The act of approaching; a coming near. 2. An approximation; nearness. 3. A way or means of approaching; access. 4. A method of beginning or accomplishing something. 5. *Often pl.* An overture of friendship, etc.; advance. [< LL *appropiare* to go nearer to] —**ap·proach′a·bil′i·ty, ap·proach′a·ble·ness** *n.* —**ap·proach′a·ble** *adj.*

ap·pro·ba·tion (ap′rə·bā′shən) *n.* 1. The act of approving; approval. 2. Sanction. —**ap·pro·ba′tive, ap·pro·ba·to·ry** (ə·prō′bə·tôr′ē) *adj.*

ap·pro·pri·ate (*adj.* ə·prō′prē·it; *v.* ə·prō′·prē·āt) *adj.* Suitable; proper; relevant. —*v.t.* **·at·ed, ·at·ing** 1. To set apart for a particular use. 2. To take for one's own use. 3. To take or use without authority. [< L *ad-* to + *proprius* one's own] —**ap·pro′pri·ate·ly** *adv.* —**ap·pro′pri·ate·ness** *n.* —**ap·pro′pri·a′tor** *n.*

ap·pro·pri·a·tion (ə·prō′prē·ā′shən) *n.* 1. The act of appropriating. 2. Money, set apart by formal action for a special use. —**ap·pro′pri·a′tive** *adj.*

ap·prov·al (ə·pro͞o′vəl) *n.* 1. The act of approving; approbation. 2. Official consent; sanction. 3. Favorable opinion; praise. —**on approval** For (a customer's) examination without obligation to purchase.

ap·prove (ə·pro͞ov′) *v.* **·proved, ·prov·ing** *v.t.* 1. To regard as worthy, proper, or right. 2. To confirm formally or authoritatively. —*v.i.* 3. To show or state approval: often with *of.* [< L *ad-* to + *probare* to approve, prove] —**ap·prov′ing·ly** *adv.*

ap·prox·i·mate (*adj.* ə·prok′sə·mit; *v.* ə·prok′sə·māt) *adj.* 1. Nearly exact, accurate, or complete. 2. Like; resembling. 3. Near; close together. —*v.* **·mat·ed, ·mat·ing** *v.t.* 1. To come close to, as in quality, degree, or quantity. 2. To cause to come near. —*v.i.* 3. To come near in quality, degree, etc. [< L *ad-* to + *proximus*, superl. of *prope* near] —**ap·prox′i·mate·ly** *adv.* —**ap·prox′i·ma′tion** *n.*

ap·pur·te·nance (ə·pûr′tə·nəns) *n.* 1. Something attached to another, more important thing. 2. *pl.* Apparatus. [< LL *appertinere* to appertain] —**ap·pur′te·nant** *adj.*

a·pri·cot (ā′pri·kot, ap′ri·kot) *n.* 1. A yellow fruit, similar to a peach. 2. The tree bearing this fruit. 3. A pinkish yellow color. [Earlier *apricock* (prob. < Pg. *albricoque*)]

A·pril (ā′prəl) *n.* The fourth month of the year, containing 30 days. [< L *Aprilis*]

a pri·o·ri (ā′ prī·ō′rī, ä′ prē·ôr′ē) 1. *Logic* Proceeding from cause to effect, or from an assumption to its logical conclusion. 2. Based on theory rather than on experience or examination. [< L, from what is before]

a·pron (ā′prən) *n.* 1. A garment worn to protect or adorn the front of a person's clothes. 2. *Mech.* Any of various overlapping pieces protecting parts of machines. 3. *Engin.* a The platform at the entrance to a dock. b The platform below a dam or in a sluiceway. 4. *Aeron.* A hard-surfaced area in front of and around a hangar or aircraft shelter. 5. The part of a theater stage in front of the curtain. [< L *mappa* cloth, napkin]

ap·ro·pos (ap′rə·pō′) *adj.* Suitable; opportune: an *apropos* remark. —*adv.* 1. With reference or regard to: with *of*: *apropos* of spring. 2. To the purpose; pertinently. [< F *à* to + *propos* purpose]

apse (aps) *n. Archit.* An extending portion of an edifice, usually semicircular with a half dome, esp. the eastern or altar end of a church. [< L *apsis* arch]

apt (apt) *adj.* 1. Inclined; liable; likely. 2. Quick to learn; intelligent. 3. Pertinent; relevant. [< L *aptus* fitted, suited] —**apt′ly** *adv.* —**apt′ness** *n.*

ap·ter·ous (ap′tər·əs) *adj. Biol.* Without wings.

ap·ter·yx (ap′tər·iks) *n.* The kiwi. [< Gk. *a-* without + *pteryx* wing]

ap·ti·tude (ap′tə·to͞od, -tyo͞od) *n.* 1. Natural or acquired ability or bent. 2. Quickness of understanding. 3. The state or quality of being apt or fitting. [< LL *aptitudo* fitness]

aq·ua (ak′wə, ā′kwə) *n. pl.* **aq·uae** (ak′wē, ā′kwē) or **aq·uas** Water. —*adj. & n.* Bluish green. [< L]

Aq·ua-Lung (ak′wə·lung′) *n.* A scuba: a trade name. Also **aq′ua·lung′.**

aq·ua·ma·rine (ak′wə·mə·rēn′) *n.* 1. A sea-green variety of precious beryl. 2. A bluish green color. —*adj.* Bluish green. [< L *aqua marina* sea water]

aq·ua·naut (ak′wə·nôt) *n.* One who is trained to live and work underwater. [< AQUA + *-naut* (< Gk. *nautēs* sailor), after *aeronaut, astronaut*]

aq·ua·plane (ak′wə·plān) *n.* A board on which one stands while being towed by a motorboat. [< AQUA + PLANE[3]] —**aq′ua·plane** *v.i.* **·planed, ·plan·ing**

aqua re·gi·a (rē′jē·ə) A mixture of nitric and hydrochloric acids, a solvent for gold and platinum. [< L, royal water]

a·quar·i·um (ə·kwâr′ē·əm) *n. pl.* **a·quar·i·ums** or **a·quar·i·a** 1. A tank, pond, or the like for the exhibition or study of aquatic animals or plants. 2. A building containing such an exhibition. [< L *aqua* water]

A·quar·i·us (ə·kwâr′ē·əs) *n.* A constellation, the Water Bearer; also, a sign of the zodiac. [< L]

a·quat·ic (ə·kwat′ik) *adj.* 1. Living or growing in or near water. 2. Performed on or in water. —*n.* 1. An aquatic animal or plant. 2. *pl.* Water sports. [< L *aqua* water]

aq·ua·tint (ak′wə·tint′) *n.* 1. A technique of engraving that gives the effect of a water color. 2. Such an engraving. [< L *aqua tincta* tinged water] —**aq′ua·tint′** *v.t.*

aq·ua·vit (ä′kwə·vēt) *n.* A clear Scandinavian liquor, flavored with caraway seeds. [< AQUA VITAE]

aqua vi·tae (vī′tē) 1. Alcohol. 2. Whisky; brandy. [< L, water of life]

aq·ue·duct (ak′wə·dukt) *n.* 1. A water conduit, esp. one for supplying water to a community from a distance. 2. A structure supporting a canal carried over a river or low ground. [< L *aqua* water + *ducere* to lead]

a·que·ous (ā′kwē·əs, ak′wē-) *adj.* 1. Of or like water; watery. 2. Made from or with water.

aqueous humor A clear fluid filling the space in the eye between the cornea and the lens.

aq·ui·cul·ture (ak′wə·kul′chər) *n.* 1. The farming of ocean plants and animals in salt water. 2. Hydroponics. Also **aq′ua·cul′ture.** [< AQUA + CULTURE, after *agriculture*]

aq·ui·line (ak′wə·līn, -lin) *adj.* 1. Of or like an eagle. 2. Curving or hooked: an *aquiline* nose. [< L *aquila* eagle]

-ar *suffix* 1. Pertaining to; like: *regular, singular.* 2. The person or thing pertaining to: *scholar.* [< OF *-er, -ier* < L *-aris* (in nouns *-are*)]

Ar·ab (ar′əb) *n.* 1. A native or inhabitant of Arabia. 2. Any of a Semitic-speaking people inhabiting Arabia. —**Ar′ab** *adj.* —**A·ra·bi·an** (ə·rā′bē·ən) *adj. & n.*

ar·a·besque (ar′ə·besk′) *n.* 1. A design, as used in Moorish architecture, of intertwined lines forming scrollwork, leaves, or flowers. 2. In ballet, a position in which the dancer extends one leg straight backward, one arm forward, and the other arm backward. —*adj.* Relating to, executed in, or resembling arabesque; fanciful; ornamental.

Ar·a·bic (ar′ə·bik) *adj.* Of or pertaining to Arabia, the Arabs, their language, culture, etc. —*n.* The Southwest Semitic language of the Arabs.

Arabic numerals The symbols 1, 2, 3, 4, 5, 6, 7, 8, 9, and 0.

ar·a·ble (ar′ə·bəl) *adj.* Capable of being plowed. —*n.* Arable land. [< L *arare* to plow] —**ar′a·bil′i·ty** *n.*

a·rach·nid (ə·rak′nid) *n.* Any of a class of arthropods, including the spiders, scorpions, mites, etc. [< Gk. *arachnē* spider] —**a·rach′ni·dan** *adj. & n.*

Ar·a·ma·ic (ar′ə·mā′ik) *n.* Any of a group of Semitic languages of Biblical times.

A·rap·a·ho (ə·rap′ə·hō) *n. pl.* **·ho** or **·hoes** A member of an Algonquian tribe. Also **A·rap′a·hoe.**

ar·ba·lest (är′bə·list) *n.* A medieval crossbow requiring a mechanical appliance to bend it. Also **ar′ba·list.** [< L *arcus* a bow + *ballista* to throw]

ar·bi·ter (är′bə·tər) *n.* 1. A chosen or appointed judge or umpire. 2. An absolute and final judge. [< L] —**ar′bi·tral** *adj.*

ar·bi·tra·ble (är′bə·trə·bəl) *adj.* Subject to, capable of, or suitable for arbitration.

ar·bit·ra·ment (är·bit′rə·mənt) *n.* 1. Arbitration. 2. The decision of an arbitrator; an award.

ar·bi·trar·y (är′bə·trer′ē) *adj.* 1. Based on or subject to opinion. 2. Absolute; despotic. 3. Capricious; not based on reason. —**ar′bi·trar′i·ly** *adv.* —**ar′bi·trar′i·ness** *n.*

ar·bi·trate (är′bə·trāt) *v.t. & v.i.* **·trat·ed, ·trat·ing** 1. To act or decide as arbitrator. 2. To submit (a dispute) to arbitration.

ar·bi·tra·tion (är′bə·trā′shən) *n.* The settlement of a dispute by the decision of a third party or court.

ar·bi·tra·tor (är′bə·trā′tər) *n.* A person chosen to decide a dispute. [< L]

ar·bor[1] (är′bər) *n.* A bower, as of latticework, supporting vines or trees. Also *Brit.* **ar′bour.** [< L *herba* grass]

ar·bor[2] (är′bər) *n.* A shaft, spindle, or axle in certain machines. [< L, tree]

ar·bo·re·al (är·bôr′ē·əl) *adj.* 1. Of or like a tree. 2. Inhabiting trees, or adapted to life in trees.

ar·bo·re·tum (är′bə·rē′təm) *n. pl.* **·tums** or **·ta** A place for study and display of trees.

arbori- *combining form* Tree. [< L *arbor* tree]

ar·bor·vi·tae (är′bər·vī′tē) *n.* An evergreen of the pine family. [< L *arbor vitae* tree of life]

ar·bu·tus (är·byōō′təs) *n.* 1. An evergreen of the heath family. 2. The trailing arbutus [< L, strawberry tree]

arc (ärk) *n.* 1. Anything in the shape of an arch, a curve, or a part of a circle. 2. *Geom.* A part of any curve. 3. The flame formed by the passage of an electric current across the gap between two conductors. —*v.i.* **arced** (ärkt) or **arcked, arc·ing** (är′king) or **arck·ing** To form an arc. [< L *arcus* bow, arch]

ar·cade (är·kād′) *n.* 1. A series of arches with supporting columns or piers. 2. A roofed passageway or street, esp. one lined with shops. [< L *arcus* bow, arch]

Ar·ca·di·a (är·kā′dē·ə) Any region of ideal rustic simplicity and contentment. Also **Ar·ca·dy** (är′kə·dē).

Ar·ca·di·an (är·kā′dē·ən) *adj.* Rural or simple; pastoral.

ar·cane (är·kān′) *adj.* Secret; esoteric. [< L *arcanus* hidden]

arch[1] (ärch) *n.* 1. A curved structure spanning an opening. 2. Any similar structure or object. 3. A bowlike curve. 4. A curved or archlike part, as of the foot. —*v.t.* 1. To cause to form an arch or arches. 2. To furnish with an arch or arches. 3. To span; extend over, as an arch. —*v.i.* 4. To form an arch or arches. [< L *arcus* bow, arch]

arch[2] (ärch) *adj.* 1. Cunning; sly. 2. Most eminent; chief. 3. Cute; playful. [< ARCH-] —**arch′ly** *adv.* —**arch′ness** *n.*

arch- *prefix* 1. Chief; principal. 2. Very great; extreme. Also *archi-*. [< Gk. *archos* ruler]

ar·chae·ol·o·gy (är′kē·ol′ə·jē) See ARCHEOLOGY.

ar·chae·op·ter·yx (är′kē·op′tər·iks) *n.* *Paleontol.* A small winged extinct animal, possibly a nonflying, feathered dinosaur. [< ARCHAEO- + Gk. *pteryx* wing]

ar·cha·ic (är·kā′ik) *adj.* 1. Old-fashioned; antiquated. 2. Characterizing a word or language no longer in current use. [< Gk. *archaios* ancient] —**ar·cha′i·cal·ly** *adv.*

ar·cha·ism (är′kē·iz′əm, -kā-) *n.* An archaic word, idiom, or style. —**ar′cha·ist** *n.* —**ar′cha·is′tic** *adj.*

arch·an·gel (ärk′ān′jəl) *n.* An angel of highest rank. [< Gk. *arch-* chief + *angelos* angel]

arch·bish·op (ärch′bish′əp) *n.* A chief bishop. —**arch′bish′op·ric** *n.*

arch·dea·con (ärch′dē′kən) *n.* A chief deacon, ranking just below a bishop.

arch·dea·con·ry (ärch′dē′kən·rē) *n. pl.* **·ries** The jurisdiction, office, or residence of an archdeacon.

arch·di·o·cese (ärch′dī′ə·sēs, -sis) *n.* The diocese or jurisdiction of an archbishop.

arch·duke (ärch′dōōk′, -dyōōk′) *n.* A chief duke, esp. a prince of the former imperial family of Austria.

archeo- *combining form* Ancient: *Archeozoic.* Also **archaeo-**. [< Gk. *archaios* ancient]

ar·che·ol·o·gy (är′kē·ol′ə·jē) *n.* The science or study of history from the remains of early human cultures. Also spelled *archaeology.* —**ar·che·o·log·i·cal** (är′kē·ə·loj′i·kəl) or **·log′ic** *adj.* —**ar′che·ol′o·gist** *n.*

arch·er·y (är′chər·ē) *n.* The art or sport of shooting with bow and arrows. —**arch′er** *n.*

ar·che·type (är′kə·tīp) *n.* An original or standard pattern or model; a prototype. [< Gk. *arche-* first + *typos* stamp, pattern] —**ar′che·typ′al, ar′che·typ′ic** (-tip′ik) or **·i·cal** *adj.*

archi- *prefix* 1. Var. of ARCH-. 2. *Biol.* Original; primitive. [See ARCH-.]

ar·chi·e·pis·co·pate (är′kē·i·pis′kə·pit, -pāt) *n.* The office or tenure of an archbishop. —**ar′chi·e·pis′co·pal** *adj.*

ar·chi·pel·a·go (är′kə·pel′ə·gō) *n. pl.* **·goes** or **·gos** 1. A sea with many islands. 2. The islands in such a sea. [< Gk. *archi-* chief + *pelagos* sea]

ar·chi·tect (är′kə·tekt) *n.* 1. One whose profession is to design and draw up the plans for buildings, etc., and supervise their construction. 2. One who devises or creates anything. [< Gk. *archi-* chief + *tektōn* worker]

ar·chi·tec·ton·ic (är′kə·tek·ton′ik) *adj.* 1. Pertaining to an architect or architecture. 2. Having architectural qualities of design and structure.

ar·chi·tec·ton·ics (är′kə·tek·ton′iks) *n.pl.* (*construed as sing.*) 1. The science of architecture. 2. Structural design, as in works of music or art.

ar·chi·tec·ture (är′kə·tek′chər) *n.* 1. The science, art, or profession of designing and constructing buildings or other structures. 2. A style or system of building. 3. Construction or structure generally. —**ar′chi·tec′tur·al** *adj.* —**ar′chi·tec′tur·al·ly** *adv.*

ar·chi·trave (är′kə·trāv) *n. Archit.* 1. The part of an entablature that rests upon the column heads and supports the frieze. 2. A molded ornament skirting the head and sides of a door or window. [< Gk. *archi-* chief + Ital. *trave* beam]

ar·chives (är′kīvz) *n.pl.* 1. A place where public records and historical documents are kept. 2. Public records, documents, etc., as kept in such a depository. [< Gk. *archeion* a public office] —**ar·chi′val** *adj.*

ar·chi·vist (är′kə·vist) *n.* A keeper of archives.

arch·way (ärch′wā′) *n.* A passage under an arch.

-archy *combining form* Rule; government. [< Gk. *archos* ruler] —**autarchy** (absolute rule) —**dyarchy** or **duarchy** (by two rulers) —**gynarchy** (by women) —**matriarchy** (rule by and descent through women) —**monarchy** (by one) —**oligarchy** (by a few) —**patriarchy** (rule by and descent through men) —**triarchy** (by three rulers)

arc lamp A lamp in which light of high intensity is produced between two electrodes. Also **arc light.**

arc·tic (ärk′tik, är′tik) *adj.* 1. Characteristic of the region of the Arctic Circle. 2. Extremely cold. [< Gk. *arktikos* of the Bear (the northern constellation Ursa Major)]

Arctic Circle The parallel at 66°33′ north latitude; the boundary of the North Frigid Zone.

-ard *suffix of nouns* One who does something to excess or who is to be disparaged: *drunkard, coward*; sometimes changed to -art: *braggart.* [< OF *-ard, -art* < G *-hard, -hart* hardy]

ar·den·cy (är′dən·sē) *n.* Ardor.

ar·dent (är′dənt) *adj.* 1. Passionate; intense. 2. Glowing. 3. Hot; burning. [< L *ardere* to burn] —**ar′dent·ly** *adv.* —**ar′dent·ness** *n.*

ar·dor (är′dər) *n.* 1. Warmth or intensity of feelings; eagerness; zeal. 2. Great heat. Also *Brit.* **ar′dour.** [< L *ardere* to burn]

ar·du·ous (är′jōō·əs) *adj.* 1. Involving great labor or hardship; difficult. 2. Toiling strenuously; energetic. 3. Steep; hard to climb or surmount. [< L *arduus* steep] —**ar′du·ous·ly** *adv.* —**ar′du·ous·ness** *n.*

are[1] (är, ər) *v.* The plural, present indicative and second person singular, of BE. [OE (Northumbrian) *aron*]

are[2] (âr, är) *n.* In the metric system, a surface measure equal to one hundred square meters; also **ar.** [< L *area* area]

ar·e·a (âr′ē·ə) *n. pl.* **ar·e·as** 1. A particular

portion of the earth's surface; region. 2. The surface included within a boundary line. 3. The extent or scope of anything. 4. A space having a particular function. [< L, an open space] —**ar′e·al** *adj.*

area code A three-digit number used in dialing long-distance telephone calls.

ar·e·a·way (âr′ē·ə·wā′) *n.* 1. A small sunken space before a basement door. 2. A passageway.

a·re·na (ə·rē′nə) *n.* 1. The oval space in a Roman amphitheater, where contests and shows were held. 2. Any place of this nature: a football *arena.* 3. A scene or sphere of action: the political *arena.* [< L, sand, sandy place]

arena theater A stage in the center of an auditorium, surrounded by seats: also called *theater-in-the-round.*

aren't (ärnt) Are not.

a·re·o·la (ə·rē′ə·lə) *n.* *pl.* **·lae** (-lē) or **·las** 1. *Bot.* An interstice in a network of leaf veins. 2. *Anat.* The colored circle about a nipple or about a vesicle. Also **ar·e·ole** (âr′ē·ōl). [< L, dim. of *area* open space]

ar·gent (är′jənt) *n. & adj.* Silver. [< L *argentum* silver]

Ar·gen·tine (är′jən·tēn, -tīn) *adj.* Of or pertaining to Argentina. —*n.* A native or citizen of Argentina: also **Ar·gen·tin·e·an** (är′jən·tin′ē·ən).

ar·gon (är′gon) *n.* A colorless, gaseous element (symbol Ar) present in the atmosphere. [< Gk., neut. of *argos* idle, inert + -ON]

ar·go·sy (är′gə·sē) *n.* *pl.* **·sies** 1. A large merchant ship. 2. A fleet of merchant vessels. [Earlier *ragusy,* after *Ragusa,* Italian name of Dubrovnik, Yugoslavia]

ar·got (är′gō, -gət) *n.* The specialized vocabulary or jargon of any class or group, as that of the underworld. [< F]

ar·gue (är′gyōō) *v.* **·gued, ·gu·ing** *v.i.* 1. To present reasons to support or contest a measure or opinion. 2. To contend in argument; quarrel. —*v.t.* 3. To present reasons for or against; discuss, as a proposal. 4. To contend or maintain, by reasoning. [< L *arguere* to prove] —**ar′gu·a·ble** *adj.* —**ar′gu·er** *n.*

ar·gu·ment (är′gyə·mənt) *n.* 1. A discussion in which there is disagreement; debate. 2. A quarrel. 3. A reason or reasons offered for or against something. 4. Discourse intended to persuade or to convince. 5. A short summary of subject matter; a brief plot synopsis.

ar·gu·men·ta·tion (är′gyə·men·tā′shən) *n.* 1. Reasoning to a conclusion. 2. Discussion; debate.

ar·gu·men·ta·tive (är′gyə·men′tə·tiv) *adj.* Given to argumentation; disputatious. —**ar′·gu·men′ta·tive·ly** *adv.* —**ar′gu·men′ta·tive·ness** *n.*

a·ri·a (ä′rē·ə) *n.* A solo vocal piece, as in an opera or oratorio, often with instrumental accompaniment. [< L *aer* air]

-arian *suffix* Used in forming adjectives and adjectival nouns denoting occupation, age, sect, beliefs, etc.: *seminarian, octogenarian.* [< L *-arius* -ary + -AN]

ar·id (ar′id) *adj.* 1. Parched; dry. 2. Lacking interest or feeling; dull. [< L *arere* to be dry] —**a·rid·i·ty** (ə·rid′ə·tē), **ar′id·ness** *n.* —**ar′·id·ly** *adv.*

Ar·ies (âr′ēz) *n.* A constellation, the Ram; also, the first sign of the zodiac. [< L]

a·right (ə·rīt′) *adv.* In a right way; correctly.

a·rise (ə·rīz′) *v.i.* **a·rose** (ə·rōz′), **a·ris·en** (ə·riz′ən), **a·ris·ing** 1. To get up. 2. To rise; ascend. 3. To come into being; originate; issue. 4. To result; proceed. [OE < *ā-* up + *rīsan* to rise]

ar·is·toc·ra·cy (ar′is·tok′rə·sē) *n.* *pl.* **·cies** 1. A hereditary nobility or privileged class. 2. Any preeminent group: the *aristocracy* of talent. [< Gk. *aristos* best + *krateein* to rule] —**a·ris·to·crat** (ə·ris′tə·krat) *n.* —**a·ris·to·crat·ic** (ə·ris′tə·krat′ik) *adj.* —**a·ris′to·crat′·i·cal·ly** *adv.*

Ar·is·to·te·li·an (ar′is·tə·tē′lē·ən, -tēl′yən) *adj.* Pertaining to or characteristic of Aristotle or his philosophy. —*n.* An adherent of Aristotle's teachings; one who tends to be scientific in his method, rather than speculative. Also **Ar′is·to·te′le·an.** —**Ar′is·to·te′li·an·ism** *n.*

a·rith·me·tic (ə·rith′mə·tik) *n.* The science of computing with numbers by addition, subtraction, multiplication, and division. [< Gk. *arithmos* number] —**a·rith·me·tic** (ar′ith·met′ik) or **·met·i·cal** *adj.* —**ar′ith·met′i·cal·ly** *adv.* —**a·rith·me·ti·cian** (ə·rith′·mə·tish′ən, ar′ith-) *n.*

arithmetic mean (ar′ith·met′ik) *Math.* The sum of a set of numbers, divided by the number of terms in the set.

arithmetic progression (ar′ith·met′ik) *Math.* A sequence of terms in which each, except the first, differs from the preceding one by a constant quantity, as 2, 4, 6, 8.

-arium *suffix of nouns* 1. A place for: *herbarium.* 2. Connected with: *honorarium.* [< L *-arius.* See -ARY[1].]

ark (ärk) *n.* 1. In the Bible: **a** The ship of Noah. *Gen.* vi–viii. **b** The chest containing the tablets bearing the Ten Commandments: also called **ark of the covenant.** *Ex.* xxv 10. 2. A large, flat-bottomed or awkward boat. [OE *arc* < L *arca* chest]

arm[1] (ärm) *n.* 1. An upper limb of the human body, from the shoulder to the hand or wrist. ◆Collateral adjective: *brachial.* 2. The forelimb of certain other vertebrates. 3. An armlike part or appendage. 4. Something intended to support or cover the human arm. 5. Power; authority. —**at arm's length** At a distance. —**with open arms** Cordially; warmly. [OE *earm, arm*]

arm[2] (ärm) *n.* 1. A weapon. 2. A distinct branch of the military service: the air *arm.* —*v.t. & v.i.* To supply or equip (oneself) with weapons. [< L *arma* weapons] —**armed** (ärmd) *adj.*

ar·ma·da (är·mä′də) *n.* A fleet of war vessels. [< Sp. < L *armare* to arm]

ar·ma·dil·lo (är′mə·dil′ō) *n.* *pl.* **·los** An American burrowing nocturnal mammal having an armorlike covering of jointed plates. [< Sp. < L *armare* to arm]

Ar·ma·ged·don (är′mə·ged′n) *n.* In Biblical prophecy, the scene of a great battle between the forces of good and evil, to occur at the end of the world. *Rev.* xvi 16.

ar·ma·ment (är′mə·mənt) *n.* 1. *Often pl.* Guns and other military equipment. 2. *Often pl.* Military strength. 3. The act of arming or equipping for war. [< L *armare* to arm]

ar·ma·ture (är′mə·cho͝or) *n.* 1. A piece of soft iron joining the poles of a magnet to prevent the loss of magnetic power. 2. *Electr.* In a dynamo or motor, the iron core carrying the coils of insulated wire to be revolved through the magnetic field. 3. *Biol.* Protective covering, as the shells of animals. 4. In sculpture, a framework to support the clay or other substance in modeling. 5. Arms; armor. [< L *armare* to arm]

arm·chair (ärm′châr′) *n.* A chair with supports for the arms.

armed forces The military, naval, and air forces of a nation.

Ar·me·ni·an (är·mē′nē·ən, -mēn′yən) *adj.* Of or pertaining to the country, people, or language of Armenia. **—Ar·me′ni·an** *n.*

arm·ful (ärm′fo͝ol′) *n. pl.* **·fuls** As much as can be held in the arm or arms.

ar·mi·stice (är′mə·stis) *n.* A temporary cessation of hostilities by mutual agreement; truce. [< L *arma* arms + *sistere* to stop, stand still]

arm·let (ärm′lit) *n.* 1. A little arm, as of the sea. 2. A band worn around the arm.

ar·moire (är·mwär′) *n.* A large, movable, often ornate cabinet or cupboard. [< F < L *armarium* a chest]

ar·mor (är′mər) *n.* 1. A defensive covering, as of metallic plates. 2. The armored vehicles of an army. 3. Any protective covering, as the shell of a turtle. **—***v.t. & v.i.* To furnish with or put on armor. Also *Brit.* **ar′mour.** [< OF *armeür* < L *armare* to arm] **—ar′·mored** *adj.*

ar·mor·er (är′mər·ər) *n.* 1. A maker or repairer of arms or armor. 2. A manufacturer of arms. Also *Brit.* **ar′mour·er.**

ar·mo·ri·al (är·môr′ē·əl) *adj.* Pertaining to heraldry.

ar·mor·y (är′mər·ē) *n. pl.* **·mor·ies** 1. A place where arms are kept; arsenal. 2. A building for the use of a body of militia, including storage for arms and equipment, drill rooms, etc. 3. An arms factory. Also *Brit.* **ar′mour·y.** [Prob. < ARMOR]

arm·pit (ärm′pit′) *n.* The cavity under the arm at the shoulder; axilla.

arms (ärmz) *n.pl.* 1. Weapons. 2. Warfare. 3. Heraldic symbols. **—up in arms** Aroused and ready to fight. [< L *arma* weapons]

ar·my (är′mē) *n. pl.* **·mies** 1. A large organized body of soldiers. 2. The total military land forces of a country. 3. The largest administrative and tactical unit of the U.S. land forces. 4. Any large body of people, animals, etc. [< L *armare* to arm]

ar·ni·ca (är′ni·kə) *n.* 1. A widely distributed, composite, herbaceous perennial. 2. A liniment prepared from this herb, used for sprains and bruises. [< NL]

a·ro·ma (ə·rō′mə) *n.* Fragrance, as from appetizing food, spices, etc.; agreeable odor. [< Gk. *arōma, -atos* spice] **—ar·o·mat·ic** (ar′ə·mat′ik) *adj. & n.*

a·rose (ə·rōz′) Past tense of ARISE.

a·round (ə·round′) *adv.* 1. On all sides; in various directions. 2. In the opposite direction: to turn *around.* 3. From place to place; here and there: to walk *around.* 4. Nearby; in the vicinity. 5. In or to a particular place: Come *around* to see us again. **—***prep.* 1. About the circumference or circuit of. 2. On all sides of; surrounding or enveloping. 3. Here and there in. 4. Somewhere near or within. 5. Somewhere near in time, amount, etc.; about.

a·rouse (ə·rouz′) *v.t.* **a·roused, a·rous·ing** 1. To awaken. 2. To excite. [< A-[2] + ROUSE] **—a·rous′al** (-zəl) *n.*

ar·peg·gi·o (är·pej′ē·ō, -pej′ō) *n. pl.* **·gi·os** *Music* 1. The sounding or playing of the notes of a chord in rapid succession. 2. A chord so played. [< Ital. *arpa* a harp]

ar·que·bus (är′kwə·bəs) *n.* A harquebus.

ar·raign (ə·rān′) *v.t.* 1. To call into court and cause to answer to an indictment. 2. To call upon for an answer; accuse. [< LL *arrationare* to call to account] **—ar·raign′er** *n.* **—ar·raign′ment** *n.*

ar·range (ə·rānj′) *v.* **·ranged, ·rang·ing** *v.t.* 1. To put in definite or proper order. 2. To plan the details of; prepare for. 3. To adjust, as a conflict or dispute. 4. *Music* To change or adapt for other instruments or voices. **—***v.i.* 5. To come to an agreement. 6. To see about the details; make plans. [< OF *arangier* to put in order] **—ar·range′ment** *n.* **—ar·rang′er** *n.*

ar·rant (ar′ənt) *adj.* Notoriously bad; unmitigated. [Var. of ERRANT]

ar·ras (ar′əs) *n.* 1. A tapestry. 2. A wall hanging of tapestry. [after *Arras,* France]

ar·ray (ə·rā′) *n.* 1. Regular or proper order, esp. of troops. 2. The persons or things arrayed. 3. Clothing; fine dress. 4. A large number; an imposing collection. **—***v.t.* 1. To set in order, as troops for battle. 2. To adorn; dress. [< OF *arei* to order]

ar·rears (ə·rirz′) *n.pl.* That which is behindhand or overdue. **—in arrears** Behind in meeting payment, completing work, etc. [< L *ad-* to + *retro* backward]

ar·rest (ə·rest′) *v.t.* 1. To stop suddenly; check. 2. To take into legal custody. 3. To attract and fix, as the attention. **—***n.* 1. The act of arresting, or the state of being arrested. 2. Seizure by legal authority. 3. A device for arresting motion. **—under arrest** In legal custody. [< L *ad-* to + *restare* to stop, remain] **—ar·rest′er** *n.*

ar·ri·val (ə·rī′vəl) *n.* 1. The act of arriving. 2. One who or that which arrives or has arrived.

ar·rive (ə·rīv′) *v.i.* **·rived, ·riv·ing** 1. To reach a place. 2. To come to a desired object, state, etc.: often with *at.* 3. To attain success or fame. 4. To come at last: The hour has *arrived.* [< L *ad-* to + *ripa* shore]

ar·ro·gant (ar′ə·gənt) *adj.* Overbearing; haughty. [< L *ad-* to + *rogare* to ask] **—ar′ro·gance** *n.* **—ar′ro·gant·ly** *adv.*

ar·ro·gate (ar′ə·gāt) *v.t.* **·gat·ed, ·gat·ing** To claim or take without right. [< L *ad-* to + *rogare* to ask] **—ar′ro·ga′tion** *n.*

ar·row (ar′ō) *n.* 1. A slender shaft, generally feathered at one end and with a pointed head at the other, to be shot from a bow. 2. Anything resembling an arrow, as a sign in the shape of an arrow, used to indicate directions. [OE *earh, arwe*]

ar·row·head (ar′ō·hed′) *n.* The sharp-pointed head of an arrow.

ar·row·root (ar′ō·ro͞ot′, -ro͝ot′) *n.* 1. A nutritious starch obtained from a tropical

American plant. 2. The plant itself. [Plant so called because used to treat arrow wounds]

ar·roy·o (ə·roiʹō) *n. pl.* **·os** (-ōz) 1. A deep, dry gully. 2. A brook. [< Sp. < L *arrugia* pit, shaft]

ar·se·nal (ärʹsə·nəl) *n.* 1. A government facility for manufacturing and storing arms and munitions. 2. A store of arms. 3. A store; collection; supply. [< Ital. < Arabic *dār aṣ-ṣinʻah* workshop]

ar·se·nic (ärʹsə·nik) *n.* A grayish white, metallic element (symbol As), forming many poisonous compounds. [< Gk. *arsenikon* yellow orpiment (a compound of arsenic)] **—ar·sen·i·cal** (är·senʹi·kəl) *adj.*

ar·son (ärʹsən) *n.* The malicious burning of a building or other property. [< L *ardere* to burn]

art[1] (ärt) *n.* 1. **a** The production of esthetically pleasing artifacts. **b** Works resulting from this activity. 2. Literature, music, and esp. painting, sculpture, drawing, etc. 3. Any system of rules and principles that facilitates skilled human accomplishment. 4. A pursuit or occupation that depends upon the skilled application of such a system of rules and principles. 5. Practical skill; dexterity. [< L *ars, artis* skill]

art[2] (ärt) *Archaic* or *Poetic* Second person singular present tense of BE: used with *thou.* [OE *eart*]

art de·co (dekʹō) A style of decoration of the late 1920's and the 1930's characterized by geometric shapes. [< F *arts decoratifs modernes* modern decorative arts]

ar·te·ri·o·scle·ro·sis (är·tirʹē·ō·sklə·rōʹsis) *n. Pathol.* The thickening and hardening of the walls of an artery. **—ar·teʹri·o·scle·rotʹic** (-rotʹik) *adj.*

ar·ter·y (ärʹtər·ē) *n. pl.* **·ter·ies** 1. Any of a large number of muscular vessels conveying blood away from the heart to every part of the body. 2. Any main channel or route. [< Gk. *artēria* windpipe] **—ar·te·ri·al** (är·tirʹē·əl) *adj.*

ar·te·sian well (är·tēʹzhən) A well at a level lower than the source of the water supply, from which the water flows out under pressure. [< F, after *Artois,* region of France]

art·ful (ärtʹfəl) *adj.* 1. Crafty; cunning. 2. Skillful; ingenious. **—artʹful·ly** *adv.* **—artʹful·ness** *n.*

ar·thri·tis (är·thrīʹtis) *n. Pathol.* Inflammation of a joint or joints. [< Gk. *arthron* joint] **—ar·thrit·ic** (är·thritʹik) *adj. & n.*

arthro- *combining form* Joint. Also, before vowels, **arthr-.** [< Gk. *arthron*]

ar·thro·pod (ärʹthrə·pod) *n. Zool.* Any of a large group of invertebrate animals having jointed legs and segmented body parts, including insects, spiders, and crabs. [< ARTHRO- + Gk. *pous, podos* foot]

ar·ti·choke (ärʹtə·chōk) *n.* A thistlelike garden plant, having an edible flower head. [< Ital. < Arabic *al-kharshūf*]

ar·ti·cle (ärʹti·kəl) *n.* 1. A particular object or substance; a thing. 2. An individual item in a class: an *article* of clothing. 3. A literary piece in a newspaper, magazine, etc. 4. A separate section in a document, as in a treaty. 5. *Gram.* An auxiliary word inserted before a noun to limit or modify it in some way, as English *a, an* (**indefinite article**) and *the* (**definite article**). [< L *artus* a joint]

ar·tic·u·lar (är·tikʹyə·lər) *adj.* Pertaining to a joint or the joints. [< L *articularis*]

ar·tic·u·late (*adj.* är·tikʹyə·lit; *v.* är·tikʹyə·lāt) *adj.* 1. Able to speak, esp. well or expressively. 2. Coherent; well presented: an *articulate* thesis. 3. Jointed; segmented, as limbs. Also **ar·ticʹu·latʹed.** **—***v.* **·lat·ed, ·lat·ing** *v.t.* 1. To utter distinctly; enunciate. 2. To express in words. 3. To joint together; unite by joints. **—***v.i.* 4. To speak distinctly. [< L *articulare* to divide into joints, utter distinctly] **—ar·ticʹu·late·ly** *adv.* **—ar·ticʹu·late·ness** *n.*

ar·tic·u·la·tion (är·tikʹyə·lāʹshən) *n.* 1. A jointing or being jointed together. 2. *Anat.* The union forming a joint, as of bones. 3. The utterance of speech sounds; enunciation. **—ar·ticʹu·laʹtive** *adj.* **—ar·ticʹu·laʹtor** *n.*

ar·ti·fact (ärʹtə·fakt) *n.* Anything made by human work or skill. [< L *ars, artis* art, skill + *facere* to make]

ar·ti·fice (ärʹtə·fis) *n.* 1. An ingenious stratagem; maneuver. 2. Subtle or deceptive craft; trickery. 3. Skill; ingenuity. [< L *ars, artis* art + *facere* to make]

ar·tif·i·cer (är·tifʹə·sər) *n.* 1. A skilled craftsman. 2. *Mil.* A skilled mechanic. 3. An inventor.

ar·ti·fi·cial (ärʹtə·fishʹəl) *adj.* 1. Produced by human art. 2. Made in imitation of something natural. 3. Not genuine; feigned; fictitious. [See ARTIFICE.] **—ar·ti·fi·ci·al·i·ty** (ärʹtə·fishʹē·alʹə·tē) *n.* **—arʹti·fiʹcial·ly** *adv.* **—arʹti·fiʹcial·ness** *n.*

artificial insemination Impregnation of the female without direct sexual contact.

artificial respiration The stimulation of breathing by forcing breath into the lungs, through the mouth, or by applying pressure to the chest cavity at regular intervals.

ar·til·ler·y (är·tilʹə·rē) *n.* 1. Guns of larger caliber than machine guns. 2. Military units armed with such guns. 3. A branch of the U.S. Army. 4. The science of gunnery. [< OF *artiller* to fortify]

ar·til·ler·y·man (är·tilʹə·rē·mən) *n. pl.* **·men** (-mən) A soldier in the artillery.

ar·ti·san (ärʹtə·zən) *n.* A skilled workman. [< L *ars, artis* art]

ar·tist (ärʹtist) *n.* 1. One skilled in any of the fine arts, esp. painting, drawing, etc. 2. One whose work exhibits skill. [< L *ars, artis* art]

ar·tiste (är·tēstʹ) *n. Chiefly Brit.* An entertainer.

ar·tis·tic (är·tisʹtik) *adj.* 1. Of or pertaining to art or artists. 2. Conforming to the principles of art; tastefully executed. 3. Fond of or sensitive to art. **—ar·tisʹti·cal·ly** *adv.*

art·ist·ry (ärʹtis·trē) *n.* 1. Artistic workmanship or ability. 2. The pursuits or occupation of an artist.

art·less (ärtʹlis) *adj.* 1. Lacking craft or deceit; guileless. 2. Natural; simple. 3. Devoid of art or skill; clumsy. **—artʹless·ly** *adv.* **—artʹless·ness** *n.*

art nou·veau (nōō·vōʹ) A style of decoration dating from the 1890's, characterized by sinuous plant shapes. [< F, new art]

art·y (ärʹtē) *adj.* Ostentatiously claiming artistic worth or interest. **—artʹi·ness** *n.*

ar·um (ârʹəm) *n.* Any of a genus of Old

World herbs, including the philodendron. [< Gk. *aron*]

-ary[1] *suffix of adjectives and nouns* 1. Connected with or pertaining to what is expressed in the root word: *elementary*. 2. A person employed as or engaged in: *apothecary*. 3. A thing connected with or a place dedicated to: *dictionary*. [< L *-arius, -arium*]

-ary[2] *suffix of adjectives* Of or pertaining to; belonging to: *military, salutary*. [< L *-aris*]

Ar·y·an (âr′ē·ən, ar′-) *n.* 1. A member or descendant of a prehistoric people who spoke Indo-European. 2. In Nazi ideology, a Caucasian gentile, esp. one of Nordic stock. [< Skt. *ārya* noble] **—Ar′y·an** *adj.*

as (az, *unstressed* əz) *adv.* To the same degree; equally. *—conj.* 1. To the same degree or extent that: often used with *as* or *so* to denote equality or identity: *as* fair *as* the sun. 2. In the way that: Do *as* I do. 3. To the degree in which: He became gentler *as* he grew older. 4. At the same time that; while. 5. Because; since. 6. For instance: used to introduce examples or illustrations: Some animals are cunning, *as* the fox. 7. Though; however: Bad *as* it was, it might have been worse. **—as for** (or **as to**) In the matter of; concerning. **—as if** (or **as though**) The same, or in the same manner, that it would be if. *—pron.* 1. That; who; which: after *same* and *such*: He lived in the same city *as* I did. 2. A fact which: He is dead, *as* everyone knows. *—prep.* 1. In the role or character of: to act *as* umpire. 2. In the manner of; like: to use a board *as* a hammer. [ME *as, als, alse*, OE *ealswā* entirely so, just as]

as·a·fet·i·da (as′ə·fet′ə·də) *n.* A strong-smelling substance prepared from certain plants of the parsley family, formerly used as an antispasmodic. Also **as′a·foet′i·da.** [< Med.L *asa* gum + L *foetida*, fem., ill-smelling]

as·bes·tos (as·bes′təs, az-) *n.* A white or light gray silicate mineral that may be woven or shaped into acid-resisting, nonconducting, and fireproof articles. Also **as·bes′tus.** [< Gk. *a-* not + *sbennynai* to quench]

as·cend (ə·send′) *v.i.* 1. To go or move upward; rise. *—v.t.* 2. To mount; climb. 3. To succeed to (a throne). [< L *ad-* to + *scandere* to climb] **—as·cen′der** *n.*

as·cen·dan·cy (ə·sen′dən·sē) *n.* The quality, fact, or state of being in the ascendant; domination. Also **as·cen′dance, as·cen′·dence, as·cen′den·cy.**

as·cen·dant (ə·sen′dənt) *adj.* 1. Ascending; rising. 2. Superior; dominant. 3. *Astron.* Coming to or above the horizon. *—n.* A position of preeminence; domination. Also **as·cen′dent. —to be in the ascendant** To approach or occupy an influential position.

as·cen·sion (ə·sen′shən) *n.* The act of ascending. **—the Ascension** *Theol.* The bodily ascent of Christ into heaven after the Resurrection, commemorated on **Ascension Day**, the fortieth day after Easter. **—as·cen′·sion·al** *adj.*

as·cent (ə·sent′) *n.* 1. The act of ascending; a rising, soaring, or climbing. 2. A rise in state, rank, or station; advancement. 3. A way or means of ascending; upward slope.

as·cer·tain (as′ər·tān′) *v.t.* To learn with certainty; find out. [< L *a-* to + CERTAIN] **—as′cer·tain′a·ble** *adj.* **—as′cer·tain′ment** *n.*

as·cet·ic (ə·set′ik) *n.* One who leads an austere and self-denying life, esp. for religious purposes. *—adj.* 1. Pertaining to ascetics or asceticism. 2. Rigidly abstinent; austere. [< Gk. *askētēs* one who practices (self-denial), a monk] **—as·cet′i·cal·ly** *adv.* **—as·cet·i·cism** (ə·set′ə·siz′əm) *n.*

a·scor·bic acid (ə·skor′bik) *Biochem.* Vitamin C. See under VITAMIN.

as·cot (as′kət, -kot) *n.* A scarflike necktie. [after *Ascot*, a village in England.]

as·cribe (ə·skrīb′) *v.t.* **·cribed, ·crib·ing** 1. To attribute or impute, as to a cause or source: I *ascribe* his conduct to insanity. 2. To consider or declare as belonging (to). [< L *ad-* to + *scribere* to write] **—as·crib′a·ble** *adj.*

as·crip·tion (ə·skrip′shən) *n.* 1. The act of ascribing. 2. That which ascribes.

-ase *suffix Chem.* Used in naming enzymes: *amylase, esterase.*

a·sep·sis (ə·sep′sis, ā-) *n. Med.* 1. Absence of pathogenic organisms. 2. The prevention of infection by the use of sterilized instruments, dressings, etc. [< A-[4] + SEPSIS]

a·sep·tic (ə·sep′tik, ā-) *adj.* Free of pathogenic organisms. **—a·sep′ti·cal·ly** *adv.*

a·sex·u·al (ā·sek′shōō·əl) *adj. Biol.* 1. Having no distinct sexual organs; without sex. 2. Occurring or performed without union of male and female gametes. **—a′sex·u·al′i·ty** (-al′ə·tē) *n.* **—a·sex′u·al·ly** *adv.*

ash[1] (ash) *n. pl.* **ash·es** 1. The powdery, whitish gray residue of a substance that has been burned. 2. *pl.* The remains of the human body after cremation or disintegration. [OE *æsce, asce*]

ash[2] (ash) *n.* 1. A tree of the olive family. 2. The light, tough, elastic wood of this tree. [OE *æsc*] **—ash** *adj.*

a·shamed (ə·shāmd′) *adj.* 1. Feeling shame. 2. Deterred by fear of shame. [OE *āscamod*, pp. of *āscamian*] **—a·sham′ed·ly** *adv.*

ash·en[1] (ash′ən) *adj.* 1. Of, pertaining to, or like ashes. 2. Pale in color; gray.

ash·en[2] (ash′ən) *adj.* Pertaining to or made of ash wood.

ash·lar (ash′lər) *n.* 1. In masonry, a rough-hewn block of stone. 2. Masonry made of such stones. [< L *axis* board, plank]

a·shore (ə·shôr′) *adv. & adj.* 1. To or on the shore. 2. On land; aground.

ash·ram (ash′rəm) *n.* 1. A secluded place for meditation by Hindus. 2. A retreat or commune. [< Skt. *ā* toward + *śrama* religious experiences]

Ash Wednesday The first day of Lent: from the application of ashes to the heads of penitents.

ash·y (ash′ē) *adj.* **ash·i·er, ash·i·est** 1. Of, pertaining to, or like ashes; ash-covered. 2. Ash-colored; ashen.

A·sian (ā′zhən, ā′shən) *adj.* Of or characteristic of Asia or its peoples. **—A′sian** *n.*

A·si·at·ic (ā′zhē·at′ik, ā′shē-) *adj. & n.* Asian: considered offensive in referring to people.

a·side (ə·sīd′) *adv.* 1. On or to one side; apart. 2. Out of thought or use: to put grief *aside*. **—aside from** 1. Apart from. 2. Excepting. *—n.* 1. A remark that is not addressed to everyone present. 2. A remark that digresses from the subject.

as·i·nine (as′ə·nīn) *adj.* Of or like an ass;

stupid; obstinate. [< L *asinus* ass] **—as′i·nine′ly** *adv.* **—as·i·nin·i·ty** (as′ə·nin′ə·tē) *n.*

ask (ask) *v.t.* 1. To put a question to. 2. To put a question about: to *ask* the time. 3. To make a request of or for; solicit. 4. To need or require. 5. To state the price of; demand. 6. To invite. *—v.i.* 7. To make inquiries: with *for, after,* or *about.* 8. To make a request: often with *for.* [OE *āscian*]

a·skance (ə·skans′) *adv.* 1. With a side glance; sidewise. 2. Disdainfully; distrustfully. [Origin unknown]

a·skew (ə·skyōō′) *adj.* Oblique. *—adv.* In an oblique position or manner; awry.

a·slant (ə·slant′) *adj.* Slanting; oblique. *—adv.* At a slant; obliquely. *—prep.* Slantingly across or over.

a·sleep (ə·slēp′) *adj.* 1. In a state of sleep; sleeping. 2. Dormant; inactive. 3. Benumbed, as an arm or leg. *—adv.* Into a sleeping condition: to fall *asleep.*

a·so·cial (ā·sō′shəl) *adj.* 1. Avoiding society; not gregarious. 2. Selfish; self-centered.

asp (asp) *n.* The common European viper. [< Gk.]

as·par·a·gus (ə·spar′ə·gəs) *n.* The succulent, edible shoots of a cultivated variety of a perennial herb of the lily family. [< Gk. *aspharagos*]

as·pect (as′pekt) *n.* 1. The look of a person; facial expression. 2. Appearance to the eye; look. 3. Appearance presented to the mind: all *aspects* of a problem. 4. A facing in a given direction. 5. The side or surface facing in a certain direction. [< L *ad-* at + *specere* to look]

asp·en (as′pən) *n.* A species of poplar of North America or Europe with leaves that tremble in the slightest breeze. *—adj.* 1. Of the aspen. 2. Shaking, like aspen leaves. [OE *æspe*]

as·per·i·ty (as·per′ə·tē) *n. pl.* **·ties** 1. Roughness or harshness, as of surface, sound, etc. 2. Sharpness of temper; acrimony. [< L *asper* rough]

as·per·sion (ə·spûr′zhən, -shən) *n.* 1. A slandering; defamation. 2. A slanderous or damaging report; calumny. [< L *ad-* to + *spargere* to sprinkle, scatter]

as·phalt (as′fôlt) *n.* 1. A solid, brownish black, combustible mixture of bituminous hydrocarbons. 2. A mixture of this with sand or gravel, used for paving, etc. *—v.t.* To pave with asphalt. [< Gk. *asphalton*] **—as·phal′tic** *adj.*

as·pho·del (as′fə·del) *n.* A plant of the lily family, bearing white, pink, or yellow flowers. [< Gk. *asphodelos*]

as·phyx·i·a (as·fik′sē·ə) *n. Pathol.* Unconsciousness caused by too little oxygen and too much carbon dioxide in the blood. [< Gk. *a-* not + *sphyzein* to beat] **—as·phyx′i·al** *adj.* **—as·phyx′i·ant** *adj. & n.*

as·phyx·i·ate (as·fik′sē·āt) *v.t. & v.i.* **·at·ed, ·at·ing** To cause or undergo asphyxia; suffocate. **—as·phyx′i·a′tion** *n.*

as·pic (as′pik) *n.* A jelly of meat or vegetable juices. [< F]

as·pi·dis·tra (as′pə·dis′trə) *n.* A stemless, Asian herb of the lily family, with large, glossy, evergreen leaves. [< Gk. *aspis, aspidos* shield + *astron* star]

as·pir·ant (ə·spīr′ənt, as′pər·ənt) *n.* One who aspires. *—adj.* Aspiring.

as·pi·rate (*v.* as′pə·rāt; *n. & adj.* as′pər·it) *v.t.* **·rat·ed, ·rat·ing** 1. To utter with a puff of breath or as if preceded by an *h* sound. 2. To follow with a puff of breath, as (p) when before a vowel. 3. *Med.* To draw out with an aspirator. *—n.* An aspirated sound. *—adj. Phonet.* Uttered with an aspirate: also **as′pi·rat′ed.** [See ASPIRE.]

as·pi·ra·tion (as′pə·rā′shən) *n.* 1. Exalted desire; high ambition. 2. The act of breathing; breath. 3. *Med.* The use of an aspirator. 4. *Phonet.* An aspirate.

as·pi·ra·tor (as′pə·rā′tər) *n. Med.* A device for drawing off fluid or gases from the body by suction.

as·pir·a·to·ry (ə·spīr′ə·tôr′ē) *adj.* Of, pertaining to, or adapted for breathing or suction.

as·pire (ə·spīr′) *v.i.* **·spired, ·spir·ing** To have an earnest desire or ambition. [< L *ad-* to + *spirare* to breathe] **—as·pir′ing** *adj.* **—as·pir′ing·ly** *adv.*

as·pi·rin (as′pər·in, -prin) *n.* A white crystalline compound, the acetyl derivative of salicylic acid, used for the relief of fever, pain, etc. [< A(CETYL) + SPIR(AEIC ACID), former name of salicylic acid, + -IN]

a·squint (ə·skwint′) *adj. & adv.* With sidelong glance.

ass (as) *n. pl.* **ass·es** 1. A long-eared quadruped related to the horse; donkey. 2. A stupid person; fool. [OE *assa* ? < L *asinus*]

as·sail (ə·sāl′) *v.t.* To attack violently, as by force, argument, etc. [< L *ad-* to + *salire* to leap] **—as·sail′a·ble** *adj.* **—as·sail′ant** *n. & adj.* **—as·sail′er** *n.*

as·sas·sin (ə·sas′in) *n.* One who kills; esp., one who murders a political figure. [< Arabic *hashshāshīn* users of hashish]

as·sas·si·nate (ə·sas′ə·nāt) *v.t.* **·nat·ed, ·nat·ing** 1. To kill by secret or surprise assault. 2. To destroy or injure by treachery, as a reputation. **—as·sas′si·na′tion** *n.*

as·sault (ə·sôlt′) *n.* 1. Any violent attack by act or words. 2. *Law* An unlawful attempt or threat to do bodily injury to another. 3. A rape. 4. *Mil.* An attack upon a fortified place. [< L *ad-* to + *salire* to leap] **—as·sault′** *v.t. & v.i.*

assault and battery *Law* The carrying out of an assault with force and violence; a beating.

as·say (*n.* ə·sā′, as′ā; *v.* ə·sā′) *n.* 1. The analysis or testing of an alloy or ore to ascertain the ingredients and their proportions. 2. Any examination or testing. *—v.t.* 1. To subject to chemical analysis. 2. To prove; test. *—v.i.* 3. To show by analysis a certain value or proportion, as of a precious metal. [< OF *assai*, var. of *essai* trial] **—as·say′er** *n.*

as·sem·blage (ə·sem′blij, *for def. 4, also Fr.* å·säṅ·bläzh′) *n.* 1. The act of assembling, or the state of being assembled. 2. Any gathering; collection; group. 3. A fitting together, as of the parts of a machine. 4. A work of art created by assembling materials and objects; also, the technique of making such works: compare COLLAGE. [< F]

as·sem·ble (ə·sem′bəl) *v.t. & v.i.* **·bled, ·bling** 1. To come or bring together; collect or congregate. 2. To fit or join together, as parts. [< L *ad-* to + *simul* together] **—as·sem′bler** *n.*

as·sem·bly (ə·sem′blē) *n. pl.* **·blies** 1. The

act of assembling, or the state of being assembled. 2. A number of persons met together for a common purpose. 3. The act or process of fitting together the parts of a machine, etc.; also, the parts themselves.

assembly line An arrangement of industrial equipment and workers in which the product passes from one specialized operation to another until completed.

as·sem·bly·man (ə·sem′blē·mən) *n. pl.* **·men** (-men′, -mən) A member of a legislative assembly. **—as·sem′bly·wom′an** (-wo͝om′ən) *n. fem.*

as·sent (ə·sent′) *v.i.* To express agreement: usu. with *to.* **—***n.* 1. Mental agreement. 2. Consent; sanction. [< L *ad-* to + *sentire* to feel]

as·sert (ə·sûrt′) *v.t.* 1. To state positively; declare. 2. To maintain as a right or claim, as by words or force. **—to assert oneself** To put forward and defend one's own rights or claims. [< L *ad-* to + *serere* to bind]

as·ser·tion (ə·sûr′shən) *n.* 1. The act of asserting. 2. A positive declaration without attempt at proof.

as·ser·tive (ə·sûr′tiv) *adj.* Confident; aggressive. **—as·ser′tive·ly** *adv.* **—as·ser′·tive·ness** *n.*

as·sess (ə·ses′) *v.t.* 1. To charge with a tax, fine, or other payment. 2. To determine the amount of, as a tax on a person or property. 3. To evaluate for taxation. [< L *assidere* to sit by (as a judge in court)] **—as·sess′a·ble** *adj.* **—as·ses′sor** *n.*

as·sess·ment (ə·ses′mənt) *n.* 1. The act of assessing. 2. An amount assessed.

as·set (as′et) *n.* 1. An item of property. 2. A useful or valuable thing or quality.

as·sets (as′ets) *n.pl.* All the property and resources of a person, business, etc., that may be used to pay debts or other obligations: opposed to *liabilities.* [< L *ad-* to + *satis* enough]

as·sev·er·ate (ə·sev′ə·rāt) *v.t.* **·at·ed, ·at·ing** To affirm or declare emphatically or solemnly. [< L *ad-* to + *severus* serious] **—as·sev′er·a′tion** *n.*

as·si·du·i·ty (as′ə·do͞o′ə·tē, -dyo͞o′-) *n. pl.* **·ties** Close application or effort; diligence.

as·sid·u·ous (ə·sij′o͞o·əs) *adj.* 1. Devoted; attentive. 2. Unremitting; persistent: *assiduous* study. [< L *ad-* to + *sedere* to sit] **—as·sid′u·ous·ly** *adv.* **—as·sid′u·ous·ness** *n.*

as·sign (ə·sīn′) *v.t.* 1. To set apart, as for a particular function; designate. 2. To appoint, as to a duty. 3. To allot as a task. 4. To ascribe or attribute. 5. *Law* To transfer, as personal property, rights, or interests. [< L *ad-* to + *signare* make a sign] **—as·sign′a·ble** *adj.* **—as·sign′er,** *Law* **as·sign·or** (ə·sīn′ər, ə·sīn′ôr′) *n.*

as·sig·na·tion (as′ig·nā′shən) *n.* 1. An appointment for meeting, esp. a secret one made by lovers. 2. An assignment. [See ASSIGN.]

as·sign·ee (ə·sī′nē′, as′ə·nē′) *n. Law* A person to whom property, rights, or powers are transferred.

as·sign·ment (ə·sīn′mənt) *n.* 1. The act of assigning. 2. Anything assigned, as a lesson or task. 3. *Law* The transfer of a claim, right, or property, or the instrument or writing of transfer.

as·sim·i·la·ble (ə·sim′ə·lə·bəl) *adj.* Capable of being assimilated. **—as·sim′i·la·bil′i·ty** *n.*

as·sim·i·late (ə·sim′ə·lāt) *v.t. & v.i.* **·lat·ed, ·lat·ing** 1. *Biol.* To take up and incorporate or be incorporated into living organisms, as food. 2. To take or be taken in; absorb or be absorbed. 3. To make or become alike or similar. [< L *ad-* to + *similare* to make like] **—as·sim′i·la′tion** *n.*

as·sist (ə·sist′) *v.t. & v.i.* To help or aid. **—***n.* 1. An act of helping. 2. A play (in baseball) that helps to put out a runner or (in hockey and basketball) helps to score a goal. [< L *ad-* to + *sistere* to cause to stand]

as·sis·tance (ə·sis′təns) *n.* The act of helping, or the help given; aid; support.

as·sis·tant (ə·sis′tənt) *n.* One who assists; a subordinate or helper. **—***adj.* 1. Subordinate or auxiliary. 2. Helping; assisting.

as·size (ə·sīz′) *n.* 1. Originally, a session of a legislative or judicial body. 2. *pl.* In England, one of the regular court sessions held in each county for the trial of civil and criminal cases by jury. [< L *assidere* to sit by (as a judge at court)]

as·so·ci·ate (*n. & adj.* ə·sō′shē·it, -sē-; *v.* ə·sō′shē·āt, -sē-) *n.* 1. A companion. 2. A partner, colleague, or fellow employee. 3. One admitted to partial membership in an association, society, or institution. 4. *cap.* A degree given by a junior college. **—***adj.* 1. Joined with another or others in a common pursuit or office. 2. Having subordinate or secondary status. 3. Existing or occurring together; concomitant. **—***v.* **·at·ed, ·at·ing** *v.t.* 1. To ally; unite. 2. To combine. 3. To connect mentally. **—***v.i.* 4. To unite for a common purpose. 5. To keep or be in company: with *with.* [< L *ad-* to + *sociare* to join]

as·so·ci·a·tion (ə·sō′sē·ā′shən, -shē-) *n.* 1. The act of associating, or the state of being associated. 2. A body of persons associated for some common purpose; society.

association football Soccer.

as·so·ci·a·tive (ə·sō′shē·ā′tiv, -sē-) *adj.* 1. Of or characterized by association. 2. Causing association.

as·so·nance (as′ə·nəns) *n.* Resemblance in sound; esp., in prosody, correspondence of accented vowels, but not of consonants, as in *main, came.* [< L *ad-* to + *sonare* to sound] **—as′so·nant** *adj. & n.*

as·sort (ə·sôrt′) *v.t.* To distribute into groups according to kinds; classify. [< OF *a-* to + *sorte* sort] **—as·sort′er** *n.*

as·sort·ed (ə·sôr′tid) *adj.* 1. Containing or arranged in various sorts or kinds; miscellaneous. 2. Classified.

as·sort·ment (ə·sôrt′mənt) *n.* 1. The act of assorting; classification. 2. A varied collection; miscellany.

as·suage (ə·swāj′) *v.t.* **·suaged, ·suag·ing** 1. To make less harsh or severe; alleviate. 2. To satisfy, as thirst. 3. To calm; pacify. [< L *ad-* to + *suavis* sweet] **—as·suage′ment** *n.*

as·sume (ə·so͞om′) *v.t.* **·sumed, ·sum·ing** 1. To take on or adopt, as a style of dress, aspect, or character. 2. To undertake, as an office or duty. 3. To usurp, as powers of state. 4. To take for granted. [< L *ad-* to + *sumere* to take] **—as·sum′a·ble** *adj.*

as·sump·tion (ə·sump′shən) *n.* 1. The act of assuming, or that which is assumed. 2. That which is taken for granted; a supposition. 3. Presumption; arrogance. **—the Assumption** A church feast, observed on August 15, commemorating the bodily ascent of the Virgin Mary into heaven. **—as·sump′tive** *adj.* **—as·sump′tive·ly** *adv.*

as·sur·ance (ə·shŏŏr′əns) *n.* 1. The act of assuring, or the state of being assured. 2. A positive statement, intended to give confidence, encouragement, etc. 3. Self-confidence; boldness. 4. *Chiefly Brit.* Insurance.

as·sure (ə·shŏŏr′) *v.t.* **·sured, ·sur·ing** 1. To make sure or secure; establish firmly. 2. To make (something) certain; guarantee. 3. To cause to feel certain; convince. 4. To promise. 5. To insure, as against loss. [< L *ad-* to + *securus* safe] **—as·sur′er** *n.*

as·sured (ə·shŏŏrd′) *adj.* 1. Made certain; guaranteed. 2. Self-possessed; confident. 3. Insured. **—as·sur′ed·ly** *adv.* **—as·sur′ed·ness** *n.*

as·ta·tine (as′tə·tēn, -tin) *n.* An unstable, radioactive, chemical element (symbol At) related to the halogens. [< Gk. *astatos* unstable + -INE[2]]

as·ter (as′tər) *n.* A composite plant having flowers with white, purple, or blue rays and a yellow disc. [< Gk. *astēr* star]

-aster *suffix* Little; inferior: *poetaster.* [< L *-aster,* dim. suffix]

as·ter·isk (as′tər·isk) *n. Printing* A starlike figure (*) used to indicate omissions, footnotes, references, etc. [< Gk. *astēr* star]

a·stern (ə·stûrn′) *adv. & adj. Naut.* 1. In the rear; at any point behind a vessel. 2. To the rear; backward.

as·ter·oid (as′tə·roid) *n. Astron.* Any of several hundred small planets between Mars and Jupiter: also called *planetoid.* [< Gk. *astēr* a star] **—as′ter·oi′dal** *adj.*

asth·ma (az′mə, as′-) *n. Pathol.* A chronic respiratory disorder characterized by recurrent paroxysmal coughing and constriction of the chest. [< Gk. *azein* to breathe hard] **—asth·mat·ic** (az·mat′ik, as-) *adj. & n.* **—asth·mat′i·cal·ly** *adv.*

as·tig·mat·ic (as′tig·mat′ik) *adj.* Of, having, or correcting astigmatism.

a·stig·ma·tism (ə·stig′mə·tiz′əm) *n.* A defect of the eye or of a lens causing imperfect focusing. [< A-[4] without + Gk. *stigma, -atos* mark, spot + -ISM]

a·stir (ə·stûr′) *adv. & adj.* Stirring; moving about.

a·ston·ish (ə·ston′ish) *v.t.* To affect with wonder and surprise; amaze. [< OF *estoner* < L *ex-* out + *tonare* to thunder] **—a·ston′·ish·ing** *adj.* **—a·ston′ish·ing·ly** *adv.*

a·ston·ish·ment (ə·ston′ish·mənt) *n.* 1. The state of being astonished. 2. A cause of such emotion.

a·stound (ə·stound′) *v.t.* To overwhelm with wonder; amaze. [See ASTONISH.] **—a·stound′·ing** *adj.* **—a·stound′ing·ly** *adv.*

as·tra·khan (as′trə·kan, -kən) *n.* The black or gray, loosely curled fur made from the pelt of certain lambs. [after *Astrakhan,* a city in Russia]

as·tral (as′trəl) *adj.* Of, pertaining to, coming from, or like the stars; starry. [< Gk. *astron* star] **—as′tral·ly** *adv.*

a·stray (ə·strā′) *adv. & adj.* Away from the right path; wandering. [< L *extra-* beyond + *vagare* to wander]

a·stride (ə·strīd′) *adv. & adj.* 1. With one leg on each side. 2. With the legs far apart. *—prep.* With one leg on each side of: *astride* a horse.

as·trin·gent (ə·strin′jənt) *adj.* 1. *Med.* Tending to contract tissues; binding. 2. Harsh; stern; austere. *—n.* An astringent substance. [< L *ad-* to + *stringere* to bind fast] **—as·trin′gen·cy** *n.* **—as·trin′gent·ly** *adj.*

astro- *combining form* 1. Star. 2. Of, pertaining to, occurring in, or characteristic of outer space: *astronautics.* [< Gk. *astron* star]

as·tro·dy·nam·ics (as′trō·dī·nam′iks) *n.pl.* (*construed as sing.*) The branch of dynamics concerned with the motions of celestial bodies.

as·tro·labe (as′trə·lāb) *n.* An instrument formerly used for obtaining the altitudes of planets and stars. [< ASTRO- + Gk. *lambanein* to take]

as·trol·o·gy (ə·strol′ə·jē) *n.* The study professing to interpret the influence of heavenly bodies upon human destiny. [< ASTRO- + Gk. *logos* discourse] **—as·trol′o·ger** *n.* **—as·tro·log·ic** (as′trə·loj′ik) or **·i·cal** *adj.* **—as′tro·log′i·cal·ly** *adv.*

as·tro·naut (as′trə·nôt) *n.* One who travels in space. [< ASTRO- + *-naut* (< Gk. *nautēs* sailor), after *aeronaut*]

as·tro·nau·tics (as′trə·nô′tiks) *n.pl.* (*construed as sing.*) The science and art of space travel. **—as′tro·nau′tic** or **·ti·cal** *adj.* **—as′tro·nau′ti·cal·ly** *adv.*

as·tro·nom·i·cal (as′trə·nom′i·kəl) *adj.* 1. Of or pertaining to astronomy. 2. Enormously or inconceivably large. Also **as′tro·nom′ic.** **—as′tro·nom′i·cal·ly** *adv.*

astronomical unit A unit of length for expressing the distances of the stars, equal to the mean distance of the earth from the sun, about 93,000,000 miles.

as·tron·o·my (ə·stron′ə·mē) *n.* The science that treats of the heavenly bodies, their motions, magnitudes, distances, and constitution. [< ASTRO- + Gk. *nomos* law] **—as·tron′o·mer** *n.*

as·tro·phys·ics (as′trō·fiz′iks) *n.pl.* (*construed as sing.*) The branch of astronomy that treats of the physical constitution and properties of the heavenly bodies. **—as′tro·phys′i·cal** *adj.* **—as′tro·phys′i·cist** (-ə·sist) *n.*

as·tute (ə·stōōt′, ə·styōōt′) *adj.* Keen in discernment; shrewd. [< L *astus* cunning] **—as·tute′ly** *adv.* **—as·tute′ness** *n.*

a·sun·der (ə·sun′dər) *adv. & adj.* 1. Apart; into pieces. 2. In or into a different place or position. [OE *on sundran*]

a·sy·lum (ə·sī′ləm) *n.* 1. An institution for the care of the mentally ill, the destitute, etc. 2. A place of refuge. 3. An inviolable shelter from arrest or punishment, as a temple or church in ancient times. [< Gk. *a-* without + *sylon* right of seizure]

a·sym·met·ric (ā′si·met′rik, as′i-) *adj.* Not symmetrical. Also **a′sym·met′ri·cal.** **—a′·sym·met′ri·cal·ly** *adv.* **—a·sym·me·try** (ā·sim′ə·trē) *n.*

as·ymp·tote (as′im·tōt) *n. Math.* A straight line that an indefinitely extended curve continually approaches as a tangent. [< Gk. *a-* not + *syn-* together + *piptein* to fall] **—as′ymp·tot′ic** (-tot′ik) or **·i·cal** *adj.* **—as′·ymp·tot′i·cal·ly** *adv.*

at (at, *unstressed* ət) *prep.* 1. In or on the position of: *at* the center. 2. Of time, on or upon the point or stroke of: *at* noon. 3. During the course of: *at* night. 4. In contact with; upon: *at* sea. 5. To or toward: Look *at* that! 6. Within the limits or region of: *at* home. 7. Engaged in: *at* work. 8. Attending: *at* a party. 9. In the state or condition of: *at* war. 10. In connection with: to cringe *at* the thought. 11. In the manner of: *at* a trot. 12. Dependent upon: *at* one's mercy. 13. According to: Act *at* your discretion. 14. Amounting to: a loan *at* two percent. [OE *æt*]

at·a·vism (at′ə·viz′əm) *n.* Occurrence in an individual of a trait from a remote ancestor; also, such an individual. [< L *at-* beyond + *avus* grandfather] **—at′a·vis′tic** *adj.*

a·tax·i·a (ə·tak′sē·ə) *n. Pathol.* Loss or failure of muscular coordination. [< Gk. *a-* not + *tattein* to arrange] **—a·tax′ic** *adj. & n.*

ate (āt) Past tense of EAT.

-ate[1] *suffix* Forming: 1. Participial adjectives equivalent to those ending in *-ated.* 2. Adjectives from nouns with the meaning "possessing or characterized by": *sectionate.* 3. *Chem.* Verbs with the meaning "combine or treat with": *chlorinate.* [< L *-atus,* pp. ending of 1st conjugation verbs]

-ate[2] *suffix* Forming: 1. Nouns denoting office, function, or agent: *magistrate.* 2. Nouns denoting the object or result of an action: *mandate.* [< L *-atus*]

at·el·ier (at′əl·yā, *Fr.* å·tə·lyā′) *n.* A workshop, esp. of an artist; studio. [< F]

a·the·ist (ā′thē·ist) *n.* One who denies or disbelieves in the existence of God. [< Gk. *a-* without + *theos* god] **—a′the·ism** *n.* **—a′the·is′tic** *adj.*

ath·e·ne·um (ath′ə·nē′əm) *n.* 1. An institution for the promotion of learning. 2. A reading room, library, etc. Also **ath′e·nae′um.**

A·the·ni·an (ə·thē′nē·ən) *adj.* Of or pertaining to Athens, or to its art or culture. **—A·the′ni·an** *n.*

ath·er·o·scle·ro·sis (ath′ər·ō·sklə·rō′sis) *n. Pathol.* Hardening of the arteries, accompanied by the deposit of fat in the inner arterial walls. [< Gk. *athērē* gruel + *sklēros* hard]

a·thirst (ə·thûrst′) *adj.* Longing; eager: with *for.* [< OE- + OE *thyrstan* to thirst]

ath·lete (ath′lēt) *n.* One trained in acts of physical strength and agility. [< Gk. *athleein* to contend for a prize]

athlete's foot Ringworm of the foot.

ath·let·ic (ath·let′ik) *adj.* 1. Of, pertaining to, or befitting an athlete or athletics. 2. Strong; vigorous. **—ath·let′i·cal·ly** *adv.* **—ath·let·i·cism** (ath·let′ə·siz′əm) *n.*

ath·let·ics (ath·let′iks) *n.pl.* Games and exercises requiring physical strength, skill, endurance, and agility; sports.

a·thwart (ə·thwôrt′) *adv.* 1. From side to side; across. 2. So as to thwart; perversely. *—prep.* 1. From side to side of. 2. Contrary to. 3. *Naut.* Across the course of.

-atic *suffix* Of; of the kind of: *erratic.* [< Gk. *-atikos*]

-ation *suffix of nouns* 1. Action or process of: *creation.* 2. Condition or quality of: *affectation.* 3. Result of: *reformation.* Also *-ion, -tion.* [< F *-ation* or L *-atio, -ationis*]

-ative *suffix* Denoting relation, tendency, or characteristic: *remunerative.* [< F *-atif,* masc., *-ative,* fem. or < L *-ativus*]

At·lan·tic (at·lan′tik) *adj.* Of, near, in, or pertaining to the Atlantic Ocean. [< Gk. *Atlantikos* after *Atlas,* a giant in Greek mythology]

at·las (at′ləs) *n.* 1. A volume of maps. 2. Any book of tables or charts.

at·man (ät′mən) *n.* In Hinduism, the soul; the divine life principle in man. **—Atman** The supreme soul, the source and goal of all individual souls. [< Skt.]

atmo- *combining form* Vapor. [< Gk. *atmos*]

at·mos·phere (at′məs·fir) *n.* 1. The body of gases surrounding the earth or a celestial body. 2. The particular climatic condition of any place or region. 3. Any surrounding or pervasive element or influence. 4. *Physics* A unit of pressure, equal to 14.69 pounds per square inch. [< Gk. *atmos* vapor + *sphaira* sphere] **—at′mos·pher′ic** (-fer′ik) *adj.* **—at′mos·pher′i·cal·ly** *adv.*

at·mos·pher·ics (at′məs·fer′iks) *n.pl.* (*construed as sing.*) In radio transmission, static.

at·oll (at′ôl, ə·tol′) *n.* A ring-shaped coral island and its associated reef, nearly or completely enclosing a lagoon. [? < Malayalam *adal* closing, uniting]

a·tom (at′əm) *n.* 1. The smallest unit of an element; one of the particles of which all matter is formed, regarded as a system of electrons organized around a nucleus. 2. A hypothetical minute entity that cannot be divided. 3. The smallest quantity or particle; iota. [< Gk. *a-* not + *temnein* to cut]

a·tom·ic (ə·tom′ik) *adj.* 1. Of or pertaining to an atom or atoms. 2. Of or pertaining to atomic energy. 3. Minute; infinitesimal. **—a·tom′i·cal·ly** *adv.*

atomic bomb A bomb of immense destructive power using the energy released by the fission of atomic nuclei: also called *A-bomb.* Also **atom bomb.**

atomic clock A high-precision instrument for the measurement of time by the vibration rate of an atomic system.

atomic energy The energy contained within the nucleus of the atom, that can be released by fission or fusion.

atomic number *Physics* A number equal to the positive charges (protons) in the atomic nucleus of an element.

atomic weight *Chem.* The average weight of an atom of an element relative to that of carbon, taken as 12.

at·om·ize (at′əm·īz) *v.t.* **·ized, ·iz·ing** 1. To reduce to atoms. 2. To spray or reduce to a spray, as by an atomizer. Also *Brit.* **at′om·ise.** **—at′om·i·za′tion** *n.*

at·om·iz·er (at′əm·ī′zər) *n.* An apparatus for producing a spray.

a·to·nal (ā·tō′nəl) *adj. Music* Without tonality; lacking key or tonal center. **—a·to·nal·i·ty** (ā′tō·nal′ə·tē) *n.* **—a·to′nal·ly** *adv.*

a·tone (ə·tōn′) *v.i.* **a·toned, a·ton·ing** To make expiation, as for sin or wrongdoing. [< earlier adverbial phrase *at one,* short for *to set at one,* i.e., reconcile] **—a·ton′a·ble** *adj.* **—a·ton′er** *n.*

a·tone·ment (ə·tōn′mənt) *n.* 1. Satisfaction, reparation, or expiation made for wrong or injury. 2. *Theol.* The reconciliation between God and man effected by Christ.

a·ton·ic (ə·ton′ik, ā-) *adj.* **1.** Not accented, as a word or syllable. **2.** Lacking tone or vigor. [< Gk. *a-* not + *teinein* to stretch]

a·top (ə·top′) *adv. & adj.* On or at the top. —*prep.* On the top of.

-ator *suffix of nouns* An agent; doer; actor; one who or that which: *arbitrator.* [< L]

-atory *suffix of adjectives* Characterized by; producing or produced by: *conciliatory.* [< L *-atorius*]

a·tri·um (ā′trē·əm) *n.* *pl.* **a·tri·a** **1.** The entrance hall or central open court of an ancient Roman house. **2.** A court or hall. **3.** *Anat.* One of the upper chambers of the heart: also called *auricle.* [< L, a hall] —**a′tri·al** *adj.*

a·tro·cious (ə·trō′shəs) *adj.* **1.** Very wicked, cruel, etc. **2.** Very bad, or in bad taste. [< L *atrox, atrocis* harsh, cruel] —**a·tro′·cious·ly** *adv.* —**a·tro′cious·ness** *n.*

a·troc·i·ty (ə·tros′ə·tē) *n.* *pl.* **·ties** **1.** The state or quality of being atrocious. **2.** An atrocious deed or act.

at·ro·phy (at′rə·fē) *n.* *pl.* **·phies** *Pathol.* A wasting or failure in development of the body or any of its parts. —*v.t. & v.i.* **·phied, ·phy·ing** To cause or undergo atrophy. [< Gk. *a-* not + *trephein* to nourish]

at·ro·pine (at′rə·pēn, -pin) *n.* A crystalline, poisonous alkaloid, found in the deadly nightshade and in certain other plants, used to relieve convulsions and to enlarge the pupil of the eye.

at·tach (ə·tach′) *v.t.* **1.** To make fast to something; fasten on; affix. **2.** To add or append, as a signature. **3.** To connect by personal ties, as of affection. **4.** To appoint officially; assign. **5.** *Law* To seize by legal process. —*v.i.* **6.** To be attached; connect. [< OF *a-* to + *tache* nail] —**at·tach′a·ble** *adj.*

at·ta·ché (at′ə·shā′, ə·tash′ā) *n.* A person officially attached to a diplomatic mission or staff in a specified capacity: military *attaché.* [< F, pp. of *attacher* to attach]

attaché case A boxlike briefcase, esp. for carrying important papers.

at·tach·ment (ə·tach′mənt) *n.* **1.** The act of attaching, or state of being attached. **2.** Something attached, as an accessory part for a machine. **3.** A bond, as of affection. **4.** *Law* Seizure of a person or property.

at·tack (ə·tak′) *v.t.* **1.** To set upon violently; begin to battle. **2.** To criticize violently; condemn. **3.** To begin work on. **4.** To harm; injure. —*v.i.* **5.** To make an attack; begin battle. —*n.* **1.** An act of attacking; assault. **2.** An approach; beginning. **3.** A seizure, as by disease. [See ATTACH.]

at·tain (ə·tān′) *v.t.* **1.** To gain by exertion of body or mind; achieve. **2.** To come to, as in time; arrive at. [< L *ad-* to + *tangere* to touch] —**at·tain′a·bil′i·ty** *n.* —**at·tain′a·ble** *adj.*

at·tain·der (ə·tān′dər) *n.* The loss of all civil rights following a sentence of death or of outlawry for a capital offense. [< OF *ataindre* to attain, strike]

at·tain·ment (ə·tān′mənt) *n.* **1.** The act of attaining. **2.** That which is attained, esp. a skill.

at·taint (ə·tānt′) *v.t.* **1.** To inflict attainder upon; condemn. **2.** To affect injuriously; disgrace; taint. —*n.* Imputation; stigma. [See ATTAIN.]

at·tar (at′ər) *n.* The fragrant essential oil extracted from the petals of flowers, esp. roses. [< Arabic *itr* perfume]

at·tempt (ə·tempt′) *v.t.* To make an effort to do or accomplish; try. —*n.* A putting forth of effort; endeavor. [< L *ad-* toward + *tendere* to stretch] —**at·tempt′a·ble** *adj.* —**at·tempt′er** *n.*

at·tend (ə·tend′) *v.t.* **1.** To be present at, as a meeting. **2.** To wait upon as an attendant. **3.** To visit or minister to (a sick person). **4.** To accompany. **5.** To give heed to; listen to. —*v.i.* **6.** To be present. **7.** To give heed; listen. [< L *ad-* toward + *tendere* to stretch]

at·ten·dance (ə·ten′dəns) *n.* **1.** The act of attending. **2.** Those who attend, collectively.

at·ten·dant (ə·ten′dənt) *n.* **1.** One who attends, esp. as a servant. **2.** A concomitant; consequence. —*adj.* Following or accompanying.

at·ten·tion (ə·ten′shən) *n.* **1.** Close or earnest attending. **2.** The power or faculty of mental concentration. **3.** Practical consideration; care. **4.** *Usu. pl.* Courteous behavior, esp. by a suitor. **5.** *Mil.* The prescribed position of readiness: to stand at *attention.*

at·ten·tive (ə·ten′tiv) *adj.* **1.** Observant. **2.** Courteous or gallant. —**at·ten′tive·ly** *adv.* —**at·ten′tive·ness** *n.*

at·ten·u·ate (ə·ten′yo͞o·āt) *v.* **·at·ed, ·at·ing** *v.t.* **1.** To make thin, small, or fine; draw out, as a wire. **2.** To weaken; lessen. —*v.i.* **3.** To become thin or less. [< L *ad-* (intensive) + *tenuare* to make thin] —**at·ten′u·a′tion** *n.*

at·test (ə·test′) *v.t.* **1.** To confirm as accurate, true, or genuine; vouch for. **2.** To certify, as by signature or oath. **3.** To be proof of. —*v.i.* **4.** To bear witness; testify. [< L *ad-* to + *testari* to bear witness] —**at·tes·ta·tion** (at′es·tā′shən) *n.*

at·tic (at′ik) *n.* A low story beneath the roof of a building; a garret. [< L *Atticus,* architectural term]

At·tic (at′ik) *adj.* **1.** Of Attica, a region surrounding ancient Athens. **2.** Of or characteristic of Athens or the Athenians. **3.** Simple and graceful. [< Gk. *Attikē* Attica]

at·tire (ə·tīr′) *v.t.* **·tired, ·tir·ing** To dress; array. —*n.* Dress or clothing. [< OF *atirer* to arrange, adorn]

at·ti·tude (at′ə·to͞od, -tyo͞od) *n.* **1.** Position of the body, as suggesting some thought or feeling. **2.** State of mind, behavior, or conduct regarding some matter. [< L *aptus* fitted, suited] —**at′ti·tu′di·nal** *adj.*

at·ti·tu·di·nize (at′ə·to͞o′də·nīz, -tyo͞o′-) *v.i.* **·nized, ·niz·ing** To assume an attitude for effect. Also *Brit.* **at′ti·tu′di·nise.**

at·tor·ney (ə·tûr′nē) *n.* A person empowered by another to act in his stead; esp., a lawyer. [< OF *atorner* to turn to, appoint] —**at·tor′·ney·ship** *n.*

attorney at law A lawyer.

attorney general *pl.* **attorneys general, attorney generals** The chief law officer of a government.

at·tract (ə·trakt′) *v.t.* **1.** To draw to or cause to come near by some physical force, as magnetism. **2.** To appeal to. —*v.i.* **3.** To exert attractive influence. [< L *ad-* toward + *trahere* to draw, drag] —**at·tract′a·bil′i·ty** *n.* —**at·trac′tor** or **at·tract′er** *n.*

at·trac·tion (ə·trak′shən) *n.* **1.** The act or

power of attracting. 2. Something that attracts. 3. *Physics* A force tending to draw objects together or prevent their separation.

at·trac·tive (ə·trak′tiv) *adj.* 1. Pleasing; charming. 2. Having the power to attract. **—at·trac′tive·ly** *adv.* **—at·trac′tive·ness** *n.*

at·trib·ute (ə·trib′yōōt) *v.t.* **·ut·ed, ·ut·ing** To ascribe as belonging to or resulting from: to *attribute* wisdom to old age. **—at·tri·bute** (at′rə·byōōt) *n.* A quality or characteristic of a person or thing. [< L *ad-* to + *tribuere* to allot, give over] **—at·trib′ut·a·ble** *adj.* **—at·trib′u·ter** or **at·trib′u·tor** *n.*

at·tri·bu·tion (at′rə·byōō′shən) *n.* 1. The act of attributing. 2. An ascribed characteristic or quality; attribute.

at·trib·u·tive (ə·trib′yə·tiv) *adj.* 1. Pertaining to or of the nature of an attribute. 2. *Gram.* Designating an adjective or its equivalent that stands before the noun it modifies. **—*n.*** *Gram.* An attributive word or phrase. **—at·trib′u·tive·ly** *adv.*

at·tri·tion (ə·trish′ən) *n.* 1. A rubbing out or grinding down, as by friction. 2. A gradual reduction or weakening, as of strength or personnel. [< L *ad-* to, against + *terere* to rub]

at·tune (ə·tōōn′, ə·tyōōn′) *v.t.* **·tuned, ·tun·ing** 1. To bring into accord; harmonize. 2. To tune.

a·typ·i·cal (ā·tip′i·kəl) *adj.* Not typical. **—a·typ′i·cal·ly** *adv.*

au·burn (ô′bûrn) *adj.* & *n.* Reddish brown. [< L *albus* white; infl. by ME *brun* brown]

au cou·rant (ō kōō·rän′) *French* Up to date; well informed.

auc·tion (ôk′shən) *n.* A public sale conducted by bidding, at which the highest bidder becomes the purchaser. [< L *augere* to increase] **—auc′tion** *v.t.*

auction bridge A variety of the game of bridge in which tricks made by the declarer in excess of the contract count toward game. Compare CONTRACT BRIDGE.

auc·tion·eer (ôk′shən·ir′) *n.* One who conducts an auction.

au·da·cious (ô·dā′shəs) *adj.* 1. Showing no fear; daring; bold. 2. Shameless; impudent. [< L *audere* to dare + -OUS] **—au·da′cious·ly** *adv.* **—au·dac·i·ty** (ô·das′ə·tē), **au·da′cious·ness** *n.*

au·di·ble (ô′də·bəl) *adj.* Loud enough to be heard. [< L *audire* to hear] **—au′di·bil′i·ty, au′di·ble·ness** *n.* **—au′di·bly** *adv.*

au·di·ence (ô′dē·əns) *n.* 1. Those who hear or see a performance or communication, esp. when assembled for the purpose. 2. A formal interview. [< L *audire* to hear]

au·di·o (ô′dē·ō) *adj.* Relating to sound waves or to their transmission, reproduction, frequency range, etc. [< L *audire* to hear]

audio- *combining form* Pertaining to hearing. Also **audi-**. [< L *audire* to hear]

au·di·o·phile (ô′dē·ə·fīl) *n.* An enthusiast for high-fidelity sound reproduction.

au·di·o·vis·u·al (ô′dē·ō·vizh′ōō·əl) *adj.* Relating to presentation of information by recorded sound and pictures.

au·dit (ô′dit) *v.t.* 1. To examine and certify financial accounts. 2. To attend (a college course) without credit. **—*v.i.*** 3. To make an audit. **—*n.*** An examination, certification, or final statement of an account. [< L *audire* to hear]

au·di·tion (ô·dish′ən) *n.* A test performance, as of an actor. [< L *audire* to hear] **—au·di′tion** *v.t.* & *v.i.*

au·di·tor (ô′də·tər) *n.* 1. One who audits accounts. 2. A listener. [< L]

au·di·to·ri·um (ô′də·tôr′ē·əm) *n.* *pl.* **·to·ri·ums** or **·to·ri·a** A room or building for the assembly of an audience. [< L, lecture room]

au·di·to·ry (ô′də·tôr′ē) *adj.* Of or pertaining to hearing or the organs or sense of hearing. **—*n.*** *pl.* **·ries** 1. An audience. 2. The nave of a church. [< L *audire* to hear]

auf Wie·der·seh·en (ouf vē′dər·zā′ən) *German* Good-by; till we meet again.

au·ger (ô′gər) *n.* A tool for boring wood. [OE *nafugār* < *nafu* nave of a wheel + *gār* borer, spear]

aught¹ (ôt) *n.* Anything; any part or item. **—*adv.*** By any chance; at all. [OE *āwiht, ōwiht* < *ā* ever + *wiht* thing]

aught² (ôt) *n.* The figure 0; a naught; nothing. [*a naught* taken as *an aught*]

aug·ment (*v.* ôg·ment′; *n.* ôg′ment) *v.t.* & *v.i.* To make or become greater, as in size, number, or amount; intensify. **—*n.*** Increase; enlargement. [< L *augere* to increase] **—aug·ment′a·ble** *adj.* **—aug′men·ta′tion** *n.* **—aug·men′ter** *n.*

au gra·tin (ō grät′n, grat′n; *Fr.* ō grȧ·taṅ′) Sprinkled with bread crumbs or grated cheese and baked. [< F]

au·gur (ô′gər, -gyər) *n.* A prophet; soothsayer. **—*v.t.* & *v.i.*** 1. To prophesy. 2. To be an omen of. [< L *augere* to increase] **—au′gu·ral** *adj.*

au·gu·ry (ô′gyə·rē) *n.* *pl.* **·ries** 1. The art or practice of divination. 2. A portent or omen.

au·gust (ô·gust′) *adj.* Inspiring admiration or reverence; majestic. [< L *augere* to increase, exalt] **—au·gust′ly** *adv.* **—au·gust′·ness** *n.*

Au·gust (ô′gəst) *n.* The eighth month of the year, containing 31 days. [< L *Augustus Caesar*]

Au·gus·tan (ô·gus′tən) *adj.* 1. Of or pertaining to Augustus Caesar or to his times. 2. Pertaining to any similar era, esp. the neoclassical period in 18th c. England.

auk (ôk) *n.* A short-winged, web-footed diving bird of northern seas; the **razor-billed auk** of the North Atlantic. [< ON *ālka*]

auld lang syne (ôld′ lang sīn′, zīn′) *Scot.* Long ago.

aunt (ant, änt) *n.* A sister of one's father or mother, or the wife of one's uncle. [< OF *aunte, ante*]

au pair (ō pâr′) *Chiefly Brit.* An arrangement whereby one receives room and board in a foreign household in exchange for doing certain chores, as caring for children: often used attributively: *au pair* girls. [< F, lit., at par, even (with)]

au·ra (ôr′ə) *n.* *pl.* **au·ras** or **au·rae** (ôr′ē) 1. An invisible emanation or exhalation. 2. A distinctive air or quality. 3. *Pathol.* Sensations preceding an epileptic attack or other neurological disorder. [< L, breeze < Gk. *aurē* breath]

au·ral (ôr′əl) *adj.* Pertaining to the ear or the sense of hearing. [< L *auris* ear + -AL¹]

au·re·ate (ôr′ē·it) *adj.* 1. Of the color of gold; golden. 2. Ornate; dazzling. [< L *aurum* gold]

au·re·ole (ôr′ē·ōl) *n.* 1. In art, a halo. 2. Any radiance or halo around a body. Also **au·re·o·la** (ô·rē′ə·lə). [< L *aureola* (*corona*) golden (crown)]

au re·voir (ō rə·vwär′) *French* Good-by; till we meet again.

au·ri·cle (ôr′i·kəl) *n.* 1. *Anat.* a An atrium of the heart. b The external ear. 2. An ear-shaped part. [< L *auricula*, dim. of *auris* ear]

au·ric·u·lar (ô·rik′yə·lər) *adj.* 1. Of or pertaining to the ear or the sense of hearing. 2. Ear-shaped. 3. Told into the ear; told privately.

au·rif·er·ous (ô·rif′ər·əs) *adj.* Containing gold. [< L *aurum* gold + *ferre* to bear]

au·ri·form (ôr′ə·fôrm) *adj.* Ear-shaped.

Au·ri·ga (ô·rī′gə) *n.* A constellation, the Charioteer, containing the bright star Capella. [< L]

au·ro·ra (ô·rôr′ə) *n.* 1. *Meteorol.* A display of arcs, bands, streamers, etc., of light occasionally seen in the skies of polar latitudes. 2. The dawn. [< L, dawn]

aurora aus·tra·lis (ôs·trā′lis) *Meteorol.* The aurora seen in far southern latitudes: also called *southern lights.* [< NL, southern aurora < L *auster* south wind]

aurora bo·re·al·is (bôr′ē·al′is, -ā′lis) *Meteorol.* The aurora seen in high northern latitudes: also called *northern lights.* [< NL, northern aurora < Gk. *boreas* north wind]

au·ro·ral (ô·rôr′əl) *adj.* 1. Pertaining to or like the dawn; roseate. 2. *Meteorol.* Of, like, or caused by an aurora.

aus·cul·tate (ôs′kəl·tāt) *v.t. & v.i.* **·tat·ed, ·tat·ing** *Med.* To examine by listening, as with a stethescope. [< L *auscultare* to listen, give ear to] **—aus′cul·ta′tion** *n.*

aus·pice (ôs′pis) *n. pl.* **aus·pi·ces** (ôs′pə·sēz) 1. *Usu. pl.* Patronage. 2. An omen, or sign. [< L *auspex* diviner]

aus·pi·cious (ôs·pish′əs) *adj.* 1. Of good omen; propitious. 2. Prosperous; fortunate. **—aus·pi′cious·ly** *adv.* **—aus·pi′cious·ness** *n.*

aus·tere (ô·stir′) *adj.* 1. Severe, grave, or stern. 2. Morally strict; ascetic. 3. Sour and astringent. 4. Severely simple; unadorned. [< Gk. *austēros* harsh, bitter] **—aus·tere′ly** *adv.* **—aus·ter·i·ty** (ô·ster′ə·tē) *n.*

aus·tral (ôs′trəl) *adj.* Southern; torrid. [< L *auster* south wind]

Aus·tral·ian (ô·strāl′yən) *adj.* Of or pertaining to Australia or to its people. **—Aus·tral′ian** *n.*

Aus·tri·an (ôs′trē·ən) *adj.* Of Austria or its people. **—Aus′tri·an** *n.*

Austro- *combining form* 1. Austrian. 2. Australian.

Aus·tro·ne·sian (ôs′trō·nē′zhən, -shən) *adj.* Of or pertaining to a family of languages of the Pacific comprising the Indonesian, Oceanic, and Polynesian subfamilies.

au·tar·chy (ô′tär·kē) *n. pl.* **·chies** 1. Absolute rule or sovereignty, or a country under such rule. 2. Autarky. [< Gk. *autos* self + *archein* to rule] **—au·tar′chic** or **·chi·cal** *adj.*

au·tar·ky (ô′tär·kē) *n.* National economic self-sufficiency. [< Gk. *autarkeia* self-sufficiency]

au·teur (ō·ter′, *Fr.* ō·tœr′) *adj.* Designating a principle of film esthetics that holds the director to be the primary creator of a motion picture. [< F, author, as the director is regarded]

au·then·tic (ô·then′tik) *adj.* 1. Authoritative; reliable. 2. Of undisputed origin; genuine. 3. *Law* Duly executed. [< Gk. *authentēs* the doer of a deed] **—au·then′ti·cal·ly** *adv.*

au·then·ti·cate (ô·then′ti·kāt) *v.t.* **·cat·ed, ·cat·ing** 1. To make authentic or authoritative. 2. To give legal validity to. 3. To establish the authenticity of. **—au·then′ti·ca′tion** *n.* **—au·then′ti·ca′tor** *n.*

au·then·tic·i·ty (ô′thən·tis′ə·tē) *n.* The state or quality of being authentic, authoritative, or genuine.

au·thor (ô′thər) *n.* 1. The writer of a book, treatise, etc.; also, one who writes as a profession. 2. One who begins or originates; creator. **—***v.t.* *Informal* To be the author of; write. [< L *auctor* originator]

au·thor·i·tar·i·an (ə·thôr′ə·târ′ē·ən, ə·thor′-) *adj.* Favoring subjection to authority as opposed to individual freedom. **—***n.* One who respects authority, esp. excessively. **—au·thor′i·tar′i·an·ism** *n.*

au·thor·i·ta·tive (ə·thôr′ə·tā′tiv, ə·thor′-) *adj.* 1. Possessing or proceeding from proper authority; duly sanctioned. 2. Exercising authority; commanding. **—au·thor′i·ta′tive·ly** *adv.*

au·thor·i·ty (ə·thôr′ə·tē, ə·thor′-) *n. pl.* **·ties** 1. The right to command and to enforce obedience. 2. Delegated right or power; authorization. 3. *pl.* Those having the power to govern or command. 4. A person, citation, etc., appealed to in support of action or belief. 5. One who has special knowledge; an expert. 6. An authoritative opinion, decision, or precedent. [< L *augere* to increase]

au·thor·ize (ô′thə·rīz) *v.t.* **·ized, ·iz·ing** 1. To confer authority upon; empower; commission. 2. To warrant; justify. 3. To sanction. [< L *auctor* originator] **—au′thor·i·za′tion** *n.* **—au′thor·iz′er** *n.*

au·thor·ship (ô′thər·ship) *n.* 1. The profession or occupation of an author. 2. Origin or source.

au·tism (ô′tiz·əm) *n.* *Psychol.* Self-absorption, as daydreaming, introspection, fantasizing, etc., in which external reality is ignored. [< AUT(O)- + -ISM] **—au·tis·tic** (ô·tis′tik) *adj.*

au·to (ô′tō) *n.* *Informal* An automobile.

auto- *combining form* 1. Arising from some process or action within the object; not induced by any stimulus from without: *autoinduction.* 2. Acting or directed upon the self: *autoanalysis.* 3. Self-propelled: *automotive.* Also, before vowels, **aut-**. [< Gk. *autos* self]

au·to·bi·og·ra·phy (ô′tə·bī·og′rə·fē) *n. pl.* **·phies** The story of a person's life written by that person. **—au′to·bi·og′ra·pher** *n.* **—au·to·bi·o·graph·ic** (ô′tə·bī′ə·graf′ik) or **·i·cal** *adj.*

au·toc·ra·cy (ô·tok′rə·sē) *n. pl.* **·cies** 1. Absolute government by an individual. 2. A state ruled by an autocrat.

au·to·crat (ô′tə·krat) *n.* 1. A supreme ruler. 2. An arrogant, dictatorial person. [< Gk. *autos* self + *kratos* power] **—au′to·crat′ic** or **·i·cal** *adj.* **—au′to·crat′i·cal·ly** *adv.*

au·to-da-fé (ô′tō·də·fā′, ou′-) *n. pl.* **au·tos-**

da-fé (ô′tōz-, ou′tōz-) The public announcement and execution of a sentence of the Inquisition; esp., the burning of heretics at the stake. [< Pg., lit., act of the faith]

au·to·gi·ro (ô′tō·jī′rō) *n.* *pl.* **·ros** An airplane that is supported in the air chiefly by freely-turning rotors but is drawn forward by a conventional propeller. Also **au′to·gy′ro.** [< AUTO- + Gk. *gyros* a circle]

au·to·graph (ô′tə·graf) *n.* 1. One's signature or handwriting. 2. A manuscript in the author's handwriting. —*v.t.* 1. To write one's name in or on. 2. To write in one's own handwriting. —*adj.* Written by one's own hand, as a will. [< Gk. *autos* self + *graphein* to write] —**au′to·graph′ic** or **·i·cal** *adj.* —**au′to·graph′i·cal·ly** *adv.*

au·to·in·tox·i·ca·tion (ô′tō·in·tok′sə·kā′·shən) *n.* Poisoning by a toxin secreted by one's own body.

au·to·mat (ô′tə·mat) *n.* A restaurant in which food is obtained from a receptacle when coins are deposited in a slot alongside.

au·to·mate (ô′tə·māt) **·mat·ed, ·mat·ing** *v.t.* To adapt, as a machine, factory, or process, for automation. [Back formation < AUTOMATION]

au·to·mat·ic (ô′tə·mat′ik) *adj.* 1. Acting from forces inherent in itself; self-moving. 2. Self-acting and self-regulating, as machinery; mechanical. 3. *Psychol.* Done from force of habit or without volition. 4. Of firearms, using the force of recoil to extract and eject the used shell and chamber the next round. —*n.* An automatic device, pistol, etc. [< Gk. *automatos* acting of oneself] —**au′to·mat′i·cal·ly** *adv.*

au·to·ma·tion (ô′tə·mā′shən) *n.* 1. The use of sophisticated, automatic machines to do work. 2. Conversion to such a system. —**au′to·ma′tive** *adj.*

au·tom·a·ton (ô·tom′ə·ton, -tən) *n.* *pl.* **·tons** or **·ta** (-tə) 1. An apparatus that functions automatically. 2. A figure, as of a person, operated by a concealed mechanism; esp., a robot. 3. A robotlike being or person. [< Gk. *automaton,* neut. of *automatos* acting of oneself, independent]

au·to·mo·bile (ô′tə·mə·bēl′, ô′tə·mə·bēl′) *n.* A four-wheeled passenger vehicle that carries its own source of power and travels on roads or streets. [< AUTO- + Gk. *mobile* moving] —**au′to·mo·bil′ist** *n.*

au·to·mo·tive (ô′tə·mō′tiv) *adj.* 1. Self-propelling. 2. Of or for automobiles.

au·to·nom·ic (ô′tə·nom′ik) *adj.* 1. Autonomous. 2. *Physiol.* Pertaining to the autonomic nervous system. Also **au′to·nom′·i·cal.** —**au′to·nom′i·cal·ly** *adv.*

autonomic nervous system A network of nerve tissue originating in the spinal column and acting to control the involuntary functions of the body, as the heart, glands, stomach, etc.

au·ton·o·mous (ô·ton′ə·məs) *adj.* Independent; self-governing. [< Gk. *autos* self + *nomos* law, rule] —**au·ton′o·mous·ly** *adv.*

au·ton·o·my (ô·ton′ə·mē) *n.* *pl.* **·mies** 1. The condition or quality of being autonomous; esp., the power or right of self-government. 2. A self-governing community or group.

au·top·sy (ô′top·sē, ô′təp-) *n.* *pl.* **·sies** Examination of a human corpse, esp. to determine cause of death. [< Gk. *autos* self + *opsis* a seeing]

au·to·sug·ges·tion (ô′tō·səg·jes′chən) *n.* *Psychol.* Suggestion emanating from one's self.

au·tumn (ô′təm) *n.* 1. The season of the year occurring between summer and winter; fall. 2. A time of maturity and incipient decline. [< L *autumnus*] —**au·tum·nal** (ô·tum′nəl) *adj.* —**au·tum′nal·ly** *adv.*

autumnal equinox See under EQUINOX.

aux·il·ia·ry (ôg·zil′yər·ē, -zil′ər-) *adj.* 1. Giving or furnishing aid. 2. Subsidiary; accessory. 3. Supplementary; reserve. —*n.* *pl.* **·ries** 1. An assistant or associate. 2. *Gram.* A verb that helps to express tense, mood, etc., as *have* in *We have gone:* also **auxiliary verb.** [< L *auxilium* help]

a·vail (ə·vāl′) *v.t.* & *v.i.* To assist or aid; benefit. —**to avail oneself of** To utilize. —*n.* Utility for a purpose; benefit; good. [< L *ad-* to + *valere* to be strong]

a·vail·a·ble (ə·vā′lə·bəl) *adj.* 1. Capable of being used; usable. 2. At hand; readily obtainable. —**a·vail′a·bil′i·ty** *n.* —**a·vail′a·bly** *adv.*

av·a·lanche (av′ə·lanch) *n.* 1. A large mass of snow, rocks, etc. falling down a slope. 2. Something like an avalanche, as in power or destructiveness. —*v.t.* & *v.i.* **·lanched, ·lanch·ing** To fall or slide upon like an avalanche. [< dial. F (Swiss) *lavenche*]

a·vant-garde (ə·vänt′gärd′, *Fr.* å·väṅ·gård′) *n.* The vanguard; esp., in art, the group regarded as most advanced or daring in technique and ideas. [< F, lit., advance guard] —**a·vant′-garde′** *adj.*

av·a·rice (av′ə·ris) *n.* Greed; miserliness. [< L *avere* to desire, crave]

av·a·ri·cious (av′ə·rish′əs) *adj.* Greedy of gain; grasping; miserly. —**av′a·ri′cious·ly** *adv.* —**av′a·ri′cious·ness** *n.*

a·vast (ə·vast′) *interj.* *Naut.* Stop! hold! [< Du. *houd vast* hold fast]

av·a·tar (av′ə·tär′) *n.* In Hinduism, the incarnation of a god. [< Skt. *avatāra* descent]

a·ve (ä′vē, ä′vā) *interj.* 1. Hail! 2. Farewell! [< L, hail, farewell]

A·ve Ma·ri·a (ä′vā mə·rē′ə, ä′vē) A Roman Catholic prayer to the Virgin Mary: also called *Hail Mary.* Also **A′ve.** [< L, Hail, Mary]

a·venge (ə·venj′) *v.t.* & *v.i.* **a·venged, a·veng·ing** To take vengeance or to punish for or in behalf of. [< L *ad-* to + *vindicare* to avenge] —**a·veng′er** *n.* —**a·veng′ing·ly** *adv.*

av·e·nue (av′ə·nōō, -nyōō) *n.* 1. A broad street, esp. one bordered with trees. 2. A mode of access or attainment. [< F < L *ad-* toward + *venire* to come]

a·ver (ə·vûr′) *v.t.* **a·verred, a·ver·ring** To declare as fact; affirm. [< L *ad-* to + *versus* true] —**a·ver′ment** *n.*

av·er·age (av′rij, av′ər·ij) *n.* 1. *Math.* An arithmetic mean. 2. A mean, ratio, etc., showing a specific standing or accomplishment: batting *average.* 3. The ordinary rank, degree, or amount; general type. —*adj.* 1. Obtained by calculating the mean of several. 2. Medium; ordinary. —*v.* **·aged, ·ag·ing** *v.t.* 1. To fix or calculate as the mean. 2. To amount to or obtain an average of. —*v.i.* 3. To be or amount to an average. [< F *avarie* damage to a ship]

a·verse (ə·vûrs′) *adj.* Opposed; unfavorable; reluctant: with *to.* [< L *aversus,* pp. of *avertere* to turn aside] **—a·verse′ly** *adv.* **—a·verse′ness** *n.*

a·ver·sion (ə·vûr′zhən, -shən) *n.* 1. Extreme dislike; opposition. 2. Something disliked.

aversion therapy Psychotherapy that seeks to change undesirable behavior by associating with it a noxious stimulus.

a·vert (ə·vûrt′) *v.t.* 1. To turn or direct away or aside. 2. To prevent or ward off, as a danger. [< L *avertere* to turn aside] **—a·vert′i·ble** *adj.*

A·ves·ta (ə·ves′tə) *n.* The sacred writings of Zoroastrianism, written in **A·ves·tan** (ə·ves′·tən), an ancient Iranian language. See ZEND–AVESTA. **—A·ves′tan** *adj.*

a·vi·ar·y (ā′vē·er′ē) *n. pl.* **·ar·ies** An enclosure or large cage for live birds. [< L *avis* bird]

a·vi·a·tion (ā′vē·ā′shən, av′ē-) *n.* The act, science, or art of flying heavier-than-air aircraft. [< L *avis* bird]

a·vi·a·tor (ā′vē·ā′tər, av′ē-) *n.* An airplane pilot. **—a′vi·a′tress** (-tris) or **a′vi·a′trix** (-triks) *n.fem.*

av·id (av′id) *adj.* Very desirous; eager; greedy. [< L *avere* to crave] **—a·vid·i·ty** (ə·vid′ə·tē) *n.* **—av′id·ly** *adv.*

a·vi·on·ics (ā′vē·on′iks, av′ē-) *n.pl.* (*construed as sing.*) The applications of electronics to aviation, astronautics, etc.

av·o·ca·do (av′ə·kä′dō, ä′və-) *n. pl.* **·dos** 1. The pear-shaped fruit of a West Indian tree: also called *alligator pear.* 2. The tree bearing this fruit. [< Nahuatl *ahuacatl*]

av·o·ca·tion (av′ə·kā′shən) *n.* An occasional occupation; hobby. [< L *ab-* away + *vocare* to call]

av·o·cet (av′ə·set) *n.* A long-legged shore bird having webbed feet and an upcurved bill. [< Ital. *avocetta*]

a·void (ə·void′) *v.t.* 1. To keep away from; shun; evade. 2. *Law* To make void. [< L *ex-* out + *viduare* to empty, deprive] **—a·void′a·ble** *adj.* **—a·void′a·bly** *adv.* **—a·void′ance** *n.*

av·oir·du·pois (av′ər·də·poiz′) *n.* 1. The ordinary system of weights of the U.S. and Great Britain in which 16 ounces avoirdupois make a pound. 2. *Informal* Weight; corpulence. [< OF *avoir de pois* goods of (i.e., sold by) weight]

a·vouch (ə·vouch′) *v.t.* 1. To vouch for; guarantee. 2. To affirm positively; proclaim. [< L *ad-* to + *vocare* to call]

a·vow (ə·vou′) *v.t.* To declare openly, as facts; frankly acknowledge. [< L *advocare* to summon] **—a·vow′a·ble** *adj.* **—a·vowed′** *adj.* **—a·vow′ed·ly** *adv.*

a·vow·al (ə·vou′əl) *n.* Frank admission or acknowledgment.

a·vun·cu·lar (ə·vung′kyə·lər) *adj.* Of, pertaining to, or like an uncle. [< L *avunculus* maternal uncle]

a·wait (ə·wāt′) *v.t.* 1. To wait for; expect. 2. To be ready or in store for. [< OF *awaitier* to watch for]

a·wake (ə·wāk′) *adj.* Not asleep; alert. **—***v.* **a·woke, a·waked, a·wak·ing** *v.t.* 1. To arouse from sleep. 2. To stir up; excite. **—***v.i.* 3. To cease to sleep; become awake. 4. To become alert or aroused. [OE *onwæcnan* rise from sleep]

a·wak·en (ə·wā′kən) *v.t. & v.i.* To awake.

a·wak·en·ing (ə·wā′kən·ing) *n.* 1. The act of waking. 2. A rousal, as of interest.

a·ward (ə·wôrd′) *v.t.* 1. To adjudge as due, as by legal decision. 2. To bestow, as a prize. **—***n.* 1. A decision, as by a judge or arbitrator. 2. That which is awarded, as a medal. [ME *awarden* to decide] **—a·ward′er** *n.*

a·ware (ə·wâr′) *adj.* Conscious; cognizant: often with *of.* [OE *gewær* watchful] **—a·ware′ness** *n.*

a·wash (ə·wosh′, ə·wôsh′) *adv. & adj.* 1. Tossed or washed about by waves. 2. Covered or overflowed by water. 3. At or just above the surface of the water.

a·way (ə·wā′) *adv.* 1. From a given place; off. 2. Far; at or to a distance. 3. In another direction; aside. 4. Out of existence: to waste *away.* 5. On and on; continuously. 6. From one's keeping: to give food *away.* 7. At once, without hesitation: Fire *away!* **—***adj.* At a distance: three blocks *away.* **—***interj.* Begone! [OE *on weg* on (one's) way]

awe (ô) *n.* Reverential fear; dread mingled with veneration. **—***v.t.* **awed, aw·ing** To inspire with awe. [< ON *agi* fear]

a·weigh (ə·wā′) *adv. Naut.* Hanging with the flukes just clear of the bottom: said of an anchor.

awe·some (ô′səm) *adj.* 1. Inspiring awe. 2. Expressing awe; reverential. **—awe′some·ly** *adv.* **—awe′some·ness** *n.*

aw·ful (ô′fəl) *adj.* 1. *Informal* Exceedingly bad or unpleasant. 2. Inspiring awe. 3. Causing fear or dread. 4. *Informal* Very great. **—aw′ful·ly** *adv.* **—aw′ful·ness** *n.*

a·while (ə·hwīl′) *adv.* For a brief time. [OE *āne hwīle* a while]

awk·ward (ôk′wərd) *adj.* 1. Ungraceful in bearing. 2. Clumsy or bungling. 3. Embarrassing or perplexing. 4. Difficult or dangerous to deal with. 5. Inconvenient. [ME *awkeward* in the wrong direction < ON *öfugr* turned the wrong way + -WARD] **—awk′ward·ly** *adv.* **—awk′ward·ness** *n.*

awl (ôl) *n.* A pointed instrument for making small holes. [ME *awel* < OE *æl*]

awn (ôn) *n. Bot.* A bristle on certain grasses, as wheat or rye. [< ON *ögn* chaff] **—awned** *adj.*

awn·ing (ô′ning) *n.* A rooflike cover, as of canvas, for protection from sun or rain. [Origin unknown]

a·woke (ə·wōk′) Past tense of AWAKE.

AWOL (*often pronounced* ā′wôl) *Mil.* Absent without leave. Also **A.W.O.L.**

a·wry (ə·rī′) *adj. & adv.* 1. Toward one side; askew. 2. Amiss; wrong.

ax (aks) *n. pl.* **ax·es** 1. A tool with a bladed head mounted on a handle, used for chopping, hewing, etc. 2. *Slang* A portable instrument for popular music, as a guitar. **—***v.t.* To cut or trim with an ax. Also **axe.** [OE *æx*]

ax·i·al (ak′sē·əl) *adj.* 1. Of, pertaining to, or forming an axis. 2. Situated on or along an axis. **—ax′i·al·ly** *adv.*

ax·il (ak′sil) *n. Bot.* The cavity or angle formed by the junction of the upper side of a leafstalk, branch, etc., with a stem or branch. [< L *axilla* armpit]

ax·il·la (ak·sil′ə) *n. pl.* **ax·il·lae** (-sil′ē) 1. *Anat.* The armpit. 2. An axil. [< L]

ax·il·lar (ak′sə·lər) *adj.* Axillary.

ax·il·lar·y (ak′sə·ler′ē) *adj.* 1. *Bot.* Of,

pertaining to, or situated in an axil. 2. *Anat.* Pertaining to the axilla.

ax·i·om (ak′sē·əm) *n.* 1. A self-evident or universally recognized truth. 2. *Logic & Math.* A self-evident proposition accepted as true without proof. [< Gk. *axioein* to think worthy] —**ax′i·o·mat′ic** or **·i·cal** *adj.* —**ax′i·o·mat′i·cal·ly** *adv.*

ax·is (ak′sis) *n. pl.* **ax·es** (ak′sēz) 1. A line around which a turning body rotates or may be supposed to rotate. 2. *Geom.* **a** A straight line through the center of a plane or solid figure. **b** A fixed line, as in a graph, along which distances are measured or to which positions are referred. 3. The central line about which the parts of a body or thing are symmetrically arranged. 4. An alliance of two or more nations. [< L, axis, axle]

ax·le (ak′səl) *n.* 1. A crossbar on which a wheel or wheels turn. 2. An axletree. [< AXLETREE] —**ax′led** *adj.*

ax·le·tree (ak′səl·trē′) *n.* A bar or beam on the ends of which the opposite wheels of a carriage or wagon revolve. [< ON *öxull* axle + *trē* tree, beam]

ax·o·lotl (ak′sə·lot′l) *n.* A North American tailed amphibian that retains its external gills and breeds in a larval state. [< Nahuatl, lit., servant of water]

ax·on (ak′son) *n. Physiol.* The central process of a nerve fiber, usu. carrying impulses away from the nerve cell. Also **ax·one** (ak′sōn). [< Gk. *axōn* axis]

a·yah (ä′yə) *n. Anglo-Indian* A nurse or lady's maid. [< Hind. *āyā* < Pg. *aia* nurse]

aye (ī) *n.* An affirmative vote or voter. —*adv.* Yes; yea. Also **ay.** [Origin unknown]

a·zal·ea (ə·zāl′yə) *n.* A flowering shrub of the heath family. [< Gk. *azein* to parch, dry up]

az·i·muth (az′ə·məth) *n.* 1. The angular distance in a horizontal plane measured clockwise from true north to a given course or celestial object. 2. *Astron.* The angle measured at the zenith, clockwise from true south to a vertical plane passing through a heavenly body. [< Arabic *as-sumūt* the ways, pl. of *samt* way] —**az·i·muth·al** (az′ə·muth′·əl) *adj.*

Az·tec (az′tek) *n.* One of a tribe of Indians, founders of an empire that was at its height when Cortés invaded Mexico in 1519. —*adj.* Of or pertaining to the Aztec Indians, their language, culture, or empire: also **Az′·tec·an.**

az·ure (azh′ər, ā′zhər) *n.* A clear, sky-blue color or pigment. [< Persian *lāzhward* lapis lazuli] —**az′ure** *adj.*

az·u·rite (azh′ə·rīt) *n.* A glassy, azure-blue copper carbonate, often used as a gemstone.

B

b, B (bē) *n. pl.* **b's** or **bs, B's** or **Bs, bees** (bēz) 1. The second letter of the English alphabet. 2. The sound represented by the letter *b*. —*symbol* 1. *Music* The seventh tone in the diatonic scale of C. 2. *Chem.* Boron (symbol B). 3. The second in a series.

baa (bä, ba) *v.i.* **baaed, baa·ing** To bleat, as a sheep. [Imit.] —**baa** *n.*

Ba·al (ba'əl, bāl) *n. pl.* **Ba·al·im** (-im) 1. Any of several ancient Semitic gods of fertility and flocks. 2. An idol or false god. [< Hebrew *ba'al* lord]

Bab·bitt (bab'it) *n.* A type of conventional American businessman; a smug, middle-class philistine. [after title character of the Sinclair Lewis novel (1922)]

Babbitt metal A soft, white, antifriction alloy of tin, copper, and antimony, used in bearings. [after Isaac *Babbitt*, 1799–1862, U.S. metallurgist]

bab·ble (bab'əl) *v.* **·bled, ·bling** *v.i.* 1. To utter inarticulate or meaningless sounds; prattle, as a baby. 2. To make a murmuring or rippling sound, as a stream. 3. To talk foolishly. —*v.t.* 4. To utter inarticulately. 5. To blurt out thoughtlessly. —*n.* 1. Inarticulate or confused speech. 2. A murmuring sound. [ME *babelen*] —**bab'bler** *n.*

babe (bāb) *n.* 1. An infant; baby. 2. *Slang* A girl or woman. [ME]

ba·bel (bā'bəl, bab'əl) *n.* A confusion of many voices or languages; tumult. Also **Ba'bel.** [after Tower of *Babel*, intended to reach to heaven but abandoned when God made the builders speak many strange languages (*Gen. xi* 9)]

ba·boon (ba·bōōn') *n.* A large terrestrial monkey of Africa and Asia, having a doglike muzzle and usu. a short tail. [< OF *babuin*]

ba·bush·ka (bə·bōōsh'kə) *n.* A woman's scarf, worn over the head. [< Russ., grandmother]

ba·by (bā'bē) *n. pl.* **·bies** 1. A very young child; an infant. 2. The youngest or smallest member of a family or group. 3. One who looks or acts like a child. 4. *Slang* A girl or woman. 5. *Slang* A pet person, thing, or project. —*adj.* 1. For a baby. 2. Like a baby. 3. Small; miniature. —*v.t.* **·bied, ·by·ing** To treat as a baby; pamper. [ME *baby*, dim. of *babe*] —**ba'by·hood'** *n.* —**ba'by·ish, ba'by·like'** *adj.*

ba·by's-breath (bā'bēz·breth') *n.* 1. An Old World perennial with clusters of small, white or pink, fragrant flowers. 2. Any of certain other fragrant herbs. Also **ba'bies'-breath.**

ba'by-sit (bā'bē·sit') *v.i.* **-sat, -sit·ting** To act as a baby sitter.

baby sitter A person who takes care of children in the absence of parents: also called *sitter*.

bac·ca·lau·re·ate (bak'ə·lôr'ē·it) *n.* 1. The degree of a bachelor of arts, bachelor of science, etc. 2. An address to a graduating class at commencement. [< Med.L *baccalaureus*, var. of *baccalaris* bachelor]

bac·ca·rat (bak'ə·rä', bak'ə·rä) *n.* A gambling game in which winnings are decided by comparing cards held by the banker with those held by the players. [< F *baccara*]

bac·cha·nal (bak·ə·nal') *n.* 1. A votary of Bacchus. 2. A drunken reveler. 3. *pl.* Bacchanalia. —*adj.* Bacchanalian. [< L *bacchanalis* of Bacchus, god of wine and revelry]

bac·cha·na·li·a (bak'ə·nā'lē·ə, -nāl'yə) *n.pl.* Drunken revelries; orgies. [< L] —**bac'cha·na'li·an** *adj.*

bac·chant (bak'ənt) *n. pl.* **bac·chants** or **bac·chan·tes** (bə·kan'tēz) 1. A votary of Bacchus. 2. A carouser; reveler. —**bac'chant** *adj.*

bac·chic (bak'ik) *adj.* Orgiastic; drunken.

bach·e·lor (bach'ə·lər, bach'lər) *n.* 1. An unmarried man. 2. One who has taken his first university or college degree. [< Med. L *baccalaris* advanced student] —**bach'e·lor·hood', bach'e·lor·ship'** *n.*

bach·e·lor's-but·ton (bach'ə·lərz·but'n, bach'lərz-) *n.* 1. Any of several plants with button-shaped flowers. 2. The cornflower.

ba·cil·lus (bə·sil'əs) *n. pl.* **·cil·li** (-sil'ī) *Bacteriol.* Any of a large class of rod-shaped bacteria, including both beneficial and pathogenic species. [< L *baculus* stick] —**bac·il·lar·y** (bas'ə·ler'ē), **ba·cil'lar** *adj.*

back¹ (bak) *n.* 1. The part of the body nearest the spine; in man the rear, in quadrupeds the upper part, extending from the neck to the base of the spine. ◆Collateral adj.: *dorsal.* 2. The backbone. 3. The rear or posterior part of anything. 4. The further or other side; the reverse. 5. The part behind or opposite to the part used: the *back* of a knife. 6. In football, a player in a position behind the line of scrimmage. —**behind one's back** 1. Secretly. 2. Treacherously. —**to turn one's back on** 1. To show contempt toward by ignoring. 2. To renounce. —*v.t.* 1. To cause to move backward; reverse the action of. 2. To furnish with a back. 3. To support, as by financing or by endorsing. 4. To bet on. —*v.i.* 5. To move backward. —**to back down** To withdraw from a position; give in. —**to back off** To retreat. —**to back out (of)** To withdraw from. —*adj.* 1. In the rear; behind. 2. Distant; remote: the *back* country. 3. Of or for an earlier date: a *back* issue. 4. In arrears; overdue: *back* taxes. [OE *bæc*]

back² (bak) *adv.* 1. At, to, or toward the rear. 2. In, to, or toward a former time, place, or condition. 3. In return or retort.

4. In reserve or concealment. 5. In check or hindrance. 6. In withdrawal or repudiation. **—to go back on** *Informal* 1. To fail to keep (an engagement, promise, etc.). 2. To desert or betray. [< ABACK]

back·bite (bak′bīt′) *v.t. & v.i.* **·bit, ·bit·ten** (*Informal* **·bit**), **·bit·ing** To revile behind one's back; slander. **—back′bit′er** *n.*

back·board (bak′bôrd′) *n.* A board forming, supporting, or at the back of something.

back·bone (bak′bōn′) *n.* 1. The spine or vertebral column. 2. Something likened to a backbone in function or appearance. 3. Strength of character. **—back′boned′** *adj.*

back·break·ing (bak′brā′king) *adj.* Physically exhausting.

back·door (bak′dôr′) *adj.* Clandestine; underhand.

back·drop (bak′drop′) *n.* A cloth hung at the rear of a stage, often depicting a scene.

back·er (bak′ər) *n.* 1. One who supports with money. 2. One who bets on a contestant.

back·field (bak′fēld′) *n.* In football, the players behind the line of scrimmage.

back·fire (bak′fīr′) *n.* 1. A premature explosion of gases in the cylinder of an internal combustion engine, or in the muffler. 2. A fire built to check a forest or prairie fire by creating a barren area in its path. **—***v.i.* **·fired, ·fir·ing** 1. To explode in a backfire. 2. To set a backfire. 3. To have an unexpected and unwelcome result: His plan *backfired.*

back formation *Ling.* 1. The creation by analogy of a new word from an existing word. 2. A word so formed, as *enthuse* from *enthusiasm.*

back·gam·mon (bak′gam′ən, bak′gam′ən) *n.* A board game for two persons, with the moves of pieces being determined by dice throws. [ME *back gamen* back game]

back·ground (bak′ground′) *n.* 1. That part in a picture against which principal subjects are represented. 2. A subordinate position; obscurity. 3. The total of one's experiences; one's history. 4. The events leading up to a situation. 5. Music or sounds subordinate to the main events in a movie, television show, etc. **—back′ground** *adj.*

back·hand (bak′hand′) *n.* 1. Handwriting that slopes toward the left. 2. A stroke of the arm made with the back of the hand forward. **—back′hand′** *adj. & adv.*

back·hand·ed (bak′hand′did) *adj.* 1. Delivered with a backhand stroke. 2. Insincere; equivocal: a *backhanded* compliment. 3. Sloping to the left, as handwriting. **—back′hand′ed·ly** *adv.* **—back′hand′ed·ness** *n.*

back·ing (bak′ing) *n.* 1. Support, assistance, or endorsement. 2. The back of anything; esp., something added as a support.

back·lash (bak′lash′) *n.* 1. A jarring recoil, as of poorly fitted parts of a machine. 2. In fishing, the tangling of line when the reel overruns the cast. 3. A negative reaction to political or social change.

back·log (bak′lôg′, -log′) *n.* 1. A large log at the back of an open fireplace. 2. A reserve supply or an accumulation.

back·pack (bak′pak′) *n.* A bag worn on the back to carry supplies on walking trips. **—***v.i.* To take a walking trip wearing a backpack.

back·rest (bak′rest′) *n.* A support for or at the back.

back·side (bak′sīd′) *n.* The rump.

back·slide (bak′slīd′) *v.i.* **·slid, ·slid** or **·slid·den, ·slid·ing** To return to wrong or sinful ways. **—back′slid′er** *n.*

back·spin (bak′spin′) *n.* Rotation of a ball that tends to retard its forward motion.

back·stage (*adv. & n.* bak′stāj′; *adj.* bak′·stāj′) *adv.* Off a theater stage, in the wings or dressing rooms. **—***n.* The wings or dressing rooms of a theater. **—***adj.* 1. Situated or occurring backstage. 2. Hidden or secret.

back·stairs (bak′stârz′) *adj.* Indirect; underhand. Also **back′stair′.**

back·stay (bak′stā′) *n.* *Naut.* A stay supporting a mast on the aft side.

back·stitch (bak′stich′) *n.* A stitch made by carrying the thread back half the length of the preceding stitch. **—back′stitch′** *v.t. & v.i.*

back·stop (bak′stop′) *n.* *Sports* A fence, screen, or the like, behind home plate, a goal, etc., to stop the ball or puck.

back·stretch (bak′strech′) *n.* That part of a racecourse farthest from the spectators, usu. a straightaway.

back·stroke (bak′strōk′) *n.* In swimming, a stroke executed while on one's back. **—***v.i.* **·stroked, ·strok·ing** To swim with a backstroke.

back talk Insolent answering back.

back·track (bak′trak′) *v.i.* 1. To retrace one's steps. 2. To withdraw from a position, undertaking, etc.

back·up (bak′up) *n.* That which is kept available as a replacement. **—back′up** *adj.*

back·ward (bak′wərd) *adv.* 1. Toward the back; to the rear. 2. With the back foremost. 3. In reverse order. 4. From better to worse. 5. To or into time past. Also **back′wards.** **—***adj.* 1. Turned to the back or rear; reversed. 2. Done the reverse or wrong way. 3. Behind in growth or development; retarded. 4. Hesitating; bashful. **—back′·ward·ly** *adv.* **—back′ward·ness** *n.*

back·wash (bak′wosh′, -wôsh′) *n.* 1. Water moved backward, as by a boat. 2. A backward current or flow.

back·wa·ter (bak′wô′tər, -wot′ər) *n.* 1. Water turned or held back, as by a dam, a current, etc. 2. Any place or condition regarded as stagnant, backward, etc.

back·woods (bak′wŏŏdz′) *n.pl.* Wild, heavily wooded, or sparsely settled districts. **—***adj.* In, from, or like the backwoods: also **back′wood′.** **—back′woods′man** (-mən) *n.*

ba·con (bā′kən) *n.* The salted and dried or smoked back and sides of the hog. **—to bring home the bacon** *Informal* To bring home money, food, etc. [< OHG *bacho, bahho* ham, side of bacon]

bac·te·ri·a (bak·tir′ē·ə) Plural of BACTERIUM.

bac·te·ri·cide (bak·tir′ə·sīd) *n.* An agent destructive of bacteria. **—bac·te′ri·ci′dal** *adj.*

bacterio- *combining form* Of or pertaining to bacteria. Also, before vowels, **bacter-.** Also **bacteri-, bactero-.** [< Gk. *baktron* rod, staff]

bac·te·ri·ol·o·gy (bak·tir′ē·ol′ə·jē) *n.* The branch of biology and medicine that deals with bacteria. **—bac·te′ri·o·log′i·cal** (-ē·ə·loj′i·kəl) *adj.* **—bac·te′ri·o·log′i·cal·ly** *adj.* **—bac·te′ri·ol′o·gist** *n.*

bac·te·ri·o·phage (bak·tir′ē·ə·fāj′, -fāzh′) *n.*

Bacteriol. A virus that can destroy certain bacteria. Also called *phage.*

bac·te·ri·um (bak·tir′ē·əm) *n. pl.* **·ri·a** Any of numerous unicellular microorganisms ranging from the harmless and beneficial to those that cause disease. [< Gk. *baktron* staff, stick] **—bac·te′ri·al** *adj.* **—bac·te′ri·al·ly** *adv.*

bad (bad) *adj.* **worse, worst** 1. Not good in any manner or degree. 2. Evil; immoral. 3. Defective; worthless. 4. Faulty; incorrect or unsound. 5. Not sufficient; inadequate. 6. Lacking skill or proficiency: a *bad* poet. 7. Distressing; unfavorable: *bad* news. 8. Disagreeable: a *bad* taste. 9. Harmful. 10. Rotted; spoiled. 11. Severe: a *bad* storm. 12. Sick; in ill health. 13. Sorry; regretful: He felt *bad* about it. **—in bad** *Informal* 1. In difficulty. 2. In disfavor. **—not bad** Rather good: also **not half bad, not so bad.** **—***n.* 1. That which is bad. 2. Those who are bad: with *the.* 3. A bad state or condition; wickedness. **—***adv. Informal* Badly. [OE *bæddel* effeminate man] **—bad′ness** *n.*

bade (bad) Past tense of BID.

badge (baj) *n.* 1. Any device worn to indicate rank, office, membership, an award, etc. 2. Any distinguishing mark or insignia. **—***v.t.* **badged, badg·ing** To decorate or provide with a badge. [ME *bage*]

badg·er (baj′ər) *n.* 1. A small, burrowing, nocturnal, carnivorous mammal, with a broad body, short legs, and long-clawed toes. 2. The fur of a badger. **—***v.t.* To harass; nag at. [Origin unknown]

bad·i·nage (bad′ə·näzh′, bad′ə·nij) *n.* Playful raillery; banter. **—***v.t.* **·naged, ·nag·ing** To tease with badinage. [< F *badin* silly, jesting]

bad·lands (bad′landz′) *n.pl.* A barren area characterized by numerous ridges, peaks, and mesas cut by erosion.

Bad Lands An arid plateau in South Dakota and Nebraska. Also **Bad′lands.**

bad·ly (bad′lē) *adv.* 1. In a bad manner; improperly, imperfectly, or grievously. 2. *Informal* Very much; greatly.

bad·min·ton (bad′min·tən) *n.* A game played by batting a shuttlecock back and forth over a high, narrow net with a light racket. [after *Badminton,* an estate in England]

bad-mouth (bad′mouth′, -mouth′) *v.t. Informal* To vilify.

bad-tem·pered (bad′tem′pərd) *adj.* Cross; irritable.

Bae·de·ker (bā′di·kər) *n.* Any of a series of travelers' guidebooks. [after Karl *Baedeker,* 1801–59, German publisher who issued them]

baf·fle (baf′əl) *v.* **·fled, ·fling** *v.t.* 1. To confuse mentally; perplex. 2. To foil or frustrate. **—***v.i.* 3. To struggle to no avail. **—***n.* A partition used to control and direct sounds, fluids, etc. [Origin uncertain] **—baf′fle·ment** *n.* **—baf′fler** *n.* **—baf′fling** *adj.* **—baf′fling·ly** *adv.*

bag (bag) *n.* 1. A sack or pouch, used as a receptacle. 2. The amount a bag will hold. 3. A woman's purse. 4. A suitcase or satchel. 5. The quantity of game caught or killed in hunting. 6. A bulging or baggy part, as of a sail. 7. *Slang* In baseball, a base. 8. *Slang* That which is especially suitable or appealing to a person: Rock music is his *bag.* **—in the bag** *Slang* Assured; certain. **—to be left holding the bag** *Informal* To be left to assume full responsibility or blame. **—***v.* **bagged, bag·ging** *v.t.* 1. To put into a bag. 2. To cause to fill out or bulge like a bag. 3. To capture or kill, as game. **—***v.i.* 4. To bulge or swell like a bag. 5. To hang loosely. [? < ON *baggi* pack, bundle]

bag and baggage *Informal* 1. With all one's possessions: He cleared out *bag and baggage.* 2. Entirely; completely.

bag·a·telle (bag′ə·tel′) *n.* 1. A trifle. 2. A game similar to billiards. [< Ital. *bagatella,* dim. of *baga* sack]

ba·gel (bā′gəl) *n.* A doughnut-shaped roll of yeast dough simmered in water and baked. [< Yiddish < G *beigen* to twist]

bag·gage (bag′ij) *n.* 1. The trunks, packages, etc., of a traveler. 2. An army's movable equipment. [< Med.L *baga* sack]

bag·ging (bag′ing) *n.* A coarse cloth for making bags.

bag·gy (bag′ē) *adj.* **bag·gi·er, bag·gi·est** Like a bag; loose; bulging. **—bag′gi·ly** *adv.* **—bag′gi·ness** *n.*

bagn·io (ban′yō, bän′-) *n. pl.* **·ios** 1. A brothel. 2. In the Orient, a prison. [< Ital.]

bag·pipe (bag′pīp′) *n.* *Often pl.* A reed musical instrument having several pipes, the air being forced through them from an inflated leather bag. **—bag′pip′er** *n.*

ba·guette (ba·get′) *n.* A gem or crystal cut in long, narrow, rectangular form. Also **ba·guet′.** [< F < L *baculum* staff, stick]

bah (bä, ba) *interj.* An exclamation of contempt or dismissal.

bail[1] (bāl) *n.* A scoop or bucket for dipping out fluids, as from a boat. **—***v.t. & v.i.* 1. To dip (water) from a boat with a bail. 2. To clear (a boat) of water by dipping out. **—to bail out** To jump with parachute from an aircraft. [< LL *baca, bacca* tub] **—bail′er** *n.*

bail[2] (bāl) *n.* 1. One who becomes surety for the debt or default of another, esp. of a person under arrest. 2. The security or guaranty given or agreed upon. 3. Release, or the privilege of release, on bail. **—***v.t.* To obtain the release of (an arrested person) by giving bail: often with *out.* [< L *bajulare* to carry] **—bail′ment** *n.*

bail[3] (bāl) *n.* 1. The semicircular handle of a pail, kettle, etc. 2. An arch-shaped support, as for a canopy. **—***v.t.* To provide with a bail or handle. [< ON *beygla* hook, ring]

bai·liff (bā′lif) *n.* 1. A court officer having custody of prisoners under arraignment. 2. A sheriff's deputy. 3. One who oversees an estate; a steward. 4. *Brit.* A subordinate magistrate with limited jurisdiction. [< L *bajalus* porter, manager]

bai·li·wick (bā′lə·wik) *n.* 1. The office, jurisdiction, or district of a bailiff. 2. A person's own area of authority or competence. [ME *bailie* bailiff + *wick* village]

bails·man (bālz′mən) *n. pl.* **·men** (-mən) One who provides bail for another.

bairn (bârn) *n. Scot.* A young child.

bait (bāt) *n.* 1. Food or any lure placed in a trap, on a hook, etc. 2. Any allurement or enticement. **—***v.t.* 1. To put food or some other lure on or in: to *bait* a trap. 2. To set dogs upon for sport: to *bait* a bear. 3. To harass; torment. 4. To lure; entice. [< ON *beita* food] **—bait′er** *n.*

baize (bāz) *n.* A plain woolen feltlike fabric, usu. dyed green, used for pool table covers, etc. [< OF *baies* brown]

bake (bāk) *v.* **baked, bak·ing** *v.t.* 1. To cook (bread, pastry, etc.) by dry heat, as in an oven. 2. To harden or vitrify by heat, as bricks or pottery. —*v.i.* 3. To bake bread, pastry, etc. 4. To become baked or hardened by heat, as soil. —*n.* A baking, or the amount baked. [OE *bacan*] **—bak′er** *n.*

Ba·ke·lite (bā′kə·līt) *n.* Any of a group of thermosetting plastics: a trade name. Also **ba′ke·lite.** [after Leo Hendrik *Baekeland*, 1863–1944, U.S. chemist]

baker's dozen Thirteen.

bak·er·y (bā′kər·ē, bāk′rē) *n. pl.* **·er·ies** 1. A place for baking bread, cake, etc.: also **bake′house′.** 2. A shop where bread, cake, etc., are sold: also **bake′shop′.**

bak·ing powder (bā′king) A finely powdered mixture of baking soda and an acid salt, used as a leavening agent in baking.

baking soda Sodium bicarbonate.

bal·a·lai·ka (bal′ə·lī′kə) *n.* A Russian stringed instrument of the guitar family. [< Russ.]

bal·ance (bal′əns) *n.* 1. *Sometimes pl.* An instrument for weighing; esp., a bar that pivots on a central point as weights are placed in the pans suspended from each end. 2. Figuratively, the scale by which deeds and principles are weighed and destinies determined. 3. The power or authority to decide and determine. 4. A state of equilibrium or equal relationship; equipoise. 5. Bodily poise. 6. Mental or emotional stability. 7. Harmonious proportion, as in the arrangement of parts in a whole. 8. Something used to produce an equilibrium; counterpoise. 9. In bookkeeping: **a** Equality between the debit and credit totals of an account. **b** A difference between such totals. 10. Whatever is left over; remainder. 11. A balance wheel. **—to strike a balance** To find or take an intermediate position; compromise. —*v.* **·anced, ·anc·ing** *v.t.* 1. To bring into or keep in equilibrium; poise. 2. To weigh in a balance. 3. To weigh (alternatives) in the mind. 4. To offset or counteract. 5. To place or keep in proportion. 6. To be equal or in proportion to. 7. In bookkeeping, to compute or adjust the difference between the debit and credit sides of (an account). —*v.i.* 8. To be or come into equilibrium. 9. To be equal. [< L *bis* two + *lanx, lancis* dish, plate] **—bal′anc·er** *n.*

balance of power A distribution of power among nations such that none may acquire a degree of strength dangerous to the others.

balance of trade The difference in value between exports and imports of a country.

balance sheet A statement in tabular form to show assets and liabilities, profit and loss, etc., of a business.

balance wheel The oscillating wheel of a watch or chronometer, that determines its rate of motion.

bal·brig·gan (bal·brig′ən) *n.* 1. A fine, unbleached, knitted cotton fabric. 2. *pl.* Underwear and hose made of this fabric. [after *Balbriggan*, Ireland]

bal·co·ny (bal′kə·nē) *n. pl.* **·nies** 1. A balustraded platform projecting from a wall of a building. 2. A projecting gallery in a theater or public building. [< OHG *balcho* beam] **—bal′co·nied** *adj.*

bald (bôld) *adj.* 1. Without hair on the head. 2. Without natural covering or growth. 3. Unadorned. 4. Without disguise; forthright. 5. *Zool.* Having white feathers or fur on the head. [? < Welsh *bāl* white] **—bald′ly** *adv.* **—bald′ness** *n.*

bal·der·dash (bôl′dər·dash) *n.* Nonsense. [Origin uncertain]

bald·head (bôld′hed′) *n.* One whose head is bald. **—bald′head′ed** *adj.*

bald·pate (bôld′pāt′) *n.* A baldheaded person. **—bald′pat′ed** *adj.*

bal·dric (bôl′drik) *n.* A belt worn over one shoulder and across the breast, to support a sword, bugle, etc. Also **bal′drick.** [< OF *baldrei*, ult. < L *balteus* belt]

bale (bāl) *n.* A large package of bulky goods, usu. corded. —*v.t.* **baled, bal·ing** To make into a bale or bales. [< OF *bale* round package] **—bal′er** *n.*

ba·leen (bə·lēn′) *n.* Whalebone. [< Gk. *phalaina* whale]

bale·ful (bāl′fəl) *adj.* 1. Hurtful; malignant. 2. Ominous. [OE *bealu* evil + -FUL] **—bale′·ful·ly** *adv.* **—bale′ful·ness** *n.*

Ba·li·nese (bä′lə·nēz′, -nēs′) *adj.* Of or pertaining to Bali, its people, or their language. —*n. pl.* **·nese** 1. A native or inhabitant of Bali. 2. The Indonesian language of Bali.

balk (bôk) *v.i.* 1. To stop short and refuse to proceed or take action. —*v.t.* 2. To render unsuccessful; thwart. —*n.* 1. A hindrance or check; disappointment. 2. An error or blunder. 3. In baseball, an illegal motion made by the pitcher, resembling a checked pitch. 4. A ridge between furrows. 5. A squared beam. Also **baulk.** [OE *balca* bank, ridge]

Bal·kan (bôl′kən) *adj.* 1. Of or pertaining to the Balkan Peninsula, its people, or their customs. 2. Of or pertaining to the Balkan Mountains.

balk·y (bô′kē) *adj.* **balk·i·er, balk·i·est** Given to balking.

ball[1] (bôl) *n.* 1. A spherical or nearly spherical body. 2. Any such object used in a number of games. 3. A game played with a ball, esp. baseball. 4. In sports, a ball moving, thrown, or struck in a specified manner. 5. In baseball, a pitch in which the ball fails to pass over the home plate between the batter's armpits and knees and is not struck at by him. 6. A roundish part of something. **—to be on the ball** *Slang* To be alert or competent. **—to have something on the ball** *Slang* To have ability. **—to play ball** 1. To begin or resume playing a ball game or some other activity. 2. *Informal* To cooperate. —*v.t. & v.i.* To form, gather, or wind into a ball. [< ON *böllr*]

ball[2] (bôl) *n.* 1. A formal social dance. 2. A good time. [< F *bal*]

bal·lad (bal′əd) *n.* 1. A narrative poem or song of popular origin in short stanzas, often with a refrain. 2. A sentimental song of several stanzas, in which usu. the melody is repeated for each stanza. [< OF *balade* dancing song] **—bal′lad·eer′** *n.* **—bal′lad·ry** *n.*

bal·last (bal′əst) *n.* 1. Any heavy substance,

as sand, stone, etc., used to steady a ship or other vessel. 2. Gravel or broken stone laid down as a stabilizer for a rail bed. 3. That which gives stability. —*v.t.* 1. To provide or fill with ballast. 2. To stabilize. [< ODan. *bar* bare, mere + *last* load]

ball bearing *Mech.* 1. A bearing in which a shaft bears on small metal balls that turn freely as it revolves. 2. A metal ball in such a bearing.

bal·le·ri·na (bal′ə·rē′nə) *n.* A female ballet dancer. [< Ital.]

bal·let (bal′ā, ba·lā′) *n.* 1. An elaborate dramatic group dance using conventionalized movements, often for narrative effect. 2. A troupe of ballet dancers. [< F, dim. of *bal* dance] —**bal·let·ic** (ba·let′ik) *adj.*

bal·let·o·mane (ba·let′ə·mān) *n.* A ballet enthusiast. [< BALLET + *-mane* (< -MANIA)]

ballistic missile A missile controlled to the apex of its trajectory, falling free thereafter.

bal·lis·tics (bə·lis′tiks) *n.pl.* (*construed as sing.*) The science that deals with the motion of projectiles. —**bal·lis′tic** *adj.* —**bal·lis·ti·cian** (bal′ə·stish′ən) *n.*

bal·loon (bə·lo͞on′) *n.* 1. A large, impermeable bag inflated with gas lighter than air, designed to rise and float in the atmosphere, and often equipped to carry passengers, instruments, etc. 2. A small, inflatable rubber bag, used as a toy. —*v.i.* 1. To increase quickly in scope or magnitude. 2. To swell out like a balloon, as a sail. 3. To ascend or travel in a balloon. —*v.t.* 4. To inflate or distend with air. [< Ital. *balla* ball, sphere] —**bal·loon′ist** *n.*

bal·lot (bal′ət) *n.* 1. A written or printed slip or ticket used in casting a secret vote. 2. The total number of votes cast in an election. 3. The system of voting secretly by ballots or by voting machines. 4. A list of candidates for office. —*v.i.* **·lot·ed, ·lot·ing** To cast a ballot in voting. [< Ital. *ballotta*, dim. of *balla* ball]

ball·park (bôl′pärk′) *n.* A baseball playing field with spectator facilities. —*adj.* Approximate, but close enough for a particular need: a *ballpark* estimate.

ball·play·er (bôl′plā′ər) *n.* A baseball player.

ball-point pen (bôl′point′) A pen having a ball bearing point that inks itself by rolling against an ink cartridge.

ball·room (bôl′ro͞om′, -ro͝om′) *n.* A large room for dancing.

ballroom dancing Social dancing for two people.

bal·ly·hoo (bal′ē·ho͞o′) *n.* *Informal* 1. Blatant or sensational advertising; noisy propaganda. 2. Clamor; uproar. —*v.t.* **·hooed, ·hoo·ing** To advocate or promote by ballyhoo. [Origin unknown]

balm (bäm) *n.* 1. An aromatic, resinous exudation from various trees or shrubs, used as medicine; balsam. 2. Any similar substance. 3. Any of various aromatic plants resembling mint. 4. A pleasing fragrance. 5. Anything that soothes. [< Gk. *balsamon* balsam tree]

balm·y (bä′mē) *adj.* **balm·i·er, balm·i·est** 1. Mild and soothing; soft. 2. Having the fragrance of balm; aromatic. 3. *Brit. Slang* Crazy. —**balm′i·ly** *adv.* —**balm′i·ness** *n.*

ba·lo·ney (bə·lō′nē) *n.* 1. *Slang* Nonsense. 2. Bologna sausage. Also spelled *boloney.* [< BOLOGNA SAUSAGE]

bal·sa (bôl′sə, bäl′-) *n.* 1. A tree of tropical America and the West Indies. 2. The very light wood of this tree. 3. A raft made of light logs. [< Sp. *balza*]

bal·sam (bôl′səm) *n.* 1. Any of a group of fragrant oleoresins obtained chiefly from the exudations of various trees. 2. Any tree yielding such a substance. 3. Any fragrant ointment. [< Gk. *balsamon* balsam] —**bal·sam·ic** (bôl·sam′ik) *adj.*

balsam fir A tree of the pine family, growing in the U.S. and Canada.

Bal·tic (bôl′tik) *adj.* Of or pertaining to the Baltic Sea or the Baltic States.

Baltimore oriole An American oriole of which the male has orange and black plumage. [after the colors of the coat of arms of Lord *Baltimore,* 1580–1632, founder of Maryland]

bal·us·ter (bal′əs·tər) *n.* One of a set of small pillars supporting a handrail. [< Ital. *balaustra* pomegranate flower]

bal·us·trade (bal′ə·strād′, bal′ə·strād) *n.* A handrail supported by balusters.

bam·bi·no (bam·bē′nō) *n.* *pl.* **·ni** (-nē) or **·nos** 1. A little child; a baby. 2. A figure of the child Jesus. [< Ital., dim. of *bambo* simple, childish]

bam·boo (bam·bo͞o′) *n.* 1. A tall, treelike or shrubby grass of tropical and semitropical regions. 2. Its tough, hollow, jointed stem, used for furniture, etc. [< Malay *bambu*]

bam·boo·zle (bam·bo͞o′zəl) *v.* **·zled, ·zling** *Informal v.t.* 1. To mislead; cheat. 2. To perplex. —*v.i.* 3. To practice trickery or deception. [Origin unknown] —**bam·boo′zle·ment** *n.* —**bam·boo′zler** *n.*

ban (ban) *v.t.* **banned, ban·ning** To proscribe or prohibit; outlaw. —*n.* 1. An official proclamation, especially of prohibition. 2. *Eccl.* An edict of excommunication or interdiction. [< OE *bannan* to proclaim and ON *banna* to curse, prohibit]

ba·nal (bā′nəl, bə·nal′) *adj.* Hackneyed; trite. [< OF *ban* feudal summons; hence, ordinary, common] —**ba·nal·i·ty** (bə·nal′ə·tē) *n.* —**ba′nal·ly** *adv.*

ba·nan·a (bə·nan′ə) *n.* 1. The elongated, edible, pulpy fruit of a herbaceous plant of tropical regions, growing in drooping clusters. 2. The plant bearing this fruit. [< native African name]

ba·nan·as (bə·nan′əz) *adj.* *Slang* Crazy.

band[1] (band) *n.* 1. A flat flexible strip of any material, often used for binding or securing. 2. A strip of fabric used to finish, strengthen, or trim an article of dress: often in combination: *hatband.* 3. Any broad stripe. 4. *Telecom.* A range of frequencies or wavelengths between two stated limits. —*v.t.* 1. To unite or tie with a band; encircle. 2. To mark by attaching a band to. [< F *bande*]

band[2] (band) *n.* 1. A company of persons associated for a common purpose; a troop or gang. 2. A group organized to play musical instruments. —*v.t. & v.i.* To unite in a band. [< MF *bande*]

band·age (ban′dij) *n.* A strip of material used in dressing wounds, etc. —*v.t.* **·aged, ·ag·ing** To bind or cover with a bandage. [< F *bande* band]

Band-Aid (band′ād′) *n.* An adhesive strip with a gauze patch for covering minor wounds: a trade name. Also **band′-aid′.**

ban·dan·na (ban·dan′ə) *n.* A large, brightly colored handkerchief. Also **ban·dan′a.** [< Hind. *bāndhnū*, a method of dyeing]

band·box (band′boks′) *n.* A light round box, usu. used for carrying hats.

ban·deau (ban·dō′, ban′dō) *n. pl.* **·deaux** (-dōz′, -dōz) 1. A narrow band, esp. for the hair. 2. A narrow brassiere. [< OF *bande* band]

ban·di·coot (ban′di·ko͞ot) *n.* 1. A large rat of India and Ceylon. 2. A small marsupial of Australia. [< Telugu *pandikokku* pig-rat]

ban·dit (ban′dit) *n. pl.* **ban·dits** or **ban·dit·ti** (ban·dit′ē) A robber; outlaw. [< Ital. *bandire* to proscribe, outlaw] **—ban′dit·ry** *n.*

band·mas·ter (band′mas′tər) *n.* The conductor of a musical band.

ban·do·leer (ban′də·lir′) *n.* A broad belt fitted with loops or cases for holding cartridges, and worn over the shoulder. Also **ban′do·lier′.** [< Ital. *banda* band]

band saw *Mech.* A saw consisting of a toothed endless belt mounted on pulleys.

band shell A bandstand having a concave hemispherical rear wall.

band·stand (band′stand′) *n.* A platform for a band of musicians.

band·wag·on (band′wag′ən) *n.* A high, decorated wagon used to carry a band in a parade. **—to climb (hop, get, etc.) on the bandwagon** *Informal* To support a principle or candidate apparently assured of success.

ban·dy (ban′dē) *v.t.* **·died, ·dy·ing** 1. To give and take; exchange, as blows or words. 2. To pass along; circulate: to *bandy* stories. [Origin uncertain]

ban·dy-leg·ged (ban′dē·leg′id, -legd′) *adj.* Bowlegged.

bane (bān) *n.* 1. Anything destructive or ruinous. 2. Poison: now only in combination: *henbane.* [OE *bana* killer] **—bane′ful** *adj.* **—bane′ful·ly** *adv.*

bang[1] (bang) *n.* 1. A heavy, noisy blow or thump. 2. A sudden, loud noise. 3. *Informal* A sudden spurt of activity. 4. *Slang* Thrill; enjoyment. **—***v.t.* 1. To strike heavily and noisily. **—***v.i.* 2. To make a loud sound. 3. To strike noisily; crash. **—***adv.* Abruptly and loudly. [< ON *banga* to hammer]

bang[2] (bang) *n.* *Usu. pl.* A fringe of hair cut straight across the forehead. [? < *bangtail* short tail]

ban·gle (bang′gəl) *n.* A bracelet or anklet. [< Hind. *bangrī* glass bracelet]

bang-up (bang′up′) *adj. Slang* Excellent.

ban·ish (ban′ish) *v.t.* 1. To compel to leave a country by political decree; exile. 2. To expel; drive away. [< LL *bannire*] **—ban′·ish·er** *n.* **—ban′ish·ment** *n.*

ban·is·ter (ban′is·tər) *n.* 1. *Often pl.* A balustrade. 2. Loosely, a baluster. Also **ban′nis·ter.** [See BALUSTER.]

ban·jo (ban′jō) *n. pl.* **·jos** or **·joes** A long-necked, usu. five-stringed musical instrument having a drumlike body and played by plucking the strings. [< a West African language] **—ban′jo·ist** *n.*

bank[1] (bangk) *n.* 1. Any moundlike formation or mass; ridge. 2. A steep slope. 3. *Often pl.* The slope of land at the edge of a watercourse or channel. 4. A raised portion of the ocean floor, a river bed, etc. 5. *Aeron.* The controlled sidewise tilt of an airplane in a turn. **—***v.t.* 1. To enclose, cover, or protect by a bank, dike, or border; embank. 2. To heap up into a bank or mound. 3. To give an upward lateral slope to, as the curve of a road. 4. To tilt (an airplane) laterally in flight. 5. To cause (a billiard ball) to rebound at an angle from a cushion. **—***v.i.* 6. To form or lie in banks. 7. To tilt laterally in flight. [ME *banke*]

bank[2] (bangk) *n.* 1. An institution for lending, borrowing, exchanging, issuing, or safeguarding money. 2. An office or building used for such purposes. 3. The funds of a gambling house. 4. A reserve supply: a blood *bank.* **—***v.t.* 1. To deposit in a bank. **—***v.i.* 2. To do business as or with a bank or banker. **—to bank on** *Informal* To rely on; be sure about. [< Ital. *banca* money-changer's table] **—bank′er** *n.* **—bank′ing** *n.*

bank[3] (bangk) *n.* 1. A set of like articles arranged in a row. 2. *Naut.* A tier of oars in a galley. **—***v.t.* To arrange in a bank. [< LL *bancus* bench]

bank account Money deposited in a bank to the credit of the depositor.

bank·book (bangk′bo͝ok′) *n.* A book kept by a depositor in which his accounts are entered: also called *passbook.*

bank note A promissory note of a bank, serving as currency. Also **bank bill.**

bank·roll (bangk′rōl′) *v.t.* **·rolled, ·roll·ing** To finance. **—***n.* A supply of money.

bank·rupt (bangk′rupt) *n.* 1. *Law* One who is judicially declared insolvent, his property being administered by a trustee. 2. Any person unable to pay his debts. 3. One ruined in some way: a spiritual *bankrupt.* **—***adj.* 1. Subject to the conditions of a bankruptcy law; insolvent. 2. Destitute; ruined. **—***v.t.* To make bankrupt. [< Ital. *bancarotte* broken bank] **—bank′rupt·cy** *n.*

ban·ner (ban′ər) *n.* 1. A flag or standard bearing a motto or device. 2. A headline extending across a newspaper page. **—***adj.* Leading; outstanding. [< LL *bandum* banner]

banns (banz) *n.pl. Eccl.* A public announcement in church of a proposed marriage. Also **bans.** [< BAN]

ban·quet (bang′kwit) *n.* 1. A sumptuous feast. 2. A formal or ceremonial dinner. **—***v.t. & v.i.* To entertain or feast at a banquet. [< MF, dim. of *banc* table] **—ban′quet·er** *n.*

ban·quette (bang·ket′) *n.* 1. *Mil.* A platform or bank behind a parapet, on which soldiers may stand and fire. 2. An upholstered bench, as along a wall. [< F < Ital. *banchetta*]

ban·shee (ban′shē, ban·shē′) *n.* In Gaelic folklore, a female spirit whose wailing foretells a death. Also **ban′shie.** [< Irish *bean* woman + *sīdhe* fairy]

ban·tam (ban′təm) *n.* 1. *Often cap.* Any of various breeds of very small domestic fowl, characterized by combativeness. 2. A small, pugnacious person. **—***adj.* Small and combative. [after *Bantam*, Java]

ban·tam·weight (ban′təm·wāt′) *n.* A boxer or wrestler who weighs between 113 and 118 pounds.

ban·ter (ban′tər) *n.* Good-humored ridicule; raillery. **—***v.t.* 1. To tease good-naturedly.

—*v.i.* 2. To exchange good-natured repartee. [Origin unknown] —**ban′ter·er** *n.*

Ban·tu (ban′to͞o) *n.* *pl.* **·tu** or **·tus** (-to͞oz) 1. A member of any of numerous Negro tribes of central and south Africa. 2. A family of languages spoken by these tribes. —**Ban′tu** *adj.*

ban·yan (ban′yən) *n.* An East Indian fig-bearing tree whose branches send down roots that develop into new trunks. [< Hindi *baniyā* merchant, from the use of the ground under the tree as a market place]

ban·zai (bän·zī) *Japanese* (May you live) ten thousand years: used as a cheer, battle cry, etc.

ba·o·bab (bā′ō·bab, bä′ō-) *n.* An African tree with a thick trunk, bearing edible fruit. [< native African name]

bap·tism (bap′tiz·əm) *n.* 1. The act of baptizing or of being baptized; esp., the Christian sacrament of initiation into the Church. 2. Any initiatory or purifying experience. [< Gk. *baptismos* immersion] —**bap·tis′mal** *adj.*

Bap·tist (bap′tist) *n.* A member of any of various Protestant denominations holding that baptism (generally by immersion) should be given only to professed believers.

bap·tis·ter·y (bap′tis·trē) *n.* *pl.* **·ter·ies** A part of a church set apart for baptism. Also **bap′tis·try.**

bap·tize (bap·tīz′, bap′tīz) *v.t.* **·tized, ·tiz·ing** 1. To immerse in water or sprinkle water on in Christian baptism. 2. To christen. 3. To cleanse or initiate. [< Gk. *baptizein* to immerse, wash] —**bap·tiz′er** *n.*

bar (bär) *n.* 1. A piece of wood, metal, etc., evenly shaped and long in proportion to its width and thickness, used as a fastening, lever, etc. 2. An oblong block of solid material, as of soap or a precious metal. 3. Any barrier or obstacle. 4. A bank, as of sand, at the entrance to a harbor or river. 5. The railing about the place in a court occupied by the judge and lawyers, or where prisoners are brought to trial. 6. A court of law. 7. Lawyers collectively; also, the legal profession. 8. *Music* **a** The vertical line that divides a staff into measures. **b** A measure. 9. A counter or establishment serving drinks and food, esp. alcoholic drinks. 10. A stripe, as of color. —*v.t.* **barred, bar·ring** 1. To fasten or secure with a bar. 2. To prevent, prohibit, or obstruct. 3. To exclude. —*prep.* Excepting: *bar* none. [< LL *barra* bar]

barb (bärb) *n.* 1. A point projecting backward on a sharp weapon, as on a fishhook or spear. 2. Any similar sharp point, as on barbed wire. 3. A stinging remark. 4. One of the threadlike processes that extend from the shaft of a feather. [< L *barba* beard] —**barb** *v.t.* —**barbed** *adj.*

bar·bar·i·an (bär·bâr′ē·ən) *n.* 1. One who belongs to a people, group, or tribe characterized by a primitive civilization. 2. A rude, coarse, or brutal person. —*adj.* Of or resembling a barbarian; uncivilized. —**bar·bar′i·an·ism** *n.*

bar·bar·ic (bär·bar′ik) *adj.* 1. Of or befitting barbarians; uncivilized. 2. Coarse; unrestrained.

bar·ba·rism (bär′bə·riz′əm) *n.* 1. The use of words or forms not standard in a language. 2. Such a word or form. 3. A primitive stage of civilization. 4. A primitive or crude trait, condition, or act.

bar·bar·i·ty (bär·bar′ə·tē) *n.* *pl.* **·ties** 1. Barbaric conduct. 2. A barbaric act. 3. Crudity in style or taste.

bar·ba·rize (bär′bə·rīz) *v.t.* & *v.i.* **·rized, ·riz·ing** To make or become barbarous or corrupt, as a language.

bar·ba·rous (bär′bər·əs) *adj.* 1. Uncivilized; primitive. 2. Lacking in refinement; coarse. 3. Cruel; brutal. 4. Rude or harsh in sound. [< Gk. *barbaros* non-Hellenic, foreign, rude] —**bar′ba·rous·ly** *adv.* —**bar′ba·rous·ness** *n.*

Bar·ba·ry ape (bär′bər·ē) A tailless monkey of North Africa and southern Spain.

bar·be·cue (bär′bə·kyo͞o) *n.* 1. A social gathering, usu. outdoors, at which meat is roasted over an open fire. 2. A whole animal carcass or any meat roasted over an open fire. 3. A grill or pit for roasting meat in this fashion. —*v.t.* **·cued, ·cu·ing** To roast (usu. beef or pork) over an open fire, often using a highly seasoned sauce. [< Sp. < Taino *barbacoa* framework of sticks]

barbed wire Fence wire having barbs.

bar·bel (bär′bəl) *n.* One of the soft threadlike appendages to the jaws, chin, or nostrils of certain fishes. [< L *barba* beard]

bar·ber (bär′bər) *n.* One who cuts hair, shaves beards, etc., as a business. ◆Collateral adjective: *tonsorial.* —*v.t.* To cut or dress the hair of; shave or trim the beard of. [< L *barba* beard]

bar·ber·ry (bär′ber′ē, -bər·ē) *n.* *pl.* **·ries** 1. A shrub bearing bright red, oblong berries. 2. Its acid berry. [< Med.L *berberis, barbaris*]

bar·ber·shop (bär′bər·shop′) *n.* The place of business of a barber.

bar·bi·can (bär′bi·kən) *n.* An outer fortification; outwork. [< OF *barbaquenne*]

bar·bi·tal (bär′bə·tôl, -tal) *n.* *Chem.* A white, odorless, bitter crystalline powder, used as a sedative and hypnotic.

bar·bit·u·rate (bär·bich′ər·it, bär′bə·to͝or′it, -tyo͝or′it) *n.* *Chem.* A salt or ester of barbituric acid, esp. one used as a sedative or sleeping pill.

bar·bi·tu·ric acid (bär′bə·to͝or′ik, -tyo͝or′-) *Chem.* A crystalline powder, from which several sedative and hypnotic drugs are derived.

bar·ca·role (bär′kə·rōl) *n.* 1. A Venetian gondolier's song. 2. A musical composition imitating this. Also **bar′ca·rolle.** [< Ital. *barcaruola* boatman's song]

bard (bärd) *n.* 1. A Celtic poet and minstrel. 2. A poet. [< Celtic] —**bard′ic** *adj.*

bare (bâr) *adj.* 1. Without clothing or covering; naked. 2. Open to view; exposed. 3. Without the usual furnishings or equipment; empty. 4. Unadorned; plain. 5. Just sufficient; mere. —*v.t.* **bared, bar·ing** To make or lay bare; reveal; expose. [OE *bær*] —**bare′ness** *n.*

bare·back (bâr′bak′) *adj.* Riding a horse without a saddle. —*adv.* Without a saddle.

bare·faced (bâr′fāst′) *adj.* 1. Having the face bare. 2. Impudent; audacious. —**bare·fac·ed·ly** (bâr′fā′sid·lē, -fāst′lē) *adv.*

bare·foot (bâr′fo͝ot′) *adj.* & *adv.* With the feet bare. Also **bare′foot′ed.**

bare·hand·ed (bâr′han′did) *adj.* & *adv.* 1. With the hands uncovered. 2. Without a weapon, tool, etc.

bare·head·ed (bâr′hed′id) *adj. & adv.* With the head bare. Also **bare′head′**.
bare·leg·ged (bâr′leg′id, -legd′) *adj. & adv.* With the legs bare.
bare·ly (bâr′lē) *adv.* 1. Only just; scarcely. 2. Openly; plainly.
barf (bärf) *v.i. Informal* To vomit. [Origin unknown]
bar·gain (bär′gən) *n.* 1. A mutual agreement between persons, esp. one to buy or sell goods. 2. That which is agreed upon or the terms of the agreement. 3. An article bought or offered at a low price. **—into the bargain** In addition; besides. **—to strike a bargain** To come to an agreement. **—***v.i.* 1. To discuss terms for selling or buying. 2. To negotiate. **—***v.t.* 3. To trade or arrange by bargaining. **—to bargain for** To expect; count on: more than I *bargained for.* [< OF *bargaine*] **—bar′gain·er** *n.*
barge (bärj) *n.* 1. A flat-bottomed freight boat or lighter for harbors and inland waters. 2. A large boat for pleasure, pageants, or state occasions. **—***v.* **barged, barg·ing** *v.t.* 1. To transport by barge. **—***v.i.* 2. To move clumsily and slowly. 3. *Informal* **a** To collide: with *into.* **b** To enter or intrude rudely or awkwardly: with *in* or *in on.* [< LL *barga*]
bar·gel·lo (bär·jel′ō) *n.* Needlework using unslanted, uncrossed stitches, usu. to form geometric patterns. [from work in the *Bargello,* a museum in Florence, Italy]
barge·man (bärj′mən) *n. pl.* **·men** (-mən) One in charge of or employed on a barge. Also *Brit.* **bar·gee** (bär·jē′).
bar·i·at·rics (bar·ē·at′riks) *n.pl.* (*construed as sing.*) The medical specialty dealing with obesity. [< Gk. *baros* weight + *iatros* physician] **—bar·i·a·tri′cian** (-ē·ə·trish′ən) *n.*
bar·ite (bâr′īt) *n.* A heavy, glassy, crystalline barium sulfate.
bar·i·tone (bar′ə·tōn) *n.* 1. A male voice of a register higher than bass and lower than tenor. 2. One having such a voice. 3. An instrument having a similar range. **—***adj.* Of or pertaining to a baritone. [< Gk. *barys* deep + *tonos* tone]
bar·i·um (bâr′ē·əm) *n.* A silver white to yellow, malleable, metallic element (symbol Ba) occurring in combination and forming salts. [< Gk. *barys* heavy]
bark[1] (bärk) *n.* 1. The short, explosive cry of a dog. 2. Any sound like this. **—***v.i.* 1. To utter a bark, as a dog, or to make a sound like a bark. 2. To speak sharply. 3. *Slang* To solicit customers at the entrance to a show. **—***v.t.* 4. To say roughly and curtly. **—to bark up the wrong tree** *Informal* To be mistaken as to one's object or the means of attaining it. [OE *beorcan*]
bark[2] (bärk) *n.* The rind or covering of a woody stem or root. **—***v.t.* 1. To remove the bark from; scrape. 2. To rub off the skin of. [< Scand.]
bark[3] (bärk) *n.* A sailing vessel of three or more masts, square-rigged on all but the mizzenmast. [< LL *barca* bark]
bar·keep·er (bär′kē′pər) *n.* 1. One who owns or manages a bar where alcoholic liquors are served. 2. A bartender. Also **bar′keep′**.
bar·ken·tine (bär′kən·tēn) *n.* A sailing vessel of three or more masts, square-rigged on the foremast and fore-and-aft-rigged on the other masts. [< BARK[3]]
bark·er (bär′kər) *n.* One who advertises a show, etc., at its entrance.
bar·ley (bär′lē) *n.* 1. A hardy cereal grass. 2. The grain borne by this grass. [OE *bærlīc*]
bar·ley·corn (bär′lē·kôrn) *n.* Barley, or a grain of barley.
Bar·ley·corn, John A personification of malt liquor, or of liquors in general.
bar·maid (bär′mād) *n.* A female bartender.
bar mitz·vah (bär mits′və) In Judaism, a boy commencing his thirteenth year, the age of religious duty; also, the ceremony celebrating this. [< Hebrew, son of the commandment]
barn (bärn) *n.* A building for storing hay, stabling livestock, etc. [OE *bern*]
bar·na·cle (bär′nə·kəl) *n.* A marine shellfish that attaches itself to rocks, ship bottoms, etc. [ME *bernacle*] **—bar′na·cled** *adj.*
barn dance A social dance held in a barn and usu. consisting of square dances.
barn owl An owl of nearly world-wide distribution, often found in barns.
barn·storm (bärn′stôrm′) *v.i. Informal* To tour rural districts, giving shows, political speeches, exhibitions of stunt flying, etc. **—barn′storm′er** *n.* **—barn′storm′ing** *adj. & n.*
barn·yard (bärn′yärd′) *n.* A yard adjoining a barn. **—***adj.* Of or fit for a barnyard; smutty.
baro- *combining form* Weight; atmospheric pressure: *barometer.* [< Gk. *baros* weight]
bar·o·gram (bar′ə·gram) *n.* The record of a barograph.
bar·o·graph (bar′ə·graf) *n.* A self-recording barometer. **—bar′o·graph′ic** *adj.*
ba·rom·e·ter (bə·rom′ə·ter) *n.* 1. An instrument for measuring atmospheric pressure. 2. Anything that indicates changes. **—bar·o·met·ric** (bar′ə·met′rik) or **·ri·cal** *adj.* **—bar′o·met′ri·cal·ly** *adv.*
bar·on (bar′ən) *n.* 1. A member of the lowest order of hereditary nobility. 2. One who has great power in a commercial field. [< LL *baro, baronis* man] **—ba·ro·ni·al** (bə·rō′nē·əl) *adj.*
bar·on·age (bar′ən·ij) *n.* 1. Barons collectively. 2. The dignity or rank of a baron.
bar·o·ness (bar′ən·is) *n.* 1. The wife or widow of a baron. 2. A woman holding a barony in her own right.
bar·on·et (bar′ən·it, bar·ə·net′) *n.* 1. A hereditary English title, below that of baron and not part of the nobility. 2. A bearer of the title. **—bar′on·et·cy** *n.*
bar·o·ny (bar′ə·nē) *n. pl.* **·nies** The rank, dignity, or domain of a baron.
ba·roque (bə·rōk′) *adj.* 1. Of or characteristic of a style of art and architecture developed in Europe in the late 16th and 17th centuries, characterized by extravagantly contorted classical forms and curvilinear ornament. 2. *Music* Of a style prevalent esp. in the 17th century, characterized by rich harmonies, ornamentation, and brilliant effects. 3. Fantastic in style; elaborately ornamented. **—***n.* The baroque style in art. [< Pg. *barroco* rough or imperfect pearl]
ba·rouche (bə·ro͞osh′) *n.* A four-wheeled carriage with folding top and an outside seat for the driver. [< L *bis* twice + *rota* wheel]
bar·racks (bar′əks) *n.pl.* (*construed as sing. or pl.*) A building or group of buildings for

the housing of soldiers. [< Ital. *baracca* soldier's tent]

bar·ra·cu·da (bar′ə·ko͞o′də) *n. pl.* **·da** or **·das** A voracious fish of tropical seas. [< Sp.]

bar·rage (bə·räzh′) *n.* 1. *Mil.* A curtain of fire designed to protect troops by impeding enemy movements. 2. Any overwhelming attack, as of words or blows. —*v.t.* & *v.i.* **·raged, ·rag·ing** To lay down or subject to a barrage. [< F]

bar·ra·try (bar′ə·trē) *n. pl.* **·tries** *Law* 1. Any willful and unlawful act by the master or crew of a ship, causing loss or injury to the owners. 2. The offense of inciting lawsuits, quarrels, etc. [< OF *barat* fraud]

barred (bärd) *adj.* 1. Having or secured with bars. 2. Prohibited. 3. Striped.

bar·rel (bar′əl) *n.* 1. A large, usu. bulging vessel usu. of wood, flat at the base and top. 2. As much as a barrel will hold. 3. Something resembling or having the form of a barrel, as the tube of a gun. —*v.* **bar·reled** or **·relled, bar·rel·ing** or **·rel·ling** *v.t.* 1. To put or pack in a barrel. —*v.i.* 2. *Slang* To move fast. [< OF *baril*]

bar·rel·house (bar′əl·hous′) *n. Slang* 1. A cheap drinking house. 2. An early style of jazz.

barrel roll A maneuver in which an airplane rolls on its longitudinal axis.

bar·ren (bar′ən) *adj.* 1. Not producing or incapable of producing offspring; sterile. 2. Not productive; unfruitful; unprofitable. 3. Lacking in interest; dull. 4. Empty; devoid. —*n. Usu. pl.* A tract of level, scrubby land. [< OF *baraigne*] —**bar′ren·ly** *adv.* —**bar′ren·ness** *n.*

bar·rette (bə·ret′) *n.* A clasp used to keep hair in place. [< F, dim. of *barre* bar]

bar·ri·cade (bar′ə·kād′, bar′ə·kād) *n.* 1. A barrier hastily built for obstruction or defense. 2. Any barrier or obstruction. —*v.t.* **·cad·ed, ·cad·ing** To enclose, obstruct, or defend with a barricade. [< Sp. *barrica* barrel; the first barricades were barrels filled with earth, stones, etc.]

bar·ri·er (bar′ē·ər) *n.* 1. A fence, wall, gate, etc., erected to bar passage. 2. Any obstacle or obstruction. [< OF *barre* bar]

barrier reef A long, narrow ridge of rock or coral parallel to the coast and close to or above the surface of the sea.

bar·ring (bär′ing) *prep.* Excepting; apart from.

bar·ri·o (bär′i·ō) *n. pl.* **·ri·os** 1. A district of a city in Spanish-speaking countries. 2. In the U.S., a district of a city inhabited by Spanish-speaking people. [< Sp.]

bar·ris·ter (bar′is·tər) *n.* In England, a member of the legal profession who argues cases in the courts.

bar·room (bär′ro͞om′, -ro͝om′) *n.* A room where alcoholic liquors are served at a bar.

bar·row[1] (bar′ō) *n.* 1. A frame or tray with handles at either end, used for transporting loads. 2. A wheelbarrow. 3. The load carried on a barrow. 4. *Brit.* A pushcart. [OE *bearwe* < *beran* to bear]

bar·row[2] (bar′ō) *n.* A mound of earth or stones built over a grave. [OE *beorg*]

bar sinister *Heraldry* A charge believed to indicate bastardy.

bar·tend·er (bär′ten′dər) *n.* One who mixes and serves alcoholic drinks over a bar.

bar·ter (bär′tər) *v.i.* 1. To trade by exchange of goods or services without use of money. —*v.t.* 2. To trade (goods or services) for something of equal value. —*n.* The act of bartering; exchange of goods. [< OF *barater* to exchange] —**bar′ter·er** *n.*

Bart·lett (bärt′lit) *n.* A pear introduced by Enoch Bartlett. Also **Bartlett pear.**

Ba·ruch (bə·ro͞ok′, bâr′ək) A book in the Old Testament Apocrypha.

ba·sal (bā′səl) *adj.* 1. Of, at, or forming the base. 2. Basic; fundamental. —**ba′sal·ly** *adv.*

basal metabolism *Physiol.* The minimum energy required by the body at rest in maintaining essential vital activities, measured by the rate (**basal metabolic rate**) of oxygen intake and heat discharge.

ba·salt (bə·sôlt′, bas′ôlt) *n.* A dense, dark volcanic rock. [< L *basaltes* dark marble] —**ba·sal′tic** *adj.*

bas·cule (bas′kyo͞ol) *n.* A mechanical apparatus used in a kind of drawbridge (**bascule bridge**) operated by a counterpoise. [< F, seesaw]

base[1] (bās) *n.* 1. The lowest or supporting part of anything; bottom. 2. An underlying principle or foundation. 3. The essential or fundamental ingredient. 4. Any point, line, or quantity from which an inference, measurement, or reckoning is made. 5. *Geom.* The side of a polygon or solid figure on which it rests. 6. *Mil.* A locality or installation from which operations are projected or supported. 7. *Chem.* A compound capable of so uniting with an acid as to neutralize it and form a salt. 8. In baseball, any of the four points of the diamond, or the bag or plate marking one of these. —**off base** *Slang* Thinking, speaking, etc., erroneously. —*v.t.* **based, bas·ing** 1. To place on a foundation or basis; ground; establish: with *on* or *upon.* 2. To form a base for. —*adj.* 1. Serving as a base. 2. Situated at or near the base. [< Gk. *bainein* to go]

base[2] (bās) *adj.* 1. Morally low; vile; contemptible. 2. Menial; degrading: *base* flattery. 3. Low in value: said of metals. 4. Debased, as money; counterfeit: *base* coin. [< LL *bassus* low] —**base′ly** *adv.* —**base′ness** *n.*

base·ball (bās′bôl′) *n.* 1. A game played with a wooden bat and a hard ball by two teams of nine players each, one team being at bat and the other in the field, alternately. 2. The ball used in this game.

base·board (bās′bôrd′) *n.* 1. A board along an interior wall, next to the floor. 2. Any board forming a base.

base·born (bās′bôrn′) *adj.* 1. Of humble birth. 2. Born out of wedlock. 3. Mean; vile.

base hit In baseball, a batted ball that enables the batter to reach a base unaided by a defensive error and without a force play: also called *hit.*

base·less (bās′lis) *adj.* Without foundation in fact; groundless. —**base′less·ness** *n.*

base line 1. In baseball, a path connecting successive bases. 2. A line, value, etc., taken as a base for measurement or comparison.

base·ment (bās′mənt) *n.* The lowest story of a building, usu. wholly or partly underground.

base runner In baseball, a member of the team at bat who has reached a base.

bash (bash) *Informal v.t.* To strike heavily; smash in. —*n.* 1. A smashing blow. 2. A lively party. [? Akin to Dan. *baske* thwack]

bash·ful (bash′fəl) *adj.* 1. Shy; timid. 2. Characterized by timid modesty: a *bashful* glance. [< ABASH + -FUL] —**bash′ful·ly** *adv.* —**bash′ful·ness** *n.*

ba·sic (bā′sik) *adj.* 1. Essential; fundamental. 2. *Chem.* Of, pertaining to, or producing a base. —**ba′si·cal·ly** *adv.*

bas·il (baz′əl, bāz′əl) *n.* An aromatic plant of the mint family, used in cooking. [< Gk. *basilikon* royal]

bas·i·lar (bas′ə·lər) *adj.* Pertaining to or situated at the base, esp. of the skull; basal. Also **bas′i·lar′y** (-ə·ler′ē).

ba·sil·i·ca (bə·sil′i·kə) *n.* 1. In ancient Rome, a rectangular building divided by columns into a nave and two side aisles, used as a place of assembly. 2. A building of this type used as a Christian church. [< Gk. *basilikē* (*stoa*) royal (hall), fem. of *basilikos*] —**ba·sil′i·can** *adj.*

bas·i·lisk (bas′ə·lisk) *n.* 1. A fabled reptile whose breath and look were said to be fatal. 2. A tropical American lizard having an erectile crest on the head. [< Gk. *basiliskos*, dim. of *basileus* king]

ba·sin (bā′sən) *n.* 1. A round, wide, shallow vessel, often with sloping sides, used for holding liquids. 2. Any vessel or depression resembling this. 3. The amount that a basin will hold. 4. A sink or washbowl. 5. *Geog.* **a** Any large depression in the earth's surface, as the bed of a lake or ocean. **b** The region drained by a river. [< LL *bacca* bowl]

ba·sis (bā′sis) *n. pl.* **·ses** (bā′sēz) 1. That on which anything rests; foundation; base. 2. Fundamental principle; groundwork. 3. The chief component of a thing. [< Gk., base, pedestal]

bask (bask) *v.i.* 1. To lie in and enjoy a pleasant warmth, as of the sun or a fire. 2. To enjoy or benefit from compliments, a favorable opinion, etc.: with *in*. [< ON *badhask* to bathe oneself]

bas·ket (bas′kit) *n.* 1. A container made of interwoven splints, rushes, strips of wood, etc. 2. Something like a basket in form or use. 3. The amount a basket will hold. 4. In basketball: **a** One of the goals, a metal ring with a cord net suspended from it. **b** A score made by throwing the ball through the basket. [ME]

bas·ket·ball (bas′kit·bôl′) *n.* 1. A game played by two teams on a court, in which the object is to throw the ball through an elevated goal (basket). 2. The ball used in this game.

bas·ket·ry (bas′kit·rē) *n.* 1. Baskets collectively; basketwork. 2. The art of making baskets.

basket weave A weave with two or more warp and filling threads woven side by side to resemble a plaited basket.

bas·ket·work (bas′kit·wûrk′) *n.* Work done in basket weave or resembling it.

ba·so·phile (bā′sə·fīl, -fil) *n. Biol.* A tissue or cell having a special affinity for basic staining dyes. [< BASIC + -PHILE] —**ba·so·phil·ic** (bā′sə·fil′ik), **ba·soph·i·lous** (bā·sof′ə·ləs) *adj.*

basque (bask) *n.* A woman's closely fitting bodice.

Basque (bask) *n.* 1. One of a people of unknown origin living in the western Pyrenees in Spain and France. 2. The language of the Basque people. —*adj.* Of the Basques.

bas-re·lief (bä′ri·lēf′, bas′-) *n.* Sculpture in which the figures project only slightly from the background. [< F < Ital. *basso* low + *rilievo* relief]

bass[1] (bas) *n. pl.* **bass** or **bass·es** Any of various spiny-finned marine and fresh-water food fishes. [OE *bærs*]

bass[2] (bās) *Music n.* 1. The lowest-pitched male singing voice. 2. The notes in the lowest register of the piano, pipe organ, etc. 3. The lowest part in vocal or instrumental music. 4. One who sings or an instrument that plays such a part. —*adj.* 1. Low in pitch; having a low musical range. 2. Of or for a bass or basses. [< OF *bas* low]

bass drum (bās) The largest of the drums, beaten on both heads and having a deep sound.

bas·set (bas′it) *n.* A hound characterized by a long, low body, long ears, and short, crooked forelegs. Also **basset hound.** [< OF, dim. of *bas* low]

bas·si·net (bas′ə·net′) *n.* A basket used as a baby's cradle, usu. with a hood over one end. [< F]

bas·so (bas′ō, bäs′ō; *Ital.* bäs′sō) *n. pl.* **bas·sos** (bas′ōz, bäs′ōz), *Ital.* **bas·si** (bäs′sē) 1. A bass singer. 2. The bass part. [< Ital., low]

bas·soon (ba·sōōn′, bə-) *n. Music* A large, low-pitched woodwind instrument. [< Ital. *basso* low]

bass viol (bās) *Music* The double bass.

bass·wood (bas′wŏŏd′) *n.* The American linden.

bast (bast) *n. Bot.* The fibrous inner bark of trees, originally of the linden, used in making cordage. [OE *bæst*]

bas·tard (bas′tərd) *n.* 1. An illegitimate child. 2. Any irregular, inferior, or counterfeit thing. 3. *Slang* A worthless or cruel man. —*adj.* 1. Born out of wedlock. 2. False; spurious. 3. Abnormal or irregular in size, shape, etc. [< OF] —**bas′tard·ly** *adj.* —**bas′tard·y** *n.*

bas·tard·ize (bas′tər·dīz) *v.t.* **·ized, ·iz·ing** 1. To prove to be or proclaim to be a bastard. 2. To make degenerate; debase. —**bas′tard·i·za′tion** *n.*

baste[1] (bāst) *v.t.* **bast·ed, bast·ing** To sew loosely together, esp. with long stitches. [< OHG *bestan* to sew with bast]

baste[2] (bāst) *v.t.* **bast·ed, bast·ing** To moisten (meat or fish) with drippings, butter, etc., while cooking. [? < OF *basser* to soak, moisten]

baste[3] (bāst) *v.t.* **bast·ed, bast·ing** *Informal* 1. To beat; thrash. 2. To attack verbally; abuse. [Prob. < Scand.]

Bas·tille (bas·tēl′, *Fr.* bȧs·tē′y′) A prison in Paris, stormed and captured in the French Revolution on July 14, 1789.

bas·ti·na·do (bas′tə·nā′dō) *n. pl.* **·does** 1. A beating with a stick, usu. on the soles of the feet. 2. A stick or cudgel. Also **bas′ti·nade′** (-nād′). [< Sp. *baston* cudgel]

bast·ing (bās′ting) *n.* 1. The act of sewing loosely together. 2. The thread used. 3. *pl.* Long, loose stitches.

bas·tion (bas′chən, -tē·ən) *n.* **1.** In fortifications, a projecting part of a rampart. **2.** Any fortified position. [< Ital. *bastire* to build] **—bas′tioned** *adj.*

bat[1] (bat) *n.* **1.** In baseball and similar games: **a** A stick or club for striking the ball. **b** The act of batting. **c** One's turn for batting. **2.** Any heavy cudgel or club. **3.** *Informal* A blow, as with a stick. **4.** *Slang* A drunken spree. **—to go to bat for** *Informal* To defend; speak up for. **—v. bat·ted, bat·ting** *v.i.* **1.** In baseball and other games, to use a bat or take a turn at bat. **—v.t. 2.** To strike with or as with a bat. [OE *batt* cudgel]

bat[2] (bat) *n.* A nocturnal flying mammal having elongated forelimbs and digits that support a thin wing membrane. **—to have bats in the belfry** *Slang* To be crazy. [ME *bakke*]

bat[3] (bat) *v.t.* **bat·ted, bat·ting** *Informal* To wink. **—not bat an eye** *Informal* Not show surprise.

batch (bach) *n.* **1.** A quantity or number taken together. **2.** The amount of bread produced at one time. **3.** Any set of things made, done, etc., at one time. [ME *bacche*]

bate (bāt) *v.t. & v.i.* **bat·ed, bat·ing** To restrain; decrease. **—with bated breath** In a state of fear, suspense, expectation, etc. [Var. of ABATE]

ba·teau (ba·tō′) *n. pl.* **·teaux** (-tōz′) A light, flat-bottomed boat. [< OF *batel*]

bat·fish (bat′fish′) *n.* **1.** A saltwater fish with a batlike appearance. **2.** A sting ray.

bath (bath) *n. pl.* **baths** (bat͟hz, baths) **1.** A washing or immersing of something, esp. the body, in water or other liquid. **2.** The liquid used for this. **3.** The container for such a liquid; a bathtub. **4.** A bathroom. **5.** *Often pl.* A set of rooms or a building equipped for bathing. **6.** *Often pl.* An establishment or resort where bathing is part of a health treatment. [OE *bæth*]

bathe (bāt͟h) *v.* **bathed, bath·ing** *v.t.* **1.** To place in liquid; immerse. **2.** To wash; wet; apply liquid to. **—v.i. 3.** To wash oneself; take a bath. **4.** To be covered or suffused as if with liquid: to *bathe* in sunshine. [OE *bathian*] **—bath′er** *n.*

bath·house (bath′hous′) *n.* **1.** A building with facilities for bathing. **2.** A building used for changing into or out of bathing suits.

bath·ing suit (bāt͟h′ing) A garment worn for swimming.

batho- *combining form* Depth. [< Gk. *bathos*]

bath·o·lith (bath′ə·lith) *n. Geol.* A large, irregular mass of igneous rock, often forming the core of mountain ranges. [< BATHO- + -LITH] **—bath′o·lith′ic** *adj.*

ba·thos (bā′thos) *n.* **1.** A descent from the lofty to the commonplace in discourse; anticlimax. **2.** Insincere pathos; sentimentality. [< Gk. *bathys* deep]

bath·robe (bath′rōb′) *n.* A long, loose garment for wear before and after bathing.

bath·room (bath′ro͞om′, -ro͝om′) *n.* **1.** A room in which to bathe. **2.** A toilet.

bath·tub (bath′tub′) *n.* A vessel in which to bathe.

bathy- *combining form* Deep; of the sea or ocean depths: *bathysphere.* [< Gk. *bathys*]

bath·y·scaph (bath′ə·skaf) *n.* A free bathysphere, capable of ocean depths below 35,000 feet. [< BATHY- + Gk. *skaphē* bowl]

bath·y·sphere (bath′ə·sfir) *n.* A spherical diving bell equipped with windows for deep-sea observations.

ba·tik (bə·tēk′, bat′ik) *n.* **1.** A process for coloring fabrics, in which the parts not to be dyed are covered with wax. **2.** The fabric so colored. [< Malay]

ba·tiste (bə·tēst′) *n.* A fine cotton fabric in plain weave. [after Jean *Baptiste,* 13th c. French linen weaver]

ba·ton (ba·ton′) *n.* **1.** A short staff or truncheon borne as an emblem of authority. **2.** *Music* A slender stick used by a conductor. [< OF *baston* < LL *bastum* stick]

ba·tra·chi·an (bə·trā′kē·ən) *adj.* Of or pertaining to a former class of amphibians, esp. to frogs and toads; amphibian. **—n.** A frog or toad. [< Gk. *batrachos* frog]

bats (bats) *adj. Slang* Batty.

bat·tal·ion (bə·tal′yən) *n.* **1.** *Mil.* **a** A unit consisting of a headquarters and two or more companies, batteries, or comparable units. **b** A body of troops. **2.** *Usu. pl.* A large group or number. [< Ital. *battaglia* battle]

bat·ten[1] (bat′n) *v.i. & v.t.* To grow or make fat, as cattle. [< ON *batna* to grow better, improve]

bat·ten[2] (bat′n) *n.* **1.** A light strip of wood, as for covering a joint between boards. **2.** *Naut.* A thin strip of wood placed in a sail to keep it flat or for fastening a tarpaulin over a hatch. **—v.t.** To fasten with battens: with *up* or *down.*

bat·ter[1] (bat′ər) *v.t.* **1.** To strike with repeated, violent blows. **2.** To damage or injure with blows or with hard usage. **—v.i. 3.** To pound or beat with blows. [< L *battuere* to beat]

bat·ter[2] (bat′ər) *n.* In baseball, the player whose turn it is to bat.

bat·ter[3] (bat′ər) *n.* A mixture, as of eggs, flour, and milk, beaten for use in cookery. [? < OF *battre* to beat]

bat·ter·ing-ram (bat′ər·ing·ram′) *n.* A long, stout beam, used in ancient warfare for battering down walls.

bat·ter·y (bat′ər·ē, ba′trē) *n. pl.* **·ter·ies** **1.** Any unit, apparatus, or grouping in which a series or set of parts or components is assembled to serve a common end. **2.** *Electr.* One or more cells operating together as a single source of direct current. **3.** *Mil.* **a** An artillery unit equivalent to an infantry company. **b** A group of guns, rockets, or related equipment forming an artillery unit. **4.** *Naval* The guns of a warship, or a specific group of them. **5.** *Law* The illegal beating or touching of another person. [< OF *battre* to beat]

bat·ting (bat′ing) *n.* Wadded cotton or wool prepared in sheets or rolls, used for interlining, stuffing mattresses, etc.

bat·tle (bat′l) *n.* **1.** A combat between hostile armies or fleets. **2.** Any fighting, conflict, or struggle. **—v. ·tled, ·tling** *v.i.* **1.** To contend in or as in battle; struggle; strive. **—v.t. 2.** To fight. [< L *battuere* to beat] **—bat′tler** *n.*

bat·tle-ax (bat′l·aks′) *n.* **1.** A large ax formerly used in battle; a broadax. **2.** *Slang* A formidable, disagreeable woman. Also **bat′tle-axe′.**

battle cruiser A war vessel having cruiser

speed, but less heavily armored than a battleship.

battle cry 1. A shout uttered by troops in battle. 2. A slogan or distinctive phrase used in any conflict or contest.

bat·tle·dore (bat′l·dôr) *n.* 1. A paddle or racket used to strike a shuttlecock. 2. A game resembling badminton: also **battledore and shuttlecock.** [? < Provençal *batedor*, an implement for beating laundry]

battle fatigue Combat fatigue.

bat·tle·field (bat′l·fēld′) *n.* The terrain on which a battle is fought. Also **bat′tle·ground′.**

bat·tle·ment (bat′l·mənt) *n.* A parapet indented along its upper line. [< OF *ba(s)tillier* to fortify]

bat·tle·ship (bat′l·ship′) *n.* A warship of great size, belonging to the class with heaviest armor and armament.

bat·ty (bat′ē) *adj.* **·ti·er, ·ti·est** *Slang* Crazy; odd.

bau·ble (bô′bəl) *n.* A worthless, showy trinket. [< OF *baubel* toy, ? < L *bellus* pretty]

baux·ite (bôk′sīt) *n.* A claylike substance containing aluminum oxide or hydroxide, the principal ore of aluminum. [after Les *Baux*, France]

Ba·var·i·an (bə·vâr′ē·ən) *n.* 1. A native or inhabitant of Bavaria. 2. The High German dialect spoken in Bavaria. —**Ba·var′i·an** *adj.*

bawd (bôd) *n.* The keeper of a brothel. [ME *bawde*]

bawd·y (bô′dē) *adj.* **bawd·i·er, bawd·i·est** Obscene; indecent. —**bawd′i·ly** *adv.* —**bawd′·i·ness** *n.*

bawd·y·house (bô′dē·hous′) *n.* A brothel.

bawl (bôl) *v.t.* 1. To call out noisily; bellow. —*v.i.* 2. To cry or sob noisily. —**to bawl out** *Slang* To berate; scold. [Prob. < Med.L *baulare* to bark] —**bawl** *n.* —**bawl′er** *n.*

bay[1] (bā) *n.* A body of water partly enclosed by land; an inlet of the sea. [< OF *baie* < LL *baia*]

bay[2] (bā) *n.* 1. *Archit.* **a** A bay window. **b** An extension or wing of a building. 2. Any opening or recess in a wall. 3. *Aeron.* A compartment in an aircraft. [< L *badare* to gape]

bay[3] (bā) *adj.* Reddish brown: said esp. of horses. —*n.* 1. A reddish brown color. 2. A horse (or other animal) of this color. [< F *bai* < L *badius*]

bay[4] (bā) *n.* A deep bark or cry, as of dogs in hunting. —**at bay** 1. Unable to escape; cornered. 2. Kept off, as by one's quarry. —*v.i.* 1. To utter a deep-throated cry, as a hound. —*v.t.* 2. To utter with or as with such a cry. [< L *badare* to gape]

bay[5] (bā) *n.* 1. A laurel wreath, bestowed as a garland of honor, esp. on a poet. 2. The bayberry. [< F *baie* < L *bacca* berry]

bay·ber·ry (bā′ber′ē, -bər·ē) *n. pl.* **·ries** 1. A tree or shrub having aromatic berries, as the wax myrtle or laurel; also, its fruit. 2. A tropical tree yielding an oil used in bay rum.

bay leaf The leaf of the laurel, used as a cooking herb.

bay·o·net (bā′ə·nit, -net, bā′ə·net′) *n.* A daggerlike weapon attachable to the muzzle of a firearm, used in close fighting. —*v.t.* **·net·ed, ·net·ing** To stab or pierce with a bayonet. [after *Bayonne*, France, where first made]

bay·ou (bī′o͞o) *n.* A marshy inlet or outlet of a lake, river, etc. [< dial. F < Choctaw *bayuk* small stream]

bay rum An aromatic liquid used in medicines and cosmetics, originally distilled from the leaves of the bayberry.

bay window A window structure projecting from the wall of a building and forming a recess within.

ba·zaar (bə·zär′) *n.* 1. An Oriental market or street of shops. 2. A shop or store for the sale of miscellaneous wares. 3. A sale of miscellaneous articles, as for charity. [< Persian *bāzār* market]

ba·zoo·ka (bə·zo͞o′kə) *n. Mil.* A tubular, portable weapon that fires an explosive rocket. [from *bazooka*, a comical musical instrument]

be (bē, *unstressed* bi) *v.i.* **been, be·ing** Present indicative: I **am**, he, she, it **is**, we, you, they **are**; past indicative: I, he, she, it **was**, we, you, they **were**; present subjunctive: **be**; past subjunctive: **were**; archaic forms: thou **art** (present), thou **wast** or **wert** (past) 1. As a substantive verb, *be* is used to mean: **a** To have existence, truth, or actuality: There *are* bears in the zoo. **b** To take place; happen: The party *is* today. **c** To stay or continue: She *was* here for one week. 2. As a copulative verb between the subject and predicate noun or adjective: Ann *is* my friend; He *is* sick. 3. As an auxiliary verb, *be* is used: **a** With the present participle of other verbs to express continued action: I *am* working. **b** With the past participle of transitive verbs to form the passive voice: He *was* injured. **c** With the past participle of intransitive verbs to form the perfect tense: I *am* finished. **d** With the infinitive or present participle to express purpose, duty, possibility, futurity, etc.: We *are* to start on Monday.

be- *prefix* Forms words meaning:

1. Around; throughout:

beclasp	**begird**
becrust	**bescreen**
bedabble	**beshroud**
bedarken	**besmother**
bedim	**bespatter**
bedrape	**bespeckle**

2. Completely; thoroughly:

beclamor	**bemadden**
bedrench	**bemuddle**
befool	**bescourge**

3. Off; away: *behead.*

4. About; over; against:

besmile	**beswarm**
bestraddle	**bethunder**

5. To provide with; cover with; affect by:

beblood	**begloom**
becharm	**bejewel**
bedrape	**beslipper**
beflower	**bewhisker**
befringe	**bewig**

6. Conspicuously furnished with:

becupided	**beringed**
becurtained	**berobed**
bedotted	**bespangled**
befrilled	**bespectacled**
bejeweled	**besteepled**
beribboned	**bewreathed**

[OE *be-*, *bi-* < *bī* near, by]

beach (bēch) *n.* The sloping shore of a body

of water, esp. a sandy shore. —*v.t.* & *v.i.* To drive or haul up (a boat or ship) on a beach; strand. [Origin unknown]

beach·comb·er (bēch′kō′mər) *n.* 1. A vagrant living on what he can find or beg around wharves and beaches. 2. A long wave rolling upon a beach.

beach·head (bēch′hed′) *n. Mil.* An area on a hostile shore established by an advance force, for the landing of troops, etc.

bea·con (bē′kən) *n.* 1. A signal, esp. a signal fire or light on a hill, building, etc., intended as a warning or guide. 2. A light, lighthouse, buoy, etc., set on a shore, shoal, or similar place to guide or warn mariners. 3. Anything that warns or signals. 4. *Aeron.* A mark, light, or radio transmitter used to plot flight courses. —*v.t.* 1. To furnish with or guide by a beacon. —*v.i.* 2. To shine as a beacon. [OE *bēacn* sign, signal]

bead (bēd) *n.* 1. A small, usually round, piece of glass, wood, stone, etc., pierced for stringing on thread or attaching to fabric as decoration. 2. *pl.* A string of beads; necklace. 3. *pl.* A rosary. 4. A drop of liquid. 5. A small knob used as the front sight of a gun. 6. *Archit.* A molding composed of a row of half-oval ornaments resembling a string of beads. —**to draw a bead on** To take careful aim at. —*v.t.* 1. To decorate with beads or beading. —*v.i.* 2. To collect in drops. [OE *gebed* prayer]

bead·ing (bē′ding) *n.* 1. Ornamentation with beads. 2. Material consisting of or ornamented with beads.

bea·dle (bēd′l) *n.* In the Church of England, a lay officer who ushers or keeps order. [< OF *bedel* messenger]

bead·work (bēd′wûrk′) *n.* 1. Decorative work made with or of beads. 2. *Archit.* A bead.

bead·y (bē′dē) *adj.* **bead·i·er, bead·i·est** 1. Small and glittering: *beady* eyes. 2. Covered with beads.

bea·gle (bē′gəl) *n.* A small, short-haired hound with short legs and drooping ears. [ME *begle*]

beak (bēk) *n.* 1. The horny, projecting mouth parts of birds. 2. A beaklike part or organ, as the horny jaws of turtles. 3. Something resembling a bird's beak, as the spout of a pitcher. [< F *bec* < LL *beccus*] —**beaked** *adj.*

beak·er (bē′kər) *n.* 1. A large, wide-mouthed drinking cup or goblet. 2. A cylindrical, flat-bottomed vessel with a lip for pouring, used in chemical analysis, etc. 3. The contents or capacity of a beaker. [< ON *bikarr*]

beam (bēm) *n.* 1. A long, heavy piece of wood, metal, or stone, shaped for use. 2. A horizontal piece forming part of the frame of a building or other structure. 3. *Naut.* **a** One of the heavy pieces of timber or iron set across a vessel to support the decks and stay the sides. **b** The greatest width of a vessel. 4. A ray of light, or a group of nearly parallel rays. 5. *Aeron.* A radio beam. 6. The widest part of anything. 7. *Slang* The hips. —**off the beam** *Informal* On the wrong track; wrong. —**on the beam** *Informal* In the right direction; just right; correct. —*v.t.* 1. To send out in beams or rays. 2. *Telecom.* To aim or transmit (a signal) in a specific direction. —*v.i.* 3. To emit light. 4. To smile radiantly. [OE *bēam* tree]

beam·ing (bē′ming) *adj.* Radiant; smiling; cheerful. —**beam′ing·ly** *adv.*

bean (bēn) *n.* 1. The oval, edible seed of any of various leguminous plants. 2. A plant that bears beans. 3. Any of several beanlike seeds or plants. 4. An immature bean pod, used as a vegetable. 5. *Slang* The head. 6. *Brit. Slang* Person; chap. —*v.t. Slang* To hit on the head. [OE *bēan*]

bean·ie (bē′nē) *n.* A small, brimless cap.

bean·pole (bēn′pōl′) *n.* A tall pole for a bean plant to climb on.

bear[1] (bâr) *v.* **bore** (*Archaic* **bare**), **borne, bear·ing** *v.t.* 1. To support; hold up. 2. To carry; convey. 3. To show visibly. 4. To conduct or guide. 5. To spread; disseminate. 6. To hold in the mind; maintain or entertain. 7. To suffer or endure; undergo. 8. To accept or acknowledge; assume, as responsibility. 9. To produce; give birth to. ◆In this sense, the participial form in the passive is **born,** except when followed by *by.* 10. To conduct, manage, or carry (oneself or a part of oneself). 11. To move by pressing against; drive. 12. To render; give: to *bear* witness. 13. To be able to withstand: to *bear* investigation. 14. To have or stand in (comparison or relation): with *to.* 15. To possess as a right or power: to *bear* title. —*v.i.* 16. To rest heavily; lean; press. 17. To produce fruit or young. 18. To move or lie in a certain direction; be pointed or aimed. 19. To be relevant; have reference: with *on* (or *upon*). —**to bear down** 1. To force down; overpower. 2. To exert oneself. —**to bear down on** (or **upon**) 1. To put pressure on. 2. To approach, esp. forcefully. —**to bear out** To support; confirm. —**to bear up** To keep up strength and spirits. [OE *beran* to carry, wear]

bear[2] (bâr) *n.* 1. A large mammal having a massive, thickly furred body and a very short tail, as the grizzly bear, polar bear, etc. ◆Collateral adjective: *ursine.* 2. Any of various other animals resembling the bear: ant *bear.* 3. A gruff, ill-mannered, or clumsy person. 4. An investor in the stock market who sells in the belief that a decline in prices is likely: opposed to *bull.* —*adj.* Of, pertaining to, or caused by stock-market bears, or a decline in prices. [OE *bera*]

bear·a·ble (bâr′ə·bəl) *adj.* Capable of being borne; endurable. —**bear′a·ble·ness** *n.* —**bear′a·bly** *adv.*

beard (bird) *n.* 1. The hair on a man's face, esp. on the chin, usu. excluding the mustache. 2. Any similar growth, as on the chin of an animal. 3. *Bot.* An awn. —*v.t.* 1. To take by the beard; pull the beard of. 2. To defy courageously. [OE] —**beard′ed** *adj.* —**beard′less** *adj.*

bear·er (bâr′ər) *n.* 1. One who or that which bears, carries, or upholds. 2. A person who bears or presents for payment a check, money order, etc. 3. A tree or vine producing fruit. 4. A carrier or porter.

bear·ing (bâr′ing) *n.* 1. Manner of conducting or carrying oneself; deportment. 2. The act, capacity, or period of producing. 3. That which is produced; crops; yield. 4. *Mech.* A part on which something rests, or in which a pin, journal, etc., turns. 5. The position or direction of an object or point. 6. *Often pl.* The situation of an object relative to that of another. 7. Reference or relation.

bear·ish (bâr′ish) *adj.* 1. Like a bear; rough; surly. 2. Tending toward, counting on, or causing low prices of stocks. —**bear′ish·ly** *adv.* —**bear′ish·ness** *n.*

bear·skin (bâr′skin′) *n.* The skin of a bear, or a coat, rug, etc., made of it.

beast (bēst) *n.* 1. Any animal except man; esp., any large quadruped. 2. Animal characteristics or animal nature. 3. A cruel, rude, or filthy person. [< L *bestia* beast]

beast·ly (bēst′lē) *adj.* **·li·er, ·li·est** 1. Resembling a beast; bestial. 2. *Informal* Disagreeable or nasty. —*adv. Brit. Slang* Very. —**beast′li·ness** *n.*

beat (bēt) *v.* **beat, beat·en** or **beat, beat·ing** *v.t.* 1. To strike repeatedly; pound. 2. To punish by blows; thrash; whip. 3. To dash or strike against. 4. To make, as one's way by or as by blows. 5. To flap; flutter, as wings. 6. To stir or mix rapidly so as to make lighter or frothier: to *beat* eggs. 7. To mark or measure as with a baton: to *beat* time. 8. To sound (a signal), as on a drum. 9. To hunt over; search. 10. To subdue or defeat. 11. To surpass; be superior to. 12. *Informal* To baffle: It *beats* me. —*v.i.* 13. To strike repeated blows or as if with blows. 14. To throb; pulsate. 15. *Physics* To alternate in intensity so as to pulsate. —**to beat about** To search. —**to beat about the bush** To approach a subject in a roundabout way. —**to beat down** To get (a seller) to accept a lower price. —**to beat it** *Slang* To depart hastily. —**to beat up (on)** *Informal* To thrash thoroughly. —*n.* 1. A stroke or blow. 2. A regular stroke, or its sound; pulsation; throb. 3. *Music* A regular pulsation; the basic unit of musical time. 4. The measured sound of verse; rhythm. 5. A line, round, or district regularly traversed, as by a sentry, policeman, or reporter. 6. *Slang* In journalism, a scoop. —*adj.* 1. *Informal* Fatigued; worn out. 2. *Informal* Of or pertaining to beatniks. [OE *bēatan*] —**beat′er** *n.*

beat·en (bēt′n) *adj.* 1. Shaped, worn down, or made thin by beating. 2. Mixed by beating. 3. Defeated; baffled. 4. Exhausted.

be·a·tif·ic (bē′ə·tif′ik) *adj.* Blissful; blessed. —**be′a·tif′i·cal·ly** *adv.*

be·at·i·fy (bē·at′ə·fī) *v.t.* **·fied, ·fy·ing** 1. To make supremely happy. 2. In the Roman Catholic Church, to declare as blessed and worthy of public honor. [< L *beatus* happy + *facere* to make] —**be·at′i·fi·ca′tion** *n.*

beat·ing (bē′ting) *n.* 1. The act of one who or that which beats. 2. Flogging. 3. Pulsation; throbbing, as of the heart. 4. A defeat.

be·at·i·tude (bē·at′ə·to͞od, -tyo͞od) *n.* Supreme blessedness or felicity. —**the Beatitudes** Eight declarations made by Jesus in the Sermon on the Mount. *Matt.* v 3–11 [< L *beatitudo* blessedness]

beat·nik (bēt′nik) *n.* *Informal* A nonconformist, or bohemian, of the 1950's.

beau (bō) *n.* *pl.* **beaus** or **beaux** (bōz) 1. A sweetheart or lover of a girl or woman. 2. A dandy. [< OF, var. of *bel* < L *bellus* fine, pretty]

Beau·fort scale (bō′fərt) *Meteorol.* A scale of wind velocities, ranging from 0 (calm) to 12 (hurricane). [after Sir Francis *Beaufort*, 1774–1857, British admiral]

beau monde (bō mônd′) *French* The fashionable world.

beau·te·ous (byo͞o′tē·əs) *adj.* Beautiful. —**beau′te·ous·ly** *adv.* —**beau′te·ous·ness** *n.*

beau·ti·cian (byo͞o·tish′ən) *n.* One who works in or operates a beauty parlor.

beau·ti·ful (byo͞o′tə·fəl) *adj.* Possessing the qualities or presenting an appearance of beauty, as in form or grace. —**beau′ti·ful·ly** *adv.*

beau·ti·fy (byo͞o′tə·fī) *v.t. & v.i.* **·fied, ·fy·ing** To make or grow beautiful. —**beau′ti·fi·ca′tion** *n.* —**beau′ti·fied** *adj.* —**beau′ti·fi′er** *n.*

beau·ty (byo͞o′tē) *n.* *pl.* **·ties** 1. The quality of objects, sounds, ideas, etc., that pleases and gratifies, as by their harmony, pattern, excellence, or truth. 2. One who or that which is beautiful, esp. a woman. 3. A special grace or charm. [< OF *biauté*, ult. < L *bellus* handsome, fine]

beauty parlor An establishment where women may go for hairdressing or other cosmetic treatment. Also **beauty salon, beauty shop.**

beauty spot 1. A small patch or mark put on the face to beautify by contrast. 2. A mole or similar natural mark. Also **beauty mark.**

beaux-arts (bō·zâr′) *n.pl. French* The fine arts. —*adj.* Of classical, decorative, usu. monumental style.

bea·ver[1] (bē′vər) *n.* 1. An amphibious rodent with a scaly, flat, oval tail and webbed hind feet, which builds dams in streams and is valued for its fur. 2. The fur of the beaver. 3. A high silk hat. [OE *beofor*]

bea·ver[2] (bē′vər) *n.* 1. A movable piece of armor covering the lower face. 2. The visor of a helmet. [< OF *bavé* saliva]

bea·ver·board (bē′vər·bôrd′) *n.* A light, stiff building material made of compressed or laminated wood pulp.

be·calm (bi·käm′) *v.t.* 1. *Naut.* To make (a sailing vessel) motionless for lack of wind. 2. To make calm; quiet.

be·came (bi·kām′) Past tense of BECOME.

be·cause (bi·kôz′) *conj.* For the reason that; on account of the fact that; since. —**because of** By reason of. [ME *bi cause* by cause]

beck (bek) *n.* A nod or other gesture of summons. —**at one's beck and call** Subject to one's slightest wish. [Short for BECKON]

beck·on (bek′ən) *v.t. & v.i.* 1. To signal or summon by sign or gesture. 2. To entice or lure. [OE *bīecnan, bēacnian* to make signs to]

be·cloud (bi·kloud′) *v.t.* To obscure with or as with clouds; darken; confuse.

be·come (bi·kum′) *v.* **·came, ·come, ·com·ing** *v.i.* 1. To come to be; grow to be. —*v.t.* 2. To be appropriate to; befit. 3. To be suitable to; show to advantage. —**to become of** To be the condition or fate of: What *became of* him? [OE *becuman* to happen, come about]

be·com·ing (bi·kum′ing) *adj.* 1. Appropriate; suitable. 2. Pleasing; attractive. —**be·com′ing·ly** *adv.*

bed (bed) *n.* 1. An article of furniture to rest or sleep on. 2. Any place or thing used for resting or sleeping. 3. A lodging, esp. for the night. 4. A heap or mass resembling a bed. 5. A plot of ground prepared for planting; also, the plants themselves. 6. The ground at the bottom of a body of water. 7. A part or surface that serves as a foundation or support. 8. *Geol.* Any layer in a mass of stratified rock; a seam. —*v.* **bed·ded, bed·ding** *v.t.* 1. To furnish with a bed. 2. To put to bed. 3. To make a bed for; provide with litter: often with *down:* to *bed* down cattle. —*v.i.* 4. To go to bed. [OE] —**bed′der** *n.*

Bed is used to make many self-explanatory words and phrases, as:

bedboard	**bed pad**
bedframe	**bedpost**
bed jacket	**bed sheet**
bed lamp	**bedstand**
bed light	**bedtime**
bedmaking	**bed tray**
bedmate	**bed warmer**

bed and board Lodging and meals.

be·daub (bi·dôb′) *v.t.* 1. To smear or daub; besmirch. 2. To ornament vulgarly or excessively.

be·daz·zle (bi·daz′əl) *v.t.* **·zled, ·zling** To confuse or blind by dazzling.

bed·bug (bed′bug′) *n.* A bloodsucking insect, infesting houses and esp. beds.

bed·clothes (bed′klōz′, -klōthz′) *n.pl.* Covering for a bed, as sheets, blankets, etc.

bed·ding (bed′ing) *n.* 1. A mattress and bedclothes. 2. Litter for animals to sleep on. 3. That which forms a bed or foundation.

be·deck (bi·dek′) *v.t.* To adorn.

be·dev·il (bi·dev′əl) *v.t.* **·iled** or **·illed, ·il·ing** or **·il·ling** 1. To harass or torment. 2. To worry or bewilder. 3. To possess with or as with a devil; bewitch. —**be·dev′il·ment** *n.*

be·dew (bi·dōō′, -dyōō′) *v.t.* To moisten with or as with dew.

bed·fel·low (bed′fel′ō) *n.* 1. One who shares a bed. 2. A companion; associate.

bed·lam (bed′ləm) *n.* 1. A place or scene of noisy confusion. 2. A lunatic asylum. [after *Bedlam,* an old London hospital for the insane]

bed linen Sheets, pillowcases, etc., for beds.

Bed·ou·in (bed′ōō·in) *n.* One of the nomadic Arabs of Syria, Arabia, etc. [< Arabic *badāwīn* desert dweller] —**Bed′ou·in** *adj.*

bed·pan (bed′pan′) *n.* 1. A shallow vessel to be used as a toilet by one confined to bed. 2. A pan for warming a bed.

be·drag·gle (bi·drag′əl) *v.t.* **·gled, ·gling** To make wet, soiled, or untidy. —**be·drag′gled** *adj.*

bed·rid·den (bed′rid′n) *adj.* Confined to bed. [OE *bed* bed + *rida* rider]

bed·rock (bed′rok′) *n.* 1. *Geol.* The solid rock underlying the looser materials of the earth's surface. 2. The lowest level; bottom. 3. Fundamental principles; foundation.

bed·roll (bed′rōl′) *n.* Bedding rolled to facilitate carrying.

bed·room (bed′rōōm′, -rŏŏm′) *n.* A room for sleeping.

bed·side (bed′sīd′) *n.* A space beside a bed, esp. of a sick person.

bed·sore (bed′sôr′) *n.* A sore caused by prolonged contact with a bed or bedclothes.

bed·spread (bed′spred′) *n.* An ornamental covering for a bed.

bed·spring (bed′spring′) *n.* The framework of springs supporting the mattress of a bed; also, any of such springs.

bed·stead (bed′sted′) *n.* A framework for supporting the springs and mattress of a bed.

bee (bē) *n.* 1. A four-winged insect feeding largely upon nectar and pollen, esp. the honeybee. 2. A social gathering for work, competition, entertainment, etc.: a quilting *bee.* [OE *bēo*]

beech (bēch) *n.* 1. A tree of temperate regions with smooth, ash-gray bark, and bearing an edible nut (**beechnut**). 2. The wood of the beech. [OE *bēce*]

beef (bēf) *n. pl.* **beeves** (bēvz) or **beefs** *for def. 2;* **beefs** *for def. 3* 1. The flesh of a slaughtered adult bovine animal. 2. An adult ox, cow, steer, bull, etc., raised for meat. 3. *Slang* A complaint. —*v.i. Slang* To complain. [< L *bos, bovis* ox]

beef·eat·er (bēf′ē′tər) *n.* 1. A yeoman of the guard, or one of the similarly uniformed warders of the Tower of London. 2. *Slang* An Englishman.

beef·steak (bēf′stāk′) *n.* A slice of beef suitable for broiling.

beef·y (bē′fē) *adj.* **beef·i·er, beef·i·est** Muscular and heavy. —**beef′i·ness** *n.*

bee·hive (bē′hīv′) *n.* 1. A hive for a colony of bees. 2. A place full of activity.

bee·keep·er (bē′kē′pər) *n.* One who keeps bees; an apiarist.

bee·line (bē′līn′) *n.* The shortest course from one place to another. —**to make a beeline for** To go straight toward.

Be·el·ze·bub (bē·el′zə·bub) The prince of the demons; the devil. [< Hebrew *ba'alzebūb* lord of flies]

been (bin, *Brit.* bēn) Past participle of BE.

beep (bēp) *n.* A short, piercing sound used as a signal or warning. —*v.i.* 1. To make such a sound. —*v.t.* 2. To sound (a horn). 3. To transmit (a message) by beeps. [Imit.]

beer (bir) *n.* 1. An alcoholic fermented beverage made from malt and hops. 2. A beverage made from various plants: ginger *beer.* [OE *bēor*]

beer·y (bir′ē) *adj.* **beer·i·er, beer·i·est** 1. Of or like beer. 2. Tipsy. —**beer′i·ness** *n.*

beest·ings (bēs′tingz) *n.pl.* (*construed as sing. or pl.*) The first milk from a cow after calving. [OE *bēost*]

bees·wax (bēz′waks′) *n.* A yellow fatty solid secreted by honeybees for honeycombs.

beet (bēt) *n.* 1. The fleshy, edible root of a plant of the goosefoot family, esp. the red beet or the sugar beet. 2. The plant itself. [< L *beta*]

bee·tle[1] (bēt′l) *n.* An insect having biting mouth parts and hard, horny front wings. —*adj.* Jutting; overhanging: a *beetle* brow: also **bee′tling.** —*v.i.* **·tled, ·tling** To jut out; overhang. [OE *bītan* to bite]

bee·tle[2] (bēt′l) *n.* 1. A heavy instrument, usu. with a wooden head, for ramming paving stones, driving wedges, etc. 2. A pestle or mallet. [OE *bīetel* mallet]

bee·tle-browed (bēt′l·broud′) *adj.* 1. Having jutting eyebrows. 2. Scowling; frowning.

beet sugar Sucrose obtained from the sugar beet.

be·fall (bi·fôl′) *v.* **·fell, ·fall·en, ·fall·ing** *v.i.* 1. To come about; happen; occur. —*v.t.* 2. To happen to. [OE *bef(e)allan* to fall]

be·fit (bi·fit′) *v.t.* **·fit·ted, ·fit·ting** To be suited to; be appropriate for. —**be·fit′ting** *adj.* —**be·fit′ting·ly** *adv.*

be·fog (bi·fôg′, -fog′) *v.t.* **·fogged, ·fog·ging** 1. To envelop in fog. 2. To confuse; obscure.

be·fore (bi·fôr′) *adv.* 1. In front; ahead. 2. Preceding in time; previously. —*prep.* 1. In front of; ahead of. 2. Earlier or sooner than. 3. In advance of in development, rank, etc. 4. In preference to; rather than. 5. In the presence of. 6. Under the consideration of: the issue *before* us. —*conj.* 1. Previous to the time when. 2. Rather than. [OE *beforan* in front of]

be·fore·hand (bi·fôr′hand′) *adv.* & *adj.* In anticipation or advance; ahead of time.

be·foul (bi·foul′) *v.t.* To make foul or dirty; sully.

be·friend (bi·frend′) *v.t.* To act as a friend to; help.

be·fud·dle (bi·fud′l) *v.t.* **·dled, ·dling** To confuse, as with liquor.

beg (beg) *v.* **begged, beg·ging** *v.t.* 1. To ask for in charity: to *beg* alms. 2. To ask for or of humbly; beseech: to *beg* forgiveness. —*v.i.* 3. To ask alms or charity. 4. To ask humbly. —**to beg off** To ask to be excused or released (from an engagement, obligation, etc.). [< OF *begard* mendicant friar]

be·gan (bi·gan′) Past tense of BEGIN.

be·get (bi·get′) *v.t.* **·got** (*Archaic* **·gat**), **·got·ten** or **·got, ·get·ting** 1. To be the father of. 2. To cause to be; initiate. [OE *begitan*] —**be·get′ter** *n.*

beg·gar (beg′ər) *n.* 1. One who lives by begging. 2. A poor person; pauper. —*v.t.* 1. To impoverish. 2. To exhaust the resources of: It *beggars* analysis. [< OF *begard* mendicant friar] —**beg′gar·y** *n.*

beg·gar·ly (beg′ər·lē) *adj.* Appropriate for a beggar; miserably poor.

be·gin (bi·gin′) *v.* **·gan, ·gun, ·gin·ning** *v.i.* 1. To start to do something. 2. To come into being; arise. —*v.t.* 3. To do the first act or part of; start to do. 4. To originate. [OE *beginnan*]

be·gin·ner (bi·gin′ər) *n.* 1. One beginning to learn a trade, study a subject, etc.; a novice. 2. Founder; originator.

be·gin·ning (bi·gin′ing) *n.* 1. The act of starting. 2. Source or first cause; origin. 3. The first part. 4. *Usu. pl.* The first or rudimentary stage. —*adj.* 1. First; opening: the *beginning* chapter. 2. Elementary; introductory: a *beginning* course in physics.

be·gon·ia (bi·gōn′yə) *n.* A plant having showy leaves and flowers. [after Michel *Bégon*, 1638–1710, French botanist]

be·got (bi·got′) Past tense and past participle of BEGET.

be·got·ten (bi·got′n) Alternative past participle of BEGET.

be·grime (bi·grīm′) *v.t.* **·grimed, ·grim·ing** To soil.

be·grudge (bi·gruj′) *v.t.* **·grudged, ·grudg·ing** 1. To envy one the possession or enjoyment of (something). 2. To give or grant reluctantly. —**be·grudg′ing·ly** *adv.*

be·guile (bi·gīl′) *v.t.* **·guiled, ·guil·ing** 1. To deceive; mislead by guile. 2. To while away pleasantly, as time. 3. To charm; divert. —**be·guil′ing** *adj.* —**be·guil′ing·ly** *adv.*

be·gum (bē′gəm) *n.* A Muslim princess or, in India, woman of rank. [< Turkish *bigim*]

be·gun (bi·gun′) Past participle of BEGIN.

be·half (bi·haf′) *n.* The interest, part, or defense: usu. preceded by *in* or *on* and followed by *of*. [OE *be healfe* by the side (of)]

be·have (bi·hāv′) *v.* **·haved, ·hav·ing** *v.i.* 1. To act; conduct oneself or itself. 2. To comport oneself properly. —*v.t.* 3. To conduct (oneself), esp. in a proper or suitable manner. [ME *be-* thoroughly + *have* to hold oneself, act]

be·hav·ior (bi·hāv′yər) *n.* 1. Manner of conducting oneself. 2. The way a person, substance, machine, etc., acts under given circumstances. Also *Brit.* **be·hav′iour.** —**be·hav′ior·al** *adj.*

be·hav·ior·ism (bi·hāv′yər·iz′əm) *n. Psychol.* The theory that the behavior of animals and man is determined by measurable external and internal stimuli. —**be·hav′ior·ist** *n.* —**be·hav′ior·is′tic** *adj.*

be·head (bi·hed′) *v.t.* To decapitate. [OE *behēafdian*]

be·held (bi·held′) Past tense and past participle of BEHOLD.

be·he·moth (bi·hē′məth, bē′ə-) *n.* 1. *cap.* In the Bible, a huge beast. *Job* xl 15. 2. Anything large. [< Hebrew *bĕhemāh* beast]

be·hest (bi·hest′) *n.* An authoritative request; command. [OE *behǣs* promise, vow]

be·hind (bi·hīnd′) *adv.* 1. In, at, or toward the rear. 2. In a place, condition, or time previously passed or departed from. 3. In arrears; late. 4. Slow, as a watch. —*prep.* 1. At the back or rear of. 2. Toward the rear of. 3. In a place or time previously passed. 4. After (a set time). 5. Not so well advanced as; inferior to. 6. Hidden by: What is *behind* your actions? 7. Backing up; supporting: to be *behind* a venture. —*n. Informal* The buttocks. [OE *behindan*]

be·hind·hand (bi·hīnd′hand′) *adv.* & *adj.* 1. Behind time; late. 2. Behind in development; backward.

be·hold (bi·hōld′) *v.t.* **·held, ·hold·ing** To look at or upon; observe. —*interj.* Look! See! [OE *beh(e)aldan* to hold] —**be·hold′er** *n.*

be·hold·en (bi·hōl′dən) *adj.* Indebted; obligated.

be·hoove (bi·ho͞ov′) *v.t.* **·hooved, ·hoov·ing** To be necessary or right for: It *behooves* me to leave. [OE *behōfian*]

beige (bāzh, bāj) *n.* Grayish tan. [< F] —**beige** *adj.*

be·ing (bē′ing) *n.* 1. Existence, as opposed to nonexistence. 2. Essential nature; substance: His whole *being* is musical. 3. A living thing. 4. A human individual; person.

be·la·bor (bi·lā′bər) *v.t.* 1. To beat soundly; assail with blows. 2. To assail verbally.

be·lat·ed (bi·lā′tid) *adj.* Late, or too late. —**be·lat′ed·ly** *adv.* —**be·lat′ed·ness** *n.*

be·lay (bi·lā′) *v.t.* & *v.i.* **·layed, ·lay·ing** 1. *Naut.* To make fast (a rope) by winding on a cleat or pin (**belaying pin**). 2. *Informal* To stop or hold: *Belay* there! [OE *belecgan*]

belch (belch) *v.i.* 1. To eject wind noisily from the stomach through the mouth; burp. 2. To issue forth in a burst or bursts; gush. 3. To emit material violently, as a volcano. —*v.t.* 4. To eject or throw forth violently. [OE *bealcian*] —**belch** *n.*

be·lea·guer (bi·lē′gər) *v.t.* 1. To surround or shut in with an armed force. 2. To surround; beset. [< Du. *be-* about + *leger* camp]

bel·fry (bel′frē) *n. pl.* **·fries** 1. A tower in which a bell is hung. 2. The part of a tower or steeple containing the bell. [< OF *berfrei* tower, infl. by BELL[1]]

Bel·gian (bel′jən, -jē·ən) *adj.* Of or pertaining to Belgium. —*n.* A native or citizen of Belgium.

Be·li·al (bē′lē·əl, bēl′yəl) In the Bible, the devil.

be·lie (bi·lī′) *v.t.* **·lied, ·ly·ing** 1. To misrepresent; disguise. 2. To prove false; contradict. 3. To fail to fulfill: to *belie* hopes. [OE *belēogan*]

be·lief (bi·lēf′) *n.* 1. Acceptance of the truth or actuality of anything. 2. Something held to be true or actual. 3. Trust in another; confidence. 4. A doctrine; creed. [ME *bi-* complete + *leafe* belief]

be·lieve (bi·lēv′) *v.* **·lieved, ·liev·ing** *v.t.* 1. To accept as true. 2. To credit (a person) with veracity. 3. To think; assume. —*v.i.* 4. To accept the truth, existence, worth, etc., of something: with *in:* to *believe* in freedom. 5. To have confidence; place one's trust: with *in.* 6. To have religious faith. 7. To think. [ME *beleven* < OE *gelēfan* to believe] —**be·liev′a·ble** *adj.* —**be·liev′er** *n.*

be·lit·tle (bi·lit′l) *v.t.* **·tled, ·tling** To cause to seem small or less; disparage.

bell[1] (bel) *n.* 1. A hollow metallic instrument, usu. cup-shaped, which rings when struck. 2. Anything in the shape of or suggesting a bell, as a flower. 3. *Naut.* A stroke on a bell every half hour to mark the periods of the watch; also, each of these periods. —*v.t.* 1. To put a bell on. 2. To shape like a bell. —*v.i.* 3. To take the shape of a bell. [OE *belle*]

bell[2] (bel) *v.i.* To cry, as a hound, etc. [OE *bellan* to bellow] —**bell** *n.*

bel·la·don·na (bel′ə·don′ə) *n.* 1. A perennial herb with purple-red flowers and black berries: also called *deadly nightshade.* 2. A poisonous alkaloid used in medicine. [< Ital. *bella donna,* lit., beautiful lady]

bell·boy (bel′boi′) *n.* A boy or man employed by a hotel to answer calls for service, carry suitcases, etc. Also **bell′hop′** (-hop′).

belle (bel) *n.* A beautiful and attractive woman or girl. [< F, fem. of *beau* beautiful]

belles-let·tres (bel′let′rə) *n.pl.* Literature having esthetic appeal, rather than instructional or informational value; poetry, drama, fiction, etc. [< F, fine letters] —**bel·let·rist** (bel′let′rist) *n.* —**bel·le·tris·tic** (bel′lə·tris′tik) *adj.*

bel·li·cose (bel′ə·kōs) *adj.* Pugnacious; warlike. [< L *bellum* war] —**bel′li·cose′ly** *adv.* —**bel′li·cos′i·ty** (-kos′ə·tē) *n.*

bel·lig·er·ence (bə·lij′ər·əns) *n.* 1. The state of being warlike. 2. Belligerency.

bel·lig·er·en·cy (bə·lij′ər·ən·sē) *n.* The condition of being at war.

bel·lig·er·ent (bə·lij′ər·ənt) *adj.* 1. Warlike; bellicose. 2. Engaged in or pertaining to warfare. —*n.* A person or nation engaged in warfare or fighting. [< L *belligerare* to wage war] —**bel·lig′er·ent·ly** *adv.*

bel·low (bel′ō) *v.i.* 1. To utter a loud, hollow cry, as a bull. 2. To roar; shout. —*v.t.* 3. To utter with a loud, roaring voice. [ME *belwen,* ? < OE *bylgian*] —**bel′low** *n.* —**bel′low·er** *n.*

bel·lows (bel′ōz) *n.pl.* (*construed as sing. or pl.*) An instrument with an air chamber and flexible sides, for drawing in air and expelling it through a nozzle or tube, used for blowing fires, filling the pipes of an organ, etc. [OE *belg, belig* bag]

bell·weth·er (bel′weth′ər) *n.* 1. A ram with a bell about its neck, that leads a flock of sheep. 2. One who leads a group. [OE *wether* a castrated ram]

bel·ly (bel′ē) *n. pl.* **·lies** 1. The abdomen in vertebrates, or the underpart of other animals. 2. The stomach. 3. The protuberance of a bulging muscle. 4. The front or underpart of anything. 5. A deep, interior cavity: the *belly* of a ship. —*v.t. & v.i.* **·lied, ·ly·ing** To swell out or fill, as a sail. [OE *belg, belig* bag]

bel·ly·ache (bel′ē·āk′) *n.* A pain in the stomach. —*v.i.* **·ached, ·ach·ing** *Slang* To complain.

bel·ly·band (bel′ē·band′) *n.* A strap or bandage passed around the belly.

bel·ly·but·ton (bel′ē·but′n) *n. Informal* The navel.

be·long (bi·lông′, -long′) *v.i.* 1. To be the property of someone: with *to.* 2. To be a part of or an appurtenance to something: with *to.* 3. To have a proper place; be suitable. 4. To have relation or be a member. [ME *be-* completely + *longen* to go along with]

be·long·ing (bi·lông′ing, -long′-) *n.* 1. That which belongs to a person or thing. 2. *pl.* Possessions; effects. 3. Affinity; a good relationship.

be·lov·ed (bi·luv′id, -luvd′) *adj.* Greatly loved. [Orig. pp. of obs. *belove* love dearly] —**be·lov′ed, ·loved′** *n.*

be·low (bi·lō′) *adv.* 1. In, on, or to a lower place. 2. Farther down or on. 3. In a lower rank or authority. —*prep.* Lower than in place, grade, degree, etc. [ME *bi-* near + *loogh* low]

belt (belt) *n.* 1. A band of leather or other flexible material worn about the waist to support clothing, tools, weapons, etc. 2. Any band resembling a belt. 3. *Mech.* An endless band of flexible material for transmitting power from one wheel or shaft to another. 4. A distinctive region or zone: a storm *belt.* 5. *Slang* A blow, as with the fist. —**below the belt** Unfair. —**to tighten one's belt** To practice thrift. —*v.t.* 1. To gird or fasten with a belt. 2. To mark with belts or bands. 3. *Slang* To strike; hit. [< L *balteus* girdle]

be·lu·ga (bə·lōō′gə) *n.* 1. A sturgeon, esp. of the Caspian Sea, a prime source of caviar. 2. A dolphin of Arctic and sub-Arctic seas: also called *white whale.* [< Russ. *byelukha*]

bel·ve·dere (bel′və·dir′) *n. Archit.* A building, or an upper story of a building, that commands a view. [< Ital., beautiful view]

be·mire (bi·mīr′) *v.t.* **·mired, ·mir·ing** 1. To soil with mud or mire. 2. To sink or stall in mud.

be·moan (bi·mōn′) *v.t.* 1. To lament, as a loss. 2. To express sympathy or pity for. [OE *bemǣnan*]

be·muse (bi·myōōz′) *v.t.* **·mused, ·mus·ing** To bewilder or preoccupy. —**be·mused′** *adj.*

bench (bench) *n.* 1. A long seat of wood, marble, etc., with or without a back. 2. A table for mechanical work. 3. The seat for judges in a court. 4. The judge, or judges collectively. 5. The office or dignity of a judge. 6. A seat for persons sitting in an

official capacity. —*v.t.* In sports, to remove (a player) from a game. [OE *benc*]
bench·mark (bench′märk′) *n.* A standard of comparison. —*adj.* Serving as a standard of reference or comparison: a *benchmark* court decision.
bench mark A geographical point on a permanent marker used for reference in surveying and mapmaking.
bench warrant *Law* A warrant issued by a judge, directing that an offender be brought into court.
bend[1] (bend) *v.* **bent, bend·ing** *v.t.* 1. To cause to take the form of a curve; crook; bow. 2. To direct or turn, as one's course, in a certain direction; deflect. 3. To subdue or cause to yield. 4. *Naut.* To make fast, as a rope or sail. —*v.i.* 5. To assume the form of a curve. 6. To take a certain direction. 7. To bow in submission or respect. —*n.* 1. An act of bending, or the state of being bent. 2. Something curved or bent. 3. *Naut.* A knot by which a rope is fastened to something else. [OE *bendan*]
bend[2] (bend) *n.* *Heraldry* A diagonal band across a shield from the upper left to the lower right. [OE *bend* strap]
bend·er (ben′dər) *n.* *Slang* A drinking spree.
bends (bendz) *n.pl.* *Informal* Caisson disease.
bend sinister *Heraldry* A band drawn diagonally from the upper right to the lower left.
be·neath (bi·nēth′) *adv.* 1. In a lower place; below. 2. Underneath; directly below. —*prep.* 1. Under; underneath; below. 2. Under the power or sway of; subdued by. 3. Lower in rank or station. 4. Unworthy of. [OE *beneothan*]
Ben·e·dic·tine (ben′ə·dik′tin, -tēn; *for n. def. 3,* -tēn) *adj.* Pertaining to St. Benedict or his order. —*n.* 1. A monk of the order established by St. Benedict, about 530. 2. A nun following the Benedictine rule. 3. A liqueur, formerly made by French Benedictines.
ben·e·dic·tion (ben′ə·dik′shən) *n.* 1. The act of blessing. 2. The invocation of divine favor upon a person. [< LL *benedicere* to bless] —**ben′e·dic′to·ry** *adj.*
ben·e·fac·tion (ben′ə·fak′shən) *n.* 1. The act of conferring a benefit. 2. A charitable deed. [< LL *benefacere* to do well]
ben·e·fac·tor (ben′ə·fak′tər, ben′ə·fak′-) *n.* One who gives help or confers a benefit. —**ben′e·fac′tress** (-tris) *n.fem.*
ben·e·fice (ben′ə·fis) *n.* *Eccl.* 1. A church office endowed with funds or property. 2. The revenue of such an office. —*v.t.* **·ficed, ·fic·ing** To invest with a benefice. [< L *beneficium* favor]
be·nef·i·cence (bə·nef′ə·səns) *n.* 1. The quality of being beneficent. 2. A beneficent act or gift.
be·nef·i·cent (bə·nef′ə·sənt) *adj.* 1. Bringing about or doing good. 2. Resulting in benefit. —**be·nef′i·cent·ly** *adv.*
ben·e·fi·cial (ben′ə·fish′əl) *adj.* Producing benefit; advantageous; helpful. [< L *beneficium* favor] —**ben′e·fi′cial·ly** *adv.*
ben·e·fi·ci·ar·y (ben′ə·fish′ē·er′ē, -fish′ər·ē) *n.* *pl.* **·ar·ies** 1. One who receives benefits or advantages. 2. *Eccl.* The holder of a benefice. 3. *Law* One entitled to income from a trust, insurance policy, or annuity. [< L *beneficium* favor]
ben·e·fit (ben′ə·fit) *n.* 1. That which is helpful; advantage; profit. 2. A charitable deed. 3. A public performance given to raise funds for a worthy cause. 4. *Often pl.* Payments made by an insurance company, etc. —*v.* **·fit·ed, ·fit·ing** *v.t.* 1. To be helpful or useful to. —*v.i.* 2. To profit; gain advantage. [< L *benefacere* to do well]
benefit of clergy Churchly approval.
be·nev·o·lence (bə·nev′ə·ləns) *n.* 1. Disposition to do good; kindliness. 2. Any act of kindness.
be·nev·o·lent (bə·nev′ə·lənt) *adj.* Disposed to do good; kindly. [< L *bene* well + *volens,* ppr. of *velle* to wish] —**be·nev′o·lent·ly** *adv.*
Ben·ga·li (ben·gô′lē, beng-) *adj.* Of or pertaining to Bengal. —*n.* 1. A native of Bengal. 2. The Indic language of Bengal.
be·night·ed (bi·nī′tid) *adj.* 1. Ignorant; unenlightened. 2. Overtaken by night. —**be·night′ed·ness** *n.*
be·nign (bi·nīn′) *adj.* 1. Of a kind disposition; kindly. 2. Gentle; mild. 3. Favorable. 4. *Med.* Nonmalignant. [< L *benignus* kindly] —**be·nign′ly** *adv.*
be·nig·nant (bi·nig′nənt) *adj.* 1. Kind; gracious, esp. to inferiors. 2. Favorable; benign. —**be·nig′nant·ly** *adv.*
be·nig·ni·ty (bi·nig′nə·tē) *n.* *pl.* **·ties** 1. The quality of being benign. Also **be·nig′nan·cy** (-nən·sē). 2. A gracious action or influence.
ben·i·son (ben′ə·zən, -sən) *n.* A benediction; blessing. [< LL *benedictio, -onis* benediction]
ben·ny (ben′ē) *n.* *pl.* **·nies** *Informal* A Benzedrine pill.
bent[1] (bent) Past tense and past participle of BEND[1]. —*adj.* 1. Not straight; crooked. 2. Set on a course; resolved. —*n.* 1. State of being bent or turned. 2. A personal inclination or penchant. 3. Limit of endurance or capacity.
bent[2] (bent) *n.* 1. A stiff, wiry grass. Also **bent grass.** 2. The stiff flower stalk of various grasses. [OE *beonet*]
be·numb (bi·num′) *v.t.* 1. To make numb; deaden. 2. To stupefy. [OE *benumen,* pp. of *beniman* to deprive]
Ben·ze·drine (ben′zə·drēn, -drin) *n.* Trademark name of a brand of amphetamine. Also **ben′ze·drine.**
ben·zene (ben′zēn, ben·zēn′) *n.* *Chem.* A colorless, flammable, liquid hydrocarbon, obtained chiefly from coal tar, used as a solvent and in organic synthesis.
ben·zine (ben′zēn, ben·zēn′) *n.* A colorless, flammable liquid derived from crude petroleum, used as a solvent, cleaner, and fuel.
ben·zo·ate (ben′zō·it, -āt) *n.* *Chem.* A salt of benzoic acid.
ben·zo·ic acid (ben·zō′ik) *Chem.* An aromatic compound, used as a food preservative and in medicine.
ben·zo·in (ben′zō·in, -zoin) *n.* A gum resin from various East Indian plants, used in medicine and as a perfume. [< Arabic *lubān jāwī* incense of Java] —**ben·zo′ic** *adj.*
ben·zol (ben′zōl, -zol) *n.* A crude benzene.
be·queath (bi·kwēth′, -kwēth′) *v.t.* 1. *Law* To give by a will. 2. To hand down. [OE *becwethan*]

be·quest (bi·kwest′) *n.* The act of bequeathing, or something bequeathed. [ME *biqueste*]
be·rate (bi·rāt′) *v.t.* **·rat·ed, ·rat·ing** To scold severely.
Ber·ber (bûr′bər) *n.* **1.** One who belongs to a group of Muslim tribes, esp. the Kabyles, of northern Africa. **2.** The Hamitic language of the Berbers. **—Ber′ber** *adj.*
ber·ceuse (ber·sœz′) *n.* *pl.* **·ceuses** (-sœz′) A lullaby. [< F]
be·reave (bi·rēv′) *v.t.* **·reaved** or **·reft, ·reav·ing** **1.** To deprive, as of hope or happiness. **2.** To leave saddened through death. [OE *berēafian*] **—be·reave′ment** *n.*
be·reft (bi·reft′) Alternative past tense and past participle of BEREAVE.
be·ret (bə·rā′, ber′ā) *n.* A soft, flat cap, usu. of wool. [< F]
berg (bûrg) *n.* An iceberg.
ber·ga·mot (bûr′gə·mot) *n.* **1.** A small tree whose fruit furnishes a fragrant essential oil. **2.** The oil itself. **3.** Any of several plants of the mint family. [? after *Bergamo*, Italy]
ber·i·ber·i (ber′ē·ber′ē) *n.* *Pathol.* A disease of the peripheral nerves resulting from the absence of B vitamins in the diet. [< Singhalese *beri* weakness]
berke·li·um (bûrk′lē·əm) *n.* An unstable radioactive element (symbol Bk). [after the *Berkeley* campus of the University of California, where discovered]
berm (bûrm) *n.* A narrow ledge, shelf, or shoulder, as on the side of a road. [< F *berme*]
Ber·mu·da shorts (bər·myōō′da) Knee-length shorts.
ber·ry (ber′ē) *n.* *pl.* **·ries** **1.** Any small, succulent fruit, as a blueberry. **2.** *Bot.* A simple fruit with the seeds in a juicy pulp, as the grape. **3.** The dry seed of certain plants, as a coffee bean, etc. **—*v.i.*** **·ried, ·ry·ing** **1.** To form or bear berries. **2.** To gather berries. [OE *berie*]
ber·serk (bər·sûrk′, bûr′sûrk) *adj.* Crazed; frenzied. [< ON *berserkr*]
ber·serk·er (bûr′sûr′kər) *n.* In Norse legend, a warrior who fought with frenzied fury.
berth (bûrth) *n.* **1.** A bunk or bed in a vessel, sleeping car, etc. **2.** *Naut.* An anchorage. **3.** Situation or employment on a vessel. **—to give a wide berth to** To avoid. **—*v.t.*** **1.** *Naut.* To bring to a berth. **2.** To provide with a berth. **—*v.i.*** **3.** *Naut.* To come to a berth. [Origin uncertain]
ber·yl (ber′əl) *n.* A glassy, variously colored white silicate of aluminum and beryllium, including the gems aquamarine and emerald. [< Gk. *bēryllos*] **—ber·yl·line** (ber′ə·lin, -līn) *adj.*
be·ryl·li·um (bə·ril′ē·əm) *n.* A hard, grayish black, noncorrosive metallic element (symbol Be). [< L *beryllus* beryl]
be·seech (bi·sēch′) *v.t.* **·sought, ·seech·ing** **1.** To implore. **2.** To beg for. [ME *bi-* greatly + *sēcan* to seek] **—be·seech′er** *n.*
be·seem (bi·sēm′) *v.i.* To be fitting or appropriate: It ill *beseems* you to speak thus. **—be·seem′ing** *adj.*
be·set (bi·set′) *v.t.* **·set, ·set·ting** **1.** To assail; harass. **2.** To hem in; encircle. **3.** To set or stud, as with gems. [OE *besettan*]
be·set·ting (bi·set′ing) *adj.* Constantly troubling: a *besetting* sin.
be·side (bi·sīd′) *prep.* **1.** At the side of; in proximity to. **2.** In comparison with. **3.** Away or apart from: *beside* the point. **4.** Other than; over and above. **—beside oneself** Out of one's senses, as from anger, fear, etc. [OE *be sidan* by the side (of)]
be·sides (bi·sīdz′) *adv.* **1.** In addition; as well. **2.** Moreover; furthermore. **3.** Apart from that mentioned; otherwise; else. **—*prep.*** **1.** In addition to; other than. **2.** Beyond; apart from: I care for nothing *besides* this.
be·siege (bi·sēj′) *v.t.* **·sieged, ·sieg·ing** **1.** To lay siege to. **2.** To crowd around. **3.** To assail. **—be·sieg′er** *n.*
be·smear (bi·smir′) *v.t.* To smear over; sully.
be·smirch (bi·smûrch′) *v.t.* **1.** To soil; stain. **2.** To sully; dim the luster of. **—be·smirch′er** *n.* **—be·smirch′ment** *n.*
be·som (bē′zəm) *n.* A bundle of twigs used as a broom. [OE *besma*]
be·sot (bi·sot′) *v.t.* **·sot·ted, ·sot·ting** **1.** To stupefy, as with drink. **2.** To infatuate.
be·sought (bi·sôt′) Past tense and past participle of BESEECH.
be·span·gle (bi·spang′gəl) *v.t.* **·gled, ·gling** To decorate with or as with spangles.
be·speak (bi·spēk′) *v.t.* **·spoke** (*Archaic* **·spake**), **·spo·ken** or **·spoke, ·speak·ing** **1.** To ask or arrange for in advance. **2.** To give evidence of. **3.** To foretell. [OE *bisprecan*]
be·spoke (bi·spōk′) Past tense and alternative past participle of BESPEAK.
be·spread (bi·spred′) *v.t.* **·spread, ·spread·ing** To cover or spread over thickly.
Bes·se·mer converter (bes′ə·mər) *Metall.* A large, pear-shaped vessel in which molten iron is converted into steel.
best (best) Superlative of GOOD, WELL². **—*adj.*** **1.** Excelling all others; of the highest quality. **2.** Most advantageous or desirable. **3.** Most; largest: the *best* part of an hour. **—*adv.*** **1.** In the most excellent way; most advantageously. **2.** To the utmost degree; most thoroughly. **—*n.*** **1.** The best thing, part, etc. **2.** Best condition or quality; utmost: Do your *best*. **—at best** Under the most favorable circumstances. **—to make the best of** To adapt oneself to the disadvantages of. **—*v.t.*** To defeat; surpass. [OE *betst*]
bes·tial (bes′chəl, best′yəl) *adj.* **1.** Of or pertaining to beasts. **2.** Brutish; depraved. [< L *bestia* beast] **—bes·ti·al·i·ty** (bes′chē·al′ə·tē, bes′tē-) *n.* **—bes′tial·ly** *adv.*
bes·tial·ize (bes′chəl·īz, best′yəl-) *v.t.* **·ized, ·iz·ing** To brutalize.
be·stir (bi·stûr′) *v.t.* **·stirred, ·stir·ring** To rouse to activity.
best man The chief attendant of a bridegroom.
be·stow (bi·stō′) *v.t.* **1.** To present as a gift. **2.** To apply; expend, as time. **3.** To give in marriage. **—be·stow′al, be·stow′ment** *n.*
be·strew (bi·strōō′) *v.t.* **·strewed, ·strewed** or **·strewn, ·strew·ing** To scatter over (a surface).
be·stride (bi·strīd′) *v.t.* **·strode, ·strid·den, ·strid·ing** **1.** To sit or stand astride of; straddle. **2.** To stride across.
best seller A book, phonograph record, etc., that sells or has sold in large numbers.
bet (bet) *n.* **1.** An agreement to risk something, on the chance of winning something else; a wager. **2.** That which is risked in a bet, as a sum of money. **—*v.*** **bet** or (less commonly) **bet·ted, bet·ting** *v.t.* **1.** To stake or

pledge (money, etc.) in a bet. **2.** To declare as in a bet: I *bet* he doesn't come. —*v.i.* **3.** To place a bet. —**you bet** *Slang* Certainly. [Origin uncertain]

be·ta (bā′tə, bē′-) *n.* The second letter of the Greek alphabet (Β, β), corresponding to English *b.* [< Gk.]

be·take (bi·tāk′) *v.t.* **·took, ·tak·en, ·tak·ing** To go; take (oneself). [ME *bitaken*]

beta rays *Physics* A stream of electrons emitted by radioactive substances.

be·ta·tron (bā′tə·tron) *n.* *Physics* An accelerator that uses a magnetic field to increase the velocity of electrons.

be·tel (bēt′l) *n.* A climbing plant of Asia, the leaves of which are chewed, esp. by natives of Malaya. [< Malay *vettila*]

be·tel·nut (bēt′l·nut′) *n.* The seed of an East Indian palm, the **betel palm** used for chewing with betel leaves and lime.

bête noire (bāt′ nwär′, *Fr.* bet′ nwȧr′) *pl.* **bêtes noires** (bāt′ nwärs′, *Fr.* bet′ nwȧr′) An object of hate or dread. [< F, black beast]

beth·el (beth′əl) *n.* **1.** A hallowed place. *Gen.* xxviii 19. **2.** A seamen's church. [< Hebrew *bēth-el* house of God]

be·think (bi·thingk′) *v.t.* **·thought, ·think·ing** To bear in mind; consider.

be·tide (be·tīd′) *v.t. & v.i.* **·tid·ed, ·tid·ing** To happen (to) or befall. [ME *bitiden*]

be·times (bi·tīmz′) *adv.* Early; also, soon. [ME *betymes* in time, seasonably]

be·to·ken (bi·tō′kən) *v.t.* To be a sign of; presage. [ME *bitacnien*] —**be·to′ken·er** *n.*

be·took (bi·to͝ok′) Past tense of BETAKE.

be·tray (bi·trā′) *v.t.* **1.** To aid an enemy of; be a traitor to. **2.** To prove faithless to. **3.** To disclose, as a secret. **4.** To reveal unwittingly. **5.** To seduce and desert. [ME *bitraien*] —**be·tray′al, be·tray′ment** *n.* —**be·tray′er** *n.*

be·troth (bi·trōth′, -trôth′) *v.t.* To engage to marry. [ME *bi-* to + *treuthe* truth]

be·troth·al (bi·trō′thəl, -trôth′əl) *n.* An engagement, or contract to marry.

be·trothed (bi·trōthd′, -trôtht′) *adj.* Engaged to be married; affianced. —*n.* A person engaged to be married.

bet·ter[1] (bet′ər) Comparative of GOOD, WELL[2]. —*adj.* **1.** Superior in quality. **2.** More advantageous or desirable. **3.** Larger; greater: the *better* part of the cake. **4.** Improved in health. —*adv.* **1.** More advantageously. **2.** To a larger degree; more thoroughly. **3.** More: *better* than a week. —**better off** In a better condition. —*v.t.* **1.** To make better; improve. **2.** To surpass; excel. —*n.* **1.** *Usu. pl.* One's superiors. **2.** Advantage. [OE *betera*]

bet·ter[2] (bet′ər) *n.* See BETTOR.

bet·ter·ment (bet′ər·mənt) *n.* Improvement or an improvement.

bet·tor (bet′ər) *n.* One who lays bets: also spelled *better.*

be·tween (bi·twēn′) *prep.* **1.** In the space that separates (two places or objects). **2.** Intermediate in relation to, as times, qualities, etc. **3.** From one to another of; connecting. **4.** By the joint action of. **5.** In the joint possession of. **6.** Regarding one or the other of: to choose *between* two offers. **7.** Being one alternative over another: to judge *between* right and wrong. —*adv.* In intervening time, space, position, or relation: few and far *between.* [Fusion of OE *bitwēonum* and *bitwēon* < *be-* by + *twā* two]

be·twixt (bi·twikst′) *adv. & prep.* *Archaic* Between. —**betwixt and between** In an intermediate or indecisive state. [OE *betweons* twofold]

BeV (bev) *n. pl.* **BeV** A unit of energy equal to one billion electron volts. Also **Bev, bev.** [< B(ILLION) E(LECTRON) V(OLTS)]

bev·el (bev′əl) *n.* **1.** Any inclination of two surfaces other than 90°, as at the edge of a timber. **2.** An adjustable instrument for measuring angles: also **bevel square.** —*adj.* Oblique; slanting. —*v.* **bev·eled** or **·elled, bev·el·ing** or **·el·ling** *v.t.* **1.** To cut or bring to a bevel. —*v.i.* **2.** To slant. [? < MF *béveau* < OF *baïf* gaping]

bevel gear *Mech.* A gear having beveled teeth.

bev·er·age (bev′rij, bev′ər·ij) *n.* That which is drunk; any drink. [< OF *bevrage*]

bev·y (bev′ē) *n. pl.* **bev·ies** **1.** A flock, esp. of quail, grouse, or larks. **2.** A group. [ME *bevey*]

be·wail (bi·wāl′) *v.t. & v.i.* To lament.

be·ware (bi·wâr′) *v.t. & v.i.* **·wared, ·war·ing** To be wary (of). [OE *wær* cautious]

be·wil·der (bi·wil′dər) *v.t.* To confuse utterly; perplex. —**be·wil′dered** *adj.* —**be·wil′der·ment** *n.*

be·witch (bi·wich′) *v.t.* **1.** To gain power over by magic. **2.** To charm; fascinate. [ME *wicchen* to enchant] —**be·witch′er** *n.* —**be·witch′ment** *n.*

be·witch·ing (bi·wich′ing) *adj.* Charming; captivating. —**be·witch′ing·ly** *adv.*

bey (bā) *n.* Formerly, the governor of a minor Turkish province or district. [< Turkish *beg* lord]

be·yond (bi·yond′) *prep.* **1.** On or to the far side of; farther on than. **2.** Later than. **3.** Outside the reach or scope of. **4.** Surpassing; superior to: lovely *beyond* description. **5.** More than; over and above. —*adv.* Farther on or away; at a distance. [OE *be-* near + *geondan* yonder]

bez·el (bez′əl) *n.* **1.** A bevel on the edge of a cutting tool. **2.** The upper part of a cut gem. [? < OF. Cf. F *biseau* bias.]

be·zique (bə·zēk′) *n.* A game of cards resembling pinochle. [Alter. of F *bésique*]

bhang (bang) *n.* **1.** Hemp (def. 1). **2.** An intoxicating, narcotic product of this plant. [< Hind. < Skt. *bhangā*]

Bhu·tan·ese (bo͞o′tən·ēz′, -ēs′) *n. pl.* **·ese** A native of Bhutan. —**Bhu′tan·ese′** *adj.*

bi- *prefix* Twice; doubly; two; esp., occurring twice or having two: *biangular.* Also: **bin-** before a vowel, as in *binaural*; **bis-** before *c, s,* as in *bissextile.* [< L *bi-* < *bis* twice]

bi·an·nu·al (bī·an′yo͞o·əl) *adj.* Occurring twice a year; semiannual. —**bi·an′nu·al·ly** *adv.*

bi·as (bī′əs) *n. pl.* **bi·as·es** **1.** A line running obliquely across a fabric: to cut on the *bias.* **2.** A mental tendency, preference, or prejudice. —*adj. & adv.* On a slant or diagonal. —*v.t.* **bi·ased** or **·assed, bi·as·ing** or **·as·sing** To influence or affect unduly or unfairly. [< MF *biais* oblique]

bi·ax·i·al (bī·ak′sē·əl) *adj.* Having two axes, as a crystal. Also **bi·ax·al** (bī·ak′səl). —**bi·ax′i·al·ly** *adv.*

bib (bib) *n.* **1.** A cloth worn under a child's

chin, esp. at meals. 2. The upper front part of an apron or of overalls. [? < L *bibere* to drink]

bib and tucker *Informal* Clothes.

bib·ber (bib′ər) *n.* A habitual drinker; tippler.

bibe·lot (bib′lō, *Fr.* bēb·lō′) *n.* A small, decorative and often rare object or trinket. [< F]

Bi·ble (bī′bəl) *n.* 1. In Christianity, the Old Testament and the New Testament. 2. In Judaism, the Old Testament. [< Gk., pl. of *biblion* book]

Bib·li·cal (bib′li·kəl) *adj.* 1. Of or in the Bible. 2. In harmony with the Bible. Also **bib′li·cal.** —**Bib′li·cal·ly** *adv.*

Bib·li·cist (bib′lə·sist) *n.* One versed in the Bible.

biblio- *combining form* Pertaining to books: *bibliophile.* [< Gk. *biblion* book]

bib·li·og·ra·phy (bib′lē·og′rə·fē) *n. pl.* **·phies** 1. A list of the works of an author, or of the literature bearing on a subject. 2. A list of books or other sources mentioned or consulted by an author. —**bib′li·og′ra·pher** *n.* —**bib·li·o·graph·ic** (bib′lē·ə·graf′ik) or **·i·cal** *adj.*

bib·li·o·ma·ni·a (bib′lē·ō·mā′nē·ə) *n.* A passion for collecting books. —**bib′li·o·ma′ni·ac** (-ak) *n. & adj.*

bib·li·o·phile (bib′lē·ə·fīl′) *n.* One who loves books.

bib·u·lous (bib′yə·ləs) *adj.* 1. Tending to drink to excess. 2. Absorbent. [< L *bibere* to drink]

bi·cam·er·al (bī·kam′ər·əl) *adj.* Consisting of two chambers, houses, or branches. [< BI- + L *camera* chamber]

bi·car·bo·nate (bī·kär′bə·nit, -nāt) *n. Chem.* A salt of carbonic acid.

bicarbonate of soda Sodium bicarbonate.

bi·cen·ten·ni·al (bī′sen·ten′ē·əl) *adj.* 1. Occurring once in 200 years. 2. Lasting or consisting of 200 years. —*n.* A 200th anniversary. Also **bi·cen·te·nar·y** (bī′sen·ten′ər·ē, bī·sen′tə·ner′ē).

bi·ceps (bī′seps) *n. pl.* **bi·ceps** *Anat.* 1. The large front muscle of the upper arm. 2. The large flexor muscle at the back of the thigh. [< L *bis* twofold + *caput* head]

bi·chlo·ride (bī·klôr′īd, -id) *n. Chem.* A salt having two atoms of chlorine for each atom of another element.

bick·er (bik′ər) *v.i.* 1. To dispute petulantly; wrangle. 2. To flicker. —*n.* A petty altercation. [ME *bikeren*] —**bick′er·er** *n.*

bi·con·cave (bī·kon′kāv, -kong′-, bī′kon·kāv′) *adj.* Concave on both sides, as a lens.

bi·con·vex (bī·kon′veks, bī′kon·veks′) *adj.* Convex on both sides, as a lens.

bi·cus·pid (bī·kus′pid) *n.* Any of eight teeth in the human jaw having two cusps or points. [< BI- + L *cuspis* point]

bi·cy·cle (bī′sik·əl) *n.* A two-wheeled vehicle driven by pedals. —*v.i.* **·cled, ·cling** To ride a bicycle. [< F < BI- + Gk. *kyklos* wheel] —**bi′cy·cler, bi′cy·clist** *n.*

bid (bid) *n.* 1. An offer to pay a price; also, the amount offered. 2. In card games, the number of tricks or points that a player engages to make; also, a player's turn to bid. 3. An effort to acquire, win, or attain. —*v.* **bid** *for defs. 1, 2, 5* or **bade** *for defs. 3, 4,* **bid·den** or **bid, bid·ding** *v.t.* 1. To make an offer of (a price). 2. In card games, to declare (the number of tricks or points one will engage to make). 3. To command; order. 4. To say to, as a greeting or farewell. —*v.i.* 5. To make a bid. —**to bid fair** To seem probable. [Fusion of OE *biddan* to ask, demand and *bēodan* to proclaim] —**bid′der** *n.*

bid·da·ble (bid′ə·bəl) *adj.* 1. Docile; obedient. 2. Worth bidding on.

bid·ding (bid′ing) *n.* 1. A command or summons. 2. Bids, or the making of bids.

bid·dy[1] (bid′ē) *n. pl.* **·dies** A hen. [Origin uncertain]

bid·dy[2] (bid′ē) *n. pl.* **·dies** A gossipy, usu. old woman. [< *Bridget*, fem. name]

bide (bīd) *v.* **bid·ed, bid·ing** *v.t.* 1. To endure; withstand. —*v.i.* 2. To dwell; abide; stay. —**to bide one's time** To await the best opportunity. [OE *bīdan*]

bi·en·ni·al (bī·en′ē·əl) *adj.* 1. Occurring every second year. 2. Lasting or living for two years. —*n. Bot.* A plant that produces flowers and fruit in its second year, then dies. [< BI- + L *annus* year] —**bi·en′ni·al·ly** *adv.*

bien·ve·nue (byaṅ·və·nü′) *n. French* A welcome.

bier (bir) *n.* A framework for carrying a corpse to the grave; also, a coffin. [OE *bǣr*]

bi·fid (bī′fid) *adj.* Cleft; forked. [< BI- + L *findere* to split]

bi·fo·cal (bī·fō′kəl) *adj. Optics* Having two foci: said of a lens ground for both near and far vision.

bi·fo·cals (bī·fō′kəlz, bī′fō·kəlz) *n.pl.* Eyeglasses with bifocal lenses.

bi·fur·cate (bī′fər·kāt, bī·fûr′kāt; *adj. also* bī·fûr′kit) *v.t. & v.i.* **·cat·ed, ·cat·ing** To divide into two branches or stems; fork. —*adj.* Forked: also **bi′fur·cat′ed** (-kā′tid), **bi·fur·cous** (bī·fûr′kəs). [< BI- + L *furca* fork] —**bi′fur·ca′tion** *n.*

big (big) *adj.* **big·ger, big·gest** 1. Of great size, extent, etc. 2. Pregnant: usu. with *with.* 3. Grown. 4. Pompous; pretentious. 5. Important; prominent. 6. Loud. 7. Generous; magnanimous. —*adv. Informal* Pompously; extravagantly: to talk *big.* [ME; origin uncertain] —**big′gish** *adj.* —**big′ness** *n.*

big·a·my (big′ə·mē) *n. Law* The criminal offense of marrying any other person while having a legal spouse living. [< BI- + Gk. *gamos* wedding] —**big′a·mist** *n.* —**big′a·mous** *adj.* —**big′a·mous·ly** *adv.*

big-bang theory *Astron.* A theory that the universe began with a huge explosion and will eventually contract again.

Big Dipper The constellation Ursa Major.

big·foot (big′fo͝ot′) *n.* The sasquatch.

big-heart·ed (big′här′tid) *adj.* Generous.

big·horn (big′hôrn) *n. pl.* **·horns** or **·horn** The Rocky Mountain sheep, having large, curved horns.

bight (bīt) *n.* 1. The loop, or middle part, of a rope. 2. A bend or curve in a shoreline, a river, etc. 3. A bay bounded by such a bend. —*v.t.* To secure with a bight. [OE *byht*]

big·no·ni·a (big·nō′nē·ə) *n.* A climbing plant having clusters of large, trumpet-shaped flowers. [after Abbé *Bignon*, 1711–1772, librarian to Louis XV]

big·ot (big′ət) *n.* An intolerant, prejudiced person. [< F] —**big′ot·ed** *adj.* —**big′ot·ed·ly** *adv.*

big·ot·ry (big′ə·trē) *n. pl.* **·ries** Bigoted behavior; intolerance.
big shot *Slang* Someone of importance. Also **big wheel.**
big top *Informal* The main tent of a circus.
big·wig (big′wig′) *n. Informal* Someone of importance.
bi·jou (bē′zhōō) *n. pl.* **bi·joux** (bē′zhōōz) A jewel or finely made trinket. [< MF]
bike (bīk) *n. Informal* A bicycle.
bi·ki·ni (bi·kē′nē) *n.* A scanty two-piece bathing suit.
bi·la·bi·al (bī·lā′bē·əl) *adj.* **1.** *Phonet.* Articulated with both lips. **2.** Having two lips. **—***n. Phonet.* A bilabial speech sound, as (b), (p), (m), and (w).
bi·la·bi·ate (bī·lā′bē·āt, -it) *adj. Bot.* Two-lipped.
bi·lat·er·al (bī·lat′ər·əl) *adj.* **1.** Pertaining to or having two sides; two-sided. **2.** On two sides. **3.** Mutually binding. **—bi·lat′er·al·ly** *adv.* **—bi·lat′er·al·ness** *n.*
bil·ber·ry (bil′ber′ē, -bər·ē) *n. pl.* **·ries** The whortleberry.
bil·bo (bil′bō) *n. pl.* **·boes** A fetter consisting of two sliding shackles attached to an iron bar. [after *Bilbao,* Spain, noted for its ironworks.]
bile (bīl) *n.* **1.** *Physiol.* A secretion from the liver that aids digestion. **2.** Anger; peevishness. [< L *bilis* bile, anger]
bile ducts *Physiol.* The excretory ducts of the gall bladder.
bilge (bilj) *n.* **1.** *Naut.* The rounded part of a ship's bottom. **2.** Bilge water. **3.** *Slang* Stupid or trivial talk or writing. [Var. of BULGE]
bilge water Foul water that collects in the bilge of a ship.
bil·i·ar·y (bil′ē·er′ē) *adj.* Pertaining to or conveying bile. [< F *biliare*]
bi·lin·gual (bī·ling′gwəl) *adj.* **1.** Written or expressed in or using two languages. **2.** Able to speak two languages. **—***n.* A bilingual person. [< BI- + L *linguis*] **—bi·lin′gual·ism** *n.* **—bi·lin′gual·ly** *adv.*
bil·ious (bil′yəs) *adj.* **1.** Affected or caused by an excess of bile. **2.** Of or containing bile. **3.** Ill-tempered. **4.** Of a sickly color. [< L *biliosus*] **—bil′ious·ly** *adv.* **—bil′ious·ness** *n.*
-bility *suffix* Forming nouns from adjectives ending in *-ble*: *probability* from *probable.* [< L *-bilitas*]
bilk (bilk) *v.t.* To cheat or swindle. [Origin unknown] **—bilk′er** *n.*
bill[1] (bil) *n.* **1.** A statement of charges for goods delivered or services rendered. **2.** A piece of paper money; a bank note. **3.** A bill of exchange; also, loosely, a promissory note. **4.** A draft of a proposed law. **5.** Any list of items or program of particulars. **6.** *Law* A formal statement of a case or a complaint. **—***v.t.* **1.** To enter in a bill or list. **2.** To present a bill to. [< LL *billa* < L *bulla* edict, document] **—bill′a·ble** *adj.*
bill[2] (bil) *n.* A beak, as of a bird. **—***v.i.* To join bills, as doves; caress. **—to bill and coo** To caress and speak lovingly. [OE *bile*]
bill[3] (bil) *n.* **1.** A hook-shaped instrument used in pruning, etc.: also **bill′hook′** (-hōōk′). **2.** A halberd. [OE]
bil·la·bong (bil′ə·bong) *n. Austral.* A stagnant backwater. [< native Australian]
bill·board (bil′bôrd′) *n.* A panel, usu. outdoors, for advertisements.
bil·let[1] (bil′it) *n.* **1.** Lodging for troops in private or nonmilitary buildings. **2.** An order for such lodging. **3.** A place assigned as quarters. **4.** A job. **—***v.t.* To lodge (soldiers, etc.) by billet. [< L *bulla* seal, document]
bil·let[2] (bil′it) *n.* **1.** A short, thick stick, as of firewood. **2.** *Metall.* A mass of iron or steel drawn into a small bar. [< OF *billete,* dim. of *bille* log]
bil·let-doux (bil′ā·dōō′, *Fr.* bē·yā·dōō′) *n. pl.* **bil·lets-doux** (bil′ā·dōōz′, *Fr.* bē·yā·dōō′) A love letter. [< F]
bill·fold (bil′fōld′) *n.* A wallet.
bil·liards (bil′yərdz) *n.pl.* (*construed as sing.*) Any of various games played with hard balls (**billiard balls**) hit by cues on an oblong, cloth-covered table (**billiard table**) having cushioned edges. [< OF *billart* cue] **—bil′liard** *adj.*
bill·ing (bil′ing) *n.* The relative eminence given to an actor or an act on a theater marquee, playbill, etc.
bil·lings·gate (bil′ingz·gāt) *n.* Vulgar or abusive language. [after *Billingsgate* fish market, London]
bil·lion (bil′yən) *n.* **1.** A thousand millions, written as 1,000,000,000. **2.** *Brit.* A million millions, written as 1,000,000,000,000: called a *trillion* in the U.S. [< F < BI- + (MI)LLION] **—bil′lionth** *n. & adj.*
bil·lion·aire (bil′yən·âr′) *n.* One whose wealth totals a billion or more. [< BILLION, on analogy with *millionaire*]
bill of exchange A written order for the payment of a given sum to a designated person.
bill of fare A menu (def. 1).
bill of health An official certificate of the health of a ship's crew.
bill of lading A written acknowledgment of goods received for transportation.
bill of rights **1.** A formal declaration of the fundamental rights of individuals. **2.** *Often cap.* The first ten amendments to the U.S. Constitution.
bill of sale An instrument attesting the transfer of property.
bil·low (bil′ō) *n.* **1.** A great wave or swell of the sea. **2.** Any wave or surge, as of sound. **—***v.t. & v.i.* To rise or cause to rise or roll in billows; surge; swell. [< ON *bylgja*]
bil·low·y (bil′ō·ē) *adj.* **·low·i·er, ·low·i·est** Swelling with or as with billows. **—bil′low·i·ness** *n.*
bill·post·er (bil′pōs′tər) *n.* A person who posts bills, notices, etc. Also **bill′stick′er** (-stik′ər). **—bill′post′ing** *n.*
bil·ly (bil′ē) *n. pl.* **·lies** A short club, esp. a policeman's. [< *Billy,* a nickname for William]
billy goat *Informal* A male goat.
bi·lo·bate (bī·lō′bāt) *adj.* Divided into or having two lobes. Also **bi·lo′bat·ed.**
bi·man·u·al (bī·man′yōō·əl) *adj.* Using or involving both hands. **—bi·man′u·al·ly** *adv.*
bi·met·al·ism (bī·met′l·iz′əm) *n.* The concurrent use of both gold and silver as the standard of currency. Also **bi·met′al·lism.**
bi·me·tal·lic (bī′mə·tal′ik) *adj.* **1.** Consisting of or relating to two metals. **2.** Of or using bimetalism.
bi·month·ly (bī·munth′lē) *adj.* **1.** Occurring

once every two months. 2. Occurring twice a month. —*n.* A bimonthly publication. —**bi·month'ly** *adv.*
bin (bin) *n.* An enclosed place or large receptacle for holding meal, coal, etc. [OE *binn* basket, crib]
bi·na·ry (bī'nər·ē) *adj.* 1. Pertaining to, characterized by, or made up of two; double; paired. 2. Permitting two possibilities only, as in a computer bit. 3. Designating a method of representing numbers using two digits, 0 and 1, with each digital position representing a successive power of 2. —*n. pl.* **·ries** 1. A combination of two things. 2. *Astron.* A binary star. [< L *binarius* < *bini* two, double]
binary star *Astron.* A pair of stars revolving about a common center of gravity.
bi·nate (bī'nāt) *adj. Bot.* Being or growing in pairs. [< L *bini* double, two]
bin·au·ral (bī·nôr'əl, bin·ôr'əl) *adj.* 1. Hearing with both ears. 2. *Electronics* Stereophonic (def. 2).
bind (bīnd) *v.* **bound, bind·ing** *v.t.* 1. To tie or fasten with a band, cord, etc. 2. To fasten around; gird. 3. To bandage; swathe: often with *up.* 4. To constrain or obligate, as by law. 5. To enclose between covers, as a book. 6. To cause to cohere; cement. 7. To constipate. 8. To apprentice or indenture: often with *out* or *over.* —*v.i.* 9. To tie up anything. 10. To cohere; stick together. 11. To have binding force; be obligatory. 12. To stiffen or harden; jam, as gears. —**to bind over** *Law* To hold on bail or under bond for future appearance in court. —*n. Informal* A difficult situation. [OE *bindan*]
bind·er (bīn'dər) *n.* 1. One who binds; esp., a bookbinder. 2. Anything used to bind, as glue. 3. A cover in which sheets of paper may be fastened. 4. *Law* A written statement binding parties to an agreement. 5. *Agric.* A machine that cuts and ties grain.
bind·er·y (bīn'dər·ē) *n. pl.* **·er·ies** A place where books are bound.
bind·ing (bīn'ding) *n.* 1. The act of one who binds. 2. Anything that binds; binder. 3. A strip sewed over an edge for protection. —*adj.* 1. Tying; restraining. 2. Obligatory. —**bind'ing·ly** *adv.* —**bind'ing·ness** *n.*
bind·weed (bīnd'wēd') *n.* Any strongly twining plant.
bine (bīn) *n.* 1. A flexible shoot or climbing stem. 2. A plant having a bine. [Var. of BIND]
binge (binj) *n. Slang* A drunken spree. [? < dial. E *binge* to soak]
bin·go (bing'gō) *n.* A gambling game resembling lotto. [Origin unknown]
bin·na·cle (bin'ə·kəl) *n. Naut.* A stand or case for a ship's compass. [Earlier *bittacle* < Pg. *bitacola*]
bin·oc·u·lar (bə·nok'yə·lər, bī-) *adj.* Using or for both eyes at once. —*n. Often pl.* An optical instrument for use by both eyes. [< L *bini* two, double + *ocularis* of the eyes]
bi·no·mi·al (bī·nō'mē·əl) *adj.* Consisting of two names or terms. —*n. Math.* An algebraic expression consisting of two terms joined by a plus or minus sign. [< LL *binominus* having two names] —**bi·no'mi·al·ly** *adv.*
bio- *combining form* Life: *biology.* [< Gk. *bios*]
bi·o·chem·is·try (bī'ō·kem'is·trē) *n.* The branch of chemistry relating to the processes and physical properties of living organisms. —**bi'o·chem'i·cal** or **bi'o·chem'ic** *adj.* —**bi'o·chem'i·cal·ly** *adv.* —**bi'o·chem'ist** *n.*
bi·o·de·grad·a·ble (bī'ō·də·grād'ə·bəl) *adj.* Capable of being decomposed by microorganisms, esp. into substances considered harmless to the environment.
bi·o·eth·ics (bī'ō·eth'iks) *n.pl.* (*construed as sing.*) The study of ethical and legal aspects of the application of medical and biological research, as in genetics, organ transplants, etc.
bi·o·feed·back (bī'ō·fēd'bak) *n.* A process of bringing unconscious functions, such as brain waves, under conscious control for healing, increased energy, tranquillity, etc.
bi·og·ra·pher (bī·og'rə·fər) *n.* A writer of biography.
bi·o·graph·i·cal (bī·ə·graf'i·kəl) *adj.* 1. Of or concerning a person's life. 2. Pertaining to biography. Also **bi'o·graph'ic.** —**bi'o·graph'i·cal·ly** *adv.*
bi·og·ra·phy (bī·og'rə·fē) *n. pl.* **·phies** An account of a person's life; also, such accounts as a form of literature. [< Gk. *bios* life + *graphein* to write]
bi·o·log·i·cal (bī'ə·loj'i·kəl) *adj.* 1. Of or pertaining to biology. 2. Used for or produced by biological research or practice. —**bi'o·log'i·cal·ly** *adv.*
biological warfare Warfare that employs bacteria and other biological agents.
bi·ol·o·gy (bī·ol'ə·jē) *n.* The science of life in all its manifestations. Its two main divisions are botany and zoology. [< BIO- + -LOGY] —**bi·ol'o·gist** *n.*
bi·on·ics (bī·on'iks) *n.pl.* (*construed as sing.*) The application of data from the functioning of biological systems to engineering problems. —**bi·on'ic** *adj.*
bi·o·phys·ics (bī'ō·fiz'iks) *n.pl.* (*construed as sing.*) The study of biological organisms and processes, using the methods of physics. —**bi'o·phys'i·cal** *adj.* —**bi'o·phys'i·cist** (-sist) *n.*
bi·op·sy (bī'op·sē) *n. pl.* **·sies** *Med.* The examination of tissue from a living subject. [< BI(O)- + Gk. *opsis* appearance] —**bi·op'sic** *adj.*
bi·o·rhythm (bī'ō·rith'əm) *n.* Theoretical cyclical patterns in biological activity or behavior. —**bi'o·rhyth'mi·cal** *adj.*
-biosis *combining form* Manner of living: *symbiosis.* [< Gk. *biōsis* < *bios* life]
bi·o·tin (bī'ə·tin) *n. Biochem.* A crystalline acid forming part of the vitamin B complex: also called *vitamin H.* [< Gk. *biotos* life]
bi·par·ti·san (bī·pär'tə·zən) *adj.* Advocated by or consisting of members of two parties. —**bi·par'ti·san·ship'** *n.*
bi·par·tite (bī·pär'tīt) *adj.* Consisting of two parts, esp. two corresponding parts. [< L *bipartire* to divide]
bi·ped (bī'ped') *n.* An animal having two feet. —*adj.* Two-footed: also **bi·ped'al.** [< L *bipes, bipedis*]
bi·pin·nate (bī·pin'āt) *adj. Bot.* Doubly pinnate, as a leaf.
bi·plane (bī'plān') *n.* A type of airplane having two wings, one above the other.
bi·po·lar (bī·pō'lər) *adj.* 1. Of or having two poles. 2. Of or belonging to both polar

regions. 3. Containing two contradictory qualities, opinions, etc. **—bi·po·lar·i·ty** (bī′pō·lar′ə·tē) *n.*

birch (bûrch) *n.* 1. A tree or shrub having the outer bark separable in thin layers: also called *white birch.* 2. A rod from this tree, used as a whip. 3. The hardwood of the birch. *—v.t.* To whip with a birch rod. [OE *birce*]

bird (bûrd) *n.* 1. A warm-blooded, feathered, egg-laying vertebrate having the forelimbs modified as wings. ◆Collateral adjective: *avian.* 2. A shuttlecock. 3. *Slang* A person, esp. one who is peculiar. [OE *bridd*]

Bird is used as a combining form to mean suitable for or used by birds, as in:

birdbath	**bird's nest**
birdhouse	**birdseed**

bird·call (bûrd′kôl′) *n.* 1. A bird's note in calling. 2. A sound imitating this, or an instrument for producing it.

bird dog A dog used in hunting game birds.

bird·ie (bûr′dē) *n.* In golf, one stroke less than par on a given hole.

bird·lime (bûrd′līm′) *n.* A sticky substance used to catch small birds.

bird of paradise A tropical bird noted for the beauty of the plumage in the male.

bird of passage A migratory bird.

bird of prey A predatory bird, as an eagle, hawk, etc.

bird's-eye (bûrdz′ī′) *adj.* 1. Marked with spots resembling birds' eyes. 2. Seen from above or from afar: a *bird's-eye* view. *—n.* A pattern or fabric having eyelike markings. Also **birds′eye′.**

bird watcher One who observes or identifies wild birds as a pastime. **—bird watching**

bi·ret·ta (bi·ret′ə) *n.* A stiff, square cap with three upright projections, worn by Roman Catholic clerics. [< Ital.]

birl (bûrl) *v.t. & v.i.* 1. To rotate (a floating log). 2. To whirl. *—n.* A droning noise.

birl·ing (bûr′ling) *n.* A sport in which two contestants try to maintain balance on a floating log spun with their feet: also called *logrolling.*

birth (bûrth) *n.* 1. The fact or act of being born. 2. The bringing forth of offspring. 3. Beginning; origin. 4. Ancestry or descent. 5. Natural talent. [ME *byrth*]

birth control The regulation of conception by preventive methods or devices.

birth·day (bûrth′dā) *n.* The day of one's birth or its anniversary.

birth·mark (bûrth′märk′) *n.* A mark or stain existing on the body from birth.

birth·place (bûrth′plās′) *n.* 1. Place of birth. 2. Place where something originates.

birth rate The number of births per a given number of individuals (usually 1,000), in a given area and in a given time period.

birth·right (bûrth′rīt′) *n.* A privilege or possession into which one is born.

birth·stone (bûrth′stōn′) *n.* A jewel identified with the month of one's birth.

bis (bis) *adv.* Twice; again. [< L]

bis·cuit (bis′kit) *n.* 1. A kind of shortened bread baked in small cakes, raised with baking powder or soda. 2. *Brit.* A thin, crisp wafer. 3. In ceramics, pottery baked once but not glazed. [< OF *bescoit*]

bi·sect (bī·sekt′, bī′sekt) *v.t.* 1. To cut or divide into two parts; halve. *—v.i.* 2. To fork, as a road. [< BI- + L *sectus,* pp. of *secare* to cut] **—bi·sec′tion** *n.* **—bi·sec′tion·al** *adj.*

bi·sec·tor (bī·sek′tər) *n.* 1. That which bisects. 2. *Geom.* A line or plane that bisects an angle or another line.

bi·sex·u·al (bī·sek′shōō·əl) *adj.* 1. Of both sexes. 2. Having the organs of both sexes; hermaphrodite. 3. Sexually attracted to both sexes. *—n.* 1. A hermaphrodite. 2. A person attracted to both sexes. **—bi·sex′u·al·ism, bi·sex′u·al′i·ty** (-al′ə·tē) *n.* **—bi·sex′u·al·ly** *adv.*

bish·op (bish′əp) *n.* 1. A prelate in the Christian church; esp., the head of a diocese. 2. A miter-shaped chess piece. [OE *biscop*]

bish·op·ric (bish′əp·rik) *n.* The office or the diocese of a bishop.

bis·muth (biz′məth) *n.* A reddish white metallic element (symbol Bi), used in medicine, alloys, etc. [< G] **—bis′muth·al** *adj.*

bi·son (bī′sən, -zən) *n. pl.* **bi·son** A bovine ruminant, closely related to the true ox; esp., the North American buffalo. [< L *bison* wild ox]

bisque[1] (bisk) *n.* 1. A thick, rich soup, esp. one made from shellfish. 2. A kind of ice cream containing crushed macaroons or nuts. [< F]

bisque[2] (bisk) *n.* Biscuit (def. 3.)

bis·ter (bis′tər) *n.* A brown pigment made from soot, used chiefly as a watercolor wash. Also **bis′tre.** [< F *bistre* dark brown]

bis·tro (bis′tro, *Fr.* bē·strō′) *n.* A small bar, tavern, or night club. [< F]

bit[1] (bit) *n.* 1. A small piece or quantity. 2. A short time. 3. A small part, as in a play or movie. 4. An amount worth 12½ cents: usu. in the expression *two bits* (a quarter). 5. *Informal* A style of behavior that conveys a message: often with *do*: do the innocent *bit.* **—to do one's bit** To make one's contribution; do one's share. *—adj.* Small; minor. [OE *bita* < *bītan* to bite]

bit[2] (bit) *n.* 1. A sharp-edged tool for boring or drilling, used with a brace, drill press, etc. 2. The sharp or cutting part of a tool. 3. The metallic mouthpiece of a bridle. 4. The part of a key that turns a lock. *—v.t.* **bit·ted, bit·ting** 1. To put a bit in the mouth of (a horse). 2. To curb; restrain. [OE *bite* a biting < *bītan* to bite]

bit[3] (bit) Past tense and alternative past participle of BITE.

bit[4] (bit) *n.* A unit of computer information equivalent to the result of a choice between two possibilities. [< BI(NARY) + (DIGI)T]

bitch (bich) *n.* 1. The female of the dog or other canine animal. 2. *Slang* A malicious or promiscuous woman. *—v.i. Slang* To complain. [OE *bicce*] **—bitch′i·ness** *n.* **—bitch′y** *adj.*

bite (bīt) *v.* **bit, bit·ten** or **bit, bit·ing** *v.t.* 1. To seize, tear, or wound with the teeth. 2. To cut or tear off with or as with the teeth: usually with *off.* 3. To puncture the skin of with a sting or fangs. 4. To cut, pierce, or corrode. 5. To grip; take hold of. 6. To cheat; deceive: usually passive. *—v.i.* 7. To seize or cut into something with the teeth. 8. To smart; sting. 9. To take hold; grip. 10. To take bait, as fish. *—n.* 1. The act of biting. 2. A wound inflicted by biting. 3. A smart;

sting. 4. A morsel of food; mouthful. 5. *Informal* A light meal; snack. 6. The grip or hold taken by a tool, etc. [OE *bītan*] **—bit′er** *n.*

bit·ing (bī′ting) *adj.* 1. Sharp; stinging. 2. Sarcastic; caustic. **—bit′ing·ly** *adv.*

bit·stock (bit′stok′) *n.* A brace for a bit.

bitt (bit) *Naut. n.* A single or double post on a ship's deck, to which cables, etc., are made fast. **—***v.t.* To wind (a cable) around a bitt. [? < ON *biti* beam]

bit·ten (bit′n) Past participle of BITE.

bit·ter (bit′ər) *adj.* 1. Having an acrid, disagreeable taste. 2. Unpleasant to accept; distasteful; painful. 3. Feeling or showing intense animosity. **—***n.* That which is bitter. [OE *biter* < *bītan* to bite] **—bit′ter·ly** *adv.* **—bit′ter·ness** *n.*

bit·tern (bit′ərn) *n.* Any of various wading birds related to the heron. [ME *bitoure*]

bit·ter·root (bit′ər·ro͞ot′, -ro͝ot′) *n.* An herb with nutritious roots and pink or white flowers.

bit·ters (bit′ərz) *n.pl.* A liquor, usu. alcoholic, made from bitter herbs, roots, etc.

bitter·sweet (bit′ər·swēt′) *n.* A shrubby or climbing plant having green flowers. **—***adj.* 1. Bitter and sweet. 2. Pleasant and unpleasant.

bi·tu·men (bi·to͞o′mən, -tyo͞o′-, bī-) *n.* 1. Any natural mixture of solid and semisolid hydrocarbons, as asphalt. 2. A brown paint made by mixing asphalt with a drying oil. [< L]

bi·tu·mi·nous (bi·to͞o′mə·nəs, -tyo͞o′-, bī-) *adj.* 1. Of, pertaining to, or containing bitumen. 2. Containing many volatile hydrocarbons, as shale.

bituminous coal A mineral coal low in carbon: also called *soft coal.*

bi·u·nique (bī′yo͞o·nēk′) *adj.* Of two sets, exhibiting a one-to-one correspondence with each other, as the set of real numbers and the points in a line. **—bi′u·nique′ness** *n.*

bi·va·lent (bī·vā′lənt) *adj. Chem.* **a** Having a valence of two. **b** Having two valences. Also *divalent.* **—bi·va′lence, bi·va′len·cy** *n.*

bi·valve (bī′valv′) *n. Zool.* A mollusk having a shell of two lateral valves hinged together, as the oyster or clam. **—***adj.* Having two valves or parts: also **bi′valved′.**

biv·ou·ac (biv′o͞o·ak, biv′wak) *n.* A temporary encampment, esp. for soldiers in the field. [< G *beiwacht* guard] **—biv′ou·ac** *v.i.* **·acked, ·ack·ing**

bi·week·ly (bī·wēk′lē) *adj.* 1. Occurring once every two weeks. 2. Occurring twice a week; semiweekly. **—***n.* A biweekly publication. **—bi·week′ly** *adv.*

bi·year·ly (bī·yir′lē) *adj.* 1. Occurring twice a year. 2. Occurring every two years. **—bi·year′ly** *adv.*

bi·zarre (bi·zär′) *adj.* Odd; fantastic; grotesque. [< F] **—bi·zarre′ly** *adv.* **—bi·zarre′ness** *n.*

blab (blab) *v.t. & v.i.* **blabbed, blab·bing** 1. To disclose indiscreetly. 2. To prattle. **—***n.* 1. One who blabs. 2. Idle chatter. Also **blab′ber.** [ME *blabbe* idle talker]

blab·ber·mouth (blab′ər·mouth′) *n.* One who talks too much and cannot keep secrets.

black (blak) *adj.* 1. Having no brightness or color; reflecting no light. 2. Destitute of light. 3. Gloomy; dismal; forbidding. 4. Belonging to a racial group characterized by dark skin; esp., Negroid. 5. Of or pertaining to black people. 6. Soiled; stained. 7. Indicating disgrace or censure. 8. Angry; threatening. 9. Evil; wicked; malignant. 10. Characterized by grotesque, savage, or morbid satire: *black* humor. 11. Of coffee, without cream or milk. **—***n.* 1. The absence of light; the darkest of all colors. 2. Something black, as soot. 3. A person with dark skin, esp. a Negro. **—***v.t.* 1. To make black; blacken. 2. To put blacking on and polish (shoes). **—***v.i.* 3. To become black. **—to black out** 1. To suffer a temporary loss of vision or consciousness. 2. To extinguish or screen all lights. [OE *blæc* dark] **—black′ness** *n.*

black-and-blue (blak′ən·blo͞o′) *adj.* Discolored: said of skin that has been bruised.

black art Necromancy; magic.

black·ball (blak′bôl′) *n.* A negative vote. **—***v.t.* 1. To vote against. 2. To ostracize; exclude. **—black′ball′er** *n.*

black bass A fresh-water game fish of the eastern U.S. and Canada.

black bear The common North American bear, having fur that varies from glossy black to cinnamon brown.

black belt 1. A rating of expert in a martial art such as judo or karate. 2. One who holds such a rating. **—black′-belt′** *adj.*

black·ber·ry (blak′ber′ē, -bər·ē) *n. pl.* **·ries** The black, edible fruit of certain shrubs of the rose family; also, the shrub.

black·bird (blak′bûrd′) *n.* Any of various birds, the male of which usu. is black.

black·board (blak′bôrd′) *n.* A blackened surface, often of slate, for drawing and writing upon with chalk.

black box A self-contained electronic device that can be inserted into a system.

black·damp (blak′damp′) *n.* A suffocating mine gas composed of carbon dioxide and nitrogen. Also called *chokedamp.*

Black Death An exceptionally virulent plague, epidemic in Asia and Europe during the 14th century: also called *plague.*

black·en (blak′ən) *v.* **·ened, ·en·ing** *v.t.* 1. To make black or dark. 2. To slander; defame. **—***v.i.* 3. To become black; darken. [ME *blaknen* < *blak* black] **—black′en·er** *n.*

Black English A dialect of English spoken by many American Negroes.

black eye 1. An eye with a black iris. 2. An eye having the adjacent surface discolored by a bruise. 3. *Informal* A bad reputation. **—black-eyed** (blak′īd′) *adj.*

black-eyed pea The cowpea.

black-eyed Susan A yellow, daisylike flower with a dark center.

black·face (blak′fās′) *n.* Exaggerated makeup for comic Negro roles.

Black·foot (blak′fo͝ot′) *n. pl.* **·feet** (-fēt′) A member of a tribe of Algonquian Indians living in Alberta and Montana. **—Black′foot′** *adj.*

black·guard (blag′ərd, -ärd) *n.* A vile scoundrel; rogue. [< BLACK + GUARD; orig., the scullions and menials of a great house or army] **—black′guard** *adj.* **—black′·guard·ly** *adj. & adv.*

black·head (blak′hed′) *n.* A plug of dried, fatty matter in a pore of the skin.

black-heart·ed (blak′här′tid) *adj.* Evil; wicked.

black hole A hypothetical astronomical body, held to be a collapsed star, small, and with an intense gravitational field.
black·ing (blak′ing) *n.* A preparation used to blacken or polish shoes, stoves, etc.
black·jack (blak′jak′) *n.* **1.** A small bludgeon with a flexible handle. **2.** A pirate's flag. **3.** A small oak of the SE U.S. **4.** Twenty-one, a card game. —*v.t.* To strike with a blackjack.
black letter *Printing* A type face characterized by heavy black letters resembling those of early printed works: also called *gothic, Old English.* —**black·let·ter** (blak′let′ər) *adj.*
black·list (blak′list′) *n.* A list of censured persons or groups to be penalized or discriminated against. —**black′list′** *v.t.*
black lung *n.* A lung disease caused by inhaling coal dust.
black·ly (blak′lē) *adv.* Darkly, gloomily, or threateningly.
black magic Witchcraft.
black·mail (blak′māl′) *n.* Extortion by threat of exposure of something secret; also, that which is so extorted, as money. —*v.t.* **1.** To level blackmail upon. **2.** To force (to do something), as by threats: with *into.* [< BLACK + OE *māl* agreement] —**black′·mail′er** *n.*
black market A system for selling goods in violation of official prices, quotas, etc.
Black Muslim A member of a sect (the **Nation of Islam**) of blacks in the U.S., which follows the practices of Islam and rejects integration.
black·out (blak′out′) *n.* **1.** The extinguishing or screening of lights, esp. as a precaution against air raids. **2.** Widespread loss of light caused by electric power failure. **3.** Partial or complete loss of vision or consciousness. **4.** A ban, as on news.
black sheep One regarded as a disgrace by his family.
black·smith (blak′smith′) *n.* **1.** One who shoes horses. **2.** One who works iron on an anvil and uses a forge.
black·snake (blak′snak′) *n.* Any of various agile, nonvenomous snakes of the eastern U.S., having smooth, black scales.
black·thorn (blak′thôrn′) *n.* **1.** A thorny European shrub of the rose family; also, its small, plumlike fruit. Also called *sloe.* **2.** A cane made from its wood.
black tie **1.** A black bow tie. **2.** A tuxedo and its correct accessories.
black widow A North American spider, esp. the venomous female.
blad·der (blad′ər) *n.* **1.** *Anat.* An expandable membranous sac in the pelvic cavity, for the temporary retention of urine. **2.** An inflatable object resembling a bladder. [OE *blǣdre*]
blad·der·wort (blad′ər·wûrt′) *n.* An aquatic herb having small sacs on the leaves for trapping food.
blade (blād) *n.* **1.** The flat cutting part of any edged tool or weapon. **2.** The thin, flat part of an oar, plow, etc. **3.** The leaf of grasses or certain other plants. **4.** A sword. **5.** A dashing young man. **6.** *Phonet.* The upper surface of the tongue behind the tip. [OE *blæd*] —**blad′ed** *adj.*
blain (blān) *n. Pathol.* An inflamed swelling; blister. [OE *blegen*]
blam·a·ble (blā′mə·bəl) *adj.* Deserving blame; culpable. Also **blame′a·ble.** —**blam′·a·ble·ness** *n.* —**blam′a·bly** *adv.*
blame (blām) *v.t.* **blamed, blam·ing** **1.** To hold responsible; accuse. **2.** To find fault with; reproach. **3.** To place the responsibility for (an action or error). —**to be to blame** To be at fault. —*n.* **1.** Expression of censure; reproof. **2.** Responsibility for something wrong; culpability. [< LL *blasphemare* to revile, reproach] —**blame′less** *adj.* —**blame′·less·ly** *adv.*
blame·wor·thy (blām′wûr′thē) *adj.* Deserving of blame. —**blame′wor′thi·ness** *n.*
blanch (blanch) *v.t.* **1.** To remove the color from; bleach. **2.** To cause to turn pale. **3.** To scald, esp. to remove the skin of. —*v.i.* **4.** To turn or become white or pale. [< F *blanc* white]
blanc·mange (blə·mänzh′) *n.* A custardlike dessert. [< OF *blanc-manger*, lit., white food]
bland (bland) *adj.* **1.** Gentle and soothing. **2.** Mild; insipid. [< L *blandus* mild] —**bland′ly** *adv.* —**bland′ness** *n.*
blan·dish (blan′dish) *v.t.* To wheedle; flatter. [< L *blandus* mild] —**blan′dish·er** *n.* —**blan′dish·ment** *n.*
blank (blangk) *adj.* **1.** Free from writing or print. **2.** Not completed or filled out, as a check. **3.** Showing no expression or interest; vacant. **4.** Lacking variety or interest. **5.** Disconcerted; bewildered. **6.** Empty or void; also, fruitless. —*n.* **1.** An empty space; void. **2.** A blank space in a printed document, to be filled in. **3.** A paper or document with such spaces. **4.** A partially prepared piece ready for forming into a finished object, as a key. **5.** A cartridge filled with powder but having no bullets: also **blank cartridge.** —*v.t.* To delete; invalidate: often with *out.* [< OF *blanc* white] —**blank′ly** *adv.* —**blank′ness** *n.*
blank check *Informal* **1.** A check bearing a signature but no specified amount. **2.** Unlimited authority or freedom.
blan·ket (blang′kit) *n.* **1.** A covering of wool or other fabric, used for warmth. **2.** Anything that covers, conceals, or protects: a *blanket* of fog. —*adj.* Covering a wide range of conditions, items, etc.: a *blanket* indictment. —*v.t.* To cover with or as with a blanket. [< OF *blankete*, dim. of *blanc* white; orig., a white or undyed woolen cloth]
blank verse Verse without rhyme.
blare (blâr) *v.t. & v.i.* **blared, blar·ing** **1.** To sound loudly, as a trumpet. **2.** To exclaim noisily. —*n.* **1.** A loud, brazen sound. **2.** Brightness or glare, as of color. [Prob. imit.]
blar·ney (blär′nē) *n.* Wheedling flattery; cajolery. [< BLARNEY STONE]
Blarney Stone A stone in a castle in Blarney, Ireland, that reputedly endows one who kisses it with skill in flattery.
bla·sé (blä·zā′, blä′zā) *adj.* Wearied or bored, as from overindulgence in pleasure. [< F *blaser* to satiate]
blas·pheme (blas·fēm′) *v.* **·phemed, ·phem·ing** *v.t.* **1.** To speak in an impious manner of (God or sacred things). **2.** To speak ill of; malign. —*v.i.* **3.** To utter blasphemy. [< Gk. *blasphēmos* evil-speaking] —**blas·phem′er** *n.*
blas·phe·my (blas′fə·mē) *n. pl.* **·mies** Impious or profane speaking of God, or of sacred persons or things. [< Gk. *blasphēmia*]

—**blas′phe·mous** *adj.* —**blas′phe·mous·ly** *adv.*

blast (blast) *v.t.* 1. To rend in pieces by or as by explosion. 2. To cause to wither or shrivel; destroy. —**to blast off** *Aerospace* To begin an ascent by means of rocket or jet propulsion. —*n.* 1. A strong wind; gust. 2. A loud, sudden sound, as of a trumpet. 3. A rush of air, steam, etc. 4. An explosion of dynamite, etc. 5. A blight. 6. *Slang* A big, enjoyable party. 7. *Slang* In baseball, a home run. —**at full blast** At capacity operation or maximum speed. [OE *blǣst*] —**blast′er** *n.*

blast·ed (blas′tid) *adj.* 1. Withered or destroyed. 2. Damned: a euphemism.

blast furnace *Metall.* A smelting furnace in which the fire is intensified by an air blast.

blast·off (blast′ôf′) *n. Aerospace* The series of events immediately before and after a rocket leaves its launching pad; also the moment of leaving.

blas·tu·la (blas′cho͞o·lə) *n. pl.* **·lae** (-lē) *Biol.* The stage of the embryo when it is a hollow sphere of one layer of cells. [< Gk. *blastos* sprout] —**blas′tu·lar** *adj.*

bla·tant (blā′tənt) *adj.* 1. Offensively loud or noisy; clamorous. 2. Obvious; obtrusive: *blatant* stupidity. [Coined by Edmund Spenser] —**bla′tan·cy** *n.* —**bla′tant·ly** *adv.*

blath·er (blath′ər) *v.t. & v.i.* To speak foolishly. [< ON *blathr* nonsense] —**blath′er** *n.* —**blath′er·er** *n.*

blaze[1] (blāz) *v.i.* **blazed, blaz·ing** 1. To burn brightly. 2. To burn as with emotion. 3. To shine. —*n.* 1. A vivid glowing flame; fire. 2. Brilliance; glow. 3. Sudden activity; outburst, as of anger. [OE *blæse*]

blaze[2] (blāz) *v.t.* **blazed, blaz·ing** 1. To mark (a tree) by or as by chipping off bark. 2. To indicate (a trail) by this means. —*n.* 1. A white spot on the face of a horse. 2. A mark to indicate a trail. [Akin to ON *blesi* white spot on a horse's face]

blaz·er (blā′zər) *n.* A lightweight jacket for informal wear. [< BLAZE[1]]

bla·zon (blā′zən) *v.t.* 1. To inscribe or adorn, as with names or symbols. 2. To describe or depict (coats of arms). 3. To proclaim; publish. —*n.* 1. A coat of arms. 2. A technical description of armorial bearings. 3. Ostentatious display. [< OF *blason* coat of arms, shield] —**bla′zon·ry** *n.*

-ble See -ABLE.

bleach (blēch) *v.t. & v.i.* To make or become colorless or white; whiten. —*n.* 1. The act of bleaching. 2. A bleaching agent. [OE *blǣcean*]

bleach·er (blē′chər) *n.* 1. One who or that which bleaches. 2. *pl.* Tiered, benchlike seats.

bleak (blēk) *adj.* 1. Exposed; bare; barren. 2. Cold; cutting. 3. Cheerless; dreary. [? < ON *bleikr* pale] —**bleak′ly** *adv.* —**bleak′ness** *n.*

blear (blir) *v.t.* 1. To dim (the eyes) with or as with tears. 2. To blur or make dim. —*adj.* Bleary. [ME *blere*]

blear·y (blir′ē) *adj.* **·i·er, ·i·est** Made dim, as by tears. —**blear′i·ly** *adv.* —**blear′i·ness** *n.*

bleat (blēt) *v.i.* 1. To utter the cry of a sheep, goat, or calf. 2. To speak or complain with a similar sound. —*v.t.* 3. To utter with a bleat. [OE *blǣtan*] —**bleat** *n.* —**bleat′er** *n.*

bleed (blēd) *v.* **bled, bleed·ing** *v.i.* 1. To lose or shed blood. 2. To feel grief or sympathy. 3. To exude sap or other fluid. 4. *Printing* To extend to or beyond the edge of a page, as an illustration. —*v.t.* 5. To draw blood from; leech. 6. *Slang* To extort money or valuables from. [OE *blēdan*]

bleed·er (blē′dər) *n.* One who bleeds profusely; esp., a hemophiliac.

bleeding heart 1. A plant having racemes of pink, drooping flowers. 2. One whose sympathy can be easily aroused.

blem·ish (blem′ish) *v.t.* To mar the perfection of; sully. —*n.* 1. A defect, esp. of the skin. 2. A moral fault. [< OF *blemir* to make livid]

blench[1] (blench) *v.i.* To shrink back; flinch. [OE *blencan* to deceive]

blench[2] (blench) *v.t. & v.i.* To make or become pale; blanch. [Var. of BLANCH]

blend (blend) *v.t.* 1. To mingle, combine, or mix thoroughly. —*v.i.* 2. To mix; intermingle. 3. To pass or shade imperceptibly into each other, as colors. 4. To harmonize. [Prob. < ON *blanda* to mix] —**blend** *n.* —**blend′er** *n.*

blende (blend) *n. Mineral.* One of a number of rather bright minerals combining sulfur with a metallic element. [< G *blendendes erz* deceptive ore]

blended whiskey Whiskey that has been blended with other whiskey or neutral spirits.

blen·ny (blen′ē) *n. pl.* **·nies** A small marine fish having an elongated body. [< Gk. *blennos* slime]

bless (bles) *v.t.* **blessed** or **blest, bless·ing** 1. To consecrate; make holy. 2. To honor and exalt; glorify. 3. To invoke God's favor upon (a person or thing). 4. To bestow prosperity upon; make happy. 5. To endow, as with a gift. 6. To guard; protect: *Bless* me! [OE *blēdsian* to consecrate (with blood) < *blōd* blood]

bless·ed (bles′id, blest) *adj.* 1. Made holy. 2. Enjoying the happiness of heaven. 3. Blissful; happy. 4. Causing happiness. Also spelled *blest.* —**bless′ed·ly** *adv.* —**bless′ed·ness** *n.*

bless·ed event (bles′id) *Informal* The birth of a baby.

bless·ing (bles′ing) *n.* 1. An invocation or benediction; grace. 2. The bestowal of divine favor. 3. That which makes happy or prosperous.

blest (blest) Alternative past participle of BLESS. —*adj.* Blessed.

blew (blo͞o) Past tense of BLOW.

blight (blīt) *n.* 1. Any of a number of destructive plant diseases, as mildew or rust. 2. Anything that withers hopes, destroys prospects, or impairs growth. —*v.t.* 1. To cause to decay; blast. 2. To ruin; frustrate. [Origin unknown]

blimp (blimp) *n. Informal* A nonrigid dirigible. [< Type *B-Limp*, a kind of British dirigible]

blind (blīnd) *adj.* 1. Unable to see. 2. Lacking in perception or judgment. 3. Acting or done without intelligent control; random. 4. Unreasoning; heedless: *blind* prejudice. 5. Concealed: a *blind* ditch. 6. Closed at one end: a *blind* alley. 7. Having no opening or outlet: a *blind* wall. 8. Done without the aid of visual reference: *blind* flying. —*n.* 1. Something that obstructs vision or shuts off light; esp., a window shade. 2. A hiding place, as for a hunter. 3. Something intended to deceive. —*adv.* 1. To the stage of insensibility: *blind* drunk. 2. By the aid of instruments only: to fly *blind.* —*v.t.* 1. To make blind. 2. To dazzle. 3. To deprive of judgment or discernment. [OE] —**blind′ing** *adj.* —**blind′ly** *adv.* —**blind′ness** *n.*

blind date *Informal* A date with a person whom one has not previously met.

blind·er (blīn′dər) *n.* 1. One who or that which blinds. 2. A flap on the side of a horse's bridle that obstructs sideways vision: also called *blinker.*

blind·fold (blīnd′fōld′) *v.t.* 1. To cover or bandage the eyes of. 2. To hoodwink; mislead. —*n.* A bandage over the eyes. [ME < *blind* blind + *fellen* to strike]

blind·man's buff (blīnd′manz′) A game in which one player is blindfolded and must catch and identify another player.

blind spot 1. *Anat.* A small area on the retina of the eye that is insensible to light because of the entrance of the optic nerve. 2. A subject about which one is ignorant, or incapable of objective thought.

blind trust A method of administering financial holdings in which the owner deprives himself of all decisions so as to avoid conflict of interest.

blink (blingk) *v.i.* 1. To wink rapidly. 2. To squint. 3. To twinkle; to flash on and off. —*v.t.* 4. To cause to wink. —**to blink at** To see but ignore. —*n.* 1. A blinking; wink. 2. A gleam. 3. A glance or glimpse. [ME *blenken*]

blink·er (blingk′ər) *n.* 1. A light that blinks. 2. *pl.* Goggles. 3. Blinder (def. 2).

blintz (blints) *n.* A thin pancake folded about a filling of cottage cheese, fruit, etc. Also **blint·ze** (blint′sə). [< Yiddish]

blip (blip) *v.t.* **blipped, blip·ping** To excise (sound, as a taboo word) from a videotape, leaving a noticeable gap in performance. —*n.* 1. A signal recorded on a radarscope. 2. The interruption in a television show, resulting from blipping. [Imit.]

bliss (blis) *n.* Gladness; joy. [OE *blīthe* joyous] —**bliss′ful** *adj.* —**bliss′ful·ly** *adv.* —**bliss′ful·ness** *n.*

blis·ter (blis′tər) *n.* 1. A thin vesicle, esp. on the skin, containing watery matter, as from rubbing, a burn, etc. 2. Any similar swelling. —*v.t.* 1. To produce a blister or blisters upon. 2. To rebuke severely. —*v.i.* 3. To become blistered. [< ON *blāstr* swelling] —**blis′·ter·y** *adj.*

blithe (blīth, blīth) *adj.* Cheerful; gay. [OE] —**blithe′ly** *adv.* —**blithe′ness** *n.*

blithe·some (blīth′səm, blīth′-) *adj.* Showing or imparting gladness. —**blithe′some·ly** *adv.* —**blithe′some·ness** *n.*

blitz (blits) *Informal n.* A sudden attack; blitzkrieg. —**blitz** *v.t.*

blitz·krieg (blits′krēg) *n.* 1. *Mil.* A swift, sudden attack by tanks, aircraft, etc.; also, warfare so waged. 2. Any sudden attack or assault. [< G *blitz* lightning + *krieg* war]

bliz·zard (bliz′ərd) *n.* A severe snowstorm. [dial. E *blizzer* sudden blow]

bloat (blōt) *v.t. & v.i.* To swell or cause to swell, as with fluid. [ME, ? < ON *blautr* soft, soaked]

blob (blob) *n.* 1. A soft, globular mass; a viscous drop. 2. A daub or spot, as of color. 3. Something shapeless or vague. [Origin unknown]

bloc (blok) *n.* A group, as of politicians or nations, joined to foster special interests. [< F]

block[1] (blok) *n.* 1. A solid piece of wood, metal, etc., usu. with one or more flat surfaces. 2. A support or form on which something is shaped or displayed. 3. A stand from which articles are sold at auction. 4. A set or section, as of tickets, etc., handled as a unit. 5. An area bounded, usu. on four sides, by streets; also, one side of such an area. 6. A pulley, or set of pulleys, in a frame with a hook or the like at one end. —*v.t.* 1. To shape into blocks. 2. To shape with a block, as a hat. 3. To support or strengthen with blocks. —**to block out** To plan broadly without details. [< F *bloc*] —**block′er** *n.*

block[2] (blok) *n.* 1. An obstacle or hindrance. 2. The act of obstructing, or the state of being obstructed. 3. *Med.* Anesthesia of a specific region. 4. *Psychol.* The inability to think or act in certain situations. —*v.t.* 1. To obstruct; hinder; stop. —*v.i.* 2. *Sports* To obstruct an opponent's actions. —**to block out** To obscure from view. [< MF *bloquer* to obstruct] —**block′age** *n.* —**block′·er** *n.*

block·ade (blo·kād′) *n.* 1. The closing by hostile ships or forces of a coast, city, etc., to traffic or communication. 2. The ships or forces used for this. 3. An obstruction to action or passage. —**to run the blockade** To elude a blockade. —*v.t.* **·ad·ed, ·ad·ing** To subject to a blockade. —**block·ad′er** *n.*

block and tackle A set of pulley blocks and ropes for pulling or hoisting.

block·bust·er (blok′bus′tər) *n.* 1. A powerful aerial bomb. 2. Something very powerful, large, or successful. 3. One who profiteers through blockbusting.

block·bust·ing (blok′bus′ting) *n.* The practice of inducing owners to sell homes quickly and at a loss, by inciting fears that a minority group will take over a neighborhood, deflating values.

block·head (blok′hed′) *n.* A stupid person; dolt.

block·house (blok′hous′) *n.* 1. A fortification, formerly of logs and heavy timbers, having loopholes from which to fire. 2. A house made of hewn logs set square.

block letter 1. Printing type cut from wood. 2. A style of letters without serifs.

block·y (blok′ē) *adj.* **block·i·er, block·i·est** 1. Unequally shaded, as if printed in blocks. 2. Short and stout; stocky.

bloke (blōk) *n. Brit. Slang* A fellow; guy.

blond (blond) *adj.* 1. Having fair hair with light eyes and skin. 2. Flaxen or golden, as hair. —*n.* A blond person. [< F]

blonde (blond) *adj. & n.* Blond: feminine form.

blood (blud) *n.* 1. *Physiol.* The red fluid that circulates through the bodies of animals, delivering oxygen and nutrients to the cells and tissues. ◆Collateral adjective: *hemal.* 2. A similar fluid, as the sap of plants. 3. The shedding of blood; murder. 4. Temperament: hot *blood.* 5. Vitality; lifeblood. 6. Descent from a common ancestor; kinship. 7. Noble descent. 8. Racial or national extraction. 9. A dashing young man. 10. People considered a source of new ideas or energy: new *blood.* **—bad blood** Enmity. **—in cold blood** 1. Deliberately; without passion. 2. Cruelly; without mercy. [OE *blōd*]

blood bank A place where blood is stored for use in transfusion.

blood bath Wanton killing; a massacre.

blood count *Med.* The number and proportion of red and white cells in a sample of blood.

blood·cur·dling (blud′kûrd′ling) *adj.* Terrifying.

blood·ed (blud′id) *adj.* 1. Having temper of a specified character: *hot-blooded.* 2. Thoroughbred.

blood group *Physiol.* One of the classes into which blood may be divided: also called *blood type.*

blood·hound (blud′hound′) *n.* A large, smooth-coated hound having a keen sense of smell and often used for tracking.

blood·less (blud′lis) *adj.* 1. Devoid of blood; pale. 2. Without bloodshed. 3. Lacking vigor; listless. 4. Coldhearted. **—blood′less·ly** *adv.* **—blood′less·ness** *n.*

blood·let·ting (blud′let′ing) *n.* 1. Bleeding for a therapeutic purpose. 2. Bloodshed.

blood money 1. *Informal* Money obtained at the cost of another's life, welfare, etc. 2. Money paid to a hired murderer. 3. Compensation paid to the kin of a murdered person.

blood plasma *Physiol.* The liquid part of the blood, without its cellular components.

blood poisoning *Pathol.* Deterioration of the blood caused by bacterial substances: also called *toxemia.*

blood pressure *Physiol.* The pressure of the blood on the walls of the arteries.

blood·shed (blud′shed′) *n.* The shedding of blood; slaughter. Also **blood′shed′ding.**

blood·shot (blud′shot′) *adj.* Suffused or shot with blood; inflamed: said of the eye.

blood·stain (blud′stān′) *n.* A spot produced by blood. **—blood′stain′** *v.t.* **—blood′stained′** *adj.*

blood·stone (blud′stōn′) *n.* A stone of green quartz flecked with red jasper: also called *heliotrope.*

blood stream The blood coursing through a living body.

blood·suck·er (blud′suk′ər) *n.* 1. An animal that sucks blood, as a leech. 2. *Informal* One who extorts or sponges.

blood·thirst·y (blud′thûrs′tē) *adj.* Murderous; cruel. **—blood′thirst′i·ly** *adv.* **—blood′·thirst′i·ness** *n.*

blood transfusion *Med.* The transfer of blood from one person or animal into another.

blood type Blood group.

blood vessel Any tubular canal, as an artery, vein, or capillary, through which the blood circulates.

blood·y (blud′ē) *adj.* **blood·i·er, blood·i·est** 1. Stained with blood. 2. Of, like, or containing blood. 3. Involving bloodshed. 4. Bloodthirsty. 5. *Brit. Slang* Damned: a vulgarism. **—*v.t.* blood·ied, blood·y·ing** To stain with blood. **—*adv.*** *Brit. Slang* Very: a vulgarism. [OE *blōdig*] **—blood′i·ly** *adv.* **—blood′i·ness** *n.*

bloom (blo͞om) *n.* 1. The flower of a plant; blossom. 2. The state of being in flower. 3. A prime condition, as of health or freshness. 4. The rosy tint of the cheeks or skin; glow. 5. *Bot.* The powdery, waxy substance on certain fruits and leaves. 6. A powdery incrustation on certain ores. **—*v.i.*** 1. To bear flowers; blossom. 2. To glow with health; flourish. [< ON *blōm* blossom] **—bloom′y** *adj.*

bloom·ers (blo͞o′mərz) *n.pl.* Formerly, loose, wide trousers gathered at the knee, worn by women as a gymnasium costume; also, an undergarment resembling these. [after Amelia Jenks *Bloomer,* 1818–94, U.S. feminist]

bloom·ing (blo͞o′ming) *adj.* 1. In flower; blossoming. 2. Flourishing.

blos·som (blos′əm) *n.* 1. A flower, esp. one of a plant yielding edible fruit. 2. The state or period of flowering; bloom. **—*v.i.*** 1. To come into blossom. 2. To prosper; thrive. [OE *blōstm*] **—blos′som·y** *adj.*

blot (blot) *n.* 1. A spot or stain, as of ink. 2. A defect or blemish. **—*v.* blot·ted, blot·ting** *v.t.* 1. To spot, as with ink; stain. 2. To disgrace; sully. 3. To obscure: usually with *out.* 4. To dry, as with blotting paper. **—*v.i.*** 5. To spread in a blot or blots, as ink. 6. To absorb. [ME *blotte*]

blotch (bloch) *n.* 1. A spot or blot. 2. An eruption on the skin. **—*v.t.* & *v.i.*** To mark or become marked with blotches. [Blend of BLOT and BOTCH] **—blotch′i·ness** *n.* **—blotch′y** *adj.*

blot·ter (blot′ər) *n.* 1. A sheet or pad of blotting paper. 2. The daily record of arrests in a police station.

blotting paper Unsized paper for absorbing excess ink.

blouse (blous, blouz) *n.* 1. A woman's garment extending from the neck to the waist or just below. 2. A loose, knee-length smock, usu. belted at the waist. 3. The service coat of the U.S. Army uniform. **—*v.t.* & *v.i.* bloused, blous·ing** To drape loosely or fully. [< F]

blow[1] (blō) *v.* **blew, blown, blow·ing** *v.i.* 1. To be in motion: said of wind or air. 2. To move in a current of air. 3. To emit a current or jet of air, steam, etc. 4. To produce sound by blowing or being blown. 5. To pant; gasp for breath. 6. To fail or become useless, as a fuse, tire, etc.: often with *out.* **—*v.t.*** 7. To drive or impel by a current of air. 8. To direct a current of air upon. 9. To sound by blowing into, as a bugle. 10. To sound (a signal): to *blow* taps. 11. To emit, as air or smoke, from the mouth. 12. To put out of breath, as a horse. 13. To form by inflating a material: to *blow* bubbles. 14. To break, shatter, or destroy by explosion: usu. with *up, down,* etc. 15. *Informal* To melt (a fuse). 16. *Slang* To spend (money) lavishly on; also, to treat or entertain. **—to blow over** 1. To pass, as a storm; subside. 2. To pass without bad result. **—*n.*** 1. A blowing, as of wind. 2. A storm or gale. [OE *blāwan*]

blow[2] (blō) *n.* 1. A sudden stroke dealt with the fist, a weapon, etc. 2. A sudden disaster. 3. A hostile act; assault. **—to come to blows** To start fighting. [ME *blaw*]

blow[3] (blō) *Archaic & Poetic* *v.t.* & *v.i.* **blew, blown, blow·ing** To bloom or cause to bloom. [OE *blōwan* to blossom]

blow·er (blō′ər) *n.* 1. One who or that which blows. 2. A device for forcing air through a building, furnace, etc.

blow·fly (blō′flī′) *n.* *pl.* **·flies** A blue or

green fly whose larvae live in carrion or in living flesh: also called *bluebottle*.

blow·gun (blō′gun′) *n.* A long tube through which a missile, as a dart, may be blown.

blow·hole (blō′hōl′) *n.* 1. *Zool.* A nasal opening in the head, as of certain whales. 2. A vent for gas and bad air, as in mines. 3. A hole in the ice to which seals, etc., come to breathe.

blown (blōn) Past participle of BLOW[1]. —*adj.* 1. Out of breath. 2. Inflated; swollen, esp. with gas.

blow·out (blō′out′) *n.* 1. A bursting, as of a tire, or the hole so made. 2. *Slang* An elaborate meal or party.

blow·pipe (blō′pīp′) *n.* 1. A tube for blowing air or gas through a flame to direct and intensify its heat. 2. A blowgun.

blow·torch (blō′tôrch′) *n.* An apparatus that produces a strong jet of intensely hot flame.

blow·up (blō′up′) *n.* 1. An explosion. 2. *Informal* A loss of self-control; also, a fight. 3. An enlargement, as of a photograph.

blow·y (blō′ē) *adj.* **blow·i·er, blow·i·est** Windy.

blowz·y (blou′zē) *adj.* **blowz·i·er, blowz·i·est** 1. Disheveled; slovenly. 2. Fat and red-faced. Also **blow′sy.** [< earlier *blowse* a fat, ruddy woman; origin uncertain]

blub·ber (blub′ər) *v.i.* 1. To weep and sob noisily. —*v.t.* 2. To utter with sobs. —*n.* 1. *Zool.* The fat of a whale or other cetacean, used as a source of oil. 2. Noisy crying. [ME *blubren*; imit.] —**blub′ber·er** *n.* —**blub′ber·y** *adj.*

blu·cher (blōō′chər, -kər) *n.* A shoe in which there is no front seam, the upper meeting above in two projecting flaps. [after G. L. *Blücher*, 1742–1819, Prussian field marshal]

bludg·eon (bluj′ən) *n.* A short club, weighted at one end, used as a weapon. —*v.t.* 1. To strike with or as with a bludgeon. 2. To coerce; bully. [Origin unknown]

blue (blōō) *adj.* **blu·er, blu·est** 1. Having the color of the clear sky seen in daylight. 2. Livid, as the skin from bruising or cold. 3. Depressed or depressing; melancholy. 4. Puritanical; strict. —**once in a blue moon** Very seldom. —*n.* 1. The color of the clear sky; azure. 2. Any pigment or dye used to impart a blue color. —**out of the blue** From an unsuspected source. —**the blue** 1. The sky. 2. The sea. —*v.t.* **blued, blu·ing** 1. To make blue. 2. To treat with bluing. [< OF *bleu*]

blue baby An infant born with bluish skin resulting esp. from a congenital heart defect.

blue·bell (blōō′bel′) *n.* Any of various plants that bear blue, bell-shaped flowers.

blue·ber·ry (blōō′ber′ē, -bər·ē) *n. pl.* **·ries** 1. An edible, blue American berry. 2. The plant that bears it.

blue·bird (blōō′bûrd′) *n.* A small American songbird with predominantly blue plumage.

blue blood 1. Aristocratic blood or descent. 2. One of aristocratic family: also **blue·blood** (blōō′blud′). —**blue′blood′ed** *adj.*

blue·bon·net (blōō′bon′it) *n.* 1. The cornflower. 2. A leguminous herb with blue flowers.

blue·bot·tle (blōō′bot′l) *n.* 1. A blowfly. 2. Any of various plants with tubular blue flowers.

blue cheese A type of cheese resembling Roquefort.

blue chip 1. In finance, the stock of a well-known company with a record of high dividends, earnings, etc. 2. A gambling chip of the highest value.

blue-col·lar (blōō′kol′ər) *adj.* Of or relating to manual laborers or their jobs.

blue·fish (blōō′fish′) *n. pl.* **·fish** or **·fish·es** A voracious food fish common along the Atlantic coast of the U.S.

blue fox A small fox of arctic regions; also, its fur.

blue·grass[1] (blōō′gras′) *n.* One of various grasses having bluish-green stems; esp., the **Kentucky bluegrass.**

blue·grass[2] (blōō′gras′) *n.* Country music of the upper South played by a string band and usu. unamplified. [after *Blue Grass Boys* < *Bluegrass State*, nickname of Kentucky]

blue jay A crested jay of North America having blue upper parts. Also **blue·jay** (blōō′jā′).

blue·jeans (blōō′jenz′) *n.pl.* Blue denim pants.

blue law A law prohibiting entertainment, business, sale of liquor, etc. on Sunday.

blue·nose (blōō′nōz′) *n. Informal* A puritanical person.

blue-pen·cil (blōō′pen′səl) *v.t.* **·ciled** or **·cilled, ·cil·ing** or **·cil·ling** To edit or cancel with or as with a blue pencil.

blue point An oyster orig. found off the shore of Long Island.

blue·print (blōō′print′) *n.* 1. A plan or drawing made by printing on sensitized paper, the drawing showing in white lines on a blue ground. 2. Any detailed plan. —**blue′print′** *v.t.*

blue-rib·bon (blōō′rib′ən) *adj.* Selected for special qualifications: a *blue-ribbon* panel.

blue ribbon The highest award; first prize.

blues (blōōz) *n.pl.* 1. Depression of spirits; melancholy. 2. A style of music originating among American Negroes and characterized by minor melodies and melancholy subjects; also, the songs sung to this music.

blue·stock·ing (blōō′stok′ing) *n.* A learned, pedantic, or literary woman. [from the informal blue stockings worn by a leading literary figure in 18th c. London]

blu·et (blōō′it) *n.* 1. One of various plants having blue flowers. 2. A delicate meadow flower of the madder family.

bluff[1] (bluf) *v.t.* & *v.i.* 1. To deceive by putting on a bold front. 2. To frighten with empty threats. —*n.* 1. The act of bluffing. 2. One who bluffs. [? < Du. *bluffen* to deceive, mislead] —**bluff′er** *n.*

bluff[2] (bluf) *n.* A steep headland or bank. —*adj.* 1. Rough and hearty in manner. 2. Having a broad, steep appearance. [? < Du. *blaf* flat] —**bluff′ness** *n.*

blu·ing (blōō′ing) *n.* A blue coloring matter used in laundering to whiten. Also **blue′ing.**

blu·ish (blōō′ish) *adj.* Somewhat blue. Also **blue′ish.**

blun·der (blun′dər) *n.* A stupid mistake. —*v.i.* 1. To act or move awkwardly; stumble. 2. To make a stupid mistake. —*v.t.* 3. To utter stupidly or confusedly: often with *out.* 4. To bungle. [ME *blondren* to mix up, confuse] —**blun′der·er** *n.* —**blun′der·ing·ly** *adv.*

blun·der·buss (blun′dər·bus) *n.* 1. An old-fashioned, short gun with large bore and flaring mouth, used for scattering shot at close range. 2. A stupid, blustering person. [Blend of BLUNDER and Du. *donderbus* thunder box]

blunt (blunt) *adj.* 1. Having a dull end or edge. 2. Abrupt in manner; brusque. 3. Slow of wit; dull. —*v.t. & v.i.* To make or become dull or less hurtful. [ME; origin unknown] —**blunt′ly** *adv.* —**blunt′ness** *n.*

blur (blûr) *v.t. & v.i.* **blurred, blur·ring** 1. To make or become vague and indistinct in outline. 2. To dim. 3. To smear; smudge. —*n.* 1. A smear; smudge. 2. Something indistinct. —**blur′ry** *adj.*

blurb (blûrb) *n.* A brief, laudatory description, esp. on a book jacket. [Coined by Gelett Burgess, 1866–1951, U.S. humorist]

blurt (blûrt) *v.t.* To utter abruptly or impulsively: often with *out.* [? Blend of BLOW¹ and SPURT]

blush (blush) *v.i.* 1. To become red in the face from modesty or confusion; flush. 2. To become red or rosy, as flowers. 3. To feel shame or regret: usually with *at* or *for.* —*n.* 1. A reddening of the face from modesty, etc. 2. A red or rosy tint. —*adj.* Reddish. [OE *blyscan* to redden] —**blush′er** *n.* —**blush′ing·ly** *adv.*

blus·ter (blus′tər) *v.i.* 1. To blow gustily with violence and noise, as the wind. 2. To talk loudly and aggressively. —*v.t.* 3. To utter noisily and threateningly. —*n.* 1. Boisterous talk or swagger. 2. A noisy blowing of the wind; blast. —**blus′ter·er** *n.* —**blus′ter·y** *adj.*

bo·a (bō′ə) *n. pl.* **bo·as** 1. Any of several nonvenomous snakes having great crushing power, esp. the **boa constrictor** of South America. 2. A long feather or fur scarf for women. [< L]

boar (bôr) *n. pl.* **boars** or **boar.** 1. A male swine. 2. The wild boar. [OE *bār*]

board (bôrd) *n.* 1. A flat, thin slab of sawed wood longer than it is wide. 2. A piece of wood or other material for a specific purpose: an ironing *board.* 3. A table set for serving food. 4. Food or meals; esp., meals furnished for pay, and often including lodging. 5. An organized official body. —**across the board** *Informal* Affecting all members or categories in the same degree: said of changes in salary, taxes, etc. —**on board** On or in a vessel or other conveyance. —**to go by the board** To fall into ruin, disuse, etc. —*v.t.* 1. To cover or enclose with boards: often with *up.* 2. To furnish with meals, or meals and lodging, for pay. 3. To place where meals and lodging are provided. 4. To get on, as a ship or train. —*v.i.* 5. To take meals, or meals and lodging. [OE *bord* board, side of a ship, table]

board·er (bôr′dər) *n.* One who pays for regular meals, or meals and lodging.

board foot *pl.* **board feet** The volume of a board 1 foot square and 1 inch thick, equal to 144 cubic inches or 2359.8 cubic centimeters.

boarding house A house where meals, or meals and lodging, can be had regularly for pay. Also **board·ing·house** (bôr′ding·hous′).

boarding school A school in which pupils are boarded.

board·walk (bôrd′wôk′) *n.* A promenade along a beach, usually of boards.

boast (bōst) *v.i.* 1. To talk in a vain or bragging manner. 2. To speak or possess with pride: with *of.* —*v.t.* 3. To be proud to possess; take pride in. —*n.* 1. A boastful speech. 2. That which is boasted about. [ME *bosten*] —**boast′er** *n.* —**boast′ful** *adj.* —**boast′ful·ly, boast′ing·ly** *adv.* —**boast′ful·ness** *n.*

boat (bōt) *n.* 1. A small, open watercraft. 2. *Informal* Any watercraft. 3. A boat-shaped object. —**in the same boat** In the same situation or condition; equally involved. —*v.i.* To travel or go out in a boat. [OE *bāt*]

boa·tel (bō·tel′) *n.* A waterside hotel, usu. with docks, serving guests who travel by boat.

boat·house (bōt′hous′) *n.* A building for storing boats.

boat·load (bōt′lōd′) *n.* 1. The amount that a boat can hold. 2. The load carried.

boat·man (bōt′mən) *n. pl.* **·men** (-mən) A man who deals in or works on boats.

boat·swain (bō′sən) *n.* A warrant officer of a naval ship, or a subordinate officer of a merchant vessel, who is in charge of the rigging, anchors, etc. Also spelled *bosun, bo's'n.* [OE *bātswegen*]

bob¹ (bob) *v.t. & v.i.* **bobbed, bob·bing** To move up and down with an irregular, jerky motion. —**to bob up** To appear or emerge suddenly. —*n.* 1. A short, jerky movement. 2. A quick bow or curtsy. 3. In fishing, a float or cork. [ME; origin uncertain] —**bob′ber** *n.*

bob² (bob) *n.* 1. A short haircut for a woman or child. 2. The docked tail of a horse. 3. A small, pendant object, as the weight on a plumb line. —*v.* **bobbed, bob·bing** *v.t.* 1. To cut short, as hair. —*v.i.* 2. To fish. [ME *bobbe*]

bob³ (bob) *n. pl.* **bob** *Brit. Informal* Formerly, a shilling. [Origin unknown]

bob·bin (bob′in) *n.* A spool or reel holding thread for spinning, weaving, or machine sewing. [< F *bobine*]

bob·by (bob′e) *n. pl.* **·bies** *Brit. Informal* A member of the police. [after Sir Robert Peel, 1788–1850, who introduced police reforms]

bobby pin A metal hairpin that clasps the hair tightly. Also **bob′bie pin.**

bobby socks *Informal* Short socks worn by girls.

bob·by·sox·er (bob′ē·sok′sər) *n.* *Informal* An adolescent girl, esp. of the 1940's and 1950's.

bob·cat (bob′kat′) *n.* The American lynx.

bob·o·link (bob′ə·lingk) *n.* A thrushlike songbird of North America. [Imit.; from its call]

bob·sled (bob′sled′) *n.* A long racing sled with a steering wheel. [Origin unknown] —**bob′sled′** *v.i.* **·sled·ded, ·sled·ding**

bob·tail (bob′tāl′) *n.* 1. A short tail or a tail cut short. 2. An animal with such a tail. —**bob′tail′** *v.t.* —**bob′tail′, bob′tailed′** *adj.*

bob·white (bob′hwīt′) *n.* A quail of North America. [Imit.; from its call]

boc·cie (boch′ē) *n.* A bowling game usu. played on a long clay court: also **boc′ce, boc′ci.** [< Ital.]

bock beer (bok) A dark, strong beer brewed in the winter and served in early spring. Also **bock.** [< G *bockbier*]

bode (bōd) *v.t.* **bod·ed, bod·ing** To foretell; presage. [OE *bodian* to announce]
bod·ice (bod′is) *n.* 1. The upper portion of a woman's dress. 2. A woman's vest. [Var. of *bodies*, pl. of BODY]
bod·ied (bod′ēd) *adj.* Having a (specified kind of) body: used in combination: **able-bodied, big-bodied, light-bodied, round-bodied, square-bodied, stout-bodied.**
bod·i·less (bod′i·lis) *adj.* Having no body; incorporeal.
bod·i·ly (bod′ə·lē) *adj.* Of or pertaining to the body. —*adv.* In the flesh; in person.
bod·kin (bod′kin) *n.* 1. A pointed instrument for piercing holes in cloth, etc. 2. A blunt needle for drawing tape through a hem. 3. A long pin for fastening the hair. [ME *boydekin* dagger]
bod·y (bod′ē) *n. pl.* **bod·ies** 1. The entire physical part of a human being, animal, or plant. 2. A corpse; carcass. 3. The torso; trunk. 4. The principal part of anything. 5. A collection of persons or things taken as a whole. 6. A distinct mass or portion: a *body* of water. 7. Density or consistency: a wine with *body*. 8. *Informal* A person. —*v.t.* **bod·ied, bod·y·ing** To furnish with or as with a body. [OE *bodig*]
bod·y·guard (bod′ē·gärd′) *n.* 1. A guard responsible for the physical safety of an individual. 2. A retinue; escort.
body language Unconscious gestures and postures considered as indications of mental and emotional states.
body shirt A close-fitting shirt, fastened at the crotch to hold it taut.
body stocking A snug, one-piece, knit undergarment, usu. for women, covering the torso.
bod·y·surf (bod′ē·sûrf′) *v.i.* To ride a breaking wave by planing with one's body.
Boer (bōr, bôr, bo͝or) *n.* A Dutch colonist or person of Dutch descent in South Africa. [< Du., farmer] —**Boer** *adj.*
bog (bog, bôg) *n.* Wet and spongy ground; marsh. —*v.i.* **bogged, bog·ging** To sink or be impeded in or as in a bog: often with *down*. [< Irish < *bog* soft] —**bog′gy** *adj.* **·gi·er, ·gi·est**
bo·gey[1] (bō′gē) *n. pl.* **·geys** In golf, one stroke over par on a hole. Also **bo′gie.** [After Col. *Bogey*, an imaginary faultless golfer] —**bo′gey** *v.t.* & *v.i.* **·geyed, ·gey·ing**
bo·gey[2] (bo′gē) See BOGY.
bog·gle (bog′əl) *v.* **·gled, ·gling** *v.i.* 1. To hesitate, as from doubt or scruples: often with *at*. 2. To start with fright. 3. To equivocate; dissemble. 4. To work clumsily. —*v.t.* 5. To bungle. [< Scot. *bogle* hobgoblin]
bo·gie (bō′gē) See BOGY.
bo·gus (bō′gəs) *adj.* Counterfeit; fake.
bo·gy (bō′gē) *n. pl.* **·gies** A goblin; bugbear: also spelled *bogey, bogie.* [? Akin to ME *bugge* scarecrow]
Bo·he·mi·an (bō·hē′mē·ən) *adj.* 1. Of or pertaining to Bohemia. 2. Leading the life of a Bohemian; unconventional. —*n.* 1. An inhabitant of Bohemia. 2. A gypsy. 3. A person, usu. of artistic or literary tastes, who lives in an unconventional manner. Also (for *adj.* def. 2, *n.* def. 3) **bo·he′mi·an.** —**Bo·he′mi·an·ism** *n.*
boil[1] (boil) *v.i.* 1. To bubble with escaping gas, usu. from the effect of heat: said of liquids. 2. To reach the boiling point. 3. To undergo the action of a boiling liquid. 4. To seethe like boiling water. 5. To be stirred by rage or passion. —*v.t.* 6. To bring to the boiling point. 7. To cook, cleanse, etc., by boiling. —**to boil down** 1. To reduce in bulk by boiling. 2. To condense; summarize. —*n.* The act or state of boiling. [< L *bullire* to boil]
boil[2] (boil) *n.* A painful, pus-filled nodule beneath the skin. [OE *byl*]
boil·er (boi′lər) *n.* 1. A closed vessel in which steam is generated for heating or power. 2. A tank for hot water.
boiling point The temperature at which a liquid boils, for water usu. 212° F. or 100° C.
bois·ter·ous (bois′tər·əs, -trəs) *adj.* 1. Noisy and unrestrained; uproarious. 2. Stormy; violent. [ME *boistous*] —**bois′ter·ous·ly** *adv.*
bo·la (bō′lə) *n.* A throwing weapon, consisting of a cord with a ball fastened to each end. Also **bo·las** (bō′ləs). [< Sp., ball]
bold (bōld) *adj.* 1. Having courage; fearless. 2. Showing or requiring courage; daring. 3. Brazen; forward. 4. Vigorous; unconventional. 5. Abrupt; steep, as a cliff. [OE *bald*] —**bold′ly** *adv.* —**bold′ness** *n.*
bold·face (bōld′fās′) *n.* *Printing* A type having thick black lines.
bole (bōl) *n.* The trunk of a tree. [< ON *bolr*]
bo·le·ro (bō·lâr′ō, bə-) *n. pl.* **·ros** 1. A short jacket open at the front. 2. A Spanish dance, usu. accompanied by castanets. 3. The music for this dance. [< Sp.]
boll (bōl) *n.* A round pod or seed capsule. —*v.i.* To form pods. [ME *bolle* bowl]
bol·lix (bol′iks) *v.t.* **·lixed, ·lix·ing** *Slang* To bungle; botch: often with *up*. [Alter. of *ballocks* testicles]
boll weevil A beetle that destroys cotton bolls.
boll·worm (bōl′wûrm′) *n.* A moth larva that feeds on cotton bolls.
bo·lo (bō′lō) *n. pl.* **·los** A large, single-edged knife of the Philippines. [< Sp. < Visayan]
Bo·lo·gna sausage (bə·lō′nē, -lō′nə, -lōn′yə) A seasoned sausage of mixed meats: also *baloney, boloney.*
bo·lo·ney (bə·lō′nē) See BALONEY.
Bol·she·vik (bōl′shə·vik, bol′-) *n. pl.* **Bol·she·viks** or **Bol·she·vi·ki** (bōl′shə·vē′kē, bol′-) 1. A member of the dominant branch of the Russian Social Democratic Party, which seized power in November 1917. 2. Loosely, any Communist or radical. Also **bol′she·vik.** [< Russian *bolshe* majority] —**Bol′she·vik** *adj.*
Bol·she·vism (bōl′shə·viz′əm, bol′-) *n.* The Marxian doctrines and policies of the Bolsheviks; also, any practice, government, etc., based on them. Also **bol′she·vism.**
Bol·she·vist (bōl′shə·vist, bol′-) *n.* A Bolshevik. Also **bol′she·vist.** —**Bol′she·vis′tic** *adj.*
bol·ster (bōl′stər) *n.* 1. A narrow, long pillow. 2. A pad used as a support or for protection. 3. Anything shaped like a bolster or used as a support. —*v.t.* To prop or reinforce: often with *up*. [OE]
bolt[1] (bōlt) *n.* 1. A sliding bar or piece for fastening a door, etc. 2. A pin or rod for holding something in place, usu. having a head at one end and threaded at the other. 3. The part of a lock that is shot or withdrawn by turning the key. 4. A sliding mechanism

that closes the breech of some small firearms. 5. An arrow, esp. for a crossbow. 6. A stroke of lightning; thunderbolt. 7. A sudden start or spring: He made a *bolt* for the door. 8. A roll of cloth, wallpaper, etc. **—a bolt from the blue** A sudden and unexpected event. *—v.i.* 1. To move, go, or spring suddenly out or away. *—v.t.* 2. To fasten or lock with or as with a bolt or bolts. 3. To break away from, as a political party. 4. To gulp, as food. **—bolt upright** Stiffly erect. [OE, arrow for a crossbow] **—bolt′er** *n.*

bolt[2] (bōlt) *v.t.* To sift. [< OF *bulter* to sift] **—bolt′er** *n.*

bo·lus (bō′ləs) *n. pl.* **·lus·es** 1. A large pill. 2. Any rounded lump or mass. [< Gk. *bōlos* a lump]

bomb (bom) *n.* 1. *Mil.* A projectile containing explosive, incendiary, or chemical material to be discharged by concussion or by a time fuse. 2. Any sudden or unexpected event. 3. *Slang* A complete failure. *—v.t.* 1. To attack with or as with bombs. *—v.i.* 2. *Slang* To fail utterly. [< F *bombe* < Gk. *bombos* hollow noise]

bom·bard (bom·bärd′) *v.t.* 1. To attack with bombs or shells. 2. To attack as with bombs. [< Gk. *bombos* hollow noise] **—bom·bard′er** *n.* **—bom·bard′ment** *n.*

bom·bar·dier (bom′bər·dir′) *n. Mil.* The member of the crew of a bomber who operates the bombsight and releases bombs. [< F]

bom·bast (bom′bast) *n.* Grandiloquent or pompous language. [< OF *bombace* padding < LL *bombax* cotton] **—bom·bas′tic** *adj.* **—bom·bas′ti·cal·ly** *adv.*

bom·ba·zine (bom′bə·zēn′, bom′bə·zēn) *n.* A twilled fabric usu. with silk warp and worsted filling. [< LL *bombax* cotton]

bombed (bombd) *adj. Slang* Drunk.

bomb·er (bom′ər) *n.* 1. An airplane designed to carry and drop bombs. 2. One who bombs.

bomb·shell (bom′shel′) *n.* 1. A bomb. 2. A surprise.

bomb·sight (bom′sīt′) *n. Mil.* An instrument on an aircraft for aiming bombs.

bo·na fide (bō′nə fīd′, fī′dē) *adj.* In good faith; authentic; genuine. [< L]

bo·nan·za (bə·nan′zə) *n.* 1. A rich mine or find of ore. 2. A source of great wealth. [< Sp., fair weather, prosperity]

bon·bon (bon′bon′, *Fr.* bôṅ·bôṅ′) *n.* A sugared candy. [< F *bon* good]

bond (bond) *n.* 1. That which binds or holds together; a band; tie. 2. A uniting force or influence. 3. A substance that cements or unites; also, the union itself. 4. *Law* An obligation in writing under seal. 5. In finance, an interest-bearing certificate of debt. 6. In insurance, a policy covering losses suffered through the acts of an employee. 7. In commerce, the condition of goods stored in a bonded warehouse until duties are paid. 8. A bondsman; also, bail; surety. 9. *Chem.* A unit of combining power between the atoms of a molecule. **—bottled in bond** Bottled under government supervision and stored in a warehouse for a stated period, as certain whiskeys. *—v.t.* 1. To put a certified debt upon; mortgage. 2. To furnish bond for; be surety for (someone). 3. To place, as goods or an employee, under bond. 4. To unite, as with glue, etc. *—v.i.* 5. To interlock or cohere. [Var. of BAND[1]] **—bond′er** *n.*

bond·age (bon′dij) *n.* 1. Involuntary servitude; slavery; serfdom. 2. Subjection to any influence or domination. [< ON *bōnde* peasant]

bond·ed (bon′did) *adj.* 1. Secured or pledged by a bond or bonds. 2. Stored in a warehouse; placed in bond.

bond·hold·er (bond′hōl′dər) *n.* One owning or holding bonds. **—bond′hold′ing** *adj. & n.*

bond·man (bond′mən) *n. pl.* **·men** (-mən) 1. A slave or serf. 2. A man bound to serve without wages. **—bond′wom′an, bonds′·wom′an** *n.fem.*

bond paper A strong grade of paper.

bond·ser·vant (bond′sûr′vənt) *n.* 1. A person bound to serve without wages. 2. A slave; serf: also **bond′slave′** (-slāv′).

bonds·man (bondz′mən) *n. pl.* **·men** (-mən) 1. One who provides bond for another. 2. A bondman.

bone (bōn) *n.* 1. *Anat.* **a** A hard, dense porous material forming the skeleton of vertebrates. **b** A piece of this material. ◆Collateral adjectives: *osseous, osteal.* 2. *pl.* The skeleton as a whole. 3. A substance resembling bone. 4. Something made of bone or similar material. **—to have a bone to pick** To have a complaint. **—to make no bones about** To be direct or straightforward about. *—v.* **boned, bon·ing** *v.t.* To remove the bones from. *—v.i. Slang* To study intensely and quickly: often with *up.* [OE *bān*]

bone·black (bōn′blak′) *n.* A black pigment made from burned bones. Also **bone black.**

bone·head (bōn′hed′) *n. Informal* A stupid person.

bone meal Pulverized bone, used as feed and fertilizer.

bon·er (bō′nər) *n. Slang* An error; blunder.

bon·fire (bon′fīr′) *n.* A large fire built in the open air. [< BONE + FIRE]

bon·go drums (bong′gō) A pair of connected drums played with the hands. Also **bon′gos.**

bon·ho·mie (bon′ə·mē′, *Fr.* bô·nô·mē′) *n.* Good nature; geniality. Also **bon′hom·mie′.** [< F]

bo·ni·to (bə·nē′tō) *n. pl.* **·to** or **·toes** A large marine food fish. [< Sp.]

bon·kers (bong′kerz) *adj. Slang* Crazy; mad. [Origin unknown]

bon mot (bôṅ mō′) *pl.* **bons mots** (bôṅ mōz′, *Fr.* mō′) A clever saying; witticism. [< F]

bon·net (bon′it) *n.* 1. A hat for women or children, typically tied under the chin. 2. *Chiefly Scot.* A cap for men and boys. [< Med.L *bonetus*]

bon·ny (bon′ē) *adj.* **·ni·er, ·ni·est** 1. Handsome or beautiful. 2. Fine; good. 3. Robust; healthy. Also **bon′nie.** [< F *bon* good]

bon·sai (bon′sī′, bon·sī′) *n. pl.* **·sai** 1. A dwarfed tree or shrub trained into a pleasing design. 2. The art of creating such trees or shrubs. [< Japanese]

bo·nus (bō′nəs) *n. pl.* **bo·nus·es** Something paid or given in addition to a usual or stipulated amount. [< L, good]

bon vi·vant (bôṅ vē·väṅ′) *pl.* **bons vi·vants** (bôṅ vē·väṅ′) *French* One who enjoys luxurious living; an epicure.

bon vo·yage (bôṅ vwȧ·yȧzh′) *French* Pleasant trip.

bon·y (bō′nē) *adj.* **bon·i·er, bon·i·est** 1. Of,

like, or full of bone or bones. 2. Having prominent bones; thin; gaunt. **—bon′i·ness** *n.*

boo (bo͞o) *n. & interj.* A vocal sound made to indicate contempt or to frighten. [Imit.] **—boo** *v.t. & v.i.* **booed, boo·ing**

boob (bo͞ob) *n. Slang* A simpleton; booby.

boo·by (bo͞o′bē) *n. pl.* **·bies** 1. A stupid person; dunce. 2. Any of several large sea birds of tropical America. [< Sp. *bobo* fool]

booby hatch 1. *Naut.* A raised hood over a small hatchway. 2. *Slang* A hospital for the mentally ill.

booby prize A mock award for a worst score or performance.

booby trap 1. A concealed bomb, mine, etc., placed so as to be detonated by the victim. 2. Any device for taking someone unawares.

boo·dle (bo͞od′l) *n. Slang* 1. Bribery money; graft. 2. Loot; plunder. [Cf. Du. *boedel* property]

boog·ie-woog·ie (bo͝og′ē·wo͝og′ē) *n.* A style of jazz piano playing. [Origin uncertain]

book (bo͝ok) *n.* 1. A bound set of printed sheets of paper, usually between covers. 2. A literary composition of some length. 3. A ledger, register, etc. 4. A main division of a literary composition: a *book* of the Bible. 5. A libretto. 6. A booklike packet, as of matches. 7. A record of bets, especially on a horse race. 8. A specific number of tricks or cards won. **—by the book** According to rule. **—like a book** Thoroughly. **—to make book** *Slang* To bet or accept bets. **—***v.t.* 1. To arrange for beforehand, as accommodations or seats. 2. To engage for performance. 3. To make a record of charges against (someone) on a police blotter. [OE]

Book is used to make many self-explanatory words and phrases, as:

bookbinder	**bookseller**
book collector	**bookselling**
book collecting	**bookshelf**
bookdealer	**bookstore**
book fair	**book-taught**

book·bind·ing (bo͝ok′bīn′ding) *n.* The art and trade of binding books.

book·case (bo͝ok′kās′) *n.* A case with shelves for books.

book end A support or prop used to hold books upright. Also **book′end.**

book·ie (bo͝ok′ē) *n. Informal* A bookmaker (def. 2).

book·ing (bo͝ok′ing) *n.* An engagement to perform, etc.

book·ish (bo͝ok′ish) *adj.* 1. Fond of books; studious. 2. Pedantic. **—book′ish·ness** *n.*

book jacket A dust jacket.

book·keep·ing (bo͝ok′kē′ping) *n.* The practice of recording business transactions systematically. **—book′keep′er** *n.*

book·let (bo͝ok′lit) *n.* A pamphlet.

book·mak·er (bo͝ok′mā′kər) *n.* 1. One who compiles, prints, or binds books. 2. One who makes a business of accepting bets.

book·mark (bo͝ok′märk′) *n.* Any object inserted in a book to mark a place.

book·mo·bile (bo͝ok′mə·bēl) *n.* A motor vehicle equipped to serve as a traveling library.

Book of Common Prayer The book of ritual used in the Anglican church.

book·rack (bo͝ok′rak′) *n.* 1. A frame to hold an open book. Also **book′rest′.** 2. A rack to hold books.

book·stall (bo͝ok′stôl′) *n.* 1. A stall or stand where books are sold. 2. *Brit.* A newsstand.

book·worm (bo͝ok′wûrm′) *n.* 1. One who spends much time reading and studying. 2. Any insect destructive to books.

boom[1] (bo͞om) *v.i.* 1. To emit a deep, resonant sound. 2. To grow rapidly; flourish. **—***v.t.* 3. To utter or sound in a deep, resonant tone: often with *out.* **—***n.* 1. A deep, reverberating sound. 2. A sudden increase; spurt. **—***adj.* Caused by a boom: *boom* prices. [Imit.]

boom[2] (bo͞om) *n.* 1. *Naut.* A spar used to extend the bottom of certain sails. 2. A long arm of a derrick, from which the objects to be lifted are suspended. [< Du. *boom* tree, beam]

boom·e·rang (bo͞o′mə·rang) *n.* 1. A curved, wooden missile originated in Australia, one form of which will return to the thrower. 2. A plan, statement, etc., that recoils upon the originator. **—***v.i.* To react harmfully on the originator. [< native Australian name]

boon[1] (bo͞on) *n.* A good thing bestowed; blessing. [< ON *bōn* petition]

boon[2] (bo͞on) *adj.* Convivial; merry: now only in the phrase **boon companion.** [< L *bonus* good]

boon·docks (bo͞on′doks′) *n.pl. Slang* An uncivilized or backwoods area: with *the.* [< Tagalog *bundok* mountain]

boon·dog·gle (bo͞on′dôg′əl, -dog′əl) *v.i.* **·gled, ·gling** *Informal* To work on wasteful or unnecessary projects. [Origin uncertain] **—boon′dog′gle** *n.* **—boon′dog′gler** *n.*

boor (bo͝or) *n.* An awkward or rude person. [< Du. *boer* farmer, rustic] **—boor′ish** *adj.* **—boor′ish·ly** *adv.* **—boor′ish·ness** *n.*

boost (bo͞ost) *v.t.* 1. To raise by pushing from beneath or behind. 2. To increase: to *boost* prices. 3. To advance by speaking well of; promote. **—***n.* 1. A lift; help. 2. An increase. [Origin uncertain]

boost·er (bo͞os′tər) *n.* 1. Any device or substance for increasing power. 2. *Informal* An enthusiastic supporter.

boot[1] (bo͞ot) *n.* 1. A covering for the foot and part or most of the leg. 2. A thick patch for the inside of a tire casing. 3. A kick. 4. In Navy and Marine Corps slang, a recent recruit. **—too big for one's boots** Proud; conceited. **—the boot** *Slang* Dismissal; discharge. **—***v.t.* 1. To put boots on. 2. To kick or to punt. 3. *Slang* To dismiss; fire. [< OF *bote*]

boot[2] (bo͞ot) *Obs. n.* Advantage. **—to boot** In addition; over and above. [OE *bōt* profit]

boot·black (bo͞ot′blak′) *n.* One whose business is shining boots and shoes.

boo·tee (bo͞o′tē) *n.* A baby's knitted boot. Also **boo′tie.**

booth (bo͞oth, bo͞oth) *n.* 1. A small compartment or cubicle. 2. A seating compartment, as in a restaurant. 3. A small stall for the display or sale of goods. [ME *bothe* < Scand.]

boot·jack (bo͞ot′jak′) *n.* A forked device for holding a boot while the foot is withdrawn.

boot·leg (bo͞ot′leg′) *v.t. & v.i.* **·legged, ·leg·ging** To make, sell, or carry for sale (liquor, etc.) illegally; smuggle. [With ref. to the smuggling of liquor in boots] **—boot′leg′** *adj. & n.* **—boot′leg′ger** *n.* **—boot′leg′ging** *n.*

boot·less (bo͞ot′lis) *adj.* Profitless; useless; unavailing. —**boot′less·ly** *adv.*
boot·lick (bo͞ot′lik′) *Slang* *v.t. & v.i.* To flatter servilely; toady. —**boot′lick′er** *n.* —**boot′lick′ing** *n. & adj.*
boo·ty (bo͞o′tē) *n. pl.* **·ties** 1. The spoil of war or any violence; plunder. 2. Any prize or gain. [< F *butin*]
booze (bo͞oz) *Informal n.* 1. Alcoholic drink. 2. A drunken spree. —*v.i.* **boozed, booz·ing** To drink to excess. [< MDu. *busen* to drink, tipple] —**booz′er** *n.*
booz·y (bo͞o′zē) *adj.* *Informal* Drunken; alcoholic. —**booz′i·ly** *adv.* —**booz′i·ness** *n.*
bop[1] (bop) *v.t.* **bopped, bop·ping** *Slang* To hit. [Imit.]
bop[2] (bop) *n.* A variety of jazz.
bo·rac·ic (bə·ras′ik) *adj.* *Chem.* Boric.
bo·rate (bôr′āt) *n.* *Chem.* A salt of boric acid. —**bo′rat·ed** *adj.*
bo·rax (bôr′aks) *n.* A white crystalline compound, used in soaps, etc. [< Persian *būrah*]
Bor·deaux (bôr·dō′) *n.* A white or red wine produced in the vicinity of Bordeaux, France.
bor·der (bôr′dər) *n.* 1. A margin, edge, or brink. 2. The frontier line or district of a country or state; boundary. 3. A decorative edging. —*adj.* Of, on, or forming the border. —*v.t.* 1. To put a border or edging on. 2. To lie along the border of; bound. —**to border on** (or **upon**) 1. To lie adjacent to. 2. To approach; verge on: That act *borders on* piracy. [< OF *bordure* edge]
bor·der·land (bôr′dər·land′) *n.* Land on or near the border of two adjoining countries.
bor·der·line (bôr′dər·līn′) *n.* A line of demarcation. Also **border line.** —*adj.* Difficult to classify; doubtful.
bore[1] (bôr) *v.* **bored, bor·ing** *v.t.* 1. To make a hole in or through, as with a drill. 2. To make (a tunnel, etc.) by or as by drilling. 3. To force (one's way). 4. To weary by being dull, etc.; tire. —*v.i.* 5. To make a hole, etc., by or as by drilling. 6. To force one's way. —*n.* 1. A hole made by or as by boring. 2. The interior diameter of a firearm or cylinder; caliber. 3. An uninteresting, tiresome person or thing. [OE *bor* auger]
bore[2] (bôr) *n.* A high, crested wave caused by the rush of a flood tide, as in the Amazon. [< ON *bāra* billow]
bore[3] (bôr) Past tense of BEAR[1].
bo·re·al (bôr′ē·əl, bō′rē-) *adj.* Of the north or the north wind. [< L *Boreas* the god of north wind]
bore·dom (bôr′dəm) *n.* The condition of being bored; tedium.
bor·er (bôr′ər) *n.* 1. A tool used for boring. 2. A beetle, moth, or worm that burrows in plants, wood, etc.
bo·ric (bôr′ik) *adj.* *Chem.* Of, pertaining to, or derived from boron: also *boracic.*
boric acid *Chem.* A white crystalline compound, used as a preservative or antiseptic.
born (bôrn) *adj.* 1. Brought forth, as offspring. 2. Natural; by birth: a *born* musician. [OE *beran* to bear]
born-a·gain (bôrn′ə·gen′) *adj.* Of a Christian, having received spiritual life, or being renewed spiritually, esp. by a personal conversion to the teachings of Christ.
borne (bôrn) Past participle of BEAR[1].
bo·ron (bôr′on) *n.* A nonmetallic element (symbol B) found only in combination.
bor·ough (bûr′ō, -ə) *n.* 1. An incorporated village or town. 2. One of the five administrative divisions of New York, N.Y. 3. *Brit.* A town with a municipal corporation and certain privileges granted by royal charter. [OE *burg, burh* fort, town]
bor·row (bor′ō, bôr′ō) *v.t.* 1. To take or obtain (something) with the promise or understanding that one will return it. 2. To adopt for one's own use, as ideas. —*v.i.* 3. To borrow something. [OE *borg* pledge] —**bor′row·er** *n.*
borscht (bôrsht) *n.* A Russian beet soup, eaten hot or cold. Also **borsch** (bôrsh). [< Russ. *borshch*]
bor·zoi (bôr′zoi) *n.* A breed of Russian hound, having a long, silky coat: also called *Russian wolfhound.* [< Russ., swift]
bosh (bosh) *n.* *Informal* Empty words; nonsense. [< Turkish, empty, worthless]
bo's'n (bō′sən) See BOATSWAIN.
Bos·ni·an (boz′nē·ən) *n.* 1. A native or inhabitant of Bosnia. 2. The Serbo-Croatian language of the Bosnians. —**Bos′ni·an** *adj.*
bos·om (bo͝oz′əm, bo͞o′zəm) *n.* 1. The breast of a human being, esp. of a woman. 2. The breast as the seat of thought and emotion. 3. Inner circle; midst. —*adj.* Close; intimate. [OE *bōsm*]
boss[1] (bôs, bos) *Informal n.* 1. One who controls and directs, as an employer, manager, etc. 2. A professional politician who controls a political organization. —*v.t.* 1. To supervise; direct. 2. To order in a high-handed manner. —*v.i.* 3. To act as boss. [< Du. *baas* master]
boss[2] (bôs, bos) *n.* A circular prominence; knob or projecting ornament. —*v.t.* To ornament with bosses. [< OF *boce* bump, knob]
bos·sa no·va (bôs′ə nō′və, bos′ə) 1. A style of music originating in Brazil and combining Latin-American and jazz elements. 2. A dance for couples done to this music. [< Pg., new bump, new trend]
boss·ism (bôs′iz·əm, bos′-) *n.* Control by political bosses.
boss·y[1] (bôs′ē, bos′ē) *adj.* **boss·i·er, boss·i·est** *Informal* Tending to boss; domineering. —**boss′i·ly** *adv.* —**boss′i·ness** *n.*
boss·y[2] (bos′ē, bôs′ē) *n.* *Informal* A cow or a calf.
Boston terrier A small terrier having a short, smooth, dark or streaked coat with white markings. Also **Boston bull.**
bo·sun (bō′sən) See BOATSWAIN.
bot (bot) *n.* The larva of a botfly. [Origin unknown]
bo·tan·i·cal (bə·tan′i·kəl) *adj.* Of or pertaining to botany or to plants. Also **bo·tan′ic.** —*n.* A drug derived from the leaves, roots, stems, etc., of a plant. [< Gk. *botanē* plant, pasture] —**bo·tan′i·cal·ly** *adv.*
bot·a·nize (bot′ə·nīz) *v.t. & v.i.* **·nized, ·niz·ing** To collect and study (plants). —**bot′a·niz′er** *n.*
bot·a·ny (bot′ə·nē) *n.* The division of biology that treats of plants, their structure, functions, classification, etc. —**bot′a·nist** *n.*
botch (boch) *v.t.* To do or make in an inept way; bungle. [ME *bocchen*] —**botch** *n.* —**botch′er** *n.* —**botch′i·ly** *adv.* —**botch′y** *adj.*
bot·fly (bot′flī′) *n. pl.* **·flies** A fly of which the larvae are parasitic in vertebrates.

both (bōth) *adj. & pron.* The two together: *Both* girls laughed. —*conj. & adv.* Equally; alike; as well: with *and.* [< ON *bādhar*]
both·er (both′ər) *v.t.* 1. To pester; give trouble to. 2. To confuse; fluster. —*v.i.* 3. To trouble or concern oneself. —*n.* 1. A state of vexation. 2. One who or that which bothers. [? dial. E (Irish)]
both·er·some (both′ər·səm) *adj.* Causing bother.
bot·tle (bot′l) *n.* 1. A vessel, usu. of glass, for holding liquids, having a neck and a narrow mouth that can be stopped. 2. As much as a bottle will hold: also **bot′tle·ful′**. —**to hit the bottle** *Slang* To drink liquor to excess. —*v.t.* **·tled, ·tling** 1. To put into a bottle or bottles. 2. To restrain: often with *up* or *in.* [< LL *buticula* flask] —**bot′tler** *n.*
bottle green A dark, dull green.
bot·tle·neck (bot′l·nek′) *n.* 1. A narrow or congested passageway. 2. Anything that retards progress.
bot·tom (bot′əm) *n.* 1. The lowest part of anything. 2. The underside or undersurface. 3. The ground beneath a body of water. 4. *Often pl.* Bottom land. 5. *Informal* The buttocks. —**at bottom** Fundamentally. —*adj.* Lowest; fundamental. —*v.t.* 1. To provide with a bottom. 2. To fathom; comprehend. —*v.i.* 3. To touch or rest on the bottom. —**to bottom out** Of a security market, to decline to a point where demand exceeds supply and prices rise. [OE]
bottom land Lowland along a river.
bot·tom·less (bot′əm·lis) *adj.* 1. Having no bottom. 2. Unfathomable; limitless; endless. 3. *Slang* Nude. —**the bottomless pit** Hell.
bottom line 1. A figure reflecting profit or loss, usu. the last line of a financial statement. 2. *Informal* Any important result, judgment, conclusion, etc.
bot·tom·ry (bot′əm·rē) *n.* A contract whereby the owner of a vessel borrows money, pledging the vessel as security.
bot·u·lism (boch′o͞o·liz′əm) *n.* Poisoning caused by a toxin produced by a bacillus sometimes present in improperly preserved food. [< L *botulus* sausage]
bou·clé (bo͞o·klā′) *n.* A woven or knitted fabric with a looped or knotted surface. [< F, pp. of *boucler* to buckle, curl]
bou·doir (bo͞o′dwär, bo͞o·dwär′) *n.* A lady's private sitting room or bedroom. [< F, lit., pouting room]
bouf·fant (bo͞o·fänt′) *adj.* Puffed-out; flaring. [< F, ppr. of *bouffer* to swell]
bough (bou) *n.* A large branch of a tree. [OE *bōg* shoulder]
bought (bôt) Past tense and past participle of BUY.
bouil·la·baisse (bo͞ol′yə·bās′, *Fr.* bo͞o·yȧ·bes′) *n.* A seafood chowder. [< F < Provençal *boui* boil + *abaisso* to settle, go down]
bouil·lon (bo͞ol′yon, -yən; *Fr.* bo͞o·yôn′) *n.* Clear soup from beef or other meats. [< F *bouillir* to boil]
boul·der (bōl′dər) *n.* A large, rounded rock. [ME *bulderston*]
boul·e·vard (bo͞ol′ə·värd, bo͞o′lə-) *n.* A broad avenue, often lined with trees. [< F]
bounce (bouns) *v.* **bounced, bounc·ing** *v.i.* 1. To move with a bound or bounds, as a ball; rebound. 2. To move suddenly; spring. 3. *Slang* To be returned by a bank as worthless: said of a check. —*v.t.* 4. To cause to bounce. 5. *Slang* To eject (a person) forcibly. —*n.* 1. A bound or rebound. 2. A sudden spring or leap. 3. *Informal* Vivacity; verve; spirit. [ME *bunsen* to thump] —**bounc′i·ly** *adv.* —**bounc′i·ness** *n.* —**bounc′y** *adj.*
bounc·er (boun′sər) *n.* *Slang* One employed, as in a bar, to eject disorderly persons.
bounc·ing (boun′sing) *adj.* Strong; active.
bound[1] (bound) *v.i.* 1. To strike and spring back from a surface, as a ball. 2. To leap; move by a series of leaps. —*n.* A leap or spring; also, a rebound. [< MF *bondir* to resound, rebound]
bound[2] (bound) *n.* 1. *Usu. pl.* A boundary; limit: out of *bounds.* 2. *pl.* The area near or within a boundary. —*v.t.* 1. To set limits to; restrict. 2. To form the boundary of. —*v.i.* 3. To adjoin; abut. [< LL *bodina* limit]
bound[3] (bound) Past tense and past participle of BIND. —*adj.* 1. Made fast; tied with bonds. 2. Having a cover or binding. 3. Morally or legally obligated. 4. Certain; sure: It's *bound* to rain. 5. *Informal* Determined; resolved.
bound[4] (bound) *adj.* Being on course for; on the way: *bound* for home. [< ON *būa* to prepare]
bound·a·ry (boun′də·rē, -drē) *n.* *pl.* **·ries** Anything indicating a limit or confine.
bound·en (boun′dən) *adj.* 1. Obligatory: our *bounden* duty. 2. Under obligation; obliged.
bound·er (boun′dər) *n.* *Brit. Informal* A cad.
bound·less (bound′lis) *adj.* Having no limit; vast. —**bound′less·ly** *adv.* —**bound′less·ness** *n.*
boun·te·ous (boun′tē·əs) *adj.* 1. Generous. 2. Abundant; plentiful. [< OF *bontif*] —**boun′te·ous·ly** *adv.* —**boun′te·ous·ness** *n.*
boun·ti·ful (boun′tə·fəl) *adj.* 1. Generous. 2. Plentiful. —**boun′ti·ful·ly** *adv.* —**boun′ti·ful·ness** *n.*
boun·ty (boun′tē) *n.* *pl.* **·ties** 1. Liberality in giving. 2. Gifts or favors. 3. A reward from a government, as for the killing of predatory animals. [< L *bonitas, -tatis* goodness]
bou·quet (bō·kā′, bo͞o·kā′) *n.* 1. A bunch of flowers. 2. Delicate odor, esp. of a wine. [< OF *boschet*]
bour·bon (bûr′bən) *n.* A whiskey distilled from a fermented mash containing at least 51 percent corn. Also **bourbon whiskey.** [after *Bourbon* County, Ky., where first made]
bour·geois (bo͝or′zhwä, bo͝or·zhwä′) *n.* *pl.* **·geois** 1. A member of the middle class, esp. a tradesman. 2. *pl.* The middle class. —*adj.* Of or characteristic of the middle class: often used disparagingly. [< F < LL *burgus* town]
bour·geoi·sie (bo͝or′zhwä·zē′) *n.* The middle class of society, esp. in France.
Bourse (bo͝ors) *n.* An exchange or money market; esp., the Paris stock exchange. [< F, purse < LL *bursa* bag]
bout (bout) *n.* 1. A contest; trial. 2. A fit or spell, as of illness. [Var. of ME *bought* bending, turn]
bou·tique (bo͞o·tēk′) *n.* A small retail shop. [< F]
bou·ton·niere (bo͞o′tən·yâr′) *n.* A bouquet or flower worn in the buttonhole. [< F]
bo·vine (bō′vīn, -vin) *adj.* 1. Of or pertaining to oxen, cows, etc. 2. Stolid; dull. —*n.* A bovine animal. [< L *bos, bovis* ox]

bow[1] (bou) *n.* The forward part of a ship, boat, etc. [< LG or Scand.] —**bow** *adj.*

bow[2] (bou) *v.* **bowed, bow·ing** *v.i.* 1. To bend the body or head, as in reverence or assent. 2. To bend or incline downward. 3. To submit; yield. —*v.t.* 4. To bend (the body, head, etc.). 5. To cause to bend or stoop. —**to bow out** To withdraw; resign. —*n.* An inclination of the body or head. [OE *būgan* to bend]

bow[3] (bō) *n.* 1. A weapon made from a strip of wood or other pliable material, bent by a string and used to project an arrow. 2. Something bent or curved; a bend. 3. A knot with a loop or loops, as of ribbon, etc. 4. A rod with fibers, as horsehair, stretched between raised ends, used for playing a stringed instrument. —*adj.* Bent; curved; bowed. —*v.t. & v.i.* **bowed, bow·ing** 1. To bend into the shape of a bow. 2. To play (a stringed instrument) with a bow. [OE *boga*]

bowd·ler·ize (boud′lər·īz) *v.t.* **·ized, ·iz·ing** To expurgate or edit prudishly. [after Dr. Thomas *Bowdler*'s "family" edition of Shakespeare (1818)] —**bowd′ler·i·za′tion** *n.*

bow·el (bou′əl, boul) *n.* 1. An intestine. 2. *pl.* The inner part of anything: the *bowels* of the earth. [< L *botellus*, dim. of *botulus* sausage]

bow·er (bou′ər) *n.* A shaded recess. —*v.t.* To enclose in or as in a bower. [OE *būr* chamber] —**bow′er·y** *adj.*

bow·ie knife (bō′ē, bōō′ē) A strong, single-edged hunting knife. [after James *Bowie*, 1799–1836, its reputed inventor]

bow·knot (bō′not′) *n.* An ornamental slipknot made with one or more loops.

bowl[1] (bōl) *n.* 1. A deep, round dish. 2. The amount a bowl will hold. 3. An amphitheater. 4. Something shaped like a bowl: the *bowl* of a pipe. [OE *bolla*]

bowl[2] (bōl) *n.* 1. A large ball used in bowling or bowls. 2. A throw of the ball in bowling. —*v.i.* 1. To play at bowls, bowling, etc. 2. To move smoothly and swiftly: usually with *along*. —*v.t.* 3. To roll or throw, as a ball. —**to bowl over** To cause to be shocked or astounded. [< F *boule* ball] —**bowl′er** *n.*

bow·leg (bō′leg′) *n.* A leg with an outward curvature at or below the knee. —**bow′·leg′ged** (-leg′id, -legd′) *adj.*

bowl·er (bō′lər) *n.* *Brit.* A derby. [after John *Bowler*, 19th c. English hatmaker]

bow·line (bō′lin, -līn′) *n.* 1. A knot tied so as to form a loop. Also **bowline knot**. 2. *Naut.* A rope to keep a sail taut.

bowl·ing (bō′ling) *n.* 1. A game played by rolling a ball down a bowling alley in an attempt to knock down ten pins set up at the other end. 2. Bowls.

bowling alley A long, narrow wooden lane for bowling, or the building containing it.

bowling green A smooth lawn for bowls.

bowls (bōlz) *n.pl.* 1. A game played by rolling balls at a stationary ball. 2. Any of various similar games.

bow·man (bō′mən) *n. pl.* **·men** (-mən) An archer.

bow·sprit (bou′sprit′, bō′-) *n.* *Naut.* A spar projecting forward from the bow of a vessel. [? < MDu. < *boeg* bow of a ship + *spriet* spear]

bow·string (bō′string′) *n.* The string of a bow.

bow tie A necktie worn in a bowknot.

box[1] (boks) *n.* 1. A receptacle or case, usu. having a lid. 2. The quantity contained in a box. 3. Something resembling a box in form or use. 4. A small booth, as for a sentry. 5. A space partitioned off for seating, as in a theater. 6. In baseball, any of several designated spaces, as for the pitcher. 7. *Mech.* An axle bearing, casing, or other enclosed cavity. 8. An enclosed space on a page. —*v.t.* 1. To place in a box. 2. *Mech.* To furnish with a bushing or box. —**to box in** To confine in, or as in, a small space. [< Gk. *pyxos* boxwood]

box[2] (boks) *v.t.* 1. To strike with the hand; cuff. 2. To fight (another) in a boxing match. —*v.i.* 3. To fight with one's fists. —*n.* A blow; cuff. [ME]

box[3] (boks) *n.* Any of a small family of evergreen shrubs and trees, used as hedges. [< Gk. *pyxos* boxwood]

box·car (boks′kär′) *n.* An enclosed freight car.

box·er[1] (bok′sər) *n.* One who fights with his fists; pugilist.

box·er[2] (bok′sər) *n.* A breed of dog, related to the bulldog.

box·ing (bok′sing) *n.* The art or practice of fighting with the fists.

boxing glove A padded mitten used for boxing.

box office 1. The ticket office of a theater, etc. 2. *Informal* Receipts at the box office.

box seat A seat in a box of a theater, stadium, etc.

box spring A mattress foundation consisting of an upholstered frame set with coil springs.

box·wood (boks′wōōd′) *n.* 1. The hard wood of box. 2. The shrub.

boy (boi) *n.* 1. A male child; lad; youth. 2. A man; fellow: a familiar use. 3. A male servant. [ME *boi*] —**boy′ish** *adj.* —**boy′·ish·ly** *adv.* —**boy′ish·ness** *n.*

boy·cott (boi′kot) *v.t.* 1. To combine together in refusing to deal or associate with, so as to punish or coerce. 2. To refuse to use or buy. [after Capt. C. *Boycott*, 1832–97, Irish landlord's agent, who was the first victim] —**boy′cott** *n.* —**boy′cot·ter** *n.*

boy friend *Informal* A preferred male companion or sweetheart. Also **boy·friend** (boi′frend′).

boy·hood (boi′hōōd) *n.* The state or period of being a boy.

boy scout A member of the **Boy Scouts of America**, an organization for boys, stressing self-reliance and good citizenship.

boy·sen·ber·ry (boi′zən·ber′ē) *n. pl.* **·ries** An edible fruit obtained by crossing the blackberry, raspberry, and loganberry. [after Rudolph *Boysen*, 20th c. U.S. horticulturist]

bra (brä) *n.* *Informal* A brassiere.

brace (brās) *v.* **braced, brac·ing** *v.t.* 1. To make firm or steady; strengthen by or as by braces. 2. To make ready to withstand pressure, shock, etc. 3. To stimulate; enliven. —*v.i.* 4. To strain against pressure. —**to brace up** *Informal* To rouse one's courage or resolution. —*n.* 1. A support, as of wood or metal, that steadies or strengthens. 2. A clasp or clamp for fastening, connecting, etc. 3. A cranklike handle for holding and turning a bit or other boring tool. 4. A pair; couple. 5. *pl.* *Brit.* Suspenders. 6. *Often pl.* *Dent.* A wire or wires fastened on irregular teeth and gradually tightened to align them. 7. *Med.* Any of various devices for supporting a joint, limb, or other part. 8. **a** A double curved line, {or}, used to connect words or items to be considered together. **b** One of two of such marks used to enclose words in a text. [< L *brachium* arm]

brace·let (brās′lit) *n.* 1. An ornamental band worn around the wrist or arm. 2. *Informal* A handcuff. [< OF, dim. of *bracel* armlet]

brac·er (brā′sər) *n.* 1. One who or that which braces or steadies. 2. *Informal* A stimulating drink, usu. containing alcohol.

bra·chi·al (brā′kē·əl, brak′ē-) *adj.* Of or pertaining to the arm or to armlike appendages. [< L *brachialis*]

brachio- *combining form* Arm; of the arm: *brachiopod.* Also, before vowels, **brachi-.** [< Gk. *brachiōn* arm]

bra·chi·o·pod (brā′kē·ə·pod′, brak′ē-) *n.* *Zool.* One of a phylum of marine animals having a bivalve shell and a pair of armlike parts on the sides of the mouth. [< NL]

bra·chi·um (brā′kē·əm, brak′ē-) *n. pl.* **·chi·a** 1. *Anat.* The arm, esp. that part above the elbow. 2. Any armlike process or appendage. [< L]

brac·ing (brā′sing) *adj.* Strengthening; invigorating. —*n.* A brace or system of braces.

brack·en (brak′en) *n.* 1. A coarse, hardy fern with very large fronds: also called *brake.* 2. A clump of such ferns. [ME *braken*]

brack·et (brak′it) *n.* 1. A piece of wood, metal, stone, etc., projecting from a wall, used to support a shelf, lamp, etc. 2. A brace used to strengthen an angle. 3. A classification according to income for tax purposes. 4. One of two marks [ ] used to enclose any part of a text. —*v.t.* 1. To support with a bracket. 2. To enclose within brackets. 3. To categorize together. [< L *bracae,* pl., breeches]

brack·ish (brak′ish) *adj.* 1. Somewhat saline; briny. 2. Distasteful. [< Du. *brak* salty] —**brack′ish·ness** *n.*

bract (brakt) *n.* *Bot.* A modified leaf situated at the base of a flower. [< L *bractea* thin metal plate] —**brac′te·al** *adj.*

brad (brad) *n.* A small, slender nail with a small head. [< ON *broddr* spike]

brae (brā) *n.* *Scot.* A bank; hillside; slope.

brag (brag) *v.t. & v.i.* **bragged, brag·ging** To boast (about oneself, one's abilities, etc.). —*n.* 1. Boastful language; boasting. 2. One who brags. [Origin uncertain] —**brag′ger** *n.*

brag·ga·do·ci·o (brag′ə·dō′shē·ō) *n. pl.* **·ci·os** 1. Pretentious boasting. 2. One who boasts; a swaggerer. [after *Braggadochio,* a boastful character in Spenser's *Faerie Queene*]

brag·gart (brag′ərt) *n.* A boastful person; bragger. [< MF *bragard* vain, flaunting]

Brah·ma (brä′mə) *n.* In Hindu religion, the supreme soul of the universe. [< Skt. *Brahmā*]

Brah·man (brä′mən) *n. pl.* **·mans** 1. A member of the highest Hindu caste, the priestly caste: also spelled *Brahmin.* 2. A breed of cattle originating in India. [< Skt., praise, worship]

Brah·min (brä min) *n.* 1. A Brahman (def. 1). 2. A person of an old, socially prominent family.

braid (brād) *v.t.* 1. To intertwine several strands of hair, etc. 2. To bind or ornament with ribbons, etc. 3. To form by braiding. —*n.* 1. A narrow, flat tape or strip for binding or ornamenting fabrics. 2. Anything braided or plaited. [OE *bregdan* to brandish, weave, braid] —**braid′ing** *n.*

Braille (brāl) *n.* A system of printing or writing for the blind in which the characters consist of raised dots to be read by the fingers; also, the characters themselves. Also **braille.** [after Louis *Braille,* 1809–52, French educator, the inventor]

brain (brān) *n.* 1. *Anat.* The large organ of the central nervous system contained in the cranium of vertebrates. 2. *Often pl.* Mind; intellect. 3. An electronic device that controls an automatic system. —*v.t.* 1. To dash out the brains of. 2. *Slang* To hit on the head. [OE *brægen*]

brain·child (brān′chīld′) *n.* *Informal* That which one has created or originated, as an idea.

brain death The condition in which brain waves are not detectable, usu. as indicated by flat tracings on an electroencephalograph.

brain·less (brān′lis) *adj.* Lacking intelligence; senseless; stupid. —**brain′less·ly** *adv.* —**brain′less·ness** *n.*

brain·storm (brān′stôrm′) *n.* *Informal* A sudden inspiration.

brain trust *Informal* A group of experts who act as consultants on matters of policy, etc. —**brain truster**

brain·wash (brān′wosh′, -wôsh′) *v.t.* To alter the convictions, beliefs, etc., of by means of intensive, coercive indoctrination. —**brain′·wash′ing** *n.*

brain wave *Physiol.* A rhythmical fluctuation of electrical potential in the brain.

brain·y (brā′nē) *adj.* **brain·i·er, brain·i·est** *Informal* Intelligent; smart. —**brain′i·ness** *n.*

braise (brāz) *v.t.* **braised, brais·ing** To cook by searing till brown and then simmering in a covered pan. [< F *braiser*]

brake[1] (brāk) *n.* A device for slowing or stopping a vehicle or wheel, esp. by friction. —*v.t. & v.i.* **braked, brak·ing** To apply a brake to or operate a brake. [< MDu. *braeke* device for breaking flax fibers] —**brake′age** *n.*

brake[2] (brāk) *n.* Bracken, a kind of fern. [ME]

brake[3] (brāk) *n.* An area covered with brushwood, briers, cane, etc.; thicket.

brake·man (brāk′mən) *n. pl.* **·men** (-mən) One who tends brakes on a railroad car or assists in operating a train.

brake shoe A rigid metal casting shaped to press against a wheel or brake when braking action is applied.

bram·ble (bram′bəl) *n.* 1. A plant of the rose family, esp. the blackberry of Europe. 2. Any prickly plant. Also **bram′ble·bush′** (-bŏŏsh′). [OE *bræmble*] —**bram′bly** *adj.*

bran (bran) *n.* The husks of cereals, separated from the flour by sifting. [< OF]

branch (branch) *n.* 1. A woody outgrowth from the trunk of a tree or other large plant; limb. 2. An offshoot, as of a deer's antlers. 3. Any separate part or division of a system, subject, etc. 4. A subordinate or local store, office, etc. 5. A division of a family, tribe, nation, etc. 6. A tributary stream of a river.

—*v.i.* 1. To put forth branches. 2. To separate into branches or subdivisions. —*v.t.* 3. To divide into branches. —**to branch out** To extend or expand, as one's business. [< OF *branche* bough]
bran·chi·ae (brang′ki·ē) *n.pl. of* **bran·chi·a** (brang′kē·ə) *Zool.* Gills, the respiratory organs of fish. [< Gk. *branchia*, pl.] —**bran′·chi·al** (-kē·əl) *adj.*
bran·chi·ate (brang′kē·it, -āt) *adj.* Having gills.
brand (brand) *n.* 1. A distinctive name or trademark identifying the product of a manufacturer. 2. The kind or make of a product: a good *brand* of coffee. 3. A mark made with a hot iron, as on cattle. 4. Any mark of disgrace; stigma. 5. A branding iron. 6. A burning piece of wood or a torch. —*v.t.* 1. To mark with a brand. 2. To stigmatize. [OE, torch, sword] —**brand′er** *n.*
branding iron An iron for burning a brand: also **brand iron.**
bran·dish (bran′dish) *v.t.* To wave or flourish triumphantly, menacingly, or defiantly. [< OF *brandir*] —**bran′dish** *n.*
brand-new (brand′no͞o′, -nyo͞o′, bran′-) *adj.* Very new; fresh and bright.
bran·dy (bran′dē) *n. pl.* **·dies** An alcoholic liquor distilled from wine or other fermented fruit juice. —*v.t.* **·died, ·dy·ing** To mix, flavor, strengthen, or preserve with brandy. [< Du. *brandewijn*, lit., distilled (burned) wine]
brash (brash) *adj.* 1. Acting hastily; rash; impetuous. 2. Impudent; saucy. [Cf. G *barsch* harsh and Sw. *barsk* impetuous] —**brash′ly** *adv.* —**brash′ness** *n.*
brass (bras) *n.* 1. An alloy essentially of copper and zinc, harder than copper, and both ductile and malleable. 2. *Sometimes pl. Music* The brass instruments of an orchestra or band collectively. 3. *Informal* Effrontery; insolence. 4. *Informal* High-ranking military officers; also any high officials. —*adj.* Made of brass; brazen. [OE *bræs*]
bras·siere (brə·zir′) *n.* A woman's undergarment to support or shape the breasts. Also **bras·sière′**. [< F]
brass·y (bras′ē) *adj.* **brass·i·er, brass·i·est** 1. Of or ornamented with brass. 2. Like brass, as in sound or color. 3. Cheap and showy. 4. *Informal* Insolent; brazen. —**brass′i·ly** *adv.* —**brass′i·ness** *n.*
brat (brat) *n.* A nasty child.
bra·va·do (brə·vä′dō) *n. pl.* **·does** or **·dos** Boastful defiance; affectation of bravery. [< Sp. *bravo* brave]
brave (brāv) *adj.* **brav·er, brav·est** 1. Having or showing courage; intrepid. 2. Making a fine display. —*v.t.* **braved, brav·ing** 1. To meet with courage and fortitude. 2. To defy; challenge. —*n.* 1. A man of courage. 2. A North American Indian warrior. [< Ital. *bravo*] —**brave′ly** *adv.* —**brave′er·y, brave′·ness** *n.*
bra·vo (brä′vō) *interj.* Good! well done! —*n. pl.* **·vos** A shout of "bravo!" [< Ital.]
bra·vu·ra (brə·vyo͝or′ə, *Ital.* brä·vo͞o′rä) *n.* 1. *Music* A brilliant or showy passage. 2. Any brilliant or daring performance. [< Ital., dash, daring] —**bra·vu′ra** *adj.*
brawl (brôl) *n.* A noisy quarrel; fight. [ME *braulen*] —**brawl** *v.i.* —**brawl′er** *n.* —**brawl′·ing·ly** *adv.*
brawn (brôn) *n.* 1. Firm or well-developed muscles. 2. Muscular power. [< OF *braon* slice of flesh, ult. < Gmc.] —**brawn′i·ness** *n.* —**brawn′y** *adj.* **brawn·i·er, brawn·i·est**
bray (brā) *n.* 1. The cry of an ass, mule, etc. 2. Any loud, harsh sound. [< OF *braire* to cry out] —**bray** *v.t. & v.i.* —**bray′er** *n.*
braze[1] (brāz) *v.t.* **brazed, braz·ing** 1. To make of brass. 2. To make like brass in hardness or appearance. 3. To ornament with or as with brass. [OE < *bræs* brass]
braze[2] (brāz) *v.t.* **brazed, braz·ing** *Metall.* To join the surfaces of (metals) with a layer of a soldering alloy applied under very high temperature. [< F *braser* solder] —**braz′er** *n.*
bra·zen (brā′zən) *adj.* 1. Made of or resembling brass. 2. Impudent; shameless. —*v.t.* To face with effrontery or impudence: with *out*. [OE < *bræs* brass] —**bra′zen·ly** *adv.* —**bra′zen·ness** *n.*
bra·zier[1] (brā′zhər) *n.* A worker in brass. [ME *brasiere*]
bra·zier[2] (brā′zhər) *n.* An open pan for holding live coals. [< F *braise* hot coals]
Bra·zil·ian (brə·zil′yən) *adj.* Of or pertaining to Brazil or its people. —**Bra·zil′ian** *n.*
Brazil nut The edible seed of a South American tree.
breach (brēch) *n.* 1. Violation of a legal obligation, promise, etc. 2. A gap or break in a dike, wall, etc. 3. A breaking up of friendly relations; estrangement. —*v.t.* To break through. [OE *bryce*]
bread (bred) *n.* 1. A food made with flour or meal, commonly leavened with yeast and baked. 2. Food in general. 3. The necessities of life. 4. *Slang* Money. —*v.t.* To roll in bread crumbs before cooking. [OE *brēad* bit, crumb] —**bread′ed** *adj.*
bread·bas·ket (bred′bas′kit) *n.* 1. A major grain-growing area. 2. *Slang* The stomach.
bread·fruit (bred′fro͞ot′) *n.* 1. A round seedless fruit that when baked resembles and tastes like bread. 2. The tropical tree bearing this fruit.
bread line A line of persons waiting to be given food as charity.
breadth (bredth, bretth) *n.* 1. Distance from side to side; width. 2. Extent or scope. 3. Broad-mindedness. [OE < *brād* broad]
bread·win·ner (bred′win′ər) *n.* One whose earnings are the principal support of a family.
break (brāk) *v.* **broke** (*Archaic* **brake**), **bro·ken** (*Archaic* **broke**), **break·ing** *v.t.* 1. To separate into pieces or fragments, as by a blow; shatter. 2. To crack. 3. To part the surface of; pierce: to *break* ground. 4. To disable; render useless. 5. To destroy the order, continuity, or completeness of: to *break* ranks. 6. To diminish the force or effect of: to *break* a fall. 7. To overcome by opposing; end: to *break* a strike. 8. To interrupt the course of, as a journey. 9. To violate: to *break* one's promise. 10. To reduce in spirit or health, as by toil. 11. To tame, as a horse. 12. To demote. 13. To give or obtain smaller units for: to *break* a dollar. 14. To make bankrupt or short of money. 15. To force (a way), as through a barrier. 16. To escape from. 17. To surpass; excel: to *break* a record. 18. To make known; tell, as news. 19. To cause to discontinue a habit. 20. *Law* To invalidate (a will) by court

action. —*v.i.* 21. To become separated into pieces or fragments; shatter; crack; snap. 22. To appear; come into being or evidence: The sun *broke* through the clouds. 23. To start or move suddenly: He *broke* from the crowd. 24. To exhibit a breach of continuity. 25. To change tone, as a boy's voice. 26. In baseball, to curve: said of a pitch. —**to break down** 1. To undergo mechanical failure. 2. To suffer physical or mental collapse. 3. To cause to yield. 4. To analyze or be analyzed. 5. To decompose. —**to break in** To train or make malleable. —**to break into** (or **in**) 1. To interrupt or intervene. 2. To enter by force. —**to break off** 1. To stop or cease, as from speaking. 2. To sever (relations); discontinue. 3. To become separate or detached. —**to break out** 1. To start unexpectedly or suddenly, as a fire or plague. 2. To have an eruption or rash. 3. To escape, as from prison. —**to break out into** (or **forth in, into,** etc.) To begin to do or perform: The birds *broke out into* song. —**to break up** 1. To disperse; end. 2. *Informal* To distress: The loss *broke up* the old man. 3. *Informal* To sever relations. —**to break with** To sever relations with. —*n.* 1. The act or result of breaking; fracture; rupture. 2. A starting or opening: the *break* of day. 3. A dash or run; esp., an attempt to escape. 4. A breach of continuity. 5. *Informal* A chance or opportunity. 6. A rupture in friendship; quarrel. 7. A sudden decline or change. [OE *brecan*] —**break′a·ble** *adj.* —**break′a·ble·ness** *n.*

break·age (brā′kij) *n.* 1. A breaking or being broken. 2. Articles broken. 3. Compensation for articles broken.

break·down (brāk′doun′) *n.* 1. A collapse or failure. 2. An analysis or summary.

break·er (brā′kər) *n.* 1. One that breaks. 2. A wave that breaks on rocks, a reef, etc.

break·fast (brek′fəst) *n.* The morning meal. —*v.i.* To eat breakfast.

break·neck (brāk′nek′) *adj.* Dangerous.

break·through (brāk′thro͞o′) *n.* 1. *Mil.* An attack that penetrates through an enemy's defenses. 2. Any sudden, important advance.

break·up (brāk′up′) *n.* 1. A dissolution or separation. 2. An ending.

break·wa·ter (brāk′wô′tər, -wot′ər) *n.* A barrier against the force of waves.

bream (brēm) *n. pl.* **breams** or **bream** Any of several fresh-water fishes with deep, compressed bodies. [< OF *bresme*]

breast (brest) *n.* 1. The front of the chest from the neck to the abdomen. 2. One of the mammary glands. 3. The breast as the seat of the emotions. —**to make a clean breast of** To confess. —*v.t.* To meet boldly. [OE *brēost*]

breast·bone (brest′bōn′) *n. Anat.* The sternum.

breast-feed (brest′fēd′) *v.t. & v.i.* **-fed, -feed·ing** To suckle.

breast·plate (brest′plāt′) *n.* Plate armor for the breast.

breast stroke In swimming, a stroke made by thrusting the arms forward simultaneously from the breast and sweeping them back.

breast·work (brest′wûrk′) *n.* A low, temporary defensive work.

breath (breth) *n.* 1. Air inhaled and exhaled in respiration. 2. Power or ability to breathe. 3. The act of breathing; also, life; existence: while *breath* remains. 4. A single respiration. 5. A slight movement of air. 6. A murmur; whisper. —**out of breath** Breathless; gasping. —**to take one's breath away** To awe or produce sudden emotion in. —**under one's breath** In a whisper or mutter. [OE *brǣth* vapor, odor]

breathe (brēth) *v.* **breathed, breath·ing** *v.i.* 1. To inhale and exhale air. 2. To be alive; live. 3. To pause for breath; rest. 4. To murmur; whisper. 5. To move gently, as breezes. —*v.t.* 6. To inhale and expel from the lungs, as air; respire. 7. To inject or infuse: to *breathe* life into a statue. 8. To express; manifest: to *breathe* confidence. 9. To allow a rest to, as for breath. [ME *breth* breath] —**breath′a·ble** *adj.*

breath·er (brē′thər) *n.* 1. *Informal* A brief rest period. 2. One who breathes in a particular manner.

breath·less (breth′lis) *adj.* 1. Gasping for breath. 2. That takes the breath away: *breathless* speed. 3. Devoid of breath; dead. —**breath′less·ly** *adv.* —**breath′less·ness** *n.*

breath·tak·ing (breth′tā′king) *adj.* Thrilling; overawing.

breath·y (breth′ē) *adj.* **breath·i·er, breath·i·est** Characterized by audible breathing. —**breath′i·ly** *adv.* —**breath′i·ness** *n.*

brec·ci·a (brech′ē·ə, bresh′-) *n. Geol.* A rock made up of angular fragments. [< Ital., gravel] —**brec′ci·at′ed** (-ā′tid) *adj.*

bred (bred) Past tense and past participle of BREED.

breech (brēch) *n.* 1. The posterior and lower part of the body; the buttocks. 2. The part of a gun, cannon, etc., that is behind the bore or barrel. [OE *brēc*]

breech·es (brich′iz) *n.pl.* 1. A man's garment covering the hips and thighs. 2. Trousers: also *britches.* [OE *brēc*]

breech·es buoy (brēch′iz) *Naut.* A lifesaving apparatus consisting of canvas breeches attached to a life buoy and run on a rope from one vessel to another or to the shore.

breech·load·er (brēch′lō′dər) *n.* A firearm loaded at the breech. —**breech′load′ing** *adj.*

breed (brēd) *v.* **bred, breed·ing** *v.t.* 1. To produce (offspring). 2. To cause. 3. To propagate (plants or animals). 4. To bring up; train. —*v.i.* 5. To procreate. 6. To increase and spread. —*n.* 1. A race or strain of animals. 2. A sort or kind. [OE *brōd* brood] —**breed′er** *n.*

breeder reactor A nuclear reactor which generates atomic energy in which the fuel is converted into more fissionable material than is consumed.

breed·ing (brē′ding) *n.* 1. The act of bearing young. 2. The rearing of the young. 3. Good manners. 4. The scientific production of varieties of plants, animals, etc.

breeze (brēz) *n.* 1. A moderate current of air; a gentle wind. 2. *Informal* Something easily done. —*v.i.* **breezed, breez·ing** *Informal* To go or act quickly and blithely. [< Sp. and Pg. *brisa, briza* northeast wind]

breeze·way (brēz′wā′) *n.* A roofed, open passageway, as between a house and garage.

breez·y (brē′zē) *adj.* **breez·i·er, breez·i·est** 1. Having breezes; windy. 2. Brisk or carefree. —**breez′i·ly** *adv.* —**breez′i·ness** *n.*

breth·ren (breth′rən) *n.pl.* 1. Brothers. 2. Members of a brotherhood. [ME]

Bret·on (bret′n) *n.* 1. A native of Brittany. 2. The Celtic language of the Bretons. —**Bret′on** *adj.*

breve (brev, brēv) *n.* 1. A mark (˘) placed over a vowel indicating a short sound, as *a* in *hat.* 2. In prosody, a similar mark (⌣) indicating a short or unstressed syllable. 3. *Music* A note equivalent to two whole notes. [< L *brevis* short]

bre·vet (brə·vet′, *esp. Brit.* brev′it) *n. Mil.* A commission advancing an officer in honorary rank without advance in pay or in command. —*v.t.* **bre·vet·ted** (brə·vet′id) or **brev·et·ed** (brev′it·id), **bre·vet·ting** (brə·vet′ing) or **brev·et·ing** (brev′it·ing) To raise in rank by brevet. [< OF *bref* letter, document] —**bre·vet′** *adj.* —**bre·vet′cy** *n.*

bre·vi·ar·y (brē′vē·er′ē, brev′ē-) *n. pl.* **·ar·ies** *Eccl.* In the Roman Catholic and Eastern Orthodox churches, a book of daily prayers. [< L *brevis* short]

brev·i·ty (brev′ə·tē) *n.* 1. Shortness of time. 2. Conciseness. [< L *brevis* short]

brew (broo) *v.t.* 1. To make, as beer or ale, by steeping, boiling, and fermenting malt, hops, etc. 2. To prepare (any beverage) as by boiling or mixing. 3. To plot; devise. —*v.i.* 4. To make ale, beer, or the like. 5. To commence to form, as a storm. —*n.* Something brewed. [OE *brēowan*] —**brew′er** *n.*

brew·er·y (broo′ər·ē) *n. pl.* **·er·ies** An establishment for brewing.

bri·ar (brī′ər) See BRIER[1].

bri·ar·root (brī′ər·root′, -root′) See BRIERROOT.

bri·ar·wood (brī′ər·wood′) *n.* Brierroot.

bribe (brīb) *n.* Any gift or emolument used corruptly to influence a person. —*v.* **bribed, brib·ing** *v.t.* 1. To give a bribe to. 2. To gain or influence by means of bribery. —*v.i.* 3. To give bribes. [< OF, piece of bread given a beggar] —**brib′a·ble** *adj.* —**brib′er** *n.*

brib·er·y (brī′bər·ē) *n. pl.* **·er·ies** The giving, offering, or accepting of a bribe.

bric-a-brac (brik′ə·brak′) *n.* Small objects of curiosity or decoration. [< F]

brick (brik) *n.* 1. A molded block of baked clay, used for building, etc. 2. Bricks collectively. 3. Any object shaped like a brick. —*v.t.* 1. To build or line with bricks. 2. To cover with bricks: with *up* or *in.* —*adj.* 1. Of brick. 2. Brick red. [< MF *brique* fragment]

brick·bat (brik′bat′) *n.* 1. A piece of a brick, esp. when used as a missile. 2. *Informal* An insulting remark.

brick·lay·er (brik′lā′ər) *n.* One who builds with bricks. —**brick′lay′ing** *n.*

brick red Dull brownish red.

bri·dal (brīd′l) *adj.* Pertaining to a bride or a wedding; nuptial. —*n.* A wedding. [OE *brȳdealo* wedding feast]

bridal wreath A flowering shrub of the rose family, with small white flowers.

bride (brīd) *n.* A newly married woman, or a woman about to be married. [OE *brȳd*]

bride·groom (brīd′groom′, -groom′) *n.* A man newly married or about to be married. [OE < *brȳd* bride + *guma* man]

brides·maid (brīdz′mād′) *n.* A young, usu. unmarried woman who attends a bride at her wedding.

bridge[1] (brij) *n.* 1. A structure erected across a waterway, ravine, road, etc., to afford passage. 2. Something that serves as a transition or connection. 3. A structure on a ship from which it is navigated and controlled. 4. The upper bony ridge of the nose. 5. The central part of a pair of spectacles. 6. In some string instruments, a thin piece of wood that raises the strings above the soundboard. 7. *Music* A transitional passage. 8. *Dent.* A mounting for false teeth. —*v.t.* **bridged, bridg·ing** 1. To construct a bridge over. 2. To make a passage over. [OE *brycg*] —**bridge′a·ble** *adj.*

bridge[2] (brij) *n.* A card game, derived from whist. See AUCTION BRIDGE, CONTRACT BRIDGE.

bridge·head (brij′hed′) *n. Mil.* A position in hostile territory, established by advance troops.

bridge·work (brij′wûrk′) *n.* 1. A dental bridge. 2. The construction of bridges.

bri·dle (brīd′l) *n.* 1. The head harness, including bit and reins, used to guide or restrain a horse. 2. Anything that restrains or limits. —*v.* **·dled, ·dling** *v.t.* 1. To put a bridle on. 2. To check or control. —*v.i.* 3. To show resentment, esp. by tossing one's head. [OE *bridel*] —**bri′dler** *n.*

bridle path A path for saddle horses.

Brie (brē) *n.* A soft-ripening cheese.

brief (brēf) *adj.* 1. Short in time or extent; quickly ending. 2. Concise. —*n.* 1. A short statement or summary. 2. *Law* A memorandum of the material facts, points of law, precedents, etc., of a case. 3. *pl.* Short underpants. —*v.t.* 1. To summarize. 2. To give a briefing to. [< L *brevis* short] —**brief′ly** *adv.* —**brief′ness** *n.*

brief·case (brēf′kās′) *n.* A rectangular case, often of leather, for carrying documents, etc.

brief·ing (brē′fing) *n.* A short lecture explaining an operation or procedure.

bri·er[1] (brī′ər) *n.* 1. A prickly bush or shrub, esp. one of the rose family. 2. A growth of such prickly bushes. 3. A thorny or prickly twig. Also spelled *briar.* [OE *brǣr, brēr*] —**bri′er·y** *adj.*

bri·er[2] (brī′ər) *n.* 1. A shrub of southern Europe whose root is used in making pipes. 2. A pipe made of brierroot. [< F *bruyère* heath]

bri·er·root (brī′ər·root′, -root′) *n.* The root of the brier. Also called *briarwood:* also spelled *briarroot.*

brig[1] (brig) *n. Naut.* A two-masted vessel, square-rigged on both masts. [Short for BRIGANTINE]

brig[2] (brig) *n.* A place of confinement, esp. on shipboard. [Origin unknown]

bri·gade (bri·gād′) *n.* 1. *Mil.* A unit of two or more groups or regiments. 2. Any body of persons more or less organized: a fire *brigade.* [< Ital. *brigare* to brawl, fight] —**bri·gade′** *v.t.* **·gad·ed, ·gad·ing**

brigadier general *Mil.* An officer ranking next above a colonel and next below a major general.

brig·and (brig′ənd) *n.* A robber. [< Ital. *brigare* to brawl, fight] —**brig′and·ish** *adj.*

brig·an·tine (brig′ən·tēn, -tīn) *n. Naut.* A two-masted vessel, square-rigged on the foremast, and fore-and-aft rigged on the mainmast. [< Ital. *brigare* to fight]

bright (brīt) *adj.* 1. Emitting or reflecting much light; full of light; shining. 2. Of brilliant color; vivid. 3. Glorious; illustrious. 4. Intelligent; quick-witted. 5. Lively; vivacious. 6. Hopeful; auspicious. —*adv.* In a bright manner; brightly. [OE *beorht, bryht*] —**bright′ly** *adv.* —**bright′ness** *n.*

bright·en (brīt′n) *v.t. & v.i.* To make or become bright or brighter. —**bright′en·er** *n.*

bril·liant (bril′yənt) *adj.* 1. Sparkling or glowing with light; very bright. 2. Splendid; illustrious. 3. Having great intellect or talent. 4. *Music* Clear; vivid; intense. —*n.* 1. A diamond of the finest cut. 2. *Printing* A very small size of type. [< F *briller* to sparkle] —**bril′liance, bril′lian·cy, bril′liant·ness** *n.* —**bril′liant·ly** *adv.*

bril·lian·tine (bril′yən·tēn) *n.* An oily hairdressing. [< F]

brim (brim) *n.* 1. The rim or upper edge of a cup, bowl, etc. 2. A projecting rim, as of a hat. 3. An edge or margin. —*v.t. & v.i.* **brimmed, brim·ming** To fill or be full to the brim. [OE *brim* seashore]

brim·ful (brim′fo͝ol′) *adj.* Full to the brim.

brim·stone (brim′stōn′) *n.* Sulfur. [OE *bryn-* burning + *stān* stone] —**brim′ston′y** *adj.*

brin·dle (brin′dəl) *adj.* Brindled. —*n.* A brindled color, or a brindled animal.

brin·dled (brin′dəld) *adj.* Tawny or grayish with irregular streaks or spots.

brine (brīn) *n.* 1. Water saturated with salt. 2. Sea water; the ocean. —*v.t.* **brined, brin·ing** To treat with or steep in brine. [OE *brȳne*] —**brin′i·ness** *n.* —**brin′ish** *adj.* —**brin′y** *adj.* **brin·i·er, brin·i·est**

bring (bring) *v.t.* **brought, bring·ing** 1. To convey or cause (a person or thing) to come with oneself to or toward a place. 2. To cause to come about; involve as a consequence. 3. To cause (a person or oneself) to adopt or admit, as a course of action. 4. To sell for: The house *brought* a good price. 5. *Law* **a** To prefer, as a charge. **b** To institute: to *bring* suit. **c** To set forth, as evidence or an argument. —**to bring about** To accomplish; cause to happen. —**to bring forth** 1. To give birth or produce. 2. To give rise to. —**to bring off** To do successfully. —**to bring on** To cause; lead to. —**to bring out** To reveal; cause to be evident. —**to bring to** To revive; restore to consciousness. —**to bring up** 1. To rear; educate. 2. To suggest or call attention to, as a subject. [OE *bringan*]

brink (bringk) *n.* The edge or verge, as of a steep place. [ME < Scand.]

brink·man·ship (bringk′mən·ship) *n.* The act or policy of taking major risks in order to achieve some end. Also **brinks′man·ship.** [< BRINK + *manship,* on analogy with *showmanship,* etc.]

bri·oche (brē·ōsh′, -osh′; *Fr.* brē·ôsh′) *n.* A soft roll. [< F]

bri·quette (bri·ket′) *n.* A block of compressed coal dust or charcoal, used for fuel. Also **bri·quet′.** [< F *brique* brick]

brisk (brisk) *adj.* 1. Quick; lively; energetic. 2. Sharp or stimulating. [? < F *brusque* abrupt, sudden] —**brisk′ly** *adv.* —**brisk′ness** *n.*

bris·ket (bris′kit) *n.* The breast of an animal, or a cut of meat from it. [< OF *bruschet*]

bris·ling (bris′ling) *n.* The sprat. [< Norw.]

bris·tle (bris′əl) *n.* Coarse, stiff hair or fiber. —*v.i.* **·tled, ·tling** 1. To erect the bristles in anger or excitement. 2. To show anger or irritation. 3. To stand or become erect, like bristles. 4. To be thickly set as if with bristles. [OE *byrst*] —**bris′tly** *adj.*

britch·es (brich′əz) *n.pl. Informal* Breeches.

Brit·i·cism (brit′ə·siz′əm) *n.* An idiom or turn of phrase peculiar to the British.

Brit·ish (brit′ish) *adj.* Pertaining to Great Britain or the United Kingdom. —*n.* The people of Great Britain: preceded by *the.* [OE *Bretisc* < *Bret* a Briton]

Brit·ish·er (brit′ish·ər) *n.* An Englishman.

British Isles Great Britain, Ireland, the Isle of Man, and the Channel Islands.

British thermal unit *Physics* The quantity of heat required to raise the temperature of one pound of water one degree Fahrenheit. Abbr. *BTU.*

Brit·on (brit′n) *n.* 1. A member of a Celtic people inhabiting ancient Britain. 2. An Englishman. [< L *Britto* < Celtic]

brit·tle (brit′l) *adj.* Liable to break or snap; fragile. [ME *britil*] —**brit′tle·ness** *n.*

broach (brōch) *v.t.* 1. To mention or suggest for the first time; introduce. 2. To pierce, as a barrel, so as to withdraw a liquid. —*n.* 1. A pointed, tapering tool for boring; a reamer. 2. A spit for roasting. [< Med.L *brocca* spike, spit] —**broach′er** *n.*

broad (brôd) *adj.* 1. Extended from side to side; wide. 2. Of great extent; vast or spacious. 3. Full; clear: *broad* daylight. 4. Of wide scope or application. 5. Liberal in spirit; tolerant. 6. Not detailed; general. 7. Obvious; clear: a *broad* hint. 8. Vulgar; unrefined. —*n. Slang* A woman. —*adv.* Completely; fully. [OE *brād*] —**broad′ly** *adv.* —**broad′ness** *n.*

Broad forms words meaning wide or extensive, as in the following list:

broad-backed	**broad-gauged**
broad-based	**broad-leaved**
broad-billed	**broad-nosed**
broad-chested	**broad-shouldered**
broad-faced	**broad-tailed**

broad·ax (brôd′aks′) *n.* An ax with a broad edge and a short handle. Also **broad′axe′.**

broad·cast (brôd′kast′) *v.* **·cast** or (*esp. for defs. 1, 4*) **·cast·ed, ·cast·ing** *v.t.* 1. To send or transmit by radio or television. 2. To scatter, as seed, over a wide area. 3. To disseminate; make public. —*v.i.* 4. To make a radio or television broadcast. —*n.* 1. The act of broadcasting. 2. A radio or television program. —**broad′cast′er** *n.*

broad·cloth (brôd′klôth′, -kloth′) *n.* 1. A fine woolen cloth used for suits, skirts, etc. 2. A closely woven fabric of silk or cotton.

broad·en (brôd′n) *v.t. & v.i.* To make or become broad.

broad jump A jump or jumping contest for distance.

broad·loom (brôd′lo͞om′) *n.* Carpet woven in widths of from 6 to 18 feet.

broad-mind·ed (brôd′mīn′did) *adj.* Liberal; tolerant. —**broad′-mind′ed·ly** *adv.* —**broad′-mind′ed·ness** *n.*

broad·side (brôd′sīd′) *n.* 1. All the guns on one side of a man-of-war, or their simultaneous discharge. 2. A volley of abuse or denunciation. 3. A wide printed sheet, formerly used esp. for political news and argument. —*adv.* With the broadside exposed.

broad·sword (brôd′sôrd′) *n.* A sword with a broad cutting blade.

broad·tail (brôd′tāl′) *n.* The lustrous black fur obtained from karakul lambs.

Broad·way (brôd′wā) A street in New York City, identified with the theater district and entertainment.

bro·cade (brō·kād′) *n.* A fabric interwoven with a raised design. —*v.t.* **·cad·ed, ·cad·ing** To weave (a cloth) with a raised design. [< Med.L *broccare* to embroider]

broc·co·li (brok′ə·lē) *n.* A variety of cauliflower, having green buds. [< Ital., pl. of *broccolo* cabbage sprout]

bro·chure (brō·shŏŏr′) *n.* A pamphlet or similar publication. [< F, lit., a stitched book < *brocher* to stitch]

bro·gan (brō′gən) *n.* A sturdy high shoe. [< Irish *brōgan*, dim. of *brōg* shoe]

brogue[1] (brōg) *n.* An Irish accent. [< Irish *barrōg* defect of speech]

brogue[2] (brōg) *n.* **1.** An oxford shoe, decorated with perforations. **2.** A shoe of untanned hide. [< Irish *brōg* a shoe]

broil (broil) *v.t.* **1.** To cook, as meat, by subjecting to direct heat. **2.** To expose to great heat; scorch. —*v.i.* **3.** To be exposed to great heat; cook. [< OF *bruller, bruillir* to burn]

broil·er (broi′lər) *n.* **1.** A device for broiling. **2.** A young chicken suitable for broiling.

broke (brōk) Past tense and archaic past participle of BREAK. —*adj.* *Informal* Having no money; bankrupt.

bro·ken (brō′kən) Past participle of BREAK. —*adj.* **1.** Forcibly separated into pieces; fractured. **2.** Violated; transgressed: *broken* vows. **3.** Interrupted; disturbed. **4.** Incomplete; fragmentary. **5.** Rough; uneven, as terrain. **6.** Humbled; crushed. **7.** Weakened or infirm. **8.** Bankrupt. **9.** Trained or made malleable: often with *in*. —**bro′ken·ly** *adv.* —**bro′ken·ness** *n.*

bro·ken-down (brō′kən·doun′) *adj.* **1.** Incapable of functioning. **2.** Ruined; decayed.

bro·ken·heart·ed (brō′kən·här′tid) *adj.* Crushed in spirit, as by grief.

bro·ker (brō′kər) *n.* **1.** One who buys and sells for another; esp., a stockbroker. **2.** An agent or mediator. [< OF *brochier* to tap, broach (a wine cask)]

bro·ker·age (brō′kər·ij) *n.* The business or commission of a broker. Also **bro′kage.**

bro·mide (brō′mīd) *n.* **1.** *Chem.* A compound of bromine. **2.** Potassium bromide, a sedative. **3.** *Informal* A platitude.

bro·mid·ic (brō·mid′ik) *adj.* *Informal* Commonplace; trite.

bro·mine (brō′mēn) *n.* A dark reddish brown, nonmetallic, fuming liquid element (symbol Br) with a suffocating odor. [< F *brome* (< Gk. *brōmos* stench) + -INE[2]]

bron·chi (brong′kī) Plural of BRONCHUS.

bron·chi·a (brong′kē·ə) *n.pl.* *Anat.* The bronchial tubes. [< Gk.] —**bron′chi·al** *adj.*

bronchial tube *Anat.* A subdivision of the trachea conveying air into the lungs.

bron·chi·tis (brong·kī′tis) *n.* *Pathol.* Inflammation of the bronchial tubes. —**bron·chit·ic** (brong·kit′ik) *adj.*

broncho- *combining form* Windpipe. Also, before vowels, **bronch-.** [< Gk. *bronchos*]

bron·cho·scope (brong′kə·skōp) *n.* *Med.* An instrument for inspecting or treating the interior of the bronchi.

bron·chus (brong′kəs) *n.* *pl.* **·chi** (-kī) *Anat.* One of the two forked branches of the trachea. [< Gk. *bronchos* windpipe]

bron·co (brong′kō) *n.* *pl.* **·cos** A small, wild or partly broken horse of the West. Also **bronc.** [< Sp. *bronco* rough]

bron·co·bust·er (brong′kō·bus′tər) *n.* *Informal* One who breaks a bronco to the saddle.

bron·to·sau·rus (bron′tə·sôr′əs) *n.* *pl.* **·rus·es** *Paleontol.* A huge, herbivorous dinosaur. Also **bron′to·saur.** [< Gk. *brontē* thunder + *sauros* lizard]

Bronx cheer (brongks) *Slang* A noisy fluttering of the lips to show contempt or derision: also called *raspberry.*

bronze (bronz) *n.* **1.** *Metall.* **a** A reddish brown alloy essentially of copper and tin. **b** A similar alloy of copper and some other metal, as aluminum. **2.** A reddish brown color or pigment. **3.** A statue, bust, etc., done in bronze. —*v.t.* & *v.i.* **bronzed, bronz·ing** To make or become bronze in color. [< Ital. *bronzo, bronzino*] —**bronz′y** *adj.*

Bronze Age *Archeol.* A stage of prehistory following the Stone Age and preceding the Iron Age, during which weapons, etc., were made of bronze.

brooch (brōch, brōōch) *n.* An ornamental pin with a clasp. [Var. of BROACH]

brood (brōōd) *n.* **1.** The young of animals, esp. of birds, produced at one time. **2.** All the young of the same mother. **3.** Kind or species. —*v.i.* **1.** To meditate moodily: usu. with *on* or *over*. **2.** To sit on eggs. —*v.t.* **3.** To sit upon or incubate (eggs). **4.** To protect (young) by covering with the wings. [OE *brōd*] —**brood′y** *adj.* **brood·i·er, brood·i·est**

brood·er (brōō′dər) *n.* **1.** A warmed structure for artificially rearing young fowl. **2.** One who or that which broods.

brook[1] (brŏŏk) *n.* A natural stream, smaller than a river or creek. [OE *brōc*]

brook[2] (brŏŏk) *v.t.* To put up with; tolerate. [OE *brūcan* to use]

brook·let (brŏŏk′lit) *n.* A little brook.

brook trout The speckled trout of eastern North America.

broom (brōōm, brŏŏm) *n.* **1.** A brush attached to a long handle for sweeping. **2.** Any of various shrubs with yellow flowers and stiff green branches. —*v.t.* To sweep. [OE *brōm*]

broom·stick (brōōm′stik′, brŏŏm′-) *n.* The handle of a broom.

broth (brôth) *n.* **1.** The water in which meat, vegetables, etc., have been boiled. **2.** A thin soup. [OE]

broth·el (broth′əl, broth′-, brôth′əl, brôth′-) *n.* A house of prostitution. [ME, a worthless person]

broth·er (bruth′ər) *n.* *pl.* **broth·ers** (*Archaic* **breth·ren**) **1.** A male individual having the same parents as another. **2.** A fellow member of a fraternity, ethnic group, etc. **3.** A comrade. **4.** One of a male religious order who is not a priest. [OE *brōthor*] —**broth′er·li·ness** *n.* —**broth′er·ly** *adj.* & *adv.*

broth·er·hood (bruth'ər·hŏŏd) *n.* 1. The relationship of or state of being brothers, esp. by blood. 2. An association of men sharing a common enterprise, profession, etc. 3. Harmony among persons of differing races or creeds.

broth·er-in-law (bruth'ər·in·lô') *n. pl.* **broth·ers-in-law** 1. A brother of one's husband or wife. 2. The husband of one's sister. 3. The husband of one's spouse's sister.

brougham (brōōm, brōō'əm, brō'əm) *n.* 1. A closed, four-wheeled carriage having a high, uncovered driver's seat. 2. A limousine with the driver's seat outside. [after Lord Henry *Brougham,* 1778–1868, British statesman]

brought (brôt) Past tense and past participle of BRING.

brou·ha·ha (brōō'hä·hä) *n.* Hubbub; uproar. [< F]

brow (brou) *n.* 1. The forehead. 2. The eyebrow. 3. The countenance in general. 4. The upper edge of a steep place: the *brow* of a hill. [OE *brū*]

brow·beat (brou'bēt') *v.t.* **·beat, ·beat·en, ·beat·ing** To intimidate; bully.

brown (broun) *adj.* 1. Of a dark color combining red, yellow, and black. 2. Dark-complexioned; tanned. —*n.* A brown color or pigment. —*v.t. & v.i.* To make or become brown. [OE *brūn*] —**brown'ish** *adj.* —**brown'·ness** *n.*

brown-bag (broun'bag') *v.i.* **-bagged, -bag·ging** *Informal* To take one's lunch to work, esp. in a brown paper bag. —**brown'-bag'ger** *n.*

brown bear 1. The black bear. 2. One of several very large bears of North America and Europe, with brownish fur.

brown Bet·ty (bet'ē) Baked pudding made of bread crumbs, apples, sugar, and spices. Also **brown bet'ty.**

Brown·i·an movement (brou'nē·ən) *Physics* The rapid oscillatory movement of small particles when suspended in fluids. Also **Brownian motion.** [after Robert *Brown,* 1773–1858, Scottish botanist, who discovered it]

brown·ie (brou'nē) *n.* 1. A small goblin or sprite, supposed to do useful work at night. 2. A small, flat chocolate cake with nuts. [< BROWN; from its color]

Brown·ie (brou'nē) *n.* A junior girl scout of the age group seven through nine.

brown·out (broun'out') *n.* A partial diminishing of lights, esp. to save energy.

brown rice Unpolished rice grains.

brown·stone (broun'stōn') *n.* A brownish red sandstone used for building; also, a house with a front of brownstone.

brown sugar Sugar that is unrefined or partly refined.

browse (brouz) *v.* **browsed, brows·ing** *v.i.* 1. To feed on leaves, shoots, etc. 2. To inspect books or merchandise casually. —*v.t.* 3. To nibble at or graze on. —*n.* Growing shoots or twigs used as fodder. [< MF *broust* bud, sprout] —**brows'er** *n.*

bru·in (brōō'in) *n.* A bear; esp., a brown bear. [< MDu.]

bruise (brōōz) *v.* **bruised, bruis·ing** *v.t.* 1. To injure, as by a blow, without breaking the surface of the skin. 2. To dent or mar the surface of. 3. To hurt or offend slightly. 4. To crush, as in a mortar. —*v.i.* 5. To become discolored as from a blow. —*n.* An injury caused by bruising. [Fusion of OE *brȳsan* to crush and OF *bruisier* to break, shatter]

bruis·er (brōō'zər) *n.* A professional boxer or the like.

bruit (brōōt) *v.t.* To noise abroad; talk about: usu. in the passive. [< F *bruire* to roar, ? < L *rugire*] —**bruit'er** *n.*

brunch (brunch) *n.* *Informal* A meal combining breakfast and lunch. [< BR(EAKFAST) + (L)UNCH]

bru·net (brōō·net') *adj.* Dark-hued; having dark complexion, hair, and eyes. —*n.* A brunet man or boy. [< F]

bru·nette (brōō·net') *adj.* Brunet: feminine form. —*n.* A brunette woman or girl. [< F]

brunt (brunt) *n.* The main force or strain of a blow, attack, etc. [? < ON *bruna* to advance quickly, as a fire]

brush[1] (brush) *n.* 1. An implement having bristles, wires, or the like, fixed in a handle or a back, and used for sweeping, painting, smoothing the hair, etc. 2. The act of brushing. 3. A light, grazing touch. 4. A brief encounter, esp. a skirmish. 5. *Electr.* A conductor for carrying current from a dynamo or through a motor. —*v.t.* 1. To sweep, paint, etc., with a brush. 2. To remove with or as with a brush. 3. To touch lightly in passing. —*v.i.* 4. To move lightly and quickly. —**to brush off** *Slang* To dismiss or refuse abruptly. —**to brush up** To refresh one's knowledge. [< OF *brosse*]

brush[2] (brush) *n.* 1. A growth of small trees and shrubs. 2. Wooded country sparsely settled. 3. Brushwood. [< OF *broche, brosse*] —**brush'y** *adj.*

brush·off (brush'ôf') *n.* *Slang* An abrupt refusal or dismissal.

brush·wood (brush'wŏŏd') *n.* 1. Bushes or branches cut or broken off. 2. A thicket.

brusque (brusk) *adj.* Rude or curt; blunt. Also **brusk.** [< F] —**brusque'ly** *adv.* —**brusque'ness** *n.*

Brussels sprouts 1. A variety of cabbage having stems covered with edible heads like little cabbages. 2. The heads themselves.

brut (brüt, brōōt) *adj.* Dry (def. 6): said of wines, esp. of champagne. [< F, lit., rough < L *brutus*]

bru·tal (brōōt'l) *adj.* 1. Like a brute; cruel; savage. 2. Rude; coarse. —**bru·tal·i·ty** (brōō·tal'ə·tē) *n.* —**bru'tal·ize** *v.t. & v.i.* **·ized, ·iz·ing** —**bru'tal·i·za'tion** *n.* —**bru'·tal·ly** *adv.*

brute (brōōt) *n.* 1. Any animal other than man. 2. A brutal person. —*adj.* 1. Incapable of reasoning. 2. Dominated by animal appetites. [< L *brutus* stupid, heavy]

brut·ish (brōō'tish) *adj.* Characteristic of a brute; stupid; gross. —**brut'ish·ly** *adv.* —**brut'ish·ness, brut'ism** *n.*

bry·o·phyte (brī'ə·fīt) *n.* *Bot.* Any moss or liverwort. [< Gk. *bryon* moss + -PHYTE] —**bry'o·phyt'ic** (-fit'ik) *adj.*

bub·ble (bub'əl) *n.* 1. A liquid globule filled with air or other gas. 2. A globule of air or other gas in a liquid or solid substance. 3. Anything unsubstantial; a delusion. 4. The process or sound of bubbling. 5. Something like a bubble, as a glass dome. —*v.* **·bled,**

·bling *v.i.* 1. To form or emit bubbles; rise in bubbles. 2. To flow with a gurgling sound. 3. To express delight in an irrepressible manner. —*v.t.* 4. To cause to bubble. 5. *Informal* To burp (a baby). [ME *buble*] —**bub′bly** *adj.*

bu·bo (byōō′bō) *n. pl.* **bu·boes** *Pathol.* An inflammatory swelling of a lymph gland in the groin or armpit. [< Gk. *boubōn* groin] —**bu·bon·ic** (byōō·bon′ik) *adj.*

bubonic plague *Pathol.* A contagious, epidemic disease, usually fatal, transmitted to man by fleas from infected rats.

buc·cal (buk′əl) *adj. Anat.* 1. Of or pertaining to the cheek. 2. Pertaining to the mouth. [< L *bucca* cheek]

buc·ca·neer (buk′ə·nir′) *n.* A pirate. [< Tupi *boucan* a frame for smoking and curing meat]

buck[1] (buk) *n.* 1. The male of certain animals, as of antelopes or deer. 2. *Informal* A young man. —*v.i.* 1. To leap upward suddenly with the back arched, as a horse. 2. *Informal* To move with jerks and jolts. —*v.t.* 3. To throw by bucking. 4. *Dial.* To butt with the head. 5. *Informal* To defy. 6. In football, to charge into (the opponent's line). —**to buck for** *Slang* To try hard to obtain (a promotion, raise, etc.). —**to buck up** *Informal* To encourage or take courage. [OE *bucca* he-goat]

buck[2] (buk) *n.* 1. A sawhorse. 2. A padded frame like a sawhorse, used for vaulting, etc. [< Du. *zaagbok* sawbuck]

buck[3] (buk) *n. Slang* A dollar bill.

buck·a·roo (buk′ə·rōō, buk′ə·rōō′) *n.* A cowboy. [Alter. of Sp. *vaquero* cowboy]

buck·board (buk′bôrd′) *n.* A light, four-wheeled, open carriage having a long, flexible board in place of body and springs.

buck·et (buk′it) *n.* 1. A deep cylindrical vessel, with a rounded handle; pail. 2. As much as a bucket will hold: also **buck′et·ful′**. [? < OF *buket* tub]

bucket seat A single seat, usu. with a rounded back, used in racing and sports cars, airplanes, etc.

buck·eye (buk′ī′) *n.* 1. The horse chestnut. 2. The glossy brown seed or nut of this tree.

buck·le[1] (buk′əl) *n.* 1. A device for fastening together two loose ends, as of a strap. 2. An ornament resembling a buckle. —*v.t. & v.i.* **·led, ·ling** To fasten or be fastened with or as with a buckle. —**to buckle down** To apply oneself. [< F *boucle* cheekstrap, boss of a shield]

buck·le[2] (buk′əl) *v.t. & v.i.* **·led, ·ling** To bend under pressure; warp; crumple. —*n.* A bend or twist. [< F *boucler* to bulge]

buck·ler (buk′lər) *n.* 1. A small, round shield. 2. A means of defense. [< OF *boucler* having a boss] —**buck′ler** *v.t.*

buck private *Slang* A private in the U.S. Army.

buck·ram (buk′rəm) *n.* A coarse cotton fabric sized with glue, used for stiffening garments, in bookbinding, etc. [< OF *boquerant* coarse cloth < *Bokhara*, Persia, where first made]

buck·saw (buk′sô′) *n.* A wood-cutting saw set in an adjustable H-shaped frame.

buck·shot (buk′shot′) *n.* Shot of a large size.

buck·skin (buk′skin′) *n.* 1. The skin of a buck. 2. A soft, strong leather, now chiefly made from sheepskins. 3. *pl.* Clothing made of such skin.

buck·tooth (buk′tōōth′) *n. pl.* **·teeth** A projecting tooth. —**buck′toothed′** *adj.*

buck·wheat (buk′hwēt′) *n.* 1. A plant yielding triangular seeds used as fodder and for flour. 2. Its seeds. 3. The flour. [OE *bōc* beech + WHEAT]

bu·col·ic (byōō·kol′ik) *adj.* Pastoral; rustic. —*n.* 1. A pastoral poem. 2. A rustic; farmer. [< Gk. *boukolos* herdsmen] —**bu·col′i·cal·ly** *adv.*

bud (bud) *n.* 1. *Bot.* **a** An undeveloped stem, branch, or shoot of a plant, with rudimentary leaves or unexpanded flowers. **b** The act or stage of budding. 2. *Zool.* A budlike projection or part. —**to nip in the bud** To stop in the initial stage. —*v.* **bud·ded, bud·ding** *v.i.* 1. To put forth buds. 2. To begin to grow or develop. —*v.t.* 3. To cause to bud. 4. To graft to another type of tree or plant. [ME *budde*; origin uncertain] —**bud′der** *n.*

Bud·dhism (bōōd′iz·əm, bōō′diz-) *n.* A mystical and ascetic religious faith of eastern Asia, which teaches that the ideal state of nirvana is reached by right living and through meditation. —**Bud′dhist** *adj. & n.* —**Bud·dhis′tic** or **·ti·cal** *adj.*

bud·ding (bud′ing) *adj.* Just beginning.

bud·dy (bud′ē) *n. pl.* **·dies** *Informal* Pal; chum.

budge (buj) *v.t. & v.i.* **budged, budg·ing** To move or stir slightly. [< F *bouger* to stir, move]

budg·er·i·gar (buj′ə·rē·gar′) *n.* A small Australian parrot, popular as a pet. Also *budgie.* [< native Australian name]

budg·et (buj′it) *n.* 1. A plan for adjusting expenditures to income. 2. A collection or stock. —*v.t.* 1. To determine in advance the expenditure of (time, money, etc.). 2. To provide for according to a budget. —*v.i.* 3. To make a budget. [< L *bulga* leather bag] —**budg·et·ar·y** (buj′ə·ter′ē) *adj.*

budg·ie (buj′ē) *n.* See BUDGERIGAR.

buff[1] (buf) *n.* 1. A thick, soft, flexible leather made from the skins of buffalo, oxen, etc. 2. Its color, a light brownish yellow. 3. A military coat made of buff. 4. *Informal* The bare skin; the nude. 5. A stick or wheel covered with soft material, used for polishing. —*adj.* 1. Made of buff. 2. Light, brownish yellow. —*v.t.* To clean or polish with or as with a buff. [< F *buffle* buffalo] —**buff′y** *adj.*

buff[2] (buf) *n.* An enthusiast or devotee. [Origin uncertain]

buf·fa·lo (buf′ə·lō) *n. pl.* **·loes** or **·los** 1. Any of various large Old World oxen. 2. The North American bison. —*v.t.* **·loed, ·lo·ing** *Slang* To intimidate; hoodwink. [< Gk. *boubalos* buffalo]

buffalo grass A low, creeping grass covering prairies east of the Rocky Mountains.

buff·er[1] (buf′ər) *n.* One who or that which buffs or polishes. [< BUFF[1], v.]

buff·er[2] (buf′ər) *n.* 1. One who or that which diminishes shock or conflict. 2. A substance that stabilizes the degree of acidity or alkalinity of a solution.

buf·fet[1] (bōō·fā′) *n.* 1. A sidebord for china, glassware, etc. 2. A counter or table for serving meals or refreshments. 3. A meal set out on a buffet table. [< F]

buf·fet[2] (buf′it) *v.t.* 1. To strike or cuff, as

with the hand. 2. To strike repeatedly; knock about. —*v.i.* 3. To fight; struggle. —*n.* A blow or cuff. [< OF *buffet*, dim. of *buffe* a blow, slap] —**buf′fet·er** *n.*

buf·foon (bu·fōōn′) *n.* 1. A clown. 2. One given to jokes, coarse pranks, etc. [< MF *bouffon*] —**buf·foon′er·y** *n.* —**buf·foon′ish** *adj.*

bug (bug) *n.* 1. Any crawling insect with sucking mouth parts, wingless or with two pairs of wings. 2. Loosely, any insect or small arthropod. 3. *Informal* A virus or germ. 4. *Slang* An enthusiast. 5. *Informal* A minor defect, as in a machine. 6. *Informal* A miniature electronic microphone, used in wiretapping, etc. —*v.* **bugged, bug·ging** *v.i.* 1. To stick out: said of eyes. —*v.t.* 2. *Slang* To annoy; pester. 3. *Informal* To fit (a room, telephone circuit, etc.) with a concealed listening device. —**to bug out** *Slang* To quit. [Origin unknown]

bug·bear (bug′bâr′) *n.* 1. A real or imaginary object of dread. 2. A hobgoblin. Also **bug·a·boo** (bug′ə·bōō).

bug-eyed (bug′īd′) *adj. Slang* With the eyes bulging.

bug·gy[1] (bug′ē) *n. pl.* **·gies** 1. A light, four-wheeled carriage. 2. A baby carriage. [Origin uncertain]

bug·gy[2] (bug′ē) *adj.* **·gi·er, ·gi·est** 1. Infested with bugs. 2. *Slang* Crazy. —**bug′gi·ness** *n.*

bu·gle (byōō′gəl) *n.* 1. A brass wind instrument resembling a trumpet, usu. without keys or valves. 2. A huntsman's horn. —*v.t. & v.i.* **·gled, ·gling** To signal with or sound a bugle. [< L *buculus*, dim. of *bos* ox] —**bu′·gler** *n.*

bug off *Slang* Go away!

build (bild) *v.* **built** (*Archaic* **build·ed**), **build·ing** *v.t.* 1. To construct, erect, or make by assembling separate parts or materials. 2. To establish and increase. 3. To found; make a basis for. —*v.i.* 4. To construct or erect a house, etc. 5. To base or develop an idea, theory, etc.: with *on* or *upon*. —**to build up** 1. To create or build by degrees. 2. To renew or strengthen; also, to increase. —*n.* 1. The manner or style of construction. 2. A person's figure; physique. [OE *byldan* < *bold* house] —**build′er** *n.*

build·ing (bil′ding) *n.* 1. A structure, as a house or barn. 2. The occupation, act, or art of constructing.

build·up (bild′up′) *n.* 1. An increase or strengthening. 2. *Informal* Extravagant publicity or praise.

built-in (bilt′in′) *adj.* 1. Built as a part of the structure. 2. Inherent: *built-in* reflexes.

bulb (bulb) *n.* 1. *Bot.* A leaf bud comprising a cluster of thickened, scalelike leaves growing usu. underground and sending forth roots, as the onion or lily. 2. Any plant growing from a bulb. 3. A rounded protuberance, as at the end of a tube. 4. An incandescent lamp. [< Gk. *bolbos* bulbous root] —**bul·bar** (bul′bər), **bul′bous** *adj.*

Bul·gar·i·an (bul·gâr′ē·ən) *n.* 1. A native or citizen of Bulgaria. 2. The Slavic language of the Bulgarians. —**Bul·gar′i·an** *adj.*

bulge (bulj) *n.* A protuberant, rounded part. —*v.t. & v.i.* **bulged, bulg·ing** To swell out. [< L *bulga*]

bulk (bulk) *n.* 1. Magnitude, volume, or size. 2. The greater or principal part. 3. A large body or mass. —*v.i.* To appear large or important; loom. [Cf. ON *bulki* heap, cargo, and Dan. *bulk* rump]

bulk·head (bulk′hed′) *n.* 1. *Naut.* An upright partition in a vessel, separating compartments. 2. A partition or wall to keep back earth, gas, etc. 3. A small structure built over an elevator shaft.

bulk·y (bul′kē) *adj.* **bulk·i·er, bulk·i·est** Large; massive; also, unwieldy. —**bulk′i·ly** *adv.* —**bulk′i·ness** *n.*

bull[1] (bŏŏl) *n.* 1. The male of a bovine animal. ◆Collateral adjective: *taurine.* 2. The male of some other animals, as of the elephant, whale, etc. 3. One likened to a bull, as in strength or manner. 4. A speculator who buys so as to profit from a rise in prices: opposed to *bear*[2]. 5. *Slang* Empty talk; nonsense. —*v.t.* 1. To push or force (a way). —*v.i.* 2. To go or push ahead. —*adj.* 1. Male; masculine. 2. Like a bull; large. 3. Marked by rising prices: a *bull* market. [ME *bule*] —**bull′ish** *adj.* —**bull′ish·ly** *adv.* —**bull′ish·ness** *n.*

bull[2] (bŏŏl) *n.* A papal edict. [< L *bulla* edict, seal]

bull·dog (bŏŏl′dôg′) *n.* A medium-sized, short-haired, powerful dog with strong jaws. —*adj.* Resembling a bulldog; tenacious. —*v.t. & v.i.* **·dogged, ·dog·ging** *Informal* To throw (a steer) by gripping its horns and twisting its neck.

bull·doze (bŏŏl′dōz′) *v.t.* **·dozed, ·doz·ing** 1. *Slang* To intimidate; bully. 2. To clear, dig, scrape, etc., with a bulldozer. [? < BULL[1], adj. + DOSE]

bull·doz·er (bŏŏl′dō′zər) *n.* A tractor with a heavy steel blade, used for moving earth, clearing wooded areas, etc.

bul·let (bŏŏl′it) *n.* 1. A small projectile for a firearm. 2. Any small ball. 3. A heavy dot (●) used in printing. [< F *boulette*, dim. of *boule* ball]

bul·le·tin (bŏŏl′ə·tən, -tin) *n.* 1. A brief, usu. unscheduled news report, as on radio. 2. A periodical publication, as of the proceedings of a society. [< Ital. *bulletino*]

bul·let·proof (bŏŏl′it·prōōf′) *adj.* Not penetrable by bullets. —**bul′let·proof′** *v.t.* —**bul′let·proof′ing** *n.*

bull·fight (bŏŏl′fīt′) *n.* A combat in an arena between men and a bull or bulls. —**bull′·fight′er** *n.* —**bull′fight′ing** *n.*

bull·finch (bŏŏl′finch′) *n.* A European songbird having a short bill and red breast.

bull·frog (bŏŏl′frog′, -frôg′) *n.* A large frog with a deep bass croak. [< BULL[1], adj. + FROG]

bull·head (bŏŏl′hed′) *n.* A fresh-water catfish.

bull·head·ed (bŏŏl′hed′id) *adj.* Stubborn.

bull·horn (bŏŏl′hôrn′) *n.* A hand-held electronic device to amplify the voice.

bul·lion (bŏŏl′yən) *n.* Gold or silver uncoined or in mass, as in bars, plates, etc. [ME]

bul·lock (bŏŏl′ək) *n.* A gelded bull; a steer or ox. [OE *bulluc*]

bull·pen (bŏŏl′pen′) *n.* 1. An enclosure for bulls. 2. *Informal* A place for temporary detention of prisoners. 3. In baseball, a place where pitchers practice during a game.

bull·ring (bŏŏl′ring′) *n.* A circular enclosure for bullfights.

bull session *Informal* An informal discussion.

bull's-eye (bo͝olz′ī′) *n.* 1. The central disk on a target; also, a shot that hits this disk. 2. Something resembling a bull's-eye.

bull terrier A white terrier having a long head and stiff coat.

bull·whip (bo͝ol′hwip′) *n.* A long, heavy whip. —*v.t.* **·whipped, ·whip·ping** To strike with a bullwhip.

bul·ly[1] (bo͝ol′ē) *n. pl.* **·lies** A swaggering, quarrelsome person who terrorizes weaker people. —*v.t. & v.i.* **·lied, ·ly·ing** To intimidate or terrorize (a person or animal). —*adj.* 1. *Informal* Excellent. 2. Jolly; dashing. —*interj.* *Informal* Well done! [? < Du. *boel* friend, lover]

bul·ly[2] (bo͝ol′ē) *n.* Canned or pickled beef. Also **bully beef.** [Prob. < F *bouillir* to boil]

bul·rush (bo͝ol′rush′) *n.* 1. A tall, rushlike plant growing in water or damp ground. 2. In the Bible, papyrus. [< BULL[1], adj. + RUSH[2]]

bul·wark (bo͝ol′wərk) *n.* 1. A defensive wall or rampart. 2. Any safeguard or defense. 3. *Usu. pl. Naut.* The raised side of a ship, above the upper deck. —*v.t.* To surround and fortify with a bulwark. [< MHG *bolwerc*]

bum (bum) *n.* *Slang* A worthless or dissolute loafer; tramp. —**the bum's rush** Forcible ejection. —*adj.* Bad; inferior. —*v.* **bummed, bum·ming** *v.i.* 1. To live by sponging. 2. To live idly and in dissipation. —*v.t.* 3. To get by begging: to *bum* a ride. [Short for *bummer*, alter. of G *bummler* loafer, dawdler]

bum·ble (bum′bəl) *v.t. & v.i.* **·bled, ·bling** To bungle, esp. in an officious manner. [? Imit.] —**bum′bling** *adj. & n.*

bum·ble·bee (bum′bəl·bē′) *n.* Any of various large, hairy bees. [< dial. E *bumble* to hum + BEE[1]]

bum·mer (bum′ər) *n.* *Slang* 1. An unpleasant situation, esp. a bad drug experience. 2. Something that fails.

bump (bump) *v.t.* 1. To come into contact with; knock into. 2. To cause to knock into or against. 3. *Slang* To displace, as from a position or seat. —*v.i.* 4. To strike heavily or with force: often with *into* or *against.* 5. To move with jerks and jolts. —**to bump off** *Slang* To kill. —*n.* 1. An impact or collision; jolt. 2. A protuberance or uneven place. [Imit.] —**bump′i·ly** *adv.* —**bump′i·ness** *n.* —**bump′y** *adj.* **bump·i·er, bump·i·est**

bump·er[1] (bum′pər) *n.* The horizontal bar at the front or rear of an automobile to absorb the shock of collision.

bump·er[2] (bum′pər) *n.* A cup or glass filled to the brim. —*adj.* Unusually full or large: a *bumper* crop. [? Alter. of F *bombarde* large cup; infl. in form by *bump*]

bump·kin (bump′kin) *n.* An awkward rustic; a lout. [? < Du. *boomkin* little tree, block]

bump·tious (bump′shəs) *adj.* Aggressively self-assertive. [Appar. < BUMP] —**bump′tious·ly** *adv.* —**bump′tious·ness** *n.*

bun (bun) *n.* 1. A small bread roll, sometimes sweetened or spiced. 2. A roll of hair shaped like a bun. [ME *bunne*]

bunch (bunch) *n.* 1. A number of things of the same kind growing, occurring, or fastened together; a cluster. 2. *Informal* A group of people. —*v.t. & v.i.* 1. To form bunches or groups. 2. To gather, as in folds. [ME *bunche*] —**bunch′i·ness** *n.* —**bunch′y** *adj.* **bunch·i·er, bunch·i·est**

bun·co (bung′kō) *n.* *Informal* A swindle; confidence game. —*v.t.* **·coed, ·co·ing** To swindle or rob. Also spelled *bunko.* [Prob. < Sp. *banco*, a card game]

bun·combe (bung′kəm) *n.* *Informal* 1. Empty speechmaking for political effect. 2. Empty talk; humbug. Also spelled *bunkum.* [after *Buncombe* County, N.C., whose congressman (1919–21) insisted on making unimportant speeches "for Buncombe"]

bun·dle (bun′dəl) *n.* 1. A number of things or a quantity of anything bound together. ◆Collateral adjective: *fascicular.* 2. A package. 3. A group; collection. —*v.* **·dled, ·dling** *v.t.* 1. To tie, roll, etc., in a bundle. 2. To send or put hastily and unceremoniously: with *away, off, out,* or *into.* —*v.i.* 3. To go hastily; hustle. 4. To lie or sleep in the same bed without undressing, formerly a courting custom in Wales and New England. —**to bundle up** To dress warmly. [< MDu. *bond* group] —**bun′dler** *n.*

bung (bung) *n.* 1. A stopper for the hole through which a cask is filled. 2. Bunghole. —*v.t.* To close with or as with a bung. [< MDu. *bonghe*]

bun·ga·low (bung′gə·lō) *n.* A small house or cottage. [< Hind. *banglā*, lit., Bengalese (house) < *Banga* Bengal]

bung·hole (bung′hōl′) *n.* A hole in a cask from which liquid is tapped. [< BUNG + HOLE]

bun·gle (bung′gəl) *v.t. & v.i.* **·gled, ·gling** To work, make, or do (something) clumsily; botch. —**bun′gle** *n.* —**bun′gler** *n.* —**bun′·gling·ly** *adv.*

bun·ion (bun′yən) *n.* A painful swelling of the foot, usu. at the base of the great toe. [< OF *bugne* swelling]

bunk[1] (bungk) *n.* 1. A narrow, built-in bed or shelf for sleeping; a berth. 2. *Informal* A bed. —*v.i.* *Informal* 1. To sleep in a bunk. 2. To go to bed.

bunk[2] (bungk) *n.* *Slang* Buncombe.

bun·ker (bung′kər) *n.* 1. A large bin, as for coal on a ship. 2. In golf, a mound of earth serving as an obstacle. 3. *Mil.* A steel and concrete fortification. [< Scot. *bonker* box]

bun·ko (bung′kō) See BUNCO.

bun·kum (bung′kəm) See BUNCOMBE.

bun·ny (bun′ē) *n. pl.* **·nies** A rabbit: a pet name. [< dial. E *bun* a rabbit]

Bun·sen burner (bun′sən) A type of gas burner producing a very hot flame. [after R. W. *Bunsen*, 1811–1899, German chemist]

bunt (bunt) *v.t. & v.i.* 1. To strike or push as with horns; butt. 2. In baseball, to bat (the ball) lightly into the infield, without swinging the bat. —*n.* 1. A push or a butt. 2. In baseball: **a** The act of bunting. **b** A ball that has been bunted. [Nasalized var. of BUTT[1]]

bunt·ing[1] (bun′ting) *n.* 1. A light wool or cotton fabric used for flags, etc. 2. Flags, banners, etc., collectively. 3. A type of sleeping bag for infants. [? ME *bonten* to sift]

bunt·ing[2] (bun′ting) *n.* One of various birds related to the finches and sparrows. [ME *bountyng*; origin unknown]

buoy (boi, bo͞o′ē) *n.* 1. *Naut.* A warning float moored on a hazard or marking a channel.

2. A device for keeping a person afloat; a life buoy. —*v.t.* 1. To keep from sinking; keep afloat. 2. To cheer; encourage: usu. with *up*. 3. *Naut.* To mark with buoys. [< L *boia* fetter]

buoy·an·cy (boi′ən·sē, bōō′yən·sē) *n.* 1. The tendency or ability to keep afloat. 2. The power of a fluid to keep an object afloat. 3. Cheerfulness. Also **buoy′ance.** [Prob. < Sp. *boyar* to float] —**buoy′ant** *adj.* —**buoy′·ant·ly** *adv.*

bur[1] (bûr) *n.* 1. *Bot.* A rough or prickly flower head or seedcase. 2. A plant that bears burs. 3. A person or thing that clings like a bur. Also spelled *burr.* [< Scand.]

bur[2] (bûr) See BURR[2].

bur·den[1] (bûr′dən) *n.* 1. Something carried; a load. 2. Something that weighs heavily, as responsibility. 3. *Naut.* The carrying capacity of a vessel. —*v.t.* To load or overload. [OE *byrthen* load]

bur·den[2] (bûr′dən) *n.* 1. Something often repeated. 2. A refrain of a song. [< LL *burdo* drone]

bur·den·some (bûr′dən·səm) *adj.* Heavy or hard to bear; oppressive. —**bur′den·some·ly** *adv.* —**bur′den·some·ness** *n.*

bur·dock (bûr′dok) *n.* A coarse weed having prickly burs. [< BUR[1] + DOCK[4]]

bu·reau (byōōr′ō) *n. pl.* **bu·reaus** or **bu·reaux** (byōōr′ōz) 1. A chest of drawers for clothing. 2. A government department. 3. An office for transacting business. [< F, desk]

bu·reau·cra·cy (byōō·rok′rə·sē) *n. pl.* **·cies** 1. Government by bureaus; also, the governing officials. 2. The undue extension of government departments and the power of their officials. 3. Rigid adherence to administrative routine. [< F < *bureau* desk, office + -CRACY]

bu·reau·crat (byōōr′ə·krat) *n.* 1. A member of a bureaucracy. 2. An official who narrowly adheres to a rigid routine. —**bu′reau·crat′ic** or **·i·cal** *adj.* —**bu′reau·crat′i·cal·ly** *adv.*

bu·rette (byōō·ret′) *n.* *Chem.* A finely graduated glass tube with a stopcock at the bottom. Also **bu·ret′.** [< F, dim. of *buire* vase, vial]

burg (bûrg) *n.* *Informal* A town; esp., a rural town. [OE *burg*]

bur·geon (bûr′jən) *v.i.* 1. To flourish; grow. 2. To bud; sprout. —*v.t.* 3. To put forth (buds, etc.). —*n.* A bud; sprout. [< OF *burjon*]

bur·gess (bûr′jis) *n.* A citizen or officer of a borough. [< OF *burgeis*]

burgh (bûrg; *Scot.* bûr′ō, -ə) *n.* In Scottish law, a chartered town. [Var. of BOROUGH] —**burgh·al** (bûr′gəl) *adj.*

burgh·er (bûr′gər) *n.* A citizen of a burgh, town, or city.

bur·glar (bûr′glər) *n.* One who commits burglary. [< OF *bourg* dwelling + *laire* robbery]

bur·gla·ry (bûr′glər·ē) *n. pl.* **·ries** The breaking and entering of a dwelling with intent to commit a crime. —**bur′glar·ize** *v.t.* **·ized, ·iz·ing**

bur·gle (bûr′gəl) *v.t. & v.i.* **·gled, ·gling** *Informal* To commit burglary (upon).

bur·go·mas·ter (bûr′gə·mas′tər) *n.* Chief magistrate or mayor of some Dutch, Flemish, or German towns. [< Du. *burgemeester*]

Bur·gun·dy (bûr′gən·dē) *n. pl.* **·dies** A dry red or white wine.

bur·i·al (ber′ē·əl) *n.* The burying of a dead body; interment. —*adj.* Of or pertaining to burial. [ME *buryel* < OE *brygels* tomb]

bu·rin (byōōr′in) *n.* A steel tool for engraving or carving.

burl (bûrl) *n.* 1. A knot or lump in wool, cloth, or thread. 2. A large wartlike growth on the trunk of a tree. —*v.t.* To dress (cloth) by removing burls. [< LL *burra* shaggy hair] —**burled** *adj.* —**burl′er** *n.*

bur·lap (bûr′lap) *n.* A coarse fabric made of jute or hemp. [Origin uncertain]

bur·lesque (bər·lesk′) *n.* 1. A satire or ludicrous imitation; parody. 2. A theatrical entertainment marked by low comedy, striptease, etc. —*v.t. & v.i.* **·lesqued, ·les·quing** To satirize, esp. with broad caricature. [< F < Ital. *burla* joke] —**bur·lesque′** *adj.* —**bur·les′quer** *n.*

bur·ly (bûr′lē) *adj.* **·li·er, ·li·est** Husky; stout. [ME *borlich*] —**bur′li·ly** *adv.* —**bur′li·ness** *n.*

Bur·mese (bər·mēz′, -mēs′) *n. pl.* **·mese** 1. A native or inhabitant of Burma. 2. The Sino-Tibetan language of Burma. —**Bur·mese′** *adj.*

burn (bûrn) *v.* **burned** or **burnt, burn·ing** *v.t.* 1. To destroy or consume by fire. 2. To set afire; ignite. 3. To injure or kill by fire. 4. To injure or damage by friction, steam, etc. 5. To produce, as a hole, by fire. 6. To brand or cauterize. 7. To finish or harden by intense heat; fire. 8. To use a light, oven, etc. 9. To cause a feeling of heat in. 10. To sunburn. 11. *Chem.* To cause to oxidize. 12. *Slang* To electrocute. —*v.i.* 13. To be on fire; blaze. 14. To be destroyed or scorched by fire. 15. To give off light, heat, etc.; shine. 16. To appear or feel hot. 17. To be excited or inflamed. 18. *Chem.* To oxidize. 19. *Slang* To be electrocuted. —**to burn down** To raze or be razed by fire. —**to burn out** 1. To become extinguished through lack of fuel. 2. To destroy or wear out by heat, friction, etc. —**to burn up** 1. To consume by fire. 2. *Slang* To make or become enraged. —*n.* 1. A burned place. 2. *Pathol.* A lesion caused by heat, corrosive chemicals, radiation, etc. 3. *Aerospace.* The firing of a rocket engine. [Fusion of OE *beornan* to be on fire, and OE *bærnan* to set afire] —**burn′a·ble** *adj.*

burn·er (bûr′nər) *n.* 1. One who or that which burns. 2. That part of a stove, lamp, etc., from which the flame comes.

burn·ing (bûr′ning) *adj.* 1. Consuming or being consumed by or as if by fire. 2. Causing intense feeling; urgent.

bur·nish (bûr′nish) *v.t. & v.i.* To polish; make or become shiny. —*n.* Polish; luster. [< OF *burnir* to polish] —**bur′nish·er** *n.* —**bur′nish·ment** *n.*

bur·noose (bər·nōōs′, bûr′nōōs) *n.* An Arab hooded cloak. Also **bur·nous′.** [< Arabic *burnus*] —**bur·noosed′** or **bur·noused′** *adj.*

burn·out (bûrn′out′) *n.* 1. A destruction or failure due to burning or to excessive heat. 2. *Aerospace* The cessation of operation in a jet or rocket engine.

burn·sides (bûrn′sīdz) *n.pl.* Full sideburns. [after A. E. *Burnside*, 1824–81, Union general in the Civil War]

burnt (bûrnt) Alternative past tense and past participle of BURN.
burnt ocher A brick red pigment.
burnt sienna A dark brown pigment.
burnt umber A reddish brown pigment.
burp (bûrp) *n. Informal* A belch. —*v.t. & v.i.* To belch or cause to belch. [Imit.]
burr[1] (bûr) *n.* 1. A rough edge or spot, esp. one left on metal in casting or cutting. 2. Any of several tools for cutting, reaming, etc. 3. A dentist's drill with a rough head. 4. A protuberant knot on a tree. —*v.t.* 1. To form a rough edge on. 2. To remove a rough edge from. Also spelled *bur.* [Var. of BUR[1]] —**burred, bur′ry** *adj.*
burr[2] (bûr) *n.* 1. A rough guttural sound of *r,* as pronounced in the Scottish dialect. 2. A dialectical pronunciation, esp. the Scottish one, featuring such a sound. 3. A buzz. Also spelled *bur.* [Imit.]
bur·ro (bûr′ō, bo͝or′ō) *n. pl.* **·ros** A small donkey. [< Sp.]
bur·row (bûr′ō) *n.* 1. A hole made in the ground, as by a rabbit. 2. Any similar place of refuge. —*v.i.* 1. To live or hide in a burrow. 2. To dig a burrow. 3. To dig into, under, or through something. —*v.t.* 4. To dig a burrow in. 5. To make by burrowing. 6. To hide (oneself) in a burrow. [ME *borow*] —**bur′row·er** *n.*
bur·sa (bûr′sə) *n. pl.* **·sae** (-sē) or **·sas** *Anat.* A pouch or saclike cavity; esp. one containing a lubricating fluid and located at joints of the body. [< Med.L, sac, pouch] —**bur′sal** *adj.*
bur·sar (bûr′sər, -sär′) *n.* A treasurer, as of a college. [< Med.L *bursa* bag, purse] —**bur·sar·i·al** (bər·sâr′ē·əl) *adj.*
bur·si·tis (bər·sī′tis) *n. Pathol.* Inflammation of a bursa.
burst (bûrst) *v.* **burst, burst·ing** *v.i.* 1. To break open or apart suddenly and violently. 2. To be full to the point of breaking open; bulge. 3. To appear or enter suddenly or violently. 4. To become audible or evident. 5. To give sudden expression to emotion. —*v.t.* 6. To cause to break open suddenly or violently. —*n.* 1. A sudden exploding or breaking forth. 2. A sudden effort or spurt; rush. 3. A crack or break. [OE *berstan*] —**burst′er** *n.*
bur·y (ber′ē) *v.t.* **bur·ied, bur·y·ing** 1. To put (a dead body) in a grave, tomb, or the sea; inter. 2. To put underground; to conceal, as by covering. 3. To embed; sink. 4. To occupy (oneself) entirely. [OE *byrgan*]
bus (bus) *n. pl.* **bus·es** or **bus·ses** A large passenger vehicle usu. following a prescribed route. —*v.t.* **bused** or **bussed, bus·ing** or **bus·sing** 1. To transport by bus. 2. To transport students by bus to achieve racially balanced school populations. —*v.i.* 3. To go by bus. 4. *Informal* To work as a bus boy. [Short form of OMNIBUS]
bus boy An employee in a restaurant who clears tables, assists the waiters, etc.
bus·by (buz′bē) *n. pl.* **·bies** A tall fur cap. [Origin uncertain]
bush[1] (bo͝osh) *n.* 1. A low, treelike or thickly branching shrub. 2. A clump of shrubs; undergrowth. 3. Wild, scrubby land; also, any rural or unsettled area. 4. Something resembling a bush, as a fox's tail. —*v.i.* 1. To grow or branch like a bush. 2. To be or become bushy. [< ON *buskr*]
bush[2] (bo͝osh) *v.t.* To put a bushing in, as a bearing. —*n.* A bushing. [< MDu. *busse* box]
bushed (bo͝osht) *adj. Informal* Exhausted.
bush·el (bo͝osh′əl) *n.* 1. A unit of dry measure. 2. A container holding this amount. [< OF *boissiel,* dim. of *boisse* box]
bush·ing (bo͝osh′ing) *n.* 1. *Mech.* A metallic lining for a hole, designed to insulate or to prevent abrasion between moving parts. 2. *Electr.* A lining in a socket to insulate an electric current. [< BUSH[2]]
bush league In baseball slang, an obscure minor league. —**bush-league** (bo͝osh′lēg) *adj.* —**bush leaguer**
bush·man (bo͝osh′mən) *n. pl.* **·men** (-mən) *Austral.* A dweller or farmer in the bush.
Bush·man (bo͝osh′mən) *n. pl.* **·men** (-mən) 1. One of a nomadic people of South Africa. 2. Their language. [Trans. of Du. *boschjesman*]
bush·mas·ter (bo͝osh′mas′tər) *n.* A venomous pit viper of Central and South America.
bush·whack (bo͝osh′hwak′) *v.t.* 1. To attack or fire upon from hiding; ambush. —*v.i.* 2. To fight as a guerrilla. [< Du. *boschwachter* forest keeper] —**bush′whack′er** *n.* —**bush′·whack′ing** *n.*
bush·y (bo͝osh′ē) *adj.* **bush·i·er, bush·i·est** 1. Covered with bushes. 2. Shaggy. —**bush′i·ly** *adv.* —**bush′i·ness** *n.*
bus·ied (biz′ēd) Past tense and past participle of BUSY.
bus·i·ly (biz′ə·lē) *adv.* In a busy manner; industriously.
busi·ness (biz′nis) *n.* 1. An occupation, trade, or profession. 2. Any of the various operations or details of trade or industry. 3. A commercial enterprise or establishment. 4. The amount or volume of trade. 5. A proper interest or concern. 6. A matter or affair. —**to give (someone) the business** *Slang* To deal with harshly or summarily. —**to mean business** *Informal* To have a serious intention. [OE *bysignis*]
busi·ness·like (biz′nis·līk′) *adj.* Methodical; systematic.
busi·ness·man (biz′nis·man′) *n. pl.* **·men** (-men′) One engaged in commercial or industrial activity. —**busi′ness·wom′an** (-wo͝om′ən) *n.fem.*
bus·kin (bus′kin) *n.* 1. A boot reaching the calf and strapped or laced to the ankle. 2. A laced half boot, worn by Greek and Roman tragic actors. 3. Tragedy. [Origin uncertain] —**bus′kined** *adj.*
bus·man's holiday (bus′mənz) A holiday spent by choice in activity similar to one's regular work.
buss (bus) *Archaic & Dial. n.* A kiss; smack. —*v.t. & v.i.* To kiss heartily. [Imit.]
bust[1] (bust) *n.* 1. The bosom of a woman. 2. A sculpture representing the human head, shoulders, and breast. [< Ital. *busto*]
bust[2] (bust) *Slang v.t.* 1. To burst. 2. To tame; train, as a horse. 3. To bankrupt. 4. To demote. 5. To punch. 6. To arrest. —*v.i.* 7. To burst. 8. To become bankrupt. —*n.* 1. Failure; bankruptcy. 2. A spree. 3. An arrest. 4. A punch. [Alter. of BURST]
bus·tard (bus′tərd) *n.* A large game bird related to the plovers and cranes. [< OF

bistarde, oustarde < L *avis tarda*, lit., slow bird]

bus·tle[1] (bus′əl) *n.* Excited activity; fuss. **—***v.t.* & *v.i.* **·tled, ·tling** To hurry or cause to hurry. [< ON *būask* to get ready]

bus·tle[2] (bus′əl) *n.* A frame or pad formerly worn under a skirt just above the buttocks.

bus·tling (bus′ling) *adj.* Active; busy. **—bus′tling·ly** *adv.*

bus·y (biz′ē) *adj.* **bus·i·er, bus·i·est** 1. Actively engaged in something; occupied. 2. Constantly active. 3. Meddling; prying. 4. Temporarily engaged, as a telephone line. **—***v.t.* **bus·ied, bus·y·ing** To make busy. [OE *bysig* active] **—bus′y·ness** *n.*

bus·y·bod·y (biz′ē·bod′ē) *n. pl.* **·bod·ies** One who meddles in the affairs of others.

bus·y·work (biz′ē·wûrk′) *n.* Nonproductive work or activity performed to keep one occupied.

but (but, *unstressed* bət) *conj.* 1. On the other hand; yet. 2. Without the result that: It never rains *but* it pours. 3. Other than; otherwise than. 4. Except: anything *but* that. 5. With the exception that: Nothing will do *but* I must leave. 6. That: We don't doubt *but* he is there. 7. That . . . not: He is not so ill *but* exercise will benefit him. 8. Who . . . not; which . . . not: Few sought his advice *but* were helped by it. **—***prep.* With the exception of. **—***adv.* Only; just: She is *but* a child. **—all but** Almost; nearly. **—but for** Were it not for. **—***n.* An objection or condition; exception: no ifs or *buts*. [OE *būtan* outside]

bu·tane (byōō′tān, byōō·tān′) *n. Chem.* A colorless, flammable, gaseous hydrocarbon of the methane series. [< L *but*(*yrum*) butter + *-ane*]

butch (bōōch) *adj. Slang* 1. Strongly masculine in style. 2. Playing the masculine role in a homosexual relationship.

butch·er (bōōch′ər) *n.* 1. One who slaughters or dresses animals for market; also, a dealer in meats. 2. One guilty of needless bloodshed. **—***v.t.* 1. To slaughter or dress for market. 2. To kill cruelly or indiscriminately. 3. To botch. [< OF *bouchier* slaughterer of bucks] **—butch′er·er** *n.*

butch·er·bird (bōōch′ər·bûrd′) *n.* The shrike.

butch·er's-broom (bōōch′ərz·brōōm′, -brōōm′) *n.* A low, evergreen shrub bearing scarlet berries. Also **butch′er·broom′**.

butch·er·y (bōōch′ər·ē) *n. pl.* **·er·ies** 1. Wanton slaughter. 2. A slaughterhouse. 3. The butcher's trade.

but·ler (but′lər) *n.* A manservant, usu. the head servant in a household. [< OF *bouteillier* bottle bearer] **—but′ler·ship** *n.*

butt[1] (but) *v.t.* 1. To strike with the head or horns; ram. 2. To push or bump, as with the head. **—***v.i.* 3. To strike or attempt to strike something with the head or horns. 4. To move or drive head foremost. 5. To project; jut. **—to butt in** *Informal* To interrupt; intrude. **—to butt out** *Informal* To cease meddling. **—***n.* A blow or push with the head. [< OF *buter* to strike, push, project] **—but′ter** *n.*

butt[2] (but) *n.* 1. A person or thing subjected to ridicule, criticism, etc. 2. A target, as on a rifle range. [< OF *but* end, goal]

butt[3] (but) *n.* 1. The larger or thicker end of anything. 2. An end or extremity. 3. An unused end, as of a cigar. 4. *Informal* The buttocks. [Akin to Dan. *but* blunt]

butt[4] (but) *n.* 1. A large cask. 2. A measure of wine, 126 U.S. gallons. [< OF *boute*]

butte (byōōt) *n.* A conspicuous hill, esp. one with steep sides and a flattened top. [< F]

but·ter (but′ər) *n.* 1. The fatty constituent of milk churned and prepared for cooking and table use. 2. Any of several substances having a semisolid consistency. **—***v.t.* 1. To put butter on. 2. *Informal* To flatter: usu. with *up*. [< Gk. *bous* cow + *tyros* cheese] **—but′ter·y** *adj.*

butter bean 1. The wax bean. 2. In the southern U.S., the lima bean.

but·ter·cup (but′ər·kup′) *n.* A plant with yellow, cup-shaped flowers.

but·ter·fat (but′ər·fat′) *n.* The fatty substance of milk, from which butter is made.

but·ter·fin·gers (but′ər·fing′gərz) *n. Informal* One who drops things easily or often. **—but′ter·fin′gered** *adj.*

but·ter·fish (but′ər·fish′) *n. pl.* **·fish** or **·fish·es** A silvery, laterally compressed fish common along the Atlantic coast.

but·ter·fly (but′ər·flī′) *n. pl.* **·flies** An insect with large, often brightly colored wings and a slender body. [OE *buttorflēoge*]

butter knife A small, blunt-edged knife.

but·ter·milk (but′ər·milk′) *n.* 1. The liquid left after the butterfat has been separated from milk or cream. 2. A form of milk made by adding bacterial cultures to skim milk.

but·ter·nut (but′ər·nut′) *n.* 1. The oily, edible nut of a walnut of North America. 2. The tree or its cathartic inner bark.

but·ter·scotch (but′ər·skoch′) *n.* 1. Hard, sticky candy made with brown sugar and butter. 2. A syrup or flavoring consisting of similar ingredients. **—but′ter·scotch′** *adj.*

but·tock (but′ək) *n.* 1. *Anat.* Either of the two fleshy prominences that form the rump. 2. *pl.* The rump. [Dim. of BUTT[3]]

but·ton (but′n) *n.* 1. A knob or disk sewn to a garment, etc., serving as a fastening or for ornamentation. 2. Anything resembling a button, as the knob for operating an electric bell. 3. *Slang* The point of the chin. **—on the button** *Informal* Exactly; precisely. **—***v.t.* & *v.i.* To fasten or be capable of being fastened with a button. [< OF *boton* button, bud] **—but′ton·er** *n.*

but·ton·hole (but′n·hōl′) *n.* A slit or loop to receive and hold a button. **—***v.t.* **·holed, ·hol·ing** 1. To work buttonholes in. 2. To seize as by the buttonhole so as to detain. **—but′ton·hol′er** *n.*

but·ton·wood (but′n·wōōd′) *n.* A plane tree of North America: also called *sycamore*.

but·tress (but′tris) *n.* 1. *Archit.* A structure built against a wall to strengthen it. 2. Any support or prop. **—***v.t.* 1. To support with a buttress. 2. To prop up; sustain. [< OF *bouter, buter* to push, thrust]

bux·om (buk′səm) *adj.* 1. Characterized by health and vigor; pleasantly plump: said of women. 2. Large-bosomed. [ME *buhsum* pliant] **—bux′om·ly** *adv.* **—bux′om·ness** *n.*

buy (bī) *v.* **bought, buy·ing** *v.t.* 1. To acquire with money; purchase. 2. To obtain by some exchange or sacrifice: to *buy* wisdom with experience. 3. To bribe; corrupt. 4. *Informal* To accept; concur. **—***v.i.* 5. To make purchases; be a purchaser. **—to buy off** To bribe. **—to buy out** To purchase the stock, interests, etc., of. **—to buy up** To purchase the entire supply of. —*n. Informal* 1. Anything bought or about to be bought. 2. A bargain. [OE *bycgan*] **—buy'a·ble** *adj.*

buy·er (bī'ər) *n.* 1. One who makes purchases. 2. A purchasing agent, as for a department store.

buzz (buz) *v.i.* 1. To make the humming, vibrating sound of the bee. 2. To talk or gossip excitedly. 3. To bustle. —*v.t.* 4. To cause to buzz. 5. To signal with a buzz. 6. *Informal* To fly an airplane very close to (something). 7. *Informal* To telephone. —*n.* 1. A vibrating hum. 2. A low murmur, as of many voices. 3. *Informal* A phone call. [Imit.]

buz·zard (buz'ərd) *n.* 1. One of several large, slow-flying hawks. 2. A turkey buzzard. [< OF *busart*]

buzz·er (buz'ər) *n.* An electric signal making a buzzing sound.

buzz saw A circular saw, so called from the sound it emits.

buzz word *Slang* A term with little meaning, used chiefly to impress or mystify.

by (bī) *prep.* 1. Next to; near. 2. Past and beyond: The train roared *by* us. 3. Through the agency of or by means of. 4. By way of: Come *by* the nearest road. 5. On the part of: a loss felt *by* all. 6. According to: *by* law. 7. In the course of; during: to travel *by* night. 8. Not later than. 9. After: day *by* day. 10. According to as a standard: to work *by* the day. 11. To the extent or amount of: insects *by* the thousands. 12. In multiplication or measurement with: Multiply 6 *by* 8. 13. With reference to: to do well *by* one's friends. 14. In the name of: *by* all that's holy. **—by the way** Incidentally. —*adv.* 1. At hand; near. 2. Up to and beyond something; past: The years go *by*. 3. Apart; aside: to lay something *by*. **—by and by** After a time; before long. **—by and large** On the whole; generally. —*adj. & n.* Bye. [OE *bī* near, about]

by- *combining form* 1. Secondary; incidental: *by-product*. 2. Near; close: *bystander*. 3. Aside; out of the way: *byway*.

by-and-by (bī'ən·bī') *n.* A future time.

bye (bī) *n.* 1. Something of minor or secondary importance. 2. In a tournament, an automatic advance to the next round. —*adj.* Secondary. Also spelled *by*. [< BY]

bye-bye (bī'bī') *interj.* Good-by.

by-e·lec·tion (bī'i·lek'shən) *n. Brit.* A special parliamentary election held to fill a vacancy.

Bye·lo·rus·sian (bī'lə·rush'ən) *n.* 1. A native or inhabitant of the Byelorussian S.S.R. 2. Their language. Also *White Russian*. **—Bye'lo·rus'sian** *adj.*

by·gone (bī'gôn', -gon') *adj.* Gone by; past. —*n. Often pl.* Something past.

by·law (bī'lô') *n.* A law adopted by a corporation, etc., and subordinate to a constitution or charter. [ME *by, bi* village + *lawe* law]

by-line (bī'līn') *n.* The line at the head of an article, giving the name of the writer **—by'lin'er** *n.*

by-pass (bī'pas') *n.* 1. Any road or route connecting two points in a course other than that normally used; a detour. 2. *Electr.* A shunt. —*v.t.* 1. To go around or avoid (an obstacle). 2. *Med.* To circumvent by surgical means.

by-path (bī'path') *n.* A secluded or indirect path.

by-play (bī'plā') *n.* Action or speech apart from the main action, as in a play.

by-prod·uct (bī'prod'əkt) *n.* A secondary product or result.

by·road (bī'rōd') *n.* A back or side road.

By·ron·ic (bī·ron'ik) *adj.* Melancholy, romantic, passionate, etc. [after Lord *Byron*, 1788–1824, an English poet]

by·stand·er (bī'stan'dər) *n.* One present but not taking part; an onlooker.

byte (bīt) *n.* A group of binary digits, usu. eight, which a computer stores and treats as a unit.

by·way (bī'wā') *n.* A branch or side road.

by·word (bī'wûrd') *n.* 1. A proverb or pet phrase. 2. A person, institution, etc., that proverbially represents a type, usu. an object of scorn.

Byz·an·tine (biz'ən·tēn, -tīn, bi·zan'tin) *adj.* 1. Of or pertaining to Byzantium or its civilization, culture, etc. 2. Pertaining to the style of architecture of Byzantium in the 5th and 6th c., characterized by rounded arches, large domes, and colored mosaics on gold. 3. Intricate, complex: the *Byzantine* file of the lawsuit. 4. Devious and surreptitious: *Byzantine* office politics. —*n.* A native or inhabitant of Byzantium. [< L *Byzantinus* < *Byzantium*, the ancient city]

Byzantine Empire The eastern part of the later Roman Empire (395–1453).

C

c, C (sē) *n. pl.* **c's** or **cs, C's** or **Cs, cees** (sēz) **1.** The third letter of the English alphabet. **2.** Any sound represented by the letter *c.* —*symbol* **1.** The Roman numeral for 100. **2.** *Chem.* Carbon (symbol C). **3.** *Music* The first tone in the diatonic scale of C. **4.** The third in sequence or class.

cab (kab) *n.* **1.** A taxicab. **2.** The operator's compartment in a truck or locomotive. [Short form of CABRIOLET]

ca·bal (kə·bal′) *n.* **1.** A number of persons secretly united for some private purpose. **2.** An intrigue; plot. —*v.i.* **·balled, ·bal·ling** To form a cabal; plot. [< MF *cabale*]

cab·a·la (kab′ə·lə, kə·bä′lə) *n.* **1.** *Often cap.* An occult system originating in a mystical interpretation of the Scriptures among certain medieval Jewish rabbis. **2.** Occultism. [< Hebrew *qābal* to receive] —**cab′a·lism** *n.* —**cab′a·list** *n. & adj.* —**cab·a·lis·tic** (kab′ə·lis′tik) *adj.* —**cab′a·lis′ti·cal·ly** *adv.*

cab·al·le·ro (kab′əl·yâr′ō) *n. pl.* **·ros** **1.** A Spanish cavalier. **2.** A horseman. [< Sp. < L *caballus* horse]

ca·ban·a (kə·ban′ə, -bä′nə) *n.* A shelter near a beach or swimming pool, used as a bathhouse. Also **ca·ba·ña** (kə·bän′yə, -ban′-). [< Sp.]

cab·a·ret (kab′ə·rā′) *n.* **1.** A restaurant that provides entertainment. **2.** The entertainment provided. [< F]

cab·bage (kab′ij) *n.* The close-leaved edible head of a plant of the mustard family. [< OF, ult. < L *caput* head]

cab·by (kab′ē) *n. pl.* **·bies** *Informal* The driver of a taxicab. Also **cab′bie.**

cab·in (kab′in) *n.* **1.** A small, rude house; a hut. **2. a** A private room on a ship. **b** An enclosed compartment on a boat. **c** A compartment for passengers on an airplane. [< LL *capanna* cabin]

cabin boy A boy who waits on the officers and passengers of a ship.

cabin class A class of accommodations for steamship passengers, higher than tourist class, lower than first class. —**cab·in-class** (kab′in·klas′) *adj. & adv.*

cabin cruiser A cruiser (def. 3).

cab·i·net (kab′ə·nit) *n.* **1.** A case or container, usually fixed to a wall and fitted with shelves and doors. **2.** A piece of furniture having shelves or drawers. **3.** *Often cap.* A body of official advisers serving a head of state. [< Ital. *gabinetto* closet, chest of drawers]

cab·i·net·mak·er (kab′ə·nit·mā′kər) *n.* One who does fine woodwork, as for cabinets, furniture, etc. —**cab′i·net·mak′ing** *n.*

cab·i·net·work (kab′ə·nit·wûrk′) *n.* Expert woodwork. —**cab′i·net·work′er** *n.*

ca·ble (kā′bəl) *n.* **1.** A heavy rope, now usu. of steel wire. **2.** A cable length. **3.** *Electr.* **a** An insulated electrical conductor or group of conductors. **b** An underwater telegraph line. **4.** A cablegram. —*v.t. & v.i.* **·bled, ·bling** To send (a cablegram). [< L *capere* to take, grasp]

cable car A car pulled on a railway by a moving cable or one suspended from a moving cable.

ca·ble·gram (kā′bəl·gram) *n.* A telegraphic message sent by underwater cable.

cable length A unit of nautical measure, in the United States 720 feet, in England 608 feet. Also **cable's length.**

cable TV Television transmission via cables, to paying subscribers.

ca·boo·dle (kə·bōōd′l) *n.* *Informal* Collection; lot: usu. in the phrase **the whole (kit and) caboodle.**

ca·boose (kə·bōōs′) *n.* A car, usu. at the rear of a freight or work train, for use by the train crew. [< MDu. *cabuse* galley]

cab·ri·o·let (kab′rē·ə·lā′, -let′) *n.* **1.** A light, one-horse carriage with two seats and a folding top. **2.** A coupe automobile. [< F < MF *cabriole* leap, caper]

ca·ca·o (kə·kā′ō, -kä′ō) *n. pl.* **·ca·os** **1.** A small evergreen tree of tropical America. **2.** Its seeds, used in making cocoa and chocolate. [< Sp. < Nahuatl *cacauatl* cacao seed]

cac·cia·to·re (käch·ə·tō′rē, -tôr′ē) *adj.* Cooked with tomatoes and herbs. [< Ital., hunter]

cache (kash) *v.t.* **cached, cach·ing** To store in a concealed place. —*n.* A concealed place for storage; also, the things stored. [< F *cacher* to hide]

ca·chet (ka·shā′, kash′ā) *n.* **1.** A seal, as for a letter. **2.** A sign of distinction, conferring prestige. **3.** A mark, slogan, etc., printed on mail. [< F *cacher* to hide]

cack·le (kak′əl) *v.* **·led, ·ling** *v.i.* **1.** To make a shrill, broken cry, as a hen that has laid an egg. **2.** To laugh or talk with a similar sound. —*v.t.* **3.** To utter in a cackling manner. [Imit.] —**cack′le** *n.* —**cack′ler** *n.*

ca·coph·o·ny (kə·kof′ə·nē) *n.* Disagreeable or discordant sound. [< Gk. *kakos* bad + *phōneein* to sound] —**ca·coph′o·nous, cac·o·phon·ic** (kak′ə·fon′ik) *adj.* —**ca·coph′o·nous·ly, cac′o·phon′i·cal·ly** *adv.*

cac·tus (kak′təs) *n. pl.* **·tus·es** or **·ti** (-tī) Any of various green, fleshy, mostly leafless and spiny plants, found in dry regions. [< Gk. *kaktos,* prickly plant]

cad (kad) *n.* An ungentlemanly or despicable fellow. —**cad′dish** *adj.* —**cad′dish·ly** *adv.* —**cad′dish·ness** *n.*

ca·dav·er (kə·dav′ər) *n.* A dead body; esp., a human body for dissection; a corpse. [< L]

ca·dav·er·ous (kə·dav′ər·əs) *adj.* Resembling or characteristic of a corpse; pale; ghastly; gaunt. —**ca·dav'er·ous·ly** *adv.* —**ca·dav'er·ous·ness** *n.*

cad·die (kad'ē) *n.* One paid to carry clubs for golf players. —*v.i.* **·died, ·dy·ing** To act as a caddie. Also spelled *caddy.*

cad·dis fly (kad'is) Any of certain four-winged insects fed upon by trout and imitated in fly-fishing lures. [Origin uncertain]

cad·dy[1] (kad'ē) *n. pl.* **·dies** A small box or case, as for tea. [< Malay *kati*, a measure of weight]

cad·dy[2] (kad'ē) *n. pl.* **·dies** A caddie.

ca·dence (kād'ns) *n.* 1. Rhythmic or measured flow, as of poetry. 2. The measure or beat of music, marching, etc. 3. Modulation, as of the voice; intonation. 4. *Music* A harmonic progression signaling the end of a phrase, movement, etc. Also **ca'den·cy.** [< L *cadere* to fall] —**ca'denced, ca'dent** *adj.*

ca·den·za (kə·den'zə, *Ital.* kä·dent'sä) *n. Music* A passage, often improvised, displaying the virtuosity of a soloist. [< Ital.]

ca·det (kə·det') *n.* 1. A student at a military or naval school. 2. A younger son or brother. [< F, ult. < L *caput* head, chief] —**ca·det'·ship** *n.*

cadge (kaj) *v.t.* **cadged, cadg·ing** *Informal* To get by begging. —**cadg'er** *n.*

cad·mi·um (kad'mē·əm) *n.* A bluish white metallic element (symbol Cd), occurring in small quantities in zinc ores. [< Gk. *kadmeia* calamine]

cad·re (kad'rē, *Fr.* kä'dr') *n.* A group of trained personnel capable of continuing an organization by training others. [< F, frame of a picture]

ca·du·ce·us (kə·dōō'sē·əs, -dyōō'-, -shəs) *n. pl.* **·ce·i** (-sē·ī) The winged, snake-entwined staff of the Greek god Hermes, used as the emblem of the medical profession. [< Gk. (Doric) *karykion* herald's staff] —**ca·du'·ce·an** *adj.*

cae- For those words not entered below, see under CE-.

cae·cum (sē'kəm) See CECUM.

Cae·sar (sē'zər) *n.* 1. The title of the Roman emperors from Augustus to Hadrian. 2. *Often not cap.* Any despot.

cae·sar·e·an (si·zâr'ē·ən) See CESAREAN.

cae·si·um (sē'zē·əm) See CESIUM.

cae·su·ra (si·zhŏŏr'ə, -zyŏŏr'ə) *n. pl.* **·su·ras** or **·su·rae** (-zhŏŏr'ē, -zyŏŏr'ē) 1. In Greek and Latin prosody, a break occurring when a word ends within a foot. 2. In modern prosody, a pause usu. near the middle of a line, indicated by two vertical lines (||). 3. *Music* A pause indicating a rhythmic division point. Also spelled *cesura.* [< L *caedere* to cut] —**cae·su'ral, cae·su'ric** *adj.*

ca·fé (ka·fā', kə-) *n.* An informal eating place, often with a bar. Also **ca·fe'.** [< F]

ca·fé au lait (kȧ·fā' ō lā') *French* 1. Coffee with scalded milk. 2. A light brown.

caf·e·te·ri·a (kaf'ə·tir'ē·ə) *n.* A restaurant where the patrons serve themselves from counters. [< Am.Sp., coffee store]

caf·feine (kaf'ēn) *n. Chem.* A stimulating alkaloid, present in coffee and tea. [< F *café* coffee]

caf·tan (kaf'tən, käf·tän') *n.* A loose, ankle-length garment, having long sleeves and a sash, worn in eastern Mediterranean countries. [< Turkish *qaftān*]

cage (kāj) *n.* 1. A boxlike structure with openwork of wires or bars, for confining birds or beasts. 2. Any cagelike structure or framework. 3. In basketball, the basket. 4. A sheer dress that hangs loose from the shoulders and is worn over a snug underdress. —*v.t.* **caged, cag·ing** To shut up in a cage; confine; imprison. [< OF, ult. < L *cavus* empty, hollow]

cage·y (kā'jē) *adj.* **cag·i·er, cag·i·est** *Informal* Wary of being duped; shrewd and careful. Also **cag'y.** [Origin uncertain] —**cag'i·ly** *adv.* —**cag'i·ness** *n.*

ca·hoots (kə·hōōts') *n.pl. Slang* Shady partnership, as in the phrase **in cahoots.** [? < F *cahute* cabin]

cai·man (kā'mən) *n.* A tropical reptile structurally related to the alligator, but resembling the crocodile. Also *cayman.* [< Sp.]

cairn (kârn) *n.* A mound or heap of stones set up as a memorial or a marker. [< Scottish Gaelic *carn* heap of stones]

cais·son (kā'sən, -son) *n.* 1. A large watertight chamber within which work is done under water, as on a bridge pier. 2. A watertight device used to raise sunken ships. 3. A two-wheeled vehicle carrying artillery ammunition. [< F, aug. of *caisse* box, chest]

caisson disease A painful, sometimes fatal disorder caused by too rapid a transition from the compressed air of caissons, diving bells, etc. to normal atmospheric pressure. Also called *the bends.*

ca·jole (kə·jōl') *v.t. & v.i.* **·joled, ·jol·ing** To coax with flattery or false promises; wheedle. [< F *cajoler*] —**ca·jol'er** *n.* —**ca·jol'er·y, ca·jole'ment** *n.* —**ca·jol'ing·ly** *adv.*

Ca·jun (kā'jən) *n.* 1. A reputed descendant of the Acadian French in Louisiana. 2. Their French dialect. [Alter. of ACADIAN]

cake (kāk) *n.* 1. A mixture of flour, milk, sugar, etc., baked in various forms and generally sweeter and richer than bread. 2. A small, usu. thin mass of dough, or other food, baked or fried: fish *cake.* 3. A mass of matter compressed or hardened into a compact form: a *cake* of soap. —*v.t. & v.i.* **caked, cak·ing** To form into a hardened mass. [< ON *kaka*]

cake·walk (kāk'wôk') *n.* A dance with a strutting step, usu. performed to syncopated music. [After a former type of dance contest, esp. among Southern Negroes, in which the winner got a cake] —**cake'walk'** *v.i.*

cal·a·bash (kal'ə·bash) *n.* 1. A tropical American tree with a gourdlike fruit. 2. The gourd fruit of this tree, used for making pipes, bowls, etc. [< Sp. *calabaza* gourd]

cal·a·boose (kal'ə·bōōs) *n. Informal* A jail; lockup. [< Sp. *calabozo*]

ca·la·di·um (kə·lā'dē·əm) *n.* Any of a genus of tropical American plants related to the arums and used for ornamental purposes. [< Malay *kelādy*]

cal·a·mine (kal'ə·mīn, -min) *n.* A mixture of zinc and iron oxides, used in the form of a lotion or ointment for skin ailments. [< Gk. *kadmeia* calamine]

ca·lam·i·ty (kə·lam'ə·tē) *n. pl.* **·ties** 1. A disaster. 2. A state of great distress. [< L *calamitas, -tatis*] —**ca·lam'i·tous** *adj.* —**ca·lam'i·tous·ly** *adv.*

cal·car·e·ous (kal·kâr'ē·əs) *adj.* 1. Com-

posed of, containing, or like limestone or calcium carbonate. 2. Containing calcium. [< L *calcarius* of lime < *calx, calcis* lime]
calci- *combining form* Lime. [< L *calx, calcis* lime]
cal·cif·er·ol (kal·sif′ər·ōl, -ol) *n. Biochem.* Vitamin D_2. See under VITAMIN. [< CALCIFER(OUS) + (ERGOSTER)OL]
cal·cif·er·ous (kal·sif′ər·əs) *adj.* Yielding or containing calcium carbonate, as rocks.
cal·ci·fy (kal′sə·fī) *v.t. & v.i.* **·fied, ·fy·ing** To make or become stony by the deposit of lime salts. **—cal·ci·fi·ca·tion** (kal′sə·fi·kā′shən) *n.*
cal·ci·mine (kal′sə·mīn, -min) *n.* A white or tinted wash for ceilings, walls, etc. —*v.t.* **·mined, ·min·ing** To apply calcimine to. [< L *calx, calcis* lime; orig. a trade name]
cal·cine (kal′sīn, -sin) *v.t.* **·cined, ·cin·ing** To heat (a calcareous substance, as bone) to a dry, powdery state. Also **cal′cin·ize.** [< Med.L *calcinare* < L *calx* lime] **—cal·ci·na·tion** (kal′sə·nā′shən) *n.*
cal·cite (kal′sīt) *n.* A widely distributed calcium carbonate mineral, including chalk, limestone, marble, etc. **—cal·cit·ic** (kal·sit′ik) *adj.*
cal·ci·um (kal′sē·əm) *n.* A silver-white, malleable, metallic element (symbol Ca), widely distributed in combination, as in chalk, gypsum, and limestone. [< L *calx, calcis* lime]
calcium carbonate *Chem.* A compound occurring naturally in bones and shells, and in marble and other limestones.
cal·cu·la·ble (kal′kyə·lə·bəl) *adj.* 1. Capable of being calculated. 2. Reliable; dependable. **—cal′cu·la·bly** *adv.*
cal·cu·late (kal′kyə·lāt) *v.t. & v.i.* **·lat·ed, ·lat·ing** 1. To determine by mathematical processes; compute. 2. To ascertain beforehand; form an estimate of. 3. *Dial.* To think; expect. **—to calculate on** To depend or rely on. [< L *calculus* pebble; with ref. to the use of pebbles in counting]
cal·cu·lat·ing (kal′kyə·lā′ting) *adj.* Using shrewd schemes, esp. for one's own interests. **—cal′cu·lat′ing·ly** *adv.*
cal·cu·la·tion (kal′kyə·lā′shən) *n.* 1. The act, process, or result of computing. 2. An estimate; forecast. 3. Forethought; prudence. **—cal′cu·la′tive** *adj.*
cal·cu·la·tor (kal′kyə·lā′tər) *n.* 1. One who calculates. 2. A machine that performs computations: also **calculating machine.**
cal·cu·lus (kal′kyə·ləs) *n. pl.* **·li** (-lī) or **·lus·es** 1. *Pathol.* A stonelike mass, as in the bladder. 2. *Math.* A method of calculating by the use of a highly specialized system of algebraic symbols. **—differential calculus** The branch of analysis that investigates the changes of varying quantities when the relations between the quantities are given. **—integral calculus** The branch of analysis that, from the relations among the variations of quantities, deduces relations among the quantities themselves. [< L, a pebble (used in counting)]
cal·de·ra (kal·der′ə) *n.* A crater of a volcano formed by collapse of the cone or by a great explosion. [< Sp., cauldron]
cal·dron (kôl′drən) See CAULDRON.
Cal·e·do·ni·a (kal′ə·dō′nē·ə, -dōn′yə) *Poetic* Scotland. [< L] **—Cal′e·do′ni·an** *adj. & n.*
cal·e·fa·cient (kal′ə·fā′shənt) *adj.* Causing heat or warmth. —*n. Med.* A remedy that produces heat. [< L *calere* to be warm + *facere* to make, cause]
cal·en·dar (kal′ən·dər) *n.* 1. Any of various systems of fixing the order, length, and subdivisions of the years and months. 2. A table showing the days, weeks, and months of a year. 3. A schedule or list, esp. one arranged in chronological order: a court *calendar.* —*v.t.* To place on a calendar; schedule. [< L *calendae* calends]
cal·en·der (kal′ən·dər) *n.* A machine for giving a gloss to cloth, paper, etc., by pressing between rollers. [< Gk. *kylindros* roller] **—cal′en·der** *v.t.*
cal·ends (kal′əndz) *n.pl.* The first day of the ancient Roman month. [< L *calendae*]
ca·len·du·la (kə·len′jo͞o·lə) *n.* An herb of the composite family, having bright orange or yellow flowers. [< NL, dim. of L *calendae* calends]
ca·les·cence (kə·les′əns) *n.* The condition of growing warm. [< L *calescere* to grow warm] **—ca·les′cent** *adj.*
calf[1] (kaf) *n. pl.* **calves** (kavz) 1. The young of the cow or various other bovine animals. 2. The young of various mammals, as the elephant, whale, etc. 3. Calfskin. [OE *cealf*]
calf[2] (kaf) *n. pl.* **calves** (kavz) The muscular rear part of the human leg below the knee. [< ON *kālfi*]
calf·skin (kaf′skin′) *n.* 1. The skin or hide of a calf. 2. Leather made from this.
cal·i·ber (kal′ə·bər) *n.* 1. The internal diameter of a tube. 2. **a** The internal diameter of the barrel of a gun, cannon, etc. **b** The diameter of a bullet. 3. Degree of personal excellence. Also *Brit.* **cal′i·bre.** [< F *calibre*]
cal·i·brate (kal′ə·brāt) *v.t.* **·brat·ed, ·brat·ing** 1. To graduate, correct, or adjust the scale of (a measuring instrument) into appropriate units. 2. To determine the reading of (such an instrument). **—cal′i·bra′tion** *n.* **—cal′i·bra′tor** *n.*
cal·i·co (kal′i·kō) *n. pl.* **·coes** or **·cos** Cotton cloth printed in a figured pattern of bright colors. —*adj.* 1. Made of calico. 2. Dappled or streaked: a *calico* cat. [after *Calicut*, India, where first obtained]
California poppy A plant of the poppy family having showy yellow flowers.
cal·i·for·ni·um (kal′ə·fôr′nē·əm) *n.* An unstable radioactive element (symbol Cf), artificially produced by bombardment of curium with alpha particles. [after the University of *California*, where first produced]
ca·lig·ra·phy (kə·lig′rə·fē) See CALLIGRAPHY.
cal·i·per (kal′ə·pər) *n. Usu. pl.* An instrument consisting of two hinged legs, used for measuring diameters. Also **caliper compass.** —*v.t. & v.i.* To measure by using calipers. Also **cal′li·per.** [< CALIBER]
ca·liph (kā′lif, kal′if) *n.* The spiritual and civil head of a Muslim state: also **ca′lif.** [< Arabic *khalīfah* successor (to Muhammad)]
cal·i·phate (kal′ə·fāt, -fit) *n.* The office, dominion, or reign of a caliph.
cal·is·then·ics (kal′is·then′iks) *n.pl.* Light, repeated exercises. [< Gk. *kalli-* beautiful + *sthenos* strength] **—cal′is·then′ic** or **·i·cal** *adj.*

calk (kôk) See CAULK.

call (kôl) *v.t.* 1. To say in a loud voice. 2. To summon. 3. To convoke; convene: to *call* a meeting. 4. To arouse, as from sleep. 5. To telephone to. 6. To lure (birds or animals) by imitating their cry. 7. To name, designate or characterize. 8. To bring to action or consideration: to *call* a case to court. 9. To demand payment of. 10. In baseball: **a** To stop or suspend (a game). **b** To designate a pitch as (a ball or strike). **c** To declare (a player) out, safe, etc. 11. In poker, to demand a show of hands by a bet equal to that of (another). —*v.i.* 12. To raise one's voice; speak loudly. 13. To make a brief visit, stop, or stay: with *at, on,* or *upon.* 14. To communicate by telephone. —**to call back** 1. To summon back; recall. 2. To call in return, as by telephone. —**to call down** 1. To invoke from heaven. 2. *Informal* To rebuke; reprimand. —**to call for** 1. To stop so as to obtain. 2. To require; need. —**to call in** 1. To collect, as debts. 2. To retire, as currency, from circulation. 3. To summon, as for consultation. —**to call off** 1. To summon away. 2. To say or read aloud. 3. To cancel. —**to call up** 1. To recollect. 2. To summon. 3. To telephone. —*n.* 1. A shout or cry. 2. A summons or invitation. 3. A demand; claim: the *call* of duty. 4. A communication by telephone. 5. An inward urge to a religious vocation. 6. A brief, often formal, visit. 7. The cry of an animal, esp. of a bird. 8. A whistle, etc., with which to imitate such a cry. 9. A need; occasion: You've no *call* to do that. 10. In sports, a referee's or judge's decision. —**on call** 1. Payable on demand. 2. Available when sent for. [< ON *kalla*]

cal·la (kal′ə) *n.* 1. A plant having a large white leaf that resembles a flower. Also **calla lily.** 2. A marsh plant bearing red berries in dense clusters. [< L]

call·back (côl′bak′) *n.* 1. The recall by a manufacturer of a product to correct a defect. 2. The product so recalled. 3. A request to return for a second audition.

call·board (kôl′bôrd′) *n.* A theater bulletin board for notices of rehearsals, etc.

call·er (kô′lər) *n.* 1. One who or that which calls. 2. One making a brief visit.

call girl A prostitute who accepts appointments principally by telephone.

cal·lig·ra·phy (kə·lig′rə·fē) *n.* 1. Beautiful penmanship. 2. Handwriting in general. Also spelled *caligraphy.* [< Gk. *kalos* beautiful + *graphein* to write] —**cal·lig′ra·pher, cal·lig′ra·phist** *n.* —**cal·li·graph·ic** (kal′ə·graf′·ik) *adj.* —**cal·li·graph′i·cal·ly** *adv.*

call·ing (kô′ling) *n.* 1. The act of speaking or crying aloud. 2. A vocation or profession. 3. An inner urge toward a vocation.

calling card A small card, printed or engraved with one's name, used to announce a visit.

cal·li·o·pe (kə·lī′ə·pē, kal′ē·ōp) *n.* A musical instrument consisting of a series of steam whistles and a keyboard. [after *Calliope,* Greek Muse of eloquence.]

call letters The code letters identifying a radio or television station. Also **call sign.**

call number A classifying number employed by libraries.

cal·los·i·ty (kə·los′ə·tē) *n. pl.* **·ties** 1. A callus. 2. Callousness of feelings; insensibility.

cal·lous (kal′əs) *adj.* 1. Thickened and hardened, as a callus. 2. Hardened in feelings; insensible. —*v.t. & v.i.* To make or become callous. [< L *callus* hard skin] —**cal′lous·ly** *adv.* —**cal′lous·ness** *n.*

cal·low (kal′ō) *adj.* Inexperienced; immature. [OE *calu* bare, bald] —**cal′low·ness** *n.*

cal·lus (kal′əs) *n. pl.* **·lus·es** 1. A thickened, hardened part of the skin: also called *callosity.* 2. The new tissue around the ends of a broken bone in the process of reuniting. 3. The tissue that forms over a cut on a plant stem. —*v.i.* **·lused, ·lus·ing** To form a callus. [< L, hard skin]

calm (käm) *adj.* 1. Free from agitation; still or nearly still. 2. Not excited by passion or emotion. —*n.* 1. Lack of wind or motion; stillness. 2. Serenity. —*v.t. & v.i.* To make or become quiet or calm: often with *down.* [< Gk. *kauma* heat; with ref. to the midday rest] —**calm′ing·ly** *adv.* —**calm′ly** *adv.* —**calm′ness** *n.*

cal·o·mel (kal′ə·mel, -məl) *n.* A chloride of mercury, used as a purgative and fungicide. [< Gk. *kalos* beautiful + *melas* black]

ca·lor·ic (kə·lôr′ik, -lor′-) *adj.* 1. Of or pertaining to heat. 2. Of or relating to calories. —*n.* Heat. [< L *calor* heat] —**cal·o·ric·i·ty** (kal′ə·ris′ə·tē) *n.*

cal·o·rie (kal′ə·rē) *n.* 1. One of two recognized units of heat. The **large** or **great calorie** is the amount of heat required to raise the temperature of one kilogram of water 1° C. The **small calorie** is the amount of heat required to raise one gram of water 1° C. 2. *Physiol.* The large calorie, a measure of the energy value of foods or the heat output of organisms. Also **cal′o·ry.** [< L *calor* heat]

cal·o·rif·ic (kal′ə·rif′ik) *adj.* Pertaining to or producing heat.

cal·o·rim·e·ter (kal′ə·rim′ə·tər) *n.* Any apparatus for measuring quantities of heat. —**cal′o·rim′e·try** *n.* —**ca·lor′i·met·ric** (kə·lôr′ə·met′rik, -lor′-) or **·ri·cal** *adj.*

cal·u·met (kal′yə·met, kal′yə·met′) *n.* A tobacco pipe with a long, ornamented stem, used in American Indian ceremonies: also called *peace pipe.* [< dial. F, pipe stem < L *calamus* reed]

ca·lum·ni·ate (kə·lum′nē·āt) *v.t. & v.i.* **·at·ed, ·at·ing** To accuse falsely; defame; slander. [< L *calumnia* slander] —**ca·lum′ni·a′tion** *n.* —**ca·lum′ni·a′tor** *n.*

cal·um·ny (kal′əm·nē) *n. pl.* **·nies** A false and malicious accusation or report. [< L *calumnia* slander] —**ca·lum·ni·ous** (kə·lum′nē·əs), **ca·lum·ni·a·to·ry** (kə·lum′nē·ə·tôr′ē) *adj.* —**ca·lum′ni·ous·ly** *adv.*

calve (kav) *v.t. & v.i.* **calved, calv·ing** To give birth to (a calf). [OE *cealfian* < *cealf* calf]

calves (kavz) Plural of CALF.

Cal·vin·ism (kal′vin·iz′əm) *n. Theol.* The doctrines of John Calvin, emphasizing predestination and characterized by an austere moral code. —**Cal′vin·ist** *n.* —**Cal′vin·is′tic** or **·ti·cal** *adj.* —**Cal′vin·is′ti·cal·ly** *adv.*

calx (kalks) *n. pl.* **calx·es** or **cal·ces** (kal′sēz) The residue from the calcination of minerals. [< L]

ca·lyp·so (kə·lip′sō) *n.* A West Indian ballad, often topical and humorous, and usu. improvised. [Origin uncertain]

ca·lyx (kā′liks, kal′iks) *n. pl.* **ca·lyx·es** or

cal·y·ces (kal′ə·sēz, kā′lə-) *Bot.* The outermost series of leaflike parts of a flower; the sepals. [< Gk. *kalyx*, husk, pod]

cam (kam) *n. Mech.* An irregularly shaped rotating piece that imparts reciprocating or variable motion to another piece bearing on it. [< Du., tooth, cog of a wheel.]

ca·ma·ra·de·rie (kä′mə·rä′dər·ē) *n.* Comradeship. [< F]

cam·ber (kam′bər) *n.* A slight upward bend, as of a timber. [< L *camera* curved roof, vault] —**cam′ber** *v.t. & v.i.*

cam·bi·um (kam′bē·əm) *n. Bot.* A layer of tissue in trees, from which new wood and bark are formed. [< LL, exchange]

Cam·bo·di·an (kam·bō′dē·ən) *adj.* Of or pertaining to Cambodia (now Khmer Republic) or its inhabitants. —**Cam·bo′di·an** *n.*

Cam·bri·an (kam′brē·ən) *adj.* Of or pertaining to Wales. —*n.* A Welshman. [< L *Cambria* name for Wales]

cam·bric (kām′brik) *n.* A fine white linen or cotton. [< Flemish *Kameryk* Cambrai, a city in France]

came (kām) Past tense of COME.

cam·el (kam′əl) *n.* A large Asian or African ruminant with a humped back, used in the desert as a beast of burden or for riding. —*adj.* Tan. [< Gk. *kamēlos* < Semitic]

ca·mel·lia (kə·mēl′yə, -mēl′ē·ə) *n.* A tropical Asian tree or shrub with glossy leaves and white, pink, red, or variegated flowers: also called *japonica.* [< NL, after G. J. *Kamel*, 1661–1706, Jesuit traveler]

camel's hair 1. The hair of the camel. 2. A soft, warm, usu. tan cloth made of camel's hair, sometimes mixed with wool. —**cam·el·hair** (kam′əl·hâr′), **cam′el's-hair′** *adj.*

Cam·em·bert (kam′əm·bâr, *Fr.* kà·mäṅ·bâr′) *n.* A rich, creamy, soft cheese.

cam·e·o (kam′ē·ō) *n. pl.* **·os** 1. A gem having a design carved in relief, often contrasting in color with the background. 2. A small part in a play or movie performed by a well-known person. [< Ital. *cammeo*; ult. origin unknown]

cam·er·a (kam′ər·ə, kam′rə) *n.* 1. An apparatus for recording an image by light focused through a lens onto a film. 2. *Telecom.* An enclosed unit containing the light-sensitive electron tube that converts optical images into electrical impulses for television transmission. —**in camera** *Law* Not in public court; privately. [< L, vaulted room < Gk. *kamara*]

cam·er·a·man (kam′ər·ə·man′, kam′rə-) *n. pl.* **·men** (-men′) The operator of a motion-picture or television camera.

cam·i·sole (kam′ə·sōl) *n.* A woman's short, sleeveless undergarment, usu. trimmed with lace. [< F < Sp. *camisola*, dim. of *camisa* shirt]

cam·o·mile (kam′ə·mīl, -mēl) *n.* A strongly scented, bitter herb whose aromatic flowers and leaves are used in medicine. Also *chamomile.* [< F < Gk. *chamai* on the ground + *mēlon* apple]

cam·ou·flage (kam′ə·fläzh, -fläj) *n.* 1. *Mil.* Measures or material used to conceal or misrepresent the identity of installations, ships, etc. 2. Any disguise or pretense. —*v.t. & v.i.* **·flaged, ·flag·ing** To hide or obscure, as with disguises. [< F *camoufler* to disguise] —**cam′ou·flag′er** *n.*

camp[1] (kamp) *n.* 1. Temporary shelter, esp. a group of tents for soldiers, hunters, or vacationers; also, the ground or area so employed. 2. The persons occupying a group of tents, etc. 3. A body of persons supporting a policy, theory, or doctrine; also, the position so upheld. —*v.i.* To set up or live in a camp; encamp. —**to camp out** To sleep in a tent; live in the open. [< L *campus* level plain]

camp[2] (kamp) *n.* 1. Exaggerated effeminacy. 2. Something so outrageous, anachronistic, etc., as to be considered amusing. [? < dial. E *camp* or *kemp* bold, impetuous fellow] —**camp** *adj.* —**camp′y** *adj.* **·i·er, ·i·est**

cam·paign (kam·pān′) *n.* 1. A series of connected military operations conducted for a common objective, in a particular area. 2. An organized series of activities designed to obtain a definite result. —*v.i.* To serve in, conduct, or go on a campaign. [< F < Ital. *campagna*] —**cam·paign′er** *n.*

cam·pa·ni·le (kam′pə·nē′lē) *n. pl.* **·les** or **·li** (-lē) A bell tower. [< Ital. < LL *campana* bell]

camp·er (kamp′ər) *n.* 1. One who sojourns in a recreational camp. 2. A vehicle affording sleeping facilities: also **camper wagon.**

cam·pes·tral (kam·pes′trəl) *adj.* Growing in or pertaining to fields or open country. [< L *campus* field]

camp·fire (kamp′fīr′) *n.* A fire in an outdoor camp, for cooking, warmth, etc.

campfire girl A girl between seven and eighteen years of age, belonging to the **Camp Fire Girls of America.**

camp follower 1. A prostitute who plies her trade near military bases. 2. A person who exploits military personnel. 3. A person who joins an organization, movement, etc. for personal gain.

camp·ground (kamp′ground′) *n.* An area used for a camp or a camp meeting.

cam·phor (kam′fər) *n.* A white, volatile, translucent crystalline compound with a penetrating odor, obtained from the camphor tree, used in medicine, etc. [< Malay *kāpūr*] —**cam·phor·ic** (kam·fôr′ik, -for′-) *adj.*

cam·phor·ate (kam′fə·rāt) *v.t.* **·at·ed, ·at·ing** To treat or saturate with camphor.

camphor tree A large evergreen tree of eastern Asia yielding camphor.

cam·pi·on (kam′pē·ən) *n.* One of various herbs of the pink family.

camp meeting A series of religious meetings usu. held in a tent; also, one such meeting.

camp·site (kamp′sīt′) *n.* A place suitable for or used for a camp, esp. one in a public or private park.

camp·stool (kamp′stōōl′) *n.* A light, folding stool.

cam·pus (kam′pəs) *n.* The grounds of a school or college. [< L, field]

cam·shaft (kam′shaft′) *n.* A shaft having one or more cams on it.

can[1] (kan, *unstressed* kən) *v.* Present **can**; past **could**; used as an auxiliary and having the following senses: 1. To be able to. 2. To know how to. 3. To have the right to. 4. To be permitted to; may. [OE *cunnan*]

can[2] (kan) *n.* 1. A vessel, usu. of tinned steel or aluminum, for holding or carrying liquids, garbage, etc. 2. A container in which fruits, tobacco, etc., are hermetically sealed; also the contents of such a container. 3. *Slang* **a** Jail. **b** A toilet. **c** The buttocks. —*v.t.* **canned,**

can·ning 1. To put in cans, jars, etc.; preserve. 2. *Slang* To record for sound or film reproduction. 3. *Slang* a To dismiss. b To cease: *Can* it! [OE *canne* cup] —**can′ner** *n.*

Canada balsam A yellowish turpentine derived from the balsam fir, used as a mounting cement in microscopy.

Canada goose The common wild goose of North America, brownish gray with black neck and head.

Canada jay A sooty gray bird of the crow family, native in Canada and the NE United States.

Ca·na·di·an (kə·nā′dē·ən) *adj.* Of or pertaining to Canada or its people. —**Ca·na′di·an** *n.*

Canadian English The English language as spoken and written in Canada.

Canadian French The French language as spoken and written in Canada.

Ca·na·di·an·ism (kə·nā′dē·ən·iz′əm) *n.* 1. A trait, custom, or tradition characteristic of the people of Canada or some of them. 2. A word, phrase, etc. characteristic of Canadian English or French.

ca·naille (kə·nāl′, *Fr.* kȧ·nä′y′) *n.* The rabble; mob. [< F < Ital. *canaglia* pack of dogs]

ca·nal (kə·nal′) *n.* 1. An artificial waterway for inland navigation, irrigation, etc. 2. *Anat.* A passage or duct; tube: the auditory *canal.* —*v.t.* **ca·nalled** or **·naled, ca·nal·ling** or **·nal·ing** To dig a canal through, or provide with canals. [< L *canalis* groove]

canal boat A long barge, used on canals.

ca·nal·ize (kə·nal′īz, kan′əl·īz) *v.t.* **·ized, ·iz·ing** 1. To convert into a canal. 2. To furnish with a canal, or a system of canals. 3. To furnish with an outlet. —**ca·nal·i·za·tion** (kə·nal′ə·zā′shən, kan′əl·ə-) *n.*

can·a·pé (kan′ə·pē, -pā; *Fr.* kȧ·nȧ·pā′) *n.* A thin piece of toast or a cracker spread with cheese, caviar, etc. [< F]

ca·nard (kə·närd′, *Fr.* kȧ·när′) *n.* A false or absurd story or rumor; a hoax. [< F, duck]

ca·nar·y (kə·nâr′ē) *n. pl.* **·nar·ies** 1. A small finch having generally yellow plumage, popular as a cage bird. 2. A bright yellow color: also **canary yellow.** [< Sp. < L *Canaria* (*Insula*) Dog (Island)]

ca·nas·ta (kə·nas′tə) *n.* A card game for two to six players, based on rummy. [< Sp., basket]

can·can (kan′kan′) *n.* An exhibition dance with high kicking performed by women. [< MF, noise]

can·cel (kan′səl) *v.* **can·celed** or **·celled, can·cel·ing** or **·cel·ling** *v.t.* 1. To mark out or off, as by drawing lines through. 2. To render null and void; annul. 3. To withdraw; call off. 4. To mark (a postage stamp) to show use. 5. To make up for; neutralize. 6. *Math.* To eliminate (a common factor) from the numerator and denominator of a fraction, or from both sides of an equation. —*v.i.* 7. To neutralize one another: with *out.* —*n.* 1. The deletion of a part. 2. The part omitted. [< L *cancellare* to cross out] —**can′cel·a·ble** or **can′cel·la·ble** *adj.* —**can·cel·la·tion** (kan′sə·lā′shən) *n.* —**can′cel·er** or **can′cel·ler** *n.*

can·cer (kan′sər) *n.* 1. Any of a group of often fatal diseases characterized by abnormal cellular growth and by malignancy. 2. A malignant tumor. 3. Any dangerous and spreading evil. [< L, crab] —**can′cer·ous** *adj.*

Can·cer (kan′sər) *n.* A constellation, the Crab; also, the fourth sign of the zodiac.

can·de·la·brum (kan′də·lä′brəm, -lā′-) *n. pl.* **·bra** or **·brums** A large, branched candlestick. Also **can′de·la′bra** *pl.* **·bras.** [< L *candela* candle]

can·des·cence (kan·des′əns) *n.* Incandescence. [< L *candere* to gleam] —**can·des′cent** *adj.* —**can·des′cent·ly** *adv.*

can·did (kan′did) *adj.* Honest and open; sincere; frank. [< L *candere* to gleam] —**can′did·ly** *adv.* —**can′did·ness** *n.*

can·di·da·cy (kan′də·də·sē) *n. pl.* **·cies** The state or position of being a candidate. Also **can·di·da·ture** (kan′də·də·cho͝or, -dā′chər), **can′di·date·ship′** (-dit·ship′).

can·di·date (kan′də·dāt, -dit) *n.* One who seeks, or is nominated for, an office, honor, or privilege. [< L *candidus* white; because office seekers in Rome wore white togas]

can·died (kan′dēd) *adj.* 1. Cooked with or in sugar. 2. Crystallized or granulated. 3. Flattering; honeyed.

can·dle (kan′dəl) *n.* 1. A cylinder of tallow, wax, or other solid fat, containing a wick, that gives light when burning. 2. *Physics* A unit of luminous intensity equal to that of 5 square millimeters of platinum at its solidification point: also called *standard candle.* —**to hold a candle to** To compare with favorably: usu. used in the negative. —*v.t.* **·dled, ·dling** To test, as eggs, by holding between the eye and a light. [< L *candere* to gleam]

can·dle·light (kan′dəl·līt′) *n.* 1. Light given by a candle; artificial light. 2. Twilight.

Can·dle·mas (kan′dəl·məs) *n.* February 2, the feast of the Purification, or of the Presentation of Christ in the temple.

can·dle·pow·er (kan′dəl·pou′ər) *n.* The illuminating power of a standard candle, used as a measure.

can·dle·stick (kan′dəl·stik′) *n.* A holder with sockets or spikes for a candle or candles.

can·dle·wick (kan′dəl·wik′) *n.* 1. The wick of a candle. 2. Tufted embroidery work.

can·dor (kan′dər) *n.* 1. Openness; frankness. 2. Impartiality; fairness. Also *Brit.* **can′dour.** [< L, sincerity]

can·dy (kan′dē) *n. pl.* **·dies** Any of numerous confections consisting chiefly of sugar. —*v.t.* **·died, ·dy·ing** 1. To cause to form into crystals of sugar. 2. To preserve by boiling or coating with sugar. 3. To render pleasant; sweeten. [< Arabic *qandī* made of sugar]

cane (kān) *n.* 1. A walking stick. 2. The jointed, woody stem of the bamboo, rattan, and certain palm trees, used as a weaving material in chairs, etc. 3. Sugarcane. 4. The stem of a raspberry or allied plant. 5. Any rod, especially one used for flogging. —*v.t.* **caned, can·ing** 1. To strike or beat with a cane. 2. To make or repair with cane, as a chair. [< Gk. *kanna* reed] —**can′er** *n.*

cane·brake (kān′brāk′) *n.* A thick growth of cane.

cane sugar Sucrose obtained from sugarcane.

ca·nine (kā′nīn) *adj.* 1. Of or like a dog. 2. *Zool.* Of the dog family. 3. Of or pertaining to a canine tooth. —*n.* 1. A dog or other canine animal. 2. *Anat.* One of the four pointed teeth situated one on either side of the upper and lower incisors. [< L *canis* dog]

Ca·nis Ma·jor (kā′nis mā′jər) A constellation containing the bright star Sirius. [< L, greater dog]

Canis Mi·nor (mī′nər) A constellation containing the bright star Procyon. [< L, lesser dog]

can·is·ter (kan′is·tər) *n.* A covered container for tea, spices, etc. [< L *canistrum* basket]

can·ker (kang′kər) *n.* 1. *Pathol.* An ulceration, chiefly of the mouth and lips. 2. Anything that causes corruption, evil, decay, etc. 3. A disease of trees, causing decay of the bark and wood. [< L *cancer* crab] —**can′ker·ous** *adj.*

can·ker·worm (kang′kər·wûrm′) *n.* An insect larva that destroys fruit and shade trees.

can·na (kan′ə) *n.* An erect, mostly tropical American plant with red or yellow irregular flowers. [< Gk. *kanna* reed] —**can·na·ceous** (kə·nā′shəs) *adj.*

can·na·bis (kan′ə·bis) *n.* 1. Hemp (def. 1). 2. The dried flowering tops of the female hemp plant. [< Gk. *kannabis* hemp]

canned (kand) *adj.* 1. Preserved in a can or jar. 2. *Slang* Recorded: *canned* music.

can·nel (kan′əl) *n.* A bituminous coal with low heating power. Also **cannel coal.**

can·ner·y (kan′ər·ē) *n. pl.* **·ner·ies** A place where foods are canned.

can·ni·bal (kan′ə·bəl) *n.* 1. One who eats human flesh. 2. An animal that devours its own species. [< Sp. *Caniables,* var. of *Caribes* Caribs] —**can′ni·bal** *adj.* —**can′ni·bal·ism′** *n.* —**can′ni·bal·is′tic** *adj.* —**can′ni·bal·is′ti·cal·ly** *adv.*

can·ni·bal·ize (kan′ə·bəl·īz′) *v.t.* **·ized, ·iz·ing** To take parts from (damaged tanks, etc.) in order to repair others. —**can′ni·bal·i·za′tion** *n.*

can·ning (kan′ing) *n.* The act, process, or business of preserving foods in hermetically sealed metal cans, glass jars, etc.

can·non (kan′ən) *n. pl.* **·nons** or **·non** 1. *Mil.* A large tubular weapon, usu. mounted on a fixed or mobile carriage, that discharges a projectile by the use of an explosive. 2. The large bone between the fetlock and knee or hock of the horse and allied animals. Also **cannon bone.** —*v.i.* 1. To fire cannon. —*v.t.* 2. To attack with cannon shot. [< Ital. *canna* tube, pipe]

can·non·ade (kan′ən·ād′) *v.* **·ad·ed, ·ad·ing** *v.t.* 1. To attack with cannon shot. —*v.i.* 2. To fire cannon repeatedly. —**can′non·ade′** *n.*

cannon ball A spherical solid shot fired from a cannon.

can·non·eer (kan′ən·ir′) *n.* An artillery gunner.

can·not (kan′ot, ka·not′) The negative of the auxiliary verb CAN.

can·ny (kan′ē) *adj. Orig. Scot.* **·ni·er, ·ni·est** 1. Cautiously shrewd. 2. Frugal; thrifty. 3. Skillful. —*adv.* In a canny manner. —**can′ni·ly** *adv.* —**can′ni·ness** *n.*

ca·noe (kə·nōō′) *n.* A small, long, narrow boat, pointed at both ends, and propelled by paddles. —*v.t. & v.i.* **·noed, ·noe·ing** To convey or travel by canoe. [< Sp. *canoa*] —**ca·noe′ist** *n.*

can of worms A situation that produces successive difficulties as it unfolds: The tax investigation opened a *can of worms.*

can·on[1] (kan′ən) *n.* 1. A rule or law; esp., a rule or body of rules of faith and practice enacted by a church council. 2. An established rule; principle. 3. A standard; criterion. 4. The books of the Bible or other sacred books. 5. A list, as of canonized saints. 6. *Often cap. Eccl.* The main portion of the Mass. 7. *Music* A composition or passage in which one or more voices follow and imitate the melody of the first voice. [< Gk. *kanōn* rule, straight rod]

can·on[2] (kan′ən) *n.* A cleric affiliated with a cathedral or collegiate church. [See CANON[1].]

ca·non·i·cal (kə·non′i·kəl) *adj.* 1. Relating or conforming to or prescribed by a canon or canons. 2. Of or contained in the canon of Scripture. 3. Authoritative; recognized. Also **ca·non′ic.** —**ca·non′i·cal·ly** *adv.*

canonical hours *Eccl.* Seven daily periods, fixed by canon, for recitation of the Divine Office.

ca·non·i·cals (kə·non′i·kəlz) *n.pl.* The habits or robes prescribed by canon to be worn by the clergy when officiating.

can·on·ist (kan′ən·ist) *n.* One skilled in canon law. —**can′on·is′tic** or **·ti·cal** *adj.*

can·on·ize (kan′ən·īz) *v.t.* **·ized, ·iz·ing** 1. To declare (a deceased person) to be a saint. 2. To glorify. —**can′on·i·za′tion** *n.*

canon law The ecclesiastical laws of a Christian church.

can·o·py (kan′ə·pē) *n. pl.* **·pies** 1. A covering suspended over a throne, bed, etc., or held over a person. 2. Any covering overhead, as the sky. 3. *Archit.* An ornamental covering over a niche, altar, or tomb. —*v.t.* **·pied, ·py·ing** To cover with or as with a canopy. [< Gk. *kōnōpeion* bed with mosquito net]

canst (kanst) *Archaic* second person singular, present tense of CAN[1]: used with *thou.*

cant[1] (kant) *n.* 1. An inclination from the vertical or horizontal; a slope or tilt. 2. A sudden motion that tilts or overturns. 3. An outer corner or angle. 4. A slant surface. —*v.t.* 1. To set slantingly; tilt. 2. To give a bevel to. 3. To throw out or off. —*v.i.* 4. To tilt; slant. —*adj.* 1. Oblique; slanting. 2. Having canted sides or corners. [< Med.L *cantus* corner, side]

cant[2] (kant) *n.* 1. Insincere talk, esp. of a religious or moralistic nature. 2. Words or phraseology peculiar to a sect, class, or calling; jargon; argot. —*v.i.* To use cant. —*adj.* Having the character of cant; hypocritical. [< L *canere* to sing]

can't (kant) Cannot.

can·ta·bi·le (kän·tä′bē·lā) *Music adj.* Melodious; flowing. —*n.* Music characterized by flowing melody. [< Ital.]

can·ta·loupe (kan′tə·lōp) *n.* A muskmelon having a rough, ribbed rind and sweet, orange flesh. Also **can′ta·loup.** [< F, after *Cantalupo,* Italian castle where first grown]

can·tank·er·ous (kan·tang′kər·əs) *adj.* Quarrelsome; ill-natured; perverse. [Prob. akin to ME *contak* strife] —**can·tank′er·ous·ly** *adv.* —**can·tank′er·ous·ness** *n.*

can·ta·ta (kən·tä′tə) *n. Music* A narrative or dramatic vocal composition, to be sung but not acted. [< Ital.]

can·teen (kan·tēn′) *n.* 1. A small flask for

carrying water or other liquids. 2. A shop at a military camp where soldiers can buy provisions, refreshments, etc. 3. A place for refreshments. [< Ital. *cantina* cellar]

can·ter (kan′tər) *n.* A moderate, easy gallop. [Short for *Canterbury gallop*; with ref. to the pace of pilgrims riding to Canterbury] **—can′ter** *v.t. & v.i.*

cant hook A lever equipped with an adjustable hook for handling logs.

can·ti·cle (kan′ti·kəl) *n.* A nonmetrical hymn, said or chanted in church. [< L *canticum* song]

can·ti·lev·er (kan′tə·lev′ər, -lē′vər) *n.* 1. *Engin.* A long structural member, as a truss, beam, or slab, lying across a support with the projecting arms in balance. 2. *Archit.* Any structural part projecting horizontally and anchored at one end only. **—***v.t. & v.i.* To project (a building member) outward and in balance beyond the base. [Origin uncertain]

cantilever bridge A bridge formed by the meeting of two freely projecting arms.

can·tle (kan′təl) *n.* The hind part of a saddle, projecting upward. [< Med.L *cantus* corner]

can·to (kan′tō) *n. pl.* **·tos** A division of a long poem. [< Ital. < L *cantus* song]

can·ton (kan′tən, -ton, kan·ton′; *for v. def. 2* kan·ton′, -tōn′, -to͞on′) *n.* A district; esp., one of the states of Switzerland. **—***v.t.* 1. To divide into cantons or districts. 2. To assign quarters to, as troops. [< OF] **—can′ton·al** *adj.*

Can·ton·ese (kan′tən·ēz′, -ēs′) *n. pl.* **·ese** 1. A native of Canton, China. 2. The Chinese language spoken in parts of southern China. **—Can′ton·ese′** *adj.*

can·tor (kan′tər, -tôr) *n.* The chief liturgical singer in a synagogue. [< L]

can·vas (kan′vəs) *n.* 1. A heavy, closely woven cloth of hemp, flax, or cotton, used for sails, tents, etc. 2. A piece of such material on which to paint, esp. in oils. 3. A painting on canvas. 4. Sails collectively. [< Gk. *kannabis* hemp]

can·vas·back (kan′vəs·bak′) *n.* A sea duck of North America.

can·vass (kan′vəs) *v.t. & v.i.* To go about (a region) or among (persons) to solicit votes, opinions, etc. **—***n.* 1. The process of canvassing. 2. A survey or poll. [< CANVAS; with ref. to its early use for sifting] **—can′·vass·er** *n.*

can·yon (kan′yən) *n.* A deep gorge or ravine, with steep sides. [< Sp. *cañón*]

caout·chouc (kou·cho͝ok′) *n.* Rubber; esp., crude rubber. [< Tupi *cahuchu*]

cap (kap) *n.* 1. A covering for the head, usu. snug, brimless, and of soft material. 2. Any headgear designed to denote rank, function, membership, etc. 3. Something suggesting a cap in form, function, or position as a bottle top, an artificial covering for a tooth etc. 4. A container holding an explosive charge. **—to set one's cap for** To try to win as a suitor or husband. **—***v.t.* **capped, cap·ping** 1. To put a cap on; cover. 2. To serve as a cap or cover to. 3. To add the final touch to. 4. To excel. [Prob. < L *caput* head]

ca·pa·bil·i·ty (kā′pə·bil′ə·tē) *n. pl.* **·ties** 1. The quality of being capable; capacity or ability. 2. *Usu. pl.* Qualities that may be used or developed; potentialities.

ca·pa·ble (kā′pə·bəl) *adj.* Able; competent. **—capable of** Having the capacity or qualities needed for. [< L *capere* to take] **—ca′pa·bly** *adv.*

ca·pa·cious (kə·pā′shəs) *adj.* Able to contain much; roomy. [< L *capere* to take] **—ca·pa′cious·ly** *adv.* **—ca·pa′cious·ness** *n.*

ca·pac·i·tance (kə·pas′ə·təns) *n. Electr.* The property of a circuit that permits it to store an electrical charge. **—ca·pac′i·tive** *adj.*

ca·pac·i·tor (kə·pas′ə·tər) *n. Electr.* A device used to increase the capacitance of an electric circuit. Also called *condenser*.

ca·pac·i·ty (kə·pas′ə·tē) *n. pl.* **·ties** 1. Ability to receive, contain, or absorb. 2. Maximum volume or content. 3. Aptitude or ability. 4. Specific position or office. 5. Maximum output or production. [< L *capax* able to hold]

cap-a-pie (kap′ə·pē′) *adv.* From head to foot. Also **cap′-à-pie′**. [< OF]

ca·par·i·son (kə·par′ə·sən) *n.* 1. An ornamental covering for a horse. 2. Rich apparel or trappings. [< LL *cappa* cape] **—ca·par′i·son** *v.t.*

cape[1] (kāp) *n.* A point of land extending into the sea or a lake. [< L *caput* head]

cape[2] (kāp) *n.* A sleeveless garment fastened at the neck and hanging loosely from the shoulders. [< LL *cappa*]

cap·e·lin (kap′ə·lin) *n. pl.* **·lin** or **·lins** A small, edible fish of northern seas, much used as bait. Also **cap′e·lan.** [< dial. F (Canadian) *capelan* < F]

ca·per[1] (kā′pər) *n.* 1. A playful leap; a skip. 2. A wild prank; antic. **—***v.i.* To leap playfully; frolic. [Short for CAPRIOLE] **—ca′per·er** *n.*

ca·per[2] (kā′pər) *n.* 1. The flower bud of a Mediterranean shrub, pickled and used as a relish. 2. The shrub itself. [< Gk. *kapparis*]

cap·il·lar·i·ty (kap′ə·lar′ə·tē) *n. pl.* **·ties** 1. The state of being capillary. 2. *Physics* A form of surface tension between the molecules of a liquid and those of a solid. When the adhesive force is stronger (**capillary attraction**) the liquid will tend to rise in a capillary tube; when cohesion dominates (**capillary repulsion**), the liquid tends to fall. [< F]

cap·il·lar·y (kap′ə·ler′ē) *adj.* 1. Of, pertaining to, or like hair; fine. 2. Having a hairlike bore, as a tube or vessel. **—***n. pl.* **·lar·ies** 1. *Anat.* A very small blood vessel, as one connecting an artery and vein. 2. Any tube with a fine bore. [< L *capillus* hair]

cap·i·ta (kap′ə·tə) Plural of CAPUT.

cap·i·tal[1] (kap′ə·təl) *n.* 1. The city or town that is the seat of government of a country, state, etc. 2. A capital letter. 3. The total amount of money or property owned or used by an individual or corporation. 4. Wealth applicable to the production of more wealth. 5. In accounting, net worth after the deduction of all liabilities. 6. Possessors of wealth as a class. **—to make capital of** To turn to advantage. **—***adj.* 1. Chief, as comprising the seat of government. 2. Standing at the head; principal. 3. Of or pertaining to funds or capital. 4. Of the first quality. 5. Punishable by or involving the death penalty: *capital* crimes. [< L *caput* head]

cap·i·tal[2] (kap′ə·təl) *n. Archit.* The upper

member of a column or pillar. [< L *caput* head]

capital gain Profit from the sale of capital investments, as stocks, real estate, etc.

cap·i·tal·ism (kap′ə·təl·iz′əm) *n.* An economic system in which the means of production and distribution are mostly privately owned and operated for private profit.

cap·i·tal·ist (kap′ə·təl·ist) *n.* 1. An owner of capital, esp. one who invests it in profit-making enterprises. 2. A supporter of capitalism. —**cap′i·tal·is′tic** *adj.* —**cap′i·tal·is′ti·cal·ly** *adv.*

cap·i·tal·i·za·tion (kap′ə·təl·ə·zā′shən, -ī·zā′-) *n.* 1. The act or process of capitalizing. 2. A sum arrived at by capitalizing. 3. The total capital employed in a business.

cap·i·tal·ize (kap′ə·təl·īz′) *v.* **·ized, ·iz·ing** *v.t.* 1. To print or write in capital letters. 2. To convert into capital. 3. To provide capital for. 4. To estimate the worth of (a business or stock) from earnings or potential earnings. —*v.i.* 5. To acquire an advantage; profit: with *on* or *by*.

capital letter The form of a letter used at the beginning of a sentence, with proper names, etc., as the A in Africa.

cap·i·tal·ly (kap′ə·təl·ē) *adv.* Admirably.

capital punishment The death penalty.

capital ship A large warship carrying heavy armament.

capital stock 1. The amount of stock a corporation is authorized to issue. 2. The total face value of such stock.

cap·i·ta·tion (kap′ə·tā′shən) *n.* An assessment on each person (or head); poll tax. [< L *caput* head]

cap·i·tol (kap′ə·təl) *n.* The building in which a state legislature convenes; a statehouse.

ca·pit·u·late (kə·pich′o͞o·lāt) *v.i.* **·lat·ed, ·lat·ing** 1. To surrender on stipulated terms. 2. To acquiesce. [< L *capitulare* to draw up in chapters] —**ca·pit′u·la′tor** *n.*

ca·pit·u·la·tion (kə·pich′o͞o·lā′shən) *n.* 1. The act of surrendering conditionally; also, the instrument containing the terms of surrender. 2. A surrender. 3. A summary of a subject. —**ca·pit′u·la·to′ry** (-lə·tôr′ē) *adj.*

ca·po (kä′pō) *n.* The leader of a group within a criminal organization. [< Ital. < L *caput* head]

ca·pon (kā′pon) *n.* A gelded rooster. [< L *capo, -onis*]

cap·puc·ci·no (kä·po͞o·chē′nō) *n.* Hot espresso coffee with cream or steamed milk, often flavored with cinnamon. [< Ital., from the color of a Capuchin monk's habit]

ca·pric·ci·o (kə·prē′chē·ō, *Ital.* kä·prēt′chō) *n. pl.* **·ci·os** or *Ital.* **ca·pric·ci** (kä·prēt′chē) 1. *Music* A lively, fanciful composition. 2. A prank; also, a caprice. [< Ital., whim < L *caper*]

ca·price (kə·prēs′) *n.* 1. A sudden, impulsive change; whim. 2. A tendency to make such changes; capriciousness. 3. *Music* A capriccio. [< Ital. *capriccio* whim]

ca·pri·cious (kə·prish′əs) *adj.* Characterized by or resulting from caprice; fickle; whimsical. —**ca·pri′cious·ly** *adv.* —**ca·pri′cious·ness** *n.*

Cap·ri·corn (kap′rə·kôrn) *n.* A constellation, the Goat; also, the tenth sign of the zodiac. [< L *caper* goat + *cornu* horn]

cap·ri·ole (kap′rē·ōl) *n.* 1. An upward leap made by a trained horse involving no forward motion. 2. A leap. [< Ital. *capriola* jump] —**cap′ri·ole** *v.i.* **·oled, ·ol·ing**

cap·si·cum (kap′si·kəm) *n.* 1. An herb or shrub of the nightshade family, producing pods prepared as a condiment. 2. The fruit of these plants; red pepper. [< L *capsa* box (from the shape of the fruit)]

cap·size (kap·sīz′, kap′sīz) *v.t.* & *v.i.* **·sized, ·siz·ing** To upset or overturn. [? < Sp. *capuzar*]

cap·stan (kap′stən) *n.* *Naut.* A drumlike apparatus, turned by bars or levers, for hoisting anchors. [< F *cabestan* < L *capere* to hold]

cap·stone (kap′stōn′) *n.* 1. Copestone (def. 1). 2. The highest point, as of achievement.

cap·sule (kap′səl, -syo͞ol) *n.* 1. A small container, usu. made of gelatin, for a dose of medicine. 2. A detachable part of an airplane, rocket, etc., containing the pilot, instruments, etc. 3. A thin covering or seal. 4. *Bot.* A dry seed vessel made up of more than one carpel. 5. *Anat.* A fibrous or membranous structure that envelops some part of the body. —*adj.* In concise form; condensed. [< L *capsula*, dim. of *capsa* box] —**cap′su·lar, cap′su·late** (-lāt), **cap′su·lat′ed** *adj.* —**cap′su·la′tion** *n.* —**cap′su·lize** *v.t.* **·ized, ·iz·ing**

cap·tain (kap′tən, -tin) *n.* 1. One at the head or in command; a chief; leader. 2. The master or commander of a vessel. 3. *Mil.* A commissioned officer ranking below a major and above a first lieutenant. 4. *Naval* A commissioned officer ranking below a rear admiral. 5. A team leader. —*v.t.* To act as captain to; command; lead. [< L *caput* head] —**cap′tain·cy, cap′tain·ship** *n.*

cap·tion (kap′shən) *n.* 1. A heading, as of a document. 2. The title and descriptive matter for an illustration. 3. A subtitle in a motion picture. [< L *capere* to take] —**cap′tion** *v.t.*

cap·tious (kap′shəs) *adj.* 1. Apt to find fault; critical. 2. Designed to ensnare or perplex. [< L *captiosus* fallacious] —**cap′tious·ly** *adv.* —**cap′tious·ness** *n.*

cap·ti·vate (kap′tə·vāt) *v.t.* **·vat·ed, ·vat·ing** To enthrall; fascinate; charm. [< LL *captivare* to capture] —**cap′ti·va′tion** *n.* —**cap′ti·va′tor** *n.*

cap·tive (kap′tiv) *n.* 1. A prisoner. 2. One enthralled by beauty, passion, etc. —*adj.* 1. Taken or held prisoner, as in war. 2. Held in restraint; confined. 3. Captivated. 4. Of or pertaining to a captive or captivity. [< L *capere* to take]

cap·tiv·i·ty (kap·tiv′ə·tē) *n. pl.* **·ties** The state of being held captive; confinement.

cap·tor (kap′tər) *n.* One who takes or holds captive.

cap·ture (kap′chər) *v.t.* **·tured, ·tur·ing** 1. To take by force, stratagem, etc., as in war. 2. To gain or win. —*n.* 1. The act of capturing; seizure. 2. The person or thing captured. [< L *capere* to take]

cap·u·chin (kap′yo͞o·chin, -shin) *n.* 1. A woman's hooded cloak. 2. A South American monkey whose head is covered with a cowl-like growth of hair. [after the cowled habit of a Capuchin monk]

ca·put (kā′pət, kap′ət) *n. pl.* **cap·i·ta** (kap′ə·tə) A head or headlike part. [< L]

car (kär) *n.* 1. An automobile. 2. Any of various wheeled vehicles. 3. The enclosed platform of an elevator. [< L *carrus* wagon]

ca·ra·ba·o (kä′rə·bä′ō) *n. pl.* **·ba·os** or **·ba·o** A Philippine water buffalo. [< Sp. < Malay *karbau*]

ca·ra·ca·ra (kä′rə·kä′rə) *n.* A large, vulture-like hawk found in South America and the southern U.S. [< Sp. *caracará*]

car·a·cole (kar′ə·kōl) *n.* A half turn to the right or left made by a trained horse. [< Sp. *caracol* snail shell] —**car′a·cole** *v.i.* **·coled, ·col·ing**

ca·rafe (kə·raf′) *n.* A glass water bottle. [< F]

car·a·mel (kar′ə·məl, -mel, kär′məl) *n.* 1. A chewy candy made of sugar, butter, milk, etc. 2. Burnt sugar, used to flavor foods. [< Med.L *canna mellis* sugarcane]

car·a·mel·ize (kar′ə·məl·īz′, kär′məl-) *v.t. & v.i.* **·ized, ·iz·ing** To convert or be converted into caramel. —**car′a·mel·i·za′tion** *n.*

car·a·pace (kar′ə·pās) *n. Zool.* A hard, bony, or horny outer case or covering, as of a turtle or lobster. [< Sp. *carapacho*]

car·at (kar′ət) *n.* 1. A unit of weight for gems, one metric carat being 200 milligrams. 2. Loosely, a karat. [< Gk. *keration* seed]

car·a·van (kar′ə·van) *n.* 1. A company of traders, pilgrims, or the like, traveling together, esp. across deserts. 2. A number of vehicles traveling together. 3. A large, covered vehicle; a van. [< Persian *kārwān*]

car·a·van·sa·ry (kar′ə·van′sə·rē) *n. pl.* **·ries** In Oriental countries, an inn enclosing a court for sheltering caravans. [< Persian *kārwān* caravan + *sarāī* inn]

car·a·vel (kar′ə·vel) *n.* A small ship of the 15th and 16th c., used esp. by the Portuguese and Spanish. Also **car′a·velle.** [< MF < Sp. *caraba* boat]

car·a·way (kar′ə·wā) *n.* An herb of the parsley family whose seeds (**caraway seeds**) are used for flavoring. [< Arabic *karwiyā* caraway]

car·bide (kär′bīd, -bid) *n. Chem.* A compound of carbon with a more electropositive element.

car·bine (kär′bīn, -bēn) *n.* A light, short-barreled rifle originally devised for mounted troops. [< F *carabine*]

carbo- *combining form* Carbon: *carbohydrate.* Also, before vowels, **carb-.** [< L *carbo* coal]

car·bo·hy·drate (kär′bō·hī′drāt) *n. Biochem.* Any of a group of compounds containing carbon combined with hydrogen and oxygen, and including sugars, starches, and cellulose.

car·bol·ic acid (kär·bol′ik) *Chem.* Phenol.

car·bo·lize (kär′bə·līz) *v.t.* **·lized, ·liz·ing** *Chem.* To treat or impregnate with carbolic acid.

car·bon (kär′bən) *n.* 1. A nonmetallic element (symbol C) found in all organic substances. 2. *Electr.* **a** A rod of carbon, used as an electrode in an arc light. **b** The negative electrode of a primary cell. 3. A piece of carbon paper. 4. A copy made with carbon paper. —*adj.* 1. Of, pertaining to, or like carbon. 2. Treated with carbon. [< L *carbo, -onis* coal]

carbon 14 *Physics* Radiocarbon.

car·bo·na·ceous (kär′bə·nā′shəs) *adj.* Of, pertaining to, or yielding carbon.

car·bon·ate (kär′bə·nāt; *for n., also* kär′bə·nit) *Chem. v.t.* **·at·ed, ·at·ing** 1. To impregnate or charge with carbon dioxide. 2. To carbonize. —*n.* A salt or ester of carbonic acid. [< F] —**car′bon·a′tion** *n.*

carbon dioxide *Chem.* A heavy, odorless, noncombustible gas taken from the atmosphere in photosynthesis and returned to it by respiration and combustion.

carboni- *combining form* Carbon; coal. [< L *carbo, -onis* coal]

car·bon·ic (kär·bon′ik) *adj.* Of, pertaining to, or obtained from carbon.

carbonic acid *Chem.* A weak, unstable acid existing only in solution.

car·bon·if·er·ous (kär′bə·nif′ər·əs) *adj.* Of, pertaining to, containing, or yielding carbon or coal.

car·bon·ize (kär′bən·īz) *v.t.* **·ized, ·iz·ing** 1. To reduce to carbon. 2. To coat with carbon, as paper. 3. To charge with carbon. —**car′bon·i·za′tion** *n.*

carbon monoxide *Chem.* A colorless, odorless gas formed by the incomplete oxidation of carbon, highly poisonous when inhaled.

carbon paper Thin paper coated with carbon or the like, used for making copies of typewritten or handwritten material.

carbon tetrachloride *Chem.* A colorless, nonflammable, poisonous liquid, used as a solvent, cleaning fluid, etc.

car·box·yl (kär·bok′sil) *n. Chem.* A univalent acid radical, the characteristic group of most organic acids.

car·boy (kär′boi) *n.* A container for corrosive acids, etc. [Alter. of Persian *qarābah* demijohn]

car·bun·cle (kär′bung·kəl) *n.* 1. An inflammation of the subcutaneous tissue, resembling a boil but larger. 2. A red garnet cut without facets. [< L *carbo, -onis* coal] —**car·bun·cu·lar** (kär·bung′kyə·lər) *adj.*

car·bu·ret (kär′bə·rāt, -byə·ret) *v.t.* **·ret·ed** or **·ret·ted, ·ret·ing** or **·ret·ting** To combine chemically with carbon; esp., to charge (air or gas) with carbon compounds. —**car′bu·re′tion** *n.*

car·bu·re·tor (kär′bə·rā′tər, -byə·ret′ər) *n.* In an internal-combustion engine, a device used to charge air or gas with volatile hydrocarbons. Also *Brit.* **car·bu·ret·tor** (kär′byə·ret′ər) or **car′bu·ret′ter.**

car·bu·rize (kär′bə·rīz, -byə-) *v.t.* **·rized, ·riz·ing** 1. To carburet. 2. *Metall.* To impregnate the surface layer of (steel) with carbon.

car·ca·jou (kär′kə·jo͞o, -zho͞o) *n. Canadian* The wolverine. [< dial. F (Canadian) < native Algonquian name]

car·cass (kär′kəs) *n.* 1. The dead body of an animal. 2. The human body, living or dead: a contemptuous or humorous use. [< Med.L *carcasium*]

car·cin·o·gen (kär·sin′ə·jən) *n. Pathol.* A substance that causes cancer. —**car·ci·no·gen·ic** (kär·sə·nō·jen′ik) *adj.*

car·ci·no·ma (kär′sə·nō′mə) *n. pl.* **·mas** or **·ma·ta** (-mə·tə) *Pathol.* A malignant epithelial tumor; cancer. [< Gk. *karkinos* cancer] —**car·ci·nom·a·tous** (kär′sə·nom′ə·təs, -nō′mə-) *adj.*

card[1] (kärd) *n.* 1. A small, usu. rectangular piece of thin pasteboard or stiff paper, used for a variety of purposes. 2. One of a pack of such pieces with figures, numbers, or other symbols, used for various games. 3. *pl.* Games played with such cards. 4. A greeting card. 5. A card certifying the identity of its owner or bearer. 6. *Informal* A witty person. **—in the cards** Likely to happen. **—to put one's cards on the table** To reveal one's intentions frankly. [< Gk. *chartēs* leaf of paper]

card[2] (kärd) *n.* A wire-toothed brush for combing and cleansing wool, etc. [< L *carduus* thistle] **—card** *v.t. & v.i.* **—card′er** *n.*

car·da·mom (kär′də·məm) *n.* 1. The aromatic seeds of either of two Asian plants of the ginger family. 2. One of the plants yielding these seeds. Also **car′da·mon** (-mən), **car′da·mum.** [< Gk. *kardamon* cress + *amōmon* spice]

card·board (kärd′bôrd′) *n.* A thin, stiff pasteboard used for making cards, boxes, etc.

car·di·ac (kär′dē·ak) *adj. Med.* Pertaining to, situated near, or affecting the heart. [< Gk. *kardia* heart]

car·di·gan (kär′də·gən) *n.* A jacket or sweater opening down the front. [after the seventh Earl of *Cardigan*, 1797–1868]

car·di·nal (kär′də·nəl, kärd′nəl) *adj.* 1. Most important; chief; principal. 2. Of a deep scarlet color. 3. Of or relating to a cardinal or cardinals. **—***n.* 1. In the Roman Catholic Church, a member of the College of Cardinals. 2. A bright red, crested finch of the eastern U.S. 3. A deep scarlet. 4. A cardinal number. [< L *cardo, cardinis* hinge, that on which something turns or depends] **—car′di·nal·ly** *adv.*

car·di·nal·ate (kär′də·nəl·āt, kärd′nəl·āt) *n.* The rank, dignity, or term of office of a cardinal. Also **car′di·nal·ship′.**

cardinal number *Math.* Any number that expresses a quantity and is used in counting, as 1, 2, 3, etc.: distinguished from *ordinal number.*

cardinal point Any of the four main points of the compass.

cardio- *combining form* Heart: *cardiogram.* Also, before vowels, **cardi-.** [< Gk. *kardia* heart]

car·di·o·gram (kär′dē·ə·gram′) *n.* The record produced by a cardiograph.

car·di·o·graph (kär′dē·ə·graf′, -gräf′) *n.* An instrument for tracing and recording the force and character of heart movements. **—car·di·og·ra·pher** (kär′dē·og′rə·fər) *n.* **—car′di·o·graph′ic** *adj.* **—car·di·og·ra·phy** (kär′dē·og′rə·fē) *n.*

car·di·ol·o·gy (kär′dē·ol′ə·jē) *n.* The branch of medicine dealing with the heart and heart disease. [< CARDIO- + -LOGY] **—car′di·ol′o·gist** *n.*

card·sharp (kärd′shärp′) *n.* One who cheats at cards, esp. as a livelihood.

care (kâr) *n.* 1. A feeling of anxiety or concern; worry. 2. A cause of worry or anxiety. 3. Watchful regard or attention; heed. 4. Charge or guardianship; custody; supervision. **—***v.i.* **cared, car·ing** 1. To have or show regard, interest, or concern. 2. To be inclined; desire: with *to.* **—to care for** 1. To look after or provide for. 2. To feel interest concerning; also, to have a fondness for; like. [OE *caru, cearu*]

ca·reen (kə·rēn′) *v.i.* 1. To lurch or twist from side to side while moving. 2. To lean sideways. **—***v.t.* 3. To turn (a ship, etc.) on one side, as for cleaning or repairing. [< L *carina* keel of a ship]

ca·reer (kə·rir′) *n.* 1. The course or progress of events, esp. in a person's life. 2. One's lifework; profession. 3. A rapid course; progress at full speed. **—***adj.* Making one's profession a lifework: *career* diplomat. **—***v.i.* To move with a swift, free motion. [< L *carrus* wagon]

ca·reer·ist (kə·rir′ist) *n.* One chiefly concerned with professional advancement. **—ca·reer′ism** *n.*

care·free (kâr′frē′) *adj.* Free of troubles.

care·ful (kâr′fəl) *adj.* 1. Exercising care; painstaking. 2. Done with care. 3. Watchful; cautious. **—care′ful·ly** *adv.* **—care′ful·ness** *n.*

care·less (kâr′lis) *adj.* 1. Not attentive; reckless. 2. Not done with care; neglectful. 3. Without care or concern; indifferent: with *about, in,* or *of.* **—care′less·ly** *adv.* **—care′less·ness** *n.*

ca·ress (kə·res′) *n.* An affectionate touch or gesture. [< L *carus* dear] **—ca·ress′** *v.t.* **—ca·ress′er** *n.* **—ca·ress′ing·ly** *adv.*

car·et (kar′ət) *n.* A sign (∧) placed below a line to indicate where something should be inserted. [< L, it is missing]

care·tak·er (kâr′tā′kər) *n.* One who takes care of a place, thing, or person; a custodian.

care·worn (kâr′wôrn′) *adj.* Showing the eeffcts of care and anxiety.

car·fare (kär′fâr′) *n.* The fare for a ride on a bus, etc.

car·go (kär′gō) *n. pl.* **·goes** or **·gos** Goods and merchandise carried by a vessel, aircraft, etc.; freight; load. [< L *carrus* wagon]

car·hop (kär′hop′) *n. Informal* A waiter or waitress at a drive-in restaurant.

Car·ib (kar′ib) *n.* 1. One of a tribe of Indians of the Lesser Antilles and northern S. America. 2. The family of languages spoken by these Indians. [< Sp. < Cariban *caribe* brave] **—Car′ib·an** *adj. & n.*

Car·ib·be·an (kar′ə·bē′ən, kə·rib′ē·ən) *adj.* 1. Of or pertaining to the Caribbean Sea. 2. Of or pertaining to the Caribs, their language or their culture.

car·i·bou (kar′ə·bo͞o) *n. pl.* **·bou** or **·bous** A North American reindeer. [< dial. F (Canadian) < Algonquian *khalibu* pawer]

car·i·ca·ture (kar′i·kə·cho͞or, -chər) *n.* 1. A picture or description in which features are exaggerated or distorted so as to produce an amusing or derisive effect. 2. The act or art of caricaturing. 3. A poor imitation. **—***v.t.* **·tured, ·tur·ing** To represent so as to make ridiculous; burlesque. [< Ital. *caricare* to load, exaggerate] **—car′i·ca·tur′ist** *n.*

car·ies (kâr′ēz) *n. Pathol.* Decay of a bone or of a tooth. [< L] **—car·i·ous** (kâr′ē·əs) *adj.*

car·il·lon (kar′ə·lon, kə·ril′yən) *n.* 1. A set of stationary bells rung by hammers operated from a keyboard or by a mechanism. 2. A melody rung on a carillon. **—***v.i.* **·lonned, ·lon·ning** To play a carillon. [< Med.L *quadrilio, -onis* set of four bells]

car·il·lon·neur (kar′ə·lə·nûr′) *n.* One who plays a carillon.

car·i·o·ca (kar′ē·ō′kə) *n.* 1. A type of South American dance, or the music for it. 2. *cap.* A native of Rio de Janeiro. Also **Car′i·o′can.**

[after Sierra de *Carioca,* a mountain range near Rio de Janeiro]

car·i·ole (kar′ē·ōl) *n.* 1. A small, open carriage. 2. A light cart. 3. *Canadian* A dog sled for one person lying down. [< F *carriole*]

car·load (kär′lōd′) *n.* The load carried in a car or freight car; also, the capacity of a car or freight car.

Car·mel·ite (kär′məl·īt) *n.* A monk or nun of the order of Our Lady of Mt. Carmel. **—Car′mel·ite** *adj.*

car·min·a·tive (kär·min′ə·tiv, kär′mə·nā′tiv) *adj. Med.* Tending to, or used to relieve flatulence. [< L *carminare* to cleanse] **—car·min′a·tive** *n.*

car·mine (kär′min, -mīn) *n.* 1. A deep red or purplish red color. 2. A crimson pigment obtained from cochineal; rouge. [< F *carmin*] **—car′mine** *adj.*

car·nage (kär′nij) *n.* Extensive and bloody slaughter, as in war; massacre. [< L *caro, carnis* flesh, meat]

car·nal (kär′nəl) *adj.* 1. Relating to bodily appetites; sensual. 2. Sexual. 3. Not spiritual; worldly. [< L *caro, carnis* flesh] **—car·nal·i·ty** (kär·nal′ə·tē) *n.* **—car′nal·ly** *adv.*

car·na·tion (kär·nā′shən) *n.* 1. The perennial flower of any of the varieties of the pink family. 2. A light pink, bright rose, or scarlet color. [< L *caro, carnis* flesh]

car·nel·ian (kär·nēl′yən) *n.* A clear red quartz, used as a gem. [< L *carnis* flesh]

car·ni·val (kär′nə·vəl) *n.* 1. A traveling amusement show, usu. presented outdoors. 2. Any gay festival. 3. A period of festivity immediately preceding Lent. [< L *carnis* flesh + *levare* to remove] **—car′ni·val·esque′** *adj.*

car·ni·vore (kär′nə·vôr) *n.* A flesh-eating mammal, as a cat, dog, etc.

car·niv·o·rous (kär·niv′ə·rəs) *adj.* 1. Eating or living on flesh. 2. Of or pertaining to carnivores. [< L *carnis* flesh + *vorare* to eat, devour] **—car·niv′o·rous·ly** *adv.* **—car·niv′o·rous·ness** *n.*

car·ol (kar′əl) *n.* A song of joy or praise; esp., a Christmas song. [< Gk. < *choros* a dance + *auleein* to play the flute] **—car′ol** *v.t. & v.i.* **·oled** or **·olled, ·ol·ing** or **·ol·ling —car′ol·er** or **car′ol·ler** *n.*

car·om (kar′əm) *n.* 1. In billiards, a shot in which the cue ball strikes against two other balls in succession. 2. Any impact followed by a rebound. [< F *carambole*] **—car′om** *v.t. & v.i.*

car·o·tene (kar′ə·tēn) *n. Biochem.* A deep yellow or red crystalline hydrocarbon found in carrots, etc., and changed in the body to vitamin A. [< L *carota* carrot]

ca·rot·id (kə·rot′id) *Anat. adj.* Of, pertaining to, or near one of the two major arteries on each side of the neck. **—***n.* A carotid artery. [< Gk. *karos* stupor]

ca·rou·sal (kə·rou′zəl) *n.* 1. A revel. 2. Boisterous merrymaking.

ca·rouse (kə·rouz′) *v.i.* **·roused, ·rous·ing** To drink freely and boisterously. **—***n.* A carousal. [< G *gar aus* (*trinken*) (to drink) all out] **—ca·rous′er** *n.*

car·ou·sel (kar′ə·sel′, -zel′) *n.* A merry-go-round (def. 1). [< Ital. *carosello*]

carp[1] (kärp) *v.i.* To find fault unreasonably. [< ON *karpa* to boast] **—carp′er** *n.* **—carp′·ing** *n. & adj.*

carp[2] (kärp) *n. pl.* **carp** or **carps** 1. A fresh-water food fish of Europe and America. 2. Any of various related fishes, as goldfish. [< LL *carpa*]

-carp *combining form* Fruit; fruit (or seed) vessel: *pericarp.* [< Gk. *karpos* fruit]

car·pal (kär′pəl) *adj. Anat.* Of, pertaining to, or near the wrist. [< Gk. *karpos* wrist]

car·pe di·em (kär′pē dē′em) *Latin* Enjoy the present; literally, seize the day.

car·pel (kär′pəl) *n. Bot.* A simple pistil or seed vessel. [< Gk. *karpos* fruit]

car·pen·ter (kär′pən·tər) *n.* A workman who builds and repairs wooden structures, as houses, ships, etc. [< L *carpentarius* carriage maker] **—car′pen·ter** *v.t. & v.i.* **—car′pen·try** *n.*

car·pet (kär′pit) *n.* 1. A heavy covering for floors; also, the fabric used for it. 2. A surface or covering suggesting this. Also **car′pet·ing.** **—on the carpet** Subjected to reproof or reprimand. [< L *carpere* to pluck, card wool] **—car′pet** *v.t.*

car·pet·bag (kär′pit·bag′) *n.* Formerly, a traveling bag made of carpeting. **—***v.i.* **·bagged, ·bag·ging** To act as a carpetbagger.

car·pet·bag·ger (kär′pit·bag′ər) *n.* One of the Northern adventurers who sought advantages in the South after the Civil War. **—car′pet·bag′ger·y** *n.*

carpet sweeper A hand-operated apparatus for sweeping carpets.

carpo- *combining form* Fruit. [< Gk. *karpos* fruit]

car·port (kär′pôrt′) *n.* A shelter for an automobile, usu. open on three sides.

-carpous *combining form* Having a certain kind or number of fruits. Also **-carpic.** [< Gk. *karpos* fruit]

car·pus (kär′pəs) *n. pl.* **·pi** (-pī) *Anat.* The wrist, or the wrist bones collectively. [< Gk. *karpos* wrist]

car·ra·geen (kar′ə·gēn) *n.* An edible seaweed known commercially as Irish moss. [after *Carragheen,* Ireland, where it grows]

car·rel (kar′əl) *n.* A small space, as among the stacks in a library, for solitary study. Also **car′rell.** [Var. of CAROL]

car·riage (kar′ij) *n.* 1. A wheeled, usu. horse-drawn vehicle for carrying persons. 2. Posture; bearing. 3. A moving portion of a machine carrying another part. 4. The act of carrying; transportation. [< L *carrus* cart]

carriage trade Wealthy patrons of a restaurant, theater, etc., so called because they formerly came in private carriages.

car·ried (kar′ēd) Past tense and past participle of CARRY.

car·ri·er (kar′ē·ər) *n.* 1. One who or that which carries. 2. A person or company that carries persons or goods for hire. 3. *Med.* A person who is immune to a disease but transmits it to others. [ME *carier* < L *carrus* cart]

carrier pigeon A homing pigeon.

carrier wave *Telecom.* A radio-frequency wave that is varied in some respect in order to transmit intelligence.

car·ri·on (kar′ē·ən) *n.* Dead and putrefying flesh. **—***adj.* 1. Feeding on carrion. 2. Like

or pertaining to carrion; putrefying. [< L *caro, carnis* flesh]
carrion crow The common crow of Europe.
car·rot (kar′ət) *n.* A long, reddish yellow root grown as a vegetable. [< Gk. *karōton* carrot]
car·rot·y (kar′ət·ē) *adj.* 1. Like a carrot, esp. in color. 2. Having red hair.
car·ry (kar′ē) *v.* **·ried, ·ry·ing** *v.t.* 1. To bear from one place to another; transport; convey. 2. To serve as a medium of conveyance for; transmit. 3. To have or bear upon or about one's person. 4. To bear the weight, burden, or responsibility of. 5. To be pregnant with. 6. To bear (the body, or a part of it) in a specified manner. 7. To conduct or comport (oneself). 8. To take by force or effort; capture; win. 9. To gain victory or acceptance for; also, to achieve success in. 10. To extend; continue. 11. To have or keep for sale. 12. To transfer, as a number or figure, to another column. 13. To maintain on one's account books for a future settlement. 14. To sing or play (a part or melody). —*v.i.* 15. To act as bearer or carrier. 16. To gain victory or acceptance: The motion *carried.* —**to carry away** To move the feelings greatly; enchant. —**to carry forward** In bookkeeping, to transfer (an item, etc.) to the next column or page. —**to carry off** 1. To cause to die. 2. To win, as a prize. 3. To succeed, as in a bluff. 4. To abduct. —**to carry on** 1. To keep up; continue. 2. To behave wildly or foolishly. 3. To engage in. —**to carry out** To accomplish; bring to completion. —**to carry through** To carry to completion or success. —*n. pl.* **·ries** 1. Range, as of a gun; also, the distance covered by a projectile, golf ball, etc. 2. A portage, as between streams. 3. The act of carrying. [< L *carrus* cart]
car·ry·all[1] (kar′ē·ôl′) *n.* A light, four-wheeled covered carriage having room for several people. [< F *carriole*]
car·ry·all[2] (kar′ē·ôl′) *n.* A large bag, handbag, etc.
carrying charge In installment buying, the interest charged on the unpaid balance.
car·ry-o·ver (kar′ē·ō′vər) *n.* 1. Something left over or kept until later. 2. In bookkeeping, a sum carried forward.
car·sick (kär′sik′) *adj.* Nauseated from riding in a car.
cart (kärt) *n.* 1. A two-wheeled vehicle, for carrying loads. 2. A light, two-wheeled vehicle with springs, used for business or pleasure. —*v.t.* To carry in or as in a cart. [< ON *kartr*] —**cart′er** *n.*
cart·age (kär′tij) *n.* The act of or charge for carting.
carte blanche (kärt′ blänsh′, *Fr.* kårt bläṅsh′) *pl.* **cartes blanches** (kärts′ blänsh′, *Fr.* kårt bläṅsh′) 1. A signed paper granting its possessor the freedom to write his own conditions. 2. Unrestricted authority. [< F, white card]
car·tel (kär·tel′, kär′təl) *n.* Two or more economic entities that exercise, or seek to exercise, monopolistic control over a particular market. [< Ital. *carta* paper]
Car·thu·sian (kär·thōō′zhən) *n.* A monk or nun of a contemplative order founded at Chartreuse in the French Alps by St. Bruno in 1084. [< Med.L *Carturissium* Chartreuse —**Car·thu′sian** *adj.*
car·ti·lage (kär′tə·lij) *n. Zool.* 1. A tough, elastic form of connective tissue in man and animals; gristle. 2. A part consisting of cartilage. [< L *cartilago* gristle]
car·ti·lag·i·nous (kär′tə·laj′ə·nəs) *adj.* 1. Of or like cartilage; gristly. 2. Having a gristly skeleton, as sharks.
car·tog·ra·phy (kär·tog′rə·fē) *n.* The art of making maps or charts. [< L *carta* map + -GRAPHY] —**car·tog′ra·pher** *n.* —**car·to·graph·ic** (kär′tə·graf′ik) or **·i·cal** *adj.*
car·ton (kär′tən) *n.* 1. A cardboard box. 2. A paper or plastic container. [< F, pasteboard]
car·toon (kär·tōōn′) *n.* 1. A humorous or satirical drawing or caricature. 2. A comic strip. 3. A motion-picture film (**animated cartoon**) made from a series of drawings. 4. A full-size sketch for a fresco, mosaic, etc. —*v.t. & v.i.* To make a caricature or cartoon of (a subject). [< L *charta* paper] —**car·toon′ist** *n.*
car·tridge (kär′trij) *n.* 1. A casing of metal, pasteboard, or the like, containing a charge of powder for a firearm and, usu., the projectile or shot and the primer. 2. Any small container or case. [< Ital. *cartoccio* < L *charta* paper]
cartridge clip A metal container holding cartridges for a rapid-fire gun.
cart·wheel (kärt′hwēl′) *n.* A sideways handspring.
carve (kärv) *v.t. & v.i.* **carved, carv·ing** 1. To make (a design, figure, etc.) by cutting, or as if by cutting. 2. To cut up (cooked meat). [OE *ceorfan*] —**carv′er** *n.*
carv·ing (kär′ving) *n.* 1. The act of one who carves. 2. Carved work; a carved figure or design.
car·y·at·id (kar′ē·at′id) *n. pl.* **·at·ids** or **·at·i·des** (-at′ə·dēz) *Archit.* A supporting column in the form of a sculptured female figure. [< Gk. *Karyatis* a Greek priestess]
ca·sa·ba (kə·sä′bə) *n.* A winter muskmelon with sweet white flesh and yellow rind. Also **casaba melon.** [after *Kasaba*, a town in western Turkey]
cas·cade (kas·kād′) *n.* 1. A fall of water over steep rocks, or one of a series of such falls. 2. Anything resembling a waterfall. —*v.i.* **·cad·ed, ·cad·ing** To fall in the form of a waterfall. [< L *cadere* to fall]
cas·car·a (kas·kâr′ə) *n.* A buckthorn of the NW United States, yielding cascara sagrada. Also **cascara buckthorn.** [< Sp. *cáscara* bark]
cascara sa·gra·da (sə·grā′də) A laxative made from dried cascara bark.
case[1] (kās) *n.* 1. A particular instance or occurrence: a *case* of mistaken identity. 2. The actual circumstance or state of affairs: Such is not the *case.* 3. An instance of disease or injury; also, a patient. 4. A set of arguments, reasons, etc.: the *case* for capital punishment. 5. A question or problem. 6. *Law* **a** An action or suit at law. **b** The set of facts offered in support of a claim. 7. *Gram.* The syntactical relationship of a noun, pronoun, or adjective to other words in a sentence. —**in any case** No matter what; regardless. —**in case** In the event that; if. —*v.t.* **cased, cas·ing** *Slang* To look over carefully, esp. with intent to rob. [< L *casus* event]
case[2] (kās) *n.* 1. A box, sheath, bag, etc., for

containing something. 2. A box and its contents. 3. A set or pair. 4. An outer or protective part, as of a watch. —*v.t.* **cased, cas·ing** To put into or cover with a case. [< L *capsa* box]

ca·se·fy (kā′sə·fī) *v.t. & v.i.* **·fied, ·fy·ing** To make or become like cheese. [< L *caseus* cheese + -FY] —**ca·se·ous** (kā′sē·əs) *adj.*

case·hard·en (kās′här′dən) *v.t.* 1. *Metall.* To harden the surface of (steel). 2. To make callous, esp. in feelings.

case history A record of a case or cases for use in medical, sociological, or similar studies. Also **case study.**

ca·se·in (kā′sē·in, -sēn) *n. Biochem.* A protein found esp. in milk and constituting the principal ingredient in cheese. [< L *caseus* cheese]

case law Law based on judicial decisions: distinguished from *common law* or *statute law.*

case·ment (kās′mənt) *n.* 1. The sash of a window that opens on hinges at the side, or a window having such sashes. 2. A case; covering. —**case′ment·ed** *adj.*

case·work (kās′wûrk′) *n.* The investigative and counseling tasks of a social worker or the like. —**case′work′er** *n.*

cash (kash) *n.* 1. Current money in hand or readily available. 2. Currency; bills and coins. —*v.t.* To convert into ready money, as a check. —**to cash in** In gambling, to turn in one's chips and receive cash. —**to cash in on** *Informal* To make a profit from or turn to advantage. [< MF *casse* money box < L *capsa* box] —**cash′a·ble** *adj.*

cash-and-car·ry (kash′ən·kar′ē) *adj.* Operated on a system of cash purchase and no delivery.

cash·book (kash′bo͝ok′) *n.* A book in which a record is kept of money taken in and paid out.

cash·ew (kash′o͞o, kə·sho͞o′) *n.* 1. A tropical American tree of the sumac family that yields a gum. 2. Its small, edible fruit: also **cashew nut.** [< Tupi *acajoba*]

cash flow accounting A measure of the worth of a business at a given point, being the net income plus bookkeeping deductions requiring no cash outlay, and usu. expressed in dollars per share of common stock.

cash·ier[1] (ka·shir′) *n.* 1. One employed to collect cash payments. 2. A bank officer responsible for the bank's assets. [See CASH.]

cash·ier[2] (ka·shir′) *v.t.* To dismiss in disgrace, as a military officer. [< LL *cassare* to annul and L *quassare* to destroy]

cash·mere (kash′mir, kazh′-) *n.* 1. A fine wool obtained from goats of India and Tibet. 2. A soft fabric made from this. [after *Kashmir,* India]

cash register A device usu. with a money drawer, that records, adds, and displays the amount of cash received.

cas·ing (kā′sing) *n.* 1. A protective case or covering. 2. A framework, as about a door.

ca·si·no (kə·sē′nō) *n. pl.* **·nos** 1. A place for dancing, gambling, etc. 2. Cassino. [< Ital., dim. of *casa* house]

cask (kask) *n.* 1. A barrel-shaped wooden vessel, bound with hoops. 2. The quantity a cask will hold. [< Sp. *casco* skull, potsherd, cask < L *quassare* to break]

cas·ket (kas′kit) *n.* 1. A coffin. 2. A small box or chest. [Orig. uncertain]

casque (kask) *n.* A helmet. [< F. Related to CASK.] —**casqued** *adj.*

Cas·san·dra (kə·san′drə) *n.* One whose predictions of disaster are disregarded. [after *Cassandra,* of Greek mythology, whose prophecies were fated by Apollo to be true but not believed]

cas·sa·va (kə·sä′və) *n.* 1. A tropical American shrub or herb, cultivated for the edible roots. 2. A starch made from these roots, the source of tapioca. [< Taino *casavi*]

cas·se·role (kas′ə·rōl) *n.* 1. A dish in which food is baked and served. 2. Any food so prepared and served. [< F]

cas·sette (kə·set′) *n.* A container of photographic film or magnetic sound tape wound on internal spools. Also **cas·ette′.** [< F, lit., small box]

cas·sia (kash′ə, kas′ē·ə) *n.* 1. A variety of cinnamon obtained from the bark of a tree native to China. 2. The tree itself. 3. Any tropical plant whose dried pods (**cassia pods**) yield a mild laxative. [< Hebrew *qātsa* to strip off bark]

cas·si·no (kə·sē′nō) *n.* A card game for two to four players.

Cas·si·o·pe·ia (kas′ē·ə·pē′ə) *n.* A constellation: also **Cassiopeia's Chair.**

cas·sock (kas′ək) *n. Eccl.* A close-fitting vestment, usu. black, reaching to the feet, and worn by clergymen. [< Ital. *casacca* greatcoat]

cas·so·war·y (kas′ə·wer′ē) *n. pl.* **·war·ies** A large, three-toed, flightless bird of Australia and New Guinea. [< Malay *kasuārī*]

cast (kast) *v.* **cast, cast·ing** *v.t.* 1. To throw or hurl with force; fling. 2. To cause to fall upon or over or in a particular direction: to *cast* a shadow. 3. To direct, as a glance of the eyes. 4. To let down; drop: to *cast* anchor. 5. To throw off; lose; also, to shed; molt. 6. To throw aside; reject or dismiss. 7. To deposit; give: He *cast* his vote. 8. To throw, as dice. 9. In the theater, movies, etc., to assign the parts of or a part in a play to (an actor). 10. To compute astrologically: to *cast* a horoscope. 11. To arrange by some system. 12. *Metall.* To shape in a mold. —*v.i.* 13. To make a throw, as with dice, a fishing line, etc. 14. To make arithmetical calculations; add. 15. *Metall.* To take shape in a mold. —**to cast about** To consider ways and means; scheme. —**to cast away** 1. To discard. 2. To shipwreck or maroon. —**to cast off** 1. To reject or discard. 2. To let go, as a ship from a dock. —*n.* 1. The act of casting or throwing; a throw. 2. The distance to which a thing may be thrown. 3. *Surg.* A rigid dressing or bandage to prevent the movement of fractured bones. 4. The performers in a play, movie, etc. 5. The act of casting or founding. 6. An impression made of anything; a mold. 7. A tinge; shade. 8. A twist to one side; squint. [< ON *kasta* to throw]

cas·ta·nets (kas′tə·nets′) *n.pl.* Two small concave disks of wood or ivory, clapped together with the fingers, as a rhythmical accompaniment to song or dance. [< Sp. < L *castanea* chestnut]

cast·a·way (kast′ə·wā′) *adj.* 1. Adrift; shipwrecked. 2. Thrown away. —*n.* One who is shipwrecked.

caste (kast) *n.* 1. In India, one of the hereditary social classes into which Hindus were traditionally divided. 2. Any rigid social class. [< L *castus* pure]

cas·tel·lat·ed (kas′tə·lā′tid) *adj.* Having battlements and turrets. [< L *castellum* castle] —**cas′tel·la′tion** *n.*

cast·er (kas′tər) *n.* 1. One who or that which casts. 2. One of a set of small, swiveling wheels or rollers, fastened under furniture, luggage, etc. to facilitate moving. 3. A cruet for condiments; also, a stand for such cruets. Also (for defs. 2 and 3) *castor.*

cas·ti·gate (kas′tə·gāt) *v.t.* **·gat·ed, ·gat·ing** To rebuke or chastise severely; criticize. [< L *castigare* to chasten] —**cas′ti·ga′tion** *n.* —**cas′ti·ga′tive** *adj.* —**cas′ti·ga′tor** *n.*

Cas·til·ian (kas·til′yən) *n.* 1. A native or citizen of Castile. 2. The standard form of Spanish as spoken in Spain, originally the dialect of Castile. —**Cas·til′ian** *adj.*

cast·ing (kas′ting) *n.* 1. The act of one who or that which casts. 2. That which is cast or formed in a mold.

cast iron A hard, nonmalleable alloy of iron, carbon, and other elements. —**cast-i·ron** (kast′ī′ərn) *adj.*

cas·tle (kas′əl) *n.* 1. In feudal times, the fortified dwelling of a prince or noble. 2. Any large, imposing house. 3. In chess, a rook. —*v.t. & v.i.* **·tled, ·tling** In chess, to move a rook to the square passed over by the king. [< L *castrum* camp, fort]

cast·off (kast′ôf′, -of′) *adj.* Thrown or laid aside. —*n.* One who or that which is no longer wanted or used.

cas·tor[1] (kas′tər) *n.* 1. An oily, odorous secretion of beavers, used in medicine and perfumery. 2. A hat of beaver or other fur. [< Gk. *kastōr* beaver]

cas·tor[2] (kas′tər) See CASTER (defs. 2 and 3).

castor bean The seed of the castor-oil plant.

castor oil A viscid oil extracted from castor beans and used as a cathartic and lubricant.

cas·tor-oil plant (kas′tər·oil′) A plant native to India, yielding the castor bean.

cas·trate (kas′trāt) *v.t.* **·trat·ed, ·trat·ing** 1. To remove the testicles from; emasculate; geld. 2. To remove the ovaries from; spay. [< L *castrare*] —**cas′trat·er** *n.* —**cas·tra′tion** *n.*

cas·u·al (kazh′o͞o·əl) *adj.* 1. Occurring by chance; accidental. 2. Without intention or plan; offhand: a *casual* question. 3. Negligent; nonchalant: a *casual* manner. 4. Designed for informal wear: *casual* clothes. [< L *casus* accident < *cadere* to fall] —**cas′u·al·ly** *adv.* —**cas′u·al·ness** *n.*

cas·u·al·ty (kazh′o͞o·əl·tē) *n. pl.* **·ties** 1. One who or that which is destroyed, injured, or otherwise made ineffective by an accident. 2. *Mil.* A soldier who is killed, wounded, captured, or otherwise lost to his command through combat action. 3. An accident, esp. a fatal or serious one.

cas·u·ist·ry (kazh′o͞o·is·trē) *n. pl.* **·ries** 1. A method of dealing with ambiguous cases of conscience or questions of right and wrong. 2. Deceptive or ambiguous reasoning, esp. in cases of conscience. [< L *casus* event, case] —**cas′u·ist** *n.* —**cas′u·is′tic** or **·ti·cal** *adj.*

ca·sus bel·li (kā′səs bel′ī) *Latin* A cause justifying war.

cat (kat) *n.* 1. A domesticated carnivorous mammal having retractile claws. 2. Any other animal of the cat family, as a lion, tiger, lynx, ocelot, etc. ◆Collateral adjective: *feline.* 3. A gossiping or backbiting woman. 4. *Slang* A man; guy. —**to let the cat out of the bag** To divulge a secret. —*v.t.* **cat·ted, cat·ting** To strike with a cat-o'-nine-tails; flog. [OE *cat, catte*] —**cat′like** *adj.*

cata- *prefix* 1. Down; against; upon. 2. Back; over. Also, before vowels, **cat-**: also **cath-**. Also spelled *kata-*. [< Gk. *kata* down, against, back]

ca·tab·o·lism (kə·tab′ə·liz′əm) *n. Biol.* The process by which living tissue breaks down into simpler and more stable substances; destructive metabolism: opposed to *anabolism.* [< Gk. *kata-* down + *ballein* to throw] —**cat·a·bol·ic** (kat′ə·bol′ik) *adj.* —**cat′a·bol′i·cal·ly** *adv.*

cat·a·clysm (kat′ə·kliz′əm) *n.* 1. Any violent upheaval or change, as a war, revolution, etc. 2. A deluge. [< Gk. *kata-* down + *klyzein* to wash] —**cat′a·clys′mic** *adj.*

cat·a·comb (kat′ə·kōm) *n. Usu. pl.* An underground place of burial, consisting of passages, small rooms, and recesses for tombs. [< LL *catacumbas*]

cat·a·falque (kat′ə·falk) *n.* A structure supporting a coffin during a funeral. [< Ital. *catafalco*]

Cat·a·lan (kat′ə·lan, -lən) *n.* 1. A native or citizen of Catalonia. 2. The Romance language of Catalonia and Valencia. —**Cat′a·lan** *adj.*

cat·a·lep·sy (kat′ə·lep′sē) *n. Psychiatry* Abnormal, intense muscular rigidity. [< Gk. *kata-* upon + *lēpsis* seizure] —**cat′a·lep′tic** *adj. & n.*

cat·a·log (kat′ə·lôg, -log) *n.* 1. A list or enumeration of names, objects, etc., usu. in alphabetical order. 2. A publication containing such a list, as of articles for sale. —*v.t. & v.i.* **·loged, ·log·ing** To make a catalog (of); enter (items) in a catalog. Also **cat′a·logue.** [< Gk. *kata-* down + *legein* to select, choose] —**cat′a·log′er, cat′a·log′ist** *n.*

ca·tal·pa (kə·tal′pə) *n.* A tree of China, Japan, and North America, having fragrant flowers and long, slender pods. [< N. Am. Ind.]

ca·tal·y·sis (kə·tal′ə·sis) *n. pl.* **·ses** (-sēz) *Chem.* An increase in the rate of a chemical reaction, caused by the addition of a substance that remains unchanged. [< Gk. *kata-* wholly, completely + *lyein* to loosen] —**cat·a·lyt·ic** (kat′ə·lit′ik) *adj. & n.* —**cat′a·lyt′i·cal·ly** *adv.*

cat·a·lyst (kat′ə·list) *n.* 1. *Chem.* Any substance that causes catalysis: also **cat·a·lyz·er** (kat′ə·līz·ər). 2. One who or that which acts as a stimulus causing something to happen. —**cat·a·lyze** (kat′ə·līz) *v.t.* **·lyzed, ·lyz·ing**

cat·a·ma·ran (kat′ə·mə·ran′) *n. Naut.* 1. A long, narrow raft of logs, often with an outrigger. 2. A boat having twin hulls. [< Tamil *kattamaran* tied wood]

cat·a·mount (kat′ə·mount) *n.* The puma; also, the lynx. [Short form of *cat of the mountain*]

cat·a·pult (kat′ə·pult) *n.* 1. An ancient military device for throwing stones, arrows, etc. 2. *Aeron.* A device for launching an airplane at flight speed, as from the deck of a ship. —*v.t.* 1. To hurl from or as from a catapult. —*v.i.* 2. To hurtle through the air. [< Gk. *kata-* down + *pallein* to brandish, hurl]

cat·a·ract (kat′ə·rakt) *n.* 1. A waterfall. 2. A downpour. 3. *Pathol.* Opacity of the lens of the eye, causing partial or total blindness. [< MF *cataracte* < Gk. *kata-* down + *arassein* to fall headlong]

ca·tarrh (kə·tär′) *n. Pathol.* Inflammation of the mucous membrane of the air passages in the throat and head, with excessive secretion of mucus. [< Gk. *kata-* down + *rheein* to flow] —**ca·tarrh′al** *adj.*

ca·tas·tro·phe (kə·tas′trə·fē) *n.* A great and sudden disaster; calamity. [< Gk. *kata-* over, down + *strephein* to turn] —**cat·a·stroph·ic** (kat′ə·strof′ik) *adj.* —**cat′a·stroph′i·cal·ly** *adv.*

Ca·taw·ba (kə·tô′bə) *n.* An American red grape; also, a wine made from it.

cat·bird (kat′bûrd′) *n.* A small, slate-colored North American songbird, having a catlike cry.

cat·boat (kat′bōt′) *n. Naut.* A small sailboat carrying a single fore-and-aft sail.

cat·call (kat′kôl′) *n.* A shrill, discordant call or whistle expressing impatience or derision. —*v.t. & v.i.* To deride or show contempt for (a person, performance, etc.) with catcalls.

catch (kach) *v.* **caught, catch·ing** *v.t.* 1. To take or seize, and hold; grasp; grip. 2. To trap; capture; ensnare. 3. To surprise in the act. 4. To stop the motion of and grasp; grab in midflight. 5. To grip; entangle. 6. To gather and retain: to *catch* rain water in a barrel. 7. To overtake. 8. To reach in time: to *catch* a train. 9. To strike. 10. To become affected with: to *catch* cold. 11. To take; get: to *catch* fire. 12. To apprehend or perceive; also, to reproduce accurately: The artist has not *caught* her expression. 13. *Informal* To see (a motion picture, television program, etc.). —*v.i.* 14. To make a movement of grasping or seizing. 15. In baseball, to act as catcher. 16. To become entangled or fastened. 17. To be communicated or communicable, as a disease. 18. To take fire; ignite. —**to catch on** *Informal* 1. To understand. 2. To become popular or fashionable. —**to catch up** 1. To regain lost ground. 2. To discover in error. 3. To absorb: *caught up* in one's work. —**to catch up with** (or **up to**) To overtake. —*n.* 1. The act of catching; a grasping and holding. 2. That which catches; a fastening. 3. That which is caught. 4. *Informal* An artful or hidden condition; trick: What's the *catch*? 5. A scrap or fragment: *catches* of song. 6. A stoppage; break, as in the voice. —*adj.* 1. Attracting or meant to attract attention: a *catch* phrase. 2. Tricky. [< L *capere* to take, hold]

catch·all (kach′ôl′) *n.* 1. A bag or the like to hold odds and ends. 2. Anything that covers a wide range of situations, etc.

catch·er (kach′ər) *n.* 1. One who or that which catches. 2. In baseball, the player stationed behind home plate.

catch·ing (kach′ing) *adj.* 1. Infectious. 2. Attractive; catchy.

catch·pen·ny (kach′pen′ē) *adj.* Designed merely to sell; cheap and showy. —*n. pl.* **·nies** A catchpenny article.

catch·up (kach′əp, kech′-) See KETCHUP.

catch·word (kach′wûrd′) *n.* 1. A word or phrase taken up and often repeated, esp. as a political slogan. Also **catch phrase.** 2. A word at the head of a page or column, identifying the first or last item on the page.

catch·y (kach′ē) *adj.* **catch·i·er, catch·i·est** 1. Attractive; also, easily remembered: *catchy* tunes. 2. Deceptive; tricky. —**catch′i·ness** *n.*

cat·e·chism (kat′ə·kiz′əm) *n.* 1. A short manual giving, in the form of questions and answers, an outline of the principles of a religious creed. 2. Any similar instructional manual. [< Gk. *katēchizein* to instruct]

cat·e·chize (kat′ə·kīz) *v.t.* **·chized, ·chiz·ing** To instruct, esp. in the principles of Christianity, by asking questions and discussing the answers. [< Gk. *katēchizein* to instruct] —**cat′e·chist** (-kist) *n.* —**cat′e·chis′tic** (-kis′tik) or **·ti·cal** *adj.*

cat·e·chu·men (kat′ə·kyo͞o′mən) *n.* One who is under instruction in the elements of Christianity.

cat·e·gor·i·cal (kat′ə·gôr′i·kəl, -gor′-) *adj.* 1. Without qualification; absolute; unequivocal. 2. Of, pertaining to, or included in a category. —**cat′e·gor′i·cal·ly** *adv.*

cat·e·go·rize (kat′ə·gə·rīz′) *v.t.* **·rized, ·riz·ing** To put into a category; classify. —**cat′e·go·ri·za′tion** *n.*

cat·e·go·ry (kat′ə·gôr′ē) *n. pl.* **·ries** A division in any system of classification; a class. [< Gk. *katēgoreein* to allege, predicate]

cat·e·nate (kat′ə·nāt) *v.t.* **·nat·ed, ·nat·ing** To connect like the links of a chain. [< L *catena* chain] —**cat′e·na′tion** *n.*

ca·ter (kā′tər) *v.i.* 1. To furnish food or entertainment. 2. To provide for the gratification of any need or taste. —*v.t.* 3. To furnish food for: to *cater* a party. [< L *ad-* toward + *captare* to grasp, seize] —**ca′ter·er** *n.*

cat·er-cor·nered (kat′ər·kôr′nərd) *adj.* Diagonal. —*adv.* Diagonally. Also *catty-cornered.* Also **cat′er-cor′ner.** [< L *quattuor* four + CORNERED]

cat·er·pil·lar (kat′ər·pil′ər) *n.* The larva of a butterfly or moth, or of certain other insects, resembling a worm. —*adj.* Moving or fitted with treads mounted on endless belts. [< L *catta* cat + *pilosus* < *pilum* hair]

Cat·er·pil·lar (kat′ər·pil′ər) *n.* A tractor that moves by means of two endless metal tracks running along each side: a trade name.

cat·er·waul (kat′ər·wôl) *v.i.* 1. To utter the discordant cry of cats at mating time. 2. To make any discordant screeching. [ME < *cater* cat + *wawen* to wail, howl] —**cat′er·waul** *n.*

cat·fish (kat′fish′) *n. pl.* **·fish** or **·fish·es** Any of numerous scaleless fishes having whiskerlike feelers around the mouth.

cat·gut (kat′gut′) *n.* A tough cord made usu. from the intestines of sheep.

ca·thar·sis (kə·thär′sis) *n.* 1. *Med.* Purgation, esp. of the alimentary canal. 2. A purifying or purging of the emotions. [< Gk. *katharos* pure]

ca·thar·tic (kə·thär′tik) *adj.* Purgative; purifying. Also **ca·thar′ti·cal.** —*n.* A laxative. [< Gk. *katharos* pure]

ca·the·dral (kə·thē′drəl) *n.* 1. The church

containing the official chair of a bishop. 2. Loosely, any large or important church.

cath·e·ter (kath′ə·tər) *n. Med.* A slender, flexible tube, esp. one to draw urine from the bladder. [< Gk. *kata-* down + *hienai* to send, let go] **—cath′e·ter·ize** *v.t.* **·ized, ·iz·ing**

cath·ode (kath′ōd) *n. Electr.* The negatively charged electrode that receives cations during electrolysis. [< Gk. *kata-* down + *hodos* road, way]

cathode rays *Physics* A stream of electrons emitted by a cathode.

cathode-ray tube *Electr.* An electron tube in which a beam of electrons is focused and then deflected onto a sensitized screen, forming an image, as in a television receiver.

cath·o·lic (kath′ə·lik, kath′lik) *adj.* 1. Broad-minded, as in belief or tastes; liberal; comprehensive; large. 2. Universal in reach; general. [< Gk. *kata-* thoroughly + *holos* whole] **—ca·thol·i·cal·ly** (kə·thol′ik·lē) *adv.* **—cath·o·lic·i·ty** (kath′ə·lis′ə·tē) *n.*

Cath·o·lic (kath′ə·lik, kath′lik) *adj.* Since the Reformation: **a** Of or pertaining to the Roman Catholic Church. **b** Designating those churches that claim to have the apostolic doctrine and sacraments of the ancient, undivided church, and including the Anglican, Old Catholic, Orthodox, and Roman Catholic churches. **—***n.* A member of any Catholic church.

Ca·thol·i·cism (kə·thol′ə·siz′əm) *n.* The doctrine, system, and practice of a Catholic church, esp. the Roman Catholic Church. Also **Cath·o·lic·i·ty** (kath′ə·lis′ə·tē).

ca·thol·i·cize (kə·thol′ə·sīz) *v.t. & v.i.* **·cized, ·ciz·ing** To make or become catholic or Catholic.

cat·i·on (kat′ī·ən) *n. Chem.* A positive ion: opposed to *anion.* [< Gk. *kata-* down + *ienai* to go] **—cat′i·on′ic** (-ī·on′ik) *adj.*

cat·kin (kat′kin) *n. Bot.* A deciduous, scaly spike of flowers, as in the willow. [< MDu. *katteken,* dim. of *katte* cat]

cat·nap (kat′nap′) *n.* A short, light nap. **—cat′nap′** *v.i.* **·napped, ·nap·ping**

cat·nip (kat′nip′) *n.* An aromatic herb of the mint family, of which cats are fond. [< CAT + dial. E *nep* catnip]

cat-o′-nine-tails (kat′ə·nīn′tālz′) *n.* A whip with nine knotted lines fastened to a handle.

cat's cradle A game played with a loop of string stretched over the fingers.

cat's-eye (kats′ī′) *n.* A gemstone showing reflections of light.

cat's-paw (kats′pô′) *n.* A person used as a tool or dupe. Also **cats′paw′.**

cat·sup (kat′səp, kech′əp) See KETCHUP.

cat·tail (kat′tāl′) *n.* A marsh plant having flowers in cylindrical terminal spikes.

cat·tle (kat′l) *n.* Domesticated bovine animals, as cows, bulls, and steers. [< L *capitale* capital, wealth]

cat·tle·man (kat′l·mən) *n. pl.* **·men** (-mən) One who raises or tends cattle.

cat·ty (kat′ē) *adj.* **·ti·er, ·ti·est** 1. Like or pertaining to cats. 2. Slyly malicious; spiteful. **—cat′ti·ly** *adv.* **—cat′ti·ness** *n.*

cat·ty-cor·nered (kat′ē·kôr′nərd) *adj.* Cater-cornered.

cat·walk (kat′wôk′) *n.* Any narrow walking space, as at the side of a bridge.

Cau·ca·sian (kô·kā′zhən, -shən) *adj.* 1. Of or pertaining to the Caucasus region, its people, and their languages. 2. Of or belonging to a major ethnic division of the human species loosely called the white race. **—***n.* 1. A native of the Caucasus region. 2. A member of the Caucasian division of the human race. Also **Cau·ca·soid** (kô′kə·soid′, -zoid′).

cau·cus (kô′kəs) *n.* A meeting of members of a political party. **—***v.i.* **cau·cused** or **·cussed, cau·cus·ing** or **·cus·sing** To meet in or hold a caucus. [after the 18th c. *Caucus* Club, Boston, Mass.]

cau·dal (kôd′l) *adj. Zool.* Of, pertaining to, or near the tail or posterior part of the body. [< L *cauda* tail] **—cau′dal·ly** *adv.*

cau·date (kô′dāt) *adj. Zool.* Having a tail or taillike appendage. Also **cau′dat·ed.** [< L *caudatus* < *cauda* tail]

caught (kôt, kot) Past tense and past participle of CATCH.

caul (kôl) *n.* A membrane that sometimes envelops the head of a child at birth. [< OF *cale* cap]

caul·dron (kôl′drən) *n.* A large kettle: also spelled *caldron.* [< L *calidus* hot]

cau·li·flow·er (kô′lə·flou′ər, kol′i-) *n.* 1. The fleshy, edible head of a variety of cabbage. 2. The plant bearing this. [< NL *cauliflora*]

cauliflower ear An ear deformed by blows.

caulk (kôk) *v.t.* To make tight, as a boat's seams, window frame, etc., by plugging with soft material, such as oakum or tar. Also spelled *calk.* [< L *calcare* to tread] **—caulk′er** *n.* **—caulk′ing** *n.*

cau·sal (kô′zəl) *adj.* Pertaining to or involving a cause. **—***n. Gram.* A form expressing cause or reason, as *therefore.* [< L *causa* cause] **—caus′al·ly** *adv.*

cau·sal·i·ty (kô·zal′ə·tē) *n. pl.* **·ties** 1. The relation of cause and effect. 2. Causal character or agency.

cau·sa·tion (kô·zā′shən) *n.* 1. The act of causing. 2. That which produces an effect; cause. 3. The relation of cause and effect. [< L *causa* cause]

caus·a·tive (kô′zə·tiv) *adj.* 1. Effective as a cause. 2. *Gram.* Expressing cause or agency. **—***n. Gram.* A form that expresses or suggests causation. [< L *causa* cause] **—caus′a·tive·ly** *adv.* **—caus′a·tive·ness** *n.*

cause (kôz) *n.* 1. The agent or force producing an effect or a result. 2. Sufficient ground; good reason. 3. An aim, object, or principle. 4. A matter under discussion or in dispute. **—***v.t.* **caused, caus·ing** To be the cause of; produce; effect. [< L *causa* cause, legal case] **—caus′er** *n.*

cause cé·lè·bre (kōz sā·leb′r′) *French* 1. A famous legal case. 2. Any well-known controversy.

cau·se·rie (kō′zə·rē′, *Fr.* kōz·rē′) *n.* 1. An informal conversation; a chat. 2. A short, chatty piece of writing. [< F]

cause·way (kôz′wā′) *n.* A raised road or way, as over marshy ground. [Earlier *causeyway* < L *calx, calcis* heel + WAY]

caus·tic (kôs′tik) *adj.* 1. Corrosive; burning, as acid or lye. 2. Sarcastic; biting. **—***n.* A caustic substance. [< Gk. *kaiein* to burn] **—caus′ti·cal·ly** *adv.* **—caus·tic·i·ty** (kôs·tis′ə·tē) *n.*

caustic soda Sodium hydroxide.

cau·ter·ize (kô′tə·rīz) *v.t.* **·ized, ·iz·ing** To

sear with a caustic agent or heated iron. **—cau′ter·i·za′tion** *n.*

cau·ter·y (kô′tər·ē) *n. pl.* **·ter·ies** *Med.* 1. The act of cauterizing. 2. A cauterizing agent. [< Gk. *kauterion* < *kaiein* to burn]

cau·tion (kô′shən) *n.* 1. Care to avoid injury or misfortune; prudence; wariness; discretion. 2. An admonition or warning. 3. *Informal* One who or that which alarms, astonishes, etc. **—***v.t.* To advise to be prudent; warn. [< L *cautio, -onis* < *cavere* to beware]

cau·tion·ar·y (kô′shən·er′ē) *adj.* Urging caution.

cau·tious (kô′shəs) *adj.* Using great care or prudence; wary. **—cau′tious·ly** *adv.* **—cau′·tious·ness** *n.*

cav·al·cade (kav′əl·kād′, kav′əl·kād) *n.* 1. A company of horsemen on the march or in procession. 2. A procession; parade. [< L *caballus* horse]

cav·a·lier (kav′ə·lir′) *n.* 1. A horseman; knight. 2. A courtly or dashing gentleman; also, a lady's escort. **—***adj.* 1. Haughty; supercilious. 2. Free and easy; offhand. [< L *caballus* horse] **—cav′a·lier′ly** *adj. & adv.*

Cav·a·lier (kav′ə·lir′) *n.* A supporter of Charles I of England; a Royalist. **—Cav′a·lier′** *adj.*

cav·al·ry (kav′əl·rē) *n. pl.* **·ries** Troops trained to fight on horseback or, more recently, in armored motor vehicles. [< L *caballus* horse] **—cav′al·ry·man** (-mən) *n.*

cave (kāv) *n.* A chamber beneath the earth, in a mountain or mountainside, etc. ◆Collateral adjective: *spelean.* **—to cave in** 1. To fall in or down, as when undermined; cause to fall in. 2. *Informal* To yield utterly; give in. [< L *cavus* hollow]

ca·ve·at (kā′vē·at) *n.* A caution or warning. [< L, let him beware]

ca·ve·at emp·tor (kā′vē·at emp′tôr) *Latin* Let the buyer beware.

cave-in (kāv′in′) *n.* A collapse or falling in, as of a mine.

cave man A prehistoric cave dweller.

cav·ern (kav′ərn) *n.* A cave, esp. one that is large or extensive. [< L *cavus* hollow] **—cav′er·nous** *adj.* **—cav′ern·ous·ly** *adv.*

cav·i·ar (kav′ē·är, kä′vē-) *n.* The salted roe of sturgeon or other fish. Also **cav′i·are.** [< Turkish *khāvyār*]

cav·il (kav′əl) *v.i.* **·iled** or **·illed, ·il·ing** or **·il·ling** To raise trivial objections; carp: with *at* or *about.* [< L *cavilla* a jeering] **—cav′il** *n.* **—cav′il·er** or **cav′il·ler** *n.* **—cav′il·ing·ly** or **cav′il·ling·ly** *adv.*

cav·i·ty (kav′ə·tē) *n. pl.* **·ties** 1. A hollow or sunken space; hole. 2. A natural hollow in the body. 3. A decayed place in a tooth. [< L *cavus* hollow]

ca·vort (kə·vôrt′) *v.i.* To prance about.

caw (kô) *v.i.* To make the high harsh sound of a crow, rook, etc. [Imit.] **—caw** *n.*

cay (kā, kē) *n.* A coastal reef or sandy islet. See KEY[2]. [< Sp. *cayo* shoal]

cay·enne pepper (kī·en′, kā-) Red pepper.

cay·man (kā′mən) See CAIMAN.

Ca·yu·ga (kā·yōō′gə, kī-) *n. pl.* **·ga** or **·gas** One of a tribe of Iroquois Indians formerly living near Cayuga Lake, N.Y.

cay·use (kī·yōōs′) *n.* An Indian pony of the western U.S.

cease (sēs) *v.* **ceased, ceas·ing** *v.t.* 1. To leave off or discontinue, as one's own actions. **—***v.i.* 2. To come to an end; stop; desist. [< L *cedere* to withdraw, yield] **—cease′less** *adj.* **—cease′less·ly** *adv.*

cease-fire (sēs′fīr′) *n.* An armistice; truce.

ce·cum (sē′kəm) *n. pl.* **ce·ca** (sē′kə) *Anat.* A pouch, or cavity, open at one end, esp. that situated between the large and small intestine: also spelled *caecum.* [< L *caecus* blind] **—ce′cal** *adj.*

ce·dar (sē′dər) *n.* 1. A large tree of the pine family, having fragrant wood. 2. The red cedar. 3. The wood of these and related trees. [< Gk. *kedros*] **—ce′dar** *adj.*

cede (sēd) *v.t.* **ced·ed, ced·ing** 1. To yield or give up. 2. To surrender title to; transfer: to *cede* land. [< L *cedere* to withdraw, yield]

ce·di (sē′dē) *n.* The monetary unit of Ghana.

ce·dil·la (si·dil′ə) *n.* A mark put under the letter *c* (ç) in some French words to indicate that it is to be sounded as (s). [< Sp.]

ceil·ing (sē′ling) *n.* 1. The overhead covering or lining of a room. 2. An upper limit; maximum.

cel·an·dine (sel′ən·dīn) *n.* 1. A plant of the poppy family, with yellow flowers. 2. A crowfoot having tuberous roots and yellow flowers. [< Gk. *chelidōn* a swallow]

-cele *combining form* Tumor or hernia. [< Gk. *kēlē* tumor]

cel·e·brate (sel′ə·brāt) *v.* **·brat·ed, ·brat·ing** *v.t.* 1. To observe, as a festival, with rejoicing. 2. To make known or famous; extol. 3. To perform (a ceremony) publicly and as ordained. **—***v.i.* 4. To observe or commemorate a day or event. [< L *celeber* famous] **—cel′e·brant** (-brənt) *n.* **—cel′e·bra′tion** *n.* **—cel·e·bra·to·ry** (sel′ə·brə·tôr′ē, sə·leb′rə-) *adj.*

cel·e·brat·ed (sel′ə·brā′tid) *adj.* Well-known; much publicized.

ce·leb·ri·ty (sə·leb′rə·tē) *n. pl.* **·ties** 1. A famous or celebrated person. 2. Fame or renown. [< L *celeber* famous]

ce·ler·i·ty (sə·ler′ə·tē) *n.* Speed; rapidity. [< L *celer* swift]

cel·er·y (sel′ər·ē, sel′rē) *n.* A biennial herb whose stems are used as a vegetable. [< dial. Ital. *selinon* parsley < Gk.]

ce·les·ta (sə·les′tə) *n.* A musical instrument having a keyboard and steel plates struck by hammers. [< F *célesta*]

ce·les·tial (sə·les′chəl) *adj.* 1. Of or pertaining to the sky or heavens. 2. Of heaven; divine. [< L *caelum* sky, heaven] **—ce·les′·tial·ly** *adv.*

celestial equator *Astron.* The great circle in which the plane of the earth's equator cuts the celestial sphere.

celestial sphere *Astron.* The imaginary spherical surface on which the heavenly bodies seem to lie.

ce·li·ac (sē′lē·ak) *adj.* Of or pertaining to the abdomen. [< L *coeliacus* < Gk. *koilos* hollow]

cel·i·ba·cy (sel′ə·bə·sē) *n.* The state of being unmarried or maintaining chastity, esp. as a religious vow. [< L *caelebs* unmarried]

cel·i·bate (sel′ə·bit, -bāt) *n.* One who remains unmarried or chaste, esp. by vow. **—cel′i·bate** *adj.*

cell (sel) *n.* 1. A small room, as for a prisoner or monk. 2. A small compartment, receptacle, or cavity. 3. A body of persons forming a single unit in an organization of similar groups. 4. *Biol.* The fundamental structural unit of plant and animal life. 5. *Electr.* The unit composing all or part of a battery, consisting of electrodes in contact with an electrolyte and in which a current is generated. [< L *cella* cell, small room]

cel·lar (sel′ər) *n.* 1. A space wholly or partly underground and usu. beneath a building, used for storage, etc. 2. A wine cellar; also, a stock of wines. —*v.t.* To put or keep in a cellar. [< L *cella* cell, small room]

cel·lar·age (sel′ər·ij) *n.* 1. Space in or for a cellar. 2. The charge for storage in a cellar.

cell-block (sel′blok′) *n.* In prisons, a unit of cells.

cel·lo (chel′ō) *n. pl.* **·los** A bass instrument of the violin family: also called *violoncello.* Also **'cel′lo.** [Short for VIOLONCELLO] —**cel′list** or **'cel′list** *n.*

cel·lo·phane (sel′ə·fān) *n.* A treated cellulose processed in thin, transparent sheets, used for moistureproof packaging.

cel·lu·lar (sel′yə·lər) *adj.* 1. Of or like a cell or cells. 2. Consisting of cells. [See CELLULE.]

cel·lule (sel′yo͞ol) *n.* A small cell. [< L *cellula,* dim. of *cella* cell, small room]

Cel·lu·loid (sel′yə·loid) *n.* A hard, elastic, flammable plastic: a trade name. Also **cel′lu·loid.**

cel·lu·lose (sel′yə·lōs) *n. Biochem.* An amorphous carbohydrate forming the fundamental material of the structure of plants. [See CELLULE.]

cellulose acetate *Chem.* A derivative of cellulose, used in making synthetic yarns and fabrics.

Cel·si·us scale (sel′sē·əs) A temperature scale in which the freezing point of water at normal atmospheric pressure is 0° and the boiling point is 100°; the centigrade scale. [after Anders *Celsius,* 1701–44, Swedish astronomer]

Celt (selt, kelt) *n.* A person of Celtic linguistic stock, esp. the Irish, Welsh, and Bretons. Also spelled *Kelt.* —**Celt′ic** *adj.*

Celt·ic (sel′tik, kel′-) *n.* A subfamily of the Indo-European family of languages, including Cornish, Welsh, and Gaelic. Also spelled *Keltic.* —**Celt′ic** *adj.*

ce·ment (si·ment′) *n.* 1. A mixture, usu. of burned limestone and clay, which hardens when dried and is used as an ingredient of mortar and concrete. 2. Any material, as glue, that will bind objects together. 3. Something that unites. 4. An adhesive material used in dental work. 5. *Anat.* A layer of bony tissue covering the roots of the teeth: also **ce·men′·tum.** —*v.t.* 1. To unite or join with or as with cement. 2. To cover or coat with cement. —*v.i.* 3. To become united by means of cement; cohere. [< OF *ciment*] —**ce·ment′er** *n.*

cem·e·ter·y (sem′ə·ter′ē) *n. pl.* **·ter·ies** A place for burying the dead; graveyard. [< L *coemeterium* < Gk. *koimaein* to put to sleep]

-cene *combining form Geol.* Recent; new: used in the names of geological periods: *Pliocene.* [< Gk. *kainos*]

ceno- *combining form* Common. Also spelled *coeno-*: also, before vowels, **cen-.** [< Gk. *koinos*]

cen·o·bite (sen′ə·bīt′) *n.* A member of a religious community. [< LL *coenobita* < Gk. *koinos* common + *bios* life] —**cen′o·bit′ic** (-bit′ik) or **·i·cal** *adj.* —**cen′o·bit·ism** *n.*

cen·o·taph (sen′ə·taf) *n.* A monument erected to the dead but not containing the remains. [< Gk. *kenos* empty + *taphos* tomb] —**cen′o·taph′ic** *adj.*

cen·ser (sen′sər) *n.* A vessel for burning incense: also called *thurible.* [< OF *censier* < Med.L *incensum* incense]

cen·sor (sen′sər) *n.* 1. An official examiner of manuscripts, plays, movies, television programs, etc., empowered to suppress them, wholly or in part, if objectionable. 2. An official who examines dispatches, letters, etc., in time of war. 3. Anyone who censures. 4. In ancient Rome, one of two magistrates who drew up the census and supervised public morals. —*v.t.* To act as censor of. [< L *censere* to judge, assess] —**cen·so·ri·al** (sen·sôr′ē·əl) *adj.*

cen·so·ri·ous (sen·sôr′ē·əs) *adj.* Given to censure; faultfinding. —**cen·so′ri·ous·ly** *adv.* —**cen·so′ri·ous·ness** *n.*

cen·sor·ship (sen′sər·ship) *n.* The action or system of censoring.

cen·sure (sen′shər) *n.* The expression of disapproval or blame; reprimand. —*v.t.* **·sured, ·sur·ing** To express disapproval of; condemn. [< L *censere* to judge] —**cen′sur·a·ble** *adj.* —**cen′sur·a·ble·ness** *n.* —**cen′·sur·a·bly** *adv.* —**cen′sur·er** *n.*

cen·sus (sen′səs) *n. pl.* **·sus·es** An official count of a population, with statistics as to age, sex, employment, etc. [< L *censere* to judge, assess] —**cen·su·al** (sen′sho͞o·əl) *adj.*

cent (sent) *n.* 1. The hundredth part of a standard monetary unit, as the dollar; also, a coin of this value: symbol ¢. 2. A hundred: used only in *percent.* [< L *centum* hundred]

cen·tare (sen′târ, *Fr.* säṅ·tȧr′) *n.* One square meter: also **cen·ti·are** (sen′tē·âr). [< F *centi-* hundredth + ARE[2].]

cen·taur (sen′tôr) *n.* In Greek mythology, one of a race of monsters, half man and half horse. [< Gk. *Kentauros*]

cen·ta·vo (sen·tä′vō) *n. pl.* **·vos** (-vōz, *Sp.* -vōs) A coin equal to one hundredth of the peso of Mexico and of other monetary units. [< Sp.]

cen·te·nar·i·an (sen′tə·nâr′ē·ən) *n.* One who is 100 years old. —*adj.* 1. Of the age of 100 years. 2. Pertaining to a period of 100 years.

cen·te·nar·y (sen·ten′ə·rē, sen′tə·ner′ē) *n. pl.* **·nar·ies** 1. A period of 100 years. 2. A centennial. [< L *centum* hundred] —**cen·te′nar·y** *adj.*

cen·ten·ni·al (sen·ten′ē·əl) *adj.* 1. Of or marking a period of 100 years or its completion. 2. Occurring every 100 years. —*n.* A 100th anniversary or its celebration. [< L *centum* hundred + *annus* year] —**cen·ten′ni·al·ly** *adv.*

cen·ter (sen′tər) *n.* 1. The point equally distant from the extremities or sides of anything. 2. A point about which a thing revolves. 3. A place or point at which activity is concentrated. 4. A point from which effects, influences, etc., proceed. 5. *Often cap.* A group, party, etc., having moderate views or tendencies. 6. In football, basketball, etc., a player who occupies a middle position. —*v.t.* 1. To place in or at

the center. 2. To direct toward one place; concentrate. 3. To determine the center of. —*v.i.* 4. To be at the center of. —*adj.* Central; middle. Also, *Brit., centre.* [< L *centrum* < Gk. *kentron* point]
cen·ter·board (sen′tər·bôrd′) *n.* A board lowered below the bottom of a sailboat to prevent leeward drift. Also *Brit.* **cen′tre·board′.**
cen·ter·fold (sen′tər·fōld′) *n.* A large, usu. folded illustration, esp. of a nude, bound into the center of a magazine.
center of gravity *Physics* The point about which a body acted upon by gravity is in equilibrium in all positions.
cen·ter·piece (sen′tər·pēs′) *n.* A piece at the center of anything; esp., a table ornament.
cen·tes·i·mal (sen·tes′ə·məl) *adj.* Pertaining to or divided into hundredths. [< L *centesimus* hundredth] —**cen·tes′i·mal·ly** *adv.*
centi- *combining form* 1. Hundred: *centipede.* 2. In the metric system, one hundredth of (a specified unit): *centiliter.* [< L *centum* hundred]
cen·ti·grade (sen′tə·grād) *adj.* Graduated to a scale of a hundred. [< F < L *centum* hundred + *gradus* step, degree]
centigrade scale The Celsius scale.
cen·ti·gram (sen′tə·gram) *n.* The hundredth part of a gram. Also *Brit.* **cen′ti·gramme.**
cen·ti·li·ter (sen′tə·lē′tər) *n.* The hundredth part of a liter. Also *esp. Brit.* **cen′ti·li′tre.**
cen·time (sän′tēm, *Fr.* säṅ·tēm′) *n.* A small coin, the hundredth part of a franc or other monetary unit. [< F < L *centesimus* hundredth]
cen·ti·me·ter (sen′tə·mē′tər) *n.* The hundredth part of a meter, equal to .3937 inch. Also *esp. Brit.* **cen′ti·me′tre.**
cen·ti·me·ter-gram-sec·ond See CGS.
cen·ti·pede (sen′tə·pēd) *n.* A wormlike animal having many pairs of legs. [< F < L *centum* hundred + *pes, pedis* foot]
cen·tral (sen′trəl) *adj.* 1. At, in, or near the center. 2. Of or constituting the center. 3. Exercising a controlling influence; dominant. 4. Most important; principal; chief. [< L *centrum* center] —**cen·tral·i·ty** (sen·tral′ə·tē) *n.* —**cen′tral·ly** *adv.*
cen·tral·ism (sen′trəl·iz′əm) *n.* A centralizing tendency or system; concentration of control in a central authority. —**cen′tral·ist** *n. & adj.* —**cen′tral·is′tic** *adj.*
cen·tral·ize (sen′trəl·īz) *v.* **·ized, ·iz·ing** *v.t.* 1. To bring to a central place or under a central authority. —*v.i.* 2. To come to a center; concentrate. —**cen′tral·i·za′tion** *n.* —**cen′tral·iz′er** *n.*
central nervous system *Anat.* That part of the nervous system consisting of the brain and spinal cord.
cen·tre (sen′tər) *Brit.* Center.
centri- *combining form* Center. Also **centro-.** Before vowels, **centr-.** [< L *centrum* < Gk. *kentron*]
cen·tric (sen′trik) *adj.* At, relating to, or having a center. Also **cen′tri·cal.** [< Gk. *kentrikos* < *kentron*] —**cen′tri·cal·ly** *adv.* —**cen·tric·i·ty** (sen·tris′ə·tē) *n.*
cen·trif·u·gal (sen·trif′yə·gəl, -trif′ə·gəl) *adj.* 1. Directed or tending away from a center; radiating. 2. Employing centrifugal force: a *centrifugal* pump. —*n.* A centrifuge. [< CENTRI- + L *fugere* to flee] —**cen·trif′u·gal·ly** *adv.*
centrifugal force *Physics* The force impelling a body to move outward from the center of rotation.
cen·tri·fuge (sen′trə·fyōōj) *n.* A machine using centrifugal force to separate substances of different densities. —*v.t.* **·fuged, ·fug·ing** To subject to the action of a centrifuge. [< F] —**cen·trif·u·ga·tion** (sen·trif′yə·gā′·shən, -ə·gā′-) *n.*
cen·trip·e·tal (sen·trip′ə·təl) *adj.* 1. Directed, tending, or drawing toward a center. 2. Acting by drawing toward a center. [< CENTRI- + L *petere* to seek] —**cen·trip′e·tal·ly** *adv.*
centripetal force *Physics* A force attracting a body toward the center of rotation.
cen·trist (sen′trist) *n.* One who takes a moderate position in politics.
cen·tu·ri·on (sen·tŏŏr′ē·ən, -tyŏŏr′-) *n.* In the ancient Roman army, a captain of a group of 100 soldiers. [< L *centurio, -onis*]
cen·tu·ry (sen′chə·rē) *n. pl.* **·ries** A period of 100 years in any system of chronology, esp. in reckoning from the first year of the Christian era. [< L *centuria* < *centum* hundred] —**cen·tu·ri·al** (sen·tŏŏr′ē·əl) *adj.*
century plant A succulent plant of the amaryllis family, flowering only once and then dying.
ce·phal·ic (sə·fal′ik) *adj.* 1. Of or pertaining to the head. 2. At, on, in, or near the head. [< Gk. *kephalē* head]
-cephalic *combining form* Head; skull: *brachycephalic.*
cephalic index *Anat.* The ratio of the width of the human head, multiplied by 100, to the greatest length.
cephalo- *combining form* Head. Also, before vowels, **cephal-.** [< Gk. *kephalē* head]
ceph·a·lo·pod (sef′ə·lə·pod′) *n. Zool.* A class of marine mollusks having a clearly defined head and eyes, ink sac, and tentacles or arms around the mouth, as squids and octopuses. —**ceph′a·lo·pod′, ceph′a·lo·pod′ic, ceph·a·lop·o·dous** (sef′ə·lop′ə·dəs) *adj.* —**ceph·a·lop·o·dan** (sef′ə·lop′ə·dən) *n. & adj.*
-cephalous *combining form* Headed: *hydrocephalous.* [< Gk. *kephalē* head]
ce·ram·ics (sə·ram′iks) *n.pl.* (*construed as sing. in def. 1.*) 1. The art of modeling and baking in clay. 2. Objects made of fired and baked clay. [< Gk. *keramos* potter's clay] —**ce·ram′ic** *adj.* —**ce·ram′i·cist** (-ə·sist), **ce·ram′ist** *n.*
ce·re·al (sir′ē·əl) *n.* 1. An edible, starchy grain, as rice, wheat, rye, oats, etc. 2. Any grain-bearing plant. 3. A breakfast food made from such a grain. [< L *Ceres,* goddess of grain]
cer·e·bel·lum (ser′ə·bel′əm) *n. pl.* **·bel·lums** or **·bel·la** (-bel′ə) *Anat.* That part of the brain serving as the coordination center of voluntary movements and equilibrium. [< L, dim. of *cerebrum* brain] —**cer′e·bel′lar** *adj.*
cer·e·bral (ser′ə·brəl, sə·rē′-) *adj.* 1. Of or pertaining to the cerebrum or the brain. 2. Appealing to or involving the intellect; intellectual. [< L *cerebrum* brain]
cerebral palsy *Pathol.* Any paralysis affecting the ability to control movement and caused by brain damage before or at birth.

cer·e·brate (ser′ə·brāt) *v.i.* **·brat·ed, ·brat·ing** To think. [< L *cerebrum* brain] **—cer′e·bra′tion** *n.*

cerebro- *combining form* Brain: *cerebrospinal.* Also, before vowels, **cerebr-.** [< L *cerebrum* brain]

cer·e·bro·spi·nal (ser′ə·brō·spī′nəl) *adj. Anat.* Of or affecting the brain and the spinal cord.

cer·e·brum (ser′ə·brəm, sə·rē′brəm) *n. pl.* **·bra** (-brə) *Anat.* The upper anterior part of the brain, constituting the seat of conscious processes. [< L] **—cer·e·bric** (ser′ə·brik, sə·rē′-) *adj.*

cere·cloth (sir′klôth′, -kloth′) *n.* Cloth treated with wax, used to wrap the dead. [Orig. *cered cloth* < L *cera* wax]

cere·ment (sir′mənt) *n. Usu. pl.* 1. A cerecloth. 2. A shroud. [< L *cera* wax]

cer·e·mo·ni·al (ser′ə·mō′nē·əl) *adj.* Of, pertaining to, or characterized by ceremony. **—*n.*** 1. A prescribed set of ceremonies for some particular occasion; ritual. 2. A rite; ceremony. **—cer′e·mo′ni·al·ism** *n.* **—cer′e·mo′ni·al·ist** *n.* **—cer′e·mo′ni·al·ly** *adv.*

cer·e·mo·ni·ous (ser′ə·mō′nē·əs) *adj.* 1. Studiously or overly polite. 2. Characterized by ceremony; formal. **—cer′e·mo′ni·ous·ly** *adv.* **—cer′e·mo′ni·ous·ness** *n.*

cer·e·mo·ny (ser′ə·mō′nē) *n. pl.* **·nies** 1. A formal act or ritual, or a series of them, performed in a prescribed manner. 2. Formal observances collectively; ritual. 3. An empty ritual. 4. Adherence to ritual forms; formality. 5. An act of formal courtesy. **—to stand on** (or **upon**) **ceremony** To insist upon formalities. [< L *caerimonia* awe]

ce·rise (sə·rēs′) *n. & adj.* Vivid red. [< F, cherry]

ce·ri·um (sir′ē·əm) *n.* A silver-white, metallic element (symbol Ce) of the lanthanide series. [after the asteroid *Ceres*]

cero- *combining form* Wax: *cerotype.* Also, before vowels, **cer-.** [< L *cera* or Gk. *kēros* wax]

cer·tain (sûr′tən) *adj.* 1. Absolutely confident. 2. Fated; destined. 3. Beyond doubt; indisputable. 4. Dependable; also, unerring. 5. Fixed; determined. 6. Not explicitly stated or identified: *certain* persons. 7. Some: a *certain* improvement. **—*n.*** An indefinite number or quantity. [< OF, ult. < L *cernere* to determine]

cer·tain·ly (sûr′tən·lē) *adv.* Without doubt; surely.

cer·tain·ty (sûr′tən·tē) *n. pl.* **·ties** 1. The state, quality, or fact of being certain. 2. A known fact.

cer·tif·i·cate (*n.* sər·tif′ə·kit; *v.* sər·tif′ə·kāt) *n.* An official or sworn document stating something to be a fact. **—*v.t.*** **·cat·ed, ·cat·ing** To furnish with or attest by a certificate. [< L *certus* certain + *facere* to make] **—cer·tif′i·ca′tor** *n.* **—cer·tif′i·ca·to′ry** *adj.*

cer·ti·fi·ca·tion (sûr′tə·fi·kā′shən) *n.* 1. The act of certifying or guaranteeing. 2. The state of being certified. 3. A certificate.

cer·ti·fied (sûr′tə·fīd) *adj.* 1. Vouched for in writing; endorsed. 2. Affirmed or guaranteed by a certificate. 3. Legally committed to a mental institution.

certified check A check issued by a bank that certifies it to be good.

cer·ti·fy (sûr′tə·fī) *v.* **·fied, ·fy·ing** *v.t.* 1. To give certain information of; attest. 2. To testify to in writing; vouch for. 3. To endorse as meeting set standards or requirements. 4. To guarantee in writing on the face of (a check) that it is good. 5. To commit to a mental institution. **—*v.i.*** 6. To make attestation; vouch (*for*) or testify (*to*). [< L *certus* certain + *facere* to make] **—cer′ti·fi′a·ble** *adj.* **—cer′ti·fi′er** *n.*

cer·ti·tude (sûr′tə·tōōd, -tyōōd) *n.* Complete confidence.

ce·ru·le·an (sə·rōō′lē·ən, -lyən) *adj. & n.* Sky blue; vivid blue. [< L *caeruleus* dark blue]

ce·ru·men (sə·rōō′mən) *n.* Earwax. [< L *cera* wax]

cer·vix (sûr′viks) *n. pl.* **cer·vix·es** or **cer·vi·ces** (sər·vī′sēz, sûr′və·sēz) *Anat.* 1. The neck. 2. The constricted neck of the uterus. 3. A necklike part. [< L] **—cer·vi·cal** (sûr′vi·kəl) *adj.*

ce·sar·e·an (si·zâr′ē·ən) *n. Surg.* The birth of a child by surgical incision of the abdominal walls and uterus. Also called **cesarean section** or **cesarean operation.** Also *caesarean.* [? after Julius *Caesar*, because he or an ancestor was born so] **—ce·sar′e·an** *adj.*

ce·si·um (sē′zē·əm) *n.* A ductile metallic element (symbol Cs) of the alkali group: also spelled *caesium.* [< L *caesius* bluish gray]

ces·sa·tion (se·sā′shən) *n.* A ceasing; stop; pause. [< L *cessare* to stop]

ces·sion (sesh′ən) *n.* The act of ceding; a giving up, as of territory or rights, to another. [< L *cessus* pp. of *cedere* to yield]

cess·pool (ses′pōōl′) *n.* 1. A covered well or pit for sewage, etc. 2. Any repository of filth. Also **cess′pit′.** [Origin uncertain]

ces·ta (ses′tə) *n.* A curved basket used as a racket in jai alai. [< Sp.]

ce·su·ra (si·zhōōr′ə, -zyōōr′ə) See CAESURA.

ce·ta·cean (si·tā′shən) *adj.* Of or belonging to the aquatic mammals, including the whales, dolphins, and porpoises. Also **ce·ta′ceous.** [< Gk. *kētos* whale] **—ce·ta′cean** *n.*

Cey·lon·ese (sel′ə·nēz′) *adj.* Of or pertaining to Ceylon (now Sri Lanka) or to its people. **—Cey′lon·ese′** *n.*

cgs The centimeter-gram-second system of measurement in which the unit of length is the centimeter, the unit of mass is the gram, and the unit of time is one second. Also **c.g.s., CGS, C.G.S.**

Cha·blis (shȧ·blē′) *n.* A dry, white wine.

Chad·i·an (chad′ē·ən) *adj.* Of Chad or its people. **—Chad′i·an** *n.*

chafe (chāf) *v.* **chafed, chaf·ing** *v.t.* 1. To abrade or make sore by rubbing. 2. To make warm by rubbing. 3. To irritate; annoy. **—*v.i.*** 4. To rub. 5. To be irritated; fret; fume: to *chafe* under the abuse. **—*n.*** 1. Soreness or wear from rubbing; friction. 2. Irritation or vexation. [< L *calere* to be warm + *facere* to make]

chaf·er (chā′fər) *n.* The cockchafer or any of various other large beetles. [OE *ceafor*]

chaff[1] (chaf) *n.* 1. The husks of grain. 2. Any trivial or worthless matter. [OE *ceaf*] **—chaff′y** *adj.*

chaff[2] (chaf) *v.t. & v.i.* To poke fun (at). **—*n.*** Good-natured raillery. [Origin uncertain] **—chaff′er** *n.*

chaf·fer (chaf′ər) *v.i.* To haggle about price;

bargain. —*n.* A haggling about terms; bargaining. [OE *cēap* bargain + *faru* going] —**chaf′fer·er** *n.*

chaf·finch (chaf′inch) *n.* A song finch of Europe.

chafing dish A vessel with a heating apparatus to cook or keep food warm at the table.

cha·grin (shə·grin′) *n.* Distress or vexation caused by disappointment, failure, etc. —*v.t.* To cause to feel chagrin. [< F]

chain (chān) *n.* **1.** A series of connected rings or links, usu. of metal, serving to bind, drag, hold, or ornament. **2.** *pl.* Anything that confines or restrains; shackles. **3.** *pl.* Bondage. **4.** Any connected series. **5.** A series of chain stores. —*v.t.* **1.** To fasten or connect with a chain. **2.** To fetter; bind. [< L *catena*]

chain gang A gang of convicts chained together while doing hard labor.

chain letter A letter intended to be sent on from one to another in a series of recipients.

chain mail Flexible armor consisting of interlinked metal chains, rings, or scales.

chain reaction **1.** *Physics* The self-sustaining fission of atomic nuclei, as in a nuclear reactor. **2.** Any causally linked succession of reactions or events.

chain saw A portable power saw with cutting teeth set on an endless chain.

chain-smoke (chān′smōk) *v.t. & v.i.* **-smoked, -smok·ing** To smoke (cigarettes) without interruption. —**chain′-smok·er** *n.* —**chain′-smok·ing** *n.*

chain store One of a number of retail stores under the same ownership and selling similar merchandise.

chair (châr) *n.* **1.** A seat, usu. having four legs and a back, for one person. **2.** A seat of office, authority, etc., as that of a professor or bishop. **3.** The office or dignity of one who presides or is in authority. **4.** A presiding officer; chairman. **5.** The electric chair; also, execution in the electric chair. —**to take the chair** To preside at or open a meeting. —*v.t.* **1.** To seat in a chair. **2.** To install in office. **3.** To preside over (a meeting). [< OF *chaiere* < L *cathedra.*]

chair lift A group of chairs suspended from a power-driven cable, used to transport people, esp. skiers, up or down mountains.

chair·man (châr′mən) *n. pl.* **·men** (-mən) One who presides over an assembly, committee, etc.: also **chair·per·son** (châr′pûr′·sən). —**chair′wom′an** (-wŏŏm′ən) *n.fem.*

chaise (shāz) *n.* **1.** A two-wheeled, one-horse vehicle for two persons, having a collapsible top. **2.** A similar carriage with four wheels. Also, *Dial.*, *shay.* [< F, var. of *chaire* chair]

chaise longue (shāz′ lông′, *Fr.* shez lông′) A couchlike chair capable of supporting the sitter's outstretched legs: also **chaise lounge.** [< F, lit., long chair]

chal·ced·o·ny (kal·sed′ə·nē, kal′sə·dō′nē) *n. pl.* **·nies** A waxy, translucent variety of quartz, often of a pale blue or grayish color. [after *Chalcedon*, an ancient Greek port]

cha·let (sha·lā′, shal′ā) *n.* **1.** A Swiss cottage with a gently sloping, projecting roof; also, any cottage built in this style. **2.** A herdsman's hut of the Alpine regions of Europe. [< F]

chal·ice (chal′is) *n.* **1.** A drinking cup or goblet. **2.** *Eccl.* In the Eucharist, a cup in which the wine is consecrated. **3.** A cup-shaped flower. [< L *calix, calicis* cup]

chalk (chôk) *n.* **1.** A soft, grayish white or yellowish compact limestone, largely composed of the shells of marine animals. **2.** A piece of limestone or similar material, used for marking, etc. **3.** A score, tally, or notation of credit given. —*v.t.* **1.** To mark, write, or draw with chalk. **2.** To treat or dress with chalk. **3.** To make pale. —**to chalk up** To score; credit. —*adj.* Made with chalk. [< L *calx* limestone] —**chalk′i·ness** *n.* —**chalk′y** *adj.*

chalk·board (chôk′bôrd′) *n.* A writing slate, as a blackboard, on which chalk is used.

chal·lenge (chal′ənj) *v.* **·lenged, ·leng·ing** *v.t.* **1.** To demand a contest with. **2.** To call in question; dispute. **3.** *Law* To object to. **4.** To claim as due; demand. **5.** *Mil.* To stop (someone) and demand identification from. **6.** To arouse interest or excitement in. —*v.i.* **7.** To present a challenge. —*n.* **1.** **a** An invitation or dare to participate in a contest. **b** An invitation to compete in a sport. **2.** *Mil.* A sentry's call, requiring one to halt and identify oneself. **3.** A calling in question; dispute. **4.** *Law* A formal objection, as to a juror. [< OF *chalenger* < L *calumnia* slander] —**chal′lenge·a·ble** *adj.* —**chal′·leng·er** *n.*

chal·lis (shal′ē) *n.* A light fabric, usu. of printed wool, rayon, etc. Also **chal′lie.** [Origin uncertain]

cham·ber (chām′bər) *n.* **1.** A room in a house; esp., a bedroom. **2.** *pl.* An office or suite of rooms, as of a judge. **3.** A hall where an assembly meets; also, the assembly itself. **4.** A council; board. **5.** An enclosed space or cavity, as in a gun. —*v.t.* **1.** To provide with a chamber. **2.** To fit into or as into a chamber. [< L *camera* vaulted room]

cham·ber·lain (chām′bər·lin) *n.* **1.** An official charged with the domestic affairs of a monarch or lord. **2.** A high officer of a royal court. **3.** A treasurer. [< OF *chamberlenc* < L *camera* vaulted room] —**cham′ber·lain·ship′** *n.*

cham·ber·maid (chām′bər·mād′) *n.* A maidservant who cleans bedrooms in a house, hotel, etc.

chamber music Music composed for a small group of instruments, as a string quartet.

chamber of commerce An association to regulate and promote business in a city or locality.

chamber pot A portable vessel used as a toilet.

cham·bray (sham′brā′) *n.* A cotton fabric woven with colored warp and white filling. [after *Cambrai*, France]

cha·me·le·on (kə·mē′lē·ən, -mēl′yən) *n.* **1.** A lizard capable of changing color. **2.** A person of changeable disposition or habits. [< Gk. *chamai* on the ground + *leōn* lion]

cham·fer (cham′fər) *v.t.* **1.** To cut away the corner of. **2.** To cut a furrow in; flute. —*n.* A surface produced by chamfering. [< F < OF *chanfraindre* to cut off an edge]

cham·ois (sham′ē, *Fr.* shȧ·mwä′) *n. pl.* **·ois** **1.** A mountain antelope of Europe and western Asia. **2.** A soft leather prepared from the skin of the chamois, sheep, goats, deer, etc. Also spelled *shammy, shamois*: also

cham′my. —*v.t.* To dress (leather or skin) like chamois. [< MF]
cham·o·mile (kam′ə·mīl) See CAMOMILE.
champ[1] (champ) *v.t.* 1. To chew noisily; munch. 2. To bite restlessly. —*v.i.* 3. To be impatient because of delay, usu. in the expression, *champ at the bit.* [Prob. imit.] —**champ** *n.*
champ[2] (champ) *n. Slang* Champion.
cham·pagne (sham·pān′) *n.* 1. A sparkling white wine made in the area of Champagne, France; also, any wine made in imitation of this. 2. A pale or greenish yellow. —**cham·pagne′** *adj.*
cham·paign (sham·pān′) *n.* Flat and open country. [< MF *champagne* < L *campus* field] —**cham·paign′** *adj.*
cham·pi·on (cham′pē·ən) *n.* 1. One who has defeated all opponents and is ranked first, esp. in a sport. 2. Anything awarded first place. 3. One who fights for another or defends a principle or cause. —*adj.* Having won first prize or rank; superior to all others. —*v.t.* To fight in behalf of; defend; support. [< LL *campio, -onis* fighter]
cham·pi·on·ship (cham′pē·ən·ship′) *n.* 1. The state of being a champion. 2. The act of championing; advocacy; defense. 3. A competition to determine a champion.
chance (chans) *n.* 1. The unknown cause of events; fortune; luck. 2. An unusual and unexplained event. 3. The probability of anything happening. 4. An opportunity. 5. A risk or gamble; hazard. 6. A ticket in a lottery. —*v.* **chanced, chanc·ing** *v.i.* 1. To occur accidentally; happen. —*v.t.* 2. To take the chance of; risk. —**to chance upon** (or **on**) To find or meet unexpectedly. —*adj.* Occurring by chance. [< OF < LL *cadentia* a falling]
chan·cel (chan′səl) *n.* The space near the altar of a church for the clergy and choir. [< L *cancelli*, pl., lattice, railing]
chan·cel·ler·y (chan′sə·lər·ē, -slər·ē) *n. pl.* **·ler·ies** 1. The office or dignity of a chancellor. 2. The building or room in which a chancellor has his office. 3. The office of an embassy or legation. Also **chan·cel·ry** (chan′səl·rē).
chan·cel·lor (chan′sə·lər, -slər) *n.* 1. In some European countries, a chief minister of state. 2. The chief secretary of an embassy. 3. A secretary, as of a nobleman or ruler. 4. The head of some universities. 5. A judge of a court of chancery or equity. Also **chan′cel·or.** [< LL *cancellarius* one who stands at the bar in a court] —**chan′cel·lor·ship′** *n.*
chan·cer·y (chan′sər·ē) *n. pl.* **·cer·ies** 1. **a** A court of equity. Also **court of chancery. b** Equity, or proceedings in equity. 2. A chancellery. 3. A court of records; archives. [See CHANCELLOR.]
chan·cre (shang′kər) *n. Pathol.* A primary syphilitic lesion. [< F < L *cancer* crab, ulcer] —**chan′crous** *adj.*
chan·croid (shang′kroid) *n. Pathol.* A nonsyphilitic venereal lesion.
chanc·y (chan′sē) *adj.* **chanc·i·er, chanc·i·est** *Informal* Risky. —**chan′ci·ly** *adv.*
chan·de·lier (shan′də·lir′) *n.* A branched light fixture, suspended from a ceiling. [< F < L *candela* candle]
chan·dler (chan′dlər) *n.* 1. A trader; dealer: ship *chandler.* 2. One who makes or sells candles. [< OF *chandelier* chandler, candlestick]
change (chānj) *v.* **changed, chang·ing** *v.t.* 1. To make different; alter. 2. To exchange: to *change* places. 3. To give or obtain the equivalent of, as money. 4. To put other garments, coverings, etc., on: to *change* the baby. —*v.i.* 5. To become different. 6. To make a change or exchange. 7. To transfer from one train, etc., to another. 8. To put on other garments. —**to change hands** To pass from one possessor to another. —*n.* 1. The act or fact of changing. 2. A substitution of one thing for another. 3. Something new or different; variety. 4. A clean or different set of clothes. 5. The amount returned when cash of greater value than the sum due has been tendered. 6. Money of lower denomination given in exchange for higher. 7. Small coins. [< LL *cambiare* to exchange] —**chang′er** *n.* —**change′ful** *adj.*
change·a·ble (chān′jə·bəl) *adj.* 1. Likely to change or vary; inconstant. 2. Capable of being changed. —**change′a·bil′i·ty, change′·a·ble·ness** *n.* —**change′a·bly** *adv.*
change·less (chānj′lis) *adj.* Free from change; enduring. —**change′less·ly** *adv.* —**change′less·ness** *n.*
change·ling (chānj′ling) *n.* A child secretly left in place of another.
change of life The menopause.
chan·nel (chan′əl) *n.* 1. The bed of a stream. 2. A wide strait. 3. *Naut.* The deep part of a river, harbor, etc. 4. A tubular passage, as for liquids. 5. The course through which anything passes. 6. *pl.* The official or proper routes of communication. 7. *Telecom.* A band of frequencies assigned for radio or television transmission. 8. A groove or furrow. —*v.t.* **chan·neled** or **·nelled, chan·nel·ing** or **·nel·ling** 1. To cut or wear channels in. 2. To direct or convey through or as through a channel. [< L *canalis* groove]
chan·son (shan′sən, *Fr.* shäṅ·sôṅ′) *n.* A song. [< F < L *canere* to sing]
chant (chant) *n.* 1. A simple melody in which a varying number of syllables are sung or intoned on each note. 2. A psalm or canticle so sung or intoned. 3. A song; melody. 4. Any repeated singing or shouting of words, as from a mob. 5. A singing intonation in speech. —*v.t. & v.i.* 1. To sing to a chant. 2. To celebrate in song. 3. To recite or say in the manner of a chant. [< OF < L *canere* to sing] —**chant′er** *n.*
chan·teuse (shäṅ·tœz′) *n. French* A woman singer, esp. of popular songs.
chant·ey (shan′tē, chan′-) *n. pl.* **·eys** A rhythmical working song of sailors: also **chan′ty.** [Alter. of F *chantez*, imperative of *chanter* to sing]
chan·ti·cleer (chan′tə·klir) *n.* A rooster. [< OF *chanter* to sing, crow + *cler* aloud]
chan·try (chan′trē) *n. pl.* **·tries** An endowment for daily masses or special prayers; also, a chapel or altar so endowed. [< L *canere* to sing]
Cha·nu·kah (khä′nōō·kə) See HANUKKAH.
cha·os (kā′os) *n.* 1. Utter disorder and confusion. 2. The supposed unformed original state of the universe. [< Gk., abyss] —**cha·ot·ic** (kā·ot′ik) *adj.* —**cha·ot′i·cal·ly** *adv.*

chap[1] (chap) *n. Informal* A fellow; lad. [Short for CHAPMAN]

chap[2] (chap) *v.t. & v.i.* **chapped, chap·ping** To split, crack, or roughen. —*n.* A crack or roughened place in the skin. [ME *chappen*]

chap·ar·ral (shap′ə·ral′) *n.* A thicket of low, thorny shrubs, particularly so called in SW U.S. [< Sp. < *chaparra* evergreen oak]

chap·book (chap′bo͝ok′) *n.* A small book containing tales, ballads, etc. [< CHAP(MAN) + BOOK]

cha·peau (sha·pō′, *Fr.* shȧ·pō′) *n. pl.* **·peaux** (-pōz′, *Fr.* -pō′) or **·peaus** (-pōz′) A hat. [< F]

chap·el (chap′əl) *n.* 1. A place of worship smaller than a church. 2. A part of a church, for special services. 3. A place in a college, school, etc., for religious services; also, the services. [< Med.L *cappa* cloak; orig., a sanctuary where the cloak of St. Martin was kept as a relic]

chap·er·on (shap′ə·rōn′) *n.* An older person who accompanies and supervises a group of young people. Also **chap′er·one′**. [< F, hood < *chape* cape] —**chap′er·on′** *v.t.* —**chap′er·on′age** *n.*

chap·lain (chap′lin) *n.* A clergyman who conducts religious services in a legislative assembly, for a military unit, etc. [< Med.L *cappa* cloak] —**chap′lain·cy, chap′lain·ship** *n.*

chap·let (chap′lit) *n.* 1. A wreath or garland for the head. 2. One third of a rosary. 3. A string of beads. [< LL *cappa* hooded cape]

chap·man (chap′mən) *n. pl.* **·men** (-mən) *Brit.* A peddler. [OE < *cēap* business + *man* man]

chaps (chaps, shaps) *n.pl.* Leather overalls without a seat, worn over trousers by cowboys to protect the legs.

chap·ter (chap′tər) *n.* 1. A main division of a book or treatise, usually numbered. 2. A branch of a society or fraternity. 3. *Eccl.* An assembly of the canons; also, the canons collectively. 4. A period of time: an important *chapter* in history. —*v.t.* To divide into chapters, as a book. [< L *capitulum*, dim. of *caput* head, capital, chapter]

char[1] (chär) *v.* **charred, char·ring** *v.t.* 1. To burn or scorch the surface of. 2. To convert into charcoal by incomplete combustion. —*v.i.* 3. To become charred. —*n.* Charcoal. [? < CHARCOAL]

char[2] (chär) *n. pl.* **chars** or **char** Any of various fishes allied to the lake trout. [< Scottish Gaelic *ceara* blood red]

char[3] (chär) *n. Brit.* A charwoman. —*v.i.* **charred, char·ring** To work as a charwoman. [OE *cerr* turn of work]

char·ac·ter (kar′ik·tər) *n.* 1. The combination of qualities or traits that distinguishes an individual or group. 2. Any distinguishing attribute. 3. Moral force; integrity. 4. A good reputation. 5. Status; capacity. 6. A person in a play, novel, etc. 7. *Informal* An eccentric or humorous person. 8. A figure engraved, written, or printed; mark; letter. 9. *Genetics* A hereditary trait. —**in (or out of) character** In keeping (or not in keeping) with the general character. [< Gk. *charaktēr* stamp, mark < *charassein* to sharpen, engrave] —**char′ac·ter·less** *adj.*

character actor An actor who portrays characters markedly different from himself in age, temperament, etc. —**character actress** *fem.*

char·ac·ter·is·tic (kar′ik·tə·ris′tik) *adj.* Distinguishing; typical. —*n.* A distinctive feature or trait. —**char′ac·ter·is′ti·cal·ly** *adv.*

char·ac·ter·ize (kar′ik·tə·rīz′) *v.t.* **·ized, ·iz·ing** 1. To describe by qualities or peculiarities. 2. To be a mark or peculiarity of. —**char′ac·ter·i·za′tion** *n.* —**char′ac·ter·iz′er** *n.*

cha·rades (shə·rādz′) *n.pl.* (*construed as sing.*) A game in which words and phrases are to be guessed from their representation in pantomime. [< F < Provençal *charrado* < *charra* to chatter]

char·coal (chär′kōl′) *n.* 1. A black, porous substance obtained by the imperfect combustion of organic matter, as wood, used as a fuel, adsorbent, filter, etc. 2. A drawing pencil made of charcoal. 3. A drawing made with such a pencil. —*v.t.* To write, draw, mark, or blacken with charcoal. [ME *charcole*; origin unknown]

chard (chärd) *n.* A variety of edible white beet cultivated for its large leaves and leafstalks. [< L *carduus* thistle]

charge (chärj) *v.* **charged, charg·ing** *v.t.* 1. To place a burden or responsibility upon. 2. To load or fill. 3. To diffuse something throughout, as water with carbon dioxide. 4. To supply (a storage battery) with a quantity of electricity. 5. To accuse; impute something to. 6. To command or exhort: to *charge* a jury. 7. To set or state as a price. 8. To make financially liable. 9. To set down or record as a debt to be paid: to *charge* a purchase. 10. To attack forcefully. —*v.i.* 11. To make an attack; rush violently. 12. To demand or fix a price. —**to charge off** To regard as a loss. —*n.* 1. A load or burden. 2. The quantity of anything that an apparatus or receptacle can hold at one time. 3. The amount of explosive to be detonated at one time. 4. The quantity of electrical energy present in a storage battery. 5. Care and custody. 6. A person or thing entrusted to one's care; a responsibility. 7. An accusation; allegation. 8. An instruction or admonition given by a judge to a jury. 9. Any cost or expense. 10. A debt or charged purchase, or an entry recording it. 11. An onslaught or attack; also, the signal for this. 12. *Slang* Excitement; thrill. 13. *Heraldry* A figure or device. —**in charge of** Having responsibility for or control of. [< OF *chargier* < LL *carricare* to carry < L *carrus* cart]

charge·a·ble (chär′jə·bəl) *adj.* 1. That may be or is liable to be charged. 2. Liable to become a public charge.

charge account A retail credit account to which purchases or services may be charged for future payment.

char·gé d'af·faires (shär·zhā′ də·fâr′, *Fr.* shȧr·zhā′ dȧ·fâr′) *pl.* **char·gés d'af·faires** (shär·zhāz′ də·fâr′, *Fr.* shȧr·zhā′ dȧ·fâr′) 1. One who temporarily heads a diplomatic mission in the absence of the ambassador or minister. 2. A diplomat of lower rank than an ambassador. Also **char·gé′**.

charge plate A stiff card used for the mechanical registration of charge-account purchases.

charg·er (chär′jər) *n.* 1. One who or that which charges. 2. A horse trained for use in battle; a war horse. 3. An apparatus for charging storage batteries.

char·i·ot (char′ē·ət) *n.* An ancient two-wheeled vehicle used in war, racing, etc —*v.t. & v.i.* To convey, ride, or drive in a chariot. [< L *carrus* cart]

char·i·o·teer (char′ē·ə·tir′) *n.* One who drives a chariot.

cha·ris·ma (kə·riz′mə) *n.* 1. *Theol.* An extraordinary grace or gift, as of healing, given by the Holy Spirit. 2. Extraordinary personal magnetism, esp. in a political leader. [< Gk., grace, favor] —**cha·ris′mal** *adj.*

char·is·mat·ic (kar′iz·mat′ik) *adj.* 1. Of or pertaining to charisma. 2. *Theol.* Of a Christian movement emphasizing spiritual charisma.

char·i·ta·ble (char′ə·tə·bəl) *adj.* 1. Generous in giving gifts to the poor; beneficent. 2. Inclined to judge others leniently. 3. Of or concerned with charity. —**char′i·ta·ble·ness** *n.* —**char′i·ta·bly** *adv.*

char·i·ty (char′ə·tē) *n. pl.* **·ties** 1. The giving of help to the needy. 2. That which is given; alms. 3. An institution, organization, or fund to help those in need. 4. Tolerance; leniency. 5. An act of good will. 6. Brotherly love. [< L *caritas, -tatis* love]

char·la·tan (shär′lə·tən) *n.* One who makes false claim to skill and knowledge; quack. [< Ital. *ciarlatano* babbler] —**char′la·tan′ic** (-tan′ik) *adj.* —**char′la·tan·ism, char′la·tan·ry** *n.*

Charles·ton (chärl′stən) *n.* A fast dance in 4/4 time, popular in the 1920's. [after *Charleston,* S.C.]

char·ley horse (chär′lē) *Informal* A muscular cramp in the arm or leg. [Origin unknown]

char·lotte russe (shär′lət ro͞os) A small sponge cake covered with whipped cream or custard. [< F, Russian charlotte]

charm (chärm) *n.* 1. The power to allure or delight; fascination. 2. Any fascinating quality or feature. 3. A small ornament worn on a necklace, bracelet, etc. 4. Something worn to ward off evil or ensure good luck; an amulet. 5. Any formula or action supposed to have magic power. 6. *Physics* A property of matter observable in high-energy collisions between subatomic particles. —*v.t. & v.i.* 1. To attract irresistibly; delight; fascinate. 2. To influence by or as if by a spell; bewitch. 3. To protect by or as by magic power. [< L *carmen* song, incantation] —**charm′er** *n.*

charm·ing (chär′ming) *adj.* Delightful; very attractive. —**charm′ing·ly** *adv.*

char·nel (chär′nəl) *n.* A room or vault where bones or bodies of the dead are placed: also **charnel house.** [< L *caro, carnis* flesh]

chart (chärt) *n.* 1. A map, esp. one for the use of mariners. 2. An outline map on which climatic data, military operations, etc., can be shown. 3. A sheet showing facts graphically or in tabular form. 4. A graph or table. —*v.t.* To lay out on a chart; map out. [< Gk. *chartēs* leaf of paper]

char·ter (chär′tər) *n.* 1. A document of incorporation of a municipality, institution, or the like. 2. A formal document by which a sovereign or government grants special rights or privileges to a person, company, or the people. 3. An authorization to establish a branch or chapter of some larger organization. 4. A contract for the lease of a vessel, bus, airplane, etc. —*v.t.* 1. To hire (an airplane, train, etc.). 2. To give a charter to. [< L *chartula,* dim. of *charta* paper] —**char′ter·age** *n.* —**char′ter·er** *n.*

charter member An original member of a corporation, order, or society.

char·treuse (shär·trœz′; *for def. 2,* also shär·tro͞oz′) *n.* 1. A yellow, pale green, or faintly green liqueur. 2. A yellowish green color. —*adj.* Of the color chartreuse. [after *La Grande Chartreuse,* the Carthusian monastery in France]

char·wom·an (chär′wo͝om′ən) *n. pl.* **·wom·en** (-wim′ən) *Brit.* A woman employed to do housework, or cleaning and scrubbing.

char·y (châr′ē) *adj.* **char·i·er, char·i·est** 1. Cautious; wary. 2. Fastidious; particular. 3. Sparing; frugal; stingy. [OE *cearig* sorrowful, sad < *cearu* care] —**char′i·ly** *adv.* —**char′i·ness** *n.*

chase[1] (chās) *v.* **chased, chas·ing** *v.t.* 1. To pursue with intent to catch or harm. 2. To follow persistently; run after. 3. To put to flight; drive. —*v.i.* 4. To follow in pursuit. 5. *Informal* To rush; go hurriedly. —*n.* 1. The act of chasing or pursuing. 2. The sport of hunting: preceded by *the.* 3. That which is pursued; prey; quarry. —**to give chase** To pursue. [< L *capere* to take]

chase[2] (chās) *n.* A groove or slot. —*v.t.* **chased, chas·ing** 1. To indent or groove. 2. To ornament by embossing; engrave. [Fusion of F *chasse* and *chas,* both ult. < L *capsa* box]

chas·er (chā′sər) *n.* 1. One who chases or pursues. 2. *Informal* Water, etc., taken after strong liquor.

chasm (kaz′əm) *n.* 1. A deep crack in the earth's surface; a gorge. 2. An abrupt interruption; a gap. 3. Any great difference of opinion. [< Gk. *chainein* to gape] —**chas′mal** *adj.*

Cha·si·dim (ha·si′dim) See HASIDIM.

chas·sis (shas′ē, chas′ē) *n. pl.* **chas·sis** (shas′ēz, chas′ēz) 1. The flat, rectangular frame that supports the body of a vehicle and includes the wheels and springs. 2. *Telecom.* The metal framework to which the components of a radio receiver, amplifier, etc., are attached. [< F. See CHASE[2].]

chaste (chāst) *adj.* 1. Not guilty of unlawful sexual intercourse; virtuous. 2. Celibate. 3. Pure in character or conduct. 4. Pure in artistic or literary style; simple. [< L *castus* pure] —**chaste′ly** *adv.* —**chaste′ness** *n.*

chas·ten (chā′sən) *v.t.* 1. To discipline by punishment or affliction; chastise. 2. To moderate; soften; temper. [< L *castigare* to correct] —**chast′en·er** *n.*

chas·tise (chas·tīz′) *v.t.* **·tised, ·tis·ing** 1. To punish, esp. by beating. 2. To scold or criticize severely. [ME *chastisen*] —**chas·tis′a·ble** *adj.* —**chas·tise′ment** *n.* —**chas·tis′er** *n.*

chas·ti·ty (chas′tə·tē) *n.* 1. The state or quality of being chaste. 2. Virginity or celibacy. [< L *castus* pure]

chas·u·ble (chaz′yə·bəl, chas′-) *n.* A long, sleeveless vestment worn over the alb by a priest when celebrating the Eucharist. [< Med.L *casubula* hooded cloak]

chat (chat) *v.i.* **chat·ted, chat·ting** To converse in an easy, informal manner. —*n.* 1. Easy, informal conversation. 2. Any of several singing birds: so called from their notes. [Short for CHATTER]

cha·teau (sha·tō′, *Fr.* shä·tō′) *n. pl.* **·teaux** (-tōz′, *Fr.* -tō′) 1. A French castle. 2. A house on a country estate. Also *French* **châ·teau′**. [< F < L *castrum* camp, fort]

chat·e·laine (shat′ə·lān) *n.* 1. A chain hanging from a woman's belt to hold small articles, as keys. 2. The mistress of a chateau or any fashionable household. [< F *châtelaine*]

chat·tel (chat′l) *n.* 1. *Law* An article of movable personal property. 2. A slave. [< OF *chatel* < L *caput* head]

chat·ter (chat′ər) *v.i.* 1. To click together rapidly, as the teeth in shivering. 2. To talk rapidly and trivially. 3. To utter a rapid series of short, inarticulate sounds, as a squirrel. —*v.t.* 4. To utter in a trivial or chattering manner. —*n.* 1. Idle or foolish talk; prattle. 2. Jabbering, as of a monkey. 3. A rattling of the teeth. [Imit.] —**chat′ter·er** *n.*

chat·ter·box (chat′ər·boks′) *n.* An incessant talker.

chat·ty (chat′ē) *adj.* **·ti·er, ·ti·est** 1. Loquacious. 2. Familiar; informal: a *chatty* style of writing. —**chat′ti·ly** *adv.* —**chat′ti·ness** *n.*

chauf·feur (shō′fər, shō·fûr′) *n.* One who drives an automobile for hire. —*v.t.* To serve as driver for. [< F, stoker < *chauffer* to warm]

chau·vin·ism (shō′vən·iz′əm) *n.* An unreasoning, often fanatical pride in, attachment to, or support for one's own nation, race, sex, etc. [after Nicholas *Chauvin*, a soldier and overzealous supporter of Napoleon Bonaparte] —**chau′vin·ist** *n.* —**chau′vin·is′tic** *adj.* —**chau′vin·is′ti·cal·ly** *adv.*

cheap (chēp) *adj.* 1. Low in price. 2. Charging low prices, as a store. 3. Inexpensive in proportion to its value. 4. Obtained with little trouble. 5. Of poor quality; inferior. 6. Mean; miserly. —*adv.* At a low price. [Earlier *good cheap* a bargain < OE *cēap* business, trade] —**cheap′ly** *adv.* —**cheap′ness** *n.*

cheap·en (chē′pən) *v.t. & v.i.* To make or become cheap or cheaper. —**cheap′en·er** *n.*

cheap·skate (chēp′skāt′) *n. Slang* A miserly person.

cheat (chēt) *v.t.* 1. To swindle or defraud. 2. To mislead or delude; trick. 3. To elude or escape; foil. —*v.i.* 4. To practice fraud or act dishonestly. 5. *Slang* To be sexually unfaithful. —*n.* 1. A fraud; swindle. 2. One who cheats or defrauds. [ME *chete*, short for *achete* to confiscate, deprive] —**cheat′er** *n.* —**cheat′ing·ly** *adv.*

check (chek) *n.* 1. A break in progress or advance; a halt. 2. One who or that which stops or controls. 3. Control or supervision. 4. A test, examination, or comparison. 5. A mark to show that something has been verified or investigated. 6. An order, in writing, upon a bank to pay a designated sum: also *Brit. cheque.* 7. A tag, slip, or the like, issued for identification. 8. A bill in a restaurant. 9. A square in a checkered surface. 10. A fabric having a checkered pattern. 11. In chess, the position of a king open to capture if it is not protected or moved. —*v.t.* 1. To bring to a stop suddenly or sharply. 2. To curb; restrain. 3. To test or verify; also, to investigate. 4. To mark with a check. 5. To mark with squares or crossed lines; checker. 6. To deposit or accept for temporary safekeeping. 7. In chess, to put (an opponent's king) in check. 8. To cause to crack. —*v.i.* 9. To come to a stop; pause. 10. To agree item for item; correspond accurately. —**to check in** To register as a guest at a hotel, etc. —**to check on** (or **up on**) To investigate. —**to check out** 1. To pay one's bill and leave, as from a hotel. 2. To investigate or confirm. 3. To be verified. —*interj.* In chess, an exclamation proclaiming that an opponent's king is in check. [< OF *eschec* defeat, check] —**check′a·ble** *adj.*

check·book (chek′bŏŏk′) *n.* A book of blank bank checks.

checked (chekt) *adj.* 1. Marked with squares. 2. Kept in check; restrained. 3. Stopped.

check·er (chek′ər) *n.* 1. A piece used in the game of checkers, usually a small disk. 2. One of the squares in a checkered surface; also, a pattern of such squares. 3. One who checks; esp., one who inspects, counts, or supervises the disposal of merchandise. 4. A cashier in a supermarket. —*v.t.* 1. To mark with squares or crossed lines. 2. To fill with variations or vicissitudes. Also, *Brit.*, *chequer.* [< OF *eschec* defeat, check]

check·er·board (chek′ər·bôrd′) *n.* A board divided into 64 squares, used in checkers or chess. Also *chessboard.*

check·ered (chek′ərd) *adj.* 1. Divided into squares. 2. Marked by light and dark patches. 3. Marked by alternations.

check·ers (chek′ərz) *n.pl.* (*construed as sing.*) A game played by two persons on a checkerboard, each player starting with twelve pieces: in England usu. called *draughts.*

check·ing account (chek′ing) A bank account against which a depositor may draw checks.

check list A list of items to be checked.

check·mate (chek′māt) *v.t.* **·mat·ed, ·mat·ing** 1. In chess, to put (an opponent's king) in check from which no escape is possible, thus winning the game. 2. To defeat by a skillful maneuver. —*n.* 1. In chess: **a** The move that checkmates a king. **b** The condition of a king when checkmated. 2. Utter defeat. Also *mate.* [< Arabic *shāh māt* the king is dead < Persian]

check·off (chek′ôf′, -of′) *n.* The deduction of trade-union dues from each worker's wages.

check-out (chek′out′) *n.* 1. The procedure or time of checking out of a hotel. 2. The itemization of goods and payment for purchases. 3. The place of payment. Also **check′out′**.

check·rein (chek′rān′) *n.* A rein from the bit to the saddle to keep a horse's head up.

check·room (chek′rōōm′, -rŏŏm′) *n.* A room in which coats, etc., may be left temporarily.

check·up (chek′up′) *n.* An examining or inspection: a physical *checkup.*

Ched·dar (ched′ər) *n.* Any of several types of white to yellow, hard, smooth cheese. Also **ched′dar, Cheddar cheese.**

cheek (chēk) *n.* 1. Either side of the face below the eye and above the mouth. 2. A side or part analogous to the side of the face.

3. *Informal* Impudent self-assurance. [OE *cēce, cēace*]
cheek·bone (chēk′bōn′) *n.* Either of two bony prominences of the cheek below the eye socket.
cheek by jowl Side by side; in close intimacy.
cheek·y (chē′kē) *adj.* **cheek·i·er, cheek·i·est** *Informal* Impudent; brazen. **—cheek′i·ly** *adv.* **—cheek′i·ness** *n.*
cheep (chēp) *v.t. & v.i.* To make, or utter with, a faint, shrill sound, as a young bird. **—***n.* A weak chirp or squeak. [Imit.] **—cheep′er** *n.*
cheer (chir) *n.* **1.** A shout of acclamation or encouragement. **2.** Gladness or gaiety. **3.** State of mind; mood. **4.** That which promotes happiness or joy; encouragement. **—***v.t.* **1.** To make cheerful; gladden: often with *up.* **2.** To acclaim with cheers. **3.** To urge; incite: often with *on.* **—***v.i.* **4.** To become cheerful or glad: often with *up.* **5.** To utter cries of encouragement, approval, etc. [< OF *chiere, chere* face] **—cheer′er** *n.* **—cheer′ing·ly** *adv.*
cheer·ful (chir′fəl) *adj.* **1.** In good spirits. **2.** Pleasant. **3.** Willing; ungrudging. **—cheer′·ful·ly** *adv.* **—cheer′ful·ness** *n.*
cheer·lead·er (chir′lē′dər) *n.* A person who leads organized cheering at an athletic event. Also **cheer leader.**
cheer·less (chir′lis) *adj.* Destitute of cheer; gloomy. **—cheer′less·ly** *adv.* **—cheer′less·ness** *n.*
cheers (chirz) *interj.* To your health: used in a toast.
cheer·y (chir′ē) *adj.* **cheer·i·er, cheer·i·est** Abounding in cheerfulness; gay. **—cheer′i·ly** *adv.* **—cheer′i·ness** *n.*
cheese (chēz) *n.* **1.** The pressed curd of milk, prepared and flavored. **2.** Any of various substances like cheese in consistency or shape. [OE *cēse* < L *caseus*]
cheese·cake (chēz′kāk′) *n.* **1.** A cake made of cream cheese or cottage cheese, eggs, milk, and sugar: also **cheese cake. 2.** *Slang* A photograph featuring a pretty girl's legs and figure.
cheese·cloth (chēz′klôth′, -kloth′) *n.* A thin, loosely woven cotton fabric.
chees·y (chē′zē) *adj.* **chees·i·er, chees·i·est** **1.** Of or like cheese. **2.** *Slang* Inferior. **—chees′i·ness** *n.*
chee·tah (chē′tə) *n.* A swift, spotted animal of the cat family, native to SW Asia and northern Africa. [< Hind. *chītā* leopard < Skt. *chitraka* speckled]
chef (shef) *n.* A head cook; also, any cook. [< F *chef* (*de cuisine*) head (of the kitchen) < OF. See CHIEF.]
che·la (kē′lə) *n. pl.* **·lae** (-lē) *Zool.* A pincer-like claw in crustaceans and arachnids. [< Gk. *chēlē* claw]
chem·i·cal (kem′i·kəl) *adj.* Of or pertaining to chemistry or its phenomena, laws, operations, or results. **—***n.* A substance obtained by or used in a chemical process. [< Med.L *alchimicus* of alchemy] **—chem′i·cal·ly** *adv.*
chemical warfare The use of gases, incendiary materials, etc., in warfare.
che·mise (shə·mēz′) *n.* **1.** A woman's loose undergarment resembling a short slip. **2.** A dress hanging straight from the shoulders. [< LL *camisia* shirt]
chem·ist (kem′ist) *n.* **1.** One versed in chemistry. **2.** *Brit.* A druggist. [< ALCHEMIST]
chem·is·try (kem′is·trē) *n. pl.* **·tries 1.** The science that treats of the structure, composition, properties, and transformations of substances. **2.** Chemical composition or processes.
chem·o·ther·a·py (kem′ō·ther′ə·pē, kḕ′mō-) *n.* *Med.* The treatment of disease by chemical means. Also **chem′o·ther′a·peu′tics** (-pyōō′tiks). **—chem′o·ther′a·peu′tic** *adj.* **—chem′o·ther′a·pist** *n.*
chem·ur·gy (kem′ər·jē) *n.* The chemical exploitation of organic raw materials to develop new products. **—chem·ur·gic** (kem·ûr′jik) or **·gi·cal** *adj.*
che·nille (shə·nēl′) *n.* **1.** A soft, fuzzy cord, used for embroidery, fringes, etc. **2.** A fabric made with this cord. [< F, caterpillar < L *canicula,* dim. of *canis* dog]
cheque (chek) *n.* *Brit.* A check (def. 6).
cheq·uer (chek′ər) *n.* *Brit.* A checker.
cher·ish (cher′ish) *v.t.* **1.** To hold dear; treat with tenderness. **2.** To entertain fondly, as a hope or an idea. [< OF *cheriss-,* stem of *cherir* to hold dear < L *carus*] **—cher′ish·er** *n.* **—cher′ish·ing·ly** *adv.*
Cher·o·kee (cher′ə·kē, cher′ə·kē′) *n. pl.* **·kee** or **·kees 1.** One of a great tribe of Iroquoian Indians formerly occupying northern Georgia and North Carolina, now dwelling in Oklahoma. **2.** The language of this tribe.
che·root (shə·rōōt′) *n.* A cigar cut square at both ends. [< Tamil *shuruttu* roll, cigar]
cher·ry (cher′ē) *n. pl.* **·ries 1.** Any of various trees of the rose family, bearing small, round or heart-shaped fruit enclosing a smooth pit; also, its wood or fruit. **2.** A bright red color resembling that of certain cherries: also **cherry red. —***adj.* **1.** Bright red. **2.** Made of or with cherries. **3.** Made of cherry wood. [ME *chery* < L *cerasus* cherry tree]
cher·ub (cher′əb) *n. pl.* **cher·ubs** or **cher·u·bim** (cher′ə·bim, -yə·bim) *for def. 1,* **cherubs** *for def. 2,* **cherubim** *for def. 3* **1.** A representation of a beautiful winged child. **2.** A beautiful child; also, a chubby, innocent-looking adult. **3.** In Scripture, a celestial being. [< Hebrew *kerūb,* an angelic being] **—che·ru·bic** (chə·rōō′bik) *adj.* **—che·ru′·bi·cal·ly** *adv.*
cher·vil (chûr′vəl) *n.* A garden herb of the parsley family. [< Gk. *chairephyllon*]
Chesh·ire cat (chesh′ər, -ir) In Lewis Carroll's *Alice's Adventures in Wonderland,* a cat that gradually faded until only its grin remained.
chess (ches) *n.* A game of skill played on a chessboard by two persons, with 16 pieces on each side. [< OF *esches,* pl. of *eschec* < Arabic *shāh* king < Persian]
chess·board (ches′bôrd′) See CHECKERBOARD.
chess·man (ches′man′, -mən) *n. pl.* **·men** (-men′, -mən) Any of the pieces used in chess.
chest (chest) *n.* **1.** The part of the body enclosed by the ribs; thorax. ◆Collateral adjective: *pectoral.* **2.** A box or cabinet for storing or protecting articles. **3.** The treasury of a public institution; also, the funds contained there. **4.** A chest of drawers. [< Gk. *kistē* basket, box]
ches·ter·field (ches′tər·fēld) *n.* A single-

breasted topcoat, generally with concealed buttons. [after a 19th c. Earl of *Chesterfield*]
chest·nut (ches′nut′, -nət) *n.* 1. The edible nut of various trees of the beech family; also, a tree that bears this nut. 2. One of certain similar trees, or their fruit, as the horse chestnut. 3. A reddish brown color. 4. A horse of this color. 5. *Informal* a A stale joke. b Anything trite, as a story, song, etc. —*adj.* Reddish brown. [< Gk. *kastanea*]
chest of drawers A piece of furniture containing a set of drawers for storing clothing, etc.
chest·y (ches′tē) *adj.* **chest·i·er, chest·i·est** *Informal* 1. Self-assertive; proud. 2. Large in the chest.
che·val glass (shə·val′) A long mirror mounted on horizontal pivots in a frame.
chev·a·lier (shev′ə·lir′) *n.* 1. A member of certain orders of knighthood or honor, as of the French Legion of Honor. 2. A knight or cavalier. 3. A chivalrous man. [< L *caballus* horse]
chev·i·ot (shev′ē·ət) *n.* A rough cloth of twill weave, used for suits, overcoats, etc.
chev·ron (shev′rən) *n.* An emblem or insignia, usu. V-shaped or inverted-V-shaped, worn on a uniform sleeve to indicate rank, length of service, etc., used by military, naval, and police forces. [< OF *chevron* rafter]
chew (cho͞o) *v.t. & v.i.* 1. To crush or grind with the teeth; masticate. 2. To meditate upon; consider carefully. —**to chew out** *Slang* To reprimand severely; berate. —*n.* 1. The act of chewing. 2. That which is chewed; a quid. [OE *cēowan*] —**chew′er** *n.*
chew·ing gum (cho͞o′ing) A preparation of natural gum, usu. chicle, flavored for chewing.
che·wink (chi·wingk′) *n.* The towhee. [Imit.]
chew·y (cho͞o′ē) *adj.* **chew·i·er, chew·i·est** Soft and requiring chewing: *chewy* caramels.
Chey·enne (shī·an′, -en′) *n. pl.* **·enne** or **·ennes** One of a tribe of North American Indians now inhabiting Montana and Oklahoma.
chi (kī) *n.* The twenty-second letter in the Greek alphabet (Χ, χ), transliterated as *ch.* [< Gk.]
chi·an·ti (kē·an′tē, *Ital.* kyän′tē) *n.* A dry red wine.
chi·a·ro·scu·ro (kē·är′ə·skyo͝or′ō) *n. pl.* **·ros** 1. The distribution and treatment of light and shade in a picture. 2. A kind of painting or drawing using only light and shade. Also **chi·a·ro-o·scu·ro** (kē·är′ə·ō·skyo͝or′ō). [< Ital. < L *clarus* clear + *obscurus* dark] —**chi·a′ro·scu′rist** *n.*
chic (shēk, shik) *n.* Originality, elegance, and taste, esp. in dress. [< F] —**chic** *adj.* —**chic′ly** *adv.*
chi·cane (shi·kān′) *v.* **·caned, ·can·ing** *v.t.* 1. To deceive or trick. 2. To quibble about. —*v.i.* 3. To resort to chicanery; use tricks. —*n.* Chicanery. [< F *chicaner*]
chi·can·er·y (shi·kā′nər·ē) *n. pl.* **·er·ies** Trickery and subterfuge.
Chi·ca·no (chi·kä′nō) *n. pl.* **·nos** A Mexican-American.
chi·chi (shē′shē) *adj. Informal* Ostentatiously stylish or elegant. [< F, frill]
chick (chik) *n.* 1. A young chicken. 2. Any young bird. 3. A child. 4. *Slang* A girl. [Short for CHICKEN]
chick·a·dee (chik′ə·dē) *n.* An American bird with the top of the head and the throat black or dark colored. [Imit. of its cry]
Chick·a·saw (chik′ə·sô) *n. pl.* **·saw** or **·saws** One of a tribe of Muskhogean North American Indians now living in Oklahoma.
chick·en (chik′ən) *n.* 1. The young of domestic fowl. 2. A cock or hen of any age. 3. The flesh of the chicken, used as food. —*adj. Slang* Afraid; cowardly. —*v.i. Slang* To lose one's nerve: often with *out.* [OE *cicen*]
chicken feed 1. *Slang* A small sum of money. 2. Food for chickens.
chicken hawk Any of various hawks that prey on poultry.
chick·en-heart·ed (chik′ən·här′tid) *adj.* Cowardly.
chicken pox *Pathol.* A contagious disease, principally of children, characterized by skin eruptions and fever.
chick·pea (chik′pē′) *n.* 1. A plant of Mediterranean regions and central Asia. 2. Its seed, widely used as a food. [ME *chichpease*]
chick·weed (chik′wēd′) *n.* Any of various weeds having seeds and leaves that birds eat.
chic·le (chik′əl) *n.* The milky juice or latex of the sapodilla, used as the basic ingredient of chewing gum. Also **chicle gum.** [< Sp. < Nahuatl *chicili*]
chic·o·ry (chik′ər·ē) *n. pl.* **·ries** 1. A perennial herb, used in salads. 2. Its dried, roasted, and ground roots, used with or as a substitute for coffee. [< Gk. *kichora*]
chide (chīd) *v.t. & v.i.* **chid·ed** or **chid** (chid), **chid·ed** or **chid** or **chid·den** (chid′n), **chid·ing** To speak reprovingly (to); scold. [OE *cīdan*] —**chid′er** *n.* —**chid′ing·ly** *adv.*
chief (chēf) *n.* 1. *Often cap.* The person highest in rank or authority, as the leader or head of a tribe, police force, etc. 2. *Usu. cap.* A ship's chief engineer; also, a chief petty officer. 3. *Slang* A boss. —**in chief** Having the highest authority: commander *in chief.* —*adj.* 1. Highest in rank or authority. 2. Most important or eminent; leading. [< OF *chef, chief* < L *caput* head]
chief justice The presiding judge of a court composed of several justices.
chief·ly (chēf′lē) *adv.* 1. Primarily; especially. 2. Principally; mainly. —*adj.* Of or like a chief.
chief of staff The principal staff officer of a division or higher level.
Chief of Staff The ranking officer in the U.S. Army or Air Force.
chief·tain (chēf′tən) *n.* 1. The head of a clan or tribe. 2. Any chief; leader. [< L *caput* head] —**chief′tain·cy, chief′tain·ship** *n.*
chif·fon (shi·fon′, shif′on) *n.* A sheer fabric, esp. of silk. —*adj.* 1. Of or pertaining to chiffon. 2. In cooking, having a fluffy texture. [< F, dim. of *chiffe* rag]
chif·fo·nier (shif′ə·nir′) *n.* A high chest of drawers, often with a mirror at the top. Also **chif′fon·nier′.** [< F < *chiffon*]
chig·ger (chig′ər) *n.* 1. The larva of various mites of the southern U.S. that attaches itself to the skin, causing intense itching. 2. The chigoe (def. 1). [Alter. of CHIGOE]
chi·gnon (shēn′yon, *Fr.* shē·nyôn′) *n.* A knot or roll of hair worn at the back of the head by women. [< F]

chig·oe (chig′ō) *n.* 1. A flea of the West Indies and South America. 2. A chigger (def. 1). [< Carib]
Chi·hua·hua (chi·wä′wä) *n.* A small, smooth-coated dog with large, pointed ears. [after *Chihuahua,* Mexico]
chil·blain (chil′blān) *n. Pathol.* An inflammation of the hands or feet caused by exposure to cold.
child (chīld) *n. pl.* **chil·dren** 1. An offspring of human parents. 2. A boy or girl, most commonly one between infancy and youth. 3. A descendant. 4. A childish person. 5. A product of a specified condition, quality, time, etc. —**with child** Pregnant. [OE *cild*] —**child′less** *adj.*
child·bear·ing (chīld′bâr′ing) *n.* The bringing forth of children.
child·birth (chīld′bûrth′) *n.* The act of giving birth to offspring.
child·hood (chīld′ho͝od) *n.* The state or time of being a child. [OE *cildhād*]
child·ish (chīl′dish) *adj.* 1. Of, like, or proper to a child. 2. Unduly like a child; immature; puerile; weak. [OE *cildisc*] —**child′ish·ly** *adv.* —**child′ish·ness** *n.*
child·like (chīld′līk′) *adj.* Like, characteristic of, or appropriate to a child; artless, docile, etc. —**child′like′ness** *n.*
chil·dren (chil′drən) Plural of CHILD.
child's play Something easy to do.
chil·i (chil′ē) *n. pl.* **chil·ies** 1. The acrid pod or fruit of the red pepper, used as a seasoning. 2. Chili con carne. Also **chil′e, chil′li.** [< Sp. < Nahuatl *chilli*]
chili con car·ne (kon kär′nē) A highly seasoned dish made with meat, chili, and often beans. [< Sp., chili with meat]
chill (chil) *n.* 1. A sensation of cold, often with shivering. 2. A moderate degree of coldness. 3. A check to enthusiasm, joy, etc. 4. A numbing sensation of dread or anxiety. —*v.t.* 1. To reduce to a low temperature. 2. To affect with cold. 3. To check, as ardor; dispirit. 4. To harden the surface of (metal) by sudden cooling. —*v.i.* 5. To become cold. 6. To be stricken with a chill. 7. To become hard by sudden cooling, as metal. —*adj.* 1. Moderately or unpleasantly cold. 2. Affected by or shivering with cold. 3. Cold in manner; distant. 4. Discouraging. [OE *ciele*] —**chill′ing·ly** *adv.* —**chill′ness** *n.*
chill·er (chil′ər) *n.* 1. That which chills. 2. A horror story or movie.
chill·y (chil′ē) *adj.* **chill·i·er, chill·i·est** 1. Causing chill; cold or chilling. 2. Feeling cold; affected by chill. 3. Disheartening; unfriendly. —**chill′i·ly** *adv.* —**chill′i·ness** *n.*
chime (chīm) *n.* 1. *Often pl.* A set of bells, as in a bell tower, tuned to a scale. 2. A single bell: the *chime* of a clock. 3. *Often pl.* The sounds or music produced by a chime. 4. Agreement; accord. —*v.* **chimed, chim·ing** *v.t.* 1. To cause to sound musically by striking; ring. 2. To announce (the hour) by the sound of bells. 3. To say rhythmically. —*v.i.* 4. To sound musically. 5. To ring chimes. 6. To harmonize; agree: with *with.* —**to chime in** 1. To join in harmoniously. 2. To join, and so interrupt, a conversation. [< L *cymbalum* cymbal] —**chim′er** *n.*
chi·me·ra (kə·mir′ə, kī-) *n.* 1. An absurd creation of the imagination. 2. In painting, etc., a grotesque monster. [< Gk. *chimaira* she-goat]
chi·mer·i·cal (kə·mer′i·kəl, kī-) *adj.* 1. Of the nature of a chimera; fantastic; imaginary. 2. Given to fanciful dreams; visionary. Also **chi·mer′ic.** —**chi·mer′i·cal·ly** *adv.*
chim·ney (chim′nē) *n.* 1. A flue to conduct gases and smoke from a fire to the outer air. 2. A structure containing such a flue, usu. vertical and rising above the roof of a building. 3. A smokestack; funnel. 4. A tube, usually of glass, for enclosing the flame of a lamp. [< OF *cheminee* ult. < Gk. *kaminos*]
chimp (chimp) *n.* A chimpanzee.
chim·pan·zee (chim′pan·zē′, chim·pan′zē) *n.* An arboreal anthropoid ape of equatorial Africa. [< native West African name]
chin (chin) *n.* 1. The lower part of the face, between the mouth and the neck. 2. *Anat.* The central and anterior part of the lower jaw. —*v.t. & v.i.* **chinned, chin·ning** To lift (oneself) while grasping an overhead bar until the chin is level with the hands. [OE *cin*]
chi·na (chī′nə) *n.* 1. Fine porcelain or ceramic ware. 2. Any crockery. Also **chi′na·ware′.**
Chi·na·town (chī′nə·toun′) The Chinese quarter of any city outside China.
chinch (chinch) *n.* 1. A small, sucking insect destructive to cereal grasses. Also **chinch bug.** 2. The bedbug. [< Sp. *chinche* < L *cimex* bug]
chin·chil·la (chin·chil′ə) *n.* 1. A small rodent native to the Andes. 2. The fur of the chinchilla. 3. A closely woven, twilled fabric having a tufted surface. [< Sp., ? alter. of Quechua *sinchi* strong]
chine (chīn) *n.* 1. The spine, backbone, or back. 2. A piece of meat including all or part of the backbone. 3. A ridge or crest. [< OF *eschine* backbone]
Chi·nese (chī·nēz′, -nēs′) *adj.* Of or pertaining to China, its people, or their languages. —*n. pl.* **·nese** 1. A native of China, or a person of Chinese ancestry. 2. The language or languages of China.
Chinese lantern A collapsible lantern made of thin paper.
chink[1] (chingk) *n.* A small, narrow cleft; crevice. —*v.t.* 1. To make cracks or fissures in. 2. To fill the cracks of, as a wall; plug up. [ME *chynke*] —**chink′y** *adj.*
chink[2] (chingk) *n.* A short, sharp, metallic sound. —*v.t. & v.i.* To make or cause to make a sharp, clinking sound. [Imit.]
chi·no (chē′nō) *n.* 1. A strong cotton fabric with a twilled weave. 2. *pl.* Trousers of this material. [< Sp., toasted; with ref. to the original tan color]
chi·nook (chi·no͞ok′, -no͝ok′) *n.* 1. A warm wind of the Oregon and Washington coasts. 2. A warm, dry wind that blows off the eastern slopes of the Rocky Mountains. [after *Chinook*]
Chi·nook (chi·no͞ok′, -no͝ok′) *n. pl.* **·nook** or **·nooks** 1. One of a tribe of North American Indians formerly occupying Oregon. 2. The language of this tribe. —**Chi·nook′an** *adj. & n.*
chintz (chints) *n.* A cotton fabric usu. glazed and printed in bright colors. Also **chints.** [< Skt. *chitra* variegated]
chintz·y (chints′ē) *adj.* **chintz·i·er, chintz·i·**

est 1. Of or relating to chintz. 2. Cheap; gaudy.

chip (chip) *n.* 1. A small piece cut or broken off. 2. A small counter used in certain games, as in poker. 3. A crack or imperfection caused by chipping. 4. A thinly sliced morsel: potato *chips.* 5. *pl. Brit.* French fried potatoes. 6. *Electronics* An integrated circuit. —**a chip off** (or **of**) **the old block** One who resembles either parent in behavior, appearance, etc. —**a chip on one's shoulder** A hostile or belligerent manner. —*v.* **chipped, chip·ping** *v.t.* 1. To break off small pieces of, as china. —*v.i.* 2. To become chipped. —**to chip in** *Informal* To contribute, as to a fund. [ME *chippe*] —**chip′per** *n.*

chip·munk (chip′mungk) *n.* Any of various small, striped North American ground-dwelling squirrels. Also **chip·muck** (chip′muk). [< N.Am.Ind.]

chipped beef (chipt) Beef smoked and sliced thin.

Chip·pen·dale (chip′ən·dāl) *adj.* Designating a graceful, highly ornamented style of furniture design that originated in 18th c. England. [after Thomas *Chippendale,* 1718–79, English cabinetmaker]

chip·per (chip′ər) *adj. Informal* 1. Brisk; cheerful. 2. Smartly dressed. [< Brit. Dial. *kipper* frisky]

Chip·pe·wa (chip′ə·wä, -wā, -wə) *n. pl.* **·wa** or **·was** Ojibwa. Also **Chip·pe·way** (chip′ə·wā).

chiro- *combining form* Hand; of or with the hand: *chirography.* Also, before vowels, **chir-.** [< Gk. *cheir, cheiros*]

chi·rog·ra·phy (kī·rog′rə·fē) *n.* The art, style, or character of handwriting; penmanship. —**chi·rog′ra·pher** *n.* —**chi·ro·graph·ic** (kī′rə·graf′ik) or **·i·cal** *adj.*

chi·rop·o·dy (kə·rop′ə·dē, kī-) *n.* The branch of medicine that deals with ailments of the foot: also called *pedicure, podiatry.* [< CHIRO- + Gk. *podos* foot] —**chi·rop′o·dist** *n.*

chi·ro·prac·tic (kī′rə·prak′tik) *n.* A therapy based on the manipulation of bodily structures, esp. the spinal column. [< CHIRO- + Gk. *praktikos* effective] —**chi′ro·prac′tor** *n.*

chirp (chûrp) *v.i.* 1. To give a short, acute cry, as a sparrow or locust. 2. To talk in a quick and shrill manner. —*v.t.* 3. To utter with a quick, sharp sound. [Var. of Scot. *chirk* < OE *cearcian* to creak] —**chirp** *n.* —**chirp′er** *n.*

chirr (chûr) *v.i.* To make a sharp trilling sound, as that of the grasshopper, cicada, and some birds. Also **chirre.** [Imit.] —**chirr** *n.*

chir·rup (chir′əp) *v.i.* 1. To chirp continuously or repeatedly, as a bird. —*v.t.* 2. To utter with chirps. [< CHIRP] —**chir′rup** *n.* —**chir′rup·y** *adj.*

chis·el (chiz′əl) *n.* A cutting tool with a beveled edge, used on metal, stone, or wood. —*v.t. & v.i.* **chis·eled** or **·elled, chis·el·ing** or **·el·ling** 1. To cut, engrave, or carve with or as with a chisel. 2. *Slang* To cheat; swindle. [< L *caedere* to cut] —**chis′el·er** or **chis′el·ler** *n.*

chit[1] (chit) *n.* A voucher of a sum owed, as for food. [< Hind. *chitthī* note]

chit[2] (chit) *n.* A pert girl. [ME *chitt*]

chit·chat (chit′chat′) *n.* 1. Small talk. 2. Gossip. —**chit′chat′** *v.i.* **·chat·ted, ·chat·ting**

chi·tin (kī′tin) *n. Biochem.* The hard, horny outer covering of insects and crustaceans. [< Gk. *chitōn* tunic] —**chi′tin·ous** *adj.*

chit·ter·lings (chit′ər·lingz) *n.pl.* The small intestines of pigs, esp. as used for food: also **chit·lins** (chit′linz), **chit·lings** (chit′lingz). [Cf. G *kutteln* entrails]

chiv·al·ric (shiv′əl·rik, shi·val′rik) *adj.* Chivalrous.

chiv·al·rous (shiv′əl·rəs) *adj.* 1. Having the qualities of the ideal knight; gallant, courteous, generous, etc. 2. Pertaining to chivalry. [< OF *chevalier* knight] —**chiv′al·rous·ly** *adv.* —**chiv′al·rous·ness** *n.*

chiv·al·ry (shiv′əl·rē) *n.* 1. The feudal system of knighthood. 2. The ideal qualities of knighthood, as courtesy, valor, skill in arms, etc. 3. A body of knights. [< OF *chevalerie,* ult. < LL *caballarius* cavalier]

chive (chīv) *n.* A perennial herb allied to the leek and onion, used in cooking. [< L *cepa* onion]

chlo·ral (klôr′əl) *n. Chem.* 1. A colorless, oily, liquid compound with a penetrating odor. 2. A white, crystalline, pungent compound used medicinally as a hypnotic and sedative: also **chloral hydrate.** [< CHLOR(INE) + AL(COHOL)]

chlo·ram·phen·i·col (klôr′am·fen′i·kōl, -kol) *n. Chem.* A crystalline nitrogenous compound, used as an antibiotic.

chlor·dane (klôr′dān) *n. Chem.* A toxic compound of chlorine, used as an insecticide.

chlo·ride (klôr′īd) *n. Chem.* A compound of chlorine. Also **chlo·rid** (klôr′id). —**chlo·rid·ic** (klə·rid′ik) *adj.*

chlo·rin·ate (klôr′ə·nāt) *v.t.* **·at·ed, ·at·ing** *Chem.* To treat or cause to combine with chlorine, as in purifying water, whitening fabrics, etc. —**chlo′rin·a′tion** *n.*

chlo·rine (klôr′ēn) *n.* A greenish yellow, poisonous, gaseous element (symbol Cl), with a suffocating odor, widely used as a bleach and disinfectant. [< Gk. *chlōros* green]

chloro- *combining form* 1. Light green: *chlorophyll.* 2. Chlorine. Also, before vowels, **chlor-.** [< Gk. *chlōros* green]

chlo·ro·form (klôr′ə·fôrm) *n. Chem.* A colorless, volatile, sweetish liquid compound, used as an anesthetic and solvent. —*v.t.* To anesthetize or kill with chloroform.

Chlo·ro·my·ce·tin (klôr′ə·mī·sē′tən) *n.* Proprietary name for a brand of chloramphenicol: also **chlo′ro·my·ce′tin.**

chlo·ro·phyll (klôr′ə·fil) *n. Biochem.* The green nitrogenous pigment found in plants, essential to photosynthesis. Also **chlo′ro·phyl.** [< CHLORO- + Gk. *phyllon* leaf] —**chlo′ro·phyl·la′ceous** (-fi·lā′shəs), **chlo′ro·phyl′lose** (-fil′ōs), **chlo′ro·phyl′lous** (-fil′əs) *adj.*

chlor·pro·ma·zine (klôr·prō′mə·zēn′, -zin′) *n.* A synthetic tranquilizing drug.

chock (chok) *n.* A block or wedge, so placed as to prevent or limit motion. —*v.t.* To make fast or fit with a chock or chocks. —*adv.* As fully or as close as possible. [< AF *choque* log]

chock-a-block (chok′ə·blok′) *adj.* Close together; jammed. —*adv.* Close; very near.

chock-full (chok′fo͞ol′) *adj.* Completely full; stuffed. [ME *chokke-fulle*]

choc·o·late (chôk′lit, chôk′ə·lit, chok′-) *n.* 1. A preparation of cacao nuts roasted and ground and usu. sweetened. 2. A beverage or confection made from this. 3. A dark, reddish-brown color. —*adj.* 1. Flavored with or made with chocolate. 2. Reddish-brown. [< Sp. < Nahuatl *chocolatl*] —**choc′o·lat·y** *adj.*

Choc·taw (chok′tô) *n. pl.* **·taw** or **·taws** 1. One of a tribe of Muskhogean North American Indians, now living in Oklahoma. 2. The language of this tribe.

choice (chois) *n.* 1. The act of choosing; selection. 2. The right or privilege of choosing; option. 3. The person or thing chosen. 4. A number or variety from which to choose. 5. An alternative. 6. The best or preferred part of anything. —*adj.* **choic·er, choic·est** 1. Select; excellent. 2. Chosen with care. [< OF *choisir* to choose] —**choice′ly** *adv.* —**choice′ness** *n.*

choir (kwīr) *n.* 1. An organized body of singers, esp. in a church. 2. The part of a church occupied by such singers. —*v.t.* & *v.i.* To sing in chorus. [< OF *cuer* < L *chorus*]

choke (chōk) *v.* **choked, chok·ing** *v.t.* 1. To stop the breathing of by obstructing the windpipe; strangle. 2. To suppress or hinder; retard the progress of. 3. To obstruct by filling; clog. 4. To lessen the air intake of the carburetor in order to enrich the fuel mixture of (a gasoline engine). —*v.i.* 5. To become suffocated or stifled. 6. To become obstructed. —**to choke up** 1. To be overcome by emotion. 2. To perform poorly because of tension, agitation, etc. —*n.* 1. The act or sound of choking. 2. A device to control the flow of air, as to a gasoline engine. [OE *acēocian*]

choke·cher·ry (chōk′cher′ē) *n. pl.* **·ries** A wild cherry of North America, or its sour fruit.

choke·damp (chōk′damp′) *n.* Blackdamp.

chok·er (chō′kər) *n.* 1. One who or that which chokes. 2. A neckcloth or necklace worn high around the throat; also, a high, tight collar.

chok·y (chō′kē) *adj.* **chok·i·er, chok·i·est** 1. Causing one to choke. 2. Somewhat choked. Also **chok′ey.**

chol·er (kol′ər) *n.* Anger; hastiness of temper. [< Gk. *cholē* bile] —**chol′er·ic** *adj.*

chol·er·a (kol′ər·ə) *n. Pathol.* An acute, infectious disease characterized principally by serious intestinal disorders. [< Gk. *cholē* bile]

cho·les·ter·ol (kə·les′tə·rōl, -rol) *n. Biochem.* A fatty, crystalline sterol derived principally from bile, present in most gallstones, and widely distributed in animal fats and tissues. Also **cho·les′ter·in** (-tə·rin). [< Gk. *cholē* bile + *stereos* solid]

choose (cho͞oz) *v.* **chose, cho·sen, choos·ing** *v.t.* 1. To select as most desirable; take by preference. 2. To prefer (to do something); decide. —*v.i.* 3. To make a choice. [OE *cēosan*] —**choos′er** *n.*

choos·y (cho͞o′zē) *adj.* **choos·i·er, choos·i·est** *Informal* Particular or fussy in one's choices. Also **choos′ey.**

chop (chop) *v.* **chopped, chop·ping** *v.t.* 1. To cut or make by strokes of a sharp tool. 2. To cut up in small pieces. 3. To make a cutting, downward stroke at (the ball), as in tennis. —*v.i.* 4. To make cutting strokes. 5. To move with sudden or violent motion. —*n.* 1. The act of chopping. 2. A cut of meat, usu. lamb, pork, or veal. 3. A sharp, downward blow or stroke, as in karate, tennis, etc. 4. A quick, broken motion of waves. [ME *choppen*]

chop·house (chop′hous′) *n.* A restaurant specializing in chops and steaks.

chop·per (chop′ər) *n.* 1. One who or that which chops, esp. a device that chops food. 2. *pl. Slang* Teeth. 3. *Slang* A helicopter. 4. *Slang* A customized motorcycle.

chop·py (chop′ē) *adj.* **·pi·er, ·pi·est** 1. Full of short, rough waves. 2. Shifting; variable. [< CHOP]

chops (chops) *n.pl.* The jaws; also the part of the face about the mouth or jaws. [ME *chaft* jaw]

chop·sticks (chop′stiks′) *n.pl.* Slender rods of ivory or wood, used in pairs in China, Japan, etc., to convey food to the mouth. [< Pidgin English *chop* quick + STICK]

chop su·ey (so͞o′ē) A Chinese-American dish made with bits of meat and vegetables, served with rice. [< Chinese *tsa-sui*, lit., mixed pieces]

cho·ral (kôr′əl) *adj.* Pertaining to, written for, or sung by a chorus or choir. —**cho′ral·ly** *adv.*

cho·rale (kô·ral′, kə-) *n.* 1. A hymn marked by a simple melody, often sung in unison. 2. A chorus or choir. Also **cho·ral′.** [< G *choral*]

chord[1] (kôrd) *n. Music* A combination of three or more tones sounded together, usu. in harmony. [Earlier *cord*, short for ACCORD]

chord[2] (kôrd) *n.* 1. A string of a musical instrument. 2. An emotional reaction. 3. *Geom.* **a** A straight line connecting the extremities of an arc. **b** The portion of a straight line contained by its intersections with a curve. 4. Any of various chordlike things, as a tendon. [< Gk. *chordē* string of a musical instrument] —**chord′al** *adj.*

chore (chôr) *n.* 1. A small or minor job. 2. An unpleasant or hard task.

cho·re·a (kô·rē′ə) *n. Pathol.* An acute nervous disease characterized by involuntary and uncontrollable muscular twitching: also called *St. Vitus's dance.* [< Gk. *choreia* dance] —**cho·re′al, cho·re′ic** *adj.*

choreo- *combining form* Dance. Also **choro-.** [< Gk. *choreia* dance]

cho·re·o·graph (kôr′ē·ə·graf′) *v.t.* To devise (ballet and other dance compositions). —**cho·re·og·ra·pher** (kôr′ē·og′rə·fər) *n.*

cho·re·og·ra·phy (kôr′ē·og′rə·fē) *n.* 1. The devising of ballets and incidental dances, esp. for the stage. 2. The written representation of figures and steps of dancing. 3. The art of dancing; ballet. 4. Stage dancing. Also **cho·reg·ra·phy** (kə·reg′rə·fē). —**cho·re·o·graph·ic** (kôr′ē·ə·graf′ik) *adj.*

chor·is·ter (kôr′is·tər, kor′-) *n.* A leader or member of a choir. [< L *chorus*]

chor·tle (chôr′təl) *v.t.* & *v.i.* **·tled, ·tling** To utter with chuckles of glee. [Blend of CHUCKLE and SNORT; coined by Lewis Carroll] —**chor′tle** *n.*

cho·rus (kôr′əs) *n.* 1. A musical composition to be sung by a large group. 2. A group of singers who perform such works. 3. A body of singers and dancers who perform together in opera, musical comedy, etc. 4. A group of persons singing or speaking something simultaneously. 5. A simultaneous utterance by many individuals. 6. A refrain, as of a song. 7. In Greek drama, a body of actors who comment upon and sometimes take part in the main action of a play. —*v.t.* & *v.i.* **cho·rused** or **·russed, cho·rus·ing** or **·rus·sing** To sing or speak all together in unison. [< Gk. *choros* dance]

chorus girl A woman in the chorus of a musical comedy, etc. —**chorus boy** *masc.*

chose (chōz) Past tense of CHOOSE.

cho·sen (chō′zən) Past participle of CHOOSE. —*adj.* 1. Made an object of choice; selected. 2. Marked or selected for special favor.

chow (chou) *n.* 1. A medium-sized dog having a thick brown or black coat: also **chow chow.** 2. *Slang* Food.

chow-chow (chou′chou′) *n.* A relish of chopped mixed vegetables pickled in mustard. [< Pidgin English]

chow·der (chou′dər) *n.* A dish usu. made of clams or fish stewed with vegetables, often in milk. [< F *chaudière* kettle < L *calidus* hot]

chow mein (mān) A Chinese-American dish made of shredded meat and vegetables, served with fried noodles. [< Chinese *ch'ao* to fry + *mein* flour]

chrism (kriz′əm) *n. Eccl.* Consecrated oil used at baptism, confirmation, etc. [< Gk. *chriein* to anoint]

Christ (krīst) *n.* Jesus of Nazareth, regarded as the Messiah foretold by the Hebrew prophets. [< Gk. *Christos* (< *chriein* to anoint); trans. of Hebrew *māshīah* anointed] —**Christ′like′** *adj.* —**Christ′like′ness, Christ′li·ness** *n.* —**Christ′ly** *adv.*

chris·ten (kris′ən) *v.t.* 1. To name in baptism. 2. To administer Christian baptism to. 3. To give a name to. 4. *Informal* To use for the first time. [See CHRIST.] —**chris′ten·ing** *n.*

Chris·ten·dom (kris′ən·dəm) *n.* 1. The Christian world. 2. Christians collectively.

Chris·tian (kris′chən) *adj.* 1. Professing or following the religion of Christ; esp., affirming the divinity of Christ. 2. Relating to or derived from Christ or his doctrine. 3. Characteristic of Christianity or Christendom. 4. *Informal* Humane; civilized. —*n.* 1. One who believes in or professes belief in the teachings of Christ; a member of any of the Christian churches. 2. *Informal* A civilized, decent, or respectable person. —**Chris′tian·ly** *adv.*

Chris·ti·an·i·ty (kris′chē·an′ə·tē) *n.* 1. The Christian religion. 2. Christians collectively. 3. The state of being a Christian.

Chris·tian·ize (kris′chən·īz) *v.t.* **·ized, ·iz·ing** 1. To convert to Christianity. 2. To imbue with Christian principles, etc. —**Chris′tian·i·za′tion** *n.* —**Chris′tian·iz′er** *n.*

Christian name 1. A baptismal name. 2. A given name; a first name.

Christian Science A religion and system of healing, founded in 1866 by Mary Baker Eddy: officially called the *Church of Christ, Scientist.* —**Christian Scientist**

chris·tie (kris′tē) *n. pl.* **·ties** A turn in skiing used for stopping or changing direction. Also **chris′ty.** [after *Christiania,* former name of Oslo]

Christ·mas (kris′məs) *n.* December 25, held as the anniversary of the birth of Jesus Christ and widely observed as a holy day or a holiday. Also **Christmas Day.**

Christ·mas·tide (kris′məs·tīd′) *n.* The season of Christmas extending from Christmas Eve to Epiphany (Jan. 6).

chro·mat·ic (krō·mat′ik) *adj.* 1. Pertaining to color. 2. *Music* Of or pertaining to a chromatic scale, or to an instrument that can play such a scale. —**chro·mat′i·cal·ly** *adv.*

chro·mat·ics (krō·mat′iks) *n.pl.* (*construed as sing.*) The science of colors.

chromatic scale *Music* A scale proceeding by semitones.

chro·ma·tog·ra·phy (krō′mə·tog′rə·fē) *n. Chem.* A method for the analysis or separation of a solution, based on selective adsorption of the constituents when passed through certain solids. —**chro·mat·o·graph·ic** (krō·mat′ə·graf′ik) *adj.* —**chro·mat′o·graph′i·cal·ly** *adv.*

chrome (krōm) *n.* 1. The yellow chromium pigment. 2. Chromium. 3. Something plated with a chromium alloy. —*v.t.* **chromed, chrom·ing** To plate with chromium. [< Gk. *chrōma* color]

chro·mi·um (krō′mē·əm) *n.* A grayish white, very hard metallic element (symbol Cr), used in making alloys and pigments. [< Gk. *chrōma* color; so called from its many brightly colored compounds] —**chro·mic** (krō′mik) *adj.*

chromo- *combining form* 1. Color; in or with color. 2. *Chem.* Chromium. Also, before vowels, **chrom-.** [< Gk. *chrōma* color]

chro·mo·some (krō′mə·sōm) *n. Biol.* A complex body found in the cell nucleus, consisting of DNA and protein molecules, containing the genes, and serving to transmit hereditary information. [< Gk. *chrōma* color + -SOME[2]] —**chro′mo·so′mal** *adj.* —**chro′·mo·so′mal·ly** *adv.*

chro·mo·sphere (krō′mə·sfir′) *n. Astron.* An incandescent, gaseous envelope that surrounds the sun or any star. —**chro′mo·spher′ic** (-sfir′ik, -sfer′-) *adj.*

chron·ic (kron′ik) *adj.* 1. Prolonged; lingering; also, recurrent: said of a disease: opposed to *acute.* 2. Given to a habit; confirmed. [< Gk. *chronos* time] —**chron′i·cal·ly** *adv.*

chron·i·cle (kron′i·kəl) *n.* A register of events in the order in which they occurred. —*v.t.* **·cled, ·cling** To record in, or in the manner of, a chronicle. [< Gk. *chronos* time] —**chron′i·cler** *n.*

Chron·i·cles (kron′i·kəlz) *n.pl.* Either of two historical books, I and II Chronicles, of the Old Testament: also, in the Douai Bible, called *I* and *II Paralipomenon.*

chrono- *combining form* Time: *chronometer.* Also, before vowels, **chron-.** [< Gk. *chronos*]

chron·o·graph (kron′ə·graf) *n.* An instrument for measuring and recording exact time intervals. [< CHRONO- + -GRAPH] —**chron′·o·graph′ic** *adj.*

chron·o·log·i·cal (kron′ə·loj′i·kəl) *adj.* 1. Arranged according to sequence in time. 2. Pertaining to chronology. Also **chron′o·log′ic.** —**chron′o·log′i·cal·ly** *adv.*

chro·nol·o·gy (krə·nol′ə·jē) *n. pl.* **·gies** 1. The science of determining the proper sequence of historical events. 2. Arrangement or relationship according to order of occurrence. 3. A chronological list or table. [< CHRONO- + -LOGY] —**chro·nol′o·ger, chro·nol′o·gist** *n.*

chro·nom·e·ter (krə·nom′ə·tər) *n.* A time-keeping instrument of high precision. [< CHRONO- + -METER] —**chron·o·met·ric** (kron′ə·met′rik) or **·ri·cal** *adj.* —**chron′o·met′ri·cal·ly** *adv.*

chro·nom·e·try (krə·nom′ə·trē) *n.* The science or method of measuring time.

chrys·a·lis (kris′ə·lis) *n. pl.* **chrys·a·lis·es** or **chry·sal·i·des** (kri·sal′ə·dēz) 1. *Entomol.* The capsule-enclosed pupa from which the butterfly or moth develops. 2. Anything in an undeveloped stage. [< Gk. *chrysos* gold] —**chrys′a·lid** *adj.*

chrys·an·the·mum (kri·san′thə·məm) *n.* 1. Any of a number of cultivated varieties of plants with large heads of showy flowers. 2. The flower. [< Gk. *chrysanthemon* golden flower]

chrys·o·lite (kris′ə·līt) *n.* A variety of olivine. [< Gk. *chrysos* gold + *lithos* stone]

chub (chub) *n. pl.* **chubs** or **chub** 1. A carplike fish common in European rivers. 2. Any of various unrelated fishes. [ME *chubbe*]

chub·by (chub′ē) *adj.* **·bi·er, ·bi·est** Plump; rounded. —**chub′bi·ness** *n.*

chuck[1] (chuk) *v.t.* 1. To pat or tap affectionately, esp. under the chin. 2. To throw or pitch. 3. *Informal* To discard. 4. *Informal* To eject forcibly: with *out.* 5. *Slang* To quit. —*n.* 1. A playful pat under the chin. 2. A throw; toss. [Cf. F *choquer* shake, jolt]

chuck[2] (chuk) *n.* 1. The cut of beef extending from the neck to the shoulder blade. 2. A clamp or wedge used to hold a tool or work, as in a lathe. [Dial. E, lump]

chuck·le (chuk′əl) *v.i.* **·led, ·ling** To laugh quietly and with satisfaction. [Freq. of CLUCK] —**chuck′le** *n.* —**chuck′ler** *n.*

chuck wagon A wagon fitted with cooking equipment and provisions for cowboys, harvest hands, etc.

chug (chug) *n.* A dull, explosive sound, as of the exhaust of an engine. —*v.i.* **chugged, chug·ging** 1. To move or operate with a series of such sounds. 2. To move laboriously. [Imit.]

chuk·ka (chu′kə) *n.* An ankle-length boot, often of suede, with four eyelets: also **chukka boot.** [after a boot worn by polo players. See CHUKKER.]

chuk·ker (chuk′ər) *n.* In polo, one of the eight periods of play. Also **chuk′kar.** [< Hind. < Skt. *chakra* wheel]

chum (chum) *n.* An intimate companion. —*v.i.* **chummed, chum·ming** 1. To associate very closely with another. 2. To share the same room. [? Short for *chamber fellow*]

chum·my (chum′ē) *adj.* **·mi·er, ·mi·est** *Informal* Friendly; intimate. —**chum′mi·ly** *adv.*

chump (chump) *n. Informal* A stupid or foolish person. [? Var. of CHUNK]

chunk (chungk) *n.* 1. A thick mass or piece of anything, as wood. 2. A considerable quantity of something. 3. *Informal* A strong, stocky person or animal. [Var. of CHUCK[2]]

chunk·y (chung′kē) *adj.* **chunk·i·er, chunk·i·est** 1. Short and thickset; stocky. 2. In chunks. —**chunk′i·ness** *n.*

church (chûrch) *n.* 1. A building for Christian worship. 2. Regular religious services; public worship. 3. A congregation of Christians. 4. *Usu. cap.* A distinct body of Christians having a common faith and discipline; a denomination. 5. All Christian believers collectively. 6. Ecclesiastical authority: the separation of *church* and state. [OE *circe,* ult. < Gk. *kyrios* Lord] —**church′ly** *adj.* —**church′li·ness** *n.*

church·go·er (chûrch′gō′ər) *n.* One who goes regularly to church. —**church′go′ing** *adj. & n.*

church·man (chûrch′mən) *n. pl.* **·men** (-mən) 1. A member of a church. 2. A clergyman. —**church′man·ly** *adj.* —**church′man·ship** *n.* —**church′wom′an** (-wŏŏm′ən) *n.fem.*

Church of Christ, Scientist See CHRISTIAN SCIENCE.

Church of England The national church of England: also called *Anglican Church.*

Church of Jesus Christ of Latter-day Saints The Mormon Church: its official name.

church·war·den (chûrch′wôr′dən) *n.* 1. In the Church of England and the Protestant Episcopal Church, an elected lay officer who assists in secular affairs of the church. 2. A long-stemmed clay pipe. Also **church warden.**

church·yard (chûrch′yärd′) *n.* The ground surrounding or adjoining a church, often used as a cemetery.

churl (chûrl) *n.* 1. A rude or surly person. 2. A stingy person. 3. A rustic; countryman. [OE *ceorl*] —**churl′ish** *adj.* —**churl′ish·ly** *adv.* —**churl′ish·ness** *n.*

churn (chûrn) *n.* 1. A vessel in which milk or cream is agitated to make butter. 2. A state of unrest or agitation. —*v.t.* 1. To stir or agitate (cream or milk), as in a churn. 2. To make in a churn, as butter. 3. To agitate violently. 4. To produce mechanically in large amount: with *out.* 5. To subject (the account of a stockbroker's client) to excessive buying and selling. —*v.i.* 6. To work a churn. 7. To move with violent agitation; seethe. [OE *cyrin*] —**churn′er** *n.*

chute (shŏŏt) *n.* 1. An inclined trough or vertical passage down which water, coal, etc., may pass. 2. A steep, narrow watercourse; a rapid. 3. A narrow pen for branding or controlling cattle. 4. A slide, as for toboggans. 5. *Informal* A parachute. [Fusion of F *chute* a fall and SHOOT, n.]

chut·ney (chut′nē) *n.* A piquant relish of fruit, spices, etc. Also **chut′nee.** [< Hind. *chatnī*]

chutz·pah (hŏŏts′pə, khŏŏts′-) *n. Slang* Brazen effrontery; gall. [< Yiddish < Hebrew]

ciao (chou) *interj.* Used in greeting and parting. [< Ital. dial. < *schiavo* I am (your) slave]

ci·ca·da (si·kā′də, -kä′-) *n. pl.* **·das** or **·dae** (-dē) A large winged insect, the male of which has vibrating membranes that produce a loud, shrill sound: often called *locust.* [< L]

cic·a·trix (sik′ə·triks) *n. pl.* **cic·a·tri·ces** (sik′ə·trī′sēz) A scar left by the healing of a wound, the fall of a leaf, etc. Also **cic·a·trice** (sik′ə·tris). [< L] —**cic·a·tri·cial** (sik′ə·trish′əl), **ci·cat·ri·cose** (si·kat′ri·kōs) *adj.*

cic·a·trize (sik′ə·trīz) *v.t. & v.i.* **·trized,**

·triz·ing To heal by the formation of a scar. **—cic′a·tri·za′tion** *n.*
cic·e·ro·ne (sis′ə·rō′nē, *Ital.* chē′chā·rō′nā) *n.* *pl.* **·nes,** *Ital.* **·ni** (-nē) A guide for tourists. [< Ital., Cicero, Roman orator]
Cic·e·ro·ni·an (sis′ə·rō′nē·ən) *adj.* Eloquent. [after the Roman orator *Cicero*]
-cidal *combining form* Killing; able to kill: *homicidal.* [< L *caedere* to kill]
-cide *combining form* 1. Killer or destroyer of: *regicide.* 2. Murder or killing of: *suicide.* [def. 1 < L *-cida* killer < *caedere* to kill; def. 2 < L *-cidium* slaughter < *caedere*]
ci·der (sī′dər) *n.* The expressed juice of apples used to make vinegar, and as a beverage before fermentation (**sweet cider**) or after fermentation (**hard cider**). [< Hebrew *shēkār* strong drink]
ci·gar (si·gär′) *n.* A small roll of tobacco leaves prepared for smoking. [< Sp. *cigarro*]
cig·a·rette (sig′ə·ret′, sig′ə·ret) *n.* A small roll of finely cut tobacco for smoking, enclosed in thin paper. Also **cig′a·ret′.** [< F, dim. of *cigare* cigar]
cig·a·ril·lo (sig′ə·ril′ō) *n.* *pl.* **·los** A small thin cigar. [< Sp. *cigarrillo*]
cil·i·a (sil′ē·ə) Plural of CILIUM.
cil·i·ar·y (sil′ē·er′ē) *adj.* *Biol.* Of, pertaining to, or like cilia. [< L *cilium* eyelid]
cil·i·um (sil′ē·əm) *n.* *pl.* **cil·i·a** 1. *Biol.* A vibratile, microscopic, hairlike process on the surface of a cell, organ, plant, etc. 2. An eyelash. [< L, eyelid] **—cil·i·ate** (sil′ē·it, -āt), **cil′i·at′ed** *adj.*
cinch (sinch) *n.* 1. A pack or saddle girth. 2. *Informal* A tight grip. 3. *Slang* Something easy or sure. **—***v.t.* 1. To fasten a saddle girth around. 2. *Slang* To get a tight hold upon. 3. *Slang* To make sure of. **—***v.i.* 4. To tighten a saddle girth. [< L *cingere* to bind]
cin·cho·na (sin·kō′nə) *n.* 1. A tropical tree or shrub the dried bark of which is a source of quinine and related alkaloids. 2. The bark itself. [after the Countess of *Chinchón,* 1576–1639] **—cin·chon·ic** (sin·kon′ik) *adj.*
cin·cho·nize (sin′kə·nīz) *v.t.* **·nized, ·niz·ing** To treat with cinchona or quinine. **—cin′cho·ni·za′tion** *n.*
cinc·ture (singk′chər) *n.* 1. A belt, cord, etc., put around the waist. 2. The act of girding or surrounding. **—***v.t.* **·tured, ·tur·ing** To encircle with or as with a cincture. [< L *cingere* to bind, gird]
cin·der (sin′dər) *n.* 1. Any partly burned substance, not reduced to ashes; esp. a tiny particle of such a substance. 2. A bit of wood, coal, etc., that can burn but without flame. 3. *pl.* Ashes. 4. Slag. 5. A fragment of volcanic lava. **—***v.t.* To burn or reduce to a cinder. [OE *sinder*] **—cin′der·y** *adj.*
Cin·der·el·la (sin′də·rel′ə) *n.* Any girl who achieves happiness or success after a period of neglect. [after the heroine of the fairy tale *Cinderella*]
cine- *combining form* Cinema. [< CINEMA]
cin·e·ma (sin′ə·mə) *n.* A motion-picture theater. **—the cinema** Motion pictures collectively; also, the art or business of making motion pictures. [Short for CINEMATOGRAPH] **—cin′e·mat′ic** (-mat′ik) *adj.* **—cin′e·mat′i·cal·ly** *adv.*
cin·e·mat·o·graph (sin′ə·mat′ə·graf) *n.* A motion-picture camera or projector. **—***v.t.* & *v.i.* To take photographs (of) with a motion-picture camera: also **cin·e·ma·tize** (sin′ə·mə·tīz′). [< Gk. *kinēma, -atos* movement + -GRAPH]
cin·e·ma·tog·ra·phy (sin′ə·mə·tog′rə·fē) *n.* The art and process of making motion pictures. **—cin′e·ma·tog′ra·pher** *n.* **—cin·e·mat·o·graph·ic** (sin′ə·mat′ə·graf′ik) *adj.* **—cin′e·mat′o·graph′i·cal·ly** *adv.*
cin·e·rar·i·a (sin′ə·râr′ē·ə) *n.* A cultivated plant having heart-shaped leaves and clusters of flowers. [< L, fem. of *cinerarius* ashy]
cin·e·rar·i·um (sin′ə·râr′ē·əm) *n.* *pl.* **·rar·i·a** A place for keeping the ashes of a cremated body. [< L] **—cin·er·ar·y** (sin′ə·rer′ē) *adj.*
cin·na·bar (sin′ə·bär) *n.* 1. A heavy, crystallized red mercuric sulfide, the chief ore of mercury. 2. Vermilion. [< Persian *zanjifrah*]
cin·na·mon (sin′ə·mən) *n.* 1. The aromatic inner bark of any of several tropical trees of the laurel family, used as a spice. 2. Any tree that yields this bark. 3. A shade of light reddish brown. [< Hebrew *quinnāmōn*]
cinque·foil (singk′foil) *n.* 1. *Archit.* A five-cusped ornament or window. 2. Any of several plants of the rose family, with five-lobed leaves. [< F < L *quinque* five + *folium* leaf]
ci·on (sī′ən) See SCION.
ci·pher (sī′fər) *n.* 1. The figure 0; zero. 2. A person or thing of no value or importance. 3. Any system of secret writing that uses a prearranged scheme or key. 4. A message in cipher; also, its key. 5. Any Arabic number. **—***v.t.* 1. To calculate arithmetically. 2. To write in characters of hidden meaning. **—***v.i.* 3. To work out arithmetical examples. [< Arabic *sifr* nothing]
cir·ca (sûr′kə) *prep.* About; around: used before approximate date or figures. [< L]
cir·ca·di·an (sər·kā′dē·ən) *adj.* Having a biorhythm of approximately daily periods. [< CIRCA + L *dies* day]
Cir·cas·sian (sər·kash′ən, -kash′ē·ən) *n.* 1. A member of a group of tribes of the Caucasus region. 2. The language of these tribes. **—Cir·cas′sian, Cir·cas·sic** (sər·kas′ik) *adj.*
cir·cle (sûr′kəl) *n.* 1. A plane figure bounded by a curved line every point of which is equally distant from the center. 2. The circumference of such a figure. 3. Something like a circle, as a crown, halo, or ring. 4. A round or spherical body; an orb. 5. A group of persons united by some common interest or pursuit. 6. The domain or scope of a special influence or action. 7. A gallery or tier of seats in a theater. 8. A series or process that finishes at its starting point or that repeats itself without end: the *circle* of the seasons. **—***v.* **·cled, ·cling** *v.t.* 1. To enclose in a circle; encompass. 2. To move around, as in a circle. **—***v.i.* 3. To move in a circle. [< L *circus* ring] **—cir′cler** *n.*
cir·clet (sûr′klit) *n.* A small ring or ring-shaped object, esp. one worn as an ornament. [< F *cercle* ring]
cir·cuit (sûr′kit) *n.* 1. A circular route or course. 2. A periodic journey from place to place, as by a judge or minister. 3. The territory visited in such a journey. 4. A group of associated theaters presenting plays, films,

etc., in turn. 5. The distance around an area; circumference; also, the area enclosed. 6. *Electr.* The entire course traversed by an electric current. 7. *Telecom.* A transmission and reception system. —*v.t. & v.i.* To go or move (about) in a circuit. [< F < CIRCUM- + L *ire* to go] —**cir′cuit·al** *adj.*

circuit breaker *Electr.* A switch or relay for interrupting a circuit under specified or abnormal conditions of current flow.

circuit court A court of law that sits in various districts under its jurisdiction.

cir·cu·i·tous (sər·kyōō′ə·təs) *adj.* Roundabout; indirect. —**cir·cu′i·tous·ly** *adv.* —**cir·cu′i·tous·ness** *n.*

circuit rider A minister who preaches at churches on a circuit or district route.

cir·cuit·ry (sur′kit·rē) *n. Electr.* The design and components of an electric circuit.

cir·cu·i·ty (sər·kyōō′ə·tē) *n. pl.* **·ties** Roundabout procedure or speech; indirectness.

cir·cu·lar (sûr′kyə·lər) *adj.* 1. Shaped like a circle; round. 2. Moving in a circle. 3. Of or referring to a circle. 4. Roundabout; indirect. 5. Addressed to several persons, or intended for general circulation. —*n.* A notice or advertisement printed for general distribution. [See CIRCLE.] —**cir·cu·lar·i·ty** (sûr′·kyə·lar′ə·tē), **cir′cu·lar·ness** *n.* —**cir′cu·lar·ly** *adv.*

cir·cu·lar·ize (sûr′kyə·lə·rīz′) *v.t.* **·ized, ·iz·ing** 1. To make circular. 2. To distribute circulars to. —**cir′cu·lar·i·za′tion** *n.* —**cir′·cu·lar·iz′er** *n.*

circular saw A disk-shaped saw having a toothed edge, rotated at high speed by a motor.

cir·cu·late (sûr′kyə·lāt) *v.* **·lat·ed, ·lat·ing** *v.i.* 1. To move by a circuitous course back to the starting point, as the blood. 2. To pass from place to place or person to person: Rumors *circulate* quickly. 3. To be in free motion, as air. —*v.t.* 4. To cause to circulate. [See CIRCLE.] —**cir′cu·la·to′ry** (-lə·tôr′ē), **cir′cu·la′tive** *adj.* —**cir′cu·la′tor** *n.*

cir·cu·la·tion (sûr′kyə·lā′shən) *n.* 1. Free movement or flow, as air. 2. Motion in a circuit, esp. the motion of the blood through the arteries and veins. 3. A transmission or spreading from one person or place to another; dissemination. 4. The extent of distribution of a periodical; also, the number of copies distributed.

circum- *prefix* 1. About; around; surrounding: **circumgyrate, circumpolar, circumnuclear, circumrotate, circumrotatory, circumsail.** 2. Revolving around: **circumlunar, circum-Martian.** [< L *circum-* around, about]

cir·cum·am·bi·ent (sûr′kəm·am′bē·ənt) *adj.* Encompassing; surrounding.

cir·cum·cise (sûr′kəm·sīz) *v.t.* **·cised, ·cis·ing** To cut off the prepuce (of a male). [< CIRCUM- + L *caedere* to cut] —**cir′cum·cis′er** *n.* —**cir′cum·ci′sion** (-sizh′ən) *n.*

cir·cum·fer·ence (sər·kum′fər·əns) *n.* 1. The boundary line of any area; esp., the boundary of a circle. 2. The length of such a line. [< CIRCUM- + L *ferre* to bear] —**cir·cum′fer·en′tial** (-fə·ren′shəl) *adj.* —**cir·cum′fer·en′·tial·ly** *adv.*

cir·cum·flex (sûr′kəm·fleks) *n.* A mark (ˆ, ˜, ˇ) written over certain letters, usu. to mark a long vowel, contraction, etc. —*adj.* 1. Pronounced or marked with the circumflex accent. 2. *Physiol.* Bent or curving around, as certain nerves. [< CIRCUM- + L *flectere* to bend]

cir·cum·lo·cu·tion (sûr′kəm·lō·kyōō′shən) *n.* An indirect, verbose way of expressing something; also, an example of this. [< CIRCUM- + L *loqui* to speak] —**cir′cum·loc′u·to′ry** (-lok′yə·tôr′ē) *adj.*

cir·cum·nav·i·gate (sûr′kəm·nav′ə·gāt) *v.t.* **·gat·ed, ·gat·ing** To go completely around, esp. to sail around. [< CIRCUM- + L *navigare* to sail] —**cir′cum·nav′i·ga·ble** (-gə·bəl) *adj.* —**cir′cum·nav′i·ga′tion** *n.* —**cir′cum·nav′i·ga′tor** *n.*

cir·cum·scribe (sûr′kəm·skrīb) *v.t.* **·scribed, ·scrib·ing** 1. To mark out the limits of; define. 2. To draw a line or figure around. 3. *Geom.* To draw (a figure) about another figure so that it touches at every possible point without intersecting. [< CIRCUM- + L *scribere* to write] —**cir′cum·scrib′a·ble** *adj.* —**cir′cum·scrib′er** *n.* —**cir′cum·scrip′tion** (-skrip′shən) *n.* —**cir′cum·scrip′tive** (-skrip′tiv) *adj.*

cir·cum·spect (sûr′kəm·spekt) *adj.* Attentive to everything; cautious. Also **cir′cum·spec′tive.** [< CIRCUM- + L *specere* to look] —**cir′cum·spec′tion** (-spek′shən), **cir′cum·spect′ness** *n.* —**cir′cum·spect′ly** *adv.*

cir·cum·stance (sûr′kəm·stans) *n.* 1. A factor connected with an act, event, or condition, either as an accessory or as a determining element. 2. *Often pl.* The conditions, influences, etc., affecting persons or actions. 3. *pl.* Financial condition in life. 4. An occurrence. 5. Formal display: pomp and *circumstance.* —**under no circumstances** Never; under no conditions. —**under the circumstances** Since such is (or was) the case. —*v.t.* **·stanced, ·stanc·ing** To place in or under limiting circumstances or conditions. [< CIRCUM- + L *stare* to stand] —**cir′cum·stanced** *adj.*

cir·cum·stan·tial (sûr′kəm·stan′shəl) *adj.* 1. Pertaining to or dependent on circumstances. 2. Incidental; not essential. 3. Full of details. —**cir′cum·stan′ti·al′i·ty** (-shē·al′ə·tē) *n.* —**cir′cum·stan′tial·ly** *adv.*

circumstantial evidence *Law* Evidence that furnishes reasonable ground for inferring the existence of a fact.

cir·cum·stan·ti·ate (sûr′kəm·stan′shē·āt) *v.t.* **·at·ed, ·at·ing** To set forth or establish by circumstances or in detail. —**cir′cum·stan′ti·a′tion** *n.*

cir·cum·vent (sûr′kəm·vent′) *v.t.* 1. To surround or entrap. 2. To gain an advantage over; outwit. 3. To go around or avoid. [< CIRCUM- + L *venire* to come] —**cir′cum·vent′er** or **cir′cum·vent′or** *n.* —**cir′cum·ven′tion** *n.* —**cir′cum·ven′tive** *adj.*

cir·cus (sûr′kəs) *n.* 1. A traveling show of acrobats, clowns, etc.; also, a performance of such a show. 2. A circular, usu. tented area used for such shows. 3. In ancient Rome, an oblong enclosure used for races, games, etc. 4. *Brit.* An open, usu. circular junction of several streets. 5. *Informal* An uproarious or disorderly exhibition. [< L, a ring, racecourse]

cir·rho·sis (si·rō′sis) *n. Pathol.* A degenerative disease of the liver. [< Gk. *kirrhos* tawny; with ref. to the color of the cirrhotic liver] —**cir·rhot·ic** (si·rot′ik) *adj.*

cirro- *combining form* Cirrus. Also **cirri-**. [< L *cirrus* curl]

cir·ro·cu·mu·lus (sir′ō·kyōōm′yə·ləs) *n.* *Meteorol.* A mass of fleecy, globular cloudlets (symbol Cc) in contact with one another.

cir·ro·stra·tus (sir′ō·strā′təs) *n.* *Meteorol.* A fine, whitish veil of cloud (symbol Cs).

cir·rus (sir′əs) *n.* *pl.* **cir·ri** (sir′ī) *Meteorol.* A type of white, wispy cloud (symbol Ci), usually consisting of ice crystals and seen in tufts or feathery bands across the sky. [< L, ringlet, curl] —**cir·rous** (sir′əs), **cir·rose** (sir′ōs) *adj.*

cis·tern (sis′tərn) *n.* 1. An artificial reservoir, as a tank, for holding water or other liquids. 2. *Anat.* A fluid-containing sac. [< L *cista* chest]

cit·a·del (sit′ə·dəl, -del) *n.* 1. A fortress commanding a city. 2. Any fortress or stronghold. [< MF < Ital. *città* city]

ci·ta·tion (sī·tā′shən) *n.* 1. A citing or quoting; also, a passage or authority so cited. 2. A public commendation for outstanding achievement. 3. A summons, as to appear in court. [See CITE.] —**ci·ta·to·ry** (sī′tə·tôr′ē) *adj.*

cite (sīt) *v.t.* **cit·ed, cit·ing** 1. To quote as authority or illustration. 2. To bring forward or refer to as proof or support. 3. *Mil.* To commend or praise, esp. for bravery. 4. To mention or enumerate. 5. To summon to appear in court. [< L *citare* < *ciere* to set in motion] —**cit′a·ble** or **cite′a·ble** *adj.*

cith·a·ra (sith′ə·rə) *n.* An ancient Greek stringed instrument resembling a lyre. [< Gk. *kithara*]

cit·i·fied (sit′i·fīd) *adj.* Having the ways, habits, fashions, etc., of city life.

cit·i·zen (sit′ə·zən) *n.* 1. A native or naturalized person owing allegiance to, and entitled to protection from, a government. 2. A resident of a city or town. 3. A civilian, as distinguished from a public officer, soldier, etc. [< AF *citesein* < L *civis* citizen]

cit·i·zen·ry (sit′ə·zən·rē) *n.* *pl.* **·ries** Citizens collectively.

citizen's band A range of radio frequencies allocated for two-way communication between private individuals by low-powered sets. Abbr. *CB* —**cit·i·zen's-band** (sit′ə·zənz·band′) *adj.*

cit·i·zen·ship (sit′ə·zən·ship′) *n.* The status of a citizen, with its rights, privileges, and duties.

cit·rate (sit′rāt, -rit) *n.* *Chem.* A salt of citric acid.

cit·ric (sit′rik) *adj.* Of or derived from citrus fruits.

citric acid *Chem.* A white, crystalline, sharply sour compound, contained in various fruits and also made synthetically.

cit·rine (sit′rin) *adj.* Lemon yellow. —*n.* 1. Citrine color. 2. A light yellow variety of quartz. [< F *citrin*]

cit·ron (sit′rən) *n.* 1. A fruit like a lemon, but larger and less acid. 2. The tree producing this fruit. 3. A watermelon with a small, hard-fleshed fruit: also **citron melon.** 4. The rind of either of these fruits, preserved and used in confections. [< L *citrus* citron tree]

cit·ron·el·la (sit′rə·nel′ə) *n.* A grass cultivated in southern Asia, yielding **citronella oil,** used in perfumes and insect repellants. Also **citronella grass.** < CITRON; so called from its odor]

cit·rus (sit′rəs) *adj.* Of or pertaining to trees bearing oranges, lemons, etc., or to their fruits. Also **cit′rous.** [< L, citron tree]

cit·y (sit′ē) *n.* *pl.* **cit·ies** 1. A place inhabited by a large, permanent community. 2. In the U.S., a state-chartered municipality, larger than a town. 3. The people of a city, collectively. [< L *civis* citizen]

city desk A department in a newspaper office handling local news.

city manager An administrator appointed by a city council to manage the city.

cit·y-state (sit′ē·stāt′) *n.* A state consisting of a city and its contiguous territories, as ancient Athens.

civ·et (siv′it) *n.* 1. A substance of musklike odor, secreted by the civet cat, used in perfumery. 2. The civet cat or its fur. [< MF *civette*]

civet cat A feline carnivore of Africa.

civ·ic (siv′ik) *adj.* Of or pertaining to a city, a citizen, or citizenship. [< L *civis* citizen]

civ·ics (siv′iks) *n.pl.* (*construed as sing.*) The division of political science dealing with the rights and duties of citizens.

civ·il (siv′əl) *adj.* 1. Of or pertaining to community life rather than military or ecclesiastical affairs. 2. Of or pertaining to citizens and their government: *civil* affairs. 3. Occurring within the state; domestic: *civil* war. 4. Of, proper to, or befitting a citizen. 5. Civilized. 6. Proper; polite. 7. *Law* Related to the rights of citizens. [< L *civis* citizen] —**civ′il·ly** *adv.*

civil defense A civilian program for the maintenance of essential services in time of emergency.

civil disobedience A nonviolent refusal to comply with certain civil laws.

civil engineer A professional engineer trained to design, build, and maintain public works, as roads, bridges, etc. —**civil engineering**

ci·vil·ian (sə·vil′yən) *n.* One who is not in the military service. —**ci·vil′ian** *adj.*

ci·vil·i·ty (sə·vil′ə·tē) *n.* *pl.* **·ties** 1. The quality of being civil; courtesy; politeness. 2. A polite act or speech.

civ·i·li·za·tion (siv′ə·lə·zā′shən, -lī·zā′-) *n.* 1. A state of human society characterized by a high level of intellectual, social, and cultural development. 2. The countries and peoples considered to have reached this stage. 3. The cultural development of a specific people, country, or region. 4. The act of civilizing, or the process of becoming civilized.

civ·i·lize (siv′ə·līz) *v.t.* **·lized, ·liz·ing** To bring into a state of civilization; bring out of savagery. Also *Brit.* **civ′i·lise.** [< L *civis* citizen] —**civ′i·liz′a·ble** *adj.* —**civ′i·liz′er** *n.*

civil law The body of laws having to do with the rights of citizens.

civil liberty A liberty guaranteed to the individual by the laws of a government.

civil marriage A marriage solemnized by a government official rather than by a clergyman.

civil rights Certain rights of citizens, esp. the right to vote, exception from servitude, and the right to equal treatment under the law.

civil service 1. The administrative branches of governmental service that are not military, legislative, or judicial. 2. Such governmental branches to which appointments are made as a result of competitive examinations. 3. The persons employed in these branches. **—civil servant**

civil war War between parties or sections of the same country.

civ·vies (siv′ēz) *n.pl.* *Informal* Civilian clothes, as distinguished from military dress.

clab·ber (klab′ər) *n.* Milk curdled by souring. **—***v.t.* & *v.i.* To curdle, as milk. [< Irish *bainne clabair*]

clack (klak) *v.i.* 1. To make a sharp, dry sound. 2. To chatter heedlessly. 3. To cluck, as a hen. **—***v.t.* 4. To cause to clack. **—***n.* 1. A short, sharp sound. 2. Something that makes a clack. 3. Chatter. [Imit.] **—clack′er** *n.*

clad (klad) Alternative past tense and past participle of CLOTHE.

claim (klām) *v.t.* 1. To demand as one's right or due; assert ownership or title to. 2. To hold to be true; assert. 3. To require or deserve: The problem *claims* our attention. **—***n.* 1. A demand or an assertion of a right. 2. An assertion of something as true. 3. A ground for claiming something. 4. That which is claimed, as a piece of land. [< L *clamere* to declare] **—claim′a·ble** *adj.* **—claim′er** *n.*

claim·ant (klā′mənt) *n.* One who makes a claim.

clair·voy·ance (klâr·voi′əns) *n.* The alleged ability to see or know things beyond the area of normal perception. [< MF] **—clair·voy′·ant** *n.* & *adj.*

clam (klam) *n.* 1. Any of various bivalve mollusks, usu. edible. 2. *Informal* A close-mouthed person. **—***v.i.* **clammed, clam·ming** To hunt for or dig clams. **—to clam up** *Slang* To become or keep silent. [< obs. *clam* a clamp]

clam·bake (klam′bāk′) *n.* 1. A picnic where clams and other foods are baked. 2. Any noisy gathering.

clam·ber (klam′bər, -ər) *v.t.* & *v.i.* To climb, mount, or descend with difficulty. [Akin to CLIMB] **—clam′ber** *n.* **—clam′ber·er** *n.*

clam·my (klam′ē) *adj.* **·mi·er, ·mi·est** Stickily soft and damp, and usu. cold. [< Du. *klam* sticky] **—clam′mi·ly** *adv.* **—clam′mi·ness** *n.*

clam·or (klam′ər) *n.* 1. A loud, repeated outcry. 2. A vehement protest or demand. 3. Any loud and continuous noise; din. **—***v.i.* & *v.t.* To make or utter with loud outcries, demands, or complaints. Also *Brit.* **clam′our.** [< L *clamare* to cry out] **—clam′or·er** *n.* **—clam′or·ous** *adj.* **—clam′or·ous·ly** *adv.* **—clam′or·ous·ness** *n.*

clamp (klamp) *n.* A device for holding objects together, securing a piece in position, etc. **—***v.t.* To hold or bind with or as with a clamp. **—to clamp down** *Informal* To become more strict. [Cf. OE *clamm*, M.Du. *klampe*]

clan (klan) *n.* 1. A united group of relatives, or families, claiming a common ancestor and having the same surname. 2. A clique; fraternity; club. [< Scottish Gaelic *clann*]

clan·des·tine (klan·des′tin) *adj.* Kept secret for a purpose; furtive. [< L *clandestinus* < *clam* in secret] **—clan·des′tine·ly** *adv.* **—clan·des′tine·ness** *n.*

clang (klang) *v.t.* & *v.i.* To make or cause to make a loud, ringing, metallic sound. **—clang** *n.*

clan·gor (klang′gər, klang′ər) *n.* Repeated clanging; clamor; din. **—***v.i.* To ring noisily. Also *Brit.* **clan′gour.** [< L *clangere* to clang] **—clan′gor·ous** *adj.* **—clan′gor·ous·ly** *adv.*

clank (klangk) *n.* A short, harsh, metallic sound. [Imit.] **—clank** *v.t.* & *v.i.*

clan·nish (klan′ish) *adj.* 1. Of or characteristic of a clan. 2. Disposed to cling together, or bound by family prejudices, traditions, etc. **—clan′nish·ly** *adv.* **—clan′nish·ness** *n.*

clans·man (klanz′mən) *n.* *pl.* **·men** (-mən) A member of a clan. **—clans′wom′an** (-wo͝om′ən) *n.fem.*

clap[1] (klap) *v.* **clapped, clap·ping** *v.i.* 1. To strike the hands together, as in applauding. 2. To make a sound, as of two boards striking together. **—***v.t.* 3. To bring (the hands) together sharply and with an explosive sound. 4. To strike with the open hand, as in greeting. 5. To put or fling quickly or suddenly: They *clapped* him into jail. **—***n.* 1. The act or sound of clapping the hands. 2. A loud, explosive sound, esp. of thunder. 3. A blow with the open hand. [OE *clæppan*]

clap[2] (klap) *n.* *Slang* Gonorrhea. [? < OF *clapier* brothel]

clap·board (klab′ərd, klap′bôrd′) *n.* A narrow board having one edge thinner than the other, used as siding on frame buildings: sometimes called *weatherboard.* **—***v.t.* To cover with clapboards. [Partial trans. of M.Du. *klapholt* barrel stave]

clap·per (klap′ər) *n.* 1. The tongue of a bell. 2. One who or that which claps.

clap·trap (klap′trap′) *n.* Pretentious language; nonsense.

claque (klak) *n.* A group of hired applauders. [< F < *claquer* to clap]

clar·et (klar′ət) *n.* 1. Any dry red wine. 2. Ruby to deep purplish red. [< OF < L *clarus* clear, bright] **—clar′et** *adj.*

clar·i·fy (klar′ə·fī) *v.t.* & *v.i.* **·fied, ·fy·ing** 1. To make or become clear or free from impurities. 2. To make or become understandable; explain. [< L *clarus* clear + *facere* to make] **—clar′i·fi·ca′tion** *n.* **—clar′i·fi′er** *n.*

clar·i·net (klar′ə·net′) *n.* A cylindrical woodwind instrument having a single-reed mouthpiece, finger holes, and keys. [< Ital. *clarinetto*] **—clar′i·net′ist** or **clar′i·net′tist** *n.*

clar·i·on (klar′ē·ən) *adj.* Clear and resounding. [< L *clarus* clear]

clar·i·ty (klar′ə·tē) *n.* Clearness; lucidity.

clash (klash) *v.t.* 1. To strike together with a harsh, metallic sound. **—***v.i.* 2. To collide with loud and confused noise. 3. To conflict; be in opposition. **—***n.* 1. A resounding, metallic noise. 2. A conflict. [Imit.]

clasp (klasp) *n.* 1. A fastening, as a hook, used to hold things or parts together. 2. A firm grasp of the hand or embrace. **—***v.t.* 1. To embrace. 2. To fasten with or as with a clasp. 3. To grasp firmly in or with the hand. [ME *claspe*] **—clasp′er** *n.*

class (klas) *n.* 1. A number of persons or things grouped together by shared characteristics. 2. The division of society by relative standing. 3. A category of objects, persons, etc., based on quality or rank: of the first *class.* 4. A group of students pursuing a study together; also, a meeting of such a group. 5. A group of students in a school or college graduating together. 6. *Biol.* A group of plants or animals standing below a phylum and above an order. 7. *Slang* Superiority; elegance. —*v.t.* To assign to a class; classify. [< L *classis*]

class action A legal action on behalf of all persons suffering the same alleged wrong. —**class-ac·tion** (klas′ak′shən) *adj.*

clas·sic (klas′ik) *adj.* 1. Belonging to the first class or highest rank; recognized as a standard of excellence. 2. Of, or in the style of, ancient Greece and Rome or their literature or art. 3. Typical: a *classic* example. 4. Of or having a style that is formal, balanced, restrained, regular, etc. —*n.* An author, artist, or work generally recognized as a standard of excellence. —**the classics** Ancient Greek and Roman literature. [< L *classis* class]

clas·si·cal (klas′i·kəl) *adj.* 1. Generally accepted as being standard and authoritative; traditional. 2. Of ancient Greece and Rome: *classical* civilization. 3. Versed in the Greek and Roman classics: a *classical* scholar. 4. *Music* Loosely, serious as distinguished from popular. —**clas′si·cal·ly** *adv.* —**clas′si·cal′i·ty** (-kal′ə·tē) *n.*

clas·si·cism (klas′ə·siz′əm) *n.* 1. A group of esthetic principles (simplicity, restraint, balance, etc.) as manifested in classical art and literature: distinguished from *romanticism.* 2. Adherence to these principles. 3. Classical scholarship. 4. A Greek or Latin idiom or form. Also **clas·si·cal·ism** (klas′i·kəl·iz′əm) *n.*

clas·si·cist (klas′ə·sist) *n.* 1. One versed in the classics. 2. An adherent or imitator of classic style. Also **clas·si·cal·ist** (klas′i·kəl·ist) *n.*

clas·si·fi·ca·tion (klas′ə·fə·kā′shən) *n.* The act, process, or result of classifying. —**clas·si·fi·ca·to·ry** (klas′ə·fə·kā′tər·ē, klə·sif′ə·kə·tôr′ē) *adj.*

classified advertisement An advertisement under any of various subject headings. Also **classified ad.**

clas·si·fy (klas′ə·fī) *v.t.* **·fied, ·fy·ing** 1. To arrange by class or category. 2. To restrict as to circulation or use, as a government document. [< L *classis* class + -FY] —**clas′si·fi′a·ble** *adj.* —**clas′si·fi′er** *n.*

class·mate (klas′māt′) *n.* A member of the same class in school or college.

class·room (klas′ro͞om′, -ro͝om′) *n.* A room in a school in which classes are held.

class·y (klas′ē) *adj.* **class·i·er, class·i·est** *Slang* Elegant.

clat·ter (klat′ər) *v.i.* 1. To make or give out short, sharp noises rapidly or repeatedly. 2. To move with a rattling noise. 3. To talk noisily; chatter. —*v.t.* 4. To cause to clatter. —*n.* 1. A rattling or clattering sound. 2. A disturbance or commotion. 3. Noisy talk; chatter. [OE *clatrunge* a clattering noise] —**clat′ter·er** *n.*

clause (klôz) *n.* 1. A distinct part of a document, as an article in a statute, treaty, etc. 2. *Gram.* A sequence of words containing a subject and a predicate, forming part of a sentence. [< L *clausus*, pp. of *claudere* to close] —**claus′al** *adj.*

claus·tro·pho·bi·a (klôs′trə·fō′bē·ə) *n.* *Psychiatry* Fear of enclosed or confined places. [< L *claustrum* a closed place + -PHOBIA] —**claus′tro·pho′bic** *adj.*

cla·vate (klā′vāt) *adj.* Club-shaped. [< L *clava* a club]

clav·i·chord (klav′ə·kôrd) *n.* A keyboard musical instrument that is a forerunner of the piano. [< L *clavis* key + *chorda* string]

clav·i·cle (klav′ə·kəl) *n.* *Anat.* The bone connecting the shoulder blade and breastbone: also called *collarbone.* [< L *clavis* key] —**cla·vic·u·lar** (klə·vik′yə·lər) *adj.*

clav·i·er (klə·vir′; for defs. 1 and 3, also klav′ē·ər) *n.* 1. A keyboard. 2. Any keyboard stringed instrument, as a harpsichord, piano, etc. 3. A dummy keyboard for silent practicing. [< F, keyboard < L *clavis* key]

claw (klô) *n.* 1. A sharp, usu. curved, horny nail on the toe of a bird, mammal, or reptile. 2. A chela or pincer of certain insects and crustaceans. 3. Anything sharp and hooked. —*v.t. & v.i.* To tear, scratch, dig, pull, etc., with or as with claws. [OE *clawu*]

clay (klā) *n.* 1. A fine-grained, variously colored earth, pliable when wet, used in the making of bricks, pottery, etc. 2. Earth. 3. The human body. —*v.t.* To mix or treat with clay. [OE *clǣg*] —**clay′ey** *adj.* —**clay′·ish** *adj.*

clay·more (klā′môr) *n.* A double-edged broadsword. [< Scot. Gaelic *claidheamh* sword + *mor* great]

clay pigeon In trapshooting, a saucer-shaped disk, as of baked clay, used as a flying target.

-cle *suffix of nouns* Small; minute: *particle, corpuscle.* [< L *-culus*, dim. suffix]

clean (klēn) *adj.* 1. Free from dirt or stain; unsoiled. 2. Morally pure; wholesome. 3. Without obstructions, encumbrances, or restrictions. 4. Thorough; complete: a *clean* getaway. 5. Clever; dexterous: a *clean* jump. 6. Trim; not ornate: *clean* lines. 7. Neat in habits. 8. Producing an explosion relatively free of radioactive fallout: said of nuclear weapons. 9. *Informal* Fair: a *clean* fight. 10. *Slang* **a** Free from drug addiction. **b** Having no illegal drugs in one's possession. —*v.t.* 1. To render free of dirt or other impurities. 2. To prepare (fowl, game, etc.) for cooking. —*v.i.* 3. To undergo or perform the act of cleaning. —**to clean out** 1. To clear of trash or rubbish. 2. To empty (a place) of contents or occupants. 3. *Informal* To leave without money. —**to clean up** 1. To clean thoroughly. 2. *Slang* To make a large profit. 3. *Informal* To complete. —*adv.* 1. In a clean manner; cleanly. 2. Wholly; completely. [OE *clǣne* clear, pure] —**clean′a·ble** *adj.* —**clean′ness** *n.*

clean-cut (klēn′kut′) *adj.* 1. Cut with smooth edge or surface; well-made. 2. Sharply defined; clear. 3. Neat in appearance.

clean·er (klē′nər) *n.* 1. A person whose work is cleaning, esp. clothing. 2. Any substance or device that cleans.

clean·ly (*adj.* klen′lē; *adv.* klēn′lē) *adj.* Habitually and carefully clean; neat; tidy. —*adv.* In a clean manner. —**clean·li·ness** (klen′lē·nis) *n.*

cleanse (klenz) *v.t.* **cleansed, cleans·ing** To free from dirt; purify. [OE *clǣnsian* < *clǣne* clean]

cleans·er (klenz′ər) *n.* One who or that which cleanses; esp., a soap or detergent.

clean·up (klēn′up′) *n.* 1. A complete cleaning. 2. *Slang* A large profit; gain.

clear (klir) *adj.* 1. Bright; unclouded. 2. Without impurity or blemish. 3. Of great transparency. 4. Free from obstructions or restrictions. 5. Understandable. 6. Plain to the eye, ear, etc. 7. Able to discern; keen: a *clear* mind. 8. Free from uncertainty; sure. 9. Free from guilt or blame. 10. Free from a financial obligation. 11. Not in contact: usu. with *of.* 12. Without deductions; net: a *clear* $5,000. —*adv.* 1. In a clear manner. 2. *Informal* All the way: *clear* through the day. —*v.t.* 1. To make clear; brighten. 2. To free from foreign matter or impurities. 3. To remove (obstacles, obstructions, etc.). 4. To free from blame or guilt. 5. To make plain. 6. To pass or get under or over without touching. 7. To free from debt by payment. 8. To settle (a debt). 9. To obtain or give clearance for. 10. To gain over and above expenses. 11. To pass (a check) through a clearing-house. —*v.i.* 12. To become free from fog, rain, clouds, etc. **—to clear away** (or **off**) To remove out of the way. **—to clear out** 1. *Informal* To go away. 2. To empty of contents. **—to clear the air** To dispel tensions; settle differences. **—to clear up** 1. To make clear. 2. To grow fair, as the weather. 3. To free from confusion or mystery. 4. To put in order; tidy. —*n.* 1. An unobstructed space. 2. Clearance. **—in the clear** 1. Free from limitations or obstructions. 2. *Informal* Free from guilt or blame. [< L *clarus*] **—clear′a·ble** *adj.* **—clear′ly** *adv.* **—clear′ness** *n.*

clear-air turbulence (klir′âr′) *Aeron.* A mass of turbulent air in an unclouded sky. Abbr. *CAT*

clear·ance (klir′əns) *n.* 1. The act or instance of clearing. 2. The space by which a moving object clears something. 3. Permission for a ship, airplane, truck, etc., to proceed.

clear-cut (klir′kut′) *adj.* 1. Distinctly and sharply outlined. 2. Plain; evident; obvious. 3. With all trees cut down: said of timberland. —*v.t.* **-cut, -cut·ting** To cut down all trees in (a tract).

clear-head·ed (klir′hed′id) *adj.* Not confused; sensible. **—clear′-head′ed·ness** *n.*

clear·ing (klir′ing) *n.* 1. A making or becoming clear. 2. That which is clear or cleared, as a tract of land.

clear·ing-house (klir′ing·hous′) *n.* 1. An office where bankers exchange drafts and checks and adjust balances. 2. A center for the storage and exchange of information. Also **clear′ing·house′.**

clear-sight·ed (klir′sī′tid) *adj.* 1. Having accurate perception and good judgment; discerning. 2. Having keen vision. **—clear′-sight′ed·ly** *adv.* **—clear′-sight′ed·ness** *n.*

clear·sto·ry (klir′stôr′ē) See CLERESTORY.

cleat (klēt) *n.* 1. A strip of wood or iron fastened across or projecting from a surface to strengthen, support, or provide a grip. 2. A piece of metal or wood with arms on which to wind or secure a rope. —*v.t.* 1. To furnish or strengthen with a cleat or cleats. 2. *Naut.* To fasten (rope, etc.) to or with a cleat. [ME *clete*]

cleav·age (klē′vij) *n.* 1. A cleaving or being cleft. 2. A split or cleft. 3. *Mineral.* A tendency in certain rocks or crystals to split in certain directions.

cleave[1] (klēv) *v.* **cleft** or **cleaved** or **clove** (*Archaic* **clave**), **cleft** or **cleaved** or **clo·ven, cleav·ing** *v.t.* 1. To split or sunder. 2. To make or achieve by cutting: to *cleave* a path. 3. To pass through; penetrate. —*v.i.* 4. To part or divide along natural lines of separation. 5. To make one's way; pass: with *through.* [OE *clēofan*] **—cleav′a·ble** *adj.*

cleave[2] (klēv) *v.i.* **cleaved** (*Archaic* **clave, clove**), **cleaved, cleav·ing** 1. To stick fast; adhere: with *to.* 2. To be faithful: with *to.* [Fusion of OE *clifan* and *clifian*]

cleav·er (klē′vər) *n.* 1. One who or that which cleaves. 2. A butcher's heavy, axlike knife. [< CLEAVE[1]]

clef (klef) *n. Music* A symbol placed on the staff to show the pitch of the notes. [< L *clavis* key]

cleft (kleft) Past tense and past participle of CLEAVE[1]. —*adj.* Divided partially or completely. —*n.* A fissure; crevice; rift. [ME *clift*]

cleft palate A congenital longitudinal fissure in the roof of the mouth.

clem·a·tis (klem′ə·tis) *n.* A perennial shrub or vine of the crowfoot family. [< Gk. *klēmatis*]

clem·en·cy (klem′ən·sē) *n. pl.* **·cies** 1. Leniency; mercy. 2. Mildness of weather. [< L *clemens* mild]

clem·ent (klem′ənt) *adj.* 1. Lenient or merciful in temperament; compassionate. 2. Mild: said of weather. [< L *clemens, -entis* mild, merciful] **—clem′ent·ly** *adv.*

clench (klench) *v.t.* 1. To grasp or grip firmly. 2. To close tightly, as the fist or teeth. 3. To clinch, as a nail. —*n.* 1. A tight grip. 2. A device that clenches or grips. [OE *-clenc(e)an* in *beclencan* to hold fast]

clere·sto·ry (klir′stôr′ē) *n. pl.* **·ries** 1. *Archit.* The highest story of the nave and choir of a church, with windows opening above the aisle roofs, etc. 2. A similar part in other structures. Also spelled *clearstory:* also **clere′sto′rey.** [< earlier *clere* clear + STORY]

cler·gy (klûr′jē) *n. pl.* **·gies** The whole body of individuals authorized to conduct religious services. [< Gk. *klēros* lot, portion]

cler·gy·man (klûr′jē·mən) *n. pl.* **·men** (-mən) One of the clergy; an ordained minister.

cler·ic (kler′ik) *adj.* Clerical. —*n.* A member of the clergy.

cler·i·cal (kler′i·kəl) *adj.* 1. Of or related to clerks or office workers or their work. 2. Belonging to or characteristic of the clergy. **—cler′i·cal·ly** *adv.*

cler·i·cal·ism (kler′i·kəl·iz′əm) *n.* Clerical influence in politics, or support for such influence. **—cler′i·cal·ist** *n.*

clerk (klûrk, *Brit.* klärk) *n.* 1. A worker in an office who attends to accounts, correspondence, etc. 2. An official or employee of a court, legislative body, or the like, charged with the care of records, etc. 3. A salesperson. —*v.i.* To work or act as clerk. [< Gk. *klēros* lot, portion] **—clerk′ly** *adj. & adv.*

clev·er (klev′ər) *adj.* 1. Mentally keen; quick-witted. 2. Physically adroit, esp. with the hands; dexterous. 3. Ingeniously made, said, done, etc. [Cf. ME *cliver* adroit] **—clev′er·ly** *adv.* **—clev′er·ness** *n.*

clev·is (klev′is) *n.* A U-shaped metal fastening pierced for a bolt, used to attach chains, cables, etc. [Akin to CLEAVE[1]]

clew (klo͞o) *n.* 1. In legends, a ball of thread that guides through a maze. 2. A clue. 3. *Naut.* A lower corner of a sail; also, a loop at the corner. [OE *cliwen*]

cli·ché (klē·shā′) *n.* A trite or hackneyed expression, action, etc. [< F, pp. of *clicher* to stereotype] **—cli·chéd′** *adj.*

click (klik) *n.* 1. A short, sharp, nonresonant metallic sound. 2. *Phonet.* A speech sound made by clicking the tongue, characteristic of certain African languages. —*v.t.* 1. To cause to make a click or clicks. —*v.i.* 2. To produce a click or clicks. 3. *Slang* To succeed. [Imit.] **—click′er** *n.*

cli·ent (klī′ənt) *n.* 1. One who engages the services of a lawyer or any professional adviser. 2. A customer. [< L *cliens, -entis* follower]

cli·en·tele (klī′ən·tel′) *n.* A body of clients, customers, etc. Also **cli·ent·age** (klī′ən·tij). [< F]

cliff (klif) *n.* A high, steep face of rock; a precipice. [OE] **—cliff′y** *adj.*

cliff·hang·er (klif′hang′ər) *n.* 1. A situation marked by suspense or uncertainty of outcome. 2. A serialized drama marked by suspense at the end of each episode. Also **cliff′-hang′er.** **—cliff′hang′ing** *adj. & n.*

cli·mac·ter·ic (klī·mak′tər·ik, klī′mak·ter′ik) *n.* 1. An age or period of life characterized by marked physiological change, as the menopause. 2. Any critical year or period. —*adj.* Pertaining to a critical year or period: also **cli′mac·ter′i·cal.** [< Gk. *klimaktēr* rung of a ladder]

cli·mac·tic (klī·mak′tik) *adj.* Pertaining to or constituting a climax. Also **cli·mac′ti·cal.**

cli·mate (klī′mit) *n.* 1. The temperature, precipitation, winds, etc., characteristic of a region. 2. A region in reference to its characteristic weather. 3. A prevailing trend or condition in human affairs: the *climate* of opinion. [< Gk. *klima, -atos* region, zone] **—cli·mat·ic** (klī·mat′ik) or **·i·cal** *adj.* **—cli·mat′i·cal·ly** *adv.*

climato- *combining form* Climate. Also, before vowels, **climat-.** [< Gk. *klima, -atos* region]

cli·ma·tol·o·gy (klī′mə·tol′ə·jē) *n.* The branch of science dealing with the phenomena of climate. **—cli·ma·to·log·ic** (klī′mə·tə·loj′ik) or **·i·cal** *adj.* **—cli′ma·tol′o·gist** *n.*

cli·max (klī′maks) *n.* 1. The point of greatest intensity or fullest development; culmination; acme. 2. In drama, fiction, etc., the scene or moment of action that determines the final outcome. 3. An orgasm. —*v.t. & v.i.* To reach or bring to a climax. [< Gk. *klimax* ladder]

climb (klīm) *v.* **climbed, climb·ing** *v.t.* 1. To ascend or mount (something), esp. by means of the hands and feet. —*v.i.* 2. To rise or advance in status, rank, etc. 3. To incline or slope upward. 4. To grow upward. **—to climb down** To descend, esp. by using the hands and feet. —*n.* 1. The act or process of climbing; ascent. 2. A place ascended by climbing. [OE *climban*] **—climb′a·ble** *adj.* **—climb′er** *n.*

clime (klīm) *n.* Climate.

clinch (klinch) *v.t.* 1. To fasten together or secure, as a driven nail or staple, by bending down the protruding point. 2. To make sure; settle. —*v.i.* 3. To grapple, as combatants. 4. *Slang* To embrace, as lovers. —*n.* 1. The act of clinching. 2. A clamp. 3. A grip or struggle at close quarters, as in boxing. 4. *Slang* A close embrace. [Var. of CLENCH]

clinch·er (klin′chər) *n.* 1. One who or that which clinches. 2. A nail made for clinching. 3. *Informal* A deciding statement, point, etc.

cling (kling) *v.i.* **clung, cling·ing** To hold fast or resist separation, either physically or emotionally. [OE *clingan*] **—cling′er** *n.*

clinging vine *Informal* A woman who displays extreme dependence on a man.

cling·stone (kling′stōn′) *n.* A variety of peach in which the pulp adheres to the stone. Also **cling peach.**

clin·ic (klin′ik) *n.* 1. An infirmary, usu. connected with a hospital or medical school, for the treatment of outpatients. 2. The teaching of medicine by treating patients in the presence of a class; also, the class itself. 3. A place where patients are studied and treated by specialists. 4. A cooperative medical group. 5. An organization that offers advice on specific problems. [< F *clinique*]

clin·i·cal (klin′i·kəl) *adj.* 1. Of or pertaining to a clinic. 2. Concerned with the observation and treatment of patients in clinics. 3. Coldly scientific or detached. **—clin′i·cal·ly** *adv.*

cli·ni·cian (kli·nish′ən) *n.* A physician trained in clinical methods, or one who gives instruction in clinics.

clink[1] (klingk) *v.t. & v.i.* To make or cause to make a short, slight, ringing sound. [Imit.] **—clink** *n.*

clink[2] (klingk) *n.* *Slang* A prison. [? after *Clink* prison in London]

clink·er (kling′kər) *n.* 1. The fused residue left by coal, etc., in burning. 2. *Slang* A mistake. [< Du. *klinckaerd* brick]

clino- *combining form* Bend; slope; incline: *clinometer.* [< Gk. *klinein* to bend]

cli·nom·e·ter (klī·nom′ə·tər, kli-) *n.* An instrument for determining angular inclination, as of guns, slopes, etc. **—cli·no·met·ric** (klī′nə·met′rik) or **·ri·cal** *adj.*

clip[1] (klip) *n.* 1. A device that clasps, grips, or holds articles together, as letters or papers. 2. A device which holds cartridges for a rifle, or ammunition for insertion into firearms. —*v.t.* **clipped, clip·ping** To fasten with or as with a clip. [OE *clyppan* to clasp]

clip[2] (klip) *v.* **clipped, clip·ping** *v.t.* 1. To cut with shears or scissors, as hair or fleece; trim. 2. To cut short; curtail. 3. *Informal* To strike with a sharp blow. 4. *Slang* To cheat or defraud. 5. In football, to block illegally. —*v.i.* 6. To cut or trim. 7. *Informal* To run or move swiftly. **—to clip the wings of** To check the aspirations or ambitions of. —*n.* 1. The act of clipping, or that which is clipped off. 2. The wool yielded at one shearing or during one season. 3. A sharp blow; punch. 4. *Informal* A quick pace. 5. In football, an illegal block. [< ON *klippa*]

clip·board (klip′bôrd′) *n.* A board providing

a writing surface, with a spring clip for holding paper.
clip·per (klip′ər) *n.* 1. *pl.* An instrument or tool for clipping or cutting. 2. A sailing vessel of the mid-19th century, built for speed: also **clipper ship.** 3. One who clips.
clip·ping (klip′ing) *n.* 1. The act of one who or that which clips. 2. That which is cut off or out by clipping: a newspaper *clipping.* —*adj.* That cuts or clips.
clique (klēk, klik) *n.* An exclusive or clannish group of people. —*v.i.* **cliqued, cli·quing** To unite in a clique. [< MF *cliquer* to click, clap] —**cli′quish** *adj.*
cli·to·ris (kli′tə·ris, klit′ə-) *n. Anat.* A small erectile organ at the upper part of the vulva. [< Gk. *kleitoris*] —**clit′o·ral** (-rəl) *adj.*
cloak (klōk) *n.* 1. A loose outer garment. 2. Something that covers or hides. —*v.t.* 1. To cover with a cloak. 2. To conceal; disguise. [< Med.L *cloca* bell, cape; so called from its bell-like shape]
cloak·room (klōk′rōōm′, -rŏŏm′) *n.* A room where hats, coats, luggage, etc., are left temporarily, as in a theater.
clob·ber (klob′ər) *v.t. Slang* 1. To beat severely; trounce. 2. To defeat utterly. [? Freq. of CLUB[1], v.]
cloche (klōsh, *Fr.* klôsh) *n.* A woman's close-fitting, bell-shaped hat. [< F, bell]
clock[1] (klok) *n.* An instrument for measuring time; esp., a mechanism that shows the hour and minute on a dial or as a digital display. —*v.t.* To ascertain the speed or the time of with a stopwatch or other device. [ME *clok* < MDu. *clocke*]
clock[2] (klok) *n.* A decoration on a stocking or sock. [Origin uncertain]
clock·wise (klok′wīz′) *adj. & adv.* Going in the direction traveled by the hands of a clock.
clock·work (klok′wûrk′) *n.* The machinery of a clock, or any similar mechanism. —**like clockwork** With regularity and precision.
clod (klod) *n.* 1. A lump of earth, clay, etc. 2. A dull, stupid person. [Var. of CLOT] —**clod′dish** *adj.* —**clod′dish·ly** *adv.* —**clod′·dish·ness** *n.*
clod·hop·per (klod′hop′ər) *n.* 1. *Informal* A rustic; hick; lout. 2. *pl.* Large, heavy shoes.
clog (klog) *n.* 1. Anything that impedes motion; an obstruction. 2. A block or weight attached, as to a horse, to hinder movement. 3. A wooden-soled shoe. —*v.* **clogged, clog·ging** *v.t.* 1. To choke up or obstruct. 2. To impede; hinder. 3. To fasten a clog to; hobble. —*v.i.* 4. To become clogged or choked. 5. To adhere in a mass; coagulate. [ME *clogge* block of wood] —**clog′gi·ness** *n.* —**clog′gy** *adj.*
cloi·son·né (kloi′zə·nā′) *n.* 1. A type of decorative enamel work. 2. The ware in this style. [< F, partitioned] —**cloi′son·né′** *adj.*
clois·ter (klois′tər) *n.* 1. A covered walk along the inside walls of buildings in a quadrangle, as in a monastery or college. 2. A monastery; convent. 3. Any place of quiet seclusion. 4. Monastic life. —*v.t.* To seclude; confine, as in a cloister. [< L *claustrum* enclosed place] —**clois′tered** *adj.* —**clois′tral** *adj.*
clone (klōn) *n.* 1. A group of organisms derived from a single individual by asexual means, including, theoretically, identical human beings from body cells. 2. One of the organisms so derived. [< Gk. *klōn* sprout, twig] —**clon′al** *adj.* —**clon′al·ly** *adv.* —**clone** *v.t.* **cloned, clon·ing**
clon·ing (klōn′ing) *n.* The production of progeny genetically identical with a progenitor.
clop (klop) *v.i.* **clopped, clop·ping** To produce a hollow percussive sound, as of a horse's hoof on pavement. [Imit.] —**clop** *n.*
close (*adj., adv., n. def. 2* klōs; *v., n. def. 1* klōz) *adj.* **clos·er, clos·est** 1. Near or together in space, time, etc. 2. Dense; compact: a *close* weave. 3. Near to the surface; short: a *close* haircut. 4. Near to the mark: a *close* shot. 5. Nearly even or equal: said of contests. 6. Fitting tightly. 7. Conforming to an original: a *close* resemblance. 8. Thorough; rigorous. 9. Bound by strong affection, loyalty, etc.: a *close* friend. 10. Confined in space; cramped: *close* quarters. 11. Strictly guarded; exclusive. 12. Uncommunicative. 13. Close-fisted; stingy. 14. Difficult to obtain: said of money or credit. 15. Stifling and humid; stuffy. —*v.* **closed, clos·ing** *v.t.* 1. To shut. 2. To obstruct, as an opening or passage. 3. To bring to an end; terminate. —*v.i.* 4. To become shut or closed. 5. To come to an end. 6. To grapple; come to close quarters. 7. To come to an agreement. 8. To be worth at the end of a business day: Stocks *closed* three points higher. —**to close down** To cease operations, as a factory. —**to close in** To advance from all sides so as to prevent escape. —**to close out** To sell all of, usu. at reduced prices. —**to close up** 1. To close completely. 2. To come nearer together, as troops. —*n.* 1. The end; conclusion. 2. An enclosed place, esp. about a cathedral or building. —*adv.* In a close manner; nearly; closely. [< L *claudere* to close] —**close·ly** (klōs′lē) *adv.* —**close·ness** (klōs′nis) *n.* —**clos·er** (klō′zər) *n.*
close call (klōs) *Informal* A narrow escape.
closed circuit (klōzd) *Telecom.* A form of television in which broadcasts are transmitted by cable to a restricted number of receivers.
closed shop An establishment where only union members are hired, by agreement with the union.
close-fist·ed (klōs′fis′tid) *adj.* Stingy; miserly. —**close′-fist′ed·ness** *n.*
close-mouthed (klōs′mouthd′, -moutht′) *adj.* Not given to idle speaking; reserved.
close quarters (klōs) 1. In fighting, an encounter at close range or hand-to-hand. 2. A small, confined space.
close shave (klōs) *Informal* A narrow escape.
clos·et (kloz′it) *n.* 1. A small room or recess for storing clothes, linen, etc. 2. A small, private room. 3. A ruler's council chamber. —*v.t.* 1. To shut up or conceal in or as in a closet: usu. reflexive. 2. To take (someone) into a room for a private interview. —*adj.* Private; confidential. [< OF, dim. of *clos* enclosure < L *claudere* to close]
close-up (klōs′up′) *n.* 1. A picture taken at close range, or with a telescopic lens. 2. A close look or view.
clo·sure (klō′zhər) *n.* 1. A closing or shutting up. 2. That which closes or shuts. 3. An end; conclusion. 4. Cloture. —*v.t. & v.i.* **·sured, ·sur·ing** To cloture. [< L *claudere* to close]
clot (klot) *n.* A thick, viscid, or coagulated

mass, as of blood. —*v.t.* & *v.i.* **clot·ted, clot·ting** To form into clots; coagulate. [OE *clott* lump, mass] —**clot′ty** *adj.*

cloth (klôth) *n.* *pl.* **cloths** (klôthz, klôths) 1. A woven, knitted, or felted fabric; also, a piece of such fabric. 2. A piece of cloth for a special use, as a tablecloth. 3. Professional attire, esp. of the clergy. —**the cloth** The clergy. [OE *clāth*]

clothe (klōth) *v.t.* **clothed** or **clad, cloth·ing** 1. To cover or provide with clothes; dress. 2. To cover as if with clothing; invest. [Fusion of OE *clāthian* and *clǣthan*]

clothes (klōz, klōthz) *n.pl.* Garments; clothing. [OE *clāthas*, pl. of *clāth* cloth]

clothes·horse (klōz′hôrs′, klōthz′-) *n.* 1. A frame on which to hang or dry clothes. 2. *Slang* A person regarded as excessively concerned with dress.

clothes·line (klōz′līn′, klōthz′-) *n.* A cord, rope, or wire on which to hang clothes to dry.

clothes·pin (klōz′pin′, klōthz′-) *n.* A forked peg or clamp for fastening clothes on a line.

clothes·press (klōz′pres′, klōthz′-) *n.* A closet; wardrobe.

cloth·ier (klōth′yər) *n.* One who makes or sells cloth or clothing.

cloth·ing (klō′thing) *n.* 1. Dress; apparel. 2. A covering.

clo·ture (klō′chər) *n.* A parliamentary device to stop debate in a legislative body in order to secure a vote. [< F *clôture*] —**clo′ture** *v.t.*

cloud (kloud) *n.* 1. A mass of visible vapor or an aggregation of watery or icy particles floating in the atmosphere. 2. Any visible collection of particles in the air. 3. A cloudlike mass of things in motion; swarm. 4. Something that darkens, obscures, or threatens. —**in the clouds** Fanciful or impractical. —**on cloud nine** In a transport of delight; elated. —**under a cloud** 1. Overshadowed by reproach or distrust. 2. Troubled or depressed. —*v.t.* 1. To cover with or as with clouds; dim; obscure. 2. To render gloomy or troubled. 3. To disgrace; sully, as a reputation. —*v.i.* 4. To become overcast: often with *up* or *over*. [OE *clūd* rocky mass, hill] —**cloud′less** *adj.*

cloud·burst (kloud′bûrst′) *n.* A sudden, heavy downpour.

cloud chamber *Physics* An apparatus used to detect the presence of ions.

cloud·y (klou′dē) *adj.* **cloud·i·er, cloud·i·est** 1. Overspread with clouds. 2. Of or like a cloud or clouds. 3. Marked with cloudlike spots. 4. Not limpid or clear. 5. Vague; confused: *cloudy* thinking. 6. Full of foreboding; gloomy. [OE *clūdig*] —**cloud′i·ly** *adv.* —**cloud′i·ness** *n.*

clout (klout) *n.* 1. *Informal* A heavy blow or cuff with the hand. 2. *Slang* Influence or power; esp., political weight. 3. In baseball slang, a long hit. —*v.t.* *Informal* To hit or strike, as with the hand. [OE *clūt*]

clove[1] (klōv) *n.* A dried flower bud of a tree of the myrtle family, used as a spice. [< OF *clou* nail-shaped bud]

clove[2] (klōv) Segment of a bulb, as of garlic. [OE *clufu*]

clo·ven (klō′vən) Alternative past participle of CLEAVE[1]. —*adj.* Parted; split.

clo·ven-hoofed (klō′vən·hoo͝ft′, -hoo͞ft′) *adj.* 1. Having the foot cleft, as cattle. 2. Satanic. Also **clo′ven-foot′ed** (-fo͝ot′id).

clo·ver (klō′vər) *n.* Any of several plants having dense flower heads and 3-parted leaves. —**in clover** In a prosperous condition. [OE *clāfre* trefoil]

clo·ver·leaf (klō′vər·lēf′) *n.* *pl.* **·leafs** A type of highway intersection resembling a four-leaf clover.

clown (kloun) *n.* 1. A professional comic performer in a play or circus; jester. 2. A coarse or vulgar person; boor. —*v.i.* To behave like a clown. [Earlier *cloune* < MLG] —**clown′er·y** *n.* —**clown′ish** *adj.* —**clown′·ish·ly** *adv.* —**clown′ish·ness** *n.*

cloy (kloi) *v.t.* 1. To gratify beyond desire; surfeit. —*v.i.* 2. To cause a feeling of surfeit. [< L *clavus* nail] —**cloy′ing** *adj.* —**cloy′ing·ly** *adv.* —**cloy′ing·ness** *n.*

club[1] (klub) *n.* 1. A stout stick or staff. 2. A stick or bat used in games. 3. A playing card bearing a black figure shaped like a three-leaf clover. —*v.t.* **clubbed, club·bing** To beat, as with a club. [< ON *klubba*]

club[2] (klub) *n.* 1. A group of persons organized for some mutual aim or pursuit, esp. a group that meets regularly. 2. The meeting place of such a group. —*v.* **clubbed, club·bing** *v.t.* 1. To contribute for a common purpose: to *club* resources. —*v.i.* 2. To combine or unite: often with *together*. [Special use of CLUB[1]]

club car A railroad passenger car furnished with armchairs, tables, a buffet or bar, etc.

club·foot (klub′fo͝ot′) *n.* *pl.* **·feet** *Pathol.* 1. Congenital distortion of the foot. 2. A foot so affected. —**club′foot′ed** *adj.*

club·house (klub′hous′) *n.* 1. The building occupied by a club. 2. Dressing rooms for an athletic team.

club moss A perennial evergreen herb allied to the ferns.

club sandwich A sandwich of three slices of toast and fillings.

club steak A small beefsteak cut from the loin.

cluck (kluk) *v.i.* 1. To give the low, guttural cry of a hen calling her chicks. 2. To utter any similar sound. —*v.t.* 3. To call by clucking. 4. To express with a like sound: to *cluck* disapproval. [OE *cloccian*; imit.] —**cluck** *n.*

clue (klo͞o) *n.* Something that leads to the solution of a problem or mystery. —*v.t.* **clued, clu·ing** *Informal* To give (someone) information. [Var. of CLEW]

clump (klump) *n.* 1. A thick cluster. 2. A heavy, dull sound, as of tramping. 3. An irregular mass; a lump. —*v.i.* 1. To walk clumsily and noisily. 2. To form clumps. —*v.t.* 3. To place or plant in a clump. [Var. of CLUB[1]] —**clump′y, clump′ish** *adj.*

clum·sy (klum′zē) *adj.* **·si·er, ·si·est** 1. Lacking dexterity, ease, or grace. 2. Ungainly or unwieldy. 3. Ill-contrived: a *clumsy* excuse. [< obs. *clumse* to be numb with cold] —**clum′si·ly** *adv.* —**clum′si·ness** *n.*

clung (klung) Past tense and past participle of CLING.

clus·ter (klus′tər) *n.* 1. A collection of similar objects growing or fastened together. 2. A group of persons or things close together. [OE *clyster*] —**clus′ter** *v.t.* & *v.i.* —**clus′tered** *adj.* —**clus′ter·y** *adj.*

clutch[1] (kluch) *v.t.* 1. To snatch, as with hands or talons. 2. To grasp and hold firmly. —*v.i.* 3. To attempt to seize, snatch, or reach: with *at*. —*n.* 1. A tight grip; grasp.

2. *pl.* Power or control. 3. *Mech.* **a** A device for coupling two working parts, as the engine and driveshaft of an automobile. **b** A lever or pedal for operating such a device. 4. A critical or crucial situation. [ME *clucchen*]

clutch[2] (kluch) *n.* 1. The number of eggs laid at one time. 2. A brood of chickens. —*v.t.* To hatch. [< ON *klekja* hatch]

clut·ter (klut′ər) *n.* 1. A disordered state or collection; litter. 2. A clatter. —*v.t.* 1. To litter, heap, or pile in a confused manner. —*v.i.* 2. To make a clatter. [Var. of earlier *clotter*]

co-[1] *prefix* With; together; joint or jointly; equally: used with verbs, nouns, adjectives, and adverbs. [< L *co-* var. of *com-* before *gn*, *h*, and vowels < *cum* with] Some self-explanatory words beginning with *co-*:

coadminister	**coestablish**
coagency	**coeternal**
coagent	**coinhabit**
coapprove	**coinheritor**
coarrange	**cointersect**
coassist	**coinventor**
coauthor	**coinvolve**
cobelligerent	**co-occupy**
coconspirator	**co-owner**
codefendant	**copartner**
coderive	**cosovereign**
codiscoverer	**cosponsor**
coeditor	**cotrustee**
coequal	**co-worker**

co-[2] *prefix* 1. *Math.* Of the complement: *cosine.* 2. *Astron.* Complement of. [< L *complementum* complement]

coach (kōch) *n.* 1. A large, four-wheeled closed carriage. 2. A passenger bus. 3. A railroad passenger car or section of an airplane offering the most economical accommodations. 4. A private tutor. 5. A trainer or director in athletics, dramatics, etc. —*v.t.* 1. To tutor or train; act as coach to. —*v.i.* 2. To act as coach. [< Hung. *kocsi* (*szeker*) (wagon) of Kocs, the village where first used]

coach-and-four (kōch′ən·fôr′) *n.* A coach drawn by four horses.

coach dog A Dalmatian.

coach·man (kōch′mən) *n. pl.* **·men** (-mən) One who drives a coach.

co·ad·ju·tant (kō·aj′ə·tənt) *adj.* Cooperating. —*n.* An assistant or co-worker. [< co-[1] + L *adjutare* to help]

co·ad·ju·tor (kō·aj′ə·tər, kō′ə·jo͞o′tər) *n.* 1. An assistant or co-worker. 2. A bishop who assists a diocesan bishop.

co·ag·u·lant (kō·ag′yə·lənt) *n.* A coagulating agent, as rennet.

co·ag·u·late (kō·ag′yə·lāt) *v.t. & v.i.* **·lat·ed, ·lat·ing** To change from a liquid into a clot or mass. [< L *coagulare* to curdle] —**co·ag′u·la·ble** (-lə·bəl) *adj.* —**co·ag′u·la′tion** *n.* —**co·ag′u·la′tive** *adj.* —**co·ag′u·la′tor** *n.*

coal (kōl) *n.* 1. A solid, dark brown to black, combustible mineral found in the earth and used as fuel and a source of hydrocarbons. 2. A piece of coal. 3. A glowing or charred fragment of wood or other fuel; an ember. —**to carry coals to Newcastle** To provide something already in abundant supply. —**to haul (rake, etc.) over the coals** To criticize severely; reprimand. —*v.t.* 1. To supply with coal. —*v.i.* 2. To take on coal. [OE *col*]

co·a·lesce (kō′ə·les′) *v.i.* **·lesced, ·lesc·ing** To grow or come together into one; blend. [< co-[1] + L *alescere* to grow up] —**co′a·les′cence** *n.* —**co′a·les′cent** *adj.*

coal gas 1. The poisonous gas produced by the combustion of coal. 2. A gas produced by the distillation of bituminous coal, used for illuminating and heating.

co·a·li·tion (kō′ə·lish′ən) *n.* 1. An alliance of persons, parties, or states. 2. A fusion into one mass. [< co-[1] + L *alescere* to grow up] —**co′a·li′tion·ist** *n.*

coal oil 1. Kerosene. 2. Crude petroleum.

coal·scut·tle (kōl′skut′l) *n.* A bucket for carrying or storing coal. Also **coal hod.**

coal tar A black, viscid liquid distilled from bituminous coal, used in making dyestuffs, drugs, plastics, etc. —**coal-tar** (kōl′tär′) *adj.*

coarse (kôrs) *adj.* 1. Lacking refinement; vulgar. 2. Inferior; base; common. 3. Composed of large parts or particles. [Adjectival use of COURSE, meaning usual, ordinary] —**coarse′ly** *adv.* —**coarse′ness** *n.*

coars·en (kôr′sən) *v.t. & v.i.* To make or become coarse.

coast (kōst) *n.* 1. The land next to the sea; the seashore. 2. A slope suitable for sliding, as on a sled; also, a slide down it. —**the Coast** That part of the United States bordering on the Pacific Ocean. —**the coast is clear** There is no danger or difficulty now. —*v.i.* 1. To slide down a slope by force of gravity alone, as on a sled. 2. To continue moving on acquired momentum alone. 3. To sail along a coast. —*v.t.* 4. To sail along, as a coast; skirt. [< L *costa* rib, flank] —**coast′al** *adj.* —**coast′al·ly** *adv.*

coast·er (kōs′tər) *n.* 1. One who or that which coasts. 2. A sled or toboggan. 3. A small disk set under a drinking glass to protect the surface beneath.

coaster brake A clutchlike brake on a bicycle, operated by back pressure on the pedals.

coast guard Naval or military coastal patrol and police. —**United States Coast Guard** A force set up to protect life and property at sea and to enforce customs, immigration, and navigation laws.

coast·line (kōst′līn′) *n.* The contour or boundary of a coast.

coast·ward (kōst′wərd) *adj.* Directed or facing toward the coast. —*adv.* Toward the coast: also **coast′wards.**

coat (kōt) *n.* 1. A sleeved outer garment. 2. A natural covering, as the fur of an animal. 3. Any layer covering a surface, as paint, ice, etc. —*v.t.* 1. To cover with a surface layer, as of paint. 2. To provide with a coat. [< OF *cote*] —**coat′ed** *adj.* —**coat′less** *adj.*

co·a·ti (kō·ä′tē) *n. pl.* **·tis** (-tēz) A small, carnivorous, raccoonlike mammal of tropical America. Also **co·a′ti-mon′di** (-mun′dē), **co·a′ti-mun′di** (-mun′dē). [< Tupi]

coat·ing (kō′ting) *n.* 1. A covering layer; coat. 2. Cloth for coats.

coat of arms 1. A shield marked with the insignia of a person or family. 2. A representation of such insignia.

coat of mail *pl.* **coats of mail** A defensive garment made of chain mail.

coat·tail (kōt′tāl′) *n.* The loose, back part of a coat below the waist; also, either half of this in a coat split at the back. —**on (one's) coattails** Dependent upon another, esp. for success in an election.

coax (kōks) *v.t.* 1. To seek to persuade by

gentleness, flattery, etc. 2. To obtain by coaxing. —*v.i.* 3. To use persuasion or cajolery. [< earlier *cokes* a fool, dupe] —**coax′er** *n.* —**coax′ing·ly** *adv.*

co·ax·i·al (kō·ak′sē·əl) *adj.* 1. Having a common axis or coincident axes. Also **co·ax·al** (kō·ak′səl). 2. Describing a cable consisting of two or more insulated conductors capable of transmitting radio or television signals or multiple telegraph or telephone messages.

cob (kob) *n.* 1. A corncob. 2. A male swan. 3. A thickset horse with short legs. [ME *cobbe*]

co·balt (kō′bôlt) *n.* A tough, lustrous, pinkish gray, metallic element (symbol Co), used as an alloy and in pigments. [< G *kobalt*, var. of *kobold* goblin] —**co·bal′tic** *adj.* —**co·bal′tous** *adj.*

cobalt blue 1. A permanent, deep blue pigment, made from oxides of cobalt and aluminum. 2. An intense blue.

cob·ble[1] (kob′əl) *n.* A cobblestone. —*v.t.* **·bled, ·bling** To pave with cobblestones. [Akin to COB]

cob·ble[2] (kob′əl) *v.t.* **·bled, ·bling** To repair, as shoes. [Origin uncertain]

cob·bler[1] (kob′lər) *n.* One who patches boots and shoes.

cob·bler[2] (kob′lər) *n.* A deep-dish fruit pie with no bottom crust. [Origin unknown]

cob·ble·stone (kob′əl·stōn′) *n.* A naturally rounded stone, formerly used for paving.

co·bra (kō′brə) *n.* A venomous snake of Asia and Africa that when excited can dilate its neck into a broad hood; esp., the **spectacled cobra** of India, and the **king cobra.** [< L *colubra* snake]

cob·web (kob′web′) *n.* 1. The network of fine thread spun by a spider; also, a single thread of this. 2. Something flimsy or entangling like a cobweb. —*v.t.* **·webbed, ·web·bing** To cover with or as with cobwebs. [ME *coppeweb* < *coppe* spider + WEB] —**cob′web′by** *adj.*

co·ca (kō′kə) *n.* 1. The dried leaves of a South American shrub, yielding cocaine and other alkaloids. 2. The shrub itself. [< Quechua *kúka*]

co·caine (kō·kān′, kō′kān) *n.* A bitter, crystalline alkaloid used as a local anesthetic and as a narcotic. Also **co·cain′, co′cain.** [< COCA + -INE[2]]

coc·cus (kok′əs) *n.* *pl.* **coc·ci** (kok′sī) *Bacteriol.* A spherical or oval-shaped bacterium. [< Gk. *kokkos* berry] —**coc·coid** (kok′oid) *adj.*

-coccus *combining form* Berry-shaped. [< Gk. *kokkos* berry]

coc·cyx (kok′siks) *n.* *pl.* **coc·cy·ges** (kok·sī′jēz) *Anat.* The small triangular bone at the base of the spine. [< Gk. *kokkyx* cuckoo; from a fancied resemblance to a cuckoo's bill] —**coc·cyg·e·al** (kok·sij′ē·əl) *adj.*

coch·i·neal (koch′ə·nēl) *n.* A brilliant scarlet dye prepared from the dried bodies of scale insects of tropical America and Java. [< Sp. *cochinilla*]

coch·le·a (kok′lē·ə) *n.* *pl.* **·le·ae** (-lē·ē, -lē·ī) *Anat.* A spiral tube in the inner ear, forming an essential part of the mechanism of hearing. [< L, snail] —**coch′le·ar** *adj.*

coch·le·ate (kok′lē·āt) *adj.* Spiralled like a snail shell. Also **coch′le·at′ed.**

cock[1] (kok) *n.* 1. A full-grown male domestic fowl; a rooster. 2. Any male bird. 3. In a firearm, the hammer; also, the condition of readiness for firing. 4. A jaunty tip or upward turn, as of a hat brim. 5. A faucet or valve. —*v.t.* 1. To set the mechanism of (a firearm) so as to be ready for firing. 2. To turn up or to one side alertly, jauntily, or inquiringly, as the head. 3. To bring to a position of readiness. —*v.i.* 4. To cock a firearm. 5. To stick up prominently. —*adj.* Male. [OE *cocc*]

cock[2] (kok) *n.* A conical pile of straw or hay. —*v.t.* To arrange in piles or cocks, as hay. [< ON *kökkr* lump, heap]

cock·ade (kok·ād′) *n.* A knot of ribbon, or the like, worn on the hat as a badge. [< MF *coq* cock] —**cock·ad′ed** *adj.*

cock·a·ma·my (kok′ə·mā′mē) *adj.* *Slang* Absurd; ridiculous. Also **cock′a·ma′mie.** [? alter. of DECALCOMANIA]

cock·a·too (kok′ə·tōō) *n.* *pl.* **·toos** Any of various brightly colored, crested parrots of the East Indies or Australia. [< Malay *kakatūa*]

cock·a·trice (kok′ə·tris) *n.* A fabulous serpent, said to be hatched from a cock's egg, deadly to those who felt its breath or met its glance. [< OF *cocatris*]

cock·boat (kok′bōt) *n.* A small boat, as a ship's rowboat: also called **cockle boat.** [< MF *coque* small boat + BOAT]

cock·chaf·er (kok′chā′fər) *n.* A large European beetle destructive to vegetation. [< COCK[1] (from def. 1, for its size) + CHAFER]

cock·crow (kok′krō′) *n.* Early morning.

cocked hat (kokt) A tricorn. —**to knock into a cocked hat** To demolish; ruin.

cock·er·el (kok′ər·əl) *n.* An immature cock.

cock·er spaniel (kok′ər) A small, sturdy spaniel of solid or variegated coloring. Also **cocker.** [? Because used in hunting woodcock]

cock·eye (kok′ī) *n.* A squinting eye.

cock·eyed (kok′īd′) *adj.* 1. Cross-eyed. 2. *Slang* Off center; askew. 3. *Slang* Absurd; ridiculous. 4. *Slang* Drunk.

cock·fight (kok′fīt′) *n.* A fight between gamecocks that are usually fitted with steel spurs. —**cock′fight′ing** *adj. & n.*

cock·horse (kok′hôrs′) *n.* A rocking horse or hobbyhorse.

cock·le[1] (kok′əl) *n.* 1. A European bivalve mollusk, esp. an edible species, with ridged shells. 2. Any of various similar mollusks. —**the cockles of one's heart** The depths of one's heart or feelings. [< Gk. *konchē* shell, mussel]

cock·le[2] (kok′əl) *n.* A weed that grows among grain, as the darnel. [OE *coccel*]

cock·le·bur (kok′əl·bûr′) *n.* 1. A coarse, branching weed having burs. 2. The burdock.

cock·le·shell (kok′əl·shel′) *n.* 1. The shell of a cockle. 2. A frail, light boat. [< COCKLE[1] + SHELL]

cock·ney (kok′nē) *n.* 1. *Often cap.* A resident of the East End of London. 2. The dialect or accent of East End Londoners: also **cock′·ney·ese′** (-ēz′, -ēs′). [ME *cokeney*, lit., pampered child, soft person, city man] —**cock′ney, cock′ney·ish** *adj.* —**cock′ney·ism** *n.*

cock·pit (kok′pit′) *n.* 1. A compartment in an airplane for the pilot and copilot. 2. A pit or ring for cockfighting.

cock·roach (kok′rōch′) *n.* Any of a large group of chiefly nocturnal insects, many of which are household pests. [< Sp. *cucaracha*]
cocks·comb (koks′kōm′) *n.* 1. The comb of a cock. 2. A plant with showy red or yellowish flowers. 3. A coxcomb.
cock·sure (kok′shŏŏr′) *adj.* 1. Absolutely sure. 2. Overly self-confident. **—cock′sure′·ness** *n.*
cock·tail (kok′tāl′) *n.* 1. Any of various chilled, usually mixed alcoholic drinks. 2. An appetizer, as chilled diced fruits or seafood seasoned with sauce. [? Alter. of F *coquetel*]
cock·y (kok′ē) *adj.* **cock·i·er, cock·i·est** *Informal* Swaggeringly self-confident; conceited. **—cock′i·ly** *adv.* **—cock′i·ness** *n.*
co·co (kō′kō) *n. pl.* **·cos** 1. The coconut palm. 2. The fruit of the coconut palm. *—adj.* Made of coconut fiber. [< Pg., grinning face]
co·coa (kō′kō) *n.* 1. A powder made from the roasted, husked seed kernels of the cacao; chocolate. 2. A beverage made from this. 3. A reddish brown color. [Alter. of CACAO]
cocoa butter A fatty substance obtained from cacao seeds, used in soap, cosmetics, etc.: also **cacao butter.**
co·co·nut (kō′kə·nut′, -nət) *n.* The fruit of the coconut palm, having white meat enclosed in a hard shell. Also **co′coa·nut′.**
coconut milk A milky fluid inside the coconut.
coconut oil An oil derived from dried coconut meat, used in soaps, foodstuffs, etc.
coconut palm A tropical palm tree bearing coconuts. Also **coco palm, coconut tree.**
co·coon (kə·kōōn′) *n.* The fibrous pupal envelope spun by the larvae of certain insects. [< F *coque* shell]
cod (kod) *n. pl.* **cod** or **cods** An important food fish of the North Atlantic. [Origin unknown]
co·da (kō′də) *n.* ***Music*** A passage at the end of a work or movement. [< Ital. < L *cauda* tail]
cod·dle (kod′l) *v.t.* **·dled, ·dling** 1. To simmer in water. 2. To baby; pamper. [? Akin to CAUDLE] **—cod′dler** *n.*
code (kōd) *n.* 1. A systematized body of law. 2. Any system of principles or regulations. 3. A set of signals, characters, or symbols used in communication. 4. A set of words, letters, or numbers, used for secrecy or brevity in sending messages. *—v.t.* **cod·ed, cod·ing** 1. To systematize, as laws. 2. To put into the symbols of a code. [< L *codex* writing tablet]
co·deine (kō′dēn′, kō′dē·in) *n.* *Chem.* A white crystalline alkaloid derived from morphine and used in medicine as a mild narcotic. Also **co′de·in, co·de·ia** (kō·dē′ə). [< Gk. *kōdeia* head of a poppy + -INE²]
co·dex (kō′deks) *n. pl.* **co·di·ces** (kō′də·sēz, kod′ə-) An ancient manuscript volume, as of Scripture. [< L, writing tablet]
codg·er (koj′ər) *n.* *Informal* An eccentric or testy man, esp. an old one. [ME *cadgear*]
cod·i·cil (kod′ə·səl) *n.* 1. *Law* A supplement to a will. 2. An appendix; addition. [< L *codex* writing tablet] **—cod·i·cil·la·ry** (kod′·ə·sil′ər·ē) *adj.*
cod·i·fy (kod′ə·fī, kō′də-) *v.t.* **·fied, ·fy·ing** To systematize, as laws. [< F *code* system, code] **—cod′i·fi·ca′tion** *n.* **—cod′i·fi′er** *n.*
cod·ling (kod′ling) *n. pl.* **·lings** (*Rare* **·ling**) 1. A young cod. 2. Any of certain related fishes. [Dim. of COD]
cod-liver oil (kod′liv′ər, kod′liv′ər) Oil from the liver of cod, a source of vitamins A and D.
co·ed (kō′ed′) *Informal n.* A woman student at a coeducational institution. *—adj.* Coeducational. Also **co′-ed′.**
co·ed·u·ca·tion (kō′ej·ōō·kā′shən) *n.* The education of both sexes in the same school. **—co′ed·u·ca′tion·al** *adj.*
co·ef·fi·cient (kō′ə·fish′ənt) *n.* 1. *Math.* A number or letter before an algebraic expression that multiplies it. 2. *Physics* A number showing the change in a substance, body, or process under given conditions. *—adj.* Acting together.
coe·la·canth (sē′lə·kanth) *n.* *Zool.* A large-bodied, hollow-spined fish, extinct except for one species. [< COEL(O)- + Gk. *akantha* spine]
coe·len·ter·ate (si·len′tə·rāt) *n.* *Zool.* Any of a phylum of invertebrate animals having a large body cavity that functions as a vascular as well as a digestive system, including sea anemones, corals, jellyfish, and hydras. [< COEL(O)- + Gk. *enteron* intestine] **—coe·len′ter·ate, coe·len·ter·ic** (sē′len·ter′ik) *adj.*
coelo- *combining form* Cavity; cavity of the body, or of an organ. Also, before vowels, **coel-.** [< Gk. *koilos* hollow]
coeno- See CENO-.
co·erce (kō·ûrs′) *v.t.* **·erced, ·erc·ing** 1. To compel by force, authority, or fear. 2. To restrain or repress by superior force. 3. To bring about by force. [< CO-¹ + L *arcere* to shut up, restrain] **—co·er′cer** *n.* **—co·er′ci·ble** *adj.* **—co·er′cive** *adj.* **—co·er′cive·ly** *adv.* **—co·er′cive·ness** *n.*
co·er·cion (kō·ûr′shən, -zhən) *n.* 1. Forcible constraint or restraint, moral or physical. 2. Government by force. **—co·er′cion·ar·y** *adj.* **—co·er′cion·ist** *n.*
co·e·val (kō·ē′vəl) *adj.* 1. Of or belonging to the same age, time, or duration. 2. Contemporary. *—n.* 1. One of the same age. 2. A contemporary. [< CO-¹ + L *aevum* age] **—co·e′val·ly** *adv.*
co·ex·ist (kō′ig·zist′) *v.i.* To exist together, in, or at the same place or time. **—co′ex·is′tence** *n.* **—co′ex·is′tent** *adj.*
co·ex·ten·sive (kō′ik·sten′siv) *adj.* Extending through the same space or time. [< CO-¹ + EXTEND] **—co′ex·ten′sive·ly** *adv.*
cof·fee (kôf′ē, kof′ē) *n.* 1. A beverage made from the roasted and ground beans of a tropical evergreen shrub. 2. The seeds or beans of this shrub: also **coffee beans.** 3. The shrub itself. 4. The brown color of coffee with cream. [< Arabic *qahwah*]
coffee cake A kind of cake to be eaten with coffee, often containing raisins or nuts. Also **cof·fee·cake** (kôf′ē·kāk′, kof′ē-).
coffee house A place where coffee is featured and people meet to talk, play chess, etc. Also **cof·fee·house** (kôf′ē·hous′, kof′ē-).
coffee shop A restaurant where coffee and food are served.
coffee table A low table, usu. placed in front of a sofa, for serving refreshments.
cof·fer (kôf′ər, kof′-) *n.* 1. A chest or box, esp. one for valuables. 2. *pl.* Financial resources; a treasury. 3. A decorative, sunken panel in a ceiling, dome, etc. 4. A lock

in a canal. 5. A cofferdam. [< Gk. *kophinos* basket]

cof·fer·dam (kôf′ər·dam, kof′-) *n.* 1. A temporary enclosure built in water and pumped dry to permit work on bridge piers and the like. 2. A watertight structure attached to a ship's side for repairs made below the water line.

cof·fin (kôf′in, kof′-) *n.* A box or case in which a corpse is buried. [< Gk. *kophinos* basket]

cog (kog) *n.* 1. *Mech.* A tooth or one of a series of teeth projecting from the surface of a wheel or gear to impart or receive motion. 2. One who plays a minor but necessary part in a large or complex process. 3. A tenon. [ME *cogge*] **—cogged** *adj.*

co·gent (kō′jənt) *adj.* Compelling assent; forcible; convincing. [< L *cogere* to compel] **—co′gen·cy** *n.* **—co′gent·ly** *adv.*

cog·i·tate (koj′ə·tāt) *v.t.* & *v.i.* **·tat·ed, ·tat·ing** To ponder; meditate. [< co-¹ + L *agitare* to consider] **—cog′i·ta′tion** *n.* **—cog′i·ta′tive** *adj.* **—cog′i·ta′tive·ly** *adv.* **—cog′i·ta′tor** *n.*

co·gnac (kōn′yak, kon′-) *n.* A kind of brandy, esp. one produced in the Cognac region of France. [< F]

cog·nate (kog′nāt) *adj.* 1. Allied by blood; kindred. 2. Allied by having the same source: said esp. of words in different languages. 3. Allied by having like characteristics; similar. [< L *cognatus* related by birth] **—cog′nate** *n.* **—cog·na′tion** *n.*

cog·ni·tion (kog·nish′ən) *n.* 1. The act or faculty of knowing or perceiving. 2. A thing known; a perception. [< L *cognoscere* to know] **—cog·ni′tion·al** *adj.* **—cog′ni·tive** *adj.*

cog·ni·zance (kog′nə·zəns, kon′ə-) *n.* Apprehension or perception of fact; knowledge; notice. **—to take cognizance of** To acknowledge; recognize. [< L *cognoscere* to know]

cog·ni·zant (kog′nə·zənt, kon′ə-) *adj.* Having knowledge; aware: with *of.*

cog·no·men (kog·nō′mən) *n.* *pl.* **·no·mens** or **·nom·i·na** (-nom′ə·nə) 1. A surname. 2. Loosely, any name, nickname, or appellation. [< co-¹ + L *nomen* name] **—cog·nom·i·nal** (kog·nom′ə·nəl) *adj.*

cog·wheel (kog′hwēl′) *n.* A wheel with cogs, used to transmit or receive motion: also called *gearwheel.*

co·hab·it (kō·hab′it) *v.i.* To live together as husband and wife, esp. without sanction of marriage. [< co-¹ + L *habitare* to live] **—co·hab′i·tant, co·hab′it·er** *n.* **—co·hab′i·ta′tion** *n.*

co·here (kō·hir′) *v.i.* **·hered, ·her·ing** 1. To stick or hold firmly together. 2. To be logically connected, as the parts of a story. [< co-¹ + L *haerere* to stick]

co·her·ence (kō·hir′ens) *n.* 1. The act or state of sticking or holding together; cohesion. 2. Logical connection or consistency. Also **co·her′en·cy.**

co·her·ent (kō·hir′ənt) *adj.* 1. Sticking together, as particles of the same substance. 2. Logical; consistent. 3. Intelligible or articulate, as speech. **—co·her′ent·ly** *adv.*

co·he·sion (kō·hē′zhən) *n.* 1. The act or state of cohering. 2. *Physics* That force by which molecules of the same kind or the same body are held together. **—co·he′sive** (-siv) *adj.* **—co·he′sive·ly** *adv.* **—co·he′sive·ness** *n.*

co·hort (kō′hôrt) *n.* 1. The tenth of an ancient Roman legion, 300 to 600 men. 2. A band or group, esp. of warriors. 3. A companion or follower. [< L *cohors, cohortis*]

coif (koif; *for n. & v. def. 2,* kwäf) *n.* 1. A close-fitting cap or hood, as that worn by nuns under the veil. 2. A hairdo. **—*v.t.*** 1. To cover with or as with a coif. 2. To style (hair). [< OF < LL *cofea*]

coif·feur (kwä·fœr′) *n.* *French* A hairdresser.

coif·fure (kwä·fyŏŏr′, *Fr.* kwȧ·für′) *n.* 1. A style of arranging the hair. 2. A headdress. **—*v.t.*** To dress (the hair). Also *coif.* [< F]

coign (koin) *n.* A projecting angle or stone; a corner. Also **coigne.** [Var. of QUOIN]

coil (koil) *n.* 1. A series of concentric rings or spirals, as that formed by winding a rope. 2. A single ring or spiral of such a series. 3. Any of several electrical devices containing a coiled wire, as an induction coil. **—*v.t.* & *v.i.*** To wind spirally or in rings. [< OF < L *colligere* to collect] **—coil′er** *n.*

coin (koin) *n.* 1. A piece of metal stamped by government authority for use as money. 2. Metal currency collectively. 3. *Archit.* A quoin. **—*v.t.*** 1. To stamp (coins) from metal. 2. To make into coins. 3. To originate or invent, as a word or phrase. [< F, wedge, die < L *cuneus* wedge] **—coin′er** *n.*

coin·age (koi′nij) *n.* 1. The act or right of making coins. 2. The coins made. 3. The system of coins of a country; currency. 4. The act of inventing a word, phrase, etc. 5. The word, phrase, etc., itself.

co·in·cide (kō′in·sīd′) *v.i.* **·cid·ed, ·cid·ing** 1. To have the same dimensions and position in space. 2. To occur at the same time. 3. To agree exactly; accord. [< co-¹ + L *incidere* to happen]

co·in·ci·dence (kō·in′sə·dəns) *n.* 1. The condition of coinciding; correspondence. 2. A remarkable concurrence of events, ideas, etc.

co·in·ci·dent (kō·in′sə·dənt) *adj.* 1. Having the same position and extent. 2. Occurring at the same time. 3. In exact agreement: with *with.* **—co·in′ci·dent·ly** *adv.*

co·in·ci·den·tal (kō·in′sə·den′təl) *adj.* Characterized by or involving coincidence. **—co·in′ci·den′tal·ly** *adv.*

co·i·tus (kō′i·təs) *n.* Sexual intercourse. Also **co·i·tion** (kō·ish′ən). [< L *coitus,* pp. of *coire* to come together]

coke (kōk) *n.* 1. A solid, carbonaceous fuel obtained by heating coal to remove its gases. 2. *Slang* Cocaine. **—*v.t.* & *v.i.*** **coked, cok·ing** To change into coke. [? ME *colke*]

col- Var. of COM-.

co·la (kō′lə) *n.* 1. A small tropical tree bearing seeds (**cola nuts**) used in making soft drinks. 2. A carbonated soft drink made from cola nuts. [< *kola,* native African name]

col·an·der (kul′ən·dər, kol′-) *n.* A perforated vessel for draining off liquids. [< L *colare* to strain]

cold (kōld) *adj.* 1. Having little or no heat. 2. Having a relatively low temperature: *cold* hands. 3. Feeling little or no warmth; chilled. 4. Dead. 5. Detached; objective: *cold* reason. 6. Lacking in affection or passion; unfriendly. 7. *Informal* Unconscious. **—cold feet** *Informal* Loss of courage; timidity. **—*adv.*** *Slang* Thoroughly; with certainty: to know it *cold.* **—*n.*** **1.** Lack of heat. **2.** The sensation caused by loss or lack of heat. **3.** An acute viral infection of the upper respiratory tract, characterized by sneezing, coughing, etc. **—out in the cold** Ignored; neglected. **—to catch (or take) cold** To become infected with a cold. [OE *cald*] **—cold′ly** *adv.* **—cold′ness** *n.*

cold-blood·ed (kōld′blud′id) *adj.* **1.** Unsympathetic; heartless. **2.** Sensitive to cold. **3.** *Zool.* Having a blood temperature that varies with that of the environment, as in reptiles. **—cold′-blood′ed·ly** *adv.* **—cold′-blood′ed·ness** *n.*

cold cream A cleansing and soothing ointment for the skin.

cold duck A blend of sparkling Burgundy and Champagne. [< G *kalte ente,* a blend of wines]

cold front *Meteorol.* The forward edge of an advancing cold air mass.

cold·heart·ed (kōld′här′tid) *adj.* Without sympathy; unkind. **—cold′heart′ed·ly** *adv.* **—cold′heart′ed·ness** *n.*

cold shoulder *Informal* A deliberate slight.

cold sore An eruption about the mouth or nostrils, often accompanying a cold or fever.

cold turkey *Slang* The abrupt and total withdrawal from a drug by an addict.

cold war An intense rivalry between nations, falling short of armed conflict.

cole (kōl) *n.* A plant related to the cabbage, esp. rape. Also **cole′wort′** (-wûrt′). [OE *cāl, cāwl* < L *caulis* cabbage]

co·le·op·ter·ous (kō′lē·op′tər·əs, kol′ē-) *adj.* Belonging to a large order of insects, including the beetles and weevils, having horny front wings that fit as cases over the hind wings. [< Gk. *koleos* sheath + *pteron* wing]

cole·slaw (kōl′slô′) *n.* A salad of shredded raw cabbage. Also **cole slaw.** Also called *slaw.* [< Du. *kool sla*]

col·ic (kol′ik) *n.* Acute abdominal pain resulting from muscular spasms. **—*adj.*** Pertaining to, near, or affecting the colon. [< Gk. *kolon* colon] **—col′ick·y** *adj.*

-coline Var. of -COLOUS.

co·lin·e·ar (kō·lin′ē·ər) *adj.* Having corresponding parts arranged in the same sequence.

col·i·se·um (kol′ə·sē′əm) *n.* A large building or stadium for exhibitions, sports events, etc. [after the *Colosseum,* a Roman amphitheater]

co·li·tis (kə·lī′tis) *n.* Inflammation of the colon.

col·lab·o·rate (kə·lab′ə·rāt) *v.i.* **·rat·ed, ·rat·ing** **1.** To work or cooperate with another, esp. in literary or scientific pursuits. **2.** To be a collaborationist. [< COM- + L *laborare* to work] **—col·lab′o·ra′tion** *n.* **—col·lab′o·ra′tive** *adj.* **—col·lab′o·ra′tor** *n.*

col·lab·o·ra·tion·ist (kə·lab′ə·rā′shən·ist) *n.* A citizen of an occupied country who cooperates with the enemy.

col·lage (kə·läzh′) *n.* An artistic composition consisting of or including flat materials pasted on a surface. Compare ASSEMBLAGE (def. 4). [< F, pasting < *colle* glue]

col·lapse (kə·laps′) *v.* **·lapsed, ·laps·ing** *v.i.* **1.** To give way; cave in. **2.** To fail utterly; come to naught. **3.** To assume a more compact form, as by being folded. **4.** To lose health, strength, etc., suddenly. **—*v.t.*** **5.** To cause to collapse. **—*n.*** **1.** The act or process of collapsing. **2.** Extreme prostration. **3.** Utter failure; ruin. [< COM- + L *labi* to fall] **—col·laps′i·ble** or **col·laps′a·ble** *adj.* **—col·laps′i·bil′i·ty** *n.*

col·lar (kol′ər) *n.* **1.** The part of a garment at the neck, often folded over. **2.** A band of leather or metal for the neck of an animal. **3.** *Mech.* Any of various devices encircling a rod or shaft, to form a connection, etc. **—*v.t.*** **1.** To provide with a collar. **2.** To grasp by the collar; capture. [< L *collum* neck]

col·lar·bone (kol′ər·bōn′) *n.* The clavicle.

col·lard (kol′ərd) *n.* *Usu. pl.* A variety of cabbage that does not form a head. [Alter. of *colewort.* See COLE.]

col·late (kə·lāt′, kol′āt) *v.t.* **·lat·ed, ·lat·ing** **1.** To compare critically, as writings or facts. **2.** To assemble (pages, etc.) in their correct order. [< COM- + L *ferre* to bear, carry] **—col·la·tor** (kə·lā′tər, kol′ā·tər) *n.*

col·lat·er·al (kə·lat′ər·əl) *adj.* **1.** Lying or running side by side; parallel. **2.** Concomitant. **3.** Tending to the same conclusion; corroborative. **4.** Subordinate; secondary. **5.** Guaranteed by stocks, property, etc.: a *collateral* loan. **6.** Descended from a common ancestor, but in a different line. **—*n.*** **1.** Security pledged for a loan or obligation. **2.** A collateral kinsman. [< COM- + L *lateralis* lateral] **—col·lat′er·al·ly** *adv.*

col·la·tion (kə·lā′shən) *n.* **1.** The act or process of collating. **2.** Any light, informal meal.

col·league (kol′ēg) *n.* A fellow member of a profession, association, etc.; an associate. [< COM- + L *legere* to choose]

col·lect[1] (kə·lekt′) *v.t.* **1.** To gather together; assemble. **2.** To bring together as a hobby: to *collect* stamps. **3.** To request and obtain (payments of money). **4.** To regain control: to *collect* one's wits. **—*v.i.*** **5.** To assemble or congregate. **6.** To accumulate. **7.** To gather payments or donations. **—*adj. & adv.*** To be paid for by the receiver. [< L *collectus,* pp. of *colligere* to choose] **—col·lect′a·ble** or **col·lect′i·ble** *adj.*

col·lect[2] (kol′ekt) *n.* *Eccl.* A short, formal prayer used in several Western liturgies. [See COLLECT[1].]

col·lect·ed (kə·lek′tid) *adj.* **1.** Gathered together. **2.** Composed; self-possessed. **—col·lect′ed·ly** *adv.* **—col·lect′ed·ness** *n.*

col·lec·tion (kə·lek′shən) *n.* **1.** The act or process of collecting. **2.** That which is collected. **3.** An accumulation. **4.** A soliciting of money; also, the money obtained.

col·lec·tive (kə·lek′tiv) *adj.* **1.** Formed or gathered together by collecting. **2.** Of, relating to, or proceeding from a number of persons or things together. **3.** *Gram.* Denoting in the singular number an aggregate of individuals: a *collective* noun. **—*n.*** A collective enterprise or body, as a farm. **—col·lec′tive·ly** *adv.* **—col·lec′tive·ness, col·lec·tiv·i·ty** (kol′ek·tiv′ə·tē) *n.*

collective bargaining Negotiation between organized workers and employers on wages, hours, etc.

col·lec·tiv·ism (kə·lek′tiv·iz′əm) *n.* A system in which the people as a whole, or the state, own and control the means of production and distribution. **—col·lec′tiv·ist** *adj. & n.* **—col·lec′tiv·is′tic** *adj.*

col·lec·tiv·ize (kə·lek′tiv·īz) *v.t.* **·ized, ·iz·ing** To organize (an agricultural settlement, industry, etc.) on a collectivist basis. **—col·lec′tiv·i·za′tion** *n.*

col·lec·tor (kə·lek′tər) *n.* One who or that which collects.

col·leen (kol′ēn, kə·lēn′) *n.* A girl. [< Irish *cailīn*]

col·lege (kol′ij) *n.* 1. A school of higher learning that grants a bachelor's degree. 2. Any of the undergraduate divisions of a university. 3. A school for instruction in a special field or a profession. 4. A building or buildings used by a college or university. 5. An association having certain rights and duties: the electoral *college.* [< L *collegium* body of associates] **—col·le·giate** (kə·lē′jit, -jē·it) *adj.*

College of Cardinals In the Roman Catholic Church, the body of cardinals who elect and advise the Pope.

col·le·gi·al·i·ty (kə·lē′jē·al′ə·tē) *n.* In the Roman Catholic Church, the principle that the bishops, acting as a body, share power with the pope in governing the church.

col·le·gian (kə·lē′jən, -jē·ən) *n.* A college student.

col·lide (kə·līd′) *v.i.* **·lid·ed, ·lid·ing** 1. To come together with violent impact; crash. 2. To come into conflict; clash. [< COM- + L *laedere* to strike]

col·lie (kol′ē) *n.* A large sheep dog with a long, narrow head and full, long-haired coat. [Prob. < Scot. Gaelic *cuilean* puppy]

col·lier (kol′yər) *n.* 1. *Chiefly Brit.* A coal miner. 2. A vessel for carrying coal. [OE *col* coal + -IER]

col·lier·y (kol′yər·ē) *n. pl.* **·lier·ies** A coal mine.

col·li·mate (kol′ə·māt) *v.t.* **·mat·ed, ·mat·ing** 1. To bring into line or make parallel, as refracted rays of light. 2. To adjust the line of sight of (a telescope, etc.). [< COM- + L *lineare* to align] **—col′li·ma′tion** *n.*

col·li·ma·tor (kol′ə·mā′tər) *n.* *Optics.* A device used to obtain parallel rays of light.

col·li·sion (kə·lizh′ən) *n.* 1. The act of colliding; a crash. 2. A clash; conflict.

col·lo·cate (kol′ō·kāt) *v.t.* **·cat·ed, ·cat·ing** To place together or in relation; arrange. [< COM- + L *locare* to place] **—col′lo·ca′tion** *n.*

col·lo·di·on (kə·lō′dē·ən) *n.* A flammable solution used as a coating for wounds and formerly for photographic plates. Also **col·lo′di·um.** [< Gk. *kolla* glue]

col·loid (kol′oid) *n.* 1. A state of matter in which finely divided particles of one substance remain suspended in another. 2. A gluelike or jellylike substance in a similar state. **—*adj.*** Of or pertaining to a colloid or the colloid state: also **col·loi·dal** (kə·loid′l). [< Gk. *kolla* glue + -OID] **—col·loi·dal·i·ty** (kol′oi·dal′ə·tē) *n.*

col·lo·qui·al (kə·lō′kwē·əl) *adj.* Of speech or writing, informal; conversational. **—col·lo′·qui·al·ly** *adv.* **—col·lo′qui·al·ness** *n.*

col·lo·qui·al·ism (kə·lō′kwē·əl·iz′əm) *n.* 1. A colloquial expression or form of speech. 2. Informal, conversational style.

col·lo·qui·um (kə·lō′kwē·əm) *n. pl.* **·qui·ums** or **·qui·a** A seminar, esp. one with several lecturers.

col·lo·quy (kol′ə·kwē) *n. pl.* **·quies** A conversation or conference, esp. a formal one. [< COM- + L *loqui* to speak] **—col′lo·quist** *n.*

col·lude (kə·lōōd′) *v.i.* **·lud·ed, ·lud·ing** To conspire. [< COM- + L *ludere* to play, trick] **—col·lud′er** *n.*

col·lu·sion (kə·lōō′zhən) *n.* Secret agreement for a wrongful purpose; conspiracy. [See COLLUDE.] **—col·lu′sive** (-siv) *adj.* **—col·lu′sive·ly** *adv.* **—col·lu′sive·ness** *n.*

colo- *combining form* *Anat.* Colon. Also, before vowels, **col-.** [< Gk. *kolon* colon]

co·logne (kə·lōn′) *n.* A toilet water consisting of alcohol scented with aromatic oils: also called *eau de Cologne.* [after *Cologne,* Germany]

co·lon¹ (kō′lən) *n. pl.* **co·lons** A punctuation mark (:), used after a word introducing a quotation, list of items, etc., after the salutation in a formal letter, and in mathematical proportions. [< Gk. *kōlon* member, limb, clause]

co·lon² (kō′lən) *n. pl.* **co·lons** or **co·la** *Anat.* The portion of the large intestine between the cecum and the rectum. [< Gk. *kolon*] **—co·lon·ic** (kə·lon′ik) *adj.*

colo·nel (kûr′nəl) *n.* *Mil.* A commissioned officer ranking next above a lieutenant colonel and next below a brigadier general. [< Ital. *colonna* column of soldiers] **—colo′·nel·cy, colo′nel·ship** *n.*

co·lo·ni·al (kə·lō′nē·əl) *adj.* 1. Of, pertaining to, or living in a colony or colonies. 2. Of or referring to the thirteen original colonies of the U.S. **—*n.*** A citizen or inhabitant of a colony. **—co·lo′ni·al·ly** *adv.*

co·lo·ni·al·ism (kə·lō′nē·əl·iz′əm) *n.* The policy of a nation seeking to acquire, extend, or retain overseas dependencies.

col·o·nist (kol′ə·nist) *n.* 1. A member or inhabitant of a colony. 2. A settler or founder of a colony.

col·o·nize (kol′ə·nīz) *v.* **·nized, ·niz·ing** *v.t.* 1. To set up a colony in; settle. 2. To establish as colonists. **—*v.i.*** 3. To establish or unite in a colony or colonies. Also *Brit.* **col′o·nise.** **—col′o·ni·za′tion** *n.* **—col′o·niz′er** *n.*

col·on·nade (kol′ə·nād′) *n.* *Archit.* A series of regularly spaced columns. [< F *colonne* column] **—col′on·nad′ed** *adj.*

col·o·ny (kol′ə·nē) *n. pl.* **·nies** 1. A body of emigrants living in a land apart from, but under the control of, the parent country. 2. The region thus settled. 3. Any territory politically controlled by a distant state. 4. A group of persons from the same country, of the same occupation, etc., living in a particular area. 5. The area itself. 6. *Biol.* A group of organisms of the same species functioning in close association, as certain bacteria. 7. *Ecol.* A group of similar plants or animals living in a particular locality. **—the Colonies** The British colonies that became the original thirteen states of the United States. [< L *colonus* farmer]

col·o·phon (kol′ə·fon, -fən) *n.* An emblematic device adopted by a publisher. [< Gk. *kolophōn* summit, finishing touch]

col·or (kul′ər) *n.* 1. A visual attribute of bodies or substances that depends upon the wavelengths of light reflected from their surfaces. 2. A paint, dyestuff, or pigment. 3. Complexion; hue of the skin. 4. Ruddy complexion; also, a blush. 5. *pl.* The ensign or flag of a nation, military or naval unit, etc. 6. A color, ribbon, badge, etc., used for identification: college *colors.* 7. A pretext; disguise: under *color* of religion. 8. Liveliness or vividness, esp. in literary work. 9. In art and literature, the use of characteristic details to produce a realistic effect: local *color.* 10. *Music* Timbre. **—to show one's (true) colors** To show one's real nature, beliefs, etc. **—*v.t.*** 1. To apply or give color to, as by painting. 2. To misrepresent or change (facts), as by exaggeration. **—*v.i.*** 3. To take on or change color. 4. To blush. Also *Brit.* **col′our.** [< L *color*] **—col′or·er** *n.*

col·or·a·tion (kul′ə·rā′shən) *n.* Arrangement of colors, as in an animal or plant; coloring.

col·or·a·tu·ra (kul′ər·ə·to͝or′ə, -tyo͝or′ə) *n.* 1. In vocal music, runs, trills, or other florid decoration. 2. Music characterized by this. 3. A coloratura soprano. [< Ital., coloration] **—col′or·a·tu′ra** *adj.*

coloratura soprano A soprano voice or a singer able to sing coloratura.

color blindness The inability to perceive chromatic color or, more commonly, to distinguish one of the three primary colors. **—col·or·blind** (kul′ər·blīnd′) *adj.*

col·or·cast (kul′ər·kast′) *v.t. & v.i.* In television, to broadcast in color. **—col′or·cast′** *n.*

col·ored (kul′ərd) *adj.* 1. Having color. 2. Of a dark-skinned race. 3. Misrepresented or distorted; biased.

col·or·fast (kul′ər·fast′) *adj.* Resistant to fading or running: *colorfast* fabrics.

col·or·ful (kul′ər·fəl) *adj.* 1. Full of colors. 2. Full of variety; vivid: a *colorful* story. 3. Picturesque. **—col′or·ful·ly** *adv.* **—col′or·ful·ness** *n.*

col·or·ing (kul′ər·ing) *n.* 1. The act or manner of applying colors. 2. A substance used to impart color. 3. Appearance of anything as to color. 4. False appearance.

col·or·ist (kul′ər·ist) *n.* One who uses color skillfully, esp. in art. **—col′or·is′tic** *adj.*

col·or·less (kul′ər·lis) *adj.* 1. Without color. 2. Weak in color; pallid. 3. Lacking vividness or variety; dull.

co·los·sal (kə·los′əl) *adj.* Of immense size or extent; enormous; huge. [< COLOSSUS] **—co·los′sal·ly** *adv.*

co·los·sus (kə·los′əs) *n.* *pl.* **co·los·si** (kə·los′ī) or **co·los·sus·es** 1. A gigantic statue. 2. Something of great size or stature. [< Gk. *kolossos* gigantic statue]

-colous *combining form* Dwelling in; inhabiting. Also *-coline.* [< L *colere* to dwell, inhabit]

colt (kōlt) *n.* A young male horse. [OE] **—colt′ish** *adj.*

col·ter (kōl′tər) *n.* A blade or disk on a plow that cuts the sod: also spelled *coulter.* [< L *culter* knife]

col·u·brine (kol′yə·brīn, -brin) *adj.* 1. Of or like a snake. 2. Of or pertaining to a family of snakes that includes the garter snake, blacksnake, etc. [< L *coluber* snake]

col·um·bine (kol′əm·bīn) *n.* A herbaceous plant with variously colored flowers of five petals. **—*adj.*** Dovelike. [< L *columba* dove]

co·lum·bi·um (kə·lum′bē·əm) *n.* Former name for the element niobium. [< *Columbia,* poetic name for the U.S.]

col·umn (kol′əm) *n.* 1. *Archit.* A post or pillar, esp. consisting of base, shaft, and capital. 2. Something suggesting a column: the spinal *column.* 3. A section of printed matter on a page, usu. narrow and enclosed by a rule or blank space. 4. A feature article that appears regularly in a newspaper or periodical. 5. *Mil. & Naval* A formation in which elements of troops, vehicles, etc., are placed one behind another. [< L *columna*] **—co·lum·nar** (kə·lum′nər), **col′umned** *adj.*

col·um·nist (kol′əm·nist, -əm·ist) *n.* One who writes or conducts a special column in a newspaper or periodical.

col·za (kol′zə) *n.* The summer rape whose seeds produce rape oil. [< Du. *kool* cabbage + *zaad* seed]

com- *prefix* With; together: *combine, compare.* Also: *co-* before *gn, h* and vowels; *col-* before *l,* as in *collide*; *con-* before *c, d, f, g, j, n, q, s, t, v,* as in *concur, confluence, connect, conspire*; *cor-* before *r,* as in *correspond.* [< L *cum*]

co·ma[1] (kō′mə) *n.* *pl.* **·mas** 1. *Pathol.* A condition of profound unconsciousness. 2. Stupor. [< Gk. *kōma* deep sleep]

co·ma[2] (kō′mə) *n.* *pl.* **·mae** (-mē) 1. *Astron.* A luminous, gaseous envelope around the nucleus of a comet. 2. *Bot.* A tuft of silky hairs, as at the end of certain seeds. [< Gk. *komē*] **—co′mal** *adj.*

Co·man·che (kō·man′chē, kə-) *n.* *pl.* **·ches** 1. A member of a tribe of Shoshonean Indians, ranging between Kansas and northern Mexico, now in Oklahoma. 2. The language of this tribe.

co·ma·tose (kō′mə·tōs, kom′ə-) *adj.* 1. Relating to or affected with coma or unconsciousness. 2. Lethargic; torpid. [< COMA[1]] **—co′ma·tose·ly** *adv.*

comb (kōm) *n.* 1. A toothed strip of hard, often flexible material, used for smoothing, dressing, or fastening the hair. 2. A thing resembling this. 3. The fleshy crest on the head of a fowl. 4. Honeycomb. **—*v.t.*** 1. To dress or smooth with or as with a comb. 2. To card, as wool or flax. 3. To search carefully. **—*v.i.*** 4. To crest and break: said of waves. [OE *camb*]

com·bat (*n.* kom′bat; *v.* kəm·bat′, kom′bat) *n.* A battle or fight; struggle. **—*v.*** **·bat·ed** or **·bat·ted, ·bat·ing** or **·bat·ting** *v.t.* 1. To fight or contend with; oppose in battle. 2. To resist. **—*v.i.*** 3. To do battle; struggle: with *with* or *against.* [< COM- + L *batuere* to fight, beat] **—com·bat′a·ble** (kəm·bat′ə·bəl) *adj.* **—com·bat·ant** (kəm·bat′nt, kom′bə·tənt) *n. & adj.* **—com·bat′er** *n.*

combat fatigue *Psychiatry* A psychoneurotic disorder characterized by anxiety, depression, etc., associated with the stresses of warfare: formerly called *shell shock*: also called *battle fatigue.*

com·bat·ive (kəm·bat′iv) *adj.* Apt or eager to fight. **—com·bat′ive·ly** *adv.* **—com·bat′ive·ness** *n.*

comb·er (kō′mər) *n.* 1. One who or that which combs. 2. A long, crested wave.

com·bi·na·tion (kom′bə·nā′shən) *n.* 1. The act of joining together or the state of being joined; union. 2. That which is formed by combining. 3. An alliance, as of persons.

4. The series of numbers or letters which when dialed on the face of a lock (**combination lock**) will open the lock. —**com′bi·na′tion·al, com′bi·na′tive** *adj.*

com·bi·na·to·ri·al (kəm·bīn′ə·tôr′ē·əl) *adj.* Of or relating to the possible arrangements of elements in a finite set.

com·bine (*v.* kəm·bīn′; *n.* kom′bīn) *v.* **·bined, ·bin·ing** *v.t.* 1. To bring together into close union; blend; merge; unite. —*v.i.* 2. To become one, or parts of a whole. 3. To associate for a purpose. —*n.* 1. A combination. 2. *Informal* A group of persons united in pursuit of selfish commercial or political ends. 3. A machine that reaps, threshes, and cleans grain while harvesting it. [< COM- + L *bini* two by two] —**com·bin′a·ble** *adj.* —**com·bin′er** *n.*

combining form The stem of a word, usu. of Greek or Latin origin, as *tele-* and *-phone* in *telephone*, or an English word unchanged, as *over* in *overeat*, used in combination with other forms to create compounds.

com·bo (kom′bō′) *n. Informal* 1. Combination. 2. A small jazz or dance band.

com·bus·ti·ble (kəm·bus′tə·bəl) *adj.* Capable of burning easily. —*n.* Any substance that will burn easily, as paper or wood. —**com·bus′ti·bil′i·ty, com·bus′ti·ble·ness** *n.* —**com·bus′ti·bly** *adv.*

com·bus·tion (kəm·bus′chən) *n.* 1. The action or operation of burning. 2. *Chem.* Oxidation. [< L *comburere* to burn up] —**com·bus′tive** *adj.*

come (kum) *v.i.* **came, come, com·ing** 1. To move to or toward the speaker; approach. 2. To arrive as the result of motion or progress. 3. To advance or move into view. 4. To arrive in due course or in orderly progression: when your turn *comes*. 5. To occur in time. 6. To reach or extend. 7. To arrive at some state or condition: to *come* to harm. 8. To happen; occur. 9. To emanate or proceed; be derived. 10. To become: The wheel *came* loose. 11. To turn out or prove to be: His prediction *came* true. 12. To be offered or produced: The car *comes* in many colors. 13. To act as the speaker wishes: used in the imperative and expressing impatience, anger, protest, etc. —**to come about** 1. To take place; happen. 2. *Naut.* To turn to the opposite tack. —**to come across** 1. To meet with or find by chance. 2. *Slang* To give or do what is requested. —**to come around** (or **round**) 1. To recover or revive. 2. To change or turn, as in direction or opinion. 3. *Informal* To pay a visit. —**to come back** 1. To return. 2. *Informal* To make a comeback. 3. *Slang* To reply sharply. —**to come by** 1. To visit. 2. To acquire; get. —**to come into** 1. To inherit. 2. To enter into; join. —**to come of** 1. To be descended from. 2. To result from. —**to come off** 1. To become detached. 2. To happen; occur. —**to come on** 1. To meet by chance. 2. To make progress; develop. 3. To enter, as on stage. 4. *Informal* To project a certain style: he *comes on* tough. —**to come out** 1. To be made public; be published. 2. To make one's debut. 3. To declare oneself. 4. To result; end. —**to come through** 1. To be successful (in). 2. To survive. 3. To wear through. 4. *Informal* To give or do what is required. —**to come to** 1. To recover; revive. 2. To amount to. 3. To result in. —**to come up to** 1. To equal; rival. 2. To reach. —**to come up with** *Informal* To propose or produce: *to come up with* an idea. [OE *cuman*]

come·back (kum′bak′) *n.* 1. *Informal* A return, as to health or lost position. 2. *Slang* A smart retort.

co·me·di·an (kə·mē′dē·ən) *n.* 1. A performer who specializes in comedy. 2. A person who writes comedy. [< F *comédien*] —**co·me′di·enne′** (-en′) *n.fem.*

come·down (kum′doun′) *n.* A humiliating or disappointing setback.

com·e·dy (kom′ə·dē) *n. pl.* **·dies** 1. A light, humorous drama or narrative having a happy ending. 2. The branch of drama in which themes are humorously treated. [< Gk. *kōmos* revel + *aeidein* to sing] —**co·me·dic** (kə·mē′dik, -med′ik) *adj.* —**co·me′di·cal·ly** *adv.*

comedy of manners A satiric comedy set in the fashionable world.

come·ly (kum′lē) *adj.* **·li·er, ·li·est** 1. Pleasing in person. 2. Suitable; becoming. [OE *cȳmlic* < *cȳme* fine] —**come′li·ness** *n.*

come-on (kum′on′, -ôn′) *n. Slang* Someone or something that lures.

com·er (kum′ər) *n.* 1. One who comes or arrives. 2. *Informal* One who or that which shows great promise.

co·mes·ti·ble (kə·mes′tə·bəl) *n.* *Usu. pl.* Food. [< L *comedere* to eat up]

com·et (kom′it) *n. Astron.* A celestial body orbiting the sun and consisting of a nucleus of condensed material, a coma, and a tail that points away from the sun. [< Gk. *komētēs* long-haired] —**com′et·ar′y, co·met·ic** (kə·met′ik) *adj.*

come·up·pance (kum′up′əns) *n. Informal* The punishment one deserves. Also **come′·up′ance.**

com·fit (kum′fit, kom′-) *n.* A sweetmeat; confection. [< L *confectus*. See CONFECTION]

com·fort (kum′fərt) *n.* 1. A state of mental or physical ease. 2. Relief from sorrow, pain, etc. 3. One who or that which brings ease. —*v.t.* 1. To cheer in time of trouble; console. 2. *Law* To aid; help. [< COM- + L *fortis* strong] —**com′fort·ing** *adj.* —**com′fort·ing·ly** *adv.*

com·fort·a·ble (kum′fər·tə·bəl, kumf′tə·bəl) *adj.* 1. Imparting comfort and satisfaction. 2. Free from distress; at ease. 3. *Informal* Moderate; adequate: a *comfortable* income. —**com′fort·a·ble·ness** *n.* —**com′fort·a·bly** *adv.*

com·fort·er (kum′fər·tər) *n.* 1. One who comforts. 2. A thick bedcover.

comfort station A public toilet.

com·ic (kom′ik) *adj.* 1. Of or pertaining to comedy. 2. Humorous; funny. —*n.* 1. A comic actor or entertainer. 2. The humorous element in art, life, etc. 3. *pl. Informal* Comic strips or a book of comic strips. [< Gk. *kōmos* revelry]

com·i·cal (kom′i·kəl) *adj.* Humorous; funny. —**com·i·cal·i·ty** (kom′ə·kal′ə·tē), **com′i·cal·ness** *n.* —**com′i·cal·ly** *adv.*

comic strip A strip of cartoons printed in a newspaper, etc.

com·ing (kum′ing) *adj.* 1. Approaching, esp. in time. 2. On the way to fame or distinction. —*n.* An approach; arrival; advent.

com·ing-out (kum′ing·out′) *n. Informal* Debut into society.

com·i·ty (kom′ə·tē) *n. pl.* **·ties** Courtesy; civility. [< L *comitas* courtesy]

comity of nations The courteous recognition that one nation accords another.

com·ma (com′ə) *n.* A punctuation mark (,) indicating a slight separation in ideas or in grammatical construction within a sentence. [< Gk. *komma* short phrase]

com·mand (kə·mand′) *v.t.* 1. To order or require with authority. 2. To control or direct. 3. To overlook, as from a height. 4. To exact: to *command* respect. —*v.i.* 5. To be in authority; rule. 6. To overlook something from above. —*n.* 1. The act of commanding. 2. The authority or power to command. 3. That which is commanded; an order. 4. Ability to control; mastery. 5. *Mil. & Naval* The unit or units under the command of one person. [< COM- + L *mandare* to order]

com·man·dant (kom′ən·dant′, -dänt′) *n.* A commanding officer, as of a military school.

com·man·deer (kom′ən·dir′) *v.t.* 1. To force into military service. 2. To seize for public use, esp. under military necessity.

com·mand·er (kə·man′dər) *n.* 1. One who commands or is in command. 2. *Naval* A commissioned officer ranking next above a lieutenant commander and next below a captain. —**com·mand′er·ship** *n.*

commander in chief *pl.* **commanders in chief** 1. *Often cap.* The supreme commander of the armed forces of a nation. 2. The commander of a major force.

com·mand·ing (kə·man′ding) *adj.* 1. Exercising command. 2. Impressive; imperious. 3. Dominating, as from a height. —**com·mand′ing·ly** *adv.*

com·mand·ment (kə·mand′mənt) *n.* 1. An edict; order; law. 2. *Sometimes cap.* One of the Ten Commandments.

com·man·do (kə·man′dō) *n. pl.* **·dos** or **·does** 1. A fighting force trained for raids into enemy territory. 2. A member of such a unit. [< Afrikaans < Pg., a group commanded]

command post The field headquarters of a military unit.

com·mem·o·rate (kə·mem′ə·rāt) *v.t.* **·rat·ed, ·rat·ing** To celebrate the memory of. Also **com·mem′o·rize.** [< COM- + L *memorare* to remember] —**com·mem′o·ra′tion** *n.* —**com·mem′o·ra′tion·al** *adj.* —**com·mem′o·ra′tor** *n.*

com·mem·o·ra·tive (kə·mem′ə·rā′tiv, -rə·tiv) *adj.* Serving to commemorate. Also **com·mem·o·ra·to·ry** (kə·mem′ər·ə·tôr′ē). —*n.* Anything that commemorates.

com·mence (kə·mens′) *v.t. & v.i.* **·menced, ·menc·ing** To start; begin; originate. [< COM- + L *initiare* to begin] —**com·menc′er** *n.*

com·mence·ment (kə·mens′mənt) *n.* 1. A beginning; origin. 2. A graduation ceremony at a college or school.

com·mend (kə·mend′) *v.t.* 1. To express approval of; praise. 2. To recommend. 3. To present the regards of. 4. To commit with confidence. [< COM- + L *mandare* to order] —**com·mend′a·ble** *adj.* —**com·mend′a·ble·ness** *n.* —**com·mend′a·bly** *adv.* —**com·men·da·tion** (kom′ən·dā′shən) *n.* —**com·mend′a·to′ry** *adj.*

com·men·sal (kə·men′səl) *adj.* 1. Eating together. 2. *Zool.* Associated in a close but nonparasitic relationship. [< COM- + L *mensa* table]

com·men·su·ra·ble (kə·men′shər·ə·bəl, -sər·ə-) *adj.* 1. Capable of being measured by a common standard or unit. 2. Fitting as to proportion. [< COM- + L *mensurabilis* measurable] —**com·men′su·ra·bil′i·ty** *n.* —**com·men′su·ra·bly** *adv.*

com·men·su·rate (kə·men′shə·rit, -sə·rit) *adj.* 1. Having the same measure or extent. 2. In proper proportion; adequate. 3. Commensurable. [< COM- + L *mensurare* to measure] —**com·men′su·rate·ly** *adv.* —**com·men′su·rate·ness** *n.* —**com·men′su·ra′tion** *n.*

com·ment (kom′ent) *n.* 1. A note of explanation, illustration, or criticism. 2. A remark made in observation or criticism. 3. Talk; conversation. —*v.i.* To make a comment or comments. [< L *comminisci* to contrive] —**com′ment·er** *n.*

com·men·tar·y (kom′ən·ter′ē) *n. pl.* **·tar·ies** 1. A series of comments. 2. *Usu. pl.* A historical narrative or memoir. [< L *comminisci* to contrive] —**com′men·tar′i·al** (-târ′ē·əl) *adj.*

com·men·ta·tor (kom′ən·tā′tər) *n.* 1. One who writes commentaries. 2. One who discusses or analyzes news events.

com·merce (kom′ərs) *n.* 1. The exchange of materials, products, etc., esp. on a large scale between states or nations; extended trade. 2. Social intercourse. [< COM- + L *merx, mercis* wares]

com·mer·cial (kə·mûr′shəl) *adj.* 1. Of, relating to, or engaged in commerce; mercantile. 2. Having financial gain as an object. —*n.* In radio and television, an advertisement. —**com·mer·ci·al·i·ty** (kə·mûr′shē·al′ə·tē) *n.* —**com·mer′cial·ly** *adv.*

com·mer·cial·ism (kə·mûr′shəl·iz′əm) *n.* The spirit or methods of commerce. —**com·mer′cial·ist** *n.* —**com·mer′cial·is′tic** *adj.*

com·mer·cial·ize (kə·mûr′shəl·īz) *v.t.* **·ized, ·iz·ing** To put on a commercial basis. —**com·mer′cial·i·za′tion** *n.*

commercial paper Any of various short-term negotiable papers.

com·min·gle (kə·ming′gəl) *v.t. & v.i.* **·gled, ·gling** To mix; mingle. [< COM- + MINGLE]

com·mi·nute (kom′ə·no͞ot, -nyo͞ot) *v.t.* **·nut·ed, ·nut·ing** To pulverize. [< COM- + L *minuere* to lessen] —**com′mi·nu′tion** *n.*

com·mis·er·ate (kə·miz′ə·rāt) *v.* **·at·ed, ·at·ing** *v.t.* 1. To feel or express sympathy for; pity. —*v.i.* 2. To express sympathy: with *with.* [< COM- + L *miserari* to feel pity] —**com·mis′er·a′tion** *n.* —**com·mis′er·a′tive** *adj.* —**com·mis′er·a′tive·ly** *adv.* —**com·mis′er·a′tor** *n.*

com·mis·sar (kom′ə·sär, kom′ə·sär′) *n.* Formerly, a Soviet official in charge of a major department of the government. [< Russ. *komissar*]

com·mis·sar·i·at (kom′ə·sâr′ē·ət) *n.* The department of an army charged with providing food and daily necessities.

com·mis·sar·y (kom′ə·ser′ē) *n. pl.* **·sar·ies** 1. A store selling food, equipment, etc., as at a camp or military post. 2. An authority delegated for a special duty. [< L *commissus* pp. of *committere.* See COMMIT.] —**com′mis·sar′i·al** (-sâr′ē·əl) *adj.* —**com′mis·sar′y·ship** *n.*

com·mis·sion (kə·mish′ən) *n.* 1. The act of committing. 2. A matter committed or entrusted; a charge. 3. Authorization or command to act as specified. 4. A written warrant conferring a particular authority. 5. *Mil.* a An official document conferring rank and authority. b The rank or authority conferred. 6. A body of persons authorized to perform certain duties. 7. The fee or percentage given an agent or salesman. —**in commission** In active service or use. —**out of commission** Not in active service or use. —*v.t.* 1. To give rank or authority to. 2. *Naval* To put into active service, as a ship. 3. To appoint; delegate. [See COMMIT.]

com·mis·sion·er (kə·mish′ən·ər) *n.* 1. One who holds a commission. 2. A member of a commission. 3. A public official in charge of a department. 4. The administrator in charge of a professional sport.

com·mit (kə·mit′) *v.t.* **·mit·ted, ·mit·ting** 1. To do; perpetrate. 2. To place in trust or charge; consign. 3. To consign for preservation. 4. To devote (oneself) unreservedly. [< L *committere* to join, entrust]

com·mit·ment (kə·mit′mənt) *n.* 1. The act of committing, or the state of being committed. 2. An engagement or pledge to do something. 3. A consignment to a prison, mental institution, etc. Also **com·mit′tal.**

com·mit·tee (kə·mit′ē) *n.* A group of people chosen to investigate, report, or act on a matter. —**in committee** Under consideration by a committee. [< AF *commettre* to entrust] —**com·mit′tee·man** (-mən) *n.* —**com·mit′·tee·wom′an** (-wŏŏm′ən) *n.fem.*

com·mode (kə·mōd′) *n.* 1. A low chest of drawers. 2. A covered washstand. 3. A toilet. [< L *commodus* convenient]

com·mo·di·ous (kə·mō′dē·əs) *adj.* Roomy; spacious. [See COMMODE.] —**com·mo′di·ous·ly** *adv.* —**com·mo′di·ous·ness** *n.*

com·mod·i·ty (kə·mod′ə·tē) *n. pl.* **·ties** 1. Something bought and sold. 2. Anything of use or profit. [< L *commoditas, -tatis* convenience]

com·mo·dore (kom′ə·dôr) *n.* 1. Formerly, in the U.S. Navy, an officer next below a rear admiral. 2. A title given to the presiding officer of a yacht club. [? < Du. *kommandeur*]

com·mon (kom′ən) *adj.* 1. Frequent or usual; unexceptional. 2. Widespread; general. 3. Shared equally. 4. Pertaining to the entire community; public. 5. Habitual; notorious. 6. Of low rank; ordinary. 7. Vulgar; low. 8. *Gram.* a Of gender, applied to either sex, as *parent.* b Of a noun, applicable to any individual of a class, as *boat, dog.* 9. *Math.* Referring to a number or quantity belonging equally to two or more quantities: a *common* denominator. —*n.* Public land open to use by all in a community. —**in common** Equally with another or others; jointly. [< L *communis* common] —**com′mon·ly** *adv.* —**com′mon·ness** *n.*

com·mon·al·ty (kom′ən·əl·tē) *n. pl.* **·ties** 1. The common people. 2. The entire mass; whole.

common carrier A company that, for a fee, transports goods or persons.

com·mon·er (kom′ən·ər) *n.* One of the common people.

common fraction *Math.* A fraction expressed by a denominator and a numerator.

common law A system of jurisprudence based on custom and precedent.

com·mon-law marriage (kom′ən·lô′) A marriage in which both members consent to live as husband and wife without undergoing a religious or civil ceremony.

common market 1. Any of several associations of nations having mutually beneficial tariff arrangements. 2. *cap.* A common market, established in 1958, which now includes Belgium, France, West Germany, Italy, Luxembourg, the Netherlands, Great Britain, Denmark, Ireland, and Greece. Also called the *European Economic Community.*

common people Ordinary people, as distinguished from the nobility, the rich, etc.

com·mon·place (kom′ən·plās′) *adj.* Not remarkable; ordinary. —*n.* 1. A trite remark. 2. Something common. —**com′mon·place′ness** *n.*

com·mons (kom′ənz) *n.pl.* *Chiefly Brit.* 1. The common people. 2. (*construed as sing.*) The dining hall of a college. 3. *cap.* (*construed as sing. or pl.*) The House of Commons.

common sense Practical understanding; sound judgment. —**com·mon-sense** (kom′ən·sens′) *adj.*

common stock Capital stock other than preferred stock.

common time *Music* A meter in which there are four quarter notes in a measure: also **common measure.**

com·mon·weal (kom′ən·wēl′) *n.* The general welfare. Also **common weal.**

com·mon·wealth (kom′ən·welth′) *n.* 1. The whole people of a state or nation. 2. A state in which sovereignty is vested in the people.

com·mo·tion (kə·mō′shən) *n.* A violent agitation; excitement. [< COM- + L *movere* to move]

com·mu·nal (kom′yə·nəl, kə·myōō′nəl) *adj.* Of, pertaining to, or belonging to a community or commune. —**com′mu·nal·ly** *adv.*

com·mu·nal·ism (kom′yə·nəl·iz′əm, kə·myōō′nəl-) *n.* A system of government based on a federation of virtually self-governing communes. —**com′mu·nal·ist** *n.* —**com′·mu·nal·is′tic** *adj.*

com·mu·nal·ize (kom′yə·nəl·īz′, kə·myōō′·nəl·īz) *v.t.* **·ized, ·iz·ing** To render communal. —**com′mu·nal·i·za′tion** *n.*

com·mune[1] (kə·myōōn′) *v.i.* **·muned, ·mun·ing** 1. To converse intimately. 2. To partake of the Eucharist. [< OF *comuner* to share]

com·mune[2] (kom′yōōn) *n.* 1. The smallest political division of France, Belgium, Italy, etc. 2. Any small, self-governing political unit. 3. Any community. 4. A group of persons, not forming a single family, sharing a home or land in common. [< L *communa* community]

com·mu·ni·ca·ble (kə·myōō′ni·kə·bəl) *adj.* Capable of being communicated, as a disease. —**com·mu′ni·ca·bil′i·ty, com·mu′ni·ca·ble·ness** *n.* —**com·mu′ni·ca·bly** *adv.*

com·mu·ni·cant (kə·myōō′nə·kənt) *n.* 1. One who communicates. 2. One who partakes or has a right to partake of the Eucharist.

com·mu·ni·cate (kə·myōō′nə·kāt) *v.* **·cat·ed, ·cat·ing** *v.t.* 1. To cause another or others to share in; impart. 2. To transmit, as a disease. —*v.i.* 3. To transmit or exchange thought or knowledge. 4. To be connected. 5. To partake of the Eucharist. [< L *communicare* to share < *communis* common] **—com·mu′·ni·ca′tor** *n.*

com·mu·ni·ca·tion (kə·myōō′nə·kā′shən) *n.* 1. The act of communicating. 2. A message. 3. A means of communicating. 4. *pl.* The science of communicating ideas, information, etc. **—com·mu·ni·ca·tive** (kə·myōō′nə·kā′·tiv, -kə·tiv) *adj.* **—com·mu′ni·ca′tive·ly** *adv.* **—com·mu′ni·ca′tive·ness** *n.*

communications satellite An artificial earth satellite used to relay radio or television signals.

com·mun·ion (kə·myōōn′yən) *n.* 1. Mutual participation or sharing. 2. Religious fellowship; also, a religious denomination. 3. *Usu. cap.* The Eucharist. [< L *communis* common]

com·mu·ni·qué (kə·myōō′nə·kā′) *n.* An official announcement or bulletin. [< F]

com·mu·nism (kom′yə·niz′əm) *n.* 1. A social system characterized by the communal sharing of goods and services. 2. *Often cap.* Marxist socialism, advocating a classless society and public ownership of almost all productive property; also, the system in force in any state based on this theory. [< F *commun* common, shared + -ISM]

com·mu·nist (kom′yə·nist) *n.* 1. *Often cap.* A member of a Communist party. 2. One who advocates communism. **—com′mu·nist, com′mu·nis′tic** *adj.* **—com′mu·nis′ti·cal·ly** *adv.*

Communist Party 1. The dominant party in the Soviet Union. 2. Any political party advocating communism.

com·mu·ni·ty (kə·myōō′nə·tē) *n. pl.* **·ties** 1. A group of people living together or in one locality and having common customs, interests, etc. 2. The district in which they live. 3. People having specified interests in common: the scientific *community*; the German-American *community*. 4. The public; society in general. 5. Common ownership or participation. 6. Identity or likeness. 7. *Ecol.* A group of plants or animals in an area living under similar conditions. [< L *communitas, -tatis* fellowship]

community chest A fund drawn upon by various charitable organizations.

community college A nonresidential two-year college supported by public funds.

com·mu·nize (kom′yə·nīz) *v.t.* **·nized, ·niz·ing** 1. To make (private property) state-owned. 2. To cause to become communistic. **—com′mu·ni·za′tion** *n.*

com·mu·tate (kom′yə·tāt) *v.t.* **·tat·ed, ·tat·ing** *Electr.* To alter or reverse the direction of (a current). **—com′mu·ta′tor** *n.*

com·mu·ta·tion (kom′yə·tā′shən) *n.* 1. A substitution, as of one kind of payment for another. 2. A payment or service substituted. 3. The act of commuting to work. 4. *Electr.* The reversing of the direction of current. 5. *Law* A reduction of a penalty or sentence. [< COM- + L *mutare* change]

commutation ticket *U.S.* A railroad or other ticket issued at a reduced rate for those who commute to work.

com·mute (kə·myōōt′) *v.* **·mut·ed, ·mut·ing** *v.t.* 1. To interchange. 2. To exchange for something less severe. 3. To pay in gross at a reduced rate. *—v.i.* 4. To serve as a substitute. 5. To make regular trips of some distance to and from work. *—n.* A trip, usu. long in time or distance, between home and work: an hour's *commute.* **—com·mut′a·ble** *adj.* **—com·mut′a·ble·ness, com·mut′a·bil′i·ty** *n.* **—com·mut′er** *n.*

com·pact[1] (*adj.* kəm·pakt′, kom′pakt; *v.* kəm·pakt′; *n.* kom′pakt) *adj.* 1. Closely united; pressed together. 2. Brief; terse. 3. Packed into a small space. *—v.t.* To pack closely; compress. *—n.* 1. A small, hinged box with a mirror, for face powder. 2. A small car. [< COM- + L *pangere* to fasten] **—com·pact′ly** *adv.* **—com·pact′ness** *n.*

com·pact[2] (kom′pakt) *n.* A covenant; agreement. [< COM- + L *pacisci* to agree]

com·pan·ion[1] (kəm·pan′yən) *n.* 1. A comrade; associate. 2. A person employed to live with or assist another. 3. One of a pair; a mate. *—v.t.* To be a companion to. [< LL *companis, -onis* < COM- + L *panis* bread] **—com·pan′ion·ship** *n.*

com·pan·ion[2] (kəm·pan′yən) *n.* A companionway; also, the covering over it. [< Du. *kampanje* quarter-deck]

com·pan·ion·a·ble (kəm·pan′yən·ə·bəl) *adj.* Friendly; sociable. **—com·pan′ion·a·bil′i·ty** *n.* **—com·pan′ion·a·bly** *adv.*

com·pan·ion·ate (kəm·pan′yən·it) *adj.* 1. Of or characteristic of companions. 2. Agreed upon; shared.

com·pan·ion·way (kəm·pan′yən·wā′) *n.* A staircase leading below from a ship's deck.

com·pa·ny (kum′pə·nē) *n. pl.* **·nies** 1. A group of people. 2. A gathering of persons for social purposes. 3. A guest or guests; visitors. 4. Companionship. 5. A business. 6. A troupe. 7. *Mil.* A body of soldiers larger than a platoon and smaller than a battalion. 8. *Naut.* The entire crew of a ship, including the officers. **—to keep company (with)** 1. To associate (with). 2. To court, as lovers. **—to part company (with)** To end friendship or association (with). *—v.t. & v.i.* **·nied, ·ny·ing** *Archaic* To keep or go in company (with). [See COMPANION[1].]

com·pa·ra·ble (kom′pər·ə·bəl) *adj.* 1. Capable of comparison. 2. Worthy of comparison. **—com′pa·ra·ble·ness, com′pa·ra·bil′i·ty** *n.* **—com′pa·ra·bly** *adv.*

com·par·a·tive (kəm·par′ə·tiv) *adj.* 1. Pertaining to, resulting from, or making use of comparison. 2. Not absolute; relative. 3. *Gram.* Expressing a degree of an adjective or adverb higher than the positive and lower than the superlative. *—n. Gram.* The comparative degree, or a word or form by which it is expressed: "Better" is the *comparative of* "good." **—com·par′a·tive·ly** *adv.*

com·pare (kəm·pâr′) *v.* **·pared, ·par·ing** *v.t.* 1. To represent as similar or equal: with *to.* 2. To examine for similarity or dissimilarity: with *with.* 3. *Gram.* To form the degrees of comparison of (an adjective or adverb). *—v.i.* 4. To be worthy of comparison: with *with.* *—n.* Comparison: usually in the phrase **beyond compare.** [< COM- + L *par* equal]

com·par·i·son (kəm·par′ə·sən) *n.* 1. A comparing or being compared. 2. Similarity. 3. *Gram.* That inflection of adjectives or adverbs that indicates the three differences of degree, as *short, shorter, shortest.*

com·part·ment (kəm·pärt′mənt) *n.* 1. A part or subdivision of an enclosed space. 2. Any separate section. [< COM- + L *partiri* to share]

com·pass (kum′pəs, kom′-) *n.* 1. An instrument for determining direction, having a magnetic needle that points toward the magnetic north. 2. Area or range; scope. 3. An enclosing boundary; circumference. 4. *Sometimes pl.* An instrument having two usu. pointed legs hinged at one end, used for taking measurements, describing circles, etc.: also **pair of compasses.** —*v.t.* 1. To go round. 2. To surround; encompass. 3. To comprehend. 4. To attain or accomplish. 5. To plot; devise. [< OF *compas* measure < COM- + L *passus* pace] —**com′pass·a·ble** *adj.*

com·pas·sion (kəm·pash′ən) *n.* Pity, with the desire to help. [< COM- + L *pati* to feel, suffer] —**com·pas′sion·ate** (-it) *adj.* —**com·pas′sion·ate·ly** *adv.*

com·pat·i·ble (kəm·pat′ə·bəl) *adj.* Capable of existing together in harmony: usu. with *with.* [< COM- + L *pati* to feel, suffer] —**com·pat′i·bil′i·ty, com·pat′i·ble·ness** *n.* —**com·pat′i·bly** *adv.*

com·pa·tri·ot (kəm·pā′trē·ət, -pat′rē·ət) *n.* A fellow countryman. —*adj.* Of the same country. [< COM- + L *patriota* countryman]

com·peer (kəm·pir′, kom′pir) *n.* 1. One of equal rank; a peer. 2. A comrade. [< COM- + L *par* equal]

com·pel (kəm·pel′) *v.t.* **·pelled, ·pel·ling** 1. To force; constrain. 2. To obtain by force; exact. [< COM- + L *pellere* to drive] —**com·pel′la·ble** *adj.* —**com·pel′la·bly** *adv.* —**com·pel′ler** *n.*

com·pen·di·ous (kəm·pen′dē·əs) *adj.* Succinct; concise. —**com·pen′di·ous·ly** *adv.* —**com·pen′di·ous·ness** *n.*

com·pen·di·um (kəm·pen′dē·əm) *n. pl.* **·di·ums** or **·di·a** A summary; abridgment. [< L, saving, shortcut]

com·pen·sate (kom′pən·sāt) *v.* **·sat·ed, ·sat·ing** *v.t.* 1. To make amends to or for; requite; reimburse. 2. To make up for; offset. —*v.i.* 3. To make amends: often with *for.* [< COM- + L *pensare,* freq. of *pendere* to weigh] —**com·pen·sa·ble** (kəm·pen′sə·bəl) *adj.* —**com′pen·sa′tion** *n.* —**com·pen·sa·tive** (kom′pən·sā′tiv, kəm·pen′sə·tiv) *adj.* —**com′pen·sa′tor** *n.* —**com·pen·sa·to·ry** (kəm·pen′sə·tôr′ē) *adj.*

com·pete (kəm·pēt′) *v.i.* **·pet·ed, ·pet·ing** To contend with another or others; engage in a contest. [< COM- + L *petere* to seek] —**com·pet·i·tor** (kəm·pet′ə·tər) *n.*

com·pe·tence (kom′pə·təns) *n.* 1. The state of being competent; ability. 2. Sufficient means for comfort. Also **com′pe·ten·cy.**

com·pe·tent (kom′pə·tənt) *adj.* 1. Able; capable. 2. Sufficient; adequate. [< L *competere* to be proper] —**com′pe·tent·ly** *adv.* —**com′pe·tent·ness** *n.*

com·pe·ti·tion (kom′pə·tish′ən) *n.* 1. A striving against another or others for some object; rivalry. 2. A contest.

com·pet·i·tive (kəm·pet′ə·tiv) *adj.* Of, pertaining to, or characterized by competition. Also **com·pet′i·to′ry.** —**com·pet′i·tive·ly** *adv.* —**com·pet′i·tive·ness** *n.*

com·pile (kəm·pīl′) *v.t.* **·piled, ·pil·ing** 1. To put together from various sources. 2. To gather (various materials) into a volume. 3. To amass; collect. [< L *compilare* to plunder] —**com·pi·la·tion** (kom′pə·lā′shən) *n.* —**com·pil′er** *n.*

com·pla·cen·cy (kəm·plā′sən·sē) *n. pl.* **·cies** Self-satisfaction; smugness. Also **com·pla′·cence.** [< COM- + L *placere* to please] —**com·pla′cent** *adj.* —**com·pla′cent·ly** *adv.*

com·plain (kəm·plān′) *v.i.* 1. To express dissatisfaction, pain, etc. 2. To make a formal accusation. [< COM- + L *plangere* to beat (the breast in grief)] —**com·plain′er** *n.*

com·plain·ant (kəm·plā′nənt) *n.* One who makes a legal complaint.

com·plaint (kəm·plānt′) *n.* 1. An expression of pain, grief, or dissatisfaction. 2. A cause for complaining; grievance. 3. An ailment. 4. *Law* A formal charge.

com·plai·sant (kəm·plā′sənt, kom′plə·zant) *adj.* Desiring to please; compliant. [See COMPLACENCY.] —**com·plai′sance** *n.* —**com·plai′sant·ly** *adv.*

com·ple·ment (*n.* kom′plə·mənt; *v.* kom′plə·ment) *n.* 1. That which fills up or completes a thing. 2. Complete number, allowance, or amount. 3. One of two parts that mutually complete each other. 4. *Geom.* An angle that when added to another angle equals 90°. 5. *Gram.* A word or phrase used after a verb to complete predication. —*v.t.* To make complete. [< COM- + L *plere* to fill] —**com′·ple·men′ta·ry** (-men′tər·ē, -trē) *adj.*

complementary color Either of a pair of spectrum colors that when combined give a white or nearly white light.

com·plete (kəm·plēt′) *adj.* 1. Having all needed or normal parts; entire; full. 2. Finished; concluded. 3. Perfect. —*v.t.* **·plet·ed, ·plet·ing** 1. To make entire or perfect. 2. To finish; end. [< COM- + L *plere* to fill] —**com·plete′ly** *adv.* —**com·plete′ness** *n.* —**com·ple′tion** *n.*

com·plex (*adj.* kəm·pleks′, kom′pleks; *n.* kom′pleks) *adj.* 1. Consisting of various connected parts; composite. 2. Complicated; involved; intricate. —*n.* 1. A whole made up of connected parts. 2. A group of structures or facilities designed for related activities: a sports *complex.* 3. *Psychoanal.* A group of interrelated feelings and ideas, which, when repressed, lead to abnormal behavior. 4. Loosely, an excessive concern; obsession. [< COM- + L *plectere* to twist] —**com·plex′ly** *adv.* —**com·plex′ness** *n.*

complex fraction *Math.* A fraction in which either the numerator or the denominator is a fraction.

com·plex·ion (kəm·plek′shən) *n.* 1. The color and appearance of the skin, esp. of the face. 2. Aspect; appearance. [< L *complexio, -onis* combination] —**com·plex′ion·al** *adj.* —**com·plex′ioned** *adj.*

com·plex·i·ty (kəm·plek′sə·tē) *n. pl.* **·ties.** 1. The state of being complex. 2. Something complex.

com·pli·a·ble (kəm·plī′ə·bəl) *adj.* Compliant. —**com·pli′a·ble·ness** *n.* —**com·pli′a·bly** *adv.*

com·pli·ance (kəm·plī′əns) *n.* 1. The act of complying or yielding. 2. A disposition to comply. Also **com·pli′an·cy.** —**in compliance with** In agreement with.

com·pli·ant (kəm·plī′ənt) *adj.* Ready or willing to comply. —**com·pli′ant·ly** *adv.*

com·pli·cate (kom′plə·kāt) *v.* **·cat·ed, ·cat·ing** *v.t.* 1. To make complex or difficult.

2. To twist; intertwine. —*v.i.* 3. To become complex or difficult. [< COM- + L *plicare* to fold] —**com′pli·ca′tion** *n.*

com·pli·cat·ed (kom′plə·kā′tid) *adj.* Difficult to separate or understand; intricate. —**com′pli·cat′ed·ly** *adv.* —**com′pli·cat′ed·ness** *n.*

com·plic·i·ty (kəm·plis′ə·tē) *n. pl.* **·ties** 1. The state of being an accomplice, as in a wrong act. 2. Complexity.

com·pli·ment (*n.* kom′plə·mənt; *v.* kom′plə·ment) *n.* 1. An expression of praise or congratulation. 2. *Usu. pl.* A formal greeting or remembrance. —*v.t.* To pay a compliment to. [< L *complementum*]

com·pli·men·ta·ry (kom′plə·men′tər·ē, -trē) *adj.* 1. Conveying, using, or like a compliment. 2. Given free. —**com′pli·men′ta·ri·ly** *adv.*

com·pline (kom′plin, -plīn) *n. Often cap. Eccl.* The last of the seven canonical hours. Also **com′plin.** [< OF *complie* < L *completa* finished. See COMPLETE.]

com·ply (kəm·plī′) *v.i.* **·plied, ·ply·ing** To conform; consent; obey: with *with.* [< L *complere* to complete] —**com·pli′er** *n.*

com·po·nent (kəm·pō′nənt) *n.* A constituent part. —*adj.* Forming a part or ingredient. [< COM- + L *ponere* to pull]

com·port (kəm·pôrt′) *v.t.* 1. To conduct or behave (oneself). —*v.i.* 2. To be compatible; agree: with *with.* [< COM- + L *portare* to carry] —**com·port′ment** *n.*

com·pose (kəm·pōz′) *v.* **·posed, ·pos·ing** *v.t.* 1. To constitute; form. 2. To make of parts; fashion. 3. To create (a literary or musical work). 4. To calm; quiet. 5. To reconcile or settle, as differences. 6. *Printing* To arrange (type) in lines; set. —*v.i.* 7. To create, as music. 8. *Printing* To set type. [< MF < COM- + *poser* to place]

com·posed (kəm·pōzd′) *adj.* Free from agitation; calm. —**com·pos′ed·ly** *adv.* —**com·pos′ed·ness** *n.*

com·pos·er (kəm·pō′zər) *n.* One who composes; esp., one who writes music.

com·pos·ite (kəm·poz′it) *adj.* 1. Made up of separate parts or elements. 2. *Bot.* Characteristic of or pertaining to a family of plants, as the dandelion, chrysanthemum, etc., whose flowers are composed of dense clusters of small flowers. —*n.* 1. That which is composed or made up of parts. 2. *Bot.* A composite plant. [< COM- + L *ponere* to put] —**com·pos′ite·ly** *adv.* —**com·pos′ite·ness** *n.*

com·po·si·tion (kom′pə·zish′ən) *n.* 1. The act of forming a whole from parts, ingredients, etc. 2. That which is so formed. 3. Constitution; make-up. 4. The act or art of creating a literary, musical, or artistic work. 5. The work so created, or its structure. 6. A short essay. 7. *Printing* The setting of type.

com·pos·i·tor (kəm·poz′ə·tər) *n.* One who sets type.

com·pos men·tis (kom′pəs men′tis) *Latin* Of sound mind.

com·post (kom′pōst) *n.* 1. A fertilizing mixture of decomposed organic matter. 2. A compound. [< OF, mixture]

com·po·sure (kəm·pō′zhər) *n.* Calmness.

com·pote (kom′pōt, *Fr.* kôn·pôt′) *n.* 1. Fruit stewed or preserved in syrup. 2. A dish for holding fruits, etc. [< F < OF *composte*]

com·pound¹ (*n.* kom′pound; *v.* kom·pound′, kəm-; *adj.* kom′pound, kom·pound′) *n.* 1. A combination of two or more elements or parts. 2. *Gram.* A word composed of two or more words, as *fly-by-night, shoestring.* 3. *Chem.* A substance resulting from the union of specific elements or radicals in fixed proportions. —*v.t.* 1. To make by combining various elements or ingredients. 2. To mix (elements). 3. To compute (interest) on both the principal and accrued interest. 4. To settle for less than the sum due, as a debt. 5. To add to; increase. —*adj.* Composed of two or more elements or parts. [< COM- + L *ponere* to put] —**com·pound′a·ble** *adj.* —**com·pound′er** *n.*

com·pound² (kom′pound) *n.* An enclosure containing buildings. [< Malay *kampong*]

compound fraction *Math.* A complex fraction.

compound interest Interest computed on the principal and its accrued interest.

compound leaf *Bot.* A leaf having several distinct blades on a common leafstalk.

compound number *Math.* A quantity having more than one unit, as 6 feet 3 inches.

com·pre·hend (kom′pri·hend′) *v.t.* 1. To understand. 2. To take in or embrace; include. —*v.i.* 3. To understand. [< COM- + L *prehendere* to grasp, seize] —**com′pre·hend′i·ble, com′pre·hen′si·ble** *adj.* —**com′pre·hen·si·bil′i·ty, com′pre·hen′si·ble·ness** *n.* —**com′pre·hen′si·bly** *adv.*

com·pre·hen·sion (kom′pri·hen′shən) *n.* 1. Understanding. 2. An including or taking in; comprehensiveness.

com·pre·hen·sive (kom′pri·hen′siv) *adj.* 1. Large in scope or content; broad. 2. Understanding; comprehending. —**com′pre·hen′sive·ly** *adv.* —**com′pre·hen′sive·ness** *n.*

com·press (*v.* kəm·pres′; *n.* kom′pres) *v.t.* To press together or into smaller space; reduce in volume; condense; compact. —*n.* 1. *Med.* A pad for applying moisture, cold, heat, or pressure to the body. 2. An apparatus for compressing bales of cotton, etc. [< COM- + L *premere* to press] —**com·pressed′** *adj.* —**com·press′i·bil′i·ty, com·press′i·ble·ness** *n.* —**com·press′i·ble** *adj.* —**com·pres′sion** (-presh′ən) *n.* —**com·press′ive** *adj.* —**com·pres′sor** *n.*

com·prise (kəm·prīz′) *v.t.* **·prised, ·pris·ing** To consist of or contain; include. [< COM- + L *premere* to press] —**com·pris′a·ble** *adj.* —**com·pri′sal** *n.*

com·pro·mise (kom′prə·mīz) *n.* 1. An adjustment or settlement by means of concessions. 2. The result of such concessions. 3. Something between, or combining the qualities of, two different things. 4. An imperiling, as of reputation. —*v.* **·mised, ·mis·ing** *v.t.* 1. To adjust by concessions. 2. To expose to risk or disrepute. —*v.i.* 3. To make a compromise. [< COM- + L *promittere* to promise] —**com′pro·mis′er** *n.*

comp·trol·ler (kən·trō′lər) See CONTROLLER (def. 2).

com·pul·sion (kəm·pul′shən) *n.* 1. The act of compelling, or the state of being compelled. 2. *Psychol.* An irresistible impulse or tendency. [< COM- + L *pellere* to drive]

com·pul·sive (kəm·pul′siv) *adj.* Compelling; compulsory. —**com·pul′sive·ly** *adv.* —**com·pul′sive·ness** *n.*

com·pul·so·ry (kəm·pul′sər·ē) *adj.* 1. Employing compulsion; coercive. 2. Required; obligatory: *compulsory* education. —**com·pul'so·ri·ly** *adv.* —**com·pul'so·ri·ness** *n.*

com·punc·tion (kəm·pungk'shən) *n.* 1. A sense of guilt or remorse. 2. A feeling of slight regret or pity. [< COM- + L *pungere* to prick, sting] —**com·punc'tious** *adj.* —**com·punc'tious·ly** *adv.*

com·pute (kəm·pyōōt') *v.t. & v.i.* **·put·ed, ·put·ing** To ascertain (an amount or number) by calculation; reckon. [< COM- + L *putare* to reckon.] —**com·put'a·bil'i·ty** *n.* —**com·put'a·ble** *adj.* —**com·pu·ta·tion** (kom'pyə·tā'shən) *n.*

com·put·er (kəm·pyōō'tər) *n.* 1. One who or that which computes. 2. An electronic machine for the high-speed performance of mathematical and logical operations, or for the processing of large masses of coded information.

com·put·er·ize (kəm·pyōōt'ər·īz') *v.t.* **·ized, ·iz·ing** 1. To control (an operation) by means of a computer. 2. To adopt the use of computers in.

com·rade (kom'rad, -rid, kum'-) *n.* 1. A companion or friend. 2. A person who shares one's occupation, interests, etc. [< MF *camarade* < L *camera* room] —**com'rade·ship** *n.*

con[1] (kon) *v.t.* **conned, con·ning** To study or memorize. [Var. of CAN[1]] —**con'ner** *n.*

con[2] (kon) *adv.* Against. —*n.* A reason, opinion, etc., to the contrary. [< L *contra* against]

con[3] (kon) *adj. Slang* Confidence: *con* man. —*v.t.* **conned, con·ning** To defraud; swindle. [< CONFIDENCE]

con[4] (kon) *n. Slang* A convict.

con- Var. of COM-.

con·cat·e·nate (kon·kat'ə·nāt) *v.t.* **·nat·ed, ·nat·ing** To connect in a series. [< COM- + L *catena* chain]

con·cat·e·na·tion (kon·kat'ə·nā'shən) *n.* 1. The act of linking. 2. A chainlike series.

con·cave (*adj.* kon·kāv', kon'kāv, kong'-; *n.* kon'kāv, kong'-; *v.* kon·kāv') *adj.* Hollow and curving inward, as the interior of a sphere or bowl. —*n.* A concave surface; hollow. —*v.t.* **·caved, ·cav·ing** To make concave. [< COM- + L *cavus* hollow] —**con·cave'ly** *adv.* —**con·cave'ness** *n.*

con·cav·i·ty (kon·kav'ə·tē) *n. pl.* **·ties** 1. The state of being concave. 2. A hollow.

con·ceal (kən·sēl') *v.t.* To keep from sight or discovery; hide. [< COM- + L *celare* to hide] —**con·ceal'a·ble** *adj.* —**con·ceal'er** *n.* —**con·ceal'ment** *n.*

con·cede (kən·sēd') *v.* **·ced·ed, ·ced·ing** *v.t.* 1. To acknowledge as correct; admit. 2. To grant; yield, as a right or privilege. —*v.i.* 3. To make a concession; yield. [< COM- + L *cedere* to yield, go away] —**con·ced'er** *n.*

con·ceit (kən·sēt') *n.* 1. Overweening self-esteem. 2. An ingenious, fanciful thought or expression. 3. In poetry, an elaborate, extended metaphor. 4. Imagination; fancy. [< CONCEIVE]

con·ceit·ed (kən·sē'tid) *adj.* Vain. —**con·ceit'ed·ly** *adv.* —**con·ceit'ed·ness** *n.*

con·ceive (kən·sēv') *v.* **·ceived, ·ceiv·ing** *v.t.* 1. To become pregnant with. 2. To form a concept of; imagine. 3. To understand. 4. To express in a particular way. —*v.i.* 5. To form a mental image; think: with *of.* 6. To become pregnant. [< COM- + L *capere* to grasp, take] —**con·ceiv'a·ble** *adj.* —**con·ceiv'a·bil'i·ty, con·ceiv'a·ble·ness** *n.* —**con·ceiv'a·bly** *adv.* —**con·ceiv'er** *n.*

con·cen·ter (kon·sen'tər) *v.t. & v.i.* To direct or come to a common point or center; focus. Also *Brit.* **con·cen'tre.** [< COM- + L *centrum* center]

con·cen·trate (kon'sən·trāt) *v.* **·trat·ed, ·trat·ing** *v.t.* 1. To direct to a common point; focus. 2. To intensify or purify; condense. —*v.i.* 3. To converge. 4. To become compacted, intensified, or more pure. 5. To direct one's entire attention: often with *on* or *upon.* —*n.* A product of concentration. —**con'cen·trat'ed** *adj.* —**con'cen·tra'tive** *adj.* —**con'cen·tra'tor** *n.*

con·cen·tra·tion (kon'sən·trā'shən) *n.* 1. The act of concentrating, or the state of being concentrated. 2. A concentrate. 3. Complete attention.

concentration camp An enclosed camp for the confinement of political prisoners, aliens, etc.

con·cen·tric (kən·sen'trik) *adj.* Having a common center, as circles. Also **con·cen'tri·cal.** —**con·cen'tri·cal·ly** *adv.* —**con·cen·tric·i·ty** (kon'sen·tris'ə·tē) *n.*

con·cept (kon'sept) *n.* A mental image; esp., an abstract idea; also, a thought or opinion. [< L *conceptus* a conceiving]

con·cep·tion (kən·sep'shən) *n.* 1. The act of conceiving or becoming pregnant, or the state of being conceived. 2. An embryo or fetus. 3. A beginning. 4. The act of forming concepts or ideas. 5. A concept, plan, or design. —**con·cep'tion·al** *adj.* —**con·cep'tive** *adj.*

con·cep·tu·al (kən·sep'chōō·əl) *adj.* Of or pertaining to conception or concepts. —**con·cep'tu·al·ly** *adv.*

con·cern (kən·sûrn') *v.t.* 1. To be of interest or importance to. 2. To occupy the attention of; engage: often used as a reflexive or in the passive. 3. To worry; trouble: often in the passive. —*n.* 1. That which concerns or affects one. 2. Anxiety or interest; care. 3. Relation or bearing. 4. A business firm. [< COM- + L *cernere* to see, discern] —**con·cerned'** *adj.*

con·cern·ing (kən·sûr'ning) *prep.* In relation to; regarding; about.

con·cern·ment (kən·sûrn'mənt) *n.* 1. Importance. 2. Concern; anxiety. 3. Anything that relates to one; affair.

con·cert (*n. & adj.* kon'sûrt; *v.* kən·sûrt') *n.* 1. A musical performance. 2. Agreement; harmony. —**in concert** In unison; all together. —*v.t. & v.i.* To make or become unified; do together; combine. —*adj.* Of or for concerts. [< Ital. *concertare* to agree]

con·cert·ed (kən·sûr'tid) *adj.* Arranged or done together; combined. —**con·cert'ed·ly** *adv.*

con·cer·ti·na (kon'sər·tē'nə) *n.* A small accordionlike musical instrument with buttons for keys. [< CONCERT + -INA]

con·cert·mas·ter (kon'sərt·mas'tər) *n.* The leader of the first violin section of an orchestra, who acts as assistant to the conductor. Also **con'cert·meis'ter** (-mīs'tər).

con·cer·to (kən·cher'tō) *n. pl.* **·tos,** *Ital.* **·ti** (-tē) *Music* A composition for a solo instrument or instruments accompanied by an orchestra. [< Ital. See CONCERT.]

concerto gros·so (grō′sō) *pl.* **concerti gros·si** (grō′sē) A concerto for a group of solo instruments and an orchestra. [< Ital., lit., big concerto]
con·ces·sion (kən·sesh′ən) *n.* 1. The act of conceding. 2. Anything so yielded. 3. A right or privilege granted by a government. 4. The right to operate a subsidiary business on certain premises. —**con·ces′sion·ar′y** *adj.* —**con·ces′sive** (-ses′iv) *adj.*
con·ces·sion·aire (kən·sesh′ən·âr′) *n.* One who holds or operates a concession. Also **con·ces′sion·ar′y, con·ces′sion·er.** [< F]
conch (kongk, konch) *n. pl.* **conchs** (kongks) or **conch·es** (kon′chiz) 1. Any of various marine mollusks having large, spiral, univalve shells. 2. Such a shell. [< Gk. *konchē* shell]
con·chol·o·gy (kong·kol′ə·jē) *n.* The study of shells and mollusks. —**con·chol′o·gist** *n.*
con·ci·erge (kon′sē·ûrzh′, *Fr.* kôn·syârzh′) *n.* A doorkeeper and custodian of a building, esp. in France. [< F]
con·cil·i·ate (kən·sil′ē·āt) *v.t.* **·at·ed, ·at·ing** 1. To placate. 2. To secure by favorable measures; win. [< L *concilium* council] —**con·cil′i·a·ble** (-ə·bəl) *adj.* —**con·cil′i·a′tion** *n.* —**con·cil′i·a′tor** *n.*
con·cil·i·a·to·ry (kən·sil′ē·ə·tôr′ē) *adj.* Tending to reconcile or conciliate. Also **con·cil′i·a′tive.** —**con·cil′i·a·to′ri·ly** *adv.* —**con·cil′i·a·to′ri·ness** *n.*
con·cise (kən·sīs′) *adj.* Terse; expressed in brief form. [< COM- + L *caedere* to cut] —**con·cise′ly** *adv.* —**con·cise′ness** *n.*
con·clave (kon′klāv, kong′-) *n.* A private or secret meeting, esp. the meeting at which the College of Cardinals elects a pope. [< COM- + L *clavis* key] —**con′clav·ist** *n.*
con·clude (kən·klōōd′) *v.* **·clud·ed, ·clud·ing** *v.t.* 1. To end; terminate. 2. To settle finally. 3. To form a judgment about; decide. 4. To resolve (to do); determine. —*v.i.* 5. To come to an end. 6. To come to a decision or agreement. [< COM- + L *claudere* to close, shut off] —**con·clud′er** *n.*
con·clu·sion (kən·klōō′zhən) *n.* 1. The end or termination of something. 2. A closing part, as of a speech. 3. A result; outcome. 4. A judgment or opinion. 5. A final decision; resolve. 6. A final settlement, as of a treaty. —**in conclusion** As a final statement.
con·clu·sive (kən·klōō′siv) *adj.* Putting an end to a question; decisive. —**con·clu′sive·ly** *adv.* —**con·clu′sive·ness** *n.*
con·coct (kon·kokt′, kən-) *v.t.* 1. To make by mixing ingredients, as a drink. 2. To make up; devise. [< COM- + L *coquere* to cook, boil] —**con·coct′er** or **con·coc′tor** *n.* —**con·coc′tion** *n.* —**con·coc′tive** *adj.*
con·com·i·tant (kon·kom′ə·tənt, kən-) *adj.* Existing or occurring together; attendant. —*n.* An attendant circumstance, state, or thing. [< COM- + L *comitari* to accompany] —**con·com′i·tance, con·com′i·tan·cy** *n.* —**con·com′i·tant·ly** *adv.*
con·cord (kon′kôrd, kong′-) *n.* 1. Unity; agreement; accord. 2. Peace. 3. A peace treaty. 4. *Music* Consonance. [< COM- + L *cor, cordis* heart]
con·cor·dance (kon·kôr′dəns, kən-) *n.* 1. Agreement; concord. 2. An alphabetical index of the important words in a book as they occur in context: a *concordance* of the Bible.
con·cor·dant (kon·kôr′dənt, kən-) *adj.* Existing in concord; agreeing; harmonious. —**con·cor′dant·ly** *adv.*
con·cor·dat (kon·kôr′dat) *n.* 1. An agreement between the papacy and a government on church affairs. 2. Any official agreement or pact.
con·course (kon′kôrs, kong′-) *n.* 1. Convergence; confluence. 2. A crowd; throng. 3. A place for the assembling or passage of crowds. [< COM- + L *currere* to run]
con·crete (kon′krēt; *for adj., n., & v. def. 2,* also kon·krēt′) *adj.* 1. Specific, as opposed to general. 2. Physically perceptible; real. 3. Constituting a composite mass; solid. 4. Made of concrete. —*n.* 1. A building material of sand and gravel or broken rock united by cement. 2. That which is concrete: often preceded by *the.* —*v.* **·cret·ed, ·cret·ing** *v.t.* 1. To bring together in one mass or body. 2. To cover with concrete. —*v.i.* 3. To coalesce; solidify. [< COM- + L *crescere* to grow] —**con·crete′ly** *adv.* —**con·crete′ness** *n.* —**con·cre·tize** (kon′kri·tīz) *v.t.* **·tized, ·tiz·ing**
con·cre·tion (kon·krē′shən) *n.* 1. The process of becoming concrete or solid. 2. A concrete mass. —**con·cre′tive** *adj.* —**con·cre′tive·ly** *adv.*
con·cu·bine (kong′kyə·bīn, kon′-) *n.* 1. A woman who cohabits with a man without being married to him. 2. In certain polygamous societies, a secondary wife. [< COM- + L *cumbere* to lie] —**con·cu·bi·nage** (kon·kyōō′bə·nij) *n.* —**con·cu·bi·nar·y** (kon·kyōō′bə·ner·ē) *adj.*
con·cu·pis·cence (kon·kyōō′pə·səns) *n.* 1. Sexual desire; lust. 2. Any immoderate desire. [< COM- + L *cupere* to desire] —**con·cu′pis·cent** *adj.*
con·cur (kən·kûr′) *v.i.* **·curred, ·cur·ring** 1. To agree or approve. 2. To cooperate. 3. To happen at the same time. 4. To converge to a point, as lines. [< COM- + L *currere* to run] —**con·cur′rence, con·cur′ren·cy** *n.*
con·cur·rent (kən·kûr′ənt) *adj.* 1. Occurring together. 2. United in action or application; cooperating. 3. *Law* Having the same authority or jurisdiction. 4. Meeting at or going toward the same point. 5. In agreement or accordance. —**con·cur′rent·ly** *adv.*
con·cus·sion (kən·kush′ən) *n.* 1. A violent shaking; shock. 2. *Pathol.* A violent shock to some organ, esp. to the brain. [< COM- + L *quatere* to strike, beat] —**con·cus·sive** (kən·kus′iv) *adj.*
con·demn (kən·dem′) *v.t.* 1. To hold to be wrong; censure. 2. To pronounce judicial sentence against. 3. To show the guilt of; convict. 4. To declare to be unfit for use, usu. by official order. 5. To appropriate for public use. [< COM- + L *damnare* to condemn] —**con·dem′na·ble** (-nə·bəl) *adj.* —**con·dem·na·tion** (kon′dem·nā′shən) *n.* —**con·dem′na·to′ry** (-nə·tôr′ē) *adj.* —**con·demn′er** *n.*
con·dense (kən·dens′) *v.* **·densed, ·dens·ing** *v.t.* 1. To compress; make dense; consolidate. 2. To abridge; make concise. 3. To change from a gas to a liquid, or from a liquid to a solid. —*v.i.* 4. To become condensed. [< COM- + L *densus* crowded, close] —**con·den′sa·ble** or **con·den′si·ble** *adj.* —**con·den·sa·tion** (kon′den·sā′shən) *n.*

condensed milk Cow's milk, sweetened, and thickened by evaporation.
con·dens·er (kən·den′sər) *n.* 1. One who or that which condenses. 2. *Electr.* A capacitor. 3. *Optics* A combination of lenses for focusing light rays.
con·de·scend (kon′di·send′) *v.i.* 1. To lower oneself (to do something); deign. 2. To behave in a patronizing manner. [< COM- + L *descendere* to stoop] —**con′de·scen′sion** (-sen′shən), **con′de·scen′dence** *n.*
con·de·scend·ing (kon′di·sen′ding) *adj.* Ostentatiously courteous toward inferiors; patronizing. —**con′de·scend′ing·ly** *adv.*
con·di·ment (kon′də·mənt) *n.* A seasoning, as a relish, spice, etc. [< L *condire* to pickle]
con·di·tion (kən·dish′ən) *n.* 1. The state or mode of existence of a person or thing. 2. State of health. 3. *Informal* An ailment. 4. Something necessary to the occurrence or existence of something else; prerequisite. 5. *Usu. pl.* The circumstances affecting an activity or a mode of existence: poor living *conditions.* 6. Social status. 7. In a will, contract, etc., a proviso. —**in** (or **out of**) **condition** Fit (or unfit), esp. for some physical activity. —**on condition that** Provided that; if. —*v.t.* 1. To be a condition or prerequisite of. 2. To specify as a condition; stipulate. 3. To render in good condition. 4. To train, as to a conditioned response. 5. To accustom (someone) to. [< COM- + L *dicere* to say] —**con·di′tion·er** *n.*
con·di·tion·al (kən·dish′ən·əl) *adj.* 1. Not absolute; tentative. 2. Expressing a condition. —**con·di′tion·al′i·ty** (-al′ə·tē) *n.* —**con·di′tion·al·ly** *adv.*
con·di·tioned response (kən·dish′ənd) *Psychol.* A learned response to a neutral stimulus that is repeatedly associated with a stimulus normally evoking the response. Also **conditioned reflex.**
con·dole (kən·dōl′) *v.i.* **·doled, ·dol·ing** To grieve or express sympathy with: with *with.* [< COM- + L *dolere* to grieve] —**con·do′la·to′ry** *adj.* —**con·do′lence** *n.* —**con·dol′er** *n.*
con·dom (kon′dəm, kun′-) *n.* A sheath for the penis, having an antivenereal or contraceptive function. [? Alter. of *Conton,* 18th c. English physician]
con·do·min·i·um (kon′də·min′ē·əm) *n.* 1. Joint sovereignty or ownership. 2. A multi-unit dwelling in which the units are owned separately; also, a unit in such a dwelling. [< COM- + L *dominium* rule]
con·done (kən·dōn′) *v.t.* **·doned, ·don·ing** To overlook (an offense); pardon. [< COM- + L *donare* to give] —**con·do·na·tion** (kon′dō·nā′shən) *n.* —**con·don′er** *n.*
con·dor (kon′dôr, -dər) *n.* A large vulture of the high Andes. [< Quechua *cuntur*]
con·duce (kən·do͞os′, -dyo͞os′) *v.i.* **·duced, ·duc·ing** To help or tend toward a result; contribute: with *to.* [< L *conducere* to bring together] —**con·du′cive, con·du′cent** *adj.* —**con·du′cive·ness** *n.*
con·duct (*v.* kən·dukt′; *n.* kon′dukt) *v.t.* 1. To accompany and show the way; guide; escort. 2. To manage or control. 3. To direct and lead, as an orchestra. 4. To convey; transmit. 5. To act or behave: used reflexively. —*v.i.* 6. To serve as a conductor. 7. To direct or lead. —*n.* 1. The way a person acts; behavior. 2. Management. [< COM- + L *ducere* to lead] —**con·duct′i·bil′i·ty** *n.* —**con·duct′i·ble** *adj.* —**con·duc′·tive** *adj.*
con·duc·tance (kən·duk′təns) *n.* *Electr.* The ability of a body to pass a current.
con·duc·tion (kən·duk′shən) *n.* 1. *Physics* The transmission of heat, sound, or electricity through matter. 2. Transmission; a conveying. 3. Conductivity.
con·duc·tiv·i·ty (kon′duk·tiv′ə·tē) *n.* The capacity to transmit sound, heat, or electricity.
con·duc·tor (kən·duk′tər) *n.* 1. One who or that which conducts. 2. One who has charge of a railroad car, bus, etc. 3. The director of an orchestra or chorus. 4. Any substance or medium that conducts electricity, heat, etc. —**con·duc′tor·ship** *n.*
con·duit (kon′dit, -do͞o·it) *n.* A channel, pipe, etc., for conveying water, electric wires, etc. [< COM- + L *ducere* to lead]
cone (kōn) *n.* 1. *Geom.* A solid figure having a circle as its base and tapering evenly on all surfaces to a point. 2. Anything cone-shaped. 3. *Bot.* A dry multiple fruit, as of the pine, composed of scales arranged symmetrically around an axis and enclosing seeds. —*v.t.* **coned, con·ing** To shape conically. [< Gk. *kōnos*]
con·el·rad (kon′əl·rad) *n.* A technique for controlling radio signals so as to prevent enemy aircraft from using them for navigation. [< CON(TROL OF) EL(ECTROMAGNETIC) RAD(IATION)]
Con·es·to·ga wagon (kon′is·tō′gə) A type of covered wagon, used by American pioneers for westward travel. [after *Conestoga,* Pa., where first made]
co·ney (kō′nē, kun′ē) See CONY.
con·fab (kon′fab) *Informal* *v.i.* **·fabbed, ·fab·bing** To converse. —*n.* A conversation.
con·fab·u·late (kən·fab′yə·lāt) *v.i.* **·lat·ed, ·lat·ing** To chat; gossip; converse. [< COM- + L *fabulari* to chat] —**con·fab′u·la′tion** *n.* —**con·fab′u·la·to′ry** (-lə·tôr′ē) *adj.*
con·fec·tion (kən·fek′shən) *n.* 1. The act or process of mixing or compounding. 2. Any of various sweet preparations, as candy or preserves. [< COM- + L *facere* to make] —**con·fec′tion·ar·y** *adj.*
con·fec·tion·er (kən·fek′shən·ər) *n.* One who makes or deals in confectionery.
confectioner's sugar A powdered sugar.
con·fec·tion·er·y (kən·fek′shən·er′ē) *n.* *pl.* **·er·ies** 1. Sweetmeats collectively. 2. A confectioner's shop, or the business of a confectioner. Also **con·fec′tion·ar′y.**
con·fed·er·a·cy (kən·fed′ər·ə·sē) *n.* *pl.* **·cies** 1. A union of states or persons; a league; alliance. 2. An unlawful combination; conspiracy. —**the Confederacy** A league of eleven southern states that seceded from the U.S. during the period from December, 1860, to May, 1861: also **Confederate States of America.**
con·fed·er·ate (*n.* & *adj.* kən·fed′ər·it; *v.* kən·fed′ə·rāt) *n.* An associate or accomplice. —*adj.* Associated in a confederacy. —*v.t.* & *v.i.* **·at·ed, ·at·ing** To form or join in a confederacy. [< COM- + L *fœdus* league] —**con·fed′er·a′tive** *adj.*
Con·fed·er·ate (kən·fed′ər·it) *n.* An

adherent of the Confederacy. —*adj.* Pertaining to the Confederate States of America.

con·fed·er·a·tion (kən·fed′ə·rā′shən) *n.* 1. The act of confederating, or the state of being confederated. 2. An association of states. —**the Confederation** The union of the American colonies, 1781–89.

con·fer (kən·fûr′) *v.* ·ferred, ·fer·ring *v.t.* 1. To grant or bestow. —*v.i.* 2. To hold a conference; consult together. [< COM- + L *ferre* to bring, carry] —**con·fer′ment** *n.* —**con·fer′ra·ble** *adj.* —**con·fer′rer** *n.*

con·fer·ee (kon′fə·rē′) *n.* One who takes part in a conference. Also **con′fer·ree′**.

con·fer·ence (kon′fər·əns, -frəns) *n.* 1. A consultation on an important matter; also, a formal meeting for this. 2. A league or association, as of athletic teams. —**con′fer·en′tial** (-fə·ren′shəl) *adj.*

con·fess (kən·fes′) *v.t.* 1. To acknowledge or admit, as a fault or sin. 2. To concede or admit to be true. 3. To acknowledge belief or faith in. 4. *Eccl.* **a** To make known (one's sins), esp. to a priest. **b** To hear the confession of: said of a priest. —*v.i.* 5. To make acknowledgment, as of fault or crime: with *to.* 6. To make confession to a priest. [< COM- + L *fateri* to own, declare] —**con·fess′ed·ly** *adv.*

con·fes·sion (kən·fesh′ən) *n.* 1. The act of confessing. 2. That which is confessed. 3. A statement in which something is confessed. 4. *Eccl.* The acknowledgment of one's sins. 5. A body of religious doctrine: also **confession of faith.** 6. A church holding a particular body of doctrine.

con·fes·sion·al (kən·fesh′ən·əl) *adj.* Of, pertaining to, or like confession. —*n.* A small enclosure where a priest hears confessions.

con·fes·sor (kən·fes′ər) *n.* 1. A priest who hears confessions. 2. One who confesses. Also **con·fess′er.**

con·fet·ti (kən·fet′ē) *n.pl.* (*construed as sing.*) Small pieces of colored paper thrown at carnivals, weddings, etc. [< Ital., pl. of *confetto* confection]

con·fi·dant (kon′fə·dant′, -dänt′, kon′fə·dant, -dänt) *n.* A person to whom secrets are confided. —**con′fi·dante′** *n.fem.*

con·fide (kən·fīd′) *v.* ·fid·ed, ·fid·ing *v.t.* 1. To reveal in trust or confidence. 2. To entrust. —*v.i.* 3. To have trust; impart secrets trustingly: with *in.* [< COM- + L *fidere* to trust] —**con·fid′er** *n.* —**con·fid′ing** *adj.* —**con·fid′ing·ly** *adv.*

con·fi·dence (kon′fə·dəns) *n.* 1. A feeling of trust; faith. 2. A relationship of trust. 3. Self-assurance; also, fearlessness. 4. A feeling of certainty. 5. A secret. —**to take into one's confidence** To trust with one's secrets. —*adj.* Of or pertaining to a swindle or swindler.

confidence game A swindle in which the victim is defrauded after his confidence has been won: also, *Slang, con game.* Also **confidence trick.**

confidence man A swindler in a confidence game. Also *con man.*

con·fi·dent (kon′fə·dənt) *adj.* 1. Having confidence; assured. 2. Self-assured; bold. —*n.* A confidant. —**con′fi·dent·ly** *adv.*

con·fi·den·tial (kon′fə·den′shəl) *adj.* 1. Secret; private. 2. Enjoying another's confidence; trusted. 3. Of or pertaining to the confiding of secrets. —**con′fi·den′ti·al′i·ty** (-shē·al′ə·tē), **con′fi·den′tial·ness** *n.* —**con′fi·den′tial·ly** *adv.*

con·fig·u·ra·tion (kən·fig′yə·rā′shən) *n.* 1. The arrangement of the parts of a thing; form; contour. 2. *Psychol.* A gestalt. [< COM- + L *figurare* to shape, fashion] —**con·fig′u·ra′tion·al, con·fig·u·ra·tive** (kən·fig′yər·ə·tiv, -yə·rā′tiv) *adj.*

con·fine (*v.* kən·fīn′; *n.* kon′fīn) *v.t.* ·fined, ·fin·ing 1. To shut in; imprison. 2. To restrain or oblige to stay within doors. 3. To restrict: to *confine* remarks. —*n.* *Usu. pl.* A boundary or border. [< COM- + L *finis* border] —**con·fin′a·ble** or **con·fine′a·ble** *adj.* —**con·fin′er** *n.*

con·fine·ment (kən·fīn′mənt) *n.* 1. The act of confining, or the state of being confined. 2. Childbirth.

con·firm (kən·fûrm′) *v.t.* 1. To verify; substantiate. 2. To strengthen. 3. To render valid by formal approval. 4. To administer the rite of confirmation. [< COM- + L *firmus* strong] —**con·firm′a·ble** *adj.* —**con·firm′a·to′ry** *adj.*

con·fir·ma·tion (kon′fər·mā′shən) *n.* 1. The act of confirming. 2. Proof. 3. A religious rite in which a person is admitted to all the privileges of a church.

con·firmed (kən·fûrmd′) *adj.* 1. Firmly established; ratified. 2. Inveterate; habitual. 3. Having received religious confirmation.

con·fis·cate (kon′fis·kāt) *v.t.* ·cat·ed, ·cat·ing 1. To seize for public use, usu. as a penalty. 2. To appropriate by or as by authority. [< COM- + L *fiscus* chest, treasury] —**con′fis·ca′tion** *n.* —**con′fis·ca′tor** *n.* —**con·fis·ca·to·ry** (kən·fis′kə·tôr′ē) *adj.*

con·fla·gra·tion (kon′flə·grā′shən) *n.* A great or extensive fire. [< COM- + L *flagare* to burn]

con·flict (*n.* kon′flikt; *v.* kən·flikt′) *n.* 1. A struggle; battle. 2. Mutual antagonism, as of ideas. 3. A clash between contradictory impulses. —*v.i.* 1. To come into collision or opposition; clash. 2. To battle; struggle. [< COM- + L *fligere* to strike] —**con·flic′tive** *adj.*

con·flu·ence (kon′flo͞o·əns) *n.* 1. A flowing together of streams; also, the place where they meet. 2. The body or stream of water so formed. 3. A coming together; crowd. Also **con·flux** (kon′fluks). [< COM- + L *fluere* to flow] —**con′flu·ent** *adj.* —**con′flu·ent·ly** *adv.*

con·form (kən·fôrm′) *v.i.* 1. To show identity or resemblance; correspond: with *to.* 2. To adhere to conventional behavior. —*v.t.* 3. To make the same or similar: with *to.* 4. To bring (oneself) into harmony or agreement: with *to.* [< COM- + L *formare* to shape] —**con·form′a·ble** *adj.* —**con·form′a·bly** *adv.* —**con·form′er** *n.*

con·for·ma·tion (kon′fôr·mā′shən) *n.* 1. Form; structure or outline. 2. The arrangement of parts. 3. The act of conforming, or the state of being conformed.

con·form·ist (kən·fôr′mist) *n.* One who conforms in behavior.

con·form·i·ty (kən·fôr′mə·tē) *n.* *pl.* ·ties 1. Correspondence; agreement. 2. The act or habit of conforming; acquiescence. Also **con·form′ance.**

con·found (kon·found′, kən-) *v.t.* 1. To confuse or amaze. 2. To confuse with something else. 3. To confuse or mingle indistinguishably. 4. To damn: used as an oath. [< COM- + L *fundere* to pour] —**con·found′ed** *adj.* —**con·found′ed·ly** *adv.* —**con·found′er** *n.*

con·frere (kon′frâr) *n.* A fellow member; a colleague. [< COM- + L *frater* brother]

con·front (kən·frunt′) *v.t.* 1. To stand face to face with; face defiantly. 2. To put face to face: with *with.* [< COM- + L *frons, frontis* face, forehead] —**con·fron·ta·tion** (kon′·frən·tā′shən) *n.* —**con·front′ment** *n.* —**con·front′er** *n.*

Con·fu·cian·ism (kən·fyo͞o′shən·iz′əm) *n.* The ethical system taught by the Chinese philosopher Confucius, emphasizing ancestor worship, devotion to family and friends, and the maintenance of justice and peace. —**Con·fu′cian·ist** *n.* —**Con·fu′cian** *n. & adj.*

con·fuse (kən·fyo͞oz′) *v.t.* **·fused, ·fus·ing** 1. To perplex or perturb; bewilder. 2. To jumble. 3. To mistake one for the other. [< COM- + L *fundere* to pour] —**con·fus′ed·ly** *adv.* —**con·fus′ed·ness** *n.* —**con·fus′ing·ly** *adv.*

con·fu·sion (kən·fyo͞o′zhən) *n.* 1. The act of confusing, or the state of being confused. 2. Disarray; disorder. 3. Perplexity of mind. 4. Embarrassment. —**con·fu′sion·al** *adj.*

con·fute (kən·fyo͞ot′) *v.t.* **·fut·ed, ·fut·ing** 1. To prove to be wrong, false, or invalid. 2. To prove (a person) to be in the wrong. [< L *confutare* to check, restrain] —**con·fu·ta·tion** (kon′fyo͞o·tā′shən) *n.* —**con·fut′er** *n.*

con·ga (kong′gə) *n.* A dance of Latin American origin in which the dancers form a winding line. [< Am. Sp.]

con game *Slang* A confidence game.

con·geal (kən·jēl′) *v.t. & v.i.* 1. To make or become solid, as by freezing or curdling. 2. To clot or coagulate, as blood. [< COM- + L *gelare* to freeze] —**con·geal′a·ble** *adj.* —**con·geal′er** *n.* —**con·geal′ment** *n.*

con·gen·ial (kən·jēn′yəl) *adj.* 1. Having similar character or tastes; sympathetic. 2. Agreeable: a *congenial* job. —**con·ge·ni·al·i·ty** (kən·jē′nē·al′ə·tē) *n.* —**con·gen′·ial·ly** *adv.*

con·gen·i·tal (kən·jen′ə·təl) *adj.* 1. Existing prior to or at birth: distinguished from *hereditary.* 2. Disposed as if by birth. [< COM- + L *genitus,* pp. of *gignere* to bear] —**con·gen′i·tal·ly** *adv.*

con·ger (kong′gər) *n.* A marine eel, used as a food fish. [< Gk. *gongros*]

con·ge·ries (kon′jə·rēz, kon·jir′ēz) *n.pl.* (*usu. construed as sing.*) A collection of things; a mass; heap. [< L *congerere* to bring together]

con·gest (kən·jest′) *v.t.* 1. To overcrowd. 2. *Pathol.* To surcharge (an organ or part) with an excess of fluid. —*v.i.* 3. To become congested. [< COM- + L *gerere* to bear, carry] —**con·ges′tion** *n.* —**con·ges′tive** *adj.*

con·glom·er·ate (*adj. & n.* kən·glom′ər·it; *v.* kən·glom′ə·rāt) *adj.* 1. Massed or clustered. 2. *Geol.* Consisting of loosely cemented heterogeneous material. —*n.* 1. A heterogeneous collection; cluster. 2. A large corporation formed by merging a number of companies, often in unrelated fields. 3. *Geol.* A conglomerate rock. —*v.t. & v.i.* **·at·ed, ·at·ing** To gather into a cohering mass. [< COM- + L *glomus, glomeris* ball] —**con·glom′er·a′tion** *n.*

con·glu·ti·nate (kən·glo͞o′tə·nāt) *v.t. & v.i.* **·nat·ed, ·nat·ing** To glue or stick together; adhere. [< COM- + L *glutinare* to stick] —**con·glu′ti·na′tion** *n.* —**con·glu′ti·na′tive** *adj.*

congo snake A tailed aquatic salamander of the SE U.S. Also **congo eel.**

con·grat·u·late (kən·grach′o͞o·lāt) *v.t.* **·lat·ed, ·lat·ing** To express pleasure in or otherwise acknowledge the achievement or good fortune of (another). [< COM- + L *gratulari* to rejoice] —**con·grat′u·la·to′ry** (-lə·tôr′ē) *adj.*

con·grat·u·la·tion (kən·grach′o͞o·lā′shən) *n.* 1. The act of congratulating. 2. *pl.* Expressions of pleasure and good wishes on another's fortune or success.

con·gre·gate (kong′grə·gāt) *v.t. & v.i.* **·gat·ed, ·gat·ing** To gather into a crowd; assemble. [< COM- + L *gregare* to collect] —**con′gre·ga′tive** *adj.* —**con′gre·ga′tor** *n.*

con·gre·ga·tion (kong′grə·gā′shən) *n.* 1. The act of congregating. 2. An assemblage. 3. A group of people worshipping together or who worship in a local church; a parish. —**con′gre·ga′tion·al** *adj.*

con·gre·ga·tion·al·ism (kong′grə·gā′shən·əl·iz′əm) *n.* A form of church government in which each local congregation is autonomous in all church matters.

Con·gre·ga·tion·al·ist (kong′grə·gā′shən·əl·ist) *n.* A member of an evangelical Protestant denomination (**Congregational Christian Churches**) practicing congregationalism. —**Con′gre·ga′tion·al** *adj.* —**Con′gre·ga′·tion·al·ism** *n.*

con·gress (kong′gris) *n.* 1. An assembly or conference. 2. A meeting. 3. The legislature of various nations, esp. of a republic. [< COM- + L *gradi* to walk]

Con·gress (kong′gris) *n.* The legislative body of the U.S., consisting of the Senate and the House of Representatives.

con·gres·sion·al (kən·gresh′ən·əl) *adj. Often cap.* Pertaining to a congress, esp. to the U.S. Congress.

con·gress·man (kong′gris·mən) *n. pl.* **·men** (-mən) *Often cap.* A member of a congress, esp. of the U.S. House of Representatives. —**con′gress·wom′an** (-wo͝om′ən) *n.fem.*

con·gru·ent (kong′gro͞o·ənt) *adj.* 1. Agreeing or conforming; congruous. 2. *Geom.* Exactly coinciding when superimposed. [< L *congruere* to agree] —**con′gru·ence, con′gru·en·cy** *n.* —**con′gru·ent·ly** *adv.*

con·gru·ous (kong′gro͞o·əs) *adj.* 1. Agreeing; harmonious. 2. Appropriate; fit. 3. *Geom.* Congruent. —**con·gru·i·ty** (kən·gro͞o′ə·tē) *n.* —**con′gru·ous·ly** *adv.* —**con′gru·ous·ness** *n.*

con·ic (kon′ik) *adj.* 1. Cone-shaped. 2. Of or formed by or upon a cone. Also **con′i·cal.** [< Gk. *kōnos* cone] —**con′i·cal·ly** *adv.*

conic section *Math.* A curve formed by the intersection of a plane with a cone; an ellipse, parabola, hyperbola, or circle.

co·nid·i·um (kō·nid′ē·əm) *n. pl.* **·nid·i·a** (-nid′ē·ə) *Bot.* An asexual spore of many species of fungi. Also **co·nid·i·o·spore** (kō·nid′ē·ə·spôr′). [< Gk. *konis* dust] —**co·nid′i·al** *adj.*

con·i·fer (kon′ə·fər, kō′nə-) *n.* Any of a

large and widely distributed family of evergreen shrubs and trees, as the pines, spruces, firs, and junipers. [< L *conus* cone + *ferre* to bear] —**co·nif·er·ous** (kō·nif′ər·əs) *adj.*

con·jec·ture (kən·jek′chər) *v.t. & v.i.* **·tured, ·tur·ing** To guess; infer. —*n.* 1. Inference from incomplete evidence. 2. A guess; surmise. [< COM- + L *jacere* to throw] —**con·jec′tur·a·ble** *adj.* —**con·jec′tur·al** *adj.* —**con·jec′tur·al·ly** *adv.* —**con·jec′tur·er** *n.*

con·join (kən·join′) *v.t. & v.i.* To join together. [< COM- + L *jungere* to join] —**con·join′er** *n.* —**con·joint′** (-joint′) *adj.* —**con·joint′ly** *adv.*

con·ju·gal (kon′jŏŏ·gəl, -jə-) *adj.* Pertaining to marriage; connubial. [< L *conjungere* to join in marriage] —**con·ju·gal·i·ty** (kon′jŏŏ·gal′ə·tē, -jə-) *n.* —**con′ju·gal·ly** *adv.*

con·ju·gate (kon′jŏŏ·gāt, -jə-; *for adj., n., also* kon′jŏŏ·git, -jə-) *v.* **·gat·ed, ·gat·ing** *v.t.* 1. *Gram.* To give the inflections of (a verb). —*v.i.* 2. To unite; join together. —*adj.* 1. Joined in pairs; coupled. 2. Kindred in origin and, usu., meaning: said of words. —*n.* 1. A conjugate word. 2. A member of any conjugate pair. [< COM- + L *jugare* to join] —**con′ju·ga′tive** *adj.* —**con′ju·ga′tor** *n.*

con·ju·ga·tion (kon′jŏŏ·gā′shən, -jə-) *n.* 1. A joining or being joined together. 2. *Gram.* **a** The inflection of verbs. **b** A schematic presentation of the entire inflection of a verb. **c** A class of verbs that are inflected in the same manner. —**con′ju·ga′tion·al** *adj.* —**con′ju·ga′tion·al·ly** *adv.*

con·junct (kən·jungkt′, kon′jungkt) *adj.* Joined together; conjoined. [See CONJOIN.] —**con·junct′ly** *adv.*

con·junc·tion (kən·jungk′shən) *n.* 1. The act of joining together, or the state of being so joined. 2. A coincidence. 3. *Astron.* **a** The position of two celestial bodies when they are in the same celestial longitude. **b** The position of a planet when it is on a direct line with the earth and the sun. 4. *Gram.* A word used to connect words, phrases, clauses, or sentences; one of the eight traditional parts of speech. —**con·junc′tion·al** *adj.* —**con·junc′tion·al·ly** *adv.*

con·junc·ti·va (kon′jungk·tī′və, kən·jungk′·tə·və) *n. pl.* **·vas** or **·vae** (-vē) *Anat.* The mucous membrane lining the eyelids and covering the front part of the eyeball. [< NL (*membrana*) *conjunctiva* connective (membrane)] —**con′junc·ti′val** *adj.*

con·junc·tive (kən·jungk′tiv) *adj.* 1. Joining; connective. 2. Joined together. 3. *Gram.* Serving as a conjunction. [See CONJOIN.] —**con·junc′tive·ly** *adv.*

con·junc·ti·vi·tis (kən·jungk′tə·vī′tis) *n.* *Pathol.* Inflammation of the conjunctiva.

con·junc·ture (kən·jungk′chər) *n.* 1. A combination of circumstances or events; juncture. 2. A critical situation; crisis. 3. Conjunction; union.

con·jure (kən·jŏŏr′ *for def. 1*; kon′jər, kun′- *for defs. 2–4*) *v.* **·jured, ·jur·ing** *v.t.* 1. To call on or appeal to solemnly; adjure. 2. To summon by magic, as a devil. 3. To accomplish by or as by magic. —*v.i.* 4. To practice magic. [< COM- + L *jurare* to swear] —**con·ju·ra·tion** (kon′jə·rā′shən, -jŏŏ-) *n.*

con·jur·er (kon′jər·ər, kun′- *for def. 1*; kən·jŏŏr′ər *for def. 2*) *n.* 1. A magician. 2. One who appeals solemnly. Also **con′jur·or.**

conk (kongk) *v.t.* *Slang* To hit on the head. —**to conk out** *Informal* To stall or fail. [? < CONCH]

con man (kon) *Slang* A confidence man.

con·nect (kə·nekt′) *v.t.* 1. To join or fasten together; link. 2. To associate as in thought. —*v.i.* 3. To join or fit. 4. To meet so that passengers can transfer: said of trains, buses, etc. [< COM- + L *nectere* to bind] —**con·nec′tor** or **con·nect′er** *n.*

connecting rod *Mech.* A rod joining a piston with a crankshaft.

con·nec·tion (kə·nek′shən) *n.* 1. The act of connecting, or the state of being connected. 2. That which joins or relates; a link. 3. Logical sequence; coherence. 4. Context. 5. Family relationship. 6. *Usually pl.* Influential friends or associates. 7. *Often pl.* A transfer or continuation from one route or vehicle to another. Also *Brit.* **con·nex′ion.** —**con·nec′tion·al** *adj.*

con·nec·tive (kə·nek′tiv) *adj.* Capable of connecting, or serving to connect. —*n.* 1. That which connects. 2. *Gram.* A connecting word or particle, as a conjunction. —**con·nec′tive·ly** *adv.* —**con·nec·tiv·i·ty** (kon′ek·tiv′ə·tē) *n.*

connective tissue *Anat.* The fibrous tissue that serves to unite and support the various organs and tissues of the body.

conning tower 1. The armored pilothouse of a warship. 2. In submarines, an observation tower, used also as an entrance.

con·nip·tion (kə·nip′shən) *n.* *Informal* A fit of hysteria, rage, etc. [Cf. dial. E *canapshus* ill-tempered]

con·nive (kə·nīv′) *v.i.* **·nived, ·niv·ing** 1. To encourage or assent to a wrong by silence or feigned ignorance: with *at.* 2. To be in collusion: with *with.* [< L *conivere* to wink, shut the eyes] —**con·niv′ance** *n.* —**con·niv′er** *n.*

con·nois·seur (kon′ə·sûr′) *n.* An expert, esp. in matters of art and taste. [< F < L *cognoscere* to know, understand] —**con′nois·seur′ship** *n.*

con·no·ta·tion (kon′ə·tā′shən) *n.* 1. The suggestive or associative significance of an expression. 2. The act of connoting. —**con′·no·ta′tive** *adj.* —**con′no·ta′tive·ly** *adv.*

con·note (kə·nōt′) *v.t.* **·not·ed, ·not·ing** To suggest or imply. [< COM- + L *notare* to mark]

con·nu·bi·al (kə·nōō′bē·əl, -nyōō′-) *adj.* Pertaining to marriage or to the married state. [< COM- + L *nubere* to marry] —**con·nu′bi·al′i·ty** *n.* —**con·nu′bi·al·ly** *adv.*

con·quer (kong′kər) *v.t.* 1. To overcome by or as by force; vanquish; surmount. —*v.i.* 2. To be victorious. [< COM- + L *quaerere* to search for, procure] —**con′quer·a·ble** *adj.* —**con′quer·or** *n.*

con·quest (kon′kwest, kong′-) *n.* 1. The act of conquering. 2. The thing conquered. 3. A winning of another's favor or love. 4. One whose favor or love has been won.

con·quis·ta·dor (kon·kwis′tə·dôr, -kis′-; *Sp.* kōng·kēs′tä·thōr′) *n. pl.* **·dors,** *Sp.* **·do·res** (-thō′rās) A conqueror; esp., any of the 16th c. Spanish conquerors of Mexico and Peru. [< Sp. < *conquistar* to conquer]

con·san·guin·e·ous (kon′sang·gwin′ē·əs) *adj.* Of the same blood or ancestry; akin. Also **con·san·guine** (kon·sang′gwin). [< COM- + L *sanguis* blood] —**con′san·guin′e·ous·ly** *adv.* —**con′san·guin′i·ty** *n.*

con·science (kon′shəns) *n.* 1. The faculty by which distinctions are made between moral right and wrong. 2. Conformity to moral standards. [< L *conscire* to know inwardly] —**con′science·less** *adj.*

con·sci·en·tious (kon′shē·en′shəs, kon′sē-) *adj.* 1. Moral; scrupulous. 2. Careful and thorough; painstaking. —**con′sci·en′tious·ly** *adv.* —**con′sci·en′tious·ness** *n.*

conscientious objector One who, on grounds of religious or moral convictions, refuses to perform military service.

con·scion·a·ble (kon′shən·ə·bəl) *adj. Rare* Moral; right; just. —**con′scion·a·bly** *adv.*

con·scious (kon′shəs) *adj.* 1. Aware of one's own existence or of external objects and conditions. 2. Aware of some object or fact. 3. Deliberate; intentional. [< L *conscius* knowing inwardly] —**con′scious·ly** *adv.*

con·scious·ness (kon′shəs·nis) *n.* 1. Awareness of oneself and one's surroundings. 2. Awareness of some object, influence, etc. 3. The mental and emotional awareness of an individual, or of a group.

con·script (*n. & adj.* kon′skript; *v.* kən·skript′) *n.* One who is compulsorily enrolled for some service. —*adj.* Conscripted. —*v.t.* To force into military or other service. [< COM- + L *scribere* to write] —**con·scrip′tion** *n.*

con·se·crate (kon′sə·krāt) *v.t.* **·crat·ed, ·crat·ing** 1. To set apart as sacred. 2. To dedicate; devote. 3. To make revered; hallow. [< COM- + L *sacer* holy] —**con′se·cra′tion** *n.* —**con′se·cra′tor** *n.* —**con·se·cra·to·ry** (kon′sə·krə·tôr′ē) *adj.*

con·sec·u·tive (kən·sek′yə·tiv) *adj.* 1. Following in uninterrupted succession; successive. 2. Characterized by logical sequence. —**con·sec′u·tive·ly** *adv.* —**con·sec′u·tive·ness** *n.*

con·sen·sus (kən·sen′səs) *n.* A collective opinion; general agreement. [< COM- + L *sentire* to feel, think]

con·sent (kən·sent′) *v.i.* To give assent; agree or acquiesce. —*n.* 1. A voluntary yielding; compliance. 2. Agreement; harmony. [See CONSENSUS.] —**con·sent′er** *n.*

con·se·quence (kon′sə·kwens, -kwəns) *n.* 1. That which naturally follows from a preceding action or condition; result. 2. A logical conclusion. 3. Importance.

con·se·quent (kon′sə·kwent, -kwənt) *adj.* 1. Following as a natural result, or as a logical conclusion. 2. Logical. —*n.* 1. That which follows something else, as in time. 2. An outcome; result. [< COM- + L *sequi* to follow]

con·se·quen·tial (kon′sə·kwen′shəl) *adj.* 1. Following as an effect or conclusion. 2. Of consequence; important. —**con′se·quen′ti·al′i·ty** (-shē·al′ə·tē), **con′se·quen′tial·ness** *n.* —**con′se·quen′tial·ly** *adv.*

con·se·quent·ly (kon′sə·kwent′lē, -kwənt·lē) *adv.* As a result; therefore.

con·ser·va·tion (kon′sər·vā′shən) *n.* 1. The act of keeping or protecting from loss or injury. 2. The preservation of natural resources, as forests, fisheries, etc. [See CONSERVE] —**con′ser·va′tion·al** *adj.* —**con′·ser·va′tion·ist** *n.*

con·ser·va·tism (kən·sûr′və·tiz′əm) *n.* Devotion to the existing order; opposition to change.

con·ser·va·tive (kən·sûr′və·tiv) *adj.* 1. Inclined to preserve the existing order of things; opposed to change. 2. Moderate; cautious: a *conservative* estimate. 3. Conserving; preservative. —*n.* 1. A conservative person. 2. A preservative. —**con·ser′va·tive·ly** *adv.* —**con·ser′va·tive·ness** *n.*

Conservative Judaism That branch of Judaism that accepts as binding the Mosaic Laws, but allows some adjustments to the changed conditions of today.

con·ser·va·to·ry (kən·sûr′və·tôr′ē) *n. pl.* **·ries** 1. A small greenhouse or glass-enclosed room for plants. 2. A school of music. Also **con·ser·va·toire** (kən·sûr′və·twär′). —*adj.* Adapted to preserve.

con·serve (kən·sûrv′; *for n., also* kon′sûrv) *v.t.* **·served, ·serv·ing** 1. To keep from loss or decay; maintain. 2. To preserve with sugar. —*n. Often pl.* A kind of jam made of several fruits. [< COM- + L *servare* to keep] —**con·serv′a·ble** *adj.* —**con·serv′er** *n.*

con·sid·er (kən·sid′ər) *v.t.* 1. To think about or deliberate upon. 2. To look upon or regard (as). 3. To believe. 4. To take into account: to *consider* the feelings of others. —*v.i.* 5. To think carefully; deliberate. [< L *considerare* to observe]

con·sid·er·a·ble (kən·sid′ər·ə·bəl) *adj.* 1. Somewhat large in amount, extent, etc. 2. Worthy of consideration. —**con·sid′er·a·bly** *adv.*

con·sid·er·ate (kən·sid′ər·it) *adj.* Thoughtful of others; kind. —**con·sid′er·ate·ly** *adv.* —**con·sid′er·ate·ness** *n.*

con·sid·er·a·tion (kən·sid′ə·rā′shən) *n.* 1. The act of considering; deliberation. 2. A circumstance to be taken into account. 3. Thoughtful or kindly feeling or treatment. 4. Something given for a service; recompense. 5. High regard; esteem. —**in consideration of** In view of, or in return for.

con·sid·er·ing (kən·sid′ər·ing) *prep.* In view of; taking into account. —*adv. Informal* Taking all the facts into account.

con·sign (kən·sīn′) *v.t.* 1. To entrust to the care of another. 2. To give up or turn over. 3. To forward or deliver, as merchandise. 4. To set apart, as for a specific use. [< COM- + L *signum* a seal] —**con·sign′a·ble** *adj.* —**con·sig·na·tion** (kon′sig·nā′shən) *n.* —**con·sign·ee** (kon′sī·nē′) *n.* —**con·sign′or** or **con·sign′er** *n.*

con·sign·ment (kən·sīn′mənt) *n.* 1. The act of consigning something. 2. That which is consigned. —**on consignment** Of goods, paid for by the retailer only after they have been sold.

con·sist (kən·sist′) *v.i.* 1. To be made up or constituted: with *of*. 2. To have as source or basis; inhere: with *in*. [< COM- + L *sistere* to stand]

con·sis·ten·cy (kən·sis′tən·sē) *n. pl.* **·cies** 1. Agreement between things, acts, or statements. 2. Firmness or thickness. Also **con·sis′tence.**

con·sis·tent (kən·sis′tənt) *adj.* 1. Not contradictory or self-contradictory. 2. Conforming to a single set of principles or to previous action or belief. [See CONSIST. —**con·sis′tent·ly** *adv.*

con·sis·to·ry (kən·sis′tər·ē) *n.* *pl.* **·ries** 1. *Eccl.* A council of the Roman Catholic Church, composed of the cardinals and usu. presided over by the Pope. 2. Any high church council. [< Med.L *consistere* to wait] —**con·sis·to·ri·al** (kon′sis·tôr′ē·əl), **con′sis·to′ri·an** (kon′sis·tôr′ē·ən) *adj.*

con·sole[1] (kən·sōl′) *v.t.* **·soled, ·sol·ing** To comfort (a person) in grief or sorrow; cheer. [< COM- + L *solari* to solace] —**con·sol′a·ble** *adj.* —**con·so·la·tion** (kon′sə·lā′shən) *n.* —**con·sol′a·to′ry** *adj.*

con·sole[2] (kon′sōl) *n.* 1. A bracket, esp. one used to support a cornice or ornamental fixture. 2. The portion of an organ containing the keyboard and stops. 3. A cabinet, as for a television set, which rests on the floor. 4. An instrument panel, esp. for controlling electronic devices. [< MF, a bracket]

con·sol·i·date (kən·sol′ə·dāt) *v.* **·dat·ed, ·dat·ing** *v.t.* 1. To make solid or coherent; strengthen. 2. To combine in one. —*v.i.* 3. To become united, solid, or firm. [< COM- + L *solidus* solid] —**con·sol′i·da′tion** *n.* —**con·sol′i·da′tor** *n.*

con·som·mé (kon′sə·mā′, *Fr.* kôṅ·sô·mā′) *n.* A clear soup made of meat and sometimes vegetables. [< F *consommer* to complete]

con·so·nance (kon′sə·nəns) *n.* 1. Agreement; accord. 2. Correspondence of sounds, esp. of consonants. 3. *Music* A combination of tones regarded as stable and not requiring resolution. Also **con′so·nan·cy.**

con·so·nant (kon′sə·nənt) *adj.* 1. Being in agreement; consistent. 2. Having consonance. 3. Consonantal. —*n.* 1. *Phonet.* A sound produced by complete or partial blockage of the breath stream, as the sounds of *b, f, k, s, t,* etc. 2. A letter representing such a sound. [< COM- + L *sonare* to sound] —**con′so·nant·ly** *adv.*

con·so·nan·tal (kon′sə·nan′təl) *adj.* 1. Of the nature of a consonant. 2. Having consonants.

con·sort (*n.* kon′sôrt; *v.* kən·sôrt′) *n.* 1. A husband or wife; spouse. 2. A companion or partner. 3. *Naut.* A vessel sailing with another. —*v.t.* & *v.i.* To associate; join. [< COM- + L *sors* share, lot]

con·sor·ti·um (kən·sôr′shē·əm) *n.* *pl.* **·ti·a** A coalition, as of banks or corporations, for a large venture. [< L, fellowship]

con·spec·tus (kən·spek′təs) *n.* *pl.* **·tus·es** 1. A general view of a subject. 2. A summary. [See CONSPICUOUS.]

con·spic·u·ous (kən·spik′yōō·əs) *adj.* Clearly visible; easily seen; striking. [< COM- + L *specere* to look at] —**con·spic′u·ous·ly** *adv.* —**con·spic′u·ous·ness** *n.*

con·spir·a·cy (kən·spir′ə·sē) *n.* *pl.* **·cies** 1. The act of conspiring secretly; also, the plan so made. 2. An acting together. —**con·spir′a·tor** *n.* —**con·spir′a·to′ri·al** *adj.*

con·spire (kən·spīr′) *v.* **·spired, ·spir·ing** *v.i.* 1. To combine secretly in an evil or unlawful enterprise. 2. To act together. —*v.t.* 3. To plan secretly; plot. [< COM- + L *spirare* to breathe] —**con·spir′er** *n.*

con·sta·ble (kon′stə·bəl, kun′-) *n.* A peace officer who arrests offenders, serves writs, etc. [< LL *comes stabuli* chief groom] —**con′sta·ble·ship′** *n.*

con·stab·u·lar·y (kən·stab′yə·ler′ē) *n.* *pl.* **·lar·ies** 1. The body of constables of a city, etc. 2. A police force organized in a military fashion. —**con·stab′u·lar′y** *adj.*

con·stan·cy (kon′stən·sē) *n.* 1. Steadiness or faithfulness. 2. Unchanging quality.

con·stant (kon′stənt) *adj.* 1. Long-continuing, or continually recurring; persistent. 2. Unchanging; invariable. 3. Steady in purpose, action, etc.; faithful. —*n.* 1. That which is permanent or invariable. 2. *Math.* A quantity that retains a fixed value. 3. In the sciences, any numerical expression of a characteristic that remains the same under specified conditions. [< COM- + L *stare* to stand] —**con′stant·ly** *adv.*

con·stel·late (kon′stə·lāt) *v.t.* & *v.i.* **·lat·ed, ·lat·ing** To group in constellations.

con·stel·la·tion (kon′stə·lā′shən) *n.* 1. *Astron.* Any of various groups of stars imagined to represent a being or thing, usu. mythological. 2. Any group of persons or things, esp. one regarded as brilliant. [< COM- + L *stella* star] —**con·stel·la·to·ry** (kən·stel′ə·tôr′ē) *adj.*

con·ster·na·tion (kon′stər·nā′shən) *n.* Sudden fear or amazement; panic. [< COM- + L *sternere* to cast down] —**con′ster·nate** *v.t.* **·nat·ed, ·nat·ing**

con·sti·pate (kon′stə·pāt) *v.t.* **·pat·ed, ·pat·ing** To cause constipation in. [< COM- + L *stipare* to press, crowd] —**con′sti·pat′ed** *adj.*

con·sti·pa·tion (kon′stə·pā′shən) *n.* A condition of the bowels characterized by suppressed or difficult evacuation.

con·stit·u·en·cy (kən·stich′ōō·ən·sē) *n.* *pl.* **·cies** 1. A body of voters who elect a representative; also, the district represented. 2. Any body of supporters.

con·stit·u·ent (kən·stich′ōō·ənt) *adj.* 1. Forming; constituting. 2. Entitled to elect a representative. 3. Having the power to frame or modify a constitution. —*n.* 1. A voter or client. 2. A necessary part or element.

con·sti·tute (kon′stə·tōōt, -tyōōt) *v.t.* **·tut·ed, ·tut·ing** 1. To be the substance or elements of; make up; compose. 2. To enact (a law, etc.). 3. To establish, as a school or an assembly, in legal form. 4. To empower; appoint. 5. To make by combining elements or parts; frame. [< COM- + L *statuere* to place, station] —**con′sti·tut′er** or **con′sti·tu′tor** *n.*

con·sti·tu·tion (kon′stə·tōō′shən, -tyōō′-) *n.* 1. The act of constituting. 2. The composition or make-up of a thing. 3. The fundamental laws and principles governing a state or association; also, a document recording such laws and principles. —**the Constitution** The Constitution of the U.S.

con·sti·tu·tion·al (kon′stə·tōō′shən·əl, -tyōō′-) *adj.* 1. Of or inherent in the constitution of a person or thing. 2. Consistent with or pertaining to the constitution of a state. 3. Controlled by a constitution. —*n.* Exercise taken for one's health. —**con′sti·tu′tion·al′i·ty** (-al′ə·tē) *n.* —**con′sti·tu′tion·al·ly** *adv.*

con·sti·tu·tive (kon′stə·tōō′tiv, -tyōō′-) *adj.* 1. Forming an essential element; basic. 2. Having power to enact or establish. —**con′sti·tu′tive·ly** *adv.*

con·strain (kən·strān′) *v.t.* 1. To compel;

coerce. 2. To confine, as by bonds. 3. To restrain. [< COM- + L *stringere* to bind] —**con·strain′a·ble** *adj.* —**con·strain′er** *n.*

con·strained (kən·strānd′) *adj.* Forced; unnatural: a *constrained* smile. —**con·strain′ed·ly** *adv.*

con·straint (kən·strānt′) *n.* 1. The use of force; coercion. 2. Confinement; restriction. 3. Unnaturalness of manner; awkwardness.

con·strict (kən·strikt′) *v.t.* To draw together by force; cause to shrink or contract; bind; cramp. [< COM- + L *stringere* to bind] —**con·stric′tion** *n.* —**con·stric′tive** *adj.*

con·stric·tor (kən·strik′tər) *n.* 1. That which constricts. 2. A serpent that coils about and crushes its prey.

con·struct (*v.* kən·strukt′; *n.* kon′strukt) *v.t.* 1. To form by combining materials or parts; build; erect. 2. To devise; form systematically. —*n.* Something constructed. [< COM- + L *struere* to build] —**con·struct′er** or **con·struc′tor** *n.*

con·struc·tion (kən·struk′shən) *n.* 1. The act of constructing; also, the business of building. 2. Something constructed; a structure or building. 3. Manner of construction. 4. Interpretation. 5. *Gram.* The arrangement of forms syntactically, as in sentences. —**con·struc′tion·al** *adj.*

con·struc·tive (kən·struk′tiv) *adj.* 1. Tending to build, improve, or advance. 2. Structural. 3. Assumed by interpretation; inferred. —**con·struc′tive·ly** *adv.* —**con·struc′tive·ness** *n.*

con·strue (kən·stro͞o′) *v.t.* **·strued, ·stru·ing** 1. To analyze the grammatical structure of; parse. 2. To interpret; also, to deduce by inference. 3. To translate orally. 4. *Gram.* To use syntactically: The noun "aerodynamics" is *construed* as singular. [< COM- + L *struere* to build up] —**con·stru′a·ble** *adj.* —**con·stru′er** *n.*

con·sul (kon′səl) *n.* 1. An officer residing in a foreign city to protect his country's commercial interests and the welfare of its citizens. 2. Either of the two chief magistrates ruling conjointly in the Roman republic. [< L] —**con′su·lar** (-sə·lər, -syə·lər) *adj.*

con·su·late (kon′sə·lit, -syə-) *n.* 1. The office or term of a consul. Also **con′sul·ship.** 2. The official place of business of a consul. 3. Government by consuls. [< L *consulatus* < *consul* consul]

consul general A consul of the highest rank.

con·sult (kən·sult′) *v.t.* 1. To ask the advice of. 2. To have regard for in deciding or acting; consider. —*v.i.* 3. To ask advice. 4. To take counsel: with *with.* 5. To give professional advice. [< L *consulere* to seek advice] —**con·sult′er** or **con·sul′tor** *n.*

con·sult·ant (kən·sul′tənt) *n.* 1. A person who gives expert advice. 2. One who consults.

con·sul·ta·tion (kon′səl·tā′shən) *n.* 1. The act of consulting. 2. A meeting of consultants. —**con·sult·a·tive** (kən·sul′tə·tiv), **con·sult·a·to·ry** (kən·sul′tə·tôr′ē) *adj.*

con·sume (kən·so͞om′) *v.* **·sumed, ·sum·ing** *v.t.* 1. To destroy, as by burning. 2. To eat, drink, or use up. 3. To engross. —*v.i.* 4. To be wasted or destroyed. [< COM- + L *sumere* to take up, use] —**con·sum′a·ble** *adj.*

con·sum·ed·ly (kən·so͞o′mid·lē) *adv.* Excessively.

con·sum·er (kən·so͞o′mər) *n.* 1. One who or that which consumes. 2. One who buys or uses an article or service.

con·sum·er·ism (kən·so͞o′mər·iz′əm) *n.* The policy or program of protecting the interests of the consumer.

con·sum·mate (*v.* kon′sə·māt; *adj.* kən·sum′it) *v.t.* **·mat·ed, ·mat·ing** 1. To complete or perfect. 2. To fulfill (a marriage) by sexual intercourse. —*adj.* Perfect; complete. [< COM- + L *summa* total] —**con·sum′mate·ly** *adv.* —**con′sum·ma′tion** *n.* —**con′sum·ma′tive** *adj.* —**con′sum·ma′tor** *n.*

con·sump·tion (kən·sump′shən) *n.* 1. The act or process of consuming. 2. The amount consumed. 3. *Econ.* The using up of goods and services. 4. Tuberculosis.

con·sump·tive (kən·sump′tiv) *adj.* 1. Of or pertaining to consumption. 2. Affected with tuberculosis. —*n.* A person affected with tuberculosis. —**con·sump′tive·ly** *adv.* —**con·sump′tive·ness** *n.*

con·tact (kon′takt) *n.* 1. A coming together or touching. 2. A potentially helpful acquaintance. 3. *Electr.* The touching or joining of conductors, permitting the flow of a current. —*v.t.* 1. To bring or place in contact; touch. 2. *Informal* To get in touch with (someone). —*v.i.* 3. To be or come in contact; touch: with *with.* [< COM- + L *tangere* to touch]

contact lens *Optics* A thin corrective lens worn directly on the eyeball.

con·ta·gion (kən·tā′jən) *n.* 1. The communication of disease by contact. 2. A communicable disease. 3. The communication of mental states, ideas, etc. [< COM- + L *tangere* to touch]

con·ta·gious (kən·tā′jəs) *adj.* 1. Transmissible by contact, as a disease. 2. Spreading contagion. 3. Exciting or tending to excite similar feelings, etc., in others; catching. —**con·ta′gious·ly** *adv.* —**con·ta′gious·ness** *n.*

con·tain (kən·tān′) *v.t.* 1. To hold or enclose. 2. To include or comprise. 3. To be capable of holding. 4. To keep within bounds; restrain. [< COM- + L *tenere* to hold] —**con·tain′a·ble** *adj.* —**con·tain′er** *n.* —**con·tain′ment** *n.*

con·tain·er·ize (kən·tā′nər·iz′) *v.t.* To place (cargo) in a container that can be transferred from one carrier to another intact. —**con·tain′er·i·za′tion** *n.*

con·tain·er·ship (kən·tā′nər·ship′) *n.* A ship designed to transport containerized cargo.

con·tam·i·nate (kən·tam′ə·nāt) *v.t.* **·nat·ed, ·nat·ing** To make impure by contact or admixture; taint; pollute. [< L *contamen* pollution] —**con·tam′i·na′tion** *n.* —**con·tam′i·na′tive** *adj.* —**con·tam′i·na′tor** *n.*

con·temn (kən·tem′) *v.t.* To despise; scorn. [< COM- + L *temnere* to slight, scorn] —**con·temn·er** (kən·tem′ər, -tem′nər) or **con·tem·nor** (kən·tem′nər) *n.*

con·tem·plate (kon′təm·plāt) *v.* **·plat·ed, ·plat·ing** *v.t.* 1. To look at attentively; gaze at. 2. To consider thoughtfully; meditate upon. 3. To intend or plan. —*v.i.* 4. To meditate; muse. [< COM- + L *templum* temple; with ref. to divination] —**con′tem·pla′tion** *n.* —**con·tem·pla·tive** (kən·tem′plə·tiv, kon′təm·plā′tiv) *adj.* & *n.* —**con·**

tem′pla·tive·ly *adv.* —**con·tem′pla·tive·ness** *n.* —**con′tem·pla′tor** *n.*

con·tem·po·ra·ne·ous (kən·tem′pə·rā′nē·əs) *adj.* Living or occurring at the same time. [< COM- + L *tempus, -oris* time] —**con·tem′po·ra·ne′i·ty** (-rə·nē′ə·tē), **con·tem′po·ra′ne·ous·ness** *n.* —**con·tem′po·ra′ne·ous·ly** *adv.*

con·tem·po·rar·y (kən·tem′pə·rer′ē) *adj.* 1. Contemporaneous. 2. Of the same age. 3. Current; modern. —*n. pl.* **·rar·ies** A contemporary person or thing. [< COM- + L *tempus, -oris* time]

con·tempt (kən·tempt′) *n.* 1. A feeling that something is vile and worthless; scorn. 2. The state of being despised. 3. *Law* Willful disrespect of authority. [< COM- + L *temnere* to scorn]

con·tempt·i·ble (kən·temp′tə·bəl) *adj.* Deserving of contempt; despicable. —**con·tempt′i·bil′i·ty, con·tempt′i·ble·ness** *n.* —**con·tempt′i·bly** *adv.*

con·temp·tu·ous (kən·temp′choo͞·əs) *adj.* Showing or feeling contempt; scornful. —**con·temp′tu·ous·ly** *adv.* —**con·temp′tu·ous·ness** *n.*

con·tend (kən·tend′) *v.i.* 1. To strive in competition; vie. 2. To argue; debate. 3. To struggle. —*v.t.* 4. To assert. [< COM- + L *tendere* to strive] —**con·tend′er** *n.*

con·tent[1] (kon′tent) *n.* 1. *Usu. pl.* That which a thing contains: the *contents* of a box. 2. Subject matter or meaning. 3. The quantity of a specified part. [See CONTAIN.]

con·tent[2] (kən·tent′) *adj.* Satisfied with what one has. —*n.* Ease of mind; satisfaction. —*v.t.* To satisfy. [See CONTAIN.] —**con·tent′ed** *adj.* —**con·tent′ed·ly** *adv.* —**con·tent′ed·ness** *n.* —**con·tent′ment** *n.*

con·ten·tion (kən·ten′shən) *n.* 1. Controversy; argument. 2. Competition; rivalry. 3. A point asserted in argument. —**in contention** Being contended over. [See CONTEND.]

con·ten·tious (kən·ten′shəs) *adj.* 1. Given to contention; quarrelsome. 2. Involving or characterized by contention. —**con·ten′tious·ly** *adv.* —**con·ten′tious·ness** *n.*

con·ter·mi·nous (kən·tûr′mə·nəs) *adj.* 1. Having a common boundary line. 2. Contained within the same limits. Also *coterminous*: also **con·ter′mi·nal.** [< COM- + L *terminus* limit] —**con·ter′mi·nous·ly** *adv.*

con·test (*n.* kon′test; *v.* kən·test′) *n.* 1. A struggling against one another; conflict. 2. A dispute. 3. A competition, game, etc. —*v.t.* 1. To fight to keep or win. 2. To call in question; challenge. —*v.i.* 3. To contend: with *with* or *against.* [< COM- + L *testari* to bear witness] —**con·test′a·ble** *adj.* —**con′tes·ta′tion** *n.* —**con·test′er** *n.*

con·test·ant (kən·tes′tənt) *n.* 1. One who enters a contest. 2. One who contests; a litigant.

con·text (kon′tekst) *n.* 1. Any phrase, sentence, or passage so closely connected to a word or words as to affect their meaning. 2. Something that surrounds and influences, as environment or circumstances. [< COM- + L *texere* to weave] —**con·tex·tu·al** (kən·teks′choo͞·əl) *adj.* —**con·tex′tu·al·ly** *adv.*

con·tig·u·ous (kən·tig′yoo͞·əs) *adj.* 1. Touching at the edge. 2. Close, but not touching. [See CONTACT.] —**con·ti·gu·i·ty** (kon′tə·gyoo͞′ə·tē), **con·tig′u·ous·ness** *n.* —**con·tig′u·ous·ly** *adv.*

con·ti·nence (kon′tə·nəns) *n.* Self-restraint, esp. sexual abstinence. Also **con′ti·nen·cy.**

con·ti·nent (kon′tə·nənt) *n.* One of the large land masses of the earth. —**the Continent** Europe, as distinct from the British Isles. —*adj.* 1. Self-restrained; moderate. 2. Abstinent, esp. sexually; chaste. [See CONTAIN.] —**con′ti·nent·ly** *adv.*

con·ti·nen·tal (kon′tə·nen′təl) *adj.* 1. Of, or of the proportions of, a continent. 2. *Often cap.* European. —*n. Usu. cap.* European.

Con·ti·nen·tal (kon′tə·nen′təl) *adj.* Pertaining to the thirteen American colonies during and just after the Revolution. —*n.* A regular soldier in the Continental army.

con·tin·gen·cy (kən·tin′jən·sē) *n. pl.* **·cies** 1. Uncertainty of occurrence; dependence upon chance or accident. 2. An unforeseen but possible occurrence. 3. Something incidental. Also **con·tin′gence.**

con·tin·gent (kən·tin′jənt) *adj.* 1. Liable to happen; possible. 2. Accidental; chance. 3. Dependent upon an uncertain event or condition: with *on* or *upon.* —*n.* 1. A contingency. 2. A proportionate quota of something to be furnished, as of troops. 3. A representative group in an assemblage. [< COM- + L *tangere* to touch] —**con·tin′gent·ly** *adv.*

con·tin·u·al (kən·tin′yoo͞·əl) *adj.* 1. Renewed frequently; often repeated. 2. Continuous (in time). [< L *continuus* hanging together] —**con·tin′u·al·ly** *adv.*

con·tin·u·ance (kən·tin′yoo͞·əns) *n.* 1. A continuing, as of an action, or a remaining, as in a place. 2. Continuation, as of a novel. 3. Duration. 4. *Law* Adjournment to a future time.

con·tin·u·a·tion (kən·tin′yoo͞·ā′shən) *n.* 1. The act of continuing or the state of being continued. 2. The extension or a carrying to a further point. 3. Addition; sequel.

con·tin·ue (kən·tin′yoo͞) *v.* **·tin·ued, ·tin·u·ing** *v.i.* 1. To go on in some action or condition; persist. 2. To resume after an interruption. 3. To remain in the same place, condition, or capacity. 4. To last; endure. —*v.t.* 5. To persevere in; carry forward. 6. To take up again after interruption. 7. To extend or prolong. 8. To cause to endure; also, to keep on, as in office. 9. *Law* To postpone. [< COM- + L *tenere* to hold] —**con·tin′u·a·ble** *adj.* —**con·tin′u·er** *n.*

con·ti·nu·i·ty (kon′tə·noo͞′ə·tē, -nyoo͞′-) *n. pl.* **·ties** 1. The state or quality of being continuous. 2. An unbroken series; succession. 3. A scenario; also, a script.

con·tin·u·ous (kən·tin′yoo͞·əs) *adj.* Uninterrupted. [< L *continuus*] —**con·tin′u·ous·ly** *adv.* —**con·tin′u·ous·ness** *n.*

con·tin·u·um (kən·tin′yoo͞·əm) *n. pl.* **·tin·u·a** (-tin′yoo͞·ə) Something continuous, with no discernible separate parts.

con·tort (kən·tôrt′) *v.t. & v.i.* To twist violently; wrench out of shape or place. [< COM- + L *torquere* to twist] —**con·tor′tion** *n.* —**con·tor′tive** *adj.*

con·tor·tion·ist (kən·tôr′shən·ist) *n.* A performer who twists into unnatural positions.

con·tour (kon′toor) *n.* The outline of a figure or body, or a line representing it. —*v.t.*

To draw the contour lines of. —*adj.* 1. *Agric.* Following the contours of land in such a way in plowing as to minimize erosion. 2. Shaped to fit the contour of something. [< COM- + L *tornare* to make round]

contour map A map having lines (**contour lines**) that connect the points of a surface having similar elevation.

contra- *prefix* Against; opposite. [< L *contra*]

con·tra·band (kon′trə·band) *n.* 1. Goods that, by law or treaty, may not be imported or exported. 2. Smuggled goods. [< Ital. < *contra* against + *bando* < LL *bannum* law] —**con′tra·band** *adj.* —**con′tra·ban′dist** *n.*

con·tra·bass (kon′trə·bās) *n. Music* The member of a family of instruments whose range is below the bass; esp., the double bass. Also **con′tra·bas′so** (-bä′sō). —*adj.* Pitched lower than the normal bass. [< Ital. *contrabasso*] —**con′tra·bass′ist** *n.*

con·tra·bas·soon (kon′trə·bə·sōōn′) *n.* The double bassoon.

con·tra·cep·tion (kon′trə·sep′shən) *n.* The deliberate prevention of fertilization of the human ovum. [< CONTRA- + (CON)CEPTION] —**con′tra·cep′tive** *n. & adj.*

con·tract (*v.* kən·trakt′; *for v. def. 2, also* kon′trakt; *n.* kon′trakt) *v.t.* 1. To cause to draw together; reduce in size. 2. To enter upon or settle by contract. 3. To acquire or become affected with, as a disease. 4. *Gram.* To shorten by contraction. —*v.i.* 5. To become smaller; shrink. 6. To make a contract. —*n.* 1. A formal agreement between two or more parties, esp. one that is legally binding. 2. The document containing such an agreement. 3. In bridge: **a** The highest and final bid of a hand, stating a denomination and the number of tricks to be made. **b** Contract bridge. [< COM- + L *trahere* to pull, draw] —**con·tract′i·bil′i·ty, con·tract′i·ble·ness** *n.* —**con·tract′i·ble** *adj.*

contract bridge A variety of the game of bridge in which tricks made by the declarer in excess of the contract do not count toward game. Compare AUCTION BRIDGE.

con·trac·tile (kən·trak′təl) *adj.* Able to contract or to induce contraction. —**con·trac·til·i·ty** (kon′trak·til′ə·tē) *n.*

con·trac·tion (kən·trak′shən) *n.* 1. The act of contracting, or the state of being contracted. 2. *Gram.* The shortening of a word or phrase by the omission of medial letters or sounds, as in *don't* for *do not*; also, the new word formed. —**con·trac′tive** *adj.*

con·trac·tor (kən·trak′tər; *for def. 1, also* kon′trak·tər) *n.* 1. One who agrees to supply materials or perform services for a sum, esp. for the construction of buildings. 2. That which contracts, as a muscle.

con·trac·tu·al (kən·trak′chōō·əl) *adj.* Connected with or implying a contract.

con·tra·dance (kon′trə·dans′, -däns′), **con·tra·danse** See CONTREDANSE.

con·tra·dict (kon′trə·dikt′) *v.t.* 1. To maintain or assert the opposite of (a statement). 2. To deny a statement of (a person). 3. To be contrary to or inconsistent with. —*v.i.* 4. To utter a contradiction. [< CONTRA- + L *dicere* to say, speak] —**con′·tra·dict′a·ble** *adj.* —**con′tra·dict′er** or **con′tra·dic′tor** *n.*

con·tra·dic·tion (kon′trə·dik′shən) *n.* 1. A denial. 2. Obvious inconsistency; discrepancy.

con·tra·dic·to·ry (kon′trə·dik′tər·ē) *adj.* 1. Inconsistent; contrary. 2. Given to contradicting. —**con′tra·dic′to·ri·ly** *adv.* —**con′tra·dic′to·ri·ness** *n.*

con·tra·dis·tinc·tion (kon′trə·dis·tingk′shən) *n.* Distinction by contrast. —**con′tra·dis·tinct′, con′tra·dis·tinc′tive** *adj.*

con·trail (kon′trāl) *n. Aeron.* A trail of condensed water vapor created by an airplane or rocket. [< CON(DENSATION) TRAIL]

con·tra·in·di·cate (kon′trə·in′də·kāt) *v.t. Med.* To indicate the danger of. —**con′tra·in′di·cant** *n.* —**con′tra·in′di·ca′tion** *n.*

con·tral·to (kən·tral′tō) *n. pl.* **·tos** or **·ti** (-tē) 1. The lowest female singing voice. 2. One having such a voice. [< Ital.] —**con·tral′to** *adj.*

con·trap·tion (kən·trap′shən) *n. Informal* A contrivance or gadget. [? < CONTRIVE]

con·tra·pun·tal (kon′trə·pun′təl) *adj. Music* Of, pertaining to, or according with the principles of counterpoint. [< Ital. *contrapunto* counterpoint] —**con′tra·pun′tal·ly** *adv.* —**con′tra·pun′tist, con′tra·pun′tal·ist** *n.*

con·tra·ri·e·ty (kon′trə·rī′ə·tē) *n. pl.* **·ties** 1. The quality or state of being contrary. 2. An inconsistency. [< L *contrarius* opposite]

con·trar·i·wise (kon′trer·ē·wīz′; *for def. 3, also* kən·trâr′ē·wīz′) *adv.* 1. On the contrary. 2. Conversely. 3. Contrarily; perversely.

con·trar·y (kon′trer·ē; *for adj. def. 4, also* kən·trâr′ē) *adj.* 1. Opposed in essence, purpose, etc. 2. Opposite as to position or direction. 3. Adverse; unfavorable. 4. Inclined to oppose and contradict; perverse. —*n. pl.* **·trar·ies** 1. One of two contrary things. 2. The opposite. —**on the contrary** As opposed to the previous statement; quite the opposite. —**to the contrary** To the opposite effect. —*adv.* In a contrary manner. [< L *contra* against] —**con′trar·i·ly** *adv.* —**con′trar·i·ness** *n.*

con·trast (*v.* kən·trast′; *n.* kon′trast) *v.t.* 1. To place in opposition so as to set off differences. 2. To set (one another) off by opposition. —*v.i.* 3. To reveal differences when set in opposition. —*n.* 1. The act of contrasting, or the state of being contrasted. 2. A dissimilarity revealed by contrasting. 3. One who or that which shows unlikeness to another. [< CONTRA- + L *stare* to stand] —**con·trast′able** *adj.*

con·tra·vene (kon′trə·vēn′) *v.t.* **·vened, ·ven·ing** 1. To come into conflict with; run counter to. 2. To oppose or contradict. [< CONTRA- + L *venire* to come] —**con′tra·ven′er** *n.* —**con·tra·ven·tion** (kon′trə·ven′·shən) *n.*

contre- *prefix* Counter; against; in opposition to. [< F < L *contra*. See CONTRA-.]

con·tre·danse (kôn·trə·däns′) *n.* A country-dance: also *contradance, contradanse*. Also **con·tre·dance** (kôn′trə·dans′, -däns′). [< F, alter. of COUNTRY-DANCE]

con·tre·temps (kôn·trə·tän′) *n. pl.* **·temps** (-tänz′, *Fr.* -tän′) An embarrassing or awkward occurrence. [< F]

con·trib·ute (kən·trib′yōōt) *v.* **·ut·ed, ·ut·ing**

v.t. 1. To give with others for a common purpose. 2. To furnish (an article, story, etc.) to a publication. —*v.i.* 3. To share in effecting a result. 4. To make a contribution. [< COM- + L *tribuere* to grant, allot] —**con·trib′ut·a·ble** *adj.* —**con·trib′u·tive** *adj.* —**con·trib′u·tive·ly** *adv.* —**con·trib′u·tor** *n.* —**con·trib′u·to′ry** *adj.* & *n.*

con·tri·bu·tion (kon′trə·byōō′shən) *n.* 1. The act of contributing. 2. Something contributed. 3. An article, story, etc., furnished to a periodical.

con·trite (kən·trīt′, kon′trīt) *adj.* Penitent; remorseful. [< COM- + L *terere* to rub] —**con·trite′ly** *adv.* —**con·trite′ness, con·tri·tion** (kən·trish′ən) *n.*

con·triv·ance (kən·trī′vəns) *n.* 1. The act or manner of contriving; also, the ability to do this. 2. A device. 3. An ingenious plan.

con·trive (kən·trīv′) *v.* **·trived, ·triv·ing** *v.t.* 1. To plan or plot. 2. To invent. 3. To manage, as by a scheme. —*v.i.* 4. To plan; plot. [< COM- + L *turbare* to stir up] —**con·triv′a·ble** *adj.* —**con·triv′er** *n.*

con·trol (kən·trōl′) *v.t.* **·trolled, ·trol·ling** 1. To exercise authority over. 2. To restrain; curb. 3. To regulate or verify, as an experiment. 4. To check, as an account, against a duplicate register. —*n.* 1. Power to regulate and direct. 2. A restraining influence. 3. A standard of comparison against which to check the results of an experiment. 4. *Often pl. Mech.* A device for operating an airplane, automobile, etc. [< CONTRA- + L *rotulus* list] —**con·trol′la·bil′i·ty, con·trol′la·ble·ness** *n.* —**con·trol′la·ble** *adj.*

con·trol·ler (kən·trō′lər) *n.* 1. One who or that which controls, regulates, or directs. 2. An officer appointed to examine and verify accounts: also spelled *comptroller.* —**con·trol′ler·ship** *n.*

control tower A structure at an airfield, from which aircraft traffic is directed.

con·tro·ver·sy (kon′trə·vûr′sē) *n. pl.* **·sies** 1. Dispute regarding a matter on which opinions differ. 2. A dispute; argument; debate. [< CONTRA- + L *versus*, pp. of *vertere* to turn] —**con′tro·ver′sial** (-shəl) *adj.*

con·tro·vert (kon′trə·vûrt) *v.t.* 1. To contradict; oppose. 2. To argue about. —**con′tro·vert′er** *n.* —**con′tro·vert′i·ble** *adj.* —**con′tro·vert′i·bly** *adv.*

con·tu·ma·cious (kon′tōō·mā′shəs, -tyōō-) *adj.* Stubbornly disobedient. —**con′tu·ma′cious·ly** *adv.* —**con′tu·ma′cious·ness** *n.*

con·tu·ma·cy (kon′tōō·mə·sē, -tyōō-) *n. pl.* **·cies** Contemptuous disobedience of authority; insubordination. [< L *contumax, -acis* stubborn]

con·tu·me·ly (kon′tōō·mə·lē, -tyōō-) *n. pl.* **·lies** 1. Insulting rudeness; insolence. 2. An insult. [< L *contumelia* reproach] —**con·tu·me·li·ous** (kon′tōō·mē′lē·əs, -tyōō-) *adj.* —**con′tu·me′li·ous·ly** *adv.* —**con′tu·me′li·ous·ness** *n.*

con·tu·sion (kən·tōō′zhən, -tyōō′-) *n.* A bruise. [< COM- + L *tundere* to beat] —**con·tuse′** (-tōōz′, -tyōōz′) *v.t.* **·tused, ·tus·ing**

co·nun·drum (kə·nun′drəm) *n.* 1. A riddle of which the answer depends on a pun. 2. Any problem or puzzle. [Origin unknown]

con·ur·ba·tion (kon′ər·bā′shən) *n.* A large metropolitan area; a cluster of suburbs, towns, and one or more cities. [< COM- + L *urbs* city + -ATION]

con·va·lesce (kon′və·les′) *v.i.* **·lesced, ·lesc·ing** To recover after illness. [< COM- + L *valere* to be strong] —**con′va·les′cence** *n.* —**con′va·les′cent** *adj.* & *n.*

con·vec·tion (kən·vek′shən) *n.* 1. *Physics* The transference of heat in a gas or liquid by currents resulting from unequal temperature and the consequent unequal densities. 2. The act of conveying. [< COM- + L *vehere* to carry] —**con·vect′** *v.t.* & *v.i.* —**con·vec′tion·al** *adj.* —**con·vec′tive** *adj.* —**con·vec′tive·ly** *adv.*

con·vene (kən·vēn′) *v.* **·vened, ·ven·ing** *v.t.* 1. To cause to assemble; convoke. 2. To summon to appear, as by judicial authority. —*v.i.* 3. To come together; assemble. [< COM- + L *venire* to come] —**con·ven′a·ble** *adj.* —**con·ven′er** *n.*

con·ven·ience (kən·vēn′yəns) *n.* 1. The quality of being convenient; suitability. 2. Personal comfort. 3. Anything that saves work. Also *Rare* **con·ven′ien·cy.** —**at one's convenience** At a time one prefers.

con·ven·ient (kən·vēn′yənt) *adj.* 1. Well suited to one's purpose or needs; conducive to ease or comfort. 2. Within easy reach; handy. [See CONVENE.] —**con·ven′ient·ly** *adv.*

con·vent (kon′vent, -vənt) *n.* 1. A religious community, esp. of nuns. 2. The building or buildings of such a community. [< L *conventus* meeting, assembly] —**con·ven·tu·al** (kən·ven′chōō·əl) *adj.*

con·ven·ti·cle (kən·ven′ti·kəl) *n.* 1. A meeting for religious worship, esp. a secret one. 2. The place of such a meeting. [See CONVENE.] —**con·ven′ti·cler** *n.*

con·ven·tion (kən·ven′shən) *n.* 1. A formal meeting of delegates or members, as for political or professional purposes. 2. The persons attending such a meeting. 3. A custom or usage. 4. Conventionality. 5. An agreement or contract.

con·ven·tion·al (kən·ven′shən·əl) *adj.* 1. Established by custom or general agreement. 2. Following approved or established practice. 3. Formal; stylized. —**con·ven′tion·al·ism** *n.* —**con·ven′tion·al·ist** *n.* —**con·ven′tion·al·ly** *adv.*

con·ven·tion·al·i·ty (kən·ven′shən·al′ə·tē) *n. pl.* **·ties** 1. Adherence to established forms, customs, or usages. 2. A conventional act, principle, custom, etc.

con·ven·tion·al·ize (kən·ven′shən·əl·īz′) *v.t.* **·ized, ·iz·ing** 1. To make conventional. 2. To represent in a conventional manner. —**con·ven′tion·al·i·za′tion** *n.*

con·verge (kən·vûrj′) *v.t.* & *v.i.* **·verged, ·verg·ing** To move or cause to move toward one point. [< COM- + L *vergere* to bend]

con·ver·gence (kən·ver′jəns) *n.* 1. The act, fact, or state of converging. 2. The degree or point of converging. Also **con·ver′gen·cy.**

con·vers·a·ble (kən·vûr′sə·bəl) *adj.* 1. Affable. 2. Fond of talking. —**con·vers′a·ble·ness** *n.* —**con·vers′a·bly** *adv.*

con·ver·sant (kən·vûr′sənt, kon′vər·sənt) *adj.* Well acquainted or familiar, as by study. [See CONVERSE[1].] —**con·ver′sance, con·ver′san·cy** *n.* —**con·ver′sant·ly** *adv.*

con·ver·sa·tion (kon′vər·sā′shən) *n.* 1. An informal talk with another or others. 2. Intimate association or social intercourse. [See CONVERSE[1].] —**con′ver·sa′tion·al** *adj.* —**con′ver·sa′tion·al·ly** *adv.*

con·ver·sa·tion·al·ist (kon′vər·sā′shən·əl·ist) *n.* One who enjoys or excels in conversation. Also **con′ver·sa′tion·ist.**

conversation piece Something, as a piece of furniture, that arouses comment.

con·verse[1] (*v.* kən·vûrs′; *n.* kon′vûrs) *v.i.* **·versed, ·vers·ing** To speak together informally. —*n.* 1. Conversation. 2. Social fellowship. [< OF *converser* to live with < COM- + L *vertere* to turn] —**con·vers′er** *n.*

con·verse[2] (*adj.* kən·vûrs′, kon′vûrs; *n.* kon′vûrs) *adj.* Turned about; reversed; contrary. —*n.* That which is in a converse relation; opposite. [< COM- + L *vertere* to turn] —**con·verse·ly** (kən·vûrs′lē, kon′·vûrs·lē) *adv.*

con·ver·sion (kən·vûr′zhən, -shən) *n.* 1. The act of converting, or the state of being converted. 2. A change in which one adopts new opinions, esp. a new religious faith. —**con·ver′sion·al, con·ver′sion·ar′y** *adj.*

con·vert (*v.* kən·vûrt′; *n.* kon′vûrt) *v.t.* 1. To change; transform. 2. To apply or adapt to a new purpose. 3. To change from one belief, religion, or course of action to another. 4. To exchange for an equivalent value, or for value of another form. 5. To assume possession of illegally. —*v.i.* 6. To become changed in character. —*n.* A person who has been converted, as from one religion to another. [See CONVERSE[2]]

con·vert·er (kən·vûr′tər) *n.* 1. One who or that which converts. 2. A Bessemer converter. Also **con·ver′tor.**

con·vert·i·ble (kən·vûr′tə·bəl) *adj.* Capable of being converted. —*n.* 1. A convertible thing. 2. An automobile with a top that folds back. —**con·vert′i·bil′i·ty, con·vert′i·ble·ness** *n.* —**con·vert′i·bly** *adv.*

con·vex (kon′veks; *for adj., also* kon·veks′) *adj.* Curving outward, as the exterior of a globe. —*n.* A convex surface or body. [< L *convexus* vaulted, curved] —**con·vex′i·ty** *n.* —**con·vex′ly** *adv.*

con·vey (kən·vā′) *v.t.* 1. To carry; transport. 2. To transmit. 3. To make known; impart. 4. To transfer ownership of. [< COM- + L *via* road, way] —**con·vey′a·ble** *adj.*

con·vey·ance (kən·vā′əns) *n.* 1. The act of conveying; communication; transportation. 2. Something used for conveying, as a truck or bus. 3. *Law* The transfer of title to property; also, the document whereby title is transferred.

con·vey·er (kən·vā′ər) *n.* 1. One who or that which conveys. 2. Any mechanical contrivance for conveying articles, as a series of rollers. Also (*esp. for def. 2*) **con·vey′or.**

con·vict (*v.* kən·vikt′; *n.* kon′vikt) *v.t.* To prove guilty; find guilty after a judicial trial. —*n.* 1. One serving a sentence in prison. 2. One found guilty of a crime. [See CONVINCE.]

con·vic·tion (kən·vik′shən) *n.* 1. The state of being convinced. 2. A firm belief. 3. The act of convincing. 4. A pronouncement of guilt. —**con·vic′tion·al, con·vic′tive** *adj.*

con·vince (kən·vins′) *v.t.* **·vinced, ·vinc·ing** To cause to believe something, as by proof; bring to belief: often with *of.* [< COM- + L *vincere* to conquer] —**con·vince′ment** *n.* —**con·vinc′er** *n.* —**con·vin′ci·ble** *adj.*

con·vinc·ing (kən·vin′sing) *adj.* 1. Tending to convince. 2. Credible or believable. —**con·vinc′ing·ly** *adv.* —**con·vinc′ing·ness** *n.*

con·viv·i·al (kən·viv′ē·əl) *adj.* 1. Fond of feasting and good fellowship; jovial. 2. Festive. [< L *convivium* a feast] —**con·viv′i·al·ist** *n.* —**con·viv·i·al·i·ty** (kən·viv′ē·al′ə·tē) *n.* —**con·viv′i·al·ly** *adv.*

con·vo·ca·tion (kon′və·kā′shən) *n.* 1. The act of convoking. 2. A meeting, esp. an ecclesiastical one. —**con′vo·ca′tion·al** *adj.* —**con′vo·ca′tor** *n.*

con·voke (kən·vōk′) *v.t.* **·voked, ·vok·ing** To call together; summon to meet. [< COM- + L *vocare* to call, summon] —**con·vok′er** *n.*

con·vo·lut·ed (kon′və·lōō′tid) *adj.* 1. Twisted or coiled up. 2. Complex; intricate. [< COM- + L *volvere* to spin, twist]

con·vo·lu·tion (kon′və·lōō′shən) *n.* 1. A coiled or convoluted state. 2. A fold or twist.

con·vol·vu·lus (kən·vol′vyə·ləs) *n.* A twining herb with large flowers, esp. the morning-glory. [< L, bindweed]

con·voy (kon′voi; *for v., also* kən·voi′) *n.* 1. A protecting escort, as for ships at sea. 2. A formation of ships, military vehicles, etc., traveling together. 3. The act of convoying, or the state of being convoyed. —*v.t.* To act as convoy to; escort. [< COM- + L *via* road]

con·vulse (kən·vuls′) *v.t.* **·vulsed, ·vuls·ing** 1. To agitate or shake. 2. To throw into convulsions or a fit, as of laughter. [< COM- + L *vellere* to pull]

con·vul·sion (kən·vul′shən) *n.* 1. *Often pl. Pathol.* A violent and involuntary contraction or series of contractions of the voluntary muscles. 2. Any violent fit or disturbance. —**con·vul′sion·ar′y** *adj. & n.* —**con·vul′sive** (-siv) *adj.* —**con·vul′sive·ly** *adv.* —**con·vul′sive·ness** *n.*

co·ny (kō′nē, kun′ē) *n. pl.* **·nies** 1. A rabbit. 2. Rabbit fur. Also spelled *coney.* [< L *cuniculus*]

coo (kōō) *v.* **cooed, coo·ing** *v.i.* 1. To utter the murmuring note of a dove. 2. To murmur amorously. —*v.t.* 3. To utter with a coo. —*n.* A murmuring sound, as of a dove. [Imit.] —**coo′er** *n.* —**coo′ing·ly** *adv.*

cook (kŏŏk) *v.t.* 1. To prepare (food) for eating by the action of heat. 2. To apply heat to. —*v.i.* 3. To act as a cook. 4. To undergo cooking. —**to cook up** *Informal* To invent; concoct. —*n.* One who prepares food for eating. [< L *coquus* a cook] —**cook′er** *n.*

cook·book (kŏŏk′bŏŏk′) *n.* A book containing recipes for cooking.

cook·er·y (kŏŏk′ər·ē) *n. pl.* **·er·ies** 1. The art or practice of cooking. 2. A place for cooking.

cook·out (kŏŏk′out′) *n. Informal* A meal cooked outdoors.

cook·y (kŏŏk′ē) *n. pl.* **cook·ies** A small, flat, dry cake, usu. sweetened. Also **cook′ey, cook′ie.** [< Du. *koekje,* dim. of *koek* cake]

cool (kōōl) *adj.* 1. Moderately cold; lacking warmth. 2. Producing a feeling of coolness: a *cool* suit. 3. Calm; composed. 4. Not cordial; chilling. 5. Suggesting coolness: said of colors. 6. *Informal* Not exaggerated; actual: a *cool* million. 7. *Slang* Excellent.

—*v.t.* & *v.i.* 1. To make or become less warm. 2. To make or become less angry, ardent, or zealous. —**to cool it** *Slang* To calm down. —*n.* 1. A cool time, thing, place, etc. 2. *Slang* Composure. [OE *cōl*] —**cool′ly** *adv.* —**cool′·ness** *n.*

cool·er (kōō′lər) *n.* 1. That which cools or keeps something cool. 2. *Slang* A jail.

cool-head·ed (kōōl′hed′id) *adj.* Calm.

coo·lie (kōō′lē) *n.* An unskilled Oriental laborer. Also **coo′ly**. [Prob. < *Kuli*, an aboriginal tribe of India]

coon (kōōn) *n.* A raccoon. [Short for RACCOON]

coop (kōōp) *n.* 1. An enclosure or box, as for fowl. 2. *Slang* A jail. —*v.t.* To put into a coop.

co-op (kō′op, kō·op′) *n.* *Informal* A cooperative.

coop·er (kōō′pər, kōōp′ər) *n.* One who makes and repairs casks, barrels, etc. —*v.t.* & *v.i.* To make or mend (casks, barrels, etc.). [ME *couper*]

coop·er·age (kōō′pər·ij, kōōp′ər-) *n.* 1. The work or workshop of a cooper. Also **coop′er·y**. 2. A cooper's fee.

co·op·er·ate (kō·op′ə·rāt) *v.i.* **·at·ed, ·at·ing** To work together for a common objective; act in combination. Also **co-op′er·ate, co·öp′er·ate.** [< co-[1] + L *operari* to work] —**co·op′er·a′tion** *n.* —**co·op′er·a′tor** *n.*

co·op·er·a·tive (kō·op′rə·tiv, -ə·rā′tiv) *adj.* 1. Cooperating or willing to cooperate. 2. Of or organized for mutual economic benefit. —*n.* A business enterprise, association, or property organized or owned by a group for its common economic benefit. Also **co-op′er·a·tive, co·öp′er·a·tive.** —**co·op′er·a·tive·ly** *adv.* —**co·op′er·a·tive·ness** *n.*

co-opt (kō·opt′) *v.t.* 1. To elect as a fellow member of a committee, etc. 2. To appoint. 3. To incorporate within the established order. [< co-[1] + L *optare* to choose] —**co′-op·ta′tion, co-op′tion** *n.* —**co′-op′ta·tive** *adj.*

co·or·di·nate (*v.* kō·ôr′də·nāt; *adj.* & *n.* kō·ôr′də·nit, -nāt) *adj.* 1. Of equal importance or rank. 2. Of or pertaining to coordinates or coordination. —*n.* 1. One who or that which is of the same order, rank, power, etc. 2. *Math.* Any of a set of magnitudes by means of which a position is determined with reference to fixed elements. —*v.* **·nat·ed, ·nat·ing** *v.t.* 1. To put in the same rank, class, or order. 2. To bring into harmonious relation or action; adjust. —*v.i.* 3. To become coordinate. 4. To act harmoniously. Also **co-or′di·nate.** [< co-[1] + L *ordinare* to set in order] —**co·or′di·nate·ly** *adv.* —**co·or′di·nate·ness** *n.* —**co·or′di·na′·tive** *adj.* —**co·or′di·na′tor** *n.*

co·or·di·na·tion (kō·ôr′də·nā′shən) *n.* 1. The act of coordinating, or the state of being coordinated. 2. Harmonious, integrated action or interaction. Also **co-or′di·na′tion.**

coot (kōōt) *n.* 1. A short-winged aquatic bird. 2. *Informal* A simpleton. [ME *cote*]

coot·ie (kōō′tē) *n.* *Slang* A louse. [? < Indonesian *kutu*, a parasitic insect]

cop (kop) *n.* *Informal* A policeman. —*v.t.* **copped, cop·ping** *Slang* 1. To steal. 2. To catch. —**to cop out** *Slang* To back down; renege. [? Var. of *cap* to catch, take]

cope[1] (kōp) *v.i.* **coped, cop·ing** To contend or strive, esp. successfully: often with *with*. [< OF *coup* blow]

cope[2] (kōp) *n.* 1. A semicircular mantle worn by priests. 2. A similar covering, as a canopy or arch. —*v.t.* **coped, cop·ing** To dress or cover in or as in a cope. [See CAP.]

Co·per·ni·can system (kô·pûr′nə·kən) *Astron.* The theory of the solar system of Copernicus that the earth and other planets revolve about the sun.

cope·stone (kōp′stōn) *n.* 1. One of the stones of a coping: also called *capstone*. 2. The final stroke; crown.

cop·i·er (kop′ē·ər) *n.* 1. An imitator. 2. One who or that which copies; esp., a machine that reproduces printed matter.

co·pi·lot (kō′pī′lət) *n.* An assistant pilot.

cop·ing (kō′ping) *n.* The top course of a wall, roof, etc. [< COPE[2].]

coping saw A narrow-bladed saw set in a recessed frame and used for cutting curved pieces from wood.

co·pi·ous (kō′pē·əs) *adj.* 1. Abundant; plentiful. 2. Diffuse; wordy. [< L *copia* abundance] —**co′pi·ous·ly** *adv.* —**co′pi·ous·ness** *n.*

cop-out (kop′out′) *n.* *Slang* 1. The act of copping out; an evasion. 2. One who cops out.

cop·per[1] (kop′ər) *n.* 1. A reddish, ductile, metallic element (symbol Cu) that is one of the best conductors of heat and electricity. 2. A coin of copper, or of bronze. 3. A lustrous, reddish brown. —*adj.* Of, or of the color of, copper. [< Gk. *Kypros* Cyprus, where copper abounded] —**cop′per·y** *adj.*

cop·per[2] (kop′ər) *n.* *Slang* A policeman. [< COP]

cop·per·as (kop′ər·əs) *n.* A green, crystalline ferrous sulfate, used in dyeing, inkmaking, etc. [< Med.L (*aqua*) *cuprosa* copper (water)]

cop·per·head (kop′ər·hed′) *n.* A venomous North American snake having reddish brown markings.

cop·per·plate (kop′ər·plāt′) *n.* 1. An engraved or etched plate of copper. 2. A print or engraving from such a plate.

cop·per·smith (kop′ər·smith′) *n.* One who works in copper.

copper sulfate A deep blue, crystalline substance used in electric batteries, etc.

cop·ra (kop′rə, kō′prə) *n.* The dried kernel of the coconut, yielding coconut oil. Also **cop·per·ah** (kop′ər·ə), **cop′rah, cop′pra.** [< Malayalam *koppara*]

copse (kops) *n.* A thicket of bushes or small trees. Also **cop·pice** (kop′is). [< OF *copeiz* < *coper* to cut]

Copt (kopt) *n.* 1. A native Egyptian of ancient Egyptian stock. 2. A member of the Coptic Church. [< Med.L *Coptus* < Coptic *gyptios* < Gk. *Aigyptios* Egyptian]

Cop·tic (kop′tik) *adj.* Of or pertaining to the Copts, or to their Hamitic language. —**Cop′·tic** *n.*

Coptic Church The principal Christian sect of Egypt.

cop·u·late (kop′yə·lāt) *v.i.* **·lat·ed, ·lat·ing** To unite in sexual intercourse. [< L *copula* a link] —**cop′u·la′tion** *n.* —**cop·u·la·to·ry** (kop′yə·lə·tôr′ē) *adj.*

cop·u·la·tive (kop′yə·lā′tiv, -lə·tiv) *adj.* 1. Serving to join. 2. *Gram.* Connecting words or clauses in a coordinate relationship. 3. Copulatory. —*n. Gram.* A copulative word. —**cop′u·la′tive·ly** *adv.*

cop·y (kop′ē) *n.*·*pl.* **cop·ies** 1. A reproduction or imitation; duplicate. 2. A single specimen of a book, print, etc. 3. Written matter, as in advertising. 4. Something to be set in type or otherwise reproduced. 5. In journalism, subject matter for an article, etc. —*v.* **cop·ied, cop·y·ing** *v.t.* 1. To make a copy of; reproduce. 2. To imitate. —*v.i.* 3. To make a copy. [< Med.L *copia* transcript] —**cop′y·ist** *n.*

cop·y·book (kop′ē·bo͝ok′) *n.* A book containing copies of good handwriting to be imitated. —*adj.* Ordinary; trite.

copy boy An errand boy in a newspaper office.

cop·y·cat (kop′ē·kat′) *n.* An imitator: a child's term.

copy desk A desk in a newspaper office where copy is edited.

cop·y·read·er (kop′ē·rē′dər) *n.* A person who edits work intended for publication.

cop·y·right (kop′ē·rīt) *n.* The exclusive statutory right of authors, composers, publishers, etc., to publish and dispose of their works for a specified period of time. —*v.t.* To secure copyright for. —*adj.* Of or protected by copyright. —**cop′y·right′a·ble** *adj.* —**cop′y·right′er** *n.*

cop·y·writ·er (kop′ē·rī′tər) *n.* One who writes copy for advertisements.

co·quet (kō·ket′) *v.i.* **·quet·ted, ·quet·ting** To flirt. [< F *coq* a cock] —**co·quet′ry** *n.*

co·quette (kō·ket′) *n.* A woman who tries to attract men; a flirt. —*v.t. & v.i.* **·quet·ted, ·quet·ting** To coquet. —**co·quet′tish** *adj.* —**co·quet′tish·ly** *adv.* —**co·quet′tish·ness** *n.*

cor- Var. of COM-.

cor·a·cle (kôr′ə·kəl, kor′-) *n.* A small boat of hide or oilcloth on a frame. [< Welsh *corwg* boat]

cor·al (kôr′əl, kor′-) *n.* 1. The calcareous skeleton secreted in or by the tissues of various marine coelenterates; also, a mass of these skeletons forming an island, reef, etc. 2. The reddish ovaries of the lobster. 3. A pinkish or yellowish red. [< Gk. *korallion* red coral] —**cor′al** *adj.*

coral reef A reef formed by coral skeletons.

coral snake A venomous snake of tropical America and the southern U.S.

cor·bel (kôr′bəl, -bel) *n. Archit.* A projection to support an overhanging weight. —*v.t.* **cor·beled** or **·belled, cor·bel·ing** or **·bel·ling** To support by or furnish with corbels. [< L *corvus* crow]

cord (kôrd) *n.* 1. A string or small rope; twine. 2. A flexible, insulated electric wire, usu. with a plug at one end. 3. A measure for wood, equaling 128 cubic feet. 4. A raised rib in fabric; also, fabric with such ribs, esp. corduroy. 5. *Anat.* A cordlike structure: spinal *cord.* —*v.t.* To bind or decorate with cord. [< Gk. *chordē* string of a musical instrument] —**cord′ed** *adj.* —**cord′er** *n.*

cord·age (kôr′dij) *n.* Ropes and cords collectively, esp. in a ship's rigging.

cor·date (kôr′dāt) *adj. Bot.* Heart-shaped, as a leaf. [< L *cordis* heart] —**cor′date·ly** *adv.*

cor·dial (kôr′jəl) *adj.* Warm and hearty; sincere. —*n.* A liqueur. [< L *cor, cordis* heart] —**cor·di·al·i·ty** (kôr′jē·al′ə·tē, -jal′-), **cor′dial·ness** *n.* —**cor′dial·ly** *adv.*

cor·dil·le·ra (kôr′dil·yâr′ə, kôr·dil′ər·ə) *n. Geog.* A system of mountain ranges roughly continuous. [< OSp. *cordilla,* dim. of *cuerda* rope] —**cor·dil·ler·an** (kôr′dil·yâr′an, kôr·dil′ər·ən) *adj.*

cord·ite (kôr′dīt) *n.* A smokeless explosive consisting of guncotton, nitroglycerin, and a mineral jelly. [< CORD; with ref. to its appearance]

cor·don (kôr′dən) *n.* 1. A line, as of men or ships, stationed so as to guard an area. 2. A ribbon or cord worn as an insignia of honor. [< F *corde* cord] —**cor′don** *adj. & v.*

cor·do·van (kôr′də·vən) *n.* A fine leather first made of goatskin or split horsehide. Also **cordovan leather.** [< OSp., of Córdoba] —**cor′do·van** *adj.*

cor·du·roy (kôr′də·roi) *n.* 1. A fabric, usu. of cotton, having a ribbed pile. 2. *pl.* Trousers made of corduroy. [? < *cord* (ribbed fabric) + obs. *duroy* coarse woolen cloth] —**cor′du·roy** *adj.*

corduroy road A road formed from logs laid transversely.

cord·wood (kôrd′wo͝od′) *n.* Firewood or pulpwood stacked or sold by the cord.

core (kôr) *n.* 1. The central or innermost part of a thing. 2. The fibrous central part of a fruit, containing the seeds. —*v.t.* **cored, cor·ing** To remove the core of. [ME; origin uncertain] —**core′less** *adj.* —**cor′er** *n.*

co·re·li·gion·ist (kō′ri·lij′ən·ist) *n.* An adherent of the same religion, church, or sect as another.

co·re·spon·dent (kō′ri·spon′dənt) *n. Law* In divorce action, one charged with having committed adultery with the defendant. —**co′re·spon′den·cy** *n.*

co·ri·an·der (kôr′ē·an′dər) *n.* 1. A plant of the parsley family. 2. The aromatic seeds of this plant. [< Gk. *koriannon*]

Co·rin·thi·an (kə·rin′thē·ən) *adj. Archit.* Of or pertaining to an order of Greek architecture characterized by capitals decorated with simulated acanthus leaves. —*n.* A native or inhabitant of the ancient Greek city of Corinth. —**Epistle to the Corinthians** Either of two letters addressed by Saint Paul to the Christians at Corinth, each forming a book of the New Testament. Also **Corinthians.**

cork (kôrk) *n.* 1. The light, porous, elastic outer bark of the cork oak. 2. Something made of cork, esp. a bottle stopper; also, a stopper made of other material. —*v.t.* To stop with a cork. [< L *quercus* oak]

cork·er (kôr′kər) *n.* 1. *Slang* Something outstanding or astonishing. 2. An argument, remark, etc., that puts an end to discussion.

cork oak An evergreen oak of southern Europe and North Africa, from whose bark cork is produced.

cork·screw (kôrk′skro͞o′) *n.* An instrument for drawing corks from bottles. —*v.t. & v.i.* To move or twist spirally. —*adj.* Shaped like a corkscrew; twisted; spiral.

cork·y (kôr′kē) *adj.* **cork·i·er, cork·i·est** 1. Of or resembling cork. 2. Tasting of cork, as wine. —**cork′i·ness** *n.*

corm (kôrm) *n. Bot.* A bulblike enlargement of the underground stem in certain plants, as the gladiolus. [< Gk. *kormos* tree trunk]

cor·mo·rant (kôr′mər·ənt) *n.* A large, voracious aquatic bird having a hooked bill and a pouch under the beak. [< L *corvus marinus* sea crow]

corn¹ (kôrn) *n.* 1. *U.S.* A tall, extensively cultivated cereal plant bearing seeds on a large ear or cob; also, the seeds of this plant: also called *Indian corn, maize.* 2. *Brit.* Any commonly cultivated cereal, esp. wheat. 3. *Slang* Anything trite or sentimental. —*v.t.* To preserve in salt or in brine. [OE]

corn² (kôrn) *n.* A horny thickening of the skin, commonly on a toe. [< L *cornu* horn]

corn borer The larva of a moth that feeds on the ears and stalks of corn.

corn·bread (kôrn′bred′) *n.* Bread made from cornmeal.

corn·cob (kôrn′kob′) *n.* The woody spike of corn on which the kernels grow.

cor·ne·a (kôr′nē·ə) *n.* *Anat.* The transparent part of the coat of the eyeball covering the iris and pupil. [< L *cornu* horn] —**cor′ne·al** *adj.*

corned (kôrnd) *adj.* Preserved in salt or brine, as beef.

cor·ner (kôr′nər) *n.* 1. The point formed by the meeting of two lines or surfaces. 2. The place where two streets meet. 3. A threatening or embarrassing position. 4. A region or place: in every *corner* of the land. 5. *Econ.* An operation in which a commodity or security is bought up by an individual or group of individuals with a view to forcing higher prices. —**to cut corners** To economize; reduce expenditures. —*v.t.* 1. To force into a corner; place in a dangerous or embarrassing position. 2. To form a corner in (a stock or commodity). —*v.i.* 3. To turn a corner. —*adj.* 1. Located on a corner. 2. Designed for a corner. [< L *cornu* horn] —**cor′nered** *adj.*

cor·ner·stone (kôr′nər·stōn′) *n.* 1. A stone uniting two walls at the corner of a building. 2. Such a stone ceremoniously laid into the foundation of an edifice. 3. Something of primary importance.

cor·net (kôr·net′) *n.* A small wind instrument of the trumpet class. [< L *cornu* horn] —**cor·net′tist** or **cor·net′ist** *n.*

corn·flow·er (kôrn′flou′ər) *n.* A hardy annual plant of the composite family, with heads of blue, purple, pink, or white flowers: also called *bachelor's-button, bluebonnet.*

cor·nice (kôr′nis) *n.* 1. *Archit.* **a** The horizontal molded projection at the top of a building. **b** The uppermost member of an entablature. 2. A molding around the walls of a room, close to the ceiling. [< Gk. *korōnis* wreath]

Cor·nish (kôr′nish) *adj.* Pertaining to Cornwall, England, or its people. —*n.* The former language of Cornwall, one of the Celtic languages. —**Cor′nish·man** (-mən) *n.*

corn·meal (kôrn′mēl′) *n.* Meal made from corn. Also **corn meal.**

corn pone *Southern U.S.* Bread made of cornmeal, water, and salt.

corn·stalk (kôrn′stôk′) *n.* A stalk of corn. Also **corn stalk.**

corn·starch (kôrn′stärch′) *n.* Starch made from corn.

corn syrup Syrup extracted from corn.

cor·nu·co·pi·a (kôr′nə·kō′pē·ə) *n.* A symbol of prosperity, represented as a curved horn overflowing with fruit, vegetables, grains, etc. Also called *horn of plenty.* [< L *cornu copiae* horn of plenty] —**cor′nu·co′pi·an** *adj.*

corn whiskey Whiskey distilled from corn.

corn·y (kôr′nē) *adj.* **corn·i·er, corn·i·est** *Slang* Trite, banal, or sentimental.

co·rol·la (kə·rol′ə) *n.* *Bot.* The petals of a flower. [< L, dim. of *corona* crown] —**cor·ol·la·ceous** (kôr′ə·lā′shəs, kor′-) *adj.* —**cor·ol·late** (kôr′ə·lāt, kor′-) *adj.*

cor·ol·lar·y (kôr′ə·ler′ē, kor′-) *n.* *pl.* **·lar·ies** 1. A proposition following so obviously from another that it requires little or no proof. 2. A natural consequence; result. [< L *corollarium* gift, orig. money paid for a garland]

co·ro·na (kə·rō′nə) *n.* *pl.* **·nas** or **·nae** (-nē) 1. A crownlike part, as the top of the head, the upper part of a tooth, etc. 2. *Astron.* **a** A luminous circle around one of the heavenly bodies, as when seen through mist. **b** The luminous envelope of ionized gases visible during a total eclipse of the sun. 3. *Bot.* A crownlike process at the top of the tube of a corolla, as in jonquils. 4. *Electr.* The luminous discharge from an electrical conductor under high voltage. [< L, crown] —**co·ro′nal** *adj.*

cor·o·nar·y (kôr′ə·ner′ē, kor′-) *adj.* 1. Coronal. 2. *Anat.* Designating either of two arteries rising from the aorta and supplying blood to the heart muscle. —*n.* Coronary thrombosis. [< L *corona* crown]

coronary thrombosis *Pathol.* The formation of a thrombus, or blood clot, in one of the coronary arteries.

cor·o·na·tion (kôr′ə·nā′shən, kor′-) *n.* The act or ceremony of crowning a monarch. [< L *corona* crown]

cor·o·ner (kôr′ə·nər, kor′-) *n.* A public officer whose principal duty is the investigation of deaths not clearly due to natural causes. [< AF *coruner* officer of the crown < L *corona* crown] —**cor′o·ner·ship′** *n.*

cor·o·net (kôr′ə·net, kor′-) *n.* 1. A small crown, denoting noble rank less than sovereign. 2. A headband ornamented with jewels, etc. [< L *corona* crown] —**cor′o·net′ed** *adj.*

cor·po·ra (kôr′pər·ə) Plural of CORPUS.

cor·po·ral¹ (kôr′pər·əl) *adj.* Belonging or related to the body. [< L *corpus, -oris* body] —**cor·po·ral·i·ty** (kôr′pə·ral′ə·tē) *n.* —**cor′po·ral·ly** *adv.*

cor·po·ral² (kôr′pər·əl, -prəl) *n.* *Mil.* A noncommissioned officer of the lowest rank. [< L *caput*]

corporal punishment Physical punishment given an offender, as flogging.

cor·po·rate (kôr′pər·it) *adj.* 1. Of or related to a corporation; incorporated. 2. Collective. [< L *corpus, -oris* body] —**cor′po·rate·ly** *adv.*

cor·po·ra·tion (kôr′pə·rā′shən) *n.* 1. A body of persons recognized by law as an individual entity, with rights, privileges, and liabilities distinct from those of its members. 2. Any group of persons acting as one body. —**cor·po·ra·tive** (kôr′pə·rā′tiv, -rə·tiv) *adj.* —**cor′po·ra′tor** *n.*

cor·po·re·al (kôr·pôr′ē·əl) *adj.* 1. Bodily; mortal. 2. Material; physical. —**cor·po·re·al·i·ty** (kôr·pôr′ē·al′ə·tē) *n.* —**cor·po′re·al·ly** *adv.* —**cor·po′re·al·ness** *n.*

cor·po·re·i·ty (kôr′pə·rē′ə·tē) *n.* Bodily or material existence. [< L *corpus, -oris* body]

corps (kôr, kōr) *n.* *pl.* **corps** (kôrz, kōrz) 1. *Mil.* a A tactical unit, intermediate between a division and an army. b A special department. 2. A number of persons acting together. [< L *corpus* body]

corps de bal·let (kôr′ də ba·lā′, *Fr.* bȧ·le′) The ballet dancers who perform as a group and have no solo parts. [< F]

corpse (kôrps) *n.* A dead body, usu. of a human being. [< L *corpus* body]

corps·man (kôr′mən, kōr′-) *n.* *pl.* **·men** (-mən) *Mil.* An enlisted man trained to give medical treatment.

cor·pu·lence (kôr′pyə·ləns) *n.* An excess of fat in the body; obesity. Also **cor′pu·len·cy.** [< L *corpus* body] **—cor′pu·lent** *adj.* **—cor′pu·lent·ly** *adv.*

cor·pus (kôr′pəs) *n.* *pl.* **·po·ra** (-pər·ə) 1. A human or animal body. 2. A collection of writings, usu. on one subject or by one author. 3. The main part of anything. [< L, body]

Cor·pus Chris·ti (kôr′pəs kris′tē, -tī) In the Roman Catholic Church, a festival honoring the Eucharist. [< L, body of Christ]

cor·pus·cle (kôr′pəs·əl, -pus′əl) *n.* 1. *Biol.* Any protoplasmic granule of distinct shape or function, esp. one of the particles forming part of the blood of vertebrates. 2. A minute particle of matter. Also **cor·pus·cule** (kôr·pus′kyo͞ol). [< L *corpus* body] **—cor·pus·cu·lar** (kôr·pus′kyə·lər) *adj.*

cor·pus de·lic·ti (kôr′pəs di·lik′tī) *Law* The essential fact of the commission of a crime, as, in a case of murder, the body of the victim. [< L, the body of the offense]

cor·ral (kə·ral′) *n.* An enclosed space or pen for livestock. **—***v.t.* **·ralled, ·ral·ling** To drive into and enclose in a corral. [< Sp.]

cor·rect (kə·rekt′) *v.t.* 1. To make free from error or mistake; set right. 2. To remedy or counteract. 3. To punish or rebuke so as to improve. 4. To adjust, as to a standard. **—***adj.* 1. True or exact; accurate. 2. Right or proper: *correct* behavior. [< COM- + L *regere* to make straight] **—cor·rect′a·ble** or **cor·rect′i·ble** *adj.* **—cor·rect′ly** *adv.* **—cor·rect′ness** *n.* **—cor·rec′tor** *n.*

cor·rec·tion (kə·rek′shən) *n.* 1. The act of correcting. 2. That which is offered or used as an improvement; an emendation. 3. Discipline or punishment. **—cor·rec′tion·al** *adj.* **—cor·rec′tive** *adj.* & *n.* **—cor·rec′tive·ly** *adv.*

cor·re·late (kôr′ə·lāt, kor′-) *v.* **·lat·ed, ·lat·ing** *v.t.* 1. To place or put in reciprocal relation. **—***v.i.* 2. To be mutually or reciprocally related. **—***adj.* Having a mutual or reciprocal relation. **—***n.* Either of two things mutually related. **—cor′re·la′tion** *n.* **—cor′re·la′tion·al** *adj.*

cor·rel·a·tive (kə·rel′ə·tiv) *adj.* 1. Having correlation or mutual relation. 2. Mutually related in grammatical or logical significance: *Either . . . or* are *correlative* conjunctions. **—***n.* 1. A correlate. 2. A correlative term. **—cor·rel′a·tive·ly** *adv.* **—cor·rel′a·tive·ness, cor·rel′a·tiv′i·ty** *n.*

cor·re·spond (kôr′ə·spond′, kor′-) *v.i.* 1. To conform in fitness or appropriateness; be in agreement; suit: often with *with* or *to.* 2. To be similar: with *to.* 3. To communicate by letters. [< COM- + L *respondere* to answer] **—cor′re·spond′ing** *adj.* **—cor′re·spond′ing·ly** *adv.*

cor·re·spon·dence (kôr′ə·spon′dəns, kor′-) *n.* 1. The act or state of corresponding; agreement; similarity. 2. Communication by letters; also, the letters written.

cor·re·spon·dent (kôr′ə·spon′dənt, kor′-) *n.* 1. One who communicates by letters. 2. A person employed to report news, etc., from a distant place. 3. A thing that corresponds; a correlative. **—***adj.* Corresponding; conforming.

cor·ri·dor (kôr′ə·dər, -dôr, kor′-) *n.* 1. A passageway, usu. having rooms opening upon it. 2. A strip of land across a foreign country, as one affording a landlocked nation access to the sea. [< L *currere* to run]

cor·ri·gen·dum (kôr′ə·jen′dəm, kor′-) *n.* *pl.* **·da** (-də) Something to be corrected, as a printer's error. [< L, gerundive of *corrigere* to correct]

cor·ri·gi·ble (kôr′ə·jə·bəl, kor′-) *adj.* Capable of being corrected or reformed. [See CORRECT.] **—cor′ri·gi·bil′i·ty** *n.* **—cor′ri·gi·bly** *adv.*

cor·rob·o·rate (kə·rob′ə·rāt) *v.t.* **·rat·ed, ·rat·ing** To strengthen or support, as conviction; confirm. [< COM- + L *robur, -oris* strength] **—cor·rob′o·ra′tion** *n.* **—cor·rob′o·ra′tive, cor·rob·o·ra·to·ry** (kə·rob′ə·rə·tôr′ē) *adj.* **—cor·rob′o·ra′tive·ly** *adv.* **—cor·rob′o·ra′tor** *n.*

cor·rode (kə·rōd′) *v.* **·rod·ed, ·rod·ing** *v.t.* 1. To eat away or destroy gradually, as by chemical action. 2. To destroy, consume, or impair. **—***v.i.* 3. To be eaten away. [< COM- + L *rodere* to gnaw] **—cor·rod′i·ble** or **cor·ro·si·ble** (kə·rō′sə·bəl) *adj.*

cor·ro·sion (kə·rō′zhən) *n.* 1. The act or process of corroding. 2. A product of this, as rust.

cor·ro·sive (kə·rō′siv) *adj.* Having the power of corroding. **—***n.* A corroding substance. **—cor·ro′sive·ly** *adv.* **—cor·ro′sive·ness** *n.*

cor·ru·gate (kôr′ə·gāt, -yə-, kor′-) *v.t.* & *v.i.* **·gat·ed, ·gat·ing** To contract into alternate ridges and furrows; wrinkle. [< COM- + L *rugare* to wrinkle] **—cor′ru·ga′tion** *n.*

cor·rupt (kə·rupt′) *adj.* 1. Open to bribery; dishonest. 2. Immoral or perverted. 3. Rotting; putrid. 4. Debased by changes or errors, as a text. [< COM- + L *rumpere* to break] **—cor·rupt′** *v.t.* & *v.i.* **—cor·rupt′er** or **cor·rup′tor** *n.* **—cor·rupt′ly** *adv.* **—cor·rupt′ness** *n.*

cor·rupt·i·ble (kə·rup′tə·bəl) *adj.* Capable of being corrupted. **—cor·rupt′i·bil′i·ty, cor·rupt′i·ble·ness** *n.* **—cor·rupt′i·bly** *adv.*

cor·rup·tion (kə·rup′shən) *n.* 1. The act of corrupting, or the state of being corrupt. 2. Dishonesty; also, bribery.

cor·sage (kôr·säzh′) *n.* A small bouquet of flowers for a woman to wear. [< OF *cors* body]

cor·sair (kôr′sâr) *n.* 1. A privateer. 2. A pirate. 3. A corsair's vessel. [< L *currere* to run]

corse·let (kôrs′lit) 1. Body armor; also, a breastplate. Also **cors′let.** 2. A light corset. [< MF, double dim. of OF *cors* body]

cor·set (kôr′sit) *n.* A close-fitting undergarment, usu. designed to support the

abdomen and back, worn chiefly by women. —*v.t.* To enclose or dress in a corset. [< OF, dim. of *cors* body]
cor·tege (kôr·tezh′, -tāsh′) *n.* 1. A train of attendants. 2. A ceremonial procession. Also **cor·tège′**. [< F < Ital. *corteggio* < *corte* court]
cor·tex (kôr′teks) *n. pl.* **·ti·ces** (-tə·sēz) 1. *Bot.* The bark of trees or the rind of fruits. 2. *Anat.* The external layer of various organs, esp. the gray matter covering the brain. [< L, bark] —**cor·ti·cal** (kôr′ti·kəl) *adj.* —**cor′ti·cal·ly** *adv.*
cor·ti·cate (kôr′ti·kit, -kāt) *adj.* Sheathed in bark or in a cortex. Also **cor′ti·cat′ed**. [< L *cortex* bark]
cor·ti·sone (kôr′tə·sōn, -zōn) *n.* A hormone of the adrenal gland, used in treating arthritis. [Short for *corticosterone*]
co·run·dum (kə·run′dəm) *n.* An aluminum oxide often used as an abrasive, varieties of which include the ruby and sapphire. [< Tamil *kurundam*]
cor·us·cate (kôr′ə·skāt, kor′-) *v.i.* **·cat·ed, ·cat·ing** To sparkle. [< L *coruscare* to glitter] —**cor′us·ca′tion** *n.*
cor·vette (kôr·vet′) *n.* A small, swift warship. Also **cor·vet′**. [< F < L *corbita* (*navis*) cargo (ship)]
cor·vine (kôr′vīn, -vin) *adj.* Of or pertaining to a crow. [< L *corvinus* < *corvus* crow]
cor·ymb (kôr′imb, -im, kor′-) *n. Bot.* A flat-topped or convex open flower cluster. [< Gk. *korymbos* flower cluster] —**co·rym·bose** (kə·rim′bōs), **co·rym·bous** (kə·rim′·bəs) *adj.* —**co·rym′bose·ly** *adv.*
co·ry·za (kə·rī′zə) *n.* A cold in the head. [< Gk. *koryza* catarrh]
co·se·cant (kō·sē′kənt, -kant) *n. Trig.* The secant of the complement of an acute angle. [< CO-[2] + SECANT]
co·sign (kō′sīn′) *v.t. & v.i.* To sign jointly, as a loan. —**co·sig·na·to·ry** (kō·sig′nə·tôr′ē) *adj. & n.* —**co′sign′er** *n.*
co·sine (kō′sīn) *n. Trig.* The sine of the complement of an acute angle. [< CO-[2] + SINE]
cos·met·ic (koz·met′ik) *adj.* Used or done to beautify or improve the appearance. Also **cos·met′i·cal**. —*n.* A cosmetic preparation. [< Gk. *kosmos* order] —**cos·met′i·cal·ly** *adv.*
cos·mic (koz′mik) *adj.* 1. Of or relating to the cosmos. 2. Limitless; vast. Also **cos′mi·cal**. —**cos′mi·cal·ly** *adv.*
cosmic rays *Physics* Streams of high-energy atomic particles from outer space.
cosmo- *combining form* The universe. Also, before vowels, **cosm-**. [< Gk. *kosmos*]
cos·mog·o·ny (koz·mog′ə·nē) *n. pl.* **·nies** 1. A theory of the origin of the universe. 2. The creation of the universe. [< Gk. *kosmos* the universe + *-gonia* < *-gon*, stem of *gignesthai* to be born] —**cos·mo·gon·ic** (koz′mə·gon′ik) or **·i·cal, cos·mog′o·nal** *adj.* —**cos·mog′o·nist** *n.*
cos·mog·ra·phy (koz·mog′rə·fē) *n. pl.* **·phies** The science that describes the universe. [< Gk. *kosmos* the universe + *graphein* to write] —**cos·mog′ra·pher, cos·mog′ra·phist** *n.* —**cos·mo·graph·ic** (koz′mə·graf′ik) or **·i·cal** *adj.*
cos·mol·o·gy (koz·mol′ə·jē) *n. pl.* **·gies** The general philosophy and science of the universe. [< Gk. *kosmos* the universe, + -LOGY] —**cos·mo·log·i·cal** (koz′mə·loj′i·kəl) or **cos′mo·log′ic** *adj.* —**cos·mol′o·gist** *n.*
cos·mo·naut (koz′mə·nôt) *n.* An astronaut, esp. from the U.S.S.R.
cos·mo·pol·i·tan (koz′mə·pol′ə·tən) *adj.* 1. Common to all the world. 2. At home in all parts of the world. —*n.* A cosmopolitan person. —**cos′mo·pol′i·tan·ism** *n.*
cos·mop·o·lite (koz·mop′ə·līt) *n.* 1. A cosmopolitan person. 2. A plant or animal widely distributed over the world. [< Gk. *kosmos* world + *politēs* citizen] —**cos·mop′o·lit·ism** *n.*
cos·mos (koz′məs, -mos) *n.* 1. The world or universe considered as an orderly system. 2. Any complete system. 3. *Bot.* A plant related to the dahlia. [< Gk. *kosmos* order, the universe]
Cos·sack (kos′ak, -ək) *n.* One of a people of the southern U.S.S.R., famous as cavalrymen. [< Russ. *kazak* < Turkic *quzzāq* freebooter]
cos·set (kos′it) *v.t.* To pamper; pet. —*n.* 1. A pet lamb. 2. Any pet. [? OE *cot-sǣta* dweller in a cottage]
cost (kôst) *v.* **cost** (*for def. 3, also* **cost·ed**), **cost·ing** *v.i.* 1. To be acquirable for a specified price. 2. To be gained by the expenditure of a specified thing, as health. —*v.t.* 3. To estimate the amount spent for the production of. —*n.* 1. The price paid for anything. 2. Loss; suffering. 3. *pl. Law* The expenses of a lawsuit in court. —**at all costs** (**or at any cost**) Regardless of cost; by any means. [ME *costen*]
cos·tal (kos′təl) *adj.* Of, on, or near a rib or the ribs.
cos·ter·mon·ger (kos′tər·mung′gər) *n. Brit.* A street hawker of vegetables, etc. Also **cos′ter**. [< *costard* a variety of apple + MONGER]
cos·tive (kos′tiv, kôs′-) *adj.* Constipated. [< OF *costivé*] —**cos′tive·ly** *adv.* —**cos′tive·ness** *n.*
cost·ly (kôst′lē, kost′-) *adj.* **·li·er, ·li·est** 1. Costing very much; expensive. 2. Sumptuous. —**cost′li·ness** *n.*
cos·tume (kos′tōōm, -tyōōm) *n.* 1. The mode of dress of a given region, time, or class. 2. Such dress as worn by actors, dancers, etc. 3. A set of garments for some occasion or activity: summer *costume*. —*v.t.* **·tumed, ·tum·ing** To furnish with costumes. [< L *consuetudo* custom]
cos·tum·er (kos·tōō′mər, -tyōō′-) *n.* One who makes or furnishes costumes. Also **cos·tum·ier** (kos·tōōm′yər, -tyōōm′-; *Fr.* kôs·tü·myā′).
cot[1] (kot) *n.* A light, narrow bed, commonly of canvas stretched on a folding frame. [< Hind. *khāt* < Skt. *khatvā*]
cot[2] (kot) *n.* A small house; cottage. [OE]
co·tan·gent (kō·tan′jənt) *n. Trig.* The tangent of the complement of an acute angle. —**co·tan·gen·tial** (kō′tan·jen′shəl) *adj.*
cote (kōt) *n.* 1. A small shelter for sheep or birds. 2. *Dial.* A hut. [OE. Akin to COT[2].]
co·te·rie (kō′tə·rē) *n.* An exclusive group of persons who share certain interests. [< F]
co·ter·mi·nous (kō·tûr′mə·nəs) See CONTERMINOUS.
co·til·lion (kō·til′yən, kə-) *n.* 1. An elaborate dance marked by frequent change of partners. 2. A formal ball at which young ladies are presented to society. [< F *cotillon* petticoat]

cot·tage (kot′ij) *n.* A small house, esp. in the country. [< COT²]

cottage cheese A soft, white cheese made of milk curds.

cot·tag·er (kot′ij·ər) *n.* 1. One who lives in a cottage. 2. *Brit.* A rural laborer.

cotter pin A key, wedge, pin, etc., that is split lengthwise so that the ends may be spread apart to hold parts of machinery together.

cot·ton (kot′n) *n.* 1. The soft, fibrous, white or yellowish material attached to the seeds of the cotton plant and widely used as a textile. 2. The plant itself. 3. Cotton cloth or thread; also, a garment of cotton cloth. —*adj.* Woven or composed of cotton cloth or thread. —**to cotton to** *Informal* To take a liking to. [< F *coton* < Arabic *qutun*] —**cot′ton·y** *adj.*

cotton belt The region of the southern U.S. in which cotton is the chief crop.

cotton flannel A soft, warm cotton fabric.

cotton gin A machine used to separate the seeds from the fiber of cotton.

cot·ton·mouth (kot′n·mouth′) *n.* The water moccasin, a snake.

cot·ton·seed (kot′n·sēd′) *n.* The seed of the cotton plant from which a pale yellow, viscid oil (**cottonseed oil**) is pressed.

cot·ton·tail (kot′n·tāl′) *n.* A small, light brown rabbit common in North America, having a short fluffy tail that is white on the underside.

cot·ton·wood (kot′n·wŏŏd′) *n.* An American poplar tree whose seeds discharge a cottony substance.

cotton wool 1. Raw cotton. 2. *Brit.* Absorbent cotton.

cot·y·le·don (kot′ə·lēd′n) *n. Bot.* A seed leaf, or one of a pair of the first leaves from a sprouting seed. [< Gk. *kotylē* a cavity] —**cot′y·le′do·nous, cot′y·le′do·nal** *adj.*

couch (kouch) *n.* A piece of furniture, usu. upholstered and having a back, on which several may sit; also, a bed. —*v.t.* & *v.i.* 1. To put into words. 2. To recline. [< OF *coucher* to put to bed]

couch·ant (kou′chənt) *adj.* Lying down. [See COUCH.]

couch grass A perennial grass having long rhizomes. [OE *cwice* + GRASS]

cou·gar (kōō′gər) *n.* The puma. [< Tupi]

cough (kôf, kof) *v.i.* 1. To expel air from the lungs in a noisy or spasmodic manner. —*v.t.* 2. To expel by a cough. —**to cough up** 1. To expel by coughing. 2. *Slang* To produce or hand over. —*n.* 1. A sudden, harsh expulsion of breath. 2. An illness in which there is frequent coughing. [ME *cozen, couzen*] —**cough′er** *n.*

cough drop A lozenge to relieve coughing.

could (kŏŏd) Past tense of CAN¹. [ME *coude*, OE *cuthe* knew how]

could·n't (kŏŏd′nt) Could not.

cou·lee (kōō′lē) *n.* A deep gulch cut by rainstorms or melting snow; gully. [< F *couler* to flow]

cou·lomb (kōō·lom′) *n.* A unit of electrical measurement: the amount conveyed by one ampere in one second. [after C. A. de *Coulomb*, 1736–1806, French physicist]

coul·ter (kōl′tər) See COLTER.

coun·cil (koun′səl) *n.* 1. An assembly convened for consultation or deliberation. 2. A body of persons elected or appointed to act in an administrative, legislative, or advisory capacity. [< COM- + L *calare* to call] —**coun′cil·man** (-mən) *n.* —**coun′cil·wom′an** (-wŏŏm′ən) *n.fem.*

coun·cil·or (koun′səl·ər, -slər) *n.* A member of a council. Also *Brit.* **coun′cil·lor.** —**coun′·cil·or·ship′** *n.*

coun·sel (koun′səl) *n.* 1. Mutual exchange of advice, opinions, etc.; consultation. 2. Advice; guidance. 3. A lawyer or lawyers. —*v.* **coun·seled** or **·selled, coun·sel·ing** or **·sel·ling** *v.t.* 1. To give advice to. 2. To recommend. —*v.i.* 3. To give or take counsel. [< L *consulere* to deliberate]

coun·sel·or (koun′səl·ər, -slər) *n.* 1. An adviser. 2. A lawyer. 3. A supervisor at a children's camp. Also **coun′sel·lor.**

count¹ (kount) *v.t.* 1. To list or call off one by one to ascertain the total. 2. To list numerals in sequence up to: to *count* ten. 3. To consider to be; judge. 4. To take note of. —*v.i.* 5. To list numbers in sequence. 6. To be of importance. 7. To be accounted or included. —**to count on (or upon)** To rely on. —*n.* 1. The act of counting. 2. The number arrived at by counting; total. 3. *Law* A charge, as in an indictment. [< COM- + L *putare* to reckon]

count² (kount) *n.* A nobleman of a rank corresponding to that of an earl in England. [< AF *counte* < L *comes* an associate]

count·down (kount′doun′) *n.* A reverse counting of time units, reaching zero at the instant when an operation, as a rocket launching, nuclear blast, etc., is to be executed.

coun·te·nance (koun′tə·nəns) *n.* 1. The face or features. 2. Facial expression. 3. An encouraging look; also, approval; support. —**out of countenance** Disconcerted. —*v.t.* **·nanced, ·nanc·ing** To approve; encourage. [< L *continere* to hang together] —**coun′te·nanc·er** *n.*

coun·ter¹ (koun′tər) *n.* 1. Something opposite or contrary. 2. A blow, thrust, or the like given in return for a similar attack. —*v.t.* 1. To return, as a blow. 2. To oppose; contradict. —*v.i.* 3. To give a blow while receiving or parrying one. 4. To make a countermove. —*adj.* Opposing; opposite; contrary. —*adv.* Contrary. [< L *contra* against]

coun·ter² (koun′tər) *n.* 1. A board, table, etc., for showing goods, transacting business, or serving refreshments. 2. A piece of wood, ivory, etc., used in a game, esp. to keep score. 3. An imitation coin. [< L *computare* to compute]

counter- *combining form*
1. Opposing; contrary; acting in response:

counteraccusation	**counterlegislation**
counteragent	**countermeasure**
counterargument	**counterplan**
counterbid	**counterplot**
counterblast	**counterproposal**
counterblow	**counterresolution**
countercharge	**countersuggestion**
counterdemand	**counterthreat**
counterforce	**counterthrust**
counterinfluence	**counterwork**

2. Done in reciprocation or exchange:

counterassurance	**counterplea**
counteroffer	**counterquestion**

3. Complementing; duplicating:

countercheck	**counterseal**
counterfugue	**counterstain**

4. Opposite in direction or position:

countercurrent	**counterpressure**
counterflow	**counterstep**
countermarch	**countertug**
counterposition	**counterturn**

[< L *contra-* against]

coun·ter·act (koun′tər·akt′) *v.t.* To act in opposition to; check. **—coun′ter·ac′tion** *n.* **—coun′ter·ac′tive** *adj.*

coun·ter·at·tack (*n.* koun′tər·ə·tak′; *v.* koun′tər·ə·tak′) *n.* An attack designed to offset another attack. **—***v.t.* & *v.i.* To make a counterattack against (an enemy fortification, etc.)

coun·ter·bal·ance (*v.* koun′tər·bal′əns; *n.* koun′tər·bal′əns) *v.t.* **·anced, ·anc·ing** To oppose with an equal weight or force; offset. **—***n.* 1. Any counterbalancing power. 2. A weight that balances another. 3. A state of equilibrium. Also *counterpoise.*

coun·ter·claim (*n.* koun′tər·klām′; *v.* koun′·tər·klām′) *n.* A claim that opposes another claim. **—***v.t.* & *v.i.* To make or plead (as) a counterclaim. **—coun′ter·claim′ant** *n.*

coun·ter·clock·wise (koun′tər·klok′wīz′) *adj.* & *adv.* Opposite to the direction taken by the hands of a clock.

coun·ter·cul·ture (koun′tər·kul′chər) *n.* A subculture, esp. among American youth in the 1960's, hostile to many prevailing social values.

coun·ter·es·pi·o·nage (koun′tər·es′pē·ə·näzh′, -nij) *n.* Measures intended to counteract enemy spying.

coun·ter·feit (koun′tər·fit) *v.t.* & *v.i.* 1. To make an imitation of (money, stamps, etc.), with the intent to defraud. 2. To copy; also, to feign: to *counterfeit* sorrow. **—***adj.* 1. Made to resemble some genuine thing; forged. 2. Pretended; feigned. **—***n.* An imitation, esp. one made for fraudulent purposes. [< CONTRA- + L *facere* to make] **—coun′ter·feit′er** *n.*

coun·ter·in·sur·gen·cy (koun′tər·in·sûr′·jən·sē) *n.* Measures to combat revolutionary guerrilla warfare.

coun·ter·in·tel·li·gence (koun′tər·in·tel′ə·jəns) *n.* Activities to oppose espionage, subversion, and sabotage.

coun·ter·man (koun′tər·mən) *n.* A man who serves food at a counter.

coun·ter·mand (*v.* koun′tər·mand′; *n.* koun′·tər·mand) *v.t.* 1. To revoke or reverse (an order). 2. To recall or order back. **—***n.* An order contrary to or revoking one previously issued. [< CONTRA- + L *mandare* to order]

coun·ter·move (*n.* koun′tər·mo͞ov′; *v.* koun′·tər·mo͞ov′) *n.* A move designed to offset another move. **—***v.t.* & *v.i.* **·moved, ·mov·ing** To move in opposition (to).

coun·ter·of·fen·sive (koun′tər·ə·fen′siv) *n.* A large-scale attack designed to stop an enemy offensive and to seize the initiative.

coun·ter·pane (koun′tər·pān′) *n.* A coverlet for a bed. [Alter. of ME *countrepoint*]

coun·ter·part (koun′tər·pärt′) *n.* Someone or something resembling another.

coun·ter·point (koun′tər·point′) *n. Music* The technique or practice of composing two or more melodic parts to be heard simultaneously. [< CONTRA- + L *punctus* point, note]

coun·ter·poise (*v.* koun′tər·poiz′; *n.* koun′tər·poiz′) *v.t.* **·poised, ·pois·ing** To balance by opposing with an equal weight, power, or force. **—***n.* Counterbalance. [< CONTRA- + L *pensare* to weigh]

coun·ter·pro·duc·tive (koun′tər·prə·duk′tiv) *adj.* Working against a desired end.

coun·ter·rev·o·lu·tion (koun′tər·rev′ə·lo͞o′·shən) *n.* 1. A revolution that counteracts a previous revolution. 2. Any movement or process to counteract revolution or revolutionaries. **—coun′ter·rev′o·lu′tion·ar′y** *adj.* & *n.* **—coun′ter·rev′o·lu′tion·ist** *n.*

coun·ter·sign (*v.* koun′tər·sīn′, koun′tər·sīn′; *n.* koun′tər·sīn′) *v.t.* To sign (a document already signed by another), as in authenticating. **—***n. Mil.* A password. [< OF *contresigner*] **—coun·ter·sig·na·ture** (koun′·tər·sig′nə·chər) *n.*

coun·ter·sink (*v.* koun′tər·singk′, koun′tər·singk′; *n.* koun′tər·singk′) *v.t.* **·sank** or **·sunk, ·sunk, ·sink·ing** 1. To cut the edges of (a hole) so that a screw, bolthead, etc., will lie flush with or below the surface. 2. To sink, as a bolt or screw, into such a depression. **—***n.* A countersunk hole.

coun·ter·ten·or (koun′tər·ten′ər) *n.* An adult male singing voice higher than the tenor. [< MF *contreteneur*]

coun·ter·vail (koun′tər·vāl′, koun′tər·vāl) *v.t.* To counteract or offset. [< L *contra valere* to avail against]

coun·ter·weight (koun′tər·wāt′) *n.* Any counterbalancing weight, force, or influence. **—coun′ter·weight′ed** *adj.*

counter word A word widely used without regard to its exact meaning, as *nice.*

count·ess (koun′tis) *n.* 1. The wife or widow of a count, or, in Great Britain, of an earl. 2. A woman equal in rank to a count or earl. [See COUNT[2].]

count·ing house (koun′ting) A building or office used esp. for bookkeeping. Also **count′ing·house′.**

count·less (kount′lis) *adj.* That cannot be counted; innumerable.

coun·tri·fied (kun′tri·fīd) *adj.* Having the appearance, manner, etc., associated with the country or with country people; provincial; rustic. Also **coun′try·fied.**

coun·try (kun′trē) *n. pl.* **·tries** 1. A land under a particular government, inhabited by a certain people, or within definite geographical limits. 2. The district outside cities and towns; rural areas. 3. A region of a specified character: sheep *country.* 4. The people of a nation. **—***adj.* Rustic. [< L *contra* on the opposite side]

country club A club in the country or suburbs, with facilities for outdoor sports.

coun·try-dance (kun′trē·dans′) *n.* A folk dance of English origin, in which the partners are in opposite lines.

coun·try·man (kun′trē·mən) *n. pl.* **·men** (-mən) 1. A man of the same country as another. 2. A rustic.

country music American popular music sung in a style associated with rural areas and usu. accompanied by plucked instruments.

coun·try·seat (kun′trē·sēt′) *n.* A country estate.

coun·try·side (kun′trē·sīd′) *n.* A rural district.
coun·ty (koun′tē) *n. pl.* **·ties** An administrative division of a state or kingdom. [< L *comes* count, companion]
county seat The seat of government of a county.
coup (ko͞o) *n. pl.* **coups** (ko͞oz, *Fr.* ko͞o) A sudden, telling blow; a masterstroke. [< F < Gk. *kolaphos* a blow with the fist]
coup de grâce (ko͞o′ də gräs′) *French* The deathblow, as delivered to a wounded enemy.
coup d'é·tat (ko͞o′dā·tá′) *French* A sudden seizure of government.
coupe (ko͞op, ko͞o·pā′) *n.* A small, closed automobile with two doors: also *coupé.* [< COUPÉ]
cou·pé (ko͞o·pā′) *n.* **1.** A low, four-wheeled, closed carriage for two, with an outside seat for the driver. **2.** A coupe. [< F, pp. of *couper* to cut]
coup·le (kup′əl) *n.* **1.** Two of a kind; a pair. **2.** Two persons of opposite sex, wedded or otherwise paired. **3.** *Informal* Approximately two: a *couple* of hours. **4.** Something joining two things together. —*v.t. & v.i.* **·led, ·ling** To join, as one thing or person to another; link; connect; pair. [< L *copula* bond]
coup·ler (kup′lər) *n.* One who or that which couples; esp., a contrivance for linking railroad cars.
coup·let (kup′lit) *n.* **1.** Two successive lines of verse, usu. rhymed. **2.** A pair.
coup·ling (kup′ling) *n.* **1.** The act of one who or that which couples. **2.** A linking device, as for joining railroad cars.
cou·pon (ko͞o′pon, kyo͞o′-) *n.* **1.** One of a number of dated certificates attached to a bond, representing interest accrued. **2.** A section of a ticket, advertisement, etc., entitling the holder to something. [< F *couper* to cut]
cour·age (kûr′ij) *n.* That quality of spirit enabling one to face danger. [< OF *corage* < L *cor* heart]
cou·ra·geous (kə·rā′jəs) *adj.* Possessing or characterized by courage; brave; daring. —**cou·ra′geous·ly** *adv.* —**cou·ra′geous·ness** *n.*
cou·ri·er (ko͝or′ē·ər, kûr′-) *n.* **1.** A messenger, esp. one on urgent official business. **2.** One who escorts tourists. [< L *currere* to run]
course (kôrs) *n.* **1.** Onward movement in a certain direction; progress. **2.** The path or ground passed over. **3.** Direction. **4.** Passage or duration in time. **5.** Natural or usual development: to run its *course.* **6.** A series of actions, events, etc. **7.** A prescribed curriculum of studies; also, any unit of study in a curriculum: a history *course.* **8.** A portion of a meal served at one time. **9.** A horizontal row or layer, as of stones in a wall. —**in due course** In the proper sequence; at the right time. —**of course 1.** As might be expected; naturally. **2.** Certainly. —*v.* **coursed, cours·ing** *v.t.* **1.** To run through or over. **2.** To pursue. **3.** To cause (hounds) to chase game. —*v.i.* **4.** To race. **5.** To hunt with hounds. [< L *currere* to run]
cours·er (kôr′sər) *n. Poetic* A fleet, spirited horse. [< L *currere* to run]
court (kôrt) *n.* **1.** A courtyard. **2.** A short street, esp. a cul de sac. **3.** The residence of a sovereign. **4.** A sovereign together with his council and retinue. **5.** A formal assembly held by a sovereign. **6.** A place where justice is administered; also, the judge or judges. **7.** The regular session of a judicial tribunal. **8.** A level space laid out for a game, as tennis. **9.** Flattering attention. **10.** Wooing; courtship. —*v.t.* **1.** To try to gain the favor of. **2.** To woo. **3.** To seek or invite: to *court* danger. —*v.i.* **4.** To engage in courtship. —*adj.* Of or pertaining to a court. [< L *cohors, cohortis* yard]
cour·te·ous (kûr′tē·əs) *adj.* Showing courtesy; polite. [< OF *corteis* befitting a court] —**cour′te·ous·ly** *adv.* —**cour′te·ous·ness** *n.*
cour·te·san (kôr′tə·zən) *n.* A prostitute. [< Ital. *cortigiana* court lady]
cour·te·sy (kûr′tə·sē) *n. pl.* **·sies 1.** Politeness; good manners. **2.** A courteous favor or act. [< OF *corteis* courteous]
court·house (kôrt′hous′) *n.* A public building occupied by judicial courts or administrative offices.
court·i·er (kôr′tē·ər, -tyər) *n.* A member of a sovereign's court.
court·ly (kôrt′lē) *adj.* **·li·er, ·li·est** Pertaining to or befitting a court; elegant. —**court′li·ness** *n.* —**court′ly** *adv.*
court-mar·tial (kôrt′mär′shəl) *n. pl.* **courts-mar·tial 1.** A military court. **2.** A trial by such a court. —*v.t.* **-mar·tialed** or **·tialled, -mar·tial·ing** or **·tial·ling** To try by court-martial.
court plaster Adhesive tape.
court·room (kôrt′ro͞om′, -ro͝om′) *n.* A room in which judicial proceedings are held.
court·ship (kôrt′ship) *n.* The act or period of courting and wooing.
court·yard (kôrt′yärd′) *n.* An enclosed yard adjoining a building or surrounded by buildings or walls; a court.
cous·in (kuz′ən) *n.* **1.** One collaterally related by descent from a common ancestor, but not a brother or sister. Children of brothers and sisters are **first cousins** to each other. **2.** One of a kindred group or nation. [< L *consobrinus* child of a maternal aunt] —**cous′in·hood, cous′in·ship** *n.* —**cous′in·ly** *adj. & adv.*
cou·tu·rier (ko͞o·tü·ryā′) *n.* A male dress designer. [< F] —**cou·tu·rière** (ko͞o·tü·ryâr′) *n.fem.*
co·va·lence (kō′vā′ləns) *n. Chem.* A bond formed by the sharing of electrons between the atoms of a compound. —**co′va′lent** *adj.*
cove (kōv) *n.* **1.** A small bay or baylike recess in a shoreline. **2.** *Archit.* A concave part, as a vault or molding. —*v.t.* **coved, cov·ing** To curve over or inward. [OE *cofa* cave]
cov·en (kuv′ən, kōv′-) *n.* A group of witches, esp. a congregation of 13. [< L *convenius* assembly]
cov·e·nant (kuv′ə·nənt) *n.* An agreement; a formal compact. [< L *convenire* to meet together, agree] —**cov′e·nant** *v.t. & v.i.*
cov·er (kuv′ər) *v.t.* **1.** To place something over or upon, as to protect or conceal. **2.** To provide or overlay with a cover or covering. **3.** To hide; conceal: often with *up.* **4.** To treat of; include. **5.** To be sufficient to pay, defray, or offset. **6.** To protect or guarantee (life, property, etc.) with insurance. **7.** To travel over. **8.** To aim directly at, as with

a firearm. **9.** *Mil.* To provide protective fire for (another person, unit, etc.). **10.** In journalism, to report the details of. **11.** In sports, to guard (an opponent); also, to protect (an area or position). —*v.i.* **12.** To spread over, as a liquid does. **13.** To protect, as with a false story: with *for.* **14.** To act as a substitute: with *for.* —*n.* **1.** That which covers or is laid over something else. **2.** Shelter; protection; concealment. **3.** A pretense or pretext. **4.** The table articles, as plate, silverware, etc., for one person. —**to break cover** To come from hiding. —**to cover up** **1.** To cover or overlay with something. **2.** To conceal, as a crime. —**under cover** **1.** Protected. **2.** Secret or secretly. [< co-[1] + L *operire* to hide] —**cov′er·er** *n.*

cov·er·age (kuv′ər·ij) *n.* The extent to which anything is covered, included, or reported.

cov·er·alls (kuv′ər·ôlz) *n.pl.* A one-piece work garment. Also **cov′er·all.**

cover charge A fixed charge added to the bill at cabarets, hotels, etc.

covered wagon A large wagon covered with canvas stretched over hoops, used esp. by American pioneers.

cov·er·ing (kuv′ər·ing) *n.* That which covers, protects, etc.

cov·er·let (kuv′ər·lit) *n.* A bedspread. Also **cov′er·lid.**

cov·ert (kuv′ərt, kō′vərt) *adj.* Concealed; secret; sheltered. —*n.* **1.** A covering. **2.** A shelter or hiding place, esp. for game. **3.** *pl. Ornithol.* Small feathers overlying the bases of tail and wing quills. [See COVER.] —**cov′ert·ly** *adv.*

co·vert cloth (kō′vərt, kuv′ərt) A twilled, chiefly woolen cloth of speckled appearance.

cov·er-up (kuv′ər·up′) *n.* The act of concealing a crime, scandal, etc.; also, a means of doing this.

cov·et (kuv′it) *v.t. & v.i.* To long for (esp. something belonging to another). [< L *cupere* to desire] —**cov′et·er** *n.*

cov·et·ous (kuv′ə·təs) *adj.* Excessively desirous (of something); greedy. [< OF *coveitus*] —**cov′et·ous·ly** *adv.* —**cov′et·ous·ness** *n.*

cov·ey (kuv′ē) *n. pl.* **·eys** **1.** A flock of quails or partridges. **2.** A company; set. [< L *cubare* to lie down]

cow[1] (kou) *n. pl.* **cows** (*Archaic* **kine**) **1.** The mature female of a bovine animal, esp. of the domesticated species. **2.** The mature female of some other animals, as of the whale, elephant, etc. [OE *cū*]

cow[2] (kou) *v.t.* To overawe; intimidate; daunt. [< ON *kūga* to tyrannize over]

cow·ard (kou′ərd) *n.* One who yields unworthily to fear. [< L *cauda* tail]

cow·ard·ice (kou′ər·dis) *n.* Lack of courage.

cow·ard·ly (kou′ərd·lē) *adj.* **1.** Lacking courage. **2.** Befitting a coward. —**cow′ard·li·ness** *n.* —**cow′ard·ly** *adv.*

cow·bell (kou′bel) *n.* A bell hung around a cow's neck to indicate her whereabouts.

cow·ber·ry (kou′ber′ē, -bər·ē) *n. pl.* **·ries** A trailing evergreen shrub of the heath family, bearing red berries.

cow·bird (kou′bûrd′) *n.* An American blackbird, often found with cattle. Also **cow blackbird.**

cow·boy (kou′boi′) *n.* A ranch worker who herds and tends cattle. —**cow′girl′** (-gûrl′) *n.fem.*

cow·catch·er (kou′kach′ər) *n.* An iron frame on the front of a locomotive or streetcar for clearing the track.

cow·er (kou′ər) *v.i.* To crouch, as in fear; tremble; quail. [ME *couren,* prob. < Scand.]

cow·hand (kou′hand′) *n.* A cowboy.

cow·hide (kou′hīd′) *n.* **1.** The skin of a cow, esp. after tanning. **2.** A heavy leather whip. —*v.t.* **·hid·ed, ·hid·ing** To whip as with a cowhide.

cowl (koul) *n.* **1.** A monk's hood; also, a hooded cloak. **2.** A hood-shaped top for a chimney, to increase the draft. **3.** *Aeron.* A cowling. **4.** The part of an automobile body to which the windshield, the instrument board, and the rear end of the hood are attached. [< L *cucullus* hood]

cowled (kould) *adj.* Wearing a cowl.

cow·lick (kou′lik′) *n.* A tuft of hair turned up.

cowl·ing (kou′ling) *n. Aeron.* The covering over or around the engine or any component of an aircraft. [< COWL]

cow·pea (kou′pē′) *n.* **1.** A twining herb of the bean family. **2.** The edible pea of this herb: also called *black-eyed pea.*

cow pony A small horse used in herding cattle.

cow·pox (kou′poks′) *n. Vet.* An acute contagious disease of cows, forming pustules containing a virus that is used in making smallpox vaccine.

cow·punch·er (kou′pun′chər) *n. Informal* A cowboy. Also **cow′poke′.**

cow·ry (kou′rē) *n. pl.* **·ries** A glossy seashell of warm seas. Also **cow′rie.** [< Hind. *kaurī*]

cow·slip (kou′slip′) *n.* **1.** An English wildflower of the primrose family. **2.** The marsh marigold of the U.S. [OE *cū* cow + *slyppe* dung]

cox (koks) *n. Informal* Coxswain. —*v.t. & v.i.* To act as coxswain to (a boat).

cox·comb (koks′kōm′) *n.* A pretentious and conceited young man. [Var. of *cockscomb*]

cox·swain (kok′sən, kok′swān′) *n.* One who steers or has charge of a small boat or a racing shell. [< COCK (BOAT) + SWAIN]

coy (koi) *adj.* **1.** Shy. **2.** Feigning shyness to attract attention. [< L *quietus* rest] —**coy′·ish** *adj.* —**coy′ly** *adv.* —**coy′ness** *n.*

coy·o·te (kī·ō′tē, kī′ōt) *n.* A small wolf of western North America. [< Nahuatl]

coy·pu (koi′po͞o) *n. pl.* **·pus** or **·pu** A South American rodent that yields a beaverlike fur known as nutria. [< native name]

coz (kuz) *n. Informal* A cousin.

coz·en (kuz′ən) *v.t. & v.i.* To cheat. [< F *cousiner* to deceive by claiming kinship. See COUSIN.] —**coz′en·age** *n.*

co·zy (kō′zē) *adj.* **·zi·er, ·zi·est** Snugly comfortable. —*n.* A padded cover for a teapot to keep it hot: also called *tea cozy.* [< dial. E *cosie*] —**co′zi·ly** *adv.* —**co′zi·ness** *n.*

crab[1] (krab) *n.* **1.** A crustacean having four pairs of legs, a pair of pincers, and a flat shell. **2.** The hermit crab. **3.** The horseshoe crab. **4.** The crab louse. —*v.t.* **crabbed, crab·bing** To take or hunt crabs. [OE *crabba*]

crab[2] (krab) *n.* An ill-tempered person. —*v.i.* **crabbed, crab·bing** *Informal* To complain. [? < Scand.]

crab apple **1.** A kind of small, sour apple. **2.** A tree bearing crab apples.

crab·bed (krab′id) *adj.* 1. Sour-tempered; surly. 2. Irregular in form; cramped. [< CRAB[2]] **—crab′bed·ly** *adv.* **—crab′bed·ness** *n.*
crab·by (krab′ē) *adj.* **·bi·er, ·bi·est** Ill-tempered; peevish. **—crab′bi·ness** *n.*
crab grass A low-growing grass, a lawn pest.
crab louse A louse that infests body hair, esp. pubic hair.
crack (krak) *v.i.* 1. To break without separation of parts; also, to break apart or to pieces. 2. To make a sharp snapping sound, as in breaking. 3. To change tone abruptly to a higher register: said of the voice. **—***v.t.* 4. To break partially or completely. 5. To cause to give forth a short, sharp sound. 6. *Informal* To break into; open. 7. *Informal* To find the solution of. 8. *Slang* To tell (a joke). **—to crack down** *Informal* To take severe repressive measures: with *on.* **—to crack up** *Informal* 1. To crash or be in a crash. 2. To have a breakdown. 3. To become convulsed with laughter. **—to crack wise** *Slang* To wisecrack. **—***n.* 1. A partial break, in which parts are not completely separated; a fissure. 2. A narrow space. 3. A sudden sharp sound. 4. *Informal* A resounding blow. 5. *Informal* A try. 6. *Informal* A witty or sarcastic remark. **—***adj. Informal* Expert: a *crack* shot. [OE *cracian*]
cracked (krakt) *adj.* 1. Having a crack or cracks. 2. Broken to pieces. 3. *Informal* Mentally deranged. 4. Uneven in tone: said of the voice.
crack·er (krak′ər) *n.* 1. A thin, crisp biscuit. 2. A firecracker. 3. A party favor that makes a popping noise. 4. A poor white of the southern U.S.: a contemptuous term.
crack·er·jack (krak′ər·jak′) *adj. Slang* Exceptional; excellent. **—***n.* An exceptional person or thing.
crack·le (krak′əl) *v.* **·led, ·ling** *v.i.* 1. To make a succession of light, sharp sounds. **—***v.t.* 2. To crush with such sounds. 3. To cover, as china, with a delicate network of cracks. **—***n.* 1. A sound of crackling. 2. A network of fine cracks. 3. Ware having such cracks: also **crack′le·ware′** (-wâr′).
crack·ling (krak′ling) *n.* 1. The giving forth of small sharp sounds. 2. The crisp browned skin of roasted pork. 3. *pl.* The crisp remains of fat after rendering.
crack·ly (krak′lē) *adj.* Likely to crackle.
crack·pot (krak′pot′) *n. Slang* An eccentric person; a crank. **—***adj.* Eccentric; insane.
crack·up (krak′up′) *n.* 1. A crash, as of an airplane or automobile. 2. *Informal* A physical or mental breakdown.
-cracy *combining form* Government or authority: *democracy.* [< Gk. *-krateia* power < *krateein* to rule]
cra·dle (krād′l) *n.* 1. A small bed for an infant, usu. on rockers. 2. A place of origin. 3. A framework for supporting something under construction or repair. 4. Any of various frames for support or protection, as a frame to protect an injured limb. 5. The holder for the receiver of a telephone. 6. A frame on a scythe to catch cut grain; also, such a scythe. 7. A framework on rockers for sifting material for gold. 8. A low frame on casters for lying on while working under an automobile. **—***v.t.* **·dled, ·dling** 1. To put into or rock in or as in a cradle; soothe. 2. To cut (grain) with a cradle. 3. To place or support in a cradle. 4. To wash, as gold-bearing gravel, in a cradle. [OE *cradol*]
cra·dle·song (krād′l·sông′) *n.* A lullaby.
craft (kraft) *n.* 1. Skill or proficiency, esp. in handwork; loosely, art. 2. Skill in deception. 3. An occupation or trade, usu. one calling for manual skill. 4. The membership of a particular trade. 5. A vessel or an aircraft: also used collectively. [OE *cræft* skill, art, strength, courage]
-craft *combining form* Skill; trade; art of: *woodcraft.*
crafts·man (krafts′mən) *n. pl.* **·men** (-mən) One skilled in a craft or art. **—crafts′man·ship** *n.*
craft union A labor union limited to workers who perform the same type of work.
craft·y (kraf′tē) *adj.* **craft·i·er, craft·i·est** Skillful in deceiving; cunning. **—craft′i·ly** *adv.* **—craft′i·ness** *n.*
crag (krag) *n.* A rough, steep, or prominently projecting rock. [ME *cragg* < Celtic]
crag·gy (krag′ē) *adj.* **·gi·er, ·gi·est** Having or resembling crags. Also **crag·ged** (krag′id). **—crag′gi·ness** *n.*
crake (krāk) *n.* Any of various small, harsh-voiced birds of the rail family. [< ON *kraka* crow]
cram (kram) *v.* **crammed, cram·ming** *v.t.* 1. To force into an inadequate space; stuff. 2. To fill or pack tightly. 3. To feed to excess. 4. To force (information) into the mind. **—***v.i.* 5. To eat greedily. 6. To study hurriedly. [OE *crammian* to stuff] **—cram′mer** *n.*
cramp[1] (kramp) *n.* 1. An involuntary, sudden, painful muscular contraction. 2. A paralysis of local muscles caused by overexertion. 3. *pl.* Acute abdominal pains. **—***v.t. & v.i.* To suffer or cause to suffer a cramp. [< OF *crampe*]
cramp[2] (kramp) *n.* An iron bar bent at both ends, used to bind two stones, timbers, etc., together. **—***v.t.* 1. To fasten with a cramp. 2. To restrain or confine; hamper. 3. To jam (a wheel) by turning too short. [< MDu. *krampe* hook.]
cram·pon (kram′pən) *n.* 1. A pair of hooked pieces of iron for raising heavy stones, etc. 2. *Usu. pl.* An iron attachment for the shoe to aid in walking on ice or in climbing. Also **cram·poon** (kram·pōōn′). [< MF *crampe* hook]
cran·ber·ry (kran′ber′ē, -bər·ē) *n. pl.* **·ries** 1. The edible, scarlet, acid berry of a plant growing in marshy land. 2. The plant itself.
crane (krān) *n.* 1. One of a family of large, long-necked, long-legged birds, as the **whooping crane.** 2. A hoisting machine, usually having a projecting movable arm, by which a heavy object can be raised and moved. **—***v.t. & v.i.* **craned, cran·ing** 1. To stretch out one's neck, as a crane does. 2. To lift or move by or as if by a crane. [OE *cran*]
crane·bill (krān′bil′) *n.* Any species of geranium. Also **cranes′bill′** (krānz′bil′), **crane′s′-bill′.**
crane fly A fly with very long, slender legs.
cranio- *combining form* Cranium; cranial. Also, before vowels, **crani-.** [< Med.L *cranium* skull]
cra·ni·ol·o·gy (krā′nē·ol′ə·jē) *n.* The branch of anatomy that treats of skulls. **—cra·ni·o·**

log·i·cal (krā′nē·ə·loj′i·kəl) *adj.* —**cra′ni·ol′o·gist** *n.*
cra·ni·um (krā′nē·əm) *n.* *pl.* **·ni·ums** or **·ni·a** (-nē·ə) The skull, esp. the part enclosing the brain. [< Med.L < Gk. *kranion* skull] —**cra′ni·al** *adj.*
crank (krangk) *n.* 1. A device for transmitting motion, usu. a handle attached at right angles to a shaft. 2. *Informal* An eccentric, hostile, or grouchy person. —*v.t.* 1. To furnish with a crank. 2. To start or operate by a crank. —*v.i.* 3. To turn a crank. [OE *cranc*]
crank·case (krangk′kās′) *n.* *Mech.* The case enclosing an engine crankshaft.
crank·shaft (krangk′shaft′) *n.* *Mech.* A shaft driven by or driving a crank.
crank·y (krang′kē) *adj.* **crank·i·er, crank·i·est** 1. Irritable; peevish. 2. Eccentric; queer. 3. *Naut.* Liable to heel: also **crank.** [< CRANK] —**crank′i·ly** *adv.* —**crank′i·ness** *n.*
cran·ny (kran′ē) *n.* *pl.* **·nies** A narrow crevice or chink, as in a wall. [? < OF *cran*, *cren* notch] —**cran′nied** *adj.*
crap (krap) *U.S.* *n.* 1. The game of craps. 2. Feces, excrement. 3. *Slang* Anything worthless. [See CRAPS]
crape (krāp) See CREPE.
crap·pie (krap′ē) *n.* *pl.* **·pies** or **·pie** An edible fresh-water fish of the central U.S.
craps (kraps) *n.pl.* (*construed as sing.*) A game of chance, played with two dice. [< E *crabs*, the lowest throw (two aces) in hazard]
crap·shoot·er (krap′sho͞o′tər) *n.* One who plays the game of craps.
crap·u·lent (krap′yo͝o·lənt) *adj.* 1. Grossly intemperate in eating or drinking. 2. Sick from such intemperance. Also **crap′u·lous.** [< Gk. *kraipalē* drunken headache] —**crap′u·lence** *n.*
crash¹ (krash) *v.i.* 1. To break to pieces with a loud noise. 2. To suffer damage or destruction, as by falling or striking something. 3. To make a loud noise of breaking. 4. To move with such a noise. 5. To fail or come to ruin. 6. *Slang* To return to normal from a drug-induced state. —*v.t.* 7. To dash to pieces; smash. 8. To cause (an airplane, automobile, etc.) to crash. 9. *Informal* To enter without invitation or without paying admission. —*n.* 1. A loud noise, as of things being violently broken. 2. A sudden failure or collapse. 3. The act of crashing. —*adj.* *Informal* Done with intensive effort, as a project or program. [Imit.]
crash² (krash) *n.* A coarse fabric used for towels, etc. [? < Russian *krashenina*]
crash helmet A heavy, padded helmet.
crash landing An emergency landing of an airplane.
crass (kras) *adj.* 1. Grossly vulgar or stupid. 2. Coarse or thick. [< L *crassus* thick] —**crass′ly** *adv.* —**crass′ness** *n.*
-crat *combining form* A supporter or member of a social class or of a type of government: *democrat*, *aristocrat*. [< F *-crate* < Gk. *-kratēs* < *krateein* to rule, govern]
crate (krāt) *n.* 1. A case or framework of slats in which to pack something for shipment. 2. *Slang* A decrepit vehicle or airplane. —*v.t.* **crat·ed, crat·ing** To pack in a crate. [Prob. < L *cratis* wickerwork] —**crat′er** *n.*
cra·ter (krā′tər) *n.* 1. A bowl-shaped depression at the outlet of a volcano. 2. Any similar cavity. [< Gk. *kratēr* bowl]
cra·vat (krə·vat′) *n.* 1. A necktie. 2. A scarf. [< F *Cravate* a Croatian; with ref. to the neckcloths worn by Croatian soldiers]
crave (krāv) *v.* **craved, crav·ing** *v.t.* 1. To long for; desire greatly. 2. To need; require. 3. To beg for. —*v.i.* 4. To desire or long: with *for* or *after*. [OE *crafian*] —**crav′er** *n.*
cra·ven (krā′vən) *adj.* Cowardly. —*n.* A base coward. [? < L *crepare* to creak, break] —**cra′ven·ly** *adv.* —**cra′ven·ness** *n.*
craw (krô) *n.* 1. The crop of a bird. 2. The stomach of any animal. [ME *crawe*. Akin to Du. *kraag* neck.]
crawl (krôl) *v.i.* 1. To move along slowly with the body on or close to the ground, esp. to move on hands and knees. 2. To move slowly or feebly. 3. To be covered with things that crawl. 4. To feel as if covered with crawling things. —*n.* 1. The act of crawling. 2. An overarm swimming stroke. [Prob. < ON *krafla* to paw] —**crawl′er** *n.*
crawl·y (krô′lē) *adj.* **crawl·i·er, crawl·i·est** *Informal* Creepy.
cray·fish (krā′fish′) *n.* *pl.* **·fish** or **·fish·es** A fresh-water crustacean resembling the lobster. Also **craw·fish** (krô′fish′). [Earlier *crevice* < OF < OHG *krebiz*]
cray·on (krā′ən, -on) *n.* A stick of colored wax, chalk, etc., for use in drawing. —*v.t.* & *v.i.* To sketch or draw with crayons. [< F, pencil]
craze (krāz) *v.t.* & *v.i.* **crazed, craz·ing** 1. To render or become insane. 2. To cover or become covered with minute cracks, as the glaze of pottery. —*n.* 1. A fad. 2. An extravagant enthusiasm. 3. A minute flaw or crack. [ME *crasen* to crack] —**crazed** *adj.*
cra·zy (krā′zē) *adj.* **·zi·er, ·zi·est** 1. Disordered in mind; insane; mad. 2. *Informal* Enthusiastic or excited. 3. *Informal* Unpredictable or strange. 4. *Slang* Wonderful; exciting. —*n.* *pl.* **·zies** 1. *Usu. pl.* Member of a 1960's radical youth group using violent acts of protest. 2. An eccentric. 3. A crazy person. —**cra′zi·ly** *adv.* —**cra′zi·ness** *n.*
crazy quilt A patchwork quilt made of pieces of various sizes, shapes, and colors.
creak (krēk) *n.* A sharp, squeaking sound, as from friction. —*v.t.* & *v.i.* To produce or cause to produce a creak. [Imit.] —**creak′i·ly** *adv.* —**creak′i·ness** *n.* —**creak′y** *adj.* **creak·i·er, creak·i·est**
cream (krēm) *n.* 1. An oily, yellowish substance contained in milk. 2. The best part. 3. The yellowish white color of cream. 4. Something made with or resembling cream. 5. An oily lotion for the skin. —*v.t.* 1. To skim cream from. 2. To take the best part from. 3. To add cream to, as coffee. 4. To beat, as butter and sugar, to a creamy consistency. 5. To cook or prepare (food) with cream or cream sauce. 6. *Slang* To defeat decisively. —*v.i.* 7. To froth or foam. [< LL *chrisma* chrism]
cream cheese Soft, white cheese made of cream or a mixture of cream and milk.
cream·er (krē′mər) *n.* 1. A pitcher for cream. 2. A device for separating cream.
cream·er·y (krē′mər·ē) *n.* *pl.* **·er·ies** A place where dairy products are prepared or sold.
cream of tartar Potassium bitartrate.

cream puff 1. A shell of pastry filled with whipped cream or custard. 2. *Slang* A sissy; weakling.

cream·y (krē′mē) *adj.* **cream·i·er, cream·i·est** 1. Containing cream. 2. Resembling cream. —**cream′i·ness** *n.*

crease (krēs) *n.* A mark or line made by folding or wrinkling. —*v.* **creased, creas·ing** *v.t.* 1. To make a crease or creases in. 2. To graze, as with a bullet. —*v.i.* 3. To become wrinkled. [ME *creaste*, ? var. of *creste* ridge] —**creas′er** *n.*

cre·ate (krē·āt′) *v.t.* **·at·ed, ·at·ing** 1. To cause to come into existence; originate. 2. To be the cause of; occasion. 3. To invest with new office, rank, etc.; appoint. [< L *creare*]

cre·a·tion (krē·ā′shən) *n.* 1. The act of creating, or the fact of being created. 2. Anything created. 3. *Usu. cap.* God's bringing of the universe into existence. 4. The universe.

cre·a·tive (krē·ā′tiv) *adj.* 1. Having the power or ability to create. 2. Characterized by originality of thought and execution. —**cre·a′tive·ly** *adv.* —**cre·a′tive·ness, cre·a·tiv·i·ty** (krē′ā·tiv′ə·tē, -ə·tiv′-) *n.*

cre·a·tor (krē·ā′tər) *n.* One who or that which creates. —**the Creator** God.

crea·ture (krē′chər) *n.* 1. A living being; esp., an animal. 2. A person. 3. One who is dependent upon something or someone; puppet; tool. [< L *creare* to create]

crèche (kresh, krāsh) *n.* A group of figures representing the scene in the stable at the Nativity. [< F, crib, cradle]

cre·dence (krēd′ns) *n.* Belief, esp. as based upon the evidence of others. [< L *credere* to believe]

cre·den·tial (kri·den′shəl) *n.* 1. That which entitles one to authority or confidence. 2. *Usually pl.* A document giving evidence of one's authority or identity. [< Med.L *credentia* belief + -AL[1]]

cre·den·za (kri·den′zə) *n.* A sideboard or buffet. [< Ital. < L *credere* to believe]

credibility gap The difference between what is said and what can be easily believed: applied esp. to public policies.

cred·i·ble (kred′ə·bəl) *adj.* 1. Believable. 2. Trustworthy; reliable. [< L *credere* to believe] —**cred′i·bil′i·ty** *n.* —**cred′i·bly** *adv.*

cred·it (kred′it) *n.* 1. Belief in someone or something; trust; faith. 2. A good reputation. 3. A source of honor: a *credit* to one's family. 4. Approval; praise. 5. *Usu. pl.* Acknowledgment of work done on a book, motion picture, etc. 6. Confidence in the ability of an individual, firm, etc., to fulfill financial obligations: to buy on *credit*. 7. The time extended for payment of a liability. 8. In bookkeeping, the entry of any amount paid by a debtor. 9. In an account, the balance in one's favor. 10. Official certification that a student has passed a course of study; also, a unit of academic study. —*v.t.* 1. To accept as true. 2. To ascribe: with *with*. 3. In bookkeeping, to give credit for or enter as credit to. [< L *credere* to believe, trust]

cred·it·a·ble (kred′it·ə·bəl) *adj.* Deserving credit or esteem; praiseworthy. —**cred′it·a·bil′i·ty** *n.* —**cred′it·a·bly** *adv.*

credit card A card entitling its holder to credit at certain places.

cred·i·tor (kred′i·tər) *n.* One to whom money is owed. [< L *credere* to believe, trust]

cre·do (krē′dō, krā′-) *n. pl.* **·dos** A set of beliefs; a creed. [< L, I believe]

cre·du·li·ty (krə·do͞o′lə·tē, -dyo͞o′-) *n.* Readiness to believe; gullibility.

cred·u·lous (krej′o͝o·ləs) *adj.* 1. Disposed to believe on slight evidence. 2. Arising from credulity. [< L *credere* to believe] —**cred′u·lous·ly** *adv.* —**cred′u·lous·ness** *n.*

Cree (krē) *n. pl.* **Cree** or **Crees** 1. One of an Algonquian tribe of North American Indians formerly dwelling in Manitoba and Saskatchewan. 2. The language of this tribe.

creed (krēd) *n.* 1. A formal statement of religious belief or doctrine. 2. Any organized system or statement of beliefs, principles, etc. —**the Creed** The Apostles' Creed. [< L *credo* I believe]

creek (krēk, krik) *n.* A stream intermediate in size between a brook and a river. [ME *creke, crike* < Scand.]

Creek (krēk) *n.* 1. A member of one of various tribes of North American Indians, once occupying parts of Georgia, Alabama, and Florida. 2. Their Muskhogean language.

creel (krēl) *n.* An angler's wicker basket for carrying fish. [Appar. related to OF *greille* grating]

creep (krēp) *v.i.* **crept, creep·ing** 1. To move with the body close to or touching the ground; crawl. 2. To move slowly or stealthily. 3. To grow along a surface or support, as a vine. 4. To have a sensation of being covered with creeping things. —*n.* 1. The act of creeping. 2. *pl. Informal* A feeling of apprehension. 3. *Slang* An unattractive person. [OE *crēopan*] —**creep′er** *n.*

creep·ing (krē′ping) *adj.* Developing too slowly to be readily apparent: *creeping* socialism.

creep·y (krē′pē) *adj.* **creep·i·er, creep·i·est** 1. Eerie; repugnant. 2. Characterized by a creeping motion. —**creep′i·ly** *adv.* —**creep′i·ness** *n.*

cre·mate (krē′māt, kri·māt′) *v.t.* **·mat·ed, ·mat·ing** To burn (a dead body) to ashes. [< L *cremare*] —**cre·ma′tion** *n.* —**cre′ma·tor** *n.*

cre·ma·to·ry (krē′mə·tôr′ē, krem′ə-) *adj.* Related to cremation. —*n. pl.* **·ries** A furnace or establishment for cremating dead bodies: also **cre′ma·to′ri·um.**

crème (krem) *n. French* Cream: used in names of sauces and liqueurs.

crème de ca·ca·o (də kə·kā′ō, -kä′ō) *French* A sweet, chocolate-flavored liqueur.

crème de menthe (də mäṅt) *French* A sweet, mint-flavored liqueur.

cre·nate (krē′nāt) *adj. Bot.* Scalloped or notched, as a leaf. Also **cre′nat·ed.** [< NL *crena* notch] —**cre′nate·ly** *adv.* —**cre·na′tion** *n.*

cren·el (kren′əl) *n.* One of the notches or indentations of a battlement. [< OF, dim. of *cren* notch]

cren·el·ate (kren′ə·lāt) *v.t.* **·lat·ed, ·lat·ing** To provide with battlements or crenels. Also *Brit.* **cren′el·late.** —**cren′el·a′tion** *n.*

Cre·ole (krē′ōl) *n.* 1. A native of Spanish America or the West Indies but of European descent. 2. A descendant of the French settlers of the southern U.S., esp. of Louisiana. 3. The French patois spoken by the Louisiana Creoles. [< F *créole* < Sp. *criollo* a native] —**Cre'ole** *adj.*

cre·o·sote (krē'ə·sōt) *n. Chem.* An oily liquid distilled from wood tar and coal tar, used as an antiseptic and preservative. —*v.t.* **·sot·ed, ·sot·ing** To treat with creosote, as shingles, etc. [< Gk. *kreas* flesh + *sōtēr* preserver]

crepe (krāp) *n.* 1. A thin, crinkled fabric. 2. Black crepe used as a sign of mourning: in this sense usu. *crape.* 3. Tissue paper resembling crepe: also **crepe paper.** 4. A thin pancake. Also **crêpe.** [< F (*tissu*) *crêpe* crinkled (cloth) < L *crispus* curled]

crêpes su·zette (krāp' sōō·zet') Thin pancakes usu. served aflame in liqueurs.

crep·i·tate (krep'ə·tāt) *v.i.* **·tat·ed, ·tat·ing** To crackle; rattle. [< L *crepitare,* freq. of *crepare* to creak] —**crep'i·tant** (-tənt) *adj.* —**crep'i·ta'tion** *n.*

crept (krept) Past tense of CREEP.

cre·pus·cu·lar (kri·pus'kyə·lər) *adj.* 1. Of or pertaining to twilight. 2. Dim; obscure. [< L *crepusculum* < *creper* dusky]

cres·cen·do (krə·shen'dō) *Music n. pl.* **·dos** A gradual increase in volume: opposed to *diminuendo.* [< Ital., ppr. of *crescere* to increase] —**cres·cen'do** *v.i.* **·doed, ·do·ing**

cres·cent (kres'ənt) *n.* 1. The visible part of the moon in its first or last quarter, having one concave edge and one convex edge. 2. Something crescent-shaped. —*adj.* 1. Increasing: said of the moon in its first quarter. 2. Shaped like the moon in its first quarter. [< L *crescens, -entis,* ppr. of *crescere* to increase]

cress (kres) *n.* One of various plants of the mustard family, as watercress. [OE *cresse*]

cres·set (kres'it) *n.* A metal holder for burning oil, wood, etc., for illumination. [< OF *craicet, craisset*]

crest (krest) *n.* 1. A comb, tuft, or projection on the head of an animal, esp. of birds. 2. The top of a wave. 3. The highest point or stage; top. 4. The projection on the top of a helmet; plume. 5. *Heraldry* A device placed above the shield in a coat of arms. —*v.t.* 1. To furnish with a crest. 2. To reach the crest of. —*v.i.* 3. To come to a crest, as a wave. [< L *crista* tuft] —**crest'ed** *adj.*

crest·fall·en (krest'fô'lən) *adj.* 1. Dejected. 2. Having a fallen or drooping crest.

cre·ta·ceous (kri·tā'shəs) *adj.* Of, containing, or resembling chalk. [< L *creta* chalk]

cre·tin (krē'tin, krēt'n) *n.* A person afflicted with cretinism. [< F *crétin,* var. of *chrétien* Christian, human being, i.e., not an animal] —**cre'tin·ous** *adj.*

cre·tin·ism (krē'tən·iz'əm) *n. Pathol.* A congenital condition associated with thyroid deficiency, marked by arrested physical development, goiter, and mental retardation.

cre·tonne (kri·ton', krē'ton) *n.* A heavy, unglazed cotton, linen, or rayon fabric printed in colored patterns. [after *Creton,* a village in Normandy]

cre·vasse (krə·vas') *n.* 1. A deep fissure or chasm, as in a glacier. 2. A breach in a levee. —*v.t.* **·vassed, ·vass·ing** To split with crevasses. [See CREVICE]

crev·ice (krev'is) *n.* A fissure or crack; cleft; chink. [< OF *crevace* < L *crepare* to crack] —**crev'iced** *adj.*

crew[1] (krōō) *n.* 1. The company belonging to one ship, aircraft, etc. 2. A group organized for a particular job: a repair *crew.* 3. A group trained to handle a racing shell. —*v.i.* To act as a member of a crew. [< L *crescere* to increase] —**crew'man** (-mən) *n.*

crew[2] (krōō) Past tense of CROW.

crew cut A closely cropped haircut.

crew·el (krōō'əl) *n.* A slackly twisted worsted yarn, used in embroidery. [Origin uncertain] —**crew'el·work'** *n.*

crib (krib) *n.* 1. A child's bed, with side railings. 2. A storage place for grain, having slat or openwork sides. 3. A rack or manger for fodder. 4. A stall for cattle. 5. A small house or room. 6. A framework of wood or metal, used to retain or support something, as in mines. 7. *Informal* A plagiarism. 8. *Informal* A translation or other unauthorized aid employed by students. —*v.* **cribbed, crib·bing** *v.t.* 1. To enclose in or as in a crib. 2. To retain or support with a crib. 3. *Informal* To plagiarize. —*v.i.* 4. *Informal* To use a crib in translating, etc. [OE *cribb*] —**crib'ber** *n.*

crib·bage (krib'ij) *n.* A game of cards for two, three, or four players, the score being kept on a pegboard.

crib death The sudden death, usu. during sleep, of a healthy baby for unknown reasons. Also *sudden infant death syndrome.*

crick (krik) *n.* A muscle cramp, as in the neck. [Origin uncertain]

crick·et[1] (krik'it) *n.* A leaping insect, the male of which makes a chirping sound. [< LG; orig. imit.]

crick·et[2] (krik'it) *n.* 1. An outdoor game played with bats, a ball, and wickets, between two sides of eleven each, popular in England. 2. *Informal* Fair play; sportsmanship. [? < MDu. *criche* stick] —**crick'·et·er** *n.*

cried (krīd) Past tense and past participle of CRY.

cri·er (krī'ər) *n.* 1. One who cries. 2. One who makes public announcements, as of news.

crime (krīm) *n.* 1. *Law* An act or omission in violation of public law; esp., a felony. 2. Any grave offense. [< L *crimen* accusation]

crim·i·nal (krim'ə·nəl) *adj.* 1. Implying or involving crime. 2. *Law* Pertaining to the administration of penal law. 3. Guilty of crime. —*n.* One who has committed a crime. —**crim'i·nal·ly** *adv.* —**crim'i·nal'i·ty** (-nal'·ə·tē) *n.*

crim·i·nol·o·gy (krim'ə·nol'ə·jē) *n.* The scientific study of crime and criminals. [< L *crimen, criminis* crime + -LOGY] —**crim·i·no·log·i·cal** (krim'ə·nə·loj'i·kəl) *adj.* —**crim'i·nol'o·gist** *n.*

crimp (krimp) *v.t.* 1. To bend or press into ridges or folds; corrugate; flute. 2. To curl or wave. —*n.* 1. Something that has been crimped. 2. *pl.* Waved or curled hair. —**to put a crimp in** *Informal* To hinder or obstruct. [< MDu. *crimpen* to wrinkle] —**crimp'er** *n.* —**crimp'y** *adj.* **crimp·i·er, crimp·i·est**

crim·son (krim'zən) *n.* A deep red color. [< Arabic *qirmiz* insect] —**crim'son** *adj.*

cringe (krinj) *v.i.* **cringed, cring·ing** 1. To shrink or crouch in fear. 2. To fawn. —*n.*

A servile crouching. [ME *cringen, crengen*] **—cring'er** *n.*
crin·kle (kring'kəl) *v.t. & v.i.* **·kled, ·kling** 1. To form or cause to form wrinkles or crimps. 2. To rustle or crackle. —*n.* A wrinkle or fold. [ME *crenklen* to curl up] **—crin'kly** *adj.*
crin·o·line (krin'ə·lin) *n.* 1. A stiff fabric, originally made of horsehair and linen. 2. A petticoat of this fabric. 3. A hoop skirt. [< L *crinis* hair + *linum* linen]
crip·ple (krip'əl) *n.* A lame or disabled person or animal. —*v.t.* **·pled, ·pling** 1. To make lame. 2. To impair or disable. [OE *crypel*] **—crip'pler** *n.*
cri·sis (krī'sis) *n. pl.* **·ses** (-sēz) 1. A crucial turning point. 2. A critical moment. 3. Any decisive change in the course of a disease, favorable or unfavorable. [< Gk. *krinein* to decide]
crisp (krisp) *adj.* 1. Brittle; easily crumbled. 2. Fresh and firm. 3. Brisk; invigorating. 4. Terse; curt. —*v.t. & v.i.* To make or become crisp. [< L *crispus* curled] **—crisp'ly** *adv.* **—crisp'ness** *n.*
crisp·y (kris'pē) *adj.* **crisp·i·er, crisp·i·est** Crisp. **—crisp'i·ness** *n.*
criss·cross (kris'krôs') *v.t.* 1. To cross with interlacing lines. —*v.i.* 2. To move in crisscrosses. —*adj.* Marked by crossings. —*n.* 1. The cross of one who cannot write. 2. A group of intersecting lines. —*adv.* Crosswise. [Alter. of *Christcross*]
cri·te·ri·on (krī·tir'ē·ən) *n. pl.* **·te·ri·a** A standard or rule by which a judgment can be made. [< Gk. *krinein* to decide]
crit·ic (krit'ik) *n.* 1. One who judges the merits of anything; esp., one who evaluates books, plays, movies, etc., professionally. 2. One who judges severely. [< Gk. *kritēs* judge]
crit·i·cal (krit'i·kəl) *adj.* 1. Given to faultfinding or severe judgments; carping. 2. Exhibiting careful judgment; analytical. 3. Of the nature of a crisis; decisive; crucial. **—crit'i·cal·ly** *adv.* **—crit'i·cal·ness** *n.*
crit·i·cism (krit'ə·siz'əm) *n.* 1. The act of criticizing. 2. A severe or unfavorable judgment. 3. The art of making discriminating judgments. 4. The occupation or profession of a critic.
crit·i·cize (krit'ə·sīz) *v.t. & v.i.* 1. To judge severely. 2. To evaluate. Also *Brit.* **crit'i·cise.** **—crit'i·ciz'a·ble** *adj.* **—crit'i·ciz'er** *n.*
cri·tique (kri·tēk') *n.* A critical review, esp. of a work of art or literature. [< F]
crit·ter (krit'ər) *n. Dial.* A creature.
croak (krōk) *v.i.* 1. To utter a hoarse, low-pitched cry, as a frog or crow. 2. To speak in a low, hoarse voice. 3. *Slang* To die. —*v.t.* 4. To utter with a croak. —*n.* A hoarse vocal sound, as of a frog. [Imit.] **—croak'er** *n.* **—croak'y** *adj.*
Cro·at (krō'at, -ət) *n.* 1. A Slavic native of Croatia. 2. The Croatian language.
Cro·a·tian (krō·ā'shən) *n.* 1. A Croat. 2. The Serbo-Croatian language of the Croats. **—Cro·a'tian** *adj.*
cro·chet (krō·shā') *n.* Needlework having looped stitches formed with a hooked needle. [< F, dim. of *croche* hook] **—cro·chet'** *v.t. & v.i.* **·cheted** (-shād'), **·chet·ing** (-shā'ing)
crock (krok) *n.* An earthenware pot or jar. [OE *croc*]
crocked (krokt) *adj. Slang* Drunk.
crock·er·y (krok'ər·ē) *n.* Earthen vessels collectively.
croc·o·dile (krok'ə·dīl) *n.* A large, lizardlike amphibious reptile of tropical regions, with long jaws and armored skin. [< Gk. *krokodilos* lizard, crocodile] **—croc·o·dil·i·an** (krok'ə·dil'ē·ən) or **croc'o·dil'e·an** *n. & adj.*
crocodile tears Hypocritical grief.
cro·cus (krō'kəs) *n. pl.* **cro·cus·es** or **cro·ci** (krō'sī) A small plant of the iris family, with long grasslike leaves and large flowers. [< Gk. *krokos*]
Croe·sus (krē'səs) *n.* A very wealthy man. [after *Croesus,* a 6th c. B.C. Lydian king noted for his wealth]
croft (krôft) *n. Brit.* 1. A small field near a house. 2. A small tenant farm. [OE, field] **—croft'er** *n.*
Cro-Mag·non (krō·mag'non) *n. Anthropol.* A member of a prehistoric European race. [after the cave in France where their remains have been found] **—Cro-Mag'non** *adj.*
crone (krōn) *n.* A withered old woman. [Prob. < OF *carogne* carcass]
cro·ny (krō'nē) *n. pl.* **·nies** A friend. [Orig. university slang < Gk. *chronios* contemporary]
crook (kro͝ok) *n.* 1. A bend or curve. 2. The curved or bent part of a thing. 3. Something with a crook in it, as a shepherd's staff. 4. *Informal* A thief. —*v.t. & v.i.* To bend. [< ON *krōkr*]
crook·ed (kro͝ok'id) *adj.* 1. Bent; not straight. 2. Tricky; dishonest. **—crook'ed·ly** *adv.* **—crook'ed·ness** *n.*
croon (kro͞on) *v.t. & v.i.* 1. To sing or hum in a low tone. 2. To sing (popular songs) in a soft and sentimental manner. —*n.* A low humming or singing. [< MDu. *kronen* to sing softly, lament] **—croon'er** *n.*
crop (krop) *n.* 1. The cultivated produce of the land, as grain or vegetables. 2. The product of a particular kind, place, or season. 3. A collection or quantity of anything. 4. A cropping, esp. of the hair. 5. An earmark, as on cattle. 6. An enlargement of the gullet, as in birds; the craw. 7. The handle of a whip. 8. A riding whip. —*v.t.* **cropped, crop·ping** 1. To cut or eat off the stems of, as grass. 2. To reap. 3. To trim or clip (the hair, ears, tail, etc.) of. **—to crop up** To develop or happen unexpectedly. [OE]
crop·per[1] (krop'ər) *n.* 1. One who or that which crops. 2. One who cultivates another's land for a share of the crop.
crop·per[2] (krop'ər) *n.* A bad fall, as over a horse's head. **—to come a cropper** 1. To fall headlong. 2. To fail. [? < dial. *neck and crop* completely]
cro·quet (krō·kā') *n.* An outdoor game played with wooden balls, mallets, and wickets. [Var. of *crochet.* See CROCHET.]
cro·quette (krō·ket') *n.* A cake of minced food, fried in deep fat. [< F *croquer* to crunch]
cro·sier (krō'zhər) *n.* A staff surmounted by a crook or cross, borne by or before a bishop or archbishop as a symbol of office. [< Med.L *crocia* bishop's crook]
cross (krôs) *n.* 1. An ancient instrument of execution, an upright with a horizontal piece

near the top, upon which the condemned persons were fastened. 2. *Often cap.* The emblem of Christianity, a representation of the cross upon which Christ died. 3. Anything in the form of a cross. 4. Any severe trial, affliction, or suffering: to bear one's *cross.* 5. The mark of one who cannot write. 6. Anything that resembles or is intermediate between two other things. 7. A hybrid. —*v.t.* 1. To move, extend, or pass from one side to the other side of; go across; traverse. 2. To intersect. 3. To make the sign of the cross upon or over. 4. To lay or place across or over: to *cross* the legs, fingers, etc. 5. To meet and pass. 6. To obstruct or hinder; thwart. 7. *Biol.* To crossbreed (plants or animals). —*v.i.* 8. To pass, move, or extend from side to side. 9. To intersect. 10. *Biol.* To crossbreed. —*adj.* 1. Peevish; ill-humored. 2. Lying across each other: *cross* streets. 3. Reciprocal. 4. Contrary; adverse: at *cross* purposes. 5. Hybrid. —*adv.* 1. Across; crosswise. 2. Adversely; contrarily. [< L *crux*] —**cross′ly** *adv.* —**cross′ness** *n.*

cross-bar (krôs′bär′) *n.* A transverse bar or line. —*v.t.* **-barred, -bar•ring** To secure or mark with crossbars.

cross•beam (krôs′bēm′) *n.* 1. A large beam or girder going from wall to wall. 2. Any beam that crosses another.

cross•bill (krôs′bil′) *n.* A finchlike bird having points on its mandibles that cross each other.

cross•bones (krôs′bōnz′) *n.* A representation of two bones crossing each other, usu. surmounted by a skull, and used as a symbol of death.

cross•bow (krôs′bō′) *n.* A medieval weapon consisting of a bow fixed transversely on a grooved stock along which arrows or stones are released. —**cross′bow′man** (-mən) *n.*

cross•breed (krôs′brēd′) *v.t. & v.i.* **•bred, •breed•ing** *Biol.* To produce (a strain or animal) by interbreeding two varieties. —*n.* A hybrid.

cross•check (krôs′chek′) *v.t. & v.i.* To confirm or make certain by using parallel or additional data.

cross-coun•try (krôs′kun′trē) *adj. & adv.* Going or moving across a country or across open country.

cross•cur•rent (krôs′kûr′ənt) *n.* A current flowing across another.

cross•cut (krôs′kut′) *v.t. & v.i.* **•cut, •cut•ting** To cut crosswise or through. —*adj.* 1. Used or made for crosscutting. 2. Cut across or on the bias. —*n.* A cut across or a shortcut.

cross-ex•am•ine (krôs′ig•zam′in) *v.t. & v.i.* **•ined, •in•ing** 1. To question anew (a witness called by the opposing party) for the purpose of testing the reliability of his previous testimony. 2. To question carefully. —**cross′-ex•am′i•na′tion** *n.* —**cross′-ex•am′in•er** *n.*

cross-eye (krôs′ī′) *n.* Strabismus in which one or both eyes are turned inward. —**cross′-eyed′** *adj.*

cross-fer•ti•li•za•tion (krôs′fûr′tə•lə•zā′shən) *n.* 1. *Biol.* The fertilization of an organism by sexually differentiated reproductive cells. 2. *Bot.* The fertilization of one plant or flower by the pollen from another. —**cross′-fer′ti•lize** *v.t.* **•lized, •liz•ing**

cross-grained (krôs′grānd′) *adj.* Having the grain running transversely.

cross•hatch (krôs′hach′) *v.t.* To shade, as a picture, by crossed lines. —**cross′hatch′ing** *n.*

cross•ing (krôs′ing) *n.* 1. The act of going across. 2. The act of hindering; opposition. 3. The place where something, as a road, may be crossed. 4. An intersection.

cross•patch (krôs′pach′) *n.* *Informal* A cranky, ill-tempered person.

cross•piece (krôs′pēs′) *n.* Any piece of material that crosses another.

cross-pol•li•nate (krôs′pol′ə•nāt) *v.t.* **•nat•ed, •nat•ing** To cross-fertilize (a plant). —**cross′-pol′li•na′tion** *n.*

cross-pur•pose (krôs′pûr′pəs) *n.* A purpose or aim in conflict with another. —**to be at cross-purposes** To misunderstand or act counter to each other's purposes.

cross-re•fer (krôs′ri•fûr′) *v.t. & v.i.* **•ferred, •fer•ring** To refer to (another passage or part).

cross-ref•er•ence (krôs′ref′rəns) *n.* A note or statement directing a reader from one part of a book, index, etc., to another part.

cross•road (krôs′rōd′) *n.* 1. A road that intersects another. 2. A road connecting one road to another.

cross•roads (krôs′rōdz′) *n.pl.* (*construed as sing.*) The place where roads meet. —**at the crossroads** At any critical point or moment.

cross section 1. A plane section of any object cut at right angles to its length. 2. A sampling meant to be characteristic of the whole.

cross-stitch (krôs′stich′) *n.* 1. A double stitch in the form of an *x*. 2. Needlework made with this stitch. —**cross′-stitch′** *v.t.*

cross-town (krôs′toun′) *adj.* Going across a town or city: a *cross-town* bus. —*adv.* Across a town or city.

cross•walk (krôs′wôk′) *n.* A lane for use by pedestrians in crossing a street.

cross•wise (krôs′wīz′) *adv.* 1. Across. 2. In the form of a cross. 3. Contrarily. Also **cross′ways′** (-wāz′).

cross•word puzzle (krôs′wûrd′) A word puzzle that reads both horizontally and vertically.

crotch (kroch) *n.* 1. The fork or angle formed by two diverging parts, as by the branches of a tree. 2. The region of the human body where the legs separate from the pelvis. [? < AF *croche* crook]

crotch•et (kroch′ət) *n.* 1. A perverse notion or whim; eccentricity. 2. A small hook or hooklike instrument. [< F *croche* hook] —**crotch′et•i•ness** *n.* —**crotch′et•y** *adj.*

cro•ton (krōt′n) *n.* 1. A tree or shrub of the spurge family, often used medicinally. 2. An ornamental tropical shrub. [< Gk. *krotōn* a tick]

crouch (krouch) *v.i.* 1. To stoop or bend low, as an animal ready to spring. 2. To cringe; cower. [? < OF *crochir* to be bent] —**crouch** *n.*

croup¹ (kro͞op) *n.* *Pathol.* A disease characterized by hoarse coughing, laryngeal spasm, and difficult breathing. [Imit.]

croup² (kro͞op) *n.* The rump, esp. of a horse. Also **croupe.** [< OF *crope*]

crou•pi•er (kro͞o′pē•ər, *Fr.* kro͞o•pyā′) *n.* One who collects the stakes lost and pays out those won at a gaming table. [< F, lit., one who rides on the croup]

croup•y (kro͞o′pē) *adj.* 1. Of or indicating

croup. 2. Having croup. Also **croup′ous.** —**crou′pi·ness** *n.*

crou·ton (kro͞o′ton, kro͞o·ton′) *n.* A small cube of toasted bread used esp. in soups. [< F]

crow[1] (krō) *n.* An omnivorous, raucous bird having glossy black plumage. ◆Collateral adjective: *corvine.* —**as the crow flies** In a straight line. —**to eat crow** *Informal* To recant; back down. [OE *crāwe*]

crow[2] (krō) *v.i.* **crowed** or (*for def. 1*) **crew, crowed, crow·ing** 1. To utter the shrill cry of a cock. 2. To exult; boast. 3. To utter sounds of delight, as an infant. —*n.* 1. The cry of a cock. 2. Any sound resembling this. [OE *crāwan*]

Crow (krō) *n.* 1. One of a tribe of Siouan Indians formerly inhabiting the region between the Platte and Yellowstone rivers. 2. The language of this tribe.

crow·bar (krō′bär′) *n.* A straight iron or steel bar with a flattened point, used as a lever.

crowd (kroud) *n.* 1. A large number of persons gathered closely together. 2. The populace; mob. 3. *Informal* A particular set of people; a clique. —*v.t.* 1. To shove or push. 2. To fill to overflowing. 3. To cram together. —*v.i.* 4. To gather in large numbers. 5. To force one's way. [OE *crūdan*] —**crowd′ed** *adj.* —**crowd′er** *n.*

crow·foot (krō′fo͝ot′) *n. pl.* **·foots** Any of a genus of plants that includes the buttercup, columbine, etc., having leaves suggestive of a bird's foot.

crown (kroun) *n.* 1. A circlet, often of precious metal set with jewels, worn on the head as a mark of sovereign power. 2. Any similar circlet. 3. A former British coin, worth five shillings. 4. The top part of the head. 5. The head itself. 6. The top or summit of something. 7. *Dent.* The part of a tooth that is covered with enamel or an artificial substitute for it. —**the Crown** 1. The sovereign ruler; monarch. 2. The power or the empire of a monarch. —*v.t.* 1. To place a crown, garland, etc., on the head of. 2. To make a monarch of. 3. To endow with honor or dignity. 4. To form the crown, ornament, or top to. 5. To finish or make complete. 6. *Informal* To strike on the head. [< L *corona*] —**crown′er** *n.*

crown prince The male heir apparent to a throne.

crown princess 1. The wife of a crown prince. 2. The female heir apparent to a throne.

crow's-foot (krōz′fo͝ot′) *n. pl.* **-feet** One of the wrinkles near the outer corner of the eye.

crow's-nest (krōz′nest′) *n.* An observation platform near the top of a ship's mast.

cru·ces (kro͞o′sēz) Alternative plural of CRUX.

cruci- *combining form* Cross. [< L *crux, crucis* cross]

cru·cial (kro͞o′shəl) *adj.* 1. Critical or decisive. 2. Difficult; severe. [< L *crux, crucis* cross, torture] —**cru′cial·ly** *adv.*

cru·ci·ble (kro͞o′sə·bəl) *n.* 1. A heat-resistant vessel for melting metals or minerals. 2. A severely trying test or experience. [< Med.L *crucibulum* earthen pot, lamp]

cru·ci·fix (kro͞o′sə·fiks) *n.* 1. A cross bearing an effigy of Christ crucified. 2. The cross as a Christian emblem. [< LL *crucifixus*, pp. of *crucifigere* to crucify]

cru·ci·fix·ion (kro͞o′sə·fik′shən) *n.* 1. The act of crucifying, or the state of being crucified. 2. A representation of the Crucifixion. —**the Crucifixion** The putting to death of Jesus Christ on the cross.

cru·ci·form (kro͞o′sə·fôrm) *adj.* Cross-shaped.

cru·ci·fy (kro͞o′sə·fī) *v.t.* **·fied, ·fy·ing** 1. To put to death by fastening to a cross. 2. To torture; destroy. [< LL *crucifigere*] —**cru′ci·fi′er** *n.*

crude (kro͞od) *adj.* **crud·er, crud·est** 1. Unrefined; raw: *crude* oil. 2. Immature; unripe. 3. Roughly made; unfinished. 4. Lacking tact, refinement, or taste. [< L *crudus* rough] —**crude′ly** *adv.* —**crude′ness** *n.*

cru·di·ty (kro͞o′də·tē) *n. pl.* **·ties** 1. The state or quality of being crude. 2. A crude act, remark, etc.

cru·el (kro͞o′əl) *adj.* **cru·el·er** or **·el·ler, cru·el·est** or **·el·lest** 1. Indifferent to or enjoying the suffering of others. 2. Causing suffering. [< L *crudelis* severe] —**cru′el·ly** *adv.*

cru·el·ty (kro͞o′əl·tē) *n. pl.* **·ties** 1. The quality or condition of being cruel. 2. That which causes suffering.

cru·et (kro͞o′it) *n.* A small glass bottle for vinegar, oil, etc. [< AF, dim. of OF *crue* pot]

cruise (kro͞oz) *v.* **cruised, cruis·ing** *v.i.* 1. To sail about, esp. for pleasure. 2. To travel about at a moderate speed. 3. To move at the optimum speed for sustained travel: said of aircraft, etc. 4. *Slang* To seek a sexual partner in a public place. —*v.t.* 5. To cruise over. 6. *Slang* To appear at (a public place) seeking a sexual partner: *cruise* the gay bars. —*n.* A cruising trip, esp. a voyage at sea. [< Du. *kruisen* to cross]

cruis·er (kro͞o′zər) *n.* 1. One who or that which cruises. 2. A fast, maneuverable warship. 3. A small power vessel equipped with living facilities: also called *cabin cruiser.*

crul·ler (krul′ər) *n.* A small cake of sweetened dough, fried in deep fat. [< Du. *krullen* to curl]

crumb (krum) *n.* 1. A tiny fragment of bread, cake, or the like. 2. A bit or scrap of anything. 3. *Slang* A contemptible person. —*v.t.* 1. To crumble. 2. In cooking, to dress or cover with bread crumbs. [OE *cruma*] —**crumb′y** *adj.* **crumb·i·er, crumb·i·est**

crum·ble (krum′bəl) *v.* **·bled, ·bling** *v.t.* 1. To break into tiny parts. —*v.i.* 2. To fall to small pieces; disintegrate. [OE *cruma* crumb]

crum·bly (krum′blē) *adj.* **·bli·er, ·bli·est** Apt to crumble; friable. —**crum′bli·ness** *n.*

crum·my (krum′ē) *adj.* **crum·mi·er, crum·mi·est** *Slang* Inferior; cheap; shabby.

crum·pet (krum′pit) *n.* A thin, leavened batter cake baked on a gridiron, then usu. toasted. [ME *crompen* to curl up]

crum·ple (krum′pəl) *v.* **·pled, ·pling** *v.t.* 1. To press into wrinkles; rumple. —*v.i.* 2. To become wrinkled; shrivel. 3. *Informal* To collapse. [Freq. of obs. *crump*, var. of CRIMP]

crunch (krunch) *v.t. & v.i.* 1. To chew with a crushing or crackling sound. 2. To move or crush with a crackling sound. —*n.* 1. A crunching, or its sound. 2. *Informal* A critical point or situation. [Imit.]

crup·per (krup′ər) *n.* 1. The strap that goes

under a horse's tail. 2. The rump of a horse. [< OF *crope* croup, rump]
cru·sade (krōō·sād′) *n.* 1. *Usu. cap.* Any of the military expeditions in the 11th, 12th, and 13th c., undertaken by Christians to recover the Holy Land from the Muslims. 2. Any expedition against heathens or heretics. 3. Any vigorous movement or cause. [< Med.L *cruciare* to mark with a cross] —**cru·sade′** *v.i.* **·sad·ed, ·sad·ing** —**cru·sad′er** *n.*
cruse (krōōz, krōōs) *n.* A small bottle, flask, or jug; cruet. [? < MDu. *cruyse* jar, pot]
crush (krush) *v.t.* 1. To press out of shape; mash. 2. To smash or grind into fine particles. 3. To extract by pressure. 4. To crowd. 5. To subdue; conquer. —*v.i.* 6. To become broken or misshapen by pressure. 7. To move ahead by pressing. —*n.* 1. The act of crushing, or the state of being crushed. 2. A crowd; jam. 3. A substance obtained by crushing: orange *crush.* 4. *Informal* An infatuation. [< MHG *krosen* to crush] —**crush′a·ble** *adj.* —**crush′er** *n.*
crust (krust) *n.* 1. The hard outer part of bread. 2. A dry, hard piece of bread. 3. The pastry shell of a pie, tart, etc. 4. Any hard, crisp surface, as of snow. 5. *Slang* Insolence; impertinence. 6. *Geol.* The exterior shell of the earth. —*v.t. & v.i.* To cover with, acquire, or form a crust. [< L *crusta*] —**crus′tal** *adj.*
crus·ta·cean (krus·tā′shən) *n.* One of a class of arthropods having crustlike shells, and generally aquatic, including lobsters, crabs, shrimps, etc. [< NL *Crustacea* < L *crusta* crust] —**crus·ta′cean, crus·ta′ceous** *adj.*
crust·y (krus′tē) *adj.* **crust·i·er, crust·i·est** 1. Like or having a crust. 2. Curt; surly. —**crust′i·ly** *adv.* —**crust′i·ness** *n.*
crutch (kruch) *n.* 1. A staff used by the lame as a support, esp. one having a crosspiece to fit under the armpit. 2. Anything that gives support. [OE *crycc*]
crux (kruks) *n.* *pl.* **crux·es** or **cru·ces** (krōō′sēz) 1. A pivotal, fundamental, or vital point. 2. A baffling problem. [< L, cross]
cry (krī) *v.* **cried, cry·ing** *v.i.* 1. To utter sobbing sounds of grief, pain, fear, etc., usu. accompanied by tears. 2. To shed tears. 3. To call out; shout: often with *out.* 4. To make characteristic calls: said of animals. —*v.t.* 5. To shout out. —*n.* *pl.* **cries** 1. A loud or emotional utterance; shout; call. 2. A fit of weeping. 3. An appeal; entreaty. 4. A rallying call; battle cry. 5. A demand; clamor. 6. The characteristic call of a bird or animal. —**a far cry** 1. A long distance away. 2. Something very unlike. —**in full cry** In full pursuit, as a pack of hounds. [< L *quiritare* to call out]
cry·ba·by (krī′bā′bē) *n.* *pl.* **·bies** A person, esp. a child, given to crying or complaining.
cry·ing (krī′ing) *adj.* 1. That cries. 2. Calling for immediate action or remedy.
cryo- *combining form* Cold; frost. [< Gk. *kryos* frost]
cry·o·gen·ics (krī′ə·jen′iks) *n.pl.* (*construed as sing.*) The branch of physics dealing with very low temperatures. —**cry′o·gen′ic** *adj.* —**cry′o·gen′i·cal·ly** *adv.*
cry·o·lite (krī′ə·līt) *n.* A fluoride of sodium and aluminum, used in the production of aluminum, soda, and glass.
crypt (kript) *n.* A chamber or vault, esp. one beneath a church, used as a place of burial. [< Gk. *kryptos* hidden]
cryp·ta·nal·y·sis (krip′tə·nal′ə·sis) *n.* *pl.* **·ses** (-sēz) The study of ciphers or codes to which the key is not known. —**cryp·tan·a·lyst** (krip·tan′ə·list) *n.* —**cryp·tan·a·lyt·ic** (krip′tan·ə·lit′ik) *adj.*
cryp·tic (krip′tik) *adj.* 1. Secret or hidden; occult. 2. Puzzling; mystifying. Also **cryp′ti·cal.** [< Gk. *kryptos* hidden]
crypto- *combining form* Hidden; secret. Also, before vowels, **crypt-.** [< Gk. *kryptos* hidden]
cryp·to·gram (krip′tə·gram) *n.* A message written in code or cipher. —**cryp′to·gram′mic** *adj.*
cryp·tog·ra·phy (krip·tog′rə·fē) *n.* 1. The art or process of writing in or reconverting cipher. 2. Any system of writing in secret characters. —**cryp·tog′ra·pher, cryp·tog′ra·phist** *n.* —**cryp·to·graph·ic** (krip′tə·graf′ik) *adj.*
crys·tal (kris′təl) *n.* 1. Colorless transparent quartz, or rock crystal. 2. *Physics* A homogeneous solid body, exhibiting a symmetrical structure, with geometrically arranged planes and faces. 3. Flint glass, or any fine clear glass; also, articles made of such glass. 4. A glass or plastic covering over the face of a watch. —*adj.* 1. Composed of crystal. 2. Like crystal; extremely clear. [< Gk. *krystallos* ice, crystal]
crys·tal·line (kris′tə·lin, -lēn) *adj.* 1. Of, pertaining to, like, or made of crystal or crystals. 2. Transparent; clear.
crys·tal·lize (kris′tə·līz) *v.* **·lized, ·liz·ing** *v.t.* 1. To cause to form crystals or become crystalline. 2. To bring to definite and permanent form. 3. To coat with sugar. —*v.i.* 4. To assume the form of crystals. 5. To assume definite and permanent form. Also **crys′ta·lize.** —**crys′tal·liz′a·ble** *adj.* —**crys′tal·li·za′tion** *n.*
crystallo- *combining form* Crystal. Also, before vowels, **crystall-.** [< Gk. *krystallos* crystal]
crys·tal·log·ra·phy (kris′tə·log′rə·fē) *n.* The science and study of crystals. —**crys′tal·log′·ra·pher** *n.*
crys·tal·loid (kris′tə·loid) *adj.* Like or having the nature of a crystal or a crystalloid. Also **crys′tal·loi′dal.** —*n.* *Chem.* One of a class of substances, usu. crystallizable, whose solutions pass easily through membranes. [< Gk. *krystalloeidēs* like crystal]
cub (kub) *n.* The young of the bear, fox, wolf, and certain other carnivores; a whelp. [Origin uncertain]
Cu·ban (kyōō′bən) *adj.* Of or pertaining to Cuba or its people. —**Cu′ban** *n.*
cub·by·hole (kub′ē·hōl′) *n.* A small, enclosed space. Also **cub′by.** [< *cubby,* dim. of dial. E *cub* shed + HOLE]
cube (kyōōb) *n.* 1. A solid bounded by six equal squares and having all its angles right angles. 2. *Math.* The third power of a quantity: the *cube* of 3 is 27, or $3^3 = 3 \times 3 \times 3 = 27$. —*v.t.* **cubed, cub·ing** 1. To raise to the third power. 2. To find the cubic capacity of. 3. To form or cut into cubes. [< Gk. *kybos* cube]

cu·beb (kyōō′beb) *n.* A berry of an East Indian shrub of the pepper family. [< Arabic *kabābah*]

cube root The number that, taken three times as a factor, produces a number called its cube: 4 is the *cube root* of 64.

cu·bic (kyōō′bik) *adj.* 1. Shaped like a cube. 2. Having three dimensions, or pertaining to three-dimensional content: a *cubic* foot. 3. *Math.* Of the third power or degree.

cu·bi·cal (kyōō′bi·kəl) *adj.* Shaped like a cube. —**cu′bi·cal·ly** *adv.* —**cu′bi·cal·ness** *n.*

cu·bi·cle (kyōō′bi·kəl) *n.* Any small partitioned area, used for sleep, study, work, etc. [< L *cubiculum* bedroom]

cubic measure A unit or system of units for measuring volume.

cu·bism (kyōō′biz·əm) *n.* A movement in early 20th c. art concerned with the abstract and geometric interpretation of form. —**cu′bist** *adj. & n.* —**cu·bis′tic** *adj.*

cu·bit (kyōō′bit) *n.* An ancient measure of length, usu. about 18 to 20 inches. [< L *cubitum* elbow]

cub reporter A young, inexperienced newspaper reporter.

cub scout A Boy Scout of eight to ten years of age.

cuck·old (kuk′əld) *n.* The husband of an unfaithful wife. —*v.t.* To make a cuckold of. [< OF *cucu* cuckoo] —**cuck′old·ry** *n.*

cuck·oo (kōōk′ōō, kōō′kōō) *n.* 1. A widely distributed bird, having a long gray body with white underneath, many forms of which deposit their eggs in the nests of other birds. 2. A simpleton; fool. 3. A cuckoo's cry. —*adj. Slang* Crazy; silly. [< OF *cucu, coucou*; imit.]

cu·cum·ber (kyōō′kum·bər) *n.* 1. The cylindrical, hard-rinded fruit of a plant of the gourd family, cultivated as a vegetable. 2. The plant. [< L *cucumis, -eris*]

cud (kud) *n.* Food forced up into the mouth from the first stomach of a ruminant and chewed over again. [OE *cwidu*]

cud·dle (kud′l) *v.* **·dled, ·dling** *v.t.* 1. To caress and embrace fondly; fondle. —*v.i.* 2. To lie close; nestle. —*n.* A caress or hug. [? < dial. E *couth* snug] —**cud′dle·some** *adj.* —**cud′dly** *adj.*

cudg·el (kuj′əl) *n.* A short, thick club. —**to take up the cudgels** To enter into a contest or controversy. —*v.t.* **cudg·eled** or **·elled, cudg·el·ing** or **·el·ling** To beat with or as with a cudgel. [OE *cycgel*] —**cudg′el·er** or **cudg′el·ler** *n.*

cue[1] (kyōō) *n.* A long, tapering rod, used in billiards or pool. —*v.t.* **cued, cu·ing** To hit with a cue. [< F *queue* tail]

cue[2] (kyōō) *n.* 1. In plays, movies, etc., any action or sound that signals the start of another action, speech, etc. 2. Any similar signal. 3. A hint or suggestion. —*v.t.* **cued, cu·ing** To call a cue to (an actor); prompt. [Earlier *Q, qu*, supposedly an abbreviation of L *quando* when]

cue ball The ball struck by the cue in billiards or pool.

cuff[1] (kuf) *n.* 1. A band or fold at the lower end of a sleeve. 2. A turned-up fold on the bottom of a trouser leg. 3. A detachable band of fabric worn about the wrist. 4. A handcuff. —**off the cuff** *Slang* Spontaneously. —**on the cuff** *Slang* On credit. [ME *cuffe, coffe*]

cuff[2] (kuf) *v.t.* To strike, as with the open hand; buffet. —*n.* A blow, esp. with the open hand. [? < Scand.]

cuff·link (kuf′lingk′) *n.* One of a pair of linked buttons or the like, used to fasten shirt cuffs.

cui·rass (kwi·ras′) *n.* A piece of armor consisting of a breastplate and backplate; also, the breastplate alone. [< L *corium* leather]

cui·ras·sier (kwi′rə·sir′) *n.* A mounted soldier wearing a cuirass.

cui·sine (kwi·zēn′) *n.* 1. The style or quality of cooking. 2. The food prepared. [< F < L *coquere* to cook]

cul-de-sac (kul′də·sak′, kōōl′-; *Fr.* kü′də·säk′) *n. pl.* **cul-de-sacs,** *Fr.* **culs-de-sac** (kü′-) A passage open only at one end; dead end. [< F, bottom of the bag]

-cule *suffix of nouns* Small; little: *animalcule.* [< L *-culus*, dim. suffix]

cu·li·nar·y (kyōō′lə·ner′ē, kul′-) *adj.* Of or pertaining to cookery or the kitchen. [< L *culina* kitchen]

cull (kul) *v.t.* 1. To pick or sort out; select. 2. To gather. —*n.* Something picked or sorted out, esp. something rejected as inferior. [< L *colligere* to collect] —**cull′er** *n.*

cul·mi·nate (kul′mə·nāt) *v.i.* **·nat·ed, ·nat·ing** 1. To reach the highest point or degree; come to a final result: with *in.* 2. *Astron.* To reach the meridian. [< L *culmen*, highest point] —**cul′mi·nant** *adj.* —**cul′mi·na′tion** *n.*

cu·lottes (kōō′lots′, kyōō′-) *n.pl.* A woman's trouserlike garment cut to resemble a skirt. [< F]

cul·pa·ble (kul′pə·bəl) *adj.* Deserving of blame or censure. [< L *culpa* fault] —**cul′pa·bil′i·ty** *n.* —**cul′pa·bly** *adv.*

cul·prit (kul′prit) *n.* 1. One guilty of some offense or crime. 2. One charged with a crime. [< AF *cul prit*, short for *culpable* guilty + *prit* ready for trial]

cult (kult) *n.* 1. A system of religious rites and observances. 2. Zealous devotion to a person, ideal, or thing. 3. The followers of a cult. [< L *cultus* care, cultivation]

cul·ti·vate (kul′tə·vāt) *v.t.* **·vat·ed, ·vat·ing** 1. To make fit for raising crops, as by plowing, fertilizing, etc.; till. 2. To raise or care for (plants, etc.). 3. To improve or develop by study, attention, or training; refine: to *cultivate* one's mind. 4. To court the friendship of. [< L *cultus*, pp. of *colere* to care for, cherish] —**cul·ti·va·bil·i·ty** (kul′tə·və·bil′ə·tē) *n.* —**cul·ti·va·ble** (kul′tə·və·bəl), **cul′ti·vat′a·ble** *adj.* —**cul′ti·vat′ed** *adj.* —**cul′ti·va′tor** *n.*

cul·ti·va·tion (kul′tə·vā′shən) *n.* 1. The act of cultivating, or the state of being cultivated. 2. Culture; refinement.

cul·ture (kul′chər) *n.* 1. The cultivation of plants or animals, esp. to improve the breed. 2. The development and refinement of mind, morals, or taste. 3. Cultivation of the soil. 4. *Anthropol.* The sum total of the attainments and learned behavior patterns of any specific period or people. 5. *Biol.* **a** The development of microorganisms in artificial media. **b** The organisms so developed. —*v.t.* **·tured, ·tur·ing** 1. To cultivate (plants or animals). 2. *Biol.* **a** To develop or grow (microorganisms) in an artificial medium. **b** To inoculate with a prepared culture. [< L *colere* to care for] **—cul′tur·al** *adj.* **—cul′·tur·al·ly** *adv.*

cul·tured (kul′chərd) *adj.* 1. Possessing or manifesting culture. 2. Created or grown by cultivation.

cul·tus (kul′təs) *n. pl.* **·tus·es** or **·ti** (-tī) A cult.

cul·ver·in (kul′vər·in) *n.* 1. A long cannon used in the 16th and 17th c. 2. An early form of musket. [< F *couleuvre* serpent]

cul·vert (kul′vərt) *n.* A conduit for water, as under a road. [Origin uncertain]

cum·ber (kum′bər) *v.t.* 1. To hinder. 2. To burden. [Cf. OF *encombrer* to hinder]

cum·ber·some (kum′bər·səm) *adj.* 1. Unwieldy; clumsy. 2. Vexatious; burdensome. **—cum′ber·some·ly** *adv.* **—cum′ber·some·ness** *n.*

cum·brance (kum′brəns) *n.* An encumbrance.

cum·brous (kum′brəs) *adj.* Cumbersome. **—cum′brous·ly** *adv.* **—cum′brous·ness** *n.*

cum·in (kum′in) *n.* 1. An annual of the parsley family. 2. Its seeds, used as a condiment. Also **cum′min.** [< Gk. *kyminon*]

cum lau·de (kum lô′dē, ko͝om lou′de) *Latin* With praise: used on diplomas to denote merit. **—magna cum laude** With high praise. **—summa cum laude** With highest praise.

cum·mer·bund (kum′ər·bund) *n.* A broad sash worn as a waistband. [< Persian *kamar* loin + *band* band]

cu·mu·la·tive (kyo͞om′yə·lā′tiv, -lə·tiv) *adj.* 1. Gathering volume, strength, or value. 2. Gained by accumulation. 3. Increasing or accruing. **—cu′mu·la′tive·ly** *adv.*

cu·mu·lo·nim·bus (kyo͞om′yə·lō·nim′bəs) *n. Meteorol.* A massive cloud formation in the shape of mountains, and producing thunder and showers.

cu·mu·lus (kyo͞om′yə·ləs) *n. pl.* **·li** (-lī) 1. A mass; pile. 2. *Meteorol.* A dense, usu. white cloud formation with dome-shaped upper surfaces and horizontal bases, seen in fair weather. [< L] **—cu′mu·lous** *adj.*

cu·ne·ate (kyo͞o′nē·it, -āt) *adj.* Wedge-shaped: said esp. of leaves. Also **cu′ne·at′ed, cu·ne·at·ic** (kyo͞o′nē·at′ik). [< L *cuneus* wedge]

cu·ne·i·form (kyo͞o·nē′ə·fôrm, kyo͞o′nē·ə·fôrm′) *adj.* Wedge-shaped, as the characters in some ancient Sumerian, Assyrian, Babylonian, and Persian inscriptions. **—***n.* Cuneiform writing. Also **cu·ni·form** (kyo͞o′·nə·fôrm). [< L *cuneus* wedge + -FORM]

cun·ning (kun′ing) *n.* 1. Skill in deception; craftiness. 2. Skill; dexterity. **—***adj.* 1. Crafty or shrewd. 2. Executed with skill; ingenious. 3. Cute; amusing. [OE < *cunnan* to know, be able] **—cun′ning·ly** *adv.* **—cun′ning·ness** *n.*

cup (kup) *n.* 1. A small, open vessel, often with a handle, used chiefly for drinking from. 2. The contents of a cup; a cupful: as a measure, equal to 8 ounces. 3. One's lot in life. 4. A cup-shaped object or part, as of a flower. 5. A cup-shaped vessel given as a prize, esp. in sports. 6. In golf, a hole, or the metal receptacle within it. **—in one's cups** Drunk. **—***v.t.* **cupped, cup·ping** 1. To shape like a cup. 2. To place in or as in a cup. 3. *Med.* To perform cupping on. [< L *cupa* tub]

cup·bear·er (kup′bâr′ər) *n.* One who serves wine, mead, etc., and refills glasses.

cup·board (kub′ərd) *n.* 1. A closet or cabinet with shelves, as for dishes. 2. Any small cabinet or closet.

cup·cake (kup′kāk′) *n.* A small individual cake.

cup·ful (kup′fo͝ol′) *n. pl.* **·fuls** The quantity held by a cup.

Cu·pid (kyo͞o′pid) *n.* 1. A representation of the god of love, Cupid, as a naked, winged boy with a bow and arrow. 2. One who helps to arrange meetings between lovers; chiefly in the phrase **to play Cupid.** [< L *Cupid*, god of love]

cu·pid·i·ty (kyo͞o·pid′ə·tē) *n.* Avarice; greed. [< L *cupiditas, -tatis*]

cu·po·la (kyo͞o′pə·lə) *Archit. n.* 1. A rounded roof; dome. 2. A small, vaulted structure, usu. hemispherical, rising above a roof. **—***v.t.* **·laed, ·la·ing** To provide with or shape like a cupola. [< L *cupa* tub]

cup·ping (kup′ing) *n. Med.* The former process of drawing blood to the surface of the skin by creating a vacuum at that point.

cu·pre·ous (kyo͞o′prē·əs) *adj.* Of or pertaining to copper. [< L *cuprum* copper]

cu·pric (kyo͞o′prik) *adj. Chem.* Of or pertaining to copper, esp. in its highest valence.

cupro- *combining form* Copper. Also, before vowels, **cupri-.**

cu·prous (kyo͞o′prəs) *adj. Chem.* Of or pertaining to copper, esp. in its lowest valence.

cu·prum (kyo͞o′prəm) *n.* Copper. [< L]

cur (kûr) *n.* 1. A mongrel dog. 2. A despicable person. [Short for earlier *kur-dogge*]

cur·a·ble (kyo͝or′ə·bəl) *adj.* Capable of being cured. **—cur′a·bil′i·ty** *n.* **—cur′a·bly** *adv.*

cu·ra·çao (kyo͝or′ə·sō′, ko͞o′rä·sou′) *n.* An orange-flavored liqueur. [after *Curaçao*, an island in the Caribbean]

cu·ra·cy (kyo͝or′ə·sē) *n. pl.* **·cies** The position, duties, or term of office of a curate.

cu·ra·re (kyo͞o·rä′rē) *n.* 1. An extract of certain South American trees, that acts to paralyze motor nerves; used as an arrow poison and, in medicine, as a muscle relaxant. 2. A plant from which this is extracted. [< Tupi]

cu·rate (kyo͝or′it) *n.* A clergyman assisting a parish priest, rector, or vicar. [< L *cura* care]

cur·a·tive (kyo͝or′ə·tiv) *adj.* Having the power to cure. **—***n.* A remedy. **—cur′a·tive·ly** *adv.* **—cur′a·tive·ness** *n.*

cu·ra·tor (kyo͞o·rā′tər) *n.* A person in charge of a museum or similar institution. [< L *cura* care] **—cu·ra′tor·ship** *n.*

curb (kûrb) *n.* 1. Anything that restrains or controls. 2. A border of concrete or stone along the edge of a street: also, *Brit.*, *kerb.* 3. A chain or strap bracing a bit against the lower jaw of a horse. **—***v.t.* 1. To control or check. 2. To provide with a curb. 3. To lead (a dog) off a curb for defecation in the street. [< L *curvus*]

curb·ing (kûr′bing) *n.* Material forming a curb.

curb·stone (kûrb′stōn′) *n.* A stone on the outer edge of a sidewalk.

curd (kûrd) *n. Often pl.* The coagulated portion of milk, of which cheese is made.

—*v.t. & v.i.* To form into or become curd. [ME] —**curd′y** *adj.*

cur·dle (kûr′dəl) *v.t. & v.i.* **·dled, ·dling** To make or become curdy; coagulate. [Freq. of CURD]

cure (kyŏŏr) *n.* 1. A restoration to a sound or healthy condition. 2. That which restores health or removes an evil. 3. A process of preserving food or other products. —*v.t.* **cured, cur·ing** 1. To restore to health. 2. To remedy or eradicate. 3. To preserve, as by salting, smoking, or aging. [< L *cura* care, cure] —**cur′er** *n.*

cu·ré (kyŏŏ·rā′) *n.* A parish priest, esp. in France. [< F]

cure-all (kyŏŏr′ôl′) *n.* A cure for all ills; panacea.

cur·few (kûr′fyōō) *n.* 1. A regulation requiring persons or certain persons to keep off the streets after a designated hour. 2. A medieval regulation requiring fires, or lights, to be put out at the tolling of a bell. 3. The bell itself; also the hour at which it was rung. [< OF *couvrir* to cover + *feu* fire]

cu·ri·a (kyŏŏr′ē·ə) *n. pl.* **cu·ri·ae** (kyŏŏr′ē·ē) 1. A court of justice. 2. *Often cap.* The collective body of officials of the papal government. [< L] —**cu′ri·al** *adj.*

cu·rie (kyŏŏr′ē, kyŏŏ·rē′) *n.* A unit of radioactivity. [after Marie *Curie*]

cu·ri·o (kyŏŏr′ē·ō) *n. pl.* **·os** A rare or curious object. [Short for CURIOSITY]

cu·ri·os·i·ty (kyŏŏr′ē·os′ə·tē) *n. pl.* **·ties** 1. Eager desire for knowledge of something. 2. Interest in the private affairs of others. 3. That which excites interest by its strangeness or rarity.

cu·ri·ous (kyŏŏr′ē·əs) *adj.* 1. Eager for information or knowledge. 2. Given to prying or meddling. 3. Rare or novel; odd; strange. [< L *curiosus* < *cura* care] —**cu′ri·ous·ly** *adv.*

u·ri·um (kyŏŏr′ē·əm) *n.* An unstable radioactive element (symbol Cm). [after Marie and Pierre *Curie*]

curl (kûrl) *v.t.* 1. To twist into ringlets or curves, as the hair. 2. To form into a curved or spiral shape. —*v.i.* 3. To form ringlets, as the hair. 4. To become curved; take a spiral shape. 5. To play at the game of curling. —*n.* 1. Something coiled or spiral, as a ringlet of hair. 2. A curled or circular shape or mark. 3. The act of curling, or the state of being curled. [Metathetic var. of ME *crull* curly] —**curl′i·ness** *n.* —**curl′y** *adj.* **curl·i·er, curl·i·est**

curl·er (kûr′lər) *n.* 1. One who or that which curls. 2. One who plays the game of curling.

cur·lew (kûr′lōō) *n.* A shore bird with a long, curved bill and long legs. [< OF *corlieu, courlieus*; orig. imit.]

curl·i·cue (kûr′li·kyōō) *n.* Any fancy curl or twist, as a flourish with a pen.

curl·ing (kûr′ling) *n.* A game played on ice in which the opposing players slide heavy, smooth, circular stones (**curling stones**) toward a goal at either end.

cur·mudg·eon (kər·muj′ən) *n.* A gruff person, esp. an old man. [Origin unknown]

cur·rant (kûr′ənt) *n.* 1. A small, round, acid berry, used for making jelly. 2. The bush producing this berry. 3. A small, seedless raisin. [< AF *(raisins de) Corauntz* (raisins from) Corinth]

cur·ren·cy (kûr′ən·sē) *n. pl.* **·cies** 1. The current medium of exchange; money. 2. General acceptance or circulation.

cur·rent (kûr′ənt) *adj.* 1. Belonging to the immediate present: the *current* year. 2. Passing from person to person; circulating, as money or news. 3. Generally accepted; prevalent. —*n.* 1. A continuous onward movement, as of water. 2. The part of any body of water or air that has a more or less steady flow in a definite direction. 3. A course or trend. 4. *Electr.* A movement or flow of electricity. [< L *currere* to run] —**cur′rent·ly** *adv.*

cur·ric·u·lum (kə·rik′yə·ləm) *n. pl.* **·lums** or **·la** (-lə) 1. All the courses of study offered at a university or school. 2. A regular or particular course of study. [< L, a race < *currere* to run] —**cur·ric′u·lar** *adj.*

cur·ry[1] (kûr′ē) *v.t.* **·ried, ·ry·ing** 1. To rub down and clean with a currycomb. 2. To dress (tanned hides) by soaking, smoothing, etc. —**to curry favor** To seek favor by flattery, etc. [< OF *correier, conreder* to prepare]

cur·ry[2] (kûr′ē) *n. pl.* **·ries** 1. A pungent sauce of East Indian origin. 2. A dish cooked with this sauce. 3. Curry powder. [< Tamil *kari* sauce] —**cur′ried** *adj.*

cur·ry·comb (kûr′ē·kōm′) *n.* A comb for grooming horses, etc. —*v.t.* To comb with a currycomb.

curry powder A condiment used in making curried dishes.

curse (kûrs) *n.* 1. An appeal to or as to God for evil or injury to befall another. 2. The evil or injury so invoked. 3. Any profane oath. 4. A source of calamity or evil. —*v.* **cursed** (kûrst) or **curst, curs·ing** *v.t.* 1. To invoke evil or injury upon; damn. 2. To swear at. 3. To cause evil or injury to; afflict. —*v.i.* 4. To utter curses; swear. [OE < OIrish *cursagim* to blame] —**curs·ed** (kûr′sid, kûrst) *adj.* —**curs′ed·ly** *adv.* —**curs′ed·ness** *n.*

cur·sive (kûr′siv) *adj.* Running; flowing: said of writing in which the letters are joined. [< L *currere* to run] —**cur′sive·ly** *adv.*

cur·so·ry (kûr′sər·ē) *adj.* Rapid and superficial. [< L *currere* to run] —**cur′so·ri·ly** *adv.* —**cur′so·ri·ness** *n.*

curt (kûrt) *adj.* Brief and abrupt; esp., rudely brief: a *curt* nod. [< L *curtus* shortened] —**curt′ly** *adv.* —**curt′ness** *n.*

cur·tail (kər·tāl′) *v.t.* To cut off or cut short; reduce. [< obs. *curtal* cut short] —**cur·tail′er** *n.* —**cur·tail′ment** *n.*

cur·tain (kûr′tən) *n.* 1. A piece or pieces of cloth, hanging in a window, doorway, etc. 2. Something that conceals or separates like a curtain: the *curtain* of darkness. 3. *pl. Slang* Ruin; death. —*v.t.* To provide, shut off, or conceal with or as with a curtain. [< LL *cortina*]

curt·sy (kûrt′sē) *n. pl.* **·sies** A bending of the knees and lowering of the body as a gesture of civility or respect, performed by women. Also **curt′sey.** [Var. of COURTESY] —**curt′sy** *v.i.* **·sied, ·sy·ing**

cur·va·ceous (kûr·vā′shəs) *adj. Informal* Having voluptuous curves: said of a woman.

cur·va·ture (kûr′və·chər) *n.* The act of curving, or the state of being curved. [< L *curvare* to bend]

curve (kûrv) *n.* 1. A line continuously bent, as the arc of a circle. 2. A curving, or something curved. 3. An instrument for drawing curves. 4. In baseball, a ball pitched with a spin that causes it to veer to one side. —*v.t. & v.i.* **curved, curv·ing** 1. To assume or cause to assume the form of a curve. 2. To move in the path of a curve. —*adj.* Curved. [< L *curvus* bent]

cur·vet (*n.* kûr′vit; *v.* kər·vet′, kûr′vit) *n.* A low leap of a horse, made so that all four legs are off the ground at one time. —*v.* **cur·vet·ted** or **·vet·ed, cur·vet·ting** or **·vet·ing** *v.i.* 1. To make a curvet. 2. To prance; frisk. —*v.t.* 3. To cause to curvet. [< L *curvus* bent]

curvi- *combining form* Curved. [< L *curvus* curved]

cur·vi·lin·e·ar (kûr′və·lin′ē·ər) *adj.* Formed or enclosed by curved lines. Also **cur′vi·lin′e·al.**

cush·ion (ko͝osh′ən) *n.* 1. A bag or casing filled with some soft or elastic material, used for lying or resting on. 2. Anything resembling a cushion in appearance or use; esp., any device to deaden an impact. —*v.t.* 1. To provide with a cushion. 2. To absorb the shock or effect of. [< F *coussin*, ult. < L *coxa* hip, thigh] —**cush′ion·y** *adj.*

cush·y (ko͝osh′ē) *adj. Slang* **cush·i·er, cush·i·est** Comfortable; agreeable; easy. [< CUSHION; orig. Brit. slang]

cusp (kusp) *n.* 1. A point or pointed end. 2. Either point of a crescent moon. 3. *Geom.* A point at which two branches of a curve meet and end, with a common tangent. [< L *cuspis, -idis* a point]

cus·pid (kus′pid) *n.* A canine tooth.

cus·pi·dor (kus′pə·dôr) *n.* A spittoon. [< COM- + L *spuere* to spit]

cuss (kus) *Informal v.t. & v.i.* To curse. —*n.* 1. A curse. 2. A perverse person or animal. [Var. of CURSE] —**cuss·ed** (kus′id) *adj.* —**cuss′ed·ly** *adv.* —**cuss′ed·ness** *n.*

cus·tard (kus′tərd) *n.* A dessert of milk, eggs, sugar, and flavoring, either boiled or baked. [< L *crusta* crust]

cus·to·di·an (kus·tō′dē·ən) *n.* A guardian; caretaker. —**cus·to′di·an·ship′** *n.*

cus·to·dy (kus′tə·dē) *n. pl.* **·dies** 1. Guardianship. 2. Restraint or confinement under guard. [< L *custos* guardian] —**cus·to·di·al** (kus·tō′dē·əl) *adj.*

cus·tom (kus′təm) *n.* 1. The habitual practice of a community or a people. 2. An ordinary or usual manner of doing or acting; habit. 3. Habitual patronage, as of a hotel, store, etc. 4. *pl.* A tariff or duty upon imported or, rarely, exported goods; also, the agency of the government that collects such duties. —*adj.* 1. Made to order. 2. Specializing in made-to-order goods. [< COM- + L *suescere* to become used to]

cus·tom·ar·y (kus′tə·mer′ē) *adj.* According to custom; usual; habitual. —**cus′tom·ar′i·ly** *adv.*

cus·tom-built (kus′təm·bilt′) *adj.* Built to order or to individual specifications.

cus·tom·er (kus′təm·ər) *n.* 1. One who buys something; esp., one who deals regularly at a given establishment. 2. *Informal* One to be dealt with: a queer *customer.*

cus·tom·house (kus′təm·hous′) *n.* The government office where duties are collected and vessels cleared. Also **cus′toms·house′.**

cus·tom·ize (kus′tə·mīz) *v.t.* To construct or alter according to individual specifications.

cus·tom-made (kus′təm·mād′) *adj.* Made to order.

cut (kut) *v.* **cut, cut·ting** *v.t.* 1. To open or penetrate with a sharp edge; gash; pierce. 2. To divide with a sharp edge. 3. To make or shape by cutting, as gems. 4. To fell or hew: often with *down.* 5. To wound with or as with a sharp edge. 6. *Informal* To pretend not to know; snub. 7. *Informal* To absent oneself from: to *cut* a class. 8. To shorten or trim, as hair, grass, etc. 9. To shorten or edit by removing parts. 10. To mow or reap (wheat, etc.) 11. To reduce or lessen: to *cut* prices. 12. To dilute or weaken, as whiskey. 13. To dissolve or break down: to *cut* grease. 14. To have (a new tooth) grow through the gum. 15. In certain games, to hit a ball so that it takes on a particular spin or is deflected. 16. To divide (a pack of cards), as before dealing. 17. To make (a recording). —*v.i.* 18. To make an incision. 19. To act as a sharp edge. 20. To penetrate like a knife. 21. To go by or be the shortest and most direct route: with *across, through,* etc. 22. To divide a pack of cards. 23. In motion pictures, television, etc., to make a quick transition from one scene to another. —**to be cut out for** To be suited for. —**to cut back** 1. To reduce or curtail. 2. To reverse one's direction. —**to cut in** 1. To move into a line abruptly or out of turn. 2. To interrupt a dancing couple so as to take the place of one partner. 3. To interrupt. —**to cut off** 1. To remove or detach by cutting. 2. To put an end to; stop. 3. To intercept. 4. To disinherit. —**to cut out** 1. To remove by cutting; excise. 2. To shape by cutting. 3. To oust. 4. *Slang* To stop doing; cease. —**to cut up** 1. To cut in pieces. 2. To affect deeply; distress. 3. *Informal* To misbehave. —*n.* 1. A severing, slashing, or piercing stroke: a clean *cut.* 2. The opening made by such a stroke; gash; cleft. 3. A part cut off; esp. the part of a meat animal. 4. A deletion or excision of a part. 5. A passage or channel that has been cut or dug out. 6. *Informal* A snub. 7. The manner in which a thing is cut; fashion; style. 8. A reduction in prices, wages, etc. 9. *Slang* A share or commission. 10. *Informal* An absence from a class at school. 11. *Printing* An engraved block or plate; also, an impression made from this. 12. A stroke imparting spin to a ball. 13. A cutting of a deck of cards. 14. A phonograph recording. —**a cut above** A degree better than. —*adj.* 1. That has been cut off, into, or through: a *cut* finger. 2. Dressed or finished by a tool, as stone or glass. 3. Reduced, as rates or prices. 4. Diluted, as whiskey. —**cut and dried** 1. Prepared or arranged according to formula. 2. Lacking interest or suspense; predictable. [ME < Scand.]

cu·ta·ne·ous (kyo͞o·tā′nē·əs) *adj.* Of or pertaining to skin. [< L *cutis* skin]

cut·a·way (kut′ə·wā′) *n.* A man's formal daytime coat, having the front corners cut slopingly away from the waist down to the tails at the back: also **cutaway coat.**

cut·back (kut′bak′) *n.* A reduction.

cute (kyōōt) *adj.* **cut·er, cut·est** *Informal* 1. Pretty or attractive. 2. Pert; appealing. 3. Clever. [Var. of ACUTE] —**cute'ly** *adv.* —**cute'ness** *n.*

cute·sy (kyōōt'sē) *adj.* Affectedly cute.

cut glass Glass that has been ornamented by cutting on an abrasive wheel.

cu·ti·cle (kyōō'ti·kəl) *n.* 1. *Anat.* The epidermis. 2. The crescent of toughened skin around the base of a fingernail or toenail. [< L *cuticula*, dim. of *cutis* skin] —**cu·tic'u·lar** *adj.*

cu·tin (kyōō'tin) *n.* *Bot.* A fatty or waxy protective cuticle of leaves, stems, etc., of plants. [< L *cutis* skin + -IN]

cut·lass (kut'ləs) *n.* A short, swordlike weapon, often curved. [< L *culter* knife]

cut·ler (kut'lər) *n.* One who makes, repairs, or deals in cutlery. [< L *cultellus*, dim. of *culter* knife]

cut·ler·y (kut'lər·ē) *n.* Cutting instruments collectively, esp. those for use at the table.

cut·let (kut'lit) *n.* 1. A thin piece of meat for frying or broiling, usu. veal or mutton. 2. A flat croquette of chopped meat, fish, etc. [< L *costa* rib]

cut·off (kut'ôf') *n.* 1. A termination or limit. 2. A short cut. 3. *Mech.* **a** The act of stopping a flow of something. **b** The mechanism that does this.

cut·out (kut'out') *n.* 1. Something cut out or intended to be cut out. 2. *Electr.* A device that cuts off the current when the flow reaches an unsafe level.

cut·purse (kut'pûrs') *n.* A pickpocket; formerly, one who cut away purses that were attached to a girdle or belt.

cut-rate (kut'rāt') *adj.* Sold or selling at reduced prices.

cut·ter (kut'ər) *n.* 1. One who cuts, esp. one who shapes or fits by cutting. 2. A device that cuts. 3. *Naut.* **a** A single-masted, fast-sailing vessel of narrow beam and deep draft. **b** A small, swift, armed vessel. **c** A ship's boat, used to discharge passengers, transport stores, etc. 4. A small sleigh.

cut·throat (kut'thrōt') *adj.* 1. Bloodthirsty. 2. Ruinous; merciless. —*n.* A murderer.

cut·ting (kut'ing) *adj.* 1. Adapted to cut; edged. 2. Sharp; chilling. 3. Unkind; sarcastic. —*n.* 1. The act of one who or that which cuts. 2. Something obtained or made by cutting, as a recording.

cut·tle·bone (kut'l·bōn') *n.* The internal calcareous plate of a cuttlefish.

cut·tle·fish (kut'l·fish') *n. pl.* **·fish** or **·fish·es** A sea mollusk having lateral fins, ten sucker-bearing arms, and a hard inner shell, and capable of ejecting an inky fluid.

cut·up (kut'up') *n.* *Informal* A person who tries to seem funny, as a practical joker.

cut·wa·ter (kut'wô'tər, -wot'ər) *n.* The forward part of the prow of a vessel.

cut·work (kut'wûrk') *n.* Openwork embroidery with cutout edges.

cut·worm (kut'wûrm') *n.* Any of several night-feeding caterpillars that cut off plants at the surface of the ground.

-cy *suffix* Forming nouns: 1. (*from adjectives*) Quality, state, or condition of: *secrecy, bankruptcy.* 2. (*from nouns*) Rank or condition of: *chaplaincy.* [< F *-cie* < L *-cia* < Gk. *-kia*]

cy·a·nide (sī'ə·nīd) *n.* *Chem.* A compound of cyanogen with a metallic element or radical, a poison.

cyano- *combining form* 1. Characterized by bluish coloring: *cyanosis.* 2. *Chem.* Cyanide. Also, before vowels, **cyan-**. [< Gk. *kyanos* dark blue]

cy·an·o·gen (sī·an'ə·jən) *n.* *Chem.* A colorless, flammable, poisonous gas, having an almondlike odor. [< F *cyanogène*] —**cy·an'ic** *adj.*

cy·a·no·sis (sī'ə·nō'sis) *n.* *Pathol.* A disordered condition due to inadequate oxygenation of the blood, causing the skin to look blue. —**cy·a·not·ic** (sī'ə·not'ik) *adj.*

cy·ber·nate (sī'bər·nāt) *v.t.* To control a process, as in manufacturing, by computers. —**cy'ber·na'tion** *n.*

cy·ber·net·ics (sī'bər·net'iks) *n.pl.* (*construed as sing.*) The science that treats of the principles of control and communication as they apply both to the operation of complex machines and the functions of organisms. [< Gk. *kybernētēs* steersman + -ICS] —**cy'·ber·net'ic** *adj.*

cyc·la·men (sik'lə·mən, -men) *n.* An Old World bulbous flowering herb of the primrose family. [< Gk. *kyklaminos, kyklamis*]

cy·cle (sī'kəl) *n.* 1. A recurring period within which certain events occur in a definite sequence. 2. A completed round of events in which there is a final return to the original state. 3. A pattern of regularly recurring events. 4. A complete series of variations or changes in electromagnetic waves of a given frequency or of alternating current; also the number of such changes per unit of time. 5. A body of poems or stories relating to the same character or subject. 6. A bicycle, tricycle, etc. —*v.i.* **·cled, ·cling** 1. To pass through cycles. 2. To ride a bicycle, tricycle, etc. [< Gk. *kyklos* circle]

cy·clic (sī'klik, sik'lik) *adj.* Pertaining to or characterized by cycles; recurring in cycles. Also **cy'cli·cal.**

cy·clist (sī'klist) *n.* One who rides a bicycle, tricycle, etc.

cyclo- *combining form* Circular. Also, before vowels, **cycl-**. [< Gk. *kyklos* circle]

cy·cloid (sī'kloid) *adj.* Resembling a circle or somewhat circular. —*n.* *Geom.* The curve described by a point on the circumference of a circle rolling along a straight line in a single plane. [< Gk. *kykloeidēs* circular] —**cy·cloi'dal** *adj.*

cy·clom·e·ter (sī·klom'ə·tər) *n.* An instrument for recording the rotations of a wheel to show speed and distance.

cy·clone (sī'klōn) *n.* 1. *Meteorol.* A system of winds circulating about a center of relatively low barometric pressure, and advancing at the earth's surface with clockwise rotation in the Southern Hemisphere, counterclockwise in the Northern. 2. Loosely, any violent storm. [< Gk. *kyklos* circle] —**cy·clon·ic** (sī·klon'ik) or **·i·cal** *adj.* —**cy·clon'i·cal·ly** *adv.*

cy·clo·pe·an (sī'klə·pē'ən) *adj.* 1. *Usu. cap.* Of or pertaining to the Cyclopes, legendary one-eyed giants. 2. Huge; massive. [< Gk. *Kyklōps* Cyclops]

cy·clo·pe·di·a (sī'klə·pē'dē·ə) *n.* An encyclopedia. Also **cy'clo·pae'di·a.** —**cy'·clo·pe'dic** *adj.* —**cy'clo·pe'dist** *n.*

cy·clo·ram·a (sī'klə·ram'ə, -rä'mə) *n.* 1. A

series of pictures on the interior of a cylindrical surface, appearing in natural perspective to a spectator standing in the center. 2. A backdrop curtain, often concave, used on theater stages. [< CYCLO- + Gk. *horama* a view] —**cy′clo·ram′ic** *adj.*
cy·clo·tron (sī′klə·tron) *n. Physics* An accelerator that obtains high-energy electrified particles by whirling them at very high speeds in a strong magnetic field.
cyg·net (sig′nit) *n.* A young swan. [< MF *cygne* swan]
cyl·in·der (sil′in·dər) *n.* 1. *Geom.* A solid figure generated by one side of a rectangle rotated about the opposite fixed side, the ends of the figure being equal, parallel circles. 2. Any object or container resembling a cylinder in form. 3. *Mech.* The piston chamber of an engine. 4. In a revolver, the rotating part that holds the cartridges. [< Gk. *kylindein* to roll] —**cy·lin·dric** (si·lin′drik) or **·i·cal** *adj.* —**cy·lin′dri·cal·ly** *adv.*
cym·bal (sim′bəl) *n.* One of a pair of concave metal plates struck together to produce a musical ringing sound. [< Gk. *kymbē* cup, hollow of a vessel] —**cym′bal·ist** *n.*
cyme (sīm) *n. Bot.* A flat-topped flower cluster in which the central flowers bloom first. [< Gk. *kyma* wave] —**cy·mose** (sī′mōs, sī·mōs′) *adj.*
cymo- *combining form* Wave. [< Gk. *kyma*]
cyn·ic (sin′ik) *n.* One who believes that all people are motivated by selfishness. [< Gk. *kyōn, kynos* dog] —**cyn′i·cal** *adj.* —**cyn′i·cal·ly** *adv.* —**cyn·i·cism** (sin′ə·siz′əm, sin′i-) *n.*
Cyn·ic (sin′ik) *n.* One of a sect of ancient Greek philosophers who held that virtue was the goal of life. Their doctrine eventually came to represent contemptuous self-righteousness. —**Cyn′ic** or **·i·cal** *adj.*
cy·no·sure (sī′nə·shŏŏr, sin′ə-) *n.* 1. An object of notice and admiration. 2. Something that guides. [< Gk. *kyōn, kynos* dog + *oura* tail; former name of the constellation Ursa Minor, containing the star Polaris]
cy·press (sī′prəs) *n.* 1. An evergreen tree of the pine family, having flat, scalelike foliage. 2. The wood of these trees. [< Gk. *kyparissos*]
cyp·ri·nid (sip′rə·nid) *adj.* Of or pertaining to the carp family of fishes. [< Gk. *kyprinos* carp]
Cyp·ri·ot (sip′rē·ət) *n.* 1. A native or inhabitant of Cyprus. 2. The ancient or modern Greek dialect of Cyprus. —*adj.* Of or pertaining to Cyprus: also **Cyp′ri·an.** Also **Cyp′ri·ote.** [< F *cypriote*]
Cy·ril·lic alphabet (si·ril′ik) A Slavic alphabet based mainly on that of the Greeks, ascribed traditionally to Saint Cyril, used for Russian and a few other languages.
cyst (sist) *n.* 1. *Pathol.* Any abnormal sac or vesicle in which matter may collect and be retained. 2. *Biol.* Any saclike organ. [< Gk. *kyein* to contain] —**cys′tic, cys′toid** *adj.*
cystic fibrosis A disease, appearing usu. in childhood, characterized by respiratory disorders and pancreatic deficiency.
cys·ti·tis (sis·tī′tis) *n. Pathol.* Inflammation of the bladder.
cysto- *combining form* Bladder; cyst. Also, before vowels, **cyst-**: also **cysti-.** [< Gk. *kystis* bladder]
-cyte *combining form* Cell: *phagocyte.* [< Gk. *kytos* hollow vessel]
cyto- *combining form* Cell. Also, before vowels, **cyt-.** [< Gk. *kytos* hollow vessel]
cy·to·ge·net·ics (sī′tō·jə·net′iks) *n.pl.* (*construed as sing.*) The study of the role of cells in heredity.
cy·tol·o·gy (sī·tol′ə·jē) *n.* The study of the structure, organization, and function of cells. —**cy·to·log·ic** (sī′tə·loj′ik) or **·i·cal** *adj.* —**cy′to·log′i·cal·ly** *adv.* —**cy·tol′o·gist** *n.*
cy·to·plasm (sī′tə·plaz′əm) *n. Biol.* All the protoplasm of a cell except that in the nucleus. —**cy′to·plas′mic** *adj.*
cy·to·sine (sīt′ə·sēn) *n. Chem.* A base that is a genetic coding constituent of DNA and RNA.
czar (zär) *n.* 1. An emperor or king; esp., one of the former emperors of Russia. 2. A despot. Also *tsar, tzar.* [< Russ. *tsar′*, ult. < L *Caesar* Caesar] —**czar′ism** *n.* —**czar′ist** *adj. & n.*
czar·e·vitch (zär′ə·vich) *n.* The eldest son of a czar: also *tsarevitch, tzarevitch.* [< Russ.]
cza·ri·na (zä·rē′nə) *n.* The wife of a czar; an empress of Russia: also *tsarina, tzarina.* Also **cza·rit·za** (zä·rit′sə). [< G *czarin*, for Russ. *tzaritsa*]
Czech (chek) *n.* 1. A member of the western branch of Slavs, including the peoples of Bohemia and Moravia. 2. The West Slavic language of the Czechs, formerly called Bohemian. —**Czech** *adj.*
Czech·o·slo·vak (chek′ə·slō′väk) *n.* A Czech or Slovak inhabiting Czechoslovakia. —**Czech′o·slo′vak** *adj.* —**Czech′o·slo·va′ki·an** *n. & adj.*

D

d, D (dē) *n.* *pl.* **d's** or **ds, D's** or **Ds, dees** (dēz) 1. The fourth letter of the English alphabet. 2. A sound represented by the letter *d.* —*symbol* 1. The Roman numeral for 500. 2. *Music* The second tone in the diatonic scale of C. 3. *Math.* Differential. 4. The fourth in a series or group. 5. Pence. 6. *Chem.* Deuterium (symbol D). 7. *Physics* Density.

dab[1] (dab) *n.* 1. Any of various flounders. 2. Any flatfish.

dab[2] (dab) *n.* 1. A soft, moist patch: a *dab* of paint. 2. A little bit. —*v.t.* & *v.i.* **dabbed, dab·bing** 1. To strike softly; tap. 2. To pat with something soft and damp. 3. To apply (paint, etc.) with light strokes. [ME *dabben*] —**dab'ber** *n.*

dab·ble (dab'əl) *v.* **·bled, ·bling** *v.i.* 1. To play in a liquid; splash gently. 2. To engage oneself slightly or superficially: to *dabble* in art. —*v.t.* 3. To wet slightly; bespatter. [Freq. of DAB[2], v.] —**dab'bler** *n.*

da ca·po (dä kä'pō) *Music* From the beginning: a direction to repeat the opening section.

dace (dās) *n.* *pl.* **dac·es** or **dace** A small fresh-water fish of the carp family. [< OF *dars*, a small fish, lit., dart]

da·cha (dä'chə) *n.* A Russian country villa, esp. a summer house. [< Russ., gift]

dachs·hund (däks'hoont') *n.* A breed of dog having a long body, short legs, and a short coat. [< G *dachs* badger + *hund* dog]

Da·cron (dā'kron, dak'ron) *n.* A synthetic polyester textile fiber: a trade name.

dac·tyl (dak'təl) *n.* In prosody, a metrical foot consisting of one long or accented syllable followed by two short or unaccented ones (—⏑⏑). [< Gk. *daktylos* finger, dactyl] —**dac·tyl·ic** (dak·til'ik) *adj.* & *n.*

dactylo- *combining form* Finger; toe. Also, before vowels, **dactyl-**. [< Gk. *daktylos* finger]

dad (dad) *n.* *Informal* Father. Also **dad·dy** (dad'ē). [Origin unknown]

da·da (dä'dä, -də) *n.* *Often cap.* A movement in art and literature, occurring in Europe about 1916–20, that protested against traditionalism and satirized all previous art. Also **da'da·ism.** [< F *dada*, a nonsense word] —**da'da·ist** *n.*

dad·dy-long·legs (dad'ē·lông'legz') *n.* *pl.* **·legs** A long-legged insect resembling a spider.

da·do (dā'dō) *n.* *pl.* **·does** 1. *Archit.* The part of a pedestal between the base and the cornice. 2. The lower part of an interior wall, often ornamented. [< Ital., a cube]

daf·fo·dil (daf'ə·dil) *n.* A plant of the amaryllis family, with solitary yellow flowers. [Var. of ME *affodile*]

daf·fy (daf'ē) *adj.* **·fi·er, ·fi·est** *Informal* Crazy; silly; zany. [< dial E *daff* fool]

daft (daft) *adj.* Foolish; crazy. [OE *gedæfte* mild, meek] —**daft'ly** *adv.* —**daft'ness** *n.*

dag·ger (dag'ər) *n.* 1. A short, pointed and edged weapon for stabbing. 2. *Printing* A reference mark (†). [? ME *dag* to stab]

da·guerre·o·type (də·ger'ə·tīp', -ē·ə·tīp') *n.* 1. An early photographic process using light-sensitive, silver-coated copper plates. 2. A picture made by this process. [after Louis *Daguerre*, 1789–1851, French inventor]

dahl·ia (dal'yə, däl'-, dāl'-) *n.* A perennial plant of the composite family, having tuberous roots and showy flowers; also, the flowers. [after Anders *Dahl*, 18th c. botanist]

dai·ly (dā'lē) *adj.* Of, occurring, or appearing every day or every weekday. —*n.* *pl.* **·lies** A daily publication. —*adv.* Day after day; on every day. [OE *dæg* day]

daily double A bet on the winners of two designated horse races.

daily dozen A set of exercises done daily.

dain·ty (dān'tē) *adj.* **·ti·er, ·ti·est** 1. Delicately pretty or graceful. 2. Fastidious; also, too fastidious. 3. Delicious; choice. —*n.* *pl.* **·ties** A delicacy. [< L *dignitas* worth, dignity] —**dain'ti·ly** *adv.* —**dain'ti·ness** *n.*

dai·qui·ri (dī'kər·ē, dak'ər·ē) *n.* A cocktail made of rum, lime or lemon juice, and sugar. [after *Daiquiri*, Cuba]

dair·y (dâr'ē) *n.* *pl.* **·ies** 1. A commercial establishment that sells milk products. 2. A room or building on a farm where milk and cream are kept and processed. 3. A dairy farm. [ME *deie* dairymaid]

dairy cattle Cows of a breed adapted for milk production.

dairy farm A farm for producing dairy products.

dair·y·ing (dâr'ē·ing) *n.* The business of a dairy.

dair·y·maid (dâr'ē·mād') *n.* A female worker in a dairy.

dair·y·man (dâr'ē·mən) *n.* *pl.* **·men** (-mən) A man who works in or owns a dairy.

da·is (dā'is, dās) *n.* A raised platform in a room or hall for a speaker, eminent guests, etc. [< OF *deis* < LL *discus* table]

dai·sy (dā'zē) *n.* *pl.* **·sies** A plant of the composite family; esp., the **oxeye daisy,** of the U.S., having a yellow disk and white rays, and the **English daisy,** having a small yellow disk and numerous white or rose rays. [OE *dægas ēage* day's eye]

Da·ko·ta (də·kō'tə) *n.* 1. A member of a Siouan tribe of North American Plains Indians. 2. The Siouan language of the Dakotas. —**Da·ko'tan** *adj.* & *n.*

Da·lai La·ma (dä·lī' lä'mə) The spiritual leader of Tibetan Lamaism, and traditional chief of state.

da·la·si (dä·lä'sē) *n.* The monetary unit of Gambia.

dale (dāl) *n.* A small valley. [OE *dæl*]

dal·ly (dal′ē) *v.* **·lied, ·ly·ing** *v.i.* 1. To make love playfully; flirt or fondle. 2. To play; trifle. 3. To waste time. —*v.t.* 4. To waste (time): with *away*. [< OF *dalier* to converse, chat] —**dal′li·ance** *n.* —**dal′li·er** *n.*

Dal·ma·tian (dal·mā′shən) *n.* 1. A large, short-haired dog, white with black spots: also called *coach dog*. 2. One of the Slavic people of Dalmatia. —*adj.* Of or pertaining to Dalmatia or its people.

dam[1] (dam) *n.* 1. A barrier to obstruct or control the flow of water. 2. The water held back by such a barrier. 3. Any obstruction. —*v.t.* **dammed, dam·ming** 1. To erect a dam in. 2. To keep back; restrain: with *up* or *in*. [ME. Akin to OE *demman* to block.]

dam[2] (dam) *n.* A female parent: said of animals. [< DAME]

dam·age (dam′ij) *n.* 1. Injury to person or property. 2. *pl. Law* Money to compensate for an injury or wrong. —*v.t. & v.i.* **·aged, ·ag·ing** To cause damage to or suffer damage. [< L *damnum* loss] —**dam′age·a·ble** *adj.*

dam·as·cene (dam′ə·sēn, dam′ə·sēn′) *v.t.* **·cened, ·cen·ing** To ornament (iron, steel, etc.) with wavy patterns or by inlaying or etching. —*adj.* Relating to damascening or to damask. —*n.* Work ornamented by damascening.

Damascus steel A steel with wavy markings, orig. used in swords made at Damascus.

dam·ask (dam′əsk) *n.* 1. A rich, reversible, elaborately patterned fabric, used for table linen, etc. 2. Damascus steel. 3. A deep pink or rose color. —*adj.* 1. Made of Damascus steel or of damask. 2. Deep pink or rose-colored. [after *Damascus*]

damask rose A large, fragrant, pink rose of the Near East.

dame (dām) *n.* 1. A mature woman; matron. 2. *Slang* A woman. 3. In Great Britain: a A title conferred on women, equivalent to that of knight. b The legal title of the wife of a knight or baronet. [< L *domina* lady]

damn (dam) *v.t.* 1. To condemn. 2. To curse or swear at. 3. *Theol.* To condemn to eternal punishment. —*v.i.* 4. To swear; curse. —*n.* 1. The saying of "damn" as an oath. 2. The smallest, most contemptible bit. —*interj.* An oath expressive of irritation, disappointment, etc. —*adj. & adv. Informal* Damned. [< L *damnare* to condemn to punishment]

dam·na·ble (dam′nə·bəl) *adj.* Meriting damnation; detestable; outrageous. [< L *damnare* to condemn] —**dam′na·bly** *adv.*

dam·na·tion (dam·nā′shən) *n.* 1. The act of damning, or the state of being damned. 2. *Theol.* Condemnation to eternal punishment; also, the punishment suffered. —*interj.* Damn.

damn·dest (dam′dist) *Informal adj.* 1. Most detestable or outrageous. 2. Most extraordinary. —*n.* The utmost: Do your *damndest*. Also **damned′est.**

damned (damd, *poetic or rhetorical* dam′nid) *adj.* 1. Doomed; condemned, esp. to eternal punishment. 2. Deserving damnation. —*adv. Informal* Very: *damned* funny.

damn·ing (dam′ing, dam′ning) *adj.* That damns or condemns; inculpating: *damning* evidence. —**damn′ing·ly** *adv.*

damp (damp) *adj.* Somewhat wet; moist. —*n.* 1. Moisture or moistness; vapor; mist. 2. Foul air or poisonous gas, esp. in a mine. —*v.t.* 1. To make damp; moisten. 2. To stifle, check, reduce, etc. [< MDu., vapor, steam] —**damp′ly** *adv.* —**damp′ness** *n.*

damp·en (dam′pən) *v.t.* 1. To make damp; moisten. 2. To check; depress. —*v.i.* 3. To become damp. —**damp′en·er** *n.*

damp·er (dam′pər) *n.* 1. One who or that which depresses or checks. 2. A plate in the flue of a stove, furnace, etc., for controlling the draft. 3. *Music* A device for stopping the vibrations of piano strings.

dam·sel (dam′zəl) *n.* A young unmarried woman; maiden. Also, *Poetic,* **dam·o·sel** (dam′ə·zəl). [< OF *dameisele* gentlewoman]

dam·son (dam′zən, -sən) *n.* 1. An oval purple plum. 2. The tree producing it. Also **damson plum.** [< L *Damascenum* from Damascus]

dan (dan) *n.* Any of several levels of expertise in the martial arts, as judo and karate. [< Japanese, grade]

dance (dans) *v.* **danced, danc·ing** *v.i.* 1. To move the body and feet rhythmically, esp. to music. 2. To move about lightly or excitedly; leap or bob about. —*v.t.* 3. To perform the steps of (a waltz, tango, etc.). 4. To cause to dance. —**to dance attendance** To wait upon another constantly. —*n.* 1. A series of regular rhythmic steps or movements, usu. performed to music. 2. A musical composition for dancing. 3. A gathering of people for dancing; a ball. [< OF *danser*] —**danc′er** *n.*

dan·de·li·on (dan′də·lī′ən, -dē-) *n.* A widespread plant having yellow flowers and toothed, edible leaves. [< F *dent de lion* lion's tooth; with ref. to the shape of the leaves]

dan·der (dan′dər) *n.* *Informal* Ruffled temper; anger. —**to get one's dander up** To become angry. [? Var. of Scottish *dunder* to ferment]

dan·di·fy (dan′də·fī) *v.t.* **·fied, ·fy·ing** To cause to resemble a dandy or fop.

dan·dle (dan′dəl) *v.t.* **·dled, ·dling** 1. To move up and down lightly on the knees or in the arms, as an infant or child. 2. To fondle; caress. [< Ital. *dandolare*] —**dan′dler** *n.*

dan·druff (dan′drəf) *n.* A fine scurf that forms on the scalp and comes off in small scales. [Origin unknown]

dan·dy (dan′dē) *n. pl.* **·dies** 1. A man who is excessively interested in an elegant appearance; a fop. 2. *Informal* Something particularly fine. —*adj.* 1. Like a dandy; foppish. 2. *Informal* Excellent; very fine. [Alter. of *Andy*, a personal name] —**dan′dy·ish** *adj.*

Dane (dān) *n.* A native or inhabitant of Denmark, or a person of Danish descent. [< ON *Danir* the Danes]

dan·ger (dān′jər) *n.* 1. Exposure to evil, injury, or loss; peril; risk. 2. A cause or instance of peril or risk. [< OF, power to harm]

dan·ger·ous (dān′jər·əs) *adj.* Attended with danger; perilous; unsafe. —**dan′ger·ous·ly** *adv.*

dan·gle (dang′gəl) *v.* **·gled, ·gling** *v.i.* 1. To hang loosely; swing to and fro. 2. To follow or hover near. 3. *Gram.* To lack clear or proper connection in a sentence. —*v.t.* 4. To hold so as to swing loosely. 5. To leave in an uncertain state. [< Scand. Cf. Dan. *dangle.*] —**dan′gler** *n.*

Dan·iel (dan′yəl) *n.* A book of the Old

Testament, containing the story and prophecies of Daniel. [after *Daniel*, a young Hebrew prophet]

Dan·ish (dā′nish) *adj.* Of or pertaining to Denmark, the Danes, or their language. —*n.* The North Germanic language of the Danes. [OE *Denisc*]

dank (dangk) *adj.* Cold and damp. [ME *danke*] —**dank′ly** *adv.* —**dank′ness** *n.*

dan·seuse (dän·sœz′) *n. pl.* **·seus·es** (-sœ′ziz, *Fr.* -sœz′) A female ballet dancer. [< F, fem. of *danseur*]

dap·per (dap′ər) *adj.* 1. Smartly dressed. 2. Small and active. [< MDu., strong]

dap·ple (dap′əl) *v.t.* **·pled, ·pling** To make spotted or variegated in color. —*adj.* Spotted; variegated: also **dap′pled.** —*n.* 1. A spot or dot, as on the skin of a horse. 2. An animal marked with spots. [Origin uncertain]

dare (dâr) *v.* **dared, dar·ing** *v.t.* 1. To have the courage or boldness to undertake. 2. To challenge (someone) to attempt something. —*v.i.* 3. To have the courage or boldness to do or attempt something; venture. —*n.* A challenge; taunt. [OE *durran*] —**dar′er** *n.*

dare·dev·il (dâr′dev′əl) *n.* One who is recklessly bold. —*adj.* Rash; reckless.

dar·ing (dâr′ing) *n.* Adventurous courage; bravery; boldness. —**dar′ing** *adj.* —**dar′ing·ly** *adv.*

dark (därk) *adj.* 1. Having or reflecting little or no light; dim. 2. Of a deep shade; black, or almost black. 3. Brunet in complexion. 4. Cheerless or disheartening. 5. Sullen; dour. 6. Unenlightened; ignorant. 7. Evil or sinister: a *dark* deed. 8. Mysterious or secret; obscure. —*n.* 1. Lack of light. 2. A place or condition of little or no light. 3. Night. 4. Obscurity; secrecy. 5. Ignorance. 6. A dark shadow or color. —**in the dark** Ignorant; uninformed. [OE *deorc*] —**dark′ness** *n.*

Dark Ages The period in European history between the fall of the Western Roman Empire (A.D. 476) and the Italian Renaissance.

dark·en (där′kən) *v.t.* 1. To make dark or darker; deprive of light. 2. To make dark in color. 3. To sadden. 4. To obscure; confuse. —*v.i.* 5. To grow dark or darker; become obscure. 6. To grow clouded. —**dark′en·er** *n.*

dark horse One who unexpectedly wins a race, contest, nomination, etc.

dark·ling (därk′ling) *Poetic adj.* Occurring or being in the dark; dim. —*adv.* In the dark. [< DARK + -LING[2]]

dark·ly (därk′lē) *adv.* 1. Obscurely. 2. Mysteriously.

dark·room (därk′ro͞om′, -ro͝om′) *n. Photog.* A room equipped to exclude light rays harmful in developing films, etc.

dark star *Astron.* An invisible or dimly shining star.

dar·ling (där′ling) *n.* 1. A person tenderly loved: often a term of address. 2. A person in great favor. —*adj.* 1. Beloved; very dear. 2. Charming; attractive. [OE *dēorling*, dim. of *dēor* dear]

darn[1] (därn) *v.t. & v.i.* To repair (a garment or a hole) by filling the gap with interlacing stitches. —*n.* A place mended by darning. [? OE *dernan* to conceal] —**darn′er** *n.*

darn[2] (därn) *v.t., adj., n., & interj. Informal* Damn: a euphemism. [Alter. of DAMN]

dar·nel (där′nəl) *n.* An annual grass often found in grain fields. [< dial. F *darnelle*]

darn·ing needle (därn′ing) 1. A large-eyed needle used in darning. 2. A dragonfly.

dart (därt) *n.* 1. A thin, pointed weapon to be thrown or shot. 2. Anything like a dart in appearance or effect. 3. A sudden, rapid motion. 4. A tapering tuck made in a garment to make it fit. —*v.i.* 1. To move suddenly; rush. —*v.t.* 2. To throw or emit suddenly or swiftly. [< Gmc.]

dart·er (där′tər) *n.* 1. One who or that which darts. 2. A small perchlike fish.

darts (därts) *n.pl.* (*construed as sing.*) A game in which darts are thrown at a target.

Dar·win·ism (där′win·iz′əm) *n.* The biological doctrine of the origin of species through descent by natural selection with variation, advocated by Charles Darwin. —**Dar·win′i·an** *n. & adj.* —**Dar′win·ist** *n. & adj.*

dash (dash) *v.t.* 1. To strike, throw, or thrust with violence, esp. so as to break or shatter. 2. To bespatter. 3. To do, write, etc., hastily: with *off* or *down.* 4. To frustrate; confound: to *dash* hopes. 5. To put to shame; abash. —*v.i.* 6. To strike or hit with violence. 7. To rush or move impetuously. —*n.* 1. A collision; impact. 2. A splashing or splash. 3. A small amount of some ingredient. 4. A hasty stroke, as with a pen. 5. A short rush. 6. A short race: the 100-yard *dash.* 7. Vigor of style; verve. 8. A horizontal line (—) used as a mark of punctuation to set off words or phrases in a sentence. 9. *Telecom.* The long sound in the Morse or similar code, used in combination with the dot to represent letters or numbers. [ME *daschen* < Scand.]

dash·board (dash′bôrd′) *n.* The instrument panel of an automobile.

dash·er (dash′ər) *n.* 1. One who or that which dashes. 2. The plunger of a churn.

da·shi·ki (dä·shē′kē) *n.* A one-piece garment that hangs loosely from the shoulders, adapted from an African garment for men. [< Yoruba]

dash·ing (dash′ing) *adj.* 1. Spirited; bold. 2. Showy or gay. —**dash′ing·ly** *adv.*

das·tard (das′tərd) *n.* A base coward; a sneak. [? ME *dased, dast,* pp. of *dasen* to daze + -ARD] —**das′tard·li·ness** *n.* —**das′·tard·ly** *adj.*

da·ta (dā′tə, dat′ə) *n.pl. of* **datum** (*often construed as sing.*) Facts or figures from which conclusions may be drawn. [< L, neut. pl. of *datus,* pp. of *dare* to give]

data bank A collection of information computerized for swift access.

data processing The operations involved in handling and storing information, using computers and other machines.

date[1] (dāt) *n.* 1. A particular point of time when something occurs. 2. An inscription giving a date, esp. when something was written or made. 3. The age or period to which a thing belongs. 4. The day of the month. 5. *Informal* A social appointment for a specified time. 6. *Informal* A person of the opposite sex with whom such an appointment is made. —**to date** Till now. —*v.* **dat·ed, dat·ing** *v.t.* 1. To furnish or mark with a date. 2. To ascertain the time or era of; assign a date to. 3. *Informal* To make an appointment or frequent appointments with (a member of the opposite sex); go out with. —*v.i.* 4. To have origin in an era or time: usually with *from:* This coin *dates* from the Renaissance. 5. *Informal* To have social engagements with members of the opposite sex. [< L *data*, fem. pp. of *dare* to give] —**dat′a·ble** or **date′a·ble** *adj.*

date[2] (dāt) *n.* 1. The sweet fruit of a palm. 2. A palm bearing this fruit: also **date palm.** [< Gk. *daktylos* finger]

dat·ed (dā′tid) *adj.* 1. Marked with a date. 2. Antiquated; old-fashioned.

date·less (dāt′lis) *adj.* 1. Bearing no date. 2. Without end or limit. 3. Of permanent interest.

date·line (dāt′līn′) *n.* The line containing the date and place of issue of a publication or of any contribution printed in it. —**date′line′** *v.t.* **·lined, ·lin·ing**

date line An imaginary line determining those points on the earth's surface where a day is dropped on crossing it from west to east and added crossing east to west.

da·tive (dā′tiv) *n. Gram.* The case of a noun, pronoun, or adjective denoting the indirect object, expressed in English by *to* or *for* with the objective or by word order, as in *I told the story to him, I told him the story.* [< L *dativus*, trans. of Gk. (*ptōsis*) *dotikē* (the case of) giving] —**da′tive** *adj.*

da·tum (dā′təm, dat′əm) Singular of DATA.

daub (dôb) *v.t. & v.i.* 1. To smear or coat (something). 2. To paint without skill. —*n.* 1. Any sticky application, as of plaster. 2. A smear or spot. 3. A poor painting. 4. An instance or act of daubing. [< L *dealbare* to whitewash] —**daub′er** *n.*

daugh·ter (dô′tər) *n.* 1. A female child, considered in relationship to either or both of her parents. 2. A female descendant. [OE *dohtor*] —**daugh′ter·ly** *adj.*

daugh·ter-in-law (dô′tər·in·lô′) *n. pl.* **daugh·ters-in-law** The wife of one's son.

daunt (dônt, dänt) *v.t.* To dishearten or intimidate; cow. [< L *domare* to tame]

daunt·less (dônt′lis, dänt′-) *adj.* Fearless; intrepid. —**daunt′less·ly** *adv.*

dau·phin (dô′fin, *Fr.* dō·faṅ′) *n.* The eldest son of a king of France. [< F, dolphin]

dav·en·port (dav′ən·pôrt) *n.* A large, upholstered sofa. [Prob. from the name of the first manufacturer]

dav·it (dav′it, dā′vit) *n. Naut.* One of a pair of small cranes on a ship's side for hoisting its boats, stores, etc. [Appar. from *David*, proper name]

Davy Jones's locker The bottom of the ocean, esp. as the grave of the drowned.

daw·dle (dôd′l) *v.t. & v.i.* **·dled, ·dling** To waste (time); idle: often with *away.* —**daw′·dler** *n.*

dawn (dôn) *n.* 1. Daybreak. ◆Collateral adjective: *auroral.* 2. A beginning or unfolding. —*v.i.* 1. To begin to grow light in the morning. 2. To begin to be understood: with *on* or *upon.* 3. To begin to expand or develop. [ME *dawenyng* daybreak]

day (dā) *n.* 1. The period of light from dawn to dark; daylight. 2. The interval represented by one rotation of the earth; twenty-four hours. ◆Collateral adjective: *diurnal.* 3. A portion of a day spent in a particular way or place: a shopping *day.* 4. The hours of a day devoted to work: a seven-hour *day.* 5. A time or period; epoch. 6. *Usu. cap.* A particular day: Labor *Day.* 7. *Often pl.* A lifetime. 8. A period of success: Your *day* will come. —**day after day** Every day. —**day by day** Each day. —**day in, day out** Every day. [OE *dæg*]

day bed A lounge or couch that can be converted into a bed.

day·book (dā′bo͝ok′) *n.* 1. In bookkeeping, the book in which transactions are recorded chronologically. 2. A diary or journal.

day·break (dā′brāk′) *n.* The time each morning when daylight replaces darkness.

day-care (dā′kâr′) *adj.* Of or relating to a facility for preschool children during the day.

day coach A railroad car without special accommodations for sleeping, dining, etc.

day·dream (dā′drēm′) *n.* A dreamlike thought; reverie. —**day′dream′** *v.i.* —**day′·dream′er** *n.*

day laborer One who works for pay by the day, esp. at unskilled manual tasks.

day·light (dā′līt′) *n.* 1. The light received from the sun; the light of day. 2. Insight into something; understanding. 3. Exposure to view; publicity. 4. The period of light during the day.

day·light-sav·ing time (dā′līt′sā′ving) Time in which clocks are set ahead of standard time, so that there is more daylight toward the end of the day.

day·long (dā′lông′, -long′) *adj.* Lasting all day. —*adv.* Through the entire day.

Day of Atonement Yom Kippur.

day school A private school for pupils who live at home.

day·time (dā′tīm′) *n.* The time of daylight.

daze (dāz) *v.t.* **dazed, daz·ing** To stupefy or bewilder; stun. —*n.* The state of being dazed. [ME *dasen*] —**daz′ed·ly** *adv.*

daz·zle (daz′əl) *v.* **·zled, ·zling** *v.t.* 1. To blind or dim the vision of by excess of light. 2. To bewilder or charm, as with magnificence. —*v.i.* 3. To be blinded by lights or glare. 4. To excite admiration. —*n.* 1. The act of dazzling, or the state of being dazzled. 2. Brightness; brilliance. [Freq. of DAZE] —**daz′zler** *n.* —**daz′zling·ly** *adv.*

D-day (dē′dā′) *n.* In military operations, the unspecified date of the launching of an attack.

DDT A powerful insecticide. [< D(I-CHLORO)D(IPHENYL)T(RICHLOROETHANE)]

de- *prefix* 1. Away; off: *deflect, decapitate.* 2. Down: *decline.* 3. Completely; utterly: *denude.* 4. The undoing, reversing, or ridding of (the action, condition or substance expressed. by the main element): *decode, decentralization.* [< L *de* from, away, down < L *dis-*]

Some self-explanatory words beginning with *de-* (def. 4):

de-Anglicize	**deflea**
decarbonate	**deforest**
dechlorinate	**deforestation**
declassify	**deglamorize**
decolorize	**destigmatize**
de-emphasize	**dewax**

dea·con (dē′kən) *n.* 1. A lay church officer or subordinate minister. 2. A clergyman ranking next below a priest. [< Gk. *diakonos* servant, minister] —**dea′con·ess** *n.fem.* —**dea′con·ry** *n.*

de·ac·ti·vate (dē·ak′tə·vāt) *v.t.* **·vat·ed, ·vat·ing** 1. To render inactive or ineffective, as an explosive, chemical, etc. 2. *Mil.* To release (a military unit, ship, etc.) from active duty; demobilize. **—de·ac′ti·va′tion** *n.*

dead (ded) *adj.* 1. Having ceased to live; lifeless. 2. Deathlike; inanimate; insensible. 3. Lacking sensation; numb. 4. Extinct: a *dead* language. 5. No longer in force: a *dead* law. 6. Not productively used: *dead* capital. 7. *Informal* Very tired. 8. Lacking activity, excitement, etc.: a *dead* town. 9. Dull: said of colors. 10. Muffled: said of sounds. 11. Without elasticity. 12. Complete; utter: *dead* silence. 13. Perfect; exact. 14. In certain games, out of play: said of the ball. **—***n.* 1. A dead person, or dead persons collectively: preceded by *the.* 2. The coldest, darkest, or most intense part: the *dead* of winter. **—***adv.* 1. Completely: to stop *dead.* 2. Directly: *dead* ahead. [OE *dēad*]

dead·beat (ded′bēt′) *n. Slang* One who avoids paying his bills or his way.

dead·en (ded′n) *v.t.* 1. To diminish the sensitivity, force, or intensity of. 2. To render soundproof. 3. To make dull or less brilliant.

dead end 1. A passage, street, etc., having no outlet. 2. A point from which no progress can be made.

dead·eye (ded′ī′) *n. Naut.* A wooden disk pierced by holes and having a grooved circumference, used to set up shrouds, stays, etc.

dead·fall (ded′fôl′) *n.* A trap operated by a weight that falls upon an animal.

dead·head (ded′hed′) *Informal n.* 1. One who is admitted, entertained, or accommodated free of charge. 2. A dull, stupid person. **—***v.t. & v.i.* To treat or go as a deadhead. **—***adj.* Traveling without passengers or freight.

dead heat A race in which two or more competitors tie.

dead letter A letter that is unclaimed or cannot be delivered because of a faulty address.

dead·line (ded′līn′) *n.* A time limit, as for the completion of newspaper copy.

dead·lock (ded′lok′) *n.* A standstill or stoppage of activity resulting from the unrelenting opposition of equally powerful forces. **—***v.t. & v.i.* To cause or come to a deadlock.

dead·ly (ded′lē) *adj.* **·li·er, ·li·est** 1. Likely or certain to cause death. 2. Implacable; mortal: a *deadly* enemy. 3. Resembling death: *deadly* pallor. 4. Ruinous; destructive. 5. Excessive. **—***adv.* 1. As in death; deathly. 2. *Informal* Very. **—dead′li·ness** *n.*

deadly nightshade Belladonna.

dead pan *Slang* A completely expressionless face. **—dead·pan** (ded′pan′) *adj. & adv.*

dead reckoning *Naut.* The computation of a vessel's position by log and compass without astronomical observations.

dead weight 1. The weight or load of something inert. 2. In transportation, the weight of a vehicle as distinguished from its load.

dead·wood (ded′wŏŏd′) *n.* 1. Wood dead on the tree. 2. A worthless person or thing.

deaf (def) *adj.* 1. Partly or completely lacking the power to hear. 2. Unwilling to listen. [OE *dēaf*] **—deaf′ly** *adv.* **—deaf′ness** *n.*

deaf·en (def′ən) *v.t.* 1. To make deaf. 2. To overwhelm, as with noise. 3. To make soundproof. **—deaf′en·ing** *adj. & n.* **—deaf′en·ing·ly** *adv.*

deaf-mute (def′myōōt′) *n.* A deaf person who cannot speak, usu. because of deafness from early life. Also **deaf mute.**

deal[1] (dēl) *v.* **dealt** (delt), **deal·ing** *v.t.* 1. To distribute or portion out. 2. To apportion to (a person). 3. To deliver or inflict, as a blow. **—***v.i.* 4. To conduct oneself: with *with.* 5. To be concerned: with *in* or *with:* to *deal* in facts. 6. To consider, discuss, or take action: with *with.* 7. To do business: with *in, with,* or *at.* 8. In card games, to act as dealer. **—***n.* 1. The act of dealing. 2. In card games: **a** The distribution of the cards to the players. **b** The right or turn to distribute the cards. **c** The cards distributed; a hand. 3. An indefinite amount, degree, extent, etc.: a great *deal* of time. 4. *Informal* A business transaction. 5. *Informal* A secret arrangement, as in politics. 6. *Informal* A plan, agreement, or treatment: a rough *deal.* [OE *dǣlan.*]

deal[2] (dēl) *n.* A fir or pine plank. [< MDu. *dele* plank] **—deal** *adj.*

deal·er (dē′lər) *n.* 1. One engaged in buying and selling: a car *dealer.* 2. In card games, one who distributes the cards.

deal·ing (dē′ling) *n.* 1. The act of distributing. 2. *Usu. pl.* Transactions or relations with others.

dealt (delt) Past tense and past participle of DEAL.

dean (dēn) *n.* 1. An officer of a college or university, having jurisdiction over a particular group of students or area of study, or acting as head of a faculty. 2. The senior member of a group. 3. The chief ecclesiastical officer of a cathedral or of a collegiate church. [< OF *deien* < LL *decanus* head of ten men] **—dean′ship** *n.*

dean·er·y (dē′nər·ē) *n. pl.* **·er·ies** The office, jurisdiction, or place of residence of a dean.

dear (dir) *adj.* 1. Beloved; precious. 2. Highly esteemed: used in letter salutations. 3. Expensive; costly. 4. Intense; earnest: our *dearest* wish. **—***n.* A darling. **—***interj.* An exclamation of regret, surprise, etc. [OE *dēore*] **—dear′ly** *adv.* **—dear′ness** *n.*

dearth (dûrth) *n.* Scarcity; lack; famine. [ME *derthe*]

dear·y (dir′ē) *n. pl.* **dear·ies** *Informal* Darling; dear. Also **dear′ie.**

death (deth) *n.* 1. The permanent cessation of all vital functions in an animal or plant. 2. The condition of being dead. 3. The extinction of anything; destruction. 4. The cause or manner of dying. ◆Collateral adjectives: *lethal, mortal.* **—to put to death** To kill; execute. [OE *dēath*]

death·bed (deth′bed′) *n.* 1. The bed on which a person dies. 2. The last hours of life.

death·blow (deth′blō′) *n.* That which causes the death or the end of a person or thing.

death·less (deth′lis) *adj.* Not liable to die; perpetual; immortal. **—death′less·ly** *adv.* **—death′less·ness** *n.*

death·ly (deth′lē) *adj.* 1. Resembling or suggesting death. Also **death′like.** 2. Causing death; fatal. **—***adv.* 1. In a deathlike manner. 2. Extremely: *deathly* ill.

death mask A cast of the face taken just after death.
death rate The number of persons per thousand of population who die within a given time.
death rattle The rattling sound of the breath of one dying.
death's-head (deths'hed') *n.* A human skull, or a representation of it, as a symbol of death.
death·trap (deth'trap') *n.* Anything unsafe or dangerous; esp., a building or structure.
death·watch (deth'woch') *n.* 1. A vigil kept at the side of one who is dying or has recently died. 2. A guard set over a condemned man before his execution. 3. A beetle that makes a ticking sound.
deb (deb) *n.* Debutante.
de·ba·cle (di·bäk'əl, -bak'-) *n.* 1. A sudden and disastrous breakdown or collapse. 2. The breaking up of ice in a river. 3. A violent flood. [< F *débâcler* to unbar]
de·bar (di·bär') *v.t.* **·barred, ·bar·ring** To bar or shut out: usu. with *from.* [< F *dé-* away + *barrer* to bar] **—de·bar'ment** *n.*
de·bark (di·bärk') *v.t. & v.i.* To put or go ashore from a ship. [< F *dé-* away + *barque* ship] **—de·bar·ka·tion** (dē'bär·kā'shən) *n.*
de·base (di·bās') *v.t.* **·based, ·bas·ing** To lower in character or worth; degrade. **—de·base'ment** *n.* **—de·bas'er** *n.*
de·bate (di·bāt') *n.* 1. A discussion of any question; argument; dispute. 2. A formal contest in argumentation. **—***v.t. & v.i.* **·bat·ed, ·bat·ing** 1. To argue; discuss. 2. To consider; deliberate, as upon alternatives. 3. To discuss (a question) in formal debate. [< OF *debatre* to strike] **—de·bat'a·ble** *adj.* **—de·bat'er** *n.*
de·bauch (di·boch', -bôch') *v.t.* 1. To corrupt in morals; seduce; deprave. **—***v.i.* 2. To indulge in debauchery; dissipate. **—***n.* An act or period of debauchery. [< OF *desbaucher* to lure from work] **—de·bauch'er** *n.* **—de·bauch'ment** *n.*
de·bauch·er·y (di·bô'chər·ē) *n. pl.* **·er·ies** Gross indulgence of one's sensual appetites.
de·ben·ture (di·ben'chər) *n.* 1. A certificate given as acknowledgment of debt. 2. A bond, usu. without security, issued by a corporation. [< L *debere* to owe]
de·bil·i·tate (di·bil'ə·tāt) *v.t.* **·tat·ed, ·tat·ing** To make feeble or languid; weaken. [< L *debilitare* to weaken] **—de·bil'i·ta'tion** *n.* **—de·bil'i·ta'tive** *adj.*
de·bil·i·ty (di·bil'ə·tē) *n. pl.* **·ties** Abnormal weakness. [< L *debilis* weak]
deb·it (deb'it) *n.* 1. An item of debt recorded in an account. 2. An entry of debt in an account, or the sum of such entries. **—***v.t.* 1. To enter (a debt) in an account. 2. To charge (someone) with a debt. [< L *debere* to owe]
deb·o·nair (deb'ə·nâr') *adj.* 1. Pleasantly gracious. 2. Cheerful; lively; gay. [< OF *de bon aire* of good mien] **—deb'o·nair'ly** *adv.*
de·bouch (di·bōōsh', -bouch') *v.i.* 1. *Mil.* To march from a narrow passage, wood, etc., into the open. 2. To come or empty forth; issue. **—***v.t.* 3. To cause to emerge. [< F *dé-* from + *bouche* mouth] **—de·bouch'ment** *n.*
de·bris (də·brē', dā'brē) *n. pl.* **·bris** (-brēz) 1. Scattered remains, as of something destroyed; ruins; rubble. 2. *Geol.* An accumulation of rock fragments. Also **dé·bris'.** [< OF *debrisier* to break away]
debt (det) *n.* 1. That which one owes, as money, goods, or services. 2. The obligation to pay or render something. 3. The condition of owing something. [< L *debere* to owe]
debt·or (det'ər) *n.* One who owes a debt.
de·bug (dē·bug') *v.t.* **·bugged, ·bug·ging** 1. To eliminate flaws in (a mechanism or system) by testing and use. 2. To rid of a hidden listening device (*bug*).
de·bunk (di·bungk') *v.t.* *Informal* To expose as false or pretentious. [< BUNK[2]]
de·but (di·byōō', dā-, dā'byōō) *n.* 1. A first public appearance. 2. A formal introduction to society. 3. The beginning, as of a career. Also **dé·but'.** [< F *débuter* to begin] **—de·but'** *v.i.*
deb·u·tante (deb'yōō·tänt, -yə-) *n.* A young woman making a debut in society. Also **dé'bu·tante'.**
deca- *combining form* 1. Ten. 2. In the metric system, *deka-*. Also, before vowels, **dec-.** [< Gk. *deka*]
dec·ade (dek'ād) *n.* A period of ten years.
dec·a·dence (dek'ə·dəns, di·kād'ns) *n.* 1. A process of deterioration; decay. 2. A condition or period of decline, as in morals. [< L *de-* down + *cadere* to fall] **—dec'a·dent** *adj. & n.* **—dec'a·dent·ly** *adv.*
dec·a·gon (dek'ə·gon) *n.* *Geom.* A polygon with ten sides and ten angles. [< DECA- + Gk. *gōnia* angle] **—de·cag·o·nal** (di·kag'ə·nəl) *adj.*
dec·a·he·dron (dek'ə·hē'drən) *n. pl.* **·drons** or **·dra** (-drə) *Geom.* A ten-sided solid figure. [< DECA- + Gk. *hedra* seat] **—dec'a·he'dral** *adj.*
de·cal (dē'kal, di·kal') *n.* A design or print prepared for transfer by decalcomania.
de·cal·ci·fy (dē·kal'sə·fī) *v.t.* **·fied, ·fy·ing** To remove lime or calcareous matter from (bones, teeth, etc.). **—de·cal'ci·fi·ca'tion** *n.*
de·cal·co·ma·ni·a (di·kal'kə·mā'nē·ə) *n.* 1. A process of transferring prints, designs, etc., from specially prepared paper to glass or other material. 2. A decal. [< F *décalquer* to transfer a tracing + *-manie* -mania]
Dec·a·logue (dek'ə·lôg, -log) *n.* The Ten Commandments. [< DECA- + Gk. *logos* word]
de·camp (di·kamp') *v.i.* 1. To break camp. 2. To leave suddenly or secretly; run away. **—de·camp'ment** *n.*
de·cant (di·kant') *v.t.* 1. To pour off (a liquid) without disturbing its sediment. 2. To pour from one container into another. [< Med.L *de-* from + *canthus* lip of a jug]
de·cant·er (di·kan'tər) *n.* A vessel for decanting; esp. a decorative bottle.
de·cap·i·tate (di·kap'ə·tāt) *v.t.* **·tat·ed, ·tat·ing** To cut off the head of; behead. [< L *de-* off + *caput* head] **—de·cap'i·ta'tion** *n.*
dec·a·pod (dek'ə·pod) *adj.* Ten-footed or ten-armed. **—***n.* *Zool.* 1. A crustacean having five pairs of legs, as a crab. 2. Any ten-armed mollusk, as a squid. [< DECA- + Gk. *pous* foot]
de·car·bu·rize (dē·kär'byə·rīz) *v.t.* **·rized, ·riz·ing** To remove carbon from (molten steel or the cylinders of an internal-combustion engine). **—de·car'bu·ri·za'tion** *n.*
de·cath·lon (di·kath'lon) *n.* An athletic

contest consisting of ten different track and field events in all of which each contestant participates. [< DEC(A)- + Gk. *athlon* a contest]

de·cay (di·kā′) *v.i.* 1. To fail slowly as in health, strength, etc. 2. To decompose; rot. 3. *Physics* To change, disintegrate, or reduce radioactivity spontaneously. —*n.* 1. A deterioration. 2. A decomposition.

de·cease (di·sēs′) *v.i.* **·ceased, ·ceas·ing** To die. —*n.* Death. [< L *de-* away + *cedere* to go]

de·ceased (di·sēst′) *adj.* Dead. —**the deceased** The dead person or persons.

de·ce·dent (di·sēd′nt) *n.* *Law* A person deceased.

de·ceit (di·sēt′) *n.* 1. The act of deceiving. 2. An instance of deception or a device that deceives; a trick. 3. The quality of being deceptive; falseness. [See DECEIVE.] —**de·ceit′ful** *adj.* —**de·ceit′ful·ly** *adv.* —**de·ceit′ful·ness** *n.*

de·ceive (di·sēv′) *v.t.* & *v.i.* **·ceived, ·ceiv·ing** To mislead by deceit; delude. [< OF *deceveir*] —**de·ceiv′er** *n.* —**de·ceiv′ing·ly** *adv.*

de·cel·er·ate (dē·sel′ə·rāt) *v.t.* & *v.i.* **·at·ed, ·at·ing** To diminish in velocity. [< L *de-* down + (AC)CELERATE] —**de·cel′er·a′tion** *n.* —**de·cel′er·a′tor** *n.*

De·cem·ber (di·sem′bər) *n.* The twelfth month of the year, having 31 days. [< L *decem* ten; December was the tenth month in the old Roman calendar]

de·cen·cy (dē′sən·sē) *n.* *pl.* **·cies** 1. The quality or state of being decent; propriety. 2. *Usu. pl.* Those things that are proper or decent.

de·cen·ni·al (di·sen′ē·əl) *adj.* 1. Of or continuing for ten years. 2. Occurring every ten years. —*n.* An anniversary observed every ten years. —**de·cen′ni·al·ly** *adv.*

de·cent (dē′sənt) *adj.* 1. Characterized by propriety of conduct, speech, or dress; respectable. 2. Adequate; satisfactory. 3. Generous; kind. 4. *Informal* Adequately or properly clothed. [< L *decere* to be fitting, proper] —**de′cent·ly** *adv.* —**de′cent·ness** *n.*

de·cen·tral·ize (dē·sen′trəl·īz) *v.t.* **·ized, ·iz·ing** To reorganize into smaller and more autonomous parts. —**de·cen′tral·i·za′tion** *n.*

de·cep·tion (di·sep′shən) *n.* 1. The act of deceiving; deceit. 2. The state of being deceived. 3. Anything that deceives or is meant to deceive; a delusion. [See DECEIVE.]

de·cep·tive (di·sep′tiv) *adj.* Having the power or tendency to deceive. —**de·cep′tive·ly** *adv.* —**de·cep′tive·ness** *n.*

deci- *combining form* In the metric system, one tenth of (a specified unit): *decimeter.* [< L *decimus* tenth]

dec·i·bel (des′ə·bəl) *n.* *Physics* A measure of sound intensity.

de·cide (di·sīd′) *v.* **·cid·ed, ·cid·ing** *v.t.* 1. To determine; settle, as a controversy. 2. To determine the outcome of. 3. To bring (someone) to a decision. —*v.i.* 4. To make a decision or render a verdict. [< L *de-* down, away + *caedere* to cut]

de·cid·ed (di·sī′did) *adj.* 1. Certain; definite. 2. Determined; emphatic. —**de·cid′ed·ly** *adv.* —**de·cid′ed·ness** *n.*

de·cid·u·ous (di·sij′o͞o·əs) *adj.* 1. *Biol.* Falling off or shed at maturity or at specific seasons, as leaves or antlers. 2. Shedding foliage annually: distinguished from *evergreen.* [< L *de-* down, away + *cadere* to fall] —**de·cid′u·ous·ly** *adv.* —**de·cid′u·ous·ness** *n.*

dec·i·gram (des′ə·gram) *n.* In the metric system, the tenth part of a gram. Also *Brit.* **dec′i·gramme.**

dec·i·li·ter (des′ə·lē′tər) *n.* In the metric system, the tenth part of a liter. Also *esp. Brit.* **dec′i·li′tre.**

dec·i·mal (des′ə·məl) *adj.* 1. Pertaining to or founded on the number 10. 2. Proceeding by tens. —*n.* A decimal fraction or one of its digits. [< L *decem* ten]

decimal fraction *Math.* A fraction whose denominator is any power of 10 and which may be expressed in decimal form, as 7/10 (0.7).

decimal point A dot used before a decimal fraction.

decimal system A system of reckoning by tens or tenths.

dec·i·mate (des′ə·māt) *v.t.* **·mat·ed, ·mat·ing** 1. To destroy or kill a large proportion of. 2. To kill one out of every ten of. [< L *decimare* to take a tenth part from] —**dec′i·ma′tion** *n.*

dec·i·me·ter (des′ə·mē′tər) *n.* In the metric system, the tenth part of a meter. Also *esp. Brit.* **dec′i·me′tre.**

de·ci·pher (di·sī′fər) *v.t.* 1. To determine the meaning of (something obscure, illegible, etc.) 2. To decode. —**de·ci′pher·a·ble** *adj.* —**de·ci′pher·er** *n.*

de·ci·sion (di·sizh′ən) *n.* 1. The act of deciding (an issue, question, etc.). 2. A conclusion or judgment reached by deciding. 3. Firmness in judgment, action, or character. [See DECIDE.]

de·ci·sive (di·sī′siv) *adj.* 1. Ending uncertainty or dispute; conclusive. 2. Firm; determined. 3. Unquestionable; unmistakable. —**de·ci′sive·ly** *adv.* —**de·ci′sive·ness** *n.*

deck (dek) *n.* 1. *Naut.* **a** A platform covering or extending horizontally across a vessel, and serving as both floor and roof. **b** The space between two such platforms. 2. Any similar flat surface, as a porch. 3. A pack of playing cards. —*v.t.* 1. To dress or decorate elegantly; adorn. 2. *Slang* To knock to the ground. [< MDu. *dek* roof, covering]

deck·er (dek′ər) *n.* Something with one or more decks, layers, levels, etc.: usu. in combination: a *double-decker.*

deck hand A common sailor employed on deck.

deck·le (dek′əl) *n.* 1. In making paper, a frame that limits the size of the sheet. 2. The ragged edge of paper so made: also **deckle edge.** [< G *decke* cover] —**deck′le-edged′** (-ejd′) *adj.*

de·claim (di·klām′) *v.i.* 1. To speak loudly and rhetorically. 2. To give a formal, set speech. 3. To attack verbally and vehemently: with *against.* —*v.t.* 4. To utter rhetorically. [< L *de-* completely + *clamare* to shout] —**de·claim′er** *n.* —**dec·la·ma·tion** (dek′lə·mā′shən) *n.* —**de·clam·a·to·ry** (di·klam′ə·tôr′ē) *adj.*

dec·la·ra·tion (dek′lə·rā′shən) *n.* 1. The act of declaring or proclaiming. 2. That which is declared. 3. A statement of goods liable to taxation. 4. In bridge, a contract.

de·clar·a·tive (di·klar′ə·tiv) *adj.* Making a declaration or statement. Also **de·clar′a·to′ry.**

de·clare (di·klâr′) *v.t.* **·clared, ·clar·ing** 1. To

make known or clear; esp. to announce formally. 2. To say emphatically; assert. 3. To reveal; prove. 4. To make full statement of, as goods liable to duty. [< L *de-* completely + *clarare* to make clear] —**de·clar′er** *n.*

dé·clas·sé (dā·klȧ·sā′) *adj. French* Fallen or lowered in social status, class, rank, etc.

de·clen·sion (di·klen′shən) *n.* 1. *Gram.* The inflection of nouns, pronouns, and adjectives according to case, number, and gender. 2. A sloping downward; descent. 3. A decline. [See DECLINE.]

dec·li·na·tion (dek′lə·nā′shən) *n.* 1. The act of inclining or bending downward. 2. Deviation, as in direction or conduct. 3. The angle formed between the direction of a compass needle and true north. 4. *Astron.* The angular distance of a heavenly body north or south from the celestial equator. 5. A polite refusal.

de·cline (di·klīn′) *v.* **·clined, ·clin·ing** *v.i.* 1. To refuse politely to accept or do something. 2. To lessen or fail gradually, as in health. 3. To draw to an end. 4. To bend or incline downward or aside. —*v.t.* 5. To refuse politely to accept or do. 6. To cause to bend or incline downward or aside. 7. *Gram.* To give the inflected forms of (a noun, pronoun, or adjective). —*n.* 1. The act or result of declining; deterioration. 2. A period of declining. 3. Mental or physical weakening or deterioration. 4. A downward slope. [< L *declinare* to lean down] —**de·clin′a·ble** *adj.* —**de·clin′er** *n.*

de·cliv·i·ty (di·kliv′ə·tē) *n. pl.* **·ties** A downward slope. [< L *de-* down + *clivus* hill, slope] —**de·cliv′i·tous** *adj.*

de·coct (di·kokt′) *v.t.* To extract by boiling; condense. [< L *de-* down + *coquere* to cook] —**de·coc′tion** *n.*

de·code (dē·kōd′) *v.t.* **·cod·ed, ·cod·ing** To convert from code into plain language. —**de·cod′er** *n.*

dé·colle·té (dā′kol·tā′) *adj.* 1. Cut low in the neck, as a gown. 2. Wearing a low-necked garment. [< F]

de·com·mis·sion (dē′kə·mish′ən) *v.t.* To take out of active service, as a ship.

de·com·pose (dē′kəm·pōz′) *v.t. & v.i.* **·posed, ·pos·ing** 1. To separate into constituent parts. 2. To decay. —**de′com·pos′a·ble** *adj.* —**de·com·po·si·tion** (dē′kom·pə·zish′ən) *n.*

de·com·press (dē′kəm·pres′) *v.t.* To free of pressure; reduce or remove the pressure on (divers, etc.). —**de′com·pres′sion** *n.*

decompression sickness Caisson disease.

de·con·tam·i·nate (dē′kən·tam′ə·nāt) *v.t.* **·nat·ed, ·nat·ing** To make (a contaminated object or area) safe.

de·con·trol (dē′kən·trōl′) *v.t.* **·trolled, ·trol·ling** To remove from control. —*n.* The removal of controls.

dé·cor (dā′kôr, dā·kôr′) *n.* The scheme or style of decoration, as of a room. Also **de′cor.** [< F *décorer* to decorate]

dec·o·rate (dek′ə·rāt) *v.t.* **·rat·ed, ·rat·ing** 1. To embellish or furnish with things beautiful; adorn. 2. To confer a decoration or medal upon. [< L *decus, decoris* grace, embellishment] —**dec·o·ra·tive** (dek′ər·ə·tiv) *adj.* —**dec′o·ra·tive·ly** *adv.* —**dec′o·ra′tor** *n.*

dec·o·ra·tion (dek′ə·rā′shən) *n.* 1. The act, process, or art of decorating. 2. A thing or group of things that decorate; ornamentation. 3. A badge, ribbon, or medal awarded for merit.

Decoration Day Memorial Day.

dec·o·rous (dek′ər·əs, di·kôr′əs) *adj.* Marked by decorum; seemly; proper. [< L *decus, decoris* grace] —**dec′o·rous·ly** *adv.* —**dec′o·rous·ness** *n.*

de·co·rum (di·kôr′əm) *n.* Conformity to the requirements of good taste or social convention; propriety in manners. [See DECOROUS.]

de·cou·page (dā·kōō·päzh′) *n.* The art and craft of decorating surfaces, as furniture, by gluing on paper designs: also **dé·cou·page′.** [< F]

de·coy (*n.* di·koi′, dē′koi; *v.* di·koi′) *n.* 1. A person or thing that lures into danger, deception, etc. 2. A bird or animal, or the likeness of one, used to lure game. 3. An enclosed place into which game may be lured. —*v.t. & v.i.* To lure or be lured into danger or a trap. [Earlier *coy* < Du. *kooi* a cage]

de·crease (*v.* di·krēs′; *n.* dē′krēs, di·krēs′) *v.t. & v.i.* **·creased, ·creas·ing** To grow, or cause to grow, gradually less or smaller; diminish. —*n.* 1. The act, process, or state of decreasing. 2. The amount or degree of decreasing. [< L *de-* down + *crescere* to grow] —**de·creas′ing·ly** *adv.*

de·cree (di·krē′) *n.* A formal and authoritative order or decision. —*v.* **·creed, ·cree·ing** *v.t.* 1. To order, adjudge, or appoint by law or edict. —*v.i.* 2. To issue an edict or decree. [< L *de-* down + *cernere* to decide]

dec·re·ment (dek′rə·mənt) *n.* 1. The act or process of decreasing. 2. The amount lost by decrease.

de·crep·it (di·krep′it) *adj.* Enfeebled or worn out by old age or excessive use. [< L *de-* completely + *crepare* to creak] —**de·crep′it·ly** *adv.* —**de·crep′i·tude** *n.*

de·crim·i·nal·ize (dē·krim′ə·nal·īz) *v.t.* **·ized, ·iz·ing** To remove from regulation by criminal laws: the state *decriminalized* marijuana use.

de·cry (di·krī′) *v.t.* **·cried, ·cry·ing** To condemn or disparage openly. [< F *dé-* down + *crier* to cry] —**de·cri′al** *n.* —**de·cri′er** *n.*

de·cum·bent (di·kum′bənt) *adj.* 1. Lying down. 2. *Bot.* Prostrate: said of stems, shoots, etc., growing along the ground. [< L *de-* down + *cumbere* to lie, recline]

de·cus·sate (di·kus′āt, -it) *adj.* 1. Crossed. 2. *Bot.* Having each pair of leaves at right angles with the pair below or above. [< L *decussare* to mark with an X]

ded·i·cate (ded′ə·kāt, -i-) *v.t.* **·cat·ed, ·cat·ing** 1. To set apart for any special use, duty, or purpose. 2. To inscribe (a work of literature, etc.) to someone. 3. To commit (oneself) to a certain course of action or thought. 4. To open or unveil (a bridge, statue, etc.) to the public. [< L *de-* down + *dicare* to proclaim]

ded·i·ca·tion (ded′ə·kā′shən, -i-) *n.* 1. The act of dedicating or the state of being dedicated. 2. An inscription dedicating a literary work, etc. —**ded′i·ca·to′ry** (-kə·tôr′ē), **ded′i·ca′tive** *adj.*

de·duce (di·dōōs′, -dyōōs′) *v.t.* **·duced, ·duc·ing** 1. To derive as a conclusion by reasoning. 2. To trace, as origin. [< L *de-* down + *ducere* to lead] —**de·duc′i·ble** *adj.*

de·duct (di·dukt′) *v.t.* To take away or subtract. [See DEDUCE.] —**de·duct′i·ble** *adj.*

de·duc·tion (di·duk′shən) *n.* 1. The act of deducing. 2. *Logic* Reasoning from the general to the particular; also, reasoning from stated premises to logical conclusions. 3. The act of deducting; also, the amount deducted. —**de·duc′tive** *adj.* —**de·duc′tive·ly** *adv.*

deed (dēd) *n.* 1. Anything done; an act. 2. A notable achievement; feat. 3. Action in general, as opposed to words. 4. *Law* Any written, sealed instrument of bond, contract, transfer, etc., esp. of real estate conveyance. —**in deed** In fact; in truth; actually. —*v.t.* To transfer by deed. [OE *dǣd*]

deem (dēm) *v.t. & v.i.* To judge; think; believe. [OE *dēman* to judge]

deep (dēp) *adj.* 1. Extending or situated far below a surface. 2. Extending far inward or backward, or to either side. 3. Having a (specified) depth or dimension: six feet *deep.* 4. Rising to the level of: used in combination: *knee-deep.* 5. Coming from or penetrating to a depth: a *deep* sigh. 6. Difficult to understand. 7. Learned; wise. 8. Profound; extreme. 9. Of intense or dark hue. 10. Of low, sonorous tone. 11. Absorbed: *deep* in thought. —*n.* 1. A place or thing of great depth; an abyss. 2. The most intense or profound part. —**the deep** *Poetic* The sea or ocean. —*adv.* 1. To great depth. 2. Far along in time. 3. *Sports* Farther than normal from the center of play: the outfield played *deep* for the slugger. [OE *dēop*] —**deep′ly** *adv.* —**deep′ness** *n.*

deep-dyed (dēp′dīd′) *adj.* Thoroughgoing; absolute.

deep·en (dē′pən) *v.t. & v.i.* To make or become deep or deeper.

deep·freeze (dēp′frēz′) *n.* A refrigerator for quick-freezing and storing food. —**deep′·freeze′** *v.t.* ·**froze** or ·**freezed,** ·**fro·zen** or ·**freezed,** ·**freez·ing**

deep-fry (dēp′frī′) *v.t.* -**fried,** -**fry·ing** To fry in deep fat.

deep-root·ed (dēp′rōō′tid, -rŏŏt′id) *adj.* 1. Having roots far below the surface. 2. Based deep within; deep-seated.

deep-seat·ed (dēp′sē′tid) *adj.* Established far within; difficult to remove.

deep-set (dēp′set′) *adj.* Deeply placed, as eyes.

deep structure *Ling.* A representation of a sentence in simple syntactic forms that reveal its semantic content.

deer (dir) *n. pl.* **deer** A ruminant animal having deciduous antlers, usu. in the male only, as the moose, elk, and reindeer. ◆Collateral adjective: *cervine.* [OE *dēor* beast]

deer·hound (dir′hound′) *n.* A breed of hunting dog, having a shaggy coat.

deer·skin (dir′skin′) *n.* A deer's hide, or leather made from it.

de-es·ca·late (dē·es′kə·lāt) *v.t. & v.i.* ·**lat·ed,** ·**lat·ing** To decrease or be decreased gradually, as in scope, effect, or intensity: to *de-escalate* a war. —**de-es′ca·la′tion** *n.*

de·face (di·fās′) *v.t.* ·**faced,** ·**fac·ing** To mar the surface or appearance of; disfigure. [< OF *des-* down, away + *face* face] —**de·face′ment** *n.*

de fac·to (dē fak′tō) Actually or really existing: distinguished from *de jure.* [< L]

de·fal·cate (di·fal′kāt) *v.i.* ·**cat·ed,** ·**cat·ing** To embezzle. [< L *de-* down, away + *falx* scythe] —**de·fal·ca·tion** (dē′fal·kā′shən) *n.* —**de·fal′ca·tor** *n.*

de·fame (di·fām′) *v.t.* ·**famed,** ·**fam·ing** To attack the good name or reputation of; slander; libel. [< L *dis-* away, from + *fama* reputation] —**def·a·ma·tion** (def′ə·mā′shən) *n.* —**de·fam·a·to·ry** (di·fam′ə·tôr′ē) *adj.* —**de·fam′er** *n.*

de·fault (di·fôlt′) *n.* A failure or neglect to fulfill an obligation or requirement, as to pay money due or finish a contest or game. [< OF *defaute*] —**de·fault′** *v.t. & v.i.* —**de·fault′er** *n.*

de·feat (di·fēt′) *v.t.* 1. To overcome in any conflict or competition; beat. 2. To prevent the success of; frustrate. —*n.* 1. The act or result of defeating; an overthrow; failure. 2. Frustration; bafflement. [< OF *des-* not + *faire* to do]

de·feat·ism (di·fē′tiz·əm) *n.* The practice of those who accept defeat as inevitable. —**de·feat′ist** *n. & adj.*

def·e·cate (def′ə·kāt) *v.* ·**cat·ed,** ·**cat·ing** *v.i.* 1. To eliminate wastes from the bowels. —*v.t.* 2. To refine; purify. [< L *de-* down, away + *faex* dregs] —**def′e·ca′tion** *n.* —**def′e·ca′tor** *n.*

de·fect (*n.* di·fekt′, dē′fekt; *v.* di·fekt′) *n.* 1. Lack of something necessary for perfection or completeness. 2. A blemish; failing; fault. —*v.i.* To desert. [< L *defectus* a lack] —**de·fec′tion** *n.* —**de·fec′tor** *n.*

de·fec·tive (di·fek′tiv) *adj.* Having a defect; imperfect; faulty. —*n.* One who or that which is imperfect. —**de·fec′tive·ly** *adv.* —**de·fec′tive·ness** *n.*

de·fend (di·fend′) *v.t.* 1. To shield from danger, attack, or injury; protect. 2. To justify or support. 3. *Law* **a** To act in behalf of (an accused). **b** To contest (a charge or suit). [< OF *defendre* to protect] —**de·fend′a·ble** *adj.* —**de·fend′er** *n.*

de·fen·dant (di·fen′dənt) *n. Law* One against whom an action is brought. —*adj.* Defending.

de·fense (di·fens′) *n.* 1. The act of defending against danger or attack. 2. Anything that serves to defend. 3. A plea or argument in justification or support of something. 4. *Law* **a** The defendant's denial of the truth of a complaint. **b** A defendant and his legal counsel, collectively. 5. The act or science of protecting oneself or a goal, as in sports. [See DEFEND.] —**de·fense′less** *adj.* —**de·fense′less·ly** *adv.*

defense mechanism *Psychoanal.* An unconscious shutting out of painful emotions and unacceptable impulses.

de·fen·si·ble (di·fen′sə·bəl) *adj.* Capable of being defended, maintained, or justified. —**de·fen′si·bil′i·ty** *n.* —**de·fen′si·bly** *adv.*

de·fen·sive (di·fen′siv) *adj.* 1. Intended or suitable for defense. 2. Carried on for the purpose of defense. 3. Having an attitude of defense. —*n.* An attitude or position of defense. —**de·fen′sive·ly** *adv.* —**de·fen′sive·ness** *n.*

de·fer[1] (di·fûr′) *v.t. & v.i.* ·**ferred,** ·**fer·ring** To delay or put off to some other time;

postpone. [See DIFFER.] —**de·fer′ra·ble** *adj.* —**de·fer′ment, de·fer′ral** *n.*

de·fer[2] (di·fûr′) *v.i.* **·ferred, ·fer·ring** To yield to the opinions or decisions of another: with *to.* [< OF *deferer* to yield] —**de·fer′rer** *n.*

def·er·ence (def′ər·əns) *n.* 1. Yielding to the will, opinions, etc., of another. 2. Respectful regard. —**def′er·ent, def·er·en·tial** (def′ə·ren′shəl) *adj.* —**def′er·en′tial·ly** *adv.*

de·ferred (di·fûrd′) *adj.* 1. Postponed. 2. With benefits or payments held back for a specific time: *deferred* stock. 3. Temporarily exempted from military draft.

de·fi·ance (di·fī′əns) *n.* 1. Bold opposition or resistance. 2. A challenge. —**de·fi′ant** *adj.* —**de·fi′ant·ly** *adv.*

de·fi·cien·cy (di·fish′ən·sē) *n. pl.* **·cies** 1. The state of being deficient. 2. A lack; insufficiency.

de·fi·cient (di·fish′ənt) *adj.* Lacking some essential; incomplete or defective. [See DEFECT.] —**de·fi′cient·ly** *adv.*

def·i·cit (def′ə·sit) *n.* The amount by which an expected or required sum of money falls short. [< L, it is lacking]

de·fi·er (di·fī′ər) *n.* One who defies.

de·file[1] (di·fīl′) *v.t.* **·filed, ·fil·ing** 1. To make foul or dirty. 2. To corrupt the purity of; sully or profane. [< OF *de-* down + *fouler* to trample] —**de·file′ment** *n.* —**de·fil′er** *n.*

de·file[2] (di·fīl′, dē′fīl) *v.i.* **·filed, ·fil·ing** To march in a line. —*n.* 1. A long, narrow pass, as between mountains. 2. A marching in file. [< MF *de-* down + *file* row]

de·fine (di·fīn′) *v.t.* **·fined, ·fin·ing** 1. To state the meaning of (a word, etc.). 2. To describe the nature or properties of; explain. 3. To determine the boundary or extent of. 4. To bring out the outline of; show clearly. 5. To specify, as the limits of power. —*v.i.* 6. To make a definition. [< L *definire* to limit] —**de·fin′a·ble** *adj.* —**de·fin′er** *n.*

def·i·nite (def′ə·nit) *adj.* 1. Having precise limits, quantity, etc.: a *definite* sum. 2. Known for certain; positive. 3. Clearly defined; precise. [< L. See DEFINE.] —**def′i·nite·ly** *adv.* —**def′i·nite·ness** *n.*

definite article *Gram.* See under ARTICLE.

def·i·ni·tion (def′ə·nish′ən) *n.* 1. The act of stating what a word, set of terms, etc., means. 2. A statement of the meaning of a word, phrase, etc. 3. The determining of the outline or limits of anything. 4. The state of being clearly outlined or determined; distinctness.

de·fin·i·tive (di·fin′ə·tiv) *adj.* 1. Sharply defining or limiting; explicit. 2. Conclusive and unalterable; final. 3. Most nearly accurate and complete: a *definitive* edition of Chaucer. —**de·fin′i·tive·ly** *adv.* —**de·fin′i·tive·ness** *n.*

de·flate (di·flāt′) *v.t.* & *v.i.* **·flat·ed, ·flat·ing** 1. To collapse by letting out air or gas. 2. To reduce in self-esteem. 3. *Econ.* To reduce or restrict (money or spending) so that prices decline. [< L *de-* down + *flare* to blow] —**de·fla′tion** *n.* —**de·fla′tion·ar′y** *adj.* —**de·fla′tor** *n.*

de·flect (di·flekt′) *v.t.* & *v.i.* To turn aside; swerve. [< L *de-* down + *flectere* to bend] —**de·flec′tor** *n.*

de·flec·tion (di·flek′shən) *n.* 1. The act of deflecting, or the state of being deflected. 2. The amount of deviation. Also *Brit.* **de·flex′ion.**

de·flow·er (di·flou′ər) *v.t.* 1. To despoil of flowers. 2. To deprive (a woman) of virginity. 3. To violate; rob of beauty, etc. Also **de·flo·rate** (di·flôr′āte). [< L *de-* down, away + *flos, floris* flower] —**def·lo·ra·tion** (def′lə·rā′shən) *n.*

de·fog (dē·fog′, -fôg′) *v.t.* **·fogged, ·fog·ging** To remove condensed moisture from, as a windshield. —**de·fog′ger** *n.*

de·fo·li·ant (dē·fō′lē·ənt) *n.* A chemical spray that causes growing plants to lose their leaves.

de·fo·li·ate (dē·fō′lē·āt) *v.* **·at·ed, ·at·ing** *v.t.* 1. To deprive or strip of leaves. —*v.i.* 2. To lose leaves. [< L *de-* down + *folium* leaf] —**de·fo′li·a′tion** *n.* —**de·fo′li·a′tor** *n.*

de·form (di·fôrm′) *v.t.* 1. To distort the form of; render misshapen. 2. To mar the beauty or excellence of. —*v.i.* 3. To become deformed. [< L *deformare* to disfigure]

de·form·a·tion (dē′fôr·mā′shən, def′ər-) *n.* 1. The act of deforming, or the state of being deformed. 2. A change in form or condition for the worse. 3. An altered form.

de·form·i·ty (di·fôr′mə·tē) *n. pl.* **·ties** 1. A deformed condition. 2. Anything deformed. [< L *deformis* misshapen]

de·fraud (di·frôd′) *v.t.* To take or withhold from by fraud; cheat; swindle. [< L *de-* completely + *fraus, fraudis* cheat] —**de·fraud′er** *n.*

de·fray (di·frā′) *v.t.* To pay (the costs, expenses, etc.). [< F *défrayer*] —**de·fray′a·ble** *adj.* —**de·fray′al, de·fray′ment** *n.*

de·frock (dē·frok′) *v.t.* To unfrock.

de·frost (dē·frôst′) *v.t.* To remove ice or frost from.

de·frost·er (dē·frôs′tər) *n.* A device that removes or prevents ice or frost formation.

deft (deft) *adj.* Neat and skillful in action; adroit. [OE *gedæfte* meek, gentle] —**deft′ly** *adv.* —**deft′ness** *n.*

de·funct (di·fungkt′) *adj.* Dead or inactive. [< L *de-* not + *fungi* to perform]

de·fuse (dē·fyo͞oz′) *v.t.* 1. To remove a fuse from, as a bomb. 2. *Informal* To remove the danger or potency from, as from a situation or argument.

de·fy (di·fī′) *v.t.* **·fied, ·fy·ing** 1. To resist, challenge, or confront openly and boldly. 2. To resist or withstand successfully. [< L *di-* not + *fidare* to be faithful]

de·gauss (di·gous′) *v.t.* To neutralize the magnetic field of, as a ship. [< L *de-* away + GAUSS]

de·gen·er·a·cy (di·jen′ər·ə·sē) *n.* 1. The process of degenerating; deterioration. 2. The state of being degenerate.

de·gen·er·ate (*v.* di·jen′ə·rāt; *adj., n.* di·jen′ər·it) *v.i.* **·at·ed, ·at·ing** 1. To become worse, or more debased; deteriorate. 2. To revert to a lower or less functional condition. —*adj.* Having become worse; degraded. —*n.* 1. A deteriorated or degraded being. 2. A morally degraded person. [< L *de-* down + *generare* to create] —**de·gen′er·ate·ly** *adv.* —**de·gen′er·a′tion** *n.* —**de·gen·er·a·tive** (di·jen′ə·rā′tiv, -ər·ə·tiv) *adj.*

de·grade (di·grād′) *v.t.* **·grad·ed, ·grad·ing** 1. To debase or lower in character, quality, etc. 2. To bring into contempt; dishonor. 3. To reduce in rank, dignity, etc. [< L *de-* down + *gradi* to step] **—deg·ra·da·tion** (deg′rə·dā′shən) *n.* **—de·grad′ed** *adj.*

de·grad·ing (di·grā′ding) *adj.* Debasing; humiliating. **—de·grad′ing·ly** *adv.*

de·gree (di·grē′) *n.* 1. One of a succession of steps or stages. 2. Relative extent, amount, or intensity. 3. Relative dignity, rank, or position. 4. Relative condition, manner, or respect. 5. An academic title conferred by an institution of learning upon completion of a course of study, or as an honorary distinction. 6. A division or unit of a scale, as of a thermometer. 7. *Law* Measure of culpability: murder in the first *degree.* 8. *Geom.* One 360th of the circumference of a circle. 9. *Geog.* A line or point of the earth's surface defined by its angular distance from a standard meridian or the equator. 10. *Gram.* One of the forms of comparison (positive, comparative, or superlative) of an adjective or adverb. **—by degrees** Little by little; gradually. **—to a degree** Somewhat. [< OF *de-* down + *gre* < L *gradus* a step]

de·hu·man·ize (dē·hyōō′mən·īz) *v.t.* **·ized, ·iz·ing** To deprive of human qualities; make mechanical. **—de·hu′man·i·za′tion** *n.*

de·hu·mid·i·fi·er (dē′hyōō·mid′ə·fī′ər) *n.* An apparatus that removes moisture from the air.

de·hu·mid·i·fy (dē′hyōō·mid′ə·fī) *v.t.* **·fied, ·fy·ing** To render less humid. **—de′hu·mid′i·fi·ca′tion** *n.*

de·hy·drate (dē·hī′drāt) *v.t. & v.i.* **·drat·ed, ·drat·ing** To lose or cause to lose water; dry out. **—de′hy·dra′tion** *n.*

de·ice (dē·īs′) *v.t.* **·iced, ·ic·ing** To free from ice. **—de·ic′er** *n.*

de·if·ic (dē·if′ik) *adj.* 1. Making, or tending to make, divine. 2. Divine.

de·i·fy (dē′ə·fī) *v.t.* **·fied, ·fy·ing** 1. To make a god of. 2. To regard or worship as a god. 3. To glorify or idealize. [< L *deus* god + *facere* to make] **—de′i·fi·ca′tion** *n.*

deign (dān) *v.t. & v.i.* To think it befitting oneself (to do something); condescend. [< L *dignus* worthy]

de·ism (dē′iz·əm) *n.* Belief in the existence of God, based solely on reason and denying the power of revelation. [< L *deus* a god + -ISM] **—de′ist** *n.* **—de·is′tic** *adj.*

de·i·ty (dē′ə·tē) *n. pl.* **·ties** 1. A god, goddess, or divine person. 2. Divine nature or status; godhead; divinity. **—the Deity** God. [< L *deus* a god]

de·ject (di·jekt′) *v.t.* To depress in spirit; dishearten. [< L *de-* down + *jacere* to throw] **—de·ject′ed** *adj.* **—de·ject′ed·ly** *adv.*

de·jec·tion (di·jek′shən) *n.* Lowness of spirits; depression; melancholy.

de ju·re (dē jōōr′ē) *Latin* By right; rightfully or legally: distinguished from *de facto.*

deka- *combining form* In the metric system, ten times (a specified unit). Also, before vowels, **dek-**. [< Gk. *deka* ten]

dek·a·gram (dek′ə·gram) *n.* In the metric system, a measure of weight equal to 10 grams. Also *Brit.* **dek′a·gramme.**

dek·a·li·ter (dek′ə·lē′tər) *n.* In the metric system, a measure of capacity equal to 10 liters. Also *esp. Brit.* **dek′a·li′tre.**

Del·a·ware (del′ə·wâr) *n.* 1. A confederacy of Algonquian tribes of North American Indians, formerly occupying the whole Delaware River valley. 2. The language of these people.

de·lay (di·lā′) *v.t.* 1. To put off to a future time; postpone. 2. To make late; detain. **—***v.i.* 3. To linger; procrastinate. **—***n.* 1. The act of delaying or state of being delayed. 2. The amount of time of delay. [< OF *delaier*] **—de·lay′er** *n.*

de·le (dē′lē) *v.t.* **·led, ·le·ing** *Printing* To take out; delete. [< L, imperative of *delere* to erase]

de·lec·ta·ble (di·lek′tə·bəl) *adj.* Giving great pleasure; delightful. [< L *delectabilis*] **—de·lec′ta·bil′i·ty** *n.* **—de·lec′ta·bly** *adv.*

de·lec·ta·tion (dē′lek·tā′shən) *n.* Delight; enjoyment.

del·e·gate (*n.* del′ə·gāt, -git; *v.* del′ə·gāt) *n.* A person sent with authority to represent or act for another or others. **—***v.t.* **·gat·ed, ·gat·ing** 1. To send as a representative, with authority to act. 2. To commit or entrust (powers, authority, etc.) to another as an agent. [< L *de-* down + *legare* to send]

del·e·ga·tion (del′ə·gā′shən) *n.* 1. The act of delegating, or the state of being delegated; deputation. 2. A person or persons appointed to represent others; delegates collectively.

de·lete (di·lēt′) *v.t.* **·let·ed, ·let·ing** To take out (written or printed matter); cancel. [< L *deletus*, pp. of *delere* to erase, destroy] **—de·le′tion** *n.*

del·e·te·ri·ous (del′ə·tir′ē·əs) *adj.* Causing moral or physical injury. [< Gk. *dēlētērios* harmful] **—del′e·te′ri·ous·ly** *adv.* **—del′e·te′ri·ous·ness** *n.*

delft (delft) *n.* A glazed earthenware, usu. white or blue, first made at Delft, Holland.

del·i (del′ē) *n. pl.* **del·is** *Informal* A delicatessen.

de·lib·er·ate (*v.* di·lib′ə·rāt; *adj.* di·lib′ər·it) *v.* **·at·ed, ·at·ing** *v.i.* 1. To consider carefully and at length. 2. To take counsel together so as to reach a decision. **—***v.t.* 3. To consider carefully; weigh. **—***adj.* 1. Carefully thought out; intentional. 2. Slow and cautious. 3. Leisurely. [< L *de-* completely + *librare* to weigh] **—de·lib′er·ate·ly** *adv.* **—de·lib′er·ate·ness** *n.*

de·lib·er·a·tion (di·lib′ə·rā′shən) *n.* 1. Careful and prolonged consideration. 2. *Often pl.* Examination and discussion of the arguments for and against a measure. 3. Slowness and care in decision or action.

de·lib·er·a·tive (di·lib′ə·rā′tiv, -rə·tiv) *adj.* Involved in or characterized by deliberation.

del·i·ca·cy (del′ə·kə·sē) *n. pl.* **·cies** 1. The quality of being delicate. 2. Frailty or weakness of body. 3. Refinement of feeling. 4. Consideration for the feelings of others. 5. Nicety of touch or execution. 6. Sensitivity in reaction, as of instruments. 7. Need of cautious, tactful treatment: a subject of great *delicacy.* 8. Something choice and dainty, as an item of food.

del·i·cate (del′ə·kit) *adj.* 1. Exquisite and fine, as in workmanship. 2. Daintily pleasing, as in taste, aroma, or color. 3. Fragile; frail. 4. Requiring tactful treatment. 5. Gentle or considerate. 6. Sensitive and subtle, as in perception or expression. 7. Refined; fastidious. 8. Sensitively accurate: a *delicate* thermometer. [< L *delicatus* pleasing] **—del′i·cate·ly** *adv.* **—del′i·cate·ness** *n.*

del·i·ca·tes·sen (del′ə·kə·tes′ən) *n.pl.* 1. (*often construed as sing.*) Ready-to-serve foods, as cooked meats, cheeses, pickles, etc. 2. (*construed as sing.*) A store that sells such foods. [< G, pl. of *delicatesse* delicacy]

de·li·cious (di·lish′əs) *adj.* Extremely pleasant or enjoyable, esp. to the taste. [< L *delicia* delight] **—de·li′cious·ly** *adv.* **—de·li′cious·ness** *n.*

de·light (di·līt′) *n.* 1. Great pleasure; gratification; joy. 2. That which gives extreme pleasure. **—***v.t. & v.i.* To give or take great pleasure. [< L *delectare* to delight] **—de·light′ed** *adj.* **—de·light′ed·ly** *adv.*

de·light·ful (di·līt′fəl) *adj.* Extremely pleasing. **—de·light′ful·ly** *adv.* **—de·light′ful·ness** *n.*

de·lim·it (di·lim′it) *v.t.* To prescribe the limits of. [< L *de-* completely + *limitare* to bound] **—de·lim′i·ta′tion** *n.*

de·lin·e·ate (di·lin′ē·āt) *v.t.* **·at·ed, ·at·ing** 1. To draw in outline. 2. To represent by a drawing. 3. To portray verbally; describe. [< L *de-* completely + *lineare* to draw a line] **—de·lin′e·a′tion** *n.* **—de·lin′e·a′tor** *n.*

de·lin·quen·cy (di·ling′kwən·sē) *n. pl.* **·cies** 1. Neglect of duty. 2. A fault; offense. 3. Juvenile delinquency.

de·lin·quent (di·ling′kwənt) *adj.* 1. Neglectful of or failing in duty or obligation; guilty of an offense. 2. Due and unpaid, as taxes. **—***n.* 1. One who fails to perform a duty or commits a fault. 2. A juvenile delinquent. [< L *delinquere* to fail, offend] **—de·lin′quent·ly** *adv.*

del·i·quesce (del′ə·kwes′) *v.i.* **·quesced, ·quesc·ing** 1. To melt away. 2. To become liquid by absorbing moisture from the air. [< L *de-* completely + *liquescere* to melt] **—del′i·ques′cence** *n.* **—del′i·ques′cent** *adj.*

de·lir·i·ous (di·lir′ē·əs) *adj.* 1. Suffering from or caused by delirium. 2. Wildly excited. **—de·lir′i·ous·ly** *adv.* **—de·lir′i·ous·ness** *n.*

de·lir·i·um (di·lir′ē·əm) *n.* 1. A temporary mental disturbance associated with fever, etc., and marked by excitement, hallucinations, and incoherence. 2. Wild emotion or excitement. [< L *delirium* madness]

delirium tre·mens (trē′mənz) A violent delirium associated with alcoholism.

de·liv·er (di·liv′ər) *v.t.* 1. To hand over; surrender. 2. To carry and distribute: to *deliver* newspapers. 3. To give forth; deal: to *deliver* a blow. 4. To utter. 5. To throw or pitch, as a ball. 6. To free, as from danger. 7. To assist in the birth of (offspring). **—***v.i.* 8. *Informal* To produce as expected or promised. **—to be delivered of** To give birth to. [< L *de-* down, away + *liberare* to set free] **—de·liv′er·ance** *n.* **—de·liv′er·er** *n.*

de·liv·er·y (di·liv′ər·ē) *n. pl.* **·er·ies** 1. The act of delivering or distributing something. 2. That which is distributed, as mail. 3. Liberation; release. 4. Transference; a handing over. 5. The bringing forth of offspring. 6. Manner of utterance. 7. The act or manner of discharging a ball, a blow, etc.

dell (del) *n.* A small, secluded, usu. wooded valley. [ME]

de·louse (dē·lous′) *v.t.* **·loused, ·lous·ing** To remove lice or other insect vermin from.

Del·phic (del′fik) *adj.* 1. Relating to the ancient city of Delphi or to the famous oracle there. 2. Oracular.

del·phin·i·um (del·fin′ē·əm) *n.* Any of a genus of perennial plants of the crowfoot family, having large, spurred flowers, usu. blue; the larkspur. [< Gk. *delphis* dolphin; so called from the shape of the nectary]

del·ta (del′tə) *n.* 1. The fourth letter in the Greek alphabet (Δ, δ), corresponding to English *d.* 2. *Geog.* A typically triangular-shaped silt deposit at or in the mouth of a river. [< Gk.]

del·toid (del′toid) *n. Anat.* A triangular muscle covering the shoulder joint. **—***adj.* Shaped like a delta; triangular. [< Gk. *delta* the letter Δ + *eidos* form]

de·lude (di·lo͞od′) *v.t.* **·lud·ed, ·lud·ing** To mislead the mind or judgment of; deceive. [< L *deludere*] **—de·lud′er** *n.* **—de·lud′ing·ly** *adv.*

del·uge (del′yo͞oj) *v.t.* **·uged, ·ug·ing** 1. To flood with water. 2. To overwhelm; destroy. **—***n.* 1. A great flood or inundation. 2. Something that overwhelms or engulfs. **—the Deluge** The flood in the time of Noah. *Gen.* vii. [< L *dis-* away + *luere* to wash]

de·lu·sion (di·lo͞o′zhən) *n.* 1. The act of deluding or state of being deluded. 2. A false belief, held in spite of evidence to the contrary.

de·lu·sive (di·lo͞o′siv) *adj.* Tending to delude; misleading. Also **de·lu·so·ry** (di·lo͞o′sər·ē). **—de·lu′sive·ly** *adv.* **—de·lu′sive·ness** *n.*

de·luxe (di·lo͝oks′, di·luks′) *adj.* Elegant and expensive; of the highest quality. [< F, lit., of luxury]

delve (delv) *v.i.* **delved, delv·ing** 1. *Archaic* To dig, as with a shovel. 2. To investigate or research carefully. [OE *delfan*] **—delv′er** *n.*

de·mag·net·ize (dē·mag′nə·tīz) *v.t.* **·ized, ·iz·ing** To deprive of magnetism.

dem·a·gogue (dem′ə·gog) *n.* One who leads the populace by appealing to prejudices and emotions. Also **dem′a·gog.** [< Gk. *dēmos* people + *agein* to lead] **—dem′a·gog′ic** (-gog′ik, -goj′ik) or **·i·cal** *adj.* **—dem′a·gog′i·cal·ly** *adv.*

dem·a·gogu·er·y (dem′ə·gog′ər·ē) *n.* The spirit, method, or conduct of a demagogue.

dem·a·go·gy (dem′ə·gog′ē, -gō′jē) *n.* 1. Demagoguery. 2. The rule of a demagogue. 3. Demagogues collectively.

de·mand (di·mand′) *v.t.* 1. To ask for boldly or preemptorily. 2. To claim as due. 3. To have need for; require. **—***v.i.* 4. To make a demand. **—***n.* 1. The act of demanding. 2. That which is demanded. 3. A claim or requirement: the *demands* on one's time. 4. *Econ.* The desire to possess combined with the ability to purchase. **—in demand** Desired; sought after. [< L *de-* down, away + *mandare* to command, order]

de·mar·cate (di·mär′kāt, dē′mär·kāt) *v.t.* **·cat·ed, ·cat·ing** 1. To mark the limits of. 2. To differentiate; separate.

de·mar·ca·tion (dē′mär·kā′shən) *n.* 1. The fixing or marking of boundaries or limits. 2. The limits or boundaries fixed. 3. A limiting or separating. [< Sp. *de-* down (< L *de-*) + *marcar* to mark a boundary]

de·mean[1] (di·mēn′) *v.t.* To behave or conduct (oneself). [< OF *demener* to conduct]

de·mean² (di·mēn′) *v.t.* To lower in dignity or reputation; debase; degrade. [< DE- + MEAN², after *debase*]
de·mean·or (di·mē′nər) *n.* The manner in which one behaves or bears oneself. Also *Brit.* **de·mean′our.**
de·ment (di·ment′) *v.t.* To make insane.
de·ment·ed (di·men′tid) *adj.* Insane. **—de·ment′ed·ly** *adv.*
de·men·tia (di·men′shə) *n.* Loss or impairment of mental powers. [< L, madness]
dementia pre·cox (prē′koks) *Psychiatry* Schizophrenia: a former name. Also **de·men′tia prae′cox.**
de·mer·it (di·mer′it) *n.* 1. A defect; fault. 2. In schools, etc., a mark for failure or misconduct. [< L *de-* down, away + *merere* to deserve]
de·mesne (di·mān′, -mēn′) *n.* 1. In law, lands held in one's own power. 2. A manor house and the adjoining lands. 3. A region; domain. [< OF *demeine, demaine*]
demi- *prefix* 1. Half; intermediate. 2. Less in size, quality, etc.; partial. [< L *dis-* from, apart + *medius* middle]
dem·i·god (dem′ē·god′) *n.* 1. A minor deity. 2. A man who is the offspring of a god. 3. A man regarded as godlike.
dem·i·john (dem′ē·jon′) *n.* A narrow-necked jug, often enclosed in wickerwork. [< F *dame-jeanne*, lit., Lady Jane]
de·mil·i·ta·rize (dē·mil′ə·tə·rīz′) *v.t.* **·rized, ·riz·ing** To free from military control.
dem·i·mon·daine (dem′ē·mon·dān′) *n.* A woman of the demimonde. [< F]
dem·i·monde (dem′ē·mond, dem′ē·mond′) *n.* 1. The class of people, esp. courtesans, who have lost social position because of sexual promiscuity. 2. Any group of doubtful respectability. [< F *demi-* half + *monde* world]
de·mise (di·mīz′) *n.* 1. Death. 2. *Law* A transfer of rights or an estate. [< L *de-* down, away + *mittere* to send]
dem·i·tasse (dem′ē·tas′, -täs′) *n.* 1. A small cup in which after-dinner coffee is served. 2. Coffee served in such a cup. [< F, a half cup]
demo- *combining form* People. [< Gk. *dēmos*]
de·mo·bi·lize (dē·mō′bə·līz) *v.t.* **·lized, ·liz·ing** To disband (an army or troops). **—de·mo′bi·li·za′tion** *n.*
de·moc·ra·cy (di·mok′rə·sē) *n. pl.* **·cies** 1. A form of government in which political power resides in all the people and is exercised by them directly or is given to elected representatives. 2. A state so governed. 3. The spirit or practice of political, legal, or social equality. [< Gk. *dēmos* people + *krateein* to rule]
dem·o·crat (dem′ə·krat) *n.* 1. One who favors a democracy. 2. One who believes in political and social equality. 3. *cap.* A member of the Democratic Party.
dem·o·crat·ic (dem′ə·krat′ik) *adj.* 1. Characterized by the principles of democracy. 2. Existing or provided for the benefit or enjoyment of all. 3. Practicing social equality. 4. *cap.* Pertaining to or belonging to the Democratic Party. **—dem′o·crat′i·cal·ly** *adv.*
Democratic Party One of the two major political parties in the United States, dating from 1828.
de·moc·ra·tize (di·mok′rə·tīz) *v.t. & v.i.* **·tized, ·tiz·ing** To make or become democratic. **—de·moc′ra·ti·za′tion** *n.*
de·mod·u·late (dē·moj′o͝o·lāt) *v.t.* **·lat·ed, ·lat·ing** *Telecom.* To reverse the effect of modulation of (a carrier wave); detect.
de·mog·ra·phy (di·mog′rə·fē) *n.* The study of vital and social statistics, as of births, deaths, disease, etc. [< DEMO- + -GRAPHY] **—de·mog′ra·pher** *n.* **—dem·o·graph·ic** (dem′ə·graf′ik) *adj.* **—dem′o·graph′i·cal·ly** *adv.*
de·mol·ish (di·mol′ish) *v.t.* 1. To tear down, as a building. 2. To destroy utterly; ruin. [< L *de-* down + *moliri* to build]
dem·o·li·tion (dem′ə·lish′ən) *n.* 1. The act or result of demolishing; destruction. 2. *pl.* Explosives. **—dem′o·li′tion·ist** *n.*
demolition derby A contest in which drivers try to eliminate competing cars by crashing into them.
de·mon (dē′mən) *n.* 1. An evil spirit; devil. 2. A very wicked or cruel person. 3. *Informal* A person of great skill or zeal. [< Gk. *daimōn*]
de·mon·e·tize (dē·mon′ə·tīz) *v.t.* **·tized, ·tiz·ing** 1. To deprive (currency) of standard value. 2. To withdraw from use, as currency. **—de·mon′e·ti·za′tion** *n.*
de·mo·ni·ac (di·mō′nē·ak) *adj.* 1. Of, like, or befitting a demon. 2. Possessed by or as by demons; frenzied. Also **de·mo·ni·a·cal** (dē′mə·nī′ə·kəl). **—***n.* One supposedly possessed by a demon. **—de′mo·ni′a·cal·ly** *adv.*
de·mon·ic (di·mon′ik) *adj.* 1. Of or like a demon. 2. Inspired, as by a demon.
de·mon·ism (dē′mən·iz′əm) *n.* 1. Belief in demons. 2. Worship of demons. 3. Demonology. **—de′mon·ist** *n.*
demono- *combining form* Demon. Also, before vowels, **demon-.** [< Gk. *daimōn* spirit, god]
de·mon·ol·o·gy (dē′mən·ol′ə·jē) *n.* The study of demons or of belief in demons. **—de′mon·ol′o·gist** *n.*
de·mon·stra·ble (di·mon′strə·bəl) *adj.* Capable of being proved. **—de·mon′stra·bil′i·ty** *n.* **—de·mon′stra·bly** *adv.*
dem·on·strate (dem′ən·strāt) *v.* **·strat·ed, ·strat·ing** *v.t.* 1. To explain or describe, as by use of examples. 2. To prove or show by reasoning. 3. To show feelings clearly. **—***v.i.* 4. To take part in a public demonstration. [< L *demonstrare* to show] **—dem′on·stra′tor** *n.*
dem·on·stra·tion (dem′ən·strā′shən) *n.* 1. The act of making known or evident. 2. Undeniable proof or evidence. 3. An explanation or showing of how something works, as a product. 4. A show or expression. 5. A display of public feeling, as a mass meeting or parade.
de·mon·stra·tive (di·mon′strə·tiv) *adj.* 1. Serving to demonstrate or point out. 2. Convincing and conclusive. 3. Inclined to strong expression, esp. of emotions. **—de·mon′stra·tive·ly** *adv.* **—de·mon′stra·tive·ness** *n.*
demonstrative pronoun *Gram.* A pronoun that indicates the person or thing referred to, as *this, those.*

de·mor·al·ize (di·môr′əl·īz, -mor′-) *v.t.* **·ized, ·iz·ing** 1. To corrupt or deprave. 2. To lower the morale of. 3. To throw into disorder. —**de·mor′al·i·za′tion** *n.* —**de·mor′al·iz′er** *n.*
de·mote (di·mōt′) *v.t.* **·mot·ed, ·mot·ing** To lower in grade or rank. —**de·mo′tion** *n.*
de·mul·cent (di·mul′sənt) *adj.* Soothing. —*n.* *Med.* A soothing substance. [< L *demulcere* to soothe]
de·mur (di·mûr′) *v.i.* **·murred, ·mur·ring** 1. To offer objections; take exception. 2. *Law* To interpose a demurrer. [< L *de-* completely + *morari* to delay] —**de·mur′** *n.*
de·mure (di·myŏŏr′) *adj.* **·mur·er, ·mur·est** 1. Grave; reserved. 2. Prim; coy. [< L *maturus* mature, discreet] —**de·mure′ly** *adv.* —**de·mure′ness** *n.*
de·mur·rage (di·mûr′ij) *n.* 1. The detention of a vessel or other commercial conveyance as a result of not loading or unloading on time. 2. Compensation for such delay.
de·mur·rer (di·mûr′ər) *n.* 1. *Law* A pleading that allows the truth of the facts stated by the opposite party, but denies that they are sufficient to constitute a good cause of action or defense in law. 2. Any objection or exception taken. 3. One who demurs. [< AF]
de·myst·i·fy (dē·mis′tə·fī) *v.t.* To remove mystery or mystification from.
den (den) *n.* 1. The cave of a wild animal; a lair. 2. A hiding place or dwelling: a *den* of thieves. 3. A small, private room for relaxation or study. [OE *denn*]
de·nar·i·us (di·nâr′ē·əs) *n.* *pl.* **·nar·i·i** (-nâr′ē·ī) 1. A silver coin of ancient Rome; the penny of the New Testament. 2. A gold coin of ancient Rome. [< L < *decem* ten]
de·na·tion·al·ize (dē·nash′ən·əl·īz′) *v.t.* **·ized, ·iz·ing** To deprive of national character, status, or rights. Also *Brit.* **de·na′tion·al·ise′.** —**de·na′tion·al·i·za′tion** *n.*
de·nat·u·ral·ize (dē·nach′ər·əl·īz′) *v.t.* **·ized, ·iz·ing** 1. To render unnatural. 2. To deprive of citizenship. Also *Brit.* **de·nat′u·ral·ise′.** —**de·nat′u·ral·i·za′tion** *n.*
de·na·ture (dē·nā′chər) *v.t.* **·tured, ·tur·ing** 1. To change the nature of. 2. To adulterate (alcohol, fat, etc.) so as to make unfit for drinking or eating without destroying other useful properties. —**de·na′tur·ant** *n.*
den·drite (den′drīt) *n.* *Physiol.* A threadlike, branching process of a nerve cell that conducts impulses toward the cell body. [< Gk. *dendron* tree] —**den·drit′ic** (-drit′ik) *adj.*
dendro- *combining form* Tree. Also **dendr-** (before vowels), **dendri-.** [< Gk. *dendron*]
-dendron *combining form* Tree. [< Gk. *dendron*]
den·gue (deng′gē, -gā) *n.* A tropical disease transmitted by the bite of a mosquito and characterized by fever, skin eruptions, and severe pains in the joints. [< Sp., ult. < Swahili]
de·ni·a·ble (di·nī′ə·bəl) *adj.* That can be denied. —**de·ni′a·bly** *adv.*
de·ni·al (di·nī′əl) *n.* 1. A contradiction, as of a statement. 2. A disowning or disavowal. 3. Refusal to grant, give, or allow.
de·ni·er[1] (di·nī′ər) *n.* One who makes denial.
den·ier[2] (den′yər, də·nir′) *n.* A unit of weight for denoting the coarseness or fineness of rayon, nylon, or silk yarns. [See DENARIUS.]
den·im (den′əm) *n.* 1. A strong, twilled cotton used for sportswear, etc. 2. *pl.* Garments made of this material. [< F (*serge*) *de Nîmes* (serge) of Nîmes]
den·i·zen (den′ə·zən) *n.* 1. An inhabitant. 2. A person, animal, or thing at home or naturalized in a region or condition not native to it. [< L *de intus* from within]
de·nom·i·nate (*v.* di·nom′ə·nāt; *adj.* di·nom′ə·nit) *v.t.* **·nat·ed, ·nat·ing** To give a name to. —*adj.* Having a specific name. [< L *de-* down + *nomen* name]
de·nom·i·na·tion (di·nom′ə·nā′shən) *n.* 1. The act of naming or calling by name. 2. A name. 3. Any specifically named class or group of things or people. 4. A religious group; a sect.
de·nom·i·na·tion·al (di·nom′ə·nā′shən·əl) *adj.* Of, pertaining to, or supported by a religious denomination or sect; sectarian.
de·nom·i·na·tion·al·ism (di·nom′ə·nā′shən·əl·iz′əm) *n.* 1. A disposition to divide into or form denominations. 2. Rigid adherence or devotion to a denomination or sect; sectarianism. —**de·nom′i·na′tion·al·ist** *n.* & *adj.*
de·nom·i·na·tive (di·nom′ə·nā′tiv, -nə·tiv) *adj.* 1. That gives or constitutes a name; appellative. 2. *Gram.* Derived from a noun or adjective, as the verb *to garden.* —*n.* *Gram.* A denominative word. —**de·nom′i·na′tive·ly** *adv.*
de·nom·i·na·tor (di·nom′ə·nā′tər) *n.* *Math.* The term below the line in a fraction indicating the number of equal parts into which the unit is divided.
de·no·ta·tion (dē′nō·tā′shən) *n.* 1. The specific meaning of a word. 2. The act of denoting.
de·note (di·nōt′) *v.t.* **·not·ed, ·not·ing** 1. To point out or make known; mark. 2. To signify; indicate. 3. To designate; mean: said of words, symbols, etc. [< L *de-* down + *notare* to mark] —**de·no·ta·tive** (di·nō′tə·tiv, dē′nō·tā′tiv) *adj.*
dé·noue·ment (dā·nōō·mäṅ′) *n.* 1. The final solution of the plot of a play, novel, etc. 2. Any final outcome. [< F, an unraveling]
de·nounce (di·nouns′) *v.t.* **·nounced, ·nounc·ing** 1. To attack or condemn openly. 2. To inform against; accuse. 3. To give formal notice of the termination of (a treaty, etc.). [< L *de-* down + *nuntiare* to announce] —**de·nounce′ment** *n.* —**de·nounc′er** *n.*
dense (dens) *adj.* **dens·er, dens·est** 1. Compact; thick; close. 2. Hard to penetrate. 3. Stupid. [< L *densus*] —**dense′ly** *adv.* —**dense′ness** *n.*
den·si·ty (den′sə·tē) *n.* *pl.* **·ties** 1. The state or quality of being dense. 2. *Sociol.* The number of specified units, as persons, families, or dwellings, per unit of area. [< L *densus* thick]
dent (dent) *n.* A small depression made by striking or pressing. —*v.t.* 1. To make a dent in. —*v.i.* 2. To become dented. [Var. of DINT]
den·tal (den′təl) *adj.* 1. Of or pertaining to the teeth. 2. Of or pertaining to dentistry. [< L *dens* tooth]

dental plate A denture.
den·tate (den′tāt) *adj.* Having teeth or toothlike processes; toothed; notched. [< L *dentatus* having teeth] —**den·ta′tion** *n.*
denti- *combining form* Tooth. Also, before vowels, **dent-**. [< L *dens* tooth]
den·ti·frice (den′tə·fris) *n.* A preparation, as a powder or paste, for cleaning the teeth. [< DENTI- + L *fricare* to rub]
den·tine (den′tēn, -tin) *n. Anat.* The hard, calcified substance forming the body of a tooth. Also **den′tin** (-tin).
den·tist (den′tist) *n.* One who practices dentistry.
den·tist·ry (den′tis·trē) *n.* 1. The branch of medicine concerned with the health and care of the teeth. 2. The work or profession of a dentist.
den·ti·tion (den·tish′ən) *n.* 1. The teething process. 2. The kind, number, and arrangement of teeth in man and other animals.
den·ture (den′chər) *n.* 1. A set of teeth. 2. A set of artificial teeth: also called *dental plate.*
de·nude (di·nōōd′, -nyōōd′) *v.t.* **·nud·ed, ·nud·ing** 1. To strip the covering from; make naked. 2. *Geol.* To expose by erosion. [< L *de-* down + *nudare* to strip] —**den·u·da·tion** (den′yōō·dā′shən, dē′nōō-, -nyōō-) *n.*
de·nun·ci·ate (di·nun′sē·āt, -shē-) *v.t. & v.i.* **·at·ed, ·at·ing** To denounce. [< L *denuntiare* to announce] —**de·nun′ci·a·to′ry** (-ə·tôr′ē) *adj.*
de·nun·ci·a·tion (di·nun′sē·ā′shən, -shē-) *n.* 1. Open disapproval or condemnation. 2. An accusation. 3. Formal notice that a treaty is to be terminated.
de·ny (di·nī′) *v.t.* **·nied, ·ny·ing** 1. To declare to be untrue; contradict. 2. To refuse to believe, as a doctrine. 3. To refuse to give or grant; withhold. 4. To refuse to acknowledge; disown. [< L *denegare* to say no, refuse]
de·o·dor·ant (dē·ō′dər·ənt) *adj.* Destroying or disguising bad odors. —**de·o′dor·ant** *n.*
de·o·dor·ize (dē·ō′dər·īz) *v.t.* **·ized, ·iz·ing** To destroy or disguise the odor of. —**de·o′dor·iz′er** *n.*
de·ox·i·dize (dē·ok′sə·dīz) *v.t.* **·dized, ·diz·ing** 1. To remove oxygen from. 2. To reduce from the state of an oxide. —**de·ox′i·di·za′·tion** *n.* —**de·ox′i·diz′er** *n.*
deoxy- *combining form* Containing less oxygen than.
de·ox·y·ri·bo·nu·cle·ic acid (dē·ok′sē·rī′bō·nōō·klē′ik, -klā′-) *Biochem.* A nucleic acid forming a principal constituent of the genes and known to play an important role in the genetic action of the chromosomes. Abbr. *DNA.*
de·part (di·pärt′) *v.i.* 1. To go away; leave. 2. To deviate: to *depart* from tradition. 3. To die. [< OF *departir* to divide]
de·part·ed (di·pär′tid) *adj.* 1. Gone; past. 2. Dead. —**the departed** The dead person, or the dead collectively.
de·part·ment (di·pärt′mənt) *n.* A distinct part, division, or administrative unit of something, as of a business, college, or government. [See DEPART.] —**de·part·men·tal** (dē′pärt·men′təl) *adj.* —**de′part·men′·tal·ly** *adv.*
de·part·men·tal·ize (dē′pärt·men′təl·īz) *v.t. & v.i.* **·ized, ·iz·ing** To divide into departments.
department store A large retail store selling various types of merchandise and service.
de·par·ture (di·pär′chər) *n.* 1. The act of going away. 2. Deviation, as from an accepted method.
de·pend (di·pend′) *v.i.* 1. To rely; trust: with *on* or *upon.* 2. To be contingent: with *on* or *upon.* 3. To hang down. [< OF *dependre* to hang from]
de·pend·a·ble (di·pen′də·bəl) *adj.* Reliable; trustworthy. —**de·pend′a·bil′i·ty** *n.* —**de·pend′a·bly** *adv.*
de·pen·dence (di·pen′dəns) *n.* 1. The state of relying on something or someone. 2. Reliance or trust. 3. Contingency. 4. An addiction. Also **de·pen′dance.**
de·pen·den·cy (di·pen′dən·sē) *n. pl.* **·cies** 1. Dependence. 2. A territory or state separate from but subject to another state or country. Also **de·pen′dan·cy.**
de·pen·dent (di·pen′dənt) *adj.* 1. Contingent upon something else. 2. Subordinate. 3. Relying on someone or something for support. 4. Hanging down. —*n.* One who depends on another. Also **de·pen′dant.**
de·pict (di·pikt′) *v.t.* 1. To portray by or as by drawing, etc. 2. To portray in words. [< L *de-* down + *pingere* to paint] —**de·pic′tion** *n.*
dep·i·late (dep′ə·lāt) *v.t.* **·lat·ed, ·lat·ing** To remove hair from. [< L *de-* away + *pilus* hair]
de·pil·a·to·ry (di·pil′ə·tôr′ē) *adj.* Having the power to remove hair. —*n. pl.* **·ries** A depilatory agent.
de·plane (dē·plān′) *v.i.* **·planed, ·plan·ing** To alight from an airplane.
de·plete (di·plēt′) *v.t.* **·plet·ed, ·plet·ing** 1. To reduce or lessen, as by use or waste. 2. To empty completely or partially. [< L *de-* not + *plere* to fill] —**de·ple′tion** *n.*
de·plor·a·ble (di·plôr′ə·bəl) *adj.* 1. To be deplored; lamentable. 2. Wretched; sad. —**de·plor′a·bly** *adv.*
de·plore (di·plôr′) *v.t.* **·plored, ·plor·ing** To have or show regret or sadness over; lament. [< L *de-* completely + *plorare* to bewail]
de·ploy (di·ploi′) *v.t. & v.i.* To place or position (forces, people, etc.) according to a plan. [< F *déployer* to unfold] —**de·ploy′·ment** *n.*
de·po·nent (di·pō′nənt) *n. Law* One who gives sworn testimony, especially in writing.
de·pop·u·late (dē·pop′yə·lāt) *v.t.* **·lat·ed, ·lat·ing** To greatly reduce the population of. [< L *depopulari* to lay waste] —**de·pop′u·la′tion** *n.*
de·port (di·pôrt′) *v.t.* 1. To expel from a country. 2. To behave or conduct (oneself). [< L *de-* away + *portare* to carry] —**de·por·ta·tion** (dē′pôr·tā′shən) *n.*
de·port·ment (di·pôrt′mənt) *n.* Conduct or behavior; demeanor; bearing.
de·pose (di·pōz′) *v.* **·posed, ·pos·ing** *v.t.* 1. To deprive of rank or office; oust. 2. *Law* To declare under oath. —*v.i.* 3. *Law* To give testimony under oath. [< OF *deposer* to put down]
de·pos·it (di·poz′it) *v.t.* 1. To set down; put. 2. To put down in a layer, as silt. 3. To entrust (money, valuables, etc.) for safe-

keeping, as in a bank. 4. To give as partial payment or security; pledge. —*v.i.* 5. To be collected; become deposited. —*n.* 1. Something entrusted for safekeeping, esp. money placed in a bank. 2. Anything given as partial payment or security. 3. That which is deposited, as sediment. 4. *Geol.* A mass of iron, coal, oil, etc. —**on deposit** In safekeeping. [< L *de-* down + *ponere* to place] —**de·pos′i·tor** *n.*

de·pos·i·tar·y (di·poz′ə·ter′ē) *n. pl.* **·tar·ies** 1. One entrusted with anything for safekeeping. 2. A depository.

dep·o·si·tion (dep′ə·zish′ən, dē′pə-) *n.* 1. The act of deposing, as from an office. 2. The act of depositing; also, that which is deposited. 3. *Law* The written testimony of a witness who is under oath.

de·pos·i·to·ry (di·poz′ə·tôr′ē) *n. pl.* **·ries** 1. A place where anything is deposited. 2. A depositary.

de·pot (dē′pō, *Mil. & Brit.* dep′ō) *n.* 1. A warehouse or storehouse. 2. A railroad station. 3. *Mil.* **a** An installation that manufactures, procures, stores, or repairs military materiel. **b** An installation for assembling and processing personnel. [See DEPOSIT.]

de·prave (di·prāv′) *v.t.* **·praved, ·prav·ing** To corrupt; pervert. [< L *de-* completely + *pravus* corrupt, wicked] —**de·prav′er** *n.*

de·prav·i·ty (di·prav′ə·tē) *n. pl.* **·ties** 1. The state of being depraved; wickedness. 2. A depraved act or habit.

dep·re·cate (dep′rə·kāt) *v.t.* **·cat·ed, ·cat·ing** To express disapproval or disparagement of. [< L *de-* away + *precari* to pray] —**dep′re·cat′ing·ly** *adv.* —**dep′re·ca′tion** *n.* —**dep′re·ca′tor** *n.* —**dep·re·ca·to·ry** (dep′rə·kə·tôr′ē) *adj.*

de·pre·ci·ate (di·prē′shē·āt) *v.* **·at·ed, ·at·ing** *v.t.* 1. To lessen the value or price of. 2. To disparage. —*v.i.* 3. To become less in value, etc. [< L *de-* down + *pretium* price] —**de·pre′ci·a′tion** *n.* —**de·pre′ci·a′tor** *n.*

dep·re·da·tion (dep′rə·dā′shən) *n.* A pillaging or plundering. [< L *de-* completely + *praeda* booty, prey]

de·press (di·pres′) *v.t.* 1. To lower the spirits of; sadden. 2. To lessen in force or energy. 3. To lower in price or value. 4. To press or push down. [< L *de-* down + *primere* to press]

de·pres·sant (di·pres′ənt) *Med. adj.* Tending to lessen nervous or functional activity. —*n.* A sedative.

de·pressed (di·prest′) *adj.* 1. Sad; dejected. 2. Pressed down; flattened. 3. Lowered even with or below the surface. 4. Reduced in power, amount, value, etc.

depressed area A region characterized by unemployment.

de·pres·sion (di·presh′ən) *n.* 1. The act of depressing, or the state of being depressed. 2. A low or depressed place or surface. 3. A severe decline in business, accompanied by unemployment, falling prices, etc. 4. *Psychiatry* Deep dejection characterized by withdrawal, lack of response to stimulation, etc. —**de·pres′sive** (-pres′iv) *adj.* —**de·pres′sive·ly** *adv.*

de·pres·sor (di·pres′ər) *n.* 1. One who or that which depresses. 2. *Physiol.* An afferent nerve connected with the heart, controlling heart rate and blood pressure.

de·prive (di·prīv′) *v.t.* **·prived, ·priv·ing** 1. To take something away from; divest. 2. To keep from acquiring, using, or enjoying something. [< L *de-* completely + *privare* to strip, remove] —**dep·ri·va·tion** (dep′rə·vā′shən), **de·priv′al** *n.*

depth (depth) *n.* 1. The state or degree of being deep. 2. Extent or distance downward, inward, or backward. 3. Profundity of thought or feeling. 4. *Usu. pl.* An extremely remote, deep, or distant part. 5. *Usu. pl.* An intense state of being or feeling. 6. Richness or intensity of color, sound, etc. 7. Lowness of pitch. [ME *depthe*]

depth charge A drum-shaped bomb that explodes under water at a desired depth. Also **depth bomb.**

dep·u·ta·tion (dep′yə·tā′shən) *n.* 1. A person or persons acting for another or others; a delegation. 2. The act of deputing, or the state of being deputed.

de·pute (di·pyōōt′) *v.t.* **·put·ed, ·put·ing** To delegate. [< L *de-* away + *putare* to think]

dep·u·tize (dep′yə·tīz) *v.t.* **·tized, ·tiz·ing** To appoint as a deputy.

dep·u·ty (dep′yə·tē) *n. pl.* **·ties** 1. One appointed to act for another: a sheriff's *deputy*. 2. A member of a legislative assembly in certain countries. —*adj.* Acting as deputy.

de·rail (dē·rāl′) *v.t. & v.i.* To run or cause (a train, etc.) to run off the rails. [< F *dé-* from + *rail* rail] —**de·rail′ment** *n.*

de·range (di·rānj′) *v.t.* **·ranged, ·rang·ing** 1. To disturb, as the working or order of. 2. To unbalance the reason of; render insane. [< F *dé-* away + *ranger* to set in line —**de·ranged′** *adj.* —**de·range′ment** *n.*

der·by (dûr′bē) *n. pl.* **·bies** A stiff felt hat with a curved, narrow brim and round crown: also *bowler*. [< DERBY]

Der·by (dûr′bē, *Brit.* där′bē) *n.* 1. An annual horse race for three-year-olds run at Epsom Downs, in England. 2. Any similar horse race, as the Kentucky Derby. [after the 12th Earl of *Derby*, the founder]

der·e·lict (der′ə·likt) *adj.* 1. Neglectful of obligation; remiss. 2. Deserted or abandoned. —*n.* 1. That which is abandoned, as a ship at sea. 2. A social outcast. [< L *de-* completely + *relinquere* to abandon]

der·e·lic·tion (der′ə·lik′shən) *n.* 1. Neglect of or failure in duty. 2. The act of abandoning, or the state of being abandoned.

de·ride (di·rīd′) *v.t.* **·rid·ed, ·rid·ing** To ridicule. [< L *de-* completely + *ridere* to laugh, mock] —**de·rid′ing·ly** *adv.*

de ri·gueur (də rē·gœr′) *French* Necessary according to rules or custom.

de·ri·sion (di·rizh′ən) *n.* Ridicule; mockery. —**de·ri·sive** (di·rī′siv), **de·ri·so·ry** (di·rī′·sər·ē) *adj.* —**de·ri′sive·ly** *adv.* —**de·ri′sive·ness** *n.*

der·i·va·tion (der′ə·vā′shən) *n.* 1. The act of deriving, or the condition of being derived. 2. That which is derived. 3. Origin or descent. —**der′i·va′tion·al** *adj.*

de·riv·a·tive (di·riv′ə·tiv) *adj.* 1. Obtained or characterized by derivation. 2. Not original. —*n.* That which is derived. —**de·riv′a·tive·ly** *adv.*

de·rive (di·rīv′) *v.* **·rived, ·riv·ing** *v.t.* 1. To draw or receive, as from a source. 2. To deduce. 3. To trace the source of (a word, etc.). 4. *Chem.* To obtain (a compound) from another, as by partial substitution. —*v.i.* 5. To originate; proceed. [< L *de-* from + *rivus* stream] —**de·riv′a·ble** *adj.* —**de·riv′er** *n.*

-derm *suffix* Skin. [< Gk. *derma*]

der·ma (dûr′mə) *n. Anat.* The dermis. [< Gk., skin] —**der′mal** *adj.*

dermato- *combining form* Skin. Also, before vowels, **dermat-**. [< Gk. *derma*]

der·ma·tol·o·gy (dûr′mə·tol′ə·jē) *n.* The branch of medical science that relates to the skin and its diseases. —**der′ma·tol′o·gist** *n.*

der·mis (dûr′mis) *n. Anat.* 1. The sensitive, vascular portion of the skin below the epidermis: also called *derma*. 2. The skin. [< Gk. *derma* skin]

dermo- *combining form* Skin. Also, before vowels, **derm-**.

der·o·gate (der′ə·gāt) **·gat·ed, ·gat·ing** *v.t.* & *v.i.* 1. To take or cause to take away; detract: with *from*. 2. To become or cause to become inferior: with *from*. [< L *de-* away + *rogare* to ask] —**der′o·ga′tion** *n.*

de·rog·a·to·ry (di·rog′ə·tôr′ē) *adj.* Belittling; disparaging: also **de·rog′a·tive.** —**de·rog′a·to′ri·ly** *adv.*

der·rick (der′ik) *n.* 1. An apparatus for hoisting and swinging heavy weights, usu. consisting of a tackle at the end of a boom or mast. 2. The framework over the mouth of an oil well. [after *Derrick*, 17th c. London hangman]

der·ring-do (der′ing·do͞o′) *n.* Courageous or daring action. [ME *dorrying don* daring to do]

der·rin·ger (der′in·jər) *n.* A pistol having a short barrel and a large bore. [after Henry *Deringer*, 19th c. U.S. gunsmith]

der·vish (dûr′vish) *n.* A member of any of various Muslim orders, some of whom express their devotion in whirling, howling, etc. [< Persian *darvēsh*]

de·salt (dē·sôlt′) *v.t.* To remove the salt from, as sea water, to make potable.

des·cant (*n.* des′kant; *v.* des·kant′, dis-) *n.* 1. A discussion or a series of remarks. 2. *Music* **a** A counterpoint above the basic melody. **b** The upper part in part music. —*v.i.* 1. To discourse at length: with *on* or *upon*. 2. *Music* To make or perform a descant. [< L *dis-* away + *cantus* a song]

de·scend (di·send′) *v.i.* 1. To move from a higher to a lower point. 2. To slope downward. 3. To lower oneself; stoop. 4. To be inherited. 5. *Biol.* To be derived by heredity. 6. To arrive or attack in great numbers. —*v.t.* 7. To go down, as stairs. [< OF *descendre* to go down] —**de·scend′er** *n.*

de·scen·dant (di·sen′dənt) *n.* One who is descended lineally from another; offspring.

de·scen·dent (di·sen′dənt) *adj.* Proceeding downward.

de·scent (di·sent′) *n.* 1. The act of descending. 2. A decline or deterioration. 3. A slope. 4. Ancestral derivation; lineage. 5. *Law* The succession of property or title by inheritance.

de·scribe (di·skrīb′) *v.t.* **·scribed, ·scrib·ing** 1. To present or depict in words. 2. To draw the figure of; outline. [< L *describere* to write down] —**de·scrib′a·ble** *adj.* —**de·scrib′er** *n.*

de·scrip·tion (di·skrip′shən) *n.* 1. The act or technique of describing. 2. An account that describes. 3. A drawing or tracing, as of an arc. 4. Sort; variety: birds of every *description*.

de·scrip·tive (di·skrip′tiv) *adj.* Characterized by or containing description. —**de·scrip′tive·ly** *adv.* —**de·scrip′tive·ness** *n.*

de·scry (di·skrī′) *v.t.* **·scried, ·scry·ing** 1. To catch sight of, as from afar. 2. To discover by observation. [< OF *descrier* to proclaim]

des·e·crate (des′ə·krāt) *v.t.* **·crat·ed, ·crat·ing** To treat sacrilegiously; profane. [< L *de-* away + *sacrare* to make holy] —**des′e·cra′tion** *n.*

de·seg·re·gate (dē·seg′rə·gāt) *v.t.* & *v.i.* **·gat·ed, ·gat·ing** To eliminate racial segregation in. —**de′seg·re·ga′tion** *n.*

de·sen·si·tize (dē·sen′sə·tīz) *v.t.* **·tized, ·tiz·ing** To make less sensitive. —**de·sen′si·ti·za′tion** *n.* —**de·sen′si·tiz′er** *n.*

des·ert[1] (dez′ərt) *n.* 1. A region greatly lacking in rainfall, moisture, and vegetation. 2. Any region that is uncultivated and desolate. —*adj.* Of or like a desert; uninhabited. [< L *deserere* to abandon]

de·sert[2] (di·zûrt′) *v.t.* 1. To forsake or abandon. 2. To forsake in violation of one's oath or orders, as a post. —*v.i.* 3. To abandon one's post, duty, etc. —**de·sert′er** *n.* —**de·ser′tion** *n.*

de·sert[3] (di·zûrt′) *n. Often pl.* That which is deserved or merited: to get one's just *deserts*. [See DESERVE.]

de·serve (di·zûrv′) *v.t.* & *v.i.* **·served, ·serv·ing** To be worthy of; merit. [< L *deservire* to serve well] —**de·serv′er** *n.*

de·served (di·zûrvd′) *adj.* Earned or merited. —**de·serv′ed·ly** *adv.*

de·serv·ing (di·zûr′ving) *adj.* Worthy; meritorious: *deserving* of praise.

des·ha·bille (dez′ə·bēl′) *n.* Dishabille.

des·ic·cant (des′ə·kənt) *adj.* Producing dryness, as a medicine. —**des′ic·cant** *n.*

des·ic·cate (des′ə·kāt) *v.t.* & *v.i.* **·cat·ed, ·cat·ing** To dry thoroughly; dehydrate. [< L *de-* completely + *siccare* to dry out] —**des′ic·ca′tion** *n.*

de·sid·er·a·tum (di·sid′ə·rā′təm) *n. pl.* **·ta** Something needed or desired. [< L]

de·sign (di·zīn′) *v.t.* 1. To draw or prepare preliminary plans or sketches of. 2. To plan and make with skill, as a work of art. 3. To form or make (plans, schemes, etc.); conceive; invent. 4. To intend; purpose. —*v.i.* 5. To be a designer. 6. To plan; conceive. —*n.* 1. A preliminary sketch or outline. 2. The arrangement and coordination of the parts or details of any object: the *design* of a jet airplane. 3. A visual pattern or composition. 4. A plan or project. 5. An object or purpose. 6. *Often pl.* A sinister scheme or plot. 7. Intelligent, purposeful, or discoverable pattern. [See DESIGNATE.] —**de·sign′er** *n.*

des·ig·nate (*v.* dez′ig·nāt; *for adj., also* dez′ig·nit) *v.t.* **·nat·ed, ·nat·ing** 1. To indicate or specify. 2. To name or entitle; characterize. 3. To select or appoint for a specific purpose, duty, etc. —*adj.* Designated; selected: the ambassador *designate*. [< L *de-* completely + *signare* to mark] —**des′ig·na′tive** *adj.* —**des′ig·na′tor** *n.*

designated hitter In baseball, a player who

bats in place of the pitcher without removal of the pitcher from the game.

des·ig·na·tion (dez′ig·nā′shən) *n.* 1. A distinctive mark or title. 2. The act of pointing out something. 3. Appointment or nomination.

de·sign·ed·ly (di·zī′nid·lē) *adv.* By design; intentionally.

des·ig·nee (dez′ig·nē′) *n.* A person designated.

de·sign·ing (di·zī′ning) *n.* 1. The act or art of making designs. 2. The act of plotting or scheming. —*adj.* Scheming, plotting, or contriving. —**de·sign′ing·ly** *adv.*

de·sir·a·ble (di·zīr′ə·bəl) *adj.* Worthy of or exciting desire. —**de·sir′a·bil′i·ty** *n.*

de·sire (di·zīr′) *v.t.* **·sired, ·sir·ing** 1. To wish or long for; crave. 2. To ask for; request. —*n.* 1. A longing or craving. 2. A request or wish. 3. An object desired. 4. Sexual passion; lust. [< OF *desirer* to long for]

de·sir·ous (di·zīr′əs) *adj.* Having a desire or craving.

de·sist (di·zist′, -sist′) *v.i.* To cease, as from an action. [< L *de-* from + *sistere* to stop]

desk (desk) *n.* 1. A table or case adapted for writing or studying. 2. A department or post in an organization: the service *desk*, the copy *desk*. [< LL *discus* table]

des·o·late (*adj.* des′ə·lit; *v.* des′ə·lāt) *adj.* 1. Destitute of inhabitants or dwellings; deserted. 2. Made unfit for habitation. 3. Gloomy; dreary. 4. Without friends; forlorn. —*v.t.* **·lat·ed, ·lat·ing** 1. To deprive of inhabitants. 2. To lay waste; devastate. 3. To make sorrowful or forlorn. [< L *de-* completely + *solus* alone] —**des′o·late·ly** *adv.* —**des′o·late·ness** *n.*

des·o·la·tion (des′ə·lā′shən) *n.* 1. The act of making desolate; a laying waste. 2. The condition of being ruined or deserted. 3. Loneliness. 4. A desolate region.

de·spair (di·spâr′) *v.i.* To lose or abandon hope: with *of.* —*n.* 1. Utter hopelessness. 2. That which causes despair. [< L *desperare* to be without hope] —**de·spair′ing** *adj.* —**de·spair′ing·ly** *adv.*

des·per·a·do (des′pə·rä′dō, -rā′dō) *n. pl.* **·does** or **·dos** A desperate or violent criminal. [< OSp. See DESPAIR.]

des·per·ate (des′pər·it) *adj.* 1. Without care for danger; reckless, as from despair. 2. Resorted to in desperation. 3. Regarded as almost hopeless; critical. 4. Extreme; very great. —**des′per·ate·ly** *adv.* —**des·per·a·tion** (des′pə·rā′shən) *n.*

des·pi·ca·ble (des′pi·kə·bəl, di·spik′ə·bəl) *adj.* That is to be despised; contemptible; vile. [See DESPISE.] —**des′pi·ca·bly** *adv.*

de·spise (di·spīz′) *v.t.* **·spised, ·spis·ing** To regard as contemptible or worthless. [< L *de-* down + *specere* to look at]

de·spite (di·spīt′) *prep.* In spite of; notwithstanding. —*n.* 1. Contemptuous defiance. 2. An act of defiance, malice, or injury. [See DESPISE.]

de·spoil (di·spoil′) *v.t.* To deprive of possessions; rob. [< L *de-* completely + *spoliare* to rob] —**de·spoil′er** *n.*

de·spond (di·spond′) *v.i.* To lose spirit, courage, or hope. [< L *despondere*] —**de·spon′dent** *adj.* —**de·spon′dent·ly** *adv.*

de·spon·den·cy (di·spon′dən·sē) *n.* Dejection of spirits from loss of hope or courage. Also **de·spon′dence.**

des·pot (des′pət, -pot) *n.* 1. An absolute monarch; autocrat. 2. A tyrant; oppressor. [< Gk. *despotēs* master] —**des·pot·ic** (di·spot′ik) *adj.* —**des·pot′i·cal·ly** *adv.* —**des′pot·ism** *n.*

des·sert (di·zûrt′) *n.* A serving of pastry, ice cream, etc., as the last course of a meal. [< F *desservir* to clear a table]

des·ti·na·tion (des′tə·nā′shən) *n.* 1. The point or place set for a journey's end, or to which something is directed. 2. The purpose for which anything is created.

des·tine (des′tin) *v.t.* **·tined, ·tin·ing** 1. To design for or appoint to a distinct purpose. 2. To determine the future of, as by destiny. [< L *destinare* to make fast, secure] —**des′·tined** *adj.*

des·ti·ny (des′tə·nē) *n. pl.* **·nies** 1. The fate to which a person or thing is destined. 2. The predetermined ordering of events. 3. The power that is thought to predetermine the course of events. [See DESTINE.]

des·ti·tute (des′tə·tōōt, -tyōōt) *adj.* 1. Not having; lacking: with *of.* 2. Extremely poor. [< L *de-* down + *statuere* to set] —**des′ti·tu′·tion** *n.*

de·stroy (di·stroi′) *v.t.* 1. To ruin utterly; consume. 2. To tear down; demolish. 3. To put an end to. 4. To kill. 5. To make ineffective or useless. [< L *de-* down + *struere* to construct]

de·stroy·er (di·stroi′ər) *n.* 1. One who or that which destroys. 2. A speedy war vessel, smaller than a cruiser.

de·struct (di·strukt′) *n.* *Aerospace* The act of destroying a defective or dangerous missile or rocket after launch. —*v.t.* & *v.i.* To destroy or be destroyed.

de·struc·ti·ble (di·struk′tə·bəl) *adj.* Capable of being destroyed. —**de·struc′ti·bil′i·ty** *n.*

de·struc·tion (di·struk′shən) *n.* 1. The act of destroying, or the state of being destroyed; demolition; ruin. 2. That which destroys.

de·struc·tive (di·struk′tiv) *adj.* 1. Causing destruction; ruinous: with *of* or *to.* 2. Tending to damage or discredit. —**de·struc′tive·ly** *adv.* —**de·struc′tive·ness** *n.*

destructive distillation *Chem.* The distillation of organic substances, as wood and coal, in such a way as to decompose them chemically and collect their volatile products: also called *dry distillation.*

des·ue·tude (des′wə·tōōd, -tyōōd) *n.* A condition of disuse. [< L *de-* away + *suescere* to be used to]

des·ul·to·ry (des′əl·tôr′ē) *adj.* 1. Passing from one thing to another; unmethodical. 2. Occurring by chance. [< L *de-* down + *sultus*, pp. of *salire* to leap] —**des′ul·to′ri·ly** *adv.*

de·tach (di·tach′) *v.t.* 1. To unfasten and separate; disconnect. 2. To send off for special duty, as a regiment. [< F *détacher* to untie] —**de·tach′a·bil′i·ty** *n.* —**de·tach′a·ble** *adj.*

de·tached (di·tacht′) *adj.* 1. Separated; disconnected. 2. Unconcerned; impartial.

de·tach·ment (di·tach′mənt) *n.* 1. The act of detaching or the state of being detached. 2. Lack of interest in surroundings or worldly affairs. 3. Absence of prejudice or partiality.

4. *Mil.* A part of a unit separated from its parent organization for duty.

de·tail (*n.* di·tāl′, dē′tāl; *v.* di·tāl′; *Mil.* dē′tāl) *n.* 1. A separately considered part or item; particular. 2. Particulars or items collectively; also, the process of dealing with particulars: to go into *detail.* 3. In art, architecture, etc., a minor or secondary part. 4. *Mil.* A small detachment designated for a particular task. **—in detail** Item by item. **—***v.t.* 1. To report or narrate minutely. 2. *Mil.* To select and send off for a special service, duty, etc. [< F *dé-* completely + *tailler* to cut up] **—de·tailed′** *adj.*

de·tain (di·tān′) *v.t.* 1. To keep from proceeding; stop; delay. 2. To hold in custody; confine. [< OF *detenir* to hold back] **—de·tain′ment** *n.*

de·tect (di·tekt′) *v.t.* 1. To perceive or find, as an error. 2. To expose or uncover, as a crime. [< L *de-* away, off + *tegere* to cover] **—de·tect′a·ble** *adj.* **—de·tec′tion** *n.* **—de·tec′tor** *n.*

de·tec·tive (di·tek′tiv) *n.* A person, often a policeman, whose work is to investigate crimes. **—***adj.* 1. Belonging or pertaining to detectives or their work. 2. Fitted for or used in detection.

dé·tente (dā·tänt′) *n.* An easing, as of discord between nations. [< F]

de·ten·tion (di·ten′shən) *n.* The act of detaining, or the state of being detained. [See DETAIN.]

de·ter (di·tûr′) *v.t.* **·terred, ·ter·ring** To prevent or discourage (someone) from acting by arousing fear, uncertainty, etc. [< L *de-* away + *terrere* to frighten]

de·ter·gent (di·tûr′jənt) *n.* A cleansing agent. [< L *detergere* to wipe away] **—de·ter′gent** *adj.*

de·te·ri·o·rate (di·tir′ē·ə·rāt′) *v.t.* & *v.i.* **·rat·ed, ·rat·ing** To make or become worse; depreciate. [< L *deterior* worse] **—de·te′ri·o·ra′tion** *n.*

de·ter·mi·nant (di·tûr′mə·nənt) *adj.* & *n.* Determinative.

de·ter·mi·nate (di·tûr′mə·nit) *adj.* 1. Definitely limited or fixed; specific. 2. Settled and conclusive; final. **—de·ter′mi·nate·ly** *adv.*

de·ter·mi·na·tion (di·tûr′mə·nā′shən) *n.* 1. The act of reaching a decision; also, the decision reached. 2. Firmness in purpose or action; resoluteness. 3. The act of determining or fixing anything; also, the result of this.

de·ter·mi·na·tive (di·tûr′mə·nā′tiv, -mə·nə·tiv) *adj.* Tending or having power to determine. **—***n.* That which determines.

de·ter·mine (di·tûr′min) *v.t.* **·mined, ·min·ing** 1. To settle or decide, as an argument. 2. To ascertain or fix. 3. To cause to reach a decision. 4. To fix or give definite form to. 5. To set bounds to; limit. 6. *Law* To limit; terminate: to *determine* a contract. [< L *de-* completely + *terminare* to end] **—de·ter′mi·na·ble** *adj.* **—de·ter′min·er** *n.*

de·ter·mined (di·tûr′mind) *adj.* Resolute; firm. **—de·ter′mined·ly** *adv.*

de·ter·min·ism (di·tûr′mə·niz′əm) *n.* *Philos.* The doctrine that every event is the inevitable result of previous conditions, and that human beings do not have free will.

de·ter·rence (dē·tûr′əns) *n.* 1. The act of deterring. 2. Maintenance of superior military power on the theory that it will deter war.

de·ter·rent (di·tûr′ənt) *adj.* Tending or serving to deter. **—***n.* Something that deters.

de·test (di·test′) *v.t.* To dislike with intensity; hate; abhor. [< L *detestari* to denounce] **—de·test′a·ble** *adj.* **—de·test′a·bly** *adv.* **—de·tes·ta·tion** (dē′tes·tā′shən) *n.* **—de·test′er** *n.*

de·throne (dē·thrōn′) *v.t.* **·throned, ·thron·ing** To remove from the throne. **—de·throne′ment** *n.*

det·o·nate (det′ə·nāt) *v.t.* & *v.i.* **·nat·ed, ·nat·ing** To explode or cause to explode. [< L *de-* down + *tonare* to thunder] **—det′o·na′tion** *n.* **—det′o·na′tor** *n.*

de·tour (dē′tŏŏr, di·tŏŏr′) *n.* A deviation from a direct route or course of action; esp., a byroad used when a main road is impassable. **—***v.t.* & *v.i.* To go or cause to go by a roundabout way. [< F *dé-* away + *tourner* to turn]

de·tox·i·fy (dē·toks′ə·fī) *v.i.* **·fied, ·fy·ing** To remove the poison or effect of poison from: also **de·tox′i·cate.** **—de·tox′i·fi·ca′tion** *n.*

de·tract (di·trakt′) *v.t.* & *v.i.* To take away (a part); diminish: with *from.* [< L *de-* away + *trahere* to pull] **—de·trac′tor** *n.*

de·train (dē·trān′) *v.t.* & *v.i.* *Chiefly Brit.* To leave or cause to leave a railroad train.

det·ri·ment (det′rə·mənt) *n.* 1. Damage or loss. 2. Something that impairs, injures, or causes loss. [< L *de-* away + *terere* to rub] **—det′ri·men′tal** (-men′təl) *adj.* **—det′ri·men′tal·ly** *adv.*

de·tri·tus (di·trī′təs) *n.* Loose fragments separated from masses of rock by erosion, glacial action, etc. [See DETRIMENT.]

de trop (də trō′) *French* Too much; superfluous.

de·tu·mes·cense (dē′tŏŏ·mes′əns) *n.* The act or process of being less swollen, as an organ.

deuce[1] (dōōs, dyōōs) *n.* 1. Two; esp., a card or side of a die having two spots. 2. In tennis, a score tied at 40 or at five or more games each. [< L *duos,* accusative of *duo* two]

deuce[2] (dōōs, dyōōs) *n.* *Informal* The devil; bad luck: a mild oath. [< LG *de duus* the deuce (throw at dice)]

deu·ced (dōō′sid, dyōō′-, dōōst, dyōōst) *Informal adj.* Confounded; excessive. **—***adv.* Devilishly. **—deu′ced·ly** *adv.*

deu·te·ri·um (dōō·tir′ē·əm, dyōō-) *n.* The isotope of hydrogen (symbol, D or H^2), having twice the mass of hydrogen: also called *heavy hydrogen.* [< Gk. *deuteros* second]

deutero- *combining form* Second; secondary. Also, **deuter-** (before vowels), **deuto-.** [< Gk. *deuteros* second]

Deu·ter·on·o·my (dōō′tə·ron′ə·mē, dyōō′-) The fifth book of the Old Testament. [< Gk. *deuteros* second + *nomos* law]

deut·sche·mark (doi′chə·märk′) *n.* The standard monetary unit of West Germany, equivalent to 100 pfennigs.

de·val·ue (dē·val′yōō) *v.t.* **·ued, ·u·ing** To reduce the value or worth of. Also **de·val′u·ate** (-āt). **—de·val′u·a′tion** *n.*

dev·as·tate (dev′ə·stāt) *v.t.* **·tat·ed, ·tat·ing** 1. To lay waste, as by war, fire, etc. 2. *Informal* To confound; crush. [< L *devastare* to lay waste] —**dev′as·tat′ing·ly** *adv.* —**dev′as·ta′tion** *n.* —**dev′as·ta′tor** *n.*

de·vel·op (di·vel′əp) *v.t.* 1. To expand or bring out the potentialities, capabilities, etc., of. 2. To enlarge upon: to *develop* an idea. 3. To bring into existence: to *develop* patience. 4. *Photog.* a To make visible (the hidden image) upon a sensitized plate that has been exposed to the action of light. b To subject (a plate or film) to a developer. —*v.i.* 5. To increase in capabilities, maturity, etc. 6. To advance to a higher stage; evolve. 7. To be disclosed; as events, a plot, etc. 8. To come into existence; grow. [< F *dé-* away + OF *voluper* to fold, wrap up]

de·vel·op·er (di·vel′əp·ər) *n.* 1. One who or that which develops. 2. *Photog.* A solution for developing photographs.

de·vel·op·ment (di·vel′əp·mənt) *n.* 1. The act of developing. 2. The state or condition of that which has been developed. 3. A result or product of developing. 4. An event or occurrence: a political *development.* —**de·vel′·op·men′tal** (-men′təl) *adj.* —**de·vel′op·men′tal·ly** *adv.*

de·vi·ant (dē′vē·ənt) *adj.* Being different, esp. from the norm. —*n.* Deviate.

de·vi·ate (*n.* dē′vē·it; *v.* dē′vē·āt) *n.* One whose actions and beliefs differ considerably from the standards of his society. —*v.i.* **·at·ed, ·at·ing** 1. To turn aside from an appointed course. 2. To differ, as in belief. [< L *de-* from + *via* road]

de·vi·a·tion (dē′vē·ā′shən) *n.* 1. The act of deviating, or its result. 2. *Stat.* The difference between one value in a series of observations and the arithmetic mean of the series.

de·vice (di·vīs′) *n.* 1. Something devised or constructed for a specific purpose. 2. A scheme or plan, esp. a crafty or evil one. 3. An ornamental design. 4. An emblem or motto. —**to leave (someone) to his own devices** To allow (someone) to do as he wishes. [< L *dividere* to divide]

dev·il (dev′əl) *n.* 1. *Sometimes cap.* In theology, the ruler of the kingdom of evil; Satan. 2. Any evil spirit; a demon. 3. A wicked person. 4. A wretched fellow. 5. A person of great energy or daring. 6. A machine for any of various purposes, as for cutting or tearing up rags. 7. A printer's apprentice: also called *printer's devil.* —*v.t.* **dev·iled** or **·illed, dev·il·ing** or **·il·ling** 1. To season highly. 2. To cut up (cloth, etc.) in a devil. 3. To annoy or harass. [< Gk. *diabolos* slanderer]

dev·il·fish (dev′əl·fish′) *n.* *pl.* **·fish** or **·fish·es** 1. The manta. 2. A cephalopod, as the octopus.

dev·il·ish (dev′əl·ish, dev′lish) *adj.* 1. Having the qualities of the devil; diabolical. 2. *Informal* Excessive. —*adv. Informal* Excessively. —**dev′il·ish·ly** *adv.* —**dev′il·ish·ness** *n.*

dev·il-may-care (dev′əl·mā·kâr′) *adj.* Careless; reckless.

dev·il·ment (dev′əl·mənt) *n.* Mischief.

dev·il's advocate (dev′əlz) 1. In the Roman Catholic Church, an official appointed to argue against a candidate for canonization. 2. One who advocates the opposite side for argument's sake.

dev·il's-food cake (dev′əlz·fo͞od′) A chocolate cake.

dev·il·try (dev′əl·trē) *n.* *pl.* **·tries** 1. Wanton mischief. 2. Wickedness or cruelty. Also *Brit.* **dev′il·ry.**

de·vi·ous (dē′vē·əs) *adj.* 1. Winding or leading away from the direct course; rambling. 2. Straying from the proper way; erring. 3. Deliberately misleading; deceitful. [< L *de-* from + *via* way] —**de′vi·ous·ly** *adv.* —**de′vi·ous·ness** *n.*

de·vise (di·vīz′) *v.* **·vised, ·vis·ing** *v.t.* 1. To form in the mind; invent; contrive; plan. 2. *Law* To transmit (real estate) by will. —*v.i.* 3. To form a plan. —*n. Law* 1. The act of bequeathing lands. 2. A gift of lands by will. 3. A will, or clause in a will, conveying real estate. [< L *dividere* to separate] —**de·vis′er** *n.*

de·vi·see (di·vī′zē′, dev′ə·zē′) *n.* *Law* The person to whom a devise is made.

de·vi·sor (di·vī′zər, -zôr) *n.* *Law* One who devises property.

de·vi·tal·ize (dē·vīt′l·īz) *v.t.* **·ized, ·iz·ing** To destroy the vitality of; make weak.

de·void (di·void′) *adj.* Not possessing; destitute; empty: with *of.* [ME *devoided,* pp. of obs. *devoid* to empty out]

de·voir (də·vwär′, dev′wär) *n.* 1. *Usu. pl.* Courteous attentions; respects. 2. Duty. [< L *debere* to owe]

de·volve (di·volv′) *v.t.* & *v.i.* **·volved, ·volv·ing** To pass or cause (authority, duty, etc.) to pass to a successor: with *on, upon,* or *to.* [< L *de-* down + *volvere* to roll] —**dev·o·lu·tion** (dev′ə·lo͞o′shən) *n.*

de·vote (di·vōt′) *v.t.* **·vot·ed, ·vot·ing** 1. To apply (attention, time, or oneself) completely to some activity, purpose, etc. 2. To dedicate. [< L *de-* completely + *vovere* to vow]

de·vot·ed (di·vō′tid) *adj.* 1. Feeling or showing devotion; devout. 2. Set apart, as by a vow; consecrated. —**de·vot′ed·ly** *adv.*

dev·o·tee (dev′ə·tē′) *n.* 1. One who is deeply devoted to anything; an enthusiast. 2. One who is marked by religious ardor.

de·vo·tion (di·vō′shən) *n.* 1. Strong attachment or affection, as to a person or cause. 2. Religious ardor or zeal. 3. *Usu. pl.* An act of worship or prayer. 4. The act of devoting, or the state of being devoted. —**de·vo′tion·al** *adj.*

de·vour (di·vour′) *v.t.* 1. To eat up greedily. 2. To destroy; waste. 3. To take in greedily with the senses or the intellect. 4. To engross. 5. To engulf; absorb. [< L *de-* down + *vorare* to gulp, swallow] —**de·vour′ing·ly** *adv.*

de·vout (di·vout′) *adj.* 1. Earnestly religious; pious. 2. Heartfelt; sincere. 3. Containing or expressing devotion. [See DEVOTE.] —**de·vout′ly** *adv.* —**de·vout′ness** *n.*

dew (do͞o, dyo͞o) *n.* 1. Moisture condensed from the atmosphere in small drops upon cool surfaces. 2. Anything moist, pure, or refreshing, as dew. —*v.t.* To wet with or as with dew. [OE *dēaw*] —**dew′i·ness** *n.* —**dew′y** *adj.* **dew·i·er, dew·i·est**

dew·ber·ry (do͞o′ber′ē, -bər·ē, dyo͞o′-) *n.* *pl.* **·ries** The fruit of several species of trailing blackberry; also, the plant.

dew·claw (do͞o′klô′, dyo͞o′-) *n.* 1. A rudimentary toe in some dogs and other mammals. 2. The false hoof above the true hoof of hogs, deer, etc. —**dew′clawed′** *adj.*

dew·drop (dōō′drop′, dyōō′-) *n.* A drop of dew.

dew·lap (dōō′lap′, dyōō′-) *n.* The pendulous skin under the throat of cattle, certain dogs, etc. [ME < *dew*, origin uncertain + *lappe* pendulous piece, lobe] —**dew′lapped′** *adj.*

dew point The temperature at which dew forms or condensation of vapor occurs.

dex·ter (dek′stər) *adj.* 1. Of or situated on the right side. 2. *Heraldry* Being on the wearer's right, and thus on the observer's left: opposed to *sinister*. [< L, right]

dex·ter·i·ty (dek·ster′ə·tē) *n.* 1. Skill in using the hands or body. 2. Mental adroitness. [< L *dexter* right]

dex·ter·ous (dek′strəs, -stər·əs) *adj.* 1. Possessing dexterity; adroit. 2. Done with dexterity. Also **dex·trous** (dek′strəs) —**dex′·ter·ous·ly** *adv.*

dex·tral (dek′stral) *adj.* 1. On the right side. 2. Right-handed. —**dex′tral·ly** *adv.*

dex·trin (dek′strin) *n. Biochem.* A gummy, water-soluble substance formed from starch, and used as an adhesive, as a size, and in syrups.

dextro- *combining form* Turned or turning to the right, or clockwise: used esp. in chemistry and physics. Also, before vowels, **dextr-**. [< L *dexter* right]

dex·trose (dek′strōs) *n. Biochem.* A sugar occurring in plants. Also **dex·tro·glu·cose** (dek′strō·glōō′kōs).

di-[1] Var. of DIS-[1].

di-[2] *prefix* 1. Twice; double. 2. *Chem.* Containing two atoms, molecules, radicals, etc. Also, before *s*, *dis-*. [< Gk. *di-* < *dis* twice]

di-[3] Var. of DIA-.

dia- *prefix* 1. Through; across; between; apart. 2. Thoroughly. Also, before vowels, *di-*. [< Gk. *dia-* through]

di·a·be·tes (dī′ə·bē′tis, -tēz) *n. Pathol.* A disease, **diabetes mel·li·tus** (mə·lī′təs), associated with deficient insulin secretion, leading to excess sugar in the blood and urine. [< Gk. *dia-* through + *bainein* to go] —**di·a·bet·ic** (dī′ə·bet′ik, -bē′tik) *adj. & n.*

di·a·bol·ic (dī′ə·bol′ik) *adj.* 1. Of or pertaining to the devil; satanic. 2. Atrociously wicked or cruel; fiendish. Also **di′a·bol′i·cal.** [< Gk. *diabolos*] —**di′a·bol′i·cal·ly** *adv.*

di·a·crit·ic (dī′ə·krit′ik) *n.* A diacritical mark. —*adj.* Diacritical. [< Gk. *dia-* between + *krinein* to distinguish]

di·a·crit·i·cal (dī′ə·krit′i·kəl) *adj.* Serving to mark a distinction, as in pronunciation of a letter. —**di′a·crit′i·cal·ly** *adv.*

diacritical mark A mark, usu. placed over a letter to indicate its pronunciation, or to distinguish it from another letter: also called *diacritic.*

di·a·dem (dī′ə·dem) *n.* 1. A crown or headband worn as a symbol of royalty or honor. 2. Regal power. [< Gk. *dia-* across + *deein* to bind]

di·aer·e·sis (dī·er′ə·sis) See DIERESIS.

di·ag·nose (dī′əg·nōs′, -nōz′) *v.t. & v.i.* **·nosed, ·nos·ing** To make a diagnosis.

di·ag·no·sis (dī′əg·nō′sis) *n. pl.* **·ses** (-sēz) 1. *Med.* **a** The act or process of recognizing diseases by their characteristic symptoms. **b** The conclusion arrived at. 2. Any similar examination, summary, and conclusion. [< Gk. *dia-* between + *gignōskein* to know] —**di·ag·nos·tic** (dī′əg·nos′tik) *adj.* —**di·ag·nos·ti·cian** (dī′əg·nos·tish′ən) *n.*

di·ag·o·nal (dī·ag′ə·nəl) *adj.* 1. Having an oblique direction from corner to corner or from side to side. 2. Marked by oblique lines, ridges, etc. —*n.* 1. *Geom.* A diagonal line or plane. 2. Anything running diagonally. [< Gk. *dia-* across + *gōnia* angle] —**di·ag′o·nal·ly** *adv.*

di·a·gram (dī′ə·gram) *n.* 1. An outline, drawing, or plan intended to represent an object or area, show the relation between parts or places, etc. 2. A graph or chart. —*v.t.* **di·a·gramed** or **·grammed, di·a·gram·ing** or **·gram·ming** To represent or illustrate by a diagram. [< Gk. *dia-* across + *graphein* to write] —**di·a·gram·mat·ic** (dī′ə·grə·mat′ik) or **·i·cal** *adj.* —**di′a·gram·mat′i·cal·ly** *adv.*

di·al (dī′əl, dīl) *n.* 1. Any graduated circular plate or face upon which pressure, temperature, time, etc., is indicated by means of a pointer or needle. 2. A knob on a radio or television set, used to tune in stations. 3. A rotating disk, used to make connections in an automatic telephone system. —*v.* **di·aled** or **·alled, di·al·ing** or **·al·ling** *v.t.* 1. To turn to or indicate by means of a dial. 2. To call by means of a dial telephone. 3. To adjust a radio or television set to (a station, program, etc.). —*v.i.* 4. To use a dial, as in telephoning. [< Med.L *dialis* daily] —**di′al·er** or **di′al·ler** *n.*

di·a·lect (dī′ə·lekt) *n.* A regional form of a spoken language: Southern *dialect.* [< Gk. *dia-* across + *legein* to speak] —**di′a·lec′tal** *adj.*

di·a·lec·tic (dī′ə·lek′tik) *n. Often pl.* The art or practice of examining statements logically, as by question and answer, to establish validity. —*adj.* Pertaining to or using dialectic: also **di′a·lec′ti·cal.** [< Gk. *dia-* across + *legein* to speak]

di·a·lec·ti·cian (dī′ə·lek·tish′ən) *n.* 1. A logician. 2. One who studies dialects.

di·a·logue (dī′ə·lôg, -log) *n.* 1. A conversation in which two or more take part. 2. The conversation in a play, novel, etc. 3. An exchange of ideas; discussion. —*v.* **·logued, ·logu·ing** *v.t.* 1. To express in dialogue form. —*v.i.* 2. To carry on a dialogue. Also **di′a·log.** [< Gk. *dialegesthai* to converse]

di·al·y·sis (dī·al′ə·sis) *n. pl.* **·ses** (-sēz) *Chem.* The separating of solutions by means of their unequal diffusion through moist membranes. [< Gk. *dia-* completely + *lyein* to loosen] —**di·a·lyt·ic** (dī′ə·lit′ik) *adj.*

di·a·mag·net·ic (dī′ə·mag·net′ik) *Physics adj.* Being repelled by both poles of a magnet and hence tending to lie at right angles to the poles. —**di′a·mag′net·ism** *n.*

di·am·e·ter (dī·am′ə·tər) *n. Math.* 1. A straight line passing through the center of a circle or sphere and terminating at the circumference or surface. 2. The length of such a line. [< Gk. *dia-* through + *metron* measure]

di·a·met·ri·cal (dī′ə·met′ri·kəl) *adj.* 1. Of, pertaining to, or coinciding with a diameter. 2. Directly opposite: *diametrical* motives. Also **di′a·met′ric.** —**di′a·met′ri·cal·ly** *adv.*

dia·mond (dī′mənd, dī′ə-) *n.* 1. A mineral of great hardness and refractive power, consisting of crystallized carbon; also, this mineral when used as a gem. 2. A figure bounded by four equal straight lines, having two of the angles acute and two obtuse. 3. A playing card bearing a red, diamond-shaped spot. 4. In baseball, the infield of a baseball field; also, the entire field. —*adj.* Made of or like diamonds. —*v.t.* To adorn with or as with diamonds. [< Gk. *adamas* adamantine]

diamond anniversary A 60th or 75th anniversary.

dia·mond·back (dī′mənd·bak′, dī′ə-) *n.* 1. An edible turtle of the southern U.S., having diamond-shaped markings on the shell. Also **diamondback terrapin.** 2. A large rattlesnake of the SE U.S., having diamond-shaped markings on the back: also **dia′mond-rat′tler** (-rat′lər).

di·a·pa·son (dī′ə·pā′sən, -zən) *n.* 1. In a pipe organ, either of two principal steps that cover the entire range of the instrument and produce its fundamental tone. 2. The entire range of an instrument or voice. [< Gk. *dia pasōn* (*chordōn*) through all (the notes)]

di·a·per (dī′ə·pər, dī′pər) *n.* 1. A folded piece of soft, absorbent fabric placed between the legs and fastened around the waist of a baby. 2. A decorative pattern of repeated figures or designs. —*v.t.* 1. To put a diaper on (a baby). 2. To decorate with a repeated figure or similar figures. [< Med.Gk. *dia-* completely + *aspros* white]

di·aph·a·nous (dī·af′ə·nəs) *adj.* Transparent; translucent. [< Gk. *diaphanēs* transparent] —**di·aph′a·nous·ly** *adv.*

di·a·pho·re·sis (dī′ə·fə·rē′sis) *n. Med.* Copious perspiration, esp. when produced artificially. [< Gk. *diaphorēsis* perspiration] —**di′a·pho·ret′ic** (-ret′ik) *adj. & n.*

di·a·phragm (dī′ə·fram) *n.* 1. *Anat.* A muscular wall separating the chest and abdominal cavities in mammals. 2. The thin, vibrating disk of a telephone receiver. 3. *Optics* A disk with an adjustable aperture that can control the amount of light passing through the lens of a camera, telescope, etc. 4. A thin, disk-shaped contraceptive, usu. of rubber, that fits over the uterine cervix. [< Gk. *dia-* across + *phragma* fence] —**di·a·phrag·mat·ic** (dī′ə·frag·mat′ik) *adj.*

di·ar·rhe·a (dī′ə·rē′ə) *n. Pathol.* A disorder of the intestine marked by abnormally frequent and fluid evacuation of the bowels. Also **di′ar·rhoe′a.** [< Gk. *dia-* through + *rheein* to flow]

di·a·ry (dī′ə·rē, dī′rē) *n. pl.* **·ries** 1. A record of daily events; esp., a personal journal. 2. A book for keeping such a record. [< L *dies* day] —**di′a·rist** *n.*

di·a·stase (dī′ə·stās) *n. Biochem.* An enzyme that converts starch into sugar. [< Gk. *diastatis* separation]

di·as·to·le (dī·as′tə·lē) *n. Physiol.* The usual rhythmic dilatation of the heart, after each contraction. Compare SYSTOLE. [< Gk. *dia-* apart + *stellein* to send, put] —**di·as·tol·ic** (dī′ə·stol′ik) *adj.*

di·as·tro·phism (dī·as′trə·fiz′əm) *n. Geol.* Any of the processes through which the earth's crust is deformed, producing continents, mountains, etc. [< Gk. *dia-* apart + *strephein* to turn] —**di·a·stroph·ic** (dī′ə·strof′ik) *adj.*

di·a·ther·my (dī′ə·thûr′mē) *n. Med.* The generation of heat in the body tissues by use of high-frequency electric currents. [< Gk. *dia-* through + *thermē* heat]

di·a·tom (dī′ə·tom, -təm) *n.* Any of various marine and fresh-water plankton whose walls contain silica. [< Gk. *dia-* through + *temnein* to cut]

di·a·ton·ic (dī′ə·ton′ik) *adj. Music* Pertaining to a major or minor scale of eight tones without the chromatic intervals. [< Gk. *dia-* through + *tenein* to stretch] —**di′a·ton′i·cal·ly** *adv.*

di·a·tribe (dī′ə·trīb) *n.* A bitter or malicious criticism or denunciation. [< L *diatriba* learned discussion]

dib·ble (dib′əl) *n.* A gardener's pointed tool for planting seeds, setting slips, etc. —*v.t.* **·bled, ·bling** To make holes in (soil) with a dibble. [ME *debylle*] —**dib′bler** *n.*

dice (dīs) *n. pl. of* **die** 1. Small cubes having the sides marked with spots from one to six. 2. A game of chance played with such cubes. —*v.* **diced, dic·ing** *v.t.* 1. To cut into small cubes. —*v.i.* 2. To play at dice. [See DIE[2]] —**dic′er** *n.*

dic·ey (dī′sē) *adj. Slang* Involving high risk.

dicho- *combining form* In two; in pairs. Also, before vowels, **dich-.** [< Gk. *dicha*]

di·chot·o·my (dī·kot′ə·mē) *n. pl.* **·mies** 1. Division into two parts. 2. *Logic* The division of a class into two mutually exclusive or opposing subclasses. [< DICHO- + Gk. *temnein* to cut] —**di·chot′o·mous** *adj.*

di·chro·mat·ic (dī′krō·mat′ik) *adj.* 1. Having two colors. 2. *Zool.* Having two color phases within the species apart from changes due to age or sex. 3. *Pathol.* Able to see only two of the three primary colors.

di·chro·ma·tism (dī·krō′mə·tiz′əm) *n.* The state of being dichromatic; esp., color blindness.

dick·er (dik′ər) *v.i.* To work toward a deal; bargain; haggle. [ME *dyker* lot of ten, esp. skins or hides]

dick·ey (dik′ē) *n. pl.* **·eys** 1. A detachable blouse or shirt front worn to fill a low-cut neckline, under a jacket, etc. 2. A driver's or servants' outside seat on a carriage. Also **dick′y.** [< *Dicky*, double dim. of *Richard*, a personal name]

di·cot·y·le·don (dī′kot·ə·lēd′n, dī·kot′-) *n. Bot.* A plant having two seed leaves: also **di′cot.** —**di′cot·y·le′do·nous** *adj.*

dic·ta (dik′tə) Plural of DICTUM.

Dic·ta·phone (dik′tə·fōn) *n.* A phonographic instrument that records and reproduces speech, used esp. for dictation: a trade name.

dic·tate (dik′tāt; *for v., also* dik·tāt′) *v.t. & v.i.* **·tat·ed, ·tat·ing** 1. To utter or read aloud (something) to be recorded. 2. To give (orders) authoritatively. —*n.* An authoritative suggestion, rule, or command: the *dictates* of reason. [< L, pp. of *dictare*, freq. of *dicere* to say, speak]

dic·ta·tion (dik·tā′shən) *n.* 1. The act of dictating material. 2. That which is dictated.

dic·ta·tor (dik′tā·tər, dik·tā′tər) *n.* 1. A person having absolute powers of government, esp. one considered to be an oppressor. 2. A person who rules, prescribes, or suggests authoritatively: a *dictator* of fashion. 3. One who dictates words to be recorded.

dic·ta·to·ri·al (dik′tə·tôr′ē·əl) *adj.* 1. Overbearing. 2. Of or pertaining to a dictator; autocratic. **—dic′ta·to′ri·al·ly** *adv.*

dic·ta·tor·ship (dik′tā·tər·ship′, dik·tā′tər·ship′) *n.* 1. The office or term of office of a dictator. 2. A state under the rule of a dictator. 3. Supreme or despotic control.

dic·tion (dik′shən) *n.* 1. The use, choice, and arrangement of words in writing and speaking. 2. The manner of speaking; enunciation. [< L *dicere* to say, speak]

dic·tion·ar·y (dik′shən·er′ē) *n. pl.* **·ar·ies** 1. A reference work containing alphabetically arranged words together with their definitions, pronunciations, etymologies, etc.; a lexicon. 2. A lexicon whose words are given in one language together with their equivalents in another. 3. A reference work containing information relating to a special branch of knowledge and arranged alphabetically. [< Med.L *dictionarium* a collection of words and phrases]

dic·tum (dik′təm) *n. pl.* **·ta** (-tə) 1. An authoritative statement; a pronouncement. 2. A popular saying; maxim. [< L *dicere* to say]

did (did) Past tense of DO[1].

di·dac·tic (dī·dak′tik, di-) *adj.* 1. Intended to instruct. 2. Morally instructive. 3. Overly inclined to teach or moralize; pedantic. [< Gk. *didaskein* to teach] **—di·dac′ti·cal·ly** *adv.*

did·dle[1] (did′l) *v.* **·dled, ·dling** *Informal v.t.* 1. To cheat. *—v.i.* 2. To dawdle; pass time idly. [? < DIDDLE[2]] **—did′dler** *n.*

did·dle[2] (did′l) *v.t. & v.i.* **·dled, ·dling** To jerk up and down or back and forth; jiggle. [? Var. of dial. *didder*, ME *diddiren* to quiver]

di·do (dī′dō) *n. pl.* **·dos** or **·does** *Informal* A caper; antic. [Origin unknown]

didst (didst) Archaic second person singular past tense of DO[1]: used with *thou*.

di·dym·i·um (dī·dim′ē·əm, di-) *n.* A mixture of the elements neodymium and praseodymium. [< Gk. *didymos* double]

die[1] (dī) *v.i.* **died, dy·ing** 1. To suffer death; expire. 2. To suffer the pains of death: The coward *dies* many times. 3. To pass gradually: with *away*, *down*, or *out*. 4. To become extinct: often with *out*. 5. *Informal* To desire exceedingly: with *to* or *for*. 6. To stop functioning, as an engine. **—to die off** To be removed one after another by death. [< ON *deyja*]

die[2] (dī) *n. pl.* **dies** *for def. 1*; **dice** *for def. 2.* 1. *Mech.* A hard metal device for stamping, shaping, or cutting out some object. 2. A small marked cube. See DICE. **—the die is cast** The choice or course of action is irrevocable. [< OF *de* one of a pair of dice]

die casting *Metall.* 1. The process of giving a metal or alloy a desired shape by forcing the molten material into a mold under pressure. 2. A metal object so made.

die-hard (dī′härd′) *n.* One who obstinately refuses to modify his views; esp., a political conservative. **—die′-hard′** or **die′hard′** *adj.*

di·e·lec·tric (dī′ə·lek′trik) *Electr. adj.* 1. Nonconducting. 2. Capable of sustaining an electric field, as by induction. Also **di′e·lec′·tri·cal.** *—n.* A dielectric substance or medium.

di·er·e·sis (dī·er′ə·sis) *n. pl.* **·ses** (-sēz) Two dots (¨) placed over the second of two adjacent vowels to indicate that they are to be pronounced separately, as in *Noël*. Also spelled *diaeresis*. [< Gk. *dia-* apart + *haireein* to take]

die·sel engine (dē′zəl) An internal-combustion engine in which fuel oil is sprayed directly into the cylinder, where it is ignited by the high temperature of the air held within the cylinder at a constant pressure. Also **Diesel engine.** [after Rudolf *Diesel*, 1858–1913, German inventor]

Di·es I·rae (dē′ās ir′ē) The name of a medieval Latin hymn on the Day of Judgment, used in masses for the dead: so called from its opening words. [< L, day of wrath]

di·e·sis (dī′ə·sis) *n. pl.* **·ses** (-sēz) *Printing* The double dagger (‡). [< Gk. *dia-* through + *hienai* to send]

di·et[1] (dī′ət) *n.* 1. A regulated course of food and drink, esp. one prescribed for reasons of health. 2. The daily fare. 3. Food, as regards its nutritive value. *—v.i.* To take food and drink according to a regimen. [< Gk. *diaita* way of living] **—di′et·er** *n.*

di·et[2] (dī′ət) *n.* A legislative assembly. [< L *dies* day]

di·e·tar·y (dī′ə·ter′ē) *adj.* Pertaining to diet. *—n. pl.* **·tar·ies** A standard or regulated allowance of food.

di·e·tet·ic (dī′ə·tet′ik) *adj.* Relating to diet or the regulation of diet.

di·e·tet·ics (dī′ə·tet′iks) *n.pl.* (*construed as sing.*) The branch of hygiene that treats of diet and dieting. **—di·e·ti·tian** (dī′ə·tish′ən) or **di′e·ti′cian** *n.*

dif- Assimilated var. of DIS-[1].

dif·fer (dif′ər) *v.i.* 1. To be unlike in quality, degree, etc.: often with *from*. 2. To disagree: often with *with*. 3. To quarrel. [< L *dis-* apart + *ferre* to carry]

dif·fer·ence (dif′ər·əns, dif′rəns) *n.* 1. The state, quality, or degree of being unlike or different. 2. A specific instance of such unlikeness. 3. A distinguishing characteristic or peculiarity. 4. A disagreement or controversy; dispute. 5. A discrimination. 6. *Math.* The amount by which one quantity differs from another. **—to make a difference** To affect or change the case or situation. *—v.t.* **·enced, ·enc·ing** To make or mark as different.

dif·fer·ent (dif′ər·ənt, dif′rənt) *adj.* 1. Marked by a difference; unlike. 2. Not the same; separate; other. 3. Not ordinary; unusual. **—dif′fer·ent·ly** *adv.*

dif·fer·en·tial (dif′ə·ren′shəl) *adj.* 1. Relating to, indicating, or exhibiting difference. 2. *Math.* Pertaining to or involving differentials or differentiation. 3. *Mech.* Of or having a construction in which a movement is obtained by the difference in two motions in the same direction. *—n.* 1. The amount, factor, or degree in which things differ. 2. *Math.* An infinitesimal increment of a quantity: symbol *d*. 3. *Mech.* A differential gear.

differential gear or **gearing** *Mech.* An arrangement of gears used to connect two or more shafts so that the wheels can move at different speeds on curves.

dif·fer·en·ti·ate (dif′ə·ren′shē·āt) *v.* **·at·ed, ·at·ing** *v.t.* 1. To constitute the difference between. 2. To perceive and indicate the differences in or between. 3. *Biol.* To develop differences in, as a species. *—v.i.*

4. To acquire a distinct character; become specialized. 5. To discriminate. **—dif′fer·en′ti·a′tion** *n.*

dif·fi·cult (dif′ə·kult, -kəlt) *adj.* 1. Hard to do, accomplish, or deal with. 2. Not easy to understand; perplexing. 3. Hard to please, persuade, etc.

dif·fi·cul·ty (dif′ə·kul′tē, -kəl-) *n. pl.* **·ties** 1. The state, fact, or quality of being difficult. 2. That which is difficult to do, overcome, or understand. 3. A dispute. 4. A trouble; worry. [< L *dis-* not + *facilis* easy]

dif·fi·dent (dif′ə·dənt) *adj.* Lacking confidence in oneself; timid. [< L *diffidens, -entis,* ppr. of *diffidere* to distrust] **—dif′fi·dence** *n.* **—dif′fi·dent·ly** *adv.*

dif·fract (di·frakt′) *v.t.* 1. To separate into parts. 2. To subject to diffraction. [< L *dis-* away + *frangere* to break] **—dif·frac′tive** *adj.*

dif·frac·tion (di·frak′shən) *n. Physics* 1. A deflection of light rays by an obstacle or when passing near the edges of an opening or through a minute hole. 2. An analogous modification of other kinds of wave motion, as of sound, electricity, X-rays, etc.

dif·fuse (*v.* di·fyo͞oz′; *adj.* di·fyo͞os′) *v.t. & v.i.* **·fused, ·fus·ing** To pour or send out so as to spread in all directions. **—***adj.* 1. Wordy or verbose. 2. Widely spread out; dispersed. [< L *dis-* from + *fundere* to pour] **—dif·fuse·ly** (di·fyo͞os′lē) *adv.* **—dif·fuse·ness** (di·fyo͞os′nis) *n.*

dif·fus·i·ble (di·fyo͞o′zə·bəl) *adj.* Capable of being diffused. **—dif·fus′i·bil′i·ty** *n.*

dif·fu·sion (di·fyo͞o′zhən) *n.* 1. The act or process of diffusing, or the state of being diffused. 2. *Physics* **a** The intermingling of molecules of fluids, gases, or solids, dependent on temperature. **b** The scattering of light rays, producing general illumination.

dif·fu·sive (di·fyo͞o′siv) *adj.* Tending to diffuse; marked by diffusion. **—dif·fu′sive·ly** *adv.*

dig (dig) *v.* **dug, dig·ging** *v.t.* 1. To break up, turn up, or remove (earth, etc.). 2. To make or form by or as by digging. 3. To obtain by digging: to *dig* clams. 4. To discover by careful effort or study: often with *up* or *out.* 5. *Slang* To understand or like. **—***v.i.* 6. To break or turn up earth, etc. 7. To force or make a way by or as by digging. **—to dig in** *Informal* 1. To entrench (oneself). 2. To begin to work intensively. 3. To begin eating. **—***n. Informal* 1. A thrust; poke. 2. A sarcastic remark; slur. 3. An archeological excavation or its site. 4. *pl. Chiefly Brit.* Living quarters. [< MF *diguer*]

di·gest (*v.* di·jest′, dī-; *n.* dī′jest) *v.t.* 1. *Physiol.* To change (food) chemically in the alimentary canal into material suitable for assimilation by the body. 2. To take in or assimilate mentally. 3. To arrange in systematic form, usu. by condensing. **—***v.i.* 4. To be assimilated, as food. 5. To assimilate food. **—***n.* A systematically arranged collection or summary of literary, scientific, legal, or other material; a synopsis. [< L *dis-* away + *gerere* to carry] **—di·gest′er** *n.* **—di·gest′i·bil′i·ty** *n.* **—di·gest′i·ble** *adj.*

di·ges·tant (di·jes′tənt, dī-) *n. Med.* Any agent that assists digestion. **—***adj.* Digestive.

di·ges·tion (di·jes′chən, dī-) *n.* 1. *Physiol.* The process or function of digesting. 2. Mental assimilation.

di·ges·tive (di·jes′tiv, dī-) *adj.* Pertaining to or promoting digestion: *digestive* tract. **—***n.* A medicine to aid digestion.

dig·ger (dig′ər) *n.* 1. One who digs. 2. Any implement or part of a machine for digging.

dig·gings (dig′ingz) *n.pl.* 1. A place of excavation; esp., a mining region. 2. The materials dug out of such a region. 3. Dig (*n.* def. 4.).

dig·it (dij′it) *n.* 1. A finger or toe. 2. Any one of the ten Arabic numeral symbols, 0 to 9. [< L *digitus* finger]

dig·i·tal (dij′ə·təl) *adj.* 1. Relating to fingers or toes. 2. Relating to numbers or calculation by numbers. 3. Providing a readout or display in numbers: a *digital* watch. **—dig′i·tal·ly** *adv.*

digital computer A computing machine that receives problems and processes the answers in digital form. Compare ANALOG COMPUTER.

dig·i·tal·is (dij′ə·tal′is, -tā′lis) *n.* 1. The foxglove. 2. The drug from dried leaves of foxglove, used as a heart stimulant. [< L *digitus* finger]

digiti- *combining form* Finger; toe. [< L *digitus*]

di·glos·si·a (di·glos′ē·ə, -glôs′-) *n.* The use of two dialects at different social levels or for different situations. [< Gk. *di-* two + *glossa* language] **—di·glos′sic** *adj.*

dig·ni·fied (dig′nə·fīd) *adj.* Characterized by or invested with dignity; stately.

dig·ni·fy (dig′nə·fī) *v.t.* **·fied, ·fy·ing** 1. To impart or add dignity to. 2. To give a high-sounding name to. [< L *dignus* worthy + -FY]

dig·ni·tar·y (dig′nə·ter′ē) *n. pl.* **·tar·ies** One having high official position.

dig·ni·ty (dig′nə·tē) *n. pl.* **·ties** 1. Stateliness and nobility of manner; gravity. 2. The state or quality of being excellent, worthy, or honorable. 3. Relative importance or position. 4. A high rank, title, or office, esp. in the church. [< L *dignus* worthy]

di·graph (dī′graf) *n.* A combination of two characters representing a single sound, as *oa* in *boat, sh* in *she.*

di·gress (di·gres′, dī-) *v.i.* To turn aside from the main subject in speaking or writing. [< L *di-* away, apart + *gradi* to go, step] **—di·gres′sion** (-gresh′ən) *n.* **—di·gres′sive** *adj.*

di·he·dral (dī·hē′drəl) *adj.* Two-sided; formed by or having two plane faces. **—***n. Aeron.* The upward or downward inclination of an airplane's supporting surfaces. [< DI-[2] + Gk. *hedra* base, face of a regular solid]

dihedral angle *Geom.* The angle formed by two intersecting planes.

dik·dik (dik′dik′) *n.* A NE African antelope about a foot tall. [< native East African name]

dike (dīk) *n.* 1. An embankment to protect low land from being flooded. 2. *Slang* A lesbian, esp. one with masculine characteristics. **—***v.t.* **diked, dik·ing** To surround or furnish with a dike. Also, *Chiefly Brit., dyke.* [OE *dīc*]

di·lap·i·date (di·lap′ə·dāt) *v.t. & v.i.* **·dat·ed, ·dat·ing** To fall or cause to fall into partial ruin or decay. [< L *dis-* away + *lapidare* to throw stones] **—di·lap′i·da′tion** *n.*

dil·a·ta·tion (dil′ə·tā′shən, dī′lə-) *n.* 1. The process of dilating, or the state of being dilated. 2. That which is dilated. 3. *Pathol.* An excessive enlargement of an organ, etc.
di·late (dī·lāt′, di-) *v.* **·lat·ed, ·lat·ing** *v.t.* 1. To make wider or larger. —*v.i.* 2. To become larger or wider. 3. To speak or write diffusely: with *on* or *upon.* [< L *dis-* apart + *latus* wide] —**di·lat′a·ble** *adj.*
di·la·tion (dī·lā′shən, di-) *n.* 1. Dilatation. 2. *Med.* The expanding of an abnormally small canal or orifice.
di·la·tor (dī·lā′tər, di-) *n.* 1. One who or that which dilates. 2. *Med.* An instrument for expanding a wound, aperture, or cavity.
dil·a·to·ry (dil′ə·tôr′ē) *adj.* 1. Given to delay; tardy; slow. 2. Tending to cause delay. [< L *dilatus,* pp. of *differe* to delay] —**dil′a·to′ri·ly** *adv.* —**dil′a·to′ri·ness** *n.*
di·lem·ma (di·lem′ə) *n.* A situation requiring a choice between equally undesirable alternatives. [< Gk. *di-* two + *lēmma* a premise]
dil·et·tan·te (dil′ə·tänt′, dil′ə·tan′tē) *n. pl.* **·ti** (-tē) or **·tes** One who interests himself in a subject superficially or for amusement; a dabbler. [< Ital., ppr. of *dilettare* to delight] —**dil′et·tan′te, dil′et·tan′tish** *adj.* —**dil′et·tan′tism** *n.*
dil·i·gent (dil′ə·jənt) *adj.* 1. Showing perseverance and application in whatever is undertaken; industrious. 2. Pursued with painstaking effort: a *diligent* search. [< L *diligere* to care for] —**dil′i·gence** *n.* —**dil′i·gent·ly** *adv.*
dill (dil) *n.* An herb of the parsley family, and its seeds or leaves, used as a spice. [OE *dile*]
dil·ly-dal·ly (dil′ē·dal′ē) *v.i.* **-dal·lied, -dal·ly·ing** To waste time, esp. in indecision. [Varied reduplication of DALLY]
di·lute (di·lōōt′, dī-; *for adj., also* dī′lōōt) *v.t.* **·lut·ed, ·lut·ing** 1. To make weaker or more fluid by adding a liquid, as water. 2. To reduce the intensity, strength, or purity of. —*adj.* Weak; diluted. [< L *dilutus,* pp. of *diluere* to wash away] —**di·lu′tion** *n.*
di·lu·vi·al (di·lōō′vē·əl) *adj.* 1. Of or pertaining to a flood, esp. the Deluge. 2. *Geol.* Produced by floods. Also **di·lu′vi·an.** [< L *diluvium* a flood]
dim (dim) *adj.* **dim·mer, dim·mest** 1. Obscured or darkened from lack of light. 2. Not clear to the senses; indistinct: a *dim* figure. 3. Not clear to the mind; vague. 4. Pessimistic. —*v.t. & v.i.* **dimmed, dim·ming** To render or grow dim. [OE *dimm, dim*] —**dim′ly** *adv.* —**dim′ness** *n.*
dime (dīm) *n.* A coin of the United States and Canada, equal to ten cents or one tenth of a dollar. [< L *decima,* fem. of *decimus* a tenth part]
dime novel A cheap, sensational novel, originally costing a dime.
di·men·sion (di·men′shən) *n.* 1. Any measurable extent, as length or thickness. 2. *Usu. pl.* Extent or magnitude: the *dimensions* of the crisis. [< L *dis-* apart + *metiri* to measure] —**di·men′sion·al** *adj.*
di·min·ish (di·min′ish) *v.t.* 1. To make smaller or less, as in size or degree. 2. To reduce, as in rank or authority. —*v.i.* 3. To dwindle; decrease. [Fusion of ME *diminuen* to lessen and OF *menusier* to make small] —**dim·i·nu·tion** (dim′ə·nōō′shən, -nyōō′-) *n.*
di·min·ished (di·min′isht) *adj. Music* One semitone smaller than the corresponding minor or perfect interval.
di·min·u·en·do (di·min′yōō·en′dō) *Music n. pl.* **·dos** A gradual lessening in volume: opposed to *crescendo.* [< Ital., ppr. of *diminuire* to lessen]
di·min·u·tive (di·min′yə·tiv) *adj.* 1. Of relatively small size. 2. *Gram.* Expressing diminished size: said of certain suffixes. —*n.* 1. *Gram.* A word formed from another to express diminished size, familiarity, affection, etc. 2. Anything very small. —**di·min′u·tive·ly** *adv.*
dim·i·ty (dim′ə·tē) *n. pl.* **·ties** A sheer cotton fabric woven with stripes, cords, or checks. [< Gk. *di-* two + *mitos* thread]
dim·mer (dim′ər) *n.* 1. A rheostat used for varying the intensity of lighting. 2. *pl.* Low-beam headlights on an automobile.
di·mor·phism (dī·môr′fiz·əm) *n.* The existence of two distinct forms of the same organ or substance. [< Gk. *di-* two + *morphē* form] —**di·mor′phic, di·mor′phous** *adj.*
dim·ple (dim′pəl) *n.* A slight depression, esp. one in the cheek or chin. —*v.t. & v.i.* **·pled, ·pling** To mark with or form dimples. [ME *dympull*] —**dim′ply** *adj.*
dim·wit (dim′wit′) *n. Slang* A stupid or simple-minded person. —**dim′wit′ted** *adj.*
din (din) *n.* A loud, continuous noise or clamor. —*v.* **dinned, din·ning** *v.t.* 1. To urge or press with repetition or insistence. —*v.i.* 2. To make a din. [OE *dyne*]
di·nar (di·när′) *n.* 1. An ancient gold coin formerly used in Muslim countries. 2. The hundredth part of the Iranian rial. 3. The monetary unit of several Middle East and North African countries and of Yugoslavia.
dine (dīn) *v.* **dined, din·ing** *v.i.* 1. To eat dinner. 2. To eat; feed: with *on* or *upon.* —*v.t.* 3. To entertain at dinner. [< OF *diner*]
din·er (dī′nər) *n.* 1. One who dines. 2. A dining car. 3. A restaurant resembling a railroad car.
di·nette (dī·net′) *n.* An alcove or small room used as a dining room.
ding (ding) *v.t. & v.i.* To sound or ring. —*n.* The sound of a bell, or a sound resembling this. [Imit.]
ding·a·ling (ding′ə·ling) *n. Slang* A silly person.
ding-dong (ding′dông′, -dong′) *n.* 1. The peal of a bell. 2. Any monotonous repetition. [Imit.]
din·ghy (ding′gē, ding′ē) *n. pl.* **·ghies** A small boat, usu. a rowboat. Also **din′gey, din′gy.** [< Hind. *dīngī*]
din·go (ding′gō) *n. pl.* **·goes** The native wild dog of Australia. [< native name]
ding·us (ding′əs) *n. Informal* A thing or device of which the name is unknown or forgotten; a gadget. [< Afrikaans < Du. *ding* thing]
din·gy (din′jē) *adj.* **·gi·er, ·gi·est** Darkened or discolored, as if soiled; dull. [Origin unknown] —**din′gi·ly** *adv.* —**din′gi·ness** *n.*
dining car A railway car in which meals are served en route.

dining room A room in which meals are served.
dink·y (ding′kē) *adj.* **dink·i·er, dink·i·est** *Informal* Small; insignificant. [< Scot. *dink* neat, tidy]
din·ner (din′ər) *n.* **1.** The principal meal of the day. **2.** A banquet in honor of a person or event. [< F *dîner* to dine]
dinner coat or **jacket** A tuxedo jacket.
din·ner·ware (din′ər·wâr′) *n.* Dishes, etc., used for meals.
di·no·saur (dī′nə·sôr) *n. Paleontol.* One of a group of extinct vertebrates of the Mesozoic period, including the largest known land animals, usu. classed as reptiles but postulated by some as warm-blooded mammals and ancestors of birds. [< Gk. *deinos* terrible + *sauros* lizard] **—di′no·sau′ri·an** *adj. & n.*
Di·no·sau·ri·a (dī·nə·sôr′ē·ə) *n. Paleontol.* A proposed new class of vertebrates that includes dinosaurs and birds.
dint (dint) *n.* **1.** Means; force: to win by *dint* of effort. **2.** A dent. [OE *dynt* a blow]
di·o·cese (dī′ə·sēs, -sis) *n.* The territory or the churches under a bishop's jurisdiction. [< Gk. < *dia-* completely + *oikeein* to dwell, manage] **—di·oc·e·san** (dī·os′ə·sən, dī′ə·sē′-) *adj. & n.*
di·ode (dī′ōd) *n. Electronics* An electron tube that permits electrons to pass in one direction only, used as a rectifier.
di·oe·cious (dī·ē′shəs) *adj. Bot.* Having the male and female organs borne by different plants. [< DI-[2] + Gk. *oikia* house]
di·op·tric (dī·op′trik) *adj. Optics* **1.** Aiding the vision by refractive lenses. **2.** Of or pertaining to dioptrics. [< Gk. *dioptra* optical instrument]
di·op·trics (dī·op′triks) *n.pl.* (*construed as sing.*) The branch of optics treating of light refraction through lenses.
di·o·ra·ma (dī′ə·rä′mə, -ram′ə) *n.* An exhibit consisting of modeled figures, etc., set in a naturalistic foreground. [< Gk. *dia-* through + *horama* a sight] **—di·o·ram·ic** (dī′ə·ram′ik) *adj.*
di·ox·ide (dī·ok′sīd, -sid) *n. Chem.* An oxide containing two atoms of oxygen to the molecule.
dip (dip) *v.* **dipped, dip·ping** *v.t.* **1.** To put or let down into a liquid momentarily. **2.** To obtain or lift up and out by scooping, bailing, etc. **3.** To lower and then raise, as a flag in salute. **4.** To plunge (animals) into a disinfectant. **5.** To make (candles) by repeatedly immersing wicks in wax or tallow. **—***v.i.* **6.** To plunge into and quickly come out of water or other liquid. **7.** To reach into a container, esp. so as to take something out: often figuratively, as to *dip* into savings. **8.** To sink or go down suddenly. **9.** To incline downward; go down; decline. **10.** *Aeron.* To drop rapidly and then climb. **11.** To engage in or read something superficially. **—***n.* **1.** An act of dipping; a brief immersion or plunge. **2.** A liquid sauce, etc., into which something is to be dipped. **3.** The quantity of something taken up at a dipping; also, the object used for dipping. **4.** A sloping downward; also, the degree of such a sloping. **5.** A hollow or depression. **6.** *Aeron.* A rapid drop of an airplane followed by a climb. **7.** *Slang* A pickpocket. [OE *dyppan*]
diph·the·ri·a (dif·thir′ē·ə, dip-) *n. Pathol.* An acute contagious disease, caused by a bacillus and characterized by the formation of a false membrane in the air passages, fever, and weakness. [< Gk. *diphthera* leather, membrane] **—diph·the′ri·al, diph·the·rit·ic** (dif′thə·rit′ik) *adj.*
diph·thong (dif′thông, -thong, dip′-) *n. Phonet.* A blend of two vowel sounds in one syllable, as *oi* in *coil*. [< Gk. *di-* two + *phthongos* sound]
diplo- *combining form* Double. Also, before vowels, **dipl-**. [< Gk. *diploos*]
dip·loid (dip′loid) *adj. Biol.* Having two sets of chromosomes.
di·plo·ma (di·plō′mə) *n.* A certificate given by a school, college, or university testifying that a student has completed a course of study. [< Gk. *diplōma* paper folded double, a letter]
di·plo·ma·cy (di·plō′mə·sē) *n. pl.* **·cies** **1.** The art, science, or practice of conducting negotiations between nations. **2.** Skill or tact in dealing with others, etc.
dip·lo·mat (dip′lə·mat) *n.* **1.** One engaged in diplomacy. **2.** Any individual possessing skill or tact in dealing with others. Also **di·plo·ma·tist** (di·plō′mə·tist). [See DIPLOMA.]
dip·lo·mat·ic (dip′lə·mat′ik) *adj.* **1.** Of or pertaining to diplomacy. **2.** Tactful in dealing with people. **—dip′lo·mat′i·cal·ly** *adv.*
diplomatic corps The corps of officials, as ambassadors and envoys, who are assigned to represent their country in another country.
diplomatic immunity Exemption of the members of a diplomatic corps from the ordinary processes of local law.
dip·per (dip′ər) *n.* **1.** One who dips. **2.** A long-handled cup used to dip liquids. **3.** Any of several American birds adept at diving.
Dip·per (dip′ər) *n.* Either of two northern constellations, the Big Dipper or the Little Dipper.
dip·so·ma·ni·a (dip′sə·mā′nē·ə) *n.* Uncontrollable craving for alcoholic drink. [< Gk. *dipsa* thirst + -MANIA] **—dip′so·ma′ni·ac** *n.*
dip·stick (dip′stik′) *n.* A graduated rod or stick indicating depth, as of oil in a crankcase.
dip·ter·ous (dip′tər·əs) *adj. Entomol.* Of or pertaining to two-winged insects. [< Gk. *di-* twice + *pteron* wing]
dire (dīr) *adj.* **dir·er, dir·est** Calamitous; dreadful; terrible. [< L *dirus* awful] **—dire′ly** *adv.* **—dire′ness** *n.*
di·rect (di·rekt′, dī-) *v.t.* **1.** To control or conduct the affairs of; manage. **2.** To order; command. **3.** *Music* To lead as a conductor. **4.** To tell (someone) the way. **5.** To cause to move in a desired direction: to *direct* one's gaze. **6.** To indicate the destination of, as a letter. **7.** To intend, as remarks, for a certain person; address. **8.** To guide or supervise (the performance of a play, film, etc.). **—***v.i.* **9.** To give commands or guidance. **10.** To act as a director of a play, film, etc. **—***adj.* **1.** Having or being the straightest course; shortest. **2.** Free from intervening agencies or conditions. **3.** Straightforward; candid; plain. **4.** Complete; absolute. **5.** In a continuous line of descent. **6.** In the exact words of the speaker or writer: a *direct* quote. **—***adv.* In a direct line or manner; directly.

[< L *dis-* apart + *regere* to guide, conduct] —**di·rect′ness** *n.*

direct current *Electr.* A current flowing in one direction.

di·rec·tion (di·rek′shən, dī-) *n.* **1.** The act of directing. **2.** The course or position of an object or point in relation to another object or point: in the *direction* of Chicago. **3.** *Usu. pl.* Instructions about how to do or use something. **4.** An order, command, or regulation. **5.** Management, control, or administration. **6.** Supervision and organization of a play, film, etc. **7.** Tendency or movement.

di·rec·tion·al (di·rek′shən·əl, dī-) *adj.* **1.** Pertaining to direction in space. **2.** *Telecom.* **a** Adapted for indicating from which of several directions signals are received. **b** Receiving radio waves more effectively from some directions than from others. **3.** Indicating direction: *directional* signals.

direction finder *Telecom.* A receiving device with which the direction of incoming radio signals may be determined.

di·rec·tive (di·rek′tiv, dī-) *n.* An order or regulation; esp., a governmental or military pronouncement.

di·rect·ly (di·rekt′lē, dī-) *adv.* **1.** In a direct line or manner. **2.** Without medium, agent, or go-between. **3.** As soon as possible; immediately. —*conj. Brit.* As soon as.

direct object See under OBJECT.

di·rec·tor (di·rek′tər, dī-) *n.* One who directs, as the head member of a corporation, the conductor of an orchestra, etc. —**di·rec′·tress** *n.fem.*

di·rec·tor·ate (di·rek′tər·it, dī-) *n.* **1.** A body of directors. **2.** The office or power of a director: also **di·rec′tor·ship.**

di·rec·to·ri·al (di·rek′tôr′ē·əl, dī-) *adj.* **1.** That directs; directive. **2.** Pertaining to a director or directorate.

di·rec·to·ry (di·rek′tər·ē, dī-) *n. pl.* **·ries** **1.** An alphabetical or classified list: a telephone *directory.* **2.** A directorate. —*adj.* Serving to direct.

direct primary *Govt.* A preliminary election in which a party chooses its candidates for public office by direct vote.

dire·ful (dīr′fo͝ol, -fəl) *adj.* Dreadful; terrible.

dirge (dûrj) *n.* **1.** A song or melody expressing mourning. **2.** A funeral hymn. [< L *dirige* (imperative of *dirigere* to direct), the first word of the antiphon (*Ps.* v 8) of matins]

dir·i·gi·ble (dir′ə·jə·bəl) *n.* A self-propelled, steerable, lighter-than-air aircraft. [< L *dirigere* to direct]

dirk (dûrk) *n.* A dagger. [Origin uncertain]

dirn·dl (dûrn′dəl) *n.* A full skirt tightly gathered at the waist. [< G *dirndl,* dim. of *dirne* girl]

dirt (dûrt) *n.* **1.** Any foul or filthy substance, as mud, dust, excrement, etc. **2.** Loose earth or soil. **3.** Something contemptible, mean, or of small worth. **4.** Obscene speech, pictures, or writing. **5.** Gossip. —*adj.* Made of earth: a *dirt* road. [ME *drit* < ON, dirt, bird droppings]

dirt-cheap (dûrt′chēp′) *adj.* Very inexpensive. —*adv.* At a very low price.

dirt·y (dûr′tē) *adj.* **dirt·i·er, dirt·i·est** **1.** Soiled with or as with dirt; unclean. **2.** Imparting dirt; making filthy. **3.** Indecent; obscene. **4.** Despicable; mean. **5.** Stormy: *dirty* weather. **6.** Not clear in color. —*v.t. & v.i.* **dirt·ied, dirt·y·ing** To make or become dirty. —**dirt′i·ness** *n.*

dis-[1] *prefix* **1.** Away from; apart: *disembody.* **2.** The reverse of or the undoing of (what is expressed in the rest of the word): *disconnect.* **3.** Deprivation of some quality, power, rank, etc.: *disable.* **4.** Not: *disloyal.* Also: *di-* before *b, d, l, m, n, r, s, v,* and usu. before *g,* as in *digress; dif-* before *f,* as in *differ.* [< L *dis-,* ult. < *duo* two]

dis-[2] *prefix* Var. of DI-[2]. [< Gk. *dis* twice]

dis·a·bil·i·ty (dis′ə·bil′ə·tē) *n. pl.* **·ties** **1.** That which disables. **2.** Legal incapacity to act.

dis·a·ble (dis·ā′bəl) *v.t.* **·bled, ·bling** **1.** To incapacitate. **2.** To render legally incapable. —**dis·a′ble·ment** *n.*

dis·a·buse (dis′ə·byo͞oz′) *v.t.* **·bused, ·bus·ing** To free from false or mistaken ideas.

dis·ad·van·tage (dis′əd·van′tij) *n.* **1.** That which produces an unfavorable condition or situation; drawback; handicap. **2.** Loss, injury, or detriment. —**at a disadvantage** In an unfavorable condition or situation. —*v.t.* **·taged, ·tag·ing** To subject to a disadvantage.

dis·ad·van·taged (dis′əd·van′tijd) *adj.* Having less than is needed for decent living.

dis·ad·van·ta·geous (dis·ad′vən·tā′jəs) *adj.* Attended with disadvantage; detrimental; inconvenient. —**dis·ad′van·ta′geous·ly** *adv.*

dis·af·fect (dis′ə·fekt′) *v.t.* To destroy or weaken the affection or loyalty of; alienate; estrange. —**dis′af·fec′tion** *n.*

dis·a·gree (dis′ə·grē′) *v.i.* **·greed, ·gree·ing** **1.** To vary in opinion; differ. **2.** To quarrel; argue. **3.** To fail to agree or harmonize, as facts. **4.** To be unacceptable or harmful: with *with.*

dis·a·gree·a·ble (dis′ə·grē′ə·bəl) *adj.* **1.** Repugnant or offensive; unpleasant. **2.** Quarrelsome; bad-tempered. —**dis′a·gree′a·ble·ness** *n.* —**dis′a·gree′a·bly** *adv.*

dis·a·gree·ment (dis′ə·grē′mənt) *n.* **1.** Failure to agree; difference. **2.** Difference in views; dissent. **3.** A quarrel; dispute.

dis·al·low (dis′ə·lou′) *v.t.* **1.** To refuse to allow. **2.** To reject as untrue or invalid. —**dis′al·low′ance** *n.*

dis·ap·pear (dis′ə·pir′) *v.i.* **1.** To pass from sight; fade away; vanish. **2.** To cease to exist. —**dis′ap·pear′ance** *n.*

dis·ap·point (dis′ə·point′) *v.t.* **1.** To fail to fulfill the expectation, hope, or desire of (a person). **2.** To prevent the fulfillment of (a hope or plan). —**dis′ap·point′ing·ly** *adv.*

dis·ap·point·ed (dis′ə·poin′tid) *adj.* Frustrated in one's expectations or hopes.

dis·ap·point·ment (dis′ə·point′mənt) *n.* **1.** The act of disappointing. **2.** The feeling of being disappointed. **3.** One who or that which disappoints.

dis·ap·pro·ba·tion (dis′ap·rə·bā′shən) *n.* Disapproval.

dis·ap·prove (dis′ə·pro͞ov′) *v.* **·proved, ·prov·ing** *v.t.* **1.** To regard with disfavor or censure. **2.** To refuse to approve; reject. —*v.i.* **3.** To have or express an unfavorable opinion: often with *of.* —**dis′ap·prov′al** *n.* —**dis′ap·prov′ing·ly** *adv.*

dis·arm (dis·ärm′) *v.t.* **1.** To deprive of weapons. **2.** To allay or reduce (suspicion,

antagonism, etc.). —*v.i.* 3. To reduce or eliminate one's military forces, equipment, etc.
dis·ar·ma·ment (dis·är′mə·mənt) *n.* The act of disarming; esp., the elimination, reduction, or limitation of armed forces, military equipment, etc.
dis·arm·ing (dis·är′ming) *adj.* Tending to overcome suspicion, etc. —**dis·arm′ing·ly** *adv.*
dis·ar·range (dis′ə·rānj′) *v.t.* **·ranged, ·rang·ing** To disturb the arrangement of; disorder. —**dis′ar·range′ment** *n.*
dis·ar·ray (dis′ə·rā′) *n.* 1. Disorder; confusion. 2. Disorder of clothing. —*v.t.* To throw into disarray.
dis·as·sem·ble (dis′ə·sem′bəl) *v.t.* **·bled, ·bling** To take apart. —**dis′as·sem′bly** *n.*
dis·as·so·ci·ate (dis′ə·sō′shē·āt, -sē·āt) *v.t.* **·at·ed, ·at·ing** To break association with. —**dis′as·so′ci·a′tion** *n.*
dis·as·ter (di·zas′tər) *n.* An event causing great distress or ruin. [< MF *desastre*]
dis·as·trous (di·zas′trəs) *adj.* Causing or accompanied by disaster; calamitous. —**dis·as′trous·ly** *adv.* —**dis·as′trous·ness** *n.*
dis·a·vow (dis′ə·vou′) *v.t.* To disclaim responsibility for or approval of. —**dis′a·vow′al** *n.*
dis·band (dis·band′) *v.t.* 1. To break up the organization of; dissolve. —*v.i.* 2. To become disbanded. —**dis·band′ment** *n.*
dis·bar (dis·bär′) *v.t.* **·barred, ·bar·ring** To expel officially from the legal profession. —**dis·bar′ment** *n.*
dis·be·lief (dis′bi·lēf′) *n.* Lack of belief.
dis·be·lieve (dis′bi·lēv′) *v.t.* & *v.i.* **·lieved, ·liev·ing** To refuse to believe. —**dis′be·liev′er** *n.*
dis·bur·den (dis·bûr′dən) *v.t.* & *v.i.* To get rid or be relieved of (a burden).
dis·burse (dis·bûrs′) *v.t.* **·bursed, ·burs·ing** To pay out; expend. [< OF *des-* away + *bourse* a purse] —**dis·burs′a·ble** *adj.* —**dis·burse′ment** *n.* —**dis·burs′er** *n.*
disc (disk) *n.* See DISK.
dis·card (*v.* dis·kärd′; *n.* dis′kärd) *v.t.* 1. To cast aside as useless or undesirable; reject. 2. In card games, to throw out (a card or cards) from one's hand; also, to play (a card, other than a trump, not of the suit led). —*v.i.* 3. In card games, to throw out a card or cards. —*n.* 1. The act of discarding, or the state of being discarded. 2. A card or cards discarded. 3. One who or that which is discarded.
dis·cern (di·sûrn′, di·zûrn′) *v.t.* 1. To perceive, as with the eyes or mind. 2. To recognize as separate and different. —*v.i.* 3. To distinguish or discriminate something. [< L *dis-* apart + *cernere* to separate] —**dis·cern′er** *n.* —**dis·cern′i·ble** *adj.* —**dis·cern′i·bly** *adv.*
dis·cern·ing (di·sûr′ning, -zûr′-) *adj.* Showing insight; discriminating. —**dis·cern′ing·ly** *adv.* —**dis·cern′ment** *n.*
dis·charge (dis·chärj′; *n. also* dis′chärj) *v.* **·charged, ·charg·ing** *v.t.* 1. To remove the contents of; unload. 2. To remove by unloading. 3. To emit (fluid). 4. To shoot or fire, as a gun. 5. To dismiss from office or employment. 6. To set at liberty. 7. To relieve of duty or obligation. 8. To perform the duties of (a trust, office, etc.). 9. To pay (a debt) or satisfy (an obligation or duty). 10. *Electr.* To free of an electrical charge. —*v.i.* 11. To get rid of a load, burden, etc. 12. To go off, as a cannon. 13. To give or send forth contents. —*n.* 1. The act of discharging or the state of being discharged. 2. The firing of a weapon or missile. 3. An issuing forth; emission. 4. Release or dismissal from service, employment, or custody. 5. Something that discharges, as a certificate separating one from military service. 6. *Electr.* The flow of electricity between the terminals of a condenser when placed in very near contact. [< OF *descharger* to unload] —**dis·charge′a·ble** *adj.* —**dis·charg′er** *n.*
dis·ci·ple (di·sī′pəl) *n.* 1. One who accepts and follows a teacher or a doctrine. 2. One of the twelve chosen companions and apostles of Jesus Christ. [< L *discere* to learn]
dis·ci·pli·nar·i·an (dis′ə·plə·nâr′ē·ən) *n.* One who administers or advocates discipline.
dis·ci·pli·nar·y (dis′ə·plə·ner′ē) *adj.* Of or relating to discipline; used for discipline.
dis·ci·pline (dis′ə·plin) *n.* 1. Training of the mental, moral, and physical powers by instruction, control, and exercise. 2. The state or condition resulting from such training. 3. Punishment or corrective action for the sake of training. 4. A system of rules, or method of practice, as of a church. 5. A branch of knowledge or instruction. —*v.t.* **·plined, ·plin·ing** 1. To train to obedience or subjection. 2. To drill; educate. 3. To punish. [< L *disciplina* instruction] —**dis′ci·plin·er** *n.*
dis·claim (dis·klām′) *v.t.* 1. To disavow any claim to, or responsibility for. 2. To reject or deny the authority of. —*v.i.* 3. *Law* To renounce a legal claim.
dis·claim·er (dis·klā′mər) *n.* 1. One who disclaims. 2. A denial.
dis·close (dis·klōz′) *v.t.* **·closed, ·clos·ing** 1. To expose to view; uncover. 2. To make known. —**dis·clos′er** *n.*
dis·clo·sure (dis·klō′zhər) *n.* 1. The act or process of disclosing. 2. That which is disclosed.
dis·co (dis′kō) *n. pl.* **·cos** Discothèque.
dis·cog·ra·phy (dis·kog′rə·fē) *n.* A systematic catalog of phonograph records, giving titles, composers, performers, dates of issue, etc.
dis·col·or (dis·kul′ər) *v.t.* 1. To change or destroy the color of; stain. —*v.i.* 2. To become discolored. Also *Brit.* **dis·col′our.** —**dis·col′or·a′tion** *n.*
dis·com·bob·u·late (dis′kəm·bob′yə·lāt) *v.t.* **·lat·ed, ·lat·ing** *Slang* To throw into confusion. [Origin uncertain]
dis·com·fit (dis·kum′fit) *v.t.* 1. To defeat the plans or purposes of; frustrate. 2. To throw into confusion. [< OF *des-* away + *confire* to prepare] —**dis·com′fi·ture** *n.*
dis·com·fort (dis·kum′fərt) *n.* 1. Lack of ease or comfort. 2. That which interferes with comfort. —*v.t.* To make uneasy; distress.
dis·com·mode (dis′kə·mōd′) *v.t.* **·mod·ed, ·mod·ing** To cause inconvenience to; trouble; disturb. [< L *dis-* not + *commodus* fit, suitable]
dis·com·pose (dis′kəm·pōz′) *v.t.* **·posed, ·pos·ing** 1. To disturb the calm of; make

uneasy. 2. To disorder or disarrange. —**dis′com·po′sure** (-pō′zhər) *n.*

dis·con·cert (dis′kən·sûrt′) *v.t.* 1. To disturb the composure of; confuse; upset. 2. To frustrate, as a plan. —**dis′con·cert′ed** *adj.* —**dis′con·cert′ed·ly** *adv.* —**dis′con·cert′ing·ly** *adv.*

dis·con·nect (dis′kə·nekt′) *v.t.* To break the connection of or between. —**dis′con·nec′tion** *n.*

dis·con·nect·ed (dis′kə·nek′tid) *adj.* 1. Not connected; disjointed. 2. Incoherent; rambling. —**dis′con·nect′ed·ly** *adv.*

dis·con·so·late (dis·kon′sə·lit) *adj.* 1. Inconsolable; dejected. 2. Producing or marked by gloominess; cheerless. [< L *disconsolatus* comfortless] —**dis·con′so·late·ly** *adv.*

dis·con·tent (dis′kən·tent′) *n.* Lack of contentment; dissatisfaction; uneasiness. —**dis′con·tent′ed** *adj.* —**dis′con·tent′ed·ly** *adv.*

dis·con·tin·ue (dis′kən·tin′yōō) *v.* **·tin·ued, ·tin·u·ing** *v.t.* 1. To break off or cease from; stop. 2. To cease using, receiving, etc. —*v.i.* 3. To come to an end; cease. —**dis′con·tin′u·a′tion** *n.*

dis·con·ti·nu·i·ty (dis′kon·tə·nōō′ə·tē, -nyōō′-) *n. pl.* **·ties** 1. Lack of continuity. 2. A gap or break.

dis·con·tin·u·ous (dis′kən·tin′yōō·əs) *adj.* Not continuous; characterized by interruptions or breaks. —**dis′con·tin′u·ous·ly** *adv.*

dis·cord (dis′kôrd) *n.* 1. Lack of agreement; conflict; strife. 2. A harsh or disagreeable mingling of noises; din. 3. *Music* Dissonance. [< L *discordare* to differ] —**dis·cor′dant** *adj.* —**dis·cor′dant·ly** *adv.*

dis·co·thèque (dis·kə·tek′) *n.* A night club offering recorded music for dancing and usu. refreshments. [< F, lit., record library]

dis·count (*v.* dis′kount, dis·kount′; *n.* dis′·kount) *v.t.* 1. To deduct (an indicated sum or percent) from the full amount; also, to reduce the cost or value of. 2. To buy, sell, or lend money on (a bill, note, or other negotiable paper), less the amount of interest to be accumulated before maturity. 3. To allow for exaggeration; minimize. —*n.* 1. A deduction of a particular sum or percent. 2. The interest deducted beforehand in buying, selling, or lending money on negotiable notes, etc. —**at a discount** Below the amount regularly charged. [< L *dis-* away + *computare* to count] —**dis′count·a·ble** *adj.* —**dis′count·er** *n.*

dis·coun·te·nance (dis·koun′tə·nəns) *v.t.* **·nanced, ·nanc·ing** 1. To disapprove of. 2. To embarrass; disconcert.

dis·cour·age (dis·kûr′ij) *v.t.* **·aged, ·ag·ing** 1. To weaken the courage or lessen the confidence of; dishearten. 2. To deter or dissuade: with *from.* 3. To attempt to repress or prevent by disapproval. [< OF *des-* away + *corage* courage] —**dis·cour′age·ment** *n.* —**dis·cour′ag·ing·ly** *adv.*

dis·course (*n.* dis′kôrs, dis·kôrs′; *v.* dis·kôrs′) *n.* A formal, extensive, oral or written treatment of a subject. —*v.i.* **·coursed, ·cours·ing** 1. To set forth one's ideas concerning a subject: with *on* or *upon.* 2. To converse; confer. [< LL *discursus* conversation] —**dis·cours′er** *n.*

dis·cour·te·ous (dis·kûr′tē·əs) *adj.* Not courteous; impolite. —**dis·cour′te·ous·ly** *adv.*

dis·cour·te·sy (dis·kûr′tə·sē) *n. pl.* **·sies** 1. Lack of courtesy. 2. A discourteous act.

dis·cov·er (dis·kuv′ər) *v.t.* To find out, get knowledge of, or come upon, esp. for the first time. [< OF *des-* away + *covrir* to cover] —**dis·cov′er·er** *n.*

dis·cov·er·y (dis·kuv′ər·ē) *n. pl.* **·er·ies** 1. The act of discovering. 2. Something discovered.

dis·cred·it (dis·kred′it) *v.t.* 1. To harm the credibility or reputation of. 2. To refuse to believe (something asserted). —*n.* 1. The state of being discredited. 2. Something that discredits. —**dis·cred′it·a·ble** *adj.*

dis·creet (dis·krēt′) *adj.* Tactful and judicious, esp. in dealing with others. [< LL *discretus*, orig. pp. of L *discernere* to discern] —**dis·creet′ly** *adv.* —**dis·creet′ness** *n.*

dis·crep·an·cy (dis·krep′ən·sē) *n. pl.* **·cies** 1. Lack of agreement or consistency. 2. An instance of this. [< L *discrepare* to sound discordantly] —**dis·crep′ant** *adj.* —**dis·crep′ant·ly** *adv.*

dis·crete (dis·krēt′) *adj.* 1. Distinct or separate. 2. Made up of distinct parts. [Var. of DISCREET] —**dis·crete′ly** *adv.* —**dis·crete′ness** *n.*

dis·cre·tion (dis·kresh′ən) *n.* 1. The quality of being discreet; tactfulness; prudence. 2. Freedom or power to make one's own judgments. [< L *discernere* to discern]

dis·cre·tion·ar·y (dis·kresh′ən·er′ē) *adj.* Left to or determined by one's discretion.

discretionary income Personal income available for items other than basic necessities.

dis·crim·i·nate (*v.* dis·krim′ə·nāt; *adj.* dis·krim′ə·nit) *v.* **·nat·ed, ·nat·ing** *v.i.* 1. To act toward someone or something with partiality or prejudice. 2. To draw a clear distinction. —*v.t.* 3. To draw or constitute a clear distinction between; differentiate. —*adj.* Discriminating. [< L *dis-* apart + *crimen* judgment] —**dis·crim′i·nate·ly** *adv.* —**dis·crim′i·na′tion** *n.* —**dis·crim′i·na′tor** *n.*

dis·crim·i·nat·ing (dis·krim′ə·nā′ting) *adj.* 1. Able to draw clear distinctions; discerning. 2. Fastidious; particular. 3. Serving to distinguish; differentiating. —**dis·crim′i·nat′ing·ly** *adv.*

dis·crim·i·na·to·ry (dis·krim′ə·nə·tôr′ē) *adj.* Showing prejudice or bias.

dis·cur·sive (dis·kûr′siv) *adj.* Passing quickly or disjointedly from one subject to another; digressive. [See DISCOURSE.] —**dis·cur′sive·ly** *adv.* —**dis·cur′sive·ness** *n.*

dis·cus (dis′kəs) *n. pl.* **dis·cus·es** or **dis·ci** (dis′ī) 1. A flat, heavy disk, as of metal or wood, hurled for distance in athletic contests. 2. Such a contest. [< Gk. *diskos*]

dis·cuss (dis·kus′) *v.t.* To talk or write about. [< L, pp. of *discutere* to discuss] —**dis·cus·sion** (dis·kush′ən) *n.*

dis·dain (dis·dān′) *v.t.* 1. To consider unworthy of one's regard or notice. 2. To refuse scornfully. —*n.* Scorn; contempt. [< OF *desdeignier* to scorn] —**dis·dain′ful** *adj.* —**dis·dain′ful·ly** *adv.*

dis·ease (di·zēz′) *n.* 1. A condition of ill health or malfunctioning in a living organism. 2. Any disordered or unwholesome condition. [< OF *des-* not + *aise* ease] —**dis·eased′** *adj.*

dis·em·bark (dis′em·bärk′) *v.t.* & *v.i.* To put or go ashore from a ship. —**dis·em′bar·ka′tion** *n.*

dis·em·bar·rass (dis′em·bar′əs) *v.t.* To free from embarrassment, entanglement, etc. —**dis′em·bar′rass·ment** *n.*

dis·em·bod·y (dis′em·bod′ē) *v.t.* **·bod·ied, ·bod·y·ing** To free from the body or from physical existence. —**dis′em·bod′i·ment** *n.*

dis·em·bow·el (dis′em·boul′) *v.t.* **·eled** or **·elled, ·el·ing** or **·el·ling** To take out the bowels or entrails of; eviscerate. —**dis′em·bow′el·ment** *n.*

dis·en·chant (dis′en·chant′) *v.t.* To free from enchantment; disillusion. —**dis′en·chant′er** *n.* —**dis′en·chant′ment** *n.*

dis·en·cum·ber (dis′en·kum′bər) *v.t.* To free from encumbrance.

dis·en·fran·chise (dis′en·fran′chīz) *v.t.* **·chised, ·chis·ing** To disfranchise. —**dis′en·fran′chise·ment** *n.*

dis·en·gage (dis′en·gāj′) *v.t. & v.i.* **·gaged, ·gag·ing** To free or become free from entanglement, obligation, occupation, etc. —**dis′en·gage′ment** *n.*

dis·en·tan·gle (dis′en·tang′gəl) *v.t. & v.i.* **·gled, ·gling** To free or become free from entanglement, confusion, etc. —**dis′en·tan′gle·ment** *n.*

dis·en·twine (dis′en·twīn′) *v.t. & v.i.* **·twined, ·twin·ing** To untwine; disentangle.

dis·es·tab·lish (dis′es·tab′lish) *v.t.* 1. To deprive of fixed or established status or character. 2. To take away government support from (a state church). —**dis′es·tab′lish·ment** *n.*

dis·es·teem (dis′es·tēm′) *v.t.* To have a low opinion of. —*n.* Lack of esteem; disfavor.

dis·fa·vor (dis·fā′vər) *n.* 1. Lack of favor; disapproval; dislike. 2. The state of being frowned upon or disliked. Also *Brit.* **dis·fa′vour.**

dis·fig·ure (dis·fig′yər) *v.t.* **·ured, ·ur·ing** To mar or destroy the appearance of; deform. —**dis·fig′ur·er** *n.* —**dis·fig′ure·ment** *n.*

dis·fran·chise (dis·fran′chīz) *v.t.* **·chised, ·chis·ing** 1. To deprive (a citizen) of a right, esp. of the right to vote. 2. To deprive of a franchise, privilege, or right. Also *disenfranchise.* —**dis·fran′chise·ment** *n.*

dis·gorge (dis·gôrj′) *v.* **·gorged, ·gorg·ing** *v.t.* 1. To throw up; vomit. 2. To pour forth; discharge. 3. To give up unwillingly. —*v.i.* 4. To discharge something; empty. [< OF *des-* from + *gorge* throat]

dis·grace (dis·grās′) *n.* 1. A condition of shame or dishonor. 2. Anything that brings about dishonor or shame. 3. A state of being out of favor. —*v.t.* **·graced, ·grac·ing** To bring reproach or shame upon. [< Ital. *dis-* away + *grazia* favor]

dis·grace·ful (dis·grās′fəl) *adj.* Characterized by or causing disgrace; shameful. —**dis·grace′ful·ly** *adv.* —**dis·grace′ful·ness** *n.*

dis·grun·tle (dis·grun′təl) *v.t.* **·tled, ·tling** To make dissatisfied; put out of humor.

dis·guise (dis·gīz′) *v.t.* **·guised, ·guis·ing** 1. To alter the appearance of so as to make unrecognizable. 2. To conceal the actual nature of. —*n.* 1. The act of disguising or the state of being disguised. 2. Something that disguises, as a mask or costume. [< OF *des-* down + *guise* manner]

dis·gust (dis·gust′) *v.t.* To cause a deep aversion or loathing in; sicken. —*n.* Strong aversion. [< MF *des-* not + *gouster* to taste] —**dis·gust′ed** *adj.* —**dis·gust′ed·ly** *adv.* —**dis·gust′ing** *adj.* —**dis·gust′ing·ly** *adv.*

dish (dish) *n.* 1. An open, concave, usu. shallow container, typically used for holding or serving food. 2. A particular preparation of food. 3. A portion of food served in a dish. 4. A hollow or depression like that in a dish. —*v.t.* 1. To put (food, etc.) into a dish; serve: usu. with *up* or *out.* 2. To hollow out (a surface). [< L *discus* disk] —**dish′like′** *adj.*

dis·ha·bille (dis′ə·bēl′) *n.* 1. A state of being partially or negligently dressed. 2. The garments worn in this state. Also *deshabille.* [< F *déshabiller* to undress]

dis·har·mo·ny (dis·här′mə·nē) *n. pl.* **·nies** Lack of harmony; discord. —**dis′har·mo′ni·ous** (-mō′nē·əs) *adj.* —**dis′har·mo′ni·ous·ly** *adv.*

dish·cloth (dish′klôth′) *n.* A cloth used in washing dishes: also called *dishrag.*

dis·heart·en (dis·här′tən) *v.t.* To discourage. —**dis·heart′en·ing·ly** *adv.*

di·shev·el (di·shev′əl) *v.t.* **di·shev·eled** or **·elled, di·shev·el·ing** or **·el·ling** To muss up or disarrange (the hair or clothing). [< MF *des-* away + *chevel* hair] —**di·shev′eled** or **·elled** *adj.* —**di·shev′el·ment** *n.*

dis·hon·est (dis·on′ist) *adj.* 1. Not honest; not trustworthy. 2. Marked by a lack of honesty; deceitful. [< LL *dis-* away + *honestus* honest] —**dis·hon′est·ly** *adv.* —**dis·hon′es·ty** *n.*

dis·hon·or (dis·on′ər) *v.t.* 1. To deprive of honor; disgrace. 2. To decline or fail to pay, as a note. —*n.* 1. Lack or loss of honor or of honorable character. 2. An insult, indignity, taint, etc. 3. Refusal or failure to pay a note, etc., when due. Also *Brit.* **dis·hon′our.** —**dis·hon′or·a·ble** *adj.* —**dis·hon′or·a·bly** *adv.*

dish·rag (dish′rag′) *n.* A dishcloth.

dish·wash·er (dish′wosh′ər, -wôsh′-) *n.* One who or that which washes dishes.

dis·il·lu·sion (dis′i·lo͞o′zhən) *v.t.* To free from illusion; disenchant. —**dis′il·lu′sion·ment, dis′il·lu′sion** *n.*

dis·in·cline (dis′in·klīn′) *v.t. & v.i.* **·clined, ·clin·ing** To make or be unwilling or averse. —**dis·in·cli·na·tion** (dis·in′klə·nā′shən) *n.*

dis·in·fect (dis′in·fekt′) *v.t.* To cleanse of disease germs; sterilize. —**dis′in·fec′tant** *n. & adj.* —**dis′in·fec′tion** *n.*

dis·in·gen·u·ous (dis′in·jen′yo͞o·əs) *adj.* Lacking simplicity, frankness, or sincerity; not straightforward; crafty. —**dis′in·gen′u·ous·ly** *adv.* —**dis′in·gen′u·ous·ness** *n.*

dis·in·her·it (dis′in·her′it) *v.t.* To deprive of an inheritance. —**dis′in·her′i·tance** *n.*

dis·in·te·grate (dis·in′tə·grāt) *v.t. & v.i.* **·grat·ed, ·grat·ing** To break up or become reduced into parts or particles. —**dis·in′te·gra′tion** *n.*

dis·in·ter (dis′in·tûr′) *v.t.* **·terred, ·ter·ring** 1. To remove from a grave; exhume. 2. To bring to light; unearth. —**dis′in·ter′ment** *n.*

dis·in·ter·est (dis·in′tər·ist, -trist) *n.* 1. Freedom from self-seeking and bias; impartiality: also **dis·in′ter·est·ed·ness.** 2. Lack of interest; indifference. —**dis·in′ter·est·ed** *adj.*

dis·join (dis·join′) *v.t.* 1. To undo or prevent the joining of; separate. —*v.i.* 2. To become divided or separated.

dis·joint (dis·joint′) *v.t.* 1. To take apart at the joints; dismember. 2. To put out of joint; dislocate. 3. To upset or destroy the coherence, connection, or sequence of. —*v.i.* 4. To come apart at the joints; fall apart.

dis·joint·ed (dis·join′tid) *adj.* 1. Separated; dismembered. 2. Disconnected; out of order; incoherent. —**dis·joint′ed·ly** *adv.* —**dis·joint′ed·ness** *n.*

dis·junct (dis·jungkt′) *adj.* Not connected; detached. [< L *dis-* not + *jungere* to join] —**dis·junc′tion** *n.*

disk (disk) *n.* 1. A fairly flat, circular plate. 2. *Anat.* Any flat, circular outgrowth, organ, or structure, as of cartilage. 3. A phonograph record. 4. A discus. Also spelled *disc.* [< L *discus* < Gk. *diskos* disk, platter]

disk jockey *Informal* A radio announcer and commentator who presents recorded music.

dis·like (dis·līk′) *v.t.* **·liked, ·lik·ing** To regard with aversion; feel repugnance for. —*n.* A feeling of repugnance or distaste.

dis·lo·cate (dis′lō·kāt, dis·lō′kāt) *v.t.* **·cat·ed, ·cat·ing** 1. To put out of proper place or order. 2. *Med.* To displace (a bone) from its normal position. —**dis′lo·ca′tion** *n.*

dis·lodge (dis·loj′) *v.t.* **·lodged, ·lodg·ing** To remove or drive out, as from a firm position.

dis·loy·al (dis·loi′əl) *adj.* Not loyal; faithless. —**dis·loy′al·ly** *adv.* —**dis·loy′al·ty** *n.*

dis·mal (diz′məl) *adj.* 1. Cheerless and depressing. 2. Devoid of joy. [ult. < L *dies mali* evil or unpropitious days] —**dis′mal·ly** *adv.*

dis·man·tle (dis·man′təl) *v.t.* **·tled, ·tling** 1. To strip of furniture or equipment. 2. To take apart. [< MF *des-* away + *manteller* to cover with a cloak] —**dis·man′tle·ment** *n.*

dis·may (dis·mā′) *v.t.* To fill with consternation or apprehension; dishearten and depress. [ME *dismayen*] —**dis·may′** *n.*

dis·mem·ber (dis·mem′bər) *v.t.* 1. To cut off or pull off the limbs or members of; tear asunder. 2. To divide forcibly into pieces; mangle. [< L *dis-* apart + *membrum* limb, member] —**dis·mem′ber·ment** *n.*

dis·miss (dis·mis′) *v.t.* 1. To discharge, as from a job. 2. To tell or allow to go or disperse. 3. To have done with quickly. 4. *Law* To put out of court without further hearing. [< L *dimissus,* pp. of *dimittere* to send away] —**dis·miss′al** *n.*

dis·mount (dis·mount′) *v.i.* 1. To get off, as from a horse; alight. —*v.t.* 2. To remove from a setting, support, etc. 3. To disassemble. 4. To knock off, as from a horse; unseat.

dis·o·be·di·ence (dis′ə·bē′dē·əns) *n.* Refusal or failure to obey. —**dis′o·be′di·ent** *adj.* —**dis′o·be′di·ent·ly** *adv.*

dis·o·bey (dis′ə·bā′) *v.t. & v.i.* To refuse or fail to obey.

dis·o·blige (dis′ə·blīj′) *v.t.* **·bliged, ·blig·ing** 1. To act contrary to the wishes of. 2. To cause inconvenience to. —**dis′o·blig′ing** *adj.*

dis·or·der (dis·ôr′dər) *n.* 1. Lack of order; disarrangement or confusion. 2. Disturbance of proper civic order; riot. 3. A sickness; ailment. —*v.t.* 1. To put out of order; disarrange. 2. To disturb or upset the normal health or functions of. —**dis·or′dered** *adj.*

dis·or·der·ly (dis·ôr′dər·lē) *adj.* 1. Devoid of order; disarranged. 2. Undisciplined and unruly: a *disorderly* mob. 3. Violating public order or decency. —**dis·or′der·li·ness** *n.* —**dis·or′der·ly** *adv.*

dis·or·gan·ize (dis·ôr′gən·īz) *v.t.* **·ized, ·iz·ing** To destroy the organization of; throw into confusion; disorder. —**dis·or′gan·i·za′tion** *n.*

dis·o·ri·ent (dis·ôr′ē·ent) *v.t.* To confuse; esp., to cause to lose one's sense of direction, place, or time. —**dis·o′ri·en·ta′tion** *n.*

dis·own (dis·ōn′) *v.t.* To refuse to acknowledge or to admit responsibility for; repudiate.

dis·par·age (dis·par′ij) *v.t.* **·aged, ·ag·ing** 1. To treat or speak of with disrespect; belittle. 2. To bring discredit upon. [< OF *desparagier* to marry below one's class] —**dis·par′age·ment** *n.* —**dis·par′ag·er** *n.* —**dis·par′ag·ing·ly** *adv.*

dis·pa·rate (dis′pər·it) *adj.* Essentially different. [< L *disparare* to separate] —**dis′pa·rate·ly** *adv.* —**dis′pa·rate·ness** *n.*

dis·par·i·ty (dis·par′ə·tē) *n. pl.* **·ties** Lack of similarity or equality, as in age or rank.

dis·pas·sion·ate (dis·pash′ən·it) *adj.* Free from passion or bias. —**dis·pas′sion** *n.* —**dis·pas′sion·ate·ly** *adv.*

dis·patch (dis·pach′) *v.t.* 1. To send off, as a messenger, to a particular destination. 2. To dispose of quickly, as a business matter. 3. To kill summarily. —*n.* 1. The act of dispatching. 2. Efficient quickness; promptness. 3. A message, usu. in writing, sent with speed. 4. A news story sent to a newspaper. [< Ital. *dispacciare* or Sp. *despachar*]

dis·patch·er (dis·pach′ər) *n.* 1. One who dispatches. 2. One who sends out trains, buses, etc., on schedule.

dis·pel (dis·pel′) *v.t.* **·pelled, ·pel·ling** To drive away by or as by scattering. [< L *dispellere*]

dis·pen·sa·ble (dis·pen′sə·bəl) *adj.* 1. That can be relinquished or dispensed with. 2. That can be removed by dispensation. —**dis·pen′sa·bil′i·ty** *n.*

dis·pen·sa·ry (dis·pen′sər·ē) *n. pl.* **·ries** A place where medicines or medical advice are given out.

dis·pen·sa·tion (dis′pən·sā′shən) *n.* 1. The act of dispensing; distribution. 2. That which is distributed. 3. A specific system of administering. 4. A special exemption, as from a law or obligation.

dis·pense (dis·pens′) *v.t.* **·pensed, ·pens·ing** 1. To give or deal out in portions. 2. To compound and give out (medicines). 3. To administer, as laws. 4. To excuse or exempt, as from an obligation, esp. a religious obligation. —**to dispense with** 1. To get along without. 2. To dispose of. [< L *dis-* away + *pendere* to weigh] —**dis·pen′ser** *n.*

dis·perse (dis·pûrs′) *v.* **·persed, ·pers·ing** *v.t.* 1. To cause to scatter in various directions. 2. To drive away; dispel. 3. To spread abroad; diffuse. —*v.i.* 4. To scatter in various directions. [< L *dis-* away + *spargere* to scatter] —**dis·per′sal** *n.* —**dis·pers′er** *n.* —**dis·per′sive** *adj.*

dis·per·sion (dis·pûr′zhən, -shən) *n.* 1. The act of dispersing, or the state of being dispersed. 2. *Physics* The separation of light into different colors by passing it through a prism. 3. *Stat.* The arrangement of a series of values around the median or mean of a distribution.

dis·pir·it·ed (dis·pir′i·tid) *adj.* Downhearted; depressed. **—dis·pir′it** *v.t.*

dis·place (dis·plās′) *v.t.* **·placed, ·plac·ing** 1. To remove or shift from the usual or proper place. 2. To take the place of; supplant. 3. To remove from a position or office; discharge. [< OF *des-* away + *placer* to place]

displaced person A person made homeless by war and forced to live in a foreign country.

dis·place·ment (dis·plās′mənt) *n.* 1. The act of displacing, or the state of being displaced. 2. *Astron.* An apparent change of position, as of a star. 3. *Physics* The weight of a fluid displaced by a floating body, being equal to the weight of the body.

dis·play (dis·plā′) *v.t.* 1. To make evident or noticeable; reveal. 2. To expose to the sight; exhibit. 3. To make a prominent or ostentatious show of. **—***n.* 1. The act of displaying. 2. That which is displayed. 3. Ostentatious show. 4. *Printing* A style or arrangement of type designed to make printed matter stand out prominently. [< LL *dis-* apart + *plicare* to fold, add]

dis·please (dis·plēz′) *v.t. & v.i.* **·pleased, ·pleas·ing** To cause displeasure or annoyance; offend. [< L *dis-* not + *placere* to please] **—dis′pleas′ing·ly** *adv.*

dis·pleas·ure (dis·plezh′ər) *n.* The state of being displeased.

dis·port (dis·pôrt′) *v.t.* 1. To divert or amuse (oneself). **—***v.i.* 2. To frisk about playfully. [< L *dis-* away + *portare* to carry]

dis·pos·a·ble (dis·pō′zə·bəl) *adj.* 1. Capable of being disposed of; esp., designed to be discarded after use. 2. Free to be used: *disposable* funds. **—dis·pos′a·ble** *n.*

dis·po·sal (dis·pō′zəl) *n.* 1. A particular ordering or arrangement; disposition. 2. A particular way of managing or settling something, as business affairs. 3. Transfer, as by gift or sale. 4. A getting rid of something. 5. Liberty to deal with or dispose of in any way.

dis·pose (dis·pōz′) *v.t.* **·posed, ·pos·ing** 1. To put into a receptive frame of mind for. 2. To make susceptible. 3. To put or set in a particular arrangement or position. **—to dispose of** 1. To deal with; settle. 2. To transfer to another, as by gift or sale. 3. To throw away. [< OF *dis-* apart + *poser* to place] **—dis·pos′er** *n.*

dis·posed (dis·pōzd′) *adj.* Having a particular frame of mind or mood: *disposed* to take offense.

dis·po·si·tion (dis′pə·zish′ən) *n.* 1. One's usual frame of mind; temperament. 2. A tendency or inclination. 3. A particular ordering or distribution, as of troops. 4. Management, as of business affairs. 5. Transfer, as by gift or sale. 6. A getting rid of something.

dis·pos·sess (dis′pə·zes′) *v.t.* To deprive of possession of something, as a house or land; oust. **—dis′pos·ses′sion** (-zesh′ən) *n.*

dis·praise (dis·prāz′) *v.t.* **·praised, ·prais·ing** To express disapproval of; disparage. **—dis·praise′** *n.* **—dis·prais′ing·ly** *adv.*

dis·proof (dis·pro͞of′) *n.* 1. The act of disproving. 2. Something that disproves.

dis·pro·por·tion (dis′prə·pôr′shən) *n.* Lack of proportion or symmetry. **—dis′pro·por′tion·al** *adj.* **—dis′pro·por′tion·al·ly** *adv.*

dis·pro·por·tion·ate (dis′prə·pôr′shən·it) *adj.* Out of proportion, as in size, form, or value. **—dis′pro·por′tion·ate·ly** *adv.*

dis·prove (dis·pro͞ov′) *v.t.* **·proved, ·proved** or **·prov·en, ·prov·ing** To prove to be false, invalid, or erroneous. [< OF *desprouver*] **—dis·prov′al** *n.*

dis·put·a·ble (dis·pyo͞o′tə·bəl) *adj.* Open to dispute; debatable. **—dis·put′a·bil′i·ty** *n.* **—dis·put′a·bly** *adv.*

dis·pu·tant (dis′pyo͝o·tənt, dis·pyo͞o′tənt) *n.* One who disputes; a debater. **—dis′pu·tant** *adj.*

dis·pu·ta·tion (dis′pyo͝o·tā′shən) *n.* 1. The act of disputing. 2. A formal debate.

dis·pu·ta·tious (dis′pyo͝o·tā′shəs) *adj.* Given to disputing; argumentative. **—dis′pu·ta′·tious·ly** *adv.* **—dis′pu·ta′tious·ness** *n.*

dis·pute (dis·pyo͞ot′) *v.* **·put·ed, ·put·ing** *v.t.* 1. To argue about. 2. To question the validity, etc., of. **—***v.i.* 3. To argue. **—***n.* 1. A debate. 2. A quarrel. [< L *dis-* away + *putare* to think] **—dis·put′er** *n.*

dis·qual·i·fy (dis·kwol′ə·fī) *v.t.* **·fied, ·fy·ing** 1. To make or pronounce unqualified or unfit. 2. In sports, to bar from competition because of rule infractions, etc. **—dis·qual′i·fi·ca′tion** *n.*

dis·qui·et (dis·kwī′ət) *n.* An unsettled or disturbed condition. **—dis·qui′et** *v.t.* **—dis·qui′et·ing** *adj.* **—dis·qui′et·ing·ly** *adv.*

dis·qui·e·tude (dis·kwī′ə·to͞od, -tyo͞od) *n.* Uneasiness.

dis·qui·si·tion (dis′kwi·zish′ən) *n.* A formal treatise or discourse. [< L *dis-* thoroughly + *quaerere* to seek]

dis·re·gard (dis′ri·gärd′) *v.t.* To pay no attention to; ignore. **—***n.* Lack of notice or due regard.

dis·re·pair (dis′ri·pâr′) *n.* The state of being in need of repair.

dis·rep·u·ta·ble (dis·rep′yə·tə·bəl) *adj.* Not in good repute; not respectable. **—dis·rep′u·ta·bly** *adv.*

dis·re·spect (dis′ri·spekt′) *n.* Lack of courtesy or respect. **—dis′re·spect′ful** *adj.* **—dis′re·spect′ful·ly** *adv.*

dis·robe (dis·rōb′) *v.t. & v.i.* **·robed, ·rob·ing** To undress.

dis·rupt (dis·rupt′) *v.t.* 1. To throw into disorder; upset. 2. To halt or impede the movement of, procedure of, etc. [< L *dis-* apart + *rumpere* to burst] **—dis·rupt′er** *n.* **—dis·rup′tion** *n.* **—dis·rup′tive** *adj.*

dis·sat·is·fy (dis·sat′is·fī) *v.t.* **·fied, ·fy·ing** To fail to satisfy; disappoint; displease. **—dis·sat′is·fied** *adj.* **—dis′sat·is·fac′tion** (-fak′shən) *n.* **—dis′sat·is·fac′to·ry** (-fak′·tər·ē) *adj.*

dis·sect (di·sekt′, dī-) *v.t.* 1. To cut apart or divide in order to examine the structure. 2. To analyze in detail. [< L *dis-* apart + *secare* to cut] **—dis·sec′tion** *n.*

dis·sect·ed (di·sek′tid, dī-) *adj.* 1. Cut in pieces. 2. *Bot.* Deeply cut into lobes or segments, as a leaf.

dis·sem·ble (di·sem′bəl) *v.* **·bled, ·bling** *v.t.* 1. To conceal or disguise the actual nature of (intentions, feelings, etc.). 2. To feign. **—***v.i.* 3. To conceal one's true intentions, etc. [< L *dissimulare* to disguise] **—dis·sem·blance** (di·sem′bləns) *n.* **—dis·sem′bler** *n.*

dis·sem·i·nate (di·sem′ə·nāt) *v.t.* **·nat·ed, ·nat·ing** To scatter, as if sowing: to dis-

seminate knowledge. [< L *disseminare* to sow] **—dis·sem'i·na'tion** *n.* **—dis·sem'i·na'tor** *n.*

dis·sen·sion (di·sen'shən) *n.* Difference of opinion, esp. arising from anger; discord.

dis·sent (di·sent') *v.i.* 1. To differ in thought or opinion: often with *from.* 2. To refuse adherence to an established church. **—***n.* 1. Difference of opinion. 2. Refusal to conform to an established church. [< L *dis-* apart + *sentire* to think, feel] **—dis·sent'er** *n.* **—dis·sen·tient** (di·sen'shənt) *n.* *& adj.*

dis·sent·ing (di·sen'ting) *adj.* Expressing disagreement: a *dissenting* opinion.

dis·sen·tious (di·sen'shəs) *adj.* Quarrelsome.

dis·ser·ta·tion (dis'ər·tā'shən) *n.* An extended formal treatise or discourse; esp., a written treatise required of a doctoral candidate. [< L *dis-* apart + *serere* to join]

dis·ser·vice (dis·sûr'vis) *n.* Ill service; injury; a harmful action. **—dis·serve'** *v.t.* **·served, ·serv·ing**

dis·sev·er (di·sev'ər) *v.t.* To divide; separate into parts. **—dis·sev'er·ance** *n.*

dis·si·dent (dis'ə·dənt) *adj.* Dissenting; differing. **—***n.* A dissenter. [< L *dis-* apart + *sedere* to sit] **—dis'si·dence** *n.*

dis·sim·i·lar (di·sim'ə·lər) *adj.* Not similar; different. **—dis·sim'i·lar·ly** *adv.*

dis·sim·i·lar·i·ty (di·sim'ə·lar'ə·tē) *n.* *pl.* **·ties** 1. Lack of similarity; difference. 2. An example of this.

dis·sim·u·late (di·sim'yə·lāt) *v.t. & v.i.* **·lat·ed, ·lat·ing** To conceal (feelings, etc.) by pretense. **—dis·sim'u·la'tion** *n.* **—dis·sim'u·la'tor** *n.*

dis·si·pate (dis'ə·pāt) *v.* **·pat·ed, ·pat·ing** *v.t.* 1. To disperse or drive away; dispel. 2. To squander. **—***v.i.* 3. To become dispersed. 4. To engage in excessive or dissolute pleasures. [< L *dis-* away + *supare* to scatter] **—dis'si·pat'ed** *adj.* **—dis'si·pa'tion** *n.*

dis·so·ci·ate (di·sō'shē·āt, -sē-) *v.t.* **·at·ed, ·at·ing** 1. To break the association or connection between. 2. To regard as separate in concept or nature. [< L *dis-* apart + *sociare* to join together] **—dis·so'ci·a'tion** *n.*

dis·so·lute (dis'ə·lo͞ot) *adj.* Not governed by moral restraints. **—dis'so·lute·ly** *adv.* **—dis'·so·lute·ness** *n.*

dis·so·lu·tion (dis'ə·lo͞o'shən) *n.* 1. Separation into parts; disintegration. 2. The breaking up of a formal or legal union, bond, or tie. 3. Dismissal of a meeting or assembly. 4. Termination or destruction. 5. End of life; death.

dis·solve (di·zolv') *v.* **·solved, ·solv·ing** *v.t.* 1. To cause to pass into solution. 2. To overcome, as by emotion. 3. To put an end to: to *dissolve* a partnership. 4. To dismiss (a meeting or assembly). **—***v.i.* 5. To pass into solution. 6. To be overcome: to *dissolve* in tears. 7. To come to an end; break up. 8. In motion pictures and television, to change gradually from one scene to another. [< L *dis-* apart + *solvere* to loosen]

dis·so·nance (dis'ə·nəns) *n.* 1. A discordant mingling of sounds. 2. Harsh disagreement; incongruity. 3. *Music* A simultaneous combination of tones that seem to clash and require resolution.

dis·so·nant (dis'ə·nənt) *adj.* 1. Harsh in sound; inharmonious. 2. Naturally hostile; incongruous. 3. *Music* Consisting of or containing a dissonance. [< L *dis-* away + *sonare* to sound] **—dis'so·nant·ly** *adv.*

dis·suade (di·swād') *v.t.* **·suad·ed, ·suad·ing** To alter the intentions of (someone) by persuasion or advice: with *from.* [< L *dis-* away + *suadere* to persuade] **—dis·suad'er** *n.* **—dis·sua'sion** (-swā'zhən) *n.* **—dis·sua'sive** (-swā'siv) *adj.*

dis·taff (dis'taf) *n.* 1. A staff that holds flax or wool for spinning by hand. 2. Women in general. 3. Woman's work or domain. [OE *dis* bundle of flax + *stæf* staff]

distaff side The maternal branch or female line of a family.

dis·tal (dis'təl) *adj.* *Anat.* Relatively remote from the center of the body or point of attachment. **—dis'tal·ly** *adv.*

dis·tance (dis'təns) *n.* 1. The extent of spatial separation between things, places, or locations. 2. The state or fact of being separated from something else in space, time, or condition. 3. Remoteness; esp., reserve or aloofness. 4. A far-off point or location.

dis·tant (dis'tənt) *adj.* 1. Far away or apart in space or time. 2. At, from, or to a distance. 3. Not closely related; remote, as to similarity, kinship, etc. 4. Reserved or unapproachable. [< L *dis-* apart + *stare* to stand] **—dis'tant·ly** *adv.*

dis·taste (dis·tāst') *n.* Dislike; aversion.

dis·taste·ful (dis·tāst'fəl) *adj.* Causing dislike; offensive; disagreeable. **—dis·taste'·ful·ly** *adv.* **—dis·taste'ful·ness** *n.*

dis·tem·per (dis·tem'pər) *n.* 1. *Vet.* Any of several infectious diseases of animals; esp., a virus disease of puppies. 2. A bad disposition; ill humor. [< L *dis-* away + *temperare* to regulate, mix]

dis·tend (dis·tend') *v.t. & v.i.* To expand by or as by pressure from within; swell. [< L *dis-* apart + *tendere* to stretch] **—dis·ten'si·ble** (-ten'sə·bəl) *adj.* **—dis·ten'tion** (-ten'·shən) or **dis·ten'sion** *n.*

dis·tich (dis'tik) *n.* In prosody, a couplet. [< Gk. *di-* two + *stichos* a row, line]

dis·till (dis·til') *v.t. & v.i.* **·tilled, ·till·ing** 1. To subject to or undergo distillation. 2. To give forth or let fall in drops. Also *Brit.* **dis·til'.** [< L *de-* down + *stillare* to drop, trickle] **—dis·till'a·ble** *adj.*

dis·til·late (dis'tə·lit, -lāt) *n.* The condensed product separated by distillation.

dis·til·la·tion (dis'tə·lā'shən) *n.* 1. The act or process of heating a substance, and collecting and condensing the vapors thus formed to purify or separate the substance into its component parts. 2. The essential or abstract quality of anything.

dis·til·ler (dis·til'ər) *n.* 1. One who distills; esp., a maker of distilled liquors. 2. A condenser for distilling.

dis·til·ler·y (dis·til'ər·ē) *n.* *pl.* **·ler·ies** An establishment for distilling, esp. alcoholic liquors.

dis·tinct (dis·tingkt') *adj.* 1. Recognizably not the same; clearly different. 2. Differentiated by individualizing features. 3. Sharp and clear to the senses or mind. [< L *distinguere* to separate] **—dis·tinct'ly** *adv.* **—dis·tinct'ness** *n.*

dis·tinc·tion (dis·tingk'shən) *n.* 1. The act of distinguishing; discrimination. 2. A difference that may be distinguished. 3. A characteristic difference or distinctive quality. 4. A mark of honor. 5. A distinguishing superiority or preeminence.

dis·tinc·tive (dis·tingk′tiv) *adj.* Serving to distinguish; characteristic. —**dis·tinc′tive·ly** *adv.* —**dis·tinc′tive·ness** *n.*

dis·tin·gué (dis′tang·gā′, *Fr.* dēs·tan·gā′) *adj.* Of distinguished appearance or bearing. [< F]

dis·tin·guish (dis·ting′gwish) *v.t.* 1. To indicate the differences of or between. 2. To be an outstanding characteristic of. 3. To bring fame or credit upon. 4. To perceive with the senses. —*v.i.* 5. To make or discern differences: often with *among* or *between.* [< L *distinguere* to separate] —**dis·tin′guish·a·ble** *adj.*

dis·tin·guished (dis·ting′gwisht) *adj.* 1. Conspicuous for qualities of excellence; eminent. 2. Dignified in appearance or demeanor.

dis·tort (dis·tôrt′) *v.t.* 1. To twist or bend out of shape. 2. To twist the meaning of; misrepresent. 3. To reproduce (sound) improperly. [< L *dis-* apart + *torquere* to twist] —**dis·tort′ed** *adj.* —**dis·tort′er** *n.* —**dis·tor′tion** *n.*

dis·tract (dis·trakt′) *v.t.* 1. To draw or divert (the mind, etc.) from something claiming attention. 2. To bewilder; confuse. 3. To make frantic; craze. [< L *dis-* away + *trahere* to draw] —**dis·tract′ed** *adj.* —**dis·tract′ed·ly** *adv.* —**dis·tract′ing** *adj.* —**dis·trac′tion** *n.*

dis·train (dis·trān′) *Law v.t. & v.i.* To seize (personal property) as security for a debt, etc. [< L *distringere* to detain, hinder] —**dis·train′or** or **dis·train′er** *n.*

dis·trait (dis·trā′, *Fr.* dēs·tre′) *adj.* Absent-minded. [< F. See DISTRACT.]

dis·traught (dis·trôt′) *adj.* 1. Worried, tense, and bewildered. 2. Driven insane; crazed. [Var. of earlier *distract*, pp. of DISTRACT]

dis·tress (dis·tres′) *v.t.* To inflict suffering upon; cause agony or worry to. —*n.* 1. Extreme suffering or its cause. 2. A state of extreme need. 3. *Law* **a** The act of distraining. **b** The goods distrained. [< L *distringere* to detain, hinder] —**dis·tress′ful** *adj.* —**dis·tress′ing** *adj.* —**dis·tress′ing·ly** *adv.*

dis·trib·u·tar·y (dis·trib′yōō·ter′ē) *n. pl.* **·tar·ies** A river branch flowing away from the main branch.

dis·trib·ute (dis·trib′yōōt) *v.t.* **·ut·ed, ·ut·ing** 1. To divide and deal out in shares. 2. To divide and classify; arrange. 3. To scatter or spread out. [< L *dis-* away, apart + *tribuere* to give, allot]

dis·tri·bu·tion (dis′trə·byōō′shən) *n.* 1. The act of distributing or the state of being distributed. 2. The manner in which something is distributed. 3. In commerce, the system of distributing goods among consumers. 4. *Stat.* The frequency of occurrence of the values of a variable. —**dis′tri·bu′tion·al** *adj.*

dis·trib·u·tive (dis·trib′yə·tiv) *adj.* 1. Pertaining to or caused by distribution. 2. Serving or tending to distribute. —**dis·trib′u·tive·ly** *adv.*

dis·trib·u·tor (dis·trib′yə·tər, -tôr) *n.* 1. One who or that which distributes or sells merchandise. 2. In a gasoline engine, a device that directs the electric current to the spark plugs.

dis·trict (dis′trikt) *n.* 1. An area, as within a city or state, set off for administrative or judicial purposes. 2. A region or locality having a distinct character or set apart for a particular purpose: business *district.* —*v.t.* To divide into districts. [< Med.L *districtus* jurisdiction]

district attorney The prosecuting officer of a judicial district.

dis·trust (dis·trust′) *v.t.* To doubt; suspect. —*n.* Doubt; suspicion. —**dis·trust′ful** *adj.*

dis·turb (dis·tûrb′) *v.t.* 1. To destroy the tranquillity or peace of. 2. To agitate the mind of; trouble. 3. To upset the order or system of. 4. To interrupt; break in on. 5. To inconvenience. [< L *dis-* completely + *turbare* to disorder]

dis·tur·bance (dis·tûr′bəns) *n.* 1. The act of disturbing, or the state of being disturbed. 2. Something that disturbs. 3. A tumult or commotion; esp., a public disorder.

dis·turbed (dis·tûrbd′) *adj.* 1. Characterized by disturbance. 2. Troubled emotionally or mentally; neurotic.

dis·u·nite (dis′yōō·nīt′) *v.* **·nit·ed, ·nit·ing** *v.t.* 1. To separate; part. —*v.i.* 2. To come apart. —**dis·un·ion** (dis·yōōn′yən), **dis·u·ni·ty** (dis·yōō′nə·tē) *n.*

dis·use (dis·yōōs′) *n.* The state of not being used; out of use.

ditch (dich) *n.* A long, narrow trench dug in the ground. —*v.t.* 1. To make a ditch in. 2. To surround with a ditch. 3. *Slang* To get rid of. —*v.i.* 4. To make a forced landing on water. [OE *dīc*] —**ditch′er** *n.*

dith·er (dith′ər) *n.* A state of nervous excitement or anxiety. —*v.i.* To be in a dither. [Var. of earlier *didder* to tremble, shake; origin uncertain]

dith·y·ramb (dith′ə·ram, -ramb) *n.* In ancient Greece, a wild, passionate choric hymn in honor of Dionysus, the god of wine, revelry etc. [< Gk. *dithyrambos*] —**dith′y·ram′bic** *adj. & n.*

dit·to (dit′ō) *n. pl.* **·tos** 1. The same (as written above or mentioned before), usually symbolized by ditto marks. 2. A duplicate or copy. 3. Ditto marks. —*adv.* As above or before; likewise. —*interj. Informal* I agree. —*v.t.* **·toed, ·to·ing** To repeat or duplicate. [< Ital. < L *dicere* to say]

ditto marks Two small marks (") placed beneath an item to indicate that it is to be repeated. Also **ditto mark.**

dit·ty (dit′ē) *n. pl.* **·ties** A short, simple song. [< OF *dittie, ditie* < L *dictatum* a thing said]

di·u·ret·ic (dī′ə·ret′ik, dī′yōō·ret′ik) *adj.* Increasing the secretion of urine. —**di′u·ret′ic** *n.*

di·ur·nal (dī·ûr′nəl) *adj.* 1. Of, belonging to, or occurring each day; daily. 2. Of or occurring during the daytime; not nocturnal. [< L *diurnus* daily] —**di·ur′nal·ly** *adv.*

di·va (dē′və) *n. pl.* **·vas** or **·ve** (-vā) A celebrated female operatic singer; a prima donna. [< Ital., fem of *divo* divine]

di·va·gate (dī′və·gāt) *v.i.* **·gat·ed, ·gat·ing** 1. To wander or stray aimlessly. 2. To digress. [< L *dis-* about + *vagari* to wander] —**di′va·ga′tion** *n.*

di·va·lent (dī·vā′lənt, div′ə-) *adj. Chem.* Bivalent.

di·van (di·van′, dī′van) *n.* A sofa or couch, usu. without arms or back. [< Turkish < Persian *dēvān* council, chamber]

dive (dīv) *v.* **dived** or **dove, dived, div·ing** *v.i.* 1. To plunge, esp. headfirst, as into water. 2. To go underwater; submerge. 3. To plunge downward at a sharp angle. 4. To dart away or leap into something. 5. To rush into and become deeply engrossed in something. —*v.t.* 6. To cause to plunge; esp., to cause (an airplane) to move swiftly downward at a sharp angle. —*n.* 1. A plunge, as into water. 2. A sharp, swift descent. 3. *Informal* A cheap, disreputable place, as a saloon. [Blend of OE *dūfan* to dive and *dȳfan* to immerse] —**div′er** *n.*

dive bomber An airplane designed to bomb a target while in a steep dive.

di·verge (di·vûrj′, dī-) *v.i.* **·verged, ·verg·ing** 1. To move or extend in different directions from a common point or from each other. 2. To deviate. 3. To differ. [< L *dis-* apart + *vergere* to incline] —**di·ver′gence** *n.* —**di·ver′gent** *adj.* —**di·ver′gent·ly** *adv.*

di·vers (dī′vərz) *adj.* 1. Several. 2. Various. [< L *diversus* different]

di·verse (di·vûrs′, dī-, dī′vûrs) *adj.* 1. Different; not alike. 2. Varied; diversified. [See DIVERS.] —**di·verse′ly** *adv.*

di·ver·si·fy (di·vûr′sə·fī, dī-) *v.t.* **·fied, ·fy·ing** 1. To make diverse; vary. 2. To make (investments) among different types of securities so as to minimize risk. —**di·ver′si·fi·ca′tion** *n.*

di·ver·sion (di·vûr′zhən, dī-) *n.* 1. The act of diverting. 2. That which diverts or entertains.

di·ver·sion·ar·y (di·vûr′zhən·er′ē) *adj.* Designed to distract attention.

di·ver·si·ty (di·vûr′sə·tē, dī-) *n. pl.* **·ties** 1. Unlikeness; difference. 2. Variety.

di·vert (di·vûrt′, dī-) *v.t.* 1. To turn aside, as from a set course; deflect. 2. To distract the attention of. 3. To amuse; entertain. [< L *dis-* apart + *vertere* to turn] —**di·vert′·ing** *adj.* —**di·vert′ing·ly** *adv.*

di·ver·ti·men·to (di·ver′ti·men′tō) *n. pl.* **·ti** (-tē) *Music* A light instrumental composition in several movements. [< Ital., diversion]

di·ver·tisse·ment (də·vûr′təs·mənt, *Fr.* dē·ver·tēs·mäṅ′) *n.* 1. A diversion; amusement. 2. *Music* A divertimento. 3. A short ballet, etc., performed during or between the parts of an opera or play. [< F]

di·vest (di·vest′, dī-) *v.t.* 1. To strip, as of clothes. 2. To deprive, as of rights or possessions. [< OF *desvestir*]

di·vest·i·ture (di·ves′tə·chər, dī-) *n.* The act of divesting, or the state of being divested. Also **di·vest′ment, di·ves′ture.**

di·vide (di·vīd′) *v.* **·vid·ed, ·vid·ing** *v.t.* 1. To separate into pieces or portions, as by cutting. 2. To distribute the pieces or portions of. 3. To separate into groups; classify. 4. To split up into opposed sides; cause dissent in. 5. To cause to be apart. 6. *Math.* To subject to the process of division. —*v.i.* 7. To become separated into parts; diverge. 8. To be at variance. 9. To perform mathematical division. —*n.* A mountain range separating one drainage system from another; watershed. [< L *dividere*] —**di·vid′a·ble** *adj.* —**di·vid′ed** *adj.*

div·i·dend (div′ə·dend) *n.* 1. *Math.* A number or quantity to be divided. 2. A sum of money to be distributed to stockholders, etc. 3. The portion of such a sum given to each individual. [< L *dividendum* thing to be divided]

di·vid·er (di·vī′dər) *n.* 1. One who or that which divides. 2. *pl.* A pair of compasses used for measuring short intervals.

div·i·na·tion (div′ə·nā′shən) *n.* 1. The act or art of knowing the future or that which is hidden or unknown. 2. A prophecy. —**di·vin·a·to·ry** (di·vin′ə·tôr′ē) *adj.*

di·vine (di·vīn′) *adj.* 1. Of, from, or pertaining to God or a god. 2. Directed or devoted to God or a god; sacred. 3. Extraordinarily perfect. 4. *Informal* Altogether delightful. —*n.* 1. A clergyman. 2. A theologian. —*v.* **·vined, ·vin·ing** *v.t.* 1. To foretell or find out by occult means. 2. To locate (water, etc.) by means of a divining rod. 3. To surmise by instinct. —*v.i.* 4. To practice divination. 5. To guess. [< L *divinus* < *deus* god] —**di·vine′ly** *adv.* —**di·vin′er** *n.*

Divine Office The prayers recited at the canonical hours.

diving bell A large, hollow, inverted vessel supplied with air under pressure, in which men may work under water.

divining rod A forked branch popularly asserted to indicate underground water or metal: also called *dowsing rod.*

di·vin·i·ty (di·vin′ə·tē) *n. pl.* **·ties** 1. The state or quality of being divine. 2. A deity. 3. Theology. 4. A soft, creamy candy. —**the Divinity** God. [< L *divinitas* godhead, deity]

di·vis·i·ble (di·viz′ə·bəl) *adj.* 1. Capable of being divided. 2. *Math.* That can be divided and leave no remainder. —**di·vis′i·bil′i·ty** *n.* —**di·vis′i·bly** *adv.*

di·vi·sion (di·vizh′ən) *n.* 1. The act of dividing, or the state of being divided. 2. One of the parts into which a thing is divided. 3. Something that divides or separates. 4. Disagreement; discord. 5. *Math.* The operation of finding how many times a number or quantity is contained in another number or quantity. 6. *Mil.* A major administrative and tactical unit that is larger than a regiment and smaller than a corps. [< L *dividere* to divide] —**di·vi′sion·al** *adj.*

division sign *Math.* The symbol (÷) that denotes a first number is to be divided by a second, as $6 \div 2 = 3$.

di·vi·sive (di·vī′siv) *adj.* Creating division, dissension, or strife.

di·vi·sor (di·vī′zər) *n.* *Math.* A number by which another number is divided.

di·vorce (di·vôrs′) *n.* 1. Dissolution of a marriage bond by legal process or by accepted custom. 2. Any radical or complete separation. —*v.* **·vorced, ·vorc·ing** *v.t.* 1. To free oneself from (one's spouse) by divorce. 2. To separate. —*v.i.* 3. To get a divorce. [< L *divertere* to divert]

di·vor·cée (di·vôr′sā′, di·vôr′sā) *n.* A divorced woman. [< F, pp. of *divorcer* to divorce] —**di·vor′cé′** *n.masc.*

div·ot (div′ət) *n.* A piece of turf torn by a golf club.

di·vulge (di·vulj′) *v.t.* **·vulged, ·vulg·ing** To tell, as a secret; disclose; reveal. [< L

dis- away + *vulgare* to make public] —**di·vulge′ment, di·vul′gence** *n.* —**di·vulg′er** *n.*
div·vy (div′ē) *Slang* *v.t.* **·vied, ·vy·ing** To divide: often with *up.* [Short for DIVIDE]
Dix·ie (dik′sē) The southern states of the U.S. Also **Dixie Land.**
Dix·ie·land (dik′sē·land′) *n.* A style of jazz originally played in New Orleans.
diz·zy (diz′ē) *adj.* **·zi·er, ·zi·est** 1. Having a feeling of whirling or unsteadiness. 2. Causing giddiness. 3. *Informal* Silly; stupid. —*v.t.* **·zied, ·zy·ing** To make giddy; confuse. [OE *dysig* foolish, stupid] —**diz′zi·ly** *adv.* —**diz′zi·ness** *n.*
DNA *Biochem.* Deoxyribonucleic acid.
do[1] (dōō) *v.* **did, done, do·ing** *v.t.* 1. To perform, as an action; produce, as a piece of work. 2. To fulfill; complete; accomplish. 3. To cause; bring about: to *do* no harm. 4. To put forth: He *did* his best. 5. To render: to *do* homage. 6. To work at. 7. To work out; solve. 8. To present (a play, opera, etc.). 9. To enact the part of. 10. To cover (a distance); travel. 11. To be sufficient for; to suit. 12. *Informal* To serve, as a term in prison. 13. To put in order; attend to. 14. To decorate or arrange. —*v.i.* 15. To exert oneself; be active: to *do* or die. 16. To conduct oneself. 17. To fare; get along. 18. To serve the purpose; suffice. —**to do away with** To kill; destroy. —**to do by** To act toward. —**to do for** 1. To provide for; care for. 2. *Informal* To ruin; kill. —**to do in** *Slang* To kill. —**to do over** 1. To do again. 2. To redecorate. —**to do up** To wrap or tie up. —**to do without** To get along without. —**to have to do with** To be involved with. —**to make do** To get along with (whatever is available). —*auxiliary* As an auxiliary, *do* is used: 1. Without specific meaning in negative, interrogative, and inverted constructions: I *do* not want it; *Do* you want to leave? 2. To add force to imperatives: *Do* hurry. 3. To express emphasis: I *do* believe you. 4. As a substitute for another verb to avoid repetition: I will not hesitate, as some *do.* —*n. pl.* **do's** or **dos** 1. *Informal* Festivity; celebration. 2. *pl.* That which ought to be done: used chiefly in the expression **do's and don'ts.** [OE *dōn*]
do[2] (dō) *n.* *Music* The first tone of the diatonic scale in solmization.
do·a·ble (dōō′ə·bəl) *adj.* Capable of being done.
do-all (dōō′ôl′) *n.* A general helper.
dob·bin (dob′in) *n.* A horse, esp. a plodding one. [after *Dobbin,* var. of *Robin* < *Robert,* a personal name]
Do·ber·man pinscher (dō′bər·mən) A large, short-haired dog. [after Ludwig *Dobermann,* its first breeder]
doc·ile (dos′əl) *adj.* Easy to manage or train. [< L *docilis* able to be taught] —**doc′ile·ly** *adv.* —**do·cil·i·ty** (do·sil′ə·tē) *n.*
dock[1] (dok) *n.* 1. The water space between two adjoining piers or wharves where ships can remain for loading, repair, etc. 2. A wharf or pier. 3. *Often pl.* A group of wharves or piers. 4. A shipping or loading platform, as for trucks. —*v.t.* 1. To bring (a vessel, truck, etc.) into or next to a dock. —*v.i.* 2. To come into a dock. 3. Of spacecraft, to be brought together in orbit and mechanically joined. [< MDu. *docke*]
dock[2] (dok) *n.* 1. The fleshy part of an animal's tail. 2. The stump of a clipped tail. —*v.t.* 1. To cut off the end of (a tail, etc.), or clip short the tail of. 2. To take a part from (wages, etc.), or take from the wages, etc., of. [Cf. ME *docken* to cut short] —**dock′er** *n.*
dock[3] (dok) *n.* An enclosed space for the defendant in a criminal court. [< Flemish *dok* cage]
dock[4] (dok) *n.* Any of various plants of the buckwheat family. [OE *docce*]
dock·age[1] (dok′ij) *n.* 1. A charge for docking (a ship, etc.). 2. Facilities for docking a vessel. 3. The act of docking.
dock·age[2] (dok′ij) *n.* 1. Curtailment, as of wages. 2. Waste matter in grain.
dock·et (dok′it) *n.* 1. A written summary. 2. *Law* **a** A record of court judgments. **b** The book in which such a record is kept. **c** A court calendar of cases pending. 3. Any calendar of things to be done. 4. A tag or label attached to a parcel, listing contents, directions, etc. —*v.t.* 1. To enter in a docket. 2. To put a tag or label on. [ME; origin uncertain]
dock·yard (dok′yärd′) *n.* An area of docks where ships are built, repaired, etc.
doc·tor (dok′tər) *n.* 1. A licensed practitioner of medicine, surgery, or any of certain other healing arts, as a dentist, veterinarian, etc. 2. A person who has received a diploma of the highest degree, as in literature. —*v.t. Informal* 1. To treat medically. 2. To repair. 3. To falsify or alter, as evidence. [< L *docere* to teach] —**doc′tor·al** *adj.*
doc·tor·ate (dok′tər·it) *n.* The degree or status of a doctor.
doc·tri·naire (dok′trə·nâr′) *adj.* 1. Theoretical. 2. Dogmatic. —*n.* An impractical, rigid theorist. —**doc′tri·nair′ism** *n.*
doc·trine (dok′trin) *n.* 1. Teachings, as of a religious group. 2. A particular principle or tenet that is taught. [< L *docere* to teach] —**doc′tri·nal** *adj.* —**doc′tri·nal·ly** *adv.*
doc·u·ment (*n.* dok′yə·mənt; *v.* dok′yə·ment) *n.* Something written or printed that furnishes conclusive information or evidence, as an official paper or record. —*v.t.* To support by conclusive information or evidence. [< L *docere* to teach] —**doc′u·men·ta′tion** (-mən·tā′shən, -men-) *n.*
doc·u·men·ta·ry (dok′yə·men′tər·ē) *adj.* 1. Pertaining to, consisting of, or based upon documents. 2. That presents factual material without fictionalizing. —*n. pl.* **·ries** A documentary motion picture or television show.
dod·der (dod′ər) *v.i.* To tremble or totter, as from age. [Cf. ME *didder* to tremble] —**dod′der·ing** *adj.*
dodeca- *combining form* Twelve; of or having twelve. Also before vowels, **dodec-.** [< Gk. *dōdeka*]
do·dec·a·gon (dō·dek′ə·gon) *n.* *Geom.* A polygon having twelve sides and twelve angles. [< Gk. *dōdekagōnon*] —**do·de·cag·o·nal** (dō′de·kag′ə·nəl) *adj.*
do·dec·a·he·dron (dō′dek·ə·hē′drən) *n. pl.* **·drons** or **·dra** *Geom.* A polyhedron bounded by twelve plane faces. —**do′dec·a·he′dral** *adj.*
dodge (doj) *v.* **dodged, dodg·ing** *v.t.* 1. To avoid, as a blow, by a sudden turn. 2. To evade, as a duty or issue. —*v.i.* 3. To avoid

something, esp. by moving suddenly. 4. To practice trickery. **—*n.*** 1. An act of dodging. 2. A trick to deceive. [Origin unknown] **—dodg′er** *n.*

do·do (dō′dō) *n. pl.* **·does** or **·dos** 1. An extinct bird about the size of a turkey, with rudimentary, functionless wings. 2. *Informal* One who is slow or dull. [< Pg. *doudo*]

doe (dō) *n.* The female of the deer, antelope, rabbit, kangaroo, and certain other animals. [OE *dā*]

do·er (do͞o′ər) *n.* One who acts, does, or performs; an agent.

does (duz) Present tense, third person singular, of DO[1].

doe·skin (dō′skin′) *n.* 1. The skin of the female deer. 2. Leather made from this.

does·n't (duz′ənt) Does not.

doff (dof, dôf) *v.t.* 1. To take off, as a hat or clothing. 2. To discard. [Contraction of *do off*] **—doff′er** *n.*

dog (dôg) *n.* 1. A domesticated, carnivorous mammal of many varieties; esp., the male of any of these. ◆Collateral adjective: *canine.* 2. A despicable person. 3. *Informal* A man; fellow. 4. *Mech.* One of several devices for gripping or holding logs, etc. 5. *pl. Slang* The feet. 6. *Slang* A complete failure. 7. *Slang* An unattractive person. **—to go to the dogs** *Informal* To go to ruin. **—to put on the dog** *Informal* To make a pretentious display. **—*v.t.* dogged, dog·ging** To pursue persistently; hound. [OE *docga*]

dog·bane (dôg′bān′) *n.* A smooth, reddish-stemmed herb having a milky juice.

dog biscuit A hard biscuit for dogs.

dog·cart (dôg′kärt′) *n.* A one-horse vehicle, usu. two-wheeled, with two seats set back to back.

dog·catch·er (dôg′kach′ər) *n.* A person employed or elected to pick up and impound stray dogs.

dog days The hot days of July and early August. [after the *Dog Star, Sirius,* which rises and sets with the sun in this period]

doge (dōj) *n.* The elective chief magistrate in the former republics of Venice and Genoa. [< Ital. < L *dux, ducis* chief]

dog·ear (dôg′ir′) *n.* A turned-down corner of a book page. **—*v.t.*** To turn down the corner of (a page). **—dog′-eared′** *adj.*

dog·face (dôg′fās′) *n. Slang* A soldier in the U.S. Army; esp., an infantryman.

dog·fight (dôg′fīt′) *n.* 1. A fight between or as between dogs. 2. *Mil.* An aerial battle between planes.

dog·fish (dôg′fish′) *n. pl.* **·fish** or **·fish·es** One of various small, littoral sharks of North American waters.

dog·ged (dôg′id) *adj.* Stubborn; obdurate. **—dog′ged·ly** *adv.* **—dog′ged·ness** *n.*

dog·ger·el (dôg′ər·əl, dog′-) *n.* Trivial, awkwardly written verse, usu. comic. **—*adj.*** Of or composed of such verse. Also **dog′grel.** [ME; origin unknown]

dog·gone (dôg′gôn′, dog′gon′) *Informal interj.* Damn!; darn!

dog·gy (dôg′ē) *n. pl.* **·gies** A dog, esp., a small dog. Also **dog′gie. —*adj.* ·gi·er, ·gi·est** Of or like a dog.

dog·house (dôg′hous′) *n.* A small house for a dog. **—in the doghouse** *Informal* In disfavor with someone.

do·gie (dō′gē) *n.* In the western U.S., a stray or motherless calf: also spelled *dogy.* [Origin unknown]

dog·ma (dôg′mə, dog′-) *n. pl.* **·mas** or **·ma·ta** (-mə·tə) A doctrine or system of doctrine, esp. one maintained by a religious body as true and necessary of belief. [< Gk. *dogma* opinion]

dog·mat·ic (dôg·mat′ik, dog-) *adj.* Marked by authoritative, often arrogant, assertion of opinions or beliefs. Also **dog·mat′i·cal. —dog·mat′i·cal·ly** *adv.*

dog·ma·tism (dôg′mə·tiz′əm, dog′-) *n.* Positive assertion, as of beliefs. **—dog′ma·tist** *n.*

dog·ma·tize (dôg′mə·tīz, dog′-) *v.i.* **·tized, ·tiz·ing** To express oneself dogmatically. **—dog′ma·ti·za′tion** *n.* **—dog′ma·tiz′er** *n.*

do-good·er (do͞o′go͝od′ər) *n. Informal* An idealistic philanthropist or reformer: a derisive term.

dog rose The wild brier of European hedges and thickets, bearing single pink flowers.

dog tag 1. A small metal plate on the collar of a dog, usu. indicating ownership. 2. *Informal* A soldier's identification tag, worn on a chain around the neck.

dog·tooth (dôg′to͞oth′) *n.* A canine tooth.

dogtooth violet 1. A European herb of the lily family. 2. One of various American plants, bearing yellow or pinkish flowers. Also **dog's-tooth violet.**

dog·trot (dôg′trot′) *n.* A regular and easy trot.

dog·watch (dôg′woch′) *n. Naut.* Either of two short watches aboard ship, from 4 to 6 or 6 to 8 P.M.

dog·wood (dôg′wo͝od′) *n.* Any of certain trees or shrubs, esp. the **flowering dogwood** or **Virginia dogwood** of the U.S., with white or pink flowers.

do·gy (dō′gē) See DOGIE.

doi·ly (doi′lē) *n. pl.* **·lies** A small, ornamental piece of lace, etc., used to protect surfaces. [after *Doily* or *Doyley,* 17th c. English draper]

do·ings (do͞o′ingz) *n.pl.* Activities or proceedings.

do·jo (dō′jō) *n.* A school for training in oriental martial arts, as judo. [< Japanese]

Dol·by (dôl′bē, dōl′-) *adj.* Designating electronic devices that eliminate noise from recorded sound: a trade name.

Dol·by·ized (dôl′bē·īzd, dōl′-) *adj.* Equipped with or recorded using a Dolby device.

dol·ce vi·ta (dōl′chə vē′tä) A life of self-indulgence. [< Ital., sweet life]

dol·drums (dol′drəmz, dōl′-) *n.pl.* 1. Those parts of the ocean near the equator where calms or baffling winds prevail. 2. A becalmed state. 3. A depressed or bored condition. [Cf. OE *dol* dull, stupid]

dole (dōl) *n.* 1. That which, as food or money, is distributed, esp. in charity. 2. A giving out of something. 3. A sum paid to an unemployed person. **—on the dole** Receiving relief payments from the government. **—*v.t.* doled, dol·ing** To dispense in small quantities; distribute: usually with *out.* [OE *dāl*]

dole·ful (dōl′fəl) *adj.* Melancholy. [< LL *dolere* to feel pain] **—dole′ful·ly** *adv.* **—dole′·ful·ness** *n.*

doll (dol) *n.* 1. A child's toy made to resemble the human figure. 2. A pretty but superficial woman. 3. A cute child. 4. *Slang* An attractive or charming person of either sex.

—*v.t. & v.i.* *Informal* To adorn or dress smartly: with *up*. [from *Doll*, nickname for *Dorothy*]
dol·lar (dol′ər) *n.* 1. The standard monetary unit of the United States, Canada, and certain other countries, equivalent to 100 cents. 2. A coin or a piece of paper currently worth one dollar. Symbol $. [< earlier *daler* < G *taler, thaler*, short for *Joachimstaler*, a coin of *Joachimstal*, a village in Bohemia]
dollar diplomacy 1. U.S. foreign policy aimed at furthering private entrepreneurial interests abroad, esp. in Latin America. 2. U.S. foreign policy using economic incentives to influence foreign leaders.
dol·lop (dol′əp) *n.* *Informal* A small serving, as of a soft substance or liquid.
dol·ly (dol′ē) *n.* *pl.* **·lies** 1. A doll: a child's term. 2. A low, flat frame set on small wheels or rollers, used for moving heavy loads. —*v.i.* **·lied, ·ly·ing** To move a motion-picture or television camera toward or away from the action.
dol·man (dōl′mən, dol′-) *n.* 1. A hussar's jacket, usu. worn as a cape. 2. A woman's coat with dolman sleeves or capelike arm pieces. [< Turkish *dōlāmān* long robe]
dolman sleeve A sleeve tapering from a wide opening at the armhole to a narrow one at the wrist.
dol·men (dōl′mən, dol-) *n.* A prehistoric monument made of a huge stone set on upright stones. [< F]
dol·o·mite (dōl′ə·mīt, dol′-) *n.* A marblelike rock. [after D. de *Dolomieu*, 1750–1801, French geologist]
do·lor (dō′lər) *n.* *Poetic* Sorrow; anguish. Also *Brit.* **do′lour.** [< L, pain]
do·lor·ous (dō′lər·əs, dol′ər-) *adj.* Sad; mournful. —**do′lor·ous·ly** *adv.*
dol·phin (dol′fin) *n.* Any of various marine mammals with beaklike snouts. [< OF *daulphin* < Gk. *delphis, -inos*]
dolt (dōlt) *n.* A stupid person. [ME *dold* stupid] —**dolt′ish** *adj.* —**dolt′ish·ly** *adv.*
-dom *suffix of nouns* 1. State or condition of being: *freedom.* 2. Domain of: *kingdom.* 3. Rank of: *earldom.* 4. The totality of those having a certain rank, state, or condition: *Christendom.* [OE *-dōm* < *dōm* state, condition]
do·main (dō·mān′) *n.* 1. A territory under a sovereign or one government. 2. A field of action, knowledge, etc. 3. A landed estate. [< L *dominus* lord]
dome (dōm) *n.* 1. A roof resembling an inverted cup or hemisphere. 2. Something shaped like this. 3. *Slang* The head. —*v.t.* **domed, dom·ing** 1. To furnish or cover with a dome. 2. To shape like a dome. [< L *domus* house]
domes·day (dōōmz′dā′) *n.* See DOOMSDAY.
do·mes·tic (də·mes′tik) *adj.* 1. Of or pertaining to the home or family. 2. Fond of things concerning the home or family. 3. Tame; domesticated. 4. Of, produced in, or pertaining to one's own country. —*n.* A household servant. [< L *domus* house] —**do·mes′ti·cal·ly** *adv.*
do·mes·ti·cate (də·mes′tə·kāt) *v.t.* **·cat·ed, ·cat·ing** 1. To tame. 2. To cause to become home-loving. Also **do·mes′ti·cize** (-sīz). —**do·mes′ti·ca′tion** *n.*
do·mes·tic·i·ty (dō′mes·tis′ə·tē) *n.* *pl.* **·ties** 1. Life at home or with one's family. 2. Devotion to home and family.
dom·i·cile (dom′ə·səl, -sīl) *n.* 1. A home, house, or dwelling. 2. The place of one's legal abode. —*v.* **·ciled, ·cil·ing** *v.t.* 1. To establish in a place of abode. —*v.i.* 2. To dwell. [< L *domus* house] —**dom·i·cil·i·ar·y** (dom′ə·sil′ē·er′ē) *adj.*
dom·i·nant (dom′ə·nənt) *adj.* 1. Dominating; ruling. 2. Conspicuously prominent. 3. *Genetics* Designating one of a pair of hereditary characters that, appearing in hybrid offspring, masks a contrasting character: opposed to *recessive.* —*n.* *Music* The fifth tone of a diatonic scale, a perfect fifth above the tonic. [See DOMINATE.] —**dom′i·nance** *n.* —**dom′i·nant·ly** *adv.*
dom·i·nate (dom′ə·nāt) *v.* **·nat·ed, ·nat·ing** *v.t.* 1. To control; govern. 2. To tower above. —*v.i.* 3. To be dominant, as in power. [< L *dominari* to rule, dominate] —**dom′i·na′tive** *adj.* —**dom′i·na′tor** *n.*
dom·i·na·tion (dom′ə·nā′shən) *n.* 1. The act of dominating, or the state of being dominated. 2. Control; authority.
dom·i·neer (dom′ə·nir′) *v.t. & v.i.* To rule arrogantly. [< L *dominus* lord] —**dom′i·neer′ing** *adj.* —**dom′i·neer′ing·ly** *adv.*
Do·min·i·can (də·min′i·kən) *n.* 1. A member of the monastic order founded by St. Dominic. 2. A native of the Dominican Republic. —**Do·min′i·can** *adj.*
do·min·ion (də·min′yən) *n.* 1. Sovereign or supreme authority. 2. A country under a particular government. [< L *dominus* lord]
dom·i·no[1] (dom′ə·nō) *n.* *pl.* **·noes** or **·nos** 1. A small mask for the eyes. 2. A loose robe, hood, and mask worn at masquerades. [< MF, hood worn by clerics]
dom·i·no[2] (dom′ə·nō) *n.* *pl.* **·noes** or **·nos** 1. A small, oblong piece of wood, plastic, etc., with the upper side marked with dots. 2. *pl.* (*construed as sing.*) A game usu. played with a set of 28 of these pieces. [? < DOMINO[1]]
domino theory The idea that one event, allowed to happen, will precipitate a series of like events. [after the fall of a row of standing dominoes]
don[1] (don) *n.* 1. A Spanish gentleman or nobleman. 2. *Brit. Informal* A head, fellow, or tutor of a college. [< L *dominus* lord]
don[2] (don) *v.t.* **donned, don·ning** To put on, as a garment. [Contraction of *do on*]
do·nate (dō′nāt, dō·nāt′) *v.t.* **·nat·ed, ·nat·ing** To give, as to a charity; contribute. [Back formation < DONATION] —**do′na·tor** *n.*
do·na·tion (dō·nā′shən) *n.* 1. The act of giving. 2. A gift. [< L *donare* to give]
done (dun) Past participle of DO[1]. —*adj.* 1. Completed; finished; ended; agreed. 2. Cooked sufficiently.
do·nee (dō·nē′) *n.* One who receives a gift.
done for *Informal* 1. Ruined; finished; exhausted. 2. Dead or about to die.
done in *Informal* 1. Utterly exhausted. 2. Killed; destroyed.
dong (dong) *n.* The monetary unit of the Socialist Republic of Vietnam.
don·jon (dun′jən, don′-) *n.* The main tower or keep of a castle. [< OF, the lord's tower]
Don Juan (don wän′) A seducer of women. [after a legendary Spanish nobleman and seducer]
don·key (dong′kē, dung′-) *n.* 1. The ass.

2. A stupid or stubborn person. [? after *Duncan*, a personal name]
don·nish (don′ish) *adj.* 1. Of or suggestive of a university don. 2. Formal; pedantic. —**don′nish·ness** *n.*
don·ny·brook (don′ē·bro͝ok′) *n.* A brawl; free-for-all. [after *Donnybrook Fair*, an event known for its brawls, held in Ireland]
do·nor (dō′nər) *n.* 1. One who gives. 2. *Med.* One who furnishes blood, skin, etc. [< L *donare* to give]
don't (dōnt) Do not.
doo·dad (do͞o′dad) *n. Informal* 1. A small ornament; bauble. 2. A doohickey. [Humorous coinage; extension of DO]
doo·dle (do͞od′l) *Informal v.t. & v.i.* **·dled, ·dling** To draw in an aimless way. —*n.* A design so made. [Cf. dial. E *doodle* to be idle, trifle] —**doo′dler** *n.*
doo·dle·bug (do͞od′l·bug′) *n.* 1. *Dial.* The larva of several insects. 2. Loosely, the tumblebug. [? < dial. E *doodle* idler, fool + BUG]
doo·hick·ey (do͞o′hik′ē) *n. pl.* **·eys** *Informal* A small object whose name is not known or remembered. [Humorous coinage; extension of DO]
doom (do͞om) *v.t.* 1. To pronounce sentence upon; condemn. 2. To destine to an unhappy fate. —*n.* 1. An unhappy fate. 2. An adverse judicial sentence. 3. Death or ruin. [OE *dōm*]
dooms·day (do͞omz′dā′) *n.* The day of the Last Judgment; the end of the world. Also spelled *domesday.* [OE *dōm* doom + *dæg* day]
door (dôr) *n.* 1. A hinged, sliding, folding, or rotating structure, used for closing or opening an entrance to a house, vehicle, etc. 2. A doorway. 3. Any means of entrance or exit. [Fusion of OE *duru* pair of doors and *dor* gate]
door·bell (dôr′bel′) *n.* A bell at a doorway.
door·jamb (dôr′jam′) *n.* A vertical piece at the side of a doorway supporting the lintel.
door·keep·er (dôr′kē′pər) *n.* A guardian or keeper of a doorway.
door·knob (dôr′nob′) *n.* A spherical handle to open a door.
door·man (dôr′man′, -mən) *n. pl.* **·men** (-men′, -mən) An attendant at the door of a hotel, apartment house, etc.
door mat A mat placed at an entrance for wiping the shoes.
door·nail (dôr′nāl′) *n.* A large-headed nail, formerly used on doors.
door·plate (dôr′plāt′) *n.* A metal plate on a door, with the occupant's name, street number, etc.
door·post (dôr′pōst′) *n.* A doorjamb.
door·sill (dôr′sil′) *n.* The sill or threshold of a door.
door·step (dôr′step′) *n.* A step or one of a series of steps leading to a door.
door·stop (dôr′stop′) *n.* A device to keep a door open.
door·way (dôr′wā′) *n.* The passage for entering and leaving a room, hall, etc.
door·yard (dôr′yärd′) *n.* A yard around, or esp. in front of, a house.
dope (dōp) *n.* 1. A usu. liquid substance having a specific purpose, as a lubricant, medication, varnish, etc. 2. *Slang* A drug or narcotic. 3. *Slang* A stupid person. 4. *Slang* Inside information. —*v.t.* **doped, dop·ing** 1. To apply dope to. 2. *Slang* To drug: often with *up.* 3. *Slang* To plan or solve: usu. with *out.* [Orig. U.S., prob. < Du. *doop* a dipping, sauce]
do·pey (dō′pē) *adj.* **·pi·er, ·pi·est** *Slang* 1. Lethargic from or as from narcotics. 2. Stupid. Also **do′py.**
Dor·ic (dôr′ik, dor′-) *adj. Archit.* Of or pertaining to the simplest of the three orders of Greek architecture characterized by heavy, fluted columns and unadorned capitals. [< Gk. *Dōrikos* < *Dōris* a region in Greece]
dorm (dôrm) *n. Informal* A dormitory.
dor·mant (dôr′mənt) *adj.* 1. Asleep or as if asleep. 2. Not active; inoperative. 3. *Biol.* Marked by partial suspension of vital processes, as many animals and plants in winter. [< L *dormire* to sleep] —**dor′man·cy** *n.*
dor·mer (dôr′mər) *n.* A vertical window set in a small gable that projects from a sloping roof. Also **dormer window.** [< OF *dormeor* < L *dormire* to sleep]
dor·mi·to·ry (dôr′mə·tôr′ē) *n. pl.* **·ries** 1. A large room with sleeping accommodations for many persons. 2. A building with sleeping and living accommodations, esp. at a school. [< L *dormire* to sleep]
dor·mouse (dôr′mous′) *n. pl.* **·mice** A small, European rodent, similar to the squirrel. [ME ? dial. E *dorm* to doze + MOUSE]
dor·sal (dôr′səl) *adj. Anat.* Of, pertaining to, on, or near the back. [< L *dorsum* back] —**dor′sal·ly** *adv.*
do·ry (dôr′ē) *n. pl.* **·ries** A deep, flat-bottomed rowboat with a sharp prow. [< native Honduran name]
dos·age (dō′sij) *n.* 1. The administering of a dose of medicine. 2. A dose.
dose (dōs) *n.* 1. A particular quantity of medicine given or prescribed to be given at one time. 2. *Informal* A particular amount of something, usu. disagreeable. —*v.t.* **dosed, dos·ing** To give medicine, etc., to in doses. [< Gk. *dosis* gift, dose]
do·sim·e·ter (dō·sim′ə·tər) *n. Med.* An instrument for measuring the total amount of radiation absorbed in a given time. [< Gk. *dosis* dose + -METER]
dos·si·er (dos′ē·ā, *Fr.* dô·syā′) *n.* A collection of papers, documents, etc., relating to a particular matter or person. [< F, bundle of papers]
dost (dust) Do: archaic or poetic second person singular, present tense of DO[1]: used with *thou.*
dot (dot) *n.* 1. A tiny, usu. round, mark; a spot or point. 2. A small amount. 3. A signal in Morse code that is of shorter duration than the dash. —**on the dot** At exactly the specified time. —*v.* **dot·ted, dot·ting** *v.t.* 1. To mark with a dot or dots. 2. To be scattered thickly over or about. —*v.i.* 3. To make a dot or dots. —**to dot one's i's and cross one's t's** To be exact or correct. [OE *dott* head of a boil]
do·tage (dō′tij) *n.* 1. Feebleness of mind as a result of old age. 2. Excessive affection.
do·tard (dō′tərd) *n.* A foolish old person.
dote (dōt) *v.i.* **dot·ed, dot·ing** 1. To lavish extreme fondness: with *on* or *upon.* 2. To be feeble-minded as a result of old age. [ME

doten] **—dot′er** *n.* **—dot′ing** *adj.* **—dot′ing·ly** *adv.*

doth (duth) Does: archaic or poetic third person singular, present tense of DO[1].

dot·ter·el (dot′ər·əl) *n.* A migratory plover of northern Europe and Asia. Also **dot′trel** (-rəl). [ME *dotrelle*]

dot·tle (dot′l) *n.* The plug of tobacco ash left in a pipe after smoking. [? Dim. of DOT]

dot·ty (dot′ē) *adj.* **·ti·er, ·ti·est 1.** Consisting of or marked with dots. **2.** *Informal* Slightly demented.

Douai Bible An English translation of the Vulgate Bible made by Roman Catholic scholars at Reims and Douai in France, and completed in 1610. Also **Douay Bible** or **Version.**

doub·le (dub′əl) *adj.* **1.** Combined with another usu. identical one; two together: a *double* scoop of ice cream. **2.** Twofold. **3.** More than one; not single. **4.** Consisting of two layers. **5.** Made for two. **6.** Twice as great, as large, as many, etc. **—***n.* **1.** Something that is twice as much. **2.** A duplicate. **3.** A person, animal, or thing that closely resembles another. **4.** A fold or pleat. **5.** *pl.* In tennis, etc., a game having two players on each side. **6.** In baseball, a fair hit that enables the batter to reach second base. **7.** In bridge, the act of challenging an opponent's bid by increasing its value and thus the penalty if the contract is not fulfilled. **—on** (or **at**) **the double 1.** In double time. **2.** *Informal* Quickly. **—***v.* **·led, ·ling** *v.t.* **1.** To make twice as great in number, size, value, force, etc. **2.** To be twice the quantity or number of. **3.** To fold or bend one part of upon another: usu. with *over, up, back.* **4.** To clench (the fist): often with *up.* **5.** *Naut.* To sail around: to *double* a cape. **6.** In bridge, to challenge (an opponent) by announcing a double. **—***v.i.* **7.** To become double; increase by an equal amount. **8.** To turn and go back on a course: often with *back.* **9.** To act or perform in two capacities. **10.** In baseball, to make a two-base hit. **11.** In bridge, to announce a double. **—to double in brass** *Slang* **1.** To be useful in another capacity apart from one's (or its) specialty. **2.** Originally, of musicians, to play a second instrument in addition to the regular one. **—to double up 1.** To bend over, as from pain or laughter. **2.** *Informal* To share one's quarters, bed, etc., with another. **—***adv.* In pairs; two-fold; doubly. [< L *duplus*]

double bass The largest and deepest-toned of the stringed instruments played with a bow: also called *bass viol.*

double bassoon A double-reed instrument pitched an octave below the ordinary bassoon: also called *contrabassoon.*

double boiler A cooking utensil consisting of two pots, one fitting into the other. Food in the upper pot is cooked by the heat from water boiling in the lower pot.

doub·le-breast·ed (dub′əl·bres′tid) *adj.* Having two rows of buttons and fastening so as to provide a double thickness of cloth across the breast: said of a coat or vest.

doub·le-cross (dub′əl·krôs′) *v.t.* *Slang* To betray by failing to act as promised. **—doub′le-cross′** *n.* **—doub′le-cross′er** *n.*

doub·le-date (doub′əl·dāt′) *v.i.* **-dat·ed, -dat·ing** *Informal* To make or go out on a social engagement of two couples. **—double date**

doub·le-deal·ing (dub′əl·dē′ling) *adj.* Treacherous; deceitful. **—***n.* Treachery; duplicity. **—doub′le-deal′er** *n.*

doub·le-deck·er (dub′əl·dek′ər) *n.* **1.** A ship, bus, etc., having two levels. **2.** *Informal* A sandwich made with three slices of bread and two layers of filling. **—doub′le-deck′er** *adj.*

doub·le-edged (dub′əl·ejd′) *adj.* **1.** Having two cutting edges. **2.** Applicable two ways.

dou·ble-en·ten·dre (dōō·bläṅ·täṅ′dr) *n.* A word or phrase of double meaning. [Alter. of F *double entente*]

double entry A method of bookkeeping in which every transaction is made to appear as both a debit and a credit.

double exposure *Photog.* The act of exposing the same film or plate twice; also, a print developed from a film or plate so exposed.

double feature A program of two motion pictures.

doub·le-head·er (dub′əl·hed′ər) *n.* In baseball, two games played on the same day by the same two teams.

double indemnity A clause in a life insurance policy by which a payment of double the face value of the policy is made in the event of accidental death.

double jeopardy The peril under which a defendant is placed when he is tried more than once for the same offense.

doub·le-joint·ed (dub′əl·join′tid) *adj.* Having very flexible joints in one's limbs, fingers, etc.

double knit A two-ply fabric knitted so that its two layers are interlocked by stitches.

doub·le-park (dub′əl·pärk′) *v.t.* & *v.i.* To park (a motor vehicle) alongside another already parked at the curb.

double play In baseball, a play in which two base runners are put out during one continuous play of the ball.

double pneumonia Pneumonia affecting both lungs.

doub·le-reed (dub′əl·rēd′) *adj.* *Music* Designating a group of wind instruments having two reeds united at the lower end and separated at the upper, as the oboe and bassoon.

double standard A moral standard that permits men greater freedom than women, esp. in sexual behavior.

doub·let (dub′lit) *n.* **1.** A short, close-fitting outer garment, with or without sleeves, worn by men during the Renaissance. **2.** A pair of like things. [< OF, something folded, orig. dim. of *double*]

double take Delayed reaction to a joke or unusual situation.

double talk 1. A flow of actual words and meaningless syllables, made to sound like talk. **2.** Ambiguous talk meant to deceive.

doub·le·think (dub′əl·thingk′) *n.* The holding of two contradictory views at the same time.

double time 1. In the U.S. Army, a fast marching step at the rate of 180 three-foot steps per minute. **2.** A wage rate that is twice one's normal pay.

doub·le·tree (dub′el·trē) *n.* A crossbar on a wagon, carriage, or plow.

doub·loon (du·blo͞on′) *n.* A former Spanish gold coin. [< Sp. *doble* double]

doub·ly (dub′lē) *adv.* 1. In twofold degree; twice. 2. In pairs. 3. In twice the quantity.

doubt (dout) *v.t.* 1. To hold the truth, validity, or reliability of as uncertain; hesitate to accept. —*v.i.* 2. To be unconvinced or mistrustful. —*n.* 1. Lack of certainty. 2. A state of affairs giving rise to uncertainty: Their fate was in *doubt.* —**beyond doubt** Unquestionably; certainly. —**no doubt** 1. Certainly. 2. Probably. —**without doubt** Certainly. [< L *dubitare*] —**doubt′er** *n.*

doubt·ful (dout′fəl) *adj.* 1. Subject to or causing doubt; uncertain; unsettled. 2. Having doubt; undecided. 3. Vague; ambiguous. 4. Of questionable character. —**doubt′ful·ly** *adv.*

doubt·less (dout′lis) *adv.* 1. Unquestionably. 2. Probably. Also **doubt′less·ly.** —*adj.* Free from uncertainty.

douche (do͞osh) *n.* 1. A jet of water, etc., directed into or onto some part of the body. 2. A cleansing or medicinal treatment of this kind. 3. A syringe or other device for administering a douche. —*v.t. & v.i.* **douched, douch·ing** To treat with or take a douche. [< F < L *ducere* to lead]

dough (dō) *n.* 1. A soft mass of moistened flour or meal and other ingredients, mixed for making bread, pastry, etc. 2. Any soft, pasty mass. 3. *Slang* Money. [OE *dāh*] —**dough′y** *adj.* **dough·i·er, dough·i·est**

dough·nut (dō′nut′) *n.* A small cake of usu. leavened and sweetened dough, fried in deep fat, and often having a hole in the center.

dough·ty (dou′tē) *adj.* **·ti·er, ·ti·est** Valiant; brave: chiefly humorous. [OE *dyhtig, dohtig*] —**dough′ti·ly** *adv.* —**dough′ti·ness** *n.*

Doug·las fir (dug′ləs) A tall evergreen timber tree, growing on the Pacific coast of the U.S. Also **Douglas hemlock, Douglas pine, Douglas spruce.** [after David *Douglas,* 1798–1834, Scottish botanist]

dour (do͝or, dour) *adj.* Forbidding and surly; morosely stern. [< L *durus* hard] —**dour′ly** *adv.* —**dour′ness** *n.*

douse[1] (dous) *v.* **doused, dous·ing** *v.t.* 1. To plunge into water or other liquid; duck. 2. To drench. —*v.i.* 3. To become drenched or immersed. Also spelled *dowse.* [Origin unknown] —**douse** *n.*

douse[2] (dous) *v.t.* **doused, dous·ing** *Informal* To put out; extinguish. [Cf. MDu. *dossen* to beat, strike]

dove[1] (duv) *n.* 1. Any bird of the pigeon family, esp. the mourning dove, turtle dove, etc. 2. A symbol of peace. 3. One who urges negotiation and compromise in a dispute: opposed to *hawk.* 4. A gentle, innocent person. [ME *duve*]

dove[2] (dōv) *Informal* Alternative past tense of DIVE.

dove·cote (duv′kōt′, -kot′) *n.* A box used for breeding pigeons. Also **dove′cot′** (-kot′).

dove·tail (duv′tāl′) *n.* 1. A tenon shaped like a wedge and designed to interlock with a mortise of similar shape. 2. A joint thus formed. —*v.t. & v.i.* To join by or as by dovetails.

dow·a·ger (dou′ə·jər) *n.* 1. In English law, a widow holding property or title derived from her deceased husband. 2. *Informal* An elderly, dignified woman. [< OF *douagiere,* ult. < L *dotare* to give]

dow·dy (dou′dē) *adj.* **·di·er, ·di·est** Not smart in dress; frumpish. —*n. pl.* **·dies** A dowdy woman. [ME *doude* slut] —**dow′·di·ly** *adv.* —**dow′di·ness** *n.*

dow·el (dou′əl) *n.* A pin or peg fitted tightly into adjacent holes of two pieces so as to hold them together. Also **dowel pin.** —*v.t.* **dow·eled** or **·elled, dow·el·ing** or **·el·ling** To furnish or fasten with dowels. [ME, ? < MLG *dovel* plug]

dow·er (dou′ər) *n.* 1. The part of a deceased man's estate that is assigned by law to his widow for life. 2. A dowry. —*v.t.* To provide with a dower. [< L *dos, dotis* dowry]

down[1] (doun) *adv.* 1. From a higher to a lower place. 2. In or on a lower place, level, etc. 3. On or to the ground. 4. To or toward the south. 5. From an upright to a prone or prostrate position. 6. To lesser bulk, amount, etc.: The mixture boiled *down.* 7. To less activity, intensity, etc.: Things quieted *down.* 8. To a lower amount, rate, etc. 9. In or into subjection or control: to put the rebels *down.* 10. In or into a depressed or prostrate physical or mental state: He came *down* with a cold. 11. From an earlier time or individual. 12. As partial payment. 13. In writing. —**down with** (Let us) do away with or overthrow. —*adj.* 1. Directed downward. 2. *Informal* Downcast; depressed. 3. Given as a partial amount. 4. In games, behind an opponent by a specified number of points, strokes, etc. 5. Ill. 6. Not working or operable. —**down and out** In a completely miserable state, as of poverty or desolation. —**down on** *Informal* Annoyed with or hostile to. —*prep.* 1. In a descending direction along, upon, or in. 2. During the course of: *down* the years. —*v.t.* 1. To knock, throw, or put down. 2. *Informal* To swallow quickly; gulp. —*n.* 1. A downward movement; descent. 2. A reverse of fortune: chiefly in the phrase **ups and downs.** 3. In football, any of the four consecutive plays during which a team must advance the ball at least ten yards to keep possession of it. [OE *dūne* < *of dūne* from the hill]

down[2] (doun) *n.* 1. The fine, soft plumage of birds under the feathers, esp. that on the breast of water birds. 2. Any similar substance. [< ON *dūnn*]

down[3] (doun) *n.* *Usu. pl.* Turf-covered, undulating tracts of upland. [OE *dūn.* Akin to DUNE.]

down·cast (doun′kast′) *adj.* 1. Directed downward. 2. Low in spirits; depressed.

down·er (doun′ər) *n.* *Slang* 1. A depressant drug. 2. A depressing situation or person.

down·fall (doun′fôl′) *n.* 1. Ruin; collapse. 2. A sudden, heavy fall of rain, etc. —**down′·fall′en** *adj.*

down·grade (doun′grād′) *n.* A descending slope, as of a hill or road. —*adj.* Downhill. —*v.t.* **·grad·ed, ·grad·ing** To reduce in status, salary, etc.

down·heart·ed (doun′här′tid) *adj.* Dejected; discouraged. —**down′heart′ed·ly** *adv.*

down·hill (*adv.* doun′hil′; *adj.* doun′hil′) *adv.* In a downward direction; toward the bottom of a hill. —**to go downhill** To decline, as in success or health. —*adj.* Descending.

down-home (doun′hōm′) *adj.* Having the earthy simplicity attributed to rural dwellers, esp. in the U.S. South.

down·pour (doun′pôr′) *n.* A heavy fall of rain.

down·right (doun′rīt′) *adj.* 1. Thorough; utter. 2. Straightforward. —*adv.* Thoroughly; utterly.

Down's syndrome Mongolism.

down·stairs (*adv.* doun′stârz′; *adj.* & *n.* doun′stârz′) *adv.* 1. Down the stairs. 2. On or to a lower floor. —*adj.* Situated on a lower floor: also **down′stair′**. —*n.* The downstairs part of a house or other building.

down·stream (*adv.* doun′strēm′; *adj.* doun′·strēm′) *adv.* Down the stream. —*adj.* In the direction of the current.

down·time (doun′tīm′) *n.* Time when a machine, factory, etc. is shut down for repairs, maintenance, etc.

down-to-earth (doun′tə·ûrth′) *adj* Realistic; practical; unaffected.

down·town (*adv.* doun′toun′; *adj.* doun′toun′) *adv.* To, toward, or in the southern or business section of a town or city. —*adj.* Located in the southern or business section of a town or city.

down·trod·den (doun′trod′n) *adj.* 1. Trampled. 2. Subjugated; oppressed. Also **down′trod′**.

down·ward (doun′wərd) *adv.* 1. From a higher to a lower level, position, etc. 2. From an earlier or more remote time, place, etc. Also **down′wards,** occasionally **down′ward·ly.** —*adj.* 1. Descending from a higher to a lower level. 2. Descending from that which is more remote.

down·y (dou′nē) *adj.* **down·i·er, down·i·est** Of, like, or covered with down. —**down′i·ness** *n.*

dow·ry (dou′rē) *n. pl.* **·ries** The money or property a wife brings to her husband at marriage. [See DOWER]

dowse[1] (dous) See DOUSE[1].

dowse[2] (douz) *v.i.* **dowsed, dows·ing** To search with a divining rod. [Origin uncertain] —**dows′er** *n.*

dows·ing rod (douz′ing) A divining rod.

dox·ol·o·gy (dok·sol′ə·jē) *n. pl.* **·gies** A hymn or verse of praise to God. [< Gk. *doxa* praise + *legein* to speak]

doze (dōz) *v.i.* **dozed, doz·ing** To sleep lightly; nap. —**to doze off** To fall into a light, brief sleep. —*n.* A light, brief sleep; nap. [< ON *dūsa* to doze]

doz·en (duz′ən) *n. pl.* **doz·ens;** *when preceded by a number,* **doz·en** A group or set of twelve things. Abbr. *doz.* [< L *duo* two + *decem* ten]

drab[1] (drab) *adj.* **drab·ber, drab·best** 1. Lacking brightness; dull and monotonous. 2. Of the color of drab. 3. Made of drab. —*n.* 1. A thick, woolen, yellowish brown cloth. 2. The yellowish brown color of this cloth. [< F *drap* cloth < LL *drappus,* ? < Celtic] —**drab′ly** *adv.* —**drab′ness** *n.*

drab[2] (drab) *n.* 1. An untidy woman. 2. A prostitute; slut. [? < Celtic]

drach·ma (drak′mə) *n. pl.* **·mas** or **·mae** (-mē) 1. An ancient Greek silver coin. 2. The standard monetary unit of Greece. 3. An ancient Greek unit of weight. [< Gk. *drachmē* a handful]

draft (draft) *n.* 1. The act or process of selecting an individual for some duty or purpose; esp., the selection of men for compulsory military service; conscription. 2. A current of air. 3. A device for controlling the airflow, as in a furnace. 4. A written order, directing the payment of money. 5. A sketch, plan, or design of something to be made. 6. A preliminary or rough version of a writing. 7. The act of drinking; also, the liquid taken at one drink. 8. The drawing of liquid from its container; also a quantity drawn for drinking. 9. The act of drawing in a fishnet; also, the amount of fish so taken. 10. The act of drawing air, smoke, etc., into the lungs; also, the air, etc., taken in. 11. The pulling of something, as a loaded wagon; also, the load pulled. 12. *pl.* Draughts. 13. *Naut.* The depth of water required for a ship to float, esp. when loaded. —**on draft** Ready to be drawn, as beer. —*v.t.* 1. To draw up in preliminary form, esp. in writing. 2. To select, as for military service. 3. To draw off or away. —*adj.* 1. Suitable to be used for pulling heavy loads: a *draft* animal. 2. Not bottled, as beer. Also *Brit. draught.* [< OE *dragan* to draw]

draft board An official board of civilians that selects men for compulsory service in the U.S. armed forces.

draft dodger One who avoids or attempts to avoid conscription into military service.

draft·ee (draf·tē′) *n.* A person drafted for service in the armed forces.

drafts·man (drafts′mən) *n. pl.* **·men** (-mən) 1. One who draws or prepares designs or plans of buildings, machinery, etc. 2. An artist skilled in drawing.

draft·y (draf′tē) *adj.* **draft·i·er, draft·i·est** Having or exposed to drafts of air. —**draft′i·ness** *n.*

drag (drag) *v.* **dragged, drag·ging** *v.t.* 1. To pull along by main force; haul. 2. To sweep or search the bottom of (a body of water); dredge. 3. To draw along heavily and wearily. 4. To continue tediously: often with *on* or *out.* —*v.i.* 5. To be pulled or hauled along. 6. To move heavily or slowly. 7. To lag behind. 8. To pass slowly. —**to drag one's feet** *Informal* To act with deliberate slowness. —*n.* 1. The act of dragging. 2. The resistance encountered in dragging. 3. A slow, heavy, usu. impeded motion or movement. 4. Something that slows down movement. 5. Something heavy that is dragged. 6. A contrivance for dragging a river, lake, etc. 7. Anything that hinders. 8. A stagecoach, with seats inside and on the top. 9. *Slang* Influence; pull. 10. *Slang* A puff on a cigarette, etc. 11. *Slang* One who or that which is tedious or boring. 12. A drag race. 13. Women's dress when worn by a man. [ME, prob. < OE *dragan*]

drag·net (drag′net′) *n.* 1. A net used in dragging a body of water. 2. An organized widespread search for a criminal.

drag·o·man (drag′ə·mən) *n. pl.* **·mans** (-mənz) or **·men** (-mən) An interpreter or guide for travelers in the Near East. [< Arabic *tarjumān* translator]

drag·on (drag′ən) *n.* A mythical, serpentlike, winged monster. [< Gk. *drakōn* serpent]

drag·on·fly (drag′ən·flī′) *n. pl.* **·flies** A predatory insect having a slender body, four wings, and strong jaws.

dra·goon (drə·gōōn′) *n.* In some European armies, a cavalryman. —*v.t.* 1. To harass by dragoons. 2. To coerce; browbeat. [< F *dragon*, a type of 17th c. firearm]

drag race A race between cars accelerating from a standstill, usu. held on a straight course (**drag strip**).

drain (drān) *v.t.* 1. To draw off (liquid) gradually. 2. To draw liquid from. 3. To empty by drinking. 4. To use up gradually; exhaust. 5. To filter. —*v.i.* 6. To flow off gradually. 7. To become dry by the flowing off of liquid. 8. To discharge waters contained: The region *drains* into the lake. —*n.* 1. A device for draining. 2. A continuous outflow, expenditure, or depletion. 3. The act of draining. [OE *drēahnian*]

drain·age (drā′nij) *n.* 1. The act or method of draining. 2. A system of drains. 3. That which is drained off. 4. A drainage basin.

drainage basin A large surface area whose waters are drained off into a principal river system.

drain·pipe (drān′pīp′) *n.* A pipe used for draining.

drake (drāk) *n.* A male duck. [ME]

dram (dram) *n.* 1. An apothecaries' weight equal to 60 grains, 3.89 grams, or one eighth of an ounce. 2. An avoirdupois measure equal to 27.34 grains, 1.77 grams, or one sixteenth of an ounce. 3. A fluid dram. 4. A small portion, esp. of alcoholic liquor. [< Gk. *drachmē* a handful]

dra·ma (drä′mə, dram′ə) *n.* 1. A literary composition written to be performed upon a stage; a play. 2. Stage plays as a branch of literature. 3. The art or profession of writing, acting, or producing plays. 4. The quality of being dramatic. [< Gk., action, drama]

dra·mat·ic (drə·mat′ik) *adj.* 1. Of, connected with, or like the drama. 2. Characterized by the spirit of the drama; theatrical. —**dra·mat′i·cal·ly** *adv.*

dra·mat·ics (drə·mat′iks) *n.pl.* (*usu. construed as sing. in def. 2*) 1. Dramatic performance, esp. by amateurs. 2. The art of staging or acting plays.

dram·a·tis per·so·nae (dram′ə·tis pər·sō′nē) *Latin* The characters of a play; also, a list of these.

dram·a·tist (dram′ə·tist) *n.* One who writes plays.

dram·a·tize (dram′ə·tīz) *v.t.* **·tized, ·tiz·ing** 1. To present in dramatic form; adapt for performance, as a play. 2. To represent or interpret (events, oneself, etc.) in a theatrical manner. Also *Brit.* **dram′a·tise.** —**dram′a·ti·za′tion** *n.*

dram·a·turge (dram′ə·tûrj) *n.* A dramatist. Also **dram′a·tur′gist.** [< Gk. *drama* play + *ergein* to work]

dram·a·tur·gy (dram′ə·tûr′jē) *n.* Dramatics (def. 2). —**dram′a·tur′gic** or **·gi·cal** *adj.*

drank (drangk) Past tense of DRINK.

drape (drāp) *v.* **draped, drap·ing** *v.t.* 1. To cover or adorn in a graceful fashion, as with drapery or clothing. 2. To arrange in graceful folds. —*v.i.* 3. To hang in folds. —*n.* 1. *pl.* Drapery. 2. The way in which cloth hangs, as in clothing. [< F *draper* to weave]

drap·er (drā′pər) *n.* *Brit.* A dealer in cloth or dry goods.

dra·per·y (drā′pər·ē) *n.* *pl.* **·per·ies** 1. Attire hanging in folds. 2. *Often pl.* Hangings or curtains arranged in loose folds. 3. Cloth.

dras·tic (dras′tik) *adj.* Vigorous; extreme. [< Gk. *drastikos* effective < *draein* to act] —**dras′ti·cal·ly** *adv.*

draught (draft) See DRAFT.

draughts (drafts) *n.pl.* (*construed as sing.*) *Brit.* The game of checkers: also spelled *drafts.* [See DRAFT.]

draw (drô) *v.* **drew, drawn, draw·ing** *v.t.* 1. To cause to move toward or to follow behind an agent exerting physical force; pull. 2. To obtain, as from a receptacle: to *draw* water. 3. To cause to flow forth, as blood. 4. To bring forth; elicit: to *draw* praise, 5. To take or pull off, on, or out, as a sword. 6. To portray with lines or words; sketch; delineate. 7. To deduce or extract by a mental process: to *draw* a conclusion. 8. To attract; entice. 9. To pull tight, as a rope. 10. To make by stretching or hammering, as wire or dies. 11. To take in, as air or a liquid, by inhaling or sucking. 12. To close or shut, as curtains. 13. To shrink or wrinkle. 14. To select or obtain, as by chance; also, to win (a prize) in a lottery. 15. To receive; earn, as a salary or interest. 16. To withdraw, as money from a bank. 17. To write out (a check). 18. *Naut.* Of a vessel, to sink to (a specified depth) in floating. —*v.i.* 19. To practice the art of drawing; sketch. 20. To exert a pulling or drawing force. 21. To approach or retreat: to *draw* near or away. 22. To exert an attracting influence. 23. To obtain by making an application to some source: with *on* or *upon*: to *draw* on one's experience. 24. To produce a current of air: This chimney *draws* well. 25. To end a contest without a decision; tie. —**to draw a blank** To be unsuccessful. —**to draw on** To approach. —**to draw oneself up** To straighten up, as in indignation. —**to draw out** 1. To prolong. 2. To cause (someone) to talk freely. —**to draw the line** To fix a limit and refuse to go further. —**to draw up** 1. To write out in proper form. 2. To bring or come to a standstill, as horses. 3. To come alongside. —*n.* 1. The act of drawing. 2. The act of drawing out a weapon for action. 3. Something drawn, as a ticket in a lottery. 4. Something that attracts a large audience. 5. A stalemate; tie. [OE *dragan*]

draw·back (drô′bak′) *n.* Anything that hinders progress, success, etc.

draw·bridge (drô′brij′) *n.* A bridge of which the whole or a part may be raised, let down, or drawn aside.

draw·er (drô′ər *for def. 1*; drôr *for def. 2*) *n.* 1. One who draws. 2. A sliding receptacle, as in a desk, that can be drawn out.

draw·ers (drôrz) *n.pl.* Underpants covering all or part of each leg.

draw·ing (drô′ing) *n.* 1. The act of one who or that which draws. 2. The art of representing something with lines and often shading, by pen, pencil, crayon, etc. 3. The picture, sketch, or design produced by this art. 4. A lottery.

drawing card Something that attracts a large audience.

drawing room 1. A room in which visitors are received and entertained. 2. A private compartment in a sleeping car on a train. [Short for *withdrawing room*]

draw·knife (drô′nīf′) *n. pl.* **·knives** (-nīvz′) A knife with a handle at each end, used for shaving a surface. Also **drawing knife.**

drawl (drôl) *v.t & v.i.* To speak or pronounce slowly, esp. with a drawing out of the vowels. [? Freq. of DRAW] **—drawl** *n.* **—drawl′er** *n.* **—drawl′ing·ly** *adv.*

drawn (drôn) Past participle of DRAW.

drawn butter Melted butter.

drawn work Ornamental open work made by pulling out threads of fabric.

dray (drā) *n.* A low, strong cart with removable sides. **—***v.t.* To transport by dray. [OE *dragan* to draw] **—dray′man** (-mən) *n.*

dread (dred) *v.t.* To anticipate with great fear or anxiety. **—***adj.* 1. Causing great fear; terrible. 2. Exciting awe. **—***n.* 1. A terrifying anticipation, as of evil or danger. 2. Awe. [OE *ondrǣdan*]

dread·ful (dred′fəl) *adj.* 1. Inspiring dread; terrible. 2. *Informal* Disgusting; very bad. **—dread′ful·ly** *adv.*

dread·nought (dred′nôt′) *n.* Any battleship of great size carrying large-caliber guns. Also **dread′naught′.**

dream (drēm) *n.* 1. A series of thoughts or images passing through the mind in sleep. 2. A daydream; reverie. 3. A cherished or vain hope. 4. Anything of dreamlike quality. **—***v.* **dreamed or dreamt** (dremt), **dream·ing** *v.t.* 1. To see or imagine in or as in a dream. 2. To spend (time) in idle reverie: with *away.* **—***v.i.* 3. To have a dream or dreams. 4. To daydream. **—to dream up** *Informal* To create, as by ingenuity. [OE *drēam* joy] **—dream′er** *n.* **—dream′ing·ly** *adv.* **—dream′·less** *adj.* **—dream′less·ly** *adv.* **—dream′like′** *adj.*

dream·y (drē′mē) *adj.* **dream·i·er, dream·i·est** 1. Of, pertaining to, or causing dreams. 2. Given to dreams; visionary. 3. *Informal* Wonderful. **—dream′i·ly** *adv.* **—dream′i·ness** *n.*

drear (drir) *adj. Poetic* Dreary.

drear·y (drir′ē) *adj.* **drear·i·er, drear·i·est** 1. Causing or manifesting sadness or gloom. 2. Dull or monotonous. [OE *dreorig* sad < *drēor* gore] **—drear′i·ly** *adv.* **—drear′i·ness** *n.*

dredge[1] (drej) *n.* 1. A large, powerful scoop or suction apparatus for removing mud or gravel from the bottoms of channels, harbors, etc. 2. Any similar, smaller device. **—***v.* **dredged, dredg·ing** *v.t.* 1. To clear or widen by means of a dredge. 2. To catch with a dredge. **—***v.i.* 3. To use a dredge. [ME *dreg*] **—dredg′er** *n.*

dredge[2] (drej) *v.t.* **dredged, dredg·ing** To dust with a powdered substance, esp. flour. [< L *tragemata* spices]

dregs (dregz) *n.pl.* 1. The sediment of liquids, esp. of beverages; lees. 2. Coarse, worthless residue. [< ON *dregg*]

drench (drench) *v.t.* 1. To wet thoroughly; soak. 2. *Vet.* To administer a potion to by force. **—***n. Vet.* A liquid medicine administered by force. [OE *drencan* to cause to drink] **—drench′er** *n.*

Dres·den (drez′dən) *n.* A china made in Dresden, Germany.

dress (dres) *v.* **dressed or drest, dress·ing** *v.t.* 1. To put clothes on; clothe. 2. To trim or decorate, as a store window. 3. To treat medicinally, as a wound. 4. To comb and arrange (hair). 5. To prepare (stone, timber, etc.) for use or sale. 6. To clean (fowl, game, etc.) for cooking. **—***v.i.* 7. To put on or wear clothing, esp. formal clothing. **—to dress down** *Informal* To rebuke severely; scold. **—to dress up** To put on or wear formal attire. **—***n.* 1. An outer garment for a woman or child, usu. in one piece with a skirt. 2. Clothing collectively. 3. External adornment or appearance. **—***adj.* 1. Of or pertaining to dress or a dress. 2. To be worn on formal occasions. [< OF *dresser* to arrange, dress]

dres·sage (dres′ij, *Fr.* dre·säzh′) *n.* The guiding of a trained horse through a set of maneuvers by imperceptible movements of the rider. [< F]

dress circle A section of seats in a theater or concert hall, usu. the first or second gallery behind and above the orchestra.

dress·er[1] (dres′ər) *n.* 1. One who dresses something. 2. One who assists another in dressing. 3. One who dresses in a particular way. 4. A tool used in dressing stone, leather, etc.

dress·er[2] (dres′ər) *n.* A chest of drawers for articles of clothing. [< OF *dresser* to dress]

dress·ing (dres′ing) *n.* 1. The act of one who or that which dresses. 2. That with which something is dressed, as medicated bandages for a wound. 3. A stuffing for poultry or roasts. 4. A sauce for salads, etc.

dress·ing-down (dres′ing·doun′) *n. Informal* A severe scolding.

dressing gown A loose gown worn while lounging at home.

dressing table A small table or stand with a mirror, used while putting on makeup, grooming the hair, etc.

dress·mak·er (dres′mā′kər) *n.* One who makes women's dresses or other articles of clothing. **—dress′mak′ing** *n.*

dress parade A formal military parade.

dress rehearsal A final rehearsal of a play, done with costumes, lighting, etc.

dress·y (dres′ē) *adj.* **dress·i·er, dress·i·est** *Informal* Elegant; stylish. **—dress′i·ness** *n.*

drew (dro͞o) Past tense of DRAW.

drib (drib) *n. Dial.* Driblet. **—dribs and drabs** Small quantities. [Var. of DRIP]

drib·ble (drib′əl) *v.t. & v.i.* **·bled, ·bling** 1. To fall or let fall in drops. 2. To drool. 3. In sports, to propel (the ball) by successive bounces or kicks. **—***n.* 1. A small quantity of a liquid falling in drops. 2. The act of dribbling. **—drib′bler** *n.*

drib·let (drib′lit) *n.* 1. A small drop of liquid. 2. A tiny quantity. Also **drib′blet.**

dried (drīd) Past tense and past participle of DRY.

dri·er (drī′ər) Comparative of DRY. **—***n.* 1. One who or that which dries. 2. A substance added to paint, etc., to make it dry more quickly. 3. A mechanical device for drying, as for drying clothes. Also spelled *dryer.*

dri·est (drī′ist) Superlative of DRY: also spelled *dryest.*

drift (drift) *n.* 1. The act of moving along, or the fact of being carried along, in or as in a current of water, air, etc. 2. A force or influence that drives something along. 3. A course, tendency, or intent: the *drift* of a conversation. 4. The rate at which a current of water moves. 5. The direction of a current of water. 6. Something driven along or heaped up by air or water currents: a snow *drift*. 7. The distance a ship, aircraft, etc., is driven from its course by wind, sea, etc. —*v.i.* 1. To move along in or as in a current. 2. To become heaped up by air currents or water currents. —*v.t.* 3. To cause to drift. [OE *drifan* to drive] —**drift′er** *n.*

drift·age (drif′tij) *n.* 1. The act or process of drifting. 2. Deviation caused by drifting. 3. Something drifting or drifted.

drift·wood (drift′wŏŏd′) *n.* Wood floated or drifted by water; esp., wood washed up on a seashore.

drill[1] (dril) *n.* 1. A tool used for boring holes in hard substances. 2. A process of training marked by fixed procedures and much repetition, as in gymnastics, in arithmetic, etc. 3. The act of teaching through such training; also, a particular exercise. —*v.t.* & *v.i.* 1. To pierce with a drill. 2. To teach (someone) or learn by drill. [< Du. *drillen* to bore] —**drill′er** *n.*

drill[2] (dril) *Agric.* *n.* A machine for planting seeds in rows. —*v.t.* & *v.i.* To sow or plant in rows.

drill[3] (dril) *n.* Heavy, twilled linen or cotton cloth. Also **drill′ing.** [< G *drillich* cloth with three threads]

drill[4] (dril) *n.* A baboon of West Africa, similar to the mandrill. [? < native name]

drill·mas·ter (dril′mas′tər) *n.* One who teaches or trains by drilling.

drill press A machine tool used in drilling holes.

dri·ly (drī′lē) See DRYLY.

drink (dringk) *v.* **drank, drunk, drink·ing** *v.t.* 1. To take into the mouth and swallow (a liquid). 2. To soak up or absorb. 3. To swallow the contents of (a glass, etc.). —*v.i.* 4. To swallow a liquid. 5. To drink alcoholic liquors, esp. to excess. 6. To drink a toast: with *to.* —**to drink the health of** To offer good wishes to by a toast. —*n.* 1. A beverage. 2. A portion of liquid swallowed. 3. Alcoholic liquor. 4. The practice of drinking alcoholic liquor to excess. [OE *drincan*] —**drink′a·ble** *adj.* —**drink′er** *n.*

drip (drip) *n.* 1. The falling of liquids in drops. 2. Liquid falling in drops; also, the sound so made. 3. Melted fat exuded from meat being roasted or fried: also **drip′pings.** 4. *Slang* A disagreeable, insipid, or inept individual. —*v.t.* & *v.i.* **dripped** or **dript, drip·ping** To fall or cause to fall in drops. [OE *dryppan*] —**drip′py** *adj.*

drip-dry (drip′drī′) *adj.* Of a garment or fabric treated to dry quickly and retain its shape after being hung while wet. —*v.i.* **-dried, -dry·ing** To dry in such a manner.

drive (drīv) *v.* **drove, driv·en, driv·ing** *v.t.* 1. To push or propel onward with force. 2. To force to work or activity. 3. To goad by force or compulsion. 4. To cause to penetrate by force. 5. To cause to go rapidly by striking. 6. To control the operation of (a vehicle). 7. To transport in a vehicle. 8. To provide the motive power for. —*v.i.* 9. To move along rapidly. 10. To strike or impel a ball, etc., with force. 11. To drive or ride in a vehicle. —**to drive home** 1. To force in all the way, as a nail. 2. To make evident with force or emphasis. —*n.* 1. The act of driving. 2. A road for driving. 3. A journey in a vehicle. 4. The gathering together of cattle, logs, etc. 5. An organized campaign. 6. *Informal* Energy; aggressiveness. 7. *Psychol.* A strong, motivating power or stimulus. 8. *Mil.* A large-scale, sustained attack. 9. *Mech.* A means of transmitting power, as from the motor of an automobile to the wheels. [OE *drīfan*]

drive-in (drīv′in′) *n.* An outdoor motion-picture theater, restaurant, etc., for patrons in cars.

driv·el (driv′əl) *v.* **·eled** or **·elled, ·el·ing** or **·el·ling** *v.i.* 1. To let saliva flow from the mouth. 2. To flow like saliva. 3. To talk foolishly. —*v.t.* 4. To let flow from the mouth. —*n.* 1. A flow of saliva from the mouth. 2. Senseless talk. [OE *dreflian*] —**driv′el·er** or **·el·ler** *n.*

driv·en (driv′ən) Past participle of DRIVE.

driv·er (drī′vər) *n.* 1. One who drives a vehicle, animals, etc. 2. In golf, a club for driving from the tee. 3. *Mech.* A part that transmits motion.

drive·way (drīv′wā′) *n.* A private road providing access to a garage, house, etc.

driz·zle (driz′əl) *v.t.* & *v.i.* **·zled, ·zling** To rain steadily in fine drops. —*n.* A light rain. [? Freq. of ME *dresen*, OE *drēosan* to fall] —**driz′zly** *adj.*

drogue (drōg) *n.* A small parachute used to slow down or stabilize a satellite or spacecraft upon re-entering earth's atmosphere. [? alter. of DRAG]

droll (drōl) *adj.* Humorously odd; comical; funny. [< MDu. *drol* a jolly man] —**drol′ly** *adv.*

droll·er·y (drō′lər·ē) *n.* *pl.* **·er·ies** 1. The quality of being droll; humor. 2. Something droll.

-drome *combining form* Place for running; racecourse. [< Gk. *dramein* to run]

drom·e·dar·y (drom′ə·der′ē) *n.* *pl.* **·dar·ies** The swift, one-humped Arabian camel trained for riding. [< L *dromas* a running]

drone[1] (drōn) *v.* **droned, dron·ing** *v.i.* 1. To make a dull, humming sound. 2. To speak monotonously. —*v.t.* 3. To utter in a monotonous tone. —*n.* A dull humming sound, as of a bee. [ME *dronen* to roar. See DRONE[2]]

drone[2] (drōn) *n.* 1. The male of the bee, esp. of the honeybee, having no sting and gathering no honey. 2. A lazy loafer. 3. *Aeron.* An unmanned airplane piloted by remote control. [ME < OE *drān*]

drool (drōōl) *v.t.* & *v.i.* To drivel; slaver. —*n.* Spittle. [Contraction of DRIVEL]

droop (drōōp) *v.i.* 1. To sink down; hang downward. 2. To lose vigor; languish. —*v.t.* 3. To let hang or sink down. [< ON *drūpa*] —**droop** *n.* —**droop′y** *adj.* **droop·i·er, droop·i·est**

drop (drop) *n.* 1. A small quantity of liquid, shaped like a tiny ball. 2. A very small amount of anything. 3. *pl.* A liquid medicine given in drops. 4. Something resembling a drop in shape, size, etc. 5. Something designed to fall, slide, or hang down, as a curtain. 6. A place for dropping or leaving something, as a slot in a mailbox. 7. The act of falling or dropping. 8. A sudden or quick downward movement or decrease. 9. The vertical distance from a higher to a lower level. 10. A falling off or away. 11. A parachuting of men or supplies. **—to have (or get) the drop on** To have (or get) the advantage over. **—v. dropped** or **dropt, drop·ping** *v.i.* 1. To fall in drops, as a liquid. 2. To fall or descend rapidly. 3. To fall down exhausted, injured, or dead. 4. To decline or decrease. 5. To fall into some state or condition. **—***v.t.* 6. To let fall by letting go of. 7. To let fall in drops. 8. To give birth to: said of animals. 9. To utter (a hint, etc.) in a casual way. 10. To write and send (a note, etc.). 11. To cause to fall, as by striking. 12. To have no more to do with. 13. To let out or deposit at a particular place. 14. To parachute (soldiers, supplies, etc.). 15. To omit, as a word, line, or stitch. 16. To move down; lower. **—to drop in** To make a casual visit. **—to drop off** 1. To decline or decrease. 2. To go to sleep. **—to drop out** To withdraw, as from membership. [OE *dropa*]

drop-kick (drop′kik′) *v.t.* & *v.i.* 1. In football, to kick (the ball) after dropping it on the ground. 2. In soccer, to drop and kick (the ball). **—drop kick** *n.*

drop·let (drop′lit) *n.* A tiny drop.

drop·out (drop′out′) *n.* A person who drops out, esp. a student who leaves school.

drop·sy (drop′sē) *n.* Edema. [< Gk. *hydrōps*] **—drop′si·cal** *adj.*

drosh·ky (drosh′kē, drôsh′-) *n. pl.* **·kies** A light, open, four-wheeled Russian carriage.

dro·soph·i·la (drō·sof′ə·lə, drə-) *n. pl.* **·lae** (-lē) The fruit fly (def. 2). [< Gk. *drosos* dew + *phileein* to love]

dross (drôs, dros) *n.* 1. *Metall.* Refuse or impurity in melted metal. 2. Waste matter; refuse. [OE *drōs*] **—dross′y** *adj.*

drought (drout) *n.* 1. Long-continued dry weather; lack of rain. 2. *Dial.* Thirst. Also **drouth** (drouth). [OE *drūgath*] **—drought′y** *adj.*

drove[1] (drōv) Past tense of DRIVE.

drove[2] (drōv) *n.* 1. A number of animals driven or herded for driving. 2. A moving crowd of human beings. **—***v.t.* **droved, drov·ing** To drive (cows, etc.) for some distance. [OE *drāf*. Akin to DRIVE.] **—drov′er** *n.*

drown (droun) *v.i.* 1. To die by suffocation with a liquid. **—***v.t.* 2. To kill by suffocation with a liquid. 3. To flood; inundate. 4. To lessen, extinguish, or muffle. [ME *drounen*]

drowse (drouz) *v.i.* **drowsed, drows·ing** To be only half awake; doze. **—***n.* The state of being half asleep; doze. [OE *drūsian* to become sluggish]

drow·sy (drou′zē) *adj.* **·si·er, ·si·est** 1. Heavy with sleepiness; dull. 2. Making sleepy; soporific. **—drow′si·ly** *adv.* **—drow′si·ness** *n.*

drub (drub) *v.t.* **drubbed, drub·bing** 1. To beat, as with a stick. 2. To vanquish; overcome. **—***n.* A blow; thump. [? < Arabic *darb* a beating] **—drub′ber** *n.*

drudge (druj) *v.i.* **drudged, drudg·ing** To work at drudgery. [OE *drēogan* work, labor] **—drudge, drudg′er** *n.* **—drudg′ing·ly** *adv.*

drudg·er·y (druj′ər·ē) *n. pl.* **·er·ies** Dull, wearisome, or menial work.

drug (drug) *n.* 1. Any chemical or biological substance, other than food, intended for use in the treatment, prevention, or diagnosis of disease. 2. A narcotic, stimulant, hallucinogen, etc. **—***v.t.* **drugged, drug·ging** 1. To mix drugs with (food, drink, etc.). 2. To administer drugs to. 3. To stupefy or poison with or as with drugs. [ME *drogge*]

drug·gist (drug′ist) *n.* 1. One who compounds prescriptions and sells drugs; a pharmacist. 2. One who operates a drugstore.

drug·store (drug′stôr′) *n.* A place where prescriptions are compounded, and drugs and miscellaneous merchandise are sold; pharmacy.

dru·id (drōō′id) *n.* *Often cap.* One of an order of priests or teachers of an ancient Celtic religion. [< L *druides* < Celtic] **—dru·id′ic** or **·i·cal** *adj.* **—dru′id·ism** *n.*

drum (drum) *n.* 1. A hollow percussion instrument, typically shaped like a cylinder or hemisphere, having a membrane stretched tightly over one or both ends, and played by beating the membrane with sticks, the hands, etc. 2. A sound produced by or as by a drum. 3. Something resembling a drum in shape; as: **a** A metal cylinder around which cable is wound. **b** A cylindrical metal container, as for oil. 4. *Anat.* The tympanic membrane. **—***v.* **drummed, drum·ming** *v.i.* 1. To beat a drum. 2. To tap or thump continuously. **—***v.t.* 3. To force upon by constant repetition. 4. To work up (business or trade) by advertising, canvassing, etc.: usu. with *up*. 5. To expel in disgrace: usu. with *out*. [Prob. < MDu. *tromme*] **—drum′mer** *n.*

drum major One who instructs or leads a band or drum corps. **—drum ma·jor·ette** (mā′jə·ret′) *fem.*

drum·stick (drum′stik′) *n.* 1. A stick for beating a drum. 2. The lower joint of the leg of a cooked fowl.

drunk (drungk) Past participle of DRINK. **—***adj.* Affected with or as with alcoholic drink; intoxicated. **—***n.* *Informal* 1. One who is drunk. 2. A drunkard. 3. A bout of drinking; binge.

drunk·ard (drungk′ərd) *n.* One who habitually drinks alcoholic beverages to excess.

drunk·en (drungk′ən) *adj.* 1. Habitually drunk. 2. Relating to or caused by a drunken state. **—drunk′en·ness** *n.* **—drunk′en·ly** *adv.*

drupe (drōōp) *n.* *Bot.* A soft, fleshy fruit, as a peach or cherry, enclosing a hard-shelled stone or seed. [< L *drupa* (*oliva*) an overripe (olive)] **—dru·pa′ceous** *adj.*

dry (drī) *adj.* **dri·er** or, occasionally, **dry·er; dri·est** or, occasionally, **dry·est.** 1. Devoid of moisture; not wet, damp, or liquid. 2. Marked by little or no rainfall. 3. Not lying under water: *dry* land. 4. Having all or nearly all the water or other liquid drained away, exhausted or evaporated. 5. Thirsty. 6. Lacking sweetness: said esp. of wines. 7. Dull; boring. 8. Crisp; quietly shrewd: *dry* humor. 9. *Informal* Opposing or prohibiting the sale of or indulgence in alcoholic beverages: a *dry* state. **—***v.* **dried, dry·ing** *v.t.* 1. To make dry. 2. To preserve (meat, fish, etc.) by removing moisture. **—***v.i.* 3. To become dry. [OE *drȳge*]

dry·ad (drī′əd, -ad) *n.* In classical mythology, a nymph dwelling in or presiding over woods and trees. [< Gk. *drys*, *dryos* tree] **—dry·ad′ic** (-ad′ik) *adj.*

dry cell *Electr.* A primary cell, the contents of which cannot be spilled.

dry-clean (drī′klēn′) *v.t.* To clean (clothing,

etc.) with solvents other than water. —**dry cleaner** —**dry cleaning**

dry dock A floating or stationary structure from which water can be removed, used for repairing and cleaning ships.

dry·er (drī′ər) Alternative comparative of DRY. —*n.* A drier.

dry·est (drī′ist) Alternative superlative of DRY.

dry-eyed (drī′īd′) *adj.* Not weeping; tearless.

dry farming In an arid country, the raising of crops without irrigation. —**dry farmer**

dry goods Textile fabrics, as distinguished from groceries, hardware, etc.

dry ice Solid carbon dioxide, having a temperature of about −110° F., widely used as a refrigerant.

dry·ly (drī′lē) *adv.* In a dry manner: also spelled *drily.*

dry measure A unit or system of units for measuring the volume of dry commodities, as fruits or grains.

dry·ness (drī′nis) *n.* The state or quality of being dry.

dry nurse A nurse who rears a child without suckling it.

dry point 1. An engraving made with a hard etching needle that incises fine lines on a metal plate without the use of acid. 2. A print made from such an engraving.

dry rot 1. A fungous disease of timber. 2. A disease of potatoes and other vegetables.

dry run 1. *Mil.* A combat exercise done without live ammunition. 2. Any trial run.

du·al (dōō′əl, dyōō′-) *adj.* 1. Denoting or relating to two. 2. Composed of two; twofold; double; binary. [< L *duo* two] —**du·al′i·ty** (-al′ə·tē) *n.*

du·al·ism (dōō′əl·iz′əm, dyōō′-) *n.* 1. The state of being twofold; duality. 2. *Philos.* The theory that the universe is composed of two principles, as mind and matter. —**du′al·ist** *n.* —**du′al·is′tic** *adj.* —**du′al·is′ti·cal·ly** *adv.*

dub[1] (dub) *v.t.* **dubbed, dub·bing** 1. To confer knighthood upon by tapping on the shoulder with a sword. 2. To name or style. [OE *dubbian*]

dub[2] (dub) *v.t.* **dubbed, dub·bing** 1. To rerecord (a record, tape, etc.) in order to make changes. 2. To insert a new sound track into (a film). [Short for DOUBLE]

du·bi·e·ty (dōō·bī′ə·tē, dyōō-) *n. pl.* **·ties** 1. The state of being dubious. 2. Something doubtful. [< L *dubius* doubtful]

du·bi·ous (dōō′bē·əs, dyōō′-) *adj.* 1. Unsettled in judgment or opinion; doubtful. 2. Causing doubt; equivocal. 3. Open to criticism, objection, or suspicion: a *dubious* reputation. [< L *dubium* doubt] —**du′bi·ous·ly** *adv.*

du·cal (dōō′kəl, dyōō′-) *adj.* Pertaining to a duke or a duchy. [< L *dux* leader]

duc·at (duk′ət) *n.* Any of several gold or silver coins, formerly used in Europe. [< Ital. *ducato* a coin with a picture of a duke]

duch·ess (duch′is) *n.* 1. The wife or widow of a duke. 2. The female sovereign of a duchy. [< L *dux* leader]

duch·y (duch′ē) *n. pl.* **duch·ies** The territory of a duke or duchess; dukedom.

duck[1] (duk) *n.* 1. Any of various aquatic birds, with webbed feet and broad bills. 2. The female of this bird. The male is called a *drake.* [OE *dūce* diver]

duck[2] (duk) *v.t.* 1. To thrust suddenly under water. 2. To lower quickly; bob, as the head. 3. *Informal* To dodge; evade; avoid. —*v.i.* 4. To submerge suddenly under water. 5. To move quickly; bob; dodge. —*n.* The act of ducking. [ME *douken, duken* to dive]

duck[3] (duk) *n.* 1. A strong linen or cotton fabric similar to canvas. 2. *pl.* Trousers made of duck. [< Du. *doek* cloth]

duck·bill (duk′bil′) *n.* A platypus.

duck·ling (duk′ling) *n.* A young duck.

duck·pin (duk′pin′) *n.* 1. A small pin used in a variation of the game of tenpins. 2. *pl.* (*construed as sing.*) The game played with such pins.

duct (dukt) *n.* 1. Any tube, canal, or passage by which a liquid, gas, etc., is conveyed. 2. *Anat.* A tubular passage by which a secretion is carried away. [< L *ducere* to lead]

duc·tile (duk′təl) *adj.* 1. Capable of being drawn out into wire or otherwise subjected to stress without breaking, as certain metals. 2. Easily molded or shaped; plastic. 3. Ready to obey; easily led. [< L *ducere* to lead] —**duc·til·i·ty** (duk·til′ə·tē) *n.*

duct·less gland (dukt′lis) *Physiol.* A gland that releases its secretions directly into the blood or lymph; an endocrine gland.

dud (dud) *n.* 1. *Mil.* A bomb or shell that fails to explode. 2. *Informal* A failure; flop. [< Du. *dood* dead]

dude (dōōd, dyōōd) *n.* 1. A dandy; fop. 2. *Informal* A city person; esp., an Easterner vacationing on a ranch. 3. *Slang* A fellow. [Origin unknown] —**dud′ish** *adj.*

dude ranch A ranch operated as a resort.

dudg·eon (duj′ən) *n.* Sullen displeasure; resentment. [Origin unknown]

duds (dudz) *n.pl. Informal* 1. Clothing. 2. Belongings in general. [ME *dudde* cloak]

due (dōō, dyōō) *adj.* 1. Subject to demand for payment, esp. because of the arrival of a stipulated date. 2. That should be rendered or given; proper. 3. Adequate; sufficient. 4. Appointed or expected to arrive, be present, or be ready: The bus is *due.* 5. That may be charged or attributed; ascribable: with *to.* —**due to** *Informal* Because of; on account of. —*n.* 1. That which is owed or rightfully required; a debt. 2. *pl.* Charge or fee. —*adv.* Directly: *due* east. [< OF *deü,* pp. of *devoir* to owe < L *debere*]

du·el (dōō′əl, dyōō′-) *n.* A prearranged combat between two persons, usu. fought with deadly weapons. —*v.t. & v.i.* **du·eled** or **·elled, du·el·ing** or **·el·ling** To fight in a duel. [< L *duellum,* earliest form of *bellum* war] —**du′el·er** or **du′el·ler, du′el·ist** or **du′el·list** *n.*

du·en·na (dōō·en′ə, dyōō-) *n.* 1. In Spain and Portugal, an elderly woman who serves as a companion and protector to a young girl. 2. A chaperon. [< Sp. < L *domina* lady]

du·et (dōō·et′, dyōō-) *n.* A musical composition for two performers. [< Ital. < L *duo* two]

duff (duf) *n.* A thick flour pudding boiled in a cloth bag. [Var. of DOUGH]

duf·fel (duf′əl) *n.* 1. A coarse woolen fabric. 2. Equipment or supplies. Also **duf′fle.** [after *Duffel,* a town near Antwerp]

duffel bag A sack used to carry clothing and personal possessions. Also **duffle bag.**

dug[1] (dug) Past tense and past participle of DIG.

dug[2] (dug) *n.* A teat or udder. [Cf. Dan. *dægge* to suckle]

du·gong (dōō′gong) *n.* A herbivorous marine mammal of warm seas, having flippers and a paddlelike tail: also called *sea cow.* [< Malay *duyong*]

dug·out (dug′out′) *n.* **1.** A canoe made by hollowing out a log. **2.** An excavated shelter for protection against storms, bombs, etc. **3.** In baseball, a structure in which team members sit when not at bat or in the field.

duke (dōōk, dyōōk) *n.* **1.** In Great Britain and certain other European countries, a nobleman ranking immediately below a prince and above a marquis. **2.** A European prince ruling over a duchy. [< L *dux* leader] **—duke′dom** *n.*

dul·cet (dul′sit) *adj.* Pleasing to the ear; soothing. [< OF dim. of *douz* sweet < L *dulcis*]

dul·ci·mer (dul′sə·mər) *n.* A stringed instrument played with two padded hammers or plucked with the fingers. [< LL *dulcis* sweet + *melos* a song]

dull (dul) *adj.* **1.** Lacking in intelligence or understanding; stupid. **2.** Without spirit; listless. **3.** Having a blunt edge or point. **4.** Exciting little or no interest; boring. **5.** Not acute or intense. **6.** Cloudy; gloomy. **7.** Not bright, clear, or vivid. **—***v.t.* & *v.i.* To make or become dull. [ME *dul*] **—dull′ish** *adj.* **—dull′ness** or **dul′ness** *n.* **—dul′ly** *adv.*

dull·ard (dul′ərd) *n.* A stupid person; dolt.

dulls·ville (dulz′vil′) *n. Slang* That which is boring.

dulse (duls) *n.* A reddish brown seaweed. [< Irish *duileasg*]

du·ly (dōō′lē, dyōō′-) *adv.* **1.** In due or proper manner; fitly. **2.** At the proper time. **3.** To an adequate degree.

dumb (dum) *adj.* **1.** Having no power of speech; mute. **2.** Temporarily speechless; silent. **3.** *Informal* Stupid. [OE] **—dumb′ly** *adv.* **—dumb′ness** *n.*

dumb·bell (dum′bel′) *n.* **1.** A gymnastic hand instrument used for exercising, consisting of a handle with a weighted ball at each end. **2.** *Slang* A stupid person.

dumb·wait·er (dum′wā′tər) *n.* A small elevator for conveying food, dishes, garbage, etc., between floors.

dum·dum bullet (dum′dum′) A bullet made to expand on impact and tear a gaping wound. [after *Dumdum,* a town near Calcutta, India, where first made]

dum·found (dum′found′) *v.t.* To strike dumb; confuse; amaze. Also **dumb′found′.** [Blend of DUMB and CONFOUND]

dum·my (dum′ē) *n. pl.* **·mies** **1.** A figure representing the human form; also, a large doll used by a ventriloquist. **2.** An imitation object. **3.** *Slang* A stupid person. **4.** One who seems to be acting for his own interests while secretly representing another. **5.** *Printing* **a** A sample book or magazine, usu. blank. **b** A model page form, made up of proofs pasted into position. **6.** In certain card games, esp. bridge, an exposed hand played in addition to his own by the person sitting opposite it. **—***adj.* Sham; counterfeit.

dump (dump) *v.t.* **1.** To drop or throw down. **2.** To empty out, as from a container. **3.** To empty (a container), as by overturning. **4.** To throw away, as rubbish. **5.** To put up (goods) for sale cheaply and in large quantities, esp. in a foreign market. **—to dump on** *Slang* To speak disparagingly of or to. **—***n.* **1.** A dumping area, as for rubbish. **2.** *Mil.* A temporary storage place for ammunition and supplies. **3.** *Slang* A shabby place. [ME < Scand.]

dump·ling (dump′ling) *n.* **1.** A ball of dough filled with fruit, ground meat, etc. and baked, steamed, or fried. **2.** A small mass of dough dropped into boiling soup or stew.

dumps (dumps) *n.pl.* A gloomy state of mind: now only in the phrase **in the dumps.** [Cf. MDu. *domp* haze]

dump truck A truck for hauling gravel, coal, etc., that unloads by tilting back the cargo bin and opening the tailboard.

dump·y (dump′ē) *adj.* **dump·i·er, dump·i·est** Short and thick; squat. **—dump′i·ness** *n.*

dun[1] (dun) *v.t.* & *v.i.* **dunned, dun·ning** To press (a debtor) for payment. **—***n.* A demand for payment. [Prob. var. of DIN]

dun[2] (dun) *adj.* Of a grayish brown or reddish brown color. [OE *dunn*] **—dun** *n.*

dunce (duns) *n.* A stupid or ignorant person. [Earlier *Dunsman,* a follower of John *Duns* Scotus]

dunce cap A conical cap, formerly placed on the head of a dull student. Also **dunce's cap.**

dun·der·head (dun′dər·hed′) *n.* A stupid person. [? < dial. E (Scot.) *dunder* thunder + HEAD] **—dun′der·head′ed** *adj.*

dune (dōōn, dyōōn) *n.* A hill of loose sand heaped up by the wind. [< MDu.]

dune buggy A motorized vehicle with broad tires permitting use on loose sand: also called *beach buggy.*

dung (dung) *n.* **1.** Animal excrement; manure. **2.** Anything foul. [OE]

dun·ga·ree (dung′gə·rē′) *n.* **1.** A coarse cotton cloth used for work clothes, tents, etc. **2.** *pl.* Trousers or overalls made of this fabric. [< Hind. *dungrī*]

dung beetle Any of various beetles that breed in dung.

dun·geon (dun′jən) *n.* **1.** A dark confining prison or cell, esp. one underground. **2.** A donjon. [< DONJON]

dung·hill (dung′hil′) *n.* A heap of manure.

dunk (dungk) *v.t.* & *v.i.* To dip (bread, etc.) into tea, coffee, etc. [< G *tunken* to dip]

dun·lin (dun′lin) *n.* A sandpiper having in summer plumage a black belly and a reddish back. [< DUN[2] + -LING[1]]

dun·nage (dun′ij) *n.* **1.** *Naut.* Mats and battens used to protect cargo. **2.** Baggage.

du·o (dōō′ō, dyōō′ō) *n. pl.* **du·os** or **du·i** (-ē) *Music* An instrumental duet. [< Ital. < L *duo* two]

duo- *combining form* Two. [< L *duo*]

du·o·dec·i·mal (dōō′ō·des′ə·məl, dyōō′-) *adj.* **1.** Pertaining to twelfth or twelfths. **2.** Reckoning by twelves. [< L *duodecim* twelve]

du·o·de·num (dōō′ə·dē′nəm, dyōō′-) *n. pl.* **·na** (-nə) *Anat.* The first section of the small intestine extending below the stomach. [< Med.L *duodenum* (*digitorum*) of twelve (fingers); with ref. to its length] **—du′o·de′nal** *adj.*

du·o·logue (do͞o′ə·lôg, -log, dyo͞o′-) *n.* 1. A dramatic piece for two performers. 2. A dialogue. Also **du′o·log.**

dupe (do͞op, dyo͞op) *n.* One who is easily deceived or misled. —*v.t.* **duped, dup·ing** To make a dupe of; deceive. [< F < MF *duppe*] —**dup′er** *n.* —**dup′er·y** *n.*

du·ple (do͞o′pəl, dyo͞o′-) *adj.* Double. [< L *duplus*]

du·plex (do͞o′pleks, dyo͞o′-) *adj.* Having two parts; twofold. —*n.* A two-floor apartment, or a two-family house. [< L *duo* two + stem of *plicare* to fold] —**du·plex′i·ty** *n.*

du·pli·cate (*adj.* & *n.* do͞o′plə·kit, dyo͞o′-; *v.* do͞o′plə·kāt, dyo͞o′-) *adj.* 1. Made like or corresponding exactly to an original: a *duplicate* key. 2. Growing or existing in pairs. —*n.* 1. An exact copy. 2. A double or counterpart. —*v.t.* **·cat·ed, ·cat·ing** 1. To copy exactly; reproduce. 2. To do a second time. [< L *duplex* twofold] —**du′pli·cate·ly** *adv.* —**du′pli·ca′tion** *n.* —**du′pli·ca′tive** *adj.*

du·pli·ca·tor (do͞o′plə·kā′tər, dyo͞o′-) *n.* A mechanical device for making duplicates.

du·plic·i·ty (do͞o·plis′ə·tē, dyo͞o-) *n. pl.* **·ties** Tricky deceitfulness. [< L *duplex* twofold]

du·ra·ble (do͝or′ə·bəl, dyo͝or′-) *adj.* Able to withstand decay or wear. [< L *durus* hard] —**du′ra·bil′i·ty** *n.*

du·ra ma·ter (do͝or′ə mā′tər, dyo͝or′ə) *Anat.* The tough fibrous membrane forming the outermost covering of the brain and spinal cord. Also **du′ra.** [< L *dura* hard + *mater* mother] —**du′ral** *adj.*

du·ra·men (do͝o·rā′min, dyo͝o-) *n. Bot.* The darker central portion of a tree trunk: also called *heartwood.* [< L, a ligneous vine branch]

dur·ance (do͝or′əns, dyo͝or′-) *n.* Forced imprisonment. [< L *durare* to endure]

du·ra·tion (do͝o·rā′shən, dyo͝o-) *n.* 1. The period of time during which anything lasts. 2. Continuance in time. [< L *durare* to endure]

du·ress (do͝o·res′, dyo͝o-) *n.* 1. Constraint by force or fear; compulsion. 2. *Law* **a** Coercion. **b** Imprisonment without full legal sanction. [< L *durus* hard]

dur·ing (do͝or′ing, dyo͝or′-) *prep.* 1. Throughout the time, existence, or action of. 2. In the course of; at some period in. [ME < ppr. of *duren* to endure]

dur·ra (do͝or′ə) *n.* A variety of sorghum of Asia and Africa: also **du′ra.** Also **durr** (do͝or). [< Arabic *dhura*]

du·rum (do͝or′əm, dyo͝or′-) *n.* A species of wheat widely grown for macaroni products. [< L *durus* hard]

dusk (dusk) *n.* The partial darkness between day and night, usu. considered darker than twilight. —*adj.* Somewhat dark or dim; shadowy. [OE *dox*]

dusk·y (dus′kē) *adj.* **dusk·i·er, dusk·i·est** 1. Dim; obscure. 2. Rather dark in shade or coloring; swarthy. 3. Gloomy. —**dusk′i·ness** *n.*

dust (dust) 1. Earthy matter reduced to particles so fine as to be easily borne in the air. 2. Any fine powder. 3. Earth, esp. as the receptacle of the dead. 4. The disintegrated remains of a human body. —**to bite the dust** To be killed or injured. —**to throw dust in someone's eyes** To deceive. —*v.t.* 1. To wipe or brush dust from. 2. To sprinkle with powder, insecticide, etc. 3. To sprinkle (powder, etc.) over something. —*v.i.* 4. To wipe or brush dust from furniture, etc. [OE *dūst*]

dust bowl An area subject to dust storms and drought.

dust·er (dus′tər) *n.* 1. One who or that which dusts. 2. An outer garment worn to protect clothing from dust.

dust jacket A removable paper cover that protects a book: also called *book jacket.*

dust·pan (dust′pan′) *n.* An implement into which dust from a floor is swept.

dust storm A windstorm of arid regions that carries clouds of dust with it.

dust·y (dus′tē) *adj.* **dust·i·er, dust·i·est** 1. Covered with or as with dust. 2. Like dust; powdery. 3. Having a grayish or dull cast: *dusty* pink. —**dust′i·ness** *n.*

Dutch (duch) *adj.* Of or relating to the Netherlands, its people, culture, or language. —*n.* 1. The people of the Netherlands: preceded by *the.* 2. The language of the Netherlands. 3. Pennsylvania Dutch. —**in Dutch** *Informal* In trouble or disgrace. —**to go Dutch** *Informal* To have each participant in a meal or entertainment pay his own expenses. [< MDu. *dutsch* Germanic]

Dutch door A door divided horizontally in the middle.

Dutch·man (duch′mən) *n. pl.* **·men** (-mən) A native of the Netherlands.

dutch·man's-breech·es (duch′mənz·brich′iz) *n. sing.* & *pl.* A low herb with widely spreading spurs. Also **dutch′mans·breech′es.**

Dutch oven A heavy pot with a tight-fitting cover, used for meats, stews, etc.

Dutch treat *Informal* An entertainment or meal at which each person pays his own bill.

Dutch uncle A very frank and severe critic or adviser.

du·te·ous (do͞o′tē·əs, dyo͞o′-) *adj.* Obedient; dutiful. —**du′te·ous·ly** *adv.*

du·ti·ful (do͞o′ti·fəl, dyo͞o′-) *adj.* 1. Performing one's duties; obedient. 2. Expressive of a sense of duty; respectful. —**du′ti·ful·ly** *adv.* —**du′ti·ful·ness** *n.*

du·ty (do͞o′tē, dyo͞o′-) *n. pl.* **·ties** 1. That which one is morally, professionally, or legally bound to do; obligation. 2. Specific obligatory service, esp. of military personnel. 3. A tax on imported or exported goods. —**off duty** Temporarily not at work. [See DUE.]

dwarf (dwôrf) *n.* A human being, animal, or plant that is stunted in its growth. —*v.t.* 1. To prevent the natural development of; stunt. 2. To cause to appear small or less by comparison. —*adj.* Diminutive; stunted. [OE *dweorh*] —**dwarf′ish** *adj.* —**dwarf′ish·ness** *n.*

dwell (dwel) *v.i.* **dwelt** or **dwelled, dwell·ing** 1. To have a fixed abode; reside. 2. To linger, as on a subject: with *on* or *upon.* 3. To continue in a state or place. [OE *dwellan* to go astray] —**dwell′er** *n.*

dwell·ing (dwel′ing) *n.* A place of residence.

dwin·dle (dwin′dəl) *v.t.* & *v.i.* **·dled, ·dling** To diminish or become less; make or become smaller. [OE *dwīnan* to waste away]

dye (dī) *v.* **dyed, dye·ing** *v.t.* 1. To fix a color in (cloth, hair, etc.), esp. by soaking in liquid coloring matter. —*v.i.* 2. To take or give color. —*n.* A coloring matter used for dyeing; also, the color so produced. [OE *dēagian* to dye < *dēag* dye] **—dy′er** *n.*

dyed-in-the-wool (dīd′in·thə·wo͝ol′) *adj.* 1. Dyed before being woven. 2. Thoroughgoing.

dye·ing (dī′ing) *n.* The act of fixing colors in cloth, etc.

dye·stuff (dī′stuff′) *n.* Any material used for dyeing.

dy·ing (dī′ing) *adj.* 1. Near death; expiring. 2. Coming to a close; destined to end. 3. Given, uttered, or manifested just before death. **—***n.* Death.

dyke (dīk) See DIKE.

dyna- *combining form* Power. Also, before vowels, **dyn-**. [< Gk. *dynamis*]

dy·nam·ic (dī·nam′ik) *adj.* 1. Of or pertaining to forces not in equilibrium, or to motion as the result of force: opposed to *static.* 2. Pertaining to dynamics. 3. Characterized by energy or forcefulness. [< Gk. *dynamis* power] **—dy·nam′i·cal·ly** *adv.*

dy·nam·ics (dī·nam′iks) *n.pl.* (*construed as sing. or pl.*) 1. The branch of physics that treats of the motion of bodies and the effects of forces in producing motion, including kinetics. 2. The forces at work in any field.

dy·na·mite (dī′nə·mīt) *n.* 1. An explosive composed of nitroglycerin held in some absorbent substance. 2. *Slang* Anything wonderful. **—***v.t.* **·mit·ed, ·mit·ing** To blow up or shatter with or as with dynamite. [< Gk. *dynamis* power]

dy·na·mo (dī′nə·mō) *n. pl.* **·mos** A generator for the conversion of mechanical energy into electrical energy.

dy·na·mom·e·ter (dī′nə·mom′ə·tər) *n.* An instrument for measuring force or power.

dy·nast (dī′nast, -nəst) *n.* A ruler, esp. a hereditary one. [< Gk. *dynasthai* to be powerful]

dy·nas·ty (dī′nəs·tē) *n. pl.* **·ties** A succession of sovereigns in one line of descent; also, the length of time during which one family is in power. **—dy·nas·tic** (dī·nas′tik) *adj.* **—dy·nas′ti·cal·ly** *adv.*

dyne (dīn) *n. Physics* The fundamental unit of force in the cgs system that, if applied to a mass of one gram, would give it an acceleration of one centimeter per second per second. [< Gk. *dynamis* power]

dys·en·ter·y (dis′ən·ter′ē) *n. Pathol.* A painful inflammation of the large intestine, attended with bloody evacuations and some fever. [< Gk. *dys-* bad + *enteron* intestine] **—dys′en·ter′ic** *adj.*

dys·pep·sia (dis·pep′shə, -sē·ə) *n.* Difficult or painful digestion. [< Gk. *dys-* hard + *peptein* to cook, digest]

dys·pep·tic (dis·pep′tik) *adj.* 1. Relating to or suffering from dyspepsia. 2. Gloomy; peevish. Also **dys·pep′ti·cal.** **—***n.* A dyspeptic person. **—dys·pep′ti·cal·ly** *adv.*

dysp·ne·a (disp′nē·ə) *n. Pathol.* Labored breathing. [< Gk. *dys-* hard + *pneein* to breathe] **—dysp·ne′al, dysp·ne′ic** *adj.*

dys·pro·si·um (dis·prō′sē·əm, -shē-) *n.* A highly magnetic element (symbol Dy) of the lanthanide series. [< Gk. *dys-* hard + *prosienai* to approach]

dys·to·pi·a (dis·tō′pē·ə) *n.* A place of utter wretchedness. [< Gk. *dys-* hard + *-topos* place, after *Utopia*]

E

e, E (ē) *n. pl.* **e's** or **es, E's** or **Es, ees** (ēz) 1. The fifth letter of the English alphabet. 2. Any sound represented by the letter *e.* —*symbol* 1. *Music* The third tone in the diatonic scale of C. 2. *Math.* The base of the system of natural logarithms, approximately 2.718.

each (ēch) *adj.* Being one of two or more that together form a group; every. —*pron.* Every one of any number or group considered individually; each one. —*adv.* For or to each person, article, etc.; apiece: one dollar *each.* [OE *ǣlc* < *ā* ever + *gelīc* alike]

each other A compound reciprocal pronoun: They saw *each other.*

ea·ger (ē′gər) *adj.* Impatiently desirous of something. [ME *egre* < L *acer* sharp] —**ea′·ger·ly** *adv.* —**ea′ger·ness** *n.*

ea·gle (ē′gəl) *n.* 1. A large bird of prey, esp. the **bald** (or **American**) **eagle,** dark brown, with the head, neck, and tail white, the national emblem of the U.S. ◆Collateral adjective: *aquiline.* 2. A former gold coin of the U.S. having a value of $10. 3. In golf, a score of two under par on any hole. [< OF *egle, aigle* < L *aquila*]

ea·gle-eyed (ē′gəl·īd′) *adj.* Having keen sight.

ea·glet (ē′glit) *n.* A young eagle.

-ean Var. of -AN.

ear[1] (ir) *n.* 1. The organ of hearing in its entirety. ◆Collateral adjective: *aural.* 2. The fleshy or cartilaginous external part of the organ of hearing. 3. The ability to perceive the refinements of music, poetry, or the like. 4. Attentive consideration; heed. 5. Something resembling the ear. [OE *ēare*]

ear[2] (ir) *n.* The fruit-bearing part of a cereal plant, as corn. —*v.i.* To form ears, as grain. [OE *ēar*]

ear·ache (ir′āk′) *n.* Pain in the middle or internal ear.

ear·drum (ir′drum′) *n.* The tympanic membrane.

eared (ird) *adj.* Having ears or earlike appendages.

earl (ûrl) *n.* A member of the British nobility next in rank above a viscount and below a marquis. [OE *eorl* nobleman] —**earl′dom** *n.*

ear lobe The fleshy lower part of the external ear.

ear·ly (ûr′lē) *adj.* **·li·er, ·li·est** 1. Coming near the beginning of a period of time or a series: an *early* American painting. 2. Belonging to a distant time or stage of development: *early* man. 3. Occurring ahead of the usual or arranged time: an *early* dinner. 4. Occurring in the near future: An *early* truce is expected. —*adv.* 1. Near the beginning of any specified period or series of things. 2. Far back in time. 3. Before the usual or arranged time. [OE *ǣrlīce*] —**ear′li·ness** *n.*

ear·mark (ir′märk′) *n.* 1. A distinctive mark made on an animal's ear to denote ownership. 2. Any mark of identification. —*v.t.* 1. To put an earmark on. 2. To set aside, as money, for a particular purpose.

earn (ûrn) *v.t.* 1. To receive or deserve as recompense for labor, service, or performance. 2. To produce as profit. [OE *earnian*]

ear·nest[1] (ûr′nist) *adj.* 1. Intent and direct in purpose; zealous: an *earnest* student. 2. Of a serious or important nature. —**in earnest** With serious intent or determination. [OE *earnoste*] —**ear′nest·ly** *adv.* —**ear′·nest·ness** *n.*

ear·nest[2] (ûr′nist) *n. Law* Money paid in advance to bind a contract. Also **earnest money.** [Prob. < OF *erres,* ult. < Hebrew *ērābōn* pledge]

earn·ings (ûr′ningz) *n.pl.* Wages or profits.

ear·phone (ir′fōn′) *n.* A radio or telephone device held at or inserted into the ear.

ear·ring (ir′ring′) *n.* An ornament worn at the ear lobe.

ear·shot (ir′shot′) *n.* The distance at which sounds may be heard.

earth (ûrth) *n.* 1. The dry land surface of the globe, as distinguished from the oceans and sky; ground. 2. Soil; dirt. 3. The planet on which man dwells. —**to run to earth** To hunt down and find, as a fox. [OE *eorthe*]

Earth (ûrth) *n.* The planet fifth in order of size, having an area of about 196 million square miles and a mass of 6.57 sextillion tons (6.57×10^{21}).

earth·bound (ûrth′bound′) *adj.* 1. Having material interests. 2. Confined to the earth.

earth·en (ûr′thən) *adj.* Made of earth or baked clay.

earth·en·ware (ûr′thən·wâr′) *n.* Dishes, pots, and the like, made of baked clay.

earth·ling (ûrth′ling) *n.* An earth dweller.

earth·ly (ûrth′lē) *adj.* 1. **a** Of or relating to the earth; terrestrial. **b** Of or relating to the material qualities of the earth; worldly; secular. 2. Possible; imaginable: of no *earthly* use. —**earth′li·ness** *n.*

earth·quake (ûrth′kwāk′) *n.* A shaking of the earth's crust. ◆Collateral adjective: *seismic.*

earth science Any of a group of sciences concerned with origin, structure, composition, and physical features of the earth, as geology, geography, etc.

earth·shak·ing (ûrth′shā′king) *adj.* Of great importance or having great effect; momentous.

earth·ward (ûrth′wərd) *adv.* Toward the

earth. Also **earth′wards.** —*adj.* Moving toward the earth.
earth·work (ûrth′wûrk′) *n.* *Mil.* A fortification made largely or wholly of earth.
earth·worm (ûrth′wûrm′) *n.* Any burrowing worm.
earth·y (ûr′thē) *adj.* **earth·i·er, earth·i·est** 1. Of or like earth. 2. Unrefined; coarse. 3. Natural; robust; lusty. —**earth′i·ness** *n.*
ear·wax (ir′waks′) *n.* A waxy secretion found in the outer ear: also called *cerumen.*
ear·wig (ir′wig′) *n.* An insect with horny forewings and a tail pair of forceps. [OE *ēarwicga*]
ease (ēz) *n.* 1. Freedom from physical discomfort or mental agitation. 2. Freedom from great effort or difficulty. 3. Naturalness; poise. —*v.* **eased, eas·ing** *v.t.* 1. To relieve or lessen pain or oppression of. 2. To lessen the pressure, weight, tension, etc., of: to *ease* an axle. 3. To make easier; facilitate. 4. To put in place slowly and carefully. —*v.i.* 5. To lessen in severity, tension, speed, etc.: often with *up* or *off.* [< OF *aise* < L *adjacens, -entis* close at hand]
ea·sel (ē′zəl) *n.* A folding frame or tripod used to support an artist's canvas, etc. [< Du. *ezel* easel, orig., an ass]
ease·ment (ēz′mənt) *n.* 1. Anything that gives ease or comfort. 2. *Law* The right to use another's property.
east (ēst) *n.* 1. The direction of the sun in relation to an observer on earth at sunrise. 2. One of the four cardinal points of the compass, directly opposite *west.* 3. *Sometimes cap.* Any region east of a specified point. —**the East** 1. Asia and its adjacent islands; the Orient. 2. The eastern U.S. —*adj.* 1. To, toward, facing, or in the east. 2. Coming from the east. —*adv.* In or toward the east. [OE *ēast*]
east·bound (ēst′bound′) *adj.* Going eastward.
East·er (ēs′tər) *n.* 1. A Christian festival commemorating the resurrection of Christ. 2. The day on which this festival is celebrated, the Sunday immediately after the first full moon that occurs on or after the spring equinox, usu. March 21: also **Easter Sunday.** [OE *Eastre* goddess of spring]
east·er·ly (ēs′tər·lē) *adj.* 1. In, of, toward, or pertaining to the east. 2. From the east, as a wind. —*adv.* Toward or from the east. —*n.* *pl.* **·lies** A wind or storm from the east.
east·ern (ēs′tərn) *adj.* 1. To, toward, or in the east. 2. Native to or inhabiting the east. 3. *Sometimes cap.* Of or like the east or the East.
Eastern Church 1. The church of the Byzantine Empire, including the patriarchates of Constantinople, Alexandria, Antioch, and Jerusalem, that separated from the Western Church in 1054. 2. The Eastern Orthodox Church.
east·ern·er (ēs′tərn·ər) *n.* 1. One who is native to or lives in the east. 2. *Usu. cap.* One who lives in or comes from the eastern U.S.
Eastern Hemisphere See under HEMISPHERE.
Eastern Orthodox Church The modern churches derived from the medieval Eastern Church, including the Greek and Russian Orthodox churches: also called *Eastern Church, Orthodox Church.*
east·ward (ēst′wərd) *adv.* Toward the east. Also **east′wards.** —*adj.* To, toward, facing, or in the east.
eas·y (ē′zē) *adj.* **eas·i·er, eas·i·est** 1. Requiring little effort; offering few difficulties: an *easy* task. 2. Free from trouble or anxiety: an *easy* mind. 3. Characterized by rest or comfort: an *easy* life. 4. Informal; relaxed: an *easy* manner. 5. Not strict; indulgent. 6. Not burdensome; moderate: to buy on *easy* terms. 7. Well-to-do; affluent: in *easy* circumstances. —**to be on easy street** *Informal* To be well-to-do; live in comfort. —*adv.* *Informal* In an easy manner. —**to go easy on** *Slang* 1. To use with moderation, as liquor. 2. To be lenient with. —**to take it easy** *Informal* 1. To relax. 2. To remain calm. [< OF *aiser* to put at ease] —**eas′i·ly** *adv.* —**eas′i·ness** *n.*
eas·y·go·ing (ē′zē·gō′ing) *adj.* Not inclined to effort or worry.
eat (ēt) *v.* **ate, eat·en, eat·ing** *v.t.* 1. To consume food. 2. To consume or destroy as by eating: usu. with *away* or *up.* 3. To make (a hole, etc.) by gnawing or corroding. —*v.i.* 4. To take food; have a meal. [OE *etan*] —**eat′er** *n.*
eau de Co·logne (ō′ də kə·lōn′) Cologne, a toilet water.
eaves (ēvz) *n.* (*orig. sing., now construed as pl.*) The lower projecting edge of a sloping roof. [OE *efes* edge]
eaves·drop (ēvz′drop′) *v.i.* **·dropped, ·drop·ping** To listen secretly, as to a private conversation. —**eaves′drop′per** *n.*
ebb (eb) *v.i.* 1. To recede, as the tide: opposed to *flow.* 2. To decline or weaken. —*n.* 1. The flowing back of tidewater to the ocean: opposed to *flood.* Also **ebb tide.** 2. A condition of decline or decay. [OE *ebbian*]
eb·on·ite (eb′ən·īt) *n.* Vulcanite, a rubber product.
eb·on·y (eb′ən·ē) *n.* *pl.* **·ies** A hard, heavy wood, usu. black; also a tropical hardwood tree yielding this wood. —*adj.* 1. Made of ebony. 2. Like ebony; black. [< Egyptian *hebni*]
e·bul·lient (i·bul′yənt) *adj.* 1. Full of enthusiasm; exuberant. 2. Boiling or bubbling up. [< L *e-* out + *bullire* to boil] —**e·bul′lient·ly** *adv.* —**e·bul′lience** *n.*
eb·ul·li·tion (eb′ə·lish′ən) *n.* 1. The bubbling of a liquid; boiling. 2. Any sudden or violent agitation, as of emotions.
ec·cen·tric (ek·sen′trik) *adj.* 1. Differing conspicuously in behavior, appearance, or opinions. 2. Not situated in the center, as an axis. 3. Deviating from a perfect circle: said chiefly of an elliptical orbit. 4. *Math.* Not having the same center. —*n.* An odd or erratic person. [< Gk. *ek-* out, away + *kentron* center] —**ec·cen′tri·cal·ly** *adv.*
ec·cen·tric·i·ty (ek′sen·tris′ə·tē) *n.* *pl.* **·ties** 1. Deviation from what is regular or expected. 2. A peculiarity.
Ec·cle·si·as·tes (i·klē′zē·as′tēz) *n.* A book of the Old Testament. [< Gk. *ekklēsiastēs,* trans. of Hebrew *qōhēleth* preacher]
ec·cle·si·as·tic (i·klē′zē·as′tik) *adj.* Ecclesiastical. —*n.* A cleric; churchman. [< Gk. *ek-* out + *kaleein* to call]

ec·cle·si·as·ti·cal (i·klē′zē·as′ti·kəl) *adj.* Of or pertaining to the church, esp. as an organized and governing power. —**ec·cle′si·as′ti·cal·ly** *adv.*

ech·e·lon (esh′ə·lon) *n.* 1. A stepped formation of troops, ships, or airplanes. 2. *Mil.* A subdivision of a military force, based on position. 3. A level in an organization; also, the persons at this level. [< F *échelon* < *échelle* ladder]

e·chid·na (i·kid′nə) *n.* *pl.* **·nae** (-nē) An egg-laying mammal of Australia, having spines and fur: also called *spiny anteater.* [< Gk., viper]

e·chi·no·derm (i·kī′nə·dûrm) *n.* A marine animal having a radial body and a hard, spiny shell, as the starfish.

ech·o (ek′ō) *n.* *pl.* **ech·oes** 1. The repetition of a sound caused by reflection; also, the sound so produced. 2. Any similar repetition or reproduction. 3. One who imitates another or repeats his words. —*v.t.* 1. To repeat or send back (sound) by echo. 2. To repeat the words, opinions, etc., of. 3. To repeat in imitation. —*v.i.* 4. To be repeated or given back. [< Gk. *ēchē* sound, noise] —**ech′o·er** *n.*

é·clair (ā·klâr′, i·klâr′) *n.* A small oblong pastry shell filled with custard or whipped cream. [< F, lit., flash of lightning]

é·clat (ā·klä′, i·klä′) *n.* 1. Brilliance of action or effect. 2. Acclaim; conspicuous success. [< F < *éclater* to burst out]

ec·lec·tic (ek·lek′tik, ik-) *adj.* 1. Selecting what is considered best from different systems or sources. 2. Composed of elements selected from diverse sources. —*n.* One who selects from various schools or methods, as in philosophy or art. [< Gk. *ek-* out + *legein* to select] —**ec·lec·ti·cism** (ek·lek′tə·siz′əm) *n.*

e·clipse (i·klips′) *n.* 1. *Astron.* The dimming or elimination of light from one heavenly body by another. A **lunar eclipse** is caused by the passage of the moon through the earth's shadow; a **solar eclipse** by the passage of the moon between the sun and the observer. 2. Any overshadowing or dimming, as of power or reputation. —*v.t.* **e·clipsed, e·clips·ing** 1. To cause an eclipse of; darken. 2. To obscure by overshadowing or surpassing. [< Gk. *ek-* out + *leipein* to leave]

e·clip·tic (i·klip′tik, ē-) *n.* *Astron.* The apparent path of the sun among the stars. —*adj.* Pertaining to eclipses or to the ecliptic: also **e·clip′ti·cal.**

ec·logue (ek′lôg, -log) *n.* A short pastoral poem. [< Gk. *ek-* out + *legein* to select]

e·co·cide (ē′kō·sīd, ek′ō-) *n.* 1. The destruction of an ecosystem. 2. That which is capable of destroying an ecosystem. [< Gk. *oikos* home + -CIDE] —**e′co·ci′dal** *adj.*

e·col·o·gy (i·kol′ə·jē, ē-) *n.* The division of biology that treats of the relations between organisms and their environment. [< Gk. *oikos* home + -LOGY] —**ec·o·log·ic** (ek′ə·loj′ik) or **·i·cal** *adj.* —**ec′o·log′i·cal·ly** *adv.* —**e·col′o·gist** *n.*

ec·o·nom·ic (ek′ə·nom′ik, ē′kə-) *adj.* 1. Of or pertaining to the development and management of the material wealth of a community. 2. Relating to the science of economics. 3. Of or pertaining to financial matters. 4. Of practical use.

ec·o·nom·i·cal (ek′ə·nom′i·kəl, ē′kə-) *adj.* 1. Frugal; thrifty. 2. Done with minimum waste of money, energy, time, etc. 3. Economic. —**ec′o·nom′i·cal·ly** *adv.*

ec·o·nom·ics (ek′ə·nom′iks, ē′kə-) *n.pl.* 1. (*construed as sing.*) The science that treats of the production, distribution, and consumption of wealth. 2. Economic matters.

e·con·o·mist (i·kon′ə·mist) *n.* A specialist in economics.

e·con·o·mize (i·kon′ə·mīz) *v.i.* **·mized, ·miz·ing** To manage thriftily. Also *Brit.* **e·con′o·mise.** —**e·con′o·miz′er** *n.*

e·con·o·my (i·kon′ə·mē) *n.* *pl.* **·mies** 1. Frugal management of money, resources, etc.; also, an example of this. 2. The administration of material resources, as of a country. 3. The distribution and interplay of resources, materials, etc., in a structure or system: the *economy* of nature. [< Gk. *oikos* house + *nemein* to manage]

e·co·sys·tem (ē′kō·sis′təm, ek′ō-) *n.* A community in nature including plants and animals and the environment, both physical and chemical, associated with them. [< Gk. *oikos* home + SYSTEM]

ec·ru (ek′rōō, ā′krōō) *adj.* Of the color of unbleached linen. Also **é′cru.** [< L *ex-* thoroughly + *crudus* raw] —**ec′ru** *n.*

ec·sta·sy (ek′stə·sē) *n.* *pl.* **·sies** 1. A state of overpowering emotion. 2. Intense delight; rapture. [< Gk. *ek-* out + *histanai* to place]

ec·stat·ic (ek·stat′ik) *adj.* 1. Of, pertaining to, or exciting to ecstasy; rapturous. 2. In a state of ecstasy; transported. —**ec·stat′i·cal·ly** *adv.*

ecto- *combining form* Outside; external: *ectoderm.* Also, before vowels, **ect-.** [< Gk. *ekto-*]

ec·to·derm (ek′tə·dûrm) *n.* *Biol.* The outermost layer in the embryo, developing into the skin, sense organs, and nervous system. —**ec′to·der′mal, ec′to·der′mic** *adj.*

ec·to·mor·phic (ek′tō·môr′fik) *adj.* Of human body types, characterized by a lean body structure. —**ec′to·morph** *n.*

-ectomy *combining form* Removal of a part by cutting out; surgical removal: *appendectomy.* [< Gk. *ek-* out + *temnein* to cut]

ec·to·plasm (ek′tə·plaz′əm) *n.* 1. *Biol.* The firm outer layer of the cytoplasm of a unicellular organism or of a plant cell. 2. A substance alleged to emanate from the body of a spiritualist medium during a trance. —**ec′to·plas′mic** *adj.*

ec·u·men·i·cal (ek′yōō·men′i·kəl) *adj.* World-wide in scope, esp. of the Christian church: an *ecumenical* council. Also **ec′u·men′ic.** [< Gk. *oikeein* to inhabit] —**ec′·u·men′i·cal·ly** *adv.*

ec·u·men·ism (ek·yōō′mən·iz′əm) *n.* The movement for world-wide unity and cooperation among all Christian churches. Also **ec·u·men·i·cal·ism** (ek′yōō·men′i·kəl·iz·əm), **ec·u·men·i·cism** (ek′yōō·men′ə·siz·əm).

ec·ze·ma (ek′sə·mə, eg′zə·mə, eg·zē′mə) *n.* *Pathol.* An inflammatory disease of the skin attended by itching, watery discharge. [< Gk. *ek-* out + *zeein* to boil]

-ed[1] *suffix* Forming the past tense of regular verbs: *walked, killed, played.* [OE *-ede, -ode, -ade*]

-ed[2] *suffix* 1. Forming the past participle of regular verbs: *washed.* 2. Forming adjectives from adjectives in *-ate*, with the same general meaning: *bipinnated.* [OE *-ed, -ad, -od*]

-ed[3] *suffix* Forming adjectives from nouns with the senses: 1. Having; characterized by: *toothed, green-eyed.* 2. Like; resembling: *bigoted.* [OE *-ede*]

E·dam (ē′dəm, ē′dam) *n.* A mild cheese in a round flattened shape, usu. coated with red paraffin.

ed·dy (ed′ē) *n. pl.* **·dies** A backward circling current of water or air. [Prob. < ON *idha*] **—ed′dy** *v.t. & v.i.* **·died, ·dy·ing**

e·del·weiss (ā′dəl·vīs) *n.* A small, perennial herb of the Alps, with white, woolly leaves. [< G *edel* noble + *weiss* white]

e·de·ma (i·dē′mə) *n. pl.* **·ma·ta** (-mə·tə) *Pathol.* An abnormal accumulation of fluid in organs, cavities, or tissues of the body; swelling. [< Gk. *oidein* to swell] **—e·dem·a·tous** (i·dem′ə·təs) *adj.*

E·den (ēd′n) *n.* 1. In the Bible, the garden that was the first home of Adam and Eve: often called *Paradise.* 2. Any delightful place or condition. [< Hebrew *ēden* delight]

e·den·tate (ē·den′tāt, i·den′-) *adj.* 1. Of or pertaining to an order of mammals, some of which lack teeth, including sloths, anteaters, and armadillos. 2. Toothless. [< L *e-* without + *dens, dentis* tooth] **—e·den′tate** *n.*

edge (ej) *n.* 1. A bounding or dividing line; also, the part along a boundary; border; margin. 2. The cutting side of a blade. 3. Sharpness; keenness. 4. *Informal* Advantage; superiority. **—on edge** 1. Tense; irritable. 2. Eager; impatient. **—***v.* **edged, edg·ing** *v.t.* 1. To sharpen. 2. To furnish with an edge or border. 3. To push sidewise or by degrees. **—***v.i.* 4. To move sidewise or by degrees. [OE *ecg*]

edge·wise (ej′wīz′) *adv.* 1. With the edge forward. 2. On, by, with, or toward the edge. Also **edge′ways′** (-wāz′).

edg·ing (ej′ing) *n.* A trimming; border.

edg·y (ej′ē) *adj.* **edg·i·er, edg·i·est** Tense, nervous, or irritable. **—edg′i·ness** *n.*

ed·i·ble (ed′ə·bəl) *adj.* Fit to eat. **—***n.* *Usu. pl.* Something fit to eat. [< L *edere* to eat] **—ed′i·bil′i·ty** *n.*

e·dict (ē′dikt) *n.* An official decree publicly proclaimed. [< L *e-* out + *dicere* to say]

ed·i·fice (ed′ə·fis) *n.* A building or other structure, esp. a large and imposing one. [< L *aedes* building + *facere* to make]

ed·i·fy (ed′ə·fī) *v.t.* **·fied, ·fy·ing** To enlighten and benefit, esp. morally or spiritually. [< L *aedes* building + *facere* to make] **—ed′i·fi·ca′tion** *n.* **—ed′i·fi′er** *n.*

ed·it (ed′it) *v.t.* 1. To prepare for publication by revising, compiling, etc. 2. To prepare (film) for viewing by selecting, cutting, etc. 3. To direct the preparation of (a newspaper, magazine, etc.). [Back formation < EDITOR]

e·di·tion (i·dish′ən) *n.* 1. The form in which a book is published: a three-volume *edition.* 2. The total number of copies of a publication issued at any one time; also, such a copy. [< L *e-* out + *dare* to give]

ed·i·tor (ed′i·tər) *n.* 1. One who edits. 2. A writer of editorials. [< L] **—ed′i·tor·ship′** *n.*

ed·i·to·ri·al (ed′i·tôr′e·əl) *n.* An article in a newspaper, magazine, etc., expressing an opinion of the editors or publishers. **—***adj.* Of, pertaining to, or written by an editor. **—ed′i·to′ri·al·ly** *adv.*

ed·i·to·ri·al·ize (ed′i·tôr′ē·əl·īz′) *v.t. & v.i.* **·ized, ·iz·ing** 1. To express opinions (on a subject) editorially. 2. To insert editorial opinions (into a news item, etc.).

ed·u·cate (ej′o͞o·kāt) *v.t.* **·cat·ed, ·cat·ing** 1. To develop or train by instruction or study; teach. 2. To form or develop (taste, special ability, etc.). 3. To provide schooling for. [< L *e-* out + *ducere* to lead] **—ed′u·ca·ble** (-kə·bəl) *adj.* **—ed′u·ca′tor** *n.*

ed·u·cat·ed (ej′o͞o·kā′tid) *adj.* 1. Developed by education; instructed; trained. 2. Having a cultivated mind, speech, manner, etc.

ed·u·ca·tion (ej′o͞o·kā′shən) *n.* 1. The act of educating; development or training of the mind, capabilities, or character, esp. through formal schooling. 2. Acquisition of knowledge or skills. 3. Knowledge, skills, or cultivation acquired through instruction or study. 4. The study of teaching methods and the learning process; pedagogy. **—ed′u·ca′·tion·al** *adj.* **—ed′u·ca′tion·al·ly** *adv.* **—ed′·u·ca′tive** *adj.*

e·duce (i·do͞os′, i·dyo͞os′) *v.t.* **e·duced, e·duc·ing** 1. To call forth; bring out; elicit. 2. To infer or develop from data; deduce. [< L *e-* out + *ducere* to lead]

-ee *suffix of nouns* 1. One who undergoes some action; opposed to *-er, -or,* as in *grantor, grantee.* 2. One who is described by the main element: *absentee.* [< AF *-é*, suffix of pp. < L *-atus*]

eel (ēl) *n. pl.* **eels or eel** A fish having a snakelike body, usu. without scales or pelvic fins. [OE *æl*] **—eel′y** *adj.*

e'en (ēn) *adv. Poetic* Even.

e'er (âr) *adv. Poetic* Ever.

-eer *suffix of nouns and verbs* One who is concerned with, works with, or makes something indicated: *engineer.* [< F *-ier* < L *-arius*]

ee·rie (ir′ē, ē′rē) *adj.* **·ri·er, ·ri·est** Inspiring fear; weird; ghostly. Also **ee′ry.** [ME *eri* timid] **—ee′ri·ly** *adv.* **—ee′ri·ness** *n.*

ef·face (i·fās′) *v.t.* **·faced, ·fac·ing** 1. To rub out; erase. 2. To obliterate. 3. To make less prominent or insignificant. [< L *ex-* out + *facies* face] **—ef·face′ment** *n.* **—ef·fac′er** *n.*

ef·fect (i·fekt′) *n.* 1. Something brought about by some cause; result; consequence. 2. Capacity to produce some result; efficacy. 3. The condition or fact of being in active force: to put a law into *effect.* 4. The state of being actually accomplished or realized. 5. The particular way in which something affects something else. 6. The overall reaction or impression produced by something. 7. A technique used to produce a certain impression. 8. Meaning; purport. 9. *pl.* Movable goods; belongings. **—in effect** 1. In actual fact. 2. For all practical purposes; virtually. 3. In active force or operation. **—***v.t.* To bring about; cause; esp., to accomplish: to *effect* an escape. [< L *ex-* out + *facere* to do, make]

ef·fec·tive (i·fek′tiv) *adj.* 1. Producing the desired or proper result. 2. Being in force, as a law. 3. Producing a striking impression. **—ef·fec′tive·ly** *adv.* **—ef·fec′·tive·ness** *n.*

ef·fec·tu·al (i·fek′cho͞o·əl) *adj.* 1. Producing

an intended effect. 2. Legally valid or binding. **—ef·fec′tu·al·ly** *adv.*
ef·fec·tu·ate (i·fek′chōō·āt) *v.t.* **·at·ed, ·at·ing** To bring about; accomplish; effect.
ef·fem·i·nate (i·fem′ə·nit) *adj.* 1. Having womanlike traits; unmanly. 2. Characterized by weakness or self-indulgence. [< L *ex-* out + *femina* a woman] **—ef·fem′·i·na·cy** *n.* **—ef·fem′i·nate·ly** *adv.*
ef·fer·ent (ef′ər·ənt) *adj. Physiol.* Carrying or carried outward: said esp. of impulses transmitted from the central nervous system to muscles, etc. [< L *ex-* out + *ferre* to carry] **—ef′fer·ent** *n.*
ef·fer·vesce (ef′ər·ves′) *v.i.* **·vesced, ·vesc·ing** 1. To give off or rise out in bubbles, as a gas. 2. To be lively or exhilarated. [< L *ex-* out + *fervescere* to boil] **—ef′fer·ves′·cence** *n.* **—ef′fer·ves′cent** *adj.*
ef·fete (i·fēt′) *adj.* 1. Having lost strength or virility. 2. Weakened; decadent. 3. Incapable of further production; barren. [< L *ex-* out + *fetus* a breeding] **—ef·fete′ly** *adv.* **—ef·fete′ness** *n.*
ef·fi·ca·cious (ef′ə·kā′shəs) *adj.* Producing an intended effect. [See EFFECT.] **—ef′·fi·ca′cious·ly** *adv.* **—ef′fi·ca′cious·ness** *n.*
ef·fi·ca·cy (ef′ə·kə·sē) *n. pl.* **·cies** Power to produce a desired or intended result.
ef·fi·cien·cy (i·fish′ən·sē) *n. pl.* **·cies** 1. The quality of being efficient. 2. The ratio of work done or energy expended to the energy supplied in the form of food or fuel.
ef·fi·cient (i·fish′ənt) *adj.* 1. Productive of results with a minimum of wasted effort. 2. Producing an effect. [See EFFECT.] **—ef·fi′cient·ly** *adv.*
ef·fi·gy (ef′ə·jē) *n. pl.* **·gies** 1. A likeness or representation; esp., a sculptured portrait. 2. A crude image of a disliked person. [< L *ex-* out + *fingere* to fashion]
ef·flo·resce (ef′lôr·es′) *v.i.* **·resced, ·resc·ing** 1. To blossom, bloom, or flower. 2. *Chem.* **a** To become powdery through evaporation of water. **b** To become covered with a powdery crust. [< L *ex-* thoroughly + *florescere* to bloom]
ef·flo·res·cence (ef′lôr·es′əns) *n.* 1. The act or season of flowering. 2. A fulfillment or culmination. 3. *Chem.* The act or process of efflorescing. 4. *Pathol.* A rash. **—ef′·flo·res′cent** *adj.*
ef·flu·ent (ef′lōō·ənt) *adj.* Flowing out. **—***n.* An outflow, as of water from a lake, industrial sewage, etc. [< L *ex-* out + *fluere* to flow] **—ef′flu·ence** *n.*
ef·flu·vi·um (i·flōō′vē·əm) *n. pl.* **·vi·a** (-vē·ə) or **·vi·ums** An invisible emanation; esp., a foul-smelling exhalation, as from decaying matter. [< L, a flowing out] **—ef·flu′vi·al** *adj.*
ef·flux (ef′luks) *n.* 1. A flowing out. 2. That which flows forth; emanation. [< L *ex-* out + *fluere* to flow]
ef·fort (ef′ərt) *n.* 1. Expenditure of physical, mechanical, or mental energy to get something done. 2. Something produced by exertion. [< L *ex-* thoroughly + *fortis* strong] **—ef′fort·less** *adj.* **—ef′fort·less·ly** *adv.*
ef·front·er·y (i·frun′tər·ē) *n. pl.* **·ies** Impudence; audacity. [< L *ex-* out + *frontis* face]
ef·ful·gent (i·ful′jənt) *adj.* Shining brilliantly; radiant; splendid. [< L *ex-* out + *fulgere* to shine] **—ef·ful′gence** *n.*
ef·fuse (i·fyōōz′) *v.i.* **·fused, ·fus·ing** 1. To pour forth. 2. To talk without stopping. [< L *ex-* out + *fundere* to pour] **—ef·fu′sion** *n.*
ef·fu·sive (i·fyōō′siv) *adj.* 1. Overflowing with sentiment; demonstrative; gushing. 2. Pouring forth; overflowing. **—ef·fu′sive·ly** *adv.* **—ef·fu′sive·ness** *n.*
e·gad (i·gad′, ē·gad′) *interj.* Used as a mild oath. Also **e·gads′**.
e·gal·i·tar·i·an (i·gal′ə·târ′ē·ən) *adj.* Of, relating to, or believing in political and social equality. **—***n.* One who believes in political and social equality. [< F *égalitaire*] **—e·gal′i·tar′i·an·ism** *n.*
egg[1] (eg) *n.* 1. The round or oval reproductive body of female birds, insects, and most reptiles and fishes, enclosed in a shell or membrane, and from which young hatch. 2. *Biol.* The reproductive cell of female animals; ovum: also **egg cell.** 3. The hen's egg as a food. 4. Something oval like a hen's egg. 5. *Slang* Person: He's a good *egg.* **—to lay an egg** *Slang* To fail completely. [< ON]
egg[2] (eg) *v.t.* To incite; urge: usu. with *on.* [< ON *eggja*]
egg·head (eg′hed′) *n. Slang* An intellectual; high-brow: often derisive.
egg·nog (eg′nog′) *n.* A drink made of beaten eggs, milk, sugar, nutmeg, and sometimes liquor.
egg·plant (eg′plant′) *n.* A widely cultivated herb with large, egg-shaped, usu. purple-skinned fruit; also the fruit, used as a vegetable.
egg·shell (eg′shel′) *n.* The hard, brittle covering of a bird's egg. **—***adj.* 1. Thin and fragile. 2. Pale yellow or ivory.
egg white The albumen of an egg.
e·gis (ē′jis) See AEGIS.
eg·lan·tine (eg′lən·tīn, -tēn) *n.* Any of various fragrant wild roses. [ME *eglentyn*]
e·go (ē′gō) *n. pl.* **e·gos** 1. The self that is aware of its distinction from the objects of its thought and perceptions. 2. *Psychoanal.* The conscious aspect of the psyche that develops through contact with the external world and resolves conflicts between the id and the superego. 3. *Informal* Self-centeredness; conceit. [< L, I]
e·go·cen·tric (ē′gō·sen′trik) *adj.* Excessively concerned with oneself. **—***n.* An egocentric person. **—e′go·cen·tric′i·ty** (-sen·tris′ə·tē) *n.*
e·go·ism (ē′gō·iz′əm) *n.* 1. Inordinate concern for oneself. 2. *Philos.* A doctrine that regards the self or self-interest as primary. **—e′go·ist** *n.* **—e′go·is′tic** or **·ti·cal** *adj.* **—e′go·is′ti·cal·ly** *adv.*
e·go·ma·ni·a (ē′gō·mā′nē·ə, -mān′yə) *n.* Abnormal or extreme egotism. **—e′go·ma′·ni·ac** *n.*
e·go·tism (ē′gə·tiz′əm) *n.* Excessive concern with or reference to oneself; conceit; selfishness. **—e′go·tist** *n.* **—e′go·tis′tic** or **·ti·cal** *adj.* **—e′go·tis′ti·cal·ly** *adv.*
ego trip *Slang* That which is self-seeking and flatters one's own vanity. **—e·go-trip** (ē′gō·trip′) *v.i.* **-tripped, -trip·ping** **—e′go-trip′per** *n.*
e·gre·gious (i·grē′jəs) *adj.* Conspicuously

bad; glaring; flagrant. [< L *e-* out + *grex, gregis* herd] —**e·gre′gious·ly** *adv.* —**e·gre′·gious·ness** *n.*

e·gress (ē′gres) *n.* 1. A going out; emergence; also, the right of going out. Also **e·gres·sion** (ē·gresh′ən). 2. A place of exit. [< L *e-* out + *gradi* to walk]

e·gret (ē′grit, eg′rit) *n.* A heron characterized in the breeding season by long and loose plumes drooping over the tail. [Var. of AIGRETTE]

E·gyp·tian (i·jip′shən) *adj.* Of or pertaining to Egypt, its people, or their culture. —*n.* 1. One of the people of Egypt. 2. The ancient Hamitic language of Egypt.

E·gyp·tol·o·gy (ē′jip·tol′ə·jē) *n.* The study of the antiquities of Egypt. —**E′gyp·tol′o·gist** *n.*

ei·der (ī′dər) *n.* A large sea duck of northern regions. [< ON *æðhr*]

ei·der·down (ī′dər·doun′) *n.* The down of the eider; also, a quilt stuffed with this down.

eight (āt) *n.* 1. The sum of seven and one: a cardinal number written 8, VIII. 2. Anything consisting of eight units. [OE *eahta*] —**eight** *adj.* —**eighth** (ātth, āth) *adj.* & *n.*

eight·een (ā′tēn′) *n.* The sum of seventeen and one: a cardinal number written 18, XVIII. [OE *eahtatiene*] —**eight′een′** *adj.* —**eight′eenth′** *adj.* & *n.*

eighth note *Music* A note having one eighth the time value of a whole note.

eight·y (ā′tē) *n. pl.* **·ies** The sum of seventy and ten: a cardinal number written 80, LXXX. [OE *eahtatig*] —**eight′y** *adj.* —**eight′i·eth** *adj.* & *n.*

ein·stein·i·um (īn·stī′nē·əm) *n.* A radioactive element (symbol, Es) artificially produced by the irradiation of plutonium. [after Albert *Einstein*]

ei·ther (ē′thər, ī′thər) *adj.* 1. One or the other of two: Use *either* foot. 2. Each of two; one and the other: They sat on *either* side of him. —*pron.* One or the other: Choose *either*. —*conj.* In one of two or more cases, indeterminately or indifferently: a disjunctive correlative used with *or*: *Either* I shall go or he will come. —*adv.* Any more so: used after the denial of an alternative, or to emphasize a preceding negative: He could not speak, and I could not *either*. [OE *ǣgther*]

e·jac·u·late (*v.* i·jak′yə·lāt; *n.* -lit) *v.* **·lat·ed, ·lat·ing** *v.t.* 1. To utter suddenly, as a brief exclamation. 2. To discharge suddenly and quickly, as seminal fluid. —*v.i.* 3. To ejaculate something. —*n.* That which is ejaculated. [< L *e-* out + *jaculari* to throw] —**e·jac′u·la′tion** *n.* —**e·jac′u·la·to′ry** (-lə·tôr′ē) *adj.*

e·ject (i·jekt′) *v.t.* 1. To throw out with sudden force; expel. 2. *Law* To dispossess; evict. [< L *e-* out + *jacere* to throw] —**e·jec′tion** *n.*

eke (ēk) *v.t.* **eked, ek·ing** 1. To supplement; extend: with *out*. 2. To make (a living) with difficulty: with *out*. [Var. of obs. *eche* to increase]

e·kis·tics (ē·kis′tiks, ə-) *n.pl.* (*construed as sing.*) The science that deals with human settlements. [< Gk. *oikizein* to colonize] —**e·kis′tic** *adj.*

e·kue·le (e·kwā′lā) *n.* The monetary unit of Equatorial Guinea.

el- Assimilated var. of EN-[2].

e·lab·o·rate (*adj.* i·lab′ər·it; *v.* i·lab′ə·rāt) *adj.* 1. Worked out with great thoroughness or in minute detail. 2. Ornate and complex. —*v.* **·rat·ed, ·rat·ing** *v.t.* 1. To work out in detail; develop carefully. —*v.i.* 2. To add details or embellishments: with *on* or *upon*. [< L *e-* out + *laborare* to work] —**e·lab′o·rate·ly** *adv.* —**e·lab′o·ra′tion** *n.*

é·lan (ā·län′) *n.* Enthusiasm; dash; vivacity. [< F]

e·land (ē′lənd) *n.* A large, oxlike African antelope with twisted horns. [< Du., elk]

e·lapse (i·laps′) *v.i.* **e·lapsed, e·laps·ing** To slip by; pass away: said of time. [< L *e-* out, away + *labi* to glide]

e·las·tic (i·las′tik) *adj.* 1. Spontaneously regaining former size or shape, after compression, extension, or other distortion. 2. Adjusting readily; flexible or resilient. —*n.* 1. A stretchable material. 2. A rubber band. [< Gk. *elaunein* to drive] —**e·las′ti·cal·ly** *adv.*

e·las·tic·i·ty (i·las′tis′ə·tē, ē′las-) *n.* The property or quality of being elastic; resilience.

e·las·to·mer (i·las′tə·mer) *n.* Any of various synthetic rubbers or plastics having elastic qualities. [< ELAST(IC) + Gk. *meros* part]

e·late (i·lāt′) *v.t.* **e·lat·ed, e·lat·ing** To raise the spirits of; make joyful; excite. [< L *ex-* out + *ferre* to bear] —**e·lat′ed** *adj.* —**e·lat′ed·ly** *adv.* —**e·lat′ed·ness, e·la′tion** *n.*

el·bow (el′bō) *n.* 1. The joint at the bend of the arm; esp., the projecting outer side of this joint. 2. The joint corresponding to an elbow in the shoulder or hock of a quadruped. 3. Something, as a pipe fitting, bent like an elbow. —**to rub elbows with** To associate closely with (celebrities, etc.). —*v.t.* 1. To push with or as with the elbows. 2. To make (one's way) by such pushing. —*v.i.* 3. To push one's way along. [OE *elnboga*]

el·bow·room (el′bō·rōōm′, -rŏŏm′) *n.* Enough room to move or work without hindrance.

eld·er[1] (el′dər) *adj.* 1. Of earlier birth; older; senior. 2. Superior or prior in rank, office, etc. 3. Earlier; former. —*n.* 1. *Often pl.* An older person; also, a forefather or predecessor. 2. An influential senior member of a family, community, etc. 3. *Eccl.* A governing or counseling officer in certain Christian churches. 4. An aged person. [OE *eldra*]

el·der[2] (el′dər) *n.* A shrub of the honeysuckle family, with white flowers and purple-black or red berries. [OE *ellæn*]

el·der·ber·ry (el′dər·ber′ē, -bər·ē) *n. pl.* **·ber·ries** 1. The berry of the elder, used to make wine. 2. The elder.

eld·er·ly (el′dər·lē) *adj.* Rather advanced in age; approaching old age; quite old.

eld·est (el′dist) *adj.* Alternative superlative of OLD.

El Do·ra·do (el də·rä′dō) A legendary place rich in gold; also any region rich in wealth or promise. Also **El′do·ra′do.**

e·lect (i·lekt′) *v.t.* 1. To choose for an office by vote. 2. To pick out; select. 3. *Theol.* To set aside by divine will for salvation. —*v.i.* 4. To make a choice. —*adj.* 1. Chosen; selected. 2. Elected to office, but not yet installed: used in compounds: president-*elect*. —*n.* An elect person or group. [< L *e-* out + *legere* to choose]

e·lec·tion (i·lek′shən) *n.* 1. The formal

choice of a person for any position, usu. by ballot. 2. A popular vote upon any question officially proposed. 3. *Theol.* Predestination to salvation.

e·lec·tion·eer (i·lek′shən·ir′) *v.i.* To work for votes for a candidate or political party.

e·lec·tive (i·lek′tiv) *adj.* 1. Of or pertaining to a choice by vote. 2. Obtained or settled by election. 3. Subject to choice; optional. —*n.* An optional subject in a school or college curriculum.

e·lec·tor (i·lek′tər) *n.* 1. One who elects; a person qualified to vote. 2. A member of the electoral college. —**e·lec′tor·al** *adj.*

electoral college A body of electors, chosen by the voters, which formally elects the president and vice president of the United States.

e·lec·tor·ate (i·lek′tər·it) *n.* 1. The whole body of voters. 2. A district of voters.

e·lec·tric (i·lek′trik) *adj.* 1. Relating to, produced by, or operated by electricity. 2. Producing or carrying electricity: an *electric* cable. 3. Thrillingly exciting. Also **e·lec′tri·cal.** [< NL *electricus* electric, being produced from amber by rubbing < Gk. *ēlektron* amber] —**e·lec′tri·cal·ly** *adv.*

electric chair A seat in which condemned prisoners are strapped and electrocuted.

electric eel An eellike, fresh-water fish of tropical America that is capable of delivering powerful electric shocks.

electric eye A photoelectric cell.

e·lec·tri·cian (i·lek′trish′ən, ē′lek-) *n.* A technician who designs, installs, operates, or repairs electrical apparatus.

e·lec·tric·i·ty (i·lek′tris′ə·tē, ē′lek-) *n.* 1. A fundamental property of matter, associated with atomic particles whose movements develop fields of force and generate kinetic or potential energy. 2. A current or charge of energy so generated. 3. The science that deals with the laws, theory, and application of electric energy. 4. A state of great tension or excitement.

e·lec·tri·fy (i·lek′trə·fī) *v.t.* **·fied, ·fy·ing** 1. To charge with or subject to electricity. 2. To equip or adapt for operation by electric power. 3. To arouse; thrill. —**e·lec′tri·fi·ca′tion** *n.*

electro- *combining form* 1. Electric; by, with, or of electricity. 2. Electrolytic. Also, before vowels, sometimes **electr-.** [< Gk. *ēlektron* amber]

e·lec·tro·car·di·o·gram (i·lek′trō·kär′dē·ə·gram′) *n. Med.* The record made by an electrocardiograph.

e·lec·tro·car·di·o·graph (i·lek′trō·kär′dē·ə·graf′) *n. Med.* An instrument for recording the electric current produced by the action of the heart muscle.

e·lec·tro·chem·is·try (i·lek′trō·kem′is·trē) *n.* The study of electricity as active in effecting chemical change. —**e·lec′tro·chem′i·cal** *adj.*

e·lec·tro·cute (i·lek′trə·kyōōt) *v.t.* **·cut·ed, ·cut·ing** 1. To execute in the electric chair. 2. To kill by electricity. —**e·lec′tro·cu′tion** *n.*

e·lec·trode (i·lek′trōd) *n. Electr.* Any terminal connecting a conductor, as copper wire, with an electrolyte.

e·lec·tro·de·pos·it (i·lek′trō·di·poz′it) *v.t.* To deposit by electrolysis. —**e·lec′tro·de·pos′it** *n.* —**e·lec′tro·dep′o·si′tion** (-dep′ə·zish′ən, -dē′pə-) *n.*

e·lec·tro·dy·nam·ics (i·lek′trō·dī·nam′iks) *n.pl.* (*construed as sing.*) The branch of physics that deals with the forces of electrical attraction and repulsion and with the energy transformations of magnetic fields and electric currents. —**e·lec′tro·dy·nam′ic** *adj.*

e·lec·tro·en·ceph·a·lo·gram (i·lek′trō·en·sef′ə·lə·gram′) *n. Med.* The record made by an electroencephalograph.

e·lec·tro·en·ceph·a·lo·graph (i·lek′trō·en·sef′ə·lə·graf′) *n. Med.* An instrument for recording the strength and character of electrical impulses in the brain. —**e·lec′tro·en·ceph′a·lo·graph′ic** *adj.*

e·lec·trol·y·sis (i·lek′trol′ə·sis) *n.* 1. The application of a direct current to an electrolyte so as to attract its positive ions to the cathode and its negative ions to the anode. 2. The removal of hair by treating the follicle with an electrically charged needle.

e·lec·tro·lyte (i·lek′trə·līt) *n.* 1. A compound that when in solution or a fluid state conducts electricity by the dissociation of its constituents into free ions. 2. A solution that conducts electricity; esp., the solution used in a cell or battery. —**e·lec′tro·lyt′ic** (-lit′ik) *adj.*

e·lec·tro·lyze (i·lek′trə·līz) *v.t.* **·lyzed, ·lyz·ing** To decompose by electric current. —**e·lec′tro·ly·za′tion** *n.*

e·lec·tro·mag·net (i·lek′trō·mag′nit) *n.* A core of soft iron that temporarily becomes a magnet when an electric current passes through a coil of wire surrounding it.

electromagnetic wave *Physics* Any of a class of waves propagated by a system of electric and magnetic fields and including all forms of radiant energy.

e·lec·tro·mag·net·ism (i·lek′trō·mag′nə·tiz′·əm) *n.* 1. Magnetism developed by electricity. 2. The science that treats of the relations between electricity and magnetism. —**e·lec′tro·mag·net′ic** (-mag·net′ik) *adj.*

e·lec·trom·e·ter (i·lek′trom′ə·tər, ē′lek-) *n.* An instrument for measuring the voltage of an electric current.

e·lec·tro·mo·tive (i·lek′trə·mō′tiv) *adj.* Producing, or tending to produce, a flow of electric current.

electromotive force 1. That which tends to produce a flow of electricity from one point to another. 2. Difference of electrical potential between two points in a circuit, a battery, etc.; voltage.

e·lec·tron (i·lek′tron) *n.* A negatively charged elementary particle existing outside the nucleus of an atom. [< Gk. *ēlektron* amber]

e·lec·tro·neg·a·tive (i·lek′trō·neg′ə·tiv) *adj.* Appearing at the positive electrode in electrolysis.

e·lec·tron·ic (i·lek′tron′ik, ē′lek-) *adj.* 1. Of or pertaining to electrons or electronics. 2. Operating or produced by the movement of free electrons, as in radio and radar. —**e·lec′tron′i·cal·ly** *adv.*

e·lec·tron·ics (i·lek′tron′iks, ē′lek-) *n.pl.* (*construed as sing.*) The study of the properties and behavior of electrons, esp. with reference to technical and industrial applications.

electron microscope A microscope that projects a greatly enlarged image of an object held in the path of a sharply focused electron beam.

electron tube A device in which a stream of electrons is conducted through a vacuum or a rarefied gas and usu. controlled by a grid: also called *vacuum tube.*

electron volt The energy acquired by an electron that passes through a potential difference of one volt.

e·lec·tro·pho·re·sis (i·lek′trō·fə·rē′sis) *n. Chem.* The movement of the electrically charged suspended particles in a fluid, when under the influence of an electric field.

e·lec·tro·plate (i·lek′trə·plāt′) *v.t.* **·plat·ed, ·plat·ing** To coat (an object) with metal by electrolysis. —*n.* An electroplated article. **—e·lec′tro·plat′er** *n.*

e·lec·tro·pos·i·tive (i·lek′trō·poz′ə·tiv) *adj.* Appearing at the negative electrode in electrolysis.

e·lec·tro·shock therapy (i·lek′trō·shok′) A treatment for mental disorders in which a coma is induced by passing an electric current through the brain.

e·lec·tro·stat·ics (i·lek′trō·stat′iks) *n.pl.* (*construed as sing.*) A branch of physics that deals with the attraction and repulsion properties of electric charges. **—e·lec′tro·stat′ic** *adj.*

e·lec·tro·type (i·lek′trə·tīp′) *n.* 1. A metallic copy, made by electrodeposition of a surface, esp. that of a page of type for printing. 2. An impression from an electrotype. —*v.t.* **·typed, ·typ·ing** To make an electrotype of. **—e·lec′tro·typ′ing** *n.*

e·lec·trum (i·lek′trəm) *n.* An alloy of native gold and silver. [< Gk. *ēlektron* amber]

el·ee·mos·y·nar·y (el′ə·mos′ə·ner′ē) *adj.* Of, pertaining to, or aided by charity or alms. [See ALMS.]

el·e·gance (el′ə·gəns) *n.* 1. The state or quality of being elegant or refined. 2. Something elegant.

el·e·gant (el′ə·gənt) *adj.* 1. Tastefully ornate in dress, furnishings, etc. 2. Marked by grace and refinement, as in style, manners, etc. [< L *e-* out + *legare* to choose] **—el′e·gant·ly** *adv.*

el·e·gi·ac (el′ə·jī′ək) *adj.* Of, pertaining to, or like an elegy. —*n. Usu. pl.* Verse composed in elegiac form.

el·e·gy (el′ə·jē) *n. pl.* **·gies** 1. A poem of mourning and praise for the dead. 2. Any meditative poem of lamentation. 3. *Music* A work of lamentation or mourning. [< Gk. *elegos* a song of lament] **—el′e·gist** *n.* **—el′e·gize** *v.t. & v.i.* **·gized, ·giz·ing**

el·e·ment (el′ə·mənt) *n.* 1. A relatively simple constituent that is a basic part of a whole; an essential part. 2. A group or class of people distinguished by belief, behavior, etc.: a rowdy *element* in a crowd. 3. One of four substances (earth, air, fire, water) anciently viewed as composing the physical universe. 4. The surrounding conditions best suited to some person or thing. 5. *pl.* Atmospheric powers or forces: the fury of the *elements.* 6. *Physics & Chem.* A substance, as oxygen, carbon, silver, etc., composed entirely of atoms having the same atomic number, and which may not be decomposed by ordinary chemical means. [< L *elementum* first principle]

el·e·men·tal (el′ə·men′təl) *adj.* 1. Of or relating to an element or elements. 2. Fundamental and relatively simple; basic. 3. Of or suggestive of the powerful forces of nature. 4. Chemically uncombined. **—el′e·men′tal·ly** *adv.*

el·e·men·ta·ry (el′ə·men′tər·ē, -men′trē) *adj.* 1. Elemental. 2. Fundamental; basic. 3. Simple and rudimentary.

elementary particle An irreducible, subatomic constituent of matter and energy, as an electron.

elementary school A school giving a course of education of six or eight years: also called *grade school, grammar school.*

el·e·phant (el′ə·fənt) *n.* A massively built, almost hairless mammal of Asia and Africa, having a flexible trunk, and long ivory tusks. [< Gk. *elephas, -antos* elephant, ivory]

el·e·phan·ti·a·sis (el′ə·fən·tī′ə·sis) *n. Pathol.* A disease caused by a parasitic worm, characterized by a hardening of the skin, and an enormous enlargement of the part affected. [< Gk. *elephas* elephant]

el·e·phan·tine (el′ə·fan′tin, -tēn, -tīn) *adj.* 1. Of or pertaining to an elephant. 2. Enormous; unwieldy; ponderous.

el·e·vate (el′ə·vāt) *v.t.* **·vat·ed, ·vat·ing** 1. To lift up; raise. 2. To raise in rank, status, etc. 3. To raise the spirits of; cheer; elate. 4. To raise the pitch or loudness of. 5. To raise the moral or intellectual level of. [< L *e-* out + *levare* to lighten, raise]

el·e·vat·ed (el′ə·vā′tid) *adj.* 1. Raised up; high. 2. Lofty in character; sublime. —*n. Informal* An overhead railroad.

el·e·va·tion (el′ə·vā′shən) *n.* 1. The act of elevating, or the state of being elevated. 2. An elevated place. 3. Height above sea level. 4. Loftiness of thought, position, etc. 5. In dancing, the ability to leap. 6. In drafting, a side, front, or rear view of a machine or other structure.

el·e·va·tor (el′ə·vā′tər) *n.* 1. One who or that which elevates. 2. A mechanism for hoisting grain. 3. A granary. 4. A movable platform or car that carries passengers or freight up and down.

e·lev·en (i·lev′ən) *n.* 1. The sum of ten and one: a cardinal number written 11, XI. 2. Anything consisting of eleven units. [OE *endleofan* one left over (after ten)] **—e·lev′en** *adj.* **—e·lev′enth** *adj. & n.*

elf (elf) *n. pl.* **elves** (elvz) In folklore, a dwarfish sprite with magical powers, usu. mischievous. [OE *ælf*] **—elf′in, elf′ish** *adj.*

e·lic·it (i·lis′it) *v.t.* 1. To draw out or forth; evoke: to *elicit* a reply. 2. To bring to light: to *elicit* the truth. [< L *e-* out + *lacere* to entice]

e·lide (i·līd′) *v.t.* **e·lid·ed, e·lid·ing** 1. To omit (a vowel or syllable) in pronunciation. 2. To suppress; omit; ignore. [< L *e-* out + *laedere* to strike]

el·i·gi·ble (el′ə·jə·bəl) *adj.* 1. Capable of and qualified for. 2. Fit for or worthy of choice. [See ELECT.] **—el′i·gi·bil′i·ty** *n.* **—el′i·gi·bly** *adv.*

e·lim·i·nate (i·lim′ə·nāt) *v.t.* **·nat·ed, ·nat·ing** 1. To get rid of. 2. To remove (a contestant, team, etc.) from further competition by defeating. 3. *Physiol.* To void; excrete. 4. *Math.* To remove (a quantity) from a system of algebraic equations. [< L *e-* out + *limen* threshold] **—e·lim′i·na′tion** *n.*

e·li·sion (i·lizh′ən) *n.* Omission of a vowel or syllable, as in "th' imperial towers." [See ELIDE.]

e·lite (ā·lēt′, i·lēt′) *n.* 1. The choicest part, as of a social group. 2. A size of typewriter type, having 12 characters to the inch. [See ELECT.] **—e·lite′** *adj.*

e·lit·ism (ā·lēt′iz′əm, i·lēt′-) *n.* 1. Rule or domination by an elite. 2. Advocacy of elite leadership. 3. Pride in belonging to an elite. **—e·lit′ist** *n. & adj.*

e·lix·ir (i·lik′sər) *n.* 1. A sweetened alcoholic medicinal preparation. 2. In ancient philosophy, a substance sought by alchemists for changing base metals into gold, or for prolonging life. 3. A cure-all. [< Arabic *al-iksīr* < Gk. *zērion* medicated powder]

E·liz·a·be·than (i·liz′ə·bē′thən) *adj.* Of or pertaining to Elizabeth I of England, or to her era. *—n.* An Englishman living during the reign of Elizabeth I.

elk (elk) *n. pl.* **elks** or **elk** 1. A large deer of northern Europe and Asia. 2. The wapiti. [OE *elh*]

ell[1] (el) *n.* A measure of length now rarely used: in England, 45 inches or 1.114 meters. [OE *eln* an arm's length]

ell[2] (el) *n.* Anything shaped like the letter L.

el·lipse (i·lips′) *n. Geom.* An oval-shaped curve; a conic section. [< L *ellipsis.* See ELLIPSIS.]

el·lip·sis (i·lip′sis) *n. pl.* **·ses** (-sēz) 1. *Gram.* The omission of a word or words necessary for the complete grammatical construction of a sentence, but not required for the understanding of it. 2. Marks (. . .) indicating omission. [< Gk. *elleipein* to leave out]

el·lip·soid (i·lip′soid) *n.* A solid of which every plane surface is an ellipse or a circle. **—el·lip′soid** or **el·lip′soi′dal** *adj.*

el·lip·tic (i·lip′tik) *adj.* 1. Of, pertaining to, or shaped like an ellipse. 2. *Gram.* Characterized by ellipsis; shortened. Also **el·lip′ti·cal.** **—el·lip′ti·cal·ly** *adv.*

elm (elm) *n.* 1. A shade tree of America, Europe, and Asia, having a broad, spreading, or overarching top. 2. The wood of this tree. [OE]

el·o·cu·tion (el′ə·kyōō′shən) *n.* The art of public speaking, including vocal delivery and gesture. [< L *e-* out + *loqui* to speak] **—el′o·cu′tion·ar′y** *adj.* **—el′o·cu′tion·ist** *n.*

e·lon·gate (i·lông′gāt) *v.t. & v.i.* **·gat·ed, ·gat·ing** To increase in length; stretch. *—adj.* Drawn out; lengthened. [< L *e-* out + *longe* far off] **—e·lon·ga·tion** (i·lông·gā′shən, ē′lông-) *n.*

e·lope (i·lōp′) *v.i.* **e·loped, e·lop·ing** To run away with a lover, usu. to get married. [< AF *aloper*] **—e·lope′ment** *n.* **—e·lop′er** *n.*

el·o·quence (el′ə·kwəns) *n.* Fluent, polished, and effective use of language.

el·o·quent (el′ə·kwənt) *adj.* 1. Possessed of or manifesting eloquence. 2. Visibly expressive of emotion: *eloquent* tears. [< L *e-* out + *loqui* to speak] **—el′o·quent·ly** *adv.*

else (els) *adv.* 1. In a different place, time, or way; instead: Where *else*? How *else*? 2. If the case or facts were different; otherwise: Hurry, or *else* you will be caught. *—adj.* Additional; different: somebody *else.* [OE *elles.* Akin to L *alius.*]

else·where (els′hwâr′) *adv.* In or to another place or places; somewhere or anywhere else.

e·lu·ci·date (i·lōō′sə·dāt) *v.t. & v.i.* **·dat·ed, ·dat·ing** To explain; clarify. [< L *e-* out + *lucidus* clear] **—e·lu′ci·da′tion** *n.*

e·lude (i·lōōd′) *v.t.* **e·lud·ed, e·lud·ing** 1. To avoid or escape from; evade. 2. To escape the notice or understanding of: The meaning *eludes* me. [< L *e-* out + *ludere* to play]

e·lu·sive (i·lōō′siv) *adj.* Tending to slip away; hard to grasp or perceive: an *elusive* fragrance. **—e·lu′sive·ly** *adv.* **—e·lu′sive·ness** *n.*

el·ver (el′vər) *n.* A young eel.

elves (elvz) Plural of ELF.

E·ly·si·um (i·lizh′ē·əm, i·liz′-) *n.* A state of bliss; paradise. [after *Elysium,* the land of the blessed dead in Greek mythology] **—E·ly·sian** (i·lizh′ən, -ē·ən) *adj.*

em (em) *n. Printing* The square of the body size of a type; esp., a pica em, about 1/6 of an inch, used as a standard unit of measurement: originally, the size of the letter M.

e·ma·ci·ate (i·mā′shē·āt) *v.t.* **·at·ed, ·at·ing** To make abnormally lean; cause to lose flesh. [< L *macies* leanness] **—e·ma′ci·at′ed** *adj.* **—e·ma′ci·a′tion** *n.*

em·a·nate (em′ə·nāt) *v.i.* **·nat·ed, ·nat·ing** To flow forth from a source; issue. [< L *e-* out + *manare* to flow] **—em′a·na′tion** *n.*

e·man·ci·pate (i·man′sə·pāt) *v.t.* **·pat·ed, ·pat·ing** To release from bondage, oppression, or authority; set free. [< L *e-* out + *manus* hand + *capere* to take] **—e·man′ci·pa′tion** *n.* **—e·man′ci·pa′tor** *n.*

e·mas·cu·late (*v.* i·mas′kyə·lāt; *adj.* i·mas′kyə·lit) *v.t.* **·lat·ed, ·lat·ing** 1. To deprive of procreative power; castrate; geld. 2. To deprive of strength and vigor; weaken. *—adj.* Emasculated; effeminate; weakened. [< L *e-* away + *masculus* male] **—e·mas′cu·la′tion** *n.* **—e·mas′cu·la′tor** *n.*

em·balm (im·bäm′) *v.t.* To preserve (a dead body) from decay by treatment with chemicals, etc. [< F *embaumer*] **—em·balm′er** *n.*

em·bank·ment (im·bangk′mənt) *n.* A mound or bank raised to hold back water, support a roadway, etc. **—em·bank′** *v.t.*

em·bar·go (im·bär′gō) *n. pl.* **·goes** 1. An order by a government restraining merchant vessels from leaving or entering its ports. 2. Authoritative stoppage of foreign commerce or of any special trade. [< Sp. < *embargar,* ult. < LL *barra* bar] **—em·bar′go** *v.t.* **·goed, ·go·ing**

em·bark (im·bärk′) *v.t.* 1. To put or take aboard a vessel. *—v.i.* 2. To go aboard a vessel for a voyage. 3. To engage in a venture. [< IN-[2] + L *barca* boat] **—em·bar·ka·tion** (em′bär·kā′shən) *n.*

em·bar·rass (im·bar′əs) *v.t.* 1. To make self-conscious and uncomfortable; disconcert. 2. To involve in financial difficulties. 3. To hamper; impede. [< F *embarrasser*] **—em·bar′rass·ing** *adj.* **—em·bar′rass·ing·ly** *adv.* **—em·bar′rass·ment** *n.*

em·bas·sy (em′bə·sē) *n. pl.* **·sies** 1. An ambassador together with his staff. 2. The mission, function, or position of an ambassador. 3. The official residence or headquarters of an ambassador. [< L *ambactus* servant]

em·bat·tle (em·bat′l) *v.t.* **·tled, ·tling** To prepare or equip for battle. [< OF *em-* in + *bataille* < L *battuere* to beat]

em·bed (im·bed′) *v.t.* **·bed·ded, ·bed·ding** To set firmly in surrounding matter.

em·bel·lish (im·bel′ish) *v.t.* 1. To ornament; decorate. 2. To heighten the interest of (a narrative) by adding fictitious details. [< OF *em-* in + *bel* beautiful] **—em·bel′lish·er** *n.* **—em·bel′lish·ment** *n.*

em·ber (em′bər) *n.* 1. A live coal or unextinguished piece of wood, as in a fire. 2. *pl.* A dying fire. [OE *ǣmerge*]

em·bez·zle (im·bez′əl) *v.t.* **·zled, ·zling** To appropriate fraudulently to one's own use, as money entrusted to one's care. [< AF *em-* in + *besiler* to destroy] **—em·bez′zle·ment** *n.* **—em·bez′zler** *n.*

em·bit·ter (im·bit′ər) *v.t.* To make bitter or unhappy. **—em·bit′ter·ment** *n.*

em·bla·zon (em·blā′zən) *v.t.* 1. To adorn magnificently, esp. with heraldic devices. 2. To decorate brilliantly with color.

em·blem (em′bləm) *n.* An object or pictorial device that serves as a symbol, as of an idea, institution, etc. [< EN-[2] + Gk. *ballein* to throw] **—em′blem·at′ic** or **·i·cal** *adj.*

em·bod·i·ment (im·bod′i·mənt) *n.* 1. The act of embodying, or the state of being embodied. 2. That which embodies, or in which something is embodied.

em·bod·y (im·bod′ē) *v.t.* **·bod·ied, ·bod·y·ing** 1. To put into visible or concrete form: to *embody* ideals in action. 2. To make part of an organized whole; incorporate.

em·bold·en (im·bōl′dən) *v.t.* To give courage to.

em·bo·lism (em′bə·liz′əm) *n.* *Pathol.* The stopping up of a vein or artery by an embolus.

em·bo·lus (em′bə·ləs) *n.* *pl.* **·li** (-lī) *Pathol.* A foreign body that forms an obstruction in a blood vessel, as a blood clot or an air bubble. [< EN-[2] + Gk. *ballein* to throw]

em·boss (im·bôs′, -bos′) *v.t.* 1. To cover with raised figures, designs, etc. 2. To raise (designs, figures, etc.) from or upon a surface. [Origin unknown] **—em·boss′er** *n.*

em·bou·chure (äm·bōō·shōōr′) *n.* 1. The mouth of a river. 2. *Music* **a** The mouthpiece of a wind instrument. **b** The position or application of the lips and tongue in playing a wind instrument. [< F *em-* in + *bouche* mouth]

em·brace (im·brās′) *v.* **·braced, ·brac·ing** *v.t.* 1. To clasp in the arms; hug. 2. To accept willingly; adopt, as a religion or doctrine. 3. To surround; encircle. 4. To include; contain. 5. To take in visually or mentally. **—*v.i.*** 6. To hug each other. **—*n.*** The act of embracing. [< OF *embracer* < L *in-* in + *bracchium* arm] **—em·brace′ment** *n.* **—em·brac′er** *n.*

em·bra·sure (em·brā′zhər) *n.* 1. *Archit.* An opening in a wall, as for a window or door, sloped so as to enlarge its interior outline. 2. An opening in a parapet, battlement, or wall used for firing of guns. [< F *embraser* to widen (an opening)]

em·broi·der (im·broi′dər) *v.t.* & *v.i.* 1. To ornament (cloth) with designs in needlework. 2. To execute (a design) in needlework. 3. To exaggerate; embellish. [< MF *broder* to stitch] **—em·broi′der·y** *n.*

em·broil (em·broil′) *v.t.* 1. To involve in dissension or strife. 2. To complicate or confuse. [< F *embrouiller* to confuse] **—em·broil′ment** *n.*

em·bry·o (em′brē·ō) *n.* *pl.* **·os** 1. *Biol.* An organism in the earliest stages of development; in the human species, the first eight weeks. 2. *Bot.* The rudimentary plant within the seed. 3. Anything in its rudimentary stage. [< Gk. *embryon* < *en-* in + *bryein* to swell] **—em·bry·on·ic** (em′brē·on′ik) *adj.*

embryo- *combining form* Embryo; embryonic. Also, before vowels, **embry-.** [< Gk. *embryon*]

em·bry·ol·o·gy (em′brē·ol′ə·jē) *n.* The science that deals with the origin, structure, and development of the embryo. **—em·bry·o·log·ic** (em′brē·ə·loj′ik) or **·i·cal** *adj.* **—em′bry·ol′o·gist** *n.*

em·cee (em′sē′) *Informal* *n.* Master of ceremonies. **—*v.t.* & *v.i.*** **·ceed, ·cee·ing** To act as master of ceremonies.

e·mend (i·mend′) *v.t.* To make corrections or changes in (a text.) [< L *e-* out + *menda* fault] **—e·mend′a·ble** *adj.* **—e·men·da·tion** (ē′men·dā′shən) *n.*

em·er·ald (em′ər·əld, em′rəld) *n.* 1. A bright green variety of beryl, valued as a jewel. 2. A rich green. [< OF *esmeralde* < Gk. *smaragdos*] **—em′er·ald** *adj.*

e·merge (i·mûrj′) *v.i.* **e·merged, e·merg·ing** 1. To come forth as from water, a hiding place, etc. 2. To come to light; become apparent. [< L *e-* out + *mergere* to dip] **—e·mer′gence** *n.* **—e·mer′gent** *adj.*

e·mer·gen·cy (i·mûr′jən·sē) *n.* *pl.* **·cies** A sudden and unexpected turn of events calling for immediate action.

e·mer·i·tus (i·mer′ə·təs) *adj.* Retired from active service, usu. because of age, but retained in an honorary position: professor *emeritus.* [< L, pp. of *emerere* to earn]

e·mer·sion (ē·mûr′shən, -zhən) *n.* An emerging.

em·er·y (em′ər·ē, em′rē) *n.* A very hard black variety of corundum, used as an abrasive. [< Gk. *smēris* emery powder]

e·met·ic (i·met′ik) *adj.* Tending to produce vomiting. [< Gk. *emeein* to vomit] **—e·met′ic** *n.*

-emia *combining form* *Med.* Blood; condition of the blood: used in names of diseases: *leukemia.* Also spelled *-aemia, -haemia, -hemia.* [< Gk. *haima* blood]

em·i·grant (em′ə·grənt) *adj.* Moving from one place or country to settle in another. **—*n.*** A person who emigrates.

em·i·grate (em′ə·grāt) *v.i.* **·grat·ed, ·grat·ing** To move away from one country, or section of a country, to settle in another. [< L *e-* out + *migrare* to move] **—em′i·gra′tion** *n.*

em·i·nence (em′ə·nəns) *n.* 1. Superiority in rank, power, achievement, etc. 2. A person having such rank or power. 3. A high place or elevation, as a hill.

em·i·nent (em′ə·nənt) *adj.* 1. Superior; outstanding; distinguished: an *eminent* scholar. 2. Noteworthy; conspicuous: *eminent* valor. 3. High; lofty. [< L *eminere* to stand out] **—em′i·nent·ly** *adv.*

eminent domain *Law* The right or power of the state to take or control private property for public use.

e·mir (ə·mir′) *n.* 1. A Muslim prince or

commander. 2. A high Turkish official. [< Arabic *amīr* ruler] —**e·mir′ate** *n.*

em·is·sar·y (em′ə·ser′ē) *n. pl.* **·sar·ies** 1. A person sent on a mission as an agent or representative of a government. 2. A secret agent; spy. —*adj.* Of, pertaining to, or serving as an emissary. [< L *emissarius* < *emittere* to send out]

e·mit (i·mit′) *v.t.* **e·mit·ted, e·mit·ting** 1. To send forth or give off (light, heat, sound, etc.); discharge. 2. To give expression to; utter, as an opinion. 3. To put into circulation, as money. [< L *e-* out + *mittere* to send] —**e·mis·sion** (i·mish′ən) *n.* —**e·mis·sive** (i·mis′iv) *adj.* —**e·mit′ter** *n.*

e·mol·lient (i·mol′yənt, -ē·ənt) *adj.* Softening or soothing, esp. to the skin. —*n. Med.* A softening or soothing medication. [< L *e-* thoroughly + *mollire* to soften]

e·mol·u·ment (i·mol′yə·mənt) *n.* A salary or fee as for a service. [< L *emolumentum* profit, gain < *e-* out + *molere* to grind]

e·mote (i·mōt′) *v.i.* **e·mot·ed, e·mot·ing** *Informal* To exhibit an exaggerated emotion, as in acting. [< EMOTION]

e·mo·tion (i·mō′shən) *n.* A strong surge of feeling, as of love, hate, or fear. [< L *emotio, -onis* < *e-* out + *movere* to move]

e·mo·tion·al (i·mō′shən·əl) *adj.* 1. Of, pertaining to, or expressive of emotion. 2. Easily or excessively affected by emotion. 3. Arousing the emotions. —**e·mo′tion·al·ly** *adv.*

e·mo·tion·al·ism (i·mō′shən·əl·iz′əm) *n.* 1. The tendency to overindulge the emotions. 2. A display of emotion. 3. Appeal to the emotions.

e·mo·tion·al·ize (i·mō′shən·əl·īz′) *v.t.* **·ized, ·iz·ing** To treat in an emotional manner.

e·mo·tive (i·mō′tiv) *adj.* Characterized by, expressing, or tending to excite emotion.

em·pa·na·da (em′pə·nä′də) *n.* A pastry filled with spiced meat. [< Sp.]

em·pan·el (im·pan′əl) See IMPANEL.

em·pa·thize (em′pə·thīz) *v.t.* & *v.i.* **·thized, ·thiz·ing** To regard with or feel empathy.

em·pa·thy (em′pə·thē) *n. Psychol.* Intellectual or imaginative apprehension of another's condition or state of mind. —**em·path·ic** (em·path′ik), **em·pa·thet·ic** (em′pə·thet′ik) *adj.* —**em·path′i·cal·ly, em′pa·thet′i·cal·ly** *adv.*

em·per·or (em′pər·ər) *n.* The sovereign of an empire. [< L *imperator* commander]

em·pha·sis (em′fə·sis) *n. pl.* **·ses** (-sēz) 1. Stress given by voice, gesture, etc., to a particular syllable, word, or phrase. 2. Force or intensity of meaning, action, etc. 3. Special importance or attention assigned to something. [< EN-² + Gk. *phainein* to show]

em·pha·size (em′fə·sīz) *v.t.* **·sized, ·siz·ing** To give emphasis to; stress.

em·phat·ic (em·fat′ik) *adj.* 1. Spoken or done with emphasis; forcibly expressive. 2. Characterized by forcefulness or intensity. 3. Striking; decisive. —**em·phat′i·cal·ly** *adv.*

em·phy·se·ma (em′fə·sē′mə) *n. Pathol.* A lung condition marked by loss of elasticity of the air sacs, causing difficulty in breathing. [< Gk. *emphysēma* inflation]

em·pire (em′pīr) *n.* 1. A state, or union of states, governed by an emperor; also, the historical period of such government. 2. A union of dispersed states and unrelated peoples under one rule. 3. Wide and supreme dominion. [< L *imperium* rule, authority]

em·pir·i·cal (em·pir′i·kəl) *adj.* Relating to or based upon direct experience or observation alone: *empirical* knowledge. Also **em·pir′ic.** [< EN-² + Gk. *peira* attempt] —**em·pir′i·cal·ly** *adv.*

em·pir·i·cism (em·pir′ə·siz′əm) *n.* 1. *Philos.* The doctrine that all knowledge is derived from sensory experience. 2. Reliance on sensory observation and experiment as the bases of knowledge. —**em·pir′i·cist** *n.*

em·place·ment (im·plās′mənt) *n.* 1. The position assigned to guns or to a battery within a fortification; also, a gun platform, the parapet, etc. 2. A setting in place; location. [< F *emplacer* to put into position]

em·ploy (im·ploi′) *v.t.* 1. To engage the services of; hire. 2. To provide work and livelihood for. 3. To make use of as a means or instrument. —*n.* The state of being employed; service. [< F *employer* < L *in-* in + *plicare* to fold] —**em·ploy′er** *n.* —**em·ploy′ment** *n.*

em·ploy·ee (im·ploi′ē, em′ploi·ē′) *n.* One who works for another for pay. Also **em·ploy′e.**

em·po·ri·um (em·pôr′ē·əm) *n. pl.* **·po·ri·ums** or **·po·ri·a** 1. A store carrying general merchandise. 2. A trading or market center. [< Gk. *emporion* market]

em·pow·er (im·pou′ər) *v.t.* 1. To authorize; delegate authority to. 2. To enable; permit.

em·press (em′pris) *n.* 1. A woman who rules an empire. 2. The wife or widow of an emperor.

emp·ty (emp′tē) *adj.* **·ti·er, ·ti·est** 1. Containing nothing: an *empty* room. 2. Without significance; unsubstantial; hollow: *empty* promises. 3. Destitute or devoid: with *of*: *empty* of compassion. 4. *Informal* Hungry. —*v.* **·tied, ·ty·ing** *v.t.* 1. To remove the contents of. 2. To transfer the contents of (a container): to *empty* a bucket. 3. To unburden; clear: with *of.* —*v.i.* 4. To discharge itself or its contents. —*n. pl.* **·ties** An empty container, vehicle, etc. [OE *ǣmetig* < *ǣmetta* leisure] —**emp′ti·ly** *adv.* —**emp′ti·ness** *n.*

emp·ty-hand·ed (emp′tē·han′did) *adj.* Carrying nothing.

em·py·re·an (em′pə·rē′ən, -pī-) *n.* 1. The highest heaven; the abode of God and the angels, anciently conceived as a region of pure fire. 2. The firmament. [< EN-² + Gk. *pyr* fire] —**em·pyr·e·al** (em·pir′ē·əl), **em′py·re′an** *adj.*

e·mu (ē′myōō) *n.* A flightless, three-toed Australian bird related to the ostrich. [Prob. < Pg. *ema* ostrich]

em·u·late (em′yə·lāt) *v.t.* **·lat·ed, ·lat·ing** To try to equal or surpass, esp. by imitating. [< L *aemulus* jealous] —**em′u·la′tion** *n.* —**em′u·lous** *adj.*

e·mul·si·fy (i·mul′sə·fī) *v.t.* **·fied, ·fy·ing** To make into an emulsion. —**e·mul′si·fi·ca′tion** *n.* —**e·mul′si·fi′er** *n.*

e·mul·sion (i·mul′shən) *n.* 1. A liquid mixture in which a fatty or resinous substance is suspended in minute globules, as butterfat in milk. 2. *Photog.* A light-sensitive coating for film, plates, etc. [< L *e-* out + *mulgere* to milk]

en (en) *n.* *Printing* A space half the width of an em.

en-[1] *prefix* Forming transitive verbs: 1. (from nouns) To cover or surround with; place into or upon: *encircle, encapsulate.* 2. (from adjectives and nouns) To make; cause to be or to resemble: *enable, enfeeble.* 3. (from verbs) Often with simple intensive force, or used to form transitive verbs from intransitives: *enact.* Also *em-* before *b, p,* and sometimes *m,* as in *embark.* Many words in *en-* or *em-* have variant forms in *in-* or *im-* respectively. [< L *in-* < *in* in, into]

en-[2] *prefix* In; into; on: *endemic.* Also *el-* before *l,* as in *ellipse; em-* before *b, m, p, ph,* as in *embolism, empathy; er-* before *r,* as in *errhine.* [< Gk. *en-* < *en* in, into]

-en[1] *suffix* Forming verbs: 1. (from adjectives) Cause to be; become: *deepen, harden.* 2. (from nouns) Cause to have; gain: *hearten, strengthen.* [OE *-nian*]

-en[2] *suffix of adjectives* Made of; resembling: *woolen.* [OE]

-en[3] *suffix* Used in the past participles of many strong verbs: *broken, beaten.* [OE]

-en[4] *suffix* Used in the plurals of certain nouns: *oxen, children.* [OE *-an*]

-en[5] *suffix* Small; little: *chicken, kitten.* [OE]

en·a·ble (in·ā′bəl) *v.t.* **·bled, ·bling** 1. To supply with adequate power or opportunity; make able. 2. To make possible or practicable.

en·act (in·akt′) *v.t.* 1. To make into a law; decree. 2. To represent in or as in a play; act the part of. **—en·act′ment** *n.*

en·am·el (in·am′əl) *n.* 1. A vitreous, usu. opaque material applied by fusion to surfaces of metal, glass, or porcelain as a decoration or a protective covering. 2. A piece executed in enamel. 3. A paint that dries to form a hard, glossy surface. 4. *Anat.* The hard, glossy, calcareous outer layer of the teeth. **—*v.t.* en·am·eled** or **·elled, en·am·el·ing** or **·el·ling** 1. To cover or inlay with enamel. 2. To surface with or as with enamel. [OF *esmail*] **—en·am′el·er, en·am′el·ist** *n.*

en·am·el·ware (in·am′əl·wâr′) *n.* Enameled kitchenware.

en·am·or (in·am′ər) *v.t.* To inflame with love; also, to charm; fascinate: chiefly in the passive, followed by *of*: He is *enamored* of his cousin. Also *Brit.* **en·am′our.** [< OF *en-* in + *amour* love] **—en·am′ored** *adj.*

en·camp (in·kamp′) *v.i.* 1. To make camp; live in a camp. **—*v.t.*** 2. To place in a camp. **—en·camp′ment** *n.*

en·cap·su·late (in·kap′sə·lāt, -syŏŏ-) *v.t.* **·lat·ed, ·lat·ing** 1. To enclose in or as in a capsule. 2. To summarize or condense. **—en·cap′su·la′tion** *n.*

en·case (in·kās′) *v.t.* **·cased, ·cas·ing** To enclose in or as in a case: also spelled *incase.* **—en·case′ment** *n.*

-ence *suffix of nouns* Forming nouns of action, quality, or condition from adjectives in *-ent,* as *prominence.* Compare -ENCY. [< L *-entia,* suffix used to form nouns from present participles]

en·ceinte (en·sānt′, *Fr.* äṅ·saṅt′) *adj.* Pregnant. [< F]

en·ceph·a·li·tis (en′sef·ə·lī′tis, en·sef′-) *n.* *Pathol.* Inflammation of the brain. **—en′·ceph·a·lit′ic** (-lit′ik) *adj.*

encephalo- *combining form* The brain. Also, before vowels, **encephal-.** [< EN-[2] + Gk. *kephalē* head]

en·chain (in·chān′) *v.t.* To bind with or as with a chain; hold fast. **—en·chain′ment** *n.*

en·chant (in·chant′) *v.t.* 1. To put a spell upon; bewitch. 2. To charm completely; delight. [< IN-[2] + L *cantare* to sing] **—en·chant′ing** *adj.* **—en·chant′ment** *n.*

en·chi·la·da (en′chi·lä′də) *n.* A rolled tortilla usu. filled with meat and served with a chili-flavored sauce. [< Sp.]

en·ci·pher (en·sī′fər) *v.t.* To convert (a message, report, etc.) from plain text into cipher.

en·cir·cle (en·sûr′kəl) *v.t.* **·cled, ·cling** 1. To form a circle around. 2. To go around. **—en·cir′cle·ment** *n.*

en·clave (en′klāv) *n.* 1. A territory completely or partially enclosed by a foreign territory to which it is not politically subject. 2. A district, as in a city, inhabited by a minority group. [< IN-[2] + L *clavis* key]

en·close (in·klōz′) *v.t.* **·closed, ·clos·ing** 1. To close in on all sides; surround. 2. To transmit within the cover of a letter. 3. To contain. Also spelled *inclose.*

en·clo·sure (in·klō′zhər) *n.* 1. The act of enclosing, or the state of being enclosed. 2. An enclosed object or area. 3. That which encloses, as a wall. Also spelled *inclosure.*

en·code (en·kōd′) *v.t.* **·cod·ed, ·cod·ing** To convert (a message, document, etc.) into code.

en·co·mi·um (en·kō′mē·əm) *n.* *pl.* **·mi·ums** or **·mi·a** A formal expression of praise; eulogy. [< Gk. *enkōmion* eulogy]

en·com·pass (in·kum′pəs, in·kom′-) *v.t.* 1. To form a circle around; surround. 2. To enclose; contain.

en·core (äṅ′kôr) *interj.* Again! once more! **—*n.*** The call by an audience for repetition of a performance or for an additional performance; also, that which is performed in response to this call. **—*v.t.* ·cored, ·cor·ing** To call for a repetition of (a performance) or by (a performer). [< F]

en·coun·ter (in·koun′tər) *n.* 1. A meeting with a person or thing, esp. when casual or unexpected. 2. A hostile meeting; contest. **—*v.t.*** 1. To meet, esp. by chance. 2. To meet in battle. 3. To be faced with or contend against (opposition, difficulties, etc.). [< IN-[2] + L *contra* against]

encounter group A group of persons seeking to develop self-awareness, sensitivity to others, etc., through uninhibited expression of feelings and physical contact.

en·cour·age (in·kûr′ij) *v.t.* **·aged, ·ag·ing** 1. To inspire with courage, hope, or resolution. 2. To help or foster. [< OF *en-* in + *corage* courage] **—en·cour′age·ment** *n.* **—en·cour′ag·ing** *adj.* **—en·cour′ag·ing·ly** *adv.*

en·croach (in·krōch′) *v.i.* To intrude stealthily or gradually: with *on* or *upon.* [< OF *en-* in + *croc* hook] **—en·croach′·ment** *n.*

en·crust (in·krust′) *v.t.* & *v.i.* To furnish with or form a crust. Also spelled *incrust.*

en·cum·ber (in·kum′bər) *v.t.* 1. To hinder in action or motion, as with a burden; impede. 2. To block up; crowd, as with obstacles. 3. To weigh down, as with debts.

Also spelled *incumber*. [< OF *en-* in + *combre* obstacle]
-ency *suffix of nouns* A variant of -ENCE, as in *decency*, used to form words expressing quality or condition. [< L *-entia*]
en·cyc·li·cal (en·sik′li·kəl, -sī′kli-) *adj.* Intended for general circulation: said of letters. —*n.* A letter addressed by the Pope to the bishops of the world. [< EN-[2] + Gk. *kyklos* circle]
en·cy·clo·pe·di·a (en·sī′klə·pē′dē·ə) *n.* A comprehensive work made up of articles covering the whole range of knowledge or treating of one particular field. Also **en·cy′clo·pae′di·a.** [< Gk. *enkyklios paideia* a general education] —**en·cy′clo·pe′dic** *adj.*
en·cy·clo·pe·dist (en·sī′klə·pē′dist) *n.* A writer for or compiler of an encyclopedia. Also **en·cy′clo·pae′dist.**
en·cyst (en·sist′) *v.t.* & *v.i.* *Biol.* To enclose or become enclosed in a cyst or sac.
end (end) *n.* 1. The terminal point or part of anything that has length: the *end* of a street. 2. The extreme limit of something; boundary: the *ends* of the earth. 3. The point in time at which something ceases. 4. The purpose of an action. 5. A conclusion; final part. 6. A natural consequence. 7. The termination of existence; death. 8. Fragment; remnant: odds and *ends*. 9. In football, a player positioned at either end of the line. —**to make (both) ends meet** To live within one's income. —*v.t.* 1. To bring to a finish or termination. 2. To be the end of. —*v.i.* 3. To come to an end. [OE *ende*]
en·dan·ger (in·dān′jər) *v.t.* To expose to danger; imperil.
en·dan·gered (in·dān′jərd) *adj.* In danger of extinction: an *endangered* species.
en·dear (in·dir′) *v.t.* To make dear or beloved. —**en·dear′ing** *adj.* —**en·dear′ing·ly** *adv.*
en·dear·ment (in·dir′mənt) *n.* 1. The act of endearing, or the state of being endeared. 2. A loving word, act, etc.
en·deav·or (in·dev′ər) *n.* An attempt or effort. —*v.t.* 1. To make an effort to do or effect; try. —*v.i.* 2. To strive. Also *Brit.* **en·deav′our.** [ME < EN-[1] + DEVOIR]
en·dem·ic (en·dem′ik) *adj.* 1. Peculiar to a particular country or people. 2. *Med.* Confined to or characteristic of a given locality: said of a disease. [< EN-[2] + Gk. *dēmos* people]
end·ing (en′ding) *n.* 1. The act of bringing or coming to an end. 2. The concluding or final part. 3. One or more concluding letters or syllables added to the base of a word, esp. to indicate an inflection.
en·dive (en′dīv, än′dēv) *n.* An herb whose leaves are used in salads. [< L *intibus*]
end·less (end′lis) *adj.* 1. Enduring forever; eternal. 2. Having no end in space; infinite. 3. Continually recurring; incessant. 4. Forming a closed loop or circle. —**end′less·ly** *adv.*
end·most (end′mōst′) *adj.* Most remote; farthest.
endo- *combining form* Within; inside. Also, before vowels, **end-**. [< Gk. *endon* within]
en·do·crine (en′dō·krin, -krēn, -krīn) *Physiol.* *adj.* 1. Secreting internally. 2. Of or pertaining to an endocrine gland or its secretion. [< ENDO- + Gk. *krinein* to separate]
endocrine gland *Anat.* A ductless gland, as the thyroid, pituitary, etc., whose secretions are released directly into the blood.
en·do·cri·nol·o·gy (en′dō·kri·nol′ə·jē, -krī-) *n.* *Med.* A science dealing with the endocrine glands. —**en′do·cri·nol′o·gist** *n.*
en·do·derm (en′dō·dûrm) *n.* *Biol.* The innermost layer of the embryo, developing into the digestive and respiratory systems.
en·dog·a·my (en·dog′ə·mē) *n.* *Anthropol.* Marriage within the group, class, caste, or tribe. —**en·dog′a·mous** *adj.*
en·dog·e·nous (en·doj′ə·nəs) *adj.* *Biol.* Originating or growing from within.
en·do·mor·phic (en′dō·môr′fik) *adj.* Of human body types, characterized by a heavy, rounded body structure. —**en′do·morph** *n.* —**en′do·mor′phy** *n.*
end organ *Physiol.* Any organ adapted for the reception or delivery of nervous stimuli.
en·dorse (in·dôrs′) *v.t.* **·dorsed, ·dors·ing** 1. To write on the back of (a paper); esp., to transfer ownership or assign payment of (a check, note, etc.). 2. To give sanction or support to. 3. To state one's personal approval of (a product) to promote its sale. Also spelled *indorse*. [< IN-[2] + L *dorsum* back] —**en·dor′see** *n.* —**en·dorse′ment** *n.* —**en·dors′er** *n.*
en·do·skel·e·ton (en′dō·skel′ə·tən) *n.* See under SKELETON.
en·do·sperm (en′dō·spûrm) *n.* *Bot.* The nutritive substance in the embryo sac of an ovule.
en·do·ther·mic (en′dō·thûr′mik) *adj.* *Chem.* Pertaining to, attended by, or produced from the absorption of heat. Also **en′do·ther′mal.** [< ENDO- + Gk. *thermē* heat]
en·dow (in·dou′) *v.t.* 1. To bestow a permanent fund or income upon. 2. To furnish or equip, as with talents: usu. with *with*. [< OF *en-* in + *douer* to give < L *dotare* to give] —**en·dow′ment** *n.*
end table A small table beside a chair, sofa, etc.
en·due (in·do͞o′, -dyo͞o′) *v.t.* **·dued, ·du·ing** To endow with some quality, power, etc. [Fusion of OF *enduire* to introduce and *enduire* to clothe]
en·dur·ance (in·do͝or′əns, -dyo͝or′-) *n.* The act or capacity of bearing up, as under hardship or prolonged stress.
en·dure (in·do͝or′, -dyo͝or′) *v.* **·dured, ·dur·ing** *v.t.* 1. To bear up under: to *endure* hardships. 2. To put up with; tolerate. —*v.i.* 3. To continue to be; last. 4. To suffer without yielding. [< IN-[2] + L *durare* to harden] —**en·dur′a·ble** *adj.* —**en·dur′a·bly** *adv.*
en·dur·ing (in·do͝or′ing, -dyo͝or′-) *adj.* 1. Lasting; permanent. 2. Long-suffering. —**en·dur′ing·ly** *adv.*
en·dur·o (en·do͝or′ō, -dyo͝or′ō) *n.* A long automobile or motorcycle race that tests endurance rather than speed.
end·wise (end′wīz′) *adv.* 1. With the end foremost or uppermost. 2. On end. 3. Lengthwise. Also **end′ways′** (-wāz′).
-ene *suffix* *Chem.* 1. Denoting a hydrocarbon compound having one double bond: *ethylene*. 2. Denoting a compound of the benzene series.
en·e·ma (en′ə·mə) *n.* *Med.* 1. A liquid injected into the rectum for cleansing or

diagnostic purposes. 2. The injection of such a liquid. [< EN-² + Gk. *hienai* to send]

en·e·my (en′ə·mē) *n. pl.* **·mies** 1. One who harbors hatred or malicious intent toward another; also, one who or that which opposes a person, cause, etc. 2. A hostile power or military force; also, a member of a hostile force. —*adj.* Of or pertaining to a hostile army or power. [< IN-¹ + L *amicus* friend]

en·er·get·ic (en′ər·jet′ik) *adj.* Having or displaying energy; forceful and efficient. —**en′er·get′i·cal·ly** *adv.*

en·er·get·ics (en′ər·jet′iks) *n.pl.* (*construed as sing.*) The pattern of energy transformations within a system, as in an ecosystem.

en·er·gize (en′ər·jīz) *v.t.* **·gized, ·giz·ing** To give energy, force, or strength to; activate. —**en′er·giz′er** *n.*

en·er·gy (en′ər·jē) *n. pl.* **·gies** 1. Vigor or intensity of action or expression. 2. Capacity or tendency for vigorous action. 3. *Physics* The capacity for doing work and for overcoming inertia. **Potential energy** is due to the position of one body relative to another, and **kinetic energy** is manifested by bodies in motion. [< EN-² + Gk. *ergon* work]

en·er·vate (en′ər·vāt) *v.t.* **·vat·ed, ·vat·ing** To weaken in body or will. [< L *e-* out + *nervus* sinew] —**en′er·va′tion** *n.* —**en′er·va′tor** *n.*

en·fee·ble (en·fē′bəl) *v.t.* **·bled, ·bling** To make feeble. —**en·fee′ble·ment** *n.*

en·fi·lade (en′fə·lād′) *n. Mil.* 1. Gunfire that can rake lengthwise a line of troops, etc. 2. A position exposed to such fire. [< F < *en-* in + *fil* thread] —**en′fi·lade′** *v.t.* **·lad·ed, ·lad·ing**

en·fold (in·fōld′) *v.t.* 1. To wrap in folds; envelop. 2. To embrace. Also *infold.*

en·force (in·fôrs′) *v.t.* **·forced, ·forc·ing** 1. To compel observance of (a law, etc.). 2. To impose (obedience, etc.) by force. [< IN-² + L *fortis* strong] —**en·force′a·ble** *adj.* —**en·force′ment** *n.* —**en·forc′er** *n.*

en·fran·chise (in·fran′chīz) *v.t.* **·chised, ·chis·ing** 1. To endow with a franchise, as with the right to vote. 2. To set free, as from bondage or legal liabilities. [< OF *en-* in + *franc* free] —**en·fran′chise·ment** *n.*

en·gage (in·gāj′) *v.* **·gaged, ·gag·ing** *v.t.* 1. To hire or employ (a person, service, etc.). 2. To reserve the use of, as lodgings. 3. To hold the interest or attention of; engross. 4. To occupy; keep busy. 5. To bind by a pledge, contract, etc. 6. To betroth: usu. in the passive. 7. To enter into conflict with: to *engage* the enemy. 8. *Mech.* To mesh or interlock with. —*v.i.* 9. To occupy oneself in an undertaking. 10. To pledge oneself; warrant. 11. To enter into combat. 12. *Mech.* To mesh. [< F *en-* in + *gager* to pledge] —**en·gaged′** *adj.*

en·ga·gé (äṅ·gà·zhā′) *adj. French* Actively committed to a cause.

en·gage·ment (in·gāj′mənt) *n.* 1. The act of engaging, or the state of being engaged. 2. Something that engages or binds, as an obligation. 3. Betrothal. 4. An appointment; date. 5. Employment, esp. for a limited period. 6. A hostile encounter; battle.

en·gag·ing (in·gā′jing) *adj.* Winning; pleasing. —**en·gag′ing·ly** *adv.*

en·gen·der (in·jen′dər) *v.t.* To cause to exist; produce. [< L *ingenerare* to create]

en·gine (en′jən) *n.* 1. A machine that converts heat energy into mechanical work. 2. A locomotive. 3. An apparatus or mechanical contrivance for producing some effect. [ME *engin* < L *in-* in + *gen-*, root of *gignere* to beget]

en·gi·neer (en′jə·nir′) *n.* 1. One versed in or practicing any branch of engineering. 2. One who operates an engine. 3. *Mil.* A member of a corps of men engaged in engineering projects. —*v.t.* 1. To put through or manage by contrivance: to *engineer* a scheme. 2. To plan and superintend as engineer.

en·gi·neer·ing (en′jə·nir′ing) *n.* 1. The art and science of designing, constructing, and operating roads, bridges, buildings, etc. 2. Clever planning or maneuvering.

Eng·lish (ing′glish) —*n.* 1. The people of England collectively: with *the.* 2. The language of England, the United States, and areas formerly controlled by England. —**Old English** or **Anglo-Saxon** The English language from about A.D. 450 to 1050. —**Middle English** The language of England after the Norman Conquest, from about 1050 to 1475. —**Modern English** The English language since 1475. 3. In billiards, a twist or spin given to a ball. [OE *Engle* the Angles] —**Eng′lish** *adj.*

English horn A double-reed instrument having a pitch a fifth lower than an oboe.

Eng·lish·man (ing′glish·mən) *n. pl.* **·men** (-mən) 1. A native or inhabitant of England. 2. An English ship.

English muffin A round, flat muffin made with little shortening, and usu. eaten toasted.

en·gorge (en·gôrj′) *v.t.* **·gorged, ·gorg·ing** 1. To fill with blood, as an artery. 2. To devour or swallow greedily. [< F *en-* in + *gorge* throat]

en·graft (en·graft′) *v.t.* 1. *Bot.* To graft. 2. To set firmly; implant.

en·gram (en′gram) *n.* A permanently altered state in the protoplasm of animal cells assumed to result from the temporary excitation of certain stimuli and to account for memory.

en·grave (in·grāv′) *v.t.* **·graved, ·grav·ing** 1. To carve or etch figures, letters, etc., into (a surface). 2. To cut (pictures, lettering, etc.) into metal, stone, or wood, for printing. 3. To print from plates so made. [< EN-¹ + OE *grafan* to dig] —**en·grav′er** *n.*

en·grav·ing (in·grā′ving) *n.* 1. The act or art of cutting designs, etc., into a surface. 2. An engraved design; plate. 3. An impression printed from an engraved plate; print.

en·gross (in·grōs′) *v.t.* 1. To occupy completely; absorb. 2. To copy legibly in a large hand, as a document. [< LL *ingrossare* to write large]

en·gross·ing (in·grō′sing) *adj.* Holding the attention or interest completely; absorbing.

en·gulf (in·gulf′) *v.t.* To flow over, bury, or overwhelm completely.

en·hance (in·hans′) *v.t.* **·hanced, ·hanc·ing** To heighten or increase, as in reputation, beauty, or quality. [< AF *en-* in, on + *haucer* to lift] —**en·hance′ment** *n.* —**en·hanc′er** *n.*

e·nig·ma (i·nig′mə) *n.* 1. An obscure or ambiguous saying. 2. Anything that puzzles or baffles. [< Gk. *ainissesthai* to speak in riddles] —**en·ig·mat·ic** (en′ig·mat′ik, ē′nig-) *adj.* —**en′ig·mat′i·cal·ly** *adv.*

en·join (in·join′) *v.t.* 1. To order or command (a person or group). 2. To impose (a condition, course of action, etc.). 3. To forbid or prohibit, esp. by judicial order. [< IN-² + L *jungere* to join]

en·joy (in·joi′) *v.t.* 1. To experience joy or pleasure in. 2. To have the use or benefit of [< OF *en-* in + *joir* to rejoice] —**en·joy′a·ble** *adj.* —**en·joy′a·bly** *adv.* —**en·joy′ment** *n.*

en·kin·dle (en·kin′dəl) *v.t.* **·dled, ·dling** 1. To set on fire. 2. To stir to action; excite.

en·large (in·lärj′) *v.* **·larged, ·larg·ing** *v.t.* 1. To make larger. —*v.i.* 2. To become larger. 3. To express oneself in greater detail or at greater length: with *on* or *upon.* —**en·large′ment** *n.*

en·light·en (in·līt′n) *v.t.* To give revealing or broadening knowledge to. —**en·light′·en·ment** *n.*

en·list (in·list′) *v.t.* 1. To engage (someone) for the armed forces. 2. To secure the active aid or participation of (a person, etc.). —*v.i.* 3. To enter military service without being drafted. 4. To join some venture, cause, etc.: with *in.* —**en·list′ment** *n.*

en·list·ed man (in·lis′tid) A member of the armed forces who is not a commissioned officer or warrant officer.

en·li·ven (in·lī′vən) *v.t.* To make lively, cheerful, or sprightly.

en masse (en mas′, *Fr.* äṅ mȧs′) All together. [< F]

en·mesh (en·mesh′) *v.t.* To ensnare in or as in a net.

en·mi·ty (en′mə·tē) *n. pl.* **·ties** Deep-seated unfriendliness; hostility. [< IN-¹ + L *amicus* friend]

en·no·ble (i·nō′bəl, en-) *v.t.* **·bled, ·bling** To make honorable or noble; dignify. —**en·no′ble·ment** *n.* —**en·no′bler** *n.*

en·nui (än·wē′, än′wē; *Fr.* äṅ·nwē′) *n.* A feeling of listless weariness and boredom. [< F]

e·nor·mi·ty (i·nôr′mə·tē) *n. pl.* **·ties** 1. Unusually great size. 2. The quality of being outrageous; heinousness. 3. An outrageous offense; atrocity. [See ENORMOUS.]

e·nor·mous (i·nôr′məs) *adj.* Far exceeding the usual size, amount, degree, etc. [< L *enormis* < *e-* out + *norma* rule] —**e·nor′·mous·ly** *adv.*

e·nough (i·nuf′) *adj.* Adequate for any demand or need; sufficient. —*n.* An ample supply; a sufficiency. —*adv.* 1. So as to be sufficient. 2. Quite; very. 3. Adequately; fairly; tolerably. [OE *genōh, genōg*]

en·plane (en·plān′) *v.i.* **·planed, ·plan·ing** To board an airplane.

en·quire (in·kwīr′) See INQUIRE.

en·rage (in·rāj′) *v.t.* **·raged, ·rag·ing** To throw into a rage.

en·rapt (in·rapt′) *adj.* Rapt; enraptured.

en·rap·ture (in·rap′chər) *v.t.* **·tured, ·tur·ing** To bring into a state of rapture; delight.

en·rich (in·rich′) *v.t.* 1. To make rich or increase the wealth of. 2. To make more productive, as soil. 3. To add attractive or desirable elements to; make better, more interesting, etc., by adding. —**en·rich′ment** *n.*

en·roll (in·rōl′) *v.t.* 1. To write or record (a name) in a roll; register; list. 2. To enlist. 3. To place on record; record. 4. To roll up; wrap. —*v.i.* 5. To enlist; register oneself. Also *Brit.* **en·rol′.**

en·roll·ment (in·rōl′mənt) *n.* 1. An enrolling or being enrolled. 2. A record of persons or things enrolled. 3. The number of persons or things enrolled. Also *Brit.* **en·rol′ment.**

en route (än ro͞ot′, en; *Fr.* äṅ ro͞ot′) On the way. [< F]

en·sconce (en·skons′) *v.t.* **·sconced, ·sconc·ing** 1. To fix securely or comfortably in some place. 2. To shelter; hide.

en·sem·ble (än·säm′bəl, *Fr.* äṅ·säṅ′bl′) *n.* 1. All the parts of a thing viewed as a whole. 2. An individual's entire costume, including accessories. 3. The entire cast of a play, ballet, etc. 4. *Music* A group of players or singers performing together. [< F < L *insimul* at the same time]

en·shrine (in·shrīn′) *v.t.* **·shrined, ·shrin·ing** 1. To place in or as in a shrine. 2. To cherish devoutly; hold sacred. —**en·shrine′ment** *n.*

en·shroud (in·shroud′) *v.t.* To shroud; conceal.

en·sign (en′sīn; *also, and always for def. 2,* en′sən) *n.* 1. A flag or banner. 2. *Naval* A commissioned officer of the lowest grade. 3. A badge, symbol, or distinguishing mark. [ME *ensigne* < L *insignia* insignia] —**en′·sign·ship, en sign·cy** *n.*

en·si·lage (en′sə·lij) *n.* 1. The process of preserving green fodder in closed pits or silos. 2. Silage. [< F] —**en·sile** (en·sīl′) *v.t.* **·siled, ·sil·ing**

en·slave (in·slāv′) *v.t.* **·slaved, ·slav·ing** 1. To make a slave of. 2. To dominate; control. —**en·slave′ment** *n.* —**en·slav′er** *n.*

en·snare (en·snâr′) *v.t.* **·snared, ·snar·ing** To catch in a snare; trick. —**en·snare′ment** *n.*

en·sue (en·so͞o′) *v.i.* **·sued, ·su·ing** 1. To follow subsequently; occur afterward. 2. To follow as a consequence; result. [< IN-² + L *sequi* to follow]

en·sure (in·sho͝or′) *v.t.* **·sured, ·sur·ing** 1. To make sure or certain; guarantee. 2. To make safe: with *from* or *against.* [< OF *en-* in + *seur* sure]

-ent *suffix of nouns and adjectives* 1. Having the quality or performing the action of (the main element): *dependent.* 2. One who or that which performs the action of (the main element): *superintendent.* [< F *-ent* < L *-ens, -entis,* suffix of present participle]

en·tab·la·ture (en·tab′lə·chər) *n. Archit.* The uppermost part of a wall or structure which is supported by columns. [< Ital. < IN-² + *tavola* base, table]

en·tail (in·tāl′) *v.t.* 1. To impose, involve, or result in by necessity. 2. *Law* To restrict or leave the inheritance of (real property) to an unalterable succession of heirs. [< OF *entaillier* to cut] —**en·tail′ment** *n.*

en·tan·gle (in·tang′gəl) *v.t.* **·gled, ·gling** 1. To catch in or as in a snare; hamper. 2. To make tangled; snarl. —**en·tan′gle·ment** *n.*

en·tente (än·tänt′, *Fr.* äṅ·täṅt′) *n.* A mutual agreement; also, the parties entering into a mutual agreement. [< F]

en·ter (en′tər) *v.t.* 1. To come or go into. 2. To penetrate; pierce. 3. To set in; insert. 4. To become a member of; join. 5. To start out upon; embark on. 6. To obtain admission to (a school, etc.). 7. To cause to be admitted.

8. To write down, as in a list. 9. To record officially. —*v.i.* 10. To come or go into a particular place. **—to enter into** 1. To start out; embark on. 2. To engage in. 3. To form a part or constituent of. 4. To consider or discuss. [< OF entrer < L *intra* within]

en·ter·ic (en·ter′ik) *adj.* Intestinal. [< Gk. *enteron* intestine]

en·ter·i·tis (en′tə·rī′tis) *n. Pathol.* Inflammation of the intestines.

en·ter·prise (en′tər·prīz) *n.* 1. Any project, undertaking, or task, especially when difficult or important. 2. Boldness and energy in practical affairs. [< OF < *entre-* between + *prendre* to take]

en·ter·pris·ing (en′tər·prī′zing) *adj.* Energetic and venturesome. **—en′ter·pris′ing·ly** *adv.*

en·ter·tain (en′tər·tān′) *v.t.* 1. To amuse; divert. 2. To extend hospitality to; receive as a guest. 3. To take into consideration, as a proposal. 4. To keep or bear in mind. —*v.i.* 5. To receive and care for guests. [< F *entre-* between + *tenir* to hold] **—en′ter·tain′er** *n.*

en·ter·tain·ing (en′tər·tā′ning) *adj.* Amusing; diverting. **—en′ter·tain′ing·ly** *adv.*

en·ter·tain·ment (en′tər·tān′mənt) *n.* 1. The act of entertaining, or the state of being entertained. 2. Something that entertains, as a play.

en·thrall (in·thrôl′) *v.t.* 1. To spellbind; fascinate. 2. To enslave. Also **en·thral′.**

en·throne (in·thrōn′) *v.t.* **·throned, ·thron·ing** 1. To put upon a throne. 2. To exalt. **—en·throne′ment** *n.*

en·thuse (in·thōōz′) *v.t. & v.i.* **·thused, ·thus·ing** *Informal* To make or become enthusiastic.

en·thu·si·asm (in·thōō′zē·az′əm) *n.* 1. Keen, animated interest in and preoccupation with something. 2. A cause or object of intense, lively interest. [< Gk. *entheos, enthous* inspired, possessed] **—en·thu′si·ast** (-ast, -ist) *n.* **—en·thu′si·as′tic** (-as′tik) *adj.* **—en·thu′si·as′ti·cal·ly** *adv.*

en·tice (in·tīs′) *v.t.* **·ticed, ·tic·ing** To attract by arousing hope of pleasure, profit, etc.; allure. [< OF *enticier* to set afire] **—en·tice′ment** *n.* **—en·tic′ing·ly** *adv.*

en·tire (in·tīr′) *adj.* 1. Having no part missing; whole; complete. 2. Not broken; in one piece; intact. [< L *integer* whole] **—en·tire′ly** *adv.*

en·tire·ty (in·tī′rə·tē, -ər·tē) *n. pl.* **·ties** 1. The state or condition of being whole or complete. 2. That which is entire.

en·ti·tle (in·tīt′l) *v.t.* **·tled, ·tling** 1. To give the right to receive, demand, or do something. 2. To give a name, title, or designation to.

en·ti·ty (en′tə·tē) *n. pl.* **·ties** 1. Something existing objectively or in the mind. 2. Existence as opposed to nonexistence. [< L ppr. of *esse* to be]

ento- *combining form* Interior. Also, before vowels, **ent-.** [< Gk. *entos* within]

en·tomb (in·tōōm′) *v.t.* To place in or as in a tomb; bury. [< OF *en-* in + *tombe* tomb] **—en·tomb′ment** *n.*

entomo- *combining form* Insect. Also, before vowels, **entom-.** [< Gk. *entoma*]

en·to·mol·o·gy (en′tə·mol′ə·jē) *n.* The branch of zoology that treats of insects. **—en′to·mol′o·gist** *n.*

en·tou·rage (än′tōō·räzh′) *n.* A group of followers or attendants; retinue. [< F < *entourer* to surround]

en·tr′acte (än·trakt′, *Fr.* äṅ·tråkt′) *n.* 1. The interval between the acts of a play, opera, etc. 2. Music, dance, etc., performed between acts. [< F]

en·trails (en′trālz, -trəlz) *n.pl.* The internal parts of a person or animal; esp., the intestines; bowels; guts. [< LL *intralia* intestines]

en·train (en·trān′) *v.t. & v.i.* To board or put aboard a train.

en·trance[1] (en′trəns) *n.* 1. The act of entering. 2. A place or passage allowing entry. 3. The right or power of entering; admittance.

en·trance[2] (in·trans′) *v.t.* **·tranced, ·tranc·ing** To delight; charm. **—en·tranc′ing·ly** *adv.*

en·trance·way (en′trəns·wā′) *n.* A means of entrance.

en·trant (en′trənt) *n.* One who enters; esp., one who enters a contest.

en·trap (in·trap′) *v.t.* **·trapped, ·trap·ping** 1. To catch in or as in a trap. 2. To trick into danger or difficulty. **—en·trap′ment** *n.*

en·treat (in·trēt′) *v.t. & v.i.* 1. To beseech with intensity; implore. 2. To request; petition. [< OF *en-* in + *traitier* to treat] **—en·treat′ing·ly** *adv.*

en·treat·y (in·trē′tē) *n. pl.* **·ies** An earnest request.

en·tre·chat (äṅ·trə·shä′) *n. French* In ballet, a leap upward in which the dancer repeatedly crosses his feet.

en·trée (än′trā, *Fr.* äṅ·trā′) *n.* 1. The act or privilege of entering; admission. 2. The principal course at a meal. Also **en′tree.** [< F, orig. pp. of *entrer.* See ENTER.]

en·trench (in·trench′) *v.t.* 1. To fortify or protect with or as with a trench. 2. To establish firmly: The idea was *entrenched* in his mind. —*v.i.* 3. To encroach: with *on* or *upon.* **—en·trench′ment** *n.*

en·tre·pre·neur (än′trə·prə·nûr′, *Fr.* äṅ·trə·prə·nœr′) *n.* One who undertakes to start and conduct an enterprise or business. [< F < *entreprendre.* See ENTERPRISE.] **—en′tre·pre·neur′i·al** *adj.*

en·tro·py (en′trə·pē) *n. Physics* 1. A measure of the amount of energy unavailable for conversion into work. 2. The irreversible tendency of a system, including the universe, toward increasing disorder; also, the final state predictable from this. [< EN-[2] + Gk. *trepein* to turn]

en·trust (in·trust′) *v.t.* 1. To give over to another for care or performance. 2. To place something in the care or trust of. Also spelled *intrust.*

en·try (en′trē) *n. pl.* **·tries** 1. The act of coming in; entrance. 2. A place of entrance. 3. The act of entering anything in a register, list, etc.; also, the item entered. 4. A contestant listed for a race, competition, etc.

en·twine (in·twīn′) *v.t. & v.i.* **·twined, ·twin·ing** To twine or twist together.

e·nu·mer·ate (i·nōō′mə·rāt, -nyōō′-) *v.t.* **·at·ed, ·at·ing** 1. To name one by one; list. 2. To ascertain the number of. [< L *e-* out + *numerare* to count] **—e·nu′mer·a′tion** *n.*

e·nun·ci·ate (i·nun′sē·āt, -shē-) *v.* **·at·ed, ·at·ing** *v.t.* 1. To articulate (speech sounds), esp. clearly. 2. To state with exactness. 3.

To announce or proclaim. —*v.i.* 4. To pronounce words, esp. clearly. [< L *e-* out + *nuntiare* to announce] —**e·nun′ci·a′tion** *n.* —**e·nun′ci·a′tor** *n.*

en·u·re·sis (en′yə·rē′sis) *n.* *Pathol.* Involuntary urination. [< EN-[2] + Gk. *oureein* to urinate]

en·vel·op (in·vel′əp) *v.t.* **·oped, ·op·ing** 1. To wrap; enclose. 2. To hide; conceal. 3. To surround. [< OF *en-* in + *voluper* to wrap] —**en·vel′op·ment** *n.*

en·ve·lope (en′və·lōp, än′-) *n.* 1. A paper case or wrapper for enclosing a letter or the like, usu. having a gummed flap for sealing. 2. Any enveloping cover or wrapper. 3. *Aeron.* The outer fabric covering of a dirigible, balloon, etc.

en·ven·om (en·ven′əm) *v.t.* 1. To impregnate with venom; poison. 2. To embitter.

en·vi·a·ble (en′vē·ə·bəl) *adj.* So admirable or desirable as to arouse envy. —**en′vi·a·bly** *adv.*

en·vi·ous (en′vē·əs) *adj.* Full of, characterized by, or expressing envy. —**en′vi·ous·ly** *adv.* —**en′vi·ous·ness** *n.*

en·vi·ron·ment (in·vī′rən·mənt, -vī′ərn-) *n.* 1. The external circumstances, conditions, and things that affect the existence and development of an individual, organism, or group. 2. Surroundings. [< OF *environ* around] —**en·vi′ron·men′tal** *adj.*

en·vi·ron·ment·al·ist (in·vī′rən·men′təl·ist, -vī′ərn-) *n.* 1. One who advocates preservation of the environment. 2. One who attaches more importance to environment than to heredity in the development of a person.

en·vi·rons (in·vī′rəns) *n.pl.* A surrounding, outlying area, as about a city; outskirts.

en·vis·age (en·viz′ij) *v.t.* **·aged, ·ag·ing** To form a mental image of; visualize; conceive of. [< EN-[1] + VISAGE]

en·vi·sion (en·vizh′ən) *v.t.* To see or foresee in the mind.

en·voy[1] (en′voi, än′-) *n.* 1. A diplomatic representative, ranking next below an ambassador. 2. A person, as a diplomat, entrusted with a mission. [< F *envoyé* < L *in-* + *via* way, road]

en·voy[2] (en′voi, än′-) *n.* The closing lines of a poem or prose work, often in the form of a dedication. Also **envoi.** [< F *envoi.* See ENVOY[1].]

en·vy (en′vē) *n.* *pl.* **·vies** 1. A feeling of resentment or discontent over another's superior attainments, endowments, or possessions. 2. Any object of envy. —*v.* **·vied, ·vy·ing** *v.t.* 1. To regard with envy; feel envy because of. —*v.i.* 2. To feel or show envy. [< IN-[2] + L *videre* to see, look]

en·zyme (en′zīm) *n.* *Biochem.* A complex, mostly protein substance able to initiate or accelerate specific chemical reactions in the metabolism of plants and animals; an organic catalyst. [< EN-[2] + Gk. *zymē* leaven] —**en·zy·mat·ic** (en′zī·mat′ik, -zi-) *adj.*

eo- *combining form* Earliest; early part of. [< Gk. *ēos* dawn, daybreak]

e·o·li·an (ē·ō′lē·ən) See AEOLIAN.

E·o·lith·ic (ē′ə·lith′ik) *adj.* *Anthropol.* Of or pertaining to a period of early human culture, known only by the rudest implements of bone and chipped stone. [< EO- + Gk. *lithos* stone]

e·on (ē′ən, ē′on) *n.* 1. An incalculable period of time. 2. *Geol.* A time interval including two or more eras. Also spelled *aeon.* [< L *aeon* < Gk. *aiōn* age]

e·o·sin (ē′ə·sin) *n.* *Chem.* A reddish coloring matter derived from coal tar. Also **e′o·sine** (-sin, -sēn). [< Gk. *ēos* morning red, dawn]

-eous *suffix* Of the nature of. [< L *-eus*]

ep·au·let (ep′ə·let) *n.* *Mil.* A shoulder ornament, usu. with a fringe, as on military and naval uniforms. Also **ep′au·lette.** [< F *épaulette* < L *spatula* shoulder blade < L *spatha* spoon, sword]

é·pée (ā·pā′) *n.* A dueling sword with a sharp point and no cutting edge. [< F < L *spatha,* spoon, sword]

e·phed·rine (i·fed′rin, ef′ə·drēn) *n.* *Chem.* An alkaloid used for relief of asthma, hay fever, nasal congestion, etc. [< NL *Ephedra,* a genus of plants]

e·phem·er·a (i·fem′ər·ə) *n.* *pl.* **·er·as** or **·er·ae** (-ə·rē) 1. A May fly. 2. Anything of very short life or duration. [< Gk. *epi-* on + *hēmera* day]

e·phem·er·al (i·fem′ər·əl) *adj.* 1. Lasting but a short time. 2. Living one day only, as certain insects. —*n.* Anything lasting for a very short time. —**e·phem′er·al·ly** *adv.*

e·phem·er·id (i·fem′ər·id) *n.* A May fly.

E·phe·sians (i·fē′zhəns) *n.pl.* (*construed as sing.*) A book of the New Testament, consisting of St. Paul's epistle to the church at Ephesus.

epi- *prefix* 1. Upon; above; among; outside: *epidermis.* 2. Besides; over; in addition to: *epilogue.* 3. Near; close to; beside. Also: **ep-,** before vowels, as in *eponym;* **eph-,** before an aspirate, as in *ephemeral.* [< Gk. *epi* upon, on, besides]

ep·ic (ep′ik) *n.* 1. A long, formal, narrative poem, typically about heroic exploits and achievements. 2. A novel, drama, etc., that in scale or subject resembles such a poem. —*adj.* 1. Of, pertaining to, or suitable as a theme for an epic. 2. Heroic; grandiose. [< L *epicus* < Gk. *epos* tale, song]

ep·i·can·thus (ep′ə·kan′thəs) *n.* *pl.* **·thi** (-thī) A small fold of skin over the inner corner of the eye, typical of Mongoloid peoples. Also **epicanthic fold.** [< Gk. *epi-* upon + *kanthos* corner of the eye] —**ep′i·can′thic** *adj.*

ep·i·cene (ep′ə·sēn) *adj.* 1. Belonging to one sex and having characteristics of the other. 2. Lacking characteristics of either sex; sexless. —*n.* An epicene person. [< Gk. *epi-* upon + *koinos* common]

ep·i·cen·ter (ep′ə·sen′tər) *n.* *Geol.* The point or area on the earth's surface directly above the focus of an earthquake.

ep·i·cure (ep′ə·kyŏŏr) *n.* One given to luxurious living; a sensualist; esp., a devotee of good food and drink. [after *Epicurus,* Greek philosopher] —**ep′i·cu·re′an** *adj.* & *n.* —**ep′i·cur·ism** *n.*

Ep·i·cu·re·an·ism (ep′ə·kyŏŏ·rē′ən·iz′əm) *n.* The doctrines of Epicurus, Greek philosopher, who taught that the chief aim of life is pleasure regulated by temperance, peace of mind, and cultural pursuits. Also **Ep′i·cur·ism.** —**Ep′i·cu·re′an** *adj.* & *n.*

ep·i·dem·ic (ep′ə·dem′ik) *adj.* Breaking out suddenly and spreading rapidly in a particular area: said esp. of contagious diseases. —*n.* 1. An epidemic disease. 2. Anything temporarily widespread, as a fad. [< Gk. *epi-* among + *dēmos* people]

ep·i·der·mis (ep′ə·dûr′mis) *n.* 1. *Anat.* The outer layer of the skin: also called *cuticle.* 2. *Bot.* The outermost covering of a plant when there are several layers of tissue. [< Gk. *epi-* upon + *derma* skin] —**ep′i·der′mal** *adj.*

ep·i·glot·tis (ep′ə·glot′is) *n.* *Anat.* A leaf-shaped, cartilaginous lid that covers the windpipe during the act of swallowing. [< Gk. *epi-* upon + *glōtta* tongue] —**ep′i·glot′tal** *adj.*

ep·i·gram (ep′ə·gram) *n.* 1. A brief, clever, pointed, usu. paradoxical remark or observation. 2. A short, witty, often satirical verse. [< Gk. *epi-* upon + *graphein* to write] —**ep·i·gram·mat·ic** (ep′i·grə·mat′ik) *adj.*

ep·i·graph (ep′ə·graf) *n.* 1. An inscription on a monument, tomb, etc. 2. A quotation prefixed to a book. [< Gk. *epi-* upon + *graphein* to write] —**ep′i·graph′ic** *adj.*

e·pig·ra·phy (i·pig′rə·fē) *n.* 1. The study of inscriptions. 2. Epigraphs collectively. —**e·pig′ra·phist** *n.*

ep·i·lep·sy (ep′ə·lep′sē) *n.* *Pathol.* A disorder of the nervous system marked by attacks of unconsciousness with or without convulsions. See GRAND MAL, PETIT MAL. [< Gk. *epi-* upon + *lambanein* to seize] —**ep′i·lep′tic** *n. & adj.*

ep·i·logue (ep′ə·lôg, -log) *n.* 1. A short section appended to a novel, poem, etc., by way of commentary. 2. A short speech appended to a play. Also **ep′i·log.** [< Gk. *epi-* in addition + *legein* to say]

ep·i·neph·rine (ep′ə·nef′rin, -rēn) *n.* *Chem.* An adrenal hormone, used as a heart stimulant: also called *adrenaline.* Also **ep′i·neph′rin** (-rin). [< Gk. *epi-* upon + *nephros* kidney]

E·piph·a·ny (i·pif′ə·nē) *n.* *Eccl.* A festival, held on January 6, commemorating the visit of the Magi to the infant Christ.

ep·i·phyte (ep′ə·fīt) *n.* *Bot.* A plant growing upon, but not receiving its nourishment from, another plant, as an orchid, moss, etc. —**ep′i·phyt′ic** (-fit′ik) *adj.*

e·pis·co·pa·cy (i·pis′kə·pə·sē) *n.* *pl.* **·cies** Government of a church by bishops. [< LL < Gk. *epi-* over + *scopein* to look]

e·pis·co·pal (i·pis′kə·pəl) *adj.* Of, pertaining to, or governed by bishops. [< LL *episcopalis* < *episcopus* bishop]

Episcopal Church The Protestant Episcopal Church.

E·pis·co·pa·li·an (i·pis′kə·pā′lē·ən, -pāl′yən) *adj.* Belonging to the Protestant Episcopal Church. —**E·pis′co·pa′li·an** *n.*

e·pis·co·pate (i·pis′kə·pit, -pāt) *n.* 1. The office, dignity, or term of office of a bishop. 2. Bishops collectively.

ep·i·sode (ep′ə·sōd) *n.* 1. A section of a novel, poem, etc., complete in itself. 2. A part of a serialized story or play; installment. 3. An event or related series of events. [< Gk. *epi-* beside + *eisodos* entrance]

ep·i·sod·ic (ep′ə·sod′ik) *adj.* 1. Of, relating to, or resembling an episode. 2. Broken up into episodes; esp., disjointed. —**ep′i·sod′i·cal·ly** *adv.*

e·pis·te·mol·o·gy (i·pis′tə·mol′ə·jē) *n.* *pl.* **·gies** The branch of philosophy that investigates the nature of human knowledge. [< Gk. *epistēmē* knowledge + -LOGY] —**e·pis·te·mo·log·i·cal** (i·pis′tə·mə·loj′i·kəl) *adj.* —**e·pis′te·mol′o·gist** *n.*

e·pis·tle (i·pis′əl) *n.* 1. A letter, esp. when long or formal. 2. *Usu. cap.* *Eccl.* **a** One of the letters written by an apostle. **b** A selection taken from one of these letters and read as part of a service. [< Gk. *epi-* to + *stellein* to send] —**e·pis·to·lar·y** (i·pis′tə·ler′ē) *adj.*

ep·i·taph (ep′ə·taf) *n.* An inscription on a tomb or monument in memory of the dead. [< Gk. *epi-* upon, at + *taphos* a tomb]

ep·i·the·li·um (ep′ə·thē′lē·əm) *n.* *pl.* **·li·ums** or **·li·a** *Biol.* A membranous tissue lining cavities and ducts of the body. [< Gk. *epi-* upon + *thēlē* nipple] —**ep′i·the′li·al** *adj.*

ep·i·thet (ep′ə·thet) *n.* 1. A descriptive word or phrase characterizing a person or thing. 2. A disparaging or abusive name. [< Gk. *epi-* upon + *tithenai* to place]

e·pit·o·me (i·pit′ə·mē) *n.* 1. A typical or extreme example; embodiment. 2. A concise summary; abridgment. [< Gk. *epi-* upon + *temnein* to cut] —**e·pit′o·mize** *v.t.* **·mized, ·miz·ing**

ep·i·zo·ot·ic (ep′ə·zō·ot′ik) *adj.* Affecting many animals within a wide area: said esp. of diseases.

e plu·ri·bus u·num (ē plŏŏr′ə·bəs yōō′nəm) *Latin* One out of many: motto of the U.S.

ep·och (ep′ək, *Brit.* ē′pok) *n.* 1. A point in time marked by the beginning of a new development or state of things. 2. An interval of time memorable for extraordinary events, important influences, etc. 3. *Geol.* A time interval less than a period. 4. *Astron.* A moment of time when a planet reaches a certain position in relation to the sun, used as a reference point. [< Gk. *epi-* upon + *echein* to hold] —**ep′och·al** *adj.*

ep·o·nym (ep′ə·nim) *n.* A real or legendary personage from whom something derives its name. [< Gk. *epi-* upon + *onyma* name] —**e·pon·y·mous** (i·pon′ə·məs) *adj.*

e·pox·y (e·pok′sē) *n.* *pl.* **·ies** Epoxy resin.

epoxy resin A thermosetting resin, with strong adhesive qualities, used in adhesives and coatings.

ep·si·lon (ep′sə·lon) *n.* The fifth letter and second vowel in the Greek alphabet (Ε, ϵ), corresponding to English short *e.* [< Gk.]

Epsom salts A hydrous magnesium sulfate, used as a purge or to reduce inflammation.

eq·ua·ble (ek′wə·bəl, ē′kwə-) *adj.* 1. Not varying greatly; even. 2. Not easily upset; tranquil. 3. Evenly proportioned; uniform. [< L *aequare* to make equal] —**eq′ua·bil′i·ty** *n.* —**eq′ua·bly** *adv.*

e·qual (ē′kwəl) *adj.* 1. Identical in size, extent, etc. 2. Having the same rights, rank, etc. 3. Having the same abilities, degree of excellence, etc. 4. Evenly proportioned; balanced. 5. Affecting or shared by all alike: *equal* rights. 6. Having the requisite ability, power, etc.: with *to: equal* to the task. —*v.t.* **e·qualed** or **e·qualled, e·qual·ing** or **e·qual·ling** 1. To be equal to; match. 2. To do or produce something equal to. —*n.* A person or thing equal to another. [< L *aequus* even] —**e·qual·i·ty** (i·kwol′ə·tē) *n.* —**e′qual·ly** *adv.*

e·qual·ize (ē′kwəl·īz) *v.t.* **·ized, ·iz·ing** To make equal or uniform. —**e′qual·iz′er** *n.*

equal sign A sign (=) denoting numbers, quantities, etc., equal to one another.

e·qua·nim·i·ty (ē′kwə·nim′ə·tē, ek′wə-) *n.* Evenness of mind or temper. [< L *aequus* even + *animus* mind]

e·quate (i·kwāt′) *v.t.* **e·quat·ed, e·quat·ing** To consider as equivalent or comparable. [< L *aequus* even]

e·qua·tion (i·kwā′zhən, -shən) *n.* 1. The act of making equal, or the state of being equal. 2. *Math.* A statement expressing (usu. by =) the equality of two quantities. 3. *Chem.* A symbolic representation of a chemical reaction.

e·qua·tor (i·kwā′tər) *n.* The great circle of the earth, an imaginary line equally distant from the North and South Poles. [< LL *aequator* equalizer] **—e·qua·to·ri·al** (ē′kwə·tôr′ē·əl, ek′wə-) *adj.*

eq·uer·ry (ek′wər·ē) *n. pl.* **·ries** 1. An officer in charge of the horses of a prince or nobleman. 2. A personal attendant of a member of the royal household of England. [Confusion of F *écurie* stable with OF *escuier* esquire]

e·ques·tri·an (i·kwes′trē·ən) *adj.* 1. Pertaining to horses or horsemanship. 2. On horseback. **—*n.*** A rider on horseback. [< L *equus* horse] **—e·ques′tri·enne′** (-en′) *n.fem.*

equi- *combining form* Equal; equally: **equiangular, equidistance, equidistant, equiprobable, equisided, equispaced, equivalued.** [< L *aequus*]

e·qui·lat·er·al (ē′kwə·lat′ər·əl) *adj.* Having sides of equal length. **—e′qui·lat′er·al** *n.*

e·qui·lib·ri·um (ē′kwə·lib′rē·əm) *n. pl.* **·ri·ums** or **·ri·a** A state of balance between two or more opposing forces. [< EQUI- + L *libra* balance]

e·quine (ē′kwīn) *adj.* Of, pertaining to, or like a horse. **—*n.*** A horse. [< L *equus* horse]

e·qui·nox (ē′kwə·noks) *n.* One of two opposite points at which the sun crosses the celestial equator, when the days and nights are equal; also, the time of this crossing (about March 21, the **vernal** or **spring equinox,** and Sept. 21, the **autumnal equinox**). [< EQUI- + L *nox* night] **—e′qui·noc′tial** (-nok′shəl) *adj.*

e·quip (i·kwip′) *v.t.* **e·quipped, e·quip·ping** To furnish or fit out with whatever is needed for any purpose or undertaking. [prob. < ON *skipa* to outfit a vessel]

eq·ui·page (ek′wə·pij) *n.* 1. The equipment for a camp, army, etc. 2. A carriage, esp. when outfitted with horses, attendants, etc.

e·quip·ment (i·kwip′mənt) *n.* 1. The act of equipping, or the state of being equipped. 2. Material with which a person or organization is provided.

e·qui·poise (ē′kwə·poiz, ek′wə-) *n.* 1. Equality of weight; equal balance. 2. A counterpoise.

eq·ui·ta·ble (ek′wə·tə·bəl) *adj.* Impartially just; fair. **—eq′ui·ta·bly** *adv.*

eq·ui·ty (ek′wə·tē) *n. pl.* **·ties** 1. Fairness or impartiality. 2. *Law* A system of jurisprudence based on concepts of fairness, administered by courts of equity, and supplementing common law. 3. In business or property, the value remaining in excess of any liability or mortgage. [< L *aequus* equal]

e·quiv·a·lent (i·kwiv′ə·lənt) *adj.* 1. Equal in value, force, meaning, effect, etc. 2. *Geom.* Equal in area. **—*n.*** That which is equivalent. [< EQUI- + L *valere* to be worth] **—e·quiv′a·lence** *n.*

e·quiv·o·cal (i·kwiv′ə·kəl) *adj.* 1. Having a doubtful meaning; ambiguous. 2. Of uncertain origin, character, value, etc.; dubious. 3. Questionable or suspicious. [< EQUI- + L *vox, vocis* voice] **—e·quiv′o·cal·ly** *adv.*

e·quiv·o·cate (i·kwiv′ə·kāt) *v.i.* **·cat·ed, ·cat·ing** To use ambiguous language with intent to mislead or deceive. **—e·quiv′o·ca′tion** *n.* **—e·quiv′o·ca′tor** *n.* **—e·quiv′o·ca·to′ry** (-kə·tôr′ē) *adj.*

-er[1] *suffix of nouns* 1. A person or thing that performs the action of the root verb: *maker, reaper.* See -EE (def. 1). 2. A person practicing a trade or profession: *geographer, hatter.* 3. One who lives in or comes from: *New Yorker, southerner.* 4. A person, thing, or action related to or characterized by: *three-decker.* [< L *-arius, -arium*]

-er[2] *suffix of nouns* A person or thing connected with: *grocer, jailer.* [< L *-arius, -arium*]

-er[3] *suffix* Forming the comparative degree of adjectives and adverbs: *harder, later.* [OE *-ra, -or*]

-er[4] *suffix of nouns* Denoting the action expressed by the root word: *rejoinder, waiver.* [< F *-er,* infinitive ending]

e·ra (ir′ə, ē′rə) *n.* 1. A period of time measured from some fixed point: the Christian *era.* 2. A period of time characterized by certain events, conditions, etc. 3. The beginning of a particular period; an epoch. 4. *Geol.* A division of geological history. [< LL *aera* counters, orig. pl. of L *aes* brass, money]

e·rad·i·cate (i·rad′ə·kāt) *v.t.* **·cat·ed, ·cat·ing** 1. To pull up by the roots. 2. To destroy. [< L *e-* out + *radix, -icis* a root] **—e·rad′i·ca·ble** (-kə·bəl) *adj.* **—e·rad′i·ca′tor** *n.*

e·rase (i·rās′) *v.t.* **e·rased, e·ras·ing** To obliterate, as by rubbing out. [< L *e-* out + *radere* to scrape] **—e·ras′a·ble** *adj.*

e·ras·er (i·rā′sər) *n.* Something used for erasing marks, as a piece of rubber, felt, etc.

e·ra·sure (i·rā′shər, -zhər) *n.* 1. The act of erasing, or the state of being erased. 2. That which is erased. 3. A mark left on a surface by erasing something.

er·bi·um (ûr′bē·əm) *n.* A metallic element (symbol Er) of the lanthanide series. [< NL *(Ytt)erby,* town in Sweden where first found]

ere (âr) *Archaic & Poetic prep.* Prior to; before in time. **—*conj.*** 1. Before. 2. Sooner than; rather than. [OE *ǣr*]

e·rect (i·rekt′) *v.t.* 1. To put up (a building, etc.). 2. To assemble the parts of; set up. 3. To set upright; raise. 4. To establish or found. 5. To work out or formulate. **—*v.i.*** 6. *Physiol.* To become rigidly upright, as through an influx of blood. **—*adj.*** Marked by a vertical position; upright. [< L *e-* out + *regere* to direct] **—e·rec′tion** *n.* **—e·rec′tor** *n.*

e·rec·tile (i·rek′təl, -tīl) *adj.* Capable of becoming erect.

er·e·mite (er′ə·mīt) *n.* A hermit, esp., a religious recluse. [< LL *eremita*]

erg (ûrg) *n. Physics* A unit of work and of energy, being the work done in moving a

body one centimeter against the force of one dyne. [< Gk. *ergon* work]
er·go (ûr′gō) *conj. & adv.* *Latin* Hence; therefore.
er·gos·ter·ol (ûr·gos′tə·rōl, -rol) *n.* A sterol found in yeast, molds, ergot, etc., and converted by ultraviolet radiation into vitamin D_2.
er·got (ûr′gət) *n.* 1. A fungus attacking rye and other cereal grasses. 2. The disease caused by this fungus. 3. A medicinal preparation, derived from this fungus, used to contract involuntary muscle and to check hemorrhage. [< F < OF *argot* spur of a cock]
E·rie (ir′ē) *n. pl.* **E·rie** or **E·ries** One of a tribe of North American Indians of Iroquoian stock, formerly inhabiting the southern shores of Lake Erie.
Er·in (âr′in, ir′in) *Chiefly Poetic* Ireland.
erl·king (ûrl′king′) *n.* In Germanic folklore, an evil spirit, malicious toward children. [< G *erlkönig*, wrong trans. of Dan. *ellerkonge, elverkonge* king of the elves]
er·mine (ûr′min) *n. pl.* **er·mine** 1. A weasel of the northern hemisphere, having brown fur that in winter turns white. 2. Its white fur. [< OF *(h)ermine*, ? < Gmc.]
erne (ûrn) *n.* A sea eagle. Also **ern.** [OE *earn*]
e·rode (i·rōd′) *v.* **e·rod·ed, e·rod·ing** *v.t.* 1. To wear away gradually by constant friction. 2. To eat into; corrode. 3. To make (a channel, gully, etc.) by wearing away or eating into. —*v.i.* 4. To become eroded. [< L *e-* off + *rodere* to gnaw] —**e·ro·sive** (i·rō′siv) *adj.*
e·rog·e·nous (i·räj′ə·nəs) *adj.* 1. Sexually sensitive: *erogenous* zones. 2. Exciting sexual feelings. Also **er·o·gen·ic** (er′ə·jen′ik). [< Gk. *erōs* love + -GENOUS]
e·ro·sion (i·rō′zhən) *n.* 1. The act of eroding, or the state of being eroded. 2. *Geol.* The wearing away of the earth's surface by the action of wind, water, glaciers, etc. —**e·ro′·sion·al** *adj.*
e·rot·ic (i·rot′ik) *adj.* 1. Of, pertaining to, or concerned with sexual love. 2. Designed to arouse sexual desire. [< Gk. *erōtikos* < *erōs* love] —**e·rot′i·cal·ly** *adv.* —**e·rot·i·cism** (i·rot′ə·siz′əm) *n.*
err (ûr, er) *v.i.* **erred, err·ing** 1. To make a mistake. 2. To go astray morally. [< L *errare* to wander]
er·rand (er′ənd) *n.* 1. A trip made to perform some task, often for someone else. 2. The business of such a trip. [OE *ǣrende* message, news]
er·rant (er′ənt) *adj.* 1. Roving or wandering, esp. in search of adventure. 2. Straying from the proper course or standard. [< L *iter* journey] —**er′rant·ly** *adv.*
er·rat·ic (i·rat′ik) *adj.* 1. Not conforming to usual standards; eccentric. 2. Lacking regularity. 3. *Geol.* Transported from the original site, as by glaciers. [< L *errare* to wander] —**er·rat′i·cal·ly** *adv.*
er·ra·tum (i·rä′təm, i·rā′təm) *n. pl.* **·ra·ta** An error, as in writing or printing. [< L]
er·ro·ne·ous (ə·rō′nē·əs, e·rō′-) *adj.* Marked by error; incorrect. —**er·ro′ne·ous·ly** *adv.*
er·ror (er′ər) *n.* 1. Something done, said, or believed incorrectly; a mistake. 2. The condition of deviating from what is correct or true. 3. In baseball, a misplay by a member of the team not batting.
er·satz (er·zäts′, er′zäts) *adj.* Substitute, and usu. inferior. [< G]
Erse (ûrs) *n.* 1. Scottish Gaelic. 2. Irish Gaelic. —*adj.* Of or pertaining to the Celts of Ireland or Scotland or their language. [Var. of IRISH]
erst (ûrst) *Archaic adv.* Formerly; long ago. [OE *ǣrest*, superl. of *ǣr* before]
erst·while (ûrst′hwīl′) *adj.* Former.
e·ruct (i·rukt′) *v.t. & v.i.* To belch. [< L *e-* out + *ructare* to belch] —**e·ruc′ta′tion** *n.*
er·u·dite (er′yoo·dīt) *adj.* Very learned; scholarly. [< L *e-* out + *rudis* untrained] —**er′u·dite·ly** *adv.* —**er′u·di′tion** (-dish′ən) *n.*
e·rupt (i·rupt′) *v.i.* 1. To cast forth lava, steam, etc., as a volcano or geyser. 2. To become suddenly and violently active. 3. To break out in a rash. —*v.t.* 4. To cast forth (lava, etc.). [< L *e-* out + *rumpere* to burst] —**e·rup′tion** *n.* —**e·rup′tive** *adj.*
-ery *suffix of nouns* 1. A business or place where something is done: *brewery.* 2. A place or residence for: *nunnery.* 3. A collection of things: *finery.* 4. The characteristics of: *snobbery.* 5. An art, trade, or profession: *cookery.* 6. A state, or condition of being: *slavery.* Also **-ry**, as in *jewelry.* [< OF *-ier* (< L *-arius*) + *-ie* (< L *-ia*)]
erythro- *combining form* Red. Also, before vowels, **erythr-**. [< Gk. *erythros*]
e·ryth·ro·cyte (i·rith′rō·sīt) *n.* *Anat.* A disk-shaped red blood cell that contains hemoglobin and transports oxygen.
es- *prefix* Out: used in words borrowed from Old French: *escape.* [< OF < L *ex*]
-es[1] An inflectional ending used to form the plural of nouns ending in *s, ss, sh, ch, x, z, zz* (*gases, brasses, crashes, witches, boxes, adzes, buzzes*), in *f* which changes to *v* (*leaves*), and in *y* which changes to *i* (*mummies*). Compare -s[1]. [OE *-as*]
-es[2] An inflectional ending used to form the third person singular present indicative of verbs ending in a vowel, in *s, sh, ch, z* (*goes, hisses, hushes, poaches, buzzes*), and in *y* which changes to *i* (*relies*). Compare -s[2]. [ME *-es*]
es·ca·drille (es′kə·dril′) *n.* 1. In France, a unit of military airplanes. 2. A squadron of naval vessels. [< F, dim. of *escadre* squadron]
es·ca·late (es′kə·lāt) *v.t. & v.i.* **·lat·ed, ·lat·ing** To increase or be increased gradually: to *escalate* a war. [Back formation < ESCALATOR] —**es′ca·la′tion** *n.*
es·ca·la·tor (es′kə·lā′tər) *n.* A moving stairway built on the conveyor-belt principle.
es·cal·lop (e·skol′əp, e·skal′-) *n.* Scallop. —*v.t.* To scallop.
es·ca·pade (es′kə·pād) *n.* A reckless, unconventional prank or adventure; fling; spree. [< F < Sp. *escapar* to escape]
es·cape (ə·skāp′, e·skāp′) *v.* **·caped, ·cap·ing** *v.i.* 1. To get free. 2. To avoid some danger or evil. 3. To seep or leak out gradually. —*v.t.* 4. To get away from (prison, captors, etc.). 5. To succeed in avoiding (capture, harm, etc.). 6. To get away from the notice or recollection of: No detail *escaped* him. 7. To slip out from unintentionally: A cry *escaped* his lips. —*n.* 1. The act of escaping,

or the fact of having escaped. 2. A means of escaping. —*adj.* 1. Escapist. 2. That provides a means of escape. [< L *ex-* out + *cappa* cloak]

es·cap·ee (es'kā·pē', ə·skā'pē, e·skā'pē) *n.* One who has escaped, as from prison.

es·cape·ment (ə·skāp'mənt, e·skāp'-) *n.* 1. *Mech.* A device used in timepieces for securing a uniform movement, consisting of a notched wheel (**escape wheel**) that is released one tooth at a time. 2. A typewriter mechanism controlling the horizontal movement of the carriage.

escape velocity *Physics* The minimum velocity a body must attain to escape a gravitational field.

es·cap·ism (ə·skā'piz·əm, e·skā'-) *n.* A desire or tendency to escape reality through diversions or daydreaming.

es·cap·ist (ə·skā'pist, e·skā'-) *adj.* Providing a means of indulging in escapism: *escapist* literature. —*n.* One given to escapism.

es·ca·role (es'kə·rōl) *n.* A variety of endive, used for salads. [< ML *escarius* fit for eating]

es·carp·ment (es·kärp'mənt) *n.* 1. A precipitous artificial slope in front of a fortification. 2. A steep slope or cliff. [< F *escarpe* < Ital. *scarpa* a slope]

-esce *suffix of verbs* To become or grow; begin to be or do (what is indicated by the main element): *phosphoresce.* [< L *-escere,* suffix of inceptive verbs]

-escence *suffix of nouns* Forming nouns of state or quality corresponding to adjectives in *-escent.* [< L *-escentia*]

-escent *suffix of adjectives* Beginning to be, have, or do (what is indicated by the main element): *effervescent.* [< L *-escens, -escentis,* suffix of ppr. of inceptive verbs]

es·cha·tol·o·gy (es'kə·tol'ə·jē) *n.* Theology that treats of death, judgment, and the future of the soul. [< Gk. *eschatos* last + -LOGY] —**es·cha·to·log·i·cal** (es'kə·tə·loj'i·kəl) *adj.* —**es'cha·to·log'i·cal·ly** *adv.*

es·cheat (es·chēt') *n.* *Law* Reversion of property to the state or to the crown in default of legal heirs or other qualified claimants. —*v.i.* & *v.t.* To revert or cause to revert to the state, etc., by escheat. [< OF *es-* out + *cheoir* to fall] —**es·cheat'a·ble** *adj.*

es·chew (es·cho͞o') *v.t.* To shun. [< OF *eschiver*] —**es·chew'al** *n.*

es·cort (*n.* es'kôrt; *v.* es·kôrt') *n.* 1. One or more people, cars, planes, etc., accompanying another to give protection, guidance, etc. 2. A man accompanying a woman. —*v.t.* To accompany as an escort. [< Ital. *scorgere* to lead]

es·cri·toire (es'kri·twär') *n.* A writing desk. [< OF < LL *scriptorium* place for writing]

es·crow (es'krō, es·krō') *n.* *Law* 1. A written deed, contract, etc., placed in the custody of a third party and effective upon fulfillment of a stipulated condition. 2. The condition of being an escrow. [< OF *escroe* scroll]

es·cu·do (es·ko͞o'dō; *Pg.* ish·ko͞o'tho͞o; *Sp.* es·ko͞o'thō) *n.* *pl.* **·dos** (-dōz; *Pg.* -tho͞os; *Sp.* -thōs) The monetary unit of Portugal, Chile, etc. [< Pg. < L *scutum* shield]

es·cutch·eon (·skuch'ən) *n.* *Heraldry* A usu. shield-shaped surface carrying armorial bearings. Also *scutcheon.* [< L *scutum* shield]

Es·dras (ez'drəs) *n.* In the Douai Bible, either of two books of the Old Testament. I Esdras corresponds to the book of Ezra and II Esdras corresponds to the book of Nehemiah. [< Gk.]

-ese *suffix of nouns and adjectives* 1. A native or inhabitant of: *Milanese.* 2. The language or dialect of: *Chinese.* 3. Originating in: *Tirolese.* 4. In the manner or style of: *journalese.* [< OF *-eis, -ese* < L *-ensis*]

Es·ki·mo (es'kə·mō) *n.* *pl.* **·mos** or **·mo** 1. One of a Mongoloid people indigenous to the Arctic coasts of North America, Greenland, and NE Siberia. 2. The language of the Eskimos. [< Dan. < N.Am.Ind., eaters of raw flesh] —**Es'ki·mo, Es'ki·mo'an** *adj.*

Eskimo dog One of a breed of large, shaggy dogs of North American origin.

e·soph·a·gus (i·sof'ə·gəs) *n.* *pl.* **·gi** (-jī) *Anat.* The tube from the mouth to the stomach; gullet. [< Gk. *oisophagos*] —**e·so·phag·e·al** (ē'sō·faj'ē·əl, i·sof'ə·jē'əl) or **e·soph'a·gal** *adj*

es·o·ter·ic (es'ə·ter'ik) *adj.* 1. Understood by or meant for a chosen few. 2. Confidential; secret. [< Gk. *esōterikos* inner] —**es'o·ter'i·cal·ly** *adv.*

ESP Extrasensory perception.

es·pa·drille (es'pə·dril') *n.* A sandal having a canvas upper part and a rubber or twisted-rope sole. [< F < Sp. *esparto* coarse grass]

es·pal·ier (es·pal'yər) *n.* 1. A flat framework on which small trees, etc., are trained to grow. 2. A tree or plant so trained. —*v.t.* To furnish with or train on an espalier. [< F < L *spatula* shoulder]

es·pe·cial (es·pesh'əl) *adj.* Preeminent; special. [< L *species* kind, type]

es·pe·cial·ly (es·pesh'əl·ē) *adv.* To a special extent or degree; particularly.

Es·pe·ran·to (es'pə·rän'tō, -ran'tō) *n.* An artificial language based on the major European languages.

es·pi·al (es·pī'əl) *n.* 1. The act of noticing, or the fact of being noticed. 2. The act of spying upon. [< OF *espier* to look]

es·pi·o·nage (es'pē·ə·näzh', -nij') *n.* 1. The practice of spying. 2. The work of spies. [< F *espionner* to spy]

es·pla·nade (es'plə·nād', -näd') *n.* A level, open stretch of land, used as a roadway or public walk. [< F < L *ex-* out + *planus* level]

es·pouse (es·pouz') *v.t.* **·poused, ·pous·ing** 1. To make one's own; support, as a cause or doctrine. 2. To take or give as a spouse; marry. [< L *spondere* to promise] —**es·pou'sal** *n.* —**es·pous'er** *n.*

es·pres·so (es·pres'ō) *n.* *pl.* **·sos** Coffee brewed from darkly roasted beans by steam pressure. [< Ital.]

es·prit (es·prē') *n.* Spirit; wit. [< F < L *spiritus*]

esprit de corps (də kôr) *French* A spirit of devotion to the common goals of a group.

es·py (es·pī') *v.t.* **·pied, ·py·ing** To catch sight of (something); see; descry. [< OF *espier* to look, spy]

-esque *suffix of adjectives* Having the manner or style of; like: *picturesque.* [< L *-iscus*]

es·quire (es·kwīr', es'kwīr) *n.* 1. *Usu. cap.*

A title of courtesy or respect: abbreviated *Esq.*: John Smith, *Esq.* 2. In England, a man ranking just below a knight. 3. A squire or young candidate for knighthood. [< LL *scutarius* shield-bearer]

-ess *suffix* Used to form the feminine of many nouns: *goddess, lioness.* [< LL *-issa*]

es·say (*n. def. 1* es′ā; *n. def. 2* es′ā, e·sā′; *v.* e·sā′) *n.* 1. A short composition dealing with a single topic and typically personal in approach. 2. An attempt; endeavor. —*v.t.* To attempt to do or accomplish; try. [< OF *essai* trial]

es·say·ist (es′ā·ist) *n.* A writer of essays.

es·sence (es′əns) *n.* 1. That in which the real nature of a thing consists; intrinsic or fundamental nature. 2. The distinctive quality of something. 3. An extract, as of a plant or food; also, an alcoholic solution of such an extract. 4. A perfume. [< L *esse* to be]

es·sen·tial (ə·sen′shəl) *adj.* 1. Of, belonging to, or constituting the essence of something. 2. Extremely important; vital; indispensable. 3. Complete, total, or absolute. —*n.* Something fundamental or indispensable. —**es·sen·ti·al·i·ty** (ə·sen′shē·al′ə·tē) *n.* —**es·sen′tial·ly** *adv.*

essential oil The volatile oil that gives to a plant its characteristic odor, flavor, etc.

-est[1] *suffix* Forming the superlative degree of adjectives and adverbs: *hardest, latest.* [OE *-ast, -est, -ost*]

-est[2] An archaic inflectional ending used in the second person singular present and past indicative, with *thou*: *eatest, walkest.* Also, in contracted forms, *-st*, as in *hast, didst.* [OE *-est, -ast*]

es·tab·lish (ə·stab′lish) *v.t.* 1. To make secure, stable, or permanent. 2. To set up, found, or institute. 3. To install: to *establish* oneself in a new home. 4. To cause to be recognized and accepted: to *establish* oneself as a writer. 5. To clear from doubt; demonstrate; prove. [< L *stabilis* stable] —**es·tab′·lish·er** *n.*

es·tab·lish·ment (ə·stab′lish·mənt) *n.* 1. The act of establishing, or the state or fact of being established. 2. Something established, as a business, residence, etc. —**the Establishment** Those collectively who occupy positions of influence and status in a society.

es·tate (ə·stāt′) *n.* 1. A usu. extensive piece of landed property or the residence built on it. 2. One's entire property and possessions. 3. A particular condition or state: man's *estate.* 4. A particular social or political class. [< L *status* a state]

es·teem (ə·stēm′) *v.t.* 1. To have a high opinion of; value greatly. 2. To think of as; rate. —*n.* 1. High regard or respect. 2. Judgment. [< L *aestimare* to value]

es·ter (es′tər) *n. Chem.* Any of a class of organic compounds formed by the reaction of an acid with an alcohol.

Es·ther (es′tər) *n.* A book of the Old Testament containing the story of Esther, the Jewish queen of Persia who saved her people from massacre.

es·thete (es′thēt) *n.* 1. One who is very responsive to beauty in art, nature, etc. 2. One who affects such sensitivity. Also spelled *aesthete.* [< Gk. *aisthētēs* one who perceives]

es·thet·ic (es·thet′ik) *adj.* 1. Of or relating to esthetics. 2. Of or relating to beauty. 3. Keenly responsive to beauty. Also spelled *aesthetic.* —**es·thet′i·cal·ly** *adv.*

es·thet·i·cism (es·thet′ə·siz′əm) *n.* 1. A theory assigning great or fundamental importance to esthetic values. 2. Keen responsiveness to beauty. Also spelled *aestheticism.*

es·thet·ics (es·thet′iks) *n.pl.* (*construed as sing.*) A branch of philosophy relating to the nature and forms of beauty in art, nature, etc., and to mental and emotional responses to it. Also spelled *aesthetics.*

es·ti·ma·ble (es′tə·mə·bəl) *adj.* Worthy of respect or admiration. —**es′ti·ma·bly** *adv.*

es·ti·mate (*v.* es′tə·māt; *n.* es′tə·mit) *v.* **·mat·ed, ·mat·ing** *v.t.* 1. To form an approximate opinion of (size, amount, number, etc.). 2. To form an opinion about; judge. —*v.i.* 3. To make or submit an estimate. —*n.* 1. A rough calculation. 2. A statement of the approximate cost for certain work. 3. A judgment or opinion. [< L *aestimare* to value] —**es′ti·ma′tor** *n.*

es·ti·ma·tion (es′tə·mā′shən) *n.* 1. The act of estimating. 2. A conclusion arrived at by estimating. 3. Esteem; regard.

es·ti·val (es′tə·vəl, es·tī′-) *adj.* Of or pertaining to summer. Also spelled *aestival.*

es·ti·vate (es′tə·vāt) *v.i.* **·vat·ed, ·vat·ing** To pass the summer in a dormant state. Also spelled *aestivate.* [< L *aestivare* to spend the summer] —**es′ti·va′tion** *n.* —**es′ti·va′tor** *n.*

Es·to·ni·an (es·tō′nē·ən) *n.* 1. One of a people inhabiting Estonia and part of Livonia. 2. The Finno-Ugric language of this people. —**Es·to′ni·an** *adj.*

es·trange (es·trānj′) *v.t.* **·tranged, ·trang·ing** 1. To make (someone previously friendly or affectionate) indifferent or hostile; alienate. 2. To remove or dissociate (oneself, etc.). [< L *extraneus* foreign] —**es·trange′ment** *n.*

es·tro·gen (es′trə·jən) *n. Biochem.* Any of various substances that influence estrus or produce changes in the sexual characteristics of female mammals. —**es′tro·gen′ic** (-jen′ik) *adj.*

es·trus (es′trəs, ēs′-) *n. Biol.* a The entire reproductive cycle of most female mammals. b The peak of the sexual cycle, culminating in ovulation; heat. [< L *oestrus* frenzy, passion < Gk. *oistros* gadfly] —**es′trous** *adj.*

es·tu·ar·y (es′chōō·er′ē) *n. pl.* **·ar·ies** A wide mouth of a river where its current meets the sea. [< L *aestus* tide] —**es′tu·ar′i·al** (-âr′ē·əl) *adj.*

-et *suffix* Small; little: *islet*: often without appreciable force, as in *sonnet.* [< F]

e·ta (ā′tə, ē′-) *n.* The seventh letter and third vowel in the Greek alphabet (Η, η), corresponding to English long *e.* [< Gk. *ēta* < Phoenician *hēth*]

et cet·er·a (et set′ər·ə, set′rə) And other things; and the rest; and so forth. Abbr. *etc.* [< L]

etch (ech) *v.t.* 1. To engrave by means of acid or other corrosive fluid, esp. on a plate for printing. 2. To produce (a drawing, design, etc.) by etching. 3. To outline or sketch by scratching lines with a pointed instrument. [< OHG *ezjan* to corrode] —**etch′er** *n.*

etch·ing (ech′ing) *n.* 1. A process of engraving in which lines are scratched on a plate covered with a coating, and the parts exposed are subjected to acid. 2. A figure or design formed by etching. 3. An impression from an etched plate.

e·ter·nal (i·tûr′nəl) *adj.* 1. Existing without beginning or end; forever existent. 2. Unending. [< L *aevum* age] **—e·ter′nal·ly** *adv.*

e·ter·ni·ty (i·tûr′nə·tē) *n. pl.* **·ties** 1. Existence without beginning or end; endless duration. 2. The endless time following death. 3. *Informal* A very long time.

e·ter·nize (i·tûr′nīz) *v.t.* **·nized, ·niz·ing** 1. To make eternal. 2. To perpetuate the fame of; immortalize. Also **e·ter′nal·ize** (-nəl·īz). **—e·ter′ni·za′tion, e·ter′nal·i·za′·tion** *n.*

-eth[1] An archaic inflectional ending used in the third person singular present indicative of some verbs: *eateth, drinketh.* Also, in contracted forms, *-th,* as in *hath, doth.* [OE *-eth, -ath*]

-eth[2] *suffix* Var. of -TH[2].

eth·ane (eth′ān) *n. Chem.* A colorless, odorless, gaseous hydrocarbon, contained in crude petroleum. [< ETHER]

eth·a·nol (eth′ə·nōl, -nol) *n. Chem.* An alcohol, obtained through fermentation, that is the intoxicant in liquors, wines, and beers: also called *ethyl alcohol, grain alcohol.* [< ETHANE + -OL]

e·ther (ē′thər) *n.* 1. Ethyl ether; also, any of a group of similar compounds. 2. A substance formerly assumed to pervade all of space: also spelled *aether.* 3. The clear, upper regions of space: also spelled *aether.* [< L *aether* sky]

e·the·re·al (i·thir′ē·əl) *adj.* 1. Resembling ether or air; airy. 2. Delicate or spiritual. 3. Of or existing in the upper regions; celestial. **—e·the′re·al·ly** *adv.* **—e·the′re·al′i·ty** (-al′ə·tē), **e·the′re·al·ness** *n.*

e·ther·ize (ē′thə·rīz) *v.t.* **·ized, ·iz·ing** To subject to the fumes of ether; anesthetize. **—e′ther·i·za′tion** *n.*

eth·ic (eth′ik) *n.* A philosophy or system of morals; ethics. **—***adj.* Ethical; moral. [< Gk. *ēthos* character]

eth·i·cal (eth′i·kəl) *adj.* 1. Pertaining to or treating of ethics and morality. 2. Conforming to right principles of conduct. **—eth′i·cal·ly** *adv.* **—eth′i·cal·ness, eth′i·cal′i·ty** (-kal′ə·tē) *n.*

eth·ics (eth′iks) *n.pl.* (*construed as sing. in def. 1*) 1. The study and philosophy of human conduct, with emphasis on the determination of right and wrong. 2. The principles of right conduct with reference to a specific profession, mode of life, etc.

E·thi·o·pi·an (ē′thē·ō′pē·ən) *adj.* Of or pertaining to Ethiopia, its people, or their language. **—E′thi·o′pi·an** *n.*

E·thi·op·ic (ē′thē·op′ik, -ō′pik) *n.* A Semitic language of ancient Ethiopia.

eth·nic (eth′nik) *adj.* Of, belonging to, or distinctive of a particular racial, cultural, or language division of mankind. [< Gk. *ethnos* nation] **—eth′ni·cal·ly** *adv.*

ethno- *combining form* Race; nation; peoples. Also, before vowels, **ethn-**.

eth·nog·ra·phy (eth·nog′rə·fē) *n. pl.* **·phies** The branch of anthropology concerned with the classification and description of regional, chiefly primitive human cultures. **—eth·nog′ra·pher** *n.* **—eth·no·graph·ic** (eth′nə·graf′ik) or **·i·cal** *adj.* **—eth′no·graph′i·cal·ly** *adv.*

eth·nol·o·gy (eth·nol′ə·jē) *n. pl.* **·gies** The branch of anthropology concerned with the study of racial and ethnic groups in their origins, distribution, and cultures. **—eth·no·log·ic** (eth′nə·loj′ik) or **·i·cal** *adj.* **—eth′·no·log′i·cal·ly** *adv.* **—eth·nol′o·gist** *n.*

e·thol·o·gy (ē·thol′ə·jē) *n.* The science of animal behavior. [< Gk. *ēthos* character + -LOGY] **—e·tho·log·i·cal** (ē·thə·loj′ə·kəl) *adj.* **—e·tho·log′i·cal·ly** *adv.* **—e·thol′o·gist** *n.*

eth·yl (eth′əl) *n. Chem.* 1. A hydrocarbon radical found in alcohol and ether. 2. Any gasoline treated to reduce knock. [< ETH(ER) + -YL] **—e·thyl·ic** (i·thil′ik) *adj.*

ethyl alcohol Ethanol.

eth·y·lene (eth′ə·lēn) *n. Chem.* A colorless, flammable, gaseous hydrocarbon, used as an anesthetic and in organic syntheses.

ethylene glycol *Chem.* A colorless, sweetish alcohol, used as an antifreeze, solvent, and lubricant.

ethyl ether *Chem.* A colorless, volatile, flammable liquid hydrocarbon, used as an anesthetic and solvent: also called *ether.*

e·ti·ol·o·gy (ē′tē·ol′ə·jē) *n. pl.* **·gies** 1. The study of causes or reasons. 2. *Med.* A theory of the cause of a disease. 3. The giving of a cause or reason for anything; also, the reason given. [< Gk. *aitia* cause + -LOGY] **—e·ti·o·log·i·cal** (ē′tē·ə·loj′i·kəl) *adj.* **—e′ti·o·log′i·cal·ly** *adv.* **—e′ti·ol′o·gist** *n.*

et·i·quette (et′ə·kət, -ket) *n.* The rules conventionally established for behavior in polite society or in official or professional life. [< F < OF *estiquette;* orig., label]

E·trus·can (i·trus′kən) *adj.* Of or relating to Etruria, its people, or their language. **—E·trus′can** *n.*

-ette *suffix of nouns* 1. Little; small: *kitchenette.* 2. Resembling: *leatherette.* 3. Feminine: *drum majorette.* [< F *-ette,* fem. of *-et,* dim. suffix]

é·tude (ā′to͞od, -tyo͞od; *Fr.* ā·tüd′) *n. Music* An exercise or composition for solo instrument or voice. [< F. See STUDY.]

et·y·mol·o·gy (et′ə·mol′ə·jē) *n. pl.* **·gies** 1. The development of a word, as shown by the histories of its antecedent forms or basic elements; also, a statement of this. 2. The study of the derivation of words. [< Gk. *etymon* true meaning + -LOGY] **—et·y·mo·log·i·cal** (et′ə·mə·loj′i·kəl) or **et′y·mo·log′ic** *adj.* **—et′y·mo·log′i·cal·ly** *adv.* **—et′y·mol′o·gist** *n.* **—et′y·mol′o·gize** *v.t. & v.i.* **·gized, ·giz·ing**

eu- *prefix* Good; well; easy; agreeable: *euphony.* [< Gk.]

eu·ca·lyp·tus (yo͞o′kə·lip′təs) *n. pl.* **·tus·es** or **·ti** (-tī) Any of a genus of large evergreen trees, yielding a volatile, pungent oil (**oil of eucalyptus**) used in medicine. [< EU- + Gk. *kalyptos* covered, from the covering of the buds]

Eu·char·ist (yo͞o′kə·rist) *n.* A Christian sacrament in which bread and wine are consecrated and received in commemoration of the Passion and the death of Jesus: also called *Communion.* [< EU- + Gk. *charizesthai* to show favor] **—Eu′cha·ris′tic** *adj.*

eu·chre (yōō′kər) *n.* A card game for two to four players, played with 32 cards. —*v.t.* **·chred, ·chring** 1. In the game of euchre, to defeat by taking three tricks. 2. *Informal* To outwit or defeat. [Origin uncertain]

Eu·clid·e·an (yōō·klid′ē·ən) *adj.* Of or relating to the geometric principles of Euclid. Also **Eu·clid′i·an**

eu·gen·ics (yōō·jen′iks) *n.pl.* (*construed as sing.*) The science of improving the physical and mental qualities of human beings through control of the factors influencing heredity. [< EU- + Gk. *genēs* born + -ICS] —**eu·gen′ic** *adj.* —**eu·gen′i·cal·ly** *adv.* —**eu·gen′i·cist** (-ə·sist) *n.*

eu·lo·gize (yōō′lə·jīz) *v.t.* **·gized, ·giz·ing** To speak or write a eulogy about. —**eu′lo·giz′er** *n.*

eu·lo·gy (yōō′lə·jē) *n. pl.* **·gies** 1. A spoken or written piece of high praise, esp. when delivered publicly. 2. Great praise. [< EU- + Gk. *legein* to speak] —**eu′lo·gist** *n.* —**eu′lo·gis′tic** *adj.*

eu·nuch (yōō′nək) *n.* A castrated man. [< Gk. *eunē* bed + *echein* to keep, guard]

eu·phe·mism (yōō′fə·miz′əm) *n.* 1. Substitution of a mild or roundabout word or expression for another felt to be too blunt or painful. 2. A word or expression so substituted, as "the departed" for "the dead." [< EU- + Gk. *phēmizein* < *phanai* to speak] —**eu′phe·mist** *n.* —**eu′phe·mis′tic** or **·ti·cal** *adj.* —**eu′phe·mis′ti·cal·ly** *adv.* —**eu′phe·mize** *v.t. & v.i.* **·mized, ·miz·ing**

eu·pho·ni·ous (yōō·fō′nē·əs) *adj.* Marked by euphony; agreeable and pleasant in sound. —**eu·pho′ni·ous·ly** *adv.*

eu·pho·ny (yōō′fə·nē) *n. pl.* **·nies** The quality of being pleasant and agreeable in sound, as in speech or music. [< EU- + Gk. *phōnē* sound] —**eu·phon·ic** (yōō·fon′ik) *adj.* —**eu·phon′i·cal·ly** *adv.*

eu·phor·bi·a (yōō·fôr′bē·ə) *n.* A plant having a milky juice: also called *spurge.* [< Gk. *euphorbion*] —**eu·phor′bi·al** *adj.*

eu·pho·ri·a (yōō·fôr′ē·ə) *n.* A feeling of well-being, relaxation, and happiness. [< EU- + Gk. *pherein* to bear] —**eu·phor′ic** *adj.*

Eur·a·sian (yōō·rā′zhən, -shən) *adj.* 1. Pertaining to Eurasia. 2. Of European and Asian descent. —**Eur·a′sian** *n.*

eu·re·ka (yōō·rē′kə) *interj.* I have found (it): an exclamation of triumph or achievement. [< Gk. *heurēka*]

Euro- *combining form* 1. European: *Eurocommunism.* 2. European and: *Eurasian.* Before vowels, **Eur-**.

Eu·ro·com·mu·nism (yōōr′ō·kom′yə·niz′əm) *n.* Nationalistic Marxism, as of Italy and France, that accepts some aspects of capitalism.

Eu·ro·dol·lar (yōōr′ō·dol′ər) *n.* A U.S. dollar held in a European bank.

Eu·ro·pe·an (yōōr′ə·pē′ən) *adj.* Relating to or derived from Europe or its inhabitants. —**Eu′ro·pe′an** *n.*

European Economic Community The Common Market.

Eu·ro·pe·an·ize (yōōr′ə·pē′ən·īz) *v.t.* **·ized, ·iz·ing** To make European, as in culture. —**Eu′ro·pe′an·i·za′tion** *n.*

European plan At a hotel, the system of paying for lodging separately from meals.

eu·ro·pi·um (yōō·rō′pē·əm) *n.* A steel-gray, malleable metallic element (symbol Eu) of the lanthanide series. [< L *Europa* Europe]

eury- *combining form* Wide; broad. [< Gk. *eurys*]

eu·ryth·mics (yōō·rith′miks) *n.pl.* (*construed as sing.*) A system for developing grace and rhythm through bodily movements done to music: also **eu·rhyth′mics.** [< EU- + Gk. *rhythmos* symmetry] —**eu·ryth′mic** or **·mi·cal** *adj.*

Eu·sta·chi·an tube (yōō·stā′shē·ən, -shən) *Anat.* A passage between the pharynx and the middle ear. [after Bartolomeo *Eustachio*, died 1574, Italian anatomist]

eu·tha·na·si·a (yōō′thə·nā′zhə, -zhē·ə) *n.* 1. Painless, peaceful death. 2. The deliberate putting to death painlessly of a person suffering from a fatal disease or the like: also called *mercy killing.* [< EU- + Gk. *thanatos* death]

eu·then·ics (yōō·then′iks) *n.pl.* (*construed as sing.*) The science of improving human beings through control of environmental factors. [< Gk. *euthēnein* to thrive]

eu·tro·phi·ca·tion (yōō′trō·fə·kā′shən) *n.* A decrease of dissolved oxygen in a body of water, such that plant life is favored over animal life. [< Gk. *eutrophein* to thrive]

e·vac·u·ant (i·vak′yōō·ənt) *adj.* Cathartic or emetic. —*n.* An evacuant medicine, drug, etc.

e·vac·u·ate (i·vak′yōō·āt) *v.* **·at·ed, ·at·ing** *v.t.* 1. To move out or withdraw (troops, inhabitants, etc.) from a threatened area or place. 2. To depart from and leave vacant; vacate. 3. To remove the contents of. 4. *Physiol.* To discharge or eject, as from the bowels. —*v.i.* 5. To withdraw, as from an area. [< L *e-* out + *vacuare* to make empty] —**e·vac′u·a′tion** *n.* —**e·vac′u·a′tor** *n.* —**e·vac′u·ee′** *n.*

e·vade (i·vād′) *v.t. & v.i.* **e·vad·ed, e·vad·ing** 1. To get away from (pursuers, etc.) by tricks or cleverness. 2. To get out of or avoid (a responsibility, question, etc.). [< L *e-* out + *vadere* to go] —**e·vad′a·ble** or **e·vad′i·ble** *adj.* —**e·vad′er** *n.*

e·val·u·ate (i·val′yōō·āt) *v.t.* **·at·ed, ·at·ing** 1. To find the amount, worth, etc., of. 2. To judge the value of. [< OF *valoir* to be worth] —**e·val′u·a′tion** *n.*

ev·a·nesce (ev′ə·nes′) *v.i.* **·nesced, ·nesc·ing** To disappear by degrees; vanish gradually. [< L *e-* out + *vanescere* to vanish] —**ev′a·nes′cence** *n.* —**ev′a·nes′cent** *adj.* —**ev′a·nes′cent·ly** *adv.*

e·van·gel·i·cal (ē′van·jel′i·kəl, ev′ən-) *adj.* 1. Of, relating to, or contained in the New Testament, esp. the Gospels. 2. Of, relating to, or maintaining the doctrine that the Bible is the only rule of faith. 3. Evangelistic. —*n.* A member of an evangelical church. Also **e′van·gel′ic.** [< EU- + Gk. *angellein* to announce] —**e′van·gel′i·cal·ism** *n.* —**e′van·gel′i·cal·ly** *adv.*

e·van·gel·ism (i·van′jə·liz′əm) *n.* The zealous preaching or spreading of the gospel.

e·van·gel·ist (i·van′jə·list) *n.* 1. *Usu. cap.* One of the four writers of the New Testament Gospels. 2. An itinerant or missionary preacher. —**e·van′gel·is′tic** *adj.* —**e·van′gel·is′ti·cal·ly** *adv.*

e·van·gel·ize (i·van′jəl·īz) *v.* **·ized, ·iz·ing**

v.t. 1. To preach the gospel to. —*v.i.* 2. To act as an evangelist; preach. —**e·van′gel·i·za′tion** *n.*

e·vap·o·rate (i·vap′ə·rāt) *v.* **·rat·ed, ·rat·ing** *v.t.* 1. To convert into vapor; vaporize. 2. To remove moisture or liquid from (milk, fruit, etc.) so as to dry or concentrate. —*v.i.* 3. To become vapor. 4. To yield vapor. 5. To vanish; disappear. [< L *e-* out, away + *vaporare* to emit vapor] —**e·vap′o·ra·ble** (-rə·bəl) *adj.* —**e·vap′o·ra′tive** *adj.* —**e·vap′o·ra′tion** *n.* —**e·vap′o·ra′tor** *n.*

evaporated milk Unsweetened canned milk thickened by the removal of water.

e·va·sion (i·vā′zhən) *n.* 1. The act of evading. 2. A means used to evade, as a vague answer.

e·va·sive (i·vā′siv) *adj.* 1. Given to or characterized by evasion; not direct and frank. 2. Elusive. —**e·va′sive·ly** *adv.* —**e·va′sive·ness** *n.*

eve (ēv) *n.* 1. *Often cap.* The evening before a holiday: Christmas *Eve.* 2. The time immediately preceding some event. 3. *Poetic* Evening. [Var. of EVEN²]

e·ven¹ (ē′vən) *adj.* 1. Flat and smooth; level. 2. Extending to the same height or depth: a tree *even* with the housetop. 3. Extending along; parallel to. 4. Equally distributed; uniform: an *even* coat of paint. 5. Calm and controlled: an *even* disposition. 6. Equally matched; balanced. 7. Being the same (score) for each side or competitor. 8. Having settled a debt. 9. Identical in quantity, number, measure, etc.: *even* portions. 10. Exactly divisible by 2: an *even* number: opposed to *odd.* —**to break even** *Informal* To end up with neither profit nor loss, as in a business deal. —**to get even** 1. To break even or settle debts. 2. To have revenge. —*adv.* 1. To all the greater extent or degree; still: an *even* better plan. 2. During the very same moment: with *as*: *Even* as they watched, the ship sank. 3. In exactly the same way: with *as*: Do *even* as I do. 4. Indeed; actually: to feel glad, *even* delighted. 5. Unlikely as it may seem: He was kind *even* to his enemies. 6. All the way; as far as: faithful *even* to death. 7. Nevertheless; notwithstanding: *Even* with that handicap, he won. 8. Not otherwise than; right: It is happening *even* now. —**even if** Although; notwithstanding. —*v.t.* & *v.i.* To make or become even: often with *up* or *off.* [OE *efen*] —**e′ven·ly** *adv.* —**e′ven·ness** *n.*

e·ven² (ē′vən) *n.* *Archaic* Evening. [OE *ǣfen*]

e·ven·fall (ē′vən·fôl′) *n.* Early evening.

e·ven·hand·ed (ē′vən·han′did) *adj.* Treating all alike; impartial. —**e′ven·hand′ed·ly** *adv.* —**e′ven·hand′ed·ness** *n.*

eve·ning (ēv′ning) *n.* 1. The latter part of day and the first part of night. ◆Collateral adjective: *vesperal.* 2. An evening's entertainment or activity. 3. The declining years of life, a career, etc. [OE *ǣfnian* to approach evening]

evening dress Formal evening wear.

evening primrose An herb with yellow flowers that open in the evening.

evening star A bright planet visible in the west just after sunset, esp. Venus.

e·vent (i·vent′) *n.* 1. Something that takes place; a happening or an incident. 2. An actual or possible situation or set of circumstances: in the *event* of failure. 3. Final outcome. 4. One of the items in a variegated program of sports. —**in any event** or **at all events** Regardless of what happens. [< L *e-* out + *venire* to come]

e·vent·ful (i·vent′fəl) *adj.* 1. Marked by important events. 2. Having important consequences: an *eventful* decision. —**e·vent′ful·ly** *adv.* —**e·vent′ful·ness** *n.*

e·ven·tide (ē′vən·tīd′) *n.* *Poetic* Evening.

e·ven·tu·al (i·ven′cho͞o·əl) *adj.* Occurring or resulting in due course of time. —**e·ven′tu·al·ly** *adv.*

e·ven·tu·al·i·ty (i·ven′cho͞o·al′ə·tē) *n.* *pl.* **·ties** A likely or possible occurrence or outcome.

e·ven·tu·ate (i·ven′cho͞o·āt) *v.i.* **·at·ed, ·at·ing** To result ultimately.

ev·er (ev′ər) *adv.* 1. At any time; on any occasion: Did you *ever* see it? 2. In any possible or conceivable way: Do it as fast as *ever* you can. 3. At all times; invariably: They remained *ever* on guard. 4. Throughout the entire course of time; always; forever: usu. followed by *since, after,* or *afterward.* —**ever so** *Informal* To a great extent or degree: It was *ever so* pleasant. [OE *ǣfre*]

ev·er·glade (ev′ər·glād) *n.* A tract of low, swampy land.

ev·er·green (ev′ər·grēn′) *adj.* Having foliage that remains green until the formation of new foliage: distinguished from *deciduous.* —*n.* An evergreen tree or plant.

ev·er·last·ing (ev′ər·las′ting) *adj.* 1. Existing or lasting forever; eternal. 2. Continuing for an indefinitely long period; perpetual. 3. Incessant; interminable. —*n.* Endless duration; eternity. [ME] —**ev′er·last′ing·ly** *adv.*

ev·er·more (ev′ər·môr′) *adv.* *Poetic* Forever; always. —**for evermore** Forever.

e·vert (i·vûrt′) *v.t.* To turn outward or inside out. [< L *e-* out + *vertere* to turn] —**e·ver·sion** (i·vûr′zhən) *n.* —**e·ver·si·ble** (i·vûr′sə·bəl) *adj.*

eve·ry (ev′rē, ev′ər·ē) *adj.* 1. Each without excepting any of a group or set. 2. Each (member or unit singled out in some way) of a series: *every* tenth man. 3. The utmost; all possible: Show him *every* consideration. —**every now and then** From time to time; occasionally. —**every other** Each alternate (specified thing). [OE *ǣfre* ever + *ǣlc* each]

eve·ry·bod·y (ev′rē·bod′ē, -bud′ē) *pron.* Every person.

eve·ry·day (ev′rē·dā′, -dā′) *adj.* 1. Happening every day; daily. 2. Commonplace; ordinary.

eve·ry·one (ev′rē·wun′) *pron.* Everybody.

every one Each individual person or thing out of the whole number, excepting none: *Every one* of the men is ill.

eve·ry·thing (ev′rē·thing′) *pron.* 1. Whatever exists; all things whatsoever. 2. Whatever is relevant, needed, or important: I have *everything.*

eve·ry·where (ev′rē·hwâr′) *adv.* At, in, or to every place.

e·vict (i·vikt′) *v.t.* To expel (a tenant) by legal process; dispossess; put out. [< L *e-* out + *vincere* to conquer] —**e·vic′tion** *n.*

ev·i·dence (ev′ə·dəns) *n.* 1. That which serves to prove or disprove something; support; proof. 2. That which serves as a ground for knowing or believing something; corroboration. 3. An indication; sign. 4. *Law* That which is properly presented before a court as a means of establishing or disproving something alleged or presumed. **—in evidence** Readily seen or noticed; present. **—to turn state's evidence** To testify in court against one's accomplices. **—*v.t.* ·denced, ·denc·ing** To show.

ev·i·dent (ev′ə·dənt) *adj.* Easily perceived or recognized; clear; plain. [< L *e-* out + *videre* to see]

ev·i·den·tial (ev′ə·den′shəl) *adj.* Relating to, serving as, or based on evidence. **—ev′i·den′tial·ly** *adv.*

ev·i·dent·ly (ev′ə·dənt·lē, -dent′-, ev′ə·dent′lē) *adv.* 1. To all appearances; apparently. 2. Quite clearly; obviously.

e·vil (ē′vəl) *adj.* 1. Morally bad; wicked. 2. Causing injury or any other undesirable result. 3. Marked by or threatening misfortune: an *evil* omen. **—*n.*** 1. That which is evil; as: **a** That which is morally bad. **b** That which is injurious. **c** That which causes suffering or misfortune. 2. Some particular act, characteristic, etc., that is evil. [OE *yfel*] **—e′vil·ly** *adv.* **—e′vil·ness** *n.*

e·vil·do·er (ē′vəl·dōō′er) *n.* One who does evil. **—e′vil·do′ing** *n.*

evil eye A glance superstitiously supposed capable of inflicting misfortune or injury.

e·vil-mind·ed (e′vəl·mīn′did) *adj.* Obsessed with vicious or depraved thoughts. **—e′vil-mind′ed·ness** *n.*

e·vince (i·vins′) *v.t.* **e·vinced, e·vinc·ing** 1. To indicate clearly; demonstrate. 2. To give an outward sign of having (a quality, feeling, etc.). [< L *e-* out + *vincere* to conquer] **—e·vin′ci·ble** *adj.*

e·vis·cer·ate (i·vis′ə·rāt) *v.t.* **·at·ed, ·at·ing** 1. To disembowel. 2. To remove the vital part of. [< L *e-* out + *viscera* entrails] **—e·vis′cer·a′tion** *n.*

e·voke (i·vōk′) *v.t.* **e·voked, e·vok·ing** 1. To call or summon forth. 2. To draw forth or produce (a response, reaction, etc.). [< L *e-* out + *vocare* to call] **—ev·o·ca·tion** (ev′ə·kā′shən) *n.* **—e·voc·a·tive** (i·vok′ə·tiv) *adj.*

ev·o·lu·tion (ev′ə·lōō′shən) *n.* 1. The process of unfolding, growing, or developing, usu. by slow stages. 2. *Biol.* **a** The theory that all forms of life originated by descent from earlier forms. **b** The series of changes, as by natural selection, mutation, etc., through which a given type of organism has acquired its present characteristics. 3. A movement or maneuver, as of troops. **—ev′o·lu′tion·ar·y** *adj.*

ev·o·lu·tion·ist (ev′ə·lōō′shən·ist) *n.* 1. A proponent of the theory of biological evolution. 2. One who advocates progress through gradual stages, as in political structure. **—*adj.*** 1. Evolutionary. 2. Of or relating to evolutionists. **—ev′o·lu′tion·ism** *n.*

e·volve (i·volv′) *v.* **e·volved, e·volv·ing** *v.t.* 1. To work out; develop gradually. 2. *Biol.* To develop to a more highly organized state: usu. in the passive. 3. To unfold or expand. **—*v.i.*** 4. To undergo the process of evolution. [< L *e-* out + *volvere* to roll] **—e·volve′ment** *n.*

ewe (yōō, *Dial.* yō) *n.* A female sheep. [OE *eowu*]

ew·er (yōō′ər) *n.* A large, wide-mouthed jug or pitcher for water. [ME]

ex-[1] *prefix* 1. Out of: *exit, exhale.* 2. Thoroughly: *exasperate.* 3. Not having; lacking. 4. Being formerly: attached with a hyphen to the word it qualifies: *ex-president.* Also: *e-* before consonants except *c, f, p, q, s, t*; *ef-* before *f.* [< L *ex* from, out of]

ex-[2] *prefix* Out of; from; forth: *exodus.* Also, before consonants, *ec-*, as in *eclipse.* [< Gk. *ex* out]

ex-[3] Var. of EXO-.

ex·ac·er·bate (ig·zas′ər·bāt) *v.t.* **·bat·ed, ·bat·ing** To make more sharp or severe; aggravate. [< L *ex-* very + *acerbus* bitter, harsh] **—ex·ac′er·ba′tion** *n.*

ex·act (ig·zakt′) *adj.* 1. Clear and complete in every detail; precise. 2. Altogether accurate. 3. Being precisely (what is specified): the *exact* amount necessary. 4. Extremely careful about detail and accuracy: an *exact* editor. 5. Rigorously demanding: an *exact* schoolmaster. **—*v.t.*** 1. To demand rigorously. 2. To obtain by or as if by force. [< L *ex-* out + *agere* to drive] **—ex·act′ness, ex·act′i·tude** *n.* **—ex·ac′tion** *n.*

ex·ac·ta (ig·zak′tə) *n.* A bet, as in horse racing, requiring selection of the first- and second-place finishers. [< Am.Sp.]

ex·act·ing (ig·zak′ting) *adj.* 1. Making rigorous demands; severe. 2. Involving constant hard work, attention, etc. **—ex·act′ing·ly** *adv.*

ex·act·ly (ig·zakt′lē) *adv.* 1. In an exact manner; accurately. 2. Precisely right; just so.

ex·ag·ger·ate (ig·zaj′ə·rāt) *v.t. & v.i.* **·at·ed, ·at·ing** To represent or look upon (something) as greater than is actually the case; overstate. [< L *ex-* out + *agger* heap] **—ex·ag′ger·at′ed** *adj.* **—ex·ag′ger·a′tion** *n.* **—ex·ag′ger·a′tor** *n.*

ex·alt (ig·zôlt′) *v.t.* 1. To raise in rank, character, honor, etc. 2. To glorify or praise. 3. To fill with delight, pride, etc.; elate. [< L *ex-* out + *altus* high] **—ex·al·ta·tion** (eg′zôl·tā′shən) *n.* **—ex·alt′ed** *adj.* **—ex·alt′ed·ly** *adv.*

ex·am (ig·zam′) *n.* *Informal* An examination.

ex·am·i·na·tion (ig·zam′ə·nā′shən) *n.* 1. The act of examining, or the state of being examined. 2. Medical scrutiny and testing. 3. A formal test of knowledge or skills.

ex·am·ine (ig·zam′in) *v.t.* **·ined, ·in·ing** 1. To inspect with care; inquire into. 2. To subject to medical scrutiny and testing. 3. To test by questions or exercises as to qualifications, fitness, etc. [< L *examinare*] **—ex·am′in·a·ble** *adj.* **—ex·am′in·er** *n.*

ex·am·ple (ig·zam′pəl) *n.* 1. A typical or representative specimen. 2. Something deserving imitation; model. 3. An instance or object of punishment, reprimand, etc., designed to warn or deter others. 4. A particular problem or exercise. **—for example** By way of illustration. [< L *ex-* out + *emere* to buy, take]

ex·as·per·ate (ig·zas′pə·rāt) *v.t.* **·at·ed, ·at·ing** 1. To make annoyed or angry; infuriate. 2. To make still worse; aggravate. [< L *ex-* out + *asper* rough] **—ex·as′per·**

at′ing *adj.* —ex·as′per·at′ing·ly *adv.* —ex·as′per·a′tion *n.*
ex·ca·vate (eks′kə·vāt) *v.t.* ·vat·ed, ·vat·ing 1. To make a hole or cavity in. 2. To form or make (a hole, tunnel, etc.) by hollowing, digging out, or scooping. 3. To remove by digging or scooping out, as soil. 4. To uncover by digging, as ruins; unearth. [< L *ex-* out + *cavus* hollow] —ex′ca·va′tion *n.* —ex′ca·va′tor *n.*
ex·ceed (ik·sēd′) *v.t.* & *v.i.* 1. To surpass or be superior. 2. To go or be beyond (a limit). [< L *ex-* out, beyond + *cedere* to go]
ex·ceed·ing (ik·sē′ding) *adj.* Greater than usual. —ex·ceed′ing·ly *adv.*
ex·cel (ik·sel′) *v.t.* & *v.i.* ·celled, ·cel·ling To surpass; outstrip; be outstanding. [< L *excellere* to rise]
Ex·cel·len·cy (ek′sə·lən·sē) *n. pl.* ·cies An honorary title or form of address: often preceded by *His, Her, Your,* etc.
ex·cel·lent (ek′sə·lənt) *adj.* Being of the very best quality; exceptionally good. —ex′cel·lence *n.* —ex′cel·lent·ly *adv.*
ex·cel·si·or (ik·sel′sē·ər) *n.* Long, fine wood shavings used as packing material.
ex·cept (ik·sept′) *prep.* With the exclusion or omission of; aside from. —*conj.* 1. Aside from the fact that: also **except that.** 2. Otherwise than. —*v.t.* 1. To exclude from consideration, enumeration, etc.; leave deliberately out of account. —*v.i.* 2. To raise an objection, esp. a formal objection: now usu. with *to.* [< L *ex-* out + *capere* to take]
ex·cept·ing (ik·sep′ting) *prep.* Barring; except.
ex·cep·tion (ik·sep′shən) *n.* 1. The act of excepting, or the state of being excepted. 2. Something excluded from or not conforming to a general class, principle, rule, etc. 3. *Law* A formal objection to the decision of a court during trial. —**to take exception** 1. To express disagreement. 2. To feel resentful.
ex·cep·tion·a·ble (ik·sep′shən·ə·bəl) *adj.* Open to exception or objection. —ex·cep′tion·a·bly *adv.*
ex·cep·tion·al (ik·sep′shən·əl) *adj.* Unusual; extraordinary. —ex·cep′tion·al·ly *adv.*
ex·cerpt (*n.* ek′sûrpt; *v.* ik·sûrpt′) *n.* An extract from a book, speech, etc. —*v.t.* To pick out and cite (a passage from a book, etc.). [< L *ex-* out + *carpere* to pluck]
ex·cess (*n.* ik·ses′, ek′ses; *adj.* ek′ses, ik·ses′) *n.* 1. The condition or fact of going beyond what is usual, necessary, allowed, proper, etc.; also, the quantity, extent, or degree of this. 2. An overabundance; superfluity. 3. Overindulgence; intemperance. —*adj.* 1. Being over and above what is expected or usual. 2. Immoderate. [See EXCEED.]
ex·ces·sive (ik·ses′iv) *adj.* Going beyond what is usual, necessary, proper, etc.; extreme. —ex·ces′sive·ly *adv.* —ex·ces′sive·ness *n.*
ex·change (iks·chānj′) *v.* ·changed, ·chang·ing *v.t.* 1. To give and receive reciprocally. 2. To give up for something taken as a replacement. 3. To transfer to another in return for the equivalent in goods or money; trade. —*v.i.* 4. To exchange something. —*n.* 1. The act of giving or receiving one thing as equivalent for another. 2. A giving and receiving in turn. 3. The substitution of one thing for another. 4. A place where brokers, etc., meet to buy, sell, or trade commodities or securities: stock *exchange.* 5. A central telephone system. 6. A bill of exchange; also, the system of using a bill of exchange, or the fee for it. 7. The mutual giving and receiving of equal sums of money, as between two countries using different currencies; also, the value of one currency relative to another. [< L *ex-* out + *cambiare* to exchange] —ex·change′a·ble *adj.*
ex·cheq·uer (iks·chek′ər, eks′chek·ər) *n.* The treasury of a state, organization, etc. [< OF *eschaquier* chessboard, then table marked in squares for keeping of accounts]
ex·cise[1] (*n.* ek′sīz, ik·sīz′; *v.* ik·sīz′) *n.* 1. An indirect tax on certain commodities produced, sold, used, or transported within a country. Also **excise tax.** 2. A license fee charged for various sports, trades, etc. —*v.t.* ·cised, ·cis·ing To levy an excise upon. [< MDu. *excijs, accijs* < OF *acceis* < L *ad-* to + *census* tax]
ex·cise[2] (ik·sīz′) *v.t.* ·cised, ·cis·ing 1. To cut out, as a growth. 2. To delete (a word, passage, etc.). [< L *ex-* out + *caedere* to cut] —ex·ci·sion (ik·sizh′ən) *n.*
ex·cit·a·ble (ik·sī′tə·bəl) *adj.* 1. Easily excited; high-strung. 2. *Physiol.* Susceptible to stimuli. —ex·cit′a·bil′i·ty *n.* —ex·cit′a·bly *adv.*
ex·cite (ik·sīt′) *v.t.* ·cit·ed, ·cit·ing 1. To arouse (a feeling, reaction, etc.) into being or activity. 2. To arouse strong feeling in; rouse. 3. To bring about; stir up; provoke. [< L *ex-* out + *ciere* to arouse] —ex·ci′tant *n.* & *adj.* —ex·ci·ta′tion *n.* —ex·cit′ed *adj.* —ex·cit′ed·ly *adv.*
ex·cite·ment (ik·sīt′mənt) *n.* 1. The state of being excited; agitation. 2. That which excites.
ex·cit·ing (ik·sī′ting) *adj.* Causing excitement; thrilling. —ex·cit′ing·ly *adv.*
ex·claim (iks·klām′) *v.t.* & *v.i.* To cry out abruptly; speak vehemently, as in surprise or anger. [< L *ex-* out + *clamare* to cry]
ex·cla·ma·tion (eks′klə·mā′shən) *n.* An abrupt or emphatic utterance, outcry, etc. —ex·clam·a·to·ry (iks·klam′ə·tôr′ē) *adj.*
exclamation point A mark (!) used in punctuation after an exclamation or interjection. Also **exclamation mark.**
ex·clude (iks·klo͞od′) *v.t.* ·clud·ed, ·clud·ing 1. To keep from entering; bar. 2. To refuse to notice, consider, or allow for; leave out. 3. To put out; eject. [< L *ex-* out + *claudere* to close] —ex·clu·sion (iks·klo͞o′zhən) *n.*
ex·clu·sive (iks·klo͞o′siv) *adj.* 1. Intended for or possessed by a single individual or group. 2. Belonging to or found in a single source: an *exclusive* news story. 3. Having no duplicate; original: an *exclusive* design. 4. Admitting or catering to only a very select group. 5. Complete and undivided: one's *exclusive* attention. 6. Inconsistent or incompatible with another: mutually *exclusive* doctrines. 7. Being the only one: the *exclusive* owner. 8. Not including: usu. with *of*: the expense *exclusive* of fees. —*n.* An exclusive news story. —ex·clu′sive·ly *adv.* —ex·clu′sive·ness *n.* —ex·clu·siv·i·ty (eks′·klo͞o·siv′ə·tē) *n.*
ex·cog·i·tate (iks·koj′ə·tāt) *v.t.* ·tat·ed, ·tat·ing To think out carefully; devise.

[< L *ex-* out + *cogitare* to think] —**ex·cog′i·ta′tion** *n.*
ex·com·mu·ni·cate (eks′kə·myōō′nə·kāt) *v.t.* **·cat·ed, ·cat·ing** To cut off by ecclesiastical authority from sharing in the sacraments, worship, privileges, or fellowship of a church. [< LL *ex-* out + *communicare* to share] —**ex′com·mu′ni·ca′tion** *n.* —**ex′com·mu′ni·ca′tor** *n.*
ex·co·ri·ate (ik·skôr′ē·āt) *v.t.* **·at·ed, ·at·ing** 1. To tear, chafe, or burn away strips of (skin, bark, etc.). 2. To upbraid or denounce scathingly. [< L *ex-* out, off + *corium* skin] —**ex·co′ri·at′ing·ly** *adv.* —**ex·co′ri·a′tion** *n.*
ex·cre·ment (eks′krə·mənt) *n.* Waste matter expelled from the body; esp., feces. —**ex′cre·men′tal** (-men′təl) *adj.*
ex·cres·cence (iks·kres′əns) *n.* 1. An unnatural or disfiguring outgrowth, as a wart. 2. Any outgrowth or addition. [< L *ex-* out + *crescere* to grow]
ex·cre·ta (iks·krē′tə) *n.pl.* Excretions, as sweat, urine, feces, etc.
ex·crete (iks·krēt′) *v.t.* **·cret·ed, ·cret·ing** To throw off or eliminate (waste matter). [< L *ex-* out + *cernere* to separate] —**ex·cre′tion** *n.* —**ex·cre·to·ry** (eks′krə·tôr′ē) *adj.*
ex·cru·ci·ate (iks·krōō′shē·āt) *v.t.* **·at·ed, ·at·ing** To inflict extreme pain or agony upon. [< L *ex-* completely + *cruciare* to torture] —**ex·cru′ci·at′ing** *adj.* —**ex·cru′ci·at′ing·ly** *adv.*
ex·cul·pate (eks′kul·pāt, ik·skul′-) *v.t.* **·pat·ed, ·pat·ing** To free from blame, or prove innocent. [< L *ex-* out + *culpare* to blame] —**ex′cul·pa′tion** *n.* —**ex·cul·pa·to·ry** (ik·skul′pə·tôr′ē) *adj.*
ex·cur·sion (ik·skûr′zhən, -shən) *n.* 1. A short trip, as for relaxation. 2. A trip on a train, etc., at reduced rates. [< L *ex-* out + *currere* to run] —**ex·cur′sion·ist** *n.*
ex·cur·sive (ik·skûr′siv) *adj.* Rambling; digressive. —**ex·cur′sive·ly** *adv.* —**ex·cur′sive·ness** *n.*
ex·cur·sus (eks·kur′səs) *n. pl.* **·sus·es** or **·sus** 1. A supplemental discussion added to a work. 2. A digression. [< L, a going out]
ex·cuse (*v.* ik·skyōōz′; *n.* ik·skyōōs′) *v.t.* **·cused, ·cus·ing** 1. To apologize for. 2. To grant pardon or forgiveness to. 3. To accept or overlook. 4. To free from censure or blame. 5. To release or exempt, as from a duty. 6. To allow to leave. —*n.* 1. A reason given as a ground for being excused. 2. A factor that frees from blame. [< L *ex-* out, away + *causa* charge, accusation] —**ex·cus·a·ble** (ik·skōōz′ə·bəl) *adj.* —**ex·cus′a·bly** *adv.*
ex·e·cra·ble (ek′sə·krə·bəl) *adj.* 1. Detestable. 2. Extremely bad. —**ex′e·cra·bly** *adv.*
ex·e·crate (ek′sə·krāt) *v.t.* **·crat·ed, ·crat·ing** 1. To call down evil upon; curse. 2. To detest; abhor. [< L *ex-* out + *sacrare* to devote to good or evil] —**ex′e·cra′tion** *n.*
ex·e·cute (ek′sə·kyōōt) *v.t.* **·cut·ed, ·cut·ing** 1. To carry out fully. 2. To put into force, as a law. 3. To put to death legally. 4. To make (a will, deed, etc.) legal or valid. 5. To perform (something demanding skill). 6. To produce or fashion. [< L *ex-* throughout + *sequi* to follow] —**ex′e·cut′er** *n.*
ex·e·cu·tion (ek′sə·kyōō′shən) *n.* 1. The act of executing, or the fact or condition of being executed. 2. The way in which something is done. 3. *Law* A judicial writ for carrying into effect a judgment or decree.
ex·e·cu·tion·er (ek′sə·kyōō′shən·ər) *n.* One who executes a death sentence.
ex·e·cu·tive (ig·zek′yə·tiv) *adj.* 1. Relating or adapted to the putting into effect of plans, projects, etc. 2. Relating or adapted to the execution of laws and the administration of judgments, decrees, etc. —*n.* 1. An individual or a group managing the administrative affairs of a nation, state, etc. 2. An individual responsible for the management of a business, etc.
ex·e·cu·tor (ig·zek′yə·tər) *n.* 1. *Law* One who is appointed to carry out the terms of a will. 2. One who executes anything; executer. —**ex·ec′u·trix** (-triks) *n.fem.*
ex·e·ge·sis (ek′sə·jē′sis) *n. pl.* **·ses** (-sēz) Critical explanation of the meaning of a literary or religious text. [< Gk. *exēgeesthai* to explain]
ex·e·gete (ek′sə·jēt) *n.* One skilled in exegesis.
ex·em·plar (ig·zem′plər, -plär) *n.* 1. A model, pattern, or original. 2. A typical example or specimen. [< LL *exemplum* a pattern]
ex·em·pla·ry (ig·zem′plər·ē) *adj.* 1. Serving as a worthy model or example. 2. Serving as a warning. —**ex·em′pla·ri·ness** *n.*
ex·em·pli·fy (ig·zem′plə·fī) *v.t.* **·fied, ·fy·ing** To show by example; illustrate. [< L *exemplum* copy + *facere* to make] —**ex·em′pli·fi·ca′tion** *n.* —**ex·em′pli·fi·ca′tive** *adj.*
ex·empt (ig·zempt′) *v.t.* To free or excuse from some obligation to which others are subject. —*adj.* Free, clear, or excused, as from some duty. [< L *ex-* out + *emere* to buy, take] —**ex·emp′tion** *n.*
ex·er·cise (ek′sər·sīz) *v.* **·cised, ·cis·ing** *v.t.* 1. To subject to drills, etc., so as to train or develop. 2. To make use of; employ. 3. To exert, as authority. 4. To make anxious or fretful. —*v.i.* 5. To perform exercises. —*n.* 1. A putting into use: an *exercise* of patience. 2. Activity performed for physical conditioning. 3. A lesson, problem, etc., designed to teach a skill. 4. *Usu. pl.* A ceremony, etc., as at a graduation. [< L *exercere* to practice] —**ex′er·cis′er** *n.*
ex·ert (ig·zûrt′) *v.t.* To put forth or into action, as force or influence. [< L *exserere* to thrust out] —**ex·er′tion** *n.*
ex·e·unt (ek′sē·ənt, -sē·ōōnt) They go out: a stage direction. [< L]
ex·fo·li·ate (eks·fō′lē·āt) *v.t. & v.i.* **·at·ed, ·at·ing** To separate or peel off in scales, layers, flakes, etc. [< L *ex-* off + *folium* leaf] —**ex·fo′li·a′tion** *n.*
ex·ha·la·tion (eks′hə·lā′shən) *n.* 1. The act of exhaling. 2. That which is exhaled.
ex·hale (eks·hāl′) *v.* **·haled, ·hal·ing** *v.i.* 1. To expel air or vapor; breathe out. 2. To pass off as a vapor or emanation. —*v.t.* 3. To breathe forth or give off, as air or an aroma. [< L *ex-* out + *halare* to breathe] —**ex·hal′a·ble** *adj.*
ex·haust (ig·zôst′) *v.t.* 1. To make extremely tired. 2. To drain of resources, strength, etc. 3. To draw off, as gas, steam, etc., from or as from a container. 4. To empty; drain. 5. To study, treat of, or develop thoroughly. —*n.* 1. The escape or discharge of waste

gases, fluid, etc.; also, the gases, etc., that escape. 2. A pipe or other engine part through which gases, etc., escape. [< L *ex-* out + *haurire* to draw] —**ex·haust'ed** *adj.* —**ex·haust'ed·ly** *adv.* —**ex·haust'i·ble** *adj.*
ex·haust·ing (ig·zôs'ting) *adj.* Extremely tiring. —**ex·haust'ing·ly** *adv.*
ex·haus·tion (ig·zôs'chən) *n.* 1. Extreme fatigue. 2. The condition of being completely used up, drained, or comprehensively studied.
ex·haus·tive (ig·zôs'tiv) *adj.* 1. That exhausts or tends to exhaust; exhausting. 2. Thorough; comprehensive. —**ex·haus'·tive·ly** *adv.* —**ex·haus'tive·ness** *n.*
ex·hib·it (ig·zib'it) *v.t.* 1. To put on view, esp. publicly. 2. To make evident; reveal. 3. *Law* To submit (evidence, etc.) formally. —*v.i.* 4. To put something on display. —*n.* 1. A putting on view; display. 2. An object or objects displayed. 3. *Law* An object submitted as evidence. [< L *ex-* out + *habere* to hold, have] —**ex·hib'i·tor** *n.*
ex·hi·bi·tion (ek'sə·bish'ən) *n.* 1. The act of exhibiting. 2. That which is exhibited. 3. A public display, as of art works.
ex·hi·bi·tion·ism (ek'sə·bish'ən·iz'əm) *n.* 1. A tendency to attract attention to oneself. 2. A tendency toward deviant sexual display. —**ex'hi·bi'tion·ist** *n.* —**ex'hi·bi'tion·is'tic** *adj.*
ex·hil·a·rate (ig·zil'ə·rāt) *v.t.* **·rat·ed, ·rat·ing** To make happy; elate. [< L *ex-* completely + *hilarare* to gladden] —**ex·hil'a·ra'tion** *n.*
ex·hort (ig·zôrt') *v.t. & v.i.* To urge by earnest appeal or argument; advise or recommend strongly. [< L *ex-* completely + *hortari* to urge] —**ex·hor·ta·tion** (eg'zôr·tā'shən, ek'sôr-) *n.* —**ex·hor'ta·tive, ex·hor'ta·to'ry** *adj.*
ex·hume (ig·zyōōm', iks·hyōōm') *v.t.* **·humed, ·hum·ing** To dig up; disinter. [< L *ex-* out + *humus* ground] —**ex·hu·ma·tion** (eks'hyōō·mā'shən) *n.*
ex·i·gen·cy (ek'sə·jən·sē) *n. pl.* **·cies** 1. Urgency. 2. A situation that requires immediate attention. 3. *Usu. pl.* A pressing need or necessity. [< L *ex-* out + *agere* to drive] —**ex'i·gent** *adj.*
ex·ig·u·ous (ig·zig'yōō·əs, ik·sig'-) *adj.* Small in amount; scanty. [< L *exiguus*] —**ex·i·gu·i·ty** (ek'sə·gyōō'ə·tē), **ex·ig'u·ous·ness** *n.*
ex·ile (eg'zīl, ek'sīl) *n.* 1. Separation from one's native country, home, etc. 2. One who is so separated. [< L *exsilium*] —**ex'ile** *v.t.* **·iled, ·il·ing**
ex·ist (ig·zist') *v.i.* 1. To have actual being or reality; be. 2. To continue to live or be. 3. To be present; occur. [< L *ex-* out + *sistere* to be located]
ex·is·tence (ig·zis'təns) *n.* 1. The state or fact of being or continuing to be. 2. Animate being; life. 3. Way or mode of living. 4. Presence; occurrence. 5. Anything or all that exists. —**ex·is'tent** *adj. & n.* —**ex·is·ten·tial** (eg'zis·ten'shəl) *adj.* —**ex'is·ten'tial·ly** *adv.*
ex·is·ten·tial·ism (eg'zis·ten'shəl·iz'əm) *n.* A philosophy that stresses existence, as opposed to essence, and the active role of the will. —**ex'is·ten'tial·ist** *adj. & n.*
ex·it (eg'zit, ek'sit) *n.* 1. A way out; egress. 2. A departure of an actor from a stage. 3. Any departure. —*v.i.* To go out; depart. [< L *ex-* out + *ire* to go]
exo- *combining form* Out; outside; external: *exogamy*. Also, before vowels, **ex-**. [< Gk. *exo-*, *ex-* < *exō* outside]
ex·o·bi·ol·o·gy (ek'sō·bī·ol'ə·jē) *n.* The study of extraterrestrial life. —**ex·o·bi·o·log·i·cal** (ek'sō·bī·ə·loj'i·kəl) *adj.* —**ex'o·bi·o·log'i·cal·ly** *adv.* —**ex'o·bi·ol'o·gist** *n.*
ex·o·dus (ek'sə·dəs) *n.* A going forth. —**the Exodus** The departure of the Israelites from Egypt, described in **Exodus**, the second book of the Old Testament. [< Gk. *ex-* out + *hodos* way]
ex of·fi·ci·o (eks ə·fish'ē·ō) *Latin* By virtue of or because of office or position.
ex·og·a·my (eks·og'ə·mē) *n.* The custom of marriage outside of the tribe, family, clan, etc. —**ex·og'a·mous** *adj.*
ex·o·gen (ek'sō·jen) *n. Bot.* A plant that increases in size by successive concentric additions beneath the bark. [< EXO- + -GEN] —**ex·og·e·nous** (eks·oj'ə·nəs) *adj.*
ex·on·er·ate (ig·zon'ə·rāt) *v.t.* **·at·ed, ·at·ing** 1. To free from accusation or blame. 2. To relieve or free from a responsibility or the like. [< L *ex-* out, away + *onus, oneris* burden] —**ex·on'er·a'tion** *n.*
ex·or·bi·tant (ig·zôr'bə·tənt) *adj.* Excessive, as in price or demand; extravagant. [< LL *exorbitare* to go astray] —**ex·or'bi·tance** *n.* —**ex·or'bi·tant·ly** *adv.*
ex·or·cise (ek'sôr·sīz) *v.t.* **·cised, ·cis·ing** 1. To cast out (an evil spirit) by prayers or incantations. 2. To free of an evil spirit. Also **ex'or·cize.** [< Gk. *ex-* out + *horkos* oath] —**ex'or·cis'er, ex'or·cist** *n.* —**ex'or·cism** *n.*
ex·or·di·um (ig·zôr'dē·əm, ik·sôr'-) *n. pl.* **·di·ums** or **·di·a** A beginning or introductory part. [< L *ex-* out + *ordiri* to begin] —**ex·or'di·al** *adj.*
ex·o·skel·e·ton (ek'sō·skel'ə·tən) *n.* See under SKELETON.
ex·o·sphere (ek'sō·sfir) *n. Meteorol.* The outer region of the earth's atmosphere.
ex·o·ther·mic (ek'sō·thûr'mik) *adj. Chem.* Pertaining to a reaction in which heat is liberated. Also **ex'o·ther'mal.**
ex·ot·ic (ig·zot'ik) *adj.* 1. Belonging to another part of the world; not native. 2. Strangely different and fascinating. [< Gk. *exōtikos* foreign] —**ex·ot'ic** *n.* —**ex·ot'i·cal·ly** *adv.* —**ex·ot·i·cism** (ig·zot'ə·siz'əm) *n.*
ex·pand (ik·spand') *v.t.* 1. To increase the range, size, etc., of. 2. To spread out by unfolding; open. 3. To develop more fully the details or form of. —*v.i.* 4. To grow larger, wider, etc. [< L *ex-* out + *pandere* to spread] —**ex·pand'a·ble, ex·pan·si·ble** (ik·span'sə·bəl) *adj.* —**ex·pan·sion** (ik·span'shən) *n.*
ex·panse (ik·spans') *n.* 1. A wide, continuous area or stretch. 2. Expansion.
ex·pan·sive (ik·span'siv) *adj.* 1. Capable of expanding or tending to expand. 2. Broad; extensive. 3. Effusive; outgoing. —**ex·pan'sive·ly** *adv.* —**ex·pan'sive·ness** *n.*
ex·pa·ti·ate (ik·spā'shē·āt) *v.i.* **·at·ed, ·at·ing** To speak or write at length; elaborate: with *on*. [< L *ex-* out + *spatiari* to walk] —**ex·pa'ti·a'tion** *n.*
ex·pa·tri·ate (eks·pā'trē·āt) *v.* **·at·ed,**

·at·ing *v.t.* 1. To banish. 2. To exile (oneself). —*v.i.* 3. To leave one's country and reside elsewhere. [< L *ex-* out + *patria* native land] —**ex·pa′tri·ate** (-it, -āt) *n.* & *adj.* —**ex·pa′tri·a′tion** *n.*

ex·pect (ik·spekt′) *v.t.* 1. To look forward to as certain or probable. 2. To look for as right, proper, or necessary. 3. *Informal* To presume; suppose. [< L *ex-* out + *spectare* to look at] —**ex·pec′ta·ble** *adj.*

ex·pec·tan·cy (ik·spek′tən·sē) *n.* *pl.* **·cies** 1. The action or state of expecting. 2. An object of expectation: life *expectancy*. Also **ex·pec′tance.**

ex·pec·tant (ik·spek′tənt) *adj.* 1. Having expectations. 2. Awaiting the birth of a child. —**ex·pec′tant·ly** *adv.*

ex·pec·ta·tion (ek′spek·tā′shən) *n.* 1. The action of expecting, or the state of mind of one who expects; anticipation. 2. The state of being expected: preceded by *in*. 3. Something expected or looked forward to.

ex·pect·ing (ik·spek′ting) *adj.* Pregnant; also, due to give birth: She is *expecting* in July.

ex·pec·to·rant (ik·spek′tər·ənt) *adj.* Promoting expectoration. —*n.* A medicine used for this purpose.

ex·pec·to·rate (ik·spek′tə·rāt) *v.t.* & *v.i.* **·rat·ed, ·rat·ing** 1. To discharge (phlegm, etc.) by spitting. 2. To spit. [< L *ex-* out + *pectus, -oris* breast] —**ex·pec′to·ra′tion** *n.*

ex·pe·di·en·cy (ik·spē′dē·ən·sē) *n.* *pl.* **·cies** 1. The state or quality of being expedient. 2. That which is expedient. 3. Adherence to what is opportune or politic. Also **ex·pe′di·ence.**

ex·pe·di·ent (ik·spē′dē·ənt) *adj.* 1. Serving to promote a desired end. 2. Pertaining to or prompted by utility, interest, or advantage rather than by what is right. —*n.* 1. Something expedient. 2. A device; makeshift. [< L *expedire* to free the feet from fetters]

ex·pe·dite (ek′spə·dīt) *v.t.* **·dit·ed, ·dit·ing** 1. To speed up the process or progress of; facilitate. 2. To do with quick efficiency. [< L *expedire* to free the feet from fetters] —**ex′pe·dit′er** *n.*

ex·pe·di·tion (ek′spə·dish′ən) *n.* 1. A journey or march for a definite purpose. 2. A group of persons engaged in such a journey, together with their equipment. —**ex′pe·di′tion·ar′y** *adj.*

ex·pe·di·tious (ek′spə·dish′əs) *adj.* Quick; speedy. —**ex′pe·di′tious·ly** *adv.*

ex·pel (ik·spel′) *v.t.* **·pelled, ·pel·ling** 1. To drive out by force. 2. To force to end attendance at a school, terminate membership, etc.; oust. [< L *ex-* out + *pellere* to drive, thrust]

ex·pend (ik·spend′) *v.t.* To pay out or use up. [< L *ex-* out + *pendere* to weigh, pay]

ex·pend·a·ble (ik·spen′də·bəl) *adj.* 1. Available for spending. 2. Denoting a thing or person that can be sacrificed. —**ex·pend′a·bil′i·ty** *n.*

ex·pen·di·ture (ik·spen′də·chər) *n.* The act of expending, or the amount expended.

ex·pense (ik·spens′) *n.* 1. Outlay or consumption of money. 2. The cost of something; money required. 3. Something that involves the spending of money. 4. *pl.* Funds allotted or spent to cover incidental costs.

ex·pen·sive (ik·spen′siv) *adj.* Involving much expense; costly. —**ex·pen′sive·ly** *adv.* —**ex·pen′sive·ness** *n.*

ex·pe·ri·ence (ik·spir′ē·əns) *n.* 1. Actual participation in or direct contact with something. 2. Knowledge or skill derived from actual participation or training. 3. The totality of whatever one has engaged in or undergone. —*v.t.* **·enced, ·enc·ing** To be personally involved in; undergo. [< L *experiri* to try out] —**ex·pe′ri·enced** *adj.*

ex·pe·ri·en·tial (ik·spir′ē·en′shəl) *adj.* Pertaining to or acquired by experience; empirical. —**ex·pe′ri·en′tial·ly** *adv.*

ex·per·i·ment (ik·sper′ə·mənt, -ment) *n.* 1. An act or operation designed to discover, test, or illustrate a truth, principle, or effect. 2. The conducting of such operations. —*v.i.* To make experiments; make a test or trial. [< L *experiri* to try out] —**ex·per′i·men·ta′tion** *n.* —**ex·per′i·ment′er** (-men′tər) *n.*

ex·per·i·men·tal (ik·sper′ə·men′təl) *adj.* 1. Pertaining to or resulting from experiment. 2. Based on experience; empirical. 3. For the purpose of experiment or testing. 4. Provisional; tentative. —**ex·per′i·men′tal·ly** *adv.*

ex·pert (ek′spûrt; *for adj., also* ik·spûrt′) *n.* One who has special skill or knowledge; a specialist. —*adj.* 1. Skillful as the result of training or experience. 2. Characteristic of or produced by an expert. [< L *expertus*, pp. of *experiri* to try out] —**ex′pert·ly** *adv.* —**ex′pert·ness** *n.*

ex·per·tise (ek′spər·tēz′) *n.* The knowledge, skill, or experience of an expert. [< F]

ex·pi·ate (ek′spē·āt) *v.t.* **·at·ed, ·at·ing** To atone for; make amends for. [< L *ex-* completely + *piare* to appease] —**ex′pi·a·ble** (-ə·bəl) *adj.* —**ex′pi·a′tion** *n.* —**ex′pi·a′tor** *n.*

ex·pi·a·to·ry (eks′pē·ə·tôr′e) *adj.* Serving to expiate; offered in atonement.

ex·pire (ik·spīr′) *v.* **·pired, ·pir·ing** *v.i.* 1. To come to an end, as a contract. 2. To exhale. 3. To die. —*v.t.* 4. To breathe out from the lungs. [< L *ex-* out + *spirare* to breathe] —**ex·pi·ra·tion** (ek′spə·rā′shən) *n.*

ex·plain (ik·splān′) *v.t.* 1. To make plain or understandable. 2. To give the meaning of; interpret. 3. To give reasons for; account for. —*v.i.* 4. To give an explanation. [< L *ex-* out + *planare* to make level] —**ex·plain′a·ble** *adj.*

ex·pla·na·tion (ek′splə·nā′shən) *n.* 1. The act or process of explaining. 2. A statement that clarifies or accounts for something. 3. The meaning given to explain something; sense. —**ex·plan·a·to·ry** (ik·splan′ə·tôr′ē) *adj.*

ex·ple·tive (eks′plə·tiv) *n.* An exclamation, often profane. [< L *ex-* completely + *plere* to fill]

ex·pli·ca·ble (eks′plĭ·kə·bəl, ik·splik′ə·bəl) *adj.* Capable of explanation.

ex·pli·cate (eks′plə·kāt) *v.t.* **·cat·ed, ·cat·ing** To explain in detail. [< L *ex-* out + *plicare* to fold] —**ex′pli·ca′tion** *n.* —**ex·pli·ca·tive** (eks′plə·kā′tiv, ik·splik′ə·tiv) *adj.* —**ex′pli·ca′tor** *n.*

ex·plic·it (ik·splis′it) *adj.* 1. Plainly expressed; clear. 2. Frank; straightforward. [See EXPLICATE.] —**ex·plic′it·ly** *adv.* —**ex·plic′it·ness** *n.*

ex·plode (ik·splōd′) *v.* **·plod·ed, ·plod·ing** *v.t.* 1. To cause to burst or blow up violently and with noise; detonate. 2. To disprove utterly; refute. 3. To cause to expand violently or pass suddenly from a solid to a gaseous state. —*v.i.* 4. To burst into pieces; blow up. 5. To be exploded, as gunpowder. 6. To break out suddenly or violently into tears, laughter, etc. [< L *ex-* out + *plaudere* to clap] —**ex·plo·sion** (ik·splō′zhən) *n.*

ex·ploit (*n.* eks′ploit, ik·sploit′; *v.* ik·sploit′) *n.* A deed or act, esp. a daring one; feat. —*v.t.* 1. To use for one's own gain or advantage: to *exploit* workers. 2. To utilize for profitable ends: to *exploit* water power. [See EXPLICATE.] —**ex·ploit′a·ble** *adj.* —**ex′ploi·ta′tion** *n.* —**ex·ploit′a·tive** *adj.* —**ex·ploi′ter** *n.*

ex·plo·ra·tion (eks′plə·rā′shən) *n.* The act of exploring; esp., the exploring of unfamiliar or unknown regions. —**ex·plor·a·to·ry** (ik·splôr′ə·tôr′ē) *adj.*

ex·plore (ik·splôr′) *v.t.* & *v.i.* **·plored, ·plor·ing** 1. To search or examine closely; scrutinize. 2. To travel through (unfamiliar territory, etc.). [< L *ex-* out + *plorare* to cry out] —**ex·plor′er** *n.*

ex·plo·sive (ik·splō′siv) *adj.* 1. Pertaining to or marked by explosion. 2. Liable to explode or to cause explosion. —*n.* Anything that, on impact or by ignition, reacts by a violent expansion of gases and the liberation of heat. —**ex·plo′sive·ly** *adv.* —**ex·plo′sive·ness** *n.*

ex·po·nent (ik·spō′nənt; *for def. 3, also* ek′spō·nənt) *n.* 1. One who or that which explains or expounds. 2. One who or that which represents or symbolizes something: an *exponent* of fair play. 3. *Math.* A number or symbol placed as a superscript to the right of a quantity to indicate a power: 2 is an *exponent* in 3^2. [< L *ex-* out + *ponere* to place]

ex·port (*v.* ik·spôrt′, eks′pôrt; *n.* & *adj.* eks′pôrt) *v.t.* To carry or send, as merchandise or raw materials, to other countries for sale or trade. —*n.* 1. The act of exporting. 2. That which is exported. —*adj.* Of or pertaining to exports. [< L *ex-* out + *portare* to carry] —**ex·port′a·ble** *adj.* —**ex′por·ta′tion** *n.* —**ex·port′er** *n.*

ex·pose (ik·spōz′) *v.t.* **·posed, ·pos·ing** 1. To lay open to criticism, ridicule, etc.: to *expose* oneself to scorn. 2. To lay open to some force, influence, etc.: to *expose* a mixture to heat. 3. To present to view by baring. 4. To reveal, as a crime. 5. To unmask (an evildoer). 6. *Photog.* To admit light to (a sensitized film or plate). [< L *ex-* out + *ponere* to place]

ex·po·sé (ek′spō·zā′) *n.* A public revelation of an evil or disgrace. [< F]

ex·po·si·tion (eks′pə·zish′ən) *n.* 1. The act of presenting, explaining, or expounding facts or ideas. 2. A presentation, commentary, or interpretation. 3. A large public display or show.

ex·pos·i·tor (ik·spoz′ə·tər) *n.* One who expounds.

ex·pos·i·to·ry (ik·spoz′ə·tôr′ē) *adj.* Of or pertaining to exposition; explanatory.

ex post fac·to (eks pōst fak′tō) *Latin* Arising or enacted after some act, occurrence, etc., and having retroactive effect: said esp. of a law.

ex·pos·tu·late (ik·spos′chōō·lāt) *v.i.* **·lat·ed, ·lat·ing** To reason earnestly, esp. to dissuade; remonstrate: usu. with *with.* [< L *ex-* out + *postulare* to demand] —**ex·pos′tu·la′tion** *n.* —**ex·pos′tu·la′tor** *n.*

ex·po·sure (ik·spō′zhər) *n.* 1. The act of exposing, or the state of being exposed. 2. Situation in relation to the sun, elements, or points of the compass: a room with southern *exposure.* 3. *Photog.* **a** The act of subjecting a sensitized plate or film to light rays, X-rays, etc. **b** The time required for this. **c** A single film or plate so acted upon.

ex·pound (ik·spound′) *v.t.* 1. To set forth in detail; state. 2. To explain; interpret. [< L *ex-* out + *ponere* to place] —**ex·pound′er** *n.*

ex·press (ik·spres′) *v.t.* 1. To formulate in words; verbalize; state. 2. To give a sign of; reveal: to *express* anger by frowning. 3. To indicate by means of a symbol, formula, etc. 4. To squeeze out (a liquid, juice, etc.); press out. 5. To send (goods, etc.) by a system of rapid delivery. —*adj.* 1. Communicated or indicated clearly; explicit. 2. Made or intended for a precise purpose. 3. Designed for or operating at high speed: an *express* train. 4. Of or relating to a system of rapid delivery of goods, etc. 5. Exact; precise. —*adv.* By rapid delivery. —*n.* 1. A system designed to convey goods, money, etc., rapidly. 2. Any means of rapid conveyance. 3. A train or other conveyance operating at high speed and making few stops. [< L *ex-* out + *pressare* to press]

ex·pres·sion (ik·spresh′ən) *n.* 1. Communication of thought, opinion, etc. 2. Outward indication of some feeling, condition, etc. 3. A conventional sign or set of signs used to indicate something; symbolization. 4. A particular cast of the features that expresses a feeling, meaning, etc. 5. The particular way in which one expresses oneself. 6. A particular word, phrase, etc., used in communication.

ex·pres·sion·ism (ik·spresh′ən·iz′əm) *n.* An early 20th c. movement in the arts, stressing the artist's highly subjective interpretation of objects and experiences. —**ex·pres′sion·ist** *n.* & *adj.* —**ex·pres′sion·is′tic** *adj.*

ex·pres·sive (ik·spres′iv) *adj.* 1. Of or characterized by expression. 2. Serving to express or indicate: a manner *expressive* of contempt. 3. Significant: an *expressive* sigh. —**ex·pres′sive·ly** *adv.* —**ex·pres′sive·ness** *n.*

ex·press·ly (ik·spres′lē) *adv.* 1. With definitely stated intent or application. 2. Exactly and unmistakably; plainly.

ex·press·way (ik·spres′wā′) *n.* A highway for rapid travel.

ex·pro·pri·ate (eks·prō′prē·āt) *v.t.* **·at·ed, ·at·ing** To take or transfer (property) from the owner, esp. for public use. [< L *ex-* out + *proprium* property] —**ex·pro′pri·a′tion** *n.*

ex·pul·sion (ik·spul′shən) *n.* The act of expelling, or the state of being expelled. —**ex·pul′sive** *adj.*

ex·punge (ik·spunj′) *v.t.* **·punged, ·pung·ing** To erase or wipe out. [< L *ex-* out + *pungere* to prick]

ex·pur·gate (eks′pər·gāt) *v.t.* **·gat·ed, ·gat·ing** 1. To take out obscene or otherwise objectionable material from: to *expurgate* a novel. 2. To remove or omit (objectionable words, lines, etc.). [< L *ex-* out + *purgare* to cleanse] **—ex′pur·ga′tion** *n.*

ex·qui·site (eks′kwi·zit, ik·skwiz′it) *adj.* 1. Marked by rare and delicate beauty, craftsmanship, etc. 2. Superb; excellent; admirable. 3. Highly sensitive; discriminating. 4. Extremely refined; fastidious. 5. Intensely keen or acute, as pleasure or pain. [< L *exquisitus*, pp. of *exquirere* to seek out] **—ex′·qui·site·ly** *adv.* **—ex′qui·site·ness** *n.*

ex·tant (ek′stənt, ik·stant′) *adj.* Still existing; not lost or destroyed; surviving. [< L *ex-* out + *stare* to stand]

ex·tem·po·ra·ne·ous (ik·stem′pə·rā′nē·əs) *adj.* Uttered, performed, or composed with little or no advance preparation; improvised; spontaneous. [< L *ex-* out + *tempus, temporis* time] **—ex·tem′po·ra′ne·ous·ly** *adv.*

ex·tem·po·re (ik·stem′pə·rē) *adj.* Extemporaneous. *—adv.* Extemporaneously. [< L *ex tempore* out of the time]

ex·tem·po·rize (ik·stem′pə·rīz) *v.t. & v.i.* **·rized, ·riz·ing** To do, make, or perform with little or no advance preparation. **—ex·tem′po·ri·za′tion** *n.* **—ex·tem′po·riz′er** *n.*

ex·tend (ik·stend′) *v.t.* 1. To open or stretch to full length. 2. To make longer. 3. To prolong; continue. 4. To spread out; expand. 5. To hold out or put forth, as the hand. 6. To give or offer to give: to *extend* hospitality. *—v.i.* 7. To be extended; stretch. [< L *ex-* out + *tendere* to stretch] **—ex·tend′ed** *adj.* **—ex·tend′i·bil′i·ty** *n.* **—ex·tend′i·ble** *adj.*

extended family Parents, their children, and their close relatives living together as a family.

ex·ten·si·ble (ik·sten′sə·bəl) *adj.* Capable of being extended. **—ex·ten′si·bil′i·ty** *n.*

ex·ten·sion (ik·sten′shən) *n.* 1. The act of extending, or the state of being extended. 2. An extended part; addition. 3. Range; extent. 4. Educational courses and programs that are offered outside the school proper: *extension* courses. 5. *Physics* That property of matter by virtue of which it occupies space. **—ex·ten′sion·al** *adj.*

ex·ten·sive (ik·sten′siv) *adj.* 1. Large in area. 2. Having a wide range; far-reaching. **—ex·ten′sive·ly** *adv.* **—ex·ten′sive·ness** *n.*

ex·ten·sor (ik·sten′sər, -sôr) *n. Anat.* A muscle that straightens out a limb.

ex·tent (ik·stent′) *n.* 1. The dimension, degree, or limit to which anything is extended; size. 2. Size within given limits; scope: the *extent* of his powers. [< L *ex-* out + *tendere* to stretch]

ex·ten·u·ate (ik·sten′yōō·āt) *v.t.* **·at·ed, ·at·ing** To represent (a fault, crime, etc.) as less blameworthy; make excuses for. [< L *ex-* out + *tenuis* thin] **—ex·ten′u·at′ing** *adj.* **—ex·ten′u·a′tion** *n.*

ex·te·ri·or (ik·stir′ē·ər) *adj.* 1. Of, pertaining to, or situated on the outside; external. 2. Coming or acting from without: *exterior* influences. *—n.* 1. That which is outside, as an external surface. 2. Outside appearance or demeanor. [< L *exterus* outside]

ex·ter·mi·nate (ik·stûr′mə·nāt) *v.t.* **·nat·ed, ·nat·ing** To destroy (living things) entirely; annihilate. [< L *ex-* out + *terminus* boundary] **—ex·ter′mi·na′tion** *n.* **—ex·ter′·mi·na′tor** *n.*

ex·ter·nal (ik·stûr′nəl) *adj.* 1. Of, pertaining to, derived from, or situated on the outside; exterior; extrinsic. 2. Pertaining to the outer self; superficial. 3. Pertaining to foreign countries. 4. Relating to, affecting, or meant for the outside of the body: *external* medication. *—n.* 1. The outside; exterior. 2. *Usu. pl.* Outward or superficial aspects, circumstances, etc. [< L *externus* outer] **—ex·ter·nal·i·ty** (ek′stər·nal′ə·tē) *n.* **—ex·ter′·nal·ly** *adv.*

ex·ter·nal·ize (ik·stûr′nəl·īz) *v.t.* **·ized, ·iz·ing** 1. To give external shape to; make external or outwardly real. 2. To attribute to causes outside the self. **—ex·ter′nal·i·za′tion** *n.*

ex·tinct (ik·stingkt′) *adj.* 1. Extinguished; inactive, as a volcano. 2. No longer existing: an *extinct* animal. [< L *ex-* completely + *stinguere* to quench] **—ex·tinc′tion** *n.*

ex·tin·guish (ik·sting′gwish, -wish) *v.t.* 1. To put out or quench, as a fire. 2. To make extinct; wipe out. 3. To obscure; eclipse. [< L *ex-* completely + *stinguere* to quench] **—ex·tin′guish·a·ble** *adj.* **—ex·tin′guish·er** *n.*

ex·tir·pate (ek′stər·pāt, ik·stûr′-) *v.t.* **·pat·ed, ·pat·ing** To root out or up; destroy wholly. [< L *ex-* out + *stirps, stirpis* stem, root] **—ex′tir·pa′tion** *n.* **—ex′tir·pa′tive** *adj.* **—ex′tir·pa′tor** *n.*

ex·tol (ik·stōl′) *v.t.* **·tolled, ·tol·ling** To praise highly; exalt. Also **ex·toll′**. [< L *ex-* out, up + *tollere* to raise] **—ex·tol′ment** or **ex·toll′ment** *n.*

ex·tort (ik·stôrt′) *v.t.* To obtain (money, etc.) from a person by threat, oppression, or abuse of authority. [< L *ex-* out + *torquere* to twist] **—ex·tor′tive** *adj.*

ex·tor·tion (ik·stôr′shən) *n.* 1. The act or practice of extorting. 2. The exaction of an exorbitant price. 3. That which has been extorted. **—ex·tor′tion·ar·y, ex·tor′tion·ate** (-it) *adj.* **—ex·tor′tion·ist, ex·tor′tion·er** *n.*

ex·tra (eks′trə) *adj.* 1. Over and above what is normal, required, expected, etc.; additional. 2. Larger or better than usual. *—n.* 1. Something beyond what is usual or required. 2. A special edition of a newspaper issued to cover important news. 3. In motion pictures, a person hired for a small part, as in a mob scene. *—adv.* Unusually: *extra* good. [< L, outside, beyond]

extra- *prefix* Beyond or outside the scope, area, or limits of. Some self-explanatory words beginning with *extra-*:

extra-atmospheric	**extraliterary**
extracanonical	**extraorbital**
extrafamilial	**extraparental**
extragalactic	**extraplanetary**
extragovernmental	**extra-Scriptural**
extrajudicial	**extraterritorial**
extralegal	**extrauterine**

ex·tract (*v.* ik·strakt′; *n.* eks′trakt) *v.t.* 1. To draw or pull out by force. 2. To derive or deduce. 3. To obtain by pressure, distillation, etc. 4. To select or copy out (a passage, etc.), as for quotation. 5. *Math.* To calculate (the root of a number). *—n.* Something extracted, as: **a** A concentrated form of a food, drug, etc. **b** A passage selected from a book. [< L *ex-* out + *trahere* to draw, pull] **—ex·trac'tor** *n.* **—ex·tract'a·ble** *adj.*

ex·trac·tion (ik·strak'shən) *n.* 1. The act of extracting, or the state of being extracted. 2. That which is extracted. 3. Lineage; descent: of European *extraction.*

ex·tra·cur·ric·u·lar (eks'trə·kə·rik'yə·lər) *adj.* Of or pertaining to organized student activities which are not part of the curriculum.

ex·tra·dite (eks'trə·dīt) *v.t.* **·dit·ed, ·dit·ing** To deliver up (an accused individual, prisoner, or fugitive) to the jurisdiction of some other state, country, etc. [< L *ex-* out + *traditio* surrender] **—ex'tra·dit'a·ble** *adj.* **—ex'tra·di'tion** (-dish'ən) *n.*

ex·tra·mar·i·tal (eks'trə·mar'ə·təl) *adj.* Adulterous.

ex·tra·mu·ral (eks'trə·myŏŏr'əl) *adj.* 1. Situated outside the walls, as of a fortified city. 2. Relating to activities taking place outside an educational institution.

ex·tra·ne·ous (ik·strā'nē·əs) *adj.* 1. Coming from without; foreign. 2. Unrelated to the matter at hand. [< L *extraneus* foreign, external] **—ex·tra'ne·ous·ly** *adv.*

ex·traor·di·nar·y (ik·strôr'də·ner'ē; *esp. for def. 3* eks'trə·ôr'də·ner'ē) *adj.* 1. Being beyond or out of the common order, course, or method. 2. Far exceeding the usual; exceptional; remarkable. 3. Employed on an exceptional occasion; special: an envoy *extraordinary.* [< L *extra* beyond + *ordo, ordinis* order] **—ex·traor'di·nar'i·ly** *adv.*

ex·trap·o·late (eks·trap'ə·lāt) *v.t. & v.i.* **·lat·ed, ·lat·ing** To infer (an unknown value, meaning, etc.) from facts that are known. [< EXTRA- + (INTER)POLATE] **—ex·trap'o·la'tion** *n.*

ex·tra·sen·so·ry (eks'trə·sen'sər·ē) *adj.* Beyond the range of normal sensory experience or capability.

ex·tra·ter·res·tri·al (eks'trə·tə·res'trē·əl) *adj.* Pertaining to the universe outside the earth.

ex·trav·a·gance (ik·strav'ə·gəns) *n.* 1. Wasteful expenditure of money. 2. Extreme lack of moderation in behavior or speech. 3. An instance of wastefulness or excess. [< F]

ex·trav·a·gant (ik·strav'ə·gənt) *adj.* 1. Overly lavish in expenditure; wasteful. 2. Immoderate; unrestrained: *extravagant* praise. 3. Flagrantly high; exorbitant: *extravagant* prices. [< L *extra* outside + *vagari* to wander] **—ex·trav'a·gant·ly** *adv.*

ex·trav·a·gan·za (ik·strav'ə·gan'zə) *n.* A lavish, spectacular theatrical production. [< Ital. *estravaganza* extravagance]

ex·tra·ve·hic·u·lar (eks'trə·vi·hik'yə·lər) *adj.* Occurring in space and outside of a spacecraft.

ex·treme (ik·strēm') *adj.* 1. Exceedingly great or severe: *extreme* danger. 2. Going far beyond the bounds of moderation: an *extreme* reactionary. 3. Very strict or drastic: *extreme* measures. 4. Outermost: the *extreme* border of a country. 5. Last; final. **—***n.* 1. The highest degree; utmost point: the *extreme* of cruelty. 2. One of the two ends or farthest limits of anything: the *extremes* of joy and sorrow. **—to go to extremes** To carry something to excess. [< L *extremus,* superl. of *exterus* outside]

ex·treme·ly (ik·strēm'lē) *adv.* Exceedingly; very.

ex·trem·ist (ik·strē'mist) *n.* 1. One who advocates extreme measures or holds extreme views. 2. One who carries something to excess. **—ex·trem'ism** *n.* **—ex·trem'ist** *adj.*

ex·trem·i·ty (ik·strem'ə·tē) *n. pl.* **·ties** 1. The utmost or farthest point. 2. The greatest degree: the *extremity* of grief. 3. *pl.* Extreme measures: to resort to *extremities.* 4. A limb or appendage of the body; esp., a hand or foot.

ex·tri·cate (eks'trə·kāt) *v.t.* **·cat·ed, ·cat·ing** To free from entanglement, hindrance, or difficulties; disentangle. [< L *ex-* out + *tricae* trifles, troubles] **—ex·tri·ca·ble** (eks'·tri·kə·bəl) *adj.* **—ex'tri·ca'tion** *n.*

ex·trin·sic (ek·strin'sik) *adj.* 1. Being outside the nature of something; not inherent: opposed to *intrinsic.* 2. External; extraneous. [< LL *exter* outside + *secus* besides] **—ex·trin'si·cal·ly** *adv.*

ex·tro·ver·sion (eks'trə·vûr'zhən) *n. Psychol.* The turning of one's interest toward objects and actions outside the self. [< L *extra* outside + *versio, -onis* a turning] **—ex'tro·vert** (-vûrt) *n. & adj.* **—ex'tro·vert'ed** *adj.*

ex·trude (ik·strōōd') *v.* **·trud·ed, ·trud·ing** *v.t.* 1. To force, thrust, or push out. 2. To shape (plastic, metal, etc.) by forcing through dies under pressure. **—***v.i.* 3. To protrude. [< L *ex-* out + *trudere* to thrust] **—ex·tru·sion** (ik·strōō'zhən) *n.* **—ex·tru·sive** (ik·strōō'siv) *adj.*

ex·u·ber·ant (ig·zōō'bər·ənt) *adj.* 1. Abounding in high spirits and vitality; full of joy and vigor. 2. Overflowing; lavish: *exuberant* praise. 3. Growing luxuriantly: *exuberant* foliage. [< L < *ex-* completely + *uberare* to be fruitful] **—ex·u'ber·ance** *n.* **—ex·u'ber·ant·ly** *adv.*

ex·ude (ig·zōōd', -zyōōd') *v.* **·ud·ed, ·ud·ing** *v.i.* 1. To ooze or trickle forth, as sweat, sap, etc. **—***v.t.* 2. To discharge gradually in this manner. 3. To manifest; display: to *exude* confidence. [< L *ex-* out + *sudare* to sweat] **—ex·u·da·tion** (eks'yōō·dā'shən) *n.*

ex·ult (ig·zult') *v.i.* To rejoice greatly, as in triumph; be jubilant. [< L *ex-* out + *salire* to leap] **—ex·ul·ta·tion** (eg'zul·tā'shən, ek'sul-) *n.* **—ex·ult'ing·ly** *adv.*

ex·ul·tant (ig·zul'tənt) *adj.* Jubilant; triumphant; elated. **—ex·ul'tant·ly** *adv.*

ex·urb (eks'ûrb') *n.* A usu. affluent residential area outside a city beyond the suburbs. [< EX-[1] + URB(AN) (on analogy with suburb)] **—ex·urb'an** *adj.* **—ex·ur'·ban·ite** *n.*

ex·ur·bi·a (eks·ûr'bē·ə) *n.* Exurbs collectively.

-ey Var. of -Y[1].

eye (ī) *n.* 1. The organ of vision in man and animals, usu. a nearly spherical mass set in the skull. 2. The area around the eye. 3. The iris of the eye, in regard to its color. 4. A look; gaze. 5. Attentive observation. 6. Sight; view: in the public *eye.* 7. Capacity to see or discern with discrimination. 8. *Often pl.* Judgment; opinion. 9. *Meteorol.* The calm central area of a hurricane or cyclone. 10. Anything resembling the human eye: the *eye* of a needle. **—to catch one's eye** To get one's attention. **—to give (someone) the eye** *Slang* To look at (someone) admiringly or invitingly. **—to keep an eye out (or peeled)** To watch for something; keep alert. **—to lay (or set) eyes on** To catch sight of. **—to make eyes at** To look at amorously or covetously. **—with an eye to** With a view to; looking to. **—*v.t.*** **eyed, ey·ing** or **eye·ing** To look at carefully. [OE *ēage*] **—eye′less** *adj.*

eye·ball (ī′bôl′) *n.* The globe or ball of the eye. **—*v.t.*** *Slang* To look at carefully; scrutinize.

eye·brow (ī′brou′) *n.* The bony ridge over the eyes; also the hair growing there.

eye·cup (ī′kup′) *n.* A small cup with a rim curved to fit the eye.

eyed (īd) *adj.* Having a specific kind or number of eyes: used in combination: *brown-eyed, one-eyed.*

eye·ful (ī′fo͝ol′) *n.* **1.** An amount of something in the eye. **2.** *Slang* **a** A good look. **b** A strikingly beautiful person.

eye·glass (ī′glas′) *n.* **1.** *pl.* A pair of corrective glass lenses mounted in a frame: also called *glasses, spectacles.* **2.** Any lens used to assist vision. **3.** An eyepiece.

eye·hole (ī′hōl′) *n.* **1.** An opening through which to pass a pin, hook, rope, etc. **2.** A peephole.

eye·lash (ī′lash′) *n.* One of the stiff, curved hairs growing from the edge of the eyelids. ◆Collateral adjective: *ciliary.*

eye·let (ī′lit) *n.* **1.** A small hole or opening, esp. one made in leather, canvas, etc., and lined with metal. **2.** A metal ring for lining such a hole. **3.** In embroidery, a small hole edged with ornamental stitches. [< F *œillet,* dim. of *œil* eye]

eye·lid (ī′lid′) *n.* Either of the movable folds of skin that close over the eyes.

eye·piece (ī′pēs′) *n.* The lens or lenses nearest the eye in a telescope, microscope, etc.

eye shadow A tinted cosmetic preparation, applied to the eyelids.

eye·sight (ī′sīt′) *n.* **1.** The power or faculty of sight. **2.** Extent or range of vision.

eye·sore (ī′sôr′) *n.* Something ugly.

eye·strain (ī′strān′) *n.* Weariness of the eyes caused by excessive or improper use.

eye·tooth (ī′to͞oth′) *n.* *pl.* **·teeth** (-tēth′) One of the upper canine teeth.

eye·wash (ī′wosh′, ī′wôsh′) *n.* **1.** A medicinal wash for the eye. **2.** *Slang* Nonsense.

eye·wit·ness (ī′wit′nis) *n.* One who has seen something happen and can give testimony about it. **—eye′wit′ness** *adj.*

ey·rie (âr′ē, ir′ē), **ey·ry** See AERIE.

E·ze·ki·el (i·zē′kē·əl, -kyəl) *n.* A book of the Old Testament written by the 6th c. B.C. Hebrew prophet Ezekiel. Also, in the Douai Bible, **E·ze′chi·el.**

Ez·ra (ez′rə) *n.* A book of the Old Testament written in part by the 5th c. B.C. Hebrew high priest Ezra. Also, in the Douai Bible, *Esdras.* [< Hebrew, help]

F

f, F (ef) *n. pl.* **f's** or **fs, F's** or **Fs, effs** (efs) 1. The sixth letter of the English alphabet. 2. The sound represented by the letter *f.* —*symbol* 1. *Music* a The fourth tone in the diatonic scale of C. b Forte. 2. *Chem.* Fluorine (symbol F).

fa (fä) *n. Music* The fourth tone of the diatonic scale in solmization.

fa·ble (fā′bəl) *n.* 1. A brief tale embodying a moral, sometimes using animals or objects as characters. 2. A legend or myth. [< L *fabula* conversation] —**fa′bled** *adj.* —**fab·u·list** (fab′yə·list) *n.*

fab·ric (fab′rik) *n.* 1. A woven, felted, or knitted material, as cloth. 2. Structure or framework: the social *fabric.* [< L *faber* workman]

fab·ri·cate (fab′rə·kāt) *v.t.* **·cat·ed, ·cat·ing** 1. To make or manufacture; build. 2. To make up or invent, as a lie or story. [< L *fabricare* to construct] —**fab′ri·ca′tion** *n.* —**fab′ri·ca′tor** *n.*

fab·u·lous (fab′yə·ləs) *adj.* 1. Beyond belief; astounding. 2. Of, like, or recorded in fable; mythical. —**fab′u·lous·ly** *adv.* —**fab′·u·lous·ness** *n.*

fa·çade (fə·säd′) *n.* 1. *Archit.* The front or principal face of a building. 2. A front or a false appearance: a *façade* of respectability. Also **fa·cade′**. [< F < L *facies* face]

face (fās) *n.* 1. The front portion of the head; countenance. 2. The expression of the countenance. 3. A grimacing expression. 4. External aspect or appearance; look. 5. *Informal* Effrontery; audacity. 6. The front or principal surface of anything: the *face* of a clock. —**in the face of** 1. Confronting. 2. In spite of. —**on the face of it** Judging by all appearances; apparently. —**to fly in the face of** To act in defiance of. —**to lose face** To lose one's dignity. —**to save face** To preserve one's dignity. —*v.* **faced, fac·ing** *v.t.* 1. To bear or turn the face toward. 2. To cause to turn in a given direction. 3. To meet face to face; confront. 4. To realize or be aware of. 5. To cover with a layer or surface of another material. —*v.i.* 6. To turn or be turned with the face in a given direction. —**to face up to** To meet with courage. [< L *facies* face] —**face′less** *adj.*

face card In playing cards, a king, queen, or jack.

face lifting 1. Plastic surgery to tighten facial tissues. 2. A slight renovation; superficial alteration. —**face-lift** (fās′lift) *n. & v.t.* —**face′-lift·ing** *adj.*

face-off (fās′ôf′) *n.* 1. A confrontation. 2. In ice hockey, the start of play when the puck is dropped between two opposing players.

fac·et (fas′it) *n.* 1. One of the small plane surfaces cut upon a gem. 2. A phase or aspect of a subject or person. —*v.t.* **fac·et·ed** or **·et·ted, fac·et·ing** or **·et·ting** To cut facets upon. [< F *facette,* dim. of *face* face]

fa·ce·tious (fə·sē′shəs) *adj.* Given to or marked by levity or flippant humor. [< L *facetiae* jests] —**fa·ce′tious·ly** *adv.* —**fa·ce′tious·ness** *n.*

face value 1. The value stated on a bond, note, etc. 2. Apparent value.

fa·cial (fā′shəl) *adj.* Of or for the face. —*n. Informal* A cosmetic treatment for the face.

fac·ile (fas′əl) *adj.* 1. Easily achieved or performed; also, superficial. 2. Ready or quick in performance; also, smooth; glib. [< L *facilis* easy to do] —**fac′ile·ly** *adv.* —**fac′ile·ness** *n.*

fa·cil·i·tate (fə·sil′ə·tāt) *v.t.* **·tat·ed, ·tat·ing** To make easy or easier. —**fa·cil′i·ta′tion** *n.* —**fa·cil′i·ta′tor** *n.*

fa·cil·i·ty (fə·sil′ə·tē) *n. pl.* **·ties** 1. Ease of performance or action. 2. Ready skill or ability. 3. *Usu. pl.* Something that makes an action or operation easier: *facilities* for research. 4. Something built or established for a particular purpose: a first-aid *facility.* [See FACILE.]

fac·ing (fā′sing) *n.* 1. A lining or covering of a garment, often sewn on lapels, cuffs, etc. 2. A fabric used for this. 3. Any ornamental or protective covering.

fac·sim·i·le (fak·sim′ə·lē) *n.* 1. An exact copy. 2. *Telecom.* A method of transmitting messages, drawings, etc., by means of radio, telegraph, etc. [< L *fac simile* make like] —**fac·sim′i·le** *adj.*

fact (fakt) *n.* 1. Something that actually exists or has occurred. 2. Something asserted to be true or to have happened. 3. Reality or actuality. 4. A criminal deed: now only in legal phrases, as **before** (or **after**) **the fact.** —**as a matter of fact, in fact, in point of fact** In reality; actually. [< L *factum* < *facere* to do]

fac·tion (fak′shən) *n.* 1. A group of people operating within, and often in opposition to, a larger group. 2. Dissension. [< L *facere* to do] —**fac′tion·al** *adj.* —**fac′tion·al·ism** *n.*

fac·tious (fak′shəs) *adj.* Given to dissension. —**fac′tious·ly** *adv.* —**fac′tious·ness** *n.*

fac·ti·tious (fak·tish′əs) *adj.* Not spontaneous; affected or artificial. [< L *factitius* artificial] —**fac·ti′tious·ly** *adv.* —**fac·ti′·tious·ness** *n.*

fac·tor (fak′tər) *n.* 1. An element or cause that contributes to a result. 2. *Math.* One or two or more quantities that, when multiplied together, produce a given quantity. 3. One who transacts business for another on a commission basis. —*v.t. Math.* To resolve into factors. [L, maker]

fac·to·ri·al (fak·tôr′ē·əl) *n. Math.* The

product of a series of consecutive positive integers from 1 to a given number. The *factorial* of four (written 4!) = 1 × 2 × 3 × 4 = 24. —*adj.* Pertaining to a factor or a factorial.

fac·to·ry (fak′tər·ē) *n. pl.* **·ries** An establishment for the manufacture or assembly of goods. [< L *facere* to make]

fac·to·tum (fak·tō′təm) *n.* An employee or servant having diverse duties. [< L *facere* to do + *totum* everything]

fac·tu·al (fak′chōō·əl) *adj.* Pertaining to, containing, or consisting of facts; literal and exact. —**fac′tu·al′i·ty** (-al′ə·tē), **fac′tu·al·ness** *n.* —**fac′tu·al·ly** *adv.*

fac·ul·ty (fak′əl·tē) *n. pl.* **·ties** 1. A natural or acquired power or ability. 2. The entire teaching staff of an educational institution. 3. A department of learning at a university: the English *faculty.* [< L *facilis* easy to do]

fad (fad) *n.* A temporary style, amusement, fashion, etc. [Origin unknown] —**fad′dish** *adj.* —**fad′dish·ness** *n.* —**fad′dist** *n.*

fade (fād) *v.* **fad·ed, fad·ing** *v.i.* 1. To lose brightness or clearness. 2. To vanish slowly. 3. To lose freshness, vigor, youth, etc. —*v.t.* 4. To cause to fade. —**to fade in or out** In television, motion pictures, and radio, to cause the picture, sound, etc., to appear or dissolve gradually. [< OF *fade* pale, insipid]

fag[1] (fag) *v.* **fagged, fag·ging** *v.t.* 1. To exhaust by hard work: usu. with *out.* —*v.i.* 2. To weary oneself by working. —*n. Slang* A cigarette. [ME *fagge* loose end]

fag[2] (fag) *Slang* A male homosexual: also **fag′got.** [Origin unknown]

fag end 1. The frayed end, as of a rope. 2. A remnant or last part. [< FAG[1]]

fag·ot (fag′ət) *n.* 1. A bundle of sticks, twigs, or branches. 2. A bundle of pieces of wrought iron or steel for working into bars, etc. —*v.t.* 1. To make a fagot of. 2. To ornament by fagoting. Also **fag′got.** [< OF]

fag·ot·ing (fag′ət·ing) *n.* Ornamental embroidery in which threads are tied in clusters and crisscrossed. Also **fag′got·ing.**

Fahr·en·heit scale (far′ən·hīt) A temperature scale in which the freezing point of water is 32° and the boiling point 212° at standard atmospheric pressure. [after G. D. *Fahrenheit,* 1686–1736, German physicist]

fail (fāl) *v.i.* 1. To be deficient or wanting, as in ability. 2. To miss doing or accomplishing something: He *failed* to make himself clear. 3. To prove inadequate; fall short; give out. 4. To decline in health or strength. 5. To go bankrupt. 6. To receive a grade of failure. —*v.t.* 7. To prove of no help to; desert. 8. **a** To receive a grade of failure in (a course or examination). **b** To assign a grade of failure to (a student). —*n.* Failure: in the phrase **without fail.** [< L *fallere* to deceive]

fail·ing (fā′ling) *n.* 1. A fault; defect. 2. The act of one who or that which fails. —*prep.* In default of. —*adj.* That fails; indicating failure.

faille (fīl) *n.* An untwilled silk dress fabric with a light grain or cord. [< F]

fail-safe (fāl′sāf′) *adj.* Designed to prevent equipment failure from causing operational failure, esp. in the case of nuclear weapons, power plants, etc.

fail·ure (fāl′yər) *n.* 1. An unsuccessful or disappointing outcome or performance. 2. A breakdown in health, efficiency, etc. 3. Nonperformance; neglect: *failure* to obey the law. 4. Bankruptcy. 5. One who or that which fails. 6. In education, a failing to pass, or the grade indicating this.

fain (fān) *adv. Archaic & Poetic* Gladly; preferably: He would *fain* depart. [OE *fægen*]

faint (fānt) *v.i.* To lose consciousness; swoon. —*adj.* 1. Feeble; weak. 2. Lacking in distinctness, brightness, etc. 3. Dizzy; weak. 4. Lacking courage; timid. —*n.* A sudden, temporary loss of consciousness. [< OF, pp. of *faindre* to shape] —**faint′ly** *adv.* —**faint′ness** *n.*

faint·heart·ed (fānt′här′tid) *adj.* Cowardly; timorous; timid. —**faint′heart′ed·ly** *adv.* —**faint′heart′ed·ness** *n.*

fair[1] (fâr) *adj.* 1. Light in coloring; not dark or sallow. 2. Pleasing to the eye; beautiful. 3. Free from blemish or imperfection. 4. Sunny; clear. 5. Just; upright. 6. According to rules, principles, etc.; legitimate: a *fair* win. 7. Properly open to attack: He is *fair* game. 8. Moderately good or large. 9. Likely; promising. 10. In baseball, within the area bounded by the foul lines; not foul. —*adv.* 1. In a fair manner. 2. Squarely; directly. [OE *fæger*] —**fair′ness** *n.*

fair[2] (fâr) *n.* 1. A periodic, usu. competitive exhibit of agricultural products, livestock, machinery, etc. 2. A large exhibition or show of products, etc.: a world's *fair.*

fair·ground (fâr′ground′) *n.* A large, open space where fairs are held: also **fair′grounds′.** [< L *feria* holiday]

fair-haired (fâr′hârd′) *adj.* 1. Having blond hair. 2. Favorite.

fair·ly (fâr′lē) *adv.* 1. Justly; equitably. 2. Moderately; somewhat. 3. Positively; completely: The crowd *fairly* roared. 4. Clearly; distinctly.

fair-mind·ed (fâr′mīn′did) *adj.* 1. Just. 2. Unprejudiced. —**fair′-mind′ed·ly** *adv.* —**fair′mind′ed·ness** *n.*

fair-trade (fâr′trād′) *v.t.* **-trad·ed, -trad·ing** To sell (a product) at no less than the minimum price set by a manufacturer. —**fair′-trade′** *adj.*

fair·way (fâr′wā′) *n.* That part of a golf course, between a tee and a putting green, where the grass is kept short.

fair-weath·er (fâr′weth′ər) *adj.* 1. Suitable for fair weather, as a racetrack. 2. Not helpful in adversity.

fair·y (fâr′ē) *n. pl.* **fair·ies** 1. An imaginary being, usu. small and having magic powers. 2. *Slang* A male homosexual. —*adj.* Of or like fairies. [< OF *faerie* fairyland]

fair·y·land (fâr′ē·land′) *n.* 1. The abode of fairies. 2. Any delightful place.

fairy tale 1. A tale about fairies. 2. A fantastic story; also, a lie.

fait ac·com·pli (fe·tà·kôṅ·plē′) *French* A thing done beyond recall or opposition; literally, an accomplished fact.

faith (fāth) *n.* 1. Confidence in or dependence on a person or thing as trustworthy. 2. Belief without need of certain proof. 3. Belief in God or religious writings. 4. A system of religious belief. 5. Allegiance. —**bad faith** Deceit; dishonesty. —**in faith**

Indeed; truly. **—in good faith** With honorable intentions. **—to break faith** 1. To betray one's principles or beliefs. 2. To break a promise. **—to keep faith** 1. To adhere to one's principles or beliefs. 2. To keep a promise. *—interj.* Indeed. [< L *fidere* to trust] **—faith′less** *adj.* **—faith′less·ly** *adv.* **—faith′less·ness** *n.*

faith·ful (fāth′fəl) *adj.* 1. True or trustworthy in the performance of duty, the fulfillment of promises, etc.; loyal. 2. True in detail or accurate in description: a *faithful* copy. **—the faithful** 1. The followers of a religious faith. 2. The loyal members of any group. **—faith′ful·ly** *adv.* **—faith′ful·ness** *n.*

faith healing The treatment of diseases by invoking divine help. **—faith healer** **—faith-heal·ing** (fāth′hēl·ing) *adj.*

fake (fāk) *Informal n.* Any person or thing not genuine. *—adj.* Not genuine; spurious. *—v.* **faked, fak·ing** *v.t.* 1. To make up and attempt to pass off as genuine: to *fake* a pedigree. 2. To simulate; feign. *—v.i.* 3. To practice faking. [? Var. of obs. *feague, feak* < G *fegen* to sweep] **—fak′er** *n.* **—fak′er·y** *n.*

fa·kir (fə·kir′, fā′kər) *n.* 1. A Muslim ascetic or religious mendicant. 2. Loosely, any Hindu yogi or religious devotee. [< Arabic *faqir* poor]

fal·chion (fôl′chən, -shən) *n.* A curved sword of the Middle Ages. [< L *falx* sickle]

fal·con (fal′kən, fôl′-) *n.* 1. A bird of prey noted for its keen vision and swiftness of attack. 2. Any other bird of the same family, having long, pointed wings, a notched bill, and strong talons. [< OF *faucon*]

fal·con·ry (fal′kən·rē, fôl′-) *n.* 1. The art of training falcons to hunt. 2. The sport of hunting with falcons. **—fal′con·er** *n.*

fal·de·ral (fal′də·ral) See FOLDEROL.

fall (fôl) *v.i.* **fell, fall·en, fall·ing** 1. To drop from a higher to a lower place or position. 2. To drop suddenly, striking the ground with some part of the body. 3. To collapse. 4. To become less in number, value, etc.: Prices *fell.* 5. To become less in rank, importance, etc. 6. To drop wounded or slain. 7. To be captured or overthrown. 8. To yield to temptation; sin. 9. To slope downward. 10. To hang down; droop. 11. To come as though descending: Night *fell.* 12. To pass into some specified condition: to *fall* asleep. 13. To come or happen by chance or lot: to *fall* among thieves. 14. To happen; occur at a specified time or place. 15. To pass by right or inheritance. 16. To be classified or divided: with *into* or *under.* **—to fall back** To recede; retreat. **—to fall back on** (or **upon**) To resort to; have recourse to; retreat to. **—to fall down on** *Informal* To fail in. **—to fall for** *Informal* 1. To be deceived by. 2. To fall in love with. **—to fall in with** To meet and accompany. **—to fall off** 1. To leave or withdraw. 2. To become less. **—to fall through** To come to nothing; fail. *—n.* 1. The act of falling; a descending. 2. That which falls. 3. The amount that falls. 4. The distance through which anything falls. 5. A sudden descent from a vertical or erect position. 6. A hanging down. 7. A downward direction or slope. 8. *Usu. pl.* A waterfall; cascade. 9. A loss or reduction in value, reputation, etc. 10. A moral lapse. 11. A surrender or downfall. 12. *Often cap.* Autumn. [OE *feallen*]

fal·la·cious (fə·lā′shəs) *adj.* 1. Deceptive or misleading. 2. Containing or involving a fallacy. **—fal·la′cious·ly** *adv.* **—fal·la′cious·ness** *n.*

fal·la·cy (fal′ə·sē) *n. pl.* **·cies** 1. A mistaken or misleading notion. 2. Unsoundness or incorrectness, as of judgment. 3. Reasoning contrary to the rules of logic. [< L *fallere* to deceive]

fall·en (fô′lən) Past participle of FALL. *—adj.* 1. Having come down by falling. 2. Brought down. 3. Overthrown; vanquished. 4. Disgraced; ruined. 5. Slain.

fall guy *Slang* One who is left to receive the blame or penalties; a dupe; scapegoat.

fal·li·ble (fal′ə·bəl) *adj.* 1. Liable to err. 2. Liable to be misled or deceived. 3. Liable to be erroneous or false. [< L *fallere* to deceive] **—fal′li·bil′i·ty** *n.* **—fal′li·bly** *adv.*

fall·ing-out (fôl′ing·out′) *n.* A quarrel.

Fal·lo·pi·an tube (fə·lō′pē·ən) *Anat.* One of a pair of long, slender passages from the ovary to the uterus: also called *oviduct.* [after Gabriello *Fallopio,* 1523–62, Italian anatomist]

fall·out (fôl′out′) *n. Physics* Airborne radioactive debris from a nuclear explosion. Also **fall′-out′.**

fal·low[1] (fal′ō) *n.* 1. Land left unseeded after plowing. 2. The process of working land and leaving it unseeded for a time. *—adj.* 1. Unseeded; uncultivated. 2. Unused; idle; dormant. [OE *fealging* fallow land] **—fal′low** *v.t. & v.i.*

fal·low[2] (fal′ō) *adj.* Light yellowish brown. [OE *fealu*]

fallow deer A small European deer spotted white in the summer.

false (fôls) *adj.* 1. Contrary to truth or fact. 2. Incorrect. 3. Not genuine; artificial. 4. Deceptive or misleading. 5. Given to lying. 6. Wanting in fidelity; faithless. *—adv.* In a false manner. [< L *falsus,* orig. pp. of *fallere* to deceive] **—false′ly** *adv.* **—false′ness** *n.* **—fal′si·ty** *n.*

false-heart·ed (fôls′här′tid) *adj.* Treacherous; deceitful.

false·hood (fôls′ho͝od) *n.* 1. Lack of accord to fact or truth. 2. An intentional untruth; lie.

fal·set·to (fôl·set′ō) *n. pl.* **·tos** 1. The register of a voice, esp. of an adult male, above its normal range. 2. A man who sings or speaks in this register: also **fal·set′tist.** [< Ital., dim. of *falso* false] **—fal·set′to** *adj. & adv.*

fal·si·fy (fôl′sə·fī) *v.* **·fied, ·fy·ing** *v.t.* 1. To tell lies about; misrepresent. 2. To alter or tamper with, esp. in order to deceive. 3. To prove to be false. *—v.i.* 4. To tell lies. [< L *falsus* false + *facere* to make] **—fal′si·fi·ca′tion** *n.* **—fal′si·fi′er** *n.*

fal·ter (fôl′tər) *v.i.* 1. To be hesitant or uncertain; waver. 2. To move unsteadily. 3. To speak haltingly. *—n.* An uncertainty or hesitation in voice or action. [? < ON *faltrask* to be encumbered] **—fal′ter·er** *n.* **—fal′ter·ing** *adj.* **—fal′ter·ing·ly** *adv.*

fame (fām) *n.* 1. Widespread and illustrious

reputation; renown. 2. Public reputation or estimation. [< L *fama* report, reputation] **—famed** *adj.*

fa·mil·ial (fə·mil′yəl) *adj.* Of, pertaining to, or associated with the family.

fa·mil·iar (fə·mil′yər) *adj.* 1. Having thorough knowledge of something: followed by *with.* 2. Well-known; customary. 3. Intimate; close. 4. Unduly intimate; forward. **—***n.* A friend or close associate. [< L *familia* family] **—fa·mil′iar·ly** *adv.*

fa·mil·i·ar·i·ty (fə·mil′ē·ar′ə·tē, -mil′yar′-) *n.* *pl.* **·ties** 1. Thorough knowledge of something. 2. Friendly closeness; intimacy. 3. Offensively familiar conduct. 4. *Often pl.* An action warranted only by intimate acquaintance.

fa·mil·iar·ize (fə·mil′yə·rīz) *v.t.* **·ized, ·iz·ing** 1. To make (oneself or someone) familiar with something. 2. To cause (something) to be familiar. **—fa·mil′iar·i·za′tion** *n.*

fam·i·ly (fam′ə·lē, fam′lē) *n.* *pl.* **·lies** 1. Parents and their children. 2. The children as distinguished from the parents. 3. **a** A group or succession of persons connected by blood, name, etc.; clan. **b** A criminal group operating within a larger criminal organization. 4. Distinguished or ancient lineage or descent. 5. Any class or group of like or related things. 6. *Biol.* A taxonomic category higher than a genus and below an order. [< L *famulus* servant] **—fam′i·ly** *adj.*

family tree A diagram showing family descent.

fam·ine (fam′in) *n.* 1. A widespread scarcity of food. 2. A great scarcity of anything; dearth. 3. Starvation. [< L *fames* hunger]

fam·ish (fam′ish) *v.t.* & *v.i.* To suffer or to cause to suffer from extreme hunger. [< F *afamer* to starve] **—fam′ished** adj.

fa·mous (fā′məs) *adj.* 1. Celebrated in history or public report; well-known; renowned. 2. *Informal* Excellent; admirable. **—fa′mous·ly** *adv.*

fan[1] (fan) *n.* 1. A hand-held device for putting the air into motion; esp., a light, flat implement, often collapsible and opening into a wedgelike shape, a circle, etc. 2. Anything shaped like a fan. 3. A machine fitted with blades that revolve rapidly about a central hub, for stirring air, etc. **—***v.* **fanned, fan·ning** *v.t.* 1. To move or stir (air) with or as with a fan. 2. To direct air upon; cool or refresh with or as with a fan. 3. To move or stir to action; excite: to *fan* someone's rage. 4. To spread like a fan. 5. In baseball, to cause (a batter) to strike out. **—***v.i.* 6. To spread out like a fan. 7. In baseball, to strike out. [OE *fann*] **—fan′ner** *n.*

fan[2] (fan) *n.* *Informal* A devotee of a sport, celebrity, etc. [? < FANATIC]

fa·nat·ic (fə·nat′ik) *n.* One who is moved by excessive enthusiasm or zeal; esp., a religious zealot. [< L *fanum* temple] **—fa·nat′ic** or **·i·cal** *adj.* **—fa·nat′i·cal·ly** *adv.* **—fa·nat·i·cism** (fə·nat′ə·siz′əm) *n.*

fan·cied (fan′sēd) *adj.* Imaginary.

fan·ci·er (fan′sē·ər) *n.* 1. One having a special taste for or interest in something. 2. A breeder of animals.

fan·ci·ful (fan′si·fəl) *adj.* 1. Produced by or existing only in the fancy. 2. Marked by fancy in design. 3. Indulging in fancies. **—fan′ci·ful·ly** *adv.*

fan·cy (fan′sē) *n.* *pl.* **·cies** 1. Imagination of a capricious or whimsical sort. 2. An odd or whimsical idea, invention, or image. 3. A caprice or whim. 4. A liking or inclination. 5. Taste or judgment in art, style, etc. **—***adj.* **·ci·er, ·ci·est** 1. Adapted to please the fancy; ornamental. 2. Coming from the fancy; imaginary. 3. Capricious; whimsical. 4. Of higher grade than the average: *fancy* fruits. 5. Exorbitant: *fancy* prices. **—***v.t.* **·cied, ·cy·ing** 1. To imagine; picture. 2. To take a fancy to. 3. To suppose. **—***interj.* An exclamation of surprise. [Contr. of FANTASY]

fan·cy·work (fan′sē·wûrk′) *n.* Ornamental needlework.

fan·dan·go (fan·dang′gō) *n.* *pl.* **·gos** 1. A Spanish dance in triple time. 2. The music for this dance. [< Sp.]

fan·fare (fan′fâr′) *n.* 1. A short, lively passage, as of trumpets. 2. A noisy or showy display. [< F]

fang (fang) *n.* 1. A long, pointed tooth or tusk of an animal for tearing at prey. 2. One of the long, hollow or grooved, usu. erectile teeth with which a venomous serpent injects its poison. [OE, a seizing] **—fanged** *adj.* **—fang′like′** *adj.*

fan-jet (fan′jet′) *n.* 1. A jet engine that draws in air at the front through fan blades, and compresses and expels it for extra thrust. 2. An airplane powered by fan-jets. **—fan′-jet′** *adj.*

fan·light (fan′līt′) *n.* *Archit.* A semicircular window, as over a door. Also **fan window.**

fan·ny (fan′ē) *n.* *pl.* **·nies** *Slang* The buttocks.

fan·tail (fan′tāl′) *n.* 1. A variety of domestic pigeon having fanlike tail feathers. 2. Any fan-shaped end or tail. 3. The after deck of a ship. **—fan′tailed′** *adj.*

fan-tan (fan′tan′) *n.* A Chinese gambling game. [< Chinese *fan t'an*]

fan·ta·si·a (fan·tā′zhə, -zhē·ə, fan′tə·zē′ə) *n.* *Music* 1. A fanciful, free-form composition. 2. A medley of various themes. [< Ital., a fancy]

fan·ta·size (fan′tə·sīz) *v.i.* **·sized, ·siz·ing** To create mental fantasies.

fan·tas·tic (fan·tas′tik) *adj.* 1. Odd, grotesque, or whimsical. 2. Wildly fanciful or exaggerated. 3. Capricious or impulsive. 4. *Informal* Wonderful; remarkable. [< Gk. *phantastēs* a boaster] **—fan·tas′ti·cal·ly** *adv.*

fan·ta·sy (fan′tə·sē, -zē) *n.* *pl.* **·sies** 1. Imagination unrestrained by reality; wild fancy. 2. An odd or unreal mental image. 3. An odd or whimsical notion. 4. An ingenious or highly imaginative creation. 5. A daydream; sequence of imagined events. 6. *Music* A fantasia. Also *phantasy.* [< Gk. *phainein* to show]

far (fär) *adv.* 1. At, to, or from a great distance. 2. To or at a particular distance, point, or degree. 3. To a great degree; very much: *far* wiser. 4. Very remotely in time, degree, quality, etc.: *far* from pleasant. **—by far** In a great degree; very much. **—far and away** Very much; decidedly. **—so far as** To the extent that. **—***adj.* **far·ther** or **fur·ther,**

far·thest or **fur·thest** 1. Very remote in space or time. 2. Extending widely or at length. 3. More distant: the *far* end of the garden. [OE *feor*]

Far as a combining form meaning at or to an extent or distance away or from:

far-advanced	**far-ranging**
far-extending	**far-reaching**
far-looking	**far-removed**
far-northern	**far-spreading**

far·ad (far′əd, -ad) *n. Electr.* The unit of capacitance; the capacitance of a condenser that retains one coulomb of charge with one volt difference of potential. [after Michael *Faraday*]

far·a·way (fär′ə·wā′) *adj.* 1. Distant. 2. Absent-minded; abstracted: a *faraway* look.

farce (färs) *n.* 1. A comedy employing ludicrous or exaggerated situations. 2. A ridiculous action or situation. [< F < L *farcire* to stuff] **—far′ci·cal** *adj.* **—far′ci·cal′i·ty** *n.* **—far′ci·cal·ly** *adv.*

far cry A long way.

fare (fâr) *v.i.* **fared, far·ing** 1. To be in a specified state; get on: He *fares* poorly. 2. To turn out: It *fared* well with him. 3. To eat and drink. **—*n.*** 1. The fee for conveyance in a vehicle, etc. 2. A passenger carried for hire. 3. Food and drink; diet. [OE *faran* to go, travel]

Far East The countries of eastern Asia, including China and Japan.

fare·well (*n.* fâr′wel′; *interj.* fâr′wel′; *adj.* fâr′wel′) *n.* 1. A parting salutation; a good-by. 2. Leave-taking. **—*interj.*** Good-by. **—*adj.*** Parting; closing. [Earlier *fare well*]

far-fetched (fär′fecht′) *adj.* Neither natural nor obvious; forced; strained.

far-flung (fär′flung′) *adj.* Extending over great distances.

fa·ri·na (fə·rē′nə) *n.* A meal or flour obtained chiefly from grain and used as a breakfast cereal or in puddings. [< L]

far·i·na·ceous (far′ə·nā′shəs) *adj.* 1. Consisting or made of farina. 2. Containing or yielding starch. 3. Mealy.

farm (färm) *n.* 1. A tract of land forming a single property and devoted to agriculture. 2. A tract of water used for the cultivation of marine life. 3. In baseball, a minor-league club used by a major-league club for training its recruits: also **farm club, farm team.** **—*v.t.*** 1. To cultivate (land). 2. To let at a fixed rental, as the authority to collect taxes, etc.: usu. with *out.* 3. To let out the services of (a person) for hire. 4. To arrange for (work) to be done outside the main organization: with *out.* **—*v.i.*** 5. To practice farming. [< L *firmare* to fix] **—farm′er** *n.*

farm hand One who works on a farm, esp. for hire.

farm·house (färm′hous′) *n.* The main house on a farm.

farm·ing (fär′ming) *n.* The business of operating a farm; agriculture. **—*adj.*** Engaged in, suitable for, or used for agriculture.

farm·stead (färm′sted) *n.* A farm and the buildings on it.

farm·yard (färm′yärd′) *n.* A space around or surrounded by farm buildings, often enclosed.

far·o (fâr′ō) *n.* A card game in which the players bet as to the order in which certain cards will appear. [Alter. of *Pharaoh*]

far-off (fär′ôf′) *adj.* Distant; remote.

far-out (fär′out′) *adj. Slang* Extremely unusual or unconventional.

far·ra·go (fə·rā′gō, -rä′-) *n. pl.* **·goes** A confused mixture; medley. [< L, mixed fodder]

far·row (far′ō) *n.* A litter of pigs. **—*v.t. & v.i.*** To give birth to (young): said of swine. [OE *fearh* young pig]

far·see·ing (fär′sē′ing) *adj.* 1. Having foresight. 2. Able to see distant objects clearly.

far·sight·ed (fär′sī′tid) *adj.* 1. Able to see things at a distance more clearly than things at hand. 2. Having foresight. **—far′·sight′ed·ly** *adv.* **—far′sight′ed·ness** *n.*

far·ther (fär′thər) Comparative of FAR. **—*adv.*** To or at a more advanced point in space or, less often, time. **—*adj.*** 1. More distant or remote. 2. Additional: in this sense usu. *further.* [ME *ferther*; var. of FURTHER]

far·ther·most (fär′thər·mōst′) *adj.* Most distant; farthest.

far·thest (fär′thist) Superlative of FAR. **—*adv.*** To or at the greatest distance. **—*adj.*** 1. Most distant or remote. 2. Longest or most extended: the *farthest* way around.

far·thing (fär′thing) *n.* A small, bronze coin, formerly used in England and worth one fourth of a penny. [OE *fēortha* a fourth]

far·thin·gale (fär′thing·gāl) *n.* The framework that extends a woman's skirt at the hips, worn esp. in the 16th and 17th c. [< OF *verdugale*, alter. of Sp. *verdugado* < *verdugo* rod, hoop]

fas·ces (fas′ēz) *n.pl.* In ancient Rome, a bundle of rods enclosing an ax, used as a symbol of power. [< L, pl. of *fascis* bundle] **—fas·ci·al** (fash′ē·əl) *adj.*

fas·ci·a (fash′ē·ə) *n. pl.* **fas·ci·ae** (fash′i·ē) 1. *Anat.* Fibrous connective tissue for enclosing or connecting muscles or internal organs. 2. Something that binds together; a band. [< L, band] **—fas′ci·al** *adj.*

fas·ci·cle (fas′i·kəl) *n.* 1. A small bundle or cluster, as of leaves. 2. One of the sections of a book that is published in installments. [< L *fascis* bundle] **—fas′ci·cled** *adj.* **—fas·cic·u·lar** (fə·sik′yə·lər) *adj.*

fas·ci·nate (fas′ə·nāt) *v.* **·nat·ed, ·nat·ing** *v.t.* 1. To attract irresistibly, as by charm; captivate. 2. To hold spellbound, as by terror. **—*v.i.*** 3. To be charming, captivating, etc. [< L *fascinum* spell] **—fas′ci·nat′ing** *adj.* **—fas′ci·nat′ing·ly** *adv.* **—fas′ci·na′tion** *n.*

fas·cism (fash′iz·əm) *n.* 1. A system of government characterized by one-party dictatorship, centralized governmental control of industry and finance, militant nationalism, and sometimes racism. 2. A political philosophy favoring such a system. [< Ital. *fascismo*] **—fas′cist** *n. & adj.* **—fa·scis·tic** (fə·shis′tik) *adj.*

fash·ion (fash′ən) *n.* 1. The mode of dress, manners, living, etc., prevailing in society. 2. A current practice or usage. 3. An object of enthusiasm among fashionable people. 4. Manner; way. 5. Kind; sort. **—after a fashion** To a limited extent. **—*v.t.*** 1. To give shape or form to. 2. To adapt; fit. [< L *factio, -onis* a (special) way of making] **—fash′ion·er** *n.*

fash·ion·a·ble (fash′ən·ə·bəl) *adj.* 1. Conforming to the current fashion. 2. Associated with, characteristic of, or patronized by persons of fashion. **—fash′ion·a·bly** *adv.*

fashion plate One who dresses in the latest fashion.

fast[1] (fast) *adj.* 1. Firm in place; not easily moved. 2. Constant; steadfast: *fast* friends. 3. Not liable to fade or run: said of colors. 4. Acting or moving quickly. 5. Performed quickly: *fast* work. 6. Permitting quick movement: a *fast* track. 7. In advance of the true time. 8. Dissipated; sexually promiscuous. **—to play fast and loose** To act in a tricky or untrustworthy fashion. **—***adv.* 1. Firmly; securely. 2. Soundly: *fast* asleep. 3. Quickly. 4. Dissipatedly: to live *fast*. [OE *fæst*]

fast[2] (fast) *n.* 1. Abstinence from food or from prescribed kinds of food, particularly as a religious duty. 2. A period prescribed for fasting. [OE *fæstan*] **—fast** *v.i.*

fast·back (fast′bak′) *n.* 1. An automobile top that slopes downward to the rear in an unbroken line. 2. An automobile with such a top.

fas·ten (fas′ən) *v.t.* 1. To attach to something else; connect. 2. To make fast; secure. 3. To direct (the attention, eyes, etc.) steadily. **—***v.i.* 4. To become attached. [OE *fæst* fixed] **—fas′ten·er** *n.*

fas·ten·ing (fas′ən·ing) *n.* 1. The act of making fast. 2. That which fastens.

fast-food (fast′fo͞od′) *adj.* Of a restaurant, specializing in swift service of a limited menu.

fas·tid·i·ous (fas·tid′ē·əs, fəs-) *adj.* Exceedingly delicate or refined; overnice; squeamish. [< L *fastidium* disgust] **—fas·tid′i·ous·ly** *adv.* **—fas·tid′i·ous·ness** *n.*

fast·ness (fast′nis) *n.* 1. A stronghold. 2. Firmness or fixedness. 3. Swiftness.

fast-talk (fast′tôk′) *v.t.* To persuade by facile or deceptive talk.

fat (fat) *adj.* **fat·ter, fat·test** 1. Having superfluous flesh or fat; obese; plump. 2. Containing much fat, oil, etc. 3. Rich or fertile, as land. 4. Abundant; plentiful: a *fat* profit. 5. Thick; broad. **—a fat chance** *Slang* Very little chance; no chance at all. **—***n.* 1. *Biochem.* An oily or greasy, solid or liquid substance widely distributed in plant and animal tissues. 2. Animal tissue containing large quantities of such compounds. 3. Any vegetable or animal fat or oil used in cooking. 4. Plumpness; corpulence. 5. The richest or most desirable part of anything. 6. Excess; superfluity. [OE *fæt*] **—fat′ness** *n.*

fa·tal (fāt′l) *adj.* 1. Resulting in or capable of causing death. 2. Ruinous; destructive. 3. Highly significant or decisive; fateful: the *fatal* hour. 4. Destined; inevitable. [< L *fatum*. See FATE.] **—fa′tal·ly** *adv.*

fa·tal·ism (fāt′l·iz′əm) *n.* 1. The doctrine that all events are predetermined and thus unalterable. 2. A disposition to accept every event or condition as inevitable. **—fa′tal·ist** *n.* **—fa′tal·is′tic** *adj.* **—fa′tal·is′ti·cal·ly** *adv.*

fa·tal·i·ty (fā·tal′ə·tē, fə-) *n. pl.* **·ties** 1. A death brought about through disaster or calamity. 2. The capability of causing death or disaster. 3. A decree of fate.

fat·back (fat′bak′) *n.* Unsmoked salt pork.

fat cat *Slang* A wealthy, influential person, esp. a heavy contributor to political parties.

fate (fāt) *n.* 1. A force viewed as determining events in advance; destiny. 2. That which inevitably happens. 3. Final result or outcome. 4. An evil destiny; esp., death or destruction. [< L *fatus*, pp. of *fari* to speak]

fat·ed (fā′tid) *adj.* 1. Controlled by fate; destined. 2. Condemned to ruin; doomed.

fate·ful (fāt′fəl) *adj.* 1. Determining destiny; momentous. 2. Brought about by or as if by fate. 3. Bringing death or disaster; fatal. 4. Ominously prophetic; portentous. **—fate′ful·ly** *adv.* **—fate′ful·ness** *n.*

Fates (fāts) In classical mythology, the three goddesses who control human destiny.

fat·head (fat′hed′) *n.* A stupid person. **—fat′head′ed** *adj.*

fa·ther (fä′thər) *n.* 1. A male parent. 2. Any male ancestor; forefather. 3. A male who founds or establishes something. 4. Any elderly man: a title of respect. 5. *Usu. cap.* One of the orthodox writers of the early Christian church. 6. A leader or elder of a council, assembly, etc. 7. *Eccl. Usu. cap.* A priest or other church dignitary. 8. *cap.* God; esp., the first person of the Trinity. **—***v.t.* 1. To beget. 2. To act as a father toward. 3. To found or make. [OE *fæder*] **—fa′ther·hood** *n.* **—fa′ther·less** *adj.* **—fa′ther·ly** *adj.*

fa·ther-in-law (fä′thər·in·lô′) *n. pl.* **fa·thers-in-law** The father of one's husband or wife.

fa·ther·land (fä′thər·land′) *n.* The land of one's birth or of one's forebears.

fath·om (fath′əm) *n. pl.* **·oms** or **·om** A measure of length, 6 feet or 1,829 meters, used principally in marine and mining measurements. **—***v.t.* 1. To find the depth of; sound. 2. To understand; interpret. [OE *fæthm* the span of two arms outstretched] **—fath′om·a·ble** *adj.* **—fath′om·less** *adj.*

fa·tigue (fə·tēg′) *n.* 1. The condition of being very tired as a result of exertion. 2. *Mech.* Structural weakness in metals, etc., produced by excessive strain. 3. *Mil.* **a** A special work assignment done by soldiers in training: also **fatigue duty**. **b** *pl.* Strong, durable clothes worn on fatigue duty. **—***v.t.* & *v.i.* **·tigued, ·ti·guing** 1. To tire out; weary. 2. To weaken, as metal. [< L *fatigare* to tire] **—fat·i·ga·ble** (fat′ə·gə·bəl) *adj.*

fat·ten (fat′n) *v.t.* 1. To cause to become fat. 2. To make (land) rich by fertilizing. 3. To add to (a sum of money, etc.) so as to make larger and more attractive. **—***v.i.* 4. to grow fatter, heavier, etc. **—fat′ten·er** *n.* **—fat′ten·ing** *adj.*

fat·ty (fat′ē) *adj.* **·ti·er, ·ti·est** 1. Containing, possessing, or made of fat. 2. Having the properties of fat; greasy; oily. **—fat′ti·ness** *n.*

fatty acid *Chem.* Any of a class of organic acids derived from hydrocarbons and occurring in plant and animal fats.

fa·tu·i·ty (fə·to͞o′ə·tē, -tyo͞o′-) *n. pl.* **·ties** 1. Smug stupidity. 2. A stupid action, remark, etc.

fat·u·ous (fach′o͞o·əs) *adj.* Foolish and silly in a self-satisfied way; inane. [< L *fatuus* foolish] **—fat′u·ous·ly** *adv.* **—fat′u·ous·ness** *n.*

fau·ces (fô′sēz) *n.pl. Anat.* The passage from the back of the mouth to the pharynx. [< L]

fau·cet (fô′sit) *n.* A fixture with an adjustable valve that controls the flow of liquids. [< OF, prob. < *fausser* to break into]

fault (fôlt) *n.* 1. Whatever impairs excellence; a flaw. 2. A mistake or blunder. 3. Responsibility for some mishap, blunder, etc.; blame. 4. *Geol.* A break in the continuity of rock strata or veins of ore. 5. In tennis, squash, etc., failure to serve the ball into the prescribed area of the opponent's court. **—to a fault** Immoderately; excessively. **—*v.t.*** To find fault with; blame. [< L *fallere* to deceive] **—fault′less** *adj.* **—fault′less·ly** *adv.* **—fault′less·ness** *n.*

fault·find·ing (fôlt′fīn′ding) *adj.* Inclined to find fault; critical; carping. **—fault′find′er** *n.* **—fault′find′ing** *n.*

fault·y (fôl′tē) *adj.* **fault·i·er, fault·i·est** Having faults; defective; imperfect. **—fault′·i·ly** *adv.* **—fault′i·ness** *n.*

faun (fôn) *n.* A satyr. [< L *Faunus*, a rural god]

fau·na (fô′nə) *n. pl.* **·nas** or **·nae** (-nē) The animal life within a given area or environment or during a stated period. [< L *Fauna*, a rural goddess] **—fau′nal** *adj.*

Faust·i·an (fous′tē·ən) *adj.* Sacrificing moral purity for knowledge, power, or material gain. [after *Faust*, a legendary scholar who sold his soul to the devil]

faux pas (fō pä′) *pl.* **faux pas** (fō päz′, *Fr.* fō pä′) A social blunder. [< F, lit., false step]

fa·vor (fā′vər) *n.* 1. A helpful or considerate act. 2. Friendliness or approval. 3. The condition of being looked upon with liking or approval. 4. Unfair partiality: to show *favor*. 5. A small gift. 6. *pl.* Consent to sexual intimacy. **—in favor of** 1. On the side of. 2. To the furtherance or advantage of. 3. Made out to the benefit of. **—*v.t.*** 1. To do a favor for; oblige. 2. To look upon with approval or liking. 3. To show special consideration to, often in an unfair way. 4. To increase the chances of success of. 5. *Informal* To show a resemblance to in features. 6. To be careful of. Also *Brit.* **fa′vour.** [< L *favere* to favor] **—fa′vor·er** *n.*

fa·vor·a·ble (fā′vər·ə·bəl) *adj.* 1. Granting something requested or hoped for. 2. Boding well; promising; approving. 3. Well-disposed or indulgent; friendly. **—fa′vor·a·bly** *adv.*

fa·vored (fā′vərd) *adj.* 1. Looked upon with favor. 2. Endowed with good qualities. 3. Having an (indicated) aspect or appearance: an *ill-favored* countenance.

fa·vor·ite (fā′vər·it) *adj.* Regarded with special favor; preferred. **—*n.*** 1. A person or thing greatly liked or preferred. 2. A contestant or candidate considered to have the best chance of winning.

favorite son A candidate favored by the political leaders of his state, esp. at a presidential nominating convention.

fa·vor·it·ism (fā′vər·ə·tiz′əm) *n.* Preferential treatment, esp. when unjust.

fawn[1] (fôn) *v.i.* 1. To show cringing fondness, as a dog: often with *on* or *upon*. 2. To show affection or seek favor in such a manner. [OE *fahnian*, var. of *fægnian* to rejoice] **—fawn′er** *n.* **—fawn′ing·ly** *adv.*

fawn[2] (fôn) *n.* 1. A young deer, esp. in its first year. 2. The light yellowish brown color of a young deer. **—*adj.*** Light yellowish brown. [< OF *foun* offspring]

fax (faks) *n.* Electronic transmission of graphic material. [< FACSIMILE]

fay (fā) *n.* A fairy. [<OF < L *fatum* fate]

faze (fāz) *v.t.* **fazed, faz·ing** *Informal* To worry; disconcert. [Var. of dial. E *fease*, OE *fēsian* to frighten]

fe·al·ty (fē′əl·tē) *n. pl.* **·ties** 1. The obligation of fidelity owed to a feudal lord by his vassal. 2. Faithfulness; loyalty. [< L *fidelitas* fidelity]

fear (fir) *n.* 1. An agitated feeling aroused by awareness of danger, trouble, etc. 2. An uneasy feeling that something may happen contrary to one's desires. 3. A feeling of deep awe and dread. **—*v.t.*** 1. To be frightened of. 2. To be uneasy or apprehensive over (an unpleasant possibility). 3. To have a deep awe of. **—*v.i.*** 4. To feel uneasy. [OE *fǣr* peril] **—fear′er** *n.* **—fear′·less** *adj.* **—fear′less·ly** *adv.* **—fear′less·ness** *n.*

fear·ful (fir′fəl) *adj.* 1. Filled with dread or terror. 2. Filled with uneasiness; apprehensive. 3. Filled with awe. 4. Causing dread or terror; terrifying; frightening. 5. Showing fear. 6. *Informal* Extremely bad. **—fear′ful·ly** *adv.* **—fear′ful·ness** *n.*

fear·some (fir′səm) *adj.* 1. Causing fear; alarming. 2. Timid; frightened. **—fear′·some·ly** *adv.* **—fear′some·ness** *n.*

fea·sance (fē′zəns) *n.* *Law* Fulfillment of a condition, obligation, etc. [< L *facere* to do]

fea·si·ble (fē′zə·bəl) *adj.* 1. Capable of being put into effect or accomplished; practicable. 2. Capable of being successfully utilized; suitable. 3. Fairly probable; likely. [< L *facere*] **—fea′si·bil′i·ty** *n.* **—fea′si·bly** *adv.*

feast (fēst) *n.* 1. A sumptuous meal. 2. Something affording great pleasure to the senses or intellect. 3. A day or days of celebration regularly set aside for a commemorative or religious purpose: also **feast day.** **—*v.t.*** 1. To give a feast for; entertain lavishly. 2. To delight; gratify. **—*v.i.*** 3. To partake of a feast; eat heartily. 4. To dwell delightedly, as on a painting. [< L *festus* joyful < *feriae* holidays]

feat (fēt) *n.* A notable act, as one displaying skill or daring. [< OF *fait* < L *factum*. See FACT.]

feath·er (feth′ər) *n.* 1. Any of the horny, elongated structures that form the plumage of birds and much of the wing surface. 2. *pl.* Plumage. 3. *pl.* Dress; attire. 4. The hairy fringe on the legs and tails of some dogs. 5. Something resembling a bird's feather, as a key, wedge, etc. 6. Class or species; kind: birds of a *feather*. **—a feather in one's cap** An achievement to be proud of. **—*v.t.*** 1. To fit with a feather, as an arrow. 2. To cover, adorn, line, or fringe with feathers. 3. To join by a tongue-and-groove joint. 4. In rowing, to turn (the oar blade) horizontally after each stroke. **—*v.i.*** 5. To grow feathers or become covered with feathers. [OE *fether*] **—feath′ered** *adj.* **—feath′er·y** *adj.*

feath·er·bed·ding (feth′ər·bed′ing) *n.* The practice of requiring the employment of more workers than are needed.

feath·er·brain (feth′ər·brān′) *n.* A flighty or stupid person. **—feath′er·brained′** *adj.*

feath·er·edge (feth′ər·ej′) *n.* A very thin, tapering edge, as of a planed board.

feath·er·weight (feth′ər·wāt′) *n.* 1. A boxer or wrestler weighing between 118 pounds and 127 pounds. 2. Any person or thing relatively light in weight or size. —*adj.* 1. Of or like a featherweight. 2. Insignificant; trivial.

fea·ture (fē′chər) *n.* 1. A distinctive part of the face, as the eyes, nose, or mouth. 2. *Usu. pl.* The overall appearance or structure of a face. 3. A distinguishing mark, part, or quality. 4. A full-length motion picture: also **feature film.** 5. Anything given special prominence, as: a A special article, department, etc., in a magazine or newspaper. b A special attraction, as on a program, etc. —*v.t.* **·tured, ·tur·ing** 1. To give special prominence to. 2. To be a distinctive characteristic of. 3. *Slang* To form an idea of; imagine. [< L *facere* to do] —**fea′ture·less** *adj.*

febri- *combining form* Fever. Also, before vowels, **febr-.** [< L *febris*]

feb·ri·fuge (feb′rə·fyo͞oj) *n.* A medicine for reducing or removing fever. [< FEBRI- + L *fugare* to drive away] —**feb′ri·fuge** *adj.*

fe·brile (fē′brəl) *adj.* Feverish.

Feb·ru·ar·y (feb′ro͞o·er′ē, -yə·wer′ē) *n. pl.* **·ar·ies** or **·ar·ys** The second month of the year, having twenty-eight, or, in leap years, twenty-nine days. Abbr. *Feb.* [< L *februa*, a Roman festival celebrated on Feb. 15]

fe·ces (fē′sēz) *n.pl.* Animal excrement; ordure. [< L *faex, faecis* sediment] —**fe′cal** (-kəl) *adj.*

feck·less (fek′lis) *adj.* 1. Devoid of energy or effectiveness; feeble. 2. Careless and irresponsible. —**feck′less·ly** *adv.* —**feck′·less·ness** *n.*

fe·cund (fē′kənd, fek′ənd) *adj.* Fruitful; prolific. [< L *fecundus* fruitful] —**fe·cun·di·ty** (fi·kun′də·tē) *n.*

fe·cun·date (fē′kən·dāt, fek′ən-) *v.t.* **·dat·ed, ·dat·ing** 1. To make fruitful. 2. To fertilize. —**fe′cun·da′tion** *n.*

fed (fed) Past tense and past participle of FEED. —**fed up** *Slang* Bored, tired, or disgusted.

fed·er·al (fed′ər·əl) *adj.* 1. Of, relating to, or formed by an agreement among two or more states, groups, etc., to merge into a union in which control of common affairs is granted to a central authority, with each member retaining jurisdiction over its own internal affairs. 2. Of or pertaining to a confederacy (def. 1). [< L *foedus, -eris* compact, league] —**fed′er·al·ly** *adv.*

Fed·er·al (fed′ər·əl) *adj.* 1. Of, relating to, or supporting the central government of a specific country, as of the U.S. 2. Of, relating to, or loyal to the Union cause in the American Civil War. —*n.* One who favored the Union cause in the Civil War. —**Fed′er·al·ly** *adv.*

fed·er·al·ism (fed′ər·əl·iz′əm) *n.* The doctrine, system, or principle of federal union or federal government. —**fed′er·al·ist** *n. & adj.*

Fed·er·al·ist Party (fed′ər·əl·ist) A political party (1787–1830) that advocated the adoption of the U.S. Constitution and the formation of a strong national government. Also **Federal Party.** —**Fed′er·al·ist** *n. & adj.* —**Fed′er·al·ism** *n.*

fed·er·al·ize (fed′ər·əl·īz′) *v.t.* **·ized, ·iz·ing** To unite in a federal union; federate. —**fed′er·al·i·za′tion** *n.*

fed·er·ate (*v.* fed′ə·rāt; *adj.* fed′ə·rit) *v.t. & v.i.* **·at·ed, ·at·ing** To unite in a federal union. —*adj.* United in a federation. [See FEDERAL.]

fed·er·a·tion (fed′ə·rā′shən) *n.* 1. The joining together of two or more states, groups, etc., into a federal union or a confederacy. 2. A league or confederacy.

fe·do·ra (fə·dôr′ə, -dō′rə) *n.* A soft hat, usu. of felt, with a curved brim and a crown creased lengthwise. [after *Fédora*, a play by V. Sardou, French dramatist]

fee (fē) *n.* A charge, compensation, or payment for something; a sum charged. [< OF *fé, fief* < Med.L *feudum* fief, property, money]

fee·ble (fē′bəl) *adj.* **·bler, ·blest** 1. Lacking strength; very weak. 2. Lacking energy, direction, or effectiveness: *feeble* efforts. [< L *flebilis* lamentable < *flere* to weep] —**fee′ble·ness** *n.* —**fee′bly** *adv.*

fee·ble-mind·ed (fē′bəl·mīn′did) *adj.* Mentally deficient. —**fee′ble-mind′ed·ness** *n.*

feed (fēd) *v.* **fed, feed·ing** *v.t.* 1. To supply with food: to *feed* a hungry family. 2. To give (something) as food or nourishment to: to *feed* carrots to rabbits. 3. To serve as food or nourishment for; also, to produce food for: acreage that will *feed* many. 4. To keep supplied, as with fuel: to *feed* a fire; also, to keep supplying: to *feed* data into a computer. 5. To keep or make more intense or greater: to *feed* suspicions. —*v.i.* 6. To eat: said chiefly of animals. —*n.* 1. Food given to animals. 2. Material supplied, as to a machine. 3. A mechanical part, as of a sewing machine, that keeps supplying material to be worked on, etc. 4. *Informal* A meal. —**off one's feed** *Slang* Having little appetite. [OE *fēdan* < *fōda* food] —**feed′er** *n.*

feed·back (fēd′bak′) *n.* 1. The return of part of the output of a system into the input, esp. to modify or control that output. 2. A response, of criticism or suggestions, to a proposal, action, process, etc.

feel (fēl) *v.* **felt, feel·ing** *v.t.* 1. To examine or explore with the hands, fingers, etc. 2. To be aware of; sense the touch of. 3. To experience consciously (an emotion, pain, etc.). 4. To perceive or be aware of through thought: to *feel* the need for reform. 5. To think; suppose; judge. 6. To experience the force or impact of. —*v.i.* 7. To have physical sensation. 8. To produce a sensory impression of being hard, soft, cold, hot, etc. 9. To experience consciously the sensation or condition of being: to *feel* joyful. 10. To produce an indicated condition, impression, or reaction: It *feels* good to be home. 11. To experience compassion or pity: with *for.* 12. To have convictions or opinions: to *feel* strongly about an issue. 13. To search by touching; grope. —**to feel like** *Informal* To have a desire or inclination for. —**to feel out** To try to learn indirectly and cautiously the viewpoint of (a person). —*n.* 1. Perception by touch or contact. 2. The quality of something as perceived by touch. 3. A sensation or impression. [OE *fēlan*]

feel·er (fē′lər) *n.* 1. Any action, hint, proposal, etc., intended to draw out the views or intentions of another. 2. *Zool.* An organ of touch.

feel·ing (fē′ling) *n.* 1. The faculty by which one perceives sensations of pain, heat, etc. 2. Any particular sensation of this sort: a *feeling* of warmth. 3. An emotion. 4. A sensation or awareness of something. 5. *pl.* Sensibilities; sensitivities: His *feelings* are easily hurt. 6. Sympathy; compassion. 7. An opinion or sentiment; also, a foreboding. —*adj.* 1. Having sensation; sentient. 2. Having warm emotions; sympathetic: a *feeling* heart. 3. Marked by or indicating emotion. —**feel′ing·ly** *adv.*

feet (fēt) Plural of FOOT. —**on one's** (or **its**) **feet** In or into a condition of health or stability: to get a business *on its feet.*

feign (fān) *v.t.* 1. To make a false show of; sham: to *feign* madness. 2. To think up (a false story) and give out as true; fabricate. [< L *fingere* to shape] —**feigned** *adj.* —**feign′er** *n.*

feint (fānt) *n.* A deceptive movement; esp., a pretended blow or attack meant to divert attention. [< F *feinte,* pp. of *feindre* < L *fingere* to shape] —**feint** *v.t.* & *v.i.*

feld·spar (feld′spär, fel′spär) *n.* Any one of a group of crystalline materials largely made up of silicates of aluminum. [< G *feld* field + *spat* spar]

fe·lic·i·tate (fə·lis′ə·tāt) *v.t.* ·**tat·ed,** ·**tat·ing** To congratulate. [< L *felix, -icis* happy] —**fe·lic′i·ta′tion** *n.*

fe·lic·i·tous (fə·lis′ə·təs) *adj.* 1. Most appropriate; apt. 2. Agreeably pertinent or effective. —**fe·lic′i·tous·ly** *adv.* —**fe·lic′i·tous·ness** *n.*

fe·lic·i·ty (fə·lis′ə·tē) *n. pl.* ·**ties** 1. Happiness; bliss. 2. A source of happiness. 3. An agreeably pertinent or effective manner or style. 4. A pleasantly appropriate remark. [< L *felix* happy]

fe·line (fē′līn) *adj.* 1. Of or relating to a cat or the cat family. 2. Catlike; stealthy. —*n.* An animal of the cat family. [< L *felis* cat] —**fe′line·ly** *adv.* —**fe′line·ness, fe·lin·i·ty** (fə·lin′ə·tē) *n.*

fell[1] (fel) Past tense of FALL.

fell[2] (fel) *v.t.* **felled, fell·ing** 1. To strike and cause to fall down. 2. To cut down (timber). 3. In sewing, to finish (a seam) by joining the edges, folding them under, and stitching flat. —*n.* 1. The timber cut down during one season. 2. In sewing, a felled seam. [OE *fellan,* causative of *feallan* to fall]

fell[3] (fel) *adj.* Cruel; vicious; inhuman. [< OF *fel* cruel]

fell[4] (fel) *n.* The skin of an animal, esp. as covered with its natural hair, wool, etc. [OE, hide]

fel·lah (fel′ə) *n. pl.* **fel·lahs** or *Arabic* **fel·la·hin, fel·la·heen** (fel′ə·hēn′) In Arabic-speaking countries, a peasant or laborer. [< Arabic *fellāh*]

fel·lat·i·o (fə·lā′shē·ō) *n.* Oral stimulation of the penis. [< NL] —**fel·late** (fel′āt) *v.t.* ·**lat·ed,** ·**lat·ing** —**fel·la′tion** *n.*

fel·low (fel′ō) *n.* 1. A man or boy: often in informal address. 2. A person; anybody; one. 3. A comrade or companion. 4. An individual belonging to the same kind, class, or group as oneself. 5. Either one of a pair; mate. 6. A member of one of several learned societies. 7. A graduate student of a university or college who is granted financial assistance to pursue further study. —*adj.* Joined through some common occupation, interests, objectives, etc.: *fellow* citizens. [OE *fēolaga* business partner]

Fellow, having the meaning companion or associate, is used to make many phrases, as:

fellow citizen	**fellow servant**
fellow creature	**fellow sufferer**
fellow passenger	**fellow worker**

fel·low·ship (fel′ō·ship) *n.* 1. Companionship; association. 2. A body of individuals joined together through similar interests, beliefs, etc. 3. The status of being a fellow at a university or college; also, the financial grant made to a fellow.

fellow traveler One who favors the ideology or program of a particular group, as of the Communist Party, without being a member.

fel·ly (fel′ē) *n. pl.* ·**lies** The rim of a wooden wheel, in which the spokes are inserted. [OE *felg*]

fel·on[1] (fel′ən) *n. Law* One who has committed a felony. [< OF *felon* base]

fel·on[2] (fel′ən) *n. Pathol.* An acute inflammation of a finger or toe in the terminal joint or at the cuticle. [? < FELON[1]]

fel·o·ny (fel′ə·nē) *n. pl.* ·**nies** *Law* A major crime, as murder, rape, arson, or burglary, for which a punishment greater than that for a misdemeanor is provided. —**fe·lo·ni·ous** (fə·lō′nē·əs) *adj.* —**fe·lo′ni·ous·ly** *adv.*

felt[1] (felt) Past tense and past participle of FEEL.

felt[2] (felt) *n.* 1. An unwoven fabric made by matting together fibers of wool, fur, or hair. 2. Something made of felt, as a hat. [OE] —**felt** *adj.*

fe·male (fē′māl) *adj.* 1. Of or pertaining to the sex that brings forth young or produces ova. 2. Characteristic of this sex; feminine. 3. *Bot.* Designating a plant that has a pistil but no stamen and that is capable of being fertilized and of producing fruit. 4. *Mech.* Denoting or having a bore or slot designed to receive a correlated inserted part, called *male,* as some electric plugs. [< L *femina* woman] —**fe′male** *n.*

fem·i·nine (fem′ə·nin) *adj.* 1. Of or pertaining to the female sex; female. 2. Typical of or appropriate to women and girls. 3. Lacking manly qualities; effeminate. 4. *Gram.* Applicable only or to persons or things classified grammatically as female. —*n. Gram.* 1. The feminine gender. 2. A word or form belonging to the feminine gender. —**fem′i·nine·ly** *adv.* —**fem′i·nin′i·ty** *n.*

fem·i·nism (fem′ə·niz′əm) *n.* 1. A doctrine advocating social, political, and economic equality for women and men. 2. A movement championing women's rights and interests. —**fem′i·nist** *n.* & *adj.*

fem·i·nize (fem′ə·nīz) *v.t.* & *v.i.* ·**nized,** ·**niz·ing** To make or become feminine or effeminate. —**fem′i·ni·za′tion** *n.*

fe·mur (fē′mər) *n. pl.* **fe·murs** or **fem·o·ra** (fem′ər·ə) *Anat.* The long bone extending from the pelvis to the knee. Also called *thighbone.* [< L, thigh] —**fem·o·ral** (fem′·ər·əl) *adj.*

fen (fen) *n.* A marsh; bog. [OE *fenn*]

fence (fens) *n.* 1. A structure of rails, stakes,

strung wire, etc., erected as an enclosure, barrier, or boundary. 2. *Slang* A dealer in stolen goods. —*v.* **fenced, fenc·ing** *v.t.* 1. To enclose with or as with a fence. 2. To cause to be separated by or as by a fence. 3. *Slang* To deal in (stolen goods). —*v.i.* 4. To practice the art of fencing. 5. To avoid giving direct answers. 6. To deal in stolen goods. [Var. of DEFENSE] —**fenc′er** *n.*

fenc·ing (fen′sing) *n.* 1. The art or practice of using a foil, sword, or similar weapon. 2. The art or practice of making parrying remarks, as in a debate. 3. Material used in making fences; also, fences collectively.

fend (fend) *v.t.* 1. To ward off; parry: usu. with *off*. —*v.i.* 2. *Informal* To provide: with *for*: to *fend* for oneself. [Var. of DEFEND]

fend·er (fen′dər) *n.* 1. One who or that which fends or wards off. 2. A part projecting over each wheel of a car or other vehicle. 3. A metal guard set before an open fire. 4. A part projecting from the front of a locomotive or streetcar.

fen·nel (fen′əl) *n.* 1. A tall herb of the parsley family. 2. The seeds of this plant. [OE < L *faeniculum*]

-fer *combining form* One who or that which bears: *conifer*. [< L *ferre* to bear]

fe·ral (fir′əl) *adj.* 1. Not domesticated; wild. 2. Of, relating to, or typical of a wild beast; savage. [< L *fera* wild beast]

fer-de-lance (fâr′də·läns′) *n.* A large, venomous snake of tropical America. [< F, lance iron]

fer·ment (*n.* fûr′ment; *v.* fər·ment′) *n.* 1. Any substance or agent producing fermentation. 2. Fermentation. 3. Excitement or agitation. —*v.t.* 1. To produce fermentation in. 2. To excite with passion; agitate. —*v.i.* 3. To undergo fermentation. 4. To be agitated, as with emotion; seethe. [< L *fervere* to boil] —**fer·ment′a·bil′i·ty** *n.* —**fer·ment′a·ble** *adj.* —**fer·ment′a·tive** *adj.*

fer·men·ta·tion (fûr′mən·tā′shən) *n.* 1. *Chem.* The decomposition of organic compounds through the action of enzymes, bacteria, etc. 2. Commotion, agitation, or excitement.

fer·mi (fer′mē, fûr′-) *n.* *Physics* A unit for the measurement of the radii of nuclear atomic particles, equal to 10^{-13} centimeter. [after E. *Fermi*]

fer·mi·um (fer′mē·əm, fûr′-) *n.* An artificially produced radioactive element (symbol Fm). [after E. *Fermi*]

fern (fûrn) *n.* A plant that bears no flowers or seeds, has large, feathery fronds, and reproduces by means of asexual spores. [OE *fearn*]

fern·er·y (fûr′nər·ē) *n.* *pl.* **·er·ies** 1. A place in which ferns are grown. 2. A standing growth or bed of ferns.

fe·ro·cious (fə·rō′shəs) *adj.* 1. Extremely savage, fierce, bloodthirsty, or cruel. 2. *Informal* Very intense. [< L *ferox, ferocis* fierce + -OUS] —**fe·ro′cious·ly** *adv.* —**fe·roc·i·ty** (fə·ros′ə·tē) *n.*

-ferous *combining form* Bearing or producing: *coniferous*. [< -FER + -OUS]

fer·ret (fer′it) *n.* A small, red-eyed polecat of Europe, often used in hunting rodents. —*v.t.* 1. To search out by careful investigation: with *out*. 2. To drive out of hiding or hunt with a ferret. —*v.i.* 3. To search. 4. To hunt by means of ferrets. [< L *fur* thief] —**fer′ret·er** *n.*

ferri- *combining form* *Chem.* Containing iron in the ferric condition. [Var. of FERRO-]

fer·ric (fer′ik) *adj.* *Chem.* 1. Pertaining to iron. 2. Pertaining to or designating compounds of iron in its higher valence. [< L *ferrum* iron + -IC]

ferric oxide A red compound of iron and oxygen, found in nature as hematite and as rust, used as a pigment and for polishing.

Fer·ris wheel (fer′is) A giant, vertical, power-driven wheel that revolves on a stationary axle and has hanging seats in which passengers ride for amusement. Also **ferris wheel.** [after G. W. G. *Ferris*, 1859–96, U.S. engineer]

ferro- *combining form* Derived from, containing, or alloyed with iron. [< L *ferrum* iron]

fer·ro·mag·net·ic (fer′ō·mag·net′ik) *adj.* *Physics* Highly magnetic, as is iron. —**fer·ro·mag·ne·tism** (fer′ō·mag′nə·tiz′əm) *n.*

fer·rous (fer′əs) *adj.* *Chem.* Of or pertaining to iron, esp. bivalent iron, where its combining value is lowest. [< L *ferrum* iron + -OUS]

fer·rule (fer′əl, -ōōl) *n.* A metal ring or cap used on or near the end of a cane, tool handle, etc., for protection or reinforcement. —*v.t.* **·ruled, ·rul·ing** To equip with a ferrule. [< L *viriae* bracelets]

fer·ry (fer′ē) *n.* *pl.* **·ries** A boat used in conveying people, cars, or merchandise across a river or other body of water. —*v.* **·ried, ·ry·ing** *v.t.* 1. To convey across a river, etc., by boat. 2. To cross (a river, etc.) in a boat. 3. To deliver (an airplane) under its own motive power. —*v.i.* 4. To cross a river, etc., by or as by a ferry. [OE *ferian* to carry, convey]

fer·ry·boat (fer′ē·bōt′) *n.* A boat used as a ferry.

fer·tile (fûr′təl) *adj.* 1. Yielding or capable of producing abundant crops or vegetation. 2. Reproducing or able to reproduce. 3. Inventive or productive: a *fertile* talent. [< L *fertilis* < *ferre* to bear] —**fer′tile·ly** *adv.* —**fer·til·i·ty** (fər·til′ə·tē) *n.*

fer·til·ize (fûr′təl·īz) *v.t.* **·ized, ·iz·ing** 1. To make fertile; cause to be productive or fruitful. 2. To cause (a female or female reproductive cell), by the introduction of the male reproductive cell or cells, to begin development of a new individual. 3. To spread manure, nitrates, or other enriching material on (land). —**fer′til·i·za′tion** *n.*

fer·til·iz·er (fûr′təl·ī′zər) *n.* Any material, as manure or nitrates, used to enrich land.

fer·ule (fer′əl, -ōōl) *n.* A flat stick or ruler sometimes used for punishing children. —*v.t.* **·uled, ·ul·ing** To punish with a ferule. [< L *ferula* whip, rod]

fer·vent (fûr′vənt) *adj.* 1. Warm or intense, as in emotion or enthusiasm; ardent. 2. *Poetic* Very hot; burning. [< L *fervere* to boil] —**fer′ven·cy, fer′vent·ness** *n.* —**fer′vent·ly** *adv.*

fer·vid (fûr′vid) *adj.* 1. Fervent; impassioned. 2. *Poetic* Very hot; burning. [< L *fervere* to boil] —**fer′vid·ly** *adv.* —**fer′vid·ness** *n.*

fer·vor (fûr′vər) *n.* 1. Great warmth or intensity, as of emotion; ardor. 2. Heat; warmth. Also *Brit.* **fer′vour.** [< L, violent heat, ardor]

fes·cue (fes′kyōō) *n.* Any of a genus of tough grasses. [< L *festuca* stalk, straw]

-fest *combining form Slang* Bout; session: *gabfest.* [< G *fest* festival]

fes·tal (fes′təl) *adj.* Typical of a celebration; festive. [< L *festum* feast] **—fes′tal·ly** *adv.*

fes·ter (fes′tər) *v.i.* 1. To develop pus; ulcerate. 2. To be or become rotten and foul. 3. To be a constant source of irritation; rankle. **—***n.* A small, ulcerous sore. [< L *fistula* ulcer]

fes·ti·val (fes′tə·vəl) *n.* 1. A particular feast, holiday, or celebration. 2. Any occasion for rejoicing or feasting. 3. A special series of performances, exhibitions, etc.: a Shakespeare *festival.* **—***adj.* Festive. [See FESTIVE.]

fes·tive (fes′tiv) *adj.* Of, relating to, or suitable for a feast or other celebration. [< L *festum* feast < *festus* joyful] **—fes′·tive·ly** *adv.* **—fes′tive·ness** *n.*

fes·tiv·i·ty (fes·tiv′ə·tē) *n. pl.* **·ties** 1. A festival. 2. Gladness and rejoicing. 3. *pl.* Festive merrymaking.

fes·toon (fes·tōōn′) *n.* 1. Flowers, colored paper, ribbon, etc., hanging in loops between two points. 2. An ornamental carving, sculpture, etc., representing this. **—***v.t.* To decorate, fashion into, or link together by festoons. [< Ital. *festa* feast] **—fes·toon′·er·y** *n.*

fe·tal (fēt′l) *adj.* Of or typical of a fetus.

fetch (fech) *v.t.* 1. To go after and bring back. 2. To draw forth; elicit. 3. To draw in (breath); also, to give forth (a sigh, groan, etc.); heave. 4. To cost or sell for. 5. *Informal* To give or deal (a blow, slap, etc.). **—***v.i.* 6. To go after something and bring it back. [OE *feccan*] **—fetch′er** *n.*

fetch·ing (fech′ing) *adj. Informal* Very attractive; charming. **—fetch′ing·ly** *adv.*

fete (fāt) *n.* 1. A festival. 2. An outdoor celebration, as a dinner, bazaar, etc. **—***v.t.* **fet·ed, fet·ing** To honor with festivities. Also **fête.** [< F *fête*]

fet·id (fet′id) *adj.* Having a foul odor; stinking. [< L *fetere* to stink] **—fet′id·ly** *adv.* **—fet′id·ness** *n.*

fet·ish (fet′ish, fē′tish) *n.* 1. An object regarded as having magical powers. 2. Something to which one is devoted excessively or irrationally. 3. *Psychiatry* Some object, not in itself erotic, which is regarded as sexually stimulating. Also **fet′ich.** [< F < Pg. *feitico* charm] **—fet′ish·ism** *n.* **—fet′·ish·ist** *n.* **—fet′ish·is′tic** *adj.*

fet·lock (fet′lok′) *n.* 1. A tuft of hair growing at the back of the leg of a horse just above the hoof. 2. The joint of the leg from which this tuft grows: also **fetlock joint.** [ME *fitlock, fetlak,* prob. < LG]

fet·ter (fet′ər) *n.* 1. A chain or other bond put about the ankles. 2. *Usu. pl.* Anything checking freedom of movement or expression. [OE *feter, fetor*] **—fet′ter** *v.t.*

fet·tle (fet′l) *n.* Proper condition of health or spirits: in fine *fettle.* [ME *fetlen* to prepare, lit., to gird up]

fet·tuc·ci·ne (fet′ōō·chē′nē, fet′ə-) *n.* Pasta in thin, narrow strips. Also **fet′tu·ci′ne, fet′tu·ci′ni.** [< Ital., little ribbons]

fe·tus (fē′təs) *n. pl.* **·tus·es** The individual organism after its embryonic stage but before birth. [< L, a bringing forth]

feud (fyōōd) *n.* Prolonged, sometimes bitter hostility between two or more individuals, families, etc. **—***v.i.* To take part in a feud. [< OHG *fehida* hatred, revenge] **—feud′ist** *n.*

feu·dal (fyōōd′l) *adj.* 1. Of, relating to, or typical of feudalism. 2. Of or relating to a fief. [< Med.L *feudum* fief] **—feu′dal·ly** *adv.*

feu·dal·ism (fyōōd′l·iz′əm) *n.* A social, political, and economic system in medieval Europe in which vassals were granted land by their lords in return for military or other services. **—feu′dal·is′tic** *adj.*

feu·da·to·ry (fyōō′də·tôr′ē) *n. pl.* **·ries** A vassal holding a fief; also, the fief held. **—***adj.* 1. Of or typical of a feudal relationship. 2. Subject to a feudal lord.

fe·ver (fē′vər) *n.* 1. A disorder marked by unduly high body temperature. 2. Any of several diseases that produce this symptom. 3. Emotional excitement or restless eagerness. ◆Collateral adjective: *febrile.* **—***v.t.* To affect with fever. [OE *fēfer* < L *febris*] **—fe′vered** *adj.*

fever blister A cold sore.

fe·ver·few (fē′vər·fyōō′) *n.* A plant bearing white flowers.

fe·ver·ish (fē′vər·ish) *adj.* 1. Having a fever, esp. a low fever. 2. Of or resembling a fever. 3. Tending to produce fever. 4. Agitated, uneasy, or restless. Also **fe′ver·ous.** **—fe′·ver·ish·ly** *adv.* **—fe′ver·ish·ness** *n.*

few (fyōō) *adj.* Small in number; not very many. **—***pron.* & *n.* A small number; not very many. **—quite a few** A considerable number. [OE *fea* little]

fey (fā) *adj.* 1. Acting as if enchanted. 2. Suggestive of a sprite. [< OF *fae* fairy]

fez (fez) *n. pl.* **fez·zes** A brimless, tapering, felt cap, usu. red and having a black tassel. [after *Fez,* a city in Morocco]

fi·an·cé (fē′än·sā′, fē·än′sā; *Fr.* fē·äṅ·sā′) *n.* A man engaged to be married. [< F]

fi·an·cée (fē′än·sā′, fē·än′sā; *Fr.* fē·äṅ·sā′) *n.* A woman engaged to be married. [< F]

fi·as·co (fē·as′ko) *n. pl.* **·coes** or **·cos** A complete or humiliating failure. [< Ital., flask]

fi·at (fē′ət, -at, fī′-) *n.* 1. A commandment or decree. 2. Authorization. [< L, let it be done]

fiat money Paper money backed solely by government authority, and not by gold or silver reserves.

fib (fib) *n.* A lie about something unimportant. **—***v.i.* **fibbed, fib·bing** To tell a fib. [? Alter. of FABLE] **—fib′ber** *n.*

fi·ber (fī′bər) *n.* 1. A fine, threadlike substance, esp. one capable of being spun or woven. 2. *Biol.* One of similar threadlike structures that together form animal or plant tissue or parts: a nerve *fiber.* 3. The particular composition or structure of something. 4. Character: moral *fiber.* Also *Brit.* **fi′bre.** [< L *fibra*] **—fi′brous** *adj.*

fi·ber·board (fī′bər·bôrd′) *n.* A tough building material made of plant fiber (as of wood).

Fi·ber·glas (fī′bər·glas′) *n.* A flexible, nonflammable material of glass spun into filaments: a trade name. Also **fi′ber·glas′, fi′ber·glass′.**

fiber optics The science of light carried by

thin glass or plastic fibers, to convey images, sound, data signals, etc. **—fi·ber-op·tic** (fī′bər·op′tik) *adj.*

fi·ber·scope (fī bər·skōp) *n.* A flexible instrument utilizing fiber optics for medical examination within internal organs.

fibr- See FIBRO-

fi·bril (fī′brəl) *n.* **1.** A minute fiber. **2.** *Bot.* A root hair. [< L *fibra* fiber] **—fi·bril·lar** (fī′brə·lər) *adj.*

fi·bril·la·tion (fib′rə·lā′shən) *n.* **1.** The formation of fibers. **2.** *Pathol.* Rapid contraction of muscle fibers of the heart.

fi·brin (fī′brin) *n.* *Biochem.* An insoluble protein that promotes the clotting of blood. **—fi·bri·nous** (fī′brə·nəs) *adj.*

fi·brin·o·gen (fī·brin′ə·jən) *n.* *Biochem.* A complex protein occurring in the formation of fibrin.

fibro- *combining form* Pertaining to or composed of fibrous tissue. Also, before vowels, *fibr-*. [< L *fibra* fiber]

fi·broid (fī′broid) *adj.* Made up of or resembling fibrous tissue.

fi·bro·sis (fī·brō′sis) *n.* An abnormal increase of fiber-containing connective tissue in the body.

fib·u·la (fib′yōō·lə) *n.* *pl.* **·lae** (-lē) or **·las** **1.** *Anat.* The outer and smaller of the two bones forming the lower part of the human leg. **2.** *Zool.* In animals, a similar bone of the hind leg. [< L, a clasp] **—fib′u·lar** *adj.*

-fic *suffix* Making, rendering, or causing: *beatific.* [< L *-ficus* < *facere* to make, render]

-fication *suffix* A causing to be (something indicated): *beatification.* [< L *facere* to make, render]

fiche (fēsh) *n.* *pl.* **fiche** or **fich·es** A microfiche.

fi·chu (fish′ōō, *Fr.* fē·shü′) *n.* A capelike piece of light material worn about the neck. [< F *ficher* to put on hastily]

fick·le (fik′əl) *adj.* Inconstant in feeling or purpose; capricious. [OE *ficol* crafty] **—fick′le·ness** *n.*

fic·tion (fik′shən) *n.* **1.** Prose works in narrative form, the characters and incidents of which are wholly or partly imaginary; also, such works collectively. **2.** Something imagined or deliberately falsified. [< L *fictio* a making < *fingere* to form] **—fic′tion·al** *adj.* **—fic′tion·al·ly** *adv.*

fic·ti·tious (fik·tish′əs) *adj.* **1.** Not corresponding to actual fact; artificially invented. **2.** Not genuine; false. **3.** Fictional. **—fic·ti′tious·ly** *adv.* **—fic·ti′tious·ness** *n.*

fic·tive (fik′tiv) *adj.* **1.** Fictitious. **2.** Relating to the creation of fiction. **—fic′tive·ly** *adv.*

-fid *combining form* **1.** Divided (into an indicated number of parts). **2.** Separated into lobes (of an indicated kind). [< L *-fidus* < *findere* to split]

fid·dle (fid′l) *n.* A violin. **—fit as a fiddle** Enjoying perfect health. **—*v.*** **·dled, ·dling** *v.i.* **1.** *Informal* To play a violin. **2.** To fidget. **—*v.t.*** **3.** To spend (time) in a careless way: usu. with *away.* [OE *fithele* < ML *fidula, fidella,* dim. of L *fides* lyre] **—fid′dler** *n.*

fiddler crab A small burrowing crab found chiefly off the Atlantic coast of the U.S., one of whose claws is, in the male, much larger than the other.

fid·dle·stick (fid′l·stik′) *n.* **1.** A bow used on a violin, etc. **2.** Something trifling. **—*interj. pl.*** Nonsense.

fi·del·i·ty (fi·del′ə·tē, fə-) *n.* *pl.* **·ties** **1.** Faithfulness to duties, vows, truth, etc. **2.** Exactness of reproductive detail. **3.** The extent to which a phonograph, tape recorder, etc., receives and transmits input signals without distortion. [< L *fides* faith]

fidg·et (fij′it) *v.i.* To make nervous or restless movements. **—*n.*** **1.** *Usu. pl.* The condition of being restless or nervous. **2.** One who fidgets: also **fidg′et·er.** [ME *fiken* to fidget]

fi·du·cial (fi·dōō′shəl, -dyōō′-) *adj.* **1.** Fiduciary. **2.** Based on trust or faith. **3.** *Physics* Fixed as a basis of measurement. [< L *fidere* to trust] **—fi·du′cial·ly** *adv.*

fi·du·ci·ar·y (fi·dōō′shē·er′ē, -shər·ē, -dyōō′-) *adj.* **1.** Of, pertaining to, or acting as a trustee. **2.** Held in trust. **3.** Consisting of fiat money. **—*n.*** *pl.* **·ar·ies** One who holds something in trust. [< L *fidere* to trust]

fie (fī) *interj.* An expression of impatience or disapproval. [< OF *fi, fy* < L *fi*]

fief (fēf) *n.* A landed estate held under feudal tenure. [< Med.L *feudum*]

field (fēld) *n.* **1.** A piece of land covered primarily with grass, weeds, or similar vegetation. ◆Collateral adjective: *campestral.* **2.** A piece of land set aside for use as pasture or for crops. **3.** A large expanse, as of open country. **4.** An area in which a natural resource is found: an oil *field.* **5.** An airport. **6.** The whole extent or a particular division of knowledge, research, or study. **7.** In sports and athletics. **a** The bounded area where a game is played or where athletic contests, exhibitions, etc., are held. **b** The members of a team, etc., engaged in active play. **c** The competitors in a contest. **8.** *Mil.* A region of active operations or maneuvers. **9.** In business, the area away from the home office. **10.** An area for active work or direct observation (**field work**), as opposed to library research, analysis of data, etc. **11.** *Physics* An extent of space within which lines of magnetic or electric force are in operation: also **field of force.** **12.** *Optics* The area within which objects are seen in a telescope, etc. **13.** The part of a painting canvas, flag, coin, etc., used for background. **—to take the field** To begin a game, military campaign, struggle, etc. **—*v.t.*** **1.** In baseball, cricket, etc., to catch or pick up (a ball) and throw to the appropriate player. **2.** To organize or put (a team) into competition. **3. a** To reply to (questions) adequately. **b** To answer (questions) extemporaneously. **—*v.i.*** **4.** In baseball, cricket, etc., to play in a field position. [OE *feld*] **—field′er** *n.*

field artillery Artillery so mounted as to be freely movable.

field day **1.** A day of military maneuvers, athletic contests, etc. **2.** A gala day.

field events The events at an athletic meet other than races.

field glass A compact, portable, binocular telescope. Also **field glasses.**

field goal **1.** In football, a goal scored by a kick from the field. **2.** In basketball, a goal scored while the ball is in active play.

field hockey See under HOCKEY.

field hospital A military hospital near a combat zone.

field magnet The magnet that produces the

magnetic field in a generator or electric motor.

field marshal In the armies of several nations, an officer of the highest rank.

field officer *Mil.* A colonel, lieutenant colonel, or major.

field·stone (fēld′stōn′) *n.* Loose stone found near a construction site and used in building. —*adj.* Consisting of or having the appearance of fieldstone: a *fieldstone* house.

field test A test to determine how a new product or process will perform with normal use. —**field-test** (fēld′test′) *v.t.*

field·work (fēld′wûrk′) *n.* A temporary fortification.

fiend (fēnd) *n.* 1. An evil spirit; devil; demon. 2. An intensely wicked or cruel person. 3. *Informal* One who is addicted to a substance, game, etc.: a bridge *fiend.* [OE *fēond* enemy, devil] —**fiend′like** *adj.*

fiend·ish (fēn′dish) *adj.* Exceedingly cruel or malicious; diabolical. —**fiend′ish·ly** *adv.* —**fiend′ish·ness** *n.*

fierce (firs) *adj.* 1. Having a violent and cruel nature. 2. Violent in action or force. 3. Vehement; intense: *fierce* anger. 4. *Slang* Very disagreeable, bad, etc. [< L *ferus* wild] —**fierce′ly** *adv.* —**fierce′ness** *n.*

fier·y (fīr′ē, fī′ər·ē) *adj.* **fier·i·er, fier·i·est** 1. Like, containing, or composed of fire. 2. Brightly glowing; blazing. 3. Passionate; impetuous. —**fier′i·ness** *n.*

fi·es·ta (fē·es′tə, *Sp.* fyes′tä) *n.* 1. A religious festival. 2. Any holiday or celebration. [< Sp. < L *festa*]

fife (fīf) *n.* A small, shrill-toned flute. —*v.t. & v.i.* **fifed, fif·ing** To play on a fife. [< G *pfeife* pipe < L *pipare* to peep, chirp] —**fif′er** *n.*

fif·teen (fif′tēn′) *n.* The sum of fourteen and one: a cardinal number written 15, XV. [OE *fīftēne*] —**fif′teen′** *adj.* —**fif′teenth′** *n. & adj.*

fifth (fifth) *adj.* 1. Next after the fourth. 2. Being one of five equal parts. —*n.* 1. One of five equal parts. 2. That which follows the fourth. 3. *Music* The interval between a tone and another tone five steps from it. 4. One fifth of a U.S. gallon, used as a measure of liquors. [OE *fīfta*] —**fifth, fifth′ly** *adv.*

fifth column In wartime, the civilians within defense lines who secretly assist the enemy. —**fifth columnist**

fifth wheel A superfluous person or thing.

fif·ty (fif′tē) *n. pl.* **·ties** The sum of forty and ten: a cardinal number written 50, L. [OE *fīftig*] —**fif′ti·eth** *n. & adj.* —**fif′ty** *adj.*

fif·ty-fif·ty (fif′tē·fif′tē) *Informal adj.* Sharing equally, as in benefits. —*adv.* Equally.

fig (fig) *n.* 1. The small, edible, pear-shaped fruit, cultivated in warm climates. 2. The tree that bears this fruit. [< L *ficus*]

fight (fīt) *v.* **fought, fight·ing** *v.t.* 1. To struggle against in battle or physical combat. 2. To struggle against in any manner. 3. To make (one's way) by struggling. —*v.i.* 4. To take part in combat. 5. To struggle in any manner. —**to fight it out** To fight until a final decision is reached. —*n.* 1. Strife or struggle; conflict; combat. 2. Power or disposition to fight; pugnacity. [OE *feohtan*]

fight·er (fī′tər) *n.* 1. One who fights. 2. *Mil.* A fast, highly maneuverable airplane for aerial fighting: also **fighter plane.**

fig·ment (fig′mənt) *n.* A fantasy or fiction; fabrication. [< L *figmentum* anything made]

fig·u·ra·tion (fig′yə·rā′shən) *n.* 1. The act of shaping something. 2. Form, shape, or outline. 3. The act of representing figuratively.

fig·ur·a·tive (fig′yər·ə·tiv) *adj.* 1. Based on, like, or containing a figure or figures of speech; metaphorical. 2. Representing by means of a form or figure. 3. Pertaining to pictorial or sculptural representation. —**fig′ur·a·tive·ly** *adv.*

fig·ure (fig′yər) *n.* 1. A character or symbol representing a number. 2. *pl.* The use of such characters in calculating. 3. An amount stated in numbers. 4. The visible form of anything; shape; outline. 5. The human form or body. 6. A personage or character, esp. a prominent one. 7. The impression that a person makes. 8. A representation or likeness, as in painting or sculpture. 9. A pattern or design, as in a fabric. 10. A printed illustration. 11. A movement or series of movements, as in a dance. 12. *Geom.* A surface or space enclosed by lines or planes. —*v.* **·ured, ·ur·ing** *v.t.* 1. To compute numerically; calculate. 2. To make a representation of; depict. 3. To ornament with a design. 4. To picture mentally; imagine. 5. To express by a figure of speech; symbolize. 6. *Informal* To believe; predict. —*v.i.* 7. To appear prominently; be conspicuous. 8. To compute; reckon. —**to figure on** (or **upon**) *Informal* 1. To count on; rely on. 2. To plan on. —**to figure out** 1. To solve; compute. 2. To make out; understand. [< L *fingere* to form] —**fig′ured** *adj.* —**fig′ur·er** *n.*

fig·ure·head (fig′yər·hed′) *n.* 1. A person having nominal leadership but no real power. 2. A carved or ornamental figure on the prow of a vessel.

figure of speech An expression that deviates from literal meaning so as to create a vivid effect, as in simile, metaphor, etc.

figure skating The art or sport of skating in prescribed patterns. —**figure skater**

fig·u·rine (fig′yə·rēn′) *n.* A small, molded or carved figure; statuette. [< Ital. *figurina*]

fig·wort (fig′wûrt′) *n.* A plant with small, dark flowers.

Fi·ji (fē′jē) *n.* 1. One of the native people of the Fiji Islands. 2. The Melanesian language of the Fijis. —**Fi·ji·an** (fē′jē·ən, fi·jē′ən) *adj. & n.*

fil·a·gree (fil′ə·grē) See FILIGREE.

fil·a·ment (fil′ə·mənt) *n.* 1. A fine thread or threadlike structure. 2. The slender wire in a light bulb or electron tube. [< L *filum* thread] —**fil′a·men′ta·ry** (-men′tər·ē), **fil·a·men′tous** (-men′təs) *adj.*

fil·bert (fil′bərt) *n.* The hazelnut, or the tree on which it grows. [after St. *Philibert*, because these nuts ripen about the time of his feast day (Aug. 22)]

filch (filch) *v.t.* To steal in small amounts; pilfer. [Origin uncertain] —**filch′er** *n.*

file[1] (fīl) *n.* 1. Any device in which papers are systematically arranged for quick reference, as a folder, drawer, or cabinet. 2. A collection of papers thus arranged. 3. A line of persons, animals, or things placed one behind another. —**on file** In a file. —*v.* **filed, fil·ing** *v.t.* 1. To store (papers, etc.) in systematic order. —*v.i.* 2. To march in file, as soldiers. 3. To put papers, etc., in a file. 4. To make an application, as for a job. [< L *filum* thread] —**fil′er** *n.*

file² (fīl) *n.* A hard steel instrument with ridged surfaces, used to abrade, smooth, or polish. —*v.t.* **filed, fil·ing** 1. To cut, smooth, or sharpen with or as with a file. 2. To remove with a file. [OE *fīl*] —**fil′er** *n.*

fi·let (fi·lā′, fil′ā) *n.* 1. Net lace having a square mesh. 2. Fillet (def. 2). —*v.t.* **fi·leted** (fi·lād′, fil′ād); **fi·let·ing** (fi·lā′ing, fil′ā·ing) To fillet. [< F]

fi·let mi·gnon (fi·lā′ min·yon′, *Fr.* fē·lā′ mē·nyôn′) A small boneless cut of beef from the inside of the loin. [< F]

fil·i·al (fil′ē·əl, fil′yəl) *adj.* Of, pertaining to, or befitting the relations of children to parents. [< L *filius* son]

fil·i·bus·ter (fil′ə·bus′tər) *n.* 1. In a legislative body, the use of delaying tactics, esp. time-consuming speeches; also, an instance of such tactics. 2. An adventurer who takes part in an unlawful military expedition. [< Sp. *filibustero* < Du. *vrijbuiter* freebooter] —**fil′i·bus′ter** *v.t.* & *v.i.*

fil·i·gree (fil′ə·grē) *n.* 1. Delicate ornamental work formed of intertwined gold or silver wire. 2. Anything fanciful and delicate. —*adj.* Resembling, made of, or adorned with filigree; ornate: also **fil′i·greed.** —*v.t.* **·greed, ·gree·ing** To adorn with or work in filigree. Sometimes spelled *filagree* or *fillagree.* [< L *filum* thread + *granum* grain]

fil·ings (fī′lingz) *n.pl.* Particles scraped off by a file.

Fil·i·pi·no (fil′ə·pē′nō) *n.* *pl.* **·nos** A native or inhabitant of the Philippine Islands. —**Fil′i·pi′no** *adj.*

fill (fil) *v.t.* 1. To supply (a container, space, etc.) with as much of something as can be contained. 2. To supply fully, as with food. 3. To occupy or pervade the whole of. 4. To stop up; plug: to *fill* a tooth. 5. To supply what is indicated in (an order, prescription, etc.). 6. To satisfy or meet (a need, requirements, etc.). 7. To occupy (an office or position). 8. To level out (an embankment, ravine, etc.) by adding stone, gravel, etc. —*v.i.* 9. To become full. —**to fill (someone) in on** *Informal* To give (someone) additional facts or details about. —**to fill out** 1. To make or become fuller or more rounded. 2. To make complete, as an application. —**to fill the bill** *Informal* To do or be what is wanted or needed. —**to fill up** To make or become full. —*n.* 1. That which fills or is sufficient to fill. 2. An embankment built up by filling in with stone, gravel, etc. [OE *fyllan* fill] —**fill′er** *n.*

fil·la·gree (fil′ə·grē) See FILIGREE.

fil·let (fil′it; *for n. def. 2 & v., also* fil′ā, fi·lā′) *n.* 1. A narrow band or ribbon for binding the hair. 2. A strip of boneless meat or fish. 3. Any narrow band. —*v.t.* To slice into fillets. [< F < L *filum* thread]

fill·ing (fil′ing) *n.* 1. That which is used to fill something; esp. the material put into a prepared cavity in a tooth. 2. The act of becoming full. 3. In weaving, the weft.

filling station A service station.

fil·lip (fil′əp) *n.* 1. The snap of a finger that has been pressed down by the thumb and suddenly released. 2. Something that excites or stimulates. —*v.t.* 1. To strike or project by or as by a fillip. 2. To stimulate; arouse. —*v.i.* 3. To make a fillip. [Var. of FLIP]

fil·ly (fil′ē) *n.* *pl.* **·lies** A young mare. [< ON *fylja* < *foli* foal]

film (film) *n.* 1. A thin covering or layer. 2. A thin haze or blur. 3. *Photog.* A sheet, roll, or strip of transparent material coated with a light-sensitive emulsion and used for making photographs. 4. A motion picture. —*v.t.* 1. To cover or obscure by or as by a film. 2. To photograph on film. 3. To make a motion picture of. —*v.i.* 4. To become covered or obscured by a film. 5. To make a motion picture. [OE *filmen* membrane]

film·og·ra·phy (film·og′rə·fē) *n.* A systematic catalog of motion pictures by performer, director, subject, etc.

film·set (film′set′) *v.t.* To prepare (text) for printing using photographically produced typographic images. —**film′set′** *adj.*

film·strip (film′strip′) *n.* A length of processed film containing frames of still pictures that are projected on a screen.

film·y (fil′mē) *adj.* **film·i·er, film·i·est** 1. Of or like film; gauzy. 2. Covered with a film or haze.

fil·ter (fil′tər) *n.* 1. A device, as paper, cloth, or charcoal, used as a strainer for clearing or purifying liquids, air, etc. 2. A device for screening out electrical oscillations or light waves of certain frequencies. —*v.t.* 1. To pass (liquids, air, etc.) through a filter; strain. 2. To separate or remove (impurities, etc.) by or as by a filter. 3. To act as a filter for. —*v.i.* 4. To pass through a filter. 5. To leak out, as news. [< Med.L *feltrum* felt (used as a filter)] —**fil′ter·a·ble** or **fil·tra·ble** (fil′trəb·əl) *adj.* —**fil′ter·er** *n.*

filth (filth) *n.* 1. Anything that is foul or dirty. 2. A foul condition. 3. Moral defilement; obscenity. [OE *fӯlth*]

filth·y (fil′thē) *adj.* **filth·i·er, filth·i·est** 1. Of the nature of or containing filth. 2. Morally foul; obscene. 3. Highly unpleasant. —**filth′i·ly** *adv.* —**filth′i·ness** *n.*

fil·trate (fil′trāt) *v.t.* **·trat·ed, ·trat·ing** To filter. —*n.* The liquid that has been separated by filtering. [< Med.L *filtrum* a filter] —**fil·tra′tion** *n.*

fin¹ (fin) *n.* 1. A membranous extension from the body of a fish or other aquatic animal, serving to propel, balance, or steer it in the water. 2. Any finlike or projecting part, appendage, or attachment, as a flipper. [OE *finn*] —**fin′less** *adj.* —**finned** *adj.*

fin² (fin) *n.* *Slang* A five-dollar bill. [< Yiddish *finf* five]

fi·na·gle (fi·nā′gəl) *v.* **·gled, ·gling** *Informal* *v.t.* 1. To get (something) by trickery or deceit. 2. To cheat or trick (someone). —*v.i.* 3. To use trickery or deceit; be sly. [Origin uncertain] —**fi·na′gler** *n.*

fi·nal (fī′nəl) *adj.* 1. Pertaining to or coming at the end; ultimate; last. 2. Precluding further action or controversy; conclusive. 3. Relating to or consisting in the end or purpose aimed at: a *final* cause. —*n.* 1. Something that is terminal or last. 2. *Often pl.* Something decisively final, as the last match in a tournament. 3. The last examination in a course. [< L *finis* end] —**fi·nal·i·ty** (fī·nal′ə·tē) *n.* —**fi′nal·ly** *adv.*

fi·na·le (fi·nä′lē, -nal′ē) *n.* The last part, as the final scene in a play. [< Ital., final]

fi·nal·ist (fī′nəl·ist) *n.* In games, contests, etc., a contestant in the finals.

fi·nal·ize (fī′nəl·īz) *v.t.* **·ized, ·iz·ing** To put into final or complete form; bring to completion. —**fi′nal·i·za′tion** *n.*

fi·nance (fi·nans′, fī′nans) *n.* 1. The science of monetary affairs. 2. *pl.* Monetary affairs; funds; revenue; income. —*v.t.* **·nanced, ·nanc·ing** 1. To supply the money for. 2. To manage the finances of. [< OF, payment] —**fi·nan′cial** (-nan′shəl) *adj.* —**fi·nan′cial·ly** *adv.*

fin·an·cier (fin′ən·sir′) *n.* One engaged or skilled in financial operations.

fin·back (fin′bak′) *n.* A rorqual. Also **finback whale.**

finch (finch) *n.* A small, seed-eating bird, as the sparrow or canary. [OE *finc*]

find (fīnd) *v.* **found, find·ing** *v.t.* 1. To come upon unexpectedly. 2. To discover after search, experience, or effort. 3. To recover (something lost). 4. To arrive at; reach. 5. To gain, or recover the use of: He *found* his tongue. 6. To determine by legal inquiry and declare. —*v.i.* 7. To express a decision after legal inquiry. —*n.* 1. The act of finding. 2. Something found or discovered; esp., a valuable discovery. [OE *findan*] —**find′a·ble** *adj.*

find·er (fīn′dər) *n.* 1. One who or that which finds. 2. A small telescope by the side of a large one, used to locate a particular object. 3. A camera attachment that shows the scene as it will appear in the photograph.

find·ing (fīn′ding) *n.* 1. The act of one who finds. 2. That which is found; a discovery or conclusion.

fine[1] (fīn) *adj.* **fin·er, fin·est** 1. Superior in quality or ability; excellent. 2. Highly satisfactory; very good. 3. Light or delicate in texture, workmanship, etc. 4. Composed of very small particles: *fine* powder. 5. Very thin: *fine* thread. 6. Keen; sharp: a *fine* edge. 7. Subtle; discriminating. 8. Elegant; polished; also, overelegant; affected. 9. Cloudless; clear. —*adv. Informal* Very well: It suits me *fine.* —*v.t. & v.i.* To make or become fine or finer. [< OF *fin* finished, perfected] —**fine′ly** *adv.* —**fine′ness** *n.*

fine[2] (fīn) *n.* A sum of money required as the penalty for an offense. —*v.t.* **fined, fin·ing** To punish by fine. [< OF *fin* settlement]

fine arts The arts of painting, drawing, sculpture, and architecture, and sometimes including literature, music, drama, and the dance.

fine-drawn (fīn′drôn′) *adj.* Drawn out to extreme fineness or subtlety.

fin·er·y (fī′nər·ē) *n.* *pl.* **·er·ies** Elaborate adornment; fine clothes or decorations.

fine-spun (fīn′spun′) *adj.* 1. Drawn or spun out to extreme fineness. 2. Excessively subtle.

fi·nesse (fi·nes′) *n.* 1. Highly refined skill; adroitness. 2. Smoothness and tact, as in handling a delicate situation; also, artful strategy. [< F < *fin.* See FINE[1].] —**fi·nesse′** *v.t. & v.i.* **·nessed, ·ness·ing**

fine-toothed comb (fīn′tōōtht′) A comb with fine teeth set very close together. Also **fine′-tooth′ comb.** —**to go over with a fine-toothed comb** To examine minutely

fin·ger (fing′gər) *n.* 1. One of the terminating members of the hand, usu. excluding the thumb. 2. That part of a glove made to fit the finger. 3. Anything that resembles or serves as a finger. 4. A unit of measure based on the width of a finger or on the length of the middle finger. —**to have** (or **put**) **a finger in the pie** 1. To take part in some matter. 2. To meddle. —**to put one's finger on** To identify or indicate correctly. —*v.t.* 1. To touch or handle with the fingers; toy with. 2. *Music* **a** To play (an instrument) with the fingers. **b** To mark the fingering of (music). 3. *Slang* To betray, as to the police. —*v.i.* 4. To touch or feel anything with the fingers. [OE] —**fin′ger·er** *n.*

fin·ger·board (fing′gər·bôrd′) *n.* In stringed instruments, the strip of wood upon which the strings are pressed by the fingers of the player.

finger bowl A bowl containing water for cleansing the fingers after eating.

fin·ger·ing (fing′gər·ing) *n.* 1. The act of touching or feeling with the fingers. 2. *Music* **a** The action or technique of using the fingers in playing an instrument. **b** The notation indicating which fingers are to be used.

fin·ger·ling (fing′gər·ling) *n.* A young, small fish.

fin·ger·nail (fing′gər·nāl′) *n.* The horny substance at the end of a finger.

fin·ger·print (fing′gər·print′) *n.* An impression of the skin pattern on the inner surface of a finger tip, used for identification. —*v.t.* To take the fingerprints of.

finger tip The extreme end of a finger.

fin·i·al (fin′ē·əl) *n.* *Archit.* An ornament at the apex of a spire, pinnacle, or the like. [< L *finis* end + -IAL]

fin·i·cal (fin′i·kəl) *adj.* Finicky. —**fin′i·cal·ly** *adv.* —**fin′i·cal·ness, fin′i·cal′i·ty** (-kal′ə·tē) *n.*

fin·ick·y (fin′i·kē) *adj.* Excessively fastidious or precise; fussy. Also **fin′ick·ing.** [< FINE[1] + -ICAL]

fin·is (fin′is, fē·nē′) *n.* *pl.* **fin·is·es** The end. [< L]

fin·ish (fin′ish) *v.t.* 1. To complete or bring to an end. 2. To use up completely. 3. To perfect (a person) in social graces, education, etc. 4. To give (fabric, wood, etc.) a particular surface quality. 5. *Informal* To kill, destroy, or defeat. —*v.i.* 6. To reach or come to an end; stop. —*n.* 1. The conclusion or last stage of anything. 2. Something that finishes, completes, or perfects. 3. Perfection or polish in manners, education, etc. 4. The surface quality or appearance of textiles, paint, etc. [< L *finis* end] —**fin′ished** *adj.* —**fin′ish·er** *n.*

fin·ish·ing school (fin′ish·ing) A school that prepares girls for entrance into society.

fi·nite (fī′nīt) *adj.* 1. Having bounds, ends, or limits. 2. That may be determined, counted, or measured. —*n.* Finite things collectively, or that which is finite. [< L *finitus* limited] —**fi′nite·ly** *adv.* —**fi′nite·ness, fin·i·tude** (fin′ə·tōōd, -tyōōd, fī′nə-) *n.*

fink (fingk) *n.* *Slang* 1. A strikebreaker. 2.

An informer. 3. Any untrustworthy or unsavory person. [? < FINGER, v. (def. 3)]

Finn (fin) *n.* 1. A native or inhabitant of Finland. 2. One whose native language is Finnish. [OE *Finnas* Finns]

fin·nan had·die (fin′ən had′ē) Smoked haddock. Also **fin′nan haddock.** [Var. of *Findhorn haddock*, after *Findhorn*, a Scottish fishing port where originally prepared]

Finn·ish (fin′ish) *adj.* Of Finland, the Finns, or their language. —*n.* The Uralic language of the Finns.

Fin·no-U·gric (fin′ō·o͞o′grik, -yo͞o′grik) *n.* A subfamily of the Uralic languages, including Finnish, Magyar, etc. Also **Fin′no-U′gri·an.** —**Fin′no-U′gric** *adj.*

fin·ny (fin′ē) *adj.* 1. Having fins. 2. Resembling a fin. 3. Of or pertaining to fish.

fiord (fyōrd) See FJORD.

fir (fûr) *n.* 1. Any of several trees of the pine family. 2. The wood of these trees. [OE *fyrh*] —**fir′ry** *adj.*

fire (fīr) *n.* 1. The visible, active phase of combustion, manifested in light and heat. 2. A burning mass of fuel, as in a fireplace. 3. A destructive burning, as of a building. 4. A flash or spark: to strike *fire.* 5. A discharge of firearms. 6. Flashing brightness; brilliance. 7. Intensity of spirit or feeling; passion. 8. Warmth or heat, as of liquor. 9. An affliction or grievous trial. —**on fire** 1. Burning; ablaze. 2. Ardent; zealous. —**to catch fire** To start to burn. —**to hang fire** 1. To fail to fire promptly, as a firearm. 2. To be delayed or undecided. —**to open fire** 1. To begin to shoot. 2. To commence. —**to play with fire** To do something rash or dangerous. —**to set fire to** or **to set on fire** 1. To make burn. 2. To inflame or excite. —**under fire** 1. Exposed to gunshot or artillery fire. 2. Subjected to severe criticism. —*v.* **fired, fir·ing** *v.t.* 1. To set on fire. 2. To tend the fire of. 3. To subject to the heat of fire. 4. To set off, as explosives. 5. To set off explosives within or near: to *fire* an oil well. 6. To discharge, as a gun or bullet. 7. *Informal* To hurl: to *fire* questions. 8. To dismiss from employment. 9. To bake, as pottery, in a kiln. 10. To inspire; excite. —*v.i.* 11. To catch fire; become ignited. 12. To go off, as a gun. 13. To set off firearms, a rocket, etc. 14. *Informal* To hurl a missile. —**to fire away** To start off and proceed energetically, esp. in asking questions. [OE *fȳr*]

fire·arm (fīr′ärm′) *n.* Any weapon, usu. small, from which a missile, as a bullet, is hurled by an explosive.

fire·ball (fīr′bôl′) *n.* 1. A luminous meteor. 2. Ball-shaped lightning. 3. A hot, incandescent sphere of air and vaporized debris, formed around the center of a nuclear explosion. 4. *Slang* A remarkably energetic person or thing.

fire·boat (fīr′bōt′) *n.* A boat equipped for fighting fires.

fire·bomb (fīr′bom′) *n.* An incendiary bomb. —**fire′bomb′** *v.t.*

fire·brand (fīr′brand′) *n.* 1. A piece of burning or glowing wood. 2. One who excites the passions of others; an agitator.

fire·break (fīr′brāk′) *n.* A strip of land plowed or cleared to prevent the spread of fire.

fire·brick (fīr′brik′) *n.* A brick made of fire clay, used for lining furnaces.

fire·bug (fīr′bug′) *n.* *Informal* A pyromaniac.

fire clay A heat-resistant material, used to make furnace linings, etc.

fire·crack·er (fīr′krak′ər) *n.* A small paper tube holding an explosive, used as a noisemaker.

fire·damp (fīr′damp′) *n.* 1. A combustible gas, chiefly methane, that enters mines from coal seams. 2. The explosive mixture formed by this gas and air.

fire engine A motor truck equipped to fight fires.

fire escape A metal stairway usu. attached to the outside of a building and furnishing a means of escape in case of fire.

fire extinguisher A portable apparatus containing fire-extinguishing chemicals.

fire·fly (fīr′flī′) *n.* *pl.* **·flies** A night-flying beetle emitting a phosphorescent light.

fire·house (fīr′hous′) *n.* A building housing fire-fighting equipment and personnel: also **fire station.**

fire·light (fīr′līt′) *n.* Light from a fire.

fire·man (fīr′mən) *n.* *pl.* **·men** (-mən) 1. A man employed to extinguish fires: also **fire fighter.** 2. One who tends fires; esp., a stoker.

fire·place (fīr′plās′) *n.* A recess or structure in which a fire is built; esp., the part of a chimney opening into a room.

fire·plug (fīr′plug′) *n.* A hydrant for supplying water in case of fire: also **fire hydrant.**

fire·pow·er (fīr′pou′ər) *n.* *Mil.* 1. Capacity for delivering fire, as from the guns of a ship, battery, etc. 2. The amount or effectiveness of fire delivered by a given weapon or unit.

fire·proof (fīr′pro͞of′) *adj.* Resistant to fire; relatively incombustible. —*v.t.* To make resistant to fire.

fire·side (fīr′sīd′) *n.* 1. The hearth or space before the fireplace. 2. Home or home life.

fire·trap (fīr′trap′) *n.* A building which is notoriously flammable or which, if on fire, is likely to trap persons inside.

fire·wa·ter (fīr′wô′tər, -wot′ər) *n.* Whiskey: term first used by the North American Indian.

fire·wood (fīr′wo͝od′) *n.* Wood cut for fuel.

fire·work (fīr′wûrk′) *n.* 1. *Usu. pl.* A device containing combustibles or explosives that, when ignited, produce brilliant light or a loud noise. 2. *pl.* A display made by or as by these devices.

firing line In combat, the front line from which gunfire is delivered.

firing pin The part of a firearm that ignites the explosive charge.

firing squad A detachment of men assigned to execute, by shooting, a person condemned to death.

firm[1] (fûrm) *adj.* 1. Relatively solid, compact, or unyielding to touch or pressure. 2. Difficult to move, loosen, etc. 3. Fixedly settled and established. 4. Constant and steadfast. 5. Full of or indicating strength; steady. —*v.t. & v.i.* To make or become firm. —*adv.* Solidly; resolutely; fixedly. [< L *firmus*] —**firm′ly** *adv.* —**firm′ness** *n.*

firm[2] (fûrm) *n.* A partnership of two or more persons for conducting business. [< L *firmus* firm]

fir·ma·ment (fûr′mə·mənt) *n.* The heavens; sky. [< L *firmare* to make firm] —**fir′ma·men′tal** (-men′təl) *adj.*

first (fûrst) *adj.* 1. Preceding all others in the order of numbering. 2. Prior to all others in time; earliest. 3. Nearest or foremost in place. 4. Highest or foremost in character, rank, etc.; chief. —**in the first place** To start with. —*n.* 1. One who or that which is first in time, rank, order, or position. 2. The beginning: from *first* to last. 3. The winning position in a race or contest. 4. *pl.* The best grade of certain merchandise, as of lumber, hosiery, etc. —**at first** At the beginning. —*adv.* 1. Before all others in order, time, place, rank, etc.: also (more formally) **firstly.** 2. For the first time. 3. In preference to something else: He would die *first.* [OE *fyrst,* superl. of *fore* before]

first aid Treatment given in an emergency before full medical care can be obtained. —**first-aid** (fûrst′ād′) *adj.*

first-born (fûrst′bôrn′) *adj.* First brought forth; eldest. —*n.* The first-born child.

first-class (fûrst′klas′) *adj.* 1. Of highest rank or best quality. 2. Of a class of sealed mail consisting wholly or partly of written matter. 3. Of the most luxurious accommodations on a ship, plane, etc. —*adv.* By first-class mail or conveyance.

first·hand (fûrst′hand′) *adj. & adv.* Direct from the original source.

first lady *Often cap.* The wife of the president of the U.S.

first lieutenant *Mil.* See under LIEUTENANT.

first·ling (fûrst′ling) *n.* The first of a kind.

first mate A ship's officer ranking next below captain.

first night The opening performance of a play, opera, etc. —**first-night** (fûrst′nīt′) *adj.* —**first′-night′er** *n.*

first person 1. A grammatical form in which the pronoun and verb (such as *I* and *am*) refer to the speaker or writer. 2. Narration using this form.

first-rate (fûrst′rāt′) *adj.* Of the finest class or quality; excellent. —*adv. Informal* Excellently.

first-string (fûrst′string′) *adj.* 1. Being the regular or preferred choice, as of a member of a team. 2. First-rate.

firth (fûrth) *n. Scot.* An arm of the sea.

fis·cal (fis′kəl) *adj.* Of or pertaining to the treasury or finances of a government; financial. [< L *fiscus* purse]

fiscal year Any twelve-month period at the end of which accounts are balanced.

fish (fish) *n. pl.* **fish** or (with reference to different species) **fish·es** 1. A vertebrate, cold-blooded aquatic animal with permanent gills, fins, and usu. scales. ◆Collateral adjective: *piscine.* 2. The flesh of fish used as food. —*v.t.* 1. To catch or try to catch fish in (a body of water). 2. To catch or try to catch (fish, eels, etc.). 3. To grope for and bring out: with *out* or *up*: to *fish* money out of one's pocket. —*v.i.* 4. To catch or try to catch fish. 5. To try to get something in an artful or indirect manner: with *for.* [OE *fisc*] —**fish′a·ble** *adj.* —**fish′·like′** *adj.*

fish and chips Fried fish fillets and French fried potatoes.

fish·bowl (fish′bōl′) *n.* A bowl, usu. of glass, serving as a small aquarium for fish.

fish cake A fried ball or cake of chopped fish. Also **fish ball.**

fish·er (fish′ər) *n.* 1. A fisherman. 2. A weasellike North American carnivore; also, its fur.

fish·er·man (fish′ər·mən) *n. pl.* **·men** (-mən) 1. One who fishes. 2. A fishing boat.

fish·er·y (fish′ər·ē) *n. pl.* **·er·ies** 1. The operation or business of catching fish or other aquatic animals. 2. A place for fishing; fishing ground. 3. A fish hatchery.

fish hatchery A place designed for the artificial propagation and nurture of fish.

fish·hook (fish′ho͝ok′) *n.* A hook, usu. barbed, for fishing.

fishing rod A slender pole with a line and usu. a reel, used for fishing: also **fishing pole.**

fishing tackle Equipment for fishing, as a rod, reel, etc.

fish·meal (fish′mēl′) *n.* Ground dried fish, used as fertilizer and feed for animals.

fish·mon·ger (fish′mung′gər, -mong′-) *n.* A dealer in fish.

fish story *Informal* An extravagant or incredible narrative.

fish·wife (fish′wīf′) *n. pl.* **·wives** (-wīvz′) 1. A woman who sells fish. 2. A coarse, abusive woman.

fish·y (fish′ē) *adj.* **fish·i·er, fish·i·est** 1. Of or like fish. 2. Abounding in fish. 3. *Informal* Improbable. —**fish′i·ly** *adv.* —**fish′i·ness** *n.*

fis·sile (fis′əl) *adj.* 1. Capable of being split or separated into layers. 2. Tending to split. [< L *fissilis* < *findere* to split] —**fis·sil·i·ty** (fi·sil′ə·tē) *n.*

fis·sion (fish′ən) *n.* 1. The act of splitting or breaking apart. 2. *Biol.* Spontaneous division of a cell or organism into new cells or organisms. 3. *Physics* The disintegration of the nucleus of an atom, leading to the release of energy. [< L *findere* to split] —**fis′sion·a·ble** *adj.*

fis·sure (fish′ər) *n.* 1. A narrow opening, cleft, or furrow. 2. The act of cleaving, or the state of being cleft. 3. *Anat.* Any cleft or furrow of the body. —*v.t. & v.i.* **·sured, ·sur·ing** To crack; split; cleave. [< L *fissura* < *findere* to split]

fist (fist) *n.* 1. The hand closed tightly, as for striking; also, grip; clutch. 2. *Printing* The index mark ☛. —*v.t.* To strike with the fist. [OE *fȳst*]

fist·ful (fist′fo͝ol) *n. pl.* **·fuls** *Informal* A handful.

fist·ic (fis′tik) *adj.* Of or pertaining to boxing; pugilistic.

fist·i·cuff (fis′ti·kuf′) *n.* 1. *pl.* A fight with the fists. 2. *pl.* The science of boxing. 3. A blow with the fist. —*v.t. & v.i.* To fight with the fists. —**fist′i·cuff′er** *n.*

fis·tu·la (fis′cho͞o·lə) *n. pl.* **·las** or **·lae** (-lē) *Pathol.* A duct or canal formed by the imperfect closing of a wound, abscess, or the like, and leading either to the body surface or from one cavity to another. [< L, a pipe] —**fis′tu·lous,** **fis′tu·lar** *adj.*

fit[1] (fit) *adj.* **fit·ter, fit·test** 1. Adapted to an end, aim, or design; suited. 2. Proper or appropriate; becoming. 3. Qualified; competent. 4. Prepared; ready. 5. In good physical condition; healthy. —*v.* **fit·ted** or **fit, fit·ting** *v.t.* 1. To be suitable or proper for. 2. To be of the right size and shape for. 3. To prepare or alter to the proper size or purpose. 4. To equip. 5. To put in place carefully or exactly. —*v.i.* 6. To be suitable or proper. 7. To be of the proper size, shape, etc. —**to fit out** (or **up**) To supply; outfit. —*n.* 1. Condition or manner of fitting. 2. Something that fits. 3. The act of fitting. [ME *fyt*] —**fit′ly** *adv.* —**fit′ness** *n.*

fit² (fit) *n.* 1. A sudden onset of a disorder, often attended by convulsions; spasm. 2. A sudden surge of emotion. 3. Impulsive and irregular exertion or action. [OE *fitt* struggle]

fitch (fich) *n.* The polecat of Europe or its fur. Also **fitch′et** (-it), **fitch′ew** (-ōō) [< MDu. *vitsche* polecat]

fit·ful (fit′fəl) *adj.* Characterized by irregular actions or moods; capricious. —**fit′·ful·ly** *adv.* —**fit′ful·ness** *n.*

fit·ting (fit′ing) *adj.* Fit; proper; appropriate. —*n.* 1. The act of one who fits. 2. A piece of equipment or an appliance used in an adjustment. 3. *pl.* Furnishings, fixtures, or decorations. —**fit′ting·ly** *adv.* —**fit′ting·ness** *n.*

five (fīv) *n.* The sum of four and one: a cardinal number written 5, V. [OE fīf] —**five** *adj.*

five-and-ten-cent store (fīv′ən·ten′sent′) A store selling relatively low-priced articles. Also **five′-and-ten′**, **five′-and-dime′** (-dīm′).

fiv·er (fī′vər) *n.* *Informal* 1. A five-dollar bill. 2. Anything counting as five.

fix (fiks) *v.t.* 1. To make firm or secure; fasten so as to be immovable. 2. To set or place permanently. 3. To render unchangeable: to *fix* color. 4. To hold or direct (the attention, gaze, etc.) steadily. 5. To determine or establish. 6. To place (blame or responsibility) on a person. 7. To adjust. 8. To repair or mend. 9. To prepare. 10. *Informal* To prearrange or influence the outcome, etc., of (a race, game, trial, etc.) as by bribery. 11. *Photog.* To bathe (a film or plate) in chemicals to remove light-sensitive substances and prevent fading. 12. *Informal* To neuter (a dog, cat, etc.) —*v.i.* 13. To become firm or stable. —*n.* 1. *Informal* A difficult situation; predicament. 2. The relative position of a ship or aircraft in transit. 3. *Slang* An outcome prearranged by bribery or other corrupt means. 4. *Slang* An injection of heroin or other narcotic. [< L *fixus*, pp. of *figere* to fasten] —**fix′a·ble** *adj.* —**fix′er** *n.*

fix·a·tion (fik·sā′shən) *n.* 1. The act of fixing, or the state of being fixed. 2. *Chem.* The conversion of free nitrogen from the air into useful compounds. 3. A preoccupation or obsession.

fix·a·tive (fik′sə·tiv) *n.* That which serves to render permanent or fixed.

fixed (fikst) *adj.* 1. Placed or fastened securely. 2. Steadily or intently directed; set. 3. Stationary or unchanging in relative position. 4. Definite and unalterable. 5. Permanent. 6. *Informal* Prearranged as to outcome or decision. —**fix·ed·ly** (fik′sid·lē) *adv.* —**fix′ed·ness** *n.*

fix·ings (fik′singz) *n.pl.* *Informal* Trimmings.

fix·i·ty (fik′sə·tē) *n.* *pl.* **·ties** 1. The state or quality of being fixed; stability; permanence. 2. That which is fixed.

fix·ture (fiks′chər) *n.* 1. Anything securely fixed or fastened into position; esp., a permanent part or appendage of a house. 2. A person or thing regarded as fixed in a particular place or job. [< ML *fixure* < L *fixus*, pp. of *figere* to fasten]

fizz (fiz) *v.i.* To make a hissing or sputtering noise. —*n.* 1. A hissing sound. 2. An effervescent beverage made with soda water liquor, flavoring, etc.: a gin *fizz.*

fiz·zle (fiz′əl) *v.i.* **·zled, ·zling** 1. To make a hissing or sputtering sound. 2. *Informal* To fail, esp. after a good start. —*n.* 1. Hissing. 2. *Informal* A failure. [Freq. of obs. *fise* to fart]

fizz·y (fiz′ē) *adj.* **fizz·i·er, fizz·i·est** Fizzing; effervescent.

fjord (fyôrd) *n.* A long, narrow arm of the sea between high, rocky cliffs or banks: also spelled *fiord.* [< Norw.]

flab·ber·gast (flab′ər·gast) *v.t.* *Informal* To astound.

flab·by (flab′ē) *adj.* **·bi·er, ·bi·est** 1. Lacking strength or firmness; soft. 2. Lacking vigor or force. —**flab′bi·ly** *adv.* —**flab′bi·ness** *n.*

flac·cid (flak′sid, flas′id) *adj.* Lacking firmness or elasticity; limp; flabby. [< L *flaccus* limp] —**flac′cid·ly** *adv.* —**flac·cid′i·ty, flac′cid·ness** *n.*

fla·con (flȧ·kôn′) *n.* *French* A stoppered bottle or flask.

flag¹ (flag) *n.* 1. A piece of cloth or bunting, usu. oblong, bearing devices and colors to designate a nation, state, organization, etc. 2. Something resembling a flag, as the bushy part of the tail of a dog. —*v.t.* **flagged, flag·ging** 1. To mark out or adorn with flags. 2. To signal with or as with a flag.

flag² (flag) *n.* Any of various irises having sword-shaped leaves.

flag³ (flag) *v.i.* **flagged, flag·ging** 1. To grow tired or weak. 2. To become limp. [? < obs. *flack* flutter]

flag⁴ (flag) *n.* A flagstone. —*v.i.* **flagged, flag·ging** To pave with flags. [< ON *flaga* slab of stone]

flag·el·late (flaj′ə·lāt) *v.t.* **·lat·ed, ·lat·ing** To whip; scourge. —*adj.* *Biol.* Having or producing whiplike processes or branches: also **flag′el·lat′ed.** —**flag′el·la′tion** *n.*

fla·gel·lum (flə·jel′əm) *n.* *pl.* **·la** (-ə) *Biol.* A lashlike appendage, as of a protozoan. [< L, whip]

flag·eo·let (flaj′ə·let′) *n.* A flutelike musical instrument. [< OF *flageol*]

flag·ging (flag′ing) *n.* 1. A pavement of flagstones; also, flagstones collectively. 2. The act of paving with flagstones.

fla·gi·tious (flə·jish′əs) *adj.* Flagrantly wicked. [< L *flagitium* disgraceful act] —**fla·gi′tious·ly** *adv.*

flag·man (flag′mən) *n.* *pl.* **·men** (-mən) 1. One who carries a flag. 2. One who signals with a flag, as on a railway.

flag·on (flag′ən) *n.* A vessel with a handle, spout, and often a hinged lid, used to serve liquids. [< Med.L *flasco*]

flag·pole (flag′pōl′) *n.* A pole on which a flag is displayed.

fla·grant (flā′grənt) *adj.* Openly disgraceful; notorious. [< L *flagrare* to blaze, burn] —**fla′gran·cy, fla′grance** *n.* —**fla′grant·ly** *adv.*

fla·gran·te de·lic·to (flə·gran′tē di·lik′tō) In

the very act of committing a crime. [< ML, lit., while the crime is blazing]

flag·ship (flag′ship′) *n.* The ship in a naval formation that carries the commander and displays his flag. —*adj.* Designating the first, largest, most important, etc., of its kind: the network's *flagship* station.

flag·staff (flag′staf′) *n. pl.* **·staffs** or **·staves** (-stāvz′) A flagpole.

flag·stone (flag′stōn′) *n.* A broad, flat stone for pavements.

flail (flāl) *n.* An implement for threshing grain by hand. —*v.t. & v.i.* To beat as with a flail. [OE *flygel*, prob. < L *flagellum* whip]

flair (flâr) *n.* 1. A talent or aptitude. 2. A sense of fashion. 3. *Informal* Dashing style. [< OF *flairer* to scent out]

flak (flak) *n.* 1. Antiaircraft fire. 2. *Slang* Severe criticism; opposition. [< G *fl(ieger)* aircraft + *a(bwehr)* defense + *k(anone)* gun]

flake (flāk) *n.* 1. A small, thin piece peeled or split off from a surface. 2. A small piece of light substance: a *flake* of snow. 3. A stratum or layer. 4. *Slang* An eccentric. —*v.t. & v.i.* **flaked, flak·ing** 1. To peel off in flakes. 2. To form into flakes. [< Scand.] —**flak′er** *n.*

flake·board (flāk′bôrd′) *n.* Particle board.

flak·y (flā′kē) *adj.* **flak·i·er, flak·i·est** 1. Resembling or consisting of flakes. 2. Splitting off or easily separated into flakes. 3. *Slang* Exhibiting odd behavior; eccentric. —**flak′i·ly** *adv.* —**flak′i·ness** *n.*

flam·beau (flam′bō) *n. pl.* **·beaux** (-bōz) or **·beaus** 1. A burning torch. 2. A large candlestick. [< F < OF *flamme*]

flam·boy·ant (flam·boi′ənt) *adj.* 1. Extravagantly ornate; showy. 2. Brilliant; resplendent. [< OF *flambeiier*] —**flam·boy′ance, flam·boy′an·cy** *n.* —**flam·boy′·ant·ly** *adv.*

flame (flām) *n.* 1. A mass of burning vapor or gas rising from a fire in streams or darting tongues of light. 2. A single tongue of flame. 3. *Often pl.* A state of bright, intensely active combustion. 4. Something resembling a flame, as in brilliance. 5. Intense passion or emotion; ardor. 6. *Informal* A sweetheart. 7. A bright, red-yellow color. —*v.i.* **flamed, flam·ing** 1. To give out flame; blaze; burn. 2. To light up or glow as if on fire; flash. 3. To become enraged or excited. [< L *flamma* flame] —**flam′ing** *adj.* —**flam′ing·ly** *adv.*

fla·men·co (flə·meng′kō, -men′-, flä-) *n.* 1. A fiery, percussive style of singing and dancing practiced esp. by the Gypsies of Andalusia. 2. A song or dance in this style. [< Sp.]

flame·out (flām′out′) *n.* A burnout.

flame thrower *Mil.* A weapon that throws a stream of an incendiary mixture.

fla·min·go (flə·ming′gō) *n. pl.* **·gos** or **·goes** A long-necked wading bird of a pink or red color, having very long legs. [< Pg. *flamengo*]

flam·ma·ble (flam′ə·bəl) *adj.* Capable of catching fire easily. —**flam′ma·bil′i·ty** *n.*

flange (flanj) *n.* 1. A projecting rim or collar on a wheel, designed to keep it on a fixed track. 2. A similar projecting part of a beam, pipe, etc., designed to aid attachment or to increase stiffness. 3. A tool used to shape flanges. —*v.t. & v.i.* **flanged, flang·ing** To provide with or take the shape of a flange. [? < OF *flangir* to bend]

flank (flangk) *n.* 1. The part between the ribs and the hip at either side of the body of an animal or human being; also, a cut of meat from such a part. 2. Loosely, the outside part of the thigh. 3. The side of something. 4. *Mil.* The right or left section of an army, fleet, fortification, etc. —*v.t.* 1. To be at the side of. 2. *Mil.* To defend, launch an attack against, or move around the flank of. —*v.i.* 3. To be located at the side of something. [< F *flanc* < Gmc.] —**flank′er** *n.*

flan·nel (flan′əl) *n.* 1. A woven fabric made of wool, or of wool and cotton. 2. A soft fabric made chiefly of cotton, with a nap on one or both sides: also **flan′nel·ette′** (-et′), **flan′nel·et′**. 3. *pl.* A garment made of flannel. [Prob. < Welsh *gwlan* wool] —**flan′nel·ly** *adj.*

flap (flap) *v.i. & v.t.* **flapped, flap·ping** 1. To move (wings, arms, etc.) vigorously up and down. 2. To move or cause to move irregularly, esp. with a noise, as a flag. 3. To slap. —*n.* 1. Something hanging loosely and usu. broad and flat, as a *flap* of an envelope, a tent, etc. 2. The motion or sound produced by a moving flap. 3. *Slang* An agitated reaction; a commotion. [ME *flappe*]

flap·jack (flap′jak′) *n.* A griddlecake.

flap·per (flap′ər) *n.* 1. One who or that which flaps. 2. *Informal* A sophisticated young woman of the 1920's.

flare (flâr) *v.* **flared, flar·ing** *v.i.* 1. To blaze up or burn with a wavering light, esp. suddenly: often with *up*. 2. To break out in sudden or violent emotion or action: often with *up* or *out*. 3. To gradually open outward, as the sides of a bell. —*v.t.* 4. To cause to flare. 5. To signal with flares. —*n.* 1. A bright, flickering light. 2. An outburst, as of emotion. 3. A spreading outward; also, that which so flares. 4. *Photog.* Excess light striking a film. 5. A signal that gives off a bright white or colored light. [Origin unknown] —**flar′ing** *adj.* —**flar′ing·ly** *adv.*

flare-up (flâr′up′) *n.* A sudden outburst of flame, anger, etc.

flash (flash) *v.i.* 1. To burst forth suddenly or repeatedly into brilliant light or fire. 2. To gleam brightly; glitter. 3. To move suddenly or with lightning speed. —*v.t.* 4. To cause to shine or glitter brightly. 5. To emit bursts of (light, fire, etc.). 6. To send or communicate with lightning speed. 7. *Informal* To show suddenly or abruptly; also, to make a display of. 8. To provide (a roof, etc.) with flashing. —*n.* 1. A quick blaze of light or fire, lasting an instant. 2. A sudden, brilliant manifestation, as of wit. 3. An instant. 4. A brief news dispatch sent by radio, etc. —*adj.* Done or occurring very quickly. [ME *flaschen*; prob. imit.] —**flash′er** *n.*

flash·back (flash′bak′) *n.* A break in the continuity of a novel, drama, motion picture, etc., to give a scene occurring earlier; also, the scene itself.

flash·bulb (flash′bulb′) *n.* *Photog.* An electrical device emitting an intense light of brief duration.

flash card A learning aid consisting of a card having words, math problems, etc. briefly displayed as by a teacher to a class.

flash·cube (flash′kyōōb′) *n.* A small, rotatable cube containing four flashbulbs.

flash flood A sudden, rushing flood.

flash-for·ward (flash′for′wərd) *n.* A break in a narrative to present a scene set in the future; also the scene itself. [by analogy with FLASHBACK]

flash gun *Photog.* A device that ignites a flashbulb.

flash·ing (flash′ing) *n.* Sheet metal used to cover joints or angles, as of a roof.

flash·light (flash′līt′) *n.* A small, portable device that emits a beam of light, usu. powered by dry batteries.

flash point The lowest temperature at which the vapors of combustible liquids will ignite.

flash·y (flash′ē) *adj.* **flash·i·er, flash·i·est** 1. Brilliant for a moment; sparkling; flashing. 2. Showy; cheap. —**flash′i·ly** *adv.* —**flash′i·ness** *n.*

flask (flask) *n.* Any of various small containers made of glass, metal, etc., with a narrow neck. [< Med.L *flasca*]

flat[1] (flat) *adj.* **flat·ter, flat·test** 1. Extended horizontally with little or no slope. 2. Smooth and regular. 3. Stretched out level or prostrate. 4. Having the front or back in full contact with an even surface. 5. Shallow: a *flat* dish. 6. Absolute and unqualified: a *flat* refusal. 7. Lifeless; insipid; dull. 8. Lacking variety or contrast. 9. Deflated: a *flat* tire. 10. *Informal* Having little or no money: also **flat broke.** 11. Fixed; uniform: a *flat* rate. 12. Exact; precise: in a minute *flat.* 13. *Music* **a** Lowered in pitch by a semitone. **b** Lower than the right, true pitch. 14. *Phonet.* Designating the vowel sound in *man,* as opposed to the sound in *calm.* —*adv.* 1. In a flat state, position, or manner. 2. Exactly. 3. In finance, without interest. 4. *Music* Below the right, true pitch. —**to fall flat** To fail to achieve a desired effect. —*n.* 1. The flat, plane surface or part of something. 2. Something that has a flat surface, as a piece of stage scenery or a level area of land. 3. A tire from which the air has escaped. 4. *pl. Informal* Women's shoes with flat heels. 5. *Music* A sign (♭) placed before a note to indicate it is at a semitone lower in pitch. —*v.t. & v.i.* **flat·ted, flat·ting** To make or become flat. [< ON *flatr*] —**flat′ly** *adv.*

flat[2] (flat) *n.* An apartment. [Var. of Scot. *flet* floor < OE *flet*]

flat·car (flat′kär′) *n.* A railroad car with no sides or roof, used for freight.

flat·fish (flat′fish′) *n. pl.* ·**fish** or ·**fish·es** A flat-bodied fish, as the halibut, flounder, or sole.

flat·foot (flat′fŏŏt′) *n.* 1. *Pathol.* A condition caused by a flattened arch. 2. *Slang* A policeman.

flat-foot·ed (flat′fŏŏt′id) *adj.* Having flat feet. —**to catch flat-footed** 1. To catch in the act of committing an offense. 2. To surprise, esp. in an unprepared state. —**flat′-foot′ed·ly** *adv.* —**flat′-foot′ed·ness** *n.*

flat·i·ron (flat′ī′ərn) *n.* An iron for pressing clothes.

flat out 1. At maximum speed. 2. Bluntly; directly.

flat·ten (flat′n) *v.t. & v.i.* To make or become flat or flatter. —**flat′ten·er** *n.*

flat·ter (flat′ər) *v.t.* 1. To praise excessively, esp. without sincerity. 2. To try to gain favor by praising. 3. To play upon the hopes or vanity of; please, as by compliments. 4. To show as more attractive. —*v.i.* 5. To flatter someone or something. [< OF *flater* to fawn] —**flat′ter·er** *n.* —**flat′ter·ing·ly** *adv.*

flat·ter·y (flat′ər·ē) *n. pl.* ·**ter·ies** 1. The act of flattering. 2. A flattering remark.

flat·top (flat′top′) *n.* A U.S. naval aircraft carrier.

flat·u·lence (flach′ŏŏ·ləns, flat′yŏŏ-) *n.* 1. Gas in the intestines. 2. Windy boastfulness. Also **flat′u·len·cy.** [< L *flatus* blowing] —**flat′u·lent** *adj.* —**flat′u·lent·ly** *adv.*

flat·ware (flat′wâr′) *n.* 1. Dishes that are flat, as plates and saucers. 2. Table utensils, as knives, forks, and spoons.

flaunt (flônt) *v.i.* 1. To make a brazen or gaudy display. 2. To wave freely. —*v.t.* 3. To display. [ME *flant*? < Norw. *flanta* to gad about] —**flaunt** *n.* —**flaunt′er** *n.* —**flaunt′ing·ly** *adv.*

flau·tist (flô′tist, flou′-) *n.* A flutist.

fla·vin (flā′vən) *n. Biochem.* One of a group of yellow pigments widely distributed in plant and animal tissues. [< L *flavus* yellow]

fla·vor (flā′vər) *n.* 1. Taste; esp., a distinctive element in the overall taste of something. 2. Flavoring. 3. A special, subtle quality pervading something. —*v.t.* To give flavor to. Also *Brit.* **fla′vour.** [< OF *flaor*] —**fla′vor·er** *n.* —**fla′vor·ful, fla′vor·ous, fla′vor·some** *adj.*

fla·vor·ing (flā′vər·ing) *n.* Something that heightens flavor or gives a distinctive taste.

flaw (flô) *n.* 1. Something missing or faulty; defect. 2. Something questionable. 3. A crack or fissure. —*v.t.* 1. To produce a flaw in. —*v.i.* 2. To become cracked or torn. [? < ON *flaga* slab of stone] —**flaw′less** *adj.*

flax (flaks) *n.* 1. An annual plant that yields the fiber used in making linen. 2. The fiber. [OE *fleax*]

flax·en (flak′sən) 1. Pertaining to or made of flax. 2. Having a light golden color. Also **flax′y.**

flax·seed (flaks′sēd′, flak′sēd′) *n.* The seed of flax: also called *linseed.*

flay (flā) *v.t.* 1. To remove the skin, bark, etc., of, esp. by or as by lashing. 2. To attack with scathing criticism. [OE *flēan*] —**flay′er** *n.*

flea (flē) *n.* A small, wingless, parasitic insect that sucks the blood of mammals and birds. [OE *flēa, flēah*]

flea-bit·ten (flē′bit′n) *adj.* 1. Bitten by or covered with fleas. 2. *Informal* Decrepit.

flea market A bazaar, usu. temporary and often outdoors, offering used articles and antiques. [< F *Marché aux Puces* in Paris]

fleck (flek) *n.* 1. A tiny streak or spot. 2. A bit; speck. —*v.t.* To mark with flecks. [Cf. ON *flekkr* spot]

fled (fled) Past tense and past participle of FLEE.

fledge (flej) *v.* **fledged, fledg·ing** *v.t.* 1. To furnish with feathers. 2. To bring up (a young bird). —*v.i.* 3. To grow enough feathers for flight. [OE *-flycge* ready to fly]

fledg·ling (flej′ling) *n.* 1. A fledged bird. 2. A beginner. Also **fledge′ling.**

flee (flē) *v.* **fled, flee·ing** *v.i.* 1. To run

away, as from danger. 2. To move swiftly; leave abruptly. —*v.t.* 3. To run away from (a person, place, etc.). [OE *flēon*] —**fle'er** *n.*

fleece (flēs) *n.* 1. The coat of wool covering a sheep or similar animal. 2. The quantity of wool sheared from a sheep. 3. Anything resembling fleece. 4. A textile fabric with a soft, silky pile. —*v.t.* **fleeced, fleec·ing** 1. To shear the fleece from. 2. To swindle; defraud. [OE *flēos*] —**fleec'er** *n.* —**fleec'i·ness** *n.* —**fleec'y** *adj.* **fleec·i·er, fleec·i·est**

fleet[1] (flēt) *n.* 1. The entire number of ships belonging to one government; navy; also, a number of ships under one command. 2. A group of aircraft, trucks, etc., organized into a unit. [OE *flēot* ship]

fleet[2] (flēt) *adj.* Swift; quick. [OE *flēotan* to float] —**fleet'ly** *adv.*

Fleet Admiral See ADMIRAL OF THE FLEET.

fleet·ing (flē'ting) *adj.* Passing quickly. —**fleet'ing·ly** *adv.* —**fleet'ing·ness** *n.*

Flem·ing (flem'ing) *n.* 1. A native of Flanders. 2. A native speaker of Flemish.

Flem·ish (flem'ish) *n.* 1. Flemings collectively. 2. The language of the Flemings, closely related to Dutch. —**Flem'ish** *adj.*

flesh (flesh) *n.* 1. The soft substance of the body of a human being or animal, esp. muscle. 2. The edible substance of animals; meat. 3. The soft, pulpy substance of fruits and vegetables. 4. The color of the skin of a white person. 5. Plumpness; weight. 6. The physical nature of man as opposed to the spiritual. 7. Kindred; kin: also **flesh and blood.** [OE *flæsc*]

flesh·ly (flesh'lē) *adj.* **·li·er, ·li·est** 1. Pertaining to the body. 2. Sensuous. 3. Worldly. —**flesh'li·ness** *n.*

flesh·pot (flesh'pot') *n.* 1. Material comfort. 2. *pl.* Places for sensual indulgence.

flesh·y (flesh'ē) *adj.* **flesh·i·er, flesh·i·est** 1. Of or resembling flesh. 2. Plump; fat. 3. Firm and pulpy. —**flesh'i·ness** *n.*

fleur-de-lis (flœr'də·lē', -lēs') *n. pl.* **fleurs-de-lis** (flœr'də·lēz') An emblem in the form of three leaves or petals bound near the base, used esp. by the former royal family of France. [< F, flower of lily]

flew (flōō) Past tense of FLY[1].

flex (fleks) *v.t. & v.i.* 1. To bend, as the arm. 2. To contract, as a muscle. [< L *flexus*, pp. of *flectere* to bend] —**flex·ion** (flek'shən) *n.* —**flex'ion·al** *adv.* —**flex'ion·less** *adj.*

flexi- *combining form* Bent. [See FLEX.]

flex·i·ble (flek'sə·bəl) *adj.* 1. Capable of being bent, twisted, etc.; pliant. 2. Yielding; tractable. 3. Able to adjust; adaptable. Also **flex·ile** (flek'sil). —**flex'i·bil'i·ty, flex'i·ble·ness** *n.* —**flex'i·bly** *adv.*

flex·or (flek'sər) *n.* *Anat.* A muscle that serves to bend a part of the body.

flex·ure (flek'shər) *n.* 1. The act of bending, or the state of being bent. 2. A turn; curve. [< L *flexura* a bending]

flib·ber·ti·gib·bet (flib'ər·tē·jib'it) *n.* An impulsive, flighty, or gossipy person. [Imit.]

flick[1] (flik) *n.* A quick, light, snapping movement or blow. —*v.t.* 1. To strike or remove with a quick, light stroke, as with a whip. 2. To cause to move or snap with a quick movement. —*v.i.* 3. To move in a darting manner. 4. To flutter.

flick[2] (flik) *n.* *Slang* A movie. [Short for FLICKER[1]]

flick·er[1] (flik'ər) *v.i.* 1. To burn or shine with an unsteady or wavering light. 2. To flash up and die away quickly, as lightning. 3. To flutter or quiver. —*v.t.* 4. To cause to flicker. —*n.* 1. A wavering or unsteady light. 2. A quivering or fluttering. 3. A slight stirring, as of emotion. [OE *flicorian* to move the wings]

flick·er[2] (flik'ər) *n.* A woodpecker of eastern North America.

flied (flīd) Past tense and past participle of FLY[1] (def. 7).

fli·er (flī'ər) *n.* 1. One who or that which flies, as an aviator. 2. One who or that which moves very fast, as an express train. 3. A big leap or jump. 4. *Informal* A risky financial investment. 5. A handbill. Also spelled *flyer*.

flight[1] (flīt) *n.* 1. The act or manner of flying; also, the power of flying. 2. Any swift movement through the air. 3. The distance traveled or the course followed by an airplane, bird, etc. 4. A journey by airplane; also, a scheduled trip by airplane. 5. A group flying through the air together. 6. A soaring or excursion. 7. A continuous series of stairs. [OE *flyht*]

flight[2] (flīt) *n.* The act of fleeing or escaping from danger.

flight·y (flī'tē) *adj.* **flight·i·er, flight·i·est** 1. Moving erratically from one idea or topic to another; giddy. 2. Impulsive; frivolous; fickle. —**flight'i·ly** *adv.* —**flight'i·ness** *n.*

flim·flam (flim'flam') *Informal v.t.* **·flammed, ·flam·ming** To swindle; hoax; trick. —*n.* 1. Nonsense; silly talk. 2. Petty trickery or deception. [Cf. Norw. *flim* lampoon]

flim·sy (flim'zē) *adj.* **·si·er, ·si·est** 1. Not strong or solid in structure. 2. Light, thin, and delicate in texture. 3. Lacking validity or effectiveness: a *flimsy* excuse. [< FILM, by metathesis] —**flim'si·ly** *adv.* —**flim'si·ness** *n.*

flinch (flinch) *v.i.* To shrink back or wince. [< OF *flechier* to bend] —**flinch** *n.* —**flinch'er** *n.* —**flinch'ing·ly** *adv.*

flin·der (flin'dər) *n.* *Usu. pl.* Small fragments; splinters. [Cf. Norw. *flindra* splinter]

fling (fling) *v.t.* **flung, fling·ing** 1. To toss or hurl, esp. with violence. 2. To throw (oneself) into something with energy. 3. To send forth, move, or put suddenly or violently. —*n.* 1. The act of casting out, down, or away. 2. A brief period of self-indulgence, unrestraint, etc. 3. *Informal* An attempt. [ME *flingen* < Scand.]

flint (flint) *n.* 1. A very hard, dull-colored variety of quartz that produces a spark when struck with steel. 2. Anything very hard or cruel. [OE] —**flint'y** *adj.* **flint·i·er, flint·i·est**

flint glass A hard glass, used for lenses, cut glass, etc.

flint·lock (flint'lok') *n.* 1. A gunlock in which a flint is used to ignite the powder. 2. An obsolete firearm that was equipped with such a gunlock.

flip (flip) *v.* **flipped, flip·ping** *v.t.* 1. To throw or move with a jerk; flick. 2. To propel, as a coin, by a fillip, or flick, of a finger. 3. To turn or toss over. —*v.i.* 4. To move with a jerk. 5. To turn over, esp. with a leap. 6. *Slang* To become angry; lose self-control. 7. *Slang* To become excited or enthusiastic. —*n.* 1. A quick, light snapping movement, as of a lash. 2. A drink made with liquor, egg, sugar, and spices. —*adj.* *Informal* Pert; impertinent. [Imit.]

flip·pan·cy (flip′ən·sē) *n.* *pl.* **·cies** 1. Impertinence; sauciness. 2. An impertinent act or remark.

flip·pant (flip′ənt) *adj.* Lacking due respect or seriousness; impertinent; saucy. [< FLIP + -ANT] —**flip′pant·ly** *adv.* —**flip′pant·ness** *n.*

flip·per (flip′ər) *n.* 1. A broad, flat limb adapted for swimming, as in seals, etc. 2. A rubber, paddlelike shoe used by skin divers and other swimmers. 3. *Slang* The hand.

flirt (flûrt) *v.i.* 1. To act in a coquettish manner; play at love. 2. To expose oneself to something carelessly or lightly: to *flirt* with danger. 3. To dart; flit. —*v.t.* 4. To move or toss quickly. —*n.* 1. One who plays at love. 2. A sudden movement. [Imit.]

flir·ta·tion (flûr·tā′shən) *n.* 1. Coquettish behavior. 2. A brief, casual love affair. —**flirt′y, flir·ta′tious** *adj.* —**flir·ta′tious·ly** *adv.*

flit (flit) *v.i.* **flit·ted, flit·ting** 1. To move or fly rapidly and lightly; dart; skim. 2. To pass away quickly. —*n.* A flitting movement. [< ON *flytja* to remove, move] —**flit′ter** *n.*

flitch (flich) *n.* 1. A salted and smoked cut of meat from a pig. 2. A piece of timber cut lengthwise. [OE *flicce*]

flit·ter (flit′ər) *v.t.* & *v.i.* *Dial.* To flutter. [Freq. of FLIT]

fliv·ver (fliv′ər) *n.* *Slang* Formerly, an old, battered car. [Origin unknown]

float (flōt) *v.i.* 1. To rest on or at the surface of a liquid. 2. To remain suspended in a liquid or gas, esp. in the atmosphere. 3. To move lightly and effortlessly. 4. To go about from one person or thing to another in a random or unstable way. —*v.t.* 5. To cause to float. 6. To put (a stock, bond, etc.) on the market. 7. To launch (a business venture, scheme, etc.). —*n.* 1. An object that floats in a liquid, as a piece of cork attached to a fishing line. 2. An anchored raft. 3. A tableau or display carried atop a wheeled platform in parades or pageants. 4. A soda or milk shake with a ball of ice cream in it. [OE *flotian*] —**float′a·ble** *adj.* —**float′er** *n.* —**float′ing** *adj.*

float·a·tion (flō·tā′shən) See FLOTATION.

floating rib A rib of either of the two lowest pairs of ribs in a human being, not attached to the sternum.

floc·cu·late (flok′yə·lāt) *v.t.* & *v.i.* **·lat·ed, ·lat·ing** To form into small, lumpy masses, as clouds. —**floc′cu·la′tion** *n.*

floc·cu·lent (flok′yə·lənt) *adj.* 1. Having soft, fluffy wool or hair. 2. Marked by or producing woolly tufts. —**floc′cu·lence** *n.* —**floc′cu·lent·ly** *adv.*

flock[1] (flok) *n.* 1. A group of animals of the same kind, esp. sheep, goats, or birds, feeding, living, or kept together. 2. A group of members of the same church or congregation. 3. Any group of persons under the care or supervision of someone. 4. A large number or assemblage of persons or things. —*v.i.* To come or go in crowds. [OE *flocc*]

flock[2] (flok) *n.* 1. Refuse wool, rags, etc., used to stuff furniture. 2. A tuft of wool, hair, etc. 3. Tiny fibers applied to fabric, wallpaper, etc., to give a velvetlike appearance: also **flock′ing.** —*v.t.* To cover or fill with flock. [Prob. < OF < L *floccus* lock of wool]

floe (flō) *n.* A large, comparatively level field of floating ice, or a detached section thereof. [< ON *flō* a layer]

flog (flog, flôg) *v.t.* **flogged, flog·ging** To beat hard with a whip, rod, strap, etc. [? < L *flagellare* to whip] —**flog′ger** *n.*

flood (flud) *n.* 1. An unusually large flow or rise of water, esp. over land not usu. covered with water; deluge. ◆Collateral adjective: *diluvial.* 2. The coming in of the tide; high tide: opposed to *ebb*: also **flood tide.** 3. Any copious flow or stream. —*v.t.* 1. To cover or inundate with a flood. 2. To fill or overwhelm as with a flood. —*v.i.* 3. To rise to a flood; overflow. 4. To flow in a flood. [OE *flōd*]

flood·gate (flud′gāt′) *n.* A gate or valve at the head of a water channel, designed to regulate the flow or depth of the water.

flood·light (flud′līt′) *n.* 1. A lamp that throws a bright, broad beam of light. 2. The light of this lamp. —*v.t.* **·light·ed** or **·lit, ·light·ing** To illuminate with a floodlight.

flood plain A plain, subject to flooding by a river, and often formed by deposits of such flooding.

floor (flôr) *n.* 1. The surface in a room or building upon which one stands or walks. 2. The area between two adjacent levels of a building; story. 3. The bottom surface of any cavity: the ocean *floor.* 4. A level structure or platform for some special purpose: a threshing *floor.* 5. The part of a legislative house, stock exchange, etc., where the members gather to conduct business. 6. The right to speak to an assembly: to be given the *floor.* 7. The lowest or minimum price for anything. —*v.t.* 1. To cover or provide with a floor. 2. To knock down, as to the floor. 3. *Informal* To confound or vanquish completely. [OE *flōr*]

floor·ing (flôr′ing) *n.* 1. Material for a floor. 2. A floor; also, floors collectively.

floor leader A party leader in either house of the U.S. Congress, who directs his party's business on the floor.

floor show Entertainment presented in a night club or cabaret.

floor·walk·er (flôr′wô′kər) *n.* In a department store, one who walks about so as to supervise the sales force, aid customers, etc.

flooz·y (flo͞o′zē) *n.* *pl.* **flooz·ies** *Slang* A loose woman or a prostitute. Also **floos′y.** [Orig. *flossy* < FLOSS]

flop (flop) *v.* **flopped, flop·ping** *v.i.* 1. To move, flap, or beat about heavily or clumsily. 2. To fall loosely and heavily. 3. *Informal* To be completely unsuccessful. —*v.t.* 4. To cause to drop or fall heavily. 5. To flap in a loose, awkward, or noisy way, as wings. —*n.* 1. The act of flopping. 2. A flopping noise. 3. *Informal* A total failure. [Var. of FLAP] —**flop′pi·ly** *adv.* —**flop′pi·ness** *n.* —**flop′py** *adj.* **·pi·er, ·pi·est**

flop·house (flop′hous′) *n.* A cheap, shabby hotel.

flo·ra (flôr′ə) *n.* *pl.* **flo·ras** or **flo·rae** (flôr′ē) The aggregate of plants growing in and usu. peculiar to a particular region or period. [< L *Flora,* goddess of flowers]

flo·ral (flôr′əl) *adj.* Of, like, or pertaining to flowers.

Flor·en·tine (flôr′ən·tēn, -tīn, flor′-) *adj.* Of or pertaining to Florence, Italy. —*n.* A native or inhabitant of Florence.

flo·res·cence (flô·res′əns) *n.* 1. The state, period, or process of blossoming. 2. A state or period of prosperity or success. [< L *florere* to bloom] —**flo·res′cent** *adj.*

flo·ret (flôr′it) *n.* 1. A little flower. 2. *Bot.* One of the small individual flowers that make up the head of a composite flower. [< OF dim. of *flor* a flower < L *flos, floris*]

flo·ri·cul·ture (flôr′ə·kul′chər) *n.* The cultivation of flowers. —**flo′ri·cul′tur·al** *adj.* —**flo′ri·cul′tur·ist** *n.*

flor·id (flôr′id, flor′-) *adj.* 1. Having a ruddy color; flushed with redness. 2. Ornate; flowery. [< L *floridus* flowery] —**flo·rid·i·ty** (flə·rid′ə·tē), **flor′id·ness** *n.* —**flor′id·ly** *adv.*

flor·in (flôr′in, flor′-) *n.* 1. A British silver coin, equal to two shillings. 2. The guilder of the Netherlands. 3. One of several former European coins. [< Ital. *fiore* flower; from the figure of a lily stamped on it]

flo·rist (flôr′ist, flor′ist) *n.* A dealer in flowers.

-florous *combining form Bot.* Having (a specified number, kind, etc., of) flowers. [< L *flos, floris* a flower]

floss (flôs, flos) *n.* One of several light, silk or silklike substances or fibers, as tassels of corn or the outside fibers on the cocoon of a silkworm. Also **floss silk.** [< OF *flosche*] —**floss′y** *adj.*

flo·ta·tion (flō·tā′shən) *n.* 1. The act or state of floating. 2. The act of financing a business undertaking, as by an issue of stocks or bonds. Also spelled *floatation.*

flo·til·la (flō·til′ə) *n.* A fleet of small vessels; also, a numerically small fleet. [< Sp., dim. of *flota* fleet]

flot·sam (flot′səm) *n.* Parts of a wrecked ship, or goods from it, found floating in the sea. [OE *flotian* to float]

flounce[1] (flouns) *n.* A gathered or pleated strip of material used for trimming skirts, etc. —*v.t.* **flounced, flounc·ing** To furnish with flounces. [Earlier *frounce* < OF *fronce* fold]

flounce[2] (flouns) *v.i.* **flounced, flounc·ing** 1. To move or go with exaggerated tosses of the body, as in anger or petulance. 2. To plunge or flounder: said of animals. [< Scand.] —**flounce** *n.*

floun·der[1] (floun′dər) *v.i.* 1. To struggle clumsily, as if mired. 2. To proceed in a stumbling or confused manner. —*n.* A stumbling or struggling motion. [? Blend of FLOUNCE[2] and FOUNDER[3]]

floun·der[2] (floun′dər) *n.* Any of certain edible flatfish. [< AF *floundre,* prob. < Scand.]

flour (flour) *n.* 1. A fine, soft, powder obtained by sifting and grinding the meal of a grain, esp. wheat. 2. Any finely powdered substance. —*v.t.* 1. To sprinkle or cover with flour. 2. To make into flour. [Var. of FLOWER] —**flour′y** *adj.*

flour·ish (flûr′ish) *v.i.* 1. To grow or fare well; thrive. 2. To be at the peak of success or development. 3. To move with sweeping motions. —*v.t.* 4. To wave about or brandish, as a weapon or flag. 5. To display ostentatiously. —*n.* 1. A brandishing, as of a sword. 2. A curved or decorative stroke in penmanship. 3. Something done primarily for display. 4. Ornate language. 5. *Music* **a** A fanfare. **b** A florid passage. [< L *florere* to bloom] —**flour′ish·er** *n.*

flout (flout) *v.t.* 1. To scoff at; defy with open contempt. —*v.i.* 2. To express contempt. —*n.* A contemptuous act or remark. [Prob. ME *flouten* to play the flute, to deride] —**flout′er** *n.* —**flout′ing·ly** *adv.*

flow (flō) *v.i.* 1. To move along steadily, as a fluid. 2. To well out or pour forth. 3. To move steadily and effortlessly. 4. To have pleasing continuity: The lines of the statue *flow.* 5. To hang in rich profusion, as hair. 6. To overflow; abound. 7. Of the tide, to rise: opposed to *ebb.* 8. To arise; derive. —*n.* 1. The act of flowing. 2. Something that flows, as a current or stream. 3. A continuous stream or outpouring. 4. The amount of that which flows. 5. The manner of flowing. 6. An overflowing. [OE *flōwan*] —**flow′ing** *adj.* —**flow′ing·ly** *adv.*

flow chart A schematic diagram showing a sequence of operations, stages, etc.

flow·er (flou′ər, flour) *n.* 1. A simple or complex cluster of petals, usu. brightly colored, and enclosing the reproductive parts of a seed-bearing plant; blossom. 2. *Bot.* The reproductive structure of any plant. 3. The condition in which the reproductive parts of a plant are mature, esp. when marked by brightly colored, open petals. 4. The stage of fullest growth, development, or vigor; prime: usu. preceded by *in.* 5. The finest or choicest part of something. 6. *pl. Chem.* A powdery substance usu. produced by heating a solid to a gaseous state and condensing the vapors: *flowers* of sulfur. —*v.i.* 1. To produce flowers; bloom. 2. To reach fullest development or vigor. [< L *flos, floris*]

flower head *Bot.* A dense cluster of florets growing directly from the main stem of a plant.

flow·er·y (flou′ər·ē, flour′ē) *adj.* **·er·i·er, ·er·i·est** 1. Full of or covered with flowers. 2. Ornate; highly embellished. 3. Having a floral pattern. —**flow′er·i·ness** *n.*

flown (flōn) Past participle of FLY[1].

flu (flōō) *n. Informal* Influenza.

flub (flub) *Informal v.t. & v.i.* **flubbed, flub·bing** To make a mess of (an opportunity, performance, etc.). —*n.* A botch or blunder. [Origin unknown]

fluc·tu·ate (fluk′chōō·āt) *v.i.* **·at·ed, ·at·ing** 1. To change or vary often and in an irregular manner; waver. 2. To undulate. [< L *fluctus* wave] —**fluc′tu·ant** *adj.* —**fluc′tu·a′tion** *n.*

flue (flōō) *n.* 1. A pipe or tube through which smoke, hot air, steam, etc., is drawn off, as from a furnace or boiler. 2. In an organ, a flue pipe. [Origin uncertain]

flu·ent (flōō′ənt) *adj.* 1. Capable of speaking or writing with effortless ease. 2. Marked by smoothness, grace, and expressiveness. 3. Running freely, as a stream of water; fluid. [< L *fluens, -entis,* ppr. of *fluere* to flow] —**flu′en·cy** *n.* —**flu′ent·ly** *adv.*

flue pipe An organ pipe in which the tone is produced by a stream of air passing over an opening in the side of the pipe.

fluff (fluf) *n.* 1. A soft, light cluster of loosely gathered fibers of wool, cotton, etc. 2. A mass of soft, fine feathers; down. 3. *Informal* An error, as by an actor, in speaking lines. —*v.t.* 1. To make (pillows, blankets, etc.) soft and light by patting or shaking. 2. *Informal* To make an error in speaking (lines). [< *flue* a soft mass + PUFF]

fluff·y (fluf′ē) *adj.* **fluff·i·er, fluff·i·est** Of, covered with, or like fluff. —**fluff′i·ness** *n.*

flu·id (flo͞o′id) *adj.* 1. Capable of flowing; not solid. 2. Consisting of or pertaining to liquids. 3. Readily changing; not fixed. —*n.* A substance capable of flowing; esp., a liquid or gas. [< L *fluere* to flow] —**flu·id′ic** *adj.* —**flu·id′i·ty** *n.* —**flu′id·ly** *adv.*

fluid dram A measure of capacity equal to $^1/_8$ of a fluid ounce.

fluid ounce A measure of capacity equal to $^1/_{16}$ of a pint.

fluke[1] (flo͞ok) *n.* 1. One of several parasitic worms having a flattened appearance. 2. A flatfish or flounder. [OE *flōc*]

fluke[2] (flo͞ok) *n.* 1. The barb of an arrowhead, harpoon, etc. 2. The triangular head at the end of either arm of an anchor. [? < FLUKE[1]]

fluke[3] (flo͞ok) *n.* 1. A lucky stroke. 2. Anything that happens by chance. [Origin unknown] —**fluk′ey** or **fluk′y** *adj.*

flume (flo͞om) *n.* 1. A narrow gap in a mountain through which a torrent passes. 2. A chute or trough for carrying water. —*v.t.* **flumed, flum·ing** To drain away, divert, or transport by means of a flume. [< L *flumen* river]

flum·mer·y (flum′ər·ē) *n.* *pl.* **·mer·ies** 1. One of several soft, light, easily digested foods, as a custard. 2. Vapid flattery. 3. Utter nonsense. [< Welsh *llymru*]

flung (flung) Past tense and past participle of FLING.

flunk (flungk) *Informal v.t.* 1. To fail in (an examination, course, etc.). 2. To give a failing grade to. —*v.i.* 3. To fail, as in an examination. —*n.* A failure, as in an examination. [Origin unknown]

flunk·y (flung′kē) *n.* *pl.* **flunk·ies** 1. A servile person. 2. A manservant in livery. Also **flunk′ey**. [? Alter. of *flanker* < FLANK, *v.*] —**flunk′y·ism** *n.*

flu·o·resce (flo͝or·es′, flo͞o·ə·res′) *v.i.* **·resced, ·resc·ing** To become fluorescent. [Back formation < FLUORESCENCE]

flu·o·res·cence (flo͝or·es′əns, flo͞o·ə·res′-) *n.* 1. The property of absorbing radiation of a particular wavelength and emitting it as light. 2. The light so produced. [< L *fluor* a flowing + -ESCENCE] —**flu·o·res′cent** *adj.*

fluorescent lamp A tubular lamp in which ultraviolet light is reradiated as visible light after striking a coating of phosphors.

fluor·i·date (flo͝or′ə·dāt, flôr′ə·dāt) *v.t.* **·dat·ed, ·dat·ing** To add sodium fluoride to (drinking water), esp. to prevent tooth decay. —**fluor′i·da′tion** *n.*

flu·o·ride (flo͝or′īd, flôr′īd) *n.* A compound of fluorine and another element.

flu·o·rine (flo͝or′ēn) *n.* A pale, greenish yellow, corrosive, and extremely reactive gaseous element (symbol F) belonging to the halogen group.

fluoro- *combining form* 1. *Chem.* Indicating the presence of fluorine in a compound. 2. Fluorescence. Also, before vowels, **fluor-**: also **fluo-**.

flu·o·ro·car·bon (flo͝or′ō·kär′bən) *n.* *Chem.* Any of a group of compounds of carbon and fluorine used as solvents, insulators, and refrigerants.

fluor·o·scope (flo͝or′ə·skōp) *n.* A device for observing the internal structure of an opaque object by means of a fluorescent screen and a beam of X-rays or other radiation. —**fluor′o·scop′ic** (-skop′ik) *adj.* —**fluor′o·scop′i·cal·ly** *adv.* —**fluor·os·co·py** (flo͝or·os′kə·pē) *n.*

flur·ry (flûr′ē) *v.* **·ried, ·ry·ing** *v.t.* 1. To bewilder or confuse. —*v.i.* 2. To move in a flurry. —*n.* *pl.* **·ries** 1. A sudden commotion or excitement. 2. A sudden, light gust of wind. 3. A light, brief rain or snowfall, accompanied by small gusts. 4. In the stock exchange, a sudden, short-lived increase in trading. [Blend of FLUTTER and HURRY]

flush[1] (flush) *v.i.* 1. To blush. 2. To glow with a reddish brightness. 3. To flow or rush suddenly and copiously. 4. To be cleansed or purified through a quick gush of water, etc. —*v.t.* 5. To wash out with a sudden gush of water. 6. To cause to glow red or blush. 7. To excite or elate: usu. in the passive: to be *flushed* with success. —*n.* 1. A heightened, reddish color. 2. A pervasive feeling of being hot. 3. A warm feeling of elation, excitement, etc. 4. Glowing bloom or freshness. 5. A sudden gush or flow of water, etc. [? < FLUSH[4]] —**flush′er** *n.*

flush[2] (flush) *adj.* 1. Even or level with another surface. 2. Of a line of print, even with the margin. 3. Having an even or unbroken surface. 4. Having plenty of money on hand. 5. Marked by prosperity. 6. Having a heightened, reddish color. 7. Of a blow, direct: a *flush* hit. —*adv.* 1. In an even position with another surface; also, in alignment with a margin. 2. In a direct manner; squarely. [? < FLUSH[1]]

flush[3] (flush) *n.* In poker, etc., a hand of cards all of one suit.

flush[4] (flush) *v.t.* 1. To drive (an animal) from cover. —*v.i.* 2. To rush out or fly from cover. [ME *flusschen*]

flus·ter (flus′tər) *v.t.* & *v.i.* To make or become confused or agitated. —*n.* Confusion or agitation of mind. [Cf. Icel. *flaustr* to hurry]

flute (flo͞ot) *n.* 1. A tubular, reedless, woodwind instrument, equipped with holes and keys, and producing tones of a high pitch and clear quality. 2. *Archit.* A rounded groove, as in a column. 3. A small groove, as in pleated cloth. [< OF *flaüte*] —**flut′ed** *adj.* —**flut′y** *adj.*

flut·ing (flo͞o′ting) *n.* Flutes or grooves collectively.

flut·ist (flo͞o′tist) *n.* A flute player: also called *flautist.*

flut·ter (flut′ər) *v.i.* 1. To wave or flap rapidly and irregularly. 2. To flap the wings rapidly in or as in erratic flight. 3. To move or proceed with irregular motion. 4. To dart about; flit. 5. To be excited or nervous. 6. To beat rapidly or unevenly, as the heart. —*v.t.* 7. To cause to flutter; agitate. 8. To excite or confuse; fluster. —*n.* 1. A vibrating or quivering motion. 2. Nervous agitation; commotion. [OE *floterian*] —**flut′ter·er** *n.* —**flut′ter·y** *adj.*

flu·vi·al (flo͞o′vē·əl) *adj.* Pertaining to,

found in, or formed by a river. Also **flu′vi·a·tile** (-ə·til).

flux (fluks) *n.* 1. A flowing or discharge. 2. Constant movement or change. 3. The flowing in of the tide. 4. *Pathol.* An abnormal discharge of fluid matter from the body. 5. The act or process of melting. 6. *Metall.* A substance that promotes the fusing of metals, as borax, or that serves to purify metals or prevent undue oxidation of metal surfaces. 7. *Physics* The rate of flow of fluids, heat, electricity, light, etc. —*v.t.* 1. To make fluid; melt. 2. To treat, as metal, with a flux. [< L *fluere* to flow] —**flux·ion** (fluk′shən) *n.*

fly[1] (flī) *v.* flew or (*for def. 7*) **flied, flown** or (*for def. 7*) **flied, fly·ing** *v.i.* 1. To move through the air on wings, as a bird. 2. To move or travel through the air by aircraft. 3. To rush or be propelled through the air, as an arrow. 4. To wave or flutter in the air. 5. To move or go by swiftly. 6. To flee; escape. 7. In baseball, to bat the ball high over the field. —*v.t.* 8. To cause to fly or float in the air. 9. To operate (an aircraft). 10. To transport by aircraft. 11. To flee from. —**to fly at** To attack suddenly. —**to fly in the face of** To defy openly. —**to fly into** To enter suddenly into (an outburst of rage, etc.). —**to fly off the handle** To lose one's temper. —**to fly out** In baseball, to be retired by batting a ball high over the field and having it caught by an opposing player. —*n. pl.* **flies** 1. A flap of material concealing the zipper or other fastening in a garment, esp. in a pair of trousers. 2. The flap at the entrance to a tent. 3. In baseball, a ball batted high over the field: also called **fly ball.** 4. A flywheel. 5. *pl.* In a theater, the space above the stage and behind the proscenium. [OE *flēogan*] —**fly′ing** *adj.*

fly[2] (flī) *n. pl.* **flies** 1. Any of various small, usu. two-winged insects; esp., the housefly. 2. A fishhook to which colored bits of material, feathers, etc., are attached to resemble an insect. —**fly in the ointment** Some small thing that detracts from the enjoyment of something. [OE *flȳge*]

fly·blown (flī′blōn′) *adj.* Spoiled or contaminated, as by eggs or larvae of flies.

fly-by (flī′bī′) *n. pl.* **-bys** A flight, usu. at low altitude, by an aircraft or spacecraft past a designated location.

fly-by-night (flī′bī·nīt′) *adj.* Financially unsound. —*n.* One who flees to cheat a creditor.

fly·catch·er (flī′kach′ər) *n.* Any of a large order of songbirds that feed on insects caught in flight.

fly·er (flī′ər) See FLIER.

fly-fish (flī′fish′) *v.i.* To fish with artificial flies as bait.

flying buttress *Archit.* A bracing structure connected to a wall by an arch to receive the outward thrust of the wall.

flying fish A fish with large pectoral fins that enable it to glide through the air.

flying jib *Naut.* A jib set out beyond the ordinary jib, on an extended boom.

flying saucer Any of various unidentified flying objects, vaguely resembling saucers.

flying squirrel A squirrel having a fold of skin connecting its front and back limbs, enabling it to glide.

fly·leaf (flī′lēf′) *n. pl.* **·leaves** (-lēvz′) A blank sheet at the beginning or end of a book, pamphlet, etc.

fly·pa·per (flī′pā′pər) *n.* A piece of paper coated with a sticky poisonous substance, placed so as to catch or kill flies.

fly·speck (flī′spek′) *n.* 1. The dot made by the excrement of a fly. 2. Any slight speck. —*v.t.* To mark with flyspecks.

fly·weight (flī′wāt′) *n.* A boxer belonging to the lightest weight class, weighing 112 pounds or less.

fly·wheel (flī′hwēl′) *n.* A wheel heavy enough to resist sudden changes of speed, used to secure uniform motion in the working parts of a machine.

F number *Photog.* A number obtained by dividing the focal length of a lens by its effective diameter: the smaller the number, the shorter the exposure required.

foal (fōl) *n.* One of the young of an animal of the horse family. —*v.t.* & *v.i.* To give birth to (a foal). [OE *fola*]

foam (fōm) *n.* 1. A frothy mass of bubbles produced on the surface of a liquid by agitation, fermentation, etc. 2. Any frothy mass. 3. *Chem.* A colloid system of gas dispersed in a liquid. —*v.i.* To become foam or become covered with foam. [OE *fām*] —**foam′i·ness** *n.* —**foam′y** *adj.* **foam·i·er, foam·i·est**

foam rubber A firm, spongy rubber produced by chemical treatment.

fob[1] (fob) *n.* 1. A small pocket at the front of trousers or a vest, designed to hold a watch. 2. A short chain or ribbon attached to a watch and worn dangling from such a pocket; also, a small ornament attached to such a chain or ribbon. [Cf. dial. G *fuppe* pocket]

fob[2] (fob) *v.t.* **fobbed, fob·bing** 1. To dispose of by fraud or trickery: with *off.* 2. To put off by lies, evasion, etc. [? < FOB[1]]

fo·cal (fō′kəl) *adj.* Of or placed at a focus. —**fo′cal·ly** *adv.*

focal length *Optics* The distance from the center of a lens or curved mirror to the point where rays from a distant object converge. Also **focal distance.**

fo'c's'le (fōk′səl) See FORECASTLE.

fo·cus (fō′kəs) *n. pl.* **·cus·es** or **·ci** (-sī) 1. *Optics* **a** The point at which light rays converge or appear to converge after being reflected or refracted. **b** The point at which such rays appear to diverge and where they would meet if their direction were reversed. 2. The adjustment of the eye, a camera lens, etc., so that a clear image is produced. 3. Focal length. 4. Any central point, as of importance or interest. 5. *Physics* The meeting point of any system of rays, beams, or waves. —*v.* **·cused** or **·cussed, ·cus·ing** or **·cus·sing** *v.t.* 1. To adjust the focus of (the eye, a lens, etc.) to receive a clear image. 2. To fix; concentrate. —*v.i.* 3. To become focused. [< L, hearth]

fod·der (fod′ər) *n.* Coarse feed for horses, cattle, etc., as the stalks and leaves of field corn. —*v.t.* To feed with fodder. [OE *fōdor*]

foe (fō) *n.* An enemy; adversary. [Fusion of OE *fāh* hostile and *gefā* enemy]

foehn (fān, *Ger.* fœn) *n.* A warm, dry wind blowing down the slopes of a mountain into the valley, esp. in the Alps. [< dial G *föhn*]

fog (fog, fôg) *n.* 1. A cloud formed at the surface of the earth by the condensation of atmospheric vapor and interfering to some extent with visibility. 2. Any hazy condition of the atmosphere. 3. A state of mental bewilderment or blurred perception. —*v.t.* & *v.i.* **fogged, fog·ging** 1. To become or cause to become foggy; mist. 2. To become or cause to become confused or bewildered. [Prob. back formation < *foggy*, in the sense "marshy"] —**fog′gi·ly** *adv.* —**fog′gi·ness** *n.* —**fog′gy** *adj.* **·gi·er, ·gi·est**

fog bank A mass of fog seen at a distance, esp. at sea.

fog·bound (fog′bound′, fôg′-) *adj.* Prevented from traveling because of fog.

fog·horn (fog′hôrn′, fôg′-) *n.* A horn or whistle for sounding a warning during a fog.

fo·gy (fō′gē) *n. pl.* **·gies** A person of old-fashioned or ultraconservative notions: usu. preceded by *old.* Also **fo′gey, fo′gie.** [? < FOGGY] —**fo′gy·ish** *adj.* —**fo′gy·ism** *n.*

foi·ble (foi′bəl) *n.* A personal weakness or failing. [< F, obs. var. of *faible* weak]

foil[1] (foil) *v.t.* To prevent the success of; thwart. [< OF *fouler, fuler* to crush]

foil[2] (foil) *n.* 1. A metal hammered or rolled into thin, pliant sheets. 2. A person or thing serving by contrast to enhance the qualities of another. 3. *Archit.* An arch, piece of tracery, etc., suggestive of a leaf. —*v.t.* 1. To apply foil to. 2. To intensify or set off by contrast. [< L *folium* leaf]

foil[3] (foil) *n.* 1. A blunted, rapierlike implement used in fencing. 2. *pl.* The art of fencing with a foil. [Origin uncertain]

foist (foist) *v.t.* 1. To impose (someone or something) slyly or wrongfully; palm off. 2. To insert or introduce fraudulently. [Prob. < dial. Du. *vuisten* hold in the hand]

fold[1] (fōld) *v.t.* 1. To turn back or bend over so that one part covers or lies alongside another. 2. To close or collapse: often with *up.* 3. To wrap up; enclose. 4. To place together and interlock: to *fold* one's hands; also, to bring (wings) close to the body. 5. To embrace; enfold. 6. To wind; coil: with *about, around,* etc. 7. In cooking, to mix into other ingredients by gently turning one part over the other: with *in.* —*v.i.* 8. To become folded. 9. *Slang* **a** To fail financially; close. **b** To collapse, as from exhaustion. —*n.* 1. One part folded over another. 2. The space between two folded parts. 3. The crease made by folding. 4. The act of folding. [OE *fealdan*]

fold[2] (fōld) *n.* 1. A pen, as for sheep. 2. The sheep enclosed in a pen. 3. A flock of sheep. 4. A group of people, as the congregation of a church, having a leader, a common purpose, etc. —*v.t.* To shut up in a fold, as sheep. [OE *fald*]

-fold *suffix* 1. Having (a specified number of) parts: a *threefold* blessing. 2. (A specified number of) times as great or as much: to reward *tenfold.* 3. An amount multiplied by (a specified number): a *hundredfold.* [OE *fealdan* to fold]

fold·a·way (fōld′ə·wā′) *adj.* Designed to be easily folded and stored.

fold·er (fōl′dər) *n.* 1. One who or that which folds. 2. A road map, timetable, etc., designed to be folded. 3. A large binder for loose papers.

fol·de·rol (fol′də·rol) *n.* 1. Nonsense. 2. A useless ornament; a trifle. Also *falderal.*

fo·li·a·ceous (fō′lē·ā′shəs) *adj.* 1. Of, pertaining to, or resembling the leaf of a plant. 2. Made up of thin, laminated sheets.

fo·li·age (fō′lē·ij) *n.* 1. The growth of leaves on a tree or other plant; also, leaves collectively. 2. An ornamental representation of leaves, flowers, and branches. [< MF *fueillage* < L *folium* leaf] —**fo′li·aged** *adj.*

fo·li·ate (fō′lē·āt; *for adj., also* fō′lē·it) *adj.* Having or resembling leaves. —*v.* **·at·ed, ·at·ing** *v.t.* 1. To roll or hammer (gold, etc.) into thin plates. —*v.i.* 2. To split into thin leaves or layers. 3. To produce leaves, as a tree.

fo·li·a·tion (fō′lē·ā′shən) *n.* 1. *Bot.* **a** The act of bursting into leaf, or the state of being in leaf. **b** The arrangement or formation of leaves in a bud. 2. *Geol.* In certain rocks, a crystalline formation into leaflike layers; also, the layers themselves. 3. The consecutive numbering of the leaves of a book.

fo·lic acid (fō′lik) A vitamin of the vitamin-B complex: also called *vitamin* B_c.

fo·li·o (fō′lē·ō) *n. pl.* **·li·os** 1. A sheet of paper folded once to form four pages (two leaves) of a book. 2. A book, manuscript, etc., having oversize pages made from such a sheet; also, the size of such a work. 3. A leaf of a book, manuscript, etc., only one side of which is numbered. 4. The number of a page. —*v.t.* **·li·oed, ·li·o·ing** To number in order the pages of (a book, manuscript, etc.).

-folious *suffix of adjectives* Leaflike or leafy. [< L *folium* leaf]

folk (fōk) *n. pl.* **folk** (*esp. def. 1*) or **folks** 1. A people; nation. 2. *Usu. pl.* People of a particular group or class: old *folks.* 3. *pl. Informal* People in general. 4. *pl. Informal* One's family, esp. one's parents. —*adj.* Originating among or characteristic of the common people. [OE *folc*]

folk etymology Popular modification of an unfamiliar word, thereby causing the word to correspond with better known forms, as *agnail* (ME, a painful nail) becoming *hangnail.*

folk·lore (fōk′lôr′) *n.* 1. The traditions, beliefs, customs, sayings, stories, etc., preserved among the common people. 2. The study of folk cultures. —**folk′lor′ic** *adj.* —**folk′lor′ist** *n.*

folk-rock (fōk′rok′) *n.* Folk music with rock-and-roll accompaniment. —**folk′-rock′** *adj.*

folk song 1. A song, usu. of unknown authorship, originating among the common people and handed down orally. 2. A song copying the style of such a song. —**folk singer** —**folk-sing·ing** (fōk′sing′ing) *n.*

folk·sy (fōk′sē) *adj.* **·si·er, ·si·est** *Informal* Friendly; unpretentious. —**folk′si·ness** *n.*

folk·ways (fōk′wāz′) *n.pl. Sociol.* The traditional habits, customs, and behavior of a group, tribe, or nation.

fol·li·cle (fol′i·kəl) *n. Anat.* A small cavity or sac in certain parts of the body, having a protective or secretory function. [< L, dim. of *follis* bag] —**fol·lic·u·lar** (fə·lik′yə·lər) *adj.*

fol·lic·u·lat·ed (fə·lik′yə·lā′tid) *adj.* 1. Having a follicle. 2. Encased in a cocoon. Also **fol·lic′u·late** (-lit).

fol·low (fol′ō) *v.t.* 1. To go or come after and in the same direction. 2. To succeed in time or order. 3. To pursue. 4. To hold to the course of: to *follow* a road. 5. To obey or conform to. 6. To imitate. 7. To watch or observe closely. 8. To work at or have an active interest in: to *follow* sports. 9. To understand. 10. To be a consequence of. 11. To be under the leadership or authority of. —*v.i.* 12. To move or come after. 13. To pay attention. 14. To understand. 15. To come as a result or consequence. —**to follow suit** 1. In card games, to play a card of the suit led. 2. To follow another's example. —**to follow through** 1. To swing to the full extent of a stroke, as in tennis or golf. 2. To perform fully. —**to follow up** 1. To bring to full completion. 2. To take further action regarding. —*n.* The act of following. [OE *folgian*]

fol·low·er (fol′ō·ər) *n.* One who or that which follows; esp., a disciple or attendant.

fol·low·ing (fol′ō·ing) *adj.* That comes next in time or sequence. —*n.* A body of adherents, attendants, or disciples.

fol·low-through (fol′ō·thrōō′) *n.* 1. In sports, the continuation and full completion of a motion. 2. Any continuing or completion.

fol·low-up (fol′ō·up′) *n.* 1. The act of following up. 2. Something, as an action, letter, etc., used in following up. —**fol′low-up′** *adj.*

fol·ly (fol′ē) *n. pl.* **·lies** 1. Foolishness. 2. A foolish idea or action. 3. A foolish or ruinous undertaking. [< F *fol* fool]

fo·ment (fō·ment′) *v.t.* 1. To stir up or instigate (rebellion, discord, etc.). 2. To treat with warm water or medicated lotions, as in applying a poultice. [< L *fomentum* poultice] —**fo′men·ta′tion** *n.* —**fo·ment′er** *n.*

fond (fond) *adj.* 1. Having affection (for someone or something specified): with *of.* 2. Loving or deeply affectionate. 3. Doting. 4. Beloved; cherished. [ME *fonned*, pp. of *fonnen* to be foolish] —**fond′ly** *adv.* —**fond′·ness** *n.*

fon·dant (fon′dənt) *n.* A soft, creamy confection. [< F, orig. ppr. of *fondre* to melt]

fon·dle (fon′dəl) *v.t.* **·dled, ·dling** To handle lovingly; caress. [Freq. of obs. *fond* to caress] —**fon′dler** *n.*

fon·due (fon·dōō′) *n.* 1. A saucelike dish of melted cheese into which pieces of bread are dipped. 2. Various other dishes served in a similar manner. [< F]

font[1] (font) *n.* 1. A basin, often of stone, for the water used in baptism. 2. A receptacle for holy water. 3. Source; origin. [< L *fons, fontis* fountain] —**font′al** *adj.*

font[2] (font) *n. Printing* An assortment of type of a particular face and size. [< F *fondre* to melt]

fon·ta·nel (fon′tə·nel′) *n.* A soft area in the fetal and infantile skull. [< F *fontanelle*]

food (fōōd) *n.* 1. That which is ingested by an organism for the maintenance of life and the growth and repair of tissues. 2. Nourishment in solid form as opposed to liquid form. 3. A particular kind of nourishment: breakfast *food.* [OE *fōda*]

food chain The sequence in an ecological system in which organisms use lower organisms as food.

food poi·son·ing (poi′zən·ing) A gastrointestinal disorder caused by eating food contaminated with bacteria, chemicals, etc.

food·stuff (fōōd′stuf′) *n.* 1. Any substance suitable for food. 2. Any substance that enters into the composition of food.

fool (fōōl) *n.* 1. A person lacking understanding, judgment, or common sense. 2. A clown formerly kept by noblemen for entertainment; jester. 3. One who has been duped or imposed upon. —*v.i.* 1. To act like a fool. 2. To act, speak, etc., in a playful or teasing manner. —*v.t.* 3. To make a fool of; deceive. —**to fool around** *Informal* 1. To waste time on trifles. 2. To play idly with. 3. To engage in casual love affairs. 4. To experiment: with *with.* —**to fool with** *Informal* 1. To meddle with. 2. To play or toy aimlessly with. —*adj. Informal* Stupid or silly. [< L *follis* a bellows; later, simpleton]

fool·er·y (fōō′lə·rē) *n. pl.* **·er·ies** Foolish behavior, speech, etc.; also, an instance of this.

fool·har·dy (fōōl′här′dē) *adj.* **·di·er, ·di·est** Bold in a foolish or reckless way. —**fool′·har′di·ly** *adv.* —**fool′har′di·ness** *n.*

fool·ish (fōō′lish) *adj.* 1. Marked by or showing a lack of good sense; silly. 2. Resulting from folly or stupidity. 3. Ridiculous; absurd. —**fool′ish·ly** *adv.* —**fool′ish·ness** *n.*

fool·proof (fōōl′prōōf′) *adj.* 1. So simple and strong as to be incapable of damage or harm even through misuse. 2. Having no weak points; infallible: a *foolproof* plan.

fools·cap (fōōlz′kap) *n.* A writing paper measuring about 13 x 16 inches.

fool's gold One of several metallic sulfides, as pyrite, resembling gold in color.

foot (fŏŏt) *n. pl.* **feet** (fēt) 1. The terminal section of the limb of a vertebrate animal, upon which it stands or moves. ◆Collateral adjective: *pedal.* 2. Any part of an animal, plant, or object corresponding in form or position to the foot. 3. The part of a boot or stocking that covers the wearer's foot. 4. The lower part of anything; base; esp.: **a** The base of a hill or mountain. **b** The part of a bed, grave, etc., where the feet rest. **c** The bottom of a page, ladder, etc. 5. The inferior part or section: the *foot* of the class. 6. A measure of length, equivalent to 12 inches: symbol (′). 7. In prosody, a group of syllables forming a major unit of poetic rhythm. —**on foot** 1. Walking or standing. 2. In progress. —**to put one's foot down** To act firmly. —*v.i.* 1. To walk or dance. —*v.t.* 2. To move on or through by foot. 3. *Informal* To pay, as a bill. 4. To add, as a column of figures: often with *up.* [OE *fōt*] —**foot′less** *adj.*

foot·age (fŏŏt′ij) *n.* 1. Length expressed in feet. 2. A segment of exposed motion-picture film or videotape, usu. containing a scene or relating to a subject.

foot·ball (fŏŏt′bôl′) *n.* 1. A game played between two teams of 11 players (12 in Canada) on a field with goals at each end. 2. The inflated, leather-covered ball with an ellipsoidal shape used in this game. 3. In Great Britain: **a** Rugby football. **b** Soccer.

foot·board (fŏŏt′bôrd′) *n.* 1. A board or small platform on which to prop or rest the feet. 2. An upright piece at the foot of a bedstead.

foot·bridge (fŏŏt′brij′) *n.* A bridge for pedestrians.

foot-can·dle (fŏŏt′kan′dəl) *n.* The illumination thrown on one square foot of surface at a distance of one foot from a uniform source of light or one candle (*def. 2*).

foot·ed (fŏŏt′id) *adj.* 1. Having a foot or feet: a *footed* goblet. 2. Having or characterized by a (specified kind of) foot or (a specified number of) feet: *light-footed; four-footed.*

foot·er (fŏŏt′ər) *n.* One who or that which has an indicated number of linear feet in height or length: a *six-footer.*

foot·fall (fŏŏt′fôl′) *n.* The sound of a footstep.

foot·hill (fŏŏt′hil′) *n.* A low hill at the base of a mountain.

foot·hold (fŏŏt′hōld′) *n.* A place on which the foot can rest securely, as in climbing.

foot·ing (fŏŏt′ing) *n.* 1. A place on which to stand, walk, or climb securely. 2. A foothold. 3. Social or professional status in relation to others; standing. 4. The adding up of a column of figures; also, the sum obtained.

foot·lights (fŏŏt′līts′) *n.pl.* In a theater, lights in a row near the front of the stage, nearly level with the performers' feet.

foot·lock·er (fŏŏt′lok′ər) *n.* A small trunk, usu. kept at the foot of a bed for storage.

foot·loose (fŏŏt′lōōs′) *adj.* Free to travel or do as one pleases; unattached.

foot·man (fŏŏt′mən) *n. pl.* **·men** (-mən) A male servant in livery who waits at table, etc.

foot·note (fŏŏt′nōt′) *n.* An explanatory note or reference to the text, usu. at the bottom of a page. **—*v.t.*** **·not·ed, ·not·ing** To furnish with footnotes.

foot·path (fŏŏt′path′) *n.* A narrow path for persons on foot.

foot-pound (fŏŏt′pound′) *n. Mech.* A unit of energy, equal to the amount of energy necessary to raise a one-pound mass through one linear foot.

foot·print (fŏŏt′print′) *n.* The outline or impression made by a foot on a surface.

foot·rest (fŏŏt′rest′) *n.* Something on which the feet can be propped or rested.

foot soldier A soldier trained and equipped to fight on foot.

foot·sore (fŏŏt′sôr′) *adj.* Having sore or tired feet.

foot·step (fŏŏt′step′) *n.* 1. The action of taking a step with the foot. 2. The distance covered by a step. 3. The sound made by a foot in stepping. 4. A footprint. 5. A step of a stairway, etc.

foot·stool (fŏŏt′stōōl′) *n.* A low stool used as a footrest.

foot·wear (fŏŏt′wâr′) *n.* Articles worn on the feet, as shoes.

foot·work (fŏŏt′wûrk′) *n.* Use or control of the feet, as in boxing or tennis.

fop (fop) *n.* A man overly concerned with fashion; a dandy. [ME, a fool. Akin to Du. *foppen* to cheat] **—fop′pish** *adj.* **—fop′pish·ly** *adv.* **—fop′pish·ness** *n.*

fop·per·y (fop′ər·ē) *n. pl.* **·per·ies** 1. The conduct or ways of a fop. 2. Something worn by or typical of a fop.

for (fôr, *unstressed* fər) *prep.* 1. To the extent of: The ground is flat *for* miles. 2. Through the duration of: *for* a week. 3. To the number or amount of: a check *for* six dollars. 4. At the cost or payment of: a hat *for* ten dollars. 5. On account of. 6. In honor of: He is named *for* his grandfather. 7. Appropriate to. 8. In place of: using a book *for* a desk. 9. In favor, support, or approval of. 10. In the interest or behalf of. 11. Directed toward: an eye *for* bargains. 12. As affecting (in a particular way): good *for* your health. 13. Sent, given, or assigned to. 14. In proportion to: big *for* his age. 15. As the equivalent to or requital of: blow *for* blow. 16. In spite of. 17. In order to reach or go toward. 18. In order to find or obtain: looking *for* a hat. 19. At (a particular time or occasion): to meet *for* the last time. 20. As being or seeming: We took him *for* an honest man. 21. In consideration of the usual characteristics of: She is tall *for* a woman. 22. With the purpose of. **—*conj.*** Inasmuch as; because. [OE]

for-[1] *prefix* 1. Away; off: *forget, forgo.* 2. Very; extremely: *forlorn.* [OE]

for-[2] See FORE-[1].

for·age (fôr′ij, for′-) *n.* 1. Food suitable for cattle or other domestic animals; fodder. 2. A search or raid to find food or supplies. **—*v.*** **·aged, ·ag·ing** *v.i.* 1. To search about, esp. for food or supplies. 2. To make a raid to get supplies. **—*v.t.*** 3. To search through for food, supplies, etc. 4. To obtain by a search or raid. 5. To provide with food or supplies. [< OF *feurre* fodder] **—for′ag·er** *n.*

fo·ra·men (fō·rā′mən) *n. pl.* **·ram·i·na** (-ram′ə·nə) *Biol.* A small opening or hole, usu. natural, as in a bone. [< L *forare* to bore]

for·as·much as (fôr′əz·much′) Inasmuch as; since.

for·ay (fôr′ā, for′ā) *v.t. & v.i.* To plunder; raid. **—*n.*** An expedition or raid, as for plunder. [< OF *forrier* plunderer] **—for′·ay·er** *n.*

for·bear[1] (fôr·bâr′) *v.* **·bore, ·borne, ·bear·ing** *v.t.* 1. To refrain or abstain from (some action). 2. To cease or desist from. **—*v.i.*** 3. To abstain. 4. To be patient. [OE] **—for·bear′ance** *n.* **—for·bear′er** *n.*

for·bear[2] (fôr′bâr′) See FOREBEAR.

for·bear·ing (fôr·bâr′ing) *adj.* Patient.

for·bid (fər·bid′, fôr-) *v.t.* **·bade** (-bad′) or **·bad, ·bid·den** (*Archaic* **·bid**), **·bid·ding** 1. To command (a person) not to do something, etc.; prohibit from doing, having, etc. 2. To prohibit the doing, use, etc., of. 3. To have the effect of preventing; hinder. [OE *forbēodan*] **—for·bid′dance** *n.*

for·bid·ding (fər·bid′ing, fôr-) *adj.* 1. Grim and unfriendly. 2. Threatening; ominous. **—for·bid′ding·ly** *adv.*

for·bore (fôr·bôr′) Past tense of FORBEAR[1].

for·borne (fôr·bôrn′) Past participle of FORBEAR[1].

force (fôrs) *n.* 1. Power or energy; strength. 2. Power exerted on any resisting person or thing; coercion. 3. Power or influence; ability to produce an effect. 4. A body of individuals belonging to one of a nation's military divisions: the armed *forces.* 5. Any body of individuals organized for some specific work: police *force.* 6. *Law* Binding effect; validity. 7. *Physics* Anything that changes or tends to change the state of rest or motion in a body. **—in (full) force** 1. Still operative. 2. With no one missing. *—v.t.* **forced, forc·ing** 1. To compel; coerce. 2. To get or obtain by or as by force. 3. To bring forth or about by or as by effort. 4. To drive or move despite resistance. 5. To assault and capture, as a fortification. 6. To open by force, as a passage or lock. 7. To press or impose upon someone as by force. 8. To stimulate the growth of artificially, as plants in a hothouse. [< L *fortis* brave, strong] **—for′ci·ble** *adj.* **—for′ci·ble·ness** *n.* **—for′·ci·bly** *adv.*

forced (fôrst) *adj.* 1. Done under force; compulsory. 2. Strained; affected: *forced* gaiety. 3. Done in an emergency.

force·ful (fôrs′fəl) *adj.* Full of or done with force; vigorous; effective. **—force′ful·ly** *adv.* **—force′ful·ness** *n.*

force·meat (fôrs′mēt′) *n.* Finely chopped, seasoned meat. [< *force*, alter. of F *farse* stuffing + MEAT]

for·ceps (fôr′səps) *n. pl.* **for·ceps** A pair of pincers used in surgery, dentistry, etc. [< L *formus* warm + *capere* to take]

ford (fôrd) *n.* A shallow place in a stream, river, etc., that can be crossed by wading. *—v.t.* To cross (a river, stream, etc.) at a shallow place. [OE] **—ford′a·ble** *adj.*

fore (fôr) *adj.* Situated at or toward the front; anterior. *—n.* 1. The front part of something. 2. *Naut.* A foremast; also, the bow of a ship. **—to the fore** 1. To or at the front part of something. 2. In or into a prominent or conspicuous position. *—interj.* In golf, a cry made to warn anyone standing in the line of a ball. *—adv. Naut.* At or toward the bow of a ship. *—prep. & conj. Archaic* or *Dial.* Before: also **'fore**. [OE, adv. & prep.]

fore-[1] *prefix*
1. Prior in time or place:

foreacquaint	**fore-exercise**
foreanswer	**foreglimpse**
foreconclude	**forenotice**
foreconclusion	**forepayment**

2. Situated at or near the front:

forebody	**forecourt**
forebrain	**foredeck**
forecabin	**fore-edge**

fore-[2] See FOR-[1].

fore-and-aft (fôr′ən·aft′) *adj. Naut.* Lying or going in the direction of a ship's length: a *fore-and-aft* sail.

fore·arm[1] (fôr′ärm′) *n.* The part of the arm between the elbow and the wrist.

fore·arm[2] (fôr·ärm′) *v.t.* To arm beforehand.

fore·bear (fôr′bâr) *n.* An ancestor: also spelled *forbear.* [Earlier *for-be-er*]

fore·bode (fôr·bōd′) *v.t. & v.i.* **·bod·ed, ·bod·ing** 1. To indicate in advance; portend. 2. To have a premonition of (something evil or harmful). [< FORE-[1] + BODE]

fore·cast (fôr′kast′) *v.t.* **·cast** or **·cast·ed, ·cast·ing** 1. To calculate beforehand, esp. to predict (weather conditions). 2. To foreshadow. *—n.* A prediction or prophecy. **—fore′cast′er** *n.*

fore·cas·tle (fōk′səl) *n. Naut.* 1. That part of the upper deck of a ship located forward of the mast nearest the bow. 2. A section of a merchant ship near the bow, in which the sailors' living quarters are located. Also spelled *fo'c's'le.*

fore·close (fôr·klōz′) *v.* **·closed, ·clos·ing** *v.t.* 1. *Law* **a** To deprive (a mortgagor in default) of the right to redeem mortgaged property. **b** To take away the power to redeem (a mortgage or pledge). 2. To shut out; exclude. *—v.i.* 3. To foreclose a mortgage. [< OF *forclore* to exclude] **—fore·clo′sure** (-klō′zhər) *n.*

fore·doom (fôr·dōōm′) *v.t.* To doom or condemn in advance.

fore·fa·ther (fôr′fä′thər) *n.* An ancestor.

fore·fin·ger (fôr′fing′gər) *n.* The index finger.

fore·foot (fôr′fōōt′) *n. pl.* **·feet** 1. A front foot of an animal. 2. *Naut.* The part of a boat where prow and keel meet.

fore·front (fôr′frunt′) *n.* 1. The very front of something. 2. The position of most prominence, activity, etc.

fore·go[1] (fôr·gō′) *v.t. & v.i.* **·went, ·gone, ·go·ing** To precede in time, place, etc. [OE *foregān*]

fore·go[2] (fôr·gō′) See FORGO.

fore·go·ing (fôr·gō′ing, fôr′gō′ing) *adj.* Previous; preceding; antecedent.

fore·gone (fôr·gôn′, fôr′gôn′) *adj.* Already gone, finished, or determined.

fore·ground (fôr′ground′) *n.* 1. The part of a landscape, picture, etc., nearest or represented as nearest to the spectator. 2. The position of most prominence or activity.

fore·hand (fôr′hand′) *adj.* 1. Of or pertaining to a stroke in tennis, etc., in which the palm of the hand faces the direction of the stroke. 2. First or foremost; leading. **—fore′hand′** *n.*

fore·hand·ed (fôr′han′did) *adj.* 1. Prudent; thrifty. 2. Done in good time. 3. Forehand (*def. 1*). **—fore′hand′ed·ness** *n.*

fore·head (fôr′id, for′-; *occasionally* fôr′hed′) *n.* The part of the face from the eyebrows to the hair. ◆Collateral adjective: *frontal.*

for·eign (fôr′in, for′-) *adj.* 1. Belonging to, located in, characteristic of, or concerned with another country, region, society, etc. 2. Unfamiliar; strange. 3. Occurring in a place or context in which it is not normally found. [< F *forain*, ult. < L *foras* out of doors]

for·eign·er (fôr′in·ər, for′-) *n.* A native or citizen of a foreign country or region; alien.

fore·judge (fôr·juj′) *v.t. & v.i.* **·judged, ·judg·ing** To judge in advance.

fore·know (fôr·nō′) *v.t.* **·knew, ·known, ·know·ing** To know beforehand. **—fore′·knowl′edge** (-nol′ij) *n.*

fore·land (fôr′land′) *n.* A projecting point of land.

fore·leg (fôr′leg′) *n.* A front leg of an animal. Also **fore′limb′** (-lim′).

fore·lock (fôr′lok′) *n.* A lock of hair growing over the forehead.

fore·man (fôr′mən) *n. pl.* **·men** (-mən) 1. The overseer of a body of workers. 2. The chairman and spokesman of a jury. **—fore′·man·ship** *n.*

fore·mast (fôr′mast′, -məst) *n. Naut.* The mast that is closest to the bow of a ship.

fore·most (fôr′mōst) *adj.* First in place, rank, etc.; chief. [OE *formest*] **—fore′most** *adv.*

fore·named (fôr′nāmd′) *adj.* Previously named or mentioned; aforesaid.

fore·noon (fôr′no͞on′) *n.* The period of daylight preceding midday; morning.
fo·ren·sic (fə·ren′sik) *adj.* Relating to, characteristic of, or used in courts of law or public debate. [< L *forensis* public < *forum* marketplace, forum] **—fo·ren′si·cal·ly** *adv.*
fore·or·dain (fôr′ôr·dān′) *v.t.* 1. To decree or appoint in advance. 2. To fix the fate of in advance. **—fore′or·dain′ment, fore·or·di·na·tion** (fôr·ôr′də·nā′shən) *n.*
fore·part (fôr′pärt′) *n.* The first part in time, place, or order. Also **fore part.**
fore·quar·ter (fôr′kwôr′tər) *n.* The front portion of a side of beef, etc.
fore·reach (fôr·rēch′) *v.t. & v.i.* To catch up with or get ahead of, as a ship.
fore·run·ner (fôr·run′ər, fôr′run′ər) *n.* 1. One who or that which precedes another; also, an ancestor. 2. One who proclaims the coming of another. 3. An omen.
fore·sail (fôr′sāl′, -səl, fō′səl) *n. Naut.* 1. The lowest sail on the foremast of a square-rigged vessel. 2. The fore-and-aft sail on a schooner's foremast.
fore·see (fôr·sē′) *v.t.* **·saw, ·seen, ·see·ing** To see or know in advance. **—fore·see′a·ble** *adj.*
fore·shad·ow (fôr·shad′ō) *v.t.* To give an advance indication of; presage.
fore·shore (fôr′shôr′) *n.* That part of a shore uncovered at low tide.
fore·short·en (fôr·shôr′tən) *v.t.* In drawing, to shorten parts of (an object) so as to create the illusion of depth and distance.
fore·sight (fôr′sīt′) *n.* 1. The act or capacity of foreseeing. 2. Prudent anticipation of the future. **—fore′sight′ed** *adj.* **—fore′sight′ed·ly** *adv.* **—fore′sight′ed·ness** *n.*
fore·skin (fôr′skin′) *n. Anat.* The prepuce.
for·est (fôr′ist, for′-) *n.* A large tract of land covered with trees; also, the trees themselves. **—*adj.*** Of, pertaining to, or inhabiting forests. **—*v.t.*** To plant with trees; make a forest of. [< Med.L (*silva*) *foresta* an unenclosed (wood)]
fore·stall (fôr·stôl′) *v.t.* 1. To hinder, prevent, or guard against in advance. 2. To deal with or realize beforehand; anticipate. [OE *foresteall* ambush]
for·est·a·tion (fôr′is·tā′shən, for′-) *n.* 1. The planting of trees so as to make a forest. 2. The science of forestry.
fore·stay (fôr′stā′) *n. Naut.* A wire or rope running from the head of the foremast to the stem.
for·est·er (fôr′is·tər, for′-) *n.* 1. One skilled in forestry. 2. An animal dwelling in a forest.
for·est·ry (fôr′is·trē, for′-) *n.* 1. The science of forest management. 2. Forest land.
fore·taste (*n.* fôr′tāst′; *v.* fôr·tāst′) *n.* An advance experiencing of something. **—*v.t.*** To taste or experience in advance.
fore·tell (fôr·tel′) *v.t. & v.i.* **·told, ·tell·ing** To tell of or about in advance; predict; prophesy. **—fore·tell′er** *n.*
fore·thought (fôr′thôt′) *n.* 1. Advance consideration. 2. Prudence; foresight.
for·ev·er (fôr·ev′ər, fər-) *adv.* 1. Throughout eternity. 2. Incessantly; constantly.
for·ev·er·more (fôr·ev′ər·môr′, fər-) *adv.* Forever: an intensive form. Also **for evermore.**
fore·warn (fôr·wôrn′) *v.t.* To warn in advance.
fore·word (fôr′wûrd′) *n.* An introductory statement preceding the text of a book.
for·feit (fôr′fit) *n.* The giving up or loss of something as a penalty for an offense, etc.; also, that which is lost. **—*v.t.*** To incur the deprivation of as a penalty. **—*adj.*** Taken away or lost as a penalty. [< OF *forfait* misdeed] **—for′feit·a·ble** *adj.* **—for′feit·er** *n.*
for·fei·ture (fôr′fi·chər) *n.* 1. The giving up or loss of something by way of penalty. 2. That which is forfeited.
for·gath·er (fôr·gath′ər) *v.i.* 1. To meet or assemble. 2. To meet by chance. 3. To associate or converse socially.
for·gave (fər·gāv′, fôr-) Past tense of FORGIVE.
forge[1] (fôrj) *n.* 1. An apparatus for heating and softening metal. 2. A place in which such an apparatus is used. 3. A furnace for melting or refining metals. **—*v.* forged, forg·ing** *v.t.* 1. To heat (metal) in a forge and work into shape; also, to produce or form as if by hammering into shape. 2. To counterfeit (a signature, etc.). **—*v.i.*** 3. To produce a fraudulent imitation of something. 4. To work at a forge. [< OF, ult. < L *fabrica* fabric] **—forg′er** *n.*
forge[2] (fôrj) *v.i.* **forged, forg·ing** To advance despite difficulties, etc. [? Alter. of FORCE]
for·ger·y (fôr′jər·ē) *n. pl.* **·ger·ies** 1. The act of making fraudulent imitations. 2. A fraudulent imitation.
for·get (fər·get′, fôr-) *v.* **·got, ·got·ten** or **·got, ·get·ting** *v.t.* 1. To be unable to recall (something). 2. To neglect (to do or take something). 3. To lose interest in or regard for. **—*v.i.*** 4. To lose remembrance of something. **—to forget oneself** 1. To be unselfish. 2. To lose self-control. 3. To be lost in thought. [OE *forgietan*] **—for·get′ta·ble** *adj.*
for·get·ful (fər·get′fəl, fôr-) *adj.* 1. Inclined to forget. 2. Neglectful; inattentive. **—for·get′ful·ly** *adv.* **—for·get′ful·ness** *n.*
for·get-me-not (fər·get′mē·not′) *n.* A small herb having blue or white flowers.
for·give (fər·giv′, fôr-) *v.* **·gave, ·giv·en, ·giv·ing** *v.t.* 1. To grant pardon for or remission of (something). 2. To cease to blame or feel resentment against. 3. To remit, as a debt. **—*v.i.*** 4. To show forgiveness; grant pardon. [OE *forgiefan*] **—for·giv′a·ble** *adj.* **—for·giv′a·bly** *adv.* **—for·give′ness** *n.* **—for·giv′er** *n.*
for·giv·ing (fər·giv′ing, fôr-) *adj.* Disposed to forgive; merciful. **—for·giv′ing·ly** *adv.* **—for·giv′ing·ness** *n.*
for·go (fôr·gō′) *v.t.* **·went, ·gone, ·go·ing** To give up or refrain from; go without. Also spelled *forego.* [OE *forgān* to pass over] **—for·go′er** *n.*
for·got (fər·got′, fôr-) Past tense and alternative past participle of FORGET.
for·got·ten (fər·got′n, fôr-) Past participle of FORGET.
fork (fôrk) *n.* 1. An implement with two or more prongs; as: **a** A utensil used at table. **b** An agricultural tool used for digging, tossing, etc. 2. The division of something into branches; also, the point at which this division begins, or any one of the parts.

—*v.t.* 1. To convey, lift, etc., with a fork. 2. To give the shape of a fork to. —*v.i.* 3. To divide into branches. [< L *furca*]

forked (fôrkt, *Poetic* fôr′kid) *adj.* Having a fork or forking parts.

fork·lift (fôrk′lift′) *n.* A powered machine that lifts and moves heavy objects by means of a two-pronged platform inserted under the object.

for·lorn (fôr·lôrn′, fər-) *adj.* 1. Left in distress; abandoned. 2. Wretched; desolate. 3. Hopeless. [OE *forlēosan* to lose] —**for·lorn′ly** *adv.* —**for·lorn′ness** *n.*

form (fôrm) *n.* 1. The shape or contour of something. 2. The body of a living being. 3. A mold, frame, etc. 4. The particular state, character, etc., in which something presents itself. 5. A specific type or species. 6. The style or manner of a poem, play, picture, etc. 7. Proper arrangement or order. 8. The manner in which something is done: diving *form.* 9. A document having spaces for the insertion of names, dates, etc. 10. Mere outward formality; convention. 11. A model formula or draft, as of a letter. —*v.t.* 1. To give shape or form to; mold. 2. To devise, as a plan. 3. To combine or organize into, as a club. 4. To develop or acquire, as a habit. 5. To be an element of. —*v.i.* 6. To take shape; assume a specific pattern or arrangement. 7. To begin to exist. [< L *forma*] —**form′less** *adj.* —**form′less·ly** *adv.* —**form′less·ness** *n.*

-form *combining form* Like; in the shape of: *cuneiform.* [< L *-formis* -like < *forma* form]

for·mal (fôr′məl) *adj.* 1. Based on established methods or conventions. 2. Requiring elaborate detail, ceremony, dress, etc. 3. Appropriate for ceremonial occasions. 4. Binding and valid: a *formal* agreement. 5. Pertaining to external appearance or structure, as of a poem. 6. Pertaining to study in regular academic institutions. 7. Of language, more elaborate or stylized than common speech. —*n.* Something formal in character, as an evening gown. —**for′mal·ly** *adv.*

for·mal·de·hyde (fôr·mal′də·hīd) *n. Chem.* A colorless, pungent gas used in solution as an antiseptic, preservative, etc. [< FORM(IC) + ALDEHYDE]

for·mal·ism (fôr′məl·iz′əm) *n.* Scrupulous observance of prescribed forms. —**for′mal·ist** *n.* —**for′mal·is′tic** *adj.*

for·mal·i·ty (fôr·mal′ə·tē) *n. pl.* **·ties** 1. The state, quality, or practice of being formal. 2. Excessive devotion to outward form. 3. A proper or customary method, practice, or observance.

for·mal·ize (fôr′məl·īz) *v.* **·ized, ·iz·ing** *v.t.* 1. To make formal. 2. To give form to. —*v.i.* 3. To be formal; act formally. —**for′·mal·i·za′tion** *n.* —**for′mal·iz′er** *n.*

for·mat (fôr′mat) *n.* 1. The form, size, and general style of a publication. 2. The general form or arrangement of anything. —*v.t.* **·mat·ted, ·mat·ting** To provide with a format; produce in a specified form. [< F < L *formare* to form]

for·ma·tion (fôr·mā′shən) *n.* 1. The act or process of forming, or the state of being formed. 2. That which is formed. 3. The manner in which a thing is shaped or formed. 4. *Mil.* The arrangement of troops, tanks, aircraft, etc. 5. *Geol.* Mineral deposits, or rock masses, having common characteristics.

form·a·tive (fôr′mə·tiv) *adj.* 1. Having power to shape or mold: a *formative* influence. 2. Of or pertaining to formation or development: *formative* years.

for·mer (fôr′mər) *adj.* 1. Being the first of two persons or things referred to: often preceded by *the.* 2. Previous: my *former* colleague. 3. Earlier: *former* times. [ME *formere*]

for·mer·ly (fôr′mər·lē) *adv.* Some time or a long time ago.

for·mic (fôr′mik) *adj.* 1. Of or pertaining to ants. 2. Designating or derived from formic acid. [< L *formica* ant]

formic acid *Chem.* A colorless, corrosive compound, with a penetrating odor.

for·mi·da·ble (fôr′mi·də·bəl) *adj.* 1. Exciting fear or dread by reason of strength, size, etc. 2. Extremely difficult. [< L *formidare* to fear] —**for′mi·da·bil′i·ty, for′mi·da·ble·ness** *n.* —**for′mi·da·bly** *adv.*

form letter One of many reproductions of a letter, etc.

For·mo·san (fôr·mō′sən) *n.* 1. A native or inhabitant of the island of Formosa (Taiwan). 2. The Indonesian language of the Malay aborigines of Formosa. —**For·mo′san** *adj.*

for·mu·la (fôr′myə·lə) *n. pl.* **·las** or **·lae** (-lē) 1. An exact or prescribed method for doing something. 2. A fixed order or form of words. 3. A prescription or recipe; also, the mixture prepared. 4. A liquid milk substitute fed to babies. 5. *Math.* A rule or combination expressed in algebraic or symbolic form. 6. *Chem.* A symbolic representation of a chemical compound, as H_2SO_4, sulfuric acid. [< L, dim. of *forma* form]

for·mu·lar·ize (fôr′myə·lə·rīz′) *v.t.* **·ized, ·iz·ing** To formulate. —**for′mu·lar·i·za′tion** *n.*

for·mu·late (fôr′myə·lāt) *v.t.* **·lat·ed, ·lat·ing** 1. To express in a formula. 2. To express in a systematic form. 3. To prepare according to a formula. 4. To devise, as a policy. —**for′·mu·la′tion** *n.* —**for′mu·la′tor** *n.*

for·ni·cate (fôr′nə·kāt) *v.i.* **·cat·ed, ·cat·ing** To commit fornication. [< L *fornix, -icis* brothel] —**for′ni·ca′tor** *n.*

for·ni·ca·tion (fôr′nə·kā′shən) *n.* Voluntary sexual intercourse between unmarried persons.

for·sake (fôr·sāk′, fər-) *v.t.* **·sook, ·sak·en, ·sak·ing** 1. To renounce or relinquish. 2. To abandon; desert. [OE *forsacan* to repudiate]

for·sooth (fôr·sōōth′, fər-) *adv.* In truth; certainly. [OE]

for·swear (fôr·swâr′) *v.* **·swore, ·sworn, ·swear·ing** *v.t.* 1. To renounce or abandon emphatically or upon oath. 2. To deny absolutely. —*v.i.* 3. To swear falsely; commit perjury. [OE *forswerian*]

for·sworn (fôr·swôrn′) *adj.* Perjured.

for·syth·i·a (fôr·sith′ē·ə, fər-) *n.* A shrub having bright yellow flowers. [after William *Forsyth,* 1737–1804, British botanist]

fort (fôrt) *n.* 1. A fortified enclosure or structure for military defense. 2. A permanent U.S. army post. [< F, orig. adj. strong]

forte[1] (fôrt, fôr′tā) *n.* That which one does with excellence. [See FORT.]
for·te[2] (fôr′tā, -tē) *adj.* *Music* Loud; forceful. [< Ital.] **—for′te** *adv.*
forth (fôrth) *adv.* 1. Forward in place, time, or order. 2. Out, as from seclusion, confinement, or inaction. 3. Away or out, as from a place of origin; abroad. **—and so forth** And the rest; and so on. [OE]
forth·com·ing (fôrth′kum′ing) *adj.* 1. Drawing near in time. 2. Ready or about to appear, arrive, etc. 3. Available or produced when expected or due. **—***n.* Arrival or appearance of something due or expected.
forth·right (fôrth′rīt′) *adj.* 1. Candid; frank. 2. Going forward in a straight line; direct. **—forth′right′ly** *adv.* **—forth′right′ness** *n.*
forth·with (fôrth′with′, -with′) *adv.* Immediately.
for·ti·fi·ca·tion (fôr′tə·fə·kā′shən) *n.* 1. The act, art, or science of fortifying. 2. That which fortifies, as walls, ditches, etc. 3. A military place of defense.
for·ti·fy (fôr′tə·fī) *v.* **·fied, ·fy·ing** *v.t.* 1. To strengthen or reinforce, esp. against attack. 2. To give physical or moral strength to. 3. To confirm. 4. To strengthen, as wine, by adding alcohol. 5. To enrich (food) by adding minerals, vitamins, etc. **—***v.i.* 6. To raise defensive works. [< L *fortis* strong + -FY] **—for′ti·fi′a·ble** *adj.* **—for′ti·fi′er** *n.*
for·tis·si·mo (fôr·tis′ə·mō, *Ital.* fôr·tēs′sē·mō) *Music adj.* Very loud. **—***adv.* Very loudly. **—***n. pl.* **·mos** A fortissimo note, chord, or passage. [< Ital., superl. of *forte* strong]
for·ti·tude (fôr′tə·to͞od, -tyo͞od) *n.* Courage and strength of mind in the face of adversity or peril. **—for′ti·tu′di·nous** (-də·nəs) *adj.*
fort·night (fôrt′nīt′, -nit′) *n.* Two weeks. [OE *fēowertēne* fourteen + *niht* nights] **—fort′night′ly** *adj. & adv.*
for·tress (fôr′tris) *n.* 1. A fortified place. 2. Any place of security. [< OF < L *fortis* strong] **—for′tress** *v.t.*
for·tu·i·tous (fôr·to͞o′ə·təs, -tyo͞o′-) *adj.* Occurring by chance rather than by design; accidental. [< L *fors, fortis* chance] **—for·tu′i·tous·ly** *adv.* **—for·tu′i·tous·ness** *n.*
for·tu·i·ty (fôr·to͞o′ə·tē, -tyo͞o′-) *n. pl.* **·ties** Chance occurrence; also, chance.
for·tu·nate (fôr′chə·nit) *adj.* 1. Happening by a favorable chance; lucky. 2. Favored with good fortune. **—for′tu·nate·ly** *adv.* **—for′tu·nate·ness** *n.*
for·tune (fôr′chən) *n.* 1. That which happens or is to happen to one, whether good or bad. 2. Luck or chance, esp. when favorable. 3. An amount of wealth or possessions. 4. A particular condition or state of life, usu. prosperous. [< L *fortuna* < *fors* chance]
for·tune·tell·er (fôr′chən·tel′ər) *n.* One who claims to foretell events in a person's future. **—for′tune·tell′ing** *n. & adj.*
for·ty (fôr′tē) *n. pl.* **·ties** The sum of thirty and ten: a cardinal number written 40, XL. [OE *fēowertig*] **—for′ty** *adj.* **—for′ti·eth** *adj. & n.*
forty winks *Informal* A short nap.
fo·rum (fôr′əm) *n. pl.* **fo·rums** or **fo·ra** 1. The public marketplace of an ancient Roman city, where legal and political business was transacted. 2. A tribunal; court. 3. An assembly for discussion of public affairs. [< L]
for·ward (fôr′wərd) *adv.* 1. Toward what is ahead or in front; onward. Also **for′wards.** 2. At or in the front part, as of a ship. 3. Out into a conspicuous position; to the forefront. **—forward of** In front of. **—***adj.* 1. Being at or near the front. 2. Moving or directed toward a point lying ahead. 3. Bold or presumptuous. 4. Developing or developed earlier than usual; precocious. 5. Extremely progressive or unconventional, as in political opinions. 6. Made or done in advance. **—***n.* In basketball, hockey, etc., a player, usu. offensive, in a forward position. **—***v.t.* 1. To help onward or ahead. 2. To send onward; esp., to send (mail) on to a new address. [OE *foreweard*] **—for′ward·er** *n.* **—for′ward·ly** *adv.* **—for′ward·ness** *n.*
fos·sil (fos′əl) *n.* 1. The remains of plants or animals, preserved in the rocks of the earth's crust. 2. Some petrified trace of the existence of an early organism, as a petrified footprint. 3. *Informal* One who or that which is out of date. [< L *fossilis* < *fodire* to dig] **—fos′sil** *adj.*
fos·sil·ize (fos′əl·īz) *v.* **·ized, ·iz·ing** *v.t.* 1. To change into a fossil; petrify. 2. To make antiquated or out of date. **—***v.i.* 3. To become a fossil. **—fos′sil·i·za′tion** *n.*
fos·ter (fôs′tər, fos′-) *v.t.* 1. To bring up (a child); rear. 2. To promote the growth or development of: to *foster* genius. 3. To keep alive (feelings, hopes, etc.) within oneself; cherish. [OE *fōstrian* nourish] **—fos′ter·age** *n.*
foster child A child reared by a foster parent or parents.
foster parent One bringing up a child not one's own by birth or adoption.
fought (fôt) Past tense and past participle of FIGHT.
foul (foul) *adj.* 1. Offensive or revolting to the senses; disgusting. 2. Full of dirt or impure matter; filthy. 3. Spoiled or rotten, as food. 4. Unfavorable; adverse: *foul* weather. 5. Obscene; vulgar. 6. Morally offensive; wicked. 7. Unjust; unfair. 8. Impeded or entangled: a *foul* anchor. 9. In baseball, etc., designating boundary lines (**foul lines**) in a playing area; also, designating a ball that falls outside these lines. 10. *Informal* Very bad; unsatisfactory. **—***n.* 1. An act of fouling, colliding, or becoming entangled. 2. In baseball, a ball batted outside of the foul lines: also **foul ball.** 3. A breach of rule in various sports. **—***v.t.* 1. To make foul or dirty. 2. To dishonor; disgrace. 3. To clog or choke, as a drain. 4. To entangle or snarl, as a rope. 5. To cover or encumber (a ship's bottom) with barnacles, seaweed, etc. 6. To collide with. 7. In sports, to commit a foul against. 8. In baseball, to bat (the ball) outside of the foul lines. **—***v.i.* 9. To become foul or dirty. 10. To become clogged or encumbered. 11. To become entangled. 12. To collide. 13. In sports, to violate a rule. 14. In baseball, to bat a foul ball. **—to foul up** *Slang* 1. To throw into disorder or confusion. 2. To blunder. [OE *fūl*] **—foul′ly** *adv.* **—foul′ness** *n.*
fou·lard (fo͞o·lärd′) *n.* 1. A lightweight,

satiny fabric, usu. with a printed design. 2. A scarf, necktie, or other article made of this fabric. [< F]
foul·mouthed (foul′mouthd′, -moutht′) *adj.* Using abusive, profane, or obscene language.
foul play 1. In games and sports, a violation of rule. 2. Any unfair or treacherous action.
foul-up (foul′up′) *n.* 1. A mix-up; a state of confusion. 2. A mechanical failure.
found[1] (found) *v.t.* 1. To originate or establish. 2. To lay the foundation of. —*v.i.* 3. To be established or based: with *on, upon.* [< L *fundus* base, bottom]
found[2] (found) *v.t.* 1. To cast, as iron, by melting and pouring into a mold. 2. To make by casting molten metal. [< L *fundere* to pour]
found[3] (found) Past tense and past participle of FIND.
foun·da·tion (foun·dā′shən) *n.* 1. The act of founding or establishing. 2. The state of being founded or established. 3. That on which anything is founded; basis. 4. A base on which a structure rests or is built. 5. A fund for the maintenance of an institution; an endowment. 6. An endowed institution. 7. A foundation garment. —**foun·da′tion·al** *adj.*
foundation garment A girdle or corset.
found·er[1] (foun′dər) *n.* One who establishes.
found·er[2] (foun′dər) *n.* One who makes metal castings.
foun·der[3] (foun′dər) *v.i.* 1. To sink after filling with water, as a boat. 2. To fall or cave in, as land or buildings. 3. To fail completely; collapse. 4. To stumble and become lame, as a horse. —*v.t.* 5. To cause to sink. —*n.* The act of foundering. [< L *fundus* bottom]
found·ling (found′ling) *n.* A deserted infant of unknown parentage. [ME *funde*, pp. of *find*]
foun·dry (foun′drē) *n. pl.* **·dries** An establishment in which metal, etc., is cast.
fount (fount) *n.* 1. A fountain. 2. Any source. [< L *fons, fontis*]
foun·tain (foun′tən) *n.* 1. A spring or jet of water issuing from the earth. 2. The origin or source of anything. 3. A jet or spray of water forced upward artificially. 4. A basinlike structure for such a jet to rise and fall in. [< LL *fontana*, orig. fem. singular of L *fontanus* of a spring]
foun·tain·head (foun′tən·hed′) *n.* 1. A spring from which a stream takes its source. 2. Any source or origin.
fountain pen A pen having a refillable reservoir of ink which feeds the writing end.
four (fôr) *n.* The sum of three and one: a cardinal number written 4, IV. —**on all fours** 1. On hands and knees. 2. On all four feet. [OE *fēower*] —**four** *adj.* —**fourth** (fôrth) *adj. & n.*
four-di·men·sion·al (fôr′di·men′shən·əl) *adj. Math.* Requiring four sets of coordinates for spatial determination.
four·flush·er (fôr′flush′ər) *n. Slang* A fake or cheat.
four·hand·ed (fôr′han′did) *adj* 1. Designed for four players. 2. Designed for performance by two persons, as a piano duet.
four hundred The most exclusive social group of a place.
four-in-hand (fôr′in·hand′) *n.* 1. A four-horse team driven by one person. 2. A vehicle drawn by such a team. 3. A necktie tied in a slip knot with the ends hanging.
four-leaf clover (fôr′lēf′) A clover with four leaflets, supposed to bring good luck.
four-post·er (fôr′pōs′tər) *n.* A bedstead with four tall posts at the corners and typically with a canopy or curtains.
four·some (fôr′səm) *n.* 1. A game, esp. of golf, in which four players take part, two on each side; also, the players in such a game. 2. Any group of four.
four·square (fôr′skwâr′) *adj.* 1. Having four equal sides; square. 2. Firm; solid. 3. Forthright; direct. —*n.* A square. —*adv.* Squarely; bluntly.
four·teen (fôr′tēn′) *n.* The sum of thirteen and one: a cardinal number written 14, XIV. [OE *fēowertēne*] —**four′teen′** *adj.* —**four′·teenth′** *adj. & n.*
fourth dimension A hypothetical dimension in addition to height, width, and thickness. —**fourth′-di·men′sion·al** *adj.*
fourth estate The public press; journalism.
fourth·ly (fôrth′lē) *adv.* In the fourth place.
Fourth of July Independence Day.
fowl (foul) *n. pl.* **fowl** or **fowls** 1. The common domestic hen or cock; a chicken. 2. Any related bird, as the duck, goose, etc. 3. The flesh of fowl. 4. Birds collectively. —*v.i.* To catch or hunt wild fowl. [OE *fugol*] —**fowl′er** *n.*
fowl·ing (fou′ling) *n.* The hunting of birds for sport.
fowling piece A light gun used for shooting birds.
fox (foks) *n.* 1. Any of several small, wild mammals of the dog family, having long, pointed muzzles, bushy tails, and erect ears, esp. the **red fox** of North America, having a reddish brown fur. ◆Collateral adjective: *vulpine.* 2. The fur of the fox. 3. A sly, crafty person. —*v.t. & v.i.* To trick; outwit; act slyly or cunningly. [OE]
fox·glove (foks′gluv′) *n.* A plant of the figwort family, cultivated as a source of digitalis.
fox·hole (foks′hōl′) *n.* A shallow pit dug as cover against enemy fire.
fox·hound (foks′hound′) *n.* A large, strong, very swift dog trained for fox hunting.
fox·tail (foks′tāl′) *n.* 1. The tail of a fox. 2. Any of various species of grass bearing a spike of flowers resembling a fox's tail.
fox terrier A small, white terrier with dark markings.
fox-trot (foks′trot′) *v.i.* **-trot·ted, -trot·ting** To do a fox trot.
fox trot A ballroom dance in 2/4 or 4/4 time.
fox·y (fok′sē) *adj.* **fox·i·er, fox·i·est** 1. Wily; cunning. 2. *Slang* Sexually attractive: said of a woman. —**fox′i·ly** *adv.* —**fox′i·ness** *n.*
foy·er (foi′ər, foi′ā; *Fr.* fwȧ·yā′) *n.* An entrance room, hall, or public lobby. [< F]
fra·cas (frā′kəs, frak′əs) *n.* A noisy disturbance or dispute; brawl. [< F < Ital. *fracassare* to shatter]
frac·tion (frak′shən) *n.* 1. A disconnected part of anything; small portion; fragment. 2. *Math.* A quantity less than a whole number, expressed as a decimal (0.25) or with numerator and denominator ($\frac{1}{2}$ or 1/4).

3. *Chem.* One of the components separated from a substance by distilling, etc. **—*v.t.*** To set or separate into fractions. [< L *fractus*, pp. of *frangere* to break] **—frac′tion·al** *adj.*

frac·tion·ate (frak′shən·āt) *v.t.* **·at·ed, ·at·ing** To separate into fractions; divide; break up. **—frac′tion·a′tion** *n.* **—frac′tion·al·ly** *adv.*

frac·tious (frak′shəs) *adj.* 1. Apt to be unruly or rebellious. 2. Easily annoyed or angered. [< FRACTION, in obs. sense of discord] **—frac′tious·ly** *adv.* **—frac′tious·ness** *n.*

frac·ture (frak′chər) *n.* 1. The act of breaking, or the state of being broken. 2. A break; crack; rupture. 3. *Med.* The breaking or cracking of a bone. **—*v.t.* & *v.i.* ·tured, ·tur·ing** To break or be broken; crack. [< L *fractura* a breaking] **—frac′tur·al** *adj.*

frag (frag) *v.t.* **fragged, frag·ging** *Mil. Slang* To kill or attempt to kill (one's superior officer). [< *frag(mentation grenade)*, a weapon so used]

frag·ile (fraj′əl) *adj.* Easily broken or damaged; frail; delicate. [< L *frangere* to break] **—frag′ile·ly** *adv.* **—fra·gil·i·ty** (frə·jil′ə·tē), **frag′ile·ness** *n.*

frag·ment (*n.* frag′mənt; *v.* frag·ment′) *n.* 1. A part broken off; a small detached portion. 2. A part or portion of something unfinished: a *fragment* of a novel. **—*v.t.* & *v.i.*** To break into fragments. [< L *fragmentum*] **—frag′·men·ta′tion** *n.* **—frag′ment·ed** *adj.*

frag·men·tar·y (frag′mən·ter′ē) *adj.* Composed of fragments; broken; incomplete. Also **frag·men′tal** (-men′təl). **—frag′men·tar′i·ly** *adv.* **—frag′men·tar′i·ness** *n.*

frag·ment·ize (frag′mən·tīz) *v.t.* & *v.i.* **·ized, ·iz·ing** To fragment.

fra·grant (frā′grənt) *adj.* Having an agreeable or sweet smell. [< L *fragrare* to smell sweet] **—fra′grance** *n.* **—fra′grant·ly** *adv.*

frail (frāl) *adj.* 1. Delicately constituted; weak. 2. Fragile. 3. Deficient in moral strength. [< L *fragilis*] **—frail′ly** *adv.* **—frail′ness** *n.*

frail·ty (frāl′tē) *n. pl.* **·ties** 1. The state or quality of being frail. 2. A moral weakness.

frame (frām) *n.* 1. A case or border made to enclose something, as a picture. 2. A supporting structure surrounding something, as around a window or door. 3. A framework; skeleton. 4. The general arrangement, structure, or constitution of a thing. 5. Bodily structure or build, esp. of the human body. 6. A machine built in the form of or utilizing a framework: a silk *frame*. 7. In bowling, one of the ten divisions of the game. 8. One of the individual pictures on a roll of motion-picture film, in a comic strip, or in a series of television images. 9. A minimal unit in a programmed instruction series, usu. requiring response from a student. **—frame of mind** Mental state; mood. **—*v.t.* framed, fram·ing** 1. To surround with or put into a frame, as a picture. 2. To put together: to *frame* a shelter. 3. To put into words; utter. 4. To conceive or devise (a theory, law, etc.). 5. *Slang* To incriminate falsely. [OE *framian* to be of service to, provide for] **—fram′er** *n.*

frame house A house built on a wooden framework covered by shingles, boards, etc.

frame-up (frām′up′) *n. Slang* A conspiracy to convict a person on a false charge.

frame·work (frām′wûrk′) *n.* 1. A structure for supporting or enclosing something; also, frames, collectively. 2. The basic structure of something: the *framework* of society.

franc (frangk) *n.* 1. The standard monetary unit of France and various other countries. 2. A coin of this denomination. [< Med.L *Franc(orum rex)* (king of the) Franks, the motto on the earliest of these coins]

fran·chise (fran′chīz) *n.* 1. The right to vote; suffrage. 2. A right or privilege granted by a governing body to an individual or a corporate group. 3. Authorization given by a manufacturer to market his products. 4. The territory over which any of these privileges or dispensations extend. [< OF *franc*, *franche* free] **—fran′chised** *adj.*

Fran·cis·can (fran·sis′kən) *n.* A member of the mendicant order founded in 1209 by St. Francis of Assisi. **—*adj.*** 1. Of or pertaining to St. Francis. 2. Belonging to a religious order following his rule.

fran·ci·um (fran′sē·əm) *n.* A radioactive element (symbol Fr), isolated from actinium. [after *France*]

Franco- *combining form* French. [< L *Francus* a Frank]

fran·gi·ble (fran′jə·bəl) *adj.* Easily broken; brittle. [< L *frangere* to break] **—fran′gi·bil′i·ty, fran′gi·ble·ness** *n.*

Fran·glais (fräṅ·glā′) *n.* French containing English words. [< F *Fran(çais)* + *(An)glais*]

frank[1] (frangk) *adj.* 1. Completely honest and unreserved; candid. 2. Unconcealed: *frank* hostility. **—*v.t.*** To mark (a letter, package, etc.) in indication that no charge is to be made for delivery; also, to send (a letter, etc.) marked in this way. **—*n.*** 1. The right to send mail without charge. 2. The mark used to indicate this right. [< OF *franc* frank, free] **—frank′ly** *adv.* **—frank′ness** *n.*

frank[2] (frangk) *n. Informal* A frankfurter.

Frank (frangk) *n.* A member of one of the Germanic tribes of the early Christian era. [< L *Francus* a Frank < Gmc., a spear]

Frank·en·stein (frangk′ən·stīn) *n.* 1. A manlike monster. 2. Anything that destroys its own creator. [after *Frankenstein*, a novel (1818) by Mary Wollstonecraft Shelley]

frank·furt·er (frangk′fər·tər) *n.* A smoked sausage made of beef or beef and pork. [after *Frankfurt*, Germany]

frank·in·cense (frangk′in·sens) *n.* An aromatic gum or resin from various trees of East Africa. [< OF *franc* pure + *encens* incense]

Frank·ish (frang′kish) *adj.* Of or pertaining to the Franks. **—*n.*** The West Germanic language of the Franks.

fran·tic (fran′tik) *adj.* 1. Nearly driven out of one's mind, as with grief, fear, or rage. 2. Madly excited. [See FRENETIC.] **—fran′ti·cal·ly** or **fran′tic·ly** *adv.*

frap·pé (fra·pā′) *adj.* Iced; chilled. **—*n.*** 1. A fruit juice or other beverage frozen to a soft, mushy consistency. 2. A liqueur or other beverage poured over shaved ice. [< F, pp. of *frapper* to chill]

frat (frat) *n. Informal* A college fraternity.

fra·ter·nal (frə·tûr′nəl) *adj.* 1. Pertaining to or befitting a brother; brotherly. 2. Of or pertaining to a brotherhood or society.

3. *Genetics* Designating either of a pair of twins that develop from separately fertilized ova: distinguished from *identical*. [< L *frater* brother] **—fra·ter′nal·ism** *n.* **—fra·ter′nal·ly** *adv.*

fra·ter·ni·ty (frə·tûr′nə·tē) *n.* *pl.* **·ties** 1. The state of being brothers; also, the spirit of fraternal regard or affection. 2. In U.S. schools, a society of male students. 3. Any brotherhood or similar society. 4. A body of people sharing the same interests, profession, etc.

frat·er·nize (frat′ər·nīz) *v.i.* **·nized, ·niz·ing** 1. To associate with someone in a comradely way. 2. To mingle intimately with one's enemies or opponents, or with citizens of a conquered country. **—frat′er·ni·za′tion** *n.* **—frat′er·niz′er** *n.*

frat·ri·cide (frat′rə·sīd) *n.* 1. The killing of one's brother. 2. One who has killed his brother. [< L *frater* brother + *caedere* to kill] **—frat′ri·ci′dal** *adj.*

Frau (frou) *n* *pl.* **Frau·en** (-ən) *German* A married woman; wife: as a title, the equivalent of *Mrs.*

fraud (frôd) *n.* 1. Willful deceit; trickery. 2. An instance of this. 3. A deceptive or spurious person or thing. [< L *fraus, fraudis* deceit]

fraud·u·lent (frô′jə·lənt) *adj.* 1. Practicing or given to fraud; dishonest or deceitful. 2. Proceeding from, obtained by, or characterized by fraud. **—fraud′u·lence, fraud′u·len·cy** *n.* **—fraud′u·lent·ly** *adv.*

fraught (frôt) *adj.* Filled; laden: with *with*: a task *fraught* with danger. [< MDu. *vrachten* freight]

Fräu·lein (froi′līn) *n. German* An unmarried woman: as a title, the equivalent of *Miss.*

fray[1] (frā) *n.* Conflict; fight; also a noisy uproar or disturbance. [< OF *effrei*]

fray[2] (frā) *v.t.* 1. To cause (cloth, rope, etc.) to become worn by friction. 2. To wear holes in (cloth, etc.) by rubbing or chafing. *—v.i.* 3. To become frayed. *—n.* A frayed place, as of a sleeve. [< F *frayer* < L *fricare* to rub]

fraz·zle (fraz′əl) *Informal* *v.t. & v.i.* **·zled, ·zling** 1. To fray, or become frayed or tattered. 2. To tire out; weary. *—n.* The state of being frazzled. [? Blend of FRAY[2] + obs. *fasel* to ravel]

freak (frēk) *n.* 1. A deformed human being, animal, or plant; monstrosity. 2. Anything unusual or bizarre. 3. A sudden whim; caprice. 4. *Slang* a A drug addict. b An enthusiast: a jazz *freak.* *—adj.* Strange; abnormal. **—to freak out** *Slang* 1. To abandon reality, esp. by taking drugs. 2. To experience hallucinations as the result of taking drugs. 3. To become extremely upset. 4. To put into a state of intense excitement: The music *freaked* him *out.* [Cf. OE *frician* to dance] **—freak′ish** *adj.* **—freak′ish·ly** *adv.* **—freak′ish·ness** *n.* **—freak′y** *adj.*

freck·le (frek′əl) *n.* A small brownish or dark-colored spot on the skin. *—v.t. & v.i.* **·led, ·ling** To mark or become marked with freckles. [< ON *freknur* freckles] **—freck′led, freck′ly** *adj.*

free (frē) *adj.* **fre·er, fre·est** 1. Having personal liberty. 2. Having civil, political, or religious liberty. 3. Not controlled by a foreign power; autonomous. 4. Not bound by impositions, restrictions, regulations: *free* trade. 5. Given or provided without charge. 6. Cleared or devoid of something: with *from, of.* 7. Not controlled or hampered by external agents or influences. 8. Not hindered by burdens, debts, discomforts, etc.: with *from, of.* 9. Not occupied; not busy. 10. Not attached; loose: the *free* end of a rope. 11. Not obstructed; unimpeded. 12. Not adhering to strict form or rule: *free* verse. 13. Not literally following the original: a *free* translation. 14. Informal; unconventional. 15. Frank and honest; candid. 16. Generous in giving; liberal: *free* with advice. 17. *Chem.* Uncombined: *free* hydrogen. **—free and clear** *Law* Held without a mortgage or other encumbrance. **—to set free** To release, as from a prison, slavery, or other restraint. *—adv.* 1. In a free manner; easily. 2. Without cost; gratuitously. **—to make free with** 1. To use freely. 2. To treat with undue familiarity. *—v.t.* **freed, free·ing** 1. To release from confinement, worry, etc. 2. To clear or rid of obstruction or hindrance. [OE *frēo*] **—free′ly** *adv.* **—free′ness** *n.*

-free *combining form* Free from: **carefree, duty-free, fat-free, frost-free, lint-free, mineral-free.**

free·bie (frē′bē) *n. Slang* Something received without cost, as a theater ticket. Also **free′bee, free′by.** [alter. of FREE]

free·boot·er (frē′bōō′tər) *n.* A pirate or plunderer. [< MDu. *vrij* free + *buit* booty]

free·dom (frē′dəm) *n.* 1. The state or condition of being free; esp., the condition of enjoying civil liberty. 2. Political autonomy, as of a nation or people. 3. Liberty from slavery or imprisonment. 4. Liberty to move, choose, act, etc., without outside interference, coercion, or restriction. 5. Release or immunity from any stated thing or condition: with *from*: *freedom* from pain. 6. Facility or ease, as in moving or acting. 7. Openness or frankness. 8. Excessive familiarity or candor. [OE *frēodōm*]

free enterprise Private ownership and operation of business with little or no governmental control.

free-for-all (frē′fər·ôl′) *n.* A generalized brawl.

free·hand (frē′hand′) *adj.* Drawn or sketched by hand without drafting instruments, etc.

free hand Full liberty to act as one sees fit.

free·hold (frē′hold′) *n. Law* 1. Tenure of an estate, office, or dignity for life or as something capable of being transferred to another. 2. The estate, office, etc., held by such tenure. **—free′hold′er** *n.*

free-lance (frē′lans′) *v.i.* **-lanced, -lanc·ing** To work as a free lance. **—free′-lance′** *adj.*

free lance A writer, artist, etc., whose services are not sold exclusively to any one buyer.

free·man (frē′mən) *n.* *pl.* **·men** (-mən) 1. A person not in bondage of any kind. 2. One having full political rights.

Free·ma·son (frē′mā′sən) *n.* A member of an extensive secret order or fraternity, the members denoting themselves **Free and Accepted Masons**: also called *Mason.* **—Free·ma·son·ic** (frē′mə·son′ik) *adj.* **—Free′ma′son·ry** *n.*

free on board Delivered, without charge to

the buyer, for shipment by a common carrier. Abbr. *F.O.B.*

free-spo·ken (frē′spō′kən) *adj.* Unreserved or frank in speech. —**free′-spo′ken·ness** *n.*

free·stone (frē′stōn′) *adj.* Having a pit from which the pulp easily separates, as a peach. —*n.* 1. Any stone, as sandstone or limestone, that can be cut in any direction without breaking. 2. A fruit easily freed from its pit.

free·style (frē′stīl′) *adj.* In swimming, using or permitting any stroke the swimmer desires. —**free′style′** *n.*

free·think·er (frē′thing′kər) *n.* One who forms opinions without regard to established authority. —**free′think′ing** *adj.* & *n.*

free trade International commerce largely or wholly free from government regulations and duties. —**free trader** *n.*

free verse Verse marked by an absence or irregularity of rhyme.

free·way (frē′wā′) *n.* A wide highway avoiding populated areas and intersections.

free·wheel·ing (frē′hwē′ling) *adj.* Unhampered or unrestricted in manner or action.

free will 1. The power of personal self-determination. 2. The doctrine that one's ability to choose is not completely determined by circumstances. —**free·will** (frē′wil′) *adj.*

freeze (frēz) *v.* **froze, fro·zen, freez·ing** *v.i.* 1. To become ice or a similar hard solid through loss of heat. 2. To become sheeted or filled with ice, as water pipes. 3. To become stiff or hard with cold, as wet clothes. 4. To adhere to something by the formation of ice. 5. To be extremely cold. 6. To be damaged or killed by great cold. 7. To become suddenly motionless, inactive, or rigid, as through fear, shock, etc. 8. To become icily aloof: often with *up.* —*v.t.* 9. To cause to become solid through loss of heat. 10. To cause ice to form on or in. 11. To make stiff or hard by freezing the moisture of. 12. To make adhere by the formation of ice. 13. To make extremely cold. 14. To damage or kill by great cold. 15. To make motionless or rigid, as through fear; paralyze. 16. To alienate. 17. To check abruptly the ardor, enthusiasm, etc., of. 18. To fix or stabilize (prices, wages, etc.) at a particular level. 19. To prohibit the continued making, use, or selling of (a raw material). 20. To prohibit the liquidation, collection, or use of (funds or other assets). —**to freeze one's blood** To fill one with terror. —**to freeze onto** (or **to**) To hold tightly to. —*n.* 1. The act of freezing, or the state of being frozen. 2. Freezing weather. [OE *frēosan*]

freeze-dry (frēz′drī′) *v.t.* **-dried, -dry·ing** To dehydrate by freezing in a high vacuum.

freez·er (frē′zər) *n.* A refrigerator unit or compartment designed to freeze and preserve food.

freezing point *Physics* The temperature at which a liquid freezes under given pressure.

freight (frāt) *n.* 1. The service of transporting commodities by land, air, or water. 2. The commodities so transported. 3. The price paid for the transportation of commodities. 4. A railroad train for carrying freight: also **freight train.** —*v.t.* 1. To load with commodities for transportation. 2. To load; burden. 3. To send or transport as or by freight. [< MDu. *vrecht*, var. of *vracht* a load]

freight·er (frā′tər) *n.* A ship used primarily for transporting cargo.

French (french) *n.* 1. The people of France collectively: preceded by *the.* 2. The Romance language of France. —**Old French** The French language from about 850 to 1400. —**Middle French** The French language from about 1400 to 1600. —**Modern French** The language of France after 1600. [OE *Frencisc*] —**French** *adj.*

French-Ca·na·di·an (french′kə·nā′dē·ən) *n.* A French settler in Canada or a descendant of French settlers. Also **French Canadian.** —*adj.* Of or pertaining to the language, culture, etc., of French-speaking people in Canada.

French cuff A cuff of a sleeve turned back and secured with a link.

French doors A pair of doors attached to opposite doorjambs and opening in the middle.

French dressing A salad dressing consisting of oil, vinegar, and spices.

French fried Cooked by frying in deep fat.

French fries Potatoes cut in strips and French fried.

French horn A valved, brass instrument with a long, coiled tube, flaring widely at the end.

French·i·fy (fren′chə·fī) *v.t.* & *v.i.* **·fied, ·fy·ing** To make or become French in form or characteristics.

French leave An informal, secret, or hurried departure.

French·man (french′mən) *n. pl.* **·men** (-mən) A native or citizen of France.

French toast Bread dipped in a batter of beaten eggs and milk and fried in shallow fat.

fre·net·ic (frə·net′ik) *adj.* Feverishly excited; frenzied; frantic. Also **fre·net′i·cal.** —*n.* A frenetic person. [ME *frenetik* < Gk. *phrenitis* delirium] —**fre·net′i·cal·ly** *adv.*

fren·zy (fren′zē) *n. pl.* **·zies** A state of extreme excitement or agitation, bordering on madness. —*v.t.* **·zied, ·zy·ing** To make frantic. [ME *frenesie* < Gk. *phrenitis* delirium] —**fren′zied** *adj.*

fre·quen·cy (frē′kwən·sē) *n. pl.* **·cies** 1. The state or fact of being frequent; repeated occurrence. 2. The number of times something occurs during a particular time. 3. *Stat.* The number of times a given case, value, or event occurs relative to the whole sample; distribution. 4. *Physics* The number of occurrences of a periodic phenomenon, as oscillation, per unit time.

frequency modulation *Telecom.* A type of modulation in which the carrier wave of a transmitter is varied in frequency rather than in amplitude. Compare AMPLITUDE MODULATION. Abbr. *FM.*

fre·quent (*adj.* frē′kwənt; *v.* frē·kwent′, frē′kwənt) *adj.* 1. Happening again and again: *frequent* relapses. 2. Showing up often; appearing repeatedly: *frequent* visitors. —*v.t.* To go to repeatedly; be in or at often: to *frequent* bars. [< L *frequens, -entis* crowded] —**fre′quen·ta′tion** *n.* —**fre·quent′er** *n.* —**fre′quent·ly** *adv.*

fres·co (fres′kō) *n. pl.* **·coes** or **·cos** 1. The art of painting on plaster that is still moist. 2. A picture so painted. —*v.t.* **·coed, ·co·ing** To paint in fresco. [< Ital., fresh]

fresh[1] (fresh) *adj.* 1. Newly made, obtained,

etc.: *fresh* coffee; *fresh* footprints. 2. New; novel: a *fresh* approach. 3. Recent; latest: *fresh* news. 4. Additional; further: *fresh* supplies. 5. Not smoked, frozen, or otherwise preserved: *fresh* vegetables. 6. Not spoiled, stale, etc. 7. Retaining original vividness, as colors or memories. 8. Not salt: *fresh* water. 9. Pure and clear: *fresh* air. 10. Appearing healthy or youthful. 11. Not fatigued; energetic. 12. Inexperienced; untrained: *fresh* recruits. [OE *fersc*, infl. by OF *freis*, both ult. < Gmc.] —**fresh′ly** *adv.* —**fresh′·ness** *n.*

fresh² (fresh) *adj. Informal* Saucy; impudent; disrespectful. [< G *frech* impudent]

fresh·en (fresh′ən) *v.t. & v.i.* To make or become fresh. —**fresh′en·er** *n.*

fresh·et (fresh′it) *n.* 1. A sudden rise or overflow of a stream. 2. A fresh-water stream emptying into the sea.

fresh·man (fresh′mən) *n. pl.* **·men** (-mən) 1. A first-year student in a high school, college, etc. 2. Any beginner.

fresh-wa·ter (fresh′wô′tər, -wot′ər) *adj.* 1. Pertaining to or living in fresh water. 2. Inland. 3. Lacking skill or experience.

fret¹ (fret) *v.* **fret·ted, fret·ting** *v.i.* 1. To be vexed, annoyed, or troubled. 2. To become worn, chafed, or corroded. 3. To eat through something by or as if by corrosion. 4. To rankle; fester. 5. To become rough or agitated, as water. —*v.t.* 6. To vex, annoy, or trouble. 7. To wear away by or as if by chafing, gnawing, or corrosion. 8. To roughen or agitate (the surface of water). —*n.* 1. Vexation. 2. The act of chafing or gnawing. 3. A worn spot. [OE *fretan* to devour]

fret² (fret) *n.* One of a series of ridges across the fingerboard of a guitar, ukulele, etc., to guide the fingers in stopping the strings. —*v.t.* **fret·ted, fret·ting** To provide (a guitar, etc.) with frets. [Cf. OF *frete* ring]

fret³ (fret) *n.* An ornamental band or border consisting of symmetrically arranged lines. —*v.t.* **fret·ted, fret·ting** To adorn with a fret. [Prob. < OF *frette* lattice, trellis]

fret·ful (fret′fəl) *adj.* Inclined to fret; peevish or restless. —**fret′ful·ly** *adv.* —**fret′ful·ness** *n.*

fret·work (fret′wûrk′) *n.* 1. Ornamental openwork, usu. composed of frets or interlaced parts. 2. A pattern, as of light and shade, resembling such openwork.

Freu·di·an (froi′dē·ən) *adj.* Of, pertaining to, or conforming to the teachings of Sigmund Freud. —*n.* An adherent of the theories of Freud. —**Freu′di·an·ism** *n.*

fri·a·ble (frī′ə·bəl) *adj.* Easily crumbled or pulverized. [< L *friare* to crumble] —**fri′a·bil′i·ty, fri′a·ble·ness** *n.*

fri·ar (frī′ər) *n.* A man who is a member of one of several religious orders, esp. the mendicant orders. [< OF *frere* < L *frater* brother]

fri·ar·y (frī′ər·ē) *n. pl.* **·ar·ies** 1. A monastery, esp. of a mendicant order. 2. A community of friars.

fric·as·see (frik′ə·sē′) *n.* A dish of meat cut small, stewed, and served with gravy. —*v.t.* **·seed, ·see·ing** To make into a fricassee. [< F *fricassé*, orig. pp. of *fricasser* to sauté]

fric·tion (frik′shən) *n.* 1. The rubbing of one object against another. 2. Conflict of opinions, differences in temperament, etc. [< L *fricare* to rub] —**fric′tion·al** *adj.*

friction tape Moisture-resistant adhesive tape, used to insulate bare electric wiring.

Fri·day¹ (frī′dē, -dā) *n.* The sixth day of the week. [OE *Frīgedæg* day of Frigg, the Norse goddess of marriage]

Fri·day² (frī′dē, -dā) *n.* Any devoted or faithful attendant or helper: man *Friday*; girl *Friday*. [after the faithful servant in Defoe's *Robinson Crusoe*]

fried (frīd) Past tense and past participle of FRY.

fried cake A small cake or doughnut fried in deep fat.

friend (frend) *n.* 1. A favored companion; intimate. 2. A valued associate or acquaintance. 3. One with whom one is united in some purpose, cause, etc. 4. A patron or supporter. [OE *frēond*] —**friend′less** *adj.* —**friend′less·ness** *n.* —**friend′ship** *n.*

Friend (frend) *n.* A member of the Society of Friends: Quaker.

friend·ly (frend′lē) *adj.* **·li·er, ·li·est** 1. Of, pertaining to, or typical of a friend. 2. Well-disposed; not antagonistic. 3. Helpful; favorable: a *friendly* wind. —**friend′li·ness** *n.* —**friend′ly** *adv.*

fri·er (frī′ər) See FRYER.

frieze (frēz) *n.* A decorative horizontal strip, as along the top of a wall of a room or building. [< Med.L *frisium*]

frig·ate (frig′it) *n.* A type of warship used from the 17th to 19th c. [< Ital. *fregata*]

fright (frīt) *n.* 1. Sudden, violent alarm or fear. 2. *Informal* One who or that which is ugly, etc. [OE *fryhto*]

fright·en (frīt′n) *v.t.* 1. To make suddenly alarmed, fearful, or terrified; scare. 2. To drive, force, etc., (away, out, into, etc.) by scaring. —*v.i.* 3. To become afraid. —**fright′·en·ing** *adj.* —**fright′en·ing·ly** *adv.*

fright·ful (frīt′fəl) *adj.* 1. Repulsive, shocking, or contemptible. 2. *Informal* Most distressing; very bad: a *frightful* headache. 3. *Informal* Very large: a *frightful* number of losses. 4. Alarming or terrifying. —**fright′·ful·ly** *adv.* —**fright′ful·ness** *n.*

frig·id (frij′id) *adj.* 1. Bitterly cold. 2. Lacking warmth of feeling; formal. 3. Habitually lacking sexual feeling or response: said of women. [< L *frigere* to be cold] —**frig′id·ly** *adv.* —**fri·gid·i·ty** (fri·jid′ə·tē), **frig′id·ness** *n.*

Frigid Zones See under ZONE.

fri·jo·le (frē′hōl, *Sp.* frē·hō′lā) *n. pl.* **fri·joles** (frē′hōlz, *Sp.* frē·hō′lās) A bean used as food, esp. by Latin Americans. Also **fri·jol′**. [< Sp.]

frill (fril) *n.* 1. An ornamental strip of lace, etc., gathered together and attached along one edge; ruffle. 2. *Informal* Any showy or superfluous detail of dress, manner, etc. —*v.t.* 1. To make into a frill. 2. To put frills on. [Origin uncertain] —**frill′y** *adv.*

fringe (frinj) *n.* 1. An ornamental border of hanging cords, threads, etc. 2. Something resembling such a border: a *fringe* of grass along a sidewalk. 3. A peripheral area: the *fringes* of a city. —*v.t.* **fringed, fring·ing** 1. To provide with or as with a fringe. 2. To constitute a fringe on or along. —*adj.* Outer; marginal: a *fringe* area. [< L *fimbria*] —**fring′y** *adj.*

fringe benefit Anything of value given an employee in addition to his salary or wages.

frip·per·y (frip′ər·ē) *n. pl.* **·per·ies** 1. Cheap, flashy dress or ornamentation. 2. Showiness or affectation in speech, manner, etc. [< OF *frepe* rag]

Fris·bee (friz′bē) *n.* A light plastic disk tossed in play: a trade name. Also **fris′bee.**

fri·sé (fri·zā′) *n.* A heavy fabric faced with a thick pile of loops. [< F, orig. pp. of *friser* to curl]

Fris·ian (frizh′ən, frizh′ē·ən) *n.* 1. A native or inhabitant of the Dutch province of Friesland or the Frisian Islands. 2. The Germanic language of the Frisians. —**Fris′ian** *adj.*

frisk (frisk) *v.i.* 1. To move or leap about playfully; frolic. —*v.t.* 2. To move with quick jerks: a lamb *frisking* its tail. 3. *Slang* To search (someone) for a concealed weapon, etc., by quickly feeling the pockets and clothing. 4. *Slang* To rob of valuables in this way. —*n.* 1. A playful skipping about. 2. *Slang* A search of someone for a weapon, etc. [< obs. *frisk* lively < F *frisque*] —**frisk′er** *n.*

frisk·y (fris′kē) *adj.* **frisk·i·er, frisk·i·est** Lively or playful. —**frisk′i·ly** *adv.* —**frisk′i·ness** *n.*

frit·ter[1] (frit′ər) *v.t.* To waste or squander little by little, as money, time, etc.: usu. with *away.* [< L *frangere* to break]

frit·ter[2] (frit′ər) *n.* A small, deep-fried cake, often containing corn, meat, fruit, etc. [< L *frigere* to fry]

friv·o·lous (friv′ə·ləs) *adj.* 1. Lacking importance or significance; petty. 2. Flippant; silly; fickle. [< L *frivolus* silly] —**fri·vol·i·ty** (fri·vol′ə·tē) *n.* —**friv′o·lous·ly** *adv.* —**friv′o·lous·ness** *n.*

frizz (friz) *v.t. & v.i.* 1. To form into tight, crisp curls, as the hair. 2. To make or form into small, tight tufts or knots, as the nap of cloth. —*n.* 1. That which is frizzed, as hair. 2. The condition of being frizzed. Also **friz.** [< F *friser* to curl] —**friz′zer** or **friz′er** *n.* —**friz′zly, frizz′y** *adj.* —**friz′zi·ness** *n.*

friz·zle[1] (friz′əl) *v.t. & v.i.* **·zled, ·zling** 1. To fry or cook with a sizzling noise. 2. To make or become curled or crisp, as by frying. [Blend of FRY and SIZZLE; ? infl. by FRIZZLE[2]]

friz·zle[2] (friz′əl) *v.t. & v.i.* **·zled, ·zling** To frizz. —*n.* A crisp curl; frizz. [? Freq. of obs. *frieze* produce a nap on < MF *friser* to curl]

fro (frō) *adv.* Away from; back: used in the phrase *to and fro.* [< ON *frā* from]

frock (frok) *n.* 1. A long, loose-fitting robe with wide sleeves worn by monks. 2. Any of several types of garments, as a dress or a worker's smock. —*v.t.* 1. To furnish with or clothe in a frock. 2. To invest with ecclesiastic office. [< OF *froc*]

frog (frog, frôg) *n.* 1. One of a genus of small, tailless, web-footed animals with short front legs and large, strong hind legs adapted to leaping. 2. One of several similar amphibians, as a tree frog. 3. A slight throat irritation producing hoarseness: also **frog in the** (or **one's**) **throat.** 4. An ornamental braid or cord, as on a jacket, often looped, so as to permit passage of a button. —*v.i.* **frogged, frog·ging** To hunt frogs. [OE *frogga*]

frog·man (frog′mən, -man′, frôg′-) *n. pl.* **·men** (-mən, -men′) An underwater reconnaissance and demolition expert.

frol·ic (frol′ik) *n.* 1. Merriness. 2. A gay occasion or diversion. 3. A playful prank. —*v.i.* **·icked, ·ick·ing** 1. To move about or behave in a frisky way. 2. To be prankish. [< MDu. *vro* glad] —**frol′ick·er** *n.*

frol·ic·some (frol′ik·səm) *adj.* Gay and lighthearted. Also **frol′ick·y.** —**frol′ic·some·ly** *adv.* —**frol′ic·some·ness** *n.*

from (frum, from; *unstressed* frəm) *prep.* 1. Starting at (a particular place or time): the plane *from* New York. 2. With (a particular person, place, or thing) as the origin or instrument: a letter *from* your mother. 3. Out of (a holder, container, etc.). 4. Out of the control of: He escaped *from* his captors. 5. Out of the totality of: to subtract 3 *from* 8. 6. At a distance in relation to: far *from* the city. 7. Beyond the possibility of: He kept her *from* falling. 8. By reason of; because of. 9. As being other or another than: He couldn't tell me *from* my brother. [OE *fram, from*]

frond (frond) *n. Bot.* 1. A leaflike expansion, as in ferns and seaweeds. 2. A large leaf of tropical plants and trees, as of the palm tree. [< L *frons, frondis* leaf]

front (frunt) *n.* 1. The part or side of an object or body that faces forward or is viewed as facing forward. 2. An area or position located directly ahead or before: He stood in *front* of her. 3. An area or position of most important activity. 4. *Mil.* **a** The lateral space from flank to flank occupied by a unit. **b** The line of contact of two opposing forces. 5. The side of a building where the main entrance is. 6. Frontage. 7. A group or movement of individuals with a common aim. 8. One chosen to head a group, movement, etc., to give it prestige, often lacking real authority. 9. An apparently respectable person, business, etc., used for cloaking objectionable or illegal activities. 10. One's bearing or attitude: to put on a bold *front.* 11. *Informal* An outward air of pretense of wealth, social importance, etc. 12. *Meteorol.* The fore part of a mass of warm or cold air; also, the line of separation between masses of warm and cold air. —*adj.* 1. Of, pertaining to, or directed toward the front. 2. Located on, in, or at the front. —*v.t.* 1. To face toward. 2. To meet face to face. 3. To provide with a front. 4. To serve as a front for. —*v.i.* 5. To face toward something: usu. with *on.* [< L *frons, frontis* forehead]

front·age (frun′tij) *n.* 1. The front part of a lot or building; also, the linear extent of this. 2. The direction in which something faces; exposure. 3. Land adjacent to a street, body of water, etc.

fron·tal (frun′təl) *adj.* 1. Of or pertaining to the front. 2. Of or pertaining to the forehead or to the bone forming the anterior part of the skull. —**fron′tal·ly** *adv.*

fron·tier (frun·tir′) *n.* 1. The part of a nation's territory lying along the border of another country. 2. The part of a settled region lying along the border of an unsettled region. 3. A new or unexplored area of thought or knowledge. [< OF *front* front] —**fron·tier′** *adj.* —**fron·tiers′man** (-tirz′·mən) *n.*

fron·tis·piece (frun′tis·pēs′, fron′-) *n.* A

picture or drawing on the page facing the title page of a book. [< L *frons, frontis* forehead + *specere* to look at]

front-page (frunt′pāj′) *adj.* Highly newsworthy.

front-run·ner (frunt′run′ər) *n.* The leading contender in a contest or selective process.

frosh (frosh) *n. pl.* **frosh** *Slang* A college freshman.

frost (frôst, frost) *n.* **1.** A feathery deposit of ice formed on surfaces by dew or water vapor that has frozen. **2.** Temperature cold enough to freeze. **3.** Coldness of manner. —*v.t.* **1.** To cover with frost. **2.** To damage or kill by frost. **3.** To produce a frostlike surface or effect on (glass, etc.). **4.** To apply frosting to. [OE] —**frost′i·ly** *adv.* —**frost′i·ness** *n.* —**frost′less** *adj.* —**frost′y** *adj.* **frost·i·er, frost·i·est**

frost·bite (frôst′bīt′, frost′-) *n.* The partial freezing of some part of the body, often resulting in gangrene. —*v.t.* **·bit, ·bit·ten, ·bit·ing** To injure, as a part of the body, by partial freezing. —**frost′bit′ten** (-bit′n) *adj.*

frost·ing (frôs′ting, fros′-) *n.* **1.** A sweet mixture used to cover cakes. **2.** A frostlike, rough, dull surface produced on metal, glass, etc. —**frost′ed** *adj.*

froth (frôth, froth) *n.* **1.** A mass of bubbles resulting from fermentation or agitation. **2.** Any foamy excretion or exudation, as of saliva. **3.** Any unsubstantial or trivial thing. —*v.t.* **1.** To cause to foam. **2.** To cover with froth. **3.** To give forth in the form of foam. —*v.i.* **4.** To form or give off froth. [< ON *frodha*] —**froth′i·ly** *adv.* —**froth′i·ness** *n.* —**froth′y** *adj.* **froth·i·er, froth·i·est**

frou·frou (fro͞o′fro͞o′) *n.* **1.** A rustling, as of silk. **2.** *Informal* Affected elegance. [< F]

fro·ward (frō′ərd, -wərd) *adj.* Disobedient; intractable. —**fro′ward·ly** *adv.* —**fro′ward·ness** *n.*

frown (froun) *v.i.* **1.** To contract the brow, as in displeasure or concentration. **2.** To look with distaste: with *on* or *upon.* —*v.t.* **3.** To make known (one's displeasure, disgust, etc.) by contracting one's brow. [< OF *froignier,* prob. < Gmc.] —**frown** *n.* —**frown′ing·ly** *adv.*

frow·zy (frou′zē) *adj.* **·zi·er, ·zi·est** **1.** Slovenly in appearance; unkempt. **2.** Having a disagreeable smell; musty. Also **frou′zy, frow′sy.** [Origin uncertain]

froze (frōz) Past tense of FREEZE.

fro·zen (frō′zən) Past participle of FREEZE. —*adj.* **1.** Changed into, covered with, or clogged with ice, as a river. **2.** Killed or damaged by cold. **3.** Preserved by freezing: *frozen* foods. **4.** Extremely cold, as a climate. **5.** Cold and unfeeling in manner. **6.** Made rigid or immobile: *frozen* with fear. **7.** *Econ.* **a** Arbitrarily maintained at a given level: said of prices, wages, etc. **b** Not readily convertible into cash: *frozen* assets. **8.** Made solid by cold.

fruc·ti·fy (fruk′tə·fī, fro͝ok′-) *v.* **·fied, ·fy·ing** *v.t.* **1.** To make fruitful; fertilize. —*v.i.* **2.** To bear fruit. [< L *fructus* fruit + -FY] —**fruc′ti·fi·ca′tion** *n.*

fruc·tose (fruk′tōs, fro͝ok′-, fro͞ok′-) *n.* *Biochem.* A very sweet sugar occurring in fruits: also **fruit sugar.** [< L *fructus* fruit + -OSE²]

fru·gal (fro͞o′gəl) *adj.* **1.** Exercising economy; saving. **2.** Costing little money: a *frugal* meal. [< L *frugalis* < *frux* fruit] —**fru·gal′i·ty** (-gal′ə·tē), **fru′gal·ness** *n.* —**fru′gal·ly** *adv.*

fruit (fro͞ot) *n.* **1.** *Bot.* **a** The pulpy, usu. edible mass covering the seeds of various plants and trees. **b** In flowering plants, the mature seed vessel and its contents. **2.** Any useful plant product. **3.** Any offspring. **4.** The outcome or result of some action, effort, etc. —*v.i. & v.t.* To produce or cause to produce fruit. [< L *fructus* < *frui* to enjoy]

fruit·cake (fro͞ot′kāk′) *n.* A rich, spiced cake containing nuts and dried fruits.

fruit fly **1.** Any of various flies whose larvae attack fruit. **2.** A fly whose larvae feed on fruit and which is used in research in genetics: also called *drosophila.*

fruit·ful (fro͞ot′fəl) *adj.* **1.** Bearing fruit or offspring abundantly. **2.** Producing results: a *fruitful* discussion. —**fruit′ful·ly** *adv.* —**fruit′ful·ness** *n.*

fru·i·tion (fro͞o·ish′ən) *n.* **1.** Accomplishment; fulfillment. **2.** The bearing of fruit. [< L *frui* to enjoy]

fruit·less (fro͞ot′lis) *adj.* **1.** Yielding no fruit; barren. **2.** Ineffectual; useless; unproductive. —**fruit′less·ly** *adv.* —**fruit′less·ness** *n.*

fruit·y (fro͞o′tē) *adj.* **fruit·i·er, fruit·i·est** Suggestive of or having the flavor of fruit. —**fruit′i·ness** *n.*

frump (frump) *n.* A dowdy, sometimes ill-tempered woman. [? < MDu. *frompelen,* var. of *verrompelen* to wrinkle] —**frump′ish** *adj.* —**frump′ish·ly** *adv.* —**frump′y** *adj.* **frump·i·er, frump·i·est**

frus·trate (frus′trāt) *v.t.* **·trat·ed, ·trat·ing** **1.** To keep (someone) from doing or achieving something; thwart. **2.** To keep, as plans or schemes, from being fulfilled. [< L *frustrari* to disappoint] —**frus·trat′ing·ly** *adv.* —**frus·tra′tion** *n.*

fry¹ (frī) *v.t. & v.i.* **fried, fry·ing** To cook in hot fat, usu. over direct heat. —*n. pl.* **fries** **1.** A dish of anything fried. **2.** A social occasion, at which foods are fried and eaten. [< F *frier* < L *frigere*]

fry² (frī) *n. pl.* **fry** **1.** Very young fish. **2.** The young of certain animals, as of frogs, when produced in very large quantities. **3.** Young children. [< ON *friō* seed]

fry·er (frī′ər) *n.* **1.** One who or that which fries. **2.** A young chicken suitable for frying. Also spelled *frier.*

fuch·sia (fyo͞o′shə, -shē·ə) *n.* **1.** A plant with drooping, four-petaled flowers. **2.** A bright bluish red. [after Leonhard *Fuchs,* 1501–66, German botanist]

fud·dle (fud′l) *v.* **·dled, ·dling** *v.t.* **1.** To confuse or stupefy. —*v.i.* **2.** To tipple. [Cf. dial. G *fuddeln* to swindle]

fud·dy-dud·dy (fud′ē·dud′ē) *n. pl.* **-dud·dies** *Informal* **1.** An old-fashioned person. **2.** A faultfinding, fussy person. [Varied reduplication, ? < dial. E *fud* the buttocks]

fudge (fuj) *n.* **1.** A soft, cooked confection made of butter, sugar, chocolate, etc. **2.** Humbug; nonsense. —*v.* **fudged, fudg·ing** *v.i.* **1.** To avoid commitment; equivocate. —*v.t.* **2.** To make, adjust, or fit together in a clumsy or dishonest manner. [Origin uncertain]

fu·el (fyo͞o′əl) *n.* **1.** Combustible matter used as a source of heat or power. **2.** Whatever sustains or heightens emotion, etc. —*v.t.* & *v.i.* **fu·eled** or **·elled, fu·el·ing** or **·el·ling** To supply with or take in fuel. [< OF *fouaille* < L *focus* hearth] —**fu′el·er** or **fu′el·ler** *n.*

fuel cell A cell that converts the chemical energy of a fuel into electrical energy.

fu·gi·tive (fyo͞o′jə·tiv) *adj.* 1. Fleeing or having fled, as from pursuit, arrest, etc. 2. Transient; fleeting. 3. Wandering about; shifting. —*n.* One who flees, as from pursuit, danger, etc.; runaway. [< L *fugere* to flee] —**fu′gi·tive·ly** *adv.* —**fu′gi·tive·ness** *n.*

fugue (fyo͞og) *n. Music* A contrapuntal composition in which a theme is introduced by one part, repeated by other parts, and subjected to complex development. [< L *fuga* flight] —**fu·gal** (fyo͞o′gəl) *adj.*

Füh·rer (fyo͝or′ər, *Ger.* fü′rər) *n. German* Leader: a title applied to Adolf Hitler: also **Fueh′rer.**

-ful *suffix* 1. Full of; characterized by: *joyful.* 2. Able to; tending to: *helpful.* 3. Having the character of: *manful.* 4. The quantity or number that will fill: *cupful.* [OE *-full, -ful* < *full* full]

ful·crum (fo͝ol′krəm) *n. pl.* **·crums** or **·cra** 1. The support on which a lever rests or about which it turns. 2. Any prop or support. [< L, bedpost < *fulcire* to prop up]

ful·fill (fo͝ol·fil′) *v.t.* **·filled, ·fill·ing** 1. To bring about the accomplishment of (something promised, hoped for, anticipated, etc.). 2. To execute or perform (something commanded or requested). 3. To come up to or satisfy (something stipulated). 4. To get through to the end of (a period of time, a task, etc.); finish up. Also *Brit.* **ful·fil′.** [OE *fullfyllan*] —**ful·fill′ment** or **ful·fil′ment** *n.*

full¹ (fo͝ol) *adj.* 1. Filled up. 2. Containing an abundant or sufficient supply. 3. Complete or entire: a *full* dozen. 4. Maximum in size, extent, degree, etc.: a *full* load; *full* speed. 5. Having had ample food or drink. 6. Of the face, figure, etc., well rounded; plump. 7. Having satisfying resonance and volume: *full* tones. 8. Of garments, cut in ample folds; flowing. —**in full cry** In close pursuit: said esp. of dogs. —*n.* The maximum size, extent, degree, etc. —**in full** 1. To the entire amount: paid *in full.* 2. Without abridgement: reprinted *in full.* —*adv.* 1. To a complete degree or extent: now chiefly in compounds: *full-fledged.* 2. Directly; straight; right: I looked him *full* in the face. [OE *ful*] —**full′ness** or **ful′ness** *n.*

full² (fo͝ol) *v.t.* & *v.i.* To shrink or thicken (cloth, yarn, etc.), as by moistening and beating or pressing. [Back formation < FULLER.]

full·back (fo͝ol′bak′) *n.* 1. In football, an offensive player usu. positioned behind the quarterback. 2. In soccer and field hockey, a player who plays a defensive position in front of the goalie.

full-blood·ed (fo͝ol′blud′id) *adj.* 1. Unmixed in race or breed. 2. Related to another through descent from the same parents. Also **full′-blood′.**

full-blown (fo͝ol′blōn′) *adj.* 1. Blooming fully. 2. Fully developed.

full-bod·ied (fo͝ol′bod′ēd) *adj.* Of beverages, having a satisfying richness and strength.

full dress Formal or ceremonial attire. —**full-dress** (fo͝ol′dres′) *adj.*

full·er (fo͝ol′ər) *n.* One who fulls cloth, etc. [OE *fullere*]

full-fledged (fo͝ol′flejd′) *adj.* 1. Having full plumage. 2. Completely developed or trained.

full gainer A dive in which one springs forward off the board and makes a complete back somersault.

full-length (fo͝ol′lengkth′) *adj.* 1. Showing the entire length of an object or figure: a *full-length* portrait. 2. Not abridged; of the usual length.

full moon 1. The moon with its whole face illuminated. 2. The time of month this occurs.

full nel·son (nel′sən) A wrestling hold in which the arms are thrust under the opponent's armpits from behind and the hands are gripped at the back of the opponent's neck.

full-scale (fo͝ol′skāl′) *adj.* 1. Scaled to actual size; not reduced. 2. All-out; unrestrained.

full swing The height of activity: a party in *full swing.*

ful·ly (fo͝ol′ē) *adv.* 1. To the fullest extent or degree; entirely: *fully* convinced. 2. Adequately; sufficiently: *fully* fed. 3. At the lowest estimate: *fully* three hundred.

ful·mi·nate (ful′mə·nāt) *v.* **·nat·ed, ·nat·ing** *v.i.* 1. To make loud or violent denunciations; inveigh. 2. To explode suddenly and violently, as a chemical. —*v.t.* 3. To issue (decrees, censures, etc.) in scathing rebuke or condemnation. 4. To cause, as a chemical, to explode with sudden violence. —*n. Chem.* Any explosive compound. [< L *fulmen, fulminis* lightning] —**ful′mi·na′tion** *n.* —**ful′mi·na·to′ry** (-nə·tôr′ē) *adj.* —**ful′mi·na′tor** *n.*

ful·some (fo͝ol′səm, ful′-) *adj.* Distastefully excessive; insincere. [< FULL¹, adj. + -SOME¹; infl. by FOUL] —**ful′some·ly** *adv.* —**ful′some·ness** *n.*

fum·ble (fum′bəl) *v.* **·bled, ·bling** *v.i.* 1. To try to locate something by groping blindly or clumsily: with *for, after.* 2. To try awkwardly to do something: with *at.* 3. In football, etc., to lose hold of the ball. —*v.t.* 4. To handle awkwardly or ineffectually; botch. 5. To drop awkwardly (a ball in one's grasp). —*n.* The act of fumbling. [Prob. < Scand. *famla* to grope] —**fum′bler** *n.*

fume (fyo͞om) *n.* 1. A gaseous exhalation or smoke, esp. when acrid or otherwise disagreeable. 2. A sharply penetrating odor. —*v.* **fumed, fum·ing** *v.i.* 1. To give off fumes. 2. To pass off in a mist or vapor. 3. To be filled with or show rage, irritation, etc. —*v.t.* 4. To subject to fumes. [< L *fumus* smoke]

fu·mi·gate (fyo͞o′mə·gāt) *v.t.* **·gat·ed, ·gat·ing** To subject to smoke or fumes, esp. to kill vermin. [< L *fumus* smoke + *agere* to drive] —**fu′mi·ga′tion** *n.* —**fu′mi·ga′tor** *n.*

fun (fun) *n.* 1. Pleasant diversion or amusement. 2. Lighthearted playfulness: full of *fun.* —**like fun** *Informal* Absolutely not; by no means. —**to make fun of** To ridicule. —*adj. Informal* Full of fun: a *fun* game. —*v.i.* **funned, fun·ning** *Informal* To behave or speak in jest. [< obs. *fonnen* to befool]

func·tion (fungk′shən) *n.* 1. The specific, natural, or proper action or activity of anything. 2. The special duties or action required of anyone in an occupation, office, or role. 3. A formal or elaborate social gathering or ceremony. 4. Any fact, quality, or thing depending upon or varying with another. 5. *Math.* A quantity whose value depends on the value of some other quantity. —*v.i.* 1. To perform as expected or required. 2. To perform the role of something else. [< L *fungi* to perform] —**func'tion·less** *adj.*

func·tion·al (fungk'shən·əl) *adj.* 1. Of or pertaining to a function or functions. 2. Designed for or suited to a particular operation or use. 3. Affecting the functions of an organ or part: *functional* disease: distinguished from *organic.* —**func'tion·al·ly** *adv.*

func·tion·al·ism (fungk'shən·əl·iz'əm) *n.* The doctrine that the use of an object should determine its design.

func·tion·ar·y (fungk'shən·er'ē) *n. pl.* **·ar·ies** One who serves in a specific capacity; esp., an official.

fund (fund) *n.* 1. A sum of money, or its equivalent, accumulated or reserved for a specific purpose. 2. *pl.* Money readily available. 3. A ready supply: a *fund* of humor. —*v.t.* 1. In finance: **a** To convert into a long-term debt. **b** To accumulate or furnish a fund for. 2. To gather up a supply of. [< L *fundus* bottom]

fun·da·ment (fun'də·mənt) *n.* The buttocks; also, the anus. [< L *fundus* bottom]

fun·da·men·tal (fun'də·men'təl) *adj.* 1. Pertaining to or constituting a foundation; basic. 2. *Music* Of or pertaining to the basic tone of a chord; root. 3. *Physics* Designating the lowest frequency harmonic component of a complex wave. —*n.* 1. Anything that serves as the basis of a system, as a truth, law, etc. 2. *Music* The basic tone of a chord. 3. *Physics* That frequency on which a harmonic or group of harmonics is based. —**fun'da·men'tal·ly** *adv.*

fun·da·men·tal·ism (fun'də·men'təl·iz'əm) *n.* 1. The belief that all statements in the Bible are to be taken literally. 2. In the U.S., a movement among Protestants holding such a belief. —**fun'da·men'tal·ist** *n. & adj.*

fu·ner·al (fyōō'nər·əl) *n.* 1. The final disposal of the body of a dead person, together with accompanying services. 2. A procession held on this occasion. —*adj.* Of, pertaining to, or suitable for a funeral. [< L *funus, funeri* burial rite] —**fu·ner·ar·y** (fyōō'nə·rer'ē) *adj.*

fu·ne·re·al (fyōō·nir'ē·əl) *adj.* 1. Depressingly sad or gloomy; doleful. 2. Pertaining to or suitable for a funeral. —**fu·ne're·al·ly** *adv.*

fungi- *combining form* Fungus. Also, before vowels, **fung-**. [< L *fungus* mushroom]

fun·gi·cide (fun'jə·sīd, fung'gə-) *n.* Something, as a chemical compound, used in destroying fungi. —**fun'gi·ci'dal** *adj.*

fun·gus (fung'gəs) *n. pl.* **fun·gus·es** or **fun·gi** (fun'jī, -gī, -gē) Any nonflowering plant that has no chlorophyll and grows on dead organic matter or lives parasitically, including mushrooms, molds, and mildews. [< L, mushroom] —**fun'gal** *adj. & n.* —**fun'gous** *adj.*

fu·nic·u·lar (fyōō·nik'yə·lər) *adj.* Moved by the pull of a cable, as a streetcar in a hilly section. —*n.* A railway along which cable cars are drawn: also **funicular railway.**

funk[1] (fungk) *n.* *Informal* 1. A state of fear or panic: esp. in the phrase **to be in a blue funk.** 2. A feeling of despondency. [Cf. Flemish *fonck* fear]

funk[2] (fungk) *n.* *Slang* Funky music.

funk·y (fung'kē) *adj.* *Slang* 1. Earthy and unpolished in style: *funky* blues. 2. Bizarre; esp., fashionably eccentric.

fun·nel (fun'əl) *n.* 1. A utensil with a wide mouth tapering to a narrow tube, through which fluids are poured into bottles, etc., having narrow necks. 2. A smokestack, as of a large ship, locomotive, etc. —*v.t. & v.i.* **fun·neled** or **·nelled, fun·nel·ing** or **·nel·ling** To pass through or as through a funnel. [Earlier *fonel,* ult. < L *infundere* to pour into]

fun·nies (fun'ēz) *n.pl.* *Informal* Comic strips, or the section of a newspaper containing them.

fun·ny (fun'ē) *adj.* **·ni·er, ·ni·est** 1. Causing one to laugh or be amused; comical. 2. *Informal* Peculiar; strange; odd. —**fun'ni·ly** *adv.* —**fun'ni·ness** *n.*

funny bone The part of the elbow which, when struck, produces an unpleasant, tingling sensation in the arm and hand.

fur (fûr) *n.* 1. The soft, fine, hairy coat covering the skin of many mammals. 2. An animal skin covered with such a coat, esp. when prepared for use in garments, rugs, etc.; also, such skins collectively. 3. A layer of foul matter, as on the tongue. —*adj.* Made of, lined with, or trimmed with fur: also **furred.** —*v.t.* **furred, fur·ring** 1. To cover, line, trim, or clothe with fur. 2. To cover, as the tongue, with a layer of foul matter. 3. To apply furring. [< OF *forrer* to line with fur < Gmc.] —**fur'ri·ness** *n.* —**fur'ry** *adj.* **fur·ri·er, fur·ri·est**

fur·be·low (fûr'bə·lō) *n.* 1. A ruffle, frill, or similar ornament. 2. Any showy bit of decoration. [< F *falbala*] —**fur'be·low** *v.t.*

fur·bish (fûr'bish) *v.t.* 1. To make bright by rubbing; burnish. 2. To restore to brightness or beauty; renovate: often with *up.* [< OHG *furban* to clean] —**fur'bish·er** *n.*

fur·cate (fûr'kāt; *for adj., also* -kit) *v.i.* **·cat·ed, ·cat·ing** To divide into branches. —*adj.* Forked: also **fur'cat·ed** (-kāt·id). [< L *furca* fork] —**fur·ca'tion** *n.*

fu·ri·ous (fyŏŏr'ē·əs) *adj.* 1. Extremely angry; raging. 2. Extremely violent or intense; fierce. 3. Pushed to the limit: a *furious* pace. [< L *furere* to rage] —**fu'ri·ous·ly** *adv.* —**fu'ri·ous·ness** *n.*

furl (fûrl) *v.t.* 1. To roll up (a sail, flag, etc.) and make secure, as to a mast or staff. —*v.i.* 2. To become furled. —*n.* 1. The act of furling, or the state of being furled. 2. A rolled-up section of a sail, flag, etc. [< F *ferler* < L *firmum* firm + *ligare* to tie]

fur·long (fûr'lông, -long) *n.* A measure of length, equal to ⅛ mile or 201.168 meters. [OE *furlang* < *furh* furrow + *lang* long]

fur·lough (fûr'lō) *n.* Permission to be absent from duty, esp. in the armed services; leave. [< Du. *verlof*] —**fur'lough** *v.t.*

fur·nace (fûr'nis) *n.* 1. An enclosed chamber designed to produce intense heat for warming a building, melting metal, etc. 2. Any intensely hot place. [< L *furnus* oven]

fur·nish (fûr'nish) *v.t.* 1. To equip, or fit out, as with fittings or furniture. 2. To supply; provide. [< OF *furnir* < OHG *frumjan* to provide] —**fur'nish·er** *n.*

fur·nish·ings (fûr′nish·ingz) *n.pl.* 1. Articles of clothing, including accessories. 2. Furniture and other fixtures for a home, office, etc.
fur·ni·ture (fûr′nə·chər) *n.* 1. The movable articles used in a home, office, etc., as sofas, tables, or mirrors. 2. Any necessary equipment, as for a factory or ship. [< F *fourniture* < OHG *frumjan* to provide]
fu·ror (fyŏŏr′ôr) *n.* 1. A great stir; commotion. 2. A state of intense excitement or enthusiasm. [< L < *furere* to rage]
fur·ri·er (fûr′ē·ər, -yər) *n.* One who deals in, processes, repairs, or stores furs.
fur·ring (fûr′ing) *n.* Strips of wood, metal, etc., affixed to a wall, floor, etc., so as to make a level surface or create air spaces.
fur·row (fûr′ō) *n.* 1. A narrow channel made in the ground by or as if by a plow. 2. Any long, narrow, deep depression, as a groove, rut, or deep wrinkle. [OE *furh*] —**fur′row** *v.t. & v.i.*
fur·ther (fûr′thər) Comparative of FAR. —*adv.* 1. At or to a more distant or remote point in time or space. 2. To a greater degree; more. 3. In addition; besides; moreover. —*adj.* 1. More distant or advanced in time or degree. 2. More distant in space; farther. 3. Additional. —*v.t.* To help forward; promote. [OE *furthra*] —**fur′ther·ance** *n.* —**fur′ther·er** *n.*
fur·ther·more (fûr′thər·môr′) *adv.* In addition; moreover.
fur·ther·most (fûr′thər·mōst′) *adj.* Furthest.
fur·thest (fûr′thist) Superlative of FAR. —*adv.* 1. At or to the most remote or distant point in space or time. 2. To the greatest degree. —*adj.* 1. Most distant, remote, or advanced in time or degree. 2. Most distant in space.
fur·tive (fûr′tiv) *adj.* 1. Done in secret; surreptitious; stealthy. 2. Evasive; shifty. [< L *fur* thief] —**fur′tive·ly** *adv.* —**fur′tive·ness** *n.*
fu·ry (fyŏŏr′ē) *n. pl.* **·ries** 1. Vehement and uncontrolled anger or rage. 2. A fit of such anger or rage. 3. Violent action or agitation; fierceness: the storm's *fury*. [< L *furia* < *furere* to rave]
furze (fûrz) *n.* A spiny evergreen shrub having many branches and yellow flowers. [OE *fyrs*] —**furz′y** *adj.*
fuse[1] (fyōōz) *n.* 1. A length of combustible material, passing into the charge of an explosive, and igniting the charge when lit. 2. *Mil.* Any device designed to detonate a bomb, projectile, etc. 3. *Electr.* A small metallic device which melts, breaking a circuit, if the current becomes excessive. —*v.t.* To attach a fuse to (a rocket, bomb, etc.). [< L *fusus* spindle]
fuse[2] (fyōōz) *v.t. & v.i.* **fused, fus·ing** 1. To liquefy by heat; melt. 2. To join by or as if by melting together. [< L *fusus*, pp. of *fundere* to pour]
fu·see (fyōō·zē′) *n.* 1. A friction match with a large head capable of burning in the wind. 2. A flare used as a railroad signal. [< F *fusée* < L *fusus* spindle]
fu·se·lage (fyōō′sə·lij, -läzh, -zə-) *n. Aeron.* The body of an airplane. [< F]
fu·si·ble (fyōō′zə·bəl) *adj.* Capable of being fused. —**fu′si·bil′i·ty, fu′si·ble·ness** *n.* —**fu′si·bly** *adv.*
fu·sil·lade (fyōō′zə·lād′) *n.* 1. A simultaneous or quickly repeated discharge of firearms. 2. Anything resembling this: a *fusillade* of hail. —*v.t.* **·lad·ed, ·lad·ing** To attack or bring down with a fusillade. Also **fu′si·lade′**. [< F < *fusiller* to shoot < *fusil* musket]
fu·sion (fyōō′zhən) *n.* 1. A melting or blending together. 2. Something formed by fusing. 3. In politics, the union of two parties or two factions within a party. 4. *Physics* A thermonuclear reaction in which the nuclei of a light element are transformed into those of a heavier element, with the release of great energy. [< L *fusio, -onis* < *fundere* to pour]
fuss (fus) *n.* 1. Nervous activity; commotion. 2. One excessively concerned with trifles: also **fuss′budg′et** (-buj′it). —*v.t. & v.i.* To bother or be bothered with trifles. [Origin unknown] —**fuss′er** *n.*
fuss·y (fus′ē) *adj.* **fuss·i·er, fuss·i·est** 1. Too much concerned with trifles; finicky. 2. Fidgety; fretful. 3. Requiring meticulous attention; fastidious. —**fuss′i·ly** *adv.* —**fuss′i·ness** *n.*
fus·tian (fus′chən) *n.* 1. A coarse, twilled cotton fabric, as corduroy. 2. Pretentious verbiage; bombast. [< L *fustis* cudgel] —**fus′tian** *adj.*
fust·y (fus′tē) *adj.* **fust·i·er, fust·i·est** 1. Musty; moldy; rank. 2. Old-fashioned; fogeyish. [< obs. *fust* moldy odor < OF, wine cask] —**fust′i·ly** *adv.* —**fust′i·ness** *n.*
fu·tile (fyōō′təl, -tīl) *adj.* 1. Being of no avail; useless. 2. Frivolous; idle. [< L *futilis* pouring out easily, useless] —**fu′tile·ly** *adv.* —**fu·til·i·ty** (fyōō·til′ə·tē), **fu′tile·ness** *n.*
fu·ture (fyōō′chər) *n.* 1. The time yet to come. 2. What will be in time to come. 3. A condition, usu. of success or prosperity, in time to come: a man with a *future*. 4. *Usu. pl.* Any commodity or security sold or bought upon agreement of future delivery. 5. *Gram.* a A verb tense denoting action that will take place at some time to come. b A verb in this tense. —*adj.* 1. Such as will be in time to come. 2. Pertaining to or expressing time to come. [< L *futurus*, future participle of *esse* to be] —**fu′tur·is′tic** *adj.* —**fu′ture·less** *adj.*
fu·tu·ri·ty (fyōō·tŏŏr′ə·tē, -tyŏŏr′-) *n. pl.* **·ties** 1. The future. 2. The state or quality of being future. 3. A future event or possibility.
fuzz (fuz) *n.* 1. Fine, loose particles, fibers, or hairs. 2. A fluffy mass of these. —*v.t. & v.i.* To become or cause to become fuzzy. [Origin unknown]
fuzz·y (fuz′ē) *adj.* **fuzz·i·er, fuzz·i·est** 1. Having fuzz. 2. Resembling fuzz. 3. Lacking sharp distinctness or clarity; blurred. —**fuzz′i·ly** *adv.* —**fuzz′i·ness** *n.*
-fy *suffix of verbs* 1. Cause to be or become: *deify*. 2. Become: *liquefy*. [< L *facere* to do, to make]

G

g, G (jē) *n. pl.* **g's** or **gs, G's** or **Gs, gees** (jēz) 1. The seventh letter of the English alphabet. 2. Any sound represented by the letter *g*. 3. *Usu. cap. Slang* One thousand dollars; a grand. **—***symbol* 1. *Music* The fifth tone in the diatonic scale of C. 2. *Physics* The acceleration of a body due to the earth's gravity, about 32 feet or 9.8 meters per second per second; also, a unit of acceleration equal to that of gravity (symbol g).

gab (gab) *Informal v.i.* **gabbed, gab·bing** To talk, esp. glibly or excessively. [Prob. < ON *gabba* to mock] **—gab** *n.* **—gab′ber** *n.*

gab·ar·dine (gab′ər·dēn, gab′ər·dēn′) *n.* 1. A firm, twilled, worsted fabric, used for coats, suits, etc. 2. A similar, softer fabric of mercerized cotton. [< Sp. *garbardina*]

gab·ble (gab′əl) *v.i.* **·bled, ·bling** 1. To talk quickly or incoherently. 2. To utter rapid, cackling sounds, as geese. **—***n.* 1. Glib, incoherent, or foolish talk. 2. Cackling sounds, as of geese. [Freq. of GAB] **—gab′bler** *n.*

gab·fest (gab′fest) *n.* An informal gathering for chatty conversation. [< GAB + G *fest* feast]

ga·ble (gā′bəl) *n. Archit.* The triangular top of an end wall of a building, formed by the sloping ends of a roof. [< OF, prob. < ON *gafl* gable] **—ga′ble** *v.t. & v.i.*

Gab·on·ese (gab·ə·nēz′) *adj.* Of Gabon or its people. **—Gab·on·ese′** *n.*

gad (gad) *v.i.* **gad·ded, gad·ding** To roam about restlessly or capriciously; ramble. [? < obs. *gadling* vagabond] **—gad** *n.* **—gad′der** *n.*

gad·a·bout (gad′ə·bout′) *n. Informal* One who goes about aimlessly, frivolously, etc.

gad·fly (gad′flī′) *n. pl.* **·flies** 1. One of various large flies that bite cattle, horses, etc. 2. A bothersome and persistently critical individual. [< ON *gaddr* goad + FLY[2]]

gadg·et (gaj′it) *n. Informal* Any small device or contrivance.

gad·o·lin·i·um (gad′ə·lin′ē·əm) *n.* A metallic element (symbol Gd) of the lanthanide series. [after John *Gadolin*, 1760–1852, Finnish chemist]

gad·wall (gad′wôl) *n. pl.* **·walls** or **·wall** A large fresh-water duck.

Gael (gāl) *n.* One of the Celts of Ireland or the Scottish Highlands. [< Scottish Gaelic *Gaidheal*]

Gael·ic (gā′lik) *adj.* Belonging or relating to the Gaels or their languages. **—***n.* 1. The languages of the Gaels. 2. The Goidelic branch of the Celtic languages.

gaff (gaf) *n.* 1. A sharp iron hook at the end of a pole, for landing a large fish; also, the pole. 2. *Naut.* A spar for extending the upper edge of a fore-and-aft sail. 3. *Slang* Loud or abusive talk. **—to stand the gaff** *Informal* To endure adversity. **—***v.t.* To strike or land with a gaff. [< OF *gaffe*, prob. < Celtic]

gaffe (gaf) *n.* A blunder; faux pas. [< F]

gaf·fer (gaf′ər) *n.* An old man. [Alter. of GODFATHER]

gag (gag) *n.* 1. Something, as a wadded cloth, forced into or over the mouth to stifle speech or outcries. 2. Any suppression of free speech, as by censorship. 3. A device to keep the jaws open, as in dentistry. 4. *Slang* A joke or hoax. **—***v.* **gagged, gag·ging** *v.t.* 1. To stifle speech by means of a gag. 2. To keep from speaking freely, as by force or authority. 3. To cause nausea in; cause to retch. **—***v.i.* 4. To heave with nausea; also, to choke on something. [ME *gaggen*] **—gag′ger** *n.*

ga·ga (gä′gä′) *adj. Slang* Foolish; crazy. [< F (slang), a foolish old man]

gage[1] (gāj) See GAUGE.

gage[2] (gāj) *n.* 1. Something given as security for an action to be performed; pledge. 2. Anything, as a glove, proffered as a challenge. 3. Any challenge. [< OF, pledge]

gag·gle (gag′əl) *v.i.* **·gled, ·gling** To cackle; gabble. **—***n.* 1. A flock of geese. 2. Any group. [ME *gagelen* to cackle]

gai·e·ty (gā′ə·tē) *n. pl.* **·ties** 1. The state of being gay; cheerfulness. 2. Bright colorfulness or showiness, as of dress. 3. *Often pl.* Fun; merrymaking.

gai·ly (gā′lē) *adv.* In a gay manner.

gain (gān) *v.t.* 1. To obtain; acquire. 2. To succeed in winning (a victory, etc.). 3. To increase: to *gain* momentum. 4. To put on (weight). 5. To earn (a living, etc.). 6. To arrive at; reach: to *gain* port. **—***v.i.* 7. To grow better: to *gain* in health. 8. To draw nearer; also, to increase one's lead: usu. with *on* or *upon*. **—***n.* 1. *Often pl.* Profits; winnings. 2. An advantage or lead. 3. An increase, as in size, amount, etc. 4. The act of gaining. [< OF *gaaignier* < Gmc.]

gain·er (gā′nər) *n.* 1. One who or that which gains. 2. A full gainer. 3. A half gainer.

gain·ful (gān′fəl) *adj.* Yielding profit; lucrative. **—gain′ful·ly** *adv.* **—gain′ful·ness** *n.*

gain·say (gān′sā′) *v.t.* **·said, ·say·ing** 1. To deny. 2. To contradict. 3. To act against; oppose. [OE *gegn-* against + SAY] **—gain′·say′er** *n.*

gait (gāt) *n.* 1. One's manner of moving along on foot. 2. One of the ways in which a horse steps or runs. **—***v.t.* To train (a horse) to take a gait. [< ON *gata* way]

gai·ter (gā′tər) *n.* 1. A covering, as of leather or canvas, worn over the leg or over the ankle and instep. 2. An old-fashioned shoe with a high top. [< F *guêtre*]

gal (gal) *n. Slang* 1. A girl. 2. A girl friend.

ga·la (gā′lə, gal′ə, gä′lə) *adj.* Appropriate to

a festive occasion; festive. —*n.* An occasion marked by joyous festivity. [< Ital., holiday dress]

Gal·a·had (gal′ə·had) *n.* A noble or gallant man. [after *Galahad*, a knight in Arthurian legend]

Ga·la·tian (gə·lā′shən) *adj.* Of ancient Galatia. —*n.* A native of Galatia. —**Epistle to the Galatians** A book of the New Testament, a letter written by the apostle Paul.

gal·ax·y (gal′ək·sē) *n. pl.* **·ax·ies** 1. *Astron.* Any very large system of stars, nebulae, or other celestial bodies. 2. *Usu. cap.* The Milky Way. 3. A brilliant group, as of persons. [< Gk. *galaxias* Milky Way] —**ga·lac·tic** (gə·lak′tik) *adj.*

gale (gāl) *n.* 1. A strong wind. 2. An outburst, as of hilarity. [Origin uncertain]

ga·le·na (gə·lē′nə) *n.* A metallic, dull gray lead sulfide compound, one of the principal ores of lead. Also **ga·le·nite** (gə·lē′nīt). [< L]

Ga·li·cian (gə·lish′ən) *n.* 1. A native of Spanish Galicia. 2. The Portuguese dialect spoken there. 3. A native of Polish Galicia. —**Ga·li′cian** *adj.*

Gal·i·le·an[1] (gal′ə·lē′ən) *n.* 1. An inhabitant of Galilee, in ancient Palestine. 2. A Christian. —**Gal′i·le′an** *adj.*

Gal·i·le·an[2] (gal′ə·lē′ən) *adj.* Of or pertaining to Galileo.

gall[1] (gôl) *n.* 1. *Physiol.* The bitter fluid secreted by the liver; bile. 2. Bitter feeling; rancor. 3. Something bitter. 4. *Slang* Impudence. [OE *gealla*]

gall[2] (gôl) *n.* 1. An abrasion or sore produced by friction. 2. Something that irritates or vexes. 3. Exasperation. —*v.t.* 1. To injure (the skin) by friction; chafe. 2. To vex or irritate. —*v.i.* 3. To become or be chafed. [Prob. < GALL[1]]

gall[3] (gôl) *n.* An abnormal plant growth that on certain oaks yields tannin. Also **gall′nut′**. [< L *galla*]

gal·lant (gal′ənt for *adj. defs. 1, 3, 4*; gə·lant′, gə·länt′ for *adj. def. 2*; *n.* gə·lant′, gə·länt′, gal′ənt) *adj.* 1. Spirited; courageous; brave. 2. Chivalrously attentive to women; also, dashingly amorous. 3. Stately; imposing. 4. Showy: *gallant* attire. —*n.* 1. A brave, spirited man. 2. A man chivalrously attentive to women or amorous in a courtly way. [< OF *galer* to rejoice] —**gal′lant·ly** *adv.* —**gal′lant·ry** *n.*

gall bladder *Anat.* A small pouch serving as a reservoir for bile conducted from the liver through the **gall duct.**

gal·le·on (gal′ē·ən) *n.* A large sailing vessel of the 15th to 17th c. [< Sp. *galeón*]

gal·er·y (gal′ər·ē) *n. pl.* **·ler·ies** 1. A roofed promenade, esp. an open-sided one, extending along an inner or outer wall of a building. 2. *Southern U.S.* A porch or veranda. 3. The topmost balcony of a theater, church, etc. 4. A group of spectators, as of those in a grandstand. 5. A part of the general public viewed as uninformed, undiscriminating, etc. 6. A room or building in which statues, paintings, etc., are displayed. 7. A room or building in which articles are sold to the highest bidder. 8. An enclosed place, as at a fair, where one shoots at targets for amusement. 9. A tunnel or underground passage, as in a mine. —**to play to the gallery** To play or cater to the common crowd. [< Med.L *galeria*]

gal·ley (gal′ē) *n. pl.* **·leys** 1. A long, low vessel used in ancient times, propelled by oars and sails. 2. A large rowboat. 3. The kitchen of a ship, trailer, etc. 4. *Printing* **a** A long tray for holding composed type. **b** A galley proof. [< OF *galee*, ult. < LGk. *galaia*]

galley proof *Printing* A proof taken from type composed in a galley and used for making corrections.

galley slave 1. A slave or convict condemned to row a galley. 2. A drudge.

gall·fly (gôl′flī) *n. pl.* **·flies** A small insect that deposits eggs in plant tissue, producing galls.

Gal·lic (gal′ik) *adj.* Of or pertaining to ancient Gaul or modern France; French. [< L *Gallus* inhabitant of Gaul]

gal·lic acid (gal′ik) *Chem.* A white, crystalline organic compound, found in plants and used in inks, paper, etc.

Gal·li·cize (gal′ə·sīz) *v.t. & v.i.* **·cized, ·ciz·ing** To make French in character or language. —**Gal′li·cism** *n.*

gal·li·na·ceous (gal′ə·nā′shəs) *adj.* Of or pertaining to an order of birds including the common hen, turkeys, partridges, etc. [< L *gallina* hen]

gall·ing (gô′ling) *adj.* Very annoying or exasperating.

gal·li·nule (gal′ə·nyōōl, -nōōl) *n.* Any of several wading birds of the rail family. [< L *gallina* hen]

gal·li·um (gal′ē·əm) *n.* A rare, bluish white, metallic element (symbol Ga) in the aluminum group. [< L *gallus* cock, trans. of *Lecoq* de Boisbaudran, 1838–1912, its discoverer] —**gal′lic** *adj.*

gal·li·vant (gal′ə·vant, gal′ə·vant′) *v.i.* To roam about capriciously; gad. [? Alter. of GALLANT]

Gallo- *combining form* Gaulish or French. [< L *Gallus*]

gal·lon (gal′ən) *n.* A liquid measure that by the U.S. standard contains 231 cubic inches or 4 quarts and by the British standard (**imperial gallon**) 277.3 cubic inches or 4 imperial quarts. [ME *galon*]

gal·lop (gal′əp) *n.* 1. The fastest gait of a horse, etc. 2. A ride at a gallop. 3. Any rapid pace. [< OF *galoper* < Gmc.] —**gal′lop** *v.i. & v.t.* —**gal′lop·er** *n.*

gal·lows (gal′ōz) *n. pl.* **·lows·es** or **·lows** An upright framework supporting a crossbeam, used for execution by hanging. [OE *galga*]

gall·stone (gôl′stōn′) *n.* *Pathol.* A small, stony mass sometimes formed in the gall bladder or bile passages.

gal·op (gal′əp) *n.* 1. A lively dance. 2. Music for this dance, written in duple meter. [< F, gallop]

ga·lore (gə·lôr′) *adv.* In great numbers or abundance. [< Irish *go leōr* enough]

ga·losh (gə·losh′) *n.* *Usu. pl.* A high overshoe worn in bad weather. [< F *galoche*]

gal·van·ic (gal·van′ik) *adj.* 1. Of or caused by electricity as produced by chemical action. 2. Stimulating; exciting.

gal·va·nism (gal′və·niz′əm) *n.* Electricity as produced by chemical action: also called *voltaism*. [after Luigi *Galvani*, 1737–98, Italian physiologist]

gal·va·nize (gal′və·nīz) *v.t.* **·nized, ·niz·ing** 1. To stimulate to muscular action by electricity. 2. To excite. 3. To plate steel, etc., with a protective coating of zinc. **—gal′va·ni·za′tion** *n.* **—gal′va·niz′er** *n.*

galvanized iron Iron coated with zinc, as for protection against rust.

galvano- *combining form* Galvanic; galvanism.

gal·va·nom·e·ter (gal′və·nom′ə·tər) *n. Electr.* An apparatus used to detect or measure an electric current. **—gal·va·no·met·ric** (gal′və·nō·met′rik, gal·van′ō-) *adj.*

gam (gam) *n. Slang* A leg, esp. of a woman.

Gam·bi·an (gam′bē·ən) *n.* A native or inhabitant of Gambia. **—Gam′bi·an** *adj.*

gam·bit (gam′bit) *n.* 1. In chess, an opening in which a player risks or sacrifices a piece to gain a favorable position. 2. Any opening move, as one to promote discussion. 3. A calculated move; a stratagem. [< OF *gambet*, a tripping up, ult. < LL *gamba* leg]

gam·ble (gam′bəl) *v.* **·bled, ·bling** *v.i.* 1. To risk or bet something of value on the outcome of a game of chance, etc. 2. To take a risk to obtain a result. **—***v.t.* 3. To wager or bet (something of value). 4. To lose by taking risks: usu. with *away*. **—***n. Informal* Any risky venture. [Cf. OE *gamenian* to sport, play] **—gam′bler** *n.*

gam·bol (gam′bəl) *v.i.* **·boled** or **·bolled, ·bol·ing** or **·bol·ling** To skip or leap about in play; frolic. [< Ital. *gamba* leg] **—gam′bol** *n.*

gam·brel roof (gam′brəl) *Archit.* A ridged roof with the slope broken on each side.

game[1] (gām) *n.* 1. A contest governed by set rules. 2. *pl.* Athletic competitions. 3. A single contest forming part of a fixed series. 4. A win, as in tennis or cards. 5. The score during a contest: The *game* was 6–6. 6. The equipment used in playing games. 7. Playing style or prowess: His *game* of golf is not good. 8. Any form of play. 9. *Informal* Any profession, business, etc.: the teaching *game*. 10. Animals, fish, etc., that are hunted or taken; also, the flesh of such animals, etc. 11. Anything hunted; quarry. 12. A target for ridicule, criticism, etc.: They were fair *game*. **—to play the game** To act in accordance with what is expected. **—***v.i.* **gamed, gam·ing** To gamble at cards, etc., for money or other stakes. **—***adj.* 1. Of hunted animals, etc., or their flesh. 2. Having a fighting spirit; plucky. 3. *Informal* Ready; willing. [OE *gamen*] **—game′ly** *adv.* **—game′·ness** *n.*

game[2] (gām) *adj. Informal* Lame: a *game* leg.

game·cock (gām′kok′) *n.* A rooster bred and trained for cockfighting.

game·keep·er (gām′kē′pər) *n.* A person having the care of game, as on an estate.

game plan A strategy designed to achieve some specified objective.

gam·ete (gam′ēt, gə·mēt′) *n. Biol.* A mature reproductive cell. [< Gk. *gamos* marriage] **—ga·met·ic** (gə·met′ik) *adj.*

game theory A mathematical theory dealing with strategies of maximizing gains and minimizing losses in games, warfare, etc.

gameto- *combining form* Gamete. [< Gk. *gamos* marriage]

gam·in (gam′in, *Fr.* gȧ·maṅ′) *n.* A homeless boy; street urchin; waif. [< F]

ga·mine (ga·mēn′, *Fr.* gȧ·mēn′) *n.* 1. A homeless girl. 2. A girl with elfin appeal. [< F]

gam·ma (gam′ə) *n.* The third letter in the Greek alphabet (Γ, γ), corresponding to *g* (as in *go*).

gamma globulin *Biochem.* A globulin present in blood plasma and rich in antibodies.

gamma rays *Physics* A type of electromagnetic radiation of great penetrating power.

gam·mer (gam′ər) *n.* An old woman. [Alter. of GODMOTHER]

gam·mon (gam′ən) *n.* In backgammon, a double victory, in which one player removes all his pieces before the other player removes any. [? ME *gamen* game] **—gam′·mon** *v.t.*

-gamous *combining form* Pertaining to marriage or union for reproduction: used in adjectives corresponding to nouns in *-gamy*: *polygamous*. [< Gk. *gamos* + -OUS]

gam·ut (gam′ət) *n.* The whole range of anything: the *gamut* of emotions. [< Med.L *gamma ut* < *gamma*, the first note of the early musical scale + *ut* (later, *do*), the topmost note (or top and bottom notes) of a scale]

gam·y (gā′mē) *adj.* **gam·i·er, gam·i·est** 1. Having the flavor or odor of game, esp. when somewhat tainted. 2. Full of pluck. Also **gam′ey**. **—gam′i·ness** *n.*

-gamy *combining form* Marriage or union for reproduction: *polygamy*. [< Gk. *gamos*]

gan·der (gan′dər) *n.* 1. A male goose. 2. *Slang* A look or glance: to take a *gander*. [OE *gandra*]

gang (gang) *n.* 1. A group of persons organized or associated together for disreputable or illegal purposes. 2. A crew of persons who work together. 3. *Informal* A group of persons associated together for some purpose. 4. A set of similar tools or other devices designed to operate as a unit. **—***v.t. & v.i.* To unite into or form a gang. **—to gang up on** To combine against or attack as a group. [OE *gangan* to go]

gan·gling (gang′gling) *adj.* Awkwardly tall and lanky. Also **gan′gly**. [Cf. dial. E *gangrel* a lanky person]

gan·gli·on (gang′glē·ən) *n. pl.* **·gli·a** or **·gli·ons** 1. *Physiol.* A bundle of nerve cells, outside of the central nervous system. 2. Any center of energy, activity, or strength. [< Gk. *ganglion* tumor] **—gan′gli·on·at′ed** *adj.*

gang·plank (gang′plangk′) *n.* A temporary bridge for passengers between a vessel and a wharf.

gan·grene (gang′grēn, gang·grēn′) *n. Pathol.* The rotting of body tissue, caused by a failure in blood circulation, as from infection, etc. [< Gk. *gangraina*] **—gan′grene** *v.t. & v.i.* **·grened, ·gren·ing —gan′gre·nous** (-grə·nəs) *adj.*

gang·ster (gang′stər) *n.* A member of a criminal gang.

gang·way (*n.* gang′wā, *interj.* gang′wā′) *n.* 1. A passageway through, into, or out of any enclosure. 2. *Naut.* **a** A passage on a ship's upper deck. **b** An opening in a ship's side for passengers or freight. **c** A gangplank. **—***interj.* Get out of the way! [OE *gangweg*]

gan·net (gan′it) *n.* Any of several large sea birds related to the pelicans and herons. [OE *ganot*]

gant·let (gônt′lit) See GAUNTLET.
gan·try (gan′trē) *n. pl.* **·tries** 1. A bridgelike framework for holding the rails of a traveling crane or for supporting railway signals. 2. A gantry scaffold. 3. A frame to support a barrel in a horizontal position. [Alter. of OF *gantier* < L *canterius* beast of burden, framework]
gantry scaffold *Aerospace* A large mobile scaffolding used to assemble and service a large rocket on its launching pad.
gaol (jāl) *n. Brit.* Jail. [Var. of JAIL] **—gaol′er** *n.*
gap (gap) *n.* 1. An opening or wide crack, as in a wall. 2. A deep notch or ravine in a mountain ridge. 3. A break in continuity; interruption. 4. A difference, as in character, opinions, etc. **—*v.t.*** **gapped, gap·ping** To make or adjust a breach or opening in. [< ON] **—gap′py** *adj.* **·pi·er, ·pi·est**
gape (gāp, gap) *v.i.* **gaped, gap·ing** 1. To stare with or as with the mouth wide open. 2. To open the mouth wide, as in yawning. 3. To be or become wide open. **—*n.*** 1. The act of gaping. 2. A wide opening. [< ON *gapa*] **—gap′er** *n.*
gar (gär) *n.* A long fresh-water fish having a spearlike snout. [Short for GARFISH]
ga·rage (gə·räzh′, -räj′) *n.* A building in which motor vehicles are stored, serviced, or repaired. **—*v.t.*** **·raged, ·rag·ing** To put or keep in a garage. [< F *garer* to protect]
garage sale A sale of used household goods held in one's garage or on one's premises. Also called *tag sale.*
garb (gärb) *n.* 1. Clothes; esp., apparel characteristic of some office, rank, etc. 2. External appearance, form, or expression. **—*v.t.*** To clothe; dress. [< MF *garbe* gracefulness]
gar·bage (gär′bij) *n.* 1. Kitchen refuse. 2. Anything worthless or useless. 3. Useless or garbled data in a computerized system. [ME, animal entrails]
gar·ble (gär′bəl) *v.t.* **·bled, ·bling** To mix up, confuse, or distort (a story, facts, etc.). **—*n.*** 1. The act of garbling. 2. That which is garbled. [< Arabic *gharbala* to sift]
gar·çon (gȧr·sôṅ′) *n. pl.* **·çons** (-sôṅ′) *French* 1. A boy or youth. 2. A waiter. 3. A male servant.
gar·den (gär′dən) *n.* 1. A place for the cultivation of flowers, vegetables, or small plants. 2. Any territory remarkable for the beauty of its vegetation. 3. *Often pl.* An area commonly used as a place of public resort. **—*adj.*** Grown or capable of being grown in a garden. **—*v.t.*** 1. To cultivate as a garden. **—*v.i.*** 2. To till or work in a garden. [< AF *gardin*] **—gar′den·er** *n.* **—gar′den·ing** *n.*
gar·de·ni·a (gär·dē′nē·ə, -dēn′yə) *n.* Any of several mainly tropical shrubs or trees with large, fragrant, yellow or white flowers. [after Alexander *Garden,* 1730–91, U.S. botanist]
garden variety Ordinary; run-of-the-mill.
gar·fish (gär′fish′) *n. pl.* **·fish** or **·fish·es** A gar. Also **gar′pike.** [OE *gar* spear + FISH]
gar·gan·tu·an (gär·gan′cho͞o·ən) *adj.* Extremely large; enormous; gigantic. [after *Gargantua,* satire (1534) by F. Rabelais]
gar·gle (gär′gəl) *v.i.* **·gled, ·gling** To rinse the throat with a liquid kept agitated by the slow expulsion of air. **—*n.*** A liquid used for gargling. [< OF *gargouille* throat]
gar·goyle (gär′goil) *n.* A waterspout, usu. made in the form of a grotesque human or animal figure, projecting from a building. [< OF *gargouille* throat]
gar·ish (gâr′ish) *adj.* Vulgarly showy or gaudy. [Cf. obs. *gaure* to stare] **—gar′ish·ly** *adv.* **—gar′ish·ness** *n.*
gar·land (gär′lənd) *n.* 1. A wreath or rope of flowers, leaves, vines, etc. 2. A collection of poems, bits of prose, etc. **—*v.t.*** To decorate with or make into a garland. [< OF *garlande*]
gar·lic (gär′lik) *n.* A plant having a compound bulb, the bulbs (or cloves) of which are used in cooking. [OE *gār* spear + *lēac* leek] **—gar′lick·y** *adj.*
gar·ment (gär′mənt) *n.* 1. An article of clothing, esp. of outer clothing. 2. *pl.* Clothes. [< OF *garnir* to garnish]
gar·ner (gär′nər) *v.t.* To gather or store; accumulate. [< L *granum* grain]
gar·net (gär′nit) *n.* 1. Any of a group of vitreous silicate minerals; esp., any of the deep red varieties, used as gems. 2. A deep red color. [< OF < Med.L *granatum* < L, pomegranate, from its red color]
gar·nish (gär′nish) *v.t.* 1. To decorate; embellish. 2. In cookery, to decorate (a dish) with flavorsome or colorful trimmings. [< OF *garnir* to prepare] **—gar′nish** *n.* **—gar·ni·ture** (gär′ni·chər) *n.*
gar·nish·ee (gär′nish·ē′) *Law v.t.* **·nish·eed, ·nish·ee·ing** To attach (a debtor's assets) by garnishment. **—*n.*** A person who has been garnisheed.
gar·nish·ment (gär′nish·mənt) *n.* 1. The act of garnishing. 2. That which garnishes; embellishment. 3. *Law* A notice to a person holding money or effects belonging to a defendant not to return or dispose of the assets pending court judgment.
gar·ret (gar′it) *n.* A room or set of rooms in an attic. [< OF *garir* to watch, defend]
gar·ri·son (gar′ə·sən) *n.* 1. The military force stationed in a fort, town, etc. 2. The place where such a force is stationed. **—*v.t.*** 1. To place troops in, as a fort or town, for defense. 2. To occupy as a garrison. [< OF *garir* to defend]
gar·rote (gə·rot′, -rōt′) *n.* A former Spanish method of execution with a cord or metal collar tightened by a screwlike device; also, the cord or collar used. **—*v.t.*** **·rot·ed, ·rot·ing** 1. To execute with a garrote. 2. To throttle in order to rob, silence, etc. Also **ga·rote′, ga·rotte′.** [< Sp. *garrote*]
gar·ru·lous (gar′ə·ləs, -yə-) *adj.* 1. Talkative; glib. 2. Rambling; wordy. [< L *garrulus* talkative] **—gar′ru·lous·ly** *adv.* **—gar·ru·li·ty** (gə·ro͞o′lə·tē), **gar′ru·lous·ness** *n.*
gar·ter (gär′tər) *n.* A band worn around the leg or a tab attached to an undergarment to hold a stocking in place. [< OF *garet* bend of the knee]
garter snake Any of various small, harmless, brightly striped snakes.
gas (gas) *n. pl.* **gas·es** or **gas·ses** 1. A form of matter having extreme molecular mobility

and capable of diffusing and expanding rapidly in all directions. 2. Any of various gases or mixtures of gases with explosive, combustive, anesthetic, or poisonous properties. 3. A noxious exhalation given off by improperly digested food in the stomach or intestines. 4. Gasoline. 5. *Slang* Long-winded talking. 6. *Slang* Something very exciting, satisfying, etc. —*v.* **gassed, gas·sing;** he, she, it **gas·ses** or **gas·es** —*v.t.* 1. To subject to or affect with gas. 2. To fill or supply with gas. —*v.i.* 3. To give off gas. 4. *Slang* To talk excessively. [Coined by J. B. van Helmont, 1577–1644, Belgian chemist, either < Du. *geest* spirit or < L < Gk. *chaos* formless mass] —**gas·e·ous** (gas′ē·əs, gas′yəs, gash′əs) *adj.* —**gas′sy** *adj.* **·si·er, ·si·est**

gash (gash) *v.t.* To make a long, deep cut in. [< OF *garser* to scratch] —**gash** *n.*

gas·ket (gas′kit) *n.* A ring or plate of rubber, asbestos, etc., used to make a joint leakproof. [Cf. Ital. *gaschetta* end of rope]

gas·light (gas′līt′) *n.* Light produced by the burning of gas. Also **gas light.**

gas mask A protective mask with an air filter worn for protection against noxious gases.

gas·o·hol (gas′ə·hôl, -hol) *n.* A mixture of gasoline and alcohol, used as a motor fuel, esp. in automobiles.

gas·o·line (gas′ə·lēn, gas′ə·lēn′) *n.* A colorless, volatile, flammable liquid hydrocarbon, made by the distillation of crude petroleum and used chiefly as a fuel. Also **gas′o·lene.**

gasp (gasp) *v.i.* 1. To take in the breath suddenly and sharply, as from fear. 2. To have great longing or desire: with *for* or *after.* —*v.t.* 3. To say or utter while gasping. [< ON *geispa* yawn] —**gasp** *n.*

gas station A service station.

gas·tric (gas′trik) *adj.* Of or pertaining to the stomach.

gastric juice *Biochem.* A fluid secreted by stomach glands, essential to digestion.

gas·tri·tis (gas·trī′tis) *n. Pathol.* Inflammation of the stomach lining. —**gas·trit·ic** (gas·trit′ik) *adj.*

gastro- *combining form* Stomach. Also, before vowels, **gastr-.** [< Gk. *gastēr*]

gas·tro·in·tes·ti·nal (gas′trō·in·tes′tə·nəl) *adj.* Of or pertaining to the stomach and intestines.

gas·tro·nome (gas′trə·nōm) *n.* A gourmet.

gas·tro·nom·ic (gas′trə·nom′ik) *adj.* Of or pertaining to gastronomes or gastronomy. Also **gas′tro·nom′i·cal.**

gas·tron·o·my (gas·tron′ə·mē) *n.* The art of good eating; epicurism. [< Gk. *gastēr* stomach + *nomos* law]

gas·tro·pod (gas′trə·pod) *n.* One of a large class of aquatic and terrestrial mollusks, usu. having a muscular creeping organ and a spiral shell with one valve. [< Gk. *gastēr* stomach + *pous, podos* foot] —**gas′tro·pod, gas·trop·o·dan** (gas·trop′ə·dən), **gas·trop·o·dous** (gas·trop′ə·dəs) *adj.*

gas·works (gas′wûrks′) *n. pl.* **·works** An establishment where gas is manufactured.

gate (gāt) *n.* 1. A movable barrier, commonly swinging on hinges, that closes or opens a passage through a wall, fence, etc. 2. A passage through a wall or fence. 3. Anything that gives access: the *gate* to success. 4. A structure or valvelike device for controlling the supply of water, oil, gas, etc. 5. The total paid attendance at a sports event, stage show, etc.; also, the money collected. [OE *gatu,* pl. of *geat* opening]

gate·crash·er (gāt′krash′ər) *n. Informal* One who enters without paying or being invited.

gate·way (gāt′wā′) *n.* 1. An entrance that is or may be closed with a gate. 2. Any means of entry or exit.

gath·er (gath′ər) *v.t.* 1. To bring together into one place or group. 2. To bring together from various places, sources, etc. 3. To harvest or pick, as crops, fruit, etc. 4. To accumulate or muster: The storm *gathered* force. 5. To clasp or enfold. 6. To wrinkle (the brow). 7. To draw into folds, as cloth on a thread. 8. To become aware of; infer. —*v.i.* 9. To come together or assemble. 10. To increase by accumulation. 11. To become wrinkled or creased, as the brow. 12. To come to a head, as a boil. —*n. Usu. pl.* A pleat or fold in cloth, secured by a thread. [OE *gadrian*] —**gath′er·er** *n.*

gath·er·ing (gath′ər·ing) *n.* 1. The action of one who or that which gathers. 2. That which is gathered. 3. An assemblage of people; group. 4. A series of gathers in cloth, etc. 5. An abscess or boil. 6. In bookbinding, a collection of printed sheets in proper order.

gauche (gōsh) *adj.* Awkward; clumsy; boorish. [< F, left]

gauche·rie (gōsh·rē′) *n.* 1. Awkward or tactless behavior. 2. An instance of this. [< F]

Gau·cho (gou′chō) *n. pl.* **·chos** A cowboy of the South American plains. [< Sp.]

gaud·y (gô′dē) *adj.* **gaud·i·er, gaud·i·est** Tastelessly bright or showy; garish. [ME *gaude* bead, trinket] —**gaud′i·ly** *adv.* —**gaud′i·ness** *n.*

gauge (gāj) *v.t.* **gauged, gaug·ing** 1. To determine the dimensions, amount, force, etc., of. 2. To determine the contents or capacity of, as a cask. 3. To estimate, appraise, or judge. 4. To make conform to a standard measurement. —*n.* 1. A standard measurement. 2. A means of comparing; criterion. 3. An instrument for measuring or recording. 4. Thickness, diameter, or fineness of something. 5. The diameter of a bore of a gun. Also spelled *gage.* [< OF *gauger* to measure] —**gaug′er** *n.*

Gaul (gôl) *n.* 1. A native of ancient Gaul. 2. A Frenchman.

Gaul·ish (gô′lish) *adj.* Of ancient Gaul, its people, or their Celtic language. —*n.* The extinct Celtic language of Gaul.

gaunt (gônt) *adj.* 1. Emaciated, as from hunger, illness, or age; haggard. 2. Desolate or gloomy in appearance: a *gaunt* region. [? < OF *gent* elegant] —**gaunt′ness** *n.*

gaunt·let[1] (gônt′lit) *n.* 1. In medieval armor, a glove covered with metal plates to protect the hand. 2. Any glove with a long, often flaring extension over the wrist. —**to take up the gauntlet** To accept a challenge. —**to throw (or fling) down the gauntlet** To challenge to combat. [< OF *gant* mitten]

gaunt·let[2] (gônt′lit) *n.* A former military punishment in which the offender ran between two lines of men, who struck him with clubs, whips, etc., as he passed. —**to run the gauntlet** 1. To undergo such punishment. 2. To suffer a barrage of problems, criticism, etc. [Earlier *gantlet* < *gantlope*, alter. of Sw. *gatlopp* a running down a lane]

gauss (gous) *n.* *Physics* The electromagnetic unit of magnetic induction. [after K. F. *Gauss*, 1777–1855, German mathematician]

gauze (gôz) *n.* 1. A lightweight, transparent fabric with an open weave, made of silk, cotton, etc. 2. Any thin, open-mesh material. [< MF *gaze*, appar. after *Gaza*, where originally made] **—gauz′y** *adj.* **—gauz′i·ness** *n.*

gave (gāv) Past tense of GIVE.

gav·el (gav′əl) *n.* A mallet used, as by a presiding officer, to call for order or attention. [< OF (Norman) *keville* pin]

ga·votte (gə·vot′) *n.* 1. A dance of French origin, popular in the 17th and 18th c. 2. Music for this dance, written in duple meter. Also **ga·vot′.** [< Provençal *gavoto* Alpine dance]

gawk (gôk) *v.i.* *Informal* 1. To stare stupidly; gape. 2. To move about or behave awkwardly. [Cf. dial. E *gawk* left-handed] **—gawk′i·ly** *adv.* **—gawk′i·ness** *n.* **—gawk′y** *adj.* **gawk·i·er, gawk·i·est**

gay (gā) *adj.* 1. Happy and carefree; merry. 2. Brightly colorful or ornamental. 3. Jaunty; sporty. 4. *Slang* Homosexual. [< OF *gai*] **—gay′ness** *n.*

gaze (gāz) *v.i.* **gazed, gaz·ing** To look steadily or fixedly at something; stare. [ME *gasen* < Scand.] **—gaze** *n.* **—gaz′er** *n.*

ga·ze·bo (gə·zē′bo, -zā′-) *n.* *pl.* **·bos** A structure, as a summerhouse, affording a view of the surrounding landscape. [< GAZE]

ga·zelle (gə·zel′) *n.* A small antelope of northern Africa and Arabia, with curved horns and large eyes. [< Arabic *ghazāl*]

ga·zette (gə·zet′) *n.* 1. A newspaper or similar periodical. 2. An official publication, as of a government or society. **—***v.t.* **·zet·ted, ·zet·ting** To publish or announce in a gazette. [< F < dial. Ital. (Venetian) *gazeta* coin]

gaz·et·teer (gaz′ə·tir′) *n.* 1. An alphabetical listing of countries, cities, rivers, etc., together with their location, size, etc. 2. A writer for or publisher of a gazette.

gear (gir) *n.* 1. *Mech.* **a** A mechanical assembly of interacting parts that serves to transmit motion or to change the rate or direction of motion. **b** A related group of parts that work together for a special purpose: steering *gear*. 2. Clothing. 3. Movable property. 4. Any equipment used for a special task: fishing *gear*. **—out of gear** 1. Not in good working order. 2. Disengaged; unconnected. **—***v.t.* 1. *Mech.* **a** To put into gear. **b** To equip with gears. **c** To connect by means of gears. 2. To regulate so as to match or suit something else: to *gear* production to demand. 3. To get ready; prepare: with *up*. 4. To put gear on; dress. **—***v.i.* 5. To come into or be in gear; to mesh. [< ON *gervi* equipment]

gear·ing (gir′ing) *n.* 1. *Mech.* Any system of gears or parts that transmit power or motion. 2. *Naut.* Rope and tackle.

gear·shift (gir′shift′) *n.* *Mech.* A device for engaging or disengaging the gears in a power-transmission system.

gear·wheel (gir′hwēl′) *n.* *Mech.* A cogwheel. Also **gear wheel.**

geck·o (gek′ō) *n.* *pl.* **·os** or **·oes** Any of a family of small lizards having toes with adhesive disks. [< Malay *gēkoq*]

gee (jē) *interj.* An exclamation expressing mild surprise, sympathy, etc. Also **gee whiz.**

geese (gēs) Plural of GOOSE.

gee·zer (gē′zər) *n.* *Slang* A fellow; guy; esp., an old man. [Var. of *guiser* mummer]

Gei·ger counter (gī′gər) *Physics* An instrument for detecting radioactive substances or cosmic rays. Also **geiger counter.** [after Hans *Geiger*, 20th c. German physicist]

gei·sha (gā′shə, gē′-) *n.* *pl.* **·sha** or **·shas** A Japanese girl trained as an entertainer and companion for men. [< Japanese]

gel (jel) *n.* *Chem.* A colloidal dispersion of a solid in a liquid, typically jellylike in consistency. **—***v.t.* & *v.i.* **gelled, gel·ling** To change into a gel. [Short for GELATIN]

gel·a·tin (jel′ə·tin) *n.* 1. A glutinous protein substance, derived from animals and used in food, drug preparations, photographic film, plastics, etc. 2. A jelly made from gelatin. Also **gel′a·tine** (-tin, -tēn). [< F *gélatine*, orig. a soup made from fish] **—ge·lat·i·nous** (ji·lat′ə·nəs) *adj.* **—ge·lat′i·nous·ly** *adv.* **—ge·lat′i·nous·ness** *n.*

ge·lat·i·nize (ji·lat′ə·nīz) *v.* **·nized, ·niz·ing** *v.t.* 1. To change into gelatin or jelly. 2. To treat or coat with gelatin. **—***v.i.* 3. To be changed into gelatin or jelly. **—ge·lat′i·ni·za′tion** *n.*

geld (geld) *v.t.* **geld·ed** or **gelt, geld·ing** To castrate or spay. [< ON *gelda*]

geld·ing (gel′ding) *n.* A castrated animal, esp. a horse.

gel·id (jel′id) *adj.* Very cold; icy; frozen. [< L *gelidus*] **—ge·lid·i·ty** (ji·lid′ə·tē) *n.* **—gel′id·ly** *adv.*

gel·ig·nite (jel′ig·nīt) *n.* An explosive compound containing nitroglycerin. [< GE(LATIN) + L *lign(um)* wood + -ITE]

gem (jem) *n.* 1. A cut and polished precious or semiprecious stone; jewel. 2. One who or that which is treasured. 3. A kind of small, light cake. **—***v.t.* **gemmed, gem·ming** To decorate or set with or as with gems. [< L *gemma* jewel]

gem·i·nate (jem′ə·nāt) *v.t.* & *v.i.* **·nat·ed, ·nat·ing** To double or become doubled. [< L *geminus* twin] **—gem′i·nate** *adj.*

Gem·i·ni (jem′ə·nī) *n.pl.* A constellation, the Twins; also, the third sign of the zodiac.

gem·ma (jem′ə) *n.* *pl.* **gem·mae** (jem′ē) *Biol.* 1. A bud. 2. A part of a plant or animal that detaches to form a new individual. [< L]

gem·mate (jem′āt) *adj.* *Biol.* Bearing or reproducing by gemmae. **—gem′mate** *v.i.* **·mat·ed, ·mat·ing** **—gem·ma′tion** *n.*

gems·bok (gemz′bok) *n.* *pl.* **·bok** or **·boks** A South African antelope having long, sharp horns and a tufted tail. [< Afrikaans < G *gemse* chamois + *bock* a buck]

gem·stone (jem′stōn′) *n.* A precious or semiprecious stone, esp. before it is cut and polished.

ge·müt·lich (gə·myōōt′lik, *Ger.* gə·müt′likh) *adj.* Agreeable; friendly. [< G]

-gen *suffix of nouns* 1. *Chem.* That which produces: *oxygen*. 2. *Biol.* That which is produced: *antigen*. [< Gk. *gen-*, stem of *gignesthai* to be born, become]

gen·darme (zhän′därm, *Fr.* zhäṅ·dȧrm′) *n.* *pl.* **·darmes** (-därmz, *Fr.* -dȧrm′) One of a corps of armed police, esp. in France. [< F < *gens d'armes* men-at-arms]

gen·der (jen′dər) *n.* 1. *Gram.* a One of two or more categories of words or affixes based upon differences of sex or sometimes upon other distinctions. b Such categories collectively, or a system of such categories. c The distinctive forms used for such categories. 2. *Informal* The quality of being male or female. [< L *genus, -eris*]

gene (jēn) *n. Biol.* A complex unit in the chromosomes that transmits hereditary characters through a specific sequence of nitrogen bases contained in DNA. [< Gk. *genea* breed, kind]

ge·ne·al·o·gy (jē′nē·al′ə·jē, jen′ē-, -nē·ol′-) *n. pl.* **·gies** 1. A family tree. 2. Descent in a direct line from a progenitor; pedigree. 3. The study of pedigrees. [< Gk. *genea* race + -LOGY] **—ge·ne·a·log·i·cal** (jē′nē·ə·loj′i·kəl, jen′ē-) *adj.* **—ge′ne·a·log′i·cal·ly** *adv.* **—ge′ne·al′o·gist** *n.*

gen·e·ra (jen′ər·ə) Plural of GENUS. [< L]

gen·er·al (jen′ər·əl) *adj.* 1. Pertaining to or of the whole; not particular. 2. Common to or current among the majority: the *general* opinion. 3. Miscellaneous: a *general* cargo. 4. Not detailed or precise: a *general* idea. 5. Not specialized: a *general* practitioner. 6. Superior in rank: a second element in some titles: attorney *general*. **—***n. Mil.* 1. In the U.S. Army and Air Force an officer of the next to highest rank, equivalent to an admiral in the navy. 2. In the U.S. Marine Corps the highest ranking officer. **—in general** 1. Without going into detail. 2. All things considered. 3. Usually; commonly. [< L *generalis* of a race or king < *genus, generis* kind]

general delivery A department of the post office in which an addressee's mail is kept until called for.

gen·er·al·is·si·mo (jen′ər·əl·is′i·mō) *n. pl.* **·mos** 1. In certain countries, one chosen as supreme commander of all the armed forces. 2. The supreme commander of several armies in a particular campaign. [< Ital.]

gen·er·al·i·ty (jen′ə·ral′ə·tē) *n. pl.* **·ties** 1. The state or quality of being general. 2. Something lacking detail or precision, as a statement or idea. 3. The greater number of a group; mass.

gen·er·al·ize (jen′ər·əl·īz′) *v.* **·ized, ·iz·ing** *v.t.* 1. To make general; as: a To make broad in application. b To avoid making detailed. c To cause to be widespread. 2. To derive a broad conclusion, principle, etc., from (particular instances, facts, etc.). **—***v.i.* 3. To write or speak without going into details, etc. Also *Brit.* **gen′er·al·ise′.** **—gen′er·al·iz′a·ble** *adj.* **—gen′er·al·i·za′·tion** *n.* **—gen′er·al·i′zer** *n.*

gen·er·al·ly (jen′ər·əl·ē) *adv.* 1. For the most part; ordinarily. 2. Without going into specific details: *generally* speaking. 3. Commonly: *generally* believed.

general officer *Mil.* Any officer ranking above a colonel.

General of the Air Force The highest ranking officer of the U.S. Air Force.

General of the Army The highest rank in the U.S. Army.

general paresis *Pathol.* Chronic paralysis of syphilitic origin. Also **general paralysis.**

general practitioner A physician whose practice is not limited to a medical specialty.

gen·er·al·ship (jen′ər·əl·ship) *n.* 1. A general's office or rank. 2. A general's military skill or management. 3. Management or leadership of any sort.

general staff 1. A body of officers who direct the military policy and strategy of a nation. 2. *Mil.* A group of officers who assist the commander in directing operations.

gen·er·ate (jen′ə·rāt) *v.t.* **·at·ed, ·at·ing** 1. To produce or cause to be; originate. 2. To beget; procreate. [< L *generatus*, pp. of *generare* to generate]

gen·er·a·tion (jen′ə·rā′shən) *n.* 1. The process of begetting offspring. 2. A successive step or degree in natural descent, or the average period between two such steps. 3. Any group of individuals born at about the same time. 4. The act or process of generating or being generated. **—gen·er·a·tive** (jen′ər·ə·tiv, -ə·rā′-) *adj.*

generative grammar A set of rules that describe the producing of grammatical sentences.

gen·er·a·tor (jen′ə·rā′tər) *n.* 1. One who or that which generates. 2. *Chem.* An apparatus designed to generate a gas. 3. Any of a class of machines for the conversion of mechanical energy into electrical energy.

ge·ner·ic (ji·ner′ik) *adj.* 1. Pertaining to a genus or class of related things. 2. Applicable to every member of a class or genus. 3. Having a wide, general application. Also **ge·ner′i·cal.** **—***n.* A generic drug. [< L *genus, -eris* race, kind + -IC]

generic drug A drug not having a trademark.

gen·er·ous (jen′ər·əs) *adj.* 1. Marked by or showing great liberality; munificent. 2. Having gracious or noble qualities: a *generous* nature. 3. Abundant and overflowing: a *generous* serving. [< L *generosus* of noble birth < *genus* race] **—gen′er·ous·ly** *adv.* **—gen·er·os·i·ty** (jen′ə·ros′ə·tē), **gen′er·ous·ness** *n.*

gen·e·sis (jen′ə·sis) *n. pl.* **·ses** (-sēz) 1. The act or mode of originating. 2. Origin. [< Gk. *genēsis*]

Gen·e·sis (jen′ə·sis) The first book of the Old Testament.

-genesis *combining form* Genesis; evolution: *biogenesis.*

gene splicing Recombinant DNA research.

ge·net·ic (jə·net′ik) *adj.* 1. Of, pertaining to, or based on genetics. 2. Of or pertaining to the origin or development of something. [< GENESIS; formed on analogy with *synthetic*, etc.] **—ge·net′i·cal·ly** *adv.*

genetic code The arrangement of the nitrogenous bases of DNA, constituting the biochemical basis of heredity.

ge·net·ics (jə·net′iks) *n.pl.* 1. (*construed as sing.*) The science of heredity. 2. The inherited characteristics of an organism. **—ge·net′i·cist** (-ə·sist) *n.*

gen·ial (jēn′yəl, jē′nē·əl) *adj.* 1. Kindly, pleasant, or cordial in disposition or manner. 2. Imparting warmth, comfort, or life. [< L *genius* tutelary spirit] **—ge·ni·al·i·ty** (jē′nē·al′ə·tē) *n.* **—gen′ial·ly** *adv.*

-genic *combining form* Related to generation or production: *biogenic.* [< -GEN + -IC]

ge·nie (jē′nē) See JINNI.

gen·i·tal (jen′ə·təl) *adj.* Of or pertaining to

reproduction or the reproductive organs. [< L *genitus*, pp. of *gignere* to beget]

gen·i·tals (jen′ə·təlz) *n.pl.* The external sexual organs. Also **gen·i·ta·li·a** (jen′ə·tā′lē·ə, -tāl′yə).

gen·i·tive (jen′ə·tiv) *adj. Gram.* Pertaining to a case in Latin, Greek, etc., corresponding in part to the English possessive. —*n. Gram.* 1. The genitive case. 2. A word in this case. [< L *gignere* to beget] —**gen′i·ti′val** (-tī′vəl) *adj.* —**gen′i·ti′val·ly** *adv.*

genito- *combining form* Genital. [< L *genitus*, pp. of *gignere* to beget]

gen·i·to·u·ri·nar·y (jen′ə·tō·yŏŏr′ə·ner′ē) *adj.* Of or pertaining to the genital and urinary organs.

gen·ius (jēn′yəs) *n. pl.* **gen·ius·es** 1. Extraordinary intelligence; also, one who possesses such intelligence. 2. An outstanding gift for a certain activity; also, one so gifted. 3. The essential spirit or distinguishing characteristics of a particular people, era, etc. 4. One who exerts a strong influence over another. [< L *gen-*, stem of *gignere* to beget]

gen·o·cide (jen′ə·sīd) *n.* The systematic extermination of an entire people or national group. [< Gk. *genos* race, tribe + -CIDE] —**gen′o·ci′dal** *adj.*

gen·o·type (jen′ə·tīp) *n. Biol.* 1. The genetic constitution of an organism. 2. A group of organisms with the same genetic constitution. 3. A type species. —**gen′o·typ′ic** (-tip′ik) or **·i·cal** *adj.* —**gen′o·typ′i·cal·ly** *adv.*

-genous *suffix of adjectives* 1. Generating; yielding. 2. Produced or generated by.

gen·re (zhän′rə, *Fr.* zhäN′r′) *n.* 1. A particular sort, kind, or category; esp., a category of art or literature. 2. A class of painting or other art depicting everyday life. [< F < L *genus, -eris* race, kind] —**gen′re** *adj.*

gens (jenz) *n. pl.* **gen·tes** (jen′tēz) *Anthropol.* A body of blood kindred having a common descent traced through the male line. [< L]

gent (jent) *n. Slang* A gentleman. [Short for GENTLEMAN]

gen·teel (jen·tēl′) *adj.* 1. Well-bred; elegant; polite. 2. Pertaining or appropriate to well-bred persons. 3. Affectedly refined. [< MF *gentil*] —**gen·teel′ly** *adv.* —**gen·teel′ness** *n.*

gen·tian (jen′shən) *n.* An annual or perennial herb with showy flowers. [< L *gentiana*, appar. after *Gentius*, an Illyrian king]

gentian violet *Chem.* A purple dye used as an antiseptic.

gen·tile (jen′tīl) *adj.* 1. Of or pertaining to a gens, tribe, or people. 2. Of or pertaining to Gentiles. [< LL *gentilis* foreign]

Gen·tile (jen′tīl) *n.* 1. Among Jews, one not a Jew. 2. Among Christians, a heathen or pagan. 3. Among Mormons, one not a Mormon. —**Gen′tile** *adj.*

gen·til·i·ty (jen·til′ə·tē) *n. pl.* **·ties** 1. The quality of being genteel; refinement. 2. Gentle birth; good extraction. 3. Well-born or well-bred persons collectively. [< L *gentilis* of good birth]

gen·tle (jen′təl) *adj.* **·tler** (-tlər), **·tlest** (-tlist) 1. Mild in nature, quality, or disposition. 2. Not steep or abrupt; gradual: a *gentle* ascent. 3. Easily managed; docile. 4. Of good family and breeding. 5. Well-behaved; polite. —*v.t.* **·tled, ·tling** To make easy to control; tame. [< L *gentilis* of good birth < *gens, gentis* race, clan] —**gen′tle·ness** *n.* —**gen′tly** (-tlē) *adv.*

gen·tle·folk (jen′təl·fōk′) *n.pl.* Persons of good family and good breeding. Also **gen′tle·folks′**.

gen·tle·man (jen′təl·mən) *n. pl.* **·men** (-mən) 1. A man of good birth and social position. 2. A courteous, considerate man. 3. Any man: in the plural, used as a form of address. —**gen′tle·man·ly** *adj.*

gen·tle·man-farm·er (jen′təl·mən·fär′mər) *n.* One who owns a farm but hires others to work it.

gen·tle·wom·an (jen′təl·wŏŏm′ən) *n. pl.* **·wom·en** (-wim′in) 1. A woman of good family or superior social position; lady. 2. A gracious, well-mannered woman.

gen·try (jen′trē) *n.* People of good family or superior social standing. [< OF *genterise* < *gentil* gentle]

gen·u·flect (jen′yə·flekt) *v.i.* To bend the knee, as in worship. [< L *genu* knee + *flectere* to bend] —**gen′u·flec′tion** *n.*

gen·u·ine (jen′yōō·in) *adj.* 1. Being of the origin, authorship, or character claimed. 2. Not spurious or counterfeit. [< L *genuinus* innate] —**gen′u·ine·ly** *adv.* —**gen′u·ine·ness** *n.*

ge·nus (jē′nəs) *n. pl.* **gen·e·ra** (jen′ər·ə) 1. *Biol.* A grouping or category of plants and animals ranking next above the species and next below the family or subfamily. 2. *Logic* A class of things divisible into two or more subordinate classes or species. 3. A particular sort, kind, or class. [< L, race, kind]

-geny *combining form* Mode of production of; generation or development of: *anthropogeny*. [< Gk. *gen-*, stem of *gignesthai* to become]

geo- *combining form* Earth; ground; soil. [< Gk. *gē* earth]

ge·o·cen·tric (jē′ō·sen′trik) *adj.* 1. Calculated or viewed relative to the earth's center. 2. Assuming that the earth is the center of the universe. Also **ge′o·cen′tri·cal**. —**ge′o·cen′tri·cal·ly** *adv.*

ge·o·chem·is·try (jē′ō·kem′is·trē) *n.* A branch of chemistry dealing with the composition of the earth's crust. —**ge′o·chem′i·cal** *adj.* —**ge′o·chem′ist** *n.*

ge·ode (jē′ōd) *n. Geol.* A rock, usually globular, having a cavity lined with crystals. [< L *geodes* a precious stone < Gk. *geōdēs* earthy] —**ge·od·ic** (jē·od′ik) *adj.*

ge·o·des·ic (jē′ə·des′ik) *adj.* 1. Of or pertaining to the geometry of geodesic lines or curved surfaces. 2. Geodetic. —*n.* A geodesic line.

geodesic dome *Archit.* A dome made of prefabricated lattice nodules and covered with a thin, strong material.

geodesic line *Math.* The shortest line connecting two points on a given, esp. a curved, surface.

ge·od·e·sy (jē·od′ə·sē) *n.* The science dealing with the determination and representation of the shape, area, and curvature of the earth. Also **ge·o·det·ics** (jē′ə·det′iks). [< Gk. *gē* earth + *daiein* to divide] —**ge·od′e·sist** *n.*

ge·o·det·ic (jē′ə·det′ik) *adj.* 1. Of or pertaining to geodesy. 2. Geodesic. Also **ge′o·det′i·cal**. —**ge′o·det′i·cal·ly** *adv.*

ge·o·dy·nam·ics (jē′ō·dī·nam′iks, -di-) *n.pl.* (*construed as sing.*) The study of the forces affecting the earth's structure.

ge·og·ra·phy (jē·og′rə·fē) *n.* *pl.* **·phies** 1. The science that describes the surface of the earth and its associated physical, biological, economic, political, and demographic characteristics. 2. The natural aspect, features, etc., of a place or area. 3. A particular work on or system of geography. [< Gk. *gē* earth + *graphein* to write, describe] **—ge·og′ra·pher** *n.* **—ge·o·graph·i·cal** (jē′ə·graf′i·kəl) or **ge′o·graph′ic** *adj.* **—ge′o·graph′i·cal·ly** *adv.*

ge·ol·o·gy (jē·ol′ə·jē) *n.* *pl.* **·gies** 1. The science that treats of the origin, structure, and history of the earth, esp. as shown by rocks and rock formations. 2. The structure of the earth in a given region. **—ge·o·log·ic** (jē′ə·loj′ik) or **·i·cal** *adj.* **—ge′o·log′i·cal·ly** *adv.* **—ge·ol′o·gist** *n.*

ge·o·met·ric (jē′ə·met′rik) *adj.* 1. Pertaining to or according to the rules and principles of geometry. 2. Forming, consisting of, or characterized by straight lines, bars, crosses, zigzags, etc., as in painting or sculpture. Also **ge′o·met′ri·cal.** **—ge′o·met′ri·cal·ly** *adv.*

ge·om·e·tri·cian (jē·om′ə·trish′ən, jē′ə·mə-) *n.* A specialist in geometry. Also **ge·om′e·ter** (-ə·tər).

geometric progression *Math.* A numerical sequence whose terms are related by a constant ratio, as 2, 4, 8, 16.

ge·om·e·try (jē·om′ə·trē) *n.* *pl.* **·tries** The branch of mathematics that treats of space and its relations, esp. as shown in the properties and measurement of points, lines, angles, surfaces, and solids. [< Gk. *gē* earth + *metreein* to measure]

ge·o·phys·ics (jē′ō·fiz′iks) *n.pl.* (*construed as sing.*) The study of the physics of the earth, including its oceans, weather, earthquakes, volcanoes, magnetic fields, and radioactivity. **—ge′o·phys′i·cal** *adj.* **—ge′o·phys′i·cist** (-ə·sist) *n.*

ge·o·pol·i·tics (jē′ō·pol′ə·tiks) *n.pl.* (*construed as sing.*) 1. The study of political and economic geography. 2. A theory that the physical geography of a country determines its political outlook. **—ge′o·po·lit′i·cal** (-pə·lit′i·kəl) *adj.* **—ge′o·po·lit′i·cal·ly** *adv.*

ge·o·ther·mal (jē′ō·thûr′məl) *adj.* Of the earth's internal heat. Also **ge′o·ther′mic.**

ge·ra·ni·um (ji·rā′nē·əm) *n.* 1. A garden plant with showy pink or red flowers: also called *cranebill.* 2. A crimson or scarlet color. [< Gk. *geranos* crane]

ger·fal·con (jûr′fal′kən, -fôl′-, -fô′-) *n.* A large falcon of the arctic regions: also spelled *gyrfalcon.* [< OHG *gir* vulture + OF *faucon* falcon]

ger·i·at·rics (jer′ē·at′riks) *n.pl.* (*construed as sing.*) 1. The branch of medicine that deals with the diseases and physiology of old age. 2. Gerontology. [< Gk. *gēras* old age + -IATRICS] **—ger′i·at′ric** *adj.* **—ger′i·a·tri′cian** (-ə·trish′ən), **ger′i·at′rist** *n.*

germ (jûrm) *n.* 1. A microorganism that causes disease; a microbe. 2. Something in its essential though rudimentary form: the *germ* of an idea. 3. *Biol.* **a** A reproductive cell. **b** An organism in its embryonic form. [< L *germen* sprig]

Ger·man (jûr′mən) *n.* 1. A native or inhabitant of Germany. 2. The language of the Germans. **—High German** The standard literary and spoken language used in Germany, Austria, and parts of Switzerland and Alsace: also called *New High German.* **—Low German** Collectively, the languages of the Low Countries, including Dutch, Flemish, and Frisian, and of the northern lowlands of Germany (*Plattdeutsch*). **—Old High German** The language of southern Germany from about 800 to 1100. **—Middle High German** The High German language from 1100 to 1450. **—Middle Low German** The Low German language from 1100 to 1450. [< L *Germanus*, prob. < Celtic] **—Ger′man** *adj.*

ger·man·der (jər·man′dər) *n.* An herb of the mint family, with pale purple flowers. [< Gk. *chamaidrys* ground oak]

ger·mane (jər·mān′) *adj.* Related to what is being discussed or considered; pertinent; relevant. [< L *germanus* closely related]

Ger·man·ic (jər·man′ik) *adj.* 1. Of or pertaining to a group of early Indo-European tribes living in the region bounded by the Rhine, Danube, and Vistula rivers, later including the Germans, English, Dutch, Flemings, Danes, Scandinavians, and German-Swiss. 2. Relating to the language or customs of any of these people. **—*n.*** A sub-family of the Indo-European family of languages, divided into **East Germanic,** including Gothic (extinct); **North Germanic** or Scandinavian, including Norwegian, Swedish, Danish, Icelandic, and Faroese; and **West Germanic,** including all the High and Low German languages and dialects.

ger·ma·ni·um (jər·mā′nē·əm) *n.* A grayish white, metallic element (symbol Ge) of the silicon group, used in electronics and optics. [< L *Germania* Germany]

German measles *Pathol.* A contagious virus disease accompanied by fever, sore throat, and a skin rash: also called *rubella.*

Germano- *combining form* German.

German shepherd A breed of dog with a large, strong body and thick, smooth coat.

germ cell *Biol.* A cell specialized for reproduction.

ger·mi·cide (jûr′mə·sīd) *n.* An agent used to destroy disease germs or other microorganisms. **—ger′mi·ci′dal** *adj.*

ger·mi·nal (jûr′mə·nəl) *adj.* 1. Of, relating to, or constituting a germ or germ cell. 2. Pertaining to the earliest stage of development. [< L *germen, -inis* sprig]

ger·mi·nate (jûr′mə·nāt) *v.* **·nat·ed, ·nat·ing** *v.i.* 1. To begin to grow or develop; sprout. **—*v.t.*** 2. To cause to sprout. [< L *germinatus*, pp. of *germinare* to sprout] **—ger′mi·na′tion** *n.* **—ger′mi·na′tive** *adj.* **—ger′mi·na′tor** *n.*

germ plasm *Biol.* The part of a germ cell that contains the chromosomes and genes.

geronto- *combining form* Old age; pertaining to old people: *gerontology.* Also, before vowels, **geront-.** [< Gk. *gerōn, gerontos* old man]

ger·on·tol·o·gy (jer′ən·tol′ə·jē) *n.* 1. The scientific study of the processes and problems of aging. 2. Geriatrics. **—ge·ron·to·log·ic** (je·ron′tə·loj′ik) or **·i·cal** *adj.* **—ger′on·tol′o·gist** *n.*

-gerous *suffix* Bearing or producing. [< L *gerere* to bear + -OUS]

ger·ry·man·der (jer′i·man′dər) *v.t.* To alter (a voting area) so as to advance unfairly the interests of a political party. —*n.* The act or result of gerrymandering. [after Elbridge *Gerry*, 1744–1814, + (SALA)MANDER: from the shape of a district formed in Massachusetts while he was governor]

ger·und (jer′ənd) *n. Gram.* A form of a verb used like a noun: in English, the *-ing* form of a verb, as *doing*, or a compound tense made with the *-ing* form of an auxiliary, as *having done*. [< L *gerere* to do]

ge·stalt (gə·shtält′, -shtôlt′) *n. pl.* **·stalts** or **·stalt·en** (-ən) A synthesis of separate elements of emotion, experience, etc., that constitutes more than the mechanical sum of the parts. Also **Ge·stalt′**. [< G, form]

gestalt psychology Psychology based on the theory of the gestalt. Also **Gestalt psychology.**

Ge·sta·po (gə·stä′pō, *Ger.* gə·shtä′pō) *n.* The German secret police under the Nazi regime, noted for their brutality. [< G *Ge(heime) Sta(ats) Po(lizei)* Secret State Police]

ges·tate (jes′tāt) *v.t.* **·tat·ed, ·tat·ing** To carry in the uterus during pregnancy. [< L *gestare* to carry] —**ges·ta′tion** *n.*

ges·tic·u·late (jes·tik′yə·lāt) *v.* **·lat·ed, ·lat·ing** *v.i.* 1. To make emphatic or expressive gestures, as in speaking. —*v.t.* 2. To express by gestures. [< L *gesticulus*, dim. of *gestus* gesture] —**ges·tic′u·la′tion** *n.* —**ges·tic′u·la′tive** *adj.* —**ges·tic′u·la′tor** *n.*

ges·ture (jes′chər) *n.* 1. A meaningful bodily motion, as of the hands in speaking. 2. Such motions collectively. 3. Something said or done as a mere formality, or for effect. [< L *gerere* to carry on, do] —**ges′ture** *v.t. & v.i.* **·tured, ·tur·ing** —**ges′tur·er** *n.*

Ge·sund·heit (gə·zŏŏnt′hīt) *interj. German* (Your) health: said to one who has just sneezed.

get (get) *v.* **got, got** or **got·ten, get·ting** *v.t.* 1. To come into possession of; obtain. 2. To go for and bring back. 3. To capture; seize. 4. To cause to come, go, etc. 5. To prepare: to *get* lunch. 6. To bring to a state or condition: to *get* the work done. 7. To persuade: *Get* her to sign the paper. 8. To find out or obtain by calculation, experiment, etc. 9. To give or receive (reward or punishment). 10. To become sick with. 11. To establish contact with: I'll *get* him on the phone. 12. To catch, as a train; board. 13. To beget: now said chiefly of animals. 14. *Informal* To come to an understanding of. 15. *Informal* To possess: with *have* or *has*: He has *got* quite a temper. 16. *Informal* To be obliged or forced (to do something specified): with *have* or *has*. 17. *Informal* To hit: The shrapnel *got* him in the arm. 18. *Slang* To puzzle or baffle. 19. *Slang* To please, irritate, etc.: That music *gets* me. —*v.i.* 20. To arrive: When does the train *get* there? 21. To come, go, or move: *Get* in here. 22. To board; enter: with *on, in*, etc. 23. To become. —**to get across** To be successful, as in projecting one's personality or conveying one's meaning. —**to get ahead** To attain success. —**to get along** 1. To leave; go: *Get along* with you! 2. To be successful, as in business. 3. To be friendly or compatible. 4. To grow old or older. —**to get around** 1. To become known, as gossip. 2. To move about. 3. To attend social or public functions, etc. 4. To dodge; circumvent. —**to get around to** To give attention to after some delay. —**to get at** 1. To arrive at; reach. 2. To intend; mean: I don't see what you're *getting at*. 3. To apply oneself to: to *get at* a problem. 4. *Informal* To prevail upon; influence. —**to get away** 1. To escape. 2. To leave; go. 3. To start, as a race horse. —**to get away with** *Slang* To do (something) without discovery, criticism, or punishment. —**to get back at** *Slang* To revenge oneself on. —**to get by** 1. To pass: This *got by* the censor. 2. *Informal* To manage to survive. —**to get down to** (business, facts, etc.) To begin to act on, investigate, or consider. —**to get in** 1. To arrive or enter. 2. To slip in (a remark, etc.). 3. To become involved or familiar with. 4. To be elected. —**to get it** *Informal* 1. To understand. 2. To be punished in some way. —**to get off** 1. To descend from; dismount. 2. To depart. 3. To be relieved or freed, as of a duty or penalty. 4. To utter: to *get off* a joke. 5. *Slang* To enjoy: with *on*. —**to get on** 1. To mount (a horse, vehicle, etc.). 2. To get along. —**to get out** 1. To depart. 2. To escape. 3. To become known, as a secret. 4. To publish. 5. To express or utter. 6. To take out. —**to get out of** 1. To obtain from. 2. To escape or evade. 3. To depart from. —**to get over** 1. To recover from (illness, surprise, anger, etc.). 2. To get across. —**to get through** (to) 1. To establish communication (with). 2. To make clear (to). —**to get to** 1. To begin. 2. To be able to (do something). 3. To get through to. —**to get together** 1. To assemble. 2. To come to an agreement. —**to get up** 1. To rise, as from sleep. 2. To climb. 3. To devise. 4. To acquire, develop, or work up. 5. *Informal* To dress up. [< ON *geta*] —**get′ta·ble** *adj.* —**get′ter** *n.*

get·a·way (get′ə·wā′) *n.* 1. An escape, as of a criminal. 2. The start, as of an automobile, race horse, etc. 3. Any departure.

get-to·geth·er (get′tə·geth′ər) *n. Informal* A gathering.

get-up (get′up′) *n. Informal* Costume.

get-up-and-go (get′up′ən·gō′) *n.* Vigorous initiative.

gew·gaw (gyōō′gô) *n.* Some little ornamental article of small value. [ME *giue-goue*]

gey·ser (gī′zər, -sər) *n.* A natural hot spring from which intermittent jets of steam, hot water, or mud are ejected in a fountainlike column. [< Icel. *geysan* to gush]

Gha·na·ian (gä′nē·ən, gä′nā-) *adj.* Of Ghana or its people. —**Gha′na·ian** *n.*

ghast·ly (gast′lē) *adj.* **·li·er, ·li·est** 1. Horrible; terrifying. 2. Deathlike in appearance; pale; wan. 3. *Informal* Very bad or unpleasant. [OE *gæstan* to terrify] —**ghast′li·ness** *n.* —**ghast′ly** *adv.*

ghat (gôt) *n. Anglo-Indian* 1. A stairway leading down to the edge of a river. 2. A mountain pass. 3. A range or chain of mountains. Also **ghaut.** [< Hind. *ghāt*]

ghee (gē) *n. Anglo-Indian* A butterlike substance, usu. made from buffalo milk. [< Hind. < Skt. *ghrta*]

gher·kin (gûr′kin) *n.* 1. A very small cucumber pickled as a relish. 2. The plant producing it. 3. Any small, immature cucumber used for pickling. [< Du. *agurk* cucumber, ult. < LGk. *angourion*]

ghet·to (get'ō) *n. pl.* **·tos** 1. An often run-down section of a city inhabited chiefly by a minority group. 2. A section in certain European cities in which Jews were required to live. [< Ital.]

ghost (gōst) *n.* 1. A disembodied spirit; a wraith, specter, or phantom. 2. A haunting recollection of something: *ghosts* from the past. 3. A mere suggestion of something: the *ghost* of a smile. 4. *Informal* A ghostwriter. 5. *Optics & Telecom.* An unwanted false or secondary image. —**to give up the ghost** To die. —*v.t.* To ghostwrite. [OE *gāst* spirit] —**ghost'li·ness** *n.* —**ghost'ly** *adj.* **·li·er, ·li·est**

ghost town A deserted town.

ghost·write (gōst'rīt') *v.t. & v.i.* **·wrote, ·writ·ten, ·writ·ing** To write (a book, article, etc.) for someone else who receives credit as author. —**ghost'writ'er** *n.*

ghoul (gōōl) *n.* 1. One who robs graves. 2. One who takes pleasure in revolting things. 3. In Muslim legend, an evil spirit who preys on corpses. [< Arabic *ghūl*] —**ghoul'ish** *adj.* —**ghoul'ish·ly** *adv.* —**ghoul'ish·ness** *n.*

GI (jē'ī') *Informal n. pl.* GIs or GI's An enlisted man in the U.S. Army. —*adj.* 1. Of or characteristic of GIs. 2. Furnished by the government for the use of the armed forces. [< G(OVERNMENT) I(SSUE)]

gi·ant (jī'ənt) *n.* 1. In legend, a manlike being of supernatural size and strength. 2. Any person or thing of great size, capability, etc. [< Gk. *gigas, -antos*] —**gi'ant** *adj.* —**gi'ant·ess** *n.fem.*

gib·ber (jib'ər, gib'-) *v.i. & v.t.* To talk rapidly and incoherently; jabber. —*n.* Gibberish.

gib·ber·ish (jib'ər·ish, gib'-) *n.* 1. Rapid or unintelligible talk; gabble. 2. Needlessly difficult or obscure language.

gib·bet (jib'it) *n.* Formerly, a gallows. —*v.t.* **gib·bet·ed** or **·bet·ted, gib·bet·ing** or **·bet·ting** 1. To execute by hanging. 2. To hold up to public contempt. [< OF *gibet* staff]

gib·bon (gib'ən) *n.* A slender, long-armed arboreal anthropoid ape of southern Asia and the East Indies. [< F]

gib·bos·i·ty (gi·bos'ə·tē) *n. pl.* **·ties** 1. The state of being gibbous or convex. 2. A rounded protuberance; hump.

gib·bous (gib'əs) *adj.* 1. Irregularly rounded or convex, as the moon when more than half full and less than full. 2. Hunchbacked. [< L *gibbus* hump] —**gib'bous·ly** *adv.*

gibe (jīb) *v.* **gibed, gib·ing** *v.i.* 1. To utter jeers or derisive remarks. —*v.t.* 2. To taunt. —*n.* A jeer. [Cf. OF *giber* to treat roughly] —**gib'er** *n.* —**gib'ing·ly** *adv.*

gib·let (jib'lit) *n. Usu. pl.* The edible heart, liver, gizzard, etc., of a fowl. [< OF *gibelet* stew made from game]

gid·dy (gid'ē) *adj.* **·di·er, ·di·est** 1. Affected by a reeling or whirling sensation; dizzy. 2. Tending to cause such a sensation. 3. Frivolous; heedless. —*v.t. & v.i.* **·died, ·dy·ing** To make or become dizzy. [OE *gydig* insane] —**gid'di·ly** *adv.* —**gid'di·ness** *n.*

gift (gift) *n.* 1. Something that is given; present. 2. The action or right of giving. 3. A natural aptitude; talent. [OE < *gifan* to give]

gift·ed (gif'tid) *adj.* Endowed with talent.

gig[1] (gig) *n.* 1. A light, two-wheeled vehicle drawn by one horse. 2. A machine for raising a nap on cloth. 3. *Naut.* A long ship's boat, usu. for the captain. [ME *gigge* spinning top]

gig[2] (gig) *n.* An arrangement of fishhooks. —*v.t. & v.i.* **gigged, gig·ging** To catch (fish) with a gig. [< earlier *fishgig* < Sp. *fisga* harpoon]

gig[3] (gig) *n. Slang* A demerit, as in the army, school, etc. —*v.t.* **gigged, gig·ging** 1. To give a demerit to. 2. To punish.

gig[4] (gig) *n. Slang* A job; esp., a musician's engagement.

giga- *combining form* A billion (10^9) times (a specified unit).

gi·gan·tic (jī·gan'tik) *adj.* 1. Of, like, or suited to a giant. 2. Tremendous; huge. [< L *gigas, -antis* giant + -IC] —**gi·gan'ti·cal·ly** *adv.*

gi·gan·tism (jī·gan'tiz·əm) *n.* Abnormal size; esp., excessive growth due to pituitary malfunction.

gig·gle (gig'əl) *v.i.* **·gled, ·gling** To laugh in a high-pitched, silly, or nervous manner. —*n.* A titter. —**gig'gler** *n.*

gig·gly (gig'lē) *adj.* **·gli·er, ·gli·est** Tending to giggle.

gig·o·lo (jig'ə·lō) *n. pl.* **·los** (-lōz) 1. A woman's paid male escort. 2. A man supported by a woman not his wife. [< F, prob. < *gigolette* prostitute]

Gi·la monster (hē'lə) A large, venomous, orange and black lizard of the North American desert.

gild (gild) *v.t.* **gild·ed** or **gilt, gild·ing** 1. To coat with a thin layer of gold. 2. To brighten or adorn. 3. To gloss over. [OE *gyldan*] —**gild'er** *n.* —**gild'ing** *n.*

gill[1] (gil) *n.* 1. *Zool.* The breathing organ of fishes, amphibians, and other aquatic vertebrates. 2. *Usu. pl.* The wattles of a fowl. —**green around the gills** Sickly in appearance. [ME *gile*]

gill[2] (jil) *n.* A liquid measure equal to ¼ pint. [< OF *gell* measure for wine]

gilt (gilt) Alternative past tense and past participle of GILD. —*adj.* Gold-colored; gilded. —*n.* A material for gilding.

gilt-edged (gilt'ejd') *adj.* 1. Having the edges gilded. 2. Of the best quality: *gilt-edged* securities. Also **gilt'-edge'**.

gim·bals (jim'bəlz, gim'-) *n.pl.* A set of three metal rings so arranged as to maintain an object supported by it, as a ship's compass, on a horizontal plane. [OF *gemelle* twin < L *geminus* twin]

gim·crack (jim'krak) *n.* A useless, gaudy object. —*adj.* Cheap and showy. —**gim'·crack·er·y** *n.*

gim·let (gim'lit) A small, sharp tool with a pointed, spiral tip for boring holes. [< OF *guimbelet*] —**gim'let** *v.t.*

gimlet eyes Sharp eyes. —**gim·let-eyed** (gim'lit·īd') *adj.*

gim·mick (gim'ik) *n. Slang* 1. A novel or clever scheme or detail. 2. A hidden or deceptive device, as one used by a magician. —**gim'mick·ry** *n.* —**gim'mick·y** *adj.*

gimp (gimp) *n. Slang* One who limps; also, a limp. —**gimp'y** *adj.*

gin[1] (jin) *n.* An aromatic alcoholic liquor, usu. flavored with juniper berries. [Short for *geneva* < Dan. *jenever* juniper]

gin[2] (jin) *n.* 1. A cotton gin. 2. A tripodlike machine for hoisting. 3. A snare or trap. —*v.t.* **ginned, gin·ning** 1. To remove the seeds from (cotton) in a gin. 2. To trap or snare. [Aphetic var. of OF *engin* ingenuity]

gin·ger (jin′jər) *n.* 1. The pungent, spicy rootstock of a tropical plant, used in medicine and cookery. 2. The plant itself. 3. A tawny, reddish brown color. 4. *Informal* Pep. [< Gk. *zingiberis*, ult. < Skt.] —**gin′ger·y** *adj.*

ginger ale A pale, effervescent soft drink lightly flavored with ginger.

ginger beer An effervescent, nonalcoholic ginger drink.

gin·ger·bread (jin′jər·bred′) *n.* 1. A dark, ginger-flavored cake or cooky. 2. Elaborate decoration or trim, as on the exterior of a house. —*adj.* Ornate, gaudy, or superfluous.

gin·ger·ly (jin′jər·lē) *adv.* In a cautious manner. —*adj.* Careful. [Cf. OF *gent* delicate] —**gin′ger·li·ness** *n.*

gin·ger·snap (jin′jər·snap′) *n.* A brittle, ginger cooky.

ging·ham (ging′əm) *n.* A cotton fabric, yarn-dyed, woven in solid colors, checks, etc. [< Malay *ginggang* striped]

gin·gi·vi·tis (jin′jə·vī′tıs) *n. Pathol.* Inflammation of the gums. [< L *gingiva* gum]

gink·go (ging′kō, jing′kō) *n. pl.* **·goes** A large tree native to China, with edible fruits and nuts. Also **ging′ko.** [< Japanese]

gin rummy A variety of rummy.

gin·seng (jin′seng) *n.* 1. An herb native to China and North America. 2. The root of this herb, used in a medicinal preparation. [< Chinese *jen shen*]

gip·sy (jip′sē), **Gip·sy** See GYPSY.

gi·raffe (jə·raf′) *n. pl.* **·raffes** or **·raffe** An African ruminant, the tallest of all mammals, having a very long neck and long slender legs. [< F, ult. < Arabic *zarāfah*]

gird (gûrd) *v.t.* **gird·ed** or **girt, gird·ing** 1. To surround or make fast with a belt or girdle. 2. To encircle; surround. 3. To prepare (oneself) for action. 4. To clothe, equip, or endow, as with some quality or attribute. [OE *gyrdan*]

gird·er (gûr′dər) *n.* A long heavy beam that supports the joists of a floor, etc.

gir·dle (gûr′dəl) *n.* 1. A belt or cord worn around the waist; sash. 2. Anything that encircles like a belt. 3. A woman's flexible undergarment worn to give support and shape. 4. An encircling cut made through the bark of a tree trunk or branch. —*v.t.* **·dled, ·dling** 1. To fasten a girdle or belt around. 2. To encircle; encompass. 3. To make an encircling cut through the bark of (a branch or tree). [OE *gyrdle*] —**gir′dler** *n.*

girl (gûrl) *n.* 1. A female infant or child. 2. A young, unmarried woman. 3. A female servant. 4. *Informal* A sweetheart. 5. *Informal* Any woman of any age. [ME *gurle*] —**girl′ish** *adj.* —**girl′ish·ly** *adv.* —**girl′ish·ness** *n.*

girl scout A member of the Girl Scouts of the United States of America, an organization for girls, stressing character development, good health practices, etc.

girth (gûrth) *n.* 1. The circumference of anything. 2. A band passed under the belly of a horse or other animal to make fast a saddle, harness, pack, etc. 3. A girdle or band. —*v.t.* 1. To bind with a girth. 2. To encircle; girdle. —*v.i.* 3. To measure in girth. [< ON *gjordh*]

gist (jist) *n.* The main idea, as of an argument, question, etc. [< OF *giste* place of rest]

give (giv) *v.* **gave, giv·en, giv·ing** *v.t.* 1. To transfer freely (what is one's own) to the permanent possession of another without asking anything in return. 2. To make available to another for temporary use; let have. 3. To put into the grasp of another: *Give* me your hand. 4. To be a source of. 5. To grant or concede, as permission. 6. To administer (a dose of medicine, a treatment, etc.). 7. To assign or allot. 8. To transmit or communicate (a disease, etc.). 9. To perform or do: to *give* a play. 10. To devote, as oneself, to a cause, etc. —*v.i.* 11. To make donations; make free gifts. 12. To move, yield, collapse, etc., as under pressure: The door *gave*. 13. To be springy, flexible, etc.: The bed *gives* comfortably. 14. To furnish a view or passage; open: with *on* or *onto*. —**to give away** 1. To bestow as a gift. 2. To present (the bride) to the bridegroom. 3. *Informal* To make known, as a secret; reveal. —**to give birth to** 1. To bear (offspring). 2. To create or originate, as an idea. 3. To result in. —**to give in** 1. To yield, as to something demanded. 2. To deliver or hand in (a report, resignation, etc.). —**to give off** To send forth, as odors; emit. —**to give out** 1. To send forth; emit. 2. To hand out or distribute. 3. To make known; publish. 4. To become completely used up or exhausted. —**to give up** 1. To surrender. 2. To stop; cease. 3. To desist from as hopeless. 4. To lose all hope for, as a sick person. 5. To devote wholly: to *give* oneself *up* to art. —**to give way** 1. To collapse, bend, fail, etc., as under pressure or force. 2. To draw back. 3. To concede or yield. 4. To abandon oneself, as to despair. —*n.* 1. Resilience; elasticity. 2. The act or process of bending or yielding. [Fusion of OE *giefan* and ON *gefa*] —**giv′er** *n.*

give-and-take (giv′ən·tāk′) *n.* The making of mutual concessions, exchanges, etc.

give·a·way (giv′ə·wā′) *n. Informal* 1. A disclosure or betrayal, generally unintentional. 2. Something given free or at a greatly reduced price. —*adj.* Offering prizes.

giv·en (giv′ən) *adj.* 1. Presented; bestowed. 2. Habitually inclined; addicted: with *to*. 3. Specified; stated: a *given* date. 4. Admitted as a fact.

given name The name bestowed on a person at birth, or shortly thereafter.

giz·mo (giz′mō) *n. Slang* A gadget.

giz·zard (giz′ərd) *n.* 1. A second stomach in birds, in which partly digested food is finely ground. 2. *Informal* The human stomach. [< L *gigeria* cooked entrails of poultry]

gla·brous (glā′brəs) *adj. Biol.* 1. Devoid of hair or down. 2. Smooth. [< L *glaber* smooth]

gla·cé (gla·sā′) *adj.* 1. Sugared or candied, as preserved fruits. 2. Having a glossy surface, as certain leathers. 3. Iced; frozen. —*v.t.* **·céed, ·cé·ing** 1. To cover with icing.

2. To make smooth and glossy. [< F *glace* ice]

gla·cial (glā′shəl) *adj.* 1. Pertaining to, caused by, or marked by the presence of glaciers. 2. Freezingly cold. 3. Indifferent. [< L *glacies* ice] —**gla′cial·ly** *adv.*

gla·ci·ate (glā′shē·āt) *v.t.* **·at·ed, ·at·ing** To cover with or subject to the action of glaciers. —**gla′ci·a′tion** *n.*

gla·cier (glā′shər) *n.* A slow-moving ice field, formed in regions of perennial frost from compacted snow. [< L *glacies* ice]

glad[1] (glad) *adj.* **glad·der, glad·dest** 1. Having a feeling of joy, pleasure, or content; gratified: often with *of* or *at.* 2. Showing joy; brightly cheerful: a *glad* face. 3. Giving reason to rejoice; bringing joy. 4. Very willing: He'd be *glad* to help. [OE *glæd* shining, glad] —**glad′ly** *adv.* —**glad′ness** *n.*

glad[2] (glad) *n. Informal* A gladiolus.

glad·den (glad′n) *v.t.* To make glad.

glade (glād) *n.* A clearing in a wood. [Prob. akin to *glad* in obs. sense of "bright, sunny"]

glad·i·a·tor (glad′ē·ā′tər) *n.* 1. In ancient Rome, a slave, captive, or paid freeman who fought other men or animals as public entertainment. 2. Any combatant. [< L *gladius* sword] —**glad·i·a·to·ri·al** (glad′ē·ə·tôr′ē·əl) *adj.*

glad·i·o·lus (glad′ē·ō′ləs) *n. pl.* **·lus·es** or **·li** (-lē, -lī) A plant of the iris family with fleshy bulbs, sword-shaped leaves, and spikes of colored flowers. Also **glad′i·o′la.**

glad·some (glad′səm) *adj.* Joyful; cheerful.

Glad·stone (glad′stōn, -stən) *n.* A suitcase hinged to open flat, forming two equal compartments. Also **Gladstone bag.** [after W. E. *Gladstone,* 1809–98, English statesman]

glam·or·ize (glam′ər·īz) *v.t.* **·ized, ·iz·ing** To make glamorous.

glam·or·ous (glam′ər·əs) *adj.* Full of glamour; alluring. —**glam′or·ous·ly** *adv.* —**glam′or·ous·ness** *n.*

glam·our (glam′ər) *n.* Alluring charm or fascination. Also **glam′or.** [< Scot. *gramarye* magic power]

glance (glans) *v.i.* **glanced, glanc·ing** 1. To take a quick look. 2. To touch briefly on some matter. 3. To be deflected at an angle after striking obliquely. —*n.* 1. A quick look. 2. A flash; glint. 3. Oblique impact and deflection. [ME *glencen* ? < OF *glacier* to slip]

gland (gland) *n. Anat.* Any of various bodily organs which secrete a substance for use or discharge. [< L *glans, glandis* acorn] —**glan·du·lar** (glan′jə·lər) *adj.*

glare (glâr) *v.* **glared, glar·ing** *v.i.* 1. To shine with a steady and dazzling intensity. 2. To gaze or stare fiercely or in hostility. 3. To be conspicuous or showy. —*v.t.* 4. To express or send forth with a glare. —*n.* 1. A dazzling, steady light or reflection. 2. An intense, piercing look or gaze, usually hostile. [ME *glaren* < LG] —**glar′ing** *adj.* —**glar′ing·ly** *adv.*

glar·y (glâr′ē) *adj.* **glar·i·er, glar·i·est** Dazzling; glaring.

glass (glas) *n.* 1. A hard, amorphous, brittle, usu. transparent substance made by fusing one or more of the oxides of silicon, boron, or phosphorus with certain basic oxides, followed by rapid cooling to prevent crystallization. ◆Collateral adjective: *vitreous.* 2. Any substance made of or resembling glass. 3. An article made wholly or partly of glass; as: **a** A windowpane, lens, mirror, tumbler, etc. **b** *pl.* A pair of eyeglasses; also, binoculars. 4. The contents of a drinking glass; glassful. —*v.t.* 1. To put in a glass container. 2. To enclose in or cover with glass. —*adj.* 1. Of, pertaining to, or consisting of glass. 2. Fitted with glass: a *glass* frame. [ME *glas* < OE *glæs*]

glass blowing The art of shaping glass by blowing air through a tube into a mass of molten glass.

glass·ful (glas′fo͝ol) *n. pl.* **·fuls** The amount contained in a drinking glass.

glass·ware (glas′wâr′) *n.* Articles made of glass.

glass wool Fibers of spun glass of woollike appearance, used for insulation, filters, etc.

glass·works (glas′wûrks′) *n.pl.* (*usu. construed as sing.*) A factory where glass is made.

glass·y (glas′ē) *adj.* **glass·i·er, glass·i·est** 1. Resembling glass. 2. Fixed, blank, and uncomprehending: a *glassy* stare. —**glass′i·ly** *adv.* —**glass′i·ness** *n.*

glau·co·ma (glô·kō′mə, glou-) *n. Pathol.* A disease of the eye characterized by pressure of fluids within the eyeball, with gradual loss of vision. [< L < Gk. *glaukos* bluish gray]

glaze (glāz) *v.* **glazed, glaz·ing** *v.t.* 1. To fit, as a window, with glass panes; also, to provide (a building, etc.) with windows. 2. To cover or coat with a thin film; as: **a** To coat (pottery) with a glasslike surface applied by fusing. **b** To cover (foods) with a thin coating of eggs, syrup, etc. **c** To cover (paintings) with a thin, transparent coating to modify the tone. —*v.i.* 3. To become covered with a thin coating or film. —*n.* 1. A thin, glossy coating; also, the substance used to make such a coating. 2. A filmy haze. [See GLASS.] —**glaz′er** *n.* —**glaz′ing** *n.*

gla·zier (glā′zhər) *n.* One who fits windows, doors, etc., with panes of glass. —**gla′zier·y** *n.*

gleam (glēm) *n.* 1. An intermittent or momentary ray or beam of light. 2. A soft radiance; glow; also, reflected light. 3. A brief manifestation, as of humor; a faint trace, as of hope. —*v.i.* 1. To shine softly; emit gleams. 2. To appear briefly as in a small burst of light. [OE *glæm*] —**gleam′y** *adj.*

glean (glēn) *v.t. & v.i.* 1. To collect (facts, etc.) by patient effort. 2. To gather (the leavings) from a field after the crop has been reaped. [< LL *glenare* < Celtic] —**glean′er** *n.*

glean·ing (glē′ning) *n. Usu. pl.* That which is gleaned.

glee (glē) *n.* 1. Lively, exuberant joy. 2. A musical composition for male voices, without accompaniment. [OE *glēo*]

glee club A group of singers organized to sing part songs.

glee·ful (glē′fəl) *adj.* Feeling or exhibiting glee; mirthful. —**glee′ful·ly** *adv.* —**glee′ful·ness** *n.*

glen (glen) *n.* A small, secluded valley. [< Scot. Gaelic *glenn*]

Glen·gar·ry (glen·gar′ē) *n.* A Scottish cap having sloping sides and streamers in back. [after *Glengarry,* a valley in Scotland]

glib (glib) *adj.* **glib·ber, glib·best** 1. Speaking

fluently; smooth in manner. 2. More facile than sincere. [< MLG *glibberich* slippery] **—glib′ly** *adv.* **—glib′ness** *n.*

glide (glīd) *v.* **glid·ed, glid·ing** *v.i.* 1. To move, slip, or flow smoothly or effortlessly. 2. To pass unnoticed or imperceptibly, as time: often with *by*. 3. *Aeron.* To descend along an oblique line gradually without motor power; also, to fly a glider. *—v.t.* 4. To cause to glide. *—n.* The act of gliding. [OE *glīdan*] **—glid′ing·ly** *adv.*

glid·er (glī′dər) *n.* 1. One who or that which glides. 2. *Aeron.* An engineless airplane, constructed to soar on air currents. 3. A swing gliding in a metal frame.

glim·mer (glim′ər) *v.i.* 1. To gleam unsteadily; flicker. 2. To appear fitfully or faintly. *—n.* 1. A faint, unsteady light. 2. A trace; inkling. [ME *glimeren* to shine] **—glim′mer·ing** *n. & adj.* **—glim′mer·ing·ly** *adv.*

glimpse (glimps) *n.* 1. A momentary view or look. 2. A faint intimation; inkling. *—v.* **glimpsed, glimps·ing** *v.t.* 1. To see for an instant; catch a glimpse of. *—v.i.* 2. To look for an instant: with *at*. [ME *glimsen* to shine faintly]

glint (glint) *v.i.* 1. To gleam; glitter. 2. To dart. *—n.* 1. A gleam. 2. A luster, as of metal. [ME *glinten* to shine < Scand.]

glis·sade (gli·säd′, -sād′) *n.* 1. The act of skillfully sliding down an icy slope. 2. A gliding dance step. *—v.i.* **·sad·ed, ·sad·ing** To execute a glissade. [< F *glisser* to slip]

glis·san·do (gli·sän′dō) *Music n. pl.* **·di** (-dē) or **·dos** A passing from one tone to another by a continuous change of pitch; also, a rapid succession of tones. [< F *glissant* slipping + Ital. *-ando*] **—glis·san′do** *adj. & adv.*

glis·ten (glis′ən) *v.i.* To shine, as reflected light. *—n.* Brightness; sparkle. [OE *glisnian* to shine]

glitch (glich) *n.* A mishap; malfunctioning. [< G *glitsche* slip]

glit·ter (glit′ər) *v.i.* 1. To sparkle brightly or brilliantly. 2. To display striking magnificence; be brilliantly showy. [< ON *glitra*] **—glit′ter** *n.* **—glit′ter·ing·ly** *adv.* **—glit′ter·y** *adj.*

gloam·ing (glō′ming) *n.* The dusk of early evening; twilight. [OE *glōmung*]

gloat (glōt) *v.i.* To take or express malicious delight: usu. with *over*. [Cf. ON *glotta* to grin]

glob (glob) *n.* 1. A small drop or ball of something. 2. A large, rounded mass of something.

glob·al (glō′bəl) *adj.* 1. Involving the whole world. 2. Spherical. **—glob′al·ly** *adv.*

globe (glōb) *n.* 1. A perfectly round body; a sphere, or anything like one. 2. The earth. 3. A spherical model of the earth or heavens. *—v.t. & v.i.* **globed, glob·ing** To form into a globe. [< L *globus* ball]

globe·fish (glōb′fish) *n. pl.* **·fish** or **·fish·es** Any of various tropical fishes that inflate their bodies into globular form.

globe·trot·ter (glōb′trot′ər) *n.* One who travels all over the world. **—globe′trot′ting** *n.*

glo·bin (glō′bin) *n. Biochem.* The protein constituent of hemoglobin. [< L *globus* ball + -IN]

glob·u·lar (glob′yə·lər) *adj.* 1. Spherical. 2. Formed of globules. Also **glob′u·lous.**

glob·ule (glob′yōōl) *n.* A tiny sphere or drop. [< L *globulus* little ball]

glob·u·lin (glob′yə·lin) *n. Biochem.* Any of various simple plant and animal proteins, insoluble in water but soluble in dilute salt solutions.

glock·en·spiel (glok′ən·spēl) *n.* A portable musical instrument with metal bars played by hammers. [< G *glocken* bells + *spiel* play]

gloom (glōōm) *n.* 1. Partial or total darkness; heavy shadow. 2. Darkness or depression of the mind or spirits. [ME *glom(b)en* to look sad]

gloom·y (glōō′mē) *adj.* **gloom·i·er, gloom·i·est** 1. Dark; dismal. 2. Melancholy; morose. 3. Producing gloom or melancholy. **—gloom′·i·ly** *adv.* **—gloom′i·ness** *n.*

glop (glop) *n. Slang* 1. Something soft and messy looking. 2. Banal sentimentality: His poetry was *glop*. [Imit.]

glo·ri·fy (glôr′ə·fī) *v.t.* **·fied, ·fy·ing** 1. To make glorious. 2. To honor; worship. 3. To give great praise to; laud. 4. To make seem more splendid than is so. [< L *gloria* glory + -FY] **—glo′ri·fi·ca′tion** *n.* **—glo′ri·fi′er** *n.*

glo·ri·ous (glôr′ē·əs) *adj.* 1. Full of glory; illustrious. 2. Bringing glory or honor. 3. Resplendent. 4. *Informal* Delightful. **—glo′ri·ous·ly** *adv.* **—glo′ri·ous·ness** *n.*

glo·ry (glôr′ē) *n. pl.* **·ries** 1. Distinguished honor or praise; exalted reputation. 2. Something bringing praise. 3. Worshipful adoration: to give *glory* to God. 4. Magnificence; splendor: the *glory* of Rome. 5. Heavenly bliss. 6. A state of extreme well-being: to be in one's *glory*. *—v.i.* **·ried, ·ry·ing** To take pride: with *in*. [< L *gloria*]

gloss[1] (glôs, glos) *n.* 1. The luster or sheen of a polished surface. 2. A deceptive or superficial appearance. *—v.t.* 1. To make lustrous, as by polishing. 2. To hide (errors, etc.) by falsehood: usu. with *over*. [< Scand. Cf. ON *glossi* blaze.] **—gloss′er** *n.*

gloss[2] (glôs, glos) *n.* 1. An explanatory note, esp. marginal or interlinear; a commentary or translation. 2. An artful or deceptive explanation to cover up a fault, etc. *—v.t.* 1. To write glosses for (a text, etc.); annotate. 2. To excuse by false explanations. [< Gk. *glōssa* foreign word]

glos·sa·ry (glos′ə·rē, glôs′-) *n. pl.* **·ries** A lexicon of the technical, obscure, or foreign words of a work or field. [< L *glossa*] **—glos·sar·i·al** (glo·sâr′ē·əl) *adj.*

glosso- *combining form* The tongue; speech; language. Also, before vowels, **gloss-.** [< Gk. *glōssa* tongue]

gloss·y (glôs′ē, glos′ē) *adj.* **gloss·i·er, gloss·i·est** 1. Having a bright sheen; lustrous. 2. Made superficially attractive. **—gloss′i·ly** *adv.* **—gloss′i·ness** *n.*

-glot *combining form* Using or able to use (a number of) languages: *polyglot*. [< Gk. *glōssa* tongue, language]

glot·tis (glot′is) *n. pl.* **glot·ti·des** (glot′ə·dēz) or **glot·tis·es** *Anat.* The cleft between the vocal cords at the upper opening of the larynx. [< Gk. *glōtta* tongue] **—glot′tal** *adj.*

glove (gluv) *n.* 1. A covering for the hand, having a separate sheath for each finger. 2. In baseball, a large leather mitt for catching the ball. 3. A boxing glove. **—to**

handle with kid gloves To use great care in dealing with. —*v.t.* **gloved, glov·ing** 1. To put gloves on. 2. To furnish with gloves. [OE *glōf*]
glov·er (gluv′ər) *n.* A maker of or dealer in gloves.
glow (glō) *v.i.* 1. To give off light, esp. without flame. 2. To be red, as from heat; flush. 3. To be animated, as with emotion, etc. —*n.* 1. The incandescence given off by a heated substance. 2. Ruddiness, as from health. 3. Strong emotion; ardor. [OE *glōwan*] —**glow′ing** *adj.* —**glow′ing·ly** *adv.*
glow·er (glou′ər) *v.i.* To stare with an angry frown; scowl sullenly. [? Obs. *glow* to stare] —**glow′er** *n.* —**glow′er·ing·ly** *adv.*
glow·worm (glō′wûrm′) *n.* A European beetle, the larva and female of which display phosphorescence.
glox·in·i·a (glok·sin′ē·ə) *n.* A plant with large, bell-shaped flowers. [after *Gloxin*, 18th c. Ger. doctor]
gloze (glōz) *v.t.* **glozed, gloz·ing** To explain away.
glu·cose (glōō′kōs) *n.* 1. *Chem.* A sugar found as dextrose in plants and animals. 2. A thick yellowish syrup used in confectionery, baking, etc. [< Gk. *glykys* sweet]
glue (glōō) *n.* 1. An adhesive made from animal substances, as skin, bones, etc. 2. An adhesive or cement made of casein or other synthetics. —*v.t.* **glued, glu·ing** To stick or fasten with or as with glue. [< OF *glu* birdlime]
glue·y (glōō′ē) *adj.* **glu·i·er, glu·i·est** 1. Having the nature of glue; sticky; viscous. 2. Covered or spread with glue.
glum (glum) *adj.* **glum·mer, glum·mest** Moody and silent; sullen. —**glum′ly** *adv.* —**glum′ness** *n.*
glut (glut) *v.t.* **glut·ted, glut·ting** 1. To feed or supply to excess; satiate. 2. To supply (the market) with an excess of goods so that the price falls. —*n.* 1. An excessive supply. 2. The act of glutting or being glutted. [< obs. *glut* glutton < OF *gloutir* to swallow]
glu·ten (glōōt′n) *n.* A tough, sticky mixture of proteins obtained from wheat flour. [< L glue] —**glu′te·nous** *adj.*
glu·te·us (glōō·tē′əs) *n.* *pl.* **·te·i** (-tē′ī) *Anat.* Any of three muscles of the buttocks. [< NL < Gk. *gloutos* rump] —**glu·te′al** *adj.*
glu·ti·nous (glōōt′n·əs) *adj.* Resembling glue; sticky. —**glu′ti·nous·ly** *adv.* —**glu′ti·nous·ness** *n.*
glut·ton (glut′n) *n.* 1. One who eats to excess. 2. One who has a great appetite or capacity for something. [< L *gluto, -onis* glutton] —**glut′ton·ous** *adj.* —**glut′ton·ous·ly** *adv.* —**glut′ton·y** *n.*
glyc·er·in (glis′ər·in) *n.* Glycerol. Also **glyc′er·ine** (-in, -ēn).
glyc·er·ol (glis′ər·ōl, -ol) *n.* *Chem.* A sweet, oily, colorless alcohol formed by decomposition of natural fats, used in medicine, industry, and the arts. [< Gk. *glykeros* sweet + -OL]
glyco- *combining form* Sweet. [< Gk. *glykys*]
gly·co·gen (glī′kə·jən) *n.* *Biochem.* A white, uncrystallized carbohydrate, contained principally in the liver and decomposable into glucose. —**gly·co·gen·ic** (glī′kə·jen′ik) *adj.*
gly·co·side (glī′kə·sīd) *n.* *Chem.* Any of a group of carbohydrates that when decomposed yield glucose or other sugar.
G-man (jē′man′) *n.* *pl.* **-men** (-men′) An agent of the Federal Bureau of Investigation. [< G(OVERNMENT) MAN]
gnarl (närl) *n.* A protuberance on a tree; a tough knot. —*v.t.* To make knotty and twisted like an old tree. —**gnarled, gnarl′y** *adj.*
gnash (nash) *v.t.* To grind or snap (the teeth) together, as in rage. [< Scand.] —**gnash** *n.*
gnat (nat) *n.* Any of various small stinging or biting flies. [OE *gnæt*]
gnaw (nô) *v.* **gnawed, gnawed** or **gnawn, gnaw·ing** *v.t.* 1. To eat away gradually with or as with the teeth; also, to bite on repeatedly. 2. To torment or oppress with fear, pain, etc. —*v.i.* 3. To bite, chew, or corrode persistently. 4. To cause constant worry, etc. [OE *gnagan*] —**gnaw′ing·ly** *adv.*
gnaw·ing (nô′ing) *n.* A dull, persistent sensation of discomfort or distress.
gneiss (nīs) *n.* A coarse-grained, banded rock like granite but having layered components. [< G] —**gneiss′ic** *adj.*
gnome (nōm) *n.* In folklore, one of a group of dwarfish, little old men, living in caves and guarding buried treasure, etc. [< NL *gnomus*] —**gnom′ish** *adj.*
gno·mic (nō′mik, nom′ik) *adj.* Consisting of or resembling maxims; aphoristic. [< Gk. *gnōmē* thought, maxim] Also **gno′mi·cal.** —**gno′mi·cal·ly** *adv.*
-gnomy *combining form* Knowledge or art of judging: *physiognomy.* [See GNOMIC.]
-gnosis *combining form* *Med.* Knowledge; recognition: *prognosis.* [< Gk. *gnōsis* knowledge]
gnos·tic (nos′tik) *adj.* Of or possessing knowledge or insight. Also **gnos′ti·cal.**
gnu (nōō, nyōō) *n.* *pl.* **gnu** or **gnus** A South African antelope having an oxlike head with curved horns, a mane, and a long tail: also called *wildebeest.* [< Xhosa *nqu*]
go[1] (gō) *v.* **went, gone, go·ing;** *3rd person sing. present* **goes** *v.i.* 1. To proceed or pass along; move. 2. To move from a place; leave; depart: often used as a command or signal, as in a race: *Go!* 3. To be in operation; also, to work or function properly. 4. To extend or reach: This pipe *goes* to the basement. 5. To emit a specified sound or act in a certain way: The chain *goes* "clank." 6. To fail, give way, or collapse; also, to disappear. 7. To have a specific place; belong: The plates *go* on the shelf. 8. To be awarded or given. 9. To pass from one person to another. 10. To pass into a condition; become: to *go* insane. 11. To be, continue, or appear in a specified state: to *go* unpunished. 12. To happen or end in a specific manner: The election *went* badly. 13. To be considered or ranked: good as lunches *go.* 14. To be suitable; harmonize; fit. 15. To have a certain form: How does the tune *go?* 16. To have recourse; resort: to *go* to court. 17. To die. 18. To pass: said of time. 19. To be abolished or given up: these expenses must *go.* 20. To be sold or bid for: with *at* or *for.* 21. To subject oneself; put oneself: He *went* to great pains. 22. To be about to: used in the progressive form and followed by the present infinitive: They are *going* to protest. —*v.t.*

23. *Informal* To furnish or provide (bail). 24. *Informal* To risk or bet; wager. **—to go about** 1. To be occupied or busy with. 2. To circulate. 3. *Naut.* To tack; turn. **—to go after** 1. To try to catch; chase. 2. To follow in sequence. **—to go around** To be enough for all to have some. **—to go at** To attack; work at. **—to go back on** 1. To be disloyal to; forsake. 2. To fail to fulfill. **—to go by** 1. To pass. 2. To conform to or be guided by. 3. To be known by. **—to go for** 1. To try to get. 2. To advocate. 3. *Informal* To attack. 4. *Informal* To be attracted by. **—to go in for** *Informal* 1. To strive for; advocate. 2. To like or participate in. **—to go into** 1. To investigate. 2. To take up, as a study or profession. **—to go off** 1. To explode or be discharged, as a gun. 2. To depart; leave. 3. *Informal* To occur. **—to go on** 1. To happen: What's *going on* here? 2. To persevere; endure. 3. In the theater, to make an entrance. **—to go (someone) better** *Informal* To surpass (someone). **—to go out** 1. To go to social gatherings, etc. 2. To be extinguished, as a light. 3. To become outdated, as fashions. 4. To go on strike. **—to go over** 1. To repeat; also, to rehearse. 2. To examine carefully. 3. *Informal* To succeed. 4. To change sides or allegiance. **—to go through with** To perform to the finish; complete. **—to go under** 1. To be overwhelmed. 2. To fail, as a business. **—to go with** 1. To harmonize with. 2. To accompany. 3. *Informal* To be sweethearts. **—to let go** 1. To release one's hold; set free. 2. To abandon. **—to let oneself go** To be uninhibited. **—*n.*** 1. The act of going. 2. *Informal* The capacity for action; He has plenty of *go*. 3. *Informal* A try: to have a *go* at something. 4. *Informal* A success: He made a *go* of it. 5. *Informal* An agreement; bargain: It's a *go*. **—no go** *Informal* Useless; hopeless; a failure. **—on the go** *Informal* In constant motion; very busy. **—*adj.*** Functioning and ready: All systems are *go*. [OE *gān*]

go[2] (gō) *n.* A Japanese board game.

goad (gōd) *n.* 1. A stick for urging on oxen, etc. 2. Something that drives. **—*v.t.*** To drive; incite. [OE *gād*]

go-a·head (gō′ə·hed′) *n.* A signal or permission to move ahead or proceed.

goal (gōl) *n.* 1. Something toward which effort or movement is directed; an end or objective. 2. The terminal point of a journey or race. 3. In some games, the point to which the players try to bring the ball, puck, etc., to score; also, the score itself. [ME *gol*]

goal·ie (gō′lē) *n.* In hockey, soccer, etc., a player whose function is to prevent the ball or puck from passing over the goal for a score. Also **goal·keep·er** (gōl′kē′pər), **goal·tend·er** (gōl′ten′dər).

goat (gōt) *n.* 1. A cud-chewing mammal related to the sheep and having hollow horns. 2. A lecherous man. 3. *Slang* One who is the butt of a joke; scapegoat. **—to get one's goat** *Slang* To move one to anger or annoyance. [OE *gāt*] **—goat′ish** *adj.* **—goat′ish·ly** *adv.* **—goat′ish·ness** *n.*

Goat (gōt) *n.* The constellation and sign of the zodiac Capricorn.

goat·ee (gō·tē′) *n.* A short, pointed beard.

goat·herd (gōt′hûrd′) *n.* One who tends goats.

goat·skin (gōt′skin′) *n.* 1. The hide of a goat. 2. Leather made from this hide.

gob[1] (gob) *n.* *Informal* 1. A piece or lump, as of a soft substance. 2. *pl.* Great quantities. [< OF *gobe* mouthful]

gob[2] (gob) *n.* *Slang* A sailor of the U.S. Navy.

gob·bet (gob′it) *n.* A piece or hunk, as of raw meat. [See GOB[1].]

gob·ble[1] (gob′əl) *v.* **·bled, ·bling** *v.t.* 1. To swallow (food) greedily. 2. *Slang* To seize in a grasping manner. **—*v.i.*** 3. To eat greedily. [< F *gover* to bolt, devour]

gob·ble[2] (gob′əl) *v.i.* **·bled, ·bling** To make the throaty sound of a male turkey. [Var. of GABBLE] **—gob′ble** *n.*

gob·ble·dy·gook (gob′əl·dē·gŏŏk′) *n.* *Informal* Unintelligible, pompous jargon. [Coined by M. Maverick, U.S. Congressman, about 1940]

gob·bler (gob′lər) *n.* A male turkey.

go-be·tween (gō′bə·twēn′) *n.* An agent or mediator.

gob·let (gob′lit) *n.* 1. A drinking vessel, typically with a base and stem. 2. A large, festive shallow drinking cup. [< OF *gobel* a drinking cup]

gob·lin (gob′lin) *n.* In folklore, an ugly elf regarded as evil or mischievous. [< OF *gobelin*]

go-cart (gō′kärt′) *n.* A small wagon for young children.

god (god) *n.* 1. One of various beings, usu. male, conceived of in polytheistic religions or mythologies as having supernatural aspects or powers. 2. Any person or thing much loved. [OE] **—god′like** *adj.*

God (god) *n.* In monotheism, the creator and ruler of life and the universe.

god·child (god′chīld′) *n.* *pl.* **·chil·dren** (-chil′drən) A child whom a person sponsors at baptism, circumcision, etc.

god·dam (god′dam′) *interj.* A strong oath used to express anger, surprise, etc. Also **God damn.**

god·damned (god′damd′) *adj.* Utterly detestable or outrageous. **—*adv.*** *Informal* To an extreme degree; very. Also **god·dam** (god′dam′).

god·daugh·ter (god′dô′tər) *n.* A female godchild.

god·dess (god′is) 1. A female god. 2. A woman adored for her beauty or charm.

god·fa·ther (god′fä′thər) *n.* A male godparent.

god-fear·ing (god′fir′ing) *adj.* 1. *Often cap.* Having reverence for God. 2. Pious; devout.

god·for·sak·en (god′fər·sā′kən) *adj.* 1. *Often cap.* Abandoned by God. 2. Wretched; desolate.

god·head (god′hed′) *n.* Divine nature or being; divinity.

God·head (god′hed′) *n.* The essential nature of God.

god·less (god′lis) *adj.* 1. Having or believing in no god. 2. Wicked. **—god′less·ly** *adv.* **—god′less·ness** *n.*

god·ly (god′lē) *adj.* **·li·er, ·li·est** Filled with love for God. **—god′li·ness** *n.*

god·moth·er (god′muth′ər) *n.* A female godparent.

god·par·ent (god′pâr′ənt) *n.* The sponsor of a child at baptism, circumcision, etc.
god·send (god′send′) *n.* Something that unexpectedly fulfills one's needs or wants.
god·son (god′sun′) *n.* A male godchild.
God·speed (god′spēd′) *n.* Best wishes for someone's journey or venture. [Shortened form of *God speed you*]
go-get·ter (gō′get′ər) *n. Informal* A hustling, energetic, aggressive person.
gog·gle (gog′əl) *n. pl.* Spectacles designed to protect the eyes against dust, sparks, wind, etc. **—*v.*** **·gled, ·gling** *v.i.* 1. To roll the eyes erratically. 2. Of the eyes, to move erratically, bulge, or be fixed in a stare. **—*v.t.*** 3. To cause (the eyes) to goggle. [ME *gogelen* to look aside] **—gog′gle-eyed′** (-īd′) *adj.*
go-go (gō′gō′) *adj.* 1. Of or describing discothèques, the dances performed there, or the women dancers. 2. Lively; energetic. 3. Modern; up-to-date. 4. Speculative, as stocks. [< F *à gogo* galore]
Goi·del·ic (goi·del′ik) *n.* The branch of the Celtic languages including Irish, the Gaelic of the Scottish Highlands, and Manx. **—*adj.*** Of or pertaining to the Gaels or their languages. [< OIrish *Goidel* Gael]
go·ing (gō′ing) *n.* 1. The act of departing or moving; leaving. 2. The condition of ground or roads as affecting walking, riding, racing, etc. **—goings on** *Informal* Actions or behavior: used chiefly to express disapproval. **—*adj.*** 1. That goes, moves, or works. 2. Continuing to function; moving ahead: a *going* concern. 3. Prevailing: the *going* rate.
goi·ter (goi′tər) *n. Pathol.* Any abnormal enlargement of the thyroid gland. Also **goi′tre.** [< F, ult. < L *guttur* throat] **—goi′trous** *adj.*
gold (gōld) *n.* 1. A precious, yellow, metallic element (symbol Au) that is highly ductile and resistant to oxidation. 2. Coin made of this metal. 3. Wealth; riches. 4. A bright yellow color. [OE] **—gold** *adj.*
gold·brick (gōld′brik′) *n. Slang* One who shirks work: said esp. of soldiers. Also **gold′brick′er.** **—gold′brick′** *v.i.*
gold digger *Slang* A woman who uses feminine wiles to get money.
gold·en (gōl′dən) *adj.* 1. Made of, containing, or resembling gold. 2. Bright yellow. 3. Happy, prosperous, etc. **—gold′en·ness** *n.*
golden age 1. In Greek and Roman legend, an early period marked by perfect innocence, peace, and happiness. 2. Any period of prosperity or excellence. 3. The later years of life, esp. over age 65.
golden ager An elderly and often retired person.
golden anniversary A fiftieth anniversary.
golden calf Riches, as unduly prized. [after a molten image worshiped by the Israelites, *Ex.* xxxii]
golden mean Moderation; avoidance of extremes.
gold·en·rod (gōl′dən·rod′) *n.* A North American herb of the composite family, having small, usu. yellow flowers.
golden rule The rule or principle of treating others as one wants to be treated.
golden wedding The fiftieth anniversary of a marriage.
gold-filled (gōld′fild′) *adj.* Filled with a base metal and covered with a layer of gold.
gold·finch (gōld′finch′) *n.* 1. A European finch having a yellow patch on each wing. 2. An American finch of which the male, in the summer, has a yellow body with black tail.
gold·fish (gōld′fish′) *n. pl.* **·fish** or **·fish·es** A small carp, usu. golden in color.
gold foil Thin sheets of gold.
gold leaf Sheets of gold hammered to extreme thinness, used in gilding, etc.
gold mine 1. A mine producing gold ore. 2. *Informal* Any source of great profit, riches, etc.
gold plate Vessels and utensils of gold, collectively.
gold reserve The quantity of gold bullion or coin owned by a country's central bank or national treasury.
gold·smith (gōld′smith′) *n.* One who makes or deals in articles of gold.
gold standard A monetary system based on gold as the unit of value.
go·lem (gō′lem, -ləm) *n.* In medieval Jewish legend, a manlike automaton. [< Hebrew, embryo, monster]
golf (golf, gôlf) *n.* An outdoor game played on a large course (**golf course**) with a small ball and a set of clubs (**golf clubs**). **—*v.i.*** To play golf. [Cf. dial. E (Scot.) *gowf* strike] **—golf′er** *n.*
Gol·go·tha (gol′gə·thə) A place near Jerusalem where Jesus was crucified; Calvary. *Matt.* xxvii 33. [< LL < Gk. < Aramaic *gogolthā* skull]
Go·li·ath (gə·lī′əth) A giant. [after the Philistine *Goliath*, slain by David, I *Sam.* xvii 4]
gol·ly (gol′ē) *interj.* An exclamation of mild surprise, impatience, etc. [Euphemistic alter. of GOD]
-gon *combining form* Having (an indicated number of) angles: *pentagon.* [< Gk. *gōnia* angle]
go·nad (gō′nad) *n. Anat.* A male or female sex gland, in which the reproductive cells develop; an ovary or testis. [< Gk. *gonos* seed] **—go·nad′al, go·nad′ic** *adj.*
gon·do·la (gon′də·lə, gon·dō′lə) *n.* 1. A long, narrow, flat-bottomed Venetian boat. 2. A large, flat-bottomed, river boat; also, a gondola car. 3. *Aeron.* The car attached below a dirigible. [< Ital. < *gondolar* to rock]
gondola car A long, shallow, open freight car.
gon·do·lier (gon′də·lir′) *n.* The boatman of a gondola.
gone (gôn, gon) Past participle of GO. **—*adj.*** 1. Moved away; left. 2. Beyond hope; ruined; lost. 3. Dead; departed. 4. Ended; past. 5. Consumed; spent.
gon·er (gôn′ər, gon′-) *n. Informal* Someone or something close to death or beyond saving.
gon·fa·lon (gon′fə·lən) *n.* A banner or ensign, usu. cut so as to end in streamers. [< Ital. *gonfalone* < OHG *gundfano* war banner]
gong (gong, gông) *n.* 1. A heavy metal disk giving a deep, resonant tone when struck. 2. A flat, saucerlike bell struck with a small mechanical hammer. [< Malay]
gono- *combining form* Procreative; sexual.

Also, before vowels, **gon-**. [< Gk. *gonos* seed]
gon·o·coc·cus (gon′ə·kok′əs) *n. pl.* **·coc·ci** (-kok′sī) The bacterium that causes gonorrhea. [< NL]
go-no-go (gō′nō′gō′) *adj.* Pertaining to that time when an action, operation, etc., must either be stopped or allowed to go to completion.
gon·or·rhe·a (gon′ə·rē′ə) *n. Pathol.* A contagious venereal infection of the genitourinary tract. Also **gon′or·rhoe′a.** [< Gk. *gonos* seed + *rheein* to flow] **—gon′or·rhe′al** *adj.*
-gony *combining form* Production of; generation: *cosmogony.* [< Gk. *gonos* seed]
goo (gōō) *n. Slang* Any sticky substance.
goo·ber (gōō′bər) *n. Southern U.S.* A peanut. Also **goober pea.** [? < Bantu *nguba*]
good (gŏŏd) *adj.* **bet·ter, best** 1. Morally excellent; virtuous. 2. Honorable; worthy: a *good* reputation. 3. Generous; loving; kind. 4. Well-behaved; tractable. 5. Proper; desirable: *good* manners. 6. Favorable: a *good* opinion. 7. Having beneficial effects; helpful: *good* advice. 8. Reliable; safe: a *good* investment. 9. Skillful; expert: He is *good* at sports. 10. Genuine; valid: a *good* excuse. 11. Backed by sufficient funds: a *good* check. 12. Excellent in quality or degree: *good* literature. 13. Orthodox; conforming. 14. Unspoiled; fresh: *good* meat. 15. Healthy: *good* lungs. 16. Attractive or striking: She looks *good* in that hat. 17. Great in amount; also, maximum; full. **—good and** *Informal* Completely; very: *good and* hot. **—good for** 1. Capable of lasting for. 2. *Informal* Able to pay, give, or produce. **—***n.* 1. That which is fitting, etc. 2. Benefit: for the *good* of mankind. 3. That which is morally or ethically desirable. **—to make good** 1. To be successful. 2. To compensate for. 3. To fulfill. 4. To prove; substantiate. **—***interj.* An exclamation of satisfaction. **—***adv. Informal* Well. [OE *gōd*] **—good′ness** *n.*
good-by (gŏŏd′bī′) *adj., n. & interj. pl.* **-bys** (-bīz′) Farewell. Also **good′bye′.** [Contraction of *God be with you*]
good-for-noth·ing (gŏŏd′fər·nuth′ing) *n.* A worthless person. **—***adj.* Of no use or value.
Good Friday The Friday before Easter, a day observed by Christians as a commemoration of the crucifixion of Jesus.
good·heart·ed (gŏŏd′här′tid) *adj.* Kind; charitable; generous. **—good′heart′ed·ly** *adv.* **—good′heart′ed·ness** *n.*
good-hu·mored (gŏŏd′hyōō′mərd, -yōō′-) *adj.* Having a cheerful temper or mood. **—good′-hu′mored·ly** *adv.*
good-look·ing (gŏŏd′lŏŏk′ing) *adj.* Handsome.
good·ly (gŏŏd′lē) *adj.* **·li·er, ·li·est** 1. Having a pleasing appearance. 2. Of fine quality. 3. Large. **—good′li·ness** *n.*
good-na·tured (gŏŏd′nā′chərd) *adj.* Having a pleasant disposition; not easily provoked. Also **good-tem·pered** (gŏŏd′tem′pərd). **—good′-na′tured·ly** *adv.* **—good′-na′tured·ness** *n.*
goods (gŏŏdz) *n.pl.* 1. Merchandise; wares. 2. Fabric; material. 3. Property, esp. when personal and movable.
Good Sa·mar·i·tan (sə·mar′ə·tən) A humane, compassionate person. [after New Testament parable, *Luke* x 30–37]
good will 1. A desire for the well-being of others; benevolence. 2. Cheerful, ready consent or willingness. 3. Intangible assets in terms of prestige and friendly relations. Also **good·will** (gŏŏd′wil′).
good·y (gŏŏd′ē) *n. pl.* **good·ies** *Informal Usu. pl.* Something tasty. **—***interj.* A childish exclamation of pleasure.
good·y-good·y (gŏŏd′ē·gŏŏd′ē) *n. pl.* **good·y-good·ies** A prissy or sanctimonious person. **—***adj.* Piously good; affectedly superior.
goof (gōōf) *Slang n.* 1. A dull-witted person; dope. 2. A mistake; blunder. **—***v.i.* 1. To blunder. **—***v.t.* 2. To make a mess of: usu. with *up.* **—to goof off** *Slang* To loaf.
goon (gōōn) *n. Slang* 1. A thug or hoodlum. 2. An oaf. [after a character created by E. C. Segar, 1894–1938, U.S. cartoonist]
goose (gōōs) *n. pl.* **geese** (gēs) 1. A subfamily of web-footed birds larger than ducks. 2. The female: distinguished from *gander.* 3. The flesh as food. 4. A fool. **—to cook one's goose** *Informal* To spoil one's chances. **—***v.t.* **goosed, goos·ing** *Slang* 1. To poke between the buttocks to startle or annoy. 2. To stimulate to activity: The ad *goosed* sales. [OE *gos*]
goose·ber·ry (gōōs′ber′ē) *n. pl.* **·ries** 1. The tart berry of a spiny shrub of the saxifrage family, used for jams, pies, etc. 2. The shrub itself.
goose flesh A taut, prickling sensation in the skin. Also **goose bumps, goose pimples.**
goose-step (gōōs′step′) *v.i.* **-stepped, -step·ping** To march along or mark time kicking stiffly and sharply. **—goose step** *n.*
go·pher (gō′fər) *n.* 1. A burrowing American rodent with large cheek pouches. 2. A North American ground squirrel. [< F *gaufre* honeycomb]
Gor·di·an knot (gôr′dē·ən) Any difficulty solved only by drastic measures. [after a legendary knot cut by Alexander the Great]
gore[1] (gôr) *n.* Blood that has been shed, esp. in copious amounts. [OE *gor* dirt] **—gor′i·ly** *adv.* **—gor′i·ness** *n.* **—gor′y** *adj.*
gore[2] (gôr) *v.t.* **gored, gor·ing** To pierce with the horns or tusks. [ME *goren*]
gore[3] (gôr) *n.* A triangular or tapering section set into a garment, sail, etc., for greater fullness. **—***v.t.* **gored, gor·ing** 1. To cut into gore-shaped pieces. 2. To furnish with gores. [OE *gāra* triangular piece of land]
gorge (gôrj) *n.* 1. A narrow, deep ravine, esp. with a stream flowing through. 2. The throat. 3. Deep or violent disgust. 4. A mass obstructing a passage. **—***v.* **gorged, gorg·ing** *v.t.* 1. To stuff with food. 2. To swallow gluttonously. **—***v.i.* 3. To stuff oneself with food. [< L *gurges* whirlpool] **—gorg′er** *n.*
gor·geous (gôr′jəs) *adj.* 1. Dazzlingly colorful; brilliant. 2. *Informal* Extremely beautiful, etc. [< OF *gorgias* elegant] **—gor′geous·ly** *adv.* **—gor′geous·ness** *n.*
gor·gon (gôr′gən) *n.* A terrifyingly ugly woman. [< Gk. *gorgos* terrible]
Gor·gon·zo·la (gôr′gən·zō′lə) *n.* A strongly flavored, white Italian cheese.
go·ril·la (gə·ril′ə) *n.* An African ape, the largest and most powerful of the anthropoids. [< Gk., appar. < African name]

gorp (gôrp) *n.* A mixture of nuts, dried fruits, grains, and sweeteners, used as a snack esp. by hikers. [Orig. unknown]
gosh (gosh) *interj.* An exclamation. [Euphemism for GOD]
gos·hawk (gos′hôk′, gôs′-) *n.* Any of various large, short-winged hawks. [OE *gōshafoc*]
gos·ling (goz′ling) *n.* A young goose. [< ON *gæslingr*]
gos·pel (gos′pəl) *n.* 1. The teachings of the Christian church as originally preached by Jesus Christ and the apostles. 2. Any information accepted as unquestionably true. [OE *godspell* good news]
Gos·pel (gos′pəl) *n.* Any of the first four books of the New Testament, attributed to Matthew, Mark, Luke, and John.
gos·sa·mer (gos′ə·mər) *n.* 1. Fine strands of spider's silk, esp. when floating in the air. 2. Any flimsy, delicate substance, as filmy, gauzelike fabric. —*adj.* Resembling gossamer; flimsy; unsubstantial. [< ME *gossomer* Indian summer, lit., goose summer]
gos·sip (gos′əp) *n.* 1. Idle, often malicious talk, esp. about others. 2. Informal talk or writing, as of personages. 3. A person who indulges in idle talk. —*v.i.* **gos·siped** or **·sipped, gos·sip·ing** or **·sip·ping** To talk idly or maliciously about others. [OE *god* + *sibb* a relative] —**gos′sip·er** *n.*
gos·sip·y (gos′əp·ē) *adj.* 1. Indulging in gossip. 2. Chatty.
got (got) Past tense and past participle of GET.
Goth (goth, gôth) *n.* A member of a Germanic people that invaded the Roman Empire in the third to fifth centuries: including the Ostrogoths (**East Goths**) and Visigoths (**West Goths**). [< Gk. *Gothoi* < Gothic]
Goth·ic (goth′ik) *adj.* 1. Of or pertaining to the Goths or to their language. 2. Of a style of European architecture, from about 1200 to 1500, characterized by pointed arches, ribbed vaulting, flying buttresses, etc. 3. *Often not cap.* Denoting a literature characterized by isolated settings and mysterious events. —*n.* 1. The extinct East Germanic language of the Goths. 2. Gothic architecture or art. 3. *Often not cap.* A gothic novel.
goth·ic (goth′ik) *n.* *Sometimes cap.* *Printing* **a** Sans serif. **b** Black letter.
got·ten (got′n) Past participle of GET.
gouache (gwosh) *n.* 1. A method of painting using opaque colors mixed with water and gum. 2. The opaque pigment so used. 3. A painting done in this medium. [< F < Ital. *guazzo* a spray < L *aqua* water]
Gou·da cheese (gou′də, gōō′-) A mild, yellow cheese similar to Edam cheese.
gouge (gouj) *n.* A chisel having a scoop-shaped blade, used for wood carving. —*v.t.* **gouged, goug·ing** 1. To cut or carve as with a gouge. 2. To scoop, force, or tear out. 3. *Informal* To cheat; esp., to charge exorbitant prices. [< LL *gulbia*] —**goug′er** *n.*
gou·lash (gōō′läsh, -lash) *n.* A stew or thick soup of meat and vegetables, seasoned with paprika, etc. [< Hung. *gulyas* (*hus*) shepherd's (meat)]
gou·ra·mi (gōō·rä′mē, gōōr′ə·mē) *n.* 1. A large, freshwater fish of SE Asia. 2. Any of various related fishes frequently kept in home aquariums, as the **dwarf gourami** and the **three-spot gourami.** [< Malay *gurami*]
gourd (gôrd, gōōrd) *n.* 1. The fruit of any of various plants, having hard, durable shells. 2. The fruit of the calabash tree. 3. A utensil, as a ladle, made from the dried shell. [ME *gourde*, ult. < L *cucurbita* gourd]
gour·mand (gōōr·mänd′, *Fr.* gōōr·män′) *n.* One who takes hearty pleasure in eating. [< F]
gour·met (gōōr·mā′, *Fr.* gōōr·me′) *n.* A devotee and connoisseur of good food and drink. [< F < OF, winetaster]
gout (gout) *n.* *Pathol.* A metabolic disease characterized by painful inflammation of the joints. [< F *goutte* drop] —**gout′y** *adj.* **gout·i·er, gout·i·est** —**gout′i·ness** *n.*
gov·ern (guv′ərn) *v.t.* 1. To rule or direct by right or authority. 2. To guide or control the action of; influence. 3. To serve as a rule or deciding factor for. 4. To keep in check. —*v.i.* 5. To exercise authority; rule. [< L *gubernare* to steer] —**gov′ern·a·ble** *adj.*
gov·ern·ance (guv′ər·nəns) *n.* Exercise of authority.
gov·ern·ess (guv′ər·nis) *n.* A woman employed in a private household to take charge of and instruct children.
gov·ern·ment (guv′ərn·mənt, -ər-) *n.* 1. The authoritative administration of the affairs of a nation, state, city, etc.; the jurisdiction exercised over the people; rule. 2. The official governing body of a nation, community, etc. 3. The system or established form by which a nation, etc., is controlled: democratic *government.* —**gov·ern·men·tal** (guv′ərn·men′təl, -ər-) *adj.* —**gov′ern·men′tal·ly** *adv.*
gov·er·nor (guv′ər·nər) *n.* 1. One who governs; as: **a** The elected chief executive of any state in the U.S. **b** An official appointed to administer a province, territory, etc. 2. *Mech.* A device for controlling speed, as of a motor. —**gov′er·nor·ship** *n.*
gown (goun) *n.* 1. A woman's dress, esp. one for formal occasions. 2. Any long, loose garment. 3. A long, loose outer robe worn by certain officials, scholars, etc. [< OF *goune* < Med.L *gunna* a loose robe] —**gown** *v.t. & v.i.* —**gowned** (gound) *adj.*
grab (grab) *v.* **grabbed, grab·bing** *v.t.* 1. To grasp or seize suddenly. 2. To take possession of by force or by dishonest means. 3. *Slang* To impress powerfully; affect: The idea *grabs* me. —*v.i.* 4. To make a sudden grasp. —*n.* 1. The act of grabbing. 2. A dishonest acquisition. 3. A mechanical apparatus used to grasp and lift. [Cf. MDu. *grabben* to grip] —**grab′ber** *n.* —**grab′by** *adj.*
grab bag A bag or other receptacle filled with unidentified articles, from which items are picked at random.
gra·ben (grä′bən) *n.* *Geol.* A depression caused by the downward faulting of a portion of the earth's crust. [< G, ditch]
grace (grās) *n.* 1. Beauty or harmony of motion, form, or manner. 2. Any attractive quality. 3. Service freely rendered; good will. 4. The act of showing favor. 5. Clemency; mercy. 6. An extension of time granted after a set date, as for paying a debt. 7. A short prayer at a meal. 8. *Theol.* **a** The love of God toward man. **b** The divine influence operating in man. —**to be in the good graces of** To be regarded with favor by. —**with good grace** In a willing manner. —*v.t.* **graced, grac·ing** 1. To add grace and beauty to; adorn. 2. To dignify; honor. [< L *gratia* favor]

Grace (grās) *n.* A title or form of address for a duke, duchess, archbishop, or bishop: preceded by *Your, His, Her,* etc.
grace·ful (grās′fəl) *adj.* Characterized by grace, elegance, or beauty. —**grace′ful·ly** *adv.* —**grace′ful·ness** *n.*
grace·less (grās′lis) *adj.* 1. Lacking grace, charm, or elegance; clumsy. 2. Having no sense of what is right or decent. —**grace′·less·ly** *adv.* —**grace′less·ness** *n.*
grace note *Music* A note played or sung as an embellishment.
gra·cious (grā′shəs) *adj.* 1. Having or showing kindness, affability, etc. 2. Full of compassion; merciful. —*interj.* An exclamation of mild surprise. [< L *gratia* favor] —**gra′cious·ly** *adv.* —**gra′cious·ness** *n.*
grack·le (grak′əl) *n.* Any of various New World blackbirds. [< L *graculus* jackdaw]
grad (grad) *n. Informal* A graduate.
gra·da·tion (grā·dā′shən) *n.* 1. An orderly and gradual progression or arrangement according to size, quality, rank, etc. 2. *Usu. pl.* A step, degree, or relative position in such a progression. 3. The act of arranging in grades. [< L *gradus* step] —**gra′date** *v.t. & v.i.* **·dat·ed, ·dat·ing** —**gra·da′tion·al** *adj.*
grade (grād) *n.* 1. A degree or step in any scale, as of quality, merit, rank, etc. 2. A stage or degree in an orderly progression, classification, or process. 3. A group or category. 4. In education: **a** A level of progress in school, usu. a year's work. **b** The pupils in such a division. 5. A rating or mark indicating the quality of school work done. 6. In the armed forces, rank or rating. 7. The degree of inclination of a road, track, or other surface. —**to make the grade** *Informal* To succeed in any undertaking. —*v.t.* **grad·ed, grad·ing** 1. To arrange or classify by grades or degrees; sort according to size, quality, type, etc. 2. To level or reduce (a road, ground, etc.) to a desirable gradient. 3. To gradate. [< L *gradus* step]
-grade *combining form* 1. Progressing or moving: *retrograde.* 2. *Zool.* Walking in a specified manner. [< L *gradi* to walk]
gra·der (grā′dər) *n.* 1. One who or that which grades. 2. A pupil in a specified school grade: a third *grader.*
grade school An elementary school.
gra·di·ent (grā′dē·ənt) *n.* 1. Degree of inclination, as in a slope; grade. 2. An incline; ramp. 3. *Physics* A rate of change, as of pressure, temperature, etc. —*adj.* Rising or descending gradually or by uniform degrees. [< L *gradiens, -entis,* ppr. of *gradi* to walk]
grad·u·al (graj′o͞o·əl) *adj.* 1. Moving, changing, etc., slowly and by degrees. 2. Having a slight degree of inclination; not abrupt or steep, as a slope. [< L *gradus* a step] —**grad′u·al·ly** *adv.* —**grad′u·al·ness** *n.*
grad·u·ate (*v.* graj′o͞o·āt; *n. & adj.* graj′o͞o·it) *v.* **·at·ed, ·at·ing** *v.i.* 1. To receive a diploma or degree upon completion of a course of study. 2. To change gradually or by degrees. —*v.t.* 3. To grant an academic diploma or degree to (someone). 4. To arrange or sort according to size, degree, etc. 5. To mark (a thermometer, scale, etc.) in units or degrees; calibrate. —*n.* 1. One who has been granted a diploma or degree by an educational institution. 2. A beaker or similar vessel marked in units or degrees. —*adj.* Denoting a graduate student or his studies. [< L *gradus* step, degree] —**grad′u·a′tion** *n.*
graduate student A college graduate working toward an advanced degree.
graf·fi·to (grə·fē′tō) *n. pl.* **·ti** (-tē) 1. *Usu. pl.* Any design or scribble drawn on a wall or other surface. 2. *Archeol.* A pictograph scratched on an escarpment, etc. [< Ital.]
graft[1] (graft) *n.* 1. A shoot (the cion) inserted into a prepared slit in a tree or plant (the stock) so as to become a living part of it. 2. *Surg.* A piece of viable tissue transplanted to another part of the body or to the body of another individual. —*v.t.* 1. To insert (a cion) into a tree or plant. 2. *Surg.* To transplant (a piece of viable tissue) as a graft. 3. To attach or incorporate, as by grafting: to *graft* new ideas on outworn concepts. [< Gk. *graphein* to write]
graft[2] (graft) *n.* 1. The act of getting personal advantage or profit by dishonest or unfair means, esp. through one's political connections. 2. Anything thus gained. —*v.i.* To practice graft. [Cf. dial. E *graft* work, livelihood] —**graft′er** *n.*
gra·ham (grā′əm) *adj.* Made of finely ground whole-wheat flour. [after Sylvester *Graham,* 1794–1851, U.S. vegetarian]
Grail (grāl) *n.* In medieval legend, the cup or dish used at the Last Supper by Jesus. [< Med.L *gradalis*]
grain (grān) *n.* 1. A hard seed or kernel; esp., that of any of the cereal plants, as wheat, oats, etc. 2. The harvested seeds of these plants. 3. These plants collectively. 4. Any very small, hard mass. 5. The smallest unit of weight used in several systems in the U.S. and Great Britain. 6. The direction or arrangement of the fibers or fibrous particles in wood, meat, etc. 7. The side of a piece of leather from which the hair has been removed; also, the characteristic texture or patterned markings of this side. 8. The comparative size or texture of the particles composing a substance, surface, or pattern: marble of fine *grain.* —**against the grain** Contrary to one's temperament or inclinations. —*v.t.* 1. To form into grains; granulate. 2. To paint or stain in imitation of the grain of wood, marble, etc. 3. To give a roughened or granular appearance or texture to. [< F < L *granum* seed] —**grain′i·ness** *n.* —**grain′y** *adj.* **grain·i·er, grain·i·est** —**grain′·er** *n.* —**grain′less** *adj.*
grain alcohol Ethanol.
grain elevator A building designed to store grain.
gram (gram) *n.* The unit of mass or weight in the metric system, equivalent to 15.432 grains, or one thousandth of a kilogram. [< Gk. *gramma* small weight]
-gram[1] *combining form* Something written or drawn: *telegram.* [< Gk. *gramma* letter, writing < *graphein* to write]
-gram[2] *combining form* A gram: used in the metric system: *kilogram.* [< GRAM]
gram·mar (gram′ər) *n.* 1. The scientific study and description of the morphology and syntax of a language or dialect. 2. A system of morphologic and syntactic rules for the regulation of a given language. 3. A treatise or book dealing with grammatical matters. 4. Speech or writing considered with regard to current standards of correctness. [< Gk.

grammatikē (*technē*) literary (art) < *grammata* literature]

gram·mar·i·an (grə·mâr′ē·ən) *n.* A specialist in grammar.

grammar school 1. An elementary school. 2. *Brit.* A secondary school.

gram·mat·i·cal (grə·mat′i·kəl) *adj.* 1. Of or pertaining to grammar. 2. Conforming to the usage of standard speech or writing. —**gram·mat′i·cal·ly** *adv.* —**gram·mat′i·cal·ness** *n.*

gram·o·phone (gram′ə·fōn) *n.* A record player.

gram·pus (gram′pəs) *n. pl.* **·pus·es** A large, dolphinlike cetacean. [Alter. of obs. *grapeys* < Med.L *crassus piscis* fat fish]

gran·a·ry (gran′ər·ē, grā′nər-) *n. pl.* **·ries** A storehouse for threshed grain. [< L *granum* grain]

grand (grand) *adj.* 1. Impressive in size, extent, or splendor. 2. In literature and the arts, lofty or sublime in subject or treatment. 3. Worthy of respect because of age, experience, or dignity. 4. Of high or highest rank or official position: a *grand* duke. 5. Principal; main: the *grand* ballroom. 6. Characterized by pomp or luxury. 7. Having a family relationship one degree more distant than: used in combination: *grandson.* 8. *Informal* Highly satisfactory; excellent. —*n.* 1. A grand piano. 2. *Slang* A thousand dollars. [< L *grandis*] —**grand′ly** *adv.* —**grand′ness** *n.*

grand·child (gran′chīld′, grand′-) *n. pl.* **·chil·dren** (-chil′drən) A child of one's son or daughter.

grand·dad (gran′dad′) *n. Informal* Grandfather. Also **grand′dad′dy.**

grand·daugh·ter (gran′dô′tər) *n.* A daughter of one's son or daughter.

grande dame (grän′ däm′) An elderly woman of commanding presence or prestige. [< F]

gran·dee (gran·dē′) *n.* 1. A Spanish or Portuguese nobleman of the highest rank. 2. Any person of high rank or great importance. [< Sp. *grande* great]

gran·deur (gran′jər, -jŏŏr) *n.* 1. The quality or condition of being grand; magnificence. 2. Greatness of character.

grand·fa·ther (gran′fä′thər, grand′-) *n.* 1. The father of one's father or mother. 2. A male ancestor. —**grand′fa′ther·ly** *adv.*

grandfather clock A clock having a pendulum and enclosed in a tall cabinet. Also **grandfather's clock.**

gran·dil·o·quent (gran·dil′ə·kwənt) *adj.* Pompous; bombastic. [< L *grandis* great + *loqui* to speak] —**gran·dil′o·quence** *n.*

gran·di·ose (gran′dē·ōs, gran′dē·ōs′) *adj.* 1. Producing an effect of grandeur; imposing. 2. Pretentiously grand; pompous; bombastic. [< F < L *grandis* great] —**gran′di·ose′ly** *adv.* —**gran′di·os′i·ty** (-os′ə·tē) *n.*

grand jury A body of persons charged with determining whether evidence of criminal misconduct warrants an indictment.

grand·ma (gran′mä′, grand′mä′, gram′mä, gram′ə) *n. Informal* Grandmother.

grand mal (grănd′ mäl′, *Fr.* grän mal′) *Pathol.* A type of epilepsy characterized by severe convulsions and loss of consciousness: distinguished from *petit mal.* [< F, lit., great sickness]

grand·moth·er (gran′muth′ər, grand′-) *n.* 1. The mother of one's father or mother. 2. A female ancestor.

grand·neph·ew (gran′nef′yōō, -nev′-, grand′-) *n.* A son of one's nephew or niece.

grand·niece (gran′nēs′, grand′-) *n.* A daughter of one's nephew or niece.

grand opera A form of opera, usu. having a serious and complex plot, in which the entire text is set to music.

grand·pa (gran′pä′, grand′-, gram′pä′, gram′·pə) *n. Informal* Grandfather.

grand·par·ent (gran′pâr′ənt, grand′-) *n.* A grandmother or grandfather.

grand piano A large piano having strings arranged horizontally in a curved, wooden case.

grand slam 1. In bridge, the winning, by the declarer, of all thirteen tricks in a round of play. 2. In baseball, a home run with the bases filled. 3. *Informal* Any great success.

grand·son (gran′sun′, grand′-) *n.* A son of one's child.

grand·stand (gran′stand′, grand′-) *n.* A raised series of seats for spectators at a racetrack, sports stadium, etc. —*v.i.* To act in a way so as to impress others or win applause. —**grand′stand′** *adj.*

grange (grānj) *n.* 1. A farm, with its outbuildings. 2. *cap.* An association of U.S. farmers. [< L *granum* grain]

grani- *combining form* Grain. [< L *granum*]

gran·ite (gran′it) *n.* 1. A hard, coarse-grained, igneous rock, much used as a building material, in sculpture, etc. 2. Great hardness, firmness, endurance, etc. [< Ital. *granito* having a grained surface, ult. < L *granum* seed] —**gra·nit·ic** (grə·nit′ik) *adj.*

gra·niv·o·rous (grə·niv′ər·əs) *adj.* Feeding on grain.

gran·ny (gran′ē) *n. pl.* **·nies** 1. Grandmother: used familiarly. 2. An old woman. 3. *Informal* A fussy, interfering person.

granny knot A knot resembling the square knot but crossed in such a way as to form an insecure fastening.

gra·no·la (grə·nō′lə) *n.* Any of various cereal foods containing whole grain products, unrefined sugars, and dried fruits.

grant (grant) *v.t.* 1. To confer or bestow, as a privilege, charter, etc. 2. To allow (someone) to have; give, as permission. 3. To admit as true, as for the sake of argument. —*n.* 1. The act of granting. 2. That which is granted, as a piece of property, a sum of money, or a special privilege. [< AF *graunter*, ult. < L *credere* to believe]

gran·tee (gran·tē′) *n.* The recipient of a grant.

grant·or (gran′tər, gran·tôr′) *n.* The person by whom a grant is made.

gran·u·lar (gran′yə·lər) *adj.* 1. Composed of, like, or containing grains or granules. 2. Having a granulated surface. —**gran′u·lar′i·ty** (-lar′ə·tē) *n.* —**gran′u·lar·ly** *adv.*

gran·u·late (gran′yə·lāt) *v.t. & v.i.* **·lat·ed, ·lat·ing** To make or become granular; form into grains or granules. —**gran′u·la′tion** *n.* —**gran′u·la′tive** *adj.*

gran·ule (gran′yōōl) *n.* A small grain or particle; tiny pellet. [< L *granum* grain]

grape (grāp) *n.* 1. One of the smooth-skinned, juicy, edible berries borne in clusters by various climbing vines or small shrubs, cultivated in many species as a fruit and for making wine. 2. Any of the vines bearing these berries. 3. A dark, purplish blue color. 4. Grapeshot. **—the grape** *Informal* Wine. [< OF, bunch of grapes]

grape·fruit (grāp′fro͞ot′) *n.* 1. A large, round citrus fruit with a yellow rind and tart, juicy pulp. 2. The tree bearing this fruit.

grape·shot (grāp′shot′) *n.* A kind of shot consisting of a cluster of iron balls, fired from cannons.

grape·vine (grāp′vīn′) *n.* 1. A climbing vine that bears grapes. 2. An informal means of relaying information, usu. from person to person.

graph (graf) *n.* A diagram representing the relationship between data using bars, curves, lines, etc. **—*v.t.*** To express or represent in the form of a graph.

-graph *combining form* 1. That which writes or records: *seismograph*. 2. A writing or record: *autograph*. [< Gk. *graphein* to write]

-grapher *combining form* Forming nouns of agency corresponding to words in *-graph* or *-graphy*: *photographer*.

graph·ic (graf′ik) *adj.* 1. Describing in full detail; vivid. 2. Of, pertaining to, or illustrated by graphs or diagrams. 3. Pertaining to, consisting of, or expressed by writing. 4. Of, pertaining to, or characteristic of the graphic arts. Also **graph′i·cal.** [< L < Gk. *graphē* writing] **—graph′i·cal·ly** or **graph′ic·ly** *adv.*

-graphic *combining form* Forming adjectives corresponding to nouns ending in *-graph*: *photographic*. Also **-graphical.**

graphic arts 1. Those visual arts involving the use of lines or strokes on a flat surface, as painting, drawing, engraving, etc. 2. Those arts that involve impressions or reproductions taken from blocks, plates, type, or the like.

graph·ite (graf′īt) *n.* A soft, black variety of carbon having a metallic luster and a slippery texture, used as a lubricant and in making pencils, etc. [< G < Gk. *graphein* to write + -ITE] **gra·phit′ic** (-fit′ik) *adj.*

graph·ol·o·gy (gra·fol′ə·jē) *n.* The study of handwriting, esp. as a method of estimating the writer's character. **—graph·o·log·i·cal** (graf′ə·loj′i·kəl) *adj.* **—graph·ol′o·gist** *n.*

-graphy *combining form* 1. A writing, recording, or process of representation: *biography, photography*. 2. A descriptive science: *petrography*. [< Gk. *graphein* to write]

grap·nel (grap′nəl) *n.* 1. A small anchor with several flukes at the end of the shank. 2. Any of various devices consisting of a hook or arrangement of hooked parts, used to seize and hold objects. [ME *grapenel* < OF *grapin*, dim. of *grape* hook]

grap·ple (grap′əl) *v.* **·pled, ·pling** *v.t.* 1. To seize or take hold of with or as with a grapnel. **—*v.i.*** 2. To struggle in close combat, as in wrestling. 3. To struggle or contend: with *with*. 4. To use a grapnel. **—*n.*** 1. A grapnel. 2. The act of grappling. [< MF *grapelle* < *grape* hook] **—grap′pler** *n.*

grappling iron A grapnel. Also **grappling hook.**

grasp (grasp) *v.t.* 1. To seize firmly with or as with the hand; grip. 2. To grab. 3. To comprehend. **—*v.i.*** 4. To make the motion of grasping or clutching. **—*n.*** 1. The act of grasping; also, a grip of the hand. 2. The power or ability to seize; reach. 3. Intellectual comprehension or mastery. [ME *graspen*, metathetic var. of *grapsen* < LG] **—grasp′a·ble** *adj.* **—grasp′er** *n.*

grasp·ing (gras′ping) *adj.* 1. Greedy. 2. That grasps. **—grasp′ing·ly** *adv.* **—grasp′ing·ness** *n.*

grass (gras) *n.* 1. Any plant of a large family having rounded, hollow jointed stems and narrow, sheathing leaves. 2. Herbage generally; esp., the herbaceous plants eaten by grazing animals. 3. Ground on which grass is growing. 4. Grazing ground; pasture. 5. *Slang* Marijuana. [OE *græs*] **—grass′i·ness** *n.* **—grass′y** *adj.* **grass·i·er, grass·i·est**

grass·hop·per (gras′hop′ər) *n.* Any of several insects, as the locust and katydid, with powerful hind legs adapted for leaping.

grass·land (gras′land′) *n.* 1. Land reserved for pasturage or mowing. 2. Land in which grasses are the predominant vegetation, as the American prairies.

grass·roots (gras′ro͞ots′, -ro͞ots) *Informal* *n.pl.* The common people, esp. the electorate of a locality. **—*adj.*** 1. Coming from, pertaining to, or directed toward the common people. 2. Basic or fundamental.

grass ski Either of a pair of devices, made of a continuous track and rollers, for gliding on grass. **—grass-ski** (gras′skē′) *v.t. & v.i.*

grate[1] (grāt) *v.* **grat·ed, grat·ing** *v.t.* 1. To reduce to fine pieces or powder by rubbing against a rough or sharp surface. 2. To rub or grind to produce a harsh sound. **—*v.i.*** 3. To produce a harsh sound or have an irritating effect. [< OF *grater* < Gmc.] **—grat′er** *n.*

grate[2] (grāt) *n.* 1. A framework of crossed or parallel bars placed over a window, drain, etc. 2. A metal framework to hold burning fuel in a furnace, etc. [< L *cratis* lattice]

grate·ful (grāt′fəl) *adj.* 1. Thankful for benefits or kindnesses; appreciative; also, expressing gratitude. 2. Giving pleasure; welcome; agreeable. [< L *gratus* pleasing] **—grate′ful·ly** *adv.* **—grate′ful·ness** *n.*

grat·i·fy (grat′ə·fī) *v.t.* **·fied, ·fy·ing** 1. To give pleasure or satisfaction to. 2. To satisfy, humor, or indulge. [< L *gratus* pleasing + -FY] **—grat·i·fi·ca·tion** (grat′ə·fə·kā′shən) *n.* **—grat′i·fi′er** *n.* **—grat′i·fy′ing** *adj.* **—grat′i·fy′ing·ly** *adv.*

grat·ing[1] (grā′ting) *n.* An arrangement of bars or slats used as a cover or screen.

grat·ing[2] (grā′ting) *adj.* 1. Harsh or disagreeable in sound; rasping. 2. Irritating; annoying. **—grat′ing·ly** *adv.*

gra·tis (grat′is, grāt′is) *adj. & adv.* Free of charge. [< L, var. of *gratiis* out of kindness]

grat·i·tude (grat′ə·to͞od, -tyo͞od) *n.* Appreciation for favors, kindness, etc. [< L *gratus* pleasing]

gra·tu·i·tous (grə·to͞o′ə·təs, -tyo͞o′-) *adj.* 1. Given or obtained without payment or return; free. 2. Lacking cause or justification; uncalled-for. [< L *gratuitus*] **—gra·tu′i·tous·ly** *adv.* **—gra·tu′i·tous·ness** *n.*

gra·tu·i·ty (grə·to͞o′ə·tē, -tyo͞o′-) *n.* *pl.* **·ties** A gift, usu. of money, given in return for services rendered; tip.

gra·va·men (grə·vā′men) *n.* *pl.* **·va·mens** or

·vam·i·na (-vam′ə·nə) 1. *Law* The burden or gist of a charge. 2. A grievance. [< L *gravis* heavy]

grave[1] (grāv, *for n. also* gräv) *adj.* 1. Of great importance; weighty: a *grave* responsibility. 2. Filled with danger; critical: a *grave* situation. 3. Solemn and dignified; sober. 4. Somber, as colors. 5. *Music* Slow and solemn. —*n.* A mark (`) used in French to indicate open *e*, or to make a distinction, as in *ou, où*: also **grave accent.** [< L *gravis* heavy] —**grave′ly** *adv.* —**grave′ness** *n.*

grave[2] (grāv) *n.* 1. A burial place for a dead body, usu. a hole in the earth. 2. A sepulcher; tomb. 3. Death. [OE *græf*]

grave[3] (grāv) *v.t.* **graved, grav·en, grav·ing** 1. To carve or sculpt. 2. To engrave or incise. 3. To impress firmly, as on the memory. [OE *grafan* to dig] —**grav′er** *n.*

grave·dig·ger (grāv′dig′ər) *n.* One who digs graves.

grav·el (grav′əl) *n.* A mixture of small, rounded pebbles or fragments of stone, often with sand. —*v.t.* **grav·eled** or **·elled, grav·el·ing** or **·el·ling** To cover or pave with gravel. [< OF *gravele* beach] —**grav′el·ly** *adj.*

grave·stone (grāv′stōn′) *n.* A stone marking a grave.

grave·yard (grāv′yärd′) *n.* A burial place; cemetery.

graveyard shift *Informal* A work shift during the night, usu. beginning at midnight.

grav·i·met·ric (grav′ə·met′rik) *adj. Chem.* 1. Determined by weight, as the constituents of a compound. 2. Pertaining to measurement by weight. Also **grav′i·met′ri·cal.** —**grav′i·met′ri·cal·ly** *adv.*

gra·vim·e·try (grə·vim′ə·trē) *n.* The measurement of weight, density, or specific gravity.

grav·i·tate (grav′ə·tāt) *v.i.* **·tat·ed, ·tat·ing** 1. To move or tend to move as a result of the force of gravity. 2. To move as though from a force or natural impulse. 3. To sink or settle to a lower level.

grav·i·ta·tion (grav′ə·tā′shən) *n.* 1. *Physics* The force whereby any two bodies attract each other. 2. The act or process of gravitating. —**grav′i·ta′tion·al** *adj.* —**grav′i·ta′·tion·al·ly** *adv.*

grav·i·ton (grav′ə·ton′) *n. Physics* A hypothetical particle thought to be the quantum of the gravitational field. [< GRAVITY + *-on* elementary particle]

grav·i·ty (grav′ə·tē) *n. pl.* **·ties** 1. *Physics* Gravitation as manifested by the tendency of material bodies to fall toward the center of the earth. 2. Weight; heaviness. 3. Great importance; seriousness. 4. Solemnity; dignified reserve. [< L *gravitas* heaviness]

gra·vure (grə·vyŏŏr′, grāv′yər) *n.* Photogravure. [< F < *graver* to engrave]

gra·vy (grā′vē) *n. pl.* **·vies** 1. The juice exuded by cooking meat; also, a sauce made from it. 2. *Slang* Money or profit easily acquired. [ME *gravey*]

gray (grā) *adj.* 1. Of a color produced by a mixture of black and white. 2. Dark or dull, as from insufficient light; dismal. 3. Having gray hair. 4. Characteristic of old age; old. —*n.* 1. A color consisting of a mixture of black and white. 2. The state of being unbleached or undyed: said of fabrics. —*v.t. & v.i.* To make or become gray. Also, *esp. Brit., grey.* [OE *grǣg*] —**gray′ness** *n.*

gray·beard (grā′bird′) *n.* An old man.

gray·ling (grā′ling) *n. pl.* **·ling** or **·lings** A troutlike fish having a large, colorful dorsal fin.

gray matter 1. *Anat.* The nerve tissue of the brain and spinal cord. 2. *Informal* Brains; intelligence.

graze[1] (grāz) *v.* **grazed, graz·ing** *v.i.* 1. To feed upon growing grass or herbage. —*v.t.* 2. To put (livestock) to feed on grass, pasturage, etc. [OE *græs* grass] —**graz′er** *n.*

graze[2] (grāz) *v.t.* **grazed, graz·ing** 1. To brush against lightly in passing. 2. To scrape or abrade slightly: The bullet *grazed* his arm. —*n.* 1. A grazing. 2. A scrape made by grazing. —**graz′ing·ly** *adv.*

graz·ing (grā′zing) *n.* Pasturage.

grease (*n.* grēs; *v.* grēs, grēz) *n.* 1. Animal fat in a soft state, as after melting or rendering. 2. Any thick fatty or oily substance, as a lubricant. —*v.t.* **greased, greas·ing** To smear or lubricate with grease or fat. [< L *crassus* fat] —**greas′er** *n.*

grease·paint (grēs′ pānt′) Theatrical makeup.

greas·y (grē′sē, -zē) *adj.* **greas·i·er, greas·i·est** 1. Smeared or spotted with grease. 2. Containing grease or fat; oily. 3. Appearing or feeling like grease; smooth; slick. —**greas′i·ly** *adv.* —**greas′i·ness** *n.*

great (grāt) *adj.* 1. Very large in bulk, volume, expanse, etc.; immense; big. 2. Large in quantity or number. 3. Prolonged in duration or extent. 4. Of unusual importance; momentous; also, renowned. 5. Marked by nobility of thought, action, etc. 6. Unusual in ability or achievement; highly gifted. 7. Impressive; remarkable. 8. Being of a relationship more remote by a single generation: used in combination: *great-uncle.* —*n.* 1. Those who are eminent, powerful, etc.: preceded by *the.* 2. *Usu. pl. Informal* An outstanding person: one of baseball's *greats.* —*adv. Informal* Very well; splendidly. [OE *grēat*] —**great′ness** *n.*

great-aunt (grāt′ant′, -änt′) *n.* An aunt of either of one's parents.

Great Bear The constellation Ursa Major.

great circle *Geom.* A circle formed on the surface of a sphere by a plane that passes through the center of the sphere.

Great Dane One of a breed of large, smooth-haired dogs.

great·er (grāt′ər) Comparative of GREAT. —*adj. Usu. cap.* Comprising a (specified) city and suburbs: *Greater* London.

great-grand·child (grāt′gran′chīld′, -grand′-) *n.* A child of a grandchild.

great-grand·daugh·ter (grāt′gran′dô′tər) *n.* A daughter of a grandchild.

great-grand·fa·ther (grāt′gran′fä′thər, -grand′-) *n.* The father of a grandparent.

great-grand·moth·er (grāt′gran′muth′ər, -grand′-) *n.* The mother of a grandparent.

great-grand·par·ent (grāt′gran′pâr′ənt, -grand′-) *n.* The father or mother of a grandparent.

great-grand·son (grāt′gran′sun′, -grand′-) *n.* A son of a grandchild.

great gross A unit of quantity equal to 12 gross.

great·heart·ed (grāt′här′tid) *adj.* 1. Noble or

generous in spirit; magnanimous. 2. High-spirited; courageous.

great horned owl A large owl having tufts of feathers that resemble horns, found chiefly in North America.

great·ly (grāt′lē) *adv.* 1. To a great degree; very much. 2. In a way characteristic of or befitting greatness.

great-un·cle (grāt′ung′kəl) *n.* An uncle of either of one's parents.

grebe (grēb) *n.* Any of a family of swimming and diving birds having partially webbed feet and very short tails; esp., the **pied-billed grebe.** [< F *grèbe*]

Gre·cian (grē′shən) *adj.* Greek. —*n.* 1. A Greek. 2. One learned in the language or literature of Greece.

Greco- *combining form* Greek.

Gre·co-Ro·man (gre kō·rō′mən) *adj.* Of or pertaining to Greece and Rome together.

greed (grēd) *n.* Selfish and grasping desire for possession, esp. of wealth; avarice; covetousness. [< GREEDY]

greed·y (grē′dē) *adj.* **greed·i·er, greed·i·est** 1. Excessively eager for acquisition or gain; covetous; grasping. 2. Having an excessive appetite for food and drink; voracious; gluttonous. [OE *grædig*] —**greed′i·ly** *adv.* —**greed′i·ness** *n.*

Greek (grēk) *n.* 1. One of the people of ancient or modern Greece. 2. The Indo-European language of ancient or modern Greece. 3. Something that is unintelligible. 4. *Slang* A member of a fraternity. [< Gk. *Graikos*] —**Greek** *adj.*

Greek Orthodox Church The established church of Greece, a branch of the Eastern Orthodox Church.

green (grēn) *adj.* 1. Of the color between blue and yellow in the spectrum, as in the foliage of growing plants. 2. Covered with or abounding in grass, growing plants, etc. 3. Consisting of edible green leaves or plant parts: a *green* salad. 4. Not fully developed; immature. 5. Not cured or ready for use. 6. Pale or sickly. —*n.* 1. The color between blue and yellow in the spectrum, characteristic of the foliage of growing plants. 2. A green pigment, dye, or substance. 3. A smooth grassy area or plot: the village *green*. 4. In golf, the area of smooth, clipped grass surrounding the hole. 5. *pl.* Freshly cut leaves, branches, vines, etc. 6. *pl.* The edible leaves and stems of certain plants, as spinach, beets, etc. —*v.t. & v.i.* To make or become green. [OE *grēne*] —**green′ness** *n.*

green·back (grēn′bak′) *n.* One of a class of U.S. notes used as legal tender.

green bean A string bean.

green·belt (grēn′belt′) *n.* An area of parks or undeveloped land surrounding or within a planned community.

green·bri·er (grēn′brī′ər) A thorny vine having small, greenish flowers.

green·er·y (grē′nər·ē) *n. pl.* **·er·ies** 1. Green plants; verdure. 2. A place where plants are grown or kept.

green-eyed (grēn′īd′) *adj.* 1. Having green eyes. 2. Jealous.

green·gage (grēn′gāj′) *n.* A variety of sweet plum.

green·gro·cer (grēn′grō′sər) *n. Brit.* A shopkeeper dealing in fresh vegetables, fruit, etc.

green·horn (grēn′hôrn′) *n.* 1. An inexperienced person; beginner. 2. A dupe.

green·house (grēn′hous′) *n.* A heated shed or building, usu. constructed chiefly of glass, in which tender or exotic plants are grown or sheltered: also called *hothouse.*

green·ing (grē′ning) *n.* One of several varieties of apples having a green skin when ripe.

green·ish (grē′nish) *adj.* Somewhat green.

green light 1. A green signal indicating that vehicles, pedestrians, etc., may proceed. 2. *Informal* Approval or authorization.

green pepper 1. The unripe fruit of the sweet pepper. 2. The unripe fruit of the red pepper, used in pickling.

green·room (grēn′ro͞om′, -ro͝om′) *n.* The waiting room in a theater used by performers when off-stage.

green·sward (grēn′swôrd′) *n.* Turf green with grass.

green tea Tea from processed but unfermented tea leaves.

green thumb A special knack for making plants thrive.

Green·wich mean time (gren′ich, -ij) Time as reckoned from the meridian at Greenwich, England. Also **Greenwich time.**

green·wood (grēn′wo͝od′) *n.* A forest in leaf.

greet (grēt) *v.t.* 1. To express friendly recognition or courteous respect to, as upon meeting. 2. To present itself to; be evident to: The warmth of a fire *greeted* us. [OE *grētan*] —**greet′er** *n.*

greet·ing (grē′ting) *n.* 1. The act of one who greets; salutation; welcome. 2. A friendly or complimentary message.

gre·gar·i·ous (gri·gâr′ē·əs) *adj.* 1. Habitually associating or found with others, as in flocks, herds, or groups. 2. Enjoying or seeking others; sociable. [< L *grex, gregis* flock] —**gre·gar′i·ous·ly** *adv.* —**gre·gar′i·ous·ness** *n.*

Gre·go·ri·an chant (gri·gôr′ē·ən) The system of plainsong associated with the liturgical reforms made by Pope Gregory I.

grem·lin (grem′lin) *n.* A mischievous, imaginary creature jokingly said to cause mechanical trouble. [Origin uncertain]

gre·nade (gri·nād′) *n.* A small explosive device, designed to be thrown by hand or projected from a rifle. [< F, pomegranate]

gren·a·dier (gren′ə·dir′) *n.* In Europe, a member of a special corps or regiment. [See GRENADE.]

gren·a·dine (gren′ə·dēn′, gren′ə·dēn) *n.* A syrup made from pomegranates or red currants, used for flavoring.

Gresh·am's law (gresh′əmz) *Econ.* The principle that bad money drives out good, since the more valuable currency is removed from circulation by hoarding. Also **Gresham's theorem.** [after Sir Thomas *Gresham*, 1519–79, English merchant]

grew (gro͞o) Past tense of GROW.

grey (grā) See GRAY.

grey·hound (grā′hound′) *n.* One of a breed of tall, slender, smooth-coated dogs noted for their speed. [OE *grīghund*]

grid (grid) *n.* 1. An arrangement of regularly spaced parallel or intersecting bars, wires, etc.; grating; gridiron. 2. A system of intersecting parallel lines dividing a map, chart, etc., into squares. 3. A network of high-tension wires transmitting electric power over a wide area. 4. *Electr.* A perforated or grooved metal plate in a storage cell or battery. 5. *Electronics* An electrode that controls the flow of electrons in an electron tube. [Back formation < GRIDIRON]

grid·dle (grid′l) *n.* A flat pan used for cooking pancakes, etc. —*v.t.* **·dled, ·dling** To cook on a griddle. [< AF *gredil*]

grid·dle·cake (grid′l·kāk′) *n.* A pancake baked on a griddle: also *flapjack.*

grid·i·ron (grid′ī′ərn) *n.* 1. A football field. 2. A metal grating set in a frame, used for broiling meat, fish, etc. [ME *gredire*, var. of *gredil* griddle]

grief (grēf) *n.* 1. Deep sorrow or mental distress caused by loss, remorse, affliction, etc. 2. A cause of such sorrow.

griev·ance (grē′vəns) *n.* 1. A real or imaginary wrong regarded as cause for complaint or resentment. 2. A feeling of resentment arising from a sense of having been wronged.

grieve (grēv) *v.* **grieved, griev·ing** *v.t.* 1. To cause to feel sorrow or grief. —*v.i.* 2. To feel sorrow or grief. [< OF < L *gravis* heavy] —**griev′er** *n.* —**griev′ing·ly** *adv.*

griev·ous (grē′vəs) *adj.* 1. Causing grief, sorrow, or misfortune. 2. Meriting severe punishment or censure: a *grievous* sin. —**griev′ous·ly** *adv.* —**griev′ous·ness** *n.*

grif·fin (grif′ən) *n.* In Greek mythology, a creature with the head and wings of an eagle and the body of a lion. Also **grif′fon.** [< Gk. *gryps*]

grift·er (grif′tər) *n.* *Slang* A petty swindler or confidence man; esp., one who operates a dishonest game of chance at a carnival or circus. [? < GRAFTER]

grill (gril) *v.t.* 1. To cook on a gridiron or similar utensil. 2. *Informal* To question or cross-examine persistently and searchingly. —*v.i.* 3. To undergo grilling. —*n.* 1. A gridiron or similar cooking utensil. 2. A meal or portion of grilled food. 3. A grillroom. 4. A grille. [< F *gril*, var. of *grille* grating] —**grilled** *adj.* —**grill′er** *n.*

grille (gril) *n.* A grating, often of decorative, open metalwork, used as a screen, divider, etc.: also spelled *grill.* [< F, ult. < L *cratis* grating, lattice]

grill·room (gril′rōōm′, -rŏŏm′) *n.* A restaurant or eating place where grilled foods are prepared and served.

grim (grim) *adj.* **grim·mer, grim·mest** 1. Stern or forbidding in appearance or character. 2. Unyielding; relentless. 3. Sinisterly ironic; ghastly: a *grim* joke. 4. Savagely destructive; fierce. [OE] —**grim′ly** *adv.* —**grim′ness** *n.*

gri·mace (grim′əs, gri·mās′) *n.* A distorted facial expression, usu. indicative of pain, annoyance, disgust, etc. —*v.i.* **·maced, ·mac·ing** To distort the features; make faces. [< Sp. *grimazo*, prob. < Gmc.] —**gri′mac·er** *n.*

gri·mal·kin (gri·mal′kin, -môl′-) *n.* 1. A cat, particularly an old female cat. 2. A shrewish old woman.

grime (grīm) *n.* Dirt, esp. soot, rubbed into or coating a surface. —*v.t.* **grimed, grim·ing** To make dirty. [< Flemish *grijm*] —**grim′i·ly** *adv.* —**grim′i·ness** *n.* —**grim′y** *adj.* **grim·i·er, grim·i·est**

grin (grin) *v.* **grinned, grin·ning** *v.i.* 1. To smile broadly. 2. To draw back the lips so as to show the teeth. —*v.t.* 3. To express by grinning. [OE *grennian*] —**grin** *n.* —**grin′ner** *n.* —**grin′ning·ly** *adv.*

grind (grīnd) *v.* **ground, grind·ing** *v.t.* 1. To reduce to fine particles, as by crushing; pulverize. 2. To sharpen, polish, or wear down by friction or abrasion. 3. To rub together or press down with a scraping or turning motion: to *grind* the teeth. 4. To oppress; crush. 5. To produce by or as by grinding. 6. To produce mechanically or laboriously: followed by *out.* —*v.i.* 7. To perform the operation or action of grinding. 8. To undergo grinding. 9. *Informal* To study or work steadily and laboriously. —*n.* 1. The act of grinding. 2. The sound made by grinding. 3. A specified state of pulverization, as of coffee. 4. *Informal* Prolonged and laborious work or study. 5. *Informal* A student who studies constantly. [OE *grindan*] —**grind′ing·ly** *adv.*

grind·er (grīn′dər) *n.* 1. One who grinds; esp., one who sharpens tools, etc. 2. A device used for grinding, as a coffee mill, etc. 3. A molar. 4. Hero (def. 5).

grind·stone (grīnd′stōn′) *n.* 1. A flat, circular stone rotated on an axle, used for sharpening tools, abrading, polishing, etc. 2. A millstone. —**to keep** (or **have**) **one's nose to the grindstone** To work hard and continuously.

grip (grip) *n.* 1. The act of seizing and holding firmly. 2. The ability to seize or maintain a hold; grasping power. 3. Control; domination. 4. Mental or intellectual grasp. 5. The manner of grasping or holding something, as a tool or implement. 6. A distinctive handclasp used in greeting. 7. The handle of an object. 8. A device or mechanical part that seizes or holds something. 9. The strength of the hand in grasping. 10. A suitcase or valise. 11. A stagehand. —**to come to grips** 1. To struggle in hand-to-hand combat. 2. To deal decisively or energetically, as with a problem. —*v.t.* **gripped, grip·ping** 1. To seize; grasp firmly. 2. To capture, as the mind or imagination; attract and hold the interest of. 3. To join or attach securely with a grip or similar device. [OE *gripan* to seize] —**grip′per** *n.*

gripe (grīp) *v.* **griped, grip·ing** *v.t.* 1. *Informal* To annoy; anger. 2. To cause sharp pain or cramps in the bowels of. —*v.i.* 3. *Informal* To complain; grumble. —*n.* 1. *Informal* A grievance. 2. *Usu. pl.* Spasmodic pain in the bowels. [OE *gripan*] —**grip′er** *n.*

grippe (grip) *n.* Influenza. [< F *gripper* to seize] —**grip′py** *adj.*

gris·ly (griz′lē) *adj.* **·li·er, ·li·est** Inspiring horror; gruesome. [OE *grislic*] —**gris′li·ness** *n.*

grist (grist) *n.* 1. Grain that is to be ground; also, a batch of such grain. 2. Ground grain. —**grist for one's mill** Something that can be used to one's advantage. [OE < *grindan* to grind]

gris·tle (gris′əl) *n.* Cartilage, esp. in meat. [OE] —**gris′tly** *adj.* —**gris′tli·ness** *n.*

grist·mill (grist′mil′) *n.* A mill for grinding grain.

grit (grit) *n.* 1. Small, rough, hard particles, as of sand, stone, etc. 2. Resolute spirit;

pluck. —*v.t.* **grit·ted, grit·ting** To grind or press together, as the teeth. [OE *grēot*] —**grit′ti·ly** *adv.* —**grit′ti·ness** *n.* —**grit′ty** *adj.* **·ti·er, ·ti·est**

grits (grits) *n.pl.* 1. Coarse meal. 2. Coarsely ground hominy: also called *hominy grits.* [OE *grytte*]

griz·zle (griz′əl) *v.t. & v.i.* **·zled, ·zling** To become or cause to become gray. —*n.* 1. The color gray, esp. when produced by intermixed hairs, specks, etc., of black and white. 2. Gray or graying hair. —*adj.* Gray. [< OF *gris* gray] —**griz′zled** *adj.*

griz·zly (griz′lē) *adj.* **·zli·er, ·zli·est** Grayish; grizzled. —*n. pl.* **·zlies** A grizzly bear.

grizzly bear A large bear of western North America.

groan (grōn) *v.i.* 1. To utter a low, prolonged sound of or as of pain, disapproval, etc. 2. To make a noise resembling such a sound; creak harshly. 3. To suffer, as from cruel or unfair treatment: usu. with *under* or *beneath.* 4. To be overburdened. —*v.t.* 5. To utter or express with or as with a groan. [OE *grānian*] —**groan** *n.* —**groan′er** *n.* —**groan′ing·ly** *adv.*

groats (grōts) *n.pl.* Hulled, usu. coarsely crushed grain, as barley, oats, or wheat. [OE *grotan*]

gro·cer (grō′sər) *n.* One who deals in foodstuffs and various household supplies. [< LL *grossus* gross]

gro·cer·y (grō′sər·ē, grōs′rē) *n. pl.* **·cer·ies** 1. A store in which foodstuffs and household supplies are sold. 2. *pl.* The merchandise sold by a grocer.

grog (grog) *n.* Any alcoholic liquor, esp. rum, mixed with water. [after Old *Grog*, nickname of Admiral E. Vernon, 1684–1757, who first rationed it to English sailors]

grog·gy (grog′ē) *adj.* **·gi·er, ·gi·est** *Informal* 1. Dazed or not fully conscious, as from a blow or exhaustion. 2. Drunk. [< GROG] —**grog′gi·ly** *adv.* —**grog′gi·ness** *n.*

groin (groin) *n.* 1. *Anat.* The fold or crease formed at the juncture of either of the thighs with the abdomen. 2. *Archit.* The curve formed by the intersection of two vaults. [? OE *grynde* abyss, hollow]

grom·met (grom′it) *n.* 1. A reinforcing eyelet of metal or other material, through which a rope, cord, or fastening may be passed. 2. *Naut.* A ring of rope or metal used to secure the edge of a sail. [< F *gourmer* to curb]

groom (grōōm, grŏŏm) *n.* 1. One employed to tend horses. 2. A bridegroom. —*v.t.* 1. To attend to the neatness or appearance of. 2. To take care of (an animal) by cleaning, combing, etc. 3. To prepare by giving special training or attention to, as for a political office. [ME *grom*]

groove (grōōv) *n.* 1. A long, narrow indentation or furrow cut into a surface, esp. by a tool. 2. Any narrow depression, channel, or rut. 3. A fixed, settled routine or habit. 4. *Anat.* Any of various furrows or depressions in an organ or part of the body. —*v.* **grooved, groov·ing** *v.t.* 1. To form a groove in. —*v.i. Slang* 2. To enjoy: often with *on.* 3. To relate successfully: Folk and rock can *groove* together. [< Du. *groeve*]

groov·y (grōō′vē) *adj.* **groov·i·er, groov·i·est** *Slang* Satisfying; delightful.

grope (grōp) *v.* **groped, grop·ing** *v.i.* 1. To feel about with or as with the hands, as in the dark; feel one's way. 2. To search bewilderedly or uncertainly. —*v.t.* 3. To seek out or find by or as by groping. [OE *grāpian*] —**grope** *n.* —**grop′er** *n.* —**grop′ing·ly** *adv.*

gros·beak (grōs′bēk′) *n.* Any of various finchlike birds having a short, stout beak. [< F < *gros* large + *bec* beak]

gros·grain (grō′grān) *n.* A strong, corded silk or rayon fabric, usu. woven as ribbon. [< F]

gross (grōs) *adj.* 1. Undiminished by deductions; total: distinguished from *net*: *gross* income. 2. Conspicuously bad or wrong: *gross* errors. 3. Excessively fat or large. 4. Coarse in composition, structure, or texture. 5. Coarse or obscene in character. —*n. pl.* **gross** *for def. 1,* **gross·es** *for def. 2* 1. A unit of quantity comprising twelve dozen. 2. The entire amount; bulk. —*v.t.* To earn or produce as total income or profit, before deductions for expenses, etc. [< LL *grossus* thick] —**gross′ly** *adv.* —**gross′ness** *n.*

gross weight Total weight.

gro·tesque (grō·tesk′) *adj.* 1. Distorted, incongruous, or fantastically ugly in appearance or style; outlandish. 2. Characterized by fantastic combinations of human and animal figures with conventional design forms. —*n.* One who or that which is grotesque. [< F < Ital. *grotta* excavation; from art found in excavations] —**gro·tesque′ly** *adv.* —**gro·tesque′ness** *n.*

grot·to (grot′ō) *n. pl.* **·toes** or **·tos** 1. A cave. 2. A cavelike structure, as for a retreat, shrine, etc. [< Ital. *grotta* < L *crypta*]

grouch (grouch) *Informal n.* 1. A discontented, grumbling person. 2. A grumbling, sulky mood. [< OF *groucher* to murmur] —**grouch** *v.t.* —**grouch′i·ly** *adv.* —**grouch′i·ness** *n.* —**grouch′y** *adj.* **grouch·i·er, grouch·i·est**

ground[1] (ground) *n.* 1. The layer of solid substances constituting the surface of the earth; land. 2. Soil, sand, etc., at or near the earth's surface. 3. *Sometimes pl.* An area or tract of land; esp., one reserved or used for a specific purpose: a burial *ground.* 4. *pl.* Private land, as the surrounding premises of a dwelling, public institution, etc. 5. *Usu. pl.* The fundamental cause, reason, or motive for an action, belief, etc.: *grounds* for suspicion: when plural, often construed as singular. 6. *pl.* Sediment; dregs; esp., the particles remaining after coffee has been brewed. 7. In various arts and crafts, the background against which colors, designs, etc., are placed. 8. *Electr.* The connection of an electrical current or circuit with the earth through a conductor. 9. *Music* A ground bass. —**to gain ground** 1. To advance; make headway. 2. To increase in favor, influence, etc. —**to hold** (or **stand**) **one's ground** To refuse to yield or retreat. —**to lose ground** 1. To fail to maintain an advantage or gain. 2. To decline in favor, influence, etc. —*adj.* 1. Being on, near, or at a level with the ground. 2. Living, growing, or active on or in the ground. —*v.t.* 1. To place on the ground. 2. To base on or as on a foundation; establish; found. 3. To teach fundamentals to. 4. *Aeron.* To confine (an aircraft, pilot, etc.) to the ground. 5. *Electr.* To place in connection with the earth or a ground, as a circuit. 6. *Naut.* To run (a vessel) aground.

—*v.i.* 7. To come or fall to the ground. [OE *grund*]

ground[2] (ground) Past tense and past participle of GRIND.

ground ball In baseball, etc., a batted ball that rolls or bounces along the ground. Also **ground•er** (groun′dər).

ground bass *Music* A short phrase in the bass, repeated continually.

ground crew *Aeron.* Those responsible for servicing and maintaining aircraft on the ground.

ground floor In a building, the floor that is level or almost level with the ground. **—to get in on the ground floor** *Informal* To enter upon a project at its beginning.

ground glass 1. Glass of which the surface has been treated so that it is not fully transparent. 2. Finely powdered glass.

ground hog The woodchuck.

ground•less (ground′lis) *adj.* Having no reason or cause; baseless. **—ground′less•ly** *adv.* **—ground′less•ness** *n.*

ground•ling (ground′ling) *n.* 1. A plant or animal living, growing, or remaining on or close to the ground. 2. A fish that keeps close to the bottom of the water. 3. A person of crude or undiscriminating tastes.

ground•nut (ground′nut′) A plant bearing edible tubers or underground nutlike seed pods, as the peanut.

ground plan 1. A diagrammatic plan of any floor of a building. 2. Any preliminary plan or basic outline.

ground•sel (ground′səl) *n.* A common herb having numerous yellow flowers. [OE *gundæswelge*, lit., that swallows pus (with ref. to its use in poultices)]

ground squirrel One of several small, terrestrial rodents of the squirrel family.

ground swell 1. A billowing of the ocean in deep waves caused by a prolonged storm, earthquake, etc. 2. A rapid, spontaneous growth, as of public opinion.

ground water Underground water, accumulating by seepage, and serving as the source of springs, wells, etc.

ground•work (ground′wûrk′) *n.* A foundation; basis.

ground zero The point on the ground vertically beneath or above the point of detonation of a nuclear bomb.

group (gro͞op) *n.* 1. A collection or assemblage of persons or things, considered as a unit. 2. A number of persons or things having in common certain characteristics, interests, etc. 3. *Biol.* A number of plants or animals considered to be related because of certain common characteristics. [< Ital. *groppo* knot, lump] **—group** *v.i.* & *v.t.*

group•er (gro͞o′pər) *n.* A food fish related to the sea basses, esp. the red grouper. [< Pg. *garupa*, appar. < S.Am.Ind.]

group•ie (gro͞op′ē) *n.* *Slang* 1. A young female fan of a rock star or group. 2. A fervid hanger-on of any celebrity: used disparagingly.

group therapy A form of therapy in which several persons discuss and analyze their problems with the aid of a person qualified to direct the discussion.

grouse[1] (grous) *n. pl.* **grouse** Any of a family of game birds characterized by rounded bodies and mottled plumage. [Origin uncertain]

grouse[2] (grous) *Informal* *v.i.* **groused, grous•ing** To grumble. **—***n.* A complaint. [? < OF *grousser* to murmur]

grove (grōv) *n.* A small wood or group of trees, esp. when cleared of underbrush. [OE *grāf*]

grov•el (gruv′əl, grov′-) *v.i.* **•eled** or **•elled, •el•ing** or **•el•ling** 1. To lie prostrate or crawl face downward, as in abjection, fear, etc. 2. To act with abject humility. 3. To take pleasure in what is base or sensual. [Back formation < *groveling* < ME *grovelynge* < *on gruf* face down] **—grov′el•er** or **grov′el•ler** *n.* **—grov′el•ing** *adj.* **—grov′el•ing•ly** *adv.*

grow (grō) *v.* **grew, grown, grow•ing** *v.i.* 1. To increase in size by the assimilation of nutriment; progress toward maturity. 2. To germinate and develop to maturity, as from a seed or spore. 3. To flourish; thrive. 4. To become: She *grew* angry. **—***v.t.* 5. To cause to grow; cultivate. 6. To produce by a natural process: to *grow* hair. 7. To cover with a growth: used in the passive. **—to grow out of** 1. To outgrow. 2. To result from. [OE *grōwan*] **—grow′er** *n.*

growl (groul) *v.i.* 1. To utter a deep, guttural sound, as that made by a hostile or agitated animal. 2. To speak gruffly and angrily. 3. To rumble, as distant thunder. **—***v.t.* 4. To utter or express by growling. [? < OF *grouler* to mumble < Gmc.] **—growl** *n.* **—growl′er** *n.*

grown (grōn) Past participle of GROW. **—***adj.* Arrived at full growth or stature; mature.

grown-up (grōn′up′) *adj.* 1. Physically or mentally mature; adult. 2. Characteristic of or appropriate to an adult. **—grown′up′** *n.*

growth (grōth) *n.* 1. The act or process of growing. 2. A gradual increase in size, influence, etc. 3. Something grown or in the process of growing: a *growth* of timber. 4. *Pathol.* An abnormal formation of tissue.

grub (grub) *v.* **grubbed, grub•bing** *v.i.* 1. To dig in the ground. 2. To lead a dreary or miserable existence; drudge. 3. To make careful or plodding search; rummage. **—***v.t.* 4. To dig from the ground; root out: often with *up* or *out*. 5. *Slang* To scrounge. **—***n.* 1. The wormlike larva of certain insects. 2. *Slang* Food. [ME *grubben*] **—grub′ber** *n.*

grub•by (grub′ē) *adj.* **•bi•er, •bi•est** 1. Dirty; sloppy. 2. Infested with grubs. **—grub′bi•ly** *adv.* **—grub′bi•ness** *n.*

grub•stake (grub′stāk′) *n.* *Informal* 1. Money, supplies, or equipment provided a prospector on condition that he share his finds with the donor. 2. Money or assistance furnished to advance any venture. **—***v.t.* **•staked, •stak•ing** To supply with a grubstake.

grudge (gruj) *n.* A feeling of ill will, rancor, or enmity, harbored for a remembered wrong, etc. **—***v.t.* **grudged, grudg•ing** 1. To be displeased or resentful because of the possessions, good fortune, etc., of (another). 2. To give or allow unwillingly and resentfully. [< OF *groucher*] **—grudg′er** *n.* **—grudg′ing•ly** *adv.*

gru•el (gro͞o′əl) *n.* A thin porridge-like food made by boiling meal in water or milk. [< OF, ult. < Med.L *grutum* coarse meal < Gmc.]

gru·el·ing (grōō′əl·ing) *adj.* Causing strain or exhaustion. Also **gru′el·ling.**

grue·some (grōō′səm) *adj.* Inspiring repugnance; frightful. [< Scot. *grue* to shudder + -SOME[1]] —**grue′some·ly** *adv.* —**grue′some·ness** *n.*

gruff (gruf) *adj.* 1. Brusque and rough in manner or speech. 2. Hoarse and guttural; harsh. [< Du. *grof* rough] —**gruff′ly** *adv.* —**gruff′ness** *n.*

grum·ble (grum′bəl) *v.* **·bled, ·bling** *v.i.* 1. To complain in a surly manner. 2. To utter low, throaty sounds; growl. 3. To rumble. —*v.t.* 4. To utter or express by grumbling. [Cf. Du. *grommelen* < *grommen* to growl] —**grum′ble** *n.* —**grum′bler** *n.* —**grum′bling·ly** *adv.* —**grum′bly** *adj.*

grump·y (grum′pē) *adj.* **grump·i·er, grump·i·est** Ill-tempered; cranky; surly. [? Blend of GRUNT and DUMP] —**grump′i·ly** *adv.* —**grump′i·ness** *n.*

grunt (grunt) *v.i.* 1. To make the deep, guttural sound of a hog. 2. To make a similar sound, as in annoyance, assent, effort, etc. —*v.t.* 3. To utter or express by grunting. —*n.* 1. A short, deep, guttural sound, as of a hog. 2. A food fish of warm American seas. [OE *grunnettan*] —**grunt′er** *n.*

Gru·yère (grē·yâr′, grōō-; *Fr.* grü·yâr′) *n.* A light yellow, whole-milk Swiss cheese having a firm texture and few or no holes.

G-string (jē′string′) *n.* 1. A narrow loincloth supported by a waistband. 2. A similar garment worn by stripteasers. 3. On musical instruments, a string tuned to G.

gua·nine (gwä′nēn) *n.* *Chem.* A base that is a genetic coding constituent of DNA and RNA.

gua·no (gwä′nō) *n. pl.* **·nos** 1. The excrement of sea birds, found on the Peruvian coast, and used as a fertilizer. 2. Any similar fertilizer. [< Sp. < Quechua *huanu* dung]

Gua·ra·ni (gwä′rä·nē′) *n. pl.* **·nis** or **·ni** 1. A member of a South American Indian tribe, formerly occupying the valleys of the Paraná and the Uruguay. 2. The Tupian language of these tribes. [< Tupi, warrior]

guar·an·tee (gar′ən·tē′) *n.* 1. A pledge or formal promise that something will meet stated specifications or that a specified act will be performed or continued: also called *warranty*. 2. A guaranty (def. 2). —*v.t.* 1. To certify; vouch for: We *guarantee* our work. 2. To accept responsibility for. 3. To give security to (a person or thing), as against loss, damage, injury, etc. [Var. of GUARANTY]

guar·an·tor (gar′ən·tər, -tôr′) *n.* One who makes or gives a guaranty.

guar·an·ty (gar′ən·tē) *n. pl.* **·ties** 1. A pledge or promise to be responsible for the contract, debt, or duty of another person in case of his default or miscarriage. 2. Something given or taken as security. —*v.t.* **·tied, ·ty·ing** To guarantee. [< OF *guarant* warrant < Gmc.]

guard (gärd) *v.t.* 1. To watch over or care for; protect. 2. To watch over so as to prevent escape, etc. 3. To maintain cautious control over. 4. To furnish (something) with a protective device or shield. —*v.i.* 5. To take precautions: followed by *against*. 6. To serve as a guard. —*n.* 1. One who guards; as: **a** A warder; keeper. **b** One who has control over a point of entry, exit, etc. 2. A group of persons serving as a ceremonial escort. 3. The act of guarding. 4. A defensive posture or stance, as in boxing or fencing. 5. In football, one of the two linemen whose position is usu. between a tackle and center. 6. In basketball, one of two players who direct the offense. —**off (one's) guard** Unprepared. —**on (one's) guard** Watchful; cautious. —**to stand guard** 1. To maintain a protective watch. 2. To serve as a sentry. [< OF *guarder*] —**guard′er** *n.*

guard·ed (gär′did) *adj.* 1. Cautious; reserved: *guarded* criticism. 2. Closely defended or kept under surveillance by a guard. 3. Needing close care: a patient in *guarded* condition. —**guard′ed·ly** *adv.* —**guard′ed·ness** *n.*

guard·house (gärd′hous′) *n.* 1. The quarters and headquarters for military guards. 2. A jail confining military personnel convicted of minor offenses, etc.

guard·i·an (gär′dē·ən) *n.* 1. One who guards or watches over something. 2. One who is legally assigned care of the person, property, etc., esp. of an infant or minor. ◆Collateral adjective: *custodial*. —*adj.* Keeping guard; protecting. —**guard′i·an·ship** *n.*

guard·room (gärd′rōōm′, -rŏŏm′) *n.* A room for the use and accommodation of military or other guards.

guards·man (gärdz′mən) *n. pl.* **·men** (-mən) 1. A guard. 2. A member of the National Guard.

gua·va (gwä′və) *n.* 1. A tree or shrub of the myrtle family, native to tropical America. 2. Its pear-shaped, edible fruit. [< Sp. *guayaba*]

gu·ber·na·to·ri·al (gōō′bər·nə·tôr′ē·əl) *adj.* Of or pertaining to a governor. [< L *gubernator* governor]

guer·don (gûr′dən) *n.* *Poetic* Reward; recompense. —*v.t.* To reward. [< OF < OHG *widar* in turn + *lōn* reward] —**guer′don·er** *n.*

Guern·sey (gûrn′zē) *n.* One of a breed of dairy cattle having fawn and white coloration.

guer·ril·la (gə·ril′ə) *n.* One of an irregular combat unit whose tactic is to neutralize the numerical superiority of the enemy through stealth and surprise. —*adj.* Of guerrillas or their warfare. Also **gue·ril′la.** [< Sp., dim. of *guerra* war]

guess (ges) *v.t.* 1. To form a judgment or opinion of (some quantity, fact, etc.) on uncertain or incomplete knowledge. 2. To conjecture correctly. 3. To suppose: I *guess* we'll be late. —*v.i.* 4. To form a judgment or opinion on uncertain or incomplete knowledge: often with *at*. 5. To conjecture correctly: How did you *guess*? [ME *gessen*] —**guess** *n.* —**guess′er** *n.*

guess·ti·mate (ges′tə·mit) *n.* *Slang* An estimate that is little better than a guess. [Blend of GUESS and ESTIMATE]

guess·work (ges′wûrk′) *n.* 1. The process of guessing. 2. Something based on a guess or guesses, as an opinion.

guest (gest) *n.* 1. One who is received and entertained by another or others, as at a party or meal, or for a visit, etc. 2. One who pays for lodging, etc., as at a hotel. —*adj.* 1. Intended for guests. 2. Acting on invitation. [OE *giest*]

guff (guf) *n.* *Slang* Empty talk; nonsense. [Imit.]

guf·faw (gə·fô′) *n.* A loud burst of boisterous laughter. —*v.i.* To utter such a laugh. [Imit.]
gui·dance (gīd′ns) *n.* 1. The act, process, or result of guiding. 2. Something that guides.
guide (gīd) *v.* **guid·ed, guid·ing** *v.t.* 1. To lead or direct, as to a destination. 2. To direct the motion or physical progress of, as a vehicle, tool, animal, etc. 3. To lead or direct the affairs, standards, opinions, etc., of. —*v.i.* 4. To act as a guide. —*n.* 1. A person who guides; esp., one who conducts others on trips, through museums, etc. 2. One who or that which is taken as a model. 3. A book that guides or explains; esp., a guidebook. 4. *Mech.* Any device that regulates or controls the operation of a part. [< OF *guider*]
guide·book (gīd′bo͝ok′) *n.* A handbook containing information for tourists, visitors, etc.
guid·ed missile (gī′did) *Mil.* An unmanned missile whose course can be altered during flight.
guide·line (gīd′līn′) *n.* 1. A line, as a rope, for guiding. 2. Any suggestion, rule, etc., intended as a guide.
guide·post (gīd′pōst′) *n.* 1. A post on which directions for travelers are given. 2. A guideline (def. 2).
gui·don (gī′don, gīd′n) *n.* *Mil.* A small flag for unit identification. [< F < Ital. *guidone*]
guild (gild) *n.* 1. In medieval times, an association of artisans or merchants. 2. Any similar association or fellowship. [Fusion of OE *gild* payment and *gegyld* association]
guil·der (gil′dər) *n.* The basic monetary unit of the Netherlands. [< Du. *gulden* golden]
guile (gīl) *n.* Treacherous cunning or craft; deceit. [< OF < Gmc.] —**guile′ful** *adj.* —**guile′ful·ly** *adv.* —**guile′less** *adj.* —**guile′less·ly** *adv.* —**guile′less·ness** *n.*
guil·lo·tine (*n.* gil′ə·tēn, gē′ə·tēn; *v.* gil′ə·tēn′, gil′ə·tēn) *n.* 1. The instrument of capital punishment in France, consisting of a weighted blade that slides down between two vertical guides and beheads the victim. 2. A similar machine for cutting paper, etc. —*v.t.* **·tined, ·tin·ing** To behead with the guillotine. [< F, after J. I. *Guillotin*, 1738–1814, French physician]
guilt (gilt) *n.* 1. The fact or condition of having committed a legal or moral offense. 2. A feeling of remorse arising from a real or imagined commission of an offense. 3. Guilty conduct. [OE *gylt*] —**guilt′less** *adj.* —**guilt′less·ly** *adv.* —**guilt′less·ness** *n.*
guilt·y (gil′tē) *adj.* **guilt·i·er, guilt·i·est** 1. Deserving of blame for some offense. 2. Convicted of some offense. 3. Involving, pertaining to, or showing guilt. —**guilt′i·ly** *adv.* —**guilt′i·ness** *n.*
guin·ea (gin′ē) *n.* Formerly, an English gold coin equal to 21 shillings.
guinea fowl A large bird, related to pheasants and turkeys, having dark gray plumage speckled with white spots. Also **guinea, guinea hen.**
guinea pig 1. A small rodent widely used in biological and medical experiments. 2. *Informal* Any person used in experimentation.
guise (gīz) *n.* 1. External appearance or aspect; semblance. 2. Assumed or false appearance; pretense. [< OF < Gmc.]
gui·tar (gi·tär′) *n.* A stringed musical instrument, plucked with the fingers or a pick. [< Sp. *guitarra*] —**gui·tar′ist** *n.*
gu·lar (go͞o′lər, gyo͞o′-) *adj.* Of or pertaining to the throat; pharyngeal. [< L *gula* throat]
gulch (gulch) *n.* A deep, narrow ravine cut out by a rushing stream. [? < dial. *gulch* to swallow greedily]
gulf (gulf) *n.* 1. A large area of ocean or sea partially enclosed by an extended sweep of land. 2. An abyss; chasm; gorge. 3. A wide or impassable separation, as in social position, education, etc. [< OF *golfe* < Gk. *kolpos* bay]
Gulf Stream A warm ocean current flowing NE along the eastern coast of North America.
gull[1] (gul) *n.* A long-winged, web-footed sea bird, usu. white and gray, and having the upper mandible hooked. [ME]
gull[2] (gul) *n.* A person easily tricked. —*v.t.* To deceive; swindle; cheat. [? < obs. *gull* swallow]
Gul·lah (gul′ə) *n.* 1. One of a group of Negroes dwelling on a narrow coastal strip of South Carolina, Georgia, and NE Florida, or on islands lying off this coast. 2. The mixed (English and African) language of these people.
gul·let (gul′it) *n.* 1. The passage from the mouth to the stomach; esophagus. 2. The throat; pharynx; also, anything resembling a throat. [< L *gula*]
gul·li·ble (gul′ə·bəl) *adj.* Easily cheated or fooled; credulous. —**gul′li·bil′i·ty** *n.* —**gul′li·bly** *adv.*
gul·ly (gul′ē) *n. pl.* **·lies** A channel, ravine, or ditch; esp., a ravine cut in the earth by running water. —*v.t.* **·lied, ·ly·ing** To cut or wear a gully in. [Var. of GULLET]
gulp (gulp) *v.t.* 1. To swallow greedily or in large amounts. 2. To choke back or stifle. —*v.i.* 3. To swallow convulsively as a sign of surprise, etc. —*n.* 1. The act of gulping. 2. The amount swallowed in gulping. [< Du. *gulpen*] —**gulp′ing·ly** *adv.*
gum[1] (gum) *n.* 1. A sticky, viscid substance exuded from various trees and plants, soluble in water and hardening on exposure to air. 2. Any similar substance, as resin. 3. A preparation made from gum and used in art, industry, etc. 4. Chewing gum. 5. Mucilage; glue. 6. The gum tree. 7. Rubber. —*v.* **gummed, gum·ming** *v.t.* 1. To smear, stiffen, or clog with gum. 2. To glue or stick together with gum. —*v.i.* 3. To become sticky or clogged with gum. —**to gum up** *Slang* To bungle. [< OF *gomme* < Gk. *kommi*] —**gum′mi·ness** *n.* —**gum′my** *adj.* **·mi·er, ·mi·est**
gum[2] (gum) *n.* *Often pl.* The fleshy tissue that covers the arches of the jaws and surrounds the necks of the teeth. —*v.t. & v.i.* **gummed, gum·ming** To chew without teeth. [OE *goma* inside of the mouth]
gum arabic The gum from various species of acacia, used in medicine, candy, ink, etc.
gum·bo (gum′bō) *n.* 1. The okra or its edible, slippery pods. 2. A thick soup or stew containing okra pods. 3. A patois of French spoken by Negroes in Louisiana. [< Bantu (Angola)]
gum·boil (gum′boil′) *n.* A small boil or abscess on the gum.

gum·drop (gum′drop′) *n.* A small, round piece of jellylike candy, usu. sugar-coated.
gump·tion (gump′shən) *n. Informal* 1. Bold, energetic initiative. 2. Shrewd common sense. [< dial. E (Scot.)]
gum resin A mixture of gum and resin that exudes from incisions in certain plants.
gum·shoe (gum′shōō′) *n. Slang* A detective.
gum tree Any of various trees that produce gum.
gun (gun) *n.* **1.** A weapon or projectile device from which a missile is thrown by the force of an explosive, by compressed air, by a spring, etc. **2.** *Mil.* **a** Any of various cannons with a flat trajectory, high muzzle velocity, and a barrel of over .25 caliber: anti-tank *gun.* **b** Any of various automatic weapons, as a machine gun. **3.** Any device resembling a gun: grease *gun.* **4.** The discharging of a firearm. **5.** *Slang* A gunman. **—big gun** *Slang* A person of influence. **—to give it the gun** *Slang* 1. To increase sharply the speed of a motor. 2. To give added speed, efficiency, etc., to some action. **—to go great guns** *Slang* To work or perform with great skill, speed, etc. **—to stick to one's guns** To continue in one's plans, opinions, etc., in spite of opposition. **—*v.* gunned, gun·ning** *v.i.* 1. To go shooting or hunting with a gun. —*v.t. Slang* 2. To open the throttle of (an engine). 3. To shoot (a person) with a gun. **—to gun for** (or **after**) *Slang* 1. To seek with intent to injure or kill. 2. To seek out in order to win favor, etc. [ME *gonne, gunne*]
gun·boat (gun′bōt′) *n.* A small, armed ship, used for patrolling rivers and coastal waters.
gun·cot·ton (gun′kot′n) *n.* A type of cellulose nitrate used as an explosive.
gun·fight (gun′fīt′) *n.* A fight between persons using guns. **—gun′fight′er** *n.*
gun·fire (gun′fīr′) *n.* 1. The firing of a gun or guns. 2. *Mil.* The use of artillery or small arms in warfare.
gung ho (gung′hō′) *Slang* Eager; enthusiastic: *gung ho* about army life. [< Chinese]
gun·lock (gun′lok′) *n.* The mechanism in certain guns by which the hammer is driven and the charge exploded.
gun·man (gun′mən) *n. pl.* **·men** (-mən) 1. A man armed with a gun; esp., an armed criminal. 2. A gunsmith.
gun-met·al (gun′met′l) *adj.* Of a dark bluish gray color.
gun·nel (gun′əl) See GUNWALE.
gun·ner (gun′ər) *n.* 1. One who operates a gun. 2. A naval warrant officer who has charge of ordnance. 3. A soldier, airman, etc., who fires or assists in firing a gun.
gun·ner·y (gun′ər·ē) *n.* The science and art of constructing and operating guns.
gun·ny (gun′ē) *n. pl.* **·nies** 1. A coarse, heavy material made of jute or hemp. 2. A bag or sack made from this material: also **gunny sack.** [< Hind. *gonī* gunny sack]
gun·pow·der (gun′pou′dər) *n.* An explosive mixture of potassium nitrate, charcoal, and sulfur, used in blasting and fireworks, and still occasionally as a propellant in guns.
gun·run·ning (gun′run′ing) *n.* The smuggling of guns and ammunition into a country. **—gun′run′ner** *n.*
gun·shot (gun′shot′) *n.* 1. The range or reach of a gun. 2. The shooting of a gun; also, the noise or the shot. **—*adj.*** Caused by a gunshot.
gun-shy (gun′shī′) *adj.* Afraid of guns or their sound.
gun·smith (gun′smith′) *n.* One who makes or repairs guns.
gun·stock (gun′stok′) *n.* The wooden stock of a gun.
gun·wale (gun′əl) *n. Naut.* The upper edge of the side of a boat: also spelled *gunnel.* [< GUN + WALE (plank)]
gup·py (gup′ē) *n. pl.* **·pies** A small, tropical, fresh-water fish. [after R. J. L. *Guppy,* British scientist]
gur·gle (gûr′gəl) *v.* **·gled, ·gling** *v.i.* 1. To flow irregularly, with a bubbling sound. 2. To make such a sound. —*v.t.* 3. To utter with a gurgling sound. [Var. of GARGLE] **—gur′gle** *n.*
gu·ru (gōō′rōō) *n.* 1. In Hinduism, a spiritual teacher or guide. 2. Anyone claiming to impart special knowledge, power, etc. [< Hind.]
gush (gush) *v.i.* 1. To pour out in volume and with sudden force. 2. To emit a sudden flow, as of blood, tears, etc. 3. *Informal* To be overly enthusiastic. —*v.t.* 4. To pour forth (blood, tears, words, etc.). —*n.* A sudden flow or outburst. [ME *guschen*] **—gush′ing·ly** *adv.*
gush·er (gush′ər) *n.* 1. One who gushes. 2. An oil well that spurts oil naturally.
gush·y (gush′ē) *adj.* **gush·i·er, gush·i·est** *Informal* Overly enthusiastic. **—gush′i·ness** *n.*
gus·set (gus′it) *n.* A triangular piece inserted into a garment, glove, shoe, etc., for added strength or roomier fit. —*v.t.* To furnish with a gusset. [< OF *gousse* pod]
gus·sy up (gus′ē) *v.t. & v.i.* **·sied, ·sy·ing** *Informal* 1. To dress up. 2. To embellish.
gust (gust) *n.* 1. A sudden, violent rush of wind or air. 2. A sudden burst or outpouring, as of emotion. **—gust′i·ly** *adv.* **—gust′i·ness** *n.* **—gust′y** *adj.* **gust·i·er, gust·i·est** [< ON *gustr*]
gus·ta·to·ry (gus′tə·tôr′ē) *adj.* Of or pertaining to the sense of taste or the act of tasting.
gus·to (gus′tō) *n.* Keen enjoyment or enthusiasm; relish. [< Ital. < L *gustus* taste]
gut (gut) *n.* 1. The alimentary canal or any part of it; esp., the stomach or intestine. 2. *pl.* Bowels; entrails. 3. The specially prepared intestines of certain animals, used as strings for musical instruments, surgical sutures, etc. 4. *pl. Slang* **a** Courage; stamina; grit. **b** Effrontery. —*v.t.* **gut·ted, gut·ting** 1. To take out the intestines of. 2. To destroy the contents of. —*adj.* 1. Basic and fundamental: a *gut* issue. 2. Involving one's emotions; not reasoned; instinctive: a *gut* reaction. 3. Not difficult: a *gut* course. [OE *guttas*]
guts·y (gut′sē) *adj.* **guts·i·er, guts·i·est** Forceful; courageous.
gut·ta·per·cha (gut′ə·pûr′chə) *n.* A coagulated, rubberlike material, used in electrical insulation, in dentistry, etc. [< Malay *getah* gum + *percha* gum tree]
gut·ter (gut′ər) *n.* 1. A channel or ditch at the side of a street, for carrying off surface

water. 2. A trough, fixed below or along the eaves of a house, for carrying off rainwater from the roof. 3. A state or condition of life, marked by poverty, filth, etc. 4. Any groove or channel. —*v.i.* To melt rapidly: said of lighted candles. [< OF *goute* drop]

gut·ter·snipe (gut′ər·snīp′) *n.* A neglected child, usu. of the slums, who spends much time in the streets.

gut·tur·al (gut′ər·əl) *adj.* 1. Pertaining to the throat. 2. Having a harsh, or muffled, grating quality. 3. *Phonet.* Produced or sounded in the throat. [< L *guttur* throat] —**gut′tur·al·ly** *adv.*

guy[1] (gī) *n. Informal* A man or boy; fellow.

guy[2] (gī) *n.* A rope, cable, wire, etc., used to steady, guide, or secure something. —*v.t.* To steady, etc., with a guy. [< OF *guider* to guide]

Guy·a·nese (gī·ə·nēz′) *adj.* Of Guyana (formerly British Guiana) or its people. —**Guy·a·nese′** *n.*

guz·zle (guz′əl) *v.t. & v.i.* **·zled, ·zling** To drink greedily or to excess. [? < OF *gosier* throat] —**guz′zler** *n.*

gym (jim) *n. Informal* 1. A gymnasium. 2. A course in physical training. [Short for GYMNASIUM]

gym·na·si·um (jim·nā′zē·əm) *n. pl.* **·si·ums** or **·si·a** (-zē·ə) A building or room equipped for certain athletic activities. [< Gk. *gymnazein* to exercise]

Gym·na·si·um (gim·nä′zē·o͝om) *n.* In Europe, esp. Germany, a secondary school to prepare students for the universities.

gym·nast (jim′nast) *n.* One skilled in gymnastics.

gym·nas·tics (jim·nas′tiks) *n.pl.* 1. Any physical exercises designed to improve strength, agility, etc. 2. (*construed as sing.*) The art or practice of such exercises. —**gym·nas′tic** *adj.* —**gym·nas′ti·cal·ly** *adv.*

gym·no·sperm (jim′nə·spûrm′) *n.* One of a class of plants whose ovules and seeds are not enclosed in a case, as certain evergreens. [< Gk. *gymnos* naked + *sperma* seed] —**gym′no·sper′mous** *adj.*

gyneco- *combining form* Female; pertaining to women. Also, before vowels, **gynec-**. [< Gk. *gynē, gynaikos* woman]

gy·ne·col·o·gy (gī′nə·kol′ə·jē, jī′nə-, jin′ə-) *n.* That branch of medicine dealing with the functions and diseases peculiar to women. —**gy·ne·co·log·i·cal** (gī′nə·kə·loj′i·kəl, jī′nə-, jin′ə-) *adj.* —**gy′ne·col′o·gist** *n.*

gyno- *combining form* 1. Woman; female. 2. *Bot. & Med.* Female reproductive organ; ovary; pistil. Also, before vowels, **gyn-**. [< Gk. *gynē* woman]

-gynous *combining form* 1. Female; of women. 2. *Biol.* Having or pertaining to female organs or pistils: *androgynous.* [< Gk. *gynē* woman]

gyp (jip) *Informal v.t. & v.i.* **gypped, gyp·ping** To cheat, swindle, or defraud. —*n.* A fraud. [? < GYPSY]

gyp·sum (jip′səm) *n.* A mineral, hydrous calcium sulfate, used in plaster of Paris, fertilizer, etc. [< Gk. *gypsos* chalk]

Gyp·sy (jip′sē) *n. pl.* **·sies** 1. A wandering, dark-skinned Caucasian people believed to have migrated to Europe from India, and known as fortunetellers, musicians, etc.: also spelled *Gipsy*: also called *Romany*. 2. Romany (def. 2). 3. *Usu. not cap.* Anyone who looks like or leads the life of a Gypsy: also spelled *gipsy.* —*v.i.* **·sied, ·sy·ing** To live or wander like a Gypsy. [Var. of *Egyptian*] —**gyp′sy** *adj.*

gypsy moth A moth having larvae destructive to foliage.

gy·rate (jī′rāt) *v.i.* **·rat·ed, ·rat·ing** 1. To rotate or revolve, usu. around a fixed point or axis. 2. To turn in a spiral motion. —*adj.* Winding or coiled about; convolute. [< L *gyrare* to gyrate < Gk. *gyros*] —**gy·ra′tion** *n.* —**gy·ra′tion·al** *adj.* —**gy·ra·tor** (jī′rā′tər, jī·rā′-) *n.* —**gy′ra·to′ry** (-rə·tôr′ē) *adj.*

gyre (jīr) *n.* A spiral or round form, as a ring or vortex; also, whirling motion. [< Gk. *gyros* circle] —**gy′ral** *adj.*

gyr·fal·con (jûr′fal′kən, -fôl′-, -fô′-) See GERFALCON.

gy·ro (jī′rō) *n.* A gyroscope or gyrocompass.

gyro- *combining form* 1. Rotating; gyrating. 2. Spiral. Also, before vowels, **gyr-**. [< Gk. *gyros* circle]

gy·ro·com·pass (jī′rō·kum′pəs, -kom′-) *n.* A compass that employs a motor-driven gyroscope so mounted that its axis of rotation maintains a constant position with reference to the true or geographic north.

gy·ro·scope (jī′rə·skōp) *n.* Any of a class of devices consisting essentially of a heavy wheel, so mounted that when set to rotate at high speeds it resists all forces tending to change the angular position of its axis of rotation. [< F] —**gy′ro·scop′ic** (-skop′ik) *adj.*

gy·ro·stat·ics (jī′rə·stat′iks) *n.pl.* (*construed as sing.*) The branch of physics that investigates the laws governing the rotation of solid bodies. —**gy′ro·stat′ic** *adj.* —**gy′ro·stat′i·cal·ly** *adv.*

H

h, H (āch) *n.* *pl.* **h's** or **hs, H's** or **Hs, aitch·es** (ā′chiz) 1. The eighth letter of the English alphabet. 2. The sound represented by the letter *h*. 3. *Slang* Heroin. —*symbol* 1. *Chem.* Hydrogen. 2. *Physics* Strength or intensity of magnetic field (symbol H). 3. *Electr.* Henry (symbol H).

ha (hä) *n. & interj.* An exclamation or sound expressing surprise, discovery, triumph, laughter, etc. Also spelled *hah.*

ha·be·as cor·pus (hā′bē·əs kôr′pəs) *Law* A writ commanding a detained person to be produced before a court, esp. to determine the lawfulness of the detention. [< L, (you) have the body]

hab·er·dash·er (hab′ər·dash′ər) *n.* A shopkeeper who deals in men's furnishings, as shirts, hats, socks, etc. [Prob. < AF *hapertas,* kind of fabric]

hab·er·dash·er·y (hab′ər·dash′ər·ē) *n.* *pl.* **·er·ies** 1. The goods sold by haberdashers. 2. A haberdasher's shop.

ha·bil·i·ment (hə·bil′ə·mənt) *n.* *Usu. pl.* Clothing; attire. [< L *habilis* fit, apt]

ha·bil·i·tate (hə·bil′ə·tāt) *v.t.* **·tat·ed, ·tat·ing** 1. To provide with clothing, equipment, or the like. 2. To train; educate. [< L *habilis* fit] —**ha·bil′i·ta′tion** *n.*

hab·it (hab′it) *n.* 1. An act or practice so frequently repeated as to become almost automatic. 2. A tendency or disposition. 3. An addiction. 4. The clothing associated with a particular profession, etc.: a monk's *habit.* 5. *Biol.* A characteristic action, aspect, or mode of growth of a plant or animal. [< L *habitus* condition, dress]

hab·it·a·ble (hab′it·ə·bəl) *adj.* Suitable for habitation. [< L *habitare* to inhabit] —**hab′it·a·bil′i·ty** *n.* —**hab′it·a·bly** *adv.*

hab·i·tant (hab′ə·tənt) *n.* An inhabitant; resident. [< L *habitare* to dwell]

hab·i·tat (hab′ə·tat) *n.* The region or environment where a plant or animal is normally found. [< NL, it dwells]

hab·i·ta·tion (hab′ə·tā′shən) *n.* 1. A place of abode; residence. 2. The act of dwelling or inhabiting.

hab·it-for·ming (hab′it·fôr′ming) *adj.* Producing a habitual practice or addiction.

ha·bit·u·al (hə·bich′o͞o·əl) *adj.* 1. Practiced or recurring by habit; customary. 2. Expected from habit or usage. [< L *habitus*] —**ha·bit′u·al·ly** *adv.*

ha·bit·u·ate (hə·bich′o͞o·āt) *v.t.* **·at·ed, ·at·ing** To accustom to a condition by repetition. [< LL *habituare* to condition] —**ha·bit′u·a′tion** *n.*

hab·i·tude (hab′ə·to͞od, -tyo͞od) *n.* A customary state or course of action.

ha·bit·u·é (hə·bich′o͞o·ā, hə·bich′o͞o·ā′) *n.* One who frequents a specific restaurant, club, etc. [< F < *habituer* to accustom

ha·ci·en·da (hä′sē·en′də, *Sp.* ä·syen′dä) *n.* In Spanish America, a landed estate; a country house. [< Am. Sp. < L *facienda* things to be done]

hack[1] (hak) *v.t.* 1. To cut or chop crudely or irregularly, as with an ax. —*v.i.* 2. To cut, strike, or thrash with heavy, crude blows. 3. To emit short, dry coughs. —**to hack it** To perform competently. —*n.* 1. A gash, cut, or nick made by or as by a sharp instrument. 2. A tool for hacking. 3. A short, dry cough. [OE *haccian* to cut] —**hack′er** *n.*

hack[2] (hak) *n.* 1. A horse for hire, as a saddle horse. 2. A worn-out horse; jade. 3. A person hired to do routine work, esp. literary work. 4. A hackney carriage. 5. *Informal* A taxicab. 6. *Informal* A hackie. —*v.i.* *Informal* To drive a taxicab. —**to hack around** To pass time idly. —*adj.* 1. For hire as a hack. 2. Of a mercenary or hackneyed nature.

hack·ie (hak′ē) *n.* *Informal* The driver of a taxicab.

hack·le (hak′əl) *n.* 1. One of the long, narrow feathers on the neck of a rooster, pigeon, etc.; also, such feathers collectively. 2. In angling: A tuft of these used in a **hackle fly.** 3. *pl.* The hairs on the neck and back of a dog, that rise in anger. —**to make (someone's) hackles rise** To make angry; infuriate. [Var. of *hatchel* a comb for flax]

hack·ney (hak′nē) *n.* *pl.* **·neys** 1. A horse of medium size used for ordinary driving and riding. 2. A carriage for hire. [< OF *haquenee* horse]

hack·neyed (hak′nēd) *adj.* Made commonplace by frequent use; trite.

hack·saw (hak′sô′) *n.* A saw with a fine-toothed, narrow blade set in a frame, used for cutting metal.

had (had) Past tense and past participle of HAVE.

had·dock (had′ək) *n.* *pl.* **·dock** or **·docks** A food fish of the North Atlantic, related to but smaller than the cod. [ME]

Ha·des (hā′dēz) In Greek mythology, the abode of the dead. [< Gk. *a-* not + *idein* to see]

hadj (haj) *n.* The pilgrimage to Mecca required of every Muslim. Also spelled *hajj.* [< Arabic *hājj* pilgrimage]

hadj·i (haj′ē) *n.* A Muslim who has made his hadj: used also as a title. Also spelled *hajji.*

ha·dron (ha′dron) *n.* *Physics* A class of strongly interacting subatomic particles, including nucleons, and believed to be complex. [< Gk. *hadros* bulky]

hadst (hadst) Archaic second person singular, past indicative, of HAVE.

hae (hā, ha) *v.t.* *Scot.* To have.

haem-, haemo- See HEMO-.

haema- See HEMA-.

haemat-, haemato- See HEMATO-.
-haemia See -EMIA.
haf·ni·um (haf′nē·əm) *n.* A metallic element (symbol Hf) found in zirconium minerals. [< NL < L *Hafnia* Copenhagen]
haft (haft) *n.* A handle of a knife, sword, etc. [OE *hæft* handle]
hag (hag) *n.* 1. A repulsive old woman. 2. A witch. [OE *hægtes* witch] —**hag′gish** *adj.*
hag·fish (hag′fish′) *n. pl.* ·**fish** or ·**fish·es** An eellike marine fish that bores into other fishes by means of a rasping mouth.
Hag·ga·dah (hə·gä′də, *Hebrew* ha·gô′dô) *n. pl.* ·**doth** (-dōth) 1. The nonlegal elements of Talmudic literature. 2. The story of the Exodus read at Passover. 3. A book containing this story. Also **Ha·ga′dah, Hag·ga′da.** [< Hebrew *higgid* to tell]
Hag·ga·i (hag′ē·ī, hag′ī) *n.* A book of the Old Testament written by the 6th c. B.C. Hebrew prophet Haggai. Also, in the Douai Bible, *Aggeus.*
hag·gard (hag′ərd) *adj.* Having a worn, gaunt look. [< OF *hagard* wild] —**hag′gard·ly** *adv.*
hag·gis (hag′is) *n.* A Scottish dish made of calf's or sheep's heart, lungs, or liver, mixed with suet, oatmeal, and onions. [ME *hagas* < *haggen* to chop + *es* food]
hag·gle (hag′əl) *v.i.* ·**gled,** ·**gling** To argue or bargain in a petty, mean way. —**hag′gle** *n.* —**hag′gler** *n.*
hagio- *combining form* Sacred: *hagiography.* Also, before vowels, **hagi-.** [< Gk. *hagios* sacred]
Hag·i·og·ra·pha (hag′ē·og′rə·fə, hā′jē-) *n.pl.* The third of the three ancient divisions of the Old Testament, containing all those books not found in the Pentateuch or the Prophets. [< Gk. *hagios* sacred + *graphein* to write]
hag·i·og·ra·phy (hag′ē·og′rə·fē, hā′jē-) *n. pl.* ·**phies** 1. The study of the lives of saints. 2. A book of such studies. —**hag′i·og′ra·pher** *n.* —**hag·i·o·graph·ic** (hag′ē·ə·graf′ik, hā′jē-) or ·**i·cal** *adj.*
hag·i·ol·o·gy (hag′ē·ol′ə·jē, hā′jē-) *n. pl.* ·**gies** 1. That part of literature dealing with the lives of the saints. 2. A book on saints' lives. 3. A list of saints. —**hag·i·o·log·ic** (hag′ē·ə·loj′ik, hā′jē-) or ·**i·cal** *adj.* —**hag′i·ol′o·gist** *n.*
hah (hä) See HA.
ha-ha (hä′hä′, hä′hä′) *n. & interj.* A sound imitating laughter. —*v.i.* To laugh. [Imit.]
hai·ku (hī′ko͞o) *n. pl.* ·**ku** A Japanese verse form of 17 syllables arranged in three lines. [< Japanese]
hail[1] (hāl) *n.* 1. Small lumps of ice that fall from the sky during a storm; hailstones. 2. A rapid or heavy showering: a *hail* of blows. —*v.i.* 1. To pour down hail. 2. To fall like hail. —*v.t.* 3. To hurl or pour like hail. [OE *hægel*]
hail[2] (hāl) *v.t.* 1. To call loudly to, as in greeting. 2. To acclaim or approve. —**to hail from** To come from, as a birthplace, residence, etc. —*n.* 1. The act of hailing. 2. A shout, as of greeting. 3. The distance a shout can be heard; earshot. [< ON *heill* hale] —**hail′er** *n.*
hail fellow A pleasant companion. Also **hail fellow well met.**
Hail Mary Ave Maria (which see).
hail·stone (hāl′stōn′) *n.* A piece of hail.
hair (hâr) *n.* 1. One of the fine, threadlike structures that grow from the skin of most mammals. ◆Collateral adjective: *capillary.* 2. Such structures collectively. 3. *Bot.* A hairlike outgrowth of the epidermis in plants. 4. Any exceedingly minute measure, etc. —**not to turn a hair** To show no reaction. —**to get in one's hair** *Slang* To annoy one. —**to let one's hair down** *Slang* To discard one's reserve. —**to make one's hair stand on end** To horrify one. —**to split hairs** To make trivial distinctions. —*adj.* 1. Like, or made of, hair. 2. For the hair. [OE *hær*] —**hair′less** *adj.*
hair·ball (hâr′bôl′) *n.* A rounded mass of hair often found in stomachs of animals that groom themselves by licking.
hair·breadth (hâr′bredth′, -bretth′) *n.* An extremely small space or margin. —*adj.* Very narrow or close. Also **hairs′breadth′.**
hair·brush (hâr′brush′) *n.* A brush for grooming the hair.
hair·cloth (hâr′klôth′) *n.* A stiff fabric of horsehair.
hair·cut (hâr′·kut′) *n.* The act of cutting the hair or the style in which it is cut.
hair·do (hâr′do͞o′) *n. pl.* ·**dos** 1. A style of arranging a woman's hair. 2. The hair so arranged.
hair·dress·er (hâr′dres′ər) *n.* One who cuts or arranges the hair, esp. women's hair. —**hair′·dres′sing** *n.*
haired (hârd) *adj.* Having a (specified kind of) hair: used in combination: *gray-haired.*
hair·line (hâr′līn′) *n.* 1. The edge of the growth of hair on the head. 2. A very thin line. 3. A tiny crack.
hair·piece (hâr′pēs′) *n.* A toupee or wig.
hair·pin (hâr′pin′) *n.* A thin, U-shaped piece of metal, bone, etc., used by women to hold the hair or a headdress in place. —*adj.* Bending sharply in a U: a *hairpin* curve.
hair-rais·er (hâr′rā′zər) *n. Informal* Something that causes excitement or fear. —**hair′-rais′ing** *adj.*
hair shirt A girdle or shirt made of haircloth, worn next to the skin by religious ascetics as a penance or mortification.
hair·split·ting (hâr′split′ing) *n.* Insistence upon minute or trivial distinctions. —**hair′·split′ter** *n.* —**hair′split′ting** *adj.*
hair·spring (hâr′spring′) *n.* The spring that regulates the balance wheel in a watch or clock.
hair trigger A trigger on a firearm which responds to very slight pressure.
hair-trig·ger (hâr′trig′ər) *adj. Informal* Responsive to the slightest provocation.
hair·y (hâr′ē) *adj.* **hair·i·er, hair·i·est** 1. Covered with or having much hair. 2. Made of hair. —**hair′i·ness** *n.*
Hai·ti·an (hā′shən) *adj.* Of or pertaining to Haiti, its people, or their culture. —*n.* 1. A native or inhabitant of Haiti. 2. A French patois spoken by the Haitians: also **Haitian Creole.**
hajj (haj) See HADJ.
hake (hāk) *n. pl.* **hake** or **hakes** Any of various marine food fish related to the cod. [OE *haca* hook]
ha·kim (hä′kēm) *n.* In Muslim countries:

1. A judge or governor. 2. A physician. [< Arabic *hakīm* wise]
hal·berd (hal′bərd) *n.* A weapon used in the 15th and 16th centuries, an ax and spear combined. [< MHG *helm* handle + *barte* broadax]
hal·cy·on (hal′sē·ən) *n.* A legendary bird supposed to calm the sea so as to be able to breed on the water. —*adj.* Calm; peaceful. [< Gk. *alkyōn* kingfisher]
hale[1] (hāl) *v.t.* **haled, hal·ing** To compel to go: to *hale* into court. [Var. of HAUL]
hale[2] (hāl) *adj.* Healthy; vigorous; robust. [OE *hāl*] —**hale′ness** *n.*
half (haf) *n. pl.* **halves** (havz) 1. Either of two equal parts into which a thing may be divided. 2. In basketball, football, etc., either of two periods into which a game is divided, between which play is suspended. —**better half** *Informal* One's spouse. —*adj.* 1. Being either of two equal parts of a thing, amount, value, etc. 2. Not complete; partial; imperfect. —*adv.* 1. To the extent of half or approximately half. 2. To a considerable extent; very nearly. 3. *Informal* To any extent; at all: used with *not*: not *half* bad. [OE *healf*]

Half, used in combinations, has the meanings:

1. Exactly half:

half-circle	**half-pint**
half-dozen	**half-price**
half-inch	**half-round**

2. Part; partly; partially:

half-afraid	**half-eaten**
half-asleep	**half-open**
half-awake	**half-right**
half-crazy	**half-serious**
half-dressed	**half-truth**

half-and-half (haf′ən·haf′) *n.* A mixture of half one thing and half another, as of porter and ale. —*adj.* Half of one thing and half of another. —*adv.* In two equal parts.
half·back (haf′bak′) *n.* 1. In football, either of two offensive players positioned behind the quarterback. 2. In soccer, field hockey, etc., a player behind the forward line.
half-baked (haf′bākt′) *adj.* 1. Incompletely baked. 2. *Informal* Stupid or immature; not fully developed.
half-breed (haf′brēd′) *n.* A person having parents of different races, esp. one of white and American Indian parentage.
half brother A brother related through only one parent.
half-caste (haf′kast′) *n.* A person having parents of different races, esp. a Eurasian.
half cock In a firearm, the position of the hammer when raised halfway and so locked. —**to go off half cock** 1. To discharge too soon. 2. *Informal* To act or speak too hastily. Also **to go off half-cocked** (haf′kokt′).
half crown Formerly, an English silver coin worth 2½ shillings.
half dollar A U.S. and Canadian coin worth fifty cents.
half gainer A dive in which one springs forward off the board, does a half back flip, and plunges into the water head first, facing the board.
half·heart·ed (haf′här′tid) *adj.* Possessing or showing little interest, enthusiasm, etc. —**half′heart′ed·ly** *adv.* —**half′heart′ed·ness** *n.*
half hitch A knot made by passing the end of a rope once around the rope, then through the loop, and then drawing the end tight.
half-hour (haf′our′) *n.* 1. Thirty minutes. 2. Thirty minutes past the beginning of an hour. —*adj.* 1. Lasting for a half-hour. 2. Occurring at the half-hour. —**half′-hour′ly** *adj. & adv.*
half life *Physics* The period of time during which half the atoms of a radioactive element or isotope will disintegrate.
half-mast (haf′mast′) *n.* The position of a flag flown about halfway up the staff, used in public mourning. Also *half-staff.*
half-moon (haf′mo͞on′) *n.* The moon when only half its disk is brightly illuminated.
half nel·son (nel′sən) A wrestling hold in which one arm is passed under the opponent's armpit, usu. from behind, and the hand pressed against the back of his neck.
half note *Music* A note having one half the time value of a whole note.
half·pen·ny (hā′pən·ē, hāp′nē) *n. pl.* **half·pence** (hā′pəns) or **half·pen·nies** (hā′pən·ēz, hāp′nēz) 1. The sum of one half of a penny. 2. A British coin equivalent to such a sum.
half sister A sister related through only one parent.
half sole The part of the sole of a boot or shoe extending from the arch to the toe.
half-staff (haf′staf′) *n.* Half-mast.
half step *Music* A semitone.
half·tone (haf′tōn′) *n.* In photoengraving, a picture whose lights and shadows are composed of minute dots obtained by photographing the original through a finely lined screen.
half tone *Music* A semitone.
half-track (haf′trak′) *n.* A vehicle propelled by caterpillar treads in the rear and wheels in front.
half·way (haf′wā′) *adv.* 1. At or to half the distance. 2. Incompletely; partially. —*adj.* 1. Midway between two points. 2. Partial; inadequate.
halfway house A facility for helping persons readjust to normal life after being released from prisons, hospitals, etc.
half-wit (haf′wit′) *n.* A feeble-minded, stupid, or foolish person. —**half′-wit′ted** *adj.*
hal·i·but (hal′ə·bət) *n. pl.* **·but** or **·buts** Either of two large flatfishes of northern seas, much esteemed as food. [ME *halybutte*, OE *halig* holy + *butte* flatfish]
hal·ide (hal′īd, -id; hā′līd, -lid) *n. Chem.* Any compound of a halogen with an element or radical.
hal·ite (hal′īt, hā′līt) *n.* A massive or granular, white or variously colored sodium chloride: also called *rock salt.*
hal·i·to·sis (hal′ə·tō′sis) *n.* Foul-smelling breath. [< L *halitus* breath + -OSIS]
hall (hôl) *n.* 1. A passage or corridor in a building. 2. A vestibule; lobby. 3. A large building or room used for public business or entertainment. 4. In a university or college, a building used for various purposes, as for dormitories, classrooms, etc. 5. In medieval times, the main room of a castle. [OE *heall*]
hal·le·lu·jah (hal′ə·lo͞o′yə) *interj.* Praise ye

the Lord! —*n.* A musical composition of praise. Also **hal′le·lu′iah.** [< Hebrew *hallelū* praise + *yāh* Jehovah]

hall·mark (hôl′märk′) *n.* 1. An official mark stamped on gold and silver articles in England to guarantee their purity. 2. Any proof of excellence. [< Goldsmiths' *Hall,* London + MARK]

hal·loo (hə·lo͞o′) *interj.* A shout to attract attention, etc. —*n.* A cry of "halloo." —*v.i. & v.t.* To shout; hail. Also **hal·lo** (hə·lō′), **hal·loa** (hə·lō′). [< OF *halloer* to pursue noisily]

hal·low (hal′ō) *v.t.* 1. To make holy; consecrate. 2. To revere; reverence. [OE *hālig* holy]

hal·lowed (hal′ōd, *in liturgical use* hal′ō·id) *adj.* 1. Made holy. 2. Honored as holy. —**hal′lowed·ness** *n.*

Hal·low·een (hal′ō·ēn′, hol′-) *n.* The evening of Oct. 31, vigil of All Saints' Day, celebrated by children with masquerading. Also **Hal′low·e′en′.** [< (ALL) HALLOW(S) E(V)EN]

hal·lu·ci·nate (hə·lo͞o′sə·nāt) *v.* **·nat·ed, ·nat·ing** *v.t.* 1. To experience as an hallucination. —*v.i.* 2. To have hallucinations. [< L *hallucinari* to wander mentally] —**hal·lu′ci·na·to′ry** (-nə·tôr′ē) *adj.*

hal·lu·ci·na·tion (hə·lo͞o′sə·nā′shən) *n.* *Psychol.* An auditory, visual, or tactile perception that has no corresponding external cause or stimulus.

hal·lu·ci·no·gen (hə·lo͞o′sə·nə·jən) *n.* Any drug or chemical capable of inducing hallucinations. —**hal·lu′ci·no·gen′ic** (-jen′ik) *adj.*

hall·way (hôl′wā′) *n.* 1. A hall or corridor. 2. A passage or room leading into the main part of a building.

ha·lo (hā′lō) *n. pl.* **·los** or **·loes** 1. In art, a disk or ring of light surrounding the head of a deity or holy person; nimbus. 2. *Meteorol.* A luminous circle around the sun or moon. —*v.t.* To enclose with a halo. [< Gk. *halōs* circular threshing floor]

hal·o·gen (hal′ə·jən) *n.* *Chem.* Any of the group of nonmetallic elements: fluorine, chlorine, bromine, iodine, and astatine. [< Gk. *hals* sea, salt + -GEN] —**hal·oid** (hal′oid, hā′loid) *adj.*

halt[1] (hôlt) *n.* A complete but temporary stop in any activity or movement. —*v.t. & v.i.* To bring or come to a halt. [< G *halten* to stop]

halt[2] (hôlt) *v.i.* 1. *Archaic* To be imperfect or defective. 2. To be in doubt; waver. —**the halt** Lame or crippled persons. [OE *healt* lame]

hal·ter (hôl′tər) *n.* 1. A strap or rope to lead or secure a horse, cow, etc. 2. A woman's upper garment designed to leave the arms and back bare, and held up by a band around the neck. 3. A rope with a noose for hanging a person. —*v.t.* 1. To catch or secure with a halter. [OE *hælftre*]

halve (hav) *v.t.* **halved, halv·ing** 1. To divide into two equal parts; share equally. 2. To lessen by half; take away half of. [< HALF]

halves (havz) Plural of HALF. —**by halves** 1. Imperfectly. 2. Half-heartedly.

hal·yard (hal′yərd) *n.* *Naut.* A rope for hoisting or lowering a sail, a yard, or a flag.

ham (ham) *n.* 1. The thigh of an animal, as of the hog. 2. The meat of a hog's thigh, used for food. 3. *pl.* The back of the thigh together with the buttocks. 4. *Slang* An actor who overacts. 5. *Informal* An amateur radio operator. —*v.t. & v.i.* **hammed, ham·ming** *Slang* To act in an exaggerated manner. [OE *hamm*] —**ham′my** *adj.*

ham·burg·er (ham′bûr′gər) *n.* 1. Ground or chopped beef. Also **ham′burg, hamburger steak.** 2. A sandwich consisting of such meat cooked, and placed between the halves of a round roll. [after *Hamburg,* Germany]

Ham·ite (ham′īt) *n.* A member of an ethnic group that includes the ancient Egyptians, inhabiting NE Africa.

Ha·mit·ic (ha·mit′ik) *adj.* 1. Of or pertaining to the Hamites. 2. Designating a group of languages spoken by the Hamites. —*n.* A North African subfamily of the Hamito-Semitic family of languages, including ancient Egyptian and the modern Berber dialects.

Ham·i·to-Se·mit·ic (ham′ə·tō·sə·mit′ik) *n.* A family of languages spoken in northern Africa and part of SW Asia. —**Ham′i·to-Se·mit′ic** *adj.*

ham·let (ham′lit) *n.* A little village. [< LL *hamellum* village]

ham·mer (ham′ər) *n.* 1. A tool usu. consisting of a handle with a metal head set crosswise at one end, used for driving nails, etc. 2. Any object or machine resembling this or used this way. 3. A mechanical part that operates by striking; as: **a** The part of a gunlock that strikes the primer or firing pin. **b** One of the levers that strike the strings of a piano. 4. *Anat.* The malleus. 5. A metal ball attached to a flexible handle, thrown for distance in athletic contests. —**to go** (or **come**) **under the hammer** To be for sale at an auction. —*v.t.* 1. To strike, beat, or drive with or as with a hammer. 2. To produce, shape, join, etc., with or as with hammer blows. —*v.i.* 3. To strike blows with or as with a hammer. 4. To work persistently: to *hammer* away. [OE *hamer*] —**ham′mer·er** *n.*

ham·mer·head (ham′ər·hed′) *n.* A voracious shark of warm seas, having a transversely elongated head with the eyes at each end.

hammer lock A wrestling hold in which an opponent's arm is twisted behind his back and upward.

ham·mock (ham′ək) *n.* A hanging bed or couch of sturdy cloth or netting, suspended from a support at each end. [< Sp. *hamaca* < native West Indian name]

ham·per[1] (ham′pər) *v.t.* To interfere with the movements of; impede. [ME *hampren*]

ham·per[2] (ham′pər) *n.* A large, usu. covered basket or basketlike container. [< OF *hanapier* a cup case]

ham·ster (ham′stər) *n.* Any of various burrowing rodents, used as a laboratory animal or as a pet. [< OHG *hamastro*]

ham·string (ham′string′) *n.* 1. One of the tendons at the back of the human knee. 2. The large tendon at the back of the hock of a quadruped. —*v.t.* **·strung, ·string·ing** To cripple by cutting the hamstring of.

hand (hand) *n.* 1. In man and other primates, the end of the forearm beyond the wrist, comprising the palm, fingers, and thumb. ◆Collateral adjective: *manual.* 2. In other organisms, a part that serves a similar function. 3. The use of the hand or hands: to launder by *hand.* 4. A characteristic mark, or kind of work: the *hand* of a master. 5. A part or role: We all had a *hand* in it. 6. Assistance. 7. *Usu. pl.* Supervisory care or authority. 8. A pledge or promise, often of marriage. 9. A position to the side: on the right *hand*. 10. A source, as of information. 11. A person, considered as producing something. 12. A manual laborer. 13. Style of handwriting. 14. Show of approval by clapping. 15. Something that resembles a hand in function, as the pointer of a clock. 16. A unit of measurement four inches long, used to state the height of horses. 17. In card games: **a** The cards held by a player in one round of a game. **b** The player. **c** The complete playing of all the cards given out at one deal. **—at hand** 1. Near by; readily available. 2. About to occur. **—at the hand** (or **hands**) **of** By the action of. **—clean hands** Freedom from guilt. **—from hand to mouth** On an income so meager it is used up immediately. **—hand in** (or **and**) **glove** In close alliance or connection. **—hands down** With ease; effortlessly. **—in hand** 1. In one's immediate possession. 2. Under control. **—off one's hands** Out of one's care or responsibility. **—on hand** 1. In one's possession; available 2. Present. **—on one's hands** In one's care or responsibility. **—out of hand** 1. Unruly; uncontrollable. 2. Finished and done with. 3. Immediately; without discussion or delay. **—to hand** 1. Within reach; readily accessible. 2. In one's possession. **—to have one's hands full** To have a great amount of work. **—to keep one's hand in** To practice or keep up with an activity or interest. **—to show one's hand** To disclose one's involvement or intentions. **—to turn** (or **put**) **one's hand to** To engage in; undertake. **—to throw up one's hands** To give up in despair. **—to wash one's hands of** To refuse further responsibility for. **—upper hand** The controlling advantage. **—with a heavy hand** 1. In a clumsy manner. 2. In an overbearing manner. **—with a high hand** In an arrogant, tyrannical manner. **—*v.t.*** To give, offer, assist, or transmit with the hand or hands. **—to hand down** 1. To transmit to one's heirs. 2. To deliver the decision of a court. **—to hand in** To submit; give. **—to hand it to** *Slang* To give praise or recognition to. **—to hand out** To distribute. **—to hand over** To give up possession of. **—*adj.*** Of or pertaining to the hand or hands; as: **a** Suitable for carrying in the hand. **b** Operated by hand. **c** Executed by hand. [OE *hand*]

hand·bag (hand′bag′) *n.* 1. A woman's purse or a similar bag. 2. A small suitcase.

hand·ball (hand′bôl′) *n.* A game in which the players hit a ball with their hands against the wall of a court.

hand·bar·row (hand′bar′ō) *n.* A flat framework for carrying loads, having handles at either end for the bearers.

hand·bill (hand′bil′) *n.* A printed advertisement or notice.

hand·book (hand′bo͝ok′) *n.* A small guidebook or book of instructions.

hand·cart (hand′kärt′) *n.* A cart pushed or pulled by hand.

hand·clasp (hand′klasp′) *n.* The act of clasping a person's hand, as in greeting, an introduction, etc.

hand·craft (hand′kraft′) *v.t.* To make or fashion by hand. **—*n.*** Handicraft.

hand·cuff (hand′kuf′) *n.* *Usu. pl.* One of a pair of metal rings joined by a chain, designed to lock around the wrist or wrists; a manacle. **—*v.t.*** To apply handcuffs to.

hand·ed (han′did) *adj.* 1. Characterized by or designed for the use of a (specified) hand: a *left-handed* batter. 2. Having or characterized by a (specified kind of) hand or (a specified number of) hands: *four-handed; empty-handed.*

hand·ful (hand′fo͝ol) *n.* *pl.* **·fuls** 1. As much or as many as a hand can hold at once. 2. A small number or quantity. 3. *Informal* Something or someone difficult to control.

hand·gun (hand′gun′) *n.* A firearm held and fired in one hand, as a pistol.

hand·i·cap (han′dē·kap) *n.* 1. A race or contest in which disadvantages or advantages are imposed on contestants, so that each may have an equal chance of winning. 2. One of the conditions stipulated. 3. Any disadvantage or disability. **—*v.t*** **·capped, ·cap·ping** 1. To serve as a hindrance or disadvantage to. 2. To assign handicaps in a race. [? < *hand in cap,* a lottery game] **—hand′i·cap·per** *n.*

hand·i·craft (han′dē·kraft′) *n.* 1. Skill in working with the hands. 2. An occupation requiring such skill. Also *handcraft.* [OE *handcræft*]

hand·i·ly (han′də·lē) *adv.* 1. In a handy manner; easily. 2. Conveniently.

hand·i·work (han′dē·wûrk′) *n.* 1. Work done by the hands; any article or articles made by hand. 2. The result or product of working or action. [OE *handgeweorc*]

hand·ker·chief (hang′kər·chif, chēf) *n.* *pl.* **·chiefs** or **·chieves** (chēvz) A piece of cloth used for wiping the nose or face.

han·dle (han′dəl) *v.* **·dled, ·dling** *v.t.* 1. To touch, hold, work, or move with the hand or hands. 2. To control; manage. 3. To dispose of; deal with. 4. To treat of or discuss. 5. To act or behave toward. 6. To trade or deal in. **—*v.i.*** 7. To respond to manipulation or control. **—*n.*** 1. That part of an object designed to be grasped in the hand. 2. Something that resembles or serves as a handle. 3. A means to achieve a desired end. 4. *Informal* A name or title. **—to fly off the handle** To become angry. [OE *hand* hand] **—han·dler** (hand′lər) *n.*

han·dle·bar (han′dəl·bär′) *n.* *Usu. pl.* 1. The curved steering bar of a bicycle, etc. 2. *Informal* A luxuriant mustache resembling handlebars: also **handlebar mustache.**

hand·made (hand′mād′) *adj.* Made by hand.

hand-me-down (hand′mē·doun′) *n.* *Informal* A used garment given to another person.

hand·out (hand′out′) *n.* 1. Any free ration of food, money, apparel, etc. 2. A prepared, distributed statement.

hand-pick (hand′pik′) *v.t.* 1. To gather by hand. 2. To choose with care.

hand·rail (hand′rāl′) *n.* A railing for grasping in the hand, on a staircase, balcony, etc.

hand·set (hand′set′) *n.* A telephone receiver and transmitter combined in a unit that may be held in one hand.

hand·shake (hand′shāk′) *n.* The act of clasping and shaking a person's hand, as in greeting, agreement, parting, etc.

hand·some (han′səm) *adj.* 1. Pleasing or well-proportioned in appearance. 2. Considerable; ample. 3. Generous; gracious. [ME *handsom* easy to handle] —**hand′·some·ly** *adv.* —**hand′some·ness** *n.*

hand·spring (hand′spring′) *n.* An acrobatic turn in which the body is supported by one or both hands while the feet are quickly passed in an arc over the head.

hand-to-hand (hand′tə·hand′) *adj.* At close quarters.

hand·work (hand′wûrk′) *n.* Work done by hand.

hand·writ·ing (hand′rī′ting) *n.* 1. Writing done by hand, as with a pen; calligraphy. 2. A characteristic style or form of writing. —**to see the handwriting on the wall** To be aware beforehand of impending misfortune, etc.

hand·y (han′dē) *adj.* **hand·i·er, hand·i·est** 1. Available; nearby. 2. Skillful. 3. Useful. —**hand′i·ness** *n.*

hand·y·man (han′dē·man′) *n.* *pl.* **·men** (-men′) A man employed to perform odd jobs.

hang (hang) *v.* **hung** or (*esp. for defs. 3, 11*) **hanged, hang·ing** *v.t.* 1. To fasten, attach, or support from above only. 2. To attach, fasten, or support off the ground, with a hinge, wire, hook, etc. 3. To kill by suspending by the neck. 4. To bend or drop downward. 5. To decorate with things suspended. 6. To fasten (wallpaper) to a wall. 7. To cause (a jury, etc.) to be unable to reach a decision. —*v.i.* 8. To be suspended; dangle. 9. To be attached so as to swing easily. 10. To fall or drape. 11. To be put to death or to die by hanging. 12. To bend or project downward; droop. 13. To keep one's hold; cling: with *on* or *onto*. 14. To hover; float in the air. 15. To be imminent; threaten: with *over*. 16. To depend; be contingent: with *on* or *upon*. 17. To be undecided. —**to be hung up** *Slang* To be halted or delayed. —**to be hung up on** *Slang* To have an emotional problem regarding. —**to hang around** *Informal* To loiter or spend one's time. —**to hang back** To be reluctant. —**to hang in** To persevere. —**to hang in the balance** To be subject to a decision. —**to hang loose** To keep calm. —**to hang on** To be tenacious. —**to hang out** *Slang* To spend one's time. —**to hang together** To be coherent or consistent. —**to hang up** 1. To end a telephone conversation by replacing the receiver. 2. To delay or suspend the progress of. —**to let it all hang out** *Slang* To hide nothing. —*n.* 1. The way in which a thing hangs. 2. *Informal* The least bit: I don't give a *hang*. —**to get the hang of** *Informal* To learn to do or understand. [Fusion of ME *hangen* and ME *henge* to cause to hang]

han·gar (hang′ər) *n.* A shelter, esp. one for aircraft. [< F]

hang·dog (hang′dog′) *adj.* Furtive or guilty.

hang·er (hang′ər) *n.* 1. A device on or from which something may be hung, esp. garments. 2. One who hangs something.

hang·er-on (hang′ər·on′, -ôn′) *n.* *pl.* **hang·ers-on** A self-seeking follower.

hang·fire (hang′fīr′) *n.* A delay in the explosion of a propelling charge, igniter, etc.

hang-glid·er (hang′glī′dər) *n.* An airfoil from which a rider hangs while gliding down from a high place. —**hang′-glide′** *v.i.*

hang·ing (hang′ing) *n.* 1. Execution by being hanged from the neck. 2. Something hung on a wall, window, etc. —**hang′ing** *adj.*

hang·man (hang′mən) *n.* *pl.* **·men** (-mən) A public executioner who hangs condemned persons.

hang·nail (hang′nāl′) *n.* Skin partially torn loose at the side or root of a fingernail.

hang·out (hang′out′) *n.* *Slang* A habitual loitering or dwelling place.

hang·o·ver (hang′ō′vər) *n.* *Informal* 1. The discomfort following overindulgence in alcoholic liquor. 2. Something or someone remaining from a past era or regime.

hang-up (hang′up′) *n.* 1. An emotional problem that can prevent action or affect judgment. 2. Any block or obstacle.

hank (hangk) *n.* 1. A skein of yarn or thread. 2. A measure of yarn or thread. 3. A loop or curl, as of hair. [ME]

han·ker (hang′kər) *v.i.* To yearn; have desire: with *after*, *for*, or *to*. [Cf. Flemish *hankeren* to long for.] —**hank′er·ing** *n.*

han·ky-pan·ky (hang′kē·pang′kē) *n.* *Slang* Deceitful or mischievous behavior. [? Formed on analogy with HOCUS-POCUS]

Han·sen's disease (han′sənz) Leprosy. [after Gerhart *Hansen*, 1841–1912, Norwegian physician]

han·som (han′səm) *n.* A low, two-wheeled, one-horse carriage, with the driver seated behind and above the cab: also **hansom cab.** [after J. A. *Hansom*, 1803–82, English inventor]

Ha·nuk·kah (khä′nŏŏ·kə, hä′-) *n.* A Jewish festival, lasting eight days, in memory of the rededication of the temple at Jerusalem in 164 B.C.: also *Chanukah*. Also **Ha′nu·kah.** [< Hebrew *hanukkah* dedication]

hap·haz·ard (hap′haz′ərd) *adj.* Accidental; random; chance. —*adv.* By chance; at random. —**hap′haz′ard·ly** *adv.*

hap·less (hap′lis) *adj.* Unfortunate; unlucky. —**hap′less·ly** *adv.* —**hap′less·ness** *n.*

hap·loid (hap′loid) *adj.* *Biol.* Having only one set of unpaired chromosomes, as a germ cell. [< Gk. *haploos* simple + -OID] —**hap′·loid** *n.*

hap·pen (hap′ən) *v.i.* 1. To take place or occur; come to pass. 2. To occur by chance. 3. To chance: We *happened* to hear him sing. —**to happen to** 1. To befall. 2. To become of. [ME *happenen*]

hap·pen·ing (hap′ən·ing) *n.* 1. An event. 2. A staged event, usu. partly improvised.

hap·pen·stance (hap′ən·stans) *n.* *Informal* A chance occurrence; accident.

hap·py (hap′ē) *adj.* **·pi·er, ·pi·est** 1. Enjoying, showing, or characterized by pleasure; joyous; contented. 2. Fortunate; lucky. 3. Produced or uttered with skill and aptness; felicitous. [ME *happi* < *hap* an occurrence] —**hap′pi·ly** *adv.* —**hap′pi·ness** *n.*

hap·py-go-luck·y (hap′ē·gō·luk′ē) *adj.* Cheerful; unconcerned; easygoing.

ha·ra-ki·ri (har′ə·kir′ē; hä′rä·kē′rē) *n.* Suicide by disembowelment, traditionally practiced by the Japanese Samurai when disgraced: also *hari-kari*. Also **ha′ra-ka′ri** (-kä′rē). [< Japanese *hara* belly + *kiri* cut]

ha·rangue (hə·rang′) *n.* A lengthy, loud, and vehement speech; tirade. —*v.t.* & *v.i.*

·rangued, ·rangu·ing To address in or deliver a harangue. [< OHG *hari* army, host + *hringa* ring] **—ha·rangu′er** *n.*

har·ass (har′əs, hə·ras′) *v.t.* 1. To trouble or pursue relentlessly; torment. 2. *Mil.* To worry by raids and small attacks. [< OF *harer* to set dogs on] **—har′ass·er** *n.* **—har′·ass·ment** *n.*

har·bin·ger (här′bin·jər) *n.* One who or that which goes before and announces the coming of something; herald. **—***v.t.* To presage; herald. [< OF *herberge* shelter]

har·bor (här′bər) *n.* 1. A sheltered place on the coast of a sea, lake, etc., used to provide protection and anchorage for ships; port. 2. Any place of refuge or rest. **—***v.t.* 1. To give refuge to; shelter. 2. To entertain in the mind; cherish. **—***v.i.* 3. To take shelter in or as in a harbor. Also *Brit.* **har′bour.** [ME < OE *here* army + *beorg* refuge]

har·bor·age (här′bər·ij) *n.* 1. A port or place of anchorage. 2. Shelter; lodging.

har·bor·mas·ter (här′bər·mas′tər) *n.* An officer in charge of enforcing the regulations of a harbor.

hard (härd) *adj.* 1. Resisting indentation or compression; solid; firm; unyielding. 2. Requiring vigorous mental or physical effort; difficult. 3. Energetic and steady; industrious. 4. Showing little mercy or feeling; stern. 5. Strict or exacting. 6. Having force or intensity; severe; violent. 7. Involving or inflicting sorrow, discomfort, poverty, etc. 8. *Informal* Verified and specific: said of facts, information, etc. 9. *Informal* Cruel or disreputable; tough. 10. Containing certain mineral salts that interfere with the cleansing action of soap: said of water. 11. Containing more than 22.5 percent alcohol: *hard* liquor. **—hard and fast** Fixed and unalterable. **—hard of hearing** Deaf or partially deaf. **—hard up** *Informal* 1. Poor; broke. 2. In need of (something): with *for.* **—to be hard on** To be severe, cruel, or damaging to. **—***adv.* 1. With great energy or force; vigorously. 2. Intently; earnestly. 3. With effort or difficulty: to breathe *hard.* 4. With resistance; reluctantly: to die *hard.* 5. Securely; tightly. 6. So as to become firm or solid. 7. In close proximity; near: with *after, by,* or *upon.* 8. *Naut.* To the extreme limit; fully: *Hard* aport. **—to be hard put** To have great difficulty. **—to go hard with** To be very painful and harsh for. [OE *heard*] **—hard′ness** *n.*

hard-bit·ten (härd′bit′n) *adj.* Tough.

hard-boiled (härd′boild′) *adj.* 1. Boiled until cooked through: said of an egg. 2. *Informal* Callous; tough.

hard cash Actual money; cash.

hard cider Cider that has fermented.

hard coal Anthracite.

hard-core (härd′kôr′) *adj.* 1. Being irreducible. 2. Of or relating to the chronically unemployed. 3. Being explicit and graphic: *hard-core* pornography. 4. Unlikely to change; inflexible.

hard·en (här′dən) *v.t. & v.i.* To make or become hard. **—hard′en·er** *n.*

hard·hat (härd′hat′) *n.* 1. A construction worker. 2. A crude, outspoken conservative or reactionary. [after the helmet worn by construction workers, and views assumed to be typical of them] **—hard′hat′** *adj.*

hard·head (härd′hed′) *n. pl.* **·heads** 1. A shrewd and practical person. 2. An obstinate person.

hard·head·ed (härd′hed′id) *adj.* 1. Shrewd and practical. 2. Stubborn; obstinate. **—hard′head′ed·ly** *adv.* **—hard′head′ed·ness** *n.*

hard·heart·ed (härd′här′tid) *adj.* Lacking pity; unfeeling. **—hard′heart′ed·ly** *adv.* **—hard′heart′ed·ness** *n.*

har·di·hood (här′dē·ho͝od) *n.* 1. Courage; boldness. 2. Audacity; impudence.

hard labor Compulsory physical labor imposed upon imprisoned criminals.

hard-line (härd′līn′) *adj.* Consistently firm in attitude or policy; undeviating. **—hard′-lin′er** *n.*

hard·ly (härd′lē) *adv.* 1. Scarcely; barely. 2. Not quite; not: *hardly* enough.

hard-nosed (härd′nōzd′) *adj.* *Slang* Hard-bitten; unyielding.

hard·pan (härd′pan′) *n.* 1. A layer of very hard, often claylike matter under soft soil. 2. Solid, unbroken ground. 3. The firm foundation of anything.

hard rubber Vulcanite.

hard sauce Butter, sugar, and flavorings creamed together and eaten on puddings, etc.

hard-shell (härd′shel′) *adj.* 1. Having a hard shell. 2. *Informal* Rigidly orthodox.

hard·ship (härd′ship) *n.* A difficult, painful condition, as from privation, suffering, etc.

hard·tack (härd′tack′) *n.* Hard, crackerlike biscuit.

hard·top (härd′top′) *n.* An automobile with the body design of a convertible, but with a rigid top.

hard·ware (härd′wâr′) *n.* 1. Manufactured articles of metal, as utensils or tools. 2. Weapons: military *hardware.* 3. Any of the machinery that makes up a digital computer installation: distinguished from *software.*

hard·wood (härd′wo͝od′) *n.* 1. Wood from deciduous trees, as distinguished from wood of coniferous trees. 2. Any hard, compact, heavy wood. 3. A tree yielding such wood.

har·dy (här′dē) *adj.* **·di·er, ·di·est** 1. Able to endure hardship; robust; tough. 2. Courageous. 3. Able to survive the winter outdoors: said of plants. [< OHG *hartjan* to make hard] **—har′di·ly** *adv.* **—har′di·ness** *n.*

hare (hâr) *n. pl.* **hares** or **hare** 1. A mammal allied to but larger than the rabbit. 2. The common American rabbit. [OE *hara*]

hare·bell (hâr′bel′) *n.* A perennial herb with blue, bell-shaped flowers. Also called *bluebell.*

hare·brained (hâr′brānd′) *adj.* Foolish; flighty; giddy.

hare·lip (hâr′lip′) *n.* A congenital fissure of the upper lip, resembling the cleft lip of a hare. **—hare′lipped′** *adj.*

har·em (hâr′əm, har′-) *n.* 1. The apartments of a Muslim household reserved for females. 2. The women occupying the harem. [< Arabic *harama* to forbid]

ha·ri-ka·ri (har′ē·kar′ē; hä′rē·kä′rē) *n.* See HARA-KIRI.

hark (härk) *v.i.* To listen; harken: usu. in the imperative. **—to hark back** To return to some previous point; revert. **—***n.* A cry used to urge on or guide hounds. [ME *herkien*]

hark·en (här′kən) *v.i.* *Poetic* To listen; heed. Also spelled *hearken.* [OE *heorcnian*]

har·le·quin (här′lə·kwin, -kin) *n.* A buffoon.

—*adj.* Like a Harlequin or his costume. [< Ital. *arlecchino*, prob. akin to OF *Herlequin*, a devil in medieval legend]

Har·le·quin (här′lə·kwin, -kin) A traditional, mischievous character in comedy and pantomime, usu. dressed in parti-colored tights, with masked face, and bearing a wooden sword.

har·lot (här′lət) *n.* A prostitute. [< OF, rogue] —**har′lot·ry** *n.*

harm (härm) *n.* 1. Injury; damage; hurt. 2. Wrong; evil. —*v.t.* To do harm to; damage; hurt. [OE *hearm* an insult]

harm·ful (härm′fəl) *adj.* Having power to injure or do harm. —**harm′ful·ly** *adv.* —**harm′ful·ness** *n.*

harm·less (härm′lis) *adj.* Inflicting no injury; not harmful; innocuous. —**harm′·less·ly** *adv.* —**harm′less·ness** *n.*

har·mon·ic (här·mon′ik) *adj.* 1. Producing, characterized by, or pertaining to harmony; consonant; harmonious. 2. *Music* Pertaining to the formation and progression of chords in musical composition. —*n.* *Music* An overtone, having a vibration rate that is an integral multiple of a given primary tone. [< Gk. *harmonia* harmony] —**har·mon′i·cal·ly** *adv.*

har·mon·i·ca (här·mon′i·kə) *n.* A wind instrument consisting of metal reeds fixed in slots in a small oblong frame: also called *mouth organ.*

har·mon·ics (här·mon′iks) *n.pl.* (*construed as sing. in def. 1*) 1. The branch of acoustics dealing with musical sounds. 2. *Music* The overtones of a fundamental.

har·mo·ni·ous (här·mō′nē·əs) *adj.* 1. Made up of sounds, colors, or other elements that combine agreeably. 2. Manifesting agreement and concord. 3. Pleasing to the ear; euphonious. —**har·mo′ni·ous·ly** *adv.* —**har·mo′ni·ous·ness** *n.*

har·mo·ni·um (här·mō′nē·əm) *n.* A type of reed organ in which air is compressed in the bellows, then driven out through the reeds; melodeon.

har·mo·nize (här′mə·nīz) *v.t. & v.i.* **·nized, ·niz·ing** 1. To make or become harmonious, suitable, or agreeable. 2. To arrange or sing in musical harmony. Also *Brit.* **har′mo·nise.** —**har′mo·ni·za′tion** *n.* —**har′mo·niz′er** *n.*

har·mo·ny (här′mə·nē) *n. pl.* **·nies** 1. Accord or agreement. 2. A state of order, agreement, or esthetically pleasing relationships among the elements of a whole. 3. Pleasing sounds; music. 4. *Music* **a** A simultaneous combination of tones, esp. a euphonious one. **b** Musical structure in terms of the relations between successive harmonies. **c** The science or study of this structure. [< Gk. *harmonia* harmony < *harmozein* to join]

har·ness (här′nis) *n.* 1. The combination of traces, straps, etc., forming the gear of a draft animal and used to attach it to a wheeled vehicle or plow. 2. Any similar arrangement of straps, cords, etc., esp. one used for attaching something, as a parachute, to the body. —**in harness** Working at one's job. —*v.t.* 1. To put harness on. 2. To make use of the power or potential of. [< OF *harneis*; ult. origin unknown]

harp (härp) *n.* A musical instrument, consisting of a frame with strings set in it, played by plucking the strings with the fingers. —*v.i.* To play a harp. —**to harp on** (or **upon**) To talk or write about persistently and vexatiously. [OE *hearpe*] —**harp′ist** *n.*

har·poon (här·po͞on′) *n.* A barbed spear, carrying a long cord, for striking whales or large fish. —*v.t.* To strike, take, or kill with or as with a harpoon. [< F *harpe* claw] —**har·poon′er, har′poon·eer′** (-ir′) *n.*

harp·si·chord (härp′sə·kôrd) *n.* A keyboard instrument, esp. of the 18th c., having the strings plucked by quills or leather points instead of struck. [< MF *harpechorde* < LL *harpa* harp + L *chorda* string]

har·py (här′pē) *n. pl.* **·pies** 1. A rapacious, predatory person, esp. a woman. 2. A shrewish woman. [< Gk. *Harpyiae*, a mythical monster with the body of a bird and the head of a woman]

har·que·bus (här′kwə·bəs) *n.* An early, large portable firearm: also *arquebus.* [< MLG *hakebusse* hooked gun]

har·ri·dan (har′ə·dən) *n.* A hateful old woman; vicious hag. [< OF *haridelle* jade]

har·ri·er (har′ē·ər) *n.* 1. A small hound used for hunting hares. 2. A cross-country runner.

har·row (har′ō) *n.* A farm implement set with spikes or disks, for leveling plowed ground, breaking clods, etc. —*v.t.* 1. To draw a harrow over. 2. To disturb painfully; distress. [ME *harwe*] —**har′row·er** *n.*

har·row·ing (har′ō·ing) *adj.* Lacerating to the feelings. —**har′row·ing·ly** *adv.*

har·ry (har′ē) *v.t.* **·ried, ·ry·ing** 1. To lay waste, as in war or invasion; pillage. 2. To harass in any way. [OE *hergian* to ravage]

harsh (härsh) *adj.* 1. Grating, rough, or unpleasant to any of the senses. 2. Ungraceful; crude. 3. Severe; cruel. [ME *harsk*] —**harsh′ly** *adv.* —**harsh′ness** *n.*

hart (härt) *n.* The male of the red deer, esp. after its fifth year. [OE *heort*]

harte·beest (härt′bēst, här′tə-) *n.* A large, grayish brown antelope of Africa. Also **hart′beest.** [< Afrikaans < Du. *hert* hart + *beest* beast]

harts·horn (härts′hôrn′) *n.* 1. The antler of a hart. 2. Ammonium carbonate or a preparation made from it, used as smelling salts.

har·um-scar·um (hâr′əm·skâr′əm) *adj.* Reckless and wild; harebrained. —*adv.* In a wild, unrestrained manner. [prob. < obs. *hare* to frighten + SCARE]

har·vest (här′vist) *n.* 1. The act of gathering or collecting a ripened crop. 2. The yield of such a crop; also, the crop itself. 3. The time of year when crops are gathered. 4. The products of any effort. —*v.t. & v.i.* To gather in (a crop). [OE *harfest* autumn, harvest]

har·vest·er (här′vis·ter) *n.* 1. One who harvests. 2. A reaping machine.

harvest moon The full moon that occurs near the autumnal equinox.

has (haz) Present indicative, third person singular, of HAVE.

has-been (haz′bin′) *n.* *Informal* One who or that which is no longer popular or effective.

hash[1] (hash) *n.* 1. Chopped meat and potatoes or other vegetables, mixed and browned. 2. A mess; jumble; mishmash. —**to make a hash of** *Informal* To bungle; spoil. —**to settle** (or **fix**) **one's hash** *Informal* To deal with punitively; subdue. —*v.t.* 1. To cut into small pieces; mince. 2. *Informal* To discuss at length: often with *over*. [< OF *hacher* to chop]

hash² (hash) *n.* Hashish.

hash house *Slang* A cheap restaurant.

hash·ish (hash′ēsh, -ish; hāsh′-) *n.* The tops of hemp, used as a narcotic and intoxicant. Also **hash′eesh.** [< Arabic *hashīsh* hemp]

Ha·si·dim (ha·si′dim, *Hebrew* khä·sē′dim) *n.pl. of* **Ha·sid** A sect of Jewish mystics: also spelled *Chasidim.* [< Hebrew, pious] —**Ha·sid′ic** *adj.* —**Ha′si·dism** *n.*

has·n't (haz′ənt) Has not.

hasp (hasp) *n.* A hinged fastening for a door, lid, etc., esp. one that passes over a staple and is secured by a padlock. [OE *hæpse*]

has·sle (has′əl) *n.* *Slang* An argument; squabble; fight. —*v.t.* **·sled, ·sling** To harass or antagonize. [? < HAGGLE + TUSSLE]

has·sock (has′ək) *n.* **1.** An upholstered stool or cushion, used for kneeling or as a footstool. **2.** A tuft of coarse grass. [OE *hassuc* coarse grass]

hast (hast) Archaic second person singular, present tense, of HAVE: used with *thou.*

haste (hāst) *n.* **1.** Swiftness of motion; rapidity. **2.** Undue or reckless hurry. **3.** The need to act quickly; urgency. —**to make haste** To hurry. [< Gmc.]

has·ten (hā′sən) *v.t. & v.i.* To move with speed; hurry. —**has′ten·er** *n.*

hast·y (hās′tē) *adj.* **hast·i·er, hast·i·est** **1.** Speedy; quick; rapid. **2.** Excessively quick; rash. **3.** Manifesting anger: *hasty* words. —**hast′i·ly** *adv.* —**hast′i·ness** *n.*

hasty pudding A boiled mush of meal and seasoning.

hat (hat) *n.* A covering for the head, esp. one with a crown and brim. —**to pass the hat** To collect contributions of money. —**to talk through one's hat** *Informal* To talk nonsense; also, to bluff. —**to throw (toss, etc.) one's hat into the ring** To enter a contest, esp. for political office. —**under one's hat** *Informal* Secret; private. [OE *hæt*]

hat·band (hat′band′) *n.* A ribbon or band of cloth around a hat just above the brim.

hatch¹ (hach) *n.* **1.** An opening in a floor, deck, etc., giving access to spaces beneath: also **hatch′way′.** **2.** A cover over such an opening: also **hatch cover.** **3.** A small opening: an escape *hatch.* [OE *hæcc* grating]

hatch² (hach) *v.t.* **1.** To bring forth (young) from (the egg) by incubation. **2.** To devise, as a plan. —*v.i.* **3.** To emerge from the egg. —*n.* **1.** The act of hatching. **2.** The brood hatched. [ME *hacchen*] —**hatch′er** *n.*

hatch³ (hach) *v.t.* To mark with close parallel or crossed lines. —*n.* Any of these lines. [< OF *hache* an ax] —**hatch′ing** *n.*

hatch·back (hach′bak′) *n.* An automobile having a sloping back that contains a rear window and that opens upward. [< HATCH¹ + BACK¹] —**hatch′back′** *adj.*

hatch·er·y (hach′ər·ē) *n. pl.* **·er·ies** A place for hatching eggs, esp. of poultry or fish.

hatch·et (hach′it) *n.* A small, short-handled ax, for use with one hand. —**to bury the hatchet** To make peace. [< F, dim. of *hache* an ax]

hatchet job *Informal* A malicious attack on someone's actions or character.

hatchet man *Informal* **1.** A professional killer. **2.** One who uses unethical or illegal means to persuade, attack, or affect adversely.

hate (hāt) *v.* **hat·ed, hat·ing** *v.t.* **1.** To regard with extreme aversion; detest. **2.** To dislike. —*v.i.* **3.** To feel hatred. —*n.* **1.** An extreme feeling of dislike or animosity; hatred. **2.** A person or thing detested. [OE *hatian*] —**hat′er** *n.*

hate·ful (hāt′fəl) *adj.* Arousing or worthy of hatred; detestable. —**hate′ful·ly** *adv.* —**hate′ful·ness** *n.*

hath (hath) Archaic or poetic third person singular, present tense, of HAVE.

ha·tred (hā′trid) *n.* Intense dislike or aversion; animosity; enmity. [ME *hate* + *-red* < OE *-rǣden* state]

hat·ter (hat′ər) *n.* One who makes, sells, or repairs hats.

haugh·ty (hô′tē) *adj.* **·ti·er, ·ti·est** Exhibiting disdain; supercilious. [< OF *haut* high] —**haugh′ti·ly** *adv.* —**haugh′ti·ness** *n.*

haul (hôl) *v.t. & v.i.* **1.** To pull or draw strongly; drag; tug. **2.** To transport or carry a load in a truck, car, etc. **3.** *Naut.* To change the course of (a ship), esp. so as to sail closer to the wind. **4.** To pull or drag; tug. —**to haul off** To draw back the arm so as to punch. —**to haul up** **1.** To compel to go: I was *hauled up* before the court. **2.** To come to a stop. **3.** *Naut.* To sail nearer the wind. —*n.* **1.** A strong pull; tug. **2.** That which is caught, won, etc., at one time. **3.** The distance over which something is hauled. **4.** That which is hauled. [< OF *haler*] —**haul′er** *n.*

haul·age (hô′lij) *n.* **1.** The act or operation of hauling. **2.** A charge for hauling.

haunch (hônch) *n.* **1.** In man and animals, the upper thigh, including the hip and buttock. **2.** The leg and loin of an animal, considered as meat. [< OF *hanche*]

haunt (hônt) *v.t.* **1.** To visit (a person or place) repeatedly; esp., to do so as a ghost or spirit. **2.** To recur persistently to the mind or memory of. **3.** To linger about; pervade. —*n.* A place often visited. [< OF *hanter*] —**haunt′er** *n.*

haunt·ed (hôn′tid) *adj.* Supposedly visited by ghosts.

haunt·ing (hôn′ting) *adj.* Recurring to the mind; difficult to forget: a *haunting* tune. —**haunt′ing·ly** *adv.*

haut·boy (hō′boi, ō′-) *n.* An oboe. Also **haut′bois.** [< F *haut* high (in tone) + *bois* wood]

haute cou·ture (ōt ko͞o·tür′) **1.** The designers of women's clothes, and their establishments, whose creations are advanced in style, exclusive, of expensive fabrics, etc. **2.** The clothes so created. [< F, high sewing]

haute cui·sine (ōt kwē·zēn′) The elaborate preparation of fine food; also the food so prepared. [< F, high cooking]

hau·teur (hō·tûr′) *n.* Haughtiness. [< F]

have (hav) *v.t.* Present indicative: I, you, we, they **have** (*Archaic* **thou hast**), he, she, it **has** (*Archaic* **hath**); past indicative **had** (*Archaic* **thou hadst**); present subjunctive **have**; past subjunctive **had**; *pp.* **had**; *ppr.* **hav·ing** **1.** To possess as property; own. **2.** To be connected with; be possessed of: to *have* a good government. **3.** To bear or possess as an attribute, quality, etc. **4.** To hold in the mind or among the feelings; entertain. **5.** To receive, take, or acquire. 6. To suffer from. 7. To engage in: to *have* a quarrel. 8. To undergo or experience. 9. To plan and carry out: to *have* a party. 10. To give birth to. 11. To manifest or exercise: to *have* patience. 12. To cause to, or cause to be: *Have* it cleaned. 13. To allow; tolerate. 14. To maintain; declare: So rumor *has* it. 15. *Informal* To catch (someone) at a disadvantage in a game, etc. 16. As an auxiliary, *have* is used: **a** With past participles to form perfect tenses expressing completed action: I *have* gone. **b** With the infinitive to express obligation or compulsion: I *have* to go. **—to have at** To attack. **—to have done** To stop; desist. **—to have it in for** *Informal* To hold a grudge against. **—to have it out** To continue a fight or discussion to a final settlement. **—to have on** To be dressed in. **—to let someone have it** *Informal* To attack or assault someone. **—*n.*** *Informal* A relatively wealthy person or country: the *haves* and the have-nots. [OE *habban*]

ha·ven (hā′vən) *n.* 1. A harbor; port. 2. A refuge; shelter. [OE *hæfen*]

have-not (hav′not′) *n.* *Informal* A person or country relatively lacking in wealth.

have·n't (hav′ənt) Have not.

hav·er·sack (hav′ər·sak) *n.* A bag for carrying rations, etc., on a march or hike. [< G *habersack* oat sack]

hav·oc (hav′ək) *n.* General carnage or destruction; ruin. [< OF *havot* to plunder < Gmc.]

haw[1] (hô) *v.i.* To hesitate in speaking: to hem and *haw.* **—*n.* & *interj.*** A hesitating sound made by a speaker.

haw[2] (hô) *n.* The hawthorn or its fruit. [OE *haga*]

Ha·wai·ian (hə·wī′yən) *n.* 1. A native or inhabitant of Hawaii. 2. The Polynesian language of Hawaii. **—Ha·wai′ian** *adj.*

Hawaiian guitar A guitar played horizontally, the chords being selected by a metal bar sliding on the strings.

hawk[1] (hôk) *n.* 1. Any of a large and widely distributed family of birds of prey, having broad, rounded wings, a long tail, and powerful talons. 2. One who urges forceful action in a dispute; an advocate of war: opposed to *dove.* **—*v.i.*** To hunt game with hawks. [OE *hafoc, hafuc*]

hawk[2] (hôk) *v.t.* & *v.i.* To cry (goods) for sale in the streets; peddle. [? < MLG *hoker* peddler] **—hawk′er** *n.*

hawk[3] (hôk) *v.t.* & *v.i.* To cough up (phlegm) with a rasping sound. [Imit.]

hawk-eyed (hôk′īd′) *adj.* Having keen eyesight.

hawk moth A large moth that flies at twilight and sucks nectar from flowers.

hawks·bill (hôks′bil′) *n.* A tropical turtle that furnishes tortoise shell of fine quality. Also **hawk's′-bill′, hawksbill turtle.**

hawk·weed (hôk′wēd′) *n.* A weedy perennial herb having small red, yellow, or orange flowers.

hawse (hôz) *n.* *Naut.* The part of a ship's bow where the hawseholes are located. [< ON *hals* neck, bow of a ship]

hawse·hole (hôz′hōl′) *n.* *Naut.* A hole in the bow of a ship, through which cables and hawsers pass.

haw·ser (hô′zər) *n.* *Naut.* A rope or cable used for mooring, towing, etc. [< OF *haucier* to lift]

haw·thorn (hô′thôrn) *n.* A shrub or tree of the rose family having a white or pink flower and a small fleshy fruit called *haw.* [OE *haguthorn*]

hay (hā) *n.* Grass, clover, or the like, cut and dried for fodder. **—to hit the hay** *Slang* To go to bed. **—to make hay while the sun shines** To take full advantage of an opportunity. **—*v.i.*** 1. To mow, cure, gather, and store hay. [OE *hēg*]

hay·cock (hā′kok′) *n.* A dome-shaped pile of hay in the field.

hay fever *Pathol.* An allergic reaction to pollen of certain plants, characterized by sneezing, runny nose, etc.

hay·loft (hā′lôft′) *n.* An open upper section of a barn or stable, used for storing hay.

hay·mak·er (hā′mā′kər) *n.* 1. One who makes hay. 2. *Slang* A powerful punch. **—hay′·mak′ing** *n.*

hay·mow (hā′mou′) *n.* 1. A mass of hay, esp. one stored in a loft or bay. 2. A hayloft.

hay·rack (hā′rak′) *n.* 1. A frame or rack mounted on a wagon body, in which hay is hauled; also, a wagon so equipped. 2. A framework for holding hay to feed livestock.

hay·seed (hā′sēd′) *n.* 1. The chaff, seeds, etc., that fall from hay. 2. *Informal* A hick; a country bumpkin.

hay·stack (hā′stak′) *n.* A pile of hay, usu. stacked and stored outdoors.

hay·wire (hā′wīr′) *adj.* *Slang* 1. Broken; broken down. 2. Crazy; nutty.

haz·ard (haz′ərd) *n.* 1. Danger of loss, injury, etc.; peril. 2. Chance; accident. 3. An obstacle or trap on a golf course. **—*v.t.*** 1. To put in danger; risk. 2. To venture (a statement, effort, etc.). 3. To gamble or gamble on. [< Arabic *al-zahr* a die]

haz·ard·ous (haz′ər·dəs) *adj.* 1. Risky; dangerous. 2. Dependent on chance; fortuitous. **—haz′ard·ous·ly** *adv.*

haze[1] (hāz) *n.* 1. A light suspension of water vapor, smoke, dust, etc., in the air. 2. Mental confusion. [< HAZY]

haze[2] (hāz) *v.t.* **hazed, haz·ing** To subject (newcomers or initiates) to pranks and humiliating horseplay. [< OF *haser* to irritate] **—haz′er** *n.* **—haz′ing** *n.*

ha·zel (hā′zəl) *n.* 1. A bushy shrub or small tree of the birch family; also, the wood of this tree. 2. The hazelnut. 3. A medium yellowish brown. [OE *hæsel*] **—ha′zel** *adj.*

ha·zel·nut (hā′zəl·nut′) *n.* The edible nut of the hazel: also called *filbert.*

haz·y (hā′zē) *adj.* **haz·i·er, haz·i·est** 1. Misty. 2. Lacking clarity; vague. [prob. < OE *hasu* gray] **—haz′i·ly** *adv.* **—haz′i·ness** *n.*

H-bomb (āch′bom′) *n.* A hydrogen bomb.

he (hē) *pron., possessive* **his,** *objective* **him;** *pl. nominative* **they,** *possessive* **their** or **theirs,** *objective* **them** 1. The nominative singular pronoun of the third person, used of the male person or animal previously mentioned. 2. That person; anyone; one. **—*n.*** *pl.* **hes** A male person or animal. [OE *hē*]

he- *combining form* Male; masculine: used in hyphenated compounds: *he-goat.* [< HE]

head (hed) *n.* *pl.* **heads** or *for def. 12* **head** 1. The part of a vertebrate animal situated at the top or front of the spinal column, containing the brain, eyes, ears, nose, and mouth. ◆Collateral adjective: *cephalic*. 2. The analogous part of other animals and organisms. 3. A part like a head: the *head* of a pin. 4. A representation of the head. 5. A leader or chief person. 6. The position or rank of a leader. 7. The front or beginning part of something. 8. The highest part of something. 9. The source, as of a river. 10. Mind; intelligence. 11. A person: two dollars a *head*. 12. Of animals, a single specimen. 13. A newspaper headline. 14. The side of a coin on which a face is struck. 15. A climax, culmination, or crisis. 16. The foam on the surface of beer or ale. 17. An amount of stored-up pressure. 18. The taut, sounding membrane of a drum, tambourine, etc. 19. The part of a tape recorder that imparts magnetic patterns to the tape or removes them from it. 20. *Naut.* A toilet. 21. *Slang* One who habitually uses a drug that distorts perception. **—head over heels** 1. End over end. 2. Rashly; impetuously. 3. Entirely; totally. **—Heads up!** *Informal* Watch out! **—out of** (or **off**) **one's head** *Informal* 1. Crazy. 2. Delirious. **—over one's head** 1. Too difficult to understand. 2. Beyond one's power to manage. 3. To a higher authority. **—to come to a head** 1. Of boils, etc., to form a core or tip of pus. 2. To reach a crisis. **—to give someone his head** To give someone freedom of action. **—to go to one's head** 1. To intoxicate one. 2. To make one conceited. **—to have rocks** (or **holes**) **in the head** *Slang* 1. To be crazy. 2. To be stupid. **—to make head or tail of** To understand: usu. used in the negative. **—to turn one's head** To make vain by praising. *—v.t.* 1. To be first or most prominent on: to *head* the list. 2. To command; preside over. 3. To direct the course of. 4. To cut off the head or top of. *—v.i.* 5. To move in a specified direction or toward a specified point. 6. To come to or form a head. 7. To originate: said of streams. **—to head off** To intercept the course of. *—adj.* 1. Principal; chief. 2. Situated at the front. 3. Bearing against the front: a *head* wind. [OE *hēafod*]

head·ache (hed′āk′) *n.* 1. A pain in the head. 2. *Informal* A difficulty or vexation. **—head′ach′y** *adj.*

head·board (hed′bôrd′) *n.* A board at the head end of a bed, grave, etc.

head·cheese (hed′chēz′) *n.* A cooked and jellied meat loaf made of the head and feet of a hog or calf.

head·dress (hed′dress′) *n.* 1. A covering or ornament for the head. 2. The style in which the hair is arranged; coiffure.

head·ed (hed′id) *adj.* 1. Having a head. 2. Having or characterized by a (specified kind of) head or (a specified number of) heads: used in combination: *clear-headed*; *two-headed*.

head·er (hed′ər) *n.* 1. One who or that which makes or puts on heads, as of nails or rivets. 2. *Agric.* A harvesting machine that cuts off the ripe ends of the grain. 3. *Informal* A fall or plunge: now only in the phrase **to take a header.**

head·first (hed′fûrst′) *adv.* 1. With the head first. 2. Recklessly. **—head′first′** *adj.*

head·gear (hed′gir′) *n.* A hat, headdress, etc.

head·hunt·er (hed′hun′tər) *n.* 1. One of a tribe that keeps heads of enemies as trophies. 2. An individual or agency that recruits people for jobs and positions.

head-hunt·ing (hed′hun′ting) *n.* Among certain savage tribes, the custom of decapitating slain enemies and preserving the heads as trophies.

head·ing (hed′ing) *n.* 1. A caption or title. 2. The front or top part of anything. 3. *Naut. & Aeron.* Direction; course.

head·land (hed′lənd *for def. 1*; hed′land′ *for def. 2*) *n.* 1. A cliff projecting into the water. 2. A strip of unplowed land.

head·light (hed′līt′) *n.* A powerful light, as at the front of a motor vehicle.

head·line (hed′līn′) *n.* 1. A summarizing word or words set in bold type, as in a newspaper. 2. A line at the top of a page, containing title, page number, etc. *—v.t.* **·lined, ·lin·ing** 1. To provide with a headline, as a news story. 2. To be a headliner in (a show, etc.).

head·lin·er (hed′lī′nər) *n.* A performer billed as the main attraction or star.

head·long (hed′lông′) *adv.* 1. Headfirst. 2. Recklessly; rashly. 3. With unbridled speed or force. *—adj.* 1. Made with the head foremost. 2. Rash.

head·mas·ter (hed′mas′tər) *n.* The principal of a school, esp. a private school.

head·mis·tress (hed′mis′tris) *n.fem.* The female principal of a school.

head·most (hed′mōst′) *adj.* Most advanced; foremost.

head-on (hed′on′) *adj. & adv.* Front end to front end.

head·phone (hed′fōn′) *n.* An earphone, usu. attached by a band passing over the head.

head·piece (hed′pēs′) *n.* 1. A hat, helmet, or other covering for the head. 2. A headset.

head·quar·ters (hed′kwôr′tərz) *n.pl.* (*construed as sing. or pl.*) 1. The place from which a chief or leader directs the operations of a military unit, police force, etc. 2. Any center of operations; also, the persons working there.

head·set (hed′set′) *n.* A pair of headphones.

head·ship (hed′ship) *n.* The position or function of a chief authority; command.

heads·man (hedz′mən) *n. pl.* **·men** (-mən) A public executioner who carries out the death sentence by decapitation.

head·stall (hed′stôl′) *n.* The part of a bridle that fits over the horse's head.

head start An advance start; also, an advantage.

head·stone (hed′stōn′) *n.* 1. The memorial stone at the head of a grave. 2. The cornerstone or keystone of a structure.

head·strong (hed′strông′, -strong′) *adj.* 1. Stubborn; determined. 2. Proceeding from willfulness or obstinacy.

head·wait·er (hed′wā′tər) *n.* A restaurant employee who supervises waiters, seats guests, takes reservations, etc.

head·wa·ters (hed′wô′tərz) *n.pl.* The tributaries or other waters that form the source of a river.

head·way (hed′wā′) *n.* 1. Forward motion; progress. 2. Overhead clearance.

head wind A wind from ahead, blowing directly opposite to one's course.

head·y (hed′ē) *adj.* **head·i·er, head·i·est** 1. Tending to affect the senses; intoxicating: a *heady* fragrance. 2. Headstrong; obstinate. **—head′i·ly** *adv.* **—head′i·ness** *n.*

heal (hēl) *v.t.* 1. To restore to health or soundness. 2. To bring about the remedy or cure of. —*v.i.* 3. To become well. 4. To perform a cure or cures. [OE *hǣlan*] —**heal′er** *n.* —**heal′a·ble** *adj.*

health (helth) *n.* 1. Freedom from defect or disease. 2. General condition of body or mind. 3. A toast wishing health or happiness. —*adj.* Of, pertaining to, connected with, or conducive to health. [OE *hǣlth* < *hāl* whole]

health·ful (helth′fəl) *adj.* Promoting health; salubrious. —**health′ful·ly** *adv.* —**health′ful·ness** *n.*

health·y (hel′thē) *adj.* **health·i·er, health·i·est** 1. Having good health. 2. Conducive to health. 3. Indicative of sound condition. —**health′i·ly** *adv.* —**health′i·ness** *n.*

heap (hēp) *n.* 1. A collection of things piled up; a pile; mound. 2. *Informal* A large number; lot. —*v.t.* 1. To assemble into a heap. 2. To fill (a container) full or more than full. 3. To bestow in great quantities. —*v.i.* 4. To form or rise in a heap or pile. [OE *hēap* crowd]

hear (hir) *v.* **heard** (hûrd), **hear·ing** *v.t.* 1. To perceive by means of the ear. 2. To listen to; give ear to. 3. To be informed of. 4. To listen officially or judicially: to *hear* a case. —*v.i.* 5. To perceive sound. 6. To be informed or made aware. —**to hear of** To approve of: usu. in the negative: He won't *hear of* it. [OE *hēran*] —**hear′er** *n.*

hear·ing (hir′ing) *n.* 1. The capacity to hear. 2. The act of perceiving sound. 3. Reach or range within which sound may be heard. 4. An opportunity to be heard, as in a court. 5. An official examination, usu. public, of an issue or person.

heark·en (här′kən) See HARKEN.

hear·say (hir′sā′) *n.* Report; rumor.

hearse (hûrs) *n.* A vehicle for conveying a dead person to the place of burial. [< F *herse* harrow]

heart (härt) *n.* 1. *Anat.* The primary organ of the circulatory system of animals, a hollow muscular structure that maintains the circulation of the blood by regular contractions. ◆Collateral adjective: *cardiac.* 2. The seat of emotion. 3. Tenderness; love. 4. Courage. 5. Enthusiasm; energy. 6. State of mind; mood. 7. The central or inner part of anything. 8. The vital or essential part. 9. Anything represented as or shaped like a heart. 10. A playing card bearing red, heart-shaped spots. —**after one's own heart** Suiting one's taste. —**at heart** In one's deepest thoughts or feelings. —**by heart** By memory. —**from (the bottom of) one's heart** With all sincerity. —**heart and soul** With complete sincerity. —**to break the heart of** To cause deep disappointment and sorrow to. —**to eat one's heart out** 1. To endure great remorse or grief. 2. To have a great longing. —**to have a heart** To be sympathetic and generous. —**to have a change of heart** To change one's opinions, attitudes, etc. —**to have the heart** To be callous or cruel enough: usu. in the negative. —**to lose heart** To become discouraged. —**to set one's heart on** To long for; crave. —**to take to heart** 1. To consider seriously. 2. To be concerned or anxious about. —**with all one's heart** 1. Willingly; fully. 2. Sincerely. [OE *heorte*]

heart·ache (härt′āk′) *n.* Mental anguish; grief; sorrow.

heart·beat (härt′bēt′) *n. Physiol.* A pulsation of the heart consisting of one full systole and diastole.

heart·break (härt′brāk′) *n.* Deep grief; overwhelming sorrow. —**heart′break′er** *n.* —**heart′break′ing** *adj.*

heart·bro·ken (härt′brō′kən) *adj.* Overwhelmingly grieved. —**heart′bro′ken·ly** *adv.*

heart·burn (härt′bûrn′) *n. Pathol.* A burning sensation in the esophagus due to acidity.

heart·ed (här′tid) *adj.* Having or characterized by a (specified kind of) heart: used in combination: *lighthearted.*

heart·en (här′tən) *v.t.* To give heart or courage to.

heart·felt (härt′felt′) *adj.* Deeply felt; most sincere.

hearth (härth) *n.* 1. The floor of a fireplace, furnace, or the like. 2. The fireside; home. [OE *heorth*]

hearth·stone (härth′stōn′) *n.* 1. A stone forming a hearth. 2. The fireside; home.

heart·i·ly (här′tə·lē) *adv.* 1. With sincerity or cordiality. 2. Abundantly and with good appetite. 3. Completely; thoroughly.

heart·land (härt′land′) *n.* In geopolitics, any central, strategically important area.

heart·less (härt′lis) *adj.* 1. Having no sympathy or kindness; pitiless. 2. Having little courage or enthusiasm; dispirited. —**heart′less·ly** *adv.* —**heart′less·ness** *n.*

heart-rend·ing (härt′ren′ding) *adj.* Causing great distress or emotional anguish; grievous.

heart·sick (härt′sik′) *adj.* Deeply disappointed or despondent. Also **heart′sore′** (-sôr′).

heart·strings (härt′stringz′) *n.pl.* The strongest feelings or affections.

heart-to-heart (härt′tə·härt′) *adj.* Marked by frankness, intimacy, and sincerity

heart·warm·ing (härt′wôr′ming) *adj.* Causing pleasant and sympathetic feelings.

heart·wood (härt′wo͝od′) *n. Bot.* The duramen.

heart·y (här′tē) *adj.* **heart·i·er, heart·i·est** 1. Full of affectionate warmth or cordiality. 2. Strongly felt. 3. Healthy and strong. 4. Supplying abundant nourishment. —*n. pl.* **heart·ies** A hearty fellow. —**heart′i·ness** *n.*

heat (hēt) *n.* 1. The state or quality of being hot; hotness; also, degree of hotness. 2. *Physics* A form of energy associated with and proportional to the molecular motions of a substance or body. ◆Collateral adjective: *thermal.* 3. The sensation produced by hotness. 4. Hot weather or climate. 5. Warmth supplied for a building, room, etc. 6. A single effort or trial, esp. in a race. 7. Great intensity of feeling. 8. The highest point of excitement or fury. 9. *Zool.* The period of sexual excitement, esp. of estrus. 10. *Slang* a Coercive pressure; also, intensive police action. b The police. —*v.t. & v.i.* 1. To make or become hot or warm. 2. To excite or become excited. [OE *hǣtu*] —**heat′ed** *adj.* —**heat′ed·ly** *adv.*

heat·er (hē′tər) *n.* An apparatus for producing heat.

heat exhaustion Mild heat stroke.

heath (hēth) *n.* 1. Any of a large genus of

hardy evergreen shrubs, including the arbutus, azalea, and rhododendron. 2. The common heather. 3. *Brit.* An area of open land overgrown with heath or coarse herbage. [OE *hǣth*]

hea·then (hē′thən) *n. pl.* **·thens** or **·then** 1. One who has not adopted Christianity, Judaism, or Islam. 2. In the Old Testament, a non-Jew; Gentile. 3. Any irreligious or uncultivated person. —*adj.* 1. Unbelieving; irreligious. 2. Of or pertaining to heathen peoples. [OE *hǣthen.* Akin to HEATH.] —**hea′then·dom** *n.* —**hea′then·ish** *adj.* —**hea′then·ism** *n.*

heath·er (heth′ər) *n.* 1. A hardy evergreen shrub related to the heath and having pinkish flowers. 2. A purplish pink color. [ME *hadder*] —**heath′er·y** *adj.*

heat lightning A fitful play of lightning without thunder, associated with hot weather.

heat prostration Heat exhaustion.

heat stroke A state of collapse, accompanied by fever, caused by excessive heat.

heat wave A period of very hot weather.

heave (hēv) *v.* **heaved** or (*esp. Naut.*) **hove, heav·ing** *v.t.* 1. To throw or hurl, esp. with great effort. 2. To raise with effort. 3. To cause to rise or bulge. 4. *Naut.* **a** To pull or haul on (a rope, cable, etc.). **b** To cause (a ship) to move in a specified direction. —*v.i.* 5. To rise or swell up; bulge. 6. To rise and fall repeatedly. 7. To vomit; retch. 8. *Naut.* **a** To move or proceed: said of ships. **b** To haul or pull, as on a rope. —**heave, ho!** *Naut.* Pull (or push) hard together! —**to heave to** 1. To bring (a ship) to a standstill by heading into the wind with the sails hauled in or shortened. 2. To lie to. —*n.* The act of heaving. [OE *hebban* to lift] —**heav′er** *n.*

heav·en (hev′ən) *n.* 1. *Theol.* The abode of God and his angels, where virtuous souls are received. 2. *Usu. pl.* The regions around and above the earth; sky. 3. Any condition of great happiness. 4. Any place resembling heaven. [OE *heofon*] —**heav′en·ly** *adj.*

Heav·en (hev′ən) God or the celestial powers.

heav·en·ward (hev′ən·wərd) *adv.* Toward heaven. Also **heav′en·wards.** —*adj.* Directed toward heaven.

heav·i·er-than-air (hev′ē·ər·thən·âr′) *adj.* Having a weight greater than that of the air it displaces: said of airplanes, etc.

heav·y (hev′ē) *adj.* **heav·i·er, heav·i·est** 1. Having great weight; hard to move. 2. Having relatively great weight in relation to size: the *heavy* metals. 3. Having more than usual quantity, volume, etc.: a *heavy* snowfall. 4. Practicing or indulging on a large scale: a *heavy* smoker. 5. Having force and severity. 6. Having great importance; grave; serious. 7. Hard to do or accomplish: *heavy* labor. 8. Hard to endure or bear; oppressive: *heavy* taxes. 9. Of food, not easily digested. 10. Giving an impression of weight; thick: *heavy* lines. 11. Despondent: a *heavy* heart. 12. Lacking animation and grace; tedious. 13. Lacking precision and delicacy: a *heavy* hand. 14. Producing massive or basic goods: *heavy* industry. 15. Pregnant. 16. *Physics* Designating an isotope having a mass greater than that of others occurring in the same element: *heavy* hydrogen. 17. *Mil.* Designating the more massive types of weapons. —*adv.* In a heavy manner. —**to hang heavy** To drag by tediously, as time. —*n. pl.* **heav·ies** 1. In the theater, the role of a villainous or tragic personage; also, the actor portraying him. 2. *Slang* A scoundrel; villain. 3. *Slang* An important person: a conference of literary *heavies.* [OE *hefig*] —**heav′i·ly** *adv.* —**heav′i·ness** *n.*

heav·y-du·ty (hev′ē·dōō′tē) *adj.* Strongly constructed for hard use.

heav·y-hand·ed (hev′ē·han′did) *adj.* 1. Bungling; clumsy. 2. Oppressive; cruel. —**heav′y-hand′ed·ly** *adv.*

heav·y-heart·ed (hev′ē·här′tid) *adj.* Melancholy; sad. —**heav′y-heart′ed·ly** *adv.* —**heav′y-heart′ed·ness** *n.*

heavy hydrogen Deuterium.

heav·y-lad·en (hev′ē·lād′n) *adj.* 1. Bearing a heavy burden. 2. Troubled; oppressed.

heav·y·weight (hev′ē·wāt′) *n.* 1. A person or animal of much more than average weight. 2. A boxer or wrestler over 175 pounds in weight. —**heav′y·weight′** *adj.*

He·bra·ic (hi·brā′ik) *adj.* Relating to or characteristic of the Hebrew people and their culture and language. [< Gk. *Hebraios* a Hebrew]

He·bra·ism (hē′brā·iz′əm, -brə-) *n.* 1. A Hebrew idiom. 2. Hebrew thought, character, practice, etc. 3. The religion of the Hebrews; Judaism. —**He′bra·ist** *n.*

He·brew (hē′brōō) *n.* 1. A member of that group of Semitic peoples claiming descent from the house of Abraham; Israelite; Jew. 2. The ancient Semitic language of the Israelites. 3. The modern Hebrew language. —**Epistle to the Hebrews** A book of the New Testament addressed to Hebrew Christians: also **Hebrews.** —*adj.* Hebraic; Jewish. [< Hebrew *'ibhri,* lit., one from beyond (Jordan)]

heck (hek) *interj. Slang* Darn: a euphemism for *hell.*

heck·le (hek′əl) *v.t.* **·led, ·ling** To try to annoy with taunts, questions, etc. [ME *hechelen*] —**heck′ler** *n.*

hec·tare (hek′târ) *n.* In the metric system, a unit of area equal to 2.47 acres.

hec·tic (hek′tik) *adj.* 1. Characterized by great excitement, turmoil, haste, etc.: a *hectic* trip. 2. Feverish, gaunt, etc., as from a wasting disease. [< Gk. *hektikos* consumptive] —**hec′ti·cal·ly** *adv.*

hecto- *combining form* In the metric system and in technical usage, a hundred times (a specified unit). Also spelled *hekto-.* Also, before vowels, **hect-.** [< F < Gk. *hekaton* hundred]

hec·to·gram (hek′tə·gram) *n.* In the metric system, a measure of weight equal to 3.5 ounces. Also *Brit.* **hec′to·gramme.**

hec·to·li·ter (hek′tə·lē′tər) *n.* In the metric system, a measure of capacity equal to 26.4 gallons. Also *Brit.* **hec′to·li′tre.**

hec·to·me·ter (hek′tə·mē′tər, hek·tom′ə·tər) *n.* In the metric system, a measure of length equal to 109.36 yards. Also *Brit.* **hec′to·me′tre.**

hec·tor (hek′tər) *v.t. & v.i.* 1. To bluster; rant. 2. To tease; torment. [after *Hector,* Trojan hero of the epic poem, the *Iliad*]

he'd (hēd) 1. He had. 2. He would.
hedge (hej) *n.* 1. A fence or barrier formed of privet or other bushes; also, any boundary or barrier. 2. The act of hedging a bet, risk, etc.; also, that which is used to hedge. —*v.* **hedged, hedg·ing** *v.t.* 1. To border or separate with a hedge. 2. To set barriers and restrictions to; hem: often with *in* or *about.* 3. To guard against undue loss from (a bet, investment, etc.) by making compensatory bets, etc. —*v.i.* 4. To make compensatory bets, etc. 5. To avoid forthright statement or action. [OE *hegg*] —**hedg'er** *n.* —**hedg'y** *adj.*
hedge·hog (hej'hôg', -hog') *n.* 1. A small, nocturnal mammal of Europe, having stout spines on the back and sides. 2. The porcupine.
hedge·hop (hej'hop') *v.i.* **·hopped, ·hop·ping** To fly close to the ground in an airplane. —**hedge'hop'per** *n.*
hedge·row (hej'rō') *n.* A dense row of bushes, trees, etc., planted as a hedge.
he·don·ism (hēd'n·iz'əm) *n.* 1. The doctrine that pleasure is the only proper goal of moral endeavor. 2. The pursuit of pleasure. [< Gk. *hēdonē* pleasure] —**he'don·ist** *n.* —**he'don·is'tic** *adj.* —**he'don·is'ti·cal·ly** *adv.*
-hedral *combining form* Having (a specified number of) sides or faces: *octahedral.*
-hedron *combining form* A figure having (a specified number of) sides or faces: *octahedron.* [< Gk. *hedra* surface]
heed (hēd) *v.t.* 1. To pay attention to. —*v.i.* 2. To pay attention; listen. —*n.* Careful attention. [OE *hēdan*] —**heed'er** *n.*
heed·ful (hēd'fəl) *adj.* Attentive; mindful. —**heed'ful·ly** *adv.* —**heed'ful·ness** *n.*
heed·less (hēd'lis) *adj.* Not showing any heed or attention; reckless. —**heed'less·ly** *adv.* —**heed'less·ness** *n.*
hee·haw (hē'hô') *n.* The braying sound of a donkey. —*v.i.* To bray. [Imit.]
heel[1] (hēl) *n.* 1. In man, the rounded posterior part of the foot in back of the ankle; also, the rounded part of the palm of the hand nearest the wrist. 2. That part of a stocking, etc., covering the heel. 3. In a shoe or boot, the built-up portion on which the rear of the foot rests. 4. Something analogous to the human heel, as the rounded end of a loaf of bread. 5. *Slang* A dishonorable person; cad. —**at heel** Close behind. —**down at the heel** 1. Having the heels of one's shoes worn down. 2. Shabby; run-down. —**on** (or **upon**) **the heels of** Right behind; quickly following. —**to cool one's heels** To be kept waiting. —**to heel** 1. To an attendant position close behind one. 2. To submission; under control. —**to kick up one's heels** 1. To have a good time. 2. To let oneself go. —**to take to one's heels** To run away; flee. —*v.t.* 1. To supply with a heel, as a shoe. 2. To pursue closely. —*v.i.* 3. To follow at one's heels. [OE *hēla*] —**heel'less** *adj.*
heel[2] (hēl) *v.t. & v.i. Naut.* To lean or cause to lean to one side; cant, as a ship. [Earlier *heeld*, OE *hieldan*] —**heel, heel'ing** *n.*
heeled (hēld) *adj.* 1. Having a certain type of heel: used in combination: *high-heeled.* *Slang* Supplied with money or a weapon.
heel·tap (hēl'tap') *n.* 1. A thickness of leather on the heel of a shoe. 2. A small quantity of liquor left in a glass.
heft (heft) *v.t.* 1. To weigh by lifting. 2. To lift. —*n.* Weight. [Akin to HEAVE]
heft·y (hef'tē) *adj.* **heft·i·er, heft·i·est** *Informal* 1. Heavy; weighty. 2. Big and powerful; muscular.
He·gel·i·an·ism (hə·gā'lē·ən·iz'əm) *n.* The philosophical doctrine of Hegel that reality is a dialectic process whereby thought passes repeatedly in ascending stages from thesis to antithesis to synthesis. Also **He·gel·ism** (hā'gəl·iz'əm). —**He·ge'li·an** *n. & adj.*
he·gem·o·ny (hə·jem'ə·nē, hej'ə·mō'nē) *n. pl.* **·nies** Domination or leadership, esp. of one state over others. [< Gk. *hēgeesthai* to lead] —**heg·e·mon·ic** (hej'ə·mon'ik) *adj.*
he·gi·ra (hi·jī'rə) *n.* 1. *Often cap.* The flight of Muhammad from Mecca in 622. 2. Any similar flight from danger. Also spelled *hejira.* [< Arabic *hijrah* departure]
heif·er (hef'ər) *n.* A young cow that has not produced a calf. [OE *heahfore*]
height (hīt) *n.* 1. The state or quality of being high or relatively high. 2. The distance from the base to the top; altitude. 3. The distance above a given level, as the sea or horizon. 4. *Often pl.* A lofty or high place; eminence. 5. The highest part of anything; summit. 6. The highest degree. [OE *hīehtho*]
height·en (hīt'n) *v.t. & v.i.* 1. To make or become high or higher; raise or lift. 2. To make or become more in degree, amount, size, etc.; intensify. —**height'en·er** *n.*
hei·nous (hā'nəs) *adj.* Extremely wicked; atrocious; odious. [< OF *haine* hatred] —**hei'nous·ly** *adv.* —**hei'nous·ness** *n.*
heir (âr) *n.* 1. Anyone inheriting or likely to inherit rank or property. 2. One who succeeds or is the beneficiary of some forerunner. [< L *heres*] —**heir'ess** *n.fem.* —**heir'less** *adj.*
heir apparent *pl.* **heirs apparent** *Law* One who must by course of law become the heir if he survives his ancestor.
heir·loom (âr'lōōm) *n.* 1. Anything that has been handed down in a family for generations. 2. *Law* Those chattels and articles that descend to an heir along with the estate.
heir presumptive *pl.* **heirs presumptive** *Law* An heir whose claim to an estate may become void by the birth of a nearer relative.
heir·ship (âr'ship) *n.* 1. The state of being an heir. 2. The right to inheritance.
heist (hīst) *Slang v.t.* To steal. —*n.* A robbery. [Var. of HOIST]
he·ji·ra (hi·jī'rə) See HEGIRA.
hekto- See HECTO-.
held (held) Past tense of HOLD.
hel·i·cal (hel'i·kəl) *adj.* Pertaining to or shaped like a helix.
hel·i·ces (hel'ə·sēz) Alternative plural of HELIX.
helico- *combining form* Spiral; helical. Also, before vowels, **helic-**. [< Gk. *helix* spiral]
hel·i·coid (hel'ə·koid) *adj.* Arranged in a spiral or flat coil, as a snail shell. Also **hel'i·coid'al.** [< Gk. *helikoeidēs* spiral-shaped] —**hel'i·coi'dal·ly** *adv.*
hel·i·cop·ter (hel'ə·kop'tər, hē'lə-) *n. Aeron.* A type of aircraft lifted by airfoil blades rotating around a vertical axis, and capable of rising and descending vertically. [< Gk. *helix, -ikos* spiral + *pteron* wing]
helio- *combining form* Sun; of the sun. Also, before vowels, **heli-**. [< Gk. *hēlios* the sun]

he·li·o·cen·tric (hē′lē·ə·sen′trik) *adj.* Having or regarding the sun as the center.
he·li·o·graph (hē′lē·ə·graf′) *n.* 1. *Astron.* An instrument for taking photographs of the sun. 2. A mirror for signaling by flashes of light. Also **he′li·o** (-lē·ō). —*v.t. & v.i.* To signal with a heliograph. —**he·li·og·ra·pher** (hē′lē·og′rə·fər) *n.* —**he′li·o·graph′ic** *adj.* —**he·li·og·ra·phy** (hē′lē·og′rə·fē) *n.*
he·li·o·trope (hē′lē·ə·trōp′, hēl′yə-) *n.* 1. An herb with white or purplish fragrant flowers. 2. The bloodstone. 3. A soft, rosy purple. [< Gk. *hēlios* sun + *trepein* to turn]
he·li·ot·ro·pism (hē′lē·ot′rə·piz′əm) *n.* *Biol.* The tendency of some organisms to move or turn toward or away from the sun. Also **he′li·ot′ro·py.** —**he·li·o·trop·ic** (hē′lē·ə·trōp′ik, -trop′-) *adj.*
hel·i·port (hel′ə·pôrt′, hē′lə-) *n.* An airport for helicopters.
he·li·um (hē′lē·əm) *n.* An inert, odorless, nonflammable, gaseous element (symbol He), used to inflate balloons, dirigibles, etc. [< Gk. *hēlios* sun]
he·lix (hē′liks) *n.* *pl.* **he·lix·es** or **hel·i·ces** (hel′ə·sēz) 1. A line, thread, wire, or the like, curved as if wound in a single layer round a cylinder; a form like a screw thread. 2. Any spiral. 3. *Anat.* The recurved bordor of the external ear. [< L, spiral < Gk. *eilyein* to roll]
hell (hel) *n.* 1. *Sometimes cap.* In various religions, the abode of the dead or the place of punishment for the wicked after death. 2. Any condition or cause of great suffering. —**a** (or **one**) **hell of a** *Slang* A remarkably bad, good, difficult, etc. (thing). —**like hell** *Slang* 1. Very much, very fast, very bad, etc.: He ran *like hell.* 2. Not at all; never: *Like hell* he will! —**to be hell on** *Slang* To be unpleasant or damaging to. —**to catch** (or **get**) **hell** *Slang* To be scolded or punished. —**to give** (**someone**) **hell** *Slang* To scold or punish (someone) severely. —**to raise hell** *Slang* To create a disturbance. —*interj.* An exclamation used as an expression of anger or impatience. [OE *hel*]
he'll (hēl) He will.
Hel·las (hel′əs) Ancient or modern Greece. [< Gk.]
hell·bend·er (hel′ben′dər) *n.* A large aquatic salamander.
hell-bent (hel′bent′) *adj.* *Slang* Determined to have or do; recklessly eager.
hell·cat (hel′kat′) *n.* 1. A shrewish woman. 2. A witch.
hel·le·bore (hel′ə·bôr) *n.* A perennial herb of the crowfoot family, having serrated leaves and large flowers. [< Gk. *helleboros*]
Hel·lene (hel′ēn) *n.* A Greek. Also **Hel·le′ni·an.** [< Gk.]
Hel·len·ic (he·len′ik, -lē′nik) *adj.* Greek; Grecian. —*n.* A group of Indo-European languages, including Greek.
Hel·len·ism (hel′ə·niz′əm) *n.* 1. Ancient Greek character, ideals, or civilization. 2. An idiom or turn of phrase peculiar to Greek. —**Hel′le·nist** *n.*
Hel·le·nis·tic (hel′ə·nis′tik) *adj.* 1. Pertaining to or characteristic of the Hellenists or Hellenism. 2. Of or pertaining to the period that began with the conquests of Alexander the Great and ended about 300 years later, characterized by the spread of Greek language and culture throughout the Near East.
Hel·le·nize (hel′ə·nīz) *v.t. & v.i.* **·nized, ·niz·ing** To make or become Greek or Hellenistic. —**Hel′le·ni·za′tion** *n.* —**Hel′le·niz′er** *n.*
hell·fire (hel′fīr′) *n.* The flames or the punishment of hell.
hel·lion (hel′yən) *n.* *Informal* A wild, mischievous person. [< HELL]
hell·ish (hel′ish) *adj.* 1. Of, like, or pertaining to hell. 2. Fiendish; horrible. —**hell′ish·ly** *adv.* —**hell′ish·ness** *n.*
hel·lo (hə·lō′) *interj.* An exclamation of greeting or surprise, or one used to gain attention. —*n.* *pl.* **·loes** The saying or calling of "hello." —*v.t. & v.i.* **·loed, ·lo·ing** To call or say "hello" to.
helm (helm) *n.* 1. *Naut.* The steering apparatus of a vessel, esp. the tiller or wheel. 2. Any place of control or responsibility. [OE *helma* rudder]
hel·met (hel′mit) *n.* A rigid, protective covering for the head, made out of metal, plastic, etc., and worn by workers, soldiers, etc. [< OF, dim. of *helme* helmet < Gmc.] —**hel′met·ed** *adj.*
helms·man (helmz′mən) *n.* *pl.* **·men** (-mən) One who steers a ship.
hel·ot (hel′ət, hē′lət) *n.* A slave; serf. [< Gk., appar. < *Helos*, a Laconian town enslaved by Sparta] —**hel′ot·ry** *n.*
help (help) *v.t.* 1. To assist or aid (someone or something). 2. To provide relief to; remedy. 3. To refrain from: I couldn't *help* laughing. 4. To serve; wait on, as a salesclerk. —*v.i.* 5. To give assistance. —**cannot help but** Cannot avoid; be obliged to. —**to help oneself** To take without requesting or being offered. —*n.* 1. The act of helping. 2. Remedy; relief. 3. One who or that which gives assistance. 4. Any hired worker or helper. [OE *helpan*] —**help′er** *n.*
help·ful (help′fəl) *adj.* Affording help; beneficial. —**help′ful·ly** *adv.* —**help′ful·ness** *n.*
help·ing (hel′ping) *n.* A single portion of food served at table.
help·less (help′lis) *adj.* 1. Unable to help oneself; powerless. 2. Without recourse to help; defenseless. —**help′less·ly** *adv.* —**help′less·ness** *n.*
help·mate (help′māt′) *n.* 1. A helper; partner. 2. A wife. Also **help·meet** (help′·mēt′).
hel·ter-skel·ter (hel′tər·skel′tər) *adv. & adj.* In or displaying a hurried and confused manner. [Imit.]
helve (helv) *n.* The handle, as of an ax or hatchet. —*v.t.* **helved, helv·ing** To furnish with a helve. [OE *helfe*]
Hel·ve·tian (hel·vē′shən) *n. & adj.* Swiss. [< L *Helvetia*, name for Switzerland]
hem[1] (hem) *n.* 1. A finished edge made on a piece of fabric or a garment by turning the raw edge under and sewing it down. 2. Any similar border or edging. —*v.t.* **hemmed, hem·ming** 1. To provide with a hem. 2. To shut in; enclose; restrict: usu. with *in.* [OE]
hem[2] (hem) *interj.* A sound made as in clearing the throat to attract attention, cover embarrassment, etc. —*v.i.* **hemmed, hem·ming** To make the sound "hem." —**to hem**

and haw To hesitate in speaking so as to keep from being explicit. [Imit.]

hem- See HEMO-.

hema- *combining form* Blood. Also spelled *haema-*. [< Gk. *haima* blood]

he·man (hē'man') *n. pl.* **·men** (-men') *Informal* A virile, muscular man.

hem·a·tite (hem'ə·tīt, hē'mə-) *n.* Red ferric oxide, a mineral which is the chief ore of iron: also called *ferric oxide*. [< Gk. *haematites* bloodlike] **—hem·a·tit·ic** (hem'ə·tit'ik, hē'mə-) *adj.*

hemato- *combining form* Blood. Also, before vowels, **hemat-**. Also spelled *haemato-*. [< Gk. *haima, haimatos*]

he·ma·tol·o·gy (hē'mə·tol'ə·jē, hem'ə-) *n.* The branch of biology that treats of the blood and its diseases. **—hem·a·to·log·ic** (hē'mə·tə·loj'ik, hem'ə-) or **·i·cal** *adj.* **—he'ma·tol'o·gist** *n.*

he·ma·to·ma (hē'mə·tō'mə, hem'ə-) *n. pl.* **·to·ma·ta** (-tō'mə·tə) *Pathol.* A tumor or swelling formed by the effusion of blood.

heme (hēm) *n.* The nonprotein, iron constituent of hemoglobin.

hemi- *prefix* Half: *hemisphere*. Also, before vowels, **hem-**. [< Gk. *hēmi-*]

-hemia See -EMIA.

hem·i·ple·gi·a (hem'i·plē'jē·ə) *n. Pathol.* Paralysis of one side of the body. [< Med.Gk. *hēmiplēgia* paralysis] **—hem'i·ple'·gic** (-plē'jik, -plej'ik) *adj. & n.*

hem·i·sphere (hem'ə·sfir) *n.* 1. A half-sphere formed by a plane passing through the center of the sphere. 2. A half of the terrestrial or celestial globe, or a map or projection of one. The world is usu. divided either at the equator into the **Northern** and **Southern Hemispheres**, or at some meridian between Europe and America into the **Eastern** and **Western Hemispheres**. [< Gk. *hēmi-* half + *sphaira* sphere] **—hem·i·spher·ic** (hem'ə·sfir'ik, -sfer'-) or **·i·cal** *adj.*

hem·i·stich (hem'i·stik) *n.* Half a line of verse.

hem·line (hem'līn') *n.* The line formed by the lower edge of a garment, as a dress.

hem·lock (hem'lok) *n.* 1. One of several evergreen trees of the pine family, having coarse, nonresinous wood used for paper pulp. 2. A large, biennial herb of the parsley family, yielding a poison: also **poison hemlock**. [OE *hymlice*]

hemo- *combining form* Blood. Also, before vowels, **hem-**. Also spelled *haemo-*. [< Gk. *haima*]

he·mo·glo·bin (hē'mə·glō'bin, hem'ə-) *n. Biochem.* The respiratory pigment in red blood corpuscles, composed of globin and heme, and serving as a carrier of oxygen from the lungs to body cells.

he·mo·phil·i·a (hē'mə·fil'ē·ə, -fil'yə, hem'ə-) *n. Pathol.* A disorder characterized by immoderate bleeding even from slight injuries. [< Gk. *haima* blood + *philia* fondness] **—he'mo·phil'i·ac** (-ē·ak) *adj. & n.*

hem·or·rhage (hem'ər·ij, hem'rij) *n.* Copious discharge of blood from a ruptured blood vessel. **—***v.i.* **·rhaged, ·rhag·ing** To bleed copiously. [< Gk. *haima* blood + *rhēgnynai* to burst] **—hem·or·rhag·ic** (hem'ə·raj'ik) *adj.*

hem·or·rhoid (hem'ə·roid, hem'roid) *n. Pathol.* A tumor or dilation of a vein in the anal region: also, in the plural, *piles*. [< Gk. *haima* blood + *rheein* to flow] **—hem'or·rhoi'dal** *adj.*

he·mo·stat (hē'mə·stat, hem'ə-) *n. Med.* A device or drug for checking the flow of blood from a ruptured vessel.

hemp (hemp) *n.* 1. A tall, annual herb of the mulberry family, native in Asia but cultivated elsewhere, with small green flowers and a tough bark: also called *bhang, cannabis, Indian hemp, marijuana*. 2. A narcotic prepared from this plant. 3. The tough, strong fiber from this plant, used for cloth and cordage. [OE *henep*] **—hemp·en** (hem'pən) *adj.*

hem·stitch (hem'stich') *n.* The ornamental finishing of a hem, made by pulling out several threads and drawing the cross threads together in groups. **—***v.t.* To embroider with a hemstitch. **—hem'stitch'er** *n.*

hen (hen) *n.* 1. The mature female of the domestic fowl and related birds. 2. The female of the lobster. [OE *henn*]

hen·bane (hen'bān) *n.* A poisonous Old World herb of the nightshade family, with sticky, malodorous foliage.

hence (hens) *adv.* 1. As a consequence; therefore. 2. From this time or date: a week *hence*. 3. Away from this place. [OE *heonan* from here]

hence·forth (hens'fôrth', hens'fôrth') *adv.* From this time on. Also **hence'for'ward** (-fôr'wərd).

hench·man (hench'mən) *n. pl.* **·men** (-mən) 1. A faithful follower. 2. A political supporter who works chiefly for personal gain. [OE *hengst* horse + *man* groom]

hen·na (hen'ə) *n.* 1. An ornamental Oriental shrub or small tree. 2. A hair dye made from its leaves. 3. A reddish brown color. **—***v.t.* **hen·naed, hen·na·ing** To dye with henna. [< Arabic *hinnā*]

hen·peck (hen'pek') *v.t.* To domineer over or harass (one's husband) by nagging, etc.

hen·pecked (hen'pekt') *adj.* Dominated by one's wife.

hen·ry (hen'rē) *n. pl.* **·ries** or **·rys** *Electr.* The unit equal to the inductance of a circuit in which the variation of a current at the rate of one ampere per second induces an electromotive force of one volt. [after Joseph *Henry*, 1797–1878, U.S. physicist]

hep (hep) *adj. Slang* Hip[3].

hep·a·rin (hep'ə·rin) *n. Biochem.* A substance found in liver and other tissues, that slows down coagulation of blood, and that is used in medicine. [< Gk. *hēpar* liver]

he·pat·ic (hi·pat'ik) *adj.* Of or like the liver. [< Gk. *hēpar* liver]

he·pat·i·ca (hi·pat'ə·kə) *n. pl.* **·cas** or **·cae** (-sē) A small perennial herb with delicate flowers: also called *liverwort*. [< L *hepaticus* of the liver]

hep·a·ti·tis (hep'ə·tī'tis) *n. Pathol.* Inflammation of the liver.

hepato- *combining form* Pertaining to the liver. Also, before vowels, **hepat-**. [< Gk. *hēpar, hēpatos* the liver]

Hep·ple·white (hep'əl·hwīt) *adj.* Denoting an English style of furniture characterized by graceful curves and light, slender woodwork. [after G. *Hepplewhite*, died 1786, the designer]

hepta- *combining form* Seven. Also, before vowels, **hept-**. [< Gk. *hepta*]

hep·tam·e·ter (hep·tam′ə·tər) *n.* In prosody, a line of verse consisting of seven metrical feet.

hep·tane (hep′tān) *n. Chem.* A colorless, flammable liquid hydrocarbon of the methane series, used as a solvent and in the determination of the octane number of motor fuels.

her (hûr) *pron.* The objective case of the pronoun *she.* —*pronominal adj.* The possessive case of *she.* [OE *hire*]

her·ald (her′əld) *n.* 1. Any bearer of important news; messenger. 2. One who or that which shows what is to follow; harbinger. —*v.t.* To announce or proclaim publicly. [< OHG *heren* to call]

he·ral·dic (hi·ral′dik) *adj.* Of heraldry or heralds.

her·ald·ry (her′əl·drē) *n. pl.* **·ries** The art or science that treats of coats of arms, genealogies, etc.

herb (ûrb, hûrb) *n.* 1. A plant without woody tissue, which withers and dies after flowering. 2. Any such plant as a medicine, seasoning, scent, etc. [< L *herba* grass, herbage] —**herb·al** (hûr′bəl, ûr′-) *adj. & n.*

her·ba·ceous (hûr·bā′shəs) *adj.* 1. Like herbs. 2. Having the semblance, color, or structure of a leaf.

herb·age (ûr′bij, hûr′-) *n.* 1. Herbs collectively, esp. pasturage. 2. The succulent parts of herbaceous plants.

herb·al·ist (hûr′bəl·ist, ûr′-) *n.* A dealer in herbs.

her·bar·i·um (hûr·bâr′ē·əm) *n. pl.* **·bar·i·ums** or **·bar·i·a** 1. A collection of dried plants scientifically arranged. 2. A room or building containing such a collection.

her·bi·cide (hûr′bə·sīd) *n.* An agent, as a chemical, that destroys plants, esp. weeds.

her·biv·o·rous (hûr·biv′ər·əs) *adj.* 1. Feeding on vegetable matter; plant-eating. 2. Belonging to a group of mammals that feed mainly on herbage, as cows, horses, camels, etc. [< L *herba* grass] —**her·biv′o·rous·ly** *adv.*

her·cu·le·an (hûr·kyōō′lē·ən, hûr′kyə·lē′ən) *adj* 1. Having great strength. 2. Requiring great strength.

her·cu·les (hûr′kyə·lēs) *n.* 1. Any man of great strength. 2. *cap.* A constellation. [< *Hercules* in Greek mythology, known for his strength]

herd (hûrd) *n.* 1. A number of cattle or other animals feeding, moving about, or kept together. 2. A large crowd of people: a contemptuous term. —*v.t. & v.i.* To bring together or move in a herd. [OE *heord*] —**herd′er** *n.*

-herd *combining form* Herdsman: *swineherd, cowherd,* etc. [OE *hierde*]

herds·man (hûrdz′mən) *n. pl.* **·men** (-mən) One who owns or tends a herd.

here (hir) *adv.* 1. In, at, or about this place: opposed to *there.* Also used to indicate or emphasize: George *here* is a good swimmer. 2. To this place; hither. 3. At this point in time, in an action, etc.: *Here* are my reasons. 4. In the present life: distinguished from *hereafter.* —*interj.* An exclamation used to answer a roll call, attract attention, etc. —**neither here nor there** Beside the point; irrelevant. —*n.* 1. This place. 2. This time; this life: the *here* and now. [OE *hēr*]

here·a·bout (hir′ə·bout′) *adv.* About this place; in this vicinity. Also **here′a·bouts′**.

here·af·ter (hir·af′tər) *adj.* 1. At some future time. 2. From this time forth. —*n.* A future state or existence, esp. after death. [OE *hēræfter*]

here·by (hir·bī′) *adv.* By means or by virtue of this.

her·e·dit·a·ment (her′ə·dit′ə·mənt) *n. Law* Every kind of property capable of being inherited.

he·red·i·tar·y (hə·red′ə·ter′ē) *adj.* 1. Derived from ancestors; inherited. 2. *Biol.* Transmitted or transmissible genetically from an animal or plant to its offspring: distinguished from *congenital.* 3. *Law* **a** Passing by inheritance to an heir. **b** Holding possession or title through inheritance.

he·red·i·ty (hə·red′ə·tē) *n. pl.* **·ties** *Biol.* 1. Genetic transmission of characteristics from parents to offspring. 2. The sum total of an individual's inherited characteristics. [< L *hereditas, -tatis* inheritance]

Her·e·ford (her′ə·fərd, hûr′fərd) *n.* One of a breed of beef cattle having a white face and a red and white coat.

here·in (hir·in′) *adv.* 1. In or into this place. 2. In this case, circumstance, etc. [OE *herinne*]

here·in·af·ter (hir′in·af′tər) *adv.* In a subsequent part of this document, contract, etc.

here·of (hir·uv′) *adv.* 1. Of this. 2. In regard to this.

here·on (hir·on′) *adv.* On this; hereupon.

her·e·sy (her′ə·sē) *n. pl.* **·sies** 1. A belief contrary to the established doctrines of a church or religious system. 2. Any belief contrary to established doctrine. 3. The holding of such a belief or opinion. [ME *heresie* < Gk. *hairesis* sect] —**he·ret·i·cal** (hə·ret′i·kəl) *adj.* —**he·ret′i·cal·ly** *adv.*

her·e·tic (her′ə·tik) *n.* 1. One who holds beliefs or opinions contrary to the established doctrines of his religion. 2. One who maintains unorthodox opinions on any subject.

here·to (hir·tōō′) *adv.* To this thing, matter, etc.

here·to·fore (hir′tə·fôr′) *adv.* Before now; previously.

here·un·to (hir·un′tōō) *adv.* To this; hereto.

here·up·on (hir′ə·pon′) *adv.* Immediately resulting from or following this.

here·with (hir·with′, -with′) *adv.* 1. Along with this. 2. By means of or through this.

her·i·ta·ble (her′ə·tə·bəl) *adj.* That can be inherited. [< OF *heriter* to inherit] —**her′i·ta·bil′i·ty** *n.* —**her′i·ta·bly** *adv.*

her·i·tage (her′ə·tij) *n.* 1. That which is inherited. 2. A cultural tradition, body of knowledge, etc., handed down from past times. 3. *Law* Property that is or can be inherited by descendants. [< OF *heriter* to inherit]

her·maph·ro·dite (hûr·maf′rə·dīt) *n.* 1. An individual having both male and female reproductive organs. 2. *Bot.* A plant having both stamens and pistils. [after *Hermaphroditus,* son of Hermes, who became united with a nymph in a single body] —**her·**

maph′ro·dite, her·maph′ro·dit′ic (-dit′ik) *adj.* —her·maph′ro·dit′ism *n.*
her·met·ic (hûr·met′ik) *adj.* 1. Airtight. 2. Of or relating to alchemy; magical; hard to understand. Also **her·met′i·cal.** [< Med.L *hermeticus*] —**her·met′i·cal·ly** *adv.*
her·mit (hûr′mit) *n.* One who lives in seclusion, often for religious reasons. [< Gk. *erēmia* desert]
her·mit·age (hûr′mə·tij) *n.* 1. The dwelling of a hermit. 2. Any secluded dwelling place.
hermit crab Any of various soft-bodied crustaceans that live in the empty shells of snails, etc.
her·ni·a (hûr′nē·ə) *n.* *pl.* **·ni·as** or **·ni·ae** (nē·ē) *Pathol.* The protrusion of a bodily part, as of the intestine, through an opening in the wall surrounding it; rupture. [< L] —**her′ni·al** *adj.*
he·ro (hir′ō, hē′rō) *n.* *pl.* **·roes** 1. A man distinguished for exceptional courage, fortitude, or bold enterprise. 2. One idealized for superior qualities or deeds of any kind. 3. The principal male character in a drama, fictional work, etc. 4. In classical mythology and legend, a man of great nobility or physical prowess. 5. A sandwich made with a long roll cut lengthwise, and usu. filled with cold cuts, cheese, etc.: also called *grinder, hoagy, submarine.* [< Gk. *hērōs*]
he·ro·ic (hi·rō′ik) *adj.* 1. Characteristic of, befitting, or resembling a hero. 2. Showing great daring or boldness; extreme in action or effect: a *heroic* attempt. 3. Grandiose in style or language. Also **he·ro′i·cal.** —*n.* 1. *Often pl.* Heroic verse. 2. *pl.* Melodramatic or extravagant behavior. —**he·ro′i·cal·ly** *adv.*
heroic couplet A verse form consisting of two rhyming lines of iambic pentameter.
heroic verse One of several verse forms used especially in epic and dramatic poetry, as the iambic pentameter of the heroic couplet and blank verse.
her·o·in (her′ō·in) *n.* An addictive, narcotic drug derived from morphine. [< G]
her·o·ine (her′ō·in) *n.fem.* 1. A woman of heroic character. 2. The principal female character of a drama, fictional work, etc. [< Gk. *hērōinē*]
her·o·ism (her′ō·iz′əm) *n.* 1. The qualities of a hero or heroine. 2. Heroic behavior.
her·on (her′ən) *n.* Any of several wading birds, having a long neck, a long, slender bill, and long legs. [< OF *hairon*, ult. < Gmc.]
hero worship Enthusiastic or extravagant admiration for heroes or other persons. —**hero worshiper**
her·pes (hûr′pēz) *n.* *Pathol.* A virus infection of the skin and mucous membranes, characterized by the eruption of blisters. [< L < Gk. *herpein* to creep]
herpes zos·ter (zos′tər) *Pathol.* Shingles. [< L, herpes + *zoster* (< Gk., girdle, belt)]
her·pe·tol·o·gy (hûr′pə·tol′ə·jē) *n.* The branch of zoology that treats of reptiles and amphibians. [< Gk. *herpeton* reptile + -LOGY] —**her·pe·to·log·i·cal** (hûr′pə·tə·loj′i·kəl) *adj.* —**her′pe·tol′o·gist** *n.*
Herr (her) *n.* *pl.* **Her·ren** (her′ən) *German* A title of address equivalent to *Mister.*
her·ring (her′ing) *n.* *pl.* **·rings** or **·ring** 1. A small food fish of the North Atlantic. 2. Any of various fish related to the herring, as the shad, sardine, etc. [OE *hæring*]
her·ring·bone (her′ing·bōn′) *n.* 1. A pattern utilizing a design, resembling the spinal structure of a herring, in which the ribs form slanting parallel lines on either side of the spine. 2. Something made in or consisting of such a pattern. —**her′ring·bone′** *adj.*
hers (hûrz) *pron.* 1. The possessive case of the pronoun *she*, used predicatively: That book is *hers.* 2. The one or ones belonging to or relating to her. [OE *hire* + *-s*]
her·self (hər·self′) *pron.* A form of the third person singular feminine pronoun, used: 1. As a reflexive: She excused *herself.* 2. As an intensive form of *she*: She *herself* called the police. 3. As a designation of a usual state: After her illness, she was *herself* again.
hertz (hûrts) *n.* A unit of frequency equal to one cycle per second. Abbr. *Hz.* [after H. R. *Hertz*]
he's (hēz) 1. He is. 2. He has.
hes·i·tant (hez′ə·tənt) *adj.* Lacking certainty or decisiveness; hesitating. —**hes′i·tan·cy** *n.* —**hes′i·tant·ly** *adv.*
hes·i·tate (hez′ə·tāt) *v.i.* **·tat·ed, ·tat·ing** 1. To be slow or doubtful in acting, making a decision, etc.; waver. 2. To be reluctant. 3. To pause. 4. To falter in speech. [< L *haesitare*, freq. of *haerere* to stick] —**hes′i·ta′tion** *n.*
he·tae·ra (hi·tir′ə, -tī′rə) *n.* *pl.* **·tae·rae** (-tir′ē, -tī′rē) In ancient Greece, a professional courtesan. [< Gk. *hetaira* companion]
hetero- *combining form* Other; different: opposed to *homo-*. Also, before vowels, **heter-**. [< Gk. *hetero-* < *heteros* other]
het·er·o·dox (het′ər·ə·doks′) *adj.* 1. At variance with accepted doctrines or beliefs. 2. Holding unorthodox opinions. [< Gk. *hetero-* other + *doxa* opinion] —**het′er·o·dox′y** *n.*
het·er·o·ge·ne·ous (het′ər·ə·jē′nē·əs) *adj.* 1. Consisting of dissimilar parts or elements; not homogeneous. 2. Differing in nature or kind; unlike. [< Gk. *hetero-* other + *genos* kind] —**het′er·o·ge′ne·ous·ly** *adv.* —**het′er·o·ge′ne·ous·ness, het′er·o·ge·ne′i·ty** (-jə·nē′ə·tē) *n.*
het·er·o·sex·u·al (het′ər·ə·sek′shōō·əl) *adj.* 1. Of or having sexual desire for those of the opposite sex. 2. *Biol.* Of or pertaining to the opposite sex or to both sexes. —**het′er·o·sex′u·al** *n.* —**het′er·o·sex′u·al′i·ty** (-al′ə·tē) *n.*
heu·ris·tic (hyōō·ris′tik) *adj.* 1. Aiding or guiding in discovery. 2. Designating an educational method by which a pupil is stimulated to make his own investigations and discoveries. [< Gk. *heuriskein* to find out]
hew (hyōō) *v.* **hewed, hewn** or **hewed, hew·ing** *v.t.* 1. To make or shape with or as with blows of an ax. 2. To fell with or as with ax blows. —*v.i.* 3. To make cutting and repeated blows, as with an ax or sword. 4. To conform, as to a principle. [OE *hēawan*] —**hew′er** *n.*
hex (heks) *n.* *Dial.* or *Informal* 1. An evil spell. 2. A witch. —*v.t.* To bewitch. [< G *hexe* witch]
hexa- *combining form* Six. Also, before vowels, **hex-**. [< Gk. *hexa-* < *hex*]

hex·a·gon (hek′sə·gon) *n. Geom.* A polygon having six sides and six angles. [< Gk. *hexagonos* six-cornered] —**hex·ag·o·nal** (hek·sag′ə·nəl) *adj.* —**hex·ag′o·nal·ly** *adv.*

hex·a·gram (hek′sə·gram) *n.* A six-pointed star made by or as by completing the equilateral triangles based on the sides of a regular hexagon.

hex·am·e·ter (hek·sam′ə·tər) *n.* 1. In prosody, a line of verse consisting of six metrical feet. 2. The dactylic verse of Greek and Latin epics. [< Gk. *hexametros*] —**hex·a·met·ric** (hek′sə·met′rik) or **·ri·cal** *adj.*

hex·a·pod (hek′sə·pod) *n.* One of the true or six-legged insects. [< Gk. *hexapous, -podos* six-footed] —**hex′a·pod** *adj.*

hey (hā) *interj.* An exclamation calling for attention or expressing surprise, etc. [ME *hei*]

hey·day (hā′dā′) *n.* Period of greatest vigor; height, as of power or prosperity. [Prob. < HIGH DAY]

hi (hī) *interj.* An exclamation of greeting. [Var. of HEY]

hi·a·tus (hī·ā′təs) *n. pl.* **·tus·es** or **·tus** 1. A gap or space from which something is missing. 2. Any break or interruption. [< L]

hi·ba·chi (hi·bä′chē) *n. pl.* **·chis** A deep container to hold burning coals, used for heating and cooking. [< Japanese]

hi·ber·nate (hī′bər·nāt) *v.i.* **·nat·ed, ·nat·ing** 1. To pass the winter in a dormant state, as certain animals. 2. To remain inactive or secluded. [< L *hibernare*] —**hi′ber·na′tion** *n.*

Hi·ber·ni·a (hī·bûr′nē·ə) Latin and poetic name for Ireland. [< L, alter. of *Iverna*] —**Hi·ber′ni·an** *n. & adj.*

hi·bis·cus (hī·bis′kəs, hi-) *n.* A shrub or tree of the mallow family, having large, showy flowers. [< Gk. *hibiskos* mallow]

hic·cup (hik′əp) *n.* 1. An involuntary contraction of the diaphragm, causing a sudden, audible inspiration of breath checked by a spasmodic closure of the glottis. 2. *pl.* A condition characterized by repetition of such spasms. Also **hic·cough** (hik′əp). [Imit.] —**hic′cup** *v.i.* **·cuped** or **·cupped, ·cup·ing** or **·cup·ping**

hick (hik) *n. Informal* One having the clumsy, unsophisticated manners, etc., supposedly typical of rural areas. [Alter. of *Richard*] —**hick** *adj.*

hick·ey (hik′ē) *n. pl.* **·eys** *Informal* 1. Any gadget or contrivance. 2. A pimple or blemish. [Origin unknown]

hick·o·ry (hik′ər·ē, hik′rē) *n. pl.* **·ries** 1. A North American tree of the walnut family, having hard, durable wood and yielding edible nuts. 2. The wood of such trees. [< Algonquian *pawcohiccoro*]

hid (hid) Past tense and alternative past participle of HIDE¹.

hi·dal·go (hi·dal′gō, *Sp.* ē·thäl′gō) *n. pl.* **·gos** (-gōz, *Sp.* -gōs) A Spanish nobleman of lower rank than a grandee. [< Sp. < *hijo de algo* son of something]

hid·den (hid′n) Past participle of HIDE¹. —*adj.* Not seen or known; concealed; obscure.

hide¹ (hīd) *v.* **hid, hid·den** or **hid, hid·ing** *v.t.* 1. To put or keep out of sight; conceal. 2. To keep secret; withhold from knowledge. 3. To block or obstruct the sight of. —*v.i.* 4. To keep oneself out of sight; be concealed. —**to hide out** *Informal* To remain in concealment, esp. as a fugitive. [OE *hȳdan*]

hide² (hīd) *n.* 1. The skin of an animal, esp. when stripped from the carcass or made into leather. 2. *Informal* The human skin. [OE *hȳd* skin]

hide-and-seek (hīd′ən·sēk′) *n.* A children's game in which those who hide are sought by one who is "it." Also **hide′-and-go-seek′**.

hide·a·way (hīd′ə·wā′) *n.* A place of concealment; hide-out.

hide·bound (hīd′bound′) *adj.* 1. Obstinately fixed in opinion; narrow-minded; bigoted. 2. Having the skin too tightly adhering to the back and ribs: said of cattle, etc.

hid·e·ous (hid′ē·əs) *adj.* 1. Extremely ugly: a *hideous* sight. 2. Morally odious or detestable; shocking. [< OF *hisde, hide* fright] —**hid′e·ous·ly** *adv.* —**hid′e·ous·ness** *n.*

hide-out (hīd′out′) *n. Informal* A place of concealment or refuge. Also **hide′out′**.

hid·ing¹ (hī′ding) *n.* 1. The act of one who or that which hides. 2. A state or place of concealment.

hid·ing² (hī′ding) *n. Informal* A flogging; whipping.

hie (hī) *v.t. & v.i.* **hied, hie·ing** or **hy·ing** To hasten; hurry: often reflexive: I *hied* myself home. [OE *hīgian*]

hi·er·ar·chy (hī′ə·rär′kē) *n. pl.* **·chies** 1. Any group of persons or things arranged in successive orders or classes. 2. A body of ecclesiastics so arranged. 3. Government or rule by such a body of ecclesiastics. —**hi′er·ar′chi·cal** (-ki·kəl) *adj.*

hiero- *combining form* Sacred; divine. Also, before vowels, **hier-**. [< Gk. *hieros* sacred]

hi·er·o·glyph·ic (hī′ər·ə·glif′ik, hī′rə·glif′ik) *n.* 1. *Usu. pl.* A picture or symbol representing an object, idea, or sound, as in the writing system of the ancient Egyptians. 2. *pl.* A system of writing using such pictures or symbols. 3. Any symbol or character having a hidden meaning. Also **hi′er·o·glyph′**. [< Gk. *hieros* sacred + *glyphein* to carve] —**hi·er·og·ly·phist** (hī′ər·og′lə·fist, hī·rog′-) *n.*

hi-fi (hī′fī′) *n.* 1. High fidelity. 2. Radio, phonograph, or recording equipment capable of reproducing sound with high fidelity. —**hi′-fi′** *adj.*

hig·gle·dy-pig·gle·dy (hig′əl·dē·pig′əl·dē) *adj.* Disordered or confused; jumbled. —*adv.* In chaotic confusion or disorder. [< obs. *higle-pigle*, a varied reduplication]

high (hī) *adj.* 1. Reaching upward to some great distance; lofty; tall. 2. Having a specified elevation: ten feet *high*. 3. Produced or extending to or from a height: a *high* jump. 4. Greater or more than is usual or normal in degree, amount, etc.: *high* fever; *high* speed. 5. Superior or exalted in quality, rank, kind, etc.: a *high* official. 6. Most important; main. 7. Having serious consequences: *high* treason. 8. Elated; joyful: *high* spirits. 9. *Informal* Feeling the effects of liquor, drugs, etc.; intoxicated. 10. Expensive; costly. 11. Luxurious or fashionable: *high* living. 12. Advanced to the fullest extent or degree: *high* tide. 13. Complex; advanced: usu. in the comparative degree: *higher* mathematics. 14. Slightly decomposed; gamy: said of meat. 15. Of sounds, having relatively short wavelengths; shrill. 16. *Music* Having relatively short wavelengths: said of vocal or instrumental tones. 17. *Mech.* Denoting a gear arrangement, as in a transmission, yielding the most rapid output speed. **—high and dry** 1. Completely above water level. 2. Stranded; helpless. **—high and mighty** *Informal* Overbearing; haughty. **—*adv.*** 1. To or at a high level, position, degree, price, rank, etc. 2. In a high manner. **—high and low** Everywhere. **—*n.*** 1. A high level, position, etc. 2. *Mech.* A gear arrangement yielding the most rapid output speed. 3. *Meteorol.* a An area of high barometric pressure. b The highest temperature, as for a day. [OE *hēah*] **—high′ly** *adv.*

high·ball (hī′bôl′) *n.* A drink of whiskey or other liquor mixed with soda, ginger ale, etc. [Prob. < HIGH + *ball*, obs., a drink of whiskey]

high·born (hī′bôrn′) *adj.* Of noble birth or ancestry.

high·boy (hī′boi′) *n.* A tall chest of drawers, usu. in two sections, the lower one mounted on legs. [Origin unknown]

high·bred (hī′bred′) *adj.* 1. Descended from fine stock; well-born. 2. Characteristic of or indicating good breeding.

high·brow (hī′brou′) *n. Informal* One who has or claims to have intellectually superior tastes. **—high′brow′** *adj.*

high·chair (hī′châr′) *n.* A baby's chair standing on tall legs.

high-class (hī′klas′) *adj. Slang* High or superior in quality, condition, status, etc.

high·er-up (hī′ər·up′) *n. Informal* A person of superior rank or position.

high·fa·lu·tin (hī′fə·lo͞ot′n) *adj. Informal* Extravagant, pompous, or high-flown in manner, speech, etc. [? < HIGH-FLOWN]

high fashion 1. Clothes that are new in style or design. 2. Haute couture.

high fidelity *Electronics* The reproduction of sound with a minimum of distortion, esp. by phonographic or tape-recording equipment: also called *hi-fi*.

high-flown (hī′flōn′) *adj.* 1. Bombastic in style, language, etc. 2. Pretentious.

high frequency *Telecom.* A radio frequency in the band from 3 to 30 megahertz.

High German See under GERMAN.

high-grade (hī′grād′) *adj.* Of superior quality.

high·hand·ed (hī′han′did) *adj.* Arbitrary and overbearing. **—high′hand′ed·ly** *adv.* **—high′·hand′ed·ness** *n.*

high-hat (hī′hat′) *v.t. Informal* **-hat·ted, -hat·ting** To snub. **—*adj.*** Snobbish. **—*n.*** A snob.

high·jack (hī′jak′) See HIJACK.

high jump In athletics, a jump for height.

high·land (hī′lənd) *n.* 1. Elevated land, as a plateau or promontory. 2. *Usu. pl.* A hilly or mountainous region. **—high′land** *adj.*

High·land·er (hī′lən·dər) *n.* 1. A native or inhabitant of the Highlands. 2. A soldier of a Highlands regiment.

High·lands (hī′ləndz) The mountainous parts of northern and western Scotland.

high·light (hī′līt′) *n.* 1. An area, as in a painting, that is brightly lighted. 2. An event, detail, etc., of special importance. **—*v.t.*** 1. *Informal* To give special emphasis to; feature. 2. To provide or emphasize with a highlight or highlights.

high-mind·ed (hī′mīn′did) *adj.* Possessing or manifesting noble thoughts or sentiments. **—high′-mind′ed·ness** *n.*

high·ness (hī′nis) *n.* 1. The state or quality of being high. 2. *cap.* A title or form of address for persons of royal rank: often preceded by *His, Her, Your*, etc.

high-pitched (hī′picht′) *adj.* 1. High in pitch; shrill. 2. Of a roof, having a steep slope.

high-pres·sure (hī′presh′ər) *adj.* 1. Using or sustaining high steam pressure, as an engine. 2. Having or showing high barometric pressure. 3. *Informal* Exerting vigorously persuasive methods or tactics. **—*v.t.* ·sured, ·sur·ing** *Informal* To persuade by aggressive or insistent methods.

high-rise (hī′rīz′) *n.* A building having many stories and requiring elevators. **—high′-rise′** *adj.*

high·road (hī′rōd′) *n.* 1. A main road. 2. An easy or sure way: the *highroad* to fame.

high school A school following elementary school or junior high school.

high seas The open waters of an ocean or sea that are beyond the territorial jurisdiction of any one nation.

high-sound·ing (hī′soun′ding) *adj.* Pretentious or imposing: *high-sounding* praise.

high-spir·it·ed (hī′spir′it·ed) *adj.* Having a courageous or fiery spirit.

high-strung (hī′strung′) *adj.* Very sensitive or nervous; excitable.

high-ten·sion (hī′ten′shən) *adj. Electr.* Having or operating under very high voltage.

high-test (hī′test′) *adj.* 1. Designating a substance or product that has passed severe tests for fitness, quality, etc. 2. Denoting a grade of gasoline with a low boiling point.

high tide 1. The maximum level reached by the incoming tide. 2. A culminating point.

high time 1. So late as to be almost past the proper time. 2. *Informal* A hilarious and enjoyable time.

high-toned (hī′tōnd′) *adj.* 1. *Informal* Stylish; modish. 2. Lofty in character.

high treason Treason against the sovereign or state.

high-wa·ter mark (hī′wô′tər, -wot′ər) 1. The highest point reached by a body of water, as during high tide, a flood, etc. 2. A point of highest achievement or development.

high·way (hī′wā′) *n.* A public road or thoroughfare.

high·way·man (hī′wā′mən) *n. pl.* **·men** (-mən) Formerly, a robber who waylaid travelers on highways.

hi·jack (hī′jak′) *v.t. Slang* 1. To seize illegally while in transit, as cargo, vehicles, etc. 2. To hold up and rob (a truck, etc.). Also spelled *highjack*. [Orig. from hoboes who hailed their victim with "Hi Jack"] **—hi′jack′er** *n.*

hike (hīk) *v.* **hiked, hik·ing** *v.i.* 1. To walk for a considerable distance. 2. To rise or be uneven, as part of a garment: often with *up*. **—*v.t.*** 3. *Informal* To increase (prices, etc.): usu. with *up*. **—*n.*** 1. A long walk. 2. *Informal* An increase. [? Var. of HITCH] **—hi′ker** *n.*

hi·lar·i·ous (hi·lâr′ē·əs, hī-) *adj.* Boisterously gay or cheerful. [< Gk. *hilaros* cheerful] —**hi·lar′i·ous·ly** *adv.* —**hi·lar′i·ous·ness** *n.*

hi·lar·i·ty (hi·lar′ə·tē, hī-) *n. pl.* **·ties** Noisy, exuberant gaiety.

hill (hil) *n.* 1. An elevation of the earth's surface, not as high as a mountain. 2. A heap or pile: often used in combination: a *molehill.* 3. A small mound of earth. —*v.t.* To surround or cover with small mounds of earth, as potatoes. [OE *hyll*] —**hill′er** *n.*

hill·bil·ly (hil′bil′ē) *n. pl.* **·lies** *Informal* A person coming from or living in the mountains or a backwoods area, esp. in the southern U.S.

hill·ock (hil′ək) *n.* A small hill or mound. —**hill′ock·y** *adj.*

hill·side (hil′sīd′) *n.* The side or slope of a hill.

hill·top (hil′top′) *n.* The summit of a hill.

hill·y (hil′ē) *adj.* **hill·i·er, hill·i·est** 1. Having many hills. 2. Steep. —**hill′i·ness** *n.*

hilt (hilt) *n.* The handle of a sword, dagger, etc. —**to the hilt** Thoroughly; fully. [OE]

him (him) *pron.* The objective case of the pronoun *he.*

him·self (him·self′) *pron.* A form of the third person singular masculine pronoun, used: 1. As a reflexive: He cut *himself.* 2. As an intensive form of *he*: He *himself* will do it. 3. As a designation of a usual state: He is not *himself.*

hind[1] (hīnd) *adj.* **hind·er, hind·most** or **hind·er·most** At or toward the rear part; posterior. [OE *hindan*]

hind[2] (hīnd) *n.* The female of the red deer, esp. when fully grown. [OE]

hind·er[1] (hin′dər) *v.t.* 1. To interfere with the progress of; impede; obstruct. 2. To prevent from acting or occurring; deter; thwart. [OE *hinder* behind] —**hin′der·er** *n.*

hind·er[2] (hīn′dər) Comparative of HIND[1]. —*adj.* Pertaining to or situated at the rear or posterior end. [OE]

Hin·di (hin′dē) *n.* 1. The principal language of northern India, belonging to the Indic branch of the Indo-Iranian languages. 2. A form of literary Hindustani used by Hindus. [< Hind. *Hind* India < OPersian *Hindu* land of the Indus < Skt. *sindhu* river, the Indus]

hind·most (hīnd′mōst′) Superlative of HIND[1]. Also **hind′er·most′** (hīn′dər-).

hind·quar·ter (hīnd′kwôr′tər) *n.* 1. One of the two back quarters of a carcass of beef, lamb, etc. 2. *pl.* The rump.

hin·drance (hin′drəns) *n.* 1. The act of hindering. 2. One who or that which hinders.

hind·sight (hīnd′sīt′) *n.* 1. The understanding of an event after it has happened. 2. The rear sight of a gun, rifle, etc.

Hin·du (hin′dōō) *n.* 1. A native of India who speaks one of the Indic languages. 2. One whose religion is Hinduism. —*adj.* Of, pertaining to, or characteristic of the Hindus or Hinduism.

Hin·du·ism (hin′dōō·iz′əm) *n.* The religion of the Hindus of India, characterized by worship of Brahma.

Hin·du·sta·ni (hin′dōō·stan′ē) *n.* The major dialect of Hindi, the official language and general medium of communication in India. —**Hin′du·sta′ni** *adj.*

hinge (hinj) *n.* 1. A device consisting of two parts that form a movable joint on which a door, gate, lid, etc., swings or turns. 2. A natural movable joint connecting two parts, as the shells of a bivalve. —*v.* **hinged, hing·ing** *v.t.* 1. To attach by or equip with a hinge. —*v.i.* 2. To depend or be contingent: with *on.* [ME *hengen*]

hin·ny (hin′ē) *n. pl.* **·nies** The hybrid offspring of a stallion and a she-ass. Compare MULE[1]. [< L *hinnus*]

hint (hint) *n.* 1. An indirect suggestion or implication. 2. A slight indication or trace. —*v.t.* 1. To suggest indirectly; imply. —*v.i.* 2. To give a slight indication or suggestion: with *at.* [OE *hentan*]

hin·ter·land (hin′tər·land′) *n.* 1. A region adjacent to a coast. 2. A region remote from urban areas. [< G]

hip[1] (hip) *n.* 1. The part of the human body projecting below the waist on either side, formed by the edge of the pelvis and the upper part of the femur. 2. An analogous part in animals. [OE *hype*]

hip[2] (hip) *n.* The ripened fruit of a rose. [OE *hēope*]

hip[3] (hip) *adj.* *Slang* Aware; informed.

hip·bone (hip′bōn′) *n.* The innominate bone.

hip·pie (hip′ē) *n.* One of a group of chiefly young people whose unconventional dress and behavior and use of drugs express withdrawal from middle-class life and indifference to its values. Also **hip′py.** [Var. of HIPSTER]

hip·po (hip′ō) *n. pl.* **·pos** *Informal* A hippopotamus.

hip·po·drome (hip′ə·drōm) *n.* 1. An arena or similar structure for horse shows, circuses, etc. 2. In ancient Greece and Rome, a course or track for horse races and chariot races. [< Gk. *hippos* horse + *dromos* running, course]

hip·po·pot·a·mus (hip′ə·pot′ə·məs) *n. pl.* **·mus·es** or **·mi** (-mī) A large, chiefly aquatic, herbivorous mammal, native to Africa, having short legs, a massive, thick-skinned, hairless body, and a very broad muzzle. [< Gk. *hippos* horse + *potamos* river]

hip·ster (hip′stər) *n.* *Slang* One who is aware or informed esp. about jazz music. [< HIP[3] + -STER]

hire (hīr) *v.t.* **hired, hir·ing** 1. To obtain the services of (a person) for payment. 2. To acquire the use of (a thing) for a fee; rent. 3. To grant the use or services of (someone or something) in return for payment: often with *out.* —**to hire out** To provide one's services in return for payment. —*n.* 1. Payment for labor, services, etc. 2. The act of hiring, or the condition of being hired. [OE *hȳr*] —**hir′er** *n.*

hire·ling (hīr′ling) *n.* One who serves for hire, esp. for mercenary reasons.

hir·sute (hûr′sōōt, hûr·sōōt′) *adj.* Covered with hair. [< L *hirsutus* rough] —**hir′·sute·ness** *n.*

his (hiz) *pron.* 1. The possessive case of the pronoun *he,* used predicatively: This room is *his.* 2. The one or ones belonging or pertaining to him: Her book is better than *his.* —*pronominal adj.* The possessive case of the pronoun *he,* used attributively: *his* book. [OE]

His·pan·ic (his·pan′ik) *adj.* Pertaining to the people, language, or culture of Spain or Latin America.

hiss (his) *v.i.* 1. To produce a sibilant sound. 2. To utter such a sound as an expression of disapproval or derision. —*v.t.* 3. To utter with a hiss. 4. To express disapproval of by hissing. [ME *hissen*, imit.] —**hiss** *n.*

his·ta·mine (his′tə·mēn) *n. Biochem.* A white, crystalline substance, found in plant and animal tissues and released in allergic reactions. —**his·ta·min·ic** (his′tə·min′ik) *adj.*

histo- *combining form* Tissue. Also, before vowels, **hist-**. [< Gk. *histos* web]

his·tol·o·gy (his·tol′ə·jē) *n. pl.* **·gies** The branch of biology that treats of the microscopic structure of tissues. —**his·tol′o·gist** *n.*

his·to·ri·an (his·tôr′ē·ən) *n.* A writer of or authority on history.

his·tor·ic (his·tôr′ik, -tor′-) *adj.* 1. Important or famous in history: *historic* dates. 2. Memorable; significant: a *historic* occasion. 3. Historical.

his·tor·i·cal (his·tôr′i·kəl, -tor′-) *adj.* 1. Belonging to history: a *historical* event. 2. Concerned with or treating the events of history: a *historical* account. 3. Based on known facts as distinct from legendary or fictitious accounts. —**his·tor′i·cal·ly** *adv.*

his·to·ri·og·ra·pher (his·tôr′ē·og′rə·fər) *n.* A historian or chronicler, esp. an official one. —**his·to′ri·og′ra·phy** *n.*

his·to·ry (his′tə·rē, his′trē) *n. pl.* **·ries** 1. That branch of knowledge concerned with past events. 2. A record or account, usu. written and in chronological order, of past events. 3. Past events in general. 4. An unusual or noteworthy past. 5. A long narrative or story. [< Gk. *histōr* knowing]

his·tri·on·ic (his′trē·on′ik) *adj.* 1. Of or pertaining to actors or acting. 2. Overly dramatic. [< L *histrio, -onis* actor] —**his′tri·on′i·cal·ly** *adv.*

his·tri·on·ics (his′trē·on′iks) *n.pl.* (*construed as sing. in def. 1*) 1. Theatrical art or performances. 2. Feigned emotional display.

hit (hit) *v.* **hit, hit·ting** *v.t.* 1. To give a blow to; strike. 2. To reach with a missile, hurled or falling object, etc. 3. To collide with. 4. To cause to make forcible contact; bump. 5. To set in motion or propel by striking. 6. To arrive at, achieve, or discover. 7. To affect adversely; cause to suffer. 8. In baseball, to succeed in making (a specified kind of base hit). 9. *Informal* To begin to journey on: to *hit* the road. 10. *Informal* To arrive at or reach (a place). —*v.i.* 11. To deliver a blow; strike. 12. To make forcible contact; bump. 13. To come or light; happen: followed by *on* or *upon*: to *hit* on the right answer. —**to hit it off** To be friendly; get along well. —*n.* 1. A blow, stroke, shot, etc., that reaches its target. 2. A forceful impact; collision. 3. A success. 4. In baseball, a base hit. 5. *Slang* A murder ordered by a criminal gang. 6. *Slang* A dose of a narcotic drug. [OE *hittan* < ON *hitta* to come upon] —**hit′ter** *n.*

hit-and-run (hit′ən·run′) *adj.* Designating or caused by the driver of a vehicle who illegally continues on his way after hitting a pedestrian or another vehicle.

hitch (hich) *v.t.* 1. To fasten or tie, esp. temporarily. 2. To harness to a vehicle: sometimes with *up*. 3. To move, pull, raise, etc., with a jerk: often with *up*. 4. *Slang* To obtain (a ride) by hitchhiking. —*v.i.* 5. To move with a jerk: to *hitch* forward. 6. To become fastened, caught, or entangled. —*n.* 1. An obstacle; halt; delay. 2. A sudden, jerking movement; tug. 3. A fastening or device used to fasten. 4. *Informal* A period of enlistment in military service. 5. *Slang* In hitchhiking, a ride. [ME *hicchen*]

hitch·hike (hich′hīk′) *v.i.* **·hiked, ·hik·ing** To travel by signaling for rides in passing vehicles. —**hitch′hik′er** *n.*

hith·er (hith′ər) *adv.* To or toward this place: Come *hither*. —*adj.* Situated toward this side; nearer. [OE *hider*]

hith·er·to (hith′ər·to͞o′) *adv.* Until this time.

hit man A professional assassin hired by a criminal gang.

hit-or-miss (hit′ər·mis′) *adj.* Haphazard; careless.

Hit·tite (hit′īt) *n.* 1. One of an ancient people who established a powerful empire in Asia Minor and northern Syria about 2000–1200 B.C. 2. Their language. [< Hebrew *Hittīm*] —**Hit′tite** *adj.*

hive (hīv) *n.* 1. An artificial structure serving as a habitation for bees; beehive. 2. A colony of bees inhabiting a hive; swarm. 3. A place astir with industrious activity. —*v.t.* **hived, hiv·ing** To induce (bees) to enter into or collect in a hive. [OE *hȳf*]

hives (hīvz) *n.pl.* (*construed as sing. or pl.*) Any of various skin disorders characterized by swellings, eruptions, itching, etc. [Origin unknown]

ho (hō) *interj.* An exclamation, often repeated, expressing exultation, derision, etc.

hoa·gy (hō′gē) *n.* Hero (def. 5). Also **hoa′gie.**

hoard (hôrd) *n.* An accumulation of something stored away for safekeeping or future use. —*v.t. & v.i.* To amass and store or hide (money, valuables, etc.). [OE *hord* treasure] —**hoard′er** *n.* —**hoard′ing** *n.*

hoar·frost (hôr′frôst′) *n.* Frost whitening the surface on which it is formed.

hoar·hound (hôr′hound′) See HOREHOUND.

hoarse (hôrs) *adj.* 1. Deep, harsh, and grating in sound. 2. Having a husky, gruff, or croaking voice. [OE *hā(r)s*] —**hoarse′ly** *adv.* —**hoarse′ness** *n.*

hoar·y (hôr′ē) *adj.* **hoar·i·er, hoar·i·est** 1. Ancient; aged. 2. Gray or white with age. 3. White or whitish in color. [OE *hār* gray-haired] —**hoar′i·ness** *n.*

hoax (hōks) *n.* A trick or deception, usu. on the public. —*v.t.* To deceive by a hoax. —**hoax′er** *n.*

hob[1] (hob) *n.* A projection on the interior of a fireplace, serving as a shelf on which to keep things warm.

hob[2] (hob) *n.* A hobgoblin or elf. —**to play (or raise) hob** To cause mischief or confusion. [Orig. a nickname for *Robert, Robin*]

hob·ble (hob′əl) *v.* **·bled, ·bling** *v.i.* 1. To move clumsily or with a limp. —*v.t.* 2. To hamper the free movement of, as a horse, by fettering the legs. —*n.* 1. A clumsy or limping gait. 2. A rope, etc., used to hobble the legs of an animal. —**hob′bler** *n.*

hob·by (hob′ē) *n. pl.* **·bies** An activity or

pursuit undertaken for pleasure during one's leisure; avocation. [< HOBBYHORSE]
hob·by·horse (hob'ē·hôrs') *n.* 1. A rocking horse. 2. A toy consisting of a stick surmounted by a horse's head. [ME *Hobby, Robbie,* common name of a draft horse]
hob·gob·lin (hob'gob'lin) *n.* 1. An imaginary cause of terror or dread. 2. A mischievous imp.
hob·nail (hob'nāl') *n.* A nail used to stud the soles of heavy shoes against wear or slipping. —**hob'nailed'** *adj.*
hob·nob (hob'nob') *v.i.* ·**nobbed,** ·**nob·bing** To associate in a friendly manner; be on intimate terms. [OE *habban* to have + *nabban* to have not]
ho·bo (hō'bō) *n. pl.* ·**boes** or ·**bos** 1. A tramp. 2. An itinerant, usu. unskilled worker. [< *Hey, Bo,* a vagabond's greeting]
hock[1] (hok) *n.* The joint of the hind leg in the horse, ox, etc., corresponding to the ankle in man. [OE *hōh* heel]
hock[2] (hok) *n.* Any white Rhine wine.
hock[3] (hok) *v.t. Informal* To pawn. —**in hock** *Informal* 1. In pawn. 2. In debt. [< Du. *hok* prison, debt]
hock·ey (hok'ē) *n.* 1. A game played on ice (**ice hockey**), in which players, wearing skates and wielding sticks, try to drive a disk (puck) into the opponent's goal. 2. A similar game played on a field (**field hockey**), in which a small ball is used instead of a puck. [< *hock* bent stick, var. of HOOK]
hock·shop (hok'shop') *n. Informal* A pawnshop. Also **hock shop.**
ho·cus-po·cus (hō'kəs·pō'kəs) *n.* 1. A verbal formula used in conjuring or sleight of hand. 2. Any trickery or deception. —*v.t. & v.i.* -**po·cused** or ·**cussed,** -**po·cus·ing** or ·**cus·sing** To trick; cheat. [A sham Latin phrase]
hod (hod) *n.* 1. A trough rested on the shoulder, to carry bricks, etc. 2. A coal-scuttle. [< OF *hotte* pannier]
hodge·podge (hoj'poj') *n.* A jumbled mixture or collection.
Hodg·kin's disease (hoj'kinz) *Pathol.* A generally fatal disease characterized by progressive enlargement of the lymph nodes, lymphoid tissue, and spleen. [after Dr. Thomas *Hodgkin,* 1798–1866, English physician, who described it]
hoe (hō) *n.* An implement for weeding, etc., having a flat blade attached to a long handle. —*v.t. & v.i.* **hoed, hoe·ing** To dig with a hoe. [< OF *hove* < OHG *houwan* to cut]
hoe-down (hō'doun') *n. Informal* A lively country dance or square dance; also, its music. [Origin uncertain]
hog (hog, hôg) *n.* 1. A pig, esp. one weighing more than 120 pounds and raised for the market. 2. *Informal* **a** A gluttonous or filthy person. **b** A selfish or greedy person. —*v.t.* **hogged, hog·ging** *Slang* To take more than one's share of; grab selfishly. [OE *hogg*] —**hog'gish** *adj.*
ho·gan (hō'gon, -gən) *n.* A Navaho Indian dwelling, made of timbers covered with earth. [< Navaho *qoghan* house]
hog·back (hog'bak', hôg'-) *n. Geol.* A sharp ridge with steep sides.
hogs·head (hogz'hed', hôgz'-) *n.* 1. A large cask, esp. one with a capacity of 63 to 140 gallons. 2. A liquid measure, esp. one equal to 63 gallons, or 8.42 cubic feet.
hog-tie (hog'tī', hôg'-) *v.t.* -**tied,** -**ty·ing** or -**tie·ing** 1. To tie together four feet, or the hands and feet of. 2. *Informal* To render (a person) ineffective or helpless. Also **hog'tie'.**
hog·wash (hog'wosh', -wôsh', hôg'-) *n.* 1. Kitchen refuse, etc., fed hogs. 2. Any nonsense; insincere talk.
hog-wild (hog'wīld') *adj.* Lacking in restraint.
hoi pol·loi (hoi' pə·loi') The common people; the masses. [< Gk., the many]
hoist (hoist) *v.t.* To raise or lift, esp. by mechanical means. —*n.* 1. Any machine for raising large objects. 2. The act of hoisting. [? < Du. *hijschen*]
ho·kum (hō'kəm) *n. Slang* Nonsense; bunk. [Alter. of HOCUS(-POCUS)]
hold[1] (hōld) *v.* **held, held, hold·ing** *v.t.* 1. To take and keep in the hand, arms, etc.; clasp. 2. To sustain, as in position; support: to *hold* one's head high. 3. To contain or enclose: The barrel *holds* ten gallons. 4. To keep under control; restrain; also, to retain possession of. 5. To keep in reserve. 6. To have the benefit or responsibilities of: to *hold* office. 7. To regard in a specified manner: to *hold* someone dear. 8. To bind by contract or duty: *Hold* him to his agreement. 9. *Law* **a** To adjudge; decide. **b** To have title to. 10. To maintain in the mind; harbor: to *hold* a grudge. 11. To engage in; carry on: to *hold* a conference. —*v.i.* 12. To maintain a grip or grasp. 13. To withstand strain or remain unbroken: The rope *holds.* 14. To remain in effect. 15. To adhere, as to a principle or purpose; cling. —**to hold back** 1. To keep in check; restrain. 2. To refrain. 3. To retain. —**to hold down** 1. To suppress; keep under control. 2. *Informal* To be employed at (a job). —**to hold forth** To preach or speak at great length. —**to hold out** 1. To stretch forth; offer. 2. To last; endure: Our supplies *held out.* 3. To continue resistance. —**to hold over** 1. To put off to a later time. 2. To remain or retain beyond the expected limit, as in office. —**to hold up** 1. To support; prop. 2. To exhibit to view. 3. To delay; stop. 4. *Informal* To endure; remain firm. 5. *Informal* To stop so as to rob. 6. *Informal* To charge too high a price. —**to hold water** *Informal* To be believable or sound, as an argument. —*n.* 1. The act or method of grasping, as with the hands. 2. A controlling force or influence. 3. *Law* A holding or tenure: used in combination: *freehold.* [OE *haldan*]
hold[2] (hōld) *n. Naut.* The space below the decks of a vessel, where cargo is stowed. [< HOLE or < MDu. *hol*]
hold·er (hōl'dər) *n.* 1. One who or that which holds. 2. An owner; possessor: chiefly in compounds: *householder.*
hold·ing (hōl'ding) *n.* 1. The act of one who or that which holds. 2. A piece of land rented. 3. *Often pl.* Property held by legal right, esp. stocks or bonds.
holding company A company that invests in the stocks of one or more other corporations, which it may thus control.
holding pattern A course flown by an aircraft over or near an airport while waiting to land.

hold·o·ver (hōld′ō′vər) *n. Informal* An incumbent continuing in office after his term has expired.

hold·up (hōld′up′) *n.* 1. Stoppage or delay. 2. *Informal* A waylaying and robbing.

hole (hōl) *n.* 1. A cavity in a solid mass or body; pit. 2. An opening in anything; aperture. 3. An animal's burrow or enclosed hiding place. 4. Any small, crowded, squalid place. 5. A defect; fault. 6. *Informal* An awkward situation. 7. In golf: **a** A small cavity into which the ball is played. **b** A division of the course, usu. one of nine or eighteen. **—hole in one** In golf, the sinking of the ball into a hole with one drive from the tee. **—in the hole** *Informal* In debt. **—*v.t.* & *v.i.* holed, hol·ing** To make a hole in. **—to hole up** To hide away; isolate oneself. [OE *hol*] **—hole′y** *adj.*

hol·i·day (hol′ə·dā) *n.* 1. A day appointed by law for suspension of business in commemoration of some event. 2. Any day of rest. 3. A day for special religious observance. 4. *pl. Chiefly Brit.* A vacation. **—*v.i.*** *Chiefly Brit.* To spend a holiday or vacation. [OE *hālig dæg* holy day]

ho·li·ness (hō′lē·nis) *n.* 1. The state or quality of being holy. 2. *cap.* A title or form of address for the Pope: preceded by *His* or *Your.*

ho·lism (hō′liz·əm) *n.* The theory that the whole, esp. a living organism, is more than the sum of its parts. **—ho·lis′tic** *adj.*

hol·lan·daise sauce (hol′ən·dāz′) A creamy sauce of butter, egg yolks, and lemon juice served with vegetables, etc. [< F, fem. of *hollandais* of Holland]

Hol·land·er (hol′ən·dər) *n.* A native or citizen of the Netherlands; a Dutchman.

hol·ler (hol′ər) *v.t.* & *v.i. Informal* To call out loudly. **—*n.*** A loud shout; yell.

hol·low (hol′ō) *adj.* 1. Having a cavity within; enclosing an empty space. 2. Having a deep opening; concave. 3. Sunken; fallen: *hollow* cheeks. 4. Deep or muffled in tone. 5. Not genuine; meaningless; empty. **—*n.*** 1. A cavity or empty space in anything; depression; hole. 2. A valley. **—*v.t.* & *v.i.*** To make or become hollow: usu. with *out.* [OE *holh*] **—hol′low·ness** *n.*

hol·low·ware (hol′ō·wâr′) *n.* Utensils, esp. of silver, that are hollow.

hol·ly (hol′ē) *n. pl.* **·lies** A tree or shrub having red berries and dark green, glossy leaves edged with spines. [OE *holen*]

hol·ly·hock (hol′ē·hok) *n.* A tall, cultivated plant of the mallow family, having spikes of showy flowers. [ME *holi* holy + *hoc* mallow]

hol·mi·um (hōl′mē·əm) *n.* A metallic element (symbol Ho) of the lanthanide series. [after *Holmia,* Latinized name of Stockholm, Sweden]

hol·o·caust (hol′ə·kôst) *n.* Wholesale destruction and loss of life, esp. by fire. **—the Holocaust** The genocidal destruction of Jews by Nazi Germany and its allies. [< Gk. *holos* whole + *kaustos* burnt]

hol·o·gram (hol′ə·gram) *n.* A picture made by holography.

hol·o·graph (hol′ə·graf) *adj.* Denoting a document, as a will, in the handwriting of the person whose signature it bears. **—*n.*** A document so written. [< Gk. *holos* entire + *graphein* to write]

hol·o·graph·ic (hol′ə·graf′ik) *adj.* 1. Pertaining to holographs. 2. Pertaining to holograms. **—hol′o·graph′i·cal·ly** *adv.*

ho·log·ra·phy (ho·log′rə·fē) *n.* A technique of producing a three-dimensional picture on photographic film using laser beams and without the aid of a camera. [< Gk. *holos* whole + -GRAPHY]

Hol·stein (hōl′stīn, -stēn) *n.* A breed of black-and-white cattle. Also **Hol′stein-Frie′sian** (-frē′zhən).

hol·ster (hōl′stər) *n.* A leather case for a pistol, generally worn on a belt or attached to a saddle. [< Du.]

ho·ly (hō′lē) *adj.* **·li·er, ·li·est** 1. Having a divine origin; associated with God; sacred. 2. Having spiritual and moral worth. 3. Designated for religious worship; consecrated: *holy* days. 4. Evoking or meriting reverence or awe: a *holy* man. [OE *hālig*]

Holy Communion The Eucharist.

Holy Ghost The third person of the Trinity. Also **Holy Spirit.**

holy orders *Eccl.* The rite of admission to the priesthood or ministry; ordination.

ho·ly·stone (hō′lē·stōn′) *n.* A piece of sandstone used to scour the decks of a ship. **—*v.t.* ·stoned, ·ston·ing** To scrub with a holystone. [Said to be used to clean decks for Sunday]

hom·age (hom′ij, om′-) *n.* 1. Respect or honor given or shown. 2. A payment, etc., indicating allegiance. [< OF *hommage* < LL *homo* vassal, man]

hom·burg (hom′bûrg) *n.* A felt hat having a brim slightly turned up at the sides, and the crown indented lengthwise. Also **Hom′·burg.** [after *Homburg,* Germany]

home (hōm) *n.* 1. A house or other dwelling where one lives. 2. A family or other group dwelling together: a happy *home.* 3. The country, region, city, etc., where one lives. 4. A peaceful or restful place; haven. 5. The natural environment of an animal. 6. The place in which something originates or is found: New Orleans is the *home* of jazz. 7. A shelter for care of the aged, orphaned, needy, etc. 8. In some games, esp. baseball, the goal or base that must be reached in order to win or score. **—*adj.*** 1. Of or pertaining to one's home, country, etc.; domestic. 2. Being at the base of operations or place of origin: the *home* office. **—*adv.*** 1. To or at one's home. 2. To the place or point intended; to the mark. 3. Deeply and intimately; to the heart. **—*v.* homed, hom·ing** *v.t.* 1. To cause (an aircraft or guided missile) to proceed toward a target by means of radio waves, radar, etc. **—*v.i.*** 2. To go home; return home. 3. To be directed toward a target by automatic devices: said of guided missiles: usu. with *in* or *in on.* [OE *hām*] **—home′less** *adj.*

home·bod·y (hōm′bod′ē) *n. pl.* **·bod·ies** One who prefers to stay at home or whose main interest is in the home.

home-brew (hōm′brōō′) *n.* An alcoholic beverage made at home, as for home use. **—home′-brewed′** *adj.*

home·com·ing (hōm′kum′ing) *n.* 1. A return to one's home. 2. In colleges, an annual alumni celebration.

home economics The science of home management.

home·land (hōm′land′) *n.* The country of one's birth or allegiance.
home·ly (hōm′lē) *adj.* **·li·er, ·li·est** 1. Having a familiar, everyday character. 2. Having plain or ugly features. 3. Lacking in refinement. **—home′li·ness** *n.*
home·made (hōm′mād′) *adj.* 1. Made at home. 2. Simply or crudely fashioned.
home·mak·er (hōm′mā′kər) *n.* One in charge of managing one's own home, as a housewife. **—home′mak′ing** *n.*
homeo- *combining form* Like; similar: *homeostasis.* [< Gk. *homoios* similar]
ho·me·op·a·thy (hō′mē·op′ə·thē) *n.* A system of therapy using minute doses of medicines that produce the symptoms of the disease treated. **—ho′me·o·path′** (-ə·path′) *n.* **—ho′me·o·path′ic** (-ə·path′ik) *adj.*
ho·me·o·sta·sis (hō′mē·ə·stā′sis) *n.* The tendency of an organism or group to maintain a uniform and beneficial physiological or social stability within and between its parts. **—ho′me·o·stat′ic** (-stat′ik) *adj.*
home plate In baseball, the marker at which a player stands when batting, and to which he returns in scoring a run.
hom·er (hō′mər) *n. Informal* 1. In baseball, a home run. 2. A homing pigeon.
home rule Self-government in local affairs.
home run In baseball, a hit that permits the batter to touch all the bases and score a run.
home·sick (hōm′sik′) *adj.* Unhappy or ill through longing for home; nostalgic. **—home′sick′ness** *n.*
home·spun (hōm′spun′) *adj.* 1. Spun at home. 2. Plain and simple; unsophisticated. 3. Made of homespun. **—***n.* 1. Fabric woven at home or by hand. 2. A rough, loosely woven fabric similar to this.
home·stead (hōm′sted) *n.* 1. A house and its land, etc. 2. A tract of public land acquired and occupied under U.S. law. **—***v.t. & v.i.* To settle on (land) under provisions described in U.S. law. **—home′stead′er** *n.*
home·stretch (hōm′strech′) *n.* 1. The straight portion of a racetrack forming the final approach to the finish. 2. The last stage of any journey or endeavor.
home·ward (hōm′wərd) *adv.* Toward home. Also **home′wards.** **—***adj.* Directed toward home.
home·work (hōm′wûrk′) *n.* Work done at home, esp. school work.
home·y (hō′mē) *adj.* **hom·i·er, hom·i·est** Suggesting the comforts of home. **—home′y·ness** or **hom′i·ness** *n.*
hom·i·cide (hom′ə·sīd, hō′mə-) *n.* 1. The killing of any human being by another. 2. A person who has killed another. [< L *homo* man + -CIDE] **—hom′i·ci′dal** *adj.*
hom·i·ly (hom′ə·lē) *n. pl.* **·lies** 1. A sermon. 2. A solemn, often lengthy speech on morals or conduct. [< Gk. *homilos* assembly] **—hom·i·let·ic** (hom′ə·let′ik) *adj.*
hom·ing (hō′ming) *adj.* 1. Returning home. 2. Helping or causing an aircraft, missile, etc., to home.
homing pigeon A pigeon capable of making its way home from great distances: also called *carrier pigeon.*
hom·i·ny (hom′ə·nē) *n.* Kernels of dried, hulled white corn, prepared as a food by boiling. [< Algonquian *rockahominie* parched corn]
hominy grits Grits (def. 2).
homo- *combining form* Same; like: opposed to *hetero-.* [< Gk. *homo-* < *homos*]
ho·mo·ge·ne·ous (hō′mə·jē′nē·əs, hom′ə-) *adj.* 1. Having the same composition, structure, or character throughout; uniform. 2. Similar or identical in nature or form; like. [< Gk. *homos* same + *genos* race] **—ho′mo·ge′ne·ous·ly** *adv.* **—ho·mo·ge·ne·i·ty** (hō′mə·jə·nē′ə·tē, hom′ə-), **ho′mo·ge′ne·ous·ness** *n.*
ho·mog·en·ize (hə·moj′ə·nīz, hō′mə·jə·nīz′) *v.t.* **·ized, ·iz·ing** 1. To make homogeneous. 2. To process, as milk, so as to break up fat globules and disperse them uniformly. **—ho·mog′en·i·za′tion** *n.* **—ho·mog′en·iz′er** *n.*
hom·o·graph (hom′ə·graf, hō′mə-) *n.* A word identical with another in spelling, but differing from it in origin, meaning, or pronunciation, as *wind,* an air current, and *wind,* to coil. [< Gk. *homos* same + *graphein* to write] **—hom′o·graph′ic** *adj.*
ho·mol·o·gous (hō·mol′ə·gəs) *adj.* 1. Similar or related in structure, position, proportion, value, etc. 2. *Biol.* Corresponding in structure or origin: The foreleg of a horse and the wing of a bird are *homologous:* distinguished from *analagous.* [< Gk. *homos* same + *logos* measure, proportion]
ho·mol·o·gy (hō·mol′ə·jē) *n. pl.* **·gies** 1. The state or quality of being homologous. 2. A homologous relationship.
hom·o·nym (hom′ə·nim) *n.* 1. A word identical with another in pronunciation but differing from it in origin, spelling, and meaning, as *fair* and *fare, read* and *reed:* also called *homophone.* 2. A word identical with another in spelling and pronunciation, but differing from it in origin and meaning, as *butter,* the food, and *butter,* one who butts. [< Gk. *homos* same + *onyma* name] **—hom′o·nym′ic** *adj.*
hom·o·phone (hom′ə·fōn) *n.* A homonym (def. 1). [< Gk. *homos* same + *phōnē* sound] **—ho·moph·o·nous** (hō·mof′ə·nəs) *adj.*
Ho·mo sa·pi·ens (hō′mō sā′pē·enz) The scientific name for modern man. [< L *homo* man + *sapiens* wise]
ho·mo·sex·u·al (hō′mə·sek′shōō·əl) *adj.* Of or having sexual desire for persons of the same sex. **—***n.* A homosexual individual. **—ho′mo·sex′u·al′i·ty** (-al′ə·tē) *n.*
ho·mun·cu·lus (hō·mung′kyə·ləs) *n. pl.* **·li** (-lī) A little man; dwarf. [< L *homo* man] **—ho·mun′cu·lar** *adj.*
hon·cho (hon′chō) *n. Slang* One in charge; a boss. [< Jap. *han* squad + *chō* leader]
hone (hōn) *n.* A fine, compact whetstone used for sharpening edged tools, razors, etc. **—***v.t.* **honed, hon·ing** To sharpen, as a razor, on a hone. [OE *hān* stone]
hon·est (on′ist) *adj.* 1. Truthful, forthright, and just; full of integrity. 2. Not false or misleading: an *honest* statement. 3. Having full worth or value; genuine. 4. Performed or earned in a conscientious manner. 5. Sincere; frank. [< L *honos* honor] **—hon′es·ty** *n.*
hon·est·ly (on′ist·lē) *adv.* 1. In an honest manner. 2. Really; truly; indeed: *Honestly,* I'll go.
hon·ey (hun′ē) *n. pl.* **hon·eys** 1. A sweet, viscous substance made by bees from nectar gathered from flowers. 2. Sweetness. 3. Dar-

ling: a term of endearment. 4. *Slang* Something regarded as a superior example of its kind: a *honey* of a car. —*v.t.* **hon·eyed** or **hon·ied, hon·ey·ing** 1. To sweeten with or as with honey. 2. To talk in a loving or flattering manner to. —*adj.* Of or like honey. [OE *hunig*]

hon·ey·bee (hun′ē·bē′) *n.* A bee that produces honey.

hon·ey·comb (hun′ē·kōm′) *n.* 1. A structure consisting of series of hexagonal wax cells, made by bees for the storage of honey, pollen, or their eggs. 2. Any similar structure. —*v.t.* To fill with small holes or cavities; riddle.

hon·ey·dew (hun′ē·dōō′) *n.* A sweetish substance secreted by aphids and other insects.

honeydew melon A melon having a smooth, white skin and sweet, greenish pulp.

hon·eyed (hun′ēd) *adj.* 1. Full of, consisting of, or resembling honey. 2. Sweet, soothing, or flattering.

honey locust A large, thorny North American tree bearing long pods.

hon·ey·moon (hun′ē·mōōn′) *n.* 1. A vacation spent by a newly married couple. 2. The first, happy period of a marriage. 3. *Informal* The early, happy period of any relationship. —*v.i.* To spend one's honeymoon.

hon·ey·suck·le (hun′ē·suk′əl) *n.* 1. A climbing shrub having white, buff, or crimson flowers. 2. Any of a number of similar fragrant plants. [OE *hunisūce*]

honk (hôngk, hongk) *n.* 1. The sound made by a goose. 2. A sound resembling this, as that of an automobile horn. [Imit.] —**honk** *v.t. & v.i.* —**honk′er** *n.*

hon·ky-tonk (hông′kē·tôngk′, hong′kē·tongk′) *n. Slang* A noisy, squalid bar or dance hall. [Prob. imit.]

hon·or (on′ər) *n.* 1. High regard, respect, or esteem. 2. Glory; fame; credit. 3. *Usu. pl.* An outward token, sign, act, etc., of regard or esteem. 4. A reputation for high standards of conduct. 5. A cause or source of esteem or pride. 6. A privilege or pleasure. 7. In bridge, one of the five highest cards of a suit. 8. *cap.* A title or form of address for a judge, mayor, etc.: preceded by *Your, His,* or *Her.* —**to do the honors** 1. To act as host or hostess. 2. To perform any of various social courtesies, as proposing toasts, etc. —*v.t.* 1. To regard with honor or respect. 2. To treat with courtesy. 3. To confer an honor upon; dignify. 4. To accept or pay, as a check or draft. Also *Brit.* **hon′our.** [< L]

hon·or·a·ble (on′ər·ə·bəl) *adj.* 1. Worthy of honor or respect. 2. Conferring honor or credit. 3. Having eminence or high rank. 4. Morally correct; upright. 5. *cap.* A formal title of courtesy for certain important officials, as cabinet members, justices of the Supreme Court, etc.: preceded by *The.* Also *Brit.* **hon′our·a·ble.** —**hon′or·a·bly** *adv.*

hon·o·rar·i·um (on′ə·râr′ē·əm) *n. pl.* **·rar·i·ums** or **·rar·i·a** (-râr′ē·ə) A payment given, as to a professional man, for services rendered when law or propriety forbids a set fee. [< L *honorarium* honorary]

hon·or·ar·y (on′ə·rer′ē) *adj.* 1. Designating an office, title, etc., bestowed as an honor, without the customary powers, duties, prerequisites, etc. 2. Bringing, conferred in, or denoting honor. [< L *honorarius*]

hon·or·if·ic (on′ə·rif′ik) *adj.* Conferring or implying honor or respect. [< L *honor* honor + *facere* to make]

hood[1] (hŏŏd) *n.* 1. A covering for the head and back of the neck, sometimes forming part of a garment. 2. Anything resembling a hood in form or use; as: **a** The movable metal cover protecting the engine of an automobile. **b** A projecting cover for a ventilator, etc. 3. *Zool.* In certain animals, as the cobra, the folds of skin near the head, capable of expansion. —*v.t.* To cover or furnish with or as with a hood. [OE *hōd*] —**hood′ed** *adj.*

hood[2] (hŏŏd) *n. Slang* A hoodlum. [< HOODLUM]

-hood *suffix of nouns* 1. Condition or quality of; state of being: *babyhood, falsehood.* 2. Class or totality of those having a certain character: *priesthood.* [OE *hād* state, condition]

hood·lum (hŏŏd′ləm) *n.* 1. A young street rowdy or tough. 2. A thug or ruffian. [? < dial. G *hodalum* rowdy]

hoo·doo (hōō′dōō) *n.* 1. Voodoo. 2. *Informal* One who or that which brings bad luck; a jinx. —*v.t. Informal* To bring bad luck to. [Var. of VOODOO]

hood·wink (hŏŏd′wingk′) *v.t.* To trick or deceive; cheat. —**hood′wink′er** *n.*

hoo·ey (hōō′ē) *n. & interj. Slang* Nonsense.

hoof (hŏŏf, hōōf) *n. pl.* **hoofs** or **hooves** (hŏŏvz, hōōvz) 1. The horny sheath encasing the foot in various mammals, as horses, cattle, etc. ◆Collateral adjective: *ungular.* 2. The entire foot of such an animal. —**on the hoof** Alive; not butchered: said of cattle. —*v.t. & v.i.* 1. To trample with the hoofs. 2. *Informal* To walk or dance: usually with *it.* [OE *hōf*] —**hoofed** (hŏŏft, hōōft) *adj.*

hoof·er (hŏŏf′ər, hōō′fər) *Slang* A professional dancer, esp. a tap dancer.

hook (hŏŏk) *n.* 1. A curved or bent implement used to catch hold of something. 2. Something resembling a hook. 3. In baseball, a curve. 4. In boxing, a short, swinging blow, with the elbow bent. 5. In golf, a stroke that sends the ball curving to the left. 6. *Naut. Slang* An anchor. —**by hook or by crook** In one way or another. —**off the hook** *Slang* Free from a troublesome situation, obligation, etc. —**on one's own hook** *Informal* By one's own efforts. —*v.t.* 1. To fasten or take hold of with or as with a hook. 2. To make (a rug, mat, etc.) by looping yarn through a backing of canvas or burlap. 3. In baseball, to pitch (the ball) in a curve. 4. In boxing, to strike with a short, swinging blow. 5. In golf, to drive (the ball) to one's left. 6. *Slang* To entrap into a bad habit. 7. *Slang* To pilfer; steal. —*v.i.* 8. To curve like a hook; bend. 9. To be fastened with or as with a hook or hooks. —**to hook up** To put together or connect. [OE *hōc*]

hook·ah (hŏŏk′ə) *n.* An Oriental tobacco pipe having a long, flexible tube that passes through a vessel of water, thus cooling the smoke. Also **hook′a.** [< Arabic *huqqah*]

hook·er (hŏŏk′ər) *n.* 1. A prostitute. 2. A drink of usu. undiluted liquor.

hook·up (hŏŏk′up′) *n. Telecom.* The arrangement of the apparatus and connections used for a radio broadcast or other electrical transmission.

hook·worm (ho͝ok′wûrm′) *n.* A nematode worm with hooked mouth parts, parasitic in the intestines.

hook·y (ho͝ok′ē) *n. Informal* Absence without leave, as from school: now only in the phrase **to play hooky,** to be a truant. [< HOOK, in dial. sense of "make off"]

hoo·li·gan (ho͞o′lə·gən) *n. Slang* A young hoodlum; petty gangster. [after *Hooligan,* name of an Irish family]

hoop (ho͞op) *n.* 1. A circular band of metal, wood, etc.; esp., such a band used to confine the staves of a barrel. 2. One of the rings of flexible metal, whalebone, etc., used to make a woman's skirt stand out. —*v.t.* To surround or fasten with a hoop or hoops. [OE *hōp*]

hoop·la (ho͞op′lä) *n. Slang* Noise and excitement.

hoo·poe (ho͞o′po͞o) *n.* An Old World bird having a long bill and an erectile crest. Also **hoo′poo.** [< L *upupa*]

hoo·ray (ho͞o·rā′, hə-, ho͞o-) See HURRAH.

hoose·gow (ho͞os′gou) *n. Slang* Jail or prison. Also **hoos′gow.** [< Sp. *juzgado* tribunal]

hoot (ho͞ot) *n.* 1. The cry of an owl. 2. A sound similar to this, as of a train whistle. 3. A loud, derisive outcry. —*v.i.* 1. To make such a sound. —*v.t.* 2. To jeer at or mock with derisive cries. [< Scand. Cf. Sw. *huta.*]

hoot·en·an·ny (ho͞ot′n·an′ē) *n. pl.* **·nies** A gathering of folk singers, especially for a public performance. Also **hoot·nan·ny** (ho͞ot′nan′ē). [Origin unknown]

hooves (ho͝ovz, ho͞ovz) Alternative plural of HOOF.

hop[1] (hop) *v.* **hopped, hop·ping** *v.i.* 1. To move by making short leaps on one foot. 2. To move in short leaps on both feet or on all four feet. 3. *Informal* To go, especially by airplane. —*v.t.* 4. To jump over, as a fence. 5. *Informal* To get on or board. —*n.* 1. The act of hopping. 2. *Informal* A dance or dancing party. 3. *Informal* A trip in an airplane. [OE *hoppian*]

hop[2] (hop) *n.* 1. A perennial climbing herb with scaly fruit. 2. *pl.* The dried cones, used medicinally and as a flavoring in beer. —**to hop up** *Slang* 1. To increase the power of, as an engine. 2. To stimulate, as with drugs. [< MDu. *hoppe*]

hope (hōp) *v.* **hoped, hop·ing** *v.t.* 1. To desire with expectation of fulfillment. 2. To wish; want. —*v.i.* 3. To have desire or expectation: usually with *for.* —*n.* 1. Desire accompanied by expectation of fulfillment. 2. That which is desired. 3. One who or that which is a cause of hopeful expectation. [OE *hopa*]

hope·ful (hōp′fəl) *adj.* 1. Full of or showing hope. 2. Affording grounds for hope; promising. —*n.* A young person who seems likely to succeed. —**hope′ful·ness** *n.*

hope·ful·ly (hōp′fə·lē) *adv.* 1. In a hopeful manner. 2. It is hoped: *Hopefully,* we can go.

hope·less (hōp′lis) *adj.* 1. Without hope; despairing. 2. Affording no ground for hope. —**hope′less·ly** *adv.* —**hope′less·ness** *n.*

hop·head (hop′hed′) *n. Slang* A drug addict.

Ho·pi (hō′pē) *n.* 1. One of a group of North American Pueblo Indians of Shoshonean stock, now living in NE Arizona. 2. Their Shoshonean language. [< Hopi *hópitu,* lit., peaceful ones]

hop·per (hop′ər) *n.* 1. One who or that which hops. 2. A jumping insect or larva. 3. A funnel-shaped receptacle for storing coal, grain, etc., that is emptied through the bottom. 4. A container in which bills to be considered by a legislative body are placed. 5. *Slang* A toilet.

hop·scotch (hop′skoch′) *n.* A children's game in which the player hops on one foot over the lines of a diagram, so as to recover a block or pebble.

horde (hôrd) *n.* A multitude, pack, or swarm, as of people, animals, etc. —*v.i.* **hord·ed, hord·ing** To gather in or live in a horde. [< Polish *horda*]

hore·hound (hôr′hound′) *n.* 1. A whitish, bitter, perennial herb of the mint family. 2. A candy or cough remedy flavored with its juice. Also spelled *hoarhound.* [OE *hārhūne*]

ho·ri·zon (hə·rī′zən) *n.* 1. The line of the apparent meeting of the sky with the earth or sea. 2. The bounds or limits of one's observation, knowledge, or experience. [< Gk. *horizein* to bound]

hor·i·zon·tal (hôr′ə·zon′təl, hor′-) *adj.* 1. Of, pertaining to, or close to the horizon. 2. Parallel to the horizon; level: opposed to *vertical.* 3. Equal and uniform: a *horizontal* tariff. —*n.* A line, plane, etc., assumed to be parallel with the horizon. —**hor′i·zon′tal·ly** *adv.*

hor·mone (hôr′mōn) *n.* 1. *Physiol.* An internal secretion produced by one of the endocrine glands, as the pituitary, thyroid, adrenals, etc., and carried by the blood stream to other parts of the body where it has a specific effect. 2. *Bot.* A similar substance in plants. [< Gk. *hormaein* to excite] —**hor·mo′nal, hor·mon·ic** (hôr·mon′ik) *adj.*

horn (hôrn) *n.* 1. A hard, permanent growth of epidermal tissue projecting from the head of various hoofed animals. 2. The substance of which animal horn is made. 3. Something made from horn: powder *horn.* 4. Something shaped like a horn or the point of a horn: a saddle *horn.* 5. A device for sounding warning signals: an automobile *horn.* 6. *Music* Any of the various brass instruments, esp. the French horn. 7. *Geog.* a One of the branches forming the delta of a stream or river. b A cape or peninsula. —**to blow one's own horn** To brag. —*adj.* Of or like horn. —**to horn in** *Slang* To intrude. [OE]

horn·bill (hôrn′bil′) *n.* A tropical bird, having a large bill with a hornlike growth surmounting it.

horn·blende (hôrn′blend) *n.* A common greenish black or black mineral, containing iron and silicate of magnesium, calcium, and aluminum; a variety of amphibole. —**horn′·blend′ic** *adj.*

horned (hôrnd) *adj.* 1. Having a horn or horns. 2. Having a projection resembling a horn.

horned owl Any of various American owls with ear tufts.

horned toad A flat-bodied, spiny lizard with a short tail and toadlike appearance. Also **horn toad.**

hor·net (hôr′nit) *n.* Any of various wasps capable of inflicting a severe sting. [OE *hyrnet*]

horn of plenty A cornucopia.

horn·pipe (hôrn′pīp′) *n.* 1. A musical

instrument resembling the clarinet. 2. A lively English dance.

hor·n·y (hôr′nē) *adj.* **horn·i·er, horn·i·est** 1. Made of horn. 2. Having horns. 3. Hard as horn; tough. 4. *Slang* Sexually excited. —**horn′i·ness** *n.*

ho·rol·o·gy (hô·rol′ə·jē) *n.* The science of the measurement of time or of the construction of timepieces. [< Gk. *hōra* time + -LOGY] —**ho·rol′o·ger, ho·rol′o·gist** *n.* —**hor·o·log·ic** (hôr′ə·loj′ik, hor′-) or **·i·cal** *adj.*

hor·o·scope (hôr′ə·skōp, hor′-) *n.* 1. In astrology, the aspect of the heavens, with special reference to the positions of the planets at any specific instant, esp. at a person's birth. 2. The diagram of the twelve divisions or houses of the heavens. [< Gk. *hōra* hour + *skopos* watcher] —**ho·ros·co·py** (hô·ros′kə·pē) *n.*

hor·ren·dous (hô·ren′dəs, hə-) *adj.* Horrible; frightful. [< L *horrere* to bristle] —**hor·ren′dous·ly** *adv.*

hor·ri·ble (hôr′ə·bəl, hor′-) *adj.* 1. Exciting or tending to excite horror; shocking. 2. *Informal* Inordinate; excessive: a *horrible* liar. 3. *Informal* Unpleasant; ugly. [< L *horrere* to bristle] —**hor′ri·ble·ness** *n.* —**hor′ri·bly** *adj.*

hor·rid (hôr′id, hor′-) *adj.* 1. Causing great aversion or horror; dreadful. 2. *Informal* Very objectionable; offensive. —**hor′rid·ly** *adv.* —**hor′rid·ness** *n.*

hor·ri·fy (hôr′ə·fī, hor′-) *v.t.* **·fied, ·fy·ing** 1. To affect or fill with horror. 2. *Informal* To shock or surprise painfully; startle. —**hor′ri·fi·ca′tion** *n.*

hor·ror (hôr′ər, hor′-) *n.* 1. A painful, strong emotion caused by extreme fear, dread, repugnance, etc. 2. One who or that which excites such an emotion. 3. *Informal* Something disagreeable, ugly, etc. [< L]

hors d'oeuvre (ôr dûrv′) *Usu. pl.* An appetizer, as olives, celery, etc. [< F]

horse (hôrs) *n. pl.* **hors·es** or **horse** 1. A large, strong, herbivorous mammal with solid hoofs and a long mane and tail, domesticated as a draft or pack animal or for riding. ◆Collateral adjective: *equine.* 2. The full-grown male horse as contrasted with the mare; a gelding or stallion. 3. Mounted soldiers; cavalry. 4. Something likened to a horse, as a sawhorse. 5. *Informal* In chess, a knight. —**to hold one's horses** *Slang* To restrain one's impetuosity or impatience. —*v.* **horsed, hors·ing** *v.t.* 1. To furnish with a horse or horses. 2. To put on horseback. —*v.i.* 3. To mount or ride on a horse. 4. *Slang* To engage in horseplay: often with *around.* [OE *hors*]

horse·back (hôrs′bak′) *n.* A horse's back. —**horse′back′** *adv.*

horse·car (hôrs′kär′) 1. A streetcar drawn by horses. 2. A car for transporting horses.

horse chestnut 1. A tree having palmate leaves, clusters of flowers, and chestnutlike fruits. 2. The fruit of this tree.

horse·flesh (hôrs′flesh′) *n.* Horses collectively.

horse·fly (hôrs′flī′) *n. pl.* **·flies** A large fly, the female of which sucks the blood of horses, cattle, etc.

horse·hair (hôrs′hâr′) *n.* 1. The hair of horses, esp. that of their manes and tails. 2. A fabric made of such hair; haircloth. —**horse′hair′** *adj.*

horse·hide (hôrs′hīd′) *n.* Leather made from a horse's hide.

horse latitudes *Naut.* A belt at about 35° north or south latitude, characterized by calms and light variable winds.

horse·laugh (hôrs′laf′) *n.* A loud, scornful laugh.

horse·man (hôrs′mən) *n. pl.* **·men** (-mən) A man skilled in riding a horse. —**horse′·man·ship** *n.*

horse·play (hôrs′plā′) *n.* Rough, boisterous play or fun.

horse·pow·er (hôrs′pou′ər) *n. Mech.* A unit of the rate of work, equal to 550 pounds lifted one foot in one second.

horse·rad·ish (hôrs′rad′ish) *n.* 1. A garden herb of the mustard family. 2. A condiment made from its root.

horse sense *Informal* Innate common sense.

horse·shoe (hôr′shōō′, hôrs′-) *n.* 1. A U-shaped piece of metal that is nailed to a horse's hoof as a protective device. 2. Something resembling a horseshoe in shape. 3. *pl.* A game in which horseshoes are thrown over or near a stake. —*v.t.* **·shoed, ·shoe·ing** To furnish with horseshoes.

horseshoe crab A large marine arthropod having a horseshoe-shaped shell: also called *king crab.*

horse·tail (hôrs′tāl′) *n.* A perennial flowerless plant.

horse·whip (hôrs′hwip′) *n.* A whip for managing horses. —*v.t.* **·whipped, ·whip·ping** To flog with a horsewhip.

horse·wom·an (hôrs′wŏŏm′ən) *n. pl.* **·wom·en** (-wim′in) A woman skilled in riding a horse.

hors·y (hôr′sē) *adj.* **hors·i·er, hors·i·est** 1. Resembling, suggesting, or having to do with a horse or horses. 2. Associated with or devoted to horses, horseracing, fox hunting, etc. Also **hors′ey.** —**hors′i·ly** *adv.* —**hors′i·ness** *n.*

hor·ta·to·ry (hôr′tə·tôr′ē) *adj.* Characterized by or giving advice or encouragement. Also **hor′ta·tive.** [< L *hortatorius*] —**hor′ta·tive·ly** *adv.*

hor·ti·cul·ture (hôr′tə·kul′chər) *n.* 1. The cultivation of a garden. 2. The art or science of growing garden vegetables, fruits, flowers, etc. [< L *hortus* garden + *cultura* cultivation] —**hor′ti·cul′tur·al** *adj.* —**hor′·ti·cul′tur·ist** *n.*

ho·san·na (hō·zan′ə) *interj.* Praised be the Lord. —*n.* 1. A cry of "hosanna." 2. Any exultant praise. [< Hebrew *hōshi āhnnā* save, we pray]

hose (hōz) *n. pl.* **hose** (*Archaic* **hos·en**) *for def. 1*; **hos·es** *for def. 2* 1. *pl.* Stockings or socks. 2. A flexible tube of rubber, plastic, etc., for conveying water and other fluids. —*v.t.* **hosed, hos·ing** To water, drench, or douse with a hose. [OE *hosa*]

Ho·se·a (hō·zē′ə, -zā′ə) *n.* A book of the Old Testament attributed to the 8th c. B.C. Hebrew prophet Hosea: also, in the Douai Bible, *Osee.*

ho·sier·y (hō′zhər·ē) *n.* Stockings and socks of all types.

hos·pice (hos′pis) *n.* A place of rest or shelter, usu. maintained by a religious order. [< L *hospitium* inn, hospitality]

hos·pi·ta·ble (hos′pi·tə·bəl, hos·pit′ə·bəl) *adj.* 1. Kind and generous. 2. Affording or expressing welcome and generosity. 3. Receptive in mind. [< L *hospitare* to entertain] —**hos′pi·ta·ble·ness** *n.* —**hos′pi·ta·bly** *adv.*

hos·pi·tal (hos′pi·təl) *n.* An institution that provides medical, surgical, or psychiatric treatment and nursing care. [< L *hospes* guest]

hos·pi·tal·i·ty (hos′pə·tal′ə·tē) *n. pl.* **·ties** The spirit, practice, or act of being hospitable.

hos·pi·tal·ize (hos′pi·təl·īz′) *v.t.* **·ized, ·iz·ing** To put in a hospital for treatment and care. —**hos′pi·tal·i·za′tion** *n.*

host[1] (hōst) *n.* 1. A man who extends hospitality to others, usu. to guests in his own home. 2. *Biol.* Any living organism from which a parasite obtains nourishment and protection. [< L *hospes* guest, host]

host[2] (hōst) *n.* 1. A large number; a multitude. 2. An army. [< L *hostis* enemy]

host[3] (hōst) *n. Eccl. Sometimes cap.* The Eucharistic bread or wafer. [< L *hostia* sacrificial victim]

hos·tage (hos′tij) *n.* A person given or held as a pledge until specified conditions are met, as in war. [< OF]

hos·tel (hos′təl) *n.* A supervised lodging house for young travelers. [< LL *hospitale* inn]

hos·tel·ry (hos′təl·rē) *n. pl.* **·ries** *Archaic* A lodging place; inn. —**hos′tel·er** or **hos′·tel·ler** *n.*

host·ess (hōs′tis) *n.* 1. A woman who performs the duties of a host. 2. A woman employed in a restaurant, etc., to greet and serve guests.

hos·tile (hos′təl) *adj.* Having or expressing enmity or opposition; unfriendly. [< L *hostilis*] —**hos′tile·ly** *adv.*

hos·til·i·ty (hos·til′ə·tē) *n. pl.* **·ties** 1. The state of being hostile. 2. A hostile act. 3. *pl.* War or acts of war.

hot (hot) *adj.* **hot·ter, hot·test** 1. Having or giving off great heat; having a high temperature. 2. Feeling abnormal bodily warmth. 3. Giving the sensation of heat or burning: *hot* pepper. 4. Carrying an electric current, esp. one of high voltage. 5. Dangerously radioactive. 6. Not far behind: in *hot* pursuit. 7. Showing strong or violent emotion: *hot* words. 8. Marked by intense activity; raging; violent: a *hot* battle. 9. *Slang* Lustful; sexy. 10. *Informal* Controversial: a *hot* issue. 11. In demand: a *hot* item. 12. *Slang* Excellent, skillful, etc.: usu. in the negative: not too *hot* an actor. 13. *Slang* Recently stolen. 14. Recent; fresh: *hot* news. [OE *hāt*] —**hot′ly** *adv.*

hot air *Slang* Empty or pretentious talk; exaggeration.

hot·bed (hot′bed′) *n.* 1. A bed of rich earth, protected by glass and used to promote the growth of plants. 2. A place or condition favoring rapid growth or great activity.

hot-blood·ed (hot′blud′id) *adj.* Easily moved or excited.

hot·box (hot′boks′) *n.* An overheated axle or shaft bearing.

hot cake A pancake.

hot cross bun A circular cake or bun marked with a cross of frosting, eaten esp. during Lent.

hot·dog (hot′dôg′) *v.i.* **·dogged, ·dog·ging** To perform showy maneuvers in skiing or surfing.

hot dog A cooked frankfurter, served in a split roll.

ho·tel (hō·tel′) *n.* An establishment or building providing lodging, food, etc., to travelers and long-term residents. [< OF *hostel* inn]

hot·head (hot′hed′) *n.* A hotheaded person.

hot·head·ed (hot′hed′id) *adj.* 1. Quick-tempered. 2. Impetuous. —**hot′head′ed·ly** *adv.* —**hot′head′ed·ness** *n.*

hot·house (hot′hous′) *n.* A greenhouse.

hot line A direct means of communication, esp. a telephone line for emergency use between Washington, D.C. and Moscow.

hot plate A small portable gas or electric stove.

hot rod *Slang* An automobile, usu. an older model, modified for high speeds.

Hot·ten·tot (hot′ən·tot) *n.* 1. A member of a South African people believed to be related to both the Bantus and the Bushmen. 2. The language of this people. —**Hot′ten·tot** *adj.*

hou·dah (hou′də) See HOWDAH.

hound (hound) *n.* 1. A dog kept for hunting, esp. one that hunts by scent and in a pack. 2. A dog of any breed. —*v.t.* 1. To hunt or pursue with or as with hounds. 2. *Informal* To nag; pester. [OE *hund* dog]

hour (our) *n.* 1. A space of time equal to $1/_{24}$ of a day; sixty minutes. ◆Collateral adjective: *horal.* 2. A time of day. 3. An indefinite period of time: The happiest *hour* of one's life. 4. *pl.* A set period of time for work or other pursuits: school *hours.* [< Gk. *hōra* time, period]

hour·glass (our′glas′) *n.* A timing device having two glass vessels connected by a narrow neck through which a quantity of sand, mercury, or water runs in a stated interval of time, usu. an hour.

hou·ri (hōō′rē, hour′ē) *n.* In Muslim belief, one of the beautiful virgins allotted to those who attain Paradise. [< Arabic *hūrīyah* black-eyed woman]

hour·ly (our′lē) *adj.* 1. Happening or done every hour. 2. Happening or done within an hour. 3. Frequent. —*adv.* 1. At intervals of an hour. 2. Hour by hour. 3. Frequently; often.

house (*n.* hous; *v.* houz) *n. pl.* **hous·es** (hou′zəz) 1. A building used as a dwelling for human beings. 2. A household; family. 3. A communal dwelling, as a dormitory. 4. A building used for any of various purposes: a *house* of correction. 5. A theater or other place of entertainment. 6. The audience in such a place of entertainment. 7. A legislative or deliberative body: *House* of Representatives. 8. A business firm or establishment: a publishing *house.* 9. In astrology: **a** One of the twelve divisions of the heavens. **b** A sign of the zodiac considered as the seat of greatest influence of a particular planet. —*v.* **housed, hous·ing** *v.t.* 1. To take or put into a house; lodge. 2. To store in a house or building. 3. To encase or enclose. —*v.i.* 4. To take shelter or lodgings; dwell. [OE *hūs*] —**house′ful** *n.*

house·boat (hous′bōt′) *n.* A barge or flat-bottomed boat fitted out as a dwelling and used in quiet waters.

house·boy (hous′boi′) *n.* A man or boy employed as a household servant.

house·break·ing (hous′brā′king) *n.* The act of breaking into and entering another's home with intent to commit theft or some other felony. —**house′break′er** *n.*

house·bro·ken (hous′brō′kən) *adj.* Trained to urinate and defecate outdoors or in a specific place, as a dog.

house·coat (hous′kōt′) *n.* A woman's garment, usu. long, for informal wear within the house.

house·fly (hous′flī′) *n. pl.* **·flies** The common fly, found in nearly all parts of the world.

house·hold (hous′hōld′) *n.* 1. A group of persons sharing a dwelling. 2. A home or the affairs of a home. —**house′hold′** *adj.*

house·hold·er (hous′hōl′dər) *n.* 1. One who owns or occupies a house. 2. The head of a family.

household word A widely familiar name.

house·keep·er (hous′kē′pər) *n.* 1. One who performs the tasks of maintaining a home. 2. A paid manager of a home. —**house′·keep′ing** *n.*

house·maid (hous′mād′) *n.* A girl or woman employed to do housework.

House of Commons 1. The lower house of the British Parliament, the members of which are elected. 2. The lower house of the Canadian Parliament.

House of Lords The upper and nonelective house of the British Parliament, made up of the peerage and the highest ranking clergy.

House of Representatives 1. The lower, larger branch of the United States Congress, and of many state legislatures, composed of members elected on the basis of population. 2. A similar legislative body, as in Australia, Mexico, etc.

house organ A publication regularly issued by a business organization for its employees and customers.

house party An entertainment of a group of guests for several days.

house·top (hous′top′) *n.* The roof of a house.

house·wares (hous′wârz′) *n.pl.* Kitchen utensils, dishes, glassware, and other wares used in the home.

house·warm·ing (hous′wôr′ming) *n.* A party held to celebrate the moving into new living quarters.

house·wife (hous′wīf′) *n. pl.* **house·wives** (-wīvz′) A married woman who manages her own household. —**house′wife′ly** *adj. & adv.*

house·work (hous′wûrk′) *n.* The chores involved in keeping house.

hous·ing (hou′zing) *n.* 1. The act of providing shelter or lodging; also, the shelter or lodging so provided. 2. Houses or dwellings collectively. 3. A structure that covers or protects.

hove (hōv) Past tense of HEAVE.

hov·el (huv′əl, hov′-) *n.* 1. A small, wretched dwelling. 2. A low, open shed for sheltering cattle, tools, etc. —*v.t.* **hov·eled** or **·elled, hov·el·ing** or **·el·ling** To shelter or lodge in a hovel. [? Dim. of OE *hof* building]

hov·er (huv′ər, hov′-) *v.i.* 1. To remain suspended in or near one place in the air. 2. To linger or remain nearby, as if watching: with *around, near,* etc. 3. To remain in an uncertain or irresolute state: with *between.* —*n.* The act or state of hovering. [< obs. *hove* to float] —**hov′er·er** *n.*

how (hou) *adv.* 1. In what way or manner. 2. To what degree, extent, or amount. 3. In what state, or condition. 4. For what reason or purpose. 5. By what name or designation. 6. *Informal* What: *How* about having lunch? —*n.* A manner or means of doing. [OE *hū*]

how·be·it (hou·bē′it) *adv. Archaic* Be that as it may.

how·dah (hou′də) *n.* A seat for riders on an elephant or camel, often fitted with a canopy. [< Hind. *haudah*]

how-do-you-do (hou′də·yə·do͞o′) *n. Informal* An embarrassing or difficult situation: usu. preceded by *fine, pretty,* etc.

how·ev·er (hou·ev′ər) *adv.* 1. In whatever manner. 2. To whatever degree or extent. —*conj.* Nevertheless; in spite of; still; yet.

how·it·zer (hou′it·sər) *n.* A cannon of medium length operating at a high angle of fire. [ult. < Czechoslovakian *houfnice* catapult]

howl (houl) *v.i.* 1. To utter the loud wail of a dog, wolf, or other animal, esp. in pain, grief, or rage. —*v.t.* 2. To utter or express with howling. [ME *houlen*] —**howl** *n.*

howl·er (hou′lər) *n.* 1. One who or that which howls. 2. *Informal* An absurd blunder.

howl·ing (hou′ling) *adj.* 1. Producing howls. 2. Characterized by or filled with howls: the *howling* wilderness. 3. *Slang* Very great: a *howling* success.

how·so·ev·er (hou′sō·ev′ər) *adv.* 1. In whatever manner. 2. To whatever degree or extent.

hoy·den (hoid′n) *n.* A boisterous or ill-mannered girl. —*adj.* Boisterous. [Origin uncertain] —**hoy′den·ish** *adj.*

hua·ra·che (hə·rä′chē, wə-) *n.* A flat sandal having a top of woven leather strips. [< Am.Sp.]

hub (hub) *n.* 1. The center part of a wheel into which the axle is inserted. 2. Any center of great activity or interest.

hub·bub (hub′ub) *n.* A loud, confused noise, as of many voices shouting or talking. [Origin unknown]

hub-cap (hub′kap′) *n.* A detachable metal cover for the hub of a wheel.

hu·bris (hyo͞o′bris) *n.* Arrogant pride. [< Gk. *hybris*]

huck·le·ber·ry (huk′əl·ber′ē) *n. pl.* **·ries** 1. The edible black or dark blue berry of any of various North American shrubs. 2. A shrub yielding this berry.

huck·ster (huk′stər) *n.* 1. A peddler of wares, esp. fruits and vegetables. 2. *Slang* One engaged in the advertising business. [< MDu. *heuken* to retail] —**huck′ster·ism** *n.*

hud·dle (hud′l) *v.* **·dled, ·dling** *v.i.* 1. To crowd or nestle together closely. 2. To draw or hunch oneself together. 3. In football, to gather in a huddle. —*v.t.* 4. To bring or crowd together closely. —*n.* 1. A number of persons or things crowded together. 2. In football, the grouping of a team before play. 3. *Informal* Any small conference. [Origin uncertain]

hue[1] (hyo͞o) *n.* 1. The attribute of a color that determines its position in the spectrum. 2. Color: the autumnal *hues.* 3. A particular tint or shade of color. [OE *hīw* appearance] —**hued** *adj.*

hue[2] (hyo͞o) *n.* A loud clamor; shouting. —**hue and cry** Any great public stir. [< OF *huer* to shout after]

huff (huf) *n.* A fit of sudden anger or irritation. —*v.i.* To puff; blow. —**huff′ish** *adj.*

huf·fy (huf′ē) *adj.* **huff·i·er, huff·i·est** 1. Touchy. 2. Petulant; sulky. —**huff′i·ly** *adv.* —**huff′i·ness** *n.*

hug (hug) *v.t.* **hugged, hug·ging** 1. To hold against the body, as in affection. 2. To cherish or cling to, as a belief. 3. To keep close to. [Prob. < ON *hugga* to console] —**hug** *n.*

huge (hyōōj) *adj.* Very great in size, quantity, extent, etc. [< OF *ahuge* high] —**huge′ly** *adv.* —**huge′ness** *n.*

hug·ger·mug·ger (hug′ər·mug′ər) *n.* Disorder; confusion. —*adj.* 1. Secret; sly. 2. Disorderly; slovenly.

hu·la (hōō′lə) *n.* A Hawaiian dance characterized by sinuous arm movements. Also **hu′la-hu′la.** [< Hawaiian]

hulk (hulk) *n.* 1. The body of an old or wrecked ship. 2. Any bulky, unwieldy object or person. —*v.i.* To appear or move as if a hulk. [Prob. < Gk. *helkein* to drag]

hulk·ing (hul′king) *adj.* Big and unwieldy. Also **hulk′y.**

hull (hul) *n.* 1. The outer covering of certain fruits or seeds. 2. Any outer covering. 3. *Naut.* The body of a ship, exclusive of the masts, etc. —*v.t.* To remove the hull of. [OE *hulu*]

hul·la·ba·loo (hul′ə·bə·lōō′) *n.* A loud, confused noise; uproar. Also **hul′la·bal·loo′.** [Imit. reduplication of *hullo,* var. of HALLOO]

hum (hum) *v.* **hummed, hum·ming** *v.i.* 1. To make a low, murmuring or droning sound. 2. To sing with the lips closed. 3. *Informal* To be very busy or active: The office *hummed.* —*v.t.* 4. To sing with closed lips without words. 5. To affect by humming: to *hum* a child to sleep. [ME *hummer*] —**hum** *n.* —**hum′mer** *n.*

hu·man (hyōō′mən) *adj.* Of, characteristic of, or having the nature or attributes of a human being. [< L *humanus*] —**hu′man** *n.* —**hu′man·ness** *n.*

human being A man, woman, or child; a person.

hu·mane (hyōō·mān′) *adj.* 1. Having kindness, sympathy, etc.; benevolent. 2. Tending to refine or civilize: *humane* learning. —**hu·mane′ly** *adv.* —**hu·mane′ness** *n.*

hu·man·ism (hyōō′mən·iz′əm) *n.* 1. The character or quality of being human. 2. A system or attitude in thought, religion, etc., in which human ideals are made central. 3. *Often cap.* The intellectual and literary movement of the Renaissance, characterized by the study of Greek and Roman classics. 4. The study of the humanities. —**hu′man·ist** *n.* —**hu′man·is′tic** *adj.* —**hu′man·is′ti·cal·ly** *adv.*

hu·man·i·tar·i·an (hyōō·man′ə·târ′ē·ən) *n.* One who seeks to promote the welfare of mankind; philanthropist. —**hu·man′i·tar′·i·an** *adj.* —**hu·man′i·tar′i·an·ism** *n.*

hu·man·i·ty (hyōō·man′ə·tē) *n.* *pl.* **·ties** 1. The human race; mankind. 2. The state of being human; human nature. 3. The state of being humane; benevolence. —**the humanities** 1. The study of classical Greek and Latin literature. 2. Literature, philosophy, the fine arts, etc., as distinguished from the sciences. [< L *humanus* human]

hu·man·ize (hyōō′mən·īz) *v.t.* **·ized, ·iz·ing** 1. To make human; give human characteristics to. 2. To make gentle, kindly, etc. —**hu′man·i·za′tion** (-ə·zā′shən, -ī·zā′-) *n.*

hu·man·kind (hyōō′mən·kīnd′) *n.* People.

hu·man·ly (hyōō′mən·lē) *adv.* 1. In a human manner. 2. Within human power or ability: Is this *humanly* possible? 3. In accordance with man's experience or knowledge.

hu·man·oid (hyōō′mən·oid) *adj.* Almost human in characteristics and form. —*n.* An almost human creature, as: **a** An early ancestor of modern man. **b** A science fiction creature.

human potentials movement The various methods of cultivating sensitivity, awareness, and creativity, of achieving tranquillity, etc., regarded collectively as a late 20th c. phenomenon.

hum·ble (hum′bəl) *adj.* **·bler, ·blest** 1. Free from pride or vanity; modest. 2. Lowly in station, condition, etc.; unpretentious. 3. Respectful. —*v.t.* **·bled, ·bling** 1. To reduce the pride of. 2. To lower in rank or dignity. [< L *humus* ground] —**hum′ble·ness** *n.* —**hum′bly** *adv.*

hum·bug (hum′bug) *n.* 1. Anything intended or used to delude; fraud. 2. One who seeks to deceive others. —*v.t.* **·bugged, ·bug·ging** To delude; trick. [Origin unknown] —**hum′·bug·ger·y** *n.*

hum·ding·er (hum′ding′ər) *n.* *Slang* One who or that which is remarkable or extraordinary.

hum·drum (hum′drum′) *adj.* Lacking interest, variety, or excitement; dull. [Reduplication of HUM]

hu·mer·us (hyōō′mər·əs) *n.* *pl.* **·mer·i** (-mər·ī) *Anat.* The bone of the upper part of the arm, from shoulder to elbow. [< L, shoulder] —**hu′mer·al** *adj.*

hu·mid (hyōō′mid) *adj.* Containing vapor or water; moist; damp. [< L *humere* to be moist] —**hu′mid·ly** *adv.*

hu·mid·i·fy (hyōō·mid′ə·fī) *v.t.* **·fied, ·fy·ing** To make moist. —**hu·mid′i·fi′er** *n.*

hu·mid·i·ty (hyōō·mid′ə·tē) *n.* Moisture; dampness, esp. of the atmosphere.

hu·mi·dor (hyōō′mə·dôr) *n.* A container in which moisture is retained, used for cigars, etc.

hu·mil·i·ate (hyōō·mil′ē·āt) *v.t.* **·at·ed, ·at·ing** To lower the pride or self-esteem of; mortify. [< L *humilis* lowly] —**hu·mil′i·a′·tion** *n.*

hu·mil·i·ty (hyōō·mil′ə·tē) *n.* The state or quality of being humble. [< L *humilitas* lowness]

hum·ming·bird (hum′ing·bûrd′) *n.* Any of a family of very small birds, having a long, slender bill and rapidly vibrating wings that produce a humming sound during flight.

hum·mock (hum′ək) *n.* A low mound of earth or rock; hillock. [Origin unknown]

hu·mor (hyōō′mər, yōō′-) *n.* 1. The quality of anything that is funny or appeals to the comic sense. 2. The ability to appreciate or express what is amusing, comic, etc. 3. Speech, writing, or actions that are amusing or comic. 4. Temperament; disposition. 5. *Physiol.* A liquid or semiliquid substance of the body, as blood, bile, lymph, etc. —*v.t.* To comply with the moods of; indulge.

Also *Brit.* **hu′mour.** [< L *umere* to be moist] **—hu′mor·less** *adj.* **—hu′mor·less·ly** *adv.* **—hu′mor·less·ness** *n.* **—hu′mor·ous** *adj.* **—hu′mor·ous·ly** *adv.* **—hu′mor·ous·ness** *n.*

hu·mor·esque (hyōō′mə·resk′, yōō′-) *n.* A playful musical composition; caprice. [< G *humoreske*]

hu·mor·ist (hyōō′mər·ist, yōō′-) *n.* 1. One who exercises a sense of humor; joker; wit. 2. A professional writer, entertainer, etc., specializing in humor or jokes. **—hu′mor·is′tic** *adj.*

hump (hump) *n.* 1. A rounded protuberance, esp. on the back, as in the camel, bison, etc., or the deformity produced in man by a curvature of the spine. 2. A low mound; hummock. **—over the hump** Beyond the most critical point. [Akin to LG *hump*]

hump·back (hump′bak′) *n.* 1. A hunchback. 2. A large whale. **—hump′backed′** *adj.*

hu·mus (hyōō′məs) *n.* The black or brown substance of the soil, formed by the decay of animal and vegetable matter, and providing nutrition for plant life. [< L, ground]

Hun (hun) *n.* 1. One of a barbarous Asian people who invaded Europe in the 5th c., led by Attila. 2. *Informal* Any barbarous or destructive person. [< LL *Hunnus*] **—Hun′nish** *adj.* **—Hun′nish·ness** *n.*

hunch (hunch) *n.* *Informal* A premonition of some coming event. **—***v.t.* & *v.i.* To bend or draw up so as to form a hump. [Origin unknown]

hunch·back (hunch′bak′) *n.* 1. A deformed back with a hump. 2. A person so deformed. **—hunch′backed′** *adj.*

hun·dred (hun′drid) *n.* The sum of ninety and ten, written as 100 or C: a cardinal number. [OE] **—hun′dred** *adj.* **—hun·dredth** (hun′dridth) *adj.* & *n.*

hun·dred·fold (hun′drid·fōld′) *n.* An amount or number a hundred times as great as a given unit. **—hun′dred·fold′** *adj.* & *adv.*

hun·dred·weight (hun′drid·wāt′) *n.* A unit of weight commonly reckoned in the United States at 100 pounds avoirdupois, in England at 112 pounds.

hung (hung) Past tense and past participle of HANG.

Hun·gar·i·an (hung·gâr′ē·ən) *n.* 1. A native or citizen of Hungary; esp., a Magyar. 2. The Finno-Ugric language of the Hungarians: also called *Magyar.* [< Med.L *Hungarus*] **—Hun·gar′i·an** *adj.*

hun·ger (hung′gər) *n.* 1. The state of discomfort or weakness caused by lack of food. 2. A desire or need for food. 3. Any strong desire or craving. **—***v.i.* 1. To be hungry. 2. To have a desire or craving: with *for* or *after.* [OE *hungor*]

hunger strike A self-imposed fast, undertaken as a means of protest.

hun·gry (hung′grē) *adj.* **·gri·er, ·gri·est** 1. Desiring or in need of food. 2. Eagerly craving: *hungry* for applause. 3. Indicating hunger: a *hungry* look. [OE *hungor*] **—hun′gri·ly** *adv.*

hunk (hungk) *n.* *Informal* A large piece or lump; chunk. [Prob. < Flemish *hunke*]

hun·ky-do·ry (hung′kē·dôr′ē) *adj.* *Slang* Fully satisfactory; all right.

hunt (hunt) *v.t.* 1. To pursue (game) for the purpose of killing or catching. 2. To range over (an area) in search of game. 3. To chase, drive away, or pursue with hostility, violence, etc. 4. To search for eagerly; seek: to *hunt* the truth. **—***v.i.* 5. To seek or pursue game. 6. To search or seek: often with *for* or *after.* **—to hunt down** 1. To pursue until caught or killed. 2. To search for until found. **—***n.* 1. The act of hunting game; chase. 2. A group of huntsmen. 3. A search; pursuit. [OE *huntian*] **—hunt′ing** *n.* & *adj.*

hunt·er (hun′tər) *n.* 1. One who hunts. 2. An animal used in hunting, as a dog or horse.

hunts·man (hunts′mən) *n.* *pl.* **·men** (-mən) 1. One who hunts game; hunter. 2. One who directs a hunt, hounds, etc.

Hu·pa (hōō′pə) *n.* 1. One of a tribe of North American Indians in NW California. 2. The language of this tribe.

hur·dle (hûr′dəl) *n.* 1. A light, portable barrier. 2. *pl.* A race in which such barriers are used: often with *the.* 3. An obstacle or difficulty to be surmounted. **—***v.t.* **·dled, ·dling** 1. To leap over (a barrier) in a race. 2. To surmount or overcome (a difficulty, etc.). [OE *hyrdel*] **—hur′dler** *n.*

hur·dy-gur·dy (hûr′dē·gûr′dē) *n.* *pl.* **·dies** A musical instrument played by turning a crank, as the barrel organ.

hurl (hûrl) *v.t.* 1. To throw, fling, or send with force. 2. To utter with vehemence. **—***n.* The act of hurling; also, a forceful throw. [ME *hurlen*] **—hurl′er** *n.*

hurl·ing (hûr′ling) *n.* An Irish game resembling field hockey. Also **hur′ley.** [< HURL]

hur·ly-bur·ly (hûr′lē·bûr′lē) *n.* Tumult; confusion; turmoil. [< earlier *hurling and burling*]

Hu·ron (hyŏŏr′ən, -on) *n.* A member of any of four tribes of North American Indians of Iroquoian stock, formerly between Lakes Huron and Ontario. [< F, ruffian]

hur·rah (hōō·rô′, hə·rä′) *n.* & *interj.* An exclamation expressing triumph, joy, encouragement, etc. Also spelled *hooray:* also **hur·ray′** (-rā′). [? < G *hurra*] **—hur·rah′** *v.t.* & *v.i.*

hur·ri·cane (hûr′ə·kān) *n.* A severe tropical cyclone, esp. one originating in the Caribbean, having a wind velocity exceeding 75 miles per hour. [< Sp. *huracán* < Carib]

hur·ried (hûr′ēd) *adj.* 1. Urged or forced to move, act, etc., in haste. 2. Done or carried on in great or too great haste: a *hurried* decision. **—hur′ried·ly** *adv.* **—hur′ried·ness** *n.*

hur·ry (hûr′ē) *v.* **·ried, ·ry·ing** *v.i.* 1. To act or move rapidly or in haste; hasten. **—***v.t.* 2. To cause or urge to act or move more rapidly. 3. To hasten the progress, etc., of, often unduly. **—***n.* 1. The act of hurrying; haste. 2. Eagerness to move, act, etc. [ME *horyen*]

hurt (hûrt) *v.* **hurt, hurt·ing** *v.t.* 1. To cause physical harm or pain to; injure. 2. To impair in some way: to *hurt* one's reputation. 3. To grieve or distress. **—***v.i.* 4. To cause discomfort, suffering, or damage. [< OF *hurter* to hit] **—hurt** *n.* **—hurt′ful** *adj.* **—hurt′ful·ly** *adv.* **—hurt′ful·ness** *n.*

hur·tle (hûr′təl) *v.* **·tled, ·tling** *v.i.* 1. To rush headlong or impetuously. **—***v.t.* 2. To hurl, throw, or drive violently. [Freq. of ME *hurten* to hit, hurt]

hus·band (huz′bənd) *n.* A married man. —*v.t.* To use or spend wisely; conserve: to *husband* one's forces. [OE *hūs* house + *bonda* freeholder]
hus·band·ry (huz′bən·drē) *n.* 1. The occupation or business of farming. 2. Careful management; economy; thrift.
hush (hush) *v.t.* 1. To make silent; cause to be quiet. 2. To keep hidden or secret: usu. with *up*. 3. To soothe or allay, as fears. —*n.* Deep silence; quiet. —*interj.* Be quiet! [Back formation < ME *husht* quiet]
hush-hush (hush′hush′) *adj. Informal* Secret.
hush·pup·py (hush′pup′ē) *n. pl.* **·pies** *Southern U.S.* A small fried ball of cornmeal.
husk (husk) *n.* 1. The outer coating of certain fruits or seeds, esp. of an ear of corn. 2. Any outer covering, esp. when comparatively worthless. —*v.t.* To remove the husk or outer covering of. [ME, prob. < Du. *huus* house]
husk·ing bee (hus′king) A social gathering of farm families to husk corn, followed by refreshments, entertainment, etc.
husk·y[1] (hus′kē) *adj.* **husk·i·er, husk·i·est** Rough or coarse in vocal quality. [< HUSK] —**husk′i·ly** *adv.* —**husk′i·ness** *n.*
husk·y[2] (hus′kē) *Informal adj.* **husk·i·er, husk·i·est** Physically strong; burly. —*n. pl.* **husk·ies** A strong or powerful person. [HUSKY[1], with ref. to toughness of husks]
Hus·ky (hus′kē) *n. pl.* **Hus·kies** A heavily furred Eskimo dog. Also **hus′ky.** [? Alter. of ESKIMO]
hus·sar (hōō·zär′) *n.* A member of a cavalry regiment found in some European armies and usu. distinguished by brilliant dress uniforms. [< Hungarian, ult. < Med.L *corsarius*]
hus·sy (huz′ē, hus′ē) *n. pl.* **·sies** 1. A brazen woman. 2. A pert or forward girl; minx. [Alter. of HOUSEWIFE]
hust·ings (hus′tingz) *n.pl.* (*usu. construed as sing.*) 1. The proceedings at an election. 2. Any place where political speeches are made. [OE < ON *hūs* house + *thing* assembly]
hus·tle (hus′əl) *v.* **·tled, ·tling** *v.t.* 1. To push about or crowd roughly; jostle. 2. To force, push, or thrust hurriedly. 3. *Informal* To cause to proceed rapidly or too rapidly; hurry. 4. *Slang* To sell or solicit (something) in an aggressive or unethical manner. —*v.i.* 5. To push or shove; elbow. 6. *Informal* To move or work with great energy. 7. *Slang* To make money by clever or unscrupulous means. 8. *Slang* To solicit clients: said of a prostitute. —*n.* 1. The act of hustling. 2. *Informal* Energetic activity; drive; push. 3. *Slang* A scheme for making money. 4. An intricate, shufflelike rock-and-roll dance. [< Du. *hutselen* to shake, toss]
hus·tler (hus′lər) *n.* 1. *Informal* An energetic, enterprising person. 2. *Slang* One who engages in petty frauds and thievery. 3. *Slang* A professional gambler. 4. *Slang* A prostitute.
hut (hut) *n.* A small, rude house or cabin; hovel. [< OHG *hutta*]
hutch (huch) *n.* 1. A coop or pen for small animals. 2. A chest, locker, or bin in which to store things; also, a cupboard for dishes. 3. A small hut or cabin. [< LL *hutica*]
hutz·pah (hōōts′pə, khōōts′-) See CHUTZPAH.
huz·za (hə·zä′) *n. & interj.* An exclamation of joy, triumph, etc. Also **huz·zah′.** [Origin uncertain] —**huz·za′** *v.i. & v.t.* **·zaed, ·za·ing**
hy·a·cinth (hī′ə·sinth) *n.* 1. A plant of the lily family, having clusters of fragrant, bell-shaped flowers. 2. A blue or purplish blue color. [< Gk. *hyakinthos*]
hy·brid (hī′brid) *n.* 1. An animal or plant produced by a male and female of different species, varieties, or breeds. 2. Anything of mixed origin. [< L *hybrida* offspring of tame sow and wild boar] —**hy′brid** *adj.* —**hy′brid·ism** *n.*
hy·brid·ize (hī′brid·īz) *v.t. & v.i.* **·ized, ·iz·ing** To produce or cause to produce hybrids. Also *Brit.* **hy′brid·ise.** —**hy′brid·i·za′tion** *n.* —**hy′brid·iz′er** *n.*
hy·dra (hī′drə) *n. pl.* **·dras** or **·drae** (-drē) Any of various small, fresh-water polyps, having a long, slender body and tentacles.
hy·dran·ge·a (hī·drān′jē·ə, -jə) *n.* A tree or shrub having large clusters of white, blue, or pink flowers. [< Gk. *hydōr* water + *angeion* vessel]
hy·drant (hī′drənt) *n.* A large, upright pipe connected to a water main, used for fire-fighting; fireplug. [< Gk. *hydōr* water + -ANT]
hy·drate (hī′drāt) *n. Chem.* A compound containing water. —*v.t.* **·drat·ed, ·drat·ing** To form a hydrate. —**hy·dra′tion** *n.*
hy·drau·lic (hī·drô′lik) *adj.* 1. Of or pertaining to hydraulics. 2. Operated by water or other liquid under pressure. 3. Hardening under water: *hydraulic* cement. [< Gk. *hydōr* water + *aulos* pipe] —**hy·drau′li·cal·ly** *adv.*
hy·drau·lics (hī·drô′liks) *n.pl.* (*construed as sing.*) The science of the laws governing the motion of water and other liquids and of their practical applications in engineering.
hy·dride (hī′drīd, -drid) *n. Chem.* A compound of hydrogen.
hydro- *combining form* 1. Water; of, related to, or resembling water. 2. *Chem.* Denoting a compound of hydrogen. Also, before vowels, **hydr-.** [< Gk. *hydōr* water]
hy·dro·car·bon (hī′drə·kär′bən) *n. Chem.* One of a large and important group of organic compounds that contain hydrogen and carbon only, as benzene, ethylene, methane, etc.
hy·dro·ceph·a·lus (hī′drə·sef′ə·ləs) *n. Pathol.* An accumulation of fluid within the brain, causing abnormal enlargement of the head. Also **hy′dro·ceph′a·ly.** [< HYDRO- + Gk. *kephalē* head] —**hy′dro·ceph′a·loid** (-loid), **hy′dro·ceph′a·lous** *adj.*
hy·dro·chlo·ric acid (hī′drə·klôr′ik) *Chem.* A corrosive acid widely used in industry, medicine, and the arts: also called *muriatic acid.*
hy·dro·chlo·ride (hī′drə·klôr′īd) *n. Chem.* A salt of hydrochloric acid with an organic base.
hy·dro·cy·an·ic acid (hī′drō·sī·an′ik) *Chem.* A colorless, volatile, very poisonous acid with a bitter odor: also called *prussic acid.*
hy·dro·dy·nam·ics (hī′drō·dī·nam′iks) *n.pl.* (*construed as sing.*) The branch of dynamics that treats of the motions and forces of

liquids, esp. water. —**hy′dro·dy·nam′ic** or **·i·cal** *adj.*
hy·dro·e·lec·tric (hī′drō·i·lek′trik) *adj.* Of or pertaining to electricity generated by the energy of running water. —**hy′dro·e·lec′tri·cal·ly** *adv.* —**hy·dro·e·lec·tric·i·ty** (hī′drō·i·lek′tris′ə·tē, -ē′lek-) *n.*
hy·dro·flu·or·ic acid (hī′drə·flo͝or′ik) *Chem.* A corrosive acid used for etching glass, treating metals, etc.
hy·dro·foil (hī′drə·foil) *n.* 1. A structure designed to lift and support the hull of a boat moving at high speed in water. 2. Such a boat. [< HYDRO- + (AIR)FOIL]
hy·dro·gen (hī′drə·jən) *n.* The lightest of the elements (symbol H), an odorless, colorless, flammable gas, occurring chiefly in combination. [< HYDRO- + -GEN] —**hy·drog·e·nous** (hī·droj′ə·nəs) *adj.*
hy·dro·gen·ate (hī·droj′ə·nāt, hī′drə·jə·nāt′) *v.t.* **·at·ed, ·at·ing** *Chem.* To combine with, treat with, or expose to the chemical action of hydrogen. —**hy·dro′gen·a′tion** *n.*
hydrogen bomb A very destructive thermonuclear weapon releasing energy by the fusion, under extremely high temperatures, of light elements, as hydrogen isotopes: also called *H-bomb.*
hydrogen peroxide *Chem.* An unstable, colorless liquid, used for bleaching, disinfecting, etc.
hy·drog·ra·phy (hī·drog′rə·fē) *n.* The science of surveying, describing, and mapping seas, lakes, rivers, etc. —**hy·drog′ra·pher** *n.* —**hy·dro·graph·ic** (hī′drə·graf′ik) or **·i·cal** *adj.* —**hy′dro·graph′i·cal·ly** *adv.*
hy·dro·ki·net·ics (hī′drō·ki·net′iks) *n.pl.* (*construed as sing.*) The branch of hydrodynamics dealing with the laws governing fluids in motion. —**hy′dro·ki·net′ic** *adj.*
hy·drol·o·gy (hī·drol′ə·jē) *n.* The branch of physical geography that deals with the waters of the earth and their distribution, characteristics, and effects in relation to human activities. —**hy·dro·log·ic** (hī′drə·loj′ik) or **·i·cal** *adj.* —**hy′dro·log′i·cal·ly** *adv.* —**hy·drol′o·gist** *n.*
hy·drol·y·sis (hī·drol′ə·sis) *n. pl.* **·ses** (-sēz) *Chem.* A chemical reaction in which a compound combines with the ions in water to produce an acid, base, or both. —**hy·dro·lyt·ic** (hī′drə·lit′ik) *adj.*
hy·dro·lyze (hī′drə·līz) *v.t. & v.i.* **·lyzed, ·lyz·ing** To undergo or cause to undergo hydrolysis. —**hy′dro·lyz′a·ble** *adj.* —**hy′dro·ly·za′tion** *n.*
hy·drom·e·ter (hī·drom′ə·tər) *n.* An instrument that determines the specific gravity or density of a liquid. —**hy·dro·met·ric** (hī′drə·met′rik) or **·ri·cal** *adj.* —**hy·drom′e·try** *n.*
hy·dro·pho·bi·a (hī′drə·fō′bē·ə) *n.* 1. Rabies. 2. Any morbid fear of water. [< HYDRO- + -PHOBIA] —**hy′dro·pho′bic** *adj.*
hy·dro·phyte (hī′drə·fīt) *n. Bot.* A plant growing in water or in wet ground. —**hy′dro·phyt′ic** (-fit′ik) *adj.*
hy·dro·plane (hī′drə·plān′) *n.* 1. A seaplane. 2. A type of motorboat designed so that its hull is raised partially out of the water when driven at high speeds. 3. A hydrofoil (def. 2). —*v.i.* **·planed, ·plan·ing** To move at great speed on the water.
hy·dro·pon·ics (hī′drə·pon′iks) *n.pl.* (*construed as sing.*) The science of growing plants with their roots in nutrient solutions rather than in soil. [< HYDRO- + Gk. *ponos* labor] —**hy′dro·pon′ic** *adj.*
hy·dro·sphere (hī′drə·sfir) *n.* 1. The total water on the surface of the earth. 2. The moisture in the earth's atmosphere. —**hy′dro·spher′ic** (-sfir′ik, -sfer′-) *adj.*
hy·dro·stat (hī′drə·stat) *n.* 1. A device for preventing the explosion of a steam boiler due to lack of water. 2. An electrical device for detecting the presence of water.
hy·dro·stat·ics (hī′drə·stat′iks) *n.pl.* (*construed as sing.*) The science that deals with the pressure and equilibrium of fluids, especially of liquids. —**hy′dro·stat′ic** or **·i·cal** *adj.* —**hy′dro·stat′i·cal·ly** *adv.*
hy·dro·ther·a·py (hī′drō·ther′ə·pē) *n.* The scientific use of water to treat various diseases.
hy·drous (hī′drəs) *adj.* 1. Watery. 2. *Chem.* Containing water of crystallization or hydration.
hy·drox·ide (hī·drok′sīd) *n. Chem.* A compound containing the **hydroxyl** group or radical, which consists of one atom each of oxygen and hydrogen.
hy·e·na (hī·ē′nə) *n.* Any of a group of wolflike, carnivorous mammals of Africa and Asia, with short hind legs, a bristly mane, and strong teeth. [< Gk. *hyaina* sow]
hy·giene (hī′jēn) *n.* The science of health. [< Gk. *hygieinos* healthful]
hy·gi·en·ic (hī′jē·en′ik, hī·jē′nik, -jen′ik) *adj.* 1. Of or pertaining to hygiene. 2. Sanitary. —**hy′gi·en′i·cal·ly** *adv.* —**hy·gi·en·ist** (hī′jē·ən·ist, hī·jēn′ist) *n.*
hygro- *combining form* Wet; moist. Also, before vowels, **hygr-**. [< Gk. *hygros*]
hy·grom·e·ter (hī·grom′ə·tər) *n.* An instrument for measuring humidity or moisture in air. —**hy·gro·met·ric** (hī′grə·met′rik) *adj.*
hy·gro·scop·ic (hī′grə·skop′ik) *adj.* Absorbing moisture from the air.
hy·men (hī′mən) *n. Anat.* A thin mucous membrane partially covering the vaginal orifice. [< Gk. *hymēn* skin, membrane]
hy·me·ne·al (hī′mə·nē′əl) *adj.* Nuptial. —*n.* A wedding song or poem. [after *Hymen,* Greek god of marriage]
hy·men·op·ter·ous (hī′mən·op′tər·əs) *adj. Entomol.* Of or belonging to an order of insects, typically having four wings, including bees, wasps, etc. [< Gk. *hymēn* membrane + *pteron* wing] —**hy′men·op′ter·an** *adj. & n.*
hymn (him) *n.* A song of praise, adoration, thanksgiving, etc., esp. one sung at a religious service. [< Gk. *hymnos* song, ode] —**hymn** *v.t. & v.i.* —**hym′nic** (-nik) *adj.* —**hym′nist** (-nist) *n.*
hym·nal (him′nəl) *n.* A book of hymns. Also **hymn′book′** (-bo͝ok′). —*adj.* Of or relating to a hymn or hymns.
hy·oid (hī oid) *n. Anat.* In man, a U-shaped bone at the base of the tongue. Also **hyoid bone.** [< F *hyoïde*] —**hy′oid** *adj.*
hype (hīp) *v.t.* **hyped, hyp·ing** *Slang* 1. To increase artificially: *hype* the profit figure. 2. To stimulate: often with *up.* 3. To deceive. 4. To publicize extravagantly. —*n.* 1. A narcotics addict. 2. A deception. 3. One who or that which is promoted by hype. [< HYP(ODERMIC)]

hyper- *prefix* 1. Over; above; excessive: **hyperaggressive, hypercautious, hyperfine, hyperslow, hypertechnical, hyperverbal.** 2. *Med.* Denoting an abnormal state of excess: *hyperglycemia.* [< Gk. *hyper* above]

hy·per·a·cid·i·ty (hī'pər·ə·sid'ə·tē) *n. Med.* An excess of acidity, as of the gastric juice.

hy·per·ac·tive (hī'pər·ak'tiv) *adj.* Abnormally active. —**hy'per·ac·tiv'i·ty** *n.*

hy·per·bar·ic (hī'pər·bar'ik) *adj.* Relating to the use of oxygen under pressure: *hyperbaric* medicine. [< HYPER- + Gk. *baros* weight] —**hy'per·bar'i·cal·ly** *adv.*

hy·per·bo·la (hī·pûr'bə·lə) *n. Math.* The curve produced by the intersection of a plane through the surface of a cone. [See HYPERBOLE.]

hy·per·bo·le (hī·pûr'bə·lē) *n.* An exaggeration or overstatement not intended to be taken literally, as: *He was centuries old.* [< Gk. *hyperbolē* a throwing beyond, excess] —**hy·per'bo·lism** *n.* —**hy·per'bo·lize** *v.i. & v.t.* ·**lized,** ·**liz·ing**

hy·per·bol·ic (hī'pər·bol'ik) *adj.* 1. Of, pertaining to, or using hyperbole. 2. *Math.* Of or pertaining to the hyperbola. Also **hy'per·bol'i·cal.** —**hy'per·bol'i·cal·ly** *adv.*

hy·per·bo·re·an (hī'pər·bôr'ē·ən) *adj.* Of or pertaining to the far north; frigid; arctic. [< Gk. *hyper* beyond + *Boreas* north wind]

hy·per·crit·i·cal (hī'pər·krit'i·kəl) *adj.* Excessively critical or carping; faultfinding. —**hy'per·crit'i·cal·ly** *adv.*

hy·per·gly·ce·mi·a (hī'pər·glī·sē'mē·ə) *n.* An abnormally high level of sugar in the blood. [< HYPER- + Gk. *glykys* sweet + -EMIA] —**hy'per·gly·ce'mic** *adj.*

hy·per·sen·si·tive (hī'pər·sen'sə·tiv) *adj.* 1. Excessively sensitive. 2. Allergic. —**hy'·per·sen'si·tive·ness, hy'per·sen'si·tiv'i·ty** *n.*

hy·per·sen·si·tize (hī'pər·sen'sə·tīz) *v.t.* ·**tized,** ·**tiz·ing** *Photog.* To increase the sensitiveness or speed of, as a film.

hy·per·son·ic (hī'pər·son'ik) *adj.* Of, pertaining to, or characterized by supersonic speeds of mach 5 or greater.

hy·per·son·ics (hī'pər·son'iks) *n.pl.* (*construed as sing.*) The branch of dynamics concerned with the design, performance, etc., of objects moving at hypersonic speeds.

hy·per·ten·sion (hī'pər·ten'shən) *n. Pathol.* High blood pressure. —**hy'per·ten'sive** (-siv) *adj.*

hy·per·thy·roid·ism (hī'pər·thī'roid·iz'əm) *n. Pathol.* 1. Excessive activity of the thyroid gland. 2. Any disorder caused by this. —**hy'per·thy'roid** *adj. & n.*

hy·per·tro·phy (hī·pûr'trə·fē) *n. Pathol.* 1. The excessive development of an organ or part. 2. The enlargement resulting from such a condition. —*v.i. & v.t.* ·**phied,** ·**phy·ing** To grow or cause to grow excessively. —**hy·per·troph·ic** (hī'pər·trof'ik, -trō'fik) or ·**i·cal** *adj.*

hy·phen (hī'fən) *n.* A mark (-) used to connect the elements of certain compound words or to show division of a word at the end of a line. —*v.t.* To hyphenate. [< Gk. *hyph' hen* under one, together]

hy·phen·ate (hī'fən·āt) *v.t.* ·**at·ed,** ·**at·ing** 1. To connect by a hyphen. 2. To write with a hyphen. —**hy'phen·a'tion** *n.*

hypno- *combining form* Of or related to sleep. Also, before vowels, **hypn-.** [< Gk. *hypnos* sleep]

hyp·no·sis (hip·nō'sis) *n. pl.* ·**ses** (-sēz) A trancelike condition that can be artificially induced, characterized by an increased responsiveness to suggestion.

hyp·no·ther·a·py (hip'nō·ther'ə·pē) *n.* The use of hypnotism in treating disease.

hyp·not·ic (hip·not'ik) *adj.* 1. Pertaining to hypnosis or hypnotism. 2. Readily hypnotized. 3. Tending to produce sleep. —*n.* 1. A drug or other agent producing sleep. 2. A hypnotized person, or one susceptible to hypnosis. [< Gk. *hypnos* sleep] —**hyp·not'i·cal·ly** *adv.*

hyp·no·tism (hip'nə·tiz'əm) *n.* The act, practice, or study of hypnosis. —**hyp'no·tist** *n.*

hyp·no·tize (hip'nə·tīz) *v.t.* ·**tized,** ·**tiz·ing** 1. To produce hypnosis in. 2. To fascinate; charm. Also *Brit.* **hyp'no·tise.** —**hyp'no·tiz'a·ble** *adj.* —**hyp'no·tiz'er** *n.*

hy·po[1] (hī'pō) *n. Photog.* Sodium thiosulfate, used as a fixing agent.

hy·po[2] (hī'pō) *n. pl.* ·**pos** *Informal* A hypodermic injection.

hypo- *prefix* 1. Under; beneath. 2. Less than. 3. *Med.* Denoting a lack of or deficiency in. Also, before vowels, **hyp-.** [< Gk. *hypo* under]

hy·po·chon·dri·a (hī'pə·kon'drē·ə) *n.* A persistent anxiety about one's health, often with imagined symptoms of illness. [< L, abdomen (once taken to be the seat of this condition)] —**hy'po·chon'dri·ac** (-ak) *adj. & n.* —**hy·po·chon·dri·a·cal·ly** (hī'pō·kən·drī'ək·lē) *adv.*

hy·poc·ri·sy (hi·pok'rə·sē) *n. pl.* ·**sies** The pretense of having feelings or characteristics one does not possess; esp., the deceitful assumption of virtue. [< Gk. *hypokrinesthai* to play a part, act]

hyp·o·crite (hip'ə·krit) *n.* One who practices hypocrisy. —**hyp'o·crit'i·cal** *adj.* —**hyp'o·crit'i·cal·ly** *adv.*

hy·po·der·mic (hī'pə·dûr'mik) *adj.* 1. Of or pertaining to the area under the skin. 2. Injected under the skin. —*n.* A hypodermic injection or syringe.

hypodermic syringe A syringe having a sharp, hollow needle for injection of substances beneath the skin.

hy·po·gly·ce·mi·a (hī'pō·glī·sē'mē·ə) *n.* An abnormally low level of sugar in the blood. [< HYPO- + Gk. *glykys* sweet + -EMIA] —**hy'po·gly·ce'mic** *adj.*

hy·pot·e·nuse (hī·pot'ə·nōōs, -nyōōs, hi-) *n. Geom.* The side of a right triangle opposite the right angle. Also **hy·poth'e·nuse** (-poth'-). [< Gk. *hypo-* under + *teinein* to stretch]

hy·po·thal·a·mus (hī'pə·thal'ə·məs) *n. pl.* ·**mi** *Anat.* A part of the brain that controls visceral activities, body temperature, and many metabolic processes. —**hy·po·tha·lam·ic** (hī'pə·thə·lam'ik) *adj.*

hy·poth·e·cate (hī·poth'ə·kāt, hi-) *v.t.* ·**cat·ed,** ·**cat·ing** *Law* To pledge (personal property) as security for debt without transfer of possession. [< LL *hypotheca* pledge] —**hy·poth'e·ca'tion** *n.* —**hy·poth'e·ca'tor** *n.*

hy·poth·e·sis (hī·poth'ə·sis, hi-) *n. pl.* ·**ses** (-sēz) 1. An unproved scientific conclusion drawn from known facts. 2. An assumption or set of assumptions provisionally accepted, esp. as a basis for further investigation. [< Gk., foundation, supposition]

hy·poth·e·size (hī·poth′ə·sīz, hi-) *v.* **·sized, ·siz·ing** *v.t.* 1. To offer or assume as a hypothesis. —*v.i.* 2. To make a hypothesis; theorize.

hy·po·thet·i·cal (hī′pə·thet′i·kəl) *adj.* Based on hypothesis; theoretical; supposed. —*n.* A hypothetical example. Also **hy′po·thet′ic.** —**hy′po·thet′i·cal·ly** *adv.*

hy·po·thy·roid·ism (hī′pō·thī′roid·iz′əm) *n.* *Pathol.* 1. Deficient functioning of the thyroid gland. 2. A disorder resulting from this, as goiter. —**hy′po·thy′roid** *adj. & n.*

hy·son (hī′sən) *n.* A green tea from China. [< Chinese]

hys·sop (his′əp) *n.* A bushy, medicinal herb of the mint family, with small clusters of blue flowers. [< Gk. *hyssōpos*]

hys·ter·ec·to·my (his′tə·rek′tə·mē) *n.* *pl.* **·mies** *Surg.* Removal of part or all of the uterus.

hys·te·ri·a (his·tir′ē·ə, -ter′-) *n.* 1. Abnormal excitement; wild emotionalism; frenzy. 2. *Psychiatry* A psychoneurotic condition characterized by emotional outbursts and sensory disturbances. Also **hys·ter′ics** (-ter′iks). [< Gk. *hystera* the womb] —**hys·ter′ic** *n. & adj.*

hys·ter·i·cal (his·ter′i·kəl) *adj.* 1. Resembling hysteria; uncontrolled; violent. 2. Characterized or caused by hysteria. 3. Inclined to hysteria. 4. *Informal* Extremely funny. —**hys·ter′i·cal·ly** *adv.*

hystero- *combining form* 1. The womb; uterine. 2. Hysteria. Also, before vowels, **hyster-.** [< Gk. *hystera* the womb]

I

i, I (ī) *n. pl.* **i's** or **is, I's** or **Is, eyes** (īz) 1. The ninth letter of the English alphabet. 2. Any sound represented by the letter *i.* —*symbol* 1. The Roman numeral for 1. 2. *Chem.* Iodine (symbol I).

I (ī) *pron., possessive* **my** or **mine,** *objective* **me;** *pl. nominative* **we,** *possessive* **our** or **ours,** *objective* **us** The nominative singular pronoun of the first person, used by a speaker or writer in referring to himself. —*n. pl.* **I's** 1. The pronoun *I* used as a noun. 2. *Philos.* The ego. [OE *ic*]

-ial *suffix of adjectives* Var. of -AL[1]: *filial, nuptial.*

i·amb (ī′amb, ī′am) *n.* 1. In prosody, a metrical foot consisting of an unaccented syllable followed by an accented one (˘ ¯). 2. A line of verse made up of such feet. [< Gk. *iambos*] —**i·am′bic** *n. & adj.*

i·am·bus (ī·am′bəs) *n. pl.* **·bi** (-bī) or **·bus·es** An iamb.

-ian *suffix of adjectives and nouns* Var. of -AN: *amphibian, Bostonian.*

-iana See -ANA.

-iasis *suffix Med.* Denoting a process and its results, esp. in diseased conditions: *psoriasis.* [Var. of -OSIS]

-iatrics *combining form* Medical treatment: *pediatrics.* [< Gk. *iatrikos* pertaining to the art of healing]

i·at·ro·gen·ic (ī·at′rə·jen′ik) *adj.* Resulting from or aggravated by medical treatment. [< Gk. *iatros* physician + -GENIC]

-iatry *combining form* Medical or curative treatment: *psychiatry.* [< Gk. *iatreia* healing]

I-beam (ī′bēm′) *n.* A beam or joist that in cross section has the shape of the letter I.

I·be·ri·an (ī·bir′ē·ən) *adj.* Of, pertaining to, or characteristic of the land, people, or culture of Spain or Portugal. —*n.* 1. One of the ancient or modern inhabitants of the peninsula comprising Spain and Portugal. 2. The language of the ancient Iberians. [< Gk. *Iberes* Spaniards]

i·bex (ī′beks) *n. pl.* **i·bex·es** or **i·bi·ces** (ī′bə·sēz, ib′ə-) One of various wild goats of Europe and Asia, with long, recurved horns.

i·bi·dem (ib′ə·dem, i·bī′dem) *adv. Latin* In the same place; in the work, chapter, etc., just mentioned. Abbr. *ibid.*

i·bis (ī′bis) *n. pl.* **i·bis·es** or **i·bis** One of various wading birds related to the heron. [< Egyptian]

-ible See -ABLE.

-ic *suffix* 1. Forming adjectives with the meanings: **a** Of, pertaining to, or connected with: *volcanic.* **b** Of the nature of; resembling: *angelic.* **c** Produced by or in the manner of: *Homeric.* **d** Consisting of; containing: *alcoholic.* **e** *Chem.* Having a higher valence than that indicated by *-ous:* said of elements in compounds: *sulfuric* acid. 2. Forming nouns by the substantive use of adjectives in *-ic: classic, lunatic.* [< F *-ique* or L *-icus* or Gk. *-ikos*]

-ical *suffix* Forming parallel adjectives from adjectives in *-ic,* often in the same sense, as *alphabetic, alphabetical,* but sometimes with extended or special senses, as *economic, economical.* [< LL *-icalis*]

ice (īs) *n.* 1. Frozen water; also a sheet, cube, etc., of this. ◆Collateral adjective: *glacial.* 2. A frozen dessert made without cream. 3. *Slang* A diamond. —**to break the ice** 1. To dispel reserve or formality, esp. at a social gathering. 2. To make a start. —**to cut no ice** *Informal* To have no influence. —**on ice** *Slang* 1. Set aside; in reserve. 2. Incommunicado. —*v.* **iced, ic·ing** *v.t.* 1. To cause to turn to ice; freeze. 2. To chill with ice. 3. To decorate with icing. —*v.i.* 4. To turn to ice. [OE *īs*] —**iced** *adj.*

-ice *suffix of nouns* Condition, quality, or act: *cowardice, notice.* [< OF < L *-itius*]

ice bag A flexible container designed to hold ice, applied to parts of the body.

ice·berg (īs′bûrg′) *n.* A large mass of glacial ice floating in the ocean. [Prob. < Du. *ijsberg*]

ice·boat (īs′bōt′) *n.* 1. A framework with skatelike runners and sails for sailing over ice. 2. An icebreaker (def. 1).

ice·bound (īs′bound′) *adj.* Surrounded or obstructed by ice.

ice·box (īs′boks′) *n.* 1. A cabinet for holding ice and perishable food. 2. Any refrigerator.

ice·break·er (īs′brā′kər) *n.* 1. A vessel used to break up ice in waterways and harbors. 2. A structure for deflecting floating ice from the base of a bridge, a pier, etc.

ice·cap (īs′kap′) *n.* A covering of ice and snow permanently overlying a tract of land.

ice cream A frozen mixture of cream, butterfat, or milk, with flavoring, and sweetening. [Orig., *iced cream*]

ice field 1. An icecap. 2. A large, flat expanse of sea ice.

ice floe 1. A mass of floating sea ice. 2. An ice cap.

ice hockey See under HOCKEY.

ice·house (īs′hous′) *n.* A building in which ice is stored.

Ice·land·ic (īs·lan′dik) *adj.* Of or pertaining to Iceland, its inhabitants, or their language. —*n.* The North Germanic language of Iceland. —**Old Icelandic** The language of Iceland before the 16th c.: sometimes called *Old Norse.*

ice·man (īs′man′, -mən) *n. pl.* **·men** (-men′, -mən) One who sells or delivers ice.

ice pack 1. A large expanse of floating ice frozen into a single mass. 2. An ice bag.

ice pick An awllike tool for chipping ice.

i·chor (ī′kôr, ī′kər) *n.* 1. In classical mythology, the ethereal fluid supposed to flow in the veins of the gods. 2. *Pathol.* A watery, acrid fluid discharged from sores. [< Gk. *ichōr*] **—i·chor·ous** (ī′kər·əs) *adj.*

ichthyo- *combining form* Fish. Also, before vowels, ichthy-. [< Gk. *ichthys*]

ich·thy·ol·o·gy (ik′thē·ol′ə·jē) *n.* The branch of zoology that treats of fishes. **—ich′thy·o·log′ic** (-ə·loj′ik) or **·i·cal** *adj.* **—ich′thy·ol′o·gist** *n.*

-ician *suffix of nouns* One skilled in or engaged in some specified field: *musician, beautician.* [< F *-icien*]

i·ci·cle (ī′si·kəl) *n.* A hanging, tapering rod of ice formed by dripping water. [OE *īsgicel*] **—i′ci·cled** *adj.*

ic·ing (ī′sing) *n.* 1. A coating made of sugar, usu. mixed with egg whites or cream, used to cover cakes, pastry, etc. 2. The formation of ice on the surface of an aircraft.

ick·y (ik′ē) *adj.* **ick·i·er, ick·i·est** 1. Sticky. 2. Unpleasant; distasteful. [Alter. of STICKY]

i·con (ī′kon) *n.* *pl.* **i·cons** or **i·co·nes** (ī′kə·nēz) 1. In the Eastern Orthodox Church, a pictorial representation of Jesus Christ or some other sacred figure. 2. An image; likeness. Also spelled *ikon.* [< Gk. *eikōn* image] **—i·con′ic** *adj.*

i·con·o·clast (ī·kon′ə·klast) *n.* 1. One who attacks cherished beliefs and institutions. 2. One who opposes the use of religious images. [< Gk. *eikōn* image + *-klastēs* breaker] **—i·con′o·clasm** *n.* **—i·con′o·clas′tic** *adj.*

-ics *suffix of nouns* 1. An art or a field of study: *mathematics.* 2. Methods, practices, or activities: *athletics.* [See -IC.]

i·cy (ī′sē) *adj.* **i·ci·er, i·ci·est** 1. Consisting of or covered with ice. 2. Like ice: *icy* green. 3. Extremely cold. 4. Forbiddingly aloof: an *icy* greeting. [OE *īsig*] **—i′ci·ly** *adv.* **—i′ci·ness** *n.*

id (id) *n.* *Psychoanal.* The unconscious part of the psyche, considered the source of fundamental impulses toward fulfilling instinctual needs. [< L *id* it, trans. of G *es*]

ID (ī′dē′) A card, document, etc. by which identity can be established. [Short for *identification*]

I'd (īd) 1. I would. 2. I should. 3. I had.

i·de·a (ī·dē′ə) *n.* 1. That which is conceived in the mind; a thought. 2. An impression or notion. 3. A conviction; belief. 4. An intention; plan. 5. *Informal* Significance; meaning: Do you get the *idea?* 6. *Philos.* The Platonic archetype, of which an existing thing is but a representation. [< Gk. *ideein* to see]

i·de·al (ī·dē′əl, ī·dēl′) *n.* 1. A concept of perfection. 2. A person or thing taken as a standard of perfection. 3. A high principle; lofty aim. 4. That which exists only as a concept of the mind. —*adj.* 1. Perfect; supremely excellent. 2. Completely satisfactory. 3. Capable of existing as a mental concept only; utopian; imaginary. 4. Pertaining to or existing in the form of an idea or ideas. [< L *idealis*]

i·de·al·ism (ī·dē′əl·iz′əm) *n.* 1. The envisioning of things as they should be or are wished to be rather than as they are; also, action based on such idealizing. 2. Pursuit of an ideal. 3. In literature and art, the idealization of subject matter. 4. *Philos.* Any of several theories that there is no reality apart from mind or consciousness. **—i·de′al·ist** *n.* **—i′de·al·is′tic** or **·ti·cal** *adj.* **—i′de·al·is′ti·cal·ly** *adv.*

i·de·al·ize (ī·dē′əl·īz) *v.* **·ized, ·iz·ing** *v.t.* 1. To consider to be ideal; hold in high esteem. 2. To glorify. —*v.i.* 3. To form an ideal or ideals. 4. To consider or represent things in their ideal form. Also *Brit.* **i·de′al·ise. —i·de′al·i·za′tion** *n.* **—i·de′al·iz′er** *n.*

i·de·al·ly (ī·dē′əl·ē, ī·dēl′ē) *adv.* 1. In conformance with an ideal; perfectly. 2. As conceived in the mind.

i·de·ate (ī′dē·āt, ī·dē′āt) *v.t.* & *v.i.* **·at·ed, ·at·ing** To form an idea or ideas of something; think. **—i′de·a′tion** *n.* **—i′de·a′tion·al** *adj.*

i·dée fixe (ē·dā′ fēks′) *French* A fixed idea; obsession.

i·dem (ī′dem) *pron.* & *adj.* *Latin* The same: used as a reference to what has been previously mentioned.

i·den·ti·cal (ī·den′ti·kəl) *adj.* 1. One and the same; the very same. 2. Alike in every respect. 3. *Genetics* Designating human twins that develop from a single fertilized ovum: distinguished from *fraternal.* [< Med.L *idem* the same] **—i·den′ti·cal·ly** *adv.* **—i·den′ti·cal·ness** *n.*

i·den·ti·fi·ca·tion (ī·den′tə·fə·kā′shən) *n.* 1. The act of identifying, or the state of being identified. 2. Anything by which identity can be established.

i·den·ti·fy (ī·den′tə·fī) *v.t.* **·fied, ·fy·ing** 1. To establish as being a particular person or thing; recognize. 2. To regard as the same. 3. To serve as a means of recognizing; be characteristic of. 4. To associate closely. 5. To consider (oneself) as like or one with another person. [< LL *identificare*] **—i·den′ti·fi′a·ble** *adj.* **—i·den′ti·fi′er** *n.*

i·den·ti·ty (ī·den′tə·tē) *n.* *pl.* **·ties** 1. The state of being identical. 2. The state of being a specific person or thing and no other. 3. The distinctive character belonging to an individual. [< L *idem* the same]

ideo- *combining form* Idea. [< Gk. *idea* form, idea]

id·e·o·gram (id′ē·ə·gram, ī′dē-) *n.* 1. A pictorial symbol of an object or idea. 2. A graphic symbol, as +, 4, $. Also **id′e·o·graph** (-graf). **—id′e·o·gram′ic** or **id′e·o·gram′mic** *adj.*

i·de·ol·o·gy (ī′dē·ol′ə·jē, id′ē-) *n.* *pl.* **·gies** 1. The ideas and objectives that influence a community, political party, or national culture, shaping its political and social procedure. 2. The science that treats of the origin, evolution, and expression of human ideas. 3. Fanciful or visionary speculation. **—i′de·o·log′ic** (-ə·loj′ik) or **·i·cal** *adj.* **—i′de·o·log′i·cal·ly** *adv.* **—i′de·ol′o·gist** *n.*

ides (īdz) *n.pl.* In the ancient Roman calendar, the 15th of March, May, July, and October, and the 13th of the other months. [< L *idus*]

idio- *combining form* One's own; individual: *idiosyncrasy.* [< Gk. *idios* own]

id·i·o·cy (id′ē·ə·sē) *n.* *pl.* **·cies** 1. The condition of being an idiot. 2. Extreme stupidity or foolishness.

id·i·om (id′ē·əm) *n.* 1. An expression peculiar to a language, not readily understandable from the meaning of its parts, as *to put up with* (tolerate, endure). 2. The language or dialect of a region or people. 3. The special terminology of a class, occupational group, etc. 4. The distinctive character of a specific language. 5. Typical style, form, or character, as in art, literature, or music. [< Gk. *idios* one's own]

id·i·o·mat·ic (id′ē·ə·mat′ik) *adj.* 1. Characteristic of a specific language. 2. Of the nature of an idiom. 3. Employing many idioms. Also **id′i·o·mat′i·cal.** —**id′i·o·mat′i·cal·ly** *adv.*

id·i·o·path·ic (id′ē·ō·path′ik) *adj.* Of unknown cause or origin: usu. said of diseases.

id·i·o·syn·cras·y (id′ē·ō·sing′krə·sē) *n. pl.* **·sies** A habit, expression, etc., peculiar to an individual; oddity. [< Gk. *idios* own + *syn* together + *krasis* mixing] —**id′i·o·syn·crat′ic** (-sin·krat′ik) *adj.* —**id′i·o·syn·crat′i·cal·ly** *adv.*

id·i·ot (id′ē·ət) *n.* 1. A person exhibiting mental deficiency in its most severe form. 2. An extremely foolish or stupid person. [ME < L *idiota*] —**id·i·ot·ic** (id′ē·ot′ik) *adj.* —**id′i·ot′i·cal·ly** *adv.*

i·dle (īd′l) *adj.* **i·dler, i·dlest** 1. Not engaged in work. 2. Not being used; not operating. 3. Unwilling to work; lazy. 4. Spent in inactivity; reserved for leisure. 5. Having no basis or effectiveness: *idle* threats. 6. Frivolous; trifling. —*v.* **i·dled, i·dling** *v.i.* 1. To be engaged in trivial activities; loaf. 2. To move or progress lazily or aimlessly; linger. 3. *Mech.* To operate without transmitting power: said of motors or machines. —*v.t.* 4. To spend (time) wastefully; fritter: often with *away.* 5. *Informal* To cause to be idle. 6. To cause to idle, as a motor. [OE *īdel* empty, useless] —**i′dle·ness** *n.* —**i′dler** *n.* —**i′dly** *adv.*

i·dol (īd′l) *n.* 1. An image representing a god, and worshiped as divine. 2. In the Christian and Jewish religions, a false god; object of heathen worship. 3. One who is loved or admired to an excessive degree. 4. A false or misleading idea. [< Gk. *eidolon*]

i·dol·a·ter (ī·dol′ə·tər) *n.* 1. One who worships an idol or idols. 2. A blindly devoted admirer. —**i·dol′a·tress** (-tris) *n.fem.*

i·dol·a·try (ī·dol′ə·trē) *n. pl.* **·tries** 1. The worship of idols. 2. Excessive admiration; blind infatuation. [< Gk. *eidolon* idol + *latreia* worship] —**i·dol′a·trous** *adj.* —**i·dol′a·trous·ly** *adv.*

i·dol·ize (īd′l·īz) *v.* **·ized, ·iz·ing** *v.t.* 1. To love or admire to excess; adore. 2. To worship as an idol. —*v.i.* 3. To worship idols. —**i′dol·i·za′tion** *n.* —**i′dol·iz′er** *n.*

i·dyl (īd′l) *n.* 1. A poem or prose piece depicting simple scenes of pastoral, domestic, or country life. 2. An event, scene, etc., suitable for an idyl. Also **i′dyll.** [< Gk. *eidyllion* form]

i·dyl·lic (ī·dil′ik) *adj.* 1. Of or having the qualities of an idyl. 2. Charmingly simple or picturesque. Also **i·dyl′li·cal.** —**i·dyl′li·cal·ly** *adv.*

-ie *suffix* Little; dear: used affectionately: *birdie.*

i.e. That is. [< L *i*(*d*) *e*(*st*)]

-ier *suffix of nouns* One who is concerned with or works with: *cashier.* Also, after *w*, **-yer:** *lawyer.* [< F]

if (if) *conj.* 1. In the event that; in case. 2. On condition that; provided that. 3. Allowing the possibility that; granting that: *If* I am wrong, I'm sorry. 4. Whether: See *if* the mail has come. 5. Even though; although: Her clothes are neat, *if* not stylish. —*n.* A possibility or condition. [OE *gif*]

if·fy (if′ē) *adj. Informal* Dependent on many uncertain factors; questionable.

ig·loo (ig′lo͞o) *n. pl.* **·loos** A dome-shaped hut used by Eskimos, usu. built of blocks of snow. [< Eskimo *igdlu* house]

ig·ne·ous (ig′nē·əs) *adj.* 1. *Geol.* Formed by the action of great heat within the earth, as rocks consolidated from a molten state. 2. Of or like fire. [< L *ignis* fire]

ig·nis fat·u·us (ig′nis fach′o͞o·əs) *pl.* **ig·nes fat·u·i** (ig′nēz fach′o͞o·ī) A flickering, phosphorescent light sometimes seen over marshes, thought to be caused by the spontaneous combustion of marsh gas. Also called *will-o'-the-wisp.* [< Med.L., foolish fire]

ig·nite (ig·nīt′) *v.* **·nit·ed, ·nit·ing** *v.t.* 1. To set on fire; make burn. 2. To enkindle; arouse. 3. *Chem.* To cause to glow with intense heat; bring to combustion. —*v.i.* 4. To start to burn. [< L *ignire* to burn] —**ig·nit′a·ble** or **ig·nit′i·ble** *adj.* —**ig·nit′a·bil′i·ty** or **ig·nit′i·bil′i·ty** *n.* —**ig·nit′er** or **ig·ni′tor** *n.*

ig·ni·tion (ig·nish′ən) *n.* 1. The act of igniting, or the state of being ignited. 2. The process of igniting the explosive mixture of fuel and air in a cylinder of an internal-combustion engine. 3. The device or system that fires this mixture. [< L *ignire* to burn]

ig·no·ble (ig·nō′bəl) *adj.* 1. Dishonorable; base. 2. Not of noble rank. 3. Of low quality; inferior. [< IN-[1] + L *gnobilis* known] —**ig′no·bil′i·ty, ig·no′ble·ness** *n.* —**ig·no′bly** *adv.*

ig·no·min·i·ous (ig′nə·min′ē·əs) *adj.* 1. Marked by or involving dishonor or disgrace; shameful. 2. Meriting disgrace; despicable. 3. Humiliating. —**ig′no·min′i·ous·ly** *adv.* —**ig′no·min′i·ous·ness** *n.*

ig·no·min·y (ig′nə·min′ē) *n. pl.* **·min·ies** 1. Disgrace; dishonor. 2. That which causes disgrace; dishonorable conduct. [< IN-[1] + L *gnomen* name, reputation]

ig·no·ra·mus (ig′nə·rā′məs, -ram′əs) *n.* An ignorant person. [< L, we do not know]

ig·no·rant (ig′nər·ənt) *adj.* 1. Having no learning or education. 2. Lacking awareness: with *of*: *ignorant* of the facts. 3. Uninformed; inexperienced: with *in.* [See IGNORE.] —**ig′no·rance** *n.* —**ig′no·rant·ly** *adv.*

ig·nore (ig·nôr′) *v.t.* **·nored, ·nor·ing** To refuse to notice or recognize; disregard. [< F *ignorer* < IN-[1] + L *gnoscere* to know] —**ig·nor′er** *n.* —**ig·nor′a·ble** *adj.*

i·gua·na (i·gwä′nə) *n.* Any of several very large tropical American lizards. [< Sp. < Carib]

i·kon (ī′kon) See ICON.

il- Assimilated var. of IN-[1] and IN-[2].

-ile *suffix* Found in adjectives derived from French and Latin, and in nouns based on such adjectives: *docile, agile, juvenile.* Also, sometimes, **-il:** *civil, fossil.* [< L *-ilis,* suffix of adjectives]

il·e·um (il′ē·əm) *n. pl.* **il·e·a** *Anat.* The lowest of the three divisions of the small intestine. [< L *ileum* groin, small intestine] **—il′e·ac** (-ak) *adj.*

i·lex (ī′leks) *n.* Any tree or shrub of the holly family. [< L, holm oak]

Il·i·ad (il′ē·əd) An ancient Greek epic poem ascribed to Homer, describing the siege of Troy. [< Gk. *Ilion* Ilium (Troy)]

il·i·um (il′ē·əm) *n. pl.* **il·i·a** *Anat.* The large upper portion of bones of the pelvis. [< L *ilia* loins] **—il′i·ac** (-ak) *adj.*

ilk (ilk) *n.* Breed; sort. [OE *ilca* same]

ill (il) *adj.* **worse, worst** 1. Not in good health; sick. 2. Destructive; harmful. 3. Hostile or malevolent. 4. Portending danger or disaster; unfavorable. 5. Morally bad; evil. 6. Not meeting accepted standards. **—***n.* 1. Evil; wrong. 2. Injury; harm. 3. A cause of unhappiness, misfortune, etc. 4. Disaster; trouble. 5. A malady; sickness. **—***adv.* 1. Not well; badly. 2. With difficulty; hardly. 3. Unsuitably; poorly. [ME < ON *illr*]

Ill, used in combination, has the meaning badly or insufficiently, as:

ill-conceived	**ill-informed**
ill-considered	**ill-placed**
ill-equipped	**ill-suited**
ill-housed	**ill-trained**

I'll (īl) 1. I will. 2. I shall.

ill-ad·vised (il′əd·vīzd′) *adj.* Not wise; rash.

ill-bred (il′bred′) *adj.* Impolite; rude.

ill-con·sid·ered (il′kən·sid′ərd) *adj.* Done with insufficient deliberation; unwise.

ill-dis·posed (il′dis·pōzd′) *adj.* 1. Unpleasant; unfriendly. 2. Disinclined; averse. **—ill′-dis·pos′ed·ly** *adv.* **—ill′-dis·pos′ed·ness** *n.*

il·le·gal (i·lē′gəl) *adj.* 1. Not legal; contrary to law. 2. Violating official rules. **—il·le·gal·i·ty** (il′ē·gal′ə·tē) *n.* **—il·le′gal·ly** *adv.*

il·leg·i·ble (i·lej′ə·bəl) *adj.* Not legible; incapable of being read. **—il·leg′i·bil′i·ty, il·leg′i·ble·ness** *n.* **—il·leg′i·bly** *adv.*

il·le·git·i·mate (il′i·jit′ə·mit) *adj.* 1. Born out of wedlock. 2. Not according to law; unlawful. 3. Contrary to good usage; incorrect. 4. Contrary to logic; unsound. **—il′le·git′i·ma·cy** *n.* **—il′le·git′i·mate·ly** *adv.*

ill-fat·ed (il′-fā′tid) *adj.* 1. Having an unhappy fate; doomed. 2. Characterized by misfortune; unlucky.

ill-fa·vored (il′fā′vərd) *adj.* 1. Homely; ugly. 2. Objectionable; disagreeable. **—ill′-fa′·vored·ly** *adv.* **—ill′-fa′vored·ness** *n.*

ill-found·ed (il′foun′did) *adj.* Based on weak or incorrect evidence or premises; unsupported.

ill-got·ten (il′got′n) *adj.* Obtained illegally or evilly.

ill-hu·mored (il′hyōō′mərd) *adj.* Irritable; cross. **—ill′-hu′mored·ly** *adv.* **—ill′-hu′·mored·ness** *n.*

il·lib·er·al (i·lib′ər·əl) *adj.* 1. Not generous; stingy. 2. Narrow-minded; intolerant. **—il·lib′er·al′i·ty** (-al′ə·tē) *n.* **—il·lib′er·al·ly** *adv.*

il·lic·it (i·lis′it) *adj.* Not permitted; unlawful. **—il·lic′it·ly** *adv.* **—il·lic′it·ness** *n.*

il·lim·it·a·ble (i·lim′it·ə·bəl) *adj.* Incapable of being limited; boundless. **—il·lim′it·a·bil′i·ty, il·lim′it·a·ble·ness** *n.* **—il·lim′it·a·bly** *adv.*

Il·li·nois (il′ə·noi′, -noiz′) *n. pl.* **·nois** A North American Indian of a tribe belonging to a confederacy of Algonquian tribes. [< F < N.Am.Ind.]

il·lit·er·ate (i·lit′ər·it) *adj.* 1. Lacking education; esp., unable to read and write. 2. Of language, characteristic of the uneducated. **—***n.* An illiterate person. **—il·lit′er·a·cy** *n.* **—il·lit′er·ate·ly** *adv.* **—il·lit′er·ate·ness** *n.*

ill-man·nered (il′man′ərd) *adj.* Bad-mannered; rude. **—ill′-man′nered·ly** *adv.*

ill nature Unpleasant disposition; surliness. **—ill-na·tured** (il′nā′chərd) *adj.* **—ill′-na′·tured·ly** *adv.*

ill·ness (il′nis) *n.* 1. The state of being in poor health; sickness. 2. An ailment.

il·log·i·cal (i·loj′i·kəl) *adj.* Not logical; neglectful of reason. **—il·log′i·cal′i·ty** (-kal′ə·tē), **il·log′i·cal·ness** *n.* **—il·log′i·cal·ly** *adv.*

ill repute Evil reputation. **—house of ill repute** Brothel.

ill-spent (il′spent′) *adj.* Wasted; misspent.

ill-starred (il′stärd′) *adj.* Unlucky.

ill temper Crossness; irritability. **—ill-tem·pered** (il′tem′pərd) *adj.* **—ill′-tem′·pered·ly** *adv.*

ill-timed (il′tīmd′) *adj.* Occurring at an unsuitable time.

ill-treat (il′trēt′) *v.t.* To act cruelly toward; maltreat.

il·lu·mi·nant (i·lōō′mə·nənt) *n.* Something that gives light.

il·lu·mi·nate (i·lōō′mə·nāt) *v.* **·nat·ed, ·nat·ing** *v.t.* 1. To give light to; light up. 2. To clarify; explain. 3. To enlighten. 4. To decorate, as a manuscript, with ornamental borders, figures, etc., often of gold. **—***v.i.* 5. To shed light; become lighted. [< L *illuminare*] **—il·lu′mi·na′tion** *n.* **—il·lu′mi·na′tive** *adj.* **—il·lu′mi·na′tor** *n.*

il·lu·mine (i·lōō′min) *v.t. & v.i.* **·mined, ·min·ing** To illuminate or be illuminated.

ill-use (*v.* il′yōōz′; *n.* il′yōōs′) *v.t.* **-used, -us·ing** To treat cruelly or unjustly; abuse. **—***n.* Bad or unjust treatment: also **ill′-us′age** (-yōō′sij, -yōō′zij) *n.*

il·lu·sion (i·lōō′zhən) *n.* 1. A false, misleading, or overly optimistic idea. 2. An impression not consistent with fact. [< L *illudere* to make sport of] **—il·lu′·sion·al, il·lu′sion·ar·y** *adj.*

il·lu·sive (i·lōō′siv) *adj.* Unreal; illusory. **—il·lu′sive·ly** *adv.* **—il·lu′sive·ness** *n.*

il·lu·so·ry (i·lōō′sər·ē) *adj.* Of the nature of illusion; deceptive. **—il·lu′so·ri·ly** *adv.* **—il·lu′so·ri·ness** *n.*

il·lus·trate (il′ə·strāt, i·lus′trāt) *v.t.* **·trat·ed, ·trat·ing** 1. To explain or make clear by means of examples, comparisons, etc. 2. To supply or accompany (a book, etc.) with pictures, as for instruction or decoration. [< IN-[2] + L *lustrare* to illuminate] **—il′lus·tra′tor** *n.*

il·lus·tra·tion (il′ə·strā′shən) *n.* 1. An example, comparison, anecdote, etc., by which a statement is explained. 2. A print, drawing, or picture in a text. 3. The act or art of illustrating. [< L *illustratio*]

il·lus·tra·tive (i·lus′trə·tiv, il′ə·strā′tiv) *adj.* Serving to illustrate. **—il·lus′tra·tive·ly** *adv.*

il·lus·tri·ous (i·lus′trē·əs) *adj.* 1. Greatly distinguished; renowned. 2. Conferring greatness or glory. [< IN-[2] + L *lustrum* light] —**il·lus′tri·ous·ly** *adv.* —**il·lus′tri·ous·ness** *n.*

ill will Hostile feeling; malevolence.

im-[1] Var. of EM-[1].

im-[2] Assimilated var. of IN-[1] and IN-[2].

I'm (īm) I am.

im·age (im′ij) *n.* 1. A representation or likeness of a real or imaginary person, creature, or object. 2. A mental picture. 3. The way in which a person or thing is popularly perceived or regarded: a politician's *image.* 4. A person or thing that closely resembles another. 5. A representative example; embodiment. 6. A literary device that evokes a mental picture, as a figure of speech. 7. *Optics* The counterpart of an object produced by reflection, refraction, or the passage of rays through a small aperture. —*v.t.* **·aged, ·ag·ing** 1. To form a mental picture of. 2. To make a visible representation of; portray. 3. To mirror; reflect. 4. To describe effectively or vividly. 5. To symbolize. [< L *imago* < *imitari* to imitate]

im·age·ry (im′ij·rē) *n. pl.* **·ries** 1. Mental images collectively. 2. The act or process of forming mental images. 3. The use of vivid descriptions or figures of speech. 4. Images used in art or decoration.

im·ag·i·nar·y (i·maj′ə·ner′ē) *adj.* Existing in the imagination only; unreal. —**im·ag′i·nar′i·ly** *adv.* —**im·ag′i·nar′i·ness** *n.*

im·ag·i·na·tion (i·maj′ə·nā′shən) *n.* 1. The process of forming mental images of the objects of perception or thought in the absence of the corresponding external stimuli. 2. The mental ability to create original and striking images and concepts. 3. Creativity or originality of any sort. 4. A creation of the mind; mental image. 5. An absurd fancy. —**im·ag′i·na′tion·al** *adj.*

im·ag·i·na·tive (i·maj′ə·nə·tiv, -nā′tiv) *adj.* 1. Endowed with imagination. 2. Given to flights of fancy. 3. Of or characterized by the creative imagination. —**im·ag′i·na·tive·ly** *adv.* —**im·ag′i·na·tive·ness** *n.*

im·ag·ine (i·maj′in) *v.t. & v.i.* **·ined, ·in·ing** 1. To form a mental picture or idea of (anything). 2. To suppose; guess. [< L *imago* image] —**im·ag′i·na·ble** *adj.*

im·a·gism (im′ə·jiz′əm) *n.* An early 20th c. movement in poetry characterized by precise images and freedom in form. [< F *Des Imagistes,* the title of the first anthology of such poetry]

i·ma·go (i·mā′gō) *n. pl.* **i·ma·goes** or **i·mag·i·nes** (i·maj′ə·nēz) *Entomol.* An insect in its adult, sexually mature stage. [< L, image]

i·mam (i·mäm′) *n.* 1. The leader of prayer in a mosque. 2. *cap.* The title of a Muslim leader; esp., a successor of Muhammad. [< Arabic *imām*]

im·bal·ance (im·bal′əns) *n.* The state of being out of balance or not coordinated.

im·be·cile (im′bə·sil) *n.* 1. A person exhibiting a degree of mental deficiency between that of the idiot and the moron. 2. A foolish or stupid person. —*adj.* 1. Mentally deficient. 2. Stupid; senseless. [< L *imbecillus* weak, feeble] —**im′be·cil′ic** *adj.* —**im′be·cil′i·ty** *n.*

im·bibe (im·bīb′) *v.* **·bibed, ·bib·ing** *v.t.* 1. To drink. 2. To suck up; absorb. 3. To take in mentally. —*v.i.* 4. To drink. [< IN-[2] + L *bibere* to drink] —**im·bib′er** *n.*

im·bri·cate (*adj.* im′brə·kit; *v.* im′brə·kāt) *adj.* 1. Arranged with overlapping edges, as shingles on a roof. 2. Covered or decorated with a design resembling overlapping scales, leaves, etc. Also **im′bri·ca′tive.** —*v.t. & v.i.* **·cat·ed, ·cat·ing** To overlap in a regular arrangement. [< L *imbrex* gutter tile < *imber* rain] —**im′bri·ca′tion** *n.*

im·bro·glio (im·brōl′yō) *n. pl.* **·glios** 1. A confused state of affairs. 2. A confused heap or tangle. [< Ital.]

im·brue (im·broo′) *v.t.* **·brued, ·bru·ing** To stain or drench, esp. with blood. [< OF *embreuver.* See IMBIBE.]

im·bue (im·byoo′) *v.t.* **·bued, ·bu·ing** 1. To pervade or permeate. 2. To wet thoroughly or saturate, as with color. [< L *imbuere* to wet, soak]

im·i·tate (im′ə·tāt) *v.t.* **·tat·ed, ·tat·ing** 1. To behave or attempt to behave in the same way as; follow the example of. 2. To mimic or impersonate. 3. To make a copy or reproduction of. 4. To have or take on the appearance of. [< L *imitari*] —**im′i·ta·ble** (-tə·bəl) *adj.* —**im′i·ta′tor** *n.*

im·i·ta·tion (im′ə·tā′shən) *n.* 1. The act of imitating. 2. That which is done by or results from imitating; copy. —*adj.* Resembling or made to resemble something superior; not genuine. [< L *imitatio, -onis*]

im·i·ta·tive (im′ə·tā′tive) *adj.* 1. Tending to imitate; characterized by imitation. 2. Patterned after or reproducing the characteristics of an original. 3. Not genuine; spurious. 4. *Ling.* Designating words that resemble natural sounds, as *buzz, swish.* —**im′i·ta′tive·ly** *adv.* —**im′i·ta′tive·ness** *n.*

im·mac·u·late (i·mak′yə·lit) *adj.* 1. Without spot or stain; unsullied. 2. Without sin; pure. 3. Without error or blemish; flawless. [< IN-[1] + L *macula* spot] —**im·mac′u·late·ly** *adv.* —**im·mac′u·late·ness** *n.*

im·ma·nent (im′ə·nənt) *adj.* 1. Existing or remaining within; indwelling. 2. Of God, pervading all creation. [< IN-[2] + L *manere* to stay] —**im′ma·nence, im′ma·nen·cy** *n.* —**im′ma·nent·ly** *adv.*

im·ma·te·ri·al (im′ə·tir′ē·əl) *adj.* 1. Of little or no importance; inconsequential. 2. Not consisting of material substance. [< IN-[1] + LL *materialis* matter] —**im′ma·te′ri·al·ly** *adv.* —**im′ma·te′ri·al·ness** *n.*

im·ma·ture (im′ə·choor′, -tyoor′, -toor′) *adj.* Not mature, ripe, or developed. —**im′ma·ture′ly** *adv.* —**im′ma·tur′i·ty, im′ma·ture′·ness** *n.*

im·meas·ur·a·ble (i·mezh′ər·ə·bəl) *adj.* Not capable of being measured; without limit; immense. —**im·meas′ur·a·bly** *adv.* —**im·meas′ur·a·bil′i·ty, im·meas′ur·a·ble·ness** *n.*

im·me·di·ate (i·mē′dē·it) *adj.* 1. Done or occurring without delay; instant. 2. Pertaining to the present moment: We have no *immediate* vacancies. 3. Very near or close. 4. Occurring or acting without an intervening agency or cause. [< IN-[1] + LL *mediatus* intermediate] —**im·me′di·a·cy, im·me′di·ate·ness** *n.* —**im·me′di·ate·ly** *adv.*

im·me·mo·ri·al (im′ə·môr′ē·əl) *adj.* Reaching back beyond memory; ancient. —**im′me·mo′ri·al·ly** *adv.*

im·mense (i·mens′) *adj.* 1. Of great size, degree, or extent; huge. 2. Having no limits; infinite. 3. *Informal* Excellent. [< IN-[1] + L *mensus*, pp. of *metiri* to measure] —**im·mense′ly** *adv.* —**im·men′si·ty** *n.*

im·men·sur·a·ble (i·men′shoor·ə·bəl, -sə·rə-) *adj.* Immeasurable. [< IN-[1] + L *mensurare* to measure] —**im·men′sur·a·bil′·i·ty** *n.*

im·merge (i·mûrj′) *v.* ·**merged**, ·**merg·ing** *v.t.* 1. To immerse. —*v.i.* 2. To plunge or sink into a liquid. [< IN-[2] + L *mergere* to dip] —**im·mer′gence** *n.*

im·merse (i·mûrs′) *v.t.* ·**mersed**, ·**mers·ing** 1. To plunge or dip into water or other fluid so as to cover completely. 2. To involve deeply; engross. 3. To baptize by plunging the entire body under water. [< L *immersus*, pp. of *immergere* to dip] —**im·mer·sion** (i·mûr′zhən) *n.*

im·mi·grant (im′ə·grənt) *n.* A person who immigrates. —*adj.* Of or pertaining to immigration or immigrants.

im·mi·grate (im′ə·grāt) *v.i.* ·**grat·ed**, ·**grat·ing** To come into a country or region of which one is not a native in order to settle there. [< IN-[2] + L *migrare* to migrate]

im·mi·gra·tion (im′ə·grā′shən) *n.* 1. The act of immigrating. 2. The total number of immigrants entering a country during a stated period. 3. Immigrants collectively. —**im·mi·gra·to·ry** (im′ə·grə·tôr′ē) *adj.*

im·mi·nent (im′ə·nənt) *adj.* About to happen; impending: said esp. of danger or catastrophe. [< IN-[2] + L *minere* to project] —**im′mi·nence**, **im′mi·nen·cy** *n.* —**im′mi·nent·ly** *adv.*

im·mis·ci·ble (i·mis′ə·bəl) *adj.* Not capable of being mixed, as oil and water. [< IN-[1] + L *miscere* to mix] —**im·mis′ci·bil′i·ty** *n.* —**im·mis′ci·bly** *adv.*

im·mo·bile (i·mō′bəl, -bēl) *adj.* 1. Incapable of being moved. 2. Not moving; motionless. [< IN-[1] + L *movere* to move] —**im′mo·bil′i·ty** *n.*

im·mo·bi·lize (i·mō′bə·līz) *v.t.* ·**lized**, ·**liz·ing** 1. To make immovable; fix in place. 2. To make unable to move or mobilize, as a body of troops. —**im·mo′bi·li·za′tion** *n.*

im·mod·er·ate (i·mod′ər·it) *adj.* Not moderate; excessive. —**im·mod′er·ate·ly** *adv.* —**im·mod′er·a·cy**, **im·mod′er·ate·ness** *n.* —**im·mod′er·a′tion** *n.*

im·mod·est (i·mod′ist) *adj.* 1. Without sense of decency; improper. 2. Lacking humility; bold. —**im·mod′est·ly** *adv.* —**im·mod′es·ty** *n.*

im·mo·late (im′ə·lāt) *v.t.* ·**lat·ed**, ·**lat·ing** To sacrifice; esp., to kill as a sacrificial victim. [< IN-[2] + L *mola* meal, after the sprinkling of victims with sacrificial meal] —**im′mo·la′tion** *n.* —**im′mo·la′tor** *n.*

im·mor·al (i·môr′əl, i·mor′-) *adj.* 1. Contrary to conscience or public morality. 2. Sexually impure; licentious. —**im·mor′·al·ly** *adv.*

im·mo·ral·i·ty (im′ə·ral′ə·tē, -ôr·al′-) *n.* *pl.* ·**ties** 1. The state or quality of being immoral; wickedness; dissoluteness. 2. Sexual impurity or misconduct. 3. An immoral act.

im·mor·tal (i·môr′təl) *adj.* 1. Not subject to death; living forever. 2. Having unending existence; eternal. 3. Pertaining to immortality or to beings or concepts that are immortal. 4. Of enduring fame. —*n.* 1. An immortal being. 2. *pl.* The gods of classical mythology. 3. A person who has gained enduring fame. —**im·mor′tal·ly** *adv.*

im·mor·tal·i·ty (im′ôr·tal′ə·tē) *n.* 1. Unending existence. 2. Eternal fame.

im·mor·tal·ize (i·môr′təl·īz) *v.t.* ·**ized**, ·**iz·ing** To make immortal; endow with perpetual fame. Also *Brit.* **im·mor′tal·ise.** —**im·mor′tal·i′zer** *n.* —**im·mor′tal·i·za′tion** *n.*

im·mov·a·ble (i·mōō′və·bəl) *adj.* 1. Incapable of being moved. 2. Unable to move; stationary. 3. Firm; unyielding. 4. Not easily aroused; impassive. —*n.pl.* *Law* Real property. —**im·mov′a·bil′i·ty**, **im·mov′a·ble·ness** *n.* —**im·mov′a·bly** *adv.*

im·mune (i·myōōn′) *adj.* 1. Protected against a disease, poison, or the like, as by inoculation. 2. Not subject to obligation, penalty, harm, etc. [< IN-[1] + L *munis* serviceable] —**im·mu′ni·ty** *n.*

im·mu·nize (im′yə·nīz) *v.t.* ·**nized**, ·**niz·ing** To make immune. —**im′mu·ni·za′tion** *n.*

im·mu·nol·o·gy (im′yə·nol′ə·jē) *n.* The branch of medical science that deals with immunity to disease. —**im·mu·no·log·i·cal** (im′yə·nə·loj′i·kəl) *adj.* —**im′mu·nol′o·gist** *n.*

im·mure (i·myŏŏr′) *v.t.* ·**mured**, ·**mur·ing** 1. To enclose within walls; imprison. 2. To entomb within a wall. [< IN-[2] + LL *murare* to wall] —**im·mure′ment** *n.*

im·mu·ta·ble (i·myōō′tə·bəl) *adj.* Not mutable; unchanging; unalterable. —**im·mu′ta·bil′i·ty**, **im·mu′ta·ble·ness** *n.* —**im·mu′ta·bly** *adv.*

imp (imp) *n.* 1. A small demon. 2. A mischievous child. [OE *impa* young shoot]

im·pact (*n.* im′pakt; *v.* im·pakt′) *n.* 1. A striking together; collision. 2. The force of such a contact; shock. 3. Strong influence; powerful effect. —*v.t.* To press or drive firmly into something. [< L *impactus*, pp. of *impingere* to impinge]

im·pact·ed (im·pak′tid) *adj.* 1. Pressed firmly together; wedged. 2. *Dent.* Denoting a tooth unable to emerge through the gum.

im·pac·tion (im·pak′shən) *n.* 1. The act of impacting, or the state of being impacted. 2. *Dent.* An impacted tooth.

im·pair (im·pâr′) *v.t.* To cause to become less in quality, power, or value; make worse. [< IN-[2] + LL *pejorare* to make worse] —**im·pair′ment** *n.*

im·pale (im·pāl′) *v.t.* ·**paled**, ·**pal·ing** 1. To fix upon a pale or a sharp stake. 2. To make helpless as if by fixing upon a stake. [< IN-[2] + L *palus* stake] —**im·pale′ment** *n.* —**im·pal′er** *n.*

im·pal·pa·ble (im·pal′pə·bəl) *adj.* 1. Not capable of being perceived by the sense of touch. 2. Not capable of being distinguished by the mind. —**im·pal′pa·bil′i·ty** *n.* —**im·pal′pa·bly** *adv.*

im·pan·el (im·pan′əl) *v.t.* **im·pan·eled** or ·**elled**, **im·pan·el·ing** or ·**el·ling** 1. To enroll upon a panel or list, as for jury duty. 2. To choose (members of a jury, etc.) from such a list. Also spelled *empanel.* —**im·pan′el·ment** *n.*

im·part (im·pärt′) *v.t.* 1. To make known; disclose. 2. To bestow a measure or quantity of. [< IN-[2] + L *partire* to share] —**im′par·ta′tion, im·part′ment** *n.* —**im·part′er** *n.*

im·par·tial (im·pär′shəl) *adj.* Free from bias; fair. —**im′par·ti·al′·i·ty** (-shē·al′·ə·tē) *n.* —**im·par′tial·ly** *adv.* —**im·par′tial·ness** *n.*

im·pass·a·ble (im·pas′ə·bəl) *adj.* That cannot be traveled over or through: an *impassable* jungle. —**im·pass′a·bil′i·ty, im·pass′a·ble·ness** *n.* —**im·pass′a·bly** *adv.*

im·passe (im′pas, im·pas′) *n.* 1. A situation in which no further progress is possible; deadlock. 2. A dead end. [< F]

im·pas·si·ble (im·pas′ə·bəl) *adj.* 1. Incapable of emotion; unfeeling. 2. Incapable of suffering pain. 3. Invulnerable. [< IN-[1] + LL *passibilis* < L *pati* to suffer] —**im·pas′si·bil′i·ty, im·pas′si·ble·ness** *n.* —**im·pas′si·bly** *adv.*

im·pas·sioned (im·pash′ənd) *adj.* Filled with passion or strong feeling; fervent. —**im·pas′sioned·ly** *adv.*

im·pas·sive (im·pas′iv) *adj.* Not feeling or tending to feel emotion; unmoved; calm. —**im·pas′sive·ly** *adv.* —**im·pas′sive·ness, im·pas·siv·i·ty** (im′pa·siv′ə·tē) *n.*

im·pas·to (im·päs′tō) *n.* 1. Painting in which the paint is applied in very heavy strokes. 2. Paint so applied. [< Ital.]

im·pa·ti·ens (im·pā′shē·enz) *n.* An herb with stems enlarged at the joints and irregular flowers. [< L, impatient; because the ripe seed pods burst open at a touch]

im·pa·tient (im·pā′shənt) *adj.* 1. Lacking patience; restless; irritable. 2. Unwilling to tolerate: with *of.* 3. Restlessly eager. 4. Exhibiting lack of patience. —**im·pa′tience** *n.* —**im·pa′tient·ly** *adv.*

im·peach (im·pēch′) *v.t.* 1. To charge (a high public official) before a legally constituted tribunal with crime or misdemeanor in office. 2. To challenge or bring discredit upon the honesty or validity of. [< IN-[2] + L *pedica* fetter] —**im·peach′a·bil′i·ty** *n.* —**im·peach′a·ble** *adj.* —**im·peach′ment** *n.*

im·pec·ca·ble (im·pek′ə·bəl) *adj.* Free from error, fault, or flaw. [< IN-[1] + L *peccare* to sin] —**im·pec′ca·bil′i·ty** *n.* —**im·pec′ca·bly** *adv.*

im·pe·cu·ni·ous (im′pə·kyōō′nē·əs) *adj.* Having no money; penniless. Also **im′pe·cu′ni·ar′y** (-nē·er′ē). [< IN-[1] + L *pecunia* money] —**im′pe·cu′ni·ous·ly** *adv.* —**im′pe·cu′ni·ous·ness, im′pe·cu′ni·os′i·ty** (-os′ə·tē) *n.*

im·ped·ance (im·pēd′ns) *n. Electr.* The total opposition to an alternating current presented by a circuit.

im·pede (im·pēd′) *v.t.* **·ped·ed, ·ped·ing** To retard or hinder; obstruct. [< L *impedire,* lit., to shackle the feet] —**im·ped′er** *n.* —**im·ped′ing·ly** *adv.*

im·ped·i·ment (im·ped′ə·mənt) *n.* 1. That which hinders or obstructs; an obstacle. 2. A physical handicap, esp. a speech defect. —**im·ped′i·men′tal** (-men′təl), **im·ped′i·men′ta·ry** (-men′tər·ē) *adj.*

im·ped·i·men·ta (im·ped′ə·men′tə) *n.pl.* 1. Cumbersome baggage or equipment. 2. Drawbacks or burdens. [< L]

im·pel (im·pel′) *v.t.* **·pelled, ·pel·ling** 1. To force or drive to an action; push; urge on. 2. To drive or push forward. [< IN-[2] + L *pellere* to drive] —**im·pel′lent** *adj. & n.* —**im·pel′ler** *n.*

im·pend (im·pend′) *v.i.* 1. To be about to occur; be imminent. 2. To be suspended: with *over.* [< IN-[2] + L *pendere* to hang] —**im·pen′dent** *adj.* —**im·pen′dence** *n.*

im·pend·ing (im·pen′ding) *adj.* 1. About to occur; imminent. 2. Overhanging.

im·pen·e·tra·ble (im·pen′ə·trə·bəl) *adj.* 1. Incapable of being penetrated; that cannot be pierced, entered, seen through, etc. 2. Incapable of being understood. —**im·pen′e·tra·bil′i·ty, im·pen′e·tra·ble·ness** *n.* —**im·pen′e·tra·bly** *adv.*

im·pen·i·tent (im·pen′ə·tənt) *adj.* Not penitent; obdurate. —**im·pen′i·tence, im·pen′i·ten·cy** *n.* —**im·pen′i·tent·ly** *adv.*

im·per·a·tive (im·per′ə·tiv) *adj.* 1. Urgently necessary; obligatory. 2. Having the nature of or expressing a command. 3. *Gram.* Designating the mood used to express commands, requests, exhortations, etc. —*n.* 1. That which is imperative. 2. *Gram.* The imperative mood. [< LL *imperare* to command] —**im·per′a·tive·ly** *adv.* —**im·per′a·tive·ness** *n.*

im·per·cep·ti·ble (im′pər·sep′tə·bəl) *adj.* 1. That can barely be perceived, as by reason of smallness, subtlety, etc. 2. Not discernible. —**im′per·cep′ti·bil′i·ty** *n.* —**im′per·cep′ti·bly** *adv.*

im·per·cep·tive (im′pər·sep′tiv) *adj.* Not perceptive; lacking the power of perception. —**im′per·cep·tiv′i·ty, im′per·cep′tive·ness** *n.*

im·per·fect (im·pûr′fikt) *adj.* 1. Falling short of perfection; faulty. 2. Wanting in completeness; deficient. 3. Denoting a tense that indicates uncompleted or continuing past action. —*n. Gram.* The imperfect tense. —**im·per′fect·ly** *adv.* —**im·per′fect·ness** *n.*

im·per·fec·tion (im′pər·fek′shən) *n.* 1. The state or quality of being imperfect. 2. A defect; flaw. [< L *imperfectus* incomplete]

im·per·fo·rate (im·pûr′fər·it) *adj.* 1. Without perforations. 2. Not separated by lines of perforations: said of stamps. Also **im·per′fo·rat′ed** (-rā′tid). —*n.* An imperforated stamp. —**im·per′fo·ra′tion** (-rā′shən) *n.*

im·pe·ri·al (im·pir′ē·əl) *adj.* 1. Of or pertaining to an empire or to the ruler of an empire. 2. Designating a nation having sovereign power over colonies or dependencies. 3. Imperious; overbearing. 4. Possessing commanding power or dignity; majestic. 5. Superior in size or quality. [< L *imperium* rule] —**im·pe′ri·al·ly** *adv.* —**im·per′i·al·ness** *n.*

imperial gallon See under GALLON.

im·pe·ri·al·ism (im·pir′ē·əl·iz′əm) *n.* 1. The creation, maintenance, or extension of an empire, comprising many nations and areas, all controlled by a central government. 2. A system of imperial government. 3. Imperial character, authority, or spirit. —**im·pe′ri·al·ist** *n. & adj.* —**im·pe′ri·al·is′tic** *adj.* —**im·pe′ri·al·is′ti·cal·ly** *adv.*

im·per·il (im·per′il) *v.t.* **im·per·iled** or **·illed, im·per·il·ing** or **·il·ling** To place in peril; endanger.

im·pe·ri·ous (im·pir′ē·əs) *adj.* 1. Commanding; domineering. 2. Urgent; imperative. —**im·pe′ri·ous·ly** *adv.* —**im·pe′ri·ous·ness** *n.*

im·per·ish·a·ble (im·per′ish·ə·bəl) *adj.* Not

perishable; enduring. —**im·per′ish·a·bil′i·ty** *n.* —**im·per′ish·a·bly** *adv.*

im·per·ma·nent (im·pûr′mə·nənt) *adj.* Not permanent; fleeting. —**im·per′ma·nence, im·per′ma·nen·cy** *n.* —**im·per′ma·nent·ly** *adv.*

im·per·me·a·ble (im·pûr′mē·ə·bəl) *adj.* 1. Not permitting passage or penetration. 2. Impervious to moisture. —**im·per′me·a·bil′i·ty** *n.* —**im·per′me·a·bly** *adv.*

im·per·mis·si·ble (im′pər·mis′ə·bəl) *adj.* Not to be permitted. —**im′per·mis′si·bil′i·ty** *n.* —**im′per·mis′si·bly** *adv.*

im·per·son·al (im·pûr′sən·əl) *adj.* 1. Not personal; objective. 2. Not having the characteristics of a person: an *impersonal* deity. 3. *Gram.* Of a verb, having no specific subject: in English the word *it* is usu. used with such verbs. —*n. Gram.* An impersonal verb. —**im·per′son·al′i·ty** (-al′ə·tē) *n.* —**im·per′son·al·ly** *adv.*

im·per·son·ate (im·pûr′sən·āt) *v.t.* **·at·ed, ·at·ing** To act the part of or pretend to be (another person), esp. for purposes of entertainment or fraud. —**im·per′son·a′tion** *n.* —**im·per′son·a′tor** *n.*

im·per·ti·nent (im·pûr′tə·nənt) *adj.* 1. Deliberately disrespectful or unmannerly; impudent. 2. Not pertinent; irrelevant. 3. Not suitable; inappropriate. —**im·per′ti·nence, im·per′ti·nen·cy** *n.* —**im·per′ti·nent·ly** *adv.*

im·per·turb·a·ble (im′pər·tûr′bə·bəl) *adj.* Incapable of being agitated; calm. —**im′per·turb′a·bil′i·ty** *n.* —**im′per·turb′a·bly** *adv.*

im·per·vi·ous (im·pûr′vē·əs) *adj.* 1. Incapable of being passed through; impermeable. 2. Not open; unreceptive. Also **im·per′vi·a·ble.** [< IN-[1] + L *per-* through + *via* way, road] —**im·per′vi·ous·ly** *adv.* —**im·per′vi·ous·ness** *n.*

im·pe·ti·go (im′pə·tī′gō) *n. Pathol.* A contagious skin disease marked by pustules. [< L *impetere* to attack]

im·pet·u·ous (im·pech′o͞o·əs) *adj.* 1. Tending to act on sudden impulse. 2. Resulting from sudden impulse; hasty. 3. Moving with violent force. [< L *impetere* to attack] —**im·pet′u·os′i·ty** (-os′ə·tē), **im·pet′u·ous·ness** *n.* —**im·pet′u·ous·ly** *adv.*

im·pe·tus (im′pə·təs) *n.* 1. The force that sets a body in motion; also, the energy with which a body moves or is driven. 2. Any motivating force; stimulus; incentive. [< IN-[2] + L *petere* to seek]

im·pi·e·ty (im·pī′ə·tē) *n. pl.* **·ties** 1. Lack of reverence for God; ungodliness. 2. Lack of respect for those to whom respect is due. 3. An impious act.

im·pinge (im·pinj′) *v.i.* **·pinged, ·ping·ing** 1. To strike; fall: with *on, upon,* or *against.* 2. To encroach; infringe: with *on* or *upon.* [< IN-[2] + L *pangere* to strike] —**im·pinge′·ment** *n.* —**im·ping′er** *n.*

im·pi·ous (im′pē·əs, im·pī′əs) *adj.* 1. Lacking in reverence for God; blasphemous. 2. Lacking in due respect. [< IN-[1] + L *pius* reverent] —**im′pi·ous·ly** *adv.*

imp·ish (imp′ish) *adj.* Characteristic of or resembling an imp; mischievous. —**imp′ish·ly** *adv.* —**imp′ish·ness** *n.*

im·pla·ca·ble (im·plā′kə·bəl, -plak′ə-) *adj.* That cannot be appeased or pacified. [< IN-[1] + L *placere* to please] —**im·pla′ca·bil′i·ty** *n.* —**im·pla′ca·bly** *adv.*

im·plant (*v.* im·plant′; *n.* im′plant′) *v.t.* 1. To fix firmly, as in the ground; embed. 2. To instill in the mind; inculcate. 3. *Med.* To insert or embed in (living tissue). —*n. Med.* A tissue or device implanted in the body. [< F *implanter*] —**im′plan·ta′tion** *n.*

im·plau·si·ble (im·plô′zə·bəl) *adj.* Not plausible; lacking the appearance of truth or trustworthiness. —**im·plau′si·bil′i·ty** *n.* —**im·plau′si·bly** *adv.*

im·ple·ment (*n.* im′plə·mənt; *v.* im′plə·ment) *n.* 1. A piece of equipment used in some form of work or activity; tool; utensil. 2. Any means or agent for the accomplishment of a purpose. —*v.t.* 1. To carry out; accomplish; fulfill. 2. To furnish with implements. [< IN-[2] + L *plere* to fill] —**im′ple·men′tal** *adj.* —**im′ple·men·ta′tion** *n.*

im·pli·cate (im′plə·kāt) *v.t.* **·cat·ed, ·cat·ing** 1. To show to be involved, as in a plot or crime. 2. To imply. [< IN-[2] + L *plicare* to fold] —**im′pli·ca′tive, im′pli·ca·to′ry** (-kə·tôr′ē) *adj.*

im·pli·ca·tion (im′plə·kā′shən) *n.* 1. The act of involving, or the state of being involved. 2. The act of implying, or the state of being implied. 3. That which is implied.

im·plic·it (im·plis′it) *adj.* 1. Unreserved; absolute. 2. Implied or understood, but not specifically expressed: *implicit* agreement. 3. Essentially contained, but not apparent; inherent: with *in.* [< L *implicare* to involve] —**im·plic′it·ly** *adv.* —**im·plic′it·ness** *n.*

im·plied (im·plīd′) *adj.* Understood, suggested, or included without being specifically expressed.

im·plode (im·plōd′) *v.t. & v.i.* **·plod·ed, ·plod·ing** To burst inward. —**im·plo·sion** (im·plō′zhən) *n.* —**im·plo·sive** (im·plō′siv) *adj.* [< IN-[2] + (EX)PLODE]

im·plore (im·plôr′) *v.t. & v.i.* **·plored, ·plor·ing** To beg humbly or urgently; beseech. [< IN-[2] + L *plorare* to cry out] —**im·plor′ing·ly** *adv.*

im·ply (im·plī′) *v.t.* **·plied, ·ply·ing** 1. To involve necessarily as a circumstance, condition, effect, etc. 2. To indicate or suggest without stating. 3. To signify. [< IN-[2] + L *plicare* to fold]

im·po·lite (im′pə·līt′) *adj.* Lacking in politeness; discourteous; rude. —**im′po·lite′ly** *adv.* —**im′po·lite′ness** *n.*

im·pol·i·tic (im·pol′ə·tik) *adj.* Not prudent; injudicious. —**im·pol′i·tic·ly** *adv.* —**im·pol′i·tic·ness** *n.*

im·pon·der·a·ble (im·pon′dər·ə·bəl) *adj.* Incapable of being estimated, calculated, or valued. —*n.* An imponderable factor. —**im·pon′der·a·bil′i·ty** *n.* —**im·pon′der·a·bly** *adv.*

im·port[1] (*v.* im·pôrt′, im′pôrt; *n.* im′pôrt) *v.t.* 1. To bring into a country from abroad for commercial purposes, as merchandise. 2. To bring in from an outside source; introduce. 3. To have as its meaning; signify. —*n.* 1. An imported commodity. 2. The act of importing. 3. That which is implied; meaning. [< IN-[2] + L *portare* to carry] —**im·port′a·ble** *adj.* —**im·port′a·bil′i·ty** *n.* —**im·port′er** *n.*

im·port[2] (*n.* im′pôrt; *v.* im·pôrt′) *n.* Importance. —*v.i.* To be of consequence; matter. [< Med.L *importare* to be important]

im·por·tance (im·pôr′təns) *n.* 1. The quality of being important; consequence; significance. 2. Worthiness of esteem; standing. 3. Pretentiousness.

im·por·tant (im·pôr′tənt) *adj.* 1. Having much significance, value, or influence. 2. Deserving of special notice or attention; noteworthy. 3. Having special relevance; mattering greatly: with *to.* 4. Pompous. —**im·por′tant·ly** *adv.*

im·por·ta·tion (im′pôr·tā′shən) *n.* 1. The act of importing. 2. That which is imported.

im·por·tu·nate (im·pôr′chə·nit) *adj.* 1. Persistent in demand; insistent. 2. Of a demand or request, repeatedly made; pressing. —**im·por′tu·nate·ly** *adv.*

im·por·tune (im′pôr·to͞on′, -tyo͞on′) *v.* **·tuned, ·tun·ing** *v.t.* 1. To harass with persistent demands or requests. 2. To ask for persistently. —*v.i.* 3. To make persistent requests or demands. —*adj.* Importunate. [< L *importunus* not blowing towards port (of a wind), hence unfavorable] —**im′por·tune′ly** *adv.* —**im′por·tun′er** *n.* —**im′por·tu′ni·ty** *n.*

im·pose (im·pōz′) *v.t.* **·posed, ·pos·ing** 1. To establish by authority as an obligation, penalty, etc.: to *impose* a fine. 2. To force (oneself, one's will, etc.) upon others. —**to impose on** (or **upon**) To take advantage of. [See IMPOST[1]] —**im·pos′a·ble** *adj.* —**im·pos′er** *n.* —**im·po·si·tion** (im′pə·zish′ən) *n.*

im·pos·ing (im·pō′zing) *adj.* Impressive; grand; stately. —**im·pos′ing·ly** *adv.*

im·pos·si·bil·i·ty (im·pos′ə·bil′ə·tē) *n. pl.* **·ties** 1. The quality of being impossible. 2. Something impossible.

im·pos·si·ble (im·pos′ə·bəl) *adj.* 1. Incapable of existing or taking place. 2. Incapable of being done or put into practice. 3. Contrary to fact or reality; inconceivable. 4. Not acceptable; intolerable. —**im·pos′si·bly** *adv.*

im·post[1] (im′pōst) *n.* A tax or customs duty. —*v.t.* To classify (imported goods) for the purpose of determining customs duties. [< L *impositus,* pp. of *imponere* to place upon]

im·post[2] (im′pōst) *n. Archit.* The top section of a pillar or wall, serving as support for an arch. [See IMPOST[1].]

im·pos·tor (im·pos′tər) *n.* One who deceives; esp., one who assumes the name of another. [< LL *impostor*]

im·pos·ture (im·pos′chər) *n.* Deception by means of false pretenses; esp., the act of posing under a false name.

im·po·tent (im′pə·tənt) *adj.* 1. Powerless to act or to accomplish anything. 2. Physically weak. 3. Incapable of sexual intercourse: said of males. [< L *impotens, -entis.* See POTENT.] —**im′po·tence, im′po·ten·cy** *n.* —**im′po·tent·ly** *adv.*

im·pound (im·pound′) *v.t.* 1. To shut up in a pound, as a stray dog. 2. To place in legal custody. 3. To collect (water) for irrigation. —**im·pound′age** *n.*

im·pov·er·ish (im·pov′ər·ish) *v.t.* 1. To reduce to poverty. 2. To exhaust the fertility of, as soil. [< L *pauperare* to impoverish] —**im·pov′er·ish·ment** *n.*

im·prac·ti·ca·ble (im·prak′ti·kə·bəl) *adj.* 1. Incapable of being carried out or put into effect; not feasible. 2. Incapable of being used for an intended purpose. —**im·prac′ti·ca·bil′i·ty** *n.* —**im·prac′ti·ca·bly** *adv.*

im·prac·ti·cal (im·prak′ti·kəl) *adj.* Not practical. —**im·prac′ti·cal′i·ty** (-kal′ə·tē) *n.*

im·pre·cate (im′prə·kāt) *v.t.* **·cat·ed, ·cat·ing** To invoke or call down (some curse or calamity). [< IN-[2] + L *precari* to pray] —**im′pre·ca′tion** *n.* —**im′pre·ca′tor** *n.* —**im′pre·ca·to′ry** (-kə·tôr′ē) *adj.*

im·preg·na·ble (im·preg′nə·bəl) *adj.* 1. Incapable of being taken by force. 2. Incapable of being overcome. [< OF *im-* not + *prendre* to take] —**im·preg′na·bil′i·ty** *n.* —**im·preg′na·bly** *adv.*

im·preg·nate (im·preg′nāt) *v.t.* **·nat·ed, ·nat·ing** 1. To make pregnant. 2. To fertilize, as an ovum. 3. To saturate or permeate. 4. To fill or imbue, as with ideas. —*adj.* Made pregnant. [< IN-[2] + L *praegnans* pregnant] —**im′preg·na′tion** *n.* —**im·preg′na·tor** *n.*

im·pre·sa·ri·o (im′prə·sä′rē·ō) *n. pl.* **·sa·ri·os** or **·sa·ri** (-sä′rē) One who manages or sponsors performers or performances for entertainment. [< Ital. < *impresa* enterprise]

im·press[1] (*v.* im·pres′; *n.* im′pres) *v.t.* 1. To produce a marked effect upon the mind or feelings of; influence. 2. To establish firmly in the mind. 3. To form or make (a mark) by pressure; stamp. 4. To form or make an imprint or mark upon. —*n.* 1. The act or process of impressing. 2. A mark produced by pressure. 3. Distinctive character or mark; stamp. [< IN-[2] + L *premere* to press] —**im·press′er** *n.*

im·press[2] (*v.* im·pres′; *n.* im′pres) *v.t.* 1. To force to enter public service, esp. naval service. 2. To seize (property) for public use. —*n.* The act of impressing. —**im·press′er** *n.* —**im·press′ment** *n.*

im·press·i·ble (im·pres′ə·bəl) *adj.* Capable of being impressed or of receiving an impression; susceptible.

im·pres·sion (im·presh′ən) *n.* 1. An effect produced on the mind, the senses, or the feelings. 2. A vague remembrance or uncertain belief. 3. A mark made by pressure. 4. The act or process of impressing. 5. An imitation of a person done for entertainment. [< L *impressio, -onis*]

im·pres·sion·a·ble (im·presh′ən·ə·bəl) *adj.* Highly receptive to impressions; readily influenced; sensitive. [< F] —**im·pres′sion·a·bil′i·ty** *n.*

im·pres·sion·ism (im·presh′ən·iz′əm) *n.* 1. In painting, a style, developed in the 19th c., that attempts to reproduce the impressions made by the actual reflection of light in pure colors. 2. In literature and music, a style that attempts to create impressions or moods. —**im·pres′sion·ist** *n. & adj.* —**im·pres′sion·is′tic** *adj.*

im·pres·sive (im·pres′iv) *adj.* Producing or tending to produce an impression; exciting emotion or admiration. —**im·pres′sive·ly** *adv.* —**im·pres′sive·ness** *n.*

im·pri·ma·tur (im′pri·mā′tər, -mä′-) *n.* 1. Official license or approval for publication of a literary work. 2. Authorization in general. [< L, let it be printed]

im·print (*v.* im·print′; *n.* im′print) *v.t.* 1. To produce (a mark) by pressure. 2. To mark or produce a mark on, as with a stamp or seal. 3. To fix firmly in the heart, mind, etc. —*n.* 1. A mark or indentation made by printing, stamping, or pressing. 2. Characteristic effect; impression; stamp. 3. The name of the publisher, place of publication, date of issue, etc., printed in a book, usu. on the title page. [< IN-² + L *premere* to press]

im·pris·on (im·priz′ən) *v.t.* 1. To put into a prison; hold in confinement. 2. To confine or restrain. —**im·pris′on·ment** *n.*

im·prob·a·bil·i·ty (im′prob·ə·bil′ə·tē) *n.* *pl.* ·ties 1. The quality of being improbable; unlikelihood. 2. An unlikely circumstance, event, or result.

im·prob·a·ble (im·prob′ə·bəl) *adj.* Not probable; unlikely. —**im·prob′a·bly** *adv.*

im·promp·tu (im·promp′to͞o) *adj.* Made, done, or uttered on the spur of the moment. —*adv.* Without preparation. [< F < L *in promptu* in readiness]

im·prop·er (im·prop′ər) *adj.* 1. Deviating from fact, truth, or established usage. 2. Deviating from accepted standards of conduct or taste. 3. Unsuitable. —**im·prop′er·ly** *adv.*

improper fraction *Math.* A fraction in which the numerator exceeds the denominator.

im·pro·pri·e·ty (im′prə·prī′ə·tē) *n.* *pl.* ·ties 1. The quality of being improper. 2. An improper action. 3. An improper usage in speech or writing.

im·prove (im·pro͞ov′) *v.* ·**proved,** ·**prov·ing** *v.t.* 1. To raise to a higher or more desirable quality, value, or condition; make better. 2. To increase the value or profit of. 3. To use to good advantage; utilize. —*v.i.* 4. To become better. —**to improve on** (or **upon**) To do or produce something better than. [< OF *en-* into + *prou* profit] —**im·prov′a·bil′i·ty** *n.* —**im·prov′a·ble** *adj.* —**im·prov′a·bly** *adv.* —**im·prov′er** *n.*

im·prove·ment (im·pro͞ov′mənt) *n.* 1. The act of making better, or the state of becoming better. 2. A modification or addition that improves something. 3. A person, thing, or process that constitutes an advance in excellence.

im·prov·i·dent (im·prov′ə·dənt) *adj.* Lacking foresight; incautious; thriftless. —**im·prov′i·dence** *n.* —**im·prov′i·dent·ly** *adv.*

im·pro·vise (im′prə·vīz) *v.* ·**vised,** ·**vis·ing** *v.t.* 1. To produce (music, verse, drama, etc.) without previous thought or preparation. 2. To contrive or construct from whatever comes to hand. —*v.i.* 3. To produce anything extemporaneously. [< IN-¹ + L *providere* to foresee] —**im·pro·vi·sa·tion** (im·prov′ə·zā′shən) *n.* —**im·pro·vi·sa·tion·al** (im·prov′ə·zā′shən·əl) *adj.* —**im′pro·vis′er, im·prov·i·sa·tor** (im·prov′ə·zā′tər) *n.*

im·pru·dent (im·pro͞od′nt) *adj.* Not prudent; lacking discretion; unwise. —**im·pru′dence** *n.*

im·pu·dent (im′pyə·dənt) *adj.* Offensively bold; insolently assured; saucy. [< IN-¹ + L *pudens* modest] —**im′pu·dence, im′pu·den·cy** *n.* —**im′pu·dent·ly** *adv.*

im·pugn (im·pyo͞on′) *v.t.* To attack (a statement, motives, etc.) with criticism or arguments; dispute the truth of. [< IN-² + L *pugnare* to strike, fight] —**im·pugn′a·ble** *adj.* —**im·pug·na·tion** (im′pəg·nā′shən), **im·pugn′ment** *n.* —**im·pugn′er** *n.*

im·pulse (im′puls) *n.* 1. A brief exertion or communication of force tending to produce motion. 2. The motion produced. 3. A sudden, unreasoned inclination to action. 4. *Physiol.* The transference of a stimulus through a nerve fiber. [See IMPEL.]

im·pul·sion (im·pul′shən) *n.* 1. The act of impelling, or the state of being impelled. 2. An impelling force.

im·pul·sive (im·pul′siv) *adj.* 1. Actuated by impulse; spontaneous. 2. Having the power of inciting to action. —**im·pul′sive·ly** *adv.* —**im·pul′sive·ness** *n.*

im·pu·ni·ty (im·pyo͞o′nə·tē) *n.* *pl.* ·ties Freedom or exemption from punishment, harm, or unpleasant consequence. [< IN-¹ + L *poena* punishment]

im·pure (im·pyo͝or′) *adj.* 1. Containing something offensive or contaminating. 2. Mixed with an inferior or worthless substance; adulterated. 3. Contrary to moral purity; sinful. 4. Having the characteristics of more than one style, period, color, language, etc.; mixed. —**im·pure′ly** *adv.*

im·pu·ri·ty (im·pyo͝or′ə·tē) *n.* *pl.* ·ties 1. The state or quality of being impure. 2. That which is impure.

im·put·a·ble (im·pyo͞o′tə·bəl) *adj.* Capable of being imputed; chargeable. —**im·put′a·bil′i·ty** *n.* —**im·put′a·bly** *adv.*

im·pute (im·pyo͞ot′) *v.t.* ·**put·ed,** ·**put·ing** 1. To attribute (a fault, crime, etc.) to a person; charge. 2. To consider as the cause or source of; ascribe: with *to*. [< IN-² + L *putare* to reckon] —**im·pu·ta·tion** (im′pyə·tā′shən) *n.* —**im·pu′ta·tive** *adj.*

in (in) *prep.* 1. Held by or within the confines of; enclosed by: apples *in* a bag. 2. Surrounded by; amidst: buried *in* mud. 3. Within the limits, area, or range of. 4. Within the category, class, or number of; belonging to: twelve inches *in* a foot. 5. Existing as a part or characteristic of: *in* the works of Shaw. 6. Affected by; under the influence of: to shout *in* rage. 7. Wearing. 8. Made of a specified color, style, or material. 9. Arranged so as to form: trees *in* a row. 10. Engaged at; occupied by: *in* business. 11. For the purpose of: to run *in* pursuit. 12. By means of: speaking *in* whispers. 13. According to: *in* my opinion. 14. With regard or respect to: Students vary *in* talent. 15. During. —**in that** For the reason that; because; since. —*adv.* 1. To or toward the inside from the outside. 2. Indoors. 3. In or into some activity; to join *in*. 4. Into some place, condition, or position: Tuck the baby *in*. 5. Into some understood substance, object, etc.: Blend *in* the oil. —**to be in for** *Informal* To be certain to experience (usu. something unpleasant). —**to have it in for** *Informal* To hold a grudge against. —*adj.* 1. That is in or remains within. 2. That has gained power or control: the *in* group. 3. Reflecting the latest trends; fashionable: an *in* resort. —*n.* 1. A member of the group in power or at an advantage. 2. *Informal* A means of entrance or access; also, a position of favor or influence: to have an *in.* **—ins and outs** The full complexities or particulars: the *ins and outs* of a business. [OE]

in-[1] *prefix* Not; without; un-; non-. Also: *i-* before *gn*, as in *ignore*; *il-* before *l*, as in *illiterate*; *im-* before *b, m, p*, as in *imbalance, immiscible, impecunious*; *ir-* before *r*, as in *irresistible.* [< L] Some self-explanatory words beginning with *in-*[1]:

inadvisability	**inedible**
inadvisable	**ineducable**
inapposite	**inelastic**
inapt	**inelasticity**
inartistic	**ineligibility**
inauthentic	**ineligible**
incapability	**inerasable**
incapable	**inexpensive**
incautious	**inexperience**
incivility	**inexperienced**
incommunicable	**inexpressive**
incomprehensive	**infertile**
incompressible	**infrangible**
inconsecutive	**inhomogeneous**
inconsonant	**insagacity**
inconversant	**insalubrious**
indemonstrable	**insobriety**
indiscoverable	**insusceptible**
inductile	**intranquillity**

in-[2] *prefix* In; into; on; within; toward: *include, incur, invade*: also used intensively, as in *inflame.* Also *il-* before *l*, as in *illuminate*; *im-* before *b, m, p*, as in *imbibe, immigrate, impress*; *ir-* before *r*, as in *irradiate.* [OE *in*; sometimes < L *in-* in, prep.]

-in *suffix Chem.* Occasionally used to denote neutral compounds, as fats, proteins, and glycerides: *stearin, albumin, lecithin.* [Var. of -INE[2]]

in·a·bil·i·ty (in′ə·bil′ə·tē) *n.* The state or quality of being unable; lack of the necessary power or means.

in ab·sen·ti·a (in ab·sen′shē·ə, -shə) *Latin* In absence (of the person concerned).

in·ac·ces·si·ble (in′ak·ses′ə·bəl) *adj.* Not accessible; incapable of being reached or closely approached. **—in′ac·ces′si·bil′i·ty** *n.* **—in′ac·ces′si·bly** *adv.*

in·ac·cu·rate (in·ak′yər·it) *adj.* Not accurate; inexact; incorrect. **—in·ac′cu·ra·cy** *n.* **—in·ac′cu·rate·ly** *adv.*

in·ac·tion (in·ak′shən) *n.* Absence of action; idleness.

in·ac·ti·vate (in·ak′tə·vāt) *v.t.* **·vat·ed, ·vat·ing** To make inactive. **—in·ac′ti·va′tion** *n.*

in·ac·tive (in·ak′tiv) *adj.* 1. Characterized by inaction; idle; inert. 2. Slow or indolent. 3. *Mil.* Not mobilized. **—in·ac′tive·ly** *adv.* **—in′ac·tiv′i·ty** *n.*

in·ad·e·quate (in·ad′ə·kwit) *adj.* Not adequate; not equal to that which is required; insufficient. **—in·ad′e·qua·cy** *n.* **—in·ad′e·quate·ly** *adv.*

in·ad·mis·si·ble (in′əd·mis′ə·bəl) *adj.* Not admissible; not to be considered, approved, or allowed. **—in′ad·mis′si·bil′i·ty** *n.* **—in′·ad·mis′si·bly** *adv.*

in·ad·ver·tent (in′əd·vûr′tənt) *adj.* 1. Not exercising due care or consideration; negligent. 2. Resulting from inattention or oversight; unintentional. **—in′ad·ver′tence, in′ad·ver′ten·cy** *n.* **—in′ad·ver′tent·ly** *adv.*

in·al·ien·a·ble (in·āl′yən·ə·bəl) *adj.* Not transferable; that cannot be rightfully taken away. **—in·al′ien·a·bil′i·ty** *n.* **—in·al′ien·a·bly** *adv.*

in·am·o·ra·ta (in·am′ə·rä′tə) *n. pl.* **·tas** A woman with whom one is in love. [< Ital.]

in·ane (in·ān′) *adj.* 1. Lacking in sense; silly. 2. Empty of meaning; pointless. [< L *inanis* empty] **—in·ane′ly** *adv.*

in·an·i·mate (in·an′ə·mit) *adj.* 1. Not living or animate. 2. Lacking animation; torpid; spiritless. **—in·an′i·mate·ly** *adv.*

in·an·i·ty (in·an′ə·tē) *n. pl.* **·ties** 1. Lack of sense or meaning; silliness; foolishness. 2. A foolish remark, action, etc. 3. Emptiness. [< L *inanis* empty]

in·ap·pli·ca·ble (in·ap′li·kə·bəl) *adj.* Not applicable; irrelevant; unsuitable. **—in·ap′·pli·ca·bil′i·ty** *n.* **—in·ap′pli·ca·bly** *adv.*

in·ap·pre·ci·a·ble (in′ə·prē′shē·ə·bəl, -shə·bəl) *adj.* Imperceptible; unnoticeable. **—in′ap·pre′ci·a·bly** *adv.*

in·ap·pro·pri·ate (in′ə·prō′prē·it) *adj.* Not appropriate; unsuitable; unfitting. **—in′ap·pro′pri·ate·ly** *adv.* **—in′ap·pro′pri·ate·ness** *n.*

in·ap·ti·tude (in·ap′tə·tōōd, -tyōōd) *n.* 1. Lack of skill. 2. Unsuitability.

in·ar·tic·u·late (in′är·tik′yə·lit) *adj.* 1. Uttered without the distinct sounds of spoken language: *inarticulate* cries. 2. Incapable of speech; dumb. 3. Unable to speak coherently. 4. Unspoken; unexpressed. **—in′·ar·tic′u·late·ly** *adv.* **—in′ar·tic′u·late·ness** *n.*

in·as·much as (in′əz·much′) 1. Considering the fact that; seeing that; because. 2. Insofar as; according as.

in·at·ten·tion (in′ə·ten′shən) *n.* Lack of attention. **—in′at·ten′tive** *adj.* **—in′at·ten′·tive·ly** *adv.*

in·au·di·ble (in·ô′də·bəl) *adj.* Incapable of being heard. **—in·au′di·bil′i·ty** *n.* **—in·au′di·bly** *adv.*

in·au·gu·ral (in·ô′gyər·əl) *adj.* Of or pertaining to an inauguration. **—***n.* A speech made at an inauguration.

in·au·gu·rate (in·ô′gyə·rāt) *v.t.* **·rat·ed, ·rat·ing** 1. To begin formally; initiate. 2. To induct into office with formal ceremony. 3. To celebrate the public opening of. [< L *inaugurare* to take omens, consecrate] **—in·au′gu·ra′tion** *n.* **—in·au′gu·ra′tor** *n.*

in·aus·pi·cious (in′ô·spish′əs) *adj.* Not auspicious; ill-omened; unfavorable. **—in′·aus·pi′cious·ly** *adv.* **—in′aus·pi′cious·ness** *n.*

in·board (in′bôrd′) *adj. & adv.* 1. *Naut.* **a** Inside the hull. **b** Toward the center line of a vessel. 2. *Aeron.* Inward from the tip of an airfoil; close to the fuselage.

in·born (in′bôrn′) *adj.* Existing from birth; natural; inherent.

in·bound (in′bound′) *adj.* Approaching a destination.

in·bred (in′bred′; *for def. 2, also* in′bred′) *adj.* 1. Inborn; innate. 2. Produced by inbreeding.

in·breed (in′brēd′, in′brēd′) *v.t.* **·bred, ·breed·ing** To breed by continual mating of closely related stock.

In·ca (ing′kə) *n.* A member of a group of Indian tribes dominant in Peru at the time of the Spanish conquest. [< Sp. < Quechua *ynca* royal prince]

in·cal·cu·la·ble (in·kal′kyə·lə·bəl) *adj.* 1. Incapable of being calculated. 2. Unpredictable. **—in·cal′cu·la·bil′i·ty** *n.* **—in·cal′cu·la·bly** *adv.*

in cam·er·a (in kam′ər·ə) In closed or secret session; privately. [< L, in a room]

In·can (ing′kən) *adj.* Of or pertaining to the Incas, their culture, or their empire. *—n.* 1. An Inca. 2. The language of the Incas; Quechua.

in·can·desce (in′kən·des′) *v.t. & v.i.* **·desced, ·desc·ing** To be or become, or cause to become, luminous with heat.

in·can·des·cent (in′kən·des′ənt) *adj.* 1. Luminous or glowing with intense heat. 2. Shining with intense brilliance. **—in′can·des′cence, in′can·des′cen·cy** *n.* **—in′can·des′cent·ly** *adv.*

incandescent lamp A lamp having a filament that is heated to incandescence by an electric current.

in·can·ta·tion (in′kan·tā′shən) *n.* 1. The uttering or intoning of words or syllables supposed to produce magical results. 2. The magic words or formula so uttered. [< L *incantare* to make an incantation]

in·ca·pac·i·tate (in′kə·pas′ə·tāt) *v.t.* **·tat·ed, ·tat·ing** 1. To deprive of ability, power, or fitness; disable. 2. *Law* To deprive of legal capacity; disqualify. **—in′ca·pac′i·ta′tion** *n.* **—in′ca·pac′i·ty** *n.*

in·car·cer·ate (*v.* in·kär′sə·rāt; *adj.* in·kär′·sər·it, -sə·rāt) *v.t.* **·at·ed, ·at·ing** 1. To put in prison; imprison. 2. To confine; enclose. *—adj.* Imprisoned. [< IN-² + L *carcer* jail] **—in·car′cer·a′tion** *n.* **—in·car′cer·a′tor** *n.*

in·car·na·dine (in·kär′nə·dīn, -din) *adj.* 1. Pink. 2. Blood-red; crimson. *—n.* An incarnadine color. *—v.t.* **·dined, ·din·ing** To color deep red or pink. [< Ital. *incarnato* flesh-colored]

in·car·nate (*adj.* in·kär′nit; *v.* in·kär′nāt) *adj.* 1. Embodied in flesh, esp. in human form. 2. Personified; exemplified. *—v.t.* **·nat·ed, ·nat·ing** 1. To give bodily form to. 2. To invest with concrete form. [< IN-² + L *caro, carnis* flesh]

in·car·na·tion (in′kär·nā′shən) *n.* 1. The assumption of bodily form, esp. human form. 2. A person, animal, or thing in which some ideal or quality is embodied. **—the Incarnation** *Theol.* The assumption by Jesus Christ of the human form and condition.

in·case (in·kās′) See ENCASE.

in·cen·di·ar·y (in·sen′dē·er′ē) *adj.* 1. Of or pertaining to the malicious burning of property. 2. Inciting to riot, rebellion, etc.; inflammatory. 3. Capable of generating intense heat. *—n. pl.* **·ar·ies** 1. One who maliciously sets fire to property. 2. One who stirs up mob violence, etc. 3. An incendiary bomb. [< L *incendere* to set on fire]

incendiary bomb A bomb designed to start a fire.

in·cense¹ (in·sens′) *v.t.* **·censed, ·cens·ing** To inflame with anger; enrage. [< L *incendere* to set on fire]

in·cense² (in′sens) *n.* 1. An aromatic substance that gives off an agreeable odor when burned. 2. The odor or smoke produced in burning such a substance. 3. Any pleasant fragrance. *—v.t.* **·censed, ·cens·ing** To perfume with incense. [< L *incendere* to set on fire]

in·cen·tive (in·sen′tiv) *n.* That which incites, or tends to incite, to action; motivating force. *—adj.* Serving to incite to action. [< L *incentivus* stimulating < *incentus,* pp. of *incinere* to set the tune]

in·cep·tion (in·sep′shən) *n.* Beginning; start. [< L *incipere* to begin]

in·cep·tive (in·sep′tiv) *adj.* Beginning; incipient; initial.

in·cer·ti·tude (in·sûr′tə·tōōd, -tyōōd) *n.* 1. Uncertainty; doubtfulness. 2. Insecurity.

in·ces·sant (in·ses′ənt) *adj.* Continuing without interruption; never ceasing. [< IN-¹ + L *cessare* to cease] **—in·ces′san·cy** *n.* **—in·ces′sant·ly** *adv.*

in·cest (in′sest) *n.* Sexual intercourse between persons so closely related that marriage between them is forbidden by law or taboo. [< IN-¹ + L *castus* chaste] **—in·ces·tu·ous** (in·ses′chōō·əs) *adj.* **—in·ces′tu·ous·ly** *adv.*

inch (inch) *n.* A measure of length equal to 1/12 of a foot: symbol ″. **—every inch** In every way; completely. *—v.t. & v.i.* To move or advance by inches or small degrees. [OE < L *uncia* the twelfth part, inch, ounce]

in·cho·ate (in·kō′it) *adj.* 1. In an early or rudimentary stage. 2. Lacking order, form, coherence, etc. [< L *incohare* to begin] **—in·cho′ate·ly** *adv.* **—in·cho′ate·ness** *n.*

in·ci·dence (in′sə·dəns) *n.* The degree of occurrence or effect: a high *incidence* of illiteracy.

in·ci·dent (in′sə·dənt) *n.* 1. A distinct event or piece of action. 2. A minor episode or event. *—adj.* 1. Naturally or usually attending: with *to*: the dangers *incident* to travel. 2. Falling or striking: *incident* rays of light. [< IN-² + L *cadere* to fall]

in·ci·den·tal (in′sə·den′təl) *adj.* 1. Occurring in the course of something. 2. Naturally or usually attending. 3. Minor; secondary. *—n.* 1. An incidental circumstance or event. 2. *pl.* Minor or casual expenses or items.

in·ci·den·tal·ly (in′sə·den′təl·ē; *for def. 2, also* in′sə·dent′lē) *adv.* 1. As a subordinate or chance occurrence along with something else. 2. By the by; by the way.

in·cin·er·ate (in·sin′ə·rāt) *v.t.* **·at·ed, ·at·ing** To consume with fire; cremate. [< IN-² + L *cinis, cineris* ashes] **—in·cin′er·a′tion** *n.*

in·cin·er·a·tor (in·sin′ə·rā′tər) *n.* An apparatus for burning refuse or for cremating.

in·cip·i·ent (in·sip′ē·ənt) *adj.* Coming into existence; just beginning to appear. [< L *incipere* to begin] **—in·cip′i·ence, in·cip′i·en·cy** *n.* **—in·cip′i·ent·ly** *adv.*

in·cise (in·sīz′) *v.t.* **·cised, ·cis·ing** 1. To cut into, or cut marks upon, with a sharp instrument. 2. To engrave; carve. [< IN-² + L *caedere* to cut] **—in·cised′** *adj.*

in·ci·sion (in·sizh′ən) *n.* 1. The act of incising. 2. A cut; gash. 3. *Surg.* A cut made in soft tissue. 4. Incisive quality; acuteness.

in·ci·sive (in·sī′siv) *adj.* 1. Sharp; keen. 2. Cutting; sarcastic. [< Med.L *incisivus*] **—in·ci′sive·ly** *adv.* **—in·ci′sive·ness** *n.*

in·ci·sor (in·sī′zər) *n.* A front tooth adapted for cutting; in man, one of eight such teeth, four in each jaw. [< NL]

in·cite (in·sīt′) *v.t.* **·cit·ed, ·cit·ing** To spur to action; urge on; instigate. [< IN-² + L *citare* to rouse] **—in′ci·ta′tion** *n.* **—in·cite′·ment** *n.* **—in·cit′er** *n.*

in·clem·ent (in·klem′ənt) *adj.* 1. Of the weather, severe; stormy. 2. Without mercy;

harsh. [< L *inclemens, -entis*] —**in·clem′en·cy** *n.* —**in·clem′ent·ly** *adv.*

in·cli·na·tion (in′klə·nā′shən) *n.* 1. A personal preference or tendency; bent; liking. 2. A tendency toward a condition; trend. 3. The act of inclining, or the state of being inclined. 4. Deviation or degree of deviation from the vertical or horizontal. 5. A sloping surface. —**in′cli·na′tion·al, in·cli·na·to·ry** (in·klī′nə·tôr′ē) *adj.*

in·cline (*v.* in·klīn′; *n.* in′klīn, in·klīn′) *v.* **·clined, ·clin·ing** *v.i.* 1. To diverge from the horizontal or vertical; slant. 2. To have a bent or preference; be disposed. 3. To tend in some quality or degree: purple *inclining* toward blue. —*v.t.* 4. To cause to bend, lean, or slope. 5. To impart a tendency or leaning to (a person); influence. 6. To bow or nod, as the head. —*n.* A gradient; slope. [< IN-[2] + L *clinare* to lean] —**in·clin′a·ble** *adj.* —**in·clined′** *adj.* —**in·clin′er** *n.*

in·close (in·klōz′) See ENCLOSE.

in·clude (in·klo͞od′) *v.t.* **·clud·ed, ·clud·ing** 1. To have as a component part or parts; comprise; contain. 2. To place in a general category, group, etc.; consider in a reckoning. 3. To have or involve as a subordinate part, quality, etc.; imply. [< IN-[2] + L *claudere* to shut] —**in·clud′a·ble** or **in·clud′i·ble** *adj.* —**in·clu·sion** (in·klo͞o′zhən) *n.*

in·clu·sive (in·klo͞o′siv) *adj.* 1. Including: with *of.* 2. Including the limits specified: from 1959 to 1964 *inclusive.* 3. Comprehensive: an *inclusive* report. [< Med.L *inclusivus*] —**in·clu′sive·ly** *adv.* —**in·clu′sive·ness** *n.*

in·cog·ni·to (in·kog′nə·tō, in′kog·nē′tō) *adj.* & *adv.* Under an assumed name or identity; in disguise. [< L *incognitus* not known]

in·cog·ni·zant (in·kog′nə·zənt) *adj.* Not cognizant; unaware: with *of.* —**in·cog′ni·zance** *n.*

in·co·her·ent (in′kō·hir′ənt) *adj.* 1. Lacking in logical connection; confused. 2. Unable to think clearly or express oneself logically. 3. Consisting of parts or ingredients that do not stick together. 4. Lacking in agreement or harmony; disorganized. —**in′co·her′ence** *n.* —**in′co·her′ent·ly** *adv.*

in·com·bus·ti·ble (in′kəm·bus′tə·bəl) *adj.* Incapable of being burned; not flammable. —*n.* An incombustible substance or material. —**in′com·bus′ti·bil′i·ty** *n.* —**in′com·bus′ti·bly** *adv.*

in·come (in′kum) *n.* Money, or sometimes its equivalent, received periodically by an individual, a corporation, etc., in return for labor or services rendered, or from property, etc.

income tax A tax levied on annual income over a specified amount.

in·com·ing (in′kum′ing) *adj.* Coming in or about to come in. —*n.* The act of coming in.

in·com·men·su·ra·ble (in′kə·men′shər·ə·bəl, -sər·ə-) *adj.* 1. Lacking a common measure or standard of comparison. 2. Greatly out of proportion; not in accordance.

in·com·men·su·rate (in′kə·men′shər·it, -sə·rit) *adj.* Inadequate; disproportionate. —**in′com·men′su·rate·ly** *adv.*

in·com·mode (in′kə·mōd′) *v.t.* **·mod·ed, ·mod·ing** To inconvenience; disturb. [< IN-[1] + L *commodus* convenient]

in·com·mo·di·ous (in′kə·mō′dē·əs) *adj.* 1. Uncomfortably small; cramped. 2. Causing discomfort; inconvenient. —**in′com·mo′di·ous·ly** *adv.* —**in′com·mo′di·ous·ness** *n.*

in·com·mu·ni·ca·do (in′kə·myo͞o′nə·kä′dō) *adj.* & *adv.* Confined without means of communication. [< Sp. < IN-[1] + L *communicare* to share]

in·com·mu·ni·ca·tive (in′kə·myo͞o′nə·kā′tiv, -kə·tiv) *adj.* Not communicative; taciturn; reserved. —**in′com·mu′ni·ca′tive·ly** *adv.*

in·com·pa·ra·ble (in·kom′pər·ə·bəl) *adj.* 1. Incapable of being equaled or surpassed; matchless. 2. Lacking in qualities or characteristics that can be compared. —**in·com′pa·ra·bil′i·ty** *n.* —**in·com′pa·ra·bly** *adv.*

in·com·pat·i·ble (in′kəm·pat′ə·bəl) *adj.* 1. Incapable of coexisting harmoniously. 2. Disagreeing in nature; conflicting. 3. *Med.* Having a harmful or undesirable effect when combined or used together. —*n.pl.* Incompatible persons, drugs, etc. —**in′com·pat′i·bil′i·ty** *n.* —**in′com·pat′i·bly** *adv.*

in·com·pe·tent (in·kom′pə·tənt) *adj.* 1. Lacking in ability or skill; inadequate to the task; unfit. 2. Reflecting a lack of skill. 3. Not legally qualified. —*n.* One who is incompetent. —**in·com′pe·tence, in·com′pe·ten·cy** *n.* —**in·com′pe·tent·ly** *adv.*

in·com·plete (in′kəm·plēt′) *adj.* 1. Not having all essential elements or parts; unfinished. 2. Not fully developed; imperfect: *incomplete* growth. —**in′com·plete′ly** *adv.* —**in′com·plete′ness, in′com·ple′tion** *n.*

in·com·pre·hen·si·ble (in′kom·pri·hen′sə·bəl, in·kom′-) *adj.* Incapable of being understood; unintelligible. —**in′com·pre·hen′si·bil′i·ty** *n.* —**in′com·pre·hen′si·bly** *adv.*

in·com·pre·hen·sion (in′kom·pri·hen′shən, in·kom′-) *n.* Lack of understanding.

in·con·ceiv·a·ble (in′kən·sē′və·bəl) *adj.* Incapable of being conceived by the mind; unbelievable. —**in′con·ceiv′a·bil′i·ty** *n.* —**in′con·ceiv′a·bly** *adv.*

in·con·clu·sive (in′kən·klo͞o′siv) *adj.* 1. Not leading to an ultimate conclusion; indeterminate; not decisive. 2. Not achieving a definite result; ineffective. —**in′con·clu′sive·ly** *adv.*

in·con·gru·ous (in·kong′gro͞o·əs) *adj.* 1. Not suitable; inappropriate. 2. Not corresponding or conforming; at odds: with *with* or *to.* 3. Consisting of elements or qualities not properly belonging together. [< IN-[1] + L *congruus* agreeing] —**in·con·gru·i·ty** (in′·kong·gro͞o′ə·tē, in′kən-) *n.* —**in·con′gru·ous·ly** *adv.*

in·con·se·quen·tial (in′kon·sə·kwen′shəl, in·kon′-) *adj.* Having little or no consequence; unimportant; trivial. —**in·con′se·quen′ti·al′i·ty** (-shē·al′ə·tē) *n.* —**in′con·se·quen′·tial·ly** *adv.*

in·con·sid·er·a·ble (in′kən·sid′ər·ə·bəl) *adj.* 1. Small in quantity, size, or value. 2. Not worth considering; trivial. —**in′con·sid′er·a·ble·ness** *n.* —**in′con·sid′er·a·bly** *adv.*

in·con·sid·er·ate (in′kən·sid′ər·it) *adj.* 1. Lacking in concern for others; thoughtless. 2. Not carefully considered or thought out. —**in′con·sid′er·ate·ly** *adv.* —**in′con·sid′er·ate·ness, in′con·sid·er·a′tion** *n.*

in·con·sis·ten·cy (in′kən·sis′tən·sē) *n.* *pl.* **·cies** 1. The quality of being inconsistent.

2. Something that is inconsistent. Also **in′con·sis′tence.**

in·con·sis·tent (in′kən·sis′tənt) *adj.* 1. Lacking in agreement or compatibility; at variance. 2. Containing contradictory elements or parts. 3. Lacking uniformity in behavior or thought; erratic; changeable. —**in′con·sis′tent·ly** *adv.*

in·con·sol·a·ble (in′kən·sō′lə·bəl) *adj.* Not to be consoled; disconsolate; dejected. —**in′con·sol′a·bil′i·ty, in′con·sol′a·ble·ness** *n.* —**in′con·sol′a·bly** *adv.*

in·con·spic·u·ous (in′kən·spik′yo͞o·əs) *adj.* Not conspicuous; not attracting attention. —**in′con·spic′u·ous·ly** *adv.* —**in′con·spic′u·ous·ness** *n.*

in·con·stant (in·kon′stənt) *adj.* Not constant; variable; fickle. —*n.* One who or that which is inconstant. —**in·con′stan·cy** *n.* —**in·con′stant·ly** *adv.*

in·con·test·a·ble (in′kən·tes′tə·bəl) *adj.* Not admitting of question; unassailable: *incontestable* evidence. —**in′con·test′a·bil′i·ty, in′con·test′a·ble·ness** *n.* —**in′con·test′a·bly** *adv.*

in·con·ti·nent (in·kon′tə·nənt) *adj.* 1. Exercising little control or restraint, esp. in sexual desires. 2. Incapable of controlling the elimination of urine or feces. 3. Unrestrained; unchecked. —**in·con′ti·nence** *n.* —**in·con′ti·nent·ly** *adv.*

in·con·trol·la·ble (in′kən·trō′lə·bəl) *adj.* Incapable of being controlled; uncontrollable. —**in′con·trol′la·bly** *adv.*

in·con·tro·vert·i·ble (in′kon·trə·vûr′tə·bəl) *adj.* Not admitting of controversy; undeniable. —**in′con·tro·vert′i·bil′i·ty** *n.* —**in′con·tro·vert′i·bly** *adv.*

in·con·ven·ience (in′kən·vēn′yəns) *n.* 1. The state or quality of being inconvenient. 2. Something that is inconvenient. —*v.t.* **·ienced, ·ienc·ing** To cause inconvenience to.

in·con·ven·ient (in′kən·vēn′yənt) *adj.* Causing or lending itself to discomfort and difficulty; troublesome; awkward. —**in′con·ven′ient·ly** *adv.*

in·cor·po·rate (*v.* in·kôr′pə·rāt; *adj.* in·kôr′·pə·rit) *v.* **·rat·ed, ·rat·ing** *v.i.* 1. To form a legal corporation or a similar association. 2. To become combined or merged as one body or whole. —*v.t.* 3. To take in, put in, or include as part of a whole. 4. To form (persons, groups, etc.) into a legal corporation or a similar association. 5. To combine or merge into a whole. —*adj.* 1. Combined into a single unit or whole. 2. Legally incorporated. [< IN-² + L *corporare* to form into a body] —**in·cor′po·ra′tion** *n.* —**in·cor·po·ra·tive** (in·kôr′pə·rā′tiv, -rə·tiv) *adj.* —**in·cor′po·ra′tor** *n.*

in·cor·po·rat·ed (in·kôr′pə·rā′tid) *adj.* 1. Forming one body or whole; combined. 2. Organized into a legal corporation: abbr. *inc., Inc.*

in·cor·po·re·al (in′kôr·pôr′ē·əl) *adj.* 1. Not consisting of matter. 2. Of or pertaining to nonmaterial things; spiritual. —**in′cor·po′re·al′i·ty** (-al′ə·tē) *n.* —**in′cor·po′re·al·ly** *adv.*

in·cor·rect (in′kə·rekt′) *adj.* 1. Inaccurate or untrue as to fact or usage; wrong. 2. Improper; unsuitable. —**in′cor·rect′ly** *adv.* —**in′cor·rect′ness** *n.*

in·cor·ri·gi·ble (in·kôr′ə·jə·bəl, -kor′-) *adj.* Incapable of being reformed or corrected. —*n.* One who is incorrigible. —**in·cor′ri·gi·bil′i·ty** *n.* —**in·cor′ri·gi·bly** *adv.*

in·cor·rupt (in′kə·rupt′) *adj.* 1. Not morally corrupt; honest; good. 2. Not spoiled or decayed; untainted; fresh. 3. Free from errors or alterations, as a literary text. Also **in′cor·rupt′ed.** —**in′cor·rupt′ly** *adv.* —**in′cor·rupt′ness** *n.*

in·cor·rupt·i·ble (in′kə·rup′tə·bəl) *adj.* 1. Not accessible to bribery; honest. 2. Incapable of corruption; not subject to decay or spoilage. —**in′cor·rupt′i·bil′i·ty** *n.* —**in′·cor·rupt′i·bly** *adv.*

in·crease (*v.* in·krēs′, *n.* in′krēs) *v.* **·creased, ·creas·ing** *v.i.* 1. To become greater, as in amount, size, degree, etc.; grow. 2. To grow in number; multiply; reproduce. —*v.t.* 3. To make greater, as in amount, size, degree, etc.; enlarge. —*n.* 1. A growing or becoming greater. 2. The amount of growth; increment. [< IN-² + L *crescere* to grow] —**in·creas′a·ble** *adj.* —**in·creas′er** *n.* —**in·creas′ing·ly** *adv.*

in·cred·i·ble (in·kred′ə·bəl) *adj.* Not credible; unbelievable. 2. Amazing; wonderful. —**in·cred′i·bly** *adv.*

in·cred·u·lous (in·krej′ə·ləs) *adj.* 1. Not willing or not disposed to believe; skeptical. 2. Characterized by or showing disbelief. —**in·cre·du·li·ty** (in′krə·do͞o′lə·tē, -dyo͞o′-) *n.* —**in·cred′u·lous·ly** *adv.*

in·cre·ment (in′krə·mənt) *n.* 1. A quantity added to another quantity. 2. The act of increasing; enlargement. [< L *increscere* to increase] —**in′cre·men′tal** (-men′təl) *adj.*

in·crim·i·nate (in·krim′ə·nāt) *v.t.* **·nat·ed, ·nat·ing** 1. To imply the wrongdoing or guilt of (a person, etc.). 2. To charge with a crime or fault. [< IN-² + LL *criminare* to accuse one of a crime] —**in·crim′i·na′tion** *n.* —**in·crim′i·na·to′ry** (-nə·tôr′ē) *adj.*

in·crust (in·krust′) See ENCRUST.

in·cu·bate (in′kyə·bāt, ing′-) *v.* **·bat·ed, ·bat·ing** *v.t.* 1. To sit upon (eggs) in order to hatch them; brood. 2. To hatch (eggs) in this manner or by artificial heat. 3. To maintain under conditions favoring optimum growth or development, as bacterial cultures. —*v.i.* 4. To undergo incubation. [< IN-² + L *cubare* to lie] —**in′cu·ba′tive** *adj.*

in·cu·ba·tion (in′kyə·bā′shən, ing′-) *n.* 1. The act of incubating, or the state of being incubated. 2. *Med.* The period between the time of exposure to an infectious disease and the appearance of the symptoms. [< L *incubatio, -onis*]

in·cu·ba·tor (in′kyə·bā′tər, ing′-) *n.* 1. An apparatus kept at a uniform warmth for artificial hatching of eggs. 2. *Bacteriol.* A device for the artificial development of microorganisms. 3. An apparatus for keeping warm a prematurely born baby. [< L, a hatcher]

in·cu·bus (in′kyə·bəs) *n. pl.* **·bus·es** or **·bi** (-bī) 1. Anything that tends to oppress or discourage. 2. A nightmare. 3. In folklore, a male demon that has sexual intercourse with sleeping women. [< LL, nightmare < L *incubare* to lie on]

in·cul·cate (in·kul′kāt, in′kul-) *v.t.* **·cat·ed, ·cat·ing** To impress upon the mind by frequent repetition or forceful admonition; instill. [< IN-[2] + L *calcare* to tread] —**in′·cul·ca′tion** *n.* —**in′cul·ca′tor** *n.*

in·cul·pate (in·kul′pāt, in′kul-) *v.t.* **·pat·ed, ·pat·ing** To involve in an accusation; incriminate. [< Med.L *inculpatus,* pp. of *inculpare* to blame] —**in′cul·pa′tion** *n.*

in·cum·ben·cy (in·kum′bən·sē) *n. pl.* **·cies** 1. The state of being incumbent. 2. That which is incumbent. 3. The holding of an office or the period in which it is held.

in·cum·bent (in·kum′bənt) *adj.* 1. Resting upon one as a moral obligation, or as necessary; obligatory. 2. Resting, leaning, or weighing upon something. —*n.* One who holds an office. [< IN-[2] + L *cubare* to lie] —**in·cum′bent·ly** *adv.*

in·cum·ber (in·kum′bər) See ENCUMBER.

in·cu·nab·u·la (in′kyōō·nab′yə·lə) *n. pl. of* **in·cu·nab·u·lum** 1. Specimens of early European printing; esp., books printed before A.D. 1500. 2. The earliest stages of development; beginnings. [< IN-[2] + L *cunabula,* dim. of *cunae* cradle] —**in′cu·nab′u·lar** *adj.*

in·cur (in·kûr′) *v.t.* **·curred, ·cur·ring** To become subject to (unpleasant consequences); bring on oneself. [< IN-[2] + L *currere* to run] —**in·cur′rence** *n.*

in·cur·a·ble (in·kyŏŏr′ə·bəl) *adj.* Not curable or remediable. —*n.* One suffering from an incurable disease. —**in·cur′a·bil′i·ty** *n.* —**in·cur′a·bly** *adv.*

in·cur·sion (in·kûr′zhən) *n.* 1. A hostile, often sudden entrance into a territory; raid. 2. A running in or against; encroachment. [< IN-[2] + L *currere* to run] —**in·cur′sive** (-siv) *adj.*

in·cus (ing′kəs) *n. pl.* **in·cu·des** (in·kyōō′dēz) *Anat.* The anvil-shaped central bone of the group of three bones in the middle ear: also called *anvil.* [< L, anvil]

in·debt·ed (in·det′id) *adj.* 1. Legally obligated to pay for value received; in debt. 2. Morally obligated to acknowledge benefits or favors. [< OF *en-* in + *dette* debt] —**in·debt′ed·ness** *n.*

in·de·cen·cy (in·dē′sən·sē) *n. pl.* **·cies** 1. The quality or condition of being indecent. 2. An indecent act, speech, etc.

in·de·cent (in·dē′sənt) *adj.* 1. Offensive to one's sense of modesty or morality. 2. Contrary to propriety or good taste; vulgar. —**in·de′cent·ly** *adv.*

in·de·ci·pher·a·ble (in′di·sī′fər·ə·bəl) *adj.* Not decipherable; unreadable.

in·de·ci·sion (in′di·sizh′ən) *n.* Inability to make decisions.

in·de·ci·sive (in′di·sī′siv) *adj.* 1. Not bringing about a definite conclusion, solution, etc. 2. Unable or unwilling to make decisions. —**in′de·ci′sive·ly** *adv.* —**in′de·ci′sive·ness** *n.*

in·de·cor·um (in′di·kôr′əm) *n.* Lack of propriety. —**in·dec·o·rous** (in·dek′ər·əs, in′di·kôr′əs) *adj.*

in·deed (in·dēd′) *adv.* In fact; in truth. —*interj.* Is that true?

in·de·fat·i·ga·ble (in′də·fat′ə·gə·bəl) *adj.* Not yielding readily to fatigue; tireless; unflagging. [< IN-[1] + L *defatigare* to tire out] —**in′de·fat′i·ga·bly** *adv.*

in·de·fea·si·ble (in′də·fē′zə·bəl) *adj.* Incapable of being annulled or set aside.

in·de·fen·si·ble (in′di·fen′sə·bəl) *adj.* 1. Incapable of being justified. 2. Incapable of being defended. —**in′de·fen′si·bil′i·ty** *n.* —**in′de·fen′si·bly** *adv.*

in·de·fin·a·ble (in′di·fī′nə·bəl) *adj.* Incapable of being defined or described; vague; ineffable. —**in′de·fin′a·bly** *adv.*

in·def·i·nite (in·def′ə·nit) *adj.* 1. Not definite or precise; vague. 2. Without a fixed number; indeterminate. 3. *Gram.* Not definite or determining. —**in·def′i·nite·ly** *adv.* —**in·def′i·nite·ness** *n.*

indefinite article See under ARTICLE.

indefinite pronoun *Gram.* A pronoun that represents an object indefinitely or generally, as *each, none, another.*

in·de·his·cent (in′də·his′ənt) *adj. Bot.* Not opening spontaneously when ripe, as certain grains and fruits. —**in′de·his′cence** *n.*

in·del·i·ble (in·del′ə·bəl) *adj.* 1. Incapable of being blotted out or effaced. 2. Leaving a mark or stain not easily erased. [< IN-[1] + L *delibilis* perishable] —**in·del′i·bil′i·ty** *n.* —**in·del′i·bly** *adv.*

in·del·i·ca·cy (in·del′ə·kə·sē) *n. pl.* **·cies** 1. The quality of being indelicate; coarseness. 2. An indelicate thing, act, etc.

in·del·i·cate (in·del′ə·kit) *adj.* 1. Lacking or offending a sense of delicacy or good taste; crude. 2. Tactless. —**in·del′i·cate·ly** *adv.*

in·dem·ni·fy (in·dem′nə·fī) *v.t.* **·fied, ·fy·ing** 1. To compensate (a person, etc.) for loss or damage sustained. 2. To make good (a loss). 3. To give security against future loss or punishment. [< L *indemnis* unhurt + -FY] —**in·dem′ni·fi·ca′tion** *n.*

in·dem·ni·ty (in·dem′nə·tē) *n. pl.* **·ties** 1. That which is given as compensation for a loss or for damage. 2. An agreement to remunerate another for loss or protect him against liability. 3. Exemption from penalties or liabilities.

in·dent[1] (in·dent′; *for n., also* in′dent) *v.t.* 1. To set in from the margin, as the first line of a paragraph. 2. To cut or mark the edge of with toothlike notches; serrate. —*v.i.* 3. To be notched or cut. 4. To set a line, paragraph, etc., in from the margin. —*n.* 1. A cut or notch on the edge of a thing. 2. An indention (def. 1). [< MF *endenter* < IN-[2] + L *dentis* tooth]

in·dent[2] (in·dent′; *for n., also* in′dent) *v.t.* To push in so as to form a dent or depression. —*n.* A dent or depression.

in·den·ta·tion (in′den·tā′shən) *n.* 1. A notch or series of notches in an edge or border. 2. The act of notching, or the condition of being notched. 3. A dent. 4. An indention.

in·den·tion (in·den′shən) *n.* 1. The setting in of a line of type, writing, etc., at the left side; also, the space thus left. 2. A dent.

in·den·ture (in·den′chər) *n.* 1. *Law* A deed or contract made between two or more parties. 2. *Usu. pl.* Such a contract between master and apprentice. —*v.t.* **·tured, ·tur·ing** To bind by indenture.

in·de·pen·dence (in′di·pen′dəns) *n.* The quality or condition of being independent.

Independence Day July 4, a holiday in the U.S. commemorating the adoption of the Declaration of Independence in 1776.

in·de·pen·den·cy (in′di·pen′dən·sē) *n. pl.* **·cies** 1. Independence. 2. An independent state or territory.

in·de·pen·dent (in′di·pen′dənt) *adj.* 1. Not subject to the authority of another; autonomous. 2. Not dependent on or part of some larger group, system, etc. 3. Not an adherent of a party or faction. 4. Not readily influenced or guided by others; self-reliant. 5. Self-supporting. 6. Having sufficient financial means to live comfortably. —*n.* One who or that which is independent; esp., one not an adherent of a party or faction. —**in′de·pen′dent·ly** *adv.*

in·de·scrib·a·ble (in′di·skrī′bə·bəl) *adj.* Incapable of being described; esp., too complex, extreme, etc., to be described. —**in′de·scrib′a·bly** *adv.*

in·de·struc·ti·ble (in′di·struk′tə·bəl) *adj.* Incapable of being destroyed; very tough and durable. —**in′de·struc′ti·bil′i·ty** *n.* —**in′de·struc′ti·bly** *adv.*

in·de·ter·mi·na·ble (in′di·tûr′mi·nə·bəl) *adj.* 1. Incapable of being ascertained. 2. Incapable of being decided. —**in′de·ter′mi·na·bly** *adv.*

in·de·ter·mi·nate (in′di·tûr′mə·nit) *adj.* 1. Not definite or precise; vague. 2. Not decided; unsettled. 3. Not fixed; inconclusive. —**in′de·ter′mi·na·cy** *n.* —**in′de·ter′mi·nate·ly** *adv.*

in·de·ter·mi·na·tion (in′di·tûr′mə·nā′shən) *n.* 1. Lack of determination. 2. The condition of being indeterminate.

in·dex (in′deks) *n. pl.* **·dex·es** or **·di·ces** (-də·sēz) 1. An alphabetical list, as at the end of a book, of topics, names, etc., and the numbers of the pages where they occur. 2. A descriptive list, as of items in a collection. 3. Anything that serves as an indicator, as a needle on a dial. 4. Anything that indicates or gives evidence of; sign: Alertness is an *index* of intelligence. 5. *Printing* A mark (☛) used to direct attention to a specific word, passage, etc.: also called *fist*. 6. A numerical expression of the ratio between one dimension or magnitude and another. 7. *Math.* A subscript or superscript. —*v.t.* 1. To provide with an index, as a book. 2. To enter in an index, as a subject. 3. To indicate. [< L, forefinger, sign] —**in′dex·er** *n.* —**in·dex′i·cal** *adj.*

In·dex (in′deks) *n.* Formerly, a list of books which the Roman Catholic Church forbade its members to read except with special permission.

index finger The finger next to the thumb: also called *forefinger*.

In·di·a ink (in′dē·ə) 1. A black pigment made from lampblack. 2. An ink made from this pigment.

In·di·an (in′dē·ən) *n.* 1. A citizen of the Republic of India. 2. A native of India or the East Indies. 3. A member of the aboriginal peoples of North America, South America, and the West Indies. 4. Loosely, any of the languages of the American Indian. —**In′di·an** *adj.*

Indian club A bottle-shaped wooden club used in gymnastics, usu. in pairs.

Indian corn Corn (def. 1).

Indian giver *Informal* One who gives a present and then wants it back.

Indian hemp 1. Hemp (def. 1). 2. A perennial American herb of the dogbane family.

Indian pipe An herb with one pipe-shaped white flower.

Indian pudding A pudding of cornmeal, milk, and molasses.

Indian summer A period of mild, warm weather occurring in late autumn.

India paper A thin, yellowish, absorbent printing paper, used in taking the finest proofs from engraved plates.

In·dic (in′dik) *adj.* Pertaining to India, its peoples, languages, and culture; Indian. —*n.* A branch of the Indo-Iranian subfamily of languages, including Sanskrit, Hindi, etc.

in·di·cate (in′də·kāt) *v.t.* **·cat·ed, ·cat·ing** 1. To be or give a sign of; signify. 2. To direct attention to; point out. 3. To make known. [< IN-[2] + L *dicare* to point out, proclaim]

in·di·ca·tion (in′də·kā′shən) *n.* 1. The act of indicating. 2. That which indicates; sign. 3. A degree or quantity shown on a measuring instrument.

in·dic·a·tive (in·dik′ə·tiv) *adj.* 1. Suggestive of; pointing out. 2. *Gram.* Denoting a mood in which an act or condition is stated or questioned as a fact. —*n. Gram.* **a** The indicative mood. **b** A verb in this mood. —**in·dic′a·tive·ly** *adv.*

in·di·ca·tor (in′də·kā′tər) *n.* 1. One who or that which indicates or points out. 2. An instrument that measures or shows position; also, its pointer or needle.

in·di·ces (in′də·sēz) Alternative plural of INDEX.

in·dict (in·dīt′) *v.t.* 1. *Law* To prefer an indictment against. 2. To charge with a crime or offense. [< AF *enditer* to make known; later infl. in form by Med.L *dictare* to accuse] —**in·dict′a·ble** *adj.* —**in·dict·ee** (in·dī·tē′) *n.* —**in·dict′er** or **in·dict′or** *n.*

in·dict·ment (in·dīt′mənt) *n.* 1. The act of indicting, or the state of being indicted. 2. *Law* A formal written charge of crime, presented by a grand jury.

in·dif·fer·ent (in·dif′ər·ənt) *adj.* 1. Having no interest or feeling; unconcerned. 2. Lacking in distinction; mediocre. 3. Only average in size, amount, etc. 4. Having little importance or significance. 5. Showing no preference; unbiased. [< L *indifferens*] —**in·dif′fer·ence** *n.* —**in·dif′fer·ent·ly** *adv.*

in·dig·e·nous (in·dij′ə·nəs) *adj.* 1. Originating or occurring naturally in the place specified; native. 2. Innate; inherent. [< L *indu-* within + *gignere* to be born]

in·di·gent (in′də·jənt) *adj.* Lacking means of subsistence; poor. [< L *indu-* within + *egere* to need] —**in′di·gence, in′di·gen·cy** *n.* —**in′di·gent·ly** *adv.*

in·di·gest·i·ble (in′də·jes′tə·bəl) *adj.* Difficult to digest; not digestible. —**in′di·gest′i·bil′i·ty** *n.* —**in′di·gest′i·bly** *adv.*

in·di·ges·tion (in′də·jes′chən) *n.* Difficulty in digesting food. [< F]

in·dig·nant (in·dig′nənt) *adj.* Feeling or showing indignation. —**in·dig′nant·ly** *adv.*

in·dig·na·tion (in′dig·nā′shən) *n.* Anger aroused by injustice or baseness. [< IN-[1] + L *dignus* worthy]

in·dig·ni·ty (in·dig′nə·tē) *n. pl.* **·ties** An act that humiliates or injures self-respect.

in·di·go (in′də·gō) *n. pl.* **·gos** or **·goes** 1. A blue coloring substance obtained from certain plants or made synthetically. 2. A deep violet blue. Also **indigo blue.** —*adj.*

Deep violet blue. [< Sp. < Gk. *Indikon* (*pharmakon*) Indian (dye)]

indigo bunting A finch of North America, the male of which is a brilliant indigo. Also **indigo bird.**

in·di·rect (in′də·rekt′) *adj.* 1. Not following a direct line, course, or procedure. 2. Not straightforward or open; underhand. 3. Not coming as an immediate result: *indirect* benefits. 4. Not expressed in the exact words of the source: an *indirect* quotation. **—in′di·rec′tion** *n.* **—in′di·rect′ly** *adv.* **—in′di·rect′·ness** *n.*

indirect lighting Lighting that is reflected, as from a white ceiling, or diffused.

indirect object See under OBJECT.

indirect tax A tax, the burden of which is ultimately passed on to another.

in·dis·cern·i·ble (in′di·sûr′nə·bəl) *adj.* Incapable of being discerned; imperceptible. **—in′dis·cern′i·bly** *adv.*

in·dis·creet (in′dis·krēt′) *adj.* Lacking discretion; imprudent. **—in′dis·creet′ly** *adv.*

in·dis·crete (in′dis·krēt′) *adj.* Not discrete; not separated; unified.

in·dis·cre·tion (in′dis·kresh′ən) *n.* 1. The state or quality of being indiscreet. 2. An indiscreet act, speech, etc.

in·dis·crim·i·nate (in′dis·krim′ə·nit) *adj.* 1. Showing no discrimination; not perceiving differences. 2. Confused; chaotic. **—in′dis·crim′i·nate·ly** *adv.* **—in′dis·crim′i·nat′ing** *adj.* **—in′dis·crim′i·na′tion** *n.* **—in′dis·crim′i·na′tive** *adj.*

in·dis·pen·sa·ble (in′dis·pen′sə·bəl) *adj.* Not to be dispensed with; essential. **—in′dis·pen′sa·bil′i·ty** *n.* **—in′dis·pen′sa·bly** *adv.*

in·dis·pose (in′dis·pōz′) *v.t.* **·posed, ·pos·ing** 1. To render unwilling; disincline. 2. To render unfit. 3. To make slightly ill or ailing. **—in′dis·po·si′tion** (-pə·zish′ən) *n.*

in·dis·posed (in′dis·pōzd′) *adj.* 1. Mildly ill; unwell. 2. Disinclined; not willing.

in·dis·put·a·ble (in′dis·pyo͞o′tə·bəl) *adj.* Incapable of being disputed. **—in′dis·put′a·bil′i·ty** *n.* **—in′dis·put′a·bly** *adv.*

in·dis·sol·u·ble (in′di·sol′yə·bəl) *adj.* 1. Incapable of being dissolved, separated into its elements, or destroyed. 2. Binding; extremely durable. **—in′dis·sol′u·bil′i·ty** *n.* **—in′dis·sol′u·bly** *adv.*

in·dis·tinct (in′dis·tingkt′) *adj.* 1. Not clearly defined or outlined; blurred. 2. Not readily distinguishable; confused. **—in′dis·tinct′ly** *adv.* **—in′dis·tinct′ness** *n.*

in·dis·tin·guish·a·ble (in′di·sting′gwish·ə·bəl) *adj.* Incapable of being perceived or distinguished. **—in′dis·tin′guish·a·bly** *adv.*

in·di·um (in′dē·əm) *n.* A soft, malleable, silver-white metallic element (symbol In). [< NL *indicum* indigo; with ref. to its spectrum color]

in·di·vid·u·al (in′də·vij′o͞o·əl) *adj.* 1. Existing as a unit; single. 2. Separate, as distinguished from others of the same kind. 3. Pertaining to or meant for a single person, animal, etc. 4. Differentiated from others by distinctive characteristics. **—***n.* 1. A single human being as distinct from others. 2. A person. [< IN-[1] + L *dividere* to divide] **—in′di·vid′u·al·ly** *adv.*

in·di·vid·u·al·ism (in′də·vij′o͞o·əl·iz′əm) *n.* 1. Personal independence in action, thought, etc. 2. The state of being individual. 3. A theory or doctrine that emphasizes the importance of the individual. **—in′di·vid′u·al·ist** *n.* **—in′di·vid′u·al·is′tic** *adj.*

in·di·vid·u·al·i·ty (in′də·vij′o͞o·al′ə·tē) *n. pl.* **·ties** 1. A quality or trait that distinguishes one person or thing from others. 2. Strikingly distinctive character or personality. 3. The state of having separate, independent existence.

in·di·vid·u·al·ize (in′də·vij′o͞o·əl·iz′) *v.t.* **·ized, ·iz·ing** 1. To make individual; distinguish. 2. To treat, mention, or consider individually. 3. To adapt to the needs of an individual. **—in′di·vid′u·al·i·za′tion** *n.*

in·di·vis·i·ble (in′də·viz′ə·bəl) *adj.* Not divisible; incapable of being divided. **—***n.* Something that is indivisible. **—in′di·vis′i·bil′i·ty** *n.* **—in′di·vis′i·bly** *adv.*

In·do·chi·nese (in′dō·chī·nēz′, -nēs′) *adj.* Of or pertaining to Indochina, its inhabitants, or their language. **—***n. pl.* **·nese** 1. A member of one of the Mongoloid peoples of Indochina. 2. The languages of these peoples, collectively.

in·doc·tri·nate (in·dok′trə·nāt) *v.t.* **·nat·ed, ·nat·ing** To instruct in doctrines; esp., to teach (someone) partisan or sectarian dogmas. [< Med.L *indoctrinare* to teach] **—in·doc′tri·na′tion** *n.*

In·do-Eu·ro·pe·an (in′dō·yo͝or′ə·pē′ən) *adj.* Designating the largest family of languages in the world, comprising most of the languages of Europe and many languages of India and SW Asia. **—In′do-Eu′ro·pe′an** *n.*

In·do-I·ra·ni·an (in′dō·i·rā′nē·ən) *adj.* Designating the subfamily of the Indo-European family of languages, consisting of Indic and Iranian branches. **—In′do-I·ra′·ni·an** *n.*

in·do·lent (in′də·lənt) *adj.* Averse to exertion or work; lazy. [< IN-[1] + L *dolere* to feel pain] **—in′do·lence** *n.* **—in′do·lent·ly** *adv.*

in·dom·i·ta·ble (in·dom′i·tə·bəl) *adj.* Not easily defeated or subdued. [< IN-[1] + L *domitare* to tame] **—in·dom′i·ta·bly** *adv.*

In·do·ne·sian (in′dō·nē′zhən, -shən) *n.* 1. An inhabitant of Indonesia. 2. The languages, collectively, spoken by the peoples native to Indonesia: also called *Malayan.* **—In′do·ne′sian** *adj.*

in·door (in′dôr′) *adj.* 1. Pertaining to or meant for the interior of a house or building. 2. Located or performed indoors. [Earlier *within-door*]

in·doors (in′dôrz′) *adv.* Inside or toward the inside of a building.

in·dorse (in·dôrs′) See ENDORSE.

in·du·bi·ta·ble (in·do͞o′bə·tə·bəl, -dyo͞o′-) *adj.* Not to be doubted. **—in·du′bi·ta·bly** *adv.*

in·duce (in·do͞os′, -dyo͞os′) *v.t.* **·duced, ·duc·ing** 1. To cause to act, speak, etc.; influence; persuade. 2. To bring on; cause. 3. To infer by inductive reasoning. [< IN-[2] + L *ducere* to lead] **—in·duc′i·ble** *adj.*

in·duce·ment (in·do͞os′mənt, -dyo͞os′-) *n.* 1. That which induces; incentive. 2. The act of inducing.

in·duct (in·dukt′) *v.t.* 1. To bring (a draftee) into military service. 2. To install formally in an office, etc. 3. To initiate in knowledge, experience, etc. 4. *Physics* To produce by induction. [See INDUCE.]

in·duc·tance (in·duk′təns) *n. Electr.* The ability of a circuit to produce induction.

in·duc·tee (in′duk·tē′) *n.* One inducted or being inducted.

in·duc·tion (in·duk′shən) *n.* 1. The act of inducting, or state of being inducted. 2. The act of inducing or causing. 3. A process of reasoning whereby a general statement is inferred from particular instances; also, the general statement itself. 4. *Electr.* The production of magnetization or electrification in a body by the mere proximity of a magnetic field or electric charge, or of an electric current in a conductor by the variation of the magnetic field in its vicinity. —**in·duc′·tion·al** *adj.*

induction coil *Electr.* A device that changes a low steady voltage into a high intermittent alternating voltage by electromagnetic induction.

in·duc·tive (in·duk′tiv) *adj.* 1. Pertaining to or resulting from induction. 2. *Electr.* Produced by or causing induction or inductance. —**in·duc′tive·ly** *adv.* —**in·duc′tive·ness** *n.*

in·dulge (in·dulj′) *v.* **·dulged, ·dulg·ing** *v.t.* 1. To yield to or gratify, as desires or whims. 2. To yield to or gratify (another); humor. —*v.i.* 3. To gratify one's own desire: with *in.* [< L *indulgere* to be kind to] —**in·dulg′er** *n.*

in·dul·gence (in·dul′jəns) *n.* 1. The act of indulging, or state of being indulgent. 2. That which is indulged in. 3. Something granted as a favor. 4. In business, permission to defer paying a bill, etc. 5. In the Roman Catholic Church, remission of temporal punishment due for a sin after it has been forgiven through sacramental absolution.

in·dul·gent (in·dul′jənt) *adj.* Prone to indulge; lenient. —**in·dul′gent·ly** *adv.*

in·du·rate (*v.* in′dŏŏ·rāt, -dyŏŏ-; *adj.* -rit) *v.t. & v.i.* **·rat·ed, ·rat·ing** 1. To make or become hard or unfeeling. 2. To make or become hardy. —*adj.* Hard; unfeeling: also **in′du·rat′ed.** [< L *indurare* to make hard] —**in′du·ra′tion** *n.* —**in′du·ra′tive** *adj.*

in·dus·tri·al (in·dus′trē·əl) *adj.* 1. Of, characteristic of, used in, or resulting from industry. 2. Having many industries: an *industrial* area. 3. Relating to workers in industry. —*n. pl.* Stocks or securities of industrial enterprises. —**in·dus′tri·al·ly** *adv.*

industrial arts The technical skills used in industry, esp. as subjects of study in schools.

in·dus·tri·al·ism (in·dus′trē·əl·iz′əm) *n.* An economic system based chiefly on large-scale industries and production of goods.

in·dus·tri·al·ist (in·dus′trē·əl·ist) *n.* An owner or manager in industry.

in·dus·tri·a·lize (in·dus′trē·əl·iz′) *v.t.* **·ized, ·iz·ing** 1. To establish large-scale industries in. 2. To make or form into an industry. —**in·dus′tri·al·i·za′tion** *n.*

in·dus·tri·ous (in·dus′trē·əs) *adj.* Hard-working. —**in·dus′tri·ous·ly** *adv.* —**in·dus′·tri·ous·ness** *n.*

in·dus·try (in′dəs·trē) *n. pl.* **·tries** 1. Any specific branch of production or manufacture. 2. Manufacturing and productive interests collectively. 3. Diligent and regular application to work or tasks. [< L *industrius* diligent]

in·dwell (in′dwel′) *v.* **·dwelt, ·dwell·ing** *v.t.* 1. To dwell in. —*v.i.* 2. To dwell. —**in′·dwell′er** *n.* —**in′dwell′ing** *n.*

-ine[1] *suffix* Like; pertaining to; of the nature of: *marine, canine.* [< F < L *-inus,* adj. suffix]

-ine[2] *suffix* 1. *Chem.* **a** Used in the names of halogens: *bromine.* **b** Used to indicate an alkaloid or basic substance: *morphine.* **c** Var. of -IN. 2. Used in names of commercial products: *brilliantine.* [Special use of -INE[1]]

-ine[3] *suffix* Used to form feminine words, names, and titles: *heroine.* [< F < L *-ina,* suffix of fem. nouns < Gk. *-inē*]

-ine[4] *suffix* Like; resembling: *crystalline.* [< L < Gk. *-inos*]

in·e·bri·ate (*v.* in·ē′brē·āt; *n. & adj.* in·ē′brē·it, -āt) *v.t.* **·at·ed, ·at·ing** To make drunk; intoxicate. —*n.* A habitual drunkard. —*adj.* Intoxicated. [< IN-[2] + L *ebriare* to make drunk] —**in·e′bri·a′ted** *adj.* —**in·e′bri·a′tion** *n.*

in·ef·fa·ble (in·ef′ə·bəl) *adj.* 1. Too overpowering to be expressed in words; indescribable. 2. Too sacred to be uttered. [< IN-[1] + L *effabilis* utterable] —**in·ef′fa·bil′i·ty** *n.* —**in·ef′fa·bly** *adv.*

in·ef·fec·tive (in′i·fek′tiv) *adj.* 1. Not effective. 2. Incompetent. —**in′ef·fec′tive·ly** *adv.* —**in′ef·fec′tive·ness** *n.*

in·ef·fec·tu·al (in′i·fek′chōō·əl) *adj.* 1. Not effectual. 2. Unsuccessful; fruitless. —**in′ef·fec′tu·al′i·ty** (-al′ə·tē) *n.* —**in′ef·fec′tu·al·ly** *adv.*

in·ef·fi·ca·cious (in′ef·ə·kā′shəs) *adj.* Not producing the effect desired or intended, as a medicine. —**in′ef·fi·ca′cious·ly** *adv.* —**in·ef′fi·ca·cy** (-kə·sē) *n.*

in·ef·fi·cient (in′i·fish′ənt) *adj.* 1. Not efficient; not performing a function economically; wasteful. 2. Incompetent. —**in′ef·fi′·cien·cy** *n.* —**in′ef·fi′cient·ly** *adv.*

in·el·e·gant (in·el′ə·gənt) *adj.* 1. Not elegant. 2. Coarse; crude. —**in·el′e·gance, in·el′e·gan·cy** *n.* —**in·el′e·gant·ly** *adv.*

in·e·luc·ta·ble (in′i·luk′tə·bəl) *adj.* Not to be escaped from or avoided; inevitable. [< IN-[1] + L *eluctabilis* resistible] —**in′e·luc′ta·bil′i·ty** *n.* —**in′e·luc′ta·bly** *adv.*

in·ept (in·ept′) *adj.* 1. Not suitable or appropriate. 2. Clumsy; awkward. [< IN-[1] + L *aptus* fit] —**in·ep′ti·tude, in·ept′ness** *n.* —**in·ept′ly** *adv.*

in·e·qual·i·ty (in′i·kwol′ə·tē) *n. pl.* **·ties** 1. The state of being unequal. 2. An instance of this. 3. Lack of evenness of proportion; variableness. 4. Disparity of social position, opportunity, justice, etc. [< L *inaequalitas*]

in·eq·ui·ta·ble (in·ek′wə·tə·bəl) *adj.* Not equitable; unfair. —**in·eq′ui·ta·bly** *adv.*

in·eq·ui·ty (in·ek′wə·tē) *n. pl.* **·ties** 1. Lack of equity; injustice. 2. An unfair act or course of action.

in·e·rad·i·ca·ble (in′i·rad′ə·kə·bəl) *adj.* Not eradicable; impossible to remove or root out. —**in′e·rad′i·ca·bly** *adv.*

in·ert (in·ûrt′) *adj.* 1. Lacking independent power to move or to resist applied force. 2. Disinclined to move or act; sluggish. 3. *Chem.* Devoid or almost devoid of active properties. [< IN-[1] + L *ars* art] —**in·ert′ly** *adv.*

in·er·tia (in·ûr′shə) *n.* 1. The state of being inert; inactivity. 2. *Physics* The tendency of any physical body to persist in its state of rest or of uniform motion until acted upon by some external force. [< L, idleness] —**in·er′tial** *adj.*

in·es·cap·a·ble (in′ə·skā′pə·bəl) *adj.* Impossible to escape; unavoidable. —**in′es·cap′a·bly** *adv.*

in·es·ti·ma·ble (in·es′tə·mə·bəl) *adj.* 1. Not to be estimated. 2. Having great value. —**in·es′ti·ma·bly** *adv.*

in·ev·i·ta·ble (in·ev′ə·tə·bəl) *adj.* That cannot be avoided or prevented from happening. [< IN-[1] + L *evitare* to avoid] —**in·ev′i·ta·bil′i·ty** *n.* —**in·ev′i·ta·bly** *adv.*

in·ex·act (in′ig·zakt′) *adj.* Not exact; not completely accurate or true. —**in′ex·act′i·tude, in′ex·act′ness** *n.* —**in′ex·act′ly** *adv.*

in·ex·cus·a·ble (in′ik·skyōō′zə·bəl) *adj.* Not excusable; impossible to excuse or justify. —**in′ex·cus′a·bil′i·ty** *n.* —**in′ex·cus′a·bly** *adv.*

in·ex·haust·i·ble (in′ig·zôs′tə·bəl) *adj.* 1. Incapable of being exhausted or used up. 2. Incapable of fatigue; tireless. —**in′ex·haust′i·bil′i·ty** *n.* —**in′ex·haust′i·bly** *adv.*

in·ex·o·ra·ble (in·ek′sər·ə·bəl) *adj.* 1. Not to be moved by entreaty or persuasion; unyielding. 2. Unalterable; relentless. [< IN-[1] + L *exorare* to move by prayer] —**in·ex′o·ra·bil′i·ty** *n.* —**in·ex′o·ra·bly** *adv.*

in·ex·pe·di·ent (in′ik·spē′dē·ənt) *adj.* Not expedient; inadvisable. —**in′ex·pe′di·ence, in′ex·pe′di·en·cy** *n.* —**in′ex·pe′di·ent·ly** *adv.*

in·ex·pert (in·ek′spûrt) *adj.* Not expert; unskilled; inept. —**in·ex′pert·ly** *adv.*

in·ex·pi·a·ble (in·ek′spē·ə·bəl) *adj.* Incapable of being expiated; unpardonable.

in·ex·pli·ca·ble (in·eks′pli·kə·bəl, in′iks·plik′ə·bəl) *adj.* Not explicable; impossible to explain. —**in·ex′pli·ca·bly** *adv.*

in·ex·press·i·ble (in′ik·spres′ə·bəl) *adj.* Incapable of being expressed or put into words. —**in′ex·press′i·bly** *adv.*

in ex·tre·mis (in iks·trē′mis) *Latin* At the point of death.

in·ex·tri·ca·ble (in·eks′tri·kə·bəl) *adj.* 1. Impossible to extricate oneself from. 2. Impossible to disentangle or undo. 3. Too intricate to be solved. —**in·ex′tri·ca·bly** *adv.*

in·fal·li·ble (in·fal′ə·bəl) *adj.* 1. Exempt from fallacy or error of judgment. 2. Not liable to fail; sure. 3. In Roman Catholic doctrine, incapable of error in matters of faith and morals. —**in·fal′li·bil′i·ty** —**in·fal′li·bly** *adv.*

in·fa·mous (in′fə·məs) *adj.* 1. Having a vile reputation. 2. Deserving or producing infamy; odious. [< IN-[1] + L *fama* fame] —**in′fa·mous·ly** *adv.*

in·fa·my (in′fə·mē) *n.* *pl.* **·mies** 1. Dishonor; disgrace. 2. The state of being infamous. 3. An infamous act.

in·fan·cy (in′fən·sē) *n.* *pl.* **·cies** 1. The state or period of being an infant; babyhood. 2. The beginnings of anything. 3. *Law* The years before attaining the age of legal majority.

in·fant (in′fənt) *n.* 1. A child in the earliest stages of life; baby. 2. *Law* One who has not attained the age of legal majority; a minor. —*adj.* 1. Of, for, or typical of infancy or infants. 2. Beginning to exist or develop. [< IN-[1] + L *fari* to speak.]

in·fan·ta (in·fan′tə) *n.* A daughter of a Spanish or Portuguese king. [< Sp., infant (fem.)]

in·fan·te (in·fan′tā) *n.* A son, except the eldest, of a Spanish or Portuguese king. [< Sp., infant (masc.)]

in·fan·ti·cide (in·fan′tə·sīd) *n.* 1. The killing of an infant, esp. at birth. 2. One who has killed an infant. [< L *infans* child + -CIDE]

in·fan·tile (in′fən·tīl, -til) *adj.* 1. Of infancy or infants. 2. Characteristic of infancy or infants; babyish. Also **in′fan·tine** (-tīn, -tin).

infantile paralysis Poliomyelitis.

in·fan·try (in′fən·trē) *n.* *pl.* **·tries** Soldiers, units, or a branch of an army trained and equipped to fight on foot. [< Ital. *infanteria* < *infante* boy, page, foot soldier < L *infans, infantis* child] —**in′fan·try·man** (-mən) *n.*

in·farct (in′färkt) *n.* An area of tissue that is dying because its supply of blood is obstructed: also **in·farc′tion.** [< IN-[2] + L *farcire* to stuff]

in·fat·u·ate (in·fach′ōō·āt) *v.t.* **·at·ed, ·at·ing** To inspire with a foolish and unreasoning love or passion. [< L *infatuare* to make a fool of] —**in·fat′u·ate** (-āt, -it), **in·fat′u·at′ed** *adj.* —**in·fat′u·a′tion** *n.*

in·fect (in·fekt′) *v.t.* 1. To affect with disease-producing organisms, as a wound. 2. To cause (a person, etc.) to contract a communicable disease. 3. To affect or inspire, as with attitudes or beliefs, esp. harmfully. [< L *inficere* to dip into, stain] —**in·fec′tor** *n.*

in·fec·tion (in·fek′shən) *n.* 1. An invasion of body tissue by disease-producing organisms. 2. A disease resulting from such an invasion. 3. The transference of a disease, idea, mood, etc.

in·fec·tious (in·fek′shəs) *adj.* 1. Liable to produce infection. 2. Denoting diseases communicable by infection. 3. Tending to excite similar reactions: *infectious* laughter. —**in·fec′tious·ly** *adv.* —**in·fec′tious·ness** *n.*

in·fec·tive (in·fek′tiv) *adj.* 1. Liable to produce infection. 2. Affecting others; infectious.

in·fe·lic·i·tous (in′fə·lis′ə·təs) *adj.* Not suitable. —**in′fe·lic′i·tous·ly** *adv.*

in·fe·lic·i·ty (in′fə·lis′ə·tē) *n.* *pl.* **·ties** 1. The state of being infelicitous. 2. That which is infelicitous, as an inappropriate remark. [< L *infelicitas*]

in·fer (in·fûr′) *v.* **·ferred, ·fer·ring** *v.t.* 1. To derive by reasoning; conclude from evidence or premises. 2. To involve as a conclusion: said of facts, statements, etc. 3. Loosely, to imply. —*v.i.* 4. To draw an inference. [< IN-[2] + L *ferre* to bring, carry] —**in·fer′a·ble** *adj.* —**in·fer′a·bly** *adv.*

in·fer·ence (in′fər·əns) *n.* 1. A conclusion. 2. The act or process of inferring. —**in·fer·en·tial** (in′fə·ren′shəl) *adj.* —**in′fer·en′·tial·ly** *adv.*

in·fer·i·or (in·fir′ē·ər) *adj.* 1. Lower in quality, worth, or adequacy. 2. Lower in rank or importance. 3. Lower in position; situated below. —*n.* A person inferior in rank or in attainments. [< L, lower] —**in·fe′ri·or′i·ty** (-ôr′ə·tē, -or′-) *n.*

in·fer·nal (in·fûr′nəl) *adj.* 1. Of or pertaining to the mythological world of the dead, or to hell. 2. Diabolical; hellish. 3. *Informal*

Damnable; hateful. [< L *infernus* situated below] —**in·fer′nal·ly** *adv.*

in·fer·no (in·fûr′nō) *n. pl.* **·nos** 1. Hell. 2. Any place comparable to hell. [< Ital.]

in·fest (in·fest′) *v.t.* 1. To overrun or occupy in large numbers so as to be annoying or dangerous. 2. To be a parasite on or in. [< L *infestare* to assail] —**in′fes·ta′tion** *n.* —**in·fest′er** *n.*

in·fi·del (in′fi·dəl) *n.* 1. One who rejects all religious belief; unbeliever. 2. One who rejects a particular religion, esp. Christianity or Islam. —*adj.* 1. Being an infidel. 2. Of or relating to infidels or unbelief. [< IN-² + L *fidelis* faithful]

in·fi·del·i·ty (in′fi·del′ə·tē) *n. pl.* **·ties** 1. Lack of fidelity. 2. A disloyal act. 3. Adultery. 4. Lack of belief in a particular religion, esp. Christianity or Islam.

in·field (in′fēld′) *n.* In baseball: **a** The playing space within or adjacent to the base lines of the field. **b** The infielders collectively.

in·field·er (in′fēld′ər) *n.* In baseball, the first baseman, second baseman, shortstop, or third baseman.

in·fil·trate (in·fil′trāt, in′fil·trāt) *v.* **·trat·ed, ·trat·ing** *v.t.* 1. To enter (an organization, etc.) secretly or stealthily in order to spy, gain control, etc. 2. To cause (a liquid or gas) to pass into or through pores. 3. To filter or move through or into. —*v.i.* 4. To pass into or through a substance. —*n.* That which infiltrates. —**in′fil·tra′tion** *n.*

in·fin·ite (in′fə·nit) *adj.* 1. Having no boundaries or limits; extending without end. 2. Very numerous or great; vast. 3. All-embracing; perfect. 4. *Math.* Of or designating a quantity conceived as always exceeding any other quantity in value. —*n.* *Math.* An infinite quantity. [< IN-¹ + L *finitus* finite] —**in′fi·nite·ly** *adv.*

in·fin·i·tes·i·mal (in′fin·ə·tes′ə·məl) *adj.* 1. Infinitely small. 2. So small as to be incalculable. —*n.* An infinitesimal quantity. [< NL *infinitus* infinite + *-esimus* (after *centesimus* hundredth)] —**in′fin·i·tes′i·mal·ly** *adv.*

in·fin·i·tive (in·fin′ə·tiv) *Gram. adj.* 1. Without limitation of person or number. 2. Of or pertaining to the infinitive. —*n.* A verb form generally used either as the principal verb of a verb phrase, most often without *to*, or as a noun, most often with *to*. [< Med.L *infinitivus*]

in·fin·i·tude (in·fin′ə·tōōd, -tyōōd) *n.* 1. The quality of being infinite or boundless. 2. An unlimited quantity.

in·fin·i·ty (in·fin′ə·tē) *n. pl.* **·ties** 1. The state of being infinite. 2. Something considered infinite, as space or time. 3. A very large amount or number.

in·firm (in·fûrm′) *adj.* 1. Feeble or weak, as from old age. 2. Lacking firmness of purpose. [< IN-¹ + L *firmus* firm] —**in·firm′ly** *adv.*

in·fir·ma·ry (in·fûr′mər·ē) *n. pl.* **·ries** A place for the treatment of the sick, esp. in a school, etc. [< L *infirmus* infirm, indisposed]

in·fir·mi·ty (in·fûr′mə·tē) *n. pl.* **·ties** 1. The state of being infirm. 2. A physical or mental defect.

in·fix (in·fiks′) *v.t.* 1. To set firmly or insert in. 2. To implant in the mind. 3. *Gram.* To insert (an infix) within a word. —*n.* *Gram.* A modifying addition inserted in the body of a word. —**in·fix′ion** (-fik′shən) *n.*

in·flame (in·flām′) *v.t. & v.i.* **·flamed, ·flam·ing** 1. To ignite; kindle. 2. To excite or become excited, esp. with rage, hate, passion, etc. 3. To increase or intensify, as a violent emotion. 4. To produce or suffer inflammation. [< IN-² + L *flamma* flame]

in·flam·ma·ble (in·flam′ə·bəl) *adj.* 1. Flammable. 2. Easily excited or aroused. —*n.* A flammable thing or substance. —**in·flam′ma·bil′i·ty** *n.* —**in·flam′ma·bly** *adv.*

in·flam·ma·tion (in′flə·mā′shən) *n.* 1. The act of inflaming, or the state of being inflamed. 2. *Pathol.* A diseased condition characterized by redness, swelling, and pain.

in·flam·ma·to·ry (in·flam′ə·tôr′ē) *adj.* 1. Tending to arouse excitement, anger, etc. 2. *Med.* Characterized by or causing inflammation.

in·flate (in·flāt′) *v.* **·flat·ed, ·flat·ing** *v.t.* 1. To cause to expand by filling with or as with gas or air. 2. To enlarge excessively; puff up. 3. *Econ.* To increase (prices, credit, etc.) in excess of usual or prior levels. —*v.i.* 4. To become inflated. [< IN-² + L *flare* to blow] —**in·flat′a·ble** *adj.* —**in·flat′er** or **in·flat′or** *n.*

in·fla·tion (in·flā′shən) *n.* 1. The act of inflating, or the state of being inflated. 2. *Econ.* An unstable rise in price levels. —**in·fla′tion·ar′y** *adj.*

in·flect (in·flekt′) *v.t.* 1. To vary the tone or pitch of (the voice); modulate. 2. To turn from a straight or usual course; bend. 3. *Gram.* To give the inflections of (a word). [< IN-² + L *flectere* to bend]

in·flec·tion (in·flek′shən) *n.* 1. The act of inflecting, or the state of being inflected. 2. An angle or bend. 3. Modulation of the voice. 4. *Gram.* **a** A change in form undergone by words to express grammatical and syntactical relations, as of case, number, tense, etc. **b** An inflected form. —**in·flec′tion·al** *adj.*

in·flex·i·ble (in·flek′sə·bəl) *adj.* 1. Incapable of being bent; rigid. 2. Unyielding; stubborn. 3. That cannot be altered; fixed. —**in·flex′i·bil′i·ty** *n.* —**in·flex′i·bly** *adv.*

in·flict (in·flikt′) *v.t.* 1. To deal; lay on: to *inflict* a blow. 2. To impose. [< IN-² + L *fligere* to strike] —**in·flict′er** or **in·flic′tor** *n.*

in·flic·tion (in·flik′shən) *n.* 1. The act of inflicting. 2. That which is inflicted, as pain, punishment, etc.

in·flo·res·cence (in′flə·res′əns) *n.* 1. A flowering; flourishing. 2. *Bot.* **a** The mode of arrangement of flowers in relation to the stem or axis. **b** A cluster of flowers. **c** A single flower. [< LL *inflorescere* to come into flower] —**in′flo·res′cent** *adj.*

in·flow (in′flō′) *n.* 1. The act of flowing in. 2. That which flows in.

in·flu·ence (in′flōō·əns) *n.* 1. The power of persons or things to produce effects on others, esp. by indirect means. 2. Power resulting from social position, wealth, etc. 3. One who or that which possesses the power to affect others. —*v.t.* **·enced, ·enc·ing** 1. To produce an effect upon the actions or thought of. 2. To have an effect upon. [< IN-² + L *fluere* to flow] —**in′flu·enc·er** *n.* —**in′flu·en′tial** (-en′shəl) *adj.* —**in′flu·en′tial·ly** *adv.*

in·flu·en·za (in′flōō·en′zə) *n. Pathol.* A contagious, infectious virus disease characterized by respiratory inflammation and fever: also called *flu, grippe.* [< Ital., influence < LL *influentia,* from the belief that illness was due to the influence of the stars]

in·flux (in′fluks′) *n.* 1. A flowing in, as of a fluid. 2. A continuous coming, as of people. 3. The mouth of a river. [< LL *influere* to flow in]

in·fo (in′fō) *n.* Information.

in·fold (in·fōld′) See ENFOLD.

in·form (in·fôrm′) *v.t.* 1. To notify. 2. To give character to: with *with* or *by.* —*v.i.* 3. To disclose information. 4. To act as an informer. [< L *informare* to give form to]

in·for·mal (in·fôr′məl) *adj.* 1. Not in the usual or prescribed form; unofficial. 2. Without formality; casual. 3. Not requiring formal attire. 4. Characteristic of or suitable to the language of ordinary conversation or familiar writing. —**in′for·mal′i·ty** (-mal′ə·tē) *n.* —**in·for′mal·ly** *adv.*

in·form·ant (in·fôr′mənt) *n.* One who gives information.

in·for·ma·tion (in′fər·mā′shən) *n.* 1. Knowledge acquired or derived; facts. 2. Timely knowledge; news. 3. The act of informing, or the state of being informed. [< L *informatio, -onis*] —**in′for·ma′tion·al** *adj.*

in·form·a·tive (in·fôr′mə·tiv) *adj.* Affording information; instructive.

in·formed (in·fôrmd′) *adj.* Having a high degree of information or education.

in·form·er (in·fôr′mər) *n.* 1. One who secretly informs authorities of criminal or disapproved acts of others; stool pigeon. 2. An informant.

infra- *prefix* Below; beneath; on the lower part. [< L]

in·frac·tion (in·frak′shən) *n.* The act of breaking or violating (a pledge, law, etc.); infringement. [< L *infractio, -onis*]

in·fra dig (in′frə) Beneath one's dignity. [< L *infra dignitatem*]

in·fra·red (in′frə·red′) *adj. Physics* Having a wavelength greater than that of visible red light, and radiating heat.

in·fra·struc·ture (in′frə·struk′chər) *n.* 1. The basic framework of a system or organization. 2. Basic technological installations, such as roads, communication systems, etc.

in·fre·quent (in·frē′kwənt) *adj.* Present or occurring at widely separated intervals; uncommon. —**in·fre′quen·cy, in·fre′quence** *n.* —**in·fre′quent·ly** *adv.*

in·fringe (in·frinj′) *v.t.* **·fringed, ·fring·ing** To break or disregard the terms of, as a law; violate. —**to infringe on** (or **upon**) To transgress or trespass on rights or privileges. [< IN-² + L *frangere* to break] —**in·fringe′·ment** *n.* —**in·fring′er** *n.*

in·fu·ri·ate (in·fyŏŏr′ē·āt) *v.t.* **·at·ed, ·at·ing** To make furious; enrage. [< Med.L *infuriare* to madden] —**in·fu′ri·at′ing·ly** *adv.*

in·fuse (in·fyōōz′) *v.t.* **·fused, ·fus·ing** 1. To instill or inculcate, as principles. 2. To inspire; imbue: with *with.* 3. To pour in. [< IN-² + L *fundere* to pour] —**in·fus′er** *n.*

in·fus·i·ble (in·fyōō′zə·bəl) *adj.* Incapable of or resisting fusion or melting.

in·fu·sion (in·fyōō′zhən) *n.* 1. The act of infusing. 2. That which is infused. 3. A liquid extract obtained by soaking a substance in water.

in·fu·sor·i·an (in′fyōō·sôr′ē·ən) *n.* One of a class of one-celled animals.

-ing¹ *suffix* 1. The act or art of doing the action expressed in the root verb: *hunting.* 2. The product or result of an action: a *painting.* 3. Material for: *flooring.* 4. That which performs the action of the root verb: a *covering.* [OE *-ung, -ing*]

-ing² *suffix* Used in the present participle of verbs and in participial adjectives: He is *talking*; an *eating* apple. [ME < OE *-ende*]

-ing³ *suffix of nouns* 1. One having the quality of: *sweeting.* 2. Small; little. [OE]

in·gen·ious (in·jēn′yəs) *adj.* Inventive; clever. [< IN-² + L *gignere* to beget] —**in·gen′ious·ly** *adv.*

in·gé·nue (an′zhə·nōō′, *Fr.* aṅ·zhā·nü′) *n. pl.* **·nues** (-nōōz′, *Fr.* -nü′) The role of a young girl in a play, film, etc.; also, an actress who plays such roles. [< F]

in·ge·nu·i·ty (in′jə·nōō′ə·tē, -nyōō′-) *n. pl.* **·ties** 1. Imaginative resources; inventiveness. 2. Originality of design or execution.

in·gen·u·ous (in·jen′yōō·əs) *adj.* 1. Straightforward; candid; frank. 2. Innocent and simple; naive. [< L *ingenuus* inborn, natural] —**in·gen′u·ous·ly** *adv.* —**in·gen′u·ous·ness** *n.*

in·gest (in·jest′) *v.t.* To take or put (food, etc.) into the body by swallowing or absorbing. [< IN-² + L *gerere* to carry] —**in·ges′·tion** *n.* —**in·ges′tive** *adj.*

in·gle·nook (ing′gəl·nŏŏk′) *n.* A corner by a fireplace.

in·glo·ri·ous (in·glôr′ē·əs) *adj.* Not reflecting honor or courage; disgraceful. —**in·glo′ri·ous·ly** *adv.*

in·go·ing (in′gō′ing) *adj.* Entering; going in.

in·got (ing′gət) *n.* A mass of cast metal from the crucible or mold. [? < IN-² + OE *geotan* to pour]

in·grain (in·grān′) *v.t.* To impress firmly on the mind.

in·grained (in·grānd′) *adj.* 1. Worked into the inmost texture; deep-rooted. 2. Thorough; inveterate.

in·grate (in′grāt) *n.* An ungrateful person. [< IN-¹ + L *gratus* pleasing]

in·gra·ti·ate (in·grā′shē·āt) *v.t.* **·at·ed, ·at·ing** To bring (oneself) deliberately into the favor or confidence of others. [< IN-² + L *gratia* favor] —**in·gra′ti·at′ing·ly** *adv.* —**in·gra′ti·a′tion** *n.* —**in·gra′ti·a·to′ry** (-ə·tôr′ē) *adj.*

in·grat·i·tude (in·grat′ə·tōōd, -tyōōd) *n.* Lack of gratitude; insensibility to kindness; thanklessness.

in·gre·di·ent (in·grē′dē·ənt) *n.* 1. Anything that enters into the composition of a mixture. 2. A component of anything. [< IN-² + L *gradi* to walk]

in·gress (in′gres) *n.* 1. A going in, as into a building: also **in·gres·sion** (in·gresh′ən). 2. A place of entrance. [< L *ingredi* to enter] —**in·gres′sive** *adj.*

in-group (in′grōōp′) *n.* Any group with strong feelings of cohesiveness, shared identity, and exclusivity.

in·grown (in′grōn′) *adj.* 1. Grown into the flesh, as a toenail. 2. Grown within; innate: *ingrown* vice. —**in′grow′ing** (-grō′ing) *adj.*

in·gui·nal (ing′gwə·nəl) *adj. Anat.* Of, pertaining to, or located in the groin. [< L *inguen, -inis* groin]

in·hab·it (in·hab′it) *v.t.* To live in; occupy as a home. [< IN-[2] + L *habitare* to dwell] **—in·hab′it·a·bil′i·ty** *n.* **—in·hab′it·a·ble** *adj.* **—in·hab′i·tant, in·hab′it·er** *n.* **—in·hab′i·ta′tion** *n.*

in·ha·la·tor (in′hə·lā′tər) *n.* A device for enabling one to inhale air, medicinal vapors, anesthetics, etc.

in·hale (in·hāl′) *v.t. & v.i.* **·haled, ·hal·ing** To draw (a substance) into the lungs; breathe in. [< IN-[2] + L *halare* to breathe] **—in·ha·la·tion** (in′hə·lā′shən) *n.*

in·hal·er (in·hāl′ər) *n.* 1. One who inhales. 2. *Med.* An inhalator. 3. A respirator.

in·har·mo·ni·ous (in′hār·mō′nē·əs) *adj.* Lacking harmony; discordant. Also **in′har·mon′ic** (-mon′ik). **—in′har·mo′ni·ous·ly** *adv.* **—in′har·mo′ni·ous·ness** *n.*

in·here (in·hir′) *v.i.* **·hered, ·her·ing** To be a permanent or essential part: with *in.* [< IN-[2] + L *haerere* to stick] **—in·her′ence** *n.*

in·her·ent (in·hir′ənt, -her′-) *adj.* Forming an essential element or quality of something. **—in·her′ent·ly** *adv.*

in·her·it (in·her′it) *v.t.* 1. To receive (property, title, etc.) by legal succession or will. 2. To derive (traits, qualities, etc.) from one's parents or ancestors. 3. To receive from one's predecessors. *—v.i.* 4. To take possession of an inheritance. [< LL *inhereditare* to appoint an heir] **—in·her′i·tor** *n.*

in·her·it·a·ble (in·her′ə·tə·bəl) *adj.* 1. Capable of being inherited. 2. Entitled to inherit. **—in·her′it·a·bly** *adv.*

in·her·i·tance (in·her′ə·təns) *n.* 1. The act of inheriting. 2. That which is legally transmissible to an heir; legacy. 3. Derivation of qualities from one's forebears; also, the qualities so derived.

in·hib·it (in·hib′it) *v.t.* To restrain; check; repress. [< IN-[2] + L *habere* to have, hold] **—in·hib′i·ter** or **in·hib′i·tor** *n.* **—in·hib′i·tive, in·hib′i·to′ry** *adj.*

in·hi·bi·tion (in′hi·bish′ən, in′i-) *n.* 1. Restraint or prohibition. 2. *Psychol.* The blocking or repression of an impulse or thought.

in·hos·pi·ta·ble (in·hos′pi·tə·bəl, in′hos·pit′·ə·bəl) *adj.* 1. Not hospitable. 2. Not affording shelter, comfort, etc. **—in·hos′pi·ta·bly** *adv.*

in-house (in′hous′) *adj.* Occurring or originating within an organization, business, group, etc.

in·hu·man (in·hyōō′mən) *adj.* 1. Not befitting human nature; bestial. 2. Not human.

in·hu·mane (in′hyōō·mān′) *adj.* Not humane; cruel.

in·hu·man·i·ty (in′hyōō·man′ə·tē) *n. pl.* **·ties** 1. Lack of human or humane qualities. 2. A cruel act, word, etc.

in·im·i·cal (in·im′i·kəl) *adj.* 1. Characterized by harmful opposition; antagonistic. 2. Behaving as an enemy; hostile. [< IN-[1] + L *amicus* friend] **—in·im′i·cal′i·ty** (-kal′ə·tē) *n.* **—in·im′i·cal·ly** *adv.*

in·im·i·ta·ble (in·im′ə·tə·bəl) *adj.* Matchless; unique. **—in·im′i·ta·bil′i·ty, in·im′i·ta·ble·ness** *n.* **—in·im′i·ta·bly** *adv.*

in·iq·ui·ty (in·ik′wə·tē) *n. pl.* **·ties** 1. Grievous violation of right or justice; wickedness. 2. A wrongful act; sin. [< IN-[1] + L *aequus* equal] **—in·iq′ui·tous** *adj.* **—in·iq′ui·tous·ly** *adv.*

in·i·tial (in·ish′əl) *adj.* 1. Standing at the beginning. 2. Of or pertaining to the beginning; first. *—n.* 1. *pl.* The first letters of one's proper name. 2. The first letter of a word, name, etc. *—v.t.* **in·i·tialed** or **·tialled, in·i·tial·ing** or **·tial·ling** To mark or sign with initials. [< L *initialis* < *initium* beginning] **—in·i′tial·ly** *adv.*

in·i·ti·ate (in·ish′ē·āt; *for adj. & n., also* in·ish′ē·it) *v.t.* **·at·ed, ·at·ing** 1. To begin; commence; originate. 2. To admit to membership in an organization, cult, etc. 3. To instruct in fundamentals. *—adj.* Initiated. *—n.* One who has been ritually admitted to an organization, cult, etc. [< L *initiare* to begin] **—in·i′ti·a′tion** *n.* **—in·i′ti·a′tor** *n.*

in·i·ti·a·tive (in·ish′ē·ə·tiv) *n.* 1. The power or right to take the first step or the next step in some action. 2. The action of commencing or originating. 3. The spirit needed to originate action. 4. In government: a The right or power to propose legislative measures. b The process by which the electorate acts to originate legislation. *—adj.* 1. Of or pertaining to initiation. 2. Serving to initiate. [< MF] **—in·i′ti·a·tive·ly** *adv.*

in·ject (in·jekt′) *v.t.* 1. To drive (a fluid, drug, etc.) into a bodily cavity, blood vessel, etc. by means of a syringe, needle, etc. 2. To introduce or interject: with *into.* [< IN-[2] + L *jacere* to throw] **—in·jec′tion** *n.*

in·ju·di·cious (in′jōō·dish′əs) *adj.* Not judicious; imprudent. **—in′ju·di′cious·ly** *adv.* **—in′ju·di′cious·ness** *n.*

in·junc·tion (in·jungk′shən) *n.* 1. The act of enjoining. 2. An authoritative order. 3. *Law* A judicial order requiring the party to do or refrain from some specified action. [< LL *injungere* to join to, enjoin] **—in·junc′tive** *adj.*

in·jure (in′jər) *v.t.* **·jured, ·jur·ing** 1. To harm, damage, or impair, esp. physically; hurt. 2. To wrong or offend. [Back formation < INJURY] **—in′jur·er** *n.*

in·ju·ry (in′jər·ē) *n. pl.* **·ries** 1. Harm, damage, or distress inflicted or suffered. 2. A particular instance of such harm. [< IN-[1] + L *jus, juris* right] **—in·ju·ri·ous** (in·jŏŏr′ē·əs) *adj.* **—in·ju′ri·ous·ly** *adv.* **—in·ju′ri·ous·ness** *n.*

in·jus·tice (in·jus′tis) *n.* 1. The fact or quality of being unjust. 2. An unjust act; wrong.

ink (ingk) *n.* 1. Any of various colored liquids used for writing, drawing, and printing. 2. The dark fluid ejected by cuttlefish, etc. *—v.t.* To stain, color, or depict with ink. [< LL *encaustum* purple ink] **—ink′er** *n.*

ink·blot test (ingk′blot′) Rorschach test.

ink·ling (ingk′ling) *n.* 1. A slight suggestion or hint. 2. A vague idea or notion. [ME < OE *inca* suspicion]

ink·stand (ingk′stand′) *n.* 1. A rack or device for holding ink, pens, etc. 2. An inkwell.

ink·well (ingk′wel′) *n.* A container for ink.

ink·y (ing′kē) *adj.* **ink·i·er, ink·i·est** 1. Resembling ink in color; dark; black. 2. Of, pertaining to, or containing ink. 3. Smeared or stained with ink. **—ink′i·ness** *n.*

in·laid (in′lād, in·lād′) *adj.* 1. Decorated with material embedded flush with the surface. 2. Inserted as an inlay.

in·land (in′lənd; *for n. and adv., also* in′land′) *adj.* 1. Remote from the sea or the border. 2. Pertaining to or located in the interior of a country. *—n.* The interior of a country. *—adv.* In or towards the interior of a land.

in-law (in′lô′) *n. Informal* A close relative by marriage.

in·lay (*v.* in·lā′, in′lā′; *n.* in′lā′) *v.t.* **·laid, ·lay·ing** 1. To set or embed (ivory, gold, etc.) flush into a surface so as to form a pattern. 2. To decorate by inserting such designs. *—n.* 1. That which is inlaid. 2. A design so produced. 3. *Dent.* A filling for a tooth.

in·let (in′let, -lit) *n.* 1. A relatively narrow channel of water, as a stream or bay leading into land. 2. An opening.

in lo·co pa·ren·tis (in lō′kō pə·ren′tis) *Latin* In the place of a parent.

in·mate (in′māt′) *n.* One who is lodged or confined with another or others, esp. in a prison, asylum, hospital, etc. [? < INN + MATE]

in me·di·as res (in mē′dē·əs rēz) *Latin* In the midst of things.

in me·mo·ri·am (in mə·môr′ē·əm) *Latin* In memory (of); as a memorial (to).

in·most (in′mōst′, -məst) *adj.* 1. Located farthest from the outside. 2. Most private or intimate. [OE *innemest*]

inn (in) *n.* A hotel, etc., where travelers may obtain meals or lodging. [OE *inn* room, house]

in·nards (in′ərdz) *n.pl. Dial. & Informal* The internal organs or parts of the body, a machine, etc.; insides.

in·nate (i·nāt′, in′āt) *adj.* Inherent in one's nature; inborn; not acquired. [< IN-[2] + L *nasci* to be born] **—in·nate′ly** *adv.* **—in·nate′ness** *n.*

in·ner (in′ər) *adj.* 1. Located or occurring farther inside or toward the center; internal; interior. 2. Pertaining to the mind or spirit; subjective. 3. More obscure; hidden; esoteric. [OE *innerra*, compar. of *inne* in (adv.)]

inner city A central part of a large city, usu. characterized by poverty.

in·ner-di·rect·ed (in′ər·di·rekt′id) *adj.* Guided by one's own standards and values.

inner ear The essential organ of hearing; the portion of the ear located in the temporal bone and containing the semicircular canals and cochlea.

in·ner·most (in′ər·mōst′) *adj.* Inmost; farthest within.

inner sole Insole.

in·ner·spring mattress (in′ər·spring′) A mattress containing built-in coiled springs.

inner tube A flexible, inflatable tube, usu. of rubber, used inside a pneumatic tire.

in·ning (in′ing) *n.* In baseball, a division of the game during which each team has a turn to bat. [OE *innung*, gerund of *innian* to put in]

inn·keep·er (in′kē′pər) *n.* The proprietor or host of an inn.

in·no·cent (in′ə·sənt) *adj.* 1. Not tainted with sin, evil, or moral wrong; pure. 2. Free from blame or guilt, esp. legally. 3. Not tending or intended to harm or injure. 4. Lacking in worldly knowledge; naive. 5. Devoid of; entirely lacking in: with *of.* *—n.* 1. One who is free from evil or sin. 2. A simple or unsuspecting person. [< IN-[1] + L *nocere* to harm] **—in′no·cence** *n.* **—in′no·cent·ly** *adv.*

in·noc·u·ous (i·nok′yōō·əs) *adj.* Having no harmful qualities or effects; harmless. [< IN-[1] + L *nocuus* harmful] **—in·noc′u·ous·ly** *adv.* **—in·noc′u·ous·ness** *n.*

in·nom·i·nate bone (i·nom′ə·nit) *Anat.* One of two large, irregular bones formed of the ileum, ischium, and pubic bones, that make up the sides of the pelvis.

in·no·vate (in′ə·vāt) *v.t. & v.i.* **·vat·ed, ·vat·ing** To introduce or bring in (something new). [< IN-[2] + L *novare* to make new] **—in′no·va′tive** *adj.* **—in′no·va′tor** *n.*

in·no·va·tion (in′ə·vā′shən) *n.* 1. Something newly introduced, as an idea, method, etc. 2. The act of introducing something new.

in·nu·en·do (in′yōō·en′dō) *n. pl.* **·does** An oblique comment, hint, or suggestion, usu. derogatory. [< IN-[2] + L *-nuere* to nod]

in·nu·mer·a·ble (i·nōō′mər·ə·bəl, i·nyōō′-) *adj.* Too numerous to be counted; numberless. Also **in·nu′mer·ous.** **—in·nu′mer·a·bly** *adv.*

in·oc·u·late (in·ok′yə·lāt) *v.t.* **·lat·ed, ·lat·ing** To inject (serum, a vaccine, etc.) into, esp. so as to produce immunity. [< L *inoculare* to put an eye or bud into] **—in·oc′u·la′tion** *n.* **—in·oc′u·la′tor** *n.*

in·of·fen·sive (in′ə·fen′siv) *adj.* Giving no offense; innocuous. **—in′of·fen′sive·ly** *adv.* **—in′of·fen′sive·ness** *n.*

in·op·er·a·ble (in·op′ər·ə·bəl) *adj.* 1. Incapable of being cured or improved by surgical operation. 2. Not practicable; unworkable. **—in·op′er·a·bil′i·ty** *n.* **—in·op′er·a·bly** *adv.*

in·op·er·a·tive (in·op′ər·ə·tiv) *adj.* 1. Not functioning. 2. Not effectual or in effect.

in·op·por·tune (in·op′ər·tōōn′, -tyōōn′) *adj.* Untimely or inappropriate; unsuitable. **—in·op′por·tune′ly** *adv.*

in·or·di·nate (in·ôr′də·nit) *adj.* Immoderate; excessive; unrestrained. [< IN-[1] + L *ordo* an order] **—in·or′di·na·cy** *n.* **—in·or′di·nate·ly** *adv.*

in·or·gan·ic (in′ôr·gan′ik) *adj.* 1. Not having the organized structure of living things; not living; inanimate. 2. Not characterized by life processes. 3. *Chem.* Designating compounds lacking carbon except in the form of carbonates, carbides, and most cyanides.

in·pa·tient (in′pā′shənt) *n.* A patient who is lodged in a hospital, clinic, etc.

in·put (in′pōōt′) *n.* 1. Energy or power delivered to a machine, circuit, etc. 2. Information put into a computer. 3. Suggestions or data to be applied in making a decision, preparing a report, etc. **—in′put′** *v.t.* **·put·ted, ·put·ting**

in·quest (in′kwest) *n.* A legal investigation into a special matter; esp., one undertaken before a jury or by a coroner. [See INQUIRE.]

in·qui·e·tude (in·kwī′ə·tōōd, -tyōōd) *n.* 1. A state of restlessness; uneasiness. 2. *pl.* Anxieties; disquieting thoughts. **—in·qui′et** *adj.* **—in·qui′et·ly** *adv.*

in·quire (in·kwīr′) *v.* **·quired, ·quir·ing** *v.i.* 1. To seek information by asking questions; ask. 2. To make an investigation: with *into.* —*v.t.* 3. To ask information about. Also spelled *enquire.* [< IN-² + L *quaerere* to seek] —**in·quir′er** *n.* —**in·quir′ing·ly** *adv.*

in·quir·y (in·kwīr′ē, in′kwər·ē) *n. pl.* **·quir·ies** 1. The act of inquiring or seeking. 2. Investigation; research. 3. A question; query. Also spelled *enquiry.*

in·qui·si·tion (in′kwə·zish′ən) *n.* 1. An investigation of the beliefs and activities of individuals or political groups for the ultimate purpose of enforcing orthodoxy. 2. *cap.* A former judicial system of the Roman Catholic Church for the discovery, examination, and punishment of heretics. 3. The act of inquiring or searching out. 4. An inquest. —**in′qui·si′tion·al** *adj.* —**in′qui·si′tion·al·ly** *adv.* —**in′qui·si′tion·ist, in·quis·i·tor** (in·kwiz′ə·tər) *n.*

in·quis·i·tive (in·kwiz′ə·tiv) *adj.* 1. Curious; prying. 2. Eager for knowledge. —**in·quis′i·tive·ly** *adv.* —**in·quis′i·tive·ness** *n.*

in·quis·i·to·ri·al (in·kwiz′ə·tôr′ē·əl) *adj.* Of, pertaining to, or resembling an inquisitor or inquisition; offensively curious. —**in·quis′i·to′ri·al·ly** *adv.*

in re (in rē′) *Law* In the matter (of); concerning. [< L]

in·road (in′rōd′) *n.* 1. *Usu. pl.* A serious encroachment; harmful trespass: with *on* or *upon.* 2. A hostile raid or foray. [< IN-² + obs. *road* riding]

in·rush (in′rush′) *n.* A sudden rushing in; invasion.

in·sane (in·sān′) *adj.* 1. Not sane; mentally deranged or unsound. 2. Characteristic of one who is not sane. 3. Extremely foolish. [< IN-¹ + L *sanus* whole] —**in·sane′ly** *adv.* —**in·san′i·ty** (-san′ə·tē) *n.*

in·sa·tia·ble (in·sā′shə·bəl, -shē·ə·bəl) *adj.* Incapable of being sated or satisfied; extremely greedy. Also **in·sa·ti·ate** (in·sā′·shē·it). —**in·sa′ti·a·bil′i·ty** *n.* —**in·sa′ti·a·bly, in·sa′ti·ate·ly** *adv.*

in·scribe (in·skrīb′) *v.t.* **·scribed, ·scrib·ing** 1. To write, mark, or engrave (words, etc.). 2. To mark (a document, etc.) with writing or engraving. 3. To enter (a name) on a formal or official list. 4. To sign or dedicate (a book, etc.) for presentation. 5. *Geom.* To draw (one figure) in another so that the latter circumscribes the former. [< IN-² + L *scribere* to write] —**in·scrib′er** *n.*

in·scrip·tion (in·skrip′shən) *n.* 1. That which is inscribed; also, the act of inscribing. 2. A durable marking or engraving on a solid object. 3. An informal written dedication. —**in·scrip′tion·al, in·scrip′tive** *adj.*

in·scru·ta·ble (in·skrōō′tə·bəl) *adj.* That cannot be searched into or understood; incomprehensible. [< IN-¹ + L *scrutare* to explore] —**in·scru′ta·bil′i·ty** *n.* —**in·scru′ta·bly** *adv.*

in·sect (in′sekt) *n.* 1. *Zool.* Any of a large class of small to minute air-breathing invertebrate animals, having six legs, a body divided into a head, thorax, and abdomen, and usu. two pairs of wings. 2. Loosely, any small invertebrate resembling an insect, as a spider, tick, etc. [< L (*animal*) *insectum* (animal) notched, alluding to their segmented bodies] —**in·sec·ti·val** (in′sek·tī′vəl, in·sek′tə-) *adj.*

in·sec·ti·cide (in·sek′tə·sīd) *n.* A substance used for killing insects.

in·sec·tiv·o·rous (in′sek·tiv′ər·əs) *adj.* Feeding or subsisting upon insects.

in·se·cure (in′sə·kyŏŏr′) *adj.* 1. Liable to break, fail, collapse, etc.; unsafe. 2. Troubled by anxiety and apprehensiveness; threatened. —**in′se·cure′ly** *adv.* —**in′se·cu′ri·ty** *n.*

in·sem·i·nate (in·sem′ə·nāt) *v.t.* **·nat·ed, ·nat·ing** 1. To make pregnant; inject semen into the vagina of. 2. To sow or implant. [< IN-² + L *seminare* to sow] —**in·sem′i·na′tion** *n.*

in·sen·sate (in·sen′sāt, -sit) *adj.* 1. Showing a lack of humane feeling; brutish. 2. Stupid; foolish. 3. Lacking physical sensation; inanimate. [< LL *insensatus*]

in·sen·si·ble (in·sen′sə·bəl) *adj.* 1. Deprived of consciousness; unconscious. 2. Incapable of feeling or perceiving. 3. So slight or gradual as to escape notice; imperceptible. —**in·sen′si·bil′i·ty** *n.* —**in·sen′si·bly** *adv.*

in·sen·si·tive (in·sen′sə·tiv) *adj.* 1. Not keenly responsive; crude; dull. 2. Without physical feeling or sensation. 3. Not affected by or aware of: with *to.* —**in·sen′si·tiv′i·ty** *n.* —**in·sen′si·tive·ly** *adv.*

in·sen·ti·ent (in·sen′shē·ənt, -shənt) *adj.* Lacking senses or consciousness; inanimate. —**in·sen′ti·ence** *n.*

in·sep·a·ra·ble (in·sep′ər·ə·bəl) *adj.* Incapable of being separated or parted. —**in·sep′a·ra·bil′i·ty** *n.* —**in·sep′a·ra·bly** *adv.*

in·sert (*v.* in·sûrt′; *n.* in′sûrt) *v.t.* 1. To put in; place; set. 2. To introduce into written matter. —*n.* 1. That which is inserted. 2. In bookbinding, illustrations, maps, etc., not part of the printed text, bound into the finished book: also called *inset.* 3. A circular, pamphlet, etc., set within a newspaper, magazine, or book. [< IN-² + L *serere* to sow, plant] —**in·sert′er** *n.*

in·ser·tion (in·sûr′shən) *n.* 1. The act of inserting. 2. That which is inserted; as: **a** A word, sentence, etc. **b** A strip of lace or embroidery sewn into plain cloth.

in·set (*v.* in·set′; *n.* in′set) *v.t.* **·set, ·set·ting** To set in; insert; implant. —*n.* 1. In bookbinding, an insert. 2. A small diagram, map, etc., inserted in the border of a larger one. 3. A piece of material let or set into a garment.

in·sheathe (in·shēth′) *v.t.* **·sheathed, ·sheath·ing** To place in or as in a sheath.

in·shore (in′shôr′) *adj.* Near or coming toward the shore. —*adv.* Toward the shore.

in·side (*n.* & *adj.* in′sīd′, -sīd′; *adv.* & *prep.* in′sīd′) *n.* 1. The part, surface, space, etc., that lies within; interior. 2. The internal nature or workings that are concealed. 3. *pl. Informal* The inner parts of the body or a machine; innards. —**inside out** Reversed so that the inside is exposed. —*adj.* 1. Situated within; internal; interior. 2. Restricted to a few; confidential. 3. Suitable for, used, or working indoors; indoor. —*adv.* 1. In or into the interior; within. 2. Indoors. —*prep.* In or into the interior of. —**inside of** *Informal* 1. Within; enclosed by. 2. Within the time or distance specified: *inside of* a year.

in·si·der (in′sī′dər) *n.* 1. A member of a given group, club, etc. 2. One close to a source, as of knowledge or influence.

in·sid·i·ous (in·sid′ē·əs) *adj.* 1. Subtly cunning or deceitful; treacherous; wily. 2. Progressing imperceptibly but harmfully: *insidious* disease. [< L *insidere* to sit in, lie in wait] —**in·sid′i·ous·ly** *adv.* —**in·sid′i·ous·ness** *n.*

in·sight (in′sīt′) *n.* Perception into the inner nature or real character of a thing. —**in·sight′ful** *adj.*

in·sig·ni·a (in·sig′nē·ə) *n. pl. of* **in·sig·ne** (in·sig′nē) 1. Badges, emblems, etc., used as marks of membership, office, or honor. 2. Marks or signs of anything. [< L]

in·sig·nif·i·cant (in′sig·nif′ə·kənt) *adj.* 1. Unimportant; trifling. 2. Meaningless. 3. Lacking size or quantity. 4. Of persons, lacking distinction, character, etc. —**in′sig·nif′i·cance** *n.* —**in′sig·nif′i·cant·ly** *adv.*

in·sin·cere (in′sin·sir′) *adj.* Not sincere; hypocritical. —**in′sin·cere′ly** *adv.* —**in′sin·cer′i·ty** (-ser′ə·tē) *n.*

in·sin·u·ate (in·sin′yōō·āt) *v.* **·at·ed, ·at·ing** *v.t.* 1. To suggest by innuendo; hint. 2. To introduce subtly and gradually. —*v.i.* 3. To give sly and indirect intimations. [< IN-[2] + L *sinuare* to curve] —**in·sin′u·at′ing·ly** *adv.* —**in·sin′u·a′tive** *adj.* —**in·sin′u·a′tor** *n.*

in·sin·u·a·tion (in·sin′yōō·ā′shən) *n.* 1. That which is insinuated; a sly hint. 2. The act of insinuating.

in·sip·id (in·sip′id) *adj.* 1. Lacking spirit and vivacity; vapid; dull. 2. Tasteless; bland. [< IN-[1] + L *sapidus* savory] —**in·si·pid·i·ty** (in′si·pid′ə·tē), **in·sip′id·ness** *n.* —**in·sip′id·ly** *adv.*

in·sist (in·sist′) *v.i.* 1. To demand or assert firmly and forcefully: with *on* or *upon.* 2. To dwell on or repeatedly emphasize: with *on* or *upon.* —*v.t.* 3. To demand or maintain forcefully: He *insisted* that the gate be opened. [< L *insistere* to stand on, tread on] —**in·sis′tence** *n.*

in·sis·tent (in·sis′tənt) *adj.* Insisting; persistent; urgent. —**in·sis′tent·ly** *adv.*

in·so·far (in′sō·fär′) *adv.* To such an extent; in such measure: followed by *as.* Also **in so far.**

in·sole (in′sōl′) *n.* 1. The inside sole of a shoe. 2. A removable sole added for warmth, comfort, etc. Also called *inner sole.*

in·so·lent (in′sə·lənt) *adj.* Overbearing or offensively impertinent; insulting; disrespectful. [< L *insolens, -entis* unusual, haughty] —**in′so·lence** *n.* —**in′so·lent·ly** *adv.*

in·sol·u·ble (in·sol′yə·bəl) *adj.* 1. Not soluble; incapable of being dissolved. 2. Not solvable; incapable of being solved: also **in·solv′a·ble** (-sol′və·bəl). —**in·sol′u·bil′i·ty** *n.* —**in·sol′u·bly** *adv.*

in·sol·vent (in·sol′vənt) *adj. Law* 1. Unable to meet the claims of creditors; bankrupt. 2. Insufficient for the payment of debts. —*n.* An insolvent person. —**in·sol′ven·cy** *n.*

in·som·ni·a (in·som′nē·ə) *n.* Chronic inability to sleep. [< IN-[1] + L *somnus* sleep] —**in·som′ni·ac** (-ak) *n.*

in·so·much (in′sō·much′) *adv.* 1. To such a degree: with *that* or *as.* 2. Inasmuch: with *as.*

in·sou·ci·ant (in·sōō′sē·ənt, *Fr.* aṅ·sōō′·syäṅ′) *adj.* Lighthearted; carefree; unconcerned. [< F] —**in·sou′ci·ance** *n.* —**in·sou′ci·ant·ly** *adv.*

in·spect (in·spekt′) *v.t.* 1. To look at or examine carefully, esp. for faults or defects. 2. To examine or review officially, as troops. [< IN-[2] + L *specere* to look] —**in·spec′tion** *n.* —**in·spec′tion·al** *adj.*

in·spec·tor (in·spek′tər) *n.* 1. One who inspects. 2. An official examiner or checker. 3. A high-ranking officer of police, firemen, etc. [< L] —**in·spec′to·ral, in′spec·to′ri·al** (-tôr′ē·əl) *adj.* —**in·spec′tor·ate** (-tə·rit), **in·spec′tor·ship** *n.*

in·spi·ra·tion (in′spə·rā′shən) *n.* 1. A creative feeling or impulse. 2. The state or quality of being inspired. 3. One who or that which acts as an inspiring influence. 4. Something that results from being inspired, as an idea. 5. The act of drawing in the breath; inhalation. —**in′spi·ra′tion·al** *adj.* —**in′spi·ra′tion·al·ly** *adv.*

in·spire (in·spīr′) *v.* **·spired, ·spir·ing** *v.t.* 1. To stir or move (a person) to creative activity or vigorous action; fill with a motivating emotion. 2. To arouse or create (a feeling, idea, etc.); generate: to *inspire* fear. 3. To direct or guide, as by special divine influence. 4. To breathe in; inhale. —*v.i.* 5. To inhale. 6. To give or provide inspiration. [< IN-[2] + L *spirare* to breathe] —**in·spir′er** *n.*

in·spir·it (in·spir′it) *v.t.* To fill with renewed spirit or life; animate. —**in·spir′it·ing·ly** *adv.*

in·sta·bil·i·ty (in′stə·bil′ə·tē) *n. pl.* **·ties** 1. Lack of stability. 2. Unsteadiness of character; unreliability.

in·stall (in·stôl′) *v.t.* 1. To fix in position and adjust for service or use. 2. To place in any office, rank, etc. 3. To establish in a place or position; settle. Also *Chiefly Brit.* **in·stal′.** [< IN-[2] + Med.L *stallum* seat < OHG *stal* seat] —**in·stall′er** *n.*

in·stal·la·tion (in′stə·lā′shən) *n.* 1. Any device or system, esp. mechanical, set in place and readied for use. 2. The act of installing, or the state of being installed. 3. *Mil.* Any large, fixed base or facility of the armed service.

in·stall·ment[1] (in·stôl′mənt) *n.* 1. A portion of a debt or sum of money made payable in specified amounts at specified intervals. 2. One of several parts, as of a serial in a newspaper or magazine. Also *Brit.* **in·stal′ment.**

in·stall·ment[2] (in·stôl′mənt) *n.* Installation.

installment plan A system of paying for goods or services in installments.

in·stance (in′stəns) *n.* 1. A case or example. 2. A step in proceedings: in the first *instance.* —**for instance** For example. —*v.t.* **·stanced, ·stanc·ing** To cite as an example. [< L *instantia* presence]

in·stant (in′stənt) *n.* 1. A very short time; moment. 2. A specific point in time. —*adj.* 1. Instantaneous; immediate. 2. Pressing; urgent. 3. Prepared quickly by the addition of water, milk, etc.: *instant* coffee. [< IN-[2] + L *stare* to stand]

in·stan·ta·ne·ous (in′stən·tā′nē·əs) *adj.*

Happening or done with no delay; immediate. [< INSTANT, on analogy with *simultaneous*] —**in′stan·ta′ne·ous·ly** *adv.* —**in′stan·ta′ne·ous·ness** *n.*

in·stant·er (in·stan′tər) *adv.* Immediately; at once. [< L]

in·stant·ly (in′stənt·lē) *adv.* Without delay; at once.

in·stead (in·sted′) *adv.* 1. In place or lieu; rather than: with *of.* 2. In the place of that just mentioned: to look for silver and find gold *instead.*

in·step (in′step′) *n.* 1. *Anat.* The arched upper part of the human foot, extending from the toes to the ankle. 2. The part of a shoe or stocking covering this.

in·sti·gate (in′stə·gāt) *v.t.* **·gat·ed, ·gat·ing** 1. To spur on or goad; incite. 2. To foment; provoke: to *instigate* treason. [< IN-[2] + L root *-stig-* to prick, goad] —**in′sti·ga′tion** *n.* —**in′sti·ga′tive** *adj.* —**in′sti·ga′tor** *n.*

in·still (in·stil′) *v.t.* 1. To introduce (a quality, feeling, idea, etc.) gradually or by degrees: to *instill* courage. 2. To pour in gradually by drops. Also *esp. Brit.* **in·stil′.** [< IN-[2] + L *stillare* to drop] —**in·stil·la·tion** (in′stə·lā′shən) *n.* —**in·still′er** *n.* —**in·still′ment** *n.*

in·stinct (in′stingkt) *n.* 1. An innate tendency or response of a given species to act in ways that are essential to its preservation. 2. A natural aptitude; knack. [< L *instinctus*, pp. of *instinguere* to impel] —**in·stinc′tive, in·stinc′tu·al** (-choo͞·əl) *adj.* —**in·stinc′·tive·ly** *adv.*

in·sti·tute (in′stə·to͞ot, -tyo͞ot) *v.t.* **·tut·ed, ·tut·ing** 1. To set up or establish; found. 2. To set in operation; initiate; start. 3. *Eccl.* To place (a clergyman) in spiritual charge of a parish: with *in* or *into.* —*n.* 1. A group or society devoted to the promotion of some particular field of knowledge or art; also, the building or buildings housing such a society. 2. In education: **a** *Usu. cap.* A college for specialized instruction, often technical. **b** A center for postgraduate study and research. 3. Something instituted, as an established principle, rule, or order. [< IN-[2] + L *statuere* to set up] —**in′sti·tut′er** or **in′sti·tu′tor** *n.*

in·sti·tu·tion (in′stə·to͞o′shən, -tyo͞o′-) *n.* 1. A principle, custom, etc., that forms part of a society or civilization. 2. A corporate body organized to perform some particular function, often in education, research, charity, etc.; also, the building or buildings housing such a body. 3. A mental hospital, prison, or other place of confinement. 4. *Informal* A familiar and characteristic object, custom, or person. 5. The act of establishing or setting in operation. —**in′sti·tu′tion·al** *adj.* —**in′sti·tu′tion·al·ly** *adv.*

in·sti·tu·tion·al·ize (in′stə·to͞o′shən·əl·īz′, -tyo͞o′-) *v.t.* **·ized, ·iz·ing** 1. To turn into or regard as an institution. 2. *Informal* To put (someone) in an institution, as for the aged. —**in′sti·tu′tion·al·i·za′tion** *n.*

in·struct (in·strukt′) *v.t.* 1. To impart knowledge or skill to, esp. by systematic method; teach. 2. To give specific orders or directions to; order. [< IN-[2] + L *struere* to build]

in·struc·tion (in·struk′shən) *n.* 1. The act of instructing or teaching. 2. Knowledge imparted; also, an item of such knowledge, as a rule, precept, or lesson. 3. *pl.* Directions; orders. 4. An order or command. —**in·struc′tion·al** *adj.*

in·struc·tive (in·struk′tiv) *adj.* Serving to instruct; informative. —**in·struc′tive·ly** *adv.*

in·struc·tor (in·struk′tər) *n.* 1. One who instructs; teacher. 2. A college teacher not having professorial rank. [< L] —**in·struc′tor·ship** *n.*

in·stru·ment (in′strə·mənt) *n.* 1. A tool or implement, esp. one used for exacting work. 2. A device for producing musical sounds. 3. An apparatus for measuring, recording, guiding, etc. 4. Anything serving to accomplish a purpose; means; agency. 5. *Law* A formal legal document, as a contract, deed, etc. [See INSTRUCT]

in·stru·men·tal (in′strə·men′təl) *adj.* 1. Serving as a means or instrument; useful; helpful. 2. Of or pertaining to an instrument or tool. 3. Of, pertaining to, composed for, or performed on musical instruments. —**in′stru·men′tal·ly** *adv.*

in·stru·men·tal·ist (in′strə·men′təl·ist) *n.* One who plays a musical instrument.

in·stru·men·tal·i·ty (in′strə·men·tal′ə·tē) *n.* *pl.* **·ties** 1. Anything serving to accomplish a purpose; means; agency. 2. The condition of being instrumental.

in·stru·men·ta·tion (in′strə·men·tā′shən) *n.* 1. The use of instruments; work performed with instruments. 2. *Music* **a** The study of the characteristics and groupings of instruments. **b** Loosely, orchestration. 3. Instrumentality.

instrument panel The panel holding the gauges and other indicators of performance in an automobile, airplane, engine room, etc. Also **instrument board.**

in·sub·or·di·nate (in′sə·bôr′də·nit) *adj.* Not obedient; rebellious. —**in′sub·or′di·nate·ly** *adv.* —**in′sub·or′di·na′tion** (-nā′shən) *n.*

in·sub·stan·tial (in′səb·stan′shəl) *adj.* 1. Not real; imaginary; illusive. 2. Not substantial, solid, or firm; flimsy. —**in′sub·stan′ti·al′i·ty** (-shē·al′ə·tē) *n.*

in·suf·fer·a·ble (in·suf′ər·ə·bəl) *adj.* Not to be endured; intolerable. —**in·suf′fer·a·bly** *adv.*

in·suf·fi·cient (in′sə·fish′ənt) *adj.* Not enough; inadequate; deficient. —**in′suf·fi′·cien·cy** *n.* —**in′suf·fi′cient·ly** *adv.*

in·su·lar (in′sə·lər, -syə-) *adj.* 1. Of or like an island. 2. Narrow or limited in customs, opinions, etc.; provincial. [< L *insula* island] —**in′su·lar′i·ty** (-lar′ə·tē) *n.*

in·su·late (in′sə·lāt, -syə-) *v.t.* **·lat·ed, ·lat·ing** 1. To surround or separate with nonconducting material in order to prevent or lessen the leakage of electricity, heat, sound, radiation, etc. 2. To isolate. [< L *insula* island] —**in′su·la′tor** *n.*

in·su·la·tion (in′sə·lā′shən, -syə-) *n.* 1. Material used for insulating. 2. The act of insulating, or the state of being insulated.

in·su·lin (in′sə·lin, -syə-) *n.* *Biochem.* 1. A hormone secreted by the pancreas, essential in regulating the metabolism of sugar. 2. A preparation of this hormone, used in treating diabetes. [< L *insula* island (of Langerhans), the endocrine cells that produce insulin]

in·sult (*v.* in·sult′; *n.* in′sult) *v.t.* To treat with insolence or contempt; disparage;

affront. —*n.* An act, remark, etc., that offends or affronts. [< IN-[2] + L *salire* to leap] —**in·sult′er** *n.* —**in·sult′ing** *adj.* —**in·sult′ing·ly** *adv.*

in·su·per·a·ble (in·sōō′pər·ə·bəl) *adj.* Not to be surmounted or overcome. [< L *insuperabilis*] —**in·su′per·a·bly** *adv.*

in·sup·port·a·ble (in′sə·pôr′tə·bəl) *adj.* 1. Not bearable; insufferable. 2. Having no grounds; unjustifiable. —**in′sup·port′a·bly** *adv.*

in·sur·ance (in·shŏŏr′əns) *n.* 1. Financial protection against risk, loss, or ruin, guaranteed by a person or company in return for the payment of premiums; also, the business of providing this protection. 2. A contract guaranteeing such protection: also **insurance policy.** 3. The payment made by the insured party. 4. The amount for which anything is insured. 5. Any safeguard against risk or harm.

in·sure (in·shŏŏr′) *v.t.* **·sured, ·sur·ing** 1. To provide insurance for or on. 2. To ensure. [< AF *en-* in + *seur* sure] —**in·sur′a·ble** *adj.*

in·sur·er (in·shŏŏr′ər) *n.* A person or company that insures against specified loss.

in·sur·gent (in·sûr′jənt) *adj.* Rising in revolt against established authority; rebellious. —*n.* An insurgent person. [< IN-[1] + L *surgere* to rise] —**in·sur′gence, in·sur′gen·cy** *n.*

in·sur·mount·a·ble (in′sər·moun′tə·bəl) *adj.* Incapable of being surmounted or overcome. —**in′sur·mount′a·bly** *adv.*

in·sur·rec·tion (in′sə·rek′shən) *n.* An organized resistance to established government. [< L *insurrectus*, pp. of *insurgere* to rise up against] —**in′sur·rec′tion·al** *adj.* —**in′sur·rec′tion·ar′y** *adj. & n.* —**in′sur·rec′tion·ist** *n.*

in·tact (in·takt′) *adj.* Remaining whole, unchanged, and undamaged; unimpaired. [< IN-[1] + L *tangere* to touch]

in·ta·glio (in·tal′yō, *Ital.* ēn·tä′lyō) *n.* *pl.* **·glios** 1. Incised carving; a sunken design. 2. The art of making such designs. 3. A work, esp. a gem, with incised carving. 4. *Printing* The process of printing from sunken or incised plates. [< Ital. < *in-* in + *tagliare* to cut]

in·take (in′tāk′) *n.* 1. The act of taking in or absorbing. 2. That which is taken in. 3. The amount or quantity taken in. 4. The place where water, a gas, etc., is drawn into a pipe or conduit.

in·tan·gi·ble (in·tan′jə·bəl) *adj.* 1. Incapable of being perceived by touch; impalpable. 2. Indefinite or vague to the mind. —*n.* That which is intangible; esp., any incorporeal asset, as good will. —**in·tan′gi·bil′i·ty** *n.* —**in·tan′gi·bly** *adv.*

in·te·ger (in′tə·jər) *n.* 1. Any of the numbers 1, 2, 3, etc., as distinguished from a fraction or mixed number: also called *whole number.* 2. A whole entity. [< L, untouched < IN-[1] + root *tag-*, of *tangere* to touch]

in·te·gral (in′tə·grəl) *adj.* 1. Being an indispensable part of a whole; essential; constituent. 2. Formed of parts that together constitute a unity: an *integral* whole. 3. Whole; entire; complete. 4. *Math.* **a** Pertaining to an integer. **b** Produced by integration. —*n.* 1. An entire thing; a whole. 2. *Math.* The result of integration. [< LL *integralis*] —**in′te·gral′i·ty** (-gral′ə·tē) *n.* —**in′te·gral·ly** *adv.*

in·te·grate (in′tə·grāt) *v.* **·grat·ed, ·grat·ing** *v.t.* 1. To bring together into a whole; unify. 2. To make the use or occupancy of (a school, neighborhood, etc.) available to persons of all races. 3. To make whole or complete by the addition of necessary parts. —*v.i.* 4. To become integrated. [< L *integratus*, pp. of *integrare* to make whole, renew] —**in′te·gra′tion** *n.* —**in′te·gra′tor** *n.*

integrated circuit A circuit of electronic components formed in or on a tiny slice of material.

in·teg·ri·ty (in·teg′rə·tē) *n.* *pl.* **·ties** 1. Uprightness of character; honesty. 2. The condition or quality of being unimpaired or sound. 3. The state of being complete or undivided. [< L *integer* untouched]

in·teg·u·ment (in·teg′yə·mənt) *n.* A covering or outer coating, as the skin of an animal, coat of a seed, etc. [< IN-[2] + L *tegere* to cover] —**in·teg′u·men′ta·ry** (-men′tə·rē) *adj.*

in·tel·lect (in′tə·lekt) *n.* 1. The power of the mind to grasp ideas and relations, and to exercise rational judgment; reason. 2. A mind or intelligence, esp. a brilliant one. 3. An intelligent person. [< L *intellectus*, pp. of *intelligere* to understand]

in·tel·lec·tu·al (in′tə·lek′chōō·əl) *adj.* 1. Of or pertaining to the intellect; mental. 2. Requiring the use of the intellect. 3. Possessing or showing intellect, esp. of a high order. —*n.* One who pursues and enjoys matters of the intellect. —**in′tel·lec′tu·al′i·ty** (-al′ə·tē) *n.* —**in′tel·lec′tu·al·ly** *adv.*

in·tel·lec·tu·al·ize (in′tə·lek′chōō·əl·īz) *v.* **·ized, ·iz·ing** *v.t.* 1. To view or express intellectually. —*v.i.* 2. To think; reason.

in·tel·li·gence (in·tel′ə·jəns) *n.* 1. The faculty of perceiving and comprehending meaning; understanding. 2. The ability to adapt to new situations. 3. The collection of secret information, as by the police or military. 4. Information that has been so collected; also, the persons so occupied.

intelligence quotient *Psychol.* A number indicating the level of a person's mental development, obtained by multiplying his mental age by 100, and dividing by his chronological age. Abbr. *IQ, I.Q.*

in·tel·li·gent (in·tel′ə·jənt) *adj.* 1. Having an active, able mind; acute. 2. Marked or characterized by intelligence. 3. Endowed with intellect or understanding; reasoning. [< L *intelligens, -entis*, ppr. of *intelligere* to understand] —**in·tel′li·gent·ly** *adv.*

in·tel·li·gent·si·a (in·tel′ə·jent′sē·ə, -gent′-) *n.pl.* Intellectual or educated people collectively. [< L *intelligentia*]

in·tel·li·gi·ble (in·tel′ə·jə·bəl) *adj.* Capable of being understood. [< L *intelligibilis*] —**in·tel′li·gi·bil′i·ty** *n.* —**in·tel′li·gi·bly** *adv.*

in·tem·per·ate (in·tem′pər·it) *adj.* 1. Lacking moderation; unrestrained. 2. Given to excessive use of alcoholic drinks. 3. Excessive or extreme, as climate. —**in·tem′per·ance** *n.* —**in·tem′per·ate·ly** *adv.*

in·tend (in·tend′) *v.t.* 1. To have as a specific aim or purpose; plan. 2. To make, design, or destine for a purpose. 3. To mean or signify; indicate. [< IN-[2] + L *tendere* to stretch]

in·tend·ed (in·ten′did) *adj.* 1. Planned; proposed. 2. Prospective: one's *intended* wife. —*n.* *Informal* Prospective husband or wife.

in·tense (in·tens′) *adj.* 1. Having great force; overpowering: *intense* feelings. 2. Performed strenuously and steadily: *intense* study. 3. Expressing or characterized by strong and earnest feelings. 4. Having its quality strongly concentrated. [< L *intensus*, pp. of *intendere* to stretch out] —**in·tense′ly** *adv.*

in·ten·si·fy (in·ten′sə·fī) *v.t. & v.i.* **·fied, ·fy·ing** 1. To make or become more intense or acute. 2. To make or become intense. —**in·ten′si·fi·ca′tion** *n.* —**in·ten′si·fi′er** *n.*

in·ten·si·ty (in·ten′sə·tē) *n. pl.* **·ties** 1. The state or quality of being intense. 2. The strength or degree of some action, quality, feeling, etc.: pain of low *intensity*. 3. Power and vehemence of thought or feeling; also, extreme effort and concentration.

in·ten·sive (in·ten′siv) *adj.* 1. Of, pertaining to, or marked by intensity. 2. Intensifying. 3. *Gram.* Adding emphasis or force. —*n.* 1. That which gives intensity or emphasis. 2. *Gram.* An intensive particle, word, or phrase. —**in·ten′sive·ly** *adv.* —**in·ten′sive·ness** *n.*

in·tent (in·tent′) *n.* 1. Purpose; aim; design. 2. The act of intending. 3. *Law* The state of mind in which or the purpose with which one does an act; also, the character that the law imputes to an act. —*adj.* 1. Firmly directed or fixed: an *intent* stare. 2. Directing one's mind or efforts steadfastly: with *on* or *upon*. [< L *intendere* to stretch out, endeavor] —**in·tent′ly** *adv.* —**in·tent′ness** *n.*

in·ten·tion (in·ten′shən) *n.* 1. Purpose; aim; goal. 2. The act of intending. 3. *pl.* *Informal* Purpose with regard to marriage.

in·ten·tion·al (in·ten′shən·əl) *adj.* Purposeful; deliberate; intended. —**in·ten′tion·al·ly** *adv.*

in·ten·tioned (in·ten′shənd) *adj.* Having or characterized by (a specified kind of) intention: used in combination: *well-intentioned*.

in·ter (in·tûr′) *v.t.* **·terred, ·ter·ring** To place in a grave; bury. [< IN-[2] + L *terra* earth]

inter- *prefix* 1. With each other; together: *intertwine*. 2. Mutual; mutually: *intercommunicate*. 3. Between or among (the units signified): *intercollegiate*. 4. Occurring or situated between: *interlinear*. [< L *inter* between, among]

in·ter·act (in′tər·akt′) *v.i.* To act on each other. —**in′ter·ac′tion** *n.* —**in′ter·ac′tive** *adj.* —**in′ter·ac·tiv′i·ty** *n.*

in·ter·breed (in′tər·brēd′) *v.* **·bred, ·breed·ing** *v.t.* 1. To breed (different stocks) together; crossbreed. 2. To produce (offspring) by crossbreeding. —*v.i.* 3. To breed genetically dissimilar stocks or individuals.

in·ter·ca·lar·y (in·tûr′kə·ler′ē) *adj.* 1. Added to the calendar. 2. Having an added day or month. 3. Interpolated.

in·ter·ca·late (in·tûr′kə·lāt) *v.t.* **·lat·ed, ·lat·ing** 1. To insert or interpolate. 2. To insert, as an additional day or month, into the calendar. [< L *inter-* between + *calare* to proclaim, call] —**in·ter′ca·la′tion** *n.*

in·ter·cede (in′tər·sēd′) *v.i.* **·ced·ed, ·ced·ing** 1. To plead or petition in behalf of another or others. 2. To come between parties in a dispute; mediate. [< L *inter-* between + *cedere* to pass, go] —**in′ter·ced′er** *n.*

in·ter·cel·lu·lar (in′tər·sel′yə·lər) *adj.* *Biol.* Situated between or among cells.

in·ter·cept (*v.* in′tər·sept′; *n.* in′tər·sept) *v.t.* 1. To stop or obstruct on the way; interrupt the course of. 2. To meet, as a moving person, ship, etc. 3. *Math.* To mark off or bound a line, plane, surface, or solid. —*n.* *Math.* An intercepted part, or a point of interception. [< L *inter-* between + *capere* to seize] —**in′ter·cep′tion** *n.* —**in′ter·cep′tive** *adj.*

in·ter·cep·tor (in′tər·sep′tər) *n.* 1. One who or that which intercepts. 2. An airplane designed for the pursuit and interception of enemy aircraft. Also **in′ter·cept′er.**

in·ter·ces·sion (in′tər·sesh′ən) *n.* The act of interceding; entreaty or prayer in behalf of others. [< L *intercessus*, pp. of *intercedere* to come between] —**in′ter·ces′sion·al** *adj.* —**in′ter·ces′sor** (-ses′ər) *n.* —**in′ter·ces′so·ry** (-ses′ər·ē) *adj.*

in·ter·change (*v.* in′tər·chānj′; *n.* in′tər·chānj′) *v.* **·changed, ·chang·ing** *v.t.* 1. To put each of (two things) in the place of the other. 2. To cause to alternate. 3. To give and receive in return, as gifts. —*v.i.* 4. To change places one with the other. —*n.* 1. A reciprocal giving in exchange. 2. An exchanging of places. 3. Alternation. 4. An intersection of a superhighway with another highway, so designed that vehicles may enter or turn off without obstructing traffic. [< OF *entre-* between + *changier* to exchange] —**in′ter·change′a·bil′i·ty** *n.* —**in′ter·change′a·ble** *adj.* —**in′ter·change′a·bly** *adv.*

in·ter·col·le·giate (in′tər·kə·lē′jit, -jē·it) *adj.* Pertaining to or involving two or more colleges.

in·ter·com (in′tər·kom′) *n.* *Informal* A telephone or radio system for intercommunication.

in·ter·com·mu·ni·cate (in′tər·kə·myōō′nə·kāt) *v.i.* **·cat·ed, ·cat·ing** To communicate with one another, esp. by a telephone system. —**in′ter·com·mu′ni·ca′tion** *n.* —**in′ter·com·mun′i·ca·tor** *n.*

in·ter·con·nect (in′tər·kə·nekt′) *v.t. & v.i.* To connect or be connected. —**in′ter·con·nec′tion** *n.*

in·ter·con·ti·nen·tal (in′tər·kon′tə·nen′təl) *adj.* Reaching from one continent to another; also, involving two or more continents.

in·ter·cos·tal (in′tər·kos′təl) *adj.* *Anat.* Situated or occurring between the ribs. [< L *inter-* between + *costa* rib]

in·ter·course (in′tər·kôrs) *n.* 1. Mutual exchange; communication; commerce. 2. Sexual connection; coitus. [< L *inter-* between + *currere* to run]

in·ter·de·nom·i·na·tion·al (in′tər·di·nom′ə·nā′shən·əl) *adj.* Of or pertaining to two or more religious denominations.

in·ter·de·pen·dent (in′tər·di·pen′dənt) *adj.* Dependent one on another; reciprocally dependent. —**in′ter·de·pen′dence, in′ter·de·pen′den·cy** *n.* —**in′ter·de·pen′dent·ly** *adv.*

in·ter·dict (*v.* in′tər·dikt′; *n.* in′tər·dikt′) *v.t.* 1. To prohibit or ban officially. 2. To restrain (someone) from doing, or forbid use of (something). 3. *Eccl.* To exclude from participation in rites and services. —*n.* An official prohibition; ban. [< L *inter-*

between + *dicere* to say] —**in′ter·dic′tion** *n.* —**in′ter·dic′tive, in′ter·dic′to·ry** *adj.* —**in′·ter·dic′tive·ly** *adv.* —**in′ter·dic′tor** *n.*

in·ter·est (in′tər·ist, -trist) *n.* 1. A feeling of curiosity or attentiveness. 2. The power to arouse curiosity or attentiveness; also, something that has such power. 3. That which is of advantage; benefit. 4. Involvement, or concern in something; also, selfish concern. 5. Payment for the use of money or credit, usu. expressed as a percentage of the amount owed or used. 6. Legal or financial claim or share, as in a business. 7. *Usu. pl.* A group of persons involved in a particular business, cause, etc.: the dairy *interests.* —**in the interest (or interests) of** In behalf of. —*v.t.* 1. To excite or hold the curiosity or attention of. 2. To cause to be concerned in; involve: with *in.* [< L *inter-* between + *esse* to be]

in·ter·est·ed (in′tər·is·tid, -tris-, -tə·res′-) *adj.* 1. Having or displaying curiosity or attention. 2. Having a concern or wish for something. 3. Having a right or share in. 4. Seeking personal advantage; biased. —**in′ter·est·ed·ly** *adv.*

in·ter·est·ing (in′tər·is·ting, -tris-, -tə·res′-) *adj.* Exciting interest; attractive; noteworthy. —**in′ter·est·ing·ly** *adv.*

in·ter·face (in′tər·fās) *n.* 1. A surface forming the common boundary between adjacent solids, spaces, etc. 2. The meeting of two systems that interact: *interface* of language and computer. —*v.i. & v.t.* To come together at an interface.

in·ter·fere (in′tər·fir′) *v.i.* **·fered, ·fer·ing** 1. To get in the way; impede: often with *with.* 2. To intervene and take part in the affairs of others, esp. without invitation or warrant; meddle. 3. In sports, to obstruct the play of an opponent illegally. [< L *inter-* between + *ferire* to strike] —**in′ter·fer′er** *n.* —**in′ter·fer′ing·ly** *adv.*

in·ter·fer·ence (in′tər·fir′əns) *n.* 1. The act of interfering. 2. In football, clearing the way for the ball carrier by blocking opponents. 3. *Physics* The effect produced by two or more sets of waves, as of light or sound, that on meeting tend to neutralize or augment each other. 4. *Telecom.* A disturbance in the reception of radio, etc., due to conflict with undesired signals.

in·ter·fold (in′tər·fōld′) *v.t. & v.i.* To fold together or one within another.

in·ter·fuse (in′tər·fyōōz′) *v.* **·fused, ·fus·ing** *v.t.* 1. To cause to permeate. 2. To permeate with something. 3. To intermix. —*v.i.* 4. To become intermixed. —**in′ter·fu′sion** (-fyōō′zhən) *n.*

in·ter·im (in′tər·im) *n.* A time between periods or events. —*adj.* For an intervening period of time; temporary. [< L, meanwhile]

in·te·ri·or (in·tir′ē·ər) *adj.* 1. Of or situated on the inside; inner. 2. Remote from the coast or border; inland. 3. Pertaining to the internal affairs of a country. 4. Not exposed to view; private. —*n.* 1. The internal part; the inside. 2. The inland region of a country, continent, etc. 3. The domestic affairs of a country. 4. A representation of the inside of a building or room. [< L *interior,* compar. of *inter* within] —**in·te′ri·or′i·ty** (-ôr′ə·tē, -or′-) *n.*

interior design The design, decoration, and furnishing of interiors, as homes, offices, etc.; also, this occupation. Also **interior decoration.** —**interior designer** *n.*

in·ter·ject (in′tər·jekt′) *v.t.* To throw or introduce in between other things: to *interject* a comment. [< L *inter-* between + *jacere* to throw]

in·ter·jec·tion (in′tər·jek′shən) *n.* 1. The act of interjecting. 2. That which is interjected. 3. *Gram.* An exclamation, as *Oh!* or *Alas!* —**in′ter·jec′tion·al** *adj.* —**in′ter·jec′tion·al·ly** *adv.*

in·ter·lace (in′tər·lās′) *v.t. & v.i.* **·laced, ·lac·ing** To join by or as by weaving together; intertwine; interlock.

in·ter·lard (in′tər·lärd′) *v.t.* 1. To vary by interjecting something different. 2. To occur frequently in. [< MF *entrelarder* to lard]

in·ter·lay (in′tər·lā′) *v.t.* **·laid, ·lay·ing** 1. To place between. 2. To decorate with something put or laid between.

in·ter·leaf (in′tər·lēf′) *n. pl.* **·leaves** (-lēvz′) An extra leaf, usu. blank, inserted between the regular leaves of a book.

in·ter·leave (in′tər·lēv′) *v.t.* **·leaved, ·leav·ing** To insert interleaves into (a book).

in·ter·line[1] (in′tər·līn′) *v.t.* **·lined, ·lin·ing** 1. To insert (words, phrases, etc.) between written or printed lines. 2. To annotate between the lines. [< L *inter-* between + *linea* line]

in·ter·line[2] (in′tər·līn′) *v.t.* **·lined, ·lin·ing** To put a lining between the usual lining and the outer fabric of (a garment). —**in′ter·lin′ing** *n.*

in·ter·lin·e·ar (in′tər·lin′ē·ər) *adj.* 1. Situated or written between the lines. 2. Having lines inserted between the lines. Also **in′ter·lin′e·al.**

in·ter·lock (in′tər·lok′) *v.t. & v.i.* To join firmly. —**in′ter·lock′er** *n.*

in·ter·loc·u·tor (in′tər·lok′yə·tər) *n.* One who takes part in a conversation. [< L *interloqui* to speak between, converse] —**in′ter·loc′u·tress** (-tris) *n.fem.*

in·ter·loc·u·to·ry (in′tər·lok′yə·tôr′ē) *adj.* 1. Having the nature of dialogue. 2. Interposed, as in a conversation. 3. *Law* Pronounced while a suit is pending; provisional.

in·ter·lope (in′tər·lōp′) *v.i.* To intrude in the affairs of others; meddle. [< INTER- + Du. *loopen* to run] —**in′ter·lo′per** *n.*

in·ter·lude (in′tər·lōōd) *n.* 1. A period that occurs in and divides some longer process. 2. In drama, a separate episode performed between the acts. 3. A short passage of instrumental music played between the stanzas of a hymn, etc. [< L *inter-* between + *ludus* game, play]

in·ter·lu·nar (in′tər·lōō′nər) *adj.* *Astron.* Pertaining to the period between old and new moon, during which the moon is invisible. Also **in′ter·lu′na·ry.**

in·ter·mar·ry (in′tər·mar′ē) *v.i.* **·ried, ·ry·ing** 1. To marry someone not a member of one's own religion, race, class, etc. 2. To become connected through the marriage of members: said of different familes, etc. —**in′ter·mar′riage** (-mar′ij) *n.*

in·ter·me·di·ar·y (in′tər·mē′dē·er′ē) *adj.* 1. Intermediate. 2. Acting as a mediator. —*n. pl.* **·ar·ies** 1. One who acts as a mediator. 2. An intermediate form, stage, or product.

in·ter·me·di·ate[1] (in′tər·mē′dē·it) *adj.* Situated or occurring between two points, places, levels, etc. —*n.* Something intermediate. [< L *inter-* between + *medius* middle] —**in′ter·me′di·ate·ly** *adv.*

in·ter·me·di·ate[2] (in′tər·mē′dē·āt) *v.i.* **·at·ed, ·at·ing** To act as an intermediary; mediate. —**in′ter·me′di·a′tion** *n.* —**in′ter·me′di·a′tor** *n.*

in·ter·ment (in·tûr′mənt) *n.* The act of interring; burial.

in·ter·mez·zo (in′tər·met′sō, -med′zō) *n. pl.* **·zos** or **·zi** (-sē, -zē) 1. A short musical offering given between the acts of a play or opera. 2. *Music* A short movement connecting the main divisions of a large musical composition. [< Ital. < L *intermedius* intermediate]

in·ter·mi·na·ble (in·tûr′mə·nə·bəl) *adj.* Having no apparent end or limit; endless. —**in·ter′mi·na·bly** *adv.*

in·ter·min·gle (in′tər·ming′gəl) *v.t. & v.i.* **·gled, ·gling** To mingle together; mix.

in·ter·mis·sion (in′tər·mish′ən) *n.* 1. An interval of time between events or activities; recess. 2. The act of intermitting, or the state of being intermitted. 3. The time between acts of a play, opera, etc. [See INTERMIT.] —**in′ter·mis′sive** (-mis′iv) *adj.*

in·ter·mit (in′tər·mit′) *v.t. & v.i.* **·mit·ted, ·mit·ting** To stop temporarily or at intervals. [< L *inter-* between + *mittere* to send, put] —**in′ter·mit′tence** *n.*

in·ter·mit·tent (in′tər·mit′ənt) *adj.* Ceasing from time to time; coming at intervals. —**in′ter·mit′tent·ly** *adv.*

in·ter·mix (in′tər·miks′) *v.t. & v.i.* To mix together. —**in′ter·mix′ture** *n.*

in·tern (*n.* in′tûrn; *v.* in·tûrn′) *n.* 1. A medical graduate serving in and living at a hospital for clinical training before being licensed to practice medicine. 2. One who is interned; internee. Also spelled *interne.* —*v.t.* 1. To confine or detain during wartime. —*v.i.* 2. To serve as an intern. [< L *internus* internal] —**in·tern′ment** *n.*

in·ter·nal (in·tûr′nəl) *adj.* 1. Of or situated on the inside; inner. 2. Belonging to or derived from the inside: *internal* evidence. 3. Pertaining to the inner self or the mind. 4. Pertaining to the domestic affairs of a country. 5. Intended to be taken or applied inwardly, as medication. [< LL *internus*] —**in·ter′nal·ly** *adv.*

in·ter·nal-com·bus·tion (in·tûr′nəl·kəm·bus′chən) *adj.* Designating a heat engine in which the fuel burns inside the engine itself, most often in a cylinder.

internal medicine The branch of medicine that is concerned with the diseases of the internal organs.

internal revenue Revenue (def. 1).

in·ter·na·tion·al (in′tər·nash′ən·əl) *adj.* 1. Existing or conducted among nations. 2. Of or affecting various nations and their peoples. —*n.* A person having ties with more than one nation. —**in′ter·na′tion·al′i·ty** (-al′ə·tē) *n.* —**in′ter·na′tion·al·ly** *adv.*

in·ter·na·tion·al·ism (in′tər·nash′ən·əl·iz′·əm) *n.* 1. The belief that cooperation among nations will advance the common welfare. 2. The state of being international. —**in′ter·na′tion·al·ist** *n.*

in·ter·na·tion·al·ize (in′tər·nash′ən·əl·īz′) *v.t.* **·ized, ·iz·ing** To place under international control; make international.

in·terne (in′tûrn) See INTERN.

in·ter·ne·cine (in′tər·nes′ēn, -in; -nēs′-) *adj.* 1. Destructive to both sides. 2. Involving great slaughter. [< L *inter-* among + *necare* to kill]

in·tern·ee (in′tûr·nē′) *n.* An interned person.

in·ter·nist (in·tûr′nist) *n.* A specialist in internal medicine.

in·ter·plan·e·tar·y (in′tər·plan′ə·ter′ē) *adj.* Between or among planets.

in·ter·play (in′tər·plā′) *n.* Reciprocal action, movement, or influence. —*v.i.* To act on each other; interact.

INTERPOL (in′tər·pōl) International Criminal Police Organization.

in·ter·po·late (in·tûr′pə·lāt) *v.* **·lat·ed, ·lat·ing** *v.t.* 1. To introduce (additions, comments, etc.) into a discourse, process, or series. 2. To interrupt with additions. 3. *Math.* **a** To compute intermediate values in (a series). **b** To insert (intermediate values) into a series. —*v.i.* 4. To make additions, insertions, interruptions, etc. [< L *inter-* between + *polire* to polish] —**in·ter′·po·la′ter** or **in·ter′po·la′tor** *n.* —**in·ter′po·la′tion** *n.*

in·ter·pose (in′tər·pōz′) *v.* **·posed, ·pos·ing** *v.t.* 1. To put between other things, esp. as a separation or barrier. 2. To put in or inject (a comment, etc.) in the course of speech or argument. 3. To exercise (authority, action, etc.) in order to intervene. —*v.i.* 4. To come between; intervene. 5. To put in a remark. —**in′ter·po′sal** *n.* —**in′ter·pos′er** *n.* —**in′ter·po·si′tion** (-pə·zish′ən) *n.*

in·ter·pret (in·tûr′prit) *v.* **·pret·ed, ·pret·ing** *v.t.* 1. To give the meaning of; explain. 2. To judge (persons, events, etc.) in a personal way. 3. To convey the meaning of (an experience, a play, etc.) by artistic representation or performance. —*v.i.* 4. To explain or construe. 5. To restate orally in one language what is said in another. [< L *interpres* agent, interpreter] —**in·ter′pret·a·ble** *adj.* —**in·ter′pret·er** *n.*

in·ter·pre·ta·tion (in·tûr′prə·tā′shən) *n.* 1. The process of interpreting. 2. The meaning assigned to actions, intentions, works of art, etc. —**in·ter′pre·ta′tion·al** *adj.*

in·ter·pre·ta·tive (in·tûr′prə·tā′tiv) *adj.* 1. Of or pertaining to interpretation. 2. Providing an interpretation; explanatory. Also **in·ter′pre·tive.** —**in·ter′pre·ta′tive·ly** *adv.*

in·ter·ra·cial (in′tər·rā′shəl) *adj.* 1. Of or for members of different races. 2. Between, among, or affecting different races, or persons of different races.

in·ter·reg·num (in′tər·reg′nəm) *n.* 1. An interval between the reigns of sovereigns. 2. Any suspension of the ruling powers of a state. 3. Any break in continuity. [< L *inter-* between + *regnum* reign]

in·ter·re·late (in′tər·ri·lāt′) *v.t. & v.i.* **·lat·ed, ·lat·ing** To have, discover, or bring about a mutual or reciprocal relation. —**in′ter·re·lat′ed·ness** *n.* —**in′ter·re·la′tion** *n.* —**in′ter·re·la′tion·ship** *n.*

in·ter·ro·gate (in·ter′ə·gāt) *v.t. & v.i.*

·gat·ed, ·gat·ing To examine formally by questioning; question. [< L *inter-* between + *rogare* to ask] **—in·ter′ro·ga′tion** *n.* **—in·ter′ro·ga′tor** *n.*

interrogation point A question mark (?). Also **interrogation mark.**

in·ter·rog·a·tive (in′tə·rog′ə·tiv) *adj.* 1. Asking or having the nature of a question. 2. *Gram.* Used to ask or indicate a question. —*n. Gram.* An interrogative word, phrase, etc. **—in′ter·rog′a·tive·ly** *adv.*

in·ter·rog·a·to·ry (in′tə·rog′ə·tôr′ē) *adj.* Of, expressing, or implying a question. —*n. pl.* **·tor·ies** A question. **—in′ter·rog′a·to′ri·ly** *adv.*

in·ter·rupt (in′tə·rupt′) *v.t.* 1. To break the continuity or regularity of. 2. To hinder or stop (someone talking, etc.) by intervening. —*v.i.* 3. To intervene abruptly. [< L *inter-* between + *rumpere* to break] **—in′ter·rup′tion** *n.* **—in′ter·rup′tive** *adj.*

in·ter·scho·las·tic (in′tər·skə·las′tik) *adj.* Between or among schools.

in·ter·sect (in′tər·sekt′) *v.t.* 1. To divide by cutting or passing across. —*v.i.* 2. To cross each other. [< L *inter-* between + *secare* to cut]

in·ter·sec·tion (in′tər·sek′shən) *n.* 1. A place of crossing; esp., a place where streets or roads cross. 2. The act of intersecting, or the state of being intersected.

in·ter·sperse (in′tər·spûrs′) *v.t.* **·spersed, ·spers·ing** 1. To scatter among other things. 2. To diversify with other things; interlard. [< L *inter-* among + *spargere* to scatter] **—in′ter·spers′ed·ly** *adv.* **—in′ter·sper′sion** (-spûr′zhən) *n.*

in·ter·state (in′tər·stāt) *adj.* Between, among, or involving different states of the U.S., or their citizens.

in·ter·stel·lar (in′tər·stel′ər) *adj.* Among the stars.

in·ter·stice (in·tûr′stis) *n. pl.* **·sti·ces** (-stə·sēz) A narrow opening or crack. [< L *intersistere* to stand between] **—in·ter·sti·tial** (in′tər·stish′əl) *adj.* **—in′ter·sti′tial·ly** *adv.*

in·ter·twine (in′tər·twīn′) *v.t. & v.i.* **·twined, ·twin·ing** To unite by twisting together or interlacing; intertwist. **—in′ter·twine′ment** *n.* **—in′ter·twin′ing·ly** *adv.*

in·ter·ur·ban (in′tər·ûr′bən) *adj.* Between or among cities.

in·ter·val (in′tər·vəl) *n.* 1. The time coming between two events, points in time, etc. 2. A space between two objects or distance between two points. 3. A break in the continuity or course of something. 4. *Music* The difference in pitch between two tones. [< L *inter-* between + *vallum* rampart]

in·ter·vene (in′tər·vēn′) *v.i.* **·vened, ·ven·ing** 1. To interfere or take a decisive role, esp. to correct or settle something. 2. To occur so as to modify an action, expectation, etc. 3. To be located between. 4. To take place between other events or times. [< L *inter-* between + *venire* to come] **—in′ter·ven′er** *n.*

in·ter·ven·tion (in′tər·ven′shən) *n.* The act of intervening, esp. in the affairs of foreign governments. **—in′ter·ven′tion·ist** *adj. & n.*

in·ter·view (in′tər·vyōō) *n.* 1. A conversation conducted, as by a reporter, with a person from whom information is sought; also, the record of such a conversation. 2. A meeting with a person applying for a job. —*v.t.* To have an interview with. [< L *inter-* between + *videre* to see] **—in′ter·view′er** *n.*

in·ter·weave (in′tər·wēv′) *v.t. & v.i.* **·wove** or **·weaved, ·wo·ven, ·weav·ing** To weave together; blend.

in·tes·tate (in·tes′tāt, -tit) *adj.* 1. Not having made a valid will before death. 2. Not legally disposed of by will. —*n.* One who dies intestate. [< IN-[1] + L *testari* to make a will] **—in·tes′ta·cy** (-tə·sē) *n.*

in·tes·tine (in·tes′tin) *n. Anat. Often pl.* The section of the alimentary canal extending from the stomach to the anus, consisting of the long, narrow small intestine and the large intestine. [< L *intestinus* internal] **—in·tes′ti·nal** *adj.* **—in·tes′ti·nal·ly** *adv.*

in·ti·mate[1] (in′tə·mit) *adj.* 1. Characterized by pronounced closeness of friendship or association. 2. Deeply personal; private. 3. Having illicit sexual relations: with *with*: a euphemism. 4. Resulting from close study. —*n.* A close or confidential friend. [< L *intimus*, superl. of *intus* within] **—in′ti·ma·cy** *n.* **—in′ti·mate·ly** *adv.*

in·ti·mate[2] (in′tə·māt) *v.t.* **·mat·ed, ·mat·ing** To make known without direct statement; hint. [< L *intimus*, superl. of *intus* within] **—in′ti·ma′tion** *n.*

in·tim·i·date (in·tim′ə·dāt) *v.t.* **·dat·ed, ·dat·ing** 1. To make timid; scare. 2. To discourage from acting by threats or violence. [< IN-[2] + L *timidus* afraid] **—in·tim′i·da′tion** *n.* **—in·tim′i·da′tor** *n.*

in·to (in′tōō) *prep.* 1. To or toward the inside of from outside: to go *into* the forest. 2. To a time in the midst of: far *into* the night. 3. To the form or condition of: to change water *into* steam. 4. Dividing: Two *into* six is three. 5. *Slang* Keenly interested in; involved with: He's *into* modern art. [OE]

in·tol·er·a·ble (in·tol′ər·ə·bəl) *adj.* Not tolerable; that cannot be borne; insufferable. **—in·tol′er·a·bil′i·ty** *n.* **—in·tol′er·a·bly** *adv.*

in·tol·er·ant (in·tol′ər·ənt) *adj.* 1. Not tolerant; bigoted. 2. Unable or unwilling to bear or endure. **—in·tol′er·ance** *n.* **—in·tol′er·ant·ly** *adv.*

in·to·na·tion (in′tō·nā′shən) *n.* 1. Way of speaking a language or utterance; esp., the meaning and melody given to speech by changing levels of pitch. 2. The act of intoning. 3. *Music* **a** The production of tones of accurate pitch. **b** Pitch or the accuracy of pitch.

in·tone (in·tōn′) *v.t.* **·toned, ·ton·ing** 1. To utter or recite in a musical monotone; chant. 2. To give particular tones or intonation to. [< Med.L *intonare* to intone, thunder] **—in·ton′er** *n.*

in to·to (in tō′tō) *Latin* In the whole; altogether; entirely.

in·tox·i·cant (in·tok′sə·kənt) *n.* That which intoxicates. —*adj.* Intoxicating.

in·tox·i·cate (in·tok′sə·kāt) *v.t.* **·cat·ed, ·cat·ing** 1. To make drunk. 2. To elate or excite to a degree of frenzy. [< IN-[2] + L *toxicum* poison] **—in·tox′i·ca′tion** *n.*

intra- *prefix* Situated or occurring within: **intra-abdominal, intracollegiate, intracon-**

tinental, intragovernmental, intramolecular, intra-union. [< L *intra* within]

in·trac·ta·ble (in·trak′tə·bəl) *adj.* 1. Not tractable; unruly. 2. Difficult to manipulate, treat, or work. —**in·trac′ta·bil′i·ty** *n.* —**in·trac′ta·bly** *adv.*

in·tra·mu·ral (in′trə·myŏŏ′rəl) *adj.* 1. Taking place within a school, college, etc.: *intramural* football. 2. Situated or occurring within the walls or limits of a city, building, organization, etc. —**in′tra·mu′ral·ly** *adv.*

in·tra·mus·cu·lar (in′trə·mus′kyə·lər) *adj.* Situated in or affecting the inside of a muscle. —**in′tra·mus′cu·lar·ly** *adv.*

in·tran·si·gent (in·tran′sə·jənt) *adj.* Refusing to compromise or come to terms; unbending. —*n.* One who is intransigent. [< IN-[1] + L *transigere* to agree] —**in·tran′si·gence, in·tran′si·gen·cy** *n.* —**in·tran′si·gent·ly** *adv.*

in·tran·si·tive (in·tran′sə·tiv) *Gram. adj.* Of or pertaining to intransitive verbs. —*n.* An intransitive verb. —**in·tran′si·tive·ly** *adv.*

intransitive verb *Gram.* A verb that has or needs no complement to complete its meaning.

in·tra·state (in′trə·stāt′) *adj.* Confined within or pertaining to a single state, esp. of the U.S.

in·tra·u·ter·ine device (in′trə·yōō′tər·in) An object inserted into and retained in the uterus to prevent conception. Abbr. *IUD.*

in·tra·ve·nous (in′trə·vē′nəs) *adj.* Situated in or affecting the inside of a vein.

in·trep·id (in·trep′id) *adj.* Unshaken by fear; bold. [< IN-[1] + L *trepidus* agitated] —**in·tre·pid·i·ty** (in′trə·pid′ə·tē) *n.* —**in·trep′id·ly** *adv.*

in·tri·cate (in′tri·kit) *adj.* 1. Perplexingly entangled, complicated, or involved. 2. Difficult to follow or understand; puzzling. [< IN-[2] + L *tricae* difficulties] —**in′tri·ca·cy** *n.* —**in′tri·cate·ly** *adv.*

in·trigue (in·trēg′; *for n., also* in′trēg) *v.* **·trigued, ·tri·guing** *v.t.* 1. To arouse the interest or curiosity of; fascinate; beguile. —*v.i.* 2. To plot; conspire. 3. To carry on a secret or illicit love affair. —*n.* 1. The act of plotting or scheming. 2. A plot or scheme. 3. A secret or illicit love affair. 4. The quality or power of arousing interest. [< L *intricare* to entangle] —**in·tri′guer** *n.*

in·trin·sic (in·trin′sik) *adj.* Belonging to or arising from the true or fundamental nature of a thing; inherent: opposed to *extrinsic.* Also **in·trin′si·cal.** [< L *intrinsecus* internally] —**in·trin′si·cal·ly** *adv.*

intro- *prefix* In; within: *introvert.* [< L *intro* inwardly]

in·tro·duce (in′trə·dōōs′, -dyōōs′) *v.t.* **·duced, ·duc·ing** 1. To make (a person or persons) acquainted face to face with another or others, usu. in a formal manner: often with *to.* 2. To bring into use or notice first; launch: to *introduce* a new technique. 3. To broach or propose. 4. To add or insert. 5. To present (a person, product, etc.) to a specific group or to the public. 6. To bring to first knowledge of something: with *to.* 7. To begin; open. [< INTRO- + L *ducere* to lead] —**in′tro·duc′er** *n.* —**in′tro·duc′i·ble** *adj.*

in·tro·duc·tion (in′trə·duk′shən) *n.* 1. The act of introducing. 2. First knowledge or acquaintance; initiation. 3. Something that introduces or leads up to what follows, as the first part of a book, or an elementary text.

in·tro·duc·to·ry (in′trə·duk′tər·ē) *adj.* Serving as an introduction; preliminary.

in·tro·it (in·trō′it) *n. Eccl.* 1. In the Roman Catholic Church, the opening act of worship in the Mass. 2. In the Anglican Church, a hymn sung at the beginning of public worship. [< INTRO- + L *ire* to go]

in·tro·spect (in′trə·spekt′) *v.i.* To practice introspection. [< INTRO- + L *specere* to look]

in·tro·spec·tion (in′trə·spek′shən) *n.* The observation and analysis of one's own mental processes and emotional states. —**in′tro·spec′tive** *adj.* —**in′tro·spec′tive·ly** *adv.*

in·tro·vert (in′trə·vûrt) *n.* 1. *Psychol.* A person whose interest is directed primarily toward the self. 2. One who is sober, reserved, and withdrawn. —*v.t.* 1. To turn inward; cause to bend in an inward direction. 2. To turn (the mind or thoughts) toward the self. —*adj.* Characterized by or tending to introversion: also **in′tro·vert′ed.** [< INTRO- + L *vertere* to turn] —**in′tro·ver′sion** (-vûr′zhən) *n.* —**in′tro·ver′sive** (-vûr′siv) *adj.*

in·trude (in·trōōd′) *v.* **·trud·ed, ·trud·ing** *v.t.* 1. To thrust or force in. —*v.i.* 2. To come in without leave or invitation: often with *upon.* [< IN-[2] + L *trudere* to thrust] —**in·trud′er** *n.*

in·tru·sion (in·trōō′zhən) *n.* 1. The act or condition of intruding; encroachment. 2. That which intrudes. —**in·tru′sive** (-siv) *adj.* —**in·tru′sive·ly** *adv.*

in·trust (in·trust′) See ENTRUST.

in·tu·it (in·tyōō′it, -tōō′-) *v.t. & v.i.* **·tu·it·ed, ·tu·it·ing** To know or discover by intuition.

in·tu·i·tion (in′tōō·ish′ən, -tyōō-) *n.* 1. A direct knowledge or awareness of something without conscious attention or reasoning. 2. Anything thus perceived. 3. The ability or quality of perceiving without conscious attention or reasoning. [< IN-[2] + L *tueri* to look] —**in·tu′i·tive** (-ə·tiv) *adj.* —**in·tu′i·tive·ly** *adv.* —**in·tu′i·tive·ness** *n.*

in·tu·mesce (in′tōō·mes′) *v.i.* **·mesced, ·mesc·ing** To swell; enlarge. [< L *intumescere* < *tumere* to swell] —**in′tu·mes′cence** *n.* —**in′tu·mes′cent** *adj.*

in·turn (in′turn′) *n.* A turning inward, as of the toes.

in·un·date (in′un·dāt) *v.t.* **·dat·ed, ·dat·ing** 1. To cover by overflowing; flood. 2. To overwhelm with abundance or excess. [< IN-[2] + L *undare* to overflow] —**in′un·da′tion** *n.* —**in′un·da′tor** *n.* —**in·un·da·to·ry** (in·un′də·tôr′ē) *adj.*

in·ure (in·yŏŏr′) *v.t.* **·ured, ·ur·ing** To cause to accept or tolerate by use or exercise; habituate. [< IN-[2] + obs. *ure* work < L *opera* work] —**in·ure′ment** *n.*

in·vade (in·vād′) *v.* **·vad·ed, ·vad·ing** *v.t.* 1. To enter by force with the intent of conquering or plundering. 2. To rush or swarm into. 3. To intrude upon. 4. To penetrate and spread through injuriously. —*v.i.* 5. To make an invasion. [< IN-[2] + L *vadere* to go] —**in·vad′er** *n.*

in·vag·i·nate (in·vaj′ə·nāt) *v.* **·nat·ed, ·nat·ing** *v.t.* 1. To put into or as into a sheath; ensheathe. 2. To infold so as to form a depression or pouch. —*v.i.* 3. To undergo invagination. [< IN-[2] + L *vagina* sheath + -ATE[1]] **—in·vag′i·na′tion** *n.*

in·va·lid[1] (in′və·lid) *n.* A sick, disabled, or bedridden person. **—***adj.* 1. Enfeebled by ill health. 2. Of or pertaining to disabled persons. **—***v.t.* 1. To cause to become an invalid; disable. 2. To release or classify (a soldier, sailor, etc.) as unfit for duty because of ill health. [< L *invalidus* not strong] **—in′va·lid·ism** *n.*

in·va·lid[2] (in·val′id) *adj.* Not valid; having no force or cogency; null; void. [< L *invalidus*] **—in·val·i·di·ty** (in′və·lid′ə·tē) *n.* **—in·val′id·ly** *adv.*

in·val·i·date (in·val′ə·dāt) *v.t.* **·dat·ed, ·dat·ing** To weaken or destroy the validity of; render invalid; annul. **—in·val′i·da′tion** *n.* **—in·val′i·da′tor** *n.*

in·val·u·a·ble (in·val′yōō·ə·bəl, -yŏŏ·bəl) *adj.* Having a value beyond estimation; priceless. **—in·val′u·a·bly** *adv.*

in·var·i·a·ble (in·vâr′ē·ə·bəl) *adj.* Not variable; not changeable; constant. **—in·var′i·a·bil′i·ty** *n.* **—in·var′i·a·bly** *adv.*

in·var·i·ant (in·vâr′ē·ənt) *adj.* Not subject to change or variation; constant. **—***n. Math.* An invariant quantity; constant. **—in·var′i·ance** *n.*

in·va·sion (in·vā′zhən) *n.* 1. The act of invading with hostile armed forces. 2. Any attack or onset of something injurious. 3. Encroachment by intrusion or trespass. 4. Entrance with intent to overrun or occupy. **—in·va′sive** (-siv) *adj.*

in·vec·tive (in·vek′tiv) *n.* Violent accusation or denunciation; abuse. [< L *invectus*, pp. of *invehere* to carry into] **—in·vec′tive** *adj.* **—in·vec′tive·ly** *adv.* **—in·vec′tive·ness** *n.*

in·veigh (in·vā′) *v.i.* To utter vehement censure or invective: with *against.* [< IN-[2] + L *vehere* to carry] **—in·veigh′er** *n.*

in·vei·gle (in·vē′gəl, -vā-) *v.t.* **·gled, ·gling** To entice or induce by guile or flattery; draw; cajole: often with *into.* [< F *aveugle* blind < L *ab-* without + *oculus* eye] **—in·vei′gle·ment** *n.* **—in·vei′gler** *n.*

in·vent (in·vent′) *v.t.* 1. To devise or create (a device, contrivance, process, etc.) by original effort. 2. To make up, as something untrue or contrary to fact. [< IN-[2] + L *venire* to come] **—in·ven′tor** *n.*

in·ven·tion (in·ven′shən) *n.* 1. The act or process of inventing. 2. A device, contrivance, etc. conceived or made by original effort. 3. The skill or ingenuity needed for inventing or contriving. 4. A fabrication of the mind.

in·ven·tive (in·ven′tiv) *adj.* 1. Skillful at invention or contrivance; ingenious. 2. Characterized by or created by invention. **—in·ven′tive·ly** *adv.* **—in·ven′tive·ness** *n.*

in·ven·to·ry (in′vən·tôr′ē) *n. pl.* **·ries** 1. A list of articles, materials, property, etc.; esp., a list of goods in stock. 2. The process of making such a list. 3. The goods or stock of a business; also, their value. **—***v.t.* **·ried, ·ry·ing** 1. To make an inventory of. 2. To insert in an inventory. [< L *inventorium*] **—in′ven·to′ri·al** *adj.*

in·ver·ness (in′vər·nes′) *n. Often cap.* 1. A type of overcoat having a detachable cape. 2. The cape itself: also called Inverness cape. [after *Inverness*, Scotland]

in·verse (in·vûrs′, in′vûrs) *adj.* 1. Reversed or opposite in order, effect, etc. 2. Turned upside down; inverted. **—***n.* That which is in direct contrast or opposition; the reverse; opposite. **—in·verse′ly** *adv.*

in·ver·sion (in·vûr′zhən) *n.* 1. The act of inverting, or the state of being inverted. 2. That which is inverted. 3. In grammar and rhetoric, a reversing of the usual word order in a phrase, clause, or sentence. **—in·ver′sive** (-siv) *adj.*

in·vert (in·vûrt′) *v.t.* 1. To turn upside-down; turn completely over. 2. To reverse the order, effect, or operation of. **—***v.i.* 3. To undergo inversion. [< IN-[2] + L *vertere* to turn] **—in·vert′i·ble** *adj.*

in·ver·te·brate (in·vûr′tə·brit, -brāt) *adj. Zool.* Not vertebrate; lacking a backbone or spinal column. Also **in·ver′te·bral** (-brəl). **—***n.* An invertebrate animal.

in·vest (in·vest′) *v.t.* 1. To commit or use (money, capital, etc.) for the purchase of property, a business, etc., with the expectation of profit. 2. To spend or use (money, time, effort, etc.) for: often with *in.* 3. To place in office formally; install. 4. To give power, authority, or rank to. 5. To array or cover with or as with a garment. **—***v.i.* 6. To make an investment or investments. [< IN-[2] + L *vestire* to clothe] **—in·ves′tor** *n.*

in·ves·ti·gate (in·ves′tə·gāt) *v.* **·gat·ed, ·gat·ing** *v.t.* 1. To search or inquire into; make a formal or official examination of. **—***v.i.* 2. To conduct a search or inquiry. [< IN-[2] + L *vestigare* to trace] **—in·ves′ti·ga·ble** (-gə·bəl) *adj.* **—in·ves′ti·ga′tion** *n.* **—in·ves′ti·ga′tive** *adj.* **—in·ves′ti·ga·to′ry** (-gə·tôr′ē) *adj.*

in·ves·ti·ga·tor (in·ves′tə·gā′tər) *n.* 1. A detective; esp., a private detective. 2. One who investigates. **—in·ves′ti·ga·to′ri·al** (-gə·tôr′ē·əl) *adj.*

in·ves·ti·tive (in·ves′tə·tiv) *adj.* 1. Of or pertaining to investiture. 2. Having the function of investing.

in·ves·ti·ture (in·ves′tə·chər) *n.* The act or ceremony of investing with an office, authority, or right.

in·vest·ment (in·vest′mənt) *n.* 1. Money or capital invested to gain profit. 2. The form of property in which one invests. 3. The act of investing, or the state of being invested. 4. Investiture.

in·vet·er·ate (in·vet′ər·it) *adj.* 1. Firmly established by long continuance; deep-rooted. 2. Confirmed or hardened: an *inveterate* bigot. [< IN-[2] + L *vetus* old] **—in·vet′er·a·cy** *n.* **—in·vet′er·ate·ly** *adv.*

in·vid·i·ous (in·vid′ē·əs) *adj.* 1. Exciting or creating ill will or dislike; offensive. 2. Provoking anger or resentment by unjust discrimination. [< L *invidia* envy] **—in·vid′i·ous·ly** *adv.*

in·vig·or·ate (in·vig′ər·āt) *v.t.* **·at·ed, ·at·ing** To give vigor and energy to; animate. [< IN-[2] + L *vigor* vigor + -ATE[1]] **—in·vig′or·at′ing·ly** *adv.* **—in·vig′or·a′tion** *n.* **—in·vig′or·a′tive** *adj.* **—in·vig′or·a′tive·ly** *adv.* **—in·vig′or·a′tor** *n.*

in·vin·ci·ble (in·vin′sə·bəl) *adj.* Not to be overcome; unconquerable. **—in·vin′ci·bil′i·ty** *n.* **—in·vin′ci·bly** *adv.*

in·vi·o·la·ble (in·vī′ə·lə·bəl) *adj.* 1. Not to be profaned, defiled, etc.; sacrosanct. 2. Not to

be violated or broken. —**in·vi′o·la·bil′i·ty** *n.* —**in·vi′o·la·bly** *adv.*
in·vi·o·late (in·vī′ə·lit) *adj.* 1. Not violated; not profaned or broken; intact. 2. Inviolable. —**in·vi′o·la·cy** *n.* —**in·vi′o·late·ly** *adv.*
in·vis·i·ble (in·viz′ə·bəl) *adj.* 1. Not visible; not capable of being seen. 2. Not in sight; concealed. 3. Not publicly or openly acknowledged. —**in·vis′i·bil′i·ty** *n.* —**in·vis′i·bly** *adv.*
in·vi·ta·tion (in′və·tā′shən) *n.* 1. The act of inviting. 2. The means or words by which one invites. 3. The act of alluring; enticement. —**in′vi·ta′tion·al** *adj.*
in·vite (*v.* in·vīt′; *n.* in′vīt) *v.t.* **·vit·ed, ·vit·ing** 1. To ask (someone) courteously to be present in some place or to perform some action. 2. To make formal or polite request for: to *invite* suggestions. 3. To present opportunity or inducement for: his opinions *invite* criticism. 4. To tempt; entice. —*n. Slang* An invitation. [< L *invitare* to entertain] —**in·vit′er** *n.*
in·vit·ing (in·vī′ting) *adj.* That invites or allures; attractive. —**in·vit′ing·ly** *adv.*
in·vo·ca·tion (in′və·kā′shən, -vō-) *n.* 1. The act of invoking. 2. A prayer, as at the opening of a ceremony. —**in·voc·a·tive** (in·vok′ə·tiv), **in·voc·a·to·ry** (in·vok′ə·tôr′ē) *adj.*
in·voice (in′vois) *n.* 1. A descriptive list of merchandise sent or services rendered to a purchaser, including quantities, costs, etc. 2. The merchandise or services so itemized. —*v.t.* **·voiced, ·voic·ing** To list on an invoice. [< F *envoyer* to send]
in·voke (in·vōk′) *v.t.* **·voked, ·vok·ing** 1. To appeal to (a deity or other agent) for aid, inspiration, protection, etc. 2. To declare relevant and operative, as a law, power, right, etc. 3. To appeal to for confirmation; quote as an authority. 4. To summon or conjure by incantation. 5. To call or petition for. [< IN-[2] + L *vocare* to call] —**in·vok′er** *n.*
in·vo·lu·cre (in′və·lo͞o′kər) *n. Bot.* A ring of bracts at the base of a compound flower. [< L *involvere* to roll up] —**in′vo·lu′cral** *adj.*
in·vol·un·tar·y (in′vol′ən·ter′ē) *adj.* 1. Done or occurring without one's consent or choice; unintentional. 2. *Physiol.* Functioning without conscious control. —**in·vol′un·tar′i·ly** *adv.*
in·vo·lute (in′və·lo͞ot) *adj.* 1. Having complications and intricacies. 2. *Bot.* Having the edges rolled inward, as a leaf. 3. *Zool.* Having whorls concealing the axis, as a shell. Also **in′vo·lut′ed.** [< L *involutus,* pp. of *involvere* to involve]
in·vo·lu·tion (in′və·lo͞o′shən) 1. A complicating or intertwining; entanglement. 2. Something involved or complicated. —**in′vo·lu′tion·al** *adj.*
in·volve (in·volv′) *v.t.* **·volved, ·volv·ing** 1. To include as a relevant or necessary aspect. 2. To have effect on; affect by drawing in or spreading. 3. To implicate; associate significantly: usu. with *in* or *with.* 4. To absorb or engross: usu. with *in.* 5. To make intricate or tangled. [< IN-[2] + L *volvere* to roll] —**in·volve′ment** *n.*
in·volved (in·volvd′) *adj.* Complicated; intricate. —**in·volv′ed·ness** *n.*
in·vul·ner·a·ble (in·vul′nər·ə·bəl) *adj.* 1. Not capable of being wounded or injured. 2. Unconquerable. —**in·vul′ner·a·bil′i·ty** *n.* —**in·vul′ner·a·bly** *adv.*
in·ward (in′wərd) *adv.* 1. Toward the inside, center, or interior. 2. In or into the mind or thoughts. Also **in′wards.** —*adj.* 1. Situated within; internal. 2. Pertaining to the mind or spirit. 3. Proceeding toward the inside: an *inward* thrust. [OE *inweard*]
in·ward·ly (in′wərd·lē) *adv.* 1. Within the mind or heart; secretly. 2. On the inside; within. 3. Toward the center or interior. 4. Essentially; intrinsically.
in·ward·ness (in′wərd·nis) *n.* 1. The state of being inward; existence within. 2. Inner quality or meaning; essence. 3. Intensity of feeling. 4. Unworldliness.
in·weave (in·wēv′) *v.t.* **·wove** or **·weaved, ·wo·ven** or *less frequently* **·wove, ·weav·ing** To weave in or together.
in·wrought (in·rôt′) *adj.* 1. Worked into a fabric, metal, etc., as a pattern. 2. Decorated with such a pattern or design. 3. Closely combined with something.
i·o·dide (ī′ə·dīd) *n. Chem.* A compound of iodine and one other element.
i·o·dine (ī′ə·dīn, -din; *in technical usage* ī′ə·dēn) *n.* 1. A grayish black nonmetallic element (symbol I), used as an antiseptic. 2. *Informal* A solution of iodine used as an antiseptic. [< Gk. *iōdēs* violetlike + -INE[2]]
i·o·dize (ī′ə·dīz) *v.t.* **·dized, ·diz·ing** To treat or combine with iodine. —**i′o·diz′er** *n.*
i·on (ī′ən, ī′on) *n. Physics* An electrically charged atom, radical, or molecule. [< Gk. *ion,* neut. of *iōn,* ppr. of *ienai* to go] —**i·on·ic** (ī·on′ik) *adj.*
-ion *suffix of nouns* 1. Action, state, quality, or process of: *communion.* 2. State or result of being: *union.* Also *-ation, -tion.* [< F < L *-io, -ionis*]
I·o·ni·an (ī·ō′nē·ən) *adj.* Of or pertaining to Ionia, the ancient coastal region of western Asia Minor, colonized by the Greeks in the 11th c. B.C. —*n.* A native of Ionia.
I·on·ic (ī·on′ik) *adj.* 1. Ionian. 2. *Archit.* Of or pertaining to an order of Greek architecture characterized by a capital having typical scroll-like ornaments. —*n.* A dialect of ancient Greek. [< Gk. *Iōnikos*]
i·o·ni·um (ī·ō′nē·əm) *n.* A radioactive isotope of thorium. [< ION + (URAN)IUM; from its ionizing action]
i·on·ize (ī′ən·īz) *v.t. & v.i.* **·ized, ·iz·ing** To convert or become converted, totally or in part, into ions. —**i′on·i·za′tion** *n.* —**i′on·iz′er** *n.*
i·on·o·sphere (ī·on′ə·sfir) *n.* The outermost region of the earth's atmosphere, consisting of several layers subject to ionization. —**i·on′o·spher′ic** (-sfir′ik, -sfer′-) *adj.*
i·o·ta (ī·ō′tə) *n.* 1. The ninth letter in the Greek alphabet (Ι, ι), corresponding to English *i.* 2. A very small or insignificant amount. [< Gk. *iōta*]
IOU A written acknowledgment of indebtedness having on it these letters (meaning *I owe you*). Also **I.O.U.**
-ious *suffix of adjectives* Characterized by; full of: occurring esp. in adjectives formed from nouns ending in *-ion: suspicious, cautious.* [< L *-iosus* full of]
ip·e·cac (ip′ə·kak) *n.* 1. Either of two plants of the madder family, yielding a medicinal

alkaloid. 2. The dried root of either of these plants. 3. An extract of this root, used as an emetic or cathartic. [< Tupi *ipe* little + *kaa* tree, herb]

ip·so fac·to (ip′sō fak′tō) *Latin* By the fact itself; by that very fact or act.

IQ Intelligence quotient. Also **I.Q.**

ir- Assimilated var. of IN-[1] and IN-[2].

I·ra·ni·an (i·rā′nē·ən) *adj.* Of or pertaining to Iran, its people, or their language. —*n.* 1. A native or inhabitant of Iran; a Persian. 2. A branch of the Indo-Iranian subfamily of Indo-European languages, including Persian, Kurdish, and Pashto. 3. Modern Persian.

I·ra·qi (i·rä′kē) *adj.* Of or pertaining to Iraq, its people, or their language. —*n.* A native or inhabitant of Iraq.

i·ras·ci·ble (i·ras′ə·bəl) *adj.* Easily angered; quick-tempered. [< LL *irasci* to be angry] —**i·ras′ci·bil′i·ty** *n.* —**i·ras′ci·bly** *adv.*

i·rate (ī·rāt′, ī′rāt) *adj.* Angry; enraged. [< L *iratus* angered] —**i·rate′ly** *adv.*

ire (īr) *n.* Wrath; anger. [< L *ira* anger] —**ire′ful** *adj.*

i·ren·ic (ī·ren′ik, ī·rē′nik) *adj.* Peaceful in purpose; conciliatory. [< Gk. *eirēnē* peace]

ir·i·des·cent (ir′ə·des′ənt) *adj.* Displaying the colors of the rainbow in shifting hues and patterns, as soap bubbles, mother-of-pearl, etc. [< Gk. *iris, iridos* rainbow] —**ir′i·des′·cence** *adj.* —**ir′i·des′cent·ly** *adv.*

i·rid·i·um (i·rid′ē·əm, ī·rid′-) *n.* A hard, brittle, silver-gray metallic element (symbol Ir) of the platinum group. [See IRIDESCENT.]

i·ris (ī′ris) *n.* *pl.* **i·ris·es** or **ir·i·des** (ir′ə·dēz, ī′rə-) 1. *Anat.* The colored, circular, contractile membrane between the cornea and the lens of the eye, having the pupil as its central aperture. 2. *Bot.* A plant with sword-shaped leaves and large handsome flowers, as the crocus, gladiolus, etc. [< Gk. *iris*]

I·rish (ī′rish) *n.* 1. The people of Ireland or of Irish ancestry: preceded by *the*. 2. The ancient or modern Celtic language of Ireland: also called **Irish Gaelic**: sometimes called *Erse*. 3. The dialect of English spoken in Ireland: also called **Irish English.** [ME *Irisc*] —**I′rish** *adj.*

Irish coffee Hot coffee with sugar, Irish whiskey, and whipped cream.

I·rish·man (ī′rish·mən) *n.* *pl.* **·men** (-mən) A man of Irish birth or ancestry.

Irish moss Carrageen, a seaweed.

Irish setter A reddish brown variety of setter.

Irish terrier A small terrier having a wiry, reddish coat.

Irish wolfhound A very large, powerful hunting dog, having a rough coat.

irk (ûrk) *v.t.* To annoy or weary; vex. [ME *irken*] —**irk·some** (ûrk′səm) *adj.* —**irk′some·ness** *n.*

i·ron (ī′ərn) *n.* 1. A tough, abundant, malleable, easily oxidized and strongly magnetic metallic element (symbol Fe). 2. That which is firm, harsh, or indestructible. 3. An implement or tool made of iron. 4. A metal appliance having a smooth, flat undersurface and a handle, and used, when heated, to press cloth, etc. 5. *pl.* Chains used to confine a prisoner; shackles. 6. A golf club having a metal head with an angled face. —**to have irons in the fire** To be engaged in various enterprises. —**to strike while the iron is hot** To act at the right moment. —*adj.* 1. Made of or consisting of iron. 2. Resembling iron. 3. Inexorable; unyielding; firm. 4. Grim; pitiless. —*v.t. & v.i.* To smooth or press (clothes, etc.) with a heated iron. —**to iron out** To remove, as difficulties. [OE *irenisen, isern*] —**i′ron·er** *n.*

Iron Age The most recent of three early stages of human progress, following the Stone Age and the Bronze Age.

i·ron·clad (ī′ərn·klad′) *adj.* 1. Covered by or in armor. 2. Strict; unbreakable, as a rule, contract, etc.

iron curtain A barrier of censorship and secrecy; esp., that imposed by the Soviet Union between its sphere of influence and the rest of the world.

i·ron·hand·ed (ī′ərn·han′did) *adj.* Exerting severe discipline; despotic.

i·ron·ic (ī·ron′ik) *adj.* 1. Of the nature of or characterized by irony. 2. Given to the use of irony. Also **i·ron′ic·al.** —**i·ron′i·cal·ly** *adv.*

i·ron·ing board (ī′ərn·ing) A board or folding table, usu. padded, on which articles of clothing, etc., are ironed.

iron lung A cabinetlike enclosure in which the respiration of a patient is artificially maintained.

iron pyrites Pyrite.

i·ron·stone (ī′ərn·stōn′) *n.* 1. Glazed, usu. white pottery. 2. Rock that is rich in iron.

i·ron·ware (ī′ərn·wâr′) *n.* Articles made of iron; hardware.

i·ron·weed (ī′ərn·wēd′) *n.* An herb or shrub having mostly purple or reddish flowers.

i·ron·wood (ī′ərn·wŏŏd′) *n.* Any of various trees having unusually hard wood; also, the wood.

i·ron·work (ī′ərn·wûrk′) *n.* 1. Parts or objects made of iron, as parts of a building. 2. The act of working in iron. —**i′ron·work′er** *n.*

i·ron·works (ī′ərn·wûrks′) *n.pl.* (*often construed as sing.*) An establishment where iron or ironwork is made.

i·ro·ny (ī′rə·nē) *n.* *pl.* **·nies** 1. A sarcastic or humorous manner of discourse in which what is said is meant to express its opposite. 2. A result, ending, etc., the reverse of what was expected. [< Gk. *eirōn* dissembler]

Ir·o·quoi·an (ir′ə·kwoi′ən) *n.* 1. A family of North American Indian languages, including Cayuga, Cherokee, Conestoga, Erie, Mohawk, Oneida, Seneca and other languages. 2. A member of a tribe speaking these languages. —**Ir′o·quoi′an** *adj.*

Ir·o·quois (ir′ə·kwoi, -kwoiz) *n.* *pl.* **·quois** 1. A member of any of several North American Indian tribes once dwelling in New York and Canada; also, these tribes collectively. 2. A member of a tribe speaking an Iroquoian language. [< F < Algonquian *Irinakoiw*, lit., real adders] —**Ir′o·quois** *adj.*

ir·ra·di·ant (i·rā′dē·ənt) *adj.* Sending forth light; shining. —**ir·ra′di·ance, ir·ra′di·an·cy** *n.*

ir·ra·di·ate (i·rā′dē·āt) *v.* **·at·ed, ·at·ing** *v.t.* 1. To light up; illuminate. 2. To make clear or understandable. 3. To send forth in or as in rays of light. 4. To subject to X-rays, ultraviolet light, or similar rays. —*v.i.* 5. To be radiant; shine. [< IN-[2] + L *radiare* to shine] —**ir·ra′di·a′tion** *n.* —**ir·ra′di·a′tive** *adj.*

ir·ra·tion·al (i·rash′ən·əl) *adj.* 1. Incapable of exercising the power of reason. 2. Contrary to reason; absurd. 3. *Math.* Denoting a number that cannot be expressed as an integer or a quotient of integers. [< L *irrationalis*] —**ir·ra′tion·al·ism** *n.* —**ir·ra′·tion·al′i·ty** (-al′ə·tē) *n.* —**ir·ra′tion·al·ly** *adv.*

ir·re·claim·a·ble (ir′i·klā′mə·bəl) *adj.* Incapable of being reclaimed. —**ir′re·claim′a·bil′i·ty** *n.* —**ir′re·claim′a·bly** *adv.*

ir·rec·on·cil·a·ble (i·rek′ən·sī′lə·bəl) *adj.* Not able or willing to be reconciled or brought into accord. —**ir·rec′on·cil′a·bil′i·ty** *n.* —**ir·rec′on·cil′a·bly** *adv.*

ir·re·cov·er·a·ble (ir′i·kuv′ər·ə·bəl) *adj.* 1. Incapable of being recovered. 2. Incapable of being remedied. —**ir′re·cov′er·a·bly** *adv.*

ir·re·deem·a·ble (ir′i·dē′mə·bəl) *adj.* 1. Incapable of being recovered, bought back, or paid off. 2. Not to be converted into coin: said of some types of paper money. 3. Beyond redemption or change; incorrigible. —**ir′re·deem′a·bly** *adv.*

ir·re·den·tist (ir′i·den′tist) *n.* A member of a party that has as its aim the acquisition of certain regions subject to other governments but historically or culturally allied to one's own nation. [after an Italian party formed in 1878] —**ir′re·den′tism** *n.* —**ir′re·den′tist** *adj.*

ir·re·duc·i·ble (ir′i·dōō′sə·bəl, -dyōō′-) *adj.* 1. Incapable of being decreased or diminished. 2. Incapable of being converted to a simpler or more basic form. —**ir′re·duc′i·bil′i·ty** *n.* —**ir′re·duc′i·bly** *adv.*

ir·ref·ra·ga·ble (i·ref′rə·gə·bəl) *adj.* That cannot be refuted or disproved. [< IN-[1] + L *refragari* to oppose] —**ir·ref′ra·ga·bil′i·ty** *n.* —**ir·ref′ra·ga·bly** *adv.*

ir·ref·u·ta·ble (i·ref′yə·tə·bəl, ir′i·fyōō′tə·bəl) *adj.* Incapable of being disproved. —**ir·ref′u·ta·bil′i·ty** *n.* —**ir·ref′u·ta·bly** *adv.*

ir·re·gard·less (ir′i·gärd′lis) *adv.* Regardless: a nonstandard or humorous usage.

ir·reg·u·lar (i·reg′yə·lər) *adj.* 1. Lacking symmetry or uniformity. 2. Occurring at unequal intervals. 3. Not according to established rules, standards, or procedure. 4. *Gram.* Not conforming to the usual pattern of inflection or conjugation. 5. *Mil.* Of troops, not belonging to a regularly organized military force. —*n.* One who or that which is irregular. —**ir·reg′u·lar′i·ty** (-lar′ə·tē) *n.* —**ir·reg′u·lar·ly** *adv.*

ir·rel·e·vant (i·rel′ə·vənt) *adj.* Not relevant; not pertinent; inapplicable. —**ir·rel′e·vance, ir·rel′e·van·cy** *n.* —**ir·rel′e·vant·ly** *adv.*

ir·re·lig·ion (ir′i·lij′ən) *n.* 1. Lack of religious faith. 2. Indifference or hostility toward religion. —**ir′re·lig′ion·ist** *n.*

ir·re·lig·ious (ir′i·lij′əs) *adj.* 1. Lacking in religious faith or piety. 2. Profane. —**ir′re·lig′ious·ly** *adv.*

ir·re·me·di·a·ble (ir′i·mē′dē·ə·bəl) *adj.* Incapable of being remedied; incurable; irreparable. —**ir′re·me′di·a·bly** *adv.*

ir·re·mis·si·ble (ir′i·mis′ə·bəl) *adj.* Not remissible; unpardonable, as a sin. —**ir′re·mis′si·bil′i·ty** *n.* —**ir′re·mis′si·bly** *adv.*

ir·re·mov·a·ble (ir′i·mōō′və·bəl) *adj.* Not removable.

ir·rep·a·ra·ble (i·rep′ər·ə·bəl) *adj.* Incapable of being repaired, rectified, or made good. —**ir·rep′a·ra·bil′i·ty** *n.* —**ir·rep′a·ra·bly** *adv.*

ir·re·place·a·ble (ir′i·plā′sə·bəl) *adj.* Not replaceable.

ir·re·pres·si·ble (ir′i·pres′ə·bəl) *adj.* Not repressible; incapable of being controlled or restrained. —**ir′re·pres′si·bil′i·ty** *n.* —**ir′re·pres′si·bly** *adv.*

ir·re·proach·a·ble (ir′i·prō′chə·bəl) *adj.* Not meriting reproach; blameless. —**ir′re·proach′a·bly** *adv.*

ir·re·sis·ti·ble (ir′i·zis′tə·bəl) *adj.* Not resistible, esp. fascinating or enchanting. —**ir′re·sis′ti·bil′i·ty** *n.* —**ir′re·sis′ti·bly** *adv.*

ir·res·o·lute (i·rez′ə·lōōt) *adj.* Not resolute or resolved; wavering; hesitating. —**ir·res′o·lute′ly** *adv.* —**ir·res′o·lu′tion** *n.*

ir·re·spec·tive of (ir′i·spek′tiv) Regardless of.

ir·re·spon·si·ble (ir′i·spon′sə·bəl) *adj.* 1. Lacking in responsibility; unreliable. 2. Free from or incapable of responsibility. —**ir′re·spon′si·bil′i·ty** *n.* —**ir′re·spon′si·bly** *adv.*

ir·re·spon·sive (ir′i·spon′siv) *adj.* Not responsive. —**ir′re·spon′sive·ness** *n.*

ir·re·triev·a·ble (ir′i·trē′və·bəl) *adj.* Not retrievable; irrecoverable; irreparable. —**ir′·re·triev′a·bil′i·ty** *n.* —**ir′re·triev′a·bly** *adv.*

ir·rev·er·ence (i·rev′ər·əns) *n.* 1. Lack of awe, veneration, or respect. 2. Behavior indicative of this. —**ir·rev′er·ent** *adj.* —**ir·rev′er·ent·ly** *adv.*

ir·re·vers·i·ble (ir′i·vûr′sə·bəl) *adj.* 1. Incapable of being turned in the opposite direction. 2. Incapable of being annulled, repealed, or undone. —**ir′re·vers′i·bil′i·ty** *n.* —**ir′re·vers′i·bly** *adv.*

ir·rev·o·ca·ble (i·rev′ə·kə·bəl) *adj.* 1. Incapable of being revoked. 2. Incapable of being brought back. —**ir·rev′o·ca·bil′i·ty** *n.* —**ir·rev′o·ca·bly** *adv.*

ir·ri·gate (ir′ə·gāt) *v.t.* **·gat·ed, ·gat·ing** 1. To supply (land) with water, as by means of ditches. 2. *Med.* To moisten or wash out with water. [< IN-[2] + L *rigare* to water] —**ir′ri·ga·ble** (-gə·bəl) *adj.* —**ir′ri·ga′tion** *n.* —**ir′ri·ga′tion·al** *adj.* —**ir′ri·ga′tor** *n.*

ir·ri·ta·ble (ir′ə·tə·bəl) *adj.* 1. Easily annoyed or angered. 2. *Biol.* Responding to stimuli. 3. *Pathol.* Influenced abnormally by the action of stimulants. —**ir′ri·ta·bil′i·ty** *n.* —**ir′ri·ta·bly** *adv.*

ir·ri·tant (ir′ə·tənt) *n.* That which irritates or causes irritation. —*adj.* Causing irritation. —**ir′ri·tan·cy** *n.*

ir·ri·tate (ir′ə·tāt) *v.t.* **·tat·ed, ·tat·ing** 1. To excite annoyance, impatience, or ill temper in; vex. 2. To make sore or inflamed. 3. *Biol.* To stimulate (a cell, tissue, or organ) to a characteristic function or action. [< L *irritare*] —**ir′ri·ta′ting** *adj.* —**ir′ri·ta′tive** *adj.* —**ir′ri·ta′ting·ly** *adv.* —**ir′ri·ta′tor** *n.*

ir·ri·ta·tion (ir′ə·tā′shən) *n.* 1. The act of irritating, or the state of being irritated; annoyance. 2. That which irritates. 3. *Pathol.* A condition of abnormal excitability or sensitivity in an organ or part.

ir·rup·tion (i·rup′shən) *n.* 1. A breaking or rushing in. 2. A violent, sudden invasion. [< IN-[2] + L *rumpere* to break] —**ir·rup′tive** *adj.*

is (iz) Present indicative, third person singular of BE. [OE]

i·sa·go·ge (ī′sə·gō′jē) *n.* An introduction,

as to a field of study. [< Gk. *eisagōgē* < *eisagein* to introduce] —**i′sa·gog′ic** (-goj′ik) *adj.*

I·sa·iah (ī·zā′ə, ī·zī′ə) *n.* A book of the Old Testament attributed to the 8th c. B.C. Hebrew prophet Isaiah. Also, in the Douai Bible, **I·sai′as** (-əs). [< Hebrew *yesha'yāhu* Salvation of God]

is·che·mi·a (is·kē′mē·ə) *n. Pathol.* A localized anemia, due to a contracted blood vessel. Also **is·chae′mi·a.** [< Gk. *ischein* to hold + *haima* blood] —**is·che′mic** *adj.*

is·chi·at·ic (is′kē·at′ik) *adj.* Of or pertaining to the ischium. Also **is′chi·ad′ic** (-ad′ik), **is·chi·al** (is′kē·əl).

is·chi·um (is′kē·əm) *n. pl.* **·chi·a** *Anat.* The lowest of the three sections composing the hipbone, or innominate bone. [< Gk. *ischion* hip]

-ise Var. of -IZE.

-ish[1] *suffix of adjectives* 1. Of or belonging to (a specified national group): *Danish.* 2. Of the nature of; like: *boyish.* 3. Having the bad qualities of: *selfish.* 4. Tending toward; inclined to: *bookish.* 5. Somewhat: *tallish.* 6. *Informal* Approximately: *fortyish.* [OE *-isc,* adjectival suffix]

-ish[2] *suffix of verbs* Appearing chiefly in verbs of French origin: *brandish, establish.* [< OF *-iss-*, stem ending of *-ir* verbs]

i·sin·glass (ī′zing·glas′, ī′zən-) *n.* 1. A preparation of nearly pure gelatin made from the swim bladders of certain fishes. 2. Mica, chiefly in the form of thin sheets. [Prob. < MDu. *huysenblas* sturgeon bladder]

Is·lam (is·läm′, is′ləm, iz′-) *n.* 1. The religion of the Muslims, that maintains that there is but one God, Allah, and that Muhammad is his prophet: also **Is·lam′·ism.** 2. Muslims collectively. 3. The areas of the world where Islam is the main religion. [< Arabic *islām* submission] —**Is·lam′ic** or **Is·lam·it·ic** (is′lə·mit′ik) *adj.*

Is·lam·ite (is′ləm·īt, iz′-) *n.* A Muslim.

is·land (ī′lənd) *n.* 1. A tract of land smaller than a continent entirely surrounded by water. 2. Something resembling an island and set apart from its surroundings. [OE *īg, īeg* island + *land*]

is·land·er (ī′lən·dər) *n.* A native or inhabitant of an island.

isle (īl) *n.* An island: used in place names or poetically. [< L *insula*]

is·let (ī′lit) *n.* A small island. [< OF *islette,* dim. of *isle*]

ism (iz′əm) *n.* A distinctive theory, doctrine, or system: usu. used disparagingly. [< -ISM]

-ism *suffix of nouns* 1. The act, process, or result of: *ostracism.* 2. The condition of being: *skepticism.* 3. The characteristic action or behavior of: *heroism.* 4. The beliefs, teachings, or system of: *Calvinism.* 5. Devotion to; adherence to the teachings of: *nationalism.* 6. A characteristic or peculiarity of: said especially of a language or idiom: *Americanism.* 7. *Med.* An abnormal condition resulting from an excess of: *alcoholism.* [< L *-ismus* < Gk. *-ismos*]

is·n't (iz′ənt) Is not.

iso- *combining form* 1. Equal; the same; identical. 2. *Chem.* Isomeric with, or an isomer of. Also, before vowels, **is-**. [< Gk. *isos* equal]

i·so·bar (ī′sə·bär) *n.* 1. *Meteorol.* A line drawn on a weather map connecting all points having the same barometric pressure for a given time or period. 2. *Physics* Any of two or more atoms having the same mass number but different atomic numbers. [< ISO- + Gk. *baros* weight] —**i·so·bar·ic** (ī′sə·bar′ik) *adj.*

i·so·late (ī′sə·lāt) *v.t.* **·lat·ed, ·lat·ing** 1. To set apart; cause to be alone. 2. *Chem.* To obtain (an element or substance) in a free or uncombined state. [< Ital. *isolare*] —**i′so·la·ble** (-lə·bəl) *adj.* —**i′so·la′tion** *n.* —**i′so·la′tor** *n.*

i·so·la·tion·ism (ī′sə·lā′shən·iz′əm) *n.* A national policy of avoiding international alliances. —**i′so·la′tion·ist** *adj. & n.*

i·so·mer (ī′sə·mər) *n.* 1. *Chem.* One of two or more compounds identical in composition, but having different structural arrangements and different properties. 2. *Physics* One of two or more nuclides having the same mass and atomic number but differing in energy characteristics. [< ISO- + Gk. *meros* part] —**i·so·mer′ic** (-mer′ik) *adj.* —**i·som·er·ism** (ī·som′ə·riz′əm) *n.*

i·so·met·ric (ī′sə·met′rik) *adj.* 1. Pertaining to or characterized by equality in dimensions or measurements. 2. Relating to isometrics. —**i′so·met′ri·cal·ly** *adv.*

i·so·met·rics (ī′sə·met′riks) *n.pl.* (*construed as sing. or pl.*) Exercises that strengthen muscles by tensing them against opposing muscles or an immovable resistance.

i·so·mor·phism (ī′sə·môr′fiz·əm) *n.* A similarity in form shown by substances of different composition, or by organisms belonging to different groups. —**i′so·morph** *n.* —**i·so·mor′phic** *adj.*

i·so·oc·tane (ī′sō·ok′tān) *n. Chem.* A hydrocarbon used in determining the octane number of motor fuels.

i·so·prene (ī′sə·prēn) *n. Chem.* A hydrocarbon obtained from crude rubber or produced synthetically, used in making synthetic rubber.

i·sos·ce·les (ī·sos′ə·lēz) *adj. Geom.* Of a triangle, having two sides of equal length. [< ISO- + Gk. *skelos* leg]

i·sos·ta·sy (ī·sos′tə·sē) *n. Geol.* The equilibrium that the earth's crust tends to assume as a result of the action of terrestrial gravitation upon rock masses. [< ISO- + Gk. *stasis* standing] —**i·so·stat·ic** (ī′sə·stat′ik) *adj.*

i·so·therm (ī′sə·thûrm) *n. Meteorol.* A line drawn on a weather map connecting all points having the same mean temperature. [< ISO- + Gk. *thermē* heat] —**i′so·ther′mal** *adj. & n.*

i·so·ton·ic (ī′sə·ton′ik) *adj. Physiol.* Having the same osmotic pressure on opposite sides of a membrane: said of solutions, esp. blood or plasma. [< ISO- + Gk. *tonos* accent]

i·so·tope (ī′sə·tōp) *n. Physics* Any of two or more forms of an element having the same atomic number and similar chemical properties but differing in mass number and radioactive behavior. [< ISO- + Gk. *topos* place] —**i·so·top·ic** (ī′sə·top′ik) *adj.* —**i·sot·o·py** (ī·sot′ə·pē) *n.*

Is·ra·el (iz′rē·əl) *n.* The Jewish people, regarded as descended from the patriarch Jacob, also called Israel. [< Hebrew *Yisrā'ēl* God persevereth]

Is·rae·li (iz·rā′lē) *adj.* Of modern Israel, its people, or their culture. —*n. pl.* ·lis A native or inhabitant of Israel.

Is·ra·el·ite (iz′rē·əl·īt′) *n.* Any of the people of ancient Israel or their descendants; a Hebrew; a Jew. —*adj.* Of or pertaining to the Hebrews; Jewish: also **Is′ra·el·it′ish** (-ī′tish), **Is′ra·el·it′ic** (-it′ik).

Is·sei (ēs·sā) *n. pl.* ·sei or ·seis A Japanese immigrant to the U.S. [< Japanese *is* first + *sei* generation]

is·sue (ish′o͞o, -yo͞o) *n.* 1. The act of giving out or publishing, esp. from an official source. 2. An item or set of items, as stamps, magazines, etc., published at a single time. 3. A result; consequence; outcome. 4. A matter of importance to be resolved. 5. An outflow; discharge. 6. Offspring; progeny. —**at issue** In question; in controversy. —**to take issue** To disagree. —*v.* ·sued, ·su·ing *v.i.* 1. To come forth; flow out; emerge. 2. To be derived or descended; originate. 3. To come as a consequence; result. 4. To terminate: often followed by *in*. 5. To be circulated or published; appear. 6. To be produced as profit. —*v.t.* 7. To publish; announce. 8. To give out; distribute, as supplies. [< L *ex-* out of + *ire* to go] —**is′su·a·ble** *adj.* —**is′su·ance** *n.* —**is′su·ant** *adj.* —**is′su·er** *n.*

-ist *suffix of nouns* 1. One who or that which does or has to do with: *catechist*. 2. One whose profession is: *pharmacist*. 3. A student or devotee of: *genealogist*. 4. One who advocates or adheres to: *socialist*. [< Gk. *-istēs*]

isth·mus (is′məs, isth′-) *n. pl.* ·mus·es or ·mi (-mī) A narrow piece of land connecting two larger land masses. [< Gk. *isthmos* narrow passage] —**isth′mi·an** *adj.* & *n.*

-istic *suffix of adjectives* Having the qualities of: formed from nouns ending in *-ist* or *-ism*: *communistic*.

is·tle (is′lē, ist′lē) *n.* A fiber derived from an agave plant, used for carpets, etc.

it (it) *pron., possessive* its; *pl. nominative* they, *possessive* their or theirs, *objective* them The nominative and objective singular neuter pronoun of the third person, used: 1. As a substitute for a specific noun. 2. To represent some implied idea, condition, action, or situation: How was *it*? 3. As the subject or predicate nominative of a verb whose logical subject is anticipated: Who is *it*? 4. As the subject of an impersonal verb: *It* rained yesterday. 5. As the indefinite subject of a verb introducing a clause or a phrase: *It* seems that he knew. 6. As the indefinite object after certain verbs in idiomatic expressions: to brazen *it* out. —*n.* In certain children's games, the player required to perform some specified act. [OE *hit*]

I·tal·ian (i·tal′yən) *n.* 1. A native or naturalized inhabitant of Italy. 2. The Romance language of Italy. —**I·tal′ian** *adj.*

i·tal·ic (i·tal′ik) *n. Usu. pl.* A style of type in which the letters slant, often used to denote emphasis: *These words are printed in italics.* —**i·tal′ic** *adj.*

I·tal·ic (i·tal′ik) *adj.* Relating to any of the peoples of ancient Italy. —*n.* A subfamily of the Indo-European languages, comprising three branches, and including Latin and the Romance languages.

i·tal·i·cize (i·tal′ə·sīz) *v.t.* & *v.i.* ·cized, ·ciz·ing To print in italics. —**i·tal′i·ci·za′·tion** *n.*

itch (ich) *v.i.* 1. To experience or produce an irritation that causes a desire to scratch or rub the affected area. 2. To have a restless desire to do something; hanker. —*n.* 1. An itching sensation. 2. Any of various skin diseases accompanied by itching. 3. A restless desire or yearning. [ME < OE *giccan*]

itch·y (ich′ē) *adj.* itch·i·er, itch·i·est Having or producing an itching sensation. —**itch′i·ness** *n.*

-ite *suffix of nouns* 1. A native or inhabitant of: *suburbanite*. 2. A follower of or sympathizer with: *Pre-Raphaelite*. 3. A descendant of: *Israelite*. 4. Resembling or related to: *dynamite*. 5. *Mineral.* A rock or mineral: *graphite*. 6. *Paleontol.* A fossil: *trilobite*. 7. *Zool.* A part of the body or of an organ: *dendrite*. [< Gk. *-ītēs*]

i·tem (ī′təm) *n.* 1. A single unit of a category, series, or enumeration. 2. An entry in an account. 3. A brief article of news, etc., as in a newspaper. —*adv.* Likewise; also. [< L, thus]

i·tem·ize (ī′təm·īz) *v.t.* ·ized, ·iz·ing To set down or specify by items. —**i′tem·i·za′tion** *n.* —**i′tem·iz′er** *n.*

it·er·ate (it′ə·rāt) *v.t.* ·at·ed, ·at·ing To state or utter again or repeatedly. [< L *iterum* again] —**it′er·a′tion** *n.* —**it′er·a′tive** *adj.*

i·tin·er·ant (ī·tin′ər·ənt, i·tin′-) *adj.* Going from place to place; wandering. —*n.* One who travels from place to place. [< LL *itineris* journey, route] —**i·tin′er·an·cy, i·tin′er·a·cy** *n.* —**i·tin′er·ant·ly** *adv.*

i·tin·er·ar·y (ī·tin′ə·rer′ē, i·tin′-) *n. pl.* ·ar·ies 1. A route followed in traveling. 2. A plan for or graphic representation of a journey. 3. A detailed account or record of a journey. [< LL *iter, itineris* journey, route] —**i·tin′er·ar′y** *adj.*

-itis *suffix Pathol.* Inflammation of: *peritonitis*. [< Gk.]

it'll (it′l) 1. It will. 2. It shall.

its (its) *pronominal adjective* The possessive case of the pronoun *it*, used attributively: *its* leaves. [< IT + *'s*, possessive case ending; written *it's* until the 19th century]

it's (its) 1. It is. 2. It has.

it·self (it·self′) *pron.* A form of the third person singular neuter pronoun, used: **a** As a reflexive or as object of a preposition in a reflexive sense: The motor started by *itself*. **b** As an intensifier or to give emphasis: simplicity *itself*. **c** As a designation for a normal or usual state: The house isn't *itself* with the children gone.

-ity *suffix of nouns* State or quality. [< L *-itas*]

IUD (ī yo͞o dē′) Intrauterine device.

IV (ī′vē′) Intravenous.

I've (īv) I have.

i·vied (ī′vēd) *adj.* Covered or overgrown with ivy.

i·vo·ry (ī′vər·ē) *n. pl.* ·ries 1. A hard, white, smooth-textured dentine, the chief substance of the tusks of elephants, walruses, etc. 2. The creamy white color of ivory. 3. *Usu.*

pl. Articles made of ivory. 4. *pl. Slang* a The teeth. b The keys of a piano. c Dice. —*adj.* 1. Made of or resembling ivory. 2. Of the color ivory. [< L *ebur, -oris* ivory]

ivory tower A condition or attitude of withdrawal from the world and reality.

i•vy (ī′vē) *n.* *pl.* **i•vies** A climbing plant, having glossy, evergreen leaves: also **English ivy.** [OE *ifig*]

-ize *suffix of verbs* 1. To cause to become or resemble: *Christianize.* 2. To subject to the action of: *oxidize.* 3. To change into: *mineralize.* 4. To act in the manner of: *sympathize.* Also *-ise.* [< Gk. *-izein*]

J

j, J (jā) *n. pl.* **j's** or **js, J's** or **Js, jays** (jāz) 1. The tenth letter of the English alphabet. 2. The sound represented by the letter *j*.

jab (jab) *v.t. & v.i.* **jabbed, jab·bing** 1. To poke or thrust sharply. 2. To punch or strike with a quick, sharp blow. —*n.* A sharp thrust or punch.

jab·ber (jab′ər) *v.t. & v.i.* To speak rapidly or without making sense. —*n.* Rapid or unintelligible talk; chatter. —**jab′ber·er** *n.*

ja·bot (zhă·bō′, *Fr.* zhȧ·bō′) *n. pl.* **·bots** (-bōz′, *Fr.* -bō′) A ruffle at the front of a blouse, shirt, or bodice. [< F, lit., gizzard]

ja·cinth (jā′sinth, jas′inth) *n.* Hyacinth. [< L *hyacinthus*]

jack (jak) *n.* 1. *Sometimes cap.* A man or boy, esp.: **a** A laborer: usu. in combination: *jack-of-all-trades*; *lumberjack.* **b** A sailor. 2. Any of various devices that perform an operation formerly done manually: often used in combinations: *bootjack.* 3. Any of various devices used for raising heavy weights through short distances, usu. by means of a lever. 4. **a** A male of certain animals: sometimes used in combination: *jackass.* **b** Any of various kinds of animals: often in combination: *jackdaw*; *jack* rabbit. 5. A playing card showing the picture of a young man; the knave. 6. A flag, flown at the bow of a ship. 7. *Slang* Money. 8. A six-pronged metal piece used in a children's game (jacks) in which the pieces are tossed and picked up. 9. *Electr.* A metallic connecting device with clips to which the wires of a circuit may be attached. —*v.t.* 1. To raise with or as with a jack: usu. with *up.* 2. *Informal* To increase, as a price: with *up.* [after *Jack*, a nickname for John]

jack·al (jak′əl, -ôl) *n.* Any of various African or Asian doglike carnivorous mammals. [< Persian *shaghal*]

jack·a·napes (jak′ə·nāps) *n.* An impertinent fellow. [< *Jack Napes*, nickname of William de la Pole, 15th c. Duke of Suffolk]

jack·ass (jak′as′) *n.* 1. A male ass. 2. A stupid person.

jack·boot (jak′bo͞ot′) *n.* A heavy topboot reaching above the knee.

jack·daw (jak′dô′) *n.* A glossy, black, crowlike bird of Europe.

jack·et (jak′it) *n.* 1. A short coat, usu. not extending below the hips. 2. An outer covering or case, as a paper cover for a book. —*v.t.* To cover or clothe with or as with a jacket. [< OF *jaque* short jacket]

Jack Frost A personification of winter.

jack·ham·mer (jak′ham′ər) *n.* A pneumatic tool for drilling rock, breaking pavements, etc.

jack-in-the-box (jak′in·thə·boks′) *n.* A toy consisting of a box containing a grotesque figure that springs up when the lid is unfastened: also **jack′-in-a-box′.**

jack-in-the-pul·pit (jak′in·thə·po͝ol′pit) *n.* An herb of the arum family whose flower resembles a canopy.

jack·knife (jak′nīf′) *n. pl.* **·knives** (-nīvz′) 1. A large pocketknife. 2. A dive in which the body is doubled forward, with the hands touching the ankles, and then straightened. —*v.t. & v.i.* **·knifed, ·knif·ing** To double up in the manner of a jackknife.

jack-of-all-trades (jak′əv·ôl′trādz′) *n.* One who is able to do many kinds of work.

jack-o'-lan·tern (jak′ə·lan′tərn) *n.* 1. A lantern made of a pumpkin hollowed and carved into a face. 2. Ignis fatuus.

jack·pot (jak′pot′) *n.* 1. In poker, a pot that accumulates until a player is dealt a pair of jacks or better, with which he may open the betting. 2. Any similar pot, pool, or prize. —**to hit the jackpot** *Informal* 1. To win the biggest possible prize. 2. To achieve a major success.

jack rabbit A large American hare.

jacks (jaks) *n.pl.* (*construed as sing.*) See JACK (def. 8).

jack·straw (jak′strô′) *n.* 1. One of a set of thin strips of wood, bone, etc., used in a game in which the players attempt to pick up each strip without moving any of the others. 2. *pl.* (*construed as sing.*) The game itself.

Jacob's ladder 1. A perennial herb, related to phlox, having blue or white bell-shaped flowers. 2. *Naut.* A rope ladder, often with wooden rungs. [after the ladder seen by *Jacob* in a dream, *Gen.* xxviii]

jade[1] (jād) *n.* 1. A hard, translucent mineral, usu. green, used as a gemstone. 2. A green color characteristic of jade. [< Sp. (*piedra de*) *ijada* (stone of) the side; because supposed to cure pain in the side]

jade[2] (jād) *n.* 1. An old or worthless horse. 2. A disreputable or ill-tempered woman; hussy. —*v.t. & v.i.* **jad·ed, jad·ing** To weary through hard work or overuse; tire. [Origin uncertain]

jad·ed (jā′did) *adj.* 1. Worn-out; exhausted. 2. Dulled or apathetic, as from overindulgence. —**jad′ed·ly** *adv.* —**jad′ed·ness** *n.*

jae·ger (yā′gər, jā′-) *n.* Any of a group of sea birds that pursue and harass gulls and terns until they drop or disgorge their prey. Also **jä′ger.** [< G, hunter]

jag[1] (jag) *n.* A sharp, projecting point; notch; tooth. —*v.t.* **jagged, jag·ging** 1. To cut notches or jags in. 2. To cut unevenly; slash. [ME *jagge*]

jag[2] (jag) *n. Slang* 1. A period of unrestrained activity. 2. A drunken spree.

jag·ged (jag′id) *adj.* Having jags or notches. —**jag′ged·ly** *adv.* —**jag′ged·ness** *n.*

jag·uar (jag wär, jag′yo͞o·är) *n.* A large, spotted leopardlike cat of Central and South America. [< Tupi *jaguara*]

jai a·lai (hī ə·lī′) A game popular in Latin America, similar to handball but played with a long, curved wicker basket strapped to the arm. [< Sp. < Basque, jolly festival]

jail (jāl) *n.* 1. A place of confinement for those guilty of minor offenses or those awaiting trial. 2. Loosely, any prison. —*v.t.* To put or hold in jail; imprison. Also, *Brit.*, *gaol.* [< OF *jaiole*, ult. < L *cavea* cave]

jail·bird (jāl′bûrd′) *n. Informal* A prisoner or ex-prisoner.

jail·er (jā′lər) *n.* The officer in charge of a jail: also, *Brit.*, *gaoler*. Also **jail′or.**

jal·ap (jal′əp) *n.* The dried root of any of several Mexican plants, used as a purgative. [< Sp. (*purga de*) *Jalapa* (medicine from) Jalapa] —**ja·lap·ic** (jə·lap′ik) *adj.*

ja·lop·y (jə·lop′ē) *n. pl.* **·lop·ies** *Informal* An old, run-down automobile. Also **ja·lop′py.** [Origin uncertain]

ja·lou·sie (jal′o͝o·sē) *n.* A window blind or shutter of overlapping horizontal slats or strips that may be tilted. [< F, lit., jealousy]

jam[1] (jam) *v.* **jammed, jam·ming** *v.t.* 1. To force or ram into or against something. 2. To pack and block up by crowding. 3. To cause to become wedged or stuck. 4. To interfere electronically with (a radio broadcast, etc.). —*v.i.* 5. To become wedged; stick. 6. To cease operation, as a machine, because parts have stuck or wedged together. 7. To take part in a jam session. —*n.* 1. A crowding together, as of people, cars, etc. 2. The act of jamming. 3. *Informal* An embarrassing or dangerous predicament. [Akin to CHAMP[1]]

jam[2] (jam) *n.* A pulpy, sweet conserve of whole fruit boiled with sugar. [? < JAM[1], v.]

Ja·mai·can (jə·mā′kən) *adj.* Of or pertaining to Jamaica and its people. —*n.* A native or inhabitant of Jamaica.

jamb (jam) *n.* A side post or side of a doorway, window, etc. [< LL *gamba* leg]

jam·bo·ree (jam′bə·rē′) *n.* 1. *Informal* A boisterous frolic. 2. A large, esp. international, assembly of Boy Scouts.

James (jāmz) *n.* A book of the New Testament consisting of the epistle attributed to James, possibly a brother of Jesus.

jam session An informal gathering of jazz musicians performing improvisations on various themes.

jan·gle (jang′gəl) *v.* **·gled, ·gling** *v.i.* 1. To make harsh sounds. 2. To wrangle; bicker. —*v.t.* 3. To cause to sound discordantly. 4. To annoy or irritate; unsettle. —*n.* 1. A discordant sound. 2. A quarrel; wrangling. [< OF *jangler*] —**jan′gler** *n.*

jan·i·tor (jan′i·tər) *n.* 1. One who is employed to care for a building, etc. 2. A doorkeeper; porter. [< L *janua* door] —**jan′i·to′ri·al** (-tôr′ē·əl) *adj.*

jan·i·zar·y (jan′ə·zer′ē) *n. pl.* **·zar·ies** *Often cap.* A soldier in the Turkish sultan's army before 1826. Also **jan′i·sar′y, jan′is·sar′y** (-ser′ē). [< Turkish *yenīcheri* new army]

Jan·u·ar·y (jan′yo͞o·er′ē) *n. pl.* **·ar·ies** or **·ar·ys** The first month of the year, containing 31 days. [< L *Januarius* < *Janus*, Roman god of portals]

Ja·nus-faced (jā′nəs·fāst′) *adj.* Two-faced; deceitful. [after *Janus*, Roman god of portals, usu. depicted as having two faces]

ja·pan (jə·pan′) *n.* 1. Any of various glossy black lacquers or varnishes, used for coating objects. 2. Ornamental objects decorated or lacquered in the Japanese manner. —*v.t.* **·panned, ·pan·ning** To enamel or lacquer with or as with japan.

Jap·a·nese (jap′ə·nēz′, -nēs′) *n. pl.* **·nese** 1. A native of Japan, or a person of Japanese ancestry. 2. The language of Japan. —**Jap′a·nese′** *adj.*

Japanese beetle A destructive beetle, introduced to the U.S. from Japan, which feeds on various plants.

jape (jāp) *Archaic v.i.* **japed, jap·ing** To joke or play tricks. —*n.* A jest or trick. [ME *jappen*] —**jap′er** *n.* —**jap′er·y** *n.*

ja·pon·i·ca (jə·pon′i·kə) *n.* 1. An Asian shrub with red flowers. 2. The camellia. [< NL, Japanese]

jar[1] (jär) *n.* 1. A wide-mouthed vessel of glass or earthenware, usu. deep and cylindrical. 2. The quantity a jar contains: also **jar′ful′**. [< Arabic *jarrah*]

jar[2] (jär) *v.* **jarred, jar·ring** *v.t.* 1. To strike against or bump so as to move or shake; jolt. 2. To disturb or shock. —*v.i.* 3. To have an unpleasant or painful effect: with *on* or *upon*. 4. To disagree or conflict; clash. 5. To bump or jolt: with *against*. 6. To make or have a disagreeable sound. —*n.* 1. A shaking, shock, or jolt. 2. A disagreeable sound or jumble of sounds. 3. A shock to the feelings. [Imit.]

jar·di·nière (jär′də·nir′, *Fr.* zhȧr·dē·nyâr′) *n.* An ornamental pot or stand for flowers or plants. [< F, fem. of *jardinier* gardener]

jar·gon (jär′gən) *n.* 1. Confused, unintelligible speech; gibberish. 2. The technical or specialized vocabulary or phraseology used by the members of a particular profession, sect, etc.: legal *jargon*. 3. A mixture of two or more languages, often serving as a lingua franca; pidgin. [< OF, a chattering]

jas·mine (jas′min, jaz′-) *n.* An ornamental plant of the olive family, with fragrant, generally white flowers. Also called *jessamine*. [< Persian *yāsmin*]

jas·per (jas′pər) *n.* An opaque, usu. red, brown, or yellow variety of quartz, admitting of a high polish: also **jas′per·ite.** [< L *jaspis*] —**jas·pid′e·an** (-pid′ē·ən), **jas·pid′e·ous** (-pid′ē·əs) *adj.*

jaun·dice (jôn′dis) *n.* 1. *Pathol.* A diseased condition of the liver due to the presence of bile pigments in the blood and characterized by yellowness of the skin and eyeballs. 2. An embittered state of mind. —*v.t.* **·diced, ·dic·ing** 1. To affect with jaundice. 2. To make bitter or biased. [< OF *jaune* yellow < L *galbus* yellow]

jaunt (jônt) *n.* A short journey, esp. for pleasure. —*v.i.* To make such a journey. [Origin unknown]

jaunt·y (jôn′tē) *adj.* **jaunt·i·er, jaunt·i·est** 1. Lively and self-confident. 2. Trim; dashing. [< F *gentil* genteel] —**jaunt′i·ly** *adv.* —**jaunt′i·ness** *n.*

ja·va (jav′ə, jä′və) *n. Sometimes cap. Slang* Coffee.

Jav·a·nese (jav′ə·nēz′, -nēs′) *n. pl.* **·nese**

1. A native or inhabitant of Java. 2. The Indonesian language of central Java, closely related to Malay. —**Jav′a·nese′** *adj.*

jave·lin (jav′lin, jav′ə·lin) *n.* 1. A light spear thrown as a weapon. 2. A long spear thrown for distance in an athletic contest. [< F, prob. < Celtic]

jaw (jô) *n.* 1. *Anat.* Either of the two bony structures forming the framework of the mouth and holding the teeth. 2. One of a pair of gripping parts capable of opening and closing, as of a tool. 3. Anything suggesting the action of the jaws. —*v.i. Informal* To talk. [< F *joue* cheek]

jaw·bone (jô′bōn′) *n.* One of the bones of the jaw, esp. that of the lower jaw.

jaw·bon·ing (jô′bō′ning) *n.* The use by one in power of persuasive talk rather than legal action. —**jaw′bone′** *v.t.* **·boned, ·bon·ing**

jaw·break·er (jô′brā′kər) *n.* 1. *Informal* A type of very hard candy. 2. A machine that crushes ore: also **jaw′crush′er** (-krush′ər). 3. *Informal* A word hard to pronounce.

jay (jā) *n.* Any of various corvine birds, usu. of brilliant coloring, as the blue jay. [< Med.L *gaius*]

jay·walk (jā′wôk′) *v.i. Informal* To cross a street recklessly, violating traffic regulations or signals. —**jay′walk′er** *n.*

jazz (jaz) *n.* 1. A kind of music that originated among black musicians in the southern U.S., and is often extemporaneous but sometimes arranged. It is characterized by melodic, harmonic, and rhythmic variation, syncopation, and a melody played against various chord patterns. 2. *Slang* Jive talk. —**and all that jazz** *Slang* Additional, related items. —*adj.* Of or pertaining to jazz. —*v.t.* 1. *Slang* a To quicken; speed up. b To jive. 2. To play or arrange (music) as jazz. —**to jazz up** *Slang* To make more exciting. [< Creole *jass* coition; from its origin in the brothels of New Orleans] —**jazz′y** *adj.* —**jazz′i·ly** *adv.*

jeal·ous (jel′əs) *adj.* 1. Fearful or suspicious of being displaced by a rival in affection or favors. 2. Vindictive toward another because of envy or rivalry. 3. Vigilant in guarding: to be *jealous* of a privilege. 4. Resulting or arising from jealousy. [< Gk. *zēlos* zeal] —**jeal′ous·ly** *adv.*

jeal·ou·sy (jel′ə·sē) *n. pl.* **·ou·sies** The attitude, feeling, or condition of being jealous.

jean (jēn) *n.* 1. A sturdy, twilled cotton cloth. 2. *pl.* Trousers or overalls made of this or a similar material. [after F *Gênes* Genoa, where it was made]

jeep (jēp) *n.* A small motorcar equipped with four-wheel drive. [< G(ENERAL) P(URPOSE) (VEHICLE)]

jeer (jir) *v.t. & v.i.* To speak or shout at in a derisive, mocking manner. —*n.* A derisive word or remark. [Origin unknown] —**jeer′er** *n.* —**jeer′ing·ly** *adv.*

Je·ho·vah (ji·hō′və) In the Old Testament, God; the Lord. [< Hebrew *JHVH* Yahweh, either Creator or Eternal] —**Je·ho′vi·an, Je·ho′vic** *adj.*

je·june (jə·jōōn′) *adj.* 1. Lacking in substance or interest; dry; barren; dull. 2. Callow; childish. [< L *jejunus* hungry; def. 2 prob. from confusion with JUVENILE] —**je·june′ly** *adv.*

je·ju·num (jə·jōō′nəm) *n. pl.* **·na** *Anat.* That portion of the small intestine that extends from the duodenum to the ileum. [< L *jejunus* hungry]

jell (jel) *v.t. & v.i. Informal* 1. To jelly; congeal. 2. To assume or cause to assume definite form. [< JELLY]

jel·lied (jel′ēd) *adj.* 1. Made gelatinous. 2. Covered with or prepared in jelly.

jel·ly (jel′ē) *n. pl.* **·lies** 1. A food made with gelatin or pectin, and having a semisolid consistency such that it quivers when shaken; esp., such a food made of boiled and sweetened fruit juice. 2. Any gelatinous substance. —*v.* **·lied, ·ly·ing** *v.t.* 1. To make into a jelly. 2. To cover or fill with jelly. —*v.i.* 3. To become jelly. [< L *gelata*, pp. of *gelare* to freeze]

jel·ly·bean (jel′ē·bēn′) *n.* A bean-shaped, gelatinous candy having a hard, colored coating.

jel·ly·fish (jel′ē·fish′) *n. pl.* **·fish** or **·fish·es** 1. Any of a number of marine animals of jellylike substance, often having umbrella-shaped bodies with trailing tentacles. 2. *Informal* One lacking determination or stamina; weakling.

jen·net (jen′it) *n.* A breed of small Spanish horses. [< Sp. *jinete* mounted soldier]

jen·ny (jen′ē) *n. pl.* **·nies** 1. A spinning jenny. 2. The female of the ass: also **jenny ass.** 3. A female wren: also **jenny wren.** [after *Jenny*, a personal name]

jeop·ard·ize (jep′ər·dīz) *v.t.* **·ized, ·iz·ing** To put in jeopardy; imperil.

jeop·ar·dy (jep′ər·dē) *n.* 1. Danger of death, loss, or injury; peril. 2. *Law* The peril in which a defendant is put when placed on trial for a crime. [< L *jocus partitus* divided play]

jer·bo·a (jər·bō′ə) *n.* Any of various nocturnal rodents of Asia and North Africa, with very long hind legs. [< Arabic *yarbu'*]

jer·e·mi·ad (jer′ə·mī′əd) *n.* A lament or tale of woe. [< F *Jérémie* Jeremiah]

Jer·e·mi·ah (jer′ə·mī′ə) *n.* The Old Testament book containing the prophecies of the 7th c. B.C. Hebrew prophet Jeremiah. Also, in the Douai Bible, **Jer′e·mi′as** (-əs). [< Hebrew *Yirmĕyāhū*, lit., God looseneth (from the womb)]

jerk¹ (jûrk) *v.t.* 1. To give a sharp, sudden pull or twist to. 2. To move or do with a sharp, suddenly arrested motion. 3. To make and serve (ice cream sodas, etc.). —*v.i.* 4. To give or move with a jerk or jerks. —*n.* 1. A sudden, sharp pull, twitch, twist, or thrust. 2. *Slang* A stupid, inept person. [? Var. of archaic *yerk*]

jerk² (jûrk) *v.t.* To cure (meat) by cutting into strips and drying. —*n.* Jerked meat, esp. beef. [< Sp. *charqui* < Quechua *echarqui* dried beef]

jer·kin (jûr′kin) *n.* A close-fitting jacket or vest, usu. sleeveless; esp., such a garment, often of leather, worn in the 16th and 17th c. [Origin unknown]

jerk·wa·ter (jûrk′wô′tər, -wot′ər) *Informal adj.* 1. Not on a main railroad line. 2. Insignificant; small. [< JERK¹ v. + WATER]

jerk·y¹ (jûrk′ē) *adj.* 1. Characterized by or

moving in jerks. 2. *Slang* Stupid or inept. —**jerk′i·ly** *adv.* —**jerk′i·ness** *n.*

jerk·y[2] *n.* Meat dried by jerking. See JERK[2].

jer·o·bo·am (jer′ə·bō′əm) *n.* A champagne bottle holding about 4/5 gallon. [after *Jeroboam* I, a 10th c. B.C. Hebrew king]

jer·ry-build (jer′ē·bild′) *v.t.* **·built, ·build·ing** To build flimsily and with inferior materials. [Origin unknown]

jer·sey (jûr′zē) *n. pl.* **·seys** 1. A ribbed elastic fabric used for clothing: also **jersey cloth.** 2. A close-fitting knit upper garment.

Jer·sey (jûr′zē) *n. pl.* **·seys** One of a breed of small cattle usu. fawn-colored, and noted for milk rich in butterfat.

jes·sa·mine (jes′ə·min) *n.* Jasmine.

jest (jest) *n.* 1. Something said or done to provoke laughter; joke. 2. Playfulness; fun. 3. An object of laughter; laughingstock. —*v.i.* 1. To make amusing remarks; quip. 2. To speak or act playfully. [< L *gesta* deeds] —**jest′ing** *n. & adj.* —**jest′ing·ly** *adv.*

jest·er (jes′tər) *n.* One who jests; esp., a court fool.

Jes·u·it (jezh′o͞o·it, jez′yo͞o-) *n.* A member of the Society of Jesus, a Roman Catholic religious order. [< L *Jesus* Jesus] —**Jes′u·it′ic** or **·i·cal** *adj.* —**Jes′u·it′i·cal·ly** *adv.*

Je·sus (jē′zəs) Founder of Christianity, 6? B.C.–29? A.D. Also **Jesus Christ, Jesus of Nazareth.**

jet[1] (jet) *n.* 1. A hard, black lignite, taking a high polish, used for jewelry, buttons, etc. 2. A deep, glossy black. —*adj.* 1. Made of or resembling jet. 2. Black as jet; jet-black. [< Gk. *gagatēs*, after *Gagai*, a Lycian town where it was mined]

jet[2] (jet) *n.* 1. A sudden spurt or gush of liquid or gas emitted from a narrow orifice. 2. A spout or nozzle. 3. An aircraft propelled by a jet engine. —*v.t. & v.i.* **jet·ted, jet·ting** To spurt forth or emit in a stream. [< L *jactare*, freq. of *jacere* to throw]

jet-black (jet′blak′) *adj. & n.* Deep black, like jet.

jet engine A reaction and heat engine that takes in outside air to oxidize fuel that it converts into the energy of a powerful jet of heated gas expelled to the rear under high pressure.

jet lag Fatigue, confusion, and other symptoms of upset of biorhythms due to long jet flights across time zones. Also **jet fatigue, jet syndrome.**

jet·sam (jet′səm) *n.* 1. Goods thrown into the sea to lighten an imperiled vessel. 2. Such goods washed ashore. [Earlier *jetson*, short for JETTISON]

jet set An international group of wealthy and fashionable persons. —**jet·set·ter** (jet′set·ər) *n.*

jet stream 1. The strong flow of gas or other fluid expelled from a jet engine, rocket motor, etc. 2. *Meteorol.* A high-velocity wind circulating, usu. from west to east, near the base of the stratosphere.

jet·ti·son (jet′ə·sən) *v.t.* 1. To throw overboard (goods or cargo). 2. To discard (something that hampers). —*n.* 1. The act of jettisoning. 2. Jetsam. [< AF *getteson*. See JET[2]]

jet·ty (jet′ē) *n. pl.* **·ties** 1. A structure of piling, rocks, etc., extending out into a body of water to protect a harbor, etc. 2. A wharf or pier. [< OF *jeter* to throw]

Jew (jo͞o) *n.* 1. A member or descendant of the Hebrew people. 2. Any person professing Judaism. 3. Originally, a member of the tribe or the kingdom of Judah. [< Hebrew *y'hudi* descendant of Judah]

jew·el (jo͞o′əl) *n.* 1. A precious stone; gem. 2. An article of jewelry. 3. A person or thing of rare excellence or value. —*v.t.* **jew·eled** or **·elled, jew·el·ing** or **·el·ling** To adorn with jewels. [< L *jocus* a joke, sport]

jew·el·er (jo͞o′əl·ər) *n.* A dealer in or maker of jewelry. Also **jew′el·ler.**

jew·el·ry (jo͞o′əl·rē) *n.* 1. Jewels, collectively. 2. Articles of personal adornment collectively, as rings, bracelets, necklaces, etc. Also *Brit.* **jew′el·ler·y.**

Jew·ish (jo͞o′ish) *adj.* Of or pertaining to Jews, their customs, religion, etc. —**Jew′ish·ness** *n.*

Jew·ry (jo͞o′rē) *n.* The Jewish people.

jew's-harp (jo͞oz′härp′) *n.* A small, lyre-shaped musical instrument held between the teeth and played by plucking a flexible steel tongue with the finger. Also **jews'-harp.**

jib[1] (jib) *n. Naut.* A triangular sail, set on a stay and extending from the foretopmast head to the jib boom or the bowsprit. —*v.t. & v.i.* **jibbed, jib·bing** *Naut.* To jibe. [? Short for GIBBET]

jib[2] (jib) *v.i.* **jibbed, jib·bing** To refuse to go forward, as a horse; move sidewise or backward; balk. [Cf. OF *giber* kick]

jib boom *Naut.* A spar forming a continuation of the bowsprit and holding a jib.

jibe[1] (jīb) *v.i.* **jibed, jib·ing** 1. *Naut.* To swing from one side of a vessel to the other, as a sail or its boom. 2. To change course so that the sails shift in this manner. Also spelled *jib.* [< Du. *gijben*]

jibe[2] (jīb) See GIBE.

jibe[3] (jīb) *v.i.* **jibed, jib·ing** *Informal* To agree; be in accordance. [Origin uncertain]

jif·fy (jif′ē) *n. pl.* **·fies** *Informal* An instant; moment. Also **jiff.** [Origin unknown]

jig (jig) *n.* 1. A fast, lively dance; also, the music for such a dance. 2. *Mech.* **a** A device for holding the material being worked or for guiding a tool. **b** Any of various devices operated by jiggling or jolting, as a sieve for cleaning coal in water. 3. In fishing, any of various lures that are jiggled. —**the jig is up** *Slang* All hope of success is gone. —*v.t. & v.i.* **jigged, jig·ging** 1. To dance or play (a jig). 2. To jiggle. 3. To make with or use a jig. [Cf. OF *gigue* a fiddle]

jig·ger (jig′ər) *n.* 1. A small glass or cup for measuring liquor, holding about one and one half ounces; also, the amount of liquor so measured. 2. A jig used in catching fish. 3. *Mech.* A jig. 4. *Naut.* **a** A small sail set in the stern of a sailing craft; also, a small boat having such a sail. **b** A light tackle. **c** A jigger mast. 5. *Informal* Any small device or thing.

jigger mast *Naut.* The aftermost mast of a four- or five-masted vessel.

jig·gle (jig′əl) *v.t. & v.i.* **·gled, ·gling** To move back and forth or up and down with quick jerks. [Freq. of JIG, v.] —**jig′gle** *n.*

jig·saw (jig′sô′) *n.* A saw having a slim blade set vertically in a frame, used for cutting curved or irregular lines.

jigsaw puzzle A puzzle consisting of a picture on wood or cardboard cut into irregular interlocking pieces for reassembly.
jilt (jilt) *v.t.* To cast off (a sweetheart). [Cf. dial. E (Scottish) *jillet* giddy girl]
Jim Crow *Slang* Racial segregation. —**Jim-Crow** (jim′krō′) *adj.* —**Jim′-Crow′ism** *n.*
jim·my (jim′ē) *n. pl.* **·mies** A burglar's crowbar. —*v.t.* **·mied, ·my·ing** To break or pry open with or as with a jimmy. [after *Jimmy*, dim. of *James*, a personal name]
jim·son·weed (jim′sən·wēd′) *n.* A tall, coarse, evil-smelling, poisonous annual weed of the nightshade family, yielding atropine and scopolamine. Also **Jimson weed.** [Alter. of *Jamestown weed* Jamestown, Va.]
jin·gle (jin′gəl) *v.t. & v.i.* **·gled, ·gling** To make or cause to make light ringing or tinkling sounds. —*n.* 1. A tinkling, clinking, or rapidly ringing sound. 2. A catchy, short song or poem, esp. one used for advertising. 3. Rapid repetition in rhyme, rhythm, alliteration, etc. [Imit.] —**jin′gly** *adj.*
jin·go (jing′gō) *n. pl.* **·goes** A boastful patriot who favors an aggressive foreign policy: also **jin′go·ist.** [Originally a magician's nonsense word] —**jin′go·ism** *n.* —**jin′go·is′tic** *adj.*
jin·ni (jin′ē, ji·nē′) *n. pl.* **jinn** (jin) In Muslim mythology, one of the supernatural beings able to assume human or animal form and often at the service of men: also spelled *genie.* Also **jin·nee′.** [< Arabic *jinnī*]
jin·rik·sha (jin·rik′shə, -shô) *n.* A small oriental two-wheeled carriage drawn by one or two men: also called *rickshaw, ricksha.* Also **jin·rick′sha, jin·rik′i·sha.** [< Japanese *jin* man + *riki* power + *sha* carriage]
jinx (jingks) *Slang n.* A person or thing supposed to bring bad luck. —*v.t.* To bring bad luck to. [< earlier *jynx* < Gk. *iynx* the wryneck (a bird anciently used in witchcraft)]
jit·ney (jit′nē) *n.* A motor vehicle that carries passengers for a small fare.
jit·ter (jit′ər) *v.i. U.S. Slang* To be nervous. —**the jitters** *Slang* Intense nervousness. —**jit′ter·y** *adj.*
jit·ter·bug (jit′ər·bug′) *Slang n.* 1. An energetic, free-moving dance for couples, done to jazz or similar popular music. 2. One who dances a jitterbug. —*v.i.* **·bugged, ·bug·ging** To dance a jitterbug.
jiu·jit·su (jo͞o·jit′so͞o), **jiu·jut·su** (jo͞o·jit′·so͞o, -jo͝ot′so͞o) See JUJITSU.
jive (jīv) *n. Slang* 1. The jargon of swing music and musicians. 2. Swing music. 3. Empty or deceptive talk. —*v.* **jived, jiv·ing** *v.t.* 1. To deceive with insincere talk. 2. To tease. —*v.i.* 3. To dance to swing music.
job (job) *n.* 1. Anything that is to be done; esp., a definite single piece of work done for a set fee; also, the thing worked on. 2. A position or situation of employment. 3. *Slang* A robbery or other criminal act. —**to lie** (or **lay**) **down on the job** *Informal* To evade work or responsibility. —*v.* **jobbed, job·bing** *v.i.* 1. To work by the job or piece. 2. To be a jobber or middleman. —*v.t.* 3. To buy and resell (goods) as a jobber. 4. To sublet (work) among separate contractors. [Origin uncertain] —**job′less** *adj.* —**job′less·ness** *n.*
Job (jōb) *n.* A book of the Old Testament concerning the sufferings of Job, a man whose faith was tested by God.
job action Disruptive action by workers short of strike, such as a slowdown, the deliberate enforcement of all rules, etc.
job·ber (job′ər) *n.* 1. One who buys goods in bulk from the manufacturer or importer and sells to the retailer; wholesaler. 2. One who works by the job, or on small jobs; pieceworker.
job·hold·er (job′hōl′dər) *n.* One who has a steady job.
job lot A collection of miscellaneous goods sold to a retailer.
jock (jok) *n. Slang* An athlete; esp., one noted for physical skills rather than intellect. [< *jockstrap*, an athletic supporter]
jock·ey (jok′ē) *n. pl.* **·eys** One employed to ride horses in races. —*v.t. & v.i.* 1. To maneuver for an advantageous position. 2. To ride (a horse) in a race. [Dim. of *Jock*, var. of the name *Jack*]
jo·cose (jō·kōs′) *adj.* Humorous; playful: joking. [< L *jocus* joke] —**jo·cose′ly** *adv.* —**jo·cose′ness, jo·cos′i·ty** (-kos′ə·tē) *n.*
joc·u·lar (jok′yə·lər) *adj.* Given to joking; also, like a joke. [< L *jocus* joke] —**joc′u·lar′i·ty** (-lâr′ə·tē) *n.* —**joc′u·lar·ly** *adv.*
jo·cund (jok′ənd, jō′kənd) *adj.* Cheerful; gay; jovial. [< LL *juvare* to delight] —**jo·cun·di·ty** (jō·kun′də·tē) *n.*
jodh·purs (jod′pərz) *n.pl.* Wide riding breeches, close-fitting from knee to ankle. [after *Jodhpur*, India]
Jo·el (jō′əl) *n* A book of the Old Testament by the Hebrew prophet Joel. [< Hebrew, the Lord is God]
jog (jog) *v.* **jogged, jog·ging** *v.i.* 1. To run, ride, or proceed at a moderate pace; trot. —*v.t.* 2. To push or touch lightly; nudge. —*n.* 1. The act of jogging. 2. A nudge. 3. A slow, jolting motion or pace. 4. An angle or projection in a surface; jag. 5. A sudden temporary turning or veering. [Prob. imit. Akin to *shog* shake < Du. *schok* shake] —**jog′ger** *n.*
jog·gle (jog′əl) *v.t. & v.i.* **·gled, ·gling** To shake slightly; jog; jiggle. [Freq. of JOG, v.] —**jog′gle** *n.*
john (jon) *n. Slang* 1. A toilet. 2. A prostitute's customer.
John (jon) *n.* 1. The fourth Gospel of the New Testament, attributed to the apostle John (also called **John the Evangelist, Saint John the Divine**). 2. One of the three New Testament epistles that bear his name.
John Bull 1. The English people. 2. A typical Englishman. [after a character in a satire (1712) by Dr. John Arbuthnot]
John Doe (dō) A name to designate a fictitious or real personage in any legal transaction or proceeding.
john·ny·cake (jon′ē·kāk′) *n.* A flat cake of cornmeal, baked on a griddle. [? < obs. *jonikin*, a type of bread]
john·ny-jump-up (jon′ē·jump′up′) *n.* 1. Any of various American spring violets. 2. The wild pansy.
joie de vi·vre (zhwä də vēv′r′) *French* Joy of living.
join (join) *v.t.* 1. To become a member of, as a club, party, etc. 2. To come to as a companion or participant. 3. To unite in act or purpose. 4. To come to a junction with.

5. To connect. 6. *Informal* To adjoin. —*v.i.* 7. To enter into association or agreement: often with *with*. 8. To take part: with *in*. 9. To come together; connect; unite. —**to join battle** To engage in a battle or conflict. —**to join up** *Informal* To enlist. —*n*. A joint or seam. [< L *jungere* to join]

join·der (join′dər) *n*. *Law* **a** A joining of causes of action or defense. **b** A joining of parties in an action.

join·er (joi′nər) *n*. 1. One who or that which joins. 2. *Informal* One who joins many clubs, lodges, etc.

joint (joint) *n*. 1. A place or point at which two or more parts of the same thing are joined together. 2. *Anat.* A place of union between two separate bones, usu. permitting movement; articulation. 3. A large cut of meat from a shoulder or leg containing the bone, used for roasting. 4. *Slang* **a** A place of low repute, as for drinking, gambling, etc. **b** A marijuana cigarette. —**out of joint** 1. Dislocated. 2. Disordered; disorganized. —*adj.* 1. Belonging to or used by two or more. 2. Produced by combined action. —*v.t.* 1. To fasten by means of a joint or joints. 2. To cut at the joints, as meat. [< L *jungere* to join]

joint·ed (join′tid) *adj.* Having a joint or joints.

joint·ly (joint′lē) *adv.* In a joint manner; unitedly.

joint-stock company (joint′stok′) An unincorporated business association of many persons, each of whom owns shares of stock which he may sell or transfer at will.

join·ture (join′chər) *n*. *Law* A settlement of property made to a woman by her husband after his death. [< L *jungere* to join]

joist (joist) *n*. Any of the parallel beams placed horizontally from wall to wall, to which the boards of a floor or the laths of a ceiling are fastened. [< L *jacere* to lie] —**joist** *v.t.*

joke (jōk) *n*. 1. Something said or done to amuse; esp., a funny story. 2. Something said or done in fun rather than in earnest. 3. One who or that which excites mirth. —*v.i.* **joked, jok·ing** To tell or make jokes; jest. [< L *jocus*] —**jok′ing·ly** *adv.*

jok·er (jō′kər) *n*. 1. One who jokes. 2. In a deck of cards, an extra card used in certain games. 3. An unobtrusive clause in a legislative bill, etc., that undermines or nullifies its original purpose.

jol·li·fy (jol′ə·fī) *v.t.* & *v.i.* **·fied, ·fy·ing** *Informal* To be or cause to be merry or jolly. —**jol′li·fi·ca′tion** *n*.

jol·ly (jol′ē) *adj.* **·li·er, ·li·est** 1. Full of good humor and high spirits. 2. Festive; merry. 3. *Brit. Informal* Extraordinary: a *jolly* bore. —*v.t.* **·lied, ·ly·ing** *Informal* To attempt to put or keep in good humor: often with *along* or *up*. —*adv. Brit. Informal* Extremely; very. [< OF *joli*] —**jol′li·ty** *n*.

Jolly Roger The pirate flag bearing the skull and crossbones.

jolt (jōlt) *v.t.* 1. To strike or knock against; jar; jostle. 2. To shake with a blow or bump. —*v.i.* 3. To move with a series of irregular bumps or jars, as over a rough road. —*n*. 1. A sudden bump or jar. 2. An unexpected surprise or emotional shock. [ME *jot* bump and *joll* bump] —**jolt′er** *n*. —**jolt′y** *adj.*

Jo·nah (jō′nə) *n*. A book of the Old Testament containing the story of the 8th or 9th c. B.C. Hebrew prophet Jonah, who survived being swallowed by a great fish: also, in the Douai Bible, **Jo′nas** (-nəs). [< Hebrew *Yōnāh*, lit., dove]

jon·gleur (jong′glər, *Fr.* zhôṅ·glœr′) *n*. A wandering minstrel of medieval England and France. [< L *joculator*]

jon·quil (jon′kwil, jong′-) *n*. A species of narcissus related to the daffodil, having fragrant, white or yellow flowers. [< F < L *juncus* a rush]

Jordan almond A large Spanish almond, frequently sugar-coated as a confection. [ME *jardyne almaunde*]

Jor·da·ni·an (jôr·dā′nē·ən) *adj.* Pertaining to Jordan or its people. —**Jor·da′ni·an** *n*.

josh (josh) *Slang v.t.* & *v.i.* To tease; banter. —*n*. A good-natured joke. [Blend of JOKE and BOSH] —**josh′er** *n*.

Josh·u·a (josh′o͞o·ə) *n*. A book of the Old Testament bearing the name of the Israelite leader Joshua. [< Hebrew *Yehōshua'* God is salvation]

joss (jos) *n*. A Chinese god. [Pidgin English < Pg. *deos* God]

joss stick A stick of perfumed paste burned as incense.

jos·tle (jos′əl) *v.t.* & *v.i.* **·tled, ·tling** To push roughly so as to shake up; elbow; shove. [Freq. of JOUST] —**jos′tle** *n*. —**jos′tler** *n*.

jot (jot) *v.t.* **jot·ted, jot·ting** To make a hasty and brief note of: usu. with *down*. —*n*. The least bit; iota. [< IOTA]

jot·ting (jot′ing) *n*. That which is jotted down; short note.

joule (jo͞ol, joul) *n*. *Physics* A unit of energy equal to 10,000,000 ergs. [after J. P. *Joule*, 1818–1889, English physicist]

jounce (jouns) *v.t.* & *v.i.* **jounced, jounc·ing** To bounce; jolt. —*n*. A shake; a bounce. [Origin unknown] —**jounc′y** *adj.*

jour·nal (jûr′nəl) *n*. 1. A diary or record of daily occurrences, as a ship's log, a bookkeeper's daybook, etc. 2. A newspaper, esp. one published daily. 3. Any periodical or magazine. [< L *diurnalis* daily]

jour·nal·ese (jûr′nəl·ēz′, -ēs′) *n*. The style of writing supposedly characteristic of newspapers, magazines, etc.: a derogatory term.

jour·nal·ism (jûr′nəl·iz′əm) *n*. The occupation, practice, and academic field concerned with writing, editing, and publishing or broadcasting news. —**jour′nal·ist** *n*. —**jour′·nal·is′tic** *adj.* —**jour′nal·is′ti·cal·ly** *adv.*

jour·ney (jûr′nē) *n*. 1. Travel from one place to another. 2. The distance traveled. —*v.i.* To make a trip; travel. [< OF *journee* a day's travel] —**jour′ney·er** *n*.

jour·ney·man (jûr′nē·mən) *n*. *pl.* **·men** (-mən) A worker who has completed his apprenticeship in a skilled trade.

joust (just, joust, jo͞ost) *n*. A combat between two mounted knights armed with lances, esp. as part of a tournament. —*v.i.* To engage in a joust. [< LL *juxtare* to approach] —**joust′er** *n*.

jo·vi·al (jō′vē·əl) *adj.* Good-natured; convivial; jolly. [< LL *Jovialis* born under the influence of Jupiter, ruler of the gods] —**jo′vi·al′i·ty** (-al′ə·tē) or **jo′vi·al·ty** *n*. —**jo′vi·al·ly** *adv.*

jowl[1] (joul, jōl) *n*. The fleshy part under the

lower jaw, esp. when fat or pendent. [ME *cholle* < OE *ceolu* throat]

jowl[2] (joul, jōl) *n.* 1. The jaw; esp., the lower jaw. 2. The cheek. [ME *chavel* < OE *ceafl*]

joy (joi) *n.* 1. A strong feeling of happiness; gladness; delight. 2. Anything that causes delight or gladness. [< L *gaudere* to rejoice] —**joy′less** *adj.* —**joy′less·ly** *adv.*

joy·ful (joi′fəl) *adj.* 1. Full of joy. 2. Showing or causing joy. —**joy′ful·ly** *adv.* —**joy′ful·ness** *n.*

joy·ous (joi′əs) *adj.* Joyful. —**joy′ous·ly** *adv.* —**joy′ous·ness** *n.*

joy ride *Informal* 1. A ride taken for pleasure. 2. A reckless ride in a stolen vehicle. —**joy rider** —**joy riding**

joy stick *Informal* The control stick of an airplane.

ju·bi·lant (jo͞o′bə·lənt) *adj.* Joyful or triumphant. [< L *jubilare* to exult] —**ju′bi·lance, ju′bi·lan·cy** *n.* —**ju′bi·lant·ly** *adv.*

ju·bi·la·tion (jo͞o′bə·lā′shən) *n.* Rejoicing; exultation. —**ju′bi·late** *v.t.* & *v.i.* **·lat·ed, ·lat·ing**

ju·bi·lee (jo͞o′bə·lē) *n.* 1. A special anniversary, esp. the 50th or 25th, of an event. 2. Any time of rejoicing. [< Hebrew *yōbēl* ram's horn, used to trumpet in a year of celebration, observed every 50 years, when slaves were freed, alienated lands returned, and fields left uncultivated]

Judaeo- See JUDEO-.

Judah (jo͞o′də) *n.* The tribe of Israel descended from Judah (*Gen.* xxix 35); also, their kingdom, geographically similar to Judea. [< Hebrew *Yehūdhāh* praised]

Ju·da·ic (jo͞o·dā′ik) *adj.* Of or pertaining to the Jews or Judaism. Also **Ju·da′i·cal.** [< L *Judaicus*]

Ju·da·ism (jo͞o′dē·iz′əm) *n.* The religious beliefs or practices of the Jews. —**Ju′da·is′tic** *adj.*

ju·das (jo͞o′dəs) *n.* *Often cap.* One who betrays another under the guise of friendship. [< *Judas*, disciple of Jesus who betrayed him]

Jude (jo͞od) *n.* A book of the New Testament by Jude, possibly a brother of Jesus.

Ju·de·a (jo͞o·dē′ə) The southern part of ancient Palestine under Persian, Greek, and Roman dominion: also **Ju·dae′a.** —**Ju·de′an, Ju·dae′an** *n.* & *adj.*

Judeo- *combining form* Jewish. Also spelled *Judaeo-*. [< L *Judaeus*]

judge (juj) *n.* 1. A public officer invested with the power to administer justice by hearing cases in a court of law. 2. One appointed to make decisions. 3. One who makes critical evaluations. 4. One appointed to rate contestants or entries, as in a horse show, essay contest, etc. —*v.* **judged, judg·ing** *v.t.* 1. To hear and decide the merits of (a case) or the guilt of (a person). 2. To decide authoritatively, as a contest. 3. To hold as judgment or opinion. 4. To form an opinion or judgment concerning. —*v.i.* 5. To act as a judge. [< L *judex, -icis* < *ius* right + *dicere* to speak]

Judg·es (juj′iz) *n.pl.* (*construed as sing.*) A book of the Old Testament, containing a history of the Jewish people.

judg·ment (juj′mənt) *n.* 1. The act of judging. 2. The decision or opinion reached through judging. 3. The ability to judge wisely. 4. *Law* **a** The sentence or decision. **b** A debt resulting from such a decision. Also **judge′ment.**

Judgment Day *Theol.* The day or time of the Last Judgment.

ju·di·ca·tor (jo͞o′də·kā′tər) *n.* One who acts as judge.

ju·di·ca·to·ry (jo͞o′də·kə·tôr′ē) *adj.* Pertaining to the administration of justice. —*n.* *pl.* **·ries** 1. Any tribunal. 2. The judicial process.

ju·di·ca·ture (jo͞o′də·kə·cho͝or) *n.* 1. The action or function of administering justice, as in courts of law. 2. The right, power, or authority of administering justice; jurisdiction. 3. A court of law; also, judges collectively.

ju·di·cial (jo͞o·dish′əl) *adj.* 1. Of or pertaining to the administering of justice, to courts of law, or to judges. 2. Decreed or enforced by a court of law. 3. Of or befitting a judge. [< L *judex, -icis* judge] —**ju·di′cial·ly** *adv.*

ju·di·ci·ar·y (jo͞o·dish′ē·er′ē, -dish′ə·rē) *adj.* Of or pertaining to courts, judges, or judgments. —*n.* *pl.* **·ar·ies** 1. The department of government that administers the law. 2. The system of courts set up to carry out this function. 3. The judges collectively.

ju·di·cious (jo͞o·dish′əs) *adj.* Having, showing, or exercising good judgment; prudent. [< L *judicium* judgment] —**ju·di′cious·ly** *adv.* —**ju·di′cious·ness** *n.*

Ju·dith (jo͞o′dith) *n.* A book in the Old Testament Apocrypha and the Douai Bible concerning a Jewish heroine, Judith, who rescued her people by slaying the Assyrian general, Holofernes. [< Hebrew *Jehūdhīth*]

ju·do (jo͞o′dō) *n.* A Japanese system of physical conditioning, based on jujitsu. [< Japanese *ju* gentle, pliant + *do* way of life]

jug (jug) *n.* 1. A pitcher or similar vessel for holding liquids. 2. *Slang* A prison or jail. —*v.t.* **jugged, jug·ging** 1. To put into a jug. 2. *Slang* To imprison; jail. [after *Jug*, a nickname for *Joan*]

ju·gate (jo͞o′git, -gāt) *adj.* 1. *Biol.* Occurring in pairs. 2. *Bot.* Having paired leaflets. [< L *jugare* to bind together]

jug·ger·naut (jug′ər·nôt) *n.* Any massive and irresistible destructive force. [< Skt. *jagannātha* lord of the universe; after an idol of the lord at Puri, India, annually drawn on a heavy cart under which devotees are said to have thrown themselves]

jug·gle (jug′əl) *v.* **·gled, ·gling** *v.t.* 1. To keep (two or more balls or other objects) continuously moving from the hand into the air. 2. To manipulate dishonestly. —*v.i.* 3. To perform as a juggler. —*n.* An act of juggling. [< L *joculari* to jest] —**jug′gler** *n.*

jug·gler·y (jug′lər·ē) *n.* *pl.* **·gler·ies** 1. The juggler's art. 2. Deception; fraud.

jug·u·lar (jug′yə·lər) *adj.* *Anat.* Of or pertaining to the throat or the jugular vein. —*n.* *Anat.* A jugular vein. [< L *jugulum* collar bone]

jugular vein *Anat.* One of the large veins on either side of the neck that returns blood from the brain, face, and neck.

juice (jo͞os) *n.* 1. The liquid part of a vegetable, fruit, or animal. 2. *Usually pl.* The fluids of the body. 3. *Slang* **a** Electricity. **b** Gasoline. **c** Alcoholic liquor. **d** Strength. [< L *jus* broth]

juic·er (jōō′sər) *n.* A device for extracting juice.
juic·y (jōō′sē) *adj.* **juic·i·er, juic·i·est** 1. Abounding with juice; moist. 2. Full of interest; spicy. —**juic′i·ly** *adv.* —**juic′i·ness** *n.*
ju·jit·su (jōō·jit′sōō) *n.* A Japanese system of hand-to-hand fighting in which surprise and a knowledge of anatomy and leverage are used: also spelled *jiujitsu, jiujutsu.* Also **ju·jut·su** (jōō·jit′sōō, -jōōt′sōō). [< Japanese *ju* pliant + *jutsu* art]
ju·jube (jōō′jōōb; *for def. 1, also* jōō′jōō·bē) *n.* 1. A gelatinous candy lozenge. 2. An Old World tree or shrub of the buckthorn family. [< F or < Med.L *jujuba*]
juke box (jōōk) A large automatic phonograph, usu. coin-operated and permitting selection of the records to be played.
juke joint *Slang* A roadhouse or barroom for drinking and dancing. [< Gullah *jook* disorderly, wicked]
ju·lep (jōō′lip) *n.* 1. A mint julep. 2. A sweetened, syrupy drink. [< Persian *gul* rose + *āb* water]
Jul·ian (jōōl′yən) *adj.* Of, pertaining to, or named after Julius Caesar.
ju·li·enne (jōō′lē·en′, *Fr.* zhü·lyen′) *adj.* Cut into thin strips. [< F]
Ju·ly (jōō·lī′, jōō-) *pl.* **·lys** The seventh month of the calendar year, having 31 days. [< L (*mensis*) *Julius* (month) of Julius Caesar]
jum·ble (jum′bəl) *v.* **·bled, ·bling** *v.t.* 1. To mix in a confused mass; put or throw together without order. —*v.i.* 2. To meet or unite confusedly. —*n.* A confused mixture or collection; hodgepodge. [Imit.]
jum·bo (jum′bō) *n. pl.* **·bos** A very large person, animal, or thing. —*adj.* Very large. [after *Jumbo*, an unusually large elephant exhibited by P. T. Barnum < ? W African]
jump (jump) *v.i.* 1. To spring from the ground, floor, etc., by using the foot and leg muscles; leap; bound. 2. To rise or move abruptly. 3. To pass suddenly, as if by leaping: to *jump* to a conclusion. 4. To start in astonishment. 5. To spring down from or out of a window, ladder, airplane, etc. 6. To skip or leap over something. —*v.t.* 7. To leap over or across. 8. To cause to leap over or across: to *jump* a horse. 9. To increase (prices, demands, etc.). 10. To pass over; skip; omit. 11. *Informal* To attack suddenly or by surprise. —**to jump at** To accept hastily. —**to jump bail** To forfeit one's bail bond by failing to appear when legally summoned. —**to jump off** *Mil.* To begin an attack. —**to jump on** (or **all over**) *Informal* To assail with abuse; scold. —**to jump the gun** *Slang* 1. To begin before the starting signal is given. 2. To start prematurely. —**to jump the track** Of a train, etc., to leave the rails. —*n.* 1. The act of jumping; a leap; spring; bound. 2. An abrupt movement upward or outward; a jerk. 3. A sudden rise or transition. 4. Something that is jumped over or across, as a hurdle. 5. A leap by parachute from an airplane. 6. In sports, a competition in jumping: broad *jump.* —**to get** (or **have**) **the jump on** *Slang* To get or have a head start on or an advantage over. [Cf. Scand. *gumpa* to jump]
jump·er[1] (jum′pər) *n.* 1. One who or that which jumps. 2. *Electr.* A short wire used to bypass or join parts of a circuit.
jum·per[2] (jum′pər) *n.* 1. A sleeveless dress, usu. worn over a blouse or sweater. 2. A loose jacket or smock worn over other clothes. [Prob. alter. of OF *juppe* jacket]
jump·ing bean (jump′ing) The seed of certain Mexican shrubs of the spurge family, which jumps about owing to the movements of a small larva inside.
jump·suit (jump′sōōt′) *n.* One-piece coveralls. Also **jump suit.** [after the garment worn by parachute jumpers]
jump·y (jum′pē) *adj.* **jump·i·er, jump·i·est** Given to startled movements; nervous. —**jump′i·ness** *n.*
jun·co (jung′kō) *n. pl.* **·cos** A North American finch having a slate-colored back and head and white underparts. [< L *juncus* rush]
junc·tion (jungk′shən) *n.* 1. The act of joining, or the state of being joined. 2. The place where lines or routes, as roads, railways, streams, etc., come together or cross.
junc·ture (jungk′chər) *n.* 1. The act of joining, or the state of being joined; junction. 2. A point or line of junction; a joint or seam. 3. A point in time; esp., a critical time. [< L *junctura* < *jungere* to join]
June (jōōn) The sixth month of the calendar year, having 30 days. [< OF *Juin* < L (*mensis*) *Junius* (month) of the Junii, a Roman family]
June bug A large, brightly colored beetle that flies in June. Also **June beetle.**
jun·gle (jung′gəl) *n.* 1. A dense tropical thicket of high grass, reeds, vines, brush, or trees, usu. inhabited by wild animals. 2. Any similar tangled growth. 3. A place of ruthless competition. [< Hind. *jangal* forest] —**jun′gly** *adj.*
jun·ior (jōōn′yər) *adj.* 1. Younger in years or lower in rank. 2. Denoting the younger of two. 3. Belonging to youth or earlier life. 4. Later in effect or tenure. 5. Pertaining to the third year of a high-school or collegiate course of four years. —*n.* 1. The younger of two. 2. One later or lower in service or standing. 3. A student in the third or junior year. Abbr. *jr., Jr.* [< L *junior*, compar. of *juvenis* young]
junior college A school giving college courses through the sophomore year.
junior high school A two- or three-year school intermediate between grammar school and high school.
ju·ni·per (jōō′nə·pər) *n.* 1. An evergreen pinaceous shrub of Europe and America. 2. The dark blue berry of this shrub, used as a flavoring. [< L *juniperus*]
junk[1] (jungk) *n.* 1. Castoff material, as scrap iron, old bottles, or paper. 2. *Informal* Rubbish; trash. 3. *Slang* Narcotics; dope. —*v.t.* *Informal* To discard as trash; scrap. [ME *jonke*]
junk[2] (jungk) *n.* A large Chinese sailing vessel with a high poop and prominent stem. [< Sp. and Pg. *junco* < Malay *djong* ship]
jun·ket (jung′kit) *n.* 1. A feast or pleasure trip. 2. A trip taken by a public official with all expenses paid from public funds. 3. A dessert made of curds or of sweetened milk and rennet. —*v.i.* 1. To have a feast;

banquet. 2. To go on a trip, esp. at public expense. [< L *juncus* rush] **—jun′ket·er** *n.*

junk·ie (jung′kē) *n. Slang* A drug addict. Also **junk′y.**

junk·man (jungk′man′) *n. pl.* **·men** (-men′) One who purchases, collects, and sells junk. Also **junk′deal′er** (-dē′lər).

Ju·no·esque (jōō′nō·esk′) *adj.* Stately and beautiful. [after *Juno,* in Roman mythology, the wife of Jupiter and queen of the gods]

jun·ta (jun′tə, *Sp.* hōōn′tä) *n.* 1. A Central or South American legislative council. 2. A group engaged in political intrigue; esp. military officers who take over a government. [< Sp. < L *jungere* to join]

Ju·pi·ter (jōō′pə·tər) *n.* The largest planet of the solar system, fifth in order from the sun. [after the Roman god *Jupiter,* ruler of all gods]

ju·rid·i·cal (jōō·rid′i·kəl) *adj.* Pertaining to the law and to the administration of justice. Also **ju·rid′ic.** [< L *juris* law + *dicere* to say, speak] **—ju·rid′i·cal·ly** *adv.*

ju·ris·dic·tion (jŏŏr′is·dik′shən) *n.* 1. Lawful right to exercise authority. 2. Those things over which such authority may be exercised. [< L *juris* law + *dicere* to say, speak] **—ju′ris·dic′tion·al** *adj.*

ju·ris·pru·dence (jŏŏr′is·prōōd′ns) *n.* 1. The philosophy or science of law. 2. A system of laws. [< L *juris* law + *prudentia* knowledge] **—ju′ris·pru·den′tial** (-prōō·den′shəl) *adj.*

ju·ris·pru·dent (jŏŏr′is·prōōd′nt) *adj.* Skilled in the law. **—***n.* One skilled in the law.

ju·rist (jŏŏr′ist) *n.* One versed in the law.

ju·ris·tic (jōō·ris′tik) *adj.* Of or pertaining to a jurist or the profession of law. Also **ju·ris′ti·cal. —ju·ris′ti·cal·ly** *adv.*

ju·ror (jŏŏr′ər) *n.* One who serves on a jury. [< L *jurare* to swear]

ju·ry[1] (jŏŏr′ē) *n. pl.* **·ries** 1. A body of persons summoned to serve on a judicial tribunal and give a verdict. 2. A committee of award in a competition. [< L *jurare* to swear]

ju·ry[2] (jŏŏr′ē) *adj. Naut.* Rigged up temporarily: a *jury* mast. [Prob. < OF *ajurie* aid < L *adjutare* to help]

ju·ry·man (jŏŏr′ē·mən) *n. pl.* **·men** (-mən) A juror.

just (just) *adj.* 1. Fair and impartial. 2. Upright; honest. 3. Legally valid; legitimate. 4. Merited; deserved. 5. True; correct; accurate. 6. Fitting; proper. **—***adv.* 1. To the exact point; precisely: *just* right. 2. Exactly now: He is *just* leaving. 3. A moment ago: He *just* left. 4. By very little; barely. 5. Only; merely. 6. *Informal* Really; very: It's *just* lovely. [< L *jus* law] **—just′ly** *adv.* **—just′ness** *n.*

jus·tice (jus′tis) *n.* 1. The quality of being just. 2. The rendering of what is due or merited; also, that which is due or merited. 3. Conformity to the law. 4. The administration of law. 5. A judge. 6. The abstract principle by which right and wrong are defined. **—to bring to justice** To arrest and try (a wrongdoer). **—to do justice to** To show appreciation of. [See JUST.]

justice of the peace A local magistrate of limited jurisdiction.

jus·ti·fi·a·ble (jus′tə·fī′ə·bəl) *adj.* Capable of being justified; defensible. **—jus′ti·fi′a·bil′i·ty** *n.* **—jus′ti·fi′a·bly** *adv.*

jus·ti·fi·ca·tion (jus′tə·fə·kā′shən) *n.* 1. The act of justifying, or the state of being justified. 2. The ground of justifying, or that which justifies.

jus·ti·fy (jus′tə·fī) *v.* **·fied, ·fy·ing** *v.t.* 1. To show to be just, right, or reasonable; vindicate. 2. To absolve. 3. To provide adequate grounds for; warrant. 4. *Printing* To adjust (lines) to the proper length by spacing. **—***v.i.* 5. *Printing* To be properly spaced; fit. [< L *justus* just + *facere* to make] **—jus′ti·fi′er** *n.*

jut (jut) *v.i.* **jut·ted, jut·ting** To extend beyond the main portion; protrude: often with *out.* **—***n.* Anything that juts; a projection. [Var. of JET[2]]

jute (jōōt) *n.* 1. A tall annual Asian herb of the linden family. 2. The tough fiber obtained from this plant, used for bags, cordage, etc. [< Skt. *jūta* braid of hair]

Jute (jōōt) *n.* A member of a Germanic tribe, some of whom invaded Britain in the fifth century. [< LL *Jutae* the Jutes] **—Jut·ish** (jōō′tish) *adj.*

ju·ve·nes·cent (jōō′və·nes′ənt) *adj.* 1. Becoming young; growing young again. 2. Making young; rejuvenating. [< L *juvenescere* to grow younger] **—ju′ve·nes′cence** *n.*

ju·ve·nile (jōō′və·nəl, -nīl) *adj.* 1. Young; youthful; also, immature. 2. Designed for young persons. **—***n.* 1. A young person. 2. An actor of youthful roles. [< L *juvenis* young person]

juvenile delinquent One who is guilty of antisocial behavior or of violations of the law but is too young to be punished as an adult criminal. **—juvenile delinquency**

ju·ve·nil·i·a (jōō′və·nil′ē·ə) *n.pl.* Works produced in youth, esp. writings or paintings.

jux·ta·pose (juks′tə·pōz′) *v.t.* **·posed, ·pos·ing** To place together; put side by side. [< L *juxta* near + F *poser* to place] **—jux′ta·po·si′tion** (-pə·zish′ən) *n.*

K

k, K (kā) *n. pl.* **k's** or **ks, K's** or **Ks, kays** (kāz) 1. The eleventh letter of the English alphabet. 2. The sound represented by the letter *k*. —*symbol Chem.* Potassium (K for *kalium*).

ka·bu·ki (kä·bo͞o′kē) *n.* A form of Japanese play on popular or comic themes, employing elaborate costume, stylized gesture, music, and dancing. [< Japanese]

Kad·dish (kä′dish) *n.* In Judaism, a prayer recited by mourners and part of the daily service. [< Aramaic, holy]

kaf·fee·klatsch (kôf′ē·kläch′, *Ger.* käf′ä·kläch′) *n. Sometimes cap.* An informal conversational gathering where coffee is drunk. [< G < *kaffee* coffee + *klatsch* chitchat]

kaf·fir (kaf′ər) *n.* A variety of sorghum grown in dry regions. Also **kaffir corn** [after *Kaffir*]

Kaf·fir (kaf′ər) *n.* A member of a group of South African Bantu tribes: usu. a derogatory term. Also **Kaf′ir.** [< Arabic *kāfir* unbeliever]

kai·ser (kī′zər) *n.* Emperor. [< G < L *Caesar* Caesar]

Kai·ser (kī′zər) Title of the emperors of the Holy Roman Empire, 962–1806; the Austrian emperors, 1804–1918; and the German emperors, 1871–1918.

kale (kāl) *n.* A variety of headless cabbage. [Var. of COLE]

ka·lei·do·scope (kə·lī′də·skōp) *n.* 1. A tube-shaped optical toy that shows constantly changing symmetrical patterns as loose bits of colored glass are moved about under a set of mirrors. 2. A swiftly changing scene, pattern, etc. [< Gk. *kalos* beautiful + *eidos* form + -SCOPE] —**ka·lei′do·scop′ic** (-skop′ik) *adj.*

kan·ga·roo (kang′gə·ro͞o′) *n. pl.* **·roos** A herbivorous marsupial of Australia and Tasmania, having short, weak forelimbs, a stout tail, and powerful hind limbs adapted for leaping. [< Austral.]

kangaroo court An unauthorized court in which the law is disregarded or willfully misinterpreted.

kangaroo rat A pouched rodent of the SW U.S. and Mexico having elongated hind limbs and tail.

ka·o·lin (kā′ə·lin) *n.* A claylike hydrous aluminum silicate used in making porcelain. Also **ka′o·line** (-lin). [< Chinese *Kao-ling,* mountain where first mined]

ka·pok (kā′pok) *n.* A cottony or silky fiber covering the seeds of the tropical **kapok tree.** [< Malay *kāpoq*]

kap·pa (kap′ə) *n.* The tenth letter in the Greek alphabet (Κ, κ), corresponding to the English *k*.

ka·put (kä·po͝ot′) *adj. Slang* Ruined; done for. [< G]

kar·a·kul (kar′ə·kəl) *n.* 1. A breed of sheep raised in the Soviet Union, Iran, Iraq, etc. 2. The black or gray, loosely curled fur made from the pelt of the karakul lamb. [after *Kara Kul,* a lake in Bukhara]

kar·at (kar′ət) *n.* 1. The twenty-fourth part by weight of gold in an article: 18-*karat* gold has 18/24 or 3/4 gold by weight. 2. Loosely, a carat. [Var. of CARAT]

ka·ra·te (kä·rä′tā, -tē) *n.* An Oriental method of hand-to-hand combat utilizing a variety of sudden, forceful blows. [< Japanese]

kar·ma (kär′mə) *n.* 1. *Hinduism & Buddhism* The spiritual force generated by one's actions, which determines one's reincarnated situation. 2. Loosely, fate. 3. Vibration (def. 3).

kart (kärt) *n.* A miniature low-powered racing car. —*v.i.* To race in karts. [< *Go-Kart,* a trade name] —**kart′ing** *n.*

karyo- *combining form Biol.* Nucleus: also spelled **caryo-.** Also, before vowels, **kary-.** [< Gk. *karyon* nut]

Kash·mi·ri (kash·mir′ē) *n.* The Indic language of the Kashmirians.

Kash·mi·ri·an (kash·mir′ē·ən) *adj.* Of or pertaining to Kashmir or its people. —*n.* A native of Kashmir.

kata- See CATA-.

ka·ty·did (kā′tē·did) *n.* A green, arboreal insect allied to the grasshoppers and crickets. [Imit., from sound produced by the males]

kau·ri (kou′rē) *n.* 1. A large timber tree of New Zealand. 2. Its wood. 3. Kauri gum. Also **kau′ry.** [< Maori]

kauri gum A resinous exudation of the kauri tree, used in varnishes, for linoleum, etc. Also **kauri copal, kauri resin.**

kay·ak (kī′ak) *n.* The hunting canoe of arctic America, made of seal skins stretched over a frame, with a hole amidships where the user sits. [< Eskimo]

kay·o ((kā′ō) *Slang v.t.* **kay·oed, kay·o·ing** In boxing, to knock out. —*n.* In boxing, a knockout. Also *KO, K.O., k.o.* [< K(NOCK) O(UT)]

ka·zoo (kə·zo͞o′) *n.* A toy instrument, an open tube with a top hole fitted with a membrane that vibrates when one hums into the tube. [? Imit.]

kedge (kej) *n. Naut.* A light anchor used in warping, freeing a vessel from shoals, etc.: also **kedge anchor.** [Origin uncertain]

keel (kēl) *n.* 1. *Naut.* The main structural member of a vessel, running fore and aft along the bottom, to which all the crosswise members are solidly fixed; the backbone of a ship. 2. Any part or object resembling a keel in shape or function. 3. *Biol.* A longitudinal ridge or process, as of the breastbone of a fowl. —**on an even keel** In equilibrium; steady. —**to keel over** 1. To turn bottom up; capsize. 2. To fall over, as in a faint or from an injury. [< ON *kjölr* or OHG *kiol*]

keel·haul (kēl′hôl′) *v.t.* 1. *Naut.* To haul (a man) under the keel of a ship as punishment. 2. To reprove severely; castigate. [< Du. *kielhalen*]

keel·son (kēl′sən) *n. Naut.* A beam running above the keel of a ship.

keen[1] (kēn) *adj.* 1. Able to cut or penetrate readily; very sharp. 2. Acute or refined, as in intelligence or perception. 3. Eager; enthusiastic. 4. Of senses or sense organs, acute; sensitive. 5. Having a piercing, intense quality or impact. 6. Fond of: with *about, for,* or *on.* 7. *Slang* Fine; excellent. [OE *cēne*] —**keen′ly** *adv.*

keen[2] (kēn) *n.* A wailing lamentation for the dead. —*v.i.* To wail loudly over the dead. [< Irish *caoinim* I wail] —**keen′er** *n.*

keep (kēp) *v.* **kept, keep·ing** *v.t.* 1. To retain possession or control of; avoid releasing or giving away: to *keep* one's earnings. 2. To hold or continue to hold in some specified state, relation, place, etc.: *Keep* the car in repair. 3. To store, hold, or confine in a regular place. 4. To maintain. 5. To be faithful to or abide by (a promise, vow, etc.). 6. To care for; tend. 7. To detain. 8. To prevent: with *from.* 9. To observe, as with rites or ceremony: to *keep* the Sabbath. 10. To write down and preserve in good order: to *keep* a diary. 11. To maintain for use or employ for service. —*v.i.* 12. To persist in; continue: often with *on.* 13. To remain; stay: *Keep* away. 14. To stay in good condition. 15. To remain good for a later time: The news will *keep.* —**to keep back** 1. To restrain. 2. To withhold. —**to keep to oneself** 1. To remain solitary. 2. To avoid revealing. —**to keep track of** (or **tabs on**) To continue to be informed about. —**to keep up** 1. To hold the pace. 2. To maintain in good condition. 3. To continue. 4. To cause to stay awake or out of bed. —**to keep up with** To stay abreast of. —*n.* 1. Means of subsistence: to earn one's *keep.* 2. Guard or custody. 3. The donjon or strongest building of a castle; also, a castle or fortress. —**for keeps** 1. Very seriously. 2. Permanently. [OE *cēpan* to observe]

keep·er (kē′pər) *n.* 1. One who keeps or guards. 2. One in charge of (a specified place, thing, etc.): used in combination: *gatekeeper.*

keep·ing (kē′ping) *n.* 1. The act of one who keeps. 2. Custody, charge, or possession. 3. Maintenance; support. —**in keeping** (**with**) In accordance (with).

keep·sake (kēp′sāk′) *n.* Anything kept, or given to be kept, for the sake of the giver; a memento.

keg (keg) *n.* A small, strong barrel. [ME *cag,* prob. < ON *kaggi*]

kelp (kelp) *n.* 1. Any of various large, coarse, brown algae; esp., the **giant kelp,** found mainly on the Pacific coast. 2. The ashes of such algae, a source of iodine. [ME *culp*]

kel·pie (kel′pē) *n. Scot.* A water sprite in the form of a horse, supposed to be an omen of drowning. Also **kel′py.**

Kelt (kelt), **Kelt·ic** (kel′tik) See CELT, CELTIC.

Kel·vin scale (kel′vin) *Physics* The absolute scale of temperature, in which zero is equal to −273° Celsius or −459.4° Fahrenheit. [after William Thompson, 1824–1907, Lord *Kelvin,* English physicist]

ken (ken) *v.t. & v.i.* **kenned** or **kent, ken·ning** 1. *Scot.* To know. 2. *Archaic* To see. —*n.* Range of sight or knowledge. [OE *cennan,* infl. by ON *kenna*]

ken·nel (ken′əl) *n.* 1. A house for a dog or for a pack of hounds. 2. *Often pl.* An establishment where dogs are bred, sold, trained, etc. 3. A pack of hounds. —*v.t.* **ken·neled** or **·nelled, ken·nel·ing** or **·nel·ling** To keep or confine in or as in a kennel. [< MF *chenil* < L *canis* dog]

ke·no (kē′nō) *n.* A game resembling bingo. [< F *quine* five winning numbers]

kep·i (kep′ē) *n.* A flat-topped military cap with a visor. [< F < dial. G käppi]

Ke·pone (kē′pōn) *n.* A chlorinated hydrocarbon, used as a pesticide: a trade name.

kept (kept) Past tense and past participle of KEEP.

ker·a·tin (ker′ə·tin) *n. Biochem.* An albuminous compound that forms the essential ingredient of horny tissue, as of horns, claws, and nails. —**ke·rat·i·nous** (kə·rat′ə·nəs) *adj.* [< Gk. *keras, -atos* horn]

ker·a·ti·tis (ker′ə·tī′tis) *n. Pathol.* Inflammation of the cornea.

kerb (kûrb) *n. Brit.* Curb (def. 2).

ker·chief (kûr′chif, chēf) *n. pl.* **·chiefs** or **·chieves** (-chēvz) A square of fabric used to cover the head or neck, or as a handkerchief. [< OF *couvrechef* head covering]

ker·mes (kûr′mēz) *n.* The dried bodies of the females of a scale insect, used as a red dyestuff. [< Arabic *qirmiz*]

ker·mis (kûr′mis) *n.* In Flanders, etc., a periodical outdoor festival: also **ker′mess** (-mis). [< Du. *kerk* church + *miss* mass]

ker·nel (kûr′nəl) *n.* 1. The entire contents of a seed or grain within its coating. 2. The edible part of a nut. 3. The central part of anything. [OE *cyrnel,* dim. of *corn* seed]

ker·o·sene (ker′ə·sēn, ker′ə·sēn′) *n.* A mixture of hydrocarbons distilled from crude petroleum and used in lamps, stoves, and some engines: also called *coal oil.* Also **ker·o·sine** (ker′ə·sēn, ker′ə·sēn′). [< Gk. *kēros* wax + -ENE]

ker·sey (kûr′zē) *n.* A coarse, ribbed, closely napped woolen cloth. [after *Kersey,* England]

kes·trel (kes′trəl) *n.* A small European falcon. [< OF *cresserelle*]

ketch (kech) *n.* A fore-and-aft rigged, two-masted vessel similar to a yawl but having the mizzen or jiggermast forward of the rudder post. [ME *cache,* prob. < CATCH, v., because used as a pursuit vessel]

ketch·up (kech′əp) *n.* A spicy sauce or condiment, usu. made of tomatoes: also spelled *catchup, catsup.* [< Malay *kēchap,* ? ult. < Chinese *ke-tsiap* brine of pickled fish]

ke·tone (kē′tōn) *n. Chem.* One of a class of organic compounds in which the carbonyl radical is attached to two carbon atoms. [< G, var. of F *acétone* acetone] —**ke·ton·ic** (ki·ton′ik) *adj.*

ket·tle (ket′l) *n.* 1. A metallic vessel for boiling or stewing. 2. A teakettle. [< L *catillus,* dim. of *catinus* a deep vessel]

ket·tle·drum (ket′l·drum′) *n.* A large drum

having a brass hemispherical shell and a parchment head that can be tuned through a small range of definite pitches.

key[1] (kē) *n. pl.* **keys** 1. An instrument for moving the bolt or tumblers of a lock in order to lock or unlock. 2. An instrument for holding and turning a screw, valve, or the like. 3. Anything serving to disclose, open, or solve something. 4. A gloss, table, or group of notes interpreting certain symbols, ciphers, problems, etc. 5. Any one of the finger levers in typewriters, computers, etc. 6. *Telecom.* A circuit breaker or opener operated by the fingers, as in a telegraph apparatus. 7. *Music* **a** In musical instruments, a lever to be pressed by the finger or thumb. **b** A system of tones in which all the tones bear a definite relationship to some specific tone (the keynote or tonic): the *key* of C. 8. The tone or pitch of the voice. 9. Level of intensity of expression or emotion. 10. *Mech.* A wedge, cotter pin, etc., used to secure various parts. —*v.t.* **keyed, key·ing** 1. To fasten with or as with a key. 2. To provide with a key or keys. 3. To provide with a cross-reference or a system of cross-references. 4. *Music* To regulate the pitch or tone of. 5. To regulate for a particular audience or in accord with a particular idea. —**to key up** To cause excitement, expectancy, etc., in. —*adj.* Of chief and decisive importance. [OE *cæg*]

key[2] (kē) *n. pl.* **keys** A low island, esp. one of coral, along a coast; cay. [< Taino, islet]

key[3] (kē) *Slang* A kilogram of an illicit drug. [Phonetic shortening of KILOGRAM]

key·board (kē′bôrd′) *n.* 1. A row of keys, as in a piano. 2. A group of keys for operating a machine, as a typewriter, a computer, etc. —*v.t.* To feed (data) into a computer by use of a keyboard. —**key′board′er** *n.*

key·hole (kē′hōl′) *n.* A hole for a key.

key·note (kē′nōt′) *n.* 1. The basic idea or principle of a political platform, literary work, etc. 2. *Music* The tonic of a key, from which it is named: also **key tone.** —*v.t.* **·not·ed, ·not·ing** 1. To sound the keynote of. 2. To deliver the keynote address of. —**key′not′er** *n.*

keynote address An opening address, esp. at a political convention, presenting basic issues and partisan principles. Also **keynote speech.**

key·punch (kē′punch′) *n.* A keyboard machine for punching holes in cards used in electronic data processing. —**key′punch′** *v.t.* —**key′punch′er** *n.*

key signature *Music* The sharps or flats following the clef sign at the beginning of each staff.

key·stone (kē′stōn′) *n.* 1. *Archit.* The uppermost and last-set stone of an arch. 2. The fundamental element, as of a science.

khak·i (kak′ē, kä′kē) *n. pl.* **khak·is** 1. A color ranging from light sand to medium brown. 2. A stout cotton cloth of this color. 3. *pl.* Trousers or a uniform made of khaki. —*adj.* Of the color khaki. [< Persian *khāk* dust]

khan (kän, kan) *n.* 1. The title of the imperial successors to the Mongol conqueror Genghis Khan. 2. A title for rulers, officials, or dignitaries in Central Asia, Iran, etc. [< Turkic *khān* lord, prince] —**khan′ate** (-āt) *n.*

kib·butz (ki·bo͞ots′) *n. pl.* **·but·zim** (-bo͞ot·sēm′) A cooperative or collective farm in Israel. [< Hebrew, gathering]

kib·itz (kib′its) *v.i. Informal* To act as a kibitzer. [Back formation < KIBITZER]

kib·itz·er (kib′it·sər) *n. Informal* One who meddles in the affairs of others; esp., a spectator who gives gratuitous advice to card players. [< Yiddish < G *kiebitzen* to look on]

kick (kik) *v.i.* 1. To strike out with the foot or feet. 2. Of firearms, to recoil. 3. In football, to kick the ball. 4. *Informal* To object or complain. —*v.t.* 5. To strike with the foot. 6. To drive or impel by striking with the foot. 7. In football, to score (a point or field goal) by kicking the ball. —**to kick around** *Informal* 1. To abuse; neglect. 2. To roam from place to place. 3. To give thought to; discuss. —**to kick back** *Slang* To pay back (part of a salary, fee, etc.) to someone, usu. as a bribe. —**to kick in** *Informal* To contribute or participate by contributing. —**to kick off** 1. In football, to put the ball in play by kicking it toward the opposing team. 2. *Slang* To die. —**to kick out** *U.S. Informal* To eject suddenly, as with a kick. —**to kick the bucket** *Slang* To die. —**to kick up** *Slang* To make or stir up (trouble, confusion, etc.). —*n.* 1. A blow or thrust with the foot. 2. *Informal* An objection or complaint. 3. *Slang* Power; force. 4. *Slang* A thrill. 5. The recoil of a firearm. 6. In football, a kicking of the ball. [ME *kike*] —**kick′er** *n.*

kick·back (kik′bak′) *n.* 1. *Informal* A recoil; repercussion. 2. *Slang* A paying back of part of a fee, etc.; also, the money so paid.

kick·off (kik′ôf′) *n.* 1. In football, the kick with which play is begun. 2. Any beginning.

kick·y (kik′ē) *adj.* **kick·i·er, kick·i·est** *Slang* Providing thrills; exciting.

kid (kid) *n.* 1. A young goat. 2. Kidskin. 3. The meat of a young goat. 4. *Informal* A child; youngster. —*adj.* 1. Made of kid. 2. *Informal* Younger: my *kid* brother. —*v.t. & v.i.* **kid·ded, kid·ding** *Slang* 1. To make fun of (someone); to tease. 2. To deceive or try to deceive (someone); fool. [ME *kide* < ON *kith*] —**kid′der** *n.*

kid·dy (kid′ē) *n. pl.* **·dies** *Slang* A small child. Also **kid′die.**

kid·nap (kid′nap) *v.t.* **·naped** or **·napped, ·nap·ing** or **·nap·ping** To seize and carry off (someone) by force or fraud, usu. so as to demand a ransom. [< KID (def. 4) + *nap*, dial. var. of NAB] —**kid′nap·er** or **kid′nap·per** *n.*

kid·ney (kid′nē) *n. pl.* **·neys** 1. *Anat.* Either of two glandular organs situated at the back of the abdominal cavity, serving to separate waste products from the blood and to excrete them as urine. ◆Collateral adjective: *renal.* 2. The meat of the kidney of certain animals, used as food. 3. Temperament, nature, or type. [Origin unknown]

kidney bean 1. A kidney-shaped bean. 2. The bean of the scarlet runner.

kidney stone *Pathol.* A hard mineral concretion formed in the kidney.

kid·skin (kid′skin′) *n.* 1. Leather tanned from the skin of a young goat, used for gloves, shoes, etc. 2. *pl.* Gloves, etc., made of kidskin.

kiel·ba·sa (kel·bäs′ə, kil-) *n. pl.* **·ba·sas** or **·ba·sy** A smoked sausage. [< Polish]

kill[1] (kil) *v.t.* 1. To cause the death of. 2. To bring to an end; destroy. 3. *Slang* To overwhelm, as with laughter, exhaustion, etc. 4. To destroy the active qualities of; neutralize. 5. To cancel by contrast, as a color. 6. To cancel or delete. 7. To turn off or stop, as a motor. 8. To pass (time) aimlessly. 9. To veto or quash (legislation). —*v.i.* 10. To cause death. 11. To murder; slay. —*n.* 1. The act of killing, esp. in hunting. 2. An animal or animals killed as prey. [ME *cullen, killen*] —**kill′er** *n.*

kill[2] (kil) *n.* A creek, stream, or channel: an element in geographical names. [< MDu. *kille*]

kill·deer (kil′dir) *n.* *pl.* **·deers** or **·deer** A North American wading bird of the plover family. Also **kill′dee** (-dē). [Imit., from its cry]

killer whale A voracious whale related to the dolphins.

kill·ing (kil′ing) *n.* 1. Homicide. 2. The act of one who or that which kills. —**to make a killing** To get or win a large amount of money. —*adj.* 1. Used to kill. 2. Likely to kill. 3. Resulting in death; fatal. 4. *Informal* a Extremely funny; hilarious. b Exhausting; destructive.

kill-joy (kil′joi′) *n.* One who spoils pleasure for others.

kiln (kil, kiln) *n.* An oven or furnace for baking, burning, or drying bricks, pottery, etc. [OE < L *culina* kitchen]

kil·o (kil′ō, kē′lō) *n.* *pl.* **kil·os** 1. A kilogram. 2. A kilometer.

kilo- *prefix* In the metric system, a thousand times (a specified unit): *kilogram.* [< Gk. *chilioi* a thousand]

kil·o·cy·cle (kil′ə·sī′kəl) *n.* Kilohertz.

kil·o·gram (kil′ə·gram) *n.* In the metric system, a thousand grams. Also *Brit.* **kil′o·gramme.**

kil·o·hertz (kil′ə·hûrtz) *n.* *pl.* **·hertz** A unit of frequency equal to one thousand hertz.

kil·o·li·ter (kil′ə·lē′tər) *n.* In the metric system, a thousand liters. Also *Brit.* **kil′o·li′tre.**

ki·lo·me·ter (ki·lom′ə·tər, kil′ə·mē′tər) *n.* In the metric system, a thousand meters. Also *Brit.* **ki·lo′me·tre.** —**kil·o·met·ric** (kil′ə·met′rik) or **·ri·cal** *adj.*

kil·o·watt (kil′ə·wät) *n.* *Electr.* A unit of power equal to 1,000 watts.

kil·o·watt-hour (kil′ə·wät·our′) *n.* The work done or the energy resulting from one kilowatt acting for one hour.

kilt (kilt) *n.* A short pleated skirt worn by Scottish Highland men and Irishmen. [ME; prob. < Scand.]

kil·ter (kil′tər) *n.* *Informal* Proper or working order: now only in the phrase **out of kilter,** out of order. [Origin uncertain]

ki·mo·no (kə·mō′nə, ki·mō′nō) *n.* *pl.* **·nos** 1. A loose robe fastened with a wide sash, worn in Japan as an outer garment. 2. Any similar robe. [< Japanese]

kin (kin) *n.* One's relatives, collectively. —**next of kin** In law, one's nearest relative or relatives. —*adj.* 1. Related by blood. 2. Similar; kindred. [OE *cyn*]

-kin *suffix* Little; small: *lambkin.* [< MDu. *-kijn, -ken*]

ki·na (kē′nä) *n.* The monetary unit of Papua, New Guinea.

kind[1] (kīnd) *adj.* Gentle and considerate; goodhearted. [OE *gecynde*]

kind[2] (kīnd) *n.* 1. A class or grouping; type. 2. The distinguishing character of something. —**in kind** 1. With a thing of the same sort. 2. In produce instead of money. —**kind of** *Informal* In a way; somewhat. —**of a kind** Inferior in quality. [OE *gecynd*]

kin·der·gar·ten (kin′dər·gär′tən) *n.* A school or class for young children, usu. from the ages of four to six. [< G]

kind·heart·ed (kīnd′här′tid) *adj.* Having or showing a kind nature. —**kind′heart′ed·ly** *adv.* —**kind′heart′ed·ness** *n.*

kin·dle (kin′dəl) *v.* **·dled, ·dling** *v.t.* 1. To cause to burn; ignite. 2. To excite, as the feelings. —*v.i.* 3. To take fire. 4. To become excited or inflamed. [ME < ON *kynda*] —**kin′dler** *n.*

kin·dling (kind′ling) *n.* Sticks, wood chips, etc., with which a fire is started.

kind·ly (kīnd′lē) *adj.* **·li·er, ·li·est** 1. Having or showing kindness; sympathetic. 2. Having a favorable effect. —*adv.* In a kind manner; good-naturedly. —**to take kindly to** To like. —**kind′li·ness** *n.*

kind·ness (kīnd′nis) *n.* 1. The quality of being kind. 2. A kind act or service; a favor.

kin·dred (kin′drid) *adj.* 1. Related by blood; akin. 2. Alike; similar. —*n.* One's relatives. [ME < OE *cynn* kin + *rǣden* condition]

kine (kīn) *n.* *Archaic* Cattle: plural of cow[1].

kin·e·mat·ics (kin′ə·mat′iks) *n.pl.* (*construed as sing.*) The branch of physics treating motion without reference to particular forces or bodies. [< Gk. *kineein* to move] —**kin′e·mat′ic** or **·i·cal** *adj.* —**kin′e·mat′i·cal·ly** *adv.*

kin·e·scope (kin′ə·skōp) *n.* 1. The cathode-ray tube of a television set, which reproduces the image recorded by the television camera: also called *picture tube.* 2. A film of a television program made from a kinescope.

kinesi- *combining form* A movement. [< Gk. *kinēsis* motion]

-kinesis *combining form* A movement; motion. [< Gk. *kinēsis* motion]

kin·es·the·si·a (kin′is·thē′zhə) *n.* *Physiol.* The perception of muscular movement, tension, etc., via afferent nerves in the muscles, skin, joints, and tendons. Also **kin′es·the′sis** (-thē′sis). [< Gk. *kineein* to move + *aisthēsis* perception] —**kin′es·thet′ic** (-thet′·ik) *adj.*

ki·net·ic (ki·net′ik) *adj.* 1. Of or pertaining to motion. 2. Producing or caused by motion: *kinetic* energy. [< Gk. *kineein* to move]

ki·ne·tics (ki·net′iks) *n.pl.* (*construed as sing.*) The branch of physics dealing with the effect of forces in the production or modification of motion in bodies.

kin·folk (kin′fōk′) *n.pl.* *Informal* Kinsfolk. Also **kin′folks′.**

king (king) *n.* 1. The sovereign male ruler of a kingdom; monarch. ◆Collateral adjective: *regal.* 2. One who is preeminent: a cattle *king.* 3. A playing card bearing the likeness of a king. 4. In chess, the principal piece, whose defense is essential. 5. In checkers, a piece that, having reached the opponent's last rank of squares, may move in any direction. [OE *cyng, cyning*]

king·bird (king′bûrd′) *n.* Any of various North American flycatchers.
king·bolt (king′bōlt′) *n.* A vertical central bolt usu. attaching the body of a wagon or similar vehicle to the fore axle, and serving as a pivot in turning: also called *kingpin.*
king crab 1. The horseshoe crab. 2. Any of a genus of usu. large crablike crustaceans common in the north Pacific, with a small, triangular body and very long legs.
king·dom (king′dəm) *n.* 1. The territory or people ruled by a king or a queen; monarchy. 2. Any area thought of as a sovereign domain. 3. Any of the three primary divisions of natural objects known as the *animal, vegetable,* and *mineral kingdoms.* [OE *cyningdom*]
king·fish (king′fish′) *n. pl.* **·fish** or **·fish·es** Any of various American food fishes.
king·fish·er (king′fish′ər) *n.* Any of several large, crested birds that feed on fish.
King James Bible An English translation of the Bible from Hebrew and Greek, proposed by James I and completed in 1611.
king·let (king′lit) *n.* Any of several small birds resembling the warblers.
king·ly (king′lē) *adj.* **·li·er, ·li·est** Of or worthy of a king; regal. —*adv.* In a kingly way. —**king′li·ness** *n.*
king·pin (king′pin′) *n.* 1. In bowling, the foremost pin. 2. In ninepins, the center pin. 3. A kingbolt. 4. *Informal* A person of central importance.
Kings (kingz) *n.pl.* (*construed as sing.*) 1. Either of two Old Testament books, I Kings and II Kings, recounting the histories of the Hebrew kings after David, the second king of Judah and Israel. 2. In the Douai version of the Old Testament, a group of four books, comprising I Samuel, II Samuel, I Kings, and II Kings.
king's English Standard English: also called *queen's English.*
king·ship (king′ship) *n.* 1. The state, power, office, or dignity of a king. 2. The monarchical type of government.
king-size (king′sīz′) *adj. Informal* Greater in size than is usual. Also **king′sized′.**
king snake A large, harmless snake of the southern U.S. that feeds on rats and mice.
kink (kingk) *n.* 1. An abrupt bend, curl, loop, or tangle in a line, wire, hair, etc. 2. A mental quirk. 3. A bizarre practice or preference, esp. sexual. 4. A painful muscular spasm; crick. —*v.i. & v.t.* To form or cause to form a kink. [< Du., twist, curl]
kink·a·jou (king′kə·jo͞o) *n.* An arboreal, carnivorous mammal of Central and South America, having large eyes, soft woolly fur, and a long tail. [< F *quincajou* < Tupi]
kink·y (kingk′ē) *adj.* **kink·i·er, kink·i·est** 1. Kinked; frizzy. 2. *Slang* Bizarre; eccentric. —**kink′i·ness** *n.*
kins·folk (kinz′fōk′) *n.pl.* One's relatives: also, *Informal, kinfolk.*
kin·ship (kin′ship) *n.* Relationship, esp. by blood.
kins·man (kinz′mən) *n. pl.* **·men** (-mən) A male blood relation. —**kins′wom′an** (-wo͝om′ən) *n.fem.*
ki·osk (kē·osk′, kē′osk, kī′-) *n.* A small, roofed structure, used as a booth, newsstand, etc. [< Persian *kūshk* palace]
kip¹ (kip) *n.* The untanned skin of a young or small animal. Also **kip′skin′** (-skin′). [ME < Du.]
kip² (kip) *n. pl.* **kip** The monetary unit of Laos.
kip·per (kip′ər) *n.* 1. A salmon or herring cured by kippering. 2. The male salmon during the spawning season. —*v.t.* To cure (fish) by splitting, salting, and drying or smoking. [? OE *cypera* spawning salmon]
kirk (kûrk) *n. Scot. & Brit. Dial.* A church.
kir·mess (kûr′mis) See KERMIS.
kir·tle (kûrt′l) *n. Archaic* A woman's skirt or gown. [OE < L *curtus* short]
kis·met (kiz′met, kis′-) *n.* Appointed lot; fate. [< Arabic *qasama* to divide]
kiss (kis) *v.t. & v.i.* 1. To touch with the lips as a sign of greeting, love, etc. 2. To meet or touch lightly. [OE *cyssan*] —**kiss** *n.*
kiss·er (kis′ər) *n.* 1. One who kisses. 2. *Slang* The mouth or the face.
kit (kit) *n.* 1. A collection of articles, tools, etc., for a special purpose. 2. A set of parts, etc., from which something is to be made. 3. One's effects or outfit, esp. for traveling. 4. A bag, knapsack, etc. [ME < MDu. *kitte* jug, vessel]
kitch·en (kich′ən) *n.* A room equipped for cooking. [OE *cycene,* ult. < L *coquere* to cook]
kitch·en·ette (kich′ən·et′) *n.* A small, compactly arranged kitchen. Also **kitch′·en·et′.**
kitchen police *Mil.* Enlisted men detailed as kitchen help; also, such duty. Abbr. *K.P.*
kitch·en·ware (kich′ən·wâr′) *n.* Kitchen utensils.
kite (kīt) *n.* 1. A light frame, covered with paper, fabric, etc., to be flown in the wind at the end of a string. 2. A long-winged bird of the hawk family. 3. In commerce, any negotiable paper not representing a genuine transaction, employed to obtain money, credit, etc. —*v.t. & v.i.* **kit·ed, kit·ing** 1. To fly, as a kite. 2. In commerce, to issue or pass (a kite). [OE *cȳta*]
kith (kith) *n. Archaic* One's friends, acquaintances, or associates: now only in **kith and kin.** [OE *cūth* known]
kitsch (kich) *n.* Art or literary works, etc., having broad popular appeal and little esthetic merit. [< G]
kit·ten (kit′ən) *n.* A young cat. [ME *kitoun* < OF *chaton* kitten]
kit·ten·ish (kit′ən·ish) *adj.* Playfully coy. —**kit′ten·ish·ness** *n.*
kit·ti·wake (kit′ē·wāk) *n.* A gull of northern seas. [Imit.]
kit·ty¹ (kit′ē) *n. pl.* **·ties** 1. Money pooled, as by card players, for any specific purpose. 2. In card games, a hand or part of a hand left over after a deal. [Origin uncertain]
kit·ty² (kit′ē) *n. pl.* **·ties** A kitten or cat.
ki·wi (kē′wē) *n.* An extinct flightless bird of New Zealand, the apteryx. [< Maori]
Klan (klan) The Ku Klux Klan. —**Klan′ism** *n.* —**Klan′ner, Klans·man** (klanz′mən) *n.*
klep·to·ma·ni·a (klep′tə·mā′nē·ə) *n.* An obsessive impulse to steal. [< Gk. *kleptēs* thief + -MANIA] —**klep′to·ma′ni·ac** (-ak) *n.*
klieg light (klēg) A powerful arc floodlight, used in making motion pictures. [after the *Kliegl* brothers, lighting pioneers]
klutz (kluts) *n.* An awkward, clumsy person. [< Yiddish] —**klutz′y** *adj.*
knack (nak) *n.* The ability to do something

readily and well; adroitness. [ME *knak, knekke*]

knap·sack (nap′sak′) *n.* A case or bag worn strapped across the shoulders, for carrying equipment or supplies; rucksack. [< Du. *knappen* to bite, eat + *zak* sack]

knave (nāv) *n.* 1. A dishonest person; rogue. 2. A playing card, the jack. [OE *cnafa* youth] —**knav′ish** *adj.*

knav·er·y (nā′vər·ē) *n. pl.* **·er·ies** 1. Deceitfulness; rascality. 2. An act of deceit.

knead (nēd) *v.t.* 1. To mix and work (dough, clay, etc.), usu. by pressing and pulling with the hands. 2. To work upon by squeezes of the hands; massage. 3. To make by kneading. [OE *cnedan*] —**knead′er** *n.*

knee (nē) *n.* 1. *Anat.* The joint of the human leg that articulates the femur with the tibia and fibula and includes the patella. 2. *Zool.* A part corresponding to the human knee. 3. Something like a bent knee, as a bent piece of metal used in construction. —*v.t.* To touch or strike with the knee. [OE *cnēow*]

knee·cap (nē′kap′) *n.* The patella.

knee-deep (nē′dēp′) *adj.* Rising or sunk to the knee.

knee·hole (nē′hōl′) *n.* A space for the knees, as in a desk.

knee-jerk (nē′jûrk′) *adj. Informal* Responding in a predictable way: *knee-jerk* liberalism. [after the reflex of the leg produced when tapped below the kneecap]

kneel (nēl) *v.i.* **knelt** or **kneeled, kneel·ing** To fall or rest on the bent knee or knees. [OE *cnēowlian*] —**kneel′er** *n.*

knell (nel) *n.* 1. The tolling of a bell, esp. one announcing a death. 2. Any sad or doleful sound. —*v.i.* 1. To sound a knell. —*v.t.* 2. To proclaim by or as by a knell. [OE *cyllan* to knock]

knelt (nelt) Past tense and past participle of KNEEL.

knew (nōō, nyōō) Past tense of KNOW.

knick·er·bock·ers (nik′ər·bok′ərz) *n.pl.* Wide, short breeches gathered below the knee: also **knick·ers** (nik′ərz). [after Diedrich *Knickerbocker*, fictitious Dutch author of Washington Irving's *History of New York* (1809)]

knick·knack (nik′nak) *n.* A trifling article; trinket; trifle. [Reduplication of KNACK]

knife (nīf) *n. pl.* **knives** (nīvz) 1. An instrument or weapon for cutting, piercing, or spreading, with one or more sharp-edged, often pointed blades, commonly set in a handle. 2. A blade for cutting. —*v.* **knifed, knif·ing** *v.t.* 1. To stab or cut with a knife. 2. *Slang* To discredit or betray behind one's back. —*v.i.* 3. To move straight and swiftly. [OE *cnīf*]

knight (nīt) *n.* 1. In medieval times: **a** A feudal tenant serving his superior as a mounted soldier. **b** A gentleman trained for mounted combat and raised to the order of chivalry. 2. In Great Britain, the holder of a nonhereditary dignity below the rank of baronet, conferred by the sovereign. 3. In chess, a piece usu. bearing a horse's head. —*v.t.* To make (a man) a knight. [OE *cniht* boy, military attendant] —**knight′hood** *n.* —**knight′ly** *adv.*

knight errant *pl.* **knights errant** A wandering knight who went forth to redress wrongs or seek adventures. —**knight-er·rant·ry** (nīt′·er′ən·trē) *n.*

knish (kə·nish′) *n.* Dough filled with potatoes, meat, etc., and baked or fried. [< Yiddish]

knit (nit) *v.t. & v.i.* **knit** or **knit·ted, knit·ting** 1. To form (a fabric or garment) by interlocking loops of yarn or thread by means of needles. 2. To unite or grow together, as broken bones. 3. To draw (the brows) together into wrinkles. —*n.* The fabric made by knitting. [OE *cnyttan*] —**knit′ter** *n.*

knit·ting (nit′ing) *n.* 1. The act of one who or that which knits. 2. The fabric produced by knitting.

knives (nīvz) Plural of KNIFE.

knob (nob) *n.* 1. A rounded protuberance, bunch, or lump. 2. A rounded handle, as of a door. 3. A rounded mountain; knoll. [ME < MLG *knobbe*] —**knobbed** *adj.* —**knob′by** *adj.* **·bi·er, ·bi·est**

knock (nok) *v.t.* 1. To deal a blow to; hit, esp. with a thumping or rapping noise. 2. To strike together. 3. To make by striking or pounding. 4. To strike or push so as to make fall: with *down, over, off*, etc. 5. *Slang* To find fault with; disparage. —*v.i.* 6. To strike a blow or blows; rap. 7. To make a pounding or clanking noise, as an engine. —**to knock around** (or **about**) 1. *Informal* To wander from place to place. 2. To treat roughly; abuse. —**to knock down** 1. To take apart for shipping or storing. 2. At auctions, to sell. 3. *Informal* To earn. 4. To reduce (a price, estimate, etc.). —**to knock off** 1. *Informal* To stop or leave off (work, talking, etc.). 2. To deduct. 3. *Informal* To do or make quickly or easily. 4. *Slang* To kill; also, to overwhelm or defeat. —**to knock (oneself) out** *Slang* 1. To make a great effort. 2. To become exhausted. —**to knock out** 1. In boxing, to defeat by knocking to the canvas for a count of ten. 2. To make unconscious. 3. *Slang* **a** To tire greatly. **b** To overwhelm or amaze. —**to knock together** To make hurriedly. —*n.* 1. A sharp blow; rap. 2. A noise made by knocking. 3. A misfortune or reversal. 4. *Slang* Hostile criticism; disparagement. [OE *cnocian*]

knock·a·bout (nok′ə·bout′) *n. Naut.* A small sailboat with no bowsprit. —*adj.* Suitable for rough or casual occasions.

knock·down (nok′doun′) *adj.* 1. Powerful enough to knock to the ground. 2. Made so as to be easily taken apart or put together.

knock·er (nok′ər) *n.* One who or that which knocks; esp., a hinged device on a door, used for knocking.

knock-knee (nok′nē′) *n.* 1. An inward curvature of the legs that causes the knees to knock or rub together in walking. 2. *pl.* Legs so curved. —**knock′-kneed′** *adj.*

knock·out (nok′out′) *adj.* Forcible enough to render unconscious. —*n.* 1. A knocking unconscious or out of action. 2. In boxing, a flooring of one fighter for a count of ten: abbr. *KO, K.O., k.o.* 3. *Slang* An impressive person or thing.

knoll (nōl) *n.* A small round hill; a mound. [OE *cnoll* hill]

knot (not) *n.* 1. An intertwining of rope, string, etc., as by passing one free end through a loop and drawing it tight; also, the lump thus made. 2. An ornamental bow of silk, braid, etc. 3. A hard, gnarled portion of the trunk of a tree, or the round mark on sawed lumber left by this. 4. A cluster or tight group. 5. An enlargement in a muscle, of a gland, etc. resembling a knot. 6. *Naut.* a A speed of a nautical mile in an hour, equivalent to 1.1516 statute miles per hour. b A nautical mile. —*v.* **knot·ted, knot·ting** *v.t.* 1. To tie in a knot. 2. To fasten by a knot. —*v.i.* 3. To become knotted or tangled. [OE *cnotta*]

knot·grass (not′gras′) *n.* A widely distributed herb with jointed stems.

knot·hole (not′hōl′) *n.* A hole in a plank or board left by the falling out of a knot.

knot·ty (not′ē) *adj.* ·ti·er, ·ti·est 1. Full of or tied in knots. 2. Difficult or intricate; puzzling. —**knot′ti·ness** *n.*

knout (nout) *n.* A whip formerly used for flogging. [< Russ. < ON *knūtr, knūta* knot] —**knout** *v.t.*

know (nō) *v.* **knew, known, know·ing** *v.t.* 1. To be cognizant of; have a concept of in the mind. 2. To be certain of. 3. To be acquainted or familiar with. 4. To be able: with *how.* 5. To recognize; distinguish. 6. To understand; have skill in. 7. To have memorized. —*v.i.* 8. To have awareness; apprehend. 9. To have understanding or certainty; be sure. —**to know better** To be aware of something truer or more correct than what one says or does. —*n. Informal* The fact of knowing: now only in the phrase **to be in the know,** to have inside information. [OE *cnāwan*] —**know′a·ble** *adj.* —**know′er** *n.*

know-how (nō′hou′) *n. Informal* Mastery of a complicated operation; technical skill.

know·ing (nō′ing) *adj.* 1. Perceptive; astute; also, hinting at having secret knowledge. 2. Conscious; intentional. 3. Having knowledge or information. —**know′ing·ly** *adv.* —**know′ing·ness** *n.*

knowl·edge (nol′ij) *n.* 1. A result or product of knowing; information or understanding acquired through experience; practical ability or skill. 2. Learning; erudition. 3. The cumulative culture of the human race. 4. The act, process, or state of knowing; cognition. 5. Any object of knowing or mental apprehension; that which is or may be known. [OE *cnāwlǣc* acknowledgement]

knowl·edge·a·ble (nol′ij·ə·bəl) *adj.* Having knowledge; well-informed; intelligent.

known (nōn) Past participle of KNOW. —*adj.* Recognized by all as the truth; understood; axiomatic: *known* facts.

knuck·le (nuk′əl) *n.* 1. One of the joints of the fingers, or the region about it; esp., one of the joints connecting the fingers to the hand. 2. The knee or hock joint of the pig, calf, etc., the flesh of which is used as food. —**to knuckle down** To apply oneself seriously. —**to knuckle under** To submit; give in. [ME *knokel*]

knuck·le·bone (nuk′əl·bōn′) *n.* One of the bones forming a knuckle.

knuck·le·head (nuk′əl·hed′) *n. Informal* A stupid person. —**knuck′le·head′ed** *adj.*

knur (nûr) *n.* A knot or knob, as on a tree trunk. [ME *knorre*]

knurl (nûrl) *n.* 1. A protuberance; lump. 2. One of a series of small ridges on the edge of a metal object, as a coin. —*v.t.* To ridge or mill, as the edge of a coin. [? Dim. of KNUR] —**knurl′y** *adj.*

KO or K.O. or k.o. Knockout (boxing).

ko·a·la (kō·ä′lə) An arboreal marsupial having gray, woolly fur and no tail. [< native Austral. name]

Ko·di·ak bear (kō′dē·ak) A very large brown bear found on Kodiak Island and adjacent islands off the Alaskan coast.

kohl·ra·bi (kōl′rä·bē, kōl·rä′-) *n. pl.* ·bies A variety of cabbage with an edible turnip-shaped stem. [< L *caulis* cabbage + *rapa* turnip]

ko·la (kō′lə), **kola nut** See COLA.

ko·lin·sky (kə·lin′skē, kō-) *n. pl.* ·skies 1. Any of several minks of Asia and Russia. 2. Their fur. [< Russ. *kolinski* of Kola]

kol·khoz (kol·khôz′) *n.* A collective farm in the Soviet Union. Also **kol·hoz′, kol·khos′.** [< Russ. *kol(lektivnoe)* collective + *khoz(yaĭstvo)* farm]

kook (kōōk) *n. Slang* An eccentric or unbalanced person. [? < CUCKOO] —**kook′y** *adj.*

ko·peck (kō′pek) *n.* A Russian bronze coin, the hundredth part of a ruble. Also **ko′pek.** [< Russ. < *kopye* lance]

Ko·ran (kō·rän′, -ran′) *n.* The sacred book of the Muslims, recording the revelations of Allah to Muhammed. [< Arabic *Qur'ān,* lit., recitation < *qar'ā* to read]

Ko·re·an (kô·rē′ən, kō-) *adj.* Of or pertaining to Korea, its inhabitants, or their language. —**Ko·re′an** *n.*

ko·ru·na (kô′rōō·nä) *n. pl.* **ko·ru·ny** (kô′rōō·nē) or **ko·run** (kô′rōōn) The monetary unit of Czechoslovakia. [< Czechoslovakian < L *corona* crown]

ko·sher (kō′shər) *adj.* 1. Permitted by or conforming to Jewish (ceremonial) law. 2. *Slang* Legitimate; proper. [< Hebrew *kāshēr* fit, proper]

kow·tow (kou′tou′) *v.i.* 1. To behave in an obsequious, servile manner. 2. To strike the forehead on the ground as a sign of reverence, etc. —*n.* The act of kowtowing. [< Chinese *k'o-t'ou,* lit., to knock the head] —**kow′tow′er** *n.*

kraal (kräl) *n.* 1. In South Africa, a village or group of native huts, usu. surrounded by a stockade. 2. A fenced enclosure for cattle or sheep, esp. in South or central Africa. [< Afrikaans < Pg. *curral* pen for cattle]

krait (krīt) *n.* Any of several venomous snakes of Asia, esp. of India. [< Hind. *karait*]

K ration A condensed food ration used by the U.S. Army in World War II.

Krem·lin (krem′lin) 1. The walled citadel of Moscow containing the government offices of the Soviet Union. 2. The government of the Soviet Union. [< Russ. *kreml'* citadel]

krill (kril) *n.* Tiny marine crustaceans, the main food of certain whales. [< Norw. *kril* very young fish]

kris (krēs) *n.* A Malay dagger or short sword with a wavy-edged blade. [< Malay]

Krish·na (krish′nə) A widely worshiped Hindu god, the eighth avatar of Vishnu. —**Krish′na·ism** *n.*

kro·na[1] (krō'nə) *n. pl.* **·nur** (-nər) The monetary unit of Iceland.

kro·na[2] (krō'nə, *Sw.* kro͞o'nə) *n. pl.* **·nor** (-nôr) The monetary unit of Sweden.

kro·ne (krō'nə) *n. pl.* **·ner** (-nər) The monetary unit of Denmark and of Norway.

kryp·ton (krip'ton) *n.* A colorless, gaseous element present in minute amounts in the atmosphere, used as a filler in incandescent and fluorescent electric lamps. [< Gk., neut. of *kryptos* hidden]

ku·chen (ko͞o'khən) *n.* A yeast-dough coffee cake usu. covered with sugar. [< G]

ku·dos (kyo͞o'dos, ko͞o'-) *n.* Glory; credit: used only in the singular. [< Gk. *kydos* glory]

ku·du (ko͞o'do͞o) *n.* A large, striped African antelope with twisted horns. [< Hottentot]

kud·zu (ko͝od'zo͞o) *n.* A rapidly-growing, perennial vine, used for forage or erosion control. [< Jap. *kuzu*]

Ku Klux Klan (ko͞o' kluks' klan', kyo͞o') 1. An anti-Negro secret society formed in the South after the Civil War. 2. Any of similarly named groups, most active in the 1920's, devoted to white Protestant supremacy. [< Gk. *kyklos* circle] —**Ku' Klux'er, Ku' Klux' Klan'ner** *n.* —**Ku' Klux'ism** *n.*

ku·lak (ko͞o·läk') *n.* Formerly, in Russia, a wealthy peasant. [< Russ., lit., fist, tight-fisted man]

ku·miss (ko͞o'mis) *n.* Fermented mare's or camel's milk, used as a beverage. Also **ku'mys.** [< Tatar *kumiz*]

küm·mel (kim'əl, *Ger.* kü'məl) *n.* A liqueur flavored with aniseed, cumin, or caraway. [< G, caraway seed]

kum·quat (kum'kwot) *n.* 1. A small, round, sour orange fruit with an edible rind. 2. The tree bearing this fruit. [< Cantonese alter. of Pekinese *chin-chü*, lit., golden orange]

kung fu (kung' fo͞o') A Chinese art of self-defense, similar to karate. [< Chinese]

Kurd (kûrd, ko͝ord) *n.* A member of a nomadic Muslim people dwelling chiefly in Kurdistan, a region partly in Turkey, Iran, and Iraq. —**Kurd'ish** *adj.*

Ku·wait·i (ko͝o·wāt'ē) *adj.* Of Kuwait or its people. —**Ku·wait'i** *n.*

kvass (kväs, kvas) *n.* A Russian fermented drink resembling sour beer. [< Russ. *kvas*]

kvetch (kvech) *v.i.* To complain habitually. [< Yiddish] —**kvetch** *n.*

kwa·cha (kwä'chä) *n.* The monetary unit of Malawi and of Zambia.

kwash·i·or·kor (kwäsh'ē·ôr'kôr) *n.* A disease of children, producing stunted growth, swelling, blotchy skin, etc., caused by a diet deficient in certain proteins. [< native name in Ghana]

kyat (kyät) *n.* The monetary unit of Burma.

L

l, L (el) *n.* *pl.* **l's** or **ls, L's** or **Ls, ells** (elz) 1. The twelfth letter of the English alphabet. 2. The sound represented by the letter *l*. 3. Anything shaped like the letter L. —*symbol* The Roman numeral 50.

la[1] (lä) *n.* *Music* The sixth tone of the diatonic scale in solmization.

la[2] (lä, lô) *interj.* An exclamation expressing surprise, emphasis, etc. [OE *lā*]

lab (lab) *n.* *Informal* Laboratory.

la·bel (lā′bəl) *n.* 1. A slip of paper, printed legend, etc., on a container or article showing its nature, producer, destination, etc. 2. A term or phrase used to classify or describe. 3. A brand; make. —*v.t.* **la·beled** or **·belled, la·bel·ing** or **·bel·ling** 1. To mark with a label. 2. To classify. [< OF, ribbon] —**la′bel·er** or **la′bel·ler** *n.*

la·bi·a (lā′bē·ə) Plural of LABIUM.

la·bi·al (lā′bē·əl) *adj.* 1. Of or pertaining to a labium or the lips. 2. *Phonet.* Articulated or modified by the lips, as are (p), (b), (m), (w), or the rounded vowels (ō) and (o͞o). —*n.* A labial sound. [< L *labium* lip]

la·bi·ate (lā′bē·āt, -it) *adj.* Having lips or liplike parts. Also **la′bi·at′ed.** [< L *labium* lip]

la·bi·um (lā′bē·əm) *n.* *pl.* **·bi·a** *Anat.* 1. A lip or liplike part. 2. One of four folds of the vulva, the outer two of skin (**labia majora**) and the inner two of mucous membrane (**labia minora**). [< L, lip]

la·bor (lā′bər) *n.* 1. Physical or manual work done for hire. 2. Arduous physical or mental exertion. 3. The working class collectively, esp. as organized into labor unions. 4. A piece of work; task. 5. *Med.* The process of childbirth. —*v.i.* 1. To work hard physically or mentally. 2. To progress with great effort or painful exertion. 3. To be oppressed or hampered. Also *Brit.* **la′bour.** [< L, toil, distress]

lab·o·ra·to·ry (lab′rə·tôr′ē, *Brit.* lə·bor′ə·trē) *n.* *pl.* **·ries** A building or room equipped for conducting scientific experiments, analyses, etc. Also, *Informal, lab.* [< L *labor* toil]

Labor Day In most States, a legal holiday, usu. the first Monday in September.

la·bored (lā′bərd) *adj.* 1. Performed with difficulty: *labored* breathing. 2. Overelaborate: *labored* prose.

la·bor·er (lā′bər·ər) *n.* One who performs physical or manual labor, esp. unskilled labor.

la·bo·ri·ous (lə·bôr′ē·əs) *adj.* 1. Requiring much labor; toilsome. 2. Diligent; industrious. —**la·bo′ri·ous·ly** *adv.* —**la·bo′ri·ous·ness** *n.*

la·bor·ite (lā′bər·īt) *n.* One who supports labor interests, esp. in politics. Also *Brit.* **la′bour·ite.**

la·bor·sav·ing (lā′bər·sā′ving) *adj.* Removing or reducing the need for manual work.

labor union An association of workers organized to improve and advance mutual interests: also called *trade union.*

la·bur·num (lə·bûr′nəm) *n.* An Old World tree with pendulous yellow flowers, and yielding a poisonous alkaloid. [< L]

lab·y·rinth (lab′ə·rinth) *n.* 1. A system of intricate, confusing passages or paths; maze. 2. Any intricate or perplexing set of difficulties. [< Gk. *labyrinthos*] —**lab′y·rin′thine** (-rin′thin, -thēn), **lab′y·rin′thi·an** *adj.*

lac (lak) *n.* A resinous deposit left on certain trees by a scale insect and used in making varnishes, paints, etc. [< Skt. *lākshā*]

lace (lās) *n.* 1. A cord or string passed through eyelets or over hooks for fastening together the edges of a shoe, garment, etc. 2. A delicate openwork fabric, usu. figured. 3. A silver or gold braid used to decorate uniforms, hats, etc. —*v.* **laced, lac·ing** *v.t.* 1. To fasten or draw together by tying the lace or laces of. 2. To trim with or as with lace. 3. To compress the waist of (a person) by tightening laces of a corset. 4. To intertwine or interlace. 5. To give added zest or flavor to: to *lace* coffee with brandy. —*v.i.* 6. To be fastened by means of laces. —**to lace into** *Informal* 1. To strike or attack. 2. To scold; berate. [< L *laqueus* noose, trap]

lac·er·ate (las′ər·āt) *v.t.* **·at·ed, ·at·ing** 1. To tear raggedly; esp., to wound (the flesh) by tearing. 2. To injure: to *lacerate* one's feelings. [< L *lacer* mangled] —**lac′er·a′tion** *n.* —**lac′er·a′tive** *adj.*

lace·wing (lās′wing′) *n.* An insect with four lacy wings.

lach·ry·mal (lak′rə·məl) *adj.* Of, pertaining to, or producing tears. —*n.* *pl.* The organs secreting tears: also **lachrymal glands.** Also **lac′ri·mal.** [< L *lacrima* tear]

lach·ry·mose (lak′rə·mōs) *adj.* 1. Tearful. 2. Provoking tears; sad. —**lach′ry·mose′ly** *adv.*

lac·ing (lā′sing) *n.* 1. A cord or string for holding together opposite parts of a shoe, etc.; lace. 2. A fastening made with lacing. 3. *Informal* A thrashing; beating. 4. An additional flavoring; dash or zest.

lack (lak) *n.* 1. Deficiency or complete absence of something. 2. That which is absent or deficient; need. —*v.t.* 1. To be without. 2. To be short by. —*v.i.* 3. To be wanting or deficient. [ME, prob. < MLG *lak* deficiency]

lack·a·dai·si·cal (lak′ə·dā′zi·kəl) *adj.* Showing lack of interest; not lively; listless. —**lack′a·dai′si·cal·ly** *adv.*

lack·ey (lak′ē) *n.* *pl.* **·eys** 1. A male servant of low status, usu. in livery; footman. 2. Any servile follower. [< Sp. *lacayo*]

lack·lus·ter (lak′lus′tər) *adj.* 1. Lacking

brightness; dull. 2. Lacking spirit; mediocre: a *lackluster* performance. Also **lack′lus′tre.**

la·con·ic (lə·kon′ik) *adj.* Brief and concise in expression. [< Gk. *Lakōn* a Spartan; with ref. to the terseness of Spartan speech] —**la·con′i·cal·ly** *adv.*

lac·quer (lak′ər) *n.* A transparent surface coating, made from resins, shellac, etc. dissolved in a volatile solvent, that dries to give a glossy finish. —*v.t.* To coat with or as with lacquer. [< MF *lacre* a kind of sealing wax < Pg. *lacca* gum lac] —**lac′quer·er** *n.*

la·crosse (lə·krôs′, -kros′) *n.* A ball game played with long, racketlike implements by two teams of ten players each. [< dial. F (Canadian) *la crosse,* lit., the crosier]

lac·tate (lak′tāt) *v.i.* **·tat·ed, ·tat·ing** To form or secrete milk. [< L *lactare* to suckle] —**lac·ta′tion** *n.*

lac·te·al (lak′tē·əl) *adj.* Of, pertaining to, or resembling milk; milky. [< L *lac, lactis* milk]

lac·tic (lak′tik) *adj.* Of, pertaining to, or derived from milk.

lactic acid *Chem.* A limpid, syrupy acid, with a bitter taste, present in sour milk.

lacto- *combining form* Milk. Also, before vowels, **lact-.** [< L *lac, lactis*]

lac·tose (lak′tōs) *n. Biochem.* A white, odorless, crystalline sugar, present in milk.

la·cu·na (lə·kyōō′nə) *n. pl.* **·nas** or **·nae** (-nē) A space from which something is missing or has been omitted, esp. in a manuscript; hiatus. Also **la·cune′** (-kyōōn′). [< L *lacus* basin, pond]

lac·y (lā′sē) *adj.* **lac·i·er, lac·i·est** Made of or resembling lace. —**lac′i·ness** *n.*

lad (lad) *n.* 1. A boy or youth. 2. Familiarly, any male. [ME *ladde*]

lad·der (lad′ər) *n.* A device of wood, metal, rope, etc., for climbing and descending, usu. consisting of two parallel side pieces connected by a series of rungs placed at regular intervals to serve as footholds. [OE *hlǣd(d)er*]

lad·die (lad′ē) *n.* A lad.

lade (lād) *v.t.* **lad·ed, lad·ed** or **lad·en, lad·ing** To load with a cargo or burden; also, to load as a cargo. [OE *hladan* to load]

lad·en¹ (lād′n) *adj.* 1. Burdened; oppressed. 2. Weighed down; loaded.

lad·en² (lād′n) *v.t. & v.i.* **lad·ened, lad·en·ing** To lade.

lad·ing (lā′ding) *n.* A load or cargo.

la·dle (lād′l) *n.* A cup-shaped vessel with a long handle, for dipping or conveying liquids. —*v.t.* **·dled, ·dling** To dip up or carry in a ladle. [OE *hladan* to lade] —**la′dler** *n.*

la·dy (lā′dē) *n. pl.* **·dies** 1. A woman showing refinement, gentility, and tact. 2. A woman of superior position in society. 3. A term of reference or address for any woman. 4. A woman at the head of a household: now only in the phrase **the lady of the house.** 5. A wife. 6. *cap.* In Great Britain, a title given to women of various ranks. [OE *hlǣfdīge,* lit., bread-kneader]

la·dy·bug (lā′dē·bug′) *n.* Any of a family of brightly colored beetles, usu. red spotted with black, that feeds on aphids and other insects. Also **lady beetle, la′dy·bird′.**

la·dy·fin·ger (lā′dē·fing′gər) *n.* A small, finger-shaped sponge cake. Also **la′dy's·fin′ger.**

lady in waiting *pl.* **ladies in waiting** A lady appointed to attend upon a queen or princess.

la·dy-kill·er (lā′dē·kil′ər) *n. Slang* A man supposed to be unusually fascinating to women.

la·dy·like (lā′dē·līk′) *adj.* Like or suitable to a lady.

la·dy·ship (lā′dē·ship) *n.* 1. The rank or condition of a Lady. 2. A title used in speaking to or of a Lady: with *Her* or *Your.*

lady's man A man attentive to and fond of the company of women. Also **ladies' man.**

lady's-slipper (lā′dēz·slip′ər) *n.* An orchid having a flower that suggests a slipper in shape. Also **la′dy·slip′per.**

la·e·trile (lā′ə·tril) *n.* A drug derived from apricot pits, sometimes used in treating cancer. [< LAE(VO-) + (MANDELONI)-TRILE]

lag (lag) *v.i.* **lagged, lag·ging** To move slowly; stay or fall behind; straggle: sometimes followed by *behind.* —*n.* 1. The condition or act of retardation or falling behind. 2. The amount or period of retardation. [? < Scand.] —**lag′ger** *n.*

la·ger (lä′gər) *n.* A beer stored for sedimentation before use. Also **lager beer.** [< G *lagerbier* < *lager* storehouse + *bier* beer]

lag·gard (lag′ərd) *n.* One who lags; straggler. —*adj.* Falling behind; loitering; slow. —**lag′gard·ly** *adv.*

la·gniappe (lan·yap′, lan′yap) *n.* 1. A small present given to the purchaser of an article by a merchant or storekeeper. 2. *Informal* Anything given beyond strict obligation; an extra. Also **la·gnappe′.** [< dial. F (Creole)]

la·goon (lə·gōōn′) *n.* A body of shallow water, as a bay, inlet, pond, or lake, usu. connecting with a river, larger lake, or the sea; esp., the water within a coral atoll. Also **la·gune′.** [< L *lacuna* pool]

la·i·cize (lā′ə·sīz) *v.t.* **·cized, ·ciz·ing** To remove from ecclesiastical control; secularize. —**la′i·ci·za′tion** *n.*

laid (lād) Past tense and past participle of LAY¹.

laid·back (lād′bak′) *adj. Slang* Relaxed.

lain (lān) Past participle of LIE¹.

lair (lâr) *n.* A resting place or den, esp. that of a wild animal. [OE *leger* bed]

laird (lârd) *n. Scot.* The proprietor of a landed estate. [Northern ME *laverd, lard*] —**laird′ly** *adj.* —**laird′ship** *n.*

lais·sez faire (les′ā fâr′) 1. The theory that the state should exercise minimal control in trade and industrial affairs. 2. Noninterference or indifference. Also **lais′ser faire′.** [< F, lit., let do]

la·i·ty (lā′ə·tē) *n. pl.* **·ties** 1. The people collectively; laymen. 2. All of those outside a specific profession or occupation.

lake¹ (lāk) *n.* 1. A sizable inland body of water. 2. A large pool of any liquid. [Fusion of OE *lacu* stream, pool and OF *lac* basin, lake]

lake² (lāk) *n.* 1. A deep red pigment made by combining cochineal with a metallic oxide. 2. Any of various bright pigments formed from dyes. [Var. of LAC]

lake trout A salmonlike fish of the Great Lakes region of North America.

lam (lam) *Slang v.i.* **lammed, lam·ming** To run away, esp. to avoid arrest; flee. —*n.*

Sudden flight or escape. **—on the lam** In flight; fleeing. [? < ON *lemja* to thrash]

la·ma (lä′mə) *n.* A Buddhist priest or monk of Tibet or Mongolia. [< Tibetan *blama*]

La·ma·ism (lä′mə·iz′əm) *n.* The form of Buddhism practiced in Tibet and Mongolia. **—La′ma·ist** *n.* **—La′ma·is′tic** *adj.*

la·ma·ser·y (lä′mə·ser′ē) *n. pl.* **·ser·ies** A Buddhist monastery for lamas. [< F *lamaserie*]

lamb (lam) *n.* 1. A young sheep. 2. The meat of a lamb used as food. 3. Any gentle or innocent person. **—the Lamb** Christ. **—*v.i.*** To give birth: said of a ewe. [OE]

lam·baste (lam·bāst′) *v.t.* **·bast·ed, ·bast·ing** *Slang* 1. To beat or thrash. 2. To scold; castigate. **—lam·bast′ing** *n.*

lamb·da (lam′də) *n.* The eleventh letter in the Greek alphabet (Λ, λ), corresponding to the English *l.* [< Gk. < Phoenician *lamed*]

lam·bent (lam′bənt) *adj.* 1. Flickering; licking: a *lambent* flame. 2. Softly radiant. 3. Lightly and playfully brilliant: *lambent* wit. [< L *lambens, -entis,* ppr. of *lambere* to lick] **—lam′ben·cy** *n.* **—lam′bent·ly** *adv.*

lamb·kin (lam′kin) *n.* 1. A little lamb. 2. A small child: a term of affection. [Dim. of LAMB]

lamb·skin (lam′skin′) *n.* 1. The dressed hide and wool of a lamb. 2. Dressed leather made from a lamb's hide.

lame (lām) *adj.* **lam·er, lam·est** 1. Crippled or disabled, esp. in the legs or feet. 2. Sore; painful: a *lame* back. 3. Weak; ineffective: a *lame* effort. **—*v.t.* lamed, lam·ing** To make lame. [OE *lama*] **—lame′ly** *adv.* **—lame′ness** *n.*

la·mé (la·mā′) *n.* A fabric woven of flat gold or silver thread, sometimes mixed with silk or other fiber. [< F]

lame duck *Informal* 1. An officeholder whose term continues for a time after his defeat for reelection. 2. An ineffectual or disabled person.

la·mel·la (lə·mel′ə) *n. pl.* **·mel·lae** (-mel′ē) A thin plate, scale, or layer, as in bone or the gills of bivalves. [< L, dim. of *lamina* plate, leaf] **—lam·el·lar** (lə·mel′ər, lam′ə·lər), **lam·el·late** (lam′ə·lāt, lə·mel′āt) *adj.*

la·mel·li·branch (lə·mel′i·brangk) *n. Zool.* One of a class of bivalve mollusks including clams, mussels, and oysters. [< LAMELLA + Gk. *branchia* gills]

la·ment (lə·ment′) *v.t.* To feel remorse or regret over. **—*v.i.*** To feel or express sorrow, grief, or regret. **—*n.*** 1. An expression of grief; lamentation. 2. An elegiac melody or writing. [< L *lamentum* wailing, weeping] **—lam·en·ta·tion** (lam′ən·tā′shən) *n.* **—la·ment′er** *n.*

lam·en·ta·ble (lam′ən·tə·bəl, lə·ment′ə-) *adj.* That warrants lamenting; deplorable: a *lamentable* failure. **—lam′en·ta·bly** *adv.*

Lam·en·ta·tions (lam′ən·tā′shənz) *n.pl.* (*construed as sing.*) A lyrical poetic book of the Old Testament, attributed to Jeremiah the prophet.

lam·en·ted (lə·men′təd) *adj.* Grieved over.

lam·i·na (lam′ə·nə) *n. pl.* **·nae** (-nē) or **·nas** 1. A thin scale or sheet. 2. A layer or coat lying over another, as in bone, minerals, armor, etc. [< L]

lam·i·nate (lam′ə·nāt) *v.* **·nat·ed, ·nat·ing** *v.t.* 1. To beat, roll, or press (metal) into thin sheets. 2. To unite layers by heat and pressure. **—*v.i.*** 3. To separate into sheets. [< L *lamina* leaf] **—lam′i·na′tion** *n.*

lam·i·nat·ed (lam′ə·nā′təd) *adj.* Made up of or arranged in thin sheets.

lamp (lamp) *n.* 1. A device for holding one or more electric light bulbs; also, an electric light bulb. 2. Any of various devices for producing light by combustion, incandescence, electric arc, or fluorescence. 3. Any of several devices for producing therapeutic heat or rays: sun *lamp.* [< Gk. *lampein* to shine]

lamp·black (lamp′blak′) *n.* A black pigment consisting of fine carbon deposited from the smoke of burning oil or gas.

lamp·light (lamp′līt′) *n.* Light from lamps.

lamp·light·er (lamp′lī′tər) *n.* One whose work is lighting lamps, esp. street lamps.

lam·poon (lam·po͞on′) *n.* A satirical attack in prose or verse directed against a person. **—*v.t.*** To satirize in a lampoon. [< MF *lampons* let's drink (a song refrain)] **—lam·poon′er, lam·poon′ist** *n.* **—lam·poon′er·y** *n.*

lamp·post (lamp′pōst′) *n.* A post supporting a lamp.

lam·prey (lam′prē) *n. pl.* **·preys** An eellike, aquatic animal having a sucking mouth with sharp rasping teeth on its inner surface. Also **lam·per eel** (lam′pər), **lamprey eel.** [< Med.L *lampreda, lampetra*]

lance (lans) *n.* 1. A spearlike weapon used by mounted soldiers or knights. 2. A lancet. **—*v.t.* lanced, lanc·ing** 1. To pierce with a lance. 2. To cut or open with a lancet. [ME < L *lancea* light spear]

lance corporal *Mil.* In the U.S. Marine Corps, an enlisted man ranking above private first class and below corporal.

lan·ce·o·late (lan′sē·ə·lit, -lāt) *adj.* Shaped like the head of a lance; tapering, as certain leaves. [< L *lanceola* small lance]

lanc·er (lan′sər) *n.* A cavalryman armed with a lance.

lan·cet (lan′sit) *n.* A small, two-edged, usu. pointed surgical knife, used to open abscesses, boils, etc. [< F *lancette,* dim. of *lance* lance]

lance·wood (lans′wo͝od′) *n.* 1. A tough, elastic wood used for fishing rods, billiard cues, etc. 2. Any of various tropical American trees yielding this wood.

land (land) *n.* 1. The solid, exposed surface of the earth as distinguished from the seas. 2. A country or region, esp. considered as a place of human habitation. 3. Ground considered with reference to its uses, location, character, etc.: pasture *land.* 4. *Law* Any tract of ground that may be owned as property together with all its resources, buildings, etc. **—*v.t.*** 1. To put ashore. 2. To bring (something in flight) down to rest. 3. To bring to some point or state: His words *landed* him in trouble. 4. To pull (a fish) out of the water; catch. 5. *Informal* To deliver (a blow). **—*v.i.*** 6. To go or come ashore from a ship or boat. 7. To descend and come to rest after a flight or jump. 8. To come to some place or state; end up: to *land* in jail. [OE]

-land *combining form* 1. A region of a certain kind: *woodland.* 2. The country of: *Scotland.* [< LAND]

lan·dau (lan′dô, -dou) *n.* 1. A former type of closed sedan having a back seat with a collapsible top. 2. A four-wheeled carriage with a collapsible top. [after *Landau,* a Bavarian city]

land·ed (lan′did) *adj.* 1. Having an estate in land: *landed* gentry. 2. Consisting in land: *landed* property.

-land·er *combining form* From or of a land.

land·fall (land′fôl′) *n.* A sighting of or coming to land; also, the land so sighted or reached.

land·fill (land′fil′) *n.* 1. Garbage or trash buried in the ground. 2. The area, usu. of low or wet ground, where landfill is buried.

land grant Government land granted to a railroad, educational institution, etc. —**land-grant** (land′grant′) *adj.*

land·hold·er (land′hōl′dər) *n.* An owner or occupant of land.

land·ing (lan′ding) *n.* 1. The act of going ashore from a craft or vessel. 2. The place where a vessel lands; pier. 3. The act of descending and settling on the ground after a flight, leap, etc. 4. The platform or floor at the top of a flight of stairs.

landing field A tract of ground selected or prepared for the landing and takeoff of aircraft.

landing gear The understructure with wheels, skids, pontoons, etc. that supports an aircraft on land or water.

land·la·dy (land′lā′dē) *n. pl.* **·dies** A woman who owns and rents out real estate.

länd·ler (lent′lər) *n.* 1. A slow Austrian country dance. 2. Music for or in the manner of this dance, in triple meter. [< dial. G *Landl* upper Austria]

land·less (land′lis) *adj.* Owning no land.

land·locked (land′lokt′) *adj.* Surrounded by land; having no seacoast.

land·lord (land′lôrd′) *n.* 1. A man who owns and rents out real estate. 2. An innkeeper. [OE *land* land + *hlaford* lord]

land·lub·ber (land′lub′ər) *n.* An awkward or inexperienced person on board a ship.

land·mark (land′märk′) *n.* 1. A fixed object serving as a boundary mark to a tract of land, as a guide to travelers, etc. 2. A prominent object in the landscape. 3. A distinguishing fact, event, etc. [OE *land* land + *mearc* boundary]

land mine *Mil.* An explosive bomb placed in the ground.

land·own·er (land′ō′nər) *n.* One who owns real estate.

land·scape (land′skāp) *n.* 1. A stretch of inland natural scenery as seen from a single point. 2. A picture representing such scenery. —*v.t.* **·scaped, ·scap·ing** To improve or change the features or appearance of a park, garden, etc. [< Du. *land* land + *-schap* -ship] —**land′scap·er** *n.*

land·slide (land′slīd′) *n.* 1. The slipping down of a mass of soil, rock, and debris on a mountain side or other steep slope. 2. The mass of soil, rock, etc., slipping down. Also *Chiefly Brit.*, **land′slip′** (-slip′). 3. An overwhelming plurality of votes for one political party or candidate in an election.

lands·man (landz′mən) *n. pl.* **·men** (-mən) One who lives and works on land.

land·ward (land′wərd) *adj. & adv.* Facing or going toward the land. Also **land′wards.**

lane (lān) *n.* 1. A narrow rural path or way, confined between fences, walls, hedges, or similar boundaries; also, a narrow city street. 2. A prescribed route for transoceanic shipping or for aircraft. 3. A marked division of a highway or road for traffic moving in the same direction. 4. Any of a set of parallel courses for contestants in races. [OE *lanu*]

lang·syne (lang′sīn′, -zīn′) *adv. Scot.* Long since; long ago.

lan·guage (lang′gwij) *n.* 1. Communication between human beings by means of speech and hearing. 2. The words used in communication among members of a single nation or group at a given period. 3. The vocabulary used in a specific business, science, etc. 4. One's characteristic use of speech. 5. **a** Any of several sets of codes and rules for programming computers. **b** Machine language. [< L *lingua* tongue, language]

lan·guid (lang′gwid) *adj.* 1. Indisposed toward physical exertion; lacking energy. 2. Feeling little interest in anything; listless. 3. Lacking in activity or quickness of movement. [< L *languere* to languish] —**lan′guid·ly** *adv.* —**lan′guid·ness** *n.*

lan·guish (lang′gwish) *v.i.* 1. To become weak or feeble; grow listless. 2. To droop gradually from restless longing; pine. 3. To pass through a period of external discomfort and mental anguish: to *languish* in prison. [< L *languere* to be weary, languish]

lan·guish·ing (lang′gwish·ing) *adj.* 1. Lacking alertness or force. 2. Melancholy. 3. Becoming weak or listless. —**lan′guish·ing·ly** *adv.*

lan·guor (lang′gər) *n.* 1. Lassitude of body; weakness; fatigue. 2. A lack of energy or enthusiasm. 3. A mood of tenderness or sentimental dreaminess.

lan·guor·ous (lang′gər·əs) *adj.* 1. Languid. 2. Producing languor. —**lan′guor·ous·ly** *adv.* —**lan′guor·ous·ness** *n.*

lank (langk) *adj.* 1. Lean; shrunken. 2. Long, flat, and straight; *lank* hair. [OE *hlanc* flexible] —**lank′ly** *adv.* —**lank′ness** *n.*

lank·y (lang′kē) *adj.* **lank·i·er, lank·i·est** Ungracefully tall and thin; loose-jointed. —**lank′i·ness** *n.*

lan·o·lin (lan′ə·lin) *n.* A fatty substance obtained from the wool of sheep and used in ointments, cosmetics, soaps, etc. Also **lan′o·line** (-lin, -lēn). [< L *lan*(*a*) wool + *ol*(*eum*) oil]

lan·tern (lan′tərn) *n.* 1. A protective, usu. portable, case with transparent or translucent sides for enclosing a light. 2. A lighthouse, esp. the top that protects the light. 3. A slide projector. [< Gk. *lampein* to shine]

lantern jaws Long, sunken jaws that make the face appear thin. —**lan·tern-jawed** (lan′tərn·jôd′) *adj.*

lan·tha·nide series (lan′thə·nīd) *Physics* The rare-earth elements having atomic numbers from 57 to 71. [< LANTHAN(UM)]

lan·tha·num (lan′thə·nəm) *n.* A dark gray metallic element (symbol La) chemically related to aluminum. [< Gk. *lanthanein* to lie concealed]

lan·yard (lan′yərd) *n.* 1. *Naut.* A small, usu. four-stranded hemp rope used on a ship for fastening riggings, etc. 2. A cord worn around the neck, used by sailors for attaching a knife. [Alter. of obs. *lanyer* < OF *lasniere* thong]

La·o (lä′ō) *n. pl.* **La·o** 1. A Buddhist people living in Laos and parts of Thailand. 2. Their Thai language.

La·o·tian (lou′shən, lā·ō′shən) *adj.* Of or pertaining to Laos. —*n.* A native or inhabitant of Laos.

lap[1] (lap) *n.* 1. The chairlike place formed by the lower torso and thighs of a person seated. 2. A place of nurture or fostering: fortune's *lap.* 3. Control, care, or custody: in the *lap* of the gods. [OE *laeppa*]

lap[2] (lap) *n.* 1. The state of overlapping. 2. A rotating disk used for grinding and polishing gems, etc. 3. One circuit of a race course. 4. The part of one thing that lies over another. —*v.* **lapped, lap·ping** *v.t.* 1. To enfold; wrap. 2. To lay (one thing) partly over or beyond another. 3. To overlap. —*v.i.* 4. To project beyond or into something else. [ME *lappen* to fold]

lap[3] (lap) *v.t. & v.i.* **lapped, lap·ping** 1. To drink (a liquid) by taking it up with the tongue, as an animal does. 2. To wash against (the shore, etc.). —**to lap up** 1. To drink by lapping. 2. *Informal* To eat or drink gluttonously. 3. To listen to eagerly. [OE *lapian*] —**lap** *n.* —**lap′per** *n.*

lap dog A dog small enough to be held on the lap.

la·pel (lə·pel′) *n.* The front of a coat, jacket, etc., that is folded back to form an extension of the collar. [< LAP[1]]

lap·i·dar·y (lap′ə·der′ē) *n. pl.* **·dar·ies** 1. One whose work is to cut, engrave, or polish precious stones: also **lap′i·dar′ist.** 2. The art of such a worker. [< L *lapidarius* of stone] —**lap′i·dar′y, lap′i·dar′i·an** *adj.*

lap·in (lap′in) *n.* Rabbit fur, usu. dyed to resemble more expensive furs. [< F]

lap·is laz·u·li (lap′is laz′yōō·lī) 1. A bluish violet gemstone. 2. A bluish violet color. Also **lap′is.** [< L *lapis* stone + Med.L *lazulus* azure]

Lapp (lap) *n.* 1. A member of a formerly nomadic Mongoloid people of Lapland, now settled largely in Sweden and Norway: also **Lap·land·er** (lap′lan·dər). 2. The Finno-Ugric language of the Lapps: also **Lap′pish.** [< Sw.]

lap·pet (lap′it) *n.* A flap or fold on a headdress or garment. [Dim. of LAP[1]]

lapse (laps) *n.* 1. A gradual passing away, as of time. 2. A pronounced fall into ruin, decay, or disuse. 3. A slip or mistake, usu. trivial. —*v.i.* **lapsed, laps·ing** 1. To sink slowly; slip: to *lapse* into a coma. 2. To fall into ruin or a state of neglect. 3. To deviate from one's principles or beliefs. 4. To become void, usually by failure to meet obligations. 5. To pass away, as time. [< L *labi* to glide, slip] —**laps′a·ble** or **laps′i·ble** *adj.*

lap·wing (lap′wing′) *n.* A ploverlike bird of the Old World, noted for its flopping flight and shrill cry. [OE *hlēapwince*]

lar·board (lär′bərd, -bôrd′) *Naut. n.* The port side of a ship. [ME *laddebord,* lit., prob., lading side]

lar·ce·ny (lär′sə·nē) *n. pl.* **·nies** *Law* The unlawful removal of the personal goods of another with intent to defraud the owner; theft. [< L *latrocinari* to rob] —**lar′cen·ist** *n.* —**lar′ce·nous** *adj.* —**lar′ce·nous·ly** *adv.*

larch (lärch) *n.* Any of several deciduous trees of the pine family; also, the wood. [< L *larix, laricis*]

lard (lärd) *n.* The semisolid fat of a hog after rendering. —*v.t.* 1. To cover or smear with lard. 2. To prepare (lean meat or poultry) by inserting strips of fat before cooking. 3. To embellish (speech or writing) with quotations, etc. [< L *lardum* lard] —**lard′y** *adj.*

lar·der (lär′dər) *n.* A room or cupboard where articles of food are stored. [< Med.L *lardum* lard]

lar·es and pe·na·tes (lâr′ēz, lā′rēz; pə·nā′tēz) 1. In ancient Rome, the household gods. 2. The belongings of one's household.

large (lärj) *adj.* **larg·er, larg·est** 1. Having considerable size, quantity, capacity, extent, etc.; big. 2. Bigger than another. 3. Sympathetic and broad in scope: to take a *large* view. —*adv.* In a size greater than usual: Print *large.* —**at large** 1. Free; at liberty. 2. In general: the people *at large.* 3. Not representing a specific district: delegate-*at-large.* [< L *largus* abundant] —**large′ness** *n.*

large·ly (lärj′lē) *adv.* 1. To a great extent; mainly; chiefly. 2. On a big scale; extensively.

large-scale (lärj′skāl′) *adj.* Of large size or scope.

lar·gess (lär·jes′; lär′jis, -jes) *n.* Liberal giving; also, something liberally given. Also **lar′gesse.** [< F *largesse*]

lar·go (lär′go) *Music adj.* Slow; broad. —*adv.* In a slow tempo. —*n. pl.* **·gos** A slow movement or passage. [< Ital., slow, large]

lar·i·at (lar′ē·ət) *n.* 1. A rope for tethering animals. 2. A lasso. [< Sp. *la reata* the rope]

lark[1] (lärk) *n.* 1. Any of numerous small singing birds, as the skylark. 2. Any similar bird, as the meadowlark. [OE *lāferce, læwerce*]

lark[2] (lärk) *n. Informal* 1. A hilarious time. 2. A prank. —*v.i.* 1. To frolic or sport. 2. To play pranks. [Origin uncertain]

lark·spur (lärk′spûr) *n.* Any of several showy herbs of the crowfoot family with clusters of white, pink, blue, or red flowers.

lar·va (lär′və) *n. pl.* **·vae** (-vē) 1. *Entomol.* The first stage of an insect after leaving the egg, as the maggot. 2. *Zool.* The immature form of any animal that must undergo metamorphosis. [< L, ghost, mask] —**lar′val** *adj.*

la·ryn·ge·al (lə·rin′jē·əl, -jəl) *adj.* Of, pertaining to, or near the larynx. [< Gk. *larynx, laryngos* larynx]

lar·yn·gi·tis (lar′ən·jī′tis) *n. Pathol.* Inflammation of the larynx. —**lar′yn·git′ic** (-jit′ik) *adj.*

lar·ynx (lar′ingks) *n. pl.* **la·ryn·ges** (lə·rin′·jēz) or **lar·ynx·es** *Anat.* An organ of the respiratory tract situated at the upper part of the trachea, and consisting of a cartilaginous box containing the vocal cords. [< Gk. *larynx*]

la·sa·gna (lə·zän′yə) *n.* Broad, flat noodles, often served baked in a meat and tomato sauce. Also **la·sa′gne.** [< Ital.]

las·civ·i·ous (lə·siv′ē·əs) *adj.* Having, manifesting, or arousing sensual desires; lustful. [< L *lascivus* lustful] —**las·civ′i·ous·ly** *adv.* —**las·civ′i·ous·ness** *n.*

la·ser (lā′zər) *n. Physics* A device that amplifies light waves to produce an intense narrow beam: also called *optical maser.* [< L(IGHT) A(MPLIFICATION BY) S(TIMULATED) E(MISSION OF) R(ADIATION)]

lash[1] (lash) *n.* 1. A whip or scourge. 2. A single whip stroke. 3. Anything that wounds the feelings. 4. An eyelash. —*v.t.* 1. To strike, punish, or command with or as with a whip; flog. 2. To switch spasmodically: The lion *lashes* his tail. 3. To assail sharply in speech or writing. —**to lash out** 1. To hit out suddenly and violently. 2. To break into angry verbal abuse. [Prob. fusion of MLG *lasch* flap and OF *laz* cord] —**lash′er** *n.*

lash[2] (lash) *v.t.* To bind or tie with rope or cord. [< L *laqueus* noose] —**lash′er** *n.*

lass (las) *n.* 1. A young woman; girl. 2. A sweetheart. 3. *Scot.* A servant girl; maid. [ME]

las·sie (las′ē) *n.* A little girl; lass. [Dim. of LASS]

las·si·tude (las′ə·tōōd, -tyōōd) *n.* A state of weariness or fatigue; languor. [< L *lassus* faint]

las·so (las′ō) *n. pl.* **·sos** or **·soes** A long rope with a running noose, used for catching horses, etc. —*v.t.* To catch with a lasso. [< Sp.] —**las′so·er** *n.*

last[1] (last) *adj.* 1. Coming after all others; final. 2. Most recent: *last* year. 3. Least probable or suitable: the *last* man for the job. 4. Conclusive; final: the *last* word. —*adv.* 1. After all others in time or order. 2. At a time next preceding the present: He was *last* seen going west. 3. In conclusion; finally. —*n.* 1. The end; final part or portion. 2. The final appearance, experience, or mention: We'll never hear the *last* of this. —**at last** At length; finally. [OE *latost* slowest]

last[2] (last) *v.i.* 1. To remain in existence; endure. 2. To continue unimpaired or unaltered. 3. To hold out: Will our supplies *last*? [OE *lǣstan*, to follow a track, continue, accomplish]

last[3] (last) *n.* A shaped form, usu. of wood, on which to make a shoe or boot. [OE *lǣste*, *lāst* footstep, track]

last·ing (las′ting) *adj.* Continuing; durable; permanent. —*n.* Endurance; continuance. [< LAST[2]] —**last′ing·ly** *adv.* —**last′ing·ness** *n.*

Last Judgment *Theol.* **a** The final judgment by God of all mankind. **b** The time of this.

last·ly (last′lē) *adv.* In the last place; in conclusion.

last rites *Eccl.* Sacraments administered to persons in peril of death.

Last Supper The last meal of Jesus Christ and his disciples before the Crucifixion.

last word 1. The final and most authoritative utterance. 2. *Informal* The most fashionable thing.

lat·a·ki·a (lat′ə·kē′ə) *n.* A Turkish smoking tobacco. [after *Latakia*, Syria]

latch (lach) *n.* A fastening for a door or gate, usu. a movable bar that falls or slides into a notch. —*v.t. & v.i.* To fasten by means of a latch; close. —**to latch on to** *Slang* To obtain, esp. something desirable. [OE *laeccean* to seize]

latch·key (lach′kē′) *n.* A key for releasing a latch.

latch·string (lach′string′) *n.* A string on the outside of a door, used for lifting the latch.

late (lāt) *adj.* **lat·er** or **lat·ter**, **lat·est** or **last** 1. Appearing or coming after the expected time; tardy. 2. Occurring at an unusually advanced time: a *late* hour. 3. Recent or comparatively recent: the *late* war. 4. Deceased: the *late* king. —*adv.* 1. After the expected time; tardily. 2. At or until an advanced time of the day, month, year, etc. —**of late** Recently. [OE *læt*] —**late′ness** *n.*

la·tent (lā′tənt) *adj.* Not visible or apparent, but capable of developing or being expressed; dormant. [< L *latere* to be hidden] —**la′ten·cy** *n.* —**la′tent·ly** *adv.*

lat·er (lā′tər) *adv.* At a subsequent time; after some time.

lat·er·al (lat′ər·əl) *adj.* Pertaining to the side or sides; situated at, occurring, or coming from the side. —*n.* Something occurring at or on the side. [< L *latus*, *lateris* side] —**lat′er·al·ly** *adv.*

la·tex (lā′teks) *n. pl.* **lat·i·ces** (lat′ə·sēz) or **la·tex·es** 1. The sticky emulsion secreted by certain plants that forms the basis of natural rubber. 2. A synthetic emulsion, used mainly as a base for paints. [< L, liquid]

lath (lath) *n.* Thin strips of wood, etc., nailed to studs or joists to support a coat of plaster, or to rafters to support shingles or slates. —*v.t.* To cover or line with laths. [Prob. fusion of OE *laett* and OE *laethth* (assumed)] —**lath′er** *n.*

lathe (lāth) *n.* A machine that holds and spins pieces of wood, metal, plastic, etc., so that they are cut and shaped when the operator holds cutting tools against them. —*v.t.* **lathed, lath·ing** To form on a lathe. [< MDu. *lade*]

lath·er (lath′ər) *n.* 1. The suds or foam formed by soap or detergents and water. 2. The foam of profuse sweating, as of a horse. —**in a lather** *Slang* In a state of intense excitement or agitation. —*v.t. & v.i.* To cover with or form lather. [OE *lēathor* washing soda, soap] —**lath′er·er** *n.* —**lath′er·y** *adj.*

lath·ing (lath′ing) *n.* Laths collectively: also **lath′work′** (-wûrk′).

Lat·in (lat′n) *adj.* 1. Pertaining to ancient Latium or ancient Rome, their inhabitants, culture, or language. 2. Pertaining to or denoting the peoples or countries with languages derived from Latin. 3. Of or belonging to Roman Catholic Church. —*n.* 1. The Indo-European, Italic language of ancient Latium and Rome. 2. A member of one of the modern Latin peoples. 3. A member of the Roman Catholic Church. 4. One of the people of ancient Latium. —**Old Latin** The language before the first century B.C. —**Classical Latin** The literary and rhetorical language of the period 80 B.C. to A.D. 200. —**Late Latin** The language from 200–600. —**Low Latin** The language of any period after the classical, such as Medieval Latin. —**Medieval Latin** The language used by the writers of the Middle Ages, from 600–1500: also called *Middle Latin.* —**New (or Neo-) Latin** A form of the language based on Latin and Greek elements, now used chiefly for scientific and taxonomic terms. —**Vulgar Latin** The popular speech of the Romans from about A.D. 200 through the medieval period. [< L *Latinus*]

Latin America The countries of the western hemisphere south of the Rio Grande, in which the official languages are derived from Latin.

—Lat·in-A·mer·i·can (lat′n·ə·mer′ə·kən) *adj.* **—Latin American** *n.*

Lat·in·ate (lat′ən·āt) *adj.* Of, like, or from Latin.

Lat·in·ism (lat′ən·iz′əm) *n.* An idiom in another language taken from or imitating Latin.

Latin Quarter A section of Paris known for its many artists and students.

lat·i·tude (lat′ə·to͞od, -tyo͞od) *n.* 1. *Geog.* Angular distance on the earth's surface northward or southward of the equator, measured in degrees along a meridian. 2. *Often pl.* A region or place considered with reference to its distance from the equator. 3. Freedom from narrow restrictions. [< L *latitudo* breadth] **—lat′i·tu′di·nal** *adj.* **—lat′i·tu′di·nal·ly** *adv.*

lat·i·tu·di·nar·i·an (lat′ə·to͞o′də·nâr′ē·ən, -tyo͞o′-) *adj.* Characterized by or tolerant of liberal or unorthodox attitudes, beliefs, etc., esp. in matters of religion. **—*n.*** One who is latitudinarian. **—lat′i·tu′di·nar′i·an·ism** *n.*

la·trine (lə·trēn′) *n.* A public toilet, as in a camp, barracks, etc. [< L *latrina* bath, privy]

-latry *combining form* Worship of; excessive devotion to: *idolatry.* [< Gk. *latreia* worship]

lat·ter (lat′ər) *adj.* 1. Being the second of two persons or things referred to: often preceded by *the*: The *latter* statement is truer than the former. 2. Later or nearer to the end: His *latter* years were happy. [OE *lætra* later]

lat·ter-day (lat′ər·dā′) *adj.* Modern: a *latter-day* martyr.

Latter-day Saint A Mormon.

lat·ter·ly (lat′ər·lē) *adv.* 1. Recently; lately. 2. At a later time; toward the end.

lat·tice (lat′is) *n.* 1. A structure consisting of strips of metal, wood, etc., crossed or interlaced to form regularly spaced openings. 2. A window, screen, gate, etc., having a lattice construction. **—*v.t.*** **·ticed, ·tic·ing** To furnish or enclose with a lattice. [< OF *latte* lath]

lat·tice·work (lat′is·wûrk′) *n.* Openwork made from or resembling a lattice. Also **lat′tic·ing.**

Lat·vi·an (lat′vē·ən) *adj.* Of or pertaining to Latvia, its people, or their language; Lettish. **—*n.*** 1. A native or inhabitant of Latvia; a Lett. 2. The Lettish language.

laud (lôd) *v.t.* To praise highly; extol. [< L *laus, laudis* praise] **—laud·a′tion** *n.*

laud·a·ble (lô′də·bəl) *adj.* Deserving approbation. **—laud′a·bil′i·ty, laud′a·ble·ness** *n.* **—laud′a·bly** *adv.*

lau·da·num (lô′də·nəm) *n.* Tincture of opium. [< L *ladanum*]

laud·a·to·ry (lô′də·tôr′ē) *adj.* Expressing or containing praise; complimentary.

laugh (laf) *v.i.* 1. To produce the characteristic sounds and physical expressions of merriment, elation, etc. 2. To express or experience amusement, satisfaction, etc. **—*v.t.*** 3. To induce, persuade, or bring about by or as by laughing: I *laughed* myself sick. **—to laugh at** 1. To express amusement at. 2. To ridicule; mock. 3. To make light of. **—to laugh away** To dispel or minimize with laughter. **—to laugh off** To rid one's self of or dismiss laughingly. **—to laugh up** (or **in**) **one's sleeve** To be covertly amused or exultant. **—*n.*** 1. An act or sound of laughing. 2. *Informal* A cause for or provocation to laughter. **—to have the last laugh** To triumph or succeed after seeming at a disadvantage. [OE *hliehhan, hlæhhan*] **—laugh′er** *n.* **—laugh′ing·ly** *adv.*

laugh·a·ble (laf′ə·bəl) *adj.* Provoking laughter; amusing. **—laugh′a·ble·ness** *n.* **—laugh′a·bly** *adv.*

laugh·ing gas (laf′ing) Nitrous oxide.

laugh·ing·stock (laf′ing·stok′) *n.* One who or that which provokes ridicule; a butt.

laugh·ter (laf′tər) *n.* The sound, expression, or action of laughing.

launch[1] (lônch) *v.t.* 1. To move (a vessel, etc.) into the water, esp. for the first time. 2. To set in flight or motion, as a rocket, missile, etc. 3. To start (a person, etc.) on a career or course of action. 4. To initiate; open: to *launch* a campaign. 5. To hurl; fling. **—*n.*** The action of launching a vessel, missile, etc. [< AF *lancher* to launch] **—launch′er** *n.*

launch[2] (lônch) *n.* An open or half-decked motor boat. [< Sp. *lancha*]

launch pad *Aerospace* The platform from which a rocket or guided missile is fired. Also **launch·ing pad** (lônch′ing).

laun·der (lôn′dər) *v.t.* 1. To wash (clothing, linens, etc.). 2. *Slang* To pass (funds) through various accounts in order to conceal their source. **—*v.i.*** 3. To undergo washing. [< L *lavare* to wash] **—laun′der·er** *n.*

laun·dress (lôn′dris) *n.* A woman paid or employed to do laundry.

laun·dro·mat (lôn′drə·mat) *n.* An establishment where laundry is washed and dried in coin-operated automatic machines. [< *Laundromat,* a trade name]

laun·dry (lôn′drē) *n. pl.* **·dries** 1. A room, commercial establishment, etc., where laundering is done. 2. Articles to be laundered. 3. The work of laundering.

laun·dry·man (lôn′drē·mən) *n. pl.* **·men** (-mən) A man who calls for and delivers laundry.

lau·re·ate (lô′rē·it) *adj.* 1. Singled out for special honor. 2. Crowned or decked with laurel as a mark of honor. **—*n.*** A person honored with a prize or award. [< L *laureatus* crowned with laurel]

lau·rel (lôr′əl, lor′-) *n.* 1. An evergreen tree or shrub related to the cinnamon, sassafras, etc. 2. *Often pl.* A crown or wreath of laurel leaves, conferred as a symbol of honor, achievement, etc. 3. *pl.* Honor or distinction gained by outstanding achievement. **—to look to one's laurels** To be on guard against losing a position of eminence, honor, etc. **—to rest on one's laurels** To be content with what one has already achieved. [< L *laurus*]

la·va (lä′və, lav′ə) *n.* 1. Molten rock that issues from an active volcano or through a fissure in the earth's crust. 2. Rock formed by the solidifying of this substance. [< Ital., orig., a stream formed by rain < *lavare* to wash]

lav·a·liere (lav′ə·lir′) *n.* An ornamental pendant worn on a thin chain around the neck. Also **lav′a·lier′,** *French* **la·val·lière** (là·và·lyâr′). [< F *la vallière,* a type of necktie]

lav·a·to·ry (lav′ə·tôr′ē) *n. pl.* **·ries** 1. A room equipped with washing and usu. toilet facilities. 2. A basin, sink, etc., used for washing. [< L *lavare* to wash]

lav·en·der (lav′ən·dər) *n.* 1. An Old World plant of the mint family, having spikes of fragrant, pale violet flowers. 2. The dried flowers and foliage of this plant, used to scent linen, clothing, etc. 3. A pale, reddish violet color. —*adj.* Pale reddish violet. [< Med.L *lavendula*]

lav·ish (lav′ish) *adj.* 1. Generous and unrestrained in giving, spending, etc.; prodigal. 2. Provided or expended in great abundance. —*v.t.* To give or bestow generously. [< OF *lavasse, lavacho* downpour of rain] —**lav′ish·ly** *adv.* —**lav′ish·ness** *n.*

law (lô) *n.* 1. A rule of conduct, recognized by custom or decreed by formal enactment, considered as binding on the members of a community, nation, etc. 2. A system or body of such rules. 3. The body of rules relating to a specified subject or activity: criminal *law*. 4. Remedial justice as administered by legal authorities: to resort to the *law*. 5. The branch of knowledge concerned with jurisprudence. 6. The legal profession. 7. *Often cap.* Divine will, command, or precept; also, a body of rules having such divine origin. 8. Any generally accepted rule, procedure, or principle governing a specified area of conduct, body of knowledge, etc. 9. In science and philosophy, a formal statement of certain regularities found in natural phenomena. —**to go to law** To engage in litigation. —**to lay down the law** To utter one's wishes, instructions, etc., in an authoritative manner. [OE < ON *lag* something laid or fixed]

law-a·bid·ing (lô′ə·bī′ding) *adj.* Obedient to the law.

law·break·er (lô′brā′kər) *n.* One who violates the law. —**law′break′ing** *n. & adj.*

law·ful (lô′fəl) *adj.* 1. Permitted by or according to law. 2. Recognized by the law: *lawful* debts. —**law′ful·ly** *adv.* —**law′ful·ness** *n.*

law·giv·er (lô′giv′ər) *n.* One who originates or institutes a law or system of laws. —**law′giv′ing** *n. & adj.*

law·less (lô′lis) *adj.* 1. Not controlled by law, authority, discipline, etc. 2. Contrary to law. —**law′less·ly** *adv.* —**law′less·ness** *n.*

law·mak·er (lô′mā′kər) *n.* One who enacts or helps to enact laws; a legislator. —**law′·mak′ing** *n. & adj.*

lawn[1] (lôn) *n.* A stretch of grassy land; esp., an area of mown grass near a house, in a park, etc. [Obs. *laund* < OF *launde* heath]

lawn[2] (lôn) *n.* A fine, thin linen or cotton fabric. [after *Laon*, France]

law·ren·ci·um (lô·ren′sē·əm) *n.* A very short-lived, artificially produced radioactive element (symbol Lw). [after E. O. *Lawrence*, 1901–58, U.S. physicist]

law·suit (lô′so͞ot′) *n.* A case, action, or proceeding brought to a court of law for settlement.

law·yer (lô′yər) *n.* A member of any branch of the legal profession; esp., one who advises and acts for clients or pleads in court.

lax (laks) *adj.* 1. Lacking strictness or discipline. 2. Lacking precision; vague. 3. Lacking firmness or rigidity. [< L *laxus* loose] —**lax′i·ty, lax′ness** *n.* —**lax′ly** *adv.*

lax·a·tive (lak′sə·tiv) *n.* A medicine taken to produce evacuation of the bowels. —*adj.* Loosening or producing evacuation of the bowels. [< F, fem. of *laxatif*]

lay[1] (lā) *v.* **laid, lay·ing** *v.t.* 1. To place in a horizontal, reclining, or low position. 2. To put or place. 3. To establish as a basis or support: to *lay* the groundwork. 4. To place or arrange in proper position: to *lay* bricks. 5. To produce internally and deposit (an egg or eggs). 6. To think out; devise: to *lay* plans. 7. To attribute or ascribe: to *lay* the blame. 8. To set forth; present: to *lay* one's claim before a court. 9. To bury, as in a grave; inter. 10. To set or prepare (a trap, etc.). 11. To twist strands so as to produce (rope, cable, etc.). —*v.i.* 12. To produce and deposit eggs. —**to lay away** 1. To store up; save. 2. To bury in or as in a grave. —**to lay into** To attack vigorously. —**to lay it on** *Informal* To be extravagant or exorbitant, esp. in praise or flattery. —**to lay low** 1. To strike down; prostrate. 2. *Slang* To go into hiding. —**to lay off** To dismiss from a job, usu. temporarily. —**to lay out** 1. To arrange or display for use, inspection, etc. 2. To arrange according to a plan; map. 3. To spend or supply (a sum of money). 4. To prepare (a corpse) for burial. —**to lay over** *Informal* To stop for a time in the course of a journey. —**to lay up** 1. To make a store of. 2. To incapacitate or confine, as by illness, injury, etc. —*n.* The manner in which something lies or is placed. [OE, pt. of *licyan* to lie, recline]

lay[2] (lā) *adj.* 1. Of or belonging to the laity; secular. 2. Not belonging to or endorsed by a learned profession: a *lay* opinion. [< Gk. *laos* the people]

lay[3] (lā) Past tense of LIE[1].

lay[4] (lā) *n.* 1. A song, ballad, or narrative poem. 2. A melody. [< OF *lai*]

lay·a·way (lā′ə·wā′) *n.* Goods kept by the seller until paid for in full.

lay·er (lā′ər) *n.* 1. A single thickness, coating, covering, etc. 2. One who or that which lays; esp., a hen considered as an egg producer. —*v.t. & v.i.* To form a layer.

layer cake A cake, usu. frosted, made in layers having a sweetened filling between them.

lay·ette (lā′et′) *n.* Clothing, bedding, etc., for a newborn infant. [< F, dim. of *laie* packing box, drawer < MDu. *lade* trunk]

lay·man (lā′mən) *n. pl.* **·men** (-mən) 1. One without training or skill in a profession or branch of knowledge. 2. One belonging to the laity, as distinguished from the clergy.

lay·off (lā′ôf′) *n.* 1. The temporary dismissal of employees. 2. A period of enforced unemployment.

lay·out (lā′out′) *n.* 1. A planned arrangement, as: a The relative positions of streets, rooms, etc. b Written matter, illustrations, etc., arranged for printing. 2. That which is laid out or provided, as equipment.

lay·o·ver (lā′ō′vər) *n.* A break in a journey.

la·zar (lā′zər, laz′ər) *n.* *Archaic* A beggar or pauper afflicted with disease; esp., a leper. [< Med.L *lazarus*, after *Lazarus*, a sick beggar mentioned in a Biblical parable (*Luke* xvi 20)]

laze (lāz) *v.t. & v.i.* **lazed, laz·ing** To loaf or idle. [< LAZY]

la·zy (lā′zē) *adj.* **·zi·er, ·zi·est** 1. Unwilling

to work or engage in energetic activity; slothful. 2. Moving or acting slowly or heavily. 3. Characterized by idleness or languor. [Prob. < MLG *lasich* loose, feeble] **—la′zi·ly** *adv.* **—la′zi·ness** *n.*

la·zy·bones (lā′zē·bōnz′) *n.* *pl.* **·bones** *Informal* A lazy person.

lazy Susan A revolving tray, often divided into compartments, used to hold condiments, etc. Also **Lazy Susan.**

lea (lē) *n.* *Chiefly Poetic* A grassy field. [OE *lēah,* orig., open ground in a wood]

leach (lēch) *v.t.* 1. To subject to the filtering action of a liquid. 2. To remove or dissolve by or as by filtering. *—v.i.* 3. To be removed or dissolved by percolation or filtration. *—n.* The process of leaching. [OE *leccan* to wet, irrigate] **—leach′er** *n.*

lead¹ (lēd) *v.* **led, lead·ing** *v.t.* 1. To go with or ahead of so as to show the way; guide. 2. To cause to progress by or as by pulling or holding: to *lead* by the hand. 3. To serve as or indicate a route for: The path *led* to the hut. 4. To control the actions or affairs of; direct. 5. To influence the ideas, conduct, or actions of. 6. To be first among. 7. To experience or live; also, to cause to experience or go through: to *lead* a merry life; They *led* him a wild chase. 8. In card games, to begin a round by playing (a specified card). *—v.i.* 9. To act as guide; conduct. 10. To afford a way or passage: The road *leads* through a swamp. 11. To be conducive; tend: followed by *to*: Delinquency *leads* to crime. 12. To have control or command. **—to lead off** 1. To make a start; begin. 2. In baseball, to be the first batter in a line-up or inning. **—to lead on** 1. To entice or tempt, esp. to wrongdoing. 2. To go first or in advance. *—n.* 1. Position in advance or at the head. 2. The distance or interval by which someone or something leads. 3. Guidance; example: Follow his *lead.* 4. Indication; clue: Give me a *lead.* 5. In dramatic presentations: **a** A starring role. **b** A performer having such a role. 6. In journalism, the introductory portion or paragraph of a news story. 7. In card games: **a** The right to play first in a game or round. **b** The card, suit, etc., thus played. 8. *Electr.* A short wire or conductor, used as a connection to a source of current. 9. A cord, leash etc., for leading an animal. [OE *lǣden* to cause to go]

lead² (led) *n.* 1. A soft, heavy, malleable, dull gray metallic element (symbol Pb). 2. Any of various objects made of lead or similar metal; esp., a weight used in sounding, etc. 3. Graphite, esp. in the form of thin rods, used as the writing material in pencils. 4. Bullets, shot, etc. 5. *Printing* A thin strip of type metal used to provide space between printed lines. *—v.t.* To cover, weight, fasten, treat, or fill with lead. [OE *lēad*]

lead·en (led′n) *adj.* 1. Dull gray, as lead. 2. Made of lead. 3. Weighty; inert: a *leaden* mass. 4. Heavy or labored in movement, etc.; sluggish. **—lead′en·ly** *adv.* **—lead′en·ness** *n.*

lead·er (lē′dər) *n.* 1. One who or that which goes ahead or in advance. 2. One who acts as a guiding force, commander, etc. 3. A pipe for draining a liquid, as rainwater.

lead·er·ship (lē′dər·ship) *n.* 1. The office, position, or capacity of a leader; guidance. 2. Ability to lead, exert authority, etc. 3. A group of leaders.

lead·ing¹ (lē′ding) *adj.* 1. Having the capacity or effect of controlling, influencing, guiding, etc. 2. Most important; chief. 3. Situated or going at the head; first. *—n.* The act of one who or that which leads; guidance.

lead·ing² (led′ing) *n.* 1. The act or process of filling, covering, or separating with lead. 2. *Printing* Spacing between lines.

lead·off (lēd′ôf′) *n.* 1. A beginning action, move, etc., as the opening play in a competitive game. 2. A player or participant who begins the action in a game or competition. **—lead′off′** *adj.*

lead poisoning (led) *Pathol.* Poisoning caused by the absorption of lead by the tissues.

leaf (lēf) *n.* *pl.* **leaves** (lēvz) 1. One of the outgrowths from the stem of a plant, commonly flat, thin, and green in color, and functioning as the principal area of photosynthesis. 2. Foliage collectively; leafage. 3. A product, as tobacco, tea, etc., in the form of gathered leaves. 4. One of the sheets of paper in a book, etc. 5. A flat piece, hinged or otherwise movable, constituting part of a table, gate, etc. 6. Metal in a very thin sheet or plate: gold *leaf.* **—to turn over a new leaf** To begin anew, esp. with the intention of improving one's ways. *—v.i.* To put forth or produce leaves. [OE *lēaf*] **—leaf′less** *adj.*

leaf·age (lē′fij) *n.* Leaves collectively; foliage.

leaf·let (lēf′lit) *n.* 1. One of the divisions of a compound leaf. 2. A small printed sheet or circular, often folded. 3. A little leaf or leaflike part.

leaf·stalk (lēf′stôk′) *n.* A petiole (def. 1).

leaf·y (lē′fē) *adj.* **leaf·i·er, leaf·i·est** 1. Bearing, covered with, or characterized by a profusion of leaves. 2. Consisting of or resembling leaves. **—leaf′i·ness** *n.*

league¹ (lēg) *n.* A measure of distance usu. reckoned as approximately 3 miles. [< LL *leuga, leuca*]

league² (lēg) *n.* 1. An association or confederation of persons, organizations, or states. 2. A compact or covenant binding such a union. 3. An association of athletic teams. **—in league** In close alliance. *—v.t. & v.i.* **leagued, lea·guing** To unite in a league. [< Ital. *legare* to bind]

leak (lēk) *n.* 1. An opening, as a crack, permitting an undesirable escape or entrance of fluid, light, etc. 2. Any condition or agency by which something is let through or escapes: a *leak* in the security system. 3. An act or instance of leaking; leakage. *—v.i.* 1. To pass, flow, or escape through a hole, crack, etc. 2. To be divulged despite secrecy: The plans *leaked* out. *—v.t.* 3. To let (a liquid, etc.) escape. 4. To disclose (information, etc.) without authorization. [< ON *leka* to drip]

leak·age (lē′kij) *n.* 1. The act or circumstance of leaking. 2. That which escapes by leaking.

leak·y (lē′kē) *adj.* **leak·i·er, leak·i·est** Having a leak; permitting leakage. **—leak′i·ness** *n.*

lean¹ (lēn) *v.i.* 1. To rest or incline for support: usu. with *against* or *on.* 2. To bend or slant from an erect position. 3. To have a tendency, preference, etc. 4. To depend for support, etc.; rely. —*v.t.* 5. To cause to incline. —*n.* The act or condition of leaning; slant. [OE *hleonian, hlinian*]

lean[2] (lēn) *adj.* 1. Not fat or plump; thin; spare. 2. Not containing fat: *lean* meat. 3. Not rich, plentiful, or satisfying; meager. —*n.* Meat or flesh having little or no fat. [OE *hlǣne* thin] —**lean′ly** *adv.* —**lean′ness** *n.*

lean·ing (lē′ning) *n.* An inclination; tendency.

lean-to (lēn′tōō′) *n. pl.* **-tos** (-tōōz′) 1. A crude hut of branches, etc., sloping to the ground from a raised support. 2. A shed or extension of a building having a sloping roof and supported by an adjoining wall or structure.

leap (lēp) *v.* **leaped** or **leapt** (lept, lēpt), **leap·ing** *v.i.* 1. To rise or project oneself by a sudden thrust from the ground; jump; spring. 2. To move, react, etc., suddenly or impulsively. 3. To make an abrupt transition. —*v.t.* 4. To traverse by a jump. —*n.* 1. The act of leaping. 2. The space traversed by leaping. 3. An abrupt transition. [OE *hlēapan*] —**leap′er** *n.*

leap·frog (lēp′frog′, -frôg′) *n.* A game in which each player leaps over another, who is bending over. —**leap′frog′** *v.t. & v.i.* **·frogged, ·frog·ging**

leap year A year of 366 days, in which a 29th day is added to February. Every year divisible by 4 (as 1980) is a leap year, except those completing a century, which must be divisible by 400 (as 2000).

learn (lûrn) *v.* **learned** or **learnt, learn·ing** *v.t.* 1. To acquire knowledge of or skill in by study, practice, etc. 2. To find out; become aware of. 3. To commit to memory; memorize. 4. To acquire by experience or example. —*v.i.* 5. To gain knowledge or acquire skill. [OE *leornian*] —**learn′er** *n.*

learn·ed (lûr′nid) *adj.* 1. Having profound or extensive knowledge. 2. Characterized by or devoted to scholarship.

learn·ing (lûr′ning) *n.* 1. Knowledge obtained by study; erudition. 2. The act of acquiring knowledge or skill.

lease (lēs) *n.* 1. A contract for the temporary occupation or use of premises, property, etc., in exchange for payment of rent. 2. The period of such occupation or use. —*v.t.* 1. To grant use of under a lease. 2. To hold under a lease. [< OF *laissier* to let go < L *laxus* loose] —**leas′a·ble** *adj.*

leash (lēsh) *n.* A thong, cord, etc., by which a dog or other animal is led or restrained. —*v.t.* To hold or secure by a leash. [< OF *laissier* to let go < L *laxus* loose]

least (lēst) Alternative superlative of LITTLE. —*adj.* Smallest in degree, value, size, etc.; slightest. —*n.* That which is smallest, slightest, or most insignificant. —**at least** 1. By the lowest possible estimate. 2. At any rate. —*adv.* In the lowest or smallest degree. [OE *lǣssa* less]

least·wise (lēst′wīz′) *adv. Informal* At least; at any rate.

leath·er (leth′ər) *n.* Animal skin, usu. with the hair removed, prepared for use by tanning. —*v.t.* To cover or equip with leather. [OE *lether*]

leath·ern (leth′ərn) *adj. Archaic* 1. Made of leather. 2. Resembling leather; leathery.

leath·er·neck (leth′ər·nek′) *n. Slang* A U.S. Marine.

leath·er·y (leth′ər·ē) *adj.* Resembling leather in texture or appearance; tough. —**leath′er·i·ness** *n.*

leave[1] (lēv) *v.* **left, leav·ing** *v.t.* 1. To go or depart from. 2. To allow to remain behind or in a specified place, condition, etc. 3. To have or cause as an aftermath: Oil *leaves* stains. 4. To commit for action, etc.; entrust: *Leave* it to me. 5. To terminate one's connection or association with. 6. To abandon; forsake. 7. To transmit as a legacy; bequeath. —*v.i.* 8. To go away; set out. —**to leave off** To stop; cease. —**to leave out** 1. To omit. 2. To exclude. [OE *lǣfan*, lit., to let remain] —**leav′er** *n.*

leave[2] (lēv) *n.* 1. Permission to do something. 2. Permission to be absent; esp., **a** Official permission to be absent from duty. **b** The period covered by such permission: also **leave of absence.** 3. Formal farewell: usu. in the phrase **to take (one's) leave.** —**on leave** Absent from work or duty with permission. [OE *lēaf* permission]

leaved (lēvd) *adj.* Having or characterized by (a specified kind or number of) leaves.

leav·en (lev′ən) *n.* 1. An agent of fermentation, as yeast, added to dough or batter to produce a light texture. 2. Any pervasive influence that produces a significant change. Also **leav′en·ing.** —*v.t.* 1. To cause fermentation in. 2. To affect in character; temper. [< L *levare* to raise]

leaves (lēvz) Plural of LEAF.

leave-tak·ing (lēv′tā′king) *n.* An act of departure.

leav·ings (lē′vingz) *n.pl.* Unused portion; remnants.

Leb·a·nese (leb′ə·nēz′, -nēs′) *adj.* Of or pertaining to Lebanon or its people. —*n.* A native or citizen of Lebanon.

lech·er·y (lech′ər·ē) *n.* Unconstrained sexual indulgence. [< OF *lechier* to live in debauchery < OHG *leccōn* to lick] —**lech′er** *n.* —**lech′er·ous** *adj.* —**lech′er·ous·ly** *adv.* —**lech′er·ous·ness** *n.*

lec·i·thin (les′ə·thin) *n.* Any of a class of fatty substances containing phosphorus, found in plant and animal tissue, and used industrially. [< Gk. *lekithos* egg yolk]

lec·tern (lek′tərn) *n.* 1. A stand on which a speaker, instructor, etc., may place books or papers. 2. In some churches, a reading desk from which certain parts of the service are read. [< LL *lectrum* < L *legere* to read]

lec·ture (lek′chər) *n.* 1. A discourse on a specific subject, delivered to an audience for instruction or information. 2. A formal reproof or lengthy reprimand. —*v.* **·tured, ·tur·ing** *v.i.* 1. To deliver a lecture or lectures. —*v.t.* 2. To deliver a lecture to. 3. To rebuke sternly or at length. [< L *lectura* reading < *legere* to read] —**lec′tur·er** *n.*

led (led) Past tense and past participle of LEAD[1].

ledge (lej) *n.* 1. A narrow, shelflike projection along the side of a rocky formation. 2. A shelf or sill projecting from or forming the top of a wall, etc. 3. An underwater or coastal ridge. [ME *legge*]

led·ger (lej′ər) *n.* An account book in which all final entries of business transactions are recorded. [ME *legger*]

lee (lē) *n.* 1. Shelter or protection, esp. from the wind. 2. *Chiefly Naut.* The side sheltered from the wind. [OE *hlēo* shelter] **—lee** *adj.*

leech (lēch) *n.* 1. Any of a class of carnivorous or blood-sucking, chiefly aquatic annelid worms; esp. the **medicinal leech**, formerly used for bloodletting. 2. One who clings to another for gain; a parasite. **—***v.t. Archaic* To treat with leeches. [OE *lǣce*, orig., physician]

leek (lēk) *n.* A culinary herb of the lily family, closely allied to the onion but having a narrow bulb and broader, dark green leaves. [OE *lēac*]

leer (lir) *n.* A sly look or sidewise glance expressing salacious desire, malicious intent, etc. [OE *hlēor* cheek, face] **—leer** *v.i.*

leer·y (lir′ē) *adj. Informal* 1. Suspicious; wary. 2. Sly.

lees (lēz) *n.pl.* Sediment, esp. in wine or liquor; dregs. [Pl. of obs. *lee* < OF *lie*]

lee·ward (lē′wərd, *Naut.* lo͞o′ərd) *adj.* Being on or toward the side sheltered from the wind. **—***n.* The side or direction toward which the wind is blowing. **—***adv.* Toward the lee. Opposed to *windward.*

lee·way (lē′wā′) *n.* 1. Additional space, time, range, etc., providing greater freedom of action. 2. *Naut.* The lateral drift of a vessel or an aircraft in motion.

left[1] (left) Past tense and past participle of LEAVE[1].

left[2] (left) *adj.* 1. Pertaining to, designating, or being on the side of the body that is toward the north when one faces east, and usu. having the weaker and less dominant hand, etc. 2. Nearest to or tending in the direction of the left side. 3. Worn on a left hand, foot, etc. 4. *Sometimes cap.* Designating a person, party, faction, etc., having liberal, socialistic, or laborite views and policies. **—***n.* 1. Any part, area, etc., on or toward the left side. 2. *Often cap.* A group, party, etc., whose views and policies are left (*adj.* def. 4). 3. In boxing, a blow with the left hand. [ME (Kentish) var. of OE *lyft* weak] **—left** *adv.*

left-hand (left′hand′) *adj.* 1. Of, for, pertaining to, or situated on the left side or the left hand. 2. Turning, opening, or swinging to the left.

left-hand·ed (left′han′did) *adj.* 1. Using the left hand habitually and more easily than the right. 2. Adapted or intended for use by the left hand. 3. Turning or moving from right to left, or counterclockwise. 4. Ironical or insincere in intent or effect: a *left-handed* compliment. **—***adv.* With the left hand. **—left′hand′ed·ness** *n.*

left·ist (lef′tist) *n.* One whose views and policies are left (*adj.* def. 4). **—***adj.* Left (*adj.* def. 4). **—left′ism** *n.*

left·o·ver (left′ō′vər) *n. Usu. pl.* An unused part, esp. of prepared food. **—left′o′ver** *adj.*

left wing *Sometimes cap.* A party, group, faction, etc., having leftist policies. **—left-wing** (left′wing′) *adj.* **—left′-wing′er** *n.*

leg (leg) *n.* 1. One of the limbs or appendages serving as a means of support and locomotion in animals and man. 2. *Anat.* **a** A lower limb of the human body, extending from the hip to the ankle. **b** The part of the lower limb between the knee and the ankle. 3. A support resembling a leg in shape, position, or function. 4. The portion of an article of clothing, as trousers, that covers a leg. 5. A division or section of a course or journey. **—on one's last legs** On the verge of collapse or death. **—to pull one's leg** *Informal* To make fun of; fool. **—to shake a leg** *Slang* To hurry. [< ON *leggr*] **—leg′less** *adj.*

leg·a·cy (leg′ə·sē) *n. pl.* **·cies** 1. Personal property, money, etc., bequeathed by will; a bequest. 2. Anything received from or passed on by an ancestor, predecessor, or earlier era. [< Med.L *legatia* the district of a legate]

le·gal (lē′gəl) *adj.* 1. Of or concerned with law: *legal* documents. 2. Established, authorized, or permitted by law. 3. Characteristic of or appropriate to those who practice law. [< L *lex, legis* law] **—le′gal·ly** *adv.*

legal age Age (*n.* def. 2).

legal holiday A day on which banks are closed and official business is suspended or limited by law.

le·gal·ism (lē′gəl·iz′əm) *n.* Strict and literal conformity to law. **—le′gal·ist** *n.* **—le′gal·is′tic** *adj.*

le·gal·i·ty (li·gal′ə·tē) *n. pl.* **·ties** 1. The condition or quality of being legal; lawfulness. 2. Adherence to law.

le·gal·ize (lē′gəl·īz) *v.t.* **·ized, ·iz·ing** To make legal. Also *Brit.* **le′gal·ise.** **—le′gal·i·za′tion** *n.*

legal tender Coin or other money that may be legally offered in payment of a debt, and that a creditor must accept.

leg·ate (leg′it) *n.* 1. An ecclesiastic appointed as an official representative of the Pope. 2. An official envoy, usu. acting as a diplomatic representative of a government. [< L *legare* to send as a deputy]

leg·a·tee (leg′ə·tē′) *n.* One to whom a legacy is bequeathed.

le·ga·tion (li·gā′shən) *n.* 1. The official residence or business premises of a diplomatic minister or envoy of lower rank than an ambassador. 2. The official staff of a foreign envoy or diplomatic mission.

le·ga·to (li·gä′tō) *adj. Music* Smooth and flowing, with unbroken transition between successive notes. [< Ital., lit., bound] **—le·ga′to** *adv.*

leg·end (lej′ənd) *n.* 1. An unauthenticated story from earlier times, preserved by tradition and popularly thought to be historical. 2. An inscription, as on a coin, banner, etc. 3. A caption or explanatory description accompanying an illustration, chart, etc. [< L *legere* to read]

leg·en·dar·y (lej′ən·der′ē) *adj.* 1. Of, presented in, or of the nature of a legend. 2. Famous; celebrated.

leg·er·de·main (lej′ər·də·mān′) *n.* 1. Sleight of hand. 2. Any artful trickery or deception. [< MF *léger de main*, lit., light of hand]

leg·ged (leg′id, legd) *adj.* Having or characterized by (a specified kind or number of) legs: *bow-legged; two-legged.*

leg·ging (leg′ing) *n.* A covering for the leg, usu. extending from the knee to the instep.

leg·gy (leg′ē) *adj.* **·gi·er, ·gi·est** 1. Having disproportionately long legs. 2. *Informal*

Having or displaying attractive, shapely legs. **—leg′gi·ness** *n.*

leg·horn (leg′hôrn, -ərn) *n.* 1. Finely plaited wheat straw. 2. A hat made from this straw. 3. One of a breed of small, hardy domestic fowl: also **Leg′horn.** [after *Leghorn,* a city in Italy]

leg·i·ble (lej′ə·bəl) *adj.* Capable of being read or deciphered; easy to read. [< L *legere* to read] **—leg′i·bil′i·ty** *n.* **—leg′i·bly** *adv.*

le·gion (lē′jən) *n.* 1. In ancient Rome, a major military unit consisting primarily of infantry troops with an auxiliary force of cavalry, altogether comprising up to 6,000 men. 2. A great number; multitude. 3. *Usu. cap.* Any of various military or honorary organizations, usu. national in character. [< L *legere* to gather] **—le′gion·ar′y** *adj.*

le·gion·naire (lē′jən·âr′) *n.* *Often cap.* A member of a legion (def. 3). [< F *légionnaire*]

legionnaires' disease A disease, resembling pneumonia, caused by a bacterium. [from an outbreak after an American Legion Convention in Philadelphia in 1976]

leg·is·late (lej′is·lāt) *v.* **·lat·ed, ·lat·ing** *v.i.* 1. To make a law or laws. **—***v.t.* 2. To effect by legislation: often with *into* or *out of.* [Back formation < LEGISLATOR]

leg·is·la·tion (lej′is·lā′shən) *n.* 1. The act or procedures of enacting laws. 2. An officially enacted law or laws.

leg·is·la·tive (lej′is·lā′tiv) *adj.* 1. Of, pertaining to, or involved in legislation. 2. Having the power to legislate: the *legislative* branch of the government. 3. Of or pertaining to a legislature. **—leg′is·la′tive·ly** *adv.*

leg·is·la·tor (lej′is·lā′tər) *n.* 1. One active in the formation and enactment of laws; a lawmaker. 2. A member of a legislature. [< L *lex, legis* law + *lator* bearer, proposer]

leg·is·la·ture (lej′is·lā′chər) *n.* A body of persons officially constituted and empowered to make and enact the laws of a nation or state; esp., in the U.S., the lawmaking body of a state, territory, etc., as distinguished from Congress.

le·git (lə·jit′) *adj.* *Slang* Legitimate.

le·git·i·mate (*adj.* lə·jit′ə·mit; *v.* lə·jit′ə·māt) *adj.* 1. In accordance with law; lawful. 2. Authentic; valid. 3. Born in wedlock. 4. According to or based on strict hereditary right. 5. In the theater, denoting drama performed by living actors before an audience. **—***v.t.* **·mat·ed, ·mat·ing** 1. To make or establish as legitimate. 2. To show reason or authorization for. [< L *legitimus* lawful < *lex, legis* law] **—le·git′i·ma·cy** (-mə·sē) *n.* **—le·git′i·mate·ly** *adv.* **—le·git′i·ma′tion** (-mā′shən) *n.*

le·git·i·mize (lə·jit′ə·mīz) *v.t.* **·mized, ·miz·ing** To legitimate. Also **le·git′i·ma·tize** (-mə·tīz). **—le·git′i·mi·za′tion** *n.*

leg·man (leg′man′) *n.* *pl.* **·men** (-men′, -mən) 1. A reporter who covers news events in person. 2. One who runs errands or collects information.

leg·ume (leg′yo͞om, lə·gyo͞om′) *n.* 1. The fruit or seed of any leguminous plant, esp. when used as food or fodder. 2. Any leguminous plant. [< L *legumen,* lit., something gathered < *legere* to gather]

le·gu·mi·nous (lə·gyo͞o′mə·nəs) *adj.* Of or belonging to a large family of plants producing seed-filled pods, including peas, beans, etc.

leg·work (leg′wûrk′) *n.* *Informal* Work, as the gathering of information, requiring physical activity.

lei (lā, lā′ē) *n.* *pl.* **leis** A festival garland of blossoms, feathers, etc., as worn in Hawaii. [< Hawaiian]

lei·sure (lē′zhər, lezh′ər) *n.* 1. Freedom from the demands of work or duty. 2. Time available for recreation or relaxation. **—at leisure** 1. Free from pressing obligation. 2. Unoccupied; not employed. 3. When one has time or opportunity: also **at one's leisure.** **—***adj.* 1. Not spent in work or necessary activity: *leisure* time. 2. Having considerable leisure: the *leisure* classes. [< L *licere* to be permitted]

lei·sure·ly (lē′zhər·lē, lezh′ər-) *adj.* Free from exertion or pressure; relaxed. Also **lei′sured.** **—lei′sure·li·ness** *n.* **—lei′sure·ly** *adv.*

leit·mo·tif (līt′mō·tēf′) *n.* *Music* A theme used for a certain person, event, or idea throughout an opera, etc. Also **leit′mo·tiv′** (-tēf′). [< G < *leiten* to lead + *motiv* motive]

lem·ming (lem′ing) *n.* Any of several small arctic rodents, having a short tail and furry feet; esp., a European species, noted for recurrent mass migrations often terminated by drowning in the ocean. [< Norw.]

lem·on (lem′ən) *n.* 1. The oval, citrus fruit having juicy, acid pulp and a yellow rind. 2. The tree bearing this fruit. 3. A bright, clear yellow. 4. *Slang* Something or someone unsatisfactory. **—***adj.* Bright, clear yellow. [< Persian *limūn*]

lem·on·ade (lem′ən·ād′) *n.* A drink made of lemon juice, water, and sugar.

lem·on·y (lem′ə·nē) *adj.* Suggestive of lemon.

lem·pi·ra (lem·pē′rä) *n.* The monetary unit of Honduras.

le·mur (lē′mər) *n.* Any of various small, arboreal, mostly nocturnal mammals related to the monkeys; esp., one having a foxlike face and soft fur, found chiefly in Madagascar. [< L *lemures* ghosts]

lend (lend) *v.* **lent, lend·ing** *v.t.* 1. To grant for temporary use or possession. 2. To grant the use of (money) at a stipulated rate of interest. 3. To impart, as an abstract quality. 4. To make available, as for aid or support. **—***v.i.* 5. To make a loan or loans. **—to lend itself (or oneself) to** To adapt or accommodate for a specific purpose. [OE *lǣn* a loan] **—lend′er** *n.*

length (lengkth, length) *n.* 1. Linear extent from end to end; usu., the longest dimension of a thing, as distinguished from its width and thickness. 2. Extent from beginning to end, as of a period of time, series, book, word, etc. 3. Duration or continuance, esp. in respect to time. 4. The measurement along, extent of, or distance equivalent to something specified: arm's *length.* 5. *Often pl.* The limit of one's efforts, ability, etc.: to go to great *lengths.* 6. In racing, the extent from front to back of a competing horse, boat, etc., used as a unit of estimating position. **—at length** 1. Finally. 2. In full. [OE *lengthu* < *lang* long]

length·en (lengk′thən, leng′-) *v.t. & v.i.* To make or become longer.

length·wise (lengkth′wīz′, length′-) *adv.* In the direction or dimension of length; longitudinally. Also **length′ways′** (-wāz′). —*adj.* According to length; longitudinal.

length·y (lengk′thē, leng′-) *adj.* **length·i·er, length·i·est** Unusually or unduly long. —**length′i·ly** *adv.* —**length′i·ness** *n.*

le·ni·ent (lē′nē·ənt, lēn′yənt) *adj.* Gentle or merciful in disposition, effect, etc.; mild. [< L *leniens, -entis,* ppr. of *lenire* to soothe] —**le′ni·en·cy, le′ni·ence** *n.* —**le′ni·ent·ly** *adv.*

len·i·tive (len′ə·tiv) *adj.* Having the power or tendency to allay pain or distress; soothing. [< L *lenitus,* pp. of *lenire* to soothe] —**len′i·tive** *n.*

len·i·ty (len′ə·tē) *n.* The state or quality of being lenient. [< L *lenitas, -tatis* softness]

lens (lenz) *n.* 1. *Optics* A piece of glass or other transparent substance, by which rays of light are made to converge or diverge. 2. Two or more such pieces in combination. 3. Any device that concentrates or disperses radiation, etc., other than light by action similar to that of an optical lens. 4. *Anat.* A transparent body situated behind the iris of the eye and serving to focus an image on the retina. [< L *lens, lentis* lentil; so called from the form]

lent (lent) Past tense and past participle of LEND.

Lent (lent) *n. Eccl.* The period of forty days, excluding Sundays, from Ash Wednesday to Easter, observed as a season of fasting, penitence, and self-denial. [Short for *Lenten* < OE *lencten, lengten* the spring] —**Len′ten** *adj.*

len·til (len′təl) *n.* 1. A leguminous plant, having broad pods containing flattish, edible seeds. 2. The seed of this plant. [< L *lenticula,* dim. of *lens, lentis* lentil]

len·to (len′tō) *Music adj.* Slow. —*adv.* Slowly. [< Ital. < L *lentus*]

Le·o (lē′ō) *n.* A constellation, the Lion; also, the fifth sign of the zodiac. [< L, lion]

le·o·ne (lē·ōn′) *n.* The monetary unit of Sierra Leone.

le·o·nine (lē′ə·nīn, -nin) *adj.* Resembling, or characteristic of a lion. [< L *leo, leonis* lion]

leop·ard (lep′ərd) *n.* 1. A large member of the cat family, native to Asia and Africa, having a tawny coat with dark brown or black spots grouped in rounded clusters: also called *panther.* 2. Any of various similar felines, as the cheetah or jaguar. 3. The fur of a leopard. [< Gk. *leopardos* < *leōn* lion + *pardos* panther]

le·o·tard (lē′ə·tärd) *n. Often pl.* A close-fitting, stretchable garment worn by dancers, acrobats, etc. [after Jules *Léotard,* 19th c. French aerialist]

lep·er (lep′ər) *n.* One afflicted with leprosy. [< Gk., orig. fem. of *lepros* scaly]

lep·i·dop·ter·ous (lep′ə·dop′tər·əs) *adj.* Belonging or pertaining to an order of insects comprising the butterflies and moths, characterized by four wings covered with minute scales. [< Gk. *lepis, -idos* scale + *pteron* wing] —**lep′i·dop′ter·ist** *n.*

lep·re·chaun (lep′rə·kôn) *n.* In Irish folklore, a tiny elf supposed to own hidden treasure. [< OIrish < *lu* little + *corpān,* dim. of *corp* body]

lep·ro·sy (lep′rə·sē) *n. Pathol.* A chronic, communicable disease caused by a microorganism and characterized by skin lesions, nerve paralysis, and physical mutilation: also called *Hansen's disease.* [See LEPER.] —**lep′rous** *adj.*

-lepsy *combining form* Seizure; attack: *epilepsy.* Also **-lepsia.** [< Gk. *lepsis* seizure]

lep·ton (lep′ton) *n. Physics* A class of weakly interacting subatomic particles believed to be elementary and including the electron, muon and neutrino. [< Gk. *leptos* small]

les·bi·an (lez′bē·ən) *n. Sometimes cap.* A homosexual woman. [< Gk. *Lesbos,* an island in the Aegean] —**les′bi·an** *adj.* —**les′bi·an·ism** *n.*

lese ma·jes·ty (lēz′ maj′is·tē) An offense against sovereign authority or a sovereign; treason. Also *Fr.* **lèse-ma·jes·té** (lez′mȧ·zhes·tā′). [< F < L *laesa majestas* injured majesty]

le·sion (lē′zhən) *n.* 1. *Pathol.* Any abnormal or harmful change in the structure of an organ or tissue. 2. An injury; damage. [< L *laesus,* pp. of *laedere* to injure]

less (les) Alternative comparative of LITTLE. —*adj.* 1. Not as great in quantity or degree; not as much. 2. Inferior in degree; smaller; lower: with *than.* —*adv.* To a smaller degree or extent. —*n.* A smaller amount or part. —*prep.* With the subtraction of; minus. [OE *lǣs*]

-less *suffix of adjectives* 1. Devoid of; without: *blameless, harmless.* 2. Deprived of; lacking: *motherless, stemless.* 3. Not able to (do something): *restless.* [OE *leas* free from]

les·see (les·ē′) *n.* One to whom a lease is granted. [< OF *lesser, laissier* to let, leave]

less·en (les′ən) *v.t.* 1. To decrease. 2. To make little of; disparage. —*v.i.* 3. To become less.

less·er (les′ər) *adj.* Not as large or important; minor.

les·son (les′ən) *n.* 1. An instance or experience from which useful knowledge may be gained. 2. An assignment to be studied or learned, as by a student. 3. A reprimand; reproof. 4. A portion of the Bible read or designated to be read at a religious service. [< L *lectio, -ionis* a reading]

les·sor (les′ôr, les·ôr′) *n.* One who grants a lease; a landlord letting property under a lease. [See LESSEE.]

lest (lest) *conj.* 1. In order to prevent the chance that (something might happen); for fear that. 2. That: after expressions denoting anxiety: We worried *lest* the money should not last. [OE (*thȳ*) *lǣs the* (by the) less that]

let[1] (let) *v.* **let, let·ting** *v.t.* 1. To allow; permit. 2. To grant or assign, as a contract for work to be performed. 3. An auxiliary verb, usu. in the imperative, signifying: **a** An exhortation or command: *Let's* go! **b** Acquiescence; inability to prevent the inevitable: *Let* it rain. **c** An assumption or suggestion: *Let* x equal the sum of two numbers. 4. *Chiefly Brit.* To rent (a house, room, etc.) to a tenant. 5. To cause to flow, as blood. —*v.i.* 6. *Chiefly Brit.* To be rented: rooms to *let.* —**to let down** 1. To cause to fall or descend; loosen, as hair. 2. To disappoint. —**to let**

loose To set free; release. —to let off 1. To emit; release, as from pressure or tension. 2. To discharge, dismiss, or excuse, as from work or obligation. —to let up 1. To grow less; abate. 2. To reduce tension. —to let up on *Informal* To cease to subject to force or severe treatment. [OE *lǣtan*]

let² (let) *n.* In tennis or similar games, a service, point, etc., that must be repeated. [OE *lettan* to make late]

-let *suffix of nouns* 1. Small; little: *booklet.* 2. A band or ornament for (a specified part of the body): *anklet.* [< OF *-let, -lette* < *-el* + *-et,* dim. suffixes]

let·down (let′doun′) *n.* 1. A decrease; slackening, as of speed, force, or energy. 2. *Informal* Disappointment.

le·thal (lē′thəl) *adj.* 1. Causing death; deadly; fatal. 2. Pertaining to or characteristic of death. [< L *lethum, letum* death]

leth·ar·gy (leth′ər·jē) *n. pl.* **·gies** 1. A state of indifference; apathy. 2. *Pathol.* Excessive drowsiness or abnormally deep sleep. [< Gk. *lēthargos* forgetful] —**le·thar·gic** (li·thär′jik) or **·gi·cal** *adj.* —**le·thar′gi·cal·ly** *adv.*

Lett (let) *n.* 1. A Latvian. 2. The Latvian language.

let·ter (let′ər) *n.* 1. A standardized character used in writing or printing to represent a speech sound. 2. A written or printed message directed to a specified person or group. 3. An official document granting certain rights or privileges to a specified person: a *letter* of credit. 4. Literal meaning: the *letter* of the law. 5. *pl.* Literature in general; literary profession: a man of *letters.* 6. An emblem in the form of the initial letter of a college, school, etc., awarded for outstanding performance in athletics. —*v.t.* 1. To inscribe letters on; mark with letters. —*v.i.* 2. To form letters, as by hand. [< L *littera* letter of the alphabet, in pl., epistle] —**let′ter·er** *n.*

let·tered (let′ərd) *adj.* 1. Versed in letters; educated. 2. Inscribed or marked with letters.

let·ter·head (let′ər·hed′) *n.* A printed heading, as a name and address, on a sheet of writing paper; also, a sheet of paper bearing this.

let·ter·ing (let′ər·ing) *n.* 1. The act or art of forming letters; process of marking or stamping with letters. 2. Letters collectively, esp. a single example.

let·ter-per·fect (let′ər·pûr′fikt) *adj.* Correct in all details. —**let′ter-per′fect** *adv.*

let·ter·press (let′ər·pres′) *n. Printing* 1. A process of printing from type or similar raised surfaces. 2. Printing so produced.

letters patent *Law* The instrument granting a patent.

Let·tish (let′ish) *adj. & n.* Latvian.

let·tuce (let′is) *n.* 1. A cultivated herb having crisp, edible leaves; also, the leaves. 2. *Slang* Paper money. [< L *lac, lactis* milk]

let·up (let′up′) *n. Informal* 1. A lessening or relaxation, as of force or intensity; lull. 2. A respite; pause; interlude.

leuco- *combining form* White; lacking color: also, before vowels, **leuc-**. Also **leuko-, leuk-**. [< Gk. *leukos* white]

leu·co·cyte (lōō′kə·sīt) *n. Physiol.* A white or colorless blood corpuscle, constituting an important agent in protection against infectious diseases. Also spelled **leu′ko·cyte.**

leu·ke·mi·a (lōō·kē′mē·ə) *n. Pathol.* A generally fatal disease of the blood and bloodmaking tissues, characterized by a marked increase in the number of leucocytes. Also **leu·kae′mi·a.** [< Gk. *leukos* white + *haima* blood]

Le·vant (lə·vant′) *n.* The regions bordering the eastern Mediterranean, between western Greece and western Egypt: usu. preceded by *the.* [< L *levare* to raise] —**Le·van·tine** (lə·van′tin, lev′ən·tīn, -tēn) *adj. & n.*

lev·ee¹ (lev′ē) *n.* 1. An embankment along the shore of a river, built for protection against floods. 2. A landing place; wharf. [< F *lever* to raise < L *levare*]

lev·ee² (lev′ē, lə·vē′) *n.* A reception, usu. held early in the day by a person of rank or distinction. [< F *levé* an arising]

lev·el (lev′əl) *n.* 1. Relative place, degree, or stage: a high *level* of development. 2. Position on a vertical scale; height: the *level* of the lower branches. 3. A horizontal line or surface: sea *level.* 4. A flat expanse, as of land. 5. Any of various devices used to find the conformity of a line or surface with the horizontal plane. —**on the level** *Informal* Without deception; fair. —*adj.* 1. Having a surface with no irregularities in height; even; flat. 2. Conforming to a horizontal plane. 3. Being at the same height as something else. 4. Measured so as to have a surface even with the edge of the container. 5. Equal to something or someone else, as in importance, development, etc. —**a level head** A calm and sensible mind. —**one's level best** *Informal* The best one can possibly do. —*v.* **lev·eled** or **·elled, lev·el·ing** or **·el·ling** *v.t.* 1. To give an even or horizontal surface to. 2. To destroy by or as by smashing to the ground. 3. To knock down. 4. To bring to a common state or condition. 5. To aim or point as a weapon. 6. To aim or direct (something) with force of emphasis: to *level* an accusation. —*v.i.* 7. To bring persons or things to a common state or condition. 8. *Slang* To be honest. —*adv.* In an even line or plane. [< OF *livel* < L *libra* a balance] —**lev′el·er** or **lev′el·ler** *n.* —**lev′el·ly** *adv.* —**lev′el·ness** *n.*

lev·el·head·ed (lev′əl·hed′id) *adj.* Characterized by common sense and cool judgment. —**lev′el·head′ed·ness** *n.*

lev·er (lev′ər, lē′vər) *n.* 1. *Mech.* A device, as a straight bar, pivoting on a fixed support (the fulcrum), and serving to impart pressure or motion from a force or effort applied at one point to a resisting force at another point. 2. Any of various tools, devices, or parts operating on the same principle, as a crowbar. 3. Any means of exerting effective power. —*v.t. & v.i.* To move or pry with or as with a lever. [< L *levare* to raise]

lev·er·age (lev′ər·ij, lē′vər-) *n.* 1. The action or mechanical effect of a lever. 2. Speculation with the use of borrowed money. 3. *Informal* The power to effect or accomplish something. —*v.t.* To speculate or cause to speculate on borrowed money.

le·vi·a·than (lə·vī′ə·thən) *n.* 1. A gigantic water beast mentioned in the Bible. 2. Any enormous creature or thing.

Le·vis (lē′vīz) *n.pl.* Close-fitting, heavy denim trousers having rivets to reinforce points of greatest strain: a registered trade mark. [after *Levi* Strauss, U.S. manufacturer]

lev·i·tate (lev′ə·tāt) *v.* **·tat·ed, ·tat·ing** *v.i.* 1. To rise and float in the air, as through buoyancy or supposed supernatural power. —*v.t.* 2. To cause to rise and float in the air. [< L *levis* light, on analogy with *gravitate*] —**lev′i·ta′tion** *n.*

Le·vit·i·cus (lə·vit′i·kəs) The third book of the Old Testament, consisting chiefly of a compilation of ceremonial laws.

lev·i·ty (lev′ə·tē) *n.* Lack of seriousness; inappropriate gaiety; frivolity. [< L *levis* light]

lev·y (lev′ē) *v.* **lev·ied, lev·y·ing** *v.t.* 1. To impose and collect by authority or force, as a tax, fine, etc. 2. To enlist or call up (troops, etc.) for military service. 3. To prepare for, begin, or wage (war). —*v.i.* 4. *Law* To seize property in order to fulfill a judgment: usu. with *on.* —*n. pl.* **lev·ies** 1. The act of levying. 2. That which is levied, as money or troops. [< L *levare* to raise]

lewd (lo͞od) *adj.* 1. Characterized by or inciting to lust or debauchery. 2. Obscene; ribald; bawdy. [OE *lǣwede* lay, unlearned] —**lewd′ly** *adv.* —**lewd′ness** *n.*

lex·i·cog·ra·phy (lek′sə·kog′rə·fē) *n.* The art or profession of compiling dictionaries. [< Gk. *lexikon* lexicon + *graphein* to write] —**lex′i·cog′ra·pher** *n.* —**lex′i·co·graph′ic** (-kō·graf′ik) or **·i·cal** *adj.*

lex·i·con (lek′sə·kon) *n.* 1. A dictionary; esp., a dictionary of Latin, Greek, or Hebrew. 2. A vocabulary of a language, a particular subject, occupation, or activity. [< Gk. *lexikos* pertaining to words]

lex·is (lek′səs) *n. pl.* **lex·es** (-sēs) Lexicon (def. 2). [< Gk., word, speech]

li·a·bil·i·ty (lī′ə·bil′ə·tē) *n. pl.* **·ties** 1. The state or condition of being liable. 2. That for which one is liable, as a debt. 3. *pl.* The debts or obligations of a business: opposed to *assets.* 4. Any obstacle or hindrance.

li·a·ble (lī′ə·bəl) *adj.* 1. Justly or legally responsible, as for damages; answerable. 2. Subject or susceptible, as to injury, illness, etc. 3. *Informal* Likely. [< L *ligare* to bind]

li·ai·son (lē′ā·zon′, lē·ā′zon, lē′ə·zon; *Fr.* lē·e·zôn′) *n.* 1. Communication or unity, as between parts of an armed force. 2. An illicit love affair. [< F < L *ligare* to bind]

li·ar (lī′ər) *n.* One who lies or utters falsehoods. [OE *lēogere*]

lib (lib) *n.* Liberation: gay *lib.*

li·ba·tion (lī·bā′shən) *n.* 1. A liquid ceremonially poured out, as in honor of a deity; also, the act of pouring such a liquid. 2. Humorously, a drink. [< L *libare* to pour out (as an offering)]

li·bel (lī′bəl) *n.* 1. *Law* **a** A written statement or graphic representation, esp. in published form, that damages a person's reputation. **b** The act or crime of publishing such a statement. 2. Any defamatory or grossly unflattering statement. —*v.t.* **li·beled** or **·belled, li·bel·ing** or **·bel·ling** To publish or perpetrate a libel against. [< L *libellus,* dim. of *liber* book] —**li′bel·er** or **li′bel·ler** *n.*

li·bel·ous (lī′bəl·əs) *adj.* Constituting, containing, or like a libel. Also *esp. Brit.* **li′bel·lous.** —**li′bel·ous·ly** *adv.*

lib·er·al (lib′ər·əl, lib′rəl) *adj.* 1. Favoring progress or reform, as in politics or religion. 2. Not intolerant or prejudiced. 3. Generous; lavish in giving. 4. Given freely or in large quantity; ample. 5. Not literal or strict. —*n.* One having liberal opinions or convictions, esp. in politics or religion. [< L *liberalis* pertaining to a freeman] —**lib′er·al·ly** *adv.*

liberal arts A group of college courses including literature, languages, history, etc., distinguished from scientific, technical, or purely practical subjects.

lib·er·al·ism (lib′ər·əl·iz′əm) *n.* Liberal beliefs or policies, esp. in regard to politics, social changes, religion, etc.

lib·er·al·i·ty (lib′ə·ral′ə·tē) *n.* 1. Generosity. 2. Broad-mindedness.

lib·er·al·ize (lib′ər·əl·īz′) *v.t. & v.i.* **·ized, ·iz·ing** To make or become liberal. —**lib′er·al·i·za′tion** (lib′ər·əl·ə·zā′shən, -ī·zā′-, lib′·rəl-) *n.*

lib·er·ate (lib′ə·rāt) *v.t.* **·at·ed, ·at·ing** 1. To set free, as from slavery or confinement. 2. To release from chemical combination, as a gas. 3. To bring about equal rights or status (for). [< L *liberatus,* pp. of *liberare* to free] —**lib′er·a′tion** *n.* —**lib′er·a′tor** *n.*

Li·be·ri·an (lī·bir′ē·ən) *adj.* Of or pertaining to Liberia or its people. —**Li·be′ri·an** *n.*

lib·er·tar·i·an (lib′ər·târ′ē·ən) *n.* One who advocates liberty of thought or conduct. —**lib′er·tar′i·an** *adj.* —**lib′er·tar′i·an·ism** *n.*

lib·er·tine (lib′ər·tēn) *n.* One lacking moral restraint; a profligate. [< L *libertus* freedman] —**lib′er·tine** *adj.* —**lib′er·tin·ism** *n.*

lib·er·ty (lib′ər·tē) *n. pl.* **·ties** 1. Freedom from oppression, tyranny, or harsh domination. 2. Freedom from confinement or slavery. 3. Freedom of thought or action, or exemption from forms of compulsion or indignity, regarded as a human right. 4. An overly free, familiar, or disrespectful act or manner. 5. In the U.S. Navy, official permission to be absent from one's ship or place of duty, usu. for less than 48 hours. —**at liberty** 1. Free; authorized or permitted (to do something). 2. Not engaged in an activity or occupation; unemployed. 3. Able to move about freely. [< L *liber* free]

li·bid·i·nous (li·bid′ə·nəs) *adj.* Characterized by or inclining toward excesses of sexual desire; lustful. —**li·bid′i·nous·ly** *adv.* —**li·bid′i·nous·ness** *n.*

li·bi·do (li·bē′dō, -bī′-) *n.* 1. Sexual desire or impulse. 2. *Psychoanal.* The instinctual craving or drive behind all human activities. [< L, lust] —**li·bid′i·nal** (-bid′ə·nəl) *adj.*

Li·bra (lī′brə, lē′-) *n.* A constellation, the Balance; also, the seventh sign of the zodiac. [< L, scales]

li·brar·i·an (lī·brer′ē·ən) *n.* 1. One who has charge of a library. 2. A person qualified by training for library service.

li·brar·y (lī′brer·ē, -brə·rē) *n. pl.* **·brar·ies** 1. A collection of books, pamphlets, etc.; esp., such a collection arranged to facilitate reference. 2. A building, room, etc., housing such a collection. 3. A commercial establishment that rents books. [< L *liber, libri* book]

li·bret·tist (li·bret′ist) *n.* The writer of a libretto.

li·bret·to (li·bret′ō) *n. pl.* **·tos** or **·ti** (-tē) 1. The verbal text of an opera or other large-scale vocal work. 2. A book containing such a text. [< Ital., little book, dim. of *libro*]

Lib·y·an (lib′ē·ən) *n.* 1. A native or inhabitant of Libya. 2. The Hamitic language of ancient Libya. —**Lib′y·an** *adj.*

lice (lis) Plural of LOUSE.

li·cense (lī′sens) *n.* 1. An official document giving permission to engage in a specified activity, perform a specified act, etc. 2. Abuse of freedom or privilege. 3. Deviation from established rules or standards, esp. for artistic effect: poetic *license.* —*v.t.* **·censed, ·cens·ing** To grant a license to or for; authorize. Also *esp. Brit.* **li′cence.** [< L *licere* to be permitted] —**li′cen·ser** or *Law* **li′cen·sor** *n.*

li·cen·see (lī′sən·sē′) *n.* One to whom a license has been granted.

li·cen·ti·ate (lī·sen′shē·it, -āt) *n.* A person licensed to practice a certain profession: a *licentiate* in dental surgery.

li·cen·tious (lī·sen′shəs) *adj.* Lacking in moral restraint; lewd. [< L *licentiosus*] —**li·cen′tious·ly** *adv.* —**li·cen′tious·ness** *n.*

li·chee (lē′chē) *n.* See LITCHI.

li·chen (lī′kən) *n.* Any of various flowerless plants composed of fungi and algae, commonly growing in flat patches on rocks, trees, etc. [< Gk., prob. < *leichein* to lick]

lic·it (lis′it) *adj.* Lawful. [< L *licere* to be allowed] —**lic′it·ly** *adv.* —**lic′it·ness** *n.*

lick (lik) *v.t.* 1. To pass the tongue over the surface of. 2. To remove or consume by taking with the tongue: often followed by *up, off,* etc. 3. To move or pass lightly over or about: The flames *licked* the coals. 4. *Informal* To defeat. 5. *Informal* To thrash; beat. —**to lick one's chops** To show pleased anticipation. —*n.* 1. A stroke of the tongue in licking. 2. A small amount. 3. A salt lick. 4. *Informal* A blow; whack. 5. *Informal* A stroke; spell, as of work. —**a lick and a promise** *Informal* Hasty washing or cleaning. [OE *liccian*]

lick·e·ty-split (lik′ə·tē·split′) *adv. Informal* At full speed.

lick·ing (lik′ing) *n. Informal* A whipping; beating.

lic·o·rice (lik′ə·ris, -rish) *n.* 1. A perennial leguminous herb of Europe. 2. The dried root of this plant, or an extract made from it, used in medicine and confections. 3. A confection flavored with this extract. Also *esp. Brit.* **liquorice.** [< LL *liquiritia* < Gk. *glykys* sweet + *rhiza* root]

lid (lid) *n.* 1. A hinged or removable cover placed at the top of a receptacle or over an opening. 2. An eyelid. [OE *hlid*] —**lid′ded** *adj.* —**lid′less** *adj.*

lie¹ (lī) *v.i.* **lay, lain, ly·ing** 1. To be in a recumbent or prostrate position. 2. To place oneself in a recumbent position; rest at full length: often with *down.* 3. To be placed upon or rest against a surface, esp. in a horizontal position. 4. To be or remain in a specified condition or state: to *lie* dormant. 5. To occupy a location; be situated. —**to lie low** *Informal* To remain in concealment; conceal one's intentions. —**to lie to** *Naut.* To maintain a vessel in a stationary position without anchoring. —*n.* The position, manner, or situation in which something lies; aspect. [OE *licgan*]

lie² (lī) *n.* 1. An untrue statement made with the intent of deceiving; a falsehood. 2. That which creates or is intended to produce a false impression. —**to give the lie (to)** To expose as false. —**white lie** A false statement made with the intent of being polite or kind. —*v.i.* **lied, ly·ing** 1. To make an untrue statement or statements, esp. with intent to deceive. 2. To give an erroneous or misleading impression: Figures don't *lie.* [OE *lyge*]

lied (lēd, *Ger.* lēt) *n. pl.* **lied·er** (lē′dər) A German song; esp., a ballad or lyric poem set to music. [< G]

lie detector A polygraph used to establish the truth or falsity of an accused person's statements.

lief (lēf) *adv.* Willingly; readily: used chiefly in the phrase **would as lief.** [OE *lēof* dear]

liege (lēj) *n.* 1. A lord or sovereign to whom allegiance or feudal service is due. 2. A vassal or subject owing allegiance to a lord or sovereign. —*adj.* Owing allegiance to a lord or sovereign; loyal. [< OF < Med.L *laeticus* free < OHG *ledig*]

lien (lēn, lē′ən) *n.* A legal right to claim or dispose of property in payment of or as security for a debt or charge. [< L *ligare* to tie]

lieu (lo͞o) *n.* Place; stead: now only in the phrase **in lieu of.** [ME *live* < L *locus* place]

lieu·ten·ant (lo͞o·ten′ənt, *Brit.* lef·ten′ənt) *n.* 1. *Mil.* A commissioned officer holding either of two ranks, **first** or **second lieutenant,** the former ranking next below a captain. 2. *Naval* A commissioned officer holding either of two ranks, **lieutenant** or **lieutenant (junior grade),** the former ranking next below a lieutenant commander and the latter next above an ensign. 3. One deputized to perform the duties of a superior. [< MF *lieu* place + *tenant,* ppr. of *tenir* to hold] —**lieu·ten′an·cy** *n.*

lieutenant colonel *Mil.* An officer ranking next above a major and next below a colonel.

lieutenant commander *Naval* An officer ranking next above a lieutenant and next below a commander.

lieutenant general *Mil.* An officer ranking next above a major general.

lieutenant governor An elected official who performs the duties of the governor of a state during his absence or disability or who replaces him in case of death or resignation.

life (līf) *n. pl.* **lives** (līvz) 1. The form of existence that distinguishes animals and plants from inorganic substances and dead organisms, characterized by metabolism, growth, reproduction, etc. 2. Existence regarded as a desirable condition: *life,* liberty, and the pursuit of happiness. 3. Living organisms collectively. 4. A living being; person: to save a *life.* 5. The period of an individual's existence between birth and death; also, a specified portion of this period. 6. A biography. 7. The period during which something continues to be effective, useful, etc.: the *life* of an engine. 8. Manner of existence; characteristic activities, as of a specified group, locality, etc.: city *life.* 9. Energetic force; animation: full of *life.* —**to bring to life** 1. To make vital; animate.

2. To recall vividly to the mind or senses. **—to come to life** 1. To regain consciousness. 2. To become animated. 3. To seem to be real or alive. **—to take life** To kill. [OE *līf*] **—life′less** *adj.*

life belt A life preserver in the form of a belt.

life·blood (līf′blud′) *n.* 1. The blood necessary to life. 2. Anything indispensable to existence; vital force.

life·boat (līf′bōt′) *n.* A boat, usu. carried on board a larger vessel, for saving lives at sea in the event of shipwreck, storm, etc.

life buoy A life preserver, often in the form of a ring.

life expectancy The probable length of life of an individual, esp. as predicted statistically.

life·guard (līf′gärd′) *n.* An expert swimmer employed at a beach, etc., to protect the safety of bathers.

life insurance Insurance on the life of an individual, providing payment to the beneficiary or beneficiaries upon the death of the insured or to the insured upon reaching a certain age. Also *Brit.* **life assurance.**

life jacket A life preserver in the form of a jacket or vest.

life·like (līf′līk′) *adj.* 1. Resembling actual life. 2. Accurately representing a person or thing. **—life′like′ness** *n.*

life line 1. A rope affording support to those in precarious situations. 2. Any route used for transporting vital supplies.

life·long (līf′lông′) *adj.* Lasting through life.

life preserver A buoyant device, either inflatable or filled with cork, kapok, etc., and made as a belt, jacket, or ring, used to keep afloat those in danger of drowning.

lif·er (lī′fər) *n.* *Slang* 1. One sentenced to prison for life. 2. One whose career is military service.

life raft A raftlike structure used as a rescue craft; esp., an inflatable rubber boat equipped with oars.

life·sav·er (līf′sā′vər) *n.* 1. One who saves, or is trained to save, another's life. 2. *Informal* One who or that which provides aid, relief, etc., in time of need. **—life′sav′ing** *n.* & *adj.*

life-size (līf′sīz′) *adj.* Having the same size as the thing or person portrayed. Also **life′-sized′.**

life span The extreme length of life regarded as biologically possible in an organism or the group to which it belongs.

life·time (līf′tīm′) *n.* 1. The period of animate existence. 2. The period of effective functioning: the *lifetime* of the car.

life·work (līf′wûrk′) *n.* The principal accomplishment of a lifetime.

lift (lift) *v.t.* 1. To take hold of and raise to a higher place or position; hoist. 2. To move, direct, or cause to rise to a higher position or level. 3. To hold up. 4. To bring to a higher or more desirable degree or condition; exalt. 5. To subject (the face) to surgery in order to remove signs of age. 6. *Informal* To take surreptitiously; steal; also, to plagiarize. **—***v.i.* 7. To exert effort in attempting to raise something. 8. To become dispersed or move away by or as by rising: the fog *lifted.* **—***n.* 1. The act of lifting or raising. 2. The ability to lift or impart upward motion. 3. The distance or degree to which something is raised. 4. A ride given to a traveler to or in the direction of his destination. 5. A feeling of exaltation, exhilaration, or well-being. 6. A mahicne or device used in lifting or hoisting. 7. *Brit.* An elevator. 8. Any of the layers of leather, etc., constituting the heel of a shoe. 9. *Aeron.* The component of aerodynamic forces acting on an aircraft, exerted perpendicular to the relative wind and generally opposing the pull of gravity. [ME < ON *lypta* to raise in the air.] **—lift′er** *n.*

lift·off (lift′ôf′) *n.* *Aerospace* The vertical ascent of a rocket or spacecraft from its launch pad.

lig·a·ment (lig′ə·mənt) *n.* *Anat.* A band of firm, fibrous tissue forming a connection between bones, or supporting an organ. [< L *ligare* to bind]

li·gate (lī′gāt) *v.t.* **·gat·ed, ·gat·ing** To bind or constrict with a ligature. [< L *ligatus*, pp. of *ligare*, to bind, tie] **—li·ga′tion** *n.*

lig·a·ture (lig′ə·cho͝or, -chər) *n.* 1. The act of tying up or constricting by binding. 2. A band, strip, etc., used to tie, bind, or constrict. 3. In printing, a character consisting of two or more connected letters, as *æ*, *ﬁ*, *ﬃ*.

light[1] (līt) *n.* 1. *Physics* **a** The form of radiant energy that makes vision possible. **b** A form of radiant energy not stimulating human vision; ultraviolet or infrared light. 2. The condition or medium that makes vision possible; illumination. 3. Any source of brightness, as a lamp, the sun, etc. 4. An emission of brightness, esp. from a particular source or direction. 5. Daylight; also the period of daylight. 6. Mental or spiritual understanding or insight. 7. Way of being regarded; aspect: to see things in a new *light.* 8. *pl.* Ability and understanding: to live according to one's own *lights.* 9. An instance of kindling; ignition. 10. An opening admitting illumination, as a window. 11. A person of authority or eminence; luminary: a lesser *light.* **—in the light of** In view of; considering. **—to see the light** 1. To come into being. 2. To be presented to public notice. 3. To become enlightened. **—***adj.* 1. Full of light; bright. 2. Diluted or combined with white, as a color; pale. **—***v.* **light·ed** or **lit, light·ing** *v.t.* 1. To ignite; kindle. 2. To illuminate or cause to illuminate. 3. To make bright, cheerful, animated, etc. 4. To guide or conduct with light. **—***v.i.* 5. To become ignited. 6. To become luminous, radiant, or bright: often with *up.* [OE *lēoht*] **—light′ness** *n.*

light[2] (līt) *adj.* 1. Having little weight; not heavy. 2. Having little weight in proportion to bulk or size. 3. Having less than standard or correct weight. 4. Not burdensome or oppressive. 5. Not difficult or arduous. 6. Having comparatively little effect; not intense, severe, etc. 7. Not great in degree or concentration; thin: a *light* fog. 8. Exerting little force or pressure; gentle: a *light* tap. 9. Not clumsy, coarse, or massive in form or appearance; delicate. 10. Intended or enjoyed as entertainment: *light* verse. 11. Slight in importance or consequence. 12. Morally unrestrained; wanton. 13. Slightly faint or delirious; giddy. 14. Easily eaten or digested. 15. Comparatively low in alcoholic content: *light* wines. 16. *Mil.* Designating the less massive types of weapons or equipment. **—to make light of** To treat or consider as trifling. —*v.i.* **light·ed** or **lit, light·ing** 1. To descend and settle down after flight, as a bird. 2. To happen or come, as by chance: with *on* or *upon*. 3. To get down, as from a horse or carriage. **—to light into** *Informal* To attack; assail. **—to light out** *Informal* To depart in haste. —*adv.* 1. Lightly. 2. Without encumbrance or excess equipment. [OE *lēoht, līht*] **—light′ness** *n.*

light·en[1] (līt′n) *v.t.* 1. To make light or bright; illuminate. —*v.i.* 2. To become light; grow brighter. 3. To emit or display lightning.

light·en[2] (līt′n) *v.t.* 1. To reduce the weight or load of; make less heavy. 2. To make less oppressive, troublesome, etc.; diminish the severity of. 3. To relieve, as of distress, uneasiness, etc. —*v.i.* 4. To become less heavy.

light·er[1] (lī′tər) *n.* One who or that which lights; esp., a device used to light cigarettes, cigars, etc.

light·er[2] (lī′tər) *n.* *Naut.* A bargelike vessel used in loading or unloading ships, or in transporting loads for short distances. [< Du. *lichten* to make light, unload]

light·face (līt′fās′) *n.* *Printing* Type having characters formed of light, thin lines.

light-fin·gered (līt′fing′gərd) *adj.* Expert at picking pockets, etc. **—light′-fin′gered·ness** *n.*

light-foot·ed (līt′fo͝ot′id) *adj.* 1. Stepping with buoyancy and grace. 2. Running lightly and swiftly. Also *Poetic* **light′foot′.** **—light′-foot′ed·ly** *adv.* **—light′-foot′ed·ness** *n.*

light·head·ed (līt′hed′id) *adj.* 1. Frivolous; giddy. 2. Dizzy. **—light′head′ed·ness** *n.*

light·heart·ed (līt′här′tid) *adj.* Free from care; blithe; gay. **—light′heart′ed·ly** *adv.* **—light′heart′ed·ness** *n.*

light·house (līt′hous′) *n.* A tower or similar structure equipped with a powerful beacon, erected at or near a dangerous place to serve as a warning or guide for ships.

light·ing (līt′ing) *n.* 1. The providing of light or the state of being lighted. 2. A system or apparatus supplying illumination, as in a public building, theater, etc. 3. The arrangement or effect of lighted areas in a painting, etc.

light·ly (līt′lē) *adv.* 1. With little weight or pressure; gently. 2. To a slight degree; moderately. 3. With a swift, buoyant step or motion. 4. In a carefree manner or spirit. 5. With insufficient seriousness or concern; frivolously: often with the negative.

light-mind·ed (līt′mīn′did) *adj.* Thoughtless; frivolous. **—light′-mind′ed·ness** *n.*

light·ning (līt′ning) *n.* A sudden flash of light caused by the discharge of atmospheric electricity between electrified regions of cloud, or between a cloud and the earth. [ME *lighten* to flash]

lightning bug A firefly.

lightning rod A pointed metal rod that protects buildings from lightning by grounding it harmlessly through a cable.

light opera Operetta.

lights (līts) *n.pl.* The lungs, esp. of animals used as food. [ME *lihtes*; so called from their light weight]

light·ship (līt′ship′) *n.* A vessel equipped with warning lights, signals, etc., and moored in dangerous waters as a guide to ships.

light·some (līt′səm) *adj.* 1. Untroubled by care; cheerful; gay. 2. Buoyant, airy, or graceful.

light·weight (līt′wāt′) *n.* 1. A person or animal of much less than average weight. 2. A boxer or wrestler weighing between 127 and 135 pounds. 3. *Informal* An unimportant, incompetent, or inadequate person. —*adj.* Of less than average or required weight.

light-year (līt′yir′) *n.* *Astron.* A unit of interstellar space measurement equal to the distance traversed by light in one year, approximately six trillion miles.

lig·ne·ous (lig′nē·əs) *adj.* Having the composition, texture, or appearance of wood. [< L *lignum* wood]

lig·nite (lig′nīt) *n.* A carbonized, brownish vegetable substance, often retaining a woodlike structure, that forms a soft coal. [< F] **—lig·nit′ic** (-nit′ik) *adj.*

lik·a·ble (lī′kə·bəl) *adj.* Of a nature to be liked; attractive; pleasing. Also **like′a·ble.** **—lik′a·ble·ness** *n.*

like[1] (līk) *v.* **liked, lik·ing** *v.t.* 1. To take pleasure in; enjoy. 2. To feel affectionately toward; be fond of. 3. To desire; prefer: I *like* that one. —*v.i.* 4. To feel disposed; choose: Do as you *like.* —*n.* *Usu. pl.* Preference; inclination. [OE *lician*]

like[2] (līk) *prep.* 1. Having a close resemblance to; similar to. 2. With the characteristics or qualities of: to smell *like* a rose. 3. Characteristic or typical of: How *like* him to behave that way! 4. Indicative of; likely to result in: It looks *like* rain. 5. Such as: a city *like* London. 6. In the manner of: He used the board *like* a hammer. —*adj.* 1. Having the same or similar characteristics; related. 2. Equal or nearly equal; equivalent. 3. Similar to what is portrayed or represented, as a portrait. —*n.* 1. Anything similar or in the same category: preceded by *the*: physics, chemistry, and the *like.* 2. One of equal value, standing, etc.: We will not see his *like* again. —*conj.* 1. *Informal* or *Illit.* As; in the manner that: It turned out *like* you said. 2. *Informal* As if: It looks *like* it's going to rain. [OE *gelīc*]

-like *suffix of adjectives* Similar to; having the characteristics of: **catlike, lemonlike, Picassolike, shell-like, wavelike.**

like·li·hood (līk′lē·ho͝od) *n.* 1. The state or quality of being probable; probability. 2. Something probable.

like·ly (līk′lē) *adj.* **·li·er, ·li·est** 1. Having or showing an apparent tendency or possibility: He is *likely* to go. 2. Seemingly about to happen; imminent; probable. 3. Apparently true; plausible; believable. 4. Suitable; appropriate: a *likely* spot. —*adv.* Probably.

lik·en (lī′kən) *v.t.* To represent as similar; compare.

like·ness (līk′nis) *n.* 1. The state or quality of being like; resemblance. 2. A pictorial representation; portrait; image. 3. Imitative form; guise.

like·wise (līk′wīz′) *adv.* 1. Moreover; also; too. 2. In like manner; similarly.

lik·ing (lī′king) *n.* 1. Feeling of attraction or affection; fondness. 2. Preference; taste.

li·lac (lī′lak, -lək, -lok) *n.* 1. A flowering shrub of the olive family, having fragrant purplish or white flowers. 2. A light pinkish purple color. —*adj.* Of a pinkish purple color. [< Persian *līlak* bluish]

lil·an·ge·ni (lil·än′gä·nē) *n.* The monetary unit of Swaziland.

lil·i·a·ceous (lil′ē·ā′shəs) *adj.* Belonging to or characteristic of the lily family. [< L *lilium* lily]

lil·li·pu·tian (lil′ə·pyōō′shən) *adj. Sometimes cap.* Extremely small; miniature or minute. [< *Lilliput,* land of tiny people in Swift's *Gulliver's Travels* (1726)]

lilt (lilt) *n.* 1. A lively quality of speech, voice, song, etc., with pronounced variations of pitch. 2. A light, buoyant motion or manner. —*v.i. & v.t.* To speak, sing, move, etc., in a cheerful rhythmic manner. [ME *lulte*]

lil·y (lil′ē) *n. pl.* **·ies** 1. Any of numerous wild or cultivated plants, having bulbs and showy, usu. funnel-shaped flowers. 2. Any of various other plants resembling a lily, as the water lily. —*adj.* Resembling a lily in whiteness, delicacy, beauty, etc. [OE < L *lilium*]

lil·y-liv·ered (lil′ē·liv′ərd) *adj.* Cowardly; fainthearted.

lily of the valley *pl.* **lilies of the valley** A perennial herb having small, fragrant white flowers.

lily pad One of the large, floating leaves of the water lily.

li·ma bean (lī′mə) 1. A species of the common bean, having large, flat, edible seeds. 2. The seed of this plant, eaten as a vegetable. Also **Lima bean.** [after *Lima,* Peru]

limb (lim) *n.* 1. A part of the animal or human body attached to but distinct from the torso, as an arm, leg, or wing. 2. One of the major divisions of a tree trunk; a large branch. 3. An extended or branching part, division, etc. —**out on a limb** *Informal* In a risky, vulnerable, or questionable position. [OE *lim*] —**limb′less** *adj.*

limbed (limd) *adj.* 1. Having limbs. 2. Having or characterized by a (specified kind of) limb or (a specified number of) limbs: used in combination: *strong-limbed; four-limbed.*

lim·ber (lim′bər) *adj.* 1. Pliant; flexible. 2. Able to bend or move easily; lithe. —*v.t.* 1. To make pliant. —*v.i.* 2. To exercise so as to become limber: with *up.* [Origin uncertain] —**lim′ber·ly** *adv.* —**lim′ber·ness** *n.*

lim·bo[1] (lim′bō) *n. pl.* **·bos** 1. *Theol.* A place for the souls of the righteous who died before the coming of Christ, and those of infants who die before baptism. 2. A place or condition for unwanted or forgotten persons, things, etc. 3. A vague state or condition. [< L *limbus* border]

lim·bo[2] (lim′bō) *n. pl.* **·bos** A West Indian acrobatic dance in which the dancer passes face up under a bar placed at successively lower levels. [Origin unknown]

Lim·burg·er cheese (lim′bûr·gər) A soft, white cheese having a strong odor and flavor. Also **Lim′burg·er.**

lime[1] (līm) *n.* A white, earthy substance, calcium oxide, used in mortars and cements. —*v.t.* **limed, lim·ing** To treat, mix, or spread with lime. [OE *līm*]

lime[2] (līm) *n.* 1. A small, green, lemonlike citrus fruit whose juice is used for flavoring, in beverages, etc. 2. The tropical tree yielding this fruit. [< Sp. *lima* < Arabic *limah*]

lime·kiln (līm′kil′, -kiln′) *n.* A kiln in which limestone, seashells, etc., are burned to produce lime.

lime·light (līm′līt′) *n.* 1. Public attention or notice. 2. A bright light used to illuminate a performer, stage area, etc., and originally produced by heating lime to incandescence.

lim·er·ick (lim′rik, -ə·rik) *n.* A humorous verse of five lines. [? from the line "Will you come up to *Limerick*"]

lime·stone (līm′stōn′) *n.* A sedimentary rock composed wholly or in part of calcium carbonate.

lim·ey (lī′mē) *n. pl.* **lim·eys** *Slang* 1. A British sailor. 2. Any Englishman. [from the former British maritime practice of drinking *lime* juice to prevent scurvy]

lim·it (lim′it) *n.* 1. The furthest extent, range, degree, etc., beyond which an activity, power, or function cannot or may not proceed: one's *limit* of endurance. 2. *Usu. pl.* The boundaries or extent of a specified area. 3. The greatest permissible amount. —**off limits** Forbidden to a specified group, as to the military, students, etc. —**the limit** *Informal* 1. One who or that which tries one's patience, credulity, etc., to the utmost. 2. To the utmost extent: usu. with *go.* —*v.t.* To set bounds to; confine; restrict. [< L *limes, limites*] —**lim′it·a·ble** *adj.* —**lim′i·ta′tion** *n.* —**lim′it·less** *adj.*

lim·it·ed (lim′it·id) *adj.* 1. Confined within or defined by a limit or limits; restricted. 2. Falling short of fullness or impressiveness: a *limited* success. 3. Having powers restricted by constitutional law or authority, as a government. 4. Of a train, bus, etc., making few stops. 5. *Chiefly Brit.* Restricted in liability to the amount invested by shareholders in its stock: a *limited* company.

limn (lim) *v.t.* To draw or paint; also, to describe in words. [ME *luminen* < L *illuminare*] —**lim·ner** (lim′nər) *n.*

Li·moges (lē·mōzh′, *Fr.* lē·môzh′) *n.* A type of fine porcelain manufactured at Limoges, France. Also **Limoges ware.**

lim·ou·sine (lim′ə·zēn′, lim′ə·zēn) *n.* 1. A large automobile or small bus, used esp. to convey passengers to and from an airport. 2. Any large, luxurious automobile, esp. one driven by a chauffeur. [< F]

limp[1] (limp) *v.i.* 1. To walk with a halting or irregular step, as with an injured leg or foot. 2. To progress in an irregular or labored manner. —*n.* The manner of walking of one who is lame. [OE *lempheallt* lame] —**limp′er** *n.*

limp[2] (limp) *adj.* 1. Lacking stiffness or firmness; flabby. 2. Lacking force or vigor; weak. [Origin uncertain] —**limp′ly** *adv.* —**limp′ness** *n.*

lim·pet (lim′pit) *n.* Any of various small marine animals having conical shells and noted for their ability to cling to rocks. [OE < LL *lampreda* limpet, lamprey]

lim·pid (lim′pid) *adj.* 1. Characterized by

crystalline clearness; transparent. 2. Characterized by clarity, lucidity, or purity, as of style. [< L *limpidus* clear] —**lim·pid′i·ty, lim′pid·ness** *n.* —**lim′pid·ly** *adv.*

lim·y (lī′mē) *adj.* **lim·i·er, lim·i·est** Containing or resembling lime.

lin·age (lī′nij) *n.* The number of lines in a piece of written or printed matter.

linch·pin (linch′pin′) *n.* A pin placed through the end of an axle in order to keep a wheel from sliding off. [OE *lynis*]

lin·den (lin′dən) *n.* Any of various shade trees having soft, white wood, heart-shaped leaves, and fragrant, cream-colored flowers: also called *basswood.* [OE *lind*]

line[1] (līn) *n.* 1. A slender, continuous mark or indentation, as that drawn by a pen, pencil, or pointed tool. 2. Any narrow band or strip resembling such a mark. 3. A wrinkle or crease in the skin. 4. A division or boundary between adjoining areas; border. 5. A demarcation or limit separating contrasting concepts, kinds of behavior, etc. 6. A row of persons or things. 7. A chronological succession of persons: the royal *line.* 8. A row of written or printed words. 9. A single row of words forming a verse, as of a stanza. 10. Course of movement or progress; route: *line* of march. 11. Course of action, thought, or performance: a *line* of thought. 12. *Often pl.* General plan or concept, as of form, content, etc.: a work on heroic *lines.* 13. Alignment; agreement; accord; to bring into *line.* 14. Scope or field of activity, ability, etc. 15. Kind of work; occupation. 16. Merchandise of a particular sort. 17. *pl.* The words of an actor's or performer's part. 18. *Slang* A glib manner of speech intended to ingratiate or persuade. 19. A pipe, conduit, or system of channels to convey liquids, gas, electricity, etc. 20. In telephonic communication, etc.: **a** A wire or cable carrying power signals. **b** A connection or channel of communication: to keep a *line* open. 21. Any system of public transportation over an established route or routes. 22. The roadbed, track, or system of tracks of a railroad. 23. A rope, string, cord, or the like, as used in fishing, measuring, etc. 24. *Math.* The theoretical trace or course of a moving point, conceived of as having length, but no other dimension. 25. *Mil.* A system of fortifications presenting an extended front. 26. In football, the players positioned at the line of scrimmage. —**in line for** Next in order for. —**out of line** 1. Not in conformity with accepted standards or practices. 2. Insubordinate; unruly. —**to get a line on** *Informal* To acquire information about. —**to hold the line** 1. To maintain a defense or opposition. 2. To wait while maintaining an open telephone connection. 3. In football, to prevent the opposing team from gaining ground. —*v.* **lined, lin·ing** *v.t.* 1. To mark with lines. 2. To place in a line. 3. To form a row or line along; border. —*v.i.* 4. To form a line; assume positions in a line: usually with *up.* —**to line up** 1. To form a line. 2. To bring into alignment. 3. To gather; marshal. [OE *līne* cord]

line[2] (līn) *v.t.* **lined, lin·ing** 1. To put a covering or facing on the inner surface of. 2. To constitute a covering or surface for: Tapestries *lined* the room. 3. To fill or stuff, as with money, food, etc. [OE *līn* flax]

lin·e·age (lin′ē·ij) *n.* 1. Line of descent from a progenitor. 2. Ancestry; family; stock. [< L *linea* line]

lin·e·al (lin′ē·əl) *adj.* 1. Being or occurring in the direct line of descent. 2. Pertaining to or based upon direct descent. 3. Consisting of lines; linear. —**lin′e·al·ly** *adv.*

lin·e·a·ment (lin′ē·ə·mənt) *n. Often pl.* 1. A facial contour or feature. 2. A distinguishing characteristic.

lin·e·ar (lin′ē·ər) *adj.* 1. Of or pertaining to a line or lines. 2. Involving or pertaining to length: *linear* measure. 3. Composed of lines. 4. Resembling a line. —**lin′e·ar·ly** *adv.*

line·back·er (līn′bak′ər) *n.* In football, a defensive player whose position is behind the line.

line drive In baseball, a batted ball that travels in an approximately horizontal trajectory: also called *liner.*

line·man (līn′mən) *n. pl.* **·men** (-mən) 1. A man who installs or repairs telephone or electric power lines: also *linesman.* 2. In football, any of the players positioned at the line of scrimmage.

lin·en (lin′ən) *n.* 1. A fabric woven from the fibers of flax. 2. Articles or garments made of linen, cotton, etc.: bed *linen.* [OE *līnen* made of flax] —**lin′en** *adj.*

line of scrimmage The imaginary line on which the ball rests and along which the opposing linemen take position at the start of play.

lin·er[1] (lī′nər) *n.* 1. A ship or airplane operated by a transportation line. 2. In baseball, a line drive.

lin·er[2] (lī′nər) *n.* 1. One who makes or fits linings. 2. Something used as a lining.

lines·man (līnz′mən) *n. pl.* **·men** (-mən) 1. In certain games, as tennis, an official making decisions on play at the lines of the court. 2. In football, the official marking the distances gained or lost in each play. 3. A lineman (def. 1).

line-up (līn′up′) *n.* 1. An arrangement of persons or things in a line. 2. In sports, a list of the team members playing at the start of a game. 3. In police work, a row of possible criminal suspects. Also **line′up′.**

ling (ling) *n. pl.* **ling** or **lings** A codlike food fish of the North Atlantic. [? < Du. *leng*]

-ling[1] *suffix of nouns* 1. Little; young: *duckling.* 2. Minor; petty: often used contemptuously: *princeling.* 3. A person or thing related to or characterized by: *worldling.* [OE]

-ling[2] *suffix* Forming adverbs and adjectives: 1. (from nouns) Toward: *sideling.* 2. (from adjectives) Being; becoming: *darkling.* Also **-lings.** [OE *-ling, -linga*]

lin·ger (ling′gər) *v.i.* 1. To stay on as if reluctant to leave. 2. To proceed in a slow manner; dawdle. 3. To pause or dwell with interest, pleasure, etc.: usu. with *over.* [Northern ME *lenger* to delay] —**lin′ger·er** *n.*

lin·ge·rie (län′zhə·rē, län′zhə·rā′, *Fr.* lañ·zhrē′) *n.* Women's light undergarments, nightgowns, etc. [< F]

lin·ger·ing (ling′gər·ing) *adj.* 1. Protracted; drawn out. 2. Long-lasting; enduring. 3. Slow. —**ling′er·ing·ly** *adv.*

lin·go (ling′gō) *n. pl.* **·goes** 1. Language: used contemptuously or humorously of a tongue one does not understand. 2. The specialized vocabulary and idiom of a profession, class, etc.: medical *lingo*. [< Pg. < L *lingua* tongue]

lin·gua fran·ca (ling′gwə frang′kə) 1. Any jargon or pidgin used as a commercial or trade language, as Pidgin English. 2. A mixture of French, Spanish, Italian, Greek, and Arabic, spoken in Mediterranean ports. [< Ital., lit., language of the Franks]

lin·gual (ling′gwəl) *adj.* Of or pertaining to the tongue or a tonguelike part. [< L *lingua* tongue]

lin·guist (ling′gwist) *n.* 1. One who is fluent in several languages. 2. A student of or specialist in linguistics.

lin·guis·tics (ling·gwis′tiks) *n.pl.* (*construed as sing.*) The scientific study of language. —**lin·guis′tic** *adj.* —**lin·guis′ti·cal·ly** *adv.*

lin·i·ment (lin′ə·mənt) *n.* A liquid rubbed on the skin to relieve pain and stiffness. [< L *linire* to anoint]

lin·ing (lī′ning) *n.* An inner surface or facing inserted in a garment, container, etc., as for protection, reinforcement, etc.; also, the material used.

link (lingk) *n.* 1. One of the loops, rings, or interlocking parts constituting a chain. 2. A single element in a series, sequence, or set: a weak *link* in his argument. 3. That which joins or connects separate parts, concepts, etc. 4. A single sausage. —*v.t.* & *v.i.* To join or connect by or as by links; interlock; couple; unite. [ME *linke* < Scand.]

link·age (ling′kij) *n.* 1. The act of linking, or the state of being linked. 2. A system of links.

links (lingks) *n.pl.* A golf course. [OE *hlinc* slope]

link·up (lingk′up′) *n.* A joining together, as of machines, groups, interests.

lin·net (lin′it) *n.* A common songbird of Europe. [< L *linum* flax; from its feeding on flax seeds]

li·no·le·um (li·nō′lē·əm) *n.* A material used as a floor covering, etc., made from oxidized linseed oil and cork pressed upon canvas or burlap. [< L *linum* flax + *oleum* oil]

Li·no·type (lī′nə·tīp) *n.* A keyboard-operated typesetting machine that casts a complete line of type on a single metal piece: a trade name. Also **li′no·type.**

li·no·typ·er (lī′nə·tīp′ər) *n.* One who operates a Linotype. Also **li′no·typ·ist.**

lin·seed (lin′sēd′) *n.* Flaxseed. [OE *līnsǣd*]

linseed oil A yellowish oil made from flaxseed and used as a drying agent in the preparation of oil paints, linoleum, etc.

lin·sey-wool·sey (lin′zē·wŏŏl′zē) *n.* *pl.* **-wool·seys** A coarse cloth woven of linen and wool or cotton and wool threads. [ME *lin* linen + *saye* cloth + WOOL]

lint (lint) *n.* 1. Bits of thread, fluff, etc. 2. A downy substance used as a surgical dressing. [ME *linnet* lint] —**lint′y** *adj.* **·i·er, ·i·est**

lin·tel (lin′təl) *n.* A horizontal part above the opening of a door or window, supporting the structure above it. [< LL *lintellus, limitellus,* dim. of *limes, limites* limit]

li·on (lī′ən) *n.* 1. A large, tawny or brownish gray carnivorous mammal of the cat family, native to Africa and SW Asia, the adult male having a shaggy mane. ◆Collateral adjective: *leonine*. 2. One of noble courage, great strength, etc. 3. A celebrity. —**the lion's share** The largest portion; an unduly large part. [< Gk. *leōn*] —**li′on·ess** (-is) *n.fem.*

li·on·heart·ed (lī′ən·härt′id) *adj.* Admirably brave.

li·on·ize (lī′ə·nīz) *v.t.* **·ized, ·iz·ing** To treat or regard as a celebrity. —**li′on·iz·a′tion** *n.* —**li′on·iz′er** *n.*

lip (lip) *n.* 1. One of the two folds of flesh that bound the mouth and serve as organs of speech. ◆Collateral adjective: *labial*. 2. A marginal part or structure resembling this. 3. The flared edge of a pitcher, bell, etc. 4. *Slang* Brash and impudent talk; sass. —**to keep a stiff upper lip** To maintain one's fortitude. —**to smack one's lips** To express anticipatory or remembered gusto; gloat. —*v.t.* **lipped, lip·ping** To touch with the lips; apply the lips to. —*adj.* 1. Of, pertaining to, or applied to the lips. 2. Made or formed by the lips or a lip; labial. [OE *lippa*] —**lipped** *adj.*

lip reading The interpretation of speech by watching the movement of the lips, as by the deaf. —**lip-read** (lip′rēd′) *v.t.* & *v.i.* **-read** (red), **-read·ing** (rēd′ing) —**lip reader**

lip service Insincere verbal assurance of assent, loyalty, etc.

lip·stick (lip′stik′) *n.* A pastelike cosmetic, usu. in the form of a small cylinder, used to color the lips.

liq·ue·fac·tion (lik′wə·fak′shən) *n.* The process of liquefying, or the state of being liquid.

liq·ue·fy (lik′wə·fī) *v.t.* & *v.i.* **·fied, ·fy·ing** To convert into or become liquid. [< L *liquere* to be liquid] —**liq′ue·fi′a·ble** *adj.* —**liq′ue·fi′er** *n.*

li·ques·cent (li·kwes′ənt) *adj.* Becoming or likely to become liquid; melting. [< L *liquere* to become liquid] —**li·ques′cence, li·ques′cen·cy** *n.*

li·queur (li·kûr′) *n.* An alcoholic beverage usu. made by adding sugar syrup and flavoring to brandy: also called *cordial*. [< OF *licur*]

liq·uid (lik′wid) *adj.* 1. Capable of flowing or of being poured. 2. Clear and flowing, as sounds. 3. Free and facile, as movement; fluent. 4. Consisting of or readily converted into cash. 5. *Physics* Not gaseous or solid. —*n.* A substance in that state in which the molecules move freely among themselves but remain in one mass; a fluid that is not a gas. [< L *liquere* to be liquid] —**li·quid·i·ty** (li·kwid′ə·tē), **liq′uid·ness** *n.* —**liq′uid·ly** *adv.*

liq·ui·date (lik′wə·dāt) *v.* **·dat·ed, ·dat·ing** *v.t.* 1. To pay off or settle, as an obligation or debt. 2. To wind up the affairs of (a business firm, etc.) by using the assets to settle debts. 3. To convert into cash, as securities. 4. *Slang* To kill or murder. —*v.i.* 5. To settle one's debts. [< Med.L *liquidare* to make liquid] —**liq′ui·da′tion** *n.*

liquid oxygen Oxygen liquefied by a reduction of temperature and an increase of pressure, used as an oxidizer in rocket fuels: also called *lox*.

liq·uor (lik′ər) *n.* 1. Any alcoholic beverage; esp., distilled spirits, as whiskey, brandy, etc. 2. A liquid such as broth, juice, etc. —*v.t.*

Slang To ply with alcoholic drink: usu. with *up*. [< L *liquor*]

li·ra (lir′ə, *Ital.* lē′rä) *n.* *pl.* **li·re** (lir′ə, *Ital.* lē′rä) or **li·ras** (lir′əz) The monetary unit of Italy and of other countries. [< Ital. < L *libra* pound]

lisle (lil) *n.* A fine, twisted cotton thread used in knitting hosiery, etc. [after *Lisle*, now Lille, France]

lisp (lisp) *n.* A speech defect or affectation in which the sibilants (s) and (z) are articulated like (th) in *thank* and (t͟h) in *this*. —*v.t. & v.i.* 1. To pronounce with a lisp. 2. To speak in a childlike manner. [OE *āwlyspiān*] —**lisp′er** *n.*

lis·some (lis′əm) *adj.* 1. Flexible; pliant. 2. Agile; lithe. Also **lis′som.** —**lis′some·ly** *adv.* —**lis′some·ness** *n.*

list[1] (list) *n.* 1. An itemized series of names, words, etc., usu. recorded in a set order. 2. A classification of persons or things belonging in the same category. —*v.t.* 1. To place on or in a list. 2. To include in a register, catalog, etc. [< OHG *līsta*] —**list′a·ble** *adj.*

list[2] (list) *v.t. & v.i.* *Naut.* Of a vessel, to lean or tilt to one side. —*n.* A leaning to one side.

list[3] (list) *Poetic* *v.t.* 1. To listen to; hear. —*v.i.* 2. To listen. [OE *hlyst* hearing]

lis·ten (lis′ən) *v.i.* 1. To make conscious use of the sense of hearing; be attentive in order to hear. 2. To pay attention; give heed. 3. To be influenced or persuaded. [OE *hlysnan*] —**lis′ten·er** *n.*

list·ing (lis′ting) *n.* 1. The act of one who or that which lists. 2. An entry in a list. 3. A list.

list·less (list′lis) *adj.* Languidly indifferent; apathetic; lackadaisical. —**list′less·ly** *adv.* —**list′less·ness** *n.*

list price The retail price of merchandise, from which a discount is sometimes made.

lists (lists) *n.pl.* In the Middle Ages, a field for tournaments or jousting. —**to enter the lists** To engage in a contest or controversy. [OE *liste* border]

lit (lit) Alternative past tense and past participle of LIGHT[1] and LIGHT[2].

lit·a·ny (lit′ə·nē) *n.* *pl.* **·nies** 1. *Eccl.* A liturgical form of prayer consisting of a series of supplications said by the clergy, with fixed responses by the congregation. 2. Any tiresome story, complaint, etc., that is frequently repeated. [< Gk. *litaneuein* to pray]

li·tchi (lē′chē) *n.* 1. The edible fruit of a tree native to China, having a hard seed and sweet pulp within a thin, brittle shell: also **litchi nut.** 2. The tree itself. Also spelled *lichee*. [< Chinese *li-chih*]

-lite *combining form* *Mineral.* Stone; stonelike. [< Gk. *lithos* stone]

li·ter (lē′tər) *n.* In the metric system, a measure of capacity equal to the volume of one kilogram of water at 4° C. and normal atmospheric pressure, or to 1.0567 liquid quarts. Also, *esp. Brit.*, *litre*.

lit·er·al (lit′ər·əl) *adj.* 1. Restricted to the exact, stated meaning; not figurative: the *literal* sense of the Scriptures. 2. Following the exact words and order of an original: a *literal* translation. 3. Tending to recognize or accept stated meanings only; matter-of-fact. [< LL *littera* letter] —**lit′er·al·ness** *n.*

lit·er·al·ly (lit′ər·ə·lē) *adv.* 1. In a literal manner; in the strictest sense. 2. Actually; really. 3. In effect; virtually.

lit·er·ar·y (lit′ə·rer′ē) *adj.* 1. Of, pertaining to, or treating of literature. 2. Characteristic of or appropriate to literature. 3. Versed in or devoted to literature. [< L *litterarius*]

lit·er·ate (lit′ər·it) *adj.* 1. Able to read and write. 2. Educated; cultured. 3. Literary. [< L *litteratus* < *littera* letter] —**lit′er·a·cy** *n.*

lit·e·ra·ti (lit′ə·rä′tē, -rā′tī) *n.pl.* 1. Scholars. 2. Literate or educated persons collectively. [< L]

lit·e·ra·tim (lit′ə·rā′tim, -rä′-) *adv.* Letter for letter; literally. [< L]

lit·er·a·ture (lit′ər·ə·cho͝or, -chər, lit′rə·chər) *n.* 1. Written works collectively, esp. those of enduring importance, exhibiting creative imagination and artistic skill. 2. Poetry, fiction, essays, etc., as distinguished from factual writing. 3. The writings pertaining to a particular subject. [< L *littera* letter]

-lith *combining form* Stone; rock. [< Gk. *lithos*]

lithe (līt͟h) *adj.* Bending easily or gracefully; supple. [OE, soft] —**lithe′ly** *adv.* —**lithe′ness** *n.*

lithe·some (līt͟h′səm) *adj.* Lithe.

-lithic *combining form* Pertaining to a (specified) anthropological stage in the use of stone implements: *Neolithic*.

lith·i·um (lith′ē·əm) *n.* A soft, silver-white element (symbol Li), the lightest of the metals. [< Gk. *lithos* stone]

litho- *combining form* Stone. Also, before vowels, **lith-**. [< Gk. *lithos*]

lith·o·graph (lith′ə·graf) *n.* A print produced by the process of lithography. —*v.t.* To produce or reproduce by lithography. —**li·thog·ra·pher** (li·thog′rə·fər) *n.* —**lith′o·graph′ic** or **·i·cal** *adj.* —**lith′o·graph′i·cal·ly** *adv.*

li·thog·ra·phy (li·thog′rə·fē) *n.* A process of printing from a flat stone or metal plate where the area to remain blank is treated with an ink-repellant material.

lith·o·sphere (lith′ə·sfir) *n.* The solid crust of the earth, as distinguished from the atmosphere and the hydrosphere.

Lith·u·a·ni·an (lith′o͞o·ā′nē·ən) *n.* 1. A native or inhabitant of Lithuania. 2. The Balto-Slavic language of the Lithuanians. —**Lith′u·a′ni·an** *adj.*

lit·i·gant (lit′ə·gənt) *n.* A participant in a lawsuit. [< L *litigare* to litigate]

lit·i·gate (lit′ə·gāt) *v.* **·gat·ed, ·gat·ing** *v.t.* 1. To bring (a dispute, claim, etc.) before a court of law for decision; contest at law. —*v.i.* 2. To engage in a lawsuit. [< L *lis*, *litis* lawsuit + *agere* to do, act] —**lit′i·ga′tion** *n.* —**lit′i·ga′tor** *n.*

li·tig·ious (li·tij′əs) *adj.* 1. Inclined to litigation; quarrelsome. 2. Subject to litigation. 3. Of or pertaining to litigation. —**li·tig′ious·ly** *adv.* —**li·tig′ious·ness** *n.*

lit·mus (lit′məs) *n.* A blue dye that is turned red by acids and remains blue when treated with an alkali. [< ON *litr* color + *mosi* moss]

litmus paper Paper dyed with litmus, used to test acidity.

li·tre (lē′tər) See LITER.

lit·ter (lit′ər) *n.* 1. Waste materials, objects,

etc., carelessly strewn about. 2. Untidy or chaotic condition; mess. 3. The young brought forth at one birth by any mammal normally having several offspring at one time. 4. A stretcher for carrying sick or wounded persons. 5. A couch carried between shafts. 6. Straw, hay, etc., spread in animal pens, or over plants as protection. —*v.t.* 1. To make untidy or unsightly by carelessly discarding trash, etc. 2. To drop or scatter carelessly. —*v.i.* 3. To give birth to a litter of young. 4. To drop or scatter refuse. [< OF *litiere* bed < L *lectus* bed]

lit·ter·bug (lit′ər·bug′) *n.* *Slang* One who litters public places, roads, etc., with trash.

lit·tle (lit′l) *adj.* **lit·tler** or (for defs. 2 and 3) **less, lit·tlest** or (for defs. 2 and 3) **least** 1. Small, or smaller compared to others, in physical size: a *little* house. 2. Not long; short; brief: a *little* time; a *little* distance away. 3. Small or relatively small in quantity or degree: *little* wealth; *little* probability. 4. Narrow or limited in viewpoint; petty: *little* minds. —*adv.* **less, least** 1. Only slightly; not much: He sleeps *little*. 2. Not at all: used before a verb: She *little* suspects. —*n.* 1. A small amount: Give me a *little*. 2. An insignificant amount: *Little* can be done about it. —**little by little** By small degrees; gradually. [OE *lȳt* small] —**lit′tle·ness** *n.*

Little Dipper The constellation Ursa Minor.

little theater An amateur or community theater group.

lit·to·ral (lit′ər·əl) *adj.* Of a shore or coastal region. —*n.* A shore and its adjacent areas. [< L < *litus, -oris* seashore]

lit·ur·gy (lit′ər·jē) *n. pl.* **·gies** In various religions, the prescribed form for public worship; religious ritual. [< Gk. *leitourgia* public duty, ult. < *laos* people + *ergon* work] —**li·tur·gi·cal** (li·tûr′ji·kəl) *adj.* —**lit′ur·gist** (-jəst) *n.*

liv·a·ble (liv′ə·bəl) *adj.* 1. Suitable or agreeable for living in. 2. Worth living; tolerable. 3. Agreeable, as for companionship. Also **live′a·ble.**

live[1] (liv) *v.* **lived, liv·ing** *v.i.* 1. To function as an animate organism; be alive. 2. To remain alive: as long as you *live*. 3. To remain or persist, as in the mind. 4. To remain valid or operative; endure. 5. To have as one's home; reside: with *in* or *at*. 6. To maintain or support oneself: with *on* or *by*: to *live* on one's income. 7. To pass life in a specified manner: to *live* in peace. 8. To enjoy a varied or satisfying life. —*v.t.* 9. To spend or pass (life, time, etc.). 10. To put into practice: to *live* one's religion. —**to live down** To live or behave so as to expiate the memory of (an error, crime, etc.). —**to live through** To survive or withstand (an experience). —**to live up to** 1. To satisfy (an ideal, expectations, etc.). 2. To fulfill (a bargain, obligation, etc.). [OE *libban, lifian*]

live[2] (līv) *adj.* 1. Functioning as an animate organism; alive. 2. Pertaining to, characteristic of, or abounding in life. 3. Of present interest and importance: a *live* issue. 4. Forceful and energetic; dynamic. 5. Burning or glowing: a *live* coal. 6. Charged with electricity: a *live* wire. 7. Capable of being detonated, as a bomb. 8. In television, radio, etc., performed by persons present at the time of transmission. 9. In sports, being in play, as a ball.

lived (līvd) *adj.* Having a (specified kind of) life or life span: used in combination: *long-lived*.

live-in (liv′in′) *adj.* Residing at one's place of employment: a *live-in* cook.

live·li·hood (līv′lē·ho͝od) *n.* Means of supporting or maintaining one's existence. [ME *liveload* < OE *līf* life + *lād* way]

live·long (liv′lông′) *adj.* Long or seemingly long in passing; entire: the *livelong* day. [ME *lefe longe*]

live·ly (līv′lē) *adj.* **·li·er, ·li·est** 1. Full of vigor or motion; energetic. 2. Arousing activity or excitement: a *lively* tune. 3. Striking and forceful to the mind: a *lively* impression. 4. Invigorating; brisk: a *lively* breeze. —*adv.* In a lively manner; briskly: now usu. in the expression **to step lively,** to hurry up. [OE *līflīce*] —**live′li·ness** *n.*

li·ven (lī′vən) *v.t.* & *v.i.* To make or become lively or cheerful: often with *up*. —**liv′en·er** *n.*

liv·er[1] (liv′ər) *n.* 1. *Anat.* The largest glandular organ of vertebrates, secreting bile and active in metabolism. ◆Collateral adjective: *hepatic*. 2. A similar digestive gland in invertebrates. 3. Food consisting of or prepared from the liver of certain animals. [OE *lifer*]

liv·er[2] (liv′ər) *n.* 1. One who lives in a specified manner: a luxurious *liver*. 2. A dweller.

liv·er·ied (liv′ər·ēd) *adj.* Dressed in livery, as a servant.

liv·er·ish (liv′ər·ish) *adj.* *Informal* Feeling or exhibiting supposed symptoms of disordered liver; bilious; irritable.

liv·er·wort (liv′ər·wûrt′) *n.* 1. A mosslike plant forming mats in damp, shady places. 2. A hepatica.

liv·er·wurst (liv′ər·wûrst′) *n.* A sausage made of ground liver. [< G *leberwurst*]

liv·er·y (liv′ər·ē) *n. pl.* **·er·ies** 1. The distinctive clothing or uniform worn by male household servants. 2. The distinguishing dress of an organization or group. 3. The stabling and care of horses for pay. 4. A livery stable. [< OF *livree* gift of clothes by a master to a servant < L *liber* free]

liv·er·y·man (liv′ər·ē·mən) *n. pl.* **·men** (-mən) A man who keeps or works in a livery stable.

livery stable A stable where horses and vehicles are cared for or kept for hire.

lives (līvz) Plural of LIFE.

live·stock (līv′stok′) *n.* Domestic farm animals, as cattle, esp. when raised for profit.

live wire 1. A wire carrying an electric current or potential. 2. *Informal* An energetic, enterprising person; a go-getter.

liv·id (liv′id) *adj.* 1. Having the skin abnormally discolored, as: **a** Flushed, purplish, etc., as from intense emotion. **b** Black-and-blue, as from contusion. 2. Having a leaden pallor; bluish gray. 3. *Informal* Furious; enraged. [< L *livere* to be livid] —**liv′id·ly** *adv.*

liv·ing (liv′ing) *adj.* 1. Alive; animate; not dead. 2. Of or characteristic of everyday life: *living* conditions. 3. Used or intended for maintaining existence: a *living* wage. 4. Having contemporary value, force, or application: *living* languages. —*n.* 1. The state of one who or that which lives. 2. Manner or conduct of life: virtuous *living.* 3. Means of supporting existence; livelihood.

living room A room designed for the general use, social activities, etc., of a household.

liz·ard (liz′ərd) *n.* 1. Any of various reptiles typically having long, scaly bodies, long tails, and four legs, as the chameleon, iguana, etc. 2. Leather made from the skin of a lizard. [< L *lacerta*]

-'ll Contracted form of SHALL or WILL[2].

lla·ma (lä′mə) *n.* A camellike, humpless ruminant of South America, having thick, woolly hair. [< Sp. < Quechua]

lla·no (lä′nō, *Sp.* lyä′nō) *n. pl.* **·nos** (-nōz, *Sp.* -nōs) A flat, treeless plain, as those of the SW U.S. and northern Latin America. [< Sp., plain, flat < L *planus*]

lo (lō) *interj.* See! observe!: *Lo* and behold! [OE *lā*]

load (lōd) *n.* 1. The weight or quantity placed upon and sustained by a vehicle, bearer, surface, etc. 2. A quantity borne or conveyed: often used in combination: *carload.* 3. A cause of physical or mental strain; burden. 4. *pl.* *Informal* An ample amount; lots: *loads* of time. 5. *Electr.* The power delivered by a generating system. —**to get a load of** *Slang* To listen to or look at. —*v.t.* 1. To place a large quantity, burden, cargo, etc., upon. 2. To place or take (cargo, people, etc.) as on a conveyance. 3. To burden, encumber, or oppress: often with *down.* 4. To charge (a firearm, etc.) with explosive or ammunition. 5. To put film or a photographic plate into (a camera). 6. To make prejudicial: to *load* the evidence. —*v.i.* 7. To put on or receive a load or cargo. 8. To charge a firearm, cartridge, etc., with ammunition. [OE *lād* way, journey] —**load′er** *n.*

load·ed (lō′did) *adj.* *Slang* 1. Wealthy. 2. Intoxicated.

load·stone (lōd′stōn′) See LODESTONE.

loaf[1] (lōf) *v.i.* 1. To loiter lazily or aimlessly. 2. To shirk or dawdle over one's work. —*v.t.* 3. To spend (time) idly: with *away.* [Back formation < LOAFER]

loaf[2] (lōf) *n. pl.* **loaves** (lōvz) 1. A rounded or elongated mass of bread baked in a single piece. 2. Any shaped mass of food, as of cake, chopped meat, etc. [OE *hlāf* bread]

loaf·er (lō′fər) *n.* 1. One who loafs; an idler or slacker. 2. A casual shoe resembling a moccasin. [Prob. < G *landläufer* idler]

loam (lōm) *n.* Loose-textured soil consisting of a mixture of sand, clay, and organic matter. [OE *lām*] —**loam′y** *adj.*

loan (lōn) *n.* 1. Something lent; esp., a sum of money lent at interest. 2. The act of lending: the *loan* of a knife. —*v.t.* & *v.i.* To lend. [ME < ON *lān*]

loan shark *Informal* One who lends money at an excessively high or illegal rate of interest.

loan-word (lōn′wûrd′) *n.* A word adopted from another language, as the English word *chauffeur,* taken from the French. Also **loan′word′.** [< G *lehnwort*]

loath (lōth) *adj.* Strongly disinclined; reluctant; unwilling: often followed by *to.* Also spelled *loth.* [OE *lāth* hateful]

loathe (lōth) *v.t.* **loathed, loath·ing** To feel great hatred or disgust for; abhor; detest. [OE *lāthian* to be hateful] —**loath′er** *n.*

loath·ing (lō′thing) *n.* Extreme dislike; abhorrence. —**loath′ing·ly** *adv.*

loath·some (lōth′səm) *adj.* Causing revulsion or disgust; repulsive. —**loath′some·ly** *adv.* —**loath′some·ness** *n.*

loaves (lōvz) Plural of LOAF.

lob (lob) *v.t.* **lobbed, lob·bing** To pitch or strike (a ball, etc.) in a high, arching curve. —*n.* In tennis, a stroke that sends the ball high into the air. [ME] —**lob′ber** *n.*

lo·bar (lō′bər, -bär) *adj.* 1. Of or pertaining to a lobe. 2. Affecting one or more lobes of the lungs. [< NL *lobaris*]

lo·bate (lō′bāt) *adj.* 1. Having or consisting of lobes. 2. Resembling a lobe. Also **lo′bat·ed.** [< NL *lobatus*]

lob·by (lob′ē) *n. pl.* **·bies** 1. An entrance hall, vestibule, or public lounge in an apartment house, hotel, theater, etc. 2. A group representing persons or organizations with a common interest, who attempt to influence the votes of legislators. —*v.i.* **·bied, ·by·ing** To attempt to influence legislators in favor of some interest. [< Med.L *lobia*] —**lob′by·ist** *n.*

lobe (lōb) *n.* 1. A rounded division, protuberance, or part, as of a leaf. 2. The soft lower part of the human ear. 3. *Anat.* Any of several well-defined, often symmetrical portions of an organ or part of the body, as of the brain. [< Gk. *lobos*] —**lobed** *adj.*

lob·lol·ly (lob′lol·ē) *n. pl.* **·lies** A pine of the southern U.S., having scaly bark and wood valuable as lumber. Also **loblolly pine.** [< dial. E *lob* bubble + *lolly* broth]

lo·bot·o·my (lō·bot′ə·mē) *n. pl.* **·mies** *Surg.* The operation of cutting into or across a lobe of the brain, esp. to relieve a mental disorder. [< Gk. *lobos* lobe + -TOMY]

lob·ster (lob′stər) *n.* 1. Any of various ten-legged marine crustaceans having the first pair of legs modified as claws, and compound eyes on flexible stalks. 2. The flesh of any of these crustaceans eaten as food. [< L *locusta* lobster, locust]

lob·ule (lob′yōōl) *n.* 1. A small lobe. 2. A subdivision of a lobe. —**lob′u·lar** *adj.*

lo·cal (lō′kəl) *adj.* 1. Pertaining to, characteristic of, or confined to a relatively small area. 2. Of or pertaining to a particular place or position in space: *local* time. 3. Stopping at all stations along its run, as a train. 4. *Med.* Relating to or affecting a specific part of the body. —*n.* 1. A branch or chapter of an organization, as a trade union. 2. A bus, train, etc., that stops at all stations. [< L *locus* place] —**lo′cal·ly** *adv.*

lo·cale (lō·kal′) *n.* 1. A place or locality, esp. with reference to some event or circumstance. 2. The setting of a literary, dramatic, or artistic work; scene. [< F]

lo·cal·ism (lō′kəl·iz′əm) *n.* A word, meaning of a word, pronunciation, etc., peculiar to a locality.

lo·cal·i·ty (lō·kal′ə·tē) *n. pl.* **·ties** 1. A place, region, etc. 2. Position, esp. in relation to surroundings, etc. [< LL *localitas*]

lo·cal·ize (lō′kəl·īz) *v.t.* **·ized, ·iz·ing** 1. To make local; confine or assign to a specific area. 2. To determine the place of origin of. —**lo′cal·iz′a·ble** *adj.* —**lo′cal·i·za′tion** *n.*

lo·cate (lō′kāt, lō·kāt′) *v.* **·cat·ed, ·cat·ing** *v.t.* 1. To discover the position of; find. 2. To establish or place at a particular site: The store is *located* on the corner. 3. To place hypothetically as to setting, a relative position, etc. —*v.i.* 4. *Informal* To settle. [< L *locus* place] —**lo·cat′a·ble** *adj.* —**lo′·ca·ter** *n.*

lo·ca·tion (lō·kā′shən) *n.* 1. The act of locating, or the state of being located. 2. A site or situation, esp. considered in regard to its surroundings. 3. Exact position or place occupied. 4. A motion picture or television locale away from the studio: usu. in the phrase **to be on location.**

loch (lokh, lok) *n. Scot.* 1. A lake. 2. An arm of the sea.

lo·ci (lō′sī) Plural of LOCUS.

lock[1] (lok) *n.* 1. A mechanical fastening device having a bolt secured or released by a key, dial, etc., and used to prevent unauthorized entry, access, or operation. 2. A section of a canal, etc., enclosed by gates, within which the water depth may be raised or lowered. 3. The mechanism that explodes the charge of a gun. 4. An interlocking, fastening, or jamming together of parts. 5. A wrestling grip or hold. —*v.t.* 1. To fasten or secure by means of a lock. 2. To keep, confine, etc., in or as in a locked enclosure: with *in, up,* or *away*. 3. To fit together securely; interlock. 4. To clasp or grip in or as in a firm hold. —*v.i.* 5. To become locked. 6. To become firmly joined or interlocked. —**to lock out** 1. To prevent (employees) from working by closing a factory, shop, etc. 2. To keep out by locking. [OE *loc* fastening, enclosure]

lock[2] (lok) *n.* 1. Strands of hair forming a curl. 2. *pl.* The hair of the head. [OE *locc*]

lock·er (lok′ər) *n.* 1. A closet, cabinet, storage space, etc., fastened with a lock, as: **a** One of a series of metal cabinets, as in a gymnasium, in which clothes, equipment, etc., are kept. **b** A cabinet in which frozen foods are kept. 2. A chest, etc., as on a ship, in which equipment or personal belongings are kept.

locker room A room having lockers for clothing, etc.

lock·et (lok′it) *n.* A small ornamental case for enclosing a picture or keepsake, usu. worn on a chain, ribbon, etc., around the neck. [< OF *loc* latch < Gmc.]

lock·jaw (lok′jô′) *n. Pathol.* A form of tetanus causing rigid closure of the jaws.

lock·out (lok′out′) *n.* The closing of a place of business by an employer in order to make employees agree to terms.

lock·smith (lok′smith′) *n.* A maker or repairer of locks.

lock step A marching style in which each marcher closely follows the one in front of him.

lock·up (lok′up′) *n.* A jail or prison cell.

lo·co (lō′kō) *adj. Informal* Crazy; insane. [< Sp., insane]

lo·co·mo·tion (lō′kə·mō′shən) *n.* The act or power of moving from one place to another. [< L *loco* from a place + *motio, -onis* movement]

lo·co·mo·tive (lō′kə·mō′tiv) *n.* An engine that moves by its own power, used to pull trains on a railroad. —*adj.* Of, pertaining to, or used in locomotion.

lo·co·weed (lō′kō·wēd′) *n.* Any of several leguminous plants of the SW U.S., often poisonous to livestock.

lo·cus (lō′kəs) *n. pl.* **·ci** (-sī) 1. A place; locality; area. 2. *Math.* A surface or curve regarded as traced by a line or point moving under specified conditions.

lo·cust[1] (lō′kəst) *n.* 1. Any of a family of winged insects resembling grasshoppers, including those of migratory habits that destroy vegetation. 2. A cicada. [< L *locusta*]

lo·cust[2] (lō kəst) *n.* 1. A leguminous tree of North America, having compound leaves and clusters of fragrant white flowers. 2. The wood of this tree. 3. Any of various similar trees, as the acacia and honey locust. [< L *locusta*]

lo·cu·tion (lō·kyōō′shən) *n.* 1. A verbal expression or phrase. 2. Manner of speech or expression. [< L *locutio, -onis* a speaking]

lode (lōd) *n. Mining* 1. A deposit of metallic ore filling fissures in native rock. 2. Any deposit of ore located between definite boundaries of associated rock. Also called *vein*. [OE *lād* way, journey]

lode·stone (lōd′stōn′) *n.* 1. Magnetite that possesses polarity. 2. Something that attracts by or as by magnetism. Also spelled *loadstone*. [ME *lode* course + STONE]

lodge (loj) *n.* 1. A local branch of a secret or fraternal society; also, the meeting place of such a society. 2. A small hut, cabin, etc., esp. one used as a base for outdoor activity. 3. An inn, hotel, motel, etc. 4. A small house on the grounds of an estate, etc. 5. The characteristic den of certain animals, as beavers. —*v.* **lodged, lodg·ing** *v.t.* 1. To furnish with temporary quarters; house. 2. To serve as a shelter or dwelling for. 3. To place or implant firmly, as by thrusting or inserting. 4. To deposit for safekeeping or storage. 5. To submit or enter (a complaint, etc.) formally. 6. To confer or invest (power, etc.): usu. with *in* or *with*. —*v.i.* 7. To take temporary quarters. 8. To become fixed or embedded. [< OHG *loub* foliage] —**lodg′er** *n.*

lodg·ing (loj′ing) *n.* 1. A temporary dwelling place. 2. *pl.* Living quarters consisting of a rented room or rooms in another's house.

lodg·ment (loj′mənt) *n.* The act of lodging, or the state of being lodged. Also **lodge′ment.**

loess (les, lō′es) *n. Geol.* A pale, yellowish silt or clay forming finely powdered, usu. wind-borne deposits. [< G *lösen* to pour, dissolve] —**loess′i·al** *adj.*

loft (lôft) *n.* 1. A floored space directly under a roof; attic. 2. A large, open workroom or storeroom on an upper story of a commercial building. 3. A hayloft. 4. An upper section or gallery, as in a church: the choir *loft*. —*v.t.* & *v.i.* To strike (a ball) so that it travels in a high arc. [< ON *lopt* air, sky]

loft·y (lôf′tē) *adj.* **loft·i·er, loft·i·est** 1. Having great or imposing height. 2. Elevated in character, quality, style, etc.; noble. 3. Arrogant; haughty. —**loft′i·ly** *adv.* —**loft′i·ness** *n.*

log[1] (log, lôg) *n.* 1. A section of a felled tree trunk, limb, etc., stripped of branches. 2. *Naut.* **a** A record of the daily progress of a vessel and of the events of a voyage. **b** Any of various devices for measuring the speed and mileage of a vessel. 3. A record of operation or progress, as of an aircraft in flight. —*v.* **logged, log·ging** *v.t.* 1. *Naut.* & *Aeron.* **a** To enter in a logbook. **b** To travel (a specified distance, etc.). —*v.i.* 2. To engage in the operation of cutting and transporting timber. [ME *logge*]

log² (log, lôg) A logarithm.

log- Var. of LOGO-.

-log (log) Var. of -LOGUE.

lo·gan·ber·ry (lō′gən·ber′ē) *n. pl.* **·ries** 1. A hybrid plant obtained by crossing the red raspberry with the blackberry. 2. The edible fruit of this plant. [after J. H. *Logan*, 1841–1928, U.S. horticulturist]

log·a·rithm (log′ə·rith′əm, lôg′-) *n. Math.* The power to which a fixed number, called the base, must be raised in order to produce a given number. [< LOG(O) + Gk. *arithmos* number] —**log′a·rith′mic** or **·mi·cal** *adj.*

log·book (log′bo͝ok′, lôg′-) *n.* The book in which the official record of a ship, aircraft, etc., is entered. Also **log book.**

loge (lōzh) *n.* A box or a section in a theater. [< F]

log·ger (log′ər, lôg′-) *n.* 1. A person engaged in logging; lumberjack. 2. A machine for hauling and loading logs.

log·ger·head (log′ər·hed, lôg′-) *n.* A large marine turtle of tropical Atlantic waters. Also **loggerhead turtle.** —**at loggerheads** Engaged in a quarrel; unable to agree. [< dial. E *logger* log tied to a horse's leg + HEAD]

log·gi·a (loj′ē·ə, lô′jə; *Ital.* lôd′jä) *n.* A roofed gallery that is open and supported by columns on one or more sides. [< Ital.]

log·ging (log′ing, lôg′-) *n.* The occupation of felling timber and transporting logs to a mill or market.

log·ic (loj′ik) *n.* 1. The science concerned with the principles of valid reasoning and correct inference. 2. Correct or sound reasoning. 3. The apparently inevitable chain of events involved in an outcome, etc. 4. The principles governing the interconnection of electronic circuits for certain computer operations; also the circuits themselves. [< Gk. *logos* word, thought] —**log′i·cal** *adj.* —**log′i·cal·ly** *adv.*

-logical *combining form* Of or related to a (specified) science or study: *biological, geological.* Also **-logic.**

lo·gi·cian (lō·jish′ən) *n.* One versed in logic.

lo·gis·tics (lō·jis′tiks) *n.pl.* (*construed as sing.*) The branch of military science dealing with supplying, equipping, and moving troops. [< F *loger* to quarter] —**lo·gis′tic** or **·ti·cal** *adj.* —**lo·gis′ti·cal·ly** *adv.*

logo- *combining form* Word; speech. Also, before vowels, *log-*. [< Gk. *logos*]

log·roll (log′rōl′, lôg′-) *v.t.* To obtain passage of (a bill) by logrolling. —*v.i.* To engage in logrolling. Also **log′-roll′.** [Back formation < LOGROLLING]

log·roll·ing (log′rō′ling, lôg′-) *n.* 1. The trading of votes and influence between politicians; also, any such trading of help or approval for one's own benefit. 2. Birling. Also **log′-roll′ing.** —**log′roll′er** *n.*

-logue *combining form* Discourse; recitation: *monologue, prologue.* Also *-log.* [< Gk. *logos* word, speech]

lo·gy (lō′gē) *adj.* **·gi·er, ·gi·est** *Informal* Dull; lethargic. [Prob. < Du. *log* dull, heavy]

-logy *combining form* 1. The science or study of. 2. Speech; discourse. [< Gk. *logos* word, study]

loin (loin) *n.* 1. *Usu. pl.* The part of the back and flanks between the lower ribs and the hipbone. ◆Collateral adjective: *lumbar.* 2. *pl.* The lower back, thighs, and groin. 3. A cut of meat from the hindquarters of beef, lamb, veal, etc. —**to gird (up) one's loins** To prepare for action. [< OF *loigne, logne* < L *lumbus*]

loin·cloth (loin′klôth′, -kloth′) *n.* A strip of cloth worn about the loins and hips.

loi·ter (loi′tər) *v.i.* 1. To linger idly or aimlessly; loaf. 2. To dawdle. —*v.t.* 3. To pass (time) idly: with *away.* [ME *lotere*] —**loi′ter·er** *n.*

loll (lol) *v.i.* 1. To lie or lean in a relaxed or languid manner; lounge. 2. To hang loosely; droop. —*v.t.* 3. To permit to droop or hang, as the tongue. —*n.* The act of lolling. [? < MDu. *lollen* to sleep] —**loll′er** *n.*

lol·la·pa·loo·za (lol′ə·pə·lo͞o′zə) *n. Slang* Something extraordinary. [Origin unknown]

lol·li·pop (lol′ē·pop′) *n.* A lump or piece of candy on the end of a stick: also called *sucker.* Also **lol′ly·pop′.** [Prob. < dial. E *lolly* tongue + POP¹]

lone (lōn) *adj.* 1. Being without companions; solitary. 2. Isolated. 3. Only; sole. [< ALONE]

lone·ly (lōn′lē) *adj.* **·li·er, ·li·est** 1. Unfrequented by human beings; deserted; desolate. 2. Sad from lack of companionship or sympathy; lonesome. 3. Characterized by or inducing loneliness. —**lone′li·ness** *n.*

lon·er (lon′ər) *n. Informal* One who prefers to work, live, etc. alone. Also **lone wolf.**

lone·some (lōn′səm) *adj.* 1. Depressed or uneasy because of being alone; lonely; forlorn. 2. Inducing a feeling of loneliness. 3. Unfrequented; secluded: a *lonesome* retreat. —**lone′some·ly** *adv.* —**lone′some·ness** *n.*

long¹ (lông) *adj.* 1. Being great in proportion to width; not short. 2. Having relatively great duration in time; prolonged. 3. Being extended: a *long* tunnel. 4. Being of a specified measurement in extent or duration: ten miles *long;* three hours *long.* 5. Having more than the usual: a *long* ton, a *long* play. 6. Slow; tedious. 7. Well supplied: *long* on excuses. 8. In gambling, denoting odds indicating little likelihood of winning. 9. *Phonet.* Denoting the vowel sounds of *Dane, dean, dine, dome, dune* as contrasted with those of *Dan, den, din, don, duck.* 10. In prosody, stressed, as in English verse. —*adv.* 1. For an extensive period of time: Will he stay *long?* 2. For a time or period (to be specified): How *long* will he stay? 3. For the whole duration (of a specified period): It rained all day *long.* 4. At a considerably distant time: *long* after midnight. —**as (or so) long as** 1. For or during the time that. 2. Inasmuch as; since. —*n.* A long syllable or sound, as in phonetics, prosody, etc. —**before long** Soon. [OE *long, lang*]

Long, meaning "for a long time," is a

combining form as in:

long-accustomed	**long-lasting**
long-awaited	**long-lived**
long-delayed	**long-lost**
long-established	**long-past**
long-forgotten	**long-settled**

long[2] (lông) *v.i.* To have a strong or eager desire; wish earnestly; yearn. [OE *langian* to grow long]

long·boat (lông′bōt′) *n. Naut.* The largest boat carried by a sailing vessel.

long·bow (lông′bō′) *n.* A large bow drawn by hand and projecting long, feathered arrows.

long-dis·tance (lông′dis′təns) *adj.* Connecting or covering relatively long distances or places. —*adv.* 1. By long-distance telephone. 2. At or to a distance.

long distance The telephone exchange, operator, or service that handles calls outside the immediate locality.

long division Arithmetical division, usu. with large numbers in which all the steps of the process are shown.

long-drawn (lông′drôn′) *adj.* Prolonged; protracted. Also **long′-drawn′-out′** (-out′).

lon·gev·i·ty (lon·jev′ə·tē) *n.* 1. Great age or length of life. 2. The tendency to live long. [< L *longus* long + *aevum* age]

long·hair (lông′hâr′) *Slang adj.* 1. Of or pertaining to intellectuals or their supposed tastes. 2. Of or pertaining to serious rather than popular music. —*n.* 1. A longhair person; intellectual. 2. Longhair music. Also **long′-hair′**.

long·hand (lông′hand′) *n.* Ordinary handwriting with the words spelled in full.

long·horn (lông′hôrn′) *n.* One of a breed of domestic cattle with long horns. Also **Texas longhorn.**

longi- *combining form* Long. [< L *longus* long]

long·ing (lông′ing) *n.* A strong, earnest, persistent craving; desire. —**long′ing** *adj.* —**long′ing·ly** *adv.*

lon·gi·tude (lon′jə·to͞od, -tyo͞od) *n. Geog.* Distance east or west on the earth's surface, usu. measured by the angle that the meridian through a particular place makes with the prime meridian that runs through Greenwich, England. [< L *longus* long]

lon·gi·tu·di·nal (lon′jə·to͞o′də·nəl, -tyo͞o′-) *adj.* 1. Of or pertaining to longitude or length. 2. Running lengthwise. —**lon′gi·tu′di·nal·ly** *adv.*

long-lived (lông′līvd′, -livd′) *adj.* Having a long life or period of existence. —**long′-lived′ness** *n.*

long-play·ing (lông′plā′ing) *adj.* LP.

long-range (lông′rānj′) *adj.* 1. Designed to shoot or move over distances. 2. Taking account of, or extending over, a long span of future time: *long-range* plans.

long·shore·man (lông′shôr′mən) *n. pl.* **·men** (-mən) A laborer employed on the waterfront to load and unload cargo. [< *alongshore* + MAN]

long shot *Informal* In betting, a race horse or other gambling choice, backed at great odds and having little chance of winning. —**not by a long shot** *Informal* Decidedly not; not at all.

long-stand·ing (lông′stan′ding) *adj.* Having existed over a ong period: a *long-standing* debt.

long-sta·ple (lông′stā′pəl) *adj.* Having a long fiber: said of fabrics, esp. cotton.

long-suf·fer·ing (lông′suf′ər·ing) *adj.* Patiently enduring injuries, misfortune, etc., for a long time. —*n.* Patient endurance of injuries, etc.

long-term (lông′tûrm′) *adj.* Involving or extending over a relatively long period of time: a *long-term* contract.

long-time (lông′tīm′) *adj.* Being such for a considerable period of time: a *long-time* friend.

long ton See under TON.

long-wind·ed (lông′win′did) *adj.* Tiresomely long in speaking or writing: a *long-winded* lecturer. —**long′-wind′ed·ly** *adv.* —**long′-wind′ed·ness** *n.*

long·wise (lông′wīz′) *adv.* Lengthwise. Also **long′ways′** (-wāz′).

look (lo͝ok) *v.i.* 1. To use one's sense of sight. 2. To turn the eyes in a specified direction. 3. To gaze so as to convey a specific feeling or meaning. 4. To use one's eyes in order to examine, repair, etc.: Let's *look* at the engine. 5. To seem: He *looks* reliable. 6. To face in a specified direction. —**to look after** To take care of. —**to look alive** *Informal* To be alert or attentive. —**to look down on (or upon)** To regard with condescension or contempt: also **to look down one's nose on (or upon).** —**to look in (or in on)** To make a short visit to. —**to look into** 1. To examine closely. 2. To make inquiries about. —**to look out for** 1. To protect. 2. To be on guard against. —**to look the other way** To ignore or avoid an unpleasant or unfavorable situation, sight, etc. —**to look to** 1. To attend to. 2. To turn to, as for help, advice, etc. —**to look up** 1. To search for and find, as in a file, book, etc. 2. *Informal* To discover the whereabouts of. 3. *Informal* To improve; become better. —**to look up to** To have respect for. —*n.* 1. The act of looking. 2. A search, examination, etc., by or as by means of one's eyes. 3. Aspect or expression: a saintly *look.* 4. *Often pl. Informal* General appearance: I like the *looks* of this place. 5. *pl. Informal* Personal appearance or attractiveness. —*interj.* 1. See! 2. Listen! [OE *lōcian*] —**look′er** *n.*

look·er-on (lo͝ok′ər·on′, -ôn′) *n. pl.* **look·ers-on** A spectator; onlooker.

look·ing glass (lo͝ok′ing) A glass mirror.

look·out (lo͝ok′out′) *n.* 1. The act of watching for someone or something. 2. A place where such a watch is kept. 3. The person or persons watching. 4. *Naut.* A crow's-nest.

loom[1] (lo͞om) *v.i.* 1. To appear or come into view indistinctly, as through a mist. 2. To appear to the mind as large or threatening. [Origin uncertain]

loom[2] (lo͞om) *n.* A machine on which thread or yarn is woven into fabric. [OE *gelōma* tool]

loon[1] (lo͞on) *n.* A diving, fish-eating waterfowl, having a weird cry. [Ult. < ON *lomr*]

loon[2] (lo͞on) *n.* 1. A stupid or crazy person. 2. A worthless person; idler. [Cf. Du. *loen* stupid fellow]

loon·y (lo͞o′nē) *Informal adj.* **loon·i·er, loon·i·est** 1. Lunatic or demented. 2. Foolish; erratic; silly. —*n. pl.* **·ies** A demented or insane person. [< LUNATIC]

loop (lo͞op) *n.* 1. A folding or doubling over of one end of a piece of thread, rope, wire, etc., so as to form an oval opening. 2. A ring or bent piece of metal, wood, thread, etc., serving as a fastener, staple, or the like. 3. Something having or suggesting the shape of a loop. 4. *Aeron.* A complete circular turn made by an aircraft flying in a vertical plane. —*v.t.* 1. To form a loop in or of. 2. To fasten or encircle by means of a loop. 3. *Aeron.* To fly (an aircraft) in a loop or loops. —*v.i.* 4. To make a loop or loops. —**to loop the loop** To make a vertical circular turn in the air, esp. in an aircraft. [ME *loupe*]

loop·hole (lo͞op′hōl′) *n.* 1. A narrow slit in a wall, esp. one in a fortification. 2. An opportunity for escaping or evading something.

loop·y (lo͞op′ē) *adj.* **loop·i·er, loop·i·est** 1. Having loops. 2. *Slang* Crazy; foolish.

loose (lo͞os) *adj.* **loos·er, loos·est** 1. Not fastened; unattached. 2. Not taut: a *loose* rein. 3. Freed from restraint. 4. Not firmly fitted or embedded. 5. Not closely fitted, as clothing. 6. Not bound or fastened together. 7. Not compact, firm, or dense: *loose* soil. 8. Not constricted; open: said of lax bowels or a cough. 9. Dissolute; unchaste. 10. Lacking in exactness or precision: a *loose* translation. —**on the loose** 1. Not confined; at large. 2. *Informal* Behaving in a free, uninhibited, and usu. dissolute manner. —*adv.* 1. In a loose manner; loosely. 2. So as to be or become loose: to break *loose.* —**to cut loose** *Informal* To behave in a free, uninhibited manner. —*v.t.* **loosed, loos·ing** 1. To set free, as from bondage, penalty, etc. 2. To untie or undo. 3. To let fly; shoot, as an arrow. [< ON *lauss*] —**loose′ly** *adv.* —**loose′ness** *n.*

loose end Something left undecided or undone, as a task, decision, etc. —**at loose ends** 1. In an unsettled state. 2. Without a job, plans, etc.

loose-joint·ed (lo͞os′join′tid) *adj.* 1. Having joints not tightly articulated. 2. Limber or flexible in movement.

loose-leaf (lo͞os′lēf′) *adj.* Having pages that are easily inserted or removed, as a notebook.

loos·en (lo͞o′sən) *v.t.* 1. To untie or undo, as bonds. 2. To set free; release. 3. To make less tight, firm, or compact. —*v.i.* 4. To become loose or looser. —**to loosen up** *Informal* 1. To relax. 2. To talk with ease; talk freely. 3. To give more generously, as money. —**loos′en·er** *n.*

loot (lo͞ot) *n.* 1. Goods taken as booty by a victorious army from a sacked city, enemy forces, etc. 2. Anything unlawfully taken. 3. *Slang* Money. —*v.t.* 1. To plunder; pillage. —*v.i.* 2. To engage in plundering. [< Hind. *lūt* < Skt. *lunt*] —**loot′er** *n.*

lop[1] (lop) *v.t.* **lopped, lop·ping** 1. To cut or trim the branches, twigs, etc., from. 2. To cut off. —*n.* A part lopped off. [Origin unknown] —**lop′per** *n.*

lop[2] (lop) *v.* **lopped, lop·ping** *v.i.* 1. To droop or hang down loosely. 2. To move about in an awkward manner. —*v.t.* 3. To permit to droop or hang down loosely. [Origin unknown]

lope (lōp) *v.t. & v.i.* **loped, lop·ing** To run or cause to run with a steady, swinging stride or gallop. —*n.* A slow, easy stride or gallop. [< ON *hlaupa* to leap, run] —**lop′er** *n.*

lop-eared (lop′ird′) *adj.* Having drooping ears.

lop·sid·ed (lop′sī′did) *adj.* Heavier, larger, or sagging on one side. —**lop′sid′ed·ly** *adv.* —**lop′sid′ed·ness** *n.*

lo·qua·cious (lō·kwā′shəs) *adj.* Characterized by continuous talking. [< L *loqui* to speak] —**lo·qua′cious·ly** *adv.* —**lo·qua′cious·ness** *n.*

lo·quac·i·ty (lō·kwas′ə·tē) *n.* Talkativeness.

lord (lôrd) *n.* 1. One possessing great power and authority. 2. In Great Britain: **a** Any one of the noblemen or peers (**lords temporal**) having the title of marquis, earl, viscount, or baron. **b** Any of the higher churchmen (**lords spiritual**). 3. In feudal law, the owner of a manor. —**to lord it (over)** To act in a domineering or arrogant manner (toward). [OE *hlāford, hlāfweard,* lit., bread keeper]

Lord (lôrd) 1. God: preceded by *the* except in direct address. 2. Jesus Christ. 3. In Great Britain, a title of honor or nobility.

lord·ly (lôrd′lē) *adj.* **·li·er, ·li·est** 1. Befitting the rank and position of a lord. 2. Noble; dignified. 3. Arrogant; haughty. —*adv.* In a lordly manner. —**lord′li·ness** *n.*

lord·ship (lôrd′ship) *n.* 1. The dominion, power, or authority of a lord. 2. *Often cap.* In Great Britain, the title by which noblemen (excluding dukes), bishops, and judges are addressed or spoken of: preceded by *Your* or *His.* [OE *hlafordscipe.* See LORD.]

lore (lôr) *n.* 1. The body of traditional, popular, often anecdotal knowledge about a particular subject: the *lore* of the woods. 2. Learning or erudition. [OE *lār*]

lor·gnette (lôr·nyet′) *n.* 1. A pair of eyeglasses with an ornamental handle. 2. An opera glass with a long handle. [< F < *lorgner* to spy, peer]

lor·ry (lôr′ē, lor′ē) *n. pl.* **·ries** 1. A low, four-wheeled wagon without sides. 2. *Brit.* A motor truck. [Prob. dial. E *lurry* to pull]

lose (lo͞oz) *v.* **lost, los·ing** *v.t.* 1. To be unable to find; mislay. 2. To fail to keep, control, or maintain: to *lose* one's footing. 3. To be deprived of; suffer the loss of: to *lose* a leg. 4. To fail to win. 5. To fail to take advantage of; miss. 6. To fail to keep in sight, memory, etc. 7. To occupy or absorb wholly; engross: usu. in the passive. 8. To squander; waste. 9. To cause (someone or something) to be or become lost. 10. To outdistance or elude. 11. To cause the loss of: His rashness *lost* him the election. 12. To bring to destruction or death; ruin: usu. in the passive. —*v.i.* 13. To suffer loss. 14. To be defeated, as in battle or a contest. —**to lose oneself** To become engrossed or absorbed. —**to lose out** *Informal* To fail or be defeated. —**to lose out on** *Informal* To fail to secure; miss. [From OE *losian* to be lost and *lēosan* to lose] —**los′er** *n.*

los·ing (lo͞o′zing) *adj.* 1. Incurring loss: a *losing* business. 2. Not winning.

loss (lôs) *n.* 1. The act of losing or the state of being lost. 2. One who or that which is lost. 3. The harm, inconvenience, etc., caused by losing something or someone. 4. *pl. Mil.* Casualties. 5. The amount by which cost exceeds selling price. —**at a loss** Perplexed. [ME]

lost (lôst) *adj.* 1. Not to be found or recovered. 2. No longer possessed, seen, or known: *lost* friends. 3. Not won, gained, or secured. 4. Having gone astray. 5. Bewildered; perplexed. 6. Not used or taken advantage of; wasted. 7. Destroyed; ruined. 8. No longer known or practiced: a *lost* art. **—to be lost in** To be absorbed or engrossed in. **—to be lost upon** (or **on**) To have no effect upon.

lot (lot) *n.* 1. That which is used in determining something by chance, as objects drawn at random from a container. 2. The share or portion that comes to one as a result of drawing lots. 3. One's portion in life as ascribed to chance, fate, custom, etc. 4. A number of things or persons considered as a single group. 5. A job lot. 6. A plot or quantity of land: a parking *lot.* 7. *Informal* A (specified) type of person: He's a bad *lot.* 8. *Often pl. Informal* A great deal: a *lot* of money; *lots* of trouble. **—a lot** (or **lots**) *Informal* Very much: He is *a lot* better; *lots* better. **—the lot** The whole of a certain number or quantity: He bought *the lot.* **—to cast** (or **draw**) **lots** To come to a decision or solution by the use of lots. **—to cast** (or **throw**) **in one's lot with** To join with and share the fortunes of. [OE *hlot*]

loth (lōth) See LOATH.

lo·tion (lō′shən) *n.* A liquid preparation used for external cleansing of the skin, eyes, etc. [< L *lotio, -onis* washing]

lot·ter·y (lot′ər·ē) *n. pl.* **·ter·ies** A drawing for prizes for which numbered tickets are sold, the winning tickets being selected by lot. [< Ital. *lotto* lottery, lot]

lot·to (lot′ō) *n.* A game of chance played by drawing numbers from a container and covering with counters the corresponding numbers on cards, the winner being the first to cover a row of numbers. [< Ital.]

lo·tus (lō′təs) *n.* 1. In Greek legend, a fruit inducing indolence and forgetfulness. 2. Any of various tropical water lilies noted for their large floating leaves and showy flowers. 3. A representation of any of these plants in art, architecture, sculpture, etc. 4. Any of a genus of herbs of the bean family. Also **lo′tos.** [< Gk. *lōtos*]

lo·tus-eat·er (lō′təs·ē′tər) *n.* Anyone considered to be living an indolent, irresponsible existence.

loud (loud) *adj.* 1. Having great volume or intensity of sound: *loud* thunder. 2. Emphatic or urgent; insistent: *loud* demands. 3. *Informal* Crude; vulgar, as manners, persons, etc. 4. *Informal* Excessively showy: a *loud* shirt. **—*adv.*** In a loud manner. [OE *hlūd*] **—loud′ly** *adv.* **—loud′ness** *n.*

loud·mouthed (loud′mouthd′, -moutht′) *adj.* Having a loud voice; offensively clamorous or talkative. **—loud′mouth′** (-mouth′) *n.*

loud·speak·er (loud′spē′kər) *n.* Any of various devices for converting an electric current into sound, as in a public-address system, radio, etc.: also called *speaker.*

lounge (lounj) *v.i.* **lounged, loung·ing** 1. To recline, walk, etc., in a relaxed, lazy manner. 2. To pass time in doing nothing. **—*n.*** 1. A couch or sofa. 2. A room in a hotel, club, train, etc., suitable for lounging and often having facilities for drinking. 3. The act of lounging; also, a period of lounging. [Origin unknown] **—loung′er** *n.*

loupe (lo͞op) *n.* A small magnifying glass, esp. one adapted as an eyepiece for jewelers or watchmakers. [< F]

louse (lous) *n. pl.* **lice** (līs) 1. A small, flat-bodied, wingless insect living as an external parasite on man and some animals. 2. Any of various other parasitic insects. 3. *Slang* A contemptible person. **—*v.t. & v.i.*** **loused, lous·ing** *Slang* To ruin; bungle: with *up.* [OE *lūs*]

lous·y (lou′zē) *adj.* **lous·i·er, lous·i·est** 1. Infested with lice. 2. *Slang* Contemptible; mean. 3. *Slang* Worthless; inferior. 4. *Slang* Having plenty (of): with *with*: *lousy* with money. **—lous′i·ly** *adv.* **—lous′i·ness** *n.*

lout (lout) *n.* An awkward fellow; oaf; boor. [? < ON *lutr* bent, stooped] **—lout′ish** *adj.*

lou·ver (lo͞o′vər) *n.* 1. An opening provided with louver boards; also, a louver board. 2. One of several narrow openings serving as an outlet for heated air. [OF *lover*] **—lou′·vered** *adj.*

louver board One of a series of horizontal, overlapping slats in a window or opening, sloped downward to shed rain while admitting light and air.

lov·a·ble (luv′ə·bəl) *adj.* Worthy of love; amiable; also, evoking love. Also **love′a·ble.** **—lov′a·bil′i·ty, lov′a·ble·ness** *n.* **—lov′·a·bly** *adv.*

love (luv) *n.* 1. A deep devotion or affection for another person or persons: *love* for one's children. 2. A strong sexual passion for another person. 3. Sexual passion in general or the gratification of it. 4. One who is beloved. 5. A very great interest in, or enjoyment of, something; also, the thing so enjoyed. 6. In tennis, a score of nothing. **—in love** Experiencing love for someone or something. **—to make love** 1. To kiss, embrace, etc. 2. To have sexual intercourse. **—*v.*** **loved, lov·ing** *v.t.* 1. To feel love or affection for. 2. To take pleasure or delight in: to *love* good food. **—*v.i.*** 3. To be in love. [OE *lufu*]

love apple A former name for the tomato.

love·bird (luv′bûrd′) *n.* One of several small parrots often kept as cage birds: so called from the affection they show.

love knot A knot tied in pledge of love and constancy; also, a representation of it, as in jewelry.

love·less (luv′lis) *adj.* 1. Having no love. 2. Receiving no love. **—love′less·ly** *adv.* **—love′less·ness** *n.*

love·lorn (luv′lôrn) *adj.* Pining for one's lover.

love·ly (luv′lē) *adj.* **·li·er, ·li·est** 1. Possessing qualities that inspire admiration or love. 2. Beautiful: a *lovely* rose. 3. *Informal* Delightful; pleasing. **—love′li·ness** *n.*

love·mak·ing (luv′mā′king) *n.* The act of making love; also, wooing; courtship.

lov·er (luv′ər) *n.* 1. One who loves: a *lover* of humanity. 2. One in love with or making love to another. 3. One who especially enjoys diversion, pursuit, etc.: a *lover* of golf.

love seat A double chair or small sofa for two persons.

love·sick (luv′sik′) *adj.* 1. Languishing with love. 2. Indicating such a state: a *lovesick* serenade. **—love′sick′ness** *n.*

lov·ing (luv′ing) *adj.* 1. Affectionate;

devoted; kind. 2. Indicative of love. **—lov′ing·ly** *adv.* **—lov′ing·ness** *n.*

loving cup 1. A wine cup, usu. with two or more handles, formerly passed around a circle of friends at a banquet. 2. An ornamental cup given as a trophy.

low[1] (lō) *adj.* 1. Having relatively little upward extension; not high or tall. 2. Located or placed below the normal or usual level: a *low* marsh. 3. Near the horizon: a *low* moon. 4. Pertaining to latitudes nearest the equator. 5. Relatively small in depth, height, amount, degree, etc. 6. Of or producing sounds of relatively long wavelengths: a *low* pitch. 7. Not loud; faint: a *low* rustle. 8. Melancholy or sad; depressed: *low* spirits. 9. Lacking vigor; feeble. 10. Not adequately provided with; short of: to be *low* on groceries. 11. *Informal* Having little or no ready cash. 12. Poor, unfavorable, or disparaging: to have a *low* estimate of one's abilities. 13. Humble or inferior, as in origin, rank, position, etc. 14. Inferior in quality: a *low* grade of tobacco. 15. Vulgar or morally base. 16. Relatively simple in structure, function, or organization: a *low* form of animal life. 17. Opposed to ritualism: *low* church. **—*adv.*** 1. In or to a low level, position, degree, etc. 2. In a low manner. 3. Softly; quietly. 4. With a low pitch. 5. In or to a humble, poor, or degraded condition. **—*n.*** 1. A low level, position, degree, etc. 2. *Meteorol.* An area of low barometric pressure. 3. *Mech.* An arrangement of gears that yields a slow or the slowest output speed. [Early ME *lah* < ON *lagr*] **—low′ness** *n.*

low[2] (lō) *v.i.* 1. To make the hollow, bellowing sound of cattle; moo. **—*v.t.*** 2. To utter by lowing. **—*n.*** The vocal sound made by cattle: also **low′ing.** [OE *hlōwan*]

low·born (lō′bôrn′) *adj.* Of humble birth.

low·boy (lō′boi) *n.* A short-legged chest of drawers of about table height.

low·bred (lō′bred′) *adj.* 1. Of humble or inferior origin or birth. 2. Vulgar; coarse.

low·brow (lō′brou′) *n. Informal* A person of uncultivated or vulgar tastes. **—*adj.*** Of or suitable for such a person: also **low′browed′.**

low·down[1] (lō′doun′) *n. Slang* The truth.

low-down[2] (lō′doun′) *adj. Informal* 1. Unethical or mean. 2. In jazz, slow, sad, or sensuous, as the blues.

low·er[1] (lou′ər) *v.i.* 1. To look sullen; scowl. 2. To appear dark and threatening, as the weather. [Cf. G *lauern* to lurk] **—low′er** *n.* **—low′er·ing** *adj.* **—low′er·ing·ly** *adv.*

low·er[2] (lō′ər) Comparative of LOW. **—*adj.*** 1. Inferior in rank, value, etc. 2. Situated below something else. 3. *Often cap. Geol.* Older; designating strata normally beneath the newer rock formations. **—*n.*** That which is beneath something else; esp., a lower berth. **—*v.t.*** 1. To bring to a lower position or level; let down, as a window. 2. To reduce in degree, quality, amount, etc. 3. To undermine or weaken. 4. To bring down in estimation, rank, etc. 5. To change (a sound) to a lower pitch or volume. **—*v.i.*** 6. To become less; decrease; sink.

lower case The small letters of the alphabet. **—low′er-case′** *adj.*

lower class The socially or economically inferior group in society. **—low·er-class** (lō′ər·klas′) *adj.*

low·er·class·man (lō′ər·klas′mən) *n. pl.* **·men** (-mən) A student in either of the first two years of a four-year course; a freshman or sophomore.

Lower House The larger and more widely representative branch of a bicameral legislative body, as the House of Representatives in the U.S. Also **Lower Chamber.**

lower world 1. The abode of the dead; hell. Also **lower regions.** 2. The earth.

low frequency *Telecom.* Radio waves having a frequency of from 30 to 300 kilohertz.

Low German See under GERMAN.

low-key (lō′kē′) *adj.* Being low in intensity; understated. Also **low′-keyed′** (-kēd′).

low·land (lō′lənd, -land′) *n. Usu. pl.* Land lying lower than the adjacent country. **—low′land** *adj.*

Low Latin See under LATIN.

low·ly (lō′lē) *adj.* **·li·er, ·li·est** 1. Humble or low in rank, origin, nature, etc. 2. Full of humility; meek. 3. Situated or lying low. **—low′li·ness** *n.*

low-mind·ed (lō′mīn′did) *adj.* Having low, vulgar, or mean thoughts, sentiments, or motives. **—low′-mind′ed·ness** *n.*

low-necked (lō′nekt′) *adj.* Having a low neckline.

low-pitched (lō′picht′) *adj.* 1. Low in tone or range of tone. 2. Having little slope, as a roof.

low-pres·sure (lō′presh′ər) *adj.* 1. Having or operating under a low degree of pressure. 2. *Meteorol.* Designating atmospheric pressure below that normal at sea level.

low profile A low-keyed or inconspicuous attitude or style.

low-rise (lō′rīz′) *n.* A building having few stories and no elevator. **—low′-rise′** *adj.*

low-spir·it·ed (lō′spir′it·id) *adj.* Despondent; melancholy. **—low′-spir′it·ed·ness** *n.*

low tide 1. The ebb tide at its lowest stage. 2. The time this lowest stage occurs.

low water A very low level of water in a stream, etc.

lox[1] (loks) *n.* A salty, smoked salmon. [< Yiddish < G *lachs* salmon]

lox[2] (loks) *n.* Liquid oxygen.

loy·al (loi′əl) *adj.* 1. Bearing true allegiance to a constituted authority, as to one's government. 2. Constant and faithful in any relation or obligation. 3. Indicating or professing loyalty. [< OF *leial* < L *legalis*] **—loy′al·ism** *n.* **—loy′al·ly** *adv.*

loy·al·ist (loi′əl·ist) *n.* One who supports and defends his government, esp. in times of crisis or war.

loy·al·ty (loi′əl·tē) *n. pl.* **·ties** The state, quality, or fact of being loyal; fidelity; allegiance.

loz·enge (loz′inj) *n.* 1. A small sweetened tablet or candy, now usu. medicated. 2. *Math.* A diamond-shaped figure. [< OF *losenge*]

LP (el′pē′) *adj.* Designating a phonograph record pressed with microgrooves and played at a speed of 33⅓ revolutions per minute: also *long-playing.* **—*n.*** An LP record: a trade mark. [< L(ONG)-P(LAYING)]

LSD (el′es′dē′) *n.* A drug that produces states similar to those of schizophrenia. [L(Y)-S(ERGIC ACID) D(IETHYLAMIDE)]

lu·au (lōō′ou) *n.* A Hawaiian feast with entertainment.

lub·ber (lub′ər) *n.* 1. An awkward, ungainly fellow. 2. A landlubber. [Origin uncertain] **—lub′ber·ly** *adj. & adv.*

lu·bri·cant (lo͞o′brə·kənt) *n.* A substance, as oil, grease, graphite, etc., used to coat moving parts in order to reduce friction and wear. —*adj.* Lubricating.

lu·bri·cate (lo͞o′brə·kāt) *v.t.* **·cat·ed, ·cat·ing** 1. To apply a lubricant to. 2. To make slippery or smooth. [< L *lubricus* slippery] **—lu′bri·ca′tion** *n.* **—lu′bri·ca′tive** *adj.* **—lu′bri·ca′tor** *n.*

lu·bric·i·ty (lo͞o·bris′ə·tē) *n. pl.* **·ties** 1. Lewdness; lasciviousness. 2. Slipperiness. [< L *lubricus* slippery]

lu·cent (lo͞o′sənt) *adj.* 1. Showing or giving off radiance. 2. Transparent or semitransparent. [< L *lucens, -entis,* ppr. of *lucere* to shine] **—lu′cen·cy** *n.* **—lu′cent·ly** *adv.*

lu·cid (lo͞o′sid) *adj.* 1. Easily understood; clear: a *lucid* explanation. 2. Mentally sound, clear, or rational: a *lucid* interval. 3. Shining; bright. [< L *lucere* to shine] **—lu·cid′i·ty, lu′cid·ness** *n.* **—lu′cid·ly** *adv.*

Lu·ci·fer (lo͞o′sə·fər) *n.* The archangel who led the revolt of the angels and fell from Heaven: identified with *Satan.* [< L, light-bearer]

luck (luk) *n.* 1. That which happens by chance; fortune; lot. 2. Good fortune; success. 3. Any object regarded as bringing good fortune. **—to try one's luck** To attempt to do something without any certainty of success. [Prob. < MDu. *luk, geluk*] **—luck′·less** *adj.*

luck·y (luk′ē) *adj.* **luck·i·er, luck·i·est** 1. Accompanied by or having good fortune. 2. Bringing or resulting in good fortune. 3. Believed to bring good fortune. **—luck′i·ly** *adv.* **—luck′i·ness** *n.*

lu·cra·tive (lo͞o′krə·tiv) *adj.* Producing or yielding gain, profit, or wealth; profitable. [< L *lucratus,* pp. of *lucrari* to gain] **—lu′cra·tive·ly** *adv.* **—lu′cra·tive·ness** *n.*

lu·cre (lo͞o′kər) *n.* Money or riches: now chiefly in the humorous phrase: **filthy lucre.** [< L *lucrum* gain]

lu·cu·bra·tion (lo͞o′kyo͝o·brā′shən) *n.* 1. Earnest and labored study. 2. The product of such study; esp., a pedantic literary composition. [< L *lucubrare* to work by candlelight] **—lu′cu·bra·to′ry** (-brə·tôr′ē) *adj.*

lu·di·crous (lo͞o′də·krəs) *adj.* Exciting laughter or ridicule; ridiculous; absurd. [< L *ludere* to play] **—lu′di·crous·ly** *adv.* **—lu′di·crous·ness** *n.*

luff (luf) *Naut. n.* The sailing of a ship close to the wind. —*v.i.* To bring the head of a vessel nearer the wind. [ME *lof, loven*]

lug[1] (lug) *n.* 1. An earlike projection for holding or supporting something. 2. *Mech.* A nut, closed at one end. [Origin uncertain]

lug[2] (lug) *v.t.* **lugged, lug·ging** To carry or pull with effort. [Prob. < Scand.]

lug·gage (lug′ij) *n.* Suitcases, trunks, etc., used for traveling; baggage. [< LUG[2]]

lug·ger (lug′ər) *n. Naut.* A one-, two-, or three-masted vessel having lugsails only.

lug·sail (lug′səl, -sāl′) *n. Naut.* A four-cornered sail having no boom and bent to a yard that hangs obliquely on the mast.

lu·gu·bri·ous (lo͞o·go͞o′brē·əs, -gyo͞o′-) *adj.* Very sad or mournful, esp. in a ludicrous manner. [< L *lugere* to mourn] **—lu·gu′bri·ous·ly** *adv.* **—lu·gu′bri·ous·ness** *n.*

Luke (lo͝ok) *n.* The third Gospel of the New Testament, attributed to Luke (also called Saint Luke), physician and companion of the apostle Paul.

luke·warm (lo͝ok′wôrm′) *adj.* 1. Moderately warm; tepid. 2. Lacking in ardor, enthusiasm, or conviction; indifferent. [Prob. OE *hlēow* warm] **—luke′warm′ly** *adv.*

lull (lul) *v.t.* 1. To quiet or put to sleep by soothing sounds or motions. 2. To calm or allay, esp. by deception: to *lull* someone's suspicions. —*n.* 1. A brief interval of calm or quiet during noise or confusion. 2. A period of diminished activity, prosperity, etc.: a *lull* in business. [Prob. imit.]

lull·a·by (lul′ə·bī) *n. pl.* **·bies** 1. A song to lull a child to sleep; a cradlesong. 2. A piece of instrumental music in the manner of a lullaby.

lum·ba·go (lum·bā′gō) *n.* Pain in the lumbar region of the back; backache, esp. in the lower part of the back.

lum·bar (lum′bər, -bär) *adj.* Pertaining to or situated near the loins. [< L *lumbus* loin]

lum·ber[1] (lum′bər) *n.* 1. Timber sawed into boards, planks, etc., of specified lengths. 2. *Chiefly Brit.* Household articles no longer used and usu. stored away. —*adj.* Made of, pertaining to, or dealing in lumber. —*v.t.* 1. To cut down (timber); also, to cut down the timber of (an area). —*v.i.* 2. To cut down or saw timber for marketing. [Var. of *Lombard* in obs. sense of "money-lender, pawnshop," hence, stored articles] **—lum′ber·ing** *n.*

lum·ber[2] (lum′bər) *v.i.* 1. To move or proceed in a heavy or awkward manner. 2. To move with a rumbling noise. —*n.* A rumbling noise. [ME *lomerer*] **—lum′ber·ing** *adj.* **—lum′ber·ing·ly** *adv.*

lum·ber·jack (lum′bər·jak) *n.* A person who fells or transports timber; a logger. [< LUMBER[1] + *jack* man, boy]

lum·ber·man (lum′bər·mən) *n. pl.* **·men** (-mən) 1. A lumberjack. 2. One who is engaged in the business of lumbering.

lum·ber·yard (lum′bər·yärd′) *n.* A yard for the storage or sale of lumber.

lu·mi·nar·y (lo͞o′mə·ner′ē) *n. pl.* **·nar·ies** 1. Any body that gives light, esp. the sun or the moon. 2. One who has achieved great eminence. [< L *lumen* light]

lu·mi·nesce (lo͞o′mə·nes′) *v.i.* **·nesced, ·nesc·ing** To be or become luminescent.

lu·mi·nes·cence (lo͞o′mə·nes′əns) *n.* An emission of light, such as fluorescence and phosphorescence, not directly attributable to the heat that produces incandescence. [< L *lumen* light + -ESCENT] **—lu′mi·nes′cent** *adj.*

lu·mi·nous (lo͞o′mə·nəs) *adj.* 1. Full of light. 2. Giving off light; shining. 3. Easily understood; clear. [< L *lumen* light] **—lu′mi·nous·ly** *adv.* **—lu′mi·nos′i·ty** (-nos′ə·tē) *n.*

lum·mox (lum′əks) *n. Informal* A stupid, clumsy person.

lump[1] (lump) *n.* 1. A shapeless, usu. small mass. 2. A swelling. 3. A mass of things thrown together; aggregate. —*adj.* Formed in a lump or lumps: *lump* sugar. —*v.t.* 1. To put together in one mass, group, etc. 2. To make lumps in or on. [ME] —lump'i·ness *n.* —lump'y *adj.* lump·i·er, lump·i·est

lump² (lump) *v.t. Informal* To put up with; endure: You can like it or *lump* it.

lump·ish (lum'pish) *adj.* 1. Like a lump. 2. Stupid; clumsy. —lump'ish·ly *adv.* —lump'ish·ness *n.*

lump sum A full or single sum of money paid at one time.

lu·na·cy (lōō'nə·sē) *n. pl.* ·cies 1. Irresponsible or senseless conduct. 2. *Law* Insanity.

lu·nar (lōō'nər) *adj.* 1. Of the moon. 2. Round or crescent-shaped like the moon. 3. Measured by the revolutions of the moon: a *lunar* month. [< L *luna* moon]

lunar month See under MONTH.

lunar year A period of twelve lunar months, one month being added at intervals to make the mean length of the astronomical year, as in the Hebrew calendar.

lu·nate (lōō'nāt) *adj.* Crescent-shaped. Also lu'nat·ed.

lu·na·tic (lōō'nə·tik) *adj.* 1. Insane. 2. Wildly foolish or irrational. 3. Of or for the insane. —*n.* An insane person. [< L *luna* moon]

lunatic fringe Extreme or fanatical followers or devotees of a movement, idea, etc.

lunch (lunch) *n.* 1. A light meal, esp. the noonday meal. 2. Food for a lunch. —*v.i.* To eat lunch. —lunch'er *n.*

lunch·eon (lun'chən) *n.* A noonday meal, esp. a formal one.

lunch·eon·ette (lun'chən·et') *n.* A restaurant where light lunches and other meals may be obtained.

lunch·room (lunch'rōōm', -rŏŏm') *n.* A restaurant serving light lunches.

lung (lung) *n. Anat.* 1. Either of two saclike organs of respiration in the thorax of man and other air-breathing vertebrates. ◆Collateral adjective: *pulmonary*. 2. An analogous organ in certain invertebrates. [OE *lungen*]

lunge (lunj) *n.* 1. A sudden pass or thrust, as with a sword, etc. 2. A quick movement or plunge forward. —*v.* lunged, lung·ing —*v.i.* 1. To make a lunge; thrust. 2. To move with a lunge. —*v.t.* 3. To cause to lunge. [< F *allonger* to prolong]

lu·pine¹ (lōō'pīn) *adj.* 1. Of, like, or related to a wolf or wolves. 2. Fierce; ravenous. [< L *lupus* wolf]

lu·pine² (lōō'pin) *n.* Any of various plants of the pea family, bearing mostly blue, white, or purple flowers, as the white lupine of Europe, whose seeds are edible. [< L *lupinus* wolflike]

lurch¹ (lûrch) *v.i.* 1. To roll suddenly to one side. 2. To stagger. —*n.* 1. A sudden swaying. 2. A reeling. [Origin unknown]

lurch² (lûrch) *n.* An embarrassing or difficult position; predicament: now only in the phrase to leave (someone) in the lurch. [< F *lourche* deceived]

lure (lŏŏr) *n.* 1. Anything that attracts or entices. 2. In angling, an artificial bait. —*v.t.* lured, lur·ing To attract or entice; allure. [< OF *leurre* < MHG *luoder* to bait] —lur'er *n.*

lu·rid (lŏŏr'id) *adj.* 1. Shocking or sensational. 2. Pale and sickly in color; livid. 3. Lighted up with a yellowish red glare or w, esp. in smoke or darkness. [< L *luridus* sallow] —lu'rid·ly *adv.* —lu'rid·ness *n.*

lurk (lûrk) *v.i.* 1. To lie hidden, as in ambush. 2. To move secretly or furtively; slink. [ME *lurken*] —lurk'er *n.* —lurk'ing·ly *adv.*

lus·cious (lush'əs) *adj.* 1. Very pleasurable to the sense of taste or smell. 2. Pleasing to any sense. —lus'cious·ly *adv.* —lus'cious·ness *n.*

lush¹ (lush) *adj.* 1. Abounding in vigorous growth. 2. Elaborate in effects, etc. [< L *laxus* loose] —lush'ness *n.*

lush² (lush) *n. Slang* A heavy drinker; drunkard.

lust (lust) *n.* 1. Sexual appetite. 2. Excessive sexual appetite, esp. that seeking immediate or ruthless satisfaction. 3. An overwhelming desire: a *lust* for power. —*v.i.* To have passionate or inordinate desire. [OE, pleasure] —lust'ful *adj.* —lust'ful·ly *adv.*

lus·ter (lus'tər) *n.* 1. Sheen; gloss. 2. Brilliance of light; radiance. 3. Splendor, glory, or distinction. 4. Any of various substances used to give a polish to a surface. Also *Brit.* lus'tre. [< L *lustrum* purification] —lus'trous *adj.* —lus'trous·ly *adv.*

lus·trate (lus'trāt) *v.t.* ·trat·ed, ·trat·ing To purify by an offering or ceremony. [< L *lustrum* purification] —lus·tra'tion *n.*

lust·y (lus'tē) *adj.* lust·i·er, lust·i·est 1. Full of vigor; robust. 2. Powerful. —lust'i·ly *adv.* —lust'i·ness *n.*

lute (lōōt) *n.* An old musical instrument having strings that are plucked by the fingers, a large body shaped like half of a pear, and a long, fretted neck. [< Arabic *al'ūd* the piece of wood] —lu·ta·nist (lōō'tə·nist) or lu'te·nist *n.*

lu·te·ti·um (lōō·tē'shē·əm, -tē'shəm) *n.* A metallic element (symbol Lu) of the lanthanide series, isolated from ytterbium. Also lu·te'ci·um.

Lu·ther·an (lōō'thər·ən) *adj.* Of or pertaining to the Lutheran Church, a Protestant denomination founded in the 16th c. by Martin Luther, or to its doctrines. —*n.* A member of the Lutheran Church. —Lu'ther·an·ism *n.*

lux·u·ri·ant (lug·zhŏŏr'ē·ənt, luk·shŏŏr'-) *adj.* 1. Growing lushly and profusely, as vegetation. 2. Abundant, exuberant, or ornate, as in design, etc. —lux·u'ri·ance *n.* —lux·u'ri·ant·ly *adv.*

lux·u·ri·ate (lug·zhŏŏr'ē·āt, luk·shŏŏr'-) *v.i.* ·at·ed, ·at·ing 1. To take great pleasure; indulge oneself fully: with *in*. 2. To live sumptuously. 3. To grow profusely. [See LUXURY.]

lux·u·ri·ous (lug·zhŏŏr'ē·əs, luk·shŏŏr'-) *adj.* 1. Characterized by or conducive to luxury or extreme comfort; opulent; sumptuous. 2. Indulging in or given to luxury. —lux·u'ri·ous·ly *adv.* —lux·u'ri·ous·ness *n.*

lux·u·ry (luk'shər·ē, lug'zhər·ē) *n. pl.* ·ries 1. Anything, usu. expensive or rare, that gives comfort or pleasure but is not a necessity to life, health, etc. 2. Free indulgence in that which is expensive, rare, or extremely gratifying. [< L *luxus* extravagance]

-ly¹ *suffix of adjectives* 1. Like; characteristic of; pertaining to: *manly, godly*. 2. Occurring every (specified interval): *weekly, daily*. [OE *-lic*]

-ly[2] *suffix of adverbs* 1. In a (specified) manner: used to form adverbs from adjectives, or (rarely) from nouns: *brightly, busily.* 2. At every (specified interval): *hourly, yearly.* [OE *-lice* < *-lic*, -LY[1]]

ly·cée (lē·sā′) *n. French* In France, a secondary school financed by the government. [See LYCEUM.]

ly·ce·um (lī·sē′əm, lī′sē·əm) *n. pl.* **·ce·ums** or **·ce·a** 1. An organization providing popular instruction by lectures, concerts, etc.; also, its building. 2. A hall for presenting lectures, concerts, etc. [< Gk. *Lykeion*, the grove near Athens where Aristotle taught]

lye (lī) *n.* A solution leached from ashes or derived from a substance containing alkali, used in making soap. [OE *lēah*]

ly·ing[1] (lī′ing) *n.* The act of telling lies; untruthfulness. **—***adj.* Deceitful or false.

ly·ing[2] (lī′ing) Present participle of LIE[1].

ly·ing-in (lī′ing·in′) *n.* The confinement of women during childbirth. **—***adj.* Of or pertaining to childbirth.

lymph (limf) *n. Physiol.* A yellowish alkaline fluid derived from the body tissues, consisting of lymphocytes and a plasma similar to that of blood. [< L *limpa* water]

lym·phat·ic (lim·fat′ik) *adj.* Pertaining to lymph or the lymph nodes. **—***n.* A vessel that conveys lymph into the veins.

lymph node *Anat.* Any of numerous glandlike bodies found in the course of the lymphatic vessels and producing lymphocytes. Also **lymph gland.**

lympho- *combining form* Lymph; of the lymph or the lymphatics. Also, before vowels, **lymph-**. [See LYMPH.]

lym·pho·cyte (lim′fə·sīt) *n. Physiol.* A variety of colorless leucocyte formed in the tissue of the lymph nodes. Also **lymph cell.**

lym·phoid (lim′foid) *adj.* Of or like lymph or the tissues of a lymph node.

lynch (linch) *v.t.* To kill (a person accused of a crime) by mob action, as by hanging, without due process of law. [? after William *Lynch*, 1742–1820, Virginia magistrate] **—lynch′er** *n.* **—lynch′ing** *n.*

lynx (lingks) *n. pl.* **lynx·es** or **lynx** A wildcat of Europe and North America having a short tail, tufted ears, and relatively long limbs. Also called *bobcat.* [< Gk.]

lynx-eyed (lingks′īd′) *adj.* Having sharp sight.

ly·on·naise (lī′ə·nāz′, *Fr.* lē·ô·nez′) *adj.* Made with finely sliced onions; esp., designating a method of preparing potatoes with fried onions. [< F, fem. of *lyonnais* of Lyon]

Ly·ra (lī′rə) *n.* A constellation, the Lyre, containing the star Vega. [< Gk.]

lyre (līr) *n.* An ancient harplike stringed instrument, used by the Greeks to accompany poetry and song. [< Gk. *lyra*]

lyre·bird (līr′bûrd′) *n.* Either of two species of Australian birds, the male of which spreads its tail feathers into the shape of a lyre.

lyr·ic (lir′ik) *adj.* 1. Of poetry, expressing the poet's inner feelings; also, pertaining to the method, personality, etc., of a writer of such verse. 2. Meant to be sung. 3. *Music* Having a singing voice of a light, flexible quality: a *lyric* soprano. Also **lyr′i·cal.** **—***n.* 1. *Usu. pl.* The words of a song. 2. A lyric poem. [< Gk. *lyra* lyre] **—lyr′i·cal·ly** *adv.*

lyr·i·cism (lir′ə·siz′əm) *n.* The quality of emotional self-expression in the arts.

lyr·i·cist (lir′ə·sist) *n.* 1. One who writes the words of a song or the lyrics for a musical play. 2. A lyric poet.

ly·ri·form (lī′rə·fôrm) *adj.* Shaped like a lyre.

ly·ser·gic acid di·eth·yl·am·ide (lī·sûr′jik as′id dī′eth·əl·am′īd, -id) *n.* LSD.

lysi- *combining form* A loosening; dissolving: *lysergic acid, lysine.* Also, before vowels, **lys-**. [< Gk. *lysis* a loosening]

ly·sine (lī′sēn, -sin) *n. Biochem.* An amino acid necessary to animal growth. Also **ly′sin.** [< LYS- + -INE[2]]

ly·sis (lī′sis) *n.* 1. *Med.* The gradual disappearing of the symptoms of a disease. 2. *Biochem.* The process of disintegration or destruction of cells, bacteria, etc. [< Gk., a loosening] **—ly·tic** (lit′ik) *adj.*

-lysis *combining form* A loosing, dissolving, etc.: *hydrolysis, paralysis.* [< Gk. *lysis* a loosening]

-lyte *combining form* A substance decomposed by a (specified) process: *electrolyte.* [< Gk. *lytos* loosened, dissolved]

-lytic *combining form* Loosing; dissolving: used in adjectives corresponding to nouns in *-lysis*: *hydrolytic, paralytic.* [< Gk. *lytikos* loosing]

-lyze *suffix of verbs* To perform, cause, or undergo: formed from nouns in *-lysis*: *electrolyze, paralyze.* Also *esp. Brit.* **-lyse.** [< -LYSIS]

M

m, M (em) *n. pl.* **m's** or **ms, M's** or **Ms** or **ems** (emz) 1. The thirteenth letter of the English alphabet. 2. The sound represented by the letter *m*. —*symbol* 1. The Roman numeral 1,000. 2. *Printing* An em.

ma'am (mam, mäm, *unstressed* məm) *n.* 1. A term of respectful address used to women; madam. 2. *Brit.* A term of respectful address used to the queen or to a royal princess.

ma·ca·bre (mə·kä′brə, -bər) *adj.* Suggesting death and decay; gruesome; ghastly. [< OF (*danse*) *macabre* (dance) of death]

mac·ad·am (mə·kad′əm) *n.* 1. A pavement or road of small stones usu. held together with tar or asphalt. 2. Broken stone used in this type of road. [after John L. *McAdam*, 1756–1836, Scottish engineer] —**mac·ad′am·ize** *v.t.* **·ized, ·iz·ing** —**mac·ad′am·i·za′tion** *n.*

mac·a·ro·ni (mak′ə·rō′nē) *n.* 1. A dried paste of wheat flour made into short tubes and prepared as a food by boiling. 2. An 18th c. English dandy. Also **mac′ca·ro′ni.** [< Ital. *maccaroni* groats]

mac·a·roon (mak′ə·ro͞on′) *n.* A small cooky made of ground almonds or sometimes coconut, egg, and sugar. [< MF *macaron*]

ma·caw (mə·kô′) *n.* Any of various large tropical American parrots with a harsh voice and brilliant plumage. [< Pg. *macao*, prob. < Tupi]

Mac·ca·bees (mak′ə·bēz) *n.pl.* Four books in the Old Testament Apocrypha treating of oppression against the Jews from 222 to 135 B.C. [after the *Maccabees*, a Jewish family that led a revolt against the Syrians]

mace[1] (mās) *n.* 1. A heavy medieval war club, usu. with a spiked metal head. 2. A club-shaped staff symbolic of office or authority. [< OF *masse, mace*]

mace[2] (mās) *n.* A spice ground from the covering between the husk and the seed of the nutmeg. [< Gk. *maker* a spicy bark from India]

Mace (mās) *n.* A chemical solution similar to tear gas that temporarily blinds or incapacitates one when sprayed in the face, used as a weapon: a trade name.

Mac·e·do·ni·an (mas′ə·dō′nē·ən) *adj.* 1. Of Macedonia (or Macedon), the ancient kingdom that became a world power under Alexander the Great. 2. Of the Balkan region including parts of Greece, Yugoslavia, and Bulgaria. —**Mac′e·do′ni·an** *n.*

mac·er·ate (mas′ə·rāt) *v.* **·at·ed, ·at·ing** *v.t.* 1. To reduce (a solid substance) to a soft mass by soaking in liquid. 2. To break down the structure of (food) in digestion. —*v.i.* 3. To become macerated. [< L *macerare* to make soft, knead] —**mac′er·a′tion** *n.*

mach (mäk) *n.* *Often cap.* A mach number.

ma·chet·e (mə·shet′ē, mə·shet′; *Sp.* mä·chā′tā) *n.* A heavy knife or cutlass used as an implement and a weapon in tropical America. [< Sp., dim. of *macho* an ax, hammer]

Mach·i·a·vel·li·an (mak′ē·ə·vel′ē·ən) *adj.* Achieving and maintaining power, esp. political power, by unprincipled means. —*n.* One who follows or subscribes to such principles. [after Niccolò *Machiavelli*, 16th c. Florentine statesman] —**Mach′i·a·vel′li·an·ism** *n.*

ma·chic·o·la·tion (mə·chik′ə·lā′shən) *n.* *Archit.* An opening between the corbels of a projecting parapet, through which missiles or boiling liquids may be dropped. [< OF *macher* to crush + *couler* to flow]

mach·i·nate (mak′ə·nāt) *v.t. & v.i.* **·nat·ed, ·nat·ing** To scheme or contrive. [< L *machinari* to contrive]

mach·i·na·tion (mak′ə·nā′shən) *n.* *Usu. pl.* A concealed working and scheming for some devious purpose.

ma·chine (mə·shēn′) *n.* 1. Any combination of interrelated parts for using or applying energy to do work. 2. A controlling political group. 3. The organization and operating principles of a complex structure: the human *machine*. 4. A motorized vehicle, esp. an automobile. —*adj.* 1. Of machines. 2. Produced by machine. —*v.t.* **·chined, ·chin·ing** To shape, mill, make, etc., by machine. [< Gk. *mēchos* a contrivance]

ma·chine-gun (mə·shēn′gun′) *v.t.* **-gunned, -gun·ning** To fire at or shoot with a machine gun.

machine gun A rapid-firing automatic gun, usu. mounted. —**machine gunner**

machine language Codes, in the form of letters and numbers, used directly by a computer.

ma·chin·er·y (mə·shē′nər·ē, -shēn′rē) *n.* 1. A collection of machines or machine parts. 2. The operating parts and principles of a complex structure: the *machinery* of the law.

machine tool A power-driven tool, partly or wholly automatic in action, for cutting, shaping, boring, milling, etc.

ma·chin·ist (mə·shē′nist) *n.* One who operates or repairs machines or machine tools.

ma·chis·mo (mä·chēz′mō, -chiz′-, -kēz′-) *n.* An exaggerated sense of masculinity. [< Sp. *macho* male]

mach number A number representing the ratio between the speed of an object moving through a fluid medium, as air, and the speed of sound in the same medium. *Mach 2* denotes a speed twice that of sound. Also **Mach number.** [after Ernst *Mach*, 1838–1916, Austrian physicist]

ma·cho (mä′chō) *adj.* Exaggeratedly masculine. [< Sp. *macho* male]
-machy *combining form* A fight between or by means of. [< Gk. *machē* a battle]
mack·er·el (mak′ər·əl) *n.* A food fish of the Atlantic, steel blue with blackish bars above, and silvery beneath. [< OF makerel]
Mack·i·naw coat (mak′ə·nô) A thick, short, double-breasted woolen coat, commonly with a plaid pattern. Also **mack′i·naw.** [after *Mackinac* Island, Michigan]
mack·in·tosh (mak′ən·tosh) *n. Chiefly Brit.* **1.** A waterproof cloak; raincoat. **2.** Thin, rubber-coated cloth. Also **mac′in·tosh.** [after Charles *Macintosh*, 1766–1843, Scottish chemist, inventor of the cloth]
mac·ra·mé (mak′rə·mā) *n.* **1.** Decoratively knotted string or cord, formed into belts, handbags, wall hangings, etc. **2.** The craft of producing macramé. [Ult. < Arabic *migramah* veil]
macro- *combining form* Large or overdeveloped: **macrocyst, macrofossil, macromolecule, macroplan, macroscale, macroworld.** Before vowels, **macr-.** [< Gk. *makros* large]
mac·ro·bi·ot·ic (mak′rō·bī·ot′ik) *adj.* Designating a usu. meatless diet, believed to promote good health and prolong life. [< Gk. *makros* long + *bios* life] **—mac′ro·bi·ot′ics** *n.*
mac·ro·cosm (mak′rə·koz′əm) *n.* The whole universe, esp. when regarded in contrast to man. [< Gk. *makros* long, great + *kosmos* world] **—mac′ro·cos′mic** *adj.*
ma·cron (mā′krən, -kron) *n.* A straight line (¯) over a vowel letter to show that it represents a long sound, as *ā* in *made.* [< Gk. *makron*, neut. of *makros* long]
mad (mad) *adj.* **mad·der, mad·dest** **1.** Suffering from or manifesting severe mental disorder; insane; psychotic. **2.** *Informal* Angry. **3.** Wildly foolish; rash: a *mad* project. **4.** Of animals, suffering from hydrophobia; rabid. **5.** *Informal* Showing a passionate infatuation with or desire for: with *about, for,* or *over.* **6.** *Informal* Flamboyant; daring. **—like mad** *Informal* Frantically. **—***n. Informal* A fit of temper: now only in the phrase **to have a mad on,** to be angry. [OE *gemǣd* insane] **—mad′ly** *adv.* **—mad′ness** *n.*
mad·am (mad′əm) *n.* *pl.* **mes·dames** (mā·däm′, *Fr.* mā·dȧm′) *for def. 1*; **mad·ams** *for def. 2.* **1.** My lady; mistress: a title of courtesy. **2.** A woman who manages a brothel. [< OF *ma dame* my lady]
mad·ame (mad′əm, *Fr.* mȧ·dȧm′) *n. pl.* **mes·dames** (mā·däm′, *Fr.* mā·dȧm′) The French title of courtesy for a married woman, equivalent to the English *Mrs.* [< F See MADAM.]
mad·cap (mad′kap′) *adj.* Wild; rattlebrained. **—***n.* One who acts wildly or rashly.
mad·den (mad′n) *v.t. & v.i.* To make or become mad or insane; inflame; infuriate. **—mad′den·ing·ly** *adv.*
mad·der[1] (mad′ər) Comparative of MAD.
mad·der[2] (mad′ər) *n.* **1.** Any of various perennial herbs, the root of which yields a brilliant red extract. **2.** The red coloring matter. [OE *mædere, mæddre*]
mad·ding (mad′ing) *adj.* Being or growing mad; delirious; raging. **—mad′ding·ly** *adv.*
made (mād) Past tense and past participle of MAKE. **—***adj.* Produced by fabrication, invention, or skill; not occurring naturally. **—to have it made** *Slang* To be sure of success.
Ma·dei·ra (mə·dir′ə, *Pg.* mə·thā′rə) *n.* A fortified dessert wine.
mad·e·moi·selle (mad′ə·mə·zel′, *Fr.* mȧd·mwȧ·zel′) *n. pl.* **mad·e·moi·selles,** *Fr.* **mes·de·moi·selles** (mād·mwȧ·zel′) The French title of courtesy for unmarried women, equivalent to *Miss.* [< F *ma* my + *demoiselle* young lady]
made-up (mād′up′) *adj.* **1.** Invented; fictitious. **2.** Adorned or altered by cosmetics. **3.** Complete; finished: a *made-up* sample. **4.** Compensated for: said of work, money, etc.
mad·house (mad′hous′) *n.* **1.** A hospital for the mentally ill; insane asylum. **2.** A place of confusion or uproar; bedlam.
mad·man (mad′man′) *n. pl.* **·men** (-men′) An insane man; lunatic.
Ma·don·na (mə·don′ə) *n.* The Virgin Mary. [< Ital. < *ma* my + *donna* lady]
ma·dras (mə·dras′, -dräs′, mad′rəs) *n.* **1.** A cotton cloth usu. striped, corded, or checked. **2.** A silk cloth, usu. striped. [after *Madras*, India, where originally made]
mad·ri·gal (mad′rə·gəl) *n.* **1.** *Music* An unaccompanied part song, often in counterpoint, popular during the 16th and 17th c. **2.** A short lyric poem. [< Ital. < LL *matricale* original, chief] **—mad′ri·gal·ist** *n.*
mad·wom·an (mad′wo͝om′ən) *n. pl.* **·wom·en** (-wim′in) An insane woman; lunatic.
mael·strom (māl′strəm) *n.* **1.** Any dangerous and irresistible force, or a place where it prevails. **2.** A whirlpool. [< Du. *malen* to whirl around + *stroom* stream]
mae·nad (mē′nad) *n.* **1.** In ancient Greece, a priestess who participated in orgiastic rites. **2.** Any woman beside herself with frenzy. Also spelled *menad.* [< Gk. *mainesthai* to rave] **—mae·nad′ic** *adj.*
ma·es·tro (mä·es′trō, mīs′trō) *n. pl.* **·tros** A master in any art; esp., an eminent conductor. [< Ital., master]
Ma·fi·a (mä′fē·ä, maf′ē·ə) *n.* **1.** A secret criminal organization believed to exist in many countries, including the U.S. **2.** *Often not cap. Informal* A dominating and often ruthless in-group. [< Ital.]
ma·fi·o·so (mä′fē·ō′sō) *n. pl.* **·si** (-sē) A member of the Mafia. [< MAFIA]
mag·a·zine (mag′ə·zēn′, mag′ə·zēn) *n.* **1.** A periodical publication, containing articles, stories, etc., by various writers. **2.** A warehouse or depot, esp. for explosives and ammunition. **3.** A supply chamber in a gun, battery, camera, etc. [< Arabic *makhāzin* storehouses]
mag·da·len (mag′də·lin) *n.* A reformed prostitute. Also **mag′da·lene** (-lēn). [after Mary *Magdalene*]
ma·gen·ta (mə·jen′tə) *n.* A purplish red color. [after *Magenta*, Italy]
mag·got (mag′ət) *n.* The legless larva of an insect, as the housefly, esp. one found in decaying matter. [Prob. alter. of ME *maddock, mathek* < ON *mathkr* worm] **—mag′got·y** *adj.*
Ma·gi (mā′jī) *n. pl. of* **Ma·gus** (mā′gəs) The three "wise men from the east" who came to Bethlehem to pay homage to the

infant Jesus. *Matt.* ii 1–12. [< Persian *magu* priest, magician]

mag·ic (maj′ik) *n.* 1. Seeming control over or foresight of natural events, forces, etc., through supernatural agencies. 2. An overpowering influence: the *magic* of his voice. 3. Sleight of hand; legerdemain. —*adj.* 1. Of or used in magic. 2. Mysteriously impressive; beautiful. [< Gk. *magikos* of the Magi] —**mag′i·cal** *adj.* —**mag′i·cal·ly** *adv.*

ma·gi·cian (mə·jish′ən) *n.* One who performs magic; esp., an entertainer who uses illusion and legerdemain.

magic lantern *Archaic* A slide projector.

mag·is·te·ri·al (maj′is·tir′ē·əl) *adj.* 1. Of or like a master; authoritative. 2. Of or pertaining to a magistrate. —**mag′is·te′ri·al·ly** *adv.*

mag·is·tra·cy (maj′is·trə·sē) *n. pl.* **·cies** The office, function, or term of a magistrate.

mag·is·trate (maj′is·trāt, -trit) *n.* 1. A public official with the power to enforce the law. 2. A minor judicial officer, as a justice of the peace. [< L *magister* master]

mag·ma (mag′mə) *n. pl.* **·ma·ta** (-mə·tə) *Geol.* The mass of molten rock from which igneous rocks are formed. [< Gk. *massein* to knead]

mag·nan·i·mous (mag·nan′ə·məs) *adj.* Manifesting generosity in forgiving insults or injuries. [< L *magnus* great + *animus* mind, soul] —**mag·na·nim·i·ty** (mag′nə·nim′ə·tē) *n.* —**mag·nan′i·mous·ly** *adv.*

mag·nate (mag′nāt) *n.* One notable or powerful, esp. in industry: a railroad *magnate.* [< LL *magnus* great]

mag·ne·sia (mag·nē′zhə, -shə, -zē·ə) *n. Chem.* Magnesium oxide, a light, white powder used in medicine as an antacid and laxative, and in refractories. [< Gk. *Magnēsia (lithos)* (stone) of Magnesia]

mag·ne·si·um (mag·nē′zē·əm, -zhē-, -shē-) *n.* A light, silver-white, malleable and ductile metallic element (symbol Mg), that burns with a very hot, bright flame and is used in lightweight alloys. [< MAGNESIA]

mag·net (mag′nit) *n.* 1. A body that has a magnetic field and therefore attracts iron and other magnetic material. 2. A lodestone. 3. One who or that which exercises a strong attraction. [< Gk. *Magnēs (lithos)* Magnesian (stone)]

mag·net·ic (mag·net′ik) *adj.* 1. Pertaining to magnetism or a magnet. 2. Capable of setting up a magnetic field. 3. Possessing personal magnetism. —**mag·net′i·cal·ly** *adv.*

magnetic field That region in the neighborhood of a magnet or current-carrying body in which magnetic forces are observable.

magnetic north The direction, usu. differing from true north, toward which the needle of a compass points.

magnetic pole 1. Either of the poles of a magnet. 2. Either of two points (**north magnetic pole** and **south magnetic pole**) on the surface of the earth where the lines of magnetic force converge.

magnetic tape *Electronics* A thin ribbon, coated with magnetic particles, for recording sound, computer data, television programs, etc.

mag·net·ism (mag′nə·tiz′əm) *n.* 1. The specific properties of a magnet. 2. The science that treats of the laws and conditions of magnetic phenomena. 3. The amount of magnetic force in a magnetized body. 4. A personal quality that attracts.

mag·net·ite (mag′nə·tīt) *n.* A black iron oxide that is an iron ore: called *lodestone* when magnetic. —**mag′net·it′ic** (-tit′ik) *adj.*

mag·net·ize (mag′nə·tīz) *v.t.* **·ized, ·iz·ing** 1. To communicate magnetic properties to. 2. To attract by personal influence. —**mag′net·i·za′tion** *n.* —**mag′net·iz′er** *n.*

mag·ne·to (mag·nē′tō) *n. pl.* **·tos** Any of various devices using a permanent magnet to generate an electric current, used esp. to produce the ignition spark in some internal-combustion engines. [Short for *magnetoelectric machine*]

magneto- *combining form* Magnetic; magnetism.

mag·ne·to·e·lec·tric·i·ty (mag·nē′tō·i·lek·tris′ə·tē) *n.* 1. Electricity generated by the inductive action of a magnet. 2. The science that treats of such electricity. —**mag·ne′to·e·lec′tric** or **·tri·cal** *adj.*

mag·ne·tom·e·ter (mag′nə·tom′ə·tər) *n.* An instrument for measuring the intensity and direction of magnetic forces.

mag·ne·to·sphere (mag·nē′tə·sfir, -net′ə-) *n. Physics* A region of the upper atmosphere forming a continuous band of ionized particles trapped by the earth's magnetic field.

magni- *combining form* Great; large; long. [< L *magnus* great]

mag·nif·i·cent (mag·nif′ə·sənt) *adj.* 1. Presenting an extraordinarily imposing appearance; splendid; beautiful. 2. Exceptionally pleasing; superb. 3. Exalted or sublime in expression or concept. —**mag·nif′i·cence** *n.* —**mag·nif′i·cent·ly** *adv.*

mag·nif·i·co (mag·nif′ə·kō) *n. pl.* **·coes** Any lordly or distinguished personage. [< Ital.]

mag·ni·fy (mag′nə·fī) *v.* **·fied, ·fy·ing** *v.t.* 1. To increase the perceived size of, as by a lens. 2. To increase the size of; enlarge. 3. To cause to seem greater or more important; exaggerate. 4. *Archaic* To extol; exalt. —*v.i.* 5. To increase or have the power to increase the apparent size of an object, as a lens. [< L *magnificus* great] —**mag′ni·fi·ca′tion** *n.* —**mag′ni·fi′er** *n.*

mag·nil·o·quent (mag·nil′ə·kwənt) *adj.* Speaking or spoken in a grandiose style; grandiloquent. [< L *magnus* great + *loqui* to speak] —**mag·nil′o·quence** *n.* —**mag·nil′o·quent·ly** *adv.*

mag·ni·tude (mag′nə·to͞od, -tyo͞od) *n.* 1. Size or extent. 2. Greatness or importance: the *magnitude* of the achievement. 3. *Astron.* The relative brightness of a star, ranging from a rating of one for the brightest to six for those just visible to the naked eye. [< L *magnus* large]

mag·no·li·a (mag·nō′lē·ə, -nōl′yə) *n.* 1. An ornamental flowering shrub or tree with large, fragrant flowers. 2. The fragrant white flower of the **evergreen magnolia.** [after Pierre *Magnol,* 1638–1715, French botanist]

mag·num (mag′nəm) *n.* A wine bottle holding about 2/5 of a gallon; also, such a quantity. [< L, neut. of *magnus* great]

magnum o·pus (ō′pəs) A great work; masterpiece; esp., the greatest single work of a writer, artist, etc. [< L]

mag·pie (mag′pī) *n.* 1. Any of various large,

noisy, long-tailed birds of the crow family, having black and white plumage. 2. A chatterbox. [< *Mag*, dim. of *Margaret*, a proper name + PIE[2]]
Ma·gus (mā′gəs) Singular of MAGI.
Mag·yar (mag′yär, mäg′-; *Hungarian* mud′·yär) *n.* 1. A member of the dominant group of the population of Hungary. 2. Hungarian, a Finno-Ugric language. —**Mag′yar** *adj.*
ma·ha·ra·ja (mä′hə·rä′jə, *Hind.* mə·hä′rä′jə) *n.* A title of certain princes of India, particularly one ruling an Indian state. Also **ma′ha·ra′jah.** [< Skt. *maha* great + *rājā* king]
ma·ha·ra·ni (mä′hə·rä′nē, *Hind.* mə·hä′rä′·nē) *n.* 1. The wife of a maharaja. 2. A sovereign princess of India. Also **ma′ha·ra′nee.** [< Hind. *maha* great + *rāni* queen]
ma·hat·ma (mə·hat′mə, -hät′-) *n. Often cap.* In some Asian religions, a title of respect for a holy man. [< Skt. *maha* great + *ātman* soul] —**ma·hat′ma·ism** *n.*
Ma·hi·can (mə·hē′kən) *n.* One of a tribe of Algonquian Indians formerly occupying the territory from the Hudson River to Lake Champlain: also called *Mohican.* [< Algonquian, lit., wolf]
mah·jong (mä′zhong′, -zhông′) *n.* A game of Chinese origin, usu. played with 144 pieces or tiles. Also **mah′-jong′, mah′jongg′.** [< Chinese *ma ch'iao* house sparrow; from the design on one of the tiles]
ma·hog·a·ny (mə·hog′ə·nē) *n. pl.* **·nies** 1. Any of various tropical trees yielding fine-grained reddish hardwood much used for furniture and cabinet work. 2. The wood itself. 3. A brownish red. —*adj.* Brownish red. [< obs. Sp. *mahogani*]
ma·hout (mə·hout′) *n.* In India and the East Indies, the keeper and driver of an elephant. [< Skt. *mahāmātra*, lit., great in measure]
maid (mād) *n.* 1. A young unmarried woman or girl; maiden. 2. A female servant. [Short for MAIDEN]
maid·en (mād′n) *n.* 1. An unmarried woman, esp. if young. 2. A virgin. —*adj.* 1. Of, pertaining to, or befitting a maiden. 2. Unmarried: said of women. 3. Of or pertaining to the first use, trial, or experience: *maiden* effort. [OE *mægden*, prob. dim. of *mægeth* virgin] —**maid′en·hood′** *n.*
maid·en·hair (mād′n·hâr′) *n.* A very delicate and graceful fern with an erect black stem, common in damp, rocky woods. Also **maidenhair fern.**
maid·en·head (mād′n·hed′) *n.* The hymen.
maid·en·ly (mād′n·lē) *adj.* Of or befitting a maiden or young girl. —**maid′en·li·ness** *n.*
maiden name A woman's surname before marriage.
maid of honor The chief unmarried attendant of a bride at a wedding.
maid·ser·vant (mād′sûr′vənt) *n.* A female servant.
mail[1] (māl) *n.* 1. Letters, printed matter, parcels, etc., sent or received through a governmental postal system. 2. The postal system itself. 3. Postal matter collected or delivered at a specified time: the morning *mail.* —*adj.* Pertaining to or used for the handling of mail. —*v.t.* To send by mail, as letters; post. [< OHG *malha* wallet] —**mail′a·ble** *adj.* —**mail′er** *n.*
mail[2] (māl) *n.* 1. Flexible armor made of interlinked rings or overlapping scales. 2. Loosely, any defensive armor. [< OF < L *macula* spot, mesh of a net]
mail·bag (māl′bag′) *n.* A bag in which mail is carried or shipped. Also **mail′pouch′** (-pouch′).
mail·box (māl′boks′) *n.* 1. A box in which letters, etc., are deposited for collection. 2. A box into which private mail is delivered.
mail·man (māl′man′, -mən) *n. pl.* **·men** (-men′, -mən) One who carries and delivers letters: also called **mail carrier.** Also *postman.*
mail order An order for merchandise to be sent by mail.
maim (mām) *v.t.* 1. To deprive of the use of a bodily part; mutilate; cripple or disable. 2. To render imperfect; make defective. [< OF *mahaignier, mayner*]
main (mān) *adj.* 1. First or chief in size, importance, etc.; leading: *main* event. 2. Fully exerted; sheer: by *main* force. —*n.* 1. A principal conduit or pipe in a system conveying gas, water, etc. 2. Utmost effort; force: now chiefly in the phrase **with might and main.** 3. The chief or most important point or part. [OE *mægen*]
main deck *Naut.* The chief deck of a vessel.
main drag *Slang* The principal business street of a town.
main·land (mān′land′, -lənd) *n.* The main part of a continent, as distinguished from an island or peninsula.
main·line (mān′līn′) *v.t. & v.i.* **·lined, ·lin·ing** To inject (a narcotic drug) into a large vein. —**main′lin′er** *n.*
main line The principal line of a railroad or highway.
main·ly (mān′lē) *adv.* Chiefly; principally.
main·mast (mān′məst, -mast′) *n. Naut.* 1. The second mast from the bow in a schooner, brig, etc. 2. The mast nearer the bow in a two-masted vessel.
main·sail (mān′səl, -sāl′) *Naut.* 1. A sail bent to the main yard of a square-rigged vessel: also **main course.** 2. The principal sail on a mainmast.
main·spring (mān′spring′) *n.* 1. The principal spring of a mechanism, as of a watch. 2. The principal or most compelling cause or agency.
main·stay (mān′stā′) *n.* 1. *Naut.* The rope from the mainmast head forward, used to steady the mast in that direction. 2. A chief support: the *mainstay* of my old age.
main·stream (mān′strēm′) *n.* The main or middle course.
main·tain (mān·tān′) *v.t.* 1. To carry on or continue; keep in existence. 2. To preserve or keep. 3. To keep in proper condition. 4. To supply with a livelihood; support. 5. To claim to be true; uphold. [< L *manus* hand + *tenere* to hold]
main·te·nance (mān′tə·nəns) *n.* 1. The act of maintaining, or the state of being maintained. 2. Means of support or subsistence; livelihood. 3. The work of keeping roads, machines, buildings, etc., in good condition.
main·top (mān′top′) *n. Naut.* A platform at the head of the lower section of the mainmast.
main yard *Naut.* The lower yard on the mainmast.
maî·tre d'hô·tel (me′tr′ dō·tel′) 1. A headwaiter or steward. Also *Informal* **mai·tre d'**

(mā′trə dē′). 2. The proprietor or manager of a hotel. [< F]

maize (māz) *n.* 1. Corn (def. 1). 2. A deep yellow color. [< Sp. < Taino *mahiz*]

ma·jes·tic (mə·jes′tik) *adj.* Stately; royal. Also **ma·jes′ti·cal.** —**ma·jes′ti·cal·ly** *adv.*

maj·es·ty (maj′is·tē) *n. pl.* **·ties** 1. Exalted dignity; stateliness; grandeur. 2. Sovereign authority: the *majesty* of the law. 3. *Cap.* A title or form of address for a sovereign: preceded by *His, Her, Your,* etc. [< OF < L *majestas, -tatis*]

ma·jol·i·ca (mə·jol′i·kə, -yol′-) *n.* A kind of glazed and colorfully decorated Italian pottery. [< Ital., prob. < *Majorca,* where formerly made]

ma·jor (mā′jər) *adj.* 1. Greater in quantity, number, or extent. 2. Having primary or greater importance, excellence, rank, etc.: a *major* writer. 3. Of, relating to, or making up a majority. 4. *Music* **a** Denoting the larger of two similarly named intervals: *major* third. **b** Denoting a triad in which the third above the fundamental is major. **c** Denoting a type of diatonic scale, or a key based on this scale. Compare MINOR. 5. In education, pertaining to the principal area of specialized study of a degree candidate in a college or university. —*n.* 1. *Mil.* An officer ranking next above a captain and next below a lieutenant colonel. 2. The principal area of specialized study of a degree candidate in a college or university. 3. *pl.* The major leagues. —*v.i.* In education, to study as a major: with *in.* [< L, compar. of *magnus* great]

ma·jor-do·mo (mā′jər·dō′mō) *n. pl.* **·mos** The chief steward or butler, esp. of a royal or noble household. [< Sp. < Med.L *major* an elder + *domus* house]

ma·jor·ette (mā′jər·et′) *n. Informal* A girl who marches and twirls a baton with a band, as in a parade.

major general *Mil.* An officer ranking next above a brigadier general.

ma·jor·i·ty (mə·jôr′ə·tē, -jor′-) *n. pl.* **·ties** 1. More than half of a given number or group; the greater part. 2. The number of votes cast for a particular candidate, bill, etc., over and above the total number of remaining votes. Distinguished from *plurality.* 3. The party or group having the most power. 4. The age when full civil and personal rights may be legally exercised. 5. The rank, commission, or office of a major. [< L *majoritas, -tatis*]

major league In baseball, either of the two main groups of professional teams in the U.S., the National League or the American League.

ma·jus·cule (mə·jus′kyōōl) *adj.* Large, as either capital or uncial letters. —*n.* A majuscule letter. [< L *majusculus,* dim. of *major* major]

make (māk) *v.* **made, mak·ing** *v.t.* 1. To produce, construct, or fashion. 2. To cause: Don't *make* trouble. 3. To bring to some state: The wind *makes* him cold. 4. To put into a specified rank or position: They *made* him president. 5. To form or create in the mind, as a plan, conclusion, or judgment. 6. To compose (a poem). 7. To utter or express, as an announcement. 8. To put forward or proffer: to *make* friendly overtures. 9. To engage in: to *make* war. 10. To earn or acquire: to *make* a fortune. 11. To amount to; add up to. 12. To draw up, enact, or frame, as laws, treaties, etc. 13. To estimate to be; reckon. 14. To prepare or arrange for use: to *make* a bed. 15. To induce or force; compel. 16. To afford or provide: Venison *makes* good eating. 17. To become through development: He will *make* a good soldier. 18. To cause the success of: His last book *made* him. 19. To perform (a specific physical movement). 20. To cover (distance) by traveling. 21. To travel at the rate of. 22. To arrive at; reach: to *make* Boston. 23. To arrive in time for. 24. *Informal* To win a place or position, as on a team; also, to achieve the rank or status of: to *make* colonel. —*v.i.* 25. To cause something to assume a specified condition: to *make* sure. 26. To act or behave in a certain manner: to *make* merry. —**to make away with** 1. To carry off; steal. 2. To get rid of; destroy. —**to make believe** To pretend; feign. —**to make do** To get along with what is available, esp. with an inferior substitute. —**to make for** 1. To go toward, esp. rapidly. 2. To rush at in order to attack. —**to make it** *Informal* To succeed in doing something. —**to make off** To leave suddenly; run away. —**to make off with** To steal. —**to make or break** To bring about the success or failure of. —**to make out** 1. To see; discern. 2. To comprehend. 3. To fill out or draw up, as a document. 4. To succeed. 5. To do well enough; get by. 6. *Slang* **a** To kiss and caress amorously. **b** To engage in sexual intercourse. —**to make over** 1. To renovate; refashion. 2. To transfer title or possession of. —**to make up** 1. To compose; compound, as a prescription. 2. To be the parts of; constitute. 3. To settle differences and become friendly again. 4. To supply what is lacking in. 5. To compensate; atone. 6. To settle; decide: to *make up* one's mind. 7. *Printing* To arrange lines of type, illustrations, etc., for (a book, etc.). 8. To put cosmetics on (the face). 9. In education: **a** To repeat (an examination or course one has failed). **b** To take (an examination one has missed). —*n.* 1. Style or type: a good *make* of car. 2. The manner in which something is made. —**on the make** *Informal* 1. Greedy for profit or advancement. 2. Eager for amorous conquest. [OE *macian*] —**mak′er** *n.*

make-be·lieve (māk′bi·lēv′) *n.* 1. Pretense; sham. 2. A pretending to believe; imagination. —*adj.* Pretended; unreal.

Ma·ker (mā′kər) *n.* God, the creator.

make·shift (māk′shift′) *n.* A temporary means devised for an emergency; stopgap. —*adj.* Having the nature of or used as a temporary substitute.

make·up (māk′up′) *n.* 1. The arrangement or combination of parts or qualities of which anything is composed. 2. The cosmetics, etc., used by an actor in a specific role. 3. Cosmetics used by women. 4. Physical or mental constitution. 5. *Printing* The arranging of composed type and cuts into pages, columns, or forms.

make·work (māk′wûrk′) *n.* Work assigned to keep one occupied.

mak·ings (mā′kingz) *n.pl.* 1. The materials or qualities from which something can be made. 2. Paper and tobacco for cigarettes.

mal- *prefix* 1. Bad; ill; wrong: *maladjustment.* 2. Defective; imperfect: *malformation.* [< L *malus* bad]

Mal·a·chi (mal′ə·kī) *n.* A book of the Old Testament containing the writings of the 5th c. B.C. Hebrew prophet Malachi. Also, in the Douai Bible, **Ma·la·chi·as** (mal·ə·kī′əs).

mal·a·chite (mal′ə·kīt) *n.* A green basic copper carbonate, a common ore of copper. [< Gk. *malachē* mallow; so called because of its color]

mal·ad·just·ed (mal′ə·jus′tid) *adj.* 1. Poorly adjusted. 2. *Psychol.* Poorly adapted to one's environment. **—mal′ad·just′ment** *n.*

mal·a·droit (mal′ə·droit′) *adj.* Lacking skill; clumsy; blundering. [< F *mal-* mal- + *adroit* clever] **—mal′a·droit′ly** *adv.* **—mal′a·droit′ness** *n.*

mal·a·dy (mal′ə·dē) *n. pl.* **·dies** 1. A disease, esp. when chronic or deep-seated. 2. Any disordered or disturbed condition. [< L *male* ill + *habere* to have]

Mal·a·ga (mal′ə·gə) *n.* A rich, sweet white wine.

mal·aise (mal·āz′, *Fr.* mȧ·lez′) *n.* A feeling of vague discomfort or lassitude, sometimes indicating the beginning of an illness. [< F *mal* ill + *aise* ease]

ma·la·mute (mä′lə·myōōt, mal′ə-) *n.* A large Alaskan sled dog with a thick, long coat: also spelled *malemute.* [Orig. name of an Innuit tribe, alter. of Eskimo *Mahlemut*]

mal·a·prop·ism (mal′ə·prop·iz′əm) *n.* 1. The absurd misuse of words. 2. An instance of this. [after Mrs. *Malaprop,* character in Sheridan's play *The Rivals* (1775)]

mal·ap·ro·pos (mal′ap·rə·pō′) *adj.* Not appropriate. **—*adv.*** Inappropriately. [< F *mal à propos* not to the point]

ma·lar·i·a (mə·lâr′ē·ə) *n. Pathol.* Any of several forms of a disease caused by certain parasites carried by the anopheles mosquito and characterized by periodic attacks of chills, fever, and profuse sweating. [< Ital. *mal' aria, mala aria,* lit., bad air] **—ma·lar′i·al** *adj.*

ma·lar·key (mə·lär′kē) *n. Slang* Insincere or senseless talk; bunk. Also **ma·lar′ky.** [Origin unknown]

mal·a·thi·on (mal′ə·thī′on, -ən) *n.* An organic phosphate insecticide with low toxicity to plants and animals.

Ma·lay (mā′lā, mə·lā′) *n.* 1. A member of a people dominant in Malaysia; a Malayan. 2. The language spoken on the Malay Peninsula and now adopted as the official language of Indonesia. **—*adj.*** Of or pertaining to the Malays; Malayan.

Ma·lay·an (mə·lā′ən) *adj.* 1. Malay. 2. Indonesian. **—*n.*** 1. A Malay (def. 1). 2. An Indonesian. 3. The Indonesian subfamily of Austronesian languages.

mal·con·tent (mal′kən·tent′) *adj.* Discontented or dissatisfied, esp. with a government or economic system. **—*n.*** One who is malcontent.

mal de mer (mȧl′ də mâr′) *French* Seasickness.

male (māl) *adj.* 1. Of or belonging to the sex that begets young or produces sperm. 2. Of, characteristic of, or suitable for members of this sex; masculine. 3. Made up of men or boys. 4. *Bot.* Designating a plant having stamens but no pistil. 5. *Mech.* Denoting a part, as in some electric plugs, etc., designed to be inserted into a correlated slot or bore known as *female.* **—*n.*** 1. A male person or animal. 2. *Bot.* A male plant. [< L *masculus*] **—male′ness** *n.*

mal·e·dic·tion (mal′ə·dik′shən) *n.* 1. The pronouncing of a curse against someone. 2. Slander; calumny. [< L *male* ill + *dicere* to speak] **—mal′e·dic′to·ry** *adj.*

mal·e·fac·tor (mal′ə·fak′tər) *n.* 1. One who commits a crime; criminal. 2. An evildoer. [< L *male* ill + *facere* to do] **—mal′e·fac′tion** *n.*

ma·lef·i·cent (mə·lef′ə·sənt) *adj.* Causing or doing evil or mischief. **—ma·lef′i·cence** *n.*

ma·le·mute (mä′lə·myōōt, mal′ə-) See MALAMUTE.

ma·lev·o·lent (mə·lev′ə·lənt) *adj.* Wishing evil toward others; malicious. [< L *male* ill + *volens, -entis* wishing] **—ma·lev′o·lence** *n.* **—ma·lev′o·lent·ly** *adv.*

mal·fea·sance (mal·fē′zəns) *n. Law* The performance of some act that is wrongful or that one has specifically contracted not to perform: said usu. of official misconduct. [< L *malus* bad + *facere* to do] **—mal·fea′·sant** *adj. & n.*

mal·for·ma·tion (mal′fôr·mā′shən) *n.* Defective structure, esp. in an organism. **—mal·formed′** (-fôrmd′) *adj.*

mal·func·tion (mal·fungk′shən) *n.* 1. Failure to function. 2. Defective functioning. **—*v.i.*** 1. To fail to function. 2. To function improperly.

mal·ice (mal′is) *n.* 1. An intention or desire to injure another; spite. 2. *Law* A willfully formed design to do another an injury: also, **malice aforethought.** [< L *malus* evil] **—ma·li·cious** (mə·lish′əs) *adj.* **—ma·li′·cious·ly** *adv.*

ma·lign (mə·līn′) *v.t.* To speak slander of; defame. **—*adj.*** 1. Having an evil disposition toward others; malevolent. 2. Tending to injure; pernicious. [< L *malignus* ill-disposed] **—ma·lign′er** *n.*

ma·lig·nant (mə·lig′nənt) *adj.* 1. *Pathol.* **a** Of tumors, rapidly growing and liable to metastasize: opposed to *benign.* **b** Becoming progressively worse; virulent. 2. Having an evil disposition toward others; malign. [< L *malignus* ill-disposed] **—ma·lig′nan·cy** *n.* **—ma·lig′nant·ly** *adv.*

ma·lig·ni·ty (mə·lig′nə·tē) *n. pl.* **·ties** 1. The state or character of being malign; intense ill will. 2. A harmful tendency; virulence. 3. *Often pl.* Something evil.

ma·lin·ger (mə·ling′gər) *v.i.* To pretend sickness so as to avoid work or duty. [< F *malingre* sickly] **—ma·lin′ger·er** *n.*

mall (môl, mal) *n.* 1. A promenade or walk, usu. public and often shaded. 2. A street of shops closed off to vehicles; also, a shopping center. [Short for *Pall-Mall,* a street in London]

mal·lard (mal′ərd) *n. pl.* **·lards** or **·lard** A wild duck, the ancestor of the domestic breeds, having brownish plumage, and, in the male, a green head. [< OF *masle* male]

mal·le·a·ble (mal′ē·ə·bəl) *adj.* 1. Capable of being hammered or rolled out without breaking: said esp. of metals. 2. Capable of adapting; flexible; pliable. [< L *malleare* to hammer] **—mal′le·a·bil′i·ty** *n.*

mal·let (mal′it) *n.* 1. A hammer having a head of wood, rubber, etc. 2. A long-handled hammer used in croquet, polo, etc. [< L *malleus* hammer]

mal·le·us (mal′ē·əs) *n. pl.* **·le·i** (-lē·ī) *Anat.* The club-shaped bone of the middle ear, articulating with the incus: also called *hammer.* [< L, hammer]

mal·low (mal′ō) *n.* Any of various herbs having roundish leaves, pale pink flowers, and disklike fruit. [OE < L *malva*]

malm·sey (mäm′zē) *n. pl.* **·seys** A rich, sweet wine.

mal·nu·tri·tion (mal′nōō·trish′ən, -nyōō-) *n.* Faulty or inadequate nutrition; undernourishment. **—mal·nour·ished** (mal·nûr′isht) *adj.*

mal·o·dor·ous (mal·ō′dər·əs) *adj.* Having a disagreeable smell. **—mal·o′dor·ous·ly** *adv.* **—mal·o′dor·ous·ness** *n.*

mal·prac·tice (mal·prak′tis) *n.* 1. In medicine or surgery, the improper, injurious, or negligent treatment of a patient. 2. Improper or immoral conduct in a professional or public position.

malt (môlt) *n.* 1. Grain, usu. barley, germinated by soaking and then kiln-dried. 2. Liquor made with malt, as beer, ale, etc. [OE *mealt*] **—malt′y** *adj.*

mal·ted milk (môl′tid) 1. A beverage made of milk, a powder of malted cereals and dried milk, and usu. ice cream: also **malt′ed.** 2. The powder used in this beverage.

Mal·tese (môl·tēz′, -tēs′) *adj.* Of or pertaining to Malta, its inhabitants, or their language. **—***n. pl.* **·tese** 1. A native or inhabitant of Malta. 2. The language of Malta.

Mal·thu·si·an (mal·thōō′zē·ən, môl′-, -zhən) *adj.* Of or pertaining to the theory that population tends to outrun its means of support, and will be checked by disaster unless births are restricted. **—***n.* A believer in this theory. [after Thomas *Malthus,* 1766–1834, English economist] **—Mal·thu′si·an·ism** *n.*

malt·ose (môl′tōs) *n. Biochem.* A white, crystalline sugar, formed by the action of enzymes on starch. Also **malt sugar.**

mal·treat (mal·trēt′) *v.t.* To treat badly, roughly, or unkindly; abuse. [< F *maltraiter*] **—mal·treat′ment** *n.*

ma·ma (mä′mə, mə·mä′) *n.* Mother: used familiarly. [Repetition of infantile syllable *ma*]

mam·bo (mäm′bō) *n. pl.* **·bos** A dance resembling the rumba; also the music for this. **—***v.i.* To dance the mambo. [< Haitian Creole]

mam·ma (mam′ə) *n. pl.* **·mae** (-mē) A mammary gland. [< L, breast]

mam·mal (mam′əl) *n.* Any of a class of vertebrates whose females have mammary glands to nourish their young. [< L *mamma* breast] **—mam·ma·li·an** (mə·mā′lē·ən, -māl′yən) *adj. & n.*

mam·ma·ry gland (mam′ər·ē) In mammals, the organ that secretes milk.

mam·mo·gram (ma′mə·gram′) *n.* An X-ray of the breast.

mam·mog·ra·phy (ma·mog′rə·fē) *n.* The X-ray examination of the breasts to detect tumors. [< L *mamma* breast + -GRAPHY]

Mam·mon (mam′ən) The personification of riches, avarice, and worldly gain. [< Aramaic *māmōnā* riches]

mam·moth (mam′əth) *n. Paleontol.* A large, now extinct elephant having a thick hairy coat and long curved tusks. **—***adj.* Huge; gigantic. [< Russian *mammot, mamant*]

mam·my (mam′ē) *n. pl.* **·mies** 1. Mother: used familiarly. 2. *Southern U.S.* A Negro nurse of white children. Also spelled **mam′mie.** [Dim. of MAMA]

man (man) *n. pl.* **men** (men) 1. An adult male human being. 2. Human beings collectively; mankind. 3. A person or individual. 4. One having pronounced masculine traits and virtues. 5. An adult male subordinate or employee; as: **a** A worker in a factory, office, etc. **b** A servant, esp. a valet. 6. A husband. 7. A piece or counter used in certain games, as chess, checkers, etc. **—the Man** *Slang* 1. The white establishment, esp. as viewed by black Americans. 2. The police. **—to a man** Unanimously. **—to be one's own man** To be independent. **—***interj. Slang* An exclamation of surprise, pleasure, etc. **—***v.t.* **manned, man·ning** 1. To supply with men, as for work, defense, etc.: to *man* the fort. 2. To take stations on, at, or in, for work, defense, etc.: *Man* the pumps! [OE *monn, mann*]

man·a·cle (man′ə·kəl) *n.* 1. *Usu. pl.* A device for restraining the hands; shackle; handcuff. 2. Anything that constrains. **—***v.t.* **·cled, ·cling** 1. To put manacles on. 2. To constrain or hamper. [< L *manus* hand]

man·age (man′ij) *v.* **·aged, ·ag·ing** *v.t.* 1. To direct or control the affairs or interests of. 2. To arrange; contrive: He *managed* to stay. 3. To cause to do one's bidding: to *manage* a crowd. 4. To handle or wield; use, as a weapon, etc. **—***v.i.* 5. To direct or control business, affairs, etc. 6. To be able to continue or thrive. [< L *manus* hand] **—man′age·a·bil′i·ty, man′age·a·ble·ness** *n.* **—man′age·a·ble** *adj.* **—man′age·a·bly** *adv.*

man·age·ment (man′ij·mənt) *n.* 1. The act, art, or practice of managing. 2. The person or persons who manage a business, etc. 3. Managers collectively, esp. in their relations with labor unions. 4. The skillful use of means.

man·ag·er (man′ij·ər) *n.* 1. One who manages; esp., one who directs an enterprise, business, etc. 2. One skilled in managing, esp. business affairs. **—man·a·ge·ri·al** (man′ə·jir′ē·əl) *adj.* **—man′ag·er·ship** *n.*

ma·ña·na (mä·nyä′nä) *n. & adv. Spanish* Tomorrow; some other time.

man-at-arms (man′ət·ärmz′) *n. pl.* **men-at-arms** (men′-) A soldier; esp., a heavily armed, mounted soldier of the Middle Ages.

man·a·tee (man′ə·tē′) *n.* An aquatic mammal of the warmer coastal waters of the Atlantic: also called *sea cow.* [< Carib *manattoui*]

-mancy *combining form* Divining or foretelling by means of: *necromancy.* [< Gk. *manteia* power of divination]

man·da·mus (man·dā′məs) *n. Law* A writ issued by a higher court to subordinate courts, corporations, etc., commanding them to do something. [< L, we command]

man·da·rin (man′də·rin) *n.* 1. A well-educated official of the Chinese Empire.

2. A powerful person; esp., an intellectual arbiter. 3. A tangerine: also **mandarin orange.** [< Skt. *mantra* counsel]

Man·da·rin (man′də·rin) *n.* The Chinese language of north and west China, including the Peking dialect upon which the official language of the country is based.

man·date (man′dāt; *for n., also* -dit) *n.* 1. In politics, an instruction from an electorate to its representative, expressed by the result of an election. 2. Formerly, a charge to a nation from the League of Nations authorizing the administration of a territory, colony, etc.; also, the territory given in charge. 3. An authoritative command; order. —*v.t.* **·dat·ed, ·dat·ing** To assign (a territory, etc.) to a specific nation under a mandate. [< L *manus* hand + *dare* to give]

man·da·to·ry (man′də·tôr′ē) *adj.* 1. Required by or as if by mandate or command; obligatory. 2. Of or pertaining to a mandate. 3. Holding a mandate.

man·di·ble (man′də·bəl) *n. Biol.* 1. The lower jaw bone. 2. Either part of the beak of a bird. [< L *mandere* to chew] —**man·dib·u·lar** (man·dib′yə·lər) *adj.*

man·do·lin (man′də·lin, man′də·lin′) *n.* A musical instrument with a fretted neck, a pear-shaped body, and eight metal strings. [< Ital. *mandola,* a type of lute]

man·drake (man′drāk) *n.* 1. A plant of the nightshade family with narcotic properties and fleshy forked roots sometimes resembling the human form. Also **man·drag·o·ra** (man·drag′ə·rə). 2. The May apple. [< Gk. *mandragoras*]

man·drel (man′drəl) *n. Mech.* 1. A shaft or spindle on which material may be fixed for working on a machine. 2. A metal bar used as a core about which wire, glass, metal, etc., may be bent, forged, or shaped. Also **man′dril.** [Prob. alter. of F *mandrin* lathe]

man·drill (man′dril) *n.* A large, ferocious West African baboon.

mane (mān) *n.* The long hair growing on and about the neck of some animals, as the horse, lion, etc. [OE *manu*] —**maned** *adj.*

man-eat·er (man′ē′tər) *n.* 1. A cannibal. 2. An animal, as a tiger, shark, etc., that devours or is said to devour human flesh. —**man′-eat′ing** *adj.*

ma·nège (ma·nezh′) *n.* The art of training and riding horses; also, a school for horsemanship. Also **man·ege′.** [< F < Ital. *maneggiare* to handle, train horses]

ma·neu·ver (mə·nōō′vər, -nyōō′-) *n.* 1. *Mil.* **a** A planned movement or shift, as of troops, warships, etc. **b** *pl.* Large-scale tactical exercises simulating war. 2. Any skillful move or stroke. —*v.t.* 1. To manage or conduct skillfully. 2. To put (troops, vessels, etc.) through a maneuver or maneuvers. —*v.i.* 3. To perform a maneuver or maneuvers. 4. To use artful moves or strokes. Also, *esp. Brit., manoeuver, manoeuvre.* [< F < L *manu operari* to work with the hand] —**ma·neu′ver·a·bil′i·ty** *n.* —**ma·neu′ver·a·ble** *adj.*

man Friday A person devoted or subservient to another; a factotum. [after *Friday,* a native servant in Daniel Defoe's novel *Robinson Crusoe* (1719)]

man·ful (man′fəl) *adj.* Having a manly spirit; sturdy. —**man′ful·ly** *adv.* —**man′ful·ness** *n.*

man·ga·nese (mang′gə·nēs, -nēz) *n. Chem.* A hard, brittle, grayish white metallic element (symbol Mn), oxidizing readily and forming an important component of certain alloys. [Alter. of Med.L *magnesia*]

mange (mānj) *n. Vet.* An itching skin disease of dogs and other domestic animals, caused by parasitic mites. [< OF *manjue* an itch, eating]

man·ger (mān′jər) *n.* A trough or box for feeding horses or cattle. [< OF *mangeoire* < *mangier* to eat < L *manducare* to chew]

man·gle[1] (mang′gəl) *v.t.* **·gled, ·gling** 1. To disfigure or mutilate by cutting, bruising, crushing, etc. 2. To mar or ruin; spoil. [< AF, appar. freq. of OF *mahaignier*] —**man′gler** *n.*

man·gle[2] (mang′gəl) *n.* A machine for smoothing and pressing fabrics by passing them between rollers. [< Du. *mangel,* ult. < Gk. *manganon* a pulley, a war machine]

man·go (mang′gō) *n. pl.* **·goes** or **·gos** 1. An edible tropical fruit having a slightly acid taste. 2. The tree producing this fruit. [< Pg. < Tamil *mān* mango tree + *kāy* a fruit]

man·grove (mang′grōv, man′-) *n.* A tropical evergreen shrub or tree, sometimes having aerial roots, growing in marshy and coastal areas. [< Sp. *mangle*]

man·gy (mān′jē) *adj.* **·gi·er, ·gi·est** 1. Affected with or resembling mange. 2. Squalid; shabby. —**man′gi·ness** *n.*

man·han·dle (man′han′dəl) *v.t.* **·dled, ·dling** To handle with rough force.

man·hole (man′hōl′) *n.* A usu. circular and covered opening by which a man may enter a sewer, boiler, etc.

man·hood (man′hŏŏd) *n.* 1. The state of being an adult male human being. 2. The masculine qualities collectively. 3. Men collectively.

man-hour (man′our′) *n.* The amount of work a man can do in an hour.

ma·ni·a (mā′nē·ə, mān′yə) *n.* 1. An extraordinary enthusiasm, craving, etc. 2. *Psychiatry* An exaggerated sense of well-being with excessive mental and physical activity. [< Gk., madness]

-mania *combining form* An exaggerated or irrational craving for or interest in: **acromania** (high places), **agoramania** (open places), **ailuromania** (cats), **cynomania** (dogs), **entomomania** (insects), **gymnomania** (nakedness), **heliomania** (exposure to sun), **hippomania** (horses), **hypnomania** (sleep), **ichthyomania** (fish), **logomania** (talking), **necromania** (death or the dead), **noctimania** (night), **ophidiomania** (reptiles), **ornithomania** (birds), **thalassomania** (sea), **xenomania** (strangers). [< Gk. *mania* madness]

ma·ni·ac (mā′nē·ak) *n.* A violently insane person; madman. —*adj.* Insane; mad. —**ma·ni·a·cal** (mə·nī′ə·kəl) *adj.* —**ma·ni′a·cal·ly** *adv.*

-maniac *combining form* Used to form nouns and adjectives from nouns ending in *-mania: kleptomaniac.*

man·ic (man′ik, mā′nik) *adj.* Of or affected by mania.

man·ic-de·pres·sive (man′ik·di·pres′iv) *adj. Psychiatry* Denoting or characteristic of a mental disorder in which periods of depression alternate with periods of excitement. —*n.* One who suffers from this disorder.

man·i·cure (man′ə·kyŏŏr) *n.* The care of the hands and fingernails. —*v.t.* & *v.i.* **·cured, ·cur·ing** To treat (the nails, etc.). [< L *manus* hand + *cura* care] —**man′i·cur′ist** *n.*

man·i·fest (man′ə·fest) *adj.* Plainly apparent; obvious. —*v.t.* 1. To reveal; show; display. 2. To prove; be evidence of. —*n.* In transportation, an itemized account or list, as of passengers or cargo. [< L *manifestus* evident, lit., struck by the hand] —**man′i·fest·ly** *adv.*

man·i·fes·ta·tion (man′ə·fes·tā′shən) *n.* 1. The act of manifesting, or the state of being manifested. 2. A sign; indication.

man·i·fes·to (man′ə·fes′tō) *n. pl.* **·toes** or **·tos** A public and formal declaration or explanation of principles, intentions, etc., usu. by a political faction or similar group.

man·i·fold (man′ə·fōld) *adj.* 1. Having many and varied forms, types, instances, etc.: *manifold* sorrows. 2. Having an assortment of features, etc. —*n.* 1. *Mech.* A pipe or chest having several or many openings, as for exhaust gas. 2. A copy made by manifolding. —*v.t.* 1. To make more than one copy of. 2. To multiply. [OE *manigfeald* varied, numerous] —**man′i·fold·ly** *adv.*

man·i·kin (man′ə·kin) *n.* 1. A little man; dwarf. 2. See MANNEQUIN. Also spelled *mannikin.* [< Du. *manneken,* dim. of *man* man]

ma·nil·a hemp (mə·nil′ə) The fiber of the abaca, a banana plant, used for making rope, etc. Also **ma·nil′a, Ma·nil′a hemp.**

Manila paper A heavy, light brown paper, originally made of manila hemp, now made of various fibers.

ma·nip·u·late (mə·nip′yə·lāt) *v.t.* **·lat·ed, ·lat·ing** 1. To manage or control (persons, figures, stocks, etc.) shrewdly and deviously for one's own profit or purposes. 2. To control, move, treat, etc., with or as with the hands; esp., to handle skillfully. [< L *manus* hand + *plere* to fill] —**ma·nip′u·la′tion** *n.* —**ma·nip′u·la′tor** *n.*

man·kind (man′kīnd; *for def. 1, also* man′·kīnd′) 1. The whole human species. 2. Men collectively, as distinguished from women.

man·ly (man′lē) *adj.* **·li·er, ·li·est** 1. Pertaining to or appropriate for a man; virile: *manly* charm. 2. Having the qualities and virtues of a man, as courage, determination, strength, etc. —**the manly art** Boxing. —**man′li·ness** *n.*

man·na (man′ə) *n.* 1. The food miraculously given to the Israelites in the wilderness as they fled from Egypt. 2. Any nourishment, help, etc., received as by divine bounty. [< Hebrew *mān* What is it?]

man·ne·quin (man′ə·kin) *n.* 1. A full-sized model of a human figure used for cutting, fitting, or displaying garments. 2. A woman who models clothing. Also spelled *manikin.* [< Du. *manneken.* See MANIKIN.]

man·ner (man′ər) *n.* 1. A way of doing or a way in which something happens or is done. 2. A style of speech and action: a grave *manner.* 3. *pl.* Social conduct; etiquette; esp., polite and civil social behavior. 4. *pl.* The modes of social behavior prevailing in a group, nation, period, etc. 5. A characteristic style in literature, music, art, etc. —**in a manner of speaking** Approximately; more or less. [OF *maniere* way of acting, ult. < L *manuarius* of the hand]

man·nered (man′ərd) *adj.* 1. Having (a specific kind of) manner or manners: used in combination: *mild-mannered.* 2. Having mannerisms in writing, speaking, etc.

man·ner·ism (man′ər·iz′əm) *n.* 1. Marked use of a distinctive style, as in writing. 2. A distinctive trait; idiosyncrasy.

man·ner·ly (man′ər·lē) *adj.* Well-behaved; polite. —**man′ner·li·ness** *n.*

man·ni·kin (man′ə·kin) See MANIKIN.

man·nish (man′ish) *adj.* Resembling a man; masculine: said of women. —**man′nish·ly** *adv.* —**man′nish·ness** *n.*

ma·noeu·ver (mə·nōō′vər, -nyōō′-), **ma·noeu·vre** See MANEUVER.

man-of-war (man′əv·wôr′, -ə·wôr′) *n. pl.* **men-of-war** (men′-) *Chiefly Archaic* A warship.

ma·nom·e·ter (mə·nom′ə·tər) *n.* Any of various instruments used to measure pressure, as of gases, liquids, or vapors. [< Gk. *manos* thin, rare + -METER] —**man·o·met·ric** (man′ə·met′rik) *adj.*

man·or (man′ər) *n.* 1. In England: **a** Formerly, a feudal domain. **b** A landed estate. 2. A mansion. 3. In colonial America, a landed estate with hereditary feudal rights. [< L *manere* to dwell] —**ma·no·ri·al** (mə·nôr′ē·əl) *adj.*

man·pow·er (man′pou′ər) *n.* 1. The force of human physical strength. 2. The number of people whose strength and skill are available to a nation, army, project, etc.; personnel.

man·qué (mäṅ·kā′) *adj. French* Lacking fulfillment; in wish only: a writer *manqué.*

man·sard (man′särd) *n. Archit.* A curb roof having the lower slope almost vertical and the upper almost horizontal, with the same profile on all four sides of the building. [after F. *Mansard,* 1598–1666, French architect]

manse (mans) *n.* A clergyman's house. [< Med.L *mansa,* pp. of L *manere* to dwell]

man·ser·vant (man′sûr′vənt) *n.* An adult male servant.

man·sion (man′shən) *n.* A large and impressive house. [< L *mansio, -onis* a dwelling]

man·slaugh·ter (man′slô′tər) *n. Law* The unlawful killing of a human being without malice.

man·ta (man′tə) *n.* 1. Any of several very large rays common in tropical American waters: also called *devilfish.* Also **manta ray.** 2. A woman's shawl made of a coarse fabric. [< Sp., blanket < LL *mantum* cloak]

man·teau (man′tō, *Fr.* mäṅ·tō′) *n. pl.* **·teaus** (-tōz) or *Fr.* **·teaux** (-tō′) A cloak or mantle. [< F. See MANTLE.]

man·tel (man′təl) *n.* 1. The shelf above a fireplace. 2. A facing of wood, brick, stone, etc., around a fireplace. Also **man′tel·piece′** (-pēs′). [< F *manteau* mantelpiece]

man·til·la (man·til′ə, -tē′yə) *n.* A light scarf, often of black lace, worn over the head and shoulders of women in Spain and Spanish America. [< Sp., dim. of *manta* blanket]

man·tis (man′tis) *n. pl.* **·tis·es** or **·tes** (-tēz)

A carnivorous, long-bodied insect, that stands with its forelegs folded as if in prayer: also called *praying mantis.* [< Gk., a prophet]

man·tle (man′təl) *n.* 1. A loose and usu. sleeveless garment worn over other garments. 2. Anything that clothes, envelops, or conceals. 3. The earth's layer beneath the crust and above the core. 4. A mantel. —*v.t.* **·tled, ·tling** To cover with or as with a mantle; conceal. [< L *mantellum*]

man·tra (man′trə) *n.* An incantation or chant, as in Hinduism. [< Skt.]

man·u·al (man′yo͞o·əl) *adj.* Involving, used, or operated by the hands. —*n.* 1. A small book of instructions. 2. An organ keyboard. 3. A prescribed drill in manipulating a rifle, flag, etc. [< L *manus* hand] —**man′u·al·ly** *adv.*

manual alphabet A series of manual signs or gestures used by the deaf and deaf-mutes as a substitute for vocal speech.

man·u·fac·ture (man′yə·fak′chər) *v.t.* **·tured, ·tur·ing** 1. To make or process a product, esp. on a large scale and with machinery. 2. To invent (a lie, alibi, etc.). —*n.* 1. The act or process of manufacturing. 2. Something that is manufactured. [< L *manus* hand + *factura* a making] —**man′u·fac′tur·er** *n.*

man·u·mit (man′yə·mit′) *v.t.* **·mit·ted, ·mit·ting** To free from bondage, as a slave. [< L *manumittere*, lit., to send forth from one's hand] —**man′u·mis′sion** (-mish′ən) *n.*

ma·nure (mə·no͝or′, -nyo͝or′) *n.* Dung, compost, etc., used to fertilize soil. —*v.t.* **·nured, ·nur·ing** To apply manure or other fertilizer to, as soil. [< AF *maynoverer* to work with the hands] —**ma·nur′er** *n.*

man·u·script (man′yə·skript) *n.* 1. A usu. typewritten copy of a book, article, document, etc., prepared or submitted for publication. 2. Something written by hand. [< L *manus* hand + *scriptus*, pp. of *scribere* to write]

Manx (mangks) *n.* 1. The people of the Isle of Man. 2. The Gaelic language of the Manx, nearly extinct. [< Scand., ult. < Celtic *Man* Isle of Man] —**Manx** *adj.*

man·y (men′ē) *adj.* **more, most** Adding up to a large number; numerous. —*n.* 1. A large number. 2. The masses: with *the.* —**many a** (**or an or another**) Many: with singular noun. —*pron.* A large number of persons or things. [OE *manig*]

Mao·ism (mou′iz·əm) *n.* The communist doctrines or practices of Mao Tse-tung. [after *Mao* Tse-tung, 1893–1976, chairman of the People's Republic of China] —**Mao′ist** *n. & adj.*

Ma·o·ri (mä′ō·rē, mou′rē) *n.* 1. One of an aboriginal people of New Zealand, chiefly Polynesian mixed with Melanesian. 2. The Polynesian language of these people. —**Ma′·o·ri** *adj.*

map (map) *n.* 1. A representation on a plane surface of any region, as of the earth's surface; a chart. 2. Anything resembling a map. —*v.t.* **mapped, map·ping** 1. To make a map of. 2. To plan in detail: often with *out.* [< Med.L *mappa*]

ma·ple (mā·pəl) *n.* 1. Any of numerous deciduous trees of the north temperate zone, with opposite leaves and a double-winged fruit, as the sugar maple. 2. The wood of these trees. 3. The flavor of the sap of the sugar maple. [OE *mapul*]

maple sugar Sugar made from the sap of the sugar maple.

maple syrup The refined sap of the sugar maple.

map·ping (map′ing) *n.* 1. The process of making a map. 2. *Math.* A concept in which each element of a set corresponds to an element of another set.

ma·quis (ma·kē′, mä-) *n.* A zone of shrubby, mostly evergreen plants in the Mediterranean region, known as cover for game, bandits, etc. [< F < Ital. *macchia* thicket]

mar (mär) *v.t.* **marred, mar·ring** 1. To damage. 2. To injure so as to deface. —*n.* A disfiguring mark; blemish. [OE *mierran* to hinder]

mar·a·bou (mar′ə·bo͞o) *n.* A stork of Africa, whose soft, white feathers are used in millinery. [< F *marabou, marabout* hermit]

ma·ra·ca (mə·rä′kə, *Pg.* mä·rä·kä′) *n.* A percussion instrument made of a gourd or gourd-shaped rattle with beans or beads inside it. [< Pg. *maracá*, ? < Tupi]

mar·a·schi·no (mar′ə·skē′nō, -shē-) *n.* A cordial distilled from the fermented juice of a small wild cherry. [< Ital. *marasca*, a wild cherry]

mar·a·thon (mar′ə·thon) *n.* 1. A footrace of 26 miles, 385 yards. 2. Any endurance contest. 3. Group therapy in which participants stay together over an extended period of time. [from a messenger's run from Marathon, Greece, to Athens to announce the decisive victory of the Athenians over the Persians at Marathon in 490 B.C.]

ma·raud (mə·rôd′) *v.i.* 1. To rove in search of plunder. —*v.t.* 2. To invade for plunder. [< F *maraud* rogue] —**ma·raud′er** *n.*

mar·ble (mär′bəl) *n.* 1. A compact, granular, partly crystallized limestone occurring in many colors, used for building, sculpture, etc. 2. A small ball of this stone, or of glass, porcelain, etc. 3. *pl.* A children's game played with balls of glass, etc. —*v.t.* **·bled, ·bling** To color or vein in imitation of marble, as book edges. [< Gk. *marmaros*, lit., sparkling stone] —**mar′ble** *adj.*

mar·bling (mär′bling) *n.* The streaked appearance of lean meat, esp. beef, caused by the intermingling of fat.

mar·cel (mär·sel′) *v.t.* **·celled, ·cel·ling** To dress (the hair) in even, continuous waves by means of special irons. [after M. *Marcel*, 19th c. French hairdresser] —**mar·cel′ler** *n.*

march[1] (märch) *v.i.* 1. To walk or proceed with measured, regular steps, as a soldier or body of troops. 2. To walk in a solemn or dignified manner. 3. To advance steadily. —*v.t.* 4. To cause to march. —*n.* 1. The act of marching. 2. A regular, measured step, as of a body of troops. 3. The distance passed over in marching: a full day's *march.* 4. Onward progress. 5. A musical composition for marching. [< MF *marcher* to walk] —**mar′·cher** *n.*

march[2] (märch) *n.* A region or district lying along a boundary line; frontier. Also **march′land′** (-land′). [< OHG *marka* mark]

March (märch) The third month of the year,

containing 31 days. [< *Mars*, Roman god of war]

mar·che·se (mär·kā′zā) *n. pl.* **·che·si** (-kā′zē) *Italian* A marquis. —**mar·che′sa** (-zä) *n.fem.*

mar·chion·ess (mär′shən·is) *n.* 1. The wife or widow of a marquis. 2. A woman having the rank corresponding to that of a marquis. [< Med.L *marchio, -onis* captain of the marches]

Mar·di gras (mär′dē grä′) The last Tuesday before Lent, often a carnival. [< F, lit., fat Tuesday]

mare[1] (mâr) *n.* The female of the horse and other equine animals. [OE *miere*]

mar·e[2] (mâr′ē) *n. pl.* **mar·i·a** (mâr′ē·ə) Any of a number of dark, seemingly flat areas of the moon's surface. [< L, sea]

mar·ga·rine (mär′jə·rin, -rēn) *n.* A substitute for butter, made from vegetable oils and sometimes milk: also called *oleomargarine*. [< F]

mar·ga·ri·ta (mär′gə·rēt′ə) *n.* A cocktail made with tequila, lime or lemon juice, and an orange liqueur. [< Sp. feminine name]

mar·gin (mär′jin) *n.* 1. The part of a page around the body of printed or written text. 2. A bounding line or surface; border. 3. An extra amount of something, as space, time, money, etc. 4. In commerce, the difference between the cost and selling price of a commodity. 5. Security deposited with a stockbroker to protect him against loss in trading. [< L *margo*]

mar·gi·nal (mär′jə·nəl) *adj.* 1. Situated or written at or on a margin. 2. *Econ.* Barely profitable. 3. Not essential; peripheral. —**mar′gin·al′i·ty** *n.* —**mar′gin·al·ly** *adv.*

mar·gi·na·li·a (mär′jə·nā′lē·ə, -nāl′yə) *n.pl.* Marginal notes.

mar·grave (mär′grāv) *n.* Formerly, the lord or governor of a German province. [< MDu. *marke* march[2] + *graf* count]

mar·i·gold (mar′ə·gōld) *n.* Any of several plants of the composite family with golden-yellow flowers. [< (VIRGIN) MARY + GOLD]

mar·i·jua·na (mar′ə·wä′nə, *Sp.* mä′rē·hwä′nä) *n.* 1. The hemp plant. 2. The dried leaves and flower tops of this plant, capable of producing disorienting or hallucinogenic effects when smoked or ingested. Also **ma′ri·hua′na.** [< Am. Sp. *marihuana, mariguana*]

ma·rim·ba (mə·rim′bə) *n.* A form of xylophone having a resonator beneath each tuned bar. [< Bantu]

ma·ri·na (mə·rē′nə) *n.* A docking area or basin for small vessels. [< Ital., seacoast < L *marinus.* See MARINE.]

mar·i·nade (mar′ə·nād′) *n.* 1. A brine pickle sometimes flavored with wine, oil, spices, etc., in which meat or fish are soaked before cooking. 2. Pickled meat or fish. —*v.t.* **·nad·ed, ·nad·ing** To marinate. [< F < Sp. *marinar* to pickle in brine]

mar·i·nate (mar′ə·nāt) *v.t.* **·nat·ed, ·nat·ing** 1. To soak (food) in marinade. 2. To allow, as salad, to soak in French dressing before serving. [< Ital. *marinare*]

ma·rine (mə·rēn′) *adj.* 1. Of, pertaining to, existing in, or formed by the sea. 2. Pertaining to the navigation or handling of ships on the sea; nautical. 3. Relating to the navy; naval. 4. Used or intended for use at sea or in navigation. —*n.* 1. A soldier trained for service at sea and on land; a member of the Marine Corps: also **Ma·rine′.** 2. Shipping vessels, shipping, or the navy collectively. [< OF < L *mare, maris* sea]

Marine Corps A branch of the U.S. armed forces within the Department of the Navy: officially the United States Marine Corps.

mar·i·ner (mar′ə·nər) *n.* One who navigates a ship; sailor; seaman. [< OF *marinier*]

mar·i·o·nette (mar′ē·ə·net′) *n.* A small jointed human or animal figure of wood, cloth, etc., animated by manipulation of strings: also called *puppet.* [< F *marionnette*, dim. of *Marion*, dim. of *Marie*]

mar·i·tal (mar′ə·təl) *adj.* Of or pertaining to marriage. [< L *maritus* husband, orig., married] —**mar′i·tal·ly** *adv.*

mar·i·time (mar′ə·tīm) *adj.* 1. Situated on or near the sea. 2. Of or pertaining to the sea or its navigation, commerce, etc. [< L *mare, maris* sea]

mar·jo·ram (mär′jər·əm) *n.* Any of several perennial herbs of the mint family, one of which, **sweet marjoram,** is used in cookery. [< OF *majorane*, ult. origin uncertain]

mark[1] (märk) *n.* 1. A visible trace, impression, or figure on something, as a line, spot, etc. 2. An identifying symbol; trademark. 3. A cross or other sign made by one who cannot write. 4. A letter or number used to rate a student's work; grade. 5. An object, point, sign, etc., serving to indicate, guide, or direct. 6. A visible indication of some quality, trait, position, etc. 7. That which is aimed at, or toward which effort is directed. 8. A standard or criterion of quality, performance, etc. 9. *Informal* A person easily duped or victimized. 10. In track sports, the starting line of the contest. 11. *Naut.* A knot, twist, etc., on a lead line indicating fathoms of depth. 12. Notice; attention; heed: worthy of *mark.* —**to make one's mark** To succeed. —**wide of the mark** 1. Striking far from the point aimed at. 2. Irrelevant. —*v.t.* 1. To make a mark on. 2. To trace the boundaries of: often with *out.* 3. To indicate or show by a mark or sign. 4. To characterize; distinguish: a year *marked* by great events. 5. To designate, appoint, or select, as if by marking: to be *marked* for death. 6. To pay attention to; notice; heed. 7. To evaluate by giving marks to. 8. To keep (record or score) in various games. 9. To produce by drawing, writing, etc. —*v.i.* 10. To take notice; pay attention; consider. —**to mark down** 1. To note down by writing. 2. To put a lower price on, as for sale. —**to mark time** 1. To keep time by moving the feet but not advancing. 2. To pause in action or progress temporarily. —**to mark up** 1. To make marks on; scar. 2. To increase the price of. [OE *mearc*, orig., boundary] —**mark′er** *n.*

mark[2] (märk) *n.* The former standard monetary unit and silver coin of Germany, superseded after World War II by the deutschemark in West Germany and the ostmark in East Germany. [OE *marc* a unit of weight]

Mark (märk) *n.* The second Gospel of the New Testament, attributed to the evangelist Mark (also called **Saint Mark.**)

mark·down (märk′doun′) *n.* 1. A lowering of price. 2. The amount of price decrease.

marked (märkt) *adj.* 1. Clearly evident; noticeable. 2. Having a mark or marks. —**a marked man** One singled out for vengeance, punishment, etc. —**mar′ked·ly** *adv.*

mar·ket (mär′kit) *n.* 1. Trade and commerce in a specific service or commodity: the boat *market*; also, trade and commerce generally: with *the.* 2. A region where one can buy or sell; also, a category of potential buyers: the college *market.* 3. A place where something is offered for sale. 4. A public gathering, often weekly, for buying and selling. —**in the market** Seeking to buy. —**on the market** Up for sale. —*v.t.* 1. To sell. —*v.i.* 2. To deal in a market. [< L *merx, mercis* merchandise]

mar·ket·a·ble (mär′kit·ə·bəl) *adj.* Suitable for sale; in demand. —**mar′ket·a·bil′i·ty** *n.*

mar·ket·place (mär′kit·plās′) *n.* 1. A market (def. 3). 2. The imagined place where ideas, opinions, etc., are tested and traded.

mark·ing (mär′king) *n.* 1. A mark or an arrangement of marks. 2. *Often pl.* The color pattern on a bird, animal, etc.

mark·ka (märk′kä) *n.* The standard monetary unit of Finland. [< Finnish < Sw. *mark*]

marks·man (märks′mən) *n. pl.* **·men** (-mən) One skilled in hitting the mark, as with a rifle or other weapon. —**marks′man·ship** *n.*

mark·up (märk′up′) *n.* 1. A raising of price. 2. The amount of price increase.

marl (märl) *n.* An earthy deposit containing lime, clay, and sand, used as fertilizer. —*v.t.* To spread with marl. [< L *marga* marl] —**marl′y** *adj.*

mar·lin (mär′lin) *n.* Any of various deep-sea game fishes; esp., the **blue marlin** of the Atlantic, and the **striped marlin** of the Pacific. [< MARLINE(SPIKE); because of its shape]

mar·line·spike (mär′lin·spīk′) *n. Naut.* A sharp-pointed iron pin used in splicing ropes. Also **mar′lin·spike′, mar′ling·spike′** (-ling-).

mar·ma·lade (mär′mə·lād) *n.* A preserve made by boiling with sugar the pulp and rind of fruits, usu. citrus fruits. [< Pg. *marmelada*]

mar·mo·re·al (mär·môr′ē·əl) *adj.* Pertaining to, made of, or resembling marble. Also **mar·mo′re·an.** [< L *marmoreus* < *marmor.* See MARBLE.]

mar·mo·set (mär′mə·zet, -set) *n.* Any of various small Central and South American monkeys with soft, woolly hair and a long, hairy tail. [< OF *marmouset* grotesque figure]

mar·mot (mär′mət) *n.* Any of various rodents, as the woodchuck. [Fusion of OF *marmotte* monkey and Romansch *murmont* marmot]

ma·roon[1] (mə·ro͞on′) *v.t.* 1. To put ashore and abandon on a desolate island or coast. 2. To abandon; leave helpless. [< Am. Sp. *cimarron* wild]

ma·roon[2] (mə·ro͞on′) *n.* A dark red color. —*adj.* Dark red. [< F *marron* chestnut]

mar·quee (mär·kē′) *n.* 1. A canopy used as a shelter over the sidewalk in front of a theater, hotel, etc. 2. A large field tent, as one used at outdoor parties. [< F *marquise* canopy]

mar·que·try (mär′kə·trē) *n.* Inlaid work of wood often interspersed with stones, ivory, etc., esp. as used in furniture. Also **mar′que·te·rie.** [< MF *marqueter* to variegate]

mar·quis (mär′kwis, mar·kē′) *n.* The title of a nobleman next in rank below a duke. Also *Brit.* **mar′quess.** [< OF < Med.L *markensis* commander of the marches]

mar·quise (mär·kēz′) *n.* 1. The wife or widow of a French marquis. 2. An ornamental hood over a door; a marquee.

mar·qui·sette (mär′ki·zet′, -kwi-) *n.* A lightweight, open-mesh fabric of cotton, silk, rayon, or nylon. [< F, dim. of *marquise* marquise]

mar·riage (mar′ij) *n.* 1. The state of being married; a legal contract, entered into by a man and a woman, to live together as husband and wife; wedlock. ◆Collateral adjective: *marital.* 2. The act of marrying; also, the accompanying rites or festivities; wedding; nuptials. 3. Any close union. [< L *maritare* to marry] —**mar′riage·a·bil′i·ty** *n.* —**mar′riage·a·ble** *adj.*

mar·ried (mar′ēd) *adj.* 1. United in matrimony; having a spouse. 2. Of or pertaining to marriage or to persons united in marriage. 3. Closely related or joined.

mar·ron (mar′ən, *Fr.* må·rôṅ′) *n. Often pl.* A large chestnut, esp. when preserved in syrup. [< F]

mar·row (mar′ō) *n.* 1. A soft, vascular tissue found in the central cavities of bones. 2. The essence of anything; pith. 3. Vitality. [OE *mearg*] —**mar′row·y** *adj.*

mar·row·bone (mar′ō·bōn′) *n.* A bone, as the shinbone, containing edible marrow.

mar·ry (mar′ē) *v.* **·ried, ·ry·ing** *v.t.* 1. To accept as husband or wife; take in marriage. 2. To join as husband and wife in marriage. 3. To unite closely. —*v.i.* 4. To take a husband or wife. 5. To join or unite closely. [< L *maritus* husband, married]

Mars (märz) *n.* The seventh largest planet of the solar system and fourth from the sun. [after L *Mars,* god of war]

Mar·sa·la (mär·sä′lä) *n.* A dark, sweet, heavy wine.

Mar·seil·laise (mär′sə·lāz′, *Fr.* mår·sā·yez′) The national anthem of France, written in 1792 by Rouget de Lisle.

marsh (märsh) *n.* A tract of low, wetland; swamp. [OE *mersc, merisc*]

mar·shal (mär′shəl) *n.* 1. In various foreign countries, a military officer of high rank, usu. just below the commander in chief: a field *marshal.* 2. *U.S.* **a** An officer of the federal courts, assigned to a judicial district and having duties similar to those of a sheriff. **b** In some cities, the chief of the police or fire department. 3. An officer authorized to organize or preside at processions, ceremonies, etc. —*v.t.* **mar·shaled** or **·shalled, mar·shal·ing** or **·shal·ling** 1. To arrange or dispose in order, as facts. 2. To array or draw up, as troops for battle. 3. To lead; usher. [< OHG *marah* horse + *scalh* servant]

marsh gas Methane.

marsh hawk A marsh-dwelling American hawk having gray or brown plumage, a white rump, and rounded wings.

marsh·mal·low (märsh′mel′ō, -mal′ō) *n.* A confection made of starch, sugar, corn syrup, and gelatin. [< MARSH MALLOW, whose root was originally used as an ingredient]

marsh mallow A plant of the mallow family growing in marshy places.

marsh marigold A showy swamp plant of the crowfoot family, having yellow flowers: also called *cowslip.*

marsh·y (mär′shē) *adj.* **marsh·i·er, marsh·i·est** 1. Of, pertaining to, or containing a marsh. 2. Swampy; boggy. 3. Growing or produced in a marsh. —**marsh′i·ness** *n.*

mar·su·pi·al (mär·sōō′pē·əl) *n.* Any member of an order of mammals, as the kangaroos, opossums, and wombats, whose females carry their undeveloped young in an abdominal pouch. [< Gk. *marsypion,* dim. of *marsipos* bag] —**mar·su′pi·al** *adj.*

mart (märt) *n.* A market. [< L *mercatus*]

mar·ten (mär′tən) *n.* 1. A weasellike carnivorous mammal, as the **pine marten** of eastern North America. 2. The valuable, dark brown fur of a marten. [< OF *martrine* of the marten]

mar·tial (mär′shəl) *adj.* 1. Of, pertaining to, or concerned with war or the military life. 2. Suggestive of or suitable for war or military operations. 3. Of or characteristic of a warrior. [< L *martialis* pertaining to Mars, god of war] —**mar′tial·ly** *adv.*

martial law Temporary jurisdiction or rule by military forces over the citizens of an area where civil law and order no longer function or exist.

Mar·tian (mär′shən) *adj. Astron.* Of or pertaining to the planet Mars. —*n.* One of the supposed inhabitants of Mars. [< L *Martius*]

mar·tin (mär′tən) *n.* Any of certain birds of the swallow family, having a tail that is less forked than that of the common swallow; esp., the **house martin** of Europe, and the **purple martin** of North America. [< F]

mar·ti·net (mär′tə·net′) *n.* One who demands rigid adherence to rules, etc. [after General Jean *Martinet,* 17th c. French drillmaster]

mar·tin·gale (mär′tən·gāl) *n.* A forked strap connecting the head gear of a horse with the bellyband, used to check upward movement of the horse's head. [< Provençal *martengalo,* appar. fem. of *martengo* an inhabitant of Martigues, miserly person]

mar·ti·ni (mär·tē′nē) *n.* *pl.* **·nis** A cocktail made of gin, or vodka, and dry vermouth. [after *Martini* and Rossi, a company making vermouth]

mar·tyr (mär′tər) *n.* 1. One who submits to death rather than renounce his religion. 2. One who dies, suffers, or sacrifices everything for a principle, cause, etc. 3. One who suffers much, as from ill health or misfortune. —*v.t.* 1. To make a martyr of. 2. To torture or persecute. [< Gk. *martyr,* Aeolic form of *martyrs, martyros* witness] —**mar′tyr·dom** *n.*

mar·vel (mär′vəl) *v.i.* **·veled** or **·velled, ·vel·ing** or **·vel·ling** To be filled with wonder, surprise, etc. —*n.* That which excites wonder; a prodigy. [< OF < L *mirabilia,* neut. pl. of *mirabilis* wonderful]

mar·vel·ous (mär′vəl·əs) *adj.* 1. Causing astonishment and wonder; amazing; extraordinary. 2. *Informal* Very good; excellent; admirable. Also **mar′vel·lous.** —**mar′vel·ous·ly** *adv.* —**mar′vel·ous·ness** *n.*

Marx·ism (märk′siz·əm) *n.* The body of socialist doctrines formulated by Karl Marx and Friedrich Engels. —**Marx′ist, Marx′i·an** *n. & adj.*

Mar·y (mâr′ē) The mother of Jesus: also *Virgin Mary.*

Mary Mag·da·lene (mag′də·lēn, mag′də·lē′nē) A woman often identified with the penitent sinner whom Jesus forgave.

mar·zi·pan (märt′sə·pan, mär′zə-) *n.* A confection of grated almonds, sugar, and egg whites, usu. made into a paste and molded into various shapes. [< Ital. *marzapane*]

-mas *combining form* Mass; a (specified) festival or its celebration: *Christmas.* [< MASS]

mas·car·a (mas·kar′ə) *n.* A cosmetic preparation used to color the eyelashes and eyebrows. [< Sp. *mascara* mask < Arabic *maskharah* buffoon]

mas·cot (mas′kot, -kət) *n.* A person, animal, or object thought to bring good luck by its presence. [< Provençal *mascot,* dim. of *masco* sorcerer, lit., mask]

mas·cu·line (mas′kyə·lin) *adj.* 1. Of or pertaining to the male sex; male. 2. Of, pertaining to, typical of, or appropriate for men or boys: *masculine* sports. 3. Applicable only to persons or things grammatically classified as male. —*n. Gram.* The masculine gender. [< L *masculus* male] —**mas′cu·lin′i·ty** *n.*

ma·ser (mā′zər) *n. Physics* Any of various devices that generate or amplify electromagnetic waves of precise frequency without loss of frequency and phase. [< M(ICROWAVE) A(MPLIFICATION BY) S(TIMULATED) E(MISSION OF) R(ADIATION)]

mash (mash) *n.* 1. A soft, pulpy mixture or mass. 2. A mixture of meal, bran, etc., and water, fed warm to horses and cattle. 3. Crushed or ground grain or malt, steeped in hot water to produce wort for making beer. —*v.t.* 1. To crush into a mash or pulp. 2. To steep (malt, grain meal, etc.) in hot water to produce wort. [OE *max-, māsc* (*wyrt*) mash (wort), infused malt] —**mash′er** *n.*

mask (mask) *n.* 1. A covering used to conceal all or part of the face as a disguise or for protection. 2. A cast of a face, usu. made of plaster. 3. That which conceals something from the sight or mind: under the *mask* of piety. 4. A masquerade. 5. See MASQUE. —*v.t.* 1. To cover (the face, head, etc.) with a mask. 2. To disguise. —*v.i.* 3. To put on a mask; assume a disguise. [Ult. < Arabic *maskharah* buffoon] —**masked** *adj.* —**mas′ker** *n.*

mask·ing tape (mas′king) An adhesive tape used to cover those parts of a surface not to be painted, sprayed, etc.

mas·o·chism (mas′ə·kiz′əm) *n.* 1. *Psychol.* A condition in which sexual gratification depends largely on undergoing physical pain or humiliation. 2. A tendency to derive pleasure from one's own suffering. [after Leopold von Sacher-*Masoch,* 1835–95, Austrian novelist, who described this condition] —**mas′o·chist** *n.* —**mas′o·chis′tic** *adj.*

ma·son (mā′sən) *n.* 1. One skilled in building with stone, brick, concrete, etc. 2. A stonecutter. 3. *cap.* Freemason. [< Med.L *matio, macio, -onis*]

ma·son·ic (mə·son′ik) *adj.* 1. Of, pertaining to, or like Freemasons or Freemasonry: also **Ma·son′ic.** 2. Of or pertaining to masons or masonry.

Ma·son jar (mā′sən) A glass jar having a tightly fitting screw top, used for canning and preserving. [after John L. *Mason*, 19th c. American inventor]

ma·son·ry (mā′sən·rē) *n. pl.* **·ries** 1. The art or work of a mason. 2. That which is built by masons. 3. *cap.* Freemasonry.

masque (mask) *n.* 1. An elaborately staged dramatic performance, popular esp. during the 17th c. in England; also, something written for this. 2. A masquerade. Also spelled *mask.* [See MASK.]

mas·quer·ade (mas′kə·rād′) *n.* 1. A social gathering in which the guests are masked and dressed in fancy costumes. 2. The costumes worn at such a gathering. 3. A false show, disguise, or pretense. Also called *mask, masque.* —*v.i.* **·ad·ed, ·ad·ing** 1. To take part in a masquerade. 2. To disguise one's true character. [See MASK.] —**mas′quer·ad′er** *n.*

mass (mas) *n.* 1. A body of matter having no definite shape but relatively large size. 2. An assemblage of individual parts or objects that collectively make up a single body. 3. A great amount or number of anything. 4. The greater part of anything; majority. 5. The volume or magnitude of a solid body; bulk; size. 6. *Physics* The measure of the inertia of a body, expressed as the quotient of the weight of the body divided by the acceleration due to gravity. —**the masses** The great body or majority of ordinary people. —*adj.* 1. Attended by, designed for, characteristic of, or affecting a large mass of people. 2. Produced in large amounts. 3. Total; allover: the *mass* effect. —*v.t. & v.i.* To form into a mass; assemble. [< L *massa*, prob. < Gk. *maza* barley cake]

Mass (mas) *n. Eccl.* 1. In the Roman Catholic and some Anglican churches, the eucharistic liturgy, consisting of various prayers and ritual ceremonies and regarded as a commemoration or repetition of Christ's sacrifice on the Cross. 2. A celebration of this liturgy. 3. A musical setting for some of the fixed portions of this liturgy. [OE < L *missa*]

Mas·sa·chu·set (mas′ə·chōō′sit) *n.* 1. One of a large tribe of Algonquian Indians, formerly inhabiting the region around Massachusetts Bay. 2. Their language. [< Algonquian (Massachuset) *mass* big + *wadchu* hill + *es*, dim. suffix + *et* at the]

mas·sa·cre (mas′ə·kər) *n.* 1. A savage and indiscriminate killing of human beings. 2. *Informal* A crushing defeat, as in sports. —*v.t.* **·cred, ·cring** 1. To kill indiscriminately or in great numbers. 2. *Informal* To defeat severely, as in sports. [< OF, ? < *mache-col* butcher] —**mas′sa·crer** (-kər·ər, -krər) *n.*

mas·sage (mə·säzh′) *n.* A manipulation of parts of the body, as by rubbing, kneading, or slapping, used to promote circulation, relax muscles, etc. —*v.t.* **·saged, ·sag·ing** To treat by massage. [< F, ? < Gk. *massein* to knead]

mas·seur (ma·sûr′, *Fr.* må·sœr′) *n.* A man who practices or gives massage. [< F] —**mas·seuse** (ma·sōōz′, -sōōs′; *Fr.* må·sœz′) *n.fem.*

mas·sive (mas′iv) *adj.* 1. Forming or constituting a large mass; having great bulk and weight. 2. Imposing or impressive in scale, scope, degree, etc. 3. *Pathol.* Extending over or affecting a large area: a *massive* swelling. [< F *massif*] —**mas′sive·ly** *adv.* —**mas′sive·ness** *n.*

mass media The various means of disseminating information to a wide public audience, as newspapers, radio, etc.

mass meeting A large public gathering for the discussion or promotion of some topic or cause, usu. political.

mass-pro·duce (mas′prə·dōōs′, -dyōōs′) *v.t.* **·duced, ·duc·ing** To manufacture or produce (goods or articles) in great quantities, usu. by machine. —**mass production**

mast[1] (mast) *n.* 1. *Naut.* A pole or spar set upright in a sailing vessel to sustain the yards, sails, etc. 2. Any large, upright pole, as of a derrick, crane, etc. —**before the mast** Serving as a common sailor. [OE *mæst*]

mast[2] (mast) *n.* The fruit of the oak, beech, etc., when used as food for swine. [OE *mæst* mast, fodder]

mast- Var. of MASTO-.

mas·tec·to·my (mas·tek′tə·mē) *n. pl.* **·mies** The surgical removal of a breast.

mas·ter (mas′tər) *n.* 1. One who has control, direction, or authority over someone or something, as over a household, an animal, etc. 2. One exceptionally gifted or skilled in an art, science, etc.: a *master* of oratory. 3. A craftsman or worker whose skill or experience qualifies him to practice his craft on his own and to train apprentices. 4. A teacher or leader in philosophy, religion, etc., who has followers or disciples. 5. *Chiefly Brit.* A male teacher. 6. One who has received a college degree beyond the bachelor's but less than the doctor's. 7. Something, as a matrix, stencil, etc., from which copies or impressions are made. 8. *Usu. cap.* A youth or boy; also, a title prefixed to a boy's name. 9. A victor or conqueror. 10. *Law* An officer of the court who assists the judge. —*v.t.* 1. To bring under control; defeat. 2. To become expert in: to *master* Greek. 3. To control or govern as a master. —*adj.* 1. Of, pertaining to, or characteristic of a master. 2. Having or exercising control. 3. Principal; main: the *master* plan. [OE < L *magnus* great] —**mas′ter·ship** *n.*

mas·ter·ful (mas′tər·fəl) *adj.* 1. Vigorously bold or authoritative in conduct, manner, etc. 2. Having or displaying the skill of a master. —**mas′ter·ful·ly** *adv.* —**mas′ter·ful·ness** *n.*

master key A key that will unlock two or more nonidentical locks.

mas·ter·ly (mas′tər·lē) *adj.* Characteristic of or befitting a master: a *masterly* performance.

mas·ter·mind (mas′tər·mīnd′) *n.* A person of great executive ability; esp., one who plans and directs at the highest levels of policy and strategy. —*v.t.* To plan and direct (a project, etc.) at the highest strategic level.

master of ceremonies A person presiding over an entertainment or dinner and introducing the performers or speakers. Also, *Informal, emcee.*

mas·ter·piece (mas′tər·pēs′) *n.* 1. Something of notable excellence; an unusually brilliant achievement. 2. Something considered the greatest achievement of its creator. Also **mas′ter·work′** (-wûrk′). [Trans. of G *meisterstück*]

master sergeant *Mil.* 1. A noncommissioned officer in the U.S. Army and U.S. Marines ranking below a sergeant major. 2. In the U.S. Air Force a noncommissioned officer ranking below a chief master sergeant.

mas·ter·stroke (mas′tər·strōk′) *n.* A masterly or decisive action or achievement.

mas·ter·y (mas′tər·ē) *n. pl.* **·ter·ies** 1. Superior knowledge or skill. 2. Victory or superiority, as in a contest. 3. The act of mastering a craft, technique, etc.

mast·head (mast′hed′) *n.* 1. *Naut.* The top of a mast. 2. The part of a periodical that gives the names of the editors, staff, and owners.

mas·tic (mas′tik) *n.* 1. A small Mediterranean evergreen tree of the cashew family. 2. The resin obtained from this tree, used in varnishes and as a flavoring agent. [< Gk. *mastichē*]

mas·ti·cate (mas′tə·kāt) *v.t.* **·cat·ed, ·cat·ing** 1. To chew. 2. To reduce, as rubber, to a pulp by crushing or kneading. [< Gk. *mastichaein* to gnash the teeth] **—mas′ti·ca′tion** *n.*

mas·tiff (mas′tif) *n.* A large hunting dog, having a thickset, heavy body, drooping ears, and pendulous lips. [< OF *mastin*]

mas·ti·tis (mas·tī′tis) *n. Pathol.* Inflammation of the breast.

masto- *combining form Med.* The breast or the mammary glands. Also, before vowels, *mast-*. [< Gk. *mastos* breast]

mas·to·don (mas′tə·don) *n. Paleontol.* Any of various large, extinct mammals resembling the elephant. [< Gk. *mastos* breast + *odous, odontos* tooth]

mas·toid (mas′toid) *adj. Anat.* Designating a nipple-shaped process of the temporal bone located behind the ear. [< Gk. *mastos* breast + *eidos* form] **—mas′toid** *n.*

mas·toid·i·tis (mas′toid·ī′tis) *n. Pathol.* Inflammation of the mastoid.

mas·tur·ba·tion (mas′tər·bā′shən) *n.* Stimulation of the sexual organs, usu. by oneself. [< L *masturbatio, -onis*] **—mas′tur·bate** *v.i.* **·bat·ed, ·bat·ing** **—mas′tur·ba′tor** *n.* **—mas′tur·ba·to′ry** (-bə·tôr′ē) *adj.*

mat[1] (mat) *n.* 1. A flat piece of material made of fiber, rubber, etc., used to cover floors. 2. A thickly padded piece of material placed on the floor for protection in various gymnastic sports. 3. A small, flat piece of material, as lace, straw, or plastic, used as a table protection, ornament, etc. 4. Any dense, twisted, or tangled mass, as of hair. **—***v.* **mat·ted, mat·ting** *v.t.* 1. To cover with or as with a mat or mats. **—***v.i.* 2. To become entangled together. [< LL *matta*]

mat[2] (mat) *n.* 1. A border of cardboard or other material, serving as the frame or part of the frame of a picture. 2. A lusterless, dull finish, as on metal or glass. **—***v.t.* **mat·ted, mat·ting** 1. To produce a dull surface on, as on metal or glass. 2. To furnish (a picture) with a mat. **—***adj.* Having a lusterless surface. [OF, defeated]

mat·a·dor (mat′ə·dôr) *n.* In bullfighting, the man who kills the bull after completing various maneuvers with a cape in order to tire the animal. [< Sp. < *matar* to slay]

match[1] (mach) *n.* 1. One who or that which is similar to another in some quality or characteristic. 2. One who or that which is exactly equal to another. 3. One who or that which is able to cope with or oppose another as an equal. 4. Either of two things that harmonize or correspond with each other. 5. A game or contest. 6. A marriage or mating; also, an agreement to marry or mate. **—***v.t.* 1. To be similar to or in accord with in quality, degree, etc. 2. To make, provide, or select as equals or as suitable for one another: to *match* pearls. 3. To compare so as to decide superiority; test. 4. To set (equal opponents) in opposition. 5. To equal; oppose successfully. 6. To place together as mates; marry. **—***v.i.* 7. To be equal or similar. [OE *gemæcca* companion] **—match′er** *n.*

match[2] (mach) *n.* A splinter of soft wood or a piece of cardboard tipped with a combustible composition that ignites by friction. [< OF *mesche* wick]

match·less (mach′lis) *adj.* Having no match or equal; peerless. **—match′less·ly** *adv.* **—match′less·ness** *n.*

match·lock (mach′lok′) *n.* An old type of musket fired by igniting the powder with a slow-burning wick.

match·mak·er[1] (mach′mā′kər) *n.* 1. One who arranges a marriage. 2. One who arranges an athletic match. **—match′mak′ing** *adj. & n.*

match·mak·er[2] (mach′mā′kər) *n.* One who makes matches for lighting. **—match′mak′ing** *adj. & n.*

mate[1] (māt) *n.* 1. Something matched, paired, or joined with another. 2. A husband or wife. 3. Either of two animals paired for propagation. 4. A companion. 5. An officer of a merchant vessel, ranking next below the captain. **—***v.t. & v.i.* **mat·ed, mat·ing** 1. To join together; pair. 2. To join in marriage. 3. To unite for breeding, as animals. [< MLG *ge-* together + *mat* meat, food]

mate[2] (māt) *v.t.* **mat·ed, mat·ing** In chess, to checkmate. **—***n.* A checkmate.

ma·te[3] (mä′tā, mat′ā) *n.* 1. An infusion of the leaves of a Brazilian holly, used as a beverage esp. in South America. 2. The plant itself. [< Sp. < Quechua *mati* calabash]

ma·te·ri·al (mə·tir′ē·əl) *n.* 1. That of which anything is composed, created, or developed. 2. *pl.* The tools, instruments, etc., for doing something. 3. Cloth or fabric. **—***adj.* 1. Of, pertaining to, or composed of matter; physical. 2. Of, related to, or affecting the body: *material* comforts. 3. Concerned with or devoted to things primarily worldly rather than spiritual or intellectual. 4. Substantial; important. [< L *materia* matter, stuff]

ma·te·ri·al·ism (mə·tir′ē·əl·iz′əm) *n.* 1. *Philos.* The doctrine that everything in the universe is reducible to matter and can be explained in terms of physical laws. 2. Undue regard for the material aspects of life. **—ma·te′ri·al·ist** *n.* **—ma·te′ri·al·is′tic** *adj.* **—ma·te′ri·al·is′ti·cal·ly** *adv.*

ma·te·ri·al·ize (mə·tir′ē·əl·īz′) *v.* **·ized, ·iz·ing** *v.t.* 1. To give material or actual form to. 2. In spiritualism, to cause (a spirit, etc.) to appear in visible form. **—***v.i.* 3. To assume material or visible form; appear. 4. To take form or shape; be realized. **—ma·te′ri·al·i·za′tion** *n.*

ma·te·ri·al·ly (mə·tir′ē·əl·ē) *adv.* 1. In an important manner or to a considerable degree. 2. Physically.

ma·te·ri·el (mə·tir′ē·el′) *n.* 1. The equipment and supplies of a military force. 2. The equipment of any organization. Also *Fr.* **ma·té·riel** (mȧ·tā·ryel′). [< F, material]

ma·ter·nal (mə·tûr′nəl) *adj.* 1. Of, pertaining to, or characteristic of a mother; motherly. 2. Derived from, related through, or connected with one's mother. [< L *mater* mother] **—ma·ter′nal·ly** *adv.*

ma·ter·ni·ty (mə·tûr′nə·tē) *n. pl.* **·ties** 1. The state of being a mother. 2. The qualities of a mother. **—***adj.* 1. Fashioned for pregnant women: *maternity* clothes. 2. Designed to accommodate women and babies during and after childbirth: a *maternity* ward. [< L *maternitas*]

math (math) *n. Informal* Mathematics.

math·e·ma·ti·cian (math′ə·mə·tish′ən) *n.* One who specializes or is expert in mathematics.

math·e·mat·ics (math′ə·mat′iks) *n.pl.* (*construed as sing.*) The study of quantity, form, arrangement, and magnitude; esp., the methods and processes for disclosing the properties and relations of quantities and magnitudes. **—math′e·mat′i·cal** *adj.* **—math′e·mat′i·cal·ly** *adv.*

mat·i·nee (mat′ə·nā′) *n.* A performance or entertainment, as a play, concert, etc., held in the daytime, usu. in the afternoon. Also **mat′i·née′.** [< F < *matin* morning]

mat·ing (mā′ting) *n.* The act of pairing or matching.

mat·ins (mat′ənz) *n.pl. Often cap. Eccl.* 1. With lauds, the first of the seven canonical hours. 2. In the Anglican Church, the order for public worship in the morning. [< L *matutinus* (*tempus*) (time) of the morning] **—mat′in, mat′in·al** *adj.*

matri- *combining form* Mother. [< L *mater*]

ma·tri·arch (mā′trē·ärk) *n.* A woman holding the position corresponding to that of a patriarch in her family or tribe. **—ma′tri·ar′chal** *adj.*

ma·tri·ar·chy (mā′trē·ar′kē) *n. pl.* **·chies** A social organization having the mother as the head of the family, in which descent is traced through the mother.

mat·ri·cide (mat′rə·sīd) *n.* 1. The killing of one's mother. 2. One who kills his mother [< L *mater* mother + *caedere* to kill] **—mat′ri·ci′dal** *adj.*

ma·tric·u·late (mə·trik′yə·lāt) *v.t. & v.i.* **·lat·ed, ·lat·ing** To register or enroll in a college or university as a candidate for a degree. [< Med.L *matriculare* to enroll < *matrix* womb] **—ma·tric′u·la′tion** *n.*

mat·ri·mo·ny (mat′rə·mō′nē) *n. pl.* **·nies** 1. The state or condition of being married. 2. The act, ceremony, or sacrament of marriage. [< L *mater* mother] **—mat′ri·mo′ni·al** *adj.* **—mat′ri·mo′ni·al·ly** *adv.*

ma·trix (mā′triks) *n. pl.* **ma·trix·es** or **ma·tri·ces** (mā′trə·sēz, mat′rə-) 1. That in which anything originates, develops, takes shape, or is contained. 2. A mold in or from which anything is cast or shaped. [< L, womb

ma·tron (mā′trən) *n.* 1. A married woman, esp. one who is mature in age or manner. 2. A female attendant or guard, as in a woman's prison, rest room, etc. 3. A female superintendent of an institution, etc. [< L *mater* mother] **—ma′tron·li·ness** *n.* **—ma′·tron·ly** *adj. & adv.*

matron of honor A married woman acting as chief attendant to a bride at a wedding.

mat·ter (mat′ər) *n.* 1. That which makes up the substance of anything; constituent material. 2. That which is material and physical, occupies space, and is perceived by the senses. 3. A specific kind of substance: organic *matter.* 4. An object of discussion, concern, etc.: a *matter* of faith. 5. Something of importance or consequence. 6. A usu. unpleasant condition or circumstance: with *the*: What's the *matter* with you? 7. The content or meaning of a book, etc., as distinguished from the style or form. 8. Pus. 9. That which is written, printed, etc.: *matter* for reading. 10. Anything sent by mail: third-class *matter.* **—***v.i.* To be of concern: It *matters* little. [< L *materia* stuff]

mat·ter-of-fact (mat′ər·əv·fakt′) *adj.* 1. Closely adhering to facts; literal. 2. Plain-spoken; blunt. **—mat′ter-of-fact′ly** *adv.*

Mat·thew (math′yo͞o) *n.* The first Gospel of the New Testament, attributed to the apostle Matthew (also called Saint Matthew).

mat·ting[1] (mat′ing) *n.* 1. A woven fabric of fiber, straw, or other material, used as a floor covering, for packing, etc. 2. Mats collectively.

mat·ting[2] (mat′ing) *n.* 1. A mat for framing a picture. 2. A dull, lusterless surface, as on metal or glass.

mat·tock (mat′ək) *n.* Either of two tools resembling a pickax, having a blade on one end and a pick on the other, or a blade on each end. [OE *mattuc*]

mat·tress (mat′rəs) *n.* A large pad made of a strong fabric and filled with a resilient material, as cotton, rubber, feathers, etc., used on or as a bed. [< Arabic *matrah* place where something is thrown]

mat·u·rate (mach′o͝o·rāt, mat′yo͞o-) *v.i.* **·rat·ed, ·rat·ing** 1. To form pus. 2. To ripen or mature. [< L *maturus* ripe, fully developed] **—mat′u·ra′tion** *n.*

ma·ture (mə·tyo͝or′, -to͝or′, -cho͝or′) *adj.* 1. Completely developed; fully ripe, as plants, fruit, or animals. 2. Highly developed in intellect, outlook, etc.: a *mature* thinker. 3. Thoroughly developed, perfected, etc.: a *mature* scheme. 4. Due and payable: a *mature* bond. **—***v.* **·tured, ·tur·ing** *v.t.* 1. To cause to ripen; bring to full development. **—***v.i.* 2. To come to full development. 3. To become due, as a note. [< L *maturus* ripe, of full age] **—ma·ture′ly** *adv.* **—ma·tur′i·ty** *n.*

ma·tu·ti·nal (mə·to͞o′tə·nəl, -tyo͞o′-, mach·ə·tī′nəl) *adj.* Of, pertaining to, or taking place in the morning; early. [< L *matutinus* early in the morning] **—ma·tu′ti·nal·ly** *adv.*

mat·zo (mät′sə) *n. pl.* **·zos** or **·zot** (-sōt) or **·zoth** (-sōth, -sōt) A large, flat piece of unleavened bread, traditionally eaten during Passover. Also **mat′zoh.** [< Hebrew *matstāh* unleavened bread]

maud·lin (môd′lin) *adj.* 1. Excessively emotional or sentimental. 2. Overly sentimental or emotional from too much liquor. [< OF *Madeleine* (Mary) Magdalen, often depicted weeping]

maul (môl) *n.* A heavy mallet for driving wedges, piles, etc. —*v.t.* 1. To beat and bruise. 2. To handle roughly; manhandle; abuse. [< L *malleus* hammer] —**maul′er** *n.*

maun·der (môn′dər) *v.i.* 1. To talk in a wandering or incoherent manner; drivel. 2. To move dreamily or idly. [? Freq. of obs. *maund* to beg] —**maun′der·er** *n.*

mau·so·le·um (mô′sə·lē′əm, -zə-) *n. pl.* **·le·ums** or **·le·a** A large, stately tomb. [< Gk. *Mausōleion*, tomb of King Mausolus at Halicarnassus]

mauve (mōv, môv) *n.* Any of various purplish rose shades. [< F, mallow]

ma·ven (mā′vən) *n.* An expert; an authority. Also **ma′vin.** [< Yiddish *meyvn*]

mav·er·ick (mav′ər·ik) *n.* 1. An unbranded or orphaned animal, as a calf. 2. *Informal* One who is unorthodox in his ideas, attitudes, etc. [after Samuel A. *Maverick*, 1803–70, Texas lawyer who did not brand his cattle]

maw (mô) *n.* 1. The jaws, mouth, or gullet of a voracious mammal or fish. 2. The craw of a bird. 3. The stomach. [OE *maga* stomach]

mawk·ish (mô′kish) *adj.* 1. Characterized by false or childish sentimentality. 2. Sickening or insipid. [< ON *mathkr* maggot] —**mawk′·ish·ly** *adv.* —**mawk′ish·ness** *n.*

max·il·la (mak·sil′ə) *n. pl.* **max·il·lae** (mak·sil′ē) In vertebrates, the upper jaw or jawbone. [< L *mala* jaw] —**max·il·lar·y** (mak′sə·ler′ē) *adj.*

max·im (mak′sim) *n.* A brief statement of a general principle, truth, or rule of conduct. [< L *maxima (sententia, propositio)* greatest (authority, premise)]

max·i·mal (mak′sə·məl) *adj.* Of or being a maximum; greatest or highest possible. —**max′i·mal·ly** *adv.*

max·i·min (mak′si·min′) *n.* In the game theory, a strategy that maximizes the smallest gains that a player can make. [< MAXI(MUM) + MIN(IMUM)] —**max′i·min′** *adj.*

max·i·mize (mak′sə·mīz) *v.t.* **·mized, ·miz·ing** To make as great as possible.

max·i·mum (mak′sə·məm) *n. pl.* **·mums** or **·ma** 1. The greatest possible quantity, amount, or degree. 2. The greatest quantity, degree, etc., reached or recorded. —**max′i·mum** *adj.* [< L *maximus*, superl. of *magnus* great]

may (mā) *v.* past: **might** A defective verb now used only in the present and past tenses as an auxiliary to express: 1. Permission or allowance: *May* I go? 2. Desire, prayer, or wish: *May* your tribe increase! 3. Contingency, esp. in clauses of result, concession, purpose, etc.: He died that we *might* live. 4. Possibility: You *may* be right. [OE *mæg*]

May (mā) *n.* 1. The fifth month of the year, containing 31 days. 2. The prime of life; youth. [< L *(mensis) Maius* (month of) May]

Ma·ya (mä′yə) *n.* 1. One of a tribe of Central American Indians, having an early advanced civilization and still living in Yucatán and parts of northern Central America. 2. The language of the Mayas. —*adj.* Of the Mayas, their culture, or their language. —**Ma′yan** *adj. & n.*

May apple A North American herb whose roots yield a purgative; also, its edible fruit. Also called *mandrake.*

may·be (mā′bē) *adv.* Perhaps; possibly. [< *(it) may be*]

May Day The first day of May, traditionally celebrated as a spring festival and, in recent times, celebrated in some countries by demonstrations honoring labor.

may·flow·er (mā′flou′ər) *n.* Any of various plants that blossom in the spring; esp., the trailing arbutus.

May fly Any of a large group of insects having transparent forewings, a relatively long nymphal life, and a short-lived adult stage: also called *ephemerid.* Also **may′fly.**

may·hem (mā′hem) *n.* 1. *Law* The offense of injuring a person's body so as to render him less able to defend himself. 2. Any situation characterized by violence, confusion, noise, etc. [< OF *mehaing, mahaym*]

may·on·naise (mā′ə·nāz′) *n.* A dressing, as for salads, made by beating together raw egg yolk, oil, lemon juice or vinegar, and condiments. [< F]

may·or (mā′ər, mâr) *n.* The chief magistrate of a city, borough, or municipal corporation. [< L *major* greater] —**may′or·al** *adj.*

may·or·al·ty (mā′ər·əl·tē, mâr′əl-) *n. pl.* **·ties** The office or term of service of a mayor. [< OF *mairalté*]

May·pole (mā′pōl′) *n.* A decorated pole around which dancing takes place on May Day. Also **may′pole′.**

maze (māz) *n.* 1. An intricate network of paths or passages; a labyrinth. 2. A state of bewilderment, uncertainty, or perplexity. [< AMAZE] —**ma′zy** *adj.*

ma·zur·ka (mə·zûr′kə, -zŏŏr′-) *n.* 1. A lively Polish dance in 3/4 time. 2. The music for such a dance. [< Polish, woman from Mazovia, a province]

Mc·Coy (mə·koi′), **the (real)** *Slang* The authentic person or thing.

Mc·In·tosh (mak′ən·tosh) *n.* A red early-autumn eating apple. Also **McIntosh red.** [after John *McIntosh*, of Ontario, who discovered it about 1796]

me (mē) *pron.* The objective case of the pronoun *I.* [OE *mē*, dat. sing.]

mead[1] (mēd) *n.* An alcoholic beverage of fermented honey and water, to which yeast and spices are added. [OE *medu*]

mead[2] (mēd) *n.* *Poetic* A meadow. [OE *mǣd*]

mead·ow (med′ō) *n.* 1. A tract of grassland, usu. used for grazing or for growing hay. 2. A low or level piece of land, as near a river, used for growing grass or hay. Also **mead′ow·land′.** [OE *mǣdwe*, oblique case of *mǣd*] —**mead′ow·y** *adj.*

mead·ow·lark (med′ō·lärk′) *n.* Any of various songbirds of North America, marked with black on a yellow breast.

mea·ger (mē′gər) *adj.* 1. Deficient in quantity or quality; scanty; inadequate. 2. Lacking in fertility, strength, or richness: *meager* soil. 3. Thin; emaciated. Also *Brit.* **mea′gre.** [< L *macer* lean] —**mea′ger·ly** *adv.*

meal[1] (mēl) *n.* 1. The edible seeds of any grain, coarsely ground and unsifted. 2. Any material having a similar texture. [OE *melu*]

meal[2] (mēl) *n.* 1. The food served or eaten regularly at certain times during the day.

2. The time or occasion of taking such food. [OE *mǣl* measure, time, meal]
meal ticket 1. A ticket or card bought for a specified price and redeemable at a restaurant for food. 2. *Slang* One who or that which provides a livelihood for another.
meal·time (mēl′tīm′) *n.* The habitual time for a meal.
meal·y (mē′lē) *adj.* **meal·i·er, meal·i·est** 1. Resembling meal; dry; powdery. 2. Containing meal. —**meal′i·ness** *n.*
meal·y-mouthed (mē′lē·moutht′, -mouthd′) *adj.* Unwilling to express facts or opinions plainly and frankly.
mean¹ (mēn) *v.* **meant** (ment), **mean·ing** *v.t.* 1. To have in mind as a purpose or intent. 2. To intend or design for some purpose, destination, etc.: Was that remark *meant* for me? 3. To have as the particular sense or significance. —*v.i.* 4. To be of specified importance: Her work *means* everything to her. —**to mean well** To have good intentions. [OE *mǣnan* to tell]
mean² (mēn) *adj.* 1. Poor or inferior in grade or quality. 2. Having little worth or consequence. 3. Ignoble in mind or character. 4. Miserly; stingy. 5. Poor in appearance; shabby. 6. Humble in birth, rank, or station. 7. *Informal* Disagreeable; nasty; vicious. 8. *Informal* Difficult; troublesome. 9. *Slang* Excellent; expert. [OE *(ge)mǣne* ordinary] —**mean′ly** *adv.* —**mean′ness** *n.*
mean³ (mēn) *n.* 1. *pl.* The medium, method, or instrument by which some end is or may be accomplished. 2. *pl.* Money; wealth. 3. The middle point or state between two extremes. 4. An average. —**by all means** Without hesitation; certainly. —**by any means** In any manner possible; at all; somehow. —**by means of** With the help of; through using. —**by no means** Most certainly not. —*adj.* 1. Intermediate or average in size, degree, quality, etc.; medium. 2. Halfway between extremes; average. [< L *medius* middle]
me·an·der (mē·an′dər) *v.i.* 1. To wind and turn in a course. 2. To wander aimlessly. —*n.* 1. *Often pl.* A tortuous or winding course. 2. Aimless wandering. [< Gk. *Maiandros*, the river Meander] —**me·an′·der·er** *n.*
mean·ing (mē′ning) *n.* 1. That which is intended; aim; purpose. 2. That which is signified; sense; interpretation. 3. Importance or significance.
mean·ing·ful (mē′ning·fəl) *adj.* Full of meaning. —**mean′ing·ful·ness** *n.* —**mean′·ing·ful·ly** *adv.*
mean·ing·less (mē′ning·lis) *adj.* Having no meaning, significance, or importance. —**mean′ing·less·ly** *adv.* —**mean′ing·less·ness** *n.*
meant (ment) Past tense and past participle of MEAN¹.
mean·time (mēn′tīm′) *n.* Intervening time. —*adv.* 1. In or during the intervening time. 2. At the same time.
mean·while (mēn′hwīl′) *n.* & *adv.* Meantime.
mea·sles (mē′zəlz) *n.pl.* (*construed as sing. or pl.*) 1. An acute, highly contagious virus disease affecting children and sometimes adults, characterized by an extensive eruption of small red spots: also called *rubeola*. 2. Any similar disease, as German measles: also called *rubella*. [ME *maseles*, pl. of *masel* blister]
mea·sly (mēz′lē) *adj.* **·sli·er, ·sli·est** *Slang* Contemptibly stingy, scanty, or petty.
meas·ur·a·ble (mezh′ər·ə·bəl) *adj.* 1. Capable of being measured or compared. 2. Notable; significant. —**meas′ur·a·bly** *adv.*
meas·ure (mezh′ər) *n.* 1. The extent, dimensions, capacity, etc., of anything. 2. A standard or unit of measurement. 3. Any standard of criticism or judgment. 4. A system of measurements: liquid *measure*. 5. An instrument for taking measurements. 6. The act of measuring. 7. A fixed or suitable limit or bound: talkative beyond all *measure*. 8. A certain amount, extent, or degree of anything: a *measure* of freedom. 9. *Often pl.* A specific action, step, or procedure. 10. A legislative bill. 11. Rhythmic movement or beat. 12. *Music* The portion of music contained between two bar lines; bar. —**for good measure** As something extra. —*v.* **·ured, ·ur·ing** *v.t.* 1. To take or ascertain the dimensions, quantity, capacity, etc., of. 2. To set apart, mark off, allot, etc., by or as by measuring: often with *off* or *out*. 3. To estimate; judge; weigh. 4. To serve as the measure of. 5. To bring into competition or comparison. —*v.i.* 6. To make or take measurements. 7. To yield a specified measurement. —**to measure up to** To fulfill or meet, as expectations. [< L *mensura* measurement] —**meas′ur·er** *n.*
meas·ured (mezh′ərd) *adj.* 1. Determined by some standard. 2. Slow and stately; rhythmical. 3. Carefully considered or weighed; deliberate.
meas·ure·less (mezh′ər·lis) *adj.* Incapable of being measured; very great; immense.
meas·ure·ment (mezh′ər·mənt) *n.* 1. The act or process of measuring anything. 2. The amount, capacity, or extent determined by measuring. 3. A system of measures.
meat (mēt) *n.* 1. The flesh of animals used as food, esp. the flesh of mammals as opposed to fish or fowl. 2. The edible part of anything. 3. The essence, gist, or main idea of something. [OE *mete*] —**meat′less** *adj.*
meat packing The commercial processing, packaging, and distribution of meat and meat products. —**meat packer**
meat·y (mē′tē) *adj.* **meat·i·er, meat·i·est** 1. Of, pertaining to, or like meat. 2. Full of meat. 3. Full of substance; significant. —**meat′i·ness** *n.*
mec·ca (mek′ə) *n.* 1. A place or attraction visited by many people. 2. The goal of one's aspirations. [after the city of *Mecca*, to which Muslims make pilgrimages]
me·chan·ic (mə·kan′ik) *n.* One who builds, operates, or repairs tools or machinery. —*adj.* 1. Involving or pertaining to manual labor or skill. 2. Mechanical. [< Gk. *mēchanē* machine]
me·chan·i·cal (mə·kan′i·kəl) *adj.* 1. Of, involving, or having to do with machinery or tools. 2. Operated or produced by a machine. 3. Of the science of mechanics. 4. Done without spontaneity or by force of habit; automatic. —**me·chan′i·cal·ly** *adv.*
mechanical drawing Drawing done with the aid of compasses, squares, etc.; also, the drawing so made.
me·chan·ics (mə·kan′iks) *n.pl.* (*construed*

as sing. in defs. 1 and 2) 1. The branch of physics that treats of motion and of the action of forces on material bodies. 2. The body of knowledge dealing with the design, operation, and maintenance of machinery. 3. The technical aspects of anything.

mech·a·nism (mek′ə·niz′əm) *n.* 1. The parts or arrangement of parts of a machine. 2. Something similar to a machine. 3. The process or technique by which something works. —**mech′a·nis′tic** *adj.* —**mech′a·nis′ti·cal·ly** *adv.*

mech·a·nize (mek′ə·nīz) *v.t.* **·nized, ·niz·ing** 1. To make mechanical. 2. To convert (an industry, etc.) to machine production. 3. *Mil.* To equip with tanks, trucks, etc. —**mech′a·ni·za′tion** *n.*

med·al (med′l) *n.* A small piece of metal bearing an image, inscription, etc., and often given as an award for some outstanding act or service. [< L *metallum* mine]

med·al·ist (med′l·ist) *n.* 1. A collector or maker of medals. 2. The recipient of a medal awarded for services or merit.

me·dal·lion (mə·dal′yən) *n.* 1. A large medal. 2. An ornamental subject usu. set in a circular or oval frame and used as a decorative element. [< F *médaillon*]

med·dle (med′l) *v.i.* **·dled, ·dling** 1. To participate or interfere officiously: often with *in* or *with.* 2. To tamper. [< OF *medler* < L *miscere* to mix] —**med′dler** *n.* —**med′dle·some** *adj.*

me·di·a (mē′dē·ə) Alternative plural of MEDIUM. —*n.* The various forms of mass communication, as broadcasting, newspapers, etc., considered collectively: often with *the.*

me·di·ae·val (mē′dē·ē′vəl, med′ē-) See MEDIEVAL.

me·di·al (mē′dē·əl) *adj.* 1. Of, pertaining to, or situated in the middle. 2. Of or pertaining to a mathematical average; mean. [< L *medius* middle] —**me′di·al·ly** *adv.*

me·di·an (mē′dē·ən) *adj.* 1. Pertaining to or situated in the middle; medial. 2. *Stat.* Designating the middle point in a series of values: 8 is the *median* of 2, 5, 8, 10, 13. —*n.* A median point, line, or number. [< L *medius* middle]

median strip A strip of land, raised pavement, etc. that divides traffic lanes.

me·di·ate (*v.* mē′dē·āt; *adj.* -it) *v.* **·at·ed, ·at·ing** *v.t.* 1. To settle or reconcile (differences) by intervening as a peacemaker. —*v.i.* 2. To act between disputing parties to bring about a settlement, etc. —*adj.* 1. Acting as an intervening agency. 2. Being in an intermediate position. [< LL *mediare* to stand between] —**me′di·a′tion** *n.* —**me′di·a′tor** *n.* —**me′di·a·to′ry** (-ə·tôr′ē) *adj.*

med·ic (med′ik) *n.* *Informal* 1. A physician or intern. 2. A corpsman.

med·i·ca·ble (med′ə·kə·bəl) *adj.* Capable of being relieved by medical treatment; curable.

med·i·caid (med′ə·kād) *n.* A state and federal program providing monetary aid for medical care to those who cannot afford it. [MEDI(CAL) + AID]

med·i·cal (med′i·kəl) *adj.* 1. Of or pertaining to medicine. 2. Having curative properties.

med·i·ca·ment (med′ə·kə·mənt, mə·dik′ə-) *n.* Any substance for the cure of disease or the alleviation of pain.

med·i·care (med′ə·kâr) *n.* A federal program that funds medical care for the aged and certain social security beneficiaries. [MEDI(CAL) + CARE]

med·i·cate (med′ə·kāt) *v.t.* **·cat·ed, ·cat·ing** 1. To treat medicinally. 2. To tincture or impregnate with medicine. [< L *medicare* to heal] —**med′i·ca′tion** *n.* —**med′i·ca′tive** *adj.*

me·dic·i·nal (mə·dis′ə·nəl) *adj.* Pertaining to or having the properties of medicine; healing, curative, or alleviating. —**me·dic′i·nal·ly** *adv.*

med·i·cine (med′ə·sən, *Brit.* med′sən) *n.* 1. Any substance used in the treatment of disease or in the relief of pain. 2. The science of the preservation and restoration of health and of treating disease, esp. as distinguished from surgery. 3. The profession of medicine. [< L *medicus* physician]

medicine ball A large, heavy, leather-covered ball, thrown and caught for physical exercise.

medicine man Among North American Indians, one professing supernatural powers of healing, etc.

med·i·co (med′ə·kō) *n.* *pl.* **·cos** *Informal* A physician or a medical student. [< Ital. or Sp., physician]

me·di·e·val (mē′dē·ē′vəl, med′ē-) *adj.* Of, like, or characteristic of the Middle Ages: also spelled *mediaeval.* [< L *medius* middle + *aevum* age] —**me′di·e′val·ly** *adv.*

me·di·e·val·ism (mē′dē·ē′vəl·iz′əm, med′ē-) *n.* 1. The spirit, beliefs, customs, and practices of the Middle Ages. 2. Devotion to the Middle Ages. 3. Any custom, idea, etc., surviving from the Middle Ages. Also spelled *mediaevalism.*

me·di·e·val·ist (mē′dē·ē′vəl·ist, med′ē-) *n.* 1. A scholar or specialist in medieval history, literature, or art. 2. One devoted to the Middle Ages. Also spelled *mediaevalist.*

Medieval Latin See under LATIN.

medio- *combining form* Middle. Also, before vowels, **medi-.** [< L *medius*]

me·di·o·cre (mē′dē·ō′kər) *adj.* Of only average quality; ordinary. [< L *medius* middle]

me·di·oc·ri·ty (mē′dē·ok′rə·tē) *n.* *pl.* **·ties** 1. The condition or quality of being mediocre. 2. Mediocre ability or performance. 3. A mediocre person.

med·i·tate (med′ə·tāt) *v.* **·tat·ed, ·tat·ing** *v.i.* 1. To engage in continuous and contemplative thought. —*v.t.* 2. To think about doing; plan. [< L *meditari* to muse, ponder] —**med′i·ta′tor** *n.* —**med′i·ta′tive** *adj.* —**med′i·ta′tion** *n.*

med·i·ter·ra·ne·an (med′ə·tə·rā′nē·ən) *adj.* Enclosed nearly or wholly by land. [< L *medius* middle + *terra* earth]

Med·i·ter·ra·ne·an (med′ə·tə·rā′nē·ən) *adj.* Of or pertaining to the Mediterranean Sea or its shores. —*n.* One who lives in a Mediterranean country.

me·di·um (mē′dē·əm) *n.* *pl.* **·di·ums** (*for def. 5*) or **·di·a** (-dē·ə) 1. An intermediate degree or condition; mean. 2. The surrounding or enveloping element; environment. 3. An intervening substance in which something may act or an effect be produced. 4. A means or agency; instrument: an advertising *medium.* 5. One through whom the spirits of the dead are believed to communicate with the material world. 6. An area or form of artistic expression, or the materials used. —*adj.* Intermediate in quantity, quality, size, etc. [< L, orig. neut. sing. of *medius* middle]

med·ley (med′lē) *n.* 1. A mingled and confused mass of elements; jumble. 2. A musical composition made up of different airs or parts of songs. [< OF *medlee*, orig. fem. pp. of *medler* to meddle]

Mé·doc (mā·dôk′) *n.* A red wine.

me·dul·la (mə·dul′ə) *n. pl.* **·lae** (-lē) *Anat.* 1. The soft inner portion of an organ or part, such as the kidney. 2. The marrow of bones. [< L, marrow, pith]

medulla ob·lon·ga·ta (ob′lông·gä′tə) *Anat.* The hindmost and lowest part of the brain, narrowing down into the spinal cord, and controlling breathing, circulation, etc.

me·du·sa (mə·dōō′sə, -zə, -dyōō′-) *n. pl.* **·sas** or **·sae** (-sē, -zē) A jellyfish. [< L]

meek (mēk) *adj.* 1. Having a patient, gentle disposition. 2. Lacking spirit or backbone; submissive. [< ON *miukr* gentle, soft] —**meek′ly** *adv.* —**meek′ness** *n.*

meer·schaum (mir′shəm, -shôm, -shoum) *n.* A tobacco pipe made of a light, heat-resisting, claylike mineral. [< G < *meer* sea + *schaum* foam]

meet[1] (mēt) *v.* **met** (met), **meet·ing** *v.t.* 1. To come upon; encounter. 2. To be at or go to the place of arrival of: to *meet* him at the station. 3. To make the acquaintance of. 4. To come into contact or conjunction with. 5. To keep an appointment with. 6. To come into the perception or recognition of (the eye, ear, etc.). 7. To oppose in battle. 8. To deal or cope with; handle. 9. To fulfill (an obligation, need, requirement, etc.). —*v.i.* 10. To come together; come face to face. 11. To assemble. 12. To make acquaintance or be introduced. 13. To come together in conflict or opposition; contend. —**to meet with** 1. To come upon; encounter. 2. To deal or confer with. 3. To experience. —*n.* An assembling for a sport or an athletic contest. [OE *mētan*]

meet[2] (mēt) *adj.* Suitable; proper. [OE *gemǣte*] —**meet′ly** *adv.*

meet·ing (mē′ting) *n.* 1. A coming together. 2. An assembly or gathering of persons; also, the persons present. 3. A joining or conjunction of things.

meeting house A house used for public meetings or worship.

mega- *combining form* 1. Great; large: **megastructure.** 2. One million times a specified unit: **megadecibel, megadyne, mega-erg, megampere, megavolt, megohm.** Before vowels, **meg-.** [< Gk. *megas* large]

meg·a·buck (meg′ə·buk) *n. Slang* A million dollars.

meg·a·cy·cle (meg′ə·sī′kəl) *n.* Megahertz.

meg·a·death (meg′ə·deth) *n.* A million dead people: used in relation to effects of a nuclear explosion.

meg·a·hertz (meg′ə·hûrtz) *n. pl.* **·hertz** A unit of frequency equal to one million hertz.

megalo- *combining form* Big; indicating excessive or abnormal size. Also, before vowels, **megal-.** [< Gk. *megas*, *megalou* big]

meg·a·lo·ma·ni·a (meg′ə·lō·mā′nē·ə, -mān′yə) *n. Psychiatry* A mental disorder in which the subject thinks himself great or exalted. —**meg′a·lo·ma′ni·ac** *adj. & n.*

meg·a·phone (meg′ə·fōn) *n.* A funnel-shaped, usu. hand-held device for amplifying or directing sound.

meg·a·ton (meg′ə·tun′) *n.* 1. One million tons. 2. A unit equal to the explosive power of one million tons of TNT.

meg·a·vi·ta·min (meg′ə·vī′tə·min) *adj.* Describing a therapy involving massive doses of vitamins.

me·gil·lah (mə·gil′ə) *n. Slang* A long, complicated account. [< Yiddish < Heb. *megillāh* scroll, volume, esp., the Book of Esther]

mei·o·sis (mī·ō′sis) *n. Biol.* The cell divisions leading to the formation of gametes in which the number of chromosomes is reduced by half. [< Gk. *meiōn* less] —**mei·ot′ic** (-ot′ik) *adj.*

mel·a·mine (mel′ə·mēn, -min) *n. Chem.* A crystalline nitrogen compound that reacts with formaldehyde to produce a high-grade thermosetting resin. [< *mel*(*am*), a chemical compound + AMINE]

mel·an·cho·li·a (mel′ən·kō′lē·ə) *n. Psychiatry* Great depression of spirits without apparent or sufficient cause. [< L] —**mel′an·cho′li·ac** *adj. & n.*

mel·an·chol·y (mel′ən·kol′ē) *adj.* 1. Excessively gloomy; sad. 2. Suggesting or promoting sadness: a *melancholy* day. —*n. pl.* **·chol·ies** Low spirits; depression. [< Gk. *melas*, *-anos* black + *cholē* bile] —**mel′an·chol′ic** *adj.*

Mel·a·ne·sian (mel′ə·nē′zhən, -shən) *n.* 1. A member of any of the dark-skinned peoples of Melanesia. 2. Any of the Austronesian languages spoken in Melanesia. —**Mel′a·ne′sian** *adj.*

mé·lange (mā·läṅzh′) *n. French* A mixture or medley.

mel·a·nin (mel′ə·nin) *n. Biochem.* A brownish black pigment contained in animal tissues, as the skin and hair.

melano- *combining form* Black; dark-colored. Also, before vowels, **melan-.** [< Gk. *melas*, *melanos* black]

Mel·ba toast (mel′bə) Thinly sliced bread toasted until brown and crisp. [after Nellie *Melba*, 1861–1931, Australian soprano]

meld (meld) *v.t. & v.i.* In pinochle and other card games, to announce or declare (a combination of cards) for inclusion in one's total score. —*n.* A group of cards to be declared, or the act of declaring them. [< G *melden* to announce]

me·lee (mā′lā, mā·lā′) *n.* A confused, general hand-to-hand fight; affray. Also *Fr.* **mê·lée** (me·lā′). [< F < OF *medlee* medley]

mel·io·rate (mēl′yə·rāt) *v.t. & v.i.* **·rat·ed, ·rat·ing** To improve, as in quality or condition; ameliorate. [< L *melior* better] —**mel′io·ra′tion** *n.* —**mel′io·ra′tive** *adj.* —**mel′io·ra′tor** *n.*

mel·lif·er·ous (mə·lif′ər·əs) *adj.* Producing or bearing honey. Also **mel·lif′ic.** [< L *mel* honey + *ferre* to bear]

mel·lif·lu·ous (mə·lif′lōō·əs) *adj.* Sweetly or smoothly flowing: *mellifluous* speech. [< L *mel* honey + *fluere* to flow] —**mel·lif′lu·ous·ly** *adv.* —**mel·lif′lu·ous·ness** *n.*

mel·low (mel′ō) *adj.* 1. Soft, sweet, and full-flavored by reason of ripeness, as fruit.

2. Well-matured, as wines. 3. Rich and soft in quality, as colors or sounds. 4. Made gentle and sympathetic by maturity or experience. —*v.t. & v.i.* To make or become mellow; soften. [ME, ? < OE *melu* meal] —**mel′low·ness** *n.*

me·lo·de·on (mə·lō′dē·ən) *n.* A small reed organ or harmonium. [A pseudo-Greek formation < MELODY]

me·lo·di·ous (mə·lō′dē·əs) *adj.* 1. Producing or characterized by melody; tuneful. 2. Pleasant to hear. —**me·lo′di·ous·ly** *adv.* —**me·lo′di·ous·ness** *n.*

mel·o·dra·ma (mel′ə·drä′mə, -dram′ə) *n.* 1. A drama in which the emotions displayed are violent or extravagantly sentimental, and the plot is made up of sensational incidents. 2. Sensational and highly emotional behavior or language. [< Gk. *melos* song + *drama* drama] —**mel′o·dra·mat′ic** (-drə·mat′ik) *adj.* —**mel′o·dra·mat′i·cal·ly** *adv.*

mel·o·dra·mat·ics (mel′ə·drə·mat′iks) *n.pl.* Melodramatic behavior.

mel·o·dy (mel′ə·dē) *n. pl.* **·dies** 1. Pleasing sounds, or an agreeable succession of such sounds. 2. *Music* An organized succession of tones, usu. in the same voice or instrument; a tune or air. [< Gk. *melos* song + *aoidos* singer] —**me·lod·ic** (mə·lod′ik) *adj.* —**me·lod′i·cal·ly** *adv.*

mel·on (mel′ən) *n.* 1. The large fruit of any of various plants of the gourd family, as the muskmelon and the watermelon. 2. Any of these plants. [< LL *melo, melonis*]

melt (melt) *v.t. & v.i.* **melt·ed, melt·ed** *Archaic* **mol·ten** (mōl′tən), **melt·ing** 1. To change from a solid to a liquid state by heat. 2. To disappear or cause to disappear: often with *away.* 3. To blend by imperceptible degrees: often with *into.* 4. To make or become softened in feeling or attitude. —*n.* 1. Something melted. 2. A single operation of fusing. [OE *meltan, mieltan*] —**melt′a·ble** *adj.* —**melt′a·bil′i·ty** *n.* —**melt′er** *n.*

melting point The temperature at which a specified solid substance melts or fuses.

mem·ber (mem′bər) *n.* 1. One who belongs to a society, club, party, etc. 2. *Usu. cap.* One who belongs to a legislative body. 3. A part or organ of an animal body, esp. a limb. 4. A part or element of a whole. [< L *membrum* limb]

mem·ber·ship (mem′bər·ship) *n.* 1. The state or fact of being a member. 2. The members of an organization, etc., collectively; also, the total number of members.

mem·brane (mem′brān) *n.* A thin, pliable layer of animal or vegetable tissue serving to cover or line an organ or part, separate adjoining cavities, or connect adjoining structures. [< L *membrana,* lit., limb coating] —**mem′bra·nous** (-brə·nəs) *adj.*

me·men·to (mə·men′tō) *n. pl.* **·tos** or **·toes** Anything that serves as a hint or reminder of the past; souvenir. [< L *meminisse* to remember]

mem·o (mem′ō) *n. pl.* **mem·os** *Informal* A memorandum.

mem·oir (mem′wär) *n.* 1. *pl.* Personal reminiscences or records; esp., a narrative of events based on the writer's personal observations and experiences. 2. *pl.* An account of the proceedings of a learned society. 3. A monograph. [< F < L *memoria* memory]

mem·o·ra·bil·i·a (mem′ə·rə·bil′ē·ə, -bil′yə) *n.pl.* Things or events worthy of remembrance and record. [< L]

mem·o·ra·ble (mem′ər·ə·bəl) *adj.* Worthy to be remembered; noteworthy. —**mem′o·ra·bil′i·ty** *n.* —**mem′o·ra·bly** *adv.*

mem·o·ran·dum (mem′ə·ran′dəm) *n. pl.* **·dums** or **·da** 1. A brief note of something to be remembered. 2. A record of transactions. 3. An informal letter, usu. sent between departments in an office. 4. *Law* A brief written outline of the terms of a transaction or contract. [< L, a thing to be remembered]

me·mo·ri·al (mə·môr′ē·əl) *adj.* 1. Serving to keep in memory a deceased person or an event; commemorative. 2. Of or pertaining to memory. —*n.* 1. Something serving to keep in remembrance a person, event, etc. 2. A written summary or presentation of facts, often in the form of a petition. [< L *memoria*]

Memorial Day A day set apart to honor the dead of any American war; in most states May 30. Formerly called *Decoration Day.*

me·mo·ri·al·ize (mə·môr′ē·əl·īz′) *v.t.* **·ized, ·iz·ing** 1. To commemorate. 2. To present a memorial to; petition. Also *Brit.* **me·mo′ri·al·ise′.** —**me·mo′ri·al·i·za′tion** *n.*

mem·o·rize (mem′ə·rīz) *v.t.* **·rized, ·riz·ing** To commit to memory. —**mem′o·ri·za′tion** *n.* —**mem′o·riz′er** *n.*

mem·o·ry (mem′ər·ē) *n. pl.* **·ries** 1. The mental capacity of recalling or recognizing previously learned behavior or past experience. 2. The total of what is remembered. 3. One who or that which is remembered. 4. The period of time covered by one's ability to remember. 5. Remembrance or commemoration. 6. Computer components that store data; also the capacity for such storage. [< L *memor* mindful]

men (men) Plural of MAN.

men·ace (men′is) *v.* **·aced, ·ac·ing** *v.t.* 1. To threaten with evil or harm. —*v.i.* 2. To make threats; appear threatening. —*n.* 1. A threat. 2. *Informal* A troublesome person; pest. [< L *minax, -acis* threatening] —**men′·ac·er** *n.* —**men′ac·ing·ly** *adv.*

me·nad (mē′nad) See MAENAD.

mé·nage (mā·näzh′, *Fr.* mā·nȧzh′) *n.* 1. The persons of a household, collectively. 2. Household management. Also **me·nage′.** [< F < L *mansio, -onis* house]

me·nag·er·ie (mə·naj′ər·ē) *n.* A collection of wild animals kept for exhibition. [< F]

mend (mend) *v.t.* 1. To make sound or serviceable again by repairing. 2. To correct errors or faults in: *Mend* your ways. —*v.i.* 3. To become better, as in health. —*n.* 1. A repairing. 2. A mended place, as on a garment. —**on the mend** Recovering health. [Var. of AMEND] —**mend′er** *n.*

men·da·cious (men·dā′shəs) *adj.* 1. Lying; deceitful. 2. Untrue; false. [< L *mendax, -acis* lying] —**men·da′cious·ly** *adv.* —**men·da′cious·ness** *n.*

men·dac·i·ty (men·das′ə·tē) *n. pl.* **·ties** 1. The quality of being mendacious. 2. A lie.

men·de·le·vi·um (men′də·lē′vē·əm) *n.* A short-lived radioactive element (symbol Md). [after D. I. *Mendeleyev,* 1834–1907, Russian chemist]

men·di·cant (men′də·kənt) *adj.* 1. Begging; depending on alms for a living. 2. Pertaining to or like a beggar. —*n.* 1. A beggar. 2. A begging friar. [< L *mendicus* needy] —**men′di·can·cy** *n.*

men·ha·den (men·hād′n) *n.* A fish of North Atlantic and West Indian waters, used as a source of oil, as fertilizer, and as bait. [Alter. of Algonquian *munnawhat* fertilizer]

me·ni·al (mē′nē·əl, mēn′yəl) *adj.* 1. Pertaining to or appropriate to servants. 2. Servile; abject. —*n.* 1. A domestic servant. 2. One who has a servile nature. [Ult. < L *mansio* house] —**me′ni·al·ly** *adv.*

me·nin·ges (mə·nin′jēz) *n. pl.* of **me·ninx** (mē′ningks) *Anat.* The three membranes enveloping the brain and spinal cord. [< Gk. *mēninx, mēningos* membrane] —**me·nin′ge·al** *adj.*

men·in·gi·tis (men′ən·jī′tis) *n. Pathol.* Inflammation of the meninges, esp. through infection.

me·nis·cus (mə·nis′kəs) *n. pl.* **·nis·cus·es** or **·nis·ci** (-nis′ī) 1. A crescent or crescent-shaped body. 2. *Optics* A lens concave on one side and convex on the other. 3. *Physics* The curved upper surface of a liquid column. [< Gk. *mēniskos* crescent, dim. of *mēnē* moon]

Men·non·ite (men′ən·īt) *n.* A member of a Protestant Christian sect founded in the 16th c. opposing the taking of oaths, the holding of public office, and military service. [after *Menno* Simons, 1492–1559, a leader of the sect]

Me·nom·i·nee (mə·nom′ə·nē) *n. pl.* **·nee** 1. One of a tribe of Algonquian Indians, inhabiting central Wisconsin. 2. The Algonquian language of this tribe. Also **Me·nom·i·ni** (-nē).

men·o·pause (men′ə·pôz) *n. Physiol.* The final cessation of menstruation, occurring normally between the ages of 45 and 50. [< Gk. *mēn* month + *pauein* to cause to cease]

Me·no·rah (mə·nôr′ə, -nō′rə) *n.* In Judaism, a candelabrum used in religious services. [< Hebrew, candlestick]

men·ses (men′sēz) *n.pl. Physiol.* Menstruation. [< L, pl. of *mensis* month]

men·stru·a·tion (men′stroo·ā′shən) *n. Physiol.* The periodic flow of bloody fluid from the uterus, occurring normally about every 28 days except during pregnancy: also called *menses.* —**men′stru·al** *adj.* —**men′·stru·ate** *v.i.* **·at·ed, ·at·ing**

men·su·ra·ble (men′shər·ə·bəl) *adj.* That can be measured. [< LL *mensurare* to measure] —**men′su·ra·bil′i·ty** *n.*

men·su·ra·tion (men′shə·rā′shən) *n.* 1. The art, act, or process of measuring. 2. The branch of mathematics having to do with determining length, area, and volume.

-ment *suffix of nouns* 1. The product or result of: *achievement.* 2. The instrument or means of: *atonement.* 3. The process or action of: *government.* 4. The quality, condition, or state of being: *astonishment.* [< L *-mentum*]

men·tal (men′təl) *adj.* 1. Of or pertaining to the mind or intellect. 2. Taking place in the mind: *mental* calculations. 3. Affected by mental illness: a *mental* patient. 4. For the care of the mentally ill: *mental* hospital. [< L *mens, mentis* mind] —**men′tal·ly** *adv.*

mental deficiency *Psychol.* Subnormal intelligence that prevents an individual from participating fully in ordinary life. Also called **mental retardation.**

men·tal·i·ty (men·tal′ə·tē) *n. pl.* **·ties** 1. The mental faculties or powers. 2. Intellectual capacity or power: an average *mentality.* 3. Cast or habit of mind.

men·thol (men′thôl, -thōl, -thol) *n. Chem.* A white, waxy, crystalline alcohol obtained from and having the odor of oil of peppermint, used as a flavoring agent, esp. in perfumery and medicine. [< L *mentha* mint] —**men′tho·lat′ed** (-thə·lā′tid) *adj.*

men·tion (men′shən) *v.t.* To refer to incidentally or briefly. —*n.* 1. The act of one who mentions. 2. Slight reference; casual allusion. [< L *mens, mentis* mind] —**men′tion·a·ble** *adj.*

men·tor (men′tər, -tôr) *n.* A wise and trusted teacher or guide. [after *Mentor,* a wise guardian in the *Odyssey*]

men·u (men′yoo, mān′-) *n.* 1. A list of dishes available or served at a meal. 2. The dishes included in it. [< F < L *minutus* small, detailed]

me·ow (mē·ou′, myou) *v.i.* To make the crying sound of a cat. [Imit.] —**me·ow′** *n.*

me·phit·ic (mə·fit′ik) *adj.* 1. Poisonous; foul. 2. Offensive to the sense of smell.

mer·can·tile (mûr′kən·til, -tīl) *adj.* Of, pertaining to, or characteristic of merchants or commerce. [< L *mercari* to traffic]

mer·ce·nar·y (mûr′sə·ner′ē) *adj.* 1. Influenced by a desire for gain or reward. 2. Serving for pay: said of soldiers hired by a foreign state. —*n. pl.* **·nar·ies** A hireling; esp., a hired soldier in foreign service. [< L *merces* reward, hire]

mer·cer·ize (mûr′sə·rīz) *v.t.* **·ized, ·iz·ing** To treat (cotton fabric) with caustic soda to make it strong, glossy, and easy to dye. [after John *Mercer,* 1791–1866, English inventor] —**mer′cer·i·za′tion** *n.*

mer·chan·dise (mûr′chən·dīz, -dīs) *n.* Anything bought and sold for profit; goods; wares. —*v.t. & v.i.* **·dised, ·dis·ing** 1. To buy and sell; trade. 2. To promote the sale of (goods) through advertising, etc. Also **mer′chan·dize.** [See MERCHANT.] —**mer′·chan·dis′er** *n.*

mer·chant (mûr′chənt) *n.* 1. One who buys and sells commodities for profit. 2. A storekeeper. —*adj.* 1. Of or pertaining to merchants or trade. 2. Of or pertaining to the merchant marine. [< L *mercari* to traffic, buy]

mer·chant·man (mûr′chənt·mən) *n. pl.* **·men** (-mən) A trading or merchant vessel.

merchant marine 1. The merchant or trading vessels of a nation, collectively. 2. The officers and men employed on these vessels.

mer·ci (mer·sē′) *interj. French* Thank you.

mer·ci·ful (mûr′sə·fəl) *adj.* Full of or characterized by mercy. —**mer′ci·ful·ly** *adv.* —**mer′ci·ful·ness** *n.*

mer·ci·less (mûr′sə·lis) *adj.* Having or showing no mercy; pitiless. —**mer′ci·less·ly** *adv.* —**mer′ci·less·ness** *n.*

mer·cu·ri·al (mər·kyoor′ē·əl) *adj.* 1. Lively; volatile; clever: a *mercurial* wit. 2. Of, containing, or caused by the action of mercury. —**mer·cu′ri·al·ly** *adv.* —**mer·cu′ri·al·ness** *n.*

mer·cu·ri·al·ize (mər·kyŏŏr′ē·əl·īz′) *v.t.* **·ized, ·iz·ing** 1. To make mercurial. 2. To treat with mercury. —**mer·cu′ri·al·i·za′tion** *n.*

mer·cu·ric (mər·kyŏŏr′ik) *adj. Chem.* Of, pertaining to, or containing mercury in its highest valence.

mer·cu·rous (mər·kyŏŏr′əs) *adj. Chem.* Of, pertaining to, or containing mercury in its lowest valence.

mer·cu·ry (mûr′kyə·rē) *n. pl.* **·ries** 1. A heavy, silver-white metallic element (symbol Hg), liquid at ordinary temperatures: also called *quicksilver*. 2. This element as used in a thermometer or barometer to indicate temperature, etc.

Mer·cu·ry (mûr′kyə·rē) *n.* The smallest planet of the solar system, and that nearest the sun. [< *Mercury*, messenger of the Roman gods]

mer·cy (mûr′sē) *n. pl.* **·cies** 1. Kind or compassionate treatment of an adversary, prisoner, etc., in one's power. 2. A disposition to be kind, forgiving, or helpful. 3. The power to show mercy or compassion. 4. A thing to be thankful for. —**at the mercy of** Wholly in the power of. [< L *merces, mercedis* payment, reward]

mercy killing Euthanasia.

mere (mir) *adj.* Being nothing more or less than: a *mere* trifle. [< L *merus* unmixed, bare] —**mere′ly** *adv.*

mer·e·tri·cious (mer′ə·trish′əs) *adj.* Artificially and vulgarly attractive. [< L *merere* to earn, gain] —**mer′e·tri′cious·ly** *adv.* —**mer′e·tri′cious·ness** *n.*

mer·gan·ser (mər·gan′sər) *n.* Any of several fish-eating ducks usu. having a crested head. [< L *mergere* to plunge + *anser* goose]

merge (mûrj) *v.t. & v.i.* **merged, merg·ing** To combine or be combined so as to lose separate identity; blend. [< L *mergere* to dip, immerse]

merg·er (mûr′jər) *n.* 1. The combining of two or more commercial interests into one. 2. The act of merging.

me·rid·i·an (mə·rid′ē·ən) *n.* 1. *Geog.* A great circle drawn from any point on the earth's surface and passing through both poles. 2. *Astron.* An analogous great circle on the celestial sphere. 3. The highest or culminating point; zenith. —*adj.* 1. Of or pertaining to a meridian. 2. Of or pertaining to midday. [< L < *medius* middle + *dies* day]

me·ringue (mə·rang′) *n.* Baked beaten egg whites and sugar, used as a topping for pies, or made into a small cake or tart shell. [< F < G *meringe*, lit., cake of Mehringen (in Germany)]

me·ri·no (mə·rē′nō) *n. pl.* **·nos** 1. A breed of sheep having fine, closely set, silky wool and heavy curled horns in the male; also, the wool of this sheep. 2. A fine fabric originally made of merino wool. —*adj.* Made of merino wool or cloth. [< Sp.]

mer·it (mer′it) *n.* 1. Worth or excellence; high quality. 2. That which deserves esteem, praise, or reward. 3. *Sometimes pl.* The quality or fact of being entitled to reward, praise, etc. 4. *pl.* The actual rights or wrongs of a matter, esp. a legal matter. —*v.t.* To earn as a reward or punishment; deserve. [< L *merere* to deserve]

mer·i·to·ri·ous (mer′ə·tôr′ē·əs) *adj.* Deserving of reward or praise. —**mer′i·to′ri·ous·ly** *adv.* —**mer′i·to′ri·ous·ness** *n.*

merle (mûrl) *n.* The European blackbird. Also **merl.** [< L *merula* blackbird]

mer·maid (mûr′mād′) *n.* A legendary marine creature having the head and upper body of a woman and the tail of a fish. [OE *mere* sea, lake + MAID]

-merous *suffix Zool.* Having (a specified number or kind of) parts. [< Gk. *meros* part, division]

mer·ri·ment (mer′i·mənt) *n.* Laughter; fun.

mer·ry (mer′ē) *adj.* **·ri·er, ·ri·est** 1. Full of mirth and laughter; joyous; gay. 2. Characterized by or conducive to mirth, cheerfulness, etc. [OE *myrige* pleasant] —**mer′ri·ly** *adv.*

mer·ry-an·drew (mer′ē·an′drōō) *n.* A clown or buffoon.

mer·ry-go-round (mer′ē·gō·round′) *n.* 1. A revolving platform fitted with wooden horses, seats, etc., on which people, esp. children ride for amusement; carousel. 2. A whirl, as of business or pleasure. Also, *Brit., roundabout.*

mer·ry·mak·ing (mer′ē·mā′king) *n.* The act of having fun and making merry. —*adj.* Festive. —**mer′ry·mak′er** *n.*

mes- Var. of MESO-.

me·sa (mā′sə, *Sp.* mā′sä) *n.* A high, flat tableland descending sharply to the surrounding plain, common in the SW U.S. [< Sp. < L *mensa* table]

mé·sal·li·ance (mā·zal′ē·əns, *Fr.* mā·zȧ·lyäṅs′) *n.* A marriage with one of inferior position; misalliance. [< F]

mes·cal (mes·kal′) *n.* 1. A spineless cactus, native to the SW U.S. and northern Mexico, whose dried tops, **mescal buttons,** are chewed by the Indians for their narcotic effect: also called *peyote*. 2. An intoxicating liquor distilled from certain species of agave. [< Sp. < Nahuatl *mexicalli*]

mes·ca·line (mes′kə·lēn, -lin) *n.* A hallucinogen extracted from mescal buttons.

mes·dames (mā·däm′, *Fr.* mā·dȧm′) Plural of MADAME.

mes·de·moi·selles (mād·mwȧ·zel′) *French* Plural of MADEMOISELLE.

mes·en·ter·y (mes′ən·ter′ē) *n. pl.* **·ter·ies** *Anat.* A membrane that connects an intestine with the posterior abdominal wall. Also **mes′en·te′ri·um** (-tir′ē·əm). [< Gk. *mesos* middle + *enteron* intestine] —**mes′en·ter′ic** *adj.*

mesh (mesh) *n.* 1. One of the open spaces between the cords of a net or the wires of a screen. 2. *pl.* The cords or wires bounding such a space or spaces. 3. A net or network. 4. *Mech.* The engagement of gear teeth. —*v.t. & v.i.* 1. To make or become entangled, as in a net. 2. To make or become engaged, as gear teeth. [< MDu. *maesche* mesh]

mesh·work (mesh′wûrk′) *n.* Meshes; network.

mes·mer·ism (mes′mə·riz′əm, mez′-) *n.* Loosely, hypnotism: also called *animal magnetism*. [after Franz Anton *Mesmer*, 1733–1815, German physician] —**mes·mer·ic** (mes·mer′ik, mez-) *adj.* —**mes′mer·ist** *n.*

mes·mer·ize (mes′mə·rīz, mez′-) *v.t.* **·ized, ·iz·ing** To hypnotize. Also *Brit.* **mes′mer·ise.** —**mes′mer·i·za′tion** *n.* —**mes′mer·iz′er** *n.*

meso- *combining form* 1. Situated in the middle. 2. Intermediate in size or degree. Also, before vowels, *mes-*. [< Gk. *mesos* middle]

mes·o·derm (mes′ə·dûrm, mē′sə-) *n.* The middle layer in the embryo of animals, developing into the skeletal and muscular systems.

mes·o·mor·phic (mes′ə·môr′fik, mē′sə-) *adj.* Of human body types, characterized by a sturdy, muscular body structure. —**mes′o·morph** *n.* —**mes′o·mor′phy** *n.*

mes·on (mē′son, mes′on) *n. Physics* Any of a group of unstable nucleons having a mass intermediate between that of the electron and the proton. [< Gk. *mesos* middle]

mes·quite (mes·kēt′, mes′kēt) *n.* A spiny, leguminous shrub of the SW U.S. and Mexico that yields sweet pods used for cattle fodder. [< Sp. < Nahuatl *mizquitl*]

mess (mes) *n.* 1. A state of disorder; esp., a condition of dirty or untidy confusion. 2. A confusing, difficult, or embarrassing situation or condition; muddle. 3. An unpleasant or confused mixture or collection; hodgepodge. 4. A quantity of food sufficient for a meal or dish. 5. A number of persons who regularly take their meals together, as in the military; also, a meal taken by them. —*v.i.* 1. To busy oneself; dabble: often with *around* or *about*. 2. To make a mess; bungle: often with *up*. 3. To eat as a member of a mess. —*v.t.* 4. To make a mess of; botch: often with *up*. 5. To make dirty: often with *up*. [< L *missus* course at a meal]

mes·sage (mes′ij) *n.* 1. A communication sent by any of various means. 2. A communication embodying important principles or counsel. [< Med.L *mittere* to send]

mes·sen·ger (mes′ən·jər) *n.* 1. One sent with a message or on an errand; esp., one whose work is running errands. 2. A bearer of official dispatches; courier. 3. *Archaic* A harbinger. [< OF *messagier*]

Mes·si·ah (mə·sī′ə) *n.* 1. In Judaism, a deliverer of Israel promised by God and expected by the Jews. 2. In Christianity, Jesus regarded as this deliverer. 3. Any expected liberator of a country, people, etc. [< Aramaic *mĕshīhā*, Hebrew *māshīah* anointed] —**Mes·si·an·ic** (mes′ē·an′ik) *adj.*

mes·sieurs (mes′ərz, *Fr.* mā·syœ′) *n.pl.* of *Fr.* MONSIEUR Sirs; gentlemen: in English in the contracted form *Messrs.*, used as plural of *Mr.*

mess kit A small, compact unit containing cooking and eating utensils, used by soldiers in the field and by campers.

mes·sy (mes′ē) *adj.* **mes·si·er, mes·si·est** Being in or causing a condition of dirt or confusion; untidy. —**mess′i·ly** *adv.* —**mess′i·ness** *n.*

mes·ti·zo (mes·tē′zō) *n. pl.* **·zos** or **·zoes** Anyone of mixed blood; in Mexico and the western U.S., a person of Spanish and Indian blood. [< Sp. < L *mixtus*, pp. of *miscere* to mix] —**mes·ti′za** (-zə) *n.fem.*

met (met) Past tense and past participle of MEET[1].

meta- *prefix* 1. Changed in place or form; reversed; altered: *metamorphosis*. 2. *Anat. & Zool.* Behind; after; on the farther side of; beyond: *metacarpus*. 3. Over; transcending: *metaphysics*. 4. *Chem.* a A modification of. b A derivative of. Also, before vowels and *h*, **met-**. [< Gk. *meta* after, beside, with]

me·tab·o·lism (mə·tab′ə·liz′əm) *n. Biol. & Physiol.* The aggregate of all chemical processes constantly taking place in a living organism, including those that use energy to convert nutritive materials into protoplasm and those that release energy for vital processes in breaking down protoplasm into simpler substances. [< Gk. *meta-* beyond + *ballein* to throw] —**met·a·bol·ic** (met′ə·bol′ik) *adj.* —**me·tab′o·lize** (-līz) *v.t. & v.i.* **·lized, ·liz·ing**

met·a·car·pus (met′ə·kär′pəs) *n. Anat.* The part of the hand between the wrist and the bones of the fingers. [< Gk. *meta-* beyond + *karpos* wrist] —**met′a·car′pal** *adj. & n.*

met·a·gal·ax·y (met′ə·gal′ək·sē) *n. pl.* **·ax·ies** *Astron.* The entire material universe, regarded esp. as a system including all the galaxies.

met·al (met′l) *n.* 1. Any of a class of elements characterized by a distinctive luster, malleability, ductility, and conductivity. 2. A composition of such metallic elements; alloy. 3. The constituent material of anything. [< Gk. *metallon*] —**me·tal·lic** (mə·tal′ik) *adj.*

met·al·lif·er·ous (met′ə·lif′ər·əs) *adj.* Yielding or containing metal.

met·al·lur·gy (met′ə·lûr′jē) *n.* 1. The science of extracting metal from ores. 2. The science of metals and alloys. [< Gk. *metallon* mine + *-ergos* working] —**met′al·lur′gi·cal** *adj.* —**met′al·lur′gist** *n.*

met·al·work (met′l·wûrk′) *n.* 1. Articles made of metal. 2. The art of making such things. —**met′al·work′er** *n.* —**met′al·work′ing** *n.*

met·a·mor·phism (met′ə·môr′fiz·əm) *n.* 1. *Geol.* The changes in the composition and texture of rocks caused by force, heat, pressure, moisture, etc. 2. Metamorphosis. —**met′a·mor′phic** *adj.*

met·a·mor·phose (met′ə·môr′fōz) *v.t.* **·phosed, ·phos·ing** 1. To change the form of. —*v.i.* 2. To undergo metamorphosis. Also **met′a·mor′phize.** [< MF *mētamorphoser*]

met·a·mor·pho·sis (met′ə·môr′fə·sis) *n. pl.* **·pho·ses** (-fə·sēz) 1. Change from one form, shape, or substance into another by any means. 2. Complete transformation of character, purpose, circumstances, etc. 3. One who or that which is metamorphosed. 4. *Biol.* Any marked change in the form and structure of an animal in its development from embryo to adult, as from tadpole to frog. [< Gk. *meta-* beyond + *morphē* form]

met·a·phor (met′ə·fôr, -fər) *n.* A figure of speech in which one object is likened to another by speaking of it as if it were that other, as *He was a lion in battle*: distinguished from *simile*. [< Gk. *meta-* beyond, over + *pherein* to carry] —**met′a·phor′i·cal** (-fôr′i·kəl, -for′i·kəl) or **met′a·phor′ic** *adj.* —**met′a·phor′i·cal·ly** *adv.*

met·a·phys·i·cal (met′ə·fiz′i·kəl) *adj.* 1. Of, pertaining to, or of the nature of metaphysics.

2. Highly abstruse; abstract. —**met′a·phys′i·cal·ly** *adv.*

met·a·phys·ics (met′ə·fiz′iks) *n.pl.* (*construed as sing.*) 1. The branch of philosophy that investigates ultimate principles of reality, esp. those principles not subject to empirical confirmation. 2. All speculative philosophy. [< Med.Gk. *ta meta ta physika* the (works) after the *Physics* of Aristotle]

me·tas·ta·sis (mə·tas′tə·sis) *n. pl.* **·ses** (-sēz) *Pathol.* 1. The transfer of a disease from one part of the body to another, as in certain types of cancer. 2. A site to which such a transfer has been made. [< Gk. *meta-* after + *histanai* to place] —**met·a·stat·ic** (met′ə·stat′ik) *adj.*

me·tas·ta·size (mə·tas′tə·sīz) *v.i.* **·sized, ·siz·ing** *Pathol.* To shift or spread from one part of the body to another, as a malignant growth.

met·a·tar·sus (met′ə·tär′səs) *n. pl.* **·si** (-sī) *Anat.* 1. In man, the part of the foot situated between the ankle and the bones of the toes. 2. An analogous part in the hind or pelvic limb of animals or birds. —**met′a·tar′sal** *adj. & n.*

me·tath·e·sis (mə·tath′ə·sis) *n. pl.* **·ses** (-sēz) The transposition of letters, syllables, or sounds in a word: Old English *bridd* became *bird* by *metathesis*. [< Gk. *meta-* over + *tithenai* to place] —**met·a·thet·ic** (met′ə·thet′ik) or **·i·cal** *adj.*

mete (mēt) *v.t.* **met·ed, met·ing** To allot or distribute by or as by measure: usu. followed by *out*. [OE *metan* to measure]

me·tem·psy·cho·sis (mə·temp′sə·kō′sis, met′əm·sī-) *n.* Transmigration of souls. [< Gk. *meta-* over + *empsychoein* to animate]

me·te·or (mē′tē·ər, -ôr) *n.* 1. *Astron.* A meteoroid that on entering the earth's atmosphere at great speed is heated to luminosity and is visible as a streak of light: also called *shooting star*. 2. Loosely, a meteorite or meteoroid. [< Gk. *meta-* beyond + *eōra* suspension]

me·te·or·ic (mē′tē·ôr′ik, -or′ik) *adj.* 1. Of, pertaining to, or consisting of meteors. 2. Resembling a meteor; brilliant, rapid, and dazzling: a *meteoric* career. —**me′te·or′i·cal·ly** *adv.*

me·te·or·ite (mē′tē·ə·rīt′) *n.* A portion of a meteor that has fallen to earth. —**me′te·or·it′ic** (-ə·rit′ik) *adj.*

me·te·or·oid (mē′tē·ə·roid′) *n. Astron.* One of the pieces of matter moving through outer space, that upon entering the earth's atmosphere form meteors.

me·te·or·ol·o·gy (mē′tē·ə·rol′ə·jē) *n.* The science that treats of atmospheric phenomena, esp. those that relate to weather. [< Gk. *meteōros* high in the air + -LOGY] —**me′te·or′o·log′i·cal** (-ôr′ə·loj′i·kəl) *adj.* —**me′te·or′o·log′i·cal·ly** *adv.* —**me′te·or·ol′o·gist** *n.*

me·ter[1] (mē′tər) *n.* An instrument or device used to measure or indicate variation in amount. —*v.t.* To measure or test by means of a meter. [< METE]

me·ter[2] (mē′tər) *n.* 1. A measured rhythm constituting one of the chief characteristics of verse. 2. *Music* The combining of rhythmic pulses into successive groups having like arrangement and duration. Also, *esp. Brit.*, *metre*. [< Gk. *metron* a measure]

me·ter[3] (mē′tər) *n.* The basic unit of length in the metric system, equivalent to 39.37 inches. Also *metre*. [< F *mètre* < Gk. *metron*]

-meter *combining form* 1. A device for measuring (a specified quality, thing, etc.). 2. Division into (a specified number of) prosodic feet: *pentameter*. 3. A (specified kind of) unit in the metric system: *kilometer*: also, *esp. Brit.*, *-metre*.

me·ter-kil·o·gram-sec·ond (mē′tər·kil′ə·gram′sek′ənd) *adj.* See MKS.

meth- *combining form Chem.* Used to indicate the presence of a methyl group in a compound. Also, before consonants, **metho-**. [< METHYL]

meth·a·done (meth′ə·dōn) *n.* A synthetic narcotic drug used as a substitute in the treatment of heroin addiction. [< (6-DI)-METH(YL)A(MINO-4,4-)D(IPHENYL-3-HEPTAN)ONE]

meth·ane (meth′ān) *n. Chem.* A colorless, odorless, flammable gas, the first member of the methane series, that is the chief constituent of firedamp and marsh gas and is obtained commercially from natural gas.

methane series *Chem.* A group of saturated hydrocarbons having the general formula C_nH_{2n+2}.

me·than·o·gen (mə·than′ə·jən, meth′ən-) *n.* An anaerobic organism that uses carbon dioxide in the air to produce methane, and is one of the earliest forms of life.

meth·a·nol (meth′ə·nōl, -nol) *n. Chem.* A colorless, flammable, highly toxic alcohol obtained by the destructive distillation of wood and widely used in industry and the arts. Also called *methyl alcohol, wood alcohol*.

meth·od (meth′əd) *n.* 1. A manner of proceeding; esp., a regular, systematic, or orderly way of doing anything. 2. System, order, or regularity in action or thought. 3. The techniques used in a particular field of knowledge, thought, practice, etc.: the scientific *method*. [< Gk. *meta-* after + *hodos* way]

me·thod·i·cal (mə·thod′i·kəl) *adj.* 1. Arranged in or performed in systematic order. 2. Orderly or systematic in habits, behavior, etc.: a *methodical* man. —**me·thod′i·cal·ly** *adv.*

Meth·od·ist (meth′əd·ist) *n.* A member of any of the Protestant denominations having their origin in a religious movement begun in England in the 18th c. by John and Charles Wesley and their followers. —**Meth′od·ism** *n.* —**Meth′od·ist** *adj.*

meth·od·ize (meth′ə·dīz) *v.t.* **·ized, ·iz·ing** To reduce to or arrange in accordance with a method; systematize.

meth·od·ol·o·gy (meth′ə·dol′ə·jē) *n. pl.* **·gies** 1. The principles, practices, etc., of orderly thought or procedure applied to a particular branch of learning. 2. The branch of logic dealing with such procedures. —**meth·od·o·log·i·cal** (meth′əd·ə·loj′i·kəl) *adj.* —**meth′od·o·log′i·cal·ly** *adv.* —**meth′·od·ol′o·gist** *n.*

meth·yl (meth′əl) *n. Chem.* An organic radical containing one atom of carbon and three atoms of hydrogen. [< Gk. *methy* wine

+ *hylē* wood] **—me·thyl·ic** (mə·thil′ik) *adj.*
methyl alcohol *Chem.* Methanol.
me·tic·u·lous (mə·tik′yə·ləs) *adj.* Extremely precise about details, esp. in minor or trivial matters. [< L *meticulosus* fearful] **—me·tic′u·lous·ly** *adv.* **—me·tic′u·lous·ness** *n.*
mé·tier (mā·tyā′) *n.* 1. One's occupation, trade, or profession. 2. Work or activity for which one is especially well suited. [< OF *mestier*]
metr- Var. of METRO-.
me·tre[1] (mē′tər) See METER[2].
me·tre[2] (mē′tər) See METER[3].
-metre See -METER (def. 3).
met·ric (met′rik) *adj.* Of, pertaining to, or using the meter as a unit of measurement. [< F *métrique*]
met·ri·cal (met′ri·kəl) *adj.* 1. Of, pertaining to, or characterized by meter; rhythmic. 2. Composed in or constituting a unit of poetic meter. 3. Of, pertaining to, or involving measurement. Also **met′ric.** **—met′ri·cal·ly** *adv.*
met·ri·cize (met′rə·sīz) *v.t.* **·cized, ·ciz·ing** To convert into the metric system. **—met·ri·ca·tion** (met′ri·kā′shən) *n.*
metric system A decimal system of weights and measures having as fundamental units the gram, the meter, and the liter.
metric ton A unit of weight equal to 1,000 kilograms, or 2,204.62 pounds avoirdupois.
met·ro (met′rō) *n.* *Often cap.* *Informal* A subway; esp., the subway system of Paris. Also **mé·tro** (mā·trō′). [< F *métro* < (*chemin de fer*) *métro*(*politain*) metro(politan railroad)]
metro- *combining form* Measure. Also, before vowels, *metr-*. [< Gk. *metron*]
met·ro·nome (met′rə·nōm) *n.* An instrument for indicating exact tempo in music, usu. producing audible clicks controlled by a reversed pendulum whose motion is regulated by a sliding weight. [< METRO- + Gk. *nomos* law] **—met′ro·nom′ic** (-nom′ik) *adj.*
me·tro·nym·ic (mē′trə·nim′ik, met′rə-) *adj.* Derived from the name of one's mother or a female ancestor. **—***n.* A metronymic name or designation. [< Gk. *mētēr* mother + *onyma* name]
me·trop·o·lis (mə·trop′ə·lis) *n.* *pl.* **·lis·es** 1. The capital or the largest or most important city of a country, state, or area. 2. An urban center of activity, culture, trade, etc. [< Gk. *mētēr* mother + *polis* city] **—met·ro·pol·i·tan** (met′rə·pol′ə·tən) *adj.* *& n.*
-metry *combining form* The process, science, or art of measuring: *geometry*. [< Gk. *metron* a measure]
met·tle (met′l) *n.* 1. Character or temperament. 2. Courage; pluck. **—on one's mettle** Aroused to one's best efforts. [Var. of METAL]
met·tle·some (met′l·səm) *adj.* Full of spirit; courageous; valiant.
mew[1] (myōō) *n.* 1. A cage in which molting hawks are kept. 2. *pl.* Stables built around a court or alley. 3. *pl.* (*construed as sing.*) *Chiefly Brit.* A narrow street or alley, often with dwellings converted from stables. **—***v.t.* To confine in or as in a cage; often with *up.* [< OF *muer* to change, molt]
mew[2] (myōō) *n.* The high-pitched, plaintive cry of a cat. [Imit.] **—mew** *v.i.*
mewl (myōōl) *v.i.* To whimper or cry feebly, as an infant. [Freq. of MEW[2]] **—mewl** *n.*
Mex·i·can (mek′sə·kən) *n.* 1. A native or inhabitant of Mexico. 2. A language indigenous to Mexico, as Nahuatl. **—Mex′i·can** *adj.*
mez·za·nine (mez′ə·nēn, -nin) *n.* 1. An intermediate story, usu. not of full width, between two main floors. 2. In a theater, the first balcony, or the front rows of the balcony. [< Ital. *mezzanino*]
mez·zo (met′sō, med′zō, mez′ō) *Music* *adj.* Half; medium; moderate: often used in combination: *mezzo-soprano*. **—***adv.* Moderately: *mezzo* forte. **—***n.* *pl.* **·zos** A mezzo-soprano. [< Ital.]
mez·zo-so·pran·o (met′sō·sə·pran′ō, -prä′nō, med′zō-, mez′ō-) *n.* *pl.* **·pran·os** 1. A female voice intermediate between a soprano and a contralto. 2. A person having such a voice. **—***adj.* Of or pertaining to such a voice. [< Ital.]
mez·zo·tint (met′sō·tint′, med′zō-, mez′ō-) *n.* 1. A method of engraving in which the roughened surface of a copper or steel plate is scraped or burnished to produce effects of light and shade. 2. A print produced from such a plate. [< Ital. *mezzo* middle + *tinto* painted] **—mez′zo·tint′er** *n.*
mi (mē) *n.* *Music* The third tone of the diatonic scale in solmization.
Mi·am·i (mī·am′ē, -am′ə) *n.* *pl.* **Mi·am·i** or **Mi·am·is** A member of a tribe of Algonquian Indians formerly inhabiting a region in Wisconsin, Indiana, and Ohio. [< N.Am.Ind.]
mi·as·ma (mī·az′mə, mē-) *n.* *pl.* **·mas** or **·ma·ta** (-mə·tə) 1. Noxious or unwholesome influence, etc. 2. The poisonous effluvium once supposed to rise from swamps, etc. Also **mi′asm** (-az·əm). [< Gk. *miainein* to stain, defile] **—mi·as′mic** *adj.*
mi·ca (mī′kə) *n.* Any of a class of silicate minerals, cleaving into tough, thin, often transparent and flexible layers: sometimes called *isinglass*. [< L, crumb] **—mi·ca·ceous** (mī·kā′shəs) *adj.*
Mi·cah (mī′kə) *n.* A book of the Old Testament. Also, in the Douai Bible, **Mi·che·as** (mī·kē′əs). [after *Micah*, 8th c. B.C. Hebrew prophet]
mice (mīs) Plural of MOUSE.
Mic·mac (mik′mak) *n.* *pl.* **·mac** or **·macs** A member of an Algonquian tribe living in Nova Scotia, New Brunswick, and Newfoundland. [< N.Am.Ind., lit., allies]
mi·cra (mī′krə) Plural of MICRON.
micro- *combining form* 1. Very small; minute: **microcrack, microexplosion, microparticle, micrometeorite, microworld.** 2. Of a science involving a microscope: **microbiology, micromechanics, microphysiology.** 3. One millionth of a specified unit: **microangstrom, microfarad, microhm, microwatt.** Before vowels, **micr-**. [< Gk. *mikros* small]
mi·crobe (mī′krōb) *n.* A microscopic organism; esp., one of the bacteria that cause disease. [< Gk. *mikros* small + *bios* life] **—mi·cro′bi·al, mi·cro′bic** *adj.*
mi·cro·cop·y (mī′krə·kop′ē) *n.* *pl.* **·cop·ies** A reduced photographic copy of a letter,

manuscript, etc. —**mi′cro·cop′y** *v.t. & v.i.* **·cop·ied, ·cop·y·ing**
mi·cro·cosm (mī′krə·koz′əm) *n.* 1. A little world; the universe in miniature. 2. Man regarded as epitomizing the universe. Also **mi′cro·cos′mos** (-koz′məs). [< Gk. *mikros cosmos*, lit., little world] —**mi′cro·cos′mic** *adj.*
mi·cro·e·lec·tron·ics (mī′krō·i·lek′tron′iks) *n.* The science dealing with miniaturized electronic circuits. —**mi′cro·e·lec′tron′ic** *adj.*
mi·cro·en·cap·su·la·tion (mī′krō·in·kap′sə·lā′shən, -syōō-) *n.* The process of forming minute portions, esp. of drugs, in tiny capsules designed for controlled release of the contents. —**mi′cro·en·cap′su·late** *v.t.* **·lat·ed, ·lat·ing** —**mi′cro·cap′sule** *n.*
mi·cro·fiche (mī′krə·fēsh′) *n. pl.* **·fiche** or **·fich·es** A sheet of microfilm containing rows of microcopy. Also *fiche.* [< MICRO- + F *fiche* card]
mi·cro·film (mī′krə·film) *n.* A photographic reproduction on film of a printed page, document, etc., highly reduced for ease in transmission and storage. —**mi′cro·film** *v.t. & v.i.*
mi·cro·gram (mī′krə·gram) *n.* In the metric system, one millionth of a gram. Also *Brit.* **mi′cro·gramme.**
mi·cro·groove (mī′krə·grōōv) *n.* 1. An extremely fine groove cut in the surface of a long-playing phonograph record. 2. *cap.* A long-playing record: a trade name.
mi·crom·e·ter (mī·krom′ə·tər) *n.* An instrument used for measuring very small distances or dimensions, as in conjunction with a microscope or telescope.
mi·crom·e·try (mī·krom′ə·trē) *n.* Measurement by means of a micrometer. —**mi·cro·met·ric** (mī′krō·met′rik) or **·ri·cal** *adj.*
mi·cron (mī′kron) *n. pl.* **·cra** (-krə) A unit of measurement equal to one thousandth of a millimeter. [< Gk. *mikros* small]
Mi·cro·ne·sian (mī′krə·nē′zhən, -shən) *n.* 1. A native of Micronesia. 2. Any of the Austronesian languages spoken in Micronesia. —**Mi′cro·ne′sian** *adj.*
mi·cro·or·gan·ism (mī′krō·ôr′gən·iz′əm) *n.* Any organism, as a bacterium or protozoan, too small to be seen without magnification. Also **mi′cro-or′gan·ism.**
mi·cro·phone (mī′krə·fōn) *n.* A device for converting sound waves into electric currents, forming the principal element of a telephone transmitter or of any sound-reproducing system, as in broadcasting. —**mi′cro·phon′ic** (-fon′ik) *adj.*
mi·cro·pho·to·graph (mī′krō·fō′tə·graf) *n.* 1. A very small or microscopic photograph, as on microfilm. 2. Loosely, a photomicrograph. —**mi′cro·pho′to·graph′ic** *adj.* —**mi′·cro·pho·tog′ra·phy** (-fə·tog′rə·fē) *n.*
mi·cro·scope (mī′krə·skōp) *n.* An optical instrument used for magnifying objects too small to be seen or clearly observed by ordinary vision. [< NL *microscopium* < MICRO- + -SCOPE]
mi·cro·scop·ic (mī′krə·skop′ik) *adj.* 1. So minute as to be visible only under a microscope. 2. Exceedingly small. 3. Of, pertaining to, or of the nature of a microscope or microscopy. —**mi′cro·scop′i·cal·ly** *adv.*
mi·cros·co·py (mī·kros′kə·pē) *n.* 1. The process or technique of using the microscope. 2. Investigation by means of the microscope. —**mi·cros′co·pist** *n.*
mi·cro·tome (mī′krə·tōm) *n.* An instrument for cutting very thin sections of organic tissue, etc., for microscopic observations. —**mi′cro·tom′ic** (-tom′ik) or **·i·cal** *adj.*
mi·cro·wave (mī′krə·wāv) *n.* An electromagnetic wave having a frequency between about 1,000 and 30,000 megahertz.
mic·tu·rate (mik′chə·rāt) *v.i.* **·rat·ed, ·rat·ing** To urinate. [< L *micturire* to desire to urinate] —**mic′tu·ri′tion** (-rish′ən) *n.*
mid[1] (mid) *adj.* Being approximately in the middle; central. [OE *midd-*]
mid[2] (mid) *prep. Chiefly Poetic* Amid; among. Also **'mid.**
mid- *combining form* Middle or middle part of: **midafternoon, mid-Atlantic, mid-century, midmonthly, midpoint, midposition.**
mid·air (mid′âr′) *n.* A point or region seemingly in the middle or midst of the air. Also **mid′-air′.**
mid·day (mid′dā′) *n.* The middle of the day; noon. —**mid′day′** *adj.*
mid·den (mid′n) *n. Brit. Dial.* A dunghill or heap of refuse. [ME *midding* < Scand.]
mid·dle (mid′l) *adj.* 1. Equally distant from the extremes, periphery, etc.; central. 2. Intermediate in position, status, etc. 3. Intervening between the earlier part and the latter part of a sequence, period of time, etc. 4. *Usu. cap.* Designating a language in a stage between an earlier and a recent form: *Middle* English. —*n.* 1. The area or point equally distant from the extremes, etc. 2. The intermediate section of anything. 3. The middle part of the body; the waist. [OE *middel*]
middle age The time of life between youth and old age, usu. thought of as the years between 40 and 60. —**mid′dle-aged′** (mid′l·ājd′) *adj.*
Middle Ages The period in European history between classical antiquity and the Renaissance, usu. regarded as extending from the downfall of Rome, in 476, to about 1450.
Middle America The conservative American middle class.
middle class The part of a society occupying a social or economic position between the laboring class and the very wealthy or the nobility. —**mid′dle-class′** *adj.*
middle ear *Anat.* The portion of the ear between the tympanic membrane and the opening of the Eustachian tube; also, the membrane itself: also called *tympanum.*
Middle East 1. The region including Egypt and the countries of SW Asia west of Pakistan. 2. Near East.
Middle English See under ENGLISH.
Middle French See under FRENCH.
Middle Latin See under LATIN.
mid·dle·man (mid′l·man′) *n. pl.* **·men** (-men′) 1. One who acts as an agent; go-between. 2. One who buys in bulk from producers and sells to retailers or consumers.
middle management The supervisors, low-ranking executives, etc. of a corporation or institution.
mid·dle·most (mid′l·mōst′) *adj.* Situated exactly or most nearly in the middle: also *midmost.*

middle of the road A moderate position or course. —**mid·dle-of-the-road** (mid′l·əv·thə·rōd′) *adj.* —**mid′dle-of-the-road′er** *n.*

mid·dle·weight (mid′l·wāt′) *n.* 1. A person or animal of average weight. 2. A boxer or wrestler weighing between 147 and 160 pounds.

mid·dling (mid′ling) *adj.* 1. Of middle size, quality, or condition. 2. Commonplace; mediocre. 3. *Informal* In fair health. —*adv.* *Informal* Fairly; moderately.

mid·dy (mid′ē) *n.* *pl.* **·dies** *Informal* A midshipman.

middy blouse A loosely fitting blouse with a sailor collar.

midge (mij) *n.* 1. A gnat or small fly. 2. An extremely small person or creature. [OE *mycge*]

midg·et (mij′it) *n.* 1. A person of abnormally small size but of normal physical proportions. 2. Anything very small of its kind. —*adj.* Very small; diminutive.

mid·land (mid′lənd) *n.* The central or interior part of a country or region. —**mid′·land** *adj.*

Mid·land (mid′lənd) *n.* The dialects of Middle English spoken in London and the Midlands; esp., **East Midland,** the direct predecessor of Modern English.

mid·most (mid′mōst′) *adj.* Middlemost. —*adv.* In the midst or middle. [OE *mydmest*]

mid·night (mid′nīt′) *n.* Twelve o'clock at night. —*adj.* 1. Of or occurring at midnight. 2. Resembling midnight; very dark. —**to burn the midnight oil** To work or study late into the night.

midnight sun The sun visible at midnight during summer at latitudes greater than 70° north or south of the equator.

mid·riff (mid′rif) *n.* The part of the body between the chest and the abdomen, in the region of the diaphragm; also, the diaphragm itself. [OE *midd* mid + *hrif* belly]

mid·ship (mid′ship′) *adj.* *Naut.* Of, pertaining to, or situated in the middle of a ship.

mid·ship·man (mid′ship′mən) *n.* *pl.* **·men** (-mən) In the U.S. Navy, a student training to be commissioned as an officer. [< *amidshipman*; so called from being amidships when on duty]

mid·ships (mid′ships′) *adv.* *Naut.* Amidships.

midst (midst) *n.* 1. The condition of being surrounded, as by people or things, or beset, as by troubles: used chiefly in the phrase **in the midst of.** 2. The central part; middle. —**in our (your, their) midst** Among us (you, them). —*prep.* Amid. [ME *middest*]

mid·sum·mer (mid′sum′ər) *n.* The middle of summer.

mid·term (mid′tûrm′) *n.* 1. The middle of a term. 2. An examination given in the middle of a school term.

mid·way (mid′wā′; *for adj. and adv., also* mid′wā′) *adv.* In the middle of the way or distance. —*adj.* Being in the middle of the way or distance. —*n.* At a fair, exposition, etc., the area where amusements, side shows, or exhibitions are situated. [OE *midweg*]

mid·week (mid′wēk′) *n.* The middle of the week.

mid·wife (mid′wīf′) *n.* *pl.* **·wives** (-wīvz′) A woman who assists women in childbirth. [OE *mid* with + *wīf* woman] —**mid′wife′ry** *n.*

mid·win·ter (mid′win′tər) *n.* The middle of winter.

mid·year (mid′yir′) *n.* 1. The middle of the year. 2. An examination given in the middle of a school year.

mien (mēn) *n.* Manner, bearing, expression, etc. [? Var. of DEMEAN]

miff (mif) *v.t.* *Informal* To cause to be offended or annoyed.

mig (mig) *n.* *Dial.* 1. A marble. 2. *pl.* The game of marbles. Also **mig·gle** (mig′əl).

might[1] (mīt) Past tense of MAY.

might[2] (mīt) *n.* 1. Power to dominate; force; strength. 2. Physical strength. —**with (all one's) might and main** With (all one's) strength or ability. [OE *miht*]

might·y (mī′tē) *adj.* **might·i·er, might·i·est** 1. Possessed of might; powerful. 2. Of great size, importance, etc. —*adv.* *Informal* Very; exceedingly. —**might′i·ly** (mī′tə·lē) *adv.* —**might′i·ness** *n.*

mi·gnon·ette (min′yən·et′) *n.* A plant having small, fragrant, yellowish green flowers. [< F]

mi·graine (mī′grān) *n.* A type of severe, recurrent headache, usu. in one side of the head. [< Gk. *hēmi* half + *kranion* skull]

mi·grant (mī′grənt) *adj.* Migrating. —*n.* One who or that which migrates, as a bird or animal, an itinerant worker, etc.

mi·grate (mī′grāt) *v.i.* **·grat·ed, ·grat·ing** 1. To move from one country, region, etc., to settle in another. 2. To move seasonally from one region or climate to another, as birds or fish. [< L *migrare* to roam, wander] —**mi′gra·tor** *n.*

mi·gra·tion (mī·grā′shən) *n.* 1. An act or instance of migrating. 2. Those participating in a single instance of migrating. —**mi′gra·to′ry** (-grə·tôr′ē) *adj.*

mi·ka·do (mi·kä′dō) *n.* *pl.* **·dos** An emperor of Japan. [< Japanese *mi* august + *kado* door]

mike (mīk) *n.* *Informal* A microphone.

mil (mil) *n.* 1. A unit of length equal to one thousandth of an inch or .0254 millimeter. 2. *Mil.* **a** A unit of angular measure equal to 1/6400 of a circle, or about 0.0560 degree. **b** A unit of angular measure equal to 0.001 radian. [< L *mille* thousand]

mi·la·dy (mi·lā′dē) *n.* *pl.* **·dies** 1. An English noblewoman or gentlewoman. 2. A fashionable woman. [< F < E *my lady*]

milch (milch) *adj.* Giving milk, as a cow. [OE *-milc*]

mild (mīld) *adj.* 1. Kind or amiable in disposition or manners. 2. Gentle or moderate: *mild* words; *mild* weather. 3. Not intense or strong: a *mild* flavor. [OE *milde*] —**mild′ly** *adv.* —**mild′ness** *n.*

mil·dew (mil′do͞o, -dyo͞o) *n.* 1. A disease of plants usu. caused by a parasitic fungus that deposits a whitish or discolored coating. 2. Any of the fungi causing such a disease. —*v.t. & v.i.* To affect or be affected with mildew. [OE *meledēaw* honeydew] —**mil′·dew·y** *adj.*

mile (mīl) *n.* A measure of distance used in the U.S. and other English-speaking countries, equal to 5,280 feet or 1.609 kilometers: also called *statute mile.* —**geographical, nautical, or air mile** One sixtieth of a degree of the earth's equator; 6,080.2 feet or

1,853.24 meters. **—international nautical mile** A unit of distance by sea equal to 1,852 meters or 6,076.103 feet. [< L *mille (passuum)* thousand (paces)]

mile·age (mī′lij) *n.* 1. Total length or distance expressed in miles. 2. Number of miles a vehicle can travel for each gallon of fuel used. 3. Period or extent of usefulness. 4. A traveling allowance estimated at a fixed amount per mile. Also **mil′age.**

mile·post (mīl′pōst′) *n.* A post or similar marker indicating distance in miles, as along a highway.

mil·er (mī′lər) *n.* A runner, racehorse, etc., trained to compete in mile races.

mile·stone (mīl′stōn′) *n.* 1. A milepost. 2. An important event or turning point.

mi·lieu (mē·lyœ′) *n.* Environment; surroundings. [< F < OF *mi* middle + *lieu* place]

mil·i·tant (mil′ə·tənt) *adj.* 1. Combative or warlike; aggressive. 2. Engaged in conflict; fighting. **—***n.* One who is militant. [< L *militare* to be a soldier] **—mil′i·tan·cy** *n.* **—mil′i·tant·ly** *adv.*

mil·i·ta·rism (mil′ə·tə·riz′əm) *n.* 1. The ideals characteristic of a military class; emphasis on martial qualities. 2. A national policy that promotes a powerful military position. **—mil′i·ta·rist** *n.* **—mil′i·ta·ris′tic** *adj.*

mil·i·ta·rize (mil′ə·tə·rīz′) *v.t.* **·rized, ·riz·ing** 1. To convert to a military system or adapt for military purposes. 2. To prepare for warfare. **—mil′i·ta·ri·za′tion** *n.*

mil·i·tar·y (mil′ə·ter′ē) *adj.* 1. Of or pertaining to the armed forces. 2. Of or characteristic of warfare. 3. Characteristic of or befitting a soldier. **—***n.* Soldiers collectively; armed forces: preceded by *the.* [< L *miles, militis* soldier] **—mil′i·tar′i·ly** *adv.*

military police Soldiers who perform police duty.

mil·i·tate (mil′ə·tāt) *v.i.* **·tat·ed, ·tat·ing** To have influence or effect: usu. with *against.* [< L *miles, militis* soldier]

mi·li·tia (mə·lish′ə) *n.* A body of citizens enrolled and drilled in military organizations other than the regular military forces, and called out only in emergencies. [< L, military service]

mi·li·tia·man (mə·lish′ə·mən) *n. pl.* **·men** (-mən) A member of the militia.

milk (milk) *n.* 1. The opaque, whitish liquid secreted by the mammary glands of female mammals for the nourishment of their young. 2. Any of various liquids resembling this, as the sap of certain plants or the liquid contained in a coconut. **—***v.t.* 1. To draw or express milk from the mammary glands of. 2. To draw or extract something from: to *milk* someone of information. 3. To exploit; take advantage of: to *milk* a client. **—***v.i.* 4. To milk a cow, cows, etc. [OE *meolc, milc*] **—milk′er** *n.* **—milk′i·ness** *n.* **—milk′y** *adv.* **milk·i·er, milk·i·est**

milk·maid (milk′mād′) *n.* A woman or girl who milks cows or works in a dairy.

milk·man (milk′man′) *n. pl.* **·men** (-men′) A man who sells or delivers milk.

milk of magnesia A white, aqueous suspension of a magnesium compound, used as a laxative and antacid.

milk·weed (milk′wēd′) *n.* Any of various herbs, shrubs, and vines having milky juice.

Milky Way A luminous band visible across the night sky, composed of distant stars and nebulae not separately distinguishable to the naked eye: also called the *Galaxy.*

mill[1] (mil) *n.* 1. A machine that grinds, crushes, shapes, cuts, etc. 2. A machine or building in which grain is ground. 3. Any of various machines that process materials: used in combination: *sawmill; windmill.* 4. A manufacturing or industrial establishment; factory. 5. A trying experience; ordeal: used chiefly in the phrase **through the mill.** **—***v.t.* 1. To grind, roll, shape, polish, etc., in or with a mill. 2. To raise, indent, or ridge the edge of (a coin, etc.). **—***v.i.* 3. To move with a circular or surging motion, as cattle. [OE *mylen* < L *mola* millstone]

mill[2] (mil) *n.* One tenth of a cent. [< L *mille* thousand]

mill·dam (mil′dam′) *n.* A dam constructed across a watercourse to raise its level sufficiently to turn a mill wheel.

mil·len·ni·um (mi·len′ē·əm) *n. pl.* **·ni·a** or **·ni·ums** 1. A period of a thousand years. 2. *Theol.* The thousand years during which Christ is to rule the world. 3. Any period of happiness, prosperity, etc. [< NL *mille* thousand + *annus* year] **—mil·len′ni·al** *adj.*

mill·er (mil′ər) *n.* 1. One who operates or tends a mill. 2. A milling machine. 3. Any of various moths having pale, dusty wings.

mil·let (mil′it) *n.* 1. A grass cultivated for forage and for its small, edible seeds. 2. The seed of these grasses. [< F, dim. of *mil* < L *milium*]

milli- *combining form* One thousandth of a specified unit: **milliampere, milliangstrom, millidegree, milliroentgen, milliwatt, millivolt.**

mil·li·gram (mil′ə·gram) *n.* A unit of weight in the metric system, equal to one thousandth of a gram. Also *Brit.* **mil′li·gramme.**

mil·li·li·ter (mil′ə·lē′tər) *n.* A unit of capacity in the metric system, equal to one thousandth of a liter. Also *Brit.* **mil′li·li′tre.**

mil·li·me·ter (mil′ə·mē′tər) *n.* A unit of length in the metric system, equal to one thousandth of a meter. Also *Brit.* **mil′li·me′tre.**

mil·li·ner (mil′ə·nər) *n.* One who makes or sells women's hats. [< *Milaner,* a dealer in woman's clothes imported from Milan, Italy]

mil·li·ner·y (mil′ə·ner′ē) *n.* 1. The articles made or sold by milliners. 2. The business of a milliner.

mil·lion (mil′yən) *n.* 1. A thousand thousands, written as 1,000,000: a cardinal number. 2. An indefinitely great number. [< Ital. *millione* < *mille* thousand] **—mil′·lion** *adj.* **—mil′lionth** *n. & adj.*

mil·lion·aire (mil′yən·âr′) *n.* One whose wealth is valued at a million or more, as of dollars, pounds, etc. Also **mil′lion·naire′.** [< F *millionnaire*]

mil·li·pede (mil′ə·pēd) *n.* Any of various wormlike animals having a rounded body divided into numerous segments, each bearing two pairs of legs. Also **mil′li·ped** (-ped). [< L *mille* thousand + *pes, pedis* foot]

mill·pond (mil′pond′) *n.* A body of water dammed up to supply power for running a mill.

mill·race (mil′rās′) *n.* 1. The current of water that operates a mill wheel. 2. The channel in which it runs.
mill·stone (mil′stōn′) *n.* 1. One of a pair of thick, heavy, stone disks used for grinding grain, etc. 2. A heavy or burdensome weight.
mill·stream (mil′strēm′) *n.* 1. A stream whose current is used to operate a mill. 2. The water in a millrace.
mill wheel A water wheel that drives a mill.
mill·work (mil′wûrk′) *n.* Objects or material finished or processed in a mill; esp., woodwork ready for use.
mill·wright (mil′rīt′) *n.* One who plans, builds, or repairs mills or mill machinery.
mi·lord (mi·lôrd′) *n.* An English nobleman or gentleman. [< F < E *my lord*]
milque·toast (milk′tōst′) *n.* A timid, meek, or very apologetic person. [after Caspar *Milquetoast,* a creation by H. T. Webster, U.S. cartoonist]
milt (milt) *n.* 1. Fish sperm. 2. The reproductive organs of a male fish when filled with seminal fluid. [OE *milte*]
mime (mīm) *n.* 1. An actor, comedian, etc., who specializes in pantomime. 2. A performance by a mime or mimes. —*v.* **mimed, mim·ing** *v.i.* 1. To play a part with gestures and usu. without words. —*v.t.* 2. To portray by pantomime. [< Gk. *mimos*] —**mim′er** *n.*
mim·e·o·graph (mim′ē·ə·graf′) *n.* A duplicating device that reproduces copies of written matter, etc., by means of a stencil wrapped around a drum: also **Mim′e·o·graph′.** —*v.t. & v.i.* To reproduce by mimeograph. [< *Mimeograph,* a trade name]
mi·met·ic (mi·met′ik, mī-) *adj.* 1. Tending to imitate or mimic; imitative. 2. Pertaining to or like mimicry. [< Gk. *mimēsis* imitation] —**mi·met′i·cal·ly** *adv.*
mim·ic (mim′ik) *v.t.* **·icked, ·ick·ing** 1. To imitate the speech or actions of. 2. To copy closely; ape. —*n.* One who mimics or imitates. [< Gk. *mimos* mime] —**mim′ick·er** *n.*
mim·ic·ry (mim′ik·rē) *n. pl.* **·ries** 1. The act, practice, or art of mimicking. 2. *Biol.* A resemblance of an organism to another or to its environment, for purposes of concealment, etc.
mi·mo·sa (mi·mō′sə, -zə) *n.* Any of a group of leguminous tropical herbs, shrubs, or trees with feathery foliage, and small, often yellow, flowers. [< L *mimus* mime]
min·a·ret (min′ə·ret′) *n.* A high, slender tower attached to a Muslim mosque and surrounded by balconies, from which a muezzin calls the summons to prayer. [< Arabic *manārah* lamp, lighthouse]
min·a·to·ry (min′ə·tôr′ē) *adj.* Conveying or expressing a threat. [< LL *minari* to threaten]
mince (mins) *v.* **minced, minc·ing** *v.t.* 1. To cut or chop into small bits, as food. 2. To moderate the force or strength of (language, ideas, etc.): He didn't *mince* words with her. —*v.i.* 3. To walk with short steps or affected daintiness. [< L *minuere* to lessen, make smaller] —**minc′er** *n.*
mince·meat (mins′mēt′) *n.* A mixture of chopped apples, raisins, spices, and often meat, used as a pie filling.
mince pie A pie filled with mincemeat.
minc·ing (min′sing) *adj.* Affectedly precise, refined, or dainty, as in manner, gait, etc. —**minc′ing·ly** *adv.*
mind (mīnd) *n.* 1. The aggregate of processes originating in or associated with the brain, involving thought, interpretation of perceptions, imagination, etc. 2. Memory: within the *mind* of man. 3. Opinion; sentiment: to change one's *mind.* 4. Desire; inclination: to have a *mind* to leave. 5. Way or state of thinking or feeling: a logical *mind.* 6. Intellectual power or capacity: He has the *mind* for such work. 7. Attention: to keep one's *mind* on a subject. —**out of one's mind** 1. Insane; mad. 2. Distracted; frantic. —**to be of one mind** To be in accord; agree. —**to blow one's mind** 1. To experience drug-induced hallucinations. 2. To excite or stimulate. —**to have a good mind** To feel strongly disposed (to do something). —**to make up one's mind** To decide; be determined. —*v.t.* 1. To pay attention to. 2. To be careful concerning: *Mind* your step. 3. To obey: *Mind* your leaders. 4. To look after; tend. 5. To object to: Do you *mind* the noise? —*v.i.* 6. To pay attention; heed: *Mind* you now, not a word. 7. To be obedient. 8. To be concerned; care; object: I don't *mind.* [OE *gemynd*] —**mind′er** *n.*
mind·blow·ing (mīnd′blō′ing) *adj.* 1. Hallucinogenic. 2. Exciting and stimulating. —**mind′blow′er** *n.*
mind·bog·gling (mīnd′bog′ling) *adj.* Amazing or overwhelming.
mind·ed (mīn′did) *adj.* 1. Having or characterized by a (specified kind of) mind: used in combination: *evil-minded.* 2. Having an inclination; disposed: often with *to.*
mind·ful (mīnd′fəl) *adj.* Keeping in mind; aware. —**mind′ful·ly** *adv.* —**mind′ful·ness** *n.*
mind·less (mīnd′lis) *adj.* 1. Devoid of intelligence; senseless. 2. Not giving heed or attention; careless. —**mind′less·ly** *adv.* —**mind′less·ness** *n.*
mind-set (mīnd′set′) *n.* Prevailing attitudes or opinions; intellectual climate.
mine[1] (mīn) *n.* 1. An excavation in the earth dug to obtain coal, precious stones, etc. 2. The site of such an excavation, together with its buildings, equipment, etc. 3. Any deposit of ore, coal, etc. 4. Any source or abundant store of something: a *mine* of talent. 5. *Mil.* An explosive charge placed in the earth or water and designed to be actuated by contact, a time fuse, or remote control. —*v.* **mined, min·ing** *v.t.* 1. To dig (coal, ores, etc.) from the earth. 2. To dig into (the earth, etc.) for coal, ores, etc. 3. To obtain useful material or information from. 4. To place an explosive mine in or under. —*v.i.* 5. To dig in a mine for coal, ores, etc. 6. To place explosive mines. [< OF] —**min′er** *n.*
mine[2] (mīn) *pron.* 1. The possessive case of the pronoun *I,* used predicatively: That book is *mine.* 2. The one relating to me: His work is better than *mine.* —**of mine** Belonging or relating to me; my. —*pronominal adj. Archaic* My: formerly used before a vowel or *h*: *mine* eyes. [OE *mīn*]
mine·field (mīn′fēld′) *n.* An area in which explosive mines have been placed.
mine·lay·er (mīn′lā′ər) *n.* A vessel provided with special equipment for laying explosive mines.

min·er·al (min′ər·əl) *n.* 1. A naturally occurring crystalline element or compound. 2. Inorganic material, esp. as distinguished from animal or vegetable matter. 3. Ore. [< Med.L *mineralis* of a mine] —**min′er·al** *adj.*

mi·ner·al·ize (min′ər·əl·īz′) *v.t.* **·ized, ·iz·ing** 1. To convert (a metal) to a mineral. 2. To convert to a mineral substance; petrify. 3. To impregnate with minerals. —**min′er·al·i·za′tion** *n.*

mineral kingdom The division of nature including all inorganic and nonliving materials, as rocks, metals, minerals, etc.

min·er·al·o·gy (min′ə·rol′ə·jē, -ral′-) *n. pl.* **·gies** 1. The science of minerals, embracing their origin, structure, characteristics, properties, and classification. 2. A treatise on minerals. —**min′er·a·log′i·cal** (-ər·ə·loj′i·kəl) *adj.* —**min′er·al′o·gist** *n.*

mineral oil Any of various oils, esp. petroleum, derived from minerals and used as fuel, in medicine, etc.

mineral water Any water impregnated with mineral salts or gases.

min·e·stro·ne (min′ə·strō′nē) *n.* A thick vegetable soup having a meat stock. [< Ital.]

mine·sweep·er (mīn′swē′pər) *n.* A ship equipped to detect, destroy, and remove marine mines.

min·gle (ming′gəl) *v.* **·gled, ·gling** *v.t.* 1. To mix together; blend. —*v.i.* 2. To be or become mixed, or closely joined. 3. To mix or associate, as with a crowd. [OE *mengan*] —**min′gler** *n.*

mini- *combining form* Small: **minibus, minicar, minicomputer, ministate.** [< L *minimus* least]

min·i·a·ture (min′ē·ə·chər, min′ə·chər) *n.* 1. A representation of anything on a small scale. 2. Reduced dimensions, form, or extent. 3. A painting done on a very small scale. —*adj.* Being on a very small or reduced scale. [< L *miniare* to color red]

min·i·a·tur·ize (min′ē·ə·chər·īz′, min′ə·chər·īz′) *v.t.* **·ized, ·iz·ing** To reduce the size of. —**min′i·a·tur′i·za′tion** *n.*

min·i·bike (min′ē·bīk′) *n.* A small motorcycle.

min·im (min′im) *n.* 1. A small liquid measure, 1/60 of a fluid dram, or about one drop. 2. *Music* A half note. 3. One who or that which is very small or insignificant. [< L *minimus* least, smallest]

min·i·mal (min′ə·məl) *adj.* Of a minimum amount, degree, etc.; least possible. —**min′i·mal·ly** *adv.*

min·i·max (min′ē·maks′) *n.* In the game theory, a strategy that minimizes the greatest loss to which a player is liable. [< MINI(MUM) + MAX(IMUM)] —**min′i·max′** *adj.*

min·i·mize (min′ə·mīz) *v.t.* **·mized, ·miz·ing** 1. To reduce to the smallest amount or degree. 2. To regard or represent as of the least possible importance, size, etc. Also *Brit.* **min′i·mise.** —**min′i·miz′er** *n.*

min·i·mum (min′ə·məm) *n. pl.* **·mums** or **·ma** 1. The least possible quantity, amount, or degree. 2. The lowest quantity, degree, number, etc., reached or recorded. [< L *minimus* smallest] —**min′i·mum** *adj.*

minimum wage The smallest wage, fixed by law or by agreement, that an employer may offer an employee.

min·ing (mī′ning) *n.* The act, process, or business of extracting coal, ores, etc., from mines.

min·ion (min′yən) *n.* A servile favorite or follower. [< F *mignon* darling]

min·i·skirt (min′ē·skûrt) *n.* A very short skirt.

min·is·ter (min′is·tər) *n.* 1. One who is authorized to preach, administer the sacraments, etc., in a church; clergyman; pastor. 2. One appointed to head an administrative department of a government. 3. A diplomat ranking next below an ambassador. 4. One who or that which acts as the agent of another. —*v.i.* 1. To provide for the wants or needs of someone. 2. To be helpful or useful. —*v.t.* 3. To administer or apply (a sacrament, medicine, etc.). [< L, attendant] —**min·is·te·ri·al** (min′is·tir′ē·əl) *adj.* —**min′is·trant** *n.* & *adj.*

min·is·tra·tion (min′is·trā′shən) *n.* 1. The act of serving. 2. *Often pl.* Help or aid. —**min′is·tra′tive** *adj.*

min·is·try (min′is·trē) *n. pl.* **·tries** 1. The profession, duties, length of service, etc., of a minister of religion. 2. The clergy. 3. *Govt.* **a** An executive or administrative department presided over by a minister; also, its building. **b** A body of ministers collectively. 4. The act of ministering.

min·i·ver (min′ə·vər) *n.* 1. A white or gray and white fur, used in the Middle Ages as trimming, etc. 2. Any white fur, as ermine. [< OF *menu vair*, lit., little spotted (fur)]

mink (mingk) *n.* 1. A semiaquatic, slender-bodied carnivorous mammal, resembling a weasel. 2. The valuable soft brown fur of this mammal. [< Scand.]

min·ne·sing·er (min′ə·sing′ər) *n.* A lyric poet and singer of medieval Germany. [< G *minne* love + *singer* singer]

min·now (min′ō) *n. pl.* **min·nows** (*Rare* **min·now**) 1. A small European fish of the carp family. 2. Any small fish. [ME *menawe*]

Mi·no·an (mi·nō′ən) *adj.* Of an advanced civilization that flourished in Crete from about 3000 to 1100 B.C.

mi·nor (mī′nər) *adj.* 1. Less in quantity, number, or extent. 2. Of secondary or lesser importance: a *minor* poet. 3. Under legal age. 4. *Music* **a** Denoting an interval smaller by a half step than the corresponding major interval. **b** Denoting a triad in which the third above the fundamental is minor. **c** Denoting a type of diatonic scale, or a key based on this scale. 5. In education, of or pertaining to an area of specialized study usu. requiring fewer class hours than a major field of study. —*n.* 1. One who is below full legal age. 2. In education, a minor subject or area of study. —*v.i.* In education, to study as a minor subject: with *in.* [< L]

mi·nor·i·ty (mə·nôr′ə·tē, -nor′-, mī-) *n. pl.* **·ties** 1. The smaller in number of two parts or groups. 2. A racial, religious, political, or national group smaller than and usu. different in some ways from the larger group. 3. The state or period of being under legal age. [< F *minorité* or L *minoritas*]

minor league Any professional sports league

not having the standing of a major league. —**mi·nor-league** (mī′nər·lēg′) *adj.*

min·ster (min′stər) *n. Chiefly Brit.* 1. A monastery church. 2. A cathedral or large church. [OE *mynster*]

min·strel (min′strəl) *n.* 1. In the Middle Ages, a wandering musician who made his living by singing and reciting poetry. 2. A performer in a minstrel show. 3. *Poetic* A poet, musician, etc. [< LL *ministerialis* servant, jester] —**min′strel·sy** *n.*

minstrel show A comic variety show of songs, dances, jokes, etc., given by a company of performers in blackface.

mint[1] (mint) *n.* 1. A place where the coin of a country is lawfully manufactured. 2. An abundant supply, esp. of money. —*v.t.* 1. To make (money) by stamping; to coin. 2. To invent or fabricate (a word, etc.). —*adj.* In original condition; unused. [< L *Moneta,* epithet of the goddess Juno, whose temple at Rome was used as a mint] —**mint′·age** *n.* —**mint′er** *n.*

mint[2] (mint) *n.* 1. Any of several aromatic herbs; esp. spearmint and peppermint, used as a flavoring, garnish, etc. 2. A mint-flavored candy. [< Gk. *mintha*]

mint julep A drink made of bourbon, crushed ice, sugar, and sprigs of fresh mint.

min·u·end (min′yo͞o·end) *n. Math.* The number from which another is to be subtracted. [< L *minuere* to lessen]

min·u·et (min′yo͞o·et′) *n.* 1. A stately dance for couples, introduced in France in the 17th c. 2. Music for or in the manner of this dance. [< L *minutus* small]

mi·nus (mī′nəs) *prep.* 1. Lessened or reduced by; less. 2. *Informal* Lacking; deprived of. —*adj.* 1. Of or denoting subtraction. 2. Negative: a *minus* value. —*n.* 1. The minus sign. 2. A minus quantity. 3. A deficit or loss. [< L, neut. of *minor* less]

mi·nus·cule (min′ə·skyo͞ol, mi·nus′kyo͞ol) *n.* Any small or lower-case letter. —*adj.* 1. Of, pertaining to, like, or composed of minuscules. 2. Very small; miniature or minimal. [< L *minusculus,* dim. of *minor* less]

minus sign A sign (−) denoting subtraction or a negative quantity.

min·ute[1] (min′it) *n.* 1. The sixtieth part of an hour; 60 seconds. 2. Any very brief period of time; moment. 3. A specific instant of time. 4. A unit of angular measure equal to the sixtieth part of a degree, indicated by the minute sign (′): also called **minute of arc.** 5. *pl.* An official record of the business discussed and transacted at a meeting, conference, etc. —*v.t.* **·ut·ed, ·ut·ing** 1. To make a brief note of; record. 2. To time to the minute. [< L *minutus* small]

mi·nute[2] (mī·no͞ot′, -nyo͞ot′, mi-) *adj.* 1. Exceedingly small; tiny. 2. Having little importance or value. 3. Demonstrating or characterized by careful, precise attention to small details. [< L *minutus* small] —**mi·nute′ly** *adv.* —**mi·nute′ness** *n.*

min·ute hand (min′it) The hand that indicates the minute on a clock or similar timepiece.

min·ute·man (min′it·man′) *n. pl.* **·men** (-men′) In the American Revolution, one of the armed citizens who volunteered to be ready for combat at a minute's notice.

mi·nu·ti·ae (mi·no͞o′shi·ē, -nyo͞o′-) *n.pl. of* **mi·nu·ti·a** (-shē·ə, -shə) Small or unimportant details; trifles. [< L]

minx (mingks) *n.* A saucy, bold, or flirtatious girl. [Prob. < LG *minsk* impudent woman]

mir·a·cle (mir′ə·kəl) *n.* 1. An event that is not explained by any known natural law and is attributed to a supernatural source. 2. Any wonderful or amazing thing, fact, or event. [< L *mirari* to wonder] —**mi·rac·u·lous** (mi·rak′yə·ləs) *adj.* —**mi·rac′u·lous·ly** *adv.*

mi·rage (mi·räzh′) *n.* 1. An optical illusion caused by reflection of light through the atmosphere. 2. Anything that appears to be real but is not. [< L *mirari* to wonder at]

mire (mīr) *n.* 1. An area of wet, yielding earth; swampy ground. 2. Deep mud or slush. —*v.* **mired, mir·ing** *v.t.* 1. To cause to sink or become stuck in mire. 2. To soil with mud; defile. 3. To entangle or entrap. —*v.i.* 4. To sink in mire; bog down. [< ON *mȳrr* swampy ground] —**mir′i·ness** *n.* —**mir′y** *adj.*

mir·ror (mir′ər) *n.* 1. Any smooth reflecting surface, as of glass backed with a coating of silver, aluminum, etc. 2. Whatever reflects or depicts truly. —*v.t.* To reflect or show an image of. [< L *mirari* to wonder at, admire]

mirth (mûrth) *n.* Spirited gaiety; social merriment. [OE *myrig* pleasant, merry] —**mirth′ful** *adj.* —**mirth′ful·ly** *adv.* —**mirth′·ful·ness** *n.*

mis-[1] *prefix* Bad; badly; wrong; wrongly; unfavorably. [OE *mis-* wrong] Some self-explanatory words beginning with *mis-*:

misact	**misclass**
misadd	**miscopy**
misaddress	**misfile**
misalphabetize	**mishear**
misbelief	**mislabel**
misbill	**mis-see**
mischarge	**misteach**
miscite	**mistranslate**

mis-[2] *prefix* Bad; amiss; not: found with negative or depreciatory force in words borrowed from Old French: *misadventure, miscreant.* [< OF *mes-* < L *minus* less]

mis-[3] Var. of MISO-.

mis·ad·ven·ture (mis′əd·ven′chər) *n.* A mishap.

mis·al·li·ance (mis′ə·lī′əns) *n.* An undesirable alliance or marriage. [< F *mésalliance*]

mis·an·thrope (mis′ən·thrōp, miz′-) *n.* One who hates or distrusts his fellow men. [< Gk. *misein* to hate + *anthrōpos* man] —**mis·an·throp·ic** (mis′ən·throp′ik) *adj.* —**mis′an·throp′i·cal·ly** *adv.* —**mis·an·thro·py** (mis·an′thrə·pē) *n.*

mis·ap·ply (mis′ə·plī′) *v.t.* **·plied, ·ply·ing** To use or apply incorrectly or wrongfully. —**mis·ap·pli·ca·tion** (mis′ap·li·kā′shən) *n.*

mis·ap·pre·hend (mis′ap·ri·hend′) *v.t.* To apprehend or interpret wrongly. —**mis′ap·pre·hen′sion** (-hen′shən) *n.*

mis·ap·pro·pri·ate (mis′ə·prō′prē·āt) *v.t.* **·at·ed, ·at·ing** To use or take improperly or dishonestly; misapply. —**mis′ap·pro′pri·a′·tion** *n.*

mis·be·have (mis′bi·hāv′) *v.i.* **·haved, ·hav·ing** To behave badly. —**mis′be·hav′ior** (-hāv′yər) *n.*

mis·be·lieve (mis′bi·lēv′) *v.i.* **·lieved, ·liev·ing** To hold a false, unorthodox, or heretical belief. —**mis′be·liev′er** *n.*

mis·cal·cu·late (mis·kal′kyə·lāt) *v.t. & v.i.* **·lat·ed, ·lat·ing** To calculate wrongly. —**mis′cal·cu·la′tion** *n.*

mis·call (mis·kôl′) *v.t.* To call by a wrong name.

mis·car·ry (mis·kar′ē) *v.i.* **·ried, ·ry·ing** 1. To fail; go wrong. 2. To bring forth a nonviable fetus prematurely. —**mis·car′riage** (-ij) *n.*

mis·cast (mis·kast′) *v.t.* **·cast, ·cast·ing** To cast (a play or an actor) inappropriately.

mis·ce·ge·na·tion (mis′i·jə·nā′shən) *n.* Interbreeding of ethnic stocks or races. [< L *miscere* to mix + *genus* race] —**mis′ce·ge·net′ic** (-jə·net′ik) *adj.*

mis·cel·la·ne·ous (mis′ə·lā′nē·əs) *adj.* 1. Composed of various and diverse things or elements; mixed. 2. Possessing diverse qualities or capabilities. [< L *miscellus* mixed] —**mis′cel·la′ne·ous·ly** *adv.*

mis·cel·la·ny (mis′ə·lā′nē) *n. pl.* **·nies** A miscellaneous collection, esp. of literary works.

mis·chance (mis·chans′) *n.* Bad luck; also, an instance of bad luck; mishap.

mis·chief (mis′chif) *n.* 1. Action, often playful, that causes some irritation, harm, or trouble. 2. The disposition to annoy, tease, or disturb. 3. Harm or injury: High winds can cause great *mischief.* 4. A source of damage, evil, etc. [< OF *meschever* to come to grief]

mis·chie·vous (mis′chi·vəs) *adj.* 1. Inclined to mischief. 2. Troubling, harmful, or annoying. 3. Having a playful, teasing nature. —**mis′chie·vous·ly** *adv.* —**mis′chie·vous·ness** *n.*

mis·ci·ble (mis′i·bəl) *adj.* Capable of being mixed. [< L *miscere* to mix] —**mis′ci·bil′i·ty** *n.*

mis·con·ceive (mis′kən·sēv′) *v.t. & v.i.* **·ceived, ·ceiv·ing** To conceive wrongly; misunderstand. —**mis′con·cep′tion** (-sep′·shən) *n.*

mis·con·duct (mis·kon′dukt) *n.* 1. Improper or immoral behavior. 2. Unlawful conduct.

mis·con·strue (mis′kən·stro͞o′) *v.t.* **·strued, ·stru·ing** 1. To interpret wrongly; misunderstand. 2. *Gram.* To construe incorrectly. —**mis′con·struc′tion** (-struk′shən) *n.*

mis·count (*v.* mis·kount′; *n.* mis′kount) *v.t. & v.i.* To count incorrectly; miscalculate. —*n.* An incorrect count or reckoning.

mis·cre·ant (mis′krē·ənt) *n.* An unscrupulous wretch; evildoer. —*adj.* Villainous; vile. [< OF *mes-* mis-[2] + *croire* to believe]

mis·cue (mis·kyo͞o′) *n. Informal* An error; slip-up. —*v.i.* **·cued, ·cu·ing** To make a miscue.

mis·deal (mis·dēl′) *v.t. & v.i.* **·dealt** (-delt′), **·deal·ing** In card games, to deal incorrectly or improperly. —*n.* An incorrect deal. —**mis·deal′er** *n.*

mis·deed (mis·dēd′) *n.* A wrong or immoral act.

mis·de·mean·or (mis′di·mē′nər) *n. Law* Any offense less serious than a felony, or for which the punishment is less severe.

mis·di·rect (mis′di·rekt′, -dī·rekt′) *v.t.* To direct or guide wrongly, as a letter, person, etc. —**mis′di·rec′tion** *n.*

mis·em·ploy (mis′im·ploi′) *v.t.* To put to a wrong or improper use. —**mis′em·ploy′ment** *n.*

mi·ser (mī′zər) *n.* One who saves or hoards avariciously, often sacrificing his own comfort. [< L, wretched] —**mi′ser·li·ness** *n.* —**mi′ser·ly** *adj.*

mis·er·a·ble (miz′ər·ə·bəl, miz′rə-) *adj.* 1. Being in a state of misery, poverty, or wretched unhappiness. 2. Causing misery or extreme discomfort: a *miserable* headache. 3. Proceeding from or exhibiting misery: a *miserable* life. 4. Meager, skimpy, or worthless. 5. Disreputable; shameful: a *miserable* scoundrel. [< L *miserari* to pity] —**mis′er·a·ble·ness** *n.* —**mis′er·a·bly** *adv.*

mis·er·y (miz′ər·ē) *n. pl.* **·er·ies** 1. A condition of great wretchedness or suffering, as caused by poverty, pain, etc. 2. Intense mental or emotional anguish; extreme unhappiness. 3. A cause or source of suffering or unhappiness. [< L *miser* wretched]

mis·fea·sance (mis·fē′zəns) *n. Law* The performance of a lawful act in an unlawful or culpable manner. [< OF *mes-* mis-[2] + *faire* to do] —**mis·fea′sor** *n.*

mis·fire (mis·fīr′) *v.i.* **·fired, ·fir·ing** 1. To fail to fire, ignite, or explode at the desired time, as a firearm, internal-combustion engine, etc. 2. To fail in achieving the proper or desired effect. —**mis′fire** *n.*

mis·fit (mis′fit′) *n.* 1. Something that fits badly. 2. One who is not well adjusted to his environment. 3. The act or condition of fitting badly.

mis·for·tune (mis·fôr′chən) *n.* 1. Adverse or ill fortune; bad luck. 2. A calamity; mishap.

mis·giv·ing (mis·giv′ing) *n.* A feeling of doubt, distrust, or apprehension.

mis·gov·ern (mis·guv′ərn) *v.t.* To govern badly; administer improperly. —**mis·gov′·ern·ment** *n.*

mis·guide (mis·gīd′) *v.t.* **·guid·ed, ·guid·ing** To guide wrongly; mislead. —**mis·guid′ance** *n.* —**mis·guid′er** *n.*

mis·guid·ed (mis·gī′did) *adj.* Guided or led wrongly in thought or action. —**mis·guid′·ed·ly** *adv.*

mis·han·dle (mis·han′dəl) *v.t.* **·dled, ·dling** To handle, treat, or manage badly; abuse.

mis·hap (mis′hap) *n.* An unfortunate accident.

mish·mash (mish′mash′, -mosh′) *n.* A confused mixture or collection of things; hodgepodge. Also **mish′-mash.**

mis·in·form (mis′in·fôrm′) *v.t.* To give false or erroneous information to. —**mis′in·for·ma′tion** (-fər·mā′shən) *n.*

mis·in·ter·pret (mis′in·tûr′prit) *v.t.* To interpret or understand incorrectly. —**mis′·in·ter′pre·ta′tion** *n.*

mis·judge (mis·juj′) *v.t. & v.i.* **·judged, ·judg·ing** To judge wrongly or unfairly. —**mis·judg′ment** *n.*

mis·lay (mis·lā′) *v.t.* **·laid, ·lay·ing** To put or lay in a place not remembered.

mis·lead (mis·lēd′) *v.t.* **·led** (-led′), **·lead·ing** 1. To guide or lead in the wrong direction. 2. To lead into error, as of judgment or conduct. —**mis·lead′ing** *adj.* —**mis·lead′·ing·ly** *adv.*

mis·man·age (mis·man′ij) *v.t.* **·aged, ·ag·ing** To manage badly or improperly. —**mis·man′age·ment** *n.* —**mis·man′ag·er** *n.*

mis·match (mis·mach′) *v.t.* To match badly or inappropriately, as in marriage. —**mis′·match** *n.*

mis·mate (mis·māt′) *v.t.* & *v.i.* **·mat·ed, ·mat·ing** To mate unsuitably.

mis·name (mis·nām′) *v.t.* **·named, ·nam·ing** To call by a wrong name.

mis·no·mer (mis·nō′mər) *n.* 1. A name wrongly applied to someone or something. 2. The act of misnaming, esp. in a legal document. [< OF *mes-* wrongly + *nomer* to name]

miso- *combining form* Hating; hatred. Also, before vowels, *mis-*. [< Gk. *misein* to hate]

mis·og·a·my (mis·og′ə·mē) *n.* Hatred of marriage. —**mis·og′a·mist** *n.*

mis·og·y·ny (mis·oj′ə·nē) *n.* Hatred of women. [< Gk. *misein* to hate + *gynē* woman] —**mis·og′y·nist** *n.* —**mis·og′y·nous** *adj.*

mis·place (mis·plās′) *v.t.* **·placed, ·plac·ing** 1. To put in a wrong place. 2. To put (confidence, faith, trust, etc.) in an unworthy or unsuitable person, thing, or idea. 3. To mislay. —**mis·place′ment** *n.*

mis·play (mis·plā′; *for n., also* mis′plā) *v.t.* & *v.i.* In games, to play badly or incorrectly. —*n.* A bad play or move.

mis·print (mis·print′) *v.t.* To print incorrectly. —**mis′print** *n.*

mis·pro·nounce (mis′prə·nouns′) *v.t.* & *v.i.* **·nounced, ·nounc·ing** To pronounce incorrectly or in an unorthodox manner. —**mis·pro·nun·ci·a·tion** (mis′prə·nun′sē·ā′·shən) *n.*

mis·quote (mis·kwōt′) *v.t.* & *v.i.* **·quot·ed, ·quot·ing** To quote incorrectly. —**mis′quo·ta′tion** *n.*

mis·read (mis·rēd′) *v.t.* **·read** (-red′), **·read·ing** To read incorrectly or with the wrong sense; misinterpret.

mis·rep·re·sent (mis′rep·ri·zent′) *v.t.* To give an incorrect or false representation of. —**mis′rep·re·sen·ta′tion** *n.* —**mis′rep·re·sent′er** *n.*

mis·rule (mis·ro͞ol′) *v.t.* **·ruled, ·rul·ing** To rule unwisely or unjustly; misgovern. —*n.* 1. Bad or unjust rule or government. 2. Disorder or confusion, as from lawlessness.

miss[1] (mis) *v.t.* 1. To fail to hit, reach, or land upon (a specified object). 2. To fail to meet or catch, as a train. 3. To fail to obtain, accomplish, or achieve: to *miss* the presidency by a few votes. 4. To fail to see, hear, perceive, etc. 5. To fail to attend, keep, perform, etc. 6. To discover the absence of, usu. belatedly: to *miss* one's wallet. 7. To feel the loss or absence of. —*v.i.* 8. To fail to hit; strike wide of the mark. 9. To be unsuccessful; fail. —*n.* A failure to hit, find, succeed, etc. [OE *missan*]

miss[2] (mis) *n.* 1. *Often cap.* A title used in speaking to a woman or girl: used without name. 2. A young girl. 3. *cap.* A title of address used before the name of a girl or unmarried woman. [Contr. of MISTRESS]

mis·sal (mis′əl) *n.* 1. A book containing all the prayers, responses, etc., for celebrating Mass throughout the year. 2. Loosely, any prayer book. [< Med.L *missalis (liber)* mass (book)]

mis·shape (mis·shāp′) *v.t.* **·shaped, ·shaped** or **·shap·en, ·shap·ing** To shape badly; deform. —**mis·shap′en** *adj.*

mis·sile (mis′əl, *Brit.* mis′īl) *n.* 1. An object, esp. a weapon, intended to be thrown or discharged, as a bullet, arrow, etc. 2. A guided missile. [< L < *missus*, pp. of *mittere* to send] —**mis′sile·ry** *n.*

miss·ing (mis′ing) *adj.* 1. Not present; absent; lacking. 2. *Mil.* Absent: said of one whose whereabouts or fate in battle has not been determined: also **missing in action.**

mis·sion (mish′ən) *n.* 1. Any body of persons sent to perform a specific work or service; esp., such a body sent to a foreign country to conduct business, negotiations, etc., on behalf of its own country. 2. The specific task that a person or body of persons is assigned to do. 3. A group of missionaries. 4. The place or establishment where missionaries carry on their work. 5. The permanent foreign office of an ambassador or envoy; embassy. 6. The particular work or goal that one is or feels destined to do or accomplish; a calling. [< L *missus*, pp. of *mittere* to send]

mis·sion·ar·y (mish′ən·er′ē) *n. pl.* **·ar·ies** 1. A person sent to propagate religion or to do educational or charitable work in some foreign country or region. 2. One who advocates or spreads any new system or doctrine. —**mis′·sion·ar′y** *adj.*

mis·sis (mis′əz) *n. Informal & Dial.* 1. A wife: often with *the*. 2. The female head of a household: with *the*. Also **mis′sus.** [Alter. of MISTRESS]

mis·sive (mis′iv) *n.* A letter, esp. one of an official nature. [< L *missus*, pp. of *mittere* to send]

Mis·sou·ri (mi·zo͝or′ē, -zo͝or′ə) *n. pl.* **·ri** One of a tribe of Siouan Indians, formerly inhabiting northern Missouri.

mis·spell (mis·spel′) *v.t.* & *v.i.* **·spelled** or **·spelt, ·spell·ing** To spell incorrectly.

mis·spell·ing (mis·spel′ing) *n.* An incorrect spelling.

mis·spend (mis·spend′) *v.t.* **·spent, ·spend·ing** To spend wrongfully or wastefully.

mis·state (mis·stāt′) *v.t.* **·stat·ed, ·stat·ing** To state wrongly or falsely. —**mis·state′ment** *n.*

mis·step (mis′step′) *n.* 1. A false step; a stumble. 2. An error or blunder, as in conduct.

mist (mist) *n.* 1. An aggregation of fine drops of water suspended in the atmosphere at or near the earth's surface. 2. *Meteorol.* A very thin fog with a horizontal visibility arbitrarily set at not more than two kilometers. 3. A film or haze before the eyes that blurs one's vision. —*v.i.* 1. To be or become dim or misty; blur. 2. To rain in very fine drops. —*v.t.* 3. To make dim or misty. [OE]

mis·take (mis·tāk′) *n.* An error or fault in action, judgment, perception, understanding, etc. —*v.t.* **·took, ·tak·en, ·tak·ing** 1. To understand wrongly; acquire a wrong conception of. 2. To take (a person or thing) to be another. [< ON *mistaka*] —**mis·tak′a·ble** *adj.* —**mis·tak′a·bly** *adv.*

mis·tak·en (mis·tā′kən) *adj.* 1. Based on or arising from error, as of judgment, understanding, perception, etc. 2. Wrong in opinion, action, etc. —**mis·tak′en·ly** *adv.*

mis·ter (mis′tər) *n.* 1. *Informal* Sir: used

without the name. 2. *cap.* Master: a title of address prefixed to the name and to some official titles of a man: commonly written *Mr.* [Var. of MASTER]

mis·time (mis·tīm′) *v.t.* **·timed, ·tim·ing** 1. To time wrongly or inappropriately. 2. To misjudge the time of.

mis·tle·toe (mis′əl·tō) *n.* A parasitic shrub having yellowish green leaves and white berries, used as a Christmas decoration. [OE *misteltān* mistletoe twig]

mis·took (mis·to͝ok′) Past tense of MISTAKE.

mis·tral (mis′trəl, *Fr.* mēs·träl′) *n.* A cold, dry, violent northerly wind blowing through Southern France and adjacent areas. [< Provençal, lit., master wind]

mis·treat (mis·trēt′) *v.t.* To treat badly or improperly. **—mis·treat′ment** *n.*

mis·tress (mis′tris) *n.* 1. A woman in a position of authority or control; as: **a** The head of a household, institution, or estate. **b** The head of a staff of servants. 2. A woman who has a sexual relationship with a man to whom she is not married, usu. over an extended period of time. 3. A woman who has mastered a skill, craft, or branch of learning. 4. *Chiefly Brit.* A female schoolteacher. 5. *cap.* Formerly, a title of address applied to women. [< OF *maistresse*, fem. of *maistre* master]

mis·tri·al (mis·trī′əl) *n. Law* 1. A trial made void because of legal errors or defects. 2. A trial terminated by the jury's inability to agree on a verdict.

mis·trust (mis·trust′) *v.t.* To regard (someone or something) with suspicion or doubt; be skeptical of. **—***n.* Lack of trust or confidence. **—mis·trust′ing·ly** *adv.*

mis·trust·ful (mis·trust′fəl) *adj.* Full of mistrust; suspicious. **—mis·trust′ful·ly** *adv.* **—mis·trust′ful·ness** *n.*

mist·y (mis′tē) *adj.* **mist·i·er, mist·i·est** 1. Consisting of, characterized by, or like mist. 2. Dimmed or obscured. 3. Lacking clarity; vague. **—mist′i·ly** *adv.* **—mist′i·ness** *n.*

mis·un·der·stand (mis′un·dər·stand′) *v.t. & v.i.* **·stood, ·stand·ing** To understand wrongly; misinterpret.

mis·un·der·stand·ing (mis′un·dər·stan′ding) *n.* 1. A failure to understand the meaning, motive, etc., of someone or something. 2. A disagreement or quarrel.

mis·un·der·stood (mis′un·dər·sto͝od′) *adj.* 1. Wrongly understood. 2. Not valued or appreciated.

mis·us·age (mis·yo͞o′sij, -zij) *n.* 1. Incorrect or improper use, as of words. 2. Maltreatment.

mis·use (*n.* mis·yo͞os′; *v.* mis·yo͞oz′) *n.* Erroneous or improper use. **—***v.t.* **·used, ·us·ing** 1. To use or apply wrongly or improperly. 2. To treat badly; abuse. **—mis·us′er** (-yo͞o′zər) *n.*

mite[1] (mīt) *n.* Any of various small arachnids, many of which are parasitic on men, animals, and plants. [OE *mīte*] **—mit′y** *adj.*

mite[2] (mīt) *n.* 1. A very small particle, object, or creature. 2. Any very small coin or sum of money. [< Du. *mijt*]

mi·ter (mī′tər) *n.* 1. A tall ornamental headdress, rising in peaks at the front and back, worn by popes, bishops, and abbots. 2. In carpentry, a miter joint. **—***v.t.* 1. To confer a miter upon; raise to the rank of bishop. 2. To make or join with a miter joint. Also **mi′tre.** [< Gk. *mitra* belt, turban]

miter joint A joint made of two pieces of material whose joined ends have been beveled at equal angles, as at the corner of a picture frame.

mit·i·gate (mit′ə·gāt) *v.t. & v.i.* **·gat·ed, ·gat·ing** To make or become milder or less severe. [< L *mitis* mild + *agere* to do, drive] **—mit′i·ga·ble** (-gə·bəl) *adj.* **—mit′i·ga′tion** *n.* **—mit′i·ga′tive** *adj.*

mi·to·sis (mī·tō′sis) *n. Biol.* A process of cell division in which the nucleus divides, producing two cells, each having the same number of chromosomes as the original cell. [< G. *mitos* thread + -OSIS] **—mi·tot·ic** (mī·tot′ik) *adj.*

mitt (mit) *n.* 1. In baseball, a large glove, used to protect the hand catching the ball. 2. A glove extending to or above the elbow but without fully covering the fingers. 3. A mitten. 4. *Slang Usu. pl.* A hand.

mit·ten (mit′n) *n.* A covering for the hand, encasing the four fingers together and the thumb separately. [< F *mitaine*]

mix (miks) *v.* **mixed** or **mixt, mix·ing** *v.t.* 1. To combine or put together in one mass or compound. 2. To make by combining ingredients: to *mix* cake batter. 3. To put or add, as an ingredient. 4. To bring into contact with; cause to mingle. **—***v.i.* 5. To become mixed or have the capacity to become mixed; mingle. 6. To associate; get along: He does not *mix* well with others. **—to mix up** 1. To mix or blend together. 2. To confuse. 3. To implicate or involve. **—***n.* 1. The act or product of mixing. 2. A mixture of ingredients, often prepared and sold commercially: a cake *mix.* 3. A mixer (def. 4). [Back formation < MIXED] **—mix′a·ble** *adj.*

mixed (mikst) *adj.* 1. Mingled or blended together in a single mass or compound. 2. Composed of different, dissimilar, or incongruous elements, qualities, classes, races, etc.: *mixed* motives. 3. Made up of or involving persons of both sexes. [< L *mixtus*, pp. of *miscere* to mix]

mixed marriage Marriage between persons of different religions or races.

mixed number A number, as 3½, 5¾, that is the sum of an integer and a fraction.

mixed-up (mikst′up′) *adj. Informal* 1. Jumbled; disordered. 2. Confused; bewildered.

mix·er (mik′sər) *n.* 1. One who or that which mixes. 2. *Informal* A person with ability to mix socially or get along well in groups. 3. *Informal* A dance or gathering for the purpose of getting acquainted. 4. A beverage, as water, soda, ginger ale, etc., used with alcoholic beverages in a drink.

mix·ture (miks′chər) *n.* 1. Something formed by or resulting from mixing. 2. Anything composed of unlike or various elements, as a blend of different kinds or qualities of tea, tobacco, etc. 3. The act of mixing, or the state of being mixed.

mix-up (miks′up′) *n.* 1. A state of confusion; also, an instance of this. 2. *Informal* A fight.

miz·zen (miz′ən) *n. Naut.* 1. A triangular sail set on the mizzenmast. 2. A mizzenmast. [< Ital. *mezzano* middle] **—miz′zen** *adj.*

miz·zen·mast (miz′ən·məst, -mast′) *n.* *Naut.* 1. The third mast aft on ships with three or more masts. 2. The mast nearest the stern on two-masted ships.

mks The meter-kilogram-second system of measurement in which the unit of length is the meter, the unit of mass is the kilogram, and the unit of time is one second. Also **m.k.s., MKS, M.K.S.**

mne·mon·ics (nē·mon′iks, ni-) *n.pl.* (*construed as sing.*) A system of principles and formulas designed to assist or improve the memory. [< Gk. < *mnasthai* to remember] —**mne·mon′ic** *adj.*

moan (mōn) *n.* 1. A low, sustained, mournful sound, as from grief or pain. 2. Any similar sound. —*v.t.* & *v.i.* 1. To utter moans or with moans. 2. To complain or lament. [Cf. OE *mǣnan* to lament, moan]

moat (mōt) *n.* A deep, wide, and usu. water-filled trench around a castle, fortress, or town, designed to discourage attempts at invasion. —*v.t.* To surround with or as with a moat. [< OF *mote* embankment]

mob (mob) *n.* 1. A disorderly or lawless crowd or throng; a rabble. 2. Any large assemblage of individuals. 3. The lower class or classes of people; the masses. 4. *Informal* A gang of thieves, hoodlums, etc. —*v.t.* **mobbed, mob·bing** 1. To attack in a mob. 2. To crowd around and jostle or molest, as from adulation or curiosity. 3. To attend or crowd into (a hall, theater, etc.). [< L *mob*(*ile vulgus*) movable crowd] —**mob′ber** *n.*

mo·bile (*adj.* mō′bəl, -bēl, -bīl; *n.* mō′bēl; *Brit.* mō′bīl) *adj.* 1. Characterized by freedom of movement. 2. Moving easily from one thing, mood, etc., to another. 3. Capable of being easily and quickly moved. 4. Capable of moving with relative ease from one social group or status to another. 5. Of, pertaining to, or like a mobile. —*n.* A form of freely moving sculpture consisting of parts that are suspended from rods, wires, etc. [< L *mobilis* movable] —**mo·bil′i·ty** (-bil′ə·tē) *n.*

mo·bi·lize (mō′bə·līz) *v.* **·lized, ·liz·ing** *v.t.* 1. To make ready for war, as an army. 2. To put into circulation or use. —*v.i.* 3. To become ready or organized, as for war. Also *Brit.* **mo′bi·lise.** [< F *mobiliser*] —**mo′bi·li·za′tion** *n.*

mob·ster (mob′stər) *n.* *Slang* A gangster.

moc·ca·sin (mok′ə·sin) *n.* 1. A heelless foot covering made of soft leather, formerly worn by North American Indians. 2. A shoe or slipper resembling a moccasin. 3. The water moccasin. [< Algonquian *mohkisson*]

mo·cha (mō′kə) *n.* 1. A choice, pungent coffee, originally brought from Mocha, Arabia. 2. A flavoring made of coffee or of coffee and chocolate.

mock (mok) *v.t.* 1. To treat or address scornfully or derisively. 2. To mimic, as in sport, derision, or contempt. 3. To deceive or disappoint; delude. 4. To defy. —*v.i.* 5. To express or show ridicule or contempt; scoff. —*adj.* Merely imitating or resembling the reality; sham. [< OF *mocquer*] —**mock′er·y** *n.* —**mock′ing·ly** *adv.*

mock·ing·bird (mok′ing·bûrd′) *n.* 1. A bird common in the southern U.S., noted for its ability to imitate the calls of other birds. 2. Any of various birds of the same family.

mock·up (mok′up′) *n.* A model, usu. full-scale, of a proposed structure, machine, apparatus, etc.

mod (mod) *adj.* Unconventional in style or manner; modern. [< MOD(ERN)]

mode (mōd) *n.* 1. Manner or form of being, doing, etc.; way. 2. Prevailing or current style or fashion, as in dress. 3. *Gram.* Mood. 4. *Music* Any of the arrangements of tones within a diatonic scale. 5. *Stat.* The value, magnitude, or score that occurs the greatest number of times in a given series of observations: also called *norm.* [< L *modus* measure, manner] —**mo′dal** *adj.* —**mo′dal·ly** *adv.*

mod·el (mod′l) *n.* 1. An object, usu. in miniature and often built according to scale, that represents something to be made or something already existing. 2. A pattern, example, or standard that is or may be used for imitation or comparison. 3. One who poses for an artist, sculptor, etc. 4. One who is employed to display or advertise merchandise; esp. one who displays articles of clothing by wearing them. 5. A representative style, plan, or design. 6. In merchandise, a particular style or design. —*v.* **mod·eled** or **·elled, mod·el·ing** or **·el·ling** *v.t.* 1. To plan or fashion after a model or pattern. 2. To shape or fashion. 3. To display by wearing. —*v.i.* 4. To pose or serve as a model. —*adj.* 1. Serving or used as a model. 2. Worthy of emulation: a *model* student. [< L *modus* measure, manner]

mod·el·ing (mod′ling, -əl·ing) *n.* 1. The act or art of making a model, esp. a sculptor's clay or wax model. 2. In painting, drawing, etc., the representation of depth or three-dimensional solidity. 3. The act or occupation of being a model (defs. 3 & 4). Also **mod′el·ling.**

mod·er·ate (*adj.* & *n.* mod′ər·it; *v.* mod′ə·rāt) *adj.* 1. Keeping or kept within reasonable limits; temperate. 2. Holding or characterized by ideas or convictions that are not extreme or radical. 3. Of medium or average quality, quantity, scope, extent, etc. —*n.* One having moderate views or practices, esp. in politics or religion. —*v.* **·at·ed, ·at·ing** *v.t.* 1. To reduce the violence, severity, etc., of. 2. To preside over. —*v.i.* 3. To become less intense or violent. [< L *moderare* to regulate] —**mod′er·ate·ly** *adv.* —**mod′er·a′tion** *n.*

mod·er·a·tor (mod′ə·rā′tər) *n.* 1. One who or that which moderates. 2. One who presides over a meeting, forum, or debate. 3. The arbitrator of a dispute.

mod·ern (mod′ərn) *adj.* 1. Of or pertaining to the present or recent time. 2. Characteristic of or serving to express the current times; up-to-date. —*n.* 1. One who lives in modern times. 2. One who has opinions, habits, prejudices, etc., characteristic of modern times. [< LL *modernus* recent] —**mo·der·ni·ty** (mə·dûr′nə·tē) *n.* —**mod′ern·ly** *adv.*

mod·ern·ism (mod′ərn·iz′əm) *n.* 1. The character or quality of thought, action, etc., that is peculiar to modern times. 2. Something characteristic of modern times, as an act, practice, idiom, attitude, etc. —**mod′ern·ist** *n.* —**mod′ern·is′tic** *adj.*

mod·ern·ize (mod′ərn·īz) *v.* **·ized, ·iz·ing** *v.t.* 1. To make modern in method, style, character, etc.; bring up to date. —*v.i.* 2. To accept or adopt modern ways, ideas, idioms, etc. **—mod′ern·i·za′tion** *n.* **—mod′ern·iz′er** *n.*

mod·est (mod′ist) *adj.* 1. Having or displaying a moderate or unexaggerated regard for oneself or one's abilities, accomplishments, etc. 2. Not showy or ostentatious. 3. Not excessive or extreme; moderate. 4. Reserved in speech, manner, dress, etc. [< L *modestus*] **—mod′est·ly** *adv.* **—mod′es·ty** *n.*

mod·i·cum (mod′i·kəm) *n.* A moderate or small amount. [< L *modicus* moderate]

mod·i·fi·er (mod′ə·fī′ər) *n.* 1. One who or that which modifies. 2. *Gram.* A word, phrase, or clause that restricts or qualifies the meaning of another word or group of words.

mod·i·fy (mod′ə·fī) *v.* **·fied, ·fy·ing** *v.t.* 1. To make somewhat different in form, character, etc. 2. To revise by making less extreme, severe, or uncompromising. 3. *Gram.* To qualify the meaning of; limit. **—***v.i.* 4. To be or become modified. [< L *modus* measure + *facere* to make] **—mod′i·fi′a·ble** *adj.* **—mod′·i·fi·ca′tion** *n.*

mod·ish (mō′dish) *adj.* Conforming to the current mode or fashion; stylish. **—mod′·ish·ly** *adv.* **—mod′ish·ness** *n.*

mo·diste (mō·dēst′) *n.* A woman who makes or deals in fashionable clothing, esp. women's hats or dresses. [< F]

mod·u·late (moj′o͞o·lāt) *v.* **·lat·ed, ·lat·ing** *v.t.* 1. To vary the tone, inflection, pitch, or volume of. 2. To regulate or adjust; modify. 3. *Telecom.* To alter some characteristic of (a radio carrier wave). **—***v.i.* 4. *Music* To change from one key to another. [< L *modulari* to regulate] **—mod′u·la′tion** *n.*

mod·ule (moj′o͞ol) *n.* 1. A standard or unit of measurement. 2. A standard structural component repeatedly used, as in a building, computer, etc. 3. A self-contained component or subassembly: a housing *module.* [< L *modulus*, dim. of *modus* measure] **—mod′u·lar** *adj.*

mo·dus op·er·an·di (mō′dəs op′ə·ran′dī) *Latin* A manner of operating or proceeding.

modus vi·ven·di (vi·ven′dī) *Latin* A manner of living.

mo·gul (mō′gul, mō·gul′) *n.* A very important, wealthy, or influential person. [after the *Moguls*, 16th c. Mongol conquerors of India]

mo·hair (mō′hâr) *n.* 1. The hair of the Angora goat. 2. A glossy, wiry fabric made of mohair and cotton in a plain or twill weave. 3. A fabric having a mohair pile, used for upholstery. [Earlier *mocayare* < Arabic *mukhayyar*]

Mo·ham·me·dan (mō·ham′ə·dən) *n. & adj.* Muhammadan. **—Mo·ham′me·dan·ism′** *n.*

Mo·ha·ve (mō·hä′vē) *n.* One of a tribe of Yuman Indians, formerly living along the Colorado River. Also spelled *Mojave.*

Mo·hawk (mō′hôk) *n.* 1. One of a tribe of Iroquoian Indians, one of the original Five Nations, formerly ranging from the Mohawk River to the St. Lawrence. 2. The language of this tribe. [< N.Am.Ind.]

Mo·he·gan (mō·hē′gən) *n.* One of a tribe of Algonquian Indians, formerly living along the Thames River in Connecticut. [< Algonquian *maingan* wolf]

Mo·hi·can (mō·hē′kən) *n.* A Mahican.

Mohs scale (mōz) *Mineral.* A qualitative scale in which the hardness of a mineral is determined by its ability to scratch, or be scratched by, any one of 15 minerals arranged in order of increasing hardness. [after Friedrich *Mohs*, 1773–1839, German mineralogist]

moi·e·ty (moi′ə·tē) *n.* *pl.* **·ties** 1. A half. 2. Any portion, part, or share. 3. *Anthropol.* Either of two basic groups that together constitute a tribe. [< MF *moité* < L *medius* half]

moil (moil) *v.i.* To work hard; toil. **—***n.* Toil; drudgery. [< OF *moillier, muiller* to wet] **—moil′er** *n.* **—moil′ing·ly** *adv.*

moi·ré (mwä·rā′) *adj.* Having a wavelike or watered appearance, as certain fabrics. **—***n.* A ribbed fabric, usu. silk or rayon, having a wavy or watered pattern: also **moire** (mwär, mōr). [< F < *moire* watered silk]

moist (moist) *adj.* 1. Slightly wet or damp. 2. Saturated with or characterized by moisture or liquid. [< OF, a fusion of L *musteus* dew + *mucidus* moldy] **—moist′ly** *adv.* **—moist′ness** *n.*

mois·ten (mois′ən) *v.t. & v.i.* To make or become moist. **—mois′ten·er** *n.*

mois·ture (mois′chər) *n.* Water or other liquid causing dampness or wetness. [< OF *moisteur*]

Mo·ja·ve (mō·hä′vē) See MOHAVE.

mo·lar (mō′lər) *n.* A grinding tooth, of which there are 12 in man, situated behind the bicuspids and having a broad, flattened crown. [< L *mola* mill] **—mo′lar** *adj.*

mo·las·ses (mə·las′iz) *n.* *pl.* **mo·las·ses** Any of various thick, dark-colored syrups obtained from sugar, sorghum, etc., during the refining process: also, *Brit.*, *treacle.* [< L *mellaceus* honeylike]

mold[1] (mōld) *n.* 1. A form or matrix that gives a particular shape to anything in a fluid or plastic condition. 2. That which is shaped or made in or on a mold. 3. General shape, form, or pattern. 4. Distinctive nature, character, or type. 5. *Archit.* A molding or set of moldings. **—***v.t.* 1. To work into a particular shape or form. 2. To shape or form in or as in a mold. 3. To influence, determine, or direct: to *mold* public sentiment. **—***v.i.* 4. To assume or come to fit a particular shape or pattern. Also, *Brit.*, *mould.* [< L *modus* measure, limit] **—mold′a·ble** *adj.* **—mold′er** *n.*

mold[2] (mōld) *n.* 1. Any of a variety of fungous growths commonly found on the surfaces of decaying food or in warm, moist places, and usu. having a woolly or furry texture. 2. A fungus producing one of these growths. **—***v.i.* To become moldy. Also *Brit.*, *mould.* [< obs. *mouled*, pp. of *moulen* to grow moldy]

mold[3] (mōld) *n.* Soft, loose earth that is rich in decaying organic matter. **—***v.t.* To cover with mold. Also, *Brit.*, *mould.* [OE *molde* earth]

mold·board (mōld′bôrd′) *n.* The curved metal plate of a plow that digs into and turns over the soil.

mold·er (mōl′dər) *v.i.* 1. To decay gradually and turn to dust; crumble. 2. To atrophy from lack of use. **—***v.t.* 3. To cause to crumble. Also, *Brit.*, *moulder.* [Freq. of obs. *mold* to crumble]

mold·ing (mōl′ding) *n.* 1. The act or process of one who or that which molds. 2. That which is molded. 3. *Archit.* A cornice or other depressed or projecting member, used to decorate the surface or angle of a building, room, etc. 4. A strip of decoratively shaped wood or other material, used to decorate or finish walls, doors, etc. Also, *Brit.*, *moulding.*

mold·y (mōl′dē) *adj.* **mold·i·er, mold·i·est** 1. Covered with or containing mold. 2. Musty, as from age, lack of use, etc. Also, *Brit.*, *mouldy.* —**mold′i·ness** *n.*

mole[1] (mōl) *n.* A small, permanent spot on the human skin, slightly protuberant and often dark and hairy. [OE *māl*]

mole[2] (mōl) *n.* Any of a number of small insectivorous mammals that live mainly underground and have soft fur, small eyes, and broad forefeet adapted for digging and burrowing. [ME *molle*]

mole[3] (mōl) *n.* A massive, usu. stone breakwater or pier, built to enclose an anchorage or harbor. [< Gk. *mylē* millstone]

mol·e·cule (mol′ə·kyōōl) *n.* *Chem.* One or more atoms constituting the smallest part of an element or compound that can exist separately without losing the characteristics of the substance. [< NL *molecula*, dim. of L *moles* mass] —**mo·lec·u·lar** (mə·lek′yə·lər) *adj.*

mole·hill (mōl′hil′) *n.* A small heap or mound of earth raised by a burrowing mole.

mole·skin (mōl′skin′) *n.* 1. The dark gray pelt of a mole, very soft and fragile and used as a fur. 2. A heavy, twilled cotton fabric with a thick, soft nap on one side.

mo·lest (mə·lest′) *v.t.* 1. To disturb or annoy by unwarranted, excessive, or malicious interference. 2. To interfere with improperly or illicitly, esp. with a sexual motive. [< L *molestus* troublesome] —**mo·les·ta·tion** (mō′les·tā′shən, mol′əs-) *n.* —**mo·lest′er** *n.*

moll (mol) *n.* *Slang* The girl friend of a gangster. [< *Moll*, dim. of *Mary*, a personal name]

mol·li·fy (mol′ə·fī) *v.t.* **·fied, ·fy·ing** 1. To make less angry, violent, or agitated; soothe. 2. To reduce the harshness, severity, or intensity of. [< L *mollis* soft + *facere* to make] —**mol′li·fi·ca′tion** *n.* —**mol′li·fi′er** *n.*

mol·lusk (mol′əsk) *n.* One of a large group of unsegmented, soft-bodied invertebrates, usu. protected by a shell of one or more pieces, and including snails, mussels, oysters, clams, and octopi. Also **mol′lusc.** [< L *molluscus* (*nux*) soft, thin-shelled (nut)] —**mol·lus·can** (mə·lus′kən) *adj.* & *n.*

mol·ly·cod·dle (mol′ē·kod′l) *n.* Any overprotected or pampered person; also, an effeminate man or boy. —*v.t.* **·dled, ·dling** To pamper; coddle. [< *Molly*, a personal name + CODDLE] —**mol′ly·cod′dler** *n.*

molt (mōlt) *v.t.* & *v.i.* To cast off or shed (feathers, horns, skin, etc.) in preparation for periodic replacement by new growth. —*n.* 1. The act or process of molting. 2. That which is molted. Also, *Brit.*, *moult.* [< L *mutare* to change] —**molt′er** *n.*

mol·ten (mōl′tən) Archaic past participle of MELT. —*adj.* 1. Made fluid by heat; melted: *molten* metal. 2. Made by melting and casting in a mold: *molten* images.

mo·lyb·de·num (mə·lib′də·nəm, mol′ib·dē′·nəm) *n.* A hard, heavy, silver-white metallic element (symbol Mo), occurring only in combination, used to harden steel. [< Gk. *molybdos* lead]

mom (mom) *n.* Mother: used familiarly. [< MAMA]

mo·ment (mō′mənt) *n.* 1. A very short or relatively short period of time. 2. A particular point in time, usu. the present time. 3. A particular period or stage in a series of events: a great *moment* in history. 4. Importance; consequence: matters of great *moment.* [< L *momentum* movement]

mo·men·tar·i·ly (mō′mən·ter′ə·lē) *adv.* 1. For a moment: *momentarily* at a loss. 2. In a moment; at any moment.

mo·men·tar·y (mō′mən·ter′ē) *adj.* 1. Lasting no more than a moment; fleeting. 2. Occurring or operating at every moment. —**mo′·men·tar′i·ness** *n.*

mo·men·tous (mō·men′təs) *adj.* Of great importance or consequence. —**mo·men′·tous·ly** *adv.* —**mo·men′tous·ness** *n.*

mo·men·tum (mō·men′təm) *n.* 1. *Physics* The quantity of motion in a body as measured by the product of its mass and velocity. 2. Impetus, as of a body in motion.

mon- *combining form* Var. of MONO-.

mon·ad (mon′ad, mō′nad) *n.* 1. An indestructible unit; a simple and indivisible substance. 2. *Biol.* A simple single-celled organism; esp. a flagellated protozoan. [< Gk. *monas* unit]

mon·arch (mon′ərk) *n.* 1. A hereditary constitutional ruler, as a king, queen, etc. 2. Formerly, a sole ruler of a state. 3. One who or that which surpasses others of the same kind. 4. *Entomol.* A large, orange and brown butterfly whose larvae feed on milkweed. [< MON(O)- + Gk. *archein* to rule] —**mo·nar·chi·cal** (mə·när′ki·kəl) *adj.*

mon·arch·ist (mon′ər·kist) *n.* One who favors monarchical government. —**mon′·arch·is′tic** *adj.*

mon·ar·chy (mon′ər·kē) *n.* *pl.* **·chies** 1. Government by a monarch; sovereign control. 2. A government or territory ruled by a monarch. —**absolute monarchy** A government in which the will of the monarch is positive law. —**constitutional** or **limited monarchy** A monarchy in which the power and prerogatives of the sovereign are limited by constitutional provisions. —**mon′·arch·ism** *n.*

mon·as·ter·y (mon′əs·ter′ē) *n.* *pl.* **·ter·ies** 1. A dwelling place occupied by monks living under religious vows and in seclusion. 2. The monks living in such a place. [< Gk. *monazein* to live alone]

mo·nas·tic (mə·nas′tik) *adj.* 1. Of, pertaining to, or characteristic of monasteries or their inhabitants; ascetic. 2. Characteristic of a life of religious seclusion. —*n.* A monk or other religious recluse. [< Gk. *monastikos*] —**mon·as′ti·cal·ly** *adv.*

mo·nas·ti·cism (mə·nas′tə·siz′əm) *n.* The monastic life or system.

mon·au·ral (mon·ôr′əl, mō·nôr′əl) *adj.* *Electronics* Designating a system of sound reproduction in which the sound is perceived as coming from one direction only.

mon·ax·i·al (mon·ak′sē·əl) *adj.* Having but one axis.

Mon·day (mun′dē, -dā) *n.* The second day of the week. [OE *mōn(an)dæg* day of the moon]

mon·e·ta·rism (mon′ə·tə·riz′əm) *n.* A theory that the economy can be controlled by regulating the flow of money. —**mon′e·ta·rist** *n. & adj.*

mon·e·tar·y (mon′ə·ter′ē, mun′-) *adj.* 1. Of or pertaining to currency or coinage. 2. Pertaining to or concerned with money. [< L *monetarius* of a mint] —**mon′e·tar′i·ly** *adv.*

mon·ey (mun′ē) *n. pl.* **mon·eys** or **mon·ies** 1. Officially issued coins and paper currency that serve as a medium of exchange and may be used as payment for goods and services and for settlement of debts. 2. Property of any type having monetary value. 3. Money of account. [< L *moneta* mint]

mon·ey·bag (mun′ē·bag) *n.* 1. A bag for holding money. 2. *pl. Slang* A wealthy person.

money belt A belt with pouches for carrying money.

mon·ey·chang·er (mun′ē·chān′jər) *n.* 1. One whose business it is to change money at a prescribed rate. 2. A device for holding and dispensing coins.

mon·eyed (mun′ēd) *adj.* 1. Possessed of money; wealthy. 2. Consisting of, arising from, or representing money or wealth: *moneyed* interests. Also spelled *monied.*

mon·ey·lend·er (mun′ē·len′dər) *n.* One whose business is the lending of money at interest.

mon·ey·mak·ing (mun′ē·mā′king) *adj.* Likely to bring in money; profitable. —*n.* The acquisition of money or wealth. —**mon′ey·mak′er** *n.*

money of account A monetary denomination used in keeping accounts, usu. not represented by a coin, as the U.S. mill.

money order An order for the payment of a specified sum of money, usu. issued at one bank or post office and payable at another.

mon·ger (mung′gər, mong′-) *n.* 1. *Brit.* A dealer or trader: chiefly in combination: *fishmonger.* 2. One who engages in discreditable matters: chiefly in compounds: a *scandalmonger.* [OE < L *mango* dealer]

Mon·gol (mong′gəl, -gōl) *n.* 1. A member of any of the native tribes of Mongolia. 2. Any of the Mongolian languages. 3. A member of the Mongoloid ethnic division. —*adj.* Mongolian. [< Mongolian *mong* brave]

Mon·go·li·an (mong·gō′lē·ən, -gōl′yən, mon-) *adj.* Of or pertaining to Mongolia, its people, or their languages. —*n.* 1. A native of Mongolia. 2. A subfamily of the Altaic languages, including the languages of the Mongols.

Mon·gol·ism (mong′gəl·iz′əm) *n.* A congenital idiocy, characterized by a broad, flat face and skull and obliquely set, narrow eyes: also called *Down's syndrome.*

Mon·go·loid (mong′gə·loid) *adj.* 1. *Anthropol.* Of, pertaining to, or belonging to a major ethnic division of the human species, characterized by yellowish skin, high cheek bones, etc. 2. Resembling, related to, or characteristic of Mongols or Mongolians. 3. Characterized by Mongolism. —*n.* A Mongoloid person.

mon·goose (mong′gōōs, mung′-) *n. pl.* **·goos·es** A small, ferretlike, carnivorous mammal that destroys rats and can kill venomous snakes. [< Marathi *mangus*]

mon·grel (mung′grəl, mong′-) *n.* 1. The progeny produced by crossing different breeds or varieties of plants or animals; esp., a dog of mixed breed. 2. Any incongruous mixture. —*adj.* Of mixed breed, origin, nature, etc.: often a contemptuous term: a *mongrel* language. [ME *mong* mixture]

'mongst (mungst) *prep. Poetic* Amongst.

mon·ied (mun′ēd) See MONEYED.

mon·i·ker (mon′ə·kər) *n. Informal* A name, signature, or nickname. Also **mon′ick·er.** [Prob. blend of MONOGRAM and MARKER]

mon·ism (mon′iz·əm, mō′niz·əm) *n. Philos.* The doctrine that there is but one principle of being or ultimate substance, as mind or matter. [< Gk. *monos* single] —**mon′ist** *n.* —**mo·nis′tic** or **·ti·cal** *adj.*

mo·ni·tion (mō·nish′ən) *n.* 1. A warning or admonition, as of impending danger. 2. An official, legal, or formal notice. [< L *monere* to warn]

mon·i·tor (mon′ə·tər) *n.* 1. In some schools, a student who helps to keep records, maintain order, etc. 2. One who or that which examines, as to maintain quality. 3. *Telecom.* A receiver, loudspeaker, or other apparatus used to check radio or television broadcasts for quality of transmission, frequency, compliance with laws, etc. —*v.t. & v.i.* 1. *Telecom.* To listen to or watch (a broadcast) with a monitor. 2. To regulate or keep track of (a performance, heartbeat, etc.). [< L *monere* to warn]

mon·i·to·ry (mon′ə·tôr′ē) *adj.* Conveying a warning; admonitory. [< L *monitor*]

monk (mungk) *n.* One who has taken the religious vows of poverty, chastity, and obedience, usu. a member of a monastic order. [OE *munuc*, ult. < Gk. *monos* alone]

mon·key (mung′kē) *n.* 1. Any of the primates, excluding humans and the anthropoid apes, having elongate limbs, and hands and feet adapted for grasping; esp., the marmosets, baboons, macaques, etc. 2. One who acts in a way suggestive of a monkey, as a mischievous child. —*v.i. Informal* To play or trifle; meddle; fool: often with *with* or *around.* [? < MLG *Moneke*, name of an ape in *Reynard the Fox*]

monkey business *Slang* Foolish tricks; deceitful or mischievous behavior.

mon·key·shine (mung′kē·shīn′) *n. Usu. pl. Slang* A mischievous or playful prank or joke.

monkey wrench A wrench having an adjustable jaw for grasping nuts, bolts, etc., of various sizes. —**to throw a monkey wrench into** *Informal* To disrupt.

monk's cloth (mungks) A sturdy cotton fabric with a basket weave used for drapes, curtains, etc.

monks·hood (mungks′ho͝od′) *n.* A plant having flowers shaped like a hood; esp., a poisonous variety.

mono- *combining form* Single; one: *monologue.* Also, before vowels, *mon-.* [< Gk. *monos* single]

mon·o·chro·mat·ic (mon′ə·krō·mat′ik) *adj.* 1. Having only one color. 2. Consisting of one wavelength. —**mon′o·chro·mat′i·cal·ly** *adv.*

mon·o·chrome (mon′ə·krōm) *n.* A painting or drawing in a single color or in various shades of the same color. [< MONO- + Gk. *chrōma* color] **—mon′o·chro′mic** *adj.* **—mon′o·chro′mist** *n.*

mon·o·cle (mon′ə·kəl) *n.* An eyeglass for one eye. [< MONO- + L *oculus* eye] **—mon′o·cled** *adj.*

mon·o·cot·y·le·don (mon′ə·kot′ə·lēd′n) *n. Bot.* Any seed plant bearing one cotyledon in the embryo. Also **mon′o·cot′**. [< NL] **—mon′o·cot′y·le′do·nous** *adj.*

mon·o·dy (mon′ə·dē) *n. pl.* **·dies** An elegy or dirge. [< MONO- + Gk. *aeidein* to sing] **—mo·nod·ic** (mə·nod′ik) *adj.* **—mon′o·dist** *n.*

mo·nog·a·my (mə·nog′ə·mē) *n.* The condition or practice of having only one wife or husband at a time. [< MONO- + Gk. *gamos* marriage] **—mo·nog′a·mist** *n.* **—mo·nog′a·mous** *adj.*

mon·o·gram (mon′ə·gram) *n.* Two or more letters combined into a design; esp., the initials of one's name. —*v.t.* **mon·o·gramed** or **·grammed, mon·o·gram·ing** or **·gram·ming** To mark with a monogram. [< MONO- + Gk. *grammē* letter]

mon·o·graph (mon′ə·graf) *n.* A book, pamphlet, or treatise on one subject or on a single aspect of a subject.

mon·o·lith (mon′ə·lith) *n.* A single block of stone, usu. very large, used in architecture and sculpture. [< MONO- + Gk. *lithos* stone]

mon·o·lith·ic (mon′ə·lith′ik) *adj.* 1. Of or resembling a monolith. 2. Having a massive, uniform structure that does not permit individual variations: a *monolithic* state.

mon·o·logue (mon′ə·lôg, -log) *n.* 1. A lengthy speech by one person. 2. A play or dramatic composition for one actor only. 3. A soliloquy. Also **mon′o·log.** [< MONO- + Gk. *logos* speech] **—mon′o·logu′ist, mo·nol·o·gist** (mə·nol′ə·jist) *n.*

mon·o·ma·ni·a (mon′ə·mā′nē·ə, -mān′yə) *n.* 1. A mental disorder in which a person is obsessed with one idea or subject. 2. An exaggerated fondness or irrational enthusiasm for something; craze. [< NL] **—mon′o·ma′ni·ac** *n.* **—mon′o·ma·ni′a·cal** (-mə·nī′ə·kəl) *adj.*

mon·o·mer (mon′ə·mər) *n. Chem.* The structural unit of a polymer. [< MONO- + Gk. *meros* part]

mo·no·mi·al (mō·nō′mē·əl) *adj.* Consisting of a single word or term. **—mo·no′mi·al** *n.*

mon·o·nu·cle·o·sis (mon′ō·nōō′klē·ō′sis, -nyōō′-) *n. Pathol.* An acute infectious disease marked by fever, swelling of the lymph nodes, and an increase of lymphocytes in the blood.

mon·o·plane (mon′ə·plān) *n. Aeron.* An airplane with only one wing or pair of wings.

mo·nop·o·lize (mə·nop′ə·līz) *v.t.* **·lized, ·liz·ing** 1. To obtain a monopoly of. 2. To assume exclusive possession or control of. **—mo·nop′o·li·za′tion** *n.* **—mo·nop′o·liz′er** *n.*

mo·nop·o·ly (mə·nop′ə·lē) *n. pl.* **·lies** 1. The exclusive control of a commodity, service, or means of production in a particular market, with the resulting power to fix prices. 2. A company having a monopoly. 3. Exclusive possession or control of anything. [< MONO- + Gk. *pōlein* to sell] **—mo·nop′o·lis′tic** *adj.*

mon·o·rail (mon′ō·rāl′) *n.* 1. A single rail serving as a track for cars either suspended from it or balanced upon it. 2. A railway using such a track.

mon·o·so·di·um glu·ta·mate (mon′ə·sō′·dē·əm glōō′tə·māt) A crystalline salt used to flavor food. Abbr. *MSG*.

mon·o·syl·la·bic (mon′ə·si·lab′ik) *adj.* 1. Having only one syllable. 2. Using or speaking in monosyllables. **—mon′o·syl·lab′i·cal·ly** *adv.*

mon·o·syl·la·ble (mon′ə·sil′ə·bəl) *n.* A word of one syllable, as *no*.

mon·o·the·ism (mon′ə·thē·iz′əm) *n.* The doctrine or belief that there is but one God. [< MONO- + THEISM] **—mon′o·the′ist** *n.* **—mon′o·the·is′tic** *adj.*

mon·o·tone (mon′ə·tōn) *n.* 1. The utterance of a succession of words, etc., in a single tone. 2. Sameness in expression, style, color, etc. 3. A single musical tone unvaried in pitch.

mo·not·o·nous (mə·not′ə·nəs) *adj.* 1. Unvaried in tone. 2. Tiresomely uniform or repetitive. [< LGk. *monotonos*] **—mo·not′o·nous·ly** *adv.* **—mo·not′o·ny** *n.*

mon·o·type (mon′ə·tīp) *n. Printing* A print from a metal plate on which a design, painting, etc., has been made.

Mon·o·type (mon′ə·tīp) *n. Printing* A machine that casts and sets type in single characters or units: a trade name.

mon·o·typ·ic (mon′ə·tip′ik) *adj. Biol.* 1. Having only one type: a *monotypic* genus. 2. Being a monotype.

mon·o·va·lent (mon′ə·vā′lənt) *adj. Chem.* Univalent. **—mon′o·va′lence, mon′o·va′·len·cy** *n.*

mon·ox·ide (mon·ok′sīd, mə·nok′-) *n. Chem.* An oxide containing a single atom of oxygen in each molecule.

Mon·sei·gneur (mon·sēn′yər; *Fr.* môṅ·se·nyœr′) *n. pl.* **Mes·sei·gneurs** (me·sen·yûrz′, *Fr.* me·se·nyœr′) My lord: a French title given to the higher nobility, bishops, etc. [< F *mon* my + *seigneur* lord]

mon·sieur (mə·syûr′, *Fr.* mə·syœ′) *n. pl.* **mes·sieurs** (mes′ərz, *Fr.* me·syœ′) The French title of courtesy for men, equivalent to *Mr.* and *sir.* [< F < *mon* my + *sieur,* short for *seigneur* lord]

Mon·si·gnor (mon·sēn′yər, *Ital.* môn′sēn·nyōr′) *n. pl.* **·gnors** or *Ital.* **·gno·ri** (-nyō′rē) In the Roman Catholic Church, a title of honor of certain prelates. [< Ital. < F *monseigneur*]

mon·soon (mon·sōōn′) *n. Meteorol.* 1. A seasonal wind of the Indian Ocean and southern Asia, blowing in winter from the northeast and in summer from the southwest. 2. The summer monsoon, characterized by heavy rains. [< Arabic *mausim* season]

mon·ster (mon′stər) *n.* 1. One who or that which is abnormal, unnatural, or hideous in form. 2. One who or that which inspires hate or horror because of cruelty, wickedness, etc. 3. A huge person or thing. —*adj.* Enormous; huge. [< L *monstrum* divine warning < *monere* to warn] **—mon′strous** *adj.* **—mon′·strous·ly** *adv.*

mon·strance (mon′strəns) *n.* In Roman Catholic ritual, a vessel in which the consecrated Host is exposed for adoration. [< L *monstrare* to show]

mon·stros·i·ty (mon·stros′ə·tē) *n. pl.* **·ties** 1. One who or that which is monstrous.

2. The condition or character of being monstrous.
mon·tage (mon·täzh′) *n.* 1. A picture made by superimposing or arranging a number of different pictorial elements; also, the art or process of making such a picture. 2. In motion pictures or television, a rapid sequence of images used to illustrate a group of associated ideas. 3. Similar techniques in radio and writing. [< F *monter* to mount]
month (munth) *n.* 1. One of the twelve parts (**calendar month**) into which the calendar year is divided. 2. A period of thirty days or four weeks. 3. The twelfth part (**solar month**) of the solar year. 4. The period (**lunar month**), equivalent to 29.53 days, during which the moon makes a complete revolution. ◆Collateral adjective: *mensal*. [OE *mōnath*]
month·ly (munth′lē) *adj.* 1. Happening, done, appearing, etc., every month. 2. Of or pertaining to a month. —*adv.* Once a month. —*n. pl.* **·lies** 1. A periodical published once a month. 2. *pl. Informal* Menstruation.
mon·u·ment (mon′yə·mənt) *n.* 1. A statue, pillar, plaque, etc., erected to perpetuate the memory of a person, event, or historical period. 2. A tombstone. 3. Any conspicuous or fine structure surviving from the past. 4. A work of art, scholarship, etc., regarded as having enduring value. [< L *monere* to remind]
mon·u·men·tal (mon′yə·men′təl) *adj.* 1. Of, pertaining to, or serving as a monument. 2. Like a monument; enduring; imposing; massive. 3. Having great significance: a *monumental* study. 4. *Informal* Very large; huge: a *monumental* bore. —**mon′u·men′·tal·ly** *adv.*
-mony *suffix of nouns* The condition, state, or thing resulting from: *parsimony*. [< L *-monia*]
moo (mōō) *v.i.* To make the deep, moaning sound of a cow. [Imit.] —**moo** *n.*
mooch (mōōch) *v.t. Slang* 1. To obtain without paying; beg; cadge. 2. To steal. [< OF *muchier* to hide, skulk] —**mooch′er** *n.*
mood[1] (mōōd) *n.* 1. A specific state of mind or feeling, esp. a temporary one. 2. An inclination or attitude; disposition. —**in the mood** Disposed; inclined. [OE *mōd* mind]
mood[2] (mōōd) *n. Gram.* The set of distinctive forms of a verb showing the attitude and understanding of the speaker regarding the action or condition expressed: also *mode*. [Var. of MODE]
mood·y (mōō′dē) *adj.* **mood·i·er, mood·i·est** 1. Given to sudden moods of moroseness. 2. Expressive of such moods. —**mood′i·ly** *adv.* —**mood′i·ness** *n.*
Moog synthesizer (mōg, mōōg) An electronic musical instrument with a keyboard. [after R. A. *Moog*, U.S. engineer, its inventor]
moon (mōōn) *n.* 1. A celestial body revolving around the earth from west to east every 29.53 days, and accompanying the earth in its yearly revolution about the sun. 2. Any satellite revolving about a planet. 3. A month; esp., a lunar month. —*v.i. Informal* To stare or wander about abstractedly. [OE *mōna*]
moon·beam (mōōn′bēm′) *n.* A ray of moonlight.
moon·light (mōōn′līt′) *n.* The light of the moon. —*adj.* Pertaining to, illuminated by, or performed by moonlight. —**moon′lit′** (-lit′) *adj.*
moon·light·ing (mōōn′līt′ing) *n. Informal* The act of one who holds a job in addition to the regular day's work. —**moon′light′** *v.i.* —**moon′light′er** *n.*
moon·shine (mōōn′shīn′) *n.* 1. Moonlight. 2. Nonsense. 3. *Informal* Smuggled or illicitly distilled whiskey, etc. —**moon′·shin′er** *n.*
moon·stone (mōōn′stōn′) *n.* A pearly, opalescent variety of feldspar, valued as a gemstone.
moon·struck (mōōn′struk′) *adj.* 1. Lunatic; deranged. 2. Romantically obsessed. Also **moon′strick′en** (-strik′ən).
moor[1] (mŏŏr) *n. Brit.* A tract of wasteland sometimes covered with heath, often elevated, marshy, and abounding in peat; a heath. [OE *mōr*]
moor[2] (mŏŏr) *v.t. & v.i.* To secure (a ship, etc.) in place by means of cables attached to shore, anchors, etc. [< MDu. *māren* to fasten] —**moor′age** *n.*
Moor (mŏŏr) *n.* 1. A Muslim of mixed Berber and Arab ancestry; esp., one of the invaders of Spain in the 8th c. 2. A native of Morocco. [< Gk. *Mauros*, lit., dark] —**Moor′ish** *adj.*
moor·ing (mŏŏr′ing) *n.* 1. A place where ships, etc., can be moored. 2. *Chiefly pl.* That which secures an object, as a cable.
moose (mōōs) *n. pl.* **moose** 1. A large, heavily built mammal of the deer family, found in northern U.S. and Canada, the male of which bears huge palmate antlers. 2. The elk (def. 1). [< Algonquian *moosu* he strips off; because it eats the bark of trees]
moot (mōōt) *adj.* 1. Open to discussion: debatable. 2. Hypothetical; academic. —*v.t.* To bring up for discussion or debate. [OE *mōt* assembly, court]
mop (mop) *n.* 1. A device for cleaning floors, consisting of a sponge, a bunch of heavy cotton yarn, etc., attached to a handle. 2. Any loosely tangled bunch, esp. of hair. —*v.t.* **mopped, mop·ping** To rub or wipe with or as with a mop. —**to mop up** *Informal* To finish. [ME *mappe*]
mope (mōp) *v.i.* **moped, mop·ing** To be gloomy, listless, or dispirited. —*n.pl.* Dejection; depression. —**mop′er** *n.* —**mop′·ish** *adj.* —**mop′ish·ness** *n.*
mo·ped (mō′ped) *n.* A motorized bicycle. [MO(TOR) + PED(AL)] —**mo′ped·al** *v.i.* **mo·ped·aled** or **·alled, mo·ped·al·ing** or **·al·ling** (mō′ped·ə·ling, mō′ped·ling) —**mo′·ped·al·ing, mo′ped·ing** *n.* —**mo′ped·al·ist** or **·al·list** *n.*
mop·pet (mop′it) *n. Informal* A child. [Dim. of MOP]
mo·raine (mə·rān′) *n. Geol.* Debris that has been carried by a glacier. [< F dial. *morēna*]
mor·al (môr′əl, mor′-) *adj.* 1. Of or related to conduct or character from the point of view of right and wrong: *moral* goodness. 2. Of good character; right or proper in behavior. 3. Sexually virtuous. 4. Arising from a sense of duty and right conduct: a *moral* obligation. 5. Acting not by physical force but by appeal to character, etc.: *moral* support. —*n.* 1. The lesson or teaching contained in or implied by a fable, poem, etc. 2. *pl.* Conduct or behavior with regard to

right and wrong, esp. in sexual matters. 3. A maxim. [< L *mores* manners, morals] **—mor′al·ly** *adv.*

mo·rale (mə·ral′, mô-) *n.* State of mind with reference to confidence, courage, hope, zeal, etc. [< F]

mor·al·ist (môr′əl·ist, mor′-) *n.* 1. A teacher of morals. 2. One who practices morality. **—mor′al·is′tic** *adj.*

mo·ral·i·ty (mə·ral′ə·tē, mô-) *n. pl.* **·ties** 1. The quality of being morally right; virtue. 2. Virtuous conduct; esp., sexual virtue. 3. A system of the principles of right and wrong conduct; ethics.

mor·al·ize (môr′əl·īz, mor′-) *v.i.* **·ized, ·iz·ing** To make moral reflections; talk about morality. [< MF *moralizer*] **—mor′al·i·za′·tion** *n.* **—mor′al·iz′er** *n.*

mo·rass (mə·ras′, mô-) *n.* 1. A tract of low-lying, soft, wet ground; marsh. 2. Anything that impedes, perplexes, or traps. [< OF *maresc* < Gmc.]

mor·a·to·ri·um (môr′ə·tôr′ē·əm, mor′-) *n. pl.* **·ri·a** or **·ri·ums** 1. A legal authorization to a debtor to suspend payments for a given period. 2. Any authorized suspension or deferment of action. [< L *morari* to delay]

Mo·ra·vi·an (mô·rā′vē·ən, mə-) *n.* 1. A native of Moravia. 2. A member of the **Moravian Church,** a Protestant denomination founded in Germany in 1722. **—Mo·ra′vi·an** *adj.*

mo·ray (môr′ā) *n.* A brightly colored, voracious eel inhabiting tropical and subtropical waters. Also **mo′ray eel.** [Origin uncertain]

mor·bid (môr′bid) *adj.* 1. Taking or showing an excessive interest in matters of a gruesome or unwholesome nature. 2. Grisly; gruesome: a *morbid* fantasy. 3. Pertaining to, arising from, or affected by disease. [< L *morbus* disease] **—mor′bid·ly** *adv.* **—mor·bid′i·ty, mor′bid·ness** *n.*

mor·dant (mor′dənt) *adj.* 1. Biting; cutting; sarcastic: a *mordant* wit. 2. Incisive; clear-cut. [< OF *modre* to bite] **—mor′dan·cy** *n.* **—mor′dant·ly** *adv.*

more (môr) *adj. superlative* **most** 1. Greater in amount, extent, degree, or number: comparative of *much* and *many.* 2. Additional: *More* coffee, please. **—*n.*** 1. A greater or additional quantity, amount, etc.: Will you have *more?* 2. That which exceeds or excels something else. **—*adv.*** 1. In or to a greater extent or degree: used to form the comparative of many adjectives and adverbs: *more* beautiful. 2. In addition; further. **—more or less** 1. In some undetermined degree. 2. Approximately. [OE *māra*]

mo·rel (mə·rel′) *n.* Any of a group of edible mushrooms resembling a sponge on a stalk. [< MF *morille*]

more·o·ver (môr·ō′vər) *adv.* Beyond what has been said; further; besides.

mo·res (môr′āz, -ēz) *n.pl. Sociol.* 1. The established, traditional customs regarded by a social group as essential to its preservation. 2. The accepted conventions of a group. [< L, pl. of *mos, moris* custom]

mor·ga·nat·ic (môr′gə·nat′ik) *adj.* Of or designating a marriage between a member of certain royal families of Europe and a person of inferior rank, in which the titles and estates are not shared by the inferior partner or their children. [< OHG *morgangeba* morning gift] **—mor′ga·nat′i·cal·ly** *adv.*

morgue (môrg) *n.* 1. A place where the bodies of dead persons are kept for identification. 2. A newspaper's files of reference material, biographical material, back issues, etc. [< F]

mor·i·bund (môr′ə·bund) *adj.* At the point of death; dying. [< L *mori* to die] **—mor′i·bun′di·ty** *n.*

mo·ri·on (môr′ē·on) *n.* A crested, visorless helmet, worn in the 16th and 17th c. [< Sp. *morra* crown of the head]

Mor·mon (môr′mən) *n.* A member of the Mormon Church; a Latter-day Saint. **—Mor′mon** *adj.* **—Mor′mon·ism** *n.*

Mormon Church The Church of Jesus Christ of Latter-day Saints, founded by Joseph Smith in 1830.

morn (môrn) *n. Poetic* The morning. [ME *morne, morwen* < OE *morgen* morning]

morn·ing (môr′ning) *n.* 1. The early part of the day; the time from midnight to noon, or from sunrise to noon. 2. The early part or stage of anything. **—*adj.*** Pertaining to or occurring in the morning. ◆Collateral adjective: *matutinal.* [ME *morwen* + *-ing* by analogy with *evening*]

morn·ing-glo·ry (môr′ning·glôr′ē) *n.* A twining plant with funnel-shaped flowers.

morning star A planet, esp. Venus, when rising in the east shortly before the sun.

Mo·roc·can (mə·rok′ən) *n.* A native or inhabitant of Morocco. **—*adj.*** Of or pertaining to Morocco.

mo·roc·co (mə·rok′ō) *n.* A fine flexible leather, made from goatskin tanned with sumac. Also **morocco leather.**

mo·ron (môr′on) *n.* 1. A person exhibiting the mildest degree of mental deficiency, permitting adequacy in simple activities. 2. Loosely, a very stupid person. [< Gk. *mōros* stupid] **—mo·ron′ic** *adj.* **—mo·ron′i·cal·ly** *adv.*

mo·rose (mə·rōs′) *adj.* Ill-humored; sullen; gloomy, as a person, mood, etc. [< L *mos, moris* manner, mood] **—mo·rose′ly** *adv.* **—mo·rose′ness** *n.*

-morph *combining form* Having the form or shape of: *polymorph.* [< Gk. *morphē* form]

mor·pheme (môr′fēm) *n. Ling.* The smallest meaningful unit of a language or dialect, whether a word, base, or affix. [< Gk. *morphē* form]

-morphic *combining form* Having the form or shape of: *anthropomorphic.* [< Gk. *morphē* form]

mor·phine (môr′fēn) *n. Chem.* A bitter, white crystalline compound, the principal alkaloid of opium, used as an analgesic and narcotic. [< L *Morpheus,* god of dreams]

morpho- *combining form* Form; shape. Also, before vowels, **morph-.** [< Gk. *morphē* form]

mor·phol·o·gy (môr·fol′ə·jē) *n. pl.* **·gies** 1. *Biol.* The study of the form and structure of plants and animals considered apart from function. 2. *Ling.* The arrangement and interrelationship of morphemes in words. **—mor·pho·log·ic** (môr′fə·loj′ik) or **·i·cal** *adj.* **—mor·phol′o·gist** *n.*

-morphous *combining form* Having a (specified) form: often equivalent to *-morphic*: *anthropomorphous.*

mor·ris (môr′is, mor′-) *n.* An old English

dance, performed esp. on May Day. [Earlier *morys, morish* Moorish]

mor·row (môr′ō, mor′ō) *n. Archaic & Poetic* **1.** The next succeeding day. **2.** A time immediately following a specified event. **3.** Formerly, morning.

Morse code A system of telegraphic signals composed of dots and dashes representing the letters of the alphabet, numerals, etc. [after Samuel F. B. *Morse,* 1791–1872, U.S. inventor]

mor·sel (môr′səl) *n.* **1.** A small fragment or bite of food. **2.** A tempting dish; tidbit. **3.** A small piece or bit of something. [< OF, dim. of *mors* bite]

mor·tal (môr′təl) *adj.* **1.** Subject to death. **2.** Of or relating to this life or world. **3.** Causing or liable to cause death. **4.** Grievous; dire: *mortal* terror. **5.** Likely to remain so until death; implacable: a *mortal* enemy. **6.** *Theol.* Incurring spiritual death unless repented of and forgiven: distinguished from *venial: mortal* sin. **—*n.*** One who is mortal; a human being. [< L *mors, mortis* death]

mor·tal·i·ty (môr·tal′ə·tē) *n. pl.* **·ties** **1.** The condition of being mortal or subject to death. **2.** The frequency of death; death rate.

mor·tal·ly (môr′təl·ē) *adv.* **1.** Fatally. **2.** After the manner of a mortal. **3.** Extremely: *mortally* offended.

mor·tar[1] (môr′tər) *n.* A bowl-shaped vessel in which substances are crushed with a pestle. [< L *mortarium* mixing trough]

mor·tar[2] (môr′tər) *n.* A mixture of lime, cement, etc., with sand and water, used in bricklaying, plastering walls, etc. [< L *mortarium* trough, mixture of sand and lime]

mor·tar[3] (môr′tər) *n. Mil.* A smooth-bored or rifled muzzleloading weapon, firing a relatively heavy shell, having a shorter range and higher trajectory than a howitzer. [< F *mortier*]

mor·tar·board (môr′tər·bôrd′) *n.* **1.** A square board with a handle, on which a mason holds mortar. **2.** An academic cap with a stiff, flat, four-cornered top, worn at graduations.

mort·gage (môr′gij) *n. Law* **1.** A transfer of property pledged as security for the repayment of a loan. **2.** The contract specifying such a pledge. **—*v.t.* ·gaged, ·gag·ing** To make over or pledge (property) by mortgage. [< OF, dead pledge]

mort·ga·gee (môr′gi·jē′) *n.* The holder of a mortgage.

mort·ga·gor (môr′gi·jər) *n.* One who mortgages his property to another as security for a loan. Also **mort′gag·er.**

mor·ti·cian (môr·tish′ən) *n.* A funeral director; undertaker. [< L *mors, mortis* death + -ICIAN]

mor·ti·fy (môr′tə·fī) *v.* **·fied, ·fy·ing** *v.t.* **1.** To humiliate. **2.** To discipline (the body, appetites, etc.) by fasting or other ascetic practices. **—*v.i.*** **3.** To practice ascetic self-discipline. [< L *mors, mortis* death + *facere* to make] **—mor′ti·fi·ca′tion** *n.* **—mor′ti·fy′ing·ly** *adv.*

mor·tise (môr′tis) *n.* A space hollowed out in a piece of timber, stone, etc., and shaped to fit a tenon to which it is to be joined. **—*v.t.* ·tised, ·tis·ing** **1.** To cut or make a mortise in. **2.** To join by a tenon and mortise. Also **mor′tice.** [< Arabic *murtazz* joined, fixed in]

mor·tu·ar·y (môr′choo·er′ē) *n. pl.* **·ar·ies** A place for the temporary reception of the dead before burial. [< L *mortuarius* of the dead]

mo·sa·ic (mō·zā′ik) *n.* **1.** Inlaid work composed of bits of stone, glass, etc., forming a pattern or picture. **2.** A design, arrangement, etc., resembling such work. [< Gk. *mouseios* of the Muses, artistic] **—mo·sa′ic** *adj.* **—mo·sa·i·cist** (mō·zā′ə·sist) *n.*

Mo·sa·ic Law (mō·zā′ik) The code of civil and religious laws contained in the Pentateuch and traditionally attributed to Moses.

Mo·selle (mō·zel′) *n.* A light, dry wine.

mo·sey (mō′zē) *v.i. Slang* To saunter or stroll; shuffle along. [Origin unknown]

Mos·lem (moz′ləm) *n. & adj.* Muslim. [See MUSLIM.]

mosque (mosk) *n.* A Muslim temple of worship. [< Arabic *masjid* < *sajada* to worship]

mos·qui·to (məs·kē′tō) *n. pl.* **·toes** or **·tos** Any of various winged insects, having in the female a long proboscis for sucking the blood of man and animals, certain species of which transmit diseases. [< Sp., dim. of *mosca* fly]

mosquito net A fine net or gauze (**mosquito netting**) placed over windows, beds, etc., to keep out mosquitoes.

moss (môs, mos) *n.* **1.** A delicate plant with a stem and distinct leaves, which grows in tufts or clusters on the ground, decaying wood, rocks, etc. **2.** Any of several similar plants, as certain lichens. [OE *mos* marsh] **—moss′i·ness** *n.* **—moss′y** *adj.*

moss·back (môs′bak′, mos′-) *n.* **1.** An old fish or turtle on whose back is a growth of algae or the like. **2.** *Slang* A very conservative or old-fashioned person; fogy.

moss rose A cultivated variety of the rose with a mossy calyx and stem.

most (mōst) *adj.* **1.** Consisting of the greatest number: superlative of *many.* **2.** Consisting of the greatest amount or degree: superlative of *much.* **3.** In the greatest number of instances: *Most* people are honest. **—for the most part** Generally; mostly. **—*n.*** **1.** (*construed as pl.*) The greatest number; the largest part. **2.** The greatest amount, quantity, or degree. **—*adv.*** **1.** In or to the greatest or highest degree, quantity, extent, etc.: used with adjectives and adverbs to form the superlative degree. **2.** Very. [OE *mǣst, māst*]

-most *suffix* Most: added to adjectives and adverbs to form superlatives: *innermost; outmost.*

most·ly (mōst′lē) *adv.* For the most part; principally.

mot (mō) *n.* A witty or pithy saying. [< F, word]

mote (mōt) *n.* A minute particle or speck, esp., of dust. [OE *mot* dust]

mo·tel (mō·tel′) *n.* A hotel for motorists, usu. having rooms directly accessible to parking facilities: also called *motor court, motor lodge.*

mo·tet (mō·tet′) *n. Music* A polyphonic vocal composition of a sacred nature, usu. unaccompanied. [< OF]

moth (môth) *n. pl.* **moths** (môthz, môths) Any of a large group of insects, usu. nocturnal, distinguished from the butterflies by smaller wings, stouter bodies, and duller coloring. [OE *moththe*]
moth·ball (môth'bôl') *adj. Mil. & Nav.* Designating ships or military equipment laid up in reserve and covered with protective materials. —*v.t.* To put in storage.
moth ball A small ball of camphor or naphthalene used to repel moths from clothing, etc., during storage.
moth-eat·en (môth'ēt'n) *adj.* 1. Eaten or damaged by moths. 2. Worn out. 3. Old-fashioned.
moth·er[1] (muth'ər) *n.* 1. A female who has borne offspring. 2. A female who adopts a child, or who otherwise holds a maternal relationship toward another. 3. Anything that creates, nurtures, or protects something else. 4. *Usu. cap.* A title given to a nun having authority. —*adj.* 1. Native: *mother* tongue. 2. Relating to or characteristic of a mother: *mother* love. 3. Holding a maternal relation: the *mother* church. —*v.t.* 1. To bring forth as a mother; produce; create. 2. To care for or protect as a mother. [OE *mōder*] —**moth'er·hood** *n.* —**moth'er·less** *adj.*
moth·er[2] (muth'ər) *n.* A slimy film composed of bacteria and yeast cells, active in the production of vinegar.
mother-in-law (muth'ər·in·lô') *n. pl.* **moth·ers-in-law** The mother of one's spouse.
moth·er·land (muth'ər·land') *n.* 1. The land of one's birth; native land. 2. The land of one's ancestors.
mother lode In mining, any principal or very rich vein.
moth·er·ly (muth'ər·lē) *adj.* Resembling, characteristic of, or like a mother. —*adv.* In the manner of a mother. —**moth'er·li·ness** *n.*
moth·er-of-pearl (muth'ər·əv·pûrl') *n.* The pearly, iridescent internal layer of certain shells, as those of the pearl oyster and abalone, used in ornamental work, for buttons, etc.: also called *nacre.* —*adj.* Of mother-of-pearl.
mother tongue One's native language.
mother wit Inherent or native intelligence; common sense.
moth·y (môth'ē) *adj.* **moth·i·er, moth·i·est** 1. Moth-eaten. 2. Full of moths.
mo·tif (mō·tēf') *n.* The underlying theme or main element in a literary or artistic work. Also *motive.* [< F]
mo·tile (mō'til, -təl) *adj. Zool.* Having the power of motion, as certain minute organisms. [See MOTION.] —**mo·til'i·ty** *n.*
mo·tion (mō'shən) *n.* 1. The act or process of changing position; movement: also, an instance of this. 2. A formal proposal or suggestion in an assembly or meeting. 3. An impulse; inclination. —**in motion** Moving; in operation. —*v.i.* 1. To make a gesture of direction or intent, as with the hand. —*v.t.* 2. To direct or guide by a gesture. [< L *motus*, pp. of *movere* to move]
motion picture 1. A sequence of pictures of moving objects photographed on a strip of film, that, when projected on a screen, gives the optical illusion of continuous movement. 2. A specific drama, story, etc., made by means of such photographs: also called *film, movie, moving picture.*
motion sickness Nausea, dizziness, etc., caused by the effects of motion, as in travel.
mo·ti·vate (mō'tə·vāt) *v.t.* **·vat·ed, ·vat·ing** To provide with a motive. [< F *motiver*] —**mo'ti·va'tion** *n.* —**mo'ti·va'tion·al** *adj.*
mo·tive (mō'tiv) *n.* 1. A conscious or unconscious need, drive, etc., that incites a person to some action or behavior; incentive; goal. 2. A motif. —*adj.* 1. Causing or having the power to cause motion. 2. Relating to or acting as a motive. [< Med.L *movere* to move]
mot·ley (mot'lē) *adj.* 1. Made up of diverse elements; heterogeneous. 2. Variegated in color. —*n.* 1. A heterogeneous mixture or collection. 2. A garment of various colors such as formerly worn by court jesters. [ME *motteley*]
mo·tor (mō'tər) *n.* 1. An engine; esp., an internal-combustion engine propelling an automobile, motor boat, etc. 2. Something that imparts or produces motion. 3. *Chiefly Brit.* A car. —*adj.* 1. Causing, producing, or imparting motion. 2. Equipped with or driven by a motor. 3. *Physiol.* Transmitting impulses from nerve centers to the muscles. —*v.i.* To travel or ride in an automobile. [< L *motus*, pp. of *movere* to move]
mo·tor·bike (mō'tər·bīk') *n. Informal* 1. A bicycle driven by a small motor. 2. A motorcycle.
mo·tor·boat (mō'tər·bōt') *n.* A boat propelled by a motor: also called *power boat.*
mo·tor·cade (mō'tər·kād) *n.* A procession of automobiles.
mo·tor·car (mō'tər·kär') *n.* An automobile.
motor court A motel.
mo·tor·cy·cle (mō'tər·sī'kəl) *n.* A two-wheeled vehicle, larger and heavier than a bicycle, propelled by an internal-combustion engine. —*v.i.* **·cled, ·cling** To travel or ride on a motorcycle. —**mo'tor·cy'clist** *n.*
mo·tor·ist (mō'tər·ist) *n.* One who drives or travels by automobile.
mo·tor·ize (mō'tər·īz) *v.t.* **·ized, ·iz·ing** 1. To equip with a motor. 2. To equip with motor-propelled vehicles. —**mo'tor·i·za'tion** *n.*
motor lodge A motel.
mo·tor·man (mō'tər·mən) *n. pl.* **·men** (-mən) One who operates an electric street car or electric railway locomotive.
motor scooter A two-wheeled vehicle similar to a child's scooter, having a driver's seat and powered by an internal-combustion engine.
motor vehicle A wheeled vehicle with a motor, as a bus or car, for use on streets or roads.
mot·tle (mot'l) *v.t.* **·tled, ·tling** To mark with spots or streaks of different colors or shades; blotch. —*n.* A spotted, blotched, or variegated appearance, as of skin or marble. [Back formation < MOTLEY] —**mot'tled** *adj.*
mot·to (mot'ō) *n. pl.* **·toes** or **·tos** 1. A word or phrase expressing a rule of conduct, principle, etc.; a maxim. 2. An appropriate or indicative phrase inscribed on something, prefixed to a literary work, etc. [< Ital. < F *mot* word]
moue (mo͞o) *n.* A pouting grimace, as of disdain. [< F]

mould (mōld) See MOLD.
moult (mōlt) See MOLT.
mound (mound) *n.* 1. A heap or pile of earth, debris, etc., either natural or artificial. 2. A small natural elevation; a hillock. 3. In baseball, the slightly raised ground from which the pitcher pitches. —*v.t.* To heap up in a mound. [Origin unknown]
mount[1] (mount) *v.t.* 1. To ascend or climb (a slope, stairs, etc.). 2. To get up on; climb upon. 3. To put or set on horseback. 4. To furnish with a horse. 5. To set, fix, or secure in or on a support, frame, etc., as for exhibition or use: to *mount* a specimen on a microscope slide. 6. To furnish with scenery, costumes, etc.: to *mount* a play. 7. *Mil.* **a** To set or raise into position, as a gun. **b** To prepare and begin: to *mount* an offensive. —*v.i.* 8. To rise or ascend; go or come up. 9. To increase in amount, number, or degree. —*n.* 1. Anything on or in which an object is placed for use, preparation, display, etc., as a setting for a jewel, etc. 2. A horse or other animal used for riding. [< OF *monter* < L *mons, montis* mountain] —**mount′ed** *adj.* —**mount′er** *n.*
mount[2] (mount) *n.* A mountain or hill: used poetically or as part of a proper name. [< L *mons, montis* mountain]
moun·tain (moun′tən) *n.* 1. A natural elevation of the earth's surface, typically having steep sides and a narrow summit, and rising higher than a hill. 2. Anything of great size: a *mountain* of a man. —*adj.* 1. Of or like a mountain. 2. Living, growing, or situated on mountains. [< L *mons, montis* mountain] —**moun′tain·ous** *adj.* —**moun′·tain·ous·ly** *adv.*
mountain ash 1. A small tree of the rose family, having white flowers and orange-red berries. 2. Any of various related trees.
moun·tain·eer (moun′tən·ir′) *n.* 1. An inhabitant of a mountainous district. 2. One who climbs mountains. —*v.i.* To climb mountains.
mountain goat The Rocky Mountain goat.
mountain laurel A low-growing evergreen shrub of the eastern U.S., having white or pink flowers.
mountain lion The puma. Also **mountain cat.**
moun·te·bank (moun′tə·bangk) *n.* 1. One who sells quack medicines at fairs. 2. Any charlatan. [< Ital. *montare* to mount + *in* upon + *banco* bench]
Moun·ty (moun′tē) *n. pl.* **·ties** *Informal* A member of the Royal Canadian Mounted Police. Also **Mount′ie.**
mourn (môrn) *v.i.* 1. To feel or express grief or sorrow, esp. for the dead; grieve. —*v.t.* 2. To lament or sorrow for (someone dead). 3. To grieve over or bemoan (misfortune, failure, etc.). [OE *murnan*] —**mourn′er** *n.*
mourn·ful (môrn′fəl) *adj.* 1. Indicating, expressing, or exciting grief. 2. Doleful; melancholy; sad. —**mourn′ful·ly** *adv.* —**mourn′ful·ness** *n.*
mourn·ing (môr′ning) *n.* 1. The act of one who mourns. 2. The manifestations of grief, as the wearing of black dress, etc. 3. The period during which one mourns. —*adj.* Of or expressive of mourning.
mourning dove A dove common in North America, having a mournful cry.
mouse (*n.* mous; *v.* mouz) *n. pl.* **mice** (mīs) 1. One of various small rodents frequenting human habitations throughout the world. ◆Collateral adjective: *murine.* 2. *Informal* A timid person. 3. *Slang* A black eye. —*v.i.* **moused, mous·ing** To hunt or catch mice. [OE *mūs*] —**mous·er** (mou′zer) *n.*
mouse·trap (mous′trap′) *n.* A trap for catching mice.
mousse (mo͞os) *n.* Any of various light desserts made with whipped cream, egg white, etc., and sugar and flavoring. [< F]
mous·tache (məs·tash′, mus′tash) See MUSTACHE.
mous·y (mou′sē, -zē) *adj.* **mous·i·er, mous·i·est** 1. Of or resembling a mouse. 2. Characterized by timidity, shyness, drabness, etc. Also **mous′ey.** —**mous′i·ness** *n.*
mouth (*n.* mouth; *v.* mouth) *n. pl.* **mouths** (mouthz) 1. The opening at which food is taken into the body; also, the cavity between the lips and throat. ◆Collateral adjective: *oral.* 2. One who needs food: so many *mouths* to feed. 3. The organ or instrument of speech: to shut one's *mouth.* 4. Something resembling a mouth; as: **a** The part of a stream where its waters are discharged into another body of water. **b** The entrance or opening of something, as a cave, mine, or jar. —**down in** (or **at**) **the mouth** *Informal* Disconsolate; dejected. —*v.t.* 1. To speak in a forced or affected manner. 2. To form (words, etc.) silently with the lips and tongue. [OE *mūth*] —**mouth·er** (mou′thər) *n.*
mouthed (mouthd, moutht) *adj.* 1. Having a mouth or mouths. 2. Having a (specified kind of) mouth or (a specified number of) mouths: used in combination: *evil-mouthed.*
mouth·ful (mouth′fo͝ol′) *n. pl.* **·fuls** (-fo͝olz′) 1. As much as can be held in the mouth. 2. *Informal* A long word or group of words difficult to say. 3. *Slang* An important or perceptive remark: chiefly in the phrase **to say a mouthful.**
mouth organ 1. A harmonica. 2. A set of panpipes.
mouth·piece (mouth′pēs′) *n.* 1. That part of a musical instrument, telephone, etc., that is used in or near the mouth. 2. One who acts as spokesman for an individual, group, belief, etc.
mouth·wash (mouth′wosh′, -wôsh′) *n.* An antiseptic and scented solution used for cleaning the mouth.
mouth·y (mou′thē, -thē) *adj.* **mouth·i·er, mouth·i·est** Garrulous; bombastic. —**mouth′i·ness** *n.*
mou·ton (mo͞o′ton) *n.* Sheepskin processed to simulate beaver or seal, used for women's coats, etc. [< F, sheep]
mov·a·ble (mo͞o′və·bəl) *adj.* 1. Capable of being moved. 2. *Eccl.* Varying in date from year to year: *movable* feast. 3. *Law* Pertaining to personal property as distinguished from real property. —*n.* 1. *Usu. pl.* Anything that can be moved; esp., an article of furniture. 2. *pl.* *Law* Personal property. Also **move′a·ble.** —**mov′a·bil′i·ty** *n.* —**mov′·a·bly** *adv.*
move (mo͞ov) *v.* **moved, mov·ing** *v.i.* 1. To change place or position; go to or from a place. 2. To change one's residence. 3. To make progress; advance. 4. To live or carry on one's life: to *move* in cultivated circles.

5. To operate, work, revolve, etc., as a machine. 6. To take or begin to take action; act. 7. To be disposed of by sale. 8. To make an application or proposal: to *move* for adjournment. 9. To evacuate: said of the bowels. —*v.t.* 10. To change the place or position of, as by carrying, pushing, pulling, etc. 11. To set or keep in motion. 12. To dislodge or force from a set position: to *move* him from his purpose. 13. To affect or arouse the emotions, sympathies, etc., of; touch. 14. To propose for action, deliberation, etc. 15. To cause (the bowels) to evacuate. —*n.* 1. An act of moving; movement. 2. An action for some purpose or design; step; maneuver. 3. A change in residence. 4. In checkers, chess, etc., the transfer of a piece. [< L *movere* to set in motion] —**mov′er** *n.*

move·ment (mo͞ov′mənt) *n.* 1. The act of moving; any change of place or position. 2. A specific instance or manner of moving: a dance *movement.* 3. The actions by individuals or organizations toward some end: the right-wing *movement.* 4. *Mech.* A particular arrangement of related moving parts. 5. *Music* One of the sections of a work, as of a symphony, string quartet, etc. 6. An emptying of the bowels. [< L *movere* to set in motion]

mov·ie (mo͞o′vē) *n.* *Informal* 1. A motion picture. 2. *pl.* The showing of a motion picture. 3. *pl.* The motion-picture industry. [Contr. of MOVING PICTURE]

mov·ing (mo͞o′ving) *adj.* 1. Going or capable of going from place to place, position to position, etc. 2. Affecting, arousing, or touching the feelings or passions. —**mov′·ing·ly** *adv.*

moving picture A motion picture.

mow[1] (mō) *v.t. & v.i.* **mowed, mowed** or **mown, mow·ing** 1. To cut down (grain, grass, etc.) with a scythe or machine. 2. To cut the grain or grass of (a field, lawn, etc.). —**to mow down** *Informal* To cut down or kill rapidly or indiscriminately. [OE *māwan*] —**mow′er** *n.*

mow[2] (mou) *n.* Hay or grain stored in a barn; also, the place of storage. —*v.t.* To store in a mow. [OE *mūga*]

mox·ie (mok′sē) *n.* *Slang* Native shrewdness or common sense.

Mo·zam·bi·can (mō′zam·bē′kən) *adj.* Of Mozambique or its people. —**Mo′zam·bi′can** *n.*

moz·za·rel·la (mot′sə·rel′ə) *n.* A soft curd cheese that is very stringy when cooked. [< Ital.]

Mr. (mis′tər) *n.* The contracted form of MISTER.

Mrs. (mis′iz) *n.* A title prefixed to the name of a married woman: a contracted form of *Mistress.*

Ms., Ms (miz) *n.* *pl.* **Mses, Mss.** or **Mss** A title of a woman that disregards marital status.

mu (myo͞o, mo͞o) *n.* 1. The twelfth letter in the Greek alphabet (M, μ), corresponding to the English *m.* 2. The micron (symbol μ).

much (much) *adj.* **more, most** Great in quantity, amount, extent, etc.: *much* noise. —*n.* 1. A considerable quantity or amount; a great deal. 2. A remarkable or important thing: It isn't *much.* —**to make much of** 1. To treat as very important. 2. To treat with great courtesy, regard, etc. —*adv.* 1. Greatly: *much* obliged. 2. For the most part; almost. [< OE *mycel*]

mu·ci·lage (myo͞o′sə·lij) *n.* 1. An aqueous solution of vegetable gum or the like, used as an adhesive. 2. Any of various gummy or gelatinous substances found in some plants. [< LL *mucilago* musty juice] —**mu·ci·lag·i·nous** (myo͞o′si·laj′ə·nəs) *adj.*

muck (muk) *n.* 1. Any wet and clinging material that soils; esp., viscid mud. 2. Moist dung mixed with decomposed vegetable matter, used as a soil fertilizer; manure. 3. A dark, rich soil consisting largely of decomposing vegetable materials. 4. A confusing or uncertain state or condition; mess. —*v.t.* 1. To fertilize with manure. 2. *Informal* To make dirty; pollute. [ME *muk*] —**muck′y** *adj.*

muck·rake (muk′rāk′) *v.i.* **·raked, ·rak·ing** To search for or expose real or alleged corruption on the part of political officials, businessmen, etc. [Back formation < *muckrakes,* slang term in late 19th c. U.S. politics] —**muck′rak′er** *n.* —**muck′rak′ing** *n.*

mu·cous (myo͞o′kəs) *adj.* 1. Secreting mucus. 2. Pertaining to, consisting of, or resembling mucus. Also **mu′cose** (-kōs). —**mu·cos′i·ty** (-kos′ə·tē) *n.*

mucous membrane *Anat.* A membrane secreting or producing mucus, that lines various body passages.

mu·cus (myo͞o′kəs) *n.* *Biol.* A viscid substance secreted by the mucous membranes. [< L]

mud (mud) *n.* 1. Soft and sticky wet earth. 2. *Informal* The most degrading place or situation: to drag one into the *mud.* —*v.t.* **mud·ded, mud·ding** To soil or cover with or as with mud. [< MLG *mudde* or MDu. *modde*]

mud·dle (mud′l) *v.* **·dled, ·dling** *v.t.* 1. To confuse or confound (the mind, speech, etc.). 2. To mess up or mismanage; bungle. 3. To make muddy or turbid. —*v.i.* 4. To act or think in a confused manner. —**to muddle through** To achieve one's object despite confusion or mistakes. —*n.* A state or condition of confusion, disorder, or uncertainty. [< MUD + freq. suffix *-le*]

mud·dle·head·ed (mud′l·hed′id) *adj.* Mentally confused; addlebrained; stupid.

mud·dy (mud′ē) *adj.* **·di·er, ·di·est** 1. Covered, spattered, or filled with mud. 2. Not clear, bright, or distinct, as color, liquid, etc. 3. Confused or obscure in thought, expression, meaning, etc. —*v.t. & v.i.* **·died, ·dy·ing** To make or become muddy. —**mud′di·ly** *adv.* —**mud′di·ness** *n.*

mud puppy A tailed amphibian found in streams and lakes of North America.

mud·sling·er (mud′sling′ər) *n.* One who casts malicious slurs, esp. at a political opponent. —**mud′sling′ing** *n.*

mud turtle Any of various turtles inhabiting muddy waters in North and Central America.

mu·ez·zin (myo͞o·ez′in) *n.* In Islam, a crier who calls the faithful to prayer. [< Arabic *mu'adhdhin* < *adhana* to call]

muff[1] (muf) *v.t. & v.i.* To perform (some act) clumsily; esp., to fail to catch (a ball). —*n.* An awkward action. [< MUFF[2]; prob. to handle as if wearing a muff]

muff[2] (muf) *n.* A pillowlike or tubular case of

fur or cloth, open at the ends, used for warming the hands. [< F *moufle* mitten]
muf·fin (muf′in) *n.* A small, cup-shaped quick bread. [Origin uncertain]
muf·fle (muf′əl) *v.t.* **·fled, ·fling** 1. To wrap up in a blanket, scarf, etc., as for warmth or concealment: often with *up.* 2. To deaden the sound of by or as by wrapping. 3. To deaden (a sound). [< F *moufle* mitten]
muf·fler (muf′lər) *n.* 1. A device to reduce noise, as from the exhaust of an engine. 2. A heavy scarf worn about the neck for warmth. [< MUFFLE]
muf·ti (muf′tē) *n.* Civilian dress, worn by one who normally wears a uniform. [< Arabic, an expounder of Muslim law]
mug[1] (mug) *n.* A large drinking cup. [Origin unknown]
mug[2] (mug) *n.* *Slang* 1. The face, esp. the mouth and chin. 2. A photograph of the face: also **mug shot.** —*v.* **mugged, mug·ging** *v.t.* 1. To assault viciously and rob. —*v.i.* 2. To make funny faces; overact to win an audience. [< MUG[1]] —**mug′ger** *n.*
mug·gy (mug′ē) *adj.* **·gi·er, ·gi·est** Warm, humid, and close; sultry. [< dial. E *mug* drizzle] —**mug′gi·ness** *n.*
mug·wump (mug′wump′) *n.* One who asserts his independence, esp. in politics. [< Algonquian *mugquomp* great man, chief] —**mug′wump′er·y** *n.*
Mu·ham·ma·dan (mo͞o·ham′ə·dən) *n.* A follower of the prophet Muhammad or a believer in Islam; a Muslim. Also called *Mohammedan*: also **Mu·ham′me·dan.** —**Mu·ham′ma·dan** *adj.* —**Mu·ham′ma·dan·ism** *n.*
mu·lat·to (mə·lat′ō, myo͞o-, -lä′tō) *n. pl.* **·toes** 1. A person having one white and one Negro parent. 2. Anyone having mixed white and Negro ancestry. —*adj.* Having the light brown color of a mulatto. [< Sp. < L *mulus* mule]
mul·ber·ry (mul′ber′ē, mul′bər·ē) *n. pl.* **·ries** 1. Any of various trees having a berrylike fruit and whose leaves are valued for silkworm culture. 2. A purplish red color. [Var. of ME *murberie*]
mulch (mulch) *n.* Any loose material, as straw, leaves, peat moss, etc., placed about the stalks of plants to protect their roots. —*v.t.* To cover with mulch. [ME *molsh* soft, OE *milisc*]
mulct (mulkt) *v.t.* 1. To defraud or cheat (someone). 2. To punish with a fine. —*n.* A fine or similar penalty. [< L *mulcta, multa* fine]
mule[1] (myo͞ol) *n.* 1. A hybrid between the ass and horse; esp., a hybrid between a jackass and mare. Compare HINNY. 2. *Informal* A stubborn person. [< L *mulus*] —**mul′ish** *adj.* —**mul′ish·ness** *n.*
mule[2] (myo͞ol) *n.* A backless lounging slipper. [< L *mulleus* reddish shoe]
mule skinner *Informal* One who drives mules.
mu·le·teer (myo͞o′lə·tir′) *n.* One who drives mules. [< MF *mulet,* dim. of OF *mul* mule]
mule train A train of mules carrying packs; also, a train of freight wagons drawn by mules.
mull[1] (mul) *v.t.* To heat and spice, as wine or cider. [Origin uncertain]
mull[2] (mul) *v.t.* To ponder: usu. with *over.* [ME *mullen* to pulverize]
mul·lein (mul′ən) *n.* Any of various herbs of the figwort family; esp., the **great mullein** and the **moth mullein.** Also **mul′len.** [< AF *moleine*]
mul·let (mul′it) *n. pl.* **·lets** or **·let** Any of various marine and fresh-water fish, as the **striped mullet** of the Atlantic and Pacific. [< L *mullus* red mullet]
mul·li·gan stew (mul′i·gən) *Slang* A meat and vegetable stew, originally made by tramps. Also **mul′li·gan.** [? from personal name]
mul·li·ga·taw·ny (mul′i·gə·tô′nē) *n.* A strongly flavored soup of the East Indies, made of meat and curry. [< Tamil *milagutannir* pepper water]
mul·lion (mul′yən) *n.* *Archit.* A vertical dividing piece in a window. —*v.t.* To divide by means of mullions. [? Var. of *monial* < L *medianus* medial]
mul·lock (mul′ək) *n.* Waste rock or earth left from mining. [ME *mull* dust] —**mul′lock·y** *adj.*
multi- *combining form* 1. Many; consisting of many: **multicolor, multihued, multipurpose, multisection, multistoried, multivalent.** 2. Having more than two (or more than one): **multicuspid, multicylinder, multinucleate, multispeed.** 3. Many times over: **multimillionaire.** Before vowels, **mult-.** [< L *multus* much]
mul·ti·col·ored (mul′ti·kul′ərd) *adj.* Having many colors.
mul·ti·far·i·ous (mul′tə·fâr′ē·əs) *adj.* Having great diversity or variety. [< LL *multifarius*] —**mul′ti·far′i·ous·ly** *adv.* —**mul′ti·far′i·ous·ness** *n.*
mul·ti·form (mul′tə·fôrm) *adj.* Having many forms or appearances.
mul·ti·lat·er·al (mul′ti·lat′ər·əl) *adj.* 1. Having many sides. 2. *Govt.* Involving more than two nations: also *multipartite.* —**mul′ti·lat′er·al·ly** *adv.*
mul·ti·lin·gual (mul′ti·ling′gwəl) *n. & adj.* Polyglot.
mul·ti·me·di·a (mul′tə·mē′dē·ə) *adj.* Involving simultaneous use of several communications media.
mul·ti·na·tion·al (mul′tə·nash′ən·əl, -nash′·nəl) *adj.* Involving more than two nations. —*n.* A corporation with significant operations in more than two nations.
mul·tip·a·rous (mul·tip′ə·rəs) *adj.* Giving birth to many at one time.
mul·ti·par·tite (mul′ti·pär′tīt) *adj.* 1. Divided into many parts. 2. *Govt.* Multilateral (def. 2).
mul·ti·ple (mul′tə·pəl) *adj.* 1. Having, consisting of, or relating to more than one part, aspect, individual, etc.; manifold. 2. Happening more than once; repeated. —*n.* *Math.* Any of the products of a given number and some other number: 8 and 12 are *multiples* of 4.
mul·ti·ple-choice (mul′tə·pəl·chois′) *adj.* Giving several answers from which the correct one is to be selected.
multiple sclerosis A degenerative disease of the nervous system, usu. affecting young people.
mul·ti·plex (mul′tə·pleks) *adj.* 1. Multiple; manifold. 2. *Telecom.* Designating a system for the simultaneous transmission of two or

more signals over the same wire or radio frequency channel. [< L *multus* much + *plicare* to fold]

mul·ti·pli·cand (mul′tə·plə·kand′) *n. Math.* A number multiplied, or to be multiplied, by another. [< L *multiplicandus* to be multiplied]

mul·ti·pli·ca·tion (mul′tə·plə·kā′shən) *n.* 1. The act of multiplying, or the state of being multiplied. 2. *Math.* The process of finding the sum of a number repeated a given number of times.

multiplication sign The symbol (×) placed between two numbers or quantities to denote a multiplication of the first by the second, as $4 \times 2 = 8$.

mul·ti·plic·i·ty (mul′tə·plis′ə·tē) *n. pl.* **·ties** 1. The condition or quality of being manifold or various. 2. A large number.

mul·ti·pli·er (mul′tə·plī′ər) *n.* 1. One who or that which multiplies or causes multiplication. 2. *Math.* The number by which a quantity is multiplied.

mul·ti·ply (mul′tə·plī) *v.t. & v.i.* **·plied, ·ply·ing** 1. To increase in number, amount, or degree. 2. *Math.* To determine the product of (two numbers) by multiplication. [< L *multus* much + *plicare* to fold] **—mul′ti·pli′a·ble** *adj.*

mul·ti·stage (mul′ti·stāj) *adj.* 1. Having or characterized by a number of definite stages in the completion of a process or action. 2. *Aerospace* Having several sections, as in a rocket, each of which fulfills a given task before burnout.

mul·ti·tude (mul′tə·tōōd, -tyōōd) *n.* A great number. **—the multitude** The common people. [< L *multus* many] **—mul′ti·tu′di·nous** *adj.*

mum[1] (mum) *adj.* Silent; saying nothing. **—*interj.*** Hush! **—mum's the word** Keep silent; be secretive. [Imit.]

mum[2] (mum) *n. Informal* A chrysanthemum.

mum·ble (mum′bəl) *v.t. & v.i.* **·bled, ·bling** To speak low and indistinctly; mutter. **—*n.*** A low, indistinct speech or sound; mutter. [ME *momelen*] **—mum′bler** *n.*

mum·ble·ty-peg (mum′bəl·tē·peg′) *n.* A game played by tossing a jackknife in various ways so that it will stick into the ground. Also **mum·ble-the-peg** (mum′bəl·thə·peg′).

mum·bo jum·bo (mum′bō jum′bō) Meaningless, complicated, or obscure ritual, observance, incantation, etc. [< *mama dyambo*, a tutelary god in certain African tribes]

mum·mer (mum′ər) *n.* 1. One who acts or makes sport in a mask or disguise. 2. An actor. **—mum′mer·y** *n.*

mum·mi·fy (mum′ə·fī) *v.* **·fied, ·fy·ing** *v.t.* 1. To make a mummy of; preserve by embalming, drying, etc. 2. To make dry and lifeless, as an idea, institution, etc. **—*v.i.*** 3. To dry up; shrivel. **—mum′mi·fi·ca′tion** *n.*

mum·my (mum′ē) *n. pl.* **·mies** A human or animal body embalmed in the ancient Egyptian manner. [< Persian *mum* wax]

mumps (mumps) *n.pl.* (*construed as sing.*) *Pathol.* A contagious virus disease usu. occurring in childhood, characterized by fever and swelling of the salivary glands. [Pl. of obs. *mump* grimace]

munch (munch) *v.t. & v.i.* To chew steadily with a crunching noise. [ME, ? < MF *manger*] **—munch′er** *n.*

mun·dane (mun·dān′, mun′dān) *adj.* 1. Pertaining to or characterized by that which is practical, routine, or ordinary: *mundane* concerns. 2. Of or relating to the world; earthly. [< L *mundus* world] **—mun·dane′ly** *adv.*

mu·nic·i·pal (myōō·nis′ə·pəl) *adj.* 1. Of or pertaining to a town or city or its local government. 2. Having local self-government. [< L *municeps, -cipis* free citizen] **—mu·nic′i·pal·ly** *adv.*

mu·nic·i·pal·i·ty (myōō·nis′ə·pal′ə·tē) *n. pl.* **·ties** An incorporated borough, town, or city.

mu·nif·i·cent (myōō·nif′ə·sənt) *adj.* Extraordinarily generous or bountiful; liberal. [< L *munus* gift + *facere* to make] **—mu·nif′i·cence** *n.* **—mu·nif′i·cent·ly** *adv.*

mu·ni·tion (myōō·nish′ən) *n. Usu. pl.* Ammunition and all other necessary war materiel. [< L *munire* to fortify]

mu·on (myōō′on) *n. Physics* A subatomic particle having the same properties as an electron but with a mass about 200 times greater.

mu·ral (myŏŏr′əl) *n.* A painting or decoration applied to a wall or ceiling. **—*adj.*** 1. Placed or executed on a wall: a *mural* painting. 2. Of, pertaining to, or resembling a wall. [< L *murus* wall] **—mu′ral·ist** *n.*

mur·der (mûr′dər) *n.* 1. The unlawful, malicious, and intentional killing of one human being by another. 2. *Informal* Something exceedingly difficult, painful, or hazardous. **—*v.t.*** 1. To kill (a human being) unlawfully and with deliberate malice. 2. To spoil or mar by a bad performance, improper pronunciation, etc. **—*v.i.*** 3. To commit murder. [OE *morthor*] **—mur′der·er** *n.* **—mur′der·ess** *n.fem.*

mur·der·ous (mûr′dər·əs) *adj.* 1. Of, pertaining to, or involving murder. 2. Capable of or given to murder. 3. Having the characteristics of or resembling murder; brutal; deadly. **—mur′der·ous·ly** *adv.*

mu·ri·at·ic acid (myŏŏr′ē·at′ik) *n.* Hydrochloric acid, esp. an impure grade used commercially. [< L *muriaticus* pickled < *muria* brine]

mu·rine (myŏŏr′īn, -in) *adj.* Of or pertaining to a family or a subfamily of rodents that includes the true mice and rats. **—*n.*** A murine rodent. [< L *mus, muris* mouse]

murk (mûrk) *n.* Darkness; gloom. [OE *mirce*]

murk·y (mûr′kē) *adj.* **mur·ki·er, mur·ki·est** 1. Dark, gloomy, or obscure: the *murky* depths. 2. Hazy, thick, or misty, as atmosphere, color, etc. 3. Not clear or distinct to the mind; confused; abstruse. **—murk′i·ness** *n.*

mur·mur (mûr′mər) *n.* 1. A low, indistinct, continuously repeated sound, as of many voices. 2. A mumbled complaint; grumbling. 3. *Med.* A soft, low sound originating in certain organs; esp., an abnormal, rasping sound produced within the heart. **—*v.i.*** 1. To make a low, indistinct sound. 2. To complain in low, muttered tones. **—*v.t.*** 3. To mutter. [< L] **—mur′mur·er** *n.* **—mur′mur·ous** *adj.*

Mur·phy's Law (mûr′fēz) The observation that whatever can go wrong, will. [Origin unknown]

mur·rain (mûr′in) *n.* A contagious disease affecting cattle. [< L *mori* to die]

mus·cat (mus′kat, -kət) *n.* Any of several varieties of musk-flavored Old World grapes. [< LL *muscus* musk]

mus·ca·tel (mus′kə·tel′) *n.* A rich, sweet wine, made from the muscat grape.

mus·cle (mus′əl) *n.* 1. *Anat.* A tissue composed of bundles of elongated fibers that produce bodily movements by expanding or contracting. 2. An organ or structure consisting of such tissue. 3. Muscular strength; brawn. —*v.i.* **·cled, ·cling** *Slang* To force one's way by or as by sheer brawn: often with *in.* [< L *musculus,* lit., little mouse] —**mus′cled** *adj.*

mus·cle-bound (mus′əl·bound′) *adj.* Having enlarged and inelastic muscles, as from excessive exercise.

mus·cu·lar (mus′kyə·lər) *adj.* 1. Pertaining to or composed of muscle. 2. Having strong muscles; brawny. —**mus′cu·lar′i·ty** (-lar′·ə·tē) *n.*

muscular dys·tro·phy (dis′trə·fē) *Pathol.* One of various diseases characterized by a progressive degeneration of muscle tissue.

mus·cu·la·ture (mus′kyə·lə·choor) *n.* 1. The arrangement of muscles in a part or organ. 2. The muscle system as a whole. [< F]

muse[1] (myooz) *n.* 1. A spirit or power regarded as inspiring artists, poets, etc. 2. *cap.* One of nine Greek goddesses presiding over the arts and sciences. [< Gk. *Mousa* Muse]

muse[2] (myooz) *v.t. & v.i.* **mused, mus·ing** To consider thoughtfully or at length; ponder; meditate. [< OF *muser* to reflect] —**muse′ful** *adj.* —**muse′ful·ly** *adv.*

mu·se·um (myoo·zē′əm) *n.* A place or building for preserving and exhibiting works of art, scientific objects, curiosities, etc. [< Gk. *mouseion* shrine of the Muses]

mush[1] (mush) *n.* 1. A thick porridge made with corn meal boiled in water or milk. 2. Anything soft and pulpy. 3. *Informal* Maudlin sentimentality. [Var. of MASH] —**mush′i·ness** *n.* —**mush′y** *adj.* **mush·i·er, mush·i·est**

mush[2] (mush) *v.i.* In arctic regions, to travel over snow with a dog sled. —*interj.* Get along!: a command to a dog team. [Prob. < F (Canadian) *marche,* the cry of voyageurs to their dogs]

mush·room (mush′room, -room) *n.* 1. Any of various fleshy, rapidly growing, umbrella-shaped fungi, esp. the common edible **field mushroom** and certain poisonous varieties loosely called toadstools. 2. Anything resembling a mushroom in shape or rapid growth. —*v.i.* To grow or spread rapidly. [ME *muscheron*]

mu·sic (myoo′zik) *n.* 1. The art of producing arrangements of sounds, usu. with reference to rhythm, pitch, and tone color. 2. Such compositions or arrangements. 3. A succession or combination of sounds, esp. if pleasing to the ear. —**to face the music** To accept the consequences of one's acts. [< Gk. *mousikē (technē),* lit., the art of the Muse]

mu·si·cal (myoo′zi·kəl) *adj.* 1. Of, pertaining to, or capable of creating music. 2. Having the nature or characteristics of music; melodious; harmonious. 3. Fond of or versed in music. 4. Set to music. —*n.* A musical comedy. —**mu′si·cal·ly** *adv.* —**mu′si·cal′i·ty** (-kal′ə·tē), **mu′si·cal·ness** *n.*

musical comedy A show with music, songs, dances, jokes, colorful staging, etc., often based on a negligible plot.

mu·si·cale (myoo′zə·kal′) *n.* A private concert or recital, as in a home. [< F *(soirée) musicale* musical (evening)]

music box A mechanism that plays tunes, usu. by means of pins that strike the tuned teeth of a comblike metal plate.

music hall 1. A public building for musical performances. 2. *Brit.* A vaudeville theater.

mu·si·cian (myoo·zish′ən) *n.* 1. A professional performer or composer of music. 2. One skilled in performing or composing music. —**mu·si′cian·ship** *n.*

mu·si·col·o·gy (myoo′zə·kol′ə·jē) *n. pl.* **·gies** The scientific and historical study of the forms, theory, methods, etc., of music. —**mu′si·co·log′i·cal** (-kə·loj′i·kəl) *adj.* —**mu′si·col′o·gist** *n.*

music stand A rack to hold music for a performer.

musk (musk) *n.* A soft, powdery secretion with a penetrating odor, obtained from the sac (**musk bag**) of the male musk deer, and used in making perfumes and in medicine. [< LGk. *moskos*] —**musk′y** *adj.*

musk deer A small, hornless deer of Asia, the male of which has a musk-secreting gland.

mus·kel·lunge (mus′kə·lunj) *n. pl.* **·lunge** or **·lung·es** A large North American pike, valued as a game fish. [< Algonquian *mas* great + *kinong* pike]

mus·ket (mus′kit) *n.* An archaic smoothbore firearm designed to be fired from the shoulder. [< Ital. *moschetto* crossbow, dart] —**mus′·ket·ry** *n.*

mus·ket·eer (mus′kə·tir′) *n.* Formerly, a soldier armed with a musket. [< F *mousquetaire*]

Mus·kho·ge·an (mus·kō′gē·ən, mus′kō·gē′ən) *n.* One of the principal North American Indian linguistic families formerly inhabiting the SE U.S. Also **Mus·ko′gi·an.**

musk·mel·on (musk′mel′ən) *n.* Any of several varieties of juicy, edible fruits of the gourd family, as the cantaloupe; also, the plant.

musk ox A shaggy, hollow-horned ruminant of arctic America and Greenland, emitting a strong odor of musk.

musk·rat (musk′rat) *n. pl.* **·rats** or **·rat** 1. An aquatic rodent of North America, having dark, glossy brown fur and a musky odor: also called *water rat.* 2. The valuable fur of this rodent. [< Algonquian *musquash*]

Mus·lim (muz′lim, mooz′-, moos′-) *n. pl.* **·lims** or **·lim** A believer in Islam; Muhammadan. —*adj.* Of or pertaining to Islam. Also called *Moslem*: also **Mus′lem.** [< Arabic, one who submits < *aslama* to surrender (to God)]

mus·lin (muz′lin) *n.* Any of several plain-weave cotton fabrics of varying fineness. [< Ital. *Mussolo* Mosul, Iraq, where it was made]

muss (mus) *n.* *Informal* 1. A state of disorder

or untidiness; mess. 2. A commotion or tumult. —*v.t.* To make messy or untidy; rumple: often with *up*. [Alter. of MESS]

mus·sel (mus′əl) *n.* 1. A bivalve marine mollusk, esp. the edible **blue mussel**. 2. Any of several fresh-water mollusks. [< L *musculus*, lit., little mouse]

Mus·sel·man (mus′əl·mən) *n. pl.* **·mans** (-mənz) or **·men** (-mən) A Muslim. [< Persian and Turkish *musulmān*]

muss·y (mus′ē) *adj. Informal* **muss·i·er, muss·i·est** Rumpled; messy. —**muss′i·ly** *adv.* —**muss′i·ness** *n.*

must[1] (must) *v. Present 3rd person sing.* **must** A defective verb now used only as an auxiliary followed by the infinitive without *to*, or elliptically with the infinitive understood, to express: **a** Compulsion: *Must* you go? **b** Requirement: You *must* be healthy to be accepted. **c** Probability or supposition: You *must* be tired. **d** Conviction or certainty: War *must* follow. —*n. Informal* Anything that is required or vital: Safety is a *must*. [OE *mōtan* to be able, to be obliged to]

must[2] (must) *n.* Mustiness; mold. [< MUSTY]

must[3] (must) *n.* The expressed unfermented juice of the grape or other fruit. [< L *mustum* (*vinum*) new (wine)]

mus·tache (məs·tash′, mus′tash) *n.* 1. The growth of hair on the upper lip. 2. The hair or bristles growing near the mouth of an animal. Also, *Chiefly Brit.*, *moustache*. [< Ital. *mostaccio* face]

mus·tang (mus′tang) *n.* A wild horse of the American plains. [< Sp. *mestengo* stray animal]

mus·tard (mus′tərd) *n.* 1. A pungent condiment prepared as a paste or powder from the seed of the mustard plant. 2. Any of several plants of a large family that also includes broccoli, cabbage, etc. 3. The yellowish or brownish color of ground mustard. [< MF *moustarde*]

mustard gas *Chem.* An oily amber liquid, having an odor of mustard or garlic, and used in warfare because of its powerful blistering effect.

mus·ter (mus′tər) *v.t.* 1. To summon or assemble (troops, etc.). 2. To collect, gather, or summon: often with *up*. —*v.i.* 3. To gather or assemble, as troops. —*n.* 1. An assembling or gathering, as of troops. 2. An official list of officers and men in a military unit or ship's crew. [< L *monstrare* to show]

must·y (mus′tē) *adj.* **must·i·er, must·i·est** 1. Having a moldy odor or flavor, as a close room. 2. Dull or stale with age. 3. Without vigor; lifeless. [? Alter. of obs. *moisty* < MOIST] —**must′i·ness** *n.*

mu·ta·ble (myōō′tə·bəl) *adj.* 1. Capable of or subject to change. 2. Liable to frequent change. [< L *mutare* to change] —**mu′ta·bil′i·ty** *n.*

mu·tant (myōō′tənt) *n.* A plant or animal organism differing from its parents in one or more characteristics that are inheritable; mutation. —**mu′tant** *adj.*

mu·tate (myōō′tāt) *v.t. & v.i.* **·tat·ed, ·tat·ing** To undergo or subject to change or mutation. [< L *mutare* to change]

mu·ta·tion (myōō·tā′shən) *n.* 1. The act or process of changing. 2. A change or modification in form, structure, function, etc. 3. *Biol.* **a** A sudden, transmissible variation in a plant or animal. **b** An individual, species, etc., resulting from such a variation. —**mu·ta′·tion·al** *adj.*

mute (myōōt) *adj.* 1. Not producing speech or sound; silent. 2. Lacking the power of speech; dumb. 3. *Phonet.* Not pronounced; silent, as the *e* in *gone*. —*n.* 1. One who is unable to speak; esp. a deaf-mute. 2. *Music* A device used to muffle the tone of an instrument. —*v.t.* **mut·ed, mut·ing** 1. To deaden the sound of (a musical instrument, etc.). 2. In art, to soften (a color, a shade, etc.). [< L *mutus* dumb] —**mute′ly** *adv.* —**mute′ness** *n.*

mu·ti·late (myōō′tə·lāt) *v.t.* **·lat·ed, ·lat·ing** 1. To deprive (a person, animal, etc.) of a limb or essential part; maim. 2. To damage or make imperfect: to *mutilate* a speech. [< L *mutilare* to maim] —**mu′ti·la′tion** *n.* —**mu′ti·la′tor** *n.*

mu·ti·ny (myōō′tə·nē) *n. pl.* **·nies** Rebellion against constituted authority; insubordination; esp., a revolt of soldiers or sailors against their commanders. —*v.i.* **·nied, ·ny·ing** To take part in a mutiny. [< MF *mutin* rebellious] —**mu′ti·neer′** (-nir′) *n.* —**mu′ti·nous** *adj.* —**mu′ti·nous·ly** *adv.*

mutt (mut) *n. Slang* A mongrel dog. [< MUTT(ONHEAD)]

mut·ter (mut′ər) *v.i.* 1. To speak in a low, indistinct tone, as in complaining. 2. To complain; grumble. 3. To make a low, rumbling sound. —*v.t.* 4. To say in a low, indistinct tone. —*n.* A low, indistinct utterance or tone. [ME *muteren*] —**mut′·ter·er** *n.*

mut·ton (mut′n) *n.* The flesh of sheep, esp. mature sheep, used as food. [< OF *molton* sheep] —**mut′ton·y** *adv.*

mut·ton·chops (mut′n·chops′) *n.pl.* Side whiskers narrow at the temples and broad at the lower cheeks.

mut·ton·head (mut′n·hed′) *n. Slang* A stupid, dense person. —**mut′ton·head′ed** *adj.*

mu·tu·al (myōō′chōō·əl) *adj.* 1. Felt, expressed, or performed for or toward each other; reciprocal: *mutual* dislike. 2. Having the same attitude toward or relationship with each other: *mutual* friends. 3. Possessed in common. [< L *mutuus* exchanged, reciprocal] —**mu′tu·al·ly** *adv.* —**mu′tu·al′i·ty** (-al′ə·tē) *n.*

mutual fund An investment company that manages the pooled capital of its investors.

muu·muu (mōō′mōō′) *n.* A loose, flowing gown for women, gathered from the neckline. [< Hawaiian]

muz·zle (muz′əl) *n.* 1. The projecting part of an animal's head, including the jaws, mouth, and snout. 2. A guard or covering for the snout. 3. The front end of the barrel of a firearm. —*v.t.* **·zled, ·zling** 1. To put a muzzle on (an animal, etc.). 2. To restrain from speaking, expressing opinions, etc.; gag. [< Med.L *musus* snout]

my (mī) *pronominal adj.* The possessive case of the pronoun *I*, used attributively: also used in certain forms of address: *my* lord; *my* good man. —*interj.* An exclamation of surprise, dismay, etc.: Oh, *my*! [OE *mīn*]

my- Var. of MYO-.

my·as·the·ni·a (mī′əs·thē′nē·ə) *n. Pathol.* Muscular debility, often accompanied by progressive exhaustion.

-mycete *combining form Bot.* A member of a class of fungi, corresponding in use to class names in *-mycetes*.

-mycetes *combining form Bot.* Used to form class names of fungi. [< Gk. *mykēs* fungus]

myco- *combining form* Fungus. Also, before vowels, myc-. [< Gk. *mykēs*]

my·col·o·gy (mī·kol′ə·jē) *n. pl.* **·gies** The branch of botany dealing with fungi. —**my·co·log·ic** (mī′kə·loj′ik) or **·i·cal** *adj.* —**my·col′o·gist** *n.*

my·e·li·tis (mī′ə·lī′tis) *n. Pathol.* Inflammation of the spinal cord or of the bone marrow.

myelo- *combining form Anat.* The spinal cord or bone marrow. Also, before vowels, **myel-**. [< Gk. *myelos* marrow]

my·na (mī′nə) *n.* Any of various starlinglike Oriental birds, some of which are taught to speak words. Also **my′nah.** [< Hind. *mainā*]

myo- *combining form* Muscle. Also, before vowels, *my-*. [< Gk. *mys, myos*]

my·o·car·di·um (mī′ō·kär′dē·əm) *n. Anat.* The muscular tissue of the heart. [< MYO- + Gk. *kardia* heart] —**my′o·car′di·al** *adj.*

my·o·pi·a (mī·ō′pē·ə) *n.* 1. *Pathol.* A visual defect in which objects are seen clearly only when close to the eye; nearsightedness. 2. Lack of insight or discernment; obtuseness. [< NL] —**my·op′ic** (-op′ik) *adj.*

myria- *combining form* 1. Very many; of great number. 2. In the metric system, ten thousand. Also, before vowels, **myri-**. [< Gk. *myrios* numberless]

myr·i·ad (mir′ē·əd) *adj.* Countless; innumerable. —*n.* A vast indefinite number. [< Gk. *myrios* numberless]

myr·i·a·pod (mir′ē·ə·pod) *n. Zool.* One of a group of arthropods whose segmented bodies bear many pairs of jointed appendages, including the centipedes. —**myr′i·ap′o·dan** (-ap′ə·dən) *adj. & n.* —**myr′i·ap′o·dous** (-ap′ə·dəs) *adj.*

myr·mi·don (mûr′mə·don, -dən) *n.* A faithful, unquestioning follower. [< *Myrmidons*, followers of Achilles in the Trojan War]

myrrh (mûr) *n.* An aromatic gum resin that exudes from certain small trees of Arabia and eastern Africa, used as incense, perfume, and in medicine. [< Gk. *myrra* < Hebrew *mōr*, *mar* bitter]

myr·tle (mûr′təl) *n.* 1. Any of a group of shrubs with evergreen leaves, white or rose-colored flowers, and black berries. 2. One of various other plants, as the periwinkle. [< Med.L *myrtillus*]

my·self (mī·self′) *pron.* A form of the first person singular pronoun, used: 1. As a reflexive or as the object of a preposition in a reflexive sense: I saw *myself* in the mirror. 2. As an emphatic or intensive form of *I*: I *myself* invented the yo-yo. 3. As a designation of a normal, proper, or usual state: Once out of uniform, I was *myself* again in no time. [OE *mē* + *sylf*]

mys·te·ri·ous (mis·tir′ē·əs) *adj.* 1. Implying or characterized by mystery. 2. Unexplained; puzzling. —**mys·te′ri·ous·ly** *adv.* —**mys·te′ri·ous·ness** *n.*

mys·ter·y (mis′tər·ē) *n. pl.* **·ter·ies** 1. Something that is not or cannot be known, understood, or explained. 2. Any action, affair, or thing that arouses curiosity or suspense because it is not fully revealed. 3. A story, play, movie, etc., narrating or dramatizing such an affair. 4. *Theol.* A truth that can be known only through divine revelation. [< Gk. *mysterion* secret rite]

mys·tic (mis′tik) *adj.* 1. Of the nature of or pertaining to mysteries. 2. Of or pertaining to mystics or mysticism. 3. Baffling or enigmatic. —*n.* One who believes in mysticism, or professes to have had mystical experiences. [< L *mysticus* pertaining to secret rites]

mys·ti·cal (mis′ti·kəl) *adj.* 1. Of the nature of a direct, intuitive, or subjective perception beyond the ordinary range of human experience, esp. one of a religious character. 2. Having a spiritual character or reality beyond human reason. 3. Mystic (defs. 1 & 2). —**mys′ti·cal·ly** *adv.*

mys·ti·cism (mis′tə·siz′əm) *n.* The belief that through contemplation and love man can achieve a direct knowledge of God or of divine truth, etc., without the use of reason or of the senses.

mys·ti·fy (mis′tə·fī) *v.t.* **·fied, ·fy·ing** 1. To confuse or perplex, esp. deliberately. 2. To make obscure or mysterious. —**mys′ti·fi·ca′tion** *n.* —**mys′ti·fy′ing·ly** *adv.*

mys·tique (mis·tēk′) *n.* A body of attitudes, opinions, or ideas that become associated with a person, thing, institution, etc., and give it a superhuman or mythical status: the *mystique* of bullfighting. [< F]

myth (mith) *n.* 1. A traditional story, usu. focusing on the deeds of gods or heroes, often in explanation of some natural phenomenon. 2. An imaginary or fictitious person, thing, event, or story. [< Gk. *mythos* word, speech, story] —**myth′i·cal** or **myth′ic** *adj.*

mytho- *combining form* Myth. Also, before vowels, **myth-**. [< Gk. *mythos* story]

my·thol·o·gy (mi·thol′ə·jē) *n. pl.* **·gies** The collective myths and legends of a particular people, person, institution, etc., and study of myths. [< Gk. *mythos* story + *logos* speech] —**myth·o·log·i·cal** (mith′ə·loj′i·kəl) *adj.* —**my·thol′o·gist** *n.*

N

n, N (en) *n. pl.* **n's** or **ns, N's** or **Ns, ens** (enz) 1. The fourteenth letter of the English alphabet. 2. The sound represented by the letter *n*. —*symbol* 1. *Printing* An en. 2. *Chem.* Nitrogen (symbol N). 3. *Math.* An indefinite number.

nab (nab) *v.t.* **nabbed, nab·bing** *Informal* 1. To catch or arrest. 2. To take or seize suddenly; snatch. [Prob. < Scand.]

na·bob (nā′bob) *n.* 1. A European who has become rich in India. 2. Any very rich or powerful man. [< Hind. *nawwāb* < Arabic *nuwwab*, pl. of *nā'ib* viceroy]

na·celle (nə·sel′) *n. Aeron.* A separate enclosure on an aircraft, esp. one for an engine. [< F, small boat]

na·cre (nā′kər) *n.* Mother-of-pearl. [< Arabic *naqqāra* drum] —**na·cre·ous** (nā′·krē·əs) *adj.*

na·dir (nā′dər, -dir) *n.* 1. The point of the celestial sphere opposite the zenith. 2. The lowest point. [< Arabic *nazīr* (*as-samt*) opposite (the zenith)]

nae (nā) *adj. & adv. Scot.* No; not.

nag[1] (nag) *v.* **nagged, nag·ging** *v.t.* 1. To annoy by repeatedly urging, scolding, carping, etc. —*v.i.* 2. To urge, scold, carp, etc., continually. 3. To be bothered by. —*n.* One who nags. [< Scand.] —**nag′ger** *n.* —**nag′·ging·ly** *adv.*

nag[2] (nag) *n.* A horse, esp. one that is old or decrepit. [ME *nagge*]

Na·hua·tl (nä′wät·l) *n.* 1. The Uto-Aztecan language of the Aztecs and certain other Indian peoples. 2. The peoples whose native language is Nahuatl. —**Na′hua·tl** *adj.*

Na·hua·tlan (nä′wät·lən) *n.* 1. A branch of the Uto-Aztecan linguistic family of North and Central American Indians, including the Aztec dialects. 2. Nahuatl. —**Na′hua·tlan** *adj.*

Na·hum (nā′əm, -hum) *n.* A book of the Old Testament containing the prophecies of a 7th c. prophet Nahum. [< Hebrew, comfort]

nai·ad (nā′ad, nī′-) *n. pl.* **·ads** or **·a·des** (-ə·dēz) 1. In classical mythology, one of the water nymphs believed to dwell in fountains, springs, rivers, lakes, and wells. 2. *Entomol.* The aquatic young of certain insects. [< Gk. *Naias, -ados.*]

nail (nāl) *n.* 1. A slender piece of metal, used esp. to hold or fasten wood, etc. 2. A thin, horny plate growing on the end of each of the fingers and toes of man and other primates. —**to hit the nail on the head** To do or say something exactly to the point. —*v.t.* 1. To hold or fasten in place with a nail or nails. 2. To make certain or definite: often with *down*. 3. *Slang* To catch or arrest. [OE *nægl*, orig., fingernail.]

nail file A small, fine file for shaping the fingernails.

nail polish A clear or colored substance applied to the nails. Also **nail enamel.**

nain·sook (nān′sŏŏk, nan′-) *n.* A soft, lightweight cotton fabric. [< Hind. *nainsukh*, lit., pleasure of the eye]

nai·ra (nī′rə) *n.* The monetary unit of Nigeria.

na·ive (nä·ēv′) *adj.* 1. Having a simple nature that lacks worldly experience; artless. 2. Uncritical: a *naive* idea. Also **na·ïve′.** [< F < L *nativus* natural, inborn] —**na·ive′ly** *adv.*

na·ive·té (nä·ēv′tā′, nä·ēv′tā) *n.* 1. The state or quality of being naive. 2. A naive incident, remark, etc. Also **na·ïve′té′.** [< F]

na·ked (nā′kid) *adj.* 1. Having no clothes on; nude. 2. Having no covering. 3. Without addition, adornment, or qualification; stark: the *naked* truth. 4. Unaided by an optical instrument: the *naked* eye. 5. Open or exposed to view: a *naked* sword. [OE *nacod*] —**na′ked·ly** *adv.* —**na′ked·ness** *n.*

nam·by-pam·by (nam′bē·pam′bē) *adj.* 1. Full of or exhibiting weak sentimentality; insipid. 2. Timid and irresolute. —*n. pl.* **·bies** One who is namby-pamby. [after the title of a satiric poem by Henry Carey, died 1743.]

name (nām) *n.* 1. A word or words by which a person, thing, animal, class, or concept is known or referred to. 2. A usu. derogatory word or phrase: to call someone *names*. 3. Popular or general reputation. —**in name only** Being such in appearance only. —**in the name of** 1. For the sake of. 2. By the authority of. —**to one's name** Of one's own: He hasn't a friend *to his name*. —*v.t.* **named, nam·ing** 1. To give a name to; call. 2. To identify. 3. To fix or determine: to *name* the day. 4. To nominate; appoint. —*adj. Informal* Famous. [OE *nama*] —**nam′er** *n.*

name day The feast day of the saint for whom one is named.

name·less (nām′lis) *adj.* 1. Undistinguished or obscure: a *nameless* multitude. 2. That cannot be named; indescribable: *nameless* terror. 3. Having no name; esp., having no legal name; illegitimate. —**name′less·ly** *adv.* —**name′less·ness** *n.*

name·ly (nām′lē) *adv.* That is to say.

name·sake (nām′sāk′) *n.* One who is named after or has the same name as another.

nan·keen (nan·kēn′) *n.* 1. A buff-colored cotton fabric. 2. *pl.* Clothes made of nankeen. Also **nan·kin′** (-kēn′). [after *Nanking*, China, where originally made]

nan·ny (nan′ē) *n. pl.* **·nies** 1. *Informal* A female goat: also **nanny goat.** 2. *Brit.* A child's nurse. [after *Nanny*, a personal name, dim. of *Ann*]

nano- *combining form* In the metric system and in technical usage, one billionth of (a specified unit): *nanosecond*. Also, before vowels, **nan-**. [< Gk. *nānos* dwarf]

nap¹ (nap) *n.* A short sleep; doze. —*v.i.* **napped, nap·ping** 1. To take a nap; doze. 2. To be unprepared. [OE *hnappian* to doze] —**nap′per** *n.*

nap² (nap) *n.* The short fibers forming a downy or fuzzy surface on certain fabrics. [< MDu. *noppe*] —**nap′less** *adj.* —**nap′py** *adj.*

na·palm (nā′päm) *n.* A jellylike mixture that is combined with gasoline to form an incendiary fuel, as in bombs, flame throwers, etc. [< *na(phthenic)* and *palm(itic) acids*, chemical compounds used in its manufacture]

nape (nāp) *n.* The back of the neck. [Origin uncertain]

na·per·y (nā′pər·ē) *n. pl.* **·per·ies** Household linen, esp. napkins, tablecloths, etc. [See NAPKIN.]

naph·tha (naf′thə, nap′-) *n.* A volatile, colorless petroleum distillate, used as a solvent, cleaning fluid, fuel, etc. [< Persian *naft* pitch]

naph·tha·lene (naf′thə·lēn, nap′-) *n. Chem.* A colorless, odorous coal-tar compound, used in the making of dyes, moth balls, etc.

naph·thol (naf′thōl, -thol, nap′-) *n. Chem.* Either of two compounds derived from naphthalene and used in making dyes.

nap·kin (nap′kin) *n.* 1. A small, usu. square cloth or paper, used at meals for wiping the hands and mouth or protecting the clothes. 2. A small piece of toweling. [< L *mappa* a cloth]

na·po·le·on (nə·pō′lē·ən) *n.* 1. A rich pastry composed of thin layers of dough filled with cream, custard, etc. 2. A former French gold coin. [after *Napoleon* Bonaparte]

Na·po·le·on·ic (nə·pō′lē·on′ik) *adj.* Characteristic of, pertaining to, or suggesting Napoleon Bonaparte.

nar·cis·sism (när′sis·iz·əm) *n.* 1. Excessive admiration for or fascination with oneself. 2. *Psychoanal.* Erotic interest in one's own body. Also **nar·cism** (när′siz·əm). [< *Narcissus*, youth of Greek mythology who fell in love with his own image.] —**nar′cis·sist** *n.* —**nar′cis·sis′tic** *adj.*

nar·cis·sus (när·sis′əs) *n. pl.* **·cis·sus·es** or **·cis·si** (-sis′ī) Any of various bulbous flowering plants of the amaryllis family, including the daffodil and jonquil.

narco- *combining form* Torpor; insensibility. Also, before vowels, **narc-**. [< Gk. *narkē* numbness]

nar·co·sis (när·kō′sis) *n.* Deep stupor produced by a drug.

nar·co·syn·the·sis (när′kō·sin′thə·sis) *n. Psychiatry* Therapy using narcotics to enable the patient to recall painful experiences.

nar·cot·ic (när·kot′ik) *n.* A drug, as opium or morphine, that relieves pain and induces sleep, but may be habit-forming. [< Gk. *narkē* torpor] —**nar·cot′ic** *adj.*

nar·co·tism (när′kə·tiz′əm) *n.* 1. Addiction to narcotics. 2. Narcosis.

nar·co·tize (när′kə·tīz) *v.t.* **·tized, ·tiz·ing** To bring under the influence of a narcotic; stupefy. —**nar′co·ti·za′tion** *n.*

nard (närd) *n.* 1. Spikenard. 2. Any of several aromatic plants or roots formerly used in medicine. [Gk. *nardos*, prob. < Semitic]

nar·es (nâr′ēz) *n. pl. of* **nar·is** (nâr′is) *Anat.* Openings into the nasal cavities; esp., the nostrils. [< L, nostrils]

Nar·ra·gan·set (nar′ə·gan′sit) *n. pl.* **·set** or **·sets** 1. One of a tribe of North American Algonquian Indians, formerly inhabiting Rhode Island. 2. The language of this tribe. Also **Nar′ra·gan′sett.**

nar·rate (nar′āt, na·rāt′) *v.* **·rat·ed, ·rat·ing** *v.t.* 1. To tell, as a story. 2. To speak in accompaniment and explanation of (a motion picture, television program, etc.). —*v.i.* 3. To tell a story, etc. [< L *narratus*, pp. of *narrare* to relate] —**nar′ra·tor** *n.*

nar·ra·tion (na·rā′shən) *n.* 1. The act of narrating. 2. A narrative. 3. An account that narrates, as in fiction, etc.

nar·ra·tive (nar′ə·tiv) *n.* 1. Something narrated. 2. The act, art, or process of narrating.

nar·row (nar′ō) *adj.* 1. Having little width. 2. Limited or small, as in extent or scope. 3. Narrow-minded. 4. Nearly unsuccessful or disastrous: a *narrow* escape. —*v.t. & v.i.* To make or become narrow or narrower, as in width or scope. —*n. Usu. pl.* A narrow passage; esp., the narrowest part of a strait, isthmus, etc. [OE *nearu*] —**nar′row·ness** *n.*

nar·row-gauge (nar′ō·gāj′) *adj.* Designed for or having a width of railroad track less than 56½ inches. Also **nar′row-gauged′.**

nar·row·ly (nar′ō·lē) *adv.* 1. Barely; hardly. 2. So as to be narrow. 3. In a narrow manner.

nar·row-mind·ed (nar′ō·mīn′did) *adj.* Having or characterized by narrow views or sentiments; illiberal; bigoted. —**nar′row-mind′ed·ly** *adv.* —**nar′row-mind′ed·ness** *n.*

nar·whal (när′wəl) *n.* A small, arctic whalelike mammal, having in the male a long, straight, spiral tusk, and valued for its oil and ivory. Also **nar′wal, nar·whale** (när′wāl′). [< Dan. or Sw. *narhval*]

na·sal (nā′zəl) *adj.* 1. Of or pertaining to the nose. 2. Produced with the voice passing through the nose. —*n.* 1. A nasal sound. 2. *Anat.* A part of the nose, as a bone. [< L *nasus* nose] —**na·sal·i·ty** (nā·zal′ə·tē) *n.* —**na′sal·ly** *adv.*

na·sal·ize (nā′zəl·īz) *v.* **·ized, ·iz·ing** *v.t.* 1. To give a nasal sound to. —*v.i.* 2. To produce nasal sounds. —**na′sal·i·za′tion** *n.*

nas·cent (nā′sənt, nas′ənt) *adj.* Beginning to exist or develop; newly conceived. [< L *nascens, -centis*, ppr. of *nasci* to be born] —**nas′cence** *n.*

naso- *combining form* 1. Nose. 2. Nasal and. [< L *nasus* nose]

na·stur·tium (nə·stûr′shəm) *n.* Any of various garden plants with funnel-shaped flowers. [< L, cress]

nas·ty (nas′tē) *adj.* **·ti·er, ·ti·est** 1. Offensive; disgusting. 2. Indecent; obscene: *nasty* language. 3. Disagreeable; unpleasant: *nasty* weather. 4. Mean; spiteful: a *nasty* remark. 5. Serious or painful: a *nasty* cut. [< Du. *nestig* or Sw. *naskug* filthy] —**nas′ti·ly** *adv.* —**nas′ti·ness** *n.*

na·tal (nāt′l) *adj.* 1. Of or pertaining to one's birth. 2. *Poetic* Native: said of a place. [< L *nasci* to be born]

Natch·ez (nach′iz) *n. pl.* **Natch·ez** One of a tribe of North American Muskhogean

Indians, formerly inhabiting the lower Mississippi valley.

na·tion (nā′shən) *n.* 1. A body of persons associated with a particular territory and organized under a government. 2. A body of persons having a common origin and language and a distinctive cultural and social way of life. 3. A tribe or federation, esp. of American Indians. [< L *nasci* to be born]

na·tion·al (nash′ən·əl) *adj.* 1. Of, belonging to, or representative of a nation as a whole. 2. Characteristic of or peculiar to a nation. —*n.* A subject or citizen of a nation. [< F] —**na′tion·al·ly** *adv.*

National Guard A militia of a state, a territory, or the District of Columbia, maintained in part by the U.S. government and subject to federal service in national emergencies.

na·tion·al·ism (nash′ən·əl·iz′əm) *n.* 1. Devotion to one's own nation. 2. A desire or movement for national independence. —**na′tion·al·ist** *adj. & n.* —**na′tion·al·is′tic** *adj.* —**na′tion·al·is′ti·cal·ly** *adv.*

na·tion·al·i·ty (nash′ən·al′ə·tē) *n. pl.* **·ties** 1. A body of people having the same traditions, language, or ethnic origin, and forming a nation. 2. The state or fact of being related to a particular nation, as by birth or citizenship. 3. National character or quality. 4. The fact or quality of existing as a nation.

na·tion·al·ize (nash′ən·əl·īz′) *v.t.* **·ized, ·iz·ing** 1. To place (industries, resources, etc.) under governmental control. 2. To make national, as in character or scope. 3. To accept as a national; naturalize. Also *Brit.* **na′tion·al·ise′**. —**na′tion·al·i·za′tion** *n.*

Nation of Islam See under BLACK MUSLIM.

na·tion-wide (nā′shən·wīd′) *adj.* Extending throughout the nation.

na·tive (nā′tiv) *adj.* 1. Born in a particular place or region. 2. Linked to a person by birth: *native* language. 3. Produced or grown in a particular region or country; indigenous. 4. Of, pertaining to, or characteristic of any particular area or its inhabitants. 5. Natural rather than acquired; inborn. 6. Occurring in nature in a pure state: *native* copper. —*n.* 1. A lifelong resident of a country or region. 2. A person or thing native to a specified country or place. [< L *nasci* to be born.] —**na′tive·ly** *adv.*

na·tive-born (nā′tiv·bôrn′) *adj.* Born in the region or country specified.

na·tiv·i·ty (nə·tiv′ə·tē, nā-) *n. pl.* **·ties** Birth, esp. with regard to the time, place, or circumstances surrounding it. —**the Nativity** 1. The birth of Christ. 2. Christmas Day. [< L *nativitas*]

NATO (nā′tō) North Atlantic Treaty Organization.

nat·ty (nat′ē) *adj.* **·ti·er, ·ti·est** Neat and smart looking. [? Akin to NEAT] —**nat′ti·ly** *adv.*

nat·u·ral (nach′ər·əl) *adj.* 1. Produced by or existing in nature; not artificial. 2. Resulting from one's nature; innate: *natural* talent. 3. Free from affectation or awkwardness: *natural* manner. 4. *Music* Not sharped or flatted. 5. Related by blood rather than through adoption: *natural* mother. 6. Born out of wedlock. —*n.* 1. *Music* **a** A note that is neither sharped nor flatted. **b** A character (♮) that cancels a sharp or flat at a specific line or space on the staff. 2. *Informal* One who or that which is naturally gifted. [< L *natura* nature, character] —**nat′u·ral·ness** *n.*

natural gas A gas consisting chiefly of methane, generated naturally in underground oil deposits and used as a fuel.

natural history The observation and study of the material universe, esp. the biological and earth sciences.

nat·u·ral·ism (nach′ər·əl·iz′əm) *n.* 1. Closeness to nature or human life, as in literature, painting, etc. 2. *Philos.* The doctrine that everything is derived from natural causes and can be explained by scientific laws. 3. Action or thought resulting only from natural desires and instincts. —**nat′u·ral·is′tic** *adj.*

nat·u·ral·ist (nach′ər·əl·ist) *n.* 1. One who is versed in natural history, as a zoologist or botanist. 2. An adherent of the doctrine of naturalism.

nat·u·ral·ize (nach′ər·əl·īz′) *v.* **·ized, ·iz·ing** *v.t.* 1. To confer the rights and privileges of citizenship upon. 2. To adapt (a foreign plant, animal, etc.) to the environment of a country or area. —*v.i.* 3. To become as if native; adapt. Also *Brit.* **nat′u·ral·ise′**. —**nat′u·ral·i·za′tion** *n.*

nat·u·ral·ly (nach′ər·əl·ē) *adv.* 1. In a natural manner. 2. By inherent nature. 3. Of course; certainly.

natural resource *Usu. pl.* A source of wealth provided by nature, as forests, minerals, and water supply.

natural science 1. The sciences collectively that deal with the physical universe. 2. Any one of these sciences, as biology, chemistry, or physics.

natural selection *Biol.* The process by which traits advantageous to an organism in a certain environment tend to be passed on to later generations; survival of the fittest forms.

na·ture (nā′chər) *n.* 1. The essential character of something: the *nature* of democracy. 2. The entire material universe and its phenomena. 3. The basic character or disposition of a person or animal. 4. Sort; kind; variety: nothing of that *nature*. 5. A wild or uncivilized condition. 6. That which is within the accepted or legal limits of morality: an act against *nature*. —**by nature** By birth or disposition. [< L *nasci* to be born]

-natured *combining form* Possessing a (specified) nature, disposition, or temperament: *good-natured*.

naught (nôt) *n.* 1. Nothing. 2. A cipher; zero; the character *0*. Also spelled *nought*. [OE *nā* not + *wiht* thing]

naugh·ty (nô′tē) *adj.* **·ti·er, ·ti·est** 1. Mischievous; disobedient; bad. 2. Indecent or improper. —**naugh′ti·ly** *adv.* —**naugh′ti·ness** *n.*

nau·se·a (nô′zē·ə, -zhə, -sē·ə, -shə) *n.* 1. A sick feeling in the stomach accompanied by an impulse to vomit. 2. Strong disgust. [< Gk. *nausia*, *nautia* seasickness] —**nau·seous** (nô′shəs, -zē·əs, -sē·əs) *adj.*

nau·se·ate (nô′zē·āt, -sē-, -shē-) *v.t. & v.i.* **·at·ed, ·at·ing** To affect with or feel nausea or disgust.

nau·ti·cal (nô′ti·kəl) *adj.* Pertaining to or involving ships, seamen, or navigation. [< Gk. *naus* ship] —**nau′ti·cal·ly** *adv.*

nautical mile See under MILE.

nau·ti·lus (nô′tə·ləs) *n. pl.* **·lus·es** or **·li** (-lī) Any of a group of mollusks with a spiral shell whose chambers are lined with mother-of-pearl; esp., the **chambered** or **pearly nautilus.** [< Gk. *nautilos* sailor]

Nav·a·ho (nav′ə·hō, näv-) *n. pl.* **·hos** or **·hoes** or **·ho** One of a tribe of North American Indians now living on reservations in Arizona, New Mexico, and Utah. Also **Nav′a·jo.**

na·val (nā′vəl) *adj.* 1. Of, involving, or having a navy. 2. Of or pertaining to ships. [< L *navis* ship]

nave (nāv) *n. Archit.* The main body of a church, situated between the side aisles. [< L *navis* ship]

na·vel (nā′vəl) *n.* The depression on the abdomen where the umbilical cord was attached. [OE *nafela*]

navel orange A seedless orange having a depression at its apex that contains a small, secondary fruit.

nav·i·ga·ble (nav′ə·gə·bəl) *adj.* 1. Broad or deep enough to admit of passage by boat. 2. Capable of being steered. **—nav′i·ga·bil′i·ty** *n.* **—nav′i·ga·bly** *adv.*

nav·i·gate (nav′ə·gāt) *v.* **·gat·ed, ·gat·ing** *v.t.* 1. To travel on or through, as by ship or aircraft. 2. To plot the course of (a ship, aircraft, etc.). **—***v.i.* 3. To guide or steer a ship, aircraft, etc. [< L *navis* boat + *agere* to direct] **—nav′i·ga′tion** *n.* **—nav′i·ga′tion·al** *adj.* **—nav′i·ga′tor** *n.*

na·vy (nā′vē) *n. pl.* **·vies** 1. *Often cap.* The entire military sea force of a country. 2. The warships of a nation, taken collectively. 3. Navy blue. [< L *navis* ship]

navy bean A small, dried, white bean related to the common kidney bean. [from its use in the U.S. Navy]

navy blue A very dark blue: also *navy.*

navy yard A government-owned dockyard for building and repairing naval vessels.

nay (nā) *adv.* 1. *Archaic* No. 2. Not exactly that, but rather. **—***n.* A negative vote or voter. [< ON *ne* not + *ei* ever]

Na·zi (nä′tsē) *n. pl.* **·zis** A member of the fascist National Socialist German Workers' Party, the ruling party in Germany from 1933 to 1945 under the dictatorship of Adolf Hitler. [< G, short for *Nationalsozialist* National Socialist] **—Na′zi** *adj.* **—Na′zism** or **Na′zi·ism** *n.*

Ne·an·der·thal man (nē·an′dər·thôl, -täl) *Anthropol.* An extinct species of man of the Stone Age. [< G *Neanderthal,* Neander valley, Germany, where the first bones of this species were found]

Ne·a·pol·i·tan (nē′ə·pol′ə·tən) *adj.* Of, relating to, or characteristic of Naples. **—***n.* A native or resident of Naples.

neap tide (nēp) A tide with minimal rise and fall occurring shortly after the first and third quarters of the moon: also **neap.** [OE *nēpflod* low tide]

near (nir) *adv.* 1. At, to, or within a little distance; not remote. 2. Nearly; almost. 3. In a close relation; intimately. 4. Stingily. **—***adj.* 1. Not distant in place, time, or degree. 2. Closely approximating; almost achieved: a *near* success. 3. Narrow; close. 4. Closely related, as by blood. 5. Intimate. 6. Stingy; miserly. **—***prep.* Close by or to. **—***v.t. & v.i.* To come or draw near (to); approach. [OE *nēar,* compar. of *nēah* nigh] **—near′ness** *n.*

near·by (nir′bī′) *adj. & adv.* Close by; near; adjacent.

Near East The countries lying east of the Mediterranean, mostly in SW Asia.

near·ly (nir′lē) *adv.* 1. Almost; practically. 2. Closely.

near·sight·ed (nir′sī′tid) *adj.* Able to see clearly at short distances only; myopic. **—near′sight′ed·ly** *adv.* **—near′sight′ed·ness** *n.*

neat (nēt) *adj.* 1. Orderly, tidy, and clean. 2. Precise. 3. Clever: a *neat* trick. 4. Undiluted, as liquor. [< OF *net* < L *nitidus* shining] **—neat′ly** *adv.* **—neat′ness** *n.*

′neath (nēth) *prep. Dial.* or *Poetic* Beneath. Also **neath.**

neat's-foot oil (nēts′fo͝ot′) A pale yellow oil obtained by boiling the shinbones and feet of cattle, used esp. as a softening agent for leather.

neb·bish (neb′ish) *n. Slang* A timid, ineffectual person. [< Yiddish *nebech* poor thing!]

neb·u·la (neb′yə·lə) *n. pl.* **·lae** (-lē) or **·las** *Astron.* Any interstellar mass of vast extent, composed of gaseous matter. [< L, vapor, mist] **—neb′u·lar** *adj.*

neb·u·los·i·ty (neb′yə·los′ə·tē) *n. pl.* **·ties** 1. The state or quality of being nebulous. 2. A nebula.

neb·u·lous (neb′yə·ləs) *adj.* 1. Vague or confused; hazy. 2. Of, pertaining to, or like a nebula. Also **neb′u·lose.** **—neb′u·lous·ly** *adv.* **—neb′u·lous·ness** *n.*

nec·es·sar·i·ly (nes′ə·ser′ə·lē) *adv.* 1. As a necessary consequence. 2. Of necessity.

nec·es·sar·y (nes′ə·ser′ē) *adj.* 1. Absolutely needed; indispensable; essential. 2. That must exist or occur; inevitable. 3. Caused by or acting under compulsion. **—***n. pl.* **·sar·ies** *Often pl.* That which is indispensable.

ne·ces·si·tate (nə·ses′ə·tāt) *v.t.* **·tat·ed, ·tat·ing** 1. To make necessary. 2. To compel or oblige. **—ne·ces′si·ta′tion** *n.* **—ne·ces′si·ta′tive** *adj.*

ne·ces·si·tous (nə·ses′ə·təs) *adj.* 1. Extremely needy; destitute. 2. Urgent; compelling.

ne·ces·si·ty (nə·ses′ə·tē) *n. pl.* **·ties** 1. *Often pl.* That which is indispensable. 2. The quality, condition, or fact of being necessary. 3. The conditions that make compulsory a particular course of action. 4. Urgent or desperate need. **—of necessity** By necessity; inevitably. [< L *necessitas*]

neck (nek) *n.* 1. *Anat.* **a** The part of an animal that connects the head with the trunk. **b** Any similarly constricted part of an organ, bone, etc. ◆Collateral adjective: *cervical.* 2. The narrowed part of an object: the *neck* of a bottle. 3. Something likened to a neck, as a narrow strip of land. 4. The part of a garment close to or covering the neck. **—neck and neck** Abreast of one another, as horses in a race. **—***v.i.* 1. *Slang* To kiss and caress in lovemaking. **—***v.t.* 2. *Slang* To make love to (someone) in such a manner. [OE *hnecca*]

necked (nekt) *adj.* 1. Having a neck or necks. 2. Having or characterized by (a specified kind of) neck: used in combination: *long-necked.*

neck·er·chief (nek′ər·chif, -chēf) *n. pl.* **·chiefs** or **·chieves** (-chēvz) A kerchief for the neck.
neck·ing (nek′ing) *n. Slang* Kissing and caressing in lovemaking.
neck·lace (nek′lis) *n.* An ornament worn around the neck.
neck·line (nek′līn′) *n.* The line formed by the fit of a garment around the neck.
neck·piece (nek′pēs′) *n.* An article of clothing, usu. of fur, worn around the neck.
neck·tie (nek′tī′) *n.* A strip of material worn around the neck and knotted under the chin.
neck·wear (nek′wâr′) *n.* Articles worn around the neck, as ties, collars, mufflers, etc.
necro- *combining form* Corpse; the dead; death. Also, before vowels, **necr-.** [< Gk. *nekros* corpse]
ne·crol·o·gy (ne·krol′ə·jē) *n. pl.* **·gies** 1. A list of persons who have died. 2. An obituary notice. —**ne·crol′o·gist** *n.*
nec·ro·man·cy (nek′rə·man′sē) *n.* 1. The art of divining the future through alleged communication with the dead. 2. Black magic; sorcery. [< Gk. *nekros* corpse + *manteia* divination] —**nec′ro·man′cer** *n.*
ne·crop·o·lis (ne·krop′ə·lis) *n.* A cemetery. [< Gk. *nekros* corpse + *polis* city]
ne·cro·sis (ne·krō′sis) *n. Pathol.* The death of tissue in a living animal, resulting from infection or burns; gangrene. [< Gk. *nekrōsis* death] —**ne·crot′ic** (-krot′ik) *adj.*
nec·tar (nek′tər) *n.* 1. In Greek mythology, the drink of the gods. 2. Any delicious drink. 3. *Bot.* The sweet secretion of plants, collected by bees to make honey. [< Gk. *nektar*] —**nec′tar·ous** *adj.*
nec·tar·ine (nek′tə·rēn′) *n.* A variety of peach having a smooth skin.
nec·ta·ry (nek′tər·ē) *n. pl.* **·ries** *Bot.* A gland that secretes nectar.
née (nā) *adj.* Born with the name of: used chiefly to note the maiden name of a married woman: Mrs. Mary Lincoln, *née* Todd. Also **nee.** [< F, pp. fem. of *naître* to be born]
need (nēd) *v.t.* 1. To have an urgent use for; want; require. —*v.i.* 2. To be in want. 3. To be obliged or compelled; have to: He *need* not go. —*n.* 1. The lack of something necessary or desirable. 2. Obligation; necessity: no *need* to be afraid. 3. Something wanted or required: modest *needs.* 4. Poverty. [OE *nīed, nēd*]
need·ful (nēd′fəl) *adj.* 1. Needed; necessary. 2. *Archaic* Needy. —**need′ful·ly** *adv.* —**need′ful·ness** *n.*
nee·dle (nēd′l) *n.* 1. A slender, pointed instrument, usu. of steel, for carrying thread through fabric in sewing. 2. A hypodermic needle. 3. A pointer, as in a gauge or compass. 4. A pointed instrument of steel, diamond, etc., that transmits sound vibrations from the grooves of a phonograph record; stylus. 5. A slender rod of steel, bone, etc., used in knitting or crocheting. 6. A needle-shaped leaf, as that of a pine tree. —*v.* **·dled, ·dling** *v.t.* 1. To sew or pierce with a needle. 2. *Informal* To tease or heckle repeatedly. —*v.i.* 3. To sew or work with a needle. [OE *nǣdle*]
nee·dle·point (nēd′l·point′) *n.* Embroidery on canvas.
need·less (nēd′lis) *adj.* Not needed or necessary. —**need′less·ly** *adv.* —**need′·less·ness** *n.*
nee·dle·wom·an (nēd′l·wŏŏm′ən) *n. pl.* **·wom·en** (-wim′in) A seamstress.
nee·dle·work (nēd′l·wûrk′) *n.* Work done with a needle.
need·n't (nēd′nt) Need not.
needs (nēdz) *adv. Archaic* Of necessity: often with *must:* He *needs* must go. [OE *nīedes*]
need·y (nē′dē) *adj.* **need·i·er, need·i·est** Being in need, want, or poverty. —**need′i·ness** *n.*
ne′er (nâr) *adv. Poetic* Never.
ne′er-do-well (nâr′dōō·wel′) *n.* A worthless, unreliable person. —**ne′er′-do-well′** *adj.*
ne·far·i·ous (ni·fâr′ē·əs) *adj.* Extremely wicked; vile. [< L *ne-* not + *fas* divine law] —**ne·far′i·ous·ly** *adv.*
ne·gate (ni·gāt′) *v.t.* **·gat·ed, ·gat·ing** 1. To render ineffective or void; nullify. 2. To deny or contradict. [< L *negatus,* pp. of *negare* to deny]
ne·ga·tion (ni·gā′shən) *n.* 1. The absence or opposite of something. 2. The act of denying or contradicting. 3. Something negative.
neg·a·tive (neg′ə·tiv) *adj.* 1. Characterized by or expressing negation, denial, or refusal. 2. Not positive or affirmative: a *negative* attitude. 3. *Math.* Less than zero; minus: usu. denoted by the minus sign (−). 4. Characterized by an excess of electrons. 5. *Med.* Not indicating the presence of a particular disease, organism, etc.: a *negative* blood test. 6. *Photog.* Having the lights and darks reversed from what they were in the original scene. —*n.* 1. *Photog.* A negative image; also, the film or plate on which it appears. 2. An expression of denial or refusal. 3. The side that denies or contradicts what the other side affirms, as in a debate. 4. *Math.* A negative symbol or quantity. 5. *Electr.* A negative pole, plate, terminal, etc. 6. *Gram.* A negative particle, as *not.* —*v.t.* **·tived, ·tiv·ing** 1. Reject; veto. 2. To deny; contradict. 3. To prove to be false. [< L *negare* to deny] —**neg′a·tive·ly** *adv.* —**neg′a·tive·ness, neg′a·tiv′i·ty** *n.*
neg·a·tiv·ism (neg′ə·tiv·iz′əm) *n.* An attitude characterized by the questioning of traditional beliefs; skepticism. —**neg′a·tiv·ist** *n. & adj.* —**neg′a·tiv·is′tic** *adj.*
neg·lect (ni·glekt′) *v.t.* 1. To fail to heed or take note of; disregard. 2. To fail to give proper attention to. 3. To fail to do or perform; leave undone. —*n.* 1. Habitual want of attention or care. 2. The act of neglecting, or the state of being neglected. [< L *nec-* not + *legere* to gather] —**neg·lect′ful** *adj.*
neg·li·gee (neg′li·zhā′) *n.* 1. A loose, flowing, usu. decorative dressing gown worn by women. 2. Any informal attire. Also **neg′li·gée′.** [< F *négligé,* pp. of *négliger* to neglect]
neg·li·gent (neg′lə·jənt) *adj.* 1. Neglecting to do what ought to be done. 2. Informal; nonchalant. [< OF] —**neg′li·gence** *n.* —**neg′li·gent ly** *adv.*
neg·li·gi·ble (neg′lə·jə·bəl) *adj.* Not worth considering. —**neg′li·gi·bly** *adv.*
ne·go·ti·a·ble (ni·gō′shē·ə·bəl, -shə·bəl) *adj.* 1. Capable of being negotiated. 2. Open to

discussion. 3. That can be legally transferred to another party. —**ne·go′ti·a·bil′i·ty** *n.*

ne·go·ti·ate (ni·gō′shē·āt) *v.* **·at·ed, ·at·ing** *v.i.* 1. To discuss or confer with another party in order to reach an agreement. —*v.t.* 2. To arrange or conclude by discussion. 3. To transfer (a note, bond, etc.) to another for a value received. 4. To manage to accomplish or cope with (something difficult): to *negotiate* a steep hill. [< L *negotiari* to do business] —**ne·go′ti·a′tion** *n.* —**ne·go′ti·a′·tor** *n.*

Ne·gri·to (ni·grē′tō) *n. pl.* **·tos** or **·toes** *Anthropol.* One of the Pygmy peoples of the Malay Peninsula, the Philippine Islands, central Africa, and southeast Asia. [< Sp., dim. of *negro* black]

ne·gri·tude (nē′grə·to͞od′) *n.* Awareness of and pride in one's black African heritage. [< L *niger* black]

Ne·gro (nē′grō) *n. pl.* **·groes** A member of the Negroid ethnic division of mankind. Also **ne′gro.** [< L *niger* black] —**Ne′gro** *adj.*

Ne·groid (nē′groid) *adj. Anthropol.* Of, pertaining to, or belonging to a major ethnic division of mankind characterized by skin color ranging from brown to almost black. —*n.* A Negroid person.

Ne·he·mi·ah (nē′hə·mī′ə) *n.* A book of the Old Testament attributed to the 5th c. B.C. Hebrew statesman Nehemiah: also, in the Douai Bible, II *Esdras.* [< Hebrew *Nehemyāh* Jehovah comforts]

neigh (nā) *v.i.* To utter the cry of a horse; whinny. [OE *hnǣgan*; imit.] —**neigh** *n.*

neigh·bor (nā′bər) *n.* 1. One who lives near another. 2. One who or that which is near another. 3. *Chiefly Dial.* Friend; mister: a term of address. —*adj.* Living nearby. —*v.t. & v.i.* To live or be near or next to. Also *Brit.* **neigh′bour.** [OE < *nēah* near + *gebur* dweller] —**neigh′bor·ing** *adj.*

neigh·bor·hood (nā′bər·ho͝od) *n.* 1. A small area or region that has some specific quality or character. 2. The people who live near one another. Also *Brit.* **neigh′bour·hood.**

neigh·bor·ly (nā′bər·lē) *adj.* Like a good neighbor; friendly; kind. —**neigh′bor·li·ness** *n.*

nei·ther (nē′thər, nī′-) *adj.* Not the one nor the other; not either. —*pron.* Not the one nor the other: *Neither* of them is here. —*conj.* 1. Not either; not: He *neither* reads nor writes. 2. Nor yet: *Neither* can he. [OE *nāhwaether*]

nemato- *combining form* Thread; filament: also, before vowels, **nemat-.** Also **nema-.** [< Gk. *nēma, -matos* thread]

nem·a·tode (nem′ə·tōd) *adj. Zool.* Of or belonging to a phylum or class of roundworms, as the hookworm. —*n.* A nematode worm. [< NL]

nem·e·sis (nem′ə·sis) *n. pl.* **·ses** (-sēz) 1. A strong and stubborn opponent. 2. An instrument of vengeance. [< Gk., retributive justice]

neo- *combining form* New; recent. Also, before vowels, usu. **ne-.** [< Gk. *neos* new]

ne·o·clas·sic (nē′ō·klas′ik) *adj.* Of, pertaining to, or denoting a revival of classical style, as in literature or art. Also **ne′o·clas′si·cal.** —**ne·o·clas·si·cism** (nē′ō·klas′ə·siz′əm) *n.* —**ne′o·clas′si·cist** (-ə·sist) *n.*

ne·o·co·lo·ni·al·ism (nē′ō·kə·lō′nē·əl·iz′əm) *n.* The use of economic and political control by a powerful nation over developing countries, former colonies, etc. —**ne′o·co·lo′ni·al·ist** *n. & adj.*

ne·o·dym·i·um (nē′ō·dim′ē·əm) *n.* A metallic element (symbol Nd) forming rose-colored salts, found in combination with cerium, etc. [< NEO- + (DI)DYMIUM]

ne·ol·o·gism (nē·ol′ə·jiz′əm) *n.* A new word or phrase. [< F *néologisme*]

ne·on (nē′on) *n.* A gaseous element (symbol Ne) occurring in the atmosphere in very small amounts. —*adj.* 1. Of or pertaining to neon. 2. Composed of or using neon. [< Gk., neut. of *neos* new]

ne·o·phyte (nē′ə·fīt) *n.* 1. A recent convert, esp. in the early Christian church. 2. Any beginner. [< Gk. *neophytos* newly planted]

ne·o·plasm (nē′ə·plaz′əm) *n. Pathol.* Any abnormal growth of tissue in the body; a tumor. —**ne′o·plas′tic** (-plas′tik) *adj.*

ne·pen·the (ni·pen′thē) *n.* 1. A drug or potion supposed by the ancient Greeks to banish pain and sorrow. 2. Anything causing oblivion. [< Gk. *nē-* not + *penthos* sorrow]

neph·ew (nef′yo͞o) *n.* The son of a brother or brother-in-law or of a sister or sister-in-law. [< L *nepos* grandson, nephew]

nepho- *combining form* Cloud. Also, before vowels, **neph-.** [< Gk. *nephos*]

ne·phrit·ic (ni·frit′ik) *adj.* 1. Of or pertaining to the kidney or kidneys; renal. 2. Of, pertaining to, or suffering from nephritis.

ne·phri·tis (ni·frī′tis) *n. Pathol.* Inflammation of the kidneys. [< Gk. *nephros* kidney]

nephro- *combining form* A kidney. Also, before vowels, **nephr-.** [< Gk. *nephros*]

ne plus ul·tra (nē plus ul′trə) *Latin* The extreme or utmost point; perfection; literally, nothing more beyond.

nep·o·tism (nep′ə·tiz′əm) *n.* Favoritism; esp. governmental patronage to relatives. [< L *nepos, -potis* grandson, nephew]

Nep·tune (nep′to͞on) *n.* The fourth largest planet and eighth in order from the sun. [< L *Neptunus*] —**Nep·tu′ni·an** *adj.*

nep·tu·ni·um (nep·to͞o′nē·əm) *n.* A radioactive element (symbol Np), artificially produced from a uranium isotope by neutron bombardment.

nerve (nûrv) *n.* 1. *Physiol.* Any of the fibers that convey impulses between the brain or spinal cord and other parts or organs. 2. Courage or boldness; daring. 3. *Informal* Impudence; brashness. 4. *Usu. pl.* Unsteadiness of mind; nervous condition; anxiety. —*v.t.* **nerved, nerv·ing** To provide with nerve or nerves. —**to nerve oneself** To summon up one's courage. [< L *nervus* sinew]

nerve cell *Physiol.* A neuron.

nerve center *Physiol.* An aggregation of neurons having a specific function, as hearing, sight, etc.

nerve·less (nûrv′lis) *adj.* 1. Lacking force; feeble. 2. Completely controlled and calm in crises; cool. 3. *Anat.* Having no nerves.

nerve-rack·ing (nûrv′rak′ing) *adj.* Extremely irritating; harrowing. Also **nerve′-wrack′ing.**

ner·vous (nûr′vəs) *adj.* 1. Characterized by or exhibiting restlessness, anxiety, tension, etc.; high-strung; excitable. 2. Neural.

3. Caused by or acting on the nerves or nervous system. **—ner′vous·ly** *adv.* **—ner′·vous·ness** *n.*

nervous breakdown Popularly, any severe mental or emotional disturbance, usu. requiring hospitalization.

nervous system *Physiol.* A system in animals that includes the brain and spinal cord, and that controls and regulates various organic activities by receiving and transmitting stimuli.

nerv·y (nûr′vē) *adj.* **nerv·i·er, nerv·i·est** 1. *Informal* Impudent; brash. 2. *Brit. Informal* Nervous; jumpy. 3. Having or requiring courage. **—nerv′i·ness** *n.*

nes·cience (nesh′əns, -ē·əns) *n.* Ignorance. [< L *ne-* not + *scire* to know]

-ness *suffix of nouns* State or quality of being. [OE *-nes(s)*, *-nis(s)*]

nest (nest) *n.* 1. The dwelling place prepared or selected by a bird for the hatching of its eggs and the rearing of its young. 2. A place used by fishes, insects, turtles, etc., for laying eggs. 3. A cozy or snug place. 4. A haunt or den. 5. A series or set of similar things designed to fit into one another, as bowls, boxes, etc. **—***v.t.* 1. To place in or as in a nest. 2. To pack or place one inside another. **—***v.i.* 3. To build or occupy a nest. [OE]

n'est-ce pas (nes pä′) *French* Isn't that so?

nest egg 1. A sum of money set aside for emergencies, etc. 2. An artificial egg kept in a nest to induce a hen to lay eggs.

nes·tle (nes′əl) *v.* **·tled, ·tling** *v.i.* 1. To lie or press closely; cuddle; snuggle. **—***v.t.* 2. To place or press snugly or lovingly. 3. To place or shelter in or as in a nest. [OE *nestlian* to nest] **—nes′tler** *n.*

nest·ling (nest′ling, nes′-) *n.* 1. A bird too young to leave the nest. 2. A young child. **—***adj.* Recently hatched.

net[1] (net) *n.* 1. A fabric of thread, rope, etc., woven to form a meshwork and used to catch fish, birds, etc. ◆Collateral adjective: *reticular*. 2. Anything that traps or entangles; a snare. 3. Something constructed with meshes: cargo *net*; tennis *net*. **—***v.t.* **net·ted, net·ting** 1. To catch in or as in a net; ensnare. 2. To cover, enclose, or shelter with a net. [OE]

net[2] (net) *adj.* 1. Obtained after deducting all expenses, losses, taxes, etc.: distinguished from *gross*. 2. Free from anything extraneous; fundamental; basic: *net* results. **—***n.* A net profit, amount, weight, etc. **—***v.t.* **net·ted, net·ting** To earn or yield as clear profit. [< F]

neth·er (neth′ər) *adj.* Situated beneath or below. [OE *nither* < Gmc.]

Neth·er·land·er (neth′ər·lan′dər, -lən-) *n.* A native or inhabitant of the Netherlands.

Neth·er·land·ish (neth′ər·lan′dish, -lən-) *adj.* Of or pertaining to the Netherlands.

neth·er·most (neth′ər·mōst′) *adj.* Lowest.

nether world 1. The world of the dead. 2. The world of punishment after death; hell.

net·ting (net′ing) *n.* 1. A net; network. 2. The act or operation of making net. 3. The right of using fishing nets.

net·tle (net′l) *n.* 1. An herb having minute stinging hairs. 2. Any of various plants having some real or fancied resemblance to this herb. **—***v.t.* **·tled, ·tling** To annoy or irritate; provoke. [OE *netle* < Gmc.]

net·tle·some (net′l·səm) *adj.* That vexes or irritates.

net·work (net′wûrk′) *n.* 1. A system of interlacing lines, tracks, or channels. 2. A meshwork fabric; netting. 3. *Telecom.* A chain of broadcasting stations. 4. Any interconnected system: an espionage *network*.

Neuf·châ·tel (noo′shə·tel′, *Fr.* nœ·shä·tel′) *n.* A soft, white cheese.

neu·ral (noor′əl) *adj.* Of or pertaining to the nerves or nervous system. [< Gk. *neuron* cord, sinew]

neu·ral·gi·a (noo·ral′jē·ə, -jə) *n. Pathol.* Acute pain along the course of a nerve. **—neu·ral′gic** *adj.*

neu·ras·the·ni·a (noor′əs·thē′nē·ə, -thēn′yə) *n.* A condition marked by debility, depression, and bodily disturbances. [< Gk. *neuron* cord, sinew + *astheneia* weakness] **—neu′ras·then′ic** (-then′ik) *adj.* & *n.*

neu·ri·tis (noo·rī′tis) *n. Pathol.* Inflammation of a nerve. **—neu·rit′ic** (-rit′ik) *adj.*

neuro- *combining form* Nerve. Also **neur-** (before vowels), **neuri-**. [< Gk. *neuron* sinew]

neu·rol·o·gy (noo·rol′ə·jē) *n.* The branch of medicine that deals with the nervous system and its disorders. [< NL *neurologia*] **—neu·ro·log·i·cal** (noor′ə·loj′i·kəl) *adj.* **—neu·rol′o·gist** *n.*

neu·ron (noor′on) *n. Physiol.* The cellular unit of the nervous system: also called *nerve cell*. [< Gk. *neuron* sinew]

neu·ro·sis (noo·rō′sis) *n. pl.* **·ses** (-sēz) *Psychiatry* Any of various emotional disturbances, usu. involving anxiety and depression: also called *psychoneurosis*. [< NL]

neu·rot·ic (noo·rot′ik) *adj.* Pertaining to or suffering from neurosis. **—***n.* A neurotic person.

neu·ter (noo′tər) *adj.* 1. *Gram.* Neither masculine nor feminine in gender. 2. *Biol.* Having nonfunctioning or imperfectly developed sex organs, as a worker bee. **—***n.* 1. *Biol.* A neuter plant or animal. 2. A castrated animal. **—***v.t.* To make neuter; castrate. [ult. < L *ne-* not + *uter* either]

neu·tral (noo′trəl) *adj.* 1. Not taking the part of either side in a dispute or war. 2. Of or belonging to neither side in a dispute or war. 3. Having no decided color; grayish. 4. *Biol.* Neuter; esp., without stamens or pistils. 5. *Chem.* Neither acid nor alkaline. 6. *Electr.* Neither positive nor negative. **—***n.* 1. One who or that which is neutral. 2. *Mech.* The state in which transmission gears are disengaged. [< L *neuter* neither] **—neu′tral·ly** *adv.*

neu·tral·ism (noo′trəl·iz′əm) *n.* In foreign affairs, the policy of not aligning a nation with any side of a power conflict. **—neu′tral·ist** *adj.* & *n.*

neu·tral·i·ty (noo·tral′ə·tē) *n. pl.* **·ties** Neutral condition, status, attitude, policy, etc., as of a nation during a war. [< Med.L *neutralitas*]

neu·tral·ize (noo′trəl·īz) *v.t.* **·ized, ·iz·ing** 1. To counteract or destroy the force, influence, or effect of. 2. To declare neutral during a war. 3. To make electrically or

chemically neutral. [< F *neutraliser*] —**neu′tral·i·za′tion** *n.* —**neu′tral·iz′er** *n.*
neu·tri·no (nōō·trē′nō) *n. Physics* A fundamental subatomic particle with no charge and a mass approaching zero. [< Ital., little neutron]
neu·tron (nōō′tron) *n. Physics* An electrically neutral particle of the atomic nucleus having a mass approximately equal to that of the proton.
neutron bomb A nuclear weapon producing great radiation but causing limited property damage.
neutron star *Astron.* A hypothetical star of great density that is a source of strong X-rays, and believed to be a collapsed large star.
nev·er (nev′ər) *adv.* 1. Not at any time; not ever. 2. Not at all. [OE *nǣfre*]
nev·er·more (nev′ər·môr′) *adv.* Never again.
nev·er·the·less (nev′ər·thə·les′) *adv.* Nonetheless; however; yet.
new (nōō) *adj.* **new·er, new·est** 1. Having recently been made, developed, or discovered. 2. Having never existed or occurred before. 3. Unfamiliar; strange. 4. Not accustomed or experienced: *new* at the job. 5. Fresh; unspoiled. 6. Repeated; renewed: a *new* plea. 7. Additional; increased: a *new* supply. 8. Rejuvenated; refreshed: a *new* man. 9. Modern; current; fashionable. 10. *cap.* Designating the most recent form or period: *New* Latin. —*adv.* Newly; freshly; recently. [OE *niwe* < Gmc.] —**new′ish** *adj.* —**new′·ness** *n.*
new·born (nōō′bôrn′) *adj.* 1. Just lately born. 2. Born anew. —*n.* A newborn infant or animal.
new·com·er (nōō′kum′ər) *n.* One who has recently arrived.
New Deal The political, economic, and social policies and principles of the administration under Franklin D. Roosevelt. —**New Dealer**
new·el (nōō′əl) *n. Archit.* 1. The post at the end of a staircase. 2. The central pillar or upright of a spiral staircase. Also **newel post.** [< OF *nouel* kernel < L *nux* nut]
new·fan·gled (nōō′fang′gəld) *adj.* Lately come into fashion; novel. [ME *newe* new + *fangel* contrivance]
New·found·land (nōō′fənd·lənd) *n.* A large dog having a broad head, square muzzle, and thick, usu. black coat.
New Latin See under LATIN.
new·ly (nōō′lē) *adv.* 1. Very recently; lately. 2. Once more; anew. 3. In a new or different way.
new·ly·wed (nōō′lē·wed′) *n.* A person recently married.
new moon The phase of the moon when its disk is invisible.
new·mown (nōō′mōn′) *adj.* Recently mown, as hay.
news (nōōz) *n.pl.* (*construed as sing.*) 1. Information of a recent event, as reported in a newspaper or on a newscast. 2. Any new or unfamiliar information. [< NEW]
news·boy (nōōz′boi′) *n.* A boy who sells or delivers newspapers.
news·cast (nōōz′kast′) *n.* A radio or television broadcast of news. —**news′cast′er** *n.*
news·let·ter (nōōz′let′ər) *n.* A specialized news report sent by mail.
news·mag·a·zine (nōōz′mag′ə·zēn, -mag′ə·zēn′) *n.* A periodical that summarizes the news.
news·man (nōōz′man′, -mən) *n. pl.* **·men** (-men′, -mən) 1. A news reporter. 2. A newsdealer. —**news·wom·an** (nōōz′wŏŏm′·ən) *n.fem.*
news·pa·per (nōōz′pā′pər) *n.* A printed publication usu. issued daily or weekly, containing news, editorials, special features, and advertisements.
news·print (nōōz′print′) *n.* The thin, unsized paper on which a newspaper is printed.
news·reel (nōōz′rēl′) *n.* A short motion picture showing current events.
news·stand (nōōz′stand′) *n.* A stand or stall where newspapers and periodicals are sold.
news·worth·y (nōōz′wûr′thē) *adj.* Important enough to be reported in a newspaper or newscast.
news·y (nōō′zē) *Informal adj.* **news·i·er, news·i·est** Full of news.
newt (nōōt) *n.* Any of various semiaquatic salamanders. [Earlier *ewt*; in ME *an ewt* was taken as a *newt*]
New Testament That portion of the Bible containing the life and teachings of Christ and his followers.
New World The Western Hemisphere.
New Year The first day of the year; January 1. Also **New Year's Day** (yirz).
New Year's Eve The night of December 31.
next (nekst) *adj.* 1. Coming directly after in time, order, or position. 2. Nearest or closest in space. 3. Adjacent or adjoining. —*adv.* 1. Immediately afterward. 2. On the first succeeding occasion: when *next* we meet. —*prep.* Nearest to: *next* his heart. —**next door** 1. The adjacent house, building, or apartment. 2. In, at, or to the adjacent house, etc. [OE *niehst*, superl. of *neah* near]
nex·us (nek′səs) *n. pl.* **·us·es** or **·us** 1. A bond or tie between the several members of a group or series; link. 2. A connected series. [< L, pp. of *nectere* to tie]
ni·a·cin (nī′ə·sin) *n.* A colorless, water-soluble compound forming part of the vitamin B complex: also called *nicotinic acid.*
nib (nib) *n.* 1. The point of a pen. 2. The projecting, pointed part of anything; tip. [OE *nebb* beak]
nib·ble (nib′əl) *v.* **·bled, ·bling** *v.t.* 1. To eat with small, quick bites. 2. To bite gently: to *nibble* an ear. —*v.i.* 3. To eat or bite, esp. with small, gentle bites: often with *at.* —*n.* A little bit or morsel. [< Gmc.] —**nib′bler** *n.*
Nic·a·ra·guan (nik′ə·rä′gwən) *adj.* Of or pertaining to Nicaragua. —*n.* A native of Nicaragua.
nice (nīs) *adj.* **nic·er, nic·est** 1. Agreeable; pleasing; suitable. 2. Friendly; kind. 3. Having or showing good breeding; respectable. 4. Having or showing discrimination; delicate or subtle. 5. Precise or accurate, as an instrument. [< OF, innocent, foolish < L *nescius* ignorant] —**nice′ly** *adv.* —**nice′ness** *n.*
ni·ce·ty (nī′sə·tē) *n. pl.* **·ties** 1. *Usu. pl.* A minute or subtle point, detail, or distinction. 2. *Usu. pl.* A delicacy or refinement:

niceties of living. 3. Precision or accuracy; exactness. **—to a nicety** Exactly.

niche (nich) *n.* 1. A recessed space in a wall. 2. Any position or purpose that is best suited: to find one's *niche.* [Prob. < F, ult. < L *nidus* nest]

Nich·o·las, (nik′ə·ləs, -lus) **Saint** See SANTA CLAUS.

nick (nik) *n.* A slight cut or notch on a surface or edge. **—in the nick of time** At the exact or crucial moment. **—nick** *v.t.*

nick·el (nik′əl) *n.* 1. A hard, silver-white metallic element (symbol Ni). 2. A five-cent coin of the U.S., made of an alloy of nickel and copper. **—***v.t.* **nick·eled** or **·elled, nick·el·ing** or **·el·ling** To plate with nickel. [< G (*kupfer*)*nickel,* lit., copper demon; because its ore looks like copper]

nick·el·o·de·on (nik′əl·ō′dē·ən) *n.* 1. A motion-picture theater charging five cents for admission. 2. A jukebox or other automatic music machine. [< NICKEL (def. 2) + *odeon* < F *odéon* theater]

nickel plate A thin layer of nickel deposited on the surface of objects by electroplating. **—nick·el-plate** (nik′əl·plāt′) *v.t.* **-plat·ed, -plat·ing**

nickel silver A white alloy of copper, nickel, and zinc, used in the manufacture of cutlery.

nick·er (nik′ər) *v.i.* 1. To neigh. 2. To snicker. [Imit.] **—nick′er** *n.*

nick·name (nik′nām′) *n.* 1. A familiar form of a proper name, as *Tom* for *Thomas.* 2. A descriptive name, as *Honest Abe.* **—***v.t.* **·named, ·nam·ing** To give a nickname to or call by a nickname. [ME *ekename* surname, *an ekename* becoming *a nickname*]

nic·o·tine (nik′ə·tēn) *n.* An acrid, poisonous, oily alkaloid contained in the leaves of tobacco. [< F, after Jean *Nicot,* 1530–1600, French courtier, who introduced tobacco into France from Portugal] **—nic′o·tin′ic** (-tin′ik) *adj.*

nicotinic acid See NIACIN.

niece (nēs) *n.* The daughter of a brother or sister. [ME *nece,* ult. < L *neptis* niece, granddaughter]

nif·ty (nif′tē) *adj.* **·ti·er, ·ti·est** *Slang* Stylish; pleasing.

Ni·ge·ri·an (nī·jir′ē·ən) *adj.* Of Nigeria or its inhabitants. **—Ni·ge′ri·an** *n.*

nig·gard (nig′ərd) *n.* A stingy person. **—***adj.* Niggardly. [< AF, ? ult. < ON *hnøggr*]

nig·gard·ly (nig′ərd·lē) *adj.* 1. Stingy. 2. Scanty. **—***adv.* In the manner of a niggard. **—nig′gard·li·ness** *n.*

nig·gle (nig′əl) *v.i.* **·gled, ·gling** To occupy oneself with trifles. [Cf. dial. Norw. *nigla*]

nig·gling (nig′ling) *adj.* 1. Fussy; overprecise. 2. Mean; petty. 3. Annoying; nagging. **—nig′gling·ly** *adv.*

nigh (nī) *Chiefly Archaic & Dial.* *adj.* **nigh·er, nigh·est** or **next** Close; near. **—***adv.* 1. Near in time or place. 2. Almost: often with *on* or *onto*: *nigh* on a year. **—***prep.* Near. [OE *nēah, nēh*]

night (nīt) *n.* 1. The period from sunset to sunrise, esp. the part that is dark. ◆Collateral adjective: *nocturnal.* 2. The period of evening. 3. Darkness; the dark. 4. A period of gloom, unhappiness, etc. [OE *niht, neaht*] **—night** *adj.*

night blindness Vision that is abnormally poor in dim light but normal in daylight.

night·cap (nīt′kap′) *n.* 1. A cap worn in bed. 2. *Informal* A drink of liquor taken just before going to bed.

night·clothes (nīt′klōz′, -klōthz′) *n.pl.* Clothes worn in bed.

night·club (nīt′klub′) *n.* A place of entertainment, providing food and drink, and open until late at night.

night crawler Any large earthworm that emerges at night.

night·fall (nīt′fôl′) *n.* The close of day.

night·gown (nīt′goun′) *n.* A loose gown worn in bed. Also **night′dress′** (-dres′).

night·hawk (nīt′hôk′) *n.* Any of various birds related to the whippoorwill.

night·in·gale (nī′tən·gāl, nī′ting-) *n.* A small, Old World thrush noted for the melodious song of the male. [OE < *niht* night + *galan* to sing]

night-life (nīt′līf′) *n.* Entertainment, as theaters and nightclubs, open at night.

night-light (nīt′līt′) *n.* A dim light kept on at night.

night·long (nīt′lông′) *adj.* Lasting through the night.

night·ly (nīt′lē) *adj.* 1. Of, pertaining to, or occurring each night. 2. Pertaining to or occurring at night. **—***adv.* Each night: to take place *nightly.*

night·mare (nīt′mâr) *n.* 1. A horrible and frightening dream. 2. Any experience or condition resembling a nightmare. [< NIGHT + MARE[2]] **—night′mar·ish** *adj.*

nights (nīts) *adv.* *Informal* At night. [OE *nihtes*]

night school A school that holds classes during the evening.

night·shade (nīt′shād′) *n.* 1. Any of various flowering plants of a family that includes tobacco, pepper, the potato, and the tomato. 2. Belladonna.

night·shirt (nīt′shûrt′) *n.* A long, loose garment worn in bed.

night·spot (nīt′spot′) *Informal* A nightclub.

night·stick (nīt′stik′) *n.* A long, heavy club carried by policemen.

night·time (nīt′tīm′) *n.* The time from sunset to sunrise, or from dark to dawn.

night watch 1. A watch or guard kept at night. 2. A night watchman. 3. A period of watch or guard.

night·wear (nīt′wâr′) *n.* Nightclothes.

night·y (nī′tē) *n.* *pl.* **night·ies** *Informal* A nightgown.

nigri- *combining form* Black. Also, before vowels, **nigr-.** [< L *niger, nigris*]

ni·hil·ism (nī′əl·iz′əm) *n.* 1. *Philos.* A doctrine that denies all traditional principles, beliefs, and institutions. 2. In politics, a doctrine advocating the destruction of all political, economic, and social institutions. **—ni′hil·ist** *n.* **—ni′hil·is′tic** *adj.*

-nik *suffix of nouns and adjectives* One who is identified with or is characterized by: **neatnik, no-goodnik, peacenik.**

nil (nil) *n.* Nothing. [< L, contr. of *nihil* nothing]

nim·ble (nim′bəl) *adj.* **·bler, ·blest** 1. Light and quick in movement; lively. 2. Characterized by a quick and ready intellect.

[OE *numel* quick at grasping] —**nim′ble·ness** *n.* —**nim′bly** *adv.*

nim·bo·stra·tus (nim′bō·strā′təs, -strat′əs) *n.* *Meteorol.* A low, dark gray cloud layer, forming rain or snow.

nim·bus (nim′bəs) *n.* *pl.* **·bus·es** or **·bi** (-bī) A light believed to surround a deity or holy person. [< L, cloud]

nin·com·poop (nin′kəm·po͞op) *n.* An idiot; fool. [Origin unknown]

nine (nīn) *n.* 1. The sum of eight and one: a cardinal number written 9, IX. 2. Anything consisting of nine units, as a baseball team, etc. [OE *nigon*] —**nine** *adj.* —**ninth** *adj.* & *n.*

nine·pins (nīn′pinz′) *n.pl.* (*construed as sing.*) A bowling game similar to tenpins, using nine large wooden pins.

nine·teen (nīn′tēn′) *n.* The sum of eighteen and one: a cardinal number written 19, XIX. [OE *nigontīene*] —**nine′teen′** *adj.* —**nine′·teenth′** *adj.* & *n.*

nine·ty (nīn′tē) *n.* *pl.* **·ties** The sum of eighty and ten: a cardinal number written 90, XC. [OE *nigontig*] —**nine′ty** *adj.* —**nine′ti·eth** *adj.* & *n.*

ni·o·bi·um (nī·ō′bē·əm) *n.* A rare, steel gray, metallic element (symbol Nb), valuable as an alloy metal: formerly called *columbium*.

nip[1] (nip) *v.* **nipped, nip·ping** *v.t.* 1. To pinch between two surfaces; bite. 2. To sever or remove by pinching, biting, or clipping: usually with *off*. 3. To check, arrest, or destroy the growth or development of. 4. To affect painfully or injuriously, as by cold. 5. *Slang* To steal. —*v.i.* 6. *Brit. Informal* To move nimbly or rapidly. —*n.* 1. The act of one who or that which nips. 2. Any small portion: a *nip* of tea. 3. Severe cold or frost. 4. A sharp, pungent flavor. —**nip and tuck** Very close or even; uncertain. [Cf. Du. *nijpen* to pinch]

nip[2] (nip) *n.* A small quantity of liquor. —*v.t.* & *v.i.* To sip (liquor). [? < earlier *nipperkin* a small liquid measure]

nip·per (nip′ər) *n.* 1. One who or that which nips. 2. *pl.* An implement used for nipping, as pliers, pincers, etc. 3. The large claw of a crab or lobster. 4. *Brit. Informal* A small boy; lad.

nip·ple (nip′əl) *n.* 1. The protuberance on the breasts of higher mammals, esp. that of the female; teat. 2. The rubber teatlike mouthpiece of a nursing bottle. [Earlier *nible*, ? dim. of NIB]

nip·py (nip′ē) *adj.* **·pi·er, ·pi·est** Biting or sharp, as cold weather. —**nip′pi·ness** *n.*

nir·va·na (nir·vä′nə, nər-) *n.* 1. In Buddhism, the state of absolute bliss attained through the annihilation of the self. 2. Freedom from care and pain; bliss. [< Skt. *nirvāna* extinction]

Ni·sei (nē·sā) *n.* *pl.* **·sei** or **·seis** A native American of immigrant Japanese parentage.

ni·si (nī′sī) *conj.* *Law* Unless: used after *order, rule, decree*, etc., signifying that it shall become effective at a certain time, unless modified or avoided. [< L]

nit (nit) *n.* 1. The egg of a louse or other parasitic insect. 2. An immature louse. [OE *hnitu*] —**nit′ty** *adj.*

ni·ter (nī′tər) *n.* Potassium or sodium nitrate; saltpeter. Also **ni′tre.** [< Gk. *nitron*]

nit-pick (nit′pik′) *Informal* *v.t.* 1. To fuss over or find fault with. —*v.i.* 2. To engage in nit-picking. Also **nit′pick.** [Back formation < NIT-PICKING] —**nit′-pick′er** *n.*

nit-pick·ing (nit′pik′ing) *n.* *Informal* A fussing over trivial details, esp. to find fault. [< NIT]

ni·trate (nī′trāt) *n.* *Chem.* 1. A salt or ester of nitric acid. 2. Niter. —*v.t.* **·trat·ed, ·trat·ing** To treat or combine with nitric acid or a compound. [See NITER.]

ni·tric (nī′trik) *adj.* *Chem.* 1. Of, pertaining to, or obtained from nitrogen. 2. Containing nitrogen in the higher valence.

nitric acid *Chem.* A colorless, highly corrosive liquid, having strong oxidising properties.

ni·tri·fy (nī′trə·fī) *v.t.* **·fied, ·fy·ing** *Chem.* 1. To treat or combine with nitrogen. 2. To treat (soil, etc.) with nitrates. [< F *nitrifier*] —**ni′tri·fi′a·ble** *adj.* —**ni′tri·fi·ca′tion** *n.*

nitro- *combining form* *Chem.* Containing the univalent radical NO_2. Also, before vowels, **nitr-.** Also **nitri-.** [< Gk. *nitron* niter]

ni·tro·gen (nī′trə·jən) *n.* An odorless, colorless gaseous element (symbol N) forming about four-fifths of the atmosphere by volume and playing a decisive role in the formation of compounds essential to life. [< F. See NITRO-, + -GEN] —**ni·trog·e·nous** (nī·troj′ə·nəs) *adj.*

ni·tro·glyc·er·in (nī′trō·glis′ər·in) *n.* *Chem.* An oily liquid, colorless to pale yellow, made by nitrating glycerol and used as an explosive, propellant, etc. Also **ni′tro, ni′tro·glyc′er·ine.** [< NITRO- + GLYCERIN]

ni·trous (nī′trəs) *adj.* *Chem.* Of, pertaining to, or derived from nitrogen: esp. applied to those compounds containing less oxygen than the nitric compounds.

nitrous oxide A gas used as an anesthetic in dental surgery: also called *laughing gas*.

nit·ty-grit·ty (nit′ē·grit′ē) *n.* *Slang* The basic questions or details; essence. —*adj.* Basic.

nit·wit (nit′wit′) *n.* A silly or stupid person.

nix (niks) *n.* *Slang* 1. Nothing. 2. No. —*adv.* No. —*v.t.* To forbid or disagree with. [< G *nichts* nothing]

no[1] (nō) *adv.* 1. Nay; not so. 2. Not at all; not in any way: *no* better than the other. 3. Not: used to express an alternative after *or*: whether or *no*. —*n.* *pl.* **noes** 1. A negative reply; a denial. 2. A negative vote or voter. [OE *nā* < *ne* not + *ā* ever]

no[2] (nō) *adj.* Not any; not one. [OE *nān* none]

no[3] (nō) *n.* *pl.* **no** *Sometimes cap.* The classical drama of Japan, tragic or noble in theme, having music and dancing: also spelled *noh*. Also **nō.** Compare KABUKI.

nob[1] (nob) *n.* *Slang* The head. [Var. of KNOB]

nob[2] (nob) *n.* *Slang* One who is rich, influential, etc.

no·be·li·um (nō·bē′lē·əm) *n.* An unstable radioactive element (symbol No) originally produced by the bombardment of curium by an isotope of carbon. [after A. B. *Nobel*]

no·bil·i·ty (nō·bil′ə·tē) *n.* *pl.* **·ties** 1. A class in society composed of persons having hereditary title, rank, and privileges. 2. In Great Britain, the peerage. 3. The state or quality of being noble.

no·ble (nō′bəl) *adj.* **·bler, ·blest** 1. Having excellence or dignity. 2. Magnificent and imposing in appearance; grand; stately. 3. Of or pertaining to the nobility; aristocratic. —*n.* 1. A nobleman. 2. In Great Britain, a peer. [< L *nobilis* noble, well-known] —**no′ble·ness** *n.* —**no′bly** *adv.*

no·ble·man (nō′bəl·mən) *n. pl.* **·men** (-mən) A man of noble rank; in Great Britain, a peer.

no·blesse o·blige (nō·bles′ ō·blēzh′) *French* The obligation of those of high birth, wealth, or social position to behave generously or nobly toward others; literally, nobility obligates.

no·ble·wom·an (nō′bəl·wŏŏm′ən) *n. pl.* **·wom·en** (-wim′in) 1. A woman of noble rank. 2. In Great Britain, a peeress.

no·bod·y (nō′bod′ē, -bəd·ē) *pron.* Not anybody. —*n. pl.* **·bod·ies** A person of no importance or influence.

nocti- *combining form* By or at night. Also, before vowels, **noct-**. [< L *nox, noctis* night]

noc·tur·nal (nok·tûr′nəl) *adj.* 1. Of, pertaining to, or occurring at night. 2. *Biol.* Active by night. [< L *nocturnus* nightly] —**noc·tur′nal·ly** *adv.*

noc·turne (nok′tûrn) *n.* 1. In painting, a night scene. 2. *Music* A composition of a pensive or romantic nature.

nod (nod) *v.* **nod·ded, nod·ding** *v.i.* 1. To lower the head forward briefly, as in agreement. 2. To let the head fall forward slightly, as when drowsy. 3. To be inattentive or careless. 4. To sway or bend, as trees. —*v.t.* 5. To lower (the head) by nodding. 6. To express or signify (assent, etc.) by nodding the head. [ME *nodden*] —**nod** *n.* —**nod′der** *n.*

nod·dy (nod′ē) *n. pl.* **·dies** 1. A dunce; a fool. 2. One of several terns of the Atlantic coast. [? < NOD]

node (nōd) *n.* 1. A knot, knob, or swelling. 2. *Bot.* A joint or knob of a stem. 3. *Astron.* Either of two points at which the orbit of a celestial object intersects the ecliptic. [< L *nodus* knot] —**nod′al** *adj.* —**nod′al·ly** *adv.*

nod·ule (noj′ōōl) *n.* 1. A little knot or node. 2. *Bot.* A tubercle. [< L *nodus* knot] —**nod′u·lar** *adj.*

no·ël (nō·el′) *n.* A Christmas carol. Also **no·el′**.

No·ël (nō·el′) *n.* Christmas. Also **No·el′**. [< F < LL (*dies*) *natalis* birthday]

no-fault (nō′ fôlt′) *adj.* Designating a system whereby claims may be settled without assigning blame to one party.

no-frills (nō′frilz′) *adj.* Eliminating nonessentials or extras: *no-frills* plane flight.

nog·gin (nog′in) *n.* 1. *Informal* A person's head. 2. A small mug or cup. 3. A measure of liquor equal to about ¼ pint or a gill. [Origin unknown]

no-good (nō′gŏŏd′) *adj.* Worthless; contemptible. —*n.* A contemptible person.

noh (nō) See NO[3].

no-hit·ter (nō′hit′ər) In baseball, a game in which the pitcher allows no base hits.

no·how (nō′hou′) *adv. Dial.* In no way.

noise (noiz) *n.* 1. Loud, confused, or disturbing sound. 2. Any random electronic disturbance. —*v.t.* **noised, nois·ing** To spread, report, or rumor: often with *about* or *abroad.* [< OF < L *nausea*]

noise·less (noiz′lis) *adj.* Causing or making little or no noise; quiet; silent. —**noise′less·ly** *adv.* —**noise′less·ness** *n.*

noise·mak·er (noiz′mā′kər) *n.* A horn, bell, etc., for making noise at celebrations. —**noise′mak′ing** *n. & adj.*

noise pollution Loud or annoying noise considered harmful to people and to the environment.

noi·some (noi′səm) *adj.* 1. Offensive or disgusting, esp. in smell. 2. Injurious; noxious. [ME < *noy* annoyance] —**noi′some·ly** *adv.* —**noi′some·ness** *n.*

nois·y (noi′zē) *adj.* **nois·i·er, nois·i·est** 1. Making a loud noise. 2. Characterized by or full of noise. —**nois′i·ly** *adv.* —**nois′i·ness** *n.*

nol·le pros·e·qui (nol′ē pros′ə·kwī) *Law* An entry in a civil or criminal case signifying that the plaintiff or prosecutor will not press it. [< L, to be unwilling to prosecute]

no-load (nō′lōd′) *adj.* Offered for sale without a sales commission added: said of mutual funds.

no·lo con·ten·de·re (nō′lō kən·ten′də·rē) *Law* A plea by a defendant in a criminal action that has the same legal effect as an admission of guilt but does not debar him from denying the truth of the charges in any other proceedings. [< L, I am unwilling to contend]

nol-pros (nol′pros′) *v.t.* **-prossed, -pros·sing** *Law* To subject to a nolle prosequi. [Short for NOLLE PROSEQUI]

no·mad (nō′mad) *n.* 1. One of a group of people that moves from place to place to find food, avoid drought, etc. 2. One who constantly moves about, usu. without purpose. [< Gk. *nemein* to graze] —**no·mad′ic** *adj.* —**no′mad·ism** *n.*

no man's land 1. A tract of wasteland. 2. In war, the land between opposing armies.

nom de plume (nom′ də plōōm′) A pen name. [< F *nom* name + *de* of + *plume* pen]

no·men·cla·ture (nō′mən·klā′chər) *n.* 1. The system of names used in science, art, etc.; terminology. 2. The specific names for the parts or stages of a device, process, etc.

nom·i·nal (nom′ə·nəl) *adj.* 1. Existing in name only; not actual. 2. Slight; trifling. [< L *nomen* name] —**nom′i·nal·ly** *adv.*

nom·i·nate (nom′ə·nāt) *v.t.* **·nat·ed, ·nat·ing** To propose as a candidate for elective office or honor. [< L *nominare* to name] —**nom′i·na′tion** *n.* —**nom′i·na′tor** *n.*

nom·i·na·tive (nom′ə·nə·tiv, -nā′-) *adj. Gram.* Designating the case of the subject of a verb. —*n. Gram.* 1. The nominative case. 2. A word in this case.

nom·i·nee (nom′ə·nē′) *n.* One who receives a nomination.

-nomy *combining form* The science or systematic study of: *astronomy, economy.* [< Gk. *nomos* law]

non- *prefix* Not. [< L *non*] The list found on page 536 contains self-explanatory words beginning with *non-*.

non·age (non′ij, nō′nij) *n.* 1. The period of legal minority. 2. A period of immaturity. [< NON- + AGE]

non·a·ge·nar·i·an (non′ə·jə·nâr′ē·ən, nō′nə-) *n.* A person between 90 and 100 years of age. [< L *nonagenarius* of ninety] —**non′a·ge·nar′i·an** *adj.*

non·a·ligned (non′ə·līnd′) *adj.* Not allied with any powerful world political bloc.

non·book (non′bŏŏk′) *n.* A book of little literary or informative value, often published to promote something.
nonce (nons) *n.* Present time or occasion: now chiefly in the phrase **for the nonce.** [ME *for then ones* for the one (occasion), misread as *for the nones*]
nonce word A word coined for a single occasion.
non·cha·lant (non′shə·länt′) *adj.* Marked by or exhibiting a lack of interest or excitement; casually indifferent. [< NON- + L *calere* to be warm] **—non′cha·lance′** *n.* **—non′cha·lant′ly** *adv.*
non·com (non′kom′) *n. Informal* A noncommissioned officer.
non·com·bat·ant (non′kəm·bat′ənt, non′·kom′bə·tənt) *n.* 1. One whose duties as a member of a military force do not entail fighting, as a chaplain or medical officer. 2. A civilian in wartime.
non·com·mis·sioned officer (non′kə·mish′·ənd) *Mil.* An enlisted man or woman appointed to any grade from corporal to sergeant major in the U.S. Army.
non·com·mit·tal (non′kə·mit′l) *adj.* Not involving or revealing a commitment to any particular attitude, opinion, etc. **—non′·com·mit′tal·ly** *adv.*
non com·pos men·tis (non kom′pəs men′tis) *Law* Not of sound mind. [< L]
non·con·duc·tor (non′kən·duk′tər) *n.* A substance that offers resistance to the passage of some form of energy, as of heat or electricity. **—non′con·duct′ing** *adj.*
non·con·form·ist (non′kən·fôr′mist) *n.* 1. One who does not conform to an approved manner of behaving or thinking. 2. *Often cap.* An English Protestant who refuses to conform to the Church of England. **—non′con·for′mi·ty** *n.*
non·co·op·er·a·tion (non′kō·op′ə·rā′shən) *n.* Failure to cooperate; esp., resistance to a government through civil disobedience. **—non′co·op′er·a·tive** (-op′rə·tiv, -op′ə·rā′·tiv) *adj.*
non·de·script (non′di·skript) *adj.* Not distinctive enough to be described; lacking individual character. [< NON- + L *describere* to describe]
none (nun) *pron.* (*construed as sing. or pl.*) 1. Not one; no one. 2. No or not one (specified person or thing); not any (of a class of things). 3. No part or portion; not any: It is *none* of my business. **—*adv.*** By no means; not at all: He is *none* too bright. [OE *ne* not + *ān* one]
non·en·ti·ty (non·en′tə·tē) *n. pl.* **·ties** 1. One who or that which is of little or no account; a nothing. 2. That which does not exist, or exists solely in the imagination.
nones (nōnz) *n.pl. Often cap. Eccl.* The fifth of the seven canonical hours. [< L *nonus* ninth]
none·such (nun′such′) *n.* 1. One who or that which has no equal; nonpareil. 2. A variety of apple.
none·the·less (nun′thə·les′) *adv.* In spite of everything; nevertheless.
non·e·vent (non′i·vent′) *n.* An event of little news interest, often contrived for publicity.
non·fat (non′fat′) *adj.* Having fat removed: *nonfat* milk.
non·fea·sance (non·fē′zəns) *n. Law* The nonperformance of some act that one is legally bound to perform. **—non·fea′sor** *n.*
non·fer·rous (non·fer′əs) *adj.* Not containing iron; esp., pertaining to metals other than iron, as copper, tin, platinum, etc.
non·fic·tion (non·fik′shən) *n.* Prose literature other than fiction, as historical works, biographies, etc. **—non·fic′tion·al** *adj.*
no·nil·lion (nō·nil′yən) *n.* A cardinal number written as 1 followed by 30 zeros. **—no·nil′lion** *adj.* **—no·nil′lionth** *adj. & n.*
non·in·ter·ven·tion (non′in·tər·ven′shən) *n.* The refusal or failure to intervene; esp., the policy or practice of a nation of not intervening in the affairs of other nations. **—non′in·ter·ven′tion·ist** *adj. & n.*
non·ju·ror (non·jŏŏr′ər) *n.* One who refuses to take an oath, as of allegiance, supremacy, or abjuration. [< NON- + JUROR, in obs. sense "one who takes an oath"]
non·met·al (non·met′l) *n. Chem.* Any element that lacks characteristics of a metal, as nitrogen, carbon, sulfur, etc.
no-no (nō′nō) *n. pl.* **no-no's** *Informal* Something forbidden or to be avoided.
non·ob·jec·tive (non′əb·jek′tiv) *adj.* Not

nonabrasive
nonabsorbent
nonacceptance
nonacid
nonaction
nonactive
nonaddictive
nonadministrative
nonadult
nonadvantageous
nonaffiliated
nonaggression
nonagreement
nonagricultural
nonalcoholic
nonallergic
nonappearance
nonappearing
nonaquatic
nonassignable
nonathletic
nonattendance
nonattributive
nonautomatic
nonbeliever
nonbelieving
nonbelligerent
nonblending
nonbreakable
nonbureaucratic
nonburnable
noncaking
noncancerous
noncandidate
noncapitalistic
nonchargeable
nonchemical
noncitizen
noncivilized
nonclassifiable
nonclerical
nonclinical
nonclotting
noncoagulating
noncognitive
noncohesive
noncollapsible
noncollectable
noncombat
noncombining
noncombustible
noncommercial
noncommunicable
non-Communist
noncompensating
noncompetitive
noncompliance
noncomplying
noncompression
nonconcurrent
nonconfidential
nonconflicting
nonconforming
noncongealing
noncongestion
nonconsecutive
nonconsenting
nonconservative
nonconstructive
nonconsular
noncontagious
noncontiguous
noncontinuous
noncontributing
noncontributory
noncontroversial
nonconventional
nonconvergent
nonconversant
nonconvertible
noncorrective
noncorroborative
noncorrosive
noncreative
noncriminal
noncritical
noncrystalline
nonculpable
noncumulative
nondecaying
nondeferential
nondeferrable

objective; esp., denoting a style of nonrepresentational art.

non·pa·reil (non′pə·rel′) *adj.* Having no equal; unrivaled. —*n.* 1. One who or that which has no equal; a paragon. 2. Any of various brilliantly colored finches of the southern U.S. [< MF *non* not + *pareil* equal]

non·par·ti·san (non·pär′tə·zən) *adj.* Not partisan; esp., not controlled by, associated with, or in support of the interests of any one political party. Also **non·par′ti·zan.**

non·per·son (non′pûr′sən) *n.* A person having no social or legal status, or no official recognition.

non·plus (non·plus′, non′plus) *v.t.* **·plused** or **·plussed, ·plus·ing** or **·plus·sing** To cause to be at a loss; baffle; perplex. [< L *non plus* no further]

non·prof·it (non·prof′it) *adj.* Not organized or maintained for the making of a profit: *nonprofit* charities.

non·rep·re·sen·ta·tion·al (non′rep′ri·zen·tā′·shən·əl) *adj.* Denoting a style of art that does not seek to represent objects as they appear in nature.

non·res·i·dent (non·rez′ə·dənt) *adj.* Not resident; esp., not residing permanently in the locality where one works, owns property, attends school, etc. —*n.* One who is nonresident. —**non·res′i·dence** *n.*

non·re·sis·tant (non′ri·zis′tənt) *adj.* 1. Not resistant; esp., incapable of resistance, as to infection. 2. Characteristic of a nonresistant. —*n.* One who is passive in the face of violence. —**non′re·sis′tance** *n.*

non·re·stric·tive (non′ri·strik′tiv) *adj.* 1. Not restrictive. 2. *Gram.* Denoting a word or word group, esp. an adjective clause, that describes its antecedent but may be omitted without loss of essential meaning, as *which is for sale* in *Our house, which is for sale, needs repairs.*

non·sec·tar·i·an (non′sek·târ′ē·ən) *adj.* Not restricted to or associated with any one religion.

non·sense (non′sens, -səns) *n.* 1. Words or actions that are meaningless or absurd. 2. Things of no importance or use; trifles. 3. Foolish or frivolous conduct. —**non·sen′si·cal** *adj.*

non seq·ui·tur (non sek′wə·tər) 1. *Logic* An inference that does not follow from the premises. 2. Any comment not relevant to what has preceded it. [< L, it does not follow]

non·skid (non′skid′) *adj.* Having a surface that resists skidding.

non·stan·dard (non·stan′dərd) *adj.* 1. Varying or deviating from the standard. 2. *Ling.* Designating those usages or varieties of a language that differ from the standard.

non·stop (non′stop′) *adj.* Making, having made, or scheduled to make no stops. —**non′stop′** *adv.*

non·sup·port (non′sə·pôrt′) *n.* Failure to provide for the support of a legal dependent.

non-U (non′yōō′) *adj.* Not U. See U.

non·un·ion (non·yōōn′yən) *adj.* 1. Not belonging to or associated with a labor union. 2. Not recognizing, contracting with, or employing the members of any union: *nonunion* shop.

non·un·ion·ism (non·yōōn′yən·iz′əm) *n.* Opposition to trade unions. —**non·un′ion·ist** *n.*

non·white (non′hwīt′) *n.* One who is not a member of the Caucasian ethnic division of mankind. —**non′white′** *adj.*

noo·dle[1] (nōōd′l) *n.* 1. A simpleton. Also **noo′dle·head′** (-hed′). 2. *Informal* The head. [? < NOD]

noo·dle[2] (nōōd′l) *n.* A thin strip of dried dough, usu. containing egg, used in soup, etc. [< G *nudel*]

nook (nŏŏk) *n.* 1. An interior corner or angle, as in a room. 2. Any narrow place, as a recess. [ME *nok* corner]

noon (nōōn) *n.* 1. The middle of the day; twelve o'clock in the daytime. 2. The highest or culminating point; zenith. —*adj.* Of, pertaining to, or occurring at or about noon. [< L *nona* (*hora*) ninth (hour)]

noon·day (nōōn′dā′) *n.* Noon. —*adj.* Of or at noon.

no one Not any person; nobody.

noon·time (nōōn′tīm′) *n.* 1. Midday. 2. The culminating point or period. Also *Archaic* **noon′tide′** (-tīd′). [OE *nōntīd*]

noose (nōōs) *n.* 1. A loop furnished with a running knot, as in a hangman's halter or a snare. 2. Anything that entraps, restrains,

nondelivery
nondemocratic
nondepartmental
nondepletion
nondepreciating
nonderivable
nonderivative
nondestructive
nondetachable
nondetonating
nondevelopment
nondiplomatic
nondirectional
nondiscountable
nondiscrimination
nondiscriminatory
nondisposal
nondistinctive
nondivergent
nondivisible
nondomesticated
nondramatic
nondrying
nonearning
nonecclesiastical
noneconomic
nonedible
noneducable
noneducational
nonelastic
nonelective
nonelectric
nonelementary
nonemotional
nonempirical
nonenforceable
nonentry
nonepicurean
nonequation
nonequatorial
nonequilibrium
nonequivalent
nonequivocating
nonerotic
nonerudite
nonessential
nonesthetic
nonethereal
nonevangelical
nonevolutionary
nonexchangeable
nonexclusive
nonexecution
nonexemplary
nonexempt
nonexistence
nonexistent
nonexpansive
nonexpendable
nonexperimental
nonexpert
nonexplosive
nonexportable
nonextended
nonextension
nonextinction
nonextradition
nonfactual
nonfading
nonfatal
nonfatalistic
nonfattening
nonfederal
nonfederated
nonfertility
nonfinancial
nonfinite
nonfiscal
nonfissionable
nonflammable
nonflowering
nonflowing
nonfluctuating
nonflying
nonfocal
nonformal
nonfulfillment
nonfunctional
nongaseous
nongelatinous
nongovernmental
nongraded

or binds. —*v.t.* **noosed, noos·ing** To capture or secure with a noose. [< L *nodus* knot]

no-par (nō′pär′) *adj.* Having no par or face value, as certain stock.

nope (nōp) *adv. Slang* No.

nor (nôr) *conj.* And not; likewise not. [Contr. of ME *nother* neither]

Nor·dic (nôr′dik) *adj. Anthropol.* Pertaining or belonging to the tall, long-headed, blond-haired subdivision of the Caucasian ethnic stock, distributed mainly in NW Europe. —*n.* A Nordic person. [< NL *nordicus*]

nor′·east·er (nôr·ēs′tər) See NORTHEASTER.

Nor·folk jacket (nôr′fək) A loose-fitting jacket with a belt and two box pleats at the back and front.

norm (nôrm) *n.* 1. A pattern, model, or standard regarded as typical of a specified group. 2. *Psychol.* The standard of performance in a given function or test, usu. the average achievement for the group concerned. 3. *Stat.* The mode. [< L *norma* rule]

nor·mal (nôr′məl) *adj.* 1. Conforming to or consisting of a pattern, process, or standard regarded as usual or typical; natural. 2. *Psychol.* **a** Well adjusted; without marked or persistent mental aberrations. **b** Of average skill, intelligence, etc. —*n.* 1. The common or natural condition, form, degree, etc. 2. The usual or accepted rule or process. [< L *norma* rule] —**nor′mal·cy, nor·mal·i·ty** (nôr·mal′ə·tē) *n.*

nor·mal·ize (nôr′məl·īz) *v.t.* **·ized, ·iz·ing** To bring into accord with a norm or standard form; make normal. —**nor′mal·i·za′tion** *n.* —**nor′mal·iz′er** *n.*

nor·mal·ly (nôr′mə·lē) *adv.* 1. As a rule; usually. 2. In a normal manner.

normal school A school that prepares secondary-school graduates to become teachers.

Nor·man (nôr′mən) *n.* 1. One of the Scandinavian people who conquered Normandy in the 10th c. 2. One of the people of mixed Scandinavian and French descent who conquered England in 1066. 3. A resident of Normandy. [< OF *Normans* Northmen] —**Nor′man** *adj.*

nor·ma·tive (nôr′mə·tiv) *adj.* 1. Of, pertaining to, or based upon a norm, esp. one regarded as a standard or rule of usage. 2. Implying, supporting, or establishing a norm.

Norse (nôrs) *adj.* 1. Scandinavian. 2. Of or pertaining to Norway, Iceland, and the Faroe Islands; West Scandinavian. —*n.* 1. The Scandinavians or West Scandinavians collectively: used with *the.* 2. The Scandinavian or North Germanic group of the Germanic languages; esp., Norwegian. 3. The West Scandinavian languages. —**Old Norse** 1. The ancestor of the North Germanic languages, best represented by Old Icelandic: also called *Old Scandinavian.* 2. Old Icelandic: see under ICELANDIC. [< MDu. *nordsch, nortsch* northern]

Norse·man (nôrs′mən) *n. pl.* **·men** (-mən) A Scandinavian of Viking times.

north (nôrth) *n.* 1. The direction to one's left when facing the sun at sunrise. 2. One of the four cardinal points of the compass, directly opposite *south.* 3. *Sometimes cap.* Any region north of a specified point. —**the North** In the U.S.: **a** The population or territory of the northern or northeastern states. **b** The states opposed to the Confederacy in the Civil War. —*adj.* 1. To, toward, facing, or in the north. 2. Coming from the north. —*adv.* In or toward the north. [OE]

North American Indian An Indian of any of the tribes inhabiting North America north of Mexico.

north·bound (nôrth′bound′) *adj.* Going northward. Also **north′-bound′.**

north·east (nôrth′ēst′, *Naut.* nôr·ēst′) *n.* 1. The direction midway between north and east. 2. Any region lying in or toward this direction. —*adj.* 1. To, toward, facing, or in the northeast. 2. Coming from the northeast. —*adv.* In or toward the northeast. —**north′·east′ern** *adj.*

north·east·er (nôrth′ēs′tər, *Naut.* nôr·ēs′tər) *n.* 1. A gale or storm from the northeast. 2. A sailor's hat with a sloping brim worn in stormy weather. Also spelled *nor'easter.*

north·east·er·ly (nôrth′ēs′tər·lē, *Naut.* nôr·ēs′tər·lē) *adj.* 1. In, of, or toward the northeast. 2. From the northeast, as a wind. —*adv.* Toward or from the northeast.

north·er (nôr′thər) *n.* 1. A gale or storm

nonhabitable
nonhabitual
nonhazardous
nonhereditary
nonheritable
nonheroic
nonhistoric
nonhuman
nonhumorous
nonidentical
nonimitative
nonimperative
nonimperial
nonimportation
nonimprovement
noninclusive
nonindependent
nonindictable
nonindividual
nonindustrial
noninfallible
noninfectious
noninflammatory
noninflected
noninformative
noninheritable
noninjurious
noninstrumental
nonintellectual
noninterference
noninternational
noninterrupted
nonintersecting
nonintoxicating
nonintuitive
nonionized
nonirritant
nonjudicial
nonjuristic
nonlegal
nonlethal
nonlicensed
nonlimiting
nonliquefying
nonliterary
nonliturgical
nonliving
nonlocal
nonloving
nonlustrous
nonmagnetic
nonmalignant
nonmalleable
nonmarital
nonmarketable
nonmarrying
nonmartial
nonmaterial
nonmaterialistic
nonmathematical
nonmechanical
nonmechanistic
nonmedical
nonmember
nonmercantile
nonmigratory
nonmilitant
nonmilitary
nonmineral
nonmobile
nonmunicipal
nonmuscular
nonmystical
nonnaval
nonnavigable
nonnegotiable
nonneutral
nonnuclear
nonnutrient
nonnutritive
nonobligatory
nonobservance
nonobservant
nonoccupational
nonoccurrence
nonofficial
nonoily
nonoperative
nonoptional
nonorthodox
nonowner
nonoxidizing

from the north. 2. A violent, cold north wind blowing over the plains of the SW states.

north·er·ly (nôr′thər·lē) *adj.* 1. In, of, toward, or pertaining to the north. 2. From the north, as a wind. —*adv.* Toward or from the north. —*n.* A wind or storm from the north. —**north′er·li·ness** *n.*

north·ern (nôr′thərn) *adj.* 1. To, toward, or in the north. 2. Native to or inhabiting the north. 3. *Sometimes cap.* Of, pertaining to, or characteristic of the north or the North. 4. From the north, as a wind.

north·ern·er (nôr′thər·nər) *n.* 1. One who is native to or lives in the north. 2. *Usu. cap.* One who lives in or comes from the North.

Northern Hemisphere See under HEMISPHERE.

northern lights The aurora borealis.

north·ern·most (nôr′thərn·mōst′) *adj.* Farthest north.

north·land (nôrth′lənd) *n.* A land or region in the north. [OE] —**north′land·er** *n.*

North Pole The northern extremity of the earth's axis.

North Star Polaris.

north·ward (nôrth′wərd, *Naut.* nôr′thərd) *adv.* Toward the north. Also **north′wards.** —*adj.* To, toward, facing, or in the north.

north·ward·ly (nôrth′wərd·lē, *Naut.* nôr′·thərd·lē) *adj. & adv.* Toward or from the north.

north·west (nôrth′west′, *Naut.* nôr·west′) *n.* 1. The direction midway between north and west. 2. Any region lying in or toward this direction. —*adj.* 1. To, facing, or in the northwest. 2. Coming from the northwest. —*adv.* In or toward the northwest. —**north′·west′ern** *adj.*

north·west·er (nôrth′wes′tər, *Naut.* nôr·wes′·tər) *n.* A gale or storm from the northwest: also **nor′·west′er.**

north·west·er·ly (nôrth′wes′tər·lē, *Naut.* nôr·wes′tər·lē) *adj.* 1. In, of, or toward the northwest. 2. From the northwest, as a wind. —*adv.* Toward or from the northwest.

Nor·we·gian (nôr·wē′jən) *n.* 1. A native or inhabitant of Norway. 2. The North Germanic language of Norway. [< ON *nor(thr)* north + *vegr* way] —**Nor·we′gian** *adj.*

nose (nōz) *n.* 1. The part of the face in man or the forward end of an animal that contains the nostrils and the organ of smell, and that in man encloses cavities used in the respiratory process. ◆Collateral adjectives: *nasal, rhinal.* 2. The sense of smell or the power of smelling. 3. The ability to perceive or discover by or as if by the sense of smell: a *nose* for scandal. 4. Something resembling a nose, as the forward part of an aircraft. —**by a nose** *Slang* By a narrow margin. —**on the nose** *Slang* Exactly; precisely. —**to pay through the nose** *Slang* To pay an excessively high price. —*v.* **nosed, nos·ing** *v.t.* 1. To nuzzle. 2. To make (one's way) carefully with the front end foremost. 3. To perceive or discover by or as if by smell; scent. —*v.i.* 4. To pry or interfere; snoop: with *around* or *about.* 5. To move forward, esp. carefully. —**to nose out** To defeat by a narrow margin. [OE *nosu*]

nose·bleed (nōz′blēd′) *n.* Bleeding from the nose.

nose cone *Aerospace* The cone-shaped forward section of a rocket or missile.

nose dive 1. A steep, downward plunge of an aircraft, nose end foremost. 2. Any steep, sudden drop. —**nose-dive** (nōz′dīv′) *v.i.* **-dived, -div·ing**

nose·gay (nōz′gā′) *n.* A small bunch of flowers; bouquet. [< NOSE + GAY, in obs. sense "a pretty thing"]

nose·piece (nōz′pēs′) *n.* Any part, as of a helmet, that covers or protects the nose.

nosh (nosh) *v.t. & v.i.* *Slang* To nibble or snack. —*n.* A snack. [< Yiddish *nashn* < OHG]

nos·tal·gi·a (nos·tal′jə, -jē·ə) *n.* 1. A longing for familiar or beloved circumstances that are now remote or irrecoverable. 2. Any longing for something far away or long ago. [< Gk. *nostos* return home + *algos* pain] —**nos·tal′gic** *adj.*

nos·tril (nos′trəl) *n.* One of the external openings of the nose. [OE *nos(u)* nose + *thyrel* hole]

nos·trum (nos′trəm) *n.* 1. A medicine of one's own preparation; also, a quack medicine. 2. A cure-all. [< L *noster* our own]

nos·y (nō′zē) *adj.* **nos·i·er, nos·i·est** *Informal* Prying; snooping; inquisitive: also spelled **nos′ey.**

not (not) *adv.* In no way, or to no extent or

nonoxygenated
nonpalatal
nonparallel
nonparasitic
nonparental
nonparliamentary
nonparochial
nonparticipant
nonpartisanship
nonpaying
nonpayment
nonperforated
nonperformance
nonperishable
nonpermanent
nonpermeable
nonpermissible
nonperseverance
nonpersistence
nonphilanthropic
nonphysical
nonphysiological
nonpigmented
nonplastic
nonpoetic
nonpoisonous
nonpolitical
nonporous
nonpredictable
nonpreferential
nonprejudicial
nonprescriptive
nonpreservative
nonpresidential
nonprevalent
nonproducer
nonproductive
nonprofessional
nonprofessorial
nonprogressive
nonprohibitive
nonprolific
nonproprietary
nonprotection
nonprotective
nonpublication
nonpuncturable
nonracial
nonradical
nonrational
nonreactive
nonreality
nonreciprocal
nonrecoverable
nonrecurrent
nonrecurring
nonredeemable
nonrefillable
nonregenerating
nonregenerative
nonregimented
nonregistered
nonreigning
nonreligious
nonremovable
nonremunerative
nonrenewable
nonrepentant
nonrepetition
nonrepetitive
nonrepresentative
nonreproductive
nonresidential
nonresinous
nonresisting
nonresonant
nonrestricted
nonretention
nonretiring
nonretractile
nonreturnable
nonreversible
nonrevolving
nonrhetorical
nonrhythmic
nonrival
nonromantic
nonrotating
nonrural
nonrusting
nonsacred
nonsacrificial

degree: used to note the absence, reverse, or opposite of something or to express negation, prohibition, or refusal. [OE *ne* not + *ā* ever + *wiht* thing however small]

no·ta·ble (nō′tə·bəl) *adj.* Worthy of note; remarkable; distinguished. —*n.* One who is distinguished, famous, etc. [< L *nota* mark] —**no′ta·bil′i·ty** *n.* —**no′ta·bly** *adv.*

no·ta·rize (nō′tə·rīz) *v.t.* **·rized, ·riz·ing** To attest to or authenticate as a notary public. —**no′ta·ri·za′tion** *n.*

no·ta·ry public (nō′tə·rē) *pl.* **no·ta·ries public** One who is legally authorized to administer oaths, certify contracts, etc. Also **notary.**

no·ta·tion (nō·tā′shən) *n.* 1. A system of signs, figures, or abbreviations used for convenience in recording a quantity, relation, process, etc.: musical *notation.* 2. A note or comment. [< L *notare* to note] —**no·ta′·tion·al** *adj.*

notch (noch) *n.* 1. A V-shaped cut in a surface. 2. A nick cut into a stick, etc., as for keeping count. 3. A narrow passage between mountains; a defile. 4. *Informal* A degree; level: He is a *notch* above the others. —*v.t.* To make a notch or notches in. [< OF *oschier* to notch]

note (nōt) *n.* 1. *Often pl.* A brief record or summary of facts set down for future study or reference: to take *notes.* 2. A brief account or jotting to aid the memory. 3. *Music* a A symbol representing a tone or sound of a given duration and pitch. b A tone or sound of a definite pitch. c A key of the keyboard. 4. A distinctive mark: a *note* of sadness. 5. A piece of paper currency issued by a government or authorized bank and negotiable as money: a bank *note.* 6. A promissory note. 7. A formal, written communication of an official or diplomatic nature. 8. A brief letter, esp. of an informal character. 9. Distinction; importance; reputation: a gentleman of *note.* 10. Notice; attention: worthy of *note.* —*v.t.* **not·ed, not·ing** 1. To become aware of; observe. 2. To pay attention to; heed carefully. 3. To set down for remembering; make a note of. [< L *nota* mark] —**no′ter** *n.*

note·book (nōt′bo͝ok′) *n.* A book with blank pages on which notes may be entered.

not·ed (nō′tid) *adj.* Well known by reputation; famous. —**not′ed·ness** *n.*

note paper Paper for writing notes or letters.

note·wor·thy (nōt′wûr′thē) *adj.* Remarkable; significant. —**note′wor′thi·ness** *n.*

noth·ing (nuth′ing) *n.* 1. Not anything; naught. 2. No part or element: He knew *nothing* of it. 3. One who or that which is of little or no importance. 4. Insignificance or unimportance: to rise from *nothing.* 5. Zero. 6. A state of nonexistence; also, that which is nonexistent. [OE *nān thing*]

noth·ing·ness (nuth′ing·nis) *n.* 1. The condition, quality, or fact of being nothing; nonexistence. 2. Utter worthlessness or insignificance. 3. Unconsciousness.

no·tice (nō′tis) *v.t.* **·ticed, ·tic·ing** 1. To pay attention to or become aware of. 2. To refer to or comment on. —*n.* 1. The act of noticing or observing. 2. Announcement; information; warning. 3. A formal announcement: to give *notice.* 4. A short advertisement or review. [< L *notitia* fame, renown]

no·tice·a·ble (nō′tis·ə·bəl) *adj.* 1. That can be noticed; perceptible. 2. Worthy of notice. —**no′tice·a·bly** *adv.*

no·ti·fy (nō′tə·fī) *v.t.* **·fied, ·fy·ing** 1. To give notice to; inform. 2. *Chiefly Brit.* To make known. [< L *notus* known + *facere* to make] —**no′ti·fi·ca′tion** *n.* —**no′ti·fi′er** *n.*

no·tion (nō′shən) *n.* 1. A general idea or impression; a vague conception. 2. An opinion, belief, or idea. 3. Intention; inclination. 4. *pl.* Small miscellaneous articles for sale. [< L *notio, -onis* < *notus* known]

no·tion·al (nō′shən·əl) *adj.* 1. Pertaining to, expressing, or consisting of notions or concepts. 2. Existing in imagination only. 3. Impulsive or capricious. —**no′tion·al·ly** *adv.*

no·to·ri·e·ty (nō′tə·rī′ə·tē) *n.* *pl.* **·ties** 1. The state or character of being notorious. 2. One who or that which is notorious.

no·to·ri·ous (nō·tôr′ē·əs) *adj.* 1. Widely known and generally disapproved of or deplored. 2. Generally known; acknowledged. [< Med.L *noscere* to know] —**no·to′ri·ous·ly** *adv.*

not·with·stand·ing (not′with·stan′ding,

nonsalaried
nonscheduled
nonscholastic
nonscientific
nonseasonal
nonsecular
nonsegmented
nonsegregated
nonselective
nonsensitive
nonsensitized
nonsensuous
nonseparable
nonsexual
nonshattering
nonshatterproof
nonshrinkable
nonsinkable
nonsmoker
nonsmoking
nonsocial
nonsocialistic
nonsolid
nonsolvent
nonsparing
nonsparkling
nonspecialized
nonspecific
nonspectral
nonspeculative
nonspiritual
nonsporting
nonstandardized
nonstarting
nonstatistical
nonstatutory
nonstrategic
nonstretchable
nonstriker
nonstriking
nonstructural
nonsubscriber
nonsupporter
nonsupporting
nonsustaining
nonsymbolic
nonsymmetrical
nonsympathizer
nonsymptomatic
nontarnishable
nontaxable
nonteaching
nontechnical
nontemporal
nontenured
nonterrestrial
nonterritorial
nontheatrical
nontheological
nontherapeutic
nonthinking
nontoxic
nontraditional
nontransferable
nontransparent
nontropical
nontypical
nonuniform
nonuniversal
nonuser
nonutilitarian
nonutilization
nonvascular
nonvegetative
nonvenomous
nonvenous
nonverbal
nonviable
nonvibratory
nonviolence
nonvirulent
nonviscous
nonvitreous
nonvocal
nonvocational
nonvolatile
nonvolition
nonvoluntary
nonvoter
nonvoting
nonworking
nonyielding

-with-) *prep.* In spite of: He left *notwithstanding* your orders. —*adv.* All the same; nevertheless: Though closely guarded, he escaped *notwithstanding.* —*conj.* In spite of the fact that; although.

nou·gat (no͞o′gət) *n.* A confection of nuts and fruits in a honey or sugar paste. [< Provençal *nogat* < L *nux, nucis* nut]

nought (nôt) See NAUGHT.

noun (noun) *n. Gram.* A word used as the name of a thing, quality, or action. [< L *nomen* name]

nour·ish (nûr′ish) *v.t.* 1. To furnish food or other material to sustain the life and promote the growth of (a living plant or animal). 2. To support; maintain; foster. [< L *nutrire* to nourish] —**nour′ish·ing** *adj.* —**nour′ish·ing·ly** *adv.*

nour·ish·ment (nûr′ish·mənt) *n.* 1. That which nourishes; nutriment. 2. The act of nourishing, or the state of being nourished.

nou·veau riche (no͞o′vō′ rēsh′) *French pl.* **nou·veaux riches** (no͞o′vō′ rēsh′) One who has recently become rich.

no·va (nō′və) *n. pl.* **·vae** (-vē) or **·vas** *Astron.* A star that suddenly brightens and then dims after a period of a few months or years. [< L, fem. of *novus* new]

nov·el (nov′əl) *adj.* New, strange, or unusual. —*n.* A fictional prose narrative of considerable length, usu. having an overall pattern or plot. [< F < L *novus* new]

nov·el·ette (nov′əl·et′) *n.* A short novel: also *novella.*

nov·el·ist (nov′əl·ist) *n.* A writer of novels.

nov·el·ize (nov′əl·īz) *v.t.* **·ized, ·iz·ing** To put into the form of a novel. —**nov′el·i·za′tion** *n.*

no·vel·la (nō·vel′ə) *n.* 1. A short tale or narrative, usu. with a moral. 2. A novelette. [< Ital. See NOVEL.]

nov·el·ty (nov′əl·tē) *n. pl.* **·ties** 1. Something novel or unusual. 2. The quality of being novel or new. 3. *Usu. pl.* A small manufactured article.

No·vem·ber (nō·vem′bər) The eleventh month of the year, containing 30 days. [< L, ninth month (of the old Roman calendar)]

no·ve·na (nō·vē′nə) *n.* In the Roman Catholic Church, devotions made on nine successive days, for some special religious purpose. [< L *novem* nine]

nov·ice (nov′is) *n.* 1. A beginner in any occupation; an inexperienced person. 2. *Eccl.* One who enters a religious order or community on probation. [< L *novicius* new]

no·vi·ti·ate (nō·vish′ē·it, -āt) *n.* 1. The state or period of being a novice. 2. *Eccl.* The period of probation of a novice in a religious order or community. 3. A novice. [< F *novicat* or Med.L *novitiatus*]

No·vo·cain (nō′və·kān) *n.* Proprietary name for a brand of procaine used as a local anesthetic. Also **No′vo·caine.**

now (nou) *adv.* 1. At once. 2. At or during the present time. 3. Nowadays. 4. At this point in the proceedings, narrative, etc.: The war was *now* virtually over. —*n.* The present time, moment, or occasion. —**now and then** From time to time; occasionally: also **now and again.** —**now that** Seeing that; since. [OE *nū*]

now·a·days (nou′ə·dāz′) *adv.* In the present time or age.

no·way (nō′wā′) *adv.* 1. In no way, manner, or degree. 2. *Dial.* By any means. Also **no′ways′.**

no·where (nō′hwâr′) *adv.* In no place; not anywhere. —*n.* No place.

no·wise (nō′wīz′) *adv.* In no manner or degree.

nox·ious (nok′shəs) *adj.* Causing or tending to cause injury to health or morals; hurtful. [< L *noxa* harm] —**nox′ious·ly** *adv.* —**nox′·ious·ness** *n.*

noz·zle (noz′əl) *n.* A projecting spout or pipe serving as an outlet, as of a teapot, hose, or rifle. [Dim. of NOSE]

nth (enth) *adj.* 1. *Math.* Representing an ordinal equivalent to *n.* 2. Infinitely or indefinitely large (or small); most extreme: to the *nth* degree.

nu (no͞o, nyo͞o) *n.* The thirteenth letter in the Greek alphabet (Ν, ν), corresponding to English *n.*

nu·ance (no͞o·äns′, no͞o′äns, nyo͞o′-) *n.* A fine or subtle variation, as in color, tone, or meaning; gradation. [< F < OF *nuer* to shade]

nub (nub) *n.* 1. A knob or protuberance. 2. A small piece, as of coal. 3. *Informal* Core; gist. [Var. of KNOB]

nub·bin (nub′in) *n.* 1. An imperfectly developed fruit or ear of corn. 2. Anything small or stunted. [< NUB]

nub·ble (nub′əl) *n.* A small protuberance or lump; nub. [Dim. of NUB] —**nub′bly** *adj.*

nu·bile (no͞o′bil, nyo͞o′-, -bīl) *adj.* Ready or suitable for marriage: said of young women. [< L *nubere* to wed] —**nu·bil′i·ty** (-bil′ə·tē) *n.*

nu·cle·ar (no͞o′klē·ər, nyo͞o′-) *adj.* 1. Of, pertaining to, or resembling a nucleus or nuclei. 2. Of or using atomic energy: *nuclear* reactor.

nuclear family A family consisting of parents and child or children considered as a discrete group.

nuclear physics The branch of physics that investigates the structure and properties of the atomic nucleus.

nu·cle·ate (no͞o′klē·āt, nyo͞o′-) *adj.* Having a nucleus. —*v.t. & v.i.* **·at·ed, ·at·ing** To form or gather into a nucleus. [< L *nucleare* to form a kernel] —**nu′cle·a′tion** *n.*

nu·cle·ic acid (no͞o·klē′ik, no͞o·klā′ik, nyo͞o-) *Biochem.* Any of a group of complex organic acids, as DNA, found esp. in cell nuclei, and made up of a carbohydrate, phosphoric acid, and organic bases.

nucleo- *combining form* Nucleus. [< L *nucleus* kernel]

nu·cle·on (no͞o′klē·on, nyo͞o′-) *n. Physics* A proton or a neutron. —**nu′cle·on′ic** *adj.*

nu·cle·on·ics (no͞o′klē·on′iks, nyo͞o′-) *n.pl.* (*usu. construed as sing.*) The branch of physics that deals with atomic nuclei.

nu·cle·o·plasm (no͞o′klē·ə·plaz′əm, nyo͞o′-) *n. Biol.* The protoplasm of a cell nucleus. —**nu′cle·o·plas′mic** *adj.*

nu·cle·o·pro·te·in (no͞o′klē·ə·prō′tē·in, -tēn, nyo͞o′-) *n. Biochem.* Any of a class of substances found in the nuclei of plant and animal cells, containing one or more protein molecules combined with nucleic acid.

nu·cle·o·tide (no͞o′klē·ə·tīd′, nyo͞o′-) *n.* *Biochem.* A compound, containing a sugar, a nitrogen base, and a phosphate group, and that is the basic unit of DNA and RNA.

nu·cle·us (no͞o′klē·əs, nyo͞o′-) *n.* *pl.* **·cle·i** (-klē·ī) 1. A central point or part around which other things are gathered; core. 2. A center of growth or development. 3. *Biol.* A complex body surrounded by a thin membrane and embedded in the protoplasm of most plant and animal cells, essential to the process of heredity and to other vital activities of the cell. 4. *Physics* The positively charged central core of an atom, containing nucleons that provide its effective mass. [< L, kernel < *nux, nucis* nut]

nu·clide (no͞o′klīd, nyo͞o′-) *n.* *Physics* A specific, relatively stable atom as defined by the composition and properties of its nucleus.

nude (no͞od, nyo͞od) *adj.* Without clothing or covering; naked. **—***n.* 1. A nude figure, esp. in painting, sculpture, etc. 2. The state of being nude. [< L *nudus* naked, bare] **—nu′di·ty** *n.*

nudge (nuj) *v.t.* **nudged, nudg·ing** To touch or push gently, as with the elbow, in order to attract attention, etc. [? < Scand.] **—nudge** *n.*

nudi- *combining form* Without covering; naked; bare. [< L *nudus*]

nud·ism (no͞o′diz·əm, nyo͞o′-) *n.* The doctrine or practice of living in the state of nudity. **—nud′ist** *adj. & n.*

nud·nik (no͞od′nik) *n.* *Slang* A pestiferous or annoying person. Also **nud′nick.** [< Yiddish]

nue·vo pe·so (nwā′vō pā′sō) The monetary unit of Uruguay.

nug·get (nug′it) *n.* A lump; esp., a lump of gold found in its native state. [? Dim. of dial. E *nug* lump]

nui·sance (no͞o′səns, nyo͞o′-) *n.* Anything that annoys, bothers, or irritates. [< F *nuire* to harm]

nuisance tax A tax on various consumer goods and services, etc., regarded as more of a bother than a burden.

null (nul) *adj.* 1. Of no legal force or effect; void; invalid. 2. Of no value; negative. 3. Of no avail; useless. **—null and void** Without legal force or effect. [< L *ne* not + *ullus* any] **—nul′li·ty** *n.*

nul·li·fy (nul′ə·fī) *v.t.* **·fied, ·fy·ing** 1. To make useless or ineffective; undo. 2. To deprive of legal force or effect. [< LL *nullus* none + *facere* to make] **—nul′li·fi·ca′tion** *n.*

numb (num) *adj.* 1. Having no sensation; without feeling. 2. Unable to move. **—***v.t.* To make numb. [OE *niman* to take] **—numb′ly** *adv.* **—numb′ness** *n.*

num·ber (num′bər) *n.* 1. A specific quantity or place in a sequence. 2. One of a series of symbols or words used to designate number; a numeral. 3. *Often pl.* A sizable collection or grouping: *numbers* of people. 4. An indefinite quantity or collection: a *number* of facts. 5. A specific sum or total count. 6. One of a series of things to which numbers are assigned: the March *number* of a magazine. 7. A part of a program of music or entertainment. 8. Quantity, as composed of units. 9. *Gram.* The representation in a language of singleness or plurality. 10. *Informal* An item or article, as of merchandise. **—any number of** A good many; rather a lot. **—beyond** (or **without**) **number** Too numerous to be counted. **—the numbers** A lottery in which bets are made on the appearance of some 3-digit number: also **numbers game, numbers pool,** *policy, policy game.* **—***v.t.* 1. To determine the total number of; reckon. 2. To assign a number to. 3. To include as one of a collection or group. 4. To amount to; total. 5. To set or limit the number of. **—***v.i.* 6. To make a count; total. [< L *numerus*] **—num′ber·er** *n.*

num·ber·less (num′bər·lis) *adj.* 1. Very numerous; countless. 2. Having no number.

Num·bers (num′bərz) *n.pl.* (*construed as sing.*) The fourth book of the Old Testament.

numb·skull (num′skul′) See NUMSKULL.

nu·mer·a·ble (no͞o′mər·ə·bəl, nyo͞o′-) *adj.* That can be numbered. [< L *numerare* to count]

nu·mer·al (no͞o′mər·əl, nyo͞o′-) *n.* A symbol, letter, or word that is used alone or in combination with others to express a number. **—***adj.* Used in expressing or representing a number. [< LL *numerus* number] **—nu′mer·al·ly** *adv.*

nu·mer·ate (no͞o′mə·rāt, nyo͞o′-) *v.t.* **·at·ed, ·at·ing** 1. To enumerate; count. 2. To read, as a numerical expression. [< L *numerare* to number] **—nu′mer·a′tion** *n.*

nu·mer·a·tor (no͞o′mə·rā′tər, nyo͞o′-) *n.* 1. *Math.* The term above the line in a fraction indicating how many of the parts of a unit are to be taken. 2. One who or that which numbers.

nu·mer·i·cal (no͞o·mer′i·kəl, nyo͞o-) *adj.* 1. Of or denoting number. 2. Numerable. 3. Represented by or consisting of numbers or figures rather than letters. [< L *numerus* number] **—nu·mer′i·cal·ly** *adv.*

nu·mer·ous (no͞o′mər·əs, nyo͞o′-) *adj.* Consisting of a great number of units; being many. **—nu′mer·ous·ly** *adv.*

nu·mis·mat·ics (no͞o′miz·mat′iks, -mis-, nyo͞o′-) *n.pl.* (*construed as sing.*) The study of coins, medals, and related objects. [< L *numisma* coin] **—nu′mis·mat′ic** *adj.* **—nu·mis′ma·tist** (-mə·tist) *n.*

num·skull (num′skul′) *n.* A blockhead; dunce: also spelled *numbskull.*

nun (nun) *n.* A woman belonging to a religious order and usu. living in a convent under vows of poverty, chastity, and obedience. [< LL *nonna*]

nun-chuck (nun′chuk) *n.* *Usu. pl.* Two hardwood sticks joined by a rope, leather, or chain, used as a weapon. Also **nun·cha·ku** (no͞on·chä·ko͞o), **nunchaku sticks.** [< Japanese]

nun·ci·o (nun′shē·ō, -sē·ō, no͞on′-) *n.* *pl.* **·ci·os** A permanent diplomatic envoy of the Pope to a foreign government. [< Ital. < L *nuntius* messenger]

nun·ner·y (nun′ər·ē) *n.* *pl.* **·ner·ies** A convent for nuns.

nup·tial (nup′shəl) *adj.* Of or pertaining to marriage or the marriage ceremony. **—***n.* *Usu. pl.* A marriage or wedding. [< L *nubere* to marry] **—nup′tial·ly** *adv.*

nurse (nûrs) *n.* 1. A person who cares for the sick, injured, or infirm; esp., one who is trained to do such work. 2. One who is a graduate of a school of nursing. 3. A nursemaid. —*v.* **nursed, nurs·ing** *v.t.* 1. To take care of (the sick, injured, or infirm). 2. To feed (an infant) at the breast; suckle. 3. To promote the growth and development of; foster; cherish. 4. To take steps to cure. 5. To preserve or prolong deliberately. —*v.i.* 6. To act or serve as a nurse. 7. To take nourishment from the breast. 8. To suckle an infant. [< L *nutrix* nursing mother] —**nurs′er** *n.*

nurse·maid (nûrs′mād′) *n.* A woman employed to care for children.

nurs·er·y (nûr′sər·ē, nûrs′rē) *n. pl.* **·er·ies** 1. A place where trees, shrubs, etc., are raised, as for sale. 2. A room or area set apart for the use of children. 3. Anything that fosters, breeds, or develops.

nurs·er·y·man (nûr′sər·ē·mən, nûrs′rē-) *n. pl.* **·men** (-mən) One who raises or cultivates plants in a nursery.

nursery school A place where children of preschool age regularly meet for training and supervised play.

nursing home A residence for persons who are unable to care for themselves, as the aged or the infirm.

nurs·ling (nûrs′ling) *n.* 1. An infant or animal in the stage of being nursed. 2. Anything that is carefully tended or supervised. Also **nurse′ling.**

nur·ture (nûr′chər) *n.* 1. That which nourishes; food; sustenance. 2. Training; breeding; education. —*v.t.* **·tured, ·tur·ing** 1. To feed or support; nourish. 2. To bring up or train; educate. [< L *nutrire* to nourish]

nut (nut) *n.* 1. A dry fruit consisting of a kernel or seed enclosed in a woody shell, as a walnut, pecan, acorn, etc. 2. A small block of metal having an internal screw thread so that it may be fitted upon a bolt, screw, or the like. 3. *Slang* A crazy, irresponsible, or eccentric person. —*v.i.* **nut·ted, nut·ting** To gather nuts. [OE *hnutu*] —**nut′ter** *n.*

nut·crack·er (nut′krak′ər) *n.* A device for cracking the hard shells of nuts.

nut·gall (nut′gôl′) *n.* A nut-shaped gall, as on an oak tree.

nut·hatch (nut′hach′) *n.* A small, short-tailed bird related to the titmouse and feeding on nuts.

nut·meg (nut′meg) *n.* The aromatic kernel of the fruit of various tropical trees that is ground and used as a spice. [< OF *nois* nut + *mugue* musk]

nu·tri·a (nōō′trē·ə, nyōō′-) *n.* The soft brown fur of the coypu, often dyed to resemble beaver. [< Sp., otter]

nu·tri·ent (nōō′trē·ənt, nyōō′-) *n.* Something that nourishes; food. [< L *nutrire* to nourish] —**nu′tri·ent** *adj.*

nu·tri·ment (nōō′trə·mənt, nyōō′-) *n.* 1. That which nourishes; food. 2. Anything that promotes development. [< L *nutrire* to nourish] —**nu′tri·men′tal** *adj.*

nu·tri·tion (nōō·trish′ən, nyōō-) *n.* 1. The processes by which food is converted into tissue in living organisms. 2. That which nourishes. —**nu·tri′tion·al** *adj.* —**nu·tri′tion·al·ly** *adv.* —**nu·tri′tion·ist** *n.*

nu·tri·tious (nōō·trish′əs, nyōō-) *adj.* Promoting growth; nourishing. Also **nu·tri·tive** (noo′trə·tiv, nyōō′-) —**nu·tri′tious·ly** *adv.* —**nu·tri′tious·ness** *n.*

nuts (nuts) *adj. Slang* 1. Crazy; demented; eccentric. 2. Extremely enthusiastic or in love: with *about.* —*interj.* An exclamation of contempt, disappointment, etc.

nut·shell (nut′shel′) *n.* The shell of a nut. —**in a nutshell** In brief and concise statement or form.

nut·ty (nut′ē) *adj.* **·ti·er, ·ti·est** 1. Having the flavor of nuts. 2. *Slang* Crazy. —**nut′ti·ly** *adv.* —**nut′ti·ness** *n.*

nuz·zle (nuz′əl) *v.* **·zled, ·zling** *v.i.* 1. To rub, press, or dig with or as with the nose. 2. To nestle or snuggle; lie close. —*v.t.* 3. To push or rub the nose, etc., into or against. [Freq. of NOSE, v.]

nycto- *combining form* Night; nocturnal. Also, before vowels, **nyct-.** [< Gk. *nyx, nyktos* night]

ny·lon (nī′lon) *n.* 1. A synthetic material of strong fibers; esp., cloth made from these fibers. 2. *pl. Informal* Stockings made of nylon. [< A trade name]

nymph (nimf) *n.* 1. In Greek and Roman mythology, any of a class of minor female divinities living in forests, fountains, etc. 2. *Chiefly Poetic.* A young woman or girl. 3. *Entomol.* The young of an insect undergoing incomplete metamorphosis, at which stage the wing pads are first evident: also **nym·pha** (nim′fə). [< Gk. *nymphē* nymph, bride] —**nymph′al, nym·phe·an** (nim·fē′·ən) *adj.*

nympho- *combining form* Nymph; bride. [< Gk. *nymphē*]

nym·pho·ma·ni·a (nim′fə·mā′nē·ə, -mān′yə) *n.* An extreme and ungovernable sexual desire in women. —**nym′pho·ma′ni·ac** *adj.* & *n.*

O

o, O (ō) *n. pl.* **o's** or **os, O's** or **Os, oes** (ōz) 1. The fifteenth letter of the English alphabet. 2. Any sound represented by the letter *o*. —*symbol Chem.* Oxygen.

o' (ō, ə) *prep.* Of: one *o*'clock, man-*o*'-war, jack-*o*'-lantern.

O (ō) *interj.* Used in direct address, as in prayer or invocation: O Lord!

oaf (ōf) *n. pl.* **oafs** or *Rare* **oaves** (ōvz) A stupid, bungling person. [< ON *ālfr* elf] —**oaf'ish** *adj.* —**oaf'ish·ly** *adv.* —**oaf'ish·ness** *n.*

oak (ōk) *n.* 1. An acorn-bearing tree or shrub of the beech family, valued for its timber. 2. The wood of the oak. [OE *āc*] —**oak'en** *adj.*

oak apple A rounded gall produced on an oak by an insect. Also **oak gall.**

oak·um (ō'kəm) *n.* Tarred rope fiber, used for caulking seams, etc. [OE *ā-* out + *cemban* to comb]

oar (ôr) *n.* An implement for propelling or steering a boat, consisting of a long shaft with a blade at one end. [OE *ār*]

oar·lock (ôr'lok') *n.* A device on the side of a boat for keeping an oar in place. Also, *Brit., rowlock.*

oars·man (ôrz'mən) *n. pl.* **·men** (-mən) One who rows.

o·a·sis (ō·ā'sis) *n. pl.* **·ses** (-sēz) An area in a desert made fertile by groundwater or by irrigation. [< Gk.]

oat (ōt) *n.* 1. *Usu. pl.* A cereal grass widely cultivated for its edible grain. 2. *Usu. pl.* The grain itself. 3. Any similar grass, as the wild oat. [OE *āte*] —**oat'en** *adj.*

oath (ōth) *n. pl.* **oaths** (ōths, ōthz) 1. A formal declaration in support of a pledge or promise, usu. based on an appeal to God. 2. A profane or vulgar utterance. [OE *āth*]

oat·meal (ōt'mēl') *n.* A cereal food made from the cooked meal of oats; also, the meal itself. Also **oat meal.**

ob- *prefix* 1. Toward; to; facing: *obverse*. 2. Against; in opposition to: *object, obstruct*. 3. Over; upon: *obliterate*. 4. Completely: *obdurate*. Also: *o-* before *m*, as in *omit*; *oc-* before *c*, as in *occur*; *of-* before *f*, as in *offend*; *op-* before *p*, as in *oppress*. [< L *ob* toward, for, against]

O·ba·di·ah (ō'bə·dī'ə) *n.* A book of the Old Testament containing the prophecies of the 6th c. B.C. minor Hebrew prophet Obadiah.

ob·bli·ga·to (ob'lə·gä'tō) *n. Music* A part or accompaniment, esp. a solo instrumental accompaniment, essential to the performance of a composition. Also **ob'li·ga'to.** [See OBLIGE.]

ob·du·rate (ob'dyə·rit) *adj.* 1. Unmoved by feelings or moral influence; hardhearted. 2. Difficult to manage; stubborn or unruly. [< L *ob-* against + *durare* to harden] —**ob'du·rate·ly** *adv.* —**ob'du·ra·cy, ob'du·rate·ness** *n.*

o·be·di·ent (ō·bē'dē·ənt) *adj.* 1. Complying with a command, restraint, etc. 2. Yielding to laws or to those in authority. [See OBEY.] —**o·be'di·ence** *n.* —**o·be'di·ent·ly** *adv.*

o·bei·sance (ō·bā'səns, ō·bē'-) *n.* Courtesy, reverence, or homage; also, an act or gesture expressing this. [< OF *obeissant*, ppr. of *obeir* to obey] —**o·bei'sant** *adj.*

ob·e·lisk (ob'ə·lisk) *n.* A four-sided shaft of stone, usu. tapering, with a pyrimidal top. [< Gk. *obelos* a spit, hence pointed pillar] —**ob'e·lis'cal, ob'e·lis'koid** *adj.*

o·bese (ō·bēs') *adj.* Very fat. [< L *obesus*, pp. of *obedere* to eat up] —**o·bese'ly** *adv.* —**o·bes'i·ty** *n.*

o·bey (ō·bā') *v.t.* 1. To comply with the command, etc., of. 2. To comply with (a command, etc.). 3. To be guided by. —*v.i.* 4. To be obedient; comply. [< L *oboedire* to give ear, obey] —**o·bey'er** *n.*

ob·fus·cate (ob·fus'kāt, ob'fəs-) *v.t.* **·cat·ed, ·cat·ing** 1. To confuse or perplex; bewilder. 2. To darken or obscure. [< L *obfuscare* to darken, obscure] —**ob'fus·ca'tion** *n.*

o·bi (ō'bē) *n.* A broad sash tied with a bow in the back, worn with a kimono. [< Japanese *ōbi*]

o·bit (ō'bit) *n. Informal* An obituary.

ob·i·ter dic·tum (ob'ə·tər dik'təm) *Latin pl.* **ob·i·ter dic·ta** An incidental remark.

o·bit·u·ar·y (ō·bich'o͞o·er'ē) *n. pl.* **·ar·ies** A published notice of a person's death. —*adj.* Of or recording a death. [< L *obitus* a going down, death]

ob·ject[1] (əb·jekt') *v.i.* 1. To feel or state opposition or disapproval. —*v.t.* 2. To offer in opposition. [< L *ob-* towards, against + *jacere* to throw] —**ob·jec'tion** *n.* —**ob·jec'tor** *n.*

ob·ject[2] (ob'jikt) *n.* 1. Anything that is apprehended by the senses. 2. The purpose or end of an action. 3. One who or that which is the focus or center of thought, action, etc. 4. *Gram.* **a** A substantive that receives or is affected by the action of the verb, called the **direct object** when it receives the direct action, as *pie* in *She gave him the pie*, and the **indirect object** when it receives the secondary action, as *him* in the same sentence. **b** A substantive following a preposition. [< Med.L *objectum* something thrown in the way]

ob·jec·ti·fy (əb·jek'tə·fī) *v.t.* **·fied, ·fy·ing** To make objective. —**ob·jec'ti·fi·ca'tion** *n.*

ob·jec·tion·a·ble (əb·jek'shən·ə·bəl) *adj.* Deserving of disapproval; offensive. —**ob·jec'tion·a·bil'i·ty** *n.* —**ob·jec'tion·a·bly** *adv.*

ob·jec·tive (əb·jek'tiv) *adj.* 1. Free from personal feelings, prejudice, etc.; unbiased. 2. Pertaining to what is independent of the mind; real. 3. Treating of or stressing actual phenomena, as distinct from inner or imaginary feelings and thoughts. 4. *Gram.* Denoting the case of the object of a transitive verb or preposition. —*n.* 1. A goal; end. 2. *Gram.* a The objective case. b A word in this case. 3. A lens or set of lenses, as in a telescope, that is nearest to the object being viewed: also called **object glass.** —**ob·jec′tive·ly** *adv.* —**ob·jec·tiv·i·ty** (ob′jek·tiv′ə·tē), **ob·jec′tive·ness** *n.*

object lesson An example of a principle or moral in a striking instance or occurrence.

ob·jet d'art (ôb·zhe′ där′) *French pl.* **ob·jets d'art** (ôb·zhe′) Any work of artistic value.

ob·jur·gate (ob′jər·gāt) *v.t.* **·gat·ed, ·gat·ing** To rebuke severely. [< L *ob-* against + *jurgare* to scold] —**ob′jur·ga′tion** *n.* —**ob′·jur·ga′tor** *n.* —**ob·jur·ga·to·ry** (ob·jûr′gə·tôr′e) *adj.* —**ob·jur′ga·to′ri·ly** *adv.*

ob·late (ob′lāt, ob·lāt′) *adj.* Flattened at the poles. [< L *ob-* towards + (*pro*)*latus* lengthened out] —**ob′late·ly** *adv.*

ob·la·tion (ob·lā′shən) *n.* Any religious or solemn offering. [< L *oblatus* presented] —**ob·la′tion·al** *adj.* —**ob·la·to·ry** (ob′lə·tôr′ē) *adj.*

ob·li·gate (ob′lə·gāt; for *adj., also* -git) *v.t.* **·gat·ed, ·gat·ing** To bind or compel, as by contract, conscience, promise, etc. —*adj.* Bound or restricted. —**ob′li·ga′tor** *n.*

ob·li·ga·tion (ob′lə·gā′shən) *n.* 1. A duty, promise, contract, etc., by which one is bound. 2. Any duty or requirement. 3. The constraining or binding power of a law, promise, conscience, etc. 4. What one owes in return for a service, favor, etc. [< L *obligare.* See OBLIGE.] —**ob·lig·a·to·ry** (ə·blig′ə·tôr′ē, ob′lə·gə-) *adj.*

o·blige (ə·blīj′) *v.t.* **o·bliged, o·blig·ing** 1. To place (one) under obligation, as for a service, favor, etc.: with *to.* 2. To compel, bind, or constrain. 3. To do a favor or service for. [< L *obligare,* orig., to tie around] —**o·blig′er** *n.*

o·blig·ing (ə·blī′jing) *adj.* Disposed to do favors. —**o·blig′ing·ly** *adv.* —**o·blig′ing·ness** *n.*

ob·lique (ə·blēk′) *adj.* 1. Deviating from the perpendicular or horizontal; slanting. 2. Not direct or straightforward in meaning, expression, etc. —*n.* An oblique thing, as a line. —*v.i.* **·liqued, ·li·quing** To deviate from the perpendicular or horizontal; slant. [< L *obleiquus*] —**ob·lique′ly** *adv.* —**ob·liq·ui·ty** (ə·blik′wə·tē), **ob·lique′ness** *n.*

oblique angle *Geom.* An angle not a right angle; an acute or obtuse angle.

ob·lit·er·ate (ə·blit′ə·rāt) *v.t.* **·at·ed, ·at·ing** 1. To destroy utterly. 2. To blot or wipe out, as writing. [< L *obliterare* to efface] —**ob·lit′er·a′tion** *n.* —**ob·lit′er·a′tive** *adj.* —**ob·lit′er·a′tor** *n.*

ob·liv·i·on (ə·bliv′ē·ən) *n.* 1. The state or fact of being completely forgotten. 2. The state or fact of forgetting completely. [< L *oblivisci* to forget]

ob·liv·i·ous (ə·bliv′ē·əs) *adj.* 1. Not conscious or aware: with *of* or *to.* 2. Forgetful. [< L *obliviosus*] —**ob·liv′i·ous·ly** *adv.* —**ob·liv′i·ous·ness** *n.*

ob·long (ob′lông) *adj.* Longer in one dimension than in another; rectangular. —*n.* An oblong figure, object, etc. [< L *oblongus* somewhat long]

ob·lo·quy (ob′lə·kwē) *n. pl.* **·quies** 1. Abusive and defamatory language; vilification. 2. Disgrace resulting from such abuse. [< LL *ob-* against + *loqui* to speak]

ob·nox·ious (əb·nok′shəs) *adj.* Highly disagreeable; offensive. [< L *ob-* towards + *noxius* harmful] —**ob·nox′ious·ly** *adv.* —**ob·nox′ious·ness** *n.*

o·boe (ō′bō) *n.* A double-reed woodwind instrument with a conical bore, having a high, penetrating tone. [< Ital. < F *hautbois* < *haut* high + *bois* wood] —**o′bo·ist** *n.*

ob·scene (əb·sēn′, ob-) *adj.* 1. Offensive to prevailing concepts of morality or decency; indecent; lewd. 2. Disgusting; loathsome; foul. [< L *obscenus* ill-omened, filthy] —**ob·scene′ly** *adv.* —**ob·scen′i·ty** (-sen′ə·tē) *n.*

ob·scur·ant·ism (əb·skyŏŏr′ən·tiz′əm) *n.* 1. The practice of purposely making matters obscure or confusing. 2. Opposition to learning and inquiry. [< L *obscurare* to darken] —**ob·scur′ant·ist** *n. & adj.*

ob·scure (əb·skyŏŏr′) *adj.* **·scur·er, ·scur·est** 1. Not clear or plain to the mind; hard to understand. 2. Not readily discovered; hidden; remote. 3. Without distinction or fame; inconspicuous. 4. Having little or no light; dark. —*v.t.* **·scured, ·scur·ing** 1. To conceal; hide. 2. To cover or darken so as to make dim, indistinct, etc. [< L *obscurus* covered over] —**ob·scure′ly** *adv.* —**ob·scu′·ri·ty** *n.*

ob·se·quies (ob′sə·kwēz) *n.pl.* Funeral rites. [< Med.L *obsequiae,* funeral rites]

ob·se·qui·ous (əb·sē′kwē·əs) *adj.* Excessively obedient or submissive; sycophantic; servile. [< L *obsequi* to comply with] —**ob·se′qui·ous·ly** *adv.* —**ob·se′qui·ous·ness** *n.*

ob·ser·vance (əb·zûr′vəns) *n.* 1. The act of observing a command, law, etc. 2. The act of celebrating a holiday, ceremony, etc. 3. A customary rite, ceremony, etc. 4. Notice; attention. 5. *Eccl.* The rule or constitution of a religious order.

ob·ser·vant (əb·zûr′vənt) *adj.* 1. Perceptive; heedful; alert. 2. Strict or careful in obeying or keeping a custom, law, etc. —**ob·ser′·vant·ly** *adv.*

ob·ser·va·tion (ob′zər·vā′shən) *n.* 1. The act of observing, or the fact of being observed. 2. Close examination for the purpose of scientific study. 3. An opinion or judgment. —**ob′ser·va′tion·al** *adj.* —**ob′ser·va′tion·al·ly** *adv.*

ob·ser·va·to·ry (əb·zûr′və·tôr′ē) *n. pl.* **·ries** A building equipped for the systematic observation of astronomical or other natural phenomena.

ob·serve (əb·zûrv′) *v.* **·served, ·serv·ing** *v.t.* 1. To see or notice; perceive. 2. To make careful observation of, esp. for scientific purposes. 3. To comment; remark. 4. To comply with (a law, custom, etc.); abide by. 5. To celebrate as a holiday. —*v.i.* 6. To look on or attend without taking part, as at a meeting. [< L *observare* to watch] —**ob·serv′a·ble** *adj.* —**ob·serv′er** *n.* —**ob·serv′·ing·ly** *adv.*

ob·sess (əb·ses′) *v.t.* To occupy or trouble the mind of; preoccupy. [< L *obsidere* to occupy, besiege] **—ob·ses′sive** *adj.* **—ob·ses′sor** *n.*

ob·ses·sion (əb·sesh′ən) *n.* 1. That which obsesses, as a persistent idea or feeling. 2. The state of being obsessed.

ob·sid·i·an (əb·sid′ē·ən) *n.* A glassy volcanic rock, usu. black. [< L *obsidianus*]

ob·so·les·cent (ob′sə·les′ənt) *adj.* Going out of use or fashion. **—ob′so·les′cence** *n.* **—ob′so·les′cent·ly** *adv.*

ob·so·lete (ob′sə·lēt′) *adj.* 1. Gone out of fashion; out-of-date. 2. No longer used or practiced. [< L *obsolescere* to wear out] **—ob′so·lete′ly** *adv.* **—ob′so·lete′ness** *n.* **—ob′so·let′ism** *n.*

ob·sta·cle (ob′stə·kəl) *n.* That which stands in the way; a hindrance or obstruction. [< L *ob-* before, against + *stare* to stand]

ob·ste·tri·cian (ob′stə·trish′ən) *n.* A medical and surgical specialist in obstetrics.

ob·stet·rics (əb·stet′riks) *n.pl.* (*construed as sing.*) The branch of medicine dealing with pregnancy and childbirth. [< L *obstetrix, -icis* midwife] **—ob·stet′ric, ob·stet′ri·cal** *adj.* **—ob·stet′ri·cal·ly** *adv.*

ob·sti·nate (ob′stə·nit) *adj.* Unreasonably fixed in one's purpose or opinion; stubborn. [< L *obstinare* to persist] **—ob′sti·na·cy** (-nə·sē) *n.* **—ob′sti·nate·ly** *adv.*

ob·strep·er·ous (əb·strep′ər·əs) *adj.* Unruly or noisy, esp. in resistance to control, advice, etc. [< L *ob-* towards + *strepere* to make noise] **—ob·strep′er·ous·ly** *adv.* **—ob·strep′er·ous·ness** *n.*

ob·struct (əb·strukt′) *v.t.* 1. To stop movement through (a way or passage) by obstacles. 2. To block or retard the progress or way of; impede. 3. To be in front of so as to prevent a clear view. [< L *ob-* before + *struere* to pile, build] **—ob·struct′er** or **ob·struc′tor** *n.* **—ob·struc′tive** *adj.* **—ob·struc′tive·ly** *adv.* **—ob·struc′tive·ness** *n.*

ob·struc·tion (əb·struk′shən) *n.* 1. That which obstructs. 2. The act of obstructing, or the state of being obstructed.

ob·struc·tion·ist (əb·struk′shən·ist) *n.* One who makes a practice of obstructing; esp., one who obstructs debate, legislation, etc. **—ob·struc′tion·ism** *n.*

ob·tain (əb·tān′) *v.t.* 1. To gain possession of, esp. by effort. **—***v.i.* 2. To be prevalent or in effect. [< L *ob-* towards + *tenere* to hold] **—ob·tain′a·ble** *adj.* **—ob·tain′er** *n.* **—ob·tain′ment** *n.*

ob·trude (əb·trōōd′) *v.* **·trud·ed, ·trud·ing** *v.t.* 1. To thrust or force (oneself, an opinion, etc.) upon another without request or warrant. 2. To push forward or out; eject. **—***v.i.* 3. To intrude oneself. [< L *ob-* towards + *trudere* to thrust] **—ob·trud′er** *n.* **—ob·tru′sion** (-trōō′zhən) *n.* **—ob·tru′sive** (-trōō′siv) *adj.* **—ob·tru′sive·ly** *adv.* **—ob·tru′sive·ness** *n.*

ob·tuse (əb·tōōs′) *adj.* 1. Lacking in sharpness of intellect; not quick-witted. 2. Not sharp; blunt or rounded. [< L *obtusus* blunt, dulled] **—ob·tuse′ly** *adv.* **—ob·tuse′·ness** *n.*

obtuse angle *Geom.* An angle greater than 90° and less than 180°.

ob·verse (ob′vûrs; *for adj., also* ob·vûrs′) *adj.* 1. Turned toward or facing one. 2. Narrower at the base than at the apex. 3. Constituting a counterpart. **—***n.* 1. The front or principal side of anything; esp., the side of a coin bearing the main design. 2. A counterpart. [< L *ob-* towards + *vertere* to turn] **—ob·verse′ly** *adv.*

ob·vi·ate (ob′vē·āt) *v.t.* **·at·ed, ·at·ing** To take care of ahead of time; make unnecessary. [< L *obviatus*, pp. of *obviare* to meet, withstand]

ob·vi·ous (ob′vē·əs) *adj.* Immediately evident. [< L *ob-* before + *via* way] **—ob′vi·ous·ly** *adv.* **—ob′vi·ous·ness** *n.*

oc- Assimilated var. of OB-.

oc·a·ri·na (ok′ə·rē′nə) *n.* A small musical instrument in the shape of a sweet potato, with a mouthpiece and finger holes. [< Ital., dim. of *oca* goose < L *auca*; so called with ref. to its shape]

oc·ca·sion (ə·kā′zhən) *n.* 1. The particular time of an event or occurrence; also, the event or occurrence itself. 2. An important or extraordinary event. 3. A favorable time or condition; opportunity. 4. The immediate cause of some action or state. **—on occasion** Now and then. **—***v.t.* To cause, esp. in an accidental or incidental manner. [< L *ob-* towards + *cadere* to fall]

oc·ca·sion·al (ə·kā′zhən·əl) *adj.* 1. Occurring, appearing, etc., now and then. 2. Made, intended, or suitable for a particular occasion: *occasional* verse. **—oc·ca′sion·al·ly** *adv.*

oc·ci·dent (ok′sə·dənt) *n.* The west. [< L *occidens, -entis* region where the sun sets.]

Oc·ci·dent (ok′sə·dənt) 1. The countries west of Asia; esp., Europe. 2. The western hemisphere.

oc·ci·den·tal (ok′sə·den′təl) *adj.* Of or belonging to the west, or to the countries constituting the Occident. **—***n.* One born or living in a western country: also **Oc′ci·den′tal.**

oc·clude (ə·klōōd′) *v.* **·clud·ed, ·clud·ing** *v.t.* 1. To shut up or close, as pores or openings. 2. To shut in, out, or off. 3. *Chem.* To take up, either on the surface or internally, but without change of properties. **—***v.i.* 4. To meet so that the corresponding cusps fit closely together: said of the teeth. [< L *ob-* against + *claudere* to close] **—oc·clu′dent** *adj.* **—oc·clu·sion** (ə·klōō′zhən) *n.* **—oc·clu′sive** (-siv) *adj.*

oc·cult (ə·kult′, ok′ult) *adj.* 1. Of or pertaining to various magical arts and practices. 2. Beyond human understanding; mysterious. 3. Not divulged or disclosed; secret. **—***n.* Occult arts or practices. [< L *occultus*, pp. of *occulere* to cover over, hide] **—oc·cult′ism** *n.* **—oc·cult′ist** *n.* **—oc·cult′ly** *adv.*

oc·cul·ta·tion (ok′ul·tā′shən) *n.* *Astron.* Concealment of one celestial body by another interposed in the line of vision.

oc·cu·pan·cy (ok′yə·pən·sē) *n.* *pl.* **·cies** The act of occupying, or the state of being occupied.

oc·cu·pant (ok′yə·pənt) *n.* 1. One who occupies a place, position, etc. 2. A tenant.

oc·cu·pa·tion (ok′yə·pā′shən) *n.* 1. One's regular, principal, or immediate business or job. 2. The act of occupying, or the state of being occupied. 3. The taking and holding of land by a military force. **—oc·cu·pa′tion·al** *adj.* **—oc·cu·pa′tion·al·ly** *adv.*

occupational therapy *Med.* The treatment of disabilities by means of work designed to promote recovery or readjustment.

oc·cu·py (ok′yə·pī) *v.t.* **·pied, ·py·ing** 1. To take and hold possession of, as by conquest. 2. To fill or take up (space or time). 3. To inhabit; dwell in. 4. To hold; fill, as an office or position. 5. To busy or engage; employ. [< L *ob-* against + *capere* to take] **—oc′cu·pi′er** *n.*

oc·cur (ə·kûr′) *v.i.* **·curred, ·cur·ring** 1. To happen or take place; come about. 2. To be found or met with; appear. 3. To suggest itself; come to mind. [< L *ob-* towards, against + *currere* to run]

oc·cur·rence (ə·kûr′əns) *n.* 1. The act or fact of occurring. 2. That which occurs; an event. **—oc·cur′rent** *adj.*

o·cean (ō′shən) *n.* 1. The great body of salt water that covers about 70 percent of the earth's surface. 2. *Often cap.* Any of the five divisions of this body of water, the Atlantic, Pacific, Indian, Arctic, and Antarctic. 3. A very large expanse or quantity. [< Gk. *ōkeanos*] **—o·ce·an·ic** (ō′shē·an′ik) *adj.*

O·ce·an·ic (ō′shē·an′ik) *n.* A subfamily of the Austronesian family of languages, including the Melanesian languages of the Solomon Islands, Fiji, New Caledonia, the New Hebrides, etc., and the Micronesian group of languages.

o·cean·og·ra·phy (ō′shən·og′rə·fē) *n.* The branch of physical geography that treats of oceanic life and phenomena. **—o′cean·og′ra·pher** *n.* **—o′cean·o·graph′ic** (-ə·graf′ik) or **·i·cal** *adj.* **—o′cean·o·graph′i·cal·ly** *adv.*

o·cel·lus (ō·sel′əs) *n.* *pl.* **·li** (-lī) *Biol.* A simple eye, as of many invertebrates. [< L, dim. of *oculus* eye] **—o·cel′lar** *adj.*

o·ce·lot (os′ə·lət, ō′sə-) *n.* A large cat of Central and South America, having a spotted yellowish or reddish gray coat. [< F, short for Nahuatl *tlaocelotl* < *tlalli* field + *ocelotl* jaguar]

o·cher (ō′kər) *n.* 1. An iron oxide mixed with various earthy materials and varying from light yellow to deep red, largely used as a pigment. 2. A dark yellow color derived from or resembling ocher. Also **o′chre.** [< Gk. *ōchra* yellow ocher < *ōchros* pale yellow] **—o′cher·ous, o·chre·ous** (ō′krē·əs), **o′cher·y, o·chry** (ō′krē) *adj.*

-ock *suffix of nouns* Small: *hillock.* [OE *-oc, -uc*]

o'clock (ə·klok′) Of or according to the clock.

oct-, octa- See OCTO-.

oc·ta·gon (ok′tə·gon) *n.* *Geom.* A polygon having eight sides and eight angles. [< OCTA- + Gk. *gōnia* angle] **—oc·tag·o·nal** (ok·tag′ə·nəl) *adj.* **—oc·tag′o·nal·ly** *adv.*

oc·ta·he·dron (ok′tə·hē′drən) *n.* *pl.* **·dra** *Geom.* A polyhedron bounded by eight plane faces. [< OCTA- + Gk. *hedra* seat] **—oc′ta·he′dral** *adj.*

oc·tane (ok′tān) *n.* *Chem.* One of a group of saturated hydrocarbons.

octane number A measure of the antiknock properties of a gasoline or other fuel.

oc·tant (ok′tənt) *n.* An eighth part of a circle; a 45° angle or arc. [< LL *octans, -antis* an eighth part] **—oc·tant′al** (-tan′təl) *adj.*

oc·tave (ok′tiv, -tāv) *n.* 1. *Music* a The interval between a tone and another having twice as many or half as many vibrations per second. b A tone at this interval above or below any other, considered in relation to that other. 2. Any group or series of eight. **—***adj.* 1. Composed of eight. 2. *Music* Producing tones an octave higher. [< L *octavus* eighth] **—oc·ta·val** (ok·tā′vəl, ok′tə-) *adj.*

oc·ta·vo (ok·tā′vō, -tä′-) *n.* *pl.* **·vos** 1. The page size (usu. 6 x 9½ inches) of a book made up of printer's sheets folded into eight leaves. 2. A book consisting of pages of this size. **—***adj.* In octavo. Also written **8vo** or **8°**. [< L *in octavo* in an eighth]

oc·tet (ok·tet′) *n.* 1. A musical composition for eight singers or instrumentalists. 2. A group of eight singers or instrumentalists. 3. Any group of eight. Also **oc·tette′.** [< L *octo* eight]

oc·til·lion (ok·til′yən) *n.* A cardinal number written as 1 followed by 27 zeros. **—oc·til′lion, oc·til′lionth** *adj.*

octo- *combining form* Eight: also, before vowels, *oct-.* Also *octa-.* [< L *octo* and Gk. *oktō* eight]

Oc·to·ber (ok·tō′bər) The tenth month of the year, containing 31 days. [< L, eighth month of early Roman calendar < *octo* eight]

oc·to·ge·nar·i·an (ok′tə·jə·nâr′ē·ən) *n.* A person between 80 and 90 years of age. **—oc′to·ge·nar′i·an** *adj.* **—oc·tog·e·nar·y** (ok·toj′ə·ner′ē) *adj. & n.* [< L *octoginta* eighty]

oc·to·pus (ok′tə·pəs) *n.* *pl.* **·pus·es** or **·pi** (-pī) or **oc·top·o·des** (ok·top′ə·dēz) 1. An eight-armed marine mollusk having a large oval head and rows of suckers along the arms. 2. Any organized power regarded as far-reaching and potentially destructive; esp., a powerful business organization. [< Gk. *oktō* eight + *pous* foot]

oc·to·roon (ok′tə·rōōn′) *n.* A person who is one-eighth Negro. [< L *octo* eight + (QUAD)ROON]

oc·u·lar (ok′yə·lər) *adj.* Of, like, or related to the eye or sight. **—***n.* The lenses forming the eyepiece of an optical instrument. [< L *oculus* eye] **—oc′u·lar·ly** *adv.*

oc·u·list (ok′yə·list) *n.* A physician skilled in treating diseases of the eye; ophthalmologist. [< L *oculus* eye]

OD (ō·dē′) *v.i.* **OD'd** or **ODed, OD'ing** To become ill or die from an overdose of a narcotic. **—***n.* 1. An overdose of a narcotic. 2. One who takes such an overdose. [< O(VER)D(OSE)]

o·da·lisque (ō′də·lisk) *n.* A female slave or concubine in an Oriental harem. Also **o′da·lisk.** [< Turkish *ōdaliq* chambermaid]

odd (od) *adj.* 1. Strange or unusual in appearance or behavior; peculiar. 2. Not part of what is regular, usual, or required: an *odd* job. 3. Being the remainder of an incomplete pair: an *odd* slipper. 4. Leaving a remainder when divided by two: opposed to *even.* 5. Additional to a stated number: seventy *odd* dollars. [< ON *oddi* point, hence, third point of a triangle, hence, odd number] **—odd′ly** *adv.* **—odd′ness** *n.*

odd·ball (od′bôl′) *n.* *Slang* An eccentric person. **—odd′ball′** *adj.*

odd·i·ty (od′ə·tē) *n.* *pl.* **·ties** 1. One who or that which is odd. 2. An odd or peculiar quality or trait; an eccentricity. 3. The state of being odd; strangeness.

odd·ment (od′mənt) *n.* *Usu. pl.* A fragment, scrap, or leftover.

odds (odz) *n.pl.* (*sometimes construed as*

sing.) 1. An equalizing allowance or advantage given to a weaker opponent. 2. A difference to the advantage of one side. **—at odds** At variance; disagreeing.

odds and ends Miscellaneous things; scraps.

odds-on (odz′on′, -ôn′) *adj.* Having a better than even chance to win.

ode (ōd) *n.* A lyric poem often in the form of an elaborate address and usually characterized by loftiness of tone, feeling, and style. [< Gk. *ōidē* song]

-ode *combining form* Way; path: *anode, cathode.* [< Gk. *hodos* way]

o·di·ous (ō′dē·əs) *adj.* Exciting hate or disgust; offensive. [< L *odium* hatred] **—o′di·ous·ly** *adv.* **—o′di·ous·ness** *n.*

o·di·um (ō′dē·əm) *n.* 1. The state of being odious. 2. Extreme dislike or aversion; hatred. 3. The reproach or disgrace associated with something hateful. [< L, hatred]

o·dom·e·ter (ō·dom′ə·tər) *n.* A device for measuring distance traveled by a vehicle. [< Gk. *hodos* way, road + *metron* a measure] **—o·dom′e·try** *n.*

o·dor (ō′dər) *n.* 1. That quality of a substance that renders it perceptible to the sense of smell; scent. 2. Regard or estimation. Also *Brit.* **o′dour.** [< L] **—o′dored** *adj.* **—o′dor·less** *adj.* **—o′dor·less·ly** *adv.* **—o′·dor·less·ness** *n.* **—o′dor·ous** *adj.* **—o′dor·ous·ly** *adv.* **—o′dor·ous·ness** *n.*

o·dor·if·er·ous (ō′də·rif′ər·əs) *adj.* Having or giving off an odor, especially a pleasant odor. [< L *odor* odor + *ferre* to bear] **—o′dor·if′er·ous·ly** *adv.* **—o′dor·if′er·ous·ness** *n.*

-odynia *combining form Med.* Pain in a part of the body. [< Gk. *odynē* pain]

Od·ys·sey (od′ə·sē) *n.* A long, wandering journey: often **od′ys·sey.** [after the *Odyssey,* an epic poem by the 9th c. B.C. Greek poet Homer]

Oed·i·pus complex (ed′ə·pəs, ē′də-) *Psychoanal.* A strong attachment of a child to the parent of the opposite sex, esp. of a son to his mother, with antagonism toward the other parent. [after *Oedipus,* legendary Greek ruler who unwittingly killed his father and married his mother] **—Oed′i·pal** *adj.*

o'er (ôr) *prep. & adv. Poetic* Over.

oeu·vre (œ′vr′) *n. pl.* **oeu·vres** (œ′vr′) *French* 1. A work, as of art or literature. 2. The totality of works, as of an author.

of (uv, ov; *unstressed* əv) *prep.* 1. Coming from: Anne *of* Cleves. 2. Included among: Is he *of* your party? 3. Located at: the Leaning Tower *of* Pisa. 4. Away or at a distance from: within six miles *of* home. 5. Named; specified as: a fall *of* ten feet. 6. Characterized by: a man *of* strength. 7. With reference to: quick *of* wit. 8. About; concerning: Good is said *of* him. 9. Because of: dying *of* cancer. 10. Possessing. 11. Belonging to: the lid *of* a box. 12. Pertaining to: the majesty *of* the law. 13. Composed of: a ship *of* steel. 14. Containing: a glass *of* water. 15. From the number or class of: six *of* the seven conspirators. 16. So as to be without: relieved *of* anxiety. 17. Produced by: the plays *of* Shakespeare. 18. Directed toward: a love *of* opera. 19. During, on, or at a specified time: *of* recent years. 20. Set aside for or devoted to: a program *of* music. 21. Before; until: used in telling time: ten minutes *of* ten. [OE, away from, off]

of- Assimilated var. of OB-.

of course 1. As expected. 2. Doubtless; certainly.

off (ôf) *adj.* 1. Farther or more distant; remote: an *off* chance. 2. In a (specified) circumstance or situation: to be well *off.* 3. Incorrect. 4. Not up to standard: an *off* season for roses. 5. No longer in effect: The deal is *off.* 6. Not on duty: *off* hours. **—*adv.*** 1. To a distance; away: My horse ran *off.* 2. To or at a (specified) future time: to put it *off* for a week. 3. So as to be no longer in place: Take *off* your hat. 4. So as to be no longer living, continuing, or in operation: to kill *off* one's enemies: to break *off* talks. 5. So as to be away from one's work or duties: to take the day *off.* 6. So as to be below standard: His game dropped *off.* **—off and on** Now and then; intermittently. **—to be off** 1. To leave; depart. 2. *Informal* To be insane. **—*prep.*** 1. So as to be distant from (a position, source, etc): twenty miles *off* course. 2. Not engaged in or occupied with: *off* duty. 3. Extending away or out from; no longer on: *off* Broadway. 4. So as to be below standard: to be *off* one's game. 5. On or from: living *off* nuts and berries. 6. *Informal* No longer using or engaging in: to be *off* drinking. [ME]

of·fal (ô′fəl) *n.* 1. The waste parts of a butchered animal. 2. Rubbish or refuse of any kind. [ME *ofall*]

off·beat (ôf′bēt′) *n. Music* Any secondary or weak beat in a measure. **—*adj.*** *Slang* Out of the ordinary; unconventional.

off-Broad·way (ôf′brôd′wā) *adj.* Pertaining to professional productions in New York outside the prime theater area, often low-budget, experimental works.

off·cast (ôf′kast′) *adj.* Rejected; castoff. **—*n.*** Anything thrown away.

off chance A bare possibility.

off-col·or (ôf′kul′ər) *adj.* 1. Unsatisfactory in color. 2. Indecent; risqué.

of·fend (ə·fend′) *v.t.* 1. To give displeasure or offense to; anger. 2. To be disagreeable to (the sense of smell, sight, etc.). **—*v.i.*** 3. To give displeasure or offense; be offensive. 4. To commit an offense. [< L *ob-* against + *fendere* to hit] **—of·fend′er** *n.*

of·fense (ə·fens′; *for defs. 4 & 5, also* ô′fens) *n.* 1. A breach of a law; crime or sin. 2. The act of offending. 3. That which offends. 4. The act of attacking or assaulting. 5. In football, hockey, etc., the team possessing the ball or puck. **—to give offense** To offend. **—to take offense** To be offended. Also *esp. Brit.* **of·fence′.**

of·fen·sive (ə·fen′siv) *adj.* 1. Unpleasant or disagreeable. 2. Giving displeasure or offense; causing anger. 3. Of, pertaining to, or characterized by attack. 4. In sports, of or relating to a team or player in possession of the ball or puck. **—*n.*** The movement, attitude, or position of offense or attack. **—of·fen′sive·ly** *adv.* **—of·fen′sive·ness** *n.*

of·fer (ô′fər) *v.t.* 1. To present for acceptance or rejection. 2. To suggest for consideration or action; propose. 3. To propose or threaten: to *offer* battle. 4. To attempt to do or inflict; also, to do or inflict. 5. To suggest as payment; bid. 6. To present for sale. —*v.i.* 7. To present itself; appear. —*n.* 1. The act of offering. 2. That which is offered. [OE *offrian* < L *ob-* before + *ferre* to bring] —**of′fer·er** or **of′fer·or** *n.*

of·fer·ing (ô′fər·ing) *n.* 1. The act of making an offer. 2. That which is offered, as a sacrifice or contribution.

of·fer·to·ry (ô′fər·tôr′ē) *n. pl.* **·ries** *Eccl.* 1. *Usu. cap.* A section of the eucharistic liturgy during which the bread and wine to be consecrated are offered. 2. Any collection taken during a religious service. 3. A hymn or anthem sung during this service. [< Med.L *offertorium* < LL, place of offerings]

off·hand (ôf′hand′) *adv.* Without preparation. Also **off′hand′ed·ly.** —*adj.* 1. Done, said, or made offhand. 2. Casual; informal; curt. Also **off′hand′ed.**

of·fice (ô′fis) *n.* 1. A place in which business is carried out; also, those working in such a place. 2. Any post or position of authority. 3. A duty, charge, or trust. 4. Any act done or intended to be done for another; favor: through his kind *offices.* 5. A prescribed religious or devotional service; also, any ceremony or rite. [< L *officium* service]

of·fice·hold·er (ô′fis·hōl′dər) *n.* One who holds an office in a government.

of·fi·cer (ô′fə·sər) *n.* 1. In the armed forces, one appointed to a certain rank and authority; esp., one holding a commission. 2. One holding a position of authority or trust. 3. On a merchant or passenger ship, the captain or any of the mates. 4. One who enforces the law, as a policeman.

of·fi·cial (ə·fish′əl) *adj.* 1. Of or relating to an office or position of authority. 2. Supported by or derived from authority. 3. Authorized to carry out some special duty. 4. Formal: *official* banquets. —*n.* One holding an office. —**of·fi′cial·ly** *adv.*

of·fi·cial·dom (ə·fish′əl·dəm) *n.* 1. Officials collectively or as a class. 2. Rigid adherence to official forms or routines: also **of·fi′cial·ism.**

of·fi·ci·ant (ə·fish′ē·ənt) *n.* One who conducts or officiates at a religious service.

of·fi·ci·ate (ə·fish′ē·āt) *v.i.* **·at·ed, ·at·ing** 1. To act or serve as a priest or minister. 2. To perform the duties or functions of any office. —**of·fi′ci·a′tion** *n.* —**of·fi′ci·a′tor** *n.*

of·fi·cious (ə·fish′əs) *adj.* Unduly forward in offering one's services or advice. [< L *officiosus* obliging < *officium* service] —**of·fi′cious·ly** *adv.* —**of·fi′cious·ness** *n.*

off·ing (ô′fing) *n.* That part of the sea visible at some distance from the shore. —**in the offing** Soon to happen.

off·ish (ô′fish) *adj.* Distant in manner; aloof. —**off′ish·ly** *adv.* —**off′ish·ness** *n.*

off-off-Broad·way (ôf′ôf′brôd′wā) *adj.* Pertaining to experimental, low-budget theatricals in New York, usu. done in cafes, lofts, etc. rather than theaters.

off-put·ting (ôf′po͝ot′ing) *adj.* That is disagreeable.

off·set (*n.* ôf′set′; *v.* ôf′set′) *n.* 1. That which balances or compensates for something else. 2. Offset printing; also, an impression made by offset printing. 3. A bend or curve made in a pipe, rod, etc., to allow it to pass an obstacle. —*v.t.* **·set, ·set·ting** 1. To balance or compensate for. 2. To reproduce by offset printing.

offset printing A method of printing in which the inked impression from a lithographic plate is transferred to a cylinder, and then onto the paper.

off·shoot (ôf′sho͞ot′) *n.* 1. *Bot.* A branch from the main stem of a plant. 2. Anything that branches off from a main source.

off·shore (ôf′shôr′) *adj.* 1. Situated away from shore. 2. Situated beyond the boundaries or control of a government. —**off′shore′** *adv.*

off·side (ôf′sīd′) *adj.* In football, in front of the ball before it is put into play. Also **off side.**

off·spring (ôf′spring′) *n. pl.* **·spring** or **·springs** The progeny of a person, animal, or plant; descendant.

off-stage (ôf′stāj′) *n.* The area behind or to the side of a stage. —*adj.* In or from this area. —*adv.* To this area.

off-the-shelf (ôf′thə·shelf′) *adj.* Designating a standard part, component, etc. ready for use.

off-track betting (ôf′trak′) Pari-mutuel betting done away from a racetrack.

off·white (ôf′hwīt′) *n.* Oyster white.

oft (ôft) *adv.* Often. [OE]

oft·en (ôf′ən) *adv.* Frequently or repeatedly. [OE *oft*]

oft·en·times (ôf′ən·tīmz′) *adv. Archaic* Frequently. Also **oft·times** (ôf′tīmz′).

o·gle (ō′gəl) *v.t. & v.i.* **o·gled, o·gling** To look at (someone) or stare in an amorous or coquettish manner. —*n.* An amorous or coquettish look. [< LG *oege* eye] —**o′gler** *n.*

o·gre (ō′gər) *n.* 1. In fairy tales, a man-eating giant or monster. 2. One who is brutal, hideous, or feared. [< F] —**o·gre·ish** (ō′gər·ish), **o·grish** (ō′grish) *adj.* —**o′gress** (-grəs) *n.fem.*

oh (ō) *interj.* An exclamation expressing surprise, sudden emotion, etc. —*n.* The interjection *oh.*

ohm (ōm) *n.* The unit of electrical resistance. [after George S. *Ohm,* 1787–1854, German physicist]

ohm·age (ō′mij) *n.* Electrical resistance of a conductor, expressed in ohms.

ohm·me·ter (ōm′mē′tər) *n.* A galvanometer for measuring ohmage.

o·ho (ō·hō′) *interj.* An exclamation expressing success, astonishment, amusement, etc.

-oid *suffix* Like; resembling; having the form of: *ovoid.* [< Gk. *eidos* form]

oil (oil) *n.* 1. A greasy, sometimes combustible liquid of vegetable, animal, or mineral origin, used as food, for lubricating, illuminating, and fuel, and in the manufacture of many substances. 2. Petroleum. 3. An oil color; also, an oil painting. 4. Anything of an oily consistency. —*v.t.* To smear, lubricate, or supply with oil. —*adj.* 1. Of or resembling oil. 2. Using, obtained from, or yielding oil. [Prob. < Gk. *elaion* olive oil]

oil·cloth (oil′klôth′) *n.* A fabric waterproofed with oils and paints, used as a covering.

oil color A color or paint made of pigment ground in oil, used chiefly by artists.

oil of vitriol Sulfuric acid.

oil painting 1. A painting done in pigments

mixed in oil. 2. The art of painting in oil colors.
oil shale A sedimentary shale impregnated with petroleum.
oil·skin (oil′skin′) *n.* Cloth made waterproof with oil, or a garment of such material.
oil slick A smooth area on water caused by a film of oil.
oil·stone (oil′stōn′) *n.* A whetstone moistened with oil.
oil well A well that is drilled to obtain petroleum.
oil·y (oi′lē) *adj.* **oil·i·er, oil·i·est** 1. Of, pertaining to, or containing oil. 2. Coated, smeared, or soaked with oil; greasy. 3. Smooth or suave in behavior, speech, etc.; unctuous. —**oil′i·ly** *adv.* —**oil′i·ness** *n.*
oint·ment (oint′mənt) *n.* A fatty or oily preparation applied to the skin as a medicine or cosmetic; unguent. [< OF *oignement*, ult. < L *unguentum* < *ungere* to anoint]
O·jib·wa (ō·jib′wā, -wə) *n. pl.* **·wa** or **·was** 1. One of a tribe of North American Indians formerly inhabiting the regions around Lake Superior. 2. Their Algonquian language. Also called *Chippewa*: also **O·jib′way.**
OK (*interj., adj., adv., & n.* ō′kā′; *v.* ō·kā′) *interj., adj., & adv.* All correct; all right: used to express approval, agreement, etc. —*v.t.* To approve, endorse, or agree to; especially, to sign with an *OK.* —*n.* Approval; agreement; endorsement. Also **O.K., o′kay′, o′keh′.** [? < *o(ll) k(orrect)*, humorous misspelling of *all correct*]
O·kie (ō′kē) *n. Slang* A migrant farmworker, originally one from Oklahoma.
o·kra (ō′krə) *n.* 1. A tall annual herb of the mallow family. 2. Its green pods, used in soups and stews, or as a vegetable. 3. Gumbo. [< West African]
-ol *suffix Chem.* Denoting an alcohol or phenol: *methanol, glycerol.*
old (ōld) *adj.* **old·er** or **eld·er, old·est** or **eld·est** 1. Existing for a long time. 2. Showing the characteristics of advanced life, age, or repeated use. 3. Having a specified age: a child two months *old.* 4. Familiar through long acquaintance or use: an *old* friend. 5. Belonging to a remote period in history; ancient. 6. *Usu. cap.* Denoting the earlier or earliest of two or more things, periods, developments, etc.; *Old* English; the *Old* Testament. —*n.* Past time: days of *old.* [OE *ald*] —**old′ish** *adj.* —**old′ness** *n.*
old country The native country of an immigrant, esp. a European country.
old·en (ōl′dən) *adj. Archaic & Poetic* Old; ancient.
Old English 1. *Printing* Black letter. 2. See under ENGLISH.
old-fash·ioned (ōld′fash′ənd) *adj.* Characteristic of or favoring former times, and old customs, beliefs, and ways.
old fashioned A cocktail of whisky, sugar, fruit, etc.
old fo·gy (fō′gē) One who is extremely conservative or old-fashioned. Also **old fo′gey.** —**old-fo·gy·ish** (ōld′fō′gē·ish) *adj.*
Old French See under FRENCH.
Old Glory The flag of the United States.
old guard The conservative element in a community, political party, etc.
old hat *Slang* Out of style; old-fashioned; obsolete.
Old High German See under GERMAN.
Old Icelandic See under ICELANDIC.
old·ie (ōld′ē) *n. Informal* Something from the past, as an old song.
old lady *Slang* 1. One's mother. 2. One's wife.
Old Latin See under LATIN.
old-line (ōld′līn′) *adj.* 1. Traditional in action or thought. 2. Long-established.
old maid 1. A spinster. 2. *Informal* One who is prim, prudish, fastidious, etc.
old man *Slang* 1. One's father. 2. One's husband. 3. Any man in a position of authority.
old master Any of the famous painters who lived between the 13th and 16th centuries; also, any of their paintings.
Old Norse See under NORSE.
old·ster (ōld′stər) *n. Informal* An old person.
old-style (ōld′stīl′) *adj.* Of a former or old-fashioned style.
Old Testament The first of the two main divisions of the Bible, divided into the Pentateuch, the Prophets, and the Hagiographa.
old-time (ōld′tīm′) *adj.* 1. Of or characteristic of a former time. 2. Of long standing; long-established.
old-tim·er (ōld′tī′mər) *n. Informal* 1. One who has been a member, resident, etc., for a long time. 2. An old-fashioned person.
old-wom·an·ish (ōld′wo͝om′ən·ish) *adj.* Characteristic of an old woman; fussy.
old-world (ōld′wûrld′) *adj.* 1. Of or pertaining to the Old World or Eastern Hemisphere. 2. Ancient; antique.
Old World The Eastern Hemisphere, including Europe, Asia and Africa; esp., Europe.
o·le·ag·i·nous (ō′lē·aj′ə·nəs) *adj.* Of or pertaining to oil; oily. [< L *olea* olive tree] —**o′le·ag′i·nous·ly** *adv.*
o·le·an·der (ō′lē·an′dər) *n.* An Old World evergreen shrub, having poisonous leaves and clusters of fragrant rose or white flowers. [< Med.L]
o·le·o (ō′lē·ō) Short for OLEOMARGARINE.
oleo- *combining form* Oil; of oil. [< L *oleum* oil]
o·le·o·mar·ga·rine (ō′lē·ō·mär′jə·rin) *n.* Margarine. Also **o′le·o·mar′ga·rin.**
o·le·o·res·in (ō′lē·ō·rez′in) *n.* A naturally occurring compound of an essential oil and a resin.
ol·fac·to·ry (ol·fak′tər·ē) *adj.* Of or pertaining to the sense of smell. —*n. pl.* **·ries** *Usu. pl.* The organ of smell. [< L *olere* to have a smell + *facere* to make]
ol·i·garch (ol′ə·gärk) *n.* A ruler in an oligarchy.
ol·i·gar·chy (ol′ə·gär′kē) *n. pl.* **·chies** 1. A form of government in which power is restricted to a few; also, a state so governed. 2. The ruling oligarchs. [< Gk. *oligos* few + *archein* to rule] —**ol′i·gar′chic, ol′i·gar′chal, ol′i·gar′chi·cal** *adj.*
ol·ive (ol′iv) *n.* 1. A small, oily fruit native to southern Europe and the Middle East. 2. The evergreen tree yielding this fruit. 3. The dull, yellowish green color of the unripe olive: also **olive green.** [< L *oliva*] —**ol′ive** *adj.*
olive branch 1. A branch of the olive tree as an emblem of peace. 2. Any peace offering.
olive drab 1. Greenish brown. 2. A woolen or cotton material of this color. 3. *Often pl.*

A uniform or a pair of trousers made of this cloth.
olive oil Oil pressed from olives.
ol·i·vine (ol′ə·vēn, -vin) *n.* A greenish, often transparent, mineral, a magnesium-iron silicate, used as a gemstone.
ol·la (ol′ə, *Sp.* ô′lyä, ô′yä) *n.* 1. A wide-mouthed pot or jar, usu. of earthenware. 2. A highly seasoned stew. [< Sp. < L *olla* pot]
O·lym·pi·ad (ō·lim′pē·ad) *n.* 1. The interval of four years between two successive celebrations of the Olympic games. 2. The modern Olympic games.
O·lym·pic games (ō·lim′pik, ə-) 1. In ancient Greece, athletic games held every four years at the plain of Olympia. 2. A modern international revival of the ancient athletic games, held every four years. Also **O·lym′pi·an games, O·lym′pics.**
-oma *suffix Med.* Tumor: *carcinoma.* [< Gk. *-ōma*]
om·buds·man (om·budz′mən) *n. pl.* **·men** (-mən) A government official appointed to investigate citizens' grievances against the government. [< Sw.]
-ome *combining form Bot.* Group; mass. [< Gk. *-ōma*]
o·me·ga (ō·mē′gə, ō·meg′ə) *n.* 1. The twenty-fourth and last letter in the Greek alphabet (Ω, ω), corresponding to English long *o.* 2. The end; the last. [< Gk. *ō mega* great o]
om·e·let (om′lit, om′ə·lit) *n.* Eggs beaten together with milk and cooked slowly over low heat. Also *Brit.* **om′e·lette.** [< F *omelette*]
o·men (ō′mən) *n.* A phenomenon or incident regarded as a prophetic sign. [< L]
om·i·cron (om′ə·kron, ō′mə-) *n.* The fifteenth letter of the Greek alphabet (O, *o*), corresponding to English short *o.* Also **om′i·kron.** [< Gk. *o mikron* little o]
om·i·nous (om′ə·nəs) *adj.* Of the nature of or foreshadowed by an evil omen; threatening. [< L *omen* omen] **—om′i·nous·ly** *adv.* **—om′i·nous·ness** *n.*
o·mit (ō·mit′) *v.t.* **o·mit·ted, o·mit·ting** 1. To leave out; fail to include. 2. To fail to do, make, etc.; neglect. [< L *omittere* to let go] **—o·mis·si·ble** (ō·mis′ə·bəl) *adj.* **—o·mis·sion** (ō·mish′ən) *n.*
omni- *combining form* All; totally: *omnipotent.* [< L *omnis* all]
om·ni·bus (om′nə·bəs) *n.* 1. A bus. 2. A printed anthology. **—***adj.* Providing for many things at the same time: an *omnibus* bill. [< L, for all]
om·nif·er·ous (om·nif′ər·əs) *adj.* Producing all kinds. [< L *omnis* all + *ferre* to bear]
om·nip·o·tent (om·nip′ə·tənt) *adj.* Almighty; not limited in authority or power. **—the Omnipotent** God. [< L *omnis* all + *potens, -entis* able, powerful] **—om·nip′o·tence** *n.* **—om·nip′o·tent·ly** *adv.*
om·ni·pres·ence (om′nə·prez′əns) *n.* The quality of being everywhere present at the same time. [< L *omnis* all + *praesens, -entis* present] **—om′ni·pres′ent** *adj.*
om·nis·cient (om·nish′ənt) *adj.* Knowing all things. **—the Omniscient** God. [< L *omnis* all + *sciens, -entis,* ppr. of *scire* to know] **—om·nis′cience** *n.* **—om·nis′cient·ly** *adv.*
om·niv·o·rous (om·niv′ər·əs) *adj.* 1. Eating both animal and vegetable food. 2. Eager and indiscriminate: an *omnivorous* eater, an *omnivorous* taste for literature. [< L *omnis* all + *vorare* to devour] **—om·niv′o·rous·ly** *adv.* **—om·niv′o·rous·ness** *n.*
on (on, ôn) *prep.* 1. Above and supported by. 2. In contact with any surface or outer part of: a blow *on* the head. 3. Attached to or suspended from: *on* a string. 4. Directed or moving along the course of. 5. Near: the cottage *on* the lake. 6. Within the duration of. 7. At the occasion of: *On* seeing her, I left. 8. At the moment or point of: *on* the hour. 9. In a state or condition of: *on* fire; *on* record. 10. By means of: *on* wheels. 11. Using as a means of sustenance, activity, etc.: living *on* fruit. 12. Following after: disease *on* the heels of famine. 13. Sustained or confirmed by: *on* good authority. 14. With reference to: to bet *on* a horse. 15. Concerning; about: a book *on* economics. 16. Engaged in: *on* a journey; *on* duty. 17. As a result of: making a profit *on* tips. 18. Directed, tending, or moving toward or against: making war *on* the enemy. 19. *Informal* With: Do you have five dollars *on* you? 20. *Informal* At the expense of: The joke is *on* them. **—to have something on** *Informal* To have knowledge, possess evidence, etc., against. **—***adv.* 1. In or into a position or condition of contact, covering, etc.: He put his hat *on.* 2. In the direction of an activity, performance, etc.: He looked *on* while they played. 3. Ahead, in space or time: later *on.* 4. In continuous course or succession: The music went *on.* 5. In or into operation, performance, or existence. **—and so on** And like what has gone before; et cetera. **—on and on** Continuously. **—to be on to** *Informal* To be aware of, informed about, or alert to. **—***adj.* 1. Being in operation, progress, or application. 2. Near. [OE *on, an*]
-on *suffix* 1. *Physics* Atomic or charged particle: *meson.* 2. *Chem.* Inert gas: *neon.*
once (wuns) *adv.* 1. One time; without repetition. 2. At or during some past time. 3. At any time; ever. **—once (and) for all** Finally. **—once in a while** Occasionally. **—***adj.* Former. **—***conj.* As soon as; whenever. **—***n.* One time. **—all at once** 1. All at the same time. 2. All of a sudden. **—at once** 1. Simultaneously. 2. Immediately. [OE *ānes,* genitive of *ān* one]
once-o·ver (wuns′ō′vər) *n. Slang* A quick glance or survey.
on·com·ing (on′kum′ing, ôn′-) *adj.* Approaching. **—***n.* An approach.
one (wun) *adj.* 1. Being a single person or thing: *one* dollar, in *one* hour. 2. Being or designating an unspecified person or thing: to go to Europe *one* day. 3. Being or designating a specified person or thing: *one* friend after another. 4. Closely united or alike; the same: *one* people. **—***n.* 1. A single unit, the first and lowest integer in the numerical series: a cardinal number written 1, I. 2. A single person or thing. **—***pron.* 1. Someone or something; anyone or anything. 2. An individual or unit among persons or things already mentioned. **—at one** In harmony or accord. **—one another** Each other. **—one by one** Singly and in succession. [OE *ān*]

one-horse (wun′hôrs′) *adj. Informal* Small; unimportant: a *one-horse* town.

O·nei·da (ō·nī′də) *n.* A member of a tribe of Iroquoian Indians originally living in New York.

one·ness (wun′nis) *n.* 1. Singleness; unity; sameness. 2. Agreement; concord. 3. Quality of being unique.

on·er·ous (on′ər·əs) *adj.* Burdensome or oppressive. [< L *onus* burden] **—on′er·ous·ly** *adv.* **—on′er·ous·ness** *n.*

one·self (wun′self′) *pron.* A form of the indefinite pronoun *one,* used as a reflexive or as object of a preposition. Also **one's self.**

one-sid·ed (wun′sī′did) *adj.* 1. Having only one side. 2. Biased; unfair. 3. Unequal or unbalanced: a *one-sided* contest. **—one′-sid′ed·ly** *adv.* **—one′-sid′ed·ness** *n.*

one-time (wun′tīm′) *adj.* Former: a *one-time* winner.

one-track (wun′trak′) *adj. Informal* Limited to a single idea or pursuit: a *one-track* mind.

one-up (wun′up′) *adj. Informal* 1. Ahead by one point, as in a game. 2. In a position of advantage. —*v.t.* **-upped, -up·ping** To gain an advantage over; best.

one-up·man·ship (wun′up′man·ship′) *n. Informal* The process of gaining or maintaining an advantage.

one-way (wun′wā′) *adj.* Moving, or permitting movement, in one direction only.

on·ion (un′yən) *n.* The edible bulb of an herb of the lily family, having a pungent odor and taste. [< L *unio* pearl, onion]

on·ion·skin (un′yən·skin′) *n.* A thin, translucent paper.

on-line (on′līn′, ôn′-) *adj.* Being in direct communication with a computer. **—on′-line′** *adv.*

on·look·er (on′lo͝ok′ər, ôn′-) *n.* One who looks on; a spectator. **—on′look′ing** *adj.*

on·ly (ōn′lē) *adv.* 1. In one manner or for one purpose alone. 2. Solely; exclusively. 3. Merely; just. —*adj.* 1. Alone in its class; sole. 2. Standing alone by reason of superior excellence. —*conj.* Except that; but. [OE *ānlic*]

on·o·mat·o·poe·ia (on′ə·mat′ə·pē′ə) *n.* 1. The formation of words in imitation of natural sounds, as *crack* or *bow-wow.* 2. An imitative word. 3. The use of such words. Also **on′o·mat′o·po·e′sis** (-pō·ē′sis), **on′o·mat′o·py** (-mat′ə·pē). [< Gk. *onoma* name + *poieein* to make] **—on′o·mat′o·poe′ic** or **·i·cal, on′o·mat′o·po·et′ic** (-pō·et′ik) *adj.* **—on′o·mat′o·poe′i·cal·ly, on′o·mat′o·po·et′i·cal·ly** *adv.*

On·on·da·ga (on′ən·dô′gə, -dā′-) *n. pl.* **·ga** or **·gas** 1. A member of a tribe of Iroquoian Indians formerly living in New York and Ontario. 2. The language of this tribe.

on·rush (on′rush′, ôn′-) *n.* An onward rush or flow.

on·set (on′set′, ôn′-) *n.* 1. An attack; assault. 2. An initial stage, as of illness. 3. Outset; start.

on·shore (on′shôr′, ôn′-) *adv. & adj.* To, toward, or on the shore.

on·slaught (on′slôt′, ôn′-) *n.* A violent assault. [< Du. *annslag* or < ON + ME *slaught* slaughter]

on-the-job (on·thə·job′, ôn-) *adj.* Pertaining to skills acquired while actually doing the job: *on-the-job* training.

on·to (on′to͞o, ôn′-) *prep.* 1. Upon the top of; to and upon. 2. *Informal* Aware of: I'm *onto* your tricks. Also **on to.**

onto- *combining form* Being; existence. Also, before vowels, **ont-.** [< Gk. *ōn, ontos* being]

on·tog·e·ny (on·toj′ə·nē) *n. pl.* **·nies** *Biol.* The history of the development of the individual organism. Also **on·to·gen·e·sis** (on′tō·jen′ə·sis). **—on·to·ge·net·ic** (on′tō·jə·net′ik), **on·to·gen·ic** (on′tō·jen′ik) *adj.* **—on·tog′e·nist** *n.*

on·tol·o·gy (on·tol′ə·jē) *n. pl.* **·gies** The branch of metaphysics dealing with the philosophical theory of reality. **—on·to·log·i·cal** (on′tə·loj′i·kəl) *adj.* **—on·tol′o·gist** *n.*

o·nus (ō′nəs) *n.* A burden or responsibility. [< L]

on·ward (on′wərd, ôn′-) *adv.* Forward in space or time; ahead. Also **on′wards.** —*adj.* Moving or tending to be forward. [ME]

on·yx (on′iks) *n.* A variety of chalcedony having layers of different colors, used as a semiprecious gemstone. [< Gk., nail, onyx]

oo·dles (o͞od′lz) *n.pl. Informal* A great deal; many. [< dial. E *oodle,* var. of HUDDLE, n.]

oo·long (o͞o′lông) *n.* A dark tea that is partly fermented before being dried. [< Chinese *wu-lung* black dragon]

ooze[1] (o͞oz) *v.* **oozed, ooz·ing** *v.i.* 1. To flow or leak out slowly or gradually. 2. To exude moisture. 3. To escape or disappear little by little. —*v.t.* 4. To give off or exude in or as in droplets or a trickle. —*n.* 1. A slow, gradual leak. 2. That which oozes. [OE *wōse* slimy mud]

ooze[2] (o͞oz) *n.* 1. Slimy mud or moist, spongy matter, esp. that deposited on the ocean bottom. 2. Muddy or marshy ground; bog. [OE *wāse* slimy mud] **—oo′zi·ly** *adv.* **—oo′zi·ness** *n.* **—oo′zy** *adj.* **oo·zi·er, oo·zi·est**

op- Assimilated var. of OB-.

o·pal (ō′pəl) *n.* An amorphous, variously colored mineral, including some iridescent varieties esteemed as gemstones. [< Gk. *opallios* < Skt. *upala* precious stone]

o·pal·es·cence (ō′pəl·es′əns) *n.* An iridescent play of brilliant or milky colors, as in an opal. **—o′pal·es′cent** *adj.*

o·pal·ine (ō′pəl·ēn, -in) *adj.* Like an opal; opalescent. —*n.* A milky variety of glass.

o·paque (ō·pāk′) *adj.* 1. Impervious to light or other forms of radiation. 2. Impervious to reason; unintelligent. 3. Having no luster; dull. 4. Unintelligible; obscure. [< L *opacus* dark] **—o·pac·i·ty** (ō·pas′ə·tē) *n.* **—o·paque′ly** *adv.* **—o·paque′ness** *n.*

op art (op) A style of art of the 1960's characterized by complex geometric patterns. [< OP(TICAL) ART]

OPEC (ō′pek) Organization of Petroleum Exporting Countries.

o·pen (ō′pən) *adj.* 1. Affording approach, view, or passage: an *open* door. 2. Public; accessible to all. 3. Not secret or hidden. 4. Expanded; unfolded: an *open* flower. 5. Not enclosed or covered: an *open* car. 6. Ready for business, appointment, etc. 7. Not settled or decided; pending: an *open* question. 8. Available: The job is still *open.* 9. Unbiased; receptive: an *open* mind; *open* to conviction. 10. Generous; liberal: an *open* hand. 11. Having openings or perforations, as needlework. 12. Not deceptive: an *open* face. 13. Without restraints or controls: *open* season. 14. Not restricted by rigid classes, control, etc.: an *open* society. —*v.t.* 1. To set open or ajar, as a door; unclose; unfasten. 2. To make passable; free from obstacles. 3. To remove the covering, lid, etc., of. 4. To bring into view; unroll; unfold. 5. To make an opening or openings into. 6. To make or declare ready for commerce, use, etc. 7. To give access. 8. To make more receptive to ideas or sentiments: to *open* the mind. 9. To reveal: to *open* one's heart. 10. To begin; start. —*v.i.* 11. To become open. 12. To come apart or break open; rupture. 13. To come into view; unroll. 14. To afford access or view: The door *opened* on a courtyard. 15. To begin, as a season, theatrical production, etc. —*n.* Any wide space not enclosed, obstructed, or covered: usu. with *the*: in the *open*. [OE] —**o'pen·er** *n.* —**o'pen·ly** *adv.* —**o'pen·ness** *n.*

o·pen-air (o'pən·âr') *adj.* Occurring, done, etc., out of doors: an *open-air* concert.

o·pen-and-shut (ō'pən·ən·shut') *adj.* *Informal* Obvious; easily determined.

open door The policy of giving to all nations the same commercial privileges. —**o·pen-door** (ō'pən·dôr') *adj.*

o·pen-eyed (ō'pən·īd') *adj.* 1. Having the eyes open; aware; watchful. 2. Amazed: in *open-eyed* wonder.

o·pen-faced (ō'pən·fāst') *adj.* 1. Having an honest face. 2. Having a face or side uncovered: an *open-faced* sandwich.

o·pen·hand·ed (ō'pən·han'did) *adj.* Giving freely.

o·pen·heart·ed (ō'pən·här'tid) *adj.* Frank; candid.

o·pen-hearth (ō'pən·härth') *adj.* *Metall.* Designating a steel-making process in which the material is melted in a shallow furnace open at each end to admit fuel and air.

o·pen-heart surgery (ō'pən·härt') Surgery during which the heart is open and its circulatory function is performed mechanically.

open house 1. A house or a social event in which hospitality is extended to all who wish to come. 2. An occasion when a school, factory, institution, etc., is open to visitors.

o·pen·ing (ō'pən·ing) *n.* 1. The act of becoming open or of causing to be open. 2. An open space. 3. The first part or stage. 4. A first time or beginning: the play's *opening*. 5. In chess, checkers, etc., a specific series of early moves. 6. An opportunity: a job *opening*.

open market A market accessible to all buyers and sellers.

o·pen-mind·ed (ō'pən·mīn'did) *adj.* Free from prejudiced conclusions; receptive. —**o'pen-mind'ed·ly** *adv.* —**o'pen·mind'ed·ness** *n.*

open shop 1. An establishment employing both union and nonunion labor. 2. An establishment whose policy is to hire only nonunion labor.

o·pen·work (ō'pən·wûrk') *n.* Any product of art or handicraft containing numerous small openings.

op·er·a (op'ər·ə, op'rə) Plural of OPUS. —*n.* 1. A form of drama set to music in which all parts are sung. 2. An opera house. [< Ital. < L, service, work < *opus* work] —**op·er·at·ic** (op'ə·rat'ik) *adj.* —**op'er·at'i·cal·ly** *adv.*

op·er·a·ble (op'ər·ə·bəl) *adj.* 1. Capable of treatment by surgical operation. 2. Practicable. —**op'er·a·bil'i·ty** *n.*

opera glass Small binoculars suitable for use at the theater. Also **opera glasses.**

opera house A theater adapted for performance of operas.

op·er·ate (op'ə·rāt) *v.* **·at·ed, ·at·ing** *v.i.* 1. To act or function; work. 2. To bring about the proper or intended effect. 3. *Surg.* To perform an operation. 4. To carry on a military or naval operation: usu. with *against*. —*v.t.* 5. To control the working of, as a machine. 6. To manage or conduct the affairs of. 7. To bring about or cause; effect. [< L *operari* to work] —**op'er·at'a·ble** *adj.*

op·er·a·tion (op'ə·rā'shən) *n.* 1. The act or process of operating. 2. A method of operating; mode of action. 3. A transaction, esp. in the stock market. 4. A course or series of acts to effect a certain purpose; process. 5. The state of being in action. 6. *Surg.* The removal or repair of diseased or injured parts of the body by means of surgery. 7. *Math.* Any procedure, as multiplication, addition, etc., that results in a change in the value or form of a quantity. 8. A military or naval campaign.

op·er·a·tion·al (op'ə·rā'shən·əl) *adj.* 1. Pertaining to an operation. 2. Checked and serviced for ready operation.

op·er·a·tive (op'ər·ə·tiv, -ə·rā'tiv) *adj.* 1. Exerting force or influence. 2. Moving or working efficiently; effective. 3. Being in operation or in force. 4. Connected with surgical operations. 5. Concerned with practical work, mechanical or manual. —*n.* 1. A skilled worker, as in a mill or factory. 2. *Informal* A detective. —**op'er·a·tive·ly** *adv.*

op·er·a·tor (op'ə·rā'tər) *n.* 1. One who operates a machine or mechanism; esp., one who operates a telephone switchboard. 2. One who runs a commercial or industrial establishment.

op·e·ret·ta (op'ə·ret'ə) *n.* A type of short, humorous opera with dialogue: also called *light opera*. [< Ital., dim. of *opera*]

o·phid·i·an (ō·fid'ē·ən) *n.* One of a group of limbless reptiles with jaws connected by elastic ligaments; a serpent or snake. —*adj.* Snakelike. [< Gk. *ophis* serpent]

oph·thal·mi·a (of·thal'mē·ə) *n.* *Pathol.* Inflammation of the eye, its membranes, or its lids. Also **oph·thal'my** (-mē). [< Gk. *ophthalmos* eye]

oph·thal·mic (of·thal'mik) *adj.* Of or pertaining to the eye.

ophthalmo- *combining form* Eye; pertaining to the eyes. [< Gk. *ophthalmos* eye]

oph·thal·mol·o·gy (of'thal·mol'ə·jē) *n.* The science dealing with the structure, functions, and diseases of the eye. —**oph·thal'mo·log'ic** (-mə·loj'ik) or **·i·cal** *adj.* —**oph'thal·mol'o·gist** *n.*

oph·thal·mo·scope (of·thal'mə·skōp) *n.* An optical instrument for viewing the center of the eye. —**oph·thal'mo·scop'ic** (-skop'ik) or **·i·cal** *adj.* —**oph·thal·mos·co·py** (of'thal·mos'kə·pē) *n.*

-opia *combining form* *Med.* A (specified)

defect of the eye, or condition of sight: *myopia.* [< Gk. *ōps, ōpos* the eye]

o·pi·ate (*n.* ō′pē·it, -āt; *v.* ō′pē·āt) *n.* 1. Medicine containing opium or one of its derivatives. 2. Something inducing relaxation or sleep. —*v.t.* **·at·ed, ·at·ing** 1. To treat with opium or an opiate. 2. To deaden; dull. —**o′pi·ate** (-it, -āt) *adj.*

o·pine (ō·pīn′) *v.t. & v.i.* **o·pined, o·pin·ing** To hold or express as an opinion: now usu. humorous. [< L *opinari* to think, suppose]

o·pin·ion (ə·pin′yən, ō-) *n.* 1. A conclusion or judgment held with confidence, but falling short of positive knowledge. 2. An expert judgment given formally. 3. An evaluation. 4. A prevailing sentiment: public *opinion.* [< L *opinari* to think]

o·pin·ion·at·ed (ə·pin′yən·ā′tid, ō-) *adj.* Obstinately attached to one's own opinion. —**o·pin′ion·at′ed·ness** *n.*

o·pi·um (ō′pē·əm) *n.* A narcotic drug obtained from the unripe capsules of the **opium poppy,** containing a mixture of alkaloids, including morphine. [< Gk. *opion* opium, dim. of *opos* vegetable juice]

o·pos·sum (ə·pos′əm, pos′əm) *n.* A tree-dwelling American marsupial, having a tail and feet adapted for grasping. [< Algonquian]

op·po·nent (ə·pō′nənt) *n.* One who opposes another, as in battle; antagonist. [< L *ob-* against + *ponere* to place] —**op·po′·nen·cy** *n.*

op·por·tune (op′ər·to͞on′, -tyo͞on′) *adj.* Timely; suitable. [< L *opportunus* favorable, lit., (a wind) blowing towards port] —**op′·por·tune′ly** *adv.* —**op′por·tune′ness** *n.*

op·por·tu·nist (op′ər·to͞o′nist, -tyo͞o′-) *n.* One who uses every opportunity to contribute to the achievement of some end, with little concern for principles or sentiment. —**op′por·tu·nis′tic** *adj.* —**op′por·tu′nism** *n.*

op·por·tu·ni·ty (op′ər·to͞o′nə·tē, -tyo͞o′-) *n. pl.* **·ties** 1. A fit or convenient time. 2. Favorable circumstance. 3. A chance for advancement in business.

op·pos·a·ble (ə·pō′zə·bəl) *adj.* 1. Capable of being placed opposite something else: said esp. of the thumb. 2. That can be opposed. —**op·pos′a·bil′i·ty** *n.*

op·pose (ə·pōz′) *v.* **·posed, ·pos·ing** *v.t.* 1. To act or be in opposition to; resist. 2. To set in opposition or contrast. 3. To place before or in front. —*v.i.* 4. To act or be in opposition. [< L *ob-* against + *ponere* to place] —**op·pos′er** *n.*

op·po·site (op′ə·zit) *adj.* 1. Situated or placed on the other side, or on each side. 2. Facing or moving the other way: *opposite* directions. 3. Contrary in tendency or character: *opposite* opinions. —*n.* Something or someone that is opposite. —*adv.* In an opposite or complementary direction or position. —*prep.* 1. Across from; facing. 2. Complementary to, as in theatrical roles: He played *opposite* her. [< L *oppositus.* See OPPOSE.] —**op′po·site·ly** *adv.* —**op′po·site·ness** *n.*

op·po·si·tion (op′ə·zish′ən) *n.* 1. The act of opposing or resisting. 2. The state of being opposite or opposed; antithesis. 3. A position confronting another or a placing in contrast. 4. That which is or furnishes an obstacle to some result. —**op′po·si′tion·al** *adj.* —**op′po·si′tion·ist** *n.*

op·press (ə·pres′) *v.t.* 1. To burden or keep down by harsh and unjust use of force or authority. 2. To lie heavily upon physically or mentally. [ult. < L *ob-* against + *premere* to press] —**op·pres′sor** *n.*

op·pres·sion (ə·presh′ən) *n.* 1. The act of oppressing, or the state of being oppressed. 2. Mental depression. 3. That which oppresses.

op·pres·sive (ə·pres′iv) *adj.* 1. Burdensome; tyrannical; harsh. 2. Producing a state of oppression. —**op·pres′sive·ly** *adv.* —**op·pres′sive·ness** *n.*

op·pro·bri·ous (ə·prō′brē·əs) *adj.* 1. Contemptuously abusive. 2. Shameful; disgraceful. —**op·pro′bri·ous·ly** *adv.* —**op·pro′bri·ous·ness** *n.*

op·pro·bri·um (ə·prō′brē·əm) *n.* 1. The state of being scornfully reproached. 2. Reproach mingled with disdain. 3. A cause of disgrace or reproach. [< L *ob-* against + *probum* disgrace]

opt (opt) *v.i.* To choose; decide. [< L *optare*]

op·tic (op′tik) *adj.* Pertaining to the eye or vision. [< Gk. *optikos*]

op·ti·cal (op′ti·kəl) *adj.* 1. Pertaining to optics. 2. Of or pertaining to eyesight. 3. Designed to assist or improve vision. —**op′ti·cal·ly** *adv.*

optical maser *Physics* A laser.

op·ti·cian (op·tish′ən) *n.* One who makes or deals in optical goods.

op·tics (op′tiks) *n.pl.* (*construed as sing.*) The science that deals with light, vision, and sight.

op·ti·mal (op′tə·məl) *adj.* Most favorable; best.

op·ti·mism (op′tə·miz′əm) *n.* 1. A disposition to look on the bright side of things. 2. The doctrine that everything is constantly tending toward a better state. [< L *optimus* best] —**op′ti·mist** (-mist) *n.* —**op′ti·mis′tic** or **·ti·cal** *adj.* —**op′ti·mis′ti·cal·ly** *adv.*

op·ti·mum (op′tə·məm) *n. pl.* **·ma** or **·mums** The condition or degree producing the best result. —*adj.* Producing the best results. [< L, neut. of *optimus* best]

op·tion (op′shən) *n.* 1. The right or power of choosing; discretion. 2. The act of choosing. 3. The purchased privilege of either buying or selling something at a specified price within a specified time. 4. A thing that is or can be chosen. [< L *optare* to choose]

op·tion·al (op′shən·əl) *adj.* Not required. —**op′tion·al·ly** *adv.*

op·tom·e·try (op·tom′ə·trē) *n.* The profession of measuring vision and prescribing corrective lenses to compensate for visual defects. —**op·tom′e·trist** *n.*

op·u·lent (op′yə·lənt) *adj.* 1. Possessing great wealth. 2. Plentiful; abundant; profuse. [< L *opulentus* < *ops, opis* power, wealth] —**op′u·lence** *n.* —**op′u·lent·ly** *adv.*

o·pus (ō′pəs) *n. pl.* **op·er·a** (op′ər·ə, op′rə) A literary or musical work or composition. [< L, work]

or (ôr, *unstressed* ər) *conj.* Introducing an alternative: stop *or* go: Will you take milk *or* coffee? [OE *oththe*]

-or[1] *suffix of nouns* The person or thing

performing the action expressed in the root verb: *competitor*. [< L *-or, -ator*]

-or[2] *suffix of nouns* Quality, state, or condition: *favor*. [< L]

or·a·cle (ôr′ə·kəl, or′-) *n.* 1. A priest who gave out prophecies inspired by a deity. 2. A person of unquestioned wisdom or knowledge. 3. A wise saying. [< L *oraculum* < *orare* to speak, pray]

o·rac·u·lar (ô·rak′yə·lər) *adj.* 1. Of or pertaining to an oracle. 2. Obscure; enigmatic. 3. Prophetic; farseeing. —**o·rac′u·lar′i·ty** (-lar′ə·tē) *n.* —**o·rac′u·lar·ly** *adv.*

o·ral (ôr′əl) *adj.* 1. Uttered through the mouth; spoken. 2. Of or pertaining to the mouth; also, situated at or near the mouth. 3. Taken by mouth. —*n. Usu. pl.* An academic examination in which the student speaks his answers aloud. [< L *os, oris* mouth] —**o′ral·ly** *adv.*

or·ange (ôr′inj, or′-) *n.* 1. A round, juicy fruit with a reddish yellow rind and a sweetish pulp. 2. Any of the evergreen trees yielding this fruit. 3. A reddish yellow color. [< OF, ult. < Persian *nārang*] —**or′ange** *adj.*

or·ange·ade (ôr′inj·ād′, or′-) *n.* A beverage made of orange juice, sugar, and water.

orange pekoe A black tea from India, Ceylon, and Java.

or·ange·wood (ôr′inj·wo͝od′, or′-) *n.* The fine-grained, yellowish wood of the orange tree, used in lathe work.

o·rang·u·tan (ə·rang′ə·tan) *n. pl.* **·tans** or **·tan** A large anthropoid ape of Borneo and Sumatra, having brownish red hair and extremely long arms. Also **o·rang′**, **o·rang′ou·tang** (-ə·tang). [< Malay *orañ* man + *utan* forest]

o·rate (ôr′āt, ô·rāt′) *v.i.* **o·rat·ed, o·rat·ing** To speak in an overly elaborate or pompous manner.

o·ra·tion (ô·rā′shən) *n.* An elaborate public speech, esp. one given at a formal occasion. [< L *orare* to speak]

or·a·tor (ôr′ə·tər, or′-) *n.* One who delivers an oration; an eloquent public speaker.

or·a·to·ri·o (ôr′ə·tôr′ē·ō, or′-) *n. pl.* **·os** A large musical composition for solo voices, chorus, and orchestra, usu. based on a sacred story. [< Ital. See ORATORY[2].]

or·a·to·ry[1] (ôr′ə·tôr′ē, or′-) *n.* 1. The art of public speaking; eloquence. 2. Eloquent language. [< L *oratoria*] —**or′a·tor′i·cal** *adj.* —**or′a·tor′i·cal·ly** *adv.*

or·a·to·ry[2] (ôr′ə·tôr′ē, or′-) *n. pl.* **·ries** A place for prayer; private chapel. [< LL *oratorium* (*templum*) (temple) for prayer]

orb (ôrb) *n.* 1. A rounded mass; a sphere. 2. Anything circular. [< L *orbis* circle]

or·bic·u·lar (ôr·bik′yə·lər) *adj.* 1. Having the form of an orb. 2. *Bot.* Circular, as a leaf. Also **or·bic′u·late** (-lit, -lāt), **or·bic′u·lat′ed**. [< L *orbiculus*, dim. of *orbis* circle] —**or·bic′u·lar′i·ty** (-lar′ə·tē) *n.* —**or·bic′u·lar·ly** *adv.*

or·bit (ôr′bit) *n.* 1. The path in space along which a heavenly body or artificial satellite moves about its center of attraction. 2. A range of influence or action. —*v.t. & v.i.* To move or cause to move in an orbit, as an artificial satellite. [< L *orbita* track of a wheel < *orbis* wheel, circle] —**or′bi·tal** *adj.*

or·bit·er (ôr′bit·ər) *n.* One who or that which orbits; esp., an artificial satellite.

or·chard (ôr′chərd) *n.* An area containing trees grown for their products, as fruit, nuts, etc.; also, the trees. [OE *ort-geard* garden]

or·ches·tra (ôr′kis·trə) *n.* 1. A comparatively large group of musicians playing together. 2. In a theater, the area in front of the stage, occupied by the musicians: also **orchestra pit**. 3. The main floor of a theater. [< Gk. *orchēstra* dancing space] —**or·ches·tral** (ôr·kes′trəl) *adj.* —**or·ches′tral·ly** *adv.*

or·ches·trate (ôr′kis·trāt) *v.t.* **·trat·ed, ·trat·ing** 1. To compose or arrange (music) for an orchestra. 2. To organize or direct (diverse elements or aspects) to produce a desired continuity: *orchestrate* a political campaign. —**or′ches·tra′tion** *n.*

or·chid (ôr′kid) *n.* 1. Any of a family of herbs of temperate regions, having bulbous roots and often very showy flowers. 2. A pale purple color. [< L *orchis* < Gk., orig., a testicle; so called because of the shape of its rootstocks]

or·dain (ôr·dān′) *v.t.* 1. To order or decree. 2. To predestine: said of God, fate, etc. 3. To invest with ministerial or priestly functions. [< L *ordinare* to set in order] —**or·dain′er** *n.*

or·deal (ôr·dēl′) *n.* A severe test of character or endurance. [OE *ordāl, ordēl* judgment < *or-* out + *dǣl* a deal]

or·der (ôr′dər) *n.* 1. A methodical, proper, or harmonious arrangement of things. 2. Established method, procedure, or condition. 3. A command, direction, or regulation. 4. A style of classical architecture; also, the architectural column representing the style. 5. A commission or instruction to supply, purchase, or sell something; also, that which is supplied or purchased. 6. A body of persons united by some common bond: the *Order* of Odd Fellows. 7. *Eccl.* **a** *Usu. pl.* Any of the various grades or degrees of the Christian ministry. **b** The rite or sacrament of ordination. 8. *Biol.* A taxonomic category ranking next below the class, and above the family. —**in order** 1. In accordance with rule or proper procedure. 2. Neat; tidy. —**in order that** So that; to the end that. —**in order to** For the purpose of. —**in short order** Quickly. —**on order** Ordered but not yet delivered. —**on the order of** Similar to. —**out of order** 1. Not in working condition. 2. Not in proper arrangement or sequence. 3. Not according to rule. 4. Not suitable or appropriate. —**to order** According to the buyer's specifications. —*v.t.* 1. To give a command or direction to. 2. To give an order that (something be done). 3. To put in an orderly arrangement. —*v.i.* 4. To give an order or orders. [< L *ordo, -inis* row, series, order] —**or′der·er** *n.*

or·der·ly (ôr′dər·lē) *adj.* 1. Having regard for arrangement, method, or system. 2. Peaceful. 3. Characterized by neatness and order. 4. Pertaining to orders. —*n. pl.* **·lies** 1. A hospital attendant. 2. A soldier detailed to carry orders. —*adv.* Methodically; regularly. —**or′der·li·ness** *n.*

or·di·nal (ôr′də·nəl) *adj.* Denoting position in an order or succession. —*n.* An ordinal number. [< L *ordo, -inis* order]

ordinal number *Math.* A number that shows the order of a unit in a given series, as first, second, third, etc.: distinguished from *cardinal number.*
or·di·nance (ôr′də·nəns) *n.* 1. An order, decree, or law of a municipal body. 2. A religious rite or ceremony. [< L *ordinare* to set in order]
or·di·nar·i·ly (ôr′də·ner′ə·lē) *adv.* 1. In ordinary cases; usually. 2. In the usual manner. 3. To the usual extent; normally.
or·di·nar·y (ôr′də·ner′ē) *adj.* 1. Of common or everyday occurrence; usual. 2. According to an established order; normal. 3. Common in rank or degree; average; commonplace. —*n. pl.* **·nar·ies** That which is usual or common. **—out of the ordinary** Not common or usual; extraordinary. [< L *ordinarius* regular, usual] **—or′di·nar′i·ness** *n.*
or·di·nate (ôr′də·nit) *adj.* Characterized by order; regular. —*n. Math.* 1. The distance of any point from the X-axis, measured on a line parallel to the Y-axis in a coordinate system. 2. The line or number indicating such distance.
or·di·na·tion (ôr′də·nā′shən) *n.* 1. *Eccl.* The rite of consecration to the ministry. 2. The state of being ordained, regulated, or settled.
ord·nance (ôrd′nəns) *n.* 1. Military weapons, ammunition, and other materiel. 2. Cannon or artillery. [Contr. of ORDINANCE]
or·dure (ôr′jər) *n.* Excrement; feces. [< OF *ord* foul, nasty < L *horridus* bristling]
ore (ôr) *n.* A natural substance, as a rock, containing a valuable metal or nonmetallic mineral. [OE *ār, ǣr* brass, copper]
o·reg·a·no (ō·reg′ə·nō) *n.* A perennial herb of the mint family, having aromatic leaves used as a seasoning. [< L *origanum* wild marjoram]
or·gan (ôr′gən) *n.* 1. A musical instrument with pipes and reeds made to sound by means of compressed air controlled by keyboards and knobs. 2. Any musical instrument resembling this. 3. Any part of a plant or animal performing some definite function. 4. A newspaper or periodical published in the interest of a special group. [< Gk. *organon* instrument]
or·gan·dy (ôr′gən·dē) *n. pl.* **·dies** A thin, crisp, transparent cotton muslin. Also **or′gan·die.** [< F *organdi*]
or·gan·ic (ôr·gan′ik) *adj.* 1. Of, pertaining to, or of the nature of animals and plants. 2. Affecting or altering the structure of an organ or part: *organic* disease: distinguished from *functional.* 3. *Chem.* Of or pertaining to compounds containing carbon. 4. Inherent in or pertaining to the fundamental structure of something. 5. Grown without artificial fertilizers, pesticides, etc. Also **or·gan′i·cal.** [< Gk. *organon* instrument] **—or·gan′i·cal·ly** *adv.*
organic chemistry The branch of chemistry dealing with compounds containing carbon.
or·gan·ism (ôr′gən·iz′əm) *n.* 1. A living animal or plant. 2. Anything similar to a living thing: the social *organism.*
or·gan·ist (ôr′gən·ist) *n.* One who plays the organ.
or·gan·i·za·tion (ôr′gən·ə·zā′shən, -ī·zā′-) *n.* 1. The act of organizing, or the state of being organized; also, that which is organized. 2. A number of individuals systematically united for some end or work. Also *Brit.* **or′gan·i·sa′tion.**
or·gan·ize (ôr′gən·īz) *v.* **·ized, ·iz·ing** *v.t.* 1. To bring together or form as a whole or combination, as for a common objective. 2. To arrange systematically; order. 3. To furnish with organic structure. 4. To enlist (workers) in a trade union. 5. To unionize the workers of (a factory, etc.). —*v.i.* 6. To form or join an organization. Also *Brit.* **or′gan·ise. —or′gan·iz′a·ble** *adj.* **—or′gan·iz′er** *n.*
or·gan·za (ôr·gan′zə) *n.* A sheer, crisp fabric of silk, rayon, etc. [Prob. var. of *Lorganza,* a trade mark]
or·gasm (ôr′gaz·əm) *n. Physiol.* The acme of excitement at the culmination of a sexual act. [< Gk. *orgaein* to swell] **—or·gas·mic** (ôr·gaz′mik) *adj.*
or·gy (ôr′jē) *n. pl.* **·gies** 1. Wild or wanton revelry. 2. A party characterized by promiscuous sexual behavior. 3. Any excessive indulgence. [Earlier *orgies,* pl. < L *orgia* < Gk., secret rites] **—or′gi·as′tic** (-as′tik) *adj.*
o·ri·el (ôr′ē·əl) *n.* A bay window, esp. one built out from a wall and resting on a bracket or similar support. [< OF *oriol* porch, gallery]
o·ri·ent (*n.* ôr′ē·ənt; *v.* ôr′ē·ent) *n.* The east. —*v.t.* 1. To cause to face or turn to the east. 2. To place or adjust, as a map, in exact relation to the points of the compass. 3. To adjust in relation to a situation, institution, etc. [< L (*sol*) *oriens, -entis* rising (sun)]
O·ri·ent (ôr′ē·ənt) 1. The countries east of Europe; esp., eastern Asia. 2. The eastern hemisphere.
o·ri·en·tal (ôr′ē·en′təl) *adj.* 1. Of or pertaining to the East, or to the countries constituting the Orient. 2. Very bright, clear, and pure: said of gems. **—o′ri·en′tal·ly** *adv.*
O·ri·en·tal (ôr′ē·en′təl) *adj.* Of or pertaining to the Orient; Eastern. —*n.* An inhabitant of Asia; an Asian.
o·ri·en·ta·tion (ôr′ē·en·tā′shən) *n.* 1. The act of orienting, or the state of being oriented. 2. A meeting or series of meetings designed to acquaint newcomers with the rules, programs, etc., of a school, business, etc.
o·ri·en·ted (ôr′ē·en·tid) *adj.* Directed or centered: Society is child *oriented.*
or·i·en·teer·ing (ôr′ē·en·tēr′ing) *n.* Cross-country racing through an unknown area guided by map and compass. [< Sw. *orientering* < F *orienter* to fix a location]
or·i·fice (ôr′ə·fis, or′-) *n.* An opening into a cavity; aperture. [< L *os, oris* mouth + *facere* to make]
or·i·flamme (ôr′ə·flam) *n.* 1. The red banner used as a battle standard by the kings of France until the 15th c. 2. Any flag or standard. [< F < OF *orie* golden + *flambe* banner]
or·i·ga·mi (ôr′i·gä′mē) *n.* The ancient Japanese art of folding single sheets of paper into the forms of animals, flowers, etc. [< Japanese]
or·i·gin (ôr′ə·jin, or′-) *n.* 1. The beginning of the existence of anything. 2. A primary source; cause. 3. Parentage; ancestry. [< L *origo, -inis* source, beginning]
o·rig·i·nal (ə·rij′ə·nəl) *adj.* 1. Of or

belonging to the beginning, origin, or first stage of existence of a thing. 2. Produced by one's own mind; not copied or imitative. 3. Able to produce new works without imitating others; creative; inventive. —*n.* 1. The first form of anything. 2. An original work, as distinct from a reproduction or copy. 3. A person of unique character or genius. —**o·rig′i·nal′i·ty** (-nal′ə·tē) *n.* —**o·rig′i·nal·ly** *adv.*

o·rig·i·nate (ə·rij′ə·nāt) *v.* **·nat·ed, ·nat·ing** *v.t.* 1. To bring into existence; create; initiate. —*v.i.* 2. To come into existence; arise. —**o·rig′i·na′tion** *n.* —**o·rig′i·na′tive** *adj.* —**o·rig′i·na′tive·ly** *adv.* —**o·rig′i·na′tor** *n.*

o·ri·ole (ôr′ē·ōl) *n.* 1. Any of a family of black and yellow birds of the Old World, related to the crows. 2. Any of various black and yellow American songbirds that build hanging nests. [< L *aureolus*, dim. of *aureus* golden]

O·ri·on (ō·rī′ən) *n.* A constellation. [after *Orion*, the hunter in Greek and Roman mythology who pursued the Pleiades]

or·i·son (ôr′i·zən, or′-) *n. Usu. pl.* A devotional prayer. [< LL *oratio, -onis* prayer]

or·mo·lu (ôr′mə·lo͞o) *n.* Any of various alloys of copper, tin, and zinc that resemble gold in appearance, used in furniture decorations, jewelry, etc. [< F *or* gold + *moulu*, pp. of *moudre* to grind]

or·na·ment (*n.* ôr′nə·mənt; *v.* ôr′nə·ment) *n.* 1. Something that adorns or beautifies; a decoration. 2. Ornaments, collectively. 3. *Music* A tone or group of tones used to embellish a melody without materially affecting its harmonic content. —*v.t.* 1. To furnish with ornaments; decorate. 2. To be an ornament to. [< L *ornare* to adorn] —**or′na·men·ta′tion** *n.* —**or′na·ment′er** *n.*

or·na·men·tal (ôr′nə·men′təl) *adj.* Of the nature of or serving as an ornament. —*n.* An ornamental object; esp., a plant used as decoration. —**or′na·men′tal·ly** *adv.*

or·nate (ôr·nāt′) *adj.* 1. Elaborately or excessively ornamented; overdecorative. 2. Florid or showy, as a style of writing. [< L *ornatus*, pp. of *ornare* to adorn] —**or·nate′ly** *adv.* —**or·nate′ness** *n.*

or·ner·y (ôr′nər·ē, ôrn′rē) *adj. Dial.* 1. Contrary or stubborn. 2. Mean; ugly. 3. Ordinary; common. [Alter. of ORDINARY] —**or′ner·i·ness** *n.*

or·ni·thol·o·gy (ôr′nə·thol′ə·jē) *n.* The branch of zoology that treats of birds. [< Gk. *ornis, ornithos* bird + -LOGY] —**or′ni·tho·log′ic** (-thə·loj′ik) or **·i·cal** *adj.* —**or′ni·tho·log′i·cal·ly** *adv.* —**or′ni·thol′o·gist** *n.*

o·rog·e·ny (ô·roj′ə·nē) *n. Geol.* The process of mountain formation. Also **or·o·gen·e·sis** (ôr′ō·jen′ə·sis). [< Gk. *oros* mountain + -GENY] —**or·o·gen·ic** (ôr′ə·jen′ik) *adj.*

o·ro·tund (ôr′ə·tund) *adj.* 1. Full, clear, rounded, and resonant: said of the voice. 2. Pompous; inflated, as a manner of speech. [< L *os, oris* mouth + *rotundus* round] —**o′ro·tun′di·ty** *n.*

or·phan (ôr′fən) *n.* A child whose parents are dead; also, less commonly, a child with one surviving parent. —*adj.* 1. That is an orphan. 2. Of or for orphans. —*v.t.* To make an orphan of. [< Gk. *orphanos* orphaned] —**or′phan·hood** *n.*

or·phan·age (ôr′fən·ij) *n.* An institution for the care of orphans or other abandoned children.

or·pine (ôr′pin) *n.* Any of a large, widely distributed family of plants, as the **common** or **garden orpine,** having succulent stems and leaves and clusters of whitish flowers. Also **or′pin.**

or·ris (ôr′is, or′-) *n.* Any of the several species of iris having a scented root. Also **or′rice.** [Prob. alter. of Ital. *ireos* < L *iris* iris]

ort (ôrt) *n. Usu. pl. Archaic* or *Dial.* A worthless scrap or leaving, as of food. [ME; ult. origin uncertain]

or·thi·con (ôr′thi·kon) *n.* A sensitive television camera tube using low-velocity electrons in scanning. Also **or·thi·con·o·scope** (or′thi·kon′ə·skōp).

ortho- *combining form* 1. Straight; in line. 2. At right angles; perpendicular. 3. Correct; proper; right: *orthography.* 4. *Med.* The correction of irregularities or deformities of: *orthopedics.* Also, before vowels, **orth-.** [< Gk. *orthos* straight]

or·tho·clase (ôr′thō·klās, -klāz) *n.* A brittle, vitreous, potassium-aluminum silicate of the feldspar group. [< ORTHO- + Gk. *klasis* fracture]

or·tho·don·tics (ôr′thə·don′tiks) *n.* The branch of dentistry concerned with the prevention and correction of irregularities of the teeth. Also **or′tho·don′tia** (-don′shə, -shē·ə). [< ORTHO- + Gk. *odous, odontos* tooth] —**or′tho·don′tic** *adj.* —**or′tho·don′tist** *n.*

or·tho·dox (ôr′thə·doks) *adj.* Holding the commonly accepted or established views or beliefs, esp. in religion; correct or sound in doctrine. [< ORTHO- + Gk. *doxa* opinion] —**or′tho·dox′ly** *adv.* —**or′tho·dox′y** *n.*

Or·tho·dox (ôr′thə·doks) *adj.* 1. Of, belonging to, or characteristic of the Eastern Orthodox Church. 2. Designating any of the bodies in this Church.

Orthodox Church The Eastern Orthodox Church.

Orthodox Judaism The branch of Judaism that accepts the Mosaic Laws and their authoritative rabbinical interpretations in the Talmud and elsewhere as binding for today.

or·thog·ra·phy (ôr·thog′rə·fē) *n. pl.* **·phies** 1. A mode or system of spelling, esp. of spelling correctly. 2. The study dealing with letters and spelling. [< Gk. *orthographos*] —**or·thog′ra·pher, or·thog′ra·phist** *n.* —**or·tho·graph·ic** (ôr′thə·graf′ik) or **·i·cal** *adj.* —**or′tho·graph′i·cal·ly** *adv.*

or·tho·pe·dics (ôr′thə·pē′diks) *n.pl.* (*construed as sing.*) The branch of surgery concerned with the correction of deformities of the skeletal system. Also **or′tho·pae′dics, or·tho·pe·dy** (ôr′thə·pē′dē). [< ORTHO- + Gk. *paideia* rearing of children] —**or′tho·pe′dic** *adj.* —**or′tho·pe′dist** *n.*

or·thop·ter·an (ôr·thop′tə·rən) *n.* An orthopterous insect. Also **or·thop′ter·on.**

or·thop·ter·ous (ôr·thop′tər·əs) *adj.* Designating any of an order of insects with membranous hind wings and leathery, usu. straight fore wings, including locusts, crickets, grasshoppers, etc. [< ORTHO- + Gk. *pteron* wing]

or·to·lan (ôr′tə·lən) *n.* A bunting of Europe, having an olive green head and a yellow throat. [< F < L *hortulus*, dim. of *hortus* garden]

-ory[1] *suffix of nouns* A place or instrument for (performing the action of the main element): *dormitory, lavatory.* [< OF *-oir, -oire.* See -ORY[2].]

-ory[2] *suffix of adjectives* Related to; like; resembling: *amatory, laudatory.* [< F *-oir, -oire* or < L *-orius, -oria, -orium*]

o·ryx (ôr′iks, or′-) *n. pl.* **o·ryx·es** or **o·ryx** Any of several long-horned antelopes, as the Arabian oryx and the gemsbok. [< Gk.]

os[1] (os) *n. pl.* **o·ra** (ôr′ə) *Anat.* A mouth or opening. [< L]

os[2] (os) *n. pl.* **os·sa** (os′ə) *Anat.* A bone. [< L]

O·sage (ō′sāj) *n.* 1. One of a tribe of Siouan Indians orig. living in the Ohio River valley. 2. The language of this tribe. [< Siouan *Wazhazhe* war people]

os·cil·late (os′ə·lāt) *v.i.* **·lat·ed, ·lat·ing** 1. To swing back and forth, as a pendulum. 2. To fluctuate; hesitate; waver. [< L *oscillare* to swing] **—os′cil·la′tion** *n.* **—os′cil·la′tor** *n.* **—os′cil·la·to′ry** (-lə·tôr′ē) *adj.*

os·cil·lo·graph (ə·sil′ə·graf) *n.* A device for recording and measuring any oscillating system convertible into wave forms, as sound, light, heartbeats, etc.

os·cil·lo·scope (ə·sil′ə·skōp) *n.* Any of various electronic instruments displaying electromagnetic waves on a fluorescent screen.

os·cine (os′in, -īn) *adj.* Of or belonging to a suborder of birds, including those having the most highly developed vocal ability, as thrushes, sparrows, etc. **—***n.* An oscine bird. [< L *oscen, oscinis* singing bird]

Os·co-Um·bri·an (os′kō·um′brē·ən) *n.* A branch of the Italic subfamily of Indo-European languages.

os·cu·late (os′kyə·lāt) *v.t.* & *v.i.* **·lat·ed, ·lat·ing** 1. To kiss: used humorously. 2. To come into close contact or union. 3. *Biol.* To have (characteristics) in common. [< L *osculari* to kiss] **—os′cu·la′tion** *n.* **—os′cu·la·to′ry** (-lə·tôr′ē) *adj.*

-ose[1] *suffix of adjectives* 1. Full of or abounding in (the main element): *verbose.* 2. Like; resembling (the main element): *grandiose.* [< L *-osus*]

-ose[2] *suffix Chem.* Indicating a sugar or other carbohydrate: *lactose, fructose.*

O·see (ō′zē, ō′sē) The Douai Bible name for HOSEA.

o·sier (ō′zhər) *n.* Any of various willows producing long, flexible shoots used in wickerwork. [< OF]

-osis *suffix of nouns* 1. The condition, process, or state of: *metamorphosis.* 2. *Med.* **a** A diseased or abnormal condition of: *neurosis.* **b** A formation of: *sclerosis.* [< Gk.]

-osity *suffix of nouns* Forming nouns corresponding to adjectives in *-ose*: *verbosity.* [< L]

os·mi·um (oz′mē·əm, os′-) *n.* A hard, brittle, extremely heavy, white metallic element (symbol Os) of the platinum group. [< Gk. *osmē* odor]

os·mo·sis (oz·mō′sis, os-) *n. Chem.* 1. The diffusion of a fluid through a semipermeable membrane, resulting in equalization of concentrations on each side. 2. The tendency of a fluid to act in such a manner. Also **os′mose.** [< Gk. *ōsmos* < *ōthein* to impel] **—os′mose** *v.i.* **·mosed, ·mos·ing —os·mot·ic** (oz·mot′ik, os-) *adj.* **—os·mot′i·cal·ly** *adv.*

os·prey (os′prē) *n.* An American hawk, brown above and white below, that preys upon fish. [ME < L *os, ossis* bone + *frangere* to break]

os·sif·er·ous (o·sif′ər·əs) *adj.* Yielding or containing bones. [< L *os, ossi(s)* + *ferre* to bear]

os·si·fy (os′ə·fī) *v.t.* & *v.i.* **·fied, ·fy·ing** 1. To convert or be converted into bone. 2. To make or become rigid or inflexible in habits, beliefs, etc.; harden. [< L *os, ossis* bone + *facere* to make] **—os·sif·ic** (o·sif′ik) *adj.* **—os′si·fi·ca′tion** *n.*

os·te·al (os′tē·əl) *adj.* Of, pertaining to, or like bone; bony. [< Gk. *osteon* bone]

os·ten·si·ble (os·ten′sə·bəl) *adj.* Offered as real or genuine; apparent. [< L *ostendere* to show] **—os·ten′si·bly** *adv.*

os·ten·sive (os·ten′siv) *adj.* Manifest; apparent; ostensible. **—os·ten′sive·ly** *adv.*

os·ten·ta·tion (os′tən·tā′shən) *n.* 1. The act of displaying vainly or pretentiously. 2. Excessive exhibition; showiness. [< L *ostendere* to show] **—os′ten·ta′tious** *adj.* **—os′ten·ta′tious·ly** *adv.* **—os′ten·ta′tious·ness** *n.*

osteo- *combining form* Bone; pertaining to bone or bones. Also, before vowels, **oste-.** [< Gk. *osteon* bone]

os·te·ol·o·gy (os′tē·ol′ə·jē) *n.* The study of the skeleton and of the structure of bones. **—os′te·o·log′i·cal** (-ə·loj′i·kəl) *adj.* **—os′te·ol′o·gist** *n.*

os·te·o·ma (os′tē·ō′mə) *n. pl.* **·o·mas** or **·o·ma·ta** (-ō′mə·tə) *Pathol.* A tumor of bony tissue. [< OSTE(O)- + -OMA]

os·te·o·my·e·li·tis (os′tē·ō·mī′ə·lī′tis) *n. Pathol.* Suppurative inflammation of the bone, sometimes involving the marrow. [< OSTEO- + MYEL(O)- + -ITIS]

os·te·op·a·thy (os′tē·op′ə·thē) *n.* A system of healing based on the theory that many diseases are the result of structural abnormalities of the body and may be cured by manipulation of the affected parts. [< OSTEO- + -PATHY] **—os·te·o·path** (os′tē·ə·path′), **os′te·op′a·thist** *n.* **—os·te·o·path·ic** (os′tē·ə·path′ik) *adj.*

ost·mark (ôst′märk′) *n.* The standard monetary unit of East Germany.

os·tra·cize (os′trə·sīz) *v.t.* **·cized, ·ciz·ing** 1. To shut out or exclude, as from society or from a particular group; banish. 2. To exile by ostracism. Also *Brit.* **os′tra·cise.** [< Gk. *ostrakizein* < *ostrakon* potsherd, shell, used in ancient Greece to vote for banishment] **—os′tra·cism** *n.*

os·trich (ôs′trich, os′-) *n. pl.* **·trich·es** or **·trich** A two-toed, flightless bird of Africa and Arabia, the largest of existing birds. [< L *avis* bird + LL *struthio* ostrich]

Os·we·go tea (os·wē′gō) A species of mint with bright red flowers.

oth·er (u*th*′ər) *adj.* 1. Different, esp. from the one or ones specified or implied. 2. Noting the remaining one of two persons or things: the *other* eye. 3. Additional; more. 4. Alternate; second: every *other* day. 5. Former: in *other* times. **—***pron.* 1. Another or different person or thing. 2. The other person or thing: this hand, not the *other.*

—*adv.* Differently; otherwise: with *than.* [OE *ōther*] —**oth′er·ness** *n.*

oth·er·wise (uth′ər·wīz′) *adv.* 1. In a different manner; by other means. 2. In other circumstances or conditions. 3. In all other respects: an *otherwise* sensible person. —*adj.* Other than supposed; different.

oth·er·world·ly (uth′ər·wûrld′lē) *adj.* Concerned with matters of the spirit or intellect, esp. to the neglect of material things. —**oth′er·world′li·ness** *n.*

-otic *suffix of adjectives* 1. *Med.* Of, related to, or affected by: corresponding to nouns in *-osis*: *sclerotic.* 2. Causing or producing: *narcotic.* [< Gk. *-ōtikos*]

o·ti·ose (ō′shē·ōs, -tē-) *adj.* 1. Being at rest; indolent; lazy. 2. Having no use or effect; futile. [< L *otiosus* idle] —**o′ti·ose′ly** *adv.* —**o′ti·os′i·ty** (-os′ə·tē) *n.*

o·ti·tis (ō·tī′tis) *n. Pathol.* Inflammation of the ear. [< Gk. *ous, ōtos* ear + -ITIS]

o·tol·o·gy (ō·tol′ə·jē) *n.* The science of the ear and its diseases. [< Gk. *ous, ōtos* ear + -LOGY] —**o·to·log·i·cal** (ō′tə·loj′i·kəl) *adj.* —**o·tol′o·gist** *n.*

Ot·ta·wa (ot′ə·wə) *n.* One of a tribe of Algonquian Indians, originally inhabiting the region around Georgian Bay, Lake Huron, and Ontario. [< dial. F *otauan*; ult. < Algonquian. Akin to Cree *atâweu* a trader.]

ot·ter (ot′ər) *n.* 1. Any of various web-footed aquatic mammals with a long, flattened tail. 2. Its dark brown fur. [OE *otor*]

ot·to·man (ot′ə·mən) *n.* 1. An upholstered, armless seat or sofa, usu. without a back. 2. A cushioned footrest. [< OTTOMAN]

Ot·to·man (ot′ə·mən) *n. pl.* **·mans** A Turk. [< Arabic *'Othmāni* of Osman, name of founder of the Ottoman dynasty, d. 1326] —**Ot′to·man** *adj.*

ou·bli·ette (o͞o′blē·et′) *n.* A secret dungeon with an entrance only through the top. [< OF < *oublier* to forget]

ouch (ouch) *interj.* An exclamation of sudden pain.

ought (ôt) *v. Present 3rd person sing.* **ought** An auxiliary followed by the infinitive with *to* expressed or understood, meaning: 1. To have a moral duty: A person *ought* to keep his promises. 2. To be advisable: You *ought* to be careful. 3. To be expected as something probable, natural, or logical: The engine *ought* to run. [OE past tense of *āgan* to owe]

ou·gui·ya (o͞o·gē′yə) *n.* The monetary unit of Mauretania.

Oui·ja (wē′jə) *n.* A board inscribed with the alphabet and other characters and over which moves a small board resting on three legs, which is thought to spell out mediumistic communications: a trade name. Also **oui′ja.**

ounce (ouns) *n.* 1. A unit of weight; $^1/_{16}$ pound avoirdupois or 28.349 grams; $^1/_{12}$ pound troy or 31.1 grams. 2. A fluid ounce. 3. A small quantity. [< L *uncia* twelfth part (of a pound or foot)]

our (our) *pronominal adj.* The possessive case of the pronoun *we*, used attributively: *our* child. [OE *ūre*, gen. of *wē*]

ours (ourz) *pron.* 1. The possessive case of the pronoun *we*, used predicatively: That dog is *ours.* 2. The one or ones belonging or relating to us: their country and *ours.* —**of ours** Belonging or relating to us.

our·self (our·self′) *pron.* Myself or ourselves, considered collectively: used in formal or regal contexts.

our·selves (our·selvz′) *pron.pl.* A form of the first person plural pronoun, used: 1. As a reflexive: We helped *ourselves.* 2. As an emphatic or intensive form of *we*: We *ourselves* want to know. 3. As a designation of a normal, proper, or usual state: We weren't *ourselves* then.

-ous *suffix of adjectives* 1. Full of; having; given to; like: *joyous, glorious.* 2. *Chem.* Having a lower valence than that indicated by *-ic*: said of elements in compounds: *nitrous* oxide. [< OF < L *-osus*]

ou·sel (o͞o′zəl) See OUZEL.

oust (oust) *v.t.* To force out or remove, as from a place or position. [< LL *ob-* against + *stare* to stand]

oust·er (ous′tər) *n.* 1. The act or condition of ousting. 2. One who ousts.

out (out) *adv.* 1. Away from the inside or center. 2. In or into the open air. 3. Away from a specified or usual place: *out* to lunch. 4. From a container or source: to pour *out* wine. 5. From among others: to pick *out.* 6. So as to remove, deplete, or exhaust: to sweep *out.* 7. Thoroughly: tired *out.* 8. Into extinction or inactivity: The excitement died *out.* 9. To a conclusion; to the end: Hear me *out.* 10. Into being or activity, or into a perceptible form: The sun came *out.* 11. In or into circulation: to bring *out* a new edition. 12. Aloud and boldly: to speak *out.* 13. So as to be extended or projecting: to lean *out.* 14. Into the care or control of another or others: to deal *out* cards. 15. Into a state of tension, irritation, etc.: to be put *out* over trifles. 16. In or into a condition of disuse or obsolescence. 17. In baseball, so as to be or count as an out. 18. *Informal* Into unconsciousness: to pass *out.* —**out and away** By far; incomparably. —**out of** 1. From the inside of; from among. 2. Beyond the limits, scope, or usual position of: *out of* sight; *out of* joint. 3. From (a material, etc.): made *out of* tin. 4. Inspired or caused by: *out of* pity. 5. Without (any): *out of* breath. —**out to** With the intention of. —*adj.* 1. External; exterior. 2. Irregular: an *out* size. 3. Not in working order. 4. At a financial loss: *out* five dollars. 5. Not to be considered: That method is altogether *out.* 6. Distant; outlying. 7. Not in office or in power. 8. No longer in use; out-of-date. —*prep.* From within; forth from: *out* the door. —*n.* 1. One who or that which is out. 2. A way of dodging responsibility or involvement: to look for an *out.* 3. In baseball, the retirement of a batter or base runner. —**on the outs** (or **at outs**) Involved in a disagreement; at odds. —*v.i.* To come out; be revealed: Murder will *out.* —*interj.* Get out! Away! [OE *ūt*]

out- *combining form* 1. Living or situated outside; away from the center; detached: *outlying, outpatient.* 2. Going forth; outward: *outbound, outstretch.* 3. To a greater extent; more; better.

Out (def. 3) is used to form compounds, as in the list below.

outact **outbeg**
outargue **outbellow**
outbalance **outblaze**
outbargain **outbluff**

outblush
outbluster
outboast
outbox
outbrag
outbrazen
outbuild
outbully
outcharm
outclimb
outcook
outcurse
outdazzle
outdress
outdrink
outeat
outfight
outflatter
outgallop
outgamble
outglitter
outgrin
outguess
outhear
outjump
outlast
outlaugh
outlearn
outlinger
outmaneuver
outmarch
outperform
outplay
outpopulate
outpreach
outprice
outproduce
outquote
outrank
outrival
outrun
outsatisfy
outscold
outscream
outshout
outshriek
outsleep
outsparkle
outstare
outstay
outstretch
outstrive
outswagger
outswear
outswindle
outtalk
outtrick
outvalue
outvoice
outvote
outweep
outwrestle
outyell
outyield

out·age (out′ij) *n.* An accidental break in operation, as of electrical power.

out-and-out (out′ən·out′) *adj.* Unqualified; outright.

out·bid (out·bid′) *v.t.* **·bid, ·bid·den** or **·bid, ·bid·ding** To offer a higher bid than.

out·board (out′bôrd′) *adj. & adv. Naut.* 1. Outside the hull. 2. Away from the center line of a vessel.

outboard motor A portable motor for attachment to the stern of a small boat.

out·bound (out′bound′) *adj.* Outward bound.

out·break (out′brāk′) *n.* A sudden bursting forth, as of an emotion or a disease; an eruption.

out·build·ing (out′bil′ding) *n.* A building separate from and subordinate to a main building, as a woodshed or barn.

out·burst (out′bûrst′) *n.* A bursting out; esp., a sudden and violent display, as of anger.

out·cast (out′kast′) *n.* 1. One who is cast out or excluded. 2. A homeless person or vagabond. 3. Anything cast out, as refuse. **—***adj.* Rejected; discarded; forlorn.

out·class (out·klas′) *v.t.* To surpass decisively.

out·come (out′kum′) *n.* Consequence or result.

out·crop (*n.* out′krop′; *v.* out·krop′) *n. Geol.* 1. The exposure at or above the surface of the ground of any rock stratum, vein, etc. 2. The rock so exposed. **—***v.i.* **·cropped, ·crop·ping** To crop out above the ground, as rocks.

out·cry (*n.* out′krī′; *v.* out·krī′) *n. pl.* **·cries** 1. A loud cry or clamor. 2. A vehement outburst of alarm, indignation, etc. **—***v.t.* **·cried, ·cry·ing** To surpass in noise or crying.

out·date (out·dāt′) *v.t.* **·dat·ed, ·dat·ing** To make obsolete or out-of-date.

out·dat·ed (out·dā′tid) *adj.* Out-of-date; old-fashioned.

out·dis·tance (out·dis′təns) *v.t.* **·tanced, ·tanc·ing** 1. To outrun, as in a race; outstrip. 2. To surpass completely.

out·do (out·do͞o′) *v.t.* **·did, ·done, ·do·ing** To exceed in performance; surpass. **—out·do′er** *n.*

out·door (out′dôr′) *adj.* 1. Being or done in the open air. 2. Intended for the outdoors. Also *out-of-door.*

out·doors (out·dôrz′) *adv.* Outside of the house; in the open air. **—***n.* The world beyond the house; the open air. Also *out-of-doors.*

out·er (ou′tər) *adj.* 1. Being on the exterior side. 2. Farther from a center or the inside.

out·er·most (ou′tər·mōst) *adj.* Most remote from the inside or inner part; farthest out.

outer space The space beyond the extreme limits of the earth's atmosphere.

out·face (out·fās′) *v.t.* **·faced, ·fac·ing** 1. To face or stare down. 2. To defy or confront fearlessly or impudently.

out·field (out′fēld′) *n.* In baseball: **a** The space beyond the infield. **b** The outfielders collectively.

out·field·er (out′fēl′dər) *n.* In baseball, any of three players whose positions are in the outfield.

out·fit (out′fit′) *n.* 1. The tools or equipment needed for any particular purpose, as a trade, etc. 2. *Informal* A group of persons regarded as a unit; esp., a military unit. 3. *Informal* A set of clothing. **—***v.t. & v.i.* **·fit·ted, ·fit·ting** To provide with or acquire an outfit. **—out′fit′ter** *n.*

out·flank (out·flangk′) *v.t.* To get around the flank of; flank.

out·flow (out′flō′) *n.* 1. That which flows out. 2. The act or process of flowing out.

out·fox (out·foks′) *v.t. Informal* To outwit.

out·go (*v.* out·gō′; *n.* out′gō′) *v.t.* **·went, ·gone, ·go·ing** To go farther than; exceed. **—***n. pl.* **·goes** 1. That which goes out; outlay. 2. The act of going out. **—out′go′er** *n.*

out·go·ing (out′gō′ing) *adj.* 1. Going out; leaving. 2. Friendly; expansive. **—***n.* The act of going out.

out-group (out′gro͞op′) *n. Sociol.* Those not in an in-group.

out·grow (out·grō′) *v.t.* **·grew, ·grown, ·grow·ing** 1. To grow too large for. 2. To lose or get rid of in the course of time or growth: to *outgrow* a habit. 3. To surpass in growth.

out·growth (out′grōth′) *n.* 1. That which grows out of something else; an excrescence. 2. A natural result or development. 3. The process of growing out.

out·house (out′hous′) *n.* An outdoor toilet.

out·ing (ou′ting) *n.* 1. A short pleasure trip; an excursion. 2. The act of going out; an airing.

out·land·er (out′lan′dər) *n.* 1. A foreigner. 2. A stranger.

out·land·ish (out·lan′dish) *adj.* 1. Strange or unfamiliar. 2. *Informal* Freakish; crazy. 3. Far-off; remote. [OE *ūtland*] **—out·land′ish·ly** *adv.* **—out·land′ish·ness** *n.*

out·law (out′lô′) *n.* 1. One who habitually breaks or defies the law; a criminal. 2. One deprived of the protection or benefit of the law. **—***v.t.* 1. To prohibit; ban. 2. To deprive of legal force or protection, as a contract.

3. To declare (a person) an outlaw. [OE < ON *ūtlagi*] **—out′law′ry** *n.*
out·lay (*n.* out′lā′; *v.* out·lā′) *n.* 1. The act of disbursing or spending. 2. The amount spent; expenditure. *—v.t.* **·laid, ·lay·ing** To expend (money, etc.).
out·let (out′let) *n.* 1. A passage or vent for escape or discharge. 2. A channel of expression or escape. 3. In commerce, a market for any commodity; also, a store handling the goods of a particular manufacturer. 4. *Electr.* The point in a wiring system at which the current is taken to supply electrical apparatus.
out·line (out′līn′) *n.* 1. *Sometimes pl.* A sketch of the principal features of a thing; general plan. 2. A systematic statement of the structure or content of an essay, etc. 3. The bordering line that defines a figure. 4. A sketch made of such lines. *—v.t.* **·lined, ·lin·ing** 1. To make an outline of. 2. To draw the outline of.
out·live (out·liv′) *v.t.* **·lived, ·liv·ing** 1. To live longer than. 2. To live through; survive.
out·look (out′lo͝ok′) *n.* 1. A point of view. 2. The prospects of a thing. 3. A place where something is viewed. 4. The expanse in view.
out·mo·ded (out·mō′did) *adj.* Out of fashion.
out·most (out′mōst′) *adj.* Farthest out; outermost.
out-of-date (out′əv·dāt′) *adj.* Old-fashioned; archaic.
out-of-door (out′əv·dôr′) *adj.* Outdoor.
out-of-doors (out′əv·dôrz′) *adv.* & *n.* Outdoors.
out-of-the-way (out′əv·thə·wā′) *adj.* 1. Remote; difficult to reach; secluded. 2. Out of the common range; odd.
out·pa·tient (out′pā′shənt) *n.* A patient treated at but not formally admitted to a hospital, dispensary, etc.
out·post (out′pōst′) *n.* 1. A detachment of troops stationed at a distance from the main body as a guard against surprise attack. 2. The station occupied by such troops. 3. Any outlying settlement, as at a frontier.
out·pour (*v.* out·pôr′; *n.* out′pôr′) *v.t.* & *v.i.* To pour out. *—n.* A free outflow. **—out′·pour′ing** *n.*
out·put (out′po͝ot′) *n.* 1. The amount of anything produced in a given time. 2. The effective work done by a machine. 3. *Electr.* The electrical energy delivered by a generator, circuit, amplifier, etc.
out·rage (*n.* out′rāj′; *v.* out·rāj′) *n.* 1. An act of shocking violence, cruelty, immorality, or indecency. 2. A profound insult or injury. 3. A state of anger over an outrageous act. *—v.t.* **·raged, ·rag·ing** 1. To commit an outrage upon. 2. To provoke to anger by an outrage. 3. To rape. [< OF *ultrage* excess, ult. < L *ultra* beyond]
out·ra·geous (out·rā′jəs) *adj.* 1. Of the nature of an outrage; awful; atrocious. 2. Heedless of authority or decency. **—out·ra′geous·ly** *adv.* **—out·ra′geous·ness** *n.*
ou·tré (o͞o·trā′) *adj.* *French* Strikingly odd; exaggerated.
out·reach (*v.* out·rēch′; *n.* out′rēch′) *v.t.* 1. To reach or go beyond; surpass. 2. To extend (something). *—v.i.* 3. To reach out. *—n.* The act or extent of reaching out.
out·ride (out·rīd′) *v.t.* **·rode, ·rid·den, ·rid·ing** To ride faster, farther, or better than.
out·rid·er (out′rī′dər) *n.* A mounted attendant who rides in advance or to one side of a carriage.
out·rig·ger (out′rig′ər) *n.* 1. A part that projects beyond a natural outline, as of a vessel or machine, esp. the projection terminating in a float, braced to the side of a canoe to prevent capsizing. 2. A boat having an outrigger.
out·right (*adj.* out′rīt′; *adv.* out′rīt′) *adj.* 1. Free from reserve or restraint; downright. 2. Complete; entire. *—adv.* 1. Without reservation or limitation; openly. 2. Entirely; utterly. 3. Without delay.
out·sell (out·sel′) *v.t.* **·sold, ·sell·ing** 1. To sell more readily than. 2. To sell more goods than.
out·set (out′set′) *n.* A beginning; start.
out·shine (out·shīn′) *v.t.* **·shone, ·shin·ing** 1. To shine brighter than. 2. To surpass.
out·side (*n., adj., & adv.* out′sīd′; *prep.* out′sīd′) *n.* 1. The outer or exterior surface or side. 2. The space beyond a bounding line or surface. 3. The part that is seen; outward appearance. 4. Mere outward display. **—at the outside** *Informal* At the farthest, longest, or most. *—adj.* 1. Pertaining to, located on, or restricted to the outside. 2. Originating, caused by, or situated beyond designated limits or boundaries. 3. Reaching the limit; extreme: an *outside* estimate. 4. Slight; slim: an *outside* possibility. *—adv.* 1. On or to the outside; externally. 2. Beyond the outside limits of. 3. Outdoors. *—prep.* 1. On or to the exterior of. 2. Beyond the limits of. **—outside of** 1. *Informal* Except. 2. Outside.
out·sid·er (out′sī′dər) *n.* One who is excluded.
out·size (out′sīz′) *n.* An irregular size, as of clothing; esp., an uncommonly large size. **—out′size′, out′sized′** *adj.*
out·skirts (out′skûrts′) *n.pl.* A place remote from the main area.
out·smart (out·smärt′) *v.t.* *Informal* To outwit; fool.
out·spo·ken (out′spō′kən) *adj.* Bold in speech; frank. **—out′spo′ken·ly** *adv.* **—out′·spo′ken·ness** *n.*
out·spread (out·spred′) *v.t.* & *v.i.* **·spread, ·spread·ing** To spread out; extend.
out·stand·ing (out·stan′ding) *adj.* 1. Prominent; excellent. 2. Still standing or unsettled, as a debt. 3. Projecting; abutting.
out·strip (out·strip′) *v.t.* **·stripped, ·strip·ping** 1. To leave behind; outrun. 2. To excel; surpass.
out·ward (out′wərd) *adj.* 1. Of, pertaining to, or leading to the outside; external. 2. Superficially evident or readily apparent: no *outward* sign of trouble. *—adv.* Toward the outside: also **out′wards.** [OE *ūtweard*] **—out′ward·ness** *n.*
out·ward·ly (out′wərd·lē) *adv.* 1. On or toward the outside. 2. In outward form or aspect; seemingly.
out·wear (out·wâr′) *v.t.* **·wore, ·worn, ·wear·ing** 1. To wear or stand use longer than; outlast. 2. To wear out.
out·weigh (out·wā′) *v.t.* 1. To weigh more than. 2. To exceed in importance, value, etc.
out·wit (out·wit′) *v.t.* **·wit·ted, ·wit·ting** To trick or baffle by superior cunning.

out·work[1] (out·wûrk′) *v.t.* **·worked** or **·wrought, ·work·ing** To work faster or better than.

out·work[2] (out′wûrk′) *n. Mil.* Any outer defense, as beyond the ditch of a fort.

out·worn (out·wôrn′) Past participle of OUTWEAR. **—*adj.*** Outmoded.

ou·zel (o͞o′zəl) *n.* One of various European thrushes, as the blackbird. Also spelled *ousel.* [OE *ōsle*]

ou·zo (o͞o′zō) *n.* A colorless, unsweetened Greek liqueur, flavored with aniseed.

o·va (ō′və) Plural of OVUM.

o·val (ō′vəl) *adj.* 1. Having the shape of an egg. 2. Resembling an ellipse. **—*n.*** An oval shape or figure. [< L *ovum* egg] **—o′val·ly** *adv.* **—o′val·ness** *n.*

o·va·ry (ō′və·rē) *n. pl.* **·ries** 1. *Zool.* The genital gland of female animals in which the ova are produced. 2. *Bot.* In plants, that organ in which the ovules are contained. [< L *ovum* egg] **—o·var·i·an** (ō·ver′ē·ən), **o·var·i·al** (ō·ver′ē·əl) *adj.*

o·vate (ō′vāt) *adj. Bot.* Egg-shaped: said of leaves. [< L *ovum* egg] **—o′vate·ly** *adv.*

o·va·tion (ō·vā′shən) *n.* A spontaneous acclamation of popularity; enthusiastic applause. [< L *ovare* to rejoice, exult] **—o·va′·tion·al** *adj.*

ov·en (uv′ən) *n.* An enclosed chamber for baking, heating, or drying. [OE *ofen*]

ov·en·bird (uv′ən·bûrd′) *n.* A North American warbler, having a grassy nest suggesting an oven.

o·ver (ō′vər) *prep.* 1. In or to a place or position above; higher than. 2. So as to pass or extend across: walking *over* a bridge. 3. On the other side of: *over* the ocean. 4. Upon the surface or exterior of. 5. Here and there upon or within: traveling *over* land and sea. 6. At or up to a level higher than: water *over* one's head. 7. So as to close or cover. 8. During or beyond: Stay *over* Christmas. 9. More than; in excess of. 10. In preference to. 11. In a position to guide or control. 12. With regard to: time wasted *over* trifles. **—over and above** In addition to; besides. **—*adv.*** 1. Above; overhead. 2. To another or opposite side, or to a specified place; across: Try to leap *over*!; Bring your friend *over*. 3. At or on the other side; at a distance in a specified direction or place: *over* in France. 4. From one side, opinion, or attitude to another. 5. From one person, condition, or custody to another. 6. So as to close, cover, or be covered: The pond froze *over*. 7. From beginning to end: I'll think the matter *over*. 8. So as to bring the underside upward. 9. From an upright position. 10. Once more; again. 11. So as to constitute a surplus: to have some left *over*. 12. Beyond or until a stated time. **—over and over** Time and again; repeatedly. **—*adj.*** 1. Finished; done; past. 2. On the other side; having got across. 3. Outer; superior; upper. 4. In excess or addition; extra. [OE *ofer*]

over- *combining form* 1. Above; superior: *overlord.* 2. Passing above; going beyond the top or limit of: *overflow.* 3. Excessively; excessive.

Over- (def. 3) is widely used to form compounds, as in the list starting below.

o·ver·act (ō′vər·akt′) *v.t. & v.i.* To act with exaggeration.

o·ver·age[1] (ō′ver·ij) *n.* In commerce, an amount of money or goods in excess of that which is listed as being on hand.

o·ver·age[2] (ō′vər·āj′) *adj.* 1. Over a specified age. 2. Too old to be of use.

o·ver·all (ō′vər·ôl′) *adj.* Including or covering everything.

o·ver·alls (ō′vər·ôlz′) *n.pl.* Loose, coarse trousers, often with suspenders and a piece extending over the breast.

o·ver·arm (ō′vər·ärm′) *adj.* Done with the arm above the level of the shoulder.

o·ver·awe (ō′vər·ô′) *v.t.* **·awed, ·aw·ing** To subdue or restrain by awe.

o·ver·bal·ance (*v.* ō′vər·bal′əns; *n.* ō′vər·bal′əns) *v.t.* **·anced, ·anc·ing** 1. To exceed in weight, importance, etc. 2. To cause to lose balance. **—*n.*** Excess of weight or value.

o·ver·bear·ing (ō′vər·bâr′ing) *adj.* 1. Arrogant; domineering. 2. Overwhelming. **—o′·ver·bear′ing·ly** *adv.*

o·ver·blown (ō′vər·blōn′) *adj.* 1. Blown up or swollen, as with conceit; bombastic. 2. Past full bloom, as a flower.

o·ver·board (ō′vər·bôrd′) *adv.* Over the side of or out of a boat or ship. **—to go overboard** *Informal* To be extremely enthusiastic about someone or something.

overabundance
overabundant
overaccentuate
overactive
overambitious
overambitiously
overanalyze
overanxious
overapprehensive
overassertive
overassess
overassessment
overattached
overattentive
overattentively
overbake
overbid
overbold
overboldly
overborrow
overbred
overbreed
overbuild
overbusy
overbuy
overcapable
overcareful
overcaring
overcautious
overcautiously
overcharitable
overcivilized
overclean
overcompensate
overcompetitive
overcomplacent
overcompliant
overconcern
overconfidence
overconfident
overconscientious
overconservative
overconsiderate
overconsumption
overcook
overcount
overcourteous
overcritical
overcrowd
overcurious
overdecorate
overdelicate
overdelicately
overdevelop
overdevoted
overdiligent
overdiscipline
overdiversify
overdramatic
overdress
overdrink
overeager
overeat
overeducated
overembellish
overemotional
overemphasis
overemphasize
overenthusiastic
overestimate
overexcitable
overexcite
overexercise
overexert
overexertion
overexpand
overexpectant
overexuberant
overfamiliar
overfastidious
overfed
overfeed
overfill
overfond
overfull
overfulness
overfurnish
overgeneralize
overgenerous
overgraze
overhastily
overhasty

o·ver·bur·den (ō′vər·bûr′dən) *v.t.* To load with too much weight, care, etc.
o·ver·cap·i·tal·ize (ō′vər·kap′i·təl·īz′) *v.t.* **·ized, ·iz·ing** 1. To invest capital in to an extent not warranted by actual prospects. 2. To affix an unjustifiable or unlawful value to the nominal capital of (a corporation). 3. To estimate the value of (a property, company, etc.) too highly. —**o′ver·cap′i·tal·i·za′tion** *n.*
o·ver·cast (ō′vər·kast′; *for v., also* ō′vər·kast′) *adj.* Covered or obscured, as with clouds. —*n.* 1. A covering or mantle, as of clouds. 2. *Meteorol.* A cloud or clouds covering more than nine-tenths of the sky. —*v.t.* & *v.i.* **·cast, ·cast·ing** To make or become overcast.
o·ver·charge (*v.* ō′vər·chärj′; *n.* ō′vər·chärj′) *v.t.* **·charged, ·charg·ing** 1. To charge too high a price. 2. To overburden. —*n.* An excessive charge.
o·ver·cloud (ō′vər·kloud′) *v.t.* & *v.i.* To cover or become covered with clouds; darken.
o·ver·coat (ō′vər·kōt′) *n.* An outdoor coat worn over a suit, etc., esp. in cold weather.
o·ver·come (ō′vər·kum′) *v.t.* **·came, ·come, ·com·ing** 1. To get the better of in a conflict; conquer. 2. To prevail over or surmount, as difficulties. 3. To render (someone) helpless, as by emotion, sickness, etc. —*v.i.* 4. To gain mastery; win. [OE *ofercuman*]
o·ver·do (ō′vər·do͞o′) *v.t.* **·did, ·done, ·do·ing** 1. To do excessively; exaggerate. 2. To overtax the strength of; exhaust. 3. To cook too much, as meat. [OE *oferdōn*]
o·ver·dose (*v.* ō′vər·dōs′; *n.* ō′vər·dōs′) *v.t.* **·dosed, ·dos·ing** To dose to excess. —*n.* An excessive dose.
o·ver·draft (ō′vər·draft′) *n.* 1. The act of overdrawing an account, as at a bank. 2. The amount by which an account is overdrawn. Also *Brit.* **o′ver·draught′.**
o·ver·draw (ō′vər·drô′) *v.t.* **·drew, ·drawn, ·draw·ing** 1. To draw against (an account) beyond one's credit. 2. To draw or strain excessively, as a bow. 3. To exaggerate.
o·ver·drive (*v.* ō′vər·drīv′; *n.* ō′vər·drīv′) *v.t.* **·drove, ·driv·en, ·driv·ing** To drive too hard or too far. —*n. Mech.* A gearing device that turns a drive shaft at a speed greater than that of the engine, thus decreasing power output.
o·ver·due (ō′vər·do͞o′, -dyo͞o′) *adj.* Past due; that should have arrived, been paid, etc., earlier.
o·ver·ex·pose (ō′vər·ik·spōz′) *v.t.* **·posed, ·pos·ing** 1. To expose excessively. 2. *Photog.* To expose (a film or plate) too long. —**o′ver·ex·po′sure** (-spō′zhər) *n.*
o·ver·flight (ō′vər·flīt′) *n.* The flight of an aircraft over a place or region, esp. for reconnaissance or espionage.
o·ver·flow (*v.* ō′vər·flō′; *n.* ō′vər·flō′) *v.* **·flowed, ·flown, ·flow·ing** *v.i.* 1. To flow or run over the brim or bank, as water, rivers, etc. 2. To be filled beyond capacity; superabound. —*v.t.* 3. To flow over the brim or bank of. 4. To flow or spread over; cover; flood. 5. To cause to overflow. —*n.* 1. The act or process of overflowing. 2. That which flows over. 3. The amount by which a capacity is exceeded; surplus. 4. An outlet for liquid. [OE *oferflōwan*]
o·ver·grow (ō′vər·grō′) *v.* **·grew, ·grown, ·grow·ing** *v.t.* 1. To grow over; cover with growth. 2. To grow too big for; outgrow. —*v.i.* 3. To increase excessively; grow too large.
o·ver·hand (ō′vər·hand′) *adj.* Executed with the hand above the level of the elbow or the shoulder. Also **o′ver·hand′ed.** —*adv.* In an overhand manner. —*n.* An overhand stroke or delivery, as in tennis.
o·ver·hang (ō′vər·hang′) *v.* **·hung, ·hang·ing** *v.t.* 1. To hang or project over; jut over. 2. To threaten; menace. —*v.i.* 3. To hang or jut over something. —*n.* An overhanging portion of a structure; also, the amount of such projection.
o·ver·haul (*v.* ō′vər·hôl′; *n.* ō′vər·hôl′) *v.t.* 1. To examine for needed repairs. 2. To repair; renovate. 3. To catch up with; gain on. —*n.* A thorough inspection and repair: also **o′ver·haul′ing.**
o·ver·head (*adj.* & *n.* ō′vər·hed′; *adv.* ō′vər·hed′) *adj.* 1. Situated or working above the level of one's head. 2. Of or relating to the overhead of a business. —*n.* The operating expenses of a business, as rent, light, heat, taxes, etc. —*adv.* Over or above the head.

overheat
overholy
overidealistic
overimaginative
overimpress
overindulge
overindulgence
overindulgent
overindustrialize
overinflate
overinsure
overinvest
overkind
overlarge
overliberal
overlofty
overlong
overloud
overluxuriant
overluxurious
overmild
overmix
overmodest
overneat
overnice
overoptimistic
overpatriotic
overpay
overpessimistic
overplump
overpopulate
overpopulated
overpraise
overpriced
overproduce
overproduction
overproductive
overprotect
overprovide
overpublicize
overpunish
overqualified
overrank
overreact
overreadiness
overrefine
overrefined
overrefinement
overreligious
overripe
oversalty
overscrupulous
overseason
overseasoned
oversensitive
overseverely
oversimplification
oversimplify
overslow
oversmall
oversolicitous
oversophistication
overspecialization
overspend
oversqueamish
overstimulate
overstimulation
overstock
overstrain
overstress
overstrict
overstrong
overstudious
oversubscribe
oversubtle
oversubtlety
oversusceptible
oversuspicious
oversuspiciously
oversweet
overtax
overtechnical
overtire
overtrain
overtrustful
overuse
overvalue
overvehement
overweight
overwide
overzeal
overzealous

o·ver·hear (ō′vər·hir′) *v.t.* **·heard, ·hear·ing** To hear (something said or someone speaking) without the knowledge or intention of the speaker. —**o′ver·hear′er** *n.*

o·ver·joy (ō′vər·joi′) *v.t.* To delight or please greatly.

o·ver·kill (ō′vər·kil′) *n.* 1. The military capacity for destruction far beyond the resources and population of an enemy. 2. Excess of any sort.

o·ver·land (ō′vər·land′) *adj. & adv.* Across, over, or via land.

o·ver·lap (*v.* ō′vər·lap′; *n.* ō′vər·lap′) *v.t. & v.i.* **·lapped, ·lap·ping** 1. To lie or extend partly over or upon (another or each other). 2. To cover and project beyond (something). —*n.* 1. The state or extent of overlapping. 2. The part that overlaps.

o·ver·lay (*v.* ō′vər·lā′; *n.* ō′vər·lā′) *v.t.* **·laid, ·lay·ing** 1. To cover, as with a decorative pattern or layer. 2. To lay or place over or upon something else. —*n.* Anything that covers or partly covers something.

o·ver·leaf (ō′vər·lēf′) *adv.* On the other side of a page.

o·ver·lie (ō′vər·lī′) *v.t.* **·lay, ·lain, ·ly·ing** To lie over or upon.

o·ver·load (*v.* ō′vər·lōd′; *n.* ō′vər·lōd′) *v.t.* To load excessively; overburden. —*n.* 1. An excessive burden. 2. *Electr.* An amperage in excess of that which can be safely carried.

o·ver·look (*v.* ō′vər·lo͝ok′; *n.* ō′vər·lo͝ok′) *v.t.* 1. To fail to notice; miss. 2. To disregard purposely or indulgently; ignore. 3. To look over or see from a higher place. 4. To afford a view of: The castle *overlooks* the harbor. 5. To supervise. 6. To inspect. —*n.* An elevated place affording a view.

o·ver·lord (ō′vər·lôrd′) *n.* 1. A superior lord or chief. 2. One who holds supremacy over others. —**o′ver·lord′ship** *n.*

o·ver·ly (ō′vər·lē) *adv.* To an excessive degree; too much; too.

o·ver·mas·ter (ō′vər·mas′tər) *v.t.* To overcome; overpower. —**o′ver·mas′ter·ing** *n. & adj.*

o·ver·match (*v.* ō′vər·mach′; *n.* ō′vər·mach′) *v.t.* To be more than a match for; surpass. —*n.* One who or that which is superior in strength, skill, etc.

o·ver·much (ō′vər·much′) *adj.* Excessive; too much. —*adv.* In too great a degree. —*n.* An excess; too much.

o·ver·night (ō′vər·nīt′) *adj.* 1. Done, happening, etc., during the night, esp. the previous night. 2. Done, happening, etc., in or as in one night: an *overnight* success. 3. Used for short trips: an *overnight* bag. —*adv.* During, in, or through the night or one night.

o·ver·pass (ō′vər·pas′) *n.* An elevated section of road crossing other lines of travel.

o·ver·play (ō′vər·plā′) *v.t.* 1. To play or act (a part or role) to excess. 2. To rely too much on the strength or value of.

o·ver·pow·er (ō′vər·pou′ər) *v.t.* To gain supremacy over; subdue; overcome. —**o′ver·pow′er·ing** *adj.* —**o′ver·pow′er·ing·ly** *adv.*

o·ver·rate (ō′vər·rāt′) *v.t.* **·rat·ed, ·rat·ing** To rate or value too highly; overestimate.

o·ver·reach (ō′vər·rēch′) *v.t.* 1. To reach over or beyond. 2. To defeat (oneself), as by attempting something beyond one's capability. 3. To miss by stretching or reaching too far. —*v.i.* 4. To reach too far. —**o′ver·reach′er** *n.*

o·ver·ride (ō′vər·rīd′) *v.t.* **·rode, ·rid·den, ·rid·ing** 1. To disregard summarily; supersede. 2. To ride over. 3. To trample down; suppress.

o·ver·rule (ō′vər·ro͞ol′) *v.t.* **·ruled, ·rul·ing** 1. To decide against or nullify; invalidate. 2. To disallow the arguments of (someone). 3. To prevail over.

o·ver·run (*v.* ō′vər·run′; *n.* ō′vər·run′) *v.* **·ran, ·run, ·run·ning** *v.t.* 1. To spread or swarm over, as vermin or invaders. 2. To overflow. 3. To pass the limit of. —*v.i.* 4. To run over; overflow. —*n.* 1. An instance of overrunning. 2. The amount of overrunning; esp., the cost of something in excess of the original estimate.

o·ver·seas (ō′vər·sēz′) *adv.* Beyond the sea; abroad. —*adj.* Situated, coming from, or for use beyond the sea; foreign: also **o′ver·sea′**.

o·ver·see (ō′vər·sē′) *v.t.* **·saw, ·seen, ·see·ing** 1. To direct; superintend. 2. To survey; watch. [OE *ofersēon*]

o·ver·se·er (ō′vər·sē′ər) *n.* One who supervises workers.

o·ver·sell (ō′vər·sel′) *v.t.* **·sold, ·sell·ing** 1. To sell with excessive enthusiasm or exaggerated claims. 2. To sell more of (a stock, etc.) than one can provide.

o·ver·sexed (ō′vər·sekst′) *adj.* Having or characterized by excessive sexual desire or interest.

o·ver·shad·ow (ō′vər·shad′ō) *v.t.* 1. To render unimportant or insignificant by comparison; dominate. 2. To throw a shadow over; obscure.

o·ver·shoe (ō′vər·sho͞o′) *n.* A shoe worn over another for protection against water, mud, etc.

o·ver·shoot (ō′vər·sho͞ot′) *v.* **·shot, ·shoot·ing** *v.t.* 1. To shoot or go over or beyond (the mark, target, etc.). 2. To exceed, as a limit. 3. To drive or force (something) beyond the proper limit. —*v.i.* 4. To shoot or go over or beyond the mark. 5. To go too far.

o·ver·shot (ō′vər·shot′) *adj.* 1. Projecting, as the upper jaw beyond the lower jaw. 2. Driven by water flowing over from above: an *overshot* wheel.

o·ver·sight (ō′vər·sīt′) *n.* 1. An inadvertent mistake or omission. 2. Watchful supervision.

o·ver·size (ō′vər·sīz′) *adj.* Larger than normal: also **o′ver·sized′**. —*n.* A large size.

o·ver·sleep (ō′vər·slēp′) *v.i.* **·slept, ·sleep·ing** To sleep too long.

o·ver·spread (ō′vər·spred′) *v.t.* **·spread, ·spread·ing** To extend over; cover completely.

o·ver·state (ō′vər·stāt′) *v.t.* **·stat·ed, ·stat·ing** To state in too strong terms; exaggerate. —**o′ver·state′ment** *n.*

o·ver·stay (ō′vər·stā′) *v.t.* To stay beyond the limits or duration of.

o·ver·step (ō′vər·step′) *v.t.* **·stepped, ·step·ping** To exceed (a limit).

o·ver·stuff (ō′vər·stuf′) *v.t.* 1. To stuff to excess. 2. To cover completely with deep upholstery: said of furniture.

o·ver·sup·ply (ō′vər·sə·plī′) *n.* *pl.* **·plies** An excessive supply. —**o′ver·sup·ply′** *v.t.* **·plied, ·ply·ing**

o·vert (ō·vûrt′, ō′vûrt) *adj.* 1. Open to view; observable. 2. *Law* Done with criminal intent. [< OF, pp. of *ovrir* to open] —**o·vert′ly** *adv.*

o·ver·take (ō′vər·tāk′) *v.t.* **·took, ·tak·en, ·tak·ing** 1. To catch up with. 2. To come upon suddenly.

o·ver-the-count·er (ō′vər·thə·koun′tər) *adj.* 1. Not sold on the floor of a stock exchange: said of stocks, bonds, etc. 2. Not requiring a prescription for sale: said of drugs, etc.

o·ver·throw (*v.* ō′vər·thrō′; *n.* ō′vər·thrō′) *v.t.* **·threw, ·thrown, ·throw·ing** 1. To bring down or remove from power by force; defeat; ruin. 2. To throw over or down; upset. —*n.* 1. The act of overthrowing; demolition. 2. In baseball, etc., a throwing of the ball over and beyond the player or base aimed at.

o·ver·time (ō′vər·tīm′) *n.* Time used in working beyond the specified hours. —**o′ver·time′** *adj.* & *adv.*

o·ver·tone (ō′vər·tōn′) *n.* 1. *Music* A partial tone heard with and above a fundamental tone. 2. A connotation, implication, etc., of language, thoughts, etc.

o·ver·ture (ō′vər·chər) *n.* 1. *Music* **a** An instrumental prelude to an opera or other large work. **b** Any of various orchestral pieces, often having programmatic content. 2. An act or proposal intended to initiate a relationship, negotiations, etc. [See OVERT.]

o·ver·turn (ō′vər·tûrn′) *v.t.* 1. To turn or throw over; upset. 2. To overthrow; defeat; ruin. —*v.i.* 3. To turn over; capsize. —**ov′er·turn′** *n.*

o·ver·view (ō′vər·vyo͞o′) *n.* A broad survey or review of a subject, activity, etc.

o·ver·ween·ing (ō′vər·wē′ning) *adj.* 1. Presumptiously proud or conceited. 2. Excessive; exaggerated. [OE *oferwēnan* to become insolent] —**o′ver·ween′ing·ly** *adv.*

o·ver·weigh (ō′vər·wā′) *v.t.* 1. To outweigh; overbalance. 2. To overburden; oppress.

o·ver·whelm (ō′vər·hwelm′) *v.t.* 1. To bury or submerge completely. 2. To defeat; crush. 3. To overcome; overpower. [ME *ofer-whelmen* to turn upside down] —**o′ver·whelm′ing** *adj.* —**o′ver·whelm′ing·ly** *adv.*

o·ver·work (*v.* ō′vər·wûrk′; *n.* ō′vər·wûrk′) *v.* **·worked** (*Archaic* **·wrought**), **·work·ing** *v.t.* 1. To cause to work too hard. 2. To work on or elaborate excessively. —*v.i.* 3. To work too hard. —*n.* Excessive work. [OE *oferwiercan*]

o·ver·write (ō′vər·rīt′) *v.t.* & *v.i.* **·wrote, ·writ·ten, ·writ·ing** 1. To write in too elaborate or labored a style. 2. To write too much about (a subject) or at too great length.

o·ver·wrought (ō′vər·rôt′) *adj.* 1. Worked up or excited excessively. 2. Too elaborate.

ovi- *combining form* Egg; of or pertaining to eggs: *oviparous.* Also **ovo-**. [< L *ovum* egg]

o·vi·duct (ō′vi·dukt) *n.* *Anat.* A Fallopian tube.

o·vip·a·rous (ō·vip′ər·əs) *adj.* *Zool.* Producing eggs or ova that mature and are hatched outside the body, as birds and most fishes and reptiles. [< OVI- + L *parere* to bring forth] —**o·vip′a·rous·ly** *adv.* —**o·vip′a·rous·ness** *n.*

o·vi·pos·i·tor (ō′vi·poz′ə·tər) *n.* *Entomol.* The tubular organ at the extremity of the abdomen in many insects by which the eggs are deposited. [< OVI- + L *ponere* to place]

o·void (ō′void) *adj.* Egg-shaped: also **o·voi′dal.** —*n.* An egg-shaped body.

o·vo·vi·vip·a·rous (ō′vō·vī·vip′ər·əs) *adj.* *Zool.* Producing eggs that are hatched within the parent's body, but without formation of a placenta, as some reptiles and fishes. [< OVO- + VIVIPAROUS] —**o′vo·vi·vip′a·rous·ly** *adv.* —**o′vo·vi·vip′a·rous·ness** *n.*

o·vu·late (ō′vyə·lāt) *v.i.* **·lat·ed, ·lat·ing** To produce ova; discharge ova from an ovary. [See OVULE.] —**o·vu·la′tion** *n.*

o·vule (ō′vyo͞ol) *n.* 1. *Bot.* The body within the ovary that upon fertilization becomes the seed. 2. *Zool.* An immature ovum. [< NL *ovulum*, dim. of L *ovum* egg] —**o·vu·lar** (ō′vyə·lər), **o·vu·lar·y** (ō′vyə·ler′ē) *adj.*

o·vum (ō′vəm) *n.* *pl.* **o·va** (ō′və) *Biol.* The female reproductive cell of animals, produced in the ovary. [< L]

owe (ō) *v.* **owed** (*Obs.* **ought**), **ow·ing** *v.t.* 1. To be indebted to the amount of. 2. To be obligated to render or offer. 3. To have by virtue of some condition or cause: with *to.* —*v.i.* 4. To be in debt. [OE *āgan* to own]

ow·ing (ō′ing) *adj.* Due; yet to be paid. —**owing to** Attributable to; on account of.

owl (oul) *n.* 1. A predatory nocturnal bird, having large eyes and head, a short, sharply hooked bill, and long powerful claws. 2. A person with nocturnal habits. [OE *ūle*] —**owl′ish** *adj.* —**owl′ish·ly** *adv.* —**owl′ish·ness** *n.*

owl·et (ou′lit) *n.* A small or young owl.

own (ōn) *adj.* 1. Belonging or relating to oneself: following the possessive as an intensive or to indicate the exclusion of others: my *own* horse. 2. Identifying the subject rather than indicating ownership: his *own* doctor. —**to come into one's own** 1. To obtain possession of one's property. 2. To achieve maturity or success. 3. To receive one's reward. —**to hold one's own** 1. To maintain one's place or position. 2. To keep up with one's work. 3. To remain undefeated. —**on one's own** Entirely dependent on one's self for support or success. —*v.t.* 1. To have or hold as one's own; possess. 2. To admit or acknowledge. —*v.i.* 3. To confess: with *to.* —**to own up** *Informal* To confess fully. [OE *āgan* to possess, have] —**own′a·ble** *adj.*

own·er (ō′nər) *n.* One who has the legal right to or has possession of a thing. —**own′er·less** *adj.* —**own′er·ship** *n.*

ox (oks) *n.* *pl.* **ox·en** (ok′sən) 1. An adult castrated male bovine, esp. of the domesticated species. 2. Any bovine quadruped, as a buffalo, bison, or yak. [OE *oxa*]

ox·al·ic acid (ok·sal′ik) *Chem.* A white, crystalline, poisonous compound found in plant tissues and made artificially, used in bleaching, dyeing, etc.

ox·blood (oks′blud′) *n.* A deep red color.

ox·bow (oks′bō′) *n.* 1. A bent piece of wood in an ox yoke, that forms a collar for the ox. 2. A bend in a river shaped like this.

ox·eye (oks′ī′) *n.* 1. Any of several plants of the composite family having large yellow heads. 2. The oxeye daisy. (See DAISY.) 3. Any of various shore birds, as the sandpiper. 4. An oval dormer window.

ox·ford (oks′fərd) *n.* 1. A low shoe laced at the instep: also **oxford shoe.** 2. A cotton cloth of basket weave, used for shirts. Also **Oxford.** [after *Oxford,* England]

oxford gray A very dark gray.

ox·heart (oks′härt′) *n.* A variety of sweet cherry.

ox·i·da·tion (ok′sə·dā′shən) *n. Chem.* 1. The process or state of undergoing combination with oxygen. 2. The process by which atoms lose electrons, thus increasing their valence.

ox·ide (ok′sīd, -sid) *n. Chem.* A compound of oxygen with another element. [< F < *ox(ygène)* oxygen + *(ac)ide* acid]

ox·i·dize (ok′sə·dīz) *v.* **·dized, ·diz·ing** *Chem. v.t.* 1. To convert (an element) into its oxide; combine with oxygen. 2. To increase the valence of an atom or group of atoms by the loss of electrons. —*v.i.* 3. To become oxidized. Also **ox·i·date** (ok′sə·dāt). Also *Brit.* **ox′i·dise.** —**ox′i·diz′a·ble** *adj.*

ox·tail (oks′tāl′) *n.* The tail of an ox, esp. when skinned for use in soup.

oxy-[1] *combining form* 1. Sharp; pointed; keen. 2. Acid: *oxygen.* [< Gk. *oxys* sharp, acid]

oxy-[2] *combining form Chem.* Oxygen; of or containing oxygen. [< OXYGEN]

ox·y·a·cet·y·lene (ok′sē·ə·set′ə·lēn) *adj.* Designating or pertaining to a mixture of acetylene and oxygen, used to obtain high temperatures, as in welding.

ox·y·gen (ok′sə·jin) *n.* A colorless, odorless gaseous element (symbol O), occurring free in the atmosphere, of which it forms about one-fifth by volume. It is an abundant and active element, essential for combustion and respiration. [< F *oxygène* < Gk. *oxys* acid]

ox·y·gen·ate (ok′sə·jən·āt′) *v.t.* **·at·ed, ·at·ing** To treat, combine, or impregnate with oxygen. —**ox′y·gen·a′tion** *n.*

oxygen mask A device worn over the nose and mouth, used for inhaling oxygen.

oxygen tent A tentlike canopy placed over a patient's head and shoulders, within which pure oxygen may be circulated.

ox·y·hy·dro·gen (ok′si·hī′drə·jən) *n.* A mixture of oxygen and hydrogen.

ox·y·mo·ron (ok′si·môr′on) *n. pl.* **·mo·ra** (-môr′ə) A figure of speech in which contradictory terms are brought together, as in the phrase, "*O heavy lightness, serious vanity!*" [< Gk. *oxys* sharp + *moros* foolish]

o·yez (ō′yes, ō′yez) *interj.* Hear! hear ye! an introductory word to call attention to a proclamation, as by a court crier. Also **o′yes.** [< OF < L *audire* to hear]

oys·ter (ois′tər) *n.* 1. A bivalve mollusk, found in salt and brackish water; esp., a common edible species of Europe and America. 2. An analogous bivalve, as the **pearl oyster.** —*v.i.* To gather or farm oysters. [< Gk. *ostreon*]

oyster bed A place where oysters breed or are grown.

oyster cracker A small biscuit or hard, salted cracker.

oyster white Any of several very light gray tints.

o·zo·ce·rite (ō·zō′kə·rīt, -sə-, ō′zō·sir′īt) *n.* A waxy, translucent mixture of natural hydrocarbons, used in candles, etc. Also **o·zo′ke·rite.** [< Gk. *ozein* to smell + *keros* wax]

o·zone (ō′zōn) *n.* 1. An unstable form of oxygen with a pungent odor, formed variously, as by the passage of electricity through the air. 2. *Informal* Fresh air. [< Gk. *ozein* to smell] —**o·zon·ic** (ō·zon′ik, ō·zō′nik), **o·zo·nous** (ō′zə·nəs) *adj.*

ozone layer A narrow layer in the stratosphere, containing a high concentration of ozone, and serving to screen out harmful ultraviolet rays from the sun. Also **o·zon·o·sphere** (ō·zon′·ə·sfir).

P

p, P (pē) *n. pl.* **p's or ps, P's or Ps, pees** (pēz) 1. The sixteenth letter of the English alphabet. 2. The sound represented by the letter *p*. —*symbol Chem.* Phosphorus (symbol P). —**to mind one's P's and Q's** To be careful of one's behavior.

pa (pä) *n. Informal* Papa.

pa'·an·ga (pä·äng'gä) *n.* The monetary unit of Tonga.

pab·u·lum (pab'yə·ləm) *n.* 1. Any substance giving nourishment; food. 2. Nourishment for the mind; food for thought. 3. A soft, bland cereal. 4. Tasteless, insipid writing. [< L, fodder; def. 3 after Pablum, a trademark] —**pab'u·lar** *adj.*

pace (pās) *n.* 1. A step in walking; also, the distance covered in one such movement, usu. considered to be three feet. 2. The manner or speed of movement in going on the legs; carriage and action, esp. of a horse. 3. Rate of speed, as in movement, work, etc. 4. A gait of a horse, etc., in which both feet on the same side are lifted and moved forward at once. —**to put (one) through his paces** To test the abilities, speed, etc., of. —*v.* **paced, pac·ing** *v.t.* 1. To walk back and forth across. 2. To measure by paces. 3. To set or make the pace for. —*v.i.* 4. To walk with regular steps or back and forth. 5. To go at a pace: said of a horse. [< L *passus*, pp. of *pandere* to stretch] —**pac'er** *n.*

pace·mak·er (pās'mā'kər) *n.* 1. One who makes or sets the pace for another in a race. 2. A mass of tissue in the heart that normally regulates the heartbeat. 3. An electronic device for regulating the heartbeat. —**pace'·mak'ing** *n. & adj.*

pach·y·derm (pak'ə·dûrm) *n.* Any of certain thick-skinned, nonruminant hoofed animals, esp. an elephant, hippopotamus, or rhinoceros. [< Gk. *pachys* thick + *derma* skin] —**pach'y·der'ma·tous** (-dûr'mə·təs), **pach'y·der'mous** *adj.*

pach·y·san·dra (pak'ə·san'drə) *n.* A hardy, evergreen plant cultivated as a ground cover. [< NL, with thick stamens]

pa·cif·ic (pə·sif'ik) *adj.* 1. Tending or leading to peace or conciliation. 2. Peaceful. Also **pa·cif'i·cal.** [See PACIFY.] —**pa·cif'i·cal·ly** *adv.*

Pa·cif·ic (pə·sif'ik) *adj.* Pertaining to the Pacific Ocean.

pac·i·fi·er (pas'ə·fī'ər) *n.* 1. One who or that which pacifies. 2. A rubber nipple or ring, for babies to suck or bite on.

pac·i·fist (pas'ə·fist) *n.* One who opposes war, usu. under all circumstances. —**pac'i·fism** *n.* —**pac'i·fis'tic** *adj.*

pac·i·fy (pas'ə·fī) *v.t.* **·fied, ·fy·ing** 1. To bring peace to (an area). 2. To calm; quiet; soothe. [< L *pax, pacis* peace + *facere* to make] —**pac'i·fi·ca'tion** *n.*

pack[1] (pak) *n.* 1. A bundle or large package, esp. one to be carried on the back. 2. A collection of anything; heap. 3. A full set of like or associated things, as cards. 4. A group of dogs, wolves, etc., that hunt together. 5. Any gang or band, esp. a criminal gang. 6. Any of various substances or materials applied as a compress, dressing, wrapping, etc.: an ice *pack*. —*v.t.* 1. To make a bundle of. 2. To place compactly in a trunk, box, etc., for storing or carrying. 3. To fill compactly. 4. To compress tightly; crowd together. 5. To fill to overflowing; cram. 6. To cover, fill, or surround so as to prevent leakage, damage, etc.: to *pack* a piston rod. 7. To prepare and place (food) in containers for storage or sale. 8. To carry or wear habitually: to *pack* a gun. 9. To send or dispatch summarily: with *off* or *away*. 10. *Slang* To be able to inflict: He *packs* a wallop. —*v.i.* 11. To place one's clothes and belongings in trunks, boxes, etc., for storing or carrying. 12. To be capable of being stowed or packed. 13. To crowd together. 14. To settle in a hard, firm mass. —**to send packing** To send away or dismiss summarily. [ME *pakke*, appar. < LG *pak*] —**pack'er** *n.*

pack[2] (pak) *v.t.* To arrange to one's own advantage: to *pack* a jury. [? < PACK[1]]

pack·age (pak'ij) *n.* 1. Something packed, as for transportation. 2. A box, case, etc., used for packing. 3. A combination of items considered as a unit: a legislative *package*. —*v.t.* **·aged, ·ag·ing** To arrange or tie into a package.

package store A store that sells liquor by the bottle.

pack animal An animal used to carry packs or burdens.

pack·et (pak'it) *n.* 1. A small package. 2. A steamship for conveying mail, passengers, and freight at stated times: also **packet boat.** [< AF *pacquet*, dim. of ME *pakke*]

pack·ing (pak'ing) *n.* 1. The act or operation of one who or that which packs. 2. Any material used in packing, closing a joint, stopping a wound, etc.

packing plant A factory where food, esp. meat, is processed and packed. Also **packing house.**

pack rat 1. A North American rat that carries off and hides small articles in its nest. 2. One who saves often unneeded items.

pack·sad·dle (pak'sad'l) *n.* A saddle for a pack animal, to which the packs are fastened.

pact (pakt) *n.* An agreement; compact. [< L *pactum* agreement]

pad[1] (pad) *n.* 1. A cushion; also, any stuffed, cushionlike thing. 2. A number of sheets of paper gummed together at one edge. 3. A large floating leaf of an aquatic plant: a lily *pad*. 4. A soft cushionlike enlargement of skin on the undersurface of the toes of many animals. 5. The foot of a fox, otter, etc. 6. The footprint of an animal. 7. A launch pad. 8. *Slang* Lodgings; living quarters. —*v.t.* **pad·ded, pad·ding** 1. To stuff, line, or protect with pads or padding. 2. To insert unnecessary matter into (a report, speech, etc.). 3. To add to (an expense account, voting register, etc.) for fraudulent purposes. [Origin unknown]

pad² (pad) *v.i.* **pad·ded, pad·ding** To walk, esp. with soft footsteps. —*n.* A dull, padded sound, as of a footstep. [Akin to *pad* path < LG]

pad·ding (pad′ing) *n.* 1. The act of one who or that which pads. 2. Material used to pad.

pad·dle (pad′l) *n.* 1. A broad-bladed implement resembling a short oar, used without a rowlock in propelling a canoe or small boat. 2. A flat board for inflicting bodily punishment. 3. A small, rounded, flat piece of wood with a handle, used in table tennis. —*v.* **·dled, ·dling** *v.i.* 1. To move a canoe, etc., by means of a paddle. 2. To swim or dabble in water with short, downward strokes. —*v.t.* 3. To convey or propel by means of a paddle or paddles. 4. To beat with a paddle; spank. —**to paddle one's own canoe** To be independent. [ME *padell*] —**pad′dler** *n.*

pad·dle·fish (pad′l·fish′) *n.* *pl.* **·fish** or **·fish·es** A large, scaleless fish with paddle-shaped snout.

paddle wheel A wheel having projecting floats or boards for propelling a vessel.

pad·dock (pad′ək) *n.* 1. A pasture, lot, or enclosure for exercising horses, adjoining a stable. 2. A grassy enclosure at a racecourse where horses are walked and saddled. [Alter. of dial. E *parrock*, OE *pearruc* enclosure]

pad·dy (pad′ē) *n.* *pl.* **·dies** 1. Rice in the husk, whether gathered or growing. 2. A rice field. [< Malay *pādi*]

paddy wagon *Slang* A patrol wagon.

pad·lock (pad′lok′) *n.* A detachable lock, having a pivoted hasp to be passed through a staple or ring and then locked. —*v.t.* To fasten with or as with a padlock. [ME]

pa·dre (pä′drā) *n.* 1. Father: a title used in Italy, Spain, and Spanish America in addressing or speaking of priests. 2. *Informal* A clergyman or chaplain. [< L *pater, patris* father]

pae·an (pē′ən) *n.* A song of joy or exultation. [< Gk. *paian* hymn]

pa·gan (pā′gən) *n.* 1. One who is neither a Christian, a Jew, nor a Muslim; a heathen. 2. An irreligious person. [< L, orig., villager < *pagus* the country] —**pa′gan** *adj.* —**pa′·gan·dom** *n.* —**pa′gan·ish** *adj.* —**pa′gan·ism** *n.*

page¹ (pāj) *n.* 1. A male attendant; esp., a youth in training for knighthood or attending a royal personage. 2. One employed to attend upon legislators while the legislature is in session. 3. One employed in a hotel, club, etc., to perform light duties. —*v.t.* **paged, pag·ing** To seek or summon (a person) by calling his name. [< Gk. *pais, paidos* boy]

page² (pāj) *n.* 1. One side of a leaf of a book, letter, etc. 2. The printing or the type used on one side. 3. *Usu. pl.* Any source or record of knowledge. —*v.* **paged, pag·ing** *v.t.* 1. To mark the pages of with numbers. —*v.i.* 2. To turn pages: usu. with *through*. [< L *pagina* written page]

pag·eant (paj′ənt) *n.* 1. An exhibition or spectacular parade devised for a public celebration. 2. A theatrical spectacle, often with historical themes. [< Med.L *pagina* scaffold of a stage]

pag·eant·ry (paj′ən·trē) *n.* *pl.* **·ries** 1. Pageants collectively. 2. Ceremonial splendor or display. 3. Empty or showy display.

pag·i·nate (paj′ə·nāt) *v.t.* **·nat·ed, ·nat·ing** To number the pages of (a book) consecutively.

pag·i·na·tion (paj′ə·nā′shən) *n.* 1. The numbering of the pages, as of a book. 2. The system of figures and marks used in paging. 3. The arrangement and number of pages.

pa·go·da (pə·gō′də) *n.* In the Far East, a sacred tower or temple, usu. pyramidal. Also **pag·od** (pag′əd, pə·god′). [< Skt. *bhagavati* belonging to a deity]

paid (pād) Past tense and past participle of PAY.

pail (pāl) *n.* 1. A cylindrical vessel with a handle, for carrying liquids, etc. 2. The amount carried in this vessel. [OE *paegel* wine measure] —**pail′ful′** *n.*

pain (pān) *n.* 1. The unpleasant sensation or feeling resulting from or accompanying a physical injury, overstrain, or disorder. 2. Any distressing or afflicting emotion. 3. *pl.* Care, effort, etc. expended on anything: with great *pains*. —**on** (or **upon** or **under**) **pain of** With the penalty of (some specified punishment). —*v.t. & v.i.* To cause pain; hurt. [< Gk. *poinē* fine, penalty] —**pain′less** *adj.* —**pain′less·ly** *adv.*

pained (pānd) *adj.* 1. Hurt or distressed. 2. Showing pain.

pain·ful (pān′fəl) *adj.* 1. Giving pain. 2. Laborious; arduous. 3. Affected with pain. —**pain′ful·ly** *adv.* —**pain′ful·ness** *n.*

pain·kill·er (pān′kil′ər) *n.* A drug that alleviates pain.

pains·tak·ing (pānz′tā′king, pān′stā′-) *adj.* Careful; assiduous. —*n.* Careful effort. —**pains′tak′ing·ly** *adv.*

paint (pānt) *n.* 1. A color or pigment, either dry or mixed with oil, water, etc. 2. A cosmetic, as rouge or greasepaint. 3. A coat of pigment applied to the surface of an object. —*v.t.* 1. In art: **a** To make a representation of in paints or colors. **b** To make (a picture) with paints or colors. 2. To describe vividly, as in words. 3. To cover, coat, or decorate with or as with paint. —*v.i.* 4. To practice the art of painting; paint pictures. 5. To apply cosmetics to the face, etc. [< L *pingere* to paint]

paint·brush (pānt′brush′) *n.* A brush for applying paint.

paint·ed bunting (pān′tid) A brilliantly colored finch widely distributed in the southern U.S. Also **painted finch.**

paint·er¹ (pān′tər) *n.* One who paints.

paint·er² (pān′tər) *n.* *Naut.* A rope with which to fasten a boat by its bow. [Prob. < L *pendere* to suspend]

paint·ing (pān′ting) *n.* 1. The act of applying paint. 2. The art of creating meaningful effects on a surface by the use of pigments. 3. A picture made with pigments.

pair (pâr) *v.t. & v.i.* 1. To bring or come together as a pair. 2. To mate. —**to pair off**

1. To separate into couples. 2. To arrange by pairs. —*n.* 1. Two persons or things of a kind, that are joined, related, or associated. 2. A single thing having two correspondent parts dependent on each other: a *pair* of scissors. [< L neut. pl. of *par* equal]

pair-bond (pâr′bond′) *n.* A mating of two animals that excludes other sexual unions; a monogamous relationship. —**pair′-bond′ing** *n.*

pais·ley (pāz′lē) *adj.* Made of a fabric patterned with curved, abstract forms. —*n.* 1. Paisley fabric. 2. A paisley shawl. Also **Pais′ley.** [after *Paisley*, a town in Scotland]

pa·ja·mas (pə·jä′məz, -jam′əz) *n.pl. of* **pa·ja·ma** 1. A garment consisting of loose trousers and jacket, used for sleeping. 2. In the Orient, similar trousers worn by both men and women. Also, *Brit.*, *pyjamas.* [< Persian *pāi* leg + *jāmāh* garment]

Pa·ki·stan·i (pä′ki·stän′ē, pak′i·stan′ē) *adj.* Of Pakistan or its inhabitants. —**Pa′ki·stan′i** *n.*

pal (pal) *n. Informal* A friend or chum. —*v.i.* **palled, pal·ling** To associate as pals. [< Romany, ult. < Skt. *bharatr* brother]

pal·ace (pal′is) *n.* 1. A royal residence, or the official residence of some high dignitary, as of a bishop. 2. Any splendid residence or stately building. [< L *Palatium* Palatine Hill at Rome, on which stood the palace of the emperor.]

pal·a·din (pal′ə·din) *n.* A knight, esp. a heroic one. [See PALACE.]

pal·an·quin (pal′ən·kēn′) *n.* A type of covered litter used as a means of conveyance in the Orient, borne by poles on the shoulders of two or more men. Also **pal′an·keen′.** [< Skt. *palyaṅka*]

pal·at·a·ble (pal′it·ə·bəl) *adj.* 1. Agreeable to the taste; savory. 2. Acceptable. —**pal′at·a·bil′i·ty** *n.* —**pal′at·a·bly** *adv.*

pal·a·tal (pal′ə·təl) *adj.* 1. Pertaining to the palate. 2. *Phonet.* **a** Produced by placing the front (not the tip) of the tongue near or against the hard palate, as *y* in English *yoke.* **b** Produced with the blade of the tongue near the hard palate, as *ch* in *child.*

pal·a·tal·ize (pal′ə·təl·īz) *v.t. & v.i.* **·ized, ·iz·ing** *Phonet.* To change (a nonpalatal sound) to a palatal one. —**pal′a·tal·i·za′tion** *n.*

pal·ate (pal′it) *n.* 1. *Anat.* The roof of the mouth, consisting of the anterior **hard palate,** having a bony skeleton, and the posterior **soft palate,** composed of muscular tissue. 2. The sense of taste. [< L *palatum*]

pa·la·tial (pə·lā′shəl) *adj.* Of, like, or befitting a palace; magnificent. —**pa·la′·tial·ly** *adv.*

pa·lat·i·nate (pə·lat′ə·nāt, -nit) *n.* A political division ruled over by a count or earl possessing certain prerogatives of royalty within his own domain.

pal·a·tine (pal′ə·tīn, -tin) *adj.* 1. Of or pertaining to a royal palace or its officials. 2. Possessing royal prerogatives: a count *palatine.* —*n.* The ruler of a palatinate. [< L *palatium* palace]

pa·lav·er (pə·lav′ər) *n.* 1. Talk intended to flatter or deceive. 2. Idle, lengthy talk. [< LL *parabola* story, word] —**pa·lav′er** *v.t. & v.i.* —**pa·lav′er·er** *n.*

pale[1] (pāl) *n.* 1. A pointed stick or stake. 2. A fence enclosing a piece of ground. 3. Any boundary or limit. 4. That which is enclosed within bounds. [< L *palus* stake]

pale[2] (pāl) *adj.* 1. Of a whitish or ashen appearance. 2. Lacking in brightness or intensity of color. 3. Feeble or weak. —*v.t. & v.i.* **paled, pal·ing** To make or turn pale; blanch. [< L < *pallere* to be pale] —**pale′ly** *adv.* —**pale′ness** *n.*

pale·face (pāl′fās′) *n.* A white person: a term allegedly originated by North American Indians.

paleo- *combining form* 1. Ancient; old. 2. Primitive. Also, before vowels, **pale-.** [< Gk. *palaios* old, ancient]

pa·le·og·ra·phy (pā′lē·og′rə·fē) *n.* The science of describing or deciphering ancient writings. [< PALEO- + -GRAPHY] —**pa′le·og′ra·pher** *n.* —**pa′le·o·graph′ic** (-ə·graf′ik) or **·i·cal** *adj.*

pa·le·ol·o·gy (pā′lē·ol′ə·jē) *n.* The study of antiquity or antiquities; archeology. [< PALEO- + -LOGY] —**pa′le·o·log′i·cal** (-ə·loj′i·kəl) *adj.* —**pa′le·ol′o·gist** *n.*

pa·le·on·tol·o·gy (pā′lē·on·tol′ə·jē) *n. pl.* **·gies** The science that treats of ancient forms of life or of fossil organisms. [< PALEO- + Gk. *ōn, ontos* being + -LOGY] —**pa′le·on′to·log′ic** (-on′tə·loj′ik) or **·i·cal** *adj.* —**pa′le·on·tol′o·gist** *n.*

Pal·es·tin·i·an (pal′is·tin′ē·ən) *adj.* 1. Of or relating to ancient Palestine or to the former modern country Palestine. 2. Of or relating to the inhabitants of ancient or modern Palestine. —**Pal′es·tin′i·an** *n.*

pa·les·tra (pə·les′trə) *n. pl.* **·trae** (-trē) In ancient Greece, a school or practice place for athletics. [< Gk. *palaiein* to wrestle] —**pa·les′tral, pa·les′tri·an** *adj.*

pal·ette (pal′it) *n.* 1. A thin board or tablet with a hole for the thumb, upon which artists lay and mix their colors. 2. The range of colors characteristic of a particular artist, painting, etc. [< L *pala* spade]

pal·frey (pôl′frē) *n. pl.* **·freys** A saddle horse; esp., a woman's saddle horse. [< OF *palefrei*]

Pa·li (pä′lē) *n.* The sacred language of the early Buddhist writings. [< Skt. *pāli* (*bhasa*) canonical (language)]

pal·imp·sest (pal′imp·sest) *n.* A parchment, manuscript, etc., written upon two or three times, the earlier writing having been wholly or partially erased. [< Gk. *palin* again + *psaein* to rub]

pal·in·drome (pal′in·drōm) *n.* A word, sentence, verse, etc., that is the same read forward or backward, as "Madam, I'm Adam." [< Gk. *palin* again + *dromos* run]

pal·ing (pā′ling) *n.* 1. One of a series of upright pales forming a fence. 2. Pales or pickets collectively. 3. A fence or enclosure made of pales or pickets.

pal·i·sade (pal′ə·sād′) *n.* 1. A barrier or fortification made of strong timbers set in the ground. 2. One of the stakes forming such a barrier. 3. *pl.* An extended cliff or rocky precipice. —*v.t.* **·sad·ed, ·sad·ing** To enclose or fortify with a palisade. [< L *palus* stake]

pall[1] (pôl) *n.* 1. A covering, usu. of black cloth, thrown over a coffin or tomb. 2. A dark, heavy covering, cloud, etc. 3. A gloomy or oppressive atmosphere, effect, etc. —*v.t.*

To cover with or as with a pall. [OE < L *pallium* cloak]

pall² (pôl) *v.i.* 1. To become insipid or uninteresting. 2. To have a dulling or displeasing effect: followed by *on.* —*v.t.* 3. To satiate; cloy. [Appar. aphetic var. of APPALL]

pal·la·di·um¹ (pə·lā′dē·əm) *n. pl.* **·di·a** Any object considered essential to the safety of a community or organization; a safeguard. [< *Pallas Athena,* goddess in Greek and Roman mythology; a statue of her was believed to afford protection.]

pal·la·di·um² (pə·lā′dē·əm) *n.* A rare, silver-white, malleable and ductile metallic element (symbol Pd). [< NL, after the asteroid *Pallas*]

pall·bear·er (pôl′bâr′ər) *n.* One who forms part of an escort for a coffin at a funeral.

pal·let¹ (pal′it) *n.* 1. *Mech.* A pawl or the like used to regulate the motion of a ratchet wheel, etc. 2. Any of various flat-bladed tools. 3. A skid (def. 2). [< L *pala* spade]

pal·let² (pal′it) *n.* 1. A small straw bed or mattress. 2. A small, hard bed. [< L *palea* chaff, straw]

pal·li·ate (pal′ē·āt) *v.t.* **·at·ed, ·at·ing** 1. To cause (a crime, fault, etc.) to appear less serious or offensive. 2. To relieve the symptoms or effects of (a disease, etc.) without curing. [< L *palliatus,* pp. of *palliare* to cloak] —**pal′li·a′tion** *n.* —**pal′li·a′tive** *adj. & n.* —**pal′li·a′tor** *n.*

pal·lid (pal′id) *adj.* Pale or wan; lacking in color. [< L *pallere* to be pale] —**pal′lid·ly** *adv.* —**pal′lid·ness** *n.*

pal·lor (pal′ər) *n.* The state of being pale or pallid; paleness. [< L *pallere* to be pale]

palm¹ (päm) *n.* The inner surface of the hand between the wrist and the base of the fingers. —*v.t.* To hide (something) in the hand, as in sleight of hand. —**to palm off** To pass off or impose fraudulently. [< F < L *palma*] —**pal·mar** (pal′mər, pä′-) *adj.*

palm² (päm) *n.* 1. Any of a large and varied group of tropical evergreen trees or shrubs, usu. having an unbranched trunk topped by a crown of large palmate or pinnate leaves. 2. A leaf or branch of the palm, used as a symbol of victory or joy. 3. Triumph; victory. [OE < L *palma* palm tree] —**pal·ma·ceous** (pal·mā′shəs, pä-) *adj.*

pal·mate (pal′māt, pä′māt) *adj.* 1. Resembling an open hand. 2. Broad and flat, with fingerlike projections, as antlers. Also **pal′mat·ed.** [< L *palmatus,* pp. of *palmare* to mark with the palm of the hand] —**pal′·mate·ly** *adv.* —**pal·ma′tion** *n.*

palm·er (pä′mər) *n.* In the Middle Ages, one who had visited Palestine. [after the palms brought back as momentos]

pal·met·to (pal·met′ō) *n. pl.* **·tos** or **·toes** Any of various palms having fanlike foliage. [< Sp. *palmito,* dim. of *palma* palm tree]

palm·is·try (pä′mis·trē) *n.* The art or practice of supposedly discovering a person's past or future from the lines and marks in the palm of the hand. [< PALM + ME *-estrie,* prob. < OF *maistrie* mastery] —**palm′ist** *n.*

palm oil A yellowish, butterlike oil obtained from the fruit of several varieties of palm.

palm sugar Sugar made from palm sap.

Palm Sunday The Sunday before Easter. [Named for Christ's triumphal entry into Jerusalem, when palm branches were strewn before him]

palm·y (pä′mē) *adj.* **palm·i·er, palm·i·est** 1. Prosperous; flourishing. 2. Abounding in palms.

pal·my·ra (pal·mī′rə) *n.* An East Indian palm having large, fan-shaped leaves. [< Pg. *palmeira* palm tree]

pal·o·mi·no (pal′ə·mē′nō) *n. pl.* **·nos** A light tan or golden brown horse with a cream-colored mane and tail. [< Am.Sp., orig., dove-colored horse < L *palumbus* ringdove]

pal·pa·ble (pal′pə·bəl) *adj.* 1. Capable of being touched or felt. 2. Readily perceived; obvious. 3. Perceptible by touching. [< L *palpare* to touch] —**pal′pa·bil′i·ty** *n.* —**pal′·pa·bly** *adv.*

pal·pate (pal′pāt) *v.t.* **·pat·ed, ·pat·ing** To feel or examine by touch, esp. for medical diagnosis. [< L *palpare* to touch] —**pal·pa′tion** *n.*

pal·pi·tate (pal′pə·tāt) *v.i.* **·tat·ed, ·tat·ing** 1. To quiver; tremble. 2. To beat more rapidly than normal; flutter: said esp. of the heart. [< L *palpitare* to tremble, freq. of *palpare* to touch] —**pal′pi·ta′tion** *n.*

pal·pus (pal′pəs) *n. pl.* **·pi** (-pī) *Zool.* A feeler, esp. one of a pair attached to the mouth parts of an arthropod: also called **palp.** [< L *palpus* feeler]

pal·sy (pôl′zē) *n. pl.* **·sies** 1. Paralysis. 2. Any impairment or loss of ability to control movement. —*v.t.* **·sied, ·sy·ing** 1. To paralyze. 2. To cause to tremble. [< L *paralysis*] —**pal′sied** *adj.*

pal·ter (pôl′tər) *v.i.* 1. To speak or act insincerely; equivocate. 2. To trifle. 3. To haggle or quibble. [Origin unknown] —**pal′·ter·er** *n.*

pal·try (pôl′trē) *adj.* **·tri·er, ·tri·est** 1. Having little or no worth or value; trifling; trivial. 2. Contemptible; petty. [< LG *palte* rag] —**pal′tri·ly** *adv.* —**pal′tri·ness** *n.*

pa·lu·dal (pə·lo͞od′l) *adj.* Pertaining to a marsh; swampy. [< L *palus, paludis* marsh]

pam·pas (pam′pəz, *Sp.* päm′päs) *n.pl.* The great treeless plains south of the Amazon river. [< Quechua *pampa* plain] —**pam·pe·an** (pam′pē·ən, pam·pē′ən) *adj. & n.*

pam·per (pam′pər) *v.t.* To treat very indulgently; coddle. [< LG *pampen* to live luxuriously] —**pam′per·er** *n.*

pam·phlet (pam′flit) *n.* A printed work stitched or pasted, but not permanently bound; esp., a brief treatise or essay on a subject of current interest published in this form. [< OF *pamphilet,* dim. of *Pamphilus,* title of a 12th c. Latin love poem]

pam·phlet·eer (pam′flə·tir′) *n.* One who writes pamphlets. —*v.i.* To write and issue pamphlets.

pan¹ (pan) *n.* 1. A wide, shallow vessel, usu. of metal, used for holding liquids or in cooking. 2. Any similar receptacle or vessel. —*v.* **panned, pan·ning** *v.t.* 1. To separate (gold) by washing (gold-bearing earth) in a pan. 2. *Informal* To criticize severely. —*v.i.* 3. To search for gold by washing earth, gravel, etc. in a pan. —**to pan out** *Informal* To succeed. [OE *panne*]

pan² (pan) *v.t.* **panned, pan·ning** To move (a motion-picture or television camera) so as to photograph an entire scene, follow a particular character, etc. [< PANORAMA]

pan- *combining form* 1. All; every; the whole: *panchromatic.* 2. Comprising, including, or applying to all: usu. capitalized when preceding proper nouns or adjectives, as in *Pan-African.* [< Gk. *pan*, neut. of *pas* all]

pan·a·ce·a (pan′ə·sē′ə) *n.* A remedy for all diseases or ills; a cure-all. [< Gk. *pan*, neut. of *pas* all + *akos* cure] **—pan′a·ce′an** *adj.*

pa·nache (pə·nash′, -näsh′) *n.* 1. A plume, esp. on a helmet. 2. Dash; verve. [< F ult. < L *penna* feather]

Pan·a·ma hat (pan′ə·mä, -mô) A hat woven from the leaves of a palmlike tree of Central and South America.

Pan·a·ma·ni·an (pan′ə·mā′nē·ən) *adj.* Of or pertaining to the Isthmus of Panama or its inhabitants. **—Pan′a·ma′ni·an** *n.*

Pan-A·mer·i·can (pan′ə·mer′ə·kən) *adj.* Including or pertaining to both North and South America, or to all Americans. Also **Pan American.**

pan·a·tel·a (pan′ə·tel′ə) *n.* A long slender cigar: also spelled *panetela, panetella.* [< Sp.]

pan-broil (pan′broil′) *v.t. & v.i.* To cook in a heavy frying pan placed over direct heat, using little or no fat.

pan·cake (pan′kāk′) *n.* 1. A thin, flat cake made from batter, fried in a pan or on a griddle. 2. A cosmetic resembling face powder: also **pancake makeup.**

pan·chro·mat·ic (pan′krō·mat′ik) *adj. Photog.* Sensitive to light of all colors of the spectrum, as film. **—pan·chro′ma·tism** (-mə·tiz′əm) *n.*

pan·cre·as (pan′krē·əs, pang′-) *n. Anat.* A large gland situated behind the lower part of the stomach, secreting digestive enzymes and producing insulin. [< PAN- + Gk. *kreas* flesh] **—pan′cre·at′ic** (-at′ik) *adj.*

pan·da (pan′də) *n. pl.* **·das** or **·da** 1. A small, raccoonlike carnivore of the SE Himalayas, with long, reddish brown fur and ringed tail. 2. A large, bearlike mammal of Tibet and China, with black-and-white coat and rings around the eyes. [Prob. < Nepalese]

pan·dem·ic (pan·dem′ik) *adj.* 1. *Med.* Widely epidemic. 2. Universal; general. *—n.* A pandemic disease. [< PAN- + Gk. *dēmos* people]

pan·de·mo·ni·um (pan′də·mō′nē·əm) *n.* 1. The abode of all demons. 2. A place marked by disorder and uproar. 3. Riotous uproar. [< PAN- + Gk. *daimōn* demon]

pan·der (pan′dər) *n.* 1. A go-between in sexual intrigues; pimp. 2. One who ministers to the passions or base desires of others. Also **pan′der·er** *—v.t. & v.i.* To act as a pander for (another or others). [< *Pandare*, character in Chaucer's *Troilus and Criseyde*]

pan·dow·dy (pan·dou′dē) *n. pl.* **·dies** A deep-dish apple pie or pudding, having only a top crust. [Origin unknown]

pane (pān) *n.* 1. One of the sections of a window, door, etc., filled with a sheet of glass. 2. A sheet of glass for such a section. 3. A panel in a door, ceiling, etc. [< L *pannus* piece of cloth]

pan·e·gyr·ic (pan′ə·jir′ik) *n.* 1. A formal public eulogy. 2. Elaborate praise. [< PAN- + Gk. *agyris* assembly] **—pan′e·gyr′i·cal** *adj.* **—pan′e·gyr′i·cal·ly** *adv.* **—pan′e·gyr′ist** *n.*

pan·e·gy·rize (pan′ə·jə·rīz′) *v.t. & v.i.* **·rized, ·riz·ing** To deliver or write a panegyric upon (someone); eulogize.

pan·el (pan′əl) *n.* 1. A rectangular or square piece forming part of a ceiling, door, etc. 2. One or more pieces of fabric inserted lengthwise in a woman's skirt. 3. *Law* **a** The official list of persons summoned for jury duty. **b** The body of persons composing a jury. 4. A small group of persons selected to hold a discussion, judge a contest, etc. 5. An instrument panel. *—v.t.* **pan·eled** or **·elled, pan·el·ing** or **·el·ling** 1. To fit, furnish, or adorn with panels. 2. To divide into panels. [< L *pannus* piece of cloth]

panel discussion A discussion before an audience of a specific topic by a group of selected speakers.

pan·el·ing (pan′əl·ing) *n.* 1. Wood or other materials used in making panels. 2. Panels collectively. Also **pan′el·ling.**

pan·el·ist (pan′əl·ist) *n.* A person serving on a panel.

panel truck A small, fully enclosed truck.

pan·e·tel·a (pan′ə·tel′ə), **pan′e·tel′la** *n.* See PANATELA.

pan fish Any little fish that can be fried whole.

pang (pang) *n.* 1. A sudden sharp pain. 2. A spasm of mental anguish. [Origin unknown]

pan·ga·mate (pan′gə·māt) *n.* A dietary supplement alleged to increase the supply of oxygen to the blood: also **pan·gam′ic acid.** Also called *vitamin* B_{15}.

pan·go·lin (pang·gō′lin) *n.* A heavily armored, typically long-tailed toothless mammal of Asia and Africa: also called *scaly anteater.* [< Malay *peng-gōling* roller, in ref. to its power of rolling itself up]

pan·han·dle¹ (pan′han′dəl) *v.i.* **·dled, ·dling** *Informal* To beg, esp. on the street. [< PAN¹ (used to receive alms) + HANDLE, v.] **—pan′han′dler** *n.*

pan·han·dle² (pan′han′dəl) *n.* 1. The handle of a pan. 2. *Usu. cap.* A narrow strip of land shaped like the handle of a pan.

pan·ic (pan′ik) *n.* 1. A sudden, unreasonable, overpowering fear, esp. when affecting a large number simultaneously. 2. An instance of such fear. *—v.t. & v.i.* **·icked, ·ick·ing** To affect or become affected with panic. [< Gk. *panikos* of Pan, the Greek god who was believed to cause sudden or groundless fear] **—pan′ick·y** *adj.*

pan·i·cle (pan′i·kəl) *n. Bot.* A loose compound flower cluster. [< L *panicula*, dim. of *panus* swelling]

pan·ic-strick·en (pan′ik·strik′ən) *adj.* Overcome by panic. Also **pan′ic-struck′** (-struk′).

pa·nic·u·late (pə·nik′yə·lāt, -lit) *adj. Bot.* Arranged in panicles. Also **pa·nic′u·lat′ed.** **—pa·nic′u·late·ly** *adv.*

pan·jan·drum (pan·jan′drəm) *n.* A self-important or pretentious official. [Coined by Samuel Foote, 1720–77, English dramatist and actor]

pan·nier (pan′yər) *n.* A basket for carrying a large load, as on the back. Also **pan′ier.** [< L *panarium* bread basket]

pa·no·cha (pə·nō′chə) *n.* A coarse Mexican sugar. Also **pa·no′che.** [< Am.Sp., dim. of Sp. *pan* < L *panis* bread]

pan·o·ply (pan′ə·plē) *n. pl.* **·plies** 1. The complete equipment of a warrior. 2. Any complete covering that protects. [< Gk. *panoplia* full armor] —**pan′o·plied** *adj.*

pan·o·ram·a (pan′ə·ram′ə, -rä′mə) *n.* **1.** A series of pictures representing a continuous scene, arranged to unroll and pass before the spectator. **2.** A complete or comprehensive view. [< PAN- + Gk. *horama* sight] —**pan′o·ram′ic** *adj.* —**pan′o·ram′i·cal·ly** *adv.*

pan·pipe (pan′pīp′) *n. Sometimes cap. Often pl.* An instrument consisting of a graduated series of short flutes, originally reeds, bound together in proper order to produce a scale.

pan·sy (pan′zē) *n. pl.* **·sies 1.** A garden violet having blossoms of a variety of colors. **2.** *Slang* An effeminate or homosexual man. [< MF *pensée* thought]

pant (pant) *v.i.* **1.** To breathe rapidly or spasmodically; gasp for breath. **2.** To gasp with desire; yearn: with *for* or *after.* —*v.t.* **3.** To breathe out or utter gaspingly. —*n.* **1.** The act of panting. **2.** A gasp. [Ult. < L *phantasiare* to have a nightmare]

pan·ta·lets (pan′tə·lets′) *n.pl.* **1.** Formerly, long ruffled or embroidered drawers extending below the hem of the skirt. **2.** Separate frilled leg coverings to be attached to drawers. Also **pan′ta·lettes′.** [Dim. of PANTALOON]

pan·ta·loons (pan′tə·lōōnz′) *n.pl.* Formerly, a tight-fitting garment for the hips and legs; trousers. [< Ital. *pantalone* clown < *Pantaleone*, popular Venetian saint]

pan·the·ism (pan′thē·iz′əm) *n.* The doctrine that the whole universe is God, or that every part of the universe is a manifestation of God. [< PAN- + Gk. *theos* god] —**pan′the·ist** *n.* —**pan′the·is′tic** *adj.*

pan·the·on (pan′thē·on) *n.* **1.** All the gods of a people collectively. **2.** A temple commemorating the great of a nation. **3.** A temple dedicated to the gods of a nation. [< PAN- + Gk. *theios* of or sacred to a god]

pan·ther (pan′thər) *n.* **1.** A leopard, esp. the black variety of Asia. **2.** The puma or cougar. **3.** The jaguar. [< Gk. *panthēr*]

pant·ies (pan′tēz) *n.pl.* A woman's or child's underpants.

pan·to·graph (pan′tə·graf) *n.* An instrument used for copying drawings, maps, etc., to any scale. [< Gk. *panto(s)* of all + -GRAPH] —**pant′o·graph′ic** or **·i·cal** *adj.* —**pan·tog·ra·phy** (pan·tog′rə·fē) *n.*

pan·to·mime (pan′tə·mīm) *n.* **1.** Any play in which the actors express their meaning by action without dialogue. **2.** Gestures without speech. —*v.t. & v.i.* **·mimed, ·mim·ing** To act or express in pantomime. [< Gk. *panto(s)* of all + *mimos* imitator] —**pan′to·mi′mist** *n.*

pan·to·then·ic acid (pan′tə·then′ik) A viscous, oily acid that is a member of the vitamin B complex and is found in plant and animal tissue.

pan·try (pan′trē) *n. pl.* **·tries** A room or closet for provisions, dishes, table linen, etc. [ME *panetrie* < L *panis* bread]

pants (pants) *n.pl.* **1.** Trousers. **2.** Underpants. [Short for PANTALOONS]

pant·suit (pant′sōōt′) *n.* A woman's two-piece garment consisting of a jacket and pants. Also **pants suit.**

pan·ty·hose (pan′tē·hōz′) *n.pl.* A one-piece garment combining panties and stockings.

pap (pap) *n.* Any soft food for babies. [Prob. akin to L *pappa*]

pa·pa (pä′pə, pə·pä′) *n.* Father: used familiarly. [< Gk. *papas*, child's word for father]

pa·pa·cy (pā′pə·sē) *n. pl.* **·cies 1.** The dignity, office, or jurisdiction of the pope. **2.** The succession of popes. **3.** The period during which a pope is in office. [< Gk. *papas* father]

Pa·pa·cy (pā′pə·sē) *n.* The Roman Catholic system of church government.

pa·pal (pā′pəl) *adj.* **1.** Of, pertaining to, or ordered by the pope. **2.** Of or pertaining to the papacy. **3.** Of or pertaining to the Roman Catholic Church.

Papal cross A cross having three crossbars or transoms, the top one the shortest and the bottom one the longest.

pa·paw (pə·pô′, pô′pô) *n.* **1.** The fleshy, edible fruit of a North American shrub or small tree. **2.** The tree. Also spelled *pawpaw.* [< PAPAYA]

pa·pa·ya (pə·pä′yə) *n.* **1.** The yellow, melonlike fruit of a tropical American evergreen tree. **2.** The tree. [< Sp. and Pg.; ult. of Carib origin]

pa·per (pā′pər) *n.* **1.** A substance made from pulp obtained from rags, wood, bark, etc., usu. formed into thin sheets for writing, printing, wrapping, etc. **2.** A sheet of this material. **3.** Wallpaper. **4.** A printed or written document, discourse, or treatise. **5.** A newspaper. **6.** In schools and colleges, a piece of written work, as an assignment, a report, etc. **7.** *pl.* Personal documents or identification; credentials. **8.** In business, negotiable written or printed pledges to pay. —**on paper 1.** In written or printed form. **2.** In theory, as distinguished from fact. —*v.t.* **1.** To cover with wallpaper. **2.** *Slang* To issue free tickets of admission to (a place of amusement). —*adj.* **1.** Made of paper. **2.** Existing only in writing. [< L *papyrus*] —**pa′per·y** *adj.*

pa·per·back (pā′pər·bak′) *adj.* Of books, having a flexible paper cover or binding. —*n.* A book so bound.

pa·per·hang·er (pā′pər·hang′ər) *n.* One whose business is to cover walls, etc., with paper. —**pa′per·hang′ing** *n.*

pa·per·knife (pā′pər·nīf′) *n. pl.* **·knives** (-nīvz′) A dull blade for opening letters, leaves of books, etc.

pa·per·weight (pā′pər·wāt′) *n.* A small, heavy object, often ornamental, placed on loose papers to secure them.

pap·er·work (pā′pər·wûrk′) *n.* Work involving the preparation or handling of reports, letters, forms, etc.

pa·pier-mâ·ché (pā′pər·mə·shā′, *Fr.* pȧ·pyā·mä·shā′) *n.* A material consisting of paper pulp mixed with size, paste, resin, etc., that can be molded when wet and that becomes hard when dry. [< F *papier* paper + *mâché*, pp. of *mâcher* to chew]

pa·pil·la (pə·pil′ə) *n. pl.* **·pil·lae** (-pil′ē) *Anat.* Any small nipplelike process of connective tissue, as on the tongue or at the root of a hair. [< L] —**pap·il·la·ry** (pap′ə·ler′ē) *adj.*

pa·pist (pā′pist) *n.* A Roman Catholic: usu. a disparaging term. [See PAPACY.] —**pa·pis·ti·cal** (pə·pis′ti·kəl) or **pa·pis′tic** *adj.* —**pa′pis·try** *n.*

pa·poose (pa·pōōs′) *n.* A North American

Indian infant or small child. Also **pap·poose′**. [< Algonquian *papoos*]

pa·pri·ka (pa·prē′kə, pap′rə·kə) *n.* A condiment made from the ripe fruit of a mild variety of red pepper. Also **pa·pri′ca.** [< Magyar, red pepper]

Pap smear (pap) A method of early detection of cervical cancer. Also **Pap test.** [after George *Papanicolaou*, 1883–1962, U.S. scientist]

pap·u·la (pap′yə·lə) *n. pl.* **·lae** (-lē) *Pathol.* A pimple. Also **pap′ule** (-yōōl). [< L, pimple] **—pap′u·lan** *adj.*

pa·py·rus (pə·pī′rəs) *n. pl.* **·ri** (-rī) 1. A tall, rushlike aquatic plant, formerly common in Egypt. 2. A type of writing paper made by the ancient Egyptians from this plant. 3. A manuscript written on this material. [< Gk. *papyros*]

par (pär) *n.* 1. An accepted standard or level used for comparison: His work is on a *par* with that of the other students. 2. The average in amount, quality, or degree: His health is up to *par*. 3. In commerce, equality between the face value and the market value of shares of stock, bonds, etc. 4. In golf, the number of strokes allotted to a hole or round when played perfectly. **—*adj.*** 1. Normal; average. 2. In commerce, having the face value normal. [< L, equal]

para-[1] *prefix* 1. Beside; along with: *paramilitary*. 2. Beyond; aside from; amiss: *paradox*. Also, before vowels and *h*, usu. **par-**. [< Gk. *para* beside]

para-[2] *combining form* Shelter or protection against: *parasol*. [< Ital. *para*, imperative of *parare* to defend]

par·a·ble (par′ə·bəl) *n.* A short narrative making a moral or religious point by comparison with natural or homely things. [< Gk. *parabolē* a placing side by side]

pa·rab·o·la (pə·rab′ə·lə) *n. Math.* The curve formed by the edges of a plane when cutting through a right circular cone at an angle parallel to one of its sides. [< Gk. *parabolē* a placing side by side] **—par·a·bol·ic** (par′ə·bol′ik) *adj.* **—par′a·bol′i·cal·ly** *adv.*

par·a·chute (par′ə·shōōt) *n.* A large, umbrella-shaped apparatus for retarding the speed of a body descending through the air, esp. from an airplane. **—*v.t. & v.i.* ·chut·ed, ·chut·ing** To drop, descend, or convey by parachute. [< PARA-[2] + F *chute* fall] **—par′a·chut′ist** *n.*

par·a·clete (par′ə·klēt) *n.* One called to the aid of another. **—the Paraclete** The Holy Spirit as a helper or comforter. [< LGk. *paraklētos* comforter, advocate]

pa·rade (pə·rād′) *n.* 1. A procession or march for ceremony, display, or inspection. 2. A ground where military reviews are held. 3. A promenade or public walk; also, the persons promenading. **—on parade** On display. **—*v.* ·rad·ed, ·rad·ing** *v.t.* 1. To walk or march through or about. 2. To display ostentatiously; flaunt. 3. To cause to assemble for military parade. **—*v.i.*** 4. To march formally. 5. To walk in public for the purpose of showing oneself. [< Sp. *parada* stopping place, exercise ground] **—pa·rad′er** *n.*

par·a·digm (par′ə·dim, -dīm) *n. Gram.* 1. A list of all the inflected forms of a word showing declension, conjugation, etc. 2. Any pattern or example. [< Gk. *paradeigma* pattern] **—par′a·dig·mat′ic** (-dig·mat′ik) *adj.*

par·a·dise (par′ə·dīs) *n.* 1. *Often cap.* Heaven or Eden. 2. A place or state of great beauty or delight. [< Gk. *paradeisos* park] **—par′a·di·sa′ic** (-di·sā′ik) or **·i·cal, par′a·dis′i·ac** (-dis′ē·ak) or **par′a·di·si′a·cal** (-di·sī′ə·kəl) *adj.*

par·a·dox (par′ə·doks) *n.* 1. A statement seemingly absurd or contradictory, yet in fact true. 2. A statement essentially self-contradictory, false, or absurd. [< Gk. *paradoxos* incredible] **—par′a·dox′i·cal** *adj.* **—par′a·dox′i·cal′i·ty, par′a·dox′i·cal·ness** *n.* **—par′a·dox′i·cal·ly** *adv.*

par·af·fin (par′ə·fin) *n. Chem.* 1. A waxy mixture of hydrocarbons distilled from petroleum and widely used for candles, as a preservative, etc. 2. Any hydrocarbon of the methane series. Also **par′af·fine** (-fin, -fēn). [< L *par(um)* too little + *affin(is)* related to; so named because it has little affinity for other substances]

paraffin wax Paraffin in its solid state.

par·a·gon (par′ə·gon) *n.* A model or pattern of excellence. [< Ital. *paragone* touchstone]

par·a·graph (par′ə·graf) *n.* 1. A distinct section of a written discourse, begun on a new line and generally containing a unified statement of a particular point. 2. A short article, item, or comment, as in a newspaper. 3. A mark (¶) used to indicate where a paragraph is to be begun. **—*v.t.*** To arrange in or into paragraphs. [< PARA-[1] + Gk. *graphein* to write] **—par′a·graph′er** *n.* **—par′a·graph′ic** or **·i·cal** *adj.*

par·a·keet (par′ə·kēt) *n.* Any of certain small parrots with long, wedge-shaped tails. [< Ital. *parrochetto*]

Par·a·li·pom·e·non (par′ə·li·pom′ə·non) *n.* The Douai Bible name for CHRONICLES.

par·al·lax (par′ə·laks) *n.* The apparent displacement of an object, esp. of a heavenly body, when it is viewed successively from two points not in the same line of sight. [< Gk. *parallassein* to deviate]

par·al·lel (par′ə·lel) *adj.* 1. Being a uniform distance away or apart throughout a certain area or extent. 2. *Geom.* Not meeting, however far extended: said of straight lines and of planes. 3. Having a close resemblance. 4. *Electr.* Connecting like terminals, as a group of cells, condensers, etc. **—*n.*** 1. An object or surface equidistant from another. 2. *Geom.* A parallel line or plane. 3. A counterpart; match. 4. Comparison: to draw a *parallel* between two things. 5. *Geog.* Any of the circles imagined as drawn parallel to the earth's equator, each of which marks a given latitude. 6. *Electr.* Connection between like terminals: usu. in the phrase **in parallel.** **—*v.t.* par·al·leled** or **·lelled, par·al·lel·ing** or **·lel·ling** 1. To make, be, go, or extend parallel to. 2. To correspond to. 3. To compare; liken. [< PAR(A)-[1] + Gk. *allēlos* one another] **—par′al·lel·ism** *n.*

parallel bars Two horizontal crossbars, parallel to each other and supported by upright posts, used for gymnastics.

par·al·lel·e·pi·ped (par′ə·lel′ə·pī′pid, -pip′id) *n.* A prism with six faces, each of which is a parallelogram. Also **par′al·lel′o·pi′ped, par′·al·lel′e·pip′e·don** (-pip′ə·don, -pī′pə-), **par′·**

al·lel′o·pip′e·don. [< Gk. *parallēlos* parallel + *epipedon* a plane surface]

par·al·lel·o·gram (par′ə·lel′ə·gram) *n.* 1. *Geom.* A four-sided plane figure whose opposite sides are parallel and equal. 2. Any area or object having such form. [< Gk. *parallēlos* parallel + *grammē* line]

pa·ral·y·sis (pə·ral′ə·sis) *n. pl.* **·ses** (-sēz) 1. *Pathol.* Partial or complete loss of motor function. 2. Cessation or crippling of normal activities. [< L < Gk. *paralyein* to disable] **—par·a·lyt·ic** (par′ə·lit′ik) *adj. & n.*

par·a·lyze (par′ə·līz) *v.t.* **·lyzed, ·lyz·ing** 1. To bring about paralysis in; make paralytic. 2. To render powerless, ineffective, or inactive. **—par′a·lyz′er** *n.* **—par′a·ly·za′tion** *n.*

par·a·me·ci·um (par′ə·mē′shē·əm, -sē·əm) *n. pl.* **·ci·a** Any of various oval-shaped protozoa having cilia. [< Gk. *paramēkēs* oblong]

par·a·med·ic (par′ə·med′ik) *n.* One trained to assist a physician. **—par′a·med′i·cal** *adj.*

pa·ram·e·ter (pə·ram′ə·tər) *n.* 1. *Math.* A constant whose values determine the operation or characteristics of a system. 2. A fixed limit or guideline. [< PARA-[1] + Gk. *metron* measure]

par·a·mil·i·tar·y (par′ə·mil′ə·ter′ē) *adj.* Having a military structure; capable of becoming or supplementing a military force. [< PARA-[1] + MILITARY]

par·a·mount (par′ə·mount) *adj.* Superior to all others; chief in importance or authority. [< OF *par* by + *à mont* up, above] **—par′a·mount·ly** *adv.*

par·a·mour (par′ə·mo͝or) *n.* A lover, esp. one who unlawfully takes the place of a spouse. [< OF *par amour* with love]

par·a·noi·a (par′ə·noi′ə) *n.* *Psychiatry* A form of mental disorder characterized by delusions of persecution or of grandeur. [< PARA-[1] + Gk. *noos, nous* mind] **—par′a·noid, par′a·noi′ac** (-ak, -ik) *adj. & n.*

par·a·nor·mal (par′ə·nôr′məl) *adj.* Not explainable scientifically.

par·a·pet (par′ə·pit, -pet) *n.* A low wall about the edge of a roof, terrace, bridge, etc. [< Ital. *parapetto*] **—par′a·pet·ed** *adj.*

par·a·pher·na·li·a (par′ə·fər·nā′lē·ə, -nāl′yə, -fə-) *n.pl.* 1. Personal effects. 2. A group of articles, esp. as used in some activity; equipment. [< Med.L *paraphernalia* (*bona*) a wife's own (goods)]

par·a·phrase (par′ə·frāz) *n.* A restatement of the meaning of a passage, work, etc., as for clarity. **—*v.t.* & *v.i.*** **·phrased, ·phras·ing** To express in or make a paraphrase. [< PARA-[1] + Gk. *phrazein* to tell] **—par′a·phras′er, par′a·phrast** (-frast) *n.* **—par′a·phras′tic** (-fras′tik) or **·ti·cal** *adj.*

par·a·ple·gi·a (par′ə·plē′jē·ə) *n.* *Pathol.* Paralysis of the lower half of the body, due to disease or injury of the spinal cord. Also **par′a·ple′gy** (-plē′jē). [< PARA-[1] + Gk. *plēssein* to strike] **—par·a·ple′gic** *adj. & n.*

par·a·pro·fes·sion·al (par′ə·prə·fesh′ə·nəl) *n.* One trained to assist professionals, as teachers.

par·a·psy·chol·o·gy (par′ə·sī·kol′ə·jē) *n.* The study of alleged psychic phenomena. **—par′a·psy·chol′o·gist** *n.*

par·a·site (par′ə·sīt) *n.* 1. *Biol.* An animal or plant that lives in or on another organism, the host, and from whom it obtains nourishment. 2. One who lives at another's expense without making proper return. [< Gk. *parasitos*, lit., one who eats at another's table] **—par′a·sit′ic** (-sit′ik) or **·i·cal** *adj.* **—par′a·sit′i·cal·ly** *adv.* **—par′a·sit′ism** *n.*

par·a·sol (par′ə·sôl, -sol) *n.* A small, light umbrella, used as protection against the sun. [< Ital. *parare* to ward off + *sole* sun]

par·a·sym·pa·thet·ic (par′ə·sim′pə·thet′ik) *adj.* *Anat.* Denoting a part of the nervous system having among its functions the constriction of the pupil, the slowing of the heart, and the dilation of the blood vessels.

par·a·thi·on (par′ə·thī′on, -ən) *n.* An organic phosphate insecticide with high toxicity to animals.

par·a·thy·roid (par′ə·thī′roid) *Anat. adj.* 1. Lying near the thyroid gland. 2. Of or pertaining to any of the small glands found near or on the thyroid gland and serving to control the amount of calcium in the blood. **—*n.*** One of the parathyroid glands.

par·a·troops (par′ə·tro͞ops) *n.pl.* Troops trained and equipped to drop behind enemy lines by parachute. **—par′a·troop′er** *n.*

par·boil (pär′boil′) *v.t.* To boil partially. [< LL *perbullire* to boil thoroughly]

par·buck·le (pär′buk′əl) *n.* A rope sling for vertically raising or lowering a heavy object. **—*v.t.*** **·led, ·ling** To raise or lower by means of a parbuckle. [Earlier *parbunkle*; origin uncertain]

par·cel (pär′səl) *n.* 1. Something that is wrapped up; package. 2. A quantity of some commodity put up for sale; lot. 3. An indefinite number of persons or things. 4. A distinct portion of land. **—*v.t.*** **par·celed** or **·celled, par·cel·ing** or **·cel·ling** To divide or distribute in parts or shares: usu. with *out.* **—*adj. & adv.*** Part; partly. [< L *pars, partis* part]

parcel post A postal service for delivering parcels not exceeding a specified weight and size.

parch (pärch) *v.t.* 1. To make extremely dry. 2. To make very thirsty. 3. To dry (corn, peas, etc.) by exposing to great heat. 4. To dry up or shrivel by exposing to cold. **—*v.i.*** 5. To become dry. 6. To become dry with thirst. [ME *parchen*; ult. origin uncertain]

parch·ment (pärch′mənt) *n.* 1. The prepared skin of sheep, goats, and other animals, used for writing or painting upon. 2. A writing on this material. 3. Paper made in imitation of parchment. [< L *pergamenus* of Pergamum, the city where it was first used]

pard[1] (pärd) *n.* *Archaic* A leopard or panther. [< Gk. *pardos*]

pard[2] (pärd) *n.* *Slang* A partner. [Short for PARDNER]

pard·ner (pärd′nər) *n.* *Dial.* Chum; friend. [Alter. of PARTNER]

par·don (pär′dən) *v.t.* 1. To remit the penalty of (an offense, insult, etc.). 2. To forgive (a person) for an offense. 3. To grant courteous allowance for or to. **—*n.*** 1. The act of pardoning; forgiveness. 2. An official warrant declaring such a remission. [< LL *per-* through + *donare* to give] **—par′don·a·ble** *adj.* **—par′don·a·bly** *adv.* **—par′don·er** *n.*

pare (pâr) *v.t.* **pared, par·ing** 1. To cut off the covering layer or part of. 2. To cut off or trim away (a covering layer or part): often with *off* or *away*. 3. To diminish gradually. [< OF *parer* to prepare, trim] **—par′er** *n.*

par·e·gor·ic (par′ə·gôr′ik, -gor′ik) *n. Med.* A camphorated tincture of opium, used primarily to treat diarrhea. [< Gk. *parēgoros* soothing]

par·ent (pâr′ənt) *n.* 1. A father or mother. 2. One exercising the functions of a father or mother. 3. A progenitor; forefather. 4. Any organism that generates another. [< L *parere* to beget] **—pa·ren·tal** (pə·ren′təl) *adj.* **—pa·ren′tal·ly** *adv.* **—par′ent·hood** *n.*

par·ent·age (pâr′ən·tij) *n.* Descent or derivation from parents; lineage; origin. [< OF]

pa·ren·the·sis (pə·ren′thə·sis) *n. pl.* **·ses** (-sēz) 1. Either of the upright curved lines ( ) used to enclose an interjected, explanatory, or qualifying remark, mathematical quantities, etc. 2. *Gram.* A word, phrase, or clause inserted in a sentence that is grammatically complete without it. [< Gk. *para* beside + *en* in + *tithenai* to place] **—par·en·thet·i·cal** (par′ən·thet′i·kəl) or **par·en·thet′ic** *adj.* **—par′en·thet′i·cal·ly** *adv.*

pa·re·sis (pə·rē′sis, par′ə·sis) *n. Pathol.* 1. Partial paralysis affecting muscular motion but not sensation. 2. General paresis (which see). [< Gk., a letting go] **—pa·ret·ic** (pə·ret′ik, -rē′tik) *adj.* **—pa·ret′i·cal·ly** *adv.*

par ex·cel·lence (pär ek′sə·läns′, *Fr.* pár ek·se·läns′) Beyond comparison; preeminently. [< F, lit., by excellence]

par·fait (pär·fā′) *n.* A frozen dessert made with eggs, sugar, whipped cream, and fruit or other flavoring. [< F, perfect]

par·he·li·on (pär·hē′lē·ən) *n. pl.* **·li·a** *Meteorol.* One of two bright images sometimes appearing on a solar halo. Also **par·he′li·um.** [< PAR(A)-¹ + Gk. *hēlios* sun] **—par·he′lic, par·he·li·a·cal** (pär′hi·lī′ə·kəl) *adj.*

pa·ri·ah (pə·rī′ə) *n.* 1. A member of an extensive low caste of southern India and Burma. 2. A social outcast. [< Tamil *paraiyon*, lit., (hereditary) drummer]

pa·ri·e·tal (pə·rī′ə·təl) *adj.* 1. *Biol.* Of, pertaining to, or forming the walls of a cavity, organ, etc. 2. Of or pertaining to the parietal bones. 3. Pertaining to residence or authority within the walls of a college. **—***n.* A parietal bone. [< L *paries* wall]

parietal bone *Anat.* Either of two bones that form a part of the top and sides of the cranium.

par·i-mu·tu·el (par′i·myōō′chōō·əl) *n.* 1. A system of betting at races in which those who have bet on the winners share in the total amount wagered. Also **par′i·mu′tu·el.** 2. A pari-mutuel machine. [< F, stake or mutual wager]

pari-mutuel machine A machine for recording pari-mutuel bets: also called *totalizator*, *totalizer*.

par·ing (pâr′ing) *n.* 1. The act of one who pares. 2. *Often pl.* The part pared off.

Paris green A poisonous green compound, used as an insecticide and as a pigment.

par·ish (par′ish) *n.* 1. *Eccl.* In the Anglican, Roman Catholic, and some other churches, a district with its own church. 2. In Louisiana, a civil district corresponding to a county. 3. The people of a parish; esp., those who worship at the same church. ◆Collateral adjective: *parochial.* [< Gk. *paroikia* neighborhood, diocese]

pa·rish·ion·er (pə·rish′ən·ər) *n.* A member of a parish.

Pa·ri·sian (pə·rizh′ən, -riz′ē·ən) *adj.* Of the city of Paris or its inhabitants. **—Pa·ri′sian** *n.*

par·i·ty (par′ə·tē) *n. pl.* **·ties** 1. Equality, as of condition, rank, value, etc.; also, a like state or degree. 2. Equality between the currency or prices of commodities of two countries or cities. 3. Perfect analogy; close resemblance. 4. A level for farm prices that gives to the farmer the same purchasing power that he averaged during each year of a chosen base period. [< MF *paritas* equality]

park (pärk) *n.* 1. A tract of land for public recreation in or near a city. 2. Land preserved by a government because of its historical, scientific, or scenic interest. 3. A large tract of land surrounding a country estate. **—***v.t. & v.i.* To place or leave (an automobile, etc.) standing for a time, as on a street. [< OF *parc* game preserve]

par·ka (pär′kə) *n.* 1. A hooded outer garment of undressed skins worn by Eskimos. 2. Any similar garment. [< Aleut]

Par·kin·son's disease (pär′kən·sənz) *Pathol.* A form of paralysis characterized by muscular rigidity, tremor, and weakness. Also **Park′·in·son·ism.** [after James *Parkinson*, 1755–1824, English physician]

Parkinson's Law The observation that work lasts as long as the time alloted to it. [after C. Northcote *Parkinson*, 1909–, English historian]

park·land (pärk′land′) *n. Often pl.* 1. Land used or designated as a park. 2. Grassland with trees.

park·way (pärk′wā) *n.* A wide thoroughfare planted with turf and trees.

par·lance (pär′ləns) *n.* Manner of speech; language. [< OF *parler* to speak]

par·lay (pär′lā, -lē) *v.t. & v.i.* To place (an original bet and its winnings) on a later race, contest, etc. **—***n.* Such a bet. [< Ital. *paroli* grand cast at dice]

par·ley (pär′lē) *n.* A conference, as with an enemy. [< F *parlée*, fem. pp. of *parler* to speak] **—par′ley** *v.i.*

par·lia·ment (pär′lə·mənt) *n.* 1. An assembly for consultation and deliberation. 2. A national legislature. [< OF *parlement* speaking]

Par·lia·ment (pär′lə·mənt) *n.* The supreme legislature of any of several countries, esp. of Great Britain and Northern Ireland.

par·lia·men·tar·i·an (pär′lə·men·târ′ē·ən) *n.* One versed in parliamentary procedure or debate.

par·lia·men·ta·ry (pär′lə·men′tər·ē) *adj.* 1. Of, pertaining to, or enacted by a parliament. 2. According to the rules of a parliament.

parliamentary procedure The rules by which meetings of deliberative assemblies, clubs, etc., are formally conducted. Also **parliamentary law.**

par·lor (par′lər) *n.* 1. A room for reception of callers or entertainment of guests. 2. A business establishment: ice-cream *parlor.* Also *Brit.* **par′lour.** [< LL *parabolare* to speak]

parlor car A railway car fitted with luxurious chairs.

par·lous (pär′ləs) *adj.* 1. Dangerous or exciting. 2. Shrewd. [Var. of PERILOUS] —**par′lous·ly** *adv.*

Par·me·san cheese (pär′mə·zan′, -zän′) A hard, dry cheese made from skim milk, usu. grated before using.

pa·ro·chi·al (pə·rō′kē·əl) *adj.* 1. Pertaining to, supported by. or confined to a parish. 2. Narrow; provincial. [See PARISH.] —**pa·ro′chi·al·ism** *n.* —**pa·ro′chi·al·ly** *adv.*

parochial school A school supported and directed by the parish of a church.

par·o·dy (par′ə·dē) *n. pl.* **·dies** A humorous or burlesque imitation of a literary or musical work or style. [< Gk. *parōidia* burlesque poem or song] —**pa·rod·ic** (pə·rod′ik) or **·i·cal** *adj.* —**par′o·dist** *n.* —**par′o·dy** *v.t.* **·died, ·dy·ing**

par·ole (pə·rōl′) *n.* 1. The conditional release of a prisoner before his sentence has expired. 2. The duration of such conditional freedom. —**on parole** Freed from prison under conditions of parole. —*v.t.* **·roled, ·rol·ing** To release (a prisoner) on parole. [< F *parole (d'honneur)* word (of honor)] —**pa·rol′ee** *n.*

pa·rot·id (pə·rot′id) *adj. Anat.* 1. Situated near the ear. 2. Designating one of the paired salivary glands in front of and below the ear. —*n.* A parotid gland. [< PAR(A)-[1] + Gk. *ous, ōtos* ear]

par·ox·ysm (par′ək·siz′əm) *n.* 1. A sudden and violent outburst, as of emotion or action. 2. *Pathol.* A sudden intensification of the symptoms of a disease, usu. occurring at intervals. [< PAR(A)-[1] + Gk. *oxynein* to goad] —**par′ox·ys′mal** *adj.* —**par′ox·ys′·mal·ly** *adv.*

par·quet (pär·kā′, -ket′) *n.* 1. Flooring of parquetry. 2. The main floor of a theater, esp. from the orchestra pit to the parquet circle: also called *orchestra.* —*v.t.* **·quet·ed** (-kād′, -ket′id), **·quet·ing** (-kā′ing, -ket′ing) To make (a floor, etc.) of parquetry. [< OF *parchet* small compartment]

parquet circle The section of theater seats at the rear of the parquet and under the balcony: also called *parterre.*

par·quet·ry (pär′kit·rē) *n. pl.* **·ries** Inlaid mosaic of wood, used esp. for floors.

parr (pär) *n.* 1. A young salmon before its first migration seaward. 2. The young of some other fishes, as the cod or pollack. [? < dial. E (Scot.)]

par·ri·cide (par′ə·sīd) *n.* 1. The killing of a parent. 2. One who has killed a parent. [< L *paricida* killer of a relative] —**par′ri·ci′dal** *adj.* —**par′ri·ci′dal·ly** *adv.*

par·rot (par′ət) *n.* Any of certain birds native in warm regions, having a hooked bill and often brilliant plumage, some of which imitate human speech and laughter. —*v.t.* To repeat or imitate by rote. [ME, var. of *Perrot* < F *Pierrot,* a personal name] —**par′rot·er** *n.*

parrot fish Any of many small fishes inhabiting warm seas and having vivid coloring and beaklike jaws.

par·ry (par′ē) *v.t. & v.i.* **·ried, ·ry·ing** To ward off or evade (a thrust in fencing, a hostile question, etc.). —*n. pl.* **·ries** A defensive stroke or diversion in or as in fencing. [< Ital. *parare* to ward off]

parse (pärs) *v.t.* **parsed, pars·ing** To analyze (a sentence) grammatically by giving the form and syntactic function of each of its words. [< L *pars, partis* part]

par·sec (pär′sek) *n. Astron.* A unit of length used in expressing stellar distances, equal to 3.26 light-years.

Par·see (pär′sē, pär·sē′) *n.* A member of a religious sect in India practicing a form of Zoroastrianism. Also **Par′si.** [< Persian *Pārsī* a Persian] —**Par′see·ism, Par′si·ism, Par′sism** *n.*

par·si·mo·ny (pär′sə·mō′nē) *n. pl.* **·nies** Undue sparingness in the expenditure of money; stinginess. [< L *parsus,* pp. of *parcere* to spare] —**par′si·mo′ni·ous** *adj.* —**par′si·mo′ni·ous·ly** *adv.*

pars·ley (pärs′lē) *n.* A cultivated herb with aromatic leaves, widely used to garnish and flavor foods. [< Gk. *petra* rock + *selinon* parsley]

pars·nip (pärs′nip) *n.* A European herb of the parsley family, with a large, sweetish, edible root. [ME < OF *pasnaie* + OE *nǣp* turnip]

par·son (pär′sən) *n.* 1. A clergyman; minister. 2. In some churches, a clergyman in charge of a parish. [< Med.L *persona* rector] —**par·son·i·cal** (pär·son′i·kəl) or **par·son′ic** *adj.*

par·son·age (pär′sən·ij) *n.* A clergyman's dwelling, esp. one provided by the church.

part (pärt) *n.* 1. A portion of a whole; segment. 2. A distinct piece or portion that fulfills a specific function in the working of the whole, as of a machine, animal body, etc. 3. *Usu. pl.* A region; territory: in foreign *parts.* 4. One's proper share, as of obligation or performance: to do one's *part.* 5. A role in a play. 6. One side in a dispute. 7. Participation in something. 8. *Usu. pl.* An endowment of mind or character: a man of *parts.* 9. The melody intended for a single voice or instrument in a concerted piece; also, the written music for this. 10. The dividing line on the scalp made by combing sections of the hair in opposite directions. —**for one's part** As far as one is concerned. —**for the most part** To the greatest extent; in general. —**in part** Partly. —**part and parcel** An essential part. —**to take part** To participate; share or cooperate: usu. with *in.* —**to take someone's part** To support someone in a contest or disagreement. —*v.t.* 1. To divide or break (something) into parts. 2. To separate; keep or move apart. 3. To comb (the hair) so as to leave a dividing line on the scalp. —*v.i.* 4. To become divided or broken into parts. 5. To go away from each other; cease associating. 6. To depart. —**to part from** To separate from; leave. —**to part with** 1. To give up; relinquish. 2. To part from. —*adv.* To some extent; partly. [< L *pars, partis*]

par·take (pär·tāk′) *v.i.* **·took, ·tak·en, ·tak·ing** 1. To take part or have a share: with *in.* 2. To receive or take a portion or share: with *of.* 3. To have something of the quality or character: with *of.* [< L *pars, partis* part + *capere* to take] —**par·tak′er** *n.*

par·terre (pär·târ′) *n.* 1. A flower garden having beds arranged in a pattern. 2. The parquet circle in a theater. [< L *per* through, all over + *terra* land]

par·the·no·gen·e·sis (pär′thə·nō·jen′ə·sis) *n. Biol.* Reproduction by means of unfertilized eggs, seeds, or spores. Also **par′the·nog′e·ny** (-noj′ə·nē). [< Gk. *parthenos* virgin + GENESIS] —**par′the·no·ge·net′ic** (-jə·net′ik), **par′the·no·gen′ic** *adj.*

par·tial (pär′shəl) *adj.* 1. Pertaining to, constituting, or involving a part only. 2. Favoring one side; biased. 3. Having a special liking: usu. with *to.* [< L *pars, partis* part] —**par·ti·al·i·ty** (pär′shē·al′ə·tē), **par′tial·ness** *n.* —**par′tial·ly** *adv.*

par·tic·i·pant (pär·tis′ə·pənt) *adj.* Sharing; taking part in. —*n.* One who participates.

par·tic·i·pate (pär·tis′ə·pāt) *v.i.* **·pat·ed, ·pat·ing** To take part or have a share in common with others: with *in.* [< L *pars, partis* part + *capere* to take] —**par·tic′i·pa′·tion, par·tic′i·pance** *n.* —**par·tic′i·pa′tor** *n.* —**par·tic′i·pa·to′ry** (-pə·tôr′ē) *adj.*

par·ti·cip·i·al (pär′tə·sip′ē·əl) *adj. Gram.* 1. Having the nature, form, or use of a participle. 2. Characterized by, consisting of, or based on a participle. —*n.* A participle.

par·ti·ci·ple (pär′tə·sip′əl) *n. Gram.* A verb form that can also function as an adjective. The **present participle** ends in *-ing* and the **past participle** commonly in *-d, -ed, -en, -n,* or *-t.* [< L *participium* a sharing, partaking]

par·ti·cle (pär′ti·kəl) *n.* 1. A minute part, piece, or portion, as of matter. 2. A very small amount or slight degree. 3. *Physics* One of the elementary components of an atom, as an electron, proton, neutron, meson, etc. 4. *Gram.* A short, uninflected part of speech, as an article, preposition, etc. [< L *particula,* dim. of *pars, partis* part]

particle board A hard board made of bonded wood chips: also *flakeboard.*

par·ti-col·ored (pär′tē·kul′ərd) *adj.* 1. Differently colored in different parts. 2. Diversified. [< F *partir,* to divide + COLORED]

par·tic·u·lar (pər·tik′yə·lər) *adj.* 1. Peculiar or pertaining to an individual person, object, or instance; not universal; specific. 2. Referring to one as distinguished from others. 3. Especially noteworthy. 4. Requiring or giving minute attention to details; fastidious. —*n.* 1. *Usu. pl.* An item; detail. 2. An individual instance; a single or separate case. —**in particular** Particularly. [< LL *particularis* concerning a part]

par·tic·u·lar·i·ty (pər·tik′yə·lar′ə·tē) *n. pl.* **·ties** 1. The state or quality of being particular. 2. That which is particular, as a circumstance, detail, or peculiarity.

par·tic·u·lar·ize (pər·tik′yə·lə·rīz′) *v.* **·ized, ·iz·ing** *v.t.* 1. To speak of or treat individually or in detail. —*v.i.* 2. To give particular details; be specific. —**par·tic′u·lar·i·za′tion** *n.* —**par·tic′u·lar·iz′er** *n.*

par·tic·u·lar·ly (pər·tik′yə·lər·lē) *adv.* 1. With specific reference; distinctly. 2. In an unusually great degree; especially. 3. Part bv part; in detail.

par·tic·u·late (pər·tik′yə·lāt) *adj.* Consisting of minute, separate particles.

part·ing (pär′ting) *adj.* 1. Given or done at parting: a *parting* glance. 2. Departing; declining. 3. Separating; dividing. —*n.* 1. The act of separating, or the state of being separated. 2. A leave-taking; esp., a final separation. 3. A place of separation.

par·ti·san (pär′tə·zən) *n.* 1. One who supports or upholds a party, cause, etc.; esp., an overly zealous adherent. 2. *Mil.* A member of a body of detached or irregular troops; a guerrilla. —*adj.* 1. Of, relating to, or characteristic of a partisan. 2. Advocated by or composed of members of one party. 3. *Mil.* Of or carried on by partisans. Also **par′ti·zan.** [< L *pars, partis* part] —**par′ti·san·ship** *n.*

par·tite (pär′tīt) *adj.* Divided into or composed of parts: used in combination: *bipartite, tripartite.* [< L *partitus,* pp. of *partire* to divide]

par·ti·tion (pär·tish′ən) *n.* 1. The act of dividing, separating, or distributing; also, the state of being divided, etc. 2. Something that divides or separates, as a light interior wall dividing a room. 3. One of the parts, sections, compartments, etc., into which a thing is divided. —*v.t.* 1. To divide into parts, sections, segments, etc. 2. To separate by a partition: often with *off.* [< L *partire* to divide] —**par·ti′tion·er** *n.* —**par·ti′tion·ment** *n.*

par·ti·tive (pär′tə·tiv) *adj.* 1. Separating into integral parts or distinct divisions. 2. *Gram.* Denoting a part as distinct from the whole. —**par′ti·tive·ly** *adv.*

part·ly (pärt′lē) *adv.* In some part; partially.

part·ner (pärt′nər) *n.* One who is united or associated with another or others in some action, enterprise, etc.; as: **a** One of the joint owners of a business. **b** A spouse. **c** One of a couple who dance together. **d** One of two or more players on the same side in a game. **e** A colleague or associate. [ME] —**part′ner·ship** *n.*

part of speech *Gram.* One of the eight traditional classes of words in English: noun, pronoun, verb, adverb, adjective, conjunction, preposition, and interjection.

par·took (pär·to͝ok′) Past tense of PARTAKE.

par·tridge (pär′trij) *n. pl.* **·tridge** or **·tridg·es** 1. Any of certain small, plump game birds of the Old World. 2. Any of various similar birds, as the ruffed grouse or the bobwhite. [< Gk. *perdix, -ikos* partridge]

part song A song of three or more parts; esp., a secular choral piece without accompaniment.

part-time (pärt′tīm′) *adj.* For, during, or by part of the time: a *part-time* student.

par·tu·ri·tion (pär′tyo͞o·rish′ən, -cho͞o-) *n.* Childbirth. [< L *parturiens, -entis* being in labor] —**par·tu·ri·ent** (pär·tyo͝or′ē·ənt, -to͝or′-) *adj.*

par·ty (pär′tē) *n. pl.* **·ties** 1. A social gathering for pleasure or entertainment. 2. A group of persons associated or gathered together for some common purpose; as: **a** A political group organized to gain control of a government through the election of its candidates to public office. **b** A small body of persons selected for some special mission or assignment: a demolition *party.* **c** A group formed for a sport or other diversion. 3. *Law* Either of the persons or groups involved in legal proceedings. 4. One who takes part or participates in an action, plan, etc.: a *party* to his crime. 5. *Informal* A person. [< OF *partir* to divide] —**par′ty** *adj.*

party line 1. A telephone line or circuit serving two or more subscribers: also **party wire.** 2. The essential beliefs or policies of a political party.

party politics Policies and acts aimed at furthering the interests of one political party.

par value The nominal or stated value of stock; face value.

par·ve·nu (par′və·nōō, -nyōō) *n.* One who has risen above his class through the sudden attainment of wealth or position; an upstart. [< F, orig., pp. of *parvenir* to arrive < L *pervenire*]

pas (pä) *n.* A dance step. [< F < L *passus* step]

pas·chal (pas′kəl) *adj.* Pertaining to Passover or to Easter. [< Hebrew *pesakh* a passing over]

pas de deux (pä də dœ′) *French* A dance or ballet figure for two persons.

pa·sha (pə·shä′, pash′ə, pä′shə) *n.* Formerly, a Turkish honorary title placed after the name of generals, governors of provinces, etc. [< Turkish *bāsh* head]

pa·sha·lik (pə·shä′lik) *n.* The province or jurisdiction of a pasha. Also **pa·sha′lic.** [< Turkish]

Pash·to (push′tō) *n.* The Iranian language dominant in Afghanistan.

pasque·flow·er (pask′flou′ər) *n.* A plant of the crowfoot family, having white, red, or purple flowers blooming about Easter: also **paschal flower, pasch′flow′er.** [< F *passe-fleur*]

pas·quin·ade (pas′kwin·ād′) *n.* An abusive or coarse personal satire posted in a public place. —*v.t.* **·ad·ed, ·ad·ing** To attack or ridicule in pasquinades; lampoon. [< Ital. *Pasquino*, a statue at Rome on which satirical verses were pasted] —**pas′quin·ad′er** *n.*

pass (pas) *v.* **passed** (*Rare*, **past**), **passed** or **past, pass·ing** *v.t.* 1. To go by or move past. 2. To succeed in meeting the requirements of (a test, trial, etc.). 3. To go beyond or surpass. 4. To spend (a specified period of time). 5. To cause or allow to move, go past, proceed, etc. 6. To approve or sanction; enact: to *pass* a bill. 7. To be approved or sanctioned by. 8. To cause or allow to get through (a test, trial, etc.). 9. To convey or transfer from one to another; transmit. 10. In football, hockey, etc., to transfer (the ball, etc.) to another player on the same team. 11. To utter or pronounce, esp. judicially: to *pass* sentence. 12. To discharge or excrete (waste). —*v.i.* 13. To go or move; proceed; advance. 14. To go by or move past. 15. To obtain or force a way: to *pass* through a crowd. 16. To lead or extend; run: The river *passes* under a bridge. 17. To go by or elapse. 18. To come to an end; terminate. 19. To change or move from one condition, place, form, etc., to another. 20. To take place; occur. 21. To be allowed or permitted without challenge, censure, etc. 22. To undergo a test, etc., successfully. 23. To be approved, sanctioned, ratified, etc. 24. To be excreted or voided. 25. *Law* To give or pronounce sentence, judgment, etc.: with *on* or *upon*. 26. In football, hockey, etc., to transfer the ball, etc., to a teammate. 27. In card games, to decline to make a play, bid, etc. —**to pass away** 1. To come to an end. 2. To die. 3. To allow (time) to elapse. —**to pass for** To be accepted or regarded as, usu. erroneously. —**to pass off** 1. To give out or circulate as genuine; palm off. 2. To be emitted, as vapor. —**to pass out** 1. To distribute or circulate. 2. *Informal* To faint. —**to pass over** To fail to notice or consider. —**to pass up** *Informal* 1. To reject or fail to take advantage of, as an offer or opportunity. 2. To pass over. —*n.* 1. A way or opening through which one can pass; esp., a narrow passage between mountains. 2. A permit, order, or license giving the bearer authority to enter, move about, depart, etc., without the usual restrictions; as: **a** *Mil.* Permission to be absent from duty; also, the period of absence covered by it. **b** A free ticket for a theater, movie, train, etc. 3. In magic, hypnotism, etc.; a movement of the hand, a wand, etc., over a person or thing. 4. A state of affairs; situation: to bring events to a critical *pass.* 5. The act of passing. —**to bring to pass** To cause to be fulfilled or accomplished. —**to come to pass** To happen. —**to make a pass at** 1. To attempt to hit. 2. *Slang* To attempt to become sexually intimate with; proposition. [< L *passus* step]

pass·a·ble (pas′ə·bəl) *adj.* 1. Capable of being passed, penetrated, crossed, etc.: *passable* rivers. 2. Fairly good or acceptable; tolerable. —**pass′a·ble·ness** *n.* —**pass′a·bly** *adv.*

pas·sage (pas′ij) *n.* 1. A portion of a writing, speech, or musical composition, usu. of small or moderate length. 2. A way, channel, duct, etc., by which a person or thing may pass. 3. A hall, corridor, etc., between apartments in a building. 4. The act of passing, changing, etc.; esp., the transition from one state or period to another. 5. A journey, esp. by sea. 6. The right, power, or freedom to pass. 7. The passing or enactment of a legislative measure. [< OF]

pas·sage·way (pas′ij·wā′) *n.* A way affording passage; esp., a hall or corridor.

pass·book (pas′bŏŏk′) *n.* A bankbook.

pas·sé (pa·sā′, pas′ā) *adj.* 1. Past the prime; faded. 2. Out-of-date; old-fashioned. [< F, orig., pp. of *passer* to pass]

pas·sel (pas′əl) *n.* A large number; a group. [Alter. of PARCEL]

pas·sen·ger (pas′ən·jər) *n.* One who travels in a conveyance. [< MF *passager*]

pas·ser-by (pas′ər·bī′) *n.* *pl.* **pas·sers-by** One who passes by, usu. casually.

pas·ser·ine (pas′ər·ēn, -in) *adj.* 1. Of or pertaining to an order of birds including all singing birds and more than half of all living birds. 2. Resembling or characteristic of a sparrow. —*n.* A passerine bird. [< L *passer* sparrow + -INE[1]]

pas·sim (pas′im) *adv.* *Latin* Here and there; in various passages.

pass·ing (pas′ing) *adj.* 1. Going by or away. 2. Transitory; fleeting. 3. Happening or occurring; current. 4. Done, said, etc., in a cursory or casual manner. 5. That serves to pass: a *passing* grade. —*n.* 1. The act of one who or that which passes. 2. Death. —**in passing** Incidentally. —*adv.* *Archaic* In a surpassing degree or manner.

pas·sion (pash′ən) *n.* 1. Any intense,

extreme, or overpowering emotion or feeling, as love, anger etc. 2. Intense sexual desire or lust. 3. An outburst of strong feeling, esp. of violence or anger. 4. A strong desire or affection for some object, cause, etc. 5. The object of such a desire or affection. [< L < *passus*, pp. of *pati* to suffer] **—pas′sion·less** *adj.*

Pas·sion (pash′ən) *n.* The sufferings of Christ, esp. after the Last Supper and on the Cross.

pas·sion·ate (pash′ən·it) *adj.* 1. Capable of or inclined to strong passion; excitable. 2. Expressing or characterized by passion or strong emotion; ardent. 3. Strong or vehement, as a feeling or emotion. **—pas′sion·ate·ly** *adv.* **—pas′sion·ate·ness** *n.*

pas·sion·flow·er (pash′ən·flou′ər) *n.* Any of various vines or shrubs having showy flowers and sometimes edible berries. [So called from the fancied resemblance of certain parts to the wounds, crown of thorns, etc., of Christ]

passion fruit The berries of the passion flower.

Passion play A religious drama representing the Passion of Christ.

pas·sive (pas′iv) *adj.* 1. Not acting, working, or operating; inactive; inert. 2. Acted upon, affected, or influenced by something external. 3. Receiving or receptive to an external force, etc. 4. Submitting or yielding without resistance or opposition; submissive. 5. *Gram.* Designating a voice of the verb that indicates that the subject is receiving the action. **—***n.* *Gram.* 1. The passive voice. 2. A verb or construction in this voice. [< L *passus*, pp. of *pati* to suffer] **—pas′sive·ly** *adv.* **—pas·siv′i·ty** *n.*

pass·key (pas′kē′) *n.* A master key.

Pass·o·ver (pas′ō′vər) *n.* A Jewish feast commemorating the deliverance of the ancient Israelites from slavery in Egypt. [Referring to the night when God, smiting the first-born of the Egyptians, "passed over" the houses of the children of Israel (*Ex.* xii)]

pass·port (pas′pôrt′) *n.* An official warrant certifying the citizenship of the bearer and affording protection to him when traveling abroad. [< MF *passer* to pass + *port* harbor]

pass·word (pas′wûrd′) *n.* 1. A secret word or phrase enabling the speaker to pass a guard or sentry. 2. Anything that gains entrance or access for one.

past (past) *adj.* 1. Ended or finished; done with. 2. Having existed in or belonging to a former time: *past* civilizations. 3. Just passed or gone by: the *past* few days. **—***n.* 1. Past or antecedent time, conditions, or events: usu. with *the.* 2. Something, as a former life or career, that is kept secret. 3. *Gram.* **a** A verb tense denoting a past action or condition. **b** A verb in this tense. **—***adv.* In such a manner as to go by: to run *past.* **—***prep.* Beyond, as in time, position, amount, or influence. [Orig. pp. of PASS]

pas·ta (päs′tə) *n.* A noodlelike paste or dough, as spaghetti, macaroni, etc. [< Ital. < LL, dough, paste]

paste (pāst) *n.* 1. A mixture used as an adhesive. 2. Any of various soft, moist, smooth preparations used as foods, in cooking, etc. 3. A vitreous composition used in making imitation gems; also, a gem made of this composition. **—***v.t.* **past·ed, past·ing** 1. To stick or fasten with or as with paste. 2. To cover by applying pasted material. [< Gk. *pastē* barley porridge] **—past′er** *n.*

paste·board (pāst′bôrd′) *n.* Paper pulp compressed, or a stiff sheet made of paper pasted together. **—***adj.* Flimsy.

pas·tel (pas·tel′, pas′tel) *n.* 1. A picture drawn with colored crayons. 2. A paste made of ground pigment in a gum solution; also, a hard crayon made of this paste. 3. A delicate, soft, or slightly grayish tint. [See PASTE.] **—pas·tel′** *adj.*

pas·tern (pas′tərn) *n.* The part of a horse's foot that is between the fetlock and the hoof. [< OF *pasture* tether for a grazing animal]

pas·teur·ize (pas′chə·rīz, -tə-) *v.t.* **·ized, ·iz·ing** To slow down fermentation and destroy disease-causing bacteria (in milk, beer, etc.) by heating. Also *Brit.* **pas′teur·ise.** [after Louis *Pasteur*, 1822–95, French chemist] **—pas′teur·i·za′tion** *n.*

pas·tiche (pas·tēsh′) *n.* A work of art, music, or literature made up of fragments from other sources. [< F]

pas·tille (pas·tēl′, -til′) *n.* 1. A compound of aromatic substances used for fumigating. 2. A troche; lozenge. Also **pas·til** (pas′til). [< F < L *pastillus* little loaf, lozenge]

pas·time (pas′tīm′) *n.* Something that serves to make time pass agreeably. [Trans. of F *passe-temps*]

pas·tor (pas′tər) *n.* A Christian clergyman who has a church or congregation under his charge. [< L *pastor*, *-oris* shepherd, lit., feeder] **—pas′tor·ship** *n.*

pas·tor·al (pas′tər·əl) *adj.* 1. Of or pertaining to shepherds, rustics, or rural life. 2. Having the characteristics usu. associated with rural life, as innocence, simplicity, etc. 3. Pertaining to a clergyman or to his duties. **—***n.* 1. A literary work, esp. a poem, dealing with rural life, scenes, etc. 2. A picture illustrating rural scenes. [< L *pastor* shepherd] **—pas′tor·al·ism** *n.* **—pas′tor·al·ist** *n.*

pas·tor·ate (pas′tər·it) *n.* 1. The office or jurisdiction of a pastor. 2. The duration of a pastoral charge.

past participle See under PARTICIPLE.

past perfect *Gram.* The verb tense indicating an action completed prior to the occurrence of some other past action, as *had finished* in *He had finished before the bell rang.* Also called *pluperfect.*

pas·tra·mi (pə·strä′mē) *n.* Heavily seasoned, smoked beef, usu. cut from the shoulder. [< Yiddish < Rumanian]

pas·try (pās′trē) *n. pl.* **·tries** Sweet, baked food, usu. made with a crust of dough, as pies, tarts, etc.

pas·tur·age (pas′chər·ij) *n.* 1. Grass and herbage for cattle. 2. Ground used or suitable for grazing.

pas·ture (pas′chər) *n.* 1. Ground for the grazing of domestic animals. 2. Grass or herbage that grazing domestic animals eat. **—***v.t.* **·tured, ·tur·ing** To put in a pasture to graze. [< L *pascere* to feed] **—pas′tur·a·ble** *adj.*

past·y[1] (pās′tē) *adj.* **past·i·er, past·i·est** Like paste. **—past′i·ness** *n.*

past·y[2] (pās′tē, *Brit.* pas′tē, päs′tē) *n. pl.* **pas·ties** A pie; esp., a meat pie. [< LL *pasta* paste]

pat (pat) *v.t.* **pat·ted, pat·ting** 1. To touch or tap lightly with something flat, esp. with the hand. 2. To shape or mold by a pat. —*n.* 1. A light, caressing stroke; a gentle tap. 2. The sound of patting or pattering. 3. A small, molded mass, as of butter. —*adj.* 1. Exactly suitable; apt. 2. Glib; facile. —*adv. Informal* Firm; steadfast: to stand *pat.* [ME *patte*] —**pat′ness** *n.* —**pat′ter** *n.*

pa·ta·ca (pä·tä′kä) *n.* The monetary unit of Macao.

patch (pach) *n.* 1. A small piece of material used to repair a garment, etc. 2. A piece of adhesive tape or the like, applied to the skin. 3. A piece of material worn over an injured eye. 4. Any small part of a surface not sharing the general character of the whole. —*v.t.* 1. To put a patch on. 2. To repair or put together, esp. hurriedly or crudely: often with *up* or *together.* 3. To make of patches, as a quilt. [ME *pacche*] —**patch′a·ble** *adj.* —**patch′er** *n.*

patch pocket A pocket sewn to the outside of a garment.

patch·work (pach′wûrk′) *n.* 1. A fabric made of patches of cloth, as for quilts, etc. 2. Work done hastily or carelessly.

patch·y (pach′ē) *adj.* **patch·i·er, patch·i·est** 1. Made up of patches. 2. Careless; jumbled. —**patch′i·ly** *adv.* —**patch′i·ness** *n.*

pate (pāt) *n.* The head or top of the head; also, the brains or intellect: usu. humorous or derogatory. [ME]

pâ·té (pä·tā′) A seasoned paste of cooked meats or poultry. [< F]

pa·tel·la (pə·tel′ə) *n. pl.* **·tel·lae** (-tel′ē) *Anat.* The flat, movable, oval bone in front of the knee joint; kneecap. [< L, dim. of *patina* pan, bowl] —**pa·tel′lar** *adj.* —**pa·tel′late** (-āt, -it) *adj.*

pat·en (pat′n) *n.* 1. A plate; esp., a plate for the eucharistic bread. 2. A thin, metallic plate or disk. [< L *patina* pan]

pat·ent (pat′nt, *Brit.* pāt′nt; *for adj. defs. 1 & 3, usu.* pāt′nt) *n.* 1. A government protection to an inventor, securing to him for a specific time the exclusive right of manufacturing and selling an invention. 2. Any official document securing a right. 3. That which is protected by a patent or its distinctive marks or features. —*v.t.* To obtain a patent on (an invention). —*adj.* 1. Manifest or apparent to everybody. 2. Open for general inspection or use. 3. *Chiefly Med.* Open; unobstructed, as an intestine. [< L *patere* to lie open] —**pa′ten·cy** *n.* —**pat′ent·a·bil′i·ty** *n.* —**pat′·ent·a·ble** *adj.*

pat·en·tee (pat′n·tē′) *n.* One who holds a patent.

patent leather Leather with a glossy, varnish-like finish.

pa·tent·ly (pāt′nt·lē, pat′nt-) *adv.* Manifestly; clearly.

pa·ter (pā′tər) *n. Brit. Informal* Father. [< L]

pa·ter·fa·mil·i·as (pā′tər·fə·mil′ē·əs) *n.* The father of a family. [< L *pater* father + *familia* family]

pa·ter·nal (pə·tûr′nəl) *adj.* 1. Of, pertaining to, or characteristic of a father; fatherly. 2. Derived from, related through, or connected with one's father. [< L *pater* father] —**pa·ter′nal·ly** *adv.*

pa·ter·nal·ism (pə·tûr′nəl·iz′əm) *n.* The care or control of a country, community, group of employees, etc., in a manner suggestive of a father looking after his children. —**pa·ter′nal·is′tic** *adj.* —**pa·ter′·nal·is′ti·cal·ly** *adv.*

pa·ter·ni·ty (pə·tûr′nə·tē) *n.* 1. The condition of being a father. 2. Parentage on the male side. 3. Origin in general.

path (path) *n. pl.* **paths** (pathz, paths) 1. A walk or way used by man or animals on foot. 2. A track or course. 3. A course of life or action. [OE *pæth*] —**path′less** *adj.*

pa·thet·ic (pə·thet′ik) *adj.* Of the nature of, expressing, or arousing sadness, pity, tenderness, etc. [< Gk. *pathos* suffering] —**pa·thet′i·cal·ly** *adv.*

path·find·er (path′fīn′dər) *n.* One skilled in leading or finding a way, esp. in unknown regions.

-pathia See -PATHY.

patho- *combining form* Suffering; disease. Also, before vowels, **path-**. [< Gk. *pathos* suffering]

path·o·gen (path′ə·jən) *n.* Any disease-producing bacterium or microorganism. —**path′o·gen′ic** (-jen′ik) *adj.*

path·o·gen·e·sis (path′ə·jen′ə·sis) *n. Med.* The production or development of any diseased condition. Also **pa·thog·e·ny** (pə·thoj′ə·nē).

path·o·log·i·cal (path′ə·loj′i·kəl) *adj.* 1. Of pathology. 2. Related to or caused by disease. —**path′o·log′i·cal·ly** *adv.*

pa·thol·o·gy (pə·thol′ə·jē) *n. pl.* **·gies** 1. The branch of medical science that treats of the origin, nature, causes, and development of disease. 2. The sum of the conditions, processes, and effects in the course of a disease. —**pa·thol′o·gist** *n.*

pa·thos (pā′thos) *n.* The quality, esp. in literature or art, that arouses feelings of pity, sorrow, compassion, etc. [< Gk., suffering]

path·way (path′wā′) *n.* A path.

-pathy *combining form* 1. Suffering; affection. 2. *Med.* Disease, or the treatment of disease: *psychopathy.* Also spelled *-pathia.* [< Gk. *pathos* suffering]

pa·tience (pā′shəns) *n.* 1. The state, quality, or fact of being patient; also, the ability to be patient. 2. *Brit.* Solitaire (def. 2).

pa·tient (pā′shənt) *adj.* 1. Possessing or demonstrating quiet, uncomplaining endurance under distress or annoyance. 2. Tolerant, tender, and forbearing. 3. Persevering; diligent. —*n.* A person undergoing treatment for disease or injury. [< L *pati* to suffer] —**pa′tient·ly** *adv.*

pat·i·na (pat′ə·nə, pə·tē′nə) *n.* A green rust that covers ancient bronzes, copper coins, medals, etc. [< L, plate]

pa·ti·o (pat′ē·ō, pät′ē·o) *n. pl.* **·ti·os** 1. An open inner court. 2. A paved area adjoining a house, used for parties, barbecues, etc. [< Sp.]

pat·ois (pat′wä, *Fr.* på·twä′) *n. pl.* **pat·ois** (pat′wäz, *Fr.* på·twä′) A type of local dialect, esp. one that is rustic or illiterate. [< F; origin uncertain]

patri- *combining form* Father: *patricide.* [< L *pater, -tris*]

pa·tri·arch (pā′trē·ärk) *n.* 1. The leader of a family or tribe who rules by paternal right. 2. A venerable man; esp., the founder of a religion, order, etc. 3. *Eccl.* In the Greek

Orthodox Church, any of the bishops of Constantinople, Alexandria, Antioch, or Jerusalem. [< Gk. *patria* family, clan + *archein* to rule] **—pa′tri·ar′chal** *adj.*

pa·tri·ar·chate (pā′trē·är′kit) *n.* The office, dominion, or residence of a patriarch.

pa·tri·ar·chy (pā′trē·är′kē) *n. pl.* **·chies** A system of government in which the father or the male heir of his choice rules.

pa·tri·cian (pə·trish′ən) *adj.* 1. Of or pertaining to the aristocracy. 2. Noble or aristocratic. *—n.* 1. An aristocrat. 2. Any one of the upper classes. [< L *pater, -tris* senator, lit., father]

pat·ri·cide (pat′rə·sīd) *n.* 1. The killing of one's father. 2. One who has killed his father. [< LL *patricidium*] **—pat′ri·ci′dal** *adj.*

pat·ri·lin·e·al (pat′rə·lin′ē·əl) *adj.* Derived from or descending through the male line.

pat·ri·mo·ny (pat′rə·mō′nē) *n. pl.* **·nies** An inheritance from a father or an ancestor; also, anything inherited. [< L *pater, -tris* father] **—pat′ri·mo′ni·al** *adj.*

pa·tri·ot (pā′trē·ət, -ot) *n.* One who loves his country and zealously guards its welfare. [< Gk. *patris* fatherland] **—pa′tri·ot′ic** (-ot′ik) *adj.* **—pa′tri·ot′i·cal·ly** *adv.* **—pa·tri·ot·ism** (pā′trē·ə·tiz′əm) *n.*

pa·tris·tic (pə·tris′tik) *adj.* Of or pertaining to the fathers of the Christian church or to their writings. **—pa·tris′ti·cal·ly** *adv.*

pa·trol (pə·trōl′) *v.t. & v.i.* **·trolled, ·trol·ling** To walk or go through or around (an area, town, etc.) for the purpose of guarding or inspecting. *—n.* 1. One or more soldiers, policemen, etc., patrolling a district. 2. A military reconnaissance or combat group. 3. The act of patrolling. [< MF *patouiller*, orig., to paddle in mud]

patrol car A squad car.

pa·trol·man (pə·trōl′mən) *n. pl.* **·men** (-mən) 1. One who patrols. 2. A policeman assigned to a beat.

patrol wagon A police wagon for conveying prisoners.

pa·tron (pā′trən) *n.* 1. One who protects, fosters, or supports some person or enterprise. 2. A regular customer. [< L *patronus* protector] **—pa′tron·ess** *n.fem.*

pa·tron·age (pā′trən·ij, pat′rən-) *n.* 1. The protection or support of a patron. 2. In the public service, the power or right to distribute offices, esp. political offices. 3. The financial support given by customers to a commercial establishment.

pa·tron·ize (pā′trən·īz, pat′rən-) *v.t.* **·ized, ·iz·ing** 1. To act as a patron toward; give support to. 2. To treat in a condescending manner. 3. To trade with as a regular customer; frequent. **—pa′tron·iz′er** *n.* **—pa′tron·iz′ing·ly** *adv.*

pat·ro·nym·ic (pat′rə·nim′ik) *n.* 1. A name derived from the name of one's father or paternal ancestor. 2. A name formed by adding a prefix or suffix to a proper name, as *Johnson*, son of John. [< Gk. *patēr* father + *onoma* name] **—pat′ro·nym′ic** *adj.*

pa·troon (pə·tro͞on′) *n.* Formerly, under Dutch law, an estate owner having some manorial rights. [< Du. < L *patronus* protector]

pat·sy (pat′sē) *n. Slang* One who is readily taken advantage of [? < Ital. *pazzo* madman]

pat·ter[1] (pat′ər) *v.i.* 1. To make a succession of light, sharp sounds. 2. To move with light, quick steps. [Freq. of PAT] **—pat′ter** *n.*

pat·ter[2] (pat′ər) *v.t. & v.i.* To speak or say glibly or rapidly; chatter. *—n.* 1. Glib and rapid talk, as used by comedians, etc. 2. Any professional jargon. [Short for *paternoster*, a prayer beginning in Latin with *pater noster* our father]

pat·tern (pat′ərn) *n.* 1. An original or model proposed for or worthy of imitation. 2. Anything shaped or designed to serve as a model or guide in making something else. 3. Any decorative design or figure. 4. The stylistic composition or design of a work of art. 5. A complex of integrated parts functioning as a whole: the behavior *pattern* of a five-year-old. 6. A representative example, sample, or instance. *—v.t.* To make after a model or pattern: with *on, upon,* or *after.* [< F *patron* patron]

pat·ty (pat′ē) *n. pl.* **·ties** 1. A small, flat piece of chopped meat, fish, etc. 2. A small pie. [< PÂTÉ]

patty shell A small pastry shell in which creamed meat, fish, vegetables, or fruit are served.

pau·ci·ty (pô′sə·tē) *n.* 1. Smallness of number or quantity. 2. Scarcity; insufficiency. [< L *paucus* few]

paunch (pônch) *n.* The abdomen or the belly, esp. if protruding. [< L *pantex, -ticis* belly] **—paunch′y** *adj.* **—paunch′i·ness** *n.*

pau·per (pô′pər) *n.* 1. One who receives, or is entitled to receive, public charity. 2. Any very poor person. [< Med.L, poor] **—pau′·per·ism** *n.* **—pau′per·ize** *v.t.* **·ized, ·iz·ing**

pause (pôz) *v.i.* **paused, paus·ing** 1. To cease action or utterance temporarily; hesitate. 2. To dwell or linger: with *on* or *upon.* *—n.* 1. A temporary ceasing of action; rest. 2. A holding back because of doubt or irresolution; hesitation. 3. A momentary cessation in speaking or music for the sake of meaning or expression. [< Gk. *pauein* to stop] **—paus′er** *n.*

pav·an (pə·van′, -vän′) *n.* A slow, stately dance of the 16th and 17th c. Also **pav·ane′.** [< MF]

pave (pāv) *v.t.* **paved, pav·ing** To cover or surface with asphalt, gravel, concrete, etc., as a road. **—to pave the way** (for) To make preparation (for); lead up (to). [< L *pavire* to ram down] **—pav′er** *n.*

pave·ment (pāv′mənt) *n.* 1. A paved road or footway. 2. The material with which a surface is paved.

pa·vil·ion (pə·vil′yən) *n.* 1. A movable or open structure, as a large tent or summerhouse. 2. A related or connected part of a principal building, as for hospital patients. 3. A canopy. *—v.t.* To provide or shelter with a pavilion. [< L *papilio, -onis* butterfly, tent]

pav·ing (pā′ving) *n.* 1. The laying of a pavement. 2. A pavement.

paw (pô) *n.* The foot of an animal having nails or claws. *—v.t. & v.i.* 1. To strike or scrape with the feet or paws: to *paw* the air. 2. *Informal* To handle or caress rudely or clumsily; maul. [< OF *powe*, prob. < Gmc.] **—paw′er** *n.*

pawl (pôl) *n. Mech.* A hinged or pivoted member shaped to engage with ratchet teeth, either to drive a ratchet wheel or to prevent its reverse motion. [Origin uncertain]

pawn[1] (pôn) *n.* 1. A chessman of lowest rank. 2. Any insignificant person used at another's will. [< OF *peon* foot soldier]

pawn[2] (pôn) *n.* 1. Something pledged as security for a loan. 2. The condition of being held as a pledge for money loaned. —*v.t.* To give as security for a loan. [< OF *pan*, var. of early Frisian *pand* pledge] —**pawn′er** *n.*

pawn·brok·er (pôn′brō′kər) *n.* One engaged in the business of lending money at interest on pledged personal property.

Paw·nee (pô·nē′) *n. pl.* **·nees** or **·nee** A member of one of four tribes of North American Indians formerly inhabiting Nebraska and Kansas.

pawn·shop (pôn′shop′) *n.* The shop of a pawnbroker.

paw·paw (pô′pô) See PAPAW.

pay (pā) *v.* **paid** or (*Obs.* except for def. 2 of *to pay out*) **payed, pay·ing** *v.t.* 1. To give (someone) what is due for a debt, purchase, etc.; remunerate. 2. To give (money, etc.) for a purchase, service rendered, etc. 3. To provide or hand over the amount of, as a debt, bill, etc. 4. To yield as return or recompense. 5. To afford profit or benefit to. 6. To render or give, as a compliment, attention, etc. 7. To make, as a call or visit. —*v.i.* 8. To make recompense or payment. 9. To be worthwhile: It *pays* to be honest. —**to pay back** To repay. —**to pay off** 1. To pay the entire amount of (a debt, mortgage, etc.). 2. To pay the wages of and discharge. 3. *Informal* To afford full return. 4. *Slang* To bribe. —**to pay out** 1. To disburse or expend. 2. *Naut.* To let out by slackening, as a rope or cable. —**to pay up** To make full payment (of). —*n.* 1. That which is given as a recompense; wages. 2. Paid employment. 3. Requital; reward; also, retribution. —*adj.* 1. Of or pertaining to payments, persons who pay, or services paid for: *pay* day. 2. Requiring payment on use: *pay* phone. [< L *pacare* to appease] —**pay′a·ble** *adj.* —**pay·ee′** *n.* —**pay′er** *n.*

pay·check (pā′chek′) *n.* 1. A check in payment of wages or salary. 2. Wages or salary.

pay dirt 1. Soil containing enough metal to be profitable to mine. 2. Anything profitable.

pay·load (pā′lōd′) *n.* 1. That part of a cargo producing revenue. 2. The warhead of a guided missile. 3. The persons, instruments, etc., carried in a spacecraft that are directly related to the objective of the flight.

pay·mas·ter (pā′mas′tər) *n.* One who has charge of paying employees.

pay·ment (pā′mənt) *n.* 1. The act of paying, or that which is paid. 2. Punishment.

pay·off (pā′ôf′) *n.* 1. *Informal* Any settlement, reward, or punishment. 2. *Informal* The climax or outcome of an incident or narrative. 3. *Slang* A bribe.

pay·roll (pā′rōl′) *n.* A list of those entitled to receive pay, with the amounts due them; also, the total sum of money needed to make the payments.

PCP Phencyclidine.

pea (pē) *n. pl.* **peas** or **pease** 1. A climbing annual leguminous herb having green pods. 2. The round edible seeds. [ME *pese*, ult. < Gk. *pison*]

peace (pēs) *n.* 1. A state of mental or physical quiet or tranquillity; calm. 2. The absence or cessation of war. 3. Public order and tranquillity. 4. A state of reconciliation after strife or enmity. —**at peace** 1. In a quiet state; tranquil. 2. In a state or condition of order and harmony. —**to hold** (or **keep**) **one's peace** To be silent. —*v.i. Obs. except as an imperative* To be or become quiet. [< L *pax, pacis*] —**peace′ful** *adj.* —**peace′·ful·ly** *adv.*

Peace Corps A U.S. government organization that sends trained volunteers to live in and aid developing countries by teaching, farming, building, etc.

peace·a·ble (pē′sə·bəl) *adj.* 1. Inclined to peace. 2. Peaceful; tranquil. —**peace′a·bly** *adv.*

peace·mak·er (pēs′mā′kər) *n.* One who effects a reconciliation between unfriendly parties.

peace pipe The calumet.

peace·time (pēs′tīm′) *n.* A time of peace. —*adj.* Of, characterized by, or used in such a time.

peach (pēch) *n.* 1. The edible fruit of a tree of the rose family, widely cultivated in many varieties. 2. The tree itself. 3. A yellowish pink color. [< Gk. *Persikon* (*mēlon*) Persian (fruit)]

peach·y (pē′chē) *adj.* **peach·i·er, peach·i·est** *Slang* Delightfully pleasant, beautiful, etc. —**peach′i·ness** *n.*

pea·cock (pē′kok′) *n.* A male peafowl, having erectile, brilliantly iridescent tail feathers marked with eyelike spots, and the neck and breast of a greenish blue. [OE *pēa, pāwa* peacock (< L *pavo*) + COCK[1]]

peacock blue A vivid greenish blue.

pea·fowl (pē′foul′) *n.* A large pheasant of Asia.

pea·hen (pē′hen′) *n.* A female peafowl.

pea jacket A short coat of thick woolen cloth, worn by seamen. Also called **pea·coat** (pē′kōt′). [< Du. *pij* coat of coarse wool + JACKET]

peak (pēk) *n.* 1. A projecting point or edge; an end terminating in a point. 2. A conspicuous or precipitous mountain; also, the summit of such a mountain. 3. The maximum development, strength, value, etc., of something. 4. *Naut.* The sharply narrowed part of a vessel at the bow or stern. —*v.t.* 1. To make into a peak or point. —*v.i.* 2. To assume the form of a peak. 3. To reach or attain a peak. [Var. of PIKE[4]]

peak·ed (pē′kid, pēkt) *adj.* Having a thin or sickly appearance. [Origin uncertain]

peal (pēl) *n.* 1. A prolonged, sonorous sound, as of a bell or thunder. 2. A set of large bells. 3. A change rung on a set of bells. —*v.t. & v.i.* To sound with a peal or peals. [< OF *apeler* to appeal]

pea·nut (pē′nut′) *n.* 1. The nutlike seed or seed pod of an annual herbaceous vine ripening underground from the flowers that bury themselves after fertilization. 2. The plant bearing this nut.

peanut butter A spread made from ground, roasted peanuts.

pear (pâr) *n.* 1. The juicy, edible, fleshy fruit of a tree of the rose family. 2. The tree. [< L *pirum*]

pearl (pûrl) *n.* 1. A smooth, rounded,

variously tinted body formed in the shells of various mollusks and largely used as a gem. 2. Something like such a jewel in form, luster, value, etc. 3. Mother-of-pearl. 4. A very pale bluish gray: also **pearl blue, pearl gray.** —*adj.* Pertaining to, consisting of, set with, or made of pearl. —*v.i.* 1. To seek or fish for pearls. —*v.t.* 2. To adorn or set with or as with pearls. [< L *perna* mussel] —**pearl'y** *adj.*

peas·ant (pez'ənt) *n.* 1. In Europe, a farmer, farm laborer, or rustic workman. 2. *Informal* A boorish, uncouth, or simple-minded person. [< OF *pais* country < LL *pagus* district]

peas·ant·ry (pez'ən·trē) *n.* 1. The peasant class; a body of peasants. 2. Rusticity.

peat (pēt) *n.* 1. A substance consisting of partially carbonized vegetable material, found usu. in bogs. 2. A block of this substance, pressed and dried for fuel: also called *turf.* [< Med.L *peta* piece of peat] —**peat'y** *adj.*

peat bog A marsh with an accumulation of peat.

peat moss A moss of which peat is largely composed.

pea·vey (pē'vē) *n. pl.* **·vies** An iron-pointed lever fitted with a movable hook and used for handling logs. Also **pea'vy.** [after Joseph *Peavey,* its inventor]

peb·ble (peb'əl) *n.* 1. A small, rounded fragment of rock, shaped by the action of water, ice, etc. 2. Quartz crystal; also, a lens made of it. —*v.t.* **·bled, ·bling** 1. To impart a rough grain to (leather). 2. To cover or pelt with pebbles. [Back formation of OE *papol(stān)* pebble(stone)] —**peb'bly** (-lē, -əl·ē) *adj.* **·bli·er, ·bli·est**

pe·can (pi·kan', -kän', pē'kan) *n.* 1. A large hickory of the central and southern U.S., with edible, oval, thin-shelled nuts. 2. The nut of this tree. [Earlier *paccan* < Algonquian (Cree) *pacan*]

pec·ca·dil·lo (pek'ə·dil'ō) *n. pl.* **·los** or **·loes** A slight or trifling sin. [< Sp., dim. of *pecado* sin < L *peccare* to sin]

pec·cant (pek'ənt) *adj.* Guilty of sin; sinful. —**pec'can·cy** *n.*

pec·ca·ry (pek'ər·ē) *n. pl.* **·ries** A hoglike animal of Central and South America. [< Carib *pakira*]

pec·ca·vi (pe·kā'vī, -kä'vē) *n. pl.* **·vis** *Latin* A confession of guilt; literally, I have sinned.

peck[1] (pek) *v.t.* 1. To strike with the beak, as a bird does, or with something pointed. 2. To make by striking thus: to *peck* a hole in a wall. 3. To pick up, as food, with the beak. —*v.i.* 4. To make strokes with the beak or with something pointed. 5. To eat in small amounts or without appetite: with *at.* —*n.* 1. A quick, sharp blow, as with a beak. 2. *Informal* A quick kiss. [Var. of PICK] —**peck'er** *n.*

peck[2] (pek) *n.* 1. A measure of capacity equal to ¼ bushel or 8.8 liters. 2. *Slang* A great quantity. [< OF *pek*]

pec·tin (pek'tin) *n. Biochem.* Any of a class of carbohydrates found in various fruits, as apples, lemons, etc., and used as a gel in fruit jellies.

pec·to·ral (pek'tər·əl) *adj.* Of or pertaining to the breast or chest. —*n.* A pectoral organ, fin, or muscle. [< L *pectus, -oris* breast]

pectoral fin *Zool.* One of the anterior paired fins of fishes, corresponding to the anterior limb of higher vertebrates.

pec·u·late (pek'yə·lāt) *v.t. & v.i.* **·lat·ed, ·lat·ing** To steal or appropriate (funds) wrongfully; embezzle. [< L *peculari* to embezzle] —**pec'u·la'tion** *n.*

pe·cul·iar (pi·kyōōl'yər) *adj.* 1. Having a character exclusively its own; specific. 2. Singular; strange or eccentric. 3. Belonging particularly or exclusively to one. [< MF *peculier* or < L *peculium* private property] —**pe·cul'iar·ly** *adv.*

pe·cu·li·ar·i·ty (pi·kyōō'lē·ar'ə·tē, -kyōōl'·yar'-) *n. pl.* **·ties** 1. A characteristic. 2. The quality of being peculiar.

pe·cu·ni·ar·y (pi·kyōō'nē·er'ē) *adj.* Consisting of or relating to money. [< L *pecunia* money]

ped-[1] Var. of PEDI-.

ped-[2] Var. of PEDO-.

-ped Var. of -PEDE.

ped·a·gog·ic (ped'ə·goj'ik, -gō'jik) *adj.* 1. Of or pertaining to the science or art of teaching. 2. Of or belonging to a pedagogue; affected with a conceit of learning. Also **ped'a·gog'i·cal.** —**ped'a·gog'i·cal·ly** *adv.*

ped·a·gogue (ped'ə·gog, -gôg) *n.* 1. A schoolmaster; educator. 2. A pedantic, narrow-minded teacher. Also **ped'a·gog.** [< Gk. *pais, paidos* child + *agōgos* leader]

ped·a·go·gy (ped'ə·gō'jē, -goj'ē) *n.* The science or profession of teaching.

ped·al (ped'l) *adj.* 1. Of or pertaining to a foot, feet, or a footlike part. 2. Of or pertaining to a pedal. —*n. Mech.* A lever operated by the foot and having various functions: a bicycle *pedal,* a piano *pedal.* —*v.t. & v.i.* **ped·aled** or **·alled, ped·al·ing** (ped'ə·ling, ped'ling) or **·al·ling** To move or operate by working pedals. [< L *pes, pedis* foot]

ped·ant (ped'ənt) *n.* One who makes needless display of his learning, or who insists upon the importance of trifling points of scholarship. [< Ital. *pedante,* prob. < Med.L *paedagogare* to teach] —**pe·dan·tic** (pi·dan'tik) *adj.* —**pe·dan'ti·cal·ly** *adv.* —**ped'·ant·ry** *n.*

ped·dle (ped'l) *v.t. & v.i.* **·dled, ·dling** 1. To travel about selling small wares. 2. To sell or dispense in small quantities. [Appar. back formation < ME *pedlere* peddler] —**ped'dler** *n.*

-pede *combining form* Footed: *centipede.* Also spelled *-ped.* [< L *pes, pedis* foot]

ped·er·as·ty (ped'ə·ras'tē, pē'də-) *n.* Sex relations between men, esp. between men and boys. [< Gk. *pais, paidos* boy + *erastēs* lover] —**ped'er·ast** *n.*

ped·es·tal (ped'is·təl) *n.* 1. A base or support for a column, statue, or vase. 2. Any foundation or support. —**to put on a pedestal** To hold in high estimation; to put in the position of an idol or hero. [< Ital. *piè, piede* foot + *di* of + *stallo* stall, standing place]

pe·des·tri·an (pə·des'trē·ən) *adj.* 1. Moving on foot; walking. 2. Pertaining to common people; plebeian. 3. Commonplace, prosaic, or dull. —*n.* One who journeys or moves from place to place on foot; a walker. [< L *pedester, -tris* on foot] —**pe·des'tri·an·ism** *n.*

pedi- *combining form* Foot; related to the foot

or feet. Also, before vowels, *ped-*. [< L *pes, pedis* foot]

pe·di·at·rics (pē′dē·at′riks) *n.pl.* (*construed as sing.*) That branch of medicine dealing with the diseases and hygienic care of children. [< PED-[2] + -IATRICS] —**pe′di·at′ric** *adj.* —**pe·di·a·tri·cian** (pē′dē·ə·trish′ən) *n.*

ped·i·cab (ped′i·kab) *n.* A three-wheeled vehicle operated by pedaling and used for public hire, esp. in Asia.

pe·dic·u·lo·sis (pə·dik′yə·lō′sis) *n. Pathol.* The condition of being infested with lice. [< L *pediculus* little louse + -OSIS] —**pe·dic′u·lous** *adj.*

ped·i·cure (ped′i·kyŏŏr) *n.* 1. Chiropody. 2. The cosmetic treatment of the feet and toenails. [< L *pes, pedis* foot + *curare* to care for] —**ped′i·cur·ist** *n.*

ped·i·gree (ped′ə·grē) *n.* 1. A line of ancestors; lineage. 2. A list or table of descent and relationship, esp. of an animal of pure breed. [< MF *pié de grue* a crane's foot; from the resemblence of its mark to a family tree] —**ped′i·greed** *adj.*

ped·i·ment (ped′ə·mənt) *n. Archit.* 1. A broad triangular part above a portico or door. 2. Any similar piece surmounting a door, screen, bookcase, etc. [Earlier *periment*, prob. alter. of PYRAMID] —**ped′i·men′tal** (-men′təl) *adj.*

pedo- *combining form* Child; children; offspring: also, before vowels, *ped-*. [< Gk. *pais, paidos* child]

pe·dom·e·ter (pi·dom′ə·tər) *n.* An instrument that records the number of steps taken by the person who carries it. [< L *pes, pedis* foot + Gk. *metron* measure]

pe·dun·cle (pi·dung′kəl) *n. Bot.* The general stalk or support of a flower or flower cluster. [< NL *pedunculus* footstalk, dim. of *pes, pedis* foot] —**pe·dun′cu·lar** (-kyə·lər) *adj.*

peek (pēk) *v.i.* To look furtively, slyly, or quickly; peep. —*n.* A peep, glance. [ME *piken*]

peel[1] (pēl) *n.* The natural coating of certain kinds of fruit, as oranges and lemons; skin; rind. —*v.t.* 1. To strip off the bark, skin, etc., of. 2. To strip off; remove. —*v.i.* 3. To lose bark, skin, etc. 4. To come off: said of bark, skin, etc. 5. *Slang* To undress. —**to keep one's eye peeled** *Informal* To keep watch; be alert. [< L *pilare* to deprive of hair] —**peel′er** *n.*

peel[2] (pēl) *n.* A long-handled implement used in moving bread, etc., about an oven. [< L *pala* shovel]

peel·ing (pē′ling) *n.* Something peeled off, as rind, skin, etc.

peen (pēn) *n.* The end of a hammer head opposite the flat, striking face, usu. shaped like a wedge. —*v.t.* To beat, bend, or shape with the peen. [< ON]

peep[1] (pēp) *v.i.* 1. To utter the small, sharp cry of a young bird or chick; chirp; cheep. 2. To speak in a weak, small voice. —*n.* 1. The cry of a chick or small bird, or of a young frog; chirp. 2. A small sandpiper. [ME *pepen*; imit.]

peep[2] (pēp) *v.i.* 1. To look through a small hole, from concealment, etc. 2. To look furtively or quickly. 3. To begin to appear; be just visible. —*n.* 1. A furtive look; a glimpse or glance. 2. The earliest appearance: the *peep* of day. [Prob. alter. of PEEK] —**peep′er** *n.*

peep·er (pē′pər) *n.* An animal that peeps, as a chick or any of several tree frogs.

peep·hole (pēp′hōl′) *n.* An aperture, as a hole or crack, through which one may peep; also, a small window in a door.

peep·ing Tom (pē′ping tom′) One who peeps in at windows. [after the legendary tailor who peeped at Lady Godiva]

peep·show (pēp′shō′) *n.* An exhibition of pictures, etc., viewed through a small orifice fitted with a magnifying lens.

peer[1] (pir) *v.i.* 1. To look narrowly or searchingly, as in an effort to see clearly. 2. To come partially into view. [Origin uncertain]

peer[2] (pir) *n.* 1. An equal, as in natural gifts or in social rank. 2. An equal before the law. 3. A noble, esp. a British duke, marquis, earl, viscount, or baron. [< OF < L *par* equal]

peer·age (pir′ij) *n.* 1. The office or rank of a peer or nobleman. 2. Peers collectively.

peer·ess (pir′is) *n.* A woman who holds a title of nobility, either in her own right or by marriage with a peer.

peer·less (pir′lis) *adj.* Of unequaled excellence. —**peer′less·ly** *adv.* —**peer′less·ness** *n.*

peeve (pēv) *v.t.* **peeved, peev·ing** *Informal* To make peevish. —*n. Informal* A complaint, annoyance, or grievance. [Back formation < PEEVISH]

pee·vish (pē′vish) *adj.* 1. Irritable or querulous; cross. 2. Showing discontent and vexation. [ME *pevische*] —**pee′vish·ly** *adv.* —**pee′vish·ness** *n.*

pee·wee (pē′wē) *n.* 1. A pewee. 2. *Informal* Anything or anyone small or diminutive. —*adj.* Tiny. [Imit.]

peg (peg) *n.* 1. A pin, usu. of wood or metal, used to fasten articles together, to stop a hole, etc. 2. A projecting pin upon which something may be hung, or which may serve to keep a score, etc. 3. A reason or excuse. 4. A degree or step, as in rank or estimation. —**to take (one) down a peg** To lower the self-esteem of (a person). —*v.* **pegged, peg·ging** *v.t.* 1. To drive or force a peg into; fasten with pegs. 2. To mark with pegs. 3. To strike or pierce with a peg or sharp instrument. 4. *Informal* To throw. —*v.i.* 5. To work or strive hard and perseveringly: usu. with *away*. [< MDu. *pegge*] —**peg** *adj.*

Peg·a·sus (peg′ə·səs) *n.* A constellation, the Winged Horse. [< Gk. *Pēgasos*]

peg·board (peg′bôrd′) *n.* Any perforated board into which pegs may be inserted for holding things, keeping score, etc.

peg leg *Informal* 1. An artificial leg of rodlike or tapering shape. 2. A person with such a leg.

peg-top (peg′top′) *adj.* Wide at the hip and narrow at the ankle: said of trousers: also **pegged.**

pei·gnoir (pān·wär′, pen-) *n.* A loose dressing gown or negligée worn by women. [< F *peigner* to comb]

pe·jo·ra·tive (pi·jôr′ə·tiv, -jor′-) *adj.* Having or giving a derogatory or disparaging meaning or sense: a *pejorative* statement. [< LL *pejorare* to make worse] —**pe·jo′ra·tive** *n.* —**pe·jo′ra·tive·ly** *adv.*

Pe·king·ese (pē′kə·nēz′ *for def. 1*; pē′king·ēz′

for defs. 2, 3) *n. pl.* **·ese** 1. A variety of a pug dog, having long, silky hair and short legs. 2. A native or inhabitant of Peking. 3. The dialect spoken in Peking. —*adj.* Of or pertaining to Peking. Also **Pe·kin·ese** (pē′kə·nēz′).

pe·koe (pē′kō, *Brit.* pek′ō) *n.* A black tea of India, Ceylon, and Java, made from the young buds of the tea plant. [< dial. Chinese *pek* white + *ho* hair]

pe·lag·ic (pə·laj′ik) *adj.* Of, pertaining to, or inhabiting the sea or ocean far from land. [< Gk. *pelagos* the sea]

pelf (pelf) *n.* Money; wealth, esp. if dishonestly acquired. [< OF *pelfre* booty]

pel·i·can (pel′i·kən) *n.* A large, gregarious, web-footed bird of warm regions, having a pouch on the lower jaw for the temporary storage of fish. [< Gk. *pelekan*]

pel·la·gra (pə·lag′rə, -lā′grə) *n. Pathol.* A disease characterized by gastric disturbance, skin eruptions, etc., caused by dietary deficiency. [< NL, prob. < Ital. *pelle agra* rough skin] —**pel·la′grous** *adj.*

pel·let (pel′it) *n.* 1. A small round ball, as of medicine or paper. 2. A small bullet. —*v.t.* To strike or hit with pellets. [< L *pila* ball]

pell-mell (pel′mel′) *adv.* 1. In a confused or disordered way. 2. In wild haste. —*adj.* Devoid of order; confused. Also **pell′mell′**. [< OF *pesle-mesle*]

pel·lu·cid (pə·lo͞o′sid) *adj.* 1. Permitting to a certain extent the passage of light. 2. Transparently clear and simple: a *pellucid* style. [< L *per-* through + *lucere* to shine] —**pel·lu′cid·ly** *adv.* —**pel·lu·cid·i·ty** (pel′o͞o·sid′ə·tē) *n.*

pe·lo·ta (pe·lō′tə) *n.* A game played in a walled court with a hard rubber ball and a curved wicker racquet. [< Sp., lit., a ball]

pelt[1] (pelt) *n.* The skin of an animal, usu. with the fur left on. [< L *pellis* skin]

pelt[2] (pelt) *v.t.* 1. To strike repeatedly with or as with blows. —*v.i.* 2. To deliver repeated blows. 3. To move rapidly; hurry. —*n.* 1. A blow. 2. A swift pace. [ME *pelten*] —**pelt′er** *n.*

pelvi- *combining form* Pelvis. [< L *pelvis* basin]

pel·vis (pel′vis) *n. pl.* **·ves** (-vēz) 1. *Anat.* The part of the skeleton that forms a bony girdle joining the lower or hind limbs to the body. 2. A basinlike structure. [< L, basin] —**pel′vic** *adj.*

pem·mi·can (pem′ə·kən) *n.* Lean meat, usu. venison, cut into strips, dried, pounded into paste with fat and a few berries, and pressed into cakes. Also **pem′i·can.** [< Algonquian (Cree) *pimekan* < *pime* fat]

pen[1] (pen) *n.* 1. An instrument for writing with fluid ink, usu. a metal point split in the middle and fitted to a holder. 2. Any of various writing instruments requiring an ink supply. 3. The quality of one's penmanship. —*v.t.* **penned, pen·ning** To write with a pen. [< L, wing, feather]

pen[2] (pen) *n.* 1. A small enclosure, as for pigs; also, the animals contained in a pen. 2. *Slang* A penitentiary. —*v.t.* **penned** or **pent, pen·ning** To enclose in or as in a pen; confine. [OE *penn*]

pe·nal (pē′nəl) *adj.* 1. Of or pertaining to punishment. 2. Liable, or rendering liable, to punishment. 3. Enacting or prescribing punishment: a *penal* code. [< L *poena* penalty]

pe·nal·ize (pē′nəl·īz, pen′əl-) *v.t.* **·ized, ·iz·ing** 1. To subject to a penalty, as for a violation. 2. To declare (an action) subject to a penalty. Also *Brit.* **pe′nal·ise.** —**pe′nal·i·za′tion** *n.*

pen·al·ty (pen′əl·tē) *n. pl.* **·ties** 1. The legal punishment for having violated a law. 2. A sum of money to be forfeited as punishment; fine. 3. The loss or suffering incurred by some act: the *penalty* of sin. 4. In sports and games, any handicap imposed for a violation of rules.

pen·ance (pen′əns) *n.* 1. *Eccl.* A sacramental rite involving contrition, confession of sins to a priest, the acceptance of penalties, and absolution. 2. Any voluntary act of atonement for sin. [< L *paenitere* to repent]

pence (pens) *Brit.* The plural of PENNY: used mostly in combination: *twopence.*

pen·chant (pen′chənt) *n.* A strong liking or inclination for something. [< F *pencher* to incline]

pen·cil (pen′səl) *n.* 1. A writing, drawing, or marking implement, usu. containing graphite. 2. A small stick of some substance: a styptic *pencil.* —*v.t.* **pen·ciled** or **·cilled, pen·cil·ing** or **·cil·ling** To mark, write, draw, or color with or as with a pencil. [< L *penicillum* paintbrush] —**pen′cil·er** or **pen′·cil·ler** *n.*

pend (pend) *v.i.* 1. To await adjustment or settlement. 2. *Dial.* To hang; depend. [< L *pendere* to hang]

pen·dant (pen′dənt) *n.* An ornament that hangs from something else. Also spelled *pendent.* —*adj.* Pendent. [See PEND.]

pen·dent (pen′dənt) *adj.* 1. Hanging downward; suspended. 2. Projecting; overhanging. 3. Undetermined; pending. Also spelled *pendant.* —*n.* A pendant. [Var. of PENDANT] —**pen′dent·ly** *adv.*

pend·ing (pen′ding) *adj.* 1. Remaining unfinished or undecided. 2. Imminent; impending. —*prep.* 1. During the process or continuance of. 2. While awaiting; until.

pen·drag·on (pen·drag′ən) *n.* In ancient Britain, a supreme ruler or chief. [< Welsh, a chief leader in war]

pen·du·lous (pen′jo͞o·ləs, -dyə-) *adj.* 1. Hanging, esp. so as to swing. 2. Undecided; wavering. [< L *pendere* to hang] —**pen′du·lous·ly** *adv.* —**pen′du·lous·ness** *n.*

pen·du·lum (pen′jo͞o·ləm, -dyə-) *n.* 1. A suspended body free to oscillate between two extremes. 2. Such a device serving to regulate the movement of a clock. [See PENDULOUS.]

pen·e·trate (pen′ə·trāt) *v.* **·trat·ed, ·trat·ing** *v.t.* 1. To force a way into or through; pierce; enter. 2. To spread or diffuse itself throughout. 3. To perceive the meaning of; understand. —*v.i.* 4. To enter or pass through something. [< L *penetrare* to put within] —**pen′e·tra·ble** (-trə·bəl) *adj.* —**pen′e·tra·bil′i·ty** *n.*

pen·e·trat·ing (pen′ə·trā′ting) *adj.* 1. Tending or having power to penetrate. 2. Acute; discerning: a *penetrating* mind. Also **pen′e·tra′tive.** —**pen′e·trat′ing·ly** *adv.*

pen·e·tra·tion (pen′ə·trā′shən) *n.* 1. The act or power of penetrating physically. 2. Ability to penetrate mentally; acuteness; discernment. 3. The depth to which something penetrates.

pen·guin (pen′gwin, peng′-) *n.* A web-footed flightless aquatic bird of the southern hemisphere, with flipperlike wings and short legs. [< Welsh *pen* head + *gwyn* white]

pen·hold·er (pen′hōl′dər) *n.* 1. A handle with a device for inserting a metallic pen. 2. A rack for pens.

pen·i·cil·lin (pen′ə·sil′in) *n.* An antibiotic found in a mold fungus, used to treat bacterial infections. [< L *penicillus* paintbrush]

pe·nin·su·la (pə·nin′sə·lə, -syə-) *n.* A piece of land almost surrounded by water, and connected with the mainland by an isthmus. [< L *paene* almost + *insula* island] **—pe·nin′su·lar** *adj.*

pe·nis (pē′nis) *n. pl.* **·nis·es** or **·nes** (-nēz) The male organ of copulation. [< L, orig., tail] **—pe′nile** (-nil, -nīl) *adj.*

pen·i·tent (pen′ə·tənt) *adj.* Affected by a sense of one's own guilt, and resolved on reform. **—***n.* One who is penitent. [< L *paenitere* to repent] **—pen′i·tence** *n.* **—pen′i·tent·ly** *adv.*

pen·i·ten·tial (pen′ə·ten′shəl) *adj.* Of or expressing penitence or penance. **—pen′i·ten′tial·ly** *adv.*

pen·i·ten·tia·ry (pen′ə·ten′shər·ē) *n. pl.* **·ries** A prison, esp. one operated by a state or federal government for those convicted of serious crimes. **—***adj.* 1. Of or pertaining to penance. 2. Relating to or used for the punishment of criminals.

pen·knife (pen′nīf′) *n. pl.* **·knives** (-nīvz′) A small pocket knife.

pen·light (pen′līt′) *n.* A flashlight which has the size and shape of a pen. Also **pen′lite′**.

pen·man (pen′mən) *n. pl.* **·men** (-mən) 1. A person considered with regard to his handwriting. 2. An author.

pen·man·ship (pen′mən·ship) *n.* 1. The art of writing. 2. The style or quality of handwriting.

pen name An author's assumed name; pseudonym; nom de plume.

pen·nant (pen′ənt) *n.* 1. A long, narrow flag, usu. triangular, used as a school emblem, etc. 2. A similar flag awarded to sports winners. [< PENNON]

-pennate *combining form* Having wings or feathers. [< L *penna* feather]

pen·ni·less (pen′i·lis) *adj.* Poverty-stricken.

pen·non (pen′ən) *n.* 1. A small, pointed flag, borne by medieval knights on their lances. 2. A wing. [< OF *penon* streamer < L *penna* feather]

Penn·syl·va·ni·a Dutch (pen′səl·vā′nē·ə, -vān′yə) 1. Descendants of immigrants from SW Germany and from Switzerland, who settled in Pennsylvania in the 17th and 18th c. 2. The language spoken by these people, a High German dialect with an admixture of English. [< early and dial. E *Dutch* (< G *Deutsch*) German] **—Penn′syl·va′ni·a-Dutch** *adj.*

pen·ny (pen′ē) *n. pl.* **pen·nies** or *Brit.* **pence** (pens) 1. In the U.S. and Canada, a cent. 2. In the United Kingdom, a coin equal in value to $^1/_{100}$ pound. **—a pretty penny** *Informal* A large amount of money. [OE *penning, penig, pending*]

-penny *combining form* Costing (a specified number of) pennies: formerly designating the cost of nails per hundred, but now denoting their length, beginning at one inch for two-penny nails. [< PENNY]

penny pincher A parsimonious person. **—pen·ny-pinch·ing** (pen′ē·pinch′ing) *adj.* & *n.*

pen·ny·roy·al (pen′ē·roi′əl) *n.* A low, erect, mintlike herb of North America yielding oil of pennyroyal, used in medicine. [Alter. of earlier *pulyole ryale*]

pen·ny·weight (pen′ē·wāt′) *n.* In troy weight, $^1/_{20}$ ounce, 24 grains, or 1.56 grams.

pen·ny-wise (pen′ē·wīz′) *adj.* Unduly economical in small matters. **—penny-wise and pound-foolish** Economical in small matters, but wasteful in large ones.

Pe·nob·scot (pə·nob′skot) *n.* One of a tribe of North American Indians of the Algonquian confederacy of 1749.

pe·nol·o·gy (pē·nol′ə·jē) *n. pl.* **·gies** The science that treats of crime and of the management of prisons. [< L *poena* penalty + -LOGY] **—pe·nol′o·gist** *n.*

pen·sile (pen′sil) *adj.* 1. Hanging loosely. 2. Constructing pensile nests: said of birds. [< L *pendere* to hang]

pen·sion (pen′shən) *n.* A periodic allowance to an individual or to his family, given when certain conditions, as age, length of service, etc., have been fulfilled. **—***v.t.* 1. To grant a pension to. 2. To dismiss with a pension: with *off.* [< L *pensio, -onis* payment] **—pen′sion·a·ble** *adj.*

pen·sion·er (pen′shən·ər) *n.* 1. One who receives a pension or is dependent on the bounty of another. 2. A boarder, as in a convent or school.

pen·sive (pen′siv) *adj.* 1. Engaged in or given to serious, quiet reflection. 2. Expressive of, suggesting, or causing a melancholy thoughtfulness. [< L *pensare* to think] **—pen′sive·ly** *adv.* **—pen′sive·ness** *n.*

pen·stock (pen′stok′) *n.* 1. A trough or conduit for carrying water to a water wheel. 2. A sluice or floodgate controlling the discharge of water, as from a pond.

pent (pent) Past participle of PEN². **—***adj.* Penned up or in; closely confined.

penta- *combining form* Five: *pentagon.* Also, before vowels, **pent-**. [< Gk. *pente*]

pen·ta·gon (pen′tə·gon) *n. Geom.* A polygon having five sides and five angles. [< Gk. *pente* five + *gōnia* angle] **—pen·tag·o·nal** (pen·tag′ə·nəl) *adj.*

pen·tam·e·ter (pen·tam′ə·tər) *n.* 1. A line of verse consisting of five metrical feet. 2. Verse comprised of pentameters. **—***adj.* Having five metrical feet. [< Gk. *pente* five + *metron* a measure]

Pen·ta·teuch (pen′tə·to͞ok, -tyo͞ok) *n.* The first five books of the Old Testament: Genesis, Exodus, Leviticus, Numbers, and Deuteronomy. [< Gk. *pente* five + *teuchos* book]

pen·tath·lon (pen·tath′lən) *n.* An athletic contest consisting of five separate events, in all of which each contestant must participate. [< Gk. *pente* five + *athlos* contest]

Pen·te·cost (pen′tə·kôst, -kost) *n.* A Christian festival, the seventh Sunday after Easter, commemorating the descent of the Holy Ghost upon the apostles: also called *Whitsunday.* [< Gk. *pentēkostē* (*hēmera*) the fiftieth (day)] **—Pen′te·cos′tal** *adj.*

pent·house (pent′hous′) *n.* An apartment or other structure on the roof of a building. [? < LL *appendicium* appendage]

pent-up (pent′up′) *adj.* Repressed: *pent-up* emotions.

pe·nult (pē′nult, pi·nult′) *n.* The syllable next to the last in a word. Also **pe·nul·ti·ma** (pi·nul′tə·mə). [< L *paene* almost + *ultimus* last]

pe·nul·ti·mate (pi·nul′tə·mit) *adj.* 1. Next to the last. 2. Of or belonging to the penult. —*n.* A penultimate part.

pe·num·bra (pi·num′brə) *n. pl.* **·brae** (-brē) or **·bras** 1. A partially lit area around a shadow, as in an eclipse. 2. The dark fringe around the central part of a sunspot. [< L *paene* almost + *umbra* shadow] —**pe·num′·bral** *adj.*

pe·nu·ri·ous (pə·no͝or′ē·əs, -nyo͝or′-) *adj.* 1. Excessively sparing in the use of money; stingy. 2. Extremely poor. [< L *penuria* want, poverty] —**pe·nu′ri·ous·ly** *adv.* —**pe·nu′ri·ous** *n.*

pen·u·ry (pen′yə·rē) *n.* Extreme poverty or want. [< L *penuria* want]

pe·on (pē′ən) *n.* 1. In Latin America, a laborer; servant. 2. Formerly, a debtor kept in servitude until he had worked off his debt. [< Sp. < LL *pedo, -onis* foot soldier] —**pe′on·age** *n.*

pe·o·ny (pē′ə·nē) *n. pl.* **·nies** 1. A plant of the crowfoot family, having large crimson, rose, or white flowers. 2. The flower. [< Gk. *Paion* Paeon, the Healer; so called from the plant's former medicinal use]

peo·ple (pē′pəl) *n. pl.* **peo·ple**; *for def. 1, also* **peo·ples** 1. The entire body of human beings living in the same country, under the same government, and speaking the same language: the *people* of England. 2. In a state or nation, the body of persons invested with political rights. 3. A group of persons having the same interests, profession, condition of life, etc.: poor *people*. 4. Persons considered collectively: *people* say. 5. Ordinary persons; the populace: usu. with *the*. 6. One's family or relatives. —*v.t.* **·pled, ·pling** To fill with inhabitants; populate. [< L *populus* populace]

pep (pep) *n. Informal* Energy and high spirits; vigorous activity. —*v.t.* **pepped, pep·ping** To fill or inspire with energy or pep: usu. with *up*. [Short for PEPPER]

pep·per (pep′ər) *n.* 1. A pungent, aromatic condiment consisting of the dried immature berries of a plant native to India. When ground entire it is **black pepper**, but when the outer coating of the seeds is removed, the product is **white pepper**. 2. The plant producing these berries. 3. Red pepper. 4. Green pepper. —*v.t.* 1. To season with pepper. 2. To sprinkle freely. 3. To shower, as with missiles; spatter; pelt. [< Gk. *peperi*]

pep·per-and-salt (pep′ər·ən·sôlt′) *adj.* Consisting of a mixture of white and black, so as to present a grayish appearance. —*n.* A pepper-and-salt cloth.

pep·per·corn (pep′ər·kôrn′) *n.* A berry of the pepper plant.

pep·per·grass (pep′ər·gras′) *n.* A plant of the mustard family having a pungent flavor and eaten in salads. Also **pep′per·wort** (-wûrt).

pepper mill A hand mill, often designed for table use, in which peppercorns are ground.

pep·per·mint (pep′ər·mint′) *n.* 1. A pungent, aromatic herb used in medicine and confectionery. 2. An oil made from this herb. 3. A confection flavored with peppermint.

pep·per·o·ni (pep′ə·rō′nē) *n. pl.* **·ni** or **·nis** A highly seasoned, hard sausage. [< Ital.]

pep·per·y (pep′ər·ē) *adj.* 1. Pertaining to or like pepper; pungent. 2. Quick-tempered; hasty. —**pep′per·i·ness** *n.*

pep·py (pep′ē) *adj.* **·pi·er, ·pi·est** *Informal* Full of energy; lively. —**pep′pi·ness** *n.*

pep·sin (pep′sin) *n.* 1. *Biochem.* An enzyme of the stomach that promotes the digestion of proteins. 2. A medicinal preparation obtained from the stomachs of various animals, used to aid digestion. Also **pep′sine** (-sin). [< Gk. *pepsis* digestion]

pep talk *Informal* A brief, vigorous talk meant to inspire confidence or enthusiasm.

pep·tic (pep′tik) *adj.* 1. Of or promotive of digestion. 2. Of or caused by pepsin. [< Gk. *pepsis* digestion]

Pe·quot (pē′kwot) *n.* One of a tribe of Algonquian Indians, formerly inhabiting southern New England.

per (pûr) *prep.* 1. By; by means of; through: used in commercial and business English: *per* bearer. 2. To or for each: ten cents *per* yard. 3. By the; every: esp. in Latin phrases: *per diem*. [< L]

per- *prefix* 1. Through; throughout: *pervade*. 2. Thoroughly: *perturb*. 3. Away: *pervert*. 4. Very: *perfervid*. 5. *Chem.* Indicating an excess amount of a specified element in a compound: hydrogen *peroxide*. [< L *per* through]

per·ad·ven·ture (pûr′əd·ven′chər) *adv. Archaic* Perhaps. [< OF *par aventure* by chance]

per·am·bu·late (pə·ram′byə·lāt) *v.* **·lat·ed, ·lat·ing** *v.t.* 1. To walk through or over. 2. To walk through or around so as to inspect, etc. —*v.i.* 3. To stroll. [< L *per* through + *ambulare* to walk] —**per·am′bu·la′tion** *n.*

per·am·bu·la·tor (pə·ram′byə·lā′tər) *n. Chiefly Brit.* A baby carriage.

per an·num (pûr an′əm) *Latin* By the year.

per·cale (pər·kāl′, -kal′) *n.* A closely woven cotton fabric without gloss. [< Persian *pergālah*]

per cap·i·ta (pûr kap′ə·tə) *Latin* For each person; literally, by heads.

per·ceive (pər·sēv′) *v.t. & v.i.* **·ceived, ·ceiv·ing** 1. To become aware of (something) through the senses; see, hear, feel, taste, or smell. 2. To come to understand. [< L *per-* thoroughly + *capere* to take] —**per·ceiv′a·ble** *adj.* —**per·ceiv′a·bly** *adv.* —**per·ceiv′er** *n.*

per·cent (pər·sent′) *n.* The number of units in proportion to one hundred: symbol, %. Also **per cent.** —*adj. & adv.* In every hundred. [Short for L *per centum* by the hundred]

per·cent·age (pər·sen′tij) *n.* 1. A proportion or part considered in its quantitative relation to the whole. 2. *Informal* Advantage; profit.

per·cen·tile (pər·sen′tīl, -til) *n. Stat.* Any of 100 points spaced at equal intervals, each point denoting that percentage of the total cases lying below it in the series.

per·cept (pûr′sept) *n. Psychol.* 1. Something

perceived. 2. Immediate knowledge derived from perceiving. [< L *percipere* to perceive]

per·cep·ti·ble (pər·sep′tə·bəl) *adj.* That can be perceived; appreciable. **—per·cep′ti·bly** *adv.*

per·cep·tion (pər·sep′shən) *n.* 1. The act or process of perceiving. 2. The result or effect of perceiving. 3. Any insight, knowledge, etc., arrived at by or as by perceiving. 4. The capacity for perceiving. **—per·cep′tu·al** (-chōō·əl) *adj.*

per·cep·tive (pər·sep′tiv) *adj.* 1. Having a quick capacity for perceiving. 2. Of or pertaining to perception. **—per·cep′tive·ly** *adv.* **—per·cep′tive·ness** *n.*

perch[1] (pûrch) *n.* 1. A horizontal staff or pole used as a roost for poultry. 2. Any place on which birds alight or rest. 3. Any place for sitting or standing, esp. if elevated. **—***v.t. & v.i.* To alight or sit on or as on a perch. [< L *pertica* pole]

perch[2] (pûrch) *n. pl.* **perch** or **perches** 1. A small, spiny-finned fresh-water food fish. 2. Any of various related fishes. [< Gk. *perkē*]

per·chance (pər·chans′) *adv.* Possibly; perhaps. [< OF *par chance* by chance]

per·cip·i·ent (pər·sip′ē·ənt) *adj.* 1. Having the power of perception. 2. Perceiving rapidly or keenly. [< L *per-* thoroughly + *capere* to take] **—per·cip′i·ence** *n.*

per·co·late (pûr′kə·lāt; *for n., also* pur′kə·lət) *v.t. & v.i.* **·lat·ed, ·lat·ing** Of a liquid, to pass or cause to pass through a porous substance; filter. **—***n.* That which has percolated. [< L *per-* through + *colare* to strain] **—per′co·la′tion** *n.*

per·co·la·tor (pûr′kə·lā′tər) *n.* A type of coffeepot in which boiling water rises to the top in a tube and then filters down through finely ground coffee to a container below.

per·cus·sion (pər·kush′ən) *n.* 1. The sharp striking of one body against another. 2. The shock, vibration, or sound produced by a striking of one body against another. **—***adj.* Of, pertaining to, or operating by percussion. [< L *per-* through + *quatere* to shake]

percussion cap A small cap of thin metal, containing a detonating compound, used in ammunition to explode the propelling charge.

percussion instrument A musical instrument whose tone is produced by striking, as the timpani, cymbals, piano, etc.

per di·em (pûr dē′əm, dī′əm) 1. By the day. 2. An allowance for expenses each day. [< L]

per·di·tion (pər·dish′ən) *n.* 1. Eternal damnation; the utter loss of a soul. 2. The place of eternal damnation; hell. [< L *per-* through, away + *dare* to give]

per·e·gri·nate (per′ə·gri·nāt′) *v.* **·nat·ed, ·nat·ing** *v.i.* 1. To travel from place to place. **—***v.t.* 2. To travel through or along. [< L *peregrinari* to travel abroad] **—per′e·gri·na′·tion** *n.*

per·emp·to·ry (pə·remp′tər·ē) *adj.* 1. Not admitting of appeal; decisive; absolute. 2. Positive in opinion, etc.; imperious. [< L *per-* entirely + *emere* to take] **—per·emp′to·ri·ly** *adv.* **—per·emp′to·ri·ness** *n.*

per·en·ni·al (pə·ren′ē·əl) *adj.* 1. Continuing or enduring through the year or through many years. 2. Perpetual; everlasting; unceasing. 3. *Bot.* Lasting more than two years. **—***n.* A plant that grows for three or more years, usu. blossoming annually. [< L *per-* through + *annus* year] **—per·en′ni·al·ly** *adv.*

per·fect (*adj. & n.* pûr′fikt; *v.* pər·fekt′) *adj.* 1. Having all the elements or qualities requisite to its nature or kind; complete. 2. Without defect; flawless. 3. Accurately corresponding to a type or original; exact: a *perfect* replica. 4. Thorough; utter: He made a *perfect* nuisance of himself. 5. *Informal* Very great: a *perfect* horror of spiders. 6. *Gram.* Denoting the tense of a verb expressing action completed in the past. 7. *Music* Denoting the three intervals whose accuracy of intonation the human ear can recognize: the **perfect octave**, the **perfect fifth**, and the **perfect fourth**. **—***n. Gram.* The perfect tense; also, a verb in this tense. **—***v.t.* 1. To bring to perfection; complete. 2. To make thoroughly skilled or accomplished: to *perfect* oneself in an art. [< L *per-* thoroughly + *facere* to do, make] **—per·fect′i·bil′i·ty** *n.* **—per·fect′i·ble** *adj.* **—per′fect·ly** *adv.* **—per′fect·ness** *n.*

per·fec·ta (pər·fek′tə) *n.* Exacta.

per·fec·tion (pər·fek′shən) *n.* 1. The state or quality of being perfect. 2. The embodiment of something that is perfect: As a hostess, she is *perfection*. 3. The highest degree of something.

per·fec·tion·ist (pər·fek′shən·ist) *n.* One who demands of himself or of others an exceedingly high degree of excellence.

per·fec·tive (pər·fek′tiv) *adj.* Tending to make perfect. **—per·fec′tive·ness** *n.*

per·fec·to (pər·fek′tō) *n. pl.* **·tos** A cigar of medium size, shaped to taper at either end. [< Sp., perfect]

perfect pitch Absolute pitch.

per·fer·vid (pər·fûr′vid) *adj.* Excessively fervid; ardent; zealous. [< L *per-* thoroughly + *fervidus* burning]

per·fi·dy (pûr′fə·dē) *n. pl.* **·dies** The act of violating faith, trust, or allegiance; treachery. [< L *per* through, under pretext of + *fides* faith] **—per·fid·i·ous** (pər·fid′ē·əs) *adj.* **—per·fid′i·ous·ly** *adv.*

per·fo·rate (*v.* pûr′fə·rāt; *adj.* pûr′fə·rit) *v.t.* **·rat·ed, ·rat·ing** 1. To make a hole or holes through, by or as by stamping or drilling. 2. To pierce with holes in rows or patterns. **—***adj.* Perforated. [< L *per-* through + *forare* to bore] **—per′fo·ra·ble** *adj.* **—per′fo·ra′tion** *n.* **—per′fo·ra′tor** *n.*

per·fo·rat·ed (pûr′fə·rā′tid) *adj.* Pierced with a hole or holes; esp., pierced with lines of holes, as sheets of stamps.

per·force (pər·fôrs′) *adv.* By or of necessity; necessarily. [< OF *par* by + *force* force]

per·form (pər·fôrm′) *v.t.* 1. To carry out in action; execute; do. 2. To fulfill; discharge, as a duty or command. 3. To act (a part) or give a performance of (a play, piece of music, etc.). **—***v.i.* 4. To carry through to completion an action, undertaking, etc. 5. To give an exhibition or performance. [< OF *par-* thoroughly + *fournir* to accomplish] **—per·form′er** *n.*

per·form·ance (pər·fôr′məns) *n.* 1. An entertainment of some kind before an audience or spectators. 2. A public presentation: The music had its first *performance* here. 3. The act or manner of performing. 4. Any act, deed, or accomplishment.

per·fume (pər·fo͞om′; *for n., usu.* pûr′·fyo͞om) *n.* 1. A fragrant substance, usu. a volatile liquid, prepared to emit a pleasant odor; scent. 2. A pleasant odor, as from flowers; fragrance. —*v.t.* **·fumed, ·fum·ing** To fill or scent with a fragrant odor. [< Ital. *per-* through + *fumare* to smoke]

per·fum·er (pər·fyo͞o′mər) *n.* 1. One who makes or deals in perfumes. 2. One who or that which perfumes.

per·fum·er·y (pər·fyo͞o′mər·ē) *n. pl.* **·er·ies** 1. The art or business of preparing perfumes. 2. Perfumes in general. 3. A place where perfumes are made.

per·func·to·ry (pər·fungk′tər·ē) *adj.* Done mechanically or superficially; careless; cursory. [< L *per-* through + *fungi* to perform] —**per·func′to·ri·ly** *adv.* —**per·func′to·ri·ness** *n.*

per·go·la (pûr′gə·lə) *n.* An arbor or covered walk made of trelliswork. [< Ital. < L *pergula* arbor]

per·haps (pər·haps′) *adv.* Maybe; possibly. [< PER + archaic *hap* chance]

peri- *prefix* 1. Around; encircling: *periphery.* 2. Situated near; adjoining: *perihelion.* [< Gk. *peri* around]

per·i·anth (per′ē·anth) *n. Bot.* The envelope of a flower, esp. one in which the calyx and corolla are so alike as to be indistinguishable. [< PERI- + Gk. *anthos* flower]

per·i·car·di·um (per′ə·kär′dē·əm) *n. pl.* **·di·a** *Anat.* A membranous bag that surrounds and protects the heart. [< PERI- + Gk. *kardia* heart] —**per′i·car′di·al** *adj.*

per·i·carp (per′ə·kärp) *n. Bot.* The wall of a ripened ovary or fruit: also called *seedcase, seed vessel.* [< PERI- + Gk. *karpos* fruit]

Per·i·cle·an (per′ə·klē′ən) *adj.* Pertaining to, characteristic of, or named after the Athenian statesman Pericles, or the period of his supremacy, 5th c. B.C., when Greek art, drama, and statesmanship are considered to have been at their height.

per·i·gee (per′ə·jē) *n. Astron.* The point in the orbit of the moon or of an artificial satellite at which it is nearest the earth: opposed to *apogee.* [< PERI- + Gk. *gē* earth] —**per′i·ge′an** *adj.*

per·i·he·li·on (per′ə·hē′lē·ən) *n. pl.* **·li·a** *Astron.* The point in the orbit of a planet or comet where it is nearest the sun: opposed to *aphelion.* [< PERI- + Gk. *hēlios* sun]

per·il (per′əl) *n.* Exposure to the chance of injury; danger; risk. —*v.t.* **per·iled** or **·illed, per·il·ing** or **·il·ling** To expose to danger; imperil. [< L *periculum* trial, danger]

per·i·lous (per′əl·əs) *adj.* Involving or attended with peril; hazardous; risky. —**per′il·ous·ly** *adv.* —**per′il·ous·ness** *n.*

per·i·lune (per′ə·lo͞on′) *n. Astron.* That point in a lunar orbit nearest to the moon. [< PERI- + F *lune* moon]

pe·rim·e·ter (pə·rim′ə·tər) *n.* 1. The boundary line of any figure of two dimensions. 2. The length of this boundary. [< PERI- + Gk. *metron* measure] —**per·i·met·ric** (per′ə·met′rik) or **·ri·cal** *adj.*

pe·ri·od (pir′ē·əd) *n.* 1. A portion of time marked or defined by certain conditions, events, etc.: a *period* of rest. 2. A portion or lapse of time, as in a process or development; a stage. 3. A portion of time into which something is divided: The school day has seven *periods.* 4. *Geol.* One of the divisions of geologic time. 5. *Physics* The time that elapses between any two successive similar phases of an oscillation or other regularly repeated cyclical motion. 6. A dot (.) placed on the line, used as a mark of punctuation after every complete declarative sentence, after most abbreviations, etc.: also called *point.* 7. An occurrence of menstruation. [< Gk. *periodos* cycle]

pe·ri·od·ic (pir′ē·od′ik) *adj.* 1. Of, pertaining to, or like a period. 2. Recurring at regular intervals. 3. Intermittent. —**pe′ri·od′i·cal·ly** *adv.* —**pe′ri·o·dic′i·ty** (-ə·dis′ə·tē) *n.*

pe·ri·od·i·cal (pir′ē·od′i·kəl) *adj.* 1. Of publications published at regular intervals. 2. Periodic. —*n.* A periodical publication.

periodic sentence A sentence so constructed as to suspend completion of both sense and structure until the close.

per·i·o·don·tics (per′ē·ə·don′tiks) *n.* The branch of dentistry dealing with diseases of the gums and the bones around the teeth. Also **per′i·o·don′ti·a** (-shə, -shē·ə). [< PERI- + Gk. *odous, odontos* tooth] —**per′i·o·don′tal** *adj.* —**per′i·o·don′tist** *n.*

per·i·os·te·um (per′ē·os′tē·əm) *n. Anat.* A tough, fibrous vascular membrane that surrounds and nourishes the bones. [< PERI- + Gk. *osteon* bone] —**per′i·os′te·al** *adj.*

per·i·pa·tet·ic (per′i·pə·tet′ik) *adj.* Walking about from place to place. —*n.* One given to walking about. [< PERI- + Gk. *pateein* to walk]

pe·riph·er·al (pə·rif′ər·əl) *adj.* 1. Of or concerning a periphery. 2. Not central; marginal: of *peripheral* importance. —**pe·riph′er·al·ly** *adv.*

pe·riph·er·y (pə·rif′ər·ē) *n. pl.* **·er·ies** 1. The outer part, surface, or boundary of something. 2. A surrounding region, area, or country. [< PERI- + Gk. *pherein* to carry]

pe·riph·ra·sis (pə·rif′rə·sis) *n. pl.* **·ses** (-sēz) A roundabout expression of something; circumlocution. [< PERI- + Gk. *phrazein* to declare] —**per·i·phras·tic** (per′ə·fras′tik) *adj.*

pe·rique (pə·rēk′) *n.* A dark, strongly flavored pipe tobacco. [after nickname of Pierre Chenet, American tobacco grower]

per·i·scope (per′ə·skōp) *n.* An optical instrument consisting of prisms or mirrors so arranged as to allow an observer to see around or over an obstacle. [< PERI- + -SCOPE] —**per′i·scop′ic** (-skop′ik) *adj.*

per·ish (per′ish) *v.i.* 1. To suffer a violent or untimely death. 2. To pass from existence. [< L *per-* away + *ire* to go]

per·ish·a·ble (per′ish·ə·bəl) *adj.* 1. Liable to perish. 2. Liable to speedy decay, as fruit in transportation. —*n. Usu. pl.* Something liable to decay, as food. —**per′ish·a·ble·ness, per′ish·a·bil′i·ty** *n.* —**per′ish·a·bly** *adv.*

per·i·stal·sis (per′ə·stôl′sis, -stal′-) *n. pl.* **·ses** (-sēz) *Physiol.* A contractile muscular movement of any hollow organ, as of the intestines, which forces the contents onward. [< PERI- + Gk. *stellein* to place] —**per′i·stal′tic** *adj.*

per·i·style (per′ə·stīl) *n. Archit.* A system of columns about a building or an internal court. [< PERI- + Gk. *stylos* pillar]

per·i·to·ne·um (per′ə·tə·nē′əm) *n. pl.* **·ne·a** *Anat.* A serous membrane that lines the abdominal cavity and serves as a covering for the viscera. [< PERI- + Gk. *teinein* to stretch] —**per′i·to·ne′al** *adj.*

per·i·to·ni·tis (per′ə·tə·nī′tis) *n. Pathol.* Inflammation of the peritoneum.

per·i·wig (per′ə·wig) *n.* A peruke or wig. [< MF *perruque*]

per·i·win·kle[1] (per′ə·wing′kəl) *n.* Any of several small marine snails, some of which are edible. [OE *pinewincle*]

per·i·win·kle[2] (per′ə·wing′kəl) *n.* A plant having shiny, evergreen leaves and blue or sometimes white flowers: also called *myrtle.* [< L *pervinca*]

per·jured (pûr′jərd) *adj.* Guilty of or constituting perjury.

per·ju·ry (pûr′jə·rē) *n. pl.* **·ries** *Law* The willful giving of false testimony or the withholding of material facts or evidence while under oath in a judicial proceeding. [< L *per-* thoroughly + *jurare* to swear] —**per′jure** *v.t.* **·jured, ·jur·ing** —**per′jur·er** *n.*

perk[1] (pûrk) *v.i.* 1. To recover one's spirits or vigor: with *up.* 2. To carry oneself or lift one's head jauntily. —*v.t.* 3. To raise quickly or smartly, as the ears: often with *up.* [ME *perken*]

perk[2] (pûrk) *v.i. Informal* To percolate.

perk·y (pûr′kē) *adj.* **perk·i·er, perk·i·est** 1. Jaunty; sprightly; pert. 2. Spirited and self-assured. —**perk′i·ly** *adv.* —**perk′i·ness** *n.*

per·ma·frost (pûr′mə·frôst, -frost) *n.* The part of the earth's surface in arctic regions that is permanently frozen.

per·ma·nent (pûr′mə·nənt) *adj.* Continuing in the same state or without essential change; enduring; durable; fixed. —*n.* A permanent wave. [< L *per-* through + *manere* to remain] —**per′ma·nence, per′ma·nen·cy** *n.* —**per′ma·nent·ly** *adv.*

permanent wave An artificial wave mechanically or chemically set in the hair and lasting several months.

per·man·ga·nate (pər·mang′gə·nāt) *n. Chem.* A dark purple salt of permanganic acid.

per·man·gan·ic acid (pûr′man·gan′ik) *Chem.* An acid that is a powerful oxidizer in aqueous solutions.

per·me·a·ble (pûr′mē·ə·bəl) *adj.* Allowing passage, esp. of fluids. —**per′me·a·bil′i·ty** *n.* —**per′me·a·bly** *adv.*

per·me·ate (pûr′mē·āt) *v.* **·at·ed, ·at·ing** *v.t.* 1. To spread thoroughly through; pervade. 2. To pass through the pores or interstices of. —*v.i.* 3. To spread itself. [< L *per-* through + *meare* to pass] —**per′me·a′tion** *n.* —**per′me·a′tive** *adj.*

per·mis·si·ble (pər·mis′ə·bəl) *adj.* That can be permitted; allowable. —**per·mis′si·bil′i·ty** *n.* —**per·mis′si·bly** *adv.*

per·mis·sion (pər·mish′ən) *n.* 1. The act of permitting or allowing. 2. Formal authorization or consent.

per·miss·ive (pər·mis′iv) *adj.* 1. Permitting; granting permission. 2. Not strict in discipline. —**per·mis′sive·ly** *adv.* —**per·mis′sive·ness** *n.*

per·mit (*v.* pər·mit′; *n.* pûr′mit) *v.* **·mit·ted, ·mit·ting** *v.t.* 1. To allow the doing of; consent to. 2. To give (someone) leave or consent; authorize. 3. To afford opportunity for. —*v.i.* 4. To afford possibility or opportunity. —*n.* 1. Permission to do something. 2. An official document or certificate authorizing performance of a specified activity; license. [< L *per-* through + *mittere* to send, let go] —**per·mit′ter** *n.*

per·mu·ta·tion (pûr′myōō·tā′shən) *n.* 1. The act of rearranging; transformation. 2. *Math.* Change in the order of sequence of elements or objects in a series.

per·mute (pər·myōōt′) *v.t.* **·mut·ed, ·mut·ing** To subject to permutation; esp., to change the order of. [< L *per-* thoroughly + *mutare* to change] —**per·mut′a·ble** *adj.*

per·ni·cious (pər·nish′əs) *adj.* 1. Having the power of destroying or injuring; deadly. 2. Malicious; wicked. [< L *per-* thoroughly + *nex, necis* death] —**per·ni′cious·ly** *adj.* —**per·ni′cious·ness** *n.*

per·nick·e·ty (pər·nik′ə·tē) *adj.* Persnickety.

per·o·rate (per′ə·rāt) *v.i.* **·rat·ed, ·rat·ing** 1. To speak at length; harangue. 2. To sum up or conclude a speech.

per·o·ra·tion (per′ə·rā′shən) *n.* The concluding portion of an oration, or the summing up of an argument. [< L *per-* through + *orare* to speak]

per·ox·ide (pə·rok′sīd) *n. Chem.* 1. An oxide having the highest proportion of oxygen for a given series. 2. Hydrogen peroxide. —*v.t.* **·id·ed, ·id·ing** To bleach with peroxide.

per·pen·dic·u·lar (pûr′pən·dik′yə·lər) *adj.* 1. Being at right angles to the plane of the horizon; upright or vertical. 2. *Math.* Meeting a given line or plane at right angles. —*n.* A perpendicular line or plane. [< L *perpendiculum* plumb line] —**per′pen·dic′u·lar′i·ty** (-lar′ə·tē) *n.* —**per′pen·dic′u·lar·ly** *adv.*

per·pe·trate (pûr′pə·trāt) *v.t.* **·trat·ed, ·trat·ing** To do, perform, or commit (a crime, etc.). [< L *per-* thoroughly + *patrare* to accomplish] —**per′pe·tra′tion** *n.* —**per′pe·tra′tor** *n.*

per·pet·u·al (pər·pech′ōō·əl) *adj.* 1. Continuing or lasting forever or for an unlimited time. 2. Incessant. [< L *perpetuus*] —**per·pet′u·al·ly** *adv.*

per·pet·u·ate (pər·pech′ōō·āt) *v.t.* **·at·ed, ·at·ing** 1. To make perpetual or enduring. 2. To cause to remain known, current, etc. —**per·pet′u·a′tion** *n.* —**per·pet′u·a′tor** *n.*

per·pe·tu·i·ty (pûr′pə·tōō′ə·tē, -tyōō′-) *n. pl.* **·ties** 1. The quality or state of being perpetual. 2. Something perpetual, as a perpetual annuity. 3. Unending or unlimited time.

per·plex (pər·pleks′) *v.t.* To cause to hesitate or become confused, as from doubt, difficulties encountered, etc.; puzzle. —**per·plex′i·ty** *n.*

per·plexed (pər·plekst′) *adj.* 1. Confused; puzzled; bewildered. 2. Of a complicated character; involved. [< L *perplexus* involved] —**per·plex′ed·ly** *adv.*

per·plex·ing (pər·plek′sing) *adj.* Confusing; puzzling. —**per·plex′ing·ly** *adv.*

per·qui·site (pûr′kwə·zit) *n.* 1. Any incidental profit, payment, etc., beyond what is earned as salary or wages. 2. Any privilege or benefit owed or claimed as one's due. [< L *perquisitum* a thing diligently sought]

per se (pûr sā′, sē′) *Latin* By itself; intrinsically.

per·se·cute (pûr′sə·kyōōt) *v.t.* **·cut·ed, ·cut·ing** 1. To annoy or harass persistently.

2. To maltreat or oppress because of race, religion, or beliefs. [< L *persequi* to pursue] —**per′se·cu′tion** *n.* —**per′se·cu′tor** *n.*

per·se·vere (pûr′sə·vir′) *v.i.* ·**vered**, ·**ver·ing** To persist in any purpose or enterprise; strive in spite of difficulties, etc. [< L *per-* thoroughly + *severus* strict] —**per′se·ver′·ance** *n.* —**per′se·ver′ing·ly** *adv.*

Per·sian (pûr′zhən) *n.* 1. A native or inhabitant of ancient Persia or modern Iran. 2. The Iranian language of the Persians. [< L *Persia* Persia] —**Per′sian** *adj.*

Persian lamb 1. The lamb of the karakul sheep. 2. Its black, gray, or brown curled fur.

per·si·flage (pûr′sə·fläzh) *n.* A light, flippant style of conversation or writing. [< F < *persifler* to banter]

per·sim·mon (pər·sim′ən) *n.* 1. A reddish orange fruit with an astringent taste when not ripe. 2. The tree bearing this fruit. [< Algonquian]

per·sist (pər·sist′, -zist′) *v.i.* 1. To continue firmly in some course, state, etc., esp. despite opposition or difficulties. 2. To continue to exist; endure. [< L *per-* thoroughly + *sistere* causative of *stare* to stand] —**per·sis′tence, per·sis′ten·cy** *n.*

per·sis·tent (pər·sis′tənt, -zis′-) *adj.* 1. Persevering or stubborn in a course or resolve. 2. Enduring; permanent. 3. Constantly repeated. —**per·sis′tent·ly** *adv.*

per·snick·e·ty (pər·snik′ə·tē) *adj. Informal* 1. Unduly fastidious; fussy. 2. Demanding minute care or pains. Also *pernickety.* [< dial. E] —**per·snick′e·ti·ness** *n.*

per·son (pûr′sən) *n.* 1. Any human being considered as a distinct entity or personality; an individual. 2. One's characteristic appearance or physical condition. 3. *Law* Any human being, corporation, or body politic having legal rights and duties. 4. *Theol.* One of the three individualities in the Trinity. 5. *Gram.* A modification of the pronoun and verb that distinguishes the speaker (**first person**), the person or thing spoken to (**second person**), and the person or thing spoken of (**third person**). —**in person** 1. Physically present. 2. Acting for oneself. [< L *persona* actor's mask, character]

per·so·na (pər·sō′nə) *n. pl.* (*for def. 1*) ·**nae** (-nē) or (*for def. 2*) ·**nas** 1. *Usu. pl.* A character in a drama, novel, etc. 2. One's personality as seen by others. [< L]

per·son·a·ble (pûr′sən·ə·bəl) *adj.* Attractive or pleasing in personal appearance. —**per′·son·a·bly** *adv.*

per·son·age (pûr′sən·ij) *n.* 1. A man or woman of importance or rank. 2. A character in fiction, drama, history, etc.

per·son·al (pûr′sən·əl) *adj.* 1. Pertaining to or concerning a particular person; not general or public. 2. Done in person: a *personal* service. 3. Of or pertaining to the body or appearance: *personal* beauty. 4. Directly referring to an individual, esp. in a disparaging manner: *personal* remarks. 5. *Law* Pertaining to property regarded as movable or temporary. 6. *Gram.* Denoting or indicating person: *personal* pronouns. —*n.* 1. *Often pl. Law* A movable or temporary article or property; chattel. 2. A paragraph or advertisement of personal reference or application. [< L *personalis*] —**per′son·al·ly** *adv.*

per·son·al·i·ty (pûr′sən·al′ə·tē) *n. pl.* ·**ties** 1. Distinctive qualities or characteristics of a person. 2. A person of outstanding or distinctive qualities. 3. *Often pl.* A remark or reference, often disparaging, of a personal nature.

per·son·al·ize (pûr′sən·əl·īz′) *v.t.* ·**ized**, ·**iz·ing** 1. To make personal. 2. To mark with one's name, initials, etc., as stationery or handkerchiefs.

personal pronoun *Gram.* A pronoun that varies in form according to person, gender, case, and number, as *we, their, him.*

per·son·al·ty (pûr′sən·əl·tē) *n. pl.* ·**ties** *Law* Personal property.

per·so·na non gra·ta (pər·sō′nə non grä′tə) *Latin* A person who is not welcome or acceptable.

per·son·ate (pûr′sən·āt) *v.t.* ·**at·ed**, ·**at·ing** *Law* To impersonate with intent to deceive. [See PERSON.] —**per′son·a′tion** *n.* —**per′son·a′tor** *n.*

per·son·i·fy (pər·son′ə·fī) *v.t.* ·**fied**, ·**fy·ing** 1. To think of or represent as having life or human qualities. 2. To represent (an abstraction or inanimate object) as a person. 3. To be the embodiment of; typify. [< L *persona* mask, person + *facere* to make] —**per·son′i·fi·ca′tion** *n.* —**per·son′i·fi′er** *n.*

per·son·nel (pûr′sə·nel′) *n.* The persons employed in a business, in military service, etc. [< F. See PERSONAL.]

per·spec·tive (pər·spek′tiv) *n.* 1. The art or theory of representing solid objects on a flat surface in such a way as to convey the impression of depth and distance. 2. The relative importance of facts or matters from any special point of view. 3. Judgment of facts, circumstances, etc., with regard to their importance. [< L *per-* through + *specere* to look]

per·spi·ca·cious (pûr′spə·kā′shəs) *adj.* 1. Keenly discerning or understanding. 2. *Archaic* Sharp-sighted. [< L *perspicax, -acis* sharp-sighted] —**per′spi·ca′cious·ly** *adv.* —**per′spi·cac′i·ty** (-kas′ə·tē) *n.*

per·spic·u·ous (pər·spik′yōō·əs) *adj.* Having clarity of expression or style; lucid. —**per·spi·cu·i·ty** (pûr′spə·kyōō′ə·tē) *n.* —**per·spic′u·ous·ly** *adv.*

per·spi·ra·tion (pûr′spə·rā′shən) *n.* 1. The act or process of perspiring. 2. The fluid excreted; sweat. 3. Arduous physical effort. —**per·spir·a·to·ry** (pər·spī′rə·tôr′ē) *adj.*

per·spire (pər·spīr′) *v.i.* ·**spired**, ·**spir·ing** To give off a saline fluid through the pores of the skin; sweat. [< L *per-* through + *spirare* to breathe]

per·suade (pər·swād′) *v.t.* ·**suad·ed**, ·**suad·ing** 1. To induce (someone) to do something. 2. To induce to a belief; convince. [< L *per-* thoroughly + *suadere* to advise] —**per·suad′a·ble** *adj.* —**per·suad′er** *n.*

per·sua·sion (pər·swā′zhən) *n.* 1. The act of persuading or of using persuasive methods. 2. Ability to persuade. 3. Settled opinion; conviction. 4. An accepted creed or belief.

per·sua·sive (pər·swā′siv) *adj.* Having power or tendency to persuade. —*n.* That which persuades or tends to persuade. —**per·sua′sive·ly** *adv.* —**per·sua′sive·ness** *n.*

pert (pûrt) *adj.* 1. Impertinent; saucy. 2. Energetic; lively. [< OF *apert* open, impudent] —**pert′ly** *adv.* —**pert′ness** *n.*

per·tain (pər·tān′) *v.i.* 1. To have reference; relate. 2. To belong as an adjunct, function, quality, etc. —**pertaining to** Having to do with; belonging or relating to. [< L *per-* through + *tenere* to hold]

per·ti·na·cious (pûr′tə·nā′shəs) *adj.* 1. Tenacious of purpose; adhering fixedly to a pursuit or opinion. 2. Stubbornly or doggedly persistent. [< L *per-* thoroughly + *tenax, -acis* tenacious] —**per′ti·na′cious·ly** *adv.* —**per′ti·nac′i·ty** (-nas′ə·tē) *n.*

per·ti·nent (pûr′tə·nənt) *adj.* Related to or properly bearing upon the matter in hand; relevant. [See PERTAIN.] —**per′ti·nence** *n.* —**per′ti·nent·ly** *adv.*

per·turb (pər·tûrb′) *v.t.* 1. To disquiet or disturb greatly; alarm; agitate. 2. To throw into disorder; cause confusion in. [< L *per-* thoroughly + *turbare* to disturb] —**per·turb′a·ble** *adj.* —**per·tur·ba·tion** (pûr′tər·bā′shən) *n.*

pe·ruke (pə·ro͞ok′) *n.* A wig, esp. one worn by men in the 17th and 18th c.: also *periwig.* [< Ital. *perrucca*]

pe·ruse (pə·ro͞oz′) *v.t.* **·rused, ·rus·ing** 1. To read carefully or attentively. 2. To read. 3. To examine; scrutinize. [< PER- + USE, v.] —**pe·rus′a·ble** *adj.* —**pe·rus′al** *n.* —**pe·rus′er** *n.*

Pe·ru·vi·an (pə·ro͞o′vē·ən) *adj.* Of or pertaining to Peru or its inhabitants. —**Pe·ru′vi·an** *n.*

per·vade (pər·vād′) *v.t.* **·vad·ed, ·vad·ing** To spread through every part of; be diffused throughout; permeate. [< L *per-* through + *vadere* to go] —**per·va′sive** (-vā′siv) *adj.* —**per·va′sive·ly** *adv.*

per·verse (pər·vûrs′) *adj.* 1. Willfully deviating from acceptable or conventional behavior, opinion, etc. 2. Refractory; capricious. 3. Petulant; cranky. [See PERVERT.] —**per·verse′ly** *adv.* —**per·verse′·ness, per·ver′si·ty** *n.*

per·ver·sion (pər·vûr′zhən, -shən) *n.* 1. The act of perverting, or the state of being perverted. 2. A perverted form, act, use, etc. 3. Deviation from the normal in sexual behavior.

per·vert (*v.* pər·vûrt′; *n.* pûr′vərt) *v.t.* 1. To turn to an improper use or purpose; misapply. 2. To turn from approved opinions or conduct; lead astray. 3. To deprave; debase; corrupt. —*n.* One characterized by or practicing sexual perversion. [< L *per-* away + *vertere* to turn]

per·vert·ed (pər·vûr′tid) *adj.* 1. Deviating widely from what is right or acceptable; distorted. 2. Characterized by viciousness, sexual perversion, etc. —**per·vert′ed·ly** *adv.*

pe·se·ta (pə·sā′tə, *Sp.* pā·sā′tä) *n.* The standard monetary unit of Spain. [< Sp., dim. of *pesa* weight]

pes·ky (pes′kē) *adj.* **·ki·er, ·ki·est** *Informal* Annoying; troublesome. [Prob. < PEST + -Y[2]] —**pes′ki·ly** *adv.*

pe·so (pā′sō) *n. pl.* **·sos** The standard monetary unit of various Spanish-speaking countries, as Argentina, Mexico, or the Philippines, equivalent to 100 centavos. [< Sp., orig., a weight]

pes·si·mism (pes′ə·miz′əm) *n.* 1. A disposition to take a gloomy or cynical view of affairs. 2. The doctrine that the world and life are essentially evil. [< L *pessimus* worst + -ISM] —**pes′si·mist** *n.* —**pes′si·mis′tic** *adj.* —**pes′si·mis′ti·cal·ly** *adv.*

pest (pest) *n.* 1. An annoying person or thing. 2. A destructive or injurious insect, plant, etc. 3. A virulent epidemic, esp. of plague. [< L *pestis* plague]

pes·ter (pes′tər) *v.t.* To harass with petty and persistent annoyances; bother; plague. [< OF *empestrer* to hobble, entangle]

pes·ti·cide (pes′tə·sīd) *n.* A chemical or other substance used to destroy plant and animal pests. —**pes′ti·ci′dal** *adj.*

pes·tif·er·ous (pes·tif′ər·əs) *adj.* 1. *Informal* Annoying; bothersome. 2. Carrying or spreading infectious disease. [< L *pestis* plague + *ferre* to bear] —**pes·tif′er·ous·ness** *n.*

pes·ti·lence (pes′tə·ləns) *n.* Any widespread, often fatal infectious or contagious disease, as cholera or the bubonic plague. —**pes′ti·len′tial** (-len′shəl) *adj.*

pes·ti·lent (pes′tə·lənt) *adj.* 1. Tending to produce pestilence. 2. Having a malign influence or effect. 3. Making trouble; vexatious. [< L *pestis* plague] —**pes′ti·lent·ly** *adv.*

pes·tle (pes′əl) *n.* An implement used for crushing, pulverizing, or mixing substances in or as in a mortar. —*v.t. & v.i.* **·tled, ·tling** To pound, grind, or mix with or as with a pestle. [< L *pistillum*]

pet[1] (pet) *n.* 1. A tame animal treated lovingly or kept as a companion or playmate. 2. A favorite: teacher's *pet.* —*adj.* 1. Tamed or kept as a pet. 2. Favorite; cherished. —*v.* **pet·ted, pet·ting** *v.t.* 1. To stroke or caress. 2. To treat indulgently; coddle. —*v.i.* 3. *Slang* To make love by kissing and caressing. [< dial. E (Scot.)]

pet[2] (pet) *n.* A fit of pique or ill temper. [Origin unknown]

pet·al (pet′l) *n. Bot.* One of the divisions or leaflike parts of a corolla. [< Gk. *petalon* leaf] —**pet′aled** or **pet′alled** *adj.*

-petal *combining form* Seeking: *centripetal.* [< L *petere* to seek]

pe·tard (pi·tärd′) *n.* 1. An explosive device used to break through walls, gates, etc. 2. A small firecracker exploding with a loud report. [< MF *péter* to break wind]

pet·cock (pet′cock′) *n. Mech.* A small valve or faucet, used for draining, releasing pressure, etc. Also **pet cock.** [? < obs. *pet* a fart + COCK[1]]

pe·ter (pē′tər) *v.i. Informal* To diminish gradually and then cease or disappear: with *out.* [Orig. U.S. mining slang; ult. origin uncertain]

Pe·ter (pē′tər) *n.* Either of the two books of the New Testament that bear the name of the apostle Peter (also called **Saint Peter**).

Peter Principle The observation that persons in an organization are promoted beyond the level of their competence. [after L. J. *Peter*, U.S. author]

pet·i·ole (pet′ē·ōl) *n. Bot.* The stem or slender stalk of a leaf; a leafstalk. [< L *petiolus*, orig. dim. of *pes, pedis* foot] —**pet′i·o·late** (-ə·lāt) *adj.*

pet·it (pet′ē) *adj. Law* Small; lesser; minor: *petit* larceny. Also spelled *petty.* [< OF, small]

pe·tite (pə·tēt′) *adj.* Diminutive; little. [< F]

pet·it four (pet′ē fôr′, *Fr.* pə·tē′fōōr′) *pl.* **pet·its fours** or **pet·it fours** (pet′ē fôrz′, *Fr.* pə·tē′fōōr′) A little, decoratively iced cake. [< F, lit., little oven]

pe·ti·tion (pə·tish′ən) *n.* 1. A formal request addressed to a person or group in authority and asking for some benefit, the redress of a grievance, etc. 2. Something formally requested or entreated. —*v.t.* 1. To make a petition to. 2. To ask for. —*v.i.* 3. To make a petition. [< L *petere* to seek] —**pe·ti′·tion·er** *n.*

pe·tit mal (pə·tē′ mäl′) *Pathol.* A mild form of epilepsy characterized by a momentary loss of consciousness: distinguished from *grand mal.* [< F, lit., little sickness]

pet·it point (pet′ē) 1. A fine tapestry stitch used in decorative needlework. 2. Needlework done in this stitch.

pet·rel (pet′rəl) *n.* Any of various small sea birds, usu. found far from shore. [? < LL *Petrellus,* dim. of *Peter,* after St. Peter]

pet·ri·fy (pet′rə·fī) *v.* **·fied, ·fy·ing** *v.t.* 1. To convert (organic material) into a substance of stony character. 2. To make fixed and unyielding. 3. To daze or paralyze with fear, surprise, etc. —*v.i.* 4. To become stone or like stone. [< L *petra* a rock + *facere* to make] —**pet′ri·fac′tion** (-fak′shən) *n.*

petro- *combining form* Rock; stone. Also, before vowels, **petr-.** [< Gk. *petros* stone]

pet·ro·chem·i·cal (pet′rō·kem′i·kəl) *n.* A chemical derived from petroleum or natural gas. —**pet′ro·chem′i·cal** *adj.*

pet·ro·chem·is·try (pet′rō·kem′is·trē) *n.* The chemistry of petroleum and its derivatives.

pe·trog·ra·phy (pə·trog′rə·fē) *n.* The systematic description and classification of rocks. —**pe·trog′ra·pher** *n.* —**pet·ro·graph·ic** (pet′rə·graf′ik) or **·i·cal** *adj.*

pet·rol (pet′rəl) *n. Brit.* Gasoline.

pet·ro·la·tum (pet′rə·lā′təm) *n.* A greasy, semisolid substance obtained from petroleum, used in ointments. Also **petroleum jelly.**

pe·tro·le·um (pə·trō′lē·əm) *n.* An oily, liquid mixture of numerous hydrocarbons, found in subterranean deposits, used in its natural state for heat and light, and as the source of gasoline, kerosene, paraffin, etc. [< L *petra* rock + *oleum* oil]

pe·trol·o·gy (pə·trol′ə·jē) *n.* The science of the origin, structure, constitution, and characteristics of rocks. —**pet·ro·log·ic** (pet′rə·loj′ik) or **·i·cal** *adj.* —**pe·trol′o·gist** *n.*

pet·ti·coat (pet′ē·kōt) *n.* 1. A skirt or skirtlike undergarment hanging from the waist. 2. Something resembling a petticoat. 3. A woman: a humorous or disparaging term. —*adj.* Of or influenced by women: *petticoat* politics.

pet·ti·fog·ger (pet′i·fog′ər, -fôg′ər) *n.* 1. An inferior lawyer, esp. one dealing with insignificant cases or resorting to tricks. 2. One who quibbles or fusses over trivialities. [< PETTY + obs. *fogger* a trickster for gain] —**pet′ti·fog** *v.i.* **·fogged, ·fog·ging** —**pet′ti·fog′ger·y** *n.*

pet·tish (pet′ish) *adj.* Capriciously ill-tempered; petulant; peevish. [Prob. < PET[2] + -ISH[1]] —**pet′tish·ly** *adv.*

pet·ty (pet′ē) *adj.* **·ti·er, ·ti·est** 1. Having little worth or importance; trifling; insignificant. 2. Having little scope or generosity; narrow-minded. 3. Mean; spiteful. 4. Having a comparatively low rank or position; minor. 5. *Law* Petit. [< F *petit* small] —**pet′ti·ly** *adv.* —**pet′ti·ness** *n.*

petty cash A supply of money kept for minor expenses, as in a business office.

petty officer *Naval* Any of a class of noncommissioned officers.

pet·u·lant (pech′ōō·lənt) *adj.* Displaying or characterized by capricious fretfulness; peevish. [< L *petulans, -antis* impudent] —**pet′u·lant·ly** *adv.* —**pet′u·lance** *n.*

pe·tu·ni·a (pə·tōō′nyə, -nē·ə) *n.* Any of various tropical American plants having variously colored funnel-shaped flowers. [< F *petun* tobacco]

pew (pyōō) *n.* A bench for seating people in church, frequently with a kneeling rack attached. [< Gk. *podion* base]

pe·wee (pē′wē) *n.* Any of various small, greenish gray flycatchers: also spelled *peewee.* [Imit.]

pew·ter (pyōō′tər) *n.* 1. An alloy, usu. of tin and lead, formerly much used for tableware. 2. A dull gray color. [< OF *peutre, pialtre*] —**pew′ter** *adj.*

pe·yo·te (pā·ō′tē, *Sp.* pā·yō′tā) *n.* Mescal. Also **pe·yo′tl** (-yot′l). [< Am.Sp. < Nahuatl *peyotl,* lit., caterpillar]

pfen·nig (fen′ig, *Ger.* pfen′ikh) *n. pl.* **·nigs** or *Ger.* **pfen·ni·ge** (pfen′i·gə) A coin of Germany, equivalent to one hundredth of a deutschemark or of an ostmark. [< G, penny]

pha·e·ton (fā′ə·tən) *n.* 1. A light, four-wheeled carriage, open at the sides, and sometimes having a top. 2. An open automobile having front and back seats. [< Gk. *Phaethōn,* son of the sun god Helios]

phage (fāj, fäzh) *n.* Bacteriophage.

-phage *combining form* One who or that which eats or consumes: *bacteriophage.* [< Gk. *phagein* to eat]

phag·o·cyte (fag′ə·sīt) *n. Physiol.* A leucocyte that ingests and destroys harmful bacteria, etc., in the blood and tissues of the body. [< Gk. *phagein* to eat + -CYTE] —**phag′o·cyt′ic** (-sit′ik) or **·i·cal** *adj.*

-phagous *combining form* Consuming; tending to eat. [< Gk. *phagein* to eat]

-phagy *combining form* The consumption or eating of. Also **-phagia.** [< Gk. *phagein* to eat]

pha·lan·ge·al (fə·lan′jē·əl) *adj.* Of, pertaining to, or resembling the phalanges of the fingers and toes. Also **pha·lan′gal** (-gəl), **pha·lan′ge·an.**

pha·lanx (fā′langks) *n. pl.* **pha·lan·ges** (fə·lan′jēz); *also for defs. 1 and 2* **pha·lanx·es** 1. In ancient Greece, a marching order of heavy infantry with close ranks and files. 2. Any massed or compact body or corps. 3. *Anat.* One of the bones articulating with the joints of the fingers or toes: also **phal·ange** (fā·lanj′, fə-). [< Gk. *phalanx, phalangos* line of battle]

phal·a·rope (fal′ə·rōp) *n.* Any of several swimming birds resembling the sandpiper, but having lobed toes. [< Gk. *phalaris* coot + *pous* foot]

phal·lus (fal′əs) *n. pl.* **·li** (-ī) 1. A representation of the male generative organ, often used as a symbol of the generative power of nature. 2. *Anat.* The penis. [< Gk. *phallos* penis] —**phal′lic** *adj.*

-phane *combining form* Something resembling or similar to (a specified substance or material): *cellophane.* [< Gk. *phainein* to show]

phan·tasm (fan′taz·əm) *n.* 1. An imaginary appearance; phantom. 2. A mental image; fancy. [< Gk. *phantasma*] —**phan·tas′mal** *adj.*

phan·tas·ma·go·ri·a (fan·taz′mə·gôr′ē·ə) *n.* 1. A changing, incoherent series of apparitions or phantasms, as in a dream. 2. An apparition. [< Gk. *phantasma* apparition + (prob.) *agora* crowd] —**phan·tas′ma·gor′ic** or **·i·cal, phan·tas′ma·go′ri·al** *adj.*

phan·ta·sy (fan′tə·sē, -zē) See FANTASY.

phan·tom (fan′təm) *n.* 1. Something that exists only in appearance. 2. An apparition; specter. 3. The visible representative of an abstract state or incorporeal person. —*adj.* Illusive; ghostlike. [< Gk. *phantasma* apparition]

-phany *combining form* Appearance; manifestation: *epiphany.* [< Gk. *phainein* to appear]

Phar·aoh (fâr′ō, fā′rō) *n.* Any one of the monarchs of ancient Egypt. [< Egyptian *pr-'ōh* the great house] —**Phar·a·on·ic** (fâr′ā·on′ik) or **·i·cal** *adj.*

Phar·i·see (far′ə·sē) *n.* 1. A member of an ancient Jewish sect that emphasized strict observance of ritual. 2. A formal, sanctimonious, hypocritical person: also **phar′i·see.** [< Aramaic *perishayā* the separated ones] —**phar′i·sa′ic** (-sā′ik) or **·i·cal** *adj.* —**phar′i·sa′i·cal·ly** *adv.*

phar·ma·ceu·ti·cal (fär′mə·sōō′ti·kəl) *adj.* Pertaining to, using, or relating to pharmacy or the pharmacopoeia: also **phar′ma·ceu′tic.** —*n.* A pharmaceutical product. [< Gk. *pharmakon* drug]

phar·ma·ceu·tics (fär′mə·sōō′tiks) *n.pl.* (*construed as sing.*) Pharmacy (def. 1).

phar·ma·cist (fär′mə·sist) *n.* A qualified druggist.

pharmaco- *combining form* A drug; of or pertaining to drugs. Also, before vowels, **pharmac-.** [< Gk. *pharmakon* drug]

phar·ma·col·o·gy (fär′mə·kol′ə·jē) *n.* The science of the nature, preparation, administration, and effects of drugs. —**phar′ma·co·log′ic** (-kə·loj′ik) or **·i·cal** *adj.* —**phar′·ma·col′o·gist** *n.*

phar·ma·co·poe·ia (fär′mə·kə·pē′ə) *n.* 1. A book, usu. published by an authority, containing standard formulas and methods for the preparation of medicines, drugs, and other remedial substances. 2. A collection of drugs. [< Gk. *pharmakon* drug + *poieein* to make]

phar·ma·cy (fär′mə·sē) *n. pl.* **·cies** 1. The art or business of compounding and identifying drugs, and of compounding and dispensing medicines: also called *pharmaceutics.* 2. A drugstore. [< Gk. *pharmakon* drug]

pharyngo- *combining form* The throat; related to the throat. Also, before vowels, **pharyng-.** [< Gk. *pharynx*]

phar·ynx (far′ingks) *n. pl.* **pha·ryn·ges** (fə·rin′jēz) or **phar·ynx·es** *Anat.* The part of the alimentary canal between the palate and the esophagus, serving as a passage for air and food. [< Gk. *pharynx, -yngos* throat] —**pha·ryn·ge·al** (fə·rin′jē·əl) *adj.*

phase (fāz) *n.* 1. The view that anything presents to the eye; any one of varying distinctive manifestations of an object. 2. *Astron.* One of the appearances or forms presented periodically by the moon and planets. 3. *Physics* Any particular stage in the complete cycle of a periodic system. 4. *Biol.* Any characteristic or decisive stage in the growth, development, or life pattern of an organism. —**in phase** Reaching corresponding phases simultaneously, as two waves. —**to phase out** (or **in**) To plan and execute the orderly and gradual completion (or initiation) of an enterprise. [< Gk. *phainein* to show] —**pha′sic** *adj.*

-phasia *combining form Med.* Defect or malfunction of speech: *dysphasia.* Also **-phasy.** [< Gk. *phanai* to speak]

pheas·ant (fez′ənt) *n.* 1. A long-tailed, mostly terrestrial bird, originally of Asia, noted for the colorful plumage of the male; esp., the **ring-necked pheasant,** common in the U.S. 2. One of various other birds, as the ruffed grouse. [< Gk. *Phasianos* (*ornis*) (bird) of the Phasis, a river in Asia]

phen·cy·cli·dine (fēn·sik′lə·dēn, -sīk′-) *n.* A nitrogen compound used as a tranquilizer for animals and in a powdered form as a hallucinogenic drug by people. Also *PCP.*

pheno- *combining form Chem.* Related to benzene; a derivative of benzene. Also, before vowels, **phen-.** [< Gk. *phaino-* shining]

phe·no·bar·bi·tal (fē′nō·bär′bə·tal, -tôl) *n. Chem.* A white, odorless, slightly bitter, crystalline powder, used as a sedative.

phe·nol (fē′nōl, -nôl) *n. Chem.* A white, crystalline, caustic compound, derived from coal tar and used as a disinfectant: also called *carbolic acid.* [< PHEN(O)- + -OL]

phe·nom·e·nal (fi·nom′ə·nəl) *adj.* 1. Pertaining to phenomena. 2. Extraordinary or marvelous. 3. *Philos.* Perceptible through the senses. —**phe·nom′e·nal·ly** *adv.*

phe·nom·e·non (fi·nom′ə·non) *n. pl.* **phe·nom·e·na** (-nə); *for defs. 2 & 3, often* **phe·nom·e·nons** 1. Something visible or directly observable, as an appearance, action, change, etc. 2. Any unusual occurrence; marvel. 3. *Informal* A person having some remarkable talent, power, or ability; prodigy. [< Gk. *phainomenon* < *phainein* to show]

phe·no·type (fē′nə·tīp) *n. Biol.* The aggregate of genetic characteristics visibly manifested by an organism. [< Gk. *phainein* to show + -TYPE] —**phe′no·typ′ic** (-tip′ik) or **·i·cal** *adj.*

pher·o·mone (fer′ə·mōn′) *n.* An animal secretion that stimulates a specific response in animals of the same species. [< Gk. *pherein* to carry + HORMONE]

phew (fyōō, fōō) *interj.* An exclamation of disgust or surprise.

phi (fī, fē) *n.* The twenty-first letter in the Greek alphabet (Φ, φ), corresponding to English *ph* and *f.*

phi·al (fī′əl) See VIAL.

phil- Var. of PHILO-.

phi·lan·der (fi·lan′dər) *v.i.* To make love without serious intentions: said of a man. —*n.* A male flirt: also **phi·lan′der·er.** [< Gk. *phileein* to love + *anēr, andros* man]

phi·lan·thro·py (fi·lan′thrə·pē) *n. pl.* **·pies** 1. The effort to promote the happiness or social elevation of mankind, as by making donations, etc. 2. Love or benevolence toward mankind in general. [< Gk. *phileein* to love + *anthropos* man] **—phil·an·throp·ic** (fil′ən·throp′ik) or **·i·cal** *adj.* **—phil′an·throp′i·cal·ly** *adv.* **—phi·lan′thro·pist** *n.*

phi·lat·e·ly (fi·lat′ə·lē) *n.* The study and collection of postage stamps, stamped envelopes, etc.; stamp collecting. [< Gk. *philos* loving + *ateleia* exemption from tax as indicated by a stamp] **—phil·a·tel·ic** (fil′ə·tel′ik) *adj.* **—phi·lat′e·list** *n.*

-phile *combining form* One who supports or is fond of; one devoted to: *bibliophile.* Also **-phil.** [< Gk. *philos* loving]

Phi·le·mon (fi·lē′mən) *n.* A book of the New Testament consisting of an epistle addressed by Saint Paul to Philemon, a Greek converted to Christianity.

phil·har·mon·ic (fil′här·mon′ik, -ər·mon′-) *adj. Sometimes cap.* Fond of music: often used in the names of musical societies. **—***n.* 1. *Sometimes cap.* A group that sponsors or supports a symphony orchestra. 2. *cap.* A symphony orchestra. [< Gk. *philos* loving + *harmonia* music]

-philia *combining form* 1. A tendency toward: *hemophilia.* 2. An excessive affection or fondness for: *necrophilia.* Also spelled *-phily.* [< Gk. *phileein* to love]

Phi·lip·pi·ans (fi·lip′ē·ənz) *n.pl.* (*construed as sing.*) A book of the New Testament consisting of an epistle of Saint Paul addressed to Christians at Philippi, an ancient Greek town.

phi·lip·pic (fi·lip′ik) *n.* An impassioned speech characterized by invective; tirade. [< Gk. *Philippikos* of Philip (of Macedon), denounced by Demosthenes in a series of speeches]

Phi·lis·tine (fil′əs·tēn, -tīn, fi·lis′tən, -tēn) *n.* An ignorant, narrow-minded person, devoid of culture and indifferent to art. Also **phi′lis·tine.** [after the *Philistines*, an ancient warlike people] **—Phi′lis·tin·ism** *n.*

philo- *combining form* Loving; fond of. Also, before vowels, *phil-.* [< Gk. *philos* loving]

phil·o·den·dron (fil′ə·den′drən) *n.* A climbing plant having glossy, evergreen leaves and cultivated as an ornamental house plant. [< Gk. *philodendros* fond of trees]

phi·lol·o·gy (fi·lol′ə·jē) *n.* 1. The study of written records, chiefly literary works, to set up accurate texts and determine their meaning. 2. Linguistics, esp. comparative and historical. [< Gk. *philologos* fond of words] **—phil·o·log·ic** (fil′ə·loj′ik) or **·i·cal** *adj.* **—phi·lol′o·gist** *n.*

phi·los·o·pher (fi·los′ə·fər) *n.* 1. A student of or specialist in philosophy. 2. One who lives, makes judgments, etc., according to a philosophy. 3. One who is calm and patient under all circumstances.

phil·o·soph·i·cal (fil′ə·sof′i·kəl) *adj.* 1. Of or founded on the principles of philosophy. 2. Proper to or characteristic of a philosopher. 3. Self-restrained; rational; thoughtful. Also **phil′o·soph′ic.** **—phil′o·soph′i·cal·ly** *adv.*

phi·los·o·phize (fi·los′ə·fīz) *v.i.* **·phized, ·phiz·ing** To speculate like a philosopher; theorize. **—phi·los′o·phiz′er** *n.*

phi·los·o·phy (fi·los′ə·fē) *n. pl.* **·phies** 1. The inquiry into the most comprehensive principles of reality in general, or of some sector of it, as human knowledge or human values. 2. The love of wisdom, and the search for it. 3. A philosophical system; also, a treatise on such a system. 4. A theory governing any field of endeavor: the *philosophy* of banking. 5. Practical wisdom; fortitude. [< Gk. *philosophos* lover of wisdom]

-philous *combining form* Loving; fond of. [< Gk. *-philos*]

phil·ter (fil′tər) *n.* 1. A charmed draft supposed to have power to excite sexual love. 2. Any magic potion. **—***v.t.* To charm with a philter. Also **phil′tre.** [< Gk. *phileein* to love]

-phily Var. of -PHILIA.

phle·bi·tis (fli·bī′tis) *n. Pathol.* Inflammation of the inner membrane of a vein. [< Gk. *phleps, phlebos* blood vessel + -ITIS] **—phle·bit′ic** (-bit′ik) *adj.*

phle·bot·o·my (fli·bot′ə·mē) *n. Surg.* The practice of opening a vein for letting blood as a remedial measure; bloodletting. [< Gk. *phleps, phlebos* blood vessel + *temnein* to cut] **—phle·bot′o·mist** *n.* **—phle·bot′o·mize** *v.t.* **·mized, ·miz·ing**

phlegm (flem) *n.* 1. *Physiol.* A viscid, stringy mucus secreted in the air passages, esp. such mucus discharged through the mouth. 2. Cold, undemonstrative temper. [< Gk., flame, phlegm]

phleg·mat·ic (fleg·mat′ik) *adj.* Not easily moved or excited. Also **phleg·mat′i·cal.** **—phleg·mat′i·cal·ly** *adv.*

phlo·em (flō′əm) *n. Bot.* The complex tissue serving for the conduction of the sap in plants. [< Gk. *phloos* bark]

phlox (floks) *n.* Any of various herbs with opposite leaves and clusters of variously colored flowers. [< Gk., wallflower, lit., flame]

-phobe *combining form* One who fears or has an aversion to. [< Gk. *phobeesthai* to fear]

pho·bi·a (fō′bē·ə) *n.* 1. A compulsive and persistent fear of any specified type of object, stimulus, or situation. 2. Any strong aversion or dislike. [< Gk. *phobos* fear] **—pho′bic** *adj.*

-phobia *combining form* An exaggerated dread of or aversion to: **acrophobia** (high places), **agoraphobia** (open spaces), **ailurophobia** (cats), **androphobia** (men), **astraphobia** (lightning), **bathophobia** (depths), **claustrophobia** (enclosed places), **ecophobia** (home), **gephyrophobia** (crossing a bridge), **gynophobia** (women), **hemophobia** (blood), **hydrophobia** (water), **musophobia** (mice), **nyctophobia** (darkness), **ophidiophobia** (reptiles), **pyrophobia** (fire), **teratophobia** (monsters), **thanatophobia** (death), **triskaidekaphobia** (13). [< Gk. *phobos* fear]

phoe·be (fē′bē) *n.* An American flycatcher having grayish brown plumage and a slightly crested head. [Imit. of its cry]

Phoe·be (fē′bē) *n. Poetic* The moon. [< Gk., bright]

Phoe·ni·cian (fə·nē′shən, -nish′ən) *n.* 1. One of the people of ancient Phoenicia or any of its colonies. 2. The Semitic language of these people. **—Phoe·ni′cian** *adj.*

phoe·nix (fē′niks) *n.* In Egyptian mythology, a bird of great beauty, said to live for 500 or 600 years and then consume itself by fire, rising from its ashes to live through another cycle. [< Gk. *phoinix*]

phon- Var. of PHONO-.

pho·nate (fō′nāt) *v.i.* **·nat·ed, ·nat·ing** To make speech sounds. [< Gk. *phōnē* voice] **—pho·na′tion** *n.*

phone (fōn) *n.* *Informal* A telephone. **—*v.t.* & *v.i.* phoned, phon·ing** To telephone. [Short for TELEPHONE]

-phone *combining form* Voice; sound: *microphone.* [< Gk. *phōnē* sound]

pho·neme (fō′nēm) *n.* *Ling.* The smallest element of speech sounds, which functions to distinguish one utterance from another, as /t/ and /p/ in the words *tin* and *pin.* [< Gk. *phōnēma* utterance] **—pho·ne′mic** *adj.* **—pho·ne′mi·cal·ly** *adv.*

pho·ne·ti·cian (fō′nə·tish′ən) *n.* A specialist in phonetics.

pho·net·ics (fə·net′iks, fō-) *n.pl.* (*construed as sing.*) The branch of linguistics dealing with the analysis, description, and classification of the sounds of speech. [< Gk. *phōnē* sound] **—pho·net′ic** *adj.* **—pho·net′i·cal·ly** *adv.*

pho·ney (fō′nē) See PHONY.

phon·ic (fon′ik, fō′nik) *adj.* Pertaining to or of the nature of sound, esp. speech sounds. **—phon′i·cal·ly** *adv.*

phon·ics (fon′iks, fō′niks) *n.pl.* (*construed as sing.*) 1. The phonetic rudiments used in teaching reading and pronunciation. 2. The science of sound; acoustics.

phono- *combining form* Sound; speech; voice. Also, before vowels, *phon-.* [< Gk. *phōnē* sound]

pho·no·graph (fō′nə·graf) *n.* A record player. **—pho′no·graph′ic** *adj.* **—pho′no·graph′i·cal·ly** *adv.*

phonograph record A grooved disk that reproduces sounds on a record player.

pho·nol·o·gy (fō·nol′ə·jē) *n.* 1. A study of the sound changes that have taken place in a language. 2. A description of such changes, as with written symbols. **—pho·no·log·ic** (fō′nə·loj′ik) or **·i·cal** *adj.* **—pho′no·log′i·cal·ly** *adv.* **—pho·nol′o·gist** *n.*

pho·ny (fō′nē) *Slang* *adj.* **·ni·er, ·ni·est** Fake; false; spurious; counterfeit. **—*n.* *pl.* ·nies** 1. Something fake or not genuine. 2. One who tries to be something he is not. Also spelled *phoney.* [? < British slang *fawney* imitation jewelry]

-phony *combining form* A (specified) type of sound or sounds: *cacophony.* [< Gk. *phōnē* sound, voice]

-phore *combining form* A bearer or producer of: *semaphore.* [< Gk. *pherein* to bear]

-phorous *combining form* Bearing or producing: found in adjectives corresponding to nouns in *-phore.*

phos·phate (fos′fāt) *n.* 1. *Chem.* A salt or ester of phosphoric acid. 2. *Agric.* Any fertilizer valued for its phosphoric acid. 3. A flavored carbonated beverage. [< F] **—phos·phat·ic** (fos·fat′ik) *adj.*

phospho- *combining form* Phosphorus; of or containing phosphorus, or any of its compounds. Also, before vowels, **phosph-.**

phos·phor (fos′fər) *n.* Any of a class of substances that will emit light under the action of certain chemicals or radiations. [< Gk. *phōs* light + *pherein* to bear]

phos·phor·es·cence (fos′fə·res′əns) *n.* 1. The emission of light without perceptible heat; also, the light so emitted. 2. The property of continuing to shine in the dark after exposure to light, shown by many mineral substances. **—phos′phor·esce′** *v.i.* **·esced, ·esc·ing** **—phos′phor·es′cent** *adj.*

phos·phor·ic (fos·fôr′ik, -for′-) *adj.* *Chem.* Derived from phosphorus, esp. in its [illegible] valence.

phosphoric acid *Chem.* One of thr[illegible] phosphorus, used as a reagent and in beverages.

phos·pho·rous (fos′fər·əs, fos·fôr′əs) *adj.* *Chem.* Derived from phosphorus, esp. in its lower valence.

phosphorous acid *Chem.* A crystalline acid obtained by the oxidation of phosphorus.

phos·pho·rus (fos′fər·əs) *n.* A soft, nonmetallic element (symbol P), found only in combination. [< Gk. *phōs* light + *pherein* to bear]

pho·tic (fō′tik) *adj.* 1. Of or relating to light or to the production of light. 2. Designating underwater regions penetrated by sunlight.

pho·to (fō′tō) *n.* *pl.* **·tos** *Informal* A photograph.

photo- *combining form* 1. Light; of, pertaining to, or produced by light. 2. Photograph; photographic: *photoengrave.* [< Gk. *phōs* light]

pho·to·cell (fō′tō·sel′) *n.* A photoelectric cell.

pho·to·chem·is·try (fō′tō·kem′is·trē) *n.* The branch of chemistry dealing with chemical reactions produced or influenced by light. **—pho′to·chem′i·cal** *adj.*

pho·to·com·po·si·tion (fō′tō·kom′pə·zish′ən) *n.* The composing of printed matter by photographic means. **—pho′to·com·pose′** (-kəm·pōz′) *v.t.*

pho·to·cop·y (fō′tō·kop′ē) *n.* *pl.* **·cop·ies** A photographic reproduction of printed or other graphic material. **—*v.* ·cop·ied, ·cop·y·ing** *v.t.* 1. To make a photocopy of. **—*v.i.*** 2. To make a photocopy. **—pho′to·cop′i·er** *n.*

pho·to·e·lec·tric (fō′tō·i·lek′trik) *adj.* Of or pertaining to the electrical or electronic effects due to the action of light. Also **pho′to·e·lec′tri·cal.** **—pho′to·e·lec′tri·cal·ly** *adv.*

photoelectric cell An electron tube, one of whose electrodes is sensitive to variations in the intensity of light, incorporated in electrical circuits as a controlling, testing, and counting device: also *electric eye, photocell.*

pho·to·e·lec·tron (fō′tō·i·lek′tron) *n.* An electron emitted from a metal surface when exposed to suitable radiation.

pho·to·e·mis·sion (fō′tō·i·mish′ən) The ejection of photoelectrons.

pho·to·en·grav·ing (fō′tō·in·grā′ving) *n.* 1. The process of producing by the aid of photography a relief block or plate for printing. 2. A plate or picture so produced. **—pho′to·en·grave′** *v.t.* **·graved, ·grav·ing** **—pho′to·en·grav′er** *n.*

photo finish 1. A race so closely contested that only a photograph of the finish can determine the winner. 2. *Informal* Any race or competition decided by a slim margin.

pho·to·flash (fō′tō·flash′) *n.* *Photog.* A flashbulb.

pho·to·flood (fō′tō·flud′) *n.* *Photog.* An electric lamp operating at excess voltage to give high illumination.

pho·to·gen·ic (fō′tō·jen′ik) *adj.* 1. Being a good subject for a photograph, esp. for esthetic reasons. 2. *Biol.* Producing phosphorescence. **—pho′to·gen′i·cal·ly** *adv.*
pho·to·graph (fō′tə·graf) *n.* A picture taken by photography. *—v.t.* 1. To take a photograph of. *—v.i.* 2. To practice photography. 3. To be depicted in photographs: He *photographs* beautifully. **—pho·tog·ra·pher** (fə·tog′rə·fər) *n.*
pho·tog·ra·phy (fə·tog′rə·fē) *n.* 1. The process of forming and fixing an image of an object by the chemical action of light and other forms of radiant energy on photosensitive surfaces. 2. The art or business of producing and printing photographs. **—pho·to·graph·ic** (fō′tə·graf′ik) *adj.* **—pho′to·graph′i·cal·ly** *adv.*
pho·to·gra·vure (fō′tō·grə·vyŏŏr′, -grāv′yər) *n.* 1. The process of making an intaglio plate from a photograph for use in printing. 2. A picture so produced. [< F]
pho·to·map (fō′tō·map′) *n.* A map composed of one or more aerial photographs.
pho·tom·e·ter (fō·tom′ə·tər) *n.* Any instrument for measuring or comparing the intensity of light. **—pho·to·met·ric** (fō′tə·met′rik) *adj.* **—pho·tom′e·try** *n.*
pho·to·mi·cro·graph (fō′tō·mī′krə·graf) *n.* A photograph taken through a microscope. **—pho·to·mi·crog·ra·phy** (fō′tō·mī·krog′rə·fē) *n.*
pho·to·mon·tage (fō′tō·mon·täzh′, -môn-) *n.* Montage produced by photography.
pho·to·mu·ral (fō′tō·myŏŏr′əl) *n.* A greatly enlarged photograph, used for wall decoration.
pho·ton (fō′ton) *n.* *Physics* A quantum of radiant energy, moving with the velocity of light. **—pho·ton′ic** *adj.*
pho·to-off·set (fō′tō·ôf′set, -of′-) *n.* Offset printing from a metal surface on which the text or design has been imprinted by photography.
pho·to·sen·si·tive (fō′tō·sen′sə·tiv) *adj.* Sensitive to light. **—pho′to·sen′si·tiv′i·ty** *n.*
pho·to·sphere (fō′tə·sfir) *n.* *Astron.* The visible shining surface of the sun. **—pho′to·spher′ic** (-sfir′ik, -sfer′-) *adj.*
pho·to·stat (fō′tə·stat) *v.t. & v.i.* **·stat·ed** or **·stat·ted, ·stat·ing** or **·stat·ting** To make a reproduction (of) with a Photostat. *—n.* The reproduction so produced. **—pho′to·stat′ic** *adj.* **—pho′to·stat′i·cal·ly** *adv.*
Pho·to·stat (fō′tə·stat) *n.* A camera designed to reproduce facsimiles of documents, drawings, etc., directly as positives: a trade name.
pho·to·syn·the·sis (fō′tō·sin′thə·sis) *n.* *Biochem.* The process by which plants form carbohydrates from carbon dioxide, inorganic salts, and water through the agency of sunlight acting upon chlorophyll. **—pho′to·syn·the′tic** (-thet′ik) *adj.*
pho·to·te·leg·ra·phy (fō′tō·tə·leg′rə·fē) *n.* The transmission of messages, photographs, etc., by facsimile; telephotography. **—pho′·to·tel′e·graph′ic** (-tel′ə·graf′ik) *adj.*
pho·to·trop·ic (fō′tə·trōp′ik, -trop′-) *adj.* *Biol.* Turning in a particular direction under the influence of light. **—pho′to·trop′i·cal·ly** *adv.* **—pho·tot·ro·pism** (fō·tot′rə·piz′əm) *n.*
phrase (frāz) *n.* 1. *Gram.* A group of two or more associated words, not containing a subject and predicate. 2. A word or group of words spoken in one breath. 3. A concise, catchy expression. 4. *Music* A brief statement, usu. comprising several measures. *—v.t. & v.i.* **·phrased, ·phras·ing** 1. To express in words or phrases. 2. To divide (a sentence, etc.) into phrases when speaking. 3. *Music* To divide (a melody) into phrases. [< Gk. *phrazein* to point out] **—phras′al** *adj.* **—phras′ing** *n.*
phra·se·ol·o·gy (frā′zē·ol′ə·jē) *n. pl.* **·gies** The choice and arrangement of words and phrases in expressing ideas. [< Gk. *phrasis* speech + *logos* word] **—phra′se·ol′o·gist** *n.*
phren·ic (fren′ik) *adj.* 1. Of or pertaining to the mind. 2. *Anat.* Of or pertaining to the diaphragm: the *phrenic* nerve. [< Gk. *phrēn, phrenos* diaphragm, mind]
phreno- *combining form* 1. Mind; brain. 2. Diaphragm; of or related to the diaphragm. Also, before vowels, **phren-**. [< Gk. *phrēn, phrenos* the diaphragm (thought to be the seat of intellect)]
phre·nol·o·gy (fri·nol′ə·jē) *n.* The doctrine that the conformation of the human skull indicates the degree of development of various mental faculties and characteristics. [< Gk. *phrēn, phrenos* mind + -LOGY] **—phren·o·log·ic** (fren′ə·loj′ik) or **·i·cal** *adj.* **—phre·nol′o·gist** *n.*
-phyceae *combining form Bot.* Seaweed: used in the names of various classes of algae. [< Gk. *phykos*]
phyco- *combining form* Seaweed; of or related to seaweed. [< Gk. *phykos*]
phy·lac·ter·y (fi·lak′tər·ē) *n. pl.* **·ter·ies** In Judaism, one of two small leather cases containing strips inscribed with Scriptural passages, and bound on the forehead or around the left arm by men during morning prayer. [< Gk. *phylaktērion* safeguard]
-phyllous *combining form* Having (a specified kind or number of) leaves. [< Gk. *phyllon* leaf]
phylo- *combining form* Tribe; race; species. Also, before vowels, **phyl-**. [< Gk. *phylē, phylon* tribe]
phy·log·e·ny (fī·loj′ə·nē) *n. pl.* **·nies** *Biol.* The history of the evolution of a species or group. [< Gk. *phylon* race + *-geneia* birth, origin]
phy·lum (fī′ləm) *n. pl.* **·la** (-lə) *Biol.* A major division of animals or plants of which the members are believed to have a common evolutionary ancestor. [< Gk. *phylon* race]
physi- Var. of PHYSIO-.
phys·ic (fiz′ik) *n.* A cathartic; a purge. *—v.t.* **·icked, ·ick·ing** 1. To treat with medicine, esp. with a cathartic. 2. To cure or relieve. [< Gk. *physikē* (*epistēmē*) (the knowledge) of nature]
phys·i·cal (fiz′i·kəl) *adj.* 1. Of or relating to the human body, as distinguished from the mind or spirit. 2. Of the nature of or pertaining to matter or material things. 3. Of or relating to the material universe or to the sciences that treat of it. 4. Of or pertaining to physics: a *physical* law. *—n.* A medical examination of one's body: also **physical examination.** [See PHYSIC.] **—phys′i·cal·ly** *adv.*
physical education Athletic training and development of the human body; also, education in hygiene.

physical geography Geography dealing with the natural features of the earth, as vegetation, land forms, drainage, ocean currents, climate, etc.: also called *physiography*.

physical science Any of the sciences that treat of inanimate matter or energy, as physics, astronomy, chemistry, or geology.

physical therapy The treatment of disability, injury, and disease by external physical means, as by electricity, heat, massage, etc.: also called *physiotherapy*. —**physical therapist**

phy·si·cian (fi·zish′ən) *n.* One who is legally authorized to practice medicine; a doctor. [See PHYSIC.]

phys·i·cist (fiz′ə·sist) *n.* A specialist in physics.

physico- *combining form* Physics. [See PHYSIC.]

phys·ics (fiz′iks) *n.pl.* (*construed as sing.*) The science that treats of motion, matter, and energy, and of their interactions.

physio- *combining form* Nature; related to natural functions or phenomena. Also, before vowels, *physi-*. [< Gk. *physis* nature]

phys·i·og·no·my (fiz′ē·og′nə·mē) *n. pl.* **·mies** 1. The face or features considered as revealing character or disposition. 2. The outward look of a thing. [< Gk. *physiognōmonia* the judging of a man's nature (by his features)] —**phys′i·og·nom′ic** (-nom′ik) or **·i·cal** *adj.* —**phys′i·og′no·mist** *n.*

phys·i·og·ra·phy (fiz′ē·og′rə·fē) *n.* 1. A description of nature. 2. Physical geography. —**phys′i·og′ra·pher** *n.* —**phys′i·o·graph′ic** (-ə·graf′ik) or **·i·cal** *adj.*

phys·i·ol·o·gy (fiz′ē·ol′ə·jē) *n. pl.* **·gies** 1. The science that treats of the processes and mechanisms by which living animals and plants function under varied conditions. 2. The aggregate of vital processes: the *physiology* of the frog. [< Gk. *physiologos* speaker on nature] —**phys′i·o·log′i·cal** (-ə·loj′i·kəl) or **phys′i·o·log′ic** *adj.* —**phys′i·o·log′i·cal·ly** *adv.* —**phys′i·ol′o·gist** *n.*

phys·i·o·ther·a·py (fiz′ē·ō·ther′ə·pē) *n.* Physical therapy.

phy·sique (fi·zēk′) *n.* The structure or appearance of the body. [< F]

-phyte *combining form* A (specified) kind of plant; a plant having a (specified) habitat. [< Gk. *phyton* plant]

pi[1] (pī) *n. pl.* **pis** 1. The sixteenth letter in the Greek alphabet (Π, π), corresponding to English *p*. 2. *Math.* **a** This letter used to designate the ratio of the circumference of a circle to its diameter. **b** The ratio itself (3.14159 . . .). [def. 2 < Gk. *p(eriphereia)* periphery]

pi[2] (pī) *n. pl.* **pies** *Printing* Type that has been thrown into disorder. —*v.t.* **pied, pie·ing** To jumble or disorder, as type. Also spelled *pie*. [Origin unknown]

pi·a·nis·si·mo (pē′ə·nis′i·mō, *Ital.* pyä·nēs′·sē·mō) *adj. & adv. Music* Very soft or very softly. —*n. pl.* **·mos** A passage so played. [< Ital.]

pi·an·ist (pē·an′ist, pē′ə·nist) *n.* One who plays the piano; esp., a professional performer on the piano. [< F *pianiste* and < Ital. *pianista*]

pi·an·o[1] (pē·an′ō) *n. pl.* **·os** A musical instrument having felt-covered hammers operated from a manual keyboard that strike upon steel wires to produce musical tones. [< Ital., short for PIANOFORTE]

pi·a·no[2] (pē·ä′nō, *Ital.* pyä′nō) *adj. & adv. Music* Soft or softly: a direction to the performer. —*n. pl.* **·nos** A passage so played. [< Ital. < L *planus* flat, soft]

pi·an·o·for·te (pē·an′ə·fôr′tā, -fôrt′) *n.* A piano. [< Ital. *piano e forte* soft and loud]

pi·as·ter (pē·as′tər) *n.* A monetary unit of various countries, as Egypt, Sudan, and Syria: the hundredth part of a pound. Also **pi·as′tre.** [< Ital. *piastra*, lit., plate of metal]

pi·az·za (pē·az′ə, *Ital.* pyät′tsä) *n.* 1. An open area or public square in a city or town, esp. in Italy. 2. A covered outer walk or gallery. [< Ital., square, marketplace]

pi·ca (pī′kə) *n.* 1. A size of type; 12-point; about $^1/_6$ inch. 2. A size of typewriter type equivalent to 12-point, with 10 characters to the inch. [< Med.L, a book of church rules]

pic·a·resque (pik′ə·resk′) *adj.* 1. Of or involving rogues or vagabonds. 2. Denoting a form of fiction involving rogues and vagabonds. [< Sp. *picaresco* roguish]

pic·a·yune (pik′i·yōōn′) *adj.* 1. Of small value; paltry; contemptible. 2. Petty; niggling; mean. Also **pic′a·yun′ish.** —*n.* Anything of trifling value. [< F *picaillon* farthing]

pic·ca·lil·li (pik′ə·lil′ē) *n.* A relish of chopped vegetables. [Prob. < PICKLE]

pic·co·lo (pik′ə·lō) *n. pl.* **·los** A small flute pitched an octave higher than the ordinary flute. [< Ital., small]

pick[1] (pik) *v.t.* 1. To choose; select, as from a group or number. 2. To detach or pluck, as with the fingers. 3. To clear (a field, tree, etc.) in such a manner. 4. To remove extraneous matter from (the teeth, etc.), as with the fingers or with a pointed instrument. 5. To touch, irritate, or remove with a fingernail, etc. 6. To nibble at or peck. 7. To break up, penetrate, or indent with or as with a pointed instrument. 8. To pull apart, as rags. 9. To seek or point out critically: to *pick* flaws. 10. To remove the contents of by stealth: to *pick* a pocket. 11. To open (a lock) by means other than the key. 12. To provoke: to *pick* a fight. —*v.i.* 13. To work with a pick. 14. To eat without appetite; nibble. 15. To select carefully. —**to pick at** 1. To eat without appetite. 2. *Informal* To nag at. —**to pick off** 1. To remove by picking. 2. To hit, as with a bullet. 3. In baseball, to catch (a base runner) off base. —**to pick on** *Informal* To tease or annoy. —**to pick out** 1. To select. 2. To distinguish (something) from its surroundings. 3. To produce the notes of (a tune, etc.) singly or slowly, as by ear. —**to pick over** To examine carefully or one by one. —**to pick up** 1. To take up, as with the hand. 2. To take up or receive into a group, vehicle, etc. 3. To acquire casually or by chance. 4. To gain speed; accelerate. 5. To be able to receive, as radio transmission. 6. *Informal* To recover spirits, health, etc.; improve. 7. *Informal* To make the acquaintance of (a stranger, esp. of the opposite sex) under casual circumstances. —*n.* 1. Right of selection; choice. 2. That which is selected, esp. the choicest part. 3. The quantity of certain crops picked by hand. 4. The act of picking. [OE *pīcan, pīcian*] **—pick′er** *n.*

pick² (pik) *n.* 1. A double-headed, pointed metal tool mounted on a wooden handle, used for breaking ground, etc. 2. Any of various implements for picking. 3. A small implement for striking the strings of a guitar, etc.: also called *plectrum.* [Appar. var. of PIKE¹]

pick·a·back (pik′ə·bak′) *adv.* Piggyback (def. 1). [Earlier *pickback, pickpack*]

pick·ax (pik′aks′) *n.* A pick with one end of the head edged like a chisel and the other pointed; also, a pick with both ends pointed. Also **pick′axe′.**

pick·er·el (pik′ər·əl, pik′rel) *n.* Various North American fresh-water fishes of the pike family, esp. the small species having a narrow snout and sharp teeth. [Dim. of PIKE²]

pick·er·el·weed (pik′ər·əl·wēd′) *n.* Any of various perennial plants found in the shallows of North American lakes.

pick·et (pik′it) *n.* 1. A pointed stick or post, used as a fence paling, tent peg, etc.; a stake. 2. A person stationed at the outside of a place affected by a strike, for the purpose of publicizing alleged grievances, etc. 3. A person engaged in public protest. 4. *Mil.* A soldier or detachment of soldiers posted to guard a camp, army, etc. **—*v.t.*** 1. To be a picket or station pickets outside of. 2. To fence or fortify with pickets. 3. To tie to a picket, as a horse. 4. *Mil.* To guard by means of a picket. **—*v.i.*** 5. To act as a picket (defs. 2 & 3). [< F *piquet* pointed stake]

pick·et·er (pik′it·ər) *n.* A picket (defs. 2 & 3).

pick·ing (pik′ing) *n.* 1. That which is or may be picked. 2. *pl.* That which is left: scanty *pickings.* 3. *Usu. pl.* That which is taken by questionable means; spoils.

pick·le (pik′əl) *n.* 1. A cucumber that has been preserved and flavored in brine or vinegar. 2. Any article of food so preserved or flavored. 3. A liquid preservative, as brine or vinegar, sometimes spiced, for meat, fish, etc. 4. *Informal* An embarrassing condition or position. **—*v.t.* ·led, ·ling** To preserve or flavor in a pickle solution. [Appar. < MDu. *pekel, peeckel*]

pick·lock (pik′lok′) *n.* 1. A special implement for opening a lock. 2. One who picks locks, esp. illegally.

pick·pock·et (pik′pok′it) *n.* One who steals from pockets.

pick·up (pik′up′) *n.* 1. Acceleration, as in the speed of an automobile, engine, etc. 2. *Electronics* A device that converts the oscillations of a needle in a record groove into electrical impulses. 3. A small, usu. open truck for light loads: also **pickup truck.** 4. *Telecom.* In television: a the scanning of an image by the electron beam. b The scanning apparatus. 5. *Informal* Renewed or increased activity: a *pickup* in business. 6. *Informal* A stranger with whom a casual acquaintance is made.

pic·nic (pik′nik) *n.* 1. An outdoor social outing for which food is usu. provided by the people participating. 2. *Slang* An easy or pleasant time or experience. **—*v.i.* ·nicked, ·nick·ing** To have or attend a picnic. [< F *pique-nique*] **—pic′nick·er** *n.*

pico- *combining form* One trillionth (10^{-12}) of a specified quantity or dimension: *picosecond.* [Prob. < Ital. *piccolo* small]

pi·cot (pē′kō) *n.* A small thread loop on ornamental edging, ribbon, etc. **—*v.t. & v.i.* ·coted** (-kōd), **·cot·ing** (-kō·ing) To sew with this edging. [< F, dim. of OF *pic* point]

pic·to·graph (pik′tə·graf) *n.* 1. A picture representing an idea, as a hieroglyph. 2. A record of such pictures. Also **pic′to·gram** (-gram). [< L *pictus* painted + -GRAPH] **—pic′to·graph′ic** *adj.* **—pic′to·graph′i·cal·ly** *adv.* **—pic·tog·ra·phy** (pik·tog′rə·fē) *n.*

pic·to·ri·al (pik·tôr′ē·əl) *adj.* 1. Pertaining to, composed of, or concerned with pictures. 2. Graphic; vivid. **—*n.*** A periodical that devotes considerable space to pictures. **—pic·to′ri·al·ly** *adv.*

pic·ture (pik′chər) *n.* 1. A visual representation of an object or scene upon a flat surface, as a painting, drawing, engraving, or photograph. 2. A vivid or graphic verbal description. 3. A mental image or impression of the nature of a situation, event, etc. 4. An overall situation. 5. One who or that which resembles or embodies another person or thing: She is the *picture* of despair. **—*v.t.* ·tured, ·tur·ing** 1. To form a mental image of. 2. To describe graphically; depict verbally. 3. To make a picture of. [< L *pictus,* pp. of *pingere* to paint]

pic·tur·esque (pik′chə·resk′) *adj.* 1. Having a striking beauty, quaintness, or charm. 2. Abounding in striking or original expression or imagery. 3. Like or suitable for a picture. **—pic′tur·esque′ness** *n.*

picture tube Kinescope.

pid·dle (pid′l) *v.* **·dled, ·dling** ***v.t.*** 1. To trifle; dawdle: usu. with *away.* **—*v.i.*** 2. To trifle; dawdle. [Origin uncertain]

pid·dling (pid′ling) *adj.* Unimportant; trivial; trifling.

pidg·in (pij′in) *n.* A mixed language combining the vocabulary and grammar of dissimilar languages. [< Chinese pronun. of *business*]

Pidgin English A jargon composed of English and elements of local non-English dialects, used as the language of commerce esp. in the Orient. Also called **Pidg′in.**

pie¹ (pī) *n.* A baked food consisting of one or two layers or crusts of pastry with a filling of fruit, custard, meat, etc. [ME]

pie² (pī) *n.* Any of various birds with speckled plumage, as the magpie. [< L *pica* magpie]

pie³ (pī) See PI².

pie·bald (pī′bôld′) *adj.* Having spots, esp. of white and black. **—*n.*** A spotted or mottled animal, esp. a horse. [< PIE² + BALD; because like a magpie's plumage]

piece (pēs) *n.* 1. A portion or quantity existing as an individual entity or mass: a *piece* of paper. 2. A small portion considered as forming a distinct part of a whole. 3. A coin: a fifty-cent *piece.* 4. An instance; example: a *piece* of luck. 5. One of a class or group: a *piece* of furniture. 6. A work of esthetic interest, as a literary or musical composition, a play, etc. 7. One of the disks or counters used in checkers, backgammon, etc. 8. A quantity or length in which an article is manufactured or sold. **—a piece of one's mind** *Informal* Criticism or censure frankly expressed. **—to go to pieces** 1. To fall apart. 2. *Informal* To lose emotional self-control. **—to have a piece of** *Slang* To have a financial interest in. **—***v.* **pieced, piec·ing** *v.t.* 1. To add or attach a piece or pieces to, as for enlargement. 2. To unite or reunite the pieces of, as in mending. 3. To unite (parts) into a whole. **—***v.i.* 4. *Dial.* To snack between meals. [< Med.L *pecia*] **—piec′er** *n.*

pièce de ré·sis·tance (pyes də rā·zē·stäns′) *French* 1. A principal or most important item. 2. The chief dish of a dinner.

piece goods Fabrics made in standard lengths.

piece·meal (pēs′mēl′) *adv. & adj.* Piece by piece; gradually. [ME *pece* piece + *-mele* a part]

piece·work (pēs′wûrk′) *n.* Work done or paid for by the piece or quantity. **—piece′·work′er** *n.*

pied (pīd) *adj.* Spotted; piebald; mottled. [< PIE[2]]

pied-à-terre (pē·äd′ə·ter′) *n.* A temporary or secondary lodging. [< F, lit., foot on the ground]

pie plant *Dial.* The common variety of rhubarb.

pier (pir) *n.* 1. A structure extending over the water, secured by piles and serving as a landing place for vessels; wharf. 2. A plain, detached mass of masonry, usu. serving as a support: the *pier* of a bridge. 3. An upright projecting portion of a wall; a buttress. [< Med.L *pera*]

pierce (pirs) *v.* **pierced, pierc·ing** *v.t.* 1. To pass into or through, with or as if with a pointed instrument; puncture; stab. 2. To force a way into or through: to *pierce* the wilderness. 3. To make an opening or hole in, into, or through. 4. To cut through as if stabbing; cleave. 5. To solve; understand: to *pierce* a mystery. **—***v.i.* 6. To enter; penetrate. [< OF *percer*] **—pierc′er** *n.* **—pierc′ing·ly** *adv.*

pier glass A large, high mirror intended to fill the space between two windows.

pi·e·tism (pī′ə·tiz′əm) *n.* 1. Piety or godliness; devotion. 2. Affected or exaggerated piety. [< G *pietismus*] **—pi′e·tis′tic** (-tis′tik) or **·ti·cal** *adj.* **—pi′e·tis′ti·cal·ly** *adv.*

pi·e·ty (pī′ə·tē) *n. pl.* **·ties** 1. Reverence toward God or the gods. 2. Honor and obedience due to parents, etc. 3. A pious act, wish, etc. [< L *pius* dutiful]

piezo- *combining form* Pressure; related to or produced by pressure. [< Gk. *piezien* to press]

pi·e·zo·e·lec·tric·i·ty (pī·ē′zō·i·lek′tris′ə·tē, -ē′lek-) *n.* Electricity or electric phenomena resulting from pressure upon certain bodies, esp. crystals. **—pi·e′zo·e·lec′tric** *adj.*

pif·fle (pif′əl) *Informal v.i.* **·fled, ·fling** To talk nonsensically; babble. **—***n.* Nonsense; babble. [? Blend of PIDDLE and TRIFLE]

pig (pig) *n.* 1. A cloven-hoofed mammal having a long, mobile snout, esp. a small, young one: also called *swine.* ◆Collateral adjective: *porcine.* 2. The flesh of a pig; pork. 3. An oblong mass of metal, esp. iron or lead, just run from the smelter and cast in a rough mold. 4. *Informal* A person who is filthy, gluttonous, or coarse. **—***v.i.* **pigged, pig·ging** To bring forth pigs. [ME *pigge*]

pig·eon (pij′ən) *n.* 1. A bird having short legs, a small head, and a sturdy body. 2. *Slang* One who is easily swindled. [< LL *pipio, -onis* young chirping bird]

pig·eon·hole (pij′ən·hōl′) *n.* 1. A hole for pigeons to nest in. 2. A small compartment, as in a desk, for filing papers. **—***v.t.* **·holed, ·hol·ing** 1. To place in a pigeonhole; file. 2. To file away and ignore. 3. To place in categories.

pig·eon-toed (pij′ən·tōd′) *adj.* Having the toes or feet turned inward.

pig·ger·y (pig′ər·ē) *n. pl.* **·ger·ies** A place for keeping or raising pigs.

pig·gish (pig′ish) *adj.* Like a pig; greedy; dirty; selfish. **—pig′gish·ly** *adv.* **—pig′gish·ness** *n.*

pig·gy (pig′ē) *n. pl.* **·gies** A little pig. Also **pig′gie.**

pig·gy·back (pig′ē·bak′) *adv.* 1. On the back or shoulders: to ride *piggyback:* also *pickaback.* 2. On a railway flat car: to ship trailers *piggyback.* **—pig′gy·back′** *adj.* **—pig′gy·back′ing** *n.*

pig·head·ed (pig′hed′id) *adj.* Stupidly obstinate. **—pig′head′ed·ly** *adv.* **—pig′·head′ed·ness** *n.*

pig iron Crude iron poured from a blast furnace into variously shaped molds of sand or the like.

pig·ment (pig′mənt) *n.* 1. Finely powdered coloring matter suitable for making paints, enamels, etc. 2. Any substance that imparts color to animal or vegetable tissues, as melanin and chlorophyll. [< L *pingere* to paint] **—pig′men·tar′y** *adj.*

pig·men·ta·tion (pig′mən·tā′shən) *n.* 1. Coloration resulting from pigment. 2. *Biol.* Deposition of pigment by cells. **—pig′·ment·ed** *adj.*

pig·my (pig′mē) See PYGMY.

pig·nut (pig′nut′) *n.* 1. The fruit of a hickory tree common in the U.S. 2. The tree.

pig·skin (pig′skin′) *n.* 1. The skin of a pig. 2. Something made of this skin, as a saddle. 3. *Informal* A football.

pig·sty (pig′stī′) *n. pl.* **·sties** A sty or pen for pigs. Also **pig′pen′** (-pen′).

pig·tail (pig′tāl′) *n.* A braid or plait of hair extending down from the back of the head.

pike[1] (pīk) *n.* A long pole having a metal spearhead. **—***v.t.* **piked, pik·ing** To run through or kill with a pike. [< MF *pique*]

pike[2] (pīk) *n.* 1. A widely distributed fresh-water food fish having a slender body and a long snout. 2. Any of several other fishes resembling the pike. [< PIKE[4], with ref. to its pointed snout]

pike[3] (pīk) *n.* A turnpike. [Short for TURNPIKE]

pike[4] (pīk) *n.* A spike or sharp point, as the end of a spear.

piked (pīkt, pī′kid) *adj.* Having a pike; pointed. [< PIKE[4]]

pik·er (pī′kər) *n. Slang* 1. One who bets or speculates in a small, niggardly way. 2. One who acts in a petty or niggling way. [Origin uncertain]

pike·staff (pīk′staf′) *n. pl.* **·staves** (-stāvz′) The wooden handle of a pike. [< PIKE[4] + STAFF]

pi·laf (pi·läf′, pē′läf) *n.* A Middle Eastern dish of rice, raisins, spice, and a meat or fowl sauce. Also **pi·laff** (pi·läf′, pē′läf), **pi·lau**

(pi·lou′, -lô′, pē′lou, -lô) **pi·law** (pi·lô′, pē′lô). [< Persian and Turkish *pilāw*]

pi·las·ter (pi·las′tər) *n.* *Archit.* A rectangular column, with capital and base, engaged in a wall. [< L *pila* column]

pil·chard (pil′chərd) *n.* A small, herringlike food fish; the sardine of Mediterranean and European Atlantic waters. [Earlier *pilcher*; origin uncertain]

pile[1] (pīl) *n.* 1. A quantity of anything gathered or thrown together in one place; a heap. 2. A funeral pyre. 3. A massive building or group of buildings. 4. *Informal* A large accumulation, quantity, or number of something. 5. *Slang* A large amount of money. **—*v.* piled, pil·ing** *v.t.* 1. To make a heap or pile of: often with *up*. 2. To cover or burden with a pile or piles: to *pile* a plate with food. **—*v.i.*** 3. To form a heap or pile. 4. To proceed or go in a confused mass: with *in*, *on*, *off*, *out*, etc. **—to pile up** To accumulate. [< L *pila* pillar, pier]

pile[2] (pīl) *n.* A column, as of wood or steel, forced into the earth to support a building, pier, etc. **—*v.t.* piled, pil·ing** 1. To drive piles into. 2. To furnish or strengthen with piles. [OE *pil* dart, pointed stake]

pile[3] (pīl) *n.* 1. The cut or uncut loops that form the surface of certain fabrics, as velvets, plushes, and corduroys. 2. Soft, fine hair; down. [< L *pilus* hair] **—piled** *adj.*

pi·le·at·ed (pī′lē·ā′tid, pil′ē-) *adj.* *Ornithol.* Having the feathers on the top of the head elongated or conspicuous; crested. Also **pi′le·ate** (-it, -āt). [< L *pileatus* capped]

pile driver A machine for driving piles.

piles (pīlz) *n.pl.* Hemorrhoids. [< LL *pila* ball]

pil·fer (pil′fər) *v.t.* & *v.i.* To steal in small quantities. [< OF *pelfrer* to rob] **—pil′·fer·age** *n.* **—pil′fer·er** *n.*

pil·grim (pil′grim) *n.* 1. One who journeys to some sacred place from religious motives. 2. Any wanderer or wayfarer. 3. *cap.* One of the English Puritans who founded Plymouth Colony in 1620. [< L *peregrinus* foreigner]

pil·grim·age (pil′grə·mij) *n.* 1. A journey made to a shrine or sacred place. 2. Any long or arduous journey.

pil·ing (pī′ling) *n.* A structure formed of piles.

pill (pil) *n.* 1. A pellet or globule containing medicine, convenient for swallowing whole. 2. *Slang* A person difficult to bear with; a bore. **—the pill or the Pill** Any of various oral contraceptive drugs in tablet form, taken by women. **—*v.t.*** 1. To form into pills. 2. To dose with pills. [< L *pila* ball]

pil·lage (pil′ij) *n.* 1. The act of taking money or property by open violence; looting. 2. Spoil; booty. **—*v.* ·laged, ·lag·ing** *v.t.* 1. To plunder. 2. To take as loot. **—*v.i.*** 3. To take plunder. [< OF *piller* to plunder] **—pil′lag·er** *n.*

pil·lar (pil′ər) *n.* 1. A vertical support, usu. slender in relation to its height; column. 2. A structure of similar form used as a decoration or monument. 3. One who strongly supports a work or cause. **—*v.t.*** To support or adorn with pillars. [< L *pila*]

pill·box (pil′boks′) *n.* 1. A small box for pills. 2. A small, round, concrete emplacement for a machine gun, antitank gun, etc.

pil·lion (pil′yən) *n.* A pad or seat behind the saddle of a horse or motorcycle for a second rider. [Appar. < Scot.Gaelic *pillean*, dim. of *pell* cushion]

pil·lo·ry (pil′ə·rē) *n.* *pl.* **·ries** A framework in which an offender was fastened by the neck and wrists and exposed to public scorn. **—*v.t.* ·ried, ·ry·ing** 1. To set in the pillory. 2. To hold up to public scorn. [< OF *pellori*]

pil·low (pil′ō) *n.* 1. A case, usu. of cloth, filled with a soft or yielding material, as feathers or foam rubber, used to cushion the head, as during sleep. 2. A small, usu. decorative cushion. **—*v.t.*** 1. To rest on or as on a pillow. 2. To act as a pillow for. **—*v.i.*** 3. To recline on or as on a pillow. [< L *pulvinus* cushion] **—pil′low·y** *adj.*

pil·low·case (pil′ō·kās′) *n.* A covering drawn over a pillow. Also **pillow slip.**

pi·lot (pī′lət) *n.* 1. One who operates or guides an aircraft or spacecraft during flight. 2. One who is licensed to conduct ships in and out of port or through certain waters difficult to navigate. 3. The helmsman of a ship. 4. Any guide. 5. A television program offered as typical of a projected series. **—*v.t.*** 1. To act as the pilot of; steer. 2. To guide or conduct, as through difficult circumstances. 3. To serve as a pilot on, over, or in. **—*adj.*** 1. Serving as a guide or control. 2. Serving as a trial situation. [< Ital. *pilota*]

pi·lot·age (pī′lət·ij) *n.* 1. The act of piloting a vessel or aircraft. 2. The fee for such service.

pilot fish An oceanic fish often seen in warm latitudes in company with sharks.

pi·lot·house (pī′lət·hous′) *n.* An enclosed structure, usu. in the forward part of a ship, containing the steering wheel and compass: also called *wheelhouse*.

pilot light A minute jet of gas kept burning for igniting an ordinary burner as soon as the gas is turned on: also **pilot burner.**

pil·sner (pil′znər) *n.* *Often cap.* 1. A light beer. 2. A long, tapered glass for beer. Also **pil′sen·er** (-zə·nər).

Pi·ma (pē′mə) *n.* *pl.* **Pi·mas** or **Pi·ma** 1. One of a tribe of North American Indians of southern Arizona and Northern Mexico. 2. The Uto-Aztecan language of this tribe.

Pi·man (pē′mən) *n.* A branch of the Uto-Aztecan language family of North American Indians. **—*adj.*** Of or pertaining to this linguistic branch.

pi·men·to (pi·men′to) *n.* *pl.* **·tos** 1. The dried, unripe, aromatic berry of a West Indian tree of the myrtle family. 2. Pimiento. [< Med.L *pigmentum* spiced drink, spice]

pimento cheese A cheese with pimientos added.

pi·mien·to (pi·myen′tō) *n.* *pl.* **·tos** A sweet pepper or its ripe fruit, used as a relish and as a stuffing in olives: also called *pimento*. [< Sp. *pimienta* pepper]

pimp (pimp) *n.* One who solicits for a prostitute in exchange for part of her earnings. **—*v.i.*** To act as a pimp. [? < L *pipire* to murmur seductively]

pim·per·nel (pim′pər·nel) *n.* A plant of the primrose family, usu. with red flowers, as the common **scarlet pimpernel.** [< Med.L *pimpernella*]

pim·ple (pim′pəl) *n.* A small swelling or elevation of the skin, with an inflamed base.

[OE *piplian* to break out in pimples] **—pim′pled, pim′ply** *adj.*

pin (pin) *n.* 1. A short, stiff piece of wire with a sharp point and a round, usu. flattened head, used for fastening together parts of clothing, sheets of paper, etc. 2. An ornament mounted on a pin or having a pin with a clasp. 3. Anything resembling a pin in form or use, as a hairpin. 4. A peg or bar, as of metal or wood, used in fastening or supporting, as the bolt of a door, a linchpin, etc. 5. In bowling and similar games, one of the rounded wooden clubs that are set up as the target. 6. In golf, a pole with a small flag attached to mark the position of a hole. 7. *pl.* *Informal* The legs. **—on pins and needles** Uneasy or anxious; nervous. **—***v.t.* **pinned, pin·ning** 1. To fasten with or as with a pin or pins. 2. To seize and hold firmly; make unable to move. 3. To transfix with a pin, spear, etc. 4. To force (someone) to make up his mind, follow a definite course of action, etc.: usu. with *down.* 5. *Slang* To hold responsible for (a wrongdoing, etc.); accuse of: with *on.* [OE *pinn* peg] **—pin′ner** *n.*

pin·a·fore (pin′ə·fôr) *n.* A sleeveless apronlike garment.

pin·ball (pin′bôl′) *n.* A game in which a ball is propelled by a spring to the top of an inclined board, and in its descent touches any of various numbered pins, holes, etc., the contacts so made determining the player's score.

pince-nez (pans′nā′, pins′-; *Fr.* pañs·nā′) *n.* *pl.* **pince-nez** (-nāz, *Fr.* -nā) Eyeglasses held upon the nose by a spring. [< F, lit., pinch-nose]

pin·cer (pin′sər) *n.* 1. *Usu. pl.* An instrument having two handles and a pair of jaws working on a pivot, used for holding objects. 2. *Zool.* A nipperlike organ, as the claw of a lobster. Also **pinch·er** (pin′chər). [< AF, to pinch] **—pin′cer·like′** *adj.*

pinch (pinch) *v.t.* 1. To squeeze between two hard edges or surfaces, as a finger and thumb, etc. 2. To bend or compress painfully. 3. To contract or make thin, as from cold or hunger. 4. To reduce in means; distress, as for lack of money. 5. *Slang* To capture or arrest. 6. *Slang* To steal. **—***v.i.* 7. To squeeze; hurt. 8. To be stingy. **—to pinch pennies** To be economical or stingy. **—***n.* 1. The act of pinching, or the state of being pinched. 2. So much of a substance as can be taken between the finger and thumb; a small amount. 3. An emergency. 4. *Slang* An arrest or raid. [< OF *pincier*] **—pinch′er** *n.*

pinch-hit (pinch′hit′) *v.i.* **-hit, -hit·ting** 1. In baseball, to go to bat in place of a regular player. 2. *Informal* To substitute for another in an emergency. **—pinch hitter**

pin·cush·ion (pin′ko͝osh′ən) *n.* A small cushion into which pins are stuck when they are not in use.

pine[1] (pīn) *n.* 1. Any of various cone-bearing trees having needle-shaped evergreen leaves growing in clusters. 2. The wood of a pine tree. [< L *pinus*]

pine[2] (pīn) *v.i.* **pined, pin·ing** 1. To grow thin or weak with longing, grief, etc. 2. To have great longing: usu. with *for.* [< L *poena* punishment]

pin·e·al body (pin′ē·əl) *Anat.* A small, reddish gray, vascular, conical body of rudimentary glandular structure found in the brain and having no known function. Also **pineal gland.** [< L *pinea* pine cone]

pine·ap·ple (pīn′ap′əl) *n.* 1. A tropical plant having spiny leaves and a cone-shaped fruit tipped with a rosette of spiked leaves. 2. Its edible fruit.

pine tar A dark, viscous tar obtained by the destructive distillation of the wood of pine trees, used to treat skin ailments.

pin·feath·er (pin′feth′ər) *n.* *Ornithol.* A rudimentary feather, esp. one just beginning to grow through the skin.

ping (ping) *n.* A brief, sharp, high-pitched sound. **—***v.i.* To make this sound. [Imit.]

Ping-Pong (ping′pong′, -pông′) *n.* The game of table tennis: a trade name.

pin·head (pin′hed′) *n.* 1. The head of a pin. 2. Any small or insignificant object. 3. *Slang* A brainless or stupid person.

pin·hole (pin′hōl′) *n.* A minute puncture made by or as by a pin.

pin·ion[1] (pin′yən) *n.* 1. The wing of a bird. 2. The outer segment of a bird's wing, bearing the flight feathers. **—***v.t.* 1. To cut off one pinion or bind the wings of (a bird) so as to prevent flight. 2. To shackle; confine. [< L *penna, pinna* feather]

pin·ion[2] (pin′yən) *n.* *Mech.* A toothed wheel driving or driven by a larger cogwheel. [< F *pignon* battlement]

pink[1] (pingk) *n.* 1. A pale red color. 2. Any of several garden plants with narrow, grasslike leaves and fragrant flowers. 3. The flower of any of these plants, as the carnation. 4. *Informal* A person who holds somewhat radical economic or political views. **—in the pink (of condition)** *Informal* In excellent health. **—***adj.* 1. Being pink in color. 2. *Informal* Moderately radical. [Origin uncertain] **—pink′ish** *adj.*

pink[2] (pingk) *v.t.* 1. To prick or stab with a pointed weapon. 2. To decorate, as cloth or leather, with a pattern of holes. 3. To cut the edges of (cloth) with a notched pattern. [ME *pynken*]

pink·eye (pingk′ī′) *n.* 1. *Pathol.* An acute, contagious conjunctivitis marked by redness of the eyeball. 2. *Vet.* A febrile, contagious corneal infection of sheep.

pink·ie (pingk′ē) *n.* *Informal* The little or fifth finger. Also **pink′y.** [Prob. < obs. *pink* small]

pink·ing shears (pingk′ing) Shears with serrated blades for scalloping the edges of fabrics.

pin money An allowance of money for minor incidental expenses.

pin·nace (pin′is) *n.* *Naut.* 1. Any ship's boat. 2. Formerly, a small vessel used as a tender, scout, etc. [< Ital. *pinaccia*]

pin·na·cle (pin′ə·kəl) *n.* 1. A small turret or tall ornament, as on a parapet. 2. Anything resembling a pinnacle, as a mountain peak. 3. The highest point or place; apex; summit. **—***v.t.* **·cled, ·cling** 1. To place on or as on a pinnacle. 2. To furnish with a pinnacle; crown. [< L *pinna* wing, pinnacle]

pin·nate (pin′āt) *adj.* 1. Like a feather. 2. *Bot.* Having leaves arranged on each side of a common axis. Also **pin′nat·ed.** [< L *pinna* feather, wing] **—pin′nate·ly** *adv.* **—pin·na′tion** *n.*

pi·noch·le (pē′nuk·əl, -nok-) *n.* A card game played with a double deck of 48 cards. Also **pi′noc·le.** [Origin uncertain]

pi·ñon (pin′yən, pēn′yōn; *Sp.* pē·nyōn′) *n.* 1. Any of various pine trees of the SW U.S., having edible seeds: also spelled *pinyon.* 2. A seed from such a tree. [< Sp. < L *pinea* pine cone]

pin·point (pin′point′) *n.* 1. The point of a pin. 2. Something extremely small. —*v.t.* To locate or define precisely.

pin·scher (pin′shər) *n.* A Doberman pinscher. [< G, terrier]

pin·stripe (pin′strīp′) *n.* A very narrow stripe, as in a fabric. —**pin′striped′** *adj.*

pint (pīnt) *n.* 1. A dry and liquid measure of capacity equal to ½ quart. The liquid pint is equal to .473 liter and the dry pint to .55 liter. 2. A container having such a capacity. [< OF *pinte*]

pin·tail (pin′tāl′) *n.* 1. A duck of the northern hemisphere, the male of which has a long, sharp tail. 2. A sharp-tailed grouse of North America.

pin·to (pin′tō) *adj. SW U.S.* Piebald; pied, as an animal. —*n. pl.* **·tos** 1. *SW U.S.* A pied animal, esp. a horse or pony. 2. A kind of spotted bean of the SW U.S.: also **pinto bean.** [< Am.Sp. < Sp., lit., painted]

pin·up (pin′up′) *n.* A picture of an attractive young woman hung on a wall. —*adj.* 1. Capable of being affixed to a wall, as a lamp. 2. Having the qualities of or suitable for a pinup: a *pinup* girl.

pin·wheel (pin′hwēl′) *n.* 1. A firework that revolves when ignited, forming a wheel of fire. 2. A child's toy resembling a windmill, revolving on a pin attached to a stick.

pin·worm (pin′wûrm′) *n.* A small worm parasitic in the lower intestines of man.

pin·y (pī′nē) *adj.* **pin·i·er, pin·i·est** Pertaining to, suggestive of, or covered with pines.

pin·yon (pin′yən) See PIÑON.

pi·o·neer (pī′ə·nir′) *n.* 1. One of the first explorers or settlers of a new country or region. 2. One of the first investigators or developers in a new field of research, enterprise, etc. —*v.t.* 1. To be a pioneer of. —*v.i.* 2. To act as a pioneer. [< OF *peonier* foot soldier < L *pes, pedis* foot]

pi·ous (pī′əs) *adj.* 1. Actuated by reverence for a supreme being; religious; godly. 2. Marked by a reverential spirit. 3. Affectedly devout or virtuous. [< L *pius* dutiful, respectful] —**pi′ous·ly** *adv.* —**pi′ous·ness** *n.*

pip[1] (pip) *n.* The seed of an apple, orange, etc. [Short for PIPPIN]

pip[2] (pip) *n.* A spot, as on a playing card, domino, or die. [Earlier *peep*; origin unknown]

pip[3] (pip) *n.* 1. *Vet.* A contagious disease of fowls. 2. *Slang* A mild human ailment. [< L *pituita* mucus, the pip]

pipe (pīp) *n.* 1. A small bowl with a hollow stem, for smoking tobacco, opium, etc. 2. A long conducting passage of wood, metal, tiling, etc., for conveying a fluid. 3. *Music* **a** A tubular flute or woodwind instrument. **b** One of the tubes of a pipe organ. **c** *pl.* The bagpipe. —*v.* **piped, pip·ing** *v.i.* 1. To play on a pipe. 2. To make a shrill sound. —*v.t.* 3. To convey by or as by means of pipes. 4. To play, as a tune, on a pipe. 5. To utter shrilly or in a high key. —**to pipe down** *Slang* To become silent; stop talking or making noise. [OE, ult. < L *pipare* to cheep]

pipe dream A groundless hope or wish; a daydream.

pipe·fit·ting (pīp′fit′ing) *n.* 1. A piece of pipe used to connect two or more pipes together. 2. The work of joining pipes together. —**pipe′fit′ter** *n.*

pipe·line (pīp′līn′) *n.* 1. A line of pipe, as for the transmission of water, oil, etc. 2. A channel for the transmission of information, usu. private or secret. —*v.t.* **·lined, ·lin·ing** To convey by pipeline.

pipe organ An organ having pipes, as distinguished from an electric organ, etc.

pip·er (pī′pər) *n.* One who plays upon a pipe, esp. a bagpipe.

pi·pette (pī·pet′, pi-) *n.* A small tube for removing or transferring measured quantities of a liquid. Also **pi·pet′.** [< F, dim. of *pipe* pipe]

pip·ing (pī′ping) *adj.* 1. Hissing or sizzling; very hot. 2. Having a shrill sound. —*n.* 1. The act of one who pipes. 2. Music of or suggesting that of pipes; a wailing or whistling sound. 3. A system of pipes, as for drainage. 4. A narrow strip of cloth folded on the bias, used for trimming edges or seams.

pip·it (pip′it) *n.* One of various larklike North American singing birds. [Prob. imit. of its call]

pip·kin (pip′kin) *n.* A small earthenware jar. [? Dim. of PIPE]

pip·pin (pip′in) *n.* 1. An apple of many varieties. 2. A seed; pip. [< OF *pepin* seed of a fruit]

pip-squeak (pip′skwēk′) *n.* A small, insignificant person.

pi·quant (pē′kənt, -känt, pē·känt′) *adj.* 1. Having an agreeably pungent or tart taste. 2. Lively and interesting. [< F, orig. ppr. of *piquer* to sting] —**pi′quan·cy** *n.*

pique (pēk) *n.* A feeling of irritation or resentment. —*v.t.* **piqued, pi·quing** 1. To excite resentment in. 2. To stimulate or arouse; provoke. [< F *piquer* to sting, prick]

pi·qué (pē·kā′) *n.* A fabric of cotton, rayon, or silk, with raised cord running lengthwise. [< F, lit., quilted]

pi·ra·cy (pī′rə·sē) *n. pl.* **·cies** 1. Robbery of craft on the high seas or in the air. 2. The unauthorized use of another's invention, idea, or literary creation.

pi·ra·nha (pi·rä′nyə, -nə) *n.* A small fish of tropical South America with massive jaws and sharp teeth, known to attack man and larger animals. [< Tupi, toothed fish]

pi·rate (pī′rit) *n.* One engaged in piracy; esp., a roving robber at sea. —*v.t. & v.i.* **·rat·ed, ·rat·ing** 1. To practice or commit piracy (upon). 2. To plagiarize. [< Gk. *peiran* to attempt] —**pi·rat·ic** (pī·rat′ik) or **·i·cal** *adj.* —**pi·rat′i·cal·ly** *adv.*

pir·ou·ette (pir′o͞o·et′) *n.* A rapid whirling upon the toes in dancing. [< F, spinning top; origin uncertain] —**pir′ou·ette′** *v.i.* **·et·ted, ·et·ting**

pis·ca·to·ri·al (pis′kə·tôr′ē·əl) *adj.* 1. Pertaining to fishes or fishing. 2. Engaged in fishing. Also **pis′ca·to′ry.** [< L *piscator* fisherman] —**pis′ca·to′ri·al·ly** *adv.*

Pis·ces (pī′sēz, pis′ez) *n.pl.* A constellation, the Fish or Fishes; also, the twelfth sign of the zodiac. [< L, pl. of *piscis* a fish]

pisci- *combining form* Fish; of or related to fish. Also, before vowels, **pisc-**. [< L *piscis*]

pis·ci·cul·ture (pis′i·kul′chər) *n.* The hatching and raising of fish. —**pis′ci·cul′tur·al** *adj.* —**pis′ci·cul′tur·ist** *n.*

pis·cine (pis′īn, -ēn, -in) *adj.* Of, pertaining to, or resembling a fish or fishes. [< L *piscis* a fish]

pis·mire (pis′mīr) *n. Archaic & Dial.* An ant. [ME *pisse* urine + *mire* an ant]

pis·ta·chi·o (pis·tä′shē·ō, -tash′ē·ō) *n. pl.* **·chi·os** A small tree bearing edible greenish nuts; also, the nut. [< Gk. *pistakē* pistachio tree, prob. < OPersian *pistah* pistachio nut]

pis·til (pis′til) *n. Bot.* The seed-bearing organ of flowering plants. [< L *pistillum* pestle] —**pis·til·late** (pis′tə·lit, -lāt) *adj.*

pis·tol (pis′təl) *n.* A small firearm having a short barrel, and fired from one hand. [< Czechoslovakian *pisťal*]

pis·ton (pis′tən) *n.* 1. *Mech.* A rigid disk fitted to slide in a cylinder, and connected with a rod for receiving the pressure of or exerting pressure upon a fluid in the cylinder. 2. A valve in a wind instrument for altering the pitch of tones. [< LL *pistare*, freq. of L *pinsere* to pound]

pit[1] (pit) *n.* 1. A cavity in the ground, esp. when wide and deep. 2. A pitfall for snaring animals; snare. 3. The usu. sunken area in front of the stage of a theater, which houses the orchestra. 4. An enclosed space in which fighting cocks, etc., are pitted against each other. 5. Any natural cavity or depression in the body: the *pit* of the stomach. 6. Any slight depression in the skin, as a pockmark. 7. A mining excavation, or the shaft of a mine. —**the pits** *Slang* An unpleasant event, situation, experience, etc. —*v.* **pit·ted, pit·ting** *v.t.* 1. To mark with dents, pits, or hollows. 2. To match as antagonists. —*v.i.* 3. To become marked with pits. [< L *puteus* a well]

pit[2] (pit) *n.* The kernel of certain fruits, as the plum. —*v.t.* **pit·ted, pit·ting** To remove pits from, as fruits. [< MDu. *pitte* kernel, pith]

pit·a·pat (pit′ə·pat′) *v.i.* **·pat·ted, ·pat·ting** To move or sound with light, quick steps or pulsations. —*n.* A tapping, or a succession of taps, steps, or similar sounds. —*adv.* With a pitapat; flutteringly. Also *pitty-pat.* [Imit.]

pitch[1] (pich) *n.* 1. A thick, viscous, dark substance obtained by boiling down tar, used in coating seams. 2. The resinous sap of pines. —*v.t.* To smear, cover, or treat with or as with pitch. [< L *pix, picis* pitch]

pitch[2] (pich) *v.t.* 1. To throw or hurl; fling. 2. To erect or set up (a tent, camp, etc.). 3. To set the level, angle, degree, etc., of. 4. In baseball, to deliver (the ball) to the batter. —*v.i.* 5. To fall or plunge forward or headlong. 6. To lurch; stagger. 7. To rise and fall alternately at the bow and stern, as a ship. 8. To incline downward; slope. 9. In baseball, to deliver the ball to the batter; act as pitcher. —**to pitch in** *Informal* 1. To work together; cooperate. 2. To start vigorously. —**to pitch into** To attack; assail. —*n.* 1. An act or manner of pitching. 2. The degree of descent or slope. 3. The frequency of a sound wave perceived by the ear; the highness or lowness of a sound. 4. Throw. 5. In baseball, the delivery of the ball by the pitcher. 6. The act of dipping or plunging downward, as a ship. 7. *Slang* A practiced talk or appeal intended to influence or persuade. 8. A level or intensity of some quality or action: activity at a high *pitch.* [ME *picchen*]

pitch-black (pich′blak′) *adj.* Intensely black, as pitch.

pitch·blende (pich′blend′) *n.* A black or brown mineral resembling pitch in luster, that is the chief source of uranium and radium. [< G *pech* pitch[1] + *blende* blende]

pitch-dark (pich′därk′) *adj.* Very dark; as black as pitch.

pitch·er[1] (pich′ər) *n.* One who pitches; esp., in baseball, the player who delivers the ball to the batter. [< PITCH[2]]

pitch·er[2] (pich′ər) *n.* A container with a spout and a handle, used for holding liquids to be poured out. [< OF *pichier*, ult. < Gk. *bikos* wine jar]

pitcher plant Any of several carnivorous plants having tubular leaves resembling pitchers that function as insect traps.

pitch·fork (pich′fôrk′) *n.* A large fork with which to handle hay, straw, etc. —*v.t.* To lift and throw with or as with a pitchfork.

pitch·man (pich′mən) *n. pl.* **·men** (-mən) One who sells small articles from a temporary stand, as at a fair, etc.; a sidewalk vender.

pitch pipe *Music* A small pipe or group of pipes that sound a particular tone when blown, used to adjust the pitch of a voice or instrument.

pitch·y (pich′ē) *adj.* **pitch·i·er, pitch·i·est** 1. Resembling pitch; intensely dark. 2. Full of or daubed with pitch. —**pitch′i·ness** *n.*

pit·e·ous (pit′ē·əs) *adj.* Exciting pity, sorrow, or sympathy. [See PITY.] —**pit′e·ous·ly** *adv.* —**pit′e·ous·ness** *n.*

pit·fall (pit′fôl′) *n.* 1. A hidden danger or unexpected difficulty. 2. A pit for entrapping wild beasts or men. [< PIT[1] + OE *fealle* a trap]

pith (pith) *n.* 1. *Bot.* The cylinder of soft, spongy tissue in the center of the stems and branches of certain plants. 2. The marrow of bones or of the spinal cord. 3. The essential part; gist. [OE *pitha*]

Pith·e·can·thro·pus (pith′ə·kan′thrə·pəs, -kan·thrō′pəs) *n. pl.* **·pi** (-pī) *n. Paleontol.* An extinct manlike primate represented by skeletal remains discovered in central Java. [< Gk. *pithēkos* ape + *anthropos* man] —**pith′e·can′thro·pine** (-pēn, -pin) *adj.*

pith helmet A topi.

pith·less (pith′lis) *adj.* Lacking force.

pith·y (pith′ē) *adj.* **pith·i·er, pith·i·est** 1. Of or like pith. 2. Terse and forceful. —**pith′i·ly** *adv.* —**pith′i·ness** *n.*

pit·i·a·ble (pit′ē·ə·bəl) *adj.* 1. Arousing or meriting pity or compassion. 2. Insignificant; contemptible. —**pit′i·a·ble·ness** *n.* —**pit′i·a·bly** *adv.*

pit·i·ful (pit′i·fəl) *adj.* 1. Calling forth pity or compassion; wretched. 2. Evoking contempt. —**pit′i·ful·ly** *adv.* —**pit′i·ful·ness** *n.*

pit·i·less (pit′i·lis) *adj.* Having no pity; ruthless. —**pit′i·less·ly** *adv.* —**pit′i·less·ness** *n.*

pit·tance (pit′əns) *n.* A small allowance of money. [< OF *pitance*, monk's food allotment]

pit·ter-pat·ter (pit′ər·pat′ər) *n.* A rapid series of light sounds or taps. [Varied reduplication of PATTER[1]]

pit·ty-pat (pit′ē·pat′) See PITAPAT.

pi·tu·i·tar·y gland (pi·to͞o′ə·ter′ē) *Anat.* A small, rounded body at the base of the brain that secretes hormones affecting growth, metabolism, and other functions of the body. [< L *pituita* mucus]

pit viper Any of various venomous snakes, as the rattlesnake, copperhead, etc., characterized by a small depression between the nostril and the eye.

pit·y (pit′ē) *n. pl.* **pit·ies** 1. Grief or pain awakened by the misfortunes of others; compassion. 2. That which arouses compassion; misfortune. —*v.t. & v.i.* **pit·ied, pit·y·ing** To feel pity (for). [< L *pietas, -tatis* dutiful conduct] —**pit′i·er** *n.* —**pit′y·ing·ly** *adv.*

piv·ot (piv′ət) *n.* 1. *Mech.* Something upon which a related part turns, oscillates, or rotates. 2. A person or thing upon which an important matter hinges or turns. —*v.t.* 1. To place on, attach by, or provide with a pivot. —*v.i.* 2. To turn on or as on a pivot; swing. [< F] —**piv′ot·al** *adj.* —**piv′ot·al·ly** *adv.*

pix·i·la·ted (pik′sə·lā′tid) *adj.* Affected by the pixies; mentally unbalanced. [Prob. alter. of dial. E (Cornish) *pixy-led* bewitched]

pix·y (pik′sē) *n. pl.* **pix·ies** A fairy or elf. Also **pix′ie.** [< dial. E *pixey, pisky*; origin uncertain]

pi·zazz (pə·zaz′) *n. Slang* 1. Exuberance; pep. 2. Dashing style. Also **piz·zazz′.** [Orig. unknown]

piz·za (pēt′sə, *Ital.* pēt′sä) *n.* An Italian food usu. consisting of a doughy crust spread with a mixture of cheese, tomatoes, spices, etc., and baked. [< Ital.]

piz·ze·ri·a (pēt′sə·rē′ə) *n.* A place where pizzas are prepared, sold, and eaten. [< Ital. < *pizza* pizza]

piz·zi·ca·to (pit′sə·kä′tō, *Ital.* pēt′tsē·kä′tō) *Music adj.* Plucked with the fingers. —*adv.* In a pizzicato manner. —*n. pl.* **·ti** (-tē) A tone or passage played in a pizzicato manner. [< Ital., pp. of *pizzicare* to pluck, pinch]

plac·ard (plak′ärd, -ərd) *n.* 1. A paper publicly displayed, as a poster. 2. A tag or plate bearing the owner's name. —*v.t.* 1. To announce by means of placards. 2. To post placards on or in. [< F *plaquer* to veneer, plate]

pla·cate (plā′kāt, plak′āt) *v.t.* **·cat·ed, ·cat·ing** To appease the anger of; pacify. [< L *placare* to appease] —**pla′ca·ble** *adj.* —**pla′·cat·er** *n.* —**pla·ca′tion** *n.*

pla·ca·to·ry (plā′kə·tôr′ē, plak′ə-) *adj.* Tending or intended to placate. Also **pla′ca·tive.**

place (plās) *n.* 1. A particular point or portion of space; a definite locality or location. 2. One's abode or quarters. 3. An open space or square in a city; also, a court or street. 4. Position in a sequence or series. 5. Station in life; rank. 6. One's employment; position. 7. Room; way: One thing gives *place* to another. 8. A particular passage or page in a book, etc. 9. The second position among the first three finishers in a race, as in a horse race. —**in place** 1. In a natural or suitable position. 2. In its original site. —**in place of** Instead of. —**to take place** To happen; occur. —*v.* **placed, plac·ing** *v.t.* 1. To put in a particular place or position. 2. To find a place, situation, home, etc., for. 3. To identify; classify. 4. To bestow or entrust. —*v.i.* 5. In racing: **a** To finish second. **b** To finish among the first three finishers. [< Gk. *plateia* street < *platys* wide]

pla·ce·bo (plə·sē′bō) *n. pl.* **·bos** or **·boes** *Med.* Any harmless substance given to humor a patient or as a test in controlled experiments. [< L *placere* to please]

place·kick (plās′kik) *n.* In football, a kick for a goal in which the ball is placed on the ground for kicking. —*v.t. & v.i.* To make or score with a placekick. —**place′kick′er** *n.*

place mat A mat on which a table setting is placed.

place·ment (plās′mənt) *n.* 1. The act of placing, or the state of being placed. 2. Relative position; arrangement. 3. The business of placing persons in jobs.

pla·cen·ta (plə·sen′tə) *n. pl.* **·tas** or **·tae** (-tē) *Anat.* In higher mammals, the vascular, spongy organ of interlocking fetal and uterine structures by which the fetus is nourished in the uterus. [< Gk. *plax, plakos* flat object] —**pla·cen′tal** *adj.*

plac·er[1] (plā′sər) *n.* One who or that which places.

plac·er[2] (plas′ər) *n. Mining* 1. An alluvial or glacial deposit of sand, gravel, etc., containing gold in particles large enough to be obtained by washing. 2. Any place where deposits are washed for valuable minerals. [Var. of Sp. *placel* sandbank < *plaza* place]

plac·id (plas′id) *adj.* Having a smooth surface or nature; unruffled; calm. [< L *placere* to please] —**pla·cid·i·ty** (plə·sid′ə·tē), **plac′id·ness** *n.* —**plac′id·ly** *adv.*

plack·et (plak′it) *n.* The opening in the upper part of a dress, blouse, or skirt to make it easy to put on and take off. [Origin unknown]

pla·gia·rize (plā′jə·rīz) *v.t. & v.i.* **·rized, ·riz·ing** To appropriate and pass off as one's own (the writings, ideas, etc., of another). [< L *plagium* kidnapping] —**pla′gia·rism** *n.* —**pla′gia·rist** *n.*

plague (plāg) *n.* 1. *Pathol.* Any of various forms of a virulent, febrile, highly contagious, and often pandemic disease; esp., the bubonic plague. 2. The Black Death. 3. *Informal* Nuisance; bother. —*v.t.* **plagued, pla·guing** 1. To vex; annoy. 2. To afflict with plague or disaster. [< L *plaga*, prob. < Gk. *plēssein* to strike]

plaice (plās) *n.* 1. A flounder of European waters. 2. Any of various American flatfishes. [< LL *platessa* flatfish < Gk. *platys* broad]

plaid (plad) *n.* 1. An oblong woolen scarf of tartan or checkered pattern, worn in the Scottish Highlands as a cloak over one shoulder; also, any fabric of this pattern. 2. A checkered pattern of vertical and horizontal stripes of varying widths. [< Scot.Gaelic *plaide* blanket] —**plaid** *adj.*

plain (plān) *adj.* 1. Open and unobstructed: *plain* view. 2. Clear; understandable. 3. Straightforward; guileless. 4. Lowly in condition or station. 5. Unadorned; without ornamentation. 6. Homely. 7. Not rich;

simple: *plain* food. —*n.* An expanse of level land; a prairie. [< L *planus* flat] —**plain′ly** *adv.* —**plain′ness** *n.*

plain·clothes man (plān′klōz′, -klōthz′) A member of a police force who does not wear a uniform while on duty; esp., a detective.

plains·man (plānz′mən) *n. pl.* **·men** (-mən) A dweller on the plains.

plain·song (plān′sông, -song) *n.* The old ecclesiastical chant, having simple melody, not governed by strict rules of meter but by accentuation of the words. Also **plain′chant** (-chant) [Trans. of Med.L *cantus planus*]

plain-spo·ken (plān′spō′kən) *adj.* Candid; frank.

plaint (plānt) *n.* 1. A lamentation. 2. A complaint. [< OF *plainte* < L *planger* to lament]

plain·tiff (plān′tif) *n. Law* The party that begins an action at law; the complaining party in an action. [See PLAINT.]

plain·tive (plān′tiv) *adj.* Expressing a subdued sadness; mournful. —**plain′tive·ly** *adv.* —**plain′tive·ness** *n.*

plait (plāt, plat) *v.t.* 1. To braid (hair, etc.). 2. To pleat. —*n.* 1. A braid, esp. of hair. 2. A pleat. [< L *plicare* to fold]

plan (plan) *n.* 1. A scheme, method, or design for the attainment of some object. 2. A drawing showing the proportion and relation of parts, as of a building. —*v.* **planned, plan·ning** *v.t.* 1. To form a scheme or method for doing, achieving, etc. 2. To make a plan of, as a building; design. —*v.i.* 3. To make plans. [< F, foundation < L *planus* flat] —**plan′ner** *n.*

plane[1] (plān) *n.* 1. *Geom.* A surface such that a straight line joining any two of its points lies wholly within the surface. 2. Any flat surface. 3. A grade of development; level: a *plane* of thought. 4. *Aeron.* A supporting surface of an airplane. 5. An airplane. —*adj.* 1. Level; flat. 2. Dealing only with flat surfaces: *plane* geometry. [< L *planus* flat] —**pla·nar** (plā′nər) *adj.*

plane[2] (plān) *n.* A tool used for smoothing boards or other surfaces of wood. —*v.* **planed, plan·ing** *v.t.* 1. To make smooth or even with a plane. 2. To remove with a plane. —*v.i.* 3. To use a plane. [< L *planare* to level] —**plan·er** (plā′nər) *n.*

plane[3] (plān) *v.i.* **planed, plan·ing** 1. To rise partly out of the water, as a power boat when driven at high speed. 2. To glide; soar. 3. To travel by airplane. [< F *planer*]

plan·et (plan′it) *n. Astron.* One of the celestial bodies revolving around the sun and shining only by reflected light. In order from the sun, the planets are: Mercury, Venus, Earth, Mars, Jupiter, Saturn, Uranus, Neptune, and Pluto. [< Gk. *planaesthai* to wander] —**plan·e·tar·y** (plan′ə·ter′ē) *adj.*

plan·e·tar·i·um (plan′ə·târ′ē·əm) *n. pl.* **·i·ums** or **·i·a** 1. An apparatus for exhibiting the features of the heavens, consisting of slide projectors or other optical equipment installed in a room having a circular dome. 2. A room or building having such an apparatus. 3. An apparatus or model representing the planetary system.

plan·e·toid (plan′ə·toid) *n. Astron.* An asteroid. —**plan′e·toi′dal** *adj.*

plane tree Any of various large deciduous trees, as the sycamore, characterized by broad, lobed leaves and spreading growth. [< Gk. *platys* broad]

plan·gent (plan′jənt) *adj.* 1. Dashing noisily; resounding, as the sound of bells. 2. Loud and mournful-sounding. [< L *plangens, -entis,* ppr. of *plangere* to lament, strike] —**plan′·gen·cy** *n.* —**plan′gent·ly** *adv.*

plan·i·sphere (plan′ə·sfir) *n.* A plane projection of the sphere; especially, a polar projection of the heavens on a chart, showing the stars visible at a given time. [< Med.L *planisphaerium* < L *planus* flat + *sphaera* sphere] —**plan′i·spher′ic** (-sfir′ik, -sfer′-) *adj.*

plank (plangk) *n.* 1. A broad piece of sawed timber, thicker than a board. 2. One of the principles of a political platform. —**to walk the plank** To walk off a plank projecting from the side of a ship, a method once used by pirates for executing prisoners. —*v.t.* 1. To cover, furnish, or lay with planks. 2. To broil or bake and serve on a plank, as fish. 3. *Informal* To put down forcibly. [< LL *planca*]

plank·ing (plangk′ing) *n.* 1. The act of laying planks. 2. Anything made of planks. 3. Planks collectively.

plank·ton (plangk′tən) *n. Biol.* The marine animal and plant organisms that drift with currents, waves, etc., unable to influence their own course and ranging in size from microorganisms to jellyfish. [< Gk. *planktos* drifting < *plazesthai* to wander] —**plank·ton′ic** (-ton′ik) *adj.*

plano-[1] *combining form* Roaming; wandering. Also, before vowels, **plan-**. [< Gk. *planos* wandering]

plano-[2] *combining form* Flat; level; plane. Also, before vowels, **plan-**. Also **plani-**. [< L *planus* flat]

pla·no-con·cave (plā′nō·kon·kāv′) *adj.* Plane on one side and concave on the other.

pla·no-con·vex (plā′nō·kon·veks′) *adj.* Plane on one side and convex on the other.

pla·nom·e·ter (plə·nom′ə·tər) *n.* A device for gauging a plane surface, esp. as used in metalworking. [< PLANO-[2] + -METER] —**pla·nom′e·try** *n.*

plant (plant) *n.* 1. A living organism of the vegetable kingdom, characterized by growth chiefly from the synthesis of simple, usu. inorganic food materials from soil, water, and air. 2. One of the smaller forms of vegetable life, as distinct from shrubs and trees. 3. A set of machines, buildings, apparatus, etc., necessary to conduct a business or other enterprise. 4. A slip or cutting from a tree or bush; sapling. —*v.t.* 1. To set in the ground for growing. 2. To furnish with plants or seed. 3. To set or place firmly; put in position. 4. To introduce into the mind. 5. To stock, as a river. 6. *Slang* To place or station for purposes of deception, observation, etc.: to *plant* evidence. [OE *plante* < L *planta* a sprout, cutting]

plan·tain[1] (plan′tin) *n.* An annual or perennial herb widely distributed in temperate regions; esp., the **common** or **greater plantain** with large, ovate, ribbed leaves. [< L *planta* sole of the foot; with ref. to the shape of the leaves]

plan·tain[2] (plan′tin) *n.* 1. A tropical, perennial herb sometimes growing to 30 feet.

2. The long, bananalike fruit of this plant, edible when cooked. [< Sp. *plátano*]

plan·tar (plan′tər) *adj.* Pertaining to the sole of the foot. [< L *planta* sole of the foot]

plan·ta·tion (plan·tā′shən) *n.* 1. A farm or estate of many acres, planted with crops and worked by resident laborers. 2. A grove cultivated for its wood. [< L *plantare* to plant]

plant·er (plan′tər) *n.* 1. One who or that which plants. 2. An early settler or colonizer. 3. An owner of a plantation. 4. A decorative container in which shrubs and flowers are planted.

plant louse Any of a family of leaping insects that infest plants and suck their juices.

plaque (plak) *n.* 1. A plate, disk, or slab of metal, porcelain, ivory, etc., artistically ornamented, as for wall decoration. 2. A whitish film, containing bacteria, that forms on teeth. [< F < MDu. *placke* flat disk, tablet]

plash (plash) *n.* A slight splash. —*v.t. & v.i.* To splash lightly. [Prob. imit.] —**plash′y** *adj.*

-plasia *combining form* Growth; development; formative action. Also **-plasis.** [< Gk. *plassein* to mold, form]

-plasm *combining form Biol.* The viscous material of an animal or vegetable cell. [< Gk. *plassein* to mold, form]

plas·ma (plaz′mə) *n.* 1. The liquid portion of nutritive animal fluids, as blood, lymph, or intercellular fluid. 2. The clear, fluid portion of blood, freed from blood cells and used for transfusions. 3. *Physics* A gas composed of ionized particles. Also **plasm** (plaz′əm). [< Gk. *plassein* to mold, form] —**plas·mat·ic** (plaz·mat′ik) *adj.*

plasmo- *combining form* Plasma; of or pertaining to plasma. Also, before vowels, **plasm-.** [See -PLASM.]

-plast *combining form* An organized living particle or cell. [< Gk. *plassein* to form]

plas·ter (plas′tər) *n.* 1. A composition of lime, sand, and water that hardens when dry, used for coating walls and partitions. 2. Plaster of Paris. 3. A viscid substance spread on cloth and applied to some part of the body, used for healing. 4. An adhesive dressing or protective bandage. —*v.t.* 1. To cover or overlay with or as with plaster. 2. To apply a plaster to, as a part of the body. 3. To apply like plaster or a plaster: to *plaster* posters on a fence. [< Gk. *en* upon, into + *plassein* to mold] —**plas′ter·er** *n.* —**plas′ter·ing** *n.* —**plas′ter·y** *adj.*

plas·ter·board (plas′tər·bôrd′) *n.* A wallboard made of gypsum or plaster and fibrous paper.

plaster cast A cast or model of a person or object made by molding plaster of Paris.

plaster of Paris Calcined gypsum, setting readily when mixed with water, useful in making molds, casts, bandages, etc. [With ref. to use of gypsum from Paris]

plas·tic (plas′tik) *adj.* 1. Giving form or fashion to matter. 2. Capable of being molded; pliable. 3. Pertaining to modeling or molding. 4. Made of plastic. 5. Artificial; synthetic. —*n.* 1. Any substance or material that may be molded. 2. *Chem.* One of a large class of synthetic organic compounds capable of being molded, extruded, cast, or drawn into filaments. [< Gk. *plastikos* moldable] —**plas′ti·cal·ly** *adv.*

-plastic *combining form* Growing; developing. [< Gk. *plastikos* plastic, moldable]

plas·tic·i·ty (plas·tis′ə·tē) *n.* 1. The quality or state of being plastic. 2. Capacity for being shaped or molded.

plastic surgery Surgery that deals with the restoration or healing of lost, wounded, or deformed parts of the body. —**plastic surgeon**

plas·tid (plas′tid) *n. Biol.* A small, specialized mass in the cytoplasm of a cell. [< G < Gk. *plassein* to mold]

-plasty *combining form Surg.* An operation involving: **a** A (specified) part of the body: *osteoplasty.* **b** Tissue from a (specified) source: *zooplasty.* **c** A (specified) process or formation: *neoplasty.* [< Gk. *-plastia* formation]

-plasy See -PLASIA.

plat (plat) *n.* 1. Plot (def. 1). 2. A map or plan, as one showing building lots. —*v.t.* **plat·ted, plat·ting** To make a map or plan of. [Var. of PLOT]

plat- Var. of PLATY-.

plate (plāt) *n.* 1. A flat, extended, rigid body of metal or any material of slight thickness. 2. A shallow vessel made of crockery, wood, etc., for serving or eating food. 3. Household articles, as trays, coated with a precious metal. 4. A portion of food served at table. 5. A piece of metal, plastic, etc., bearing a design or inscription or intended for reproduction. 6. An impression from an engraving, woodcut, etc., as reproduced in a book. 7. *Dent.* A piece of plastic or other material fitted to the mouth and holding one or more artificial teeth. 8. A thin part of the brisket of beef. 9. *Photog.* A sensitized sheet, as of glass, for taking photographs. 10. In baseball, home plate. 11. A dish used in taking up collections, as in churches; also, a collection. —*v.t.* **plat·ed, plat·ing** 1. To coat with a thin layer of gold, silver, etc. 2. To cover or sheathe with metal plates for protection. [< LL *plattus* flat] —**plat′er** *n.*

pla·teau (pla·tō′, *esp. Brit.* plat′ō) *n. pl.* **·teaus** or **·teaux** (-tōz′) 1. An extensive stretch of elevated and comparatively level land; mesa. 2. A stage or period of leveling off in the development of something. [< F < OF *plat* flat]

plate·ful (plāt′fo͝ol′) *n. pl.* **·fuls** The quantity that fills a plate.

plate glass Glass in clear, thick sheets, suitable for mirrors, display windows, etc.

plat·en (plat′n) *n. Mech.* 1. The part of a printing press, typewriter, or the like, on which the paper is supported to receive the impression. 2. In a machine tool, the adjustable table that carries the work. [See PLATE.]

plate tectonics The theory that the earth's crust consists of a few huge plates and that their drifting determines land masses and earthquakes.

plat·form (plat′fôrm) *n.* 1. Any floor or flat surface raised above the adjacent level, as a stage or a walk upon which railroad passengers alight. 2. A formal scheme of principles; esp., the document stating the principles of a political party. [< MF *plate* flat + *forme* form]

plat·ing (plā′ting) *n.* 1. A layer or coating of metal. 2. A sheathing of metal plates, as armor. 3. The act or process of sheathing or coating something with plates or metal.

platino- *combining form* Platinum; of or containing platinum. Also, before vowels, **platin-**.

plat·i·num (plat′ə·nəm) *n.* 1. A heavy, steel gray, malleable and ductile metallic element (symbol Pt) that is very infusible, resistant to most acids, and that has a high electrical resistance. 2. A color resembling that of platinum. [< Sp. *plata* silver]

platinum blond 1. A very light, almost white blond. 2. One having platinum blond hair.

plat·i·tude (plat′ə·to͞od, -tyo͞od) *n.* A flat, dull, or commonplace statement; an obvious truism. [< F *plat* flat] **—plat′i·tu′di·nous** *adj.*

pla·ton·ic (plə·ton′ik) *adj.* *Often cap.* Purely spiritual, or devoid of sensual feeling. [after *Plato,* 4th c. B.C. Gk. philosopher] **—pla·ton′i·cal·ly** *adv.*

pla·toon (plə·to͞on′) *n.* 1. A subdivision of a company, troop, or other military unit, commanded by a lieutenant. 2. A company of people; esp., in football, a defensive or offensive unit. **—***v.t.* In football, to use as or in a platoon. [< F *peloton* ball, group of men]

platoon sergeant In the U.S. Army, a noncommissioned officer ranking below a first sergeant.

plat·ter (plat′ər) *n.* 1. A large shallow dish for serving meat, etc. 2. *Informal* A phonograph record. [< AF *plat* dish]

platy- *combining form* Flat. Also, before vowels, *plat-*. [< Gk. *platys*]

plat·y·pus (plat′ə·pəs) *n.* A burrowing, egg-laying, aquatic mammal of Australia, having a ducklike bill: also called *duckbill.* [< Gk. *platus* flat + *pous* foot]

plau·dit (plô′dit) *n.* An expression of applause; praise. [< L *plaudite,* pl. imperative of *plaudere* to applaud]

plau·si·ble (plô′zə·bəl) *adj.* Seeming to be likely, trustworthy, believable, etc. [< L *plausibilis* deserving applause] **—plau′si·bil′i·ty** *n.* **—plau′si·bly** *adv.*

play (plā) *v.i.* 1. To engage in sport or diversion; amuse oneself. 2. To take part in a game of skill or chance. 3. To act in a way that is not to be taken seriously. 4. To act or behave in a specified manner: to *play* false. 5. To behave lightly or insincerely: with *with.* 6. To move quickly or irregularly as if frolicking: lights *playing* along a wall. 7. To perform on a musical instrument. 8. To give forth musical sounds. 9. To be performed or exhibited. 10. To act on or as on a stage; perform. **—***v.t.* 11. To engage in (a game etc.). 12. To perform sportively: to *play* a trick. 13. To oppose in a game or contest. 14. To move or employ in a game. 15. To cause: to *pla* havoc. 16. To perform upon (a musical instrument). 17. To perform or produce, as a piece of music, a play, etc. 18. To act the part of on or as on the stage. 19. In angling, to let (a hooked fish) tire itself by maintaining pressure on the line. 20. To bet or bet on. **—to play at** To pretend to be doing; do half-heartedly. **—to play down** To minimize. **—to play into the hands of** To act to the advantage of (a rival or opponent). **—to play off** 1. To oppose against one another. 2. To decide (a tie) by playing one more game. **—to play on** 1. To take unscrupulous advantage of (another's hopes, emotions, etc.). 2. To continue. **—to play out** 1. To come to an end; be exhausted. 2. To continue to the end. **—to play the game** To behave in a fair manner. **—to play up** *Informal* To emphasize. **—to play up to** *Informal* To flatter. **—***n.* 1. A dramatic composition; drama. 2. Exercise or action for recreation or diversion. 3. A maneuver or turn in a game. 4. Manner of playing, dealing, acting, etc.: rough *play.* 5. In sports, a state of being actively and legitimately in use or motion: in *play.* 6. The act of playing a game, esp. gambling. 7. Fun; joking. 8. Action or operation that is light, free, and unencumbered. 9. Light, quick, fitful movement. **—to make a play for** *Informal* 1. To attempt to gain. 2. To attempt to seduce. [OE *plegan*] **—play′a·ble** *adj.*

play·back (plā′bak′) *n.* 1. The act of reproducing a sound recording. 2. A method or machine for reproducing sound recordings.

play·bill (plā′bil′) *n.* 1. A bill or poster advertising a play. 2. A program of a play.

play·boy (plā′boi′) *n.* *Informal* A wealthy, frivolous man who constantly seeks pleasure.

play-by-play (plā′bī·plā′) *adj.* Dealing with each play or event as it happens.

play·er (plā′ər) *n.* 1. One who takes part or specializes in a game. 2. An actor. 3. A performer on a musical instrument.

player piano A piano having a mechanical device by which it may be played automatically.

play·fel·low (plā′fel′ō) *n.* An associate in play; playmate.

play·ful (plā′fəl) *adj.* 1. Lightly humorous; joking. 2. High-spirited; frolicsome. **—play′ful·ly** *adv.* **—play′ful·ness** *n.*

play·go·er (plā′gō′ər) *n.* One who goes often to the theater.

play·ground (plā′ground′) *n.* An outdoor area for playing, usu. used by children.

play·house (plā′hous′) *n.* 1. A theater. 2. A small house for children to play in.

playing card One of a pack of cards used in playing various games, the pack usu. consisting of four suits (spades, hearts, diamonds, clubs) of 13 cards each.

play·let (plā′lit′) *n.* A short play.

play·mate (plā′māt′) *n.* A companion in sports or in play.

play·off (plā′ôf′) *n.* In sports, a decisive game or series of games to decide a championship, award, etc.

play·pen (plā′pen′) *n.* A small, usu. collapsible enclosure for a baby or small child.

play·thing (plā′thing′) *n.* A thing to play with; a toy.

play·wright (plā′rīt′) *n.* A writer of plays.

pla·za (plā′zə, plaz′ə) *n.* An open square or marketplace in a town or city. [< Sp. < L *platea* wide street]

plea (plē) *n.* 1. An appeal or entreaty. 2. An excuse, pretext, or justification. 3. *Law* **a** An allegation made by either party in a cause. **b** A statement made by or for a defendant concerning the charge against him. [< L *placitum* opinion, orig. pp. of *placere* to please]

plead (plēd) *v.* **plead·ed** or **pled** (pled), **plead·ing** *v.i.* 1. To make earnest entreaty;

beg. 2. *Law* To present a case or plea. —*v.t.* 3. To allege as an excuse or defense. 4. *Law* To argue (a case). [See PLEA.] —**plead′a·ble** *adj.* —**plead′er** *n.*

plead·ing (plē′ding) *n.* 1. The act of making a plea. 2. *Law* a The art or system of preparing pleas. b *Usu. pl.* Any one of such pleas. —**plead′ing·ly** *adv.*

pleas·ant (plez′ənt) *adj.* 1. Pleasing; enjoyable. 2. Agreeable in manner, appearance, etc. [< L *placere* to please] —**pleas′·ant·ly** *adv.* —**pleas′ant·ness** *n.*

pleas·an·try (plez′ən·trē) *n. pl.* **·tries** An amusing or good-natured remark or trick.

please (plēz) *v.* **pleased, pleas·ing** *v.t.* 1. To give pleasure to; be agreeable to. 2. To be the wish or will of. 3. To be so kind as to; be willing to: usu. in the imperative: *Please* pass the bread. —*v.i.* 4. To give satisfaction or pleasure. 5. To have the will or preference; wish: Go when you *please.* [< L *placere* to please]

pleas·ing (plē′zing) *adj.* Affording pleasure. —**pleas′ing·ly** *adv.* —**pleas′ing·ness** *n.*

pleas·ur·a·ble (plezh′ər·ə·bəl) *adj.* Gratifying; pleasant; satisfying. —**pleas′ur·a·ble·ness** *n.* —**pleas′ur·a·bly** *adv.*

pleas·ure (plezh′ər) *n.* 1. An agreeable or delightful sensation or emotion; enjoyment. 2. Something that gives such a feeling. 3. Amusement or diversion. 4. One's preference; choice. [See PLEASE.]

pleat (plēt) *n.* A fold of cloth doubled on itself and pressed or sewn in place. —*v.t.* To make a pleat in. Also *plait.* [Var. of PLAIT] —**pleat′er** *n.*

plebe (plēb) *n.* A member of the freshman class in a military or naval academy. [Short for PLEBEIAN]

ple·be·ian (pli·bē′ən) *adj.* 1. Of or pertaining to the common people. 2. Common or vulgar. —*n.* 1. One of the common people, esp. of ancient Rome. 2. Anyone who is coarse or vulgar. [< L *plebs* the common people] —**ple·be′ian·ism** *n.*

pleb·i·scite (pleb′ə·sīt, -sit) *n.* An expression of the popular will by means of a vote by the whole people. [< L *plebs* common people + *scitum* decree] —**ple·bis·ci·tar·y** (plə·bis′ə·ter′ē) *adj.*

plec·trum (plek′trəm) *n. pl.* **·trums** or **·tra** (-trə) Pick[2] (def. 3). Also **plec′tron** (-tron). [< Gk. *plessein* to strike]

pled (pled) Alternate past tense and past participle of PLEAD.

pledge (plej) *v.t.* **pledged, pledg·ing** 1. To give or deposit as security for a loan, etc. 2. To bind by or as by a pledge. 3. To promise solemnly. 4. To offer (one's word, life, etc.) as a guaranty or forfeit. 5. To drink a toast to. —*n.* 1. A promise or agreement to perform or fulfill some act, contract, or duty. 2. The drinking of a toast to one's health, etc. 3. A person or thing given as security for a debt or obligation. 4. The state of being given or held as security: to put property in *pledge.* [< OF *plege* guarantee] —**pledg′er** *n.*

pledg·ee (plej·ē′) *n.* 1. One to whom something is pledged. 2. One with whom a pledge is deposited.

pledg·or (plej′ər) *n.* *Law* One who gives a pledge. Also **pledge′or.**

-plegia *combining form* *Pathol.* A (specified) kind of paralysis or paralytic condition: *hemiplegia.* Also **-plegy.** [< Gk. *plēgē* stroke]

Plei·a·des (plē′ə·dēz, plī′-) *n.pl.* *Astron.* A loose cluster of many stars in the constellation Taurus, six of which are visible to ordinary sight. [after the seven daughters of Atlas in Greek mythology, set by Zeus among the stars]

ple·na·ry (plē′nə·rē, plen′ə-) *adj.* 1. Full in all respects or requisites; complete. 2. Fully or completely attended, as an assembly. [< L *plenus* full] —**ple′na·ri·ly** *adv.* —**ple′·na·ri·ness** *n.*

plen·i·po·ten·ti·ar·y (plen′i·pə·ten′shē·er′ē, -shə·rē) *adj.* Possessing or conferring full powers. —*n. pl.* **·ar·ies** A person fully empowered to represent a government. [< L *plenus* full + *potens* powerful]

plen·i·tude (plen′ə·tōōd, -tyōōd) *n.* The state of being full, complete, or abounding.

plen·te·ous (plen′tē·əs) *adj.* 1. Amply sufficient. 2. Yielding an abundance. —**plen′te·ous·ly** *adv.* —**plen′te·ous·ness** *n.*

plen·ti·ful (plen′ti·fəl) *adj.* 1. Existing in great quantity; abundant. 2. Yielding or containing plenty; affording ample supply. —**plen′ti·ful·ly** *adv.* —**plen′ti·ful·ness** *n.*

plen·ty (plen′tē) *n.* 1. The state of being sufficient and in abundance. 2. As much as can be required; an abundance or sufficiency: I have *plenty.* —*adj.* Existing in abundance; plentiful. —*adv.* *Informal* In a sufficient degree: *plenty* large enough. [< L *plenus* full]

ple·num (plē′nəm) *n. pl.* **·nums** or **·na** 1. Space fully occupied by matter: opposed to *vacuum.* 2. A meeting attended by all members, as of a legislature. [< L *plenus* full]

ple·o·nasm (plē′ə·naz′əm) *n.* 1. The use of needless words; redundancy; also, an instance of it. 2. A redundant word or phrase. 3. Superabundance. [< Gk. *pleōn* more] —**ple′o·nas′tic** (-nas′tik) *adj.* —**ple′o·nas′·ti·cal·ly** *adv.*

pleth·o·ra (pleth′ər·ə) *n.* A state of excessive fullness; superfluity. [< Gk. *plēthein* to be full] —**ple·thor·ic** (plə·thôr′ik) *adj.* —**ple·thor′i·cal·ly** *adv.*

pleu·ra (plōōr′ə) *n. pl.* **pleu·rae** (plōōr′ē) *Anat.* The serous membrane that envelops the lungs. [< Gk. *pleura* side] —**pleu′ral** *adj.*

pleu·ri·sy (plōōr′ə·sē) *n.* *Pathol.* Inflammation of the pleura. —**pleu·rit·ic** (plōō·rit′ik) *adj.*

pleuro- *combining form* 1. Of or pertaining to the side. 2. *Med.* Of, related to, or affecting the pleura. Also, before vowels, **pleur-.** [< Gk. *pleura* side]

Plex·i·glas (plek′si·glas′) *n.* A lightweight, transparent thermoplastic acrylic resin: a trade name.

plex·us (plek′səs) *n. pl.* **plex·us·es** or **plex·us** 1. A network or complicated interlacing of parts. 2. *Anat.* A network of cordlike structures, as blood vessels or nerves. [< L, pp. of *plectere* to intertwine]

pli·a·ble (plī′ə·bəl) *adj.* 1. Easily bent or twisted; flexible. 2. Easily persuaded or controlled; tractable. —**pli′a·bil′i·ty** *n.* —**pli′a·bly** *adv.*

pli·ant (plī′ənt) *adj.* 1. Capable of being bent or twisted with ease. 2. Easily yielding to influence; compliant. [< L *plicare* to fold] **—pli′an·cy** *n.* **—pli′ant·ly** *adv.*

pli·cate (plī′kāt) *adj.* Folded or pleated, as a fan. Also **pli′cat·ed.** **—pli′cate·ness** *n.* **—pli′cate·ly** *adv.* **—pli·ca′tion, plic·a·ture** (plik′ə·cho͝or) *n.*

pli·er (plī′ər) *n.* 1. *pl.* Small pincers for bending, holding, or cutting: also **pair of pliers.** 2. One who or that which plies.

plight[1] (plīt) *n.* A condition, state, or circumstance, usu. of a dangerous or complicated nature. [< AF *plit* fold, condition]

plight[2] (plīt) *v.t.* To pledge or promise. **—to plight one's troth** 1. To pledge one's solemn word. 2. To promise oneself in marriage. [OE *plihtan* to expose to danger] **—plight′er** *n.*

plinth (plinth) *n.* *Archit.* 1. The slab, block, or stone, usu. square, on which a column, pedestal, or statue rests. 2. A thin course, as of slabs, usu. projecting beneath a wall: also **plinth course.** [< Gk. *plinthos* brick]

plod (plod) *v.* **plod·ded, plod·ding** *v.i.* 1. To walk heavily or laboriously. 2. To work in a steady, laborious manner. **—***v.t.* 3. To walk along heavily or laboriously. **—***n.* 1. The act of plodding. 2. The sound of a heavy step. [Imit.] **—plod′der** *n.* **—plod′ding·ly** *adv.*

-ploid *combining form* *Biol.* Having a (specified) number of chromosomes: *polyploid.* Corresponding nouns end in **-ploidy.** [< Gk. *-ploos* fold + -OID]

plop (plop) *v.t. & v.i.* **plopped, plop·ping** To drop with a sound like that of something striking water heavily. **—***adv.* Suddenly with a plopping sound. [Imit.] **—plop** *n.*

plo·sion (plō′zhən) *n.* *Phonet.* The sudden release of breath after closure of the oral passage in the articulation of a stop consonant, as after the *p* in *pat.* [< EXPLOSION]

plo·sive (plō′siv) *adj.* *Phonet.* Designating a sound produced by plosion. **—plo′sive** *n.*

plot (plot) *n.* 1. A piece or patch of ground, usu. used for some special purpose. 2. A chart or diagram, as of a building; also, a surveyor's map. 3. A secret plan; conspiracy. 4. The scheme or pattern of the events and situations of a story, play, etc. **—***v.* **plot·ted, plot·ting** *v.t.* 1. To make a map, chart, or plan of. 2. To plan for secretly. 3. To arrange the plot of (a novel, etc.). 4. *Math.* To represent graphically the position of. **—***v.i.* 5. To form a plot; scheme. [OE] **—plot′ter** *n.*

plov·er (pluv′ər, plō′vər) *n.* Any of various shore birds, having long, pointed wings and a short tail. [< OF *plovier* < L *pluvia* rain]

plow (plou) *n.* 1. An implement for cutting, turning over, stirring, or breaking up the soil. 2. Any implement that operates like a plow: often in combination: a *snowplow.* **—***v.t.* 1. To turn up the surface of (land) with a plow. 2. To make or form (a furrow, one's way, etc.) by or as by means of a plow. 3. To dig out or remove with a plow: with *up* or *out.* 4. To move or cut through (water). **—***v.i.* 5. To turn up soil with a plow. 6. To move or proceed as a plow does: usu. with *through* or *into.* 7. To advance laboriously; plod. **—to plow into** *Informal* 1. To hit hard. 2. To undertake vigorously to accomplish, finish, or solve (a meal, problem, etc.). Also *esp. Brit.* **plough.** [OE *plōh,* prob. < ON *plōgr*] **—plow′a·ble** *adj.* **—plow′er** *n.*

plow·boy (plou′boi′) *n.* 1. A boy who plows land. 2. A country boy.

plow·man (plou′mən) *n.* *pl.* **·men** (-mən) 1. One who plows land. 2. A farmer; rustic.

plow·share (plou′shâr′) *n.* The blade of a plow.

ploy (ploi) *n.* A maneuver or stratagem, as in a game or conversation. [< EMPLOY]

pluck (pluk) *v.t.* 1. To pull out or off; pick. 2. To pull out the feathers, hair, etc., of. 3. To give a twitch or pull to, as a sleeve. 4. To cause the strings of (a musical instrument) to sound by quickly pulling or picking them. **—***v.i.* 5. To give a sudden pull; tug: with *at.* **—to pluck up** To rouse (one's courage). **—***n.* 1. Courage; nerve. 2. A sudden pull; twitch. **—pluck′er** *n.* [OE *pluccian* to pick out]

pluck·y (pluk′ē) *adj.* **pluck·i·er, pluck·i·est** Brave and spirited; courageous. **—pluck′i·ly** *adv.* **—pluck′i·ness** *n.*

plug (plug) *n.* 1. Anything, as a piece of wood or a cork, used to stop a hole. 2. *Electr.* A pronged device attached to the end of a wire or cable and inserted in a socket or jack to make a connection. 3. A spark plug. 4. A fireplug. 5. A flat cake or piece of tobacco. 6. *Informal* An old, worn-out horse. 7. *Slang* A favorable piece of publicity for someone or something. **—***v.* **plugged, plug·ging** *v.t.* 1. To stop or close, as a hole, by inserting a plug: often with *up.* 2. *Slang* To shoot a bullet into. 3. *Slang* To hit or punch. 4. *Slang* To advertise frequently or insistently. **—***v.i.* 5. *Informal* To work doggedly. 6. *Slang* To hit or shoot. 7. *Slang* To favor or work for a cause, person, etc.: usu. with *for.* **—to plug in** To insert the plug of (a lamp, etc.) in an electrical outlet. [< MDu. *plugge*] **—plug′ger** *n.*

plug-ug·ly (plug′ug′lē) *n.* *pl.* **·lies** *Slang* A gangster, ruffian, or rowdy.

plum (plum) *n.* 1. The edible fruit of any of various trees of the rose family; also the tree itself. 2. The plumlike fruit of any of various other trees; also, a tree bearing such fruit. 3. A raisin, esp. as used in cooking. 4. A dark, reddish purple. 5. Something desirable, as a post or appointment. [OE *plūme* < L *prunum* < Gk. *prounon*]

plum·age (plo͞o′mij) *n.* The feathers of a bird. [< F *plume* plume]

plumb (plum) *n.* A lead weight (**plumb bob**) on the end of a line (**plumb line**) used to find the exact perpendicular, to sound the depth of water, etc. **—off** (or **out of**) **plumb** Not in alignment. **—***adj.* 1. Conforming to a true vertical or perpendicular. 2. *Informal* Sheer; absolute. **—***adv.* 1. In a vertical line; vertically. 2. *Informal* Utterly; completely. **—***v.t.* 1. To test the perpendicularity of with a plumb. 2. To test the depth of; sound. 3. To reach the lowest level or extent of. [< L *plumbum* lead]

plumb·er (plum′ər) *n.* One whose occupation is the installing or repairing of plumbing.

plumb·er's friend (plum′ərz) A plunger (def. 2).

plumb·ing (plum′ing) *n.* 1. The art or trade of putting into buildings the tanks, pipes, etc., for water, gas, sewage, etc. 2. The pipe system of a building.

plumbo- *combining form* Lead; of or containing lead. Also, before vowels, **plumb-**. [< L *plumbum* lead]

plume (plōōm) *n.* 1. A feather, esp. when long and ornamental. 2. *Biol.* A featherlike form or part. 3. Anything resembling a plume. 4. A decoration of honor. —*v.t.* **plumed, plum·ing** 1. To furnish with or as with plumes. 2. To smooth (itself or its feathers); preen. 3. To congratulate or pride (oneself): with *on* or *upon*. [< L *pluma*]

plum·met (plum′it) *n.* 1. A plumb bob. 2. Something that oppresses or weighs down. —*v.i.* To drop straight down; plunge. [< L *plumbum* lead]

plu·mose (plōō′mōs) *adj.* 1. Bearing feathers or plumes. 2. Plumelike; feathery. [< L *pluma* feather] —**plu′mose·ly** *adv.* —**plu·mos·i·ty** (plōō·mos′ə·tē) *n.*

plump[1] (plump) *adj.* 1. Somewhat fat; chubby. 2. Well filled or rounded out. —*v.t. & v.i.* To make or become plump: often with *up* or *out*. [< MDu., var. of *plomp* blunt] —**plump′ly** *adv.* —**plump′ness** *n.*

plump[2] (plump) *v.i.* 1. To fall suddenly or heavily; drop. 2. To give one's complete support: with *for*. —*v.t.* 3. To drop or throw down heavily or all at once. —*n.* 1. The act of plumping or falling. 2. The sound made by this. —*adj.* Blunt; downright. —*adv.* 1. With a sudden impact or fall. 2. Straightforwardly; bluntly. 3. Straight down. [< MDu. *plompen*; ult. imit.] —**plump′er** *n.* —**plump′ly** *adv.*

plum·y (plōō′mē) *adj.* **plum·i·er, plum·i·est** 1. Made of, covered with, or adorned with feathers. 2. Like a plume or feather. —**plum′i·ness** *n.*

plun·der (plun′dər) *v.t.* 1. To rob of goods or property by open violence, as in war; pillage. 2. To despoil by robbery or fraud. —*v.i.* 3. To take plunder. —*n.* 1. That which is taken by plundering; booty. 2. The act of plundering or robbing. [< MHG *plundern*, orig., to remove household goods] —**plun′der·er** *n.*

plunge (plunj) *v.* **plunged, plung·ing** *v.t.* 1. To thrust or force suddenly into a fluid, penetrable substance, hole, etc. 2. To force into some condition or state: to *plunge* a nation into debt. —*v.i.* 3. To dive, jump, or fall into a body of water, chasm, etc. 4. To move suddenly or violently forward or downward. 5. To descend abruptly or steeply, as a road or cliff. 6. *Informal* To gamble or speculate heavily. —*n.* 1. The act of plunging; a leap; dive. 2. A swim. 3. A heavy or extravagant bet, expenditure, or speculation. [< OF *plongier* < L *plumbum* lead]

plung·er (plun′jər) *n.* 1. One who or that which plunges. 2. A cuplike device made of rubber and attached to a stick, used to clean out clogged drains, etc.: also called *plumber's friend*. 3. *Mech.* Any appliance having a plunging motion, as a piston.

plunk (plungk) *v.t.* *Informal* 1. To pluck; strum. 2. To place or throw heavily: with *down*. —*v.i.* 3. To emit a twanging sound. 4. To fall heavily. —*n.* A twang or thump. —*adv.* Directly; exactly. [Imit.]

plu·per·fect (plōō·pûr′fikt) *n.* *Gram.* The past perfect. [< L *plus quam perfectus*, lit., more than completed]

plu·ral (plŏŏr′əl) *adj.* 1. Containing, consisting of, or designating more than one. 2. *Gram.* Of or designating a linguistic form that denotes more than one. [< L *plus, pluris* more] —**plu′ral** *n.* —**plu′ral·ly** *adv.*

plu·ral·ism (plŏŏr′əl·iz′əm) *n.* 1. The condition of being plural. 2. A social condition in which disparate religious, ethnic, and racial groups are part of a common community. 3. *Philos.* The doctrine that there are several ultimate substances. —**plu′ral·ist** *n.* —**plu′ral·is′tic** *adj.*

plu·ral·i·ty (plōō·ral′ə·tē) *n.* *pl.* **·ties** 1. In U.S. politics: a The number of votes cast for a candidate over and above the number cast for his nearest opponent. b In a contest having more than two candidates, the greatest number of votes cast for any one candidate but not more than half the total number of votes cast. Distinguished from *majority*. 2. The larger or greater portion of anything. 3. The state or condition of being plural or numerous.

plu·ral·ize (plŏŏr′əl·īz) *v.t.* **·ized, ·iz·ing** 1. To make plural. 2. To express in the plural. —**plu′ral·i·za′tion** *n.*

pluri- *combining form* More; many; several. [< L *plus, pluris* more]

plus (plus) *prep.* 1. Added to: Three *plus* two equals five. 2. Increased by. —*adj.* 1. Of, pertaining to, or involving addition. 2. Extra; supplemental. 3. Positive: a *plus* quantity. 4. *Informal* More of something specified: He has personality *plus*. —*n.* *pl.* **plus·es** 1. The plus sign. 2. An addition or an extra quantity. 3. A positive quantity. [< L, more]

plus fours Knickerbockers cut very full and bagging below the knees. [Orig. tailor's cant; because they were four inches longer than ordinary knickerbockers]

plush (plush) *n.* A pile fabric having a deeper pile than velvet. —*adj.* 1. Of plush. 2. *Slang* Luxurious. [< L *pilus* hair]

plush·y (plush′ē) *adj.* **plush·i·er, plush·i·est** Of or resembling plush. —**plush′i·ly** *adv.* —**plush′ness** *n.*

plus sign A sign (+) denoting addition or a positive quantity.

Plu·to (plōō′tō) *n.* A planet of the solar system, ninth in order from the sun. [< L < Gk. *Ploutōn*, god of the dead]

plu·toc·ra·cy (plōō·tok′rə·sē) *n.* *pl.* **·cies** 1. Government by the wealthy. 2. A wealthy class that controls the government. [< Gk. *ploutos* wealth + *krateein* to rule]

plu·to·crat (plōō′tə·krat) *n.* 1. A member of a plutocracy. 2. *Informal* Any wealthy person. —**plu′to·crat′ic** or **·i·cal** *adj.* —**plu′·to·crat′i·cal·ly** *adv.*

plu·ton·ic (plōō·ton′ik) *adj.* *Geol.* Deeply subterranean in original position: said of igneous rocks. [< L *Pluto*, god of the dead]

plu·to·ni·um (plōō·tō′nē·əm) *n.* A radioactive element (symbol Pu), formed by the decay of neptunium. [< NL < *Pluto* (the planet)]

plu·vi·al (plōō′vē·əl) *adj.* 1. Of or pertaining to rain. 2. Caused by the action of rain. [< L *pluvia* rain]

pluvio- *combining form* Pertaining to rain. Also before vowels, **pluvi-**. [< L *pluvia* rain]

ply[1] (plī) *v.t.* **plied, ply·ing** To bend; mold; shape. —*n.* *pl.* **plies** 1. A layer, fold, or thickness, as of cloth, plywood, etc. 2. One of the folds, twists, or strands of which rope, yarn, etc. is composed. [< L *plicare* to fold]

ply[2] (plī) *v.* **plied, ply·ing** *v.t.* 1. To use in working, fighting, etc.; wield; employ. 2. To work at; be engaged in. 3. To supply with or offer repeatedly: to *ply* a person with drink. 4. To address or assail repeatedly. 5. To traverse regularly. —*v.i.* 6. To make regular trips; sail: usu. with *between.* 7. To work steadily. [< APPLY]

ply·wood (plī′wo͝od′) *n.* A structural material consisting of layers of wood glued together.

pneu·mat·ic (no͞o·mat′ik) *adj.* 1. Pertaining to pneumatics. 2. Operated by compressed air. 3. Pertaining to or containing air or gas. Also **pneu·mat′i·cal.** —*n.* A tire inflated with compressed air. [< Gk. *pneuma* breath, wind] —**pneu·mat′i·cal·ly** *adv.*

pneu·mat·ics (no͞o·mat′iks) *n.pl.* (*construed as sing.*) The branch of physics that treats of the mechanical properties of air and other gases.

pneumo- *combining form* Lung; related to the lungs; respiratory. Also **pneum-** (before vowels), **pneumono-.** [< Gk. *pneumōn, pneumonos* a lung]

pneu·mo·coc·cus (no͞o′mə·kok′əs) *n. pl.* **·coc·ci** (-kok′sī) Any of a group of bacteria that inhabit the respiratory tract. —**pneu′·mo·coc′cal, pneu′mo·coc′cic** (-kok′sik) *adj.*

pneu·mo·co·ni·o·sis (no͞o′mō·kō′nē·ō′sis) *n.* A disease of the lungs caused by inhalation of irritants such as asbestos.

pneu·mo·nia (no͞o·mōn′yə) *n. Pathol.* Inflammation of the lungs, a disease of bacterial or viral origin occurring in many forms, as **bronchial pneumonia** or **lobar pneumonia.** [< Gk. *pneumōn* lung]

pneu·mon·ic (no͞o·mon′ik) *adj.* 1. Of or affected with pneumonia. 2. Pulmonary.

poach[1] (pōch) *v.t.* To cook (eggs, fish, etc.) in boiling water or other liquid. [< OF *poche* pocket, pouch; because the egg white forms a pouch around the yolk]

poach[2] (pōch) *v.t. & v.i.* 1. To trespass (on another's property, etc.), esp. for the purpose of taking game or fish. 2. To take (game or fish) unlawfully. [< OF *pocher* to thrust, encroach upon] —**poach′er** *n.*

pock (pok) *n.* 1. A pustule in an eruptive disease, as in smallpox. 2. A pockmark. [OE *pocc*] —**pock′y** *adj.* **·i·er, ·i·est**

pock·et (pok′it) *n.* 1. A small pouch inserted in a garment, for carrying money, etc. 2. Any opening, receptacle, or container. 3. Money, means, or financial interests. 4. An air pocket. 5. A region or area, usu. small and differentiated in some way from the surrounding area. —**in one's pocket** Under one's influence or control. —*adj.* 1. That can be put in a pocket; diminutive. 2. Pertaining to, for, or carried in a pocket. —*v.t.* 1. To put into or confine in a pocket. 2. To appropriate as one's own, esp. dishonestly. 3. To conceal or suppress: *Pocket* your pride. [< AF *pokete,* dim. of OF *poque, poche* pouch] —**pock′et·a·ble** *adj.*

pocket billiards Pool[2] (def. 4).

pock·et·book (pok′it·bo͝ok′) *n.* 1. A purse or handbag. 2. A book, usu. paperbound and smaller than standard size: also **pocket book.** 3. Money or financial resources.

pock·et·ful (pok′it·fo͝ol′) *n. pl.* **·fuls** As much as a pocket will hold.

pock·et·knife (pok′it·nīf′) *n. pl.* **·knives** (-nīvz′) A knife having one or more blades that fold into the handle.

pocket money Money for small expenses.

pocket veto An act whereby the President, on being presented a bill by Congress for his signature of approval, retains ("pockets") it unsigned until the session has adjourned, thus causing it to fail, without a direct veto.

pock·mark (pok′märk′) *n.* A pit or scar left on the skin by smallpox or a similar disease. —**pock′-marked′** *adj.*

po·co (pō′kō) *adv. Music* Slightly; a little. [< Ital.]

pod[1] (pod) *n.* 1. A seed vessel or capsule, esp. of a leguminous plant. 2. *Aeron.* A separate enclosure on an aircraft, esp. one beneath the wing for a jet engine. —*v.i.* **pod·ded, pod·ding** To produce pods. [Origin unknown]

pod[2] (pod) *n.* A group of animals, esp. of seals, whales, or walruses. [Origin unknown]

-pod *combining form* 1. One who or that which has (a specified number or kind of) feet: *arthropod.* 2. A (specified kind of) foot. Also **-pode.** [< Gk. *pous, podos* foot]

podg·y (poj′ē) *adj.* **podg·i·er, podg·i·est** Pudgy. [< dial. *podge* to walk slowly and heavily] —**podg′i·ness** *n.*

po·di·a·try (pə·dī′ə·trē, pō-) *n.* Chiropody. [< Gk. *pous, podos* foot + -IATRY] —**po·di′a·trist** *n.*

po·di·um (pō′dē·əm) *n. pl.* **·di·ums** or **·di·a** 1. A small platform or dais for the conductor of an orchestra, a speaker, etc. 2. *Zool.* A foot, or any footlike structure. [< L < Gk. *podion,* dim. of *pous, podos* foot]

-podium *combining form* A footlike part. [< NL < Gk. *podion,* dim. of *pous, podos* a foot]

po·em (pō′əm) *n.* A composition in verse, characterized by the imaginative treatment of experience and a condensed use of language. [< Gk. *poieein* to make]

po·e·sy (pō′ə·sē, -zē) *n. pl.* **·sies** *Poetic* 1. Poetry taken collectively. 2. The art of writing poetry.

po·et (pō′it) *n.* 1. One who writes poems. 2. One who is highly skilled and creative. —**po′et·ess** *n.fem.*

po·et·as·ter (pō′it·as′tər) *n.* An inferior poet. [< NL]

po·et·ic (pō·et′ik) *adj.* 1. Of or pertaining to a poet or poetry. 2. Having the nature or quality of or expressed in poetry. Also **po·et′i·cal.**

poetic justice The ideal distribution of rewards to the good and punishment to the evil.

poetic license The departure from fact or rigid rule for the sake of an artistic effect.

po·et·ics (pō·et′iks) *n.pl.* (*usu. construed as sing.*) The nature, principles, and forms of poetry or, by extension, of any art.

po·et·ize (pō′it·īz) *v.t. & v.i.* **·ized, ·iz·ing** To write or express in poetry. —**po′et·iz′er** *n.*

poet laureate *pl.* **poets laureate** In Great Britain, the official poet of the realm, charged with writing verses for particular occasions.

po·et·ry (pō′it·rē) *n.* 1. The art or craft of writing poems. 2. Poems collectively. 3. The quality, effect, or spirit of a poem.

po·go stick (pō′gō) A toy consisting of a pole with a spring at the base and two projections for the feet, on which a person may stand and hop.

po·grom (pō′grəm, pō·grom′) *n.* An organized and often officially instigated local massacre, esp. one directed against the Jews. [< Russ., destruction]

po·gy (pō′gē) *n. pl.* **·gies** or **·gy** The menhaden, a fish. [< Algonquian *pauhagen*]

poi (poi, pō′ē) *n.* A native Hawaiian food made from the root of the taro. [< Hawaiian]

-poietic *combining form* Making; producing; creating. [< Gk. *poiētikos* forming < *poieein* to make]

poign·ant (poin′yənt) *adj.* 1. Painful and afflicting to the feelings; profoundly moving. 2. Sharp; penetrating: *poignant wit.* [< F < L *pungere* to prick] **—poign′an·cy** *n.* **—poign′ant·ly** *adv.*

poi·lu (pwä·lü′) *French adj.* Hairy. **—***n.* A French soldier, esp. of World War I.

poin·ci·a·na (poin′sē·a′nə) *n.* 1. A tropical tree or shrub of the bean family. 2. A similar tree, the **royal poinciana,** having bright orange and scarlet flowers. [< NL, after M. de *Poinci,* a 17th c. governor of the West Indies]

poin·set·ti·a (poin·set′ē·ə) *n.* Any of various American plants of the spurge family, having large, showy red bracts. [after J. R. *Poinsett,* 1779–1851, U.S. statesman]

point (point) *n.* 1. The sharp, tapering end of a thing. 2. Something sharp or tapering, as a needle or dagger. 3. In printing or writing, a dot or similar mark, esp. a period. 4. That which is conceived to have position, but not parts, dimension, or extent, as the extremity of a line. 5. A spot, place, or locality. 6. A tapering tract of land extending into water. 7. A fixed place from which position and distance are reckoned. 8. A particular degree, state, or limit reached or determined: the boiling *point.* 9. One of the 32 equal divisions that indicate direction on a mariner's compass card, each division equal to an angular distance of 11° 15′, reckoning from north at 0°. 10. A particular moment of time. 11. The important or main idea or purpose. 12. An important, striking, or effective fact, idea, etc.: good *points* in an argument. 13. Any single item or particular; detail. 14. A prominent or distinguishing feature. 15. *pl.* The extremities of an animal, as a horse. 16. A spike or prong on the antler of a deer. 17. A unit, as in measuring, evaluating, rating, scoring, etc.: A touchdown equals six *points.* 18. *Printing* A unit of type size, about $^1/_{72}$ of an inch. 19. In commerce, one dollar: used in quoting prices of stocks, etc. 20. *Electr.* A contact or conducting part for making or breaking a circuit, as in a distributor, relay, etc. 21. The act of pointing. **—at** (or **on, upon**) **the point of** On the verge of. **—beside the point** Irrelevant. **—in point** Pertinent. **—in point of** In the matter of; as regards. **—to make a point of** To treat as vital or essential. **—to see the point** To understand the purpose or meaning of something. **—to stretch a point** To interpret a rule, definition, etc., broadly, so as to make an exception. **—to the point** Relevant; apt. **—***v.t.* 1. To direct or aim, as a finger or weapon. 2. To indicate; direct attention to: often with *out.* 3. To give force to; emphasize: often with *up.* 4. To shape or sharpen to a point. 5. To punctuate, as writing. 6. To mark or separate with points, as decimal fractions: with *off.* 7. In hunting, to indicate the presence of (game) by standing rigid and directing the muzzle toward it: said of dogs. 8. In masonry, to fill and finish the joints of (brickwork) with mortar. **—***v.i.* 9. To call attention or indicate direction by or as by extending the finger: usually with *at* or *to.* 10. To be directed; tend; face: with *to* or *toward.* 11. To point game: said of hunting dogs. [< OF *point* dot and *pointe* sharp tip]

point·blank (point′blangk′) *adj.* 1. Aimed directly at the mark; in gunnery, fired horizontally. 2. Close enough to aim directly at the mark: *pointblank* range. 3. Direct; plain: a *pointblank* question. **—***adv.* 1. In a straight line; from close range. 2. Directly; bluntly. [? < F *de pointe en blanc* from a point into the white (of a target)]

point·ed (poin′tid) *adj.* 1. Having a point. 2. Sharply precise and cutting, as an epigram. 3. Directed or aimed, as at a particular person. **—point′ed·ly** *adv.* **—point′ed·ness** *n.*

point·er (poin′tər) *n.* 1. One who or that which points. 2. An arrow or other indicator, as on a scale. 3. A long, tapering rod used to point out things. 4. One of a breed of smooth-haired dogs trained to scent and point out game. 5. *Informal* A hint; tip.

poin·til·lism (pwan′tə·liz′əm) *n.* In painting, a method of producing effects of light by placing small spots of varying hues close together on a surface. [< F *pointiller* to mark with dots] **—poin′til·list** *n.*

point·less (point′lis) *adj.* 1. Having no point; blunt. 2. Having no relevance or meaning. 3. Having no points scored. **—point′less·ly** *adv.* **—point′less·ness** *n.*

point of honor Something that vitally affects one's honor.

point of no return That stage in any enterprise, action, etc., beyond which there can be no return to the starting point.

point of order A question as to whether or not the correct parliamentary procedure is being observed.

point of view 1. The place or position from which one views an object, situation, etc. 2. An attitude or viewpoint.

poise (poiz) *v.* **poised, pois·ing** *v.t.* 1. To bring into or hold in balance; maintain in equilibrium. 2. To hold; support, as in readiness. **—***v.i.* 3. To be balanced or suspended; hover. **—***n.* 1. The state or quality of being balanced; equilibrium. 2. Repose and dignity of manner; self-possession. 3. Physical ease or balance. [< OF *pois* < L *pendere* to weigh, suspend]

poi·son (poi′zən) *n.* 1. Any substance that acts chemically upon the tissues of an organism in such a way as to harm or destroy them. 2. Anything that tends to harm, destroy, or corrupt. **—***v.t.* 1. To administer poison to; kill or injure with poison. 2. To put poison into or on. 3. To corrupt; pervert. [< OF < L *potio, -onis* drink, esp. a poisonous one] **—poi′son·er** *n.* **—poi′son·ous** *adj.* **—poi′son·ous·ly** *adv.*

poison ivy A climbing shrub related to sumac, having glossy, variously notched, trifoliate leaves, greenish flowers, and whitish berries, and that may cause a skin rash in one who touches its leaves.

poison oak 1. Any of various shrubs related to poison ivy or poison sumac. 2. A species of poison ivy common in the western U.S.

poison sumac A shrub or small tree growing in swamps, having smooth, entire leaflets and greenish yellow berries, and that may cause a skin rash in one who touches its leaves.

poke[1] (pōk) *v.* **poked, pok·ing** *v.t.* 1. To push or prod, as with the end of a stick; jab. 2. To make by or as by thrusting. 3. To thrust or push in, out, through, from, etc.: to *poke* one's head from a window. —*v.i.* 4. To make thrusts, as with a stick: often with *at*. 5. To intrude or meddle; pry. 6. To proceed slowly; dawdle: often with *along*. —**to poke one's nose into** To meddle in. —**to poke fun at** To ridicule. —*n.* 1. A push; prod. 2. A slowpoke; dawdler. 3. *Informal* A jab or punch. [< MLG *poken*]

poke[2] (pōk) *n.* A pocket or small bag. [< OF *poke, poque*]

poke[3] (pōk) *n.* A large bonnet with projecting front or brim. Also **poke bonnet.** [Prob. < POKE[1]]

poke·ber·ry (pōk′ber′ē) *n.* *pl.* **·ries** 1. A berry of the pokeweed. 2. The pokeweed plant.

pok·er[1] (pō′kər) *n.* 1. One who or that which pokes. 2. A metal rod for poking a fire.

po·ker[2] (pō′kər) *n.* Any of several games of cards in which the players bet on the value of the cards dealt to them. [Cf. G *pochspiel*, lit., boast game < *pochen* to boast]

poker face *Informal* A face that reveals nothing, as the face of a skillful poker player.

poke·weed (pōk′wēd′) *n.* A stout perennial North American herb, having purple berries, edible shoots, and a medicinal root: also called *pokeberry*. Also **poke′root′** (-ro͞ot′, -ro͝ot′). [< Algonquian (Virginian) *pakon* weed used for staining < *pak* blood]

pok·y (pō′kē) *adj.* **pok·i·er, pok·i·est** *Informal* 1. Dull; slow. 2. Shabby or dowdy. 3. Cramped; stuffy. Also **poke′y.**

pol (pol) *n.* *Informal* A politician.

po·lar (pō′lər) *adj.* 1. Of the poles of a sphere, magnet, etc. 2. Of, from, or near the North or South Pole. 3. Directly opposite in character, etc. [< Gk. *polos* pivot, pole]

polar bear A large, white bear of arctic regions.

Po·lar·is (pō·lar′is, -lâr′-) *n.* One of the brightest stars, used in navigation as an indicator of north: also called *polestar, North Star*. [< L]

po·lar·i·scope (pō·lar′ə·skōp) *n.* An optical instrument for exhibiting or measuring the polarization of light, or for examining substances in polarized light.

po·lar·i·ty (pō·lar′ə·tē) *n.* *pl.* **·ties** 1. The quality or condition of having poles. 2. *Physics* The possession by a body of opposite magnetic poles. 3. The quality or condition of being attracted to one pole and repelled from the other. 4. The possession of two contrary qualities, tendencies, etc.

po·lar·i·za·tion (pō′lər·ə·zā′shən) *n.* 1. The act of polarizing, or the state of being polarized. 2. *Physics* A condition of electromagnetic waves, most noticeable in light, in which one component of its oscillation is limited to a certain plane.

po·lar·ize (pō′lə·rīz) *v.* **·ized, ·iz·ing** *v.t.* 1. To develop polarization in. —*v.i.* 2. To acquire polarity. 3. To separate into or concentrate around two opposing viewpoints, groups, etc. —**po′lar·iz′a·ble** *adj.* —**po′lar·iz′er** *n.*

pole[1] (pōl) *n.* 1. Either of the two extremities of the axis of a sphere or any spheroidal body. 2. One of the two points where the earth's axis of rotation meets the surface, called the North Pole and the South Pole. 3. *Physics* One of the two points at which opposite qualities or forces are concentrated, as in a magnet. 4. Either of two diametrically opposite forces, tendencies, etc. —**to be poles apart** To differ greatly. [Gk. *polos*]

pole[2] (pōl) *n.* 1. A long, comparatively slender piece of wood or metal. 2. A unit of linear measure, usu. equal to 16.5 feet. —*v.t. & v.i.* **poled, pol·ing** To propel or push (a boat, raft, etc.) with a pole. [OE < L *palus* stake]

Pole (pōl) *n.* A native or inhabitant of Poland.

pole·ax (pōl′aks′) *n.* A battle-ax set on a pole. Also **pole′axe′.** [ME *pol* poll + AX] —**pole′ax′** *v.t.*

pole·cat (pōl′kat′) *n.* 1. A European carnivore allied to the weasel, noted for its offensive odor. 2. A skunk. [< F *poule* pullet + CAT; from its predacity]

po·lem·ic (pō·lem′ik) *adj.* Of or pertaining to controversy; disputatious. Also **po·lem′i·cal.** —*n.* 1. An argument or controversy. 2. One who engages in argument or controversy. 3. *pl.* (*construed as sing.*) The art or practice of disputation. [< Gk. *polemos* war] —**po·lem′i·cist** (-ə·sist) *n.*

pole·star (pōl′stär′) *n.* Polaris.

pole vault An athletic event in which a vault or jump over a high, horizontal bar is made with the help of a long pole. —**pole-vault** (pol′vôlt′) *v.i.* —**pole′-vault′er** *n.*

po·lice (pə·lēs′) *n.* 1. An official civil force organized to maintain order, prevent and detect crime, and enforce law. 2. (*construed as pl.*) The members of such a force. 3. In the U.S. Army: **a** The cleaning of a camp or garrison. **b** A group of soldiers assigned to some specific duty: kitchen *police*. —*v.t.* **·liced, ·lic·ing** 1. To protect, regulate, etc., with or as with police. 2. To make clean or orderly. [< Gk. *politēs* citizen]

police dog A German shepherd dog.

po·lice·man (pə·lēs′mən) *n.* *pl.* **·men** (-mən) A member of a police force. —**po·lice′wom′an** (-wo͝om′ən) *n.fem.*

police state A country whose citizens are rigidly supervised by a national police.

pol·i·clin·ic (pol′i·klin′ik) *n.* The department of a hospital in which outpatients are treated. [< Gk. *polis* city + *klinik* clinic]

pol·i·cy[1] (pol′ə·sē) *n.* *pl.* **·cies** 1. Any plan of action, esp. in governmental or business administration. 2. Prudence, wisdom, or shrewdness, as in the management of one's affairs. [< Gk. *politeia* polity]

pol·i·cy[2] (pol′ə·sē) *n.* *pl.* **·cies** 1. A written contract of insurance. 2. The numbers. See under NUMBER. [< Gk. *apodeiknynai* to show forth] —**pol′i·cy·hol′der** (-hōl′dər) *n.*

policy game The numbers. See under NUMBER.

po·li·o (pō′lē·ō) *n. Informal* Poliomyelitis.

polio- *combining form Med.* Of or pertaining to the gray matter of the brain or the spinal cord. [< Gk. *polios* gray]

po·li·o·my·e·li·tis (pō′lē·ō·mī′ə·lī′tis) *n. Pathol.* An acute, infectious virus disease, occurring esp. in children, and characterized by inflammation of the gray matter of the spinal cord, followed by paralysis: also called *infantile paralysis.* [< POLIO- + Gk. *myelos* marrow + -ITIS]

pol·ish (pol′ish) *n.* 1. Smoothness or glossiness of surface. 2. A substance used to produce a smooth or glossy surface. 3. Refinement or elegance. 4. The act of polishing. —*v.t.* 1. To make smooth or lustrous, as by rubbing. 2. To perfect or refine. —*v.i.* 3. To take a gloss. —**to polish off** 1. To do or finish completely. 2. To dispose of. —**to polish up** To improve. [< L *polire* to smooth] —**pol′·ished** *adj.* —**pol′ish·er** *n.*

Po·lish (pō′lish) *adj.* Of or pertaining to Poland, its inhabitants, or their language. —*n.* The West Slavic language of the Poles.

po·lite (pə·līt′) *adj.* **·lit·er, ·lit·est** 1. Courteous; mannerly. 2. Refined; cultured. [< L *polire* to polish] —**po·lite′ly** *adv.* —**po·lite′ness** *n.*

pol·i·tic (pol′ə·tik) *adj.* 1. Skillful, ingenious, or shrewd. 2. Wise, prudent, or expedient. [< Gk. *politēs* citizen < *polis* city] —**pol′i·tic·ly** *adv.*

po·lit·i·cal (pə·lit′i·kəl) *adj.* 1. Of or concerned with government. 2. Of, relating to, or involved in politics. 3. Having an organized system of government. [< Gk. *politēs* citizen] —**po·lit′i·cal·ly** *adv.*

political science The science of the form, principles, and conduct of civil government. —**political scientist**

pol·i·ti·cian (pol′ə·tish′ən) *n.* One who is engaged in politics, esp. professionally.

po·lit·i·co (pə·lit′i·kō) *n. pl.* **·cos** A politician. [< Sp. < L *politicus*]

pol·i·tics (pol′ə·tiks) *n.pl.* (*Usu. construed as sing.*) 1. The science or art of government. 2. The activities or policies of those controlling or seeking to control a government; also, the profession or area of activity of such persons. 3. The acts or practices of those who seek any position of power or advantage. [< Gk. *politēs* citizen]

pol·i·ty (pol′ə·tē) *n. pl.* **·ties** 1. The form or method of government of a nation, state, church, etc. 2. Any community living under some definite form of government. [< Gk. *politeia*]

pol·ka (pōl′kə, pō′-) *n.* 1. A lively dance consisting of three quick steps and a hop. 2. Music for this dance. —*v.i.* **·kaed, ·ka·ing** To dance the polka. [< Czech *pulka* half step]

polka dot 1. One of a series of round dots decorating a textile fabric. 2. A pattern or fabric made up of such dots.

poll (pōl) *n.* 1. The voting at an election. 2. The total number of votes cast. 3. *pl.* The place where votes are cast and counted. 4. A survey of public opinion on a given subject. 5. A list of persons. 6. The head; esp., the top or back of the head where hair grows. —*v.t.* 1. To receive (a specified number of votes). 2. To enroll, as for voting; register. 3. To cast (a vote). 4. To canvass in a poll. 5. To cut off or trim, as hair, horns, etc. 6. To cut off or trim the hair, horns, top, etc., of: to *poll* cattle. [< MDu. *polle* top of the head] —**poll′er** *n.*

pol·lack (pol′ək) *n.* A food fish of the North Atlantic: also **pol′lock.** [< Scot. *podlok*]

pol·len (pol′ən) *n.* The male or fertilizing element in a seed plant, consisting of fine yellowish powder formed within the anther of the stamen. [< L, fine flour]

pollen count A measure of the relative concentration of pollen grains in the atmosphere.

pol·li·nate (pol′ə·nāt) *v.t.* **·nat·ed, ·nat·ing** *Bot.* To supply or convey pollen to. Also **pol′len·ate.** —**pol′li·na′tion** *n.*

pol·li·wog (pol′ē·wog) *n.* A tadpole. Also **pol′ly·wog.** [ME *polwygle*]

poll·ster (pōl′stər) *n.* One who takes polls.

poll tax A tax on a person, esp. as a prerequisite for voting.

pol·lute (pə·lo͞ot′) *v.t.* **·lut·ed, ·lut·ing** To make unclean or impure; contaminate. [< L *polluere* to defile] —**pol·lut′er** *n.* —**pol·lu′tion** *n.*

Pol·ly·an·na (pol′ē·an′ə) *n.* One who persistently finds good in everything. [after a character in stories by Eleanor H. Porter, 1868–1920]

po·lo (pō′lō) *n.* 1. A hockeylike game played on horseback with a ball and mallets. 2. A similar game played on ice, in the water, etc. [Prob. < Tibetan *pulu* ball]

pol·o·naise (pol′ə·nāz′, pō′lə-) *n.* 1. A stately, marchlike Polish dance. 2. Music for this dance. [< F (*danse*) *polonaise* Polish (dance)]

po·lo·ni·um (pə·lō′nē·əm) *n.* A radioactive element (symbol Po). [named by its discoverers, Pierre and Marie Curie, after *Poland*, Mme. Curie's birthplace]

pol·ter·geist (pōl′tər·gīst) *n.* A rambunctious ghost. [< G, lit., noisy ghost]

pol·troon (pol·tro͞on′) *n.* A mean-spirited coward; dastard. [< Ital. *poltrone* < *poltro* colt] —**pol·troon′** *adj.* —**pol·troon′er·y** *n.*

poly- *combining form* 1. Many; several; much: *polygamy.* 2. Excessive; abnormal. [< Gk. *polys* much, many]

pol·y·an·dry (pol′ē·an′drē) *n.* The condition or practice of having more than one husband at the same time. [< POLY- + Gk. *anēr, andros* man, husband] —**pol′y·an′drous** *adj.*

pol·y·clin·ic (pol′i·klin′ik) *n.* A hospital or clinic in which all forms of diseases are treated.

pol·y·es·ter (pol′ē·es′tər) *n.* A complex ester used in making fibers and plastics.

pol·y·eth·y·lene (pol′ē·eth′ə·lēn) *n.* A tough, flexible thermoplastic resin, used in making moisture-proof plastics for packaging.

po·lyg·a·my (pə·lig′ə·mē) *n.* 1. The condition or practice of having more than one wife or husband at the same time. 2. *Zool.* The state of having more than one mate at the same time. [< POLY- + Gk. *gamos* marriage] —**po·lyg′a·mist** *n.* —**po·lyg′a·mous** *adj.* —**po·lyg′a·mous·ly** *adv.*

pol·y·glot (pol′i·glot) *adj.* Expressed in or speaking several languages; multilingual. —*n.* 1. A polyglot book or person. 2. A mixture of several languages. [< POLY- + Gk. *glotta* tongue] —**pol′y·glot′ism** *n.*

pol·y·gon (pol′i·gon) *n. Geom.* A closed plane figure bounded by straight lines, esp. by more than four. [< POLY- + Gk. *gonia* angle] —**po·lyg·o·nal** (pə·lig′ə·nəl), **po·lyg·o·nous** (pə·lig′ə·nəs) *adj.* —**po·lyg′o·nal·ly** *adv.*

pol·y·graph (pol′i·graf) *n.* An electrical device for simultaneously recording variations in heartbeat, blood pressure, etc., sometimes used as a lie detector. [< Gk. *polygraphos* writing much] —**pol′y·graph′ic** or **·i·cal** *adj.* —**po·lyg·ra·phy** (pə·lig′rə·fē) *n.*

po·lyg·y·ny (pə·lij′ə·nē) *n.* The condition or practice of having more than one wife at the same time. [< POLY- + Gk. *gyne* woman] —**po·lyg′y·nous** *adj.*

pol·y·he·dron (pol′i·hē′drən) *n. pl.* **·dra** or **·drons** *Geom.* A solid bounded by plane faces, esp. by more than four. [< POLY- + Gk. *hedra* base, side] —**pol′y·he′dral** *adj.*

pol·y·math (pol′i·math′) *n.* A person of extensive and diversified learning. [< Gk. *polymathēs* knowing much]

pol·y·mer (pol′i·mər) *n.* A compound of high molecular weight formed by the chemical combination of two or more molecules of the same kind. [< POLY- + Gk. *meros* part] —**po·lym·er·i·za·tion** (pə·lim′·ər·ə·zā′shən) *n.* —**po·lym·er·ize** (pə·lim′ə·rīz) *v.t. & v.i.* **·ized, ·iz·ing**

pol·y·morph (pol′i·môrf) *n.* A substance or organism that passes through several forms, characters, or styles. [< POLY- + Gk. *morphē* form] —**pol′y·morph′ic, pol′y·mor′·phous** *adj.* —**pol′y·morph′ism** *n.*

Pol·y·ne·sian (pol′i·nē′zhən, -shən) *n.* 1. An inhabitant of Polynesia. 2. A subfamily of the Austronesian family of languages. —**Pol′·y·ne′sian** *adj.*

pol·y·no·mi·al (pol′i·nō′mē·əl) *adj.* Of or consisting of many names or terms. —*n. Math.* An expression, as in algebra, containing two or more terms. [< POLY- + L *nomen* name]

pol·yp (pol′ip) *n.* 1. *Pathol.* A smooth growth found in mucous membrane. 2. *Zool.* A hydra. [< POLY- + Gk. *pous* foot] —**pol′y·pous** *adj.*

pol·y·pet·al·ous (pol′i·pet′əl·əs) *adj. Bot.* Having the petals free and distinct. [< POLY- + Gk. *petalon* leaf]

pol·y·phon·ic (pol′i·fon′ik) *adj.* 1. Consisting of many sounds or voices. 2. *Music* Designating or involving the simultaneous combination of two or more independent melodic parts. Also **po·lyph·o·nous** (pə·lif′ə·nəs). [< POLY- + Gk. *phōnē* voice]

po·lyph·o·ny (pə·lif′ə·nē, pol′i·fō′nē) *n. pl.* **·nies** 1. Multiplicity of sounds. 2. Polyphonic music.

pol·y·ploid (pol′i·ploid′) *adj. Genetics* Having more than twice the normal number of chromosomes. —**pol′y·ploid′** *n.*

pol·y·pus (pol′i·pəs) *n. pl.* **·pi** (-pī) *Pathol.* A polyp.

pol·y·sty·rene (pol′ē·stī′rēn) *n.* A clear thermoplastic, used esp. in foams and in molded and sheet forms.

pol·y·syl·lab·ic (pol′i·si·lab′ik) *adj.* 1. Having or pertaining to several syllables, esp. to more than three. 2. Characterized by words of more than three syllables. Also **pol′y·syl·lab′i·cal.** [< POLY- + Gk. *syllabē* syllable]

pol·y·syl·la·ble (pol′i·sil′ə·bəl) *n.* A polysyllabic word.

pol·y·tech·nic (pol′i·tek′nik) *adj.* Embracing many arts: also **pol′y·tech′ni·cal.** —*n.* A school of applied science and the industrial arts. [< POLY- + Gk. *technē* craft, art]

pol·y·the·ism (pol′i·thē·iz′əm) *n.* The belief in and worship of more gods than one. [< POLY- + THEISM] —**pol′y·the′ist** *n.* —**pol′y·the·is′tic** or **·ti·cal** *adj.*

pol·y·un·sat·u·rate (pol′i·un·sach′ə·rit) *n.* An unsaturated fat or oil. —**pol′y·un·sat′u·rat′ed** (-ə·rāt′id) *adj.*

pom·ace (pum′is) *n.* The pulpy substance of apples or similar fruit after grinding. [< Med.L *pomacium* cider]

po·ma·ceous (pō·mā′shəs) *adj.* 1. Relating to or made of apples. 2. Of or pertaining to a pome. [< L *pomum* apple]

po·made (pä·mād′, pō-) *n.* A perfumed dressing for the hair or scalp. —*v.t.* **·mad·ed, ·mad·ing** To anoint with pomade. [< L *pomum* apple]

pome (pōm) *n. Bot.* A fleshy fruit with a core. [< OF, apple < L *pomum*]

pome·gran·ate (pom′gran·it, pom′ə-) *n.* 1. The fruit of a tropical Asian and African tree, about the size of an orange and having many seeds. 2. The tree itself. [< OF *pome* apple + *grenate* (< L *granatum* seeded)]

Pom·e·ra·ni·an (pom′ə·rā′nē·ən) *n.* One of a breed of small dogs with pointed ears, a bushy tail, and a long, straight, silky coat.

pom·mel (pum′əl, pom′-) *n.* 1. A knob, as on the hilt of a sword. 2. A knob at the front and top of a saddle. —*v.t.* **pom·meled** or **·melled, pom·mel·ing** or **·mel·ling** To beat with or as with the fists or a pommel. Also spelled *pummel.* [< OF *pomel* rounded knob]

po·mol·o·gy (pō·mol′ə·jē) *n.* The science that deals with fruits and fruit culture. [< L *pomum* apple, fruit + -LOGY] —**po·mo·log·i·cal** (pō′mə·loj′i·kəl) *adj.* —**po·mol′o·gist** *n.*

pomp (pomp) *n.* 1. Magnificent display; splendor. 2. Ostentatious display. [< Gk. *pompē* procession]

pom·pa·dour (pom′pə·dôr) *n.* A style of arranging hair by puffing it over the forehead. [after the Marquise de *Pompadour,* 1721–64]

pom·pa·no (pom′pə·nō) *n. pl.* **·nos** A spiny-finned food fish of warm seas. [< Sp. *pámpano*]

pom-pom (pom′pom) *n.* A tuft or ball, as of wool, worn on hats, etc. [Alter. of POMPON]

pom·pon (pom′pon, *Fr.* pôn·pôn′) *n.* 1. A pom-pom. 2. A small, compact variety of chrysanthemum or dahlia. [< F]

pom·pous (pom′pəs) *adj.* 1. Marked by exaggerated dignity or self-importance. 2. Bombastic and florid, as speech. [See POMP.] —**pom·pos·i·ty** (pom·pos′ə·tē), **pom′pous·ness** *n.* —**pom′pous·ly** *adv.*

pon·cho (pon′chō) *n. pl.* **·chos** 1. A cloak like a blanket with a hole in the middle for the head. 2. A similar waterproofed garment. [< Sp.]

pond (pond) *n.* A body of still water, smaller than a lake. [ME *ponde,* var. of POUND[2]]

pon·der (pon′dər) *v.t. & v.i.* To weigh (a matter) in the mind; consider carefully. [< L *ponderare* to weigh] —**pon′der·er** *n.*

pon·der·a·ble (pon′dər·ə·bəl) *adj.* Capable of being weighed; having appreciable weight. —**pon′der·a·bil′i·ty** *n.*

pon·der·o·sa pine (pon′də·rō′sə) A tall yellow pine of North America; also its wood.

pon·der·ous (pon′dər·əs) *adj.* 1. Having great weight; also, huge. 2. Dull; lumbering. [< L *pondus, ponderis* weight] —**pon′der·os′i·ty** (-də·ros′ə·tē), **pon′der·ous·ness** *n.* —**pon′der·ous·ly** *adv.*

pond lily Any of various plants of the water-lily family.

pone (pōn) *n.* Corn pone.

pon·gee (pon·jē′) *n.* A thin, natural, unbleached silk with a rough weave. [? < Chinese *pen chi* home loom]

pon·iard (pon′yərd) *n.* A dagger. —*v.t.* To stab with a poniard. [< OF *poing* fist]

pon·tiff (pon′tif) *n.* In the Roman Catholic Church: **a** The Pope. **b** Any bishop. [< MF *pontife* < L *pontifex* high priest]

pon·tif·i·cal (pon·tif′i·kəl) *adj.* 1. Of, pertaining to, or suitable for a pope or bishop. 2. Haughty; pompous; dogmatic. —**pon·tif′i·cal·ly** *adv.*

pon·tif·i·cate (*n.* pon·tif′ə·kit, -kāt′; *v.* -kāt′) *v.i.* **·cat·ed, ·cat·ing** 1. To act or speak pompously or dogmatically. 2. To perform the office of a pontiff. —*n.* The office or term of a pontiff.

pon·toon (pon·tōōn′) *n.* 1. *Mil.* A flat-bottomed boat, metal cylinder, or the like, used in the construction of temporary floating bridges. 2. Either of the floats on the landing gear of a seaplane. [< L *pons, pontis* bridge]

pontoon bridge A bridge supported on pontoons.

po·ny (pō′nē) *n. pl.* **·nies** 1. One of a breed of very small horses, esp. not over 14 hands high. 2. Any small horse. 3. *Slang* A translation used to prepare foreign language lessons: also called *trot.* 4. *Informal* A very small glass for liquor, or its contents. —*v.t. & v.i.* **·nied, ·ny·ing** *Slang* To pay (money) that is due: with *up.* [< dial. E (Scot.) *powney*]

pony express A former postal system by which mail was relayed by horseback riders.

po·ny·tail (pō′nē·tāl′) *n.* 1. A style of arranging long hair by gathering it tightly at the back of the head and letting it hang down like a pony's tail. 2. Hair so worn.

pooch (pōōch) *n. Slang* A dog; esp., a small mongrel. [? < dial. E, var. of POUCH]

poo·dle (pōōd′l) *n.* One of a breed of dogs with long, curly hair. [< G *pudel* < *pudeln* to splash in water]

pooh (pōō) *interj.* An exclamation of contempt, disdain, etc.

Pooh-Bah (pōō′bä′) *n. Informal* A pompous official. [after a character in Gilbert and Sullivan's *The Mikado* (1885)]

pooh-pooh (pōō′pōō′) *v.t.* To reject or speak of disdainfully. [Reduplication of POOH] —**pooh′-pooh′er** *n.*

pool¹ (pōōl) *n.* 1. A small body of fresh water, as a spring. 2. A deep place in a stream. 3. Any small, isolated body of liquid: a *pool* of blood. 4. A swimming pool. [OE *pōl*]

pool² (pōōl) *n.* 1. In certain gambling games, a collective stake. 2. In business or finance, any combination formed for mutual advantage, as for price fixing or a speculative operation. 3. Any combining of efforts or resources: a typists' *pool.* 4. Any of various games played on a six-pocket billiard table: also *pocket billiards.* —*v.t. & v.i.* To combine in a mutual fund or pool. [< L *pulla* stake]

pool·room (pōōl′rōōm′, -rŏŏm′) *n.* A commercial establishment or room equipped for the playing of pool, billiards, etc.

pool table A six-pocket billiard table for playing pool.

poop¹ (pōōp) *n. Naut.* 1. The after part or stern of a ship. 2. A short deck built over the main deck at the stern of a ship: also **poop deck.** [< L *puppis*]

poop² (pōōp) *v.t. Slang* To tire: usu. in the passive. [Origin unknown]

poop³ (pōōp) *n. Slang* Information. —*adj.* Supplying information: *poop* sheet.

poor (pŏŏr) *adj.* 1. Lacking means of comfortable subsistence; needy. 2. Characterized by poverty. 3. Not abundant; scanty; meager. 4. Lacking in fertility; sterile: *poor* soil. 5. Inferior in quality. 6. Feeble; frail: *poor* health. 7. Lacking proper ability; unsatisfactory. 8. Deserving of pity. [< L *pauper*] —**poor′ly** *adv. & adj.* —**poor′ness** *n.*

poor·house (pŏŏr′hous′) *n.* A public establishment maintained as a dwelling for paupers.

poor-mouth (pŏŏr′mouth′) *v.* **-mouthed, -mouth·ing** *v.t.* 1. To disparage; belittle. —*v.i.* 2. To complain of or claim poverty. —**poor′-mouth′** *adj.* —**poor′-mouth′er** (-mouth′ər) *n.*

poor-spir·it·ed (pŏŏr′spir′it·ed) *adj.* Having little spirit or courage. —**poor′-spir′it·ed·ness** *n.*

pop¹ (pop) *v.* **popped, pop·ping** *v.i.* 1. To make a sharp, explosive sound. 2. To burst open or explode with such a sound. 3. To move or go suddenly or quickly: with *in, out,* etc. 4. To bulge: His eyes *popped.* —*v.t.* 5. To cause to burst or explode, as kernels of corn. 6. To thrust or put suddenly: with *in, out,* etc. 7. *Slang* To take (drugs): to *pop* pills. —**to pop the question** *Informal* To make a proposal of marriage. —*n.* 1. A sharp, explosive noise. 2. A shot. 3. Soda (def. 2). —*adv.* 1. Like or with the sound of a pop. 2. Suddenly. [Imit.]

pop² (pop) *n. Slang* 1. Papa. 2. A familiar term of address for an old man. [Short for *poppa,* var. of PAPA]

pop³ (pop) *adj.* 1. Featuring popular or light classical music: a *pop* concert. 2. Of or relating to mass culture: *pop* styles. [Short for POPULAR]

pop art *Sometimes cap.* A style of art of the 1960's influenced by popular commercial art.

pop·corn (pop′kôrn′) *n.* A variety of maize, the kernels of which explode when heated, forming white, puffy balls; also, the corn after popping.

pope (pōp) *n. Often cap.* In the Roman Catholic Church, the bishop of Rome and the head of the Church. [OE < Gk. *pappas* father] —**pope′dom** *n.*

pop·er·y (pō′pər·ē) *n.* The practices, doctrines, etc., of the Roman Catholic Church: an offensive term.

pop·eyed (pop′īd′) *adj.* 1. Having bulging eyes. 2. Astonished; amazed.

pop·gun (pop′gun′) *n.* A child's toy gun that makes a popping sound when it expels a pellet.

pop·in·jay (pop′in·jā) *n.* A vain, conceited person. [< OF *papegai* < Arabic *babaghā*]

pop·ish (pō′pish) *adj.* Pertaining to popes or popery: an offensive term. —**pop′ish·ly** *adv.* —**pop′ish·ness** *n.*

pop·lar (pop′lər) *n.* 1. A tree related to the willow, having soft wood and usu. upturned branches. 2. The wood of this tree. [< L *populus*]

pop·lin (pop′lin) *n.* A durable silk, cotton, or rayon fabric with a ribbed surface. [< Ital. *papalina* papal; because made in Avignon, a papal residence]

pop·o·ver (pop′ō′vər) *n.* A very light egg muffin.

pop·per (pop′ər) *n.* 1. One who or that which pops. 2. A device for popping corn.

pop·py (pop′ē) *n. pl.* **·pies** 1. Any of various plants having showy red, violet, orange, or white flowers, as the **opium poppy.** 2. The bright scarlet color of certain poppy blossoms: also **poppy red.** [OE *popig* < L *papaver*]

pop·py·cock (pop′ē·kok) *n. Informal* Pretentious talk; humbug; nonsense. [< Dial. Du. *pappekak*, lit., soft dung]

poppy seed The small, black seed of the poppy plant, used to flavor and top rolls, bread, etc.

pop·u·lace (pop′yə·lis) *n.* The common people; the masses. [< L *populus* the people]

pop·u·lar (pop′yə·lər) *adj.* 1. Approved of, admired, or liked by most people. 2. Having many friends. 3. Of or pertaining to the people at large. 4. Suited to ordinary people. [< L *popularis* of the people] —**pop′u·lar′i·ty** (-lar′ə·tē) *n.* —**pop′u·lar·ly** *adv.*

popular front A coalition of leftist, labor, and liberal parties.

pop·u·lar·ize (pop′yə·lə·rīz′) *v.t.* **·ized, ·iz·ing** To make popular. Also *Brit.* **pop′u·lar·ise′.** —**pop′u·lar·i·za′tion** *n.* —**pop′u·lar·iz′er** *n.*

pop·u·late (pop′yə·lāt) *v.t.* **·lat·ed, ·lat·ing** 1. To furnish with inhabitants; people. 2. To inhabit. [< L *populus* the people]

pop·u·la·tion (pop′yə·lā′shən) *n.* 1. The total number of persons living in a specified area. 2. The total number of persons of a particular group, class, etc., residing in a place. 3. *Stat.* A group of items or individuals. [< L *populus* the people]

pop·u·list (pop′yə·list) *n.* One who supports broad-based social and political reforms similar to those advocated by the Populists. —**pop′u·lism** *n.* —**pop′u·list** *adj.*

Pop·u·list (pop′yə·list) *n.* A member of the Populist or People's Party, formed in the U.S. in 1891 and advocating public control of railways, an income tax, and limitation of ownership of land. —**Pop′u·lism** *n.* —**Pop′u·list** *adj.*

pop·u·lous (pop′yə·ləs) *adj.* Containing many inhabitants; thickly settled. —**pop′u·lous·ly** *adv.* —**pop′u·lous·ness** *n.*

porce·lain (pôrs′lin, pôr′sə-) *n.* A white, hard, translucent ceramic ware, usu. glazed; chinaware. [< Ital. *porcellana* shell] —**por·ce·la·ne·ous** (pôr′sə·lā′nē·əs) or **por′cel·la′ne·ous** *adj.*

porch (pôrch) *n.* A covered structure or recessed space at the entrance to a building; a veranda. [< L *porticus* colonnade < *porta* gate]

por·cine (pôr′sīn, -sin) *adj.* Of, pertaining to, or characteristic of swine. [< L *porcus* pig]

por·cu·pine (pôr′kyə·pīn) *n.* Any of various large rodents covered with erectile spines or quills: also called *hedgehog.* [< L *porcus* pig + *spina* thorn]

pore[1] (pôr) *v.i.* **pored, por·ing** 1. To gaze steadily or intently. 2. To study or read with care: with *over.* [ME *pouren*]

pore[2] (pôr) *n.* 1. A minute orifice or opening, as in the skin or a leaf, serving as an outlet for perspiration or as a means of absorption. 2. Any similar opening, as in rock. [< Gk. *poros*]

por·gy (pôr′gē) *n. pl.* **·gies** or **·gy** Any of various salt-water food fishes, esp. the **red porgy** of Mediterranean and European waters. [Origin uncertain]

pork (pôrk) *n.* The flesh of swine used as food. [< L *porcus* pig]

pork barrel *Slang* A government appropriation for some local enterprise that will favorably impress a representative's constituents.

pork·er (pôr′kər) *n.* A pig or hog.

pork·pie (pôrk′pī) *n.* 1. A pie filled with pork. 2. A man's hat with a low, flat crown. Also **pork pie.**

pork·y (pôr′kē) *adj.* **pork·i·er, pork·i·est** 1. Of or like pork. 2. Obese; fat.

porn (pôrn) *adj. Slang* Pornographic. —*n.* Pornography. Also **por·no** (pôr′nō).

por·nog·ra·phy (pôr·nog′rə·fē) *n. pl.* **·phies** Obscene books, movies, etc. [< Gk. *pornē* prostitute + *graphein* to write] —**por·nog′ra·pher** *n.* —**por·no·graph·ic** (pôr′nə·graf′ik) *adj.*

po·rous (pôr′əs) *adj.* 1. Having pores. 2. Permeable by fluids or light. —**po·ros·i·ty** (pô·ros′ə·tē) *n.* —**po′rous·ly** *adv.* —**po′rous·ness** *n.*

por·phy·ry (pôr′fə·rē) *n. pl.* **·ries** An igneous rock that has a fine-grained or glassy base enclosing crystals of feldspar or quartz. [< Gk. *porphyros* purple]

por·poise (pôr′pəs) *n. pl.* **·pois·es** or **·poise** 1. A dolphinlike whale with a blunt, rounded snout. 2. Loosely, any small cetacean, as the common dolphin. [< L *porcus pisces*, lit., hog fish]

por·ridge (pôr′ij, por-) *n. Chiefly Brit.* Oatmeal or other meal cooked in water or milk. [Alter. of POTTAGE]

por·rin·ger (pôr′in·jər, por′-) *n.* A small, relatively shallow bowl for porridge or soup. [< MF *potager* soup bowl]

port[1] (pôrt) *n.* 1. A city or place of customary entry and exit of ships, esp. for commerce. 2. A harbor or haven. [OE < L *portus* harbor]

port[2] (pôrt) *n. Naut.* The left side of a vessel as one faces the front or bow: opposed to *starboard.* —*v.t.* & *v.i.* To put or turn to the port side. —*adj.* Left. [Prob. < PORT[1]]

port[3] (pôrt) *n.* 1. *Naut.* **a** A porthole. **b** A covering for a porthole. 2. *Mech.* An orifice for the passage of air, gas, etc. [Prob. < L *porta* gate]

port[4] (pôrt) *n.* A sweet wine, usu. dark red.

port[5] (pôrt) *v.t. Mil.* To carry (a rifle, saber, etc.) diagonally across the body and sloping to the left shoulder. —*n.* Manner of carrying oneself; bearing. [< L *portare* to carry]

port·a·ble (pôr′tə·bəl) *adj.* That can be readily carried or moved. —*n.* Something portable, as a typewriter or radio. [< L *portare* to carry] —**port′a·bil′i·ty** *n.* —**port′a·bly** *adv.*

port·age (pôr′tij, pôr·täzh′) *n.* 1. The act of transporting (canoes, boats, etc.) from one navigable water to another; also, that which is transported. 2. The route over which such transportation is made. 3. The charge for transportation. —*v.t.* & *v.i.* **·taged, ·tag·ing** To carry (boats, etc.) over a portage.

por·tal (pôr′təl) *n.* *Often pl.* An entrance, door, or gate, esp. one that is grand and imposing. [< L *porta* gate]

port authority An official body in charge of the coordination of all traffic of a port.

port·cul·lis (pôrt·kul′is) *n.* A grating that can be let down to close the gateway of a fortified place. [< OF *porte* gate + fem. of *coleis*, pp. of *couler* to slide]

porte-co·chère (pôrt′kō·shâr′, *Fr.* pôrt·kô·shâr′) *n.* 1. A large covered gateway leading into a courtyard. 2. A porch over a driveway at the entrance of a building. [< F, coach door]

por·tend (pôr·tend′) *v.t.* To warn of as an omen; forebode. [< L *pro-* forth + *tendere* to stretch]

por·tent (pôr′tent) *n.* 1. A sign of what is to happen, esp. of something momentous; omen. 2. Ominous significance. —**por·ten′tous** *adj.* —**por·ten′tous·ly** *adv.* —**por·ten′tous·ness** *n.*

por·ter[1] (pôr′tər) *n.* 1. One who carries travelers' luggage, etc., for hire. 2. An attendant in a railroad car. [< L *portare* to carry]

por·ter[2] (pôr′tər) *n.* A keeper of a door or gate; janitor. [< L *porta* gate, door]

por·ter[3] (pôr′tər) *n.* A dark brown, heavy English liquor resembling ale. [< PORTER[1]; so called because formerly drunk chiefly by porters]

por·ter·house (pôr′tər·hous′) *n.* 1. Formerly, a place where porter, ale, etc., were sold; also, a restaurant or chophouse. 2. A choice cut of beefsteak including a part of the tenderloin, usu. next to the sirloin: also **porterhouse steak.**

port·fo·li·o (pôrt·fō′lē·ō) *n.* *pl.* **·li·os** 1. A portable case for holding drawings, papers, etc. 2. The office of a minister of state or a cabinet member. 3. A list of investments, securities, etc., of a bank or investor. [< L *portare* to carry + *folium* leaf, sheet of paper]

port·hole (pôrt′hōl′) *n.* 1. A small, usu. round opening in a ship's side. 2. Any similar opening, as in an aircraft.

por·ti·co (pôr′ti·kō) *n.* *pl.* **·coes** or **·cos** An open space with a roof upheld by columns; a porch. [< Ital. < L *porticus* < *porta* door] —**por′ti·coed** *adj.*

por·tière (pôr·tyâr′) *n.* A curtain for a doorway, used instead of a door. Also **por·tiere′.** [< F]

por·tion (pôr′shən) *n.* 1. A part of a whole. 2. An allotment or share. 3. The quantity of food usu. served to one person. —*v.t.* 1. To divide into shares for distribution; parcel: usu. with *out.* 2. To assign; allot. [< L *portio, -onis*] —**por′tion·a·ble** *adj.* —**por′·tion·less** *adj.*

por·tion·er (pôr′shən·ər) *n.* One who divides in shares or holds a share or shares.

port·ly (pôrt′lē) *adj.* **·li·er, ·li·est** 1. Corpulent; stout. 2. Stately; impressive. [< PORT[5]] —**port′li·ness** *n.*

port·man·teau (pôrt·man′tō) *n.* *pl.* **·teaus** or **·teaux** (-tōz) A large, leather suitcase, having two distinct compartments. [< MF < *porter* to carry + *manteau* coat]

portmanteau word A word formed from parts of two related words, as *brunch* from *breakfast* and *lunch.*

port of call A port where vessels put in for supplies, repairs, taking on of cargo, etc.

port of entry *Law* A place, whether on the coast or inland, designated as a point at which persons or merchandise may enter or leave a country: also called *port.*

por·trait (pôr′trit, -trāt) *n.* 1. A likeness of a person, esp. of the face, by an artist or photographer. 2. A vivid word description, esp. of a person. [See PORTRAY.] —**por′trait·ist** *n.*

por·trai·ture (pôr′tri·chər) *n.* 1. The art or practice of making portraits. 2. Portraits collectively.

por·tray (pôr·trā′) *v.t.* 1. To represent by drawing, painting, etc. 2. To describe or depict in words. 3. To represent, as in a play; act. [< L *pro-* forward + *trahere* to draw] —**por·tray′a·ble** *adj.* —**por·tray′al** *n.* —**por·tray′er** *n.*

Por·tu·guese (pôr′chə·gēz′, -gēs′) *n.* 1. A native or inhabitant of Portugal. 2. The Romance language of Portugal and Brazil. —**Por′tu·guese′** *adj.*

Portuguese man-of-war Any of several large marine animals, having long, stinging tentacles hanging down from a bladderlike float.

por·tu·lac·a (pôr′chə·lak′ə) *n.* A succulent plant having flowers of many colors. [< L, purslane]

pose[1] (pōz) *n.* 1. The position of the whole or part of the body, esp. such a position assumed for or represented by an artist or photographer. 2. A mode of behavior, role, attitude, etc., adopted for effect. —*v.* **posed, pos·ing** *v.i.* 1. To assume or hold a pose, as for a portrait. 2. To affect an attitude, role, etc.: to *pose* as an expert. —*v.t.* 3. To cause to assume a pose, as an artist's model. 4. To state or propound; put forward as a question, etc. [< OF, fusion of LL *pausare* to place and L *pos-*, stem of *ponere* to put]

pose[2] (pōz) *v.t.* **posed, pos·ing** To puzzle or confuse by asking a difficult question. [< obs. *appose*, var. of OPPOSE]

pos·er[1] (pō′zər) *n.* One who poses. [< POSE[1], v.]

pos·er[2] (pō′zər) *n.* A question that baffles. [< POSE[2]]

po·seur (pō·zœr′) *n.* One who affects an attitude, mode of behavior, etc., to make an impression on others. [< F]

posh (posh) *adj.* Luxurious; fashionable. [Origin unknown]

pos·it (poz′it) *v.t.* 1. To put; place. 2. To assume as a fact or basis of argument; postulate. [< L *positus*, pp. of *ponere* to place]

po·si·tion (pə·zish′ən) *n.* 1. The manner in which a thing is placed. 2. Disposition of the body or parts of the body. 3. The locality or place occupied by a person or thing. 4. The proper or appropriate place: in *position.* 5. An attitude or point of view; stand. 6. Relative social standing; status; also, high social standing. 7. Employment; job. 8. In sports, the assignment of an area covered by a particular player. **—to be in a position to** To have the means or opportunity. —*v.t.* To place in a particular or appropriate position. [< L *ponere* to place] **—po·si'tion·al** *adj.*

pos·i·tive (poz'ə·tiv) *adj.* 1. That is or may be directly affirmed; actual. 2. Characterized by or expressing affirmation: a *positive* attitude. 3. Openly and plainly expressed: a *positive* denial. 4. Not admitting of doubt or denial. 5. *Math.* Greater than zero; plus: said of quantities and usu. denoted by the sign (+). 6. *Med.* Denoting the presence of a specific condition or organism. 7. *Photog.* Having the lights and darks in their original relation, as in a print made from a negative. 8. *Electr.* Characterized by a deficiency of electrons. —*n.* 1. That which is positive or capable of being directly or certainly affirmed. 2. *Math.* A positive symbol or quantity. 3. *Electr.* A positive pole, terminal, etc. 4. *Photog.* A positive picture or print. 5. *Gram.* The uncompared degree of an adjective or adverb; also, a word in this degree. [< OF, fem. of *positif* < L *ponere* to place] **—pos'i·tive·ly** *adv.* **—pos'i·tive·ness** *n.*

pos·i·tiv·ism (poz'ə·tiv·iz'əm) *n.* A way of thinking that regards nothing as ascertained or ascertainable beyond the facts of physical science or of sense. **—pos'i·tiv·ist** *n.* **—pos'i·tiv·is'tic** *adj.*

pos·i·tron (poz'ə·tron) *n.* *Physics* The positive counterpart of an electron.

pos·se (pos'ē) *n.* A force of men deputized by a sheriff to assist him. [< Med.L *posse* (*comitatus*) power (of the county)]

pos·sess (pə·zes') *v.t.* 1. To have as property; own. 2. To have as a quality, attribute, skill, etc. 3. To enter and exert control over; dominate: often used passively: The idea *possessed* him. 4. To have sexual intercourse with. [< L *potis* master + *sedere* to sit (as)]

pos·sessed (pə·zest') *adj.* 1. Having; owning. 2. Controlled by or as if by evil spirits; frenzied.

pos·ses·sion (pə·zesh'ən) *n.* 1. The act or fact of possessing. 2. The state of being possessed. 3. That which is possessed or owned. 4. *pl.* Property; wealth. 5. Self-possession.

pos·ses·sive (pə·zes'iv) *adj.* 1. Of or pertaining to possession or ownership. 2. Having a strong desire to dominate another person. 3. *Gram.* Designating a case of the noun or pronoun that denotes possession, origin, or the like. In English, this is usu. formed in nouns by adding *'s*. —*n.* *Gram.* 1. The possessive case. 2. A possessive form or construction. **—pos·ses'·sive·ness** *n.*

pos·set (pos'it) *n.* A drink of hot milk curdled with wine or ale, sweetened and spiced. [ME *poshote, possot*]

pos·si·bil·i·ty (pos'ə·bil'ə·tē) *n.* *pl.* **·ties** 1. The fact or state of being possible. 2. That which is possible.

pos·si·ble (pos'ə·bəl) *adj.* 1. Capable of happening or proving true. 2. Capable of being done or of coming about; feasible. 3. That may or may not happen. [< L *posse* to be able] **—pos'si·bly** *adv.*

pos·sum (pos'əm) *n.* *Informal* An opossum. **—to play possum** To feign death, illness, etc. [< OPOSSUM]

post[1] (pōst) *n.* An upright piece of timber or other material; as: **a** A support for a sign. **b** A bearing or framing member in a building. **c** An indicator of the starting or finishing point of a racecourse, etc. —*v.t.* 1. To put up (a poster, etc.) in some public place. 2. To fasten posters upon. 3. To announce by or as by a poster: to *post* a reward. 4. To publish the name of on a list. [OE < L *postis* door post]

post[2] (pōst) *n.* 1. A position or employment; esp., a public office. 2. *Mil.* **a** A place occupied by a detachment of troops. **b** The buildings and grounds of such a place. 3. An assigned beat, position, or station, as of a sentry, policeman, etc. 4. A trading post or settlement. —*v.t.* To assign to a particular post; station, as a sentry. [< L *positum*, pp. neut. of *ponere* to place]

post[3] (pōst) *n.* 1. *Chiefly Brit.* A single delivery of mail to a home, office, etc.; also, the mail itself. 2. *Chiefly Brit.* An established, usu. government, system for transporting the mails; also, a local post office. —*v.t.* 1. *Chiefly Brit.* To mail. 2. To inform. 3. In bookkeeping, to transfer (items or accounts) to the ledger. —*v.i.* 4. To travel with speed; hasten. 5. To ride to a horse's trot by raising and lowering oneself in rhythm with the gait. —*adv.* Speedily; rapidly. [< Ital. *posta*, orig., a station < L *ponere* to place]

post- *prefix* After in time, order, or position; following: *postdate, postwar.* [< L *post* behind, after]

post·age (pōs'tij) *n.* 1. The charge levied on mail. 2. Stamps, etc., representing payment of this charge.

postage stamp A small, printed label issued and sold by a government to be used in payment of postage.

pos·tal (pōs'təl) *adj.* Pertaining to the mails or to mail service. —*n.* A postal card.

postal card A card, issued officially, for carrying a message through the mails.

post-bel·lum (pōst'bel'əm) *adj.* Occurring after a war, esp. after the Civil War. [< POST- + L *bellum* war]

post card 1. A postal card. 2. A similar, unofficial card, usu. having a picture on one side.

post·date (pōst'dāt') *v.t.* **·dat·ed, ·dat·ing** 1. To assign or fix a date later than the actual date to (a check, document, etc.). 2. To follow in time.

post·er (pōs'tər) *n.* A placard or bill used for advertising, public information, etc., to be posted on a wall or other surface. [< POST[1]]

pos·te·ri·or (pos·tir'ē·ər) *adj.* 1. Situated behind or toward the hinder part. 2. Subsequent in time; later. —*n.* *Sometimes pl.* The buttocks. [< L, compar. of *posterus* coming after < *post* after, behind] **—pos·te'ri·or'i·ty** (-ôr'ə·tē, -or'ə-) *n.* **—pos·te'ri·or·ly** *adv.*

pos·ter·i·ty (pos·ter'ə·tē) *n.* 1. Future generations taken collectively. 2. All of one's descendants. [< L *posterus* coming after]

pos·tern (pōs'tərn, pos'-) *n.* A small back

gate or door, esp. in a fortification or castle. —*adj.* Situated at the back or side. [< LL *postera* back door, gate]

post exchange *Mil.* An establishment for the sale of merchandise and services to military personnel. Abbr. *PX*

post·grad·u·ate (post′graj′o͞o·it) *adj.* Of or pertaining to studies pursued beyond the bachelor's degree. —*n.* One who pursues such studies.

post·haste (pōst′hāst′) *n. Archaic* Great haste or speed. —*adv.* With utmost speed.

post·hu·mous (pos′cho͞o·məs) *adj.* 1. Denoting a child born after the father's death. 2. Published after the author's death, as a book. 3. Arising or continuing after one's death. [< L *postumus* latest, last] —**post′·hu·mous·ly** *adv.*

pos·til·ion (pōs·til′yən, pos-) *n.* One who guides a team drawing a carriage by riding the lead horse. Also **pos·til′lion.** [< Ital. *posta* post, station]

post·im·pres·sion·ism (pōst′im·presh′ən·iz′·əm) *n.* The theories and practice of a group of expressionist painters of the late 19th c., who rejected the objective naturalism of the impressionists and emphasized the subjective view of the artist. —**post′im·pres′sion·ist** *n. & adj.* —**post′im·pres′sion·is′tic** *adj.*

post·lude (pōst′lo͞od) *n. Music* 1. An organ solo concluding a church service. 2. Loosely, a coda.

post·man (pōst′mən) *n. pl.* **·men** (-mən) A mailman.

post·mark (pōst′märk′) *n.* Any official mark stamped on mail to cancel stamps. —**post′·mark′** *v.t.*

post·mas·ter (pōst′mas′tər) *n.* An official having charge of a post office. —**post′mis′·tress** (-mis′tris) *n.fem.*

postmaster general *pl.* **postmasters general** The executive head of the postal service of a government.

post·me·rid·i·an (pōst′mə·rid′ē·ən) *adj.* Pertaining to or occurring in the afternoon. [< POST- + L *meridies* noon]

post me·rid·i·em (pōst mə·rid′ē·əm) After noon. Abbr. *p.m., P.M.* [< L]

post-mor·tem (pōst·môr′təm) *adj.* 1. Happening or performed after death. 2. Of or pertaining to a post-mortem examination. —*n.* 1. A post-mortem examination. 2. *Informal* An analysis or discussion of an accomplished fact. [< L *post mortem* after death]

post-mortem examination *Med.* A thorough examination of a human body after death: also called *autopsy.*

post·na·tal (pōst·nāt′l) *adj.* Occurring after birth.

post office 1. The branch of a government charged with delivering the mails. 2. Any local office that delivers mail, sells stamps, etc.

post·op·er·a·tive (pōst·op′ər·ə·tiv) *adj. Surg.* Occurring or done after a surgical operation.

post·paid (pōst′pād′) *adj.* Having postage prepaid.

post·par·tum (pōst′pär′təm) *adj. Med.* After childbirth. [< POST- + L *partus* childbirth]

post·pone (pōst·pōn′) *v.t.* **·poned, ·pon·ing** To put off to a future time; defer; delay. [< POST- + L *ponere* to put] —**post·pon′a·ble** *adj.* —**post·pone′ment** *n.* —**post·pon′er** *n.*

post·pran·di·al (pōst·pran′dē·əl) *adj.* After-dinner. [< POST- + L *prandium* lunch]

post road A road built for the transportation of mail.

post·script (pōst′skript′) *n.* A sentence or other addition at the end of a letter or other document. Abbr. *p.s., P.S.* [< L *postscriptum*, pp. of *postscribere* to write after]

pos·tu·lant (pos′chə·lənt) *n. Eccl.* An applicant for admission into a religious order. [< L *postulare* to demand] —**pos′tu·lan·cy** *n.*

pos·tu·late (*v.* pos′chə·lāt; *n.* pos′chə·lit) *v.t.* **·lat·ed, ·lat·ing** To assume the truth or reality of. —*n.* A principle assumed to be true and used as the basis for further reasoning. —**pos′tu·la′tion** *n.* —**pos′tu·la′tor** *n.*

pos·ture (pos′chər) *n.* 1. The position or carriage of the body or parts of the body. 2. A mental attitude; frame of mind. 3. A situation or condition, esp. if a consequence of policy: national defense *posture.* —*v.i.* **·tured, ·tur·ing** To assume or adopt a bodily pose or a character not natural to one. [< L *positura* position] —**pos′tur·al** *adj.* —**pos′tur·er** *n.*

post·war (pōst′wôr′) *adj.* Being or happening after a war.

po·sy (pō′zē) *n. pl.* **·sies** A single flower or a bouquet. [Contr. of POESY]

pot (pot) *n.* 1. A round, fairly deep vessel of metal, earthenware, or glass, generally having a handle, used for cooking and other domestic purposes. 2. The amount a pot will hold. 3. In card games, esp. poker, the amount of stakes wagered or played for. 4. *Slang* Marijuana. —**to go to pot** To deteriorate. —*v.* **pot·ted, pot·ting** *v.t.* 1. To put into a pot or pots: to *pot* plants. 2. To preserve (meat, etc.) in pots or jars. 3. To shoot or kill with a pot shot. —*v.i.* 4. To take a pot shot; shoot. [OE *pott*]

po·ta·ble (pō′tə·bəl) *adj.* Suitable for drinking: said of water. —*n. Often pl.* Something drinkable; a drink. [< LL *potare* to drink]

po·tage (pō·täzh′) *n. French* Any thick soup.

pot·ash (pot′ash′) *n.* 1. Crude potassium carbonate. 2. Any of various potassium compounds. [< Du. *potasch*]

po·tas·si·um (pə·tas′ē·əm) *n.* A bluish white, highly reactive metallic element (symbol K), never found free in nature, but yielding many compounds of great practical value in industry, medicine, etc. [< POTASH] —**po·tas′sic** *adj.*

potassium bi·tar·trate (bī·tär′trāt) *Chem.* A white crystalline compound that is an ingredient of baking powder: also called *cream of tartar.*

potassium bromide *Chem.* A crystalline compound, used in photography and as a sedative.

potassium carbonate *Chem.* A white, strongly alkaline compound, used in making soap and glass.

potassium nitrate *Chem.* A crystalline white salt, used in gunpowder, fertilizers, and in medicine. Also called *niter, saltpeter.*

po·ta·tion (pō·tā′shən) *n.* 1. The act of drinking; also, a drink, esp. of an alcoholic beverage. 2. A drinking bout. [< L *potare* to drink]

po·ta·to (pə·tā'tō) *n. pl.* **·toes** 1. One of the edible tubers of a plant of the nightshade family. 2. The plant. 3. The sweet potato. [< Sp. *patata*]

potato beetle A beetle that feeds on the leaves of the potato, tomato, and similar plants. Also **potato bug.**

potato chip A very thin slice of potato, fried crisp and salted.

pot·bel·ly (pot'bel'ē) *n. pl.* **·lies** 1. A protuberant belly. 2. An upright wood- or coal-burning stove with bulging sides: also **potbellied stove.** —**pot'bel'lied** *adj.*

pot·boil·er (pot'boi'ler) *n. Informal* A usu. inferior literary or artistic work produced simply for money.

po·tent (pōt'nt) *adj.* 1. Physically powerful. 2. Having great authority. 3. Exerting great influence on mind or morals; very convincing: a *potent* argument. 4. Of a drug, liquor, etc., strong in its physical and chemical effects. 5. Sexually competent: said of the male. [< L *potens, -entis* powerful < *posse* to be able] —**po'ten·cy** *n.* —**po'tent·ly** *adv.*

po·ten·tate (pōt'n·tāt) *n.* One having great power or sway; a sovereign. [< LL *potentatus*]

po·ten·tial (pə·ten'chəl) *adj.* 1. Possible but not actual. 2. Having capacity for existence, but not yet existing; latent. —*n.* 1. A possible development; potentiality. 2. *Electr.* The charge on a body as referred to another body or to a given standard, as the earth, considered as having zero potential. [< LL *potentialis*] —**po·ten'tial·ly** *adv.*

potential energy See under ENERGY.

po·ten·ti·al·i·ty (pə·ten'chē·al'ə·tē) *n. pl.* **·ties** 1. Inherent capacity for development or accomplishment. 2. That which is potential or capable of being realized.

poth·er (poth'ər) *n.* Excitement mingled with confusion; fuss. —*v.t. & v.i.* To worry; bother.

pot·herb (pot'ûrb', -hûrb') *n.* Any plant or herb, esp. greens, the leaves or stems of which are cooked as a vegetable or are used to flavor foods.

pot·hole (pot'hōl') *n.* A deep hole, as in a road.

pot·hook (pot'hŏŏk') *n.* A curved or hooked piece of iron for lifting or hanging pots.

po·tion (pō'shən) *n.* A draft, as a large dose of liquid medicine: often used of a magic or poisonous draft. [< L *potare* to drink]

pot·luck (pot'luk') *n.* Whatever food may have been prepared: usu. in the phrase **to take potluck.**

pot·pie (pot'pī') *n.* 1. A meat pie baked in a deep dish. 2. Meat stewed with dumplings.

pot·pour·ri (pō'pōō·rē') *n.* 1. A mixture of dried flower petals kept in a jar and used to perfume a room. 2. A musical medley or literary miscellany. [< F, lit., rotten pot]

pot roast Meat braised and cooked in a covered pot.

pot·sherd (pot'shûrd) *n.* A bit of broken earthenware.

pot shot 1. A shot fired to kill, without regard to the rules of sports. 2. A shot fired, as from ambush, at a person or animal within easy range.

pot·tage (pot'ij) *n.* A thick broth or stew of vegetables with or without meat. [< OF *pot* pot]

pot·ted (pot'id) *adj.* 1. Placed or kept in a pot. 2. Cooked or preserved in a pot. 3. *Slang* Drunk.

pot·ter[1] (pot'ər) *v.t. & v.i. Chiefly Brit.* To putter. [Freq. of dial. *pote* to poke] —**pot'·ter·er** *n.*

pot·ter[2] (pot'ər) *n.* One who makes earthenware or porcelain vessels.

potter's field A burial ground for the destitute and the unknown.

pot·ter·y (pot'ər·ē) *n. pl.* **·ter·ies** 1. Ware molded from clay and hardened by intense heat. 2. The art of making earthenware or porcelain. 3. A place where pottery is made. [< Med.L *pot* pot]

pouch (pouch) *n.* 1. A small bag, sack, or other container, used for carrying money, pipe tobacco, ammunition, etc. 2. *Zool.* A saclike structure of certain animals, as the kangaroo, for carrying and nurturing young. 3. A mailbag. —*v.t.* 1. To put in a pouch. —*v.i.* 2. To form a pouchlike cavity. [< OF *poche*] —**pouch'y** *adj.*

poul·tice (pōl'tis) *n.* A hot, soft mass applied to a sore part of the body. —*v.t.* **·ticed, ·tic·ing** To cover with a poultice. [< L *puls* porridge]

poul·try (pōl'trē) *n.* Domestic fowls, generally or collectively, as hens. [< OF *poule* hen]

pounce (pouns) *v.i.* **pounced, pounc·ing** To swoop or spring in or as in seizing prey: with *on, upon,* or *at.* [ME *pownce* talon] —**pounce** *n.*

pound[1] (pound) *n.* 1. A unit of weight varying in different countries and at different periods. 2. In Great Britain and the U.S., either of two legally fixed units, the avoirdupois pound and the troy pound. 3. The standard monetary unit of the United Kingdom, equivalent to 100 pence: also **pound sterling.** Symbol £. 4. A standard monetary unit of various other countries. [< L *pondus* weight]

pound[2] (pound) *n.* 1. A place, enclosed by authority, in which stray animals, seized property, etc., are left until claimed or redeemed. 2. A place of confinement for lawbreakers. —*v.t.* To confine in a pound; impound. [OE *pund-*]

pound[3] (pound) *v.t.* 1. To strike heavily and repeatedly; beat. 2. To reduce to a pulp or powder by beating. —*v.i.* 3. To strike heavy, repeated blows: with *on, at,* etc. 4. To move or proceed heavily. 5. To throb heavily or resoundingly. —*n.* 1. A heavy blow. 2. The act of pounding. [OE *pūnian* to bruise]

pound cake A rich cake originally made with ingredients equal in weight, as a pound each of flour, butter, and sugar, with eggs added.

pound·er[1] (poun'dər) *n.* One who or that which pounds, beats, or strikes.

pound·er[2] (poun'dər) *n.* One who or that which weighs a given number of pounds: used in combination: an *eight-pounder.*

pound-fool·ish (pound'fōō'lish) *adj.* Extravagant with large sums, but watching small sums closely.

pour (pôr) *v.t.* 1. To cause to flow in a continuous stream, as water, sand, etc. 2. To emit or utter profusely or continuously. —*v.i.* 3. To flow in a continuous stream; gush. 4. To rain heavily. 5. To move in great numbers; swarm. —*n.* A pouring, flow, or downfall. [ME *pouren*] —**pour′er** *n.* —**pour′ing·ly** *adv.*

pout (pout) *v.i.* 1. To thrust out the lips, esp. in ill humor. 2. To be sullen; sulk. —*v.t.* 3. To thrust out (the lips, etc.). 4. To utter with a pout. [ME *pouten*] —**pout** *n.*

pout·er (pou′tər) *n.* 1. One who pouts. 2. A breed of pigeon having the habit of puffing out the crop.

pov·er·ty (pov′ər·tē) *n.* 1. The condition or quality of being poor. 2. Scantiness of essential elements: a *poverty* of imagination. [< OF *poverte* < L *pauper* poor]

pov·er·ty-strick·en (pov′er·tē·strik′ən) *adj.* Suffering from poverty; destitute.

pow·der (pou′dər) *n.* 1. A finely ground or pulverized mass of loose particles formed from a solid substance in the dry state. 2. Any of various substances prepared in this form, as a cosmetic, medicine, or explosive. —*v.t.* 1. To reduce to powder; pulverize. 2. To sprinkle or cover with or as with powder. —*v.i.* 3. To be reduced to powder. [< OF *poudre* < L *pulvis* dust] —**pow′der·er** *n.* —**pow′der·y** *adj.*

powder blue A soft medium blue.

pow·er (pou′ər) *n.* 1. Ability to act; capability. 2. Potential capacity. 3. Strength or force actually put forth. 4. The right, ability, or capacity to exercise control; legal authority. 5. An important and influential sovereign nation. 6. *Often pl.* A mental or physical faculty. 7. Any form of energy available for doing work; esp., electrical energy. 8. *Physics* The time rate at which energy is transferred, or converted into work. 9. *Math.* The number of times a number is to be multiplied by itself, expressed as an exponent. 10. *Optics* Magnifying capacity, as of a lens. —*v.t.* To supply with power; esp., to provide with means of propulsion. [< L *posse* to be able]

power boat A motorboat.

pow·er·ful (pou′ər·fəl) *adj.* 1. Possessing great force or energy; strong. 2. Exercising great authority, or manifesting high qualities. 3. Having great effect on the mind. —*adv.* *Dial.* Very. —**pow′er·ful·ly** *adv.*

pow·er·house (pou′ər·hous′) *n.* 1. *Electr.* A station where electricity is generated: also **power plant.** 2. *Informal* A forceful, powerful, or energetic person.

pow·er·less (pou′ər·lis) *adj.* 1. Destitute of power; unable to accomplish an effect; impotent. 2. Without authority. —**pow′er·less·ly** *adv.* —**pow′er·less·ness** *n.*

power of attorney *Law* 1. The authority or power to act conferred upon an agent. 2. The document conferring such authority.

pow·wow (pou′wou′) *n.* 1. *Informal* Any meeting or conference. 2. A North American Indian ceremony to cure the sick, effect success in war, etc. 3. A conference with or of American Indians. —*v.i.* To hold a powwow. [< Algonquian (Massachusetts) *pauwaw*, lit., he dreams]

pox (poks) *n.* 1. Any disease characterized by purulent eruptions: *chickenpox.* 2. *Archaic* Syphilis. [Var. of *pocks*, pl. of POCK]

prac·ti·ca·ble (prakt′i·kə·bəl) *adj.* 1. That can be put into practice; feasible. 2. That can be used; usable. [< Gk. *prassein* to do] —**prac′ti·ca·bil′i·ty** *n.* —**prac′ti·ca·bly** *adv.*

prac·ti·cal (prak′ti·kəl) *adj.* 1. Pertaining to actual use and experience, as contrasted with speculation. 2. Trained by or derived from practice or experience. 3. Applicable to use. 4. Manifested in practice. 5. Being such to all intents and purposes; virtual. [< Gk. *praktikos* < *prassein* to do] —**prac′ti·cal′i·ty** (-kal′ə·tē), **prac′ti·cal·ness** *n.*

practical joke A trick having a victim or victims.

prac·ti·cal·ly (prak′tik·lē) *adv.* 1. In a practical manner. 2. In effect; virtually.

practical nurse One who has training in nursing but who is not a registered nurse.

prac·tice (prak′tis) *v.* **·ticed, ·tic·ing** *v.t.* 1. To make use of habitually or often: to *practice* economy. 2. To apply in action; make a practice of. 3. To work at as a profession. 4. To do or perform repeatedly in order to acquire skill or training; rehearse. —*v.i.* 5. To repeat or rehearse something in order to acquire skill or proficiency. 6. To work at a profession. —*n.* 1. Any customary action or proceeding; habit. 2. An established custom or usage. 3. The act of doing or performing, as distinguished from theory. 4. The regular prosecution of a profession. 5. Frequent and repeated exercise in any matter. 6. *pl.* Stratagems or schemes for bad purposes; tricks. Also **prac′tise.** [See PRACTICAL.] —**prac′tic·er** *n.*

prac·ticed (prak′tist) *adj.* 1. Expert by practice; experienced. 2. Acquired by practice. Also **prac′tised.**

prac·ti·tion·er (prak·tish′ən·ər) *n.* One who practices an art or profession.

prae- See PRE-.

praeter- See PRETER-.

prae·tor (prē′tər) *n.* A city magistrate of ancient Rome: also spelled *pretor.* [< L < *praeire* to go before] —**prae·to·ri·al** (pri·tôr′ē·əl) *adj.* —**prae·to·ri·an** (pri·tôr′ē·ən) *adj. & n.* —**prae′tor·ship** *n.*

prag·mat·ic (prag·mat′ik) *adj.* 1. Pertaining to or concerned with events or everyday occurrences; practical. 2. *Philos.* Pertaining to pragmatism. Also **prag·mat′i·cal.** [< Gk. *pragma, pragmatos* thing done] —**prag·mat′i·cal·ly** *adv.*

prag·ma·tism (prag′mə·tiz′əm) *n.* *Philos.* The doctrine that ideas have value only in terms of their practical consequences. —**prag′ma·tist** *n.*

prai·rie (prâr′ē) *n.* A tract of grassland; esp., the broad, grassy plain of central North America. [< L *pratum* meadow]

prairie chicken Either of two large, chiefly terrestrial game birds inhabiting the plains of western North America. Also **prairie hen.**

prairie dog A burrowing rodent of the plains of North America. Also **prairie squirrel.**

prairie schooner A covered wagon used for travel by pioneers.

praise (prāz) *n.* 1. An expression of approval or commendation. 2. The glorifying and honoring of a god, ruler, hero, etc. —*v.t.* **praised, prais·ing** 1. To express approval and commendation of; applaud. 2. To express adoration of; glorify, esp. in song. [< LL *pretiare* to prize] —**prais′er** *n.*

praise·wor·thy (prāz′wûr′thē) *adj.* Worthy of praise. —**praise′wor′thi·ly** *adv.* —**praise′wor′thi·ness** *n.*

Pra·krit (prä′krit) *n.* Any of several vernacular languages of ancient India. [< Skt. *prakrtā* natural]
pra·line (prä′lēn, prā′-) *n.* A confection made of pecans or other nuts browned in boiling sugar. [< F, after Marshal Duplessis-*Praslin*, 1598–1675, whose cook invented it]
pram (pram) *n.* *Chiefly Brit. Informal* A baby carriage. [Short for PERAMBULATOR]
prance (prans) *v.* **pranced, pranc·ing** *v.i.* 1. To move proudly with high steps, as a spirited horse; spring from the hind legs; also, to ride a horse moving thus. 2. To move in an arrogant or elated manner; swagger. —*v.t.* 3. To cause to prance. —*n.* The act of prancing; caper. [ME *prauncen*] —**pranc′er** *n.*
pran·di·al (pran′dē·əl) *adj.* Of or pertaining to a meal. [< L *prandium* breakfast or lunch]
prank (prangk) *n.* A mischievous or frolicsome act; a trick. —*v.i.* To play pranks or tricks. [Origin uncertain] —**prank′ish** *adj.* —**prank′ster** *n.*
pra·se·o·dym·i·um (prā′zē·ō·dim′ē·əm, prā′sē-) *n.* A yellowish white metallic element (symbol Pr), having olive-green salts. [< Gk. *prasios* light green + (DI)DYMIUM]
prate (prāt) *v.t.* & *v.i.* **prat·ed, prat·ing** To talk or utter idly and at length; chatter. —*n.* Idle talk; prattle. [< MDu. *praten*] —**prat′er** *n.* —**prat′ing·ly** *adv.*
prat·fall (prat′fôl′) *n.* *Slang* A fall on the buttocks.
prat·tle (prat′l) *v.t.* & *v.i.* **·tled, ·tling** To talk or utter in a foolish or childish way. —*n.* Childish or foolish talk. [See PRATE.] —**prat′tler** *n.*
prawn (prôn) *n.* Any of various shrimplike crustaceans of tropical and temperate waters, used as food. —*v.i.* To fish for prawns. [ME *prane, prayne*]
pray (prā) *v.i.* 1. To address prayers to a deity, idol, etc. 2. To make earnest request or entreaty; beg. —*v.t.* 3. To say prayers to. [< L *prex, precis* request, prayer]
prayer[1] (prâr) *n.* 1. A devout request or petition to a deity. 2. The act of praying, esp. to God. 3. *Often pl.* A religious service. 4. Something prayed for. 5. Any earnest request.
pray·er[2] (prā′ər) *n.* One who prays.
prayer book (prâr) A book of prayers for divine service.
prayer·ful (prâr′fəl) *adj.* Inclined or given to prayer; devotional. —**prayer′ful·ly** *adv.* —**prayer′ful·ness** *n.*
praying mantis The mantis (which see).
pre- *prefix*
1. Before in time; preceding:

pre-Christian	**premarital**
predawn	**prerevolutionary**
preglacial	**preschooler**
preinaugural	**preteen**
prekindergarten	**prewar**

2. Before in position: **precardiac, precerebral, prevertebral**
3. Preliminary to; preparing for: **precollege, predoctorate**
4. Beforehand; in advance:

prearrange	**prechill**
prearm	**precool**
preexamine	**preplan**
preheat	**presalt**
prepackage	**preset**

Also *prae-*. [< L *prae* before]
preach (prēch) *v.t.* 1. To advocate or recommend urgently. 2. To proclaim or expound upon: to *preach* the gospel. 3. To deliver (a sermon, etc.). —*v.i.* 4. To deliver a sermon. 5. To give advice, esp. in an officious or moralizing manner. [< L *praedicare* to proclaim]
preach·er (prē′chər) *n.* One who preaches; esp., a clergyman.
preach·ment (prēch′mənt) *n.* A sermon or moral lecture, esp. a tedious one.
preach·y (prē′chē) *adj.* **preach·i·er, preach·i·est** Given to preaching; sanctimonious. —**preach′i·ness** *n.*
pre·am·ble (prē′am·bəl) *n.* 1. An introductory statement or preface. 2. An introductory act, event, fact, etc. [< L *prae-* before + *ambulare* to walk] —**pre·am′bu·lar′y** (-byə·ler′ē) *adj.*
pre·am·pli·fi·er (prē·am′plə·fī′ər) *n.* In a sound reproduction system, an auxiliary amplifier used to reinforce very weak signals before sending them into the main amplifier. Also **pre′amp.**
preb·end (preb′ənd) *n.* 1. A stipend allotted from the revenues of a cathedral or conventual church to a clergyman. 2. The land or tithe yielding the stipend. [< L *praebere* to supply] —**preb′en·dal** *adj.*
preb·en·dar·y (preb′ən·der′ē) *n. pl.* **·dar·ies** A canon or clergyman who holds a prebend.
pre·can·cel (prē·kan′səl) *v.t.* **·celed** or **·celled, ·cel·ing** or **·cel·ling** To cancel (stamps) before use on mail. —*n.* A precanceled stamp.
pre·car·i·ous (pri·kâr′ē·əs) *adj.* 1. Subject to continued risk; uncertain. 2. Subject or exposed to danger; hazardous. [< L *precarius* obtained by prayer]
pre·cau·tion (pri·kô′shən) *n.* 1. A step or preparation taken to avoid a possible danger, evil, etc. 2. Preparation for a possible emergency. [< L *prae-* before + *cavere* to take care] —**pre·cau′tion·ar′y** *adj.*
pre·cede (pri·sēd′) *v.* **·ced·ed, ·ced·ing** *v.t.* 1. To go or be before in order, place, rank, time, etc. 2. To preface; introduce. —*v.i.* 3. To go or be before; take precedence. [< L *prae-* before + *cedere* to go]
pre·ce·dence (pres′ə·dəns, pri·sēd′əns) *n.* The act, right, or state of preceding in place, time, or rank.
prec·e·dent (*n.* pres′ə·dənt; *adj.* pri·sēd′nt) *n.* An act or instance capable of being used as a guide or standard in evaluating future actions. —*adj.* Former; preceding. —**prec·e·den·tial** (pres′ə·den′shəl) *adj.*
pre·ced·ing (pri·sē′ding) *adj.* Going before, as in time, place, or rank; earlier; foregoing. —**the preceding** That which precedes or has been mentioned before.
pre·cen·tor (pri·sen′tər) *n.* One who leads the singing of a church choir or congregation. [< L *prae-* before + *canere* to sing] —**pre·cen·to·ri·al** (prē′sen·tôr′ē·əl) *adj.* —**pre·cen′tor·ship** *n.*
pre·cept (prē′sept) *n.* A rule for guiding conduct or action; a maxim. [< L *praecipere* to prescribe] —**pre·cep·tive** (pri·sep′tiv) *adj.*

pre·cep·tor (pri·sep′tər) *n.* A teacher. [< L *praeceptor*] —**pre·cep·to·ri·al** (prē′sep·tôr′·ē·əl) *adj.* —**pre·cep′tress** (-tris) *n. fem.*

pre·ces·sion (pri·sesh′ən) *n.* The act of preceding. —**pre·ces′sion·al** *adj.*

pre·cinct (prē′singkt) *n.* 1. An election district of a town, township, county, etc. 2. A subdivision of a city or town under the jurisdiction of a police unit. 3. A place marked off by fixed limits; also, the boundary of such a place. 4. *pl.* Neighborhood; environs. [< L *prae-* before + *cingere* to encircle]

pre·ci·os·i·ty (presh′ē·os′ə·tē) *n. pl.* **·ties** Extreme fastidiousness or affected refinement, as in speech, style, etc.

pre·cious (presh′əs) *adj.* 1. Highly priced or prized; valuable: a *precious* stone. 2. Greatly esteemed or cherished. 3. Affectedly delicate or sensitive, as a style of writing. —*n.* Precious one; sweetheart. —*adv.* Extremely; very. [< L *pretium* price] —**pre′cious·ly** *adv.* —**pre′cious·ness** *n.*

precious stone A valuable, rare gem, as the diamond, ruby, sapphire, or emerald.

prec·i·pice (pres′i·pis) *n.* A high vertical or overhanging face of rock; the brink of a cliff. [< L *prae-* before + *caput* head]

pre·cip·i·tate (pri·sip′ə·tāt; *for adj. & n., also* pri·sip′ə·tit) *v.* **·tat·ed, ·tat·ing** *v.t.* 1. To hasten the occurrence of. 2. To hurl from or as from a height. 3. *Meteorol.* To cause (vapor, etc.) to condense and fall as dew, rain, etc. 4. *Chem.* To separate (a substance) in solid form, as from a solution. —*v.i.* 5. *Meteorol.* To fall as condensed vapor, etc. 6. *Chem.* To separate and settle, as a substance held in solution. —*adj.* 1. Moving speedily or hurriedly; rushing headlong. 2. Lacking due deliberation; hasty; rash. —*n. Chem.* A deposit of solid matter formed by precipitation. [< L *praeceps.* See PRECIPICE.] —**pre·cip′i·tate·ly** *adv.* —**pre·cip′i·tate·ness** *n.* —**pre·cip′i·ta′tor** *n.*

pre·cip·i·ta·tion (pri·sip′ə·tā′shən) *n.* 1. *Meteorol.* **a** The depositing of moisture from the atmosphere upon the surface of the earth. **b** The amount of rain, snow, etc., deposited. 2. *Chem.* The process of separating in the form of a solid any of the constituents of a solution. 3. Rash haste or hurry.

pre·cip·i·tous (pri·sip′ə·təs) *adj.* 1. Like a precipice; very steep. 2. Having many precipices. 3. Hasty. —**pre·cip′i·tous·ly** *adv.* —**pre·cip′i·tous·ness** *n.*

pré·cis (prā′sē, prā·sē′) *n. pl.* **pré·cis** (prā′sēz, prā·sēz′) A concise summary of a book, article, or document; abstract. [< F]

pre·cise (pri·sīs′) *adj.* 1. Sharply and clearly determined or defined. 2. No more and no less than; exact in amount. 3. Scrupulously observant of rule. [< L *prae-* before + *caedere* to cut] —**pre·cise′ly** *adv.* —**pre·cise′ness** *n.*

pre·ci·sion (pri·sizh′ən) *n.* The state or quality of being precise; accuracy. —*adj.* Designed for extremely accurate measurement: *precision* instruments. —**pre·ci′sion·ist** *n.*

pre·clude (pri·klōōd′) *v.t.* **·clud·ed, ·clud·ing** 1. To make impossible or ineffectual by prior action. 2. To shut out; exclude. [< L *prae-* before + *claudere* to shut] —**pre·clu′sion** (-klōō′zhən) *n.* —**pre·clu′sive** (-klōō′siv) *adj.* —**pre·clu′sive·ly** *adv.*

pre·co·cious (pri·kō′shəs) *adj.* Unusually developed or advanced for one's age. [< L *prae-* beforehand, early + *coquere* to cook] —**pre·co′cious·ly** *adv.* —**pre·co′cious·ness, pre·coc′i·ty** (-kos′ə·tē) *n.*

pre·con·ceive (prē′kən·sēv′) *v.t.* **·ceived, ·ceiv·ing** To conceive in advance; form an idea or opinion of beforehand. —**pre′con·cep′tion** (-sep′shən) *n.*

pre·con·di·tion (prē′kən·dish′ən) *n.* A condition that must be met before a certain result is attained; prerequisite.

pre·cur·sor (pri·kûr′sər) *n.* One who or that which precedes and suggests the course of future events. [< L *prae-* before + *currere* to run] —**pre·cur′so·ry** *adj.*

pre·da·cious (pri·dā′shəs) *adj.* Living by preying upon others, as a beast or bird; raptorial: also *predatory.* Also **pre·da′ceous.** [< L *praeda* prey] —**pre·da′cious·ness, pre·dac′i·ty** (-das′ə·tē) *n.*

pre·date (prē′dāt′) *v.t.* **·dat·ed, ·dat·ing** 1. To date before the actual time. 2. To precede in time.

pred·a·to·ry (pred′ə·tôr′ē) *adj.* 1. Of, relating to, or characterized by plundering. 2. Predacious. [< L *praeda* prey] —**pred′a·tor** (-tər) *n.* —**pred′a·to′ri·ly** *adv.* —**pred′a·to′ri·ness** *n.*

pre·de·cease (prē′di·sēs′) *v.t.* **·ceased, ·ceas·ing** To die before (someone else).

pred·e·ces·sor (pred′ə·ses′ər) *n.* 1. One who goes or has gone before another in time. 2. A thing succeeded by something else. 3. An ancestor. [< LL *prae-* before + *decessor* withdrawer]

pre·des·ti·na·tion (prē·des′tə·nā′shən) *n. Theol.* The foreordination of all things by God, including the salvation or damnation of men. [< L *prae-* before + *destinare* to determine] —**pre·des′ti·nate** *v.t.* **·nat·ed, ·nat·ing**

pre·des·tine (prē·des′tin) *v.t.* **·tined, ·tin·ing** To destine or decree beforehand; foreordain.

pre·de·ter·mine (prē′di·tûr′min) *v.t.* **·mined, ·min·ing** To determine beforehand; foreordain. —**pre′de·ter′mi·nate** (-mə·nit, -nāt) *adj.* —**pre′de·ter′mi·na′tion** *n.*

pred·i·ca·ble (pred′i·kə·bəl) *adj.* Capable of being predicated or affirmed. —**pred′i·ca·bil′i·ty, pred′i·ca·ble·ness** *n.*

pre·dic·a·ment (pri·dik′ə·mənt) *n.* A trying or embarrassing situation; plight. [< LL *praedicare* to proclaim]

pred·i·cate (*v.* pred′i·kāt; *n.* pred′i·kit) *v.* **·cat·ed, ·cat·ing** *v.t.* 1. To found or base (an argument, proposition, etc.): with *on* or *upon.* 2. To affirm as a quality or attribute of something. —*v.i.* 3. To make a statement or affirmation. —*n. Gram.* The verb in a sentence or clause together with its complements and modifiers. [< L *praedicare* to proclaim] —**pred·i·ca′tion** *n.* —**pred′i·ca′tive** *adj.* —**pred′i·ca′tive·ly** *adv.*

pre·dict (pri·dikt′) *v.t.* 1. To make known beforehand; prophesy. 2. To assert on the basis of data, theory, or experience but in advance of proof. —*v.i.* 3. To make a prediction. [< L *prae-* before + *dicere* to say]

—**pre·dict′a·ble** *adj.* —**pre·dict′a·bly** *adv.* —**pre·dic′tor** *n.*

pre·dic·tion (pri·dik′shən) *n.* 1. The act of predicting. 2. Something predicted. —**pre·dic′tive** *adj.* —**pre·dic′tive·ly** *adv.*

pre·di·gest (prē′di·jest′, -dī-) *v.t.* To treat (food) by a process of partial digestion before introduction into the stomach. —**pre′di·ges′tion** *n.*

pre·di·lec·tion (pred′ə·lek′shən, prē′də-) *n.* A preference or bias in favor of something; a partiality: with *for.* [< L *prae-* before + *diligere* to love, choose]

pre·dis·pose (prē′dis·pōz′) *v.t.* ·**posed,** ·**pos·ing** To give a tendency or inclination to; make susceptible.

pre·dom·i·nant (pri·dom′ə·nənt) *adj.* Superior in power, influence, effectiveness, number, or degree. —**pre·dom′i·nance, pre·dom′i·nan·cy** *n.* —**pre·dom′i·nant·ly** *adv.*

pre·dom·i·nate (pri·dom′ə·nāt) *v.i.* ·**nat·ed,** ·**nat·ing** 1. To have governing influence or control; be in control: often with *over.* 2. To be superior to all others. 3. To prevail. —**pre·dom′i·na′tion** *n.*

pre·em·i·nent (prē·em′ə·nənt) *adj.* Distinguished above all others; outstanding. [< L *prae-* before + *eminere* to stand out] —**pre·em′i·nence** *n.* —**pre·em′i·nent·ly** *adv.*

pre·empt (prē·empt′) *v.t.* 1. To acquire or appropriate beforehand. 2. To occupy (public land) so as to acquire by preemption. 3. To take the place of; replace. —**pre·emp′tor** *n.* —**pre·emp′to·ry** *adj.*

pre·emp·tion (prē·emp′shən) *n.* 1. The right to purchase something before others; also, the act of so purchasing. 2. Public land obtained by exercising this right. [< L *prae-* before + *emptus,* pp. of *emere* to buy] —**pre·emp′tive** *adj.*

preen (prēn) *v.t.* 1. To trim and dress (feathers, etc.) with the beak, as a bird. 2. To dress or adorn (oneself) carefully. 3. To pride or congratulate (oneself): with *on.* —*v.i.* 4. To primp. [ME *prene*]

pre·ex·ist (prē′ig·zist′) *v.t.* & *v.i.* To exist before. —**pre′ex·is′tence** *n.* —**pre′ex·is′tent** *adj.*

pre·fab (prē′fab′) *n.* A prefabricated structure or part.

pre·fab·ri·cate (prē·fab′rə·kāt) *v.t.* ·**cat·ed,** ·**cat·ing** To manufacture in standard sections that can be rapidly assembled. —**pre·fab′ri·ca′tion** *n.*

pref·ace (pref′is) *n.* 1. A statement or brief essay, included in the front matter of a book, etc., and dealing primarily with the purpose and scope of the work. 2. Any introductory speech, writing, etc. —*v.t.* ·**aced,** ·**ac·ing** 1. To furnish with a preface. 2. To serve as a preface for. [< L *prae-* before + *fari* to speak] —**pref·a·to·ry** (pref′ə·tôr′ē) *adj.*

pre·fect (prē′fekt) *n.* 1. In ancient Rome, any of various civil and military officials. 2. Any magistrate, chief official, etc. [< L *praeficere* to set over] —**pre·fec·ture** (prē′·fek·chər) *n.*

pre·fer (pri·fûr′) *v.t.* ·**ferred,** ·**fer·ring** 1. To hold in higher regard or esteem; value more. 2. To choose (something or someone) over another or others; like better. 3. To give priority to, as certain securities over others. [< L *prae-* before + *erre* to carry] —**pre·fer′rer** *n.*

pref·er·a·ble (pref′ər·ə·bəl) *adj.* That is preferred; more desirable. —**pref′er·a·ble·ness, pref′er·a·bil′i·ty** *n.* —**pref′er·a·bly** *adv.*

pref·er·ence (pref′ər·əns) *n.* 1. The choosing of one person or thing over another or others; also, the privilege of so choosing. 2. One who or that which is preferred. 3. The granting of special advantage to one over others.

pref·er·en·tial (pref′ə·ren′shəl) *adj.* 1. Showing or arising from preference or partiality. 2. Giving preference, as in tariffs. —**pref′er·en′tial·ism** *n.* —**pref′er·en′tial·ly** *adv.*

pre·fer·ment (pri·fûr′mənt) *n.* 1. The act of promoting to higher office; advancement. 2. A position, rank, or office of social prestige or profit. 3. The act of preferring.

preferred stock Stock on which dividends must be paid before dividends can be paid on common stocks, usu. also receiving preference in the distribution of assets on liquidation.

pre·fig·ure (prē·fig′yər) *v.t.* ·**ured,** ·**ur·ing** 1. To serve as an indication or suggestion of; foreshadow. 2. To imagine or picture to oneself beforehand. [< L *prae-* before + *figurare* to form] —**pre·fig′ur·a′tion** *n.*

pre·fix (*n.* prē′fiks; *v.* prē·fiks′) *n. Gram.* An addition at the beginning of a word, altering or modifying its meaning, as *re-* in *renew.* —*v.t.* To put or attach before or at the beginning; add as a prefix. [< L *prae-* before + *figere* to fasten, fix]

preg·na·ble (preg′nə·bəl) *adj.* 1. Capable of being captured, as a fort. 2. Open to attack; vulnerable; assailable. [< L *prehendere* to seize] —**preg′na·bil′i·ty** *n.*

preg·nan·cy (preg′nən·sē) *n. pl.* ·**cies** 1. The state of being pregnant. 2. An instance of being pregnant.

preg·nant (preg′nənt) *adj.* 1. Carrying a growing fetus in the uterus. 2. Having considerable weight or significance; full of meaning. [< L *prae-* before + *gnasci* to be born] —**preg′nant·ly** *adv.*

pre·hen·sile (pri·hen′sil) *adj.* Adapted for grasping or holding, as the tail of a monkey. [See PREHENSION.] —**pre·hen·sil·i·ty** (prē′·hen·sil′ə·tē) *n.*

pre·hen·sion (pri·hen′shən) *n.* The act of grasping, physically or mentally. [< L *prehendere* to seize]

pre·his·tor·ic (prē′his·tôr′ik, -tor′-) *adj.* Of or belonging to the period before written history. Also **pre′his·tor′i·cal.** —**pre′his·tor′i·cal·ly** *adv.*

pre·his·to·ry (prē·his′tə·rē) *n. pl.* ·**ries** The history of mankind in the period preceding written records.

pre·judge (prē·juj′) *v.t.* ·**judged,** ·**judg·ing** To judge beforehand or without proper inquiry. —**pre·judg′er** *n.* —**pre·judg′ment** or **pre·judge′ment** *n.*

prej·u·dice (prej′o͞o·dis) *n.* 1. A judgment or opinion formed before the facts are known; esp., an unfavorable, irrational opinion. 2. Hatred of or dislike for a particular group, race, religion, etc. 3. Injury or damage to a person arising from a hasty and unfair judgment by others. —*v.t.* ·**diced,** ·**dic·ing** 1. To cause to have a prejudice; bias; influence. 2. To damage or impair by some act, judgment, etc. [< L *prae-* before + *judicium* judgment]

prej·u·di·cial (prej′o͞o·dish′əl) *adj.* Tending to prejudice or injure; detrimental. **—prej′u·di′cial·ly** *adv.*

prel·ate (prel′it) *n.* An ecclesiastic of high rank, as a bishop, archbishop, etc. [< L *praelatus* set over] **—prel′a·cy** *n.*

pre·lim·i·nar·y (pri·lim′ə·ner′ē) *adj.* Before or introductory to the main event, proceeding, or business. **—***n. pl.* **·nar·ies** 1. A preparatory step or act. 2. A preliminary examination. 3. In sports, a minor, introductory event, as a boxing match. [< L *prae-* before + *limen, liminis* threshold] **—pre·lim′i·nar′i·ly** *adv.*

prel·ude (prel′yo͞od, prē′lo͞od, prā′lo͞od) *n.* 1. *Music* **a** An instrumental composition of moderate length, in a free style. **b** An opening section or movement of a musical composition. 2. Any introductory or opening performance or event. **—***v.t.* **·ud·ed, ·ud·ing** 1. To introduce with a prelude. 2. To serve as a prelude to. [< L *prae-* before + *ludere* to play] **—pre·lud·er** (prē·lo͞o′dər, prā-, prel′yə·dər) *n.*

pre·ma·ture (prē′mə·cho͝or′, -to͝or′, -tyo͝or′) *adj.* Existing, happening, or developed before the natural or proper period; untimely. [< L *prae-* before + *maturus* ripe] **—pre′ma·ture′ly** *adv.* **—pre′ma·ture′ness, pre′ma·tu′ri·ty** *n.*

pre·med·i·cal (prē·med′i·kəl) *adj.* Preparatory to or preparing for the study of medicine. Also *Informal* **pre′med′.**

pre·med·i·tate (prē·med′ə·tāt) *v.t. & v.i.* **·tat·ed, ·tat·ing** To plan or consider beforehand. [< L *prae-* before + *meditari* to muse, ponder] **—pre·med′i·tat′ed·ly** *adv.* **—pre·med′i·ta′tion** *n.* **—pre·med′i·ta′tive** *adj.* **—pre·med′i·ta′tor** *n.*

pre·mi·er (pri·mir′, -myir′) *adj.* 1. First in rank or position; principal. 2. First in order of occurrence; senior. **—***n.* Prime minister. [< L *primus* first] **—pre·mi·er′ship** *n.*

pre·mière (pri·mir′, *Fr.* prə·myâr′) *n.* The first performance of a play, movie, etc. **—***v.t. & v.i.* **·mièred, ·mièr·ing** To give the first performance of (a play, movie, etc.). Also **pre·miere′.** [< F, fem. of *premier* first]

prem·ise (prem′is; *for v., also* pri·mīz′) *n.* 1. A proposition that serves as a ground for argument or for a conclusion. 2. *pl.* A definite portion of real estate; land with its appurtenances; also, a building or part of a building. **—***v.* **·mised, ·mis·ing** *v.t.* 1. To state or assume as a premise or basis of argument. **—***v.i.* 2. To make a premise. [< L *prae-* before + *mittere* to send]

pre·mi·um (prē′mē·əm) *n.* 1. An object or service offered free as an inducement to buy, rent, or contract for another object or service. 2. The amount paid or payable for insurance, usu. in periodical installments. 3. An extra amount or bonus paid in addition to a fixed price, wage, etc. 4. High regard or value. 5. A reward or prize awarded in a competition. **—at a premium** 1. Valuable and in demand. 2. Above par. [< L *prae-* before + *emere* to take]

pre·mo·lar (prē·mō′lər) *adj.* Situated in front of the molar teeth. **—pre·mo′lar** *n.*

pre·mo·ni·tion (prē′mə·nish′ən, prem′ə-) *n.* 1. A presentiment of the future not based on information received; an instinctive foreboding. 2. A warning of something yet to occur. [< LL *prae-* before + *monere* to advise] **—pre·mon·i·to·ry** (pri·mon′ə·tôr′ē) *adj.* **—pre·mon′i·to′ri·ly** *adv.*

pre·na·tal (prē·nāt′l) *adj.* Prior to birth: *prenatal* care. **—pre·na′tal·ly** *adv.*

pre·oc·cu·pied (prē·ok′yə·pīd) *adj.* 1. Engrossed in thought or in some action. 2. Previously occupied.

pre·oc·cu·py (prē·ok′yə·pī) *v.t.* **·pied, ·py·ing** 1. To engage fully; engross the mind. 2. To occupy or take possession of first. [< L *praeoccupare* to seize beforehand] **—pre·oc′u·pan·cy** (-pən·sē), **pre·oc′cu·pa′tion** *n.*

pre·or·dain (prē′ôr·dān′) *v.t.* To ordain beforehand; foreordain. **—pre′or·di·na′tion** (-də·nā′shən) *n.*

prep (prep) *Informal adj.* Preparatory: a *prep* school. **—***v.t.* **prepped, prep·ping** To prepare for an examination, for surgery, etc.

prep·a·ra·tion (prep′ə·rā′shən) *n.* 1. The act or process of preparing. 2. An act or proceeding undertaken in advance of some event; provision. 3. The fact or state of being prepared. 4. Something made or prepared, as a medicine.

preparatory school A private school that prepares students for college admission: also **prep school.**

pre·pare (pri·pâr′) *v.* **·pared, ·par·ing** *v.t.* 1. To make ready, fit, or qualified; put in readiness. 2. To provide with what is needed; equip: to *prepare* an expedition. 3. To bring to a state of completeness: to *prepare* a meal. **—***v.i.* 4. To make preparations; get ready. [< L *prae-* before + *parare* to produce] **—pre·par·a·to·ry** (pri·par′ə·tôr′ē) *adj.* **—pre·par′ed·ly** *adv.* **—pre·par′er** *n.*

pre·par·ed·ness (pri·pâr′id·nis, -pârd′-) *n.* Readiness; esp., military readiness for war.

pre·pay (prē·pā′) *v.t.* **·paid, ·pay·ing** To pay or pay for in advance. **—pre·pay′ment** *n.*

pre·pon·der·ant (pri·pon′dər·ənt) *adj.* Having superior force, weight, importance, quantity, etc. **—pre·pon′der·ance, pre·pon′der·an·cy** *n.* **—pre·pon′der·ant·ly** *adv.*

pre·pon·der·ate (pri·pon′də·rāt) *v.i.* **·at·ed, ·at·ing** To be of greater power, importance, quantity, etc.; predominate; prevail. [< L *prae-* before + *ponderare* to weigh] **—pre·pon′der·a′tion** *n.*

prep·o·si·tion (prep′ə·zish′ən) *n. Gram.* In some languages, a word, as *by, for, from,* that combines with a noun to form an adjectival or adverbial modifier. [< L *prae-* before + *ponere* to place] **—prep′o·si′tion·al** *adj.* **—prep′o·si′tion·al·ly** *adv.*

pre·pos·sess (prē′pə·zes′) *v.t.* 1. To preoccupy to the exclusion of other ideas, beliefs, etc. 2. To impress or influence beforehand or at once, esp. favorably. **—pre′pos·ses′sion** *n.*

pre·pos·sess·ing (prē′pə·zes′ing) *adj.* Inspiring a favorable opinion; pleasing. **—pre′pos·sess′ing·ly** *adv.*

pre·pos·ter·ous (pri·pos′tər·əs) *adj.* Contrary to nature or common sense; utterly absurd. [< L *prae-* before + *posterus* last] **—pre·pos′ter·ous·ly** *adv.* **—pre·pos′ter·ous·ness** *n.*

pre·puce (prē′pyo͞os) *n. Anat.* The fold of skin covering the glans of the penis or clitoris: also called *foreskin.* [< L *praeputium*] **—pre·pu·tial** (pri·pyo͞o′shəl) *adj.*

pre·req·ui·site (prē·rek′wə·zit) *adj.* Required for something that follows. —*n.* Something prerequisite.

pre·rog·a·tive (pri·rog′ə·tiv) *n.* An exclusive and unquestionable right belonging to a person or body of persons; esp., a hereditary or official right. [< L *prae-* before + *rogare* to ask]

pres·age (*n.* pres′ij; *v.* pri·sāj′) *n.* 1. An indication of something to come; omen. 2. A presentiment; foreboding. —*v.* **·saged, ·sag·ing** *v.t.* 1. To give a presage or portent of; foreshadow. 2. To predict; foretell. —*v.i.* 3. To make a prediction. [< L *prae-* before + *sagire* to perceive keenly] —**pre·sag′er** *n.*

pres·by·ter (prez′bə·tər, pres′-) *n.* *Eccl.* 1. In various hierarchical churches, a priest. 2. In the Presbyterian church: **a** An ordained clergyman. **b** A layman who is a member of the governing body of a congregation. [< Gk. *presbyteros* elder] —**pres′by·te′ri·al** (-tir′ē·əl) *adj.* —**pres′by·te′ri·al·ly** *adv.*

Pres·by·te·ri·an (prez′bə·tir′ē·ən, pres′-) *adj.* Pertaining to any of various Protestant churches that have church government by presbyters. —**Pres′by·te′ri·an** *n.* —**Pres′by·te′ri·an·ism** *n.*

pres·by·ter·y (prez′bə·ter′ē, pres′-) *n.* *pl.* **·ter·ies** 1. In the Presbyterian church, a court composed of the ministers and one or two presbyters of each church in a district. 2. That part of a church set apart for the clergy. [< LL *presbyterium* assembly of elders]

pre·school (prē′skōōl′) *adj.* Of, intended for, or designating a child past infancy but under school age.

pre·sci·ence (prē′shē·əns, presh′ē-) *n.* Knowledge of events before they take place; foreknowledge. [< L *prae-* before + *scire* to know] —**pre′sci·ent** *adj.* —**pre′sci·ent·ly** *adv.*

pre·scribe (pri·skrīb′) *v.* **·scribed, ·scrib·ing** *v.t.* 1. To set down as a direction or rule to be followed. 2. *Med.* To order the use of (a medicine, treatment, etc.). —*v.i.* 3. To lay down laws or rules; give directions. [< L *prae-* before + *scribere* to write] —**pre·scrib′er** *n.* —**pre·scrip′tive** (-skrip′tiv) *adj.*

pre·scrip·tion (pri·skrip′shən) *n.* 1. *Med.* **a** A physician's order for a medicine, including directions for its use. **b** The remedy so prescribed. 2. The act of prescribing. 3. That which is prescribed.

pres·ence (prez′əns) *n.* 1. The state or fact of being present. 2. The area immediately surrounding a person, esp. one of superior rank, as a sovereign; also, the person or personality of a sovereign, ruler, etc. 3. Personal appearance; esp., a pleasing or dignified bearing. 4. An invisible spirit or influence felt to be near.

pres·ent[1] (prez′ənt) *adj.* 1. Now going on; not past or future. 2. Of or pertaining to time now occurring; current. 3. Being in the place or company referred to. 4. Being actually considered, written, discussed, etc.: the *present* issue. 5. *Gram.* Denoting a tense or verb form that expresses a current or habitual action or state. —*n.* 1. Present time; the time being; now. 2. *Gram.* The present tense. —**at present** Now. [< L *praeesse* to be before]

pre·sent[2] (*v.* pri·zent′; *n.* prez′ənt) *v.t.* 1. To bring into the presence or acquaintance of another; introduce, esp. to one of higher rank. 2. To exhibit to view or notice. 3. To suggest to the mind: This *presents* a problem. 4. To put forward for consideration or action; submit, as a petition. 5. To make a gift or presentation of or to, usu. formally. —**to present arms** *Mil.* To salute by holding a gun vertically in front of one's body with the muzzle up and the trigger facing forward. —*n.* Something presented or given; a gift. [< OF *presenter*] —**pre·sent′er** *n.*

pre·sent·a·ble (pri·zen′tə·bəl) *adj.* 1. Fit to be presented; in suitable condition or attire for company. 2. Capable of being offered, exhibited, or bestowed. —**pre·sent′a·bil′i·ty, pre·sent′a·ble·ness** *n.* —**pre·sent′a·bly** *adv.*

pres·en·ta·tion (prez′ən·tā′shən, prē′zən-) *n.* 1. The act of presenting or proffering for acceptance, approval, etc., or the state of being presented. 2. An exhibition or representation, as of a play.

pres·ent-day (prez′ənt·dā′) *adj.* Modern; current.

pre·sen·ti·ment (pri·zen′tə·mənt) *n.* A prophetic sense of something to come; a foreboding. [< L *prae-* before + *sentire* to perceive]

pres·ent·ly (prez′ənt·lē) *adv.* 1. After a little time; shortly. 2. At the present time; now.

pre·sent·ment (pri·zent′mənt) *n.* The act of presenting; also, the state or manner of being presented or exhibited.

present participle See under PARTICIPLE.

pre·ser·va·tive (pri·zûr′və·tiv) *adj.* Serving or tending to preserve. —*n.* A preservative agent; esp., a chemical substance added to food to retard spoilage.

pre·serve (pri·zûrv′) *v.* **·served, ·serv·ing** *v.t.* 1. To keep in safety; guard: May the gods *preserve* you. 2. To keep intact or unimpaired; maintain. 3. To prepare (food) for future consumption, as by boiling with sugar or by salting. 4. To keep from decomposition or change, as by chemical treatment. —*v.i.* 5. To make preserves, as of fruit. —*n.* 1. *Usu. pl.* Fruit that has been cooked, usu. with sugar, to prevent its fermenting. 2. An area set apart for the protection of wildlife, forests, etc. [< L *prae-* before + *servare* to keep] —**pre·serv′a·bil′i·ty** *n.* —**pre·serv′a·ble** *adj.* —**pres·er·va·tion** (prez′ər·vā′shən) *n.* —**pre·serv′er** *n.*

pre-shrunk (prē′shrungk′) *adj.* Shrunk during manufacture to minimize later shrinkage during washing or cleaning.

pre·side (pri·zīd′) *v.i.* **·sid·ed, ·sid·ing** 1. To sit in authority, as over a meeting; act as chairman or president. 2. To exercise direction or control. [< L *prae-* before + *sedere* to sit] —**pre·sid′er** *n.*

pres·i·den·cy (prez′ə·dən·sē) *n.* *pl.* **·cies** The office, function, or term of office of a president.

pres·i·dent (prez′ə·dənt) *n.* 1. One who is chosen to preside over an organized body. 2. *Often cap.* The chief executive of a republic. 3. The chief executive officer of a government department, corporation, society, or similar body. [See PRESIDE.] —**pres′i·den′tial** (-den′shəl) *adj.* —**pres′i·dent·ship′** *n.*

pre·sid·i·o (pri·sid′ē·ō) *n.* *pl.* **·sid·i·os**

A garrisoned post; fortified settlement. [< Am.Sp.]

pre·sid·i·um (pri·sid′ē·əm) *n. pl.* **·i·a, ·i·ums** *Often cap.* An executive committee in a Communist country that acts for a larger governmental body.

press[1] (pres) *v.t.* **1.** To act upon by weight or pressure: to *press* a button. **2.** To compress so as to extract the juice: to *press* grapes. **3.** To exert pressure upon so as to smooth, shape, make compact, etc. **4.** To smooth or shape by heat and pressure, as clothes; iron. **5.** To embrace closely; hug. **6.** To distress or harass; place in difficulty. **7.** To urge persistently; entreat: They *pressed* me for an answer. **8.** To put forward insistently: to *press* a claim. **9.** To produce (a phonograph record) from a matrix. —*v.i.* **10.** To exert pressure; bear heavily. **11.** To advance forcibly or with speed. **12.** To crowd; cram. **13.** To be urgent or importunate. —*n.* **1.** Newspapers or periodicals collectively, or the persons concerned with such publications, as editors, reporters, etc. **2.** Criticism, news, etc., in newspapers and periodicals. **3.** The place of business where printing is carried on. **4.** A printing press. **5.** An apparatus by which pressure is applied, as for crushing grapes. **6.** The act of crowding together. **7.** Hurry or pressures of affairs. **8.** The proper creases in a pressed garment. **9.** A movable upright closet. [< L *pressare*, freq. of *premere* to press] —**press′er** *n.*

press[2] (pres) *v.t.* To force into military or naval service. [< L *prae-* before + *stare* to stand]

press agent A person employed to advance the interests of another by means of publicity.

press conference An interview granted by a celebrity, official, etc., to a number of journalists at the same time.

press·ing (pres′ing) *adj.* Demanding immediate attention; urgent. —**press′ing·ly** *adv.*

press·man (pres′mən) *n. pl.* **·men** (-mən) **1.** One in charge of a press, as a printing press. **2.** *Brit.* A journalist.

press release A bulletin prepared by a public relations department, etc., announcing an event, decision, etc.

pres·sure (presh′ər) *n.* **1.** The act of pressing, or the state of being pressed. **2.** Any force that acts against an opposing force. **3.** Urgent demands on one's time or strength. **4.** The oppressive influence or depressing effect of something hard to bear; weight. **5.** *Physics* The force acting upon a surface per unit of area. —*v.t.* **·sured, ·sur·ing** *Informal* To compel, as by forceful persuasion. [See PRESS[1].]

pressure cabin *Aeron.* An enclosed compartment in an aircraft in which air is pressurized.

pressure cooker A strong, airtight pot for cooking food at high temperature under pressure.

pressure group A group that seeks to influence legislators and public opinion in behalf of its own special interests.

pres·sur·ize (presh′ər·īz) *v.t.* **·ized, ·iz·ing** **1.** To subject to high pressure. **2.** To establish normal atmospheric pressure (in an aircraft, etc.) when at high altitudes. —**pres′sur·i·za′tion** *n.*

pres·ti·dig·i·ta·tion (pres′tə·dij′ə·tā′shən) *n.* The practice of sleight of hand. [< LL *praestus* nimble + *digitus* finger] —**pres′ti·dig′i·ta′tor** *n.*

pres·tige (pres·tēzh′, pres·tēj′) *n.* Authority or importance based on past achievements, reputation, power, etc. [< L *praestigium* illusion]

pres·tig·ious (pres·tij′əs, -tē′jəs) *adj.* Having prestige; honored or well-known; illustrious. —**pres·tig′ious·ly** *adv.* —**pres·tig′ious·ness** *n.*

pres·to (pres′tō) *adj. Music* Quick; faster than allegro. —*adv.* **1.** *Music* In a presto manner. **2.** At once; speedily. —*n. Music* A presto movement or passage. [< Ital.]

pre·stressed concrete (prē′strest′) Concrete containing steel cables under tension to increase its strength and counteract external stresses.

pre·sum·a·ble (pri·zōō′mə·bəl) *adj.* That may be assumed; reasonable. —**pre·sum′a·bly** *adv.*

pre·sume (pri·zōōm′) *v.* **·sumed, ·sum·ing** *v.t.* **1.** To assume to be true until disproved. **2.** To take upon oneself without permission; venture: usu. with *to*. **3.** To indicate the probability of: A concealed weapon *presumes* the intent to commit a crime. —*v.i.* **4.** To act presumptuously or overconfidently. [< L *prae-* before + *sumere* to take] —**pre·sum′ed·ly** *adv.* —**pre·sum′er** *n.*

pre·sump·tion (pri·zump′shən) *n.* **1.** Offensively forward or arrogant conduct or speech; insolence. **2.** The act of presuming; also, something presumed. **3.** That which may be logically assumed true until disproved. **4.** *Law* The inference of a fact from circumstances that usually or necessarily attend such a fact.

pre·sump·tive (pri·zump′tiv) *adj.* **1.** Creating or affording reasonable grounds for belief. **2.** Based upon presumption: an heir *presumptive*. —**pre·sump′tive·ly** *adv.*

pre·sump·tu·ous (pri·zump′chōō·əs) *adj.* Unduly confident or bold; audacious; arrogant. —**pre·sump′tu·ous·ly** *adv.* —**pre·sump′tu·ous·ness** *n.*

pre·sup·pose (prē′sə·pōz′) *v.t.* **·posed, ·pos·ing** **1.** To assume beforehand. **2.** To imply as a necessary antecedent condition. —**pre·sup·po·si·tion** (prē′sup·ə·zish′ən) *n.*

pre·tend (pri·tend′) *v.t.* **1.** To assume or display a false appearance of; feign. **2.** To claim or assert falsely. **3.** To feign in play; make believe. —*v.i.* **4.** To make believe, as in play or deception. **5.** To put forward a claim: with *to*. [< L *prae-* before + *tendere* to spread out] —**pre·tend′ed** *adj.*

pre·tend·er (pri·ten′dər) *n.* **1.** One who advances a claim or title; a claimant to a throne. **2.** One who pretends.

pre·tense (pri·tens′, prē′tens) *n.* **1.** A pretended claim; pretext. **2.** A false assumption of a character or condition. **3.** The act or state of pretending. Also *Brit.* **pre·tence′**. —**pre·ten′sion** (-ten′shən) *n.*

pre·ten·tious (pri·ten′shəs) *adj.* **1.** Making an ambitious outward show; ostentatious. **2.** Making claims, esp. when exaggerated or false. [< F *prétentieux*] —**pre·ten′tious·ly** *adv.* —**pre·ten′tious·ness** *n.*

preter- *prefix* Beyond; past; more than: also spelled *praeter-*. [< L *praeter* beyond]

pret·er·it (pret′ər·it) *adj. Gram.* Signifying past time or completed past action. —*n.* The tense that expresses absolute past time; also, a verb in this tense. Also **pret′er·ite.** [< L *praeter-* beyond + *ire* to go]

pre·ter·nat·u·ral (prē′tər·nach′ər·əl) *adj.* 1. Diverging from or exceeding the common order of nature; unusual or abnormal. 2. Outside the natural order. **—pre′ter·nat′u·ral·ism** *n.* **—pre′ter·nat′u·ral·ly** *adv.*

pre·text (prē′tekst) *n.* 1. A fictitious reason or motive advanced to conceal a real one. 2. A specious excuse or explanation. [< L *prae-* before + *texere* to weave]

pre·tor (prē′tər), **pre·to·ri·an** (pri·tôr′ē·ən) See PRAETOR, etc.

pret·ti·fy (prit′i·fī) *v.t.* **·fied, ·fy·ing** To make pretty; embellish overmuch. **—pret′ti·fi·ca′tion** *n.* **—pret′ti·fi′er** *n.*

pret·ty (prit′ē) *adj.* **·ti·er, ·ti·est** 1. Characterized by delicacy, gracefulness, or proportion rather than by striking beauty. 2. Pleasant; attractive: a *pretty* melody. 3. *Informal* Rather large in size or degree; considerable. **—*adv.*** To a fair extent; rather: He looked *pretty* well. **—sitting pretty** *Informal* In good circumstances. **—*n.*** *pl.* **·ties** A pretty person or thing. [OE *prættig* sly, cunning] **—pret′ti·ly** *adv.* **—pret′ti·ness** *n.*

pret·zel (pret′səl) *n.* A glazed, salted biscuit, usu. baked in the form of a loose knot. [< G *brezel*]

pre·vail (pri·vāl′) *v.i.* 1. To gain mastery; triumph. 2. To be effective or efficacious. 3. To use persuasion or influence successfully: with *on*, *upon*, or *with*. 4. To be or become a predominant feature or quality; be prevalent. [< L *prae-* before + *valere* to be strong]

pre·vail·ing (pri·vā′ling) *adj.* 1. Current; prevalent. 2. Having effective power or influence; efficacious. **—pre·vail′ing·ly** *adv.* **—pre·vail′ing·ness** *n.*

prev·a·lent (prev′ə·lənt) *adj.* 1. Of wide extent or frequent occurrence; common. 2. Predominant; superior. **—prev′a·lence** *n.* **—prev′a·lent·ly** *adv.*

pre·var·i·cate (pri·var′ə·kāt) *v.i.* **·cat·ed, ·cat·ing** To speak or act in a deceptive or evasive manner; lie. [< L *prae-* before + *varicare* to straddle] **—pre·var′i·ca′tion** *n.* **—pre·var′i·ca′tor** *n.*

pre·vent (pri·vent′) *v.t.* 1. To keep from happening, as by previous preparations; preclude; thwart. 2. To keep from doing something; forestall; hinder. [< L *prae-* before + *venire* to come] **—pre·vent′a·ble** or **pre·vent′i·ble** *adj.* **—pre·vent′a·bil′i·ty** or **pre·vent′i·bil′i·ty** *n.* **—pre·vent′er** *n.* **—pre·ven′tion** *n.*

pre·ven·tive (pri·ven′tiv) *adj.* Intended or serving to ward off harm, disease, etc.: *preventive* medicine. **—*n.*** That which prevents or hinders. Also **pre·vent·a·tive** (pri·ven′tə·tiv). **—pre·ven′tive·ly** *adv.* **—pre·ven′tive·ness** *n.*

pre·view (prē′vyōō) *n.* 1. An advanced showing, as of a motion picture, esp. before public viewing. 2. A showing of scenes from a motion picture, television show, etc., as advertising: also **pre′vue.** 3. A preliminary view; foretaste. **—*v.t.*** To view in advance.

pre·vi·ous (prē′vē·əs) *adj.* 1. Existing or taking place before something else in time or order. 2. *Informal* Acting or occurring too soon; premature. **—previous to** Antecedent to; before. [< L *prae-* before + *via* way] **—pre′vi·ous·ly** *adv.* **—pre′vi·ous·ness** *n.*

pre·vi·sion (prē·vizh′ən) *n.* 1. The act or power of foreseeing; prescience; foresight. 2. An anticipatory vision.

prey (prā) *n.* 1. Any animal seized by another for food. 2. A victim of a harmful or hostile person or influence. **—*v.i.*** 1. To seek or take prey for food. 2. To make someone a victim, as by cheating. 3. To exert a wearing or harmful influence. Usu. with *on* or *upon*. [< L *praeda* booty] **—prey′er** *n.*

price (prīs) *n.* 1. The amount of money, goods, etc., for which something is bought or sold. 2. The cost at which something is obtained. 3. Value; worth. 4. A reward for the capture or death of someone. **—*v.t.*** **priced, pric·ing** 1. To set a price on; establish a price for. 2. *Informal* To ask the price of. [< L *pretium*]

price fixing 1. The establishment and maintenance of a scale of prices by specified groups of producers or distributors. 2. The establishing by law of maximum or minimum or fixed prices for certain goods and services. **—price′-fix·ing** (prīs′fik′sing) *adj.*

price·less (prīs′lis) *adj.* 1. Beyond price or valuation; invaluable. 2. *Informal* Wonderfully amusing or absurd.

prick (prik) *v.t.* 1. To pierce slightly, as with a sharp point; puncture. 2. To affect with a sharp mental sting; spur. 3. To outline or indicate by punctures. 4. To urge on with or as with a spur; goad. **—*v.i.*** 5. To have or cause a stinging or piercing sensation. **—to prick up one's (or its) ears** 1. To raise the ears erect. 2. To listen attentively. **—*n.*** 1. The act of pricking; also, the sensation of being pricked. 2. A mental sting or spur. 3. A slender, sharp-pointed thing, as a thorn or weapon. [OE *prica* point, dot] **—prick′er** *n.*

prick·le (prik′əl) *n.* 1. A small, sharp point, as on a plant. 2. A tingling or stinging sensation. **—*v.*** **·led, ·ling** *v.t.* 1. To prick; pierce. 2. To cause a tingling or stinging sensation in. **—*v.i.*** 3. To have a stinging sensation; tingle. [OE *pricel*]

prick·ly (prik′lē) *adj.* 1. Furnished with prickles. 2. Stinging, as if from a prick or sting.

prickly heat A rash characterized by redness, itching, and small eruptions.

prickly pear 1. A flat-stemmed cactus bearing a prickly pear-shaped fruit. 2. The fruit itself.

pride (prīd) *n.* 1. An undue sense of one's own superiority; arrogance; conceit. 2. A proper sense of personal dignity and worth. 3. That of which one is justly proud. 4. The best time or the flowering of something: the *pride* of summer. 5. A group or company: said of lions. **—*v.t.*** **prid·ed, prid·ing** To take pride in (oneself) for something: with *on* or *upon*. [OE *prūt* proud]

pride·ful (prīd′fəl) *adj.* Full of pride; haughty; disdainful.

prie-dieu (prē·dyœ′) *n.* A small desk with a shelf for a book, at which to kneel at prayers. [< F, pray God]

pri·er (prī′ər) *n.* One who pries: also spelled *pryer*.

priest (prēst) *n.* 1. One consecrated to the service of a divinity, and serving as mediator between the divinity and his worshipers.

2. In the Anglican, Greek, and Roman Catholic churches, a clergyman ranking next below a bishop, and having authority to administer the sacraments. [< L *presbyter*] **—priest′ess** *n.fem.* **—priest′li·ness** *n.* **—priest′ly** *adj.*

priest·hood (prēst′hŏŏd) *n.* 1. The priestly office or character. 2. Priests collectively.

prig (prig) *n.* A formal and narrow-minded person who assumes superior virtue and wisdom. [Origin uncertain] **—prig′gish** *adj.* **—prig′gish·ly** *adv.* **—prig′gish·ness** *n.*

prim (prim) *adj.* Minutely or affectedly precise and formal; stiffly proper and neat. **—***v.t.* **primmed, prim·ming** To fix (the face, mouth, etc.) in a precise or prim expression. [Origin uncertain] **—prim′ly** *adv.* **—prim′ness** *n.*

pri·ma·cy (prī′mə·sē) *n. pl.* **·cies** 1. The state of being first, as in rank or excellence. 2. The office or province of a primate; archbishopric: also **pri′mate·ship** (-mit·ship). 3. In the Roman Catholic Church, the office of the Pope. [< LL *primas, primatis* one of the first]

pri·ma don·na (prē′mə don′ə) 1. A leading female singer, as in an opera company. 2. *Informal* A temperamental or vain person. [< Ital., lit., first lady]

pri·ma fa·ci·e (prī′mə fā′shi·ē, fā′shē) *Latin* At first view; so far as at first appears. **—pri′ma-fa′ci·e** *adj.*

prima-facie evidence Evidence that, if unexplained or uncontradicted, would establish the fact alleged.

pri·mal (prī′məl) *adj.* 1. Being at the beginning or foundation; first; original. 2. Most important; chief. [< L *primus* first]

pri·ma·ri·ly (prī·mâr′ə·lē) *adv.* In the first place; originally; essentially.

pri·ma·ry (prī′mer·ē, -mər·ē) *adj.* 1. First in time or origin; primitive. 2. First in a series or sequence. 3. First in rank or importance; chief. 4. Constituting the fundamental or original elements of which a whole is composed; basic; elemental. 5. Of the first stage of development; elementary; lowest: *primary* school. **—***n. pl.* **·ries** 1. That which is first in rank, dignity, or importance. 2. *Usu. pl.* A direct primary election. 3. One of the primary colors. [< L *primus* first]

primary accent See under ACCENT.

primary cell *Electr.* Any of several devices consisting of two electrodes immersed in an electrolyte and capable of generating a current by chemical action when the electrodes are in contact through a conducting wire. Also called *voltaic cell.*

primary colors Any set of colors considered basic to all other colors, as red, yellow, and blue or red, green, and blue.

primary election A direct primary election.

primary school A school for very young pupils, usu. the first four grades of elementary school.

pri·mate (prī′mit, *esp. for def. 2* -māt) *n.* 1. The prelate highest in rank in a nation or province. 2. Any of an order of mammals including the monkeys, apes, and man. [< L *primus* first] **—pri·ma·tial** (prī·mā′·shəl) *adj.*

prime[1] (prīm) *adj.* 1. First in rank or importance. 2. First in value or quality; first-rate. 3. First in time or order; original; primitive. 4. *Math.* Divisible by no whole number except itself and 1. **—***n.* 1. The period of full vigor, beauty, and power succeeding youth and preceding age. 2. The period of full perfection in anything. 3. The beginning of anything; dawn. 4. The best of anything. 5. *Math.* A number that cannot be divided except by itself or by 1. 6. A mark or accent (′) written above and to the right of a letter or figure; also, an inch, a minute, etc., as indicated by that sign. **—***v.* **primed, prim·ing** *v.t.* 1. To prepare; make ready. 2. To put a primer into (a gun, etc.) preparatory to firing. 3. To pour water into (a pump) so as to displace air and promote suction. 4. To cover (a surface) with sizing, a first coat of paint, etc. 5. To supply beforehand with information; brief. **—***v.i.* 6. To make something ready, as for firing, pumping, etc. [< L *primus* first] **—prime′ly** *adv.* **—prime′·ness** *n.*

prime[2] (prīm) *n. Often cap. Eccl.* The second of the seven canonical hours. [< LL *prima (hora)* first (hour)]

prime meridian A meridian from which longitude is reckoned, now, generally, the one that passes through Greenwich, England.

prime minister The chief minister and head of a cabinet, and often the chief executive of a government.

prim·er[1] (prim′ər) *n.* 1. An elementary textbook; esp., a beginning reading book. 2. An introductory book on any subject. [< L *primus* first]

prim·er[2] (prī′mər) *n.* 1. Any device, as a cap, tube, etc., used to detonate the main charge of a gun, mine, etc. 2. Any substance used in priming, as the first layer of paint applied to a surface.

pri·me·val (prī·mē′vəl) *adj.* Belonging to the first ages; primitive. [< L *primus* first + *aevum* age] **—pri·me′val·ly** *adv.*

primi- *combining form* First. [< L *primus*]

prim·i·tive (prim′ə·tiv) *adj.* 1. Pertaining to the beginning or origin; earliest; primary. 2. Resembling the manners or style of early times; simple; crude. 3. *Anthropol.* Of or pertaining to the earliest anthropological forms or civilizations. 4. *Biol.* Being or occurring at an early stage of development or growth; rudimentary. **—***n.* 1. An artist, or a work of art, belonging to an early period; also, a work resembling such art, or an artist producing it. 2. One who or that which is primitive. [< L *primus* first] **—prim′i·tive·ly** *adv.* **—prim′i·tive·ness, prim′i·tiv′i·ty** *n.*

pri·mo·gen·i·tor (prī′mə·jen′ə·tər) *n.* An earliest ancestor; a forefather. [< L *primo* first + *genitor* father]

pri·mo·gen·i·ture (prī′mə·jen′ə·chər) *n.* 1. The state of being the first-born child. 2. The exclusive right of the eldest son to inherit the property, title, etc., of a parent. [< L *primo* first + *gignere* to beget]

pri·mor·di·al (prī·môr′dē·əl) *adj.* 1. First in time; original; elemental. 2. *Biol.* First in order or appearance in the growth or development of an organism. [< L *primus* first + *ordiri* to begin a web] **—pri·mor′di·al·ly** *adv.*

primp (primp) *v.t. & v.i.* To dress up, esp. with superfluous attention to detail.

prim·rose (prim′rōz) *n.* 1. A perennial herb with tufted leaves and variously colored flowers. 2. A pale yellow color. [ME *primerole*; infl. by ROSE[1]]

prince (prins) *n.* 1. A nonreigning male member of a royal family; esp., the son of a sovereign. 2. A male monarch or sovereign. 3. One of the highest rank of any class: a merchant *prince*. [< L *primus* first + stem of *capere* to take]

prince consort The husband of a reigning female sovereign.

prince·ling (prins′ling) *n.* A young or subordinate prince. Also **prince′let** (-lit).

prince·ly (prins′lē) *adj.* **·li·er, ·li·est** 1. Liberal; generous. 2. Like or suitable for a prince. 3. Having the rank of a prince. —*adv.* In a princely manner. —**prince′li·ness** *n.*

prin·cess (prin′sis, -ses) *n.* 1. A nonreigning female member of a royal family; esp., the daughter of a sovereign. 2. The consort of a prince.

prin·cesse (prin·ses′, prin′sis) *adj.* Designating a woman's close-fitting garment hanging in an unbroken line from shoulder to flared hem. Also **prin′cess.** [< F, princess]

princess royal The eldest daughter of a sovereign.

prin·ci·pal (prin′sə·pəl) *adj.* First in rank, character, or importance. —*n.* 1. One who takes a leading part in some action. 2. *Law* **a** The perpetrator of a crime, or one present aiding and abetting. **b** The employer of one who acts as an agent. **c** One primarily liable for whom another has become surety. 3. The head teacher, master, or officer of a school. 4. Property or capital, as opposed to interest or income. [< L *princeps* first, principal] —**prin′ci·pal·ly** *adv.* —**prin′ci·pal·ship′** *n.*

prin·ci·pal·i·ty (prin′sə·pal′ə·tē) *n. pl.* **·ties** The territory of a reigning prince.

principal parts The inflected forms of a verb.

prin·ci·ple (prin′sə·pəl) *n.* 1. A general truth or law, basic to other truths. 2. A rule of personal conduct. 3. Moral standards collectively: a man of *principle*. 4. A primary source or fundamental cause. 5. An established mode of action or operation in natural phenomena: the *principle* of relativity. [< L *principium* a beginning]

prin·ci·pled (prin′sə·pəld) *adj.* Having or characterized by ethical principles: often in combination: *high-principled*.

prink (pringk) *v.t.* & *v.i.* 1. To dress (oneself) for show. —**prink′er** *n.*

print (print) *n.* 1. An impression with ink from type, plates, etc.; printed characters collectively; also, any printed matter. 2. Anything printed from an engraved plate or lithographic stone. 3. A mark made by pressure; imprint. 4. Any fabric stamped with a design. 5. *Photog.* A positive picture made from a negative. —**in print** Printed; also, for sale in printed form. —**out of print** No longer on sale, the edition being exhausted: said of books, etc. —*v.t.* 1. To mark, as with inked type, a stamp, die, etc. 2. To fix as if by impressing: The scene is *printed* on my memory. 3. To produce (a book, newspaper, etc.) by the application of inked type, plates, etc., to paper or similar material. 4. To cause to be put in print; publish. 5. To write in letters similar to those used in print. 6. *Photog.* To produce (a positive picture) by transmitting light through a negative onto a sensitized surface. —*v.i.* 7. To take or give an impression in printing. 8. To form letters similar to printed ones. [< L *premere* to press] —**print′a·ble** *adj.* —**prin′ter** *n.*

printer's devil Devil (def. 7).

print·ing (prin′ting) *n.* 1. The making and issuing of printed matter. 2. The act of reproducing a design upon a surface. 3. The number of copies of anything printed at one time. 4. Writing that resembles printed matter.

printing press A mechanism for printing from an inked surface, operating by pressure.

print·out (print′out′) *n.* Material printed automatically, as by a computer.

pri·or[1] (prī′ər) *adj.* Preceding in time, order, or importance. —**prior to** Before. [< L, earlier, superior]

pri·or[2] (prī′ər) *n.* A monastic officer next in rank below an abbot. [< L] —**pri′or·ate** (-it) *n.*

pri·or·ess (prī′ər·is) *n.* A woman holding a position corresponding to that of a prior; a nun next below an abbess.

pri·or·i·ty (prī·ôr′ə·tē, -or′-) *n. pl.* **·ties** 1. Antecedence; precedence. 2. A first right established on emergency or need.

pri·or·y (prī′ər·ē) *n. pl.* **·or·ies** A monastic house presided over by a prior or prioress. [< Med.L *prioria*]

prism (priz′əm) *n.* 1. *Geom.* A solid whose ends are equal and parallel plane figures, and whose lateral faces are parallelograms. 2. *Optics* A transparent prism, usu. having triangular ends, used to produce a spectrum or to refract light beams. [< Gk. *prizein* to saw] —**pris·mat′ic** (-mat′ik) or **·i·cal** *adj.* —**pris·mat′i·cal·ly** *adv.*

pris·on (priz′ən) *n.* 1. A public building for the safekeeping of persons in legal custody; a penitentiary. 2. A place or state of confinement. [< OF *prisun* < L *prehendere* to seize]

pris·on·er (priz′ən·ər, priz′nər) *n.* One who is confined in a prison or whose liberty is forcibly restrained.

pris·sy (pris′ē) *Informal adj.* **·si·er, ·si·est** Effeminate; overprecise; prim. [Blend of PRIM or PRECISE + SISSY]

pris·tine (pris′tēn, -tin) *adj.* 1. Of or pertaining to the earliest state or time; primitive. 2. Extremely pure; untouched; unspoiled. [< L *pristinus* primitive]

prith·ee (prith′ē) *interj. Archaic* I pray thee.

pri·va·cy (prī′və·sē) *n. pl.* **·cies** 1. The condition of being private; seclusion. 2. The state of being secret; secrecy.

pri·vate (prī′vit) *adj.* 1. Removed from public view; secluded. 2. Not for public or common use. 3. Having no official rank, character, office, etc.: a *private* citizen. 4. Not generally known; secret. 5. Individual; personal: one's *private* opinion. —*n.* 1. *Mil.* An enlisted man or woman ranking below a corporal. 2. *pl.* The genitals. —**in private** In secret. [< L *privatus* apart from the state] —**pri′vate·ly** *adv.* —**pri′vate·ness** *n.*

private detective A detective employed by a private citizen, business enterprise, etc., rather than by a city or state.

pri·va·teer (prī′və·tir′) *n.* 1. A vessel owned and commanded by private persons, but carrying on maritime war under government authorization. 2. The commander or one of

the crew of a privateer. —*v.i.* To cruise in or as a privateer. —**pri′va·teer′ing** *n.*
private eye *Informal* A private detective.
private first class A soldier ranking next above a private and below a corporal.
pri·va·tion (prī·vā′shən) *n.* The state of lacking something necessary or desirable; esp., want of the common comforts of life. [< L *privare* to set apart] —**priv·a·tive** (priv′ə·tiv) *adj.*
priv·et (priv′it) *n.* An ornamental, bushy shrub of the olive family, with white flowers and black berries, used for hedges. [Earlier *primet*; origin unknown]
priv·i·lege (priv′ə·lij, priv′lij) *n.* 1. A special or peculiar benefit, favor, or advantage. 2. An exemption or immunity by virtue of one's office or station. 3. A fundamental civil, legal, or political right: the *privilege* of voting. —*v.t.* **·leged, ·leg·ing** To grant a privilege to. [< L *privus* one's own + *lex* law]
priv·i·leged (priv′ə·lijd, priv′lijd) *adj.* Having or enjoying a privilege.
priv·y (priv′ē) *adj.* Knowing about a secret transaction: with *to.* —*n. pl.* **priv·ies** 1. *Law* One who is concerned with another in a matter affecting the interests of both. 2. A small toilet or outhouse. [< L *privatus.* See PRIVATE] —**priv′i·ly** *adv.*
prix fixe (prē fēks′) A meal served at a fixed price. [< F, fixed price]
prize[1] (prīz) *n.* 1. That which is offered or won as a reward, as in a contest or lottery. 2. Anything to be striven for. —*adj.* 1. Offered or awarded as a prize: a *prize* medal. 2. Highly valued or esteemed. —*v.t.* **prized, priz·ing** 1. To value highly. 2. To estimate the value of; appraise. [Var. of PRICE]
prize[2] (prīz) *n.* Property, as a vessel and cargo, captured by a belligerent at sea. —*v.t.* **prized, priz·ing** 1. To seize as a prize, as a ship. 2. To raise or force with a lever; pry. [< F *prise* something taken, booty < L *prehendere* to seize]
prize fight A fight between professional boxers for a prize. —**prize fighter** —**prize fighting**
pro[1] (prō) *n. pl.* **pros** 1. An argument or vote in favor of something. 2. *Usu. pl.* One who votes for or favors a proposal. —*adv.* In behalf of; in favor of; for. [< L, for]
pro[2] (prō) *n. pl.* **pros** *Informal* 1. A professional athlete. 2. An expert in any field.
pro-[1] *prefix* 1. Forward; toward the front from a position behind: *project.* 2. Forward in time or direction: *proceed.* 3. In behalf of: *prolocutor.* 4. In place of; substituted for: *proconsul.* 5. In favor of: *pro-Russian.* [< L *pro* before, forward, for]
pro-[2] *prefix* 1. Prior; occurring earlier in time: *prognosis.* 2. Situated in front; forward; before: *prognathous.* [< Gk. *pro* before, in front]
prob·a·bil·i·ty (prob′ə·bil′ə·tē) *n. pl.* **·ties** 1. The state or quality of being probable; likelihood. 2. A probable event, statement, condition, etc.
prob·a·ble (prob′ə·bəl) *adj.* 1. Likely to be true or to happen, but leaving room for doubt. 2. That renders something worthy of belief, but falls short of demonstration: *probable* evidence. [< L *probare* to prove, test]
prob·a·bly (prob′ə·blē) *adv.* In all probability.
pro·bate (prō′bāt) *adj.* 1. Of or pertaining to a probate court. 2. Pertaining to making proof. —*v.t.* **·bat·ed, ·bat·ing** To establish legal proof of, as a will. [< L *probare* to prove]
probate court A court having jurisdiction of the proof of wills, of guardianships, and of the settlement of estates.
pro·ba·tion (prō·bā′shən) *n.* 1. *Law* A method of allowing a convicted person to go at large but usu. under supervision. 2. A proceeding or period designed to test character, qualifications, etc., as of a new employee. —**pro·ba′tion·al, pro·ba′tion·ar′y** *adj.*
pro·ba·tion·er (prō·bā′shən·ər) *n.* One on probation.
pro·ba·tive (prō′bə·tiv) *adj.* 1. Serving to prove or test. 2. Pertaining to probation; proving. Also **pro′ba·to′ry.**
probe (prōb) *v.* **probed, prob·ing** *v.t.* 1. To explore with a probe. 2. To investigate or examine thoroughly. —*v.i.* 3. To penetrate; search. —*n.* 1. *Surg.* An instrument for exploring cavities, wounds, etc. 2. A searching investigation or inquiry, esp. into crime. [< LL *proba* proof] —**prob′er** *n.*
pro·bi·ty (prō′bə·tē, prob′ə-) *n.* Virtue or integrity; honesty. [< L *probus* good, honest]
prob·lem (prob′ləm) *n.* 1. A perplexing question or situation, esp. when difficult or uncertain of solution. 2. Any puzzling or difficult circumstance or person. [< Gk. *pro-* forward + *ballein* to throw] —**prob′lem** *adj.*
prob·lem·at·ic (prob′ləm·at′ik) *adj.* Constituting or involving a problem; questionable; contingent. Also **prob′lem·at′i·cal.** —**prob′lem·at′i·cal·ly** *adv.*
pro·bos·cis (prō·bos′is) *n. pl.* **·bos·cis·es** or **·bos·ci·des** (-bos′ə·dēz) *Zool.* **a** A long, flexible snout, as of the tapir. **b** The trunk of an elephant. [< Gk. *pro-* before + *boskein* to feed]
pro·caine (prō·kān′, prō′kān) *n.* A white crystalline compound, used as a local anesthetic. [< PRO-[1] + (CO)CAINE]
pro·ce·dure (prə·sē′jər) *n.* 1. A manner of proceeding or acting in any course of action. 2. The methods or forms of conducting a business, parliamentary affairs, etc. —**pro·ce′du·ral** *adj.*
pro·ceed (prə·sēd′) *v.i.* 1. To go on or forward, esp. after a stop. 2. To begin and carry on an action or process. 3. To issue or come, as from some source: with *from.* [< L *pro-* forward + *cedere* to go] —**pro·ceed′er** *n.*
pro·ceed·ing (prə·sē′ding) *n.* 1. An act or course of action; also, a particular act or course of action. 2. The act of one who or that which proceeds. 3. *pl.* The records or minutes of the meetings of a society, etc. 4. *Law* Any action instituted in a court.
pro·ceeds (prō′sēdz) *n.pl.* The amount derived from the disposal of goods, work, or the use of capital; return; yield.
proc·ess (pros′es, *esp. Brit.* prō′ses) *n.* 1. A course or method of operations in the production of something. 2. A series of continuous actions that bring about a particular result: the *process* of growth. 3. A forward movement; advance; course. 4. *Law* **a** Any judicial writ, esp. an order to bring a defendant into court. **b** The whole

course of proceedings in a cause. 5. *Biol.* An outgrowth of an organism. —*adj.* Produced by a special method: *process* cheese. —*v.t.* 1. To subject to a routine procedure: to *process* an application. 2. To treat or prepare by a special method. [See PROCEED.] —**proc′es·sor** *n.*

pro·ces·sion (prə·sesh′ən, prō-) *n.* An array, as of persons or vehicles, arranged in succession and moving in a formal manner; a parade; also, any continuous course: the *procession* of the stars. [See PROCEED.]

pro·ces·sion·al (prə·sesh′ən·əl) *adj.* Of, pertaining to, or moving in a procession. —*n.* 1. A hymn sung at the opening of a church service, during the entrance of the choir, etc. 2. The music played or sung during a procession. —**pro·ces′sion·al·ly** *adv.*

pro·claim (prō·klām′) *v.t.* 1. To announce or make known publicly or officially; declare. 2. To make plain; manifest. [< L *pro-* before + *clamare* to call] —**pro·claim′er** *n.* —**proc·la·ma·tion** (prok′lə·mā′shən) *n.*

pro·cliv·i·ty (prō·kliv′ə·tē) *n. pl.* **·ties** Natural tendency. [< L *pro-* before + *clivus* slope]

pro·con·sul (prō·kon′səl, prō′kon′-) *n.* 1. In ancient Rome, an official who exercised authority over a province or an army. 2. A governor of a dependency; a viceroy. [< L] —**pro·con′su·lar** (-sə·lər, -syə-) *adj.* —**pro·con′su·late** (-sə·lit, -syə-), **pro·con′·sul·ship** *n.*

pro·cras·ti·nate (prō·kras′tə·nāt) *v.* **·nat·ed, ·nat·ing** *v.i.* 1. To put off taking action until a future time; be dilatory. —*v.t.* 2. To defer or postpone. [< L *procrastinare*] —**pro·cras′ti·na′tion** *n.* —**pro·cras′ti·na′tor** *n.*

pro·cre·ate (prō′krē·āt) *v.t.* & *v.i.* **·at·ed, ·at·ing** To engender or beget (offspring). [< L *pro-* before + *creare* to create] —**pro′·cre·a′tive, pro′cre·ant** *adj.* —**pro′cre·a′tion** *n.* —**pro′cre·a′tor** *n.*

Pro·crus·te·an (prō·krus′tē·ən) *adj.* Ruthlessly or violently bringing about conformity. [< *Procrustes*, giant of Greek mythology, who stretched or maimed captives to fit his iron bed]

procto- *combining form Med.* Related to or affecting the rectum. Also, before vowels, **proct-**. [< Gk. *proktos* anus]

proc·tol·o·gy (prok·tol′ə·jē) *n.* The branch of medicine that treats of the diseases of the rectum. —**proc·to·log·i·cal** (prok′tə·loj′i·kəl) *adj.* —**proc·tol′o·gist** *n.*

proc·tor (prok′tər) *n.* One charged with maintaining order, supervising examinations, etc. —*v.t.* & *v.i.* To supervise (an examination). [ME *proketour, procutour*] —**proc·to·ri·al** (prok·tôr′ē·əl) *adj.*

pro·cum·bent (prō·kum′bənt) *adj. Bot.* Lying on the ground; trailing. [< L *pro-* forward + *cumbere* to lie down]

proc·u·ra·tor (prok′yə·rā′tər) *n.* An administrator; esp., in ancient Rome, one who had charge of a province. [See PROCURE.] —**proc′u·ra·to′ri·al** (-rə·tôr′ē·əl) *adj.* —**proc′u·ra′tor·ship** *n.*

pro·cure (prō·kyŏŏr′) *v.* **·cured, ·cur·ing** *v.t.* 1. To obtain by some effort or means; acquire. 2. To bring about; cause. 3. To obtain (women) for the sexual gratification of others. —*v.i.* 4. To be a procurer. [< L *pro-* on behalf of + *curare* to attend to] —**pro·cur′a·ble** *adj.* —**pro·cure′ment** *n.*

pro·cur·er (prō·kyŏŏr′ər) *n.* One who procures for another, as to gratify lust; a pimp.

prod (prod) *v.t.* **prod·ded, prod·ding** 1. To punch or poke with or as with a pointed instrument. 2. To arouse mentally; goad. —*n.* 1. Any pointed instrument used for prodding; a goad. 2. A thrust or poke. 3. A reminder. [Origin unknown] —**prod′der** *n.*

prod·i·gal (prod′ə·gəl) *adj.* 1. Addicted to wasteful expenditure, as of money, time, or strength; extravagant. 2. Yielding in profusion; bountiful. —*n.* One who is wasteful or profligate; a spendthrift. [< L *prodigus* wasteful] —**prod′i·gal′i·ty** (-gal′·ə·tē) *n.* —**prod′i·gal·ly** *adv.*

pro·dig·ious (prə·dij′əs) *adj.* 1. Enormous or extraordinary in size, quantity, or degree; vast. 2. Marvelous; amazing. [< L *prodigium* omen] —**pro·dig′ious·ly** *adv.* —**pro·dig′·ious·ness** *n.*

prod·i·gy (prod′ə·jē) *n. pl.* **·gies** 1. A person having remarkable qualities or powers: a violin *prodigy*. 2. Something extraordinary. [< L *prodigium*]

pro·duce (*v.* prə·dōōs′, -dyōōs′; *n.* prod′ōōs, -yōōs, prō′dōōs, -dyōōs) *v.* **·duced, ·duc·ing** *v.t.* 1. To bring forth or bear; yield, as young or a natural product. 2. To bring forth by mental effort; compose, write, etc. 3. To bring about: His words *produced* a violent reaction. 4. To bring to view; exhibit: to *produce* evidence. 5. To manufacture; make. 6. To bring to performance before the public, as a play. —*v.i.* 7. To yield or generate an appropriate product or result. —*n.* That which is produced; a product; esp., farm products collectively. [< L *pro-* forward + *ducere* to lead] —**pro·duc′er** *n.* —**pro·duc′i·ble** *adj.*

prod·uct (prod′əkt, -ukt) *n.* 1. Anything produced or obtained as by generation, growth, labor, study, or skill. 2. *Math.* The result obtained by multiplication.

pro·duc·tion (prə·duk′shən) *n.* 1. The act or process of producing. 2. Any tangible result of industrial, artistic, or literary effort.

pro·duc·tive (prə·duk′tiv) *adj.* 1. Producing; creative, as of artistic things. 2. Producing profits or increase in quantity, quality, or value. 3. Causing; resulting in: with *of.* —**pro·duc′tive·ly** *adv.* —**pro·duc·tiv·i·ty** (prō′duk·tiv′ə·tē, prod′uk-), **pro·duc′tive·ness** *n.*

pro·em (prō′əm) *n.* An introductory statement; preface. [< Gk. *prooimion* overture] —**pro·e·mi·al** (prō·ē′mē·əl) *adj.*

pro·fane (prə·fān′, prō-) *v.t.* **·faned, ·fan·ing** 1. To treat (something sacred) with irreverence or abuse; desecrate; pollute. 2. To put to an unworthy or degrading use; debase. —*adj.* 1. Manifesting irreverence or disrespect toward the Deity or sacred things. 2. Not religious or concerned with religious things; secular. 3. Vulgar; common; coarse. [< L *profanus* before or outside the temple] —**prof·a·na·tion** (prof′ə·nā′shən) *n.* —**pro·fan·a·to·ry** (prə·fan′ə·tôr′ē) *adj.* —**pro·fane′ly** *adv.* —**pro·fan′er** *n.* —**pro·fane′ness** *n.*

pro·fan·i·ty (prə·fan′ə·tē) *n. pl.* **·ties** 1. The state of being profane. 2. Profane speech or action.

pro·fess (prə·fes′) *v.t.* 1. To declare openly; avow; affirm. 2. To assert, usu. insincerely: to *profess* remorse. 3. To declare or affirm faith in. 4. To have as one's profession: to *profess* the law. —*v.i.* 5. To make open declaration; avow. [< L *pro-* before + *fateri* to confess]

pro·fess·ed·ly (prə·fes′id·lē) *adv.* 1. By open profession; avowedly. 2. Pretendedly.

pro·fes·sion (prə·fesh′ən) *n.* 1. An occupation that properly involves a liberal, scientific, or artistic education. 2. The collective body of those following such occupations. 3. The act of professing or declaring; declaration. 4. That which is avowed or professed; a declaration.

pro·fes·sion·al (prə·fesh′ən·əl) *adj.* 1. Connected with, preparing for, engaged in, appropriate to, or conforming to a profession. 2. Of or pertaining to an occupation pursued for gain: a *professional* ball player. —*n.* 1. One who pursues as a business some vocation or occupation. 2. One who engages for money to compete in sports. —**pro·fes′·sion·al·ism** *n.* —**pro·fes′sion·al·ly** *adv.*

pro·fes·sor (prə·fes′ər) *n.* A teacher of the highest rank in a university or college. —**pro·fes·so·ri·al** (prō′fə·sôr′ē·əl, prof′ə-) *adj.* —**pro·fes′sor·ship** *n.*

prof·fer (prof′ər) *v.t.* To offer for acceptance. [< L *pro-* in behalf of + *offere* to offer] —**prof′fer** *n.* —**prof′fer·er** *n.*

pro·fi·cient (prə·fish′ənt) *adj.* Thoroughly versed, as in an art or science. —*n.* An expert. [< L *pro-* forward + *facere* to do] —**pro·fi′cien·cy** *n.* —**pro·fi′cient·ly** *adv.*

pro·file (prō′fīl, *esp. Brit.* prō′fēl) *n.* 1. The outline of a human face or figure as seen from the side; also, a drawing of this outline. 2. Any outline or contour. 3. A short biographical sketch. —*v.t.* **·filed, ·fil·ing** 1. To draw a profile of. 2. To write or make a profile of. [< Ital. *proffilare* to draw in outline]

prof·it (prof′it) *n.* 1. Any advantage or gain; benefit. 2. *Often pl.* Excess of returns over outlay or expenditure. 3. The return from the employment of capital after deducting the amount paid for raw material and for wages, rent, interest, etc. —**gross profit** The excess of receipts from sales over expenditures for production or purchase. —**net profit** The surplus remaining after all necessary deductions, as for interest, bad debts, etc. —*v.i.* 1. To be of advantage or benefit. 2. To derive gain or benefit. —*v.t.* 3. To be of profit or advantage to. [< L *proficere* to go forward] —**prof′it·less** *adj.*

prof·it·a·ble (prof′it·ə·bəl) *adj.* Bringing profit or gain; advantageous. —**prof′it·a·bil′i·ty, prof′it·a·ble·ness** *n.* —**prof′it·a·bly** *adv.*

prof·i·teer (prof′ə·tir′) *v.i.* To seek or obtain excessive profits. —*n.* One who is given to making excessive profits, esp. to the detriment of others. —**prof′i·teer′ing** *n.*

prof·li·ga·cy (prof′lə·gə·sē) *n. pl.* **·cies** The state or quality, or an instance of being profligate.

prof·li·gate (prof′lə·git, -gāt) *adj.* 1. Lost or insensible to principle, virtue, or decency. 2. Recklessly extravagant; in great profusion. —*n.* 1. A depraved or dissolute person. 2. A reckless spendthrift. [< L *profligare* to destroy] —**prof′li·gate·ly** *adv.* —**prof′li·gate·ness** *n.*

pro·found (prə·found′, prō-) *adj.* 1. Intellectually deep or penetrating. 2. Reaching to, arising from, or affecting the depth of one's nature: *profound* respect. 3. Situated far below the surface; unfathomable. 4. Thorough; exhaustive: *profound* changes. [< L *pro-* very + *fundus* deep] —**pro·found′ly** *adv.* —**pro·found′ness** *n.*

pro·fun·di·ty (prə·fun′də·tē, prō-) *n. pl.* **·ties** 1. The state or quality of being profound. 2. A profound or abstruse statement, theory, etc.

pro·fuse (prə·fyōōs′, prō-) *adj.* 1. Giving or given forth lavishly; liberal; extravagant. 2. Copious; overflowing; abundant: *profuse* vegetation. [< L *pro-* forward + *fundere* to pour] —**pro·fuse′ly** *adv.* —**pro·fuse′ness** *n.*

pro·fu·sion (prə·fyōō′zhən, prō-) *n.* 1. A lavish supply or condition: a *profusion* of ornaments. 2. The act of pouring forth or supplying in great abundance; prodigality.

pro·gen·i·tor (prō·jen′ə·tər) *n.* A forefather or parent. [< L *pro-* forth + *gignere* to beget]

prog·e·ny (proj′ə·nē) *n. pl.* **·nies** Offspring.

prog·na·thous (prog′nə·thəs, prog·nā′thəs) *adj.* Having abnormally projecting jaws. Also **prog·nath·ic** (prog·nath′ik). [< Gk. *pro-* before + *gnathos* jaw] —**prog′na·thism** *n.*

prog·no·sis (prog·nō′sis) *n. pl.* **·ses** (-sēz) 1. *Med.* A prediction or conclusion regarding the course of a disease and the probability of recovery. 2. Any prediction or forecast. [< Gk. *pro-* before + *gignōskein* to know]

prog·nos·tic (prog·nos′tik) *adj.* 1. Of, pertaining to, or serving as a prognosis. 2. Predicting or foretelling. —*n.* A sign of some future occurrence; an omen.

prog·nos·ti·cate (prog·nos′tə·kāt) *v.t.* **·cat·ed, ·cat·ing** To foretell (future events, etc.) by present indications. —**prog·nos′ti·ca′tion** *n.* —**prog·nos′ti·ca′tor** *n.*

pro·gram (prō′gram, -grəm) *n.* 1. A performance or show, esp. one given at a scheduled time on television or radio. 2. A printed announcement or schedule of events, esp. one for a theatrical performance. 3. Any prearranged, proposed, or desired plan or course of proceedings. 4. Coded instructions for the sequence of operations to be performed by a computer. Also *Brit.* **pro′gramme.** —*v.t.* **pro·gramed** or **·grammed, pro·gram·ing** or **·gram·ming** 1. To arrange or include in a program. 2. To make up a program for (a radio station, a computer, etc.). [< Gk. *pro-* before + *graphein* to write]

pro·gram·mat·ic (pro′grə·mat′ik) *adj.* 1. Of or pertaining to a program or programs. 2. Of or pertaining to program music or its references. Also **pro′gram·a′tic.**

pro·gram·mer (prō′gram·ər) *n.* One who makes up a computer program. Also **pro′gram·er.**

program music Music intended to suggest a story, an event, or an idea.

prog·ress (*n.* prog′res, *esp. Brit.* prō′gres;

v. prə·gres′) *n.* 1. Movement forward nearer a goal. 2. Advancement toward maturity or completion; improvement. —*v.i.* 1. To move forward or onward. 2. To advance toward completion or fuller development. [< L *pro-* forward + *gradi* to walk]

pro·gres·sion (prə·gresh′ən) *n.* 1. The act of progressing; advancement. 2. Any sequence or succession of numbers, musical chords, etc. —**pro·gres′sion·al** *adj.*

pro·gres·sive (prə·gres′iv) *adj.* 1. Moving forward; advancing. 2. Proceeding gradually or step by step. 3. Aiming at or characterized by progress. 4. Spreading from one part to others; increasing: said of a disease: *progressive* paralysis. 5. Striving for or favoring progress or reform, esp. social, political, educational, or religious. —*n.* One who believes in progress or in progressive methods; esp., one who favors or promotes reforms, as in politics or religion. —**pro·gres′sive·ly** *adv.* —**pro·gres′sive·ness** *n.* —**pro·gres′siv·ism** *n.* —**pro·gres′siv·ist** *n.*

pro·hib·it (prō·hib′it) *v.t.* 1. To forbid, esp. by authority or law; interdict. 2. To prevent or hinder. [< L *pro-* before + *habere* to have] —**pro·hib′it·er** *n.*

pro·hi·bi·tion (prō′ə·bish′ən) *n.* 1. The act of prohibiting, preventing, or stopping; also, a decree or order forbidding anything. 2. The forbidding of the manufacture, transportation, and sale of alcoholic liquors as beverages. —**pro′hi·bi′tion·ist** *n.*

pro·hib·i·tive (prō·hib′ə·tiv) *adj.* 1. Prohibiting or tending to prohibit. 2. Preventing the sale, purchase, etc., of something: *prohibitive* costs. Also **pro·hib′i·to′ry.** —**pro·hib′i·tive·ly** *adv.*

proj·ect (*n.* proj′ekt; *v.* prə·jekt′) *n.* 1. Something proposed; a plan. 2. An organized or assigned undertaking. —*v.t.* 1. To cause to extend forward or out. 2. To throw forth or forward, as missiles. 3. To cause (an image, shadow, etc.) to fall on a surface. 4. To propose or plan. 5. To use or produce (one's voice, words, etc.) so as to be heard clearly and at a distance. —*v.i.* 6. To protrude. 7. *Psychol.* To attribute one's own ideas, impulses, etc., to others. [< L *pro-* before + *jacere* to throw] —**pro·jec′tion** *n.*

pro·jec·tile (prə·jek′təl, *esp. Brit.* -tīl) *adj.* 1. Projecting, or impelling forward. 2. Capable of being or intended to be projected or shot forth. —*n.* 1. A body projected or thrown forth by force. 2. *Mil.* A missile for discharge from a gun or cannon. [< L *projectus* thrown out]

pro·jec·tion·ist (prə·jek′shən·ist) *n.* One who operates a motion-picture or slide projector.

pro·jec·tor (prə·jek′tər) *n.* An apparatus for throwing illuminated images or motion pictures upon a screen.

pro·le·gom·e·non (prō′lə·gom′ə·non) *n. pl.* **·na** (-nə) *Often pl.* Introductory remarks; a preface. [< Gk. *pro-* before + *legein* to say] —**pro′le·gom′e·nous** (-nəs) *adj.*

pro·le·tar·i·an (prō′lə·târ′ē·ən) *adj.* Of or pertaining to the proletariat. —*n.* A member of the proletariat. [< L *proletarius*, the lowest class of the Roman state] —**pro′le·tar′i·an·ism** *n.*

pro·le·tar·i·at (prō′lə·târ′ē·ət) *n.* The working class: a term used esp. in Marxism.

pro·lif·er·ate (prō·lif′ə·rāt) *v.t. & v.i.* **·at·ed, ·at·ing** To produce, reproduce, or grow, esp. with rapidity, as cells in tissue formation. —**pro·lif′er·a′tion** *n.* —**pro·lif′er·a′tive** *adj.*

pro·lif·ic (prō·lif′ik) *adj.* 1. Producing abundantly, as offspring or fruit; fertile. 2. Producing results abundantly: a *prolific* writer. [< L *proles, prolis* offspring + stem of *facere* to make] —**pro·lif′i·ca·cy, pro·lif′ic·ness** *n.* —**pro·lif′i·cal·ly** *adv.*

pro·lix (prō′liks, prō·liks′) *adj.* Unduly long and verbose. [< L *pro-* before + stem of *liquere* to flow] —**pro·lix′i·ty, pro′lix·ness** *n.* —**pro′lix·ly** *adv.*

pro·logue (prō′lôg, -log) *n.* 1. A prefatory statement to a poem, discourse, or performance; esp., an introduction spoken or sung before a play or opera. 2. Any anticipatory act or event. —*v.t.* **·logued, ·lo·guing** To introduce with a prologue or preface. Also **pro′log.** [< Gk. *pro-* before + *logos* discourse]

pro·long (prə·lông′) *v.t.* To extend in time or space; continue; lengthen. Also **pro·lon′gate** (-lông′gāt). [< L *pro-* forth + *longus* long] —**pro·lon·ga·tion** (prō′lông·gā′shən) *n.* —**pro·long′er** *n.* —**pro·long′ment** *n.*

prom (prom) *n. Informal* A formal college or school dance. [Short for PROMENADE]

prom·e·nade (prom′ə·nād′, -näd′) *n.* 1. A walk for amusement or exercise, or as part of a formal or social entertainment. 2. A place for promenading. 3. A concert or ball opened with a formal march; also, the march. —*v.* **·nad·ed, ·nad·ing** *v.i.* 1. To take a promenade. —*v.t.* 2. To take a promenade through or along. [< LL *pro-* before + *minare* to drive (cattle)] —**prom′e·nad′er** *n.*

pro·me·thi·um (prə·mē′thē·əm) *n.* A radioactive element (symbol Pm) belonging to the lanthanide series. [< *Prometheus*, a Titan of Greek mythology who stole fire from heaven for mankind]

prom·i·nence (prom′ə·nəns) *n.* 1. The state of being prominent. 2. That which is prominent. 3. *Astron.* One of the great flames shooting out from the sun's surface, seen during total eclipses.

prom·i·nent (prom′ə·nənt) *adj.* 1. Jutting out; projecting. 2. Conspicuous in position, character, or importance. 3. Well-known; eminent. [< L *prominere* to project] —**prom′i·nent·ly** *adv.*

pro·mis·cu·ous (prə·mis′kyōō·əs) *adj.* 1. Composed of individuals or things confusedly or indiscriminately mingled. 2. Indiscriminate, esp. in sexual relations. 3. *Informal* Lacking plan or purpose; casual; random. [< L *pro-* thoroughly + stem of *miscere* to mix] —**pro·mis·cu·i·ty** (prō′mis·kyōō′·ə·tē, prom′is-) *n.* —**pro·mis′cu·ous·ly** *adv.* —**pro·mis′cu·ous·ness** *n.*

prom·ise (prom′is) *n.* 1. An assurance given by one person to another that a specified act will or will not be performed. 2. Reasonable ground for hope or expectation, esp. of future excellence or satisfaction. 3. Something promised. —*v.* **·ised, ·is·ing** *v.t.* 1. To engage or pledge by a promise: used with the infinitive or a clause. 2. To make a promise of (something) to someone. 3. To give reason for expecting. 4. *Informal* To assure (someone). —*v.i.* 5. To make a promise. [< L *pro-* forth + *mittere* to send] —**prom′·is·ee** *n.* —**prom′is·er** *n.*

prom·is·ing (prom′is·ing) *adj.* Giving promise of good results: a *promising* sign. **—prom′is·ing·ly** *adv.*

prom·is·so·ry (prom′ə·sôr′ē) *adj.* Containing or of the nature of a promise.

promissory note A written promise to pay a certain sum of money at a specified time, or upon demand.

prom·on·to·ry (prom′ən·tôr′ē) *n. pl.* **·ries** A high point of land extending into the sea; headland. [< L *promunturium*]

pro·mote (prə·mōt′) *v.t.* **·mot·ed, ·mot·ing** 1. To contribute to the progress, development, or growth of; further; encourage. 2. To advance to a higher position, grade, or honor. 3. To work in behalf of; advocate actively. 4. To seek to make (a commercial product, business venture, etc.) popular or successful, as by securing capital or by advertising. [< L *pro-* forward + *movere* to move] **—pro·mot′er** *n.* **—pro·mo′tion** *n.* **—pro·mo′tion·al** *adj.* **—pro·mo′tive** *adj.*

prompt (prompt) *v.t.* 1. To incite to action; instigate. 2. To suggest or inspire (an act, thought, etc.). 3. To remind; give a cue to. *—v.i.* 4. To give help or suggestions. *—adj.* 1. Acting or ready to act at the moment; punctual. 2. Done readily; taking place at the appointed time. *—n.* An act of prompting. [< L *pro-* forth + *emere* to take] **—prompt′er** *n.* **—prompt′ly** *adv.* **—prompt′ness** *n.*

promp·ti·tude (promp′tə·to͞od, -tyo͞od) *n.* The quality, habit, or fact of being prompt.

pro·mul·gate (prom′əl·gāt, prō·mul′gāt) *v.t.* **·gat·ed, ·gat·ing** To make known or announce formally; put into effect by public proclamation, as a law or dogma. [< L *pro-* forth + *vulgus* people] **—pro′mul·ga′tion** *n.* **—pro′mul·ga·tor** *n.*

prone (prōn) *adj.* 1. Lying flat, esp. with the face, front, or palm downward; prostrate. 2. Mentally inclined or predisposed: with *to.* [< L *pronus* prostrate] **—prone′ly** *adv.* **—prone′ness** *n.*

prong (prông, prong) *n.* 1. A pointed end of an instrument, as the tine of a fork. 2. Any pointed, projecting part, as the end of an antler. *—v.t.* To prick or stab with or as with a prong. [ME *pronge*]

prong·horn (prông′hôrn′, prong′-) *n. pl.* **·horns** or **·horn** A ruminant of western North America, resembling an antelope and having branched horns.

pronominal adjective The possessive case of a personal pronoun used attributively, as *my, your, his, her,* etc.

pro·noun (prō′noun) *n. Gram.* A word that may be used instead of a noun, as *who, which, he,* or *that.* [< L *pro-* in place of + *nomen* name, noun] **—pro·nom′i·nal** (-nom′ə·nəl) *adj.*

pro·nounce (prə·nouns′) *v.* **·nounced, ·nounc·ing** *v.t.* 1. To utter or deliver officially or solemnly; proclaim: to *pronounce* judgment. 2. To assert; declare, esp. as one's judgment. 3. To utter the constituent sounds of (a word or phrase) in a particular sequence or with a particular accentual pattern. 4. To utter (the sound of a letter). *—v.i.* 5. To make a judgment or pronouncement. [< L *pro-* forth + *nuntiare* to announce] **—pro·nounce′a·ble** *adj.* **—pro·nounc′er** *n.*

pro·nounced (prə·nounst′) *adj.* Of marked or clearly indicated character. **—pro·nounc′ed·ly** *adv.*

pro·nounce·ment (prə·nouns′mənt) *n.* 1. The act of pronouncing. 2. A formal declaration or announcement.

pron·to (pron′tō) *adv. Informal* Quickly; promptly; instantly. [< Sp. < L *promptus* brought forth]

pro·nun·ci·a·men·to (prə·nun′sē·ə·men′tō, -shē·ə-) *n. pl.* **·tos** A public announcement; proclamation; manifesto. [< Sp.]

pro·nun·ci·a·tion (prə·nun′sē·ā′shən) *n.* The act or manner of uttering words.

proof (pro͞of) *n.* 1. The act or process of proving; esp., the establishment of a fact by evidence or a truth by other truths. 2. A trial of strength, truth, excellence, etc. 3. Evidence and argument sufficient to induce belief. 4. *Law* Anything that serves to determine a verdict. 5. The standard of strength of alcoholic liquors. 6. *Printing* A trial sheet printed from metal type or a plate. 7. *Photog.* A trial print from a negative. 8. *Math.* A process to check a computation by using its result; also, a demonstration. *—adj.* 1. Capable of resisting successfully: with *against.* 2. Of standard alcoholic strength, as liquors. [< LL *probare* to test]

-proof *combining form* 1. Impervious to; able to withstand: *bombproof.* 2. Protected against: *mothproof.* Adjectives formed with *-proof* may also be used as verbs. [< PROOF, adj.]

proof·read (pro͞of′rēd′) *v.t. & v.i.* **·read** (-red′), **·read·ing** (-rē′ding) To read and correct (printers' proofs). **—proof′read′er** *n.* **—proof′read′ing** *n.*

prop[1] (prop) *n.* A rigid object, as a beam or pole, that bolsters or sustains weight. *—v.t.* **propped, prop·ping** 1. To support or keep from falling with or as with a prop. 2. To lean or place: usu. with *against.* [< MDu. *proppe* a support]

prop[2] (prop) *n.* A stage property.

prop·a·gan·da (prop′ə·gan′də) *n.* 1. A systematic effort to persuade a body of people to support or adopt a particular opinion, attitude, or course of action. 2. Any selection of facts, ideas, or allegations forming the basis of such an effort. [See PROPAGATE.] **—prop′a·gan′dism** *n.* **—prop′a·gan′dist** *n. & adj.* **—prop′a·gan′dize** *v.t. & v.i.* **·dized, ·diz·ing**

prop·a·gate (prop′ə·gāt) *v.* **·gat·ed, ·gat·ing** *v.t.* 1. To cause (animals, plants, etc.) to multiply by natural reproduction. 2. To spread from person to person, as a doctrine or belief; disseminate. 3. To transmit through a medium: to *propagate* heat. *—v.i.* 4. To have offspring; breed. [< L *propagare*] **—prop′a·ga·ble** (-gə·bəl) *adj.* **—prop′a·ga′tion** *n.* **—prop′a·ga′tive** *adj.* **—prop′a·ga′tor** *n.*

pro·pane (prō′pān) *n. Chem.* A gaseous hydrocarbon obtained from petroleum and used as a fuel gas.

pro·pel (prə·pel′) *v.t.* **·pelled, ·pel·ling** To cause to move forward or ahead; drive or urge forward. [< L *pro-* forward + *pellere* to drive]

pro·pel·lant (prə·pel′ənt) *n.* One who or that which propels, as an explosive, a rocket fuel, etc. Also **pro·pel′lent.** —**pro·pel′lant** or **pro·pel′lent** *adj.*

pro·pel·ler (prə·pel′ər) *n.* Any device for propelling a craft through water or air, esp. one having blades mounted on a shaft that produce a thrust by their rotary action: also *screw propeller.*

pro·pen·si·ty (prə·pen′sə·tē) *n. pl.* **·ties** A natural disposition or tendency; bent. [< L *pro-* forward + *pendere* to hang]

prop·er (prop′ər) *adj.* **1.** Specially suited or adapted for some end; appropriate. **2.** Conforming to a prevalent standard of conduct or manners; fitting. **3.** Understood in a strict or literal sense: usu. following the noun modified: part of the book *proper.* **4.** Naturally belonging to a particular person, thing, or class. **5.** Modest; decent. **6.** *Brit. Informal* Thorough; unmitigated: a *proper* bore. [< L *propius* one's own] —**prop′er·ly** *adv.* —**prop′er·ness** *n.*

proper noun *Gram.* A noun that names a particular person, place, or thing, and is always capitalized, as *Paul, Venice, U.S.S. Nautilus.*

prop·er·tied (prop′ər·tēd) *adj.* Owning property.

prop·er·ty (prop′ər·tē) *n. pl.* **·ties** **1.** Any object of value that a person may lawfully acquire and hold; that which may be owned, as stocks, land, etc. **2.** The legal right to the possession, use, enjoyment, and disposal of a thing. **3.** A parcel of land. **4.** Any of the qualities or characteristics that together make up the nature or basic structure of a thing. **5.** In the theater, any portable article used in a performance other than scenery and costumes: also called *prop.* [< L *proprius* one's own.] —**prop′er·ty·less** *adj.*

proph·e·cy (prof′ə·sē) *n. pl.* **·cies** **1.** A prediction made under divine influence and direction. **2.** Any prediction. [< Gk. *prophētēs* < *pro* before + *phanai* to speak]

proph·e·sy (prof′ə·sī) *v.* **·sied, ·sy·ing** *v.t.* **1.** To utter or foretell with or as with divine inspiration. **2.** To predict (a future event). —*v.i.* **3.** To speak by divine influence, or as a medium between God and man. **4.** To foretell the future. [See PROPHECY.] —**proph′e·si′er** *n.*

proph·et (prof′it) *n.* **1.** One who delivers divine messages or interprets the divine will. **2.** One who foretells the future; esp., an inspired predictor. **3.** A religious leader. —**the Prophet** According to Islam, Muhammad. —**the Prophets** The second of the three ancient divisions of the Old Testament. [< Gk. *pro-* before + *phanai* to speak] —**proph′et·ess** *n.fem.*

pro·phet·ic (prə·fet′ik) *adj.* **1.** Of or pertaining to a prophet or prophecy. **2.** Pertaining to or involving prediction or presentiment; predictive. Also **pro·phet′i·cal.** —**pro·phet′i·cal·ly** *adv.* —**pro·phet′i·cal·ness** *n.*

pro·phy·lac·tic (prō′fə·lak′tik, prof′ə-) *adj.* Tending to protect against or ward off something, esp. disease; preventive. —*n.* A prophylactic medicine or appliance. [< Gk. *pro-* before + *phylassein* to guard]

pro·phy·lax·is (prō′fə·lak′sis, prof′ə-) *n.* Preventive treatment for disease.

pro·pin·qui·ty (prō·ping′kwə·tē) *n.* **1.** Nearness in place or time. **2.** Kinship. [< L *prope* near]

pro·pi·ti·ate (prō·pish′ē·āt) *v.t.* **·at·ed, ·at·ing** To cause to be favorably disposed; conciliate. [See PROPITIOUS.] —**pro·pi′ti·a·ble** (-ə·bəl) *adj.* —**pro·pi′ti·at′ing·ly** *adv.* —**pro·pi′ti·a′tion** *n.* —**pro·pi′ti·a′tive, pro·pi′ti·a·to′ry** (-ə·tôr′ē) *adj.* —**pro·pi′ti·a′tor** *n.*

pro·pi·tious (prō·pish′əs) *adj.* **1.** Attended by favorable circumstances; auspicious. **2.** Kindly disposed; gracious. [< L, favorable] —**pro·pi′tious·ly** *adv.* —**pro·pi′tious·ness** *n.*

prop·jet (prop′jet′) *n. Aeron.* A turboprop.

pro·po·nent (prə·pō′nənt) *n.* One who advocates or supports a cause or doctrine. [< L *pro-* forth + *ponere* to put]

pro·por·tion (prə·pôr′shən) *n.* **1.** Relative magnitude, number, or degree, as existing between parts, a part and a whole, etc. **2.** Fitness and harmony; symmetry. **3.** A proportionate or proper share. **4.** An equality or identity between ratios. **5.** *pl.* Size; dimensions. [< L *pro-* for + *portio, -onis* share] —**pro·por′tion** *v.t.* —**pro·por′tion·a·ble** *adj.* —**pro·por′tion·a·bly** *adv.* —**pro·por′tion·er** *n.* —**pro·por′tion·ment** *n.*

pro·por·tion·al (prə·pôr′shən·əl) *adj.* Of or being in proportion. —*n.* Any quantity or number in proportion to another or others. —**pro·por′tion·al·ly** *adv.* —**pro·por′tion·al′i·ty** (-al′ə·tē) *n.*

pro·por·tion·ate (*adj.* prə·pôr′shən·it; *v.* prə·pôr′shən·āt) *adj.* Being in due proportion; proportional. —*v.t.* **·at·ed, ·at·ing** To make proportionate. —**pro·por′tion·ate·ly** *adv.* —**pro·por′tion·ate·ness** *n.*

pro·pose (prə·pōz′) *v.* **·posed, ·pos·ing** *v.t.* **1.** To put forward for acceptance or consideration. **2.** To intend; aim. **3.** To suggest the drinking of (a toast). —*v.i.* **4.** To form or announce a plan or design. **5.** To make an offer, as of marriage. [< OF *pro-* forth + *poser* to put down, rest] —**pro·po′sal** *n.* —**pro·pos′er** *n.*

prop·o·si·tion (prop′ə·zish′ən) *n.* **1.** A scheme or proposal offered for consideration or acceptance. **2.** *Informal* Any matter to be dealt with. **3.** A subject or statement presented for discussion or proof. [< L *pro-* forth + *ponere* to put] —**prop′o·si′tion** *v.t.* —**prop′o·si′tion·al** *adj.* —**prop′o·si′tion·al·ly** *adv.*

pro·pound (prə·pound′) *v.t.* To put forward for consideration, solution, etc.; submit. [< L *proponere* to set forth] —**pro·pound′er** *n.*

pro·pri·e·tar·y (prə·prī′ə·ter′ē) *adj.* **1.** Of or belonging to a proprietor. **2.** Designating an article, as a medicine, protected by copyright, patent, secrecy, etc. —*n. pl.* **·tar·ies** A proprietor or proprietors collectively. [< L *proprius* one's own]

pro·pri·e·tor (prə·prī′ə·tər) *n.* A person having the exclusive title to anything. —**pro·pri′e·tor·ship′** *n.* —**pro·pri′e·tress** *n. fem.*

pro·pri·e·ty (prə·prī′ə·tē) *n. pl.* **·ties** The character or quality of being proper; esp., accordance with recognized usage or principles. —**the proprieties** The standards of good society. [See PROPER]

pro·pul·sion (prə·pul′shən) *n.* **1.** The act or operation of propelling. **2.** A propelling force. —**pro·pul′sive** (-siv) *adj.*

pro ra·ta (prō rā′tə, rat′ə, rä′tə) In proportion. [< L *pro rata* (*parte*) according to the calculated (share)]

pro·rate (prō·rāt′, prō′rāt′) *v.t. & v.i.* **·rat·ed, ·rat·ing** To distribute or divide proportionately. [< PRO RATA] **—pro·rat′a·ble** *adj.* **—pro·ra′tion** *n.*

pro·rogue (prō·rōg′) *v.t.* **·rogued, ·ro·guing** To discontinue a session of (an assembly). [< L *pro-* forward + *rogare* to ask] **—pro′ro·ga′tion** (-rō·gā′shən) *n.*

pro·sa·ic (prō·zā′ik) *adj.* 1. Commonplace; dull. 2. Of or like prose. Also **pro·sa′i·cal.** [< L *prosa* prose] **—pro·sa′i·cal·ly** *adv.* **—pro·sa′ic·ness** *n.*

pro·sce·ni·um (prō·sē′nē·əm) *n. pl.* **·ni·a** The part of a theater stage in front of the curtain. [< Gk. *pro-* before + *skēnē* stage, tent]

proscenium arch The arch that frames the stage.

pro·scribe (prō·skrīb′) *v.t.* **·scribed, ·scrib·ing** 1. To denounce or condemn; prohibit. 2. To outlaw or banish. [< L *proscribere* to write publicly] **—pro·scrib′er** *n.* **—pro·scrip′tion** (-skrip′shən) *n.* **—pro·scrip′tive** (-skrip′tiv) *adj.*

prose (prōz) *n.* Speech or writing without metrical structure: distinguished from *verse.* **—*v.t. & v.i.*** **prosed, pros·ing** To write or speak in prose. [< L *prosa* (*oratio*) straightforward (discourse)] **—prose** *adj.*

pros·e·cute (pros′ə·kyōōt) *v.* **·cut·ed, ·cut·ing** *v.t.* 1. To go on with so as to complete. 2. *Law* **a** To bring suit against. **b** To seek to enforce, as a claim, by legal process. **—*v.i.*** 3. To begin and carry on a legal proceeding. [< L *pro-* forward + *sequi* to follow] **—pros′e·cu·tor** *n.*

prosecuting attorney The attorney acting in behalf of the state, county, or national government in prosecuting for penal offenses.

pros·e·cu·tion (pros′ə·kyōō′shən) *n.* 1. The act or process of prosecuting. 2. *Law* The instituting and carrying forward of a judicial or criminal proceeding; also, the party instituting and conducting it.

pros·e·lyte (pros′ə·līt) *n.* One who has been brought over to any opinion, belief, sect, or party, esp. from one religious belief to another. **—*v.t. & v.i.*** **·lyt·ed, ·lyt·ing** To proselytize. [< Gk. *proselytos,* orig., a newcomer] **—pros′e·lyt′ism** (-lə·tiz′əm, -līt′iz·əm) *n.*

pros·e·lyt·ize (pros′ə·lit·īz′) *v.t. & v.i.* **·ized, ·iz·ing** To try to convert (someone) to another opinion, religion, etc. Also *Brit.* **pros′e·lyt·ise′.** **—pros′e·lyt·iz′er** *n.*

pros·o·dy (pros′ə·dē) *n. pl.* **·dies** The study of poetical forms, including accent of syllables, meter, and versification. [< Gk. *prosōidia* a song sung to music] **—pro·sod·ic** (prō·sod′ik) or **·i·cal** *adj.* **—pros′o·dist** *n.*

pros·pect (pros′pekt) *n.* 1. *Often pl.* A future probability; the chance for future success. 2. An extended view. 3. An exposure; outlook. 4. A prospective buyer. **—*v.t. & v.i.*** To explore (a region) for gold, oil, etc. [< L *pro-* forward + *specere* to look] **—pros′pec·tor** *n.*

pro·spec·tive (prə·spek′tiv) *adj.* 1. Anticipated. 2. Looking toward the future. **—pro·spec′tive·ly** *adv.*

pro·spec·tus (prə·spek′təs) *n. pl.* **·tus·es** 1. A paper containing information of a proposed undertaking. 2. A summary; outline. [< L *pro-* forward + *specere* to look]

pros·per (pros′pər) *v.i.* To be prosperous; thrive; flourish. [< L *prosperus* favorable, prosperous]

pros·per·i·ty (pros·per′ə·tē) *n.* The state of being prosperous; material well-being.

pros·per·ous (pros′pər·əs) *adj.* 1. Successful; flourishing. 2. Auspicious or favorable. [< L *prosperus*] **—pros′per·ous·ly** *adv.* **—pros′per·ous·ness** *n.*

pros·tate (pros′tāt) *n.* *Anat.* A partly muscular gland at the base of the bladder and surrounding the urethra in male mammals, providing some of the chemicals necessary to maintain the sperm for reproduction. Also **prostate gland.** [< Gk. *prostatēs* stander before] **—pros′tate, pro·stat·ic** (prō·stat′ik) *adj.*

pros·the·sis (pros′thə·sis, pros·thē′-) *n. pl.* **·ses** (-sēz) An artificial part fitted to the body, as an artificial limb, false tooth, etc. [< Gk. *pros-* to + *tithenai* to put] **—pros·thet′ic** (-thet′ik) *adj.*

pros·thet·ics (pros·thet′iks) *n.pl.* (*construed as sing.*) The branch of surgery that specializes in artificial parts. **—pros′the·tist** (-thə·tist) *n.*

pros·ti·tute (pros′tə·tōōt, -tyōōt) *n.* 1. A woman who offers her body for hire for purposes of sexual intercourse. 2. One who sells his services for unworthy purposes. **—*v.t.*** **·tut·ed, ·tut·ing** 1. To apply (talent, etc.) to unworthy purposes. 2. To offer (oneself or another) for sexual relations, esp. for money. [< L *pro-* forward + *statuere* to place] **—pros′ti·tu′tion** *n.* **—pros′ti·tu′tor** *n.*

pros·trate (pros′trāt) *adj.* 1. Lying prone, or with the face to the ground, as in adoration or subjection. 2. Brought low in mind or spirit. 3. *Bot.* Trailing along the ground. **—*v.t.*** **·trat·ed, ·trat·ing** 1. To bow or cast (oneself) down, as in adoration or pleading. 2. To throw flat; lay on the ground. 3. To overcome; make helpless. [< L *pro-* before + *sternere* to stretch out] **—pros·tra′tion** *n.*

pros·y (prō′zē) *adj.* **pros·i·er, pros·i·est** 1. Like prose; prosaic. 2. Dull; tedious. **—pros′i·ly** *adv.* **—pros′i·ness** *n.*

prot- Var. of PROTO-.

pro·tac·tin·i·um (prō′tak·tin′ē·əm) *n.* A radioactive metallic element (symbol Pa) of the actinide series.

pro·tag·o·nist (prō·tag′ə·nist) *n.* 1. The actor who played the chief part in a Greek drama. 2. Any leading character, contender, etc. [< Gk. *prōtos* first + *agōnistēs* actor]

pro·te·an (prō′tē·ən, prō·tē′ən) *adj.* Readily assuming different forms or various aspects; changeable. [< *Proteus,* sea god of Greek mythology who assumed many forms]

pro·tect (prə·tekt′) *v.t.* To shield or defend from attack, harm, or injury. [< L *pro-* before + *tegere* to cover] **—pro·tect′ing·ly** *adv.*

pro·tec·tion (prə·tek′shən) *n.* 1. The act of protecting, or the state of being protected. 2. *Econ.* A system aiming to protect the industries of a country by imposing duties. **—pro·tec′tive** *adj.* **—pro·tec′tive·ly** *adv.*

pro·tec·tion·ism (prə·tek′shən·iz′əm) *n.* The economic doctrine or system of protection. **—pro·tec′tion·ist** *n.*

protective tariff A tariff that protects domestic industries against foreign competition.

pro·tec·tor (prə·tek′tər) *n.* 1. One who protects; a defender. 2. In English history, one appointed as a regent of the kingdom during minority or incapacity of the sovereign. Also **pro·tect′er.** —**pro·tec′tress** *n.fem.* —**pro·tec′tor·ship** *n.*

pro·tec·tor·ate (prə·tek′tər·it) *n.* 1. A relation of protection and partial control by a strong nation over a weaker power. 2. A country or region under the protection of another. 3. The office, or period of office, of a protector of a kingdom.

pro·té·gé (prō′tə·zhā, *Fr.* prô·tā·zhā′) *n.* One specially cared for by another who is older or more powerful. [< F < L *protegere* to protect] —**pro′té·gée** *n.fem.*

pro·te·in (prō′tēn, prō′tē·in) *n.* *Biochem.* Any of a class of highly complex nitrogenous organic compounds that are made up of amino acids and are essential in animal metabolism. [< Gk. *prōtos* first]

pro tem·po·re (prō tem′pə·rē) *Latin* For the time being.

pro·test (*n.* & *adj.* prō′test; *v.* prə·test′) *n.* 1. A solemn or formal objection or declaration. 2. A public expression of dissent. —*adj.* Of or relating to public protest: *protest* demonstrations. —*v.t.* 1. To assert earnestly or positively. 2. To make a protest against; object to. —*v.i.* 3. To make solemn affirmation. 4. To make a protest; object. [< L *pro-* forth + *testari* to testify] —**pro·test′er** *n.* —**pro·test′ing·ly** *adv.*

prot·es·tant (prot′is·tənt, prə·tes′-) *n.* One who makes a protest. [< L *protestari*]

Prot·es·tant (prot′is·tənt) *n.* One who belongs to a Christian church or sect other than the Roman Catholic and Eastern Orthodox Churches. —**Prot′es·tant** *adj.* —**Prot′es·tant·ism** *n.*

Protestant Episcopal Church A religious body in the U.S. that is descended from the Church of England: also called *Episcopal Church.*

prot·es·ta·tion (prot′is·tā′shən) *n.* 1. The act of protesting; also, that which is protested. 2. A formal declaration of dissent. 3. Any solemn or urgent avowal.

proto- *combining form* 1. First in rank or time; chief; typical. 2. Primitive; original: *prototype.* Also, before vowels, *prot-.* [< Gk. *prōtos* first]

pro·to·col (prō′tə·kôl, -kol) *n.* 1. The rules of diplomatic and state etiquette and ceremony. 2. The preliminary draft of diplomatic negotiation or of an official document. —*v.i.* **pro·to·coled** or **·colled, pro·to·col·ing** or **·col·ling** To write or form protocols. [< LGk. *prōtokollon* the first sheet glued to a papyrus roll, enumerating the contents]

pro·ton (prō′ton) *n.* *Physics* One of the elementary particles in the nucleus of an atom, having a positive electrical charge. [< Gk. *prōtos* first]

pro·to·plasm (prō′tə·plaz′əm) *n.* *Biol.* A complex colloid that forms the essential living matter of plant and animal cells. [< Gk. *prōtos* first + *plasma* form] —**pro′to·plas′mic** *adj.*

pro·to·type (prō′tə·tīp) *n.* 1. *Biol.* A primitive or ancestral organism; an archetype. 2. An original model on which subsequent forms are to be based. [< Gk. *prōtos* first + *typos* form] —**pro′to·typ′al, pro′to·typ′ic** (-tip′ik)·or **·i·cal** *adj.*

pro·to·zo·an (prō′tə·zō′ən) *n.* *pl.* **·zo·a** Any of a phylum of microscopic single-celled organisms, largely aquatic and including many parasites. Also **pro′to·zo′on.** [< Gk. *prōtos* first + *zōion* animal] —**pro′to·zo′an, pro′to·zo′ic** *adj.*

pro·tract (prō·trakt′) *v.t.* 1. To extend in time; prolong. 2. *Anat.* To protrude or extend. [< L *pro-* forward + *trahere* to draw] —**pro·trac′tion** *n.* —**pro·trac′tive** *adj.*

pro·trac·tile (prō·trak′til) *adj.* Capable of being protracted or protruded.

pro·trac·tor (prō·trak′tər) *n.* 1. An instrument for measuring and laying off angles. 2. *Anat.* A muscle that extends a limb or moves it forward.

pro·trude (prō·trōōd′) *v.t.* & *v.i.* **·trud·ed, ·trud·ing** To push or thrust out; project outward. [< L *pro-* forward + *trudere* to thrust] —**pro·tru′sion** (-trōō′zhən) *n.*

pro·tru·sive (prō·trōō′siv) *adj.* 1. Tending to protrude; protruding. 2. Pushing or driving forward. —**pro·tru′sive·ly** *adv.* —**pro·tru′sive·ness** *n.*

pro·tu·ber·ance (prō·tōō′bər·əns, -tyōō′-) *n.* 1. Something that protrudes; a knob; prominence. 2. The state of being protuberant. [< L *pro-* forth + *tuber* swelling] —**pro·tu′ber·ant** *adj.* —**pro·tu′ber·ant·ly** *adv.*

proud (proud) *adj.* 1. Actuated by, possessing, or manifesting pride; arrogant; also, self-respecting. 2. Sensible of honor and personal elation: generally followed by *of* or by a verb in the infinitive. 3. High-mettled, as a horse. 4. Being a cause of honorable pride, as a distinction. [OE *prūd*] —**proud′ly** *adv.*

prove (prōōv) *v.* **proved, proved** or **prov·en, prov·ing** *v.t.* 1. To show to be true or genuine, as by evidence or argument. 2. To determine the quality or genuineness of; test: to *prove* a gun. 3. *Math.* To verify the accuracy of (a calculation, etc.). —*v.i.* 4. To be shown to be by the result or outcome; turn out to be. [< L *probus* upright] —**prov′a·ble** *adj.* —**prov′er** *n.*

prov·e·nance (prov′ə·nəns) *n.* Provenience. [< F See PROVENIENCE.]

Pro·ven·çal (prō′vən·säl′, *Fr.* prō·väṅ·säl′) *n.* 1. A native or resident of Provence, France. 2. The Romance language of Provence, used esp. in the 12th and 13th c. in the lyric literature of the troubadours. —**Pro′ven·çal′** *adj.*

prov·en·der (prov′ən·dər) *n.* 1. Food for cattle, esp. dry food, as hay. 2. Provisions generally. —*v.t.* To provide with food, as cattle. [< L *praebere* to supply]

pro·ve·ni·ence (prō·vēn′yəns) *n.* Origin or source. [< L *pro-* forth + *venire* to come]

prov·erb (prov′ərb) *n.* A pithy saying, esp. one condensing the wisdom of experience; adage; saw; maxim. [< L *pro-* before + *verbum* word] —**pro·ver′bi·al** *adj.* —**pro·ver′bi·al·ly** *adv.*

Prov·erbs (prov′ərbz) *n.pl.* (*construed as sing.*) An Old Testament book of moral sayings.

pro·vide (prə·vīd′) *v.* **·vid·ed, ·vid·ing** *v.t.* 1. To supply or furnish. 2. To afford; yield. 3. To prepare, make ready, or procure beforehand. —*v.i.* 4. To take measures in advance: with *for* or *against.* 5. To furnish means of subsistence: usu. with *for*. **6.** To make a stipulation. [< L *pro-* before + *videre* to see] **—pro·vid′er** *n.*

pro·vid·ed (prə·vī′did) *conj.* On condition; if: He will get the loan *provided* he offers good security. Also **pro·vid′ing.**

prov·i·dence (prov′ə·dəns) *n.* **1.** The care exercised by God over the universe. **2.** The exercise of foresight and care for the future. **3.** *cap.* God; the Deity. [< L *providere* to foresee]

prov·i·dent (prov′ə·dənt) *adj.* Anticipating and making ready for future wants. **—prov′i·dent·ly** *adv.*

prov·i·den·tial (prov′ə·den′shəl) *adj.* **1.** Resulting from or involving God's providence. **2.** Lucky; opportune. **—prov′i·den′tial·ly** *adv.*

prov·ince (prov′ins) *n.* **1.** Any large administrative division of a country. **2.** *pl.* Regions lying at a distance from the capital or most populous part of a country. **3.** A sphere of knowledge, activity, or endeavor. [< L *provincia*]

pro·vin·cial (prə·vin′shəl) *adj.* **1.** Of or pertaining to a province. **2.** Confined to a province; rustic. **3.** Narrow; uncultured. **—pro·vin′cial** *n.* **—pro·vin′cial·ly** *adv.*

pro·vin·cial·ism (prə·vin′shəl·iz′əm) *n.* **1.** The quality of being provincial. **2.** A provincial custom, esp. of speech.

pro·vi·sion (prə·vizh′ən) *n.* **1.** The act of providing, or the state of being provided. **2.** Measures taken or means made ready in advance. **3.** *pl.* Food or a supply of food. **4.** The part of an agreement, instrument, etc., referring to one specific thing; a stipulation. **—***v.t.* To provide with food or provisions. [< L *pro-* before + *videre* to see] **—pro·vi′sion·er** *n.*

pro·vi·sion·al (prə·vizh′ən·əl) *adj.* Provided for a present service or temporary necessity; adopted tentatively. **—pro·vi′sion·al·ly** *adv.*

pro·vi·so (prə·vī′zō) *n.* *pl.* **·sos** or **·soes** A stipulation or clause, as in a contract, limiting, modifying, or rendering conditional its operation. [< Med.L, it being provided]

prov·o·ca·tion (prov′ə·kā′shən) *n.* **1.** The act of provoking. **2.** An incitement to action.

pro·voc·a·tive (prə·vok′ə·tiv) *adj.* Serving to provoke; stimulating. **—***n.* That which provokes or tends to provoke. **—pro·voc′a·tive·ly** *adv.* **—pro·voc′a·tive·ness** *n.*

pro·voke (prə·vōk′) *v.t.* **·voked, ·vok·ing** **1.** To stir to anger or resentment; vex. **2.** To arouse or stimulate to some action. **3.** To stir up or bring about: to *provoke* a quarrel. [< L *pro-* forth + *vocare* to call] **—pro·vok′ing·ly** *adv.*

pro·vo·lo·ne (prō′və·lō′nē) *n.* A hard smooth cheese that is molded into various shapes and is often smoked. [< Ital.]

prov·ost (prō′vōst, prov′əst) *n.* **1.** A high-ranking official or authority. **2.** In some English and American colleges, the head of the faculty. [Ult. < L *praepositus* chief] **—prov′ost·ship** *n.*

pro·vost marshal (prō′vō) A military or naval officer exercising police functions.

prow (prou) *n.* The fore part of the hull of a vessel; the bow. [< Gk. *prōira*]

prow·ess (prou′is) *n.* **1.** Strength, skill, and courage, esp. in battle. **2.** Exceptional ability. [< OF *prou* brave]

prowl (proul) *v.t. & v.i.* To roam about stealthily, as in search of prey or plunder. **—***n.* The act of prowling. [ME *prollen* to search] **—prowl′er** *n.*

prowl car A police patrol car.

prox·i·mate (prok′sə·mit) *adj.* Being in immediate relation with something else; next. [< L *proximus* nearest] **—prox′i·mate·ly** *adv.*

prox·im·i·ty (prok·sim′ə·tē) *n.* The state or fact of being near or next; nearness.

proximity fuse A fuse in a projectile, usu. activated by an electronic device, that detonates by simple proximity to the target.

prox·i·mo (prok′sə·mō) *adv.* In or of the next or coming month. [See PROXIMATE.]

prox·y (prok′sē) *n.* *pl.* **prox·ies** **1.** A person empowered by another to act for him. **2.** The office or right to so act, or the instrument conferring it.. [ME *prokecie*]

prude (prōōd) *n.* A person who makes an affected display of modesty and propriety, esp. in matters relating to sex. [< F *preude* (*femme*) strong, hence, modest (woman)] **—prud′er·y, prud′ish·ness** *n.* **—prud′ish** *adj.* **—prud′ish·ly** *adv.*

pru·dent (prōōd′nt) *adj.* **1.** Cautious; discreet. **2.** Exercising sound judgment. **3.** Not extravagant. [< L *prudens, -entis* knowing, foreseeing] **—pru′dence** *n.* **—pru·den·tial** (prōō·den′shəl) *adj.* **—pru·den′·tial·ly, pru′dent·ly** *adv.*

prune[1] (prōōn) *n.* The dried fruit of the plum. [< L *prunum*]

prune[2] (prōōn) *v.t. & v.i.* **pruned, prun·ing** To trim or cut branches or parts from (trees, etc.) so as to improve growth, appearance, etc. [< OF *proöignier, proignier*] **—prun′er** *n.*

pru·ri·ent (prŏŏr′ē·ənt) *adj.* **1.** Having lustful cravings or desires. **2.** Lewd. [< L *prurire* to itch] **—pru′ri·ence** *n.* **—pru′ri·ent·ly** *adv.*

Prus·sian (prush′ən) *adj.* **1.** Of or pertaining to Prussia, its inhabitants, or their language. **2.** Militaristic; overbearing. **—***n.* A native or inhabitant of Prussia.

prus·sic acid (prus′ik) Hydrocyanic acid.

pry[1] (prī) *v.i.* **pried, pry·ing** To look or peer carefully, curiously, or slyly; snoop. **—***n.* *pl.* **pries** **1.** A sly and searching inspection. **2.** One who pries; an inquisitive, prying person. [ME *prien*] **—pry′ing·ly** *adv.*

pry[2] (prī) *v.t.* **pried, pry·ing** **1.** To raise, move, or open by means of a lever; prize. **2.** To obtain by effort. **—***n.* A lever, as a bar, stick, or beam; also, leverage. [< PRIZE[2]]

pry·er (prī′ər) See PRIER.

psalm (säm) *n.* **1.** *Often cap.* A sacred song or lyric contained in the Old Testament Book of Psalms. **2.** Any sacred song. **—***v.t.* To celebrate or praise in psalms. [< Gk. *psalmos* song accompanied by a harp] **—psalm′ist** *n.*

psalm·o·dy (sä′mə·dē, sal′-) *n.* *pl.* **·dies** **1.** The use of psalms in divine worship. **2.** A collection of psalms. [< Gk. *psalmos* psalm + *aeidein* to sing]

Psalms (sämz) A book of the Old Testament, containing 150 hymns. Also **Book of Psalms.**

psal·ter (sôl′tər) *n.* The psalms appointed to be read or sung at any given service. [See PSALTERY.] **—psal·te·ri·an** (sôl·tir′ē·ən, sal-) *adj.*

Psal·ter (sôl′tər) *n.* The Book of Psalms,

esp. for use in religious services. Also **Psal′ter·y.**

psal·ter·y (sôl′tər·ē) *n. pl.* **·ter·ies** An ancient stringed instrument played by plucking with a pick. [< Gk. *psallein* to pluck]

pseu·do (sōō′dō) *adj.* Pretended; sham.

pseudo- *combining form* False; pretended. Also, before vowels, **pseud-**. [< Gk. *pseudēs* false]

pseu·do·nym (sōō′də·nim) *n.* A fictitious name; pen name. [< Gk. *pseudēs* false + *onoma* name] **—pseu·don·y·mous** (sōō·don′ə·məs) *adj.* **—pseu·don′y·mous·ly** *adv.* **—pseu·don′y·mous·ness, pseu′do·nym′i·ty** *n.*

pshaw (shô) *interj.* An exclamation of annoyance, disapproval, disgust, or impatience. —*v.t. & v.i.* To exclaim *pshaw* at (a person or thing).

psi (sī, psī, psē) *n.* The twenty-third letter in the Greek alphabet (Ψ, ψ), equivalent to English *ps*.

pso·ri·a·sis (sə·rī′ə·sis) *n. Pathol.* A noncontagious, inflammatory skin disease, characterized by reddish patches and white scales. [< Gk. *psōra* an itch]

psych (sīk) *v.t. & v.i. Informal* 1. To become or cause to become emotionally aroused or prepared: also **psych up.** 2. To lose or cause to lose courage, resolve, etc.: also **psych out.**

psy·che (sī′kē) *n.* 1. The human soul. 2. *Psychoanal.* The mind, often regarded as an entity functioning apart from or independently of the body. [< Gk. *psychē* soul]

psy·che·del·ic (sī′kē·del′ik) *adj.* 1. Causing or having to do with an abnormal stimulation of consciousness or perception. 2. Resembling the effects of taking psychedelic drugs: *psychedelic* art. [< Gk. *psychē* soul + *del* (*os*) manifest]

psy·chi·a·try (si·kī′ə·trē, si-) *n.* The branch of medicine that deals with the diagnosis and treatment of mental disorders. **—psy·chi·at·ric** (sī′kē·at′rik) *adj.* **—psy·chi′a·trist** *n.*

psy·chic (sī′kik) *adj.* 1. Pertaining to the mind. 2. Pertaining to mental phenomena that appear to be independent of normal sensory stimuli, as clairvoyance, telepathy, and extrasensory perception. 3. Sensitive to mental or occult phenomena. Also **psy′chi·cal.** —*n.* One sensitive to extrasensory phenomena. [See PSYCHE.] **—psy′chi·cal·ly** *adv.*

psy·cho (sī′kō) *n. pl.* **·chos** One who is mentally disturbed.

psycho- *combining form* Mind; soul; spirit: *psychosomatic.* Also, before vowels, **psych-**. [< Gk. *psychē*]

psy·cho·a·nal·y·sis (sī′kō·ə·nal′ə·sis) *n.* A system of psychotherapy that seeks to alleviate neuroses and other mental disorders by the analysis of unconscious factors as revealed in dreams, free association, etc. **—psy′cho·an′a·lyst** (-an′ə·list) *n.* **—psy′cho·an′a·lyt′ic** (-an′ə·lit′ik) or **·i·cal** *adj.* **—psy′cho·an′a·lyt′i·cal·ly** *adv.*

psy·cho·an·a·lyze (sī′kō·an′ə·līz) *v.t.* **·lyzed, ·lyz·ing** To treat by psychoanalysis. Also *Brit.* **psy′cho·an′a·lyse.**

psy·cho·chem·i·cal (sī′kō·kem′i·kəl) *n. Chem.* A drug or compound that affects consciousness and behavior. **—psy′cho·chem′i·cal** *adj.*

psy·cho·gen·ic (sī′kō·jen′ik) *adj.* Having mental origin, or being affected by mental conflicts and states.

psy·cho·his·to·ry (sī′kō·his′tə·rē) *n.* History of great persons or events from a psychological point of view. **—psy′cho·his·tor′i·cal** (-his·tôr′i·kəl) *adj.* **—psy′cho·his·to′ri·an** (-his·tôr′ē·ən) *n.*

psy·chol·o·gize (sī·kol′ə·jīz) *v.* **·gized, ·giz·ing** —*v.t.* 1. To interpret by means of psychology. —*v.i.* 2. To theorize on psychology.

psy·chol·o·gy (sī·kol′ə·jē) *n. pl.* **·gies** 1. The science of the human mind in any of its aspects, operations, powers, or functions. 2. The behavior patterns regarded as characteristic of an individual, type, group, etc. **—psy·cho·log·i·cal** (sī′kə·loj′i·kəl) *adj.* **—psy′cho·log′i·cal·ly** *adv.* **—psy·chol′o·gist** *n.*

psy·cho·neu·ro·sis (sī′kō·nōō·rō′sis, -nyōō-) *n. pl.* **·ses** (-sēz) *Psychiatry* Neurosis. **—psy′cho·neu·rot′ic** (-rot′ik) *adj. & n.*

psy·cho·path (sī′kō·path) *n.* One who is mentally unstable, esp. in a criminal or antisocial manner.

psy·chop·a·thy (sī·kop′ə·thē) *n.* Mental disorder. **—psy·cho·path·ic** (sī′kō·path′ik) *adj.*

psy·cho·sis (sī·kō′sis) *n. pl.* **·ses** (-sēz) *Psychiatry* A severe mental disorder, often involving disorganization of the total personality. [< Gk. *psychoein* to animate]

psy·cho·so·mat·ic (sī′kō·sō·mat′ik) *adj.* Of or pertaining to the effect of emotional states upon the body, with special reference to certain disorders.

psy·cho·ther·a·py (sī′kō·ther′ə·pē) *n. pl.* **·pies** The treatment of mental disorders by psychological methods, as hypnosis, re-education, psychoanalysis, etc. **—psy′cho·ther′a·peu′tic** (-pyōō′tik) *adj.* **—psy′cho·ther′a·pist** *n.*

psy·chot·ic (sī·kot′ik) *n.* One suffering from a psychosis. —*adj.* Of or characterized by a psychosis.

psychro- *combining form* Cold. [< Gk. *psychros*]

ptar·mi·gan (tär′mə·gən) *n. pl.* **·gans** or **·gan** A grouse of the northern hemisphere, having a white winter plumage and feathered toes. [< Scot. Gaelic *tarmachan*]

PT boat A small, highly maneuverable vessel, armed with torpedoes. [< P(ATROL) T(ORPEDO)]

ptero- *combining form* Wing; feather; winglike. Also, before vowels, **pter-**. [< Gk. *pteron* wing]

pter·o·dac·tyl (ter′ə·dak′til) *n. Paleontol.* Any of a genus of extinct flying reptiles. [< Gk. *pteron* wing + *daktylos* finger]

-pterous *combining form* Having (a specified number or kind of) wings: *dipterous.* [< Gk. *pteron* wing]

pto·maine (tō′mān, tō·mān′) *n. Biochem.* Any of a class of basic nitrogenous compounds, some of which are poisonous, derived from decomposing animal or vegetable protein. [< Gk. *ptōma* corpse]

ptomaine poisoning An erroneous term for food poisoning.

pub (pub) *n. Brit. Informal* A public house; inn; tavern.

pu·ber·ty (pyōō′bər·tē) *n. pl.* **·ties** The period during which an individual becomes physiologically capable of reproduction. [< L *pubes, puberis* an adult]

pu·bes·cent (pyōō·bes′ənt) *adj.* 1. Arriving or having arrived at puberty. 2. Having a growth of soft, fine hairs, as certain plants. [< L *pubescere* to grow hair, attain puberty] **—pu·bes′cence** *n.*

pu·bic (pyōō′bik) *adj.* Of or pertaining to the region in the lower part of the abdomen.

pu·bis (pyōō′bis) *n. pl.* **·bes** (-bēz) *Anat.* Either of the two bones that join with a third to form an arch on either ventral side of the pelvis. [See PUBERTY.]

pub·lic (pub′lik) *adj.* 1. Of, pertaining to, or affecting the people at large or the community. 2. Maintained by or for the public: *public* parks. 3. Participated in by the people: a *public* demonstration. 4. Well-known; open; notorious: a *public* scandal. 5. Acting before or for the community: a *public* official. **—***n.* 1. People as a whole; the community. 2. An audience; esp., the admirers of an actor or other celebrity. [< L *publicus*] **—pub′lic·ly** *adv.* **—pub′lic·ness** *n.*

pub·li·can (pub′lə·kən) *n.* 1. *Brit.* The keeper of a public house. 2. In ancient Rome, a tax collector. [< L *publicum* public revenue]

pub·li·ca·tion (pub′lə·kā′shən) *n.* 1. The act of publishing. 2. Any printed work placed on sale or otherwise distributed or offered for distribution. [See PUBLISH.]

public domain Lands owned by a government; public lands. **—in the public domain** Available for unrestricted use: said of material on which copyright or patent right has expired.

public enemy A person, esp. a criminal, regarded as a menace to the public.

public house 1. An inn or hotel. 2. *Brit.* A place licensed to sell intoxicating liquors; a saloon.

pub·li·cist (pub′lə·sist) *n.* 1. A writer on international law or on topics of public interest. 2. One engaged in public relations work; a publicity agent.

pub·lic·i·ty (pub·lis′ə·tē) *n.* 1. Information or personal news intended to promote the interests of individuals, institutions, etc. 2. The attention or interest of the public gained by any method.

pub·li·cize (pub′lə·sīz) *v.t.* **·cized, ·ciz·ing** To advertise.

public opinion The prevailing ideas, beliefs, and aims of the people, collectively.

public relations The activities and techniques used by organizations and individuals to establish favorable attitudes and responses in their behalf; also, the occupation of establishing such attitudes and responses.

public school 1. *U.S.* A school maintained by public funds for the free education of the children of the community, usu. covering elementary and secondary grades. 2. *Brit.* A private or endowed school, esp. one that prepares students for the universities.

public utility A business organization or industry that supplies water, electricity, gas, etc., to the public, and is subject to particular governmental regulations.

public works Works or improvements built with public money, as parks, roads, etc.

pub·lish (pub′lish) *v.t.* 1. To print and issue (a book, magazine, map, etc.) to the public. 2. To make known or announce publicly; promulgate; proclaim. [< L *publicare* to make public] **—pub′lish·a·ble** *adj.* **—pub′lish·er** *n.*

puce (pyōōs) *adj.* Of a dark brown or purplish brown. [< F, flea color, flea]

puck[1] (puk) *n.* An evil sprite or hobgoblin. [OE *pūca*]

puck[2] (puk) *n.* The hard, black rubber disk used in playing ice hockey. [? < dial. E, to strike]

puck·er (puk′ər) *v.t. & v.i.* To gather or draw up into small folds or wrinkles. **—***n.* A wrinkle or group of wrinkles. [Appar. freq. of POKE[2]] **—puck′er·y** *adj.*

puck·ish (puk′ish) *adj.* Mischievous; impish.

pud·ding (pōōd′ing) *n.* 1. A sweetened and flavored dessert of soft food, usu. made of boiled milk, flavoring, a thickening agent, etc. 2. A sausage of seasoned minced meat usu. boiled or broiled. [ME *poding*]

pud·dle (pud′l) *n.* 1. A small pool of water, esp. dirty water. 2. A small pool of any liquid. **—***v.t.* **·dled, ·dling** *Metall.* To convert (molten pig iron) into wrought iron by melting and stirring in the presence of oxidizing substances. [ME *podel*, dim. of OE *pudd* ditch] **—pud′dler** *n.* **—pud′dly** *adj.*

pud·dling (pud′ling) *n. Metall.* The operation or business of making wrought iron from pig iron.

pudg·y (puj′ē) *adj.* **pudg·i·er, pudg·i·est** Short and fat; dumpy; chubby: also *podgy.* [< Scot.] **—pudg′i·ness** *n.*

pueb·lo (pweb′lō *for def. 1*; pwā′blō *for def. 2*) *n. pl.* **·los** 1. A communal adobe or stone building or group of buildings of the Indians of the SW U.S. 2. A town or village of Indians or Spanish Americans, as in Mexico. [< Sp., village]

Pueb·lo (pweb′lō) *n.* A member of one of the Indian tribes of Mexico and the SW U.S., as a Zuñi, Hopi, etc.

pu·er·ile (pyōō′ər·il, pyōō′rəl, -rīl, pwer′əl, -īl) *adj.* 1. Pertaining to or characteristic of childhood; juvenile. 2. Immature; weak; silly: a *puerile* suggestion. [< L *puer* boy, child] **—pu′er·ile·ly** *adv.* **—pu′er·il′i·ty** *n.*

pu·er·per·al (pyōō·ûr′pər·əl) *adj. Med.* Of or connected with childbirth. [< L *puer* child + *parere* to bear]

Puer·to Ri·can (pôr′tō rē′kən, pwer′-) *adj.* Of Puerto Rico or its inhabitants. **—Puerto Rican** *n.*

puff (puf) *n.* 1. A breath emitted suddenly and with force; also, a sudden emission, as of air, smoke, or steam. 2. A light, air-filled piece of pastry. 3. A light ball or pad for dusting powder on the hair or skin. 4. Excessive praise, as in a newspaper or advertisement. **—***v.i.* 1. To blow in puffs, as the wind. 2. To breathe hard, as after violent exertion. 3. To smoke a cigar, etc., with puffs. 4. To move, act, or exert oneself while emitting puffs: with *away, up,* etc. 5. To swell or distend: with *up* or *out.* **—***v.t.* 6. To send forth or emit with short puffs or breaths. 7. To smoke, as a pipe or cigar, with puffs. 8. To swell or distend. [ME *puf*] **—puff′er** *n.*

puff·ball (puf′bôl′) *n.* Any of various globular fungi that puff out dustlike spores when broken open.

puf·fin (puf′in) *n.* A sea bird allied to the auk and having a deep, compressed, highly colored bill. [ME *poffin*]

puff·y (puf′ē) *adj.* **puff·i·er, puff·i·est** 1. Swollen with or as with air, etc. 2. Inflated in manner; bombastic. 3. Blowing in puffs. —**puff′i·ly** *adv.* —**puff′i·ness** *n.*

pug¹ (pug) *n.* Clay worked with water, for molding pottery or bricks. —*v.t.* **pugged, pug·ging** To knead or work (clay) with water, as in brickmaking. [Origin unknown]

pug² (pug) *n.* 1. A breed of dog characterized by a short, square body, upturned nose, curled tail, and short, smooth coat. 2. A pug nose. [Prob. alter. of PUCK¹]

pug³ (pug) *n. Slang* A professional boxer. [Short for PUGILIST]

pu·gi·lism (pyōō′jə·liz′əm) *n.* The art or practice of boxing or fighting with the fists. [< L *pugil* boxer] —**pu′gi·list** *n.* —**pu′gi·lis′tic** *adj.*

pug·na·cious (pug·nā′shəs) *adj.* Disposed or inclined to fight; quarrelsome. [< L *pugnare* to fight] —**pug·na′cious·ly** *adv.* —**pug·nac′i·ty** (-nas′ə·tē), **pug·na′cious·ness** *n.*

pug nose A short nose tilted upward at the end. [< PUG²] —**pug-nosed** (pug′nōzd′) *adj.*

pu·is·sant (pyōō′ə·sənt, pyōō·is′ənt, pwis′·ənt) *adj.* Powerful; mighty. [< L *posse* to be able] —**pu′is·sance** *n.* —**pu′is·sant·ly** *adv.*

puke (pyōōk) *v.t. & v.i.* **puked, puk·ing** To vomit or cause to vomit. —*n.* Vomit. [Origin unknown]

puk·ka (puk′ə) *adj. Anglo-Indian* 1. Made of good materials; substantial. 2. Genuine; superior. [< Hind. *pakkā* substantial, cooked, ripe]

pul·chri·tude (pul′krə·tōōd, -tyōōd) *n.* Beauty; grace; physical charm. [< L *pulcher* beautiful] —**pul′chri·tu′di·nous** *adj.*

pule (pyōōl) *v.i.* **puled, pul·ing** To cry plaintively, as a child; whimper; whine. [Prob. imit.] —**pul′er** *n.*

pull (pōōl) *v.t.* 1. To apply force so as to cause motion toward; drag; tug. 2. To draw or remove from a fixed place. 3. To give a pull or tug to. 4. To pluck, as a fowl. 5. To rip; tear; rend. 6. To strain so as to cause injury. 7. *Slang* To put into effect; carry out: often with *off.* 8. *Slang* To draw out so as to use. 9. *Printing* To make or obtain by impression from type: to *pull* a proof. 10. In boxing, to deliver (a punch, etc.) with less than one's full strength. —*v.i.* 11. To use force in hauling, dragging, moving, etc. 12. To move: with *out, in, away, ahead,* etc. 13. To drink or inhale deeply. 14. To propel a boat with oars; row. —**to pull for** 1. To strive in behalf of. 2. *Informal* To declare one's allegiance to. —**to pull off** *Informal* To accomplish. —**to pull oneself together** To regain one's composure. —**to pull out** To withdraw, as from established position. —**to pull through** To manage to succeed, recover, etc. —*n.* 1. The act or result of pulling. 2. Something that is pulled, as the handle of a drawer. 3. An impression made by pulling the lever of a hand press. 4. A long swallow, or a deep puff. 5. Any steady, continuous effort. 6. *Slang* A means of influencing those in power; influence. 7. The amount of resistance met in drawing a bowstring, pulling a trigger, etc., usu. measured in pounds. [OE *pullian* to pluck] —**pull′er** *n.*

pull·back (pōōl′bak′) *n.* A planned withdrawal of military forces.

pul·let (pōōl′it) *n.* A young hen, or one not fully grown. [< OF *poule* hen]

pul·ley (pōōl′ē) *n. pl.* **·leys** 1. A wheel grooved to receive a rope, and usu. mounted in a block, used to increase the mechanical advantage of an applied force. 2. A block with its pulleys or tackle. 3. A wheel driving, carrying, or being driven by a belt. [Prob. < Gk. *polos* axis]

Pull·man (pōōl′mən) *n.* A sleeping car or chair car on a passenger train: a trade name. Also **Pullman car.** [after George M. *Pullman,* 1831–97, U.S. inventor]

pull·out (pōōl′out′) *n.* 1. A withdrawal, as of troops. 2. *Aeron.* The maneuver of an airplane in passing from a dive to horizontal flight.

pull·o·ver (pōōl′ō′vər) *n.* A garment put on by being drawn over the head, as a sweater. —**pull′o′ver** *adj.*

pulmo- *combining form* Lung. [< L *pulmo, -onis*]

pul·mo·nar·y (pul′mə·ner′ē) *adj.* 1. Of, pertaining to, or affecting the lungs: also *pneumonic.* 2. Having lunglike organs. [< L *pulmo, -onis* lung]

Pul·mo·tor (pul′mō′tər, pōōl′-) *n.* An apparatus for producing artificial respiration by forcing oxygen into the lungs: a trade name. Also **pul′mo′tor.** [< PUL(MO)- + MOTOR]

pulp (pulp) *n.* 1. A moist, soft, slightly cohering mass of matter, as the succulent part of fruit. 2. The moist mixture of ground wood fibers or rags that forms the substance of paper. 3. A magazine printed on rough, unglazed paper, and usu. having contents of a cheap, sensational nature. 4. *Dent.* The soft tissue of vessels and nerves that fills the central cavity of a tooth. [< L *pulpa* flesh, pulp of fruit, pith] —**pulp** *v.t. & v.i.* —**pulp′i·ness** *n.* —**pulp′y** *adj.* **·i·er, ·i·est**

pul·pit (pōōl′pit) *n.* An elevated stand or desk for a preacher in a church. [< L *pulpitum* scaffold, stage]

pulp·wood (pulp′wōōd′) *n.* The soft wood of certain trees, as the spruce, used in the manufacture of paper.

pul·sar (pul′sär′) *n.* A rotating, collapsed neutron star, a source of regularly pulsing radio waves. [< PULSE + QUASAR]

pul·sate (pul′sāt) *v.i.* **·sat·ed, ·sat·ing** 1. To move or throb with rhythmical impulses, as the pulse or heart. 2. To vibrate; quiver. [< L *pulsus,* pp. of *pellere* to beat] —**pul·sa′tion** *n.* —**pul′sa·tive** (-sə·tiv) *adj.* —**pul·sa′tor** *n.* —**pul′sa·to′ry** (-sə·tôr′ē) *adj.*

pulse (puls) *n.* 1. *Physiol.* The rhythmical beating of the arteries resulting from the successive contractions of the heart. 2. *Telecom.* A brief surge of electrical or electromagnetic energy, usu. transmitted as a signal in communication. —*v.i.* **pulsed, puls·ing** To pulsate; throb. [< L *pulsus* (*venarum*) the beating (of the veins)] —**pulse′less** *adj.*

pul·ver·ize (pul′və·rīz) *v.* **·ized, ·iz·ing** *v.t.* 1. To reduce to powder or dust, as by crushing. 2. To demolish; annihilate. —*v.i.* 3. To become reduced to powder or dust. Also *Brit.* **pul′ver·ise.** [< L *pulvis, pulveris* powder, dust] —**pul′ver·iz′a·ble** *adj.* —**pul′·ver·i·za′tion** *n.* —**pul′ver·iz′er** *n.*

pu·ma (pyo͞o′mə) *n.* A reddish carnivore of the cat family: also called *cougar, mountain cat, mountain lion.* [< Peruvian]

pum·ice (pum′is) *n.* Spongy volcanic lava, used as an abrasive and polishing material, esp. when powdered. Also **pumice stone.** —*v.t.* **·iced, ·ic·ing** To smooth, polish, or clean with pumice. [< L *pumex, pumicis*] —**pu·mi·ceous** (pyo͞o·mish′əs) *adj.*

pum·mel (pum′əl) *v.t.* See POMMEL.

pump[1] (pump) *n.* A mechanical device for raising, circulating, exhausting, or compressing a liquid or gas. —*v.t.* 1. To raise with a pump, as water. 2. To remove the water, etc., from. 3. To inflate with air by means of a pump. 4. To force from or as if from a pump. 5. To obtain information from persistently or subtly: to *pump* a witness. —*v.i.* 6. To work a pump; raise water or other liquid with a pump. 7. To move up and down like a pump handle. [Prob. < MDu. *pompe*] —**pump′er** *n.*

pump[2] (pump) *n.* A low-cut shoe without a fastening. [Origin uncertain]

pum·per·nick·el (pum′pər·nik′əl) *n.* A coarse, dark, sour bread made from unsifted rye. [< G]

pump·kin (pump′kin, pung′-) *n.* A large, round, edible, yellow-orange fruit borne by a coarse trailing vine with heart-shaped leaves. [< Gk. *pepon* melon].

pun (pun) *n.* The humorous use of a word having two different, more or less incongruous meanings. —*v.i.* **punned, pun·ning** To make a pun. [Origin uncertain] —**pun′ning·ly** *adv.*

punch[1] (punch) *n.* A tool for perforating, stamping, shaping, or indenting. —*v.t.* To perforate, shape, indent, etc., with a punch. [Prob. ult. < L *pungere* to prick]

punch[2] (punch) *v.t.* 1. To strike sharply, esp. with the fist. 2. To operate; work; use: to *punch* a time clock. 3. In the West, to drive (cattle). —*n.* 1. A swift blow with the fist. 2. *Slang* Vitality; force: an editorial with *punch.* [ME *punchen*] —**punch′er** *n.*

punch[3] (punch) *n.* A beverage having wine or spirits, milk, tea, or fruit juices as a basic ingredient, sweetened, and sometimes spiced. [? < Skt. *pañchan* five; from the five original ingredients]

punch card In data processing, a card with punched holes that convey information by their position on the card. Also **punched card.**

punch-drunk (punch′drungk′) *adj.* 1. Groggy; slow in movement, speech, etc., from repeated blows to the head: said of prize fighters. 2. Confused; dazed.

pun·cheon (pun′chən) *n.* A liquor cask of variable capacity, from 72 to 120 gallons. [< OF *ponçon, poinchon*]

punch·ing bag (pun′ching) An inflated or stuffed ball, usu. suspended, that is punched with the fists for exercise.

punc·til·i·o (pungk·til′ē·ō) *n. pl.* **·til·i·os** 1. A fine point of etiquette. 2. Preciseness in the observance of etiquette. [< Ital. *puntiglio* < L *punctum* point]

punc·til·i·ous (pungk·til′ē·əs) *adj.* 1. Very careful in the observance of forms of etiquette, etc. 2. Very precise. —**punc·til′i·ous·ly** *adv.* —**punc·til′i·ous·ness** *n.*

punc·tu·al (pungk′cho͞o·əl) *adj.* 1. Acting or arriving promptly. 2. Done or made precisely at an appointed time. [< L *punctus* pricking, point] —**punc′tu·al′i·ty** (-al′ə·tē) *n.* —**punc′tu·al·ly** *adv.*

punc·tu·ate (pungk′cho͞o·āt) *v.* **·at·ed, ·at·ing** *v.t.* 1. To divide or mark with punctuation. 2. To interrupt at intervals. 3. To emphasize; stress. —*v.i.* 4. To use punctuation. [< L *punctus* point] —**punc′·tu·a′tor** *n.*

punc·tu·a·tion (pungk′cho͞o·ā′shən) *n.* The use of marks in written or printed matter to indicate the separation of the words into sentences, clauses, and phrases, and to aid in the better comprehension of the meaning; also, the marks so used (**punctuation marks**). The chief punctuation marks are:

period (point)	.	braces	{ }
colon	:	dash (em-dash)	—
semicolon	;	(en-dash)	–
comma	,	hyphen	-
question mark	?	quotation marks	“ ”
exclamation point	!	single quotation marks	‘ ’
apostrophe	’	ellipsis	...
parentheses	( )	slash (solidus)	/
brackets	[ ]		

punc·ture (pungk′chər) *v.t. & v.i.* **·tured, ·tur·ing** To pierce or be pierced, as with a sharp point. —*n.* 1. A small hole made by piercing with a sharp point. 2. The act of puncturing. [< L *pungere* to prick]

pun·dit (pun′dit) *n.* 1. A learned man; esp., in India, one versed in laws and religion of the Hindus. 2. An authority. [< Skt. *pandita*]

pun·gent (pun′jənt) *adj.* 1. Sharp or acrid to taste or smell; keen; penetrating: a *pungent* odor. 2. Caustic; biting: *pungent* sarcasm. [< L *pungere* to prick] —**pun′gence, pun′gen·cy** *n.* —**pun′gent·ly** *adv.*

Pu·nic (pyo͞o′nik) *adj.* Of or pertaining to ancient Carthage or the Carthaginians. —*n.* The language of the Carthaginians. [< L *Poenus* Carthaginian, Phoenician]

pun·ish (pun′ish) *v.t.* 1. To subject (a person) to pain, confinement, or other penalty for a crime or fault. 2. To impose a penalty on. 3. To use roughly; injure. [< L *punire*] —**pun′ish·a·ble** *adj.* —**pun′ish·a·bil′i·ty** *n.* —**pun′ish·er** *n.*

pun·ish·ment (pun′ish·mənt) *n.* 1. A penalty imposed, as for transgression of law. ◆Collateral adjective: *penal.* 2. Any ill suffered in consequence of wrongdoing. 3. The act of punishing. 4. *Informal* Rough handling, as in a prize fight.

pu·ni·tive (pyo͞o′nə·tiv) *adj.* Pertaining to or inflicting punishment: *punitive* measures. —**pu′ni·tive·ly** *adv.* —**pu′ni·tive·ness** *n.*

Pun·ja·bi (pun·jä′bē) *n.* 1. A native of the Punjab. 2. The Sanskritic language of the Punjab.

punk[1] (pungk) *n.* 1. Wood decayed through the action of a fungus, useful as tinder. 2. An artificial preparation that will smolder without flame. [< Algonquian]

punk[2] (pungk) *Slang n.* 1. A petty hoodlum. 2. A young, inexperienced person: a contemptuous term. —*adj.* 1. Worthless. 2. Unwell. [Origin uncertain]

pun·ster (pun′stər) *n.* One who puns. Also **pun′ner.**

punt[1] (punt) *n.* A flat-bottomed, square-ended boat, often propelled by a pole, used in shallow waters. —*v.t.* 1. To propel (a boat) by pushing with a pole against the bottom of a shallow stream, lake, etc. —*v.i.* 2. To go or hunt in a punt. [< L *ponto, -onis*] —**punt′er** *n.*

punt[2] (punt) *n.* In football, a kick made by dropping the ball from the hands and kicking it before it strikes the ground. [? Var. of BUNT] —**punt** *v.t. & v.i.* —**punt′er** *n.*

pu·ny (pyōō′nē) *adj.* **·ni·er, ·ni·est** Of small and feeble development or importance; weak and insignificant. [< OF *puis* afterwards + *né* born] —**pu′ni·ly** *adv.* —**pu′ni·ness** *n.*

pup (pup) *n.* 1. A puppy (def. 1). 2. The young of the seal, the shark, and certain other animals. —*v.i.* **pupped, pup·ping** To bring forth pups. [Short for PUPPY]

pu·pa (pyōō′pə) *n. pl.* **·pae** (-pē) *Entomol.* The quiescent stage in the development of an insect, following the larval and preceding the adult stage. [< L, girl, doll, puppet] —**pu′pal** *adj.*

pu·pil[1] (pyōō′pəl) *n.* A person of any age under the care of a teacher; learner. [< L *pupillus*]

pu·pil[2] (pyōō′pəl) *n. Anat.* The contractile opening in the iris of the eye, through which light reaches the retina. [< L *pupilla*]

pup·pet (pup′it) *n.* 1. A small figure of a person, animal, etc., animated by the hand. 2. A marionette. 3. One slavishly subject to the will of another. —*adj.* 1. Of or pertaining to puppets. 2. Not autonomous: a *puppet* state. [< L *pupa* girl, doll, puppet]

pup·pet·eer (pup′i·tir′) *n.* One who manipulates puppets.

pup·py (pup′ē) *n. pl.* **·pies** 1. A young dog: also called *pup.* 2. A pup (def. 2). [< L *pupa* girl, doll] —**pup′py·ish** *adj.*

puppy love Sentimental, adolescent love or infatuation.

pup tent A small wedge-shaped portable tent.

pur·blind (pûr′blīnd′) *adj.* 1. Partly blind. 2. Having little or no insight or understanding. [ME] —**pur′blind′ly** *adv.* —**pur′blind′·ness** *n.*

pur·chase (pûr′chəs) *v.t.* **·chased, ·chas·ing** 1. To acquire by paying money or its equivalent; buy. 2. To obtain by exertion, sacrifice, flattery, etc. —*n.* 1. Something purchased. 2. The act of purchasing. 3. A firm grasp or hold on something so as to prevent slipping, etc. 4. A device that gives a mechanical advantage, as a tackle or lever; also, leverage. [< OF *porchacier* to seek for] —**pur′chas·a·ble** *adj.* —**pur′chas·er** *n.*

pur·dah (pûr′də) *n. Anglo-Indian* 1. A curtain or screen used to seclude women. 2. The state or system of such seclusion. [< Persian *pardah*]

pure (pyŏŏr) *adj.* **pur·er, pur·est** 1. Free from anything that weakens, impairs, or pollutes. 2. Free from adulteration; clear; clean. 3. Free from moral defilement; innocent; chaste. 4. Abstract; nonobjective: *pure* form. 5. Concerned with fundamental research, as distinguished from practical application; theoretical: said of sciences. 6. Nothing but; sheer: *pure* luck. [< L *purus*] —**pure′ness** *n.*

pure·bred (*adj.* pyŏŏr′bred′; *n.* pyŏŏr′bred′) *adj. Biol.* Bred from stock having had no admixture for many generations: said esp. of livestock. —*n.* A purebred animal.

pu·rée (pyōō·rā′, pyŏŏr′ā) *n.* A thick pulp, usu. of vegetables, boiled and strained. [< F < L *purare* to purify]

pure·ly (pyŏŏr′lē) *adv.* 1. So as to be free from admixture, taint, or any harmful substance. 2. Completely; totally. 3. Merely; simply.

pur·ga·tive (pûr′gə·tiv) *adj.* Tending to purge; esp., precipitating a bowel movement. —*n.* A purgative agent.

pur·ga·to·ry (pûr′gə·tôr′ē) *n. pl.* **·ries** 1. In Roman Catholic theology, a state or place where the souls of those who have died penitent are made fit for paradise. 2. Any place or state of temporary banishment, suffering, or punishment. [See PURGE] —**pur′ga·to′ri·al** *adj.*

purge (pûrj) *v.* **purged, purg·ing** *v.t.* 1. To cleanse of what is impure or extraneous; purify. 2. To rid (a group, nation, etc.) of elements regarded as undesirable or inimical, esp. by killing. 3. To cleanse or rid of sin, fault, or defilement. 4. *Med.* To cause evacuation of (the bowels, etc.). —*v.i.* 5. To become clean or pure. —*n.* 1. The act or process of purging: also **pur·ga·tion** (pûr·gā′shən). 2. That which purges, esp. a cathartic. [< L *purgare* to cleanse] —**purg′er** *n.* —**purg′ing** *n.*

pu·ri·fy (pyŏŏr′ə·fī) *v.* **·fied, ·fy·ing** *v.t.* 1. To make pure or clean. 2. To free from sin. —*v.i.* 3. To become pure or clean. [< L *purus* pure + *facere* to make] —**pu′ri·fi·ca′·tion** *n.* —**pu·rif·i·ca·to·ry** (pyōō·rif′ə·kə·tôr′ē) *adj.* —**pu′ri·fi′er** *n.*

pur·ist (pyŏŏr′ist) *n.* One who believes in or practices exact or meticulous usage, as of a language, style, etc. —**pur′ism** *n.* —**pu·ris′tic** *adj.*

pu·ri·tan (pyŏŏr′ə·tən) *n. Sometimes cap.* One who is scrupulously strict or exacting in his religious or moral life: often used disparagingly. —*adj.* Puritanical. —**pu′ri·tan·ism** *n.*

Pu·ri·tan (pyŏŏr′ə·tən) *n.* One of a group of English Protestants who in the 16th and 17th c. advocated simpler forms of creed and ritual in the Church of England. [< L *purus* pure] —**Pu′ri·tan** *adj.* —**Pu′ri·tan·ism** *n.*

pu·ri·tan·i·cal (pyŏŏr′ə·tan′i·kəl) *adj.* 1. Rigidly scrupulous or exacting in religious observance or morals; strict. 2. *Often cap.* Of or characteristic of the Puritans. —**pu′ri·tan′i·cal·ly** *adv.* —**pu′ri·tan′i·cal·ness** *n.*

pu·ri·ty (pyŏŏr′ə·tē) *n.* 1. The quality or state of being pure. 2. Saturation: said of a color.

purl[1] (pûrl) *v.i.* 1. To whirl; turn. 2. To flow with a bubbling sound. 3. To move in eddies. —*n.* A circling movement of water; an eddy. [Cf. Norw. *purla* to gush out]

purl[2] (pûrl) *n.* In knitting, the inversion of the knit stitch, giving a horizontal rib effect. [Earlier *pyrle* < *pyrl* twist] —**purl** *v.t. & v.i.*

pur·lieu (pûr′lōō) *n.* 1. *pl.* The outlying districts or outskirts of any place. 2.

Formerly, ground unlawfully taken for a royal forest, but afterward restored to its rightful owners. [< OF *puraler* to go through]

pur·loin (pûr·loin′) *v.t. & v.i.* To steal; filch. [< OF *porloignier* to remove, put far off] **—pur·loin′er** *n.*

pur·ple (pûr′pəl) *n.* 1. A bluish red color. 2. Royal power or dignity: usu. in the phrase **born to the purple.** *—v.t. & v.i.* **·pled, ·pling** To make or become purple. *—adj.* 1. Of the color of purple. 2. Imperial; regal. 3. Ornate; flowery: a *purple* passage of prose. [< L *purpura,* orig., shellfish yielding a purple dye] **—pur′plish** *adj.*

pur·port (pûr′pôrt; *for v., also* pər·pôrt′) *v.t.* 1. To have as its meaning; signify; imply. 2. To claim or profess (to be), esp. falsely. *—n.* 1. That which is suggested as the meaning or intention; import. 2. The substance of a statement, etc.; gist. [< L *pro-* forth + *portare* to carry] **—pur·port′·ed·ly** *adv.*

pur·pose (pûr′pəs) *n.* 1. An idea or ideal kept before the mind as an end of effort or action; design; aim. 2. Practical advantage or result; use: words to little *purpose.* 3. Settled resolution; determination. **—on purpose** Intentionally. *—v.t. & v.i.* **·posed, ·pos·ing** To have the intention of doing or accomplishing (something); intend; aim. [< OF *pro-* forth + *poser* to put] **—pur′pose·ful** *adj.* **—pur′pose·ful·ly** *adv.* **—pur′pose·ful·ness** *n.* **—pur′pose·less** *adj.* **—pur′pose·less·ly** *adv.*

pur·pose·ly (pûr′pəs·lē) *adv.* For a purpose; intentionally.

pur·po·sive (pûr′pə·siv) *adj.* Pertaining to, having, or indicating purpose. **—pur′po·sive·ly** *adv.* **—pur′po·sive·ness** *n.*

purr (pûr) *n.* A murmuring sound, such as a cat makes when pleased. *—v.i.* 1. To make such a sound. *—v.t.* 2. To express by or as by purring. [Imit.]

purse (pûrs) *n.* 1. A small bag or pouch, esp. one for carrying money. 2. Available resources or means; treasury: the public *purse.* 3. A sum of money offered as a prize. *—v.t.* **pursed, purs·ing** To contract into wrinkles or folds: to *purse* the lips. [< Gk. *byrsa* skin, hide]

purs·er (pûr′sər) *n.* An officer having charge of the accounts, etc., of a vessel.

purs·lane (pûrs′lin, -lān) *n.* A common garden herb with reddish green stem and leaves, used as a salad. [< L *porcilaca*]

pur·su·ance (pər·sōō′əns) *n.* The act of pursuing; a following up; prosecution: usu. in the phrase **in pursuance of.**

pur·su·ant (pər·sōō′ənt) *adj.* Done in accordance with or by reason of something. *—adv.* In accordance: usu. with *to*: also **pur·su′ant·ly.**

pur·sue (pər·sōō′) *v.* **·sued, ·su·ing** *v.t.* 1. To follow in an attempt to overtake or capture; chase. 2. To seek or attain. 3. To advance along the course of. 4. To apply one's energies to or have as one's chief interest: to *pursue* one's studies. *—v.i.* 5. To follow; chase. [< L *pro-* forth + *sequi* to follow] **—pur·su′a·ble** *adj.* **—pur·su′er** *n.*

pur·suit (pər·sōōt′) *n.* 1. The act of pursuing; a chase. 2. That which is followed as a continued employment, pastime, etc.

pu·ru·lent (pyŏŏr′ə·lənt, -yə·lənt) *adj.* Consisting of or secreting pus. [< L *pus, puris* pus] **—pu′ru·lence** *n.* **—pu′ru·lent·ly** *adv.*

pur·vey (pər·vā′) *v.t. & v.i.* To furnish (provisions, etc.). [< L *providere*] **—pur·vey′ance** *n.* **—pur·vey′or** *n.*

pur·view (pûr′vyōō) *n.* 1. Extent, sphere, or scope of anything, as of official authority. 2. Range of view, experience, or understanding; outlook. [< AF *purveu* provided]

pus (pus) *n.* A yellowish secretion from inflamed tissues. [< L]

push (pŏŏsh) *v.t.* 1. To exert force upon or against (an object) for the purpose of moving. 2. To force (one's way), as through a crowd, jungle, etc. 3. To urge, advocate, or promote vigorously and persistently: to *push* a new product. 4. To bear hard upon; harass: I am *pushed* for time. 5. *Slang* To sell (illegal narcotics). *—v.i.* 6. To exert steady pressure against something so as to move it. *—n.* 1. The act of pushing; a shove. 2. Determined activity; energy. [< L *pusare* to beat]

push button A button or knob that on being pushed opens or closes a circuit in an electric system. **—push·but·ton** (pŏŏsh′but′n) *adj.*

push·cart (pŏŏsh′kärt′) *n.* A cart pushed by hand, used by venders, peddlers, etc.

push·er (pŏŏsh′ər) *n.* 1. One who or that which pushes; esp., an active, energetic person. 2. *Slang* One who illegally sells narcotics to addicts.

push·ing (pŏŏsh′ing) *adj.* 1. Possessing enterprise and energy. 2. Aggressive; impertinent. **—push′ing·ly** *adv.*

push·o·ver (pŏŏsh′ō′vər) *n.* *Slang* 1. One who is easily defeated, taken advantage of, etc. 2. Anything that can be done with little or no effort.

push-pull (pŏŏsh′pŏŏl′) *adj.* *Electronics* Designating a circuit or system that uses two similar components operating in opposite phase.

push-up (pŏŏsh′up′) *n.* An exercise in which a prone person pushes his body up from the floor with his arms. Also **push′up′.**

push·y (pŏŏsh′ē) *adj.* **·i·er, ·i·est** *Informal* Offensively aggressive; bossy. **—push′i·ly** *adv.* **—push′i·ness** *n.*

pu·sil·lan·i·mous (pyōō′sə·lan′ə·məs) *adj.* Lacking courage or spirit; cowardly. [< L *pusillus* very little + *animus* soul] **—pu′sil·la·nim′i·ty** (-lə·nim′ə·tē) *n.* **—pu′sil·lan′i·mous·ly** *adv.* **—pu′sil·lan′i·mous·ness** *n.*

puss[1] (pŏŏs) *n.* *Informal* A cat. [< LG *puus,* name for a cat]

puss[2] (pŏŏs) *n.* *Slang* The mouth; face. [< Irish *pus* mouth]

pus·sy[1] (pus′ē) *adj.* Filled with or discharging pus.

pus·sy[2] (pŏŏs′ē) *n. pl.* **·sies** *Informal* A cat. Also **pus′sy·cat′** (-kat′). [Dim. of PUSS[1]]

pus·sy·foot (pŏŏs′ē·fŏŏt′) *v.i.* 1. To move softly and stealthily, as a cat does. 2. To act or proceed without committing oneself or revealing one's intentions.

pus·sy willow (pŏŏs′ē) A small American willow with silky catkins in early spring.

pus·tu·late (pus′chŏŏ·lāt; *for adj., also* pus′chŏŏ·lit) *v.t. & v.i.* **·lat·ed, ·lat·ing** To form into or become pustules. —*adj.* Covered with pustules. —**pus'tu·la'tion** *n.*

pus·tule (pus'chōōl) *n. Pathol.* A small elevation of the skin with an inflamed base containing pus; pimple. [< L *pustula* a blister] —**pus'tu·lar** (-chə·lər), **pus'tu·lous** (-chə·ləs) *adj.*

put (pōōt) *v.* **put, put·ting** *v.t.* 1. To bring into or set in place or position; lay. 2. To bring into a specified state: to *put* a prisoner to death. 3. To bring to bear; apply: *Put* your back into it! 4. To impose. 5. To ascribe or attribute, as the wrong interpretation on a remark. 6. To place according to one's estimation: I *put* the time at five o'clock. 7. To throw with a pushing motion of the arm: to *put* the shot. 8. To bring forward for debate, answer, consideration, etc. 9. To subject. 10. To express in words: That's *putting* it mildly. —*v.i.* 11. To go; proceed: to *put* to sea. —**to put aside** (or **away** or **by**) 1. To place in reserve; save. 2. To thrust aside; discard. —**to put down** 1. To repress; crush. 2. To write down; record. 3. *Slang* To disparage. —**to put forth** 1. To extend, as the arm or hand. 2. To grow, as shoots or buds. 3. To exert. —**to put forward** To advance; urge, as a claim. —**to put in** 1. To interpolate; interpose. 2. *Informal* To devote; expend, as time. 3. To advance (a claim, etc.). —**to put off** 1. To delay; postpone. 2. To evade. —**to put on** 1. To don. 2. To simulate; pretend. 3. To give a representation of; stage. 4. *Slang* To deceive; mock. —**to put out** 1. To extinguish. 2. To expel; eject. 3. To inconvenience. 4. In baseball, to retire (a batter or base runner). —**to put over** 1. To place in command or charge. 2. *Informal* To accomplish successfully. —**to put through** 1. To bring to successful completion. 2. To cause to undergo. —**to put up** 1. To erect; build. 2. To preserve or can. 3. To wager; bet. 4. To provide (money, capital, etc.). 5. To sheathe, as a weapon. 6. To shelter; house. —**to put upon** To take advantage of. —**to put up with** To endure. —*n.* The act of putting, as a throw. —*adj. Informal* Fixed; settled: My hat won't stay *put*. [Fusion of OE *pūtian* to instigate, *potian* to push, and *pȳtan* to put out]

pu·ta·tive (pyōō'tə·tiv) *adj.* Supposed; reputed. [< L *putare* to think] —**pu'ta·tive·ly** *adv.*

put-on (pōōt'on') *n. Slang* A hoax or deception.

put·out (pōōt'out') *n.* In baseball, the act of causing an out, as of a batter or base runner.

pu·tre·fy (pyōō'trə·fī) *v.t. & v.i.* **·fied, ·fy·ing** 1. To decay or cause to decay with a fetid odor; rot. 2. To make or become gangrenous. [< L *putrere* to decay + *facere* to make] —**pu'tre·fac'tion** (-fak'shən) *n.* —**pu'tre·fac'tive** (-fak'tiv) *adj.* —**pu'tre·fi'er** *n.*

pu·tres·cent (pyōō·tres'ənt) *adj.* 1. Becoming putrid. 2. Pertaining to putrefaction. —**pu·tres'cence** *n.*

pu·trid (pyōō'trid) *adj.* 1. Being in a state of putrefaction; rotten. 2. Indicating or produced by putrefaction: a *putrid* smell. 3. Rotten; corrupt. [< L *putrere* to decay] —**pu·trid'i·ty** *n.* —**pu'trid·ly** *adv.* —**pu'trid·ness** *n.*

putsch (pōōch) *n.* An outbreak or rebellion; an attempted *coup d'etat*. [< G]

putt (put) *n.* In golf, a light stroke made to place the ball in or near the hole. [Var. of PUT] —**putt** *v.t. & v.i.*

put·tee (put'ē, pu·tē') *n.* A strip of cloth wound spirally about the leg from knee to ankle; also, a leather gaiter strapped around the leg. Also **put'ty**. [< Skt. *patta* strip of cloth]

put·ter[1] (put'ər) *n.* 1. In golf, one who putts. 2. An upright, stiff-shafted golf club.

put·ter[2] (put'ər) *v.i.* 1. To act or work in a dawdling manner. —*v.t.* 2. To waste (time, etc.) in dawdling. [Var. of POTTER[1]]

put·ty (put'ē) *n.* Whiting mixed with linseed oil to the consistency of dough, used for filling cracks in surfaces, securing panes of glass in the sash, etc. —*v.t.* **·tied, ·ty·ing** To fill, stop, fasten, etc., with putty. [< OF *potée*, lit., potful] —**put'ti·er** *n.*

put-up (pōōt'up') *adj. Informal* Prearranged or contrived in an artful manner: a *put-up* job.

puz·zle (puz'əl) *v.* **·zled, ·zling** *v.t.* 1. To confuse or perplex. 2. To solve by investigation and study, as something perplexing: with *out*. —*v.i.* 3. To be perplexed or confused. —**to puzzle over** To attempt to understand or solve. —*n.* 1. Something that puzzles; enigma. 2. A toy, word game, etc., designed to test one's ingenuity or patience. [Origin unknown] —**puz'zler** *n.* —**puz'zle·ment** *n.*

py·e·mi·a (pī·ē'mē·ə) *n. Pathol.* A type of blood poisoning characterized by many abscesses. [< Gk. *pyon* pus + *haima* blood] —**py·e'mic** *adj.*

pyg·my (pig'mē) *adj.* 1. Diminutive; dwarfish. 2. Trivial; unimportant. —*n. pl.* **·mies** A small person or thing regarded as insignificant. Also spelled *pigmy*. [< Gk. *pygmē* the length from elbow to knuckles]

Pyg·my (pig'mē) *n. pl.* **·mies** 1. A member of a Negroid people of equatorial Africa, ranging in height from four to five feet. 2. Any of the Negrito peoples of the Philippines, Andaman Islands, and Malaya. Also *Pigmy*.

py·ja·mas (pə·jä'məz, -jam'əz) See PAJAMAS.

py·lon (pī'lon) *n.* 1. *Archit.* An entrance to an Egyptian temple, consisting of a central gateway flanked on each side by a truncated pyramidal tower. 2. A stake marking the course in an airport or turning point in an air race. 3. One of the steel towers supporting a high-tension electric power line. [< Gk. *pylōn* gateway]

py·or·rhe·a (pī'ə·rē'ə) *n. Pathol.* An inflammation of the gums, usu. with a discharge of pus. [< Gk. *pyon* pus + *rheein* to flow] —**py'or·rhe'al** *adj.*

pyr·a·mid (pir'ə·mid) *n.* 1. *Archit.* A large structure of masonry, typically having a square base and triangular sides meeting in an apex, used as tombs or temples in ancient Egypt. 2. *Geom.* A solid consisting of a polygonal base and triangular sides with a common vertex. —*v.t. & v.i.* 1. To arrange or form in the shape of a pyramid. 2. To buy or sell (stock) with paper profits, and to continue so buying or selling. [< Gk. *pyramis, -idos*] —**py·ram·i·dal** (pi·ram'ə·

dəl), **pyr′a·mid′ic** or **·i·cal** *adj.* —**py·ram′i·dal·ly** *adv.*

pyre (pīr) *n.* A heap of combustibles arranged esp. for burning a dead body. [< Gk. *pyr* fire]

py·reth·rum (pī·rē′thrəm) *n.* The powdered flowers of a chrysanthemum, used as an insecticide. [< Gk. *pyrethron*]

py·ret·ic (pī·ret′ik) *adj.* 1. Affected with or relating to fever. 2. Remedial in fevers. [< Gk. *pyretos* fever]

Py·rex (pī′reks) *n.* A type of heat-resisting glass having a high silica content: a trade name. Also **py′rex.**

pyr·i·dox·ine (pir′ə·dok′sēn, -sin) *n.* Vitamin B_6. See under VITAMIN.

py·rite (pī′rīt) *n.* *pl.* **py·ri·tes** (pī·rī′tēz) A metallic, pale yellow iron disulfide, a source of sulfuric acid: also called *fool's gold, iron pyrites.* [< Gk. *pyritēs* (*lithos*) fire (stone)] —**py·rit′ic** (-rit′ik) or **·i·cal** *adj.*

py·ri·tes (pī·rī′tēz) *n.pl.* Any of various metallic sulfides.

pyro- *combining form* Fire; heat. Also, before vowels, **pyr-**. [< Gk. *pyr, pyros* fire]

py·rol·y·sis (pī·rol′ə·sis) *n. Chem.* Decomposition of compounds by the action of heat. [< Gk. *pyr, pyros* fire + *lysis* loosing] —**py·ro·lit·ic** (pī′rə·lit′ik, pir′ə-) *adj.*

py·ro·mag·net·ic (pī′rō·mag·net′ik) *adj.* Pertaining to changes in magnetic properties caused by change of temperature.

py·ro·ma·ni·a (pī′rə·mā′nē·ə, -mān′yə) *n.* A compulsion to set things on fire. —**py′ro·ma′ni·ac** (-mā′nē·ak) *adj. & n.* —**py′ro·ma·ni·a·cal** (-mə·nī′ə·kəl) *adj.*

py·rom·e·ter (pī·rom′ə·tər) *n.* An instrument for measuring high degrees of heat. —**py·ro·met·ric** (pī′rə·met′rik, pir′ə-) or **·ri·cal** *adj.* —**py·rom′e·try** *n.*

py·ro·tech·nics (pī′rə·tek′niks) *n.pl.* (*construed as sing. in def. 1*) 1. The art of making or using fireworks. 2. A display of fireworks. 3. An ostentatious display, as of oratory. [< Gk. *pyr, pyros* fire + *technē* art] —**py′ro·tech′nic** or **·ni·cal** *adj.* —**py′ro·tech′nist** *n.*

py·ro·tox·in (pī′rə·tok′sin) *n. Biochem.* Any of various toxins found in the body and inducing a rise of bodily temperature.

Pyr·rhic victory (pir′ik) A victory gained at a ruinous loss. [after the victory of *Pyrrhus,* king of Epirus, over the Romans in 279 B.C.]

Py·thag·o·re·an theorem (pi·thag′ə·rē′ən) *Geom.* The theorem of Pythagoras that the sum of the squares of the legs of a right triangle is equal to the square of the hypotenuse.

py·thon (pī′thon, -thən) *n.* 1. A large, nonvenomous serpent that crushes its prey. 2. Any nonvenomous constrictor. [< Gk. *Python,* a serpent slain by Apollo]

pyx (piks) *n. Eccl.* A vessel or casket, usu. of precious metal, in which the Host is preserved. [< Gk. *pyxos* box]

Q

q, Q (kyo͞o) *n. pl.* **q's** or **qs, Q's** or **Qs** (kyo͞oz) **1.** The seventeenth letter of the English alphabet. **2.** The sound represented by the letter *q*.

qua (kwā, kwä) *adv.* In the capacity of; insofar as. [< L]

quack[1] (kwak) *v.i.* To utter a harsh, croaking cry, as a duck. [Imit.] —**quack** *n.*

quack[2] (kwak) *n.* **1.** A pretender to medical knowledge or skill. **2.** One who falsely poses as an expert. —*v.i.* To play the quack. [Short for QUACKSALVER] —**quack** *adj.* —**quack′er·y** *n.* —**quack′ish** *adj.* —**quack′·ish·ly** *adv.*

quack·sal·ver (kwak′sal′vər) *n.* A medical quack. [< MDu. < *quacken* quack[1] + *salf* salve]

quad[1] (kwod) *n. Informal* A quadrangle, as of a college.

quad[2] (kwod) *n. Printing* A piece of type metal of less height than the letters, used for spacing.

quad·ran·gle (kwod′rang·gəl) *n.* **1.** *Geom.* A plane figure having four sides and four angles. **2.** A court, either square or oblong; also, the buildings that surround such a court. [< L *quattuor* four + *angulus* angle] —**quad·ran′gu·lar** (-gyə·lər) *adj.*

quad·rant (kwod′rənt) *n.* **1.** A quarter section of a circle, subtending an arc of 90°; also, the arc subtended. **2.** An instrument used in navigation, surveying, and astronomy for measuring altitudes. [< L *quattuor* four] —**quad·ran·tal** (kwod·ran′təl) *adj.*

quad·ra·phon·ic (kwod′rə·fon′ik) *adj.* Relating to a system of recording and reproducing sound through four tracks. [< QUADRI- + PHONIC]

quad·rat·ic (kwod·rat′ik) *adj.* **1.** Of or like a square. **2.** *Math.* Pertaining to an equation, curve, surface, etc., involving quantities raised to no higher power than a square. —*n. Math.* A quadratic equation, curve, etc.

quad·rat·ics (kwod·rat′iks) *n.pl.* (*construed as sing.*) The branch of algebra dealing with quadratic equations.

quad·ren·ni·al (kwod·ren′ē·əl) *adj.* **1.** Occurring once in four years. **2.** Lasting four years. —**quad·ren′ni·al·ly** *adv.*

quadri- *combining form* Four: *quadrilateral.* Also **quadru-**; before vowels, **quadr-**. [< L *quattuor* four]

quad·ri·lat·er·al (kwod′rə·lat′ər·əl) *adj.* Formed or bounded by four lines; four-sided. —*n. Geom.* A plane figure having four sides and four angles. [< L *quattuor* four + *latus* side]

qua·drille (kwə·dril′) *n.* A square dance for four couples, having five figures. [< F < L *quattuor* four]

quad·ril·lion (kwod·ril′yən) *n.* **1.** A thousand trillions, written as 1 followed by 15 zeros: a cardinal number. **2.** *Brit.* A million trillions (def. 2), written as 1 followed by 24 zeros: a cardinal number. —**quad·ril′lion** *adj.* —**quad·ril′lionth** *adj. & n.*

quad·roon (kwod·ro͞on′) *n.* A person having one Negro grandparent. [< Sp. *cuarto* fourth]

quad·ru·ped (kwod′ro͞o·ped) *n.* An animal having four feet; esp., a four-footed mammal. [< L *quattuor* four + *pes* foot] —**quad′·ru·ped, quad·ru·pe·dal** (kwod·ro͞o′pə·dəl, kwod′ro͞o·ped′l) *adj.*

quad·ru·ple (kwod·ro͞o′pəl, -ro͞o′-) *v.t. & v.i.* **·pled, ·pling** To multiply by four; make or become four times larger. —*adj.* Consisting of or multiplied by four. —*n.* A number four times as great as another. [< L *quadruplus*]

quad·ru·plet (kwod·ro͞o′plit, -ro͞o′-) *n.* **1.** A group of four things or objects, usu. of the same kind. **2.** One of four offspring born at one birth.

quad·ru·pli·cate (*adj. & n.* kwod·ro͞o′plə·kit *v.* -kāt) *adj.* Quadruple; fourfold. —*n.* One of four like things. —*v.t. & v.i.* **·cat·ed, ·cat·ing** To make or become quadruple. [< L *quattuor* four + stem of *plicare* to fold] —**quad·ru′pli·cate·ly** *adv.* —**quad·ru′pli·ca′tion** *n.*

quaff (kwof, kwaf) *v.t. & v.i.* To drink, esp. copiously or with relish. —*n.* A drink; swallow. —**quaff′er** *n.*

quag·mire (kwag′mīr′, kwog′-) *n.* **1.** Marshy ground that gives way under the foot. **2.** A difficult situation. [< obs. *quag* to shake + MIRE] —**quag′mired′** *adj.* —**quag′mir′y** *adj.*

qua·hog (kwô′hôg, -hog; kō′-, kwō′-) *n.* An edible, hard-shelled American clam. Also **qua′haug.** [< Algonquian (Narraganset) *poquauhock*]

quail[1] (kwāl) *n.* Any of various small American game birds related to the partridge; esp., the bobwhite. [< OF *quaille*]

quail[2] kwāl) *v.i.* To shrink with fear; lose heart or courage. [ME *quailen*]

quaint (kwānt) *adj.* Pleasingly odd or old-fashioned. [< OF *cointe* < L *cognoscere* to ascertain] —**quaint′ly** *adv.* —**quaint′ness** *n.*

quake (kwāk) *v.i.* **quaked, quak·ing** **1.** To shake, as with violent emotion or cold. **2.** To tremble, as ground during an earthquake. —*n.* **1.** The act of quaking. **2.** An earthquake. [OE *cwacian* to shake] —**quak′y** *adj.* **·i·er, ·i·est**

Quak·er (kwā′kər) *n.* A member of the Society of Friends. [< QUAKE, v.; with ref. to their founder's admonition to tremble at the word of the Lord] —**Quak′er·ism** *n.* —**Quak′er·ly** *adj. & adv.*

qual·i·fi·ca·tion (kwol′ə·fə·kā′shən) *n.* 1. The act of qualifying, or the state of being qualified. 2. Any ability, training, etc., that fits a person for a specific office, role, position, etc. 3. A restriction or modification.

qual·i·fied (kwol′ə·fīd) *adj.* 1. Competent or fit. 2. Restricted or modified. —**qual′i·fied′ly** *adv.*

qual·i·fy (kwol′ə·fī) *v.* **·fied, ·fy·ing** *v.t.* 1. To make fit or capable, as for an office, occupation, or privilege. 2. To make legally capable. 3. To limit or restrict. 4. To make less strong or extreme. 5. *Gram.* To modify. —*v.i.* 6. To meet the requirements, as for entering a race. [< L *qualis* of such a kind + *facere* to make] —**qual′i·fi′a·ble** *adj.* —**qual′i·fi′er** *n.*

qual·i·ta·tive (kwol′ə·tā′tiv) *adj.* Of or pertaining to quality: distinguished from *quantitative.* [< L *qualis* of such a kind] —**qual′i·ta′tive·ly** *adv.*

qual·i·ty (kwol′e·tē) *n. pl.* **·ties** 1. A distinguishing element or characteristic. 2. The basic or essential character, nature, etc., of something. 3. Excellence. 4. The degree of excellence. 5. *Archaic* High social rank or birth. [< L *qualis* of such a kind]

qualm (kwäm, kwôm) *n.* 1. A feeling of sickness. 2. A twinge of conscience; moral scruple. 3. A sensation of fear or misgiving. [? OE *cwealm* death] —**qualm′ish** *adj.* —**qualm′ish·ly** *adv.* —**qualm′ish·ness** *n.* —**qualm′y** *adj.*

quan·da·ry (kwon′dər·ē) *n. pl.* **·da·ries** A state of hesitation or perplexity.

quan·ta (kwon′tə) Plural of QUANTUM.

quan·ti·ta·tive (kwon′tə·tā′tiv) *adj.* Of or pertaining to quantity: distinquished from *qualitative.* —**quan′ti·ta′tive·ly** *adv.* —**quan′·ti·ta′tive·ness** *n.*

quan·ti·ty (kwon′tə·tē) *n. pl.* **·ties** 1. An amount, number, weight, etc. 2. *Often pl.* A large amount: abundance. [< L *quantus* how much]

quan·tize (kwon′tīz) *v.t.* **·tized, ·tiz·ing** *Physics* 1. To restrict the possible values of (an observable quantity or magnitude). 2. To express as multiples of a given quantity or quantum. —**quan′ti·za′tion** *n.*

quan·tum (kwon′təm) *n. pl.* **·ta** *Physics* A fundamental unit of energy. [< L, neuter of *quantus* how much]

quantum theory *Physics* The theory that energy is not a smoothly flowing continuum but is manifested by the emission from radiating bodies of discrete particles or *quanta.*

quar·an·tine (kwôr′ən·tēn, kwor′-) *n.* 1. The enforced isolation in port for a fixed period of time of ships suspected of carrying a contagious disease. 2. A place designated for the enforcement of such interdiction. 3. The enforced isolation of any person or place infected with contagious disease. 4. Any enforced isolation. —*v.t.* **·tined, ·tin·ing** To isolate by or as by quarantine. [< L *quadraginta* forty (days)]

quark (kwärk, kwôrk) *n. Physics* A hypothetical elementary particle. [after "Three *quarks* for Muster Mark" in James Joyce's *Finnegan's Wake*]

quar·rel (kwôr′əl, kwor′-) *n.* 1. An unfriendly, angry, or violent dispute. 2. The cause for dispute. —*v.i.* **quar·reled** or **·relled, quar·rel·ing** or **·rel·ling** To engage in a quarrel. [< L *queri* to complain] —**quar′·rel·er** or **quar′rel·ler** *n.*

quar·rel·some (kwôr′əl·səm, kwor′-) *adj.* Inclined to quarrel. —**quar′rel·some·ly** *adv.* —**quar′rel·some·ness** *n.*

quar·ry¹ (kwôr′ē, kwor′ē) *n. pl.* **·ries** 1. A beast or bird hunted or killed, as in the chase. 2. Anything hunted, slaughtered, or pursued. [< L *corium* hide]

quar·ry² (kwôr′ē, kwor′ē) *n. pl.* **·ries** An excavation from which stone is cut, blasted, etc. —*v.t.* **·ried, ·ry·ing** To cut, dig, or take from or as from a quarry. [< L *quadrus* square] —**quar′ri·er** *n.*

quart (kwôrt) *n.* 1. A measure of capacity equal to ¼ gallon, or two pints. In the U.S., the dry quart is equal to 1.10 liters and the liquid quart is equal to 0.946 liter. 2. A container having such a capacity. [< L *quartus* fourth]

quar·ter (kwôr′tər) *n.* 1. One of four equal parts into which anything is or may be divided. 2. A coin having the value of 25 cents. 3. Fifteen minutes or the fourth of an hour. 4. Three months or a fourth of a year. 5. *Astron.* A fourth part of the moon's revolution about the earth. 6. A particular district or locality, as of a city: the native *quarter.* 7. *Usu. pl.* Proper or assigned station, as of officers and crew on a warship. 8. *pl.* A place of lodging or residence. 9. Mercy shown to a vanquished enemy. —**at close quarters** Close by; at close range. —*adj.* 1. Being one of four equal parts. 2. Having one fourth of a standard value. —*v.t.* 1. To divide into four equal parts. 2. To divide into a number of parts or pieces. 3. To furnish with quarters or shelter; lodge. —*v.i.* 4. To be stationed or lodged. [< L *quartus* fourth]

quar·ter·back (kwôr′tər·bak′) *n.* In football, the back who directs offensive play.

quar·ter-deck (kwôr′tər·dek′) *n. Naut.* The rear part of a ship's upper deck, reserved for officers.

quarter horse A strong, fast horse, prized for its endurance as a riding horse.

quar·ter·ly (kwôr′tər·lē) *adj.* 1. Containing or being a fourth part. 2. Occurring at intervals of three months. —*n. pl.* **·lies** A publication issued once every three months. —*adv.* 1. Once in a quarter of a year. 2. In or by quarters.

quar·ter·mas·ter (kwôr′tər·mas′tər) *n.* 1. *Usu. cap. Mil.* An officer responsible for the supply of food, fuel, clothing, etc. 2. On shipboard, a petty officer responsible for steering and related functions.

quarter note *Music* A note having one fourth the time value of a whole note.

quar·ter·staff (kwôr′tər·staf′) *n. pl.* **·staves** (-stāvz′) A stout, iron-tipped staff about 6½ feet long, formerly used as a weapon.

quar·tet (kwôr·tet′) *n.* 1. A composition for four voices or instruments; also the four persons performing it. 2. Any group or set of four things of a kind. Also **quar·tette′.** [< Ital. *quartetto* < *quarto* fourth]

quar·to (kwôr′tō) *adj.* Having four leaves or eight pages to the sheet: a *quarto* book. —*n. pl.* **·tos** A book or pamphlet having pages the size of a fourth of a sheet: often

written 4to or 4°. [< L (*in*) *quarto* (in) fourth]
quartz (kwôrts) *n.* A hard, vitreous mineral, silicon dioxide, usu. transparent and colorless. [< G *quarz*]
qua·sar (kwā′zär) *n.* A galaxy-like formation in remote space that emits radio waves and vast energy. [< QUAS(I-STELL)AR (RADIO SOURCE)]
quash (kwosh) *v.t.* 1. *Law* To make void or set aside, as an indictment; annul. 2. To put down or suppress forcibly or summarily: to *quash* a rebellion. [< L *quassare* to shatter]
qua·si (kwā′sī, -zī; kwā′sē, -zi) *adj.* Resembling but not exactly of the same kind. [< L, as if]
quasi- *prefix* Resembling; nearly; in some degree: *quasi-official.*
qua·ter·na·ry (kwot′ər·ner′ē) *adj.* 1. Consisting of four. 2. Fourth in order. —*n. pl.* ·ries The number four; a group of four things. [< L *quaternarius* < *quaterni* by fours]
quat·rain (kwot′rān) *n.* A stanza or poem of four lines. [< F < *quatre* four]
quat·re·foil (kat′ər·foil′, kat′rə-) *n.* 1. A leaf, etc., having four leaflets. 2. *Archit.* An ornament with four lobes. [< OF *quatre* four + *foil* leaf]
quat·tro·cen·to (kwot′rō·chen′tō) *n.* The 15th c. as connected with the revival of art and literature, esp. in Italy. [< Ital.] —**quat′tro·cen′to** *adj.*
qua·ver (kwā′vər) *v.i.* 1. To tremble or shake: said usu. of the voice. 2. To produce trills or quavers in singing or in playing a musical instrument. —*v.t.* 3. To utter or sing in a tremulous voice. —*n.* 1. A quivering or tremulous motion. 2. A trill. [Freq. of obs. *quave*, ME *cwafian* to tremble] —**qua′·ver·y** *adj.*
quay (kē, kā) *n.* A wharf where vessels may load or unload. [< OF *cai* wall]
quean (kwēn) *n.* A brazen or ill-behaved woman; prostitute. [OE *cwene* prostitute]
quea·sy (kwē′zē) *adj.* ·si·er, ·si·est 1. Sick at the stomach. 2. Easily nauseated. [ME *coisy*; origin unknown] —**quea′si·ly** *adv.* —**quea′si·ness** *n.*
Quech·ua (kech′wä) *n.* 1. One of a tribe of South American Indians. 2. Their language: also called *Incan.* —**Quech′uan** (-wən) *adj. & n.*
queen (kwēn) *n.* 1. The wife of a king. 2. A female sovereign or monarch. 3. A woman preeminent in a given sphere. 4. In chess, the most powerful piece, capable of moving any number of squares in a straight or diagonal line. 5. A playing card bearing a picture of a queen. 6. *Entomol.* The single fully developed female in a colony of bees, ants, etc. —*v.t.* 1. To make a queen of. 2. In chess, to make a queen of (a pawn) by moving it to the eighth row. —*v.i.* 3. To reign as or play the part of a queen. [OE *cwēn* woman, queen]
Queen Anne's lace The wild carrot.
queen consort The wife of a reigning king, who does not share his sovereignty.
queen dowager The widow of a king.
queen·ly (kwēn′lē) *adj.* ·li·er, ·li·est 1. Of or like a queen. 2. Fit for a queen. —*adv.* In the manner of a queen. —**queen′li·ness** *n.*
queen mother A queen dowager who is mother of a reigning sovereign.
queen's English King's English.
queer (kwir) *adj.* 1. Unusual; strange. 2. Eccentric. 3. *Slang* Counterfeit. 4. *Slang* Homosexual. —*n. Slang* 1. Counterfeit money. 2. A homosexual person. —*v.t. Slang* To jeopardize or spoil. [Origin unknown] —**queer′ly** *adv.* —**queer′ness** *n.*
quell (kwel) *v.t.* 1. To put down or suppress by force; extinguish. 2. To quiet; allay, as pain. [OE *cwellan* to kill]
quench (kwench) *v.t.* 1. To put out or extinguish, as a fire. 2. To put an end to; subdue. 3. To slake or satisfy (thirst). 4. To cool, as heated iron or steel, by thrusting into water or other liquid. [OE *cwincan* to grow less, disappear] —**quench′a·ble** *adj.* —**quench′er** *n.* —**quench′less** *adj.*
quer·u·lous (kwer′ə·ləs, -yə·ləs) *adj.* 1. Disposed to complain or be fretful. 2. Of a complaining or whining manner. [< LL *queri* to complain] —**quer′u·lous·ly** *adv.* —**quer′u·lous·ness** *n.*
que·ry (kwir′ē) *v.t. & v.i.* ·ried, ·ry·ing To question. —*n. pl.* ·ries An inquiry or question. [< L *quaerere* to ask]
quest (kwest) *n.* 1. The act of looking for something; a search. 2. An adventure or expedition. —*v.t. & v.i.* To go on a quest or to search for (something). [< L *quaerere* to ask, seek] —**quest′er** *n.*
ques·tion (kwes′chən) *n.* 1. An interrogative sentence calling for an answer; an inquiry. 2. A subject of inquiry or debate; a matter to be decided; problem. 3. Possibility of disagreement or dispute; doubt: no *question* about it. —**out of the question.** Not to be thought of; impossible. —*v.t.* 1. To put a question to; interrogate. 2. To be uncertain of; doubt. 3. To make objection to; challenge; dispute. —*v.i.* 4. To ask a question. [< L *quaerere* to ask] —**ques′tion·er** *n.*
ques·tion·a·ble (kwes′chən·ə·bəl) *adj.* 1. Characterized by doubtful integrity, honesty, respectability, etc. 2. Liable to be called in question; debatable. —**ques′tion·a·bil′i·ty, ques′tion·a·ble·ness** *n.* —**ques′·tion·a·bly** *adv.*
question mark A mark of punctuation (?) indicating that the sentence it closes is a direct question: also called *interrogation point.*
ques·tion·naire (kwes′chə·nâr′) *n.* A written or printed series of questions submitted to a number of persons to obtain information.
quet·zal (ket·säl′) *n. pl.* ·zal·es (-sä′lās) 1. A bird of long, brilliant plumage, the national symbol of Guatemala. 2. The standard monetary unit of Guatemala. Also **que·zal** (kā·säl′). [< Sp.]
queue (kyōō) *n.* 1. A pigtail. 2. A line of persons or vehicles. —*v.i.* **queued, queu·ing** *Brit.* To form a line: usu. with *up.* [< L *cauda* a tail]
quib·ble (kwib′əl) *n.* 1. An evasion of a point or question. 2. A trivial distinction or objection; cavil. —*v.i.* ·bled, ·bling To raise trivial objections. [< obs. *quib* < L *quibus*, ablative pl. of *qui* who, which] —**quib′bler** *n.*

quick (kwik) *adj.* 1. Done or occurring in a short time; rapid; swift. 2. Responding readily to impressions or instruction: a *quick* mind. 3. Easily aroused or excited; hasty: a *quick* temper. 4. Nimble: *quick* fingers. —*n.* 1. Those who are alive: chiefly in the phrase **the quick and the dead.** 2. The living flesh, esp. the tender flesh under a fingernail. 3. The feelings: cut to the *quick.* —*adv.* Rapidly. [OE *cwic* alive] —**quick'ly** *adv.* —**quick'ness** *n.*

quick bread Any bread, biscuits, etc., whose leavening agent makes immediate baking possible.

quick·en (kwik'ən) *v.t.* 1. To cause to move or act more rapidly. 2. To give or restore life to. 3. To excite or arouse; stimulate. —*v.i.* 4. To move or act more rapidly. 5. To come or return to life; revive. 6. To begin to manifest signs of life: said of the fetus. —**quick'en·er** *n.*

quick-freeze (kwik'frēz') *v.t.* **-froze, -fro·zen, -freez·ing** To subject (food) to rapid freezing for storage.

quick·ie (kwik'ē) *n. Slang* Anything done hastily, as by short cuts or makeshift methods.

quick·lime (kwik'līm') *n.* A product obtained by the calcining of limestone.

quick march A march in quick time; quickstep.

quick·sand (kwik'sand') *n.* A deep bed of water-soaked sand that engulfs anything upon it.

quick·sil·ver (kwik'sil'vər) *n.* 1. Mercury in its liquid form. 2. An amalgam of tin, used for the backs of mirrors. [OE *cwicseolfor.* Trans. of L *argentum vivum.*]

quick·step (kwik'step') *n.* A march or dance written in a rapid tempo; also, a quick march.

quick-tem·pered (kwik'tem'pərd) *adj.* Easily angered.

quick time A marching step of 120 paces a minute, each pace of 30 inches.

quick-wit·ted (kwik'wit'id) *adj.* Having a ready wit or quick discernment; keen; alert. —**quick'-wit'ted·ly** *adv.* —**quick'-wit'ted·ness** *n.*

quid[1] (kwid) *n.* 1. A small portion of chewing tobacco. 2. A cud, as of a cow. [OE *cwudu.* Var. of CUD.]

quid[2] (kwid) *n. pl.* **quid** *Brit. Slang* A pound sterling, or a sovereign. [? < QUID PRO QUO]

quid pro quo (kwid' prō kwō') *Latin* Something for something; an equivalent in return.

qui·es·cent (kwī·es'ənt) *adj.* Being in a state of repose or inaction; quiet; still. [< L *quiescere* to be quiet] —**qui·es'cence** *n.* —**qui·es'cent·ly** *adv.*

qui·et (kwī'ət) *adj.* 1. Making little or no noise. 2. Having little or no motion; still; calm. 3. Characterized by silence; also, retired or secluded: a *quiet* nook. 4. Free from excessive activity, turmoil, or vexation: a *quiet* day. 5. Gentle; mild: a *quiet* temperament. 6. Not showy or pretentious; modest. 7. In commerce, not busy or active. —*n.* The quality or condition of being quiet; peace, tranquillity. —*v.t. & v.i.* To make or become quiet: often with *down.* —*adv.* In a quiet or peaceful manner. [< L *quies, quietis* rest, repose] —**qui'et·ly** *adv.* —**qui'et·ness** *n.*

qui·e·tude (kwī'ə·tōōd, -tyōōd) *n.* A condition of calm or tranquillity; repose; rest.

qui·e·tus (kwī·ē'təs) *n.* 1. Anything that kills, as a blow; also, death itself. 2. A final discharge, as of a debt. [< L *quietus est* he is quit]

quill (kwil) *n.* 1. *Ornithol.* One of the large, strong flight feathers or tail feathers of a bird. 2. Something made from a quill, as a pen. 3. *Zool.* One of the large, sharp spines of a porcupine or hedgehog. [ME *quil*]

quilt (kwilt) *n.* 1. A bedcover made by stitching together firmly two layers of cloth or patchwork with some soft and warm substance (as wool or cotton) between them. 2. Any bedcover, esp. if thick. —*v.t.* 1. To stitch together (two pieces of material) with a soft substance between. 2. To pad or line with something soft. —*v.i.* 3. To make a quilt or quilted work. [< OF *cuilte* < L *culcita* bed, cushion]

quince (kwins) *n.* The hard, acid, applelike fruit of a small tree of the rose family, used for preserves. [ME *quynes* quinces, ult. < Gk. *kydōnion*]

qui·nine (kwī'nīn, *esp. Brit.* kwi·nēn') *n. Chem.* A white, very bitter, amorphous or slightly crystalline alkaloid, contained in cinchona barks, the salts of which are used in medicine esp. in the treatment of malaria. [< Sp. *quina* cinchona bark]

quinine water A carbonated beverage flavored with quinine: also called *tonic.*

quin·sy (kwin'zē) *n. Pathol.* An inflammation of the tonsils. [< Gk. *kynanchē* dog's collar]

quint (kwint) *n.* 1. A fifth. 2. A set of five. 3. *Informal* A quintuplet. [< L *quintus* fifth]

quin·tal (kwin'təl) *n.* 1. A hundredweight. 2. In the metric system, 100 kilograms. [< Arabic *quintar* ult. < LL *centarium* one hundred]

quin·tes·sence (kwin·tes'əns) *n.* 1. An extract from anything, containing in concentrated form its most essential principle. 2. The purest example of something. [< Med.L *quinta essentia* fifth essence] —**quin·tes·sen·tial** (kwin'tə·sen'shəl) *adj.*

quin·tet (kwin·tet') *n.* 1. A musical composition for five voices or instruments; also, the five persons performing it. 2. Any group of five persons or things. Also **quin·tette'.** [< Ital. *quintetto* < *quinto* fifth]

quin·til·lion (kwin·til'yən) *n.* 1. A thousand quadrillions, written as 1 followed by 18 zeros: a cardinal number. 2. *Brit.* A million quadrillions (def. 2), written as 1 followed by 30 zeros: a cardinal number. —**quin·til'lion** *adj.* —**quin·til'lionth** *adj. & n.*

quin·tu·ple (kwin·tup'əl, -tōō'pəl) *v.t. & v.i.* **·pled, ·pling** To multiply by five; make or become five times larger. —*adj.* Consisting of or multiplied by five. —*n.* A number five times as great as another. [< LL *quintuplex* fivefold]

quin·tu·plet (kwin·tup'lit, -tōō'plit) *n.* 1. Five things of a kind used or occurring together. 2. One of five born at one birth.

quin·tu·pli·cate (*adj. & n.* kwin·tōō'plə·kit; *v.* -kāt) *adj.* 1. Fivefold. 2. Raised to the fifth power. —*v.t.* & *v.i.* **·cat·ed, ·cat·ing** To multiply by five; quintuple. —*n.* One of five identical things. —**quin·tu′pli·cate·ly** *adv.* —**quin·tu′pli·ca′tion** *n.*

quip (kwip) *n.* A sarcastic or witty jest or retort. —*v.i.* **quipped, quip·ping** To make a witty remark; jest. [Prob. < L *quippe* indeed] —**quip′pish** *adj.* —**quip′ster** *n.*

quire (kwīr) *n.* The twentieth part of a ream of paper; 24 (or 25) sheets. —*v.t.* **quired, quir·ing** To fold or separate into quires. [< OF *quaer*, ult. < L *quaterni* a set of four]

quirk (kwûrk) *n.* 1. A personal peculiarity, mannerism, or caprice. 2. A sharp turn or twist. [Origin uncertain] —**quirk′i·ness** *n.* —**quirk′y** *adj.*

quirt (kwûrt) *n.* A short-handled riding whip with a braided lash. —*v.t.* To strike with a quirt. [< Am.Sp. *cuarta*]

quis·ling (kwiz′ling) *n.* One who betrays his country to the enemy and is then given political power by the conquerors. [after Vidkum *Quisling*, 1887–1945, Norwegian Nazi party leader and traitor] —**quis′ling·ism** *n.*

quit (kwit) *v.* **quit** or **quit·ted, quit·ting** *v.t.* 1. To cease or desist from; discontinue. 2. To give up; renounce. 3. To go away from; leave. —*v.i.* 4. To stop; cease; discontinue. 5. *Informal* To resign from a position, etc. —*adj.* Released, relieved, or absolved from something; clear; free; rid. —*n.* The act of quitting. —**to be quits** To be even (with another). —**to call it quits** 1. To stop working. 2. To end a friendship or other association. [< OF *quitter*, ult. < L *quietus* at rest]

quit·claim (kwit′klām′) *n.* *Law* A full release and acquittance given by one to another in regard to a certain demand, suit, or right of action. Also **quit′claim′ance.** —*v.t.* To relinquish or give up claim or title to; release from a claim. [< MF *quite clamer* to declare quit or free]

quite (kwīt) *adv.* 1. To the fullest extent; totally: *quite* dead. 2. Really; truly. 3. *Informal* To a great or considerable extent; noticeably; very; *quite* ill. ◆The phrase *quite a* is used to indicate considerable but indefinite number, size, quantity, etc., as in **quite a lot** (a good deal), **quite a few** (many), **quite a while** (a long while). [ME; var. of QUIT, adj.]

quit·tance (kwit′ns) *n.* 1. Discharge or release, as from a debt or obligation. 2. A recompense or repayment. [See QUIT.]

quit·ter (kwit′ər) *n.* One who quits needlessly; a shirker.

quiv·er[1] (kwiv′ər) *v.i.* To shake with a slight, tremulous motion; vibrate; tremble. —*n.* The act or fact of quivering; a trembling or shaking. [Var. of QUAVER]

quiv·er[2] (kwiv′ər) *n.* A portable case for arrows; also, its contents. [< AF *quivier* < OF *cuivre* < OHG *kochar*]

quix·ot·ic (kwik·sot′ik) *adj.* Ridiculously chivalrous or romantic; having high but impractical sentiments, aims, etc. [after *Don Quixote*, hero of a Cervantes novel (1605, 1615)] —**quix·ot′·i·cal·ly** *adv.* —**quix·ot·ism** (kwik′sə·tiz′əm) *n.*

quiz (kwiz) *n.* 1. The act of questioning; esp., an informal oral or written examination of a class or individual. 2. An eccentric person or thing. 3. A hoax; practical joke. —*v.t.* **quizzed, quiz·zing** To examine by asking questions. [Origin unknown] —**quiz′·zer** *n.*

quiz·zi·cal (kwiz′i·kəl) *adj.* 1. Given to chaffing or bantering. 2. Queer; odd. 3. Questioning; puzzled: a *quizzical* smile. —**quiz′zi·cal·ly** *adv.*

quoin (koin, kwoin) *n.* 1. An external angle or corner of a building. 2. A stone or stones forming such an angle. —*v.t.* To provide, secure, or support with a quoin or quoins. [Var. of COIN]

quoit (kwoit, *esp. Brit.* koit) *n.* 1. A ring of metal, rope, etc., thrown in a game at a short stake, either encircling it or coming as close to it as possible. 2. *pl.* (*construed as sing.*) The game so played. [< MF *coite*, ? flat stone < OF *cuilte* quilt]

quon·dam (kwon′dəm) *adj.* Having been formerly; former. [< L]

quo·rum (kwôr′əm) *n.* The number of members of any deliberative or corporate body as is necessary for the legal transaction of business; commonly, a majority. [< L, genitive plural of *qui* who]

quo·ta (kwō′tə) *n.* The proportional part or share required for making up a certain number or quantity. [< L *quotus* how many]

quot·a·ble (kwō′tə·bəl) *adj.* Suitable for quotation. —**quot′a·bil′i·ty** *n.*

quo·ta·tion (kwō·tā′shən) *n.* 1. The act of quoting. 2. The words quoted or cited. 3. A price quoted or current, as of securities, etc. —**quo·ta′tion·al** *adj.* —**quo·ta′tion·al·ly** *adv.*

quotation mark Either of a pair of punctuation marks (" or ' and " or ') used to enclose a quotation, the single marks being used to set off a quotation within a quotation.

quote (kwōt) *v.t.* **quot·ed, quot·ing** 1. To reproduce the words of. 2. To repeat or cite (a rule, author, etc.), as for authority or illustration. 3. In commerce: **a** To state (a price). **b** To give the current or market price of. —*n.* 1. Loosely, a quotation. 2. A quotation mark. [< Med.L *quotare* to distinguish by number < L *quot* how many] —**quot′er** *n.* —**quote′wor′thy** (-wûr′thē) *adj.* —**quot′ing·ly** *adv.*

quoth (kwōth) *v.t.* *Archaic* Said or spoke; uttered. [OE *cwæth*, pt. of *cwethan* to say]

quo·tid·i·an (kwō·tid′ē·ən) *adj.* 1. Recurring or occurring every day. 2. Ordinary; commonplace. [< OF, or < L *quotidianus* daily]

quo·tient (kwō′shənt) *n.* *Math.* The result obtained by division; a number indicating how many times one quantity is contained in another. [< L *quotiens* how often]

R

r, R (är) *n. pl.* **r's** or **rs, R's** or **Rs, ars** (ärz) 1. The eighteenth letter of the English alphabet. 2. The sound represented by the letter *r*. —**the three R's** Reading, writing, and arithmetic regarded as the essential elements of a primary education.

Ra (rä) The supreme Egyptian deity, the sun god.

rab·bet (rab'it) *n.* A recess or groove in or near the edge of one piece of wood, etc., cut so as to receive the edge of another piece. —*v.* **·bet·ed, ·bet·ing** *v.t.* 1. To cut a rabbet in. 2. To unite in a rabbet. —*v.i.* 3. To be jointed by a rabbet. [< OF *rabattre* to beat down]

rab·bi (rab'ī) *n. pl.* **·bis** or **·bies** In Judaism: a The spiritual head of a Jewish community, authorized to perform religious duties. b Master; teacher: a title for one learned in the Law. Also **rab'bin** (-in). [< Hebrew *rabbī* my master] —**rab·bin·ic** (ra·bin'ik) or **·i·cal** *adj.* —**rab·bin'i·cal·ly** *adv.*

rab·bin·ate (rab'in·āt) *n.* 1. The office or term of office of a rabbi. 2. Rabbis collectively.

rab·bit (rab'it) *n.* 1. Any of a family of various small, long-eared mammals allied to but smaller than the hare, as the common American cottontail. 2. The pelt of a rabbit or hare. —*v.i.* To hunt rabbits. [Akin to Walloon *robett*, Flemish *robbe*] —**rab'bit·er** *n.*

rabbit fever Tularemia.

rabbit punch A short chopping blow at the base of the skull or back of the neck.

rab·ble (rab'əl) *n.* A disorderly crowd or mob. —**the rabble** The populace or lower classes: a contemptuous term. —*v.t.* **·bled, ·bling** To mob. [? < Du. *rabbelen* to speak indistinctly] —**rab'ble** *adj.*

rab·ble-rous·er (rab'əl·rou'zər) *n.* One who incites mobs by arousing prejudices and passions.

Rab·e·lai·si·an (rab'ə·lā'zē·ən, -zhən) *adj.* Bawdy and boisterous. [after François *Rabelais*, 1494–1553, French satirist] —**Rab'·e·lai'si·an·ism, Rab'e·la'ism** *n.*

rab·id (rab'id) *adj.* 1. Affected with rabies. 2. Fanatical; violent. 3. Furious; raging. Also **rab'ic.** [< L *rabere* to be mad] —**rab'·id·ly** *adv.* —**rab'id·ness** *n.*

ra·bies (rā'bēz) *n.* An acute, infectious, usu. fatal disease of certain animals, esp. of dogs, readily transmissible to man by the bite of an affected animal: also called *hydrophobia.* [< L, madness]

rac·coon (ra·ko͞on') *n.* 1. A North American nocturnal carnivore, grayish brown with a black cheek patch and a black-and-white-ringed bushy tail. 2. The fur of this animal. [Alter. of Algonquian *arakunem* hand-scratcher]

race[1] (rās) *n.* 1. One of the major subdivisions of mankind, regarded as having a common origin and exhibiting a relatively constant set of physical traits. 2. A nation, tribe, ethnic group, etc.: the German *race.* 3. A genealogical or family stock; clan. 4. Pedigree; lineage. 5. *Biol.* A group of plants or animals, having distinct characteristics that are passed on to offspring. [< Ital. *razza*; origin uncertain]

race[2] (rās) *n.* 1. A contest to determine the relative speed of the contestants. 2. Any contest. 3. Duration of life; course; career. 4. A swift current of water or its channel. 5. A sluice or channel by which to conduct water to or from a water wheel or around a dam. —*v.* **raced, rac·ing** *v.i.* 1. To take part in a contest of speed. 2. To move at great or top speed. 3. To move at an accelerated or too great speed: said of machinery. —*v.t.* 4. To contend against in a race. 5. To cause to race. [< ON *rās*]

race·course (rās'kôrs') *n.* A racetrack.

race·horse (rās'hôrs') *n.* A horse bred and trained for contests of speed.

ra·ceme (rā·sēm', rə-) *n. Bot.* An inflorescence in which the flowers are arranged singly at intervals on a common axis. [< L *racemus* cluster] —**rac·e·mose** (ras'ə·mōs), **rac'e·mous** (-məs) *adj.*

rac·er (rā'sər) *n.* 1. One who races. 2. Anything designed or used for racing, as a car, yacht, etc. 3. One of various nonvenomous snakes, as the blacksnake.

race·track (rās'trak') *n.* A track or course over which a horse race, dog race, etc., is run: also called *racecourse.*

race·way (rās'wā') *n.* 1. A channel for conducting water. 2. A racetrack for trotting horses.

ra·chi·tis (rə·kī'tis) *n. Pathol.* Rickets. [< Gk. *rachis* spine] —**ra·chit'ic** (-kit'ik) *adj.*

ra·cial (rā'shəl) *adj.* Of, pertaining to, or characteristic of a race, races, or descent. —**ra'cial·ly** *adv.*

ra·cism (rā'siz·əm) *n.* 1. An irrational belief in the superiority of a given people or nation, usu. one's own. 2. Action or policy based upon such a belief. Also **ra·cial·ism** (rā'shəl·iz'əm). —**ra'cist** *n. & adj.*

rack[1] (rak) *n.* 1. An open grating, framework, or the like, in or on which articles may be placed. 2. *Mech.* A bar or the like having teeth that engage with those of a gearwheel, pinion, or worm gear. 3. An instrument of torture that stretches the limbs of victims. —*v.t.* 1. To place or arrange in or on a rack. 2. To torture on or as on the rack. 3. To strain, as with the effort of thinking: to *rack* one's brains. —**to**

rack up *Informal* To achieve: to *rack up* a perfect score. [< MDu. *recken* to stretch] —**rack′er** *n.*

rack[2] (rak) *n.* Thin, flying, or broken clouds. —*v.i.* To move rapidly, as clouds before the wind. [< Scand.]

rack[3] (rak) *n.* See WRACK. —**to rack up** *Slang* To wreck.

rack·et[1] (rak′it) *n.* 1. A nearly elliptical hoop of bent wood, usu. strung with catgut or nylon, and having a handle, used in striking a tennis ball, etc. 2. *Often pl.* (*construed as sing.*) A game played with a ball and rackets in a court with four walls. Also **rac′quet.** [< Arabic *rāha* palm of the hand]

rack·et[2] (rak′it) *n.* 1. A clattering or confused noise. 2. *Informal* A scheme for getting money or other benefits by fraud, intimidation, or other illegitimate means. 3. *Slang* Any business or occupation. —*v.i.* To make a loud, clattering noise. —**to racket around** To frequent parties, nightclubs, etc. [Prob. imit.]

rack·et·eer (rak′ə·tir′) *n.* One engaged in a racket; mobster. —**rack′et·eer′ing** *n.*

rack·et·y (rak′it·ē) *adj.* Making a racket; noisy.

rac·on·teur (rak′on·tûr′, *Fr.* râ·kôn·tœr′) *n.* A skilled storyteller.

rac·y (ra′sē) *adj.* **rac·i·er, rac·i·est** 1. Having a spirited or pungent interest; spicy. 2. Having a characteristic flavor assumed to be indicative of origin, as wine. 3. Suggestive; slightly immodest: a *racy* story. [< RACE] —**rac′i·ly** *adv.* —**rac′i·ness** *n.*

ra·dar (rā′där) *n. Telecom.* An electronic device that locates objects by beaming radio-frequency impulses that are reflected back from the object. [< RA(DIO) D(ETECTION) A(ND) R(ANGING)]

radar beacon *Telecom.* The part of a radar that transmits radio-frequency waves. Also **ra·con** (rā′kon).

ra·dar·scope (rā′där·skōp) *n. Telecom.* The oscilloscope of a radar set.

rad·dle (rad′l) *v.t.* **·dled, ·dling** To intertwine or weave together. [< MHG *reidel* stout stick]

ra·di·al (rā′dē·əl) *adj.* 1. Of, pertaining to, or resembling a ray or radius. 2. *Anat.* Denoting the radius. —*n.* A radiating part. —**ra′di·al·ly** *adv.*

radial engine A multicylinder internal-combustion engine having its cylinders arranged like the spokes in a wheel.

radial tire An automotive tire having cords perpendicular to the wheel rim. Also **ra·di·al-ply tire** (rā′dē·əl·plī).

ra·di·an (rā′dē·ən) *n. Math.* 1. An arc equal in length to the radius of the circle of which it is a part. 2. The angle subtended by such an arc.

ra·di·ance (rā′dē·əns) *n.* The quality or state of being radiant; brightness. Also **ra′di·an·cy.**

ra·di·ant (rā′dē·ənt) *adj.* 1. Emitting rays of light or heat. 2. Beaming with light or brightness, kindness, or love. 3. Resembling rays. 4. Consisting of or transmitted by radiation. —*n.* That which radiates. [< L *radians, -antis,* ppr. of *radiare* to emit rays] —**ra′di·ant·ly** *adv.*

radiant energy *Physics* The energy transmitted in the form of waves, esp. electromagnetic waves, as heat, light, X-rays, etc.

ra·di·ate (*v.* rā′dē·āt; *adj.* rā′dē·it) *v.* **·at·ed, ·at·ing** *v.i.* 1. To emit rays or radiation; be radiant. 2. To issue forth in rays, as light from the sun. 3. To spread out from a center, as the spokes of a wheel. —*v.t.* 4. To send out or emit in or as in rays. —*adj.* Having rays; radiating. —**ra′di·a′tive** *adj.*

ra·di·a·tion (rā′dē·ā′shən) *n.* 1. The act of radiating, or the state of being radiated. 2. *Physics* The emission and propagation of radiant energy, esp. by radioactive substances capable of affecting living tissue.

radiation sickness *Pathol.* A condition due to absorption of excess radiation and marked by fatigue, vomiting, internal hemorrhage, and progressive tissue breakdown.

ra·di·a·tor (rā′dē·ā′tər) *n.* 1. A chamber, coil, etc., through which is passed steam or hot water for warming a building or apartment. 2. In engines, a nest of tubes for cooling water flowing through them. 3. *Physics* A source of radiation or radioactivity. —**ra′di·a·to′ry** (-ə·tôr′ē) *adj.*

rad·i·cal (rad′i·kəl) *adj.* 1. Of, proceeding from, or pertaining to the root or foundation; fundamental. 2. Thoroughgoing; extreme. 3. *Math.* Pertaining to the root or roots of a number. 4. Of or pertaining to political radicals. —*n.* 1. One who advocates widespread changes and reforms in government, social institutions, etc., at the earliest opportunity. 2. *Math.* **a** A quantity that is the root of another quantity. **b** The radical sign. 3. *Chem.* A group of atoms that acts as a unit in a compound and may pass unchanged through a series of reactions. [< LL *radicalis* having roots] —**rad′i·cal·ly** *adv.* —**rad′i·cal·ness** *n.*

rad·i·cal·ism (rad′i·kəl·iz′əm) *n.* 1. The state of being radical. 2. Advocacy of radical measures.

radical sign *Math.* The symbol √ placed before a quantity to indicate that a designated root is to be taken.

rad·i·cle (rad′i·kəl) *n.* 1. *Bot.* **a** The embryonic root below the cotyledon of a plant. **b** A small root or rootlet. 2. *Anat.* A rootlike part, as the initial fiber of a nerve. [< L *radicula,* dim. of *radix, -icis* root]

ra·di·i (rā′dē·ī) Plural of RADIUS.

ra·di·o (rā′dē·ō) *n. pl.* **·os** 1. The science and technique of communicating by means of electromagnetic waves that have been modulated to carry information in the form either of sound or of a code. 2. A receiver, transmitter, or other radio apparatus. 3. The radio business and industry. —*v.t. & v.i.* **ra·di·oed, ra·di·o·ing** 1. To transmit (a message, etc.) by radio. 2. To communicate with (someone) by radio. Also, *Brit., wireless.* [< RADIO(TELEGRAPHY)] —**ra′·di·o** *adj.*

radio- *combining form* 1. Radial. 2. Radio; produced or obtained by or related to radio. 3. Radioactive. 4. Radiation. [< L *radius* ray]

ra·di·o·ac·tiv·i·ty (rā′dē·ō·ak·tiv′ə·tē) *n. Physics* The spontaneous nuclear disintegration of certain elements, as uranium, with the emission of radiation in the form of particles or rays. —**ra′di·o·ac′tive** *adj.*

radio astronomy The branch of astronomy and astrophysics that studies celestial objects by the analysis of radio waves received.

radio beacon A stationary radio transmitter that sends out characteristic signals for the guidance of ships and aircraft.

radio beam *Aeron.* A continuous radio signal along an airway to guide aircraft.

ra·di·o·bi·ol·o·gy (rā′dē·ō·bī·ol′ə·jē) *n.* The study of the effects of radiation upon living organisms.

ra·di·o·broad·cast (rā′dē·ō·brôd′kast′) *v.t. & v.i.* **·cast** or **·cast·ed, ·cast·ing** To broadcast by radio. —*n.* A broadcast. —**ra′di·o·broad′cast′er** *n.* —**ra′di·o·broad′cast′ing** *n.*

ra·di·o·car·bon (rā′dē·ō·kär′bən) *n. Physics* The radioactive isotope of carbon of mass 14 with a half life of about 5570 years, used in the dating of fossils, artifacts, etc.: also called *carbon 14.*

radio compass *Aeron.* A directional radio receiver that indicates the bearing of a radio transmitting station.

ra·di·o·dat·ing (ra′dē·ō·dā′ting) *n.* The technique of dating objects by measuring their radioactivity.

radio frequency Any frequency lying between the audio sound waves and infrared light portion of the frequency spectrum, used in radio and television transmission.

ra·di·o·gram (rā′dē·ō·gram′) *n.* 1. A message sent by radio. 2. A radiograph.

ra·di·o·graph (rā′dē·ō·graf′) *n.* A picture made by means of radioactivity; an X-ray photograph. —*v.t.* To make a radiograph of. —**ra′di·og′ra·pher** (-og′rə·fər) *n.* —**ra′di·o·graph′ic** or **·i·cal** *adj.* —**ra′di·og′ra·phy** (-og′rə·fē) *n.*

ra·di·o·i·so·tope (rā′dē·ō·ī′sə·tōp) *n. Physics* A radioactive isotope.

ra·di·ol·o·gy (rā′dē·ol′ə·jē) *n.* The branch of science that relates to radiant energy and its applications, esp. in the diagnosis and treatment of disease. —**ra′di·o·log′i·cal** (-ə·loj′i·kəl) or **ra′di·o·log′ic** *adj.* —**ra′di·ol′o·gist** *n.*

ra·di·om·e·ter (rā′dē·om′ə·tər) *n.* An instrument for detecting and measuring radiant energy by converting it into mechanical energy. —**ra′di·o·met′ric** (-ō·met′rik) *adj.* —**ra′di·om′e·try** *n.*

ra·di·o·phone (rā′dē·ō·fōn′) *n.* 1. Any device for the production or transmission of sound by radiant energy. 2. A radiotelephone. —**ra′di·o·phon′ic** (-fon′ik) *adj.* —**ra′di·oph′o·ny** (-of′ə·nē) *n.*

ra·di·o·pho·tog·ra·phy (rā′dē·ō·fə·tog′rə·fē) *n.* The transmission of a photograph by radio waves. —**ra′di·o·pho′to·graph** (-fō′tə·graf) *n.*

ra·di·o·scope (rā′dē·ō·skōp′) *n.* An apparatus for detecting radioactivity or X-rays.

ra·di·os·co·py (rā′dē·os′kə·pē) *n.* Examination of opaque bodies with the aid of X-rays or some other form of radiant energy. —**ra′di·o·scop′ic** (-ō·skop′ik) or **·i·cal** *adj.*

ra·di·o·sonde (rā′dē·ō·sond′) *n. Meteorol.* An airborne device, usu. attached to a balloon, that radios meteorological data to the ground. [< F *radio* radio + *sonde* sounding]

radio star Any of a large number of stars that may be identified and studied by means of the radio waves they emit.

ra·di·o·tel·e·gram (rā′dē·ō·tel′ə·gram) *n.* A message sent by radiotelegraphy.

ra·di·o·te·leg·ra·phy (rā′dē·ō·tə·leg′rə·fē) *n.* Telegraphic communication using radio waves. —**ra′di·o·tel′e·graph′ic** (-tel′ə·graf′ik) *adj.* —**ra′di·o·tel′e·graph** (-tel′ə·graf) *n.*

ra·di·o·tel·e·phone (rā′dē·ō·tel′ə·fōn) *n.* A telephone that operates by means of radio waves. —**ra′di·o·tel′e·phon′ic** (-fon′ik) *adj.* —**ra′di·o·te·leph′o·ny** (-tə·lef′ə·nē) *n.*

radio telescope *Astron.* A radio receiver designed to receive radio waves from outer space.

ra·di·o·ther·a·py (rā′dē·ō·ther′ə·pē) *n. Med.* The treatment of disease by X-rays and other forms of radioactivity.

radio wave Any electromagnetic wave having a radio frequency.

rad·ish (rad′ish) *n.* The pungent, edible root of an herb of the mustard family; also, the herb. [OE *rædic* < L *radix, radicis* root]

ra·di·um (rā′dē·əm) *n.* A powerfully radioactive metallic element (symbol Ra). [< L *radius* ray]

radium therapy The treatment of diseases, esp. of cancer, by means of radium.

ra·di·us (ra′dē·əs) *n. pl.* **·di·i** (-dē·ī) 1. A straight line from the center of a circle or sphere to the circumference or surface. 2. *Anat.* The outer bone of the two long bones of the forearm, located on the same side as the thumb. 3. A circular area or boundary measured by the length of its radius. 4. Sphere, scope, or limit, as of activity. [< L, rod, spoke of a wheel]

radius vector *pl.* **radius vectors** or **ra·di·i vec·to·res** (rā′dē·ī vek·tôr′ēz) *Math.* The straight-line distance from a fixed origin to any point of a curve.

ra·dix (rā′diks) *n. pl.* **rad·i·ces** (rad′ə·sēz, rā′də-) or **ra·dix·es** 1. *Math.* A number or symbol used as the basis of a scale of enumeration. 2. *Bot.* The root of a plant. [< L, root]

ra·dome (rā′dōm) *n.* A protective housing for the antenna of a radar assembly. [< RA(DAR) + DOME]

ra·don (rā′don) *n.* A heavy, gaseous, radioactive element (symbol Rn), formed by the disintegration of radium.

raff (raf) *n.* The rabble; riffraff. [< dial. *raff* to rake]

raf·fi·a (raf′ē·ə) *n.* 1. A cultivated palm of Madagascar, the leafstalks of which furnish fiber for making hats, mats, baskets, etc. 2. Its fiber. [< Malagasy]

raff·ish (raf′ish) *adj.* 1. Tawdry; gaudy; flashy. 2. Disreputable.

raf·fle (raf′əl) *n.* A form of lottery in which one buys a chance on a prize. —*v.t.* **·fled, ·fling** To dispose of by a raffle: often with *off.* [< OF *rafle* a game of dice] —**raf′fler** *n.*

raft[1] (raft) *n.* 1. A float of logs, planks, etc., fastened together for transportation by water. 2. Any similar float, as one anchored for use by swimmers. 3. A life raft. —*v.t.* 1. To transport on a raft. —*v.i.* 2. To travel by raft. [< ON *raptr* rafter]

raft[2] (raft) *n. Informal* A large number or collection of any kind. [< RAFF]

raft·er (raf′tər) *n.* A beam giving form, slope, and support to a roof. [OE *ræfter*]

rag[1] (rag) *v.t.* **ragged, rag·ging** *Slang* 1. To tease or annoy. 2. To scold. [Origin uncertain]

rag[2] (rag) *n.* 1. A torn or discarded piece of cloth. 2. A small cloth used for washing, cleaning, etc. 3. *pl.* Cotton or linen textile remnants used in the making of rag paper. 4. *pl.* Tattered or shabby clothing. —**glad rags** *Slang* One's best clothes. [OE < ON *rögg* tuft]

rag[3] (rag) *v.t.* **ragged, rag·ging** To compose or play in ragtime. —*n.* Ragtime.

ra·ga (rä′gə) *n.* Any of the traditional melody patterns in Indian music on which improvisations are made. [< Skt., color]

rag·a·muf·fin (rag′ə·muf′in) *n.* Anyone, esp. a child, wearing ragged clothes. [after *Ragamoffyn*, demon in William Langland's *Piers Plowman* (1393)]

rage (rāj) *n.* 1. Violent anger; wrath; fury. 2. Any great violence or intensity. 3. Extreme eagerness or emotion; great enthusiasm. 4. Something popular or in demand; a fad. —*v.i.* **raged, rag·ing** 1. To speak or act with great anger. 2. To act or proceed with violence or intensity. [< L *rabere* to rage] —**rag′ing·ly** *adv.*

rag·ged (rag′id) *adj.* 1. Torn or worn into rags; frayed. 2. Wearing worn, frayed, or shabby garments. 3. Of rough or uneven character or aspect. —**rag′ged·ly** *adv.* —**rag′ged·ness** *n.*

rag·lan (rag′lən) *n.* An overcoat with sleeves extending in one piece up to the collar. —*adj.* 1. Denoting a garment with such sleeves. 2. Denoting such sleeves. [after Lord *Raglan*, 1788–1855, English field marshal]

rag·man (rag′man′) *n.* *pl.* **·men** (-men′) One who gathers and sells rags and other junk for a living. Also **rag′pick′er.**

ra·gout (ra·gōō′) *n.* A highly seasoned dish of stewed meat and vegetables. —*v.t.* **ra·gouted** (-gōōd′), **ra·gout·ing** (-gōō′ing) To make into a ragout. [< F]

rag·time (rag′tīm′) *n.* 1. A kind of American dance music, developed from about 1890 to 1920, characterized by highly syncopated rhythm in fast time. 2. The rhythm of this music. Also called *rag.* [< *ragged time*]

rag·weed (rag′wēd′) *n.* A coarse, very common annual or perennial herb, the pollen of which induces hay fever.

rag·wort (rag′wûrt′) *n.* An herb of the composite family, with bright yellow flowers.

rah (rä) *interj.* Hurrah.

raid (rād) *n.* 1. A hostile or predatory incursion by a rapidly moving body of troops or an armed vessel; a foray. 2. An air raid. 3. Any sudden invasion, capture, or seizure. —*v.t.* 1. To make a raid on. —*v.i.* 2. To participate in a raid. [< Scot. form of OE *rād* a riding] —**raid′er** *n.*

rail[1] (rāl) *n.* 1. A bar of wood, metal, etc., resting on supports, as in a fence, at the side of a stairway, etc.; a railing. 2. One of a series of parallel bars of iron or steel resting upon crossties and forming a support and guide for wheels, as of a railroad. 3. A railroad considered as a means of transportation: to ship by *rail.* —*v.t.* To furnish or shut in with rails; fence. [< L *regula* wooden ruler]

rail[2] (rāl) *n.* Any of numerous marsh birds having long legs and a short, turned-up tail. [< OF *raale*]

rail[3] (rāl) *v.i.* To use abusive language; scold: with *at* or *against.* [< Provençal *ralhar* to jest at] —**rail′er** *n.*

rail·ing (rā′ling) *n.* 1. A series of rails; a balustrade. 2. Rails, or material from which rails are made.

rail·ler·y (rā′lər·ē) *n.* *pl.* **·ler·ies** Merry jesting or teasing; banter. [< F *raillerie* jesting]

rail·road (rāl′rōd′) *n.* 1. A graded road having metal rails supported by ties, for the passage of trains or rolling stock drawn by locomotives. 2. The system of tracks, stations, etc., used in transportation by rail. 3. The corporation or persons owning or operating such a system. —*v.t.* 1. To transport by railroad. 2. *Informal* To rush or force with great speed or without deliberation. 3. *Slang* To cause to be imprisoned on false charges or without fair trial. —*v.i.* 4. To work on a railroad. —**rail′road′er** *n.* —**rail′road′ing** *n.*

rail·way (rāl′wā′) *n.* 1. *Chiefly Brit.* A railroad. 2. Any track or set of rails similar to those of a railroad.

rai·ment (rā′mənt) *n.* *Archaic* Wearing apparel; clothing; garb. [< ARRAY + -MENT]

rain (rān) *n.* 1. The condensed water vapor of the atmosphere falling in drops. ◆ Collateral adjective: *pluvial.* 2. The fall of such drops. 3. A fall or shower of anything. 4. A rainstorm. 5. *pl.* The rainy season, as in a tropical country. —*v.i.* 1. To fall from the clouds in drops of water: usu. with *it* as the subject. 2. To fall like rain, as tears. —*v.t.* 3. To send down like rain; shower. —**to rain out** To cause (an outdoor event) to be canceled or postponed because of rain. [OE *regn*] —**rain′y** *adj.* **·i·er, ·i·est**

rain·bow (rān′bō′) *n.* An arch of prismatic colors formed in the sky opposite the sun and caused by refraction, reflection, and dispersion of light in raindrops falling through the air. [OE *regnboga*]

rain check 1. The stub of a ticket to an outdoor event, as a baseball game, entitling the holder to admission at a future date if the event is called off. 2. A postponed invitation.

rain·coat (rān′kōt′) *n.* A coat, often waterproof, intended to be worn in rainy weather.

rain·fall (rān′fôl′) *n.* 1. A fall of rain. 2. *Meteorol.* The amount of water, measured in inches, precipitated in a given region over a stated time, as rain, hail, snow, or the like.

rain forest A dense tropical forest on which 100 inches or more of rain falls each year.

rain gauge An instrument for measuring the amount of rainfall at a given place or time. Also **rain gage.**

rain·mak·ing (rān′mā′king) *n.* Production of rain, or an attempt to produce it, esp. by seeding clouds. —**rain′mak′er** *n.*

rain·proof (rān′prōōf′) *adj.* Shedding rain, as garments.

rain·storm (rān′stôrm′) *n.* A storm accompanied by rain.

rain·wa·ter (rān′wô′tər) *n.* Water that falls

or has fallen in the form of rain. Also **rain water.**

rainy day *Informal* A time of need.

raise (rāz) *v.* **raised, rais·ing** *v.t.* 1. To cause to move upward or to a higher level; elevate. 2. To place erect; set up. 3. To construct or build. 4. To make greater in amount, size, or value: to *raise* prices. 5. To advance or elevate in rank, estimation, etc. 6. To increase the strength, intensity, or degree of. 7. To breed; grow. 8. To rear (children, a family, etc.). 9. To cause; occasion. 10. To stir to action or emotion; animate. 11. To gather together; obtain or collect. 12. To bring up for consideration, as a question. 13. To cause to swell or become lighter; leaven. 14. To put an end to, as a siege. 15. In poker, to bet more than. —*v.i.* 16. In poker, to make a raise. —**to raise the devil** (or **the dickens, hell, the roof, a rumpus,** etc.) *Informal* To make a great disturbance; stir up confusion. —*n.* 1. The act of raising. 2. An increase, as of wages or a bet. [< ON *risa* to rise] —**rais′er** *n.*

raised (rāzd) *adj.* 1. Elevated. 2. Made with yeast or leaven.

rai·sin (rā′zən) *n.* A grape dried for eating. [< L *racemus* bunch of grapes]

rai·son d'ê·tre (re·zôn′ de′tr′) *French* Reason or excuse for existing; literally, reason for being.

raj (räj) *n.* In India, sovereignty; rule. [< Hind. *rāj*]

ra·jah (rä′jə) *n.* A Hindu prince or chief of a tribal state in India; also, a Malay or Javanese ruler: often used as a courtesy title. Also **ra′ja.** [< Skt. *rājan* king]

rake[1] (rāk) *n.* A toothed implement for drawing together loose material, loosening the surface of the soil, etc. —*v.* **raked, rak·ing** *v.t.* 1. To scrape or gather together with or as with a rake. 2. To smooth, clean, or prepare with a rake. 3. To direct heavy gunfire along the length of, as a ship or column of troops. —*v.i.* 4. To use a rake. —**to rake in** *Informal* To earn or acquire (money, etc.) in large quantities. [OE *raca*] —**rak′er** *n.*

rake[2] (rāk) *v.t. & v.i.* **raked, rak·ing** To lean or cause to lean from the perpendicular, as a ship's masts; incline. —*n.* Inclination from the perpendicular or horizontal. [Origin uncertain]

rake[3] (rāk) *n.* A dissolute, lewd man; a roué. [Earlier *rakehell* < ME *rakel* rash, wild]

rake·off (rāk′ôf′) *n. Slang.* 1. A share, as of profits; commission. 2. A rebate, usu. illegitimate.

rak·ish[1] (rā′kish) *adj.* 1. Dashing; jaunty; smart. 2. *Naut.* Having the masts unusually inclined, so as to suggest speed. [< RAKE[2]] —**rak′ish·ly** *adv.* —**rak′ish·ness** *n.*

rak·ish[2] (rā′kish) *adj.* Characteristic of a rake; dissolute; profligate. —**rak′ish·ly** *adv.* —**rak′ish·ness** *n.*

râle (räl) *n. Pathol.* A sound additional to that of normal respiration, indicative of disease. [< F, rattle]

ral·len·tan·do (ral′ən·tan′dō, *Ital.* räl′len·tän′dō) *Music adj. & adv.* Gradually slower. [< Ital.

ral·ly[1] (ral′ē) *n. pl.* **·lies** 1. A meeting of persons for a common purpose. 2. A rapid recovery, as after exhaustion. 3. A return, as of scattered troops, to order or action. 4. In tennis, etc., the interchange of several strokes. 5. A driving competition or procession, as for sports cars, antique automobiles, etc. —*v.* **·lied, ·ly·ing** *v.t.* 1. To bring together and restore to normal order, as troops. 2. To summon up or revive. 3. To bring together for common action. —*v.i.* 4. To return to discipline or action. 5. To unite for common action. 6. To make a return to a normal condition; improve. 7. In tennis, etc., to engage in a rally. [< F *re-* again + *allier* to join] —**ral′li·er** *n.*

ral·ly[2] (ral′ē) *v.t. & v.i.* **·lied, ·ly·ing** To mock or tease with raillery; banter. [< F *railler* to banter] —**ral′li·er** *n.*

ram (ram) *n.* 1. A male sheep. 2. A device for driving, forcing, or crushing by heavy blows or thrusts. —*v.t.* **rammed, ram·ming** 1. To strike with or as with a ram; dash against. 2. To drive or force down or into something. [OE *ramm*] —**ram′mer** *n.*

ram·ble (ram′bəl) *v.i.* **·bled, ·bling** 1. To walk about freely and aimlessly; roam. 2. To write or talk aimlessly. 3. To proceed with turns and twists; meander. —*n.* 1. An aimless stroll. 2. A meandering path. [? ME *romblen*, freq. of *romen* to roam]

ram·bler (ram′blər) *n.* 1. One who or that which rambles. 2. A climbing rose.

ram·bunc·tious (ram·bungk′shəs) *adj. Informal* Boisterous; rough. [Prob. var. of *robustious* < ROBUST]

ram·e·kin (ram′ə·kin) *n.* 1. A small dish for baking eggs, macaroni, etc. 2. A serving of eggs, etc., baked in such a dish. Also **ram′e·quin.** [< F *ramequin*]

ram·ie (ram′ē) *n.* The fiber yielded by a shrubby Chinese and East Indian perennial of the nettle family, used for cordage and certain textiles. Also **ram′ee.** [< Malay *rami*]

ram·i·fi·ca·tion (ram′ə·fə·kā′shən) *n.* 1. The act or process of ramifying. 2. A result, consequence, etc., stemming from a main source.

ram·i·form (ram′ə·fôrm) *adj.* 1. Branch-shaped. 2. Branched. [< L *ramus* branch]

ram·i·fy (ram′ə·fī) *v.t. & v.i.* **·fied, ·fy·ing** To divide or spread out into or as into branches; branch out. [< L *ramus* branch + *facere* to make]

ra·mose (rā′mōs, rə·mōs′) *adj.* 1. Branching. 2. Consisting of or having branches. [< L *ramus* branch]

ra·mous (rā′məs) *adj.* 1. Of or like branches. 2. Ramose. [See RAMOSE]

ramp (ramp) *n.* 1. An inclined passageway, roadway, or runway. 2. A movable stairway by which passengers enter or leave an airplane. [< OF *ramper* to climb]

ram·page (*n.* ram′pāj; for *v.*, also ram·pāj′) *n.* Violent action or excitement. —*v.i.* **·paged, ·pag·ing** 1. To rush or act violently. 2. To storm; rage. [Orig. Scot., ? < OF *ramper* to climb] —**ram′pag·er** *n.* —**ram·pa′geous** *adj.*

ram·pant (ram′pənt) *adj.* 1. Exceeding all bounds; wild; widespread. 2. Standing on the hind legs; rearing. [< OF, ppr. of *ramper* to climb] **—ram′pan·cy** *n.* **—ram′·pant·ly** *adv.*

ram·part (ram′pärt, -pərt) *n.* 1. The embankment surrounding a fort, on which the parapet is raised. 2. A bulwark or defense. *—v.t.* To supply with or as with ramparts; fortify. [< F *remparer* to fortify]

ram·rod (ram′rod′) *n.* 1. A rod used to drive home the charge of a muzzleloading gun or pistol. 2. A similar rod used for cleaning the barrel of a rifle, etc.

ram·shack·le (ram′shak′əl) *adj.* Likely to go to pieces, as from age or neglect. [< *ransackle*, freq. of RANSACK]

ran (ran) Past tense of RUN.

ranch (ranch) *n.* 1. An establishment for raising or grazing cattle, sheep, horses, etc., in large herds. 2. The buildings, personnel, and lands connected with it. 3. A large farm. *—v.i.* To manage or work on a ranch. [< Sp. *rancho* soldiers' mess] **—ranch′er, ranch′man** (-mən) *n.*

ranch house 1. The main building of a ranch. 2. A one-story house, usu. having a low roof with a wide overhang.

ran·cid (ran′sid) *adj.* 1. Having an unpleasant taste or smell; rank. 2. Spoiled, as food. [< L *rancere* to be rank] **—ran·cid′i·ty, ran′cid·ness** *n.*

ran·cor (rang′kər) *n.* Bitter enmity; spitefulness. Also *Brit.* **ran′cour.** [< L *rancere* to be rank] **—ran′cor·ous** *adj.* **—ran′cor·ous·ly** *adv.* **—ran′cor·ous·ness** *n.*

rand (rand, ränd) *n. pl.* **rand** The monetary unit of South Africa, Lesotho, and Botswana. [< The *Rand*, or Witwatersrand, a region of Transvaal, South Africa]

ran·dom (ran′dəm) *n.* Lack of definite aim or intention: now chiefly in the phrase **at random,** without definite purpose or aim; haphazardly. *—adj.* Done at random. [< OF *random* rapidity, impetuosity] **—ran′dom·ly** *adv.*

rang (rang) Past tense of RING².

range (rānj) *n.* 1. The area over which anything moves, operates, or is distributed. 2. An extensive tract of land over which cattle, sheep, etc., roam and graze. 3. Extent or scope. 4. The extent of variation of anything: the temperature *range.* 5. A line, row, or series, as of mountains. 6. A place for shooting at a mark: a rifle *range.* 7. A large cooking stove. *—adj.* Of or pertaining to a range. *—v.* **ranged, rang·ing** *v.t.* 1. To arrange in definite order, as in rows. 2. To assign to a class, division, or category. 3. To move about or over (a region, etc.). *—v.i.* 4. To move over an area in a thorough, systematic manner. 5. To rove; roam. 6. To extend or proceed. 7. To exhibit variation within specified limits. [< OF *ranc* row]

rang·er (rān′jər) *n.* 1. One who or that which ranges; a rover. 2. One of an armed band designed to protect large tracts of country. 3. A warden employed in patrolling forest tracts. 4. *Often cap.* One of a select group of U.S. soldiers trained for raiding action on enemy territory. **—rang′er·ship** *n.*

rang·y (rān′jē) *adj.* **rang·i·er, rang·i·est** Having long, slender limbs, as a person. **—rang′i·ness** *n.*

ra·ni (rä′nē) *n.* 1. The wife of a raja or prince. 2. A reigning Hindu queen or princess. Also **ra′nee.** [< Skt. *rājnī*, fem. of *rajan* king]

rank¹ (rangk) *n.* 1. A series of objects ranged in a line or row; a range. 2. Relative standing or position, as in the armed forces; status; grade. 3. A line of soldiers drawn up side by side in close order. 4. *pl.* An army; also, the mass of soldiery. 5. High degree or position: a lady of *rank.* *—v.t.* 1. To arrange in a rank or ranks. 2. To place in a class, order, etc. *—v.i.* 3. To hold a specified place or rank. 4. To have the highest rank or grade. [< OF *ranc*]

rank² (rangk) *adj.* 1. Very vigorous and flourishing in growth, as vegetation. 2. Strong and disagreeable to the taste or smell. 3. Utter; complete: *rank* injustice. [OE *ranc* strong] **—rank′ly** *adv.* **—rank′·ness** *n.*

rank and file 1. The common soldiers of an army. 2. The ordinary members of any group.

rank·ing (rangk′ing) *adj.* Superior in rank; taking precedence over others.

ran·kle (rang′kəl) *v.* **·kled, ·kling** *v.i.* 1. To cause continued resentment, irritation, etc.; fester. *—v.t.* 2. To irritate; embitter. [< OF *rancler* to fester]

ran·sack (ran′sak) *v.t.* To search through every part of for or as if for plunder; pillage. [< ON *rannsaka* to search a house] **—ran′·sack·er** *n.*

ran·som (ran′səm) *v.t.* To secure the release of (a person, property, etc.) for a required price, as from captivity. *—n.* The payment for such a release. [< L *re-* back + *emere* to buy] **—ran′som·er** *n.*

rant (rant) *v.i.* 1. To speak in loud, violent, or extravagant language; rave. *—v.t.* 2. To utter in a ranting manner. *—n.* Bombastic talk. [< MDu. *ranten* rave] **—rant′er** *n.*

rap¹ (rap) *v.* **rapped, rap·ping** *v.t.* 1. To strike sharply and quickly; hit. 2. To utter in a sharp manner: with *out.* 3. *Slang* To criticize severely. *—v.i.* 4. To strike sharp, quick blows. 5. *Slang* To have a frank discussion; talk. *—n.* 1. A sharp blow. 2. A knocking or tapping sound. 3. *Slang* A charge of wrongdoing; blame. 4. *Slang* A talk; discussion. [ME, prob. imit.] **—rap′per** *n.*

rap² (rap) *n.* The least bit: I don't care a *rap.* [< RAPT]

ra·pa·cious (rə·pā′shəs) *adj.* 1. Given to plunder or rapine. 2. Grasping; greedy. 3. Subsisting on prey seized alive, as hawks, etc. [< L *rapere* to seize] **—ra·pa′cious·ly** *adv.* **—ra·pa′cious·ness** *n.* **—ra·pac′i·ty** (-pas′ə·tē) *n.*

rape¹ (rāp) *v.* **raped, rap·ing** *v.t.* To commit rape upon; ravish. *—n.* 1. Illegal, esp. forcible, sexual intercourse with a woman or girl. 2. Forcible sexual relations, whether with a female or male. [< L *rapere* to seize] **—rap′ist** *n.*

rape² (rāp) *n.* A plant related to the cabbage, having seeds (**rapeseeds**) that yield an oil (**rape oil**). [< L *rapum* turnip]

rap·id (rap′id) *adj.* Having, moving, or done with great speed; swift. *—n.* *Usu. pl.* A swift-running descent in a river. [< L *rapere* to seize, rush] **—ra·pid·i·ty** (rə·pid′·ə·tē), **rap′id·ness** *n.* **—rap′id·ly** *adv.*

rapid eye movement Rapid movement of

the closed eyes during sleep, associated with dreaming and a characteristic pattern of electrical activity of the brain. Also *REM*.

rap·id-fire (rap′id·fīr′) *adj.* 1. Firing or designed for firing shots in rapid succession. 2. Characterized by speed.

ra·pi·er (rā′pē·ər, rāp′yər) *n.* 1. A long, straight, two-edged sword, used chiefly for thrusting. 2. A shorter straight sword without cutting edge, used for thrusting only. [< MF *rapière*]

rap·ine (rap′in) *n.* The taking of property by force, as in war; pillage. [< L *rapere* to seize]

rap·port (rə·pôr′) *n.* Harmony or sympathy of relation; agreement; accord. [< F < *rapporter* to bring back]

rap·proche·ment (rá·prôsh·mäṅ′) *n. French* A state of harmony or reconciliation.

rap·scal·lion (rap·skal′yən) *n.* A rogue; rascal. [< earlier *rascallion*, extension of RASCAL]

rapt (rapt) *adj.* 1. Carried away with lofty emotion; enraptured; transported. 2. Engrossed; intent. [< L *rapere* to seize]

rap·to·ri·al (rap·tôr′ē·əl) *adj.* 1. Seizing prey; predatory. 2. Having talons adapted for seizing prey, as hawks, vultures, eagles, etc. [< L *rapere* to seize]

rap·ture (rap′chər) *n.* 1. The state of being rapt or transported; ecstatic joy; ecstasy. 2. *Often pl.* An act or expression of excessive delight. —*v.t.* **·tured, ·tur·ing** *Poetic* To enrapture. [< RAPT] —**rap′tur·ous** *adj.* —**rap′tur·ous·ly** *adv.*

rare[1] (râr) *adj.* rar·er, rar·est 1. Infrequent in occurrence, distribution, etc. 2. Highly esteemed; exceptional. 3. Rarefied. [< L *rarus*] —**rare′ness** *n.*

rare[2] (râr) *adj.* Partially cooked, as broiled meat, so as to retain its redness and juices. [OE *hrēre*]

rare·bit (râr′bit) *n.* Welsh rabbit.

rare-earth element (râr′urth′) *Chem.* Any of a group of metallic elements constituting the lanthanide series. Also **rare-earth metal**.

rar·e·fy (râr′ə·fī) *v.t. & v.i.* **·fied, ·fy·ing** To make or become thin, less solid, or less dense. [< L *rarus* rare + *facere* to make] —**rar′e·fac′tion** (-fak′shən) *n.* —**rar′e·fac′tive** (-fak′tiv) *adj.* —**rar′e·fi′a·ble** *adj.*

rare·ly (râr′lē) *adv.* 1. Not often; infrequently. 2. Exceptionally.

rar·ing (râr′ing) *adj. Informal* Extremely eager or enthusiastic. [< Pres. part of *rare*, dial. of REAR[2]]

rar·i·ty (râr′ə·tē) *n. pl.* **·ties** 1. That which is exceptionally valued because of scarceness. 2. The state of being rare.

ras·cal (ras′kəl) *n.* A rogue; knave: sometimes used playfully. [< OF *rascaille* rabble] —**ras·cal′i·ty** (-kal′ə·tē) *n.* —**ras′·cal·ly** *adj. & adv.*

rase (rāz) *v.t.* rased, ras·ing See RAZE.

rash[1] (rash) *adj.* Acting or done without due caution; reckless. [Prob. < OHG *rasc* lively] —**rash′ly** *adv.* —**rash′ness** *n.*

rash[2] (rash) *n.* 1. A superficial eruption of the skin, often localized. 2. A great number of instances within a short period. [< L *radere* to scratch]

rash·er (rash′ər) *n.* A thin slice of meat, esp. bacon.

rasp (rasp) *n.* 1. A file having coarse projections for abrasion. 2. The act or sound of rasping. —*v.t.* 1. To scrape or rub with or as with a rasp. 2. To utter in a rough voice. —*v.i.* 3. To grate; scrape. 4. To make a rough, harsh sound. [< OF *rasper* to scrape] —**rasp′er** *n.* —**rasp′y** *adj.*

rasp·ber·ry (raz′ber′ē) *n. pl.* **·ries** 1. The round fruit of certain brambles of the rose family. 2. Any plant yielding this fruit. 3. *Slang* A Bronx cheer. [< earlier *raspis* (*berry*)]

rat (rat) *n.* 1. A destructive and injurious rodent of worldwide distribution, larger and more aggressive than the mouse. 2. *Slang* A person who deserts or betrays his associates. 3. A pad over which a woman's hair is combed. —**to smell a rat** To suspect that something is wrong. —*v.i.* rat·ted, rat·ting 1. To hunt rats. 2. *Slang* To inform; betray: with *on*. [OE *ræt*]

ratch·et (rach′it) *n.* 1. A mechanism consisting of a notched wheel, the teeth of which engage with a pawl, permitting motion of the wheel in one direction only. 2. The pawl or the wheel thus used. Also **ratchet wheel**. [< F *rochet* bobbin]

rate[1] (rāt) *n.* 1. The measure of a variable in relation to some fixed unit. 2. Degree of value; price; also, the unit cost of a commodity or service. 3. Comparative rank or class. 4. *Brit.* A local tax on property. 5. A fixed allowance, amount, or ratio. —**at any rate** In any case; anyhow. —*v.* **rat·ed, rat·ing** *v.t.* 1. To estimate the value or worth of; appraise. 2. To place in a certain rank or grade. 3. To consider; regard. 4. *Informal* To deserve. —*v.i.* 5. To have rank, rating, or value. [< L *reri* to calculate] —**rat′a·ble** or **rate′a·ble** *adj.* —**rat′er** *n.*

rate[2] (rāt) *v.t. & v.i.* **rat·ed, rat·ing** To reprove with vehemence; rail at.

rath·er (rath′ər) *adv.* 1. More willingly. 2. With more reason, wisdom, etc. 3. More precisely, strictly, or accurately. 4. Somewhat: *rather* cold. 5. On the contrary. —*interj. Brit.* Yes indeed! [OE *hrathor*, compar. of *hrathe* soon, quickly]

raths·kel·ler (rath′skel·ər, räts′kel·ər) *n.* A beer hall or similar restaurant, usu. located in a cellar. [< G *rat* town hall + *keller* cellar]

rat·i·fy (rat′ə·fī) *v.t.* **·fied, ·fy·ing** To give sanction to, esp. official sanction; confirm. [< L *ratus* fixed, calculated + *facere* to make] —**rat′i·fi·ca′tion** *n.* —**rat′i·fi′er** *n.*

rat·i·né (rat·ə·nā′) *n.* A heavy, loosely woven fabric with a nubby surface. [< F *ratiner* to make nubby]

rat·ing (rā′ting) *n.* 1. Classification according to a standard; grade; rank. 2. An evaluation, as of the financial standing of a business. 3. A numerical index of the size of the audience of a television or radio broadcast, estimated from a sample poll.

ra·tio (rā′shō, -shē·ō) *n. pl.* **·tios** 1. Relation of degree, number, etc.; proportion; rate. 2. The relation of two quantities, esp. the quotient of the first divided by the second. [< L *reri* to think]

ra·ti·oc·i·nate (rash′ē·os′ə·nāt, rat′ē-) *v.i.* **·nat·ed, ·nat·ing** To make a deduction from premises; reason. [< L *reri* to think] —**ra′ti·oc′i·na′tion** *n.* —**ra′ti·oc′i·na′tive** *adj.* —**ra′ti·oc′i·na′tor** *n.*

ra·tion (rash′ən, rā′shən) *n.* 1. A portion;

share. 2. *Often pl.* A fixed allowance or portion of food, etc., allotted in time of scarcity. 3. *Mil.* Food for one person for one day. —*v.t.* 1. To issue rations to. 2. To give out or allot in rations. [< L *ratio, -onis*] —**ra′·tion·ing** *n.*

ra·tion·al (rash′ən·əl) *adj.* 1. Possessing the faculty of reasoning. 2. Not delirious, mad, etc.; sane. 3. Reasonable; judicious; sensible. 4. Attained by reasoning. 5. *Math.* Denoting an algebraic expression containing no variables within irreducible radicals. [See RATIO.] —**ra′tion·al′i·ty** (-al′ə·tē) *n.* —**ra′tion·al·ly** *adv.*

ra·tion·ale (rash′ən·al′) *n.* 1. The rational or logical basis of something. 2. A rational explanation of principles.

ra·tion·al·ism (rash′ən·əl·iz′əm) *n.* 1. The formation of opinions by reason alone. 2. *Philos.* The theory that truth and knowledge are attainable through reason rather than by empirical means. —**ra′tion·al·ist** *n.* —**ra′tion·al·is′tic** or **·ti·cal** *adj.* —**ra′tion·al·is′ti·cal·ly** *adv.*

ra·tion·al·ize (rash′ən·əl·iz′) *v.* **·ized, ·iz·ing** *v.t.* 1. *Psychol.* To explain or base (one's behavior) on grounds ostensibly rational but not in accord with the actual or unconscious motives. 2. To explain or treat from a rationalistic point of view. 3. To make rational or reasonable. —*v.i.* 4. *Psychol.* To devise ostensibly rational grounds for one's behavior. 5. To think in a rational or rationalistic manner. Also *Brit.* **ra′tion·al·ise′.** —**ra′tion·al·i·za′tion** *n.* —**ra′tion·al·iz′er** *n.*

rat·ite (rat′īt) *n.* Any of a group of flightless birds including ostriches, kiwis, emus, etc. [< L *ratis* raft] —**rat′ite** *adj.*

rat·line (rat′lin) *n.* *Naut.* One of the small ropes fastened across the shrouds of a ship, used as a ladder. Also **rat′lin** (-lin). [Origin unknown]

rat race *Slang* A frantic, usu. fruitless, struggle.

rat's nest *Informal* A cluttered and messy place.

rat·tan (ra·tan′) *n.* 1. The long, tough, flexible stem of various tropical palms, used in making wickerwork, light furniture, etc. 2. The palm itself. [< Malay *rotan*]

rat·ter (rat′ər) *n.* 1. A dog or cat that catches rats. 2. *Slang* A deserter; traitor.

rat·tle (rat′l) *v.* **·tled, ·tling** *v.i.* 1. To make a series of sharp noises in rapid succession, as of hard objects striking one another. 2. To move or act with such noises. 3. To talk rapidly and foolishly; chatter. —*v.t.* 4. To cause to rattle. 5. To utter or perform rapidly or noisily. 6. *Informal* To confuse; disconcert. —*n.* 1. A series of short, sharp sounds in rapid succession. 2. A plaything, implement, etc., made to produce a rattling noise. 3. Any of the jointed horny rings in the tail of a rattlesnake. [Imit.]

rat·tle·brain (rat′l·brān′) *n.* A talkative, flighty person; foolish chatterer. Also **rat′tle·head′** (-hed′), **rat′tle·pate′** (-pāt′). —**rat′tle·brained′** *adj.*

rat·tle·snake (rat′l·snāk′) *n.* Any of several venomous American snakes with a tail ending in a series of horny, loosely connected, modified joints that make a rattling noise when the tail is vibrated. Also **rat′tler.**

rat·tle·trap (rat′l·trap′) *n.* A vehicle, etc., that is rickety, clattering, or worn out.

rat·trap (rat′trap′) *n.* 1. A trap for catching rats. 2. A rundown building. 3. Any hopeless or involved predicament.

rat·ty (rat′ē) *adj.* **·ti·er, ·ti·est** 1. Ratlike. 2. Abounding in rats. 3. *Slang* Disreputable; shabby. —**rat′ti·ness** *n.*

rau·cous (rô′kəs) *adj.* 1. Rough in sound; harsh. 2. Boisterous; unruly. [< L *raucus*] —**rau′cous·ly** *adv.* —**rau′cous·ness** *n.*

raun·chy (rôn′chē) *adj.* **·chi·er, ·chi·est** *Slang* 1. Dirty; sloppy. 2. Risqué; obscene. 3. Lustful; lecherous. [Origin unknown]

rau·wol·fi·a (rou·wo͝ol′fē·ə) *n.* Any of a genus of tropical trees or shrubs, several of which have medicinal properties. [after Leonard *Rauwolf*, 17th c. German botanist]

rav·age (rav′ij) *v.* **·aged, ·ag·ing** *v.t.* 1. To lay waste, as by pillaging; despoil. —*v.i.* 2. To wreak havoc; be destructive. —*n.* Destructive action, or its result; ruin. [See RAVISH] —**rav′ag·er** *n.*

rave (rāv) *v.i.* **raved, rav·ing** 1. To speak wildly or incoherently. 2. To praise extravagantly. —*n.* 1. The act or state of raving; a frenzy. 2. Enthusiastic praise. *adj.* *Informal* Extravagantly enthusiastic. [< OF *raver* to be delirious]

rav·el (rav′əl) *v.t.* & *v.i.* **rav·eled** or **·elled, rav·el·ing** or **·el·ling** To separate into parts; unravel; fray. —*n.* 1. A broken or loose thread; also **rav′el·ing.** 2. A tangle. [< MDu. *ravelen* to tangle] —**rav′el·er** or **rav′el·ler** *n.*

ra·ven[1] (rā′vən) *n.* A large bird, related to the crow, having lustrous black plumage. —*adj.* Black and shining, like a raven. [OE *hræfn*]

rav·en[2] (rav′ən) *v.t.* 1. To devour hungrily or greedily. —*v.i.* 2. To search for prey or plunder. 3. To eat voraciously. —*n.* The act of plundering; pillage. [< OF *raviner* < L *rapere* to seize] —**rav′en·er** *n.*

rav·en·ing (rav′ən·ing) *adj.* 1. Seeking prey; rapacious. 2. Devouring; voracious.

rav·en·ous (rav′ən·əs) *adj.* Violently voracious or hungry. [See RAVEN[2]] —**rav′en·ous·ly** *adv.* —**rav′en·ous·ness** *n.*

ra·vine (rə·vēn′) *n.* A deep gorge or gully, esp. one worn by a flow of water. [< F]

rav·ing (rā′ving) *adj.* 1. Delirious; frenzied. 2. *Informal* Outstanding. —*adv.* Extremely; wildly. —*n.* Furious or irrational utterance.

ra·vi·o·li (rav′ē·ō′lē) *n.pl.* Little envelopes of dough filled with meat or cheese. [< Ital., pl. of *raviolo* little turnip]

rav·ish (rav′ish) *v.t.* 1. To fill with strong emotion, esp. delight; enrapture. 2. To commit a rape upon. [< L *rapere* to seize] —**rav′ish·er** *n.* —**rav′ish·ment** *n.*

rav·ish·ing (rav′ish·ing) *adj.* Filling with delight; enchanting. —**rav′ish·ing·ly** *adv.*

raw (rô) *adj.* 1. Not changed or prepared by cooking; uncooked. 2. Having the skin irritated or abraded. 3. Bleak; chilling: a *raw* wind. 4. In a natural state; crude. 5. Inexperienced; undisciplined. 6. Obscene; coarse. 7. Harshly unfair; ruthless. —*n.* A sore or abraded spot: with *the.* —**in the raw** 1. In a raw or unrefined state. 2. *In-*

formal Naked; nude. [OE *hrēaw*] **—raw′ly** *adv.* **—raw′ness** *n.*

raw·boned (rô′bōnd′) *adj.* Bony; gaunt.

raw·hide (rô′hīd′) *n.* 1. A hide dressed without tanning. 2. A whip made of such hide.

ray[1] (rā) *n.* 1. A narrow beam of light. 2. Anything representing or suggesting this. 3. A slight manifestation; glimmer; hint. 4. *Geom.* One of several straight lines emerging from a point. 5. *Zool.* A radiating part, as of a starfish. 6. *Physics* **a** A line of propagation of any form of radiant energy. **b** A stream of particles spontaneously emitted by a radioactive substance. **—*v.i.*** 1. To emit rays; shine. 2. To issue forth as rays; radiate. **—*v.t.*** 3. To send forth as rays. [< L *radius* rod]

ray[2] (rā) *n.* Any of various fishes having a flattened body with expanded pectoral fins and gill openings on the lower surface. [< L *raia*]

ray·on (rā′on) *n.* 1. A synthetic fiber produced from cellulose. 2. A fabric made from such fibers. [Coined from RAY[1]]

raze (rāz) *v.t.* **razed, raz·ing** 1. To demolish, as a building. 2. To scrape or shave off. Also spelled *rase*. [< L *radere* to scrape]

ra·zor (rā′zər) *n.* A sharp cutting implement used for shaving off the beard or hair, etc. [< LL *rasorium* scraper]

ra·zor·back (rā′zər·bak′) *n.* A lean, long-legged, half-wild hog, common in the SE U.S.

ra·zor-backed (rā′zər·bakt′) *adj.* Having a narrow, ridged back or top, as a razorback hog.

razz (raz) *Slang* *n.* A Bronx cheer. **—*v.t.*** To heckle; deride. [< RASPBERRY]

raz·zle-daz·zle (raz′əl·daz′əl) *n.* *Slang* Bewildering, exciting, or dazzling activity or performance. Also **razz·ma·tazz** (raz′mə·taz′). [Varied reduplication of DAZZLE]

re[1] (rā) *n.* *Music* The second tone of the diatonic scale in solmization.

re[2] (rē) *prep.* Concerning; about: used in business letters, law, etc. [< L, ablative of *res* thing]

re- *prefix* 1. Back: *rebound, remit.* 2. Again; anew; again and again. [< L *re-*, *red-* back, again]

The list starting below contains self-explanatory words beginning with *re-* (def. 2).

reach (rēch) *v.t.* 1. To stretch out or forth, as the hand; extend. 2. To be able to touch or grasp: Can you *reach* the top shelf? 3. To arrive at or come to by motion or progress. 4. To achieve communication with; gain access to. **—*v.i.*** 5. To stretch the hand, foot, etc., out or forth. 6. To attempt to touch or grasp something. 7. To have extent in space, time, etc. **—*n.*** 1. The act or power of reaching. 2. The distance one is able to reach, as with the hand, an instrument, etc. 3. Extent of thought, influence, etc.; scope. 4. An unbroken stretch; a vista or expanse. [OE *rǣcan*] **—reach′er** *n.*

re·act (rē·akt′) *v.i.* 1. To act in response, as to a stimulus. 2. To act in a manner contrary to some preceding act. 3. *Physics* To exert an opposite and equal force on an acting or impinging body. 4. *Chem.* To undergo a reaction.

re·ac·tance (rē·ak′təns) *n.* *Electr.* In a circuit, the opposition to an alternating current caused by inductance and capacitance.

re·ac·tion (rē·ak′shən) *n.* 1. Responsive action, attitude, etc. 2. Tendency toward a former state of things; esp., a trend toward an earlier social, political, or economic policy or condition. 3. The action of a muscle, nerve, organ, etc., in response to a stimulus; reflex action. 4. *Physics* **a** The equal and opposite force exerted on an agent by the body acted upon. **b** A nuclear reaction. 5. *Chem.* The interaction of substances, resulting in a chemical change. 6. *Med.* Response, esp. adverse, to a drug, serum, etc.

re·ac·tion·ar·y (rē·ak′shən·er′ē) *adj.* Pertaining to, favoring, or characterized by reaction (def. 2). **—*n.*** *pl.* **·ar·ies** One who favors political or social reaction.

re·ac·ti·vate (rē·ak′tə·vāt) *v.t.* **·vat·ed,**

reabsorb
reabsorption
reaccept
reaccommodate
reacquire
readapt
readdress
readjourn
readjournment
readjust
readjustment
readmission
readmit
readmittance
readopt
readoption
readorn
reaffirm
reaffirmation
realign
realignment
reallocate
reallocation
reanalysis
reanalyze
reannex
reannexation
reannoint
reappear
reappearance
reapplication
reapply
reappoint
reappointment
reapportion
reapportionment
reappraisal
reappraise
reargue
rearrest
reascend
reascension
reascent
reassail
reassemble
reassembly
reassert
reassertion
reassess
reassessment
reassign
reassimilate
reassimilation
reassort
reassume
reassumption
reattach
reattack
reattempt
reauthorize
reavow
reawake
reawaken
rebaptism
rebaptize
rebid
rebind
rebloom
reblossom
reboil
reborn
rebuild
rebuilt
rebury
recalculate
recapitalize
rechallenge
rechange
rechannel
recharge
recharter
recheck
rechristen
recircle
recirculate
reclasp
reclean
reclothe
recoat
recoin
recoinage
recolonization
recolonize
recolor
recomb
recombination
recombine
recommence
recommission
recompose

·vat·ing To make active or effective again. **—re·ac′ti·va′tion** *n.*

re·ac·tive (rē·ak′tiv) *adj.* Reacting or tending to react. **—re′ac·tiv′i·ty** *n.*

re·ac·tor (rē·ak′tər) *n.* 1. One who or that which reacts. 2. *Electr.* A device for introducing reactance into a circuit, as for starting motors, controlling current, etc. 3. *Physics* Any of various assemblies for the generation and control of a chain reaction with nuclear materials.

read (*v. & n.* rēd; *adj.* red) *v.* **read** (red), **read·ing** (rē′ding) *v.t.* 1. To apprehend the meaning of (a book, writing, etc.) by perceiving the form and relation of the printed or written characters. 2. To utter aloud (something printed or written). 3. To understand the significance, intent, etc., of as if by reading. 4. To discover the true nature of (a person, character, etc.) by observation or scrutiny. 5. To interpret (something read) in a specified manner. 6. To take as the meaning of something read. 7. To have as its wording: The passage *reads* "principal," not "principle." 8. To indicate or register, as an instrument. 9. To bring into a specified condition by reading: I *read* her to sleep. **—***v.i.* 10. To apprehend written or printed characters, as of words, music, etc. 11. To utter aloud the words or contents of a book, etc. 12. To gain information by reading: with *of* or *about.* 13. To have a specified wording: How does the contract *read*? 14. To admit of being read in a specified manner; also, to have the quality of a specified style of writing: His work *reads* well. It *reads* like poetry. 15. To give a public reading or recital. **—to read between the lines** To perceive what is not expressed or obvious. **—to read up** (or **up on**) To learn by reading. **—***adj.* Informed by books: well *read.* [OE *rǣdan* to read]

read·a·ble (rē′də·bəl) *adj.* 1. Legible. 2. Interesting or enjoyable to read. **—read′a·bil′i·ty** *n.* **—read′a·bly** *adv.*

read·er (rē′dər) *n.* 1. One who reads. 2. A textbook containing exercises in reading. 3. An anthology of writings on a particular subject.

read·er·ship (rē′dər·ship) *n.* The readers, collectively, of a publication or type of publication.

read·ing (rē′ding) *n.* 1. The act or practice of one who reads. 2. A public or formal recital of something written. 3. Matter that is read or is designed to be read. 4. The indication of a meter, dial, etc. 5. The form in which any passage or word appears in any copy of a work. 6. A specific interpretation. **—***adj.* 1. Pertaining to or suitable for reading. 2. Of or pertaining to a reader or readers.

read·out (rēd′out′) *n.* 1. Data or information from a computer in a readable form, usu. as a printed sheet or as a display on a screen. 2. The process of producing information in such a form. **—read′out′** *v.i.*

read·y (red′ē) *adj.* **read·i·er, read·i·est** 1. Prepared for use or action. 2. Prepared in mind; willing. 3. Likely or liable: with *to: ready* to sink. 4. Quick to act, follow, occur, or appear; prompt. 5. Immediately available or at hand; convenient; handy. **—***n.* The position in which a rifle is held before aiming. **—***v.t.* **read·ied, read·y·ing** To make ready; prepare. [OE *rǣde*] **—read′i·ly** *adv.* **—read′i·ness** *n.*

read·y-made (red′ē·mād′) *adj.* 1. Not made to order; prepared or kept on hand for general demand: said esp. of clothing. 2. Prepared beforehand. **—read′y-made′** *n.*

read·y-mix (red′ē·miks) *adj.* Ready to use after adding liquid, etc.: *ready-mix* pancake flour.

ready money Money on hand; cash.

read·y-to-wear (red′ē·tə·wâr′) *adj.* Ready-made: said of clothing.

re·a·gent (rē·ā′jənt) *n. Chem.* Any substance that takes part in a chemical reaction.

real[1] (rēl, rē′əl) *adj.* 1. Having existence or actuality as a thing or state; not imaginary: a *real* event. 2. Not artificial or counterfeit; genuine. 3. Unaffected; unpretentious: a *real* person. 4. *Law* Pertaining to property regarded as immovable or permanent, as

recompute
reconcentrate
recondensation
recondense
reconduct
reconfine
reconfirm
reconfirmation
reconnect
reconquer
reconquest
reconsecrate
reconsolidate
recontaminate
recontamination
reconvene
recook
recopy
recouple
recrown
recrystallize
recultivate
recultivation
recut
rededicate
rededication
redefine
redemand
redemonstrate
redeploy
redeployment
redescent
redesign
redetermine
redip
rediscover
rediscovery
redissolve
redistill
redistribute
redistribution
redivide
redivision
redo
redrive
redye
reedit
reelect
reelection
reembark
reembodiment
reembody
reembrace
reemerge
reemergence
reemphasis
reemphasize
reemploy
reemployment
reenact
reenactment
reencouragement
reendow
reengage
reengagement
reenlist
reenlistment
reenslave
reenter
reentrance
reequip
reerect
reestablish
reestablishment
reexamination
reexamine
reexchange
reexhibit
reexpel
reexperience
reexport
reexpulsion
reface
refashion
refasten
refertilize
refigure
refilm
refinance
refinish
refire
reflower
refocus
refold
reforge
reformulate
refortification
refortify
reframe
refreeze

land or buildings. —*adv. Informal* Very; extremely. [< LL *realis* < L *res* thing] —**real′ness** *n.*

re·al² (rē′əl, *Sp.* rā·äl′) *n. pl.* **re·als** or **re·a·les** (rā·ä′lās) *for def. 1,* **reis** (rās) *for def. 2* 1. A former small silver coin of Spain and various Latin-American countries. 2. A former Portuguese and Brazilian coin. [< Sp., lit., royal]

real estate Land, including whatever is made part of or attached to it by man or nature, as trees, houses, etc. —**real-es·tate** (rēl′ə·stāt′, rē′əl-) *adj.*

re·al·ism (rē′əl·iz′əm) *n.* 1. The tendency to be concerned with and act in accordance with actual facts rather than ideals, feelings, etc. 2. In literature and art, the treatment of subject matter in conformance with nature or real life. —**re′al·ist** *n.* —**re′al·is′tic** *adj.* —**re·al·is′ti·cal·ly** *adv.*

re·al·i·ty (rē·al′ə·tē) *n. pl.* **·ties** 1. The fact, state, or quality of being real or genuine. 2. That which is real; an actual thing, situation, or event. 3. The sum or totality of real things. [< L *realis* real]

re·al·ize (rē′əl·īz, rē′līz) *v.* **·ized, ·iz·ing** *v.t.* 1. To understand or appreciate fully. 2. To make real or concrete. 3. To cause to appear real. 4. To obtain as a profit or return. —*v.i.* 5. To sell property for cash. Also *Brit.* **re′al·ise.** —**re′al·iz′a·ble** *adj.* —**re′al·i·za′tion** *n.*

re·al-life (rē′əl·līf′, rēl′-) *adj. Informal* Actual; true.

real·ly (rē ə·lē, rē′lē) *adv.* 1. In reality; as a matter of fact; actually; indeed. 2. Honestly; truly: used for emphasis.

re-al·ly (rē′ə·lī′) *v.t. & v.i.* **-al·lied, -al·ly·ing** To ally again.

realm (relm) *n.* 1. A kingdom or domain. 2. The scope or range of any power or influence. [< OF *realme*]

re·al·po·li·tik (rā·äl′pō·li·tēk′) *n.* Practical or realistic politics; ruthless pursuit of national or party interests, without regard for ethical principles. Also **Re·al′po·li·tik′.** [< G]

real-time operation (rēl′tīm′) The use by a computer of incoming data to control a process as it happens. —**real′-time′** *adj.*

Re·al·tor (rē′əl·tər, -tôr) *n.* A realty broker who is a member of the National Association of Real Estate Boards: a trade name. Also **re′al·tor.**

re·al·ty (rē′əl·tē) *n. pl.* **·ties** *Law* Real estate or real property in any form.

ream¹ (rēm) *n.* 1. A unit of quantity of paper consisting of 480 sheets (**short ream**), 500 sheets (**long ream**), or 516 sheets (**printer's** or **perfect ream**). 2. *Usu. pl. Informal* A prodigious amount. [< Arabic *rizmah* bundle]

ream² (rēm) *v.t.* 1. To increase the size of (a hole). 2. To enlarge or taper (a hole) with a rotating cutter or reamer. [? OE *ryman* to enlarge]

ream·er (rē′mər) *n.* 1. A finishing tool with a rotating cutting edge for reaming: sometimes called *rimmer.* 2. A device with a ridged cone for extracting juice from citrus fruits.

re·an·i·mate (rē·an′ə·māt) *v.t.* **·mat·ed, ·mat·ing** 1. To bring back to life; resuscitate. 2. To give renewed strength or vigor to; revive. —**re′an·i·ma′tion** *n.*

reap (rēp) *v.t.* 1. To harvest or gather (a crop) with a scythe, reaper, etc. 2. To obtain as the result of action or effort; receive as a return or result. —*v.i.* 3. To harvest grain, etc. 4. To receive a return or result. [OE *rēopan, ripan*] —**reap′a·ble** *adj.*

reap·er (rē′pər) *n.* 1. One who reaps. 2. A machine for harvesting grain.

rear¹ (rir) *n.* 1. The back or hind part. 2. A place or position behind any person or thing. 3. The portion of a military force that is farthest from the front. —*adj.* Being in the rear. [Var. of ARREAR]

rear² (rir) *v.t.* 1. To place upright; raise. 2. To build; erect. 3. To care for and bring to maturity. 4. To breed or grow. —*v.i.* 5. To rise upon the hind legs, as a horse. 6. To rise high; tower, as a mountain. [OE *rǣran*, causative of *rīsan* to rise] —**rear′er** *n.*

rear admiral *Naval* A commissioned officer ranking next below a vice admiral.

refuel
refurnish
regather
regear
regild
reglaze
reglue
regrade
regraft
regrant
regroup
rehandle
rehear
rehearing
reheat
reheel
rehire
reignite
reimplant
reimpose
reimposition
reimpress
reimprint
reimprison
reimprisonment
reinaugurate
reincorporate
reincur
reinduce
reinfect
reinfection
reinflame
reinfuse
reinoculate
reinoculation
reinscribe
reinsert
reinsertion
reinspect
reinspection
reinstall
reinstruct
reintegrate
reintegration
reinter
reinterment
reinterpret
reinterpretation
reintroduce
reintroduction
reinvent
reinvest
reinvestigate
reinvestigation
reinvestment
reinvigorate
reinvigoration
reinvolve
rejudge
rekindle
reknit
relabel
relace
relaunch
relaunder
relearn
relight
reline
relive
reload
reloan
remade
remake
remarriage
remarry
rematch
remeasure
remelt
remigrate
remigration
remilitarization
remilitarize
remix
remodification
remodify
remold
rename
renavigate
renegotiate
renegotiation
renominate
renomination
renumber
reoccupation
reoccupy
reoccur
reoccurrence
reopen
reoppose
reordination

rear guard A body of troops to protect the rear of an army.

re·arm (rē·ärm′) *v.t. & v.i.* 1. To arm again. 2. To arm with more modern weapons. —**re·ar′ma·ment** (-är′mə·mənt) *n.*

rear·most (rir′mōst′) *adj.* Coming or stationed last.

re·ar·range (rē′ə·rānj′) *v.t. & v.i.* **·ranged, ·rang·ing** To arrange again or in some new way. —**re′ar·range′ment** *n.*

rear·ward (rir′wərd) *adj.* Coming last or toward the rear; hindward. —*adv.* Toward or at the rear; backward: also **rear′wards.** —*n.* Hindward position; the rear; end.

rea·son (rē′zən) *n.* 1. A motive or cause for an action, belief, thought, etc. 2. An explanation for or defense of an action, belief, etc.; justification. 3. The faculty of thinking logically. 4. Good judgment; common sense. 5. A normal state of mind; sanity. —**by reason of** Because of. —**it stands to reason** It is logical or reasonable. —**with reason** Justifiably; properly. —*v.i.* 1. To think logically; obtain inferences or conclusions from known or presumed facts. 2. To talk or argue logically. —*v.t.* 3. To think out carefully and logically; analyze: with *out.* [< OF *raison* < L *reri* to think] —**rea′son·er** *n.* —**rea′son·less** *adj.*

rea·son·a·ble (rē′zən·ə·bəl) *adj.* 1. Conformable to reason; sensible. 2. Having the faculty of reason; rational. 3. Governed by reason. 4. Moderate, as in price; fair. —**rea′·son·a·bil′i·ty, rea′son·a·ble·ness** *n.* —**rea′·son·a·bly** *adv.*

rea·son·ing (rē′zən·ing) *n.* The mental process of drawing conclusions from known or presumed facts.

re·as·sure (rē′ə·shŏŏr′) *v.t.* **·sured, ·sur·ing** 1. To restore to courage or confidence. 2. To assure again. —**re′as·sur′ance** *n.* —**re′as·sur′ing·ly** *adv.*

re·bate (rē′bāt) *v.t.* **·bat·ed, ·bat·ing** 1. To allow as a deduction. 2. To make a deduction from. —*n.* A deduction from a gross amount; discount: also **re·bate′ment.** [< OF *rabattre* to beat down] —**re′bat·er** *n.*

re·bec (rē′bek) *n.* An early violinlike instrument. Also **re′beck.** [< F, alter. of OF *rebebe* < Arabic *rabāb*]

re·bel (*v.* ri·bel′; *n. & adj.* reb′əl) *v.i.* **·belled, ·bel·ling** 1. To rise in armed resistance, esp. against a government or ruler. 2. To resist any authority or established usage. 3. To react with violent aversion: usu. with *at.* —*n.* One who rebels. —*adj.* Rebellious; refractory. [< L *re-* again + *bellare* to make war]

re·bel·lion (ri·bel′yən) *n.* 1. The act of rebelling. 2. Organized resistance to a lawful government or authority.

re·bel·lious (ri·bel′yəs) *adj.* 1. Being in a state of rebellion; insubordinate. 2. Of or pertaining to a rebel or rebellion. —**re·bel′·lious·ly** *adv.* —**re·bel′lious·ness** *n.*

re·birth (rē·bûrth′, rē′bûrth′) *n.* 1. A new birth. 2. A revival or renaissance.

re·bound (ri·bound′; *for n., also* rē′bound′) *v.t. & v.i.* To bound back or cause to bound back; recoil. —*n.* 1. The act or state of rebounding; recoil. 2. Something that rebounds or resounds. [< F *re-* back + *bondir* to bound]

re·broad·cast (rē·brôd′kast′) *v.t.* **·cast** or **·cast·ed, ·cast·ing** 1. To broadcast more than once. 2. To broadcast (a program received from another station). —*n.* A program so broadcast.

re·buff (ri·buf′) *v.t.* 1. To reject or refuse abruptly or rudely. 2. To drive or beat back; repel. —*n.* 1. A sudden repulse; curt denial. 2. A sudden check; defeat. 3. A beating back. [< Ital. *ribuffare* to reprimand]

re·buke (ri·byōōk′) *v.t.* **·buked, ·buk·ing** To reprove sharply; reprimand. —*n.* A strong expression of disapproval. [< OF *re-* back + *buchier* to beat] —**re·buk′a·ble** *adj.* —**re·buk′er** *n.*

re·bus (rē′bəs) *n. pl.* **·bus·es** A puzzle representing a word, phrase, sentence, etc., by letters, numerals, pictures, etc. [< L, ablative pl. of *res* thing]

re·but (ri·but′) *v.t.* **·but·ted, ·but·ting** To refute by contrary evidence or proof; disprove. [< OF *re-* back + *bouter* to strike, push] —**re·but′tal** (-but′l) *n.* —**re·but′ter** *n.*

reorient
repacify
repack
repackage
repaint
repaper
repass
repave
rephotograph
replant
replay
repledge
repolish
repopulate
repopulation
repour
reprocess
republication
republish
repurchase
repurify
reread
rerecord
reroll
reroute
resaddle
resail
reseal
reseat
reseed
resegregate
reseize
reseizure
resell
resend
resettle
resettlement
resew
reshape
resharpen
reship
reshipment
reshuffle
resift
resilver
resolder
resow
respell
respread
restack
restaff
restock
restraighten
restrengthen
restrike
restring
restructure
restudy
restuff
resubject
resubjection
resubmit
resummon
resummons
resupply
resurvey
resynthesize
reteach
retell
retest
rethink
retie
retool
retrain
retranslate
retransmit
retraverse
retrim
retype
reunification
reunify
revaluate
revaluation
revalue
revarnish
reverification
reverify
revindicate
revindication
revisit
revitalize
rewarm
rewash
rewater
reweave
rewed
reweigh
rewind
rework
rezone

re·cal·ci·trant (ri·kal′sə·trənt) *adj.* Not complying; obstinate; rebellious. —*n.* One who is recalcitrant. [< L *re-* back + *calcitrare* to kick < *calx* heel] —**re·cal′ci·trance, re·cal′ci·tran·cy** *n.*

re·call (ri·kôl′; *for n., also* rē′kôl) *v.t.* 1. To call back; order or summon to return. 2. To recollect; remember. 3. To take back; revoke. —*n.* 1. A summons to come back. 2. The ability to remember. 3. Revocation. 4. A system whereby officials may be removed from office by popular vote. 5. A request by a manufacturer for the return of a possibly defective product. 6. The ability of a computer to retrieve stored data.

re·cant (ri·kant′) *v.t. & v.i.* To withdraw formally one's belief in (something previously believed or maintained). [< L *re-* back + *cantare* to sing] —**re·can·ta·tion** (rē′kan·tā′shən) *n.* —**re·cant′er** *n.*

re·cap[1] (*v.* rē′kap′, rē·kap′; *n.* rē′kap′) *v.t.* **·capped, ·cap·ping** To recondition the tread of (an automobile tire) with new rubber. —*n.* A tire that has been recapped.

re·cap[2] (rē′kap) *n. Informal* A recapitulation; summary. —**re′cap** *v.t. & v.i.* **·capped, ·cap·ping**

re·ca·pit·u·late (rē′kə·pich′ōō·lāt) *v.t. & v.i.* **·lat·ed, ·lat·ing** To review briefly (a discussion, report, etc.); sum up. [< L *re-* again + *capitulare* to draw up in chapters] —**re′ca·pit′u·la′tion** *n.* —**re′ca·pit′u·la′·tive, re′ca·pit′u·la·to′ry** (-lə·tôr′ē) *adj.*

re·cap·ture (rē·kap′chər) *v.t.* **·tured, ·tur·ing** 1. To capture again. 2. To recall; remember. —*n.* 1. The act of retaking. 2. Anything recaptured.

re·cast (*v.* rē·kast′; *n.* rē′kast′) *v.t.* **·cast, ·cast·ing** 1. To form anew; cast again. 2. To calculate anew. —*n.* Something that has been recast.

re·cede (ri·sēd′) *v.i.* **·ced·ed, ·ced·ing** 1. To move back, as flood waters. 2. To slope backward. 3. To become more distant. [< L *re-* back + *cedere* to go]

re·ceipt (ri·sēt′) *n.* 1. The act or state of receiving anything. 2. *Usu. pl.* That which is received: cash *receipts.* 3. A written acknowledgment of payment, delivery, etc. 4. *Dial.* A recipe. —*v.t.* To give a receipt for the payment of. [< L *re-* back + *capere* to take]

re·ceiv·a·ble (ri·sē′və·bəl) *adj.* 1. Capable of being received; fit to be received, as legal tender. 2. Maturing for payment: said of a bill.

re·ceiv·a·bles (ri·sē′və·bəlz) *n. pl.* Outstanding accounts listed among the assets of a business.

re·ceive (ri·sēv′) *v.* **·ceived, ·ceiv·ing** *v.t.* 1. To take into one's hand or possession; acquire. 2. To gain knowledge of: to *receive* good news. 3. To bear; support. 4. To experience; undergo. 5. To contain; hold. 6. To allow entrance to; admit; greet. —*v.i.* 7. To welcome visitors. 8. *Telecom.* To convert radio waves into sounds or images. [< L *re-* back + *capere* to take]

re·ceiv·er (ri·sē′vər) *n.* 1. One who receives; a recipient. 2. *Law* A person appointed by a court to have charge of the property or funds of another pending judicial action. 3. Something that receives; a receptacle. 4. *Telecom.* **a** An instrument serving to receive and reproduce signals transmitted from another part of a circuit: a telephone *receiver.* **b** Any of various electronic devices that convert radio waves into sounds or images: also **receiving set.** 5. In football, an offensive player designated to receive a forward pass.

re·ceiv·er·ship (ri·sē′vər·ship) *n.* 1. The office and functions pertaining to a receiver under appointment of a court. 2. The state of being in the hands of a receiver.

re·cent (rē′sənt) *adj.* Pertaining to, or formed, developed, or created in time not long past; modern. [< L *recens*] —**re′cent·ly** *adv.* —**re′cen·cy, re′cent·ness** *n.*

re·cep·ta·cle (ri·sep′tə·kəl) *n.* 1. Anything that serves to contain or hold something else. 2. *Bot.* The base to which the parts of the flower, fruit, or seeds are fixed. [< L *re-* back + *capere* to take] —**re·cep·tac·u·lar** (rē′sep·tak′yə·lər) *adj.*

re·cep·tion (ri·sep′shən) *n.* 1. The act of receiving, or the state of being received. 2. A formal social entertainment of guests. 3. The manner of receiving: a warm *reception.* 4. *Telecom.* The act or process of receiving, or the quality of reproduction achieved. [< L *re-* back + *capere* to take]

re·cep·tion·ist (ri·sep′shən·ist) *n.* One employed to receive callers at the entrance to an office.

re·cep·tive (ri·sep′tiv) *adj.* 1. Able or inclined to receive, as truths or impressions. 2. Able to take in or hold. —**re·cep′tive·ly** *adv.* —**re·cep·tiv·i·ty** (rē′sep·tiv′ə·tē), **re·cep′tive·ness** *n.*

re·cep·tor (ri·sep′tər) *n. Anat.* A nerve ending that receives stimuli and transmits them to the spinal cord and brain. [< OF or L, receiver]

re·cess (*n.* ri·ses′, rē′ses; *for def. 2., usu.* rē′ses; *v.* ri·ses′) *n.* 1. A depression or indentation in any surface, esp. in a wall; niche. 2. A time of cessation from employment or occupation. 3. *Usu pl.* A secluded spot; withdrawn or inner place. —*v.t.* 1. To place in or as in a recess. 2. To make a recess in. 3. To adjourn for a recess. —*v.i.* 4. To take a recess. [< L *re-* back + *cedere* to go]

re·ces·sion (ri·sesh′ən) *n.* 1. The act of receding; a withdrawal. 2. The procession of the clergy, choir, etc., after a church service. 3. An economic setback in commercial and industrial activity.

re·ces·sion·al (ri·sesh′ən·əl) *adj.* Of or pertaining to recession. —*n.* A hymn sung as the choir or clergy leave the chancel after service.

re·ces·sive (ri·ses′iv) *adj* 1. Having a tendency to recede or go back; receding. 2. *Genetics* Designating one of a pair of hereditary characters that, appearing in an offspring, is masked by a contrasting character: opposed to *dominant.* —**re·ces′sive·ly** *adv.*

re·cher·ché (rə·sher·shā′) *adj. French* 1. Rare and exquisite; choice. 2. Elegant and refined; also, overrefined.

re·cid·i·vism (rə·sid′ə·viz′əm) *n.* Repetition of criminal acts by an offender, or the tendency to do so. [< L *recidivus* relapsing]

—re·cid′i·vist *n.* —re·cid′i·vis′tic, re·cid′i·vous *adj.*
rec·i·pe (res′ə·pē) *n.* 1. A formula or list of ingredients of a mixture, giving proper directions for compounding, cooking, etc. 2. A method prescribed for attaining a desired result. [< L *re-* back + *capere* to take]
re·cip·i·ent (ri·sip′ē·ənt) *adj.* Receiving or ready to receive; receptive. —*n.* One who or that which receives. [< L *re-* back + *capere* to take] —**re·cip′i·ence** *n.*
re·cip·ro·cal (ri·sip′rə·kəl) *adj.* 1. Done or given by each of two to the other; mutual. 2. Mutually interchangeable. 3. Alternating; moving to and fro. 4. *Gram.* Expressive of mutual relationship or action. 5. *Math.* Of or pertaining to various types of mutual relations between two quantities. —*n.* 1. That which is reciprocal. 2. *Math.* The quotient obtained by dividing 1 by a number or expression, as $^1/_x$ is the *reciprocal* of *x*. [< L *reciprocus*] —**re·cip′ro·cal′i·ty** (-kal′ə·tē) *n.* —**re·cip′ro·cal·ly** *adv.*
re·cip·ro·cate (ri·sip′rə·kāt) *v.t. & v.i.* ·**cat·ed**, ·**cat·ing** 1. To move backward and forward alternately. 2. To give and receive mutually; interchange. 3. To make a return (of an emotion, response, etc.) in kind. [< L *reciprocus* reciprocal] —**re·cip′ro·ca′tion** *n.* —**re·cip′ro·ca′tive** *adj.* —**re·cip′ro·ca′tor** *n.* —**re·cip′ro·ca·to′ry** (-kə·tôr′ē) *adj.*
rec·i·proc·i·ty (res′ə·pros′ə·tē) *n.* Reciprocal obligation, action, or relation.
re·ci·sion (ri·sizh′ən) *n.* A cancellation; annulment. [< L *re-* back + *caedere* to cut]
re·cit·al (ri·sīt′l) *n.* 1. A telling over in detail, or that which is thus told. 2. A public delivery of something previously memorized. 3. A musical program performed usu. by one person or several appearing as soloists.
rec·i·ta·tion (res′ə·tā′shən) *n.* 1. The act of repeating from memory. 2. The reciting of a lesson, or the meeting of a class for that purpose.
rec·i·ta·tive (res′ə·tə·tēv′, rə·sit′ə·tiv) *n.* *Music* 1. Language uttered in the phrasing of ordinary speech, but set to music. 2. This style of singing, or a passage so rendered. [< Ital. *recitativo*]
re·cite (ri·sīt′) *v.* ·**cit·ed**, ·**cit·ing** *v.t.* 1. To declaim or say from memory, esp. formally, as a lesson in class. 2. To tell in detail; relate. —*v.i.* 3. To declaim from memory. 4. To repeat a lesson in class. [< L *re-* again + CITE] —**re·cit′er** *n.*
reck·less (rek′lis) *adj.* Foolishly heedless of danger; rash; careless. [OE *recceléas*] —**reck′less·ly** *adv.* —**reck′less·ness** *n.*
reck·on (rek′ən) *v.t.* 1. To count; compute; calculate. 2. To look upon as being; regard. —*v.i.* 3. To make computation; count up. 4. To think; figure. 5. To rely or depend: with *on* or *upon*. —**to reckon with** 1. To settle accounts with. 2. To take into consideration. [OE *recenian* to explain] —**reck′on·er** *n.*
reck·on·ing (rek′ən·ing) *n.* 1. The act of counting; computation; a settlement of accounts. 2. Account; score; bill.
re·claim (ri·klām′) *v.t.* 1. To bring (swamp, desert, etc.) into arable condition, as by draining or irrigating. 2. To obtain (a substance) from used or waste products. 3. To cause to return from sinful ways. —*n.* The act of reclaiming, or state of being reclaimed. [< L *re-* back + *clamare* to cry out] —**re·claim′a·ble** *adj.* —**re·claim′ant**, **re·claim′er** *n.* —**rec′la·ma′tion** (rek′la·mā′shən) *n.*
re-claim (rē·klām′) *v.t.* To claim again.
re·cline (ri·klīn′) *v.t. & v.i.* ·**clined**, ·**clin·ing** To assume or cause to assume a recumbent position; lie or lay down or back. [< L *re-* back + *clinare* to lean] —**re·clin′er** *n.*
re·cluse (ri·klo͞os′; *for n., also* rek′lo͞os) *n.* One who lives in retirement or seclusion. —*adj.* Secluded or retired from the world. [< L *re-* back + *claudere* to shut] —**re·clu′sion** (-klo͞o′zhən) *n.* —**re·clu′sive** *adj.*
rec·og·ni·tion (rek′əg·nish′ən) *n.* 1. The act of recognizing, or the state of being recognized. 2. Acknowledgment of a fact or claim. [< L *re-* again + *cognoscere* to know]
re·cog·ni·zance (ri·kog′nə·zəns, -kon′ə-) *n.* *Law* An obligation of record, with condition to do some particular act, as to appear and answer. [See RECOGNITION.] —**re·cog′ni·zant** *adj.*
rec·og·nize (rek′əg·nīz) *v.t.* ·**nized**, ·**niz·ing** 1. To perceive or be aware of as known previously. 2. To identify, as by previous experience: I *recognize* poor poetry when I see it. 3. To perceive as true; realize. 4. To acknowledge the independence and validity of, as a government. 5. To indicate appreciation of. 6. To regard as valid or genuine. 7. To give (someone) permission to speak, as in a legislative body. [Back formation < RECOGNIZANCE] —**rec′og·niz′a·ble** *adj.* —**rec′og·niz′a·bly** *adv.* —**rec′og·niz′er** *n.*
re·coil (*v.* ri·koil′; *n.* rē′koil′) *v.i.* 1. To start back, as in fear or loathing; shrink. 2. To spring back, as from force of discharge or impact. 3. To rebound; react: with *on* or *upon*. —*n.* A backward movement, as of a gun at the moment of firing; also, a shrinking. [< OF *reculer*] —**re·coil′er** *n.*
re-coil (rē′koil′) *v.t. & v.i.* To coil again.
rec·ol·lect (rek′ə·lekt′) *v.t. & v.i.* To call (something) back to the mind; remember. [< RE- + COLLECT]
re-col·lect (rē′kə·lekt′) *v.t.* 1. To collect again, as things scattered. 2. To collect or compose (one's thoughts or nerves); recover (oneself). —**re′-col·lec′tion** *n.*
rec·ol·lec·tion (rek′ə·lek′shən) *n.* 1. The act or power of remembering. 2. Something remembered. —**rec′ol·lec′tive** *adj.* —**rec′ol·lec′tive·ly** *adv.*
recombinant DNA research Work that involves the introduction of new characteristics into an organism by recombining or splicing together genetic material: also called *gene splicing*.
re·com·bi·na·tion (rē′kom·bə·nā′shən) *n.* *Genetics* An interchange of genetic material that produces an organism having different characteristics than the parent organism. —**re·com′bi·nant** *adj.*
rec·om·mend (rek′ə·mend′) *v.t.* 1. To commend with favorable representations. 2. To make attractive or acceptable. 3. To advise; urge. 4. To give in charge; commend. [< RE- + COMMEND] —**rec′om·mend′er** *n.*
rec·om·men·da·tion (rek′ə·men·dā′shən) *n.*

1. The act of recommending. 2. Something recommended. 3. A letter, statement, etc., recommending a person.

re·com·mit (rē′kə·mit′) *v.t.* **·mit·ted, ·mit·ting** 1. To commit again. 2. To refer back to a committee, as a bill. —**re′com·mit′tal** *n.*

rec·om·pense (rek′əm·pens) *v.t.* **·pensed, ·pens·ing** 1. To give compensation to; pay or repay; reward. 2. To compensate for, as a loss. —*n.* An equivalent for anything given or done; payment; compensation. [< RE- + COMPENSATE]

rec·on·cil·a·ble (rek′ən·sī′lə·bəl) *adj.* Capable of being reconciled, adjusted, or harmonized. —**rec′on·cil′a·bil′i·ty** *n.* —**rec′on·cil′a·bly** *adv.*

rec·on·cile (rek′ən·sīl) *v.t.* **·ciled, ·cil·ing** 1. To bring back to friendship after estrangement. 2. To settle or adjust, as a quarrel. 3. To bring to acquiescence, acceptance, or submission. 4. To make or show to be consistent or congruous; harmonize: often with *to* or *with*. [< L *re-* again + *conciliare* to unite] —**rec′on·cile′ment** *n.* —**rec′on·cil′er** *n.* —**rec′on·cil′i·a′tion** (-sil′ē·ā′·shən) *n.*

rec·on·dite (rek′ən·dīt, ri·kon′dīt) *adj.* 1. Remote from ordinary or easy perception; abstruse; secret. 2. Hidden. [< L *recondere* to hide] —**rec′on·dite′ly** *adv.* —**rec′on·dite′ness** *n.*

re·con·di·tion (rē′kən·dish′ən) *v.t.* To put into good or working condition, as by making repairs; overhaul.

re·con·nais·sance (ri·kon′ə·səns, -säns) *n.* 1. A preliminary survey, as of the territory and resources of a country. 2. *Mil.* The act of obtaining information, esp. regarding the position, strength, and movement of enemy forces. Also **re·con′nois·sance.** [< F]

re·con·noi·ter (rē′kə·noi′tər, rek′ə-) *v.t.* To examine or survey. —*v.i.* To make a reconnaissance. [< L *re-* again + *cognoscere* to know] —**re′con·noi′ter·er** *n.*

re·con·sid·er (rē′kən·sid′ər) *v.t. & v.i.* To consider again, esp. with a view to a reversal of previous action. —**re′con·sid′er·a′tion** *n.*

re·con·sti·tute (rē·kon′stə·tōōt, -tyōōt) *v.t.* **·tut·ed, ·tut·ing** To constitute again; make over. —**re·con′sti·tu′tion** *n.*

re·con·struct (rē′kən·strukt′) *v.t.* To build again; rebuild.

re·con·struc·tion (rē′kən·struk′shən) *n.* 1. The act of reconstructing, or the state of being reconstructed. 2. *Usu. cap.* The restoration of the seceded states as members of the Union following the Civil War; also, the period of and following this restoration: also called **Reconstruction period.** —**re′con·struc′tive** *adj.*

re·con·vert (rē′kən·vûrt′) *v.t.* 1. To change back to a state or form previously possessed. 2. To convert back to a previously held religious belief. —**re′con·ver′sion** *n.*

rec·ord (*n. & adj.* rek′ərd; *v.* ri·kôrd′) *n.* 1. An account in written or other permanent form serving as a memorial or evidence of a fact or event. 2. Information preserved and handed down: the heaviest rainfall on *record.* 3. The known career or performance of a person, organization, etc. 4. The best listed achievement, as in a competitive sport. 5. A phonograph record. —**off the record** 1. Unofficially or unofficial. 2. Not for quotation or publication. —**on the record** 1. Official or officially. 2. For quotation or publication. —*adj.* Surpassing any previously recorded achievement, amount, etc. —*v.t.* 1. To write down or otherwise inscribe or preserve as a record. 2. To indicate; register. 3. To make a tape or phonograph record of. —*v.i.* 4. To record something. [< L *recordari* to remember]

re·cord·er (ri·kôr′dər) *n.* 1. One who or that which records. 2. Any of a group of flutes having eight finger holes. 3. A tape or wire recorder.

re·cord·ing (ri·kôr′ding) *n.* 1. *Telecom.* The registration of a physical record of sounds or other communicable signals. 2. A phonograph record.

record player A motor-driven turntable with a pickup attachment and auxiliary equipment for the playing of phonograph records: also called *gramophone, phonograph.*

re·count (ri·kount′) *v.t.* To narrate in detail; relate. [< OF *reconter* to relate]

re·count (rē·kount′; *for n., also* rē′kount′) *v.t.* To count again. —*n.* A repetition of a count; esp., a second count of votes cast.

re·coup (ri·kōōp′) *v.t.* 1. To recover or make up, as a loss. 2. To reimburse for a loss; indemnify. —*n.* The act or process of recouping. [< OF *re-* back + *couper* to cut] —**re·coup′a·ble** *adj.* —**re·coup′ment** *n.*

re·course (rē′kôrs, ri·kôrs′) *n.* 1. Resort to or application for help or security. 2. One who or that which is resorted to for help or supply. [< L *re-* back + *currere* to run]

re·cov·er (ri·kuv′ər) *v.t.* 1. To regain after losing; retrieve. 2. To reclaim, as land. 3. *Law* To gain or regain in legal proceedings. —*v.i.* 4. To regain health, composure, etc. [< L *re-* back + *capere* to take] —**re·cov′er·a·ble** *adj.* —**re·cov′er·er** *n.*

re·cov·er (rē·kuv′ər) *v.t.* To cover again.

re·cov·er·y (ri·kuv′ər·ē) *n. pl.* **·er·ies** 1. The act or process of recovering. 2. Restoration from sickness, misfortune, etc. 3. The retrieval of a balloon, space vehicle, etc., after it has fallen to earth.

rec·re·ant (rek′rē·ənt) *adj.* 1. Unfaithful to a cause or pledge; false. 2. Craven; cowardly. —*n.* A coward; also, a deserter. [< L *re-* back + *credere* to believe] —**rec′re·ant·ly** *adv.*

rec·re·ate (rek′rē·āt) *v.* **·at·ed, ·at·ing** *v.t.* 1. To impart fresh vigor to; refresh. —*v.i.* 2. To take recreation. [< L *re-* again + *creare* to create] —**rec′re·a′tive** *adj.*

re-cre·ate (rē′krē·āt′) *v.t.* **·at·ed, ·at·ing** To create anew. —**re′-cre·a′tion** *n.*

rec·re·a·tion (rek′rē·ā′shən *n.* Refreshment of body or mind; diversion; amusement. —**rec′re·a′tion·al** *adj.*

re·crim·i·nate (ri·krim′ə·nāt) *v.t. & v.i.* **·nat·ed, ·nat·ing** To accuse (someone) in return. [< L *re-* again + *criminare* to accuse of crime] —**re·crim′i·na′tion** *n.* —**re·crim′i·na′tive, re·crim′i·na·to′ry** (-nə·tôr′ē) *adj.* —**re·crim′i·na′tor** *n.*

re·cru·desce (rē′krōō·des′) *v.i.* **·desced, ·desc·ing** To break out afresh. [< L *re-* again + *crudescere* to become raw] —**re′cru·des′cence** *n.* —**re′cru·des′cent** *adj.*

re·cruit (ri·krōōt′) *v.t. & v.i.* 1. To enlist (personnel) for military service; also to raise (an army) by enlistment. 2. To seek

or hire (new members, employees, etc.). —*n.* A newly enlisted member of an organization, esp. of the armed forces. [< L *re-* again + *crescere* to grow] —**re·cruit′er** *n.* —**re·cruit′ment** *n.*
rec·tal (rek′təl) *adj.* *Anat.* Of, for, or in the rectum.
rec·tan·gle (rek′tang′gəl) *n.* A parallelogram with all its angles right angles. [< L *rectus* straight + *angulus* angle] —**rec·tan′gu·lar** (-gyə·lər) *adj.* —**rec·tan′gu·lar′i·ty** (-gyə·lar′ə·tē) *n.* —**rec·tan′gu·lar·ly** *adv.*
recti- *combining form* Straight: *rectilinear.* Also, before vowels, **rect-.** [< L *rectus* straight < *regere* to guide]
rec·ti·fi·er (rek′tə·fī′ər) *n.* 1. One who or that which rectifies. 2. *Electr.* A device used to convert an alternating current into a direct current.
rec·ti·fy (rek′tə·fī) *v.t.* **·fied, ·fy·ing** 1. To make right; correct; amend. 2. *Electr.* To change (an alternating current) into a direct current. [< L *rectus* straight] —**rec′ti·fi′a·ble** *adj.* —**rec′ti·fi·ca′tion** *n.*
rec·ti·lin·e·ar (rek′tə·lin′ē·ər) *adj.* Pertaining to, consisting of, moving in, or bounded by a straight line or lines; straight. Also **rec′ti·lin′e·al.** —**rec′ti·lin′e·ar·ly** *adv.*
rec·ti·tude (rek′tə·tōōd, -tyōōd) *n.* 1. Uprightness in principles and conduct. 2. Correctness, as of judgment. [< L *rectus* straight]
rec·to (rek′tō) *n.* *pl.* **·toes** A right-hand page, as of a book: opposed to *verso.* [< L *recto (folio)* on the right (page)]
recto- *combining form* *Anat.* Rectal; pertaining to or located in the rectum. Also, before vowels **rect-.** [See RECTUM]
rec·tor (rek′tər) *n.* 1. A clergyman in charge of a church, congregation, or parish. 2. The head of a seminary or university. [< L *regere* to guide, rule] —**rec′tor·ate** (-it) *n.* —**rec·to·ri·al** (rek·tôr′ē·əl) *adj.*
rec·to·ry (rek′tər·ē) *n.* *pl.* **·ries** A rector's dwelling.
rec·tum (rek′təm) *n.* *pl.* **·ta** *Anat.* The terminal portion of the large intestine, connecting the colon with the anus. [< NL *rectum (intestinum)* straight (intestine)]
re·cum·bent (ri·kum′bənt) *adj.* 1. Lying down, wholly or partly. 2. *Biol.* Tending to rest upon or extend from a surface. [< L *re-* back + *-cumbere* < *cubare* to lie down] —**re·cum′bence, re·cum′ben·cy** *n.* —**re·cum′bent·ly** *adv.*
re·cu·per·ate (ri·kōō′pə·rāt, -kyōō′-) *v.* **·at·ed, ·at·ing** *v.i.* 1. To regain health or strength. 2. To recover from loss, as of money. —*v.t.* 3. To obtain again after loss; recover. [< L *re-* back + *capere* to take] —**re·cu′per·a′tion** *n.* —**re·cu′per·a′tive, re·cu′per·a·to′ry** (-pər·e·tôr′ē) *adj.*
re·cur (ri·kûr′) *v.i.* **·curred, ·cur·ring** 1. To happen again or repeatedly, esp. at regular intervals. 2. To come back or return; esp., to return to the mind. [< L *re-* back + *currere* to run] —**re·cur′rence** *n.* —**re·cur′rent** *adj.* —**re·cur′rent·ly** *adv.*
re·cur·vate (ri·kûr′vit, -vāt) *adj.* Bent back. —**re·cur′va·ture** (-və·chər) *n.*
re·curve (ri·kûrv′) *v.t.* & *v.i.* **·curved, ·curv·ing** To curve or bend back or down. [< L *re-* back + *curvus* curved] —**re·cur·va·tion** (rē′kûr·vā′shən) *n.*
re·cy·cle (rē·sī′kəl) *v.t.* **·cy·cled, ·cy·cling** To reclaim (waste materials, as newsprint) by using in the manufacture of new products. —**re·cy′cla·ble** *adj.*
red (red) *adj.* **red·der, red·dest** 1. Being of or having a bright color resembling that of blood. 2. *Often cap.* Leftist; esp., communistic. —*n.* 1. One of the primary colors, occurring at the opposite end of the spectrum from violet; the color of blood. 2. *Often cap.* An ultraradical in political views, esp. a communist. —**in the red** *Informal* Operating at a loss; owing money. —**to see red** *Informal* To be very angry. [OE *rēad*] —**red′dish** *adj.* —**red′ly** *adv.* —**red′ness** *n.*
re·dact (ri·dakt′) *v.t.* 1. To prepare, as for publication; edit; revise. 2. To draw up or frame, as an edict. [< L *re-* back + *agere* to drive] —**re·dac′tion** *n.* —**re·dac′tor** *n.*
red algae Any of a class of algae of a reddish color.
red·bird (red′bûrd′) *n.* Any of several birds, as the cardinal, scarlet tanager, etc., that are predominately red-colored.
red blood cell An erythrocyte.
red-blood·ed (red′blud′id) *adj.* Having vitality and vigor.
red·breast (red′brest′) *n.* A bird having a red breast, as the robin.
red·cap (red′kap′) *n.* A railroad porter.
red carpet Ceremonious or luxurious treatment. [after the practice of rolling out a red carpet to welcome dignitaries] —**red-car·pet** (red′kär′pit) *adj.*
red cedar 1. An American juniper tree of the cypress family, having a fine-grained, durable wood of a red color, resembling cedar. 2. The wood of this tree.
red·coat (red′kōt′) *n.* A British soldier of the period when a red coat was part of the uniform, esp. during the American Revolution and the War of 1812.
Red Cross An international organization founded in 1864 to care for the sick and wounded.
red deer 1. The common European and Asian stag. 2. The white-tailed deer in its dull red summer coat.
red·den (red′n) *v.t.* 1. To make red. —*v.i.* 2. To grow red; flush; blush.
re·dec·o·rate (ri·dek′ə·rāt) *v.t.* & *v.i.* **·rat·ed, ·rat·ing** To renovate or remodel (an apartment). —**re′dec′o·ra′tion** *n.*
re·deem (ri·dēm′) *v.t.* 1. To regain possession of, as mortgaged property, by paying a price. 2. To pay off; receive back and satisfy, as a promissory note. 3. To turn in and receive a specified value for (a coupon, etc.). 4. *Theol.* To rescue from sin and its penalties. 5. To fulfill, as an oath or promise. 6. To compensate for; atone for. 7. To save; restore, as to favor. [< L *re-* back + *emere* to buy] —**re·deem′a·ble, re·demp′ti·ble** (-demp′tə·bəl) *adj.*
re·deem·er (ri·dē′mər) *n.* One who redeems. —**The Redeemer** Jesus Christ.
re·deem·ing (ri·dē′ming) *adj.* Compensating for faults, lacks, poor quality, etc.
re·de·liv·er (rē′di·liv′ər) *v.t.* 1. To deliver again. 2. To give back; return. —**re′de·liv′er·y, re′de·liv′er·ance** *n.*
re·demp·tion (ri·demp′shən) *n.* 1. The act of redeeming, or the state of being redeemed.

2. That which redeems. —**re·demp′tive, re·demp′to·ry** *adj.*
Red Ensign The Canadian flag, bearing both the Union Jack and the arms of Canada.
re·de·vel·op (rē′di·vel′əp) *v.t.* 1. To develop again. 2. *Photog.* To intensify with chemicals and put through a second developing process. —*v.i.* 3. To develop again. —**re′de·vel′op·ment** *n.* —**re′de·vel′op·er** *n.*
red·eye (red′ī′) *n.* 1. *Informal* The danger signal in a railroad semaphore system. 2. *Slang* Inferior whisky.
red·fin (red′fin′) *n. pl.* ·**fins** or ·**fin** A small freshwater fish related to the carp.
red-hand·ed (red′han′did) *adj. & adv.* In the act of committing, or having just committed, a crime or misdeed.
red·head (red′hed′) *n.* A person with red hair. —**red′head′ed** *adj.*
red herring 1. Herring dried and smoked to a reddish color. 2. Something that diverts attention from the main subject, question, etc.
red-hot (red′hot′) *adj.* 1. Extremely hot. 2. New; very recent.
red·in·gote (red′ing·gōt) *n.* An outer coat with long, full skirts. [< F *rédingote,* alter. of E *riding coat*]
re·di·rect[1] (rē′di·rekt′) *v.t.* To direct again or anew: to *redirect* a letter. —**re′di·rec′tion** *n.*
re·di·rect[2] (rē′di·rekt′) *adj. Law* Designating the examination of a witness, after cross-examination, by the party who first examined him.
re·dis·trict (rē·dis′trikt) *v.t. & v.i.* To district again; esp., to redraw the election districts of (an area).
red-let·ter day (red′let′ər) A memorable occasion. [from the use on calendars of red letters to indicate holidays]
red light A red traffic or signal light meaning "stop."
red-light district (red′līt′) A part of a city or town in which brothels are numerous.
red·lin·ing (red′līn′ing) *n.* The practice by banks of refusing to grant mortgages in deteriorating neighborhoods. [from the supposed red line on maps that define such areas] —**red′line′** *v.t. & v.i.*
red oak Any of several oaks having a dense, cross-grained wood; also, the wood.
red·o·lent (red′ə·lənt) *adj.* Pleasantly fragrant. [< L *red-* thoroughly + *olere* to smell] —**red′o·lence** *n.* —**red′o·lent·ly** *adv.*
re·doub·le (rē·dub′əl) *v.t. & v.i.* ·**led,** ·**ling** 1. To make or become double. 2. To increase greatly. 3. In bridge, to double (an opponent's double). —*n.* In bridge, the doubling of an opponent's double.
re·doubt (ri·dout′) *n.* An enclosed fortification, esp. a temporary one of any form. [< L *reductus* secret place, pp. of *reducere* to reduce]
re·doubt·a·ble (ri·dou′tə·bəl) *adj.* 1. Inspiring fear; formidable. 2. Deserving respect or deference. Also **re·doubt′ed** (-dou′tid). [< L *re-* thoroughly + *dubitare* to doubt] —**re·doubt′a·bly** *adv.*
re·dound (ri·dound′) *v.i.* To have an effect, as by reaction, on the original agent; accrue. —*n.* A return by way of consequence; requital. [< L *red-* back + *undare* to surge]
red pepper A herb of the nightshade family, the dried pods of which are ground and used as a condiment: also called *cayenne pepper*.
red·poll (red′pōl′) *n.* Any of various small finches having a reddish crown.
re·draft (rē′draft′) *n.* A second draft or copy. —**re·draft′** *v.t. & v.i.*
re·dress (ri·dres′; *for n., also* rē′dres) *v.t.* 1. To set right, as a wrong, by compensation or by punishment of the wrong doer; make reparation for. 2. To make reparation to; compensate. 3. To remedy; correct. 4. To adjust, as balances. —*n.* 1. Satisfaction for wrong done; reparation; amends. 2. A restoration; correction. [< F *re-* again + *dresser* to arrange] —**re·dress′er** or **re·dres′·sor** *n.*
re-dress (rē·dres′) *v.t. & v.i.* To dress again.
red salmon The sockeye.
red·skin (red′skin′) *n.* A North American Indian: usu. considered offensive.
red snapper A reddish fish found in Atlantic waters and esteemed as a food fish.
red·start (red′stärt′) *n.* 1. A small European singing bird allied to the warblers, having a black throat, white forehead, and rust-red breast, sides, and tail. 2. A small fly-catching warbler of eastern North America, with bright orange-red patches against black and white.
red tape Rigid official procedure involving delay or inaction. [from the tying of public documents with red tape]
re·duce (ri·dōōs′, -dyōōs′) *v.* ·**duced,** ·**duc·ing** *v.t.* 1. To make less in size, amount, number, intensity, etc.; diminish. 2. To bring to a lower condition; degrade. 3. To bring to submission; conquer. 4. To bring to a specified condition or state: with *to.* 5. To thin (paint, etc.) with oil or turpentine. 6. *Math.* To change (an expression) to a more elementary form. 7. *Surg.* To restore (displaced parts) to normal position. —*v.i.* 8. To become less in any way. 9. To decrease one's weight, as by dieting. [< L *re-* back + *ducere* to lead] —**re·duc′er** *n.* —**re·duc′i·bil′i·ty** *n.* —**re·duc′i·ble** *adj.* —**re·duc′i·bly** *adv.*
re·duc·tion (ri·duk′shən) *n.* 1. The act or process of reducing. 2. Something made by reducing. 3. The amount by which something is reduced. —**re·duc′tion·al** *adj.* —**re·duc′tive** *adj.*
re·dun·dan·cy (ri·dun′dən·sē) *n. pl.* ·**cies** 1. Something that is redundant. 2. The condition or quality of being redundant. Also **re·dun′dance.**
re·dun·dant (ri·dun′dənt) *adj.* 1. Being more than is required; constituting an excess. 2. Unnecessarily verbose; tautological. [< L *redundans, -antis,* ppr. of *redundare* to overflow] —**re·dun′dant·ly** *adv.*
re·du·pli·cate (*v.* ri·dōō′plə·kāt, -dyōō′-; *adj.* ri·dōō′plə·kit, -dyōō′-) *v.* ·**cat·ed,** ·**cat·ing** *v.t.* 1. To repeat again and again; redouble; iterate. 2. *Ling.* To affix a reduplication to. —*v.i.* 3. To undergo reduplication. —*adj.* Repeated again and again; duplicated. [< L *re-* again + *duplicare* to double] —**re·du′·pli·ca′tive** *adj.*
re·du·pli·ca·tion (ri·dōō′plə·kā′shən, -dyōō′-) *n.* 1. The act of reduplicating, or the state of being reduplicated; a redoubling. 2. *Ling.* **a** The repetition of an initial element

in a word. b The doubling of all or part of a word, often with vowel or consonant change, as in *razzle-dazzle.*

red·wing (red′wing′) *n.* An American blackbird with bright scarlet patches on the wings of the male. Also **red′-winged′ black-bird.**

red·wood (red′wo͝od′) *n.* 1. A sequoia. 2. Its durable reddish wood.

re·ech·o (rē·ek′ō) *v.t. & v.i.* To echo back or again. —**re·ech′o** *n.*

reed (rēd) *n.* 1. The slender, frequently jointed stem of certain tall grasses growing in wet places, or the grasses themselves. 2. A thin, elastic plate of reed, wood, or metal nearly closing an opening, used in oboes, clarinets, etc., to produce a musical tone. 3. A musical pipe made of the hollow stem of a plant. —*v.t.* 1. To fashion into or decorate with reeds. 2. To thatch with reeds. [OE *hrēod*]

reed organ A keyboard musical instrument sounding by means of free reeds vibrated by air currents.

re·ed·u·cate (rē·ej′o͞o·kāt) *v.t.* **·cat·ed, ·cat·ing** 1. To educate again. 2. To rehabilitate, as a criminal, by education. —**re′ed·u·ca′tion** *n.*

reed·y (rē′dē) *adj.* **reed·i·er, reed·i·est** 1. Full of reeds. 2. Like a reed. 3. Having a thin, sharp tone, like a reed instrument. —**reed′i·ness** *n.*

reef[1] (rēf) *n.* A ridge of sand or rocks, or esp. of coral, at or near the surface of the water. [< ON *rif*] —**reef′y** *adj.*

reef[2] (rēf) *Naut. n.* The part of a sail that is taken in or let out in regulating its size on the mast. —*v.t.* 1. To reduce (a sail) by folding a part and fastening it to a yard or boom. 2. To shorten or lower, as a topmast by taking part of it in. [< ON *rif* rib]

reef·er[1] (rē′fər) *n.* 1. One who reefs. 2. A close-fitting jacket of heavy material.

reef·er[2] (rē′fər) *n.* *Slang* A marijuana cigarette. [Origin uncertain]

reek (rēk) *v.i.* 1. To give off a strong, offensive smell. 2. To be pervaded with anything offensive. —*v.t.* 3. To give off or emit (fumes, an odor, etc.) [OE *rēocan* to smoke] —**reek′er** *n.* —**reek′y** *adj.*

reel[1] (rēl) *n.* 1. A rotary device or frame for winding rope, film, etc. 2. Motion picture film wound on one reel, used as a unit of length. 3. A wooden spool for wire, thread, etc. —*v.t.* 1. To wind on a reel or bobbin, as a line. 2. To pull by reeling a line: with *in.* 3. To say, do, etc., easily and fluently: with *off.* [OE *hrēol*] —**reel′a·ble** *adj.* —**reel′er** *n.*

reel[2] (rēl) *v.i.* 1. To stagger, sway, or lurch, as when giddy or drunk. 2. To whirl round and round. 3. To have a sensation of giddiness or whirling. 4. To waver or fall back, as attacking troops. —*n.* A staggering motion; giddiness. [< REEL[1]] —**reel′er** *n.*

reel[3] (rēl) *n.* A lively dance, chiefly Scottish or Irish; also, the music for this dance. [? < REEL[1]]

re·en·force (rē′en·fôrs′), **re·en·force·ment** (rē′en·fôrs′mənt) See REINFORCE, etc.

re·en·try (rē·en′trē) *n. pl.* **·tries** 1. The act of entering again. 2. *Aerospace* The return of a rocket or other object to the atmosphere of the earth.

re·e·val·u·ate (rē′i·val′yo͞o·āt) *v.t.* **·at·ed, ·at·ing** To consider anew. —**re′e·val′u·a′tion** *n.*

reeve (rēv) *v.t.* **reeved** or **rove, reev·ing** *Naut.* To pass, as a rope or rod, through a hole, block, or aperture. [Origin uncertain]

ref (ref) *Informal n.* A referee. —*v.t. & v.i.* **reffed, ref·fing** To referee.

re·fec·tion (ri·fek′shən) *n.* 1. Refreshment with food and drink. 2. A light meal. [< L *re-* again + *facere* to make]

re·fec·to·ry (ri·fek′tə·rē) *n. pl.* **·ries** A dining hall, esp. in a religious house.

re·fer (ri·fûr′) *v.* **·ferred, ·fer·ring** *v.t.* 1. To direct or send for information, assistance, etc. 2. To submit for consideration, settlement, etc. 3. To assign to a source, class, period, etc. —*v.i.* 4. To make reference; allude. 5. To turn, as for information, help, or authority. [< L *re-* back + *ferre* to carry] —**ref·er·a·ble** (ref′ər·ə·bəl, ri·fûr′-) or **re·fer′ra·ble** *adj.* —**re·fer′ral** *n.* —**re·fer′·rer** *n.*

ref·e·ree (ref′ə·rē′) *n.* 1. A person to whom something is referred for arbitration. 2. In certain sports, a supervisory official. —*v.t. & v.i.* **·reed, ·ree·ing** To judge as a referee.

ref·er·ence (ref′ər·əns, ref′rəns) *n.* 1. The act of referring. 2. An allusion or direction of the attention: *reference* to a recent event. 3. A note or other indication in a book, referring to some other book or passage. 4. One who or that which is or may be referred to. 5. The state of being referred or related: used in the phrase **with** (or **in**) **reference to.** 6. A person to whom one seeking employment may refer for recommendation. —**ref′er·enc·er** *n.*

ref·er·en·dum (ref′ə·ren′dəm) *n. pl.* **·dums** or **·da** 1. The submission of a proposed law to a vote of the people for ratification or rejection. 2. The vote in such a procedure. [< L, gerund of *referre* to refer]

ref·er·ent (ref′ər·ənt) *n.* The object, concept, etc., to which reference is made.

re·fill (*v.* rē·fil′; *n.* rē′fil′) *v.t.* To fill again. —*n.* Any commodity packaged to fit and fill a container originally containing that commodity.

re·fine (ri·fīn′) *v.* **·fined, ·fin·ing** *v.t.* 1. To free from impurities or extraneous matter. 2. To make polished or cultured. 3. To improve or change by subtle or precise alterations. —*v.i.* 4. To become fine or pure. [< RE- + FINE[1], v.] —**re·fin′er** *n.*

re·fined (ri·fīnd′) *adj.* 1. Characterized by refinement; cultivated; polished. 2. Free from impurity. 3. Exceedingly precise.

re·fine·ment (ri·fīn′mənt) *n.* 1. Fineness of thought, taste, language, etc.; culture. 2. The act, effect, or process of refining. 3. A nice distinction; subtlety. 4. Fastidiousness.

re·fin·er·y (ri·fī′nər·ē) *n. pl.* **·er·ies** A place where crude material, as sugar or petroleum, is purified.

re·fit (rē·fit′, *for n. also* rē′fit′) *v.t. & v.i.* **·fit·ted, ·fit·ting** To make or be made fit or ready again, as by repairs, replacement of equipment, etc. —*n.* The repair of damages or wear, esp. of a ship.

re·flect (ri·flekt′) *v.t.* 1. To turn or throw back, as waves of light, heat, or sound. 2. To give back an image of; mirror. 3. To manifest as a result of influence, imitation, etc. —*v.i.* 4. To send back rays, as of light or heat. 5. To give back an image. 6. To think carefully; ponder. 7. To bring blame, discredit, etc.: with *on* or *upon.* [< L *re-* back + *flectere* to bend] **—re·flec′tion** *n.* **—re·flec′tive** *adj.* **—re·flec′tive·ly** *adv.* **—re·flec′tive·ness** *n.* **—re′flec·tiv′i·ty** *n.*

re·flec·tor (ri·flek′tər) *n.* 1. That which reflects. 2. A polished surface for reflecting light, heat, sound, etc. 3. A telescope that transmits an image from a reflecting surface.

re·flex (*adj. & n.* rē′fleks; *v.* ri·fleks′) *adj.* 1. *Physiol.* Of, pertaining to, or produced by involuntary response to a stimulus. 2. Turned or directed backward or in the opposite direction. 3. Bent back; reflexed. —*n. Physiol.* An involuntary movement or response to a stimulus, as in sneezing, shivering, etc.: also **reflex action.** —*v.t.* To bend back; turn back or reflect. [See REFLECT.]

re·flex·ive (ri·flek′siv) *adj. Gram.* **a** Of verbs, having an object that is identical with the subject, as "dresses" in "He dresses himself." **b** Of pronouns in the objective case, being identical with the subject, as "herself" in "She hurt herself." **—re·flex′ive** *n.* **—re·flex′·ive·ly** *adv.* **—re·flex′ive·ness** *n.*

re·flux (rē′fluks′) *n.* A flowing back; ebb. —*v.t.* To heat so that vapors condense and are reheated. [< L *refluxus,* pp. of *refluere* to flow back]

re·for·est (rē·fôr′ist, -for′-) *v.t. & v.i.* To replant (an area) with trees. **—re′for·es·ta′tion** *n.*

re·form (ri·fôrm′) *v.t.* 1. To make better by removing abuses, altering, etc. 2. To improve morally; persuade or educate to a better life. —*v.i.* 3. To give up sin or error; become better. —*n.* An act or result of reformation; change for the better. [< L *re-* again + *formare* to form] **—re·form′a·tive** *adj.* **—re·form′er, re·form′ist** *n.*

re-form (rē′fôrm′) *v.t. & v.i.* To form again. **—re′for·ma′tion** *n.*

ref·or·ma·tion (ref′ər·mā′shən) *n.* 1. The act of reforming, or the state of being reformed; esp., moral improvement. 2. *cap.* The 16th c. religious revolution that established Protestantism.

re·for·ma·to·ry (ri·fôr′mə·tôr′ē) *n. pl.* **·ries** An institution for the reformation and instruction of juvenile offenders. Also **reform school.** —*adj.* Tending to reform.

re·formed (ri·fôrmd′) *adj.* 1. Restored to a better state. 2. Improved in conduct, habits, etc.

Reform Judaism The branch of Judaism that interprets traditional law and ritual in relation to modern times.

re·fract (ri·frakt′) *v.t.* 1. To deflect (a ray) by refraction. 2. *Optics* To determine the degree of refraction of (an eye or lens). [< L *refringere* to turn aside]

re·frac·tion (ri·frak′shən) *n. Physics* The change of direction of a ray, as of light or heat, in passage from one medium to another of different density. **—re·frac′tive** *adj.* **—re·frac′tive·ly** *adv.* **—re·frac′tive·ness, re·frac·tiv·i·ty** (rē′frak·tiv′ə·tē) *n.*

re·frac·tor (ri·frak′tər) *n.* 1. That which refracts. 2. A telescope focused primarily by means of a lens: also **refracting telescope.**

re·frac·to·ry (ri·frak′tər·ē) *adj.* 1. Not amenable to control; unmanageable; obstinate. 2. Resisting heat or ordinary methods of reduction, as an ore. —*n. pl.* **·ries** 1. One who or that which is refractory. 2. Any of various materials highly resistant to the action of great heat, as fire clay. [See REFRACT.] **—re·frac′to·ri·ly** *adv.* **—re·frac′to·ri·ness** *n.*

re·frain[1] (ri·frān′) *v.i.* To keep oneself back; abstain from action. [< L *refrenare* to curb] **—re·frain′er** *n.*

re·frain[2] (ri·frān′) *n.* A phrase or strain in a poem or song repeated at the end of each stanza. [< L *refringere* to turn aside]

re·fresh (ri·fresh′) *v.t.* 1. To make fresh or vigorous again, as by food or rest; reinvigorate; revive. 2. To make fresh, clean, cool, etc. 3. To stimulate, as the memory. —*v.i.* 4. To become fresh again; revive. 5. To take refreshment.

re·fresh·er (ri·fresh′ər) *adj.* Reviewing material previously studied. —*n.* One who or that which refreshes.

re·fresh·ing (ri·fresh′ing) *adj.* 1. Serving to refresh. 2. Enjoyably novel or unusual. **—re·fresh′ing·ly** *adv.*

re·fresh·ment (ri·fresh′mənt) *n.* 1. The act of refreshing, or the state of being refreshed. 2. That which refreshes. 3. *pl.* Food, or food and drink.

re·frig·er·ate (ri·frij′ə·rāt) *v.t.* **·at·ed, ·at·ing** 1. To keep or make cold. 2. To freeze or chill (foodstuffs, etc.) for preservation. [< L *re-* thoroughly + *frigerare* to cool] **—re·frig′er·ant** (-ər·ənt) *n. & adj.* **—re·frig′er·a′tion** *n.* **—re·frig′er·a′tive** *adj. & n.*

re·frig·er·a·tor (ri·frij′ə·rā′tər) *n.* A box, cabinet, room, etc., equipped with a cooling apparatus for preserving perishable foods, etc.

ref·uge (ref′yo͞oj) *n.* 1. Shelter or protection as from danger or distress. 2. One who or that which shelters or protects. 3. A safe place; asylum. [< L *re-* back + *fugere* to flee]

ref·u·gee (ref′yo͝o·jē′, ref′yo͝o·jē′) *n.* One who flees to another country to escape from invasion, persecution, or political danger.

re·ful·gent (ri·ful′jənt) *adj.* Shining brilliantly; radiant. [< L *re-* back + *fulgere* to shine] **—re·ful′gence** *n.* **—re·ful′gent·ly** *adv.*

re·fund (*v.* ri·fund′; *n.* rē′fund) *v.t. & v.i.* To give or pay back (money, etc.); repay. —*n.* A repayment; also, the amount repaid. [< L *re-* back + *fundere* to pour] **—re·fund′er** *n.*

re·fur·bish (ri·fûr′bish) *v.t.* To renovate or freshen; polish up; brighten.

re·fuse[1] (ri·fyo͞oz′) *v.* **·fused, ·fus·ing** *v.t.* 1. To decline to do, permit, take, or yield. 2. To decline to jump over: said of a horse at a ditch, hedge, etc. —*v.i.* 3. To decline to do, permit, take, or yield something. [< L *refusus,* pp. of *refundere* to refund] **—re·fus′al** *n.*

ref·use[2] (ref′yo͞os) *n.* Anything worthless; rubbish. —*adj.* Rejected as worthless. [See REFUSE[1].]

re·fute (ri·fyo͞ot′) *v.t.* **·fut·ed, ·fut·ing** 1. To

prove the incorrectness or falsity of (a statement). 2. To prove (a person) to be in error; confute. [< L *refutare* to repulse] —**re·fut′a·bil′i·ty** *n.* —**re·fut′a·ble** *adj.* —**re·fut′a·bly** *adv.* —**ref·u·ta·tion** (ref′·yōō·tā′shən) *n.* —**re·fut′er** *n.*

re·gain (ri·gān′) *v.t.* 1. To get possession of again, as something lost; recover. 2. To get back to: He *regained* the street. —**re·gain′er** *n.*

re·gal (rē′gəl) *adj.* 1. Of a king; royal. 2. Stately. [< L *rex, regis* king] —**re·gal·i·ty** (ri·gal′ə·tē) *n.* —**re′gal·ly** *adv.*

re·gale (ri·gāl′) *v.* **·galed, ·gal·ing** *v.t.* 1. To give unusual pleasure to; delight. 2. To entertain sumptuously; feast. —*v.i.* 3. To feast. [< F *ré-* again + OF *gale* pleasure] —**re·gale′ment** *n.*

re·ga·li·a (ri·gā′lē·ə, -gāl′yə) *n. pl.* 1. The insignia and emblems of royality, as the crown, scepter, etc. 2. The distinctive symbols, insignia, etc., of any society, order, or rank. 3. Fine clothes; fancy trappings. [See REGAL.]

re·gard (ri·gärd′) *v.t.* 1. To look at or observe closely. 2. To think of in a certain manner: I *regard* him as a friend. 3. To take into account; consider. 4. To have relation or pertinence to; concern. —*v.i.* 5. To pay attention. —*n.* 1. Careful attention or notice; heed; consideration. 2. Esteem; respect. 3. *Usu. pl.* Good wishes; affection. [< OF *re-* again + *garder* to guard, heed] —**re·gard′ful** *adj.* —**re·gard′·ful·ly** *adv.*

re·gard·ing (ri·gär′ding) *prep.* In reference to; concerning.

re·gard·less (ri·gärd′lis) *adj.* Having no regard or consideration; heedless; negligent: often with *of.* —*adv. Informal* In spite of everything. —**re·gard′less·ly** *adv.*

re·gat·ta (ri·gat′ə, -gä′tə) *n.* A boat race, or a series of such races. [< Ital.]

re·gen·cy (rē′jən·sē) *n. pl.* **·cies** 1. The government or office of a regent or body of regents. 2. The period during which a regent governs. 3. A body of regents.

re·gen·er·ate (*v.* ri·jen′ə·rāt; *adj.* ri·jen′ər·it) *v.* **·at·ed, ·at·ing** *v.t.* 1. To cause complete moral and spiritual reformation in. 2. To produce or form anew; recreate; reproduce. 3. *Biol.* To grow or form (new tissue). —*v.i.* 4. To form anew; be reproduced. 5. To become spiritually regenerate. —*adj.* 1. Having new life; restored. 2. Spiritually renewed. —**re·gen′er·a·cy, re·gen′er·a′tion** *n.* —**re·gen·er·a·tive** (ri·jen′ə·rā′tiv, -ər·ə·tiv) *adj.* —**re·gen′er·a′tive·ly** *adv.* —**regen′er·a′tor** *n.*

re·gent (rē′jənt) *n.* 1. One who rules in the name and place of a sovereign. 2. One of various educational officers, as of a state. —*adj.* Exercising authority in another's place. [< L *regere* to rule]

reg·gae (re′gā′) *n.* A type of Jamaican popular music, influenced by American soul music, and usu. with accents on the second and fourth beats. [< *reggay*, term coined by Frederick "Toots" Hibbert in "Do the Reggay," recorded in 1966 < ? RAGGEDNESS]

reg·i·cide (rej′ə·sīd) *n.* 1. The killing of a king or sovereign. 2. One who has killed a king or sovereign. [< L *rex, regis* king + -CIDE] —**reg′i·ci′dal** *adj.*

re·gime (ri·zhēm′) *n.* 1. System of government or administration. 2. A social system. 3. Regimen. Also **ré·gime′** (rā-). [< F. See REGIMEN.]

reg·i·men (rej′ə·mən) *n.* A systematized course of living, as to food, clothing, etc.: also *regime.* [< L *regere* to rule]

reg·i·ment (rej′ə·mənt) *n.* 1. *Mil.* An administrative and tactical unit of infantry, artillery, etc., comprising several battalions. 2. Any large body of persons. —*v.t.* 1. To form into a regiment or regiments; organize. 2. To systematize or make uniform. [< L *regere* to rule] —**reg′i·men′tal** *adj.* —**reg′i·men·ta′tion** *n.*

reg·i·men·tals (rej′ə·men′təlz) *n.pl.* 1. A military uniform. 2. The uniform worn by a regiment.

re·gion (rē′jən) *n.* 1. An indefinite portion of territory or space, usu. of considerable extent. 2. A particular area or place: the delta *region* of the Nile. [< L *regere* to rule]

re·gion·al (rē′jən·əl) *adj.* 1. Of or pertaining to a particular region; sectional; local: *regional* planning. 2. Of or pertaining to an entire region or section. —**re′gion·al·ly** *adv.*

reg·is·ter (rej′is·tər) *n.* 1. A formal or official record or account, as of names or transactions; also, a book containing such a record. 2. Any of various devices for counting or recording: a cash *register.* 3. A device by which heated or cooled air is admitted to a room. 4. The act of recording or registering; registry. —*v.t.* 1. To enter in or as in a register; record officially or exactly. 2. To indicate, as on a scale. 3. To express; show: His face *registered* shock. 4. To cause (mail) to be recorded, on payment of a fee, when deposited with the postal system, so as to insure delivery. —*v.i.* 5. To enter one's name in a register. 6. To cause one's name to be included on a list of eligible voters. 7. *Informal* To have effect; make an impression. [< L *re-* back + *gerere* to carry] —**reg′is·tered** *adj.* —**reg·is·tra·ble** (rej′is·trə·bəl) *adj.* —**reg′is·trant** *n.*

registered nurse A graduate nurse licensed to practice by the appropriate state authority.

reg·is·trar (rej′is·trär) *n.* An authorized keeper of a register or of records; esp., a college or university officer who records the enrollment of students, their grades, etc.

reg·is·tra·tion (rej′is·trā′shən) *n.* 1. The act of entering in a registry; also, such an entry. 2. The registering of voters; also, the number of voters registered. 3. Enrollment in a school, college, or university.

reg·is·try (rej′is·trē) *n. pl.* **·tries** 1. The act of registering; registration. 2. A register, or the place where it is kept.

reg·nant (reg′nənt) *adj.* 1. Reigning in one's own right. 2. Dominant. [< L *regnum* reign] —**reg′nan·cy** *n.*

re·gress (*n.* rē′gres; *v.* ri·gres′) *n.* 1. Passage back; return. 2. The power or right of passing back. 3. Withdrawal; retrogression. —*v.i.* To go back; move backward; return. [< L *re-* back + *gradi* to walk] —**re·gres′·sive** *adj.* —**re·gres′sive·ly** *adv.* —**re·gres′sor** *n.*

re·gres·sion (ri·gresh′ən) *n.* 1. The act of regressing. 2. *Psychoanal.* A retreat to earlier and less mature forms of behavior.

re·gret (ri·gret′) *v.* **·gret·ted, ·gret·ting** —*v.t.* 1. To look back upon with a feeling of distress or loss. —*v.i.* 2. To feel sorrow or grief. —*n.* 1. Distress of mind over loss or circumstances beyond one's control. 2. Remorseful sorrow; compunction. 3. *pl.* A polite refusal in response to an invitation. [< OF *regreter* < Gmc.] —**re·gret′ful** *adj.* —**re·gret′ful·ly** *adv.* —**re·gret′ful·ness** *n.* —**re·gret′ta·ble** *adj.* —**re·gret′ta·bly** *adv.* —**re·gret′ter** *n.*

reg·u·lar (reg′yə·lər) *adj.* 1. Made according to rule; symmetrical; normal. 2. Acting according to rule; methodical; orderly: *regular* habits. 3. Constituted, appointed, or conducted in the proper manner; duly authorized: a *regular* meeting. 4. *Gram.* Undergoing the inflection that is normal or most common. 5. *Mil.* Pertaining or belonging to the permanent military services. 6. In politics, adhering loyally to a party organization or platform. 7. *Geom.* Having equal sides and angles. 8. *Informal* Thorough; unmitigated; absolute. —*n.* 1. A regular soldier. 2. *Informal* One regularly employed or engaged; also, a habitual customer. 3. A person loyal to a certain political party. [< L *regula* rule] —**reg′u·lar′i·ty** (-lar′ə·tē) *n.* —**reg′u·lar·ly** *adv.* —**reg′u·lar·ness** *n.*

reg·u·lar·ize (reg′yə·lə·rīz′) *v.t.* **·ized, ·iz·ing** To make regular. Also *Brit.* **reg′u·lar·ise′**. —**reg′u·lar·i·za′tion** *n.*

reg·u·late (reg′yə·lāt) *v.t.* **·lat·ed, ·lat·ing** 1. To direct or control according to certain rules, principles, etc. 2. To adjust according to a standard, degree, etc.: to *regulate* currency. 3. To adjust to accurate operation. 4. To put in order. [< LL *regulare* to rule] —**reg′u·la′tive, reg′u·la·to′ry** (-lə·tôr′ē) *adj.* —**reg′u·la′tor** *n.*

reg·u·la·tion (reg′yə·lā′shən) *n.* 1. The act of regulating, or the state of being regulated. 2. A rule of conduct.

re·gur·gi·tate (ri·gûr′jə·tāt) *v.* **·tat·ed, ·tat·ing** *v.i.* 1. To rush, pour, or surge back. —*v.t.* 2. To cause to surge back, as partially digested food; vomit. [< L *re-* back + *gurgitare* to swallow, engulf] —**re·gur′gi·tant** (-tənt) *adj.* —**re·gur′gi·ta′tion** *n.*

re·ha·bil·i·tate (rē′hə·bil′ə·tāt) *v.t.* **·tat·ed, ·tat·ing** 1. To restore to a former state, capacity, privilege, rank, etc.; reinstate. 2. To restore to a state of health, useful activity, etc., through training, therapy, or guidance. 3. To put back into good condition. [< L *re-* back + *habilis* fit] —**re′ha·bil′i·ta′tion** *n.*

re·hash (*v.* rē·hash′; *n.* rē′hash′) *v.t.* To work into a new form; go over again. —*n.* Something rehashed.

re·hear·ing (rē·hir′ing) *n.* A new hearing, as in court.

re·hears·al (ri·hûr′səl) *n.* 1. A practice session as preparation for public performance. 2. The act of telling over again; recital.

re·hearse (ri·hûrs′) *v.* **·hearsed, ·hears·ing** *v.t.* 1. To perform privately in preparation for public performance, as a play or song. 2. To instruct by rehearsal. 3. To say over again; repeat aloud; recite. —*v.i.* 4. To rehearse a play, song, etc. [< OF *re-* again + *hercier* to harrow] —**re·hears′er** *n.*

Reich (rīkh) *n.* Germany or its government; esp., the **Third Reich**, the Nazi state under Adolf Hitler, 1933–45. [< G, realm]

reign (rān) *n.* 1. The possession or exercise of supreme power, esp. royal power; sovereignty. 2. The time or duration of a sovereign's rule. —*v.i.* 1. To hold and exercise sovereign power. 2. To prevail: Winter *reigns.* [< L *regnum* rule]

re·im·burse (rē′im·bûrs′) *v.t.* **·bursed, ·burs·ing** To pay back. [< RE- + obs. *imburse* to pay] —**re′im·burs′a·ble** *adj.* —**re′im·burse′ment** *n.* —**re′im·burs′er** *n.*

rein (rān) *n.* 1. *Usu. pl.* A strap attached to the bit to control a horse or other draft animal. 2. Any means of restraint or control; a check. —*v.t.* 1. To guide, check, or halt with or as with reins. —*v.i.* 2. To check or halt a horse by means of reins. [< L *retinere* to retain]

re·in·car·na·tion (rē′in·kär·nā′shən) *n.* A rebirth of the soul in successive bodies; also, the belief in such rebirth. —**re′in·car′nate** *v.t.* **·nat·ed, ·nat·ing**

rein·deer (rān′dir′) *n. pl.* **·deer** A deer of northern regions, having branched antlers in both sexes and used as a pack animal. [< ON *hreinn* reindeer + *dȳr* deer]

re·in·force (rē′in·fôrs′) *v.t.* **·forced, ·forc·ing** 1. To give new force or strength to. 2. *Mil.* To strengthen with additional personnel or equipment. 3. To add some strengthening part or material to. Also spelled *reenforce.* [< RE- + *inforce,* var. of ENFORCE]

reinforced concrete Concrete containing metal rods or netting to increase its tensile strength and durability.

re·in·force·ment (rē′in·fôrs′mənt) *n.* 1. The act of reinforcing. 2. *Often pl. Mil.* A fresh body of troops or additional vessels. Also spelled *reenforcement.*

re·in·state (rē′in·stāt′) *v.t.* **·stat·ed, ·stat·ing** To restore to a former state, position, etc. —**re′in·state′ment** *n.*

re·is·sue (rē·ish′o͞o) *n.* A second printing of postage stamps from the same plates. —*v.t.* **·sued, ·su·ing** To issue again.

re·it·er·ate (rē·it′ə·rāt) *v.t.* **·at·ed, ·at·ing** To say or do again and again. [< L *re-* again + ITERATE] —**re·it′er·a′tion** *n.* —**re·it′er·a′tive** *adj.* —**re·it′er·a′tive·ly** *adv.*

re·ject (*v.* ri·jekt′; *n.* rē′jekt) *v.t.* 1. To refuse to accept, recognize, believe, etc. 2. To refuse to grant; deny, as a petition. 3. To cast away as worthless; discard. —*n.* One who or that which has been rejected. [< L *re-* back + *jacere* to throw] —**re·ject′er** or **re·jec′tor** *n.* —**re·jec′tion** *n.*

re·joice (ri·jois′) *v.* **·joiced, ·joic·ing** *v.i.* 1. To feel joyful; be glad. —*v.t.* 2. To fill with joy; gladden. [< OF *re-* again + *esjoir* to be joyous] —**re·joic′er** *n.* —**re·joic′ing** *n. & adj.*

re·join[1] (ri·join′) *v.t.* 1. To say in reply; answer. —*v.i.* 2. To answer. [< F *rejoindre*]

re·join[2] (rē·join′) *v.t.* 1. To come again into company with. 2. To join together again; reunite. —*v.i.* 3. To come together again.

re·join·der (ri·join′dər) *n.* An answer to a reply; also, any reply or retort.

re·ju·ve·nate (ri·jo͞o′və·nāt) *v.t.* **·nat·ed, ·nat·ing** To give new vigor or youthfulness to. [< RE- + L *juvenis* young] **—re·ju′ve·na′tion** *n.* **—re·ju′ve·na′tor** *n.*

re·lapse (ri·laps′; *for n., also* rē′laps) *v.i.* **·lapsed, ·laps·ing** 1. To lapse back, as into a disease. 2. To return to bad habits or ways; backslide. **—***n.* The act or condition of relapsing. [< L *re-* back + *labi* to slide] **—re·laps′er** *n.*

re·late (ri·lāt′) *v.* **·lat·ed, ·lat·ing** *v.t.* 1. To tell the particulars of; narrate. 2. To bring into connection or relation. **—***v.i.* 3. To have relation: with *to.* 4. To have reference: with *to.* [< L *relatus,* pp. of *referre* to refer] **—re·lat′er** *n.*

re·lat·ed (ri·lā′tid) *adj.* 1. Standing in relation; connected. 2. Connected by blood or marriage. 3. Narrated; told. **—re·lat′ed·ness** *n.*

re·la·tion (ri·lā′shən) *n.* 1. The fact or condition of being related or connected in some way. 2. Connected by blood or marriage; kinship. 3. A person connected by blood or marriage; kinsman. 4. Reference; regard; allusion: in *relation* to that matter. 5. *pl.* Conditions or connections between or among individuals; also, any conditions or connections by which one country may come into contact with another politically and commercially. 6. The act of narrating; also, that which is narrated. **—re·la′tion·al** *adj.*

re·la·tion·ship (ri·lā′shən·ship) *n.* The state of being related; connection.

rel·a·tive (rel′ə·tiv) *adj.* 1. Having connection; pertinent: an inquiry *relative* to one's health. 2. Resulting from or depending upon relation; comparative. 3. Intelligible only in relationship. 4. Referring to an antecedent term: a *relative* pronoun. **—***n.* One who is related; a kinsman. **—rel′a·tive·ly** *adv.* **—rel′a·tive·ness** *n.*

rel·a·tiv·i·ty (rel′ə·tiv′ə·tē) *n.* 1. The quality or condition of being relative. 2. *Physics* The principle of the interdependence of matter, energy, space, and time, as mathematically formulated by Albert Einstein.

re·lax (ri·laks′) *v.t.* 1. To make lax or loose; make less tight or firm. 2. To make less stringent or severe, as discipline. 3. To abate; slacken, as efforts. 4. To relieve from strain or effort. **—***v.i.* 5. To become lax or loose; loosen. 6. To become less stringent or severe. 7. To rest; repose. [< L *re-* again + *laxare* to loosen] **—re·lax′a·ble** *adj.* **—re·lax·a·tion** (rē′lak·sā′shən) *n.* **—re·lax′er** *n.*

re·lax·ant (ri·laks′ənt) *n.* A drug, therapy, etc., that relaxes the muscles or reduces nervous tension. **—***adj.* Of or causing relaxation.

re·lay (rē′lā, *for v. also* ri·lā′) *n.* 1. A fresh set, as of men, horses, or dogs, to replace or relieve a tired set. 2. A relay race, or one of its laps or legs. 3. *Electr.* A device that utilizes variations in the condition of a current in a circuit to effect the operation of similar devices in the same or another circuit. **—***v.t.* 1. To send onward by or as by relays. 2. *Electr.* To operate or retransmit by means of a relay. [< MF *relaier* to release]

re-lay (rē·lā′) *v.t.* **-laid, -lay·ing** To lay again.

relay race A race between teams each member of which races a set part of the course and is relieved by a teammate.

re·lease (ri·lēs′) *v.t.* **·leased, ·leas·ing** 1. To set free; liberate. 2. To deliver from worry, pain, obligation, etc. 3. To free from something that holds, binds, etc. 4. To permit the circulation, sale, performance, etc., of, as a phonograph record or news item. **—***n.* 1. The act of releasing or the state of being released. 2. A discharge from responsibility or penalty, as from a debt. 3. *Law* A document by which one relinquishes all claim to something. 4. Anything formally released to the public, as news, a motion picture, etc. [< L *relaxare* to relax] **—re·leas′er** *n.*

re-lease (rē′lēs′) *v.t.* **-leased, -leas·ing** To lease again.

rel·e·gate (rel′ə·gāt) *v.t.* **·gat·ed, ·gat·ing** 1. To send off or consign, as to an obscure position or place. 2. To assign, as to a particular class or sphere. 3. To refer (a matter) to someone for decision. 4. To banish; exile. [< L *re-* back + *legare* to send] **—rel′e·ga′tion** *n.*

re·lent (ri·lent′) *v.i.* To soften in temper; become less severe. [< L *re-* again + *lentus* soft]

re·lent·less (ri·lent′lis) *adj.* 1. Unremitting; continuous. 2. Indifferent to the pain of others; pitiless. **—re·lent′less·ly** *adv.* **—re·lent′less·ness** *n.*

rel·e·vant (rel′ə·vənt) *adj.* Pertinent; applicable: usu. with *to.* [< Med.L. *relevare* to bear upon] **—rel′e·vance, rel′e·van·cy** *n.* **—rel′e·vant·ly** *adv.*

re·li·a·ble (ri·lī′ə·bəl) *adj.* That may be relied upon; worthy of confidence; trustworthy. **—re·li′a·bil′i·ty, re·li′a·ble·ness** *n.* **—re·li′a·bly** *adv.*

re·li·ance (ri·lī′əns) *n.* 1. The act of relying, or the condition of being reliant. 2. Something or someone relied upon. **—re·li′ant** *adj.*

rel·ic (rel′ik) *n.* 1. Some remaining portion or fragment of that which has vanished or been destroyed. 2. A keepsake or memento. 3. The body or part of the body of a saint; also, any sacred memento. [< L *relinquiae* remains, leavings]

re·lief (ri·lēf′) *n.* 1. The act of relieving, or the state of being relieved. 2. That which relieves. 3. Charitable aid, as food or money. 4. The release, as from one's post or duty, and the substitution of someone else; also, the one so substituted. 5. In architecture and sculpture, the projection of a figure, ornament, etc., from a surface. 6. *Geog.* The elevations and unevenness of land surface. [See RELIEVE.]

re·lieve (ri·lēv′) *v.t.* **·lieved, ·liev·ing** 1. To free from pain, embarrassment, etc. 2. To lessen or alleviate, as pain or anxiety. 3. To release from duty, as a sentinel, by providing or serving as a substitute. 4. To make less monotonous, harsh, or unpleasant; vary. 5. To bring into relief or prominence. [< L *re-* again + *levare* to lift, raise] **—re·liev′a·ble** *adj.* **—re·liev′er** *n.*

re·lig·ion (ri·lij′ən) *n.* The beliefs, attitudes,

emotions, behavior, etc., constituting man's relationship with the powers and principles of the universe, esp. with a deity or deities. [< L *re-* back + *ligare* to bind]

re·lig·i·os·i·ty (ri·lij′ē·os′ə·tē) *n.* Religiousness; also, pious sentimentality. [< Med.L *religiositas*]

re·lig·ious (ri·lij′əs) *adj.* 1. Feeling and manifesting religion; devout; pious. 2. Of or pertaining to religion: a *religious* teacher. 3. Strict in performance; conscientious: a *religious* loyalty. —*n. pl.* **·ious** A monk or nun. —**re·lig′ious·ly** *adv.* —**re·lig′ious·ness** *n.*

re·lin·quish (ri·ling′kwish) *v.t.* 1. To give up; abandon. 2. To renounce: to *relinquish* a claim. 3. To let go (a hold, etc.). [< L *re-* back, from + *linquere* to leave] —**re·lin′quish·er** *n.* —**re·lin′quish·ment** *n.*

rel·i·quar·y (rel′ə·kwer′ē) *n. pl.* **·quar·ies** A repository for religious relics. [< L *re-* back, from + *linguere* to leave]

rel·ish (rel′ish) *n.* 1. Appetite; appreciation; liking. 2. The flavor, esp. when agreeable, in food and drink. 3. The quality in anything that lends spice or zest: Danger gives *relish* to adventure. 4. Something taken with food to lend it flavor, as chopped pickles. —*v.t.* 1. To like the savor of; enjoy. —*v.i.* 2. To have an agreeable flavor; afford gratification. [< OF *relaissier* to leave behind] —**rel′ish·a·ble** *adj.*

re·lo·cate (rē′lō′kāt, rē·lō·kāt′) *v.t. & v.i.* **·cat·ed, ·cat·ing** To locate again or anew; esp., to move to a new residence, city, or region.

re·luc·tance (ri·luk′təns) *n.* 1. The state of being reluctant. 2. *Electr.* Capacity for opposing magnetic induction. Also **re·luc′tan·cy.**

re·luc·tant (ri·luk′tənt) *adj.* Marked by unwillingness, or performed unwillingly. [< L *re-* back + *luctari* to fight] —**re·luc′tant·ly** *adv.*

re·ly (ri·lī′) *v.i.* **·lied, ·ly·ing** To place trust or confidence: with *on* or *upon.* [< L *re-* again + *ligare* to bind] —**re·li′er** *n.*

REM (rem) *n.* Rapid eye movement.

re·main (ri·mān′) *v.i.* 1. To stay or be left behind after the removal of other persons or things. 2. To continue in one place, condition, or character: He *remained* in office. 3. To be left as something to be done, dealt with, etc.: It *remains* to be proved. 4. To endure or last; abide. [< L *re-* back + *manere* to stay]

re·main·der (ri·mān′dər) *n.* 1. That which remains after a subtraction, expenditure, or passing over of a part. 2. *Math.* The quantity left after subtraction or division. 3. A copy of a book sold at reduced price by a publisher after sales have slowed. —*adj.* Left over. —*v.t.* To sell (books, etc.) as a remainder.

re·mains (ri·mānz′) *n. pl.* 1. That which is left after a part has been removed or destroyed. 2. The body of a deceased person. 3. Writings of an author published after his death.

re·mand (ri·mand′) *v.t.* 1. To order or send back. 2. *Law* To recommit to custody, as an accused person after a preliminary examination. —*n.* A remanding, or being remanded. [< L *re-* back + *mandare* to order]

re·mark (ri·märk′) *n.* 1. An oral or written comment or saying; a casual observation. 2. The act of observing or noticing; observation; notice. —*v.t.* 1. To say or write by way of comment. 2. To take particular notice of. —*v.i.* 3. To make remarks: with *on* or *upon.* [< F *re-* again + *marquer* to mark] —**re·mark′er** *n.*

re·mark·a·ble (ri·mär′kə·bəl) *adj.* 1. Worthy of notice. 2. Extraordinary; unusual; conspicuous; distinguished. —**re·mark′a·ble·ness** *n.* —**re·mark′a·bly** *adv.*

re·me·di·a·ble (ri·mē′dē·ə·bəl) *adj.* Capable of being cured or remedied. —**re·me′di·a·ble·ness** *n.* —**re·me′di·a·bly** *adv.*

re·me·di·al (ri·mē′dē·əl) *adj.* Of the nature of or adapted to be used as a remedy: *remedial* help in spelling. —**re·me′di·al·ly** *adv.*

rem·e·dy (rem′ə·dē) *n. pl.* **·dies** 1. That which cures or affords relief to bodily disease or ailment; a medicine; also, remedial treatment. 2. A means of counteracting or removing an error, evil, etc. —*v.t.* **·died, ·dy·ing** To serve as a remedy for. [< L *re-* again + *mederi* to heal]

re·mem·ber (ri·mem′bər) *v.t.* 1. To bring back or recall again to the mind or memory. 2. To keep in mind carefully, as for a purpose. 3. To bear in mind as worthy of a reward, gift, etc. —*v.i.* 4. To have or use one's memory. —**to remember (one) to** To inform a person of the regard of: *Remember* me *to* your wife. [< L *re-* again + *memorare* to bring to mind] —**re·mem′ber·er** *n.*

re·mem·brance (ri·mem′brəns) *n.* 1. The act or power of remembering, or the state of being remembered. 2. That which is remembered. 3. *Often pl.* A memento; keepsake. 4. Mindful regard. [< OF]

re·mind (ri·mīnd′) *v.t.* To bring to (someone's) mind; cause to remember. —**re·mind′er** *n.* —**re·mind′ful** *adj.*

rem·i·nis·cence (rem′ə·nis′əns) *n.* 1. The recalling to mind of past incidents and events. 2. The narration of past experiences. [< L *re-* again + *memini* to remember] —**rem′i·nisce′** *v.i.* **·nisced, ·nisc·ing** —**rem′i·nis′cent** *adj.* —**rem′i·nis′cent·ly** *adv.*

re·miss (ri·mis′) *adj.* Slack or careless in matters requiring attention; negligent. [< L *re-* back + *mittere* to send] —**re·miss′·ness** *n.*

re·mis·sion (ri·mish′ən) *n.* 1. The act of remitting, or the state of being remitted. 2. Deliverance from penalty, debt, or obligation. 3. *Med.* Temporary abatement of a disease or pain. Also **re·mit·tal** (ri·mit′l). [See REMIT.]

re·mit (ri·mit′) *v.* **·mit·ted, ·mit·ting** *v.t.* 1. To send, as money in payment for goods; transmit. 2. To refrain from exacting or inflicting, as a penalty. 3. To pardon; forgive, as a sin or crime. 4. To abate; relax, as vigilance. 5. To refer or submit for judgment, settlement, etc. —*v.i.* 6. To send money, as in payment. 7. To diminish; abate. [< L *re-* back + *mittere* to send] —**re·mit′ta·ble** *adj.* —**re·mit′ter** or **re·mit′tor** *n.*

re·mit·tance (ri·mit′əns) *n.* The act of

sending money or credit; also, the money or credit so sent.

rem·nant (rem′nənt) *n.* 1. That which remains. 2. The piece of cloth, etc., left over after the last cutting. [< L *re-* back + *manere* to stay, remain]

re·mod·el (rē·mod′l) *v.t.* **·eled** or **·elled, ·el·ing** or **·el·ling** To make over or anew.

re·mon·strance (ri·mon′strəns) *n.* The act of remonstrating; protest; expostulation.

re·mon·strant (ri·mon′strənt) *adj.* Having the character of a remonstrance; expostulatory. —*n.* One who presents or signs a remonstrance.

re·mon·strate (ri·mon′strāt) *v.* **·strat·ed, ·strat·ing** *v.t.* 1. To say or plead in protest. —*v.i.* 2. To urge strong reasons against any course or action; protest; object. [< L *re-* again + *monstrare* to show] —**re·mon·stra·tion** (rē′mon·strā′shən, rem′ən-) *n.* —**re·mon′stra·tive** (-strə·tiv) *adj.* —**re·mon′stra·tor** (-strā·tər) *n.*

re·morse (ri·môrs′) *n.* The keen or hopeless anguish caused by a sense of guilt; distressing self-reproach. [< L *re-* again + *mordere* to bite] —**re·morse′ful** *adj.* —**re·morse′·ful·ly** *adv.* —**re·morse′ful·ness** *n.* —**re·morse′less** *adj.* —**re·morse′less·ly** *adv.* —**re·morse′less·ness** *n.*

re·mote (ri·mōt′) *adj.* **·mot·er, mot·est** 1. Located far from a specified place. 2. Distant in time. 3. Having slight relation or connection: a *remote* cousin. 4. Not obvious; slight. 5. Distant in manner; aloof. [< L *re-* again + *movere* to move] —**re·mote′ly** *adv.* —**re·mote′ness** *n.*

re·move (ri·mōōv′) *v.* **·moved, ·mov·ing** *v.t.* 1. To take or move away, as from one place to another. 2. To take off; doff, as a hat. 3. To get rid of; do away with: to *remove* abuses. 4. To displace or dismiss, as from office. 5. To take out; extract: with *from.* —*v.i.* 6. To change one's place of residence or business. 7. *Poetic* To go away. —*n.* 1. The act of removing, as one's business or belongings. 2. The space moved over in changing an object from one position to another. [< L *re-* again + *movere* to move] —**re·mov′a·bil′i·ty, re·mov′a·ble·ness** *n.* —**re·mov′a·ble** *adj.* —**re·mov′a·bly** *adv.* —**re·mov′al** *n.* —**re·mov′er** *n.*

re·moved (ri·mōōvd′) *adj.* Separated, as by intervening space, time, or relationship, or by difference in kind: a cousin twice *removed.* —**re·mov′ed·ness** *n.*

re·mu·ner·ate (ri·myōō′nə·rāt) *v.t.* **·at·ed, ·at·ing** To make just or adequate return to or for; pay or pay for. [< L *re-* again + *munus* gift] —**re·mu′ner·a·bil′i·ty** *n.* —**re·mu′ner·a·ble** *adj.* —**re·mu′ner·a′tion** *n.* —**re·mu·ner·a·tive** (ri·myōō′nə·rā′tiv, -nər·ə·tiv) *adj.* —**re·mu′ner·a′tive·ly** *adv.*

ren·ais·sance (ren′ə·säns′, -zäns′, ri·nā′·səns; *Fr.* rə·ne·säns′) *n.* 1. A new birth; resurrection; renascence. 2. *cap.* The revival of letters and art in Europe, marking the transition from medieval to modern history, roughly from the 14th through 16th c.: also *Renascence.* —*adj. cap.* Of or characteristic of the Renaissance. [< F < L *re-* again + *nasci* to be born]

re·nal (rē′nəl) *adj.* Of, pertaining to, affecting, or near the kidneys. [< L *renes* kidneys]

re·nas·cence (ri·nas′əns, -nās′-) *n.* 1. A rebirth; revival. 2. *cap.* The Renaissance. [< L *re-* again + *nasci* to be born] —**re·nas′cent** *adj.*

rend (rend) *v.* **rent** or **rend·ed, rend·ing** *v.t.* 1. To tear apart forcibly. 2. To pull or remove forcibly: with *away, from, off,* etc. 3. To pass through (the air) violently and noisily. 4. To distress (the heart, etc.). —*v.i.* 5. To split; part. [OE *rendan* to tear] —**rend′er** *n.*

ren·der (ren′dər) *v.t.* 1. To present for action, approval, payment, etc. 2. To provide; give: to *render* aid to the poor. 3. To give as due: to *render* obedience. 4. To perform: to *render* great service. 5. To represent or depict, as in painting. 6. To cause to be: to *render* a ship seaworthy. 7. To translate. 8. To melt and clarify, as lard. [< L *re-* back + *dare* to give] —**ren′der·a·ble** *adj.* —**ren′der·er** *n.*

ren·dez·vous (rän′dā·vōō, -də-; *Fr.* rän·dā·vōō′) *n. pl.* **·vous** (-vōōz, *Fr.* -vōō′) 1. An appointed place of meeting. 2. A meeting or an appointment to meet. —*v.t. & v.i.* **·voused** (-vōōd), **·vous·ing** (-vōō′ing) To assemble at a certain place or time. [< F < *se rendre* to betake oneself]

ren·di·tion (ren·dish′ən) *n.* 1. The interpretation of a text; a translation. 2. Artistic, dramatic, or musical interpretation. 3. The act of rendering; also, that which is rendered. [< obs. F < *rendre* to render]

ren·e·gade (ren′ə·gād) *n.* 1. One who forsakes his faith, etc. 2. A traitor; deserter. [< L *re-* again + *negare* to deny] —**ren′e·gade** *adj.*

re·nege (ri·nig′, -neg′) *v.i.* **·neged, ·neg·ing** 1. In card games, to fail to follow suit when able and required by the rules to do so; revoke. 2. *Informal* To fail to fulfill a promise. [See RENEGADE.] —**re·neg′er** *n.*

re·new (ri·nōō′, -nyōō′) *v.t.* 1. To make new or as if new again; restore to a former or sound condition. 2. To begin again; resume. 3. To repeat: to *renew* an oath. 4. To cause to continue in effect; extend. 5. To replenish or replace, as provisions. —*v.i.* 6. To become new again. [< RE- + NEW] —**re·new′a·ble** *adj.* —**re·new′al** *n.* —**re·new′ed·ly** *adv.*

ren·net (ren′it) *n.* 1. The mucous membrane lining the stomach of a suckling calf or sheep. 2. *Biochem.* A substance that yields rennin, obtained from the stomach of such an animal. [ME *rennen* to cause to run]

ren·nin (ren′in) *n. Biochem.* A milk-curdling enzyme present in rennet. [< RENNET]

re·nounce (ri·nouns′) *v.t.* **·nounced, ·nounc·ing** 1. To give up, esp. by formal statement. 2. To disown; repudiate. [< L *re-* back, against + *nuntiare* to report] —**re·nounce′·ment** *n.* —**re·nounc′er** *n.*

ren·o·vate (ren′ə·vāt) *v.t.* **·vat·ed, ·vat·ing** 1. To make as good as new; repair. 2. To renew; refresh. [< L *re-* again + *novare* to make new] —**ren′o·va′tion** *n.* —**ren′o·va′tor** *n.*

re·nown (ri·noun′) *n.* Exalted reputation; celebrity; fame. [< L *re-* again + *nominare* to name] —**re·nowned′** *adj.*

rent[1] (rent) *n.* 1. Compensation paid to a landlord or owner for the use of land, buildings, etc. 2. Similar payment for the use of any property, movable or fixed. 3. *Econ.*

Income derived by the owner from the use or cultivation of his land or property. —*v.t.* 1. To obtain temporary possession and use of for a rent. 2. To grant such temporary possession and use. —*v.i.* 3. To be let for rent. [< L *re-* back + *dare* to give] —**rent′·a·ble** *adj.* —**rent′er** *n.*

rent[2] (rent) Alternative past tense and past participle of REND. —*n.* 1. A hole or slit made by rending or tearing. 2. A violent separation; schism.

rent·al (ren′təl) *n.* 1. The revenue from rented property; also the property rented. 2. The act of renting. —*adj.* Of or for rent. [< AF]

re·nun·ci·a·tion (ri·nun′sē·ā′shən, -shē-) *n.* The act of renouncing or disclaiming; a repudiation. [< L *renunciatio, -onis* proclamation] —**re·nun′ci·a′tive** *adj.* . —**re·nun′ci·a·to′ry** (-ə·tôr′ē) *adj.*

re·or·der (rē·ôr′dər) *v.t.* 1. To order (goods) again. 2. To put back into order; rearrange. —*n.* Goods ordered again.

re·or·gan·ize (rē·ôr′gən·īz) *v.t. & v.i.* **·ized, ·iz·ing** To organize anew. —**re′or·gan·i·za′tion** *n.* —**re·or′gan·iz′er** *n.*

rep (rep) *n.* A fabric having a crosswise rib: also spelled *repp.* [< F *reps,* prob. < E *ribs*]

re·pair[1] (ri·pâr′) *v.t.* 1. To restore to sound or good condition after damage, injury, etc. 2. To make up, as a loss; compensate for. —*n.* 1. The act or process of repairing. 2. Condition after use or after repairing: in good *repair.* [< L *re-* again + *parare* to prepare] —**re·pair′er** *n.*

re·pair[2] (ri·pâr′) *v.i.* To betake oneself; go: to *repair* to the garden. [< L *re-* again + *patria* native land]

re·pair·man (ri·pâr′man′, -mən) *n. pl.* **·men** (-men′, -mən) One whose work is to make repairs.

rep·a·ra·ble (rep′ər·ə·bəl) *adj.* Capable of being repaired. Also **re·pair·a·ble** (ri·pâr′ə·bəl). —**rep′a·ra·bil′i·ty** *n.* —**rep′a·ra·bly** *adv.*

rep·a·ra·tion (rep′ə·rā′shən) *n.* 1. The act of making amends; atonement. 2. *pl.* Indemnities paid by defeated countries for acts of war. [See REPAIR[1].] —**re·par·a·tive** (ri·par′ə·tiv) *adj.*

rep·ar·tee (rep′ər·tē′, -är-, -tā′) *n.* 1. Conversation marked by quick and witty replies. 2. A witty or quick reply; a sharp rejoinder. [< OF *repartir* to depart again, reply]

re·past (ri·past′) *n.* 1. Food taken at a meal. 2. A meal. [< L *re-* again + *pascere* to feed]

re·pa·tri·ate (*v.* rē·pā′trē·āt; *n.* -it) *v.t.* **·at·ed, ·at·ing** To return to one's own country or to the place of one's citizenship. —*n.* One who has been repatriated. [< L *re-* again + *patria* native land] —**re·pa′tri·a′tion** *n.*

re·pay (ri·pā′) *v.* **·paid, ·pay·ing** *v.t.* 1. To pay back; refund. 2. To pay back or refund something to. 3. To give a reward or inflict a penalty for. —*v.i.* 4. To make repayment or requital. —**re·pay′a·ble** *adj.* —**re·pay′ment** *n.*

re·peal (ri·pēl′) *v.t.* To rescind, as a law; revoke. —*n.* The act of repealing; revocation. [< OF *re-* back, again + *apeler* to call] —**re·peal′a·ble** *adj.* —**re·peal′er** *n.*

re·peat (ri·pēt′) *v.t.* 1. To say again; iterate. 2. To recite from memory. 3. To do, make, or experience again. —*v.i.* 4. To say or do something again. —*n.* 1. The act of repeating; a repetition. 2. Anything repeated. [< L *re-* again + *petere* to seek, demand] —**re·peat′a·ble** *adj.*

re·peat·ed (ri·pē′tid) *adj.* Occurring or spoken again and again; reiterated. —**re·peat′ed·ly** *adv.*

re·peat·er (ri·pē′tər) *n.* 1. One who or that which repeats. 2. A firearm that can shoot several bullets without reloading. 3. One who has been repeatedly imprisoned.

re·pel (ri·pel′) *v.* **·pelled, ·pel·ling** *v.t.* 1. To force or drive back; repulse. 2. To reject; refuse, as a suggestion. 3. To cause to feel distaste or aversion. 4. To push or keep away; resist. —*v.i.* 5. To act so as to drive something back or away. [< L *re-* back + *pellere* to drive] —**re·pel′ler** *n.*

re·pel·lent (ri·pel′ənt) *adj.* 1. Serving, tending, or having power to repel. 2. Repugnant; repulsive. —*n.* Something that repels. —**re·pel′len·cy** *n.*

re·pent (ri·pent′) *v.t. & v.i.* To feel remorse or regret for (an action, etc.). [< L *re-* again + *poenitere* to cause to repent] —**re·pen′tance** *n.* —**re·pen′tant** *adj.* —**re·pen′tant·ly** *adv.* —**re·pent′er** *n.*

re·peo·ple (rē·pē′pəl) *v.t.* **·pled, ·pling** 1. To people anew. 2. To provide again with animals; restock.

re·per·cus·sion (rē′pər·kush′ən) *n.* 1. A stroke or blow given in return; also, the recoil after impact. 2. The indirect result of something; aftereffect. [< L *re-* again + *percutere* to strike] —**re′per·cus′sive** (-kus′iv) *adj.*

rep·er·toire (rep′ər·twär, -twôr) *n.* The songs, plays, operas, or the like, that a person or company is prepared to perform: also called *repertory.* [See REPERTORY.]

rep·er·to·ry (rep′ər·tôr′ē) *n. pl.* **·ries** 1. Repertoire. 2. A repository. 3. The presentation of several plays, often alternately, by a theatrical company in one season. [< LL *repertorium* inventory]

rep·e·ti·tion (rep′ə·tish′ən) *n.* 1. The doing, making, or saying of something again. 2. That which is repeated. —**re·pet·i·tive** (ri·pet′ə·tiv) *adj.* —**re·pet′i·tive·ly** *adv.*

rep·e·ti·tious (rep′ə·tish′əs) *adj.* Characterized by or containing repetition, esp. useless or tedious repetition. —**rep′e·ti′tious·ly** *adv.* —**rep′e·ti′tious·ness** *n.*

re·phrase (rē·frāz′) *v.t.* **·phrased, ·phras·ing** To express in a new way.

re·pine (ri·pīn′) *v.i.* **·pined, ·pin·ing** To be discontented or fretful; complain. [< RE- + PINE[2]] —**re·pin′er** *n.*

re·place (ri·plās′) *v.t.* **·placed, ·plac·ing** 1. To put back in place. 2. To take or fill the place of; supersede. 3. To refund; repay. —**re·place′a·ble** *adj.* —**re·place′ment** *n.* —**re·plac′er** *n.*

re·plen·ish (ri·plen′ish) *v.t.* 1. To fill again, as something wholly or partially emptied. 2. To supply again; restock. [< L *re-* again + *plenus* full] —**re·plen′ish·er** *n.* —**re·plen′ish·ment** *n.*

re·plete (ri·plēt′) *adj.* 1. Full or supplied to the uttermost. 2. Gorged with food or drink; sated. [< L *re-* again + *plere* to fill] **—re·ple′tion** *n.*

rep·li·ca (rep′lə·kə) *n.* Any close copy or reproduction, esp. of a work of art. [< Ital. < L *replicare* to reply]

rep·li·cate (rep′lə·kāt) *v.t.* **·cat·ed, ·cat·ing** 1. To make a replica of; reproduce. 2. To fold over. [See REPLY.]

rep·li·ca·tion (rep′lə·kā′shən) *n.* 1. A reply. 2. A copy or duplicate. **—rep′li·ca′tive** *adj.*

re·ply (ri·plī′) *v.* **·plied, ·ply·ing** *v.i.* 1. To give an answer orally or in writing. 2. To respond by some act, gesture, etc. *—v.t.* 3. To say in answer: often with a clause as object. *—n. pl.* **·plies** Something said, written, or done by way of answer. [< L *replicare* to fold back, answer to] **—re·pli′er** *n.*

re·port (ri·pôrt′) *v.t.* 1. To make or give an account of, often formally. 2. To relate, as information obtained by investigation. 3. To complain about, esp. to a superior. *—v.i.* 4. To make a report. 5. To act as a reporter. 6. To present oneself, as for duty. *—n.* 1. That which is reported. 2. A statement or record of an investigation, transaction, etc. 3. Common talk; rumor. 4. An explosive sound. [< L *re-* back + *portare* to carry] **—re·port′a·ble** *adj.*

re·port·age (ri·pôr′tij, rep′ər·täzh′) *n.* 1. The act, process, or style of reporting news. 2. Writing in journalistic form.

report card A periodic statement of a pupil's scholastic record.

re·port·ed·ly (ri·pôr′tid·lē) *adv.* According to report.

re·port·er (ri·pôr′tər) *n.* 1. One who reports; esp., one who reports news for a newspaper, magazine, etc. 2. One who reports cases in court for official publication. **—rep·or·to·ri·al** (rep′ər·tôr′ē·əl) *adj.*

re·pose[1] (ri·pōz′) *n.* 1. The act of taking rest, or the state of being at rest. 2. Calm; peace. 3. Ease of manner; graceful and dignified calmness. *—v.* **·posed, ·pos·ing** *v.t.* 1. To lay or place in a position of rest. *—v.i.* 2. To lie at rest. [< LL *re-* again + *pausare* to pause] **—re·pos′al** *n.* **—re·pose′ful** *adj.* **—re·pose′ful·ly** *adv.* **—re·pos′er** *n.*

re·pose[2] (ri·pōz′) *v.t.* **·posed, ·pos·ing** To place, as confidence or hope: with *in.* [< L *reponere* to put back]

re·pos·i·to·ry (ri·poz′ə·tôr′ē) *n. pl.* **·ries** 1. A place in which goods are or may be stored. 2. A person to whom a secret is entrusted. 3. A receptacle for relics. [< L *re-* back, again + *ponere* to place]

re·pos·sess (rē′pə·zes′) *v.t.* To have possession of again; regain possession of, esp. in default of payment. **—re′pos·ses′sion** (-zesh′ən) *n.*

repp (rep) See REP.

rep·re·hend (rep′ri·hend′) *v.t.* To criticize sharply; blame or censure. [< L *re-* back + *prehendere* to hold] **—rep′re·hen′sion** (-hen′shən) *n.* **—rep′re·hen′sive** (-hen′siv) *adj.* **—rep′re·hen′sive·ly** *adv.*

rep·re·hen·si·ble (rep′ri·hen′sə·bəl) *adj.* Deserving blame or censure. **—rep′re·hen′si·bil′i·ty, rep′re·hen′si·ble·ness** *n.* **—rep′re·hen′si·bly** *adv.*

rep·re·sent (rep′ri·zent′) *v.t.* 1. To serve as the symbol, expression, or designation of; symbolize. 2. To depict; portray, as in painting or sculpture. 3. To act the part of; impersonate. 4. To serve as or be the delegate, agent, etc., of. 5. To describe: They *represented* him as a genius. 6. To serve as an example, specimen, type, etc., of. [< L *re-* again + *praesentare* to exhibit] **—rep′re·sent′a·ble** *adj.* **—rep′re·sent′a·bil′i·ty** *n.*

rep·re·sen·ta·tion (rep′ri·zen·tā′shən) *n.* 1. The act of representing or the state of being represented. 2. Anything that represents, as a picture, a statue, etc. 3. A dramatic performance. 4. The right of acting authoritatively for others, esp. in a legislative body. 5. Representatives collectively. 6. A formal statement setting forth a proposal, objection. etc. **—rep′re·sen·ta′tion·al** *adj.*

rep·re·sen·ta·tive (rep′ri·zen′tə·tiv) *adj.* 1. Typifying or typical of a group or class. 2. Acting as a qualified agent. 3. Made up of representatives. 4. Based on or pertaining to the political principle of representation. *—n.* 1. One who or that which is fit to stand as a type; a typical instance. 2. One who is a qualified agent of any kind. 3. A member of a legislative body, esp. of the lower house. **—rep′re·sen′ta·tive·ly** *adv.* **—rep′re·sen′ta·tive·ness** *n.*

re·press (ri·pres′) *v.t.* 1. To keep under restraint or control. 2. To put down; quell, as a rebellion. 3. *Psychoanal.* To effect the repression of, as fears, impulses, etc. [< L *repressus*, pp. of *reprimere* to press back, curb] **—re·press′i·ble** *adj.* **—re·pres′sive** *adj.* **—re·pres′sive·ly** *adv.* **—re·pres′sive·ness** *n.* **—re·pres′sor** *n.*

re·pres·sion (ri·presh′ən) *n.* 1. The act of repressing or the condition of being repressed. 2. *Psychoanal.* The exclusion from consciousness of painful or unacceptable memories, etc.

re·prieve (ri·prēv′) *v.t.* **·prieved, ·priev·ing** 1. To suspend temporarily the execution of a sentence upon. 2. To relieve for a time from suffering, danger, or trouble. *—n.* 1. The temporary suspension of a sentence, or the document ordering it. 2. Temporary relief of pain or ill. 3. The act of reprieving, or the state of being reprieved. [< earlier *repry* < F *rependre* to take back] **—re·priev′a·ble** *adj.*

rep·ri·mand (rep′rə·mand) *v.t.* To reprove sharply or formally. *—n.* Severe reproof or censure. [< F *réprimande* reproof]

re·print (*n.* rē′print′; *v.* rē·print′) *n.* Printed work that is a reproduction of the original. *—v.t.* To print a new edition or copy of. **—re·print′er** *n.*

re·pri·sal (ri·prī′zəl) *n.* 1. A retaliatory act by one nation against another; also, an instance of such an act. 2. Any act of retaliation. [< L *re-* back + *prehendere* to hold]

re·prise (rə·prēz′, -prīz′) *n.* *Music* A repeated phrase; also, the repetition of a performance. [See REPRISAL.]

re·proach (ri·prōch′) *v.t.* 1. To charge with or blame for something wrong; rebuke; censure. 2. To bring discredit or disgrace upon. *—n.* 1. The act of reproaching; censure; rebuke. 2. A cause of blame or disgrace. 3. Disgrace; discredit. [< OF *reprochier*] **—re·proach′a·ble** *adj.* **—re·**

proach′a·ble·ness *n.* —**re·proach′a·bly** *adv.* —**re·proach′er** *n.* —**re·proach′ful** *adj.* —**re·proach′ful·ly** *adv.* —**re·proach′ful·ness** *n.*

rep·ro·bate (rep′rə·bāt) *adj.* Having lost all sense of duty; depraved. —*n.* A depraved or profligate person. [See REPROVE.] —**rep′ro·ba′tion** *n.* —**rep′ro·ba′tive** *adj.*

re·pro·duce (rē′prə·dōōs′, -dyōōs′) *v.* **·duced, ·duc·ing** *v.t.* 1. To make a copy, image, or reproduction of. 2. *Biol.* To produce (offspring) by sexual or asexual generation. 3. To produce again. —*v.i.* 4. To produce offspring. 5. To undergo copying, reproduction, etc. —**re′pro·duc′er** *n.* —**re′pro·duc′i·ble** *adj.*

re·pro·duc·tion (rē′prə·duk′shən) *n.* 1. The act or power of reproducing. 2. *Biol.* The process by which an animal or plant generates another of its kind. 3. That which is reproduced, as a copy of a picture. —**re′pro·duc′tive** *adj.* —**re′pro·duc′tive·ly** *adv.*

re·proof (ri·prōōf′) *n.* 1. The act of reproving. 2. A rebuke; blame; censure. Also **re·prov·al** (ri·prōō′vəl).

re·prove (ri′prōōv′) *v.t.* **·proved, ·prov·ing** 1. To censure, as for a fault; rebuke. 2. To express disapproval of (an act). [< LL *re-* again + *probare* to test] —**re·prov′a·ble** *adj.* —**re·prov′er** *n.* —**re·prov′ing·ly** *adv.*

rep·tile (rep′til, -tīl) *n.* Any of a class of cold-blooded, air-breathing vertebrates, including the snakes, crocodiles, lizards, and turtles. —*adj.* Of or resembling a reptile. [< LL *repere* to creep] —**rep·til′i·an** (-til′ē·ən) *adj. & n.*

re·pub·lic (ri·pub′lik) *n.* A state in which the sovereignty resides in the people and the legislative and administrative powers are lodged in officers elected by them. [< L *respublica* commonwealth]

re·pub·li·can (ri·pub′li·kən) *adj.* 1. Of, like, or suitable for a republic. 2. Supporting republican government. 3. *cap.* Pertaining to or belonging to the Republican Party. —*n.* 1. One who advocates a republican form of government. 2. *cap.* A member of the Republican Party.

re·pub·li·can·ism (ri·pub′li·kən·iz′əm) *n.* 1. The theory or principles of republican government. 2. Advocacy of or adherence to republican principles. 3. *cap.* The policy and principles of the Republican Party.

Republican Party One of the two major political parties of the U.S., founded in 1854 in opposition to the extension of slavery.

re·pu·di·ate (ri·pyōō′dē·āt) *v.t.* **·at·ed, ·at·ing** 1. To refuse to accept as valid or binding; reject. 2. To cast off; disown, as a son. [< L *repudiare* to divorce] —**re·pu′di·a′tion** *n.* —**re·pu′di·a′tive** *adj.* —**re·pu′di·a′tor** *n.*

re·pug·nant (ri·pug′nənt) *adj.* Offensive to taste or feeling; exciting aversion or repulsion. [< L *re-* back + *pugnare* to fight] —**re·pug′nance, re·pug′nan·cy** *n.*

re·pulse (ri·puls′) *v.t.* **·pulsed, ·puls·ing** 1. To drive back; repel, as an attacking force. 2. To repel by coldness, discourtesy, etc.; reject; rebuff. —*n.* 1. The act of repulsing or the state of being repulsed. 2. Rejection; refusal. [< L *repulsus*, pp. of *repellere* to repel] —**re·puls′er** *n.*

re·pul·sion (ri·pul′shən) *n.* 1. The act of repelling, or the state of being repelled. 2. Aversion; repugnance. 3. *Physics* The mutual action of two bodies that tends to drive them apart.

re·pul·sive (ri·pul′siv) *adj.* 1. Exciting feelings of dislike, disgust, or horror; grossly offensive. 2. Such as to forbid approach or familiarity; forbidding. 3. Acting to repel or force back: *repulsive* forces. —**re·pul′sive·ly** *adv.* —**re·pul′sive·ness** *n.*

rep·u·ta·ble (rep′yə·tə·bəl) *adj.* Having a good reputation; estimable; honorable. —**rep′u·ta·bil′i·ty** *n.* —**rep′u·ta·bly** *adv.*

rep·u·ta·tion (rep′yə·tā′shən) *n.* 1. The general estimation in which a person or thing is held by others. 2. The state of being in high regard or esteem. [See REPUTE.]

re·pute (ri·pyōōt′) *v.t.* **·put·ed, ·put·ing** To consider to be as specified; esteem: They are *reputed* to be an intelligent people. —*n.* 1. Reputation or regard. 2. Public opinion; general report. [< L *reputare* to reckon, be reputed]

re·put·ed (ri·pyōō′tid) *adj.* Generally supposed: a *reputed* criminal. —**re·put′ed·ly** *adv.*

re·quest (ri·kwest′) *v.t.* 1. To express a desire for. 2. To ask (a person) to do a favor, answer an inquiry, etc. —*n.* 1. The act of requesting; petition. 2. That which is requested. —*adj.* Having been asked for: a *request* program. [See REQUIRE.]

re·qui·em (rek′wē·əm, rāk′-) *n.* 1. Any musical composition or service for the dead. 2. *Often cap. Eccl.* In the Roman Catholic Church, a solemn mass sung for the dead: also **Requiem mass.** 3. *Often cap.* A musical setting for such a mass. [< L *requies* rest]

re·quire (ri·kwīr′) *v.* **·quired, ·quir·ing** *v.t.* 1. To have need of; find necessary. 2. To demand authoritatively; insist upon. —*v.i.* 3. To make demand or request. [< L *re-* again + *quaerere* to ask, seek] —**re·quire′ment** *n.*

req·ui·site (rek′wə·zit) *adj.* Required by the nature of things or by circumstances; indispensable. [See REQUEST.] —**req′ui·site** *n.* —**req′ui·site·ly** *adv.* —**req′ui·site·ness** *n.*

req·ui·si·tion (rek′wə·zish′ən) *n.* 1. A formal request or demand, as for supplies. 2. The state of being required. —*v.t.* To demand or take upon requisition. [See REQUIRE.]

re·quite (ri·kwīt′) *v.t.* **·quit·ed, ·quit·ing** 1. To make equivalent return for, as kindness, service, or injury; make up for. 2. To avenge; retaliate. [< RE- + *quite*, obs. var. of QUIT] —**re·quit′al** *adj.* —**re·quit′er** *n.*

rere·dos (rir′dos) *n.* *Chiefly Brit.* An ornamental screen behind an altar. [< AF *rere* rear + *dos* back]

re·run (*n.* rē′run; *v.* rē·run′) *n.* The presenting of a motion picture, television show, etc., after its original run; also, the picture, show, etc., so presented. —*v.t.* **·ran, ·run·ning** To run again or a second time.

re·sale (rē′sāl, rē·sāl′) *n.* The act of selling again. —**re·sal′a·ble** *adj.*

re·scind (ri·sind′) *v.t.* To make void, as an act; abrogate; repeal. [< L *re-* back + *scindere* to cut] —**re·scind′a·ble** *adj.* —**re·scind′er** *n.* —**re·scis·sion** (ri·zish′ən) *n.*

res·cue (res′kyōō) *v.t.* **·cued, ·cu·ing** To save or free from danger, captivity, evil, etc.;

deliver. —*n.* The act of rescuing; deliverance. [< OF *re-* back + *escorre* to move, shake] —**res′cu·a·ble** *adj.* —**res′cu·er** *n.*

re·search (ri·sûrch′, rē′sûrch) *n.* 1. Diligent, protracted investigation; studious inquiry. 2. A systematic investigation of some phenomenon. —*v.t.* & *v.i.* To undertake research (on). [< F *re-* back + *chercher* to seek] —**re·search′er** *n.*

re·sec·tion (ri·sek′shən) *n. Surg.* The removal of part of a bone, organ, etc.

re·sem·blance (ri·zem′bləns) *n.* The quality of similarity in nature, form, etc.; likeness.

re·sem·ble (ri·zem′bəl) *v.t.* **·bled, ·bling** To be similar to in appearance, quality, or character. [< OF *re-* again + *sembler* to seem] —**re·sem′bler** *n.*

re·sent (ri·zent′) *v.t.* To feel or show resentment at; be indignant at. [< F *re-* again + *sentir* to feel] —**re·sent′ful** *adj.* —**re·sent′ful·ly** *adv.* —**re·sent′ful·ness** *n.*

re·sent·ment (ri·zent′mənt) *n.* Anger and ill will in view of real or fancied wrong or injury.

re·ser·pine (ri·sûr′pēn, -pin) *n.* A drug originally prepared from alkaloids found in rauwolfia, used as a tranquilizer. [< NL *Rauwolfia serpentina*, genus name + -INE[2]]

res·er·va·tion (rez′ər·vā′shən) *n.* 1. The act of reserving. 2. That which is reserved, kept back, or withheld. 3. A qualification or condition, as to an opinion or commitment. 4. An arrangement to reserve a seat on a train, hotel room, etc., in advance. 5. A tract of government land reserved for a special purpose, as for the use and occupancy of an Indian tribe. [< LL *reservatio, -onis*]

re·serve (ri·zûrv′) *v.t.* **·served, ·serv·ing** 1. To hold back or set aside for special or future use. 2. To keep as one's own; retain. 3. To arrange for ahead of time; have set aside for one's use. —*n.* 1. Something stored up for future use or set apart for a particular purpose. 2. A reservation of land. 3. In banking, the amount of funds reserved in order to meet anticipated demands. 4. The act of reserving. 5. Silence or reticence as to one's feelings, opinions, or affairs. 6. *Usu. pl.* A fighting force held back from action to meet possible emergencies. 7. A branch of the armed forces composed of persons subject to call in emergencies. —*adj.* Held in reserve; constituting a reserve. [< L *re-* back + *servare* to keep] —**re·serv′·a·ble** *adj.* —**re·serv′er** *n.*

re·served (ri·zûrvd′) *adj.* 1. Characterized by reserve of manner; distant; undemonstrative. 2. Retained; kept back. —**re·serv′·ed·ly** *adv.* —**re·serv′ed·ness** *n.*

re·serv·ist (ri·zûr′vist) *n.* A member of a military reserve.

res·er·voir (rez′ər·vwôr, -vwär, -vôr) *n.* A lake, either natural or artificial, for collecting and containing a supply of water, as for use in a city. [< F *réservoir*]

re·set (rē·set′) *v.t.* **·set, ·set·ting** To set again. —**re′set′** *n.*

re·side (ri·zīd′) *v.i.* **·sid·ed, ·sid·ing** 1. To dwell for a considerable time; make one's home; live. 2. To exist as an attribute or quality: with *in*. 3. To be vested: with *in*. [< L *residere* to abide]

res·i·dence (rez′ə·dəns) *n.* 1. The place or the house where one resides. 2. The act of residing. 3. The length of time one resides in a place. Also *residency.* [< LL *residentia*]

res·i·den·cy (rez′ə·dən·sē) *n. pl.* **·cies** 1. Residence. 2. An official abode of the representative of a government. 3. *Med.* The period of clinical training served by a physician in his chosen specialty.

res·i·dent (rez′ə·dənt) *n.* 1. One who resides or dwells in a place. 2. A diplomatic representative residing at a foreign seat of government. 3. *Med.* One serving a residency. —*adj.* 1. Having a residence. 2. Abiding in a place in connection with one's official work: a *resident* physician. 3. Not migratory: said of certain birds.

res·i·den·tial (rez′ə·den′shəl) *adj.* 1. Of, pertaining to, or restricted to residences. 2. Consisting of or suitable for residences or living quarters.

re·sid·u·al (ri·zij′o͞o·əl) *adj.* 1. Having the nature of a remainder. 2. Left over as a residue. —*n.* 1. Something that remains. 2. A payment to a writer, actor, etc., for each showing of a television commercial or program.

res·i·due (rez′ə·do͞o, -dyo͞o) *n.* 1. A remainder or surplus after a part has been separated or otherwise treated. 2. *Chem.* Insoluble matter left after filtration or separation from a liquid. 3. *Law* The portion of an estate that remains after all charges, debts, and particular bequests have been satisfied: also **re·sid·u·um** (ri·zij′o͞o·əm). [< L *re-* back + *sedere* to sit]

re·sign (ri·zīn′) *v.t.* 1. To give up, as a position, office, or trust. 2. To give over (oneself, one's mind, etc.), as to fate or domination. —*v.i.* 3. To resign a position, etc. [< L *re-* back + *signare* to seal] —**re·sign′er** *n.*

res·ig·na·tion (rez′ig·nā′shən) *n.* 1. The act of resigning, as a position or office. 2. A written declaration of such intent. 3. The quality of being submissive or acquiescent.

re·signed (ri·zīnd′) *adj.* Characterized by resignation; submissive. —**re·sign′ed·ly** *adv.*

re·sil·ient (ri·zil′yənt) *adj.* Springing back to a former shape, position, or state. [< L *re-* back + *salire* to leap] —**re·sil′ience, re·sil′ien·cy** *n.* —**re·sil′ient·ly** *adv.*

res·in (rez′in) *n.* 1. A yellowish substance exuded from certain plants and trees. 2. Any similar synthetic substance, esp. one used in the making of plastics. 3. Rosin. —*v.t.* To apply resin to. [< Gk. *rhētinē*] —**res′i·nous** *adj.*

re·sist (ri·zist′) *v.t.* 1. To strive against; act counter to. 2. To be proof against; withstand. —*v.i.* 3. To offer opposition. [< L *resistere* to withstand] —**re·sist′er** *n.* —**re·sist′i·bil′i·ty** *n.* —**re·sist′i·ble** *adj.* —**re·sist′i·bly** *adv.* —**re·sist′less** *adj.* —**re·sist′less·ly** *adv.*

re·sis·tance (ri·zis′təns) *n.* 1. The act of resisting. 2. Any force tending to hinder motion. 3. *Electr.* The opposition that a conductor offers to the passage of a current, resulting from the conversion of energy into heat, light, etc. 4. The underground and guerrilla movement opposing an occupying power. —**re·sis′tant** *n.*

re·sis·tive (ri·zis′tiv) *adj.* Having or exercising the power of resistance. —**re·sis′·tive·ly** *adv.*

re·sis·tiv·i·ty (rē′zis·tiv′ə·tē) *n. pl.* **·ties** The capacity to resist, or the degree of that capacity.

re·sis·tor (ri·zis′tər) *n. Electr.* A device, as a coil of wire, for introducing resistance into an electrical circuit.

re·sole (rē·sōl′) *v.t.* **·soled, ·sol·ing** To sole (a shoe, etc.) again.

res·o·lute (rez′ə·lo͞ot) *adj.* 1. Having a fixed purpose; determined. 2. Bold; unflinching. [See RESOLVE.] —**res′o·lute·ly** *adv.* —**res′o·lute·ness** *n.*

res·o·lu·tion (rez′ə·lo͞o′shən) *n.* 1. The act of resolving. 2. The state of being resolute; active fortitude. 3. The purpose or course resolved upon. 4. The separation of anything into component parts. 5. A proposition offered to or adopted by an assembly. —**res′o·lu′tion·er, res′o·lu′tion·ist** *n.*

re·solve (ri·zolv′) *v.* **·solved, ·solv·ing** *v.t.* 1. To decide or determine (to do something). 2. To cause to decide or determine. 3. To separate or break down into constituent parts. 4. To make clear; explain or solve, as a problem. 5. To explain away; remove (doubts, etc.). 6. To state or decide by vote, as in a legislative assembly. 7. *Optics* To make distinguishable the structure or parts of, as in a microscope or telescope. —*v.i.* 8. To make up one's mind; arrive at a decision: with *on* or *upon.* —*n.* 1. Fixity of purpose; resolution. 2. A fixed determination; a resolution. [< L *re-* again + *solvere* to loosen] —**re·solv′a·bil′i·ty** *n.* —**re·solv′a·ble** *adj.* —**re·solv′er** *n.*

re·solved (ri·zolvd′) *adj.* Fixed or set in purpose; determined. —**re·solv′ed·ly** *adv.*

res·o·nant (rez′ə·nənt) *adj.* 1. Sending back or prolonging sound. 2. Resounding. 3. Intensifying sound. [< L *re-* again + *sonare* to sound] —**res′o·nance** *n.* —**res′o·nant·ly** *adv.*

res·o·nate (rez′ə·nāt) *v.i.* **·nat·ed, ·nat·ing** 1. To exhibit enhanced or intensified sound. 2. To manifest sympathetic vibration, as a resonator. [See RESONANT.]

res·o·na·tor (rez′ə·nā′tər) *n.* Any device that resounds or increases sounds by resonance. [< NL]

re·sort (ri·zôrt′) *v.i.* 1. To go frequently or habitually; repair. 2. To have recourse; apply or betake oneself for relief or aid: with *to.* —*n.* 1. A place frequented for recreation or rest. 2. The use of something as a means; a recourse. [< OF *re-* again + *sortir* to go out] —**re·sort′er** *n.*

re·sound (ri·zound′) *v.i.* 1. To be filled with sound; echo; reverberate. 2. To make a loud, prolonged, or echoing sound. 3. To become reknown or be extolled. —*v.t.* 4. To give back (a sound, etc.). [< L *resonare* to echo]

re·sound·ing (ri·zound′ing) *adj.* 1. Reverberating. 2. Emphatic; unmistakable: a *resounding* success.

re·source (ri·sôrs′, -zors′, rē′sôrs) *n.* 1. That which is resorted to for aid or support; resort. 2. *pl.* Available means or property; any natural advantages or products. 3. Skill or ingenuity in meeting any situation; resourcefulness. [< L *resurgere* to rise again]

re·source·ful (ri·sôrs′fəl, -zors′-) *adj.* Capable of dealing with problems. —**re·source′ful·ly** *adv.* —**re·source′ful·ness** *n.*

re·spect (ri·spekt′) *v.t.* 1. To have deferential regard for; esteem. 2. To regard as inviolable; avoid intruding upon. 3. To have relation or reference to; concern. —*n.* 1. Regard for and appreciation of worth; honor and esteem. 2. *pl.* Expressions of consideration or esteem; compliments: to pay one's *respects.* 3. Conformity to duty or obligation: *respect* for the law. 4. The condition of being honored or respected. 5. Reference or relation: usu. with *to*: with *respect* to profits. [< L *re-* again + *specere* to look] —**re·spect′er** *n.* —**re·spect′ful** *adj.* —**re·spect′ful·ly** *adv.*

re·spect·a·ble (ri·spek′tə·bəl) *adj.* 1. Deserving of respect; also, respected. 2. Being of moderate size or excellence; average. 3. Having a good appearance; presentable. 4. Conventionally correct or socially acceptable in conduct. —**re·spect′a·bil′i·ty** *n.* —**re·spect′a·bly** *adv.*

re·spect·ing (ri·spek′ting) *prep.* In relation to; regarding.

re·spec·tive (ri·spek′tiv) *adj.* Individual; separate or particular: our *respective* careers.

re·spec·tive·ly (ri·spek′tiv·lē) *adv.* In the order designated: The first three go to John, James, and William *respectively.*

res·pi·ra·tion (res′pə·rā′shən) *n.* 1. The act of inhaling and exhaling; breathing. 2. The process by which an organism takes in oxygen and gives off carbon dioxide and other products of oxidation. [< L *re-* again + *spirare* to breathe] —**re·spir·a·to·ry** (res′pər·ə·tôr′ē, ri·spīr′ə·tôr′ē) *adj.* —**res·pire** (ri·spīr′) *v.i. & v.t.* **·spired, ·spir·ing**

res·pi·ra·tor (res′pə·rā′tər) *n.* 1. A screen, as of fine gauze, worn over the mouth or nose as a protection against dust, etc. 2. A device worn over the nose and mouth for the inhalation of oxygen, etc. 3. An apparatus for artificial respiration.

res·pite (res′pit) *n.* 1. Postponement; delay. 2. An interval of rest. —*v.t.* **·pit·ed, ·pit·ing** 1. To relieve by a pause or rest. 2. To grant delay in the execution of (a penalty, sentence, etc.). [< L *respectus* regard, refuge]

re·splen·dent (ri·splen′dənt) *adj.* Shining with brilliant luster; splendid; gorgeous. [< L *re-* back + *splendere* to shine] —**re·splen′dence, re·splen′den·cy** *n.* —**re·splen′dent·ly** *adv.*

re·spond (ri·spond′) *v.i.* 1. To give an answer; reply. 2. To act in reply or return; react. —*v.t.* 3. To say in answer; reply. —*n. Archit.* A pilaster or similar feature placed against a wall to receive an arch. [< L *re-* back + *spondere* to pledge] —**re·spon′der** *n.*

re·spon·dent (ri·spon′dənt) *adj.* Answering; responsive. —*n.* 1. One who responds or answers. 2. *Law* A defendant. —**re·spon′dence, re·spon′den·cy** *n.*

re·sponse (ri·spons′) *n.* 1. The act of responding, or that which is responded; reply; reaction. 2. *Eccl.* A portion of a liturgy or church service said or sung by the congregation or choir in reply to the officiating priest. 3. *Biol.* The behavior of an organism resulting from a stimulus or influence; a reaction.

re·spon·si·bil·i·ty (ri·spon′sə·bil′ə·tē) *n.*

pl. **·ties** 1. The state of being responsible or accountable: also **re·spon′si·ble·ness.** 2. That for which one is answerable; a duty or trust.

re·spon·si·ble (ri·spon′sə·bəl) *adj.* 1. Answerable legally or morally for the discharge of a duty, trust, or debt. 2. Having capacity to distinguish between right and wrong. 3. Having sufficient property or means for the payment of debts. 4. Involving accountability or obligation. [See RESPOND.] **—re·spon′si·bly** *adv.*

re·spon·sive (ri·spon′siv) *adj.* 1. Inclined or ready to respond. 2. Constituting, or of the nature of, response or reply. 3. Characterized by or containing responses. **—re·spon′sive·ly** *adv.* **—re·spon′sive·ness** *n.*

rest[1] (rest) *v.i.* 1. To cease working, exerting oneself, etc., so as to refresh oneself. 2. To obtain ease or refreshment by lying down, sleeping, etc. 3. To be at peace; be tranquil. 4. To remain unchanged. 5. To be supported; stand, lean, lie, or sit: with *against, on,* or *upon.* 6. To be founded or based: with *on* or *upon.* 7. To be placed as a burden or responsibility: with *on* or *upon.* 8. To be or lie in a specified place. 9. *Law* To cease presenting evidence in a case. —*v.t.* 10. To give rest to; refresh by rest. 11. To put, lay, lean, etc., as for support or rest. 12. To direct (the gaze, eyes, etc.). 13. *Law* To cease presenting evidence in (a case). —*n.* 1. The act or state of resting; repose. 2. Freedom from disturbance or disquiet; tranquillity. 3. Sleep. 4. That on which anything rests; a support. 5. A place of repose or quiet; a stopping place; abode. 6. *Music* A pause or interval of silence that corresponds to the time value of a note. 7. In prosody, a pause in a verse. [OE *restan*] **—rest′er** *n.*

rest[2] (rest) *n.* 1. That which remains or is left over; a remainder. 2. (*construed as pl.*) Those remaining or not enumerated; the others. —*v.i.* To be and remain; stay: *Rest* content. [< L *re-* back + *stare* to stand]

re·state (rē·stāt′) *v.t.* **·stat·ed, ·stat·ing** To state again or anew. **—re·state′ment** *n.*

res·tau·rant (res′tər·ənt, -tə·ränt) *n.* A place where refreshments or meals are bought; a public dining room. [< F, lit., restoring]

res·tau·ra·teur (res′tər·ə·tûr′) *n.* The proprietor or keeper of a restaurant. [< F]

rest·ful (rest′fəl) *adj.* 1. Full of or giving rest; affording freedom from disturbance, work, or trouble. 2. Being at rest or in repose; quiet. **—rest′ful·ly** *adv.* **—rest′ful·ness** *n.*

rest home A nursing home.

res·ti·tu·tion (res′tə·tōō′shən, -tyōō′-) *n.* 1. The act of restoring something that has been taken away or lost. 2. The act of making good or rendering an equivalent for injury or loss. [< L *re-* again + *statuere* to set up]

res·tive (res′tiv) *adj.* 1. Impatient of control; unruly. 2. Restless; fidgety. [< L *restare* to stand] **—res′tive·ly** *adv.* **—res′tive·ness** *n.*

rest·less (rest′lis) *adj.* 1. Having no rest; never quiet. 2. Unable or disinclined to rest. 3. Constantly seeking change; discontented. **—rest′less·ly** *adv.* **—rest′less·ness** *n.*

res·to·ra·tion (res′tə·rā′shən) *n.* 1. The act of restoring a person or thing to a former place or condition. 2. The reconstruction or repair of something so as to restore it to its original or former state; also, an object that has been so restored. **—the Restoration** The return of Charles II to the English throne in 1660; also, the following period until 1685.

re·sto·ra·tive (ri·stôr′ə·tiv) *n.* That which restores; esp., something to restore good health or consciousness. **—re·sto′ra·tive** *adj.*

re·store (ri·stôr′) *v.t.* **·stored, ·stor·ing** 1. To bring into existence or effect again. 2. To bring back to a former or original condition, appearance, etc., as a painting. 3. To bring back to health and vigor. 4. To give back (something lost or taken away). [< L *restaurare*] **—re·stor′er** *n.*

re·strain (ri·strān′) *v.t.* 1. To hold back from acting, proceeding, or advancing; repress. 2. To deprive of freedom or liberty, as by placing in a prison. 3. To restrict or limit. [< L *re-* back + *stringere* to draw tight] **—re·strain′a·ble** *adj.* **—re·strain′ed·ly** *adv.* **—re·strain′er** *n.*

re·straint (ri·strānt′) *n.* 1. The act of restraining. 2. The state of being restrained; confinement. 3. That which restrains; a restriction. 4. Self-repression; constraint.

re·strict (ri·strikt′) *v.t.* To hold or keep within limits or bounds. [< L *restrictus,* pp. of *restringere* to restrain] **—re·stric′tive** *adj.* **—re·stric′tive·ly** *adv.*

re·strict·ed (ri·strik′tid) *adj.* 1. Limited; confined. 2. Not available to the general public; limited to a specific group: *restricted* information. **—re·strict′ed·ly** *adv.*

re·stric·tion (ri·strik′shən) *n.* 1. The act of restricting, or the state of being restricted. 2. That which restricts.

rest room A toilet and washroom in a public building.

re·sult (ri·zult′) *n.* 1. The outcome of an action, course, process, or agency; consequence; effect; conclusion. 2. *Math.* A quantity or value ascertained by calculation. —*v.i.* To be a result or outcome; be a physical or logical consequent; follow: with *from.* [< L *re-* back + *salire* to leap]

re·sul·tant (ri·zul′tənt) *adj.* Arising or following as a result. —*n.* That which results; a consequence.

re·sume (ri·zōōm′) *v.* **·sumed, ·sum·ing** *v.t.* 1. To take up again after cessation or interruption; begin again. 2. To take or occupy again. —*v.i.* 3. To continue after cessation or interruption. [< L *re-* again + *sumere* to take] **—re·sum′a·ble** *adj.* **—re·sum′er** *n.* **—re·sump·tion** (ri·zump′shən) *n.*

ré·su·mé (rez′ōō·mā, rez′ōō·mā′) *n.* A summary, as of one's employment record. Also **re′su·me, re′su·mé.** [< F]

re·sur·face (rē·sûr′fis) *v.t.* **·faced, ·fac·ing** To provide with a new surface.

re·surge (ri·sûrj′) *v.i.* **·surged, ·surg·ing** 1. To rise again into life or activity. 2. To surge or sweep back again, as the tide. [< L *re-* again + *surgere* to rise] **—re·sur′gence** *n.* **—re·sur′gent** *adj.*

res·ur·rec·tion (rez′ə·rek′shən) *n.* 1. A rising again from the dead. 2. Any revival or renewal, as of a practice or custom, after disuse, decay, etc.; restoration. —**the Resurrection** *Theol.* The rising of Christ from the dead. [See RESURGE.] —**res′ur·rect′** *v.t. & v.i.* —**res′ur·rec′tion·al** *adj.* —**res′ur·rec′tion·ar·y** *adj.*

re·sus·ci·tate (ri·sus′ə·tāt) *v.t. & v.i.* **·tat·ed, ·tat·ing** To bring or come back to life; revive from unconsciousness. [< L *re-* again + *suscitare* to revive] —**re·sus′ci·ta′tion** *n.* —**re·sus′ci·ta′tive** *adj.* —**re·sus′ci·ta′tor** *n.*

ret (ret) *v.t.* **ret·ted, ret·ting** To steep or soak, as flax, to separate the fibers. [ME < MDu. *reten*]

re·tail (*n. & adj.* rē′tāl; *for v., also* ri·tāl′) *n.* The selling of goods in small quantities, esp. to the ultimate consumer: distinguished from *wholesale.* —*adj.* Involving or engaged in the sale of goods at retail. —*v.t.* 1. To sell at retail. 2. To repeat, as gossip. —*v.i.* 3. To be sold at retail. [< OF *re-* back + *tailler* to cut] —**re′tail·er** *n.*

re·tain (ri·tān′) *v.t.* 1. To keep or continue to keep in one's possession; hold. 2. To keep in a fixed condition or place. 3. To hire; also, to engage (an attorney or other representative) by paying a retainer. [< L *re-* back + *tenere* to hold] —**re·tain′a·ble** *adj.*

re·tain·er[1] (ri·tā′nər) *n.* 1. A servant. 2. One who retains or keeps.

re·tain·er[2] (ri·tā′nər) *n.* A fee paid to a lawyer, etc., to retain his services. [< OF *retenir* to hold back, used as noun]

re·take (*v.* rē·tāk′; *n.* rē′tāk′) *v.t.* **·took, ·tak·en, ·tak·ing** 1. To take back; receive again. 2. To recapture. 3. To photograph again. —*n.* A motion-picture or television scene, part of a musical or other recording, etc., done again.

re·tal·i·ate (ri·tal′ē·āt) *v.* **·at·ed, ·at·ing** *v.i.* 1. To return like for like; esp., to repay evil with evil. —*v.t.* 2. To repay (an injury, wrong, etc.) in kind; revenge. [< L *re-* back + *talio* punishment in kind] —**re·tal′i·a′tion** *n.* —**re·tal′i·a′tive** *adj.* —**re·tal′i·a·to′ry** (-ə·tôr′ē) *adj.*

re·tard (ri·tärd′) *v.t.* 1. To cause to move or proceed slowly; delay. —*v.i.* 2. To be delayed. —*n.* The act of retarding; delay. [< L *re-* back + *tardare* to make slow] —**re·tard′ant** *n. & adj.* —**re·tar·da·tion** (rē′tär·dā′shən) *n.* —**re·tard′a·tive** (-ə·tiv) *adj. & n.* —**re·tard′er** *n.*

re·tard·ate (ri·tär′dāt) *n.* One who is mentally retarded.

re·tard·ed (ri·tär′did) *adj. Psychol.* Slowed down or backward in mental development.

retch (rech) *v.i.* To make an effort to vomit; strain; heave. [OE *hrǣcan* to clear one's throat]

re·ten·tion (ri·ten′shən) *n.* 1. The act of retaining, or the state of being retained. 2. The ability to remember. 3. The capacity or ability to retain.

re·ten·tive (ri·ten′tiv) *adj.* Having the power or tendency to retain. —**re·ten·tiv·i·ty** (rē′ten·tiv′ə·tē) *n.* —**re·ten′tive·ness** *n.*

ret·i·cent (ret′ə·sənt) *adj.* Habitually silent or reserved in utterance. [< L *re-* again + *tacere* to be silent] —**ret′i·cence, ret′i·cen·cy** *n.* —**ret′i·cent·ly** *adv.*

re·tic·u·late (ri·tik′yə·lāt; *for adj., also* ri·tik′yə·lit) *v.* **·lat·ed, ·lat·ing** *v.t.* 1. To make a network of. 2. To cover with or as with lines of network. —*v.i.* 3. To form a network. —*adj.* Having the form or appearance of a network. [< L *reticulum* network] —**re·tic′u·la′tion** *n.*

ret·i·na (ret′ə·nə, ret′nə) *n. pl.* **·nas** or **·nae** (-nē) *Anat.* The light-sensitive inner membrane at the back of the eyeball that receives the image. [< L *rete* net] —**ret′i·nal** *adj.*

ret·i·nue (ret′ə·no͞o, -nyo͞o) *n.* The body of retainers attending a person of rank; entourage. [< F *retenir* to retain]

re·tire (ri·tīr′) *v.* **·tired, ·tir·ing** *v.i.* 1. To go away or withdraw, as for privacy, shelter, or rest. 2. To go to bed. 3. To withdraw oneself from business, public life, or active service. 4. To fall back; retreat, as troops under attack. —*v.t.* 5. To remove from active service. 6. In baseball, etc., to put out (a batter or side). [< MF *re-* back + *tirer* to draw] —**re·tire′ment** *n.*

re·tired (ri·tīrd′) *adj.* 1. Withdrawn from public view; solitary; secluded: a *retired* life. 2. Withdrawn from active service, business, office, etc.

re·tir·ing (ri·tīr′ing) *adj.* Shy; modest; reserved.

re·tort[1] (ri·tôrt′) *v.t.* 1. To direct (a word or deed) back upon the originator. 2. To reply to, as an accusation or argument, by a similar accusation, etc. —*v.i.* 3. To make answer, esp. sharply. —*n.* 1. A keen rejoinder or retaliatory speech; caustic repartee. 2. The act of retorting. [< L *re-* back + *torquere* to twist] —**re·tort′er** *n.*

re·tort[2] (ri·tôrt′) *n. Chem.* A vessel with a bent tube for the heating of substances or for distillation. [< L *retortus* bent back]

re·touch (rē·tuch′; *for n., also* rē′tuch) *v.t.* 1. To modify; revise. 2. *Photog.* To change or improve, as a print. —*n.* An additional touch, as to a picture, model, or other work of art. —**re·touch′er** *n.*

re·trace (ri·trās′) *v.t.* **·traced, ·trac·ing** 1. To go back over; follow backward, as a path. 2. To trace the whole story of, from the beginning. —**re·trace′a·ble** *adj.*

re-trace (rē·trās′) *v.t.* **-traced, -trac·ing** To trace again, as an engraving, drawing, or map.

re·tract (ri·trakt′) *v.t. & v.i.* 1. To take back or disavow (an assertion, admission, etc.); recant. 2. To draw back or in, as the claws of a cat. [< L *re-* again + *tractare* to handle] —**re·tract′a·ble** or **·i·ble** *adj.* —**re·trac′tion** *n.* —**re·trac′tive** *adj.*

re·trac·tile (ri·trak′til) *adj. Zool.* Capable of being drawn back or in, as a cat's claws. —**re·trac·til·i·ty** (rē′trak·til′ə·tē) *n.*

re·trac·tor (ri·trak′tər) *n.* 1. One who or that which retracts. 2. *Surg.* An instrument used to hold apart the edges of a wound, incision, etc.

re·tread (*n.* rē′tred′; *v.* rē·tred′) *n.* A pneumatic tire furnished with a new tread. —*v.t.* **·tread·ed, ·tread·ing** To fit or furnish (an automobile tire) with a new tread.

re·treat (ri·trēt′) *v.i.* 1. To go back or backward; withdraw; retire. 2. To curve or slope backward. —*n.* 1. The act of retreating. 2. The retirement of a military force from a position of danger or from an enemy. 3. *Mil.* A signal, as by bugle, for the lowering of the flag at sunset. 4. Retirement; seclusion; solitude. 5. A place of retirement, quiet, or security; a refuge; haunt. **—to beat a retreat** 1. To give a signal for retreat, as by the beat of drums. 2. To turn back; flee. [< L *re-* back + *trahere* to draw]

re·trench (ri·trench′) *v.t.* 1. To cut down or reduce; curtail (expenditures). *—v.i.* 2. To reduce expenses; economize. [< MF *re-* back + *trencher* to cut] **—re·trench′·ment** *n.*

re·tri·al (rē·trī′əl) *n.* A second or succeeding trial, as of a judicial case.

ret·ri·bu·tion (ret′rə·byōō′shən) *n.* 1. The act of requiting; esp., impartial infliction of punishment. 2. That which is done or given in requital, as a reward or punishment. [< L *re-* back + *tribuere* to divide, grant] **—re·trib·u·tive** (ri·trib′yə·tiv), **re·trib·u·to·ry** (ri·trib′yə·tôr′ē) *adj.*

re·trieve (ri·trēv′) *v.* **·trieved, ·triev·ing** *v.t.* 1. To get back; regain. 2. To restore; revive, as flagging spirits. 3. To find and bring in (wounded or dead game): said of dogs. 4. *Electronics* To obtain or extract (specific information) from the storage unit of an electronic computer. *—v.i.* 5. To retrieve game. *—n.* The act of retrieving; recovery. [< OF *re-* again + *trouver* to find] **—re·triev′a·bil′i·ty** *n.* **—re·triev′a·ble** *adj.* **—re·triev′a·bly** *adv.* **—re·triev′al** *n.*

re·triev·er (ri·trē′vər) *n.* 1. A sporting dog specifically trained to retrieve game. 2. One who retrieves.

retro- *prefix* 1. Back; backward. 2. Behind. [< L *retro* back, backward]

ret·ro·ac·tive (ret′rō·ak′tiv) *adj.* Taking effect at a (usu. specified) time prior to its enactment, ratification, etc., as a provision in a law or contract. **—ret′ro·ac′tive·ly** *adv.* **—ret′ro·ac·tiv′i·ty** *n.*

ret·ro·fire (ret′rō·fīr) *v.t.* *Aerospace* **·fired, ·fir·ing** To ignite (a retrorocket). **—ret′ro·fire** *n.*

ret·ro·grade (ret′rə·grād) *adj.* 1. Going or tending backward; reversed. 2. Declining to or toward a worse state or character. 3. Reversed; inverted. *—v.* **·grad·ed, ·grad·ing** *v.i.* 1. To move or appear to move backward. 2. To degenerate. *—v.t.* 3. To cause to move backward; reverse. [< RETRO- + L *gradi* to walk] **—ret′ro·gra·da′tion** *n.*

ret·ro·gress (ret′rə·gres) *v.i.* To go back to an earlier or worse state. [< RETRO- + L *gradi* to walk]

ret·ro·gres·sion (ret′rə·gresh′ən) *n.* 1. The act or process of retrogressing. 2. *Biol.* Return to or toward an earlier form or structure. **—ret′ro·gres′sive** (-gres′iv) *adj.*

ret·ro·rock·et (ret′rō·rok′it) *n.* *Aerospace* An auxiliary rocket whose reverse thrust decelerates a rocket or spaceship.

ret·ro·spect (ret′rə·spekt) *n.* A view or contemplation of something past. [< RETRO- + L *specere* to look] **—ret′ro·spec′tion** *n.*

ret·ro·spec·tive (ret′rə·spek′tiv) *adj.* 1. Looking back on the past. 2. Applying retroactively, as legislation. *—n.* An exhibition of past work, as of an artist. **—ret′ro·spec′tive·ly** *adv.*

ret·rous·sé (ret′rōō·sā′, *Fr.* rə·trōō·sā′) *adj.* Turned up at the end: said of a nose. [< F, pp. of *retrousser* to turn up]

re·try (rē·trī′) *v.t.* **·tried, ·try·ing** To try again, as a judicial case.

re·turn (ri·tûrn′) *v.i.* 1. To come or go back, as to or toward a former place or condition. 2. To revert to a former owner. 3. To answer; respond. *—v.t.* 4. To bring, carry, send, or put back; replace. 5. To repay or requite, esp. with an equivalent: to *return* a compliment. 6. To yield or produce, as a profit or interest. 7. To send back; reflect, as light or sound. 8. To report or announce officially. *—n.* 1. The act, process, state, or result of coming back or returning. 2. That which is returned. 3. That which accrues, as from investments, labor, or use; profit. 4. A report, list, etc.; esp., a formal or official report. 5. *pl.* A set of tabulated statistics: election *returns.* *—adj.* 1. Of, pertaining to, or for a return: a *return* ticket. 2. Given, taken, or done in return: a *return* visit. 3. Reversing direction; doubling back, as a U-shaped bend. [< OF *re-* back + *torner* to turn] **—re·turn′a·ble** *adj.* **—re·turn′er** *n.*

re·un·ion (rē·yōōn′yən) *n.* 1. The act of reuniting. 2. A gathering of persons who have been separated.

re·u·nite (rē′yōō·nīt′) *v.t.* & *v.i.* **·nit·ed, ·nit·ing** To unite, cohere, or combine again after separation. **—re′u·nit′er** *n.*

rev (rev) *n.* A revolution, as of a motor. *—v.t.* & *v.i.* **revved, rev·ving** To alter the speed of (a motor): usu. with *up.*

re·vamp (rē·vamp′) *v.t.* To patch up; make over; renovate.

re·veal (ri·vēl′) *v.t.* 1. To make known; disclose; divulge. 2. To make visible; expose to view; show. [< L *re-* back + *velum* veil] **—re·veal′a·ble** *adj.* **—re·veal′er** *n.* **—re·veal′ment** *n.*

rev·eil·le (rev′i·lē) *n.* 1. A morning signal by drum or bugle, notifying soldiers or sailors to rise. 2. The hour at which this signal is sounded. [< F, ult. < L *re-* again + *vigilare* to keep watch]

rev·el (rev′əl) *v.i.* **·eled** or **·elled, ·el·ing** or **·el·ling** 1. To take delight: with *in*: He *revels* in his freedom. 2. To engage in boisterous festivities; make merry. *—n.* 1. Merrymaking; carousing. 2. *Often pl.* An occasion of boisterous festivity; a celebration. [< OF *reveler* to make an uproar] **—rev′el·er** or **rev′el·ler** *n.*

rev·e·la·tion (rev′ə·lā′shən) *n.* 1. The act or process of revealing. 2. That which is or has been revealed. 3. *Theol.* The act of revealing or communicating divine truth, esp. by divine agency. **—rev·e·la·to·ry** (rev′ə·lə·tôr′ē) *adj.*

Rev·e·la·tion (rev′ə·lā′shən) *n.* *Often pl.* The last book of the New Testament; the Apocalypse: in full, **The Revelation of Saint John the Divine.**

rev·el·ry (rev′əl·rē) *n.* *pl.* **·ries** Noisy or boisterous merriment.

re·venge (ri·venj′) *v.t.* **·venged, ·veng·ing** 1. To inflict punishment, injury, or loss in return for. 2. To take or seek vengeance in behalf of. *—n.* 1. The act of revenging. 2. A means of avenging oneself or others. 3. A desire for vengeance. [< OF *re-* again

+ *vengier* to take vengeance] —**re·venge′ful** *adj.* —**re·venge′ful·ly** *adv.* —**re·venge′ful·ness** *n.* —**re·veng′er** *n.*

rev·e·nue (rev′ə·nyōō, -nōō) *n.* 1. Total current income of a government, except duties on imports: also called *internal revenue.* 2. Income from any form of property. [< L *re-* back + *venire* to come]

re·ver·ber·ate (ri·vûr′bə·rāt) *v.t. & v.i.* **·at·ed, ·at·ing** 1. To resound; reecho, as a sound. 2. To reflect or be reflected. [< L *re-* back + *verberare* to beat]

re·ver·ber·a·tion (ri·vûr′bə·rā′shən) *n.* 1. The act or process of reverberating. 2. That which is reverberated. 3. The rebound or reflection of light, heat, or sound waves. —**re·ver′ber·ant** (-bər·ənt), **re·ver′ber·a′tive** *adj.* —**re·ver′ber·a·to′ry** (-bər·ə·tôr′ē) *adj.*

re·vere (ri·vir′) *v.t.* **·vered, ·ver·ing** To regard with reverence; venerate. [< L *re-* again + *vereri* to fear] —**re·ver′er** *n.*

rev·er·ence (rev′ər·əns) *n.* 1. A feeling of profound respect often mingled with awe and affection; veneration. 2. An act of respect; an obeisance. 3. *cap.* A title or form of address for clergymen: often preceded by *His, Your,* etc. —*v.t.* **·enced, ·enc·ing** To regard with reverence.

rev·er·end (rev′ər·ənd) *adj.* 1. Worthy of reverence. 2. *Often cap.* A title of respect often used with the name of a clergyman. —*n. Informal* A clergyman; minister. [See REVERE.]

rev·er·ent (rev′ər·ənt) *adj.* 1. Feeling reverence. 2. Expressing reverence: also **rev·er·en·tial** (rev′ə·ren′shəl). [See REVERE.] —**rev′er·ent·ly, rev′er·en′tial·ly** *adv.*

rev·er·ie (rev′ə·rē) *n. pl.* **·er·ies** 1. Abstracted musing; dreaming. 2. A product of such musing. Also **rev′er·y.** [< F < MF *resver* to dream]

re·vers (rə·vir′, -vâr′) *n. pl.* **·vers** (-virz′, -vârz′) A part of a garment folded over to show the inside, as the lapel of a coat. Also **re·vere′.** [< OF. See REVERSE.]

re·verse (ri·vûrs′) *adj.* 1. Having a contrary or opposite direction, character, order, etc.; turned backward. 2. Causing backward motion: the *reverse* gear of an automobile. —*n.* 1. That which is directly opposite or contrary. 2. The back or secondary side of anything. 3. A change for the worse; a check or partial defeat. 4. *Mech.* A reversing gear or movement. —*v.* **·versed, ·vers·ing** *v.t.* 1. To turn upside down or inside out. 2. To turn in an opposite direction. 3. To set aside; annul: to *reverse* a decree. 4. *Mech.* To cause to have an opposite motion or effect. —*v.i.* 5. To move or turn in the opposite direction. 6. To reverse its action, as an engine. [< L *re-* back + *vertere* to turn] —**re·ver′sal** *n.* —**re·verse′ly** *adv.* —**re·vers′er** *n.*

re·vers·i·ble (ri·vûr′sə·bəl) *adj.* 1. Capable of being reversed in direction or position. 2. Capable of going either forward or backward, as a chemical reaction or physiological process. 3. Capable of being used or worn inside out or backward, as a coat. —*n.* A reversible coat. —**re·vers′i·bil′i·ty, re·vers′i·ble·ness** *n.* —**re·vers′i·bly** *adv.*

re·ver·sion (ri·vûr′zhən) *n.* 1. A return to or toward some former state, condition, practice, or belief. 2. *Biol.* The reappearance in an individual of characteristics that had not been evident for two or more generations. 3. *Law* The right of succession to an estate. [See REVERT.] —**re·ver′sion·al, re·ver′sion·ar′y** *adj.*

re·vert (ri·vûrt′) *v.i.* 1. To go or turn back to a former place, condition, attitude, etc. 2. *Biol.* To return to or show characteristics of an earlier type. 3. *Law* To return to the former owner or his heirs. [< L *re-* back + *vertere* to turn] —**re·vert′i·ble** *adj.* —**re·vert′ive** *adj.*

re·view (ri·vyōō′) *v.t.* 1. To go over or examine again; look at or study again. 2. To look back upon; think of retrospectively. 3. To make an inspection of, esp. formally. 4. To write or make a critical review of, as a new book. 5. *Law* To reexamine (something done or adjudged by a lower court). —*v.i.* 6. To write reviews, as for a magazine. —*n.* 1. A new view or study of something; a retrospective survey. 2. A lesson studied or recited again. 3. Critical study or examination. 4. An article containing a critical discussion of some work. 5. A periodical devoted to essays in criticism and on general subjects. 6. A formal inspection, as of troops. 7. *Law* A judicial revision by a superior court of the order or decree of a subordinate court. [< L *re-* again + *videre* to see]

re·view·er (ri·vyōō′ər) *n.* One who reviews; esp., one who critically reviews new books, plays, movies, etc.

re·vile (ri·vīl′) *v.t.* **·viled, ·vil·ing** To assail with abusive or contemptuous language; vilify; abuse. [< OF *reviler* to despise] —**re·vile′ment** *n.* —**re·vil′er** *n.* —**re·vil′ing·ly** *adv.*

re·vise (ri·vīz′) *v.t.* **·vised, ·vis·ing** 1. To read over so as to correct errors, make changes, etc. 2. To change; alter. —*n.* The act or result of revising; a revision. [< L *re-* again + *visere* to scrutinize] —**re·vis′er** or **re·vi′sor** *n.* —**re·vi·so·ry** (ri·vī′zər·ē) *adj.*

re·vi·sion (ri·vizh′ən) *n.* 1. The act or process of revising. 2. Something revised, as a new version of a book. —**re·vi′sion·al, re·vi′sion·ar′y** *adj.*

re·vi·val (ri·vī′vəl) *n.* 1. The act of reviving, or the state of being revived. 2. A restoration, as after neglect or obscurity. 3. A series of evangelical meetings to reawaken faith.

re·vi·val·ist (ri·vī′vəl·ist) *n.* A preacher or leader in a religious revival movement. —**re·vi′val·ism** *n.* —**re·vi′val·ist, re·vi′val·is′tic** *adj.*

re·vive (ri·vīv′) *v.* **·vived, ·viv·ing** *v.t.* 1. To bring back to life or to consciousness. 2. To give new health, etc., to. 3. To bring back into use. 4. To produce again, as an old play. —*v.i.* 5. To come back to life again. 6. To assume new vigor, health, etc. 7. To come back into use. [< L *re-* again + *vivere* to live] —**re·viv′er** *n.*

re·viv·i·fy (ri·viv′ə·fī) *v.t.* **·fied, ·fy·ing** To give new life to; revive. [< L *re-* again + *vivus* alive + *facere* to make] —**re·viv′i·fi·ca′tion** *n.*

rev·o·ca·ble (rev′ə·kə·bəl) *adj.* Capable of being revoked. Also **re·vok·a·ble** (ri·vō′kə·bəl). —**rev′o·ca·bil′i·ty** *n.* —**rev′o·ca·bly** *adv.*

rev·o·ca·tion (rev′ə·kā′shən) *n.* The act of revoking, or the state of being revoked; repeal.

re·voke (ri·vōk′) *v.* **·voked, ·vok·ing** *v.t.* 1. To annul or make void by recalling; cancel; rescind. —*v.i.* 2. In card games, to fail to follow suit. —*n.* In card games, a renege. [< L *re-* back + *vocare* to call] —**re·vok′er** *n.*

re·volt (ri·vōlt′) *n.* 1. An uprising against authority; rebellion. 2. An act of protest, refusal, or disgust. 3. The state of a person or persons who revolt: to be in *revolt.* —*v.i.* 1. To rise in rebellion against constituted authority; mutiny. 2. To turn away in disgust: with *against, at,* or *from.* —*v.t.* 3. To cause to feel disgust; repel. [<L *re-* back + *volvere* to roll] —**re·volt′er** *n.*

re·volt·ing (ri·vōl′ting) *adj.* Abhorrent; loathsome; nauseating. —**re·volt′ing·ly** *adv.*

rev·o·lu·tion (rev′ə·lo͞o′shən) *n.* 1. A motion in a closed curve around a center, or a complete circuit made by a body in such a course. 2. *Mech.* Rotation about an axis. 3. *Astron.* The movement of a planet around the sun or of any celestial body around a center of attraction. 4. A cycle of successive events or changes. 5. The overthrow and replacement of a government or political system by those governed. 6. A drastic change in a condition, method, idea, etc. [See REVOLVE.]

rev·o·lu·tion·ar·y (rev′ə·lo͞o′shən·er′ē) *adj.* 1. Pertaining to, causing, or of the nature of revolution, esp. political. 2. Rotating; revolving. —*n. pl.* **·ar·ies** One who advocates or participates in a political revolution.

rev·o·lu·tion·ize (rev′ə·lo͞o′shən·īz) *v.t.* **·ized, ·iz·ing** To effect a radical change in the character, operation, etc., of.

re·volve (ri·volv′) *v.* **·volved, ·volv·ing** *v.i.* 1. To move in an orbit about a center. 2. To spin around on an axis; rotate. 3. To recur periodically. —*v.t.* 4. To cause to move in a circle or orbit. 5. To turn over mentally; consider. [< L *re-* back + *volvere* to roll] —**re·volv′a·ble** *adj.*

re·volv·er (ri·vol′vər) *n.* A pistol having a revolving cylinder designed to hold several cartridges that may be fired in succession without reloading.

re·vue (ri·vyo͞o′) *n.* A show consisting of songs, dances, and skits that satirize contemporary people and events. [< F]

re·vul·sion (ri·vul′shən) *n.* 1. A sudden change of or strong reaction in feeling. 2. A feeling of disgust. [< L *re-* back + *vellere* to pull] —**re·vul′sive** (-siv) *adj.*

re·ward (ri·wôrd′) *n.* 1. Something given or done in return; esp., a gift, prize, etc., for merit, service, or achievement. 2. Money offered for information, for the return of lost goods, etc. —*v.t.* 1. To give a reward to or for. 2. To be a reward for. [< OF *re-* back + *warder* to guard] —**re·ward′er** *n.*

re·wire (rē·wīr′) *v.t.* **·wired, ·wir·ing** To wire again, as a house or a machine.

re·word (rē·wûrd′) *v.t.* To say again in other words; express differently.

re·write (*v.* rē·rīt′; *n.* rē′rīt′) *v.t.* **·wrote, ·writ·ten, ·writ·ing** 1. To write over again. 2. In journalism, to put into publishable form (a story submitted by a reporter). —*n.* A news item written in this manner.

rex (reks) *n. pl.* **re·ges** (rē′jēs) *Usu. cap. Latin* King.

-rhage, -rhagia, -rhagy See -RRHAGIA.

rhap·so·dize (rap′sə·dīz) *v.t. & v.i.* **·dized, ·diz·ing** To express or exclaim rhapsodically. —**rhap′so·dist** *n.*

rhap·so·dy (rap′sə·dē) *n. pl.* **·dies** 1. A series of disconnected and often extravagant utterances composed under excitement. 2. *Music* An instrumental composition of irregular form, often suggestive of improvisation. [< Gk. *rhaptein* to stitch together + *oidē* song] —**rhap·sod·ic** (rap·sod′ik) or **·i·cal** *adj.* —**rhap·sod′i·cal·ly** *adv.*

rhe·a (rē′ə) *n.* A flightless three-toed bird of the plains of South America, similar to but smaller than the African ostrich. [< Gk.]

-rhea See -RRHEA.

rhe·ni·um (rē′nē·əm) *n.* A heavy, lustrous, rare metallic element (symbol Re) of the manganese group. [< L *Rhenus* Rhine]

rheo- *combining form* Current or flow, as of water or electricity. [< Gk. *rheos* a current]

rhe·o·stat (rē′ə·stat) *n. Electr.* A variable resistor used to control current and voltage strength in a circuit. [< RHEO- + Gk. *statos* standing] —**rhe′o·stat′ic** *adj.*

rhe·sus (rē′səs) *n.* A monkey with a short tail, common throughout India and widely used in biological and medical research. [after *Rhesus,* a mythical king mentioned in the *Iliad*]

rhet·o·ric (ret′ə·rik) *n.* 1. The art of discourse, both written and spoken. 2. Affected and exaggerated display in the use of language. [< Gk. *rhētōr* public speaker] —**rhet′o·ri′cian** (-rish′ən) *n.*

rhe·tor·i·cal (ri·tôr′i·kəl, -tor′-) *adj.* 1. Pertaining to rhetoric; oratorical. 2. Designed for showy oratorical effect. —**rhe·tor′i·cal·ly** *adv.* —**rhe·tor′i·cal·ness** *n.*

rhetorical question A question put only for oratorical or literary effect, the answer being implied in the question.

rheum (ro͞om) *n. Pathol.* A thin, watery discharge from the nose and eyes. [< Gk. *rheuma* stream] —**rheum′y** *adj.*

rheumatic fever *Pathol.* An infectious disease chiefly affecting children, characterized by painful inflammation around the joints, fever, and inflammation of the heart valves.

rheu·ma·tism (ro͞o′mə·tiz′əm) *n. Pathol.* 1. A painful inflammation and stiffness of the muscles, joints, etc. 2. Rheumatoid arthritis. [< Gk. *rheuma* a stream] —**rheu·mat′ic** (-mat′ik) *adj. & n.* —**rheu′ma·toid** (-toid), **rheu′ma·toi′dal** (-toid′l) *adj.*

rheumatoid arthritis *Pathol.* A persisting inflammatory disease of the joints, marked by atrophy, weakening of the bones, and deformities.

Rh factor (är′āch′) *Biochem.* A property present in the blood of most persons (who are said to be **Rh positive**) and that may cause antigenic reactions under certain conditions, as during pregnancy or following transfusions with persons lacking this factor (who are said to be **Rh negative**). [< RH(ESUS)]

rhi·nal (rī′nəl) *adj.* Of or pertaining to the nose; nasal.

rhine·stone (rīn′stōn′) *n.* A refractive, colorless glass or paste, used as an imitation gemstone. [Trans. of F *caillou du Rhin*]

rhi·ni·tis (rī·nī′tis) *n. Pathol.* Inflammation of the mucous membranes of the nose.

rhi·no (rī′nō) *n. pl.* **·nos** A rhinoceros.

rhino- *combining form* Nose; nasal. Also, before vowels, **rhin-**. [< Gk. *rhis, rhinos* nose]

rhi·noc·e·ros (rī·nos′ər·əs) *n. pl.* **·ros·es** or **·ros** A large, herbivorous mammal of Africa and Asia, having one or two horns on the snout and a very thick hide. [< Gk. *rhis, rhinos* nose + *keras* horn]

rhi·zome (rī′zōm) *n. Bot.* A subterranean rootlike stem, producing roots from its lower surface and leaves or shoots from its upper surface: also called *rootstalk, rootstock.* Also **rhi·zo·ma** (rī·zō′mə). [< Gk. *rhiza* root] —**rhi·zom·a·tous** (rī·zom′ə·təs, -zō′mə-) *adj.*

rho (rō) *n.* The seventeenth letter in the Greek alphabet (Ρ, ρ), corresponding to the English *r*. [< Gk. *rhō*]

Rho·de·sian (rō·dē′zhən) *adj.* Of Rhodesia or its inhabitants. —**Rho·de′sian** *n.*

rho·di·um (rō′dē·əm) *n.* A whitish gray, metallic element (symbol Rh) of the platinum group, whose salts are for the most part rose-colored, used in electroplating to prevent corrosion. [< Gk. *rhodon* rose]

rho·do·den·dron (rō′də·den′drən) *n.* Any of a genus of evergreen shrubs or small trees of the heath family, with clusters of white, pink, or purple flowers. [< Gk. *rhodon* rose + *dendron* tree]

-rhoea See -RRHEA.

rhom·boid (rom′boid) *n. Geom.* A parallelogram having opposite sides and opposite angles equal but having no right angle. [< F *rhomboïde*] —**rhom′boid, rhom·boi′dal** *adj.*

rhom·bus (rom′bəs) *n. pl.* **·bus·es** or **·bi** (-bī) *Geom.* An equilateral parallelogram having the angles usu., but not necessarily, oblique. Also **rhomb** (rom, romb). [< Gk. *rhombos* spinning top] —**rhom′bic** or **·bi·cal** *adj.*

rhu·barb (rōō′bärb) *n.* 1. A stout, coarse, perennial herb having large leaves and small clusters of flowers on tall stalks, esp. one whose acid leafstalks are used in cooking. 2. *Slang* A heated argument or quarrel. [< Gk. *rha* rhubarb + L *barbarus* foreign]

rhum·ba (rum′bə) See RUMBA.

rhyme (rīm) *n.* 1. A correspondence of sounds in two or more words, esp. at the ends of lines of poetry. 2. Poetry; verse. —*v.* **rhymed, rhym·ing** *v.i.* 1. To make rhymes or verses. 2. To correspond in sound or in terminal sounds. —*v.t.* 3. To put or write in rhyme or verse. Also spelled *rime.* [< OF *rime*] —**rhym′er** *n.*

rhyme·ster (rīm′stər) *n.* A writer of jingles: also spelled *rimester.*

rhythm (rith′əm) *n.* 1. The recurrence or repetition of stress, beat, sound, accent, motion, etc., usu. occurring in a regular or harmonious pattern or manner. 2. *Music* The relative duration and accent of musical sounds. 3. In painting, sculpture, etc., a regular or harmonious recurrence of lines, forms, colors, etc. [< Gk. *rhythmos* < *rheein* to flow] —**rhyth·mic** (rith′mik), **rhyth·mi·cal** (rith′mə·kəl) *adj.* —**rhyth′mi·cal·ly** *adv.*

rhythm method Birth control by sexual abstinence during the woman's period of fertility.

ri·al (rī′al) *n.* The monetary unit of Iran, Oman, and Yemen. [< OF *rial, real* royal]

ri·al·to (rē·al′tō) *n. pl.* **·tos** A market or place of exchange. [after *Rialto*, the ancient business quarter of Venice]

rib (rib) *n.* 1. *Anat.* One of the series of bony rods attached to the spine of most vertebrates, and nearly encircling the thorax. In man there are twelve ribs on each side. ◆Collateral adjective: *costal.* 2. Something resembling a rib: the *rib* of an umbrella. 3. A curved side timber bending away from the keel in a boat or ship. 4. A raised wale or stripe in cloth or knit goods. —*v.t.* **ribbed, rib·bing** 1. To make with ridges: to *rib* a piece of knitting. 2. *Slang* To make fun of; tease. [OE]

rib·ald (rib′əld) *adj.* Pertaining to or indulging in coarse language or vulgar jokes. —*n.* One who uses coarse or abusive language. [< OF *ribauld*] —**rib′ald·ry** *n.*

rib·and (rib′ənd) *n. Archaic* A decorative ribbon.

rib·bing (rib′ing) *n.* An arrangement or collection of ribs, as in ribbed cloth, etc.

rib·bon (rib′ən) *n.* 1. A narrow strip of fine fabric, having finished edges and used as trimming. 2. *Often pl.* A narrow strip; a shred: torn to *ribbons.* 3. An inked strip of cloth for giving the impression in a typewriter or similar device. 4. A colored strip of cloth worn as a military badge, etc. —*v.t.* To ornament with ribbons; also, to form or tear into ribbons. [< MF *riban*]

ri·bo·fla·vin (rī′bō·flā′vin) *n. Biochem.* A member of the vitamin B complex, vitamin B_2, an orange-yellow, crystalline compound, found in milk, leafy vegetables, egg yolk, and meats, and also made synthetically. [< RIBO(SE) + FLAVIN]

ri·bo·nu·cle·ic acid (rī′bō·nōō·klē′ik, -klā-) *Biochem.* A complex nucleic acid associated with DNA in the synthesis of cell proteins. Abbr. *RNA.*

ri·bose (rī′bōs) *n. Chem.* A sugar occurring in certain nucleic acids. [< G *ribonsäure*, arbitrary alteration of *arabinose* + -OSE[2]]

ri·bo·some (rī′bə·sōm) *n. Biol.* A minute particle found in the cytoplasm of plant and animal cells, associated with ribonucleic acid and concerned with protein synthesis. —**ri·bo·so′mal** *adj.*

-ric *combining form* Realm or jurisdiction of: *bishopric.* [OE *rīce* kingdom, realm]

rice (rīs) *n.* 1. The edible seeds of an annual cereal grass, rich in carbohydrates and forming a staple food throughout the world. 2. The grass itself. [< Gk. *oryza*]

rich (rich) *adj.* 1. Having large possessions, as of money, goods, or lands; wealthy; opulent. 2. Composed of rare or precious materials; costly: *rich* fabrics. 3. Luscious to the taste, often implying an excess of fats, flavoring, etc. 4. Full, satisfying, and pleasing, as a tone, voice, color, etc. 5. Luxuriant; abundant: *rich* hair; *rich* crops. 6. Abundantly supplied: often with *in* or *with*. [Fusion of OE *rīce* powerful, rich and OF *riche*] **—rich′ly** *adv.* **—rich′ness** *n.*

rich·es (rich′iz) *n. pl.* 1. Abundant possessions; wealth. 2. Abundance of whatever is precious.

Rich·ter scale (rikh′tər) A scale for measuring the magnitude of earthquakes. [after C. F. *Richter*, born 1900, U.S. seismologist]

rick (rik) *n.* A stack, as of hay, having the top covered to protect the interior from rain. **—*v.t.*** To pile in ricks. [OE *hrēac*]

rick·ets (rik′its) *n. Pathol.* A disease of early childhood, chiefly due to a deficiency of calcium salts or vitamin D, characterized by softening of the bones and consequent deformity: also called *rachitis*. [? Alter. of Gk. *rachitis* inflammation of the spine]

rick·ett·si·a (rik·et′sē·ə) *n. pl.* **·si·as** or **·si·ae** (-si·ē) Any of a genus of microorganisms typically parasitic in ticks and lice, but transmissible to other animals and to man, causing typhus, Rocky Mountain spotted fever, etc. [after Howard T. *Ricketts*, 1871–1910, U.S. pathologist] **—rick·ett′si·al** *adj.*

rick·et·y (rik′it·ē) *adj.* **·et·i·er, ·et·i·est** 1. Ready to fall; tottering. 2. Affected with or like rickets. 3. Feeble; infirm; unsteady. **—rick′et·i·ly** *adv.* **—rick′et·i·ness** *n.*

rick·rack (rik′rak′) *n.* Flat braid in zigzag form; also, the openwork trimming made with this braid. [Reduplication of RACK[1]]

rick·shaw (rik′shô) *n.* A jinriksha. Also **rick′sha.**

ric·o·chet (rik′ə·shā′, -shet′) *v.i.* **·cheted** (-shād′) or **·chet·ted** (-shet′id), **·chet·ing** (-shā′ing) or **·chet·ting** (-shet′ing) To glance from a surface, as a stone thrown over the water; make a series of skips or bounds. **—*n.*** A bounding, as of a projectile over or off a surface. [< F]

rid (rid) *v.t.* **rid** or **rid·ded, rid·ding** To free, as from a burden or annoyance: usu. with *of.* **—*adj.*** Free; clear; quit: with *of*: We are well *rid* of him. [< ON *rythja* to clear land] **—rid·dance** (rid′ns) *n.*

rid·den (rid′n) Past participle of RIDE.

rid·dle[1] (rid′l) *v.t.* **·dled, ·dling** 1. To perforate in numerous places, as with shot. 2. To sift through a coarse sieve. **—*n.*** A coarse sieve. [OE *hriddel* sieve] **—rid′dler** *n.*

rid·dle[2] (rid′l) *n.* 1. A puzzling question stated as a problem to be solved by clever ingenuity; a conundrum. 2. Any puzzling object or person. **—*v.*** **·dled, ·dling** *v.t.* 1. To solve; explain. **—*v.i.*** 2. To utter or solve riddles. [OE *rǣdels* advice, interpretation]

ride (rīd) *v.* **rode, rid·den, rid·ing** *v.i.* 1. To sit on and be borne along by a horse or other animal. 2. To travel or be carried on or in a vehicle or other conveyance. 3. To be supported in moving: The wheel *rides* on the shaft. 4. To carry a rider in a specified manner: This car *rides* easily. 5. *Naut.* To lie at anchor, as a ship. 6. To work or move upward out of place: with *up*. 7. *Slang* To continue unchanged: Let it *ride*. **—*v.t.*** 8. To sit on and control the motion of (a horse, bicycle, etc.). 9. To overlap or overlie. 10. To travel or traverse (an area, etc.) on horseback, in an automobile, etc. 11. To control imperiously or oppressively. 12. To accomplish by riding: to *ride* a race. 13. *Informal* To tease or harass by ridicule or petty criticisms; tyrannize. **—to ride out** To survive; endure successfully. **—*n.*** 1. An excursion by any means of conveyance, as on horseback, by car, etc. 2. A road intended for riding. [OE *rīdan*] **—rid′a·ble** *adj.*

rid·er (rī′dər) *n.* 1. One who or that which rides. 2. One who breaks in horses. 3. Any device that rides upon or weighs down something else. 4. A separate piece of writing or print added to a document, record, or the like.

ridge (rij) *n.* 1. A long, relatively narrow elevation of land. 2. That part of a roof at the top where the rafters meet. 3. Any raised strip, as on fabric, etc. **—*v.t.* & *v.i.*** **ridged, ridg·ing** To form into or mark with ridges. [OE *hrycg*] **—ridg′y** *adj.*

ridge·pole (rij′pōl′) *n.* A horizontal timber at the ridge of a roof. Also **ridge beam, ridge piece, ridge plate.**

rid·i·cule (rid′ə·kyōōl) *n.* Language or actions calculated to make a person or thing the object of contemptuous or humorous derision or mockery. **—*v.t.*** **·culed, ·cul·ing** To make fun of; deride. [< L *ridiculum* a joke] **—rid′i·cul′er** *n.*

ri·dic·u·lous (ri·dik′yə·ləs) *adj.* Exciting ridicule; absurd and unworthy of consideration. **—ri·dic′u·lous·ly** *adv.* **—ri·dic′u·lous·ness** *n.*

rid·ing (rī′ding) *n.* The act of one who rides; a ride. **—*adj.*** Suitable for riding.

ri·el (rē·el′) The monetary unit of Cambodia.

rife (rīf) *adj.* 1. Great in number or quantity; abundant. 2. Prevalent; current. [OE *rȳfe*]

riff (rif) *n.* In jazz music, a melodic phrase or motif played repeatedly as background or used as the main theme. [? Back formation < REFRAIN[2]]

rif·fle (rif′əl) *n.* 1. A shoal or rocky obstruction lying beneath the surface of a river or other stream. 2. A stretch of shallow, choppy water caused by such a shoal. **—*v.t.* & *v.i.*** **·fled, ·fling** 1. To cause or form a rapid. 2. To shuffle (cards). 3. To thumb through (the pages of a book). [? Alter. of RUFFLE[1]]

riff·raff (rif′raf′) *n.* 1. The populace; rabble. 2. Miscellaneous rubbish. [ME *riff and raff* one and all]

ri·fle[1] (rī′fəl) *n.* 1. A firearm having a spirally grooved bore, fired from the shoulder. 2. An artillery piece having a spirally grooved bore. 3. *pl.* A body of soldiers equipped with rifles. **—*v.t.*** **·fled, ·fling** To cut a spirally grooved bore in (a firearm, etc.). [< F *rifler* to file, scrape]

ri·fle[2] (rī′fəl) *v.t.* **·fled, ·fling** To search through and rob, as a safe. [< OF *rifler* to plunder] **—ri′fler** *n.*

ri·fle·man (rī′fəl·mən) *n. pl.* **·men** (-mən) One armed or skilled with the rifle.

ri·fling (rī′fling) *n.* 1. The operation of forming the grooves in a rifle. 2. The grooves of a rifle collectively.

rift (rift) *n.* 1. An opening made by riving

or splitting; a cleft; fissure. 2. Any disagreement or lack of harmony, as between friends, nations, etc. —*v.t.* & *v.i.* To rive; burst open; split. [< Scand.]

rig[1] (rig) *v.t.* **rigged, rig·ging** 1. To fit out; equip. 2. *Naut.* To fit, as a ship, with rigging. 3. *Informal* To dress; clothe, esp. in finery. 4. To make or construct hurriedly: often with *up.* —*n.* 1. *Naut.* The arrangement of sails, rigging, spars, etc., on a vessel. 2. *Informal* A style of dress; costume. 3. *Informal* A horse or horses and vehicle. 4. Any apparatus, gear, or tackle: an oil-well *rig.* [< Scand.]

rig[2] (rig) *v.t.* **rigged, rig·ging** To control fraudulently; manipulate: to *rig* an election. [Origin uncertain]

rig·ger (rig′ər) *n.* 1. One who rigs. 2. A ship having a specified rig: used in combination: a *square-rigger.*

rig·ging (rig′ing) *n. Naut.* The entire cordage system of a vessel.

right (rīt) *adj.* 1. Done in accordance with moral law; equitable; just; righteous. 2. Conformable to truth or fact. 3. Conformable to a standard of propriety; proper. 4. Most desirable or preferable; also, fortunate. 5. Pertaining to, designating, or situated on the side of the body that is toward the south when one faces east. 6. Properly placed, disposed, or adjusted; well-regulated; orderly. 7. Sound in mind or body; healthy; well. 8. Designed to be worn outward or when in use placed toward an observer. 9. *Sometimes cap.* Designating a person, party, faction, etc., having conservative or reactionary views and policies. —**to rights** In a proper or orderly condition: to put a room *to rights.* —*adv.* 1. In accordance with justice or moral principle. 2. According to the fact or truth; correctly. 3. In a straight line; directly. 4. Very: used in some titles: *Right* Reverend. 5. Suitably; properly. 6. Precisely; just; also, immediately. 7. Toward the right. 8. Completely. The house burned *right* to the ground. —**right on** An exclamation of agreement, encouragement, etc. —*n.* 1. That which is right; moral rightness; also, justice. 2. *Often pl.* A just and proper claim or title. 3. The right hand, side, or direction. 4. *Often cap.* A group, party, etc., whose views and policies are predominantly conservative. 5. In boxing, a blow delivered with the right hand. —*v.t.* 1. To restore to an upright or normal position. 2. To put in order; set right. 3. To make correct or in accord with facts. 4. To make reparation for. —*v.i.* 5. To regain an upright or normal position. [OE *riht*] —**right′ness** *n.*

right·a·bout (rīt′ə·bout′) *n.* 1. The opposite direction. 2. A turning in or to the opposite direction.

right angle *Geom.* An angle whose sides are perpendicular to each other; an angle of 90°. —**right-an·gled** (rīt′ang′gəld) *adj.*

right·eous (rī′chəs) *adj.* 1. Conforming to a standard of right and justice; virtuous. 2. Morally right; equitable: a *righteous* act. [OE *riht* right + *wis* wise] —**right′eous·ly** *adv.* —**right′eous·ness** *n.*

right·ful (rīt′fəl) *adj.* 1. Characterized by or conforming to a right or just claim: *rightful* heritage. 2. Consonant with moral right or with justice and truth. 3. Proper; fitting. 4. Upright; just. [OE *rihtful*] —**right′·ful·ly** *adv.* —**right′ful·ness** *n.*

right-hand (rīt′hand′) *adj.* 1. Of, for, pertaining to, or situated on the right side or right hand. 2. Chiefly depended on: *right-hand* man. 3. Toward the right.

right-hand·ed (rīt′han′did) *adj.* 1. Using the right hand more easily than the left. 2. Done with or adapted for the right hand. 3. Moving from left to right, as the hands of a clock. —**right′-hand′ed·ness** *n.*

right·ist (rī′tist) *n.* One whose views and policies are conservative. —*adj.* Conservative or reactionary. —**right′ism** *n.*

right·ly (rīt′lē) *adv.* 1. Correctly. 2. Honestly; uprightly. 3. Properly; aptly.

right-mind·ed (rīt′mīn′did) *adj.* Having correct or proper feelings or opinions. —**right′mind′ed·ly** *adv.* —**right′mind′ed·ness** *n.*

right of way 1. *Law* The right of a person to pass over the land of another; also, the piece of land used. 2. The strip of land over which a railroad lays its tracks, on which a public highway is built, or above which a high-tension power line is built. 3. The legal or customary precedence which allows one vehicle or vessel to cross in front of another. Also **right-of-way** (rīt′əv·wā).

right triangle A triangle containing one right angle.

right wing *Sometimes cap.* A party, group, faction, etc., having rightist policies. —**right-wing** (rīt′wing′) *adj.* —**right′-wing′er** *n.*

rig·id (rij′id) *adj.* 1. Resisting change of form; stiff. 2. Rigorous; inflexible; severe. 3. Not moving; fixed. 4. Strict; exact, as reasoning. [< L *rigere* to be stiff] —**rig′·id·ly** *adv.* —**ri·gid·i·ty** (rə·jid′ə·tē), **rig′id·ness** *n.*

rig·ma·role (rig′mə·rōl) *n.* 1. Incoherent talk or writing; nonsense. 2. Any complicated procedure. Also **rig′a·ma·role′** (-ə·mə-). [Alter. of *ragman roll* deed on parchment]

rig·or (rig′ər) *n.* 1. The condition of being stiff or rigid. 2. Stiffness of opinion or temper; harshness. 3. Exactness without allowance or indulgence; inflexibility; strictness. 4. Inclemency, as of the weather; hardship. Also *Brit.* **rig′our.** [< L *rigere* to be stiff] —**rig′or·ist** *n.* —**rig′or·ous** *adj.* —**rig′or·ous·ly** *adv.* —**rig′or·ous·ness** *n.*

rig·or mor·tis (rig′ər môr′tis, rī′gər) The muscular rigidity that ensues shortly after death. [< L, stiffness of death]

rile (rīl) *v.t.* **riled, ril·ing** *Informal* 1. To vex; irritate. 2. To make (a liquid) muddy. [Var. of ROIL]

rill (ril) *n.* A small stream; brook. [Prob. < LG *rille*]

rim (rim) *n.* 1. The edge of a usu. circular object. 2. The peripheral part of a wheel, connected to the hub by spokes. 3. The frame of a pair of spectacles, surrounding the lenses. —*v.t.* **rimmed, rim·ming** 1. To provide with a rim; border. 2. In sports, to roll around the edge of (the basket, cup, etc.) without falling in. [OE *rima*]

rime[1] (rīm) See RHYME.

rime[2] (rīm) *n.* 1. A milky white, granular

deposit of ice formed on objects by fog or water vapor that has frozen. 2. Frost. —*v.t. & v.i.* **rimed, rim·ing** To cover with or congeal into rime. [OE *hrīm* frost] —**rim′y** *adj.*

rime·ster (rīm′stər) See RHYMESTER.

rim·mer (rim′ər) *n.* A reamer (def. 1).

rind (rīnd) *n.* The skin or outer coat that may be peeled or taken off, as of bacon, fruit, cheese, etc. [OE, bark]

ring[1] (ring) *n.* 1. Any circular object, line, arrangement, etc. 2. A circular band, usu. of precious metal, worn on a finger. 3. Any metal or wooden band used for holding or carrying something. 4. A group of persons, as in a conspiracy. 5. One of a series of concentric layers of wood in the trunk of a tree, formed by annual growth. 6. An area or arena, as that used for circuses or boxing matches. 7. Political competition or rivalry: He tossed his hat into the *ring.* —**the ring** Prize fighting in general. —**to run rings around** *Informal* To be superior to in some way. —*v.t.* **ringed, ring·ing** 1. To surround with a ring; encircle. 2. To form into a ring or rings. 3. In certain games, to cast a ring over (a peg or pin). [OE *hring*] —**ringed** *adj.*

ring[2] (ring) *v.* **rang, rung, ring·ing** *v.i.* 1. To give forth a resonant, sonorous sound, as a bell when struck. 2. To reverberate or resound. 3. To cause a bell or bells to sound. 4. To have or suggest a specified quality: His story *rings* true. 5. To have a continued sensation of ringing or buzzing: My ears *ring.* —*v.t.* 6. To cause (a bell, etc.) to ring. 7. To produce, as a sound, by or as by ringing. 8. To announce or proclaim by ringing: to *ring* the hour. 9. To summon, escort, usher, etc., in this manner: with *in* or *out*: to *ring* out the old year. 10. To call on the telephone: often with *up.* —**to ring up** 1. To total, esp. on a cash register. 2. To score. —*n.* 1. The sound produced by a bell or other vibrating, sonorous object. 2. The act of sounding a bell. 3. A telephone call. 4. Characteristic sound or impression: the *ring* of truth. [OE *hringan*]

ring·er[1] (ring′ər) *n.* 1. One who or that which rings (a bell or chime). 2. *Slang* An athlete, horse, etc., illegally entered in a contest by concealing disqualifying facts, as age, professional status, etc. 3. *Slang* A person who bears a marked resemblance to another: You are a *ringer* for Jones.

ring·er[2] (ring′ər) *n.* 1. One who or that which encircles. 2. A quoit or horseshoe that falls around one of the posts.

ring·git (ring′git) *n.* The monetary unit of Malaysia.

ring·lead·er (ring′lē′dər) *n.* A leader or organizer of any undertaking, esp. of an unlawful one, as a riot.

ring·let (ring′lit) *n.* A long, spiral lock of hair; a curl.

ring·mas·ter (ring′mas′tər) *n.* One who has charge of the performances in a circus ring.

ring·side (ring′sīd′) *n.* The space or seats immediately surrounding a ring, as at a prize fight.

ring·worm (ring′wûrm′) *n. Pathol.* Any of several contagious skin diseases caused by certain fungi and marked by the appearance of discolored, scaly patches on the skin.

rink (ringk) *n.* 1. A smooth, artificial surface of ice, used for ice-skating or hockey. 2. A smooth floor used for roller-skating. 3. A building containing a surface for skating. [< Scot., course, race]

rinse (rins) *v.t.* **rinsed, rins·ing** 1. To remove soap from by putting through clear water. 2. To wash lightly, as by dipping in water or by running water over or into. —*n.* 1. The act of rinsing, or the solution in which something is rinsed. 2. A hair coloring agent. [< L *recens* fresh] —**rins′er** *n.*

rins·ing (rin′sing) *n.* 1. A rinse. 2. The liquid in which anything is rinsed. 3. That which is removed by rinsing.

ri·ot (rī′ət) *n.* 1. A disturbance consisting of wild and turbulent conduct of a large number of persons, as a mob. 2. A brilliant or sometimes confusing display: a *riot* of color. 3. Boisterous festivity; revelry. 4. *Slang* An uproariously amusing person, thing, or performance. —**to run riot** 1. To act or move wildly and without restraint. 2. To grow profusely or luxuriantly, as vines. —*v.i.* To take part in a riot or public disorder. [< OF *rioter* to quarrel] —**ri′ot·er** *n.* —**ri′ot·ous** *adj.* —**ri′ot·ous·ly** *adv.* —**ri′ot·ous·ness** *n.*

riot act Any forceful or vigorous warning or reprimand. —**to read the riot act to** To reprimand bluntly and severely.

riot squad A group of policemen specially trained, armed, and equipped to deal with riots.

rip[1] (rip) *v.* **ripped, rip·ping** *v.t.* 1. To tear or cut apart roughly or violently; slash. 2. To tear or cut from something else in a rough or violent manner: with *off, away, out,* etc. 3. To saw or split (wood) in the direction of the grain. —*v.i.* 4. To be torn or cut apart; split. 5. *Informal* To rush headlong. —**to rip off** *Slang* 1. To steal or steal from. 2. To swindle. —*n.* A place torn or ripped open; a tear. [Prob. < MDu. *rippen*] —**rip′per** *n.*

rip[2] (rip) *n.* A ripple; a rapid in a river. [Origin uncertain]

ri·par·i·an (ri·pâr′ē·ən, rī-) *adj.* Of or growing on a bank of a river or stream. [< L *ripa* river bank]

rip·cord (rip′kôrd′) *n. Aeron.* The cord, together with the handle and fastening pins, that when pulled releases a parachute from its pack.

ripe (rīp) *adj.* 1. Grown to maturity and fit for food, as fruit or grain. 2. Brought by keeping and care to a condition for use, as wine or cheese. 3. In full readiness to do or try; prepared; ready. [OE *rīpe*] —**ripe′ly** *adv.* —**ripe′ness** *n.*

rip·en (rī′pən) *v.t. & v.i.* To make or become ripe; mature.

rip-off (rip′ôf′) *n. Slang* 1. An act of stealing or cheating. 2. Anything dishonest, illegal, or exploitative.

ri·poste (ri·pōst′) *n.* 1. A return thrust, as in fencing. 2. A quick, clever reply; repartee. Also **ri·post′.** [< Ital. *risposta* reply] —**ri·poste′** *v.i.* **·post·ed, ·post·ing**

rip·ple (rip′əl) *v.* **·pled, ·pling** *v.i.* 1. To become slightly agitated on the surface, as water blown on by a light breeze. 2. To make a sound like that of water flowing in small waves. —*v.t.* 3. To cause to form ripples. —*n.* 1. One of the wavelets on the surface of water. 2. Any sound like that made by rippling. [? Fusion of RIFFLE + RIP[2]] —**rip′pler** *n.* —**rip′ply** *adj.*

rip-roar·ing (rip′rôr′ing) *adj. Slang* Good and lively; boisterous.

rip·saw (rip′sô′) *n.* A coarse-toothed saw used for cutting wood in the direction of the grain.

rip·tide (rip′tīd′) *n.* Water agitated and made dangerous for swimmers by conflicting tides or currents. Also **rip current.**

rise (rīz) *v.i.* **rose, ris·en, ris·ing** 1. To move upward; go from a lower to a higher position. 2. To slope gradually upward. 3. To gain elevation in rank, status, etc. 4. To swell up: Dough *rises.* 5. To become greater in force, intensity, height, etc.; also, to become higher in pitch, as the voice. 6. To become greater in amount, value, etc. 7. To stand up. 8. To get out of bed. 9. To revolt; rebel. 10. To appear above the horizon: said of the sun, moon, etc. 11. To have origin; begin. —**to rise above** To prove superior to; show oneself indifferent to. —*n.* 1. The act of rising; ascent. 2. Degree of ascent; elevation; also, an ascending course. 3. A beginning; an origin. 4. An elevated place; a small hill. 5. Increase or advance, as in price or value. 6. Advance or elevation, as in rank, prosperity, or importance. 7. The height of a stair step. 8. *Informal* An emotional reaction; a response or retort. 9. *Brit.* An increase in salary. [OE *rīsan*]

ris·en (riz′ən) Past participle of RISE.

ris·er (rī′zər) *n.* 1. One who rises or gets up, as from bed: He is an early *riser.* 2. The vertical part of a step or stair.

ris·i·bil·i·ty (riz′ə·bil′ə·tē) *n. pl.* **·ties** 1. A tendency to laughter. 2. *pl.* Impulses to laughter: also **ris′i·bles.**

ris·i·ble (riz′ə·bəl) *adj.* 1. Having the power of laughing. 2. Exciting laughter; funny. 3. Pertaining to laughter. [< L *ridere* to laugh] —**ris′i·bly** *adv.*

ris·ing (rī′zing) *adj.* 1. Increasing in wealth, power, or distinction. 2. Ascending; also, sloping upward: a *rising* hill. 3. Advancing to adult years; growing: the *rising* generation. —*n.* 1. That which rises above the surrounding surface. 2. An insurrection or revolt.

risk (risk) *n.* 1. A chance of encountering harm or loss; hazard; danger. 2. In insurance: **a** The hazard or chance of loss. **b** An insurance applicant who is considered a hazard to the insurer. —*v.t.* 1. To expose to a chance of injury or loss. 2. To incur the risk of. [< Ital. *risco*] —**risk′er** *n.*

risk·y (ris′kē) *adj.* **risk·i·er, risk·i·est** Attended with risk; hazardous; dangerous. —**risk′i·ness** *n.*

ris·qué (ris·kā′) *adj.* Bordering on or suggestive of impropriety; bold; off-color: a *risqué* story. [< F, pp. of *risquer* to risk]

rite (rīt) *n.* 1. A solemn or religious ceremony performed in an established or prescribed manner; also, the words or acts constituting or accompanying it. 2. Any formal practice or custom. [< L *ritus*]

rit·u·al (rich′o͞o·əl) *n.* A prescribed form or method for the performance of a religious or solemn ceremony; any body of rites or ceremonies. [< L *ritus* rite] —**rit′u·al** *adj.* —**rit′u·al·ly** *adv.*

rit·u·al·ism (rich′o͞o·əl·iz′əm) *n.* 1. Adherence to ritual. 2. Excessive concern with ritual. —**rit′u·al·ist** *n.* —**rit′u·al·is′tic** *adj.* —**rit′u·al·is′ti·cal·ly** *adv.*

ritz·y (rit′sē) *adj.* **ritz·i·er, ritz·i·est** *Slang* Smart; elegant; classy. [after the *Ritz-Carlton Hotel, New York*]

ri·val (rī′vəl) *n.* 1. One who strives to equal or excel another or is in pursuit of the same object as another; a competitor. 2. One equaling or nearly equaling another, in any respect. —*v.t.* **ri·valed** or **·valled, ri·val·ing** or **·val·ling** 1. To strive to equal or excel; compete with. 2. To be the equal of or a match for. —*adj.* Being a rival; competing. [< L *rivales* those living near the same stream]

ri·val·ry (rī′vəl·rē) *n. pl.* **·ries** The act or state of being a rival or rivals; competition.

rive (rīv) *v.t. & v.i.* **rived, rived** or **riv·en** (riv′ən), **riv·ing** 1. To split asunder by force; cleave. 2. To break, as the heart. [< ON *rifa*] —**riv·er** (rī′vər) *n.*

riv·er (riv′ər) *n.* 1. A large, natural stream of water, usu. fed by converging tributaries along its course and discharging into a larger body of water, as the ocean, a lake, or another stream. ◆Collateral adjective: *fluvial.* 2. A large stream of any kind. [< OF *rivière*]

riv·er·side (riv′ər·sīd′) *n.* The space alongside of or adjacent to a river.

riv·et (riv′it) *n.* A short, soft metal bolt, having a head on one end, used to join objects, as metal plates, by passing the shank through holes and flattening out the headless end. —*v.t.* 1. To fasten with or as with a rivet. 2. To batter the headless end of (a bolt, etc.) so as to make fast. 3. To engross or attract (the eyes, attention, etc.). [< OF *river* to clench] —**riv′·et·er** *n.*

riv·u·let (riv′yə·lit) *n.* A small stream or brook; streamlet. [< L. *rivulus*, dim. of *rivus* stream]

ri·yal (rē′yôl) *n.* The monetary unit of Saudi Arabia and Qatar.

RNA Ribonucleic acid.

roach[1] (rōch) *n.* A European fresh-water fish of the carp family, with a greenish back. [< OF *roche*]

roach[2] (rōch) *n.* 1. A cockroach. 2. *Slang* The butt of a marijuana cigarette.

road (rōd) *n.* 1. An open way for public passage; esp., a highway. 2. Any way of advancing or progressing: the *road* to fame. 3. *Usu. pl.* A roadstead. —**on the road** 1. On tour: said of theatrical companies, etc. 2. Traveling, as a salesman. 3. Living the life of a hobo. [OE *rād* journey]

road·bed (rōd′bed′) *n.* 1. The graded foundation of gravel, etc., on which the ties, rails, etc., of a railroad are laid. 2. The graded foundation or surface of a road.

road·block (rōd′blok′) *n.* An obstruction in a road, esp. one for blocking passage of enemy troops, fugitives, etc.

road·house (rōd′hous′) *n.* A restaurant, dance hall, etc., located at the side of the road in a rural area.

road metal Broken stone or the like, used for making or repairing roads.
road runner A long-tailed ground cuckoo of SW North America, that can run swiftly.
road·side (rōd′sīd′) *n.* The area along the side of a road. —*adj.* Situated on the side of a road.
road·stead (rōd′sted) *n.* *Naut.* A place of anchorage offshore, less sheltered than a harbor. [< ROAD + *stead*, a place]
road·ster (rōd′stər) *n.* A light, open automobile, usu. with a single seat for two people.
road·way (rōd′wā′) *n.* A road, esp. that part over which vehicles pass.
road·work (rōd′wûrk′) *n.* Outdoor running as a form of exercise.
roam (rōm) *v.t. & v.i.* To move or wander about (an area, place, etc.); rove; range. —*n.* The act of roaming. [ME *romen*] —**roam′er** *n.*
roan (rōn) *adj.* Of a horse, having a color consisting of bay, sorrel, or chestnut, thickly interspersed with gray or white. —*n.* 1. A roan color. 2. An animal of a roan color. [< Sp. *roano*]
roar (rôr) *v.i.* 1. To utter a deep, prolonged cry, as of rage or distress. 2. To make a loud noise, as the sea or a cannon. 3. To laugh loudly. —*v.t.* 4. To utter or express by roaring. —*n.* 1. A full, deep, resonant cry, as of a lion or an enraged person. 2. Any loud, prolonged sound. [OE *rārian*] —**roar′er** *n.*
roast (rōst) *v.t.* 1. To cook (meat, etc.) by subjecting to the action of heat, as in an oven. 2. To cook before an open fire or on embers, etc. 3. *Informal* To criticize or ridicule severely. —*v.i.* 4. To roast food in an oven, etc. 5. To be cooked by this method. 6. *Informal* To be uncomfortably hot. —*n.* 1. Something roasted; esp., a piece of roasted meat. 2. A piece of meat adapted or prepared for roasting. 3. The act of roasting. 4. A gathering at which a person is ridiculed in a spirit of fun. —*adj.* Roasted. [< OF *rostir*]
roast·er (rōs′tər) *n.* 1. One who or that which roasts. 2. A pan or contrivance for roasting something. 3. Something suitable for roasting.
rob (rob) *v.* **robbed, rob·bing** *v.t.* 1. To seize and carry off the property of by unlawful violence or threat of violence. 2. To deprive of something belonging or due. 3. To steal from. —*v.i.* 4. To commit robbery. [< OF *robe* booty] —**rob′ber** *n.* —**rob′ber·y** *n.*
robber baron One of the powerful and unscrupulous financial adventurers of the late 19th c.
robe (rōb) *n.* 1. A long, loose, flowing garment, worn over other dress; a gown. 2. *pl.* Such a garment worn as a badge of office or rank. 3. A bathrobe. 4. A blanket or covering, as for use in an automobile: lap *robe.* —*v.t. & v.i.* **robed, rob·ing** To dress in a robe. [< OF, orig., booty]
rob·in (rob′in) *n.* 1. A large North American thrush with a reddish brown breast and underparts. 2. A small European thrush, with the cheeks and breast yellowish red. Also **robin redbreast.** [< OF *Robin*, dim. of *Robert*]
rob·in's-egg blue (rob′inz·eg′) A light greenish blue.
ro·bot (rō′bət, -bät) *n.* 1. A manlike machine. 2. One who works mechanically; automaton. 3. Any mechanism that operates automatically or is remotely controlled. [< Czechoslovakian *robota* forced labor]
ro·bust (rō·bust′, rō′bust) *adj.* Strong and healthy; rugged. [< L *robur* oak, hence, strength] —**ro·bust′ly** *adv.* —**ro·bust′ness** *n.*
roc (rok) *n.* In Arabian and Persian legend, an enormous and powerful bird of prey. [< Persian *rukh*]
Ro·chelle salt (rō·shel′) A white crystalline tartrate of potassium and sodium, used as a cathartic. [after La *Rochelle*, city in France]
rock[1] (rok) *n.* 1. A large mass of stone or stony material. 2. A fragment of rock; stone. 3. *Geol.* The material forming the essential part of the earth's crust. 4. Something resembling or suggesting a rock, as a firm support, source of strength, etc. 5. *Slang* A gemstone, esp., a large diamond. —**on the rocks** *Informal* 1. Ruined; also, destitute or bankrupt. 2. Served with ice cubes but without soda or water. —*adj.* Made or composed of rock. [< OF *roque, roche*]
rock[2] (rok) *v.t. & v.i.* 1. To move backward and forward or from side to side; sway. 2. To reel or stagger; shake. —*n.* 1. The act of rocking; a rocking motion. 2. Rock-and-roll. [OE *roccian*]
rock·a·by (rok′ə·bī) *interj.* Go to sleep: from a nursery song intended to lull a child to slumber. —*n.* A lullaby. Also **rock′a·bye, rock′-a-bye.**
rock-and-roll (rok′ən·rōl′) *adj.* Denoting a form of popular music derived from hillbilly styles, characterized by repetitious melody and insistent rhythms. —*n.* Rock-and-roll music: also *rock 'n' roll.*
rock bottom The lowest possible level: Prices hit *rock bottom.* —**rock-bot·tom** (rok′bot′əm) *adj.*
rock-bound (rok′bound′) *adj.* Encircled by or bordered with rocks.
rock candy Large crystals of sugar.
rock crystal Colorless transparent quartz.
rock dove The wild pigeon of Europe, the parent of domestic varieties.
rock·er (rok′ər) *n.* 1. One who or that which rocks. 2. One of the curved pieces on which a rocking chair, etc., rocks. 3. A rocking chair. 4. A rocking horse. —**off one's rocker** *Slang* Mentally unbalanced.
rock·et (rok′it) *n.* 1. A firework, projectile, missile, or other device, usu. cylindrical in form, that is propelled by the reaction of escaping gases produced during flight. 2. A type of vehicle operated by rocket propulsion and designed for space travel. —*v.i.* 1. To move like a rocket. —*v.t.* 2. To propel by means of a rocket. [< Ital. *rocchetta*, dim. of *rocca* distaff < Gmc.]
rock·et·eer (rok′ə·tir′) *n.* One who designs or launches rockets.
rocket engine A reaction engine fueled by a liquid or solid propellant containing its own oxidizing agent.
rocket gun Any gunlike device used for the discharge of rocket projectiles, as a bazooka.
rock·et·ry (rok′it·rē) *n.* The science, art,

and technology of rocket flight, design, construction, etc.

rocket ship Rocket (def. 2).

rock·et·sonde (rok′it·sond′) *n. Meteorol.* A radiosonde adapted for use on high-altitude rockets.

rock·fish (rok′fish′) *n. pl.* **·fish** or **·fish·es** Any of several spiny-finned fishes of the Pacific coast of North America.

rock garden A garden with flowers and plants growing among rocks.

rocking chair A chair having the legs set on rockers.

rocking horse A large toy horse mounted on rockers: also called *hobbyhorse*.

rock lobster The spiny lobster.

rock maple The sugar maple.

rock 'n' roll See ROCK-AND-ROLL.

rock·oon (rok·o͞on′) *n.* A small rocket equipped with various meteorological recording devices and attached to a balloon, from which it is released at predetermined altitudes. [< ROCK(ET) + (BALL)OON]

rock-ribbed (rok′ribd′) *adj.* 1. Having rocky ridges. 2. Unyielding; inflexible.

rock salt Halite.

rock·shaft (rok′shaft′) A shaft in an engine made to rock on its bearings.

rock wool A fibrous, woollike material made from molten rock, used as insulation.

rock·y[1] (rok′ē) *adj.* **rock·i·er, rock·i·est** 1. Consisting of, abounding in, or resembling rocks. 2. Tough; unfeeling; hard. —**rock′i·ness** *n.*

rock·y[2] (rok′ē) *adj.* **rock·i·er, rock·i·est** 1. Inclined to rock or shake; unsteady. 2. *Informal* Dizzy or weak. —**rock′i·ness** *n.*

Rocky Mountain goat A goatlike, shaggy white ruminant with short black horns, found in the mountains of NW North America: also called *mountain goat*.

Rocky Mountain sheep The bighorn.

Rocky Mountain spotted fever *Pathol.* An acute infectious disease caused by a microorganism transmitted by the bite of certain ticks, and marked by skin eruptions.

ro·co·co (rə·kō′kō) *n.* 1. A very ornate style of art and architecture that developed in France in the 18th c. 2. Florid, fantastic, or odd style. —*adj.* 1. In the rococo style. 2. Overelaborate; florid. [< F, alter. of *rocaille* shellwork]

rod (rod) *n.* 1. A straight, slim piece of wood, metal, or other material. 2. A switch or several switches together, used as an instrument of punishment. 3. Discipline; correction: with *the.* 4. A scepter or badge of office; a wand. 5. A bar, typically of metal, forming part of a machine: a connecting *rod.* 6. A measure of length equal to 5.5 yards; also, a square rod. 7. One of the rodlike bodies of the retina sensitive to faint light. 8. A rod-shaped bacterium. 9. *Slang* A pistol. [OE *rodd*]

rode (rōd) Past tense of RIDE.

ro·dent (rōd′nt) *n.* Any of a large order of gnawing mammals, having in each jaw two (rarely four) prominent incisors, as a squirrel, beaver, or rat. —*adj.* 1. Gnawing; corroding. 2. Of or pertaining to a rodent or rodents. [< L *rodens, -entis,* ppr. of *rodere* to gnaw]

ro·de·o (rō′dē·ō, rō·dā′ō) *n. pl.* **·os** 1. The driving of cattle together to be branded, inspected, etc.; a roundup. 2. A public spectacle featuring the riding of broncos, lariat throwing, etc. [< Sp. *rodear* to go around < L *rota* wheel]

roe[1] (rō) *n.* The spawn or eggs of female fish. [Var. of dial. *roan,* appar. < ON *hrogn* or MDu. *roch*]

roe[2] (rō) *n.* A small, graceful deer of Europe and western Asia. Also **roe deer.** [OE *rā*]

roe·buck (rō′buk′) *n.* The male of the roe deer.

roent·gen (rent′gən, *Ger.* rœnt′gən) *n.* A measure of the intensity of gamma or X-rays. [after Wilhelm Konrad *Roentgen*]

roent·gen·o·gram (rent′gən·ə·gram′) *n.* An X-ray photograph. Also **roent′gen·o·graph′** (-graf′).

roent·gen·og·ra·phy (rent′gən·og′rə·fē) *n. Med.* Photography by means of X-rays. —**roent′gen·o·graph′ic** (-ə·graf′ik) *adj.* —**roent′gen·o·graph′i·cal·ly** *adv.*

roent·gen·ol·o·gy (rent′gən·ol′ə·jē) *n.* The science of X-rays, esp. of their use in the diagnosis and treatment of disease. —**roent′·gen·o·log′ic** (-ə·log′ik) *adj.* —**roent′·gen·ol′o·gist** *n.*

Roentgen rays X-rays.

rog·er (roj′ər) *interj.* 1. *Often cap.* Message received: used in radio communication. 2. *Informal* All right; O.K. [after *Roger,* personal name representing *r* in telecommunication]

rogue (rōg) *n.* 1. A dishonest and unprincipled person; rascal. 2. One who is innocently mischievous. 3. A fierce and dangerous animal, as an elephant, separated from the herd. —*v.t.* **rogued, ro·guing** To practice roguery upon; defraud. [Origin uncertain] —**ro·guer·y** (rō′gər·ē) *n.* —**ro·guish** (rō′gish) *adj.* —**ro′guish·ly** *adv.* —**ro′·guish·ness** *n.*

rogues' gallery A collection of photographs of criminals.

roil (roil) *v.t.* 1. To make muddy or turbid, as by stirring up sediment. 2. To vex; irritate; rile. [< F *rouiller, ruiler*]

roil·y (roi′lē) *adj.* **roil·i·er, roil·i·est** Turbid; muddy.

roist·er (rois′tər) *v.i.* 1. To bluster; swagger. 2. To engage in tumultuous merrymaking; revel. [< L *rusticus* rustic] —**roist′er·er** *n.*

role (rōl) *n.* 1. A part or character taken by an actor. 2. Any assumed character or function. Also **rôle.** [< F *rôle*]

roll (rōl) *v.i.* 1. To move forward on a surface by turning round and round, as a ball or wheel. 2. To move or be moved on wheels or rollers. 3. To move or appear to move in undulations or swells, as waves. 4. To assume the shape of a ball or cylinder by turning over and over, as a ball of yarn, or by curling up, as an animal: often with *up.* 5. To pass; elapse: with *on* or *by.* 6. To make a prolonged sound, as thunder. 7. To rotate wholly or partially. 8. To sway or move from side to side, as a ship. 9. To walk with a swaying motion. 10. To move ahead; progress. —*v.t.* 11. To cause to move along a surface by turning round and round, as a ball, log, etc. 12. To move, push forward, etc., on wheels or rollers. 13. To wrap round and round upon itself or on an axis: often with *up.* 14. To spread or make flat by pressing with a roller or rollers, as dough. 15. To wrap or envelop in or as in a covering. 16. To rotate, as the eyes. 17. To utter, emit, etc., with a trilling or rumbling sound: to *roll* one's r's. 18. To cast (dice). 19. *Slang* To rob (a drunk or a person who is asleep). **—to roll back** 1. To force back; push or pull back. 2. In commerce, to cause (prices, wages, etc.) to return to a previous, lower level, as by government direction. **—to roll in** *Informal* 1. To arrive, esp. in numbers or large amounts. 2. To wallow; luxuriate: to *roll in* money. —*n.* 1. Anything rolled up in cylindrical form. 2. A register or list of names. 3. Any food rolled up in preparation for use; also, a small, individually shaped portion of bread. 4. A rolling gait or movement, as of a ship. 5. A reverberating, rumbling, or trilling sound. 6. A swell or undulation of a surface, as of land or water. 7. *Slang* A wad of paper money. 8. The act of rolling, or the state of being rolled. 9. *Aeron.* A complete rotation of an airplane about its longitudinal axis without change in the direction of flight. [< L *rotula* < *rota* wheel]

roll·a·way (rōl′ə·wā′) *adj.* Mounted on rollers for easy movement into storage.

roll·back (rōl′bak′) *n.* 1. The act of rolling back, or the state of being rolled back. 2. A return to a lower price or wage level.

roll bar An overhead metal bar to protect passengers should a vehicle overturn.

roll call The act of calling a roll or list of the names of a number of persons, as soldiers, to determine which are present.

roll·er (rō′lər) *n.* 1. One who or that which rolls. 2. Any of various cylindrical devices that roll or rotate. 3. The wheel of a caster or roller skate. 4. A heavy cylinder for rolling, smoothing, or crushing something: a steam *roller.* 5. One of a series of long, swelling waves that break on a coast, esp. after a storm. 6. *Ornithol.* a Any of various European birds remarkable for their rolling and tumbling flight. b A canary having a trilling song.

roller bearing A bearing employing steel rollers to lessen friction between the parts of a mechanism.

roller coaster A railway with small, open cars run over a route of steep inclines and sharp turns, common at amusement parks.

roller derby A contest between two teams of roller skaters on a banked oval track.

roller skate A skate having wheels instead of a runner. **—roll·er-skate** (rō′lər·skāt′) *v.i.* **-skat·ed, -skat·ing**

rol·lick (rol′ik) *v.i.* To move or behave in a careless, frolicsome manner. [? Blend of ROLL and FROLIC] **—rol′lick·ing, rol′lick·some, rol′lick·y** *adj.*

roll·ing (rō′ling) *adj.* 1. Turning round and round, esp. so as to move forward on a surface. 2. Having a succession of sloping elevations and depressions: *rolling* hills. 3. Turning on or as if on wheels; rotating. 4. Of sounds, trilling, rumbling or reverberating; resounding. 5. Recurring; elapsing. —*n.* The act of one who or that which rolls or is rolled.

rolling mill 1. An establishment in which metal is rolled into sheets, bars, etc. 2. A machine used to roll metal.

rolling pin A cylindrical device, usu. of wood and with a handle at each end, for rolling out dough, etc.

rolling stock The wheeled transportation equipment of a railroad.

roll-top (rōl′top′) *adj.* Designating a type of desk having a flexible, slatted cover that rolls back out of the way.

ro·ly-po·ly (rō′lē·pō′lē) *adj.* Short and fat; pudgy; dumpy. —*n. pl.* **-po·lies** A roly-poly person or thing. [Reduplication of ROLL]

Ro·ma·ic (rō·mā′ik) *n.* Modern Greek, esp. the popular spoken form. [< Gk. *Rhōmaikos* Roman] **—Ro·ma′ic** *adj.*

ro·maine (rō·mān′) *n.* A variety of lettuce characterized by long, crisp leaves. [< F, fem. of *romain* Roman]

ro·man (rō′mən) *Sometimes cap. n.* A common style of type or lettering characterized by vertical rather than slanted strokes: This line is set in roman. —*adj.* Pertaining to, designating, or printed in roman. [< ROMAN]

Ro·man (rō′mən) *adj.* 1. Of, pertaining to, or characteristic of modern or ancient Rome or its people. 2. Of or belonging to the Roman Catholic Church. 3. Of or pertaining to the Latin language. —*n.* 1. A native or citizen of ancient or modern Rome. 2. The language of ancient Rome; Latin. [< L *Roma* Rome]

Roman candle A firework consisting of a tube that discharges colored sparks of fire.

Roman Catholic A member of the Roman Catholic Church. **—Roman Catholicism**

Roman Catholic Church The Christian church that recognizes the Pope as its supreme head.

ro·mance (rō·mans′; *for n., also* rō′mans) *n.* 1. A love affair. 2. A kind of love between the sexes, characterized by high ideals of devotion, strong ardor, etc. 3. Adventurous, heroic, or exotic nature: the *romance* of faraway places. 4. A long narrative, sometimes in verse, presenting chivalrous ideals and heroes. 5. Any fictitious narrative about adventure and love. —*v.* **·manced, ·manc·ing** *v.i.* 1. To tell or write romances. 2. To think or act in a romantic manner. 3. *Informal* To make love. —*v.t.* 4. *Informal* To make love to; woo. [< OF *romans* story written in French < L *Romanicus* Roman] **—ro·manc′er** *n.*

Ro·mance (rō·mans′, rō′mans) *adj.* Pertaining or belonging to one or more, or all, of the languages that have developed from Latin, including French, Italian, and Spanish.

Roman Empire The empire of ancient Rome, established in 27 B.C. and continuing until A.D. 395.

Ro·man·esque (rō′mən·esk′) *adj.* Of, pertaining to, or designating a style of Western architecture that prevailed from the 5th to the 12th c., characterized by round arches and general massiveness. —*n.* The Romanesque style of architecture.

Roman holiday 1. Enjoyment or profit derived from the suffering of others. 2. A day of gladiatorial and other contests in ancient Rome.

Ro·man·ic (rō·man′ik) *adj.* 1. Roman. 2. Romance.

Ro·man·ism (rō′mən·iz′əm) *n.* The dogmas, forms, etc., of the Roman Catholic Church: often used disparagingly. —**Ro′man·ist** *n.*

Ro·man·ize (rō′mən·īz) *v.t. & v.i.* ·**ized,** ·**iz·ing** 1. To make or become Roman or Roman Catholic. 2. To write in the Roman style, language, etc. —**Ro′man·i·za′tion** *n.*

Roman nose An aquiline nose.

Roman numerals The letters used by the ancient Romans as symbols in arithmetical notation. The basic letters are I (1), V (5), X (10), L (50), C (100), D (500), and M (1000).

Ro·man·o (rō·mä′nō) *n.* A hard, sharp cheese.

Ro·mans (rō′mənz) *n.pl.* (*construed as sing.*) One of the books of the New Testament, in the form of a letter from the apostle Paul to the Christians at Rome: in full; **Epistle to the Romans.**

ro·man·tic (rō·man′tik) *adj.* 1. Of, characterized by, or of the nature of romance. 2. Characterized by or given to feelings of romance. 3. Suitable for or conducive to love or amorousness. 4. Visionary; impractical. 5. Of or pertaining to romanticism. —*n.* One who is romantic. [< F *romantique* < *romant* romance, novel] —**ro·man′ti·cal·ly** *adv.*

ro·man·ti·cism (rō·man′tə·siz′əm) *n.* 1. *Usu. cap.* A movement in art, music, and literature originating in Europe in the late 18th c., characterized by a revolt against neoclassic rules, forms, and traditions and by an exalting of the feelings and individualism: distinguished from *classicism.* Also **Romantic Movement.** 2. Romantic quality. —**ro·man′ti·cist** *n.*

ro·man·ti·cize (rō·man′tə·sīz) *v.t.* ·**cized,** ·**ciz·ing** To regard or interpret in a romantic manner.

Rom·a·ny (rom′ə·nē, rō′mə-) *n. pl.* ·**nies** 1. A Gypsy (def. 1). 2. The Indic language of the Gypsies: also called *Gypsy.* Also **Rom′ma·ny** (rom′ə·nē). [< Romany *rom* man] —**Rom′a·ny** *adj.*

Rome (rōm) 1. Capital of the former Roman republic, of the Roman Empire and of modern Italy. 2. The Roman Catholic Church.

Ro·me·o (rō′mē·ō) 1. A man who is an ardent lover. 2. A philanderer. [after the hero of Shakespeare's *Romeo and Juliet*]

romp (romp) *v.i.* 1. To play boisterously. 2. To win easily. —*n.* 1. One who romps, esp. a girl. 2. Noisy, exciting frolic or play. 3. *Informal* An easy win. —**romp′ish** *adj.* —**romp′ish·ly** *adv.* —**romp′ish·ness** *n.*

romp·er (rom′pər) *n.* 1. One who romps. 2. *pl.* A garment combining a waist and bloomers, worn by young children.

ron·deau (ron′dō, ron·dō′) *n. pl.* ·**deaux** (ron′dōz, ron·dōz′) A poem of usu. 13 lines with only two rhymes, and in which the opening words are repeated in two places as an unrhymed refrain. [< F *rond* round]

ron·del (ron′dəl, -del) *n.* A verse form consisting of usu. 14 lines, the first two lines being repeated as a refrain in other lines. [< F *rond* round]

ron·do (ron′dō, ron·dō′) *n. Music* A composition or movement having a main theme and several contrasting episodes, the main theme being repeated after each subordinate theme. [< Ital. < F *rond* round]

rood (rōōd) *n.* 1. A cross or crucifix. 2. A land measure equivalent to ¼ acre, or 40 square rods: also **square rood.** [OE *rōd* rod, measure of land, cross]

roof (rōōf, rŏŏf) *n.* 1. The exterior upper covering of a building: also **roof′top** (-top). 2. Any top covering, as of a car. 3. The most elevated part of anything. —*v.t.* To cover with or as with a roof. [OE *hrōf*] —**roof′less** *adj.*

roof·er (rōō′fər, rŏŏf′ər) *n.* One who makes or repairs roofs.

roof garden 1. A garden on a roof. 2. A restaurant, etc., on a roof, having plants or a garden.

roof·ing (rōō′fing, rŏŏf′ing) *n.* 1. Material for roofs. 2. A roof: covering.

roof·tree (rōōf′trē′, rŏŏf′-) *n.* Ridgepole.

rook[1] (rŏŏk) *n.* 1. An Old World crow. 2. A trickster or cheat. —*v.t. & v.i.* To cheat; defraud. [OE *hrōc*]

rook[2] (rŏŏk) *n.* A castle-shaped chessman that can move any number of unoccupied squares parallel to the sides of the board: also called *castle.* [< Persian *rukh*]

rook·er·y (rŏŏk′ər·ē) *n. pl.* ·**er·ies** 1. A colony or breeding place of rooks. 2. A breeding place of sea birds, seals, etc.

rook·ie (rŏŏk′ē) *n. Slang* A recruit or novice. [Prob. alter. of RECRUIT]

room (rōōm, rŏŏm) *n.* 1. An extent of space used for some implied or specified purpose. 2. A space for occupancy or use enclosed on all sides, as in a building. 3. *pl.* Lodgings. —*v.i.* To occupy a room; lodge. [OE *rūm* space]

room·er (rōō′mər, rŏŏm′ər) *n.* A lodger, esp. one who eats elsewhere.

room·ette (rōō·met′, rŏŏm·et′) *n.* A small compartment in a railroad sleeping car.

room·ful (rōōm′fŏŏl′, rŏŏm′-) *n. pl.* ·**fuls** 1. As many or as much as a room will hold. 2. A number of persons present in a room.

room·ing house (rōō′ming, rŏŏm′ing) A house for roomers.

room·mate (rōōm′māt′, rŏŏm′-) *n.* One who shares lodgings with another or others.

room·y (rōō′mē, rŏŏm′ē) *adj.* **room·i·er, room·i·est** Having abundant room; spacious. —**room′i·ness** *n.*

roor·back (rōōr′bak) *n.* A slanderous report circulated for political purposes. [after *Roorback,* purported author of a (nonexistent) book cited as authority for certain defamatory charges against President Polk]

roost (rōōst) *n.* 1. A perch or place where birds rest at night. 2. Any temporary resting place. —*v.i.* 1. To perch upon a roost. 2. To come to rest; settle. [OE *hrōst*]

roost·er (rōōs′tər) *n.* A male chicken; cock.

root[1] (rōōt, rŏŏt) *n.* 1. The underground portion of a plant, that absorbs moisture, obtains or stores nourishment, and provides support. 2. Any underground growth, as a tuber or bulb. 3. That from which anything derives origin, growth, or support. 4. A rootlike part of an organ or structure, as of a tooth. 5. *Ling.* A base to which affixes may be added to form words. 6. *Math.* A quantity that, multiplied by itself a specified number of times, will give a given quantity: 3 is the square *root* of 9. 7. *Music* The fundamental tone of a chord. —*v.i.* 1. To put forth roots. 2. To be or become firmly fixed. —*v.t.* 3. To fix by or as by roots. 4. To pull, dig, or tear up by or as by the roots: with *up* or *out.* [OE *rōt* < ON] —**root′less** *adj.* —**root′y** *adj.*

root[2] (rōōt, rŏŏt) *v.t.* 1. To dig up with the snout, as swine do. —*v.i.* 2. To turn up the earth with the snout. 3. To search; rummage. [OE *wrōtan* to root up] —**root′er** *n.*

root[3] (rōōt, rŏŏt) *v.i. Informal* To cheer for or encourage a contestant, team, etc.: with *for.* [Prob. var. of ROUT[2]] —**root′er** *n.*

root beer A beverage made with yeast and root extracts.

root hair *Bot.* Hairlike outgrowths of plant roots.

root·let (rōōt′lit, rŏŏt′-) *n.* A small root.

root·stalk (rōōt′stôk′, rŏŏt′-) *n. Bot.* A rhizome.

root·stock (rōōt′stok′, rŏŏt′-) *n.* 1. Original source; origin. 2. *Bot.* A rhizome.

rope (rōp) *n.* 1. A construction of twisted fibers, as of hemp, so intertwined in strands as to form a thick cord. 2. A collection of things united in a line. 3. A slimy or glutinous filament or thread. 4. A cord or halter used in hanging. 5. A lasso. —**to give (one) plenty of rope** To allow (a person) to pursue unchecked a course that will end in disaster. —**to know the ropes** *Informal* To be familiar with all the conditions in any sphere of activity. —*v.t.* **roped, rop·ing** 1. To tie or fasten with or as with rope. 2. To enclose or divide with a rope: usu. with *off.* 3. To catch with a lasso. [OE *rāp*]

rope·danc·er (rōp′dan′sər) *n.* A tightrope walker: also **rope′walk′er** (-wô′kər).

rope·walk (rōp′wôk′) *n.* A long alley or building used for the spinning of rope yarn.

rop·y (rō′pē) *adj.* **rop·i·er, rop·i·est** 1. Stringy; viscous. 2. Resembling ropes. —**rop′i·ly** *adv.* —**rop′i·ness** *n.*

Roque·fort cheese (rōk′fərt, *Fr.* rôk·fôr′) A strong cheese with a blue mold, made from ewe's and goat's milk.

ror·qual (rôr′kwəl) *n.* A whalebone whale of the Atlantic and Pacific oceans: also called *finback.* [< Norw. *röyrkval*]

Ror·schach test (rôr′shäk) *Psychol.* A test of personality characteristics based on analysis of the subject's interpretation of standard patterns formed by inkblots. [after Hermann *Rorschach,* 1884–1922, Swiss psychiatrist]

ro·sa·ceous (rō·zā′shəs) *adj.* 1. *Bot.* Of or pertaining to the rose family of plants. 2. Resembling a rose. [< L *rosa* rose]

ro·sa·ry (rō′zə·rē) *n. pl.* **·ries** *Eccl.* 1. A series of prayers. 2. A string of beads for keeping count of these prayers. [< L *rosa* rose]

rose[1] (rōz) *n.* 1. Any of a large genus of erect or climbing shrubs, with rodlike, prickly stems. 2. The flower of such a shrub, usu. white, yellow, pink, or red. 3. Any of various similar plants or flowers. 4. A light pinkish red. —**bed of roses** A peaceful or carefree time, place, or condition. —*v.t.* **rosed, ros·ing** To redden; flush. [< L *rosa,* prob. < Gk. *rhodea*]

rose[2] (rōz) Past tense of RISE.

ro·sé (rō·zā′) *n.* A pink wine. [F, lit., pink]

ro·se·ate (rō′zē·it, -āt) *adj.* 1. Rosy; rose-colored. 2. Cheerful; optimistic. [< L *roseus*] —**ro′se·ate·ly** *adv.*

rose·bud (rōz′bud′) *n.* The bud of a rose.

rose·bush (rōz′bŏŏsh′) *n.* A rose-bearing shrub or vine.

rose campion An herbaceous plant, cultivated for its pink or crimson flowers.

rose chafer A hairy, fawn-colored beetle injurious to roses: also **rose beetle, rose bug.**

rose-col·ored (rōz′kul′ərd) *adj.* Pink or crimson, as a rose. —**to see through rose-colored glasses** To see things in an unduly favorable light.

rose fever *Pathol.* A variety of hay fever, assumed to be caused by rose pollen. Also **rose cold.**

rose·mar·y (rōz′mâr′ē) *n. pl.* **·mar·ies** A fragrant Old World evergreen shrub of the mint family. [ME < L *ros* dew + *marinus* of the sea]

rose of Sharon 1. A hardy shrub of the mallow family. 2. A species of St. Johnswort having large, yellow flowers.

rose quartz A semitransparent variety of quartz, pink or rose in color.

Ro·set·ta stone (rō·zet′ə) A tablet inscribed with Egyptian hieroglyphics and in Greek, found near Rosetta, Egypt, in 1799. It was the key to the ancient inscriptions of Egypt.

ro·sette (rō·zet′) *n.* A circular ornament or badge having some resemblance to a rose. [< F, dim. of *rose*]

rose water A fragrant preparation made from rose petals or rose oil and water.

rose window A circular window filled with tracery, often radiating from the center.

rose·wood (rōz′wŏŏd′) *n.* A hard, dark-colored, fragrant wood yielded by certain tropical American trees; also, a tree yielding this wood.

Rosh Ha·sha·na (rosh hə·shä′nə, rōsh) The Jewish New Year, celebrated in September or October. Also **Rosh Ha·sho′nah** (-shō′-). [< Hebrew *rōsh* head + *hash-shānāh* of the year]

ros·in (roz′in) *n.* The hard, amber-colored resin forming the residue after the distillation of oil from crude turpentine: also called *resin.* —*v.t.* To apply rosin to. [Alter. of RESIN] —**ros′in·y** *adj.*

ros·ter (ros′tər) *n.* 1. A list of officers and men enrolled for duty; also, a list of active military organizations. 2. Any list of names. [< Du. *rooster* list, lit. gridiron]

ros·trum (ros′trəm) *n. pl.* **·trums** or **·tra** *for def. 1,* **·tra** *for def. 2* 1. A pulpit or platform. 2. In ancient Rome: **a** A beaklike part on the prow of a ship. **b** The orators' platform in the Roman forum, embellished with such parts. [< L, beak] —**ros′tral, ros′trate** (-trāt) *adj.*

ros·y (rō′zē) *adj.* **ros·i·er, ros·i·est** 1. Like a rose; rose red; blushing. 2. Bright, pleasing, or flattering. 3. Auguring success; optimistic. —**ros′i·ly** *adv.* —**ros′i·ness** *n.*

rot (rot) *v.* **rot·ted, rot·ting** *v.i.* 1. To undergo decomposition; decay. 2. To become morally rotten. —*v.t.* 3. To cause to decompose. —*n.* 1. The process of rotting or the state of being rotten. 2. That which is rotten. 3. Any of various diseases involving decay in humans, plants, and animals. 4. *Informal* Nonsense; rubbish. —*interj.* Nonsense. [OE *rotian*]

ro·ta·ry (rō′tər·ē) *adj.* 1. Turning or designed to turn around its axis, like a wheel. 2. Having some part that turns on its axis. —*n. pl.* **·ries** A rotary device or part. [< L *rota* wheel]

rotary engine *Mech.* 1. An engine in which rotary motion is directly produced, as in a turbine. 2. A radial engine revolving about a fixed crankshaft.

rotary press A printing press using curved type plates that revolve against the paper.

ro·tate (rō′tāt) *v.t. & v.i.* **·tat·ed, ·tat·ing** 1. To turn or cause to turn on or as on its axis. 2. To alternate in a definite order or succession. [< L *rotare* to turn < *rota* wheel] —**ro′tat·a·ble, ro·ta·tive** (rō′tə·tiv) *adj.* —**ro·ta′tion** *n.* —**ro·ta′tion·al** *adj.* —**ro′ta·tor** *n.*

ro·ta·to·ry (rō′tə·tôr′ē) *adj.* 1. Having, pertaining to, or producing rotation. 2. Following in succession. 3. Alternating or recurring.

rote (rōt) *n.* Mechanical routine, as the repetition of words, with slight attention to the sense. —**by rote** Mechanically; without intelligent attention. [ME; origin uncertain]

ro·te·none (rō′tə·nōn) *n. Chem.* A crystalline compound used as an insecticide and fish poison. [Origin unknown]

rot·gut (rot′gut′) *Informal* An inferior raw whisky.

ro·ti·fer (rō′tə·fər) *n.* One of a division of microscopic organisms having rings of cilia. [< L *rota* wheel + *ferre* to bear] —**ro·tif′er·al** (-tif′ər·əl), **ro·tif′er·ous** (-tif′ər·əs) *adj.*

ro·tis·se·rie (rō·tis′ər·ē) *n.* 1. A restaurant or shop specializing in roasted meat. 2. A rotating device for roasting meat, etc. [< F < *rôtir* to roast]

ro·to·gra·vure (rō′tə·grə·vyŏŏr′, -grāv′yər) *n.* 1. The process of printing from cylinders etched from photographic plates and run through a rotary press. 2. A picture printed by this process. 3. The section of a newspaper containing such pictures. [< L *rota* wheel + GRAVURE]

ro·tor (rō′tər) *n.* 1. The rotating section of a motor, turbine, etc. 2. *Aeron.* The horizontally rotating unit of a helicopter or autogiro, consisting of the airfoils and hub. [Contraction of ROTATOR]

rot·ten (rot′n) *adj.* 1. Decomposed by natural process; putrid. 2. Untrustworthy; treacherous. 3. Corrupt; venal. 4. Liable to break; unsound. 5. *Informal* Worthless. [< ON *rotinn*] —**rot′ten·ly** *adv.* —**rot′ten·ness** *n.*

rot·ter (rot′ər) *n. Chiefly Brit. Slang* A worthless or objectionable person; scoundrel.

ro·tund (rō·tund′) *adj.* 1. Rounded out; plump. 2. Full-toned; sonorous. [< L *rotundus* round] —**ro·tun′di·ty** *n.* —**ro·tund′ly** *adv.* —**ro·tund′ness** *n.*

ro·tun·da (rō·tun′də) *n.* A circular building or an interior hall, surmounted with a dome. [< Ital. See ROTUND.]

rou·ble (rōō′bəl) See RUBLE.

rou·é (rōō·ā′) *n.* A sensualist; debauchee [< F, broken on the wheel]

rouge (rōōzh) *n.* 1. Any cosmetic used for coloring the cheeks or lips pink or red. 2. A ferric oxide used in polishing metals and glass. —*v.t. & v.i.* **rouged, roug·ing** To use rouge on (the cheeks, lips, etc.). [< F < L *rubeus* ruby]

rough (ruf) *adj.* 1. Having an uneven surface; not smooth or polished. 2. Coarse in texture. 3. Disordered or ragged; shaggy. 4. Harsh; rude; violent. 5. Boisterous or tempestuous; stormy. 6. Not refined or cultured; crude. 7. Done or made hastily and without attention to details, as a drawing. —*n.* 1. A low, violent fellow. 2. A crude, incomplete, or unpolished object, material, or condition. 3. Any part of a golf course on which tall grass, bushes, etc., grow. —**in the rough** In a crude or unpolished state. —*v.t.* 1. To make rough; roughen. 2. To treat roughly. 3. To make, cut, or sketch roughly: with *in* or *out.* —**to rough it** To live, camp, or travel under rough or hard conditions. —*adv.* In a rude manner; roughly. [OE *rūh*] —**rough′ly** *adv.* —**rough′ness** *n.*

rough·age (ruf′ij) *n.* 1. Any coarse or tough substance. 2. Food material containing a high percentage of indigestible constituents, as cellulose.

rough-and-read·y (ruf′ən·red′ē) *adj.* Crude but competent or effective.

rough-and-tum·ble (ruf′ən·tum′bəl) *adj.* Marked by the disregard of rules; scrambling; disorderly. —*n.* A rough-and-tumble fight or scuffle.

rough·cast (ruf′kast′) *v.t.* **·cast, ·cast·ing** To shape or prepare in a preliminary or incomplete form. —*n.* A roughcast form or model. —**rough′cast′er** *n.*

rough·draw (ruf′drô′) *v.t.* **·drew, ·drawn, ·draw·ing** To sketch hastily or crudely.

rough·dry (ruf′drī′) *v.t.* **·dried, ·dry·ing** To dry without ironing, as washed clothes.

rough·en (ruf′ən) *v.t. & v.i.* To make or become rough.

rough·hew (ruf′hyōō′) *v.t.* **·hewed, ·hewed** or **·hewn, ·hew·ing** 1. To hew or shape roughly or irregularly. 2. To make crudely; roughcast.

rough·house (ruf′hous′) *Slang n.* A boisterous or violent game; rough play. —*v.* **·housed, ·hous·ing** *v.i.* 1. To engage in horseplay or violence. —*v.t.* 2. To treat roughly.

rough·neck (ruf′nek′) *n. Slang* A rowdy.

rough·rid·er (ruf′rī′dər) *n.* One skilled in breaking broncos or performing dangerous feats in horsemanship.

rough·shod (ruf′shod′) *adj.* Shod with rough shoes to prevent slipping, as a horse. —**to ride roughshod (over)** To act overbearingly.

rou·lette (rōō·let′) *n.* 1. A game of chance, played at a table having a rotating disk (**roulette wheel**) on which a ball is rolled until it drops into a numbered space. 2. An engraver's disk of tempered steel, as for tracing points on a copperplate; also, a draftsman's wheel for making dotted lines. —*v.t.* **·let·ted, ·let·ting** To perforate or mark with a roulette. [< F, small wheel]

round (round) *adj.* 1. Having a contour

that is circular or approximately so; spherical, ring-shaped, or cylindrical. 2. Having a curved contour or surface; not angular or flat. 3. Liberal; ample; large. 4. Easy and free, as in motion; brisk. 5. Of full cadence; full-toned. 6. Made without reserve; outspoken. 7. Open; just. 8. Formed or moving in rotation or a circle. 9. Returning to the point of departure. 10. Of a number, increased or decreased by a relatively small amount for the sake of simplicity. 11. *Phonet.* Formed or spoken with the lips rounded. —*n.* 1. Something round, as a portion of the thigh of a beef. 2. *Often pl.* A circular course; circuit; beat. 3. A single revolution; also revolving motion. 4. A series of recurrent movements; routine: the daily *round* of life. 5. One of a series of concerted actions performed in succession: a *round* of applause. 6. One of the divisions of a boxing match. 7. In golf, a number of holes or an interval of play in a match. 8. *Music* A short canon in which each voice enters in turn and returns to the beginning upon reaching the end. 9. A single shot or complete unit of ammunition. **—to go** (or **make**) **the rounds** 1. To take a usual walk or tour, as of inspection. 2. To pass from person to person of a certain group. —*v.t.* 1. To make round or full. 2. To bring to completion; perfect: usu. with *off* or *out.* 3. *Phonet.* To utter (a vowel) with the lips in a rounded position. 4. To travel or go around. —*v.i.* 5. To become round or plump. 6. To come to completeness or perfection. 7. To turn around. **—to round off** 1. To make round. 2. To make into a round number. **—to round up** 1. To collect (cattle, etc.) in a herd, as for driving to market. 2. *Informal* To assemble. —*adv.* 1. On all sides. 2. With a circular or rotating motion. 3. Through a circle or circuit, as from point to point. 4. In circumference. 5. From one view or position to another; to and fro. —*prep.* 1. Enclosing; encircling. 2. On every side of, or from every side toward; surrounding. 3. Toward every side from; about. [< L *rotundus* round] **—round′ed** *adj.* **—round′ish** *adj.* **—round′ish·ness** *n.* **—round′ness** *n.*

round·a·bout (round′ə·bout′) *adj.* 1. Circuitous; indirect. 2. Encircling. —*n.* 1. A jacket. 2. *Brit.* A merry-go-round.

roun·de·lay (roun′də·lā) *n.* 1. A simple melody. 2. A musical setting of a poem with a recurrent refrain. [< OF *rond* round]

round·er (roun′dər) *n.* 1. A tool for rounding. 2. *Slang* A drunkard, drifter, or petty criminal. 3. *pl.* (*construed as sing.*) An English game somewhat resembling baseball.

round·house (round′hous′) *n.* 1. A cabin on the after part of the quarter-deck of a vessel. 2. A round building with a turntable in the center for housing and switching locomotives.

round·ly (round′lē) *adv.* 1. In a round manner or form; circularly; spherically. 2. Severely; thoroughly. 3. Frankly; bluntly.

round number A number expressed to the nearest ten, hundred, thousand, etc. Also **round figure.**

round robin 1. A tournament, as in tennis or chess, in which each player meets every other player. 2. A letter circulated among the members of a group. 3. A number of signatures, as to a petition, written in a circle so as to avoid giving prominence to any one name.

round-shoul·dered (round′shōl′dərd) *adj.* Having the upper back rounded or the shoulders stooping.

round table 1. A meeting place for conference. 2. Any discussion group. **—round-ta·ble** (round′tā′bəl) *adj.*

round-the-clock (round′thə·klok′) *adj.* Through all 24 hours of the day.

round trip A trip to a place and back again; a two-way trip. **—round-trip** (round′trip′) *adj.*

round·up (round′up′) *n.* 1. The bringing together of cattle, etc., scattered over a range. 2. The cowboys, horses, etc., employed in this work. 3. *Informal* A bringing together of persons or things.

round·worm (round′wûrm′) *n.* A nematode worm, esp. one parasitic in the human intestines.

rouse (rouz) *v.t. & v.i.* **roused, rous·ing** 1. To awaken. 2. To excite or become excited. 3. To flush or start from cover: said of game. —*n.* The act of rousing. [Orig. technical term in hawking and hunting] **—rous′er** *n.*

rous·ing (rou′zing) *adj.* 1. Able to rouse or excite. 2. Lively; vigorous.

roust (roust) *v.t. & v.i. Informal* To arouse and drive (a person or thing); stir up: usu. with *out.* [< ROUSE]

roust·a·bout (rous′tə·bout′) *n.* A casual or unskilled laborer for heavy work, as on the waterfront, on a cattle ranch, or in a circus.

rout[1] (rout) *n.* 1. A disorderly and overwhelming defeat or flight. 2. A boisterous crowd. —*v.t.* To defeat disastrously; put to flight. [< L *rumpere* to break]

rout[2] (rout) *v.i.* 1. To root, as swine. 2. To search; rummage. —*v.t.* 3. To turn up with the snout. 4. To dig up; discover; disclose: with *out.* 5. To hollow or scrape, as with a scoop. 6. To drive or force out. [Var. of ROOT[2]]

route (ro͞ot, rout) *n.* 1. A course, road, or way taken in traveling. 2. The specific course followed, as in delivering mail. —*v.t.* **rout·ed, rout·ing** To dispatch or send by a certain way, as passengers, goods, etc. [< L *rupta* (*via*) broken (road), fem. of *ruptus.* See ROUT[1].]

rout·er (rou′tər) *n.* 1. One who or that which scoops or routs. 2. A plane for working a molding around a circular sash. [< ROUT[2]]

rou·tine (ro͞o·tēn′) *n.* 1. A detailed method of procedure, regularly followed. 2. Habitual methods or actions. —*adj.* 1. Customary; adhering to procedure. 2. Commonplace. [< F *route* way, road] **—rou·tine′ly** *adv.*

rou·tin·ism (ro͞o·tē′niz·əm) *n.* Adherence to routine. **—rou·tin′ist** *n.*

rou·tin·ize (ro͞o·tē′niz) *v.t.* **·ized, ·i·zing** To reduce or fit to a routine.

roux (ro͞o) *n. French* Butter and flour mixed and cooked together as a thickening agent.

rove[1] (rōv) *v.* **roved, rov·ing** *v.i.* 1. To wander from place to place. —*v.t.* 2. To roam over, through, or about. —*n.* The act

of roving; a ramble. [ME *roven*] **—rov′er** *n.*
rove[2] (rōv) Alternate past tense and past participle of REEVE.
row[1] (rō) *n.* 1. An arrangement or series of persons or things in a continued line; a rank; file. 2. A line of seats, as in a theater. **—a long row to hoe** A hard undertaking. *—v.t.* To arrange in a row: with *up.* [OE *rāw*, var. of *rǣw* line]
row[2] (rō) *v.i.* 1. To use oars, etc., in propelling a boat. *—v.t.* 2. To propel or transport by rowing. *—n.* 1. The act of rowing. 2. A trip in a rowboat. [OE *rōwan*]
row[3] (rou) *n.* 1. A noisy disturbance or quarrel; a brawl. 2. Any dispute or disturbance. *—v.t. & v.i.* To engage in a row or brawl. [Origin uncertain]
row·an (rō′ən) A small mountain ash native to Europe, having bright orange berries.
row·boat (rō′bōt′) *n.* A boat propelled by oars.
row·dy (rou′dē) *n. pl.* **·dies** A rough, disorderly person. *—adj.* **·di·er, ·di·est** Rough and loud; disorderly. [Origin unknown] **—row′dy·ish** *adj.* **—row′di·ness, row′dy·ism** *n.*
row·el (rou′əl) *n.* A spiked or toothed wheel, as on a spur. *—v.t.* **row·eled** or **·elled, row·el·ing** or **·el·ling** To prick with a rowel; spur. [< OF *roele* < L *rota* wheel]
row·lock (rō′lok′) *n.* An oarlock.
roy·al (roi′əl) *adj.* 1. Pertaining to a monarch. 2. Connected with or under the authority of a monarch. 3. Like or befitting a monarch; regal. [< L *regalis* kingly] **—roy′al·ly** *adv.*
royal blue A brilliant blue, often with reddish overtones.
Royal Canadian Mounted Police The federal police force of Canada.
roy·al·ist (roi′əl·ist) *n.* A supporter of a royal dynasty. *—adj.* Of or pertaining to royalists: also **roy′al·is′tic.**
Roy·al·ist (roi′əl·ist) *n.* 1. In English history, a Cavalier or adherent of King Charles I. 2. In French history, a supporter of various claimants to the throne since 1793. 3. In the American Revolution, a Tory.
royal palm Any of various tall, handsome palms native in tropical America.
royal purple 1. A very deep violet color. 2. Originally, a rich crimson.
roy·al·ty (roi′əl·tē) *n. pl.* **·ties** 1. The rank, birth, or lineage of a king or queen. 2. A royal personage; also, royal persons collectively. 3. A share of proceeds paid to a proprietor, author, or inventor. [< OF *roialte*]
-rrhagia *combining form Pathol.* An abnormal or violent discharge or flow; an eruption: also *-rhage, -rhagia, -rhagy.* Also **-rrhage, -rrhagy.** Corresponding adjectives are formed with **-rrhagic.** [< Gk. *rrhag-*, root of *rrhēgnynai* to burst]
-rrhaphy *combining form* A sewing together; a suture. [< Gk. *rhaptein* to sew together]
-rrhea *combining form Pathol.* An abnormal or excessive flow or discharge: also spelled *-rhea, -rhoea.* Also **-rrhoea.** [< Gk. *-rrhoia* < *rheein* to flow]
rub (rub) *v.* **rubbed, rub·bing** *v.t.* 1. To move or pass over the surface of with pressure and friction. 2. To cause (something) to move in this way. 3. To cause to become worn or sore from friction. 4. To clean, shine, etc., by means of pressure and friction. 5. To apply or spread by this means. 6. To remove or erase by friction: with *off* or *out.* *—v.i.* 7. To move along a surface with friction; scrape. 8. To exert pressure and friction. 9. To become worn or sore from friction; chafe. 10. To undergo removal by rubbing: with *off, out,* etc. **—to rub it in** *Slang* To harp on someone's errors, faults, etc. **—to rub out** *Slang* To kill. **—to rub the wrong way** *Slang* To irritate; annoy. *—n.* 1. A rubbing. 2. A hindrance, doubt, etc. [ME *rubben*, prob. < LG]
ru·ba·to (ro͞o·bä′tō) *Music adj.* Denoting the lengthening of one note at the expense of another. *—n. pl.* **·tos** A rubato modification. [< Ital., robbed] **—ru·ba′to** *adv.*
rub·ber[1] (rub′ər) *n.* 1. A resinous elastic material obtained from the latex of certain tropical plants, and also made synthetically. 2. Anything used for rubbing, erasing, etc. 3. An article made of rubber, as an overshoe. 4. One who or that which rubs. *—adj.* Made of rubber. [< RUB] **—rub′ber·y** *adj.*
rub·ber[2] (rub′ər) *n.* In some card games, a series of two or three games terminated when one side has won two games; also, the odd game that breaks a tie. [Origin unknown]
rubber check *Slang* A worthless check.
rub·ber·ize (rub′ər·īz) *v.t.* **·ized, ·iz·ing** To coat, impregnate, or cover with rubber.
rub·ber·neck (rub′ər·nek′) *Slang n.* One who cranes his neck in order to see something. *—v.i.* To gape.
rubber plant 1. Any of several plants yielding rubber. 2. A house plant of the mulberry family, having large, glossy, leathery leaves.
rub·ber-stamp (rub′ər·stamp′) *v.t.* 1. To mark or approve with a rubber stamping device. 2. *Informal* To approve as a matter of routine.
rub·bish (rub′ish) *n.* 1. Waste refuse; trash. 2. Nonsense; rot. [ME *rubbous*] **—rub′·bish·y** *adj.*
rub·ble (rub′əl; *for def. 3, also* ro͞o′bəl) *n.* 1. Rough pieces of broken stone. 2. The debris to which buildings, walls, etc., are reduced by earthquakes, bombings, etc. 3. Rough pieces of stone for use in construction; also, masonry composed of such pieces. [Origin uncertain] **—rub′bly** *adj.*
rub·down (rub′doun′) *n.* A massage.
rube (ro͞ob) *n. Slang* A farmer; rustic. [Abbreviation of *Reuben*, a personal name]
ru·bel·la (ro͞o·bel′ə) *n.* German measles. [< NL, neut. pl. of L *rubellus* reddish]
ru·be·o·la (ro͞o·bē·ō′lə, ro͞o·bē′ə·lə) *n.* Measles (def. 1). [< L *rubeus* red] **—ru·be·o′lar** *adj.*
ru·bi·cund (ro͞o′bə·kənd) *adj.* Red; rosy. [< L *rubicundus* red] **—ru′bi·cun′di·ty** (-kun′də·tē) *n.*
ru·bid·i·um (ro͞o·bid′ē·əm) *n.* A soft, silvery white, rare metallic element (symbol Rb) resembling potassium. [< L *rubidus* red]
ru·ble (ro͞o′bəl) *n.* 1. A standard monetary unit of the U.S.S.R.: also spelled *rouble.* 2. Formerly, a Russian silver coin.
ru·bric (ro͞o′brik) *n.* 1. A part of an early book that appears in red, as an initial

letter. 2. *Eccl.* A direction in a religious service. 3. A heading or title. 4. Any direction or rule of conduct. —*adj.* 1. Red. 2. Written in red. [< L *rubrica* red earth] —**ru′bri·cal** *adj.* —**ru′bri·cal·ly** *adv.*

ru·bri·cate (ro͞o′brə·kāt) *v.t.* **·cat·ed, ·cat·ing** To mark or illuminate with red, as a book. [< L *rubricare* to redden] —**ru′bri·ca′tion** *n.* —**ru′bri·ca′tor** *n.*

ru·by (ro͞o′bē) *n. pl.* **·bies** 1. A translucent, deep red variety of corundum, valued as a gemstone. 2. A red color. —*v.t.* **·bied, ·by·ing** To redden. [< L *rubeus* red] —**ru′by** *adj.*

ruche (ro͞osh) *n.* Frilled or ruffled fabric at the neck or wrists of a costume. [< F, beehive, frill]

ruch·ing (ro͞o′shing) *n.* Material for ruches; also, ruches collectively.

ruck[1] (ruk) *n.* 1. A mass of ordinary things; heap. 2. The ordinary run of people or things. 3. Trash; rubbish. [ME < Scand. Cf. Norw. *ruka* heap, crowd]

ruck[2] (ruk) *v.t. & v.i.* To wrinkle; rumple. —*n.* A wrinkle; crease. [< ON *hrukka* wrinkle]

ruck·sack (ruk′sak′) *n.* A canvas knapsack. [< G *rücken* back + *sack* sack]

ruck·us (ruk′əs) *n. Slang* An uproar; commotion. [Prob. blend of RUMPUS and RUCTION]

ruc·tion (ruk′shən) *n.* A riotous outbreak; uproar. [Prob. alter. of INSURRECTION]

rud·der (rud′ər) *n.* A broad, flat, movable device at the rear of a vessel or aircraft for steering. [OE *rōthor* oar, scull]

rud·dy (rud′ē) *adj.* **·di·er, ·di·est** 1. Tinged with red. 2. Having a healthy glow; rosy. 3. *Brit. Slang* Bloody: a euphemism. [OE *rudig*] —**rud′di·ly** *adv.* —**rud′di·ness** *n.*

ruddy duck A small North American duck having stiffened tail feathers and, in the adult male, a bright chestnut-colored body.

rude (ro͞od) *adj.* **rud·er, rud·est** 1. Offensively blunt or uncivil; impudent. 2. Lacking refinement; uncouth. 3. Crudely made or done; rough. 4. Startling; sudden: *rude* awakening. [< L *rudis* rough] —**rude′ly** *adv.* —**rude′ness** *n.*

ru·di·ment (ro͞o′də·mənt) *n.* 1. A first principle, step, stage, or condition. 2. Something undeveloped or only partially developed. [< L *rudimentum*] —**ru′di·men′ta·ri·ly** *adv.* —**ru′di·men′ta·ri·ness** *n.* —**ru′di·men′ta·ry** (-men′tər·ē) *adj.*

rue[1] (ro͞o) *v.t. & v.i.* **rued, ru·ing** To feel sorrow or remorse for (something). —*n.* Sorrowful remembrance; regret. [OE *hrēowan* to be sorry] —**rue·ful** (ro͞o′fəl) *adj.* —**rue′·ful·ly** *adv.* —**rue′ful·ness** *n.* —**ru′er** *n.*

rue[2] (ro͞o) *n.* 1. A small, bushy herb with bitter, acrid leaves, formerly much used in medicine. 2. Any bitter draft. [< L *ruta* < Gk. *rhytē*]

ruff[1] (ruf) *n.* 1. A pleated, round, heavily starched collar popular in the 16th c. 2. Ruffle[1] (def. 1). 3. A natural collar of projecting feathers or hair around the neck of a bird or mammal. [Short for RUFFLE[1]] —**ruffed** *adj.*

ruff[2] (ruf) *v.t. & v.i.* To trump (a card). [< OF *roffle*] —**ruff** *n.*

ruffed grouse A North American grouse: called *partridge* in the northern and *pheasant* in the southern U.S.

ruf·fi·an (ruf′ē·ən, ruf′yən) *n.* A lawless, brutal man; a tough. —*adj.* Brutal or cruel. [< OF] —**ruf′fi·an·ism** *n.* —**ruf′fi·an·ly** *adj.*

ruf·fle[1] (ruf′əl) *n.* 1. A pleated strip or frill of fabric, lace, etc.: also *ruff.* 2. A slight disturbance, as a ripple. —*v.* **·fled, ·fling** *v.t.* 1. To disturb the smoothness of; wrinkle or rumple. 2. To draw into ruffles; gather. 3. To erect (the feathers) in a ruff. 4. To irritate; upset. —*v.i.* 5. To be or become rumpled or disordered. 6. To become disturbed or irritated. [< RUFFLE[2]]

ruf·fle[2] (ruf′əl) *n.* A low, continuous beat of a drum. [Earlier *ruff*; prob. imit.] —**ruf′fle** *v.t.* **·fled, ·fling**

ru·fous (ro͞o′fəs) *adj.* Dull red. [< L *rufus* red]

rug (rug) *n.* 1. A heavy piece of fabric to cover a portion of a floor. 2. A cover, coverlet, or lap robe. [< Scand.]

rug·by football (rug′bē) *Usu. cap. Brit.* Football in which the ball is propelled toward the opponents' goal by kicking or carrying.

rug·ged (rug′id) *adj.* 1. Having a surface broken into irregular points or crags; uneven. 2. Shaggy; unkempt. 3. Harsh; rough; severe. 4. Having strongly marked features. 5. Lacking refinement; rude. 6. Robust; sturdy; hale. [< Scand.] —**rug′·ged·ly** *adv.* —**rug′ged·ness** *n.*

ru·gose (ro͞o′gōs) *adj.* Full of wrinkles, as some leaves. Also **ru′gous** (-gəs). [< L *ruga* wrinkle]

ru·in (ro͞o′in) *n.* 1. Total destruction of value or usefulness. 2. Loss of honor, wealth, etc. 3. *Often pl.* The remains of something demolished or decayed. 4. A condition of desolation or destruction; also, the cause of this. —*v.t. & v.i.* To bring to or fall into ruin. [< L *ruere* to fall] —**ru′in·a·ble** *adj.* —**ru′in·a′tion** *n.* —**ru′in·er** *n.*

ru·in·ous (ro͞o′in·əs) *adj.* 1. Causing or tending to ruin. 2. Falling to ruin; decayed. —**ru′in·ous·ly** *adv.* —**ru′in·ous·ness** *n.*

rule (ro͞ol) *n.* 1. Controlling power, or its possession and exercise; dominion; authority. 2. A prescribed method or procedure: the *rules* of a game. 3. Regulations laid down by or for a religious order. 4. An established form or method, as for grammatical usage. 5. Something belonging to the ordinary course of events or condition of things. 6. *Law* A judicial decision on some motion or special application. 7. A ruler (def. 2). —**as a rule** Ordinarily; usually. —*v.t. & v.i.* **ruled, rul·ing** 1. To control or govern; have authority over. 2. To decide or determine a matter judicially or authoritatively. 3. To mark (a paper, etc.) with straight, parallel lines. [< L *regula* ruler, rule] —**rul′a·ble** *adj.*

rule of thumb A rough, practical measure, rather than a scientific one.

rul·er (ro͞o′lər) *n.* 1. One who rules or governs. 2. A straight-edged instrument for use in measuring or in drawing lines.

rul·ing (ro͞o′ling) *adj.* Controlling; predominant. —*n.* A decision, as of a judge.

rum[1] (rum) *n.* 1. An alcoholic liquor distilled from fermented molasses or cane juice. 2. Any alcoholic liquor. [? Short for obs. *rumbullion* rum]

rum² (rum) *adj. Brit. Slang* Queer; strange; peculiar. [? < Romany *rom* man]

Ru·ma·ni·an (ro͞o·mā′nē·ən, -mān′yən) *n.* 1. A native or inhabitant of Rumania. 2. The Romance language of the Rumanians. —**Ru·ma′ni·an** *adj.*

rum·ba (rum′bə, *Sp.* ro͞om′bä) *n.* 1. A dance of Cuban origin. 2. Music for or in the manner of such a dance. Also spelled *rhumba.* [< Am.Sp.]

rum·ble (rum′bəl) *v.* **·bled, ·bling** *v.i.* 1. To make a low, heavy, rolling sound, as thunder. 2. To move or proceed with such a sound. —*v.t.* 3. To cause to make a low, heavy, rolling sound. 4. To utter with such a sound. —*n.* 1. A rumbling sound. 2. A seat or baggage compartment in the rear of a carriage. 3. A folding seat in the back of a coupé or roadster: in full **rumble seat.** 4. *Slang* A gang fight, usu. involving teenagers. [ME *romblen*] —**rum′bler** *n.* —**rum′·bling·ly** *adv.* —**rum′bly** *adj.*

ru·men (ro͞o′men) *n. pl.* **ru·mi·na** (ro͞o′·mə·nə) The first stomach or the cud of a ruminant. [< L, gullet]

ru·mi·nant (ro͞o′mə·nənt) *n.* One of a division of cud-chewing mammals, as the deer, cow, camel, etc., having a stomach with four cavities. —*adj.* 1. Chewing the cud. 2. Of or pertaining to a ruminant. 3. Meditative. [< L *ruminare* to chew over]

ru·mi·nate (ro͞o′mə·nāt) *v.t. & v.i.* **·nat·ed, ·nat·ing** 1. To chew (the cud). 2. To meditate or reflect upon (an issue, etc.); ponder. [See RUMINANT.] —**ru′mi·nat′ing·ly** *adv.* —**ru′mi·na′tion** *n.* —**ru′mi·na′tive** *adj.* —**ru′mi·na′tive·ly** *adv.* —**ru′mi·na′tor** *n.*

rum·mage (rum′ij) *v.t. & v.i.* **·maged, ·mag·ing** To search through (a place, box, etc.) by disarranging the contents; ransack. [< MF *arrumer* to stow cargo] —**rum′mage** *n.* —**rum′mag·er** *n.*

rummage sale A sale of second-hand or unwanted objects, esp. to obtain money for charity.

rum·my¹ (rum′ē) *n.* A card game in which the object is to obtain sets of three or four cards of the same denomination, or sequences of three or more cards of the same suit. [? < Brit. slang *rummy,* queer]

rum·my² (rum′ē) *n. pl.* **·mies** *Slang* A drunkard. —*adj.* **·mi·er, ·mi·est** Of or resembling rum: a *rummy* flavor.

ru·mor (ro͞o′mər) *n.* 1. An unverified or unfounded report circulating from person to person. 2. Common gossip; hearsay. —*v.t.* To tell or spread as a rumor. Also *Brit.* **ru′mour.** [< L]

rump (rump) *n.* 1. The rounded or fleshy upper part of the hind quarters of an animal. 2. The analogous region in man; the buttocks. 3. A cut of beef between the loin and the round. 4. A last, often undesirable remnant. [ME *rumpe*]

rum·ple (rum′pəl) *v.t. & v.i.* **·pled, ·pling** To crease; wrinkle; ruffle. —*n.* An untidy wrinkling or ruffling. [< MDu. *rumpelen*]

rum·pus (rum′pəs) *n. Informal* A row; wrangle; to-do. [Origin uncertain]

rumpus room A room for games, informal gatherings, etc.

rum·run·ner (rum′run′ər) *n.* A person or ship illicitly transporting alcoholic liquors across a border.

run (run) *v.* **ran** (*Archaic* or *Dial.* **run**), **run, run·ning** *v.i.* 1. To move by rapid steps, faster than walking, in such a manner that both feet are off the ground for a portion of each step. 2. To move rapidly; go swiftly. 3. To flee; take flight. 4. To make a brief or rapid journey. 5. To make regular trips. 6. To be a candidate or contestant. 7. To finish a race in a specified position. 8. To move or pass easily; flow. 9. To elapse; pass. 10. To proceed in direction or extent: This road *runs* north. 11. To move in or as in a stream; flow. 12. To become liquid and flow, as wax; also, to spread, as colors when wet. 13. To move or pass into a specified condition: to *run* into trouble. 14. To climb or grow in long shoots, as vines. 15. To become torn by unraveling. 16. To suppurate. 17. To leak. 18. To continue or proceed: The conversation *ran* on and on. 19. To be in operation; work. 20. To continue in existence, effect, action, etc.; extend in time. 21. To proceed; go: The story *runs* as follows. 22. To migrate, as salmon from the sea. 23. To incline; tend. —*v.t.* 24. To lay, build, draw, etc., in or as in a particular course: to *run* a road through a wilderness. 25. To go along by running, as a route, course, or path. 26. To make one's way over, through, or past: to *run* rapids. 27. To perform or accomplish by or as by running: to *run* an errand. 28. To enter (a horse, candidate, etc.) in a race. 29. To drive or force: with *out of, off, into, through,* etc. 30. To move (the eye, hand, etc.) quickly or lightly. 31. To cause to move, slide, etc., as into a specified position. 32. To transport or convey. 33. To smuggle. 34. To cause to flow. 35. To give forth a flow of; emit: Her eyes *ran* tears. 36. To operate, as a machine vehicle, etc. 37. To direct; oversee. 38. To become liable to; incur: to *run* a risk. 39. To publish in a magazine or newspaper: to *run* an ad. 40. To suffer from (a fever, etc.). —**to run across** To meet by chance. —**to run down** 1. To pursue and overtake, as a fugitive. 2. To strike down while moving. 3. To speak of disparagingly; decry. 4. To find the source of; search out. 5. To cease to operate, as a watch. —**to run in** 1. To insert; include. 2. *Printing* To print without a paragraph or break. 3. *Slang* To arrest and place in confinement. —**to run into** 1. To meet by chance. 2. To collide with. —**to run off** 1. To make copies, as with a duplicator, printing press, etc. 2. To decide (a tied race, game, etc.) by the outcome of another, subsequent race, game, etc. 3. To flee or escape; elope. —**to run out** To come to an end; be exhausted, as supplies. —**to run out of** To exhaust one's supply of. —**to run over** 1. To ride or drive over; run down. 2. To overflow. 3. To go over or examine hastily or quickly; rehearse. —**to run through** 1. To spend wastefully; squander. 2. To stab or pierce. 3. To run over (def. 3). —**to run up** 1. To allow to continue or mount up, as a bill. 2. To produce; make hurriedly, as on a sewing machine. —*n.* 1. An act or instance of running or going rapidly. 2. The movement or gait of running: to break into a *run.* 3. A distance covered by running. 4. A habitual course or route. 5. A rapid, brief journey. 6. A steep course, as for skiing. 7. A swift stream or current. 8. The privilege of free use or access: to have the *run* of the place. 9. A series, succession, or sequence, as of playing cards in consecutive order. 10. A continuous spell of a specified condition: a *run* of luck. 11. A continuous period of performances, action, effect, etc. 12. An unusually great or sustained demand, as for a commodity. 13. A broadly inclusive category: the general *run* of readers. 14. A period of continuous operation, as of a machine or factory. 15. The output during such a period. 16. A continuous length or extent of something: a *run* of pipe. 17. A lengthwise rip in knitted fabric. 18. Mass migration or movement of animals, esp. of fish to spawn. 19. An enclosure for animals or poultry. 20. *Music* A rapid succession of tones. 21. In baseball, the scoring of a point by a player's making a complete circuit of the bases; also, a point so scored. 22. *Mining* A vein of ore or rock. **—a run for one's money** A successful or satisfactory instance of activity, esp. in competition. **—in the long run** As the ultimate outcome. *—adj.* 1. Made liquid; melted. 2. Made by a process of melting and casting or molding: *run* metal; *run* butter. [OE *rinnan*]

run·a·bout (run′ə·bout′) *n.* 1. A small, open automobile. 2. A light, open wagon. 3. A small motorboat.

run·a·round (run′ə·round′) *n.* *Slang* Artful deception; evasion.

run·a·way (run′ə·wā′) *adj.* 1. Escaping or escaped; fugitive. 2. Brought about by running away. 3. Easily won, as a horse race. 4. Characterized by a rapid rise, as of prices. *—n.* 1. One who or that which runs away. 2. A horse whose driver has lost control. 3. *Informal* An easily won victory, as in a race.

run·down (run′doun′) *n.* A summary.

run-down (run′doun′) *adj.* 1. Debilitated; tired out. 2. Dilapidated. 3. Stopped because not wound: said of a timepiece.

rune (rōōn) *n.* 1. Any of the characters in the runic alphabet. 2. *pl.* Old Norse lore expressed in or as in runes. 3. Any obscure or mystic poem, saying, etc. [< OE and ON *rūn* mystery] **—ru′nic** *adj.*

rung[1] (rung) *n.* 1. A round crosspiece forming one of the steps of a ladder. 2. A crosspiece used in chairs to support the legs or back. 3. The spoke of a wheel. [OE *hrung* staff]

rung[2] (rung) Past principle of RING[2].

runic alphabet An old Germanic alphabet, consisting originally of 24 characters.

run-in (run′in′) *n.* 1. A quarrel. 2. *Printing* Inserted matter. *—adj. Printing* Inserted.

run·nel (run′əl) *n.* A rivulet. [OE *rynel* < *rinnan* to run]

run·ner (run′ər) *n.* 1. One who or that which runs. 2. That part on which an object slides: the *runner* of a skate. 3. *Mech.* A device to assist sliding motion. 4. Any of various fishes of warm and temperate seas. 5. *Bot.* **a** A slender, trailing stem rooting at the end and nodes, as in the strawberry. **b** Any of various twining plants. 6. A long, narrow rug. 7. A narrow strip of cloth, used on tables, etc.

run·ner-up (run′ər·up′) *n.* *pl.* **·ners-up** or **·ner-ups** A contestant or team finishing in second place.

run·ning (run′ing) *adj.* 1. Moving or going rapidly. 2. Creeping or clinging, as a plant. 3. Flowing or oozing. 4. Slipping, moving, pulling, etc., easily and freely. 5. Being or able to be in operation: a *running* engine. 6. Liquid or fluid. 7. In a straight line: three feet *running.* 8. Current, as an account. 9. Continuous; repeated. 10. Accomplished or performed with a run. 11. Of or pertaining to a trip or run. *—adv.* Without intermission; in succession. *—n.* 1. The act of one who or that which runs. 2. That which runs or flows. 3. The amount or quantity that runs. 4. Competition or race: He is out of the *running.*

running board A footboard on the side of a locomotive, street car, automobile, etc.

running gear *Mech.* The wheels and axles of any vehicle and their immediate attachments.

running knot A knot made so as to slip along a rope, etc. and tighten when pulled upon: also called *slipknot.*

running light One of the lights displayed at night by a ship or aircraft.

running mate The candidate for the lesser of two related offices; esp., a vice-presidential candidate.

running title *Printing* A title or headline repeated at the head of every page or every other page of a book or chapter. Also **running head.**

run·ny (run′ē) *adj.* **·ni·er, ·ni·est** 1. Flowing; liquid: *runny* custard. 2. Discharging mucous, tears, etc.

run·off (run′ôf′) *n.* 1. The part of the rainfall that is drained off in rills or streams. 2. A special contest held to break a tie.

run-of-the-mill (run′əv·thə·mil′) *adj.* Average; ordinary. Also **run-of-the-mine.**

run-on (run′on′) *n.* *Printing* Appended matter.

runt (runt) *n.* 1. A small or stunted animal or plant. 2. A small person: often a contemptuous term. [< Scot., old cow] **—runt′·i·ness** *n.* **—runt′y** *adj.* **runt·i·er, runt·i·est**

run·way (run′wā′) *n.* 1. A way or path over or through which something runs. 2. A pathway extending from a stage into the audience. 3. A channel, chute, track, etc., along or in which something runs. 4. *Aeron.* A roadlike surface used for the takeoff and landing of aircraft.

ru·pee (rōō·pē′) *n.* The monetary unit of various countries, as of India and Pakistan. [< Skt. *rūpya* coined silver]

rup·ture (rup′chər) *n.* 1. The act of breaking apart, or the state of being broken apart. 2. *Pathol.* Hernia. 3. Breach of friendship or concord. *—v.t. & v.i.* **·tured, ·tur·ing** 1. To break apart; separate into parts. 2. To cause or suffer a rupture. [< Med.L. *ruptura* < *rumpere* to break] **—rup′tur·a·ble** *adj.*

ru·ral (rŏŏr′əl) *adj.* 1. Of or pertaining to the country; rustic. 2. Of or pertaining to farming or agriculture. [< L < *rus, ruris* country] **—ru′ral·ism** *n.* **—ru′ral·ist** *n.* **—ru·ral·i·ty** (rŏŏ·ral′ə·tē) *n.* **—ru′ral·ly** *adv.*

rural free delivery A government service of

house-to-house free mail delivery in rural districts. Abbr. *RFD, R.F.D.*

ru·ral·ize (ro͝or′əl·īz) *v.t. & v.i.* **·ized, ·iz·ing** To make or become rural; rusticate. —**ru′ral·i·za′tion** *n.*

ruse (ro͞oz) *n.* An action intended to mislead or deceive. [< MF *ruser* to turn aside.]

rush[1] (rush) *v.i.* 1. To move or go swiftly or with violence. 2. To make an attack; charge: with *on* or *upon.* 3. To proceed recklessly or rashly; plunge: with *in* or *into.* 4. To come, surge, flow, etc., suddenly. —*v.t.* 5. To drive or push with haste or violence; hurry. 6. To do or perform hurriedly. 7. To make a sudden assault upon; also, to capture by such an assault. 8. To consider for membership in a fraternity or sorority. —*n.* 1. The act of rushing. 2. A state of impatient activity; hurry. 3. A sudden surge, flow, or outpouring. 4. A sudden pressing demand. 5. A sudden or urgent flow or press of traffic, business, etc. 6. *pl.* In motion pictures, the first film prints of a scene or series of scenes. 7. *Slang* The sudden pleasurable feeling experienced after taking a drug; also, any sudden pleasurable feeling. —*adj.* 1. Requiring urgency or haste: a *rush* order. 2. Characterized by much traffic, business, etc. [< OF *ruser, reuser* to push back < L *recusare* to refuse] —**rush′er** *n.*

rush[2] (rush) *n.* 1. Any one of various grasslike, usu. aquatic herbs, growing in marshy ground and having pliant, cylindrical, leafless stems, often used for making mats, etc. 2. A rushlight. [OE *risc*] —**rush′y** *adj.* **rush·i·er, rush·i·est**

rush hour A time when traffic or business is at its height. —**rush-hour** (rush′our′) *adj.*

rush·light (rush′līt′) *n.* A candle made by dipping a rush in tallow. Also **rush candle.**

rusk (rusk) *n.* Bread or cake that has been crisped and browned in an oven. [< Sp. *rosca,* twisted loaf of bread]

rus·set (rus′it) *n.* 1. A reddish or yellowish brown. 2. Coarse homespun cloth or clothing of this color. 3. A winter apple of greenish color, mottled with brown. —*adj.* 1. Of the color russet. 2. Made of russet cloth; also, coarse; homespun. [< L *russus* red]

Rus·sian (rush′ən) *n.* 1. A native or citizen of the Soviet Union or the former Russian Empire. 2. The East Slavic language of the Russian people. —**Rus′sian** *adj.*

Russian dressing Mayonnaise dressing to which chili sauce, pimientos, chopped pickles, etc., have been added.

Rus·sian·ize (rush′ən·iz) *v.t.* **·ized, ·iz·ing** To make Russian in manner, character, etc. —**Rus·sian·i·za′tion** *n.*

Russian leather A smooth, high-grade leather of calfskin or light cattle hide.

Russian Orthodox Church An autonomous branch of the Eastern Orthodox Church in the Soviet Union, under the patriarch of Moscow.

Russian roulette A suicidal stunt in which one spins the cylinder of a revolver containing only one cartridge, aims at one's head, and pulls the trigger.

Russian wolfhound The borzoi.

Russo- *combining form* Russia; pertaining to the Russians.

rust (rust) *n.* 1. The reddish or yellow coating formed on iron and steel by exposure to air and moisture. 2. Any film formed on the surface of a metal by oxidation. 3. A fungus disease of plants, characterized by orange or reddish brown spots. 4. Any coating or accretion formed by a corrosive or degenerative process. 5. Any of several shades of reddish brown. —*v.t. & v.i.* 1. To become or cause to become rusty. 2. To contract or cause to contract rust. 3. To become or cause to become weakened or impaired because of inactivity or disuse. 4. To make or become rust-colored. [OE *rūst*]

rus·tic (rus′tik) *adj.* 1. Typical of or appropriate to simple country life. 2. Plain; simple; homely. 3. Uncultured; rude. 4. Unaffected; artless. —*n.* 1. One who lives in the country. 2. A country person of simple manners or character; also, a coarse or clownish person. [< L *rus* country] —**rus′ti·cal·ly** *adv.* —**rus·tic′i·ty** (-tis′ə·tē) *n.*

rus·ti·cate (rus′tə·kāt) *v.* **·cat·ed, ·cat·ing** *v.i.* 1. To go to the country. 2. To stay or live in the country. —*v.t.* 3. To send or banish to the country. 4. To make rustic. —**rus′ti·ca′tion** *n.* —**rus′ti·ca′tor** *n.*

rus·tic·work (rus′tik·wûrk′) *n.* 1. Masonry having rough surfaces. 2. Furniture, etc., made of the natural limbs and roots of trees. Also **rustic work.**

rus·tle[1] (rus′əl) *v.t. & v.i.* **·tled, ·tling** To fall, move, or cause to move with a quick succession of small, light, sounds, as dry leaves. —*n.* A rustling sound. [ME *rustel,* alter. of OE *hrūxlian* to make a noise] —**rus′tler** *n.* —**rus′tling·ly** *adv.*

rus·tle[2] (rus′əl) *v.t. & v.i.* **·tled, ·tling** *Informal* 1. To act with or obtain by energetic or vigorous action. 2. To steal (cattle, etc.). [Blend of RUSH and HUSTLE] —**rus′tler** *n.*

rust·y (rus′tē) *adj.* **rust·i·er, rust·i·est** 1. Covered or affected with rust. 2. Having the color of rust. 3. Impaired by inaction or want of exercise; also, stiff. 4. Ineffective or weakened through neglect; also, having lost skill for want of practice. —**rust′i·ly** *adv.* —**rust′i·ness** *n.*

rut[1] (rut) *n.* 1. A sunken track worn by a wheel, as in a road; also, a groove forming a path for anything. 2. A settled habit or course of procedure; routine. —*v.t.* **rut·ted, rut·ting** To wear or make a rut or ruts in. [Var. of ROUTE]

rut[2] (rut) *n.* 1. The sexual excitement of various animals, esp. of deer and other ruminants; estrus. 2. The period during which this excitement lasts. —*v.i.* **rut·ted, rut·ting** To be in rut. [< L *rugire* to roar]

ru·ta·ba·ga (ro͞o′tə·bā′gə) *n.* 1. A cultivated plant allied to the turnip. 2. Its edible root. [< dial. Sw. *rotabagge*]

Ruth (ro͞oth) *n.* The book of the Old Testament that tells the story of Ruth, a widow, who left her own people and went with her mother-in-law to Bethlehem.

ru·the·ni·um (ro͞o·thē′nē·əm) *n.* A gray, brittle, rare metallic element (symbol Ru) of the platinum group. [< NL, after *Ruthenia,* a region in the U.S.S.R.]

ruth·less (ro͞oth′lis) *adj.* Having no compassion; merciless. [ME *reuthe* pity < OE *hrēow* sad] **—ruth′less·ly** *adv.* **—ruth′less·ness** *n.*

rut·tish (rut′ish) *adj.* Disposed to rut; lustful; libidinous.

rut·ty (rut′ē) *adj.* **·ti·er, ·ti·est** Full of ruts. **—rut′ti·ness** *n.*

Rwan·dan (rwän′dən, ro͞o·än′-) *adj.* Of Rwanda or its inhabitants. **—Rwan′dan** *n.*

-ry Var. of -ERY.

rye (rī) *n.* **1.** The grain or seeds of a hardy cereal grass closely allied to wheat. **2.** The grass. **3.** Whiskey distilled from rye or partly from rye. [OE *ryge*]

S

s, S (es) *n. pl.* **s's** or **ss, S's** or **Ss, ess·es** (es′iz) 1. The nineteenth letter of the English alphabet. 2. The sound represented by the letter *s*, usu. a voiceless sibilant, but often voiced between vowels, as in *easy*. —*symbol* 1. Anything shaped like an S. 2. *Chem.* Sulfur (symbol S).

-s[1] A variant of *-es*[1], inflectional ending of the plurals of nouns: *books, words, cars.* Compare -ES[1].

-s[2] An inflectional ending used to form the third person singular present indicative of verbs: *reads, walks, sings.* Compare -ES[2].

-s[3] *suffix* On; of a; at: *nights, Mondays, always, towards.* [OE *-es*]

-'s[1] An inflectional ending used to form the possessive of singular nouns and of plural nouns not ending in *-s*: a *man's* home, *women's* fashions.

-'s[2] Contraction of: **a** Is: *He's* here. **b** Has: *She's* left. **c** Us: *Let's* go.

Sab·bath (sab′əth) *n.* **1.** The seventh day of the week (Saturday), a day of rest observed by Jews and some Christians. 2. Sunday, the day of rest and worship observed by most Christians. 3. The institution or observance of a day of rest. [< Hebrew *shābath* to rest] —**Sab·bat·ic** (sə·bat′ik) or **·i·cal** *adj.* —**Sab·bat′i·cal·ly** *adv.*

sab·bat·i·cal (sə·bat′i·kəl) *adj.* Offering rest: also **sab·bat′ic.** —*n.* A year's vacation awarded to teachers in some American educational institutions every seven years: also **sabbatical year.** [See SABBATH.]

sa·ber (sā′bər) *n.* 1. A heavy one-edged cavalry sword with a thick-backed blade, often curved. 2. In fencing, a light swordlike instrument, used for both thrusting and slashing. —*v.t.* To strike, wound, or kill with a saber. Also *Brit.* **sa′bre.** [Prob. < Hung. *szabni* to cut]

sable (sā′bəl) *n.* 1. A carnivore of northern Asia and Europe, related to the marten and prized for its valuable fur. 2. The dressed fur of a sable. 3. *pl.* Garments made wholly or partly of this fur. 4. The color black; also, mourning or a mourning garment. —*adj.* 1. Black, esp. as the color of mourning. 2. Made of or having the color of sable fur; dark brown. [< Med.L *sabelum*]

sab·o·tage (sab′ə·täzh) *n.* 1. Deliberate destruction, as of installations, railways, etc., by enemy agents during a war, or of employer's property by workers on strike. 2. Any act performed to hamper or obstruct. —*v.* **·taged, ·tag·ing** *v.i.* 1. To engage in sabotage. —*v.t.* 2. To damage or destroy by sabotage. [< F < *sabot* a wooden shoe; with ref. to damage done to machinery with these shoes]

sab·o·teur (sab′ə·tûr′) *n.* One who engages in sabotage. [< F]

sa·bra (sä′brə) *n.* A native-born Israeli. [< Hebrew, cactus]

sac (sak) *n. Biol.* A pouch or receptacle in an animal or plant, as for containing a liquid: the ink *sac* of a squid. [< L *saccus* sack[1]]

sac·cha·rin (sak′ər·in) *n. Chem.* A white crystalline coal-tar compound, used as a noncaloric sweetening agent. [< Gk. *sakcharon*, ult. < Skt. *sharkarā* grit, sugar]

sac·cha·rine (sak′ər·in) *adj.* Cloyingly sweet: a *saccharine* manner. —*n.* Saccharin. —**sac′cha·rine·ly** *adv.* —**sac′cha·rin′i·ty** *n.*

sac·er·do·tal (sas′ər·dōt′l) *adj.* 1. Pertaining to a priest or priesthood; priestly. 2. Believing in the divine authority of the priesthood. [< L *sacerdos, -dotis* priest] —**sac′er·do′tal·ism** *n.* —**sac′er·do′tal·ly** *adv.*

sa·chem (sā′chəm) *n.* A North American Indian hereditary chief. [< Algonquian (Narraganset)]

sa·chet (sa·shā′) *n.* A small ornamental bag for perfumed powder. [< MF, dim. of *sac* sack]

sack[1] (sak) *n.* 1. A bag for holding bulky articles. 2. A loose jacketlike garment, worn by women and babies: also **sacque.** 3. *Slang* Dismissal: esp. in the phrases **to get the sack, to give (someone) the sack.** 4. *Slang* A bed; mattress. —**to hit the sack** *Slang* To go to bed. —**to sack out** *Slang* To go to bed. —*v.t.* 1. To put into a sack or sacks. 2. To dismiss. [< Hebrew *saq* sack, sackcloth]

sack[2] (sak) *v.t.* To plunder or pillage (a town or city) after capturing. —*n.* 1. The pillaging of a captured town or city. 2. Loot or booty obtained by pillage. [< Ital. *sacco*, orig., plunder < L *saccus* sack[1]] —**sack′er** *n.*

sack[3] (sak) *n.* Light-colored Spanish dry wine; also, any strong white wine from southern Europe. [Earlier *(wyne) seck* < F *(vin) sec* dry (wine) < L *siccus* dry]

sack·cloth (sak′klôth′) *n.* 1. A coarse cloth used for making sacks. 2. Coarse cloth or haircloth worn in penance.

sack·ful (sak′fŏŏl′) *n. pl.* **·fuls** Enough to fill a sack.

sack·ing (sak′ing) *n.* A coarse cloth made of hemp or flax and used for sacks.

sack race A race run with the feet in a sack.

sa·cral[1] (sā′krəl) *adj.* Of, pertaining to, or situated near the sacrum. —*n.* A sacral vertebra or nerve.

sa·cral[2] (sā′krəl) *adj.* Pertaining to sacred rites. [< L *sacrum* rite < *sacer* sacred]

sac·ra·ment (sak′rə·mənt) *n.* 1. *Eccl.* Any of certain rites ordained by Christ or by the church, as baptism or the Eucharist. 2. *Often cap. Eccl.* The Eucharist. [< L *sacrare* to consecrate] —**sac′ra·men′tal** *adj.* —**sac′ra·men′tal·ly** *adv.*

sa·cred (sā′krid) *adj.* 1. Set apart or dedicated to religious use; hallowed. 2. Pertaining or related to a deity or religion. 3. Consecrated or dedicated to a person or purpose. 4. Entitled to reverence or respect. [< L *sacrare* to treat as sacred] **—sa′cred·ly** *adv.* **—sa′cred·ness** *n.*

sacred cow *Informal* Something or someone regarded as above criticism or reproach.

sac·ri·fice (sak′rə·fīs) *n.* 1. The act of making an offering to a deity, in worship or atonement; also, that which is so offered. 2. A giving up of something valued for the sake of something else; also, that which is so given up. 3. In baseball, a sacrifice hit. **—*v.* ·ficed, ·fic·ing** *v.t.* 1. To make an offering or sacrifice of, as to a god or deity. 2. To give up (something valued) for the sake of something else. **—*v.i.*** 3. To make a sacrifice. 4. To make a sacrifice hit. [< L *sacer* sacred + *facere* to perform, do] **—sac′ri·fic′er** *n.* **—sac′ri·fi′cial** (-fish′əl) *adj.* **—sac′ri·fi′cial·ly** *adv.*

sacrifice fly In baseball, a fly ball hit with less than two out that enables a runner on third base to score after the catch.

sacrifice hit In baseball, a bunt made with less than two out that enables a runner or runners to advance a base while the batter is being retired. Also **sacrifice bunt.**

sac·ri·lege (sak′rə·lij) *n.* The act of violating or profaning anything sacred. [< L *sacer, sacris* sacred + *legere* to gather, steal] **—sac′ri·le′gious** (-lij′əs, -lē′jəs) *adj.* **—sac′ri·le′gious·ly** *adv.* **—sac′ri·le′gious·ness** *n.*

sac·ris·tan (sak′ris·tən) *n.* An officer having charge of the sacristy of a church. [< L *sacer, sacris* sacred]

sac·ris·ty (sak′ris·tē) *n. pl.* **·ties** A room in a religious house for the sacred vessels and vestments; vestry.

sac·ro·il·i·ac (sak′rō·il′ē·ak) *adj. Anat.* Pertaining to the sacrum and the ilium and to the joints or ligaments connecting them.

sac·ro·sanct (sak′rō·sangkt) *adj.* Extremely sacred; inviolable. [< L *sacrum* rite + *sanctus,* pp. of *sancire* to make holy, inviolable] **—sac′ro·sanc′ti·ty** *n.*

sa·crum (sā′krəm) *n. pl.* **·cra** *Anat.* A composite bone formed by the union of five vertebrae, constituting the dorsal part of the pelvis. [< L *(os) sacrum* sacred (bone); from its use in sacrifices]

sad (sad) *adj.* **sad·der, sad·dest** 1. Sorrowful or depressed. 2. Causing sorrow or pity; unfortunate. 3. Dark-hued; somber. [OE *sæd,* orig., sated] **—sad′ly** *adv.* **—sad′ness** *n.*

sad·den (sad′n) *v.t. & v.i.* To make or become sad.

sad·dle (sad′l) *n.* 1. A seat or pad, usu. of leather, for a rider, as on the back of a horse. 2. The two hindquarters of a carcass, as of mutton, veal, or venison. **—in the saddle** In control. **—*v.t.* ·dled, ·dling** 1. To put a saddle on. 2. To load, as with a burden. [OE *sadol*]

sad·dle·bag (sad′l·bag) *n.* One of a pair of pouches connected by a strap or band and slung over an animal's back or attached to a saddle.

sad·dle·cloth (sad′l·klôth′) *n.* A cloth placed under and attached to a saddle.

saddle horse A horse used with or trained for the saddle.

saddle soap A softening and preserving soap for leather, containing pure white soap and neat's-foot oil.

Sad·du·cee (saj′o͞o·sē, sad′yo͞o·sē) *n.* A member of an ancient Jewish sect that adhered to the written Mosaic law but repudiated oral tradition. [Appar. ult. after *Zadok,* a high priest (*Ezek.* xl 46)] **—Sad′du·ce′an, Sad′du·cae′an** *adj.* **—Sad′du·cee′ism** *n.*

sad·i·ron (sad′ī′ərn) *n.* An iron for pressing clothes.

sad·ism (sā′diz·əm, sad′iz·əm) *n.* A tendency to take delight in being cruel. [after Comte Donatien de *Sade,* 1740–1814, French writer] **—sad·ist** (sā′dist, sad′ist) *n. & adj.* **—sa·dis·tic** (sə·dis′tik, sā-) *adj.* **—sa·dis′ti·cal·ly** *adv.*

sad sack *Slang* A blundering, pitiable person.

sa·fa·ri (sə·fä′rē) *n. pl.* **·ris** An expedition or journey, often on foot. [< Arabic *safara* to travel]

safe (sāf) *adj.* **saf·er, saf·est** 1. Free from danger or evil. 2. Having escaped injury or damage; unharmed. 3. Not involving risk or loss. 4. Conferring safety; also, not likely to cause or do harm or injury. 5. In baseball, having reached base without being retired. **—*n.*** A strong metal receptacle for protecting valuables. [< L *salvus* whole, healthy] **—safe′ly** *adv.* **—safe′ness** *n.*

safe-con·duct (sāf′kon′dukt) *n.* An official document assuring protection on a journey or voyage, as in time of war; a passport.

safe·crack·er (sāf′krak′ər) *n.* One who breaks into safes to rob them. **—safe′crack′ing** *n.*

safe·guard (sāf′gärd′) *n.* One who or that which guards or protects against accident or injury. **—*v.t.*** To defend; protect; guard.

safe·keep·ing (sāf′kē′ping) *n.* The act or state of keeping or being kept in safety; protection.

safe·ty (sāf′tē) *n. pl.* **·ties** 1. Freedom from danger or injury. 2. A device or catch designed as a safeguard, as in a firearm. 3. In football: **a** A defensive player positioned deep in the backfield. **b** A play in which the ball is grounded by the offense behind its own goal line, the opponent scoring two points. [< L *salvus* sound]

safety belt 1. A strap or strong belt encircling the user and fastened to a fixed object, worn as a safeguard against falling. 2. A seat belt.

safety glass Two sheets of glass having a film of transparent, adhesive plastic tightly pressed between them.

safety lamp A miner's lamp having the flame surrounded by fine wire gauze that prevents the ignition of explosive gases.

safety match A match that will ignite only when struck upon a chemically prepared surface.

safety pin A pin whose point springs into place within a protecting sheath.

safety razor A razor provided with a guard for the blade to prevent accidental gashing of the skin.

safety valve 1. *Mech.* A valve in a steam boiler, etc., for automatically relieving excessive pressure. 2. Any outlet for pent-up energy or emotion.

saf·flow·er (saf′lou′ər) *n.* A thistlelike herb, the seeds of which yield an edible oil (**safflower oil**). [< Du. *saffloer*]

saf·fron (saf′rən) *n.* 1. An autumn-flowering species of crocus. 2. The dried orange-colored stigmas of this plant, used as a flavoring and coloring for food. 3. A deep yellow-orange: also **saffron yellow**. —*adj.* Yellow-orange. [< Arabic *za'farān*]

sag (sag) *v.* **sagged, sag·ging** *v.i.* 1. To bend or sink downward, esp. in the middle. 2. To hang unevenly. 3. To weaken, as from exhaustion or depression: His spirits *sagged*. —*v.t.* 4. To cause to sag. —*n.* 1. A sagging. 2. A sagging or sunken place or part. [ME *saggen*]

sa·ga (sä′gə) *n.* 1. A medieval Icelandic story dealing with legendary or historical Scandinavian heroes and their exploits. 2. A long story, often telling the history of a family. [< ON]

sa·ga·cious (sə·gā′shəs) *adj.* Characterized by discernment, shrewdness, and wisdom. [< L *sagax*] —**sa·ga′cious·ly** *adv.* —**sa·gac′i·ty** (-gas′ə·tē), **sa·ga′cious·ness** *n.*

sag·a·more (sag′ə·môr) *n.* A chief among the Algonquian Indians of North America, usu. inferior to a sachem. [< Algonquian (Penobscot) *sagamo* he prevails]

sage[1] (sāj) *n.* A man of wisdom and prudence. —*adj.* **sag·er, sag·est** Wise; prudent. [Ult. < LL *sapius* prudent, wise] —**sage′ly** *adv.* —**sage′ness** *n.*

sage[2] (sāj) *n.* 1. A plant of the mint family, having gray-green leaves used for flavoring meats. 2. The leaves of this plant. 3. The sagebrush. [< L *salvus* safe; from its reputed healing powers]

sage·brush (sāj′brush′) *n.* A small, aromatic shrub, widely distributed on the plains of the western U.S.

sage hen A large grouse of the western U.S.

sag·it·tal (saj′ə·təl) *adj.* Of, pertaining to, or resembling an arrow or arrowhead. [< L *sagitta* arrow] —**sag′it·tal·ly** *adv.*

Sag·it·ta·ri·us (saj′ə·târ′ē·əs) *n.* A constellation, the Archer; also, the ninth sign of the zodiac. [< L *sagitta* arrow]

sag·it·tate (saj′ə·tāt) *adj. Bot.* Shaped like an arrowhead, as certain leaves.

sa·go (sā′gō) *n. pl.* **·gos** 1. An East Indian palm. 2. The pith of this palm, used as a thickening agent in puddings, etc. [< Malay *sāgū*]

sa·gua·ro (sə·gwä′rō, -wä′-) *n. pl.* **·ros** A large desert cactus with an erect, columnar trunk, strong spines, and flowering tops. Also **sa·hua′ro** (-wä′-). [< Sp. < Piman]

Sa·hib (sä′ib, -hib) *n.* Master; sir: used in India and Pakistan for people of rank and, esp. formerly, for Europeans. Also **Sa′heb**. [< Hindi < Arabic *sāhib* lord, companion]

said (sed) Past tense and past participle of SAY.

sail (sāl) *n. pl.* **sails**; *for def. 2, often* **sail** 1. *Naut.* A piece of strong material attached to a vessel's mast for propulsion by catching the wind. 2. A sailing vessel or craft. 3. A trip in any watercraft. 4. Anything resembling a sail. —*v.i.* 1. To move across the water by the action of wind or mechanical power. 2. To travel over water in a ship or boat. 3. To manage a sailing craft. 4. To glide or float in the air. —*v.t.* 5. To move or travel across the surface of (a body of water) in a ship or boat. 6. To navigate (a ship, etc.). [OE *segl*] —**sail′a·ble** *adj.*

sail·boat (sāl′bōt′) *n.* A small boat propelled by a sail or sails.

sail·cloth (sāl′klôth′) *n.* A very strong cotton canvas suitable for sails.

sail·fish (sāl′fish′) *n. pl.* **·fish** or **·fish·es** A fish having a large dorsal fin likened to a sail.

sail·or (sā′lər) *n.* A seaman; mariner.

saint (sānt) *n.* 1. A holy or godly person. 2. In certain churches, such a person who has died and been canonized. 3. Any one of the blessed in heaven. 4. A very patient, unselfish person. —*adj.* Holy; canonized. [< L *sancire* to make sacred] —**saint′ed** *adj.* —**saint′hood, saint′ship** *n.*

Saint For entries not found under *Saint*, see under ST.

Saint Bernard A working dog of great size and strength, used formerly to rescue travelers.

saint·ly (sānt′lē) *adj.* **·li·er, ·li·est** Like, concerned with, or suitable for a saint. —**saint′li·ness** *n.*

Saint Patrick's Day March 17, a day celebrated by the Irish in honor of their patron saint.

Saint Valentine's Day February 14, the anniversary of the martyrdom of St. Valentine, and a day when valentines are exchanged.

saith (seth, sā′əth) *Archaic* Present indicative third person singular of SAY.

sake[1] (sāk) *n.* 1. Purpose; aim; intent. 2. Interest; account; advantage: for your own *sake*. [OE *sacu* lawsuit]

sa·ke[2] (sä′kē) *n.* A fermented liquor made in Japan from rice. Also **sa′ki**. [< Japanese]

sal (sal) *n.* Salt. [< L]

sa·laam (sə·läm′) *n.* 1. An oriental greeting made with a low bow, the palm of the right hand being held to the forehead. 2. A respectful or ceremonious greeting. —*v.t. & v.i.* To greet with or make a salaam. [< Arabic *salām* peace, a salutation]

sal·a·ble (sā′lə·bəl) *adj.* Such as can be sold; marketable: also spelled *saleable*. —**sal′a·bil′i·ty, sal′a·ble·ness** *n.*

sa·la·cious (sə·lā′shəs) *adj.* 1. Lustful; lewd. 2. Obscene: a *salacious* joke. [< L *salire* to leap] —**sa·la′cious·ly** *adv.* —**sa·la′cious·ness, sa·lac′i·ty** (-las′ə·tē) *n.*

sal·ad (sal′əd) *n.* 1. Green herbs or vegetables, served with a dressing. 2. Cold meat or fish, eggs, etc. served with a dressing. 3. A similar dish made with fruit. [< Provençal *salada* < *salar* to salt < L *sal* salt]

sal·a·man·der (sal′ə·man′dər) *n.* A lizardlike amphibian having a smooth, moist skin. [< Gk.]

sa·la·mi (sə·lä′mē) *n.* A salted, spiced sausage, originally Italian. [< Ital., < L *sal* salt]

sal ammoniac *Chem.* A white, crystalline, soluble compound, used in medicine and industry. [< L *sal Ammoniacum*, lit., salt of Ammon]

sal·a·ry (sal′ər·ē, sal′rē) *n. pl.* **·ries** A periodic, fixed payment for services or work. —*v.t.* **·ried, ·ry·ing** To pay a salary to. [< L *salarium* money paid Roman soldiers to buy salt] —**sal′a·ried** *adj.*

sale (sāl) *n.* 1. The exchange or transfer of

property for money. 2. An auction. 3. The selling of something at bargain prices. 4. Opportunity of selling; market. [OE *sala* < ON]
sale·a·ble (sā′lə·bəl) See SALABLE.
sales·girl (sālz′gûrl′) *n.* A saleswoman.
sales·man (sālz′mən) *n. pl.* **·men** (-mən) A man hired to sell goods, stock, etc.
sales·man·ship (sālz′mən·ship) *n.* 1. The work or profession of a salesman. 2. Ability or skill in selling.
sales·peo·ple (sālz′pē′pəl) *n.pl.* Salespersons.
sales·per·son (sālz′pûr′sən) *n.* A person hired to sell merchandise in a store.
sales·room (sālz′rōōm′, -rŏŏm′) *n.* A room where merchandise is displayed for sale.
sales tax A tax on money received from sale of goods.
sales·wom·an (sālz′wŏŏm′ən) *n. pl.* **·wom·en** (-wim′in) A woman or girl hired to sell merchandise in a store. Also **sales′la′dy** (-lā′dē).
sal·i·cyl·ic acid (sal′ə·sil′ik) *Chem.* A white crystalline compound occurring in many plants and also manmade, one form of which is widely known as aspirin.
sa·li·ent (sā′lē·ənt) *adj.* 1. Standing out prominently; conspicuous. 2. Protruding; projecting. —*n.* The part of a fortification or line of defense that protrudes most towards the enemy. [< L salire to leap] —**sa′li·ence** *n.* —**sa′li·ent·ly** *adv.* —**sa′li·ent·ness** *n.*
sa·line (sā′līn, -lēn) *adj.* Made of, characteristic of, or containing salt; salty. —*n.* 1. A metallic salt. 2. A salt solution. [< L *sal, salis* salt] —**sa·lin·i·ty** (sə·lin′ə·tē) *n.*
Salis·bur·y steak (sôlz′ber·ē, -brē) Hamburger (def. 1).
sa·li·va (sə·lī′və) *n. Physiol.* The fluid, secreted by the glands of the mouth, that promotes digestion. [< L] —**sal·i·var·y** (sal′ə·ver′ē) *adj.*
sal·i·vate (sal′ə·vāt) *v.* **·vat·ed, ·vat·ing** *v.i.* To secrete saliva. —*v.t.* To produce an abnormally increased flow of saliva in. —**sal′i·va′tion** *n.*
sal·low (sal′ō) *adj.* Of an unhealthy yellowish color: *sallow* skin. [OE *salu*] —**sal′low·ish, sal′low·y** *adv.* —**sal′low·ness** *n.*
sal·ly (sal′ē) *v.i.* **·lied, ·ly·ing** 1. To rush out suddenly. 2. To set out energetically. —*n. pl.* **·lies** 1. A rushing forth, as of troops against besiegers; sortie. 2. A bantering remark or witticism. 3. A walk or other short excursion. [< L *salire* to leap]
sal·ma·gun·di (sal′mə·gun′dē) *n.* 1. A saladlike dish of chopped meat, anchovies, eggs, onions, oil, etc. 2. Any medley or mixture. Also **sal′ma·gun′dy.** [< F *salmigondis*]
salm·on (sam′ən) *n.* 1. Any of various food fishes with pinkish flesh inhabiting the North Atlantic coastal waters. 2. A reddish or pinkish orange color: also **salmon pink.** —*adj.* Having a salmon color. [< L *salmo, -onis,* prob. akin to *salire* to leap] —**sal·mo·noid** (sal′mə·noid) *adj. & n.*
sa·lon (sə·lon′, *Fr.* sȧ·lôn′) *n.* 1. A room in which guests are received; a drawing room. 2. The periodic gathering of noted persons. 3. An establishment devoted to some specific purpose: a beauty *salon.* [< F < Ital. *sala* hall < Gmc.]
sa·loon (sə·lōōn′) *n.* 1. A place where alcoholic drinks are sold; a bar. 2. A large apartment or room for assemblies, etc. [< F *salon* salon]
sa·loon·keep·er (sə·lōōn′kē′pər) *n.* One who owns or manages a saloon (def. 1).
sal soda Sodium carbonate.
salt (sôlt) *n.* 1. A crystalline compound used as a seasoning and preservative; sodium chloride. ◆Collateral adjective: *saline.* 2. *Chem.* Any compound consisting of the positive ion of a base and the negative ion of an acid. 3. *pl.* A salt used as a laxative or cathartic; also, smelling salts. 4. *Informal* A sailor: an old *salt.* 5. A saltcellar. —**to take with a grain of salt** To have doubts about. —*adj.* 1. Flavored with salt; briny. 2. Cured or preserved with salt. —*v.t.* 1. To season, preserve, or cure with salt. 2. To furnish with salt: to *salt* cattle. —**to salt away** *Informal* To store up; save. [OE *sealt*] —**salt′ed** *adj.* —**salt′i·ness, salt′ness** *n.* —**salt′y** *adj.* **·i·er, ·i·est**
salt·cel·lar (sôlt′sel′ər) *n.* A small receptacle for salt. [ME *salt* + F *salière* saltcellar]
sal·tine (sôl·tēn′) *n.* A crisp, salty cracker.
salt lick A place, as a salt spring or dried salt pond, to which animals go to lick salt.
salt·pe·ter (sôlt′pē′tər) *n.* Potassium nitrate. —**Chile saltpeter** Mineral sodium nitrate, found chiefly in Chile. [< L *sal* salt + *petra* a rock]
salt·shak·er (sôlt′shā′kər) *n.* A container with small holes for sprinkling salt.
salt-wa·ter (sôlt′wô′tər, -wot′ər) *adj.* Of composed of, or living in salty water.
sa·lu·bri·ous (sə·lōō′brē·əs) *adj.* Conducive to health. [< L *salus* health] —**sa·lu′bri·ous·ly** *adv.* —**sa·lu′bri·ous·ness, sa·lu′bri·ty** (-brə·tē) *n.*
sal·u·tar·y (sal′yə·ter′ē) *adj.* 1. Beneficial. 2. Salubrious. [< L *salus, salutis* health] —**sal′u·tar′i·ly** *adv.* —**sal′u·tar′i·ness** *n.*
sal·u·ta·tion (sal′yə·tā′shən, -yōō-) *n.* 1. The act of saluting. 2. Any form of greeting. 3. The opening words of a letter, as *Dear Sir.*
sa·lute (sə·lōōt′) *n.* 1. A greeting by display of military or other official honors. 2. The act of or attitude assumed in giving a military salute. 3. A gesture of greeting. —*v.* **·lut·ed, ·lut·ing** *v.t.* 1. To greet with a sign of welcome, respect, etc. 2. To honor in some prescribed way, as by raising the hand to the cap. —*v.i.* 3. To make a salute. [< L *salus, salutis* health] —**sa·lut′er** *n.*
sal·va·ble (sal′və·bəl) *adj.* Capable of being saved or salvaged. [< L *salvus* safe] —**sal′va·bil′i·ty** *n.*
sal·vage (sal′vij) *v.t.* **·vaged, ·vag·ing** To save from loss or destruction. —*n.* 1. The saving of a ship, cargo, etc., from loss. 2. Any act of saving property. 3. Compensation to persons who save a vessel, her cargo, or the lives of those belonging to her. 4. That which is saved, as from a fire. [< L *salvus* safe] —**sal′vage·a·ble** *adj.* —**sal′vag·er** *n.*
sal·va·tion (sal·vā′shən) *n.* 1. The process or state of being saved. 2. *Theol.* Deliverance from sin and its penalty. 3. That which saves. [< L *salvus* safe]
Salvation Army A religious and charitable organization on military lines, founded by William Booth in 1865.
salve[1] (sav) *n.* An ointment for local ailments.

—*v.t.* **salved, salv·ing** 1. To dress with ointment. 2. To soothe; appease. [OE *sealf*]
salve[2] (salv) *v.t.* **salved, salv·ing** To save from loss; salvage. [< Med.L *salvare*]
sal·ver (sal′vər) *n.* A tray. [< Sp. *salva* the foretasting of food, as for a king < *salvar* to taste, save]
sal·vo (sal′vō) *n. pl.* **·vos** or **·voes** A simultaneous discharge of artillery. [< Ital. *salva* salute]
sa·mar·i·um (sə·mâr′ē·əm) *n.* A hard, brittle, yellowish gray metallic element (symbol Sm) of the lanthanide series. [< NL *samarskite*, a vitreous, black mineral]
sam·ba (sam′bə, säm′bä) *n.* 1. A popular dance of Brazil. 2. Music for this dance. —*v.i.* To dance the samba. [< Pg. < native African name]
same (sām) *adj.* 1. Having specific identity as the very one; identical: with *the.* 2. Similar in kind, quality, or quantity; equivalent. —*pron.* The identical person, thing, etc. —*adj.* In like manner; equally: with *the.* [< ON *samr*] —**same′ness** *n.*
sa·mite (sā′mīt, sam′it) *n.* A rich medieval fabric of silk, often interwoven with gold or silver. [< Gk. *hex* six + *mitos* thread]
Sa·mo·an (sə·mō′ən) *n.* 1. A native of Samoa. 2. The Polynesian language of the Samoans. —**Sa·mo′an** *adj.*
sam·o·var (sam′ə·vär) *n.* A metal urn for heating water, as for making tea. [< Russ., lit., self-boiler]
Sam·o·yed (sam′ə·yed′) *n.* 1. One of a Mongoloid people inhabiting the Arctic coasts of Siberia. 2. A large dog having a thick coat of long, white hair. —*adj.* Of the Samoyeds or their language; Samoyedic. Also **Sam′o·yede′** (-yed′). [< Russ., lit., self-eater]
Sam·o·yed·ic (sam′ə·yed′ik) *n.* A subfamily of the Uralic languages.
sam·pan (sam′pan) *n.* A small flat-bottomed boat or skiff used along rivers and coasts of China and Japan. [< Chinese *san* three + *pan* board, plank]
sam·ple (sam′pəl) *n.* A portion, part, or piece shown as a representative of the whole. —*v.t.* **·pled, ·pling** To test or examine by means of a sample. [See EXAMPLE.]
sam·pler[1] (sam′plər) *n.* One who tests by sampling.
sam·pler[2] (sam′plər) *n.* A piece of needlework, originally designed to show a beginner's skill. [See EXAMPLE.]
sam·pling (sam′pling) *n.* A small part of something selected for analysis in order to estimate the nature of the whole.
Sam·u·el (sam′yōō·əl) *n.* Either of two historical books, I and II Samuel, of the Old Testament.
sam·u·rai (sam′ōō·rī) *n. pl.* **·rai** Under the Japanese feudal system, a member of the soldier class of the lower nobility; also, the class itself. [< Japanese]
san·a·tive (san′ə·tiv) *adj.* Healing; health-giving. [< L *sanare* to heal]
san·a·to·ri·um (san′ə·tôr′ē·əm) *n. pl.* **·ri·ums** or **·ri·a** 1. An institution for the treatment and care of invalids and convalescents. 2. A health resort. Also called *sanitarium.* [< L *sanare* to heal]
sanc·ti·fy (sangk′tə·fī) *v.t.* **·fied, ·fy·ing** 1. To set apart as holy; consecrate. 2. To purify or make holy. [< L *sanctus* holy + *facere* to make] —**sanc′ti·fi·ca′tion** *n.* —**sanc′ti·fi′er** *n.*
sanc·ti·mo·ni·ous (sangk′tə·mō′nē·əs) *adj.* Making a display of holiness or devoutness. —**sanc′ti·mo′ni·ous·ly** *adv.* —**sanc′ti·mo′ni·ous·ness** *n.*
sanc·ti·mo·ny (sangk′tə·mō′nē) *n.* A display of holiness or devoutness. [< L *sanctimonia* holiness]
sanc·tion (sangk′shən) *v.t.* 1. To approve; confirm. 2. To countenance; allow. —*n.* 1. Approval; confirmation. 2. *Usu. pl.* Measures adopted to force a nation that is violating international law to desist. [< L < *sancire* to render sacred, inviolable]
sanc·ti·ty (sangk′tə·tē) *n. pl.* **·ties** 1. The state of being sanctified; holiness. 2. Sacredness.
sanc·tu·ar·y (sangk′chōō·er′ē) *n. pl.* **·ar·ies** 1. A holy or sacred place. 2. The most sacred place in a sacred structure. 3. A place of refuge; also, immunity. [< L *sanctus* holy]
sanc·tum (sangk′təm) *n. pl.* **·tums** or **·ta** A private room where one is not to be disturbed. [< L, neut. of *sanctus* holy]
sand (sand) *n.* 1. A hard, granular rock material. 2. *pl.* Stretches of sandy beach, desert, etc. 3. *pl.* Sandy grains in an hourglass. —*v.t.* 1. To sprinkle or cover with sand. 2. To smooth or polish with sandpaper or other abrasive. [OE] —**sand′er** *n.* —**sand′i·ness** *n.* —**sand′y** *adj.*
san·dal (san′dəl) *n.* 1. A foot covering, consisting of a sole held to the foot by thongs. 2. A light slipper. 3. An overshoe of rubber, cut very low. [< Gk. *sandalon*] —**san′daled, san′dalled** *adj.*
san·dal·wood (san′dəl·wŏŏd′) *n.* 1. The fine-grained, fragrant wood of any of several East Indian trees. 2. The similar wood of other trees, whose dark red wood is used as a dyestuff. [< Med.L *sandalum*, ult. < Skt. *candana*]
sand·bag (sand′bag′) *n.* A bag filled with sand, used for building fortifications, for ballast, etc. —*v.t.* **·bagged, ·bag·ging** To fill or surround with sandbags. —**sand′bag′ger** *n.*
sand·bar (sand′bär′) *n.* A ridge of sand in rivers, along beaches, etc., formed by the action of currents or tides.
sand·blast (sand′blast′) *n.* A fine jet of sand, propelled under pressure and used to clean, grind, or decorate hard surfaces. —*v.t.* To clean or engrave by means of a sandblast.
sand·box (sand′boks′) *n.* A box of sand for children to play in.
sand-cast (sand′kast′) *v.t.* **-cast, -cast·ing** To make (a casting) by pouring metal into a mold of sand.
sand flea Any of various fleas that live in sand, as the chigoe.
sand·hog (sand′hôg′, -hog′) *n.* One who works in a caisson to build underwater tunnels.
sand-lot (sand′lot′) *adj.* Of or in a vacant lot: *sand-lot* baseball.
sand·man (sand′man′) *n.* In nursery lore, a person supposed to make children sleepy by casting sand in their eyes.
sand·pa·per (sand′pā′pər) *n.* Heavy paper coated with sand for smoothing or polishing. —*v.t.* To rub or polish with sandpaper.
sand·pi·per (sand′pī′pər) *n.* A small wading

bird related to the snipe and frequenting seashores. Also **sand′peep′** (-pēp′).

sand·stone (sand′stōn′) *n.* A rock consisting chiefly of quartz sand cemented with silica, feldspar, lime, or clay.

sand·storm (sand′stôrm′) *n.* A high wind that propels masses of sand or dust.

sand·wich (sand′wich, san′-) *n.* 1. Two slices of bread with meat, cheese, etc., between them. 2. Any combination of dissimilar things pressed together. —*v.t.* To place between two layers or objects. [after John Montagu, fourth Earl of *Sandwich*, 1718–92, who originated it]

sane (sān) *adj.* 1. Mentally sound; not deranged. 2. Proceeding from a sound mind. [< L *sanus* whole, healthy] —**sane′ly** *adv.* —**sane′ness** *n.*

sang (sang) Past tense of SING.

sang-froid (säṅ·frwä′) *n.* Calmness amid trying circumstances; coolness; composure. [< F, lit., cold blood]

san·gri·a (säng·grē′ə) *n.* Red wine flavored with fruit juices. [< Sp. *sangría*, lit., bleeding]

san·gui·nar·y (sang′gwə·ner′ē) *adj.* 1. Involving bloodshed. 2. Bloodthirsty. —**san′·gui·nar′i·ly** *adv.* —**san′gui·nar′i·ness** *n.*

san·guine (sang′gwin) *adj.* 1. Full of hope and cheer. 2. Ruddy; robust. [< L *sanguis, -inis* blood] —**san′guine·ly** *adv.* —**san′·guine·ness** *n.*

san·i·tar·i·um (san′ə·târ′ē·əm) *n. pl.* **·tar·i·ums** or **·tar·i·a** A sanatorium. [< L *sanitas* health]

san·i·tar·y (san′ə·ter′ē) *adj.* 1. Having to do with health. 2. Favorable to health; clean. [< L *sanitas* health] —**san′i·tar′i·ly** *adv.*

sanitary napkin An absorbent pad worn by women during menstruation.

san·i·ta·tion (san′ə·tā′shən) *n.* The use of sanitary measures; to make favorable to health.

san·i·ta·tion·man (san′i·tā′shən·man′) *n. pl.* **·men** (-mən, -men′) A person whose work is the collection of refuse and trash.

san·i·tize (san′ə·tīz) *v.t.* **·tized, ·tiz·ing** To make sanitary.

san·i·ty (san′ə·tē) *n. pl.* **·ties** The state of being sane; soundness of mind.

sank (sangk) Past tense of SINK.

sans (sanz, *Fr.* säṅ) *prep.* Without. [<F < OF *sanz*]

San·sei (sän·sā′) *n. pl.* **·sei** or **·seis** An American citizen of Japanese descent whose grandparents settled in the U.S. [< Japanese, third generation]

San·skrit (san′skrit) *n.* The ancient and classical language of the Hindus of India, belonging to the Indic branch of the Indo-Iranian subfamily of Indo-European languages. Also **San′scrit.** [< Skt. *saṁskṛta* artificial, highly cultivated] —**San·skrit′ic** *adj.*

sans ser·if (san ser′if, sanz′) *Printing* A type face without serifs: also called *gothic.*

San·ta Claus (san′tə klôz′) In lore, a fat, jolly old man who brings presents at Christmas time. [< Du. *Sant Nikolaas* Saint Nicholas]

sap¹ (sap) *n.* 1. In plants, the juices that contain and transport the materials necessary to growth. 2. Any vital fluid. 3. *Slang* A foolish or gullible person. [OE *sæp*] —**sap′less** *adj.*

sap² (sap) *v.t.* **sapped, sap·ping** 1. To weaken or destroy gradually; exhaust. 2. To undermine (an enemy fortification) by digging a trench or tunnel. [< Ital. *zappa* spade, goat] —**sap′per** *n.*

sa·pi·ent (sā′pē·ənt) *adj.* Wise; sagacious. [< L *sapere* to have good taste] —**sa′pi·ence, sa′pi·en·cy** *n.* —**sa′pi·ent·ly** *adv.*

sap·ling (sap′ling) *n.* 1. A young tree. 2. A youth. [Dim. of SAP¹]

sap·o·dil·la (sap′ə·dil′ə) *n.* 1. A large evergreen tree of the West Indies and tropical America. 2. Its edible fruit, a source of chicle: also **sapodilla plum.** Also **sa·po·ta** (sə·pō′tə), **sap′a·dil′lo, sap′o·dil′lo.** [< Sp. < Nahuatl *tzapotl*]

sap·o·na·ceous (sap′o·nā′shəs) *adj.* Soapy.

sa·pon·i·fy (sə·pon′ə·fī) *v.t.* **·fied, ·fy·ing** *Chem.* To convert (a fat or oil) into soap by the action of an alkali. [< L *sapo, saponis* soap + *facere* to make] —**sa·pon′i·fi′a·ble** *adj.* —**sa·pon′i·fi·ca′tion** *n.* —**sa·pon′i·fi′er** *n.*

sap·phire (saf′īr) *n.* 1. A hard, translucent, deep blue variety of corundum, used as a gem. 2. Deep, pure blue. [< Gk. *sappheiros*]

sap·py (sap′ē) *adj.* **·pi·er, ·pi·est** 1. Full of sap; juicy. 2. *Slang* Immature; silly. —**sap′pi·ly** *adv.* —**sap′pi·ness** *n.*

sap·ro·phyte (sap′rə·fīt) *n.* A vegetable organism, such as a fungus or bacterium, that lives on dead or decaying organic matter. [< Gk. *sapros* rotten + -PHYTE] —**sap′ro·phyt′ic** (-fit′ik) *adj.*

sap·suck·er (sap′suk′ər) *n.* A small black and white woodpecker that damages orchard trees by exposing and drinking the sap.

sap·wood (sap′wo͝od′) *n. Bot.* The new wood next to the bark of a tree.

sar·a·band (sar′ə·band) *n.* 1. A slow, stately dance of the 17th and 18th c. 2. Music for this dance. Also **sar′a·bande.** [< Persian *sarband* a kind of dance and song]

Sar·a·cen (sar′ə·sən) *n.* 1. Originally, a nomad Arab of the Syrian-Arabian desert. 2. A Moslem, esp. during the Crusades. [< LGk. *Sarakēnos*] —**Sar′a·cen′ic** (-sen′ik) or **·i·cal** *adj.*

sar·casm (sär′kaz·əm) *n.* An ironical or scornful utterance; contemptuous and taunting language. [< Gk. *sarkazein* to tear flesh, sneer < *sarx, sarkos* flesh] —**sar·cas′tic** (-kas′tik) or **·ti·cal** *adj.* —**sar·cas′ti·cal·ly** *adv.*

sarce·net (särs′nit) See SARSENET.

sar·co·ma (sär·kō′mə) *n. pl.* **·ma·ta** (-mə·tə) *Pathol.* A tumor, often malignant, made up of cells resembling those of embryonic connective tissue. [< Gk. *sarx, sarkos* flesh] —**sar·co′ma·toid, sar·co′ma·tous** *adj.*

sar·coph·a·gus (sär·kof′ə·gəs) *n. pl.* **·gi** (-jī) A stone coffin, often large and ornamental. [< Gk. *sarx, sarkos* flesh + *phagein* to eat]

sar·dine (sär·dēn′) *n.* A small, herringlike fish commonly preserved in oil as a food. [< Gk. *sardēnē*, ? < *Sardo* Sardinia]

sar·don·ic (sär·don′ik) *adj.* Scornful or derisive; mocking. [< Gk. *sardanios* bitter, scornful] —**sar·don′i·cal·ly** *adv.* —**sar·don·i·cism** (sär·don′ə·siz′əm) *n.*

sar·gas·so (sär·gas′ō) *n.* An olive-brown

seaweed having small air bladders on its stalks, native in tropical American waters. Also **sar·gas′sum** (-əm). [< Pg. *sarga*, ? < L *salicastrum*]

sa·ri (sä′rē) *n. pl.* **·ris** The principal garment of Hindu women, made of a long piece of cloth and worn round the body from the head or shoulder to the feet. Also **sa′ree.** [< Hind. *sarī* < Skt. *śāṭī*]

sa·rong (sə·rong′) *n.* A skirtlike garment of colored silk or cotton cloth worn by both sexes in the Malay Archipelago, etc. [< Malay *sārung*, prob. < Skt. *sāranga* variegated]

sar·sa·pa·ril·la (sas′pə·ril′ə) *n.* 1. The dried roots of certain tropical American climbing plants of the lily family. 2. A medicinal preparation or a beverage made from such roots. [< Sp. *zarza* bramble + *parilla*, dim. of *parra* vine]

sarse·net (särs′nit) *n.* A fine, thin silk, used for linings: also spelled *sarcenet*. [< AF, dim. of ME *sarzin* Saracen]

sar·to·ri·al (sär·tôr′ē·əl) *adj.* 1. Pertaining to a tailor or his work. 2. Pertaining to men's clothes. [< L *sartor* patcher, mender] **—sar·to′ri·al·ly** *adv.*

sash[1] (sash) *n.* An ornamental band or scarf worn around the waist or over the shoulder. [< Arabic *shāsh* muslin, turban]

sash[2] (sash) *n.* A frame, as of a window, in which glass is set. **—*v.t.*** To furnish with a sash. [Alter. of CHASSIS, taken as a pl.]

sa·shay (sa·shā′) *v.i. Informal* To move with a swinging or gliding motion. [Alter. of *chassé*, a dance motion]

sa·shi·mi (sä·shē′mē) *n.* A dish of sliced raw fish. [< Jap.]

sas·quatch (sas′kwäch′) *n.* A large manlike animal reportedly sighted in the forests of NW North America: also called *bigfoot*. [< Salish, wild man of the woods]

sass (sas) *n. Informal* Impudence; back talk. **—*v.t.*** To talk to impudently or disrespectfully. [Dial. alter. of SAUCE]

sas·sa·fras (sas′ə·fras) *n.* 1. A tree of the laurel family. 2. The root bark of this tree, used for flavoring and yielding a volatile oil. [< Sp. *sasafrás*, prob. < N.Am.Ind. name]

sas·sy (sas′ē) *adj.* **·si·er, ·si·est** *Dial.* Saucy; impertinent.

sat (sat) Past tense of SIT.

Sa·tan (sā′tən) In the Bible, the great adversary of God and tempter of mankind; the Devil: identified with *Lucifer*. Also **Sa′than** (sā′tən), **Sath·a·nas** (sath′ə·nəs). [< Hebrew *sātān* enemy]

sa·tan·ic (sā·tan′ik, sə-) *adj.* Devilish; infernal; wicked. Also **sa·tan′i·cal. —sa·tan′i·cal·ly** *adv.*

satch·el (sach′əl) *n.* A small handbag or suitcase. [< L *sacellus*, dim. of *saccus* sack]

sate (sāt) *v.t.* **sat·ed, sat·ing** To satisfy the appetite of; satiate. [Prob. < SATIATE]

sa·teen (sa·tēn′) *n.* A cotton fabric woven so as to give it a satin surface. [Alter. of SATIN]

sat·el·lite (sat′ə·līt) *n.* 1. *Astron.* A smaller body revolving round a larger one; a moon. 2. Any obsequious attendant. 3. A small nation that is dependent on a great power. 4. Any manmade object revolving around the earth. [< L *satelles, satellitis* attendant, guard]

sa·ti·a·ble (sā′shē·ə·bəl) *adj.* Capable of being satiated. **—sa′ti·a·bil′i·ty, sa′ti·a·ble·ness** *n.* **—sa′ti·a·bly** *adv.*

sa·ti·ate (*v.* sā′shē·āt; *adj.* -it) *v.t.* **·at·ed, ·at·ing** 1. To satisfy the appetite or desire of; gratify. 2. To fill or gratify beyond natural desire; glut. **—*adj.*** Filled to satiety; satiated. [< L *satis* enough] **—sa′ti·a′tion** *n.*

sa·ti·e·ty (sə·tī′ə·tē) *n. pl.* **·ties** The state of being satiated.

sat·in (sat′ən) *n.* A silk, cotton, rayon, or acetate fabric of thick texture, with glossy face and dull back. **—*adj.*** Of or resembling satin; glossy; smooth. [< Med.L *satinus, setinus*, ult. < L *seta* silk] **—sat′in·y** *adj.*

sat·in·wood (sat′ən·wo͝od′) *n.* 1. The satinlike wood of an East Indian tree of the mahogany family. 2. The tree itself.

sat·ire (sat′īr) *n.* 1. Sarcasm, irony, or wit used to ridicule or expose abuses or follies. 2. A written composition in which satire is used. [< L *satira, satura* satire, orig., medley] **—sa·tir·ic** (sə·tir′ik) or **·i·cal** *adj.* **—sa·tir′i·cal·ly** *adv.* **—sa·tir′i·cal·ness** *n.* **—sat′i·rist** (-ə·rist) *n.* **—sat′i·rize** (-ə·rīz) *v.t.* **—sat′i·riz′er** *n.*

sat·is·fac·tion (sat′is·fak′shən) *n.* 1. The act of satisfying, or the state of being satisfied; gratification. 2. The making of amends, reparation, or payment. 3. That which satisfies.

sat·is·fac·to·ry (sat′is·fak′tər·ē) *adj.* Giving satisfaction; answering all requirements. **—sat′is·fac′to·ri·ly** *adv.* **—sat′is·fac′to·ri·ness** *n.*

sat·is·fy (sat′is·fī) *v.* **·fied, ·fy·ing** *v.t.* 1. To supply fully with what is desired, expected, or needed; gratify. 2. To free from doubt or anxiety; convince. 3. To give what is due to. 4. To pay or discharge (a debt, obligation, etc.). 5. To answer sufficiently or convincingly, as a question or objection. 6. To fulfill the conditions or requirements of. **—*v.i.*** 7. To give satisfaction. [< L *satis* enough + *facere* to do] **—sat′is·fi′er** *n.* **—sat′is·fy′ing·ly** *adv.*

sa·trap (sā′trap, sat′rap) *n.* 1. A governor of a province in ancient Persia. 2. A subordinate, often despotic, ruler or governor. [< OPersian *shathraparan*, lit., protector of a province]

sa·trap·y (sā′trə·pē, sat′rə·pē) *n. pl.* **·trap·ies** The territory or the jurisdiction of a satrap. Also **sa·trap·ate** (sā′trə·pit, sat′rə-).

sat·u·rate (sach′ə·rāt) *v.t.* **·rat·ed, ·rat·ing** 1. To soak thoroughly. 2. To fill or charge (something) to capacity. [< L *saturare* to fill up] **—sat·u·ra·ble** (sach′ər·ə·bəl) *adj.* **—sat′u·ra′ter** or **sat′u·ra′tor** *n.* **—sat′u·ra′tion** *n.*

Sat·ur·day (sat′ər·dē, -dā) *n.* The seventh day of the week; the Sabbath day as observed by Jews and certain Christians. [OE *Sæterdæg, Sæternesdæg*]

Sat·urn (sat′ərn) *n.* The second largest planet of the solar system and sixth in order from the sun. [after *Saturn*, Roman god of agriculture] **—Sa·tur·ni·an** (sə·tûr′nē·ən) *adj.*

sat·ur·na·li·a (sat′ər·nā′lē·ə, -nāl′yə) *n.pl.* (*Usu. construed as sing.*) Any season or period of license or revelry. [< L *Saturnalia*, feast in honor of the god Saturn] **—sat′ur·na′li·an** *adj.*

sat·ur·nine (sat′ər·nīn) *adj.* Having a grave, gloomy, or morose disposition or character. [< Med.L *Saturnus* lead, Saturn]

sat·yr (sat′ər, sā′tər) *n.* 1. In classical mythology, a lecherous woodland deity in human form, having pointed ears, goat's legs, and budding horns. 2. A lascivious man. [< Gk. *satyros*] —**sa·tyr·ic** (sə·tir′ik) or **·i·cal** *adj.*

sauce (sôs) *n.* 1. A dressing or liquid relish for food. 2. A dish of fruit pulp stewed and sweetened. 3. *Informal* Pert or impudent language. —*v.t.* **sauced, sauc·ing** 1. To flavor with sauce; season. 2. To give zest to. 3. *Informal* To be saucy to. [< OF < LL *salsa*, orig. fem. of L *salsus* salted]

sauce·pan (sôs′pan′) *n.* A pan with projecting handle, for cooking food.

sau·cer (sô′sər) *n.* A small dish for holding a cup. [< OF *sauce* sauce]

sau·cy (sô′sē) *adj.* **·ci·er, ·ci·est** 1. Disrespectful to superiors; impudent. 2. Piquant; sprightly; amusing. —**sau′ci·ly** *adv.* —**sau′ci·ness** *n.*

Sau·di (sou′dē, sä·o͞o′dē) *adj.* Of Saudi Arabia or its inhabitants. —**Sau′di** *n.* —**Sau′di A·ra′bi·an** *n. & adj.*

sauer·bra·ten (sour′brätn) *n.* Beef marinated in vinegar before being braised. [< G *sauer* sour + *braten* to roast]

sauer·kraut (sour′krout′) *n.* Shredded and salted cabbage fermented in its own juice. [< G *sauer* sour + *kraut* cabbage]

Sauk (sôk) *n.* One of a tribe of Algonquian Indians, formerly occupying Michigan.

sau·na (sou′nə) *n.* 1. A room or house for taking steam baths in steam produced by throwing water on hot stones; also, such a steam bath. 2. A dry heat bath; also, the room for such baths. [< Finnish]

saun·ter (sôn′tər) *v.i.* To walk in a leisurely way; stroll. —*n.* 1. A slow, aimless manner of walking. 2. An idle stroll. [ME *santren* to muse, meditate]

sau·sage (sô′sij) *n.* Finely chopped and highly seasoned meat, commonly stuffed into the cleaned entrails of some animal or into casings. [< LL *salsicia*, ult. < L *salsus* salted]

sau·té (sō·tā′, sô-) *v.t.* **·téed, ·té·ing** To fry quickly in a little fat. [< F, pp. of *sauter* to leap] —**sau·té** *adj. & n.*

sau·terne (sō·tûrn′) *n.* A sweet, white French wine. Also **sau·ternes′** (-tûrn′).

sav·age (sav′ij) *adj.* 1. Having a wild nature; not domesticated. 2. Ferocious; fierce. 3. Primitive or uncivilized: *savage* tribes. 4. Vicious; cruel. —*n.* 1. A primitive or uncivilized human being. 2. A brutal, fierce, and cruel person. —*v.t.* **·aged, ·ag·ing** To attack savagely, esp. with the teeth. [< L *salvaticus, silvaticus* of the woods < *silva* a wood] —**sav′age·ly** *adv.* —**sav′age·ness** *n.* —**sav′age·ry** *n.*

sa·van·na (sə·van′ə) *n.* Tropical or subtropical grassland, with trees and spiny shrubs. Also **sa·van′nah.** [Earlier *zavana* < Carib]

sa·vant (sə·vänt′, sav′ənt) *n.* A man of exceptional learning. [< F < L *sapere* to be wise]

save[1] (sāv) *v.* **saved, sav·ing** *v.t.* 1. To preserve or rescue from danger, harm, wear, etc. 2. To keep from being spent or lost. 3. To set aside for future use; accumulate. 4. *Theol.* To rescue from sin and its penalties; redeem. —*v.i.* 5. To avoid waste; be economical. [< L *salvus* safe] —**sav′a·ble** or **save′a·ble** *adj.* —**sav′a·ble·ness** *n.* —**sav′er** *n.*

save[2] (sāv) *prep. & conj.* Except; but. [< OF *sauf* being excepted, orig., safe < L *salvus*]

sav·ing (sā′ving) *adj.* That saves. —*n.* 1. Preservation from loss or danger. 2. Avoidance of waste; economy. 3. The extent of something saved. 4. *pl.* Sums of money not spent. —*prep.* With the exception of; save. —*conj.* Save; but. —**sav′ing·ly** *adv.* —**sav′ing·ness** *n.*

savings account A sum of money deposited in a bank and drawing interest.

sav·ior (sāv′yər) *n.* One who saves. Also *Brit.* **sav′iour.** [< OF *savëour* < L *salvare* to save]

Sav·ior (sāv′yər) *n.* Jesus Christ. Also **Sav′iour.**

sa·voir-faire (sȧ·vwȧr·fâr′) *French* Ability to say and do the right thing; tact.

sa·vor (sā′vər) *n.* 1. Flavor or odor. 2. Specific quality. 3. Relish; zest. —*v.i.* 1. To have a specified flavor, odor, or quality: with *of.* —*v.t.* 2. To give flavor to; season. 3. To taste or enjoy with pleasure; relish. Also *Brit.* **sa′vour.** [< OF *savour* < L *sapor* taste < *sapere* to taste, know] —**sa′vor·er** *n.* —**sa′vor·ous** *adj.*

sa·vor·less (sā′vər·lis) *adj.* Tasteless; insipid.

sa·vor·y[1] (sā′vər·ē) *adj.* 1. Of an agreeable flavor and odor; appetizing. 2. Piquant to the taste. 3. In good repute; respectable. —*n.* *Brit.* A small, hot serving of food eaten at the end or beginning of a dinner. Also *Brit.* **sa′vour·y.** [< OF *savouré*, pp. of *savourer* to taste] —**sa′vor·i·ly** *adv.* —**sa′vor·i·ness** *n.*

sa·vor·y[2] (sā′vər·ē) *n.* A hardy, annual, aromatic herb of the mint family, used for seasoning. Also **summer savory.** [OE < L *satureia*]

sa·voy (sə·voi′) *n.* A variety of cabbage with wrinkled leaves. [< F (*chou de*) *Savoie* (cabbage of) Savoy]

sav·vy (sav′ē) *Slang* *v.i.* **·vied, ·vy·ing** To understand. —*n.* Understanding; good sense. [Alter. of Sp. *¿Sabe* (*usted*)*?* Do (you) know? < L *sapere* to know]

saw[1] (sô) *n.* A cutting instrument having pointed teeth along the blade, used to cut wood, etc. —*v.* **sawed, sawed** or **sawn, saw·ing** *v.t.* 1. To cut, shape, or fashion with a saw. —*v.i.* 2. To use a saw. 3. To be cut with a saw: This wood *saws* easily. [OE *sagu*] —**saw′er** *n.*

saw[2] (sô) *n.* A proverbial or familiar saying; old maxim. [OE *sagu*]

saw[3] (sô) Past tense of SEE[1].

saw·bones (sô′bōnz′) *n.* *Slang* A surgeon.

saw·buck (sô′buk′) *n.* 1. A sawhorse with two X-shaped ends joined by a bar or bars. 2. *Slang* A ten-dollar bill. [Trans. of Du. *zaagbok*]

saw·dust (sô′dust′) *n.* Small particles of wood produced by sawing.

sawed-off (sôd′ôf′) *adj.* 1. Having one end sawed off. 2. *Slang* Short.

saw·fish (sô′fish′) *n.* *pl.* **·fish** or **·fish·es**

A sharklike tropical fish with the snout prolonged into a flat blade with teeth on each edge.

saw·horse (sô′hôrs′) *n.* A frame on which to rest wood, etc., for sawing.

saw·mill (sô′mil′) *n.* An establishment for sawing logs with power-driven machinery.

sawn (sôn) Alternative past participle of SAW[1].

saw-toothed (sô′tōōtht′) *adj.* Toothed or notched like a saw; serrate.

saw·yer (sô′yər) *n.* One whose occupation is the sawing of wood. [Alter. of SAWER]

sax (saks) *n. Informal* A saxophone.

sax·i·frage (sak′sə·frij) *n.* Any of a genus of herbaceous plants growing in rocky places and bearing small white, yellow, or purplish flowers. [< L (*herba*) *saxifraga*, lit., stone-breaking (herb)]

Sax·on (sak′sən) *n.* 1. A member of a Germanic tribe that formerly inhabited northwestern Germany and invaded England in the fifth and sixth centuries A.D. 2. An Anglo-Saxon. **—***adj.* 1. Of or pertaining to the Saxons or their language. 2. Anglo-Saxon; English. [< F < L *Saxo, Saxonis* < WGmc.]

sax·o·phone (sak′sə·fōn) *n.* A metal wind instrument having a single reed. [after A. J. *Sax*, 1814–94, Belgian instrument maker] **—sax′o·phon′ist** *n.*

say (sā) *v.t.* **said, say·ing** 1. To pronounce or utter; speak. 2. To declare or express in words. 3. To state positively or as an opinion: *Say* which you prefer. 4. To report; allege. 5. To assume; suppose. **—that is to say** In other words. **—***n.* 1. Right or turn to speak: to have one's *say*. 2. Authority: to have the final *say* in the matter. **—***interj. Informal* An exclamation to command attention, show surprise, etc.: also *Brit.* I say. [OE *secgan*] **—say′er** *n.*

say·ing (sā′ing) *n.* 1. A maxim; adage. 2. Something said.

says (sez) Third person singular, present indicative of SAY.

say-so (sā′sō′) *n. Informal* 1. An assertion or decision. 2. Right or power to make decisions.

scab (skab) *n.* 1. A crust formed on the surface of a wound or sore. 2. *Vet.* Scabies. 3. A plant disease characterized by a roughened or warty appearance. 4. *Informal* A workman who will not join or act with a labor union; esp., a strikebreaker. **—***v.i.* **scabbed, scab·bing** 1. To form or become covered with a scab. 2. *Informal* To take the job of a striker. [Fusion of ON *skabbr* (assumed) and OE *sceabb*]

scab·bard (skab′ərd) *n.* A sheath for a weapon, as for a bayonet or a sword. [< OF *escalberc*, prob. < OHG *scar* sword + *bergan* to hide, protect]

scab·by (skab′ē) *adj.* **·bi·er, ·bi·est** 1. Having, consisting of, or resembling a scab or scabs. 2. Having scabies. 3. *Informal* Contemptible. **—scab′bi·ly** *adv.* **—scab′bi·ness** *n.*

sca·bies (skā′bēz) *n.* 1. A skin disease caused by the itch mite; itch. 2. *Vet.* A similar skin disease of sheep: also called *scab*. [< L, roughness, an itch < *scabere* to scratch, scrape] **—sca·bi·et·ic** (skā′bē·et′ik) *adj.*

sca·brous (skab′rəs, skā′brəs) *adj.* 1. Roughened with minute points; scurfy. 2. Off-color; risqué. [< LL *scabere* to scratch] **—sca′brous·ly** *adv.* **—sca′brous·ness** *n.*

scads (skadz) *n.pl. Informal* A large amount or quantity. [? Var. of dial E *scald* a large amount, great number]

scaf·fold (skaf′əld, -ōld) *n.* 1. A structure for the support of workmen, materials, etc., as in building. 2. A platform for the execution of criminals. **—***v.t.* To furnish or support with a scaffold. [< OF (*e*)*schaffaut*]

scaf·fold·ing (skaf′əl·ding) *n.* A scaffold or system of scaffolds, or the materials for constructing them. Also **scaf′fold·age** (-dij).

scal·a·wag (skal′ə·wag) *n. Informal* A worthless person; scamp. Also **scal′la·wag, scal′ly·wag** (-ē·wag). [Origin uncertain]

scald (skôld) *v.t.* 1. To burn with or as with hot liquid or steam. 2. To cleanse or treat with boiling water. 3. To heat (a liquid) to a point just short of boiling. **—***v.i.* 4. To be or become scalded. **—***n.* 1. A burn to the skin by a hot liquid. 2. A destructive parasitic disease of plants. [< AF *escalder* < L *ex-* very + *calidus* hot]

scale[1] (skāl) *n.* 1. One of the thin, horny, membranous or bony outgrowths of the skin of various animals, as most fishes. 2. Any similar thin formation, piece, or part. 3. *Metall.* The coating of oxide that forms on heated iron, etc. **—***v.* **scaled, scal·ing** *v.t.* 1. To strip or clear of scales. **—***v.i.* 2. To come off in scales; peel. [< OF *escale* husk < Gmc.] **—scal′er** *n.*

scale[2] (skāl) *n.* 1. An instrument bearing accurately spaced lines or gradations for use in measurement. 2. Any system of designating units of measurement: the Celsius *scale*. 3. A fixed proportion used in determining measurements or dimensions: a *scale* of one inch to the mile. 4. *Music* An arrangement of tones in ascending or descending order through the interval of an octave. **—***v.* **scaled, scal·ing** *v.t.* 1. To climb to the top of. 2. To make according to a scale. 3. To regulate or adjust according to a scale or ratio. **—***v.i.* 4. To climb; ascend. 5. To rise in steps or stages. [< Ital. *scala* ladder < L *scandere* to climb] **—scal′a·ble** *adj.* **—scal′er** *n.*

scale[3] (skāl) *n.* 1. Any weighing machine. 2. A pan, platform, etc., that holds something to be weighed in a balance. 3. *Usu. pl.* A balance (defs. 1 & 2). **—to turn the scales** To determine; decide. **—***v.t. & v.i.* **scaled, scal·ing** To weigh or be weighed in scales. [< ON *skāl* bowl, in pl., a weighing balance]

scale insect One of numerous small insects that feed on plants and as adults have a scalelike, protective shield.

sca·lene (skā′lēn, skā·lēn′) *adj. Geom.* Designating a triangle having no two sides equal. [< Gk. *skalēnos* uneven]

scal·lion (skal′yən) *n.* 1. A young, tender onion with a small white bulb. 2. A shallot or leek. [< L (*caepa*) *Ascalonia* (onion) of Ashkelon, a Palestinian seaport]

scal·lop (skal′əp, skol′-) *n.* 1. A bivalve mollusk having a rounded, ridged shell whose valves are snapped together in swimming. 2. An edible muscle of certain species of this mollusk. 3. One of a series of semicircular curves along an edge, as for ornament. **—***v.t.*

1. To shape the edge of with scallops. 2. To bake (food) in a casserole. Also *escallop, scollop.* [< OF *escalope* < Gmc.] **—scal′·lop·er** *n.*

scalp (skalp) *n.* The skin of the top and back of the human skull, usu. covered with hair. **—***v.t.* 1. To cut or tear the scalp from. 2. *Informal* To buy and resell (tickets) at prices exceeding the established rate. **—***v.i.* 3. *Informal* To scalp tickets, etc. [ME, prob. < Scand.] **—scalp′er** *n.*

scal·pel (skal′pəl) *n.* A small pointed knife with a very sharp, thin blade, used in dissections and in surgery. [< L *scalpere* to cut]

scal·y (skā′lē) *adj.* **scal·i·er, scal·i·est** Having or resembling scales. **—scal′i·ness** *n.*

scaly anteater A pangolin.

scamp (skamp) *n.* A rogue; good-for-nothing. [< obs. *scamp* to roam, contr. of SCAMPER] **—scamp′ish** *adj.*

scam·per (skam′pər) *v.i.* To run quickly or hastily. **—***n.* A hurried run. [AF *escamper,* ult. < L *ex* out from + *campus* plain, battlefield] **—scam′per·er** *n.*

scam·pi (scam′pē) *n.pl.* Large shrimp or similar shellfish, usu. broiled and served with a garlic sauce. [< Ital., pl. of *scampo* prawn]

scan (skan) *v.* **scanned, scan·ning** *v.t.* 1. To examine in detail. 2. To pass the eyes over quickly; glance at. 3. To separate (verse) into metrical feet. 4. *Telecom.* To pass a beam of light or electrons rapidly over. **—***v.i.* 5. To conform to metrical rules: said of verse. [< L *scandere* climb] **—scan′na·ble** *adj.* **—scan′ner** *n.*

scan·dal (skan′dəl) *n.* 1. Heedless or malicious gossip. 2. Disgrace caused by shameful or dishonorable conduct; ignominy. [< Gk. *skandalon* snare]

scan·dal·ize (skan′dəl·īz) *v.t.* **·ized, ·iz·ing** To shock the moral feelings of. **—scan′dal·i·za′tion** *n.* **—scan′dal·iz′er** *n.*

scan·dal·mong·er (skan′dəl·mung′gər, -mong′-) *n.* One who spreads scandal.

scan·dal·ous (skan′dəl·əs) *adj.* 1. Causing or tending to cause scandal; disgraceful. 2. Consisting of or spreading scandal. **—scan′dal·ous·ly** *adv.* **—scan′dal·ous·ness** *n.*

Scan·di·na·vi·an (skan′də·nā′vē·ən) *adj.* Of or pertaining to Scandinavia, its people, or their languages. **—***n.* 1. A native or inhabitant of Scandinavia. 2. The North Germanic group of languages: see under GERMANIC. Also *Norse.* **—Old Scandinavian** Old Norse. See under NORSE.

scan·di·um (skan′dē·əm) *n.* A metallic element (symbol Sc) of the lanthanide series. [< L *Scandia* Scandinavia]

scant (skant) *adj.* 1. Scarcely enough; meager. 2. Being just short of the measure specified: a *scant* five yards. **—***v.t.* To limit or restrict; stint. [< ON *skammr* short] **—scant′ly** *adv.* **—scant′ness** *n.*

scant·ling (skant′ling) *n.* A piece of lumber of small or moderate cross section, used for studding, etc. [< OF *eschantillon* cornerpiece]

scant·y (skan′tē) *adj.* **scant·i·er, scant·i·est** Limited or restricted; meager. **—scant′i·ly** *adv.* **—scant′i·ness** *n.*

scape·goat (skāp′gōt′) *n.* A person or group that bears the blame for others. [< (E)SCAPE + GOAT (*Lev.* xvi)]

scape·grace (skāp′grās′) *n.* A mischievous person; rogue.

scap·u·la (skap′yə·lə) *n.* *pl.* **·lae** (-lē) *Anat.* Either of a pair of large, flat, triangular bones in the back of the shoulder in man: also called *shoulder blade.* [< L *scapulae* shoulder blades] **—scap′u·lar** *adj.*

scar (skär) *n.* 1. The mark left on the skin after the healing of a wound or sore. 2. Any mark, damage, or lasting effect resulting from past injury, stress, etc. **—***v.t. & v.i.* **scarred, scar·ring** To mark or become marked with a scar. [< LL *eschara* scab < Gk.]

scar·ab (skar′əb) *n.* 1. A large, black beetle held sacred by the ancient Egyptians. 2. A gem or ornament representing this beetle. [< L *scarabaeus*]

scarce (skârs) *adj.* **scarc·er, scarc·est** 1. Rarely seen or found. 2. Not plentiful. **—to make oneself scarce** *Informal* To go away or stay away. [< OF *eschars* scanty, ult. < L *excerpere* to pick out] **—scarce′ness** *n.* **—scar·ci·ty** (skâr′sə·tē) *n.*

scarce·ly (skârs′lē) *adv.* 1. Only just; barely. 2. Not quite; hardly.

scare (skâr) *v.* **scared, scar·ing** *v.t.* 1. To strike with sudden fear; frighten. 2. To drive or force by frightening: with *off* or *away.* **—***v.i.* 3. To become scared. **—***n.* 1. Sudden fright. 2. Panic. [< ON *skirra* to frighten < *skiarr* shy] **—scar′er** *n.* **—scar′ing·ly** *adv.*

scare·crow (skâr′krō′) *n.* 1. Any crude figure of a person set up to scare crows and other birds away from growing crops. 2. A person of ragged or disreputable appearance.

scarf (skärf) *n.* *pl.* **scarfs** or **scarves** (skärvz) 1. A band or square of cloth worn about the head, neck, etc. 2. A necktie, cravat, kerchief, etc. **—***v.t.* To cover or decorate with or as with a scarf. [< OF *escharpe*]

scar·i·fy (skar′ə·fī) *v.t.* **·fied, ·fy·ing** 1. To scratch or make slight incisions in, as the skin in surgery. 2. To criticize severely. [< Gk. *skariphasthai* to scratch an outline < *skariphos* stylus] **—scar′i·fi′er** *n.* **—scar′i·fi·ca′tion** *n.*

scar·la·ti·na (skär′lə·tē′nə) *n.* *Pathol.* A mild form of scarlet fever. [< Ital. See SCARLET.]

scar·let (skär′lit) *n.* A brilliant red. [< Persian *saqalāt* a rich, scarlet cloth] **—scar′let** *adj.*

scarlet fever *Pathol.* An acute infectious disease characterized by a scarlet rash.

scarlet runner A tall climbing bean of tropical America, having vivid red flowers and long seed pods.

scarlet tanager An American tanager, the male of which has brilliant red plumage with black wings and tail.

scarp (skärp) *n.* 1. A steep slope. 2. An embankment or wall at the outer part of a fortification. [< Ital. *scarpa*]

scarves (skärvz) Alternative plural of SCARF.

scar·y (skâr′ē) *adj.* **scar·i·er, scar·i·est** *Informal* 1. Easily scared; timid. 2. Causing fear or alarm; frightening.

scat (skat) *v.i.* **scat·ted, scat·ting** *Informal* To go away: usu. in the imperative. [? < SCATTER]

scathe (skāth) *v.t.* **scathed, scath·ing** 1. To criticize severely. 2. To injure severely. **—***n.*

Severe injury. [< ON *skathi* to harm] **—scathe′ful** *adj.* **—scathe′less** *adj.*

scath·ing (skā′thing) *adj.* Mercilessly severe: a *scathing* rebuke. **—scath′ing·ly** *adv.*

sca·tol·o·gy (skə·tol′ə·jē) *n.* 1. The study of, or a preoccupation with, excrement. 2. Interest in obscene matters, esp. in literature. **—scat·o·log·ic** (skat′ə·loj′ik) or **·i·cal** *adj.* **—sca·tol′o·gist** *n.*

scat·ter (skat′ər) *v.t.* 1. To throw about; sprinkle. 2. To separate and drive away; disperse. *—v.i.* 3. To separate and go in different directions. [ME *scateren* to squander] **—scat′ter·er** *n.*

scat·ter·brain (skat′ər·brān′) *n.* A flighty or forgetful person. **—scat′ter·brained′** *adj.*

scatter rug A small rug used to cover only part of a floor.

scav·enge (skav′inj) *v.* **·enged, ·eng·ing** *v.t.* 1. To remove filth, rubbish, and refuse from. *—v.i.* 2. To act as a scavenger. 3. To search or rummage, as for food. [Back formation < SCAVENGER]

scav·en·ger (skav′in·jər) *n.* 1. An animal that feeds on carrion, as the buzzard. 2. One who searches refuse, garbage, etc., for usable material. [< AF *scawage* inspection < Flemish *scauwen* to see]

sce·nar·i·o (si·nâr′ē·ō, -nä′rē·ō) *n.* *pl.* **·nar·i·os** 1. The written plot and arrangement of incidents of a motion picture. 2. A plan of a projected series of actions or events. [< Ital. See SCENE.]

scene (sēn) *n.* 1. A locality as presented to view. 2. The place in which the action of a drama is supposed to occur; setting. 3. The place and surroundings of any event. 4. A division of an act of a play. 5. An event, situation, or continuous related action in a motion picture, play, etc. 6. Scenery (def. 2). 7. A display of excited feeling. 8. *Slang* A place or realm of a currently popular activity: the pop music *scene.* **—behind the scenes** 1. Out of sight of a theater audience. 2. Privately; in secret. [< L *scena* < Gk. *skēnē* tent, stage]

scen·er·y (sē′nər·ē) *n.* *pl.* **·er·ies** 1. The appearance of a landscape, locality, etc. 2. The settings, backdrops, etc., of a theatrical production.

sce·nic (sē′nik) *adj.* 1. Of or pertaining to natural scenery; picturesque. 2. Relating to stage scenery. Also **sce′ni·cal.** **—sce′ni·cal·ly** *adv.*

scent (sent) *n.* 1. An odor or smell, esp. a pleasant one. 2. An animal's odor by which it can be tracked. 3. A trail, trace, or clue. 4. A perfume. 5. The sense of smell. 6. A suggestion; hint. *—v.t.* 1. To smell. 2. To get a hint of. 3. To make fragrant; perfume. [< OF *sentir* to sense, feel] **—scent′less** *adj.*

scep·ter (sep′tər) *n.* A staff carried by a ruler as a symbol of authority. [< Gk. *skēptron* staff]

scep·tic (skep′tik), **scep·ti·cal** See SKEPTIC, etc.

sched·ule (skej′o͞ol, -əl, -o͞o·əl; *Brit.* shed′·yo͞ol) *n.* 1. A list of details or items: a *schedule* of postal rates. 2. A timetable. 3. A detailed and timed plan; program: a production *schedule.* **—behind schedule** Not on time; late. **—on schedule** According to plan; on time. *—v.t.* **·uled, ·ul·ing** 1. To place on a schedule. 2. To plan for a specified time. [< L *scida, scheda* leaf of paper]

sche·ma (skē′mə) *n.* *pl.* **·ma·ta** (-mə·tə) A plan or diagram of a process, etc. Also **sche·mat·ic** (skē·mat′ik). [< Gk. See SCHEME.] **—sche·mat′ic** or **·i·cal** *adj.* **—sche·mat′i·cal·ly** *adv.*

sche·ma·tize (skē′mə·tīz) *v.t.* **·tized, ·tiz·ing** 1. To form into or arrange according to a plan or design. 2. To depict in a diagram.

scheme (skēm) *n.* 1. A plan for doing something. 2. A systematic arrangement or design. 3. A secret or underhand plot. 4. An outline or sketch; diagram. *—v.t. & v.i.* **schemed, schem·ing** To plan or plot, esp. in an underhand manner. [< Gk. *schema, -atos* a form, plan] **—schem′er** *n.*

scher·zo (sker′tsō) *n.* *pl.* **·zos** or **·zi** (-tsē) *Music* A playful movement, as in a symphony. [< Ital., a jest]

Schick test (shik) A test to determine one's susceptibility to diphtheria. [after Dr. Béla *Schick,* 1877–1967]

schil·ling (shil′ing) *n.* The standard monetary unit of Austria. [< G]

schism (siz′əm) *n.* 1. A division or split, esp. in a religious group. 2. The offense of causing such division. 3. Discord within a group; dissension. [< Gk. *schizein* to split] **—schis·mat·ic** (siz·mat′ik) or **·i·cal** *adj.*

schist (shist) *n.* *Geol.* A rock that readily splits into parallel layers: also spelled *shist.* [< Gk. *schizein* to split] **—schist·ous** (shis′təs), **schist′ose** (-tōs) *adj.*

schiz·o (skit′sō) *n.* *Slang* One who suffers from schizophrenia.

schizo- *combining form* Split; divided. Before vowels, **schiz-.** [< Gk. *schizein* to split]

schiz·oid (skit′soid, skiz′oid) *Psychiatry* *n.* One who suffers from schizophrenia. *—adj.* Of or pertaining to schizophrenia.

schiz·o·phre·ni·a (skit′sō·frē′nē·ə, skiz′ō-) *n.* *Psychiatry* Any of a group of psychotic disorders characterized by delusions, withdrawal, conflicting emotions, and deterioration of the personality. [< SCHIZO- + Gk. *phrēn* mind] **—schiz′o·phren′ic** (-fren′ik) *adj. & n.*

schle·miel (shlə·mēl′) *n.* *Slang* An inept, easily duped person; bungler; dolt. Also **schle·mihl′.** Also *shlemiel.* [< Yiddish]

schlep (shlep) *Slang* *v.* **schlepped, schlep·ping** *v.t.* 1. To drag awkwardly; lug. *—v.i.* 2. To proceed wearily or heavily. *—n.* 1. A difficult journey. 2. A stupid, awkward person. Also **schlepp.** Also *shlep.* [< Yiddish < G *schleppen* to drag] **—schlep′per** *n.*

schlock (shlok) *Slang* *n.* Shoddy, inferior merchandise. *—adj.* Of inferior quality. Also *shlock.* [< Yiddish < G *schlacke* slag] **—schlock′y** *adj.*

schmaltz (shmälts) *n.* *Slang* Sentimental music, literature, etc. Also *shmaltz.* [< Yiddish < G *schmalz* rendered fat] **—schmaltz′y** *adj.*

schmo (shmō) *n.* *pl.* **schmoes** or **schmos** *Slang* A stupid or foolish person. Also *shmo.* [< Yiddish]

schnapps (shnäps, shnaps) *n.* *pl.* **schnapps** Any strong liquor, esp. a type of gin. Also **schnaps.** [< G < Du. *snaps* gulp, mouthful]

schnau·zer (shnou′zər) *n.* A terrier having a wiry coat. [< G *schnauze* snout]
schol·ar (skol′ər) *n.* 1. A learned or erudite person. 2. One considered an authority in a specific field, esp. in the humanities. 3. A student or pupil. [See SCHOOL[1].] —**schol′ar·ly** *adj.*
schol·ar·ship (skol′ər·ship) *n.* 1. The knowledge and qualities of a scholar; learning; erudition. 2. Scholarly inquiry or research. 3. Money awarded to a student to help him pay for his education; stipend.
scho·las·tic (skō·las′tik, skə-) *adj.* 1. Of or characteristic of scholars, education, or schools. 2. *Often cap.* Of or characteristic of medieval scholasticism. Also **scho·las′ti·cal.** —*n. Often cap.* An advocate of scholasticism. [< Gk. *scholazein* to devote leisure to study] —**scho·las′ti·cal·ly** *adv.*
scho·las·ti·cism (skō·las′tə·siz′əm, skə-) *n.* *Often cap.* The systematized logic, philosophy, and theology of medieval Christian scholars.
school[1] (sko͞ol) *n.* 1. An institution for instructing students in certain skills, a particular field, etc.; also, the classrooms and buildings of such an institution. 2. The students and teachers of an educational institution. 3. A subdivision of a university: the *school* of medicine. 4. A group following the same system, methods, or style; also, the system, etc., of such a group. —*v.t.* 1. To instruct in or as in a school; train; educate. 2. To subject to rule or discipline. [< Gk. *scholē* leisure, school]
school[2] (sko͞ol) *n.* A large number of fish, whales, etc., of the same kind swimming together; shoal. —*v.i.* To swim together in a school. [< Du., a crowd, school of fishes]
school board A committee in charge of a local school system.
school·book (sko͞ol′bo͝ok′) *n.* A book for use in school; textbook.
school·boy (sko͞ol′boi′) *n.* A boy attending school.
school·girl (sko͞ol′gûrl′) *n.* A girl attending school.
school·house (sko͞ol′hous′) *n.* A building used as a school.
school·ing (sko͞o′ling) *n.* Instruction given at school.
school·man (sko͞ol′mən) *n. pl.* ·**men** (-mən) One of the theologians of the Middle Ages; a scholastic.
school·marm (sko͞ol′märm′) *n. Informal* 1. A woman schoolteacher. 2. Any person who is strict, prudish, or old-fashioned. Also **school′ma'am′** (-mam′).
school·mas·ter (sko͞ol′mas′tər) *n.* A man who teaches in or directs a school.
school·mate (sko͞ol′māt′) *n.* A fellow pupil. Also **school′fel′low** (-fel′ō).
school·mis·tress (sko͞ol′mis′tris) *n.* A woman schoolteacher.
school·room (sko͞ol′ro͞om′, -ro͝om′) *n.* A room in which classes are held.
school·teach·er (sko͞ol′tē′chər) *n.* One who teaches in a school, esp. below the college level.
school year The part of the year during which school is in session.
schoon·er (sko͞o′nər) *n.* 1. A fore-and-aft rigged vessel having two or more masts. 2. A large beer glass. [< dial. *scoon* to skim on water]
schot·tische (shot′ish) *n.* A round dance similar to the polka; also, the music for this dance. [< G *schottisch* Scottish]
schuss (sho͞os) *n.* In skiing, a straight, fast downhill run; also, a straight, steep downhill course. —*v.i.* To execute a schuss. [< G, lit., shot]
schuss·boom·er (sho͞os′bo͞om′ər) *n.* One who skies at great speed, usu. straight downhill.
schwa (shwä) *n. Phonet.* A weak, neutral sound occurring in most unstressed syllables in English, as the *a* in *alone* or the *u* in *circus*: written ə. [< G < Hebrew *shewa*]
sci·at·ic (sī·at′ik) *adj.* Of or affecting the hip or the sciatic nerve. [< Gk. *ischion* hip]
sci·at·i·ca (sī·at′i·kə) *n. Pathol.* 1. Neuralgia affecting the sciatic nerve. 2. Any painful affection of the hip or thighs. [See SCIATIC.]
sciatic nerve A long nerve extending down the back of the thigh and leg.
sci·ence (sī′əns) *n.* 1. Any branch of knowledge, such as biology or chemistry, characterized by close observation, experimentation, classification of data, and the establishment of verifiable principles. 2. The body of systematized knowledge based on such methods. 3. Techniques that use a systematic approach: the *science* of cooking. [< L *sciens, -entis,* ppr. of *scire* to know]
science fiction Fiction in which scientific facts or theories are imaginatively employed.
sci·en·tif·ic (sī′ən·tif′ik) *adj.* 1. Of, discovered by, derived from, or used in science. 2. Agreeing with or using the principles or methods of science; systematic; exact. [< L *scientia* knowledge + *facere* to make] —**sci′en·tif′i·cal·ly** *adv.*
scientific method The method used in the sciences for obtaining knowledge, in which hypotheses are tested by experimentation and observation.
sci·en·tist (sī′ən·tist) *n.* A person engaged in biology, chemistry, or other science as a profession.
scil·i·cet (sil′ə·set) *adv.* Namely; to wit; that is to say. [< L *scire licet* it is permitted to know]
scim·i·tar (sim′ə·tər) *n.* A curved Oriental sword or saber. Also **scim′e·tar, scim′i·ter.** [< Ital. *scimitarra*]
scin·til·la (sin·til′ə) *n.* A spark; trace; iota: a *scintilla* of truth. [< L]
scin·til·late (sin′tə·lāt) *v.i.* ·**lat·ed,** ·**lat·ing** 1. To give off sparks. 2. To be brilliant, exciting, or witty; sparkle. 3. To twinkle, as a star. [< L *scintilla* spark] —**scin′til·lant** (-lənt) *adj.* —**scin′til·lat′ing·ly** *adv.* —**scin′·til·la′tion** *n.*
sci·o·lism (sī′ə·liz′əm) *n.* Superficial knowledge; charlatanism. [< L *scius* < *scire* to know] —**sci′o·lis′tic** *adj.*
sci·on (sī′ən) *n.* 1. Descendant; heir. 2. A twig or shoot cut from a plant or tree, esp. for grafting: also spelled *cion.* [< L *secare* to cut]
scis·sile (sis′il) *adj.* Capable of being cut or split easily and evenly. [< L *scindere* to cut]
scis·sion (sizh′ən, sish′-) *n.* The act of cutting or splitting; division. [< LL *scissus,* pp. of *scindere* to cut]

scis·sor (siz′ər) *v.t. & v.i.* To cut with scissors.

scis·sors (siz′ərz) *n.pl.* (*construed as sing. in def. 2*) 1. A cutting implement with a pair of blades pivoted face to face so that the opposed edges may be brought together. Also **pair of scissors**. 2. In wrestling, a hold secured by clasping the legs about the body or head of the opponent. [< LL *cisorium* cutting instrument]

scle·ra (sklir′ə) *n. Anat.* The hard, white, fibrous outer coat of the eyeball. Also **scle·rot·i·ca** (sklə·rot′i·kə). [< Gk. *sklēros* hard]

sclero- *combining form* Hardness; hard. Also, before vowels, **scler-**. [< Gk. *sklēros* hard]

scle·ro·sis (sklə·rō′sis) *n. pl.* **·ses** (-sēz) *Pathol.* The thickening and hardening of body tissue. [< Gk. *sklēros* hard] —**scle·rose′** (-rōz′, -rōs′) *v.t. & v.i.* —**scle·rot′ic** (-rot′ik) *adj.*

scoff (skôf, skof) *v.i.* To speak with contempt or derision; jeer: often with *at*. —*n.* An expression of contempt or derision. [ME *scof*, prob. < Scand.] —**scoff′er** *n.* —**scoff′ing·ly** *adv.*

scoff·law (skôf′lô′, skof′-) *n. Informal* A habitual violator of traffic laws.

scold (skōld) *v.t. & v.i.* To find fault with (someone) harshly. —*n.* One who scolds, esp. a shrewish woman. [Appar. < ON *skāld* poet, satirist] —**scold′er** *n.* —**scold′·ing·ly** *adv.*

scol·lop (skol′əp) See SCALLOP.

sconce (skons) *n.* An ornamental wall bracket for holding a candle or other light. [< L *abscondere* to hide]

scone (skōn, skon) *n.* A round tea cake or biscuit. [? < MDu. *schoonbrot* fine bread]

scoop (sko͞op) *n.* 1. A small shovellike implement for taking up flour, sugar, etc. 2. An implement for dispensing spherical portions of ice cream, etc. 3. The large, deep bucket of a steam shovel or dredge. 4. A scoopful. 5. A long, sweeping movement. 6. *Informal* In journalism, a news story published ahead of rival papers. —*v.t.* 1. To take out with or as with a scoop. 2. To hollow out. 3. To form with or as with a scoop. 4. To gather up with a low, sweeping motion. 5. *Informal* To publish a news story before (a rival). [Fusion of MDu. *schope* bucket, and *schoppe* shovel] —**scoop′er** *n.*

scoop·ful (sko͞op′fo͝ol) *n.* The amount held by a scoop.

scoot (sko͞ot) *v.i. Informal* To go quickly; dart off. [Prob. < Scand.]

scoot·er (sko͞o′tər) *n.* 1. A child's foot-operated vehicle consisting of a footboard mounted between two tandem wheels and steered by an upright handle. 2. A motor scooter.

scope (skōp) *n.* 1. The range, area, or sphere in which an activity takes place. 2. The range of one's views or abilities. 3. Opportunity for development, expression, etc. [< Gk. *skopeein* to look at]

-scope *combining form* An instrument for viewing: *telescope*. [< Gk. *skopeein* to watch]

sco·pol·a·mine (skō·pol′ə·mēn, -min) *n. Chem.* A drug used as a hypnotic and sedative. [after G. A. *Scopoli*, 1723–88, Italian naturalist]

-scopy *combining form* Observation; viewing: *microscopy*. [< Gk. *skopeein* to look at]

scor·bu·tic (skôr·byo͞o′tik) *adj.* Of or affected with scurvy: also **scor·bu′ti·cal**. [< Med.L *scorbutus* scurvy] —**scor·bu′ti·cal·ly** *adv.*

scorch (skôrch) *v.t.* 1. To burn or char the surface of. 2. To wither or shrivel by heat. 3. To criticize severely. —*v.i.* 4. To become scorched. —*n.* A superficial burn. [Prob. < ON *skorpna* to dry up, shrivel] —**scorch′ing** *adj.* —**scorch′ing·ly** *adv.*

scorched-earth policy (skôrcht′ûrth′) The military strategy of destroying all crops, industrial equipment, etc., so as to leave nothing useful for the enemy.

scorch·er (skôr′chər) *n. Informal* An extremely hot day.

score (skôr) *n.* 1. The number of points made in a game or contest; also, the act of making such points. 2. Grade or rating in a test. 3. A debt. 4. An account of grievances. 5. A notch or groove cut in something. 6. A set of twenty. 7. *pl.* An indefinitely large number. 8. *Music* The notation for a composition, showing the various instrumental or vocal parts. 9. Music for a motion picture or theatrical production. —**to know the score** *Informal* To be aware of the facts of a situation. —*v.* **scored, scor·ing** *v.t.* 1. To mark with notches, cuts, or lines. 2. To make or gain (points, runs, etc.) in a game or contest; also, to record such points, runs, etc. 3. To grade (a test); also, to make a grade of in a test. 4. To achieve (a victory, success, etc.). 5. *Music* To compose or arrange (music) for an orchestra or for an instrument. —*v.i.* 6. To make points, runs, etc., as in a game. 7. To keep score in a game. 8. To win an advantage or success. [< ON *skor* notch, tally] —**score′less** *adj.* —**scor′er** *n.*

sco·ri·a (skôr′ē·ə) *n. pl.* **·ri·ae** (-ē·ē, -ē·ī) 1. Refuse remaining after metal has been smelted; slag. 2. Loose, clinkerlike lava. [< Gk. *skōria* refuse] —**sco′ri·a′ceous** (-ā′shəs) *adj.*

scorn (skôrn) *n.* A feeling of contempt or loathing; disdain. —*v.t.* 1. To treat with contempt; despise. 2. To reject with contempt; spurn. [< OF *escarn* < Gmc.] —**scorn′er** *n.* —**scorn′ful** *adj.* —**scorn′ful·ly** *adv.* —**scorn′ful·ness** *n.*

Scor·pi·o (skôr′pē·ō) *n.* A constellation, the Scorpion, containing the bright star Antares; also, the eighth sign of the zodiac. Also **Scor′pi·us** (-əs). [< L]

scor·pi·on (skôr′pē·ən) *n.* An arachnid with a long, segmented tail ending in a poisonous sting. [< Gk. *skorpios*]

Scot (skot) *n.* 1. A native of Scotland. 2. One of a Gaelic people who migrated in the 6th c. to Scotland from Ireland. [OE *Scottas*, pl., the Irish < LL *Scotus, Scoti*]

scotch (skoch) *v.t.* 1. To maim or cripple. 2. To crush or suppress. [Origin uncertain]

Scotch (skoch) *n.* 1. The people of Scotland: with *the*. 2. Scots. 3. A smoky-flavored liquor made in Scotland from malted barley: also **Scotch whisky**. —*adj.* Of or pertaining to Scotland, its people, or their language.

Scotch·man (skoch′mən) *n. pl.* **·men** (-mən) A native of Scotland.

Scotch tape Transparent cellulose tape with adhesive on one side: a trade name.
Scotch terrier A Scottish terrier.
scot-free (skot′frē′) *adj.* Without injury, punishment, or loss; unharmed. [OE, payment < ON *skot* tax + -FREE]
Scot·land Yard (skot′land) The London police department; also, its headquarters.
Scots (skots) *n.* The dialect of English spoken in Scotland. [Earlier *Scottis*, var. of SCOTTISH]
Scots·man (skots′mən) *n. pl.* **·men** (-mən) A native of Scotland.
Scot·tish (skot′ish) *n. & adj.* Scotch. [OE *Scottisc*]
Scottish Gaelic The language of the Scottish Highlands: also called *Erse.*
Scottish terrier A small, short-legged terrier, having a large head and a wiry coat: also *Scotch terrier.* Also *Informal* **Scot·tie** (skot′ē), **Scot′ty.**
scoun·drel (skoun′drəl) *n.* A mean, unprincipaled rascal; rogue. [? < L *ex-* off + *condere* to hide] —**scoun′drel·ly** *adj.*
scour[1] (skour) *v.t. & v.i.* 1. To clean or brighten by thorough washing and rubbing. 2. To clear by means of a strong current of water; flush. [Prob. < L *ex-* out + *curare* to take care of] —**scour′er** *n.*
scour[2] (skour) *v.t.* To go over thoroughly, as in making a search. [ME *scoure*] —**scour′er** *n.*
scourge (skûrj) *n.* 1. A whip for inflicting punishment. 2. Any means for inflicting punishment or suffering. 3. A cause of suffering or trouble. —*v.t.* **scourged, scourg·ing** 1. To whip severely; flog. 2. To punish severely; afflict. [< LL *excoriare* to flay] —**scourg′er** *n.*
scout[1] (skout) *n.* 1. A soldier sent out to gather information about enemy troop movements, terrain, etc. 2. A talent scout. 3. A Boy or Girl Scout. —*v.t.* 1. To survey in order to gain information: to *scout* the area. —*v.i.* 2. To go or act as a scout. —**to scout around** To go in search. [< L *auscultare* to listen] —**scout′er** *n.*
scout[2] (skout) *v.t. & v.i.* To mock; jeer. [< Scand.]
scout car An armored car for reconnaissance work.
scout·ing (skout′ing) *n.* The activities of a scout, esp. of a Boy Scout or Girl Scout.
scout·mas·ter (skout′mas′tər) *n.* The adult leader of a scout troop.
scow (skou) *n.* A large, flat-bottomed boat with square ends, used for carrying loads and often towed. [< Du. *schouw* boat propelled by a pole]
scowl (skoul) *n.* A lowering of the brows, as in anger, disapproval, or sullenness. —*v.i.* 1. To express anger, etc., with such a look. —*v.t.* 2. To express by scowling. [ME *skoul*, prob. < Scand.] —**scowl′er** *n.* —**scowl′ing·ly** *adv.*
scrab·ble (skrab′əl) *v.i.* **·bled, ·bling** 1. To scratch, scrape, or paw, as with the hands. 2. To clamber; scramble. 3. To struggle or strive. [< Du. *schrabbelen*, freq. of *schrabben* to scratch]
scrag·gly (skrag′lē) *adj.* **·gli·er, ·gli·est** Unkempt; shaggy. [? < Scand.]
scrag·gy (skrag′ē) *adj.* **·gi·er, ·gi·est** 1. Rough. 2. Scrawny. —**scrag′gi·ly** *adv.* —**scrag′gi·ness** *n.*
scram (skram) *v.i.* **scrammed, scram·ming** *Slang* To leave quickly. [Prob. short for SCRAMBLE]
scram·ble (skram′bəl) *v.* **·bled, ·bling** *v.i.* 1. To climb or crawl quickly; clamber. 2. To move hurriedly; rush. 3. To struggle or compete in a disorderly way. —*v.t.* 4. To mix together haphazardly. 5. To fry (eggs) with the yolks and whites stirred together. 6. *Telecom.* To alter or garble (a signal) so that it is unintelligible in transit. —*n.* 1. A disorderly struggle. 2. A difficult climb or trek. [Prob. nasalized var. of SCRABBLE] —**scram′bler** *n.*
scrap[1] (skrap) *n.* 1. A small piece; bit; fragment. 2. *pl.* Discarded or leftover bits of food. 3. Used or discarded material; esp., metal that can be reclaimed. —*v.t.* **scrapped, scrap·ping** 1. To break up into scrap. 2. To discard. [< ON *skrapa* to scrape]
scrap[2] (skrap) *v.i.* **scrapped, scrap·ping** *Slang* To fight; quarrel. —*n.* A quarrel or fight. [< SCRAPE (n. def. 2)] —**scrap′per** *n.*
scrap·book (skrap′bo͝ok′) *n.* A blank book in which pictures, clippings, etc., are pasted as mementos.
scrape (skrāp) *v.* **scraped, scrap·ing** *v.t.* 1. To clean or make smooth by rubbing with something sharp or rough. 2. To remove thus: with *off, away,* etc. 3. To rub (a rough or sharp object) across a surface. 4. To rub roughly across or against (a surface). 5. To form by scratching or digging. 6. To gather with effort or difficulty: usu. with *up* or *together.* —*v.i.* 7. To scrape something. 8. To manage or get along with difficulty. —*n.* 1. A mark or harsh sound made by scraping. 2. A difficult situation; predicament. [Prob. fusion of OE *scrapian* and ON *skrapa* to scrape, erase] —**scrap′er** *n.*
scrap·heap (skrap′hēp′) *n.* A pile of used or discarded things.
scrap iron Iron suitable for reworking.
scrap·ple (skrap′əl) *n.* A boiled mixture of pork scraps, meal, and seasonings, which is allowed to set and then fried. [Dim. of SCRAP[1]]
scrap·py[1] (skrap′ē) *adj.* **·pi·er, ·pi·est** Not connected; fragmentary. —**scrap′pi·ly** *adv.* —**scrap′pi·ness** *n.*
scrap·py[2] (skrap′ē) *adj.* **·pi·er, ·pi·est** Eager to fight; pugnacious. —**scrap′pi·ly** *adv.* —**scrap′pi·ness** *n.*
scratch (skrach) *v.t.* 1. To tear or mark the surface of with something sharp or rough. 2. To scrape lightly to relieve itching. 3. To rub with a grating sound; scrape. 4. To write or draw awkwardly or hurriedly. 5. To erase or cancel. 6. To withdraw (an entry) from a race, game, etc. —*v.i.* 7. To use the nails or claws, as in fighting or digging. 8. To scrape the skin to relieve itching. 9. To make a harsh, grating noise. 10. To manage or get along with difficulty. —*n.* 1. A mark or cut made by scratching. 2. A slight flesh wound. 3. A harsh, grating sound. —**from scratch** From the beginning; from nothing. —**up to scratch** *Informal* Up to standard. —*adj.* 1. Done by chance; haphazard: a *scratch* hit. 2. Used for quick notes, etc.: a *scratch* pad. [Prob. blend of ME *scratte* and *cracchen*] —**scratch′er** *n.*
scratch test *Med.* A test to determine the

substances to which a person is allergic by rubbing allergens into small scratches made in the skin.

scratch·y (skrach′ē) *adj.* ·i·er, ·i·est 1. Making a grating noise. 2. Uneven; shaggy; rough. 3. That scratches or irritates. —**scratch′i·ly** *adv.* —**scratch′i·ness** *n.*

scrawl (skrol) *v.t. & v.i.* To write hastily or illegibly. —*n.* Irregular or careless writing. [? < dial. E, var. of CRAWL] —**scrawl′y** *adj.* ·i·er, ·i·est

scraw·ny (skrô′nē) *adj.* ·ni·er, ·ni·est Skinny; thin. [< dial. E *scranny*, ? < Scand.] —**scraw′ni·ness** *n.*

scream (skrēm) *v.i.* 1. To utter a loud, piercing cry, as of pain or terror. 2. To make a prolonged, piercing sound. 3. To laugh loudly and wildly. 4. To speak loudly; shout. 5. To make a frantic demand. —*v.t.* 6. To utter with a scream. —*n.* 1. A loud, shrill cry or sound. 2. *Slang* A very funny person or situation. [ME *scraemen*] —**scream′er** *n.*

screech (skrēch) *n.* A shrill, harsh cry or sound; shriek. —*v.t. & v.i.* To utter with or make such a sound. [Var. of obs. *scritch*; prob. imit.] —**screech′er** *n.* —**screech′y** *adj.* ·i·er, ·i·est

screech owl 1. Any of various owls common from Canada to Brazil; esp. a small, gray species of the eastern U.S. 2. The barn owl of England.

screen (skrēn) *n.* 1. A partition, curtain, etc., used to conceal, separate, or protect. 2. Anything having a similar purpose: a smoke *screen.* 3. A wire mesh or netting forming a partition or panel in a window, door, etc. 4. A sieve for sifting. 5. A surface on which motion pictures, etc., may be shown. 6. In television sets, radar apparatus, etc., the surface on which the image is displayed. 7. The motion-picture industry. —*v.t.* 1. To shield, protect, etc., with or as with a screen. 2. To sift through a screen. 3. To show or exhibit on a screen, as a motion picture. 4. To determine the competence or eligibility of (an individual) for a specified task. [Prob. < OF *escren*, prob. < OHG *skirm*] —**screen′a·ble** *adj.* —**screen′er** *n.*

screen·ing (skrē′ning) *n.* 1. The showing of a motion picture. 2. Mesh for window screens, etc.

screen play (skrēn′plā′) *n.* A motion-picture script.

screw (skrōō) *n.* 1. A naillike fastening device with a spiraling thread. 2. A similar device of cylindrical form, for insertion into a corresponding grooved part. 3. Anything having the form of a screw. —**to have a screw loose** *Slang* To be mentally deranged, eccentric, etc. —**to put the screws on** (or **to**) *Slang* To exert pressure or force upon. —*v.t.* 1. To tighten, attach, etc., by or as by a screw. 2. To turn or twist. 3. To twist out of shape; contort. 4. *Slang* To cheat or harm. —*v.i.* 5. To twist or turn as a screw. 6. To be attached or become detached by means of screws: with *on, off*, etc. —**to screw up** *Slang* To make a mess of; botch. [Appar. < OF *escroue* nut, female screw] —**screw′er** *n.*

screw·ball (skrōō′bôl′) *n.* *Slang* 1. An odd or erratic person. 2. In baseball, a pitch that travels in a direction opposite to that of a curve ball.

screw·driv·er (skrōō′drī′vər) *n.* 1. A tool for turning screws. 2. A cocktail consisting of vodka and orange juice.

screw propeller A propeller.

screw·y (skrōō′ē) *adj.* **screw·i·er, screw·i·est** *Slang* Weird; eccentric; crazy.

scrib·ble (skrib′əl) *v.t. & v.i.* ·bled, ·bling 1. To write hastily and carelessly. 2. To make or cover with illegible or meaningless marks. —*n.* Scribbled writing; scrawl. [< L *scribere* to write] —**scrib′bler** *n.*

scribe (skrīb) *n.* 1. One who copies manuscripts and other documents. 2. Among the ancient Hebrews, a teacher or interpreter of the Mosaic law. 3. A writer; a journalist. [< L *scribere* to write] —**scrib′al** *adj.*

scrim (skrim) *n.* A light, loosely woven cloth, used esp. in the theater as a stage backdrop or semitransparent curtain. [Origin unknown]

scrim·mage (skrim′ij) *n.* 1. A rough-and-tumble contest; fracas. 2. In football: **a** The entire play from the pass from the center to the downing of the ball. **b** A practice session. —*v.i.* ·maged, ·mag·ing To engage in a scrimmage. [Alter. of *scrimish*, var. of SKIRMISH]

scrimp (skrimp) *v.i.* To spend little money; be frugal; economize. [Prob. akin to OE *scrimman* to shrink, shrivel] —**scrimp′i·ness** *n.* —**scrimp′y** *adj.* **scrimp·i·er, scrimp·i·est**

scrim·shaw (skrim′shô) *n.* Carved or engraved articles made of bone, ivory, etc., esp. those made of whalebone by American whalers.

scrip (skrip) *n.* 1. A provisional document certifying that the holder is entitled to receive something else, as shares of stock or land. 2. Any money substitute that can be exchanged for goods or services. 3. Paper money for an amount less than a dollar. [< SCRIPT]

script (skript) *n.* 1. Handwriting. 2. Printing resembling handwriting. 3. The text of a play, motion picture, broadcast, etc. —*v.t.* *Informal* To prepare a script for (a motion picture, etc.). [< L *scribere* to write]

scrip·ture (skrip′chər) *n.* 1. *Often pl.* The books of the Old and New Testaments, including often the Apocrypha. 2. Any sacred writings. —**scrip′tur·al** *adj.* —**scrip′tur·al·ly** *adv.* —**scrip′tur·al·ness** *n.*

script·writ·er (skript′rī′tər) *n.* A writer who prepares scripts for motion pictures, television plays, etc.

scriv·en·er (skriv′ən·ər, skriv′nər) *n.* *Archaic* One who prepares deeds, contracts, etc.; scribe. [< L *scribere* to write]

scrod (skrod) *n.* A young codfish, esp. when split and prepared for broiling. [? < MDu. *schrode* piece cut off]

scrof·u·la (skrof′yə·lə) *n.* *Pathol.* Tuberculosis of the lymph glands, esp. those of the neck. [< LL *scrofulae* swelling of glands] —**scrof′u·lous** *adj.* —**scrof′u·lous·ly** *adv.* —**scrof′u·lous·ness** *n.*

scroll (skrōl) *n.* 1. A roll of parchment, paper, etc., esp. one containing or intended for writing. 2. An ornament or design resembling a parchment roll. [< AF *escrowe*]

scroll·work (skrōl′wûrk′) *n.* Ornamental work of scroll-like patterns.

scro·tum (skrō′təm) *n. pl.* **·ta, ·tums** *Anat.* The pouch of skin that contains the testicles in most mammals. [< L] **—scro′tal** *adj.*

scrounge (skrounj) *Slang v.t. & v.i.* **scrounged, scroung·ing** 1. To hunt about in order to take (something); pilfer. 2. To mooch; sponge; beg. **—***n.* One who scrounges: also **scroung′er.** [? < dial. E *scrunge* to steal]

scrub[1] (skrub) *v.* **scrubbed, scrub·bing** *v.t.* 1. To rub vigorously in washing. 2. To remove (dirt, etc.) by such action. 3. *Informal* To cancel; call off. **—***v.i.* 4. To rub something vigorously, as in washing. **—***n.* The act of scrubbing. [? < Scand. Cf. Dan. *skrubbe,* MDu. *shrubben.*] **—scrub′ber** *n.*

scrub[2] (skrub) *n.* 1. A thicket of stunted trees or shrubs. 2. A poor, insignificant person. 3. In sports, a player not on the varsity or regular team. **—***adj.* 1. Undersized or stunted. 2. Made up or played by players not on the varsity or regular team: a *scrub* game. [Dial. var. of SHRUB]

scrub·by (skrub′ē) *adj.* **·bi·er, ·bi·est** 1. Of stunted growth. 2. Covered with scrub or underbrush. **—scrub′bi·ness** *n.*

scrub oak Any of various dwarf oaks of the U.S.

scrub pine Any of several stunted American pines.

scruff (skruf) *n.* The nape of the neck. [Earlier *scuff,* ? < ON *skopt* hair]

scrump·tious (skrump′shəs) *adj. Informal* Delightful, esp. to one's taste; delectable. [Prob. alter. of SUMPTUOUS]

scrunch (skrunch) *v.t.* 1. To crush; crunch. 2. To crumble. **—***v.i.* 3. To crouch. 4. To make a crunching sound. **—***n.* 1. A crunching sound. 2. A crouch. [Imit. alter. of CRUNCH]

scru·ple (skrōō′pəl) *n.* 1. Doubt or uncertainty regarding a question of moral right or duty. 2. An apothecaries' weight of 20 grains. 3. A minute quantity. **—***v.i.* **·pled, ·pling** To hesitate over scruples. [< L *scrupulus* small sharp stone]

scru·pu·lous (skrōō′pyə·ləs) *adj.* 1. Morally strict; conscientious; honest. 2. Careful of small details; painstaking; precise. **—scru′·pu·lous·ly** *adv.* **—scru′pu·los′ity** (-los′ə·tē), **scru′pu·lous·ness** *n.*

scru·ti·nize (skrōō′tə·nīz) *v.t.* **·nized, ·niz·ing** To examine in detail; inspect closely. Also *Brit.* **scru′ti·nise. —scru′ti·niz′er** *n.* **—scru′·ti·niz′ing·ly** *adv.*

scru·ti·ny (skrōō′tə·nē) *n. pl.* **·nies** Close and careful examination. [< L *scrutari* to examine]

scu·ba (skōō′bə, skyōō′-) *n.* An underwater breathing apparatus consisting of compressed-air tanks connected by hoses to the swimmer's mouthpiece: also called *Aqua-Lung, aqualung.* [<S(ELF)-C(ONTAINED) U(NDERWATER) B(REATHING) A(PPARATUS)]

scud (skud) *v.i.* **scud·ded, scud·ding** 1. To move, run, or fly swiftly. 2. *Naut.* To run rapidly before the wind. **—***n.* Light clouds driven rapidly before the wind. [Prob. < Scand.]

scuff (skuf) *v.i.* 1. To walk with a dragging movement; shuffle. 2. To become scratched or marred by scraping or wear. **—***v.t.* 3. To scratch or mar the surface of by scraping or wear. **—***n.* 1. A mark or sound made by scuffing. 2. A flat slipper having no covering for the heel. [Prob. < ON *skūfa* to shove]

scuf·fle (skuf′əl) *v.i.* **·fled, ·fling** 1. To struggle roughly or confusedly. 2. To drag one's feet; shuffle. **—***n.* 1. A disorderly struggle. 2. The sound of shuffling feet. [Prob. freq. of SCUFF] **—scuf′fler** *n.*

scull (skul) *n.* 1. A long oar worked from side to side over the stern of a boat. 2. A light, short-handled oar, used in pairs by one person. 3. A light racing boat or shell propelled by sculls. **—***v.t. & v.i.* To propel (a boat) by a scull or sculls. [ME *sculle, skulle;* origin unknown] **—scull′er** *n.*

scul·ler·y (skul′ər·ē) *n. pl.* **·ler·ies** A room where kitchen utensils are kept and cleaned, vegetables washed, etc. [< OF *escuelerie* care of dishes]

scul·lion (skul′yən) *n. Archaic* 1. A servant who does messy kitchen chores. 2. A base, contemptible person. [< OF *escouillon* mop < *escouve* broom]

sculpt (skulpt) *v.t. & v.i. Informal* To sculpture.

sculp·tor (skulp′tər) *n.* One who creates sculpture.

sculp·ture (skulp′chər) *n.* 1. The art of creating three-dimensional figures and designs, as by carving or molding. 2. A figure or design created this way; also, such figures and designs collectively. **—***v.t.* **·tured, ·tur·ing** 1. To create (a statue, bust, or other work of sculpture). 2. To represent or portray in sculpture. 3. To embellish with sculpture. 4. To change, as a canyon, by erosion and deposition. [< L *sculpere* to carve in stone] **—sculp′tur·al** *adj.*

scum (skum) *n.* 1. A thin layer of impurities, vegetation, etc., on the surface of a liquid. 2. A vile, despicable person; also, a group of such persons. **—***v.* **scummed, scum·ming** *v.t.* 1. To take scum from; skim. **—***v.i.* 2. To become covered with or form scum. [< MDu. *schuum*] **—scum′mer** *n.* **—scum′·my** *adj.* **·mi·er, ·mi·est**

scup (skup) *n. pl.* **scup** or **scups** A food fish of the eastern coast of the U.S.: also called *porgy.* Also **scup·paug** (skup′ôg, skə·pôg′). [< Algonquian (Narraganset) *mishcup* thickscaled]

scup·per (skup′ər) *n. Naut.* A hole along the side of a ship's deck to let water run off. [? Short for *scupper hole* < OF *escope* bailing scoop]

scurf (skûrf) *n.* 1. Dry, scaly skin, as dandruff. 2. Any scaly matter. [OE] **—scurf′y** *adj.*

scur·ri·lous (skûr′ə·ləs) *adj.* Grossly and offensively abusive; coarse. Also **scur·rile** (skûr′il), **scur′ril.** [< L *scurrilis* buffoonlike] **—scur·ril·i·ty** (skə·ril′ə·tē) *n.* **—scur′ri·lous·ly** *adv.* **—scur′ri·lous·ness** *n.*

scur·ry (skûr′ē) *v.i.* **·ried, ·ry·ing** To move or go hurriedly; scamper. **—***n. pl.* **·ries** The act or sound of scurrying. [Short for *hurry-scurry,* a reduplication of HURRY]

scur·vy (skûr′vē) *adj.* **·vi·er, ·vi·est** Low or contemptible; base. **—***n. Pathol.* A disease caused by lack of vitamin C in the diet, characterized by bleeding gums, weakness, etc. [< SCURF] **—scur′vi·ly** *adv.* **—scur′vi·ness** *n.*

scu·tate (skyōō′tāt) *adj.* 1. *Zool.* Covered with horny, shieldlike plates or scales. 2. *Bot.* Shaped like a shield. [< L *scutum* shield]

scutch·eon (skuch′ən) *n.* An escutcheon.

scut·tle[1] (skut′l) *n.* 1. A small opening with a cover, esp. on the deck of a ship. 2. The lid closing such an opening. —*v.t.* **·tled, ·tling** To sink (a ship) by making holes in the bottom. [< MF *escoutille* hatchway]

scut·tle[2] (skut′l) *n.* A metal vessel or hod for coal. [OE *scutel* dish, platter < L *scutella*]

scut·tle[3] (skut′l) *v.i.* **·tled, ·tling** To run in haste; scurry. —*n.* A hurried run or departure. [? Var. of SCUD]

scut·tle·butt (skut′l·but) *n.* 1. A drinking fountain aboard ship. 2. *Slang* Rumor; gossip. [Orig. *scuttled butt* a lidded cask for drinking water]

scythe (sīth, *sometimes* sī) *n.* An implement used for mowing, reaping, etc., consisting of a long, curved blade fixed at an angle to a long bent handle. —*v.t.* **scythed, scyth·ing** To cut or mow with or as with a scythe. [OE *sīthe*]

sea (sē) *n.* 1. The great body of salt water covering the larger portion of the earth's surface; the ocean. 2. A large body of salt water partly enclosed by land. 3. A large inland body of water, salt or fresh. 4. The swell or surface of the ocean: a calm *sea.* 5. Anything that suggests the sea, as something vast. —**at sea** 1. On the ocean. 2. At a loss; bewildered. —**to follow the sea** To become a sailor. —**to go to sea** 1. To become a sailor. 2. To take an ocean voyage. —**to put to sea** To start on an ocean voyage. [OE *sǣ*]

sea anemone Any of various marine animals that attach themselves to rocks, etc., suggesting flowers by their coloring and outspread tentacles.

sea bass Any of various large-mouthed food fishes of Atlantic waters; esp., the **black sea bass.**

sea·board (sē′bôrd′) *n.* The land near the sea; seashore or seacoast. —*adj.* Bordering on the sea. [ME < SEA + *board* border, OE *bord*]

sea·coast (sē′kōst′) *n.* The seashore; seaboard.

sea cow Any aquatic mammal, as the manatee or the dugong.

sea cucumber Any of a group of marine animals shaped like a cucumber and having long branched tentacles.

sea dog 1. The sea lion. 2. An old or experienced sailor.

sea duck Any of various diving ducks, esp. the eider.

sea·far·er (sē′fâr′ər) *n.* A seaman; mariner.

sea·far·ing (sē′fâr′ing) *n.* 1. Travel by sea. 2. The profession of a seaman. —**sea′far′ing** *adj.*

sea·food (sē′fōōd′) *n.* Edible marine fish or shellfish.

sea·fowl (sē′foul′) *n.* A sea bird, or sea birds collectively.

sea front Land or buildings that border on the sea.

sea·girt (sē′gûrt′) *adj.* Surrounded by the sea.

sea·go·ing (sē′gō′ing) *adj.* 1. Adapted for use on the ocean. 2. Of or related to the sea.

sea green A deep bluish green.

sea gull Any gull or large tern.

sea horse A marine fish, having a prehensile tail and a head like that of a horse.

seal[1] (sēl) *n.* 1. A device for making an impression on wax or other soft substance; also, the impression made. 2. Such an impression affixed to a document as a proof of authenticity. 3. Anything used to fasten, secure, or close a letter, door, etc. 4. Anything that confirms or ratifies; pledge. 5. An ornamental stamp for packages, etc. —*v.t.* 1. To affix a seal to, in order to attest to weight, quality, authenticity, etc. 2. To fasten or close with or as with a seal. 3. To establish or settle finally; determine. 4. To secure, set, or fill up, as with plaster. [< L *sigillum* small picture, seal] —**seal′a·ble** *adj.* —**seal′er** *n.*

seal[2] (sēl) *n.* 1. Any of a group of carnivorous sea mammals mostly of northern latitudes. 2. Sealskin. —*v.i.* To hunt seals. [OE *seolh*]

seal·ant (sēl′ənt) *n.* A substance that seals a surface, seam, etc.

sea legs *Informal* The ability to walk aboard ship, esp. in rough seas, without losing one's balance.

sea level The assumed mean level of the ocean surface, esp. as used in determining elevation on maps, etc.

sea lion Any of various large seals of the Pacific Ocean, esp., the **California sea lion:** also called *sea dog.*

seal·skin (sēl′skin′) *n.* 1. The fur of a seal. 2. A coat, etc., made of this fur.

Sea·ly·ham terrier (sē′lē·ham, -əm) A breed of terrier having short legs and a white, wiry coat.

seam (sēm) *n.* 1. A line of junction between parts, esp. the edges of two pieces of cloth sewn together. 2. A mark like this, as a crack, fissure, or scar. 3. A thin stratum of rock. —*v.t.* 1. To unite by means of a seam. 2. To mark with a cut, furrow, wrinkle, etc. [OE *sēam*] —**seam′er** *n.* —**seam′less** *adj.*

sea·man (sē′mən) *n. pl.* **·men** (-mən) 1. A sailor. 2. *Naval* An enlisted person of any of the lowest grades. —**sea′man·like′** (-līk′) *adj.* —**sea′man·ly** *adj. & adv.*

sea·man·ship (sē′mən·ship) *n.* The skill and ability of a seaman.

seam·stress (sēm′stris) *n.* A woman whose occupation is sewing. Also *sempstress.* [OE *sēamestre* seamster + -ESS]

seam·y (sē′mē) *adj.* **seam·i·er, seam·i·est** Degraded; squalid; sordid. —**seam′i·ness** *n.*

sé·ance (sā′äns) *n.* A meeting of persons seeking contact with the spirits of the dead. [< F < OF *seoir* to sit < L *sedere*]

sea otter A large marine animal of the north Pacific coast, having dark brown fur.

sea·plane (sē′plān′) *n.* An airplane equipped to land on or take off from the water.

sea·port (sē′pôrt′) *n.* 1. A harbor or port for seagoing ships. 2. A town on such a harbor.

sear (sir) *v.t.* 1. To wither; dry up. 2. To burn the surface of; scorch. 3. To burn, as with a hot iron; brand. —*adj.* Sere[1]. [OE *sēarian* to wither]

search (sûrch) *v.t.* 1. To look through or explore carefully in order to find something. 2. To examine (a person), as for concealed weapons. 3. To examine closely; probe.

4. To learn by investigation: with *out.* —*v.i.* 5. To make a search. —*n.* The act of searching. [< L *circare* to go round, explore] —**search′a·ble** *adj.* —**search′er** *n.*
search·ing (sûr′ching) *adj.* 1. Investigating minutely. 2. Keenly penetrating: a *searching* gaze. —**search′ing·ly** *adv.*
search·light (sûrch′līt′) *n.* 1. An apparatus for throwing a strong beam of light; also, the beam of light. 2. A flashlight.
search warrant A warrant authorizing the search of a house, etc., for things alleged to be unlawfully concealed there.
sea·scape (sē′skāp′) *n.* 1. An ocean view. 2. A picture presenting a marine view. [< SEA + (LAND)SCAPE]
sea·shell (sē′shel′) *n.* The shell of any marine mollusk.
sea·shore (sē′shôr′) *n.* Land bordering on the ocean.
sea·sick·ness (sē′sik′nis) *n.* Nausea, dizziness, etc., caused by the motion of a vessel at sea. —**sea′sick′** *adj.*
sea·side (sē′sīd′) *n.* The seashore, esp. as a place of resort.
sea·son (sē′zən) *n.* 1. One of the four divisions of the year: spring, summer, autumn, or winter. 2. A special period: the hunting *season.* 3. A fit or suitable time. —**in season** 1. In condition and obtainable for use. 2. Legally permitted to be killed or taken, as game. —*v.t.* 1. To increase the flavor of (food), as by adding spices. 2. To add zest to. 3. To render more suitable for use. 4. To make accustomed or inured; harden. —*v.i.* 5. To become seasoned. [< LL *satio, -onis* sowing time] —**sea′son·er** *n.*
sea·son·a·ble (sē′zən·ə·bəl) *adj.* 1. In keeping with the season. 2. Done at the proper time; timely. —**sea′son·a·ble·ness** *n.* —**sea′son·a·bly** *adv.*
sea·son·al (sē′zən·əl) *adj.* Characteristic of, affected by, or occurring at a certain season. —**sea′son·al·ly** *adv.*
sea·son·ing (sē′zən·ing) *n.* 1. The process by which something, as lumber, is rendered fit for use. 2. A spice, herb, etc., added to food to give relish; esp., a condiment. 3. Anything that adds enjoyment, zest, etc.
season ticket A ticket or pass for a series of sporting events, concerts, etc.
seat (sēt) *n.* 1. A chair, bench, or other thing to sit on. 2. The part of a chair, garment, etc., on which one sits; also, the buttocks. 3. The place where anything is situated or established. 4. The right of membership in a legislative body, etc. —*v.t.* 1. To cause to sit down. 2. To have seats for. 3. To locate, settle, or center. [< ON *sæti.* Akin to SIT.]
seat belt An anchored strap in an airplane or car designed to protect the passenger against sudden stops, accidents, etc.
seat·ing (sē′ting) *n.* 1. Fabric for upholstering seats. 2. The arrangement of seats in an auditorium, etc.
sea urchin A marine animal having a soft rounded body covered with a shell bearing numerous movable spines.
sea wall A wall or an embankment to prevent the erosion of the shore, etc.
sea·ward (sē′wərd) *adj.* 1. Going toward the sea. 2. Blowing, as wind, from the sea. —*adv.* In the direction of the sea: also **sea′wards** (-wərdz).
sea·way (sē′wā′) *n.* An inland waterway that receives ocean shipping.
sea·weed (sē′wēd′) *n.* Any of various sea plants, including the kelps, etc.
sea·wor·thy (sē′wûr′thē) *adj.* In fit condition for a voyage: said of a vessel. —**sea′wor′thi·ness** *n.*
se·ba·ceous (si·bā′shəs) *adj. Physiol.* 1. Of or like fat; oily. 2. Designating any of the glands in the skin that secrete sebum. [< L *sebum* tallow]
se·bum (sē′bəm) *n. Physiol.* A fatty matter secreted by the sebaceous glands. [< L, tallow]
sec (sek) *adj. French* Dry (def. 6): said of wines.
se·cant (sē′kənt, -kant) *adj.* Cutting, esp. into two parts; intersecting. —*n.* 1. *Geom.* A straight line intersecting a given curve. 2. *Trig.* A function of an acute angle, equal to the ratio of the hypotenuse to the side adjacent to the angle when the angle is included in a right triangle. [< L *secans, -antis,* ppr. of *secare* to cut]
se·cede (si·sēd′) *v.i.* **·ced·ed, ·ced·ing** To withdraw formally, esp. from a political or religious organization. [< L *se-* apart + *cedere* to go] —**se·ced′er** *n.*
se·ces·sion (si·sesh′ən) *n.* 1. The act of seceding. 2. *Usu. cap.* The withdrawal of the Southern States from the Union in 1860–61. —**se·ces′sion·al** *adj.* —**se·ces′sion·ist** *adj. & n.*
se·clude (si·klōōd′) *v.t.* **·clud·ed, ·clud·ing** 1. To remove and keep apart from others; isolate. 2. To screen or shut off, as from view. [< L *se-* apart + *claudere* to shut] —**se·clud′ed** *adj.* —**se·clud′ed·ly** *adv.* —**se·clud′ed·ness** *n.*
se·clu·sion (si·klōō′zhən) *n.* A secluding or the state of being secluded; solitude. —**se·clu′sive** (-siv) *adj.* —**se·clu′sive·ly** *adv.* —**se·clu′sive·ness** *n.*
sec·ond[1] (sek′ənd) *n.* 1. A unit of time, $^1/_{60}$ of a minute. 2. A very short amount of time; instant. 3. *Geom.* A unit of angular measure, $^1/_{60}$ of a minute of arc. [< OF *seconde*]
sec·ond[2] (sek′ənd) *adj.* 1. Next in order, responsibility, etc., after the first: the ordinal of *two.* 2. Ranking below the first or best; secondary; subordinate. 3. Like another or preceding one; another. —*n.* 1. The one next after the first in position, rank, etc. 2. An attendant who supports or aids another, as in a duel. 3. *pl.* Imperfect or inferior merchandise. 4. In a car, bus, etc., the forward gear next after the first or low gear. 5. Formal endorsement of an initial proposal or motion. —*v.t.* 1. To give aid or encouragement to. 2. To support formally, as a motion. —*adv.* In the second order, place, or rank. [< L *secundus* following]
sec·on·dar·y (sek′ən·der′ē) *adj.* 1. Of second rank, grade, or influence; subordinate; auxiliary. 2. Depending on what is primary or original: *secondary* sources. —*n. pl.* **·dar·ies** One who helps or supports; an assistant. —**sec′on·dar′i·ly** *adv.*
secondary accent See under ACCENT.
secondary education High school or prepara-

tory school education between the elementary and college levels.

secondary school A high school or preparatory school intermediate between the elementary school and college.

sec·ond-best (sek′ənd·best′) *adj.* Next to the best.

second childhood Senility; dotage.

sec·ond-class (sek′ənd·klas′) *adj.* 1. Less than the best; inferior. 2. Of or pertaining to travel accommodations below first class. 3. Of or pertaining to a class of mail including printed periodicals. —*adv.* By second-class ticket, mail, etc.

second fiddle Any secondary or inferior status, esp. in the phrase **to be (or play) second fiddle.**

sec·ond-guess (sek′ənd·ges′) *v.t. & v.i.* To conjecture about (something) after it has occurred.

sec·ond·hand (sek′ənd·hand′) *adj.* 1. Having been previously owned, worn, or used by another; not new. 2. Received from another: *secondhand* information. 3. Handling or dealing in merchandise that is not new. —*adv.* In a secondhand manner.

second hand The hand that marks the seconds on a clock or a watch.

second lieutenant See under LIEUTENANT.

second nature An acquired trait that is deeply fixed in one's personality.

sec·ond-rate (sek′ənd·rāt′) *adj.* Of inferior quality, size, etc.; second-class. —**sec′ond-rat′er** *n.*

second sight The alleged power of seeing events occurring at distant places, in the future, etc.; clairvoyance.

sec·ond·sto·ry man (sek′ənd·stôr′ē) *Slang* A burglar.

second-string (sek′ənd·string′) *adj. Informal* In sports, playing as a substitute, as on a football team.

second wind 1. A return of easy breathing while one is running, exercising, etc., and after one has been winded. 2. Any similar restoration of energy.

se·cre·cy (sē′krə·sē) *n. pl.* **·cies** 1. The condition or quality of being secret. 2. The character of being secretive. Also **se·cret·ness** (sē′krit·nis).

se·cret (sē′krit) *adj.* 1. Kept separate or hidden from view or knowledge; concealed. 2. Beyond normal comprehension; obscure. 3. Known or revealed only to the initiated: *secret* rites. —*n.* 1. Something not to be told. 2. A thing undiscovered or unknown. 3. An underlying reason; key. —**in secret** In private. [< L *se-* apart + *cernere* to separate] —**se′cret·ly** *adv.*

sec·re·tar·i·at (sek′rə·târ′ē·it, -at) *n.* 1. The administrative department of an organization, esp. of the United Nations. 2. A secretarial staff. Also **sec′re·tar′i·ate.**

sec·re·tar·y (sek′rə·ter′ē) *n. pl.* **·tar·ies** 1. A person employed to deal with correspondence and handle clerical business for an organization or person. 2. One who heads a department of government. 3. A writing desk. [< L *secretum* secret] —**sec′re·tar′i·al** (-târ′ē·əl) *adj.*

secretary general *pl.* **secretaries general** A chief administrative officer. —**sec′re·tar′y-gen′er·al·cy** (-jen′ər·əl·sē) *n.*

se·crete (si·krēt′) *v.t.* **·cret·ed, ·cret·ing** 1. To conceal; hide. 2. *Physiol.* To produce (a secretion). [See SECRET.] —**se·cre′tor** *n.*

se·cre·tion (si·krē′shən) *n. Physiol.* 1. The process, generally glandular, by which milk, hormones, etc., are produced in the body. 2. The substance secreted. [See SECRET.] —**se·cre′to·ry** (-tər·ē) *adj.*

se·cre·tive (si·krē′tiv; *for def. 1, also* sē′krə·tiv) *adj.* 1. Inclined to secrecy; reticent. 2. *Physiol.* Producing or causing secretion. —**se·cre′tive·ly** *adv.* —**se·cre′tive·ness** *n.*

secret service The secret or espionage work of various government agencies in time of war.

Secret Service A section of the Department of the Treasury concerned with counterfeiting, the protection of the President of the United States, etc.

sect (sekt) *n.* 1. A body of persons distinguished by peculiarities of faith and practice, esp., the adherents of a particular religious creed. 2. Any number of persons united in opinion or beliefs. [< L *sequi* to follow]

-sect *combining form* To cut; divide (in a specified manner): *vivisect, bisect.* [< L *secare* to cut]

sec·tar·i·an (sek·târ′ē·ən) *adj.* 1. Pertaining to or belonging to a particular sect. 2. Adhering or confined to a specific group, party, etc.; partisan. —*n.* A member of a sect, esp. if bigoted. —**sec·tar′i·an·ism** *n.*

sec·ta·ry (sek′tər·ē) *n. pl.* **·ries** 1. A sectarian. 2. A dissenter from an established church; a nonconformist. Also **sec′ta·rist.** [See SECT.]

sec·tion (sek′shən) *n.* 1. A separate part or division, as a portion of a book or a chapter. 2. A distinct part of a country, community, etc. 3. A picture of a building, geological formation, etc., as if cut by an intersecting plane; cross section. 4. The act of cutting; division by cutting. —*v.t.* To cut or divide into sections. [< L *secare* to cut]

-section *combining form* The act or process of cutting or dividing: *vivisection.* [See SECTION.]

sec·tion·al (sek′shən·əl) *adj.* 1. Pertaining to a section, as of a country; local: a *sectional* dialect. 2. Dividing or alienating one section from another. 3. Made up of sections. —*n.* A sofa having several separate units. —**sec′·tion·al·ly** *adv.*

sec·tion·al·ism (sek′shən·əl·iz′əm) *n.* Undue concern for a particular section of the country. —**sec′tion·al·ist** *n.*

sec·tor (sek′tər) *n.* 1. *Geom.* A part of a circle or ellipse bounded by two radii and the arc subtended by them. 2. A part or portion. 3. *Mil.* A defined area for which a unit is responsible. —*v.t.* To divide into sectors. [< L *secare* to cut] —**sec·to·ri·al** (sek·tôr′e·al) *adj.*

sec·u·lar (sek′yə·lər) *adj.* 1. Of this world or the present life; temporal; worldly. 2. Not under the control of the church; civil. 3. Not concerned with religion. 4. Not bound by monastic vows. —*n.* 1. One in holy orders who is not bound by monastic vows. 2. A layman. [< L *saeculum* generation, an age]

sec·u·lar·ism (sek′yə·lə·riz′əm) *n.* 1. Adherence to nonreligious values, as in morality. 2. The view that religion should not be introduced into public education or civil affairs. —**sec′u·lar·ist** *n.*

sec·u·lar·ize (sek′yə·lə·rīz′) *v.t.* **·ized, ·iz·ing** 1. To convert from sacred to secular uses. 2. To make worldly. —**sec′u·lar·i·za′tion** *n.*

se·cure (si·kyŏŏr′) *adj.* 1. Guarded against or not likely to be exposed to danger; safe. 2. Free from fear, worry, etc. 3. Fixed firmly in place. 4. So strong or well-made as to render loss, escape, or failure impossible. 5. Assured; certain. —*v.* **·cured, ·cur·ing** *v.t.* 1. To make secure; protect. 2. To make firm or tight; fasten. 3. To make certain; ensure. 4. To obtain; get. —*v.i.* 5. To be or become secure: with *against*, etc. [< L *se-* without + *cura* care] —**se·cur′a·ble** *adj.* —**se·cure′ly** *adv.* —**se·cure′ment** *n.* —**se·cure′ness** *n.* —**se·cur′er** *n.*

se·cur·i·ty (si·kyŏŏr′ə·tē) *n. pl.* **·ties** 1. The state of being secure. 2. One who or that which secures or guarantees. 3. Something deposited or pledged as a guarantee for payment. 4. *pl.* Stocks, bonds, notes, etc. 5. Protection of secrecy, as in wartime.

Security Council A permanent organ of the United Nations charged with the maintenance of international peace.

se·dan (si·dan′) *n.* 1. A closed automobile having two or four doors and a front and back seat. 2. A sedan chair. [? Ital. *sedere* to sit]

sedan chair A portable, enclosed chair, usu. for one passenger, carried by means of poles at the front and back.

se·date (si·dāt′) *adj.* 1. Composed; unhurried; calm. 2. Sober and decorous. [< L *sedere* to sit] —**se·date′ly** *adv.* —**se·date′ness** *n.*

se·da·tion (si·dā′shən) *n.* The act of administering sedatives; also their effect.

sed·a·tive (sed′ə·tiv) *adj.* Allaying irritation; assuaging pain. —*n.* Any means, as a medicine, of soothing distress or allaying pain.

sed·en·tar·y (sed′ən·ter′ē) *adj.* 1. Characterized by or requiring much sitting. 2. Settled in one place. [< L *sedere* to sit] —**sed′en·tar′i·ness** *n.*

Se·der (sā′dər) *n. pl.* **Se·ders** or **Se·dar·im** (sə·där′im) In Judaism, the Passover feast commemorating the departure of the Israelites from Egypt. [< Hebrew *sedher* service]

sedge (sej) *n.* Any of various grasslike herbs widely distributed in marshy places. [OE *secg*] —**sedg′y** *adj.*

sed·i·ment (sed′ə·mənt) *n.* 1. Matter that settles to the bottom of a liquid; dregs. 2. *Geol.* Fragmentary material deposited by water or air. [< L *sedere* to sit, settle] —**sed′i·men′ta·ry, sed′i·men′tal** *adj.*

se·di·tion (si·dish′ən) *n.* 1. Language or conduct directed against public order and the safety of the state. 2. The clandestine incitement of such disorder. 3. Dissension; revolt. [< L *sed-* aside + *itio, -onis* a going] —**se·di′tion·ar·y, se·di′tion·ist** *adj.* & *n.* —**se·di′tious** (-əs) *adj.* —**se·di′tious·ly** *adv.*

se·duce (si·dŏŏs′, -dyŏŏs′) *v.t.* **·duced, ·duc·ing** 1. To lead astray; entice into wrong. 2. To induce to engage in illicit sexual intercourse. [< L *se-* apart + *ducere* to lead] —**se·duc′er** *n.* —**se·duc′i·ble** or **se·duce′a·ble** *adj.* —**se·duc′tion** (-duk′shən) *n.* —**se·duc′tive** (-duk′tiv) *adj.* —**se·duc′tive·ly** *adv.* —**se·duc′tive·ness** *n.*

sed·u·lous (sej′ŏŏ·ləs) *adj.* Diligent; assiduous. [< L *sedulus* careful] —**se·du·li·ty** (si·dŏŏ′lə·tē, -dyŏŏ′-), **sed′u·lous·ness** *n.* —**sed′u·lous·ly** *adv.*

se·dum (sē′dəm) *n.* Any of a large genus of chiefly perennial plants, having very thick leaves and usu. white, yellow, or pink flowers. [< L, houseleek]

see[1] (sē) *v.* **saw, seen, see·ing** *v.t.* 1. To perceive with the eyes. 2. To perceive with the mind; understand. 3. To find out or ascertain. 4. To have experience of. 5. To encounter; chance to meet. 6. To visit or receive as a guest, patient, etc. 7. To attend as a spectator; view. 8. To accompany; escort. 9. To take care; be sure: *See* that you do it! —*v.i.* 10. To have or exercise the power of sight. 11. To find out; inquire. 12. To understand. 13. To consider. —**to see about** 1. To inquire into. 2. To take care of; attend to. —**to see (someone) off** To accompany to a point of departure, as for a journey. —**to see (someone) through** To aid or protect, as throughout a period of difficulty or danger. —**to see through** To penetrate, as a disguise or deception. —**to see to** To be responsible for; give one's attention to. [OE *sēon*]

see[2] (sē) *n.* The local seat from which a bishop, archbishop, or pope exercises jurisdiction; also such jurisdiction, authority, rank, or office. —**Holy See** The Pope's jurisdiction or office. [< L *sedes* seat]

seed (sēd) *n.* 1. The fertilized ovule from which a plant may be reproduced. 2. Origin; source. 3. Offspring; children. 4. The male fertilizing element; semen; sperm. 5. Seeds collectively. —**to go to seed** 1. To develop and shed seed. 2. To deteriorate. —*v.t.* 1. To sow with seed. 2. To remove the seeds from. 3. In sports, to arrange the matches of (players) in a tournament, so that the more skilled meet only in the later events. 4. To intersperse (clouds) with silver iodide or other particles in order to produce rainfall. —*v.i.* 5. To sow seed. 6. To grow to maturity and produce or shed seed. [OE *sǣd*] —**seed′er** *n.* —**seed′less** *adj.*

seed bud *Bot.* The germ within a seed; also, the ovule.

seed cake A sweet cake containing aromatic seeds.

seed·case (sēd′kās′) *n.* *Bot.* A pericarp.

seed leaf *Bot.* A cotyledon.

seed·ling (sēd′ling) *n.* 1. *Bot.* A plant grown from seed. 2. A very young tree or plant.

seed oyster A young oyster, esp. one transplanted to another bed.

seed pearl A small pearl.

seeds·man (sēdz′mən) *n. pl.* **·men** (-mən) 1. A dealer in seeds. 2. A sower. Also **seed′man.**

seed vessel *Bot.* A pericarp.

seed·y (sē′dē) *adj.* **seed·i·er, seed·i·est** 1. Full of seeds. 2. Gone to seed. 3. Poor; shabby. 4. *Informal* Feeling or looking wretched. —**seed′i·ly** *adv.* —**seed′i·ness** *n.*

see·ing (sē′ing) *n.* The act of seeing; vision; sight. —*conj.* Since; in view of the fact.

seek (sēk) *v.* **sought, seek·ing** *v.t.* 1. To go in search of; look for. 2. To strive for; try to obtain. 3. To endeavor or try. 4. To ask for; request. —*v.i.* 5. To make a search or inquiry. [OE *sēcan*] —**seek′er** *n.*

seem (sēm) *v.i.* 1. To give the impression of being; appear. 2. To appear to oneself: I *seem* to hear voices. 3. To be evident or apparent: It *seems* to be raining. [ME *sēmen* < ON *sǣma* to conform to]

seem·ing (sē′ming) *adj.* Apparent but not necessarily actual. —*n.* Appearance; semblance; esp., false show. —**seem′ing·ly** *adv.* —**seem′ing·ness** *n.*

seem·ly (sēm′lē) *adj.* **·li·er, ·li·est** Proper; decorous. —*adv.* Becomingly; decently; appropriately. [< ON *sœmr* fitting] —**seem′·li·ness** *n.*

seen (sēn) Past participle of SEE.

seep (sēp) *v.i.* To soak through pores or cracks; percolate; ooze. —*n.* A small spring or a place out of which water, oil, etc., oozes. [Alter. of OE *sypian* to soak] —**seep·age** (sē′pij) *n.*

seer (sē′ər *for def. 1*; *also* sir *for def. 2*) *n.* 1. One who sees. 2. A prophet. [< SEE[1] + -ER] —**seer′ess** *n.fem.*

seer·suck·er (sir′suk′ər) *n.* A thin fabric, usu. striped in colors, with a crinkled surface. [< Persian *shīr o shakkar*, lit., milk and sugar]

see·saw (sē′sô′) *n.* 1. A balanced board made to move alternately up and down by persons at opposite ends: also called *teeter.* 2. Any up-and-down movement or change. —*v.t. & v.i.* To move or cause to move on or as if on a seesaw. —*adj.* Moving to and fro; vacillating. [Reduplication of SAW[1]]

seethe (sēth) *v.* **seethed, seeth·ing** *v.i.* 1. To boil. 2. To foam or bubble as if boiling. 3. To be agitated, as by rage. —*v.t.* 4. To soak in liquid; steep. —*n.* The act or condition of seething; turmoil. [OE *sēothan*]

seg·ment (seg′mənt) *n.* 1. A part cut off or divided from the other parts; a section. 2. *Geom.* **a** A part of a figure, esp., of a circle, cut off by a line or plane. **b** A finite part of a line. —*v.t. & v.i.* To divide into segments. [< L *secare* to cut] —**seg·men′tal, seg′men·tar′y** *adj.* —**seg·men′tal·ly** *adv.* —**seg′men·ta′tion** *n.*

se·go (sē′gō) *n. pl.* **·gos** 1. A perennial herb of the lily family, having white flowers. 2. Its edible bulb. [< Shoshonean (Ute) *sīgo*]

seg·re·gate (seg′rə·gāt; *for adj. also* seg′rə·git) *v.t.* **·gat·ed, ·gat·ing** 1. To place (a person or thing) apart from others or the rest; isolate. 2. To subject to segregation. —*adj.* Set apart from others. [< L *se-* apart + *grex, gregis* flock] —**seg′re·ga′tive** *adj.*

seg·re·ga·tion (seg′rə·gā′shən) *n.* 1. The act or process of segregating. 2. The practice of requiring separate facilities, for use by different racial groups. —**seg′re·ga′tion·ist** *n.*

seign·ior (sēn′yər) *n.* A feudal lord; noble. Also **sei·gneur** (sēn·yûr′). [< L *senior* older] —**sei·gnio·ri·al** (sēn·yôr′ē·əl) *adj.*

seign·ior·y (sēn′yər·ē) *n. pl.* **·ies** The territory or jurisdiction of a seignior; a manor. Also **sei′gneur·y.**

seine (sān) *n.* A long fishnet hanging vertically in the water and having floats at the top edge and weights at the bottom. —*v.t. & v.i.* **seined, sein·ing** To fish or catch with a seine. [< Gk. *sagēnē* fishnet]

seis·mic (sīz′mik) *adj.* Of, characteristic of, or produced by earthquakes. Also **seis′mal, seis′mi·cal, seis·mat·i·cal** (sīz·mat′ə·kəl) [< Gk. *seiein* to shake]

seismic sea wave A tsunami.

seismo- *combining form* Earthquake. Also, before vowels, **seism-.** [< Gk. *seismos* earthquake]

seis·mo·gram (sīz′mə·gram) *n.* The record made by a seismograph.

seis·mo·graph (sīz′mə·graf) *n.* An instrument for recording automatically the intensity, direction, and duration of an earthquake shock. —**seis′mo·graph′ic** *adj.* —**seis·mog·ra·pher** (sīz·mog′rə·fər) *n.*

seis·mog·ra·phy (sīz·mog′rə·fē) *n.* The study and recording of earthquake phenomena.

seis·mol·o·gy (sīz·mol′ə·jē) *n.* The science of earthquake phenomena. —**seis·mo·log·ic** (sīz′mə·loj′ik) or **·i·cal** *adj.* —**seis′mo·log′i·cal·ly** *adv.* —**seis·mol′o·gist** *n.*

seize (sēz) *v.* **seized, seiz·ing** *v.t.* 1. To take hold of suddenly and forcibly. 2. To take possession of by authority or right. 3. To take possession of by force. 4. To take prisoner; arrest. 5. To act upon with sudden and powerful effect: Terror *seized* him. —*v.i.* 6. To take a sudden or forcible hold. [< Med.L *sacire*] —**seiz′a·ble** *adj.* —**seiz′er** *n.*

sei·zure (sē′zhər) *n.* 1. The act of seizing. 2. A sudden or violent attack, as of epilepsy; fit.

se·la·chi·an (si·lā′kē·ən) *adj.* Of or belonging to a group of fishes including the sharks, skates, and rays. [< Gk. *selachos* shark] —**se·la′chi·an** *n.*

sel·dom (sel′dəm) *adv.* At widely separated intervals; infrequently. [OE *seldum*]

se·lect (si·lekt′) *v.t.* 1. To take in preference to another or others. —*v.i.* 2. To make a choice. —*adj.* 1. Chosen in preference to others; choice. 2. Exclusive. 3. Very particular in selecting. [< L *se-* apart + *legere* to choose] —**se·lect′ness** *n.* —**se·lec′tor** *n.*

se·lec·tee (si·lek′tē′) *n.* One selected; esp., one drafted for military or naval service.

se·lec·tion (si·lek′shən) *n.* 1. The act of selecting; choice. 2. Anything selected. 3. A thing or collection of things chosen with care. 4. *Biol.* Natural selection.

se·lec·tive (si·lek′tiv) *adj.* Pertaining to selection; tending to select. —**se·lec′tiv′i·ty, se·lec′tive·ness** *n.*

selective service Compulsory military service according to specified conditions of age, fitness, etc.

se·lect·man (si·lekt′mən) *n. pl.* **·men** (-mən) In New England, one of a board of town officers.

sel·e·nite (sel′ə·nīt) *n.* A pearly, usu. transparent variety of gypsum. [< Gk. *selēnītēs* (*lithos*) moonstone]

se·le·ni·um (si·lē′nē·əm) *n.* A gray, crystalline, nonmetallic element (symbol Se) of the sulfur group, varying greatly in electrical resistance under the influence of light. [< Gk. *selēnē* the moon]

selenium cell A photoelectric cell in which

plates of selenium respond to the action of light upon them.

seleno- *combining form* Moon; pertaining to the moon; lunar. Also, before vowels, selen-. [< Gk. *selēnē* the moon]

self (self) *n. pl.* **selves** 1. An individual known or considered as the subject of his own consciousness. 2. Personal interest or advantage. 3. Any thing, class, or attribute that, abstractly considered, maintains a distinct and characteristic individuality or identity. —*adj.* 1. Being of the same color, substance, etc., throughout; uniform. 2. Of a part, accessory, etc., made of the same material as that with which it is used. [OE]

Self as a combining form has the meanings:

1. Of the self (the object of the root word), as in:

self-abasement
self-abhorrence
self-accusation
self-admiration
self-adornment
self-adulation
self-advancement
self-advertisement
self-advertising
self-affliction
self-aggrandizement
self-analysis
self-annihilation
self-appreciation
self-approval
self-asserting
self-awareness
self-betrayal
self-blame
self-condemnation
self-condemning
self-confinement
self-conserving
self-consideration
self-consuming
self-contempt
self-contradicting
self-correction
self-corruption
self-criticism
self-cure
self-deceiving
self-defeating
self-degradation
self-delusion
self-deprecating
self-depreciation
self-destroying
self-destruction
self-destructive
self-direction
self-disclosure
self-discovery
self-doubt
self-enriching
self-examination
self-expansion
self-exploiting
self-exposure
self-flattery
self-folding
self-forgetful
self-giving
self-glorification
self-gratification
self-guidance
self-harming
self-humbling
self-humiliation
self-hypnosis
self-idolatry
self-idolizing
self-ignorant
self-image
self-immolation
self-impairment
self-improvement
self-incriminating
self-indignation
self-indulging
self-inspection
self-instruction
self-insurer
self-justification
self-justifying
self-knowledge
self-laudatory
self-limitation
self-limiting
self-maintenance
self-martyrdom
self-mastery
self-mutilation
self-neglect
self-opinion
self-perceptive
self-perfection
self-perpetuating
self-perpetuation
self-persuasion
self-pleasing
self-praise
self-preparation
self-presentation
self-preserving
self-protecting
self-protection
self-punishment
self-realization
self-regulation
self-representation
self-repressing
self-reproach
self-restriction
self-revealing
self-revelation
self-scrutinizing
self-searching
self-soothing
self-study
self-tolerant
self-torment
self-torture
self-trust
self-trusting
self-valuing
self-vindication
self-worship

2. By or from oneself or itself, as in:

self-administered
self-apparent
self-approved
self-arising
self-authorized
self-blinded
self-caused
self-complete
self-condemned
self-conducted
self-confessed
self-constituted
self-declared
self-defining
self-deluded
self-deprived
self-derived
self-determined
self-devised
self-doomed
self-elected
self-employed
self-explained
self-explanatory
self-exposed
self-forbidden
self-fulfilling
self-furnished
self-generated
self-healing
self-imposed
self-inclusive
self-incurred
self-induced
self-inflicted
self-initiated
self-instructed
self-invited
self-issuing
self-judged
self-justified
self-limited
self-moving
self-named
self-ordained
self-originating
self-paid
self-perpetuated
self-posed
self-proclaimed
self-professed
self-punished
self-refuting
self-reliance
self-reliant
self-renewing
self-repressed
self-restoring
self-restrained
self-restraint
self-revealed
self-rewarding
self-schooled
self-stimulated
self-sustained
self-sustaining

3. To, toward, in, for, or with oneself, as in:

self-absorbed
self-addressed
self-aid
self-amusement
self-assumed
self-assuming
self-benefit
self-care
self-complacency
self-conflict
self-consistency
self-consistent
self-content
self-contented
self-deception
self-delight
self-dependence
self-dependent
self-directed
self-disgust
self-enclosed
self-gain
self-help
self-injurious
self-injury
self-liking
self-loathing
self-love
self-occupied
self-preference
self-prescribed
self-pride
self-produced
self-purifying
self-relying
self-repellent
self-reproof
self-resentment
self-resigned
self-respectful

4. Independent, as in:

self-agency
self-authority
self-credit
self-entity
self-existence
self-ownership
self-rule
self-sovereignty

5. In technology, automatic or automatically, as in:

self-acting
self-adapting
self-adjustable
self-adjusting
self-aligning
self-burning
self-charging
self-checking
self-cleaning
self-closing
self-cocking
self-cooled

self-defrosting
self-emptying
self-feeding
self-filling
self-focusing
self-inking
self-lighting
self-locking
self-lubricating
self-moving
self-oiling
self-priming
self-recording
self-registering
self-regulated
self-regulating
self-righting
self-winding

self-ab·ne·ga·tion (self′ab′ni·gā′shən) *n.* The complete putting aside of oneself and one's own claims for the sake of others.

self-ab·sorp·tion (self′ab·sôrp′shən, -zôrp′-) *n.* Absorption in or concentration on one's own affairs, work, interests, etc.

self-ap·point·ed (self′ə·poin′təd) *adj.* Appointed by oneself rather than by others: a *self-appointed* boss.

self-as·ser·tion (self′ə·sûr′shən) *n.* The asserting or putting forward of oneself, one's opinions, claims, or rights. **—self′-as·ser′tive** *adj.* **—self′-as·ser′tive·ly** *adv.*

self-as·sured (self′ə·shŏŏrd′) *adj.* Confident in one's own abilities; self-reliant. **—self′-as·sur′ance** *n.*

self-cen·tered (self′sen′tərd) *adj.* Concerned chiefly with one's own affairs and interests, often with a lack of consideration for others. **—self′-cen′tered·ness** *n.* **—self′-cen′tered·ly** *adv.*

self-com·mand (self′kə·mand′) *n.* The state of having all the faculties and powers fully at command.

self-con·ceit (self′kən·sēt′) *n.* An unduly high opinion of oneself; vanity. **—self′-con·ceit′ed** *adj.*

self-con·fi·dence (self′kon′fə·dəns) *n.* Confidence in oneself, one's judgment, etc. **—self′-con′fi·dent** *adj.* **—self′-con′fi·dent·ly** *adv.*

self-con·scious (self′kon′shəs) *adj.* 1. Unduly conscious that one is observed by others; ill at ease. 2. Manifesting embarrassment. **—self′-con′scious·ly** *adv.* **—self′-con′scious·ness** *n.*

self-con·tained (self′kən·tānd′) *adj.* 1. Keeping one's thoughts and feelings to oneself. 2. Exercising self-control. 3. Complete and independent. 4. Having all parts needed for working order.

self-con·tra·dic·tion (self′con′trə·dik′shən) *n.* 1. The act or state of contradicting oneself or itself. 2. That which contradicts itself. **—self′-con′tra·dic′to·ry** *adj.*

self-con·trol (self′kən·trōl′) *n.* The act, power, or habit of keeping one's faculties or energies under control of the will.

self-de·fense (self′di·fens′) *n.* Defense of oneself, one's property, or one's reputation. **—self′-de·fen′sive** *adj.*

self-de·ni·al (self′di·nī′əl) *n.* The act or power of denying oneself gratification. **—self′-de·ny′ing** *adj.* **—self′-de·ny′ing·ly** *adv.*

self-de·struct (self′di·strukt′) *v.i.* To destroy itself: The rocket is designed to *self-destruct.*

self-de·ter·mi·na·tion (self′di·tûr′mə·nā′·shən) *n.* 1. The principle of free will; decision by oneself. 2. Decision by the people of a country or section as to its future political status. **—self′-de·ter′min·ing** *adj. & n.*

self-dis·ci·pline (self′dis′ə·plin) *n.* The discipline or training of oneself.

self-ed·u·cat·ed (self′ej′ŏŏ·kā′tid) *adj.* Educated through one's own efforts without the aid of instructors. **—self′-ed′u·ca′tion** *n.*

self-ef·face·ment (self′i·fās′mənt) *n.* The keeping of oneself in the background. **—self′-ef·fac′ing** *adj.*

self-es·teem (self′ə·stēm′) *n.* A good opinion of oneself.

self-ev·i·dent (self′ev′ə·dənt) *adj.* Requiring no proof or explanation. **—self′-ev′i·dence** *n.* **—self′-ev′i·dent·ly** *adv.*

self-ex·pres·sion (self′ik·spresh′ən) *n.* Expression of one's own temperament or emotions.

self-fer·til·i·za·tion (self′fûr′təl·ə·zā′shən) *n.* *Biol.* Fertilization of an ovum by sperm from the same animal or of a plant ovule by its own pollen.

self-gov·ern·ment (self′guv′ərn·mənt, -ər·mənt) *n.* Government of a country or region by its own people. **—self′-gov′erned, self′-gov′ern·ing** *adj.*

self·heal (self′hēl′) *n.* Any of various weedy, perennial herbs with violet flowers.

self·hood (self′hŏŏd) *n.* The state of being an individual; personality.

self-im·por·tance (self′im·pôr′təns) *n.* Pompous self-conceit. **—self′-im·por′tant** *adj.*

self-in·dul·gence (self′in·dul′jəns) *n.* The indulgence or gratification of one's own desires, weaknesses, etc. **—self′-in·dul′gent** *adj.* **—self′-in·dul′gent·ly** *adv.*

self-in·ter·est (self′in′tər·ist, -in′trist) *n.* Personal interest or advantage, or the pursuit of it; selfishness. **—self′-in′ter·est·ed** *adj.*

self·ish (sel′fish) *adj.* 1. Caring chiefly for oneself or one's own interests or comfort, esp. to the point of disregarding the welfare or wishes of others. 2. Proceeding from or characterized by undue love of self. **—self′·ish·ly** *adv.* **—self′ish·ness** *n.*

self·less (self′lis) *adj.* Regardless of self; unselfish. **—self′less·ly** *adv.* **—self′less·ness** *n.*

self-load·ing (self′lō′ding) *adj.* Of firearms, utilizing a portion of the force of the exploding gas or of recoil to eject the empty case and load the next round.

self-made (self′mād′) *adj.* 1. Having attained honor, wealth, etc., by one's own efforts. 2. Made by oneself.

self-pit·y (self′pit′ē) *n.* The act or state of pitying oneself. **—self′-pit′y·ing** *adj.* **—self′-pit′y·ing·ly** *adv.*

self-pol·li·na·tion (self′pol′ə·nā′shən) *n.* *Bot.* The transfer of pollen from stamens to pistils of the same flower. **—self′-pol′li·nat·ed** *adj.*

self-pos·ses·sion (self′pə·zesh′ən) *n.* 1. Control of one's powers or faculties. 2. Presence of mind; self-command. **—self′-pos·sessed′** *adj.*

self-pres·er·va·tion (self′prez′ər·vā′shən) *n.* 1. The protection of oneself from destruction. 2. The urge to protect oneself, regarded as an instinct.

self-pro·pelled (self′prə·peld′) *adj.* 1. Able to propel itself. 2. Having the means of propulsion contained within itself, as an automobile.

self-re·gard (self′ri·gärd′) *n.* 1. Regard or consideration for oneself or one's own interests. 2. Estimation of self.

self-re·spect (self′ri·spekt′) *n.* Proper respect for oneself and one's own character. **—self′-re·spect′ing** *adj.*

self-right·eous (self′rī′chəs) *adj.* Righteous in one's own estimation. **—self′-right′eous·ly** *adv.* **—self′-right′eous·ness** *n.*

self-ris·ing (self′rī′zing) *adj.* 1. That rises of itself. 2. Having the leaven already added, as some flours.

self-sac·ri·fice (self′sak′rə·fīs) *n.* The sacrifice of one's self or one's personal welfare or wishes for the sake of duty or for the good of others. **—self′-sac′ri·fic′ing** *adj.*

self·same (self′sām′) *adj.* Exactly the same; identical. **—self′same′ness** *n.*

self-sat·is·fac·tion (self′sat′is·fak′shən) *n.* Satisfaction with one's own actions and characteristics; conceit; complacency. **—self′-sat′is·fied** *adj.* **—self′-sat′is·fy′ing** *adj.*

self-seek·ing (self′sē′king) *adj.* Selfish. **—***n.* Actions, motives, etc., characteristic of a self-seeking person. **—self′-seek′er** *n.*

self-ser·vice (self′sûr′vis) *adj.* Designating a restaurant, store, etc., where patrons serve themselves.

self-ser·ving (self′sûr′ving) *adj.* Tending to advance one's own interests.

self-start·er (self′stär′tər) *n.* A starter (def. 2).

self-styled (self′stīld′) *adj.* Characterized (as such) by oneself: a *self-styled* gentleman.

self-suf·fi·cient (self′sə·fish′ənt) *adj.* Able to maintain oneself without aid from others. Also **self′-suf·fic′ing** (-sə·fī′sing). **—self′-suf·fi′cien·cy** *n.*

self-sup·port (self′sə·pôrt′) *n.* The act or state of supporting oneself entirely by one's own efforts. **—self′-sup·port′ed, self′-sup·port′ing** *adj.*

self-taught (self′tôt′) *adj.* Taught by oneself or through one's own efforts.

self-will (self′wil′) *n.* Strong or tenacious adherence to one's own will or wish; obstinacy. **—self′-willed′** *adj.*

sell (sel) *v.* **sold, sell·ing** *v.t.* 1. To transfer (property) to another for money or for some other consideration. 2. To deal in; offer for sale. 3. To deliver, surrender, or betray for a price or reward. 4. To promote the sale of. 5. *Informal* To cause to accept or approve something: with *on*: They *sold* him on the scheme. 6. *Informal* To cause the acceptance or approval of. **—***v.i.* 7. To transfer ownership for money, etc.; engage in selling. 8. To be on sale; be sold. 9. *Informal* To attract buyers. 10. *Informal* To gain acceptance or approval. **—to sell off** To get rid of by selling. **—to sell out** 1. To sell all one's merchandise, possessions, etc. 2. *Informal* To betray. [OE *sellan* to give] **—sell′a·ble** *adj.* **—sell′er** *n.*

sell·out (sel′out′) *n.* *Informal* 1. A performance for which all seats have been sold. 2. A betrayal.

selt·zer (selt′sər) *n.* An effervescing mineral water. Also **seltzer water.** [Alter. of G *Selterser*, from *Nieder Selters*, a village in SW Prussia]

sel·vage (sel′vij) *n.* The edge of a woven fabric so finished that it will not ravel. Also **sel′vedge.** [< SELF + EDGE, trans. of MDu. *selfegghe*]

selves (selvz) Plural of SELF.

se·man·tic (si·man′tik) *adj.* 1. Of or pertaining to meaning. 2. Of or relating to semantics. **—se·man′ti·cal·ly** *adv.*

se·man·ti·cist (si·man′tə·sist) *n.* A specialist in semantics.

se·man·tics (si·man′tiks) *n.pl.* (*construed as sing.*) 1. *Ling.* The study of the meanings of words. 2. *Logic* The relation between signs or symbols and what they signify or denote. [< Gk. *sēmainein* to signify]

sem·a·phore (sem′ə·fôr) *n.* An apparatus for making signals, as with movable arms. [< Gk. *sēma* a sign + -PHORE] **—sem′a·phor′ic** or **·i·cal** *adj.*

sem·blance (sem′bləns) *n.* 1. A mere show without reality; pretense. 2. Outward appearance. 3. A likeness or resemblance. [< L *simulare, similare* to simulate]

se·men (sē′mən) *n.* The impregnating fluid of male humans and animals that contains spermatozoa; seed. [< L *serere* to sow]

se·mes·ter (si·mes′tər) *n.* In colleges, etc., a period of instruction, usu. lasting 17 or 18 weeks. [< L *semestris* six months] **—se·mes′tral** *adj.*

sem·i (sem′ī) *Informal* A semitrailer.

semi- *prefix* 1. Not fully; partially; partly: *semiautomatic.* 2. Exactly half: *semicircle.* 3. Occurring twice (in the periods specified): *semiweekly.* [< L]

Semi- (def. 1) appears as a prefix in many words, as in the list below.

semiagricultural
semialcoholic
semianimated
semiarid
semiattached
semiautonomous
semibald
semibarbaric
semibarren
semiblind
semicivilized
semicoagulated
semicollapsible
semiconfident
semiconfinement
semiconscious
semiconservative
semicooperative
semidangerous
semidarkness
semideaf
semidelirious
semidependent
semideveloped
semidigested
semidomesticated
semidry
semienclosed
semifailure
semifeudalism
semifictional
semiflexed
semifluid
semiformal
semigloss
semi-Gothic
semihard
semihistorical
semihumorous
semi-idle
semi-independent
semi-intoxicated
semi-invalid
semiliberal
semiliquid
semiliterate
semimilitary
semimobile
semimodern
semimute
semiofficial
semiorganized
semiparalysis
semipastoral
semiperishable
semipermanent
semiplastic
semipolitical
semipublic
semiradical
semireactionary
semireligious
semirespectable
semiretired
semiretirement
semirustic
semisacred
semisatirical
semiscientific
semiserious
semiskilled
semisoft
semisolid
semisuccessful
semisweet
semitechnical
semitrained
semitransparent
semivoluntary
semiwild

sem·i·an·nu·al (sem′ē·an′yōō·əl) *adj.* Issued or occurring twice a year; half-yearly. —*n.* A publication issued twice a year. —**sem′i·an′nu·al·ly** *adv.*

sem·i·au·to·mat·ic (sem′ē·ô′tə·mat′ik) *adj.* 1. Partly automatic. 2. Of firearms, self-loading but firing once at each pull on the trigger.

sem·i·cir·cle (sem′ē·sûr′kəl) *n.* 1. A half-circle. 2. Anything formed or arranged in a half-circle. —**sem′i·cir′cu·lar** (-kyə·lər) *adj.*

semicircular canal *Anat.* One of the three tubular structures in the inner ear, serving as the organ of equilibrium.

sem·i·co·lon (sem′ē·kō′lən, sem′ə-) *n.* A mark (;) of punctuation, indicating a greater degree of separation than the comma.

sem·i·con·duc·tor (sem′ē·kən·duk′tər) *n.* *Physics* One of a class of substances whose electrical conductivity at ordinary temperatures is between that of a metal and an insulator. —**sem′i·con·duct′ing** *adj.*

sem·i·de·tached (sem′ē·di·tacht′) *adj.* Joined to another on one side only; esp., designating a house having one wall in common with another house.

sem·i·fi·nal (sem′ē·fī′nəl) *n.* In sports, a competition that precedes the final event. —*adj.* Next before the final. —**sem′i·fi′nal·ist** *n.*

sem·i·month·ly (sem′ē·munth′lē) *adj.* Taking place twice a month. —*n.* *pl.* **·lies** A publication issued twice a month. —*adv.* At half-monthly intervals.

sem·i·nal (sem′ə·nəl) *adj.* 1. Of, pertaining to, or containing seeds or semen. 2. Having productive power; germinal. 3. Not developed; rudimentary. [< L *semen, seminis* semen, seed] —**sem′i·nal·ly** *adv.*

sem·i·nar (sem′ə·när) *n.* 1. A group of advanced students meeting regularly with a professor for discussion of research problems. 2. The course thus conducted.

sem·i·nar·y (sem′ə·ner′ē) *n.* *pl.* **·nar·ies** A special school, as one for training the clergy or a private school for girls. [< L *seminarium* seed plot]

sem·i·na·tion (sem′ə·nā′shən) *n.* 1. The act of sowing or spreading. 2. Propagation; reproduction. [< L *seminare* to sow]

Sem·i·nole (sem′ə·nōl) *n.* One of a Florida tribe of Muskhogean Indians, now chiefly in Oklahoma. [< Muskhogean (Creek) *Simanóle*, lit., separatist, runaway]

sem·i·per·me·a·ble (sem′ē·pûr′mē·ə·bəl) *adj.* Partially permeable, as a membrane that allows some but not all molecules to pass through it.

sem·i·pre·cious (sem′ē·presh′əs) *adj.* Designating gemstones, that are somewhat less rare or valuable than precious stones.

sem·i·pri·vate (sem′ē·prī′vit) *adj.* Partly but not wholly private, as a hospital room for two or several patients.

sem·i·pro·fes·sion·al (sem′ē·prə·fesh′ən·əl) *adj.* Engaged in a sport for profit, but not as a full-time occupation. —*n.* A semiprofessional athlete. Also *Informal* **sem′i·pro′** (-prō′). —**sem′i·pro·fes′sion·al·ly** *adv.*

Sem·ite (sem′īt) *n.* One of a people of Caucasian stock, now represented by the Jews and Arabs, but originally including the ancient Babylonians, Assyrians, Phoenicians, etc. [< Hebrew *Shēm* Shem, a son of Noah]

Se·mit·ic (sə·mit′ik) *adj.* Of or pertaining to the Semites, or to any of their languages. —*n.* The Semitic subfamily of languages.

sem·i·tone (sem′ē·tōn′) *n.* *Music* The smallest interval of the chromatic scale; a tone at an interval a half step from another: also called *half step, half tone.* —**sem′i·ton′ic** (-ton′ik) *adj.*

sem·i·trail·er (sem′ē·trā′lər) *n.* A trailer having wheels only at the rear, the front end resting on the tractor.

sem·i·week·ly (sem′ē·wēk′lē) *adj.* Issued or occurring twice a week. —*n.* *pl.* **·lies** A publication issued twice a week. —*adv.* At half-weekly intervals.

sem·i·year·ly (sem′ē·yir′lē) *adj.* Issued or occurring twice a year. —*n.* *pl.* **·lies** A semi-yearly occurrence. —*adv.* At half-yearly intervals.

sem·o·li·na (sem′ə·lē′nə) *n.* The gritty or grainlike portions of wheat retained after the fine flour has been sifted out. [< L *simila* fine flour]

sem·per fi·de·lis (sem′pər fi·dā′lis) *Latin* Always faithful: motto of the U.S. Marine Corps.

sem·per pa·ra·tus (sem′pər pə·rā′təs) *Latin* Always prepared: motto of the U.S. Coast Guard.

semp·stress (semp′stris, sem′-) *n.* A seamstress.

sen·ate (sen′it) *n.* 1. The governing body of some universities and institutions of learning. 2. A council or legislative body. 3. *cap.* The upper branch of national or state legislative bodies of the U.S., Canada, France, and other governments. [< L *senatus*, lit., council of old men]

sen·a·tor (sen′ə·tər) *n.* *Often cap.* A member of a senate.

sen·a·to·ri·al (sen′ə·tôr′ē·əl) *adj.* Of, pertaining to, or befitting a senator or senate. —**sen′a·to′ri·al·ly** *adv.*

send (send) *v.* **sent, send·ing** *v.t.* 1. To cause or direct (a person) to go; dispatch. 2. To cause to be taken or directed to another place; transmit: sometimes with *off.* 3. To cause to issue; emit or discharge, as heat, light, smoke, etc. 4. To throw or drive by force; impel. 5. *Slang* To make rapturous with joy. —*v.i.* 6. To dispatch an agent, messenger, or message. —**to send for** To summon. —**to send packing** To dismiss quickly and forcefully. —**to send up** *Informal* To sentence to prison. [OE *sendan*] —**send′er** *n.*

send·off (send′ôf′) *n.* 1. The act of sending off; a start. 2. A celebration or demonstration at parting. 3. Encouragement, as in starting a career.

Sen·e·ca (sen′ə·kə) *n.* One of a tribe of Iroquoian Indians formerly inhabiting western New York. [< Algonquian *A′sinnika*]

Sen·e·ga·lese (sen′ga·lēz′, -lēs′) *adj.* Of Senegal or its people. —**Sen′e·ga·lese′** *n.*

se·nes·cent (si·nes′ənt) *adj.* 1. Growing old. 2. Characteristic of old age. [< L *senescere* to grow old] —**se·nes′cence** *n.*

se·nile (sē′nīl, sen′īl) *adj.* 1. Pertaining to, proceeding from, or characteristic of old age. 2. Infirm; weak; doting. [< L *senex* old] —**se′nile·ly** *adv.* —**se·nil·i·ty** (si·nil′ə·tē) *n.*

sen·ior (sēn′yər) *adj.* 1. Older in years or higher in rank. 2. Denoting the older of two.

3. Belonging to maturity or later life. 4. Pertaining to the last year of a four-year high school or college course. —*n.* 1. The older of two. 2. One longer in service or higher in standing. 3. A student in the senior year of a high school, college, or university. [< L, compar. of *senex* old]

senior citizen An elderly person, esp. one of or over the age of retirement.

senior high school A high school, in the U.S. typically comprising grades 10, 11, and 12.

sen·ior·i·ty (sēn·yôr′ə·tē, -yor′-) *n. pl.* **·ties** 1. The state of being senior; priority of age or rank. 2. Precedence or priority due to length of service.

sen·na (sen′ə) *n.* The dried leaflets of any of several leguminous plants, used medicinally as purgatives. [< Arabic *sanā*]

se·ñor (sā·nyôr′) *n. pl.* **·ño·res** (-nyō′rās) *Spanish* 1. A gentleman. 2. Sir; Mr.: used as a title of address.

se·ño·ra (sā·nyō′rä) *n. Spanish* 1. A lady. 2. Mrs.: used as a title of address.

se·ño·ri·ta (sā′nyō·rē′tä) *n. Spanish* 1. A young, unmarried lady. 2. Miss: used as a title of address.

sen·sate (sen′sāt) *adj.* Perceived by the senses. Also **sen′sat·ed.** —*v.t.* **·sat·ed, ·sat·ing** To perceive by the senses. [< L *sensus* sense]

sen·sa·tion (sen·sā′shən) *n.* 1. The consciousness of external stimulation, in the form of hearing, taste, touch, smell, or sight. 2. *Physiol.* The capacity to respond to such stimulation. 3. That which produces great interest or excitement. 4. An excited condition: to cause a *sensation.*

sen·sa·tion·al (sen·sā′shən·əl) *adj.* 1. Pertaining to physical sensation or emotional excitement. 2. Causing excitement; startling. —**sen·sa′tion·al·ly** *adv.*

sen·sa·tion·al·ism (sen·sā′shən·əl·iz′əm) *n.* The use of sensational or melodramatic methods, words, etc. —**sen·sa′tion·al·ist** *n.* —**sen·sa′tion·al·is′tic** *adj.*

sense (sens) *n.* 1. The faculty of sensation; sense perception. 2. Any of certain agencies by or through which an individual receives impressions of the external world, as taste, touch, hearing, smell, or sight. 3. Rational perception accompanied by feeling: a *sense* of wrong. 4. *Often pl.* Normal power of mind or understanding; sound judgment: She is coming to her *senses.* 5. Signification; import; meaning. 6. Sound reason or judgment; wisdom. 7. Capacity to perceive or appreciate: a *sense* of color. —*v.t.* **sensed, sens·ing** 1. To become aware of through the senses. 2. *Informal* To comprehend; understand. [< L *sensus* perception]

sense·less (sens′lis) *adj.* 1. Devoid of sense; making no sense; irrational. 2. Unconscious. 3. Incapable of feeling or perception. —**sense′less·ly** *adv.* —**sense′less·ness** *n.*

sen·si·bil·i·ty (sen′sə·bil′ə·tē) *n. pl.* **·ties** 1. The capability of sensation; power to perceive or feel. 2. The capacity of sensation and rational emotion, as distinguished from intellect and will. 3. *Often pl.* Susceptibility or sensitiveness to outside influences or mental impressions. 4. Discerning judgment.

sen·si·ble (sen′sə·bəl) *adj.* 1. Possessed of good practical judgment; exhibiting sound sense and understanding. 2. Capable of physical sensation. 3. Emotionally or mentally sensitive. 4. Great enough to be perceived. [< L *sentire* to feel, perceive] —**sen′si·ble·ness** *n.* —**sen′si·bly** *adv.*

sen·si·tive (sen′sə·tiv) *adj.* 1. Easily affected by outside influences; excitable or impressionable; touchy. 2. Reacting readily to external agents or forces: paper *sensitive* to light. 3. Closing or moving when touched or irritated, as certain plants. 4. Capable of indicating minute changes or differences; delicate. 5. Of, relating to, or dealing with secret or delicate matters: a *sensitive* federal job. [See SENSIBLE.] —**sen′si·tive·ly** *adv.* —**sen′si·tive·ness** *n.*

sen·si·tiv·i·ty (sen′sə·tiv′ə·tē) *n. pl.* **·ties** The state or degree of being sensitive.

sen·si·tize (sen′sə·tīz) *v.t.* **·tized, ·tiz·ing** 1. To render sensitive. 2. *Photog.* To make sensitive to light, as a plate or film. —**sen′si·ti·za′tion** *n.* —**sen′si·tiz′er** *n.*

sen·sor (sen′sər) *n.* That which receives and responds to a stimulus or signal; esp., an instrument or device designed to detect and respond to some force, change, or radiation.

sen·so·ry (sen′sər·ē) *adj.* 1. Of or pertaining to sensation. 2. Conveying or producing sense impulses. Also **sen·so·ri·al** (sen·sôr′ē·əl).

sen·su·al (sen′shōō·əl) *adj.* 1. Unduly indulging the physical appetites as for sex, food, etc. 2. Pertaining to the body or to the physical senses. [< L *sensus* sense] —**sen′·su·al′i·ty** (-al′ə·tē) *n.* —**sen′su·al·ist** *n.* —**sen′su·al·is′tic** *adj.* —**sen′su·al·ly** *adv.*

sen·su·al·ize (sen′shōō·əl·īz′) *v.t.* **·ized, ·iz·ing** To make sensual. Also *Brit.* **sen′su·al·ise′.** —**sen′su·al·i·za′tion** *n.*

sen·su·ous (sen′shōō·əs) *adj.* 1. Pertaining or appealing to or derived from the senses. 2. Keenly appreciative of and aroused by beauty, refinement, or luxury. —**sen′su·ous·ly** *adv.* —**sen′su·ous·ness** *n.*

sent (sent) Past tense and past participle of SEND.

sen·tence (sen′təns) *n.* 1. *Gram.* A group of words containing a subject and a predicate, as declarative, interrogative, imperative, and exclamatory sentences, or a single word in the case of the simple imperative. 2. *Law* A penalty pronounced upon a person convicted. —*v.t.* **·tenced, ·tenc·ing** To pass sentence upon. [< L *sentire* to feel, be of opinion] —**sen′tenc·er** *n.* —**sen·ten·tial** (sen·ten′shəl) *adj.*

sen·ten·tious (sen·ten′shəs) *adj.* 1. Abounding in or using terse, laconic, or aphoristic language. 2. Pompously formal; moralizing. [< L *sententia* an opinion] —**sen·ten′tious·ly** *adv.* —**sen·ten′tious·ness** *n.*

sen·ti·ent (sen′shē·ənt, -shənt) *adj.* Possessing powers of sense or sense perception; having sensation or feeling. —*n.* A sentient person or thing. [< L *sentiens, -entis*] —**sen′ti·ence** *n.* —**sen′ti·ent·ly** *adv.*

sen·ti·ment (sen′tə·mənt) *n.* 1. Noble, tender, or artistic feeling; sensibility. 2. A mental attitude or response to a person, object, or idea, based on feeling instead of reason. 3. *Often pl.* An opinion or judgment. [< L *sentire* to feel]

sen·ti·men·tal (sen′tə·men′təl) *adj.* 1. Characterized by sentiment or emotion. 2. Experiencing, displaying, or given to sentiment, often in an extravagant or mawkish manner: a *sentimental* novel. —**sen′ti·men′·tal·ly** *adv.*

sen·ti·men·tal·i·ty (sen′tə·men·tal′ə·tē) *n. pl.* **·ties** 1. The state or quality of being mawkishly sentimental. 2. Any expression of sentiment. Also **sen′ti·men′tal·ism** (-təl·iz′əm). —**sen′ti·men′tal·ist** (-təl·ist) *n.*

sen·ti·men·tal·ize (sen′tə·men′təl·īz) *v.* **·ized, ·iz·ing** *v.t.* 1. To make sentimental. 2. To cherish sentimentally. —*v.i.* 3. To behave sentimentally. Also *Brit.* **sen′ti·men′·tal·ise.**

sen·ti·nel (sen′tə·nəl) *n.* 1. A sentry. 2. Any watcher or guard. —*v.t.* **·neled** or **·nelled, ·nel·ing** or **·nel·ling** To watch over as a sentinel. [< LL *sentinare* to avoid danger]

sen·try (sen′trē) *n. pl.* **·tries** 1. A soldier placed on guard to see that only authorized persons pass his post and to warn of danger. 2. The watch or guard kept by a sentry. [? Var. of SENTINEL]

se·pal (sē′pəl) *n. Bot.* One of the individual leaves of a flower calyx. [< L *sep(aratus)* separate + *(pet)alum* petal]

sep·a·ra·ble (sep′ər·ə·bəl, sep′rə-) *adj.* Capable of being separated. —**sep′a·ra·bil′i·ty, sep′a·ra·ble·ness** *n.* —**sep′a·ra·bly** *adv.*

sep·a·rate (*v.* sep′ə·rāt; *adj.* sep′ər·it, sep′rit) *v.* **·rat·ed, ·rat·ing** *v.t.* 1. To set asunder; disunite or disjoin; sever. 2. To occupy a position between; serve to keep apart. 3. To divide into components, parts, etc. —*v.i.* 4. To become divided or disconnected; draw apart. 5. To part company; withdraw from association or combination. —*adj.* 1. Existing or considered apart from others; individual. 2. Disunited from the body; disembodied. 3. Separated; disjoined. [< L *se-* apart + *parare* to prepare] —**sep′a·rate·ly** *adv.* —**sep′a·rate·ness** *n.* —**sep·a·ra·tive** (sep′ə·rā′tiv, sep′rə-), **sep·a·ra·to·ry** (sep′·ər·ə·tôr′ē, sep′rə-). —**sep′a·ra′tor** *n.*

sep·a·ra·tion (sep′ə·rā′shən) *n.* 1. The act or process of separating; division. 2. The state of being disconnected or apart. 3. Something that separates. 4. *Law* Relinquishment of cohabitation between husband and wife by mutual consent.

sep·a·ra·tist (sep′ər·ə·tist, sep′rə-) *n.* One who advocates or upholds separation, esp. one who secedes. Also **sep′a·ra′tion·ist.** —**sep′a·ra·tism** *n.*

se·pi·a (sē′pē·ə) *n.* A reddish brown pigment prepared from the inky secretion of the cuttlefish. [< Gk. *sēpia* cuttlefish] —**se′pi·a** *adj.*

sep·sis (sep′sis) *n. Pathol.* Infection by pathogenic microorganisms. [< Gk. *sēpein* to make putrid]

sep·ta (sep′tə) Plural of SEPTUM.

Sep·tem·ber (sep·tem′bər) The ninth month of the year, containing 30 days. [< L *septem* seven]

sep·ten·ni·al (sep·ten′ē·əl) *adj.* 1. Recurring every seven years. 2. Continuing or capable of lasting seven years. [< L *septem* seven + *annus* year] —**sep·ten′ni·al·ly** *adv.*

sep·tet (sep·tet′) *n.* 1. A group of seven persons, things, etc. 2. *Music* A composition for seven singers or instrumentalists. Also **sep·tette′.** [< L *septem* seven]

septi- *combining form* Seven. Also, before vowels, **sept-.** [< L *septem*]

sep·tic (sep′tik) *adj.* 1. Of, pertaining to, or caused by sepsis. 2. Producing sepsis; infective. Also **sep′ti·cal.** —*n.* Any agent producing sepsis. [See SEPSIS.] —**sep·tic·i·ty** (sep·tis′ə·tē) *n.*

sep·ti·ce·mi·a (sep′tə·sē′mē·ə) *n. Pathol.* An infection of the blood by pathogenic microorganisms; blood poisoning. Also **sep′ti·cae′mi·a.** [< Gk. *sēptikos* putrefactive + *haima* blood] —**sep′ti·ce′mic** (-sē′mik) *adj.*

septic tank A tank in which sewage is kept until purified by bacterial action.

sep·til·lion (sep·til′yən) *n.* A cardinal number written as 1 followed by 24 zeros. —**sep·til′lion, sep·til′lionth** *adj.*

sep·tu·a·ge·nar·i·an (sep′chōō·ə·jə·nâr′ē·ən, sep′tōō-) *n.* A person between 70 and 80 years of age. [< L *septuaginta* seventy] —**sep′tu·a·ge·nar′i·an** *adj.* —**sep′tu·ag′e·nar′y** (-aj′ə·ner′ē) *adj. & n.*

Sep·tu·a·gint (sep′chōō·ə·jint′, sep′tōō-) *n.* An old Greek version of the Old Testament Scriptures. [< L *septuaginta* seventy]

sep·tum (sep′təm) *n. pl.* **·ta** (-tə) *Biol.* A dividing wall between two cavities: the nasal *septum.* [< L *sepire* to enclose] —**sep′tal, sep′tate** (-tāt) *adj.*

sep·ul·cher (sep′əl·kər) *n.* 1. A burial place; tomb; vault. 2. A receptacle for relics, esp. in an altar slab. —*v.t.* **·chered** or **·chred, ·cher·ing** or **·chring** To place in a sepulcher; bury. Also *Brit.* **sep′ul·chre** (-kər). [< L *sepulcrum* burial place, tomb]

se·pul·chral (si·pul′krəl) *adj.* 1. Pertaining to a sepulcher. 2. Suggestive of the grave; dismal. 3. Unnaturally low and hollow in tone, as a voice. —**se·pul′chral·ly** *adv.*

sep·ul·ture (sep′əl·chər) *n.* 1. The act of entombing; burial. 2. *Archaic* A sepulcher.

se·quel (sē′kwəl) *n.* 1. Something that follows and serves as a continuation; a development from what went before. 2. A narrative discourse that, though complete in itself, develops from a preceding one. 3. A consequence; upshot; result. [< L *sequi* to follow]

se·quence (sē′kwəns) *n.* 1. The process or fact of following in space, time, or thought; succession or order. 2. Order of succession; arrangement. 3. A number of things following one another, considered collectively; a series. 4. An effect or consequence. 5. A section of motion-picture film presenting a single episode, without time lapses or interruptions. [< L *sequi* to follow] —**se·quen·tial** (si·kwen′shəl) *adj.* —**se·quen′tial·ly** *adv.*

se·quent (sē′kwənt) *adj.* 1. Following in the order of time; succeeding. 2. Consequent; resultant. [See SEQUENCE.]

se·ques·ter (si·kwes′tər) *v.t.* 1. To place apart; separate. 2. To seclude; withdraw: often used reflexively. [< LL *sequestrare* to remove, lay aside] —**se·ques′tra·ble** *adj.* —**se·ques′tered** *adj.*

se·ques·trate (si·kwes′trāt) *v.t.* **·trat·ed, ·trat·ing** 1. To seize, esp. for the use of the government; confiscate. 2. To seclude; sequester. —**se·ques·tra·tion** (sē′kwes·trā′·shən, sek′wəs-) *n.* —**se·ques·tra·tor** (sē′·kwes·trā′tər, si·kwes′trā·tər) *n.*

se·quin (sē′kwin) *n.* A small coinlike

ornament sewn on clothing. [< Arabic *sikka* coining-die]

se·quoi·a (si·kwoi′ə) *n.* 1. A gigantic evergreen tree of the western U.S.: also called *redwood.* 2. A closely related tree of the Sierra Nevada mountains of California, sometimes reaching a height of 300 feet. [after *Sequoyah,* 1770?–1843, a Cherokee Indian who invented the Cherokee alphabet]

ser- Var. of SERO-.

se·ra (sir′ə) Plural of SERUM.

se·ra·glio (si·ral′yō, -räl′-) *n.* The portion of a Muslim house reserved for the wives and concubines; a harem. Also **se·rail** (se·räl′). [< Ital. *serraglio* enclosure]

se·ra·pe (sə·räp′ē) *n.* A blanketlike outer garment worn in Latin America, esp. in Mexico. [< Am.Sp.]

ser·aph (ser′əf) *n. pl.* **ser·aphs** or **ser·a·phim** (ser′ə·fim) An angel having three pairs of wings. [Back formation < *seraphim,* pl. < Hebrew] —**se·raph·ic** (si·raf′ik) or **·i·cal** *adj.* —**se·raph′i·cal·ly** *adv.*

ser·a·phim (ser′ə·fim) *n.* 1. Plural of SERAPH: also **ser′a·phin** (-fin). 2. *pl.* **·phims** A seraph: an erroneous usage.

Ser·bo-Cro·a·tian (sûr′bō·krō·ā′shən) *n.* 1. The South Slavic language of Yugoslavia. 2. One whose native tongue is Serbo-Croatian. Also **Ser′bo-Cro′at** (-krō′at, -ət). —**Ser′bo-Cro·a′tion** *adj.*

sere[1] (sir) *adj.* Dried up; withered. Also spelled *sear.*

sere[2] (sir) *n. Ecol.* The series of changes found in a given plant formation from the initial to the ultimate stage. [Back formation < SERIES] —**ser′al** *adj.*

ser·e·nade (ser′ə·nād′) *n.* An evening song, usu. that of a lover beneath his sweetheart's window. —*v.t. & v.i.* **·nad·ed, ·nad·ing** To entertain with a serenade. [< L *serenus* clear, serene] —**ser′e·nad′er** *n.*

ser·e·na·ta (ser′ə·nä′tə) *n. pl.* **·tas** or **·te** (-tā) *Music* A dramatic cantata on any subject, often composed for a royal personage. [< Ital. See SERENADE.]

ser·en·dip·i·ty (ser′ən·dip′ə·tē) *n.* The faculty of happening upon fortunate discoveries when not in search of them. [Coined by Horace Walpole (1754), in *The Princes of Serendip* (Ceylon)] —**ser′en·dip′i·tous** *adj.*

se·rene (si·rēn′) *adj.* 1. Clear; calm: a *serene* sky. 2. Marked by peaceful repose; tranquil; placid: a *serene* spirit. 3. Of exalted rank, chiefly in titles: His *Serene* Highness. [< L *serenus*] —**se·rene′ly** *adv.* —**se·rene′·ness** *n.*

se·ren·i·ty (si·ren′ə·tē) *n. pl.* **·ties** 1. The state or quality of being serene; peacefulness; repose. 2. Clearness; brightness. 3. *Usu. cap.* A title of honor given to certain members of royal families: preceded by *His, Your,* etc.

serf (sûrf) *n.* 1. In feudal times, a person bound in servitude on an estate. 2. A slave. [< L *servus* slave] —**serf′age, serf′dom, serf′hood** *n.*

serge (sûrj) *n.* A strong twilled fabric, characterized by a diagonal rib on both sides of the cloth. [< L *serica* (*lana*) (wool) of the Seres, an eastern Asian people]

ser·geant (sär′jənt) *n.* 1. *Mil.* Any of several noncommissioned officer grades. 2. A police officer ranking next below a captain (sometimes lieutenant). Also, *esp. Brit., serjeant.* [< L *servire* to serve] —**ser′gean·cy, ser′geant·cy, ser′geant·ship** *n.*

sergeant at arms *pl.* **sergeants at arms** An executive officer in a legislative body who enforces order.

sergeant major *pl.* **sergeants major** A noncommissioned officer in the highest enlisted grade of the U.S. Army and Marine Corps.

se·ri·al (sir′ē·əl) *adj.* 1. Of the nature of a series. 2. Published in a series at regular intervals. 3. *Music* Relating to or composed by serialism. —*n.* A novel or other story presented in successive installments, as in a magazine, on television, etc. [< L *series* row, order] —**se′ri·al·ize′** *v.t.* **·ized, ·iz·ing** —**se′ri·al·i·za′tion** *n.* —**se′ri·al·ly** *adv.*

se·ri·al·ism (sir′ē·əl·iz′əm) *n. Music* The theory and practice of composition that uses all the tones of the twelve-tone scale in various sequences.

ser·i·cul·ture (sir′ə·kul′chər) *n.* The raising and care of silkworms for the production of raw silk. [< L *sericum* silk + *cultura* a raising, culture] —**ser′i·cul′tur·al** *adj.* —**ser′i·cul′tur·ist** *n.*

se·ries (sir′ēz) *n. pl.* **se·ries** 1. An arrangement of one thing after another; a connected succession of persons, things, data, etc. on the basis of like relationships. 2. *Electr.* An arrangement of sources or utilizers of electricity in which the positive electrode of one is connected with the negative electrode of another. [< L *serere* to join, weave together]

ser·if (ser′if) *n. Printing* A light line or stroke crossing or projecting from the end of a main line or stroke in a letter. [< L *scribere* to write]

ser·i·graph (ser′ə·graf) *n.* A handmade silk screen print designed and executed entirely by the artist. [< L *sericum* silk + -GRAPH] —**se·rig·ra·pher** (sə·rig′rə·fər) *n.* —**ser′i·graph′ic** *adj.* —**se·rig·ra·phy** (sə·rig′rə·fē) *n.*

se·ri·o·com·ic (sir′ē·ō·kom′ik) *adj.* Mingling the serious with the comic. Also **se′ri·o·com′·i·cal.**

se·ri·ous (sir′ē·əs) *adj.* 1. Grave and earnest in quality, feeling, or disposition; sober. 2. Said, planned, or done with full practical intent; being or done in earnest. 3. Of grave importance: a *serious* problem. 4. Attended with considerable danger or loss: a *serious* accident. [< L *serius*] —**se′ri·ous·ly** *adv.* —**se′ri·ous·ness** *n.*

ser·jeant (sär′jənt) See SERGEANT.

ser·mon (sûr′mən) *n.* 1. A discourse based on a passage or text of the Bible, delivered as part of a church service. 2. Any speech of a serious or solemn kind, as a formal exhortation. [< L *sermo, -onis* talk] —**ser·mon′ic** (-mon′ik) or **·i·cal** *adj.*

ser·mon·ize (sûr′mən·īz) *v.t. & v.i.* **·ized, ·iz·ing** 1. To compose or deliver a sermon (to). 2. To address at length in a moralizing manner. —**ser′mon·iz′er** *n.*

sero- *combining form* Connected with or related to serum. Also, before vowels, *ser-.* [< L *serum* whey]

se·rol·o·gy (si·rol′ə·jē) *n.* The science of serums and their actions. —**se·ro·log·i·cal** (sir′ə·loj′i·kəl) *adj.*

se·rous (sir′əs) *adj.* Pertaining to, containing or resembling serum. [< L *serum* whey]

serous membrane A membrane lining large cavities of the body.

ser·pent (sûr′pənt) *n.* 1. A scaly, limbless reptile; a snake. 2. Anything of serpentine form or appearance. [< L *serpere* to creep]

ser·pen·tine (sûr′pən·tēn, -tīn) *adj.* 1. Pertaining to or like a serpent; sinuous. 2. Sly; cunning. —*n.* A mottled green or yellow mineral, used as a source of asbestos, and as architecturally decorative stonework.

ser·rate (ser′āt, -it) *adj.* 1. Toothed or notched like a saw. 2. *Bot.* Having notched edges, as certain leaves. Also **ser·rat·ed** (sə·rā′tid). [< L *serra* saw] —**ser·ra·tion** (sə·rā′shən) *n.*

ser·ried (ser′ēd) *adj.* Compacted in rows or ranks, as soldiers in company formation. [< MF *serrer* to tighten]

se·rum (sir′əm) *n. pl.* **se·rums** or **se·ra** (sir′ə) 1. The clear, slightly yellow portion of an animal liquid, as blood, after separation from its solid constituents. 2. Loosely, an antiserum. [< L, whey, watery fluid]

ser·vant (sûr′vənt) *n.* A person hired to work for another, esp. to assist in domestic matters.

serve (sûrv) *v.* **served, serv·ing** *v.t.* 1. To work for, esp. as a servant; be in the service of. 2. To promote the interests of; aid. 3. To obey and give homage to: to *serve* God. 4. To satisfy the requirements of. 5. To perform the duties connected with, as a public office. 6. To go through (a period of enlistment, etc.). 7. To furnish or provide, as with a regular supply. 8. To offer or bring food or drink to (a guest, etc.). 9. In tennis, etc., to put (the ball) in play by hitting it to one's opponent. 10. *Law* a To deliver (a summons or writ) to a person. b To deliver a summons or writ to. —*v.i.* 11. To work as or perform the functions of a servant. 12. To wait at table; distribute food or drink. 13. To go through a term of service, as in the army or navy. 14. To be suitable or usable, as for a purpose. —*n.* 1. In tennis, etc., the delivering of the ball by striking it toward an opponent. 2. The turn of the server. [< L *servus* slave] —**serv′er** *n.*

ser·vice (sûr′vis) *n.* 1. Assistance or benefit afforded another. 2. The manner in which one is waited upon or served: The *service* in this restaurant is only fair. 3. A system of labor and material aids for the public or a portion of it: telephone *service*. 4. A division of public employment devoted to a particular function: the diplomatic *service*. 5. A public duty or function: jury *service*. 6. Any branch of the armed forces. 7. Military duty or assignment. 8. A formal and public exercise of worship. 9. A ritual prescribed for a particular ministration or observance: a marriage *service*. 10. The music for a liturgical office or rite. 11. The state or position of a servant, esp. a domestic servant. 12. A set of tableware for a specific purpose. 13. Installation, maintenance, and repair of an article provided a buyer by a seller. 14. In tennis, etc., the act or manner of serving a ball. —*adj.* 1. Pertaining to or for service. 2. For the use of servants or tradespeople: a *service* entrance. 3. Of, pertaining to, or belonging to a military service. —*v.t.* **·viced, ·vic·ing** 1. To maintain or repair. 2. To supply service to. [See SERVE.

ser·vice·a·ble (sûr′vis·ə·bəl) *adj.* 1. That can be made of service; beneficial; usable. 2. Capable of rendering long service; durable. —**ser′vice·a·bil′i·ty, ser′vice·a·ble·ness** *n.* —**ser′vice·a·bly** *adv.*

ser·vice·man (sûr′vis·man′) *n. pl.* **·men** (-men′) 1. A member of one of the armed forces. 2. A man who performs services of maintenance, supply, repair, etc. —**ser′vice·wom′an** (-wo͝om′ən) *n.fem.*

service station A place for supplying automobiles, trucks, etc., with gasoline, oil, water, etc. Also called *filling station, gas station.*

ser·vi·ette (sûr′vē·et′, -vyet′) *n. Brit.* A table napkin. [< MF, prob. < *servir* to serve]

ser·vile (sûr′vil, -vīl) *adj.* 1. Having the spirit of a slave; abject: a *servile* flatterer. 2. Being in a condition of servitude. [< L *servus* slave] —**ser′vile·ly** *adv.* —**ser′vile·ness, ser·vil·i·ty** (sûr·vil′ə·tē) *n.*

serv·ing (sûr′ving) *n.* A portion of food for one person. —*adj.* Used for serving food at table: a *serving* platter.

ser·vi·tor (sûr′və·tər) *n.* One who waits upon and serves another; esp. a male attendant; servant. —**ser′vi·tor·ship′** *n.*

ser·vi·tude (sûr′və·to͞od, -tyo͞od) *n.* 1. The condition of a slave; bondage. 2. Enforced service as a punishment for crime: penal *servitude.*

ser·vo (sûr′vō) *n. pl.* **·vos** Any of various relay devices used in the automatic control of a complex machine, instrument, operation, or process. Also **ser′vo·mech′a·nism** (-mek′·ə·niz′əm). [< L *servus* slave]

servo- *combining form* In technical use, auxiliary. [< L *servus* slave]

ser·vo·mo·tor (sûr′vō·mō′tər) *n.* An electric motor connected with and supplying power for a servo.

ses·a·me (ses′ə·mē) *n.* 1. An East Indian plant. 2. The seeds of this plant, used as food and as a source of **sesame oil,** an emollient: also **sesame seeds.** [< Gk. *sēsamon, sēsamē*]

sesqui- *prefix* One and a half; one and a half times: *sesquicentennial.* [< L *semis* half + *que* and]

ses·qui·cen·ten·ni·al (ses′kwi·sen·ten′ē·əl) *n.* A 150th anniversary, or its celebration. —**ses′qui·cen·ten′ni·al** *adj.*

ses·sile (ses′il) *adj. Bot.* Attached by its base, without a stalk, as a leaf. [< L *sessus*, pp. of *sedere* to sit] —**ses·sil′i·ty** *n.*

ses·sion (sesh′ən) *n.* 1. A meeting or series of meetings of a group of persons, convened for a specific purpose or activity. 2. A division of a school year; term. 3. A part of a day during which classes meet in a school. [< L *sessio, -onis* < *sedere* to sit] —**ses′·sion·al** *adj.*

set[1] (set) *v.* **set, set·ting** *v.t.* 1. To put in a certain place or position; place. 2. To put into a fixed or immovable position or state: to *set* one's jaw. 3. To bring to a specified state: to *set* a boat adrift. 4. To restore to proper position for healing, as a broken bone. 5. To place in readiness for operation or use: to *set* a trap. 6. To adjust (an instrument, dial, clock, etc.) to a particular calibration or position. 7. To place knives, forks, etc., on (a table) in preparing for a meal. 8. To appoint or establish: to *set* a date. 9. To assign to some specific duty or function;

station: to *set* a guard. 10. To cause to sit. 11. To present or perform so as to be copied or emulated: to *set* a bad example. 12. To direct: He *set* his course for the Azores. 13. To place in a mounting or frame, as a gem. 14. To arrange (hair) in waves, curls, etc., while moist. 15. To place (a hen) on eggs to hatch them. 16. To place (a price or value): with *by* or *on*. 17. *Printing* To arrange (type) for printing; compose. 18. *Music* To arrange an accompaniment for (words or music). 19. To describe (a scene) as taking place: to *set* the scene in Monaco. 20. In some games, as bridge, to defeat. —*v.i.* 21. To go or pass below the horizon, as the sun. 22. To wane; decline. 23. To sit on eggs, as fowl. 24. To become hard or firm; congeal. 25. To begin a journey; start: with *forth, out, off,* etc. 26. *Bot.* To begin development or growth, as a rudimentary fruit. 27. *Dial.* or *Illit.* To sit. —**to set about** To start doing; begin. —**to set aside** 1. To place apart or to one side. 2. To reject; dismiss. —**to set back** To reverse; hinder. —**to set down** 1. To place on a surface. 2. To write or print; record. 3. To judge or consider. —**to set forth** To state or declare; express. —**to set in** 1. To begin to occur: Rigor mortis *set in*. 2. To blow or flow toward shore, as wind or tide. —**to set off** 1. To serve as a contrast or foil for. 2. To cause to explode. —**to set out** 1. To present to view; exhibit. 2. To plant. 3. To start a journey, enterprise, etc. —**to set up** 1. To place in an upright position. 2. To place in power, authority, etc. 3. To construct or build; assemble. 4. To provide with the means to start a new business. 5. *Informal* To pay for the drinks, etc., of; treat. —*adj.* 1. Established by authority or agreement; appointed: a *set* time; a *set* method. 2. Customary; conventional: a *set* phrase. 3. Fixed and motionless; rigid. 4. Fixed in opinion or disposition. 5. Formed; made: with a qualifying adverb: *deep-set* eyes. 6. Ready; prepared: to get *set*. —*n.* 1. The act or condition of setting. 2. Permanent change of form, as by chemical action, cooling, pressure, etc. 3. The arrangement, tilt, or hang of a garment, sail, etc. 4. Carriage or bearing: the *set* of his shoulders. 5. The direction of a current or wind. 6. A young plant for setting out; a cutting, slip, or seedling. 7. A group of games constituting a division of a tennis match. [OE *settan* to cause to sit]

set² (set) *n.* 1. A number of persons regarded as associated through status, common interests, special characteristics, etc. 2. A number of things belonging together and customarily used together: a *set* of dishes. 3. A group of volumes issued together. 4. In motion pictures, television, etc., the properties, structures, etc., required in a scene. 5. Radio or television receiving equipment assembled for use. 6. *Math.* An array of objects, quantities, magnitudes, etc.: the *set* of integers. [< L *secta* sect]

se·ta (sē′tə) *n. pl.* **·tae** (-tē) 1. A bristle, or slender, bristlelike part, as a spine or prickle. 2. A coarse, rigid hair. [< L] —**se·ta·ceous** (si·tā′shəs) *adj.*

set·back (set′bak′) *n.* 1. An unexpected reverse or relapse. 2. *Archit.* In tall buildings, the stepping of upper sections so that they progressively recede from the street line.

seti- *combining form* A bristle. Also, before vowels, **set-**. [< L *seta*]

set·screw (set′skrōō′) *n.* A screw used as a clamp, esp. one used to screw through one part and slightly into another to bind the parts tightly.

set·tee (se·tē′) *n.* 1. A long wooden seat with a high back. 2. A sofa suitable for two or three people. [< SET¹ or SET(TLE), n. + -*ee*, dim. suffix]

set·ter (set′ər) *n.* One of a breed of medium-sized, silky-coated, lithe hunting dogs trained to indicate the presence of game birds by standing rigid.

set·ting (set′ing) *n.* 1. That in which something is set; a frame or mounting. 2. The music adapted to a song or poem. 3. The scene or background of a play or narrative. 4. The apparent sinking of the sun, etc., below the horizon. 5. The tableware set out for one person.

set·tle (set′l) *v.* **·tled, ·tling** *v.t.* 1. To put in order; set to rights. 2. To put firmly in place: He *settled* himself on the couch. 3. To free of agitation or disturbance; quiet: to *settle* one's nerves. 4. To make clear or transparent, as by causing sediment to sink. 5. *Informal* To make quiet or orderly: One blow *settled* him. 6. To decide or determine finally, as an argument. 7. To pay, as a debt; satisfy, as a claim. 8. To establish residents or residence in (a country, town, etc.). 9. To establish in a permanent occupation, home, etc. 10. To decide (a suit at law) by agreement between the litigants. 11. *Law* To make over or assign (property) by legal act: with *on* or *upon*. —*v.i.* 12. To come to rest, as after moving about or flying. 13. To sink or come to rest, as dust or sediment. 14. To become more firm or compact. 15. To become clear or transparent, as by the sinking of sediment. 16. To take up residence. 17. To come to a decision; resolve: with *on, upon,* or *with*. 18. To pay a bill, etc. —**to settle down** To start living a regular, orderly life, esp. after a period of wandering or irresponsibility. —*n.* A long seat or bench, generally of wood, with a high back. [OE *setl* seat, *setlan* to seat]

set·tle·ment (set′l·mənt) *n.* 1. The act of settling, or the state of being settled; esp., an adjustment of affairs by public authority. 2. The settling of a new region; colonization. 3. An area of country newly occupied by those who intend to live and labor there; a colony. 4. An accounting; adjustment; liquidation in regard to amounts. 5. The conveyance of property in such form as to provide for financial support, etc.; also, the property so settled. 6. A welfare institution established in a city, that conducts educational and recreational activities for the community: also **settlement house**.

set·tler (set′lər) *n.* One who settles; esp., one who establishes himself in a colony or new country; a colonist.

set-to (set′tōō′) *n. pl.* **-tos** A bout at fighting, arguing, etc.

set·up (set′up′) *n.* 1. *Informal* The overall scheme or pattern of organization or construction; circumstances. 2. *Slang* A contest or match arranged to result in an easy victory.

3. *Informal* Ice, soda water, etc., provided for use in alcoholic drinks.

sev·en (sev′ən) *n.* The sum of six and one: a cardinal number written 7, VII. [OE *seofon*] **—sev′en** *adj.*

sev·en·teen (sev′ən·tēn′) *n.* The sum of sixteen and one: a cardinal number written 17, XVII. [OE *seofontiene*] **—sev′en·teen′** *adj.* **—sev′en·teenth′** *adj. & n.*

sev·en·teen-year locust (sev′ən·tēn′yir′) A dark-bodied, wedge-shaped cicada native to the eastern U.S., having an underground nymphal stage of from 13 to 17 years.

sev·enth (sev′ənth) *adj.* 1. Next after the sixth: the ordinal of *seven.* 2. Being one of seven equal parts. **—***n.* 1. One of seven equal parts. 2. That which follows the sixth. 3. *Music* The interval between any tone and the seventh tone above it in the diatonic scale. **—***adv.* In the seventh order, place, or rank: also, in formal discourse, **sev′enth·ly.**

sev·enth-day (sev′ənth·dā′) *adj.* 1. Pertaining to the seventh day of the week. 2. *Often cap.* Advocating the observance of this day as the Sabbath: a *Seventh-Day* Adventist.

Seventh-Day Adventist See under ADVENTIST.

sev·en·ty (sev′ən·tē) *n. pl.* **·ties** The sum of sixty and ten: a cardinal number written 70, LXX. [OE *(hund-) seofontig*] **—sev′en·ti·eth** *adj. & n.* **—sev′en·ty** *adj.*

sev·er (sev′ər) *v.t. & v.i.* To divide; separate; break off. [< L *separare* to separate] **—sev′er·a·ble** *adj.*

sev·er·al (sev′ər·əl, sev′rəl) *adj.* 1. More than two, yet not many. 2. Considered individually; single; separate. 3. Individually different; various or diverse. **—***n.* Several persons or things. [< L *separ* separate] **—sev′er·al·ly** *adv.*

sev·er·ance (sev′ər·əns, sev′rəns) *n.* 1. The act of severing, or the condition of being severed. 2. Separation; partition. 3. The additional money given an employee when he leaves a job: also **severance pay.**

se·vere (si·vir′) *adj.* **·ver·er, ·ver·est** 1. Rigorous in the treatment of others; unsparing. 2. Serious and austere in disposition or manner. 3. Causing extreme anguish or hardship: a *severe* pain; a *severe* storm. [< L *severus*] **—se·vere′ly** *adv.* **—se·vere′·ness** *n.*

se·ver·i·ty (si·ver′ə·tē) *n. pl.* **·ties** 1. The quality of being severe. 2. Harshness or cruelty of disposition or treatment. 3. Seriousness; austerity. 4. Strict conformity to truth or law.

sew (sō) *v.* **sewed, sewed** or **sewn, sew·ing** *v.t.* 1. To make, mend, or fasten with needle and thread. **—***v.i.* 2. To work with needle and thread. **—to sew up** *Informal* To conclude (a deal, etc.). [OE *siwian*] **—sew′er** *n.*

sew·age (sōō′ij) *n.* The waste matter from domestic, commercial, and industrial establishments carried off in sewers.

sew·er (sōō′ər) *n.* 1. A conduit, usu. laid underground, to carry off drainage and wastes. 2. Any large public drain. [< MF *essewer* to drain]

sew·er·age (sōō′ər·ij) *n.* 1. A system of sewers. 2. Systematic draining by sewers. 3. Sewage.

sew·ing (sō′ing) *n.* 1. The act or occupation of one who sews. 2. That which is sewed.

sewing machine A machine for stitching or sewing.

sewn (sōn) Alternative past participle of SEW.

sex (seks) *n.* 1. Either of two divisions, male and female, by which organisms are distinguished with reference to the reproductive functions. 2. The character of being male or female. 3. *Informal* Sexual intercourse. [< OF < L, prob. orig. < *secare* to divide] **—sex′less** *adj.* **—sex′less·ness** *n.*

sex- *combining form* Six: also **sexi-.** [< L *sex*]

sex·a·ge·nar·i·an (sek′sə·jə·nâr′ē·ən) *n.* A person between 60 and 70 years of age. [< L *sexaginta* sixty] **—sex′a·ge·nar′i·an** *adj.* **—sex·ag·e·nar·y** (seks·aj′ə·ner′ē) *adj. & n.*

sex chromosome *Genetics* A chromosome whose presence in the reproductive cells of certain plants and animals is associated with the determination of the sex of offspring.

sex·ism (seks′iz·əm) *n.* Prejudice against either sex, esp. against women. [< SEX + -ISM, on analogy with *racism*] **—sex′ist** *n. & adj.*

sext (sekst) *n. Often cap. Eccl.* The fourth of the seven canonical hours. [< L *sexta (hora)* the sixth (hour)]

sex·tant (seks′tənt) *n.* An instrument for measuring angular distance between two objects, as a heavenly body and the horizon, used esp. in determining latitude at sea. [< L *sextus* sixth]

sex·tet (seks·tet′) *n.* 1. *Music* A group of six singers or players; also, a musical composition for six performers. 2. Any collection of six persons or things. Also **sex·tette′.**

sex·til·lion (seks·til′yən) *n.* A cardinal number written as 1 followed by 21 zeros. **—sex·til′lion, sex·til′lionth** *adj. & n.*

sex·ton (seks′tən) *n.* One having charge of the maintenance of church property. [< Med.L *sacristanus*] **—sex′ton·ship** *n.*

sex·tu·ple (seks·tup′əl, -tōō′pəl) *v.t. & v.i.* **·pled, ·pling** To multiply by six; make or become six times larger. **—***adj.* 1. Consisting of or multiplied by six. 2. *Music* Having six beats to the measure. **—***n.* A number six times as great as another. [< L *sex* six, on analogy with *quadruple*]

sex·tu·plet (seks·tup′lit, -tōō′plit) *n.* One of six offspring produced at a single birth. [< SEXTUPLE, on analogy with *triplet*]

sex·u·al (sek′shōō·əl) *adj.* 1. Of, pertaining to, or characteristic of sex, the sexes, or the organs or functions of sex. 2. *Biol.* Designating a type of reproduction involving both sexes. [< L *sexus* sex] **—sex′u·al′i·ty** (-al′ə·tē) *n.* **—sex′u·al·ly** *adv.*

sexual intercourse Sexual connection, esp. of humans; copulation.

sex·y (sek′sē) *adj.* **sex·i·er, sex·i·est** *Slang* Provocative of sexual desire; erotic. **—sex′i·ness** *n.*

shab·by (shab′ē) *adj.* **·bi·er, ·bi·est** 1. Threadbare; ragged. 2. Wearing worn or seedy garments. 3. Mean; paltry. [OE *sceabb* scab] **—shab′bi·ly** *adv.* **—shab′bi·ness** *n.*

shack (shak) *n. Informal* A rude cabin, as of logs. [? < dial. Sp. (Mexican) *jacal* wooden hut]

shack·le (shak′əl) *n.* 1. A ring, clasp, or braceletlike fastening for encircling and fettering a limb. 2. Impediment or restraint. 3. One of various forms of fastenings. —*v.t.* **·led, ·ling** To restrain or confine with or as with shackles. [OE *sceacul*] —**shack′ler** *n.*

shad (shad) *n. pl.* **shad** Any of several food fishes related to the herring. [OE *sceadd*]

shade (shād) *v.* **shad·ed, shad·ing** *v.t.* 1. To screen from light by intercepting its rays. 2. To make dim; darken. 3. To screen or protect with or as with a shade. 4. To cause to change by gradations. 5. In graphic arts: **a** To represent (degrees of shade, colors, etc.) by gradations of light or dark lines or shading. **b** To represent varying shades, colors, etc., in (a picture, etc.) thus. —*v.i.* 6. To change or vary by degrees. —*n.* 1. Relative obscurity due to interception of the rays of light. 2. A shady place; secluded retreat. 3. A screen that shuts off light, heat, dust, etc. 4. A gradation of color; also, slight degree; minute difference. 5. A disembodied spirit; ghost. 6. *pl. Slang* Sunglasses. [OE *sceadu*] —**shade′less** *adj.*

shad·ing (shā′ding) *n.* The lines, dots, etc., by which degrees of darkness, color, or depth are represented in a picture.

shad·ow (shad′ō) *n.* 1. A comparative darkness within an illuminated area, esp. that caused by the interception of light by a body. 2. The dark image thus produced representing the approximate shape of the intercepting body. 3. The shaded portion of a picture. 4. A delusive image or semblance. 5. A phantom; ghost; shade. 6. A remnant; vestige. 7. Gloom; a saddening influence. 8. An inseparable companion. —*v.t.* 1. To cast a shadow upon. 2. To darken; make gloomy. 3. To follow closely or secretly. 4. To shade in painting, etc. [OE *sceadu* shade] —**shad′ow·er** *n.* —**shad′ow·less** *adj.*

shad·ow·box (shad′ō·boks′) *v.i.* To spar with an imaginary opponent as a form of exercise. —**shad′ow·box′ing** *n.*

shad·ow·y (shad′ō·ē) *adj.* **·ow·i·er, ·ow·i·est** 1. Full of or providing shadow. 2. Vague; dim. 3. Unsubstantial or illusory. —**shad′ow·i·ness** *n.*

shad·y (shā′dē) *adj.* **shad·i·er, shad·i·est** 1. Full of shade; casting a shade. 2. Shaded, sheltered, or hidden. 3. *Informal* Questionable as to honesty or legality; dubious. —**on the shady side of** Older than; past the age of. —**shad′i·ly** *adv.* —**shad′i·ness** *n.*

shaft[1] (shaft) *n.* 1. The long narrow rod of an arrow, spear, etc. 2. An arrow. 3. Anything resembling a missile in appearance or effect: *shafts* of ridicule. 4. A beam of light. 5. A long handle, as of a hammer, etc. 6. *Mech.* A long bar, esp. if rotating and transmitting motive power. 7. *Archit.* The portion of a column between capital and base. 8. An obelisk or memorial column. 9. One of two poles by which a horse is harnessed to a vehicle. [OE *sceat*]

shaft[2] (shaft) *n.* 1. A narrow, vertical or inclined, excavation connected with a mine. 2. An opening through the floors of a building, as for an elevator. [< LG *schacht* rod, shaft]

shag (shag) *n.* 1. A rough coat or mass, as of hair. 2. Cloth having a rough or long nap. 3. A coarse, strong tobacco: also **shag tobacco.** —*v.t.* **shagged, shag·ging** To make shaggy; roughen. [OE *sceacga* rough hair, wool]

shag·gy (shag′ē) *adj.* **·gi·er, ·gi·est** 1. Having, consisting of, or resembling rough hair or wool; rugged; rough. 2. Covered with any rough, tangled growth; fuzzy; scrubby. 3. Unkempt. —**shag′gi·ly** *adv.* —**shag′gi·ness** *n.*

shah (shä) *n.* An eastern king or ruler, esp. of Iran. [< Persian *shāh*]

shake (shāk) *v.* **shook, shak·en, shak·ing** *v.t.* 1. To cause to move to and fro or up and down with short, rapid movements. 2. To affect in a specified manner by or as by vigorous action: with *off, out, from,* etc. 3. To cause to tremble or quiver; vibrate. 4. To weaken or disturb: I could not *shake* his determination. 5. To agitate or rouse: often with *up.* 6. *Slang* To get rid of or away from. —*v.i.* 7. To move to and fro or up and down in short, rapid movements. 8. To be affected in a specified way by vigorous action: with *off, out, from,* etc. 9. To tremble or quiver, as from cold or fear. —**to shake down** 1. To cause to fall by shaking; bring down. 2. To cause to settle. 3. *Slang* To extort money from. —**to shake off** To rid oneself of by or as by shaking. —**to shake up** 1. To shake, mix, or stir. 2. *Informal* To shock or jar mentally or physically. —*n.* 1. A shaking; agitation; jolt. 2. The state of being shaken. 3. *pl. Informal* Trembling, as with a chill or fever. 4. *Informal* Treatment: a fair *shake.* —**no great shakes** *Informal* Of no great importance; mediocre. [OE *scacan*] —**shak′a·ble, shake′a·ble** *adj.*

shake·down (shāk′doun′) *n. Slang* A swindle; extortion. —*adj. Informal* For the purpose of adjusting mechanical parts or habituating people: a *shakedown* cruise.

shak·er (shā′kər) *n.* 1. One who or that which shakes. 2. A container for shaking or pouring something: cocktail *shaker.*

Shak·er (shā′kər) *n.* One of a sect practicing celibacy and communal living: so called from their characteristic bodily movements during religious meetings. —**Shak′er** *adj.* —**Shak′er·ism** *n.*

Shake·spear·e·an (shāk·spir′ē·ən) *adj.* Of, pertaining to, or characteristic of Shakespeare, his work, or his style. —*n.* A specialist on Shakespeare or his writings. Also **Shake·spear′i·an.** —**Shake·spear′e·an·ism** *n.*

shake·up (shāk′up′) *n.* A radical change of personnel or organization, as in a business office, etc.

shak·y (shā′kē) *adj.* **shak·i·er, shak·i·est** 1. Habitually shaking or tremulous; tottering; weak; unsound. 2. Wavering; unreliable. —**shak′i·ly** *adv.* —**shak′i·ness** *n.*

shale (shāl) *n.* A claylike rock resembling slate. —**shal′y** *adj.*

shall (shal) *v.* Present **shall;** past **should** A defective verb having a past tense that is now used only as an auxiliary to express simple futurity, determination, command, etc.

shal·lop (shal′əp) *n.* An open boat propelled by oars or sails. [< Du. *sloep*]

shal·lot (shə·lot′) *n.* An onionlike vegetable, allied to garlic but having milder bulbs that are used in seasoning. [< OF *eschalotte*]

shal·low (shal′ō) *adj.* 1. Having the bottom not far below the surface; lacking depth. 2. Lacking intellectual depth; not wise; superficial. —*n.* A shallow place in a body of water; shoal. —*v.t.* & *v.i.* To make or become shallow. [ME *schalowe*] —**shal′·low·ly** *adv.* —**shal′low·ness** *n.*

shalt (shalt) Archaic or poetic second person singular, present tense of SHALL: used with *thou.*

sham (sham) *v.* **shammed, sham·ming** *v.t.* 1. To assume or present the appearance of; counterfeit; feign. 2. To represent oneself as; pretend to be. —*v.i.* 3. To make false pretenses. —*adj.* False; counterfeit. —*n.* 1. A pretense; imposture; deception. 2. One who simulates a certain character; a pretender: also **sham′mer.** 3. A deceptive imitation. [Prob. dial. var. of SHAME]

sha·man (shä′mən, shā′-) *n.* A North American Indian medicine man. [< Skt. *śamana* ascetic] —**sha′man, sha·man·ic** (shə·man′ik) *adj.*

sham·ble (sham′bəl) *v.i.* **·bled, ·bling** To walk with shuffling or unsteady gait. —*n.* A shambling walk. [Origin uncertain]

sham·bles (sham′bəlz) *n.pl.* (*usu. construed as sing.*) 1. A place where butchers kill animals; slaughterhouse. 2. A place marked by great destruction or disorder. [< L *scamnum* bench, stool]

shame (shām) *n.* 1. A painful sense of guilt or degradation caused by consciousness of guilt or of anything degrading, unworthy, or immodest. 2. A state of dishonor or disgrace. —**to put to shame** 1. To disgrace; make ashamed. 2. To surpass or eclipse. —*v.t.* **shamed, sham·ing** 1. To make ashamed; cause to feel shame. 2. To bring shame upon; disgrace. [OE *scamu*] —**shame′ful** *adj.* —**shame′ful·ly** *adv.* —**shame′ful·ness** *n.*

shame·faced (shām′fāst′) *adj.* Easily abashed; showing shame or bashfulness in one's face; modest; bashful. [OE *scamfæst* abashed] —**shame·face·ed·ly** (shām′fā′·sid·lē, shām′fāst′lē) *adv.* —**shame′fac′ed·ness** *n.*

shame·less (shām′lis) *adj.* 1. Impudent; brazen; immodest. 2. Done without shame; indicating a want of pride or decency. —**shame′less·ly** *adv.* —**shame′less·ness** *n.*

sham·my (sham′ē), **sham·ois** (sham′ē) See CHAMOIS.

sham·poo (sham·pōō′) *n.* 1. A liquid preparation of soap, detergent, etc., used to cleanse the hair and scalp. 2. The act or process of shampooing. —*v.t.* To cleanse (the hair and scalp) with a shampoo. [< Hind. *chāmpnā* to press] —**sham·poo′er** *n.*

sham·rock (sham′rok) *n.* A plant with three leaflets, accepted as the national emblem of Ireland. [< Irish *seamar* trefoil]

shang·hai (shang′hī, shang·hī′) *v.t.* **·haied, ·hai·ing** 1. To drug or render unconscious and kidnap for service aboard a ship. 2. To cause to do something by force or deception. [after *Shanghai*, China]

Shan·gri-la (shang′gri·lä′) *n.* Any imaginary hidden utopia or paradise. [after the locale of James Hilton's novel *Lost Horizon* (1933)]

shank (shangk) *n.* 1. The part of the leg between the knee and the ankle. 2. A cut of meat from the leg of an animal; the shin. 3. The part of a tool connecting the handle with the working part. 4. The chief or best part: the *shank* of the evening. [OE *scanca*]

shan't (shant, shänt) Shall not.

shan·tung (shan′tung, shan·tung′) *n.* A fabric with a rough, nubby surface, originally of wild silk. [after *Shantung*, China]

shan·ty (shan′tē) *n. pl.* **·ties** A hastily built shack or cabin; a ramshackle dwelling. [< F (Canadian) *chantier* lumberer's shack]

shape (shāp) *n.* 1. Outward appearance or construction. 2. A developed expression or definite formulation; cast: to put an idea into *shape.* 3. A phantom. 4. A pattern or mold; in millinery, a stiff frame. 5. The lines of a person's body; figure. 6. Condition: Everything is in good *shape.* —**to take shape** To have or assume a definite form. —*v.* **shaped, shap·ing** *v.t.* 1. To give shape to; mold. 2. To adjust or adapt; modify. 3. To devise; prepare. 4. To give direction or character to. —*v.i.* 5. To take shape; develop; form: often with *up* or *into.* —**to shape up** *Informal* 1. To proceed satisfactorily or favorably. 2. To improve one's behavior, work, etc. [OE *sceippan* to create] —**shaped** *adj.* —**shap′er** *n.*

shape·less (shāp′lis) *adj.* Having no definite shape; lacking symmetry. —**shape′less·ly** *adv.* —**shape′less·ness** *n.*

shape·ly (shāp′lē) *adj.* **·li·er, ·li·est** Having a pleasing shape; well-formed; graceful. —**shape′li·ness** *n.*

shard (shärd) *n.* A broken piece of a brittle substance, as of an earthen vessel; a potsherd; a fragment: also called *sherd.* [OE *sceard*]

share (shâr) *n.* 1. A portion; allotted or equitable part. 2. One of the equal parts into which the capital stock of a company or corporation is divided. —**to go shares** To partake equally, as in an enterprise. —*v.* **shared, shar·ing** *v.t.* 1. To divide and give out in shares or portions; apportion. 2. To enjoy or endure in common; participate in. —*v.i.* 3. To have a part; participate: with *in.* [OE *scieran* to shear] —**shar′er** *n.*

share·crop·per (shâr′krop′ər) *n.* A tenant farmer who pays a share of his crop as rent for his land.

share·hold·er (shâr′hōl′dər) *n.* One who owns stock in a company.

shark[1] (shärk) *n.* One of a group of generally large marine fishes, having dun-colored bodies covered with platelike scales. [Origin uncertain]

shark[2] (shärk) *n.* A greedy and dishonest person: a loan *shark.* Also **shark′er.** —*v.i.* To live by trickery. [Prob. < G *schürke* scoundrel; infl. by SHARK[1]]

shark·skin (shärk′skin′) *n.* A fabric with a smooth, almost shiny surface.

sharp (shärp) *adj.* 1. Having a keen edge or an acute point. 2. Keen of perception or discernment; also, shrewd and artful. 3. Affecting the mind or senses, as if by cutting or piercing; poignant; acrimonious. 4. Shrill. 5. Pinching; cutting, as cold. 6. Having an acrid or pungent taste. 7. Distinct, as an outline. 8. *Music* **a** Raised in pitch by a semitone. **b** Above the right, true pitch. —*adv.* 1. In a sharp manner; sharply. 2. Promptly; exactly: at 4 o'clock *sharp.* 3. *Music* Above the proper pitch. —*n.* 1. *Music* A sign (♯) placed before a note to indicate that the note is sharped. 2. A cheat:

a *cardsharp.* —*v.t. Music* To raise in pitch, as by a half step. [OE *scearp*] —**sharp′ly** *adv.* —**sharp′ness** *n.*

sharp·en (shär′pən) *v.t. & v.i.* To make or become sharp. —**sharp′en·er** *n.*

sharp·er (shär′pər) *n.* A swindler; cheat.

sharp·ie (shär′pē) *n.* 1. A long, sharp, flat-bottomed sailboat having a centerboard and one or two masts, each having a triangular sail, originally used for fishing. 2. *Informal* An alert, intelligent person: also **sharp′y.** [< SHARP]

sharp·shoot·er (shärp′shōō′tər) *n.* A skilled marksman, esp. in the use of the rifle. —**sharp′shoot′ing** *n.*

shat·ter (shat′ər) *v.t.* 1. To break into pieces suddenly, as by a blow. 2. To break the health or tone of, as the body or mind. —*v.i.* 3. To break into pieces; burst. [ME *schateren*]

shave (shāv) *v.* **shaved, shaved** or **shav·en, shav·ing** *v.i.* 1. To cut hair, esp. the beard, close to the skin with a razor. —*v.t.* 2. To remove hair from (the face, head, etc.) with a razor. 3. To cut thin slices from, as in preparing the surface; pare; plane. 4. To cut into thin slices. 5. To touch or scrape in passing; graze; come close to. —*n.* 1. The act or operation of cutting off the beard with a razor. 2. A knife or blade, mounted between two handles, as for shaving wood: also **draw shave, spoke shave.** —**a close shave** *Informal* A narrow escape. [OE *scafan*]

shave·ling (shāv′ling) *n.* A youth.

shav·en (shā′vən) Alternative past participle of SHAVE. —*adj.* 1. Shaved; also, tonsured. 2. Trimmed closely.

shav·ing (shā′ving) *n.* 1. The act of one who or that which shaves. 2. A thin paring shaved from anything, as a board.

shawl (shôl) *n.* A wrap, as a square cloth, or large scarf, worn over the upper part of the body. [< Persian *shāl*]

Shaw·nee (shô·nē′) *n.* One of a tribe of Algonquian Indians, now living in Oklahoma. [< Algonquian (Shawnee) *Shawunogi* southerners]

shay (shā) See CHAISE.

she (shē) *pron., possessive* **her** or **hers,** *objective* **her;** *pl. nominative* **they,** *possessive* **their** or **theirs,** *objective* **them** The nominative singular pronoun of the third person, used of the female person or animal previously mentioned, or of things conventionally regarded as feminine, as ships. —*n. pl.* **shes** A female person or animal. [OE *sēo, sīo*]

she- *combining form* Female; feminine: in hyphenated compounds: a *she-lion; she-devil.*

sheaf (shēf) *n. pl.* **sheaves** (shēvz) 1. A quantity of the stalks of cut grain or the like, bound together. 2. Any collection of things, as papers, tied together. 3. A quiverful of arrows. —*v.t.* To bind in a sheaf. [OE *scēaf*]

shear (shir) *n.* 1. *Physics* A deformation of a solid body, equivalent to a sliding over each other of adjacent layers: also **shearing stress.** 2. The act or result of shearing. —*v.* **sheared, sheared** or **shorn, shear·ing** *v.t.* 1. To cut the hair, fleece, etc., from. 2. To deprive; strip, as of wealth. 3. To cut or clip with or as with shears. —*v.i.* 4. To use shears. 5. To proceed by or as by cutting a way: with *through.* [OE *scieran* to shear] —**shear′er** *n.*

shears (shirz) *n.pl.* 1. Any large cutting or clipping instrument worked by the crossing of cutting edges. Also **pair of shears.** 2. The ways or guides, as of a lathe. [See SHEAR.]

sheath (shēth) *n. pl.* **sheaths** (shē*th*z, shēths) 1. An envelope or case, as for a sword; scabbard. 2. A close-fitting dress having straight, unbroken lines. —*v.t.* To sheathe. [OE *scæth*] —**sheath′less** *adj.*

sheathe (shē*th*) *v.t.* **sheathed, sheath·ing** 1. To put into a sheath. 2. To encase or protect with a covering. [< SHEATH]

sheath·ing (shē′*th*ing) *n.* 1. A protective covering, as of a ship's hull. 2. The covering or waterproof material on outside walls or roofs.

sheave[1] (shēv) *v.t.* **sheaved, sheav·ing** To gather into sheaves; collect. [< SHEAF]

sheave[2] (shēv) *n.* A grooved pulley wheel; also, a pulley wheel and its block. [ME *schive*]

sheaves (shēvz) Plural of SHEAF.

she·bang (shi·bang′) *n. Slang* Matter; affair: tired of the whole *shebang.*

shed[1] (shed) *v.* **shed, shed·ding** *v.t.* 1. To pour forth in drops; emit, as tears. 2. To cause to pour forth. 3. To send forth; radiate. 4. To throw off without allowing to penetrate, as rain; repel. 5. To cast off by natural process, as hair, etc. 6. To rid oneself of. —*v.i.* 7. To cast off or lose skin, etc., by natural process. —**to shed blood** To kill. —*n.* That which sheds, as a sloping surface or watershed. [OE *scēadan* to separate, part] —**shed′der** *n.*

shed[2] (shed) *n.* 1. A small low building, often with front or sides open; also, a lean-to: a wagon *shed.* 2. *Brit.* A barn. [Var. of SHADE]

she'd (shēd) 1. She had. 2. She would.

sheen (shēn) *n.* A glistening brightness, as if from reflection. —*v.i.* To shine; glisten. [OE *sciene* beautiful] —**sheen′y** *adj.*

sheep (shēp) *n. pl.* **sheep** 1. A medium-sized, domesticated, even-toed ruminant, bred in many varieties for its flesh, wool, and skin. ◆Collateral adjective: *ovine.* 2. A meek, bashful, or timid person. [OE *scēap*]

sheep dip A liquid disinfectant into which sheep are immersed.

sheep dog A dog trained to guard and control sheep, often a collie, but also an **Old English sheep dog,** a rough-coated, heavy, bobtailed dog much used by drovers in England: also called *shepherd dog, shepherd's dog.*

sheep·fold (shēp′fōld′) *n.* A pen for sheep.

sheep·herd·er (shēp′hûr′dər) *n.* A herder of sheep. —**sheep′herd′ing** *n.*

sheep·ish (shē′pish) *adj.* Foolish, as a sheep; awkwardly diffident; abashed. —**sheep′ish·ly** *adv.* —**sheep′ish·ness** *n.*

sheep's eyes (shēps) Bashful or amorous glances.

sheep·skin (shēp′skin′) *n.* 1. The skin of a sheep, tanned or untanned, or anything made from it. 2. A document written on parchment, as an academic diploma.

sheer[1] (shir) *v.i.* 1. To swerve from a course; turn aside. —*v.t.* 2. To cause to swerve. —*n.* A swerving course. [< SHEAR]

sheer[2] (shir) *adj.* 1. Having no modifying conditions; pure, absolute: *sheer* folly. 2. Exceedingly thin and fine: said of fabrics. 3. Perpendicular; steep. —*n.* Any very thin fabric used for clothes. —*adv.* Steeply;

perpendicularly. [ME *schere*] **—sheer′ness** *n.* **—sheer′ly** *adv.*
sheet (shēt) *n.* 1. A very thin and broad piece of any substance; as: **a** A large rectangular piece of bed linen. **b** A newspaper. **c** A piece of metal or other substance hammered, rolled, or cut very thin. 2. A broad, flat surface; superficial expanse: a *sheet* of water. 3. *Naut.* **a** A rope or chain from a lower corner of a sail to extend it or move it. **b** *pl.* In an open boat, the space at the bow and stern not occupied by the thwarts. **c** A sail. **—three sheets in (or to) the wind** *Slang* Drunk. **—*v.t.*** To cover with a sheet. [OE *scȳte* linen cloth]
sheet·ing (shē′ting) *n.* Cotton, muslin, etc., used for making sheets for beds.
sheet lightning Lightning appearing in sheetlike form as a momentary and broadly diffused radiance in the sky, caused by the reflection of a distant lightning flash.
sheet metal Metal rolled and pressed into sheets.
sheet music Music printed on unbound sheets of paper.
sheik (shēk, *also for def. 1* shāk) *n.* 1. A Muslim high priest or a venerable man; also, the chief or head of an Arab tribe or family. 2. *Slang* A man who fascinates women. Also **sheikh.** [< Arabic *sheikh, shaykh,* lit., an elder, chief]
sheik·dom (shēk′dəm, shāk′-) *n.* The land ruled by a sheik. Also **sheikh′dom.**
shek·el (shek′əl) *n.* 1. An Assyrian, Babylonian, and, later, Hebrew unit of weight and money; also, a coin having this weight. 2. *pl. Slang* Money. [< Hebrew *shāqal* to weigh]
shelf (shelf) *n. pl.* **shelves** (shelvz) 1. A board or slab set horizontally against a wall, in a bookcase, etc., to support articles, as books. 2. Contents of a shelf. 3. Any flat projecting ledge, as of rock. 4. A reef; shoal. **—on the shelf** No longer in use. [< LG *schelf* set of shelves]
shell (shel) *n.* 1. Any of various hard structures encasing an animal, as a mollusk or other shellfish. 2. The relatively hard covering of a fruit, nut, egg, etc. 3. A hollow structure or vessel, generally thin and weak; also, a case or mold for holding something: a pie *shell.* 4. A very light, long, and narrow racing rowboat. 5. A hollow metallic projectile filled with an explosive or chemical. 6. A shape or outline that merely simulates a reality; hollow form; external semblance. **—*v.t.*** 1. To divest of or remove from a shell. 2. To separate from the cob, as corn. 3. To bombard with shells, as a fort. **—*v.i.*** 4. To shed the shell or pod. **—to shell out** *Informal* To hand over, as money. [OE *sciell*] **—shell′er** *n.* **—shell′y** *adj.*
she'll (shēl) She will.
shel·lac (shə·lak′) *n.* 1. A purified lac in the form of thin flakes, extensively used in varnish, sealing wax, insulators, etc. 2. A varnishlike solution of flake shellac, used for coating floors, woodwork, etc. **—*v.t.*** **·lacked, ·lack·ing** 1. To cover or varnish with shellac. 2. *Slang* To defeat utterly. Also **shel·lack′.** [< SHELL + LAC]
shel·lack·ing (shə·lak′ing) *n. Slang* 1. A beating; assault. 2. A thorough defeat.
shell·fire (shel′fīr′) *n.* The firing of artillery shells.
shell·fish (shel′fish′) *n. pl.* **·fish** or **·fish·es** Any aquatic animal having a shell, as a clam.
shell game 1. A swindling game in which the victim bets on the location of a pea covered by one of three nutshells. 2. Any game in which the victim cannot win.
shell·proof (shel′pro͞of′) *adj.* Built to resist the destructive effect of projectiles and bombs.
shell shock Formerly, combat fatigue. **—shell-shock** (shel′shok′) *v.t.* **—shell′-shocked′** *adj.*
shel·ter (shel′tər) *n.* That which covers or shields from exposure or danger; a place of safety. **—*v.t.*** 1. To provide protection or shelter for; shield, as from danger or inclement weather. **—*v.i.*** 2. To take shelter. [? OE *scēld-truma* a body of men armed with shields] **—shel′ter·er** *n.* **—shel′ter·less** *adj.*
shelve (shelv) *v.* **shelved, shelv·ing** *v.t.* 1. To place on a shelf. 2. To postpone indefinitely; put aside. 3. To retire. 4. To provide or fit with shelves. **—*v.i.*** 5. To incline gradually; slope. [< SHELF] **—shelv′y** *adj.*
shelves (shelvz) Plural of SHELF.
shelv·ing (shel′ving) *n.* 1. Shelves collectively. 2. Material for shelves.
she·nan·i·gan (shi·nan′ə·gən) *n. Usu. pl.* 1. Trickery. 2. Questionable behavior. 3. Mischief; nonsense. [? < Irish *sionnach* fox]
shep·herd (shep′ərd) *n.* 1. A keeper or herder of sheep. 2. A pastor, leader, or guide. **—*v.t.*** To watch and tend as a shepherd. [OE *scēaphyrde*] **—shep′herd·ess** (-is) *n.fem.*
shepherd dog A sheep dog. Also **shepherd's dog.**
shep·herd's purse A weed bearing small white flowers and notched triangular pods.
sher·bet (shûr′bit) *n.* 1. A frozen dessert, usu. fruit-flavored, and sometimes containing milk. 2. *Brit.* A drink made of sweetened fruit juice. [< Turkish]
sherd (shûrd) *n.* A shard: often in combination: *potsherd.* [Var. of SHARD]
she·rif (she·rēf′) *n.* An Arab chief. [< Arabic *sharīf* noble]
sher·iff (sher′if) *n.* The chief administrative officer of a county, who executes the mandates of courts, enforces order, etc. [OE *scīr-gerēfa* high official of a shire] **—sher′iff·dom** *n.*
Sher·pa (shûr′pə) *n. pl.* **·pas** or **·pa** One of a Tibetan tribe living on the southern slopes of the Himalayas in Nepal.
sher·ry (sher′ē) *n. pl.* **·ries** A fortified wine. [after *Jerez,* Spain]
she's (shēz) 1. She is. 2. She has.
Shet·land pony (shet′lənd) A small, hardy, shaggy breed of pony.
shew (shō) *v.t. & v.i.* **shewed, shewn, shew·ing** *Archaic* To show. **—shew′er** *n.*
shib·bo·leth (shib′ə·leth) *n.* 1. A pet phrase; a watchword; a slogan. 2. A custom or use of language regarded as distinctive of a particular social class, profession, etc. [< Hebrew *shibbōleth* ear of grain, used as a password]
shied (shīd) Past tense and past participle of SHY.
shield (shēld) *n.* 1. A broad piece of defensive armor, commonly carried on the left arm. 2. Something that protects or defends. 3. *Heraldry* An escutcheon. **—*v.t.*** 1. To

protect from danger as with a shield; defend; guard. —*v.i.* 2. To act as a shield or safeguard. [OE *scild*] —**shield′er** *n.*

shi·er (shī′ər) Comparative of SHY. —*n.* A horse in the habit of shying. Also spelled *shyer.*

shift (shift) *v.t.* 1. To change or move from one position, place, etc., to another. 2. To change for another or others of the same class. 3. To change (gears) from one arrangement to another. —*v.i.* 4. To change position, opinion, etc. —**to shift for oneself** To do the best one can to provide for one's needs. —*n.* 1. The act of shifting. 2. A dodge; artifice; trick. 3. *Archaic* or *Dial.* An undergarment; chemise. 4. A straight, loosely hanging woman's garment, as a dress. 5. A change of position, place, direction, or form: a *shift* in the wind. 6. A relay of workers; also, the working time of each group. [OE *sciftan* to divide] —**shift′er** *n.*

shift·less (shift′lis) *adj.* 1. Unable or unwilling to shift for oneself; inefficient or lazy. 2. Showing lack of energy or resource. —**shift′less·ly** *adv.* —**shift′less·ness** *n.*

shift·y (shif′tē) *adj.* **shift·i·er, shift·i·est** Artful; tricky; crafty or devious. —**shift′i·ly** *adv.* —**shift′i·ness** *n.*

shill (shil) *n.* *Slang* The assistant of a sidewalk peddler or gambler, who makes a purchase or bet to encourage onlookers to buy or bet. [Origin unknown]

shil·le·lagh (shi·lā′lē, -lə) *n.* In Ireland, a stout cudgel made of oak or blackthorn. Also **shil·e′lah.** [after *Shillelagh,* Ireland]

shil·ling (shil′ing) *n.* 1. The monetary unit of Kenya, Somalia, Tanzania, and Uganda. 2. A former British monetary unit equivalent to $^{1}/_{20}$ pound. [OE *scilling*]

shil·ly-shal·ly (shil′ē·shal′ē) *v.i.* **·lied, ·ly·ing** To act with indecision; be irresolute; vacillate. —*adj.* Weak; hesitating. —*n.* Weak or foolish vacillation; irresolution. —*adv.* In an irresolute manner. [Reduplication of *shall I?*] —**shil′ly-shal′li·er** *n.*

shim (shim) *n.* A piece of metal or other material used to fill out space, for leveling, etc. —*v.t.* **shimmed, shim·ming** To fill out by inserting a shim. [Origin unknown]

shim·mer (shim′ər) *v.i.* To shine faintly; glimmer. —*n.* A tremulous shining or gleaming; glimmer. [OE *scimerian*] —**shim′·mer·y** *adj.*

shim·my (shim′ē) *n.* *pl.* **·mies** 1. *Informal* A chemise. 2. Unusual vibration, as in automobile wheels. —*v.i.* **·mied, ·my·ing** To vibrate or wobble. [Alter. of CHEMISE]

shin (shin) *n.* 1. The front part of the leg below the knee; also, the shinbone. 2. The lower foreleg: a *shin* of beef. —*v.t.* & *v.i.* **shinned, shin·ning** To climb (a pole) by gripping with the hands or arms and the shins or legs: usu. with *up.* [OE *scinu*]

shin·bone (shin′bōn′) *n.* The tibia.

shin·dig (shin′dig) *n.* *Slang* A dance or noisy party. [< *shindy* uproar]

shine (shīn) *v.i.* **shone** or (*esp. for def. 5*) **shined, shin·ing** 1. To emit light; beam; glow. 2. To gleam, as by reflected light. 3. To excel or be conspicuous in splendor, beauty, etc. —*v.t.* 4. To cause to shine. 5. To brighten by rubbing or polishing. —**to shine up to** *Slang* To try to please. —*n.* 1. The state or quality of being bright or shining; radiance; luster. 2. Fair weather; sunshine. 3. *Informal* A liking or fancy. 4. A shoeshine. —**to take a shine to** *Informal* To become fond of. [OE *scīnan*]

shin·er (shī′nər) *n.* 1. One of various silvery fresh-water fishes related to the minnows. 2. *Slang* A black eye (def. 2).

shin·gle[1] (shing′gəl) *n.* 1. A thin, tapering, oblong piece of wood or other material, used in rows to cover roofs. 2. A small sign bearing the name of a doctor, lawyer, etc., and placed outside his office. —*v.t.* **·gled, ·gling** To cover (a roof, building, etc.) with or as with shingles. [ME < L *scandula*] —**shin′gler** *n.*

shin·gle[2] (shing′gəl) *n.* Rounded, waterworn gravel, found on the seashore. [Cf. Norw. *singl* coarse gravel] —**shin′gly** *adj.*

shin·gles (shing′gəlz) *n.pl.* (*construed as sing. or pl.*) *Pathol.* An acute, painful, inflammatory virus disease characterized by blisters along the course of the affected nerves: also called *herpes zoster.* [< L *cingulum* girdle]

shin·ing (shī′ning) *adj.* 1. Emitting or reflecting a continuous light; gleaming; luminous. 2. Of unusual brilliance or excellence; conspicuous. —**shin′ing·ly** *adv.*

shin·ny (shin′ē) *v.i.* **·nied, ·ny·ing** *Informal* To climb using one's shins: usu. with *up.*

Shin·to (shin′tō) *n.* A religion of Japan, consisting chiefly in ancestor worship, nature worship, and, formerly, a belief in the divinity of the Emperor. Also **Shin′to·ism.** [< Japanese, way of the gods] —**Shin′to·ist** *n.*

shin·y (shī′nē) *adj.* **shin·i·er, shin·i·est** 1. Glistening; glossy; polished. 2. Bright; clear. —**shin′i·ness** *n.*

ship (ship) *n.* 1. Any vessel suitable for deep-water navigation; also, its personnel. 2. An airship, airplane, or spacecraft. —*v.* **shipped, ship·ping** *v.t.* 1. To transport by ship or other mode of conveyance. 2. *Informal* To get rid of. 3. To set or fit in a prepared place on a boat or vessel, as a mast, or a rudder. —*v.i.* 4. To go on board ship; embark. 5. To undergo shipment: Raspberries do not *ship* well. 6. To enlist as a seaman: usu. with *out.* [OE *scip*] —**ship′pa·ble** *adj.* —**ship′per** *n.*

-ship *suffix of nouns* 1. The state, condition, or quality of: *friendship.* 2. Office, rank, or dignity of: *kingship.* 3. The art or skill of: *marksmanship.* [OE *-scipe*]

ship·board (ship′bôrd′) *n.* 1. The side or deck of a ship. 2. A vessel: used only in the phrase **on shipboard.**

ship·build·er (ship′bil′dər) *n.* One whose work is the building of vessels. —**ship′·build′ing** *adj.* & *n.*

ship·load (ship′lōd′) *n.* The quantity that a ship carries or can carry; a cargo.

ship·mate (ship′māt′) *n.* A fellow sailor.

ship·ment (ship′mənt) *n.* 1. The act of shipping. 2. That which is shipped.

ship·ping (ship′ing) *n.* 1. Ships collectively; also, tonnage. 2. The business of transporting goods.

ship·shape (ship′shāp′) *adj.* Well arranged, orderly, and neat. —**ship′shape′** *adv.*

ship·wreck (ship′rek′) *n.* 1. The partial or total destruction of a ship at sea. 2. Utter or practical destruction; ruin. —*v.t.* 1. To

wreck, as a vessel. 2. To bring to disaster; ruin.
ship·wright (ship′rīt′) *n.* One who builds or repairs ships.
ship·yard (ship′yärd′) *n.* A place where ships are built or repaired.
shire (shīr) *n.* A territorial division of Great Britain; a county. [OE *scīr*]
shirk (shûrk) *v.t. & v.i.* To avoid doing (something that should be done). —*n.* One who shirks: also **shirk′er.** [? < G *schürke* rascal]
shirr (shûr) *v.t.* 1. To draw (fabric) into parallel rows of gathers. 2. To bake with crumbs in a buttered dish, as eggs. [Origin unknown]
shirr·ing (shûr′ing) *n.* The gathering of fabric into parallel rows using short stitches or elastic thread.
shirt (shûrt) *n.* 1. A garment for the upper part of the body, usu. having collar and cuffs and a front closing. 2. A closely fitting undergarment. —**to lose one's shirt** *Slang* To lose everything. [OE *scyrte*] —**shirt′less** *adj.*
shirt·ing (shûr′ting) *n.* Closely woven fabric of cotton, silk, etc., used for making shirts, blouses, dresses, etc.
shirt·waist (shûrt′wāst′) *n.* 1. A woman's tailored, sleeved blouse or shirt. 2. A woman's tailored dress having a bodice like a shirtwaist: also **shirtwaist dress.**
shish ke·bab (shish′ kə·bob′) Meat roasted or broiled in small pieces on skewers. [< Turkish *shish* skewer + *kebap* roast meat]
shist (shist) See SCHIST.
shiv·er[1] (shiv′ər) *v.i.* 1. To tremble; shake; quiver. —*v.t.* 2. *Naut.* To cause to flutter in the wind, as a sail. —*n.* The act of shivering; a tremble. [ME *chivere*] —**shiv′er·y** *adj.*
shiv·er[2] (shiv′ər) *v.t. & v.i.* To break suddenly into fragments; shatter. —*n.* A splinter; sliver. [ME *schivere*] —**shiv′er·y** *adj.*
shle·miel (shlə·mēl′) See SCHLEMIEL.
shlep (shlep) See SCHLEP.
shlock (shlok) See SCHLOCK.
shmaltz (shmälts) See SCHMALTZ.
shmo (shmō) See SCHMO.
shoal[1] (shōl) *n.* 1. A shallow place in any body of water. 2. A sandbank or bar, esp. one seen at low water. —*v.i.* 1. To become shallow. —*v.t.* 2. To sail into a lesser depth of (water): said of a ship. —*adj.* Shallow. [OE *sceald* shallow] —**shoal′i·ness** *n.* —**shoal′y** *adj.* ·i·er, ·i·est
shoal[2] (shōl) *n.* 1. An assemblage or multitude; throng. 2. A school of fish. —*v.i.* To throng in multitudes. [OE *scolu* troop, multitude]
shock[1] (shok) *n.* 1. A violent collision or concussion; impact; blow. 2. A sudden and severe agitation of the mind or emotions, as in horror or great sorrow. 3. *Pathol.* Prostration of bodily functions, as from sudden injury. 4. The physical reactions produced by the passage of a strong electric current through the body. —*v.t.* 1. To shake by sudden collision; jar. 2. To disturb the emotions or mind of; horrify; disgust. 3. To give an electric shock to. [< F *choquer*] —**shock′er** *n.*
shock[2] (shok) *n.* A number of sheaves of grain, stalks of corn, etc., stacked for drying upright in a field. —*v.t. & v.i.* To gather (grain) into a shock. [ME *schokke*] —**shock′·er** *n.*
shock[3] (shok) *adj.* Shaggy; bushy. —*n.* A coarse, tangled mass, as of hair. [Back formation < *shock dog* a shaggy dog]
shock absorber *Mech.* A device designed to absorb the force of shocks, as the springs of an automobile.
shock·ing (shok′ing) *adj.* 1. Causing a mental or emotional shock, as with horror or disgust. 2. *Informal* Terrible; awful. —**shock′ing·ly** *adv.* —**shock′ing·ness** *n.*
shock therapy *Psychiatry* The treatment of certain psychotic disorders by the use of drugs, or electrical shocks, both methods inducing coma, with or without convulsions.
shod (shod) Past tense and alternative past participle of SHOE.
shod·dy (shod′ē) *n. pl.* ·dies 1. Wool obtained from used woolens; also, cloth made of such wool. 2. Any inferior goods. —*adj.* **shod·di·er, shod·di·est** 1. Poorly made or inferior. 2. Sham. [Origin uncertain] —**shod′di·ly** *adv.* —**shod′di·ness** *n.*
shoe (sho͞o) *n. pl.* **shoes** 1. An outer covering, usu. of leather, for the human foot. 2. A rim or plate of iron to protect the hoof of an animal. 3. The part of the brake that presses upon a wheel or drum. 4. The tread or outer covering of a pneumatic tire, as for an automobile. —*v.t.* **shod, shod** or **shod·den, shoe·ing** 1. To furnish with shoes or the like. 2. To furnish with a guard of metal, wood, etc., for protection, as against wear. [OE *scōh*] —**sho′er** *n.*
shoe·horn (sho͞o′hôrn′) *n.* A smooth curved implement used to help put on a shoe.
shoe·lace (sho͞o′lās′) *n.* A lace or cord for fastening shoes.
shoe·mak·er (sho͞o′mā′kər) *n.* One who makes or repairs shoes, boots, etc. —**shoe′·mak′ing** *n.*
shoe·shine (sho͞o′shīn′) *n.* The waxing and polishing of a pair of shoes.
shoe·string (sho͞o′string′) *n.* A shoelace. —**on a shoestring** With a small sum of money with which to begin a business, etc.
shoe·tree (sho͞o′trē′) *n.* A form for inserting in a shoe to preserve its shape or to stretch it.
sho·far (shō′fär) *n.* A ram's horn used as a trumpet by the ancient Hebrews on solemn occasions and in war, now sounded in the synagogue on Rosh Hashana and Yom Kippur. [< Hebrew *shōphār*]
sho·gun (shō′gun, -go͞on) *n.* Any of the hereditary military dictators who ruled Japan until the 19th century. [< Jap. < Chinese *chiang-chün* leader of an army]
sho·ji (shō′jē) *n.* A translucent paper screen forming a partition, wall, or sliding door. [< Jap.]
shone (shōn) Past tense and past participle of SHINE.
shoo (sho͞o) *interj.* Begone! be off!: used in driving away fowls, etc. —*v.t.* 1. To drive away, as by crying "shoo." —*v.i.* 2. To cry "shoo." [Imit.]
shoo-in (sho͞o′in′) *n.* *Informal* A contestant, candidate, etc., who is certain to win.
shook (sho͝ok) Past tense of SHAKE.
shoot (sho͞ot) *v.* **shot, shoot·ing** *v.t.* 1. To hit, wound, or kill with a missile discharged from a weapon. 2. To discharge (a weapon): often with *off*: to *shoot* a cannon. 3. To send forth

as if from a weapon, as questions, glances, etc. 4. To pass over or through swiftly: to *shoot* rapids. 5. To emit, as rays of light. 6. To photograph; film. 7. To cause to stick out or protrude; extend. 8. To send forth (buds, leaves, etc.). 9. To push into or out of the fastening, as the bolt of a door. 10. To propel, discharge, or dump, as down a chute or from a container. 11. In games: a To score (a goal, point, etc.) by kicking or otherwise forcing the ball, etc., to the objective. b To play (golf, craps, pool, etc.). c To play (marbles). d To cast (the dice). 12. *Slang* To inject (a drug, esp. a narcotic). —*v.i.* 13. To discharge a missile from a bow, firearm, etc. 14. To go off; discharge. 15. To move swiftly; dart. 16. To jut out; extend or project. 17. To put forth buds, leaves, etc.; germinate; sprout. 18. To take a photograph. 19. In games, to make a play by propelling the ball, puck, etc., in a certain manner. —**to shoot at** (or **for**) *Informal* To strive for; attempt to attain or obtain. —*n.* 1. A young branch or sucker of a plant; offshoot. 2. An inclined passage down which anything may be shot; a chute. 3. The act of shooting; a shot. 4. A shooting match, hunting party, etc. [OE *scēotan*] —**shoot′er** *n.*

shoot·ing star (sho͞o′ting) 1. A meteor. 2. Any of certain small perennial herbs, having clusters of white, rose, or crimson flowers.

shoot-out (sho͞ot′out′) *n.* An exchange of gunfire.

shop (shop) *n.* 1. A place for the sale of goods at retail: also **shoppe.** 2. A place for making or repairing any article. —**to talk shop** To talk about one's work, often with others involved in similar work. —*v.i.* **shopped, shop·ping** To visit shops or stores to purchase or look at goods. [OE *sceoppa* booth] —**shop′per** *n.* —**shop′ping** *n.*

shop·keep·er (shop′kē′pər) *n.* One who runs a shop or store; a tradesman.

shop·lift·er (shop′lif′tər) *n.* One who steals goods exposed for sale in a shop. —**shop′lift** *v.t. & v.i.* —**shop′lift′ing** *n.*

shopping bag A paper or plastic bag with handles for carrying things.

shopping center A group of retail stores, restaurants, etc., including an ample parking area, usu. built as a unit.

shop steward A union worker chosen by fellow workers to represent them to management in seeking redress of grievances, etc. Also **shop chairman.**

shop·talk (shop′tôk′) *n.* Conversation limited to one's job or profession.

shop·worn (shop′wôrn′) *adj.* 1. Soiled or otherwise deteriorated from much handling in a store. 2. Worn out, as from overuse; stale.

shore[1] (shôr) *n.* 1. The coast or land adjacent to an ocean, sea, lake, or large river. ◆Collateral adjective: *littoral.* 2. Land: to be on *shore.* —**in shore** Near or toward the shore. —*v.t.* **shored, shor·ing** 1. To set on shore. 2. To surround as with a shore. [ME *schore*] —**shore′less** *adj.*

shore[2] (shôr) *v.t.* **shored, shor·ing** To prop or brace: usu., with *up.* —*n.* A beam set endwise as a prop or temporary support. [Cf. Du. *schoor* prop, ON *skortha* stay]

shore·line (shôr′līn′) *n.* The contour of a shore.

shore patrol A detail of the U.S. Navy, Coast Guard, or Marine Corps assigned to police duties ashore.

shore·ward (shôr′wərd) *adj. & adv.* Toward or at the shore. Also **shore′wards.**

shor·ing (shôr′ing) *n.* 1. The operation of supporting or propping. 2. Shores, collectively.

shorn (shôrn) Alternative past participle of SHEAR.

short (shôrt) *adj.* 1. Having little linear extension; not long; of no great distance. 2. Being below the average stature; not tall. 3. Having little extension in time; of limited duration; brief. 4. Abrupt in manner or spirit; cross. 5. Not reaching or attaining a requirement, result, or mark; inadequate: often with *of.* 6. Having little scope or breadth: a *short* view. 7. Of or pertaining to stocks or commodities not in possession of the seller: *short* sales. 8. Not comprehensive or retentive; in error: a *short* memory. 9. Breaking easily; crisp. 10. *Phonet.* Denoting the vowel sounds of *Dan, den, din, don, duck,* as contrasted with those of *Dane, dean, dine, dome, dune.* 11. Concise; compressed. —*n.* 1. Anything that is short. 2. A deficiency, as in a payment. 3. A short contract or sale. 4. *pl.* Trousers with legs extending part way to the knees. 5. *pl.* A man's undergarment covering the loins and often a portion of the legs. 6. In baseball slang, shortstop. 7. *Electr.* A short circuit. —**for short** For brevity: Edward was called Ed *for short.* —**in short** In a word; briefly. —*adv.* 1. Abruptly: to stop *short.* 2. Curtly; crossly. 3. So as not to reach or extend to a certain point, condition, etc.: to fall *short.* —*v.t. & v.i.* To short-circuit. [OE *sort*] —**short′ness** *n.*

short·age (shôr′tij) *n.* The amount by which anything is short; deficiency.

short·bread (shôrt′bred′) *n.* A rich, dry cake or cooky made with shortening.

short·cake (shôrt′kāk′) *n.* 1. A cake made short and crisp with butter or other shortening. 2. Cake or biscuit served with fruit; strawberry *shortcake.*

short·change (shôrt′chānj′) *v.t.* **·changed, ·chang·ing** *Informal* To give less change than is due to; also, to cheat or swindle. —**short′chang′er** *n.*

short circuit *Electr.* 1. A path of low resistance established between any two points in an electric circuit. 2. Any defect in an electric circuit or apparatus that may result in a leakage of current. —**short-cir·cuit** (shôrt′·sûr′kit) *v.t. & v.i.*

short·com·ing (shôrt′kum′ing) *n.* A failure or deficiency in character, action, etc.

short cut 1. A way between two places that is shorter than the regular way. 2. Anything that saves distance or time.

short·en (shôr′tən) *v.t. & v.i.* To make or become shorter. —**short′en·er** *n.*

short·en·ing (shôr′tən·ing) *n.* 1. A fat, such as lard or butter, used to make pastry crisp. 2. An abbreviation.

short·hand (shôrt′hand′) *n.* Any system of rapid writing, usu. employing symbols other than letters, words, etc. —**short′hand′** *adj.*

short-hand·ed (shôrt′han′did) *adj.* Not having a sufficient or the usual number of assistants, workmen, etc.

short·horn (shôrt′hôrn′) *n.* One of a breed of

cattle with short horns, originally from northern England.
short-lived (shôrt′līvd′, -livd′) *adj.* Living or lasting but a short time.
short·ly (shôrt′lē) *adv.* 1. In a short time; soon. 2. In few words; briefly; abruptly.
short order Food requiring little time to prepare. —**in short order** Without any delay; quickly; abruptly.
short shrift 1. A short time in which to confess before dying. 2. Little consideration, as in dealing with a person. —**to make short shrift of** To dispose of quickly.
short-sight·ed (shôrt′sī′tid) *adj.* 1. Unable to see clearly at a distance; near-sighted. 2. Lacking foresight. 3. Resulting from or characterized by lack of foresight. —**short′-sight′ed·ly** *adv.* —**short′-sight′ed·ness** *n.*
short-spo·ken (shôrt′spō′kən) *adj.* Characterized by shortness or curtness of speech or manner; abrupt; gruff.
short·stop (shôrt′stop′) *n.* In baseball, an infielder stationed between second and third bases; also, his position.
short story A narrative prose story shorter than a novel.
short-tem·pered (shôrt′tem′pərd) *adj.* Easily angered.
short-term (shôrt′tûrm′) *adj.* In finance, due or payable within a short time, usu. one year: said of loans, etc.
short ton See under TON.
short waves Electromagnetic waves that are 60 meters or less in length. —**short-wave** (shôrt′wāv′) *adj.*
short-wind·ed (shôrt′win′did) *adj.* Becoming easily out of breath.
Sho·sho·ne (shō·shō′nē) *n.* 1. One of a large tribe of Shoshonean Indians, formerly occupying parts of Wyoming, Idaho, Nevada, and Utah. 2. The Shoshonean language of this tribe. Also **Sho·sho′ni.**
Sho·sho·ne·an (shō·shō′nē·ən, shō′shə·nē′ən) *n.* The largest branch of the Uto-Aztecan language family of North American Indians, including the Comanche, Ute, and Shoshone plateau tribes, and the Hopi Indians. —*adj.* Of or pertaining to this linguistic branch. Also **Sho·sho′ni·an.**
shot[1] (shot) *n. pl.* **shots;** *for def. 1* **shot** 1. A solid missile, as a ball of iron or a bullet or pellet of lead, to be discharged from a firearm; also, such pellets collectively. 2. The act of shooting; any stroke, hit, or blow. 3. One who shoots; a marksman. 4. *Informal* The firing of a rocket, etc., that is directed toward a specific target: a moon *shot.* 5. A stroke, esp. in certain games, as in billiards. 6. An attempted performance. 7. In a distance contest, a metal sphere that a competitor puts, pushes, or slings. 8. *Informal* A hypodermic injection of a drug. 9. *Informal* A drink of liquor. 10. A single action or scene recorded on motion-picture or television film or tape. 11. A photograph or a snapshot. —*v.t.* **shot·ted, shot·ting** To load or weight with shot. [OE *scot*]
shot[2] (shot) Past tense and past participle of SHOOT. —*adj.* 1. Streaked or mixed irregularly with other colors: a sky *shot* with pink. 2. *Informal* Completely done for; ruined or worn out.
shot·gun (shot′gun′) *n.* A light, smoothbore gun, either single or double barreled, adapted for the discharge of shot at short range. —*adj.* Coerced with, or as with, a shotgun: a *shotgun* wedding.
shot-put (shot′po͝ot′) *n.* An athletic contest in which a shot is thrown, or put, for distance. —**shot′-put′ter** *n.* —**shot′-put′ting** *n.*
should (sho͝od) Past tense of SHALL, expressing a wide range of feelings and attitudes: 1. Obligation: You *should* write that letter; *Should* we tell him the truth about his condition? 2. Condition: **a** Simple contingency: If I *should* go, he would go too. **b** Assumption: *Should* the space platform prove practicable, as seems almost certain, a trip to the moon will be easy. 3. Surprise: When I reached the station, whom *should* I run into but the detective! 4. Expectation: I *should* be at home by noon. 5. *Informal* Irony: He'll be fined heavily, but with all his money he *should* (*need not*) worry! [OE *scolde*, pt. of *sculan* to owe]
shoul·der (shōl′dər) *n.* 1. The part of the trunk between the neck and the free portion of the arm or forelimb; also, the joint connecting the arm or forelimb with the body. 2. Anything that supports, bears up, or projects like a shoulder. 3. The forequarter of various animals. 4. Either edge of a road or highway. —**shoulder to shoulder** 1. Side by side and close together. 2. With united effort; in cooperation. —**straight from the shoulder** *Informal* Candidly; straightforwardly. —**to cry on (one's) shoulder** To seek sympathy and understanding from (one). —**to give the cold shoulder to** To treat with scorn, contempt, or coldness. —**to put (one's) shoulder to the wheel** To work with great vigor and purpose. —*v.t.* 1. To assume as something to be borne; sustain; bear. 2. To push with or as with the shoulders. —*v.i.* 3. To push with the shoulders. —**to shoulder arms** To rest a rifle against the shoulder, holding the butt with the hand. [OE *sculdor*]
shoulder blade *Anat.* The scapula.
should·n't (sho͝od′nt) Should not.
shouldst (sho͝odst) Archaic second person singular of SHALL: used with *thou.* Also **should·est** (sho͝od′ist).
shout (shout) *n.* A sudden and loud outcry, often expressing joy, anger, etc., or used as a call or command. —*v.t.* 1. To utter with a shout; say or express loudly. —*v.i.* 2. To utter a shout. [Cf. ON *skūta* a taunt] —**shout′er** *n.*
shove (shuv) *v.t. & v.i.* **shoved, shov·ing** 1. To push, as along a surface. 2. To press forcibly (against); jostle. —**to shove off** 1. To push along or away, as a boat. 2. *Informal* To depart. —*n.* The act of pushing or shoving. [OE *scūfan*] —**shov′er** *n.*
shov·el (shuv′əl) *n.* A somewhat flattened scoop with a handle, as for digging or lifting earth, snow, etc. —*v.* **shov·eled** or **·elled, shov·el·ing** or **·el·ling** *v.t.* 1. To take up and move with a shovel. 2. To toss hastily or in large quantities as if with a shovel. 3. To clear with a shovel, as a path. —*v.i.* 4. To work with a shovel. [OE *scofl*]
shov·el·er (shuv′əl·ər, shuv′lər) *n.* 1. One who or that which shovels. 2. A large river duck with a broad, flat bill: also called *spoonbill:* also **shov·el·bill** (shuv′əl·bil′). Also **shov′el·ler.**
show (shō) *v.* **showed, shown** or, sometimes,

showed, show·ing *v.t.* 1. To cause or permit to be seen; exhibit, display. 2. To give in a marked or open manner; bestow: to *show* favor. 3. To cause or allow (something) to be understood or known; reveal. 4. To cause (someone) to understand or see; teach. 5. To make evident; demonstrate. 6. To guide; introduce, as into a room or building: with *in* or *up*. 7. To indicate: The thermometer *shows* the temperature. 8. To enter in a show or exhibition. —*v.i.* 9. To become visible or known. 10. To make one's or its appearance; be present. 11. In racing, to finish third. —**to show off** 1. To exhibit proudly or ostentatiously. 2. To make an ostentatious display of oneself or of one's accomplishments. —**to show up** 1. To expose or be exposed, as faults. 2. To be evident or prominent. 3. To make an appearance. 4. *Informal* To be better than; outdo. —*n.* 1. An entertainment or performance. 2. Anything shown or manifested. 3. An elaborate display: a *show* of wealth. 4. A pretense or semblance: a *show* of piety. 5. Any public exhibition, contest, etc.: an art *show*. 6. The third position among the first three winners of a race. [OE *scēawian*] —**show′er** *n.*

show bill A poster announcing a play or show.

show·boat (shō′bot′) *n.* A boat on which a traveling troupe gives a theatrical performance.

show·case (shō′kās′) *n.* A glass case for exhibiting and protecting articles for sale. —*v.t.* **·cased, ·cas·ing** To put on display.

show·down (shō′doun′) *n.* Any action or disclosure that brings an issue to a head.

show·er (shou′ər) *n.* 1. A fall of rain, hail, or sleet. 2. A copious fall, as of tears, sparks, etc. 3. A bath in which water is sprayed from an overhead nozzle: also **shower bath.** 4. An abundance or profusion of something. 5. A party for the bestowal of gifts, as to a bride; also, the gifts. —*v.t.* 1. To sprinkle or wet with water. 2. To discharge in a shower; pour out. 3. To bestow liberally. —*v.i.* 4. To fall as in a shower. 5. To bathe under a shower. [OE *scūr*] —**show′er·y** *adj.*

show·ing (shō′ing) *n.* 1. A show or display, as of a quality. 2. A presentation or statement, as of a subject.

show·man (shō′mən) *n. pl.* **·men** (-mən) 1. One who exhibits or owns a show. 2. One who is skilled in presenting something. —**show′man·ship** *n.*

shown (shōn) Past participle of SHOW.

show·off (shō′ôf′) *n. Informal* 1. The act of showing off; ostentatious display. 2. One who shows off.

show·piece (shō′pēs′) *n.* 1. A prized object considered worthy of special exhibit. 2. An object on display.

show·y (shō′ē) *adj.* **show·i·er, show·i·est** 1. Making a great or brilliant display. 2. Conspicuous; ostentatious. —**show′i·ly** *adv.* —**show′i·ness** *n.*

shrank (shrangk) Past tense of SHRINK.

shrap·nel (shrap′nəl) *n. pl.* **·nel** *Mil.* 1. A field artillery projectile for use against personnel, containing metal balls that are expelled by an explosion in mid-air. 2. Shell fragments. [after Henry *Shrapnel*, 1761–1842, British artillery officer]

shred (shred) *n.* 1. A small irregular strip torn or cut off. 2. A bit; fragment. —*v.t.* **shred·ded** or **shred, shred·ding** To tear or cut into shreds. [OE *scrēade*] —**shred′der** *n.*

shrew (shrōō) *n.* 1. A small chiefly insectivorous mammal, having a long pointed snout and soft fur. Also **shrew′mouse′** (-mous′). 2. A scolding or nagging woman. [OE *scrēawa*]

shrewd (shrōōd) *adj.* 1. Sharp or wise; sagacious. 2. Artful; sly. [ME *shrew* malicious person] —**shrewd′ly** *adv.* —**shrewd′·ness** *n.*

shrew·ish (shrōō′ish) *adj.* Ill-tempered; nagging. —**shrew′ish·ly** *adv.* —**shrew′·ish·ness** *n.*

shriek (shrēk) *v.t. & v.i.* To utter (a shrill outcry). [ME] —**shriek** *n.* —**shriek′er** *n.*

shrift (shrift) *n.* 1. The act of shriving. 2. Confession or absolution, as to or from a priest. [OE *scrift*]

shrike (shrīk) *n.* Any of numerous predatory birds with hooked bill, short wings, and long tail. [OE *scrīc* thrush]

shrill (shril) *adj.* 1. Having a high-pitched and piercing tone quality. 2. Emitting a sharp, piercing sound. —*v.t.* 1. To cause to utter a shrill sound. —*v.i.* 2. To make a shrill sound. [< Gmc.] —**shrill, shril′ly** *adv.* —**shrill′ness** *n.*

shrimp (shrimp) *n. pl.* **shrimp** or **shrimps** *for def. 1,* **shrimps** *for def. 2* 1. Any of numerous small, long-tailed, principally marine animals, some species of which are used as food. 2. *Slang* A small or unimportant person. [Akin to OE *scrimman* to shrink]

shrine (shrīn) *n.* 1. A receptacle for sacred relics. 2. A place, as a tomb or a chapel, sacred to some holy personage. —*v.t.* **shrined, shrin·ing** *Rare & Poetic* To enshrine. [< L *scrinium* case, chest]

shrink (shringk) *v.* **shrank** or **shrunk, shrunk** or, sometimes, **shrunk·en, shrink·ing** *v.i.* 1. To draw together; contract. 2. To diminish. 3. To draw back, as from disgust, horror, or timidity; recoil: with *from*. —*v.t.* 4. To cause to shrink, contract, or draw together. —*n.* 1. The act of shrinking. 2. *Slang* A psychiatrist. [OE *scrincan*] —**shrink′a·ble** *adj.* —**shrink′er** *n.*

shrink·age (shringk′ij) *n.* 1. The act or fact of shrinking; contraction. 2. The amount lost by such shrinking. 3. Decrease in value; depreciation.

shrive (shrīv) *v.* **shrove** or **shrived, shriv·en** or **shrived, shriv·ing** *v.t.* 1. To receive the confession of and give absolution to. —*v.i.* 2. To make confession. [OE *scrīfan*, ult. < L *scribere* to write, prescribe] —**shriv′er** *n.*

shriv·el (shriv′əl) *v.t. & v.i.* **shriv·eled** or **·elled, shriv·el·ing** or **·el·ling** 1. To contract into wrinkles; shrink and wrinkle: often with *up*. 2. To make or become impotent; wither. [Origin uncertain]

shroud[1] (shroud) *n.* 1. A dress or garment for the dead. 2. Something that envelops or conceals like a garment: the *shroud* of night. —*v.t.* To envelop, as with a garment. [OE *scrūd* garment] —**shroud′less** *adj.*

shroud[2] (shroud) *n. Naut.* One of a set of ropes, often of wire, stretched from a masthead to the sides of a ship, serving as means of ascent and as a support for the masts. [< SHROUD[1]]

shrub (shrub) *n.* A woody perennial plant of low stature, having stems and branches springing from the base. [OE *scrybb* brushwood] —**shrub′bi·ness** *n.* —**shrub′by** *adj.* **·bi·er, ·bi·est**

shrub·ber·y (shrub′ər·ē) *n. pl.* **·ber·ies** 1. Shrubs collectively. 2. A collection of shrubs, as in a garden.

shrug (shrug) *v.t. & v.i.* **shrugged, shrug·ging** To draw up (the shoulders), as in displeasure, doubt, surprise, etc. —**to shrug off** To dismiss casually from one's attention. —*n.* The act of shrugging the shoulders. [ME *shrugge*]

shrunk (shrungk) Alternative past tense and past participle of SHRINK.

shrunk·en (shrungk′ən) Alternative past participle of SHRINK. —*adj.* Contracted and atrophied.

shuck (shuk) *n.* 1. A husk, shell, or pod. 2. A shell of an oyster or a clam. —*v.t.* 1. To remove the husk or shell from (corn, oysters, etc.). 2. *Informal* To take off or cast off, as clothes. [Origin unknown] —**shuck′er** *n.*

shucks (shuks) *interj. Informal* A mild exclamation of annoyance, disgust, etc.

shud·der (shud′ər) *v.i.* To tremble or shake, as from fright or cold; shiver; quake. —*n.* The act of shuddering. [ME *shodder*]

shuf·fle (shuf′əl) *v.t. & v.i.* **·fled, ·fling** 1. To mix or change the order of (playing cards). 2. To move (the feet) along the ground with a dragging gait. 3. To change from one place to another. 4. To dance by pushing one's foot along the floor at each step. [Prob. < LG *schuffeln*] —**shuf′fle** *n.* —**shuf′fler** *n.*

shuf·fle·board (shuf′əl·bôrd′) *n.* 1. A game in which disks are slid by means of a pronged cue along a smooth surface toward numbered spaces. 2. The board or surface on which the game is played.

shun (shun) *v.t.* **shunned, shun·ning** To keep clear of; avoid; refrain from. [OE *scunian*] —**shun′ner** *n.*

shunt (shunt) *n.* 1. The act of shunting. 2. A railroad switch. 3. *Electr.* A conductor serving to divert part of the current to an auxiliary circuit; also called *by-pass.* —*v.t.* 1. To turn aside. 2. To switch, as a train or car, from one track to another. 3. *Electr.* To distribute by means of shunts. 4. To evade by turning away from; put off on someone else, as a task. —*v.i.* 5. To move to one side; be diverted. [ME *schunten*] —**shunt′er** *n.*

shush (shush) *v.t.* To quiet, as by making the sound "sh."

shut (shut) *v.* **shut, shut·ting** *v.t.* 1. To bring into such position as to close an opening or aperture; close, as a door, lid, or valve. 2. To close and fasten securely, as with a latch or lock. 3. To forbid entrance into or exit from. 4. To keep from entering or leaving: with *in, out, from,* etc. 5. To close, fold, or bring together, as extended, expanded, or unfolded parts: to *shut* an umbrella. —*v.i.* 6. To be or become closed or in a closed position. —**to shut down** To cease from operating, as a factory or mine. —**to shut one's eyes to** To ignore. —**to shut out** In sports, to keep (an opponent) from scoring during the course of a game. —**to shut up** 1. *Informal* To stop talking or cause to stop talking. 2. To imprison; confine. —*adj.* Made fast or closed. —*n.* 1. The act of shutting. 2. The time or place of shutting or closing. [OE *scyttan*]

shut·down (shut′doun′) *n.* The stopping of work, as in a factory.

shut-in (shut′in′) *n.* An invalid who is unable to go out. —*adj.* Obliged to stay at home.

shut·out (shut′out′) *n.* In sports, a game in which one side is prevented from scoring.

shut·ter (shut′ər) *n.* 1. That which shuts out or excludes; esp., a cover or screen, usu. hinged, for closing a window. 2. *Photog.* Any of various mechanisms for momentarily admitting light through a camera lens to the film or plate. —*v.t.* To furnish, close, or divide off with shutters.

shut·tle (shut′l) *n.* 1. A device used in weaving to carry the weft to and fro between the warp threads. 2. A similar rotating or other device, as in a sewing machine. 3. A transport system operating between two nearby points. —*v.t. & v.i.* **·tled, ·tling** To move to and fro, like a shuttle. [OE *scytel* missile]

shut·tle·cock (shut′l·kok′) *n.* A rounded piece of cork, with a crown of feathers, as used in badminton. —*v.t.* To send or knock back and forth like a shuttlecock.

shy[1] (shī) *v.i.* **shied, shy·ing** 1. To start suddenly aside, as in fear: said of a horse. 2. To draw back, as from doubt or caution: with *off* or *away.* —*adj.* **shi·er** or **shy·er, shi·est** or **shy·est** 1. Easily frightened or startled; timorous. 2. Bashful; coy. 3. Circumspect, as from motives of caution; wary: with *of.* 4. *Informal* Short; lacking. —*n. pl.* **shies** A starting aside, as in fear. [OE *scēoh* timid] —**shy′ness** *n.*

shy[2] (shī) *v.t. & v.i.* **shied, shy·ing** To throw with a swift sidelong motion. —*n. pl.* **shies** A careless throw or fling. [Origin unknown]

shy·er (shī′ər) *n.* 1. One who shies. 2. See SHIER.

Shy·lock (shī′lok) *n. Slang* Any relentless creditor. [after Shylock, character in Shakespeare's *Merchant of Venice*]

shy·ly (shī′lē) *adv.* In a shy manner.

shy·ster (shīs′tər) *n. Slang* Anyone, esp. a lawyer, who conducts his business in an unscrupulous manner. [Origin uncertain]

Si·a·mese (sī′ə·mēz′, -mēs′) *n.* 1. *pl.* **·mese** A native of Thailand (formerly Siam). 2. The Thai language of the people of Siam, now officially called *Thai.* —**Si′a·mese′** *adj.*

Siamese twins Any twins joined together at birth. [after such a pair of twins born in Siam in 1811]

sib·i·lant (sib′ə·lənt) *adj.* 1. Hissing. 2. *Phonet.* Denoting those consonants produced by the frictional passage of breath through a narrow opening in the front part of the mouth, as (s), (z), (sh), and (zh). —*n. Phonet.* A sibilant consonant. [< L *sibilare* to hiss] —**sib′i·lance, sib′i·lan·cy** *n.* —**sib′i·lant·ly** *adv.*

sib·ling (sib′ling) *n.* A brother or sister. [OE, a relative]

sib·yl (sib′əl) *n.* A fortuneteller; sorceress. [< Gk. *sibylla*] —**sib′yl·line** (-īn, -ēn, -in), **si·byl·ic** (si·bil′ik), **si·byl′lic** *adj.*

sic[1] (sik) *adv.* So; thus; inserted in brackets after a quotation to indicate that it is accurately reproduced even though it may seem questionable or incorrect. [< L]
sic[2] (sik) *v.t.* **sicked, sick·ing** See SICK[2].
Si·cil·i·an (si·sil′ē·ən, -sil′yən) *adj.* Of or pertaining to Sicily or its people. —**Si·cil′i·an** *n.*
sick[1] (sik) *adj.* 1. Affected with disease; ill. 2. Of or used by ill persons: often used in combination: *sickbed.* 3. Affected by nausea. 4. Expressive of or experiencing disgust or unpleasant emotion. 5. Impaired or unsound from any cause. 6. Mentally unsound. 7. Pallid; wan. 8. Disinclined by reason of satiety or disgust; surfeited: with *of.* 9. Sadistic or macabre; morbid: *sick* jokes. —*n.* Sick people collectively: with *the.* [OE *sēoc*] —**sick′ness** *n.*
sick[2] (sik) *v.t.* 1. To attack: used in the imperative as an order to a dog. 2. To urge to attack: I'll *sick* the dog on you. Also spelled *sic.* [Var. of SEEK]
sick·bay (sik′bā′) *n.* That part of a ship or of a naval base set aside for the care of the sick.
sick·bed (sik′bed′) *n.* The bed a sick person lies on.
sick call *Mil.* The daily period during which all nonhospitalized sick or injured personnel report to the medical officer.
sick·en (sik′ən) *v.t. & v.i.* To make or become sick or disgusted. —**sick′en·er** *n.*
sick·en·ing (sik′ən·ing) *adj.* Disgusting; revolting; nauseating. —**sick′en·ing·ly** *adv.*
sick·le (sik′əl) *n.* An implement with a curved or crescent-shaped blade mounted on a short handle, used for cutting tall grass, grains, etc. —*v.t.* **·led, ·ling** To cut with a sickle, as grass. [< L *secare* to cut]
sickle cell A crescent-shaped red blood corpuscle containing a genetically transmitted type of hemoglobin in which the oxygen concentration is below normal, and causing an anemia (**sickle cell anemia**) occurring chiefly among Negroes.
sick·ly (sik′lē) *adj.* **·li·er, ·li·est** 1. Habitually indisposed; ailing; unhealthy. 2. Nauseating; disgusting. 3. Pertaining to or characteristic of sickness: a *sickly* appearance. 4. Weak; faint. —*adv.* In a sick manner; poorly. —*v.t.* **·lied, ·ly·ing** To make sickly, as in color or complexion. —**sick′li·ness** *n.*
side (sīd) *n.* 1. Any one of the bounding lines of a surface or of the bounding surfaces of a solid object; also, a particular line or surface other than top or bottom: the *side* of a mountain. 2. Either of the two surfaces of a piece of paper, cloth, etc.; also, a specific surface: the rough *side* of sandpaper. 3. One of two or more contrasted directions, parts, or places: the east *side* of town. 4. A distinct party or body of competitors or partisans. 5. An opinion, aspect, or point of view: my *side* of the question. 6. Family connection, esp. by descent through one parent. 7. Either half of the human body. 8. The space beside someone. 9. In sports, a team. —**side by side** Beside or next to each other. —**to take sides** To support a particular opinion, point of view, etc. —*adj.* 1. Situated on one side: a *side* window. 2. Being from one side: a *side* glance. 3. Directed towards one side: a *side* blow. 4. Not primary; subordinate: a *side* issue. —*v.t.* **sid·ed, sid·ing** To provide with sides, as a building. —**to side with** To support or take the part of. [OE *sīde*]
side·arm (sīd′ärm) *adj.* Executed with the hand level with the elbow, as a pitch. —*adv.* In a sidearm manner.
side arms Weapons worn at the side, as pistols, etc.
side·board (sīd′bôrd′) *n.* A piece of dining-room furniture for holding tableware.
side·burns (sīd′bûrnz′) *n.pl.* The hair growing on the sides of a man's face below the hairline, esp. when worn as whiskers. [Alter. of *burnsides*, side whiskers or mutton-chops]
sid·ed (sī′did) *adj.* Having or characterized by (a specified kind or number of) sides: used in combination: *one-sided.*
side effect A secondary, usu. injurious effect, as of a drug.
side·kick (sīd′kik′) *n.* *Slang* A close friend; buddy.
side·light (sīd′līt′) *n.* Incidental facts or information.
side·line (sīd′līn′) *n.* 1. An auxiliary line of goods sold by a store or a commercial traveler. 2. Any secondary work differing from one's main job. 3. One of the lines bounding the two sides of a football field, tennis court, etc. —*v.t.* **·lined, ·lin·ing** To prevent or remove (someone) from active participation.
side·long (sīd′lông′) *adj.* 1. Inclining, tending, or directed to one side. 2. Indirect; sly. —*adv.* In a lateral or oblique direction.
si·de·re·al (sī·dir′ē·əl) *adj.* 1. Of or pertaining to stars. 2. Measured by means of the stars: *sidereal* year. [< L *sidus* star] —**si·de′re·al·ly** *adv.*
sidereal year The period of 365 days, 6 hours, 9 minutes, and 9 seconds in which the sun apparently returns to the same position among the stars.
sidero-[1] *combining form* Of or pertaining to iron. Also, before vowels, **sider-**. [< Gk. *sidēros* iron]
sidero-[2] *combining form* Star; stellar. Also, before vowels, **sider-**. [< L *sidus* star]
side show 1. A small show incidental to but connected with a larger or more important one: a circus *side show.* 2. Any subordinate issue or attraction.
side·slip (sīd′slip′) *v.i.* **·slipped, ·slip·ping** To slip or skid sideways. —*n.* 1. A lateral skid. 2. *Aeron.* A downward, sideways slipping of an airplane along the lateral axis.
side·split·ting (sīd′split′ing) *adj.* 1. Hearty and uproarious, as laughter. 2. Causing great laughter or hilarity.
side·step (sīd′step′) *v.* **·stepped, ·step·ping** *v.i.* 1. To step to one side. —*v.t.* 2. To avoid, as an issue, or postpone, as a decision; evade.
side·swipe (sīd′swīp′) *n.* A sweeping blow along the side. —*v.t. & v.i.* **·swiped, ·swip·ing** To strike or collide with such a blow.
side·track (sīd′trak′) *v.t. & v.i.* 1. To move to a siding, as a railroad train. 2. To divert or distract from the main issue or subject. —*n.* A railroad siding; also, a branch line.
side·walk (sīd′wôk′) *n.* A path or pavement

at the side of the street, for the use of pedestrians.

side·wall (sīd′wôl′) *n.* The side surface of a tire.

side·ways (sīd′wāz′) *adv.* 1. From the side. 2. So as to incline toward the side, or with the side forward: Hold it *sideways.* 3. Toward one side; obliquely. —*adj.* Moving to or from one side. Also **side′way′, side′·wise′** (-wīz′).

side·wind·er (sīd′wīn′dər) *n.* A small rattlesnake found in the SW U.S., so called because of its characteristic lateral movement.

sid·ing (sī′ding) *n.* 1. A railway track by the side of the main track. 2. The boarding that covers the side of a house, etc.

si·dle (sīd′l) *v.i.* **·dled, ·dling** To move sideways, esp. in a cautious or stealthy manner. [Back formation < obs. *sidling* sidelong] —**si′dle** *n.* —**si′dler** *n.*

siege (sēj) *n.* 1. The act of surrounding any fortified area with the intention of capturing it. 2. The time during which one undergoes a protracted illness or difficulty. —**to lay siege to** To attempt to capture or gain; besiege. —*v.t.* **sieged, sieg·ing** To lay siege to. [< L *sedere* to sit]

sie·mens (sē′mənz) *n. pl.* **sie·mens** A unit of electrical conductance equal to one ampere per volt. [after Werner von *Siemens,* 1816–1892, Ger. physicist]

si·en·na (sē·en′ə) *n.* 1. A brownish yellow clay containing oxides of iron and manganese, used as a pigment. 2. A brownish yellow color. [< Ital. (*terra di*) *Siena* (earth of) Siena]

si·er·ra (sē·er′ə) *n.* A mountain range having a jagged outline. [< Sp. < L *serra* saw]

Si·er·ra Le·on·e·an (sē·er′ə lē·ō′nē·ən) *adj.* Of Sierra Leone or its inhabitants. —**Si·er′ra Le·on′e·an** *n.*

si·es·ta (sē·es′tə) *n.* A midday or afternoon nap. [< Sp. < L *sexta* (*hora*) sixth (hour)]

sieve (siv) *n.* A utensil for straining or sifting, consisting of a frame with a bottom of wire mesh, etc. —*v.t. & v.i.* **sieved, siev·ing** To pass through a sieve. [OE *sife*]

sift (sift) *v.t.* 1. To pass through a sieve. 2. To scatter as by a sieve. 3. To examine carefully. 4. To separate; distinguish: to *sift* fact from fiction. —*v.i.* 5. To use a sieve. [OE *siftan*] —**sift′er** *n.*

sigh (sī) *v.i.* 1. To draw in and exhale a deep, audible breath, as in expressing sorrow, weariness, etc. 2. To make a sound suggestive of a sigh, as the wind. 3. To yearn; long: with *for.* —*v.t.* 4. To express with a sigh. —*n.* The act or sound of sighing. [OE *sīcan*]

sight (sīt) *n.* 1. The act or fact of seeing. 2. That which is seen; a view. 3. *pl.* Things worth seeing: the *sights* of the town. 4. The faculty of seeing; vision. 5. The range or scope of vision. 6. A device to assist aim, as on a gun, etc. 7. *Informal* Something unusual or ugly to look at: He was a *sight.* —**at** (or **on**) **sight** As soon as seen. —**sight unseen** Without ever having seen the object in question. —*v.t.* 1. To perceive with the eyes; observe. 2. To take a sight of. —*v.i.* 3. To take aim. [OE *gesiht*]

sight·less (sīt′lis) *adj.* 1. Lacking sight; blind. 2. Invisible. —**sight′less·ly** *adv.* —**sight′less·ness** *n.*

sight·ly (sīt′lē) *adj.* **·li·er, ·li·est** 1. Pleasant to the view; comely. 2. Affording a fine view. —**sight′li·ness** *n.*

sight·see·ing (sīt′sē′ing) *n.* The visiting of places of interest. —**sight′se′er** *n.*

sig·ma (sig′mə) *n.* The eighteenth letter in the Greek alphabet (Σ, σ), corresponding to English *s* in *so.*

sign (sīn) *n.* 1. A motion or action indicating a thought, desire, command, etc. 2. A board, placard, etc., generally bearing an inscription conveying information of some kind: a street *sign.* 3. Any arbitrary mark, symbol, or token: a *sign* of mourning. 4. Any indication or evidence: *signs* of poverty. 5. Any omen or miraculous occurrence. 6. One of the twelve equal divisions of the zodiac. —*v.t.* 1. To write one's signature or initials on. 2. To mark with a sign. 3. To engage by obtaining the signature of to a contract; also, to hire (oneself) out for work: often with *on.* 4. To dispose of or transfer title to by signature: with *off, over,* or *away.* —*v.i.* 5. To make signs or signals. 6. To write one's signature or initials. —**to sign off** *Telecom.* To cease broadcasting. —**to sign up** To enlist, as in a military service. [< L *signum*] —**sign′er** *n.*

sig·nal (sig′nəl) *n.* 1. A sign or means of communication agreed upon or understood, used to convey information, a command, etc. 2. *Telecom.* An electromagnetic impulse that transmits information, whether direct or in code. —*adj.* 1. Notable; conspicuous. 2. Used to signal. —*v.t. & v.i.* **sig·naled** or **·nalled, sig·nal·ing** or **·nal·ling** 1. To make signals (to). 2. To communicate by signals. [< L *signum* sign] —**sig′nal·er** or **sig′·nal·ler** *n.*

sig·nal·ize (sig′nəl·īz) *v.t.* **·ized, ·iz·ing** 1. To render noteworthy. 2. To point out with care.

sig·nal·ly (sig′nəl·ē) *adv.* In a signal manner; eminently.

sig·nal·man (sig′nəl·mən) *n. pl.* **·men** (-mən) One who sends or interprets signals, esp. railroad signals.

sig·na·to·ry (sig′nə·tôr′ē) *adj.* Bound by the terms of a signed document; having signed: *signatory* powers. —*n. pl.* **·ries** One who has signed or is bound by a document; esp., a nation so bound. [< L *signum* sign]

sig·na·ture (sig′nə·chər) *n.* 1. The name of a person written by himself; also, the act of signing one's name. 2. A distinctive mark, characteristic, etc. 3. *Printing* A large printed sheet that, when folded, forms four, or a multiple of four, pages of a book. 4. *Music* A symbol or group of symbols at the beginning of a staff, indicating meter or key. [< L *signum* sign]

sign·board (sīn′bôrd′) *n.* A board on which a sign, direction, or advertisement is displayed.

sig·net (sig′nit) *n.* A seal, esp. one used to authenticate documents, etc. [< L *signum* sign]

sig·nif·i·cance (sig·nif′ə·kəns) *n.* 1. The character or state of being significant. 2. Meaning. 3. Importance; consequence. Also **sig·nif′i·can·cy.**

sig·nif·i·cant (sig·nif′ə·kənt) *adj.* 1. Having or expressing a meaning. 2. Conveying or having some covert meaning: a *significant* look. 3. Important; weighty; momentous. [< L *signum* sign + *facere* to do, make] —**sig·nif′i·cant·ly** *adv.*

sig·ni·fy (sig′nə·fī) *v.* **·fied, ·fy·ing** *v.t.* 1. To make known by signs or words; express. 2. To betoken in any way; import. 3. To amount to; mean. —*v.i.* 4. To have some meaning or importance; matter. —**sig′ni·fi·ca′tion** *n.* —**sig′ni·fi′er** *n.*

sign language A system of communication by means of signs, largely manual.

si·gno·ra (sē·nyō′rä) *n. pl.* **·re** (-rā) *Italian* The title for a married woman, equivalent to *Mrs.*

si·gno·re (sē·nyō′rē) *n. pl.* **·ri** (-rē) *Italian* The title for a man, equivalent to *Mr.*, *sir.*

si·gno·ri·na (sē′nyō·rē′nä) *n. pl.* **·ne** (-nā) *Italian* The title for an unmarried woman, equivalent to *Miss.*

sign·post (sīn′pōst′) *n.* 1. A post bearing a sign. 2. Any sign, clue, or indication.

Sikh (sēk) *n.* One of a religious and military sect founded in India in the 16th c. [< Hind., lit., disciple] —**Sikh** *adj.* —**Sikh′ism** *n.*

si·lage (sī′lij) *n.* Fodder, grain, etc., stored in a silo and allowed to ferment, used as feed for livestock. [< ENSILAGE]

si·lence (sī′ləns) *n.* 1. The state or quality of being silent. 2. Absence of sound or noise; stillness. 3. A failure to mention something; secrecy. —*v.t.* **·lenced, ·lenc·ing** 1. To make silent. 2. To force (guns, etc.) to cease firing, as by bombing, etc. —*interj.* Be silent.

si·lenc·er (sī′lən·sər) *n.* A tubular device attached to the muzzle of a firearm to reduce the sound of the report.

si·lent (sī′lənt) *adj.* 1. Not making any sound or noise; noiseless; still; mute. 2. Not given to speech; taciturn. 3. Unspoken or unuttered: *silent* grief. [< L *silere* to be silent] —**si′lent·ly** *adv.* —**si′lent·ness** *n.*

si·lex (sī′leks) *n.* Silica. [< L, flint]

sil·hou·ette (sil′o͞o·et′) *n.* 1. A profile drawing or portrait having its outline filled in with uniform color, commonly black. 2. The outline of a solid figure. —*v.t.* **·et·ted, ·et·ting** To cause to appear in silhouette. [after Etienne de *Silhouette*, 1709–67, French minister of finance]

sil·i·ca (sil′i·kə) *n.* A white or colorless, very hard, crystalline silicon compound, the principal constituent of quartz and sand: also called *silex.* [< L *silex, silicis* flint]

sil·i·cate (sil′i·kit) *n. Chem.* A compound of silica.

si·li·ceous (si·lish′əs) *adj.* 1. Pertaining to, resembling, or containing silica. 2. Growing or living on soil rich in silica. Also **si·li′cious.**

silico- *combining form* Silicon; of, related to, or containing silicon. Also, before vowels, **silic-.** [< L *silex, silicis* flint]

sil·i·con (sil′ə·kən, -kon) *n.* A widely distributed nonmetallic element (symbol Si). [< L *silex, silicis* flint]

sil·i·cone (sil′ə·kōn) *n. Chem.* An organic silicon compound, used in lubricants, insulating resins, waterproofing materials, etc.

sil·i·co·sis (sil′ə·kō′sis) *n. Pathol.* A pulmonary disease caused by the inhalation of finely powdered silica or quartz.

silk (silk) *n.* 1. The creamy-white or yellowish, very fine natural fiber produced by silkworms. 2. A similar threadlike material spun by other insects. 3. Cloth, thread, or garments made of silk. 4. Anything resembling silk. —**to hit the silk** *Slang* To parachute from an aircraft. —*adj.* 1. Consisting of silk. 2. Resembling silk. —*v.t.* 1. To clothe or cover with silk. —*v.i.* 2. To produce the portion of the flower called silk: said of corn. [< L *sericus* silken]

silk·en (sil′kən) *adj.* 1. Made of silk. 2. Like silk; glossy; delicate; smooth. 3. Luxurious.

silk-screen process (silk′skrēn′) A stencil process that prints designs by forcing ink through the open meshes of a silk screen.

silk-stock·ing (silk′stok′ing) *adj. Informal* Wealthy; luxurious. —*n.* A member of the wealthy class.

silk·worm (silk′wûrm′) *n.* Certain moth larvae that spin a dense silken cocoon; esp., the **common silkworm,** yielding commercial silk.

silk·y (sil′kē) *adj.* **silk·i·er, silk·i·est** 1. Made of or resembling silk; soft; lustrous. 2. Gentle or insinuating in manner. —**silk′i·ly** *adv.* —**silk′i·ness** *n.*

sill (sil) *n. Archit.* A horizontal, lower member of something, as the bottom of a door or window casing. [OE *syll*]

sil·ly (sil′ē) *adj.* **·li·er, ·li·est** 1. Destitute of ordinary good sense; foolish. 2. Stupid; absurd. —*n. pl.* **·lies** *Informal* A silly person. [OE *sǣsig* happy] —**sil′li·ly** *adv.* —**sil′li·ness** *n.*

si·lo (sī′lō) *n. pl.* **·los** 1. A pit or tower in which fodder, grain, or other food is stored green to be fermented and used as feed for cattle, etc. 2. A similar structure, built underground, for the housing or launching of missiles, esp. nuclear missiles. —*v.t.* **·loed, ·lo·ing** To put or preserve in a silo; turn into silage. [< Gk. *siros* pit for corn]

silt (silt) *n.* An earthy sediment consisting of fine particles of rock and soil suspended in and carried by water. —*v.i.* 1. To become filled or choked with silt: usu. with *up.* 2. To ooze; drift. —*v.i.* 3. To fill or choke with silt or mud: usu. with *up.* [ME *cylte*] —**silt′y** *adj*

sil·ver (sil′ver) *n.* 1. A white malleable metallic element (symbol Ag) of high electric conductivity, used in medicine, industry, and the arts. 2. Silver regarded as a commodity or as a standard of currency. 3. Silver coin; cash or change; money in general. 4. Silver plate; silverware. 5. A lustrous, pale gray color resembling that of silver. —*adj.* 1. Made of or coated with silver. 2. Of, containing, or producing silver. 3. Having a silvery luster. 4. Having the soft, clear tones of a silver bell. 5. Persuasive; eloquent. 6. White or gray, as the hair. —*v.t.* 1. To coat or plate with silver or with a silverlike substance. —*v.i.* 2. To become silver or white. [OE *seolfor*] —**sil′ver·er** *n.*

silver anniversary A 25th anniversary.

sil·ver·fish (sil′vər·fish′) *n. pl.* **·fish** or **·fish·es** Any of numerous flat-bodied,

wingless insects that damage books, papers, etc.
silver fox 1. A color phase of the red fox of North America, having fur interspersed with white-tipped hairs. 2. The fur of this animal.
silver gray A light, slightly bluish gray.
silver nitrate *Chem.* A poisonous crystalline compound, widely used in industry, photography, and medicine.
silver plate Articles, as table utensils, made of silver or metal plated with silver.
sil·ver·smith (sil′vər·smith′) *n.* A worker in silver; a maker of silverware.
sil·ver-tongued (sil′vər·tungd′) *adj.* Eloquent.
sil·ver·ware (sil′vər·wâr′) *n.* Articles, esp. for table use, made of silver.
sil·ver·y (sil′vər·ē) *adj.* 1. Containing or adorned with silver. 2. Resembling silver, as in luster or hue. 3. Soft and clear in sound. —**sil′ver·i·ness** *n.*
sim·i·an (sim′ē·ən) *adj.* Pertaining to, resembling, or characteristic of apes and monkeys. —*n.* An ape or monkey. [< L *simia* ape]
sim·i·lar (sim′ə·lər) *adj.* 1. Bearing resemblance to one another or to something else; like, but not completely identical. 2. Of like characteristics, nature, or degree; of the same scope, order, or purpose. [< L *similis* like] —**sim′i·lar·ly** *adv.*
sim·i·lar·i·ty (sim′ə·lar′ə·tē) *n. pl.* ·**ties** 1. The quality or state of being similar. 2. The point in which the objects compared are similar.
sim·i·le (sim′ə·lē) *n.* A figure of speech expressing comparison or likeness by the use of such terms as *like, as, so,* etc.: distinguished from *metaphor.* [< L, neut. of *similis* similar]
si·mil·i·tude (si·mil′ə·to͞od, -tyo͞od) *n.* 1. Similarity. 2. A counterpart or likeness. [< L *similis* like]
sim·mer (sim′ər) *v.i.* 1. To boil gently; be or stay at or just below the boiling point. 2. To be on the point of breaking forth, as with rage. —*v.t.* 3. To keep at or just below the boiling point. —**to simmer down** *Informal* To subside from a state of anger or excitement. —*n.* The state or process of simmering. [< obs. *simper* to boil]
si·mon-pure (sī′mən·pyo͝or′) *adj.* Real; genuine; authentic. [after *Simon Pure,* a character impersonated by another in the play *A Bold Stroke for a Wife* (1718)]
si·mo·ny (sī′mə·nē, sim′ə-) *n.* The purchase or sale of a church office. [< *Simon (Magus),* who offered Peter money for the gift of the Holy Spirit] —**si′mon·ist** *n.*
si·moom (si·mo͞om′, sī-) *n. Meteorol.* A hot dry wind of the desert in northern Africa, Arabia, etc. Also **si·moon′** (-mo͞on′). [< Arabic *samma* poison]
sim·per (sim′pər) *v.i.* 1. To smile in a silly, self-conscious manner; smirk. —*v.t.* 2. To say with a simper. —*n.* A silly, self-conscious smile. [< Scand.] —**sim′per·er** *n.* —**sim′per·ing·ly** *adv.*
sim·ple (sim′pəl) *adj.* ·**pler,** ·**plest** 1. Consisting of one thing; single; uncombined. 2. Not complex or complicated; easy. 3. Without embellishment; plain; unadorned. 4. Free from affectation; artless. 5. Of humble rank; lowly. 6. Silly; feeble-minded. 7. Lacking luxury; frugal. 8. Having nothing added; mere. 9. *Bot.* Not divided; entire. —*n.* 1. That which is simple; an uncomplex, or natural thing. 2. A simpleton. [< L *simplex*]
sim·ple-mind·ed (sim′pəl·mīn′did) *adj.* 1. Artless or unsophisticated. 2. Mentally defective. 3. Stupid; foolish. —**sim′ple-mind′ed·ly** *adv.* —**sim′ple-mind′ed·ness** *n.*
sim·ple·ton (sim′pəl·tən) *n.* A weak-minded or silly person.
simplici- *combining form* Simple. Also, before vowels, simplic-. [< L *simplex, simplicis*]
sim·plic·i·ty (sim·plis′ə·tē) *n. pl.* ·**ties** 1. The state of being simple; freedom from complexity or complication. 2. Sincerity; unaffectedness. 3. Lack of intelligence or good sense. [< L *simplicitas*]
sim·pli·fy (sim′plə·fī) *v.t.* ·**fied,** ·**fy·ing** To make more simple or less complex. [< L *simplex* simple + *facere* to make] —**sim′pli·fi·ca′tion** *n.* —**sim′pli·fi′er** *n.*
sim·plis·tic (sim·plis′tik) *adj.* Tending to ignore complications or details. —**sim′plism** *n.* —**sim·plis′ti·cal·ly** *adv.*
sim·ply (sim′plē) *adv.* 1. In a simple manner; intelligibly. 2. Without ostentation or extravagance. 3. Merely; only. 4. Really; absolutely: *simply* charming.
sim·u·late (sim′yə·lāt) *v.t.* ·**lat·ed,** ·**lat·ing** 1. To have the appearance or form of, without the reality; counterfeit; imitate. 2. To make a pretense of. [< L *similis* like] —**sim′u·lat′ed** *adj.* —**sim′u·la′tor** *n.*
sim·u·la·tion (sim′yə·lā′shən) *n.* 1. The act of simulating; counterfeit; sham. 2. The taking on of a particular aspect or form. —**sim′u·la′tive, sim′u·la·to′ry** (-lə·tôr′ē) *adj.* —**sim′u·la′tive·ly** *adv.*
si·mul·cast (sī′məl·kast′) *v.t.* ·**cast** or ·**cast·ed,** ·**cast·ing** To broadcast by radio and television simultaneously. [< SIMUL(TANEOUS) + (BROAD)CAST] —**si′mul·cast′** *n.*
si·mul·ta·ne·ous (sī′məl·tā′nē·əs, sim′əl-) *adj.* Occurring, done, or existing at the same time. [< L *simul* at the same time] —**si′mul·ta′ne·ous·ly** *adv.* —**si′mul·ta′ne·ous·ness, si′mul·ta·ne′i·ty** (-tə·nē′ə·tē) *n.*
sin (sin) *n.* 1. A transgression, esp., when deliberate, of a religious law. 2. Any offense against a standard: a literary *sin.* —*v.i.* **sinned, sin·ning** 1. To commit sin; transgress the divine law. 2. To violate any requirement of right, duty, etc.; do wrong. [OE *synn*]
since (sins) *adv.* 1. From a past time, mentioned or referred to, up to the present. 2. At some time between a certain past time or event and the present. 3. In time before the present; ago; before now. —*prep.* 1. During or within the time after: *since* you left. 2. Continuously throughout the time after: *since* noon. —*conj.* 1. Continuously from the time when. 2. Because of or following upon the fact that; inasmuch as. [OE *siththan* afterwards]
sin·cere (sin·sir′) *adj.* 1. Being in reality as it is in appearance; genuine. 2. Free from hypocrisy; honest. [< L *sin-* without + stem of *caries* decay] —**sin·cere′ly** *adv.* —**sin·cer′i·ty** (-ser′ə·tē), **sin·cere′ness** *n.*
sine (sīn) *n. Trig.* In a right triangle, a

function of an acute angle, equal to the ratio of the side opposite the angle to the hypotenuse. [< L *sinus* a bend]

si·ne·cure (sī′nə·kyŏŏr, sin′ə-) *n.* An office or position for which pay is received, but involving few or no duties. [< L *sine* without + *cura* care] **—si′ne·cur·ism** *n.* **—si′ne·cur·ist** *n.*

si·ne di·e (sī′nē dī′ē) *Latin* Without setting a day for reassembling; literally, without a day.

si·ne qua non (sī′nē kwā non′) *Latin* That which is indispensable; an essential; literally, without which not.

sin·ew (sin′yōō) *n.* 1. A tendon or similar fibrous cord. 2. Strength, or that which supplies strength. **—***v.t.* To strengthen or knit together. [OE *seono*] **—sin′ew·less** *adj.*

sin·ew·y (sin′yōō·ē) *adj.* 1. Strong; brawny. 2. Forceful; vigorous: a *sinewy* style.

sin·ful (sin′fəl) *adj.* Characterized by, suggestive of, or tainted with sin; wicked; immoral. [OE *synfull*] **—sin′ful·ly** *adv.* **—sin′ful·ness** *n.*

sing (sing) *v.* **sang, sung, sing·ing** *v.i.* 1. To produce word sounds that differ from speech in that vowels are lengthened and pitches are clearly defined. 2. To use the voice in this manner for musical rendition or performance. 3. To produce melodious sounds, as a bird. 4. To make a melodious sound suggestive of singing, as a teakettle. 5. *Slang* To give evidence. **—***v.t.* 6. To render (a song, etc.) by singing. 7. To chant, intone, or utter in a songlike manner. 8. To bring to a specified condition by singing: *Sing* me to sleep. 9. To relate in or as in song; acclaim: they *sing* his fame. **—to sing out** *Informal* To call out loudly; shout. **—***n. Informal* A gathering for general participation in singing. [OE *singan*] **—sing′a·ble** *adj.*

singe (sinj) *v.t.* **singed, singe·ing** 1. To burn slightly or superficially; scorch. 2. To remove bristles or feathers from by passing through flame. 3. To burn the ends of (hair, etc.). **—***n.* 1. The act of singeing, esp. as performed by a barber. 2. A superficial burn; scorch. [OE *sengan* to scorch, hiss]

sing·er (sing′ər) *n.* 1. One who sings, esp. as a profession. 2. A songbird.

Sin·gha·lese (sing′gə·lēz′, -lēs′) *n.* 1. One of the Singhalese people who inhabit Sri Lanka. 2. The Indic language of the Singhalese. Also *Sinhalese.* [< Skt. *Siṅhala* Ceylon] **—Sin′gha·lese′** *adj.*

sin·gle (sing′gəl) *adj.* 1. Consisting of one only; individual. 2. Without another; alone. 3. Unmarried. 4. Consisting of only one part. 5. Designed for use by only one person: a *single* bed. **—***n.* 1. One person or thing. 2. In baseball, a base hit that enables the batter to reach first base. 3. A hotel room for one person. 4. *pl.* In tennis, etc., a game having one player on each side. 5. *Informal* A one-dollar bill. 6. *Usu. pl.* An unmarried person: a resort for *singles.* **—***v.* **·gled, ·gling** *v.t.* 1. To select from others: usu. with *out.* **—***v.i.* 2. In baseball, to make a one-base hit. [< L *singulus*] **—sin′gle·ness** *n.*

sin·gle-breast·ed (sing′gəl·bres′tid) *adj.* Fastening in front with a single set of buttons, loops, etc., as a coat or jacket.

single file A line of persons or things one behind the other.

sin·gle-hand·ed (sing′gəl·han′did) *adj.* 1. Without help; unaided. 2. Having or using but one hand. **—sin′gle-hand′ed, sin′gle-hand′ed·ly** *adv.* **—sin′gle-hand′ed·ness** *n.*

sin·gle-mind·ed (sing′gəl·mīn′did) *adj.* Having but one purpose or aim. **—sin′gle-mind′ed·ly** *adv.* **—sin′gle-mind′ed·ness** *n.*

sin·gle-phase (sin′gəl·fāz′) *adj. Electr.* Designating an alternating-current circuit having one phase at any given instant.

sin·gle·ton (sing′gəl·tən) *n.* A single card of a suit in a card player's hand.

sin·gle·tree (sing′gəl·trē′) *n.* A whiffletree.

sin·gly (sing′glē) *adv.* 1. Without help; unaided. 2. One by one; separately.

sing·song (sing′sông′) *n.* Monotonous cadence in speaking or reading. **—***adj.* Monotonous; droning.

sin·gu·lar (sing′gyə·lər) *adj.* 1. Extraordinary; remarkable. 2. Odd; peculiar. 3. Being the only one of its type; unique. 4. *Gram.* Of or designating a word form that denotes one person or thing. **—***n. Gram.* The singular number or form of a word. [< L *singulus* single] **—sin′gu·lar′i·ty** (-lar′ə·tē) *n.* **—sin′gu·lar·ly** *adv.* **—sin′gu·lar·ness** *n.*

Sin·ha·lese (sin′hə·lēz′, -lēs′) *n. & adj.* Singhalese.

sin·is·ter (sin′is·tər) *adj.* 1. Malevolent; evil; wicked. 2. Threatening or tending toward disaster; ominous. 3. *Heraldry* Being on the wearer's left, and hence on the observer's right: opposed to *dexter.* [< L, left] **—sin′is·ter·ly** *adv.* **—sin′is·ter·ness** *n.*

sin·is·tral (sin′is·trəl) *adj.* 1. On the left side. 2. Left-handed. **—sin′is·tral·ly** *adv.*

sink (singk) *v.* **sank, sunk** (*Obs.* **sunk·en**), **sink·ing** *v.i.* 1. To go beneath the surface of water or other liquid. 2. To descend or appear to descend to a lower level. 3. To fail, as from ill health; approach death. 4. To become less in force, volume, or degree: His voice *sank* to a whisper. 5. To become less in value, price, etc. 6. To decline in moral level, prestige, wealth, etc. 7. To permeate: The oil *sank* into the wood. 8. To become hollow; cave in, as the cheeks. 9. To be impressed or fixed, as in the mind: with *in.* **—***v.t.* 10. To cause to go beneath the surface or to the bottom. 11. To cause to fall or drop; lower. 12. To force or drive into place: to *sink* a fence post. 13. To make (a mine shaft, well, etc.) by digging or excavating. 14. To reduce in force, volume, or degree. 15. To invest and subsequently lose. **—***n.* 1. A box-shaped or basinlike receptacle with a drainpipe and usu. with a water supply. 2. A cesspool or sewer. 3. A basin or other depression in the earth's surface where water collects. [OE *sincan*] **—sink′a·ble** *adj.*

sink·er (singk′ər) *n.* A weight for sinking a fishing line.

sink·hole (singk′hōl′) *n.* A natural cavity, esp. a drainage cavity, as a hole worn by water.

sinking fund A fund established to wipe out a debt.

sin·less (sin′lis) *adj.* Having no sin; guiltless; innocent. **—sin′less·ly** *adv.* **—sin′less·ness** *n.*

sin·ner (sin′ər) *n.* One who has sinned.

Sino- *combining form* Chinese. [< LL *Sinae* the Chinese]

sin·ter (sin′tər) *v.t. & v.i.* *Metall.* To make or become cohesive by the combined action of heat and pressure. [< G, dross of iron] —**sin′ter** *n.*

sin·u·ous (sin′yo͞o·əs) *adj.* Characterized by bends, curves, or folds; winding; undulating. [< L *sinus* bend] —**sin′u·os′i·ty** (-os′ə·tē) *n.* —**sin′u·ous·ly** *adv.* —**sin′u·ous·ness** *n.*

si·nus (sī′nəs) *n.* 1. An opening or cavity. 2. *Anat.* Any of the air-filled cavities in the cranial bones, connected to the nostrils. [< L]

si·nu·si·tis (sī′nə·sī′tis) *n.* *Pathol.* Inflammation of a sinus or sinuses.

Siou·an (so͞o′ən) *n.* A large family of North American Indian languages formerly spoken from the west banks of the Mississippi to the Rocky Mountains. —**Siou′an** *adj.*

Sioux (so͞o) *n.* *pl.* **Sioux** One of a group of North American Indian tribes formerly occupying the Dakotas and parts of Minnesota and Nebraska: also called *Dakota.*

sip (sip) *v.t. & v.i.* **sipped, sip·ping** To drink (a liquid) a little at a time. —*n.* A small amount sipped. [OE *sypian* to absorb] —**sip′per** *n.*

si·phon (sī′fən) *n.* 1. A bent or flexible tube through which liquids may be passed from a higher to a lower level over an intervening elevation by making use of atmospheric pressure. 2. A siphon bottle. —*v.t.* To draw off through a siphon. [< Gk. *siphōn*] —**si′phon·al** *adj.*

siphon bottle A bottle containing carbonated water that can be expelled by pressure.

sir (sûr) *n.* 1. The term of respectful address to men, not followed by a proper name. 2. *cap.* A title of baronets and knights, used before the name. [< SIRE]

sire (sīr) *n.* 1. A father; begetter: sometimes used in combination: *grandsire.* 2. The male parent of a mammal. 3. A form of address used in speaking to a king. —*v.t.* **sired, sir·ing** To beget. [< L *senior* older]

si·ren (sī′rən) *n.* 1. A fascinating, dangerous woman. 2. A device that emits a loud, wailing sound, used chiefly as a warning signal. [< Gk. *seirēn*]

sir·loin (sûr′loin) *n.* A loin of beef, esp. the upper portion. [< OF *sur-* over, above + *longe* loin]

si·roc·co (si·rok′ō) *n.* *pl.* **·cos** *Meteorol.* A hot, dry, dusty wind blowing from northern Africa to southern Europe. [< Ital. < Arabic *sharq* the east, the rising sun]

sir·rah (sir′ə) *n.* *Archaic* Fellow; sir: a term of address expressing contempt or annoyance. [Var. of SIR]

sir·up (sir′əp) See **SYRUP.**

sis (sis) *n.* *Informal* Sister.

si·sal (sī′səl, sī′zəl, sis′əl) *n.* 1. A strong fiber obtained from the leaves of an agave of the West Indies. 2. The plant yielding this fiber. Also **sisal grass, sisal hemp.** [after *Sisal,* town in Yucatán, Mexico]

sis·sy (sis′ē) *n.* *pl.* **·sies** *Informal* 1. An effeminate man or boy. 2. A coward or weakling. [< SIS] —**sis′sy·ish** *adj.*

sis·ter (sis′tər) *n.* 1. A female having the same parents as another. 2. A female fellow member of a club, sorority, etc. 3. A nun. 4. *Brit.* A head nurse in a hospital ward. —*adj.* Bearing the relationship of a sister or one suggestive of sisterhood. [OE *sweostor*] —**sis′ter·li·ness** *n.* —**sis′ter·ly** *adv.*

sis·ter·hood (sis′tər·ho͝od) *n.* 1. The relationship between sisters. 2. A body of women united by some bond of fellowship or sympathy.

sis·ter-in-law (sis′tər·in·lô′) *n.* *pl.* **sis·ters-in-law** 1. A sister of a husband or wife. 2. A brother's wife. 3. The wife of a spouse's brother.

sit (sit) *v.* **sat, sat, sit·ting** *v.i.* 1. To rest with the buttocks on a supporting surface. 2. To perch or roost, as a bird; also, to cover eggs for hatching. 3. To remain passive or inactive. 4. To pose, as for a portrait. 5. To meet in assembly; hold a session. 6. To occupy a seat in a deliberative body. 7. To fit or be adjusted; suit: That hat *sits* well. 8. To be located: The wind *sits* in the east. 9. To baby-sit, serve as company for someone ill, etc. —*v.t.* 10. To ride (a horse). 11. To seat. —**to sit in** To join or take part. —**to sit out** 1. To remain till the end of. 2. To sit aside during: They *sat out* a dance. —**to sit tight** *Informal* To wait for the next move. [OE *sittan*] —**sit′ter** *n.*

si·tar (si·tär′) *n.* An East Indian stringed instrument resembling a guitar. [< Hind. *sitār*]

sit-down strike (sit′doun′) A strike during which strikers refuse to leave their place of employment until agreement is reached. Also **sit′-down′.**

site (sīt) *n.* A location or position; scene. [< L *situs* position]

sit-in (sit′in′) *n.* A demonstration of protest, in which participants enter and remain seated in a public place, commercial establishment, etc.

sito- *combining form* Food. [< Gk. *sitos*]

sit·ting (sit′ing) *adj.* 1. Being in a seated position. 2. Used for sitting: *sitting* room. —*n.* 1. A single period of remaining seated for a specific purpose. 2. A session or term.

sitting duck *Informal* Any easy target.

sitting room A parlor; living room.

sit·u·ate (sich′o͞o·āt) *v.t.* **·at·ed, ·at·ing** To place in a certain position or place; locate. [< Med.L. *situare* to place]

sit·u·at·ed (sich′o͞o·ā′tid) *adj.* 1. Having a fixed place or location; placed. 2. Placed in (usu. specified) circumstances: He is *well* situated.

sit·u·a·tion (sich′o͞o·ā′shən) *n.* 1. Condition; state of affairs; status. 2. A location or position; place. 3. One's job. —**sit′u·a′tion·al** *adj.*

sit-up (sit′up) *n.* An exercise in which one rises from a supine to a sitting position without bending the legs.

six (siks) *n.* The sum of five and one: a cardinal number written 6, VI. —**at sixes and sevens** 1. In a state of confusion. 2. At odds; estranged. [OE] —**six** *adj.*

six-pack (siks′pak′) *n.* Six cans or bottles, esp. of beer, packaged and sold as a unit.

six·pence (siks′pəns) *n.* A former British silver coin worth six pennies.

six·pen·ny (siks′pen′ē, -pən·ē) *adj.* 1.

Worth or sold for sixpence. 2. Paltry; trashy.
six-shoot·er (siks′shōō′tər) *n.* *Informal* A revolver firing six times without reloading.
six·teen (siks′tēn′) *n.* The sum of fifteen and one: a cardinal number written 16, XVI. [OE *sixtȳne*] **—six′teen′** *adj.* **—six′·teenth′** *adj. & n.*
sixteenth note *Music* A note having one sixteenth the time value of a whole note.
sixth (siksth) *adj.* 1. Next after the fifth: the ordinal of *six.* 2. Being one of six equal parts. *—n.* 1. One of six equal parts. 2. That which follows the fifth. 3. *Music* The interval between any tone and another tone five steps from it in a diatonic scale. *—adv.* In the sixth order, place, etc.
sixth sense Intuitive perception; intuition.
six·ty (siks′tē) *n. pl.* **·ties** The sum of fifty and ten: a cardinal number written 60, LX. [OE *sixtig*] **—six′ti·eth** *adj. & n.* **—six′ty** *adj.*
siz·a·ble (sī′zə·bəl) *adj.* Quite large. Also **size′a·ble.** **—siz′a·ble·ness** *n.* **—siz′a·bly** *adv.*
size¹ (sīz) *n.* 1. Measurement or extent of a thing as compared with some standard. 2. Comparative magnitude or bulk. 3. One of a series of graded measures, as of hats, shoes, etc. 4. A standard of measurement; specified quantity. 5. *Informal* State of affairs; true situation: That's the *size* of it. *—v.t.* **sized, siz·ing** To distribute or classify according to size. **—to size up** *Informal* 1. To form an estimate or opinion of. 2. To meet a standard. [< F *assise* to assize]
size² (sīz) *n.* A pasty substance, as glue or casein, used to glaze paper, coat walls, etc.: also called *sizing.* *—v.t.* **sized, siz·ing** To treat with size. [< OItal. *sisa* painter's glue]
sized (sīzd) *adj.* Of a specified size: often used in combination: *good-sized.* Also **size:** life-*size.*
siz·ing (sī′zing) *n.* 1. Size². 2. The process of adding or applying size to a fabric, surface, etc.
siz·zle (siz′əl) *v.i.* **·zled, ·zling** 1. To burn, fry, etc., with a hissing sound. 2. To be extremely hot. *—n.* A sizzling sound. [Imit.]
siz·zler (siz′lər) *n.* *Informal* A very hot day. [< SIZZLE]
skate¹ (skāt) *n.* 1. A metal runner attached to the sole of a shoe, used for gliding over ice. 2. A roller skate. *—v.i.* **skat·ed, skat·ing** To move over a surface on skates. [< OF *escache* stilt] **—skat′er** *n.*
skate² (skāt) *n.* Any of various ray fishes having large pectoral fins and a pointed snout. [< ON *skata*]
skate·board (skāt′bôrd′) *n.* A narrow platform on roller-skate wheels. *—v.i.* To ride or perform on a skateboard. **—skate′board·er** *n.* **—skate′board·ing** *n.*
ske·dad·dle (ski·dad′l) *v.i.* **·dled, ·dling** *Informal* To flee in haste. [Origin unknown]
skeet (skēt) *n.* Trapshooting in which targets are fired at from various angles. [< ON *skjota* to shoot]
skein (skān) *n.* A quantity of yarn, thread, etc., in a loose coil. [< OF *escaigne*]
skel·e·ton (skel′ə·tən) *n.* 1. The supporting or protective framework of a human or animal body, consisting of the bones and connective cartilage (**endoskeleton**) in man and the vertebrates, or of a hard outer structure (**exoskeleton**), as in crustaceans, insects, etc. 2. An outline, as of a play; sketch. 3. A very thin or emaciated person or animal. **—skeleton in the closet** A secret source of shame or discredit. *—adj.* 1. Of or like a skeleton. 2. Consisting merely of a few workers, a crude outline, etc.: a *skeleton* crew. [< Gk. *skeleton* (*sōma*) dried (body), mummy < *skeletos* dried up] **—skel′e·tal** *adj.*
skeleton key A key used to open a number of different locks.
skep·tic (skep′tik) *n.* 1. One who doubts, disbelieves, or disagrees with generally accepted ideas. 2. One who questions the doctrines of a religion. Also spelled *sceptic.* [< LGk. *skeptikos* reflective]
skep·ti·cal (skep′ti·kəl) *adj.* Doubting; questioning; disbelieving. Also spelled *sceptical.* **—skep′ti·cal·ly** *adv.* **—skep′ti·cal·ness** *n.*
skep·ti·cism (skep′tə·siz′əm) *n.* 1. A doubting or disbelieving attitude. 2. *Philos.* The doctrine that absolute knowledge is unattainable. Also spelled *scepticism.*
sketch (skech) *n.* 1. A rough or rapid drawing or outline. 2. A short or light story, play, comedy act, etc. *—v.t. & v.i.* To make a rough drawing or outline (of). [< Gk. *schedios* improvisation] **—sketch′a·ble** *adj.* **—sketch′er** *n.*
sketch·book (skech′bo͝ok′) *n.* 1. A pad used for sketching. 2. A set or collection of literary sketches.
sketch·y (skech′ē) *adj.* **sketch·i·er, sketch·i·est** 1. Roughly suggested without detail. 2. Incomplete. **—sketch′i·ly** *adv.* **—sketch′i·ness** *n.*
skew (skyōō) *v.i.* 1. To take an oblique direction; swerve. *—v.t.* 2. To give an oblique direction or form to; slant. 3. To twist the meaning of; distort. *—adj.* Placed or turned obliquely; twisted. *—n.* A deviation from symmetry or straightness; slant. [< OF *eschiuver* to shun < Gmc.]
skew·er (skyōō′ər) *n.* A pin thrust into meat to hold it together while cooking. *—v.t.* To run through or fasten with or as with a skewer. [< ON *skifa* a slice]
ski (skē) *n. pl.* **skis** One of a pair of wooden or metal runners attached to the feet and used in sliding over snow. *—v.i.* **skied** (skēd), **ski·ing** To glide on skis, esp. as a sport. [< Norw. < ON *skith* snowshoe] **—ski′er** *n.*
skid (skid) *n.* 1. The act of skidding or slipping. 2. A platform for moving or storing loads: also called *pallet.* 3. A log, rail, etc., used as a track in sliding heavy articles about. 4. A device to stop a wheel from turning. 5. *Aeron.* A runner in an airplane's landing gear. *—v.i.* **skid·ded, skid·ding** To slide or slip, as a car on ice. [? < ON *skith* piece of wood]
skid road A road along which logs are hauled.
skid row *Slang* An urban section inhabited by vagrants and derelicts. [< SKID ROAD]
skiff (skif) *n.* A light rowboat or small, open sailing vessel. [< OHG *scif* ship]
ski·ing (skē′ing) *n.* The act or sport of one who skis.

ski jump A course that allows skiers to make high jumps.
ski lift A motor-driven conveyor for transporting skiers to the top of a slope. Also called *ski tow*.
skill (skil) *n.* 1. Proficiency or ability in any task. 2. A developed art, trade, or technique. [< ON *skil* knowledge] **—skilled** *adj.* **—skill′ful** *adj.* **—skill′ful·ly** *adv.* **—skill′ful·ness** *n.*
skil·let (skil′it) *n.* A frying pan. [? < OF *esculette* dish]
skim (skim) *v.* **skimmed, skim·ming** *v.t.* 1. To remove floating matter from the surface of: to *skim* milk. 2. To remove thus: to *skim* cream. 3. To move lightly and quickly over. 4. To read hastily or superficially. **—***v.i.* 5. To move quickly and lightly over a surface; glide. 6. To do something hastily or superficially: with *over* or *through*. [Var. of SCUM]
skim·mer (skim′ər) *n.* 1. A flat ladle or other utensil for skimming. 2. A hat having a shallow crown and a wide, round brim.
skim milk Milk from which the cream has been removed. Also **skimmed milk.**
skimp (skimp) *v.t.* & *v.i.* To scrimp or scamp. **—***adj.* Scant; meager. [Prob. < ON *skemma* to shorten]
skimp·y (skim′pē) *adj.* **skimp·i·er, skimp·i·est** Hardly enough; scanty; meager. **—skimp′i·ly** *adv.* **—skimp′i·ness** *n.*
skin (skin) *n.* 1. The tissue covering the body of an animal; integument. ◆Collateral adjectives: *cutaneous, dermal.* 2. The pelt of an animal. 3. An outside layer, as the rind of a fruit. 4. One's life: to save one's *skin.* **—by the skin of one's teeth** Very closely or narrowly; barely. **—to get under one's skin** To be provoking or irritating. **—***v.t.* **skinned, skin·ning** To remove the skin of; flay; peel. [< ON *skinn*]
skin-deep (skin′dēp′) *adj.* Superficial.
skin-dive (skin′dīv′) *v.i.* **-dived** (*Informal* **-dove**), **-dived, -div·ing** To engage in skin diving.
skin diving Underwater swimming with goggles, foot fins, and scuba or snorkel. **—skin diver**
skin·flick (skin′flik′) *n.* *Slang* A pornographic motion picture.
skin·flint (skin′flint) *n.* A stingy person; miser.
skin game A crooked gambling game; also, any swindle.
skin·ner (skin′ər) *n.* 1. One who deals in pelts and hides. 2. *Slang* A mule driver.
skin·ny (skin′ē) *adj.* **·ni·er, ·ni·est** Very thin; lean. **—skin′ni·ness** *n.*
skin·ny-dip (skin′ē dip′) *v.i.* **-dipped, -dip·ping** *Informal* To swim nude.
skin·tight (skin′tīt′) *adj.* Fitting tightly.
skip (skip) *v.* **skipped, skip·ping** *v.i.* 1. To move with light springing steps; caper. 2. To bounce or ricochet. 3. *Informal* To leave hurriedly; flee. 4. To be advanced in school beyond the next grade in order. **—***v.t.* 5. To leap lightly over. 6. To cause to bounce or ricochet. 7. To pass over or by; omit. 8. *Informal* To leave (a place) hurriedly. **—***n.* 1. A light bound or hop. 2. A passing over without notice. [Prob. < Scand. Cf. Sw. *sku ppa* to skip.]
ski pants Close-fitting pants worn for skiing.
skip·jack (skip′jak′) *n.* Any of various fishes that leap from or skip along the surface of the water, as the bonito.
skip·per[1] (skip′ər) *n.* Any of a family of small butterflies.
skip·per[2] (skip′ər) *n.* The captain of a ship. [< Du. *schip* ship] **—skip′per** *v.t.*
skir·mish (skûr′mish) *n.* 1. A brief, minor battle in a war. 2. Any minor conflict or argument. **—***v.i.* To engage in a skirmish. [< OF *eskermir* to fence, fight] **—skir′·mish·er** *n.*
skirt (skûrt) *n.* A garment or part of a garment that hangs below the waist. **—***v.t.* 1. To lie along or form the edge of; to border. 2. To bypass. 3. To evade or avoid (a subject, issue, etc.). **—***v.i.* 4. To pass or be near the edge or border of something. [ON *skyrt* shirt]
ski run A course or slope for skiing.
skit (skit) *n.* A short, humorous dramatic sketch. [? < ON *skjota* to shoot]
ski tow A ski lift.
skit·ter (skit′ər) *v.i.* To glide or skim along a surface.
skit·tish (skit′ish) *adj.* 1. Easily frightened, as a horse. 2. Capricious; uncertain; unreliable. [< dial. E *skit* to caper, as a horse] **—skit′tish·ly** *adv.* **—skit′tish·ness** *n.*
skit·tle (skit′l) *n.* 1. *pl.* A game of ninepins, in which a flattened ball or thick rounded disk is thrown to knock down the pins. 2. One of the pins used in this game. **—beer and skittles** Carefree existence; drink and play. [Prob. < Dan. *skyttel* a child's earthen ball]
Skiv·vies (skiv′ēz) *n.pl.* 1. A man's short-sleeved undershirt: also **skiv′vy shirt.** 2. Men's underwear. A trade name.
skoal (skōl) *interj.* To your good health: a toast. [< Scand.]
skul·dug·ger·y (skul·dug′ər·ē) *n.* Trickery; underhandedness. [Origin uncertain]
skulk (skulk) *v.i.* To move about furtively; slink. [< Scand.] **—skulk′er** *n.*
skull (skul) *n.* 1. The bony framework of the head of a vertebrate animal; cranium. 2. The head considered as the seat of brain; the mind. [< Scand.]
skull and crossbones A representation of the human skull over two crossed bones, used as a symbol of death or as a warning label on poison.
skull·cap (skul′kap′) *n.* A small, snug, brimless cap.
skunk (skungk) *n.* 1. A carnivorous mammal of North America, usu. black with a white stripe and a bushy tail, and ejecting at will a malodorous liquid. 2. *Informal* A hateful or contemptible person. **—***v.t.* *Slang* To defeat utterly in a game or contest. [< Algonquian *seganku*]
skunk cabbage A perennial plant of the arum family, emitting a strong odor. Also **skunk·weed** (skungk′wēd′).
sky (skī) *n.* *pl.* **skies** 1. The region of the upper air; firmament. 2. *Often pl.* Atmospheric condition: cloudy *skies.* 3. Heaven. **—***v.t.* **skied, sky·ing** *Informal* To bat or throw (a ball, etc.) high into the air. [< ON *sky* cloud] **—sky·ey** (skī′ē) *adj.*
sky blue A blue like the color of the sky on a clear day. **—sky-blue** (skī′blo͞o′) *adj.*

sky·cap (skī′kap′) *n.* A porter at an airline terminal.
sky·div·ing (skī′dī′ving) *n.* The sport of jumping from an airplane and performing various maneuvers before opening the parachute. —**sky diver**
Skye terrier (skī) A small terrier having a long body, short legs, and long, straight hair.
sky-high (skī′hī′) *adj. & adv.* Extremely high.
sky·jack (skī′jak′) *v.t.* To seize control of (an aircraft). [< SKY + (HI)JACK] —**sky′·jack′er** *n.* —**sky′jack′ing** *n.*
sky·lark (skī′lärk′) *n.* A lark of the Old World that sings as it rises in flight. —*v.i.* To frolic boisterously. —**sky′lark′er** *n.*
sky·light (skī′līt′) *n.* A window in a roof or ceiling.
sky·line (skī′līn′) *n.* 1. The horizon. 2. The outline of buildings, etc., seen against the sky.
sky marshal A federal security officer assigned to prevent skyjackings.
sky·rock·et (skī′rok′it) *n.* A fireworks rocket projected so as to explode high in the air. —*v.i.* To rise rapidly or suddenly.
sky·scrap·er (skī′skrā′pər) *n.* A very high building.
sky·ward (skī′wərd) *adv.* Toward the sky. Also **sky′wards.** —*adj.* Moving or directed toward the sky.
sky·writ·ing (skī′rī′ting) *n.* 1. The forming of words in the air by the release of vapor from an airplane. 2. The words or letters thus formed. —**sky′writ′er** *n.*
slab (slab) *n.* A flat, thick piece or slice. —*v.t.* **slabbed, slab·bing** To make or form into slabs. [ME]
slack[1] (slak) *adj.* 1. Hanging or extended loosely. 2. Careless; remiss; slovenly. 3. Slow; sluggish. 4. Lacking activity; not busy: a *slack* season. —*v.t.* 1. To slacken. 2. To slake, as lime. —*v.i.* 3. To be or become slack. —**to slack off** To slow down; be less diligent. —*n.* 1. A part of a rope, sail, etc., that is slack or loose. 2. Slack condition; looseness. 3. A period of inactivity. —*adv.* In a slack manner. [OE *sleac*] —**slack′ly** *adv.* —**slack′ness** *n.*
slack[2] (slak) *n.* Small pieces of coal left after screening. [Cf. Flemish *slecke*, LG *slacke*]
slack·en (slak′ən) *v.i.* 1. To become less active, productive, etc. 2. To become less tense or tight. —*v.t.* 3. To become slow, negligent, or remiss in: to *slacken* one's efforts. 4. To loosen.
slack·er (slak′ər) *n.* One who shirks his duties or avoids military service in wartime; shirker.
slacks (slaks) *n.pl.* Trousers worn by men or women.
slag (slag) *n.* 1. *Metall.* The waste left after a metal is separated from its ore in the smelting process. 2. Volcanic lava in small, cinderlike pieces. —*v.t. & v.i.* **slagged, slag·ging** To form into slag. [< MLG *slagge*] —**slag′gy** *adj.*
slain (slān) Past participle of SLAY.
slake (slāk) *v.* **slaked, slak·ing** *v.t.* 1. To quench or satisfy, as thirst. 2. To cause (lime) to heat and crumble by mixing it with water. —*v.i.* 3. Of lime, to crumble. [OE *slacian* to retard < *sleac* slack[1]]
slaked lime Lime treated with water.
sla·lom (slä′ləm) *n.* In skiing, a downhill race over a zigzag course. —*v.i.* To ski in such a course. [< Norw.]
slam[1] (slam) *v.* **slammed, slam·ming** *v.t.* 1. To shut, hit, throw, etc., forcefully and noisily. 2. *Slang* To criticize harshly. —*v.i.* 3. To close, swing, etc., with force and noise. —*n.* 1. The act or noise of slamming. 2. *Slang* Harsh criticism; abuse. [< Scand. Cf. dial. Norw. *slamra* slam.]
slam[2] (slam) *n.* In bridge, the winning of all (**grand slam**) or all but one (**little** or **small slam**) of the tricks in a round of play; also, a bid to do so. [Origin uncertain]
slam·mer (slam′ər) *n.* *Slang* A jail or prison.
slan·der (slan′dər) *n.* A false statement that damages another's reputation. —*v.t.* 1. To make such a statement against. —*v.i.* 2. To utter slander. [< L *scandalum* cause of stumbling] —**slan′der·er** *n.* —**slan′der·ous** *adj.* —**slan′der·ous·ly** *adv.* —**slan′der·ous·ness** *n.*
slang (slang) *n.* Language of a vigorous, colorful, or taboo nature, invented for specific occasions or uses or derived from the unconventional use of the standard vocabulary. [Origin uncertain]
slang·y (slang′ē) *adj.* **slang·i·er, slang·i·est** Containing or using slang. —**slang′i·ness** *n.*
slant (slant) *v.t.* 1. To give an oblique or sloping direction to; incline. 2. To write or utter so as to express a special attitude, bias, or opinion. —*v.i.* 3. To have or take an oblique direction; slope. —*adj.* Lying at an angle; sloping. —*n.* 1. A slanting direction, course, or plane; slope. 2. A bent, bias, or leaning. 3. Point of view; attitude. [< Scand. Cf. Norw. *slenta* slope.] —**slant′ing·ly** *adv.*
slant·wise (slant′wīz′) *adj.* Slanting; oblique. —*adv.* At a slant or slope; obliquely. Also **slant′ways′** (-wāz′).
slap (slap) *n.* 1. A blow delivered with the open hand or something flat. 2. A sharp rebuke; insult; slur. —*v.* **slapped, slap·ping** *v.t.* 1. To hit or strike with the open hand or something flat. —*v.i.* 2. To strike or beat as if with slaps. [< LG *slapp*] —**slap′·per** *n.*
slap·dash (slap′dash′) *adj.* Done or acting in a reckless way; impetuous; careless. —**slap′dash′** *adv.*
slap·hap·py (slap′hap′ē) *adj.* **·pi·er, ·pi·est** *Slang* Dazed or giddy from or as from repeated blows. —**slap′hap′pi·ness** *n.*
slap·stick (slap′stick′) *n.* Boisterous, loud comedy. —*adj.* Using or like slapstick.
slash (slash) *v.t.* 1. To cut violently with sweeping strokes. 2. To make gashes or slits in. 3. To reduce sharply, as prices. —*v.i.* 4. To make sweeping strokes with or as with a knife. —*n.* 1. A slit or gash. 2. A slanting line (/) used to indicate two alternatives (and/or), to express *per* (feet/sec.), to form fractions (3/8), etc.: also called *solidus, virgule.* [? < OF *esclachier* to break] —**slash′er** *n.*
slash·ing (slash′ing) *adj.* Driving or falling hard: a *slashing* snowstorm. —**slash′ing·ly** *adv.*

slat (slat) *n.* A thin, narrow strip, as in a window blind. —*v.t.* **slat·ted, slat·ting** To provide or make with slats. [< OF *esclat* splinter]

slate (slāt) *n.* 1. A compact, fine-grained rock that splits readily into thin layers. 2. A piece of slate used for roofing, writing upon, etc. 3. A list of candidates for election. 4. A dull bluish gray color. —**a clean slate** A record free of misdeeds, past performances, etc. —*adj.* 1. Made of slate. 2. Having the color of slate. —*v.t.* **slat·ed, slat·ing** 1. To roof with slate. 2. To designate for candidacy, appointment, action, etc. [< OF *esclate*, fem. of *esclat* chip, splinter] —**slat'er** *n.* —**slat'y** *adj.*

slath·er (slath'ər) *Informal v.t.* To daub thickly or use profusely. [Origin uncertain]

slat·tern (slat'ərn) *n.* An untidy or slovenly woman. [< dial. E *slatter* to slop, spill] —**slat'tern·li·ness** *n.* —**slat'tern·ly** *adj. & adv.*

slaugh·ter (slô'tər) *n.* 1. The butchering of cattle and other animals for market. 2. Wanton or savage killing of human beings; massacre; carnage. —*v.t.* 1. To kill for the market; butcher. 2. To kill wantonly or savagely. [< ON *slātr* butcher's meat] —**slaugh'ter·er** *n.* —**slaugh'ter·ous** *adj.* —**slaugh'ter·ous·ly** *adv.*

slaugh·ter·house (slô'tər·hous') *n.* A place where animals are butchered.

Slav (släv, slav) *n.* A member of any of the Slavic-speaking peoples of northern or eastern Europe.

slave (slāv) *n.* 1. A person who is the property of another; bondman; serf. 2. A person who is dominated by a habit, vice, etc.: a *slave* to drink. 3. *Informal* A drudge. —*v.i.* **slaved, slav·ing** To work like a slave. [< Med.L *slavus, sclavus*]

slave driver 1. A person who oversees slaves at work. 2. Any severe or exacting employer.

slave·hold·er (slāv'hōl'dər) *n.* An owner of slaves. —**slave'hold'ing** *adj. & n.*

slav·er[1] (slav'ər) *v.i.* To dribble saliva; drool. —*n.* Saliva dribbling from the mouth. [Prob. < ON *slafra*] —**slav'er·er** *n.*

slav·er[2] (slā'vər) *n.* A person or vessel engaged in the slave trade.

slav·er·y (slā'vər·ē, slāv'rē) *n.* 1. The holding of human beings as property; also, the condition of a slave. 2. Drudgery; toil.

slave trade The business of dealing in slaves. —**slave trader**

slav·ey (slā'vē, slav'ē) *n. pl.* **slav·eys** *Brit. Informal* A female servant.

Slav·ic (slä'vik, slav'ik) *adj.* Of or pertaining to the Slavs or their languages. —*n.* A branch of the Balto-Slavic sub-family of the Indo-European language family, including Russian, Czech, Polish, and Bulgarian.

slav·ish (slā'vish) *adj.* 1. Of or like a slave; servile; base. 2. Dependent; imitative. —**slav'ish·ly** *adv.* —**slav'ish·ness** *n.*

Sla·von·ic (slə·von'ik) *adj. & n.* Slavic.

slaw (slô) *n.* Coleslaw.

slay (slā) *v.t.* **slew, slain, slay·ing** To kill violently. [OE *slēan*] —**slay'er** *n.*

slea·zy (slē'zē) *adj.* **·zi·er, ·zi·est** Of poor quality; cheap; shoddy. [Origin uncertain] —**slea'zi·ly** *adv.* —**slea'zi·ness** *n.*

sled (sled) *n.* A vehicle on runners moving over snow and ice; sledge. —*v.t. & v.i.* **sled·ded, sled·ding** To ride or convey on a sled. [< MLG *sledde*] —**sled'der** *n.*

sledge[1] (slej) *n.* A sled. —*v.t. & v.i.* **sledged, sledg·ing** To travel or convey on a sledge. [< MDu. *sleedse*]

sledge[2] (slej) *n.* A heavy hammer wielded with both hands, for breaking stone, etc. Also **sledge hammer.** —*v.t.* **sledged, sledg·ing** To strike with a sledge. [OE *slecg*]

sleek (slēk) *adj.* 1. Smooth and glossy; slick. 2. Looking prosperous and well-fed. —*v.t.* To make smooth or glossy. [Var. of SLICK] —**sleek'ly** *adv.* —**sleek'ness** *n.*

sleep (slēp) *n.* 1. A period of rest, accompanied by a complete or partial unconsciousness. 2. Any state like sleep, such as a trance or coma. —*v.* **slept, sleep·ing** *v.i.* 1. To be or fall asleep; slumber. 2. To be in a state, such as death, that resembles sleep. 3. To be dormant. —*v.t.* 4. To provide sleeping quarters for: a cabin that *sleeps* four. —**to sleep away** (or **off** or **out**) To pass or get rid of by or as by sleep: to *sleep off* a hangover. —**to sleep on** To postpone a decision upon. —**to sleep with** To have sexual relations with. [OE *slǣp*] —**sleep'less** *adj.* —**sleep'less·ness** *n.*

sleep·er (slē'pər) *n.* 1. One who sleeps. 2. A passenger railroad car with accommodations for sleeping: also **sleeping car.** 3. *Informal* A play, book, etc., that achieves unexpected success.

sleeping bag A large bag with a warm lining, used for sleeping outdoors.

sleeping pill A pill taken to induce sleep.

sleeping sickness *Pathol.* A usu. fatal disease transmitted by the tsetse fly, prevalent in tropical Africa, and marked by lethargy, fever, and headaches.

sleep·walk·ing (slēp'wô'king) *n.* The act of one who walks while asleep. —**sleep'walk'er** *n.*

sleep·y (slē'pē) *adj.* **sleep·i·er, sleep·i·est** 1. Inclined to sleep; drowsy. 2. Inactive or sluggish. —**sleep'i·ly** *adv.* —**sleep'i·ness** *n.*

sleep·y·head (slē'pē·hed') *n.* A sleepy person. —**sleep'y·head'ed** *adj.*

sleet (slēt) *n.* 1. A mixture of snow and rain. 2. Partly frozen rain. [Akin to MLG *slōte* hail] —**sleet** *v.i.* —**sleet'y** *adj.*

sleeve (slēv) *n.* 1. The part of a garment that covers the arms. 2. *Mech.* A tube surrounding a shaft, etc., for protection or connection. —**up one's sleeve** Hidden but ready for use. [OE *slīefe*] —**sleeve'less** *adj.*

sleigh (slā) *n.* A vehicle, usu. horse-drawn, with runners for use on snow and ice. —*v.i.* To travel in a sleigh. [< Du. *slee*, contr. of *slede* sledge] —**sleigh'ing** *n.*

sleight (slīt) *n.* 1. Skillful manipulation; dexterity. 2. Craft; cunning. [< ON *slǣgth* slyness]

sleight of hand A trick, as in magic, requiring skillful manipulation: also called *legerdemain.*

slen·der (slen'dər) *adj.* 1. Long and thin; slim. 2. Small or inadequate; meager. [ME *slendre*] —**slen'der·ly** *adv.* —**slen'der·ness** *n.*

slen·der·ize (slen'də·rīz) *v.t. & v.i.* **·ized, ·iz·ing** To make or become slender.

slept (slept) Past tense and past participle of SLEEP.

sleuth (slōōth) *n. Informal* A detective. —*v.t.* 1. To follow; track. —*v.i.* 2. To play the detective. [< ON *slōth* track, trail]
slew[1] (slōō) Past tense of SLAY.
slew[2] (slōō) See SLOUGH[1] (def. 2).
slew[3] (slōō) *n. Informal* A large number or amount: also spelled *slue.* [Cf. Irish *sluagh* crowd]
slew[4] (slōō) See SLUE[1].
slice (slīs) *n.* 1. A thin, broad piece cut off from something. 2. *Informal* Part or share. 3. In golf, a stroke that causes the ball to veer to the right. —*v.* **sliced, slic·ing** *v.t.* 1. To cut from a larger piece: often with *off.* 2. To cut into broad, thin pieces. 3. To hit (a golf ball) so that it veers to the right. —*v.i.* 4. In golf, to slice a ball. [< OHG *slizan* to slit] —**slic′er** *n.*
slick (slik) *adj.* 1. Smooth; slippery; sleek. 2. Crafty; wily: a *slick* operator. 3. Smart and clever, but often of little depth. —*n.* 1. A smooth area on a surface of water, as from oil. 2. A magazine printed on glazed paper. —*v.t.* To make smooth, glossy, or oily. [ME *slike,* ? < OE *nīgslȳcod* glossy]
slick·er (slik′ər) *n.* 1. A waterproof overcoat. 2. *Informal* A clever, shifty person.
slide (slīd) *v.* **slid** (slid), **slid·ing** *v.i.* 1. To slip along on ice or other smooth surface. 2. To move easily or smoothly; glide. 3. To slip or fall. 4. In baseball, to throw oneself along the ground toward a base. —*v.t.* 5. To cause to slide, as over a surface. 6. To move, put, enter, etc., with quietness or dexterity: with *in* or *into.* —*n.* 1. An act of sliding. 2. The fall of a mass of earth, snow, etc.; avalanche. 3. An inclined plane for children to slide upon. 4. A small glass plate on which a specimen is mounted and examined through a microscope. 5. A small plate bearing an image for projection on a screen. [OE *slīdan*]
slide fastener A zipper.
slide projector An optical device for projecting images from transparent slides onto a screen.
slid·er (slid′ər) *n.* 1. One who or that which slides. 2. In baseball, a curve ball that breaks only slightly.
slide rule A ruler with a sliding piece, both of which are graduated in a logarithmic scale to permit rapid calculations.
sliding scale A schedule of prices, wages, etc., that varies under certain conditions.
slight (slīt) *adj.* 1. Of small importance; trifling. 2. Small in quantity, intensity, etc.; meager. 3. Slender; frail; flimsy. —*v.t.* 1. To treat with disrespect; also, to ignore discourteously. 2. To perform carelessly. 3. To treat as trivial or insignificant. —*n.* An act of disrespect; a discourtesy. [ME] —**slight′ing** *adj.* —**slight′ing·ly** *adv.* —**slight′ly** *adv.* —**slight′ness** *n.*
sli·ly (slī′lē) See SLYLY.
slim (slim) *adj.* **slim·mer, slim·mest** 1. Slender; slight; thin. 2. Insufficient; meager: a *slim* attendance. —*v.t.* & *v.i.* **slimmed, slim·ming** To make or become thin. [< Du. *slim* bad] —**slim′ly** *adv.* —**slim′ness** *n.*
slime (slīm) *n.* Any moist, soft, sticky substance. —*v.t.* **slimed, slim·ing** To smear or cover with slime. [OE *slīm*]
slim·y (slī′mē) *adj.* **slim·i·er, slim·i·est** 1. Covered with slime. 2. Offensive; foul. —**slim′i·ly** *adv.* —**slim′i·ness** *n.*
sling (sling) *n.* 1. A strap with strings attached for hurling a stone or other missile. 2. A strap or rope, as for supporting an injured limb, carrying a rifle, etc. —*v.t.* **slung, sling·ing** 1. To throw with force; hurl. 2. To place or hang in a sling. [OE *slingan*] —**sling′er** *n.*
sling·shot (sling′shot′) *n.* A forked stick with an elastic strip for hurling stones, etc.
slink (slingk) *v.i.* **slunk, slink·ing** To creep or steal along furtively or stealthily, as in fear. [OE *slincan* to creep] —**slink′ing·ly** *adv.*
slink·y (slingk′ē) *adj.* **slink·i·er, slink·i·est** 1. Sneaking; stealthy. 2. *Slang* Sinuous or catlike in movement or form. —**slink′i·ly** *adv.* —**slink′i·ness** *n.*
slip[1] (slip) *v.* **slipped** or **slipt, slip·ping** *v.t.* 1. To cause to glide or slide. 2. To put on or off easily, as a loose garment. 3. To convey slyly or secretly. 4. To get away from; elude. 5. To escape or pass unobserved: It *slipped* my mind. —*v.i.* 6. To lose one's footing. 7. To fail to hold: It *slipped* out of his hand. 8. To make a mistake; err. 9. To move smoothly and easily. 10. To go or come stealthily or unnoticed: often with *off, away,* or *from.* 11. To fall below one's usual level of performance. —**to let slip** To say without intending to. —**to slip one over on** *Informal* To cheat; hoodwink. —*n.* 1. A loss of one's footing. 2. A lapse or error; a slight mistake. 3. A space between two wharves; berth. 4. A woman's undergarment, usu. the length of a dress. 5. A pillowcase. —**to give (someone) the slip** To elude (someone). [< MLG *slippen*]
slip[2] (slip) *n.* 1. A cutting from a plant for planting or grafting; scion. 2. A small piece of paper, esp. one used for a record: a sales *slip.* —*v.t.* **slipped, slip·ping** To cut off for planting. [< MDu. *slippen* to cut]
slip·case (slip′kās′) *n.* A protective container for a book, having one open end.
slip·cov·er (slip′kuv′ər) *n.* A removable fitted cover for a chair, sofa, etc.
slip·knot (slip′not′) *n.* 1. A knot having part of the material drawn through in a loop so that it is easily untied. 2. A running knot.
slip-on (slip′on′) *n.* A garment, as a blouse, that is easily slipped on or off.
slip·o·ver (slip′ō′vər) *n.* A sweater that is donned by drawing it over the head.
slip·per (slip′ər) *n.* A low, light shoe that is easily slipped on or off the foot. —**slip′·pered** *adj.*
slip·per·y (slip′ər·ē) *adj.* **·per·i·er, ·per·i·est** 1. Having a surface so smooth that objects slip or slide easily on it. 2. Unreliable; elusive; tricky. —**slip′per·i·ness** *n.*
slip·shod (slip′shod′) *adj.* Carelessly done; sloppy; slovenly.
slip-stream (slip′strēm′) *n. Aeron.* The stream of air driven backwards by the propeller of an aircraft.
slip-up (slip′up′) *n. Informal* A mistake; error.
slit (slit) *n.* A long, narrow cut or opening; slash. —*v.t.* **slit, slit·ting** 1. To make a

slit in; slash. 2. To cut into strips. [ME *slitten* to cut] —**slit′ter** *n.*

slith·er (slith′ər) *v.i.* To glide, as a snake. [OE *slīdan* to slide] —**slith′er·y** *adj.*

sliv·er (sliv′ər) *n.* A slender piece cut or torn off; splinter. —*v.t.* & *v.i.* To cut or split into slivers. [< dial. E *slive* to cleave < OE *tōflifan*] —**sliv′er·er** *n.*

slob (slob) *n.* *Informal* A stupid, careless, or unclean person. [< Irish *slab* mud]

slob·ber (slob′ər) *v.i.* To dribble saliva from the mouth; drivel; slaver. —*n.* 1. Drivel; slaver. 2. Gushing, sentimental talk. [ME *sloberen*. Akin to LG *slubberen*] —**slob′ber·er** *n.* —**slob′ber·y** *adj.*

sloe (slō) *n.* 1. The plumlike fruit of the blackthorn. 2. Any of various related plants. [OE *slāh*]

sloe-eyed (slō′īd′) *adj.* Having dark or almond-shaped eyes.

sloe gin A cordial made of gin flavored with sloes.

slog (slog) *v.t.* & *v.i.* **slogged, slog·ging** To plod (one's way), as through deep mud. [Origin uncertain] —**slog′ger** *n.*

slo·gan (slō′gən) *n.* A catchword or motto adopted by a group, as a political party. [< Scot. Gaelic *sluagh* army + *gairm* yell]

sloop (sloo͞p) *n.* *Naut.* A single-masted, fore-and-aft rigged sailing vessel carrying at least one jib. [< Du. *sloep*]

slop (slop) *v.* **slopped, slop·ping** *v.i.* 1. To splash or spill. —*v.t.* 2. To cause (a liquid) to spill or splash. 3. To feed (hogs) with slops. —**to slop over** To overflow and splash. —*n.* 1. Slush; watery mud. 2. *pl.* Unappetizing liquid or watery food. 3. *Usu. pl.* Refuse liquid. 4. *pl.* Waste food or swill, used to feed pigs, etc. [ME *sloppe*]

slope (slōp) *v.* **sloped, slop·ing** *v.i.* 1. To be inclined; slant. —*v.t.* 2. To cause to slope. —*n.* Any slanting surface or line; also, the degree of inclination. [OE *āslūpan* to slip away] —**slop′er** *n.* —**slop′ing·ly** *adv.* —**slop′ing·ness** *n.*

slop·py (slop′ē) *adj.* **·pi·er, ·pi·est** 1. Slushy; splashy; wet. 2. *Informal* Messy; slovenly; untidy. 3. *Informal* Slipshod; careless. —**slop′pi·ly** *adv.* —**slop′pi·ness** *n.*

slop sink A deep sink for washing out mops, etc.

slosh (slosh) *v.t.* 1. To throw about, as a liquid. —*v.i.* 2. To splash; flounder: to *slosh* through a pool. [Var. of SLUSH] —**slosh′y** *adj.*

slot (slot) *n.* 1. A long narrow groove or opening; slit: the *slot* of a mailbox. 2. A job opening. 3. A place in a sequence. —*v.t.* **slot·ted, slot·ting** 1. To cut a slot in; groove. 2. *Informal* To place in a schedule or series. [< OF *esclot* the hollow between the breasts]

sloth (slôth, slōth) *n.* 1. Indolence; laziness. 2. A slow-moving tree-dwelling mammal of tropical America. [ME *slouthe* < OE *slǣwth*]

sloth·ful (slôth′fəl, slōth′-) *adj.* Sluggish; lazy; indolent. —**sloth′ful·ly** *adv.* —**sloth′ful·ness** *n.*

slot machine A vending or gambling machine operated by dropping a coin in a slot.

slouch (slouch) *v.i.* To have a downcast or drooping gait, look, or posture; slump. —*n.* 1. A drooping gait or posture. 2. An awkward or incompetent person: usu. in the negative: He's no *slouch* at baseball. [Origin uncertain] —**slouch′i·ness** *n.* —**slouch′y** *adj.*

slough[1] (slou *for defs. 1 & 3*; sloo͞ *for def. 2*) *n.* 1. A place of deep mud or mire; bog. 2. A stagnant swamp or backwater: also spelled *slew, slue*. 3. A state of despair. [OE *slōh*] —**slough′y** *adj.*

slough[2] (sluf) *n.* Any layer or covering, as a snake's skin, that has been shed or cast off. —*v.t.* To cast off; discard; shed: with *off*. Also spelled *sluff*. [ME *slouh*] —**slough′y** *adj.*

Slo·vak (slō′vak, -väk) *n.* 1. One of a Slavic people of eastern Czechoslovakia. 2. The West Slavic language of the Slovaks. [< Czech *slovák* Slav] —**Slo′vak** *adj.* —**Slo·vak′i·an** *n.* & *adj.*

slov·en (sluv′ən) *n.* A sloppy person.

Slo·vene (slō′vēn) *n.* 1. One of a group of Slavs now living in NW Yugoslavia. 2. The language of the Slovenes. [< G] —**Slo′vene** *adj.* —**Slo·ve′ni·an** *adj.* & *n.*

slov·en·ly (sluv′ən·lē) *adj.* **·li·er, ·li·est** Of or like a sloven; sloppy; untidy; careless. —**slov′en·li·ness** *n.* —**slov′en·ly** *adv.*

slow (slō) *adj.* 1. Having relatively small velocity; not quick in motion, performance, or occurrence. 2. Behind the standard time: said of a timepiece. 3. Not precipitate or hasty: *slow* to anger. 4. Dull or stupid; mentally sluggish. 5. *Informal* Dull or tedious in character. 6. Inactive: Business is *slow* today. —*v.t.* & *v.i.* To make, go, or become slow or slower: often with *up* or *down*. —*adv.* In a slow or cautious manner or speed. [OE *slāw*] —**slow′ly** *adv.* —**slow′ness** *n.*

slow-mo·tion (slō′mō′shən) *adj.* Pertaining to or designating a motion picture filmed at greater than standard speed so that the action appears slow in normal projection.

slow·poke (slō′pōk′) *n.* *Informal* A person who works or moves slowly; a laggard.

sludge (sluj) *n.* 1. Soft mud; mire. 2. Muddy or pasty refuse, as that produced by sewerage purification. [Earlier *slutch*] —**sludg′y** *adj.*

slue[1] (sloo͞) *v.t.* & *v.i.* **slued, slu·ing** To move or cause to move sideways, as if some portion were pivoted. —*n.* The act of sluing around sideways. Also spelled *slew*. [Origin unknown]

slue[2] (sloo͞) See SLEW[3].

slue[3] (sloo͞) See SLOUGH[1] (def. 2).

sluff (sluf) *n.* & *v.* See SLOUGH[2].

slug[1] (slug) *n.* 1. A bullet or shot of irregular or oblong shape. 2. *Printing* A strip of type metal for spacing matter, etc. 3. Any small chunk of metal; esp., one used as a counterfeit coin. [Origin uncertain]

slug[2] (slug) *n.* Any of various elongated mollusks related to the snail and having a rudimentary shell. [ME *slugge* sluggard]

slug[3] (slug) *Informal* *n.* 1. A heavy blow, as with the fist. 2. A drink of undiluted liquor. —*v.i.* **slugged, slug·ging** To strike heavily; hit hard. [Origin uncertain] —**slug′ger** *n.*

slug·gard (slug′ərd) *n.* A person habitually lazy or idle; a drone. —*adj.* Lazy; sluggish.

slug·gish (slug′ish) *adj.* 1. Slow; inactive;

torpid. 2. Idle and lazy. —**slug′gish·ly** *adv.* —**slug′gish·ness** *n.*

sluice (slōōs) *n.* 1. An artificial channel for conducting water, equipped with a valve or gate (**sluice gate**) to regulate the flow. 2. Any artificial channel. 3. A trough through which water is run to separate gold ore, to float logs, etc. —*v.* **sluiced, sluic·ing** *v.t.* 1. To wet, water, or wash by or as by means of a sluice. 2. To draw out or conduct by or through a sluice. —*v.i.* 3. To flow out or issue from a sluice. [< L *exclusa*, pp. fem of *excludere* to shut out]

slum (slum) *n. Often pl.* A squalid section of a city, marked by poverty and poor living conditions. —*v.i.* **slummed, slum·ming** To visit slums, disreputable establishments, etc., for amusement. [Origin uncertain] —**slum′mer** *n.*

slum·ber (slum′bər) *v.i.* 1. To sleep, esp. lightly or quietly. 2. To be inactive; stagnate. —*v.t.* 3. To spend or pass in sleeping. —*n.* 1. Sleep. 2. A state of inactivity or quiescence. [OE *slūma*] —**slum′ber·er** *n.* —**slum′ber·ing·ly** *adv.* —**slum′ber·less** *adj.*

slum·ber·ous (slum′bər·əs) *adj.* 1. Inducing sleep. 2. Sleepy; drowsy. 3. Torpid; inactive. Also **slum′ber·y, slum′brous** (-brəs). —**slum′ber·ous·ly** *adv.* —**slum′ber·ous·ness** *n.*

slum·lord (slum′lôrd′) *n.* A landlord, esp. of a slum tenement, who profiteers by neglecting upkeep. [< SLUM + (LAND)LORD]

slump (slump) *v.i.* 1. To fall down or collapse suddenly. 2. To decrease suddenly, as in value or quality. 3. To stand or walk with a stooping posture. —*n.* The act of slumping; a fall, failure, or decline.

slung (slung) Past tense and past participle of SLING.

slunk (slungk) Past tense and past participle of SLINK.

slur (slûr) *v.t.* **slurred, slur·ring** 1. To slight; disparage; depreciate. 2. To pass over lightly or hurriedly. 3. To weaken and elide (speech sounds) by hurried articulation. 4. *Music* To sing or play as indicated by the slur. —*n.* 1. A disparaging remark. 2. *Music* A curved line (⌣ or ⌢) indicating that tones so tied are to be sung to the same syllable or performed without a break between them. 3. A slurred articulation. [< dial. E, orig., fluid mud]

slush (slush) *n.* 1. Soft, sloppy material, as melting snow. 2. Overly sentimental talk or writing; drivel. [? Scand.] —**slush′y** *adj.*

slush fund *Slang* Money collected or spent for corrupt purposes, as bribery.

slut (slut) *n.* 1. A slatternly woman. 2. A woman of loose character; hussy. [ME *slutte*] —**slut′tish** *adj.* —**slut′tish·ly** *adv.* —**slut′tish·ness** *n.*

sly (slī) *adj.* **sli·er** or **sly·er, sli·est** or **sly·est** 1. Artful in doing things secretly; cunning. 2. Playfully clever; mischievous. 3. Done with or marked by cunning and secrecy. —**on the sly** In a stealthy way. [< ON *slœgr*] —**sly′ness** *n.*

sly·ly (slī′lē) *adv.* In a sly manner: also spelled *slily.*

smack¹ (smak) *n.* 1. A quick, sharp sound, as of the lips when separated rapidly. 2. A sounding blow or slap. 3. *Informal* A kiss. —*v.t. & v.i.* To give or make a smack.

smack² (smak) *v.i.* To have a taste or flavor: usu. with *of.* —*n.* A taste or flavor. [OE *smæc* the taste]

smack³ (smak) *n.* A small vessel used chiefly for fishing. [< Du. *smak*]

smack·ing (smak′ing) *adj.* Brisk; lively.

small (smôl) *adj.* 1. Comparatively less in size, quantity, extent, etc.; diminutive. 2. Being of slight importance. 3. Narrow; ignoble; mean; paltry. 4. Transacting business in a limited way. 5. Lacking in power or strength. —*n.* A small or slender part: the *small* of the back. [OE *smæl*] —**small** *adv.* —**small′ness** *n.*

small arms Firearms of small caliber, as pistols, rifles, and machine guns.

small change Coins of small denomination.

small craft Small boats or vessels collectively.

small fry 1. Small, young fish. 2. Young children.

small hours The early hours of the morning.

small-mind·ed (smôl′mīn′did) *adj.* Petty; intolerant. —**small′-mind′ed·ly** *adv.* —**small′-mind′ed·ness** *n.*

small potatoes *Informal* Insignificant persons or things.

small·pox (smôl′poks′) *n. Pathol.* An acute, highly contagious virus disease, characterized by fever and pustules.

small talk Unimportant or trivial conversation.

small·time (smôl′tīm′) *adj. Slang* Petty; unimportant: a *smalltime* hoodlum.

smart (smärt) *v.i.* 1. To experience a stinging sensation, generally superficial, either bodily or mental. 2. To cause a stinging sensation. —*v.t.* 3. To cause to smart. —*adj.* 1. Quick in thought or action; bright; clever. 2. Impertinently witty: often used contemptuously. 3. Vigorous; emphatic; severe; brisk. 4. Sharp, as at trade; shrewd. 5. Stylish; fashionable. —*n.* 1. An acute stinging sensation, as from a scratch or an irritant. 2. Any distress. [OE *smeortan*] —**smart′ly** *adv.* —**smart′·ness** *n.*

smart al·eck (al′ik) *Informal* A cocky, offensively conceited person. Also **smart al′ec.** —**smart-al·eck·y** (smärt′al′ik·ē) *adj.*

smart bomb A bomb that is guided to a target by electronic means.

smart·en (smär′tən) *v.t. & v.i.* To make or become smart: often with *up.*

smart set Fashionable society.

smart·weed (smärt′wēd′) *n.* A widely distributed marsh plant whose leaves cause itching.

smash (smash) *v.t.* 1. To break in many pieces suddenly, as by a blow, pressure, or collision. 2. To flatten; crush; destroy. 3. To dash or fling violently so as to crush or break. 4. To strike with a sudden, forceful blow. —*v.i.* 5. To come into violent contact so as to crush or be crushed; collide. —*n.* 1. An act or instance of smashing, or the state of being smashed. 2. In tennis, etc., a strong overhand shot. 3. *Informal* Something striking or acclaimed: The play was a *smash.* [Prob. imit.] —**smash′er** *n.*

smash·ing (smash′ing) *adj. Informal* Extremely impressive; overwhelmingly good.

smash·up (smash′up′) *n.* A smash; a disastrous collision.
smat·ter·ing (smat′ər·ing) *n.* A superficial knowledge of something. Also **smat′ter.** [ME *smateren*] —**smat′ter·ing·ly** *adv.*
smear (smir) *v.t.* 1. To spread, rub, or cover with grease, paint, dirt, etc. 2. To apply in a thick layer or coating. 3. To defame; slander. 4. *Slang* To defeat utterly. —*v.i.* 5. To be or become smeared. —*n.* 1. A spoiled spot; stain. 2. A small quantity of material, as blood, sputum, etc., placed on a microscope slide for analysis. 3. A slanderous attack; defamation. [OE *smeoru* grease]
smear·y (smir′ē) *adj.* **smear·i·er, smear·i·est** Greasy, viscous, or staining; also, smeared. —**smear′i·ness** *n.*
smell (smel) *v.* **smelled** or **smelt, smell·ing** *v.t.* 1. To perceive by means of the nose and its olfactory nerves; scent. 2. To discover or detect as if by smelling: often with *out.* —*v.i.* 3. To emit an odor or perfume: frequently with *of*; also, to give indications of, as if by odor: to *smell* of treason. 4. To be malodorous. 5. To use the sense of smell. —*n.* 1. The special sense by means of which odors are perceived. 2. That which is directly perceived by this sense; an odor. 3. A hint; trace. [ME *smellen*] —**smell′er** *n.*
smelling salts Pungent or aromatic salts, used as a stimulant usu. to relieve faintness.
smel·ly (smel′ē) *adj.* **·li·er, ·li·est** *Informal* Having an unpleasant smell; malodorous. —**smel′li·ness** *n.*
smelt[1] (smelt) *v.t. Metall.* 1. To reduce (ores) by fusion in a furnace. 2. To obtain (a metal) from the ore by a process including fusion. —*v.i.* 3. To melt or fuse, as a metal. [< MDu. *smelten* to melt]
smelt[2] (smelt) *n. pl.* **smelts** or **smelt** Any of various small silvery food fishes of north Atlantic and Pacific waters. [OE]
smelt[3] (smelt) Alternative past tense and past participle of SMELL.
smelt·er (smel′tər) *n.* 1. One engaged in smelting ore. 2. An establishment for smelting: also **smelt′er·y.**
smidg·en (smij′ən) *n. Informal* A tiny bit or part.
smi·lax (smī′laks) *n.* 1. Any of various vines of the lily family, having thorny stems. 2. A delicate twining greenhouse plant of the lily family, with greenish flowers. [< Gk. *smilax* yew]
smile (smīl) *n.* A pleased or amused expression of the face, characterized by a raising up of the corners of the mouth. —*v.* **smiled, smil·ing** *v.i.* 1. To give a smile; wear a cheerful aspect. 2. To show approval or favor: often with *upon.* —*v.t.* 3. To express by means of a smile. [ME *smilen*] —**smil′er** *n.* —**smil′ing·ly** *adv.* —**smil′ing·ness** *n.*
smirch (smûrch) *v.t.* 1. To soil, as with grime; smear. 2. To defame; degrade. [ME *smorchen* < OF *esmorcher* to hurt] —**smirch** *n.*
smirk (smûrk) *v.i.* To smile in a silly, self-complacent, or affected manner. —*n.* An affected or artificial smile. [OE *smearcian*] —**smirk′er** *n.* —**smirk′ing·ly** *adv.*
smite (smīt) *v.* **smote, smit·ten** or **smote, smit·ing** *v.t.* 1. To strike (something). 2. To strike with disaster; afflict. 3. To affect powerfully with sudden feeling. 4. To affect as if by a blow; strike. 5. To kill by a sudden blow. —*v.i.* 6. To come with sudden force; also, to knock against something. [OE *smītan*] —**smit′er** *n.*
smith (smith) *n.* 1. One who shapes metals by hammering: *goldsmith, tinsmith.* 2. A blacksmith. [OE]
smith·er·eens (smith′ə·rēnz′) *n.pl. Informal* Fragments. Also **smith′ers** (-ərz). [Cf. dial. E (Irish) *smidirin* fragment]
smith·y (smith′ē, smith′ē) *n. pl.* **smith·ies** A blacksmith's shop; a forge. [< ON *smithja*]
smit·ten (smit′n) Alternative past participle of SMITE. —*adj.* 1. Struck with sudden force; gravely afflicted. 2. Having the affections suddenly attracted.
smock (smok) *n.* A loose outer garment of light material worn to protect one's clothes. —*v.t.* 1. To clothe in a smock. 2. To decorate with smocking. [OE *smoc*]
smock·ing (smok′ing) *n.* Needlework in which the material is stitched into very small pleats or gathers.
smog (smog) *n.* A combination of smoke and fog. [Blend of SM(OKE) and (F)OG]
smoke (smōk) *n.* 1. The volatilized products of burning substances, as coal, wood, etc. 2. The act of smoking a pipe, cigar, etc. 3. *Informal* A cigarette, cigar, or pipeful of tobacco. —*v.* **smoked, smok·ing** *v.i.* 1. To emit or give out smoke. 2. To inhale and exhale the smoke from a pipe, cigarette, etc. —*v.t.* 3. To inhale and exhale the smoke of (tobacco, opium, etc.); also, to use (a pipe, etc.) for this purpose. 4. To cure (meat, fish, etc.) by treating with smoke. 5. To force into the open with or as with smoke: with *out.* [OE *smoca*] —**smoke′less** *adj.*
smoke·house (smōk′hous′) *n.* A building or closed room in which meat, fish, hides, etc., are cured by smoke.
smok·er (smō′kər) *n.* 1. One who or that which smokes. 2. A place where one can smoke, as a railroad car. 3. A social gathering.
smoke screen 1. A dense cloud of smoke used to prevent enemy observation of a place, force, or operation. 2. Something designed to obscure or mislead.
smoke·stack (smōk′stak′) *n.* An upright pipe or funnel through which combustion gases from a furnace are discharged into the air.
smoking jacket A short coat worn instead of a regular suit coat as a lounging jacket.
smok·y (smō′kē) *adj.* **smok·i·er, smok·i·est** 1. Giving forth smoke. 2. Mixed with smoke: *smoky* air. 3. Discolored with smoke. 4. Smoke-colored; dark gray. —**smok′i·ly** *adv.* —**smok′i·ness** *n.*
smol·der (smōl′dər) *v.i.* 1. To burn with little smoke and no flame. 2. To exist in a latent or suppressed state. —*n.* Smoke. Also spelled *smoulder.* [ME *smoldren*]
smolt (smōlt) *n.* A young salmon on its first descent from the river to the sea. [? Akin to SMELT[2]]
smooch (smōōch) *Slang n.* A kiss. —*v.i.* To kiss or neck. [<dial. *smouch*]

smooth (smōōth) *adj.* 1. Having a surface without irregularities; not rough; continuously even. 2. Having no impediments or obstructions; easy; free from shocks or jolts. 3. Calm; bland; mild. 4. Suave, as in speech: often implying deceit. 5. Free from hair; beardless. 6. Without lumps. —*adv.* Calmly; evenly. —*v.t.* 1. To make smooth or even. 2. To make easy or less difficult. 3. To free from or remove obstructions. 4. To render less harsh; soften; palliate: often with *over.* 5. To make calm; mollify. —*v.i.* 5. To become smooth. —**to smooth one's ruffled feathers** To mollify. —*n.* The smooth portion or surface of anything. [OE *smōth*] —**smooth′er** *n.* —**smooth′ly** *adv.* —**smooth′ness** *n.*

smooth·bore (smōōth′bôr′) *n.* A firearm with an unrifled bore. Also **smooth bore.** —**smooth′bored′** *adj.*

smooth·en (smōō′thən) *v.t. & v.i.* To smooth.

smör·gås·bord (smôr′gəs·bôrd, *Sw.* smœr′·gōs·bōrd) *n.* 1. A variety of hors d'oeuvres such as meats, cheeses, fish, etc. 2. A meal containing many dishes and served buffet-style. Also **smor′gas·bord.** [< Sw.]

smote (smōt) Past tense of SMITE.

smoth·er (smuth′ər) *v.t.* 1. To prevent the respiration of; suffocate; stifle. 2. To cover or coat. 3. To hide or suppress. —*v.i.* 4. To suffocate, as from lack of air, etc. —*n.* 1. That which smothers, as stifling vapor or dust. 2. The state of being smothered; suppression. [Earlier *smorther*] —**smoth′er·y** *adj.*

smoul·der (smōl′dər) See SMOLDER.

smudge (smuj) *v.* **smudged, smudg·ing** *v.t.* 1. To smear; soil. —*v.i.* 2. To cause a smudge. 3. To be smudged. —*n.* 1. A soiling, as of soot; smear; stain. 2. A smoky fire or its smoke for driving away insects, preventing frost, etc. [Var. of SMUTCH]

smudg·y (smuj′ē) *adj.* **smudg·i·er, smudg·i·est** Full of or causing smudges. —**smudg′·i·ly** *adv.* —**smudg′i·ness** *n.*

smug (smug) *adj.* **smug·ger, smug·gest** Self-satisfied; complacent. [Cf. LG *smuk* neat] —**smug′ly** *adv.* —**smug′ness** *n.*

smug·gle (smug′əl) *v.* **·gled, ·gling** *v.t.* 1. To take (goods) into or out of a country without payment of lawful duties. 2. To bring in illicitly. —*v.i.* 3. To practice smuggling. [< LG *smuggeln*] —**smug′gler** *n.* —**smug′·gling** *n.*

smut (smut) *n.* 1. The blackening made by soot, smoke, etc. 2. Obscenity; obscene language. 3. A fungus disease of plants, in which the affected part changes into a dusty black powder. —*v.* **smut·ted, smut·ting** *v.t.* 1. To blacken or stain, as with soot or smoke. 2. To affect with smut, as growing grain. —*v.i.* 3. To give off smut. 4. To be or become stained. [< LG *schmutt* dirt]

smutch (smuch) *v.t.* To smudge; soil. —*n.* A smear; smudge. [Cf. MHG *smutzen* to smear] —**smutch′y** *adj.*

smut·ty (smut′ē) *adj.* **·ti·er, ·ti·est** 1. Soiled with smut. 2. Affected with smut: *smutty* corn. 3. Obscene. —**smut′ti·ly** *adv.* —**smut′·ti·ness** *n.*

snack (snak) *n.* A light, hurried meal. —*v.i.* To eat a light meal; also, to eat between meals. [< MDu. *snacken* to bite]

snaf·fle (snaf′əl) *n.* A horse's bit without a curb, jointed in the middle. Also **snaf′fle·bit′** (-bit′). —*v.t.* **·fled, ·fling** To control with a snaffle. [Cf. Du. *snavel* muzzle]

sna·fu (sna·fōō′, sna′fōō) *Slang n.* A state of utter confusion. —*v.t.* **·fued, ·fu·ing** To put into confusion. [Acronym for "Situation normal, all fouled up"]

snag (snag) *n.* 1. A jagged protuberance; esp., the stumpy base of a branch. 2. A tear or pulled-out loop in fabric. 3. The trunk of a tree fixed in the bottom of a river, etc. 4. Any obstacle or difficulty. —*v.t.* **snagged, snag·ging** To injure, destroy, or impede by or as by a snag. [Prob. < Scand.] —**snag′gy** *adj.*

snag·gle·tooth (snag′əl·tōōth′) *n. pl.* **·teeth** A tooth that is broken, projecting, or out of alignment with the others. —**snag′·gle·toothed′** (-tōōtht′, -tōōthd′) *adj.*

snail (snāl) *n.* 1. Any of a large class of slow-moving mollusks of aquatic and terrestrial habits, having a spiral shell. 2. A slow or lazy person. [OE *snægl*]

snail pace A very slow gait or forward movement. Also **snail's pace.** —**snail-paced** (snāl′pāst′) *adj.*

snake (snāk) *n.* 1. Any of a large order of scaly, legless reptiles with long, slim bodies and tapering tails, some kinds having poisonous bites. 2. A flexible, resilient wire used to clean clogged drains. —*v.* **snaked, snak·ing** *v.t.* 1. To drag by pulling from one end. 2. To pull with jerks. —*v.i.* 3. To move like a snake. [OE *snaca*] —**snak′y** *adj.* **·i·er, ·i·est**

snake·bite (snāk′bīt′) *n.* The bite of a snake; also the poisoning it causes.

snake·root (snāk′rōōt′, -rŏŏt′) *n.* Any of various plants having roots reputed to be effective against snakebite.

snap (snap) *v.* **snapped, snap·ping** *v.i.* 1. To make a sharp, quick sound. 2. To break suddenly with a cracking noise. 3. To fly off or give way quickly, as when tension is suddenly relaxed. 4. To make the jaws come suddenly together in an effort to bite: often with *up* or *at.* 5. To seize or snatch suddenly: often with *up* or *at.* 6. To speak sharply, harshly, or irritably: often with *at.* 7. To close, fasten, etc., with a click. —*v.t.* 8. To seize suddenly or eagerly, with or as with the teeth: often with *up.* 9. To sever with a snapping sound. 10. To utter harshly, abruptly, or irritably. 11. To close, fasten, etc., with a snapping sound. 12. To cause to move suddenly, neatly, etc. 13. To photograph with a camera. —**to snap out of it** *Informal* To recover quickly, as from a state of depression. —*n.* 1. The act of snapping, or a sharp, quick sound produced by it. 2. A sudden breaking, or the sound so produced. 3. A fastener or other similar device. 4. A sudden seizing or effort to seize with or as with the teeth. 5. A small, thin, crisp cake or cooky. 6. Brisk energy; vigor. 7. A brief spell; a sudden turn: said chiefly of cold weather. 8. *Informal* Any task easy to perform. 9. A snapshot. —*adj.* 1. Made or done suddenly and without consideration; offhand. 2.

Fastening with a snap. 3. *Informal* Easy; requiring little work. [< MDu. *snappen* to bite at]
snap bean A bean with an edible pod, esp. the string bean.
snap·drag·on (snap′drag′ən) *n.* A plant of the figwort family having solitary flowers likened to dragons' heads.
snap·per (snap′ər) *n.* 1. One who or that which snaps. 2. A large food fish of the Gulf Coast, as the **red snapper**.
snapping turtle A large, voracious, fresh-water turtle of North America, used as food.
snap·pish (snap′ish) *adj.* 1. Apt to speak crossly or tartly. 2. Disposed to snap, as a dog. —**snap′pish·ly** *adv.* —**snap′pish·ness** *n.*
snap·py (snap′ē) *adj.* **·pi·er, ·pi·est** 1. *Informal* Brisk; energetic. 2. *Informal* Smart; stylish. 3. Snappish. —**make it snappy** *Informal* Hurry up! —**snap′pi·ly** *adv.* —**snap′pi·ness** *n.*
snap·shot (snap′shot′) *n.* A photograph taken quickly with a small hand-held camera.
snare[1] (snâr) *n.* 1. A device, as a noose, for catching birds or other animals; a trap. 2. Anything that entangles or entraps. —*v.t.* **snared, snar·ing** 1. To catch with a snare. 2. To capture by trickery; entice. [OE < ON *snara*] —**snar′er** *n.*
snare[2] (snâr) *n.* 1. One of the cords or wires stretched across one of the heads of a snare drum to increase the resonance. 2. A snare drum. [< MDu., a string]
snare drum A small drum having snares on one head.
snarl[1] (snärl) *n.* A sharp, harsh, angry growl or utterance. —*v.i.* 1. To growl harshly, as a dog. 2. To speak angrily. —*v.t.* 3. To utter or express with a snarl. [Freq. of obs. *snar* to growl] —**snarl′er** *n.* —**snarl′·ing·ly** *adv.* —**snarl′y** *adj.*
snarl[2] (snärl) *n.* 1. A tangle, as of hair or yarn. 2. Any complication or entanglement. —*v.t.* & *v.i.* To put or get into a snarl or tangle. [< SNARE[1]] —**snarl′er** *n.* —**snarl′y** *adj.*
snatch (snach) *v.t.* 1. To seize suddenly, hastily, or eagerly. 2. To take or remove suddenly. 3. To take or obtain as the opportunity arises. 4. *Slang* To kidnap. —*v.i.* 5. To attempt to seize swiftly and suddenly: with *at*. —*n.* 1. An act of snatching. 2. A brief period. 3. A small amount. 4. *Slang* A kidnaping. [ME *snacchen*] —**snatch′er** *n.*
snatch·y (snach′ē) *adj.* **snatch·i·er, snatch·i·est** Interrupted; spasmodic.
sneak (snēk) *v.i.* 1. To move or go in a stealthy manner. 2. To act with cowardice or servility. —*v.t.* 3. To put, give, move, etc., secretly or stealthily. —*n.* 1. One who sneaks. 2. An act of sneaking. —*adj.* Stealthy; covert. [OE *snīcan* to creep] —**sneak′i·ly** *adv.* —**sneak′i·ness** *n.* —**sneak′y** *adj.* **·i·er, ·i·est**
sneak·er (snē′kər) *n.* *Informal* A rubber-soled canvas shoe, used esp. for sports.
sneak·ing (snē′king) *adj.* 1. Acting in an underhand way. 2. Secret: a *sneaking* suspicion. —**sneak′ing·ly** *adv.*
sneak preview The showing of a new motion picture before its date of release.
sneer (snir) *n.* A grimace of contempt or derision made by slightly raising the upper lip. —*v.i.* 1. To make a sneer. 2. To express derision. [ME *sneren*] —**sneer′er** *n.* —**sneer′ing·ly** *adv.*
sneeze (snēz) **sneezed, sneez·ing** *v.i.* To drive air forcibly and audibly out of the mouth and nose by a spasmodic involuntary action. —**not to be sneezed at** *Informal* Worthy of consideration. [Alter. of ME *fnese*, OE *fnēosan* to sneeze] —**sneeze** *n.* —**sneez′er** *n.* —**sneez′y** *adj.*
snick (snik) *n.* A small cut. —*v.t.* To cut a nick in. [See SNICKERSNEE.]
snick·er (snik′ər) *n.* A half-suppressed laugh, often of derision. —*v.i.* To utter a snicker. [Imit.]
snick·er·snee (snik′ər·snē′) *n.* A swordlike knife. [Alter. of earlier *snick or snee* to thrust or cut]
snide (snīd) *adj.* Malicious or derogatory; nasty: *snide* comments. [Origin unknown]
sniff (snif) *v.i.* 1. To breathe through the nose in short, quick, audible inhalations. 2. To express contempt, etc., by or as by sniffing: often with *at*. —*v.t.* 3. To breathe in through the nose; inhale. 4. To smell with sniffs. —*n.* 1. An act or the sound of sniffing. 2. That which is inhaled by sniffing. [Appar. back formation < SNIVEL]
snif·fle (snif′əl) *v.i.* **·fled, ·fling** 1. To breathe through the nose noisily. 2. To snivel or whimper. —**the sniffles** *Informal* A head cold or the sniffling that results. [Freq. of SNIFF] —**snif′fle** *n.* —**snif′fler** *n.*
snif·ter (snif′tər) *n.* A pear-shaped liquor glass. [< *snift*, var. of SNIFF]
snig·ger (snig′ər) *n.* A snicker. —*v.t.* & *v.i.* To snicker. [Var. of SNICKER] —**snig′ger·er** *n.*
snip (snip) *v.t.* & *v.i.* **snipped, snip·ping** To clip or cut with a light stroke of shears: often with *off*. —*n.* 1. An act of snipping. 2. A small piece snipped off. 3. *Informal* A small or insignificant person or thing. [< Du. *snippen*]
snipe (snīp) *n.* *pl.* **snipe** or **snipes** Any of various long-billed shore or marsh birds, allied to the woodcock. —*v.i.* **sniped, snip·ing** 1. To hunt or shoot snipe. 2. To shoot at a person or persons from hiding. [< ON *snīpa*]
snip·er (snī′pər) *n.* One who shoots a person or persons from hiding.
snip·pet (snip′it) *n.* 1. A small piece snipped off. 2. A small portion or share.
snip·py (snip′ē) *adj.* **·pi·er, ·pi·est** *Informal* 1. Pert; impertinent. 2. Fragmentary; scrappy. Also **snip′pet·y** (-ət·ē).
snitch (snich) *Slang* *v.t.* 1. To grab quickly; steal; swipe. —*v.i.* 2. To turn informer: with *on*. [Origin unknown]
sniv·el (sniv′əl) *v.i.* **·eled** or **·elled, ·el·ing** or **·el·ling** 1. To cry in a snuffling manner. 2. To whine. 3. To run at the nose. [OE *snyflung* mucus from the nose] —**sniv′el·er** or **sniv′el·ler** *n.*
snob (snob) *n.* One who delights in feeling that he is a member of an elite circle, esp. in high society. [Origin uncertain] —**snob′·ber·y** *n.* —**snob′bish** *adj.* —**snob′bish·ly** *adv.* —**snob′bish·ness** *n.*
snood (snōōd) *n.* A small, meshlike cap or

bag, worn by women to keep the hair in place. [OE *snōd*]

snoop (snōōp) *Informal v.i.* To look or pry into things with which one has no business. [< Du. *snoepen* to eat goodies on the sly] —**snoop, snoop'er** *n.* —**snoop'i·ly** *adv.* —**snoop'i·ness** *n.* —**snoop'y** *adj.* ·**i·er,** ·**i·est**

snoot (snōōt) *n. Informal* The nose or face. [Var. of SNOUT]

snoot·y (snoo'tē) *adj.* **snoot·i·er, snoot·i·est** *Informal* Conceited or supercilious. —**snoot'i·ly** *adv.* —**snoot'i·ness** *n.*

snooze (snōōz) *Informal v.i.* **snoozed, snooz·ing** To sleep lightly; doze. —*n.* A short nap. [Origin uncertain]

snore (snôr) *v.i.* **snored, snor·ing** To breathe in sleep with a hoarse, rough noise, usu. with the mouth open. —*n.* An act or the noise of snoring. [ME *snoren*] —**snor'er** *n.*

snor·kel (snôr'kəl) *n.* 1. A mouth tube permitting a skin diver to breathe while swimming on the surface with his face under water. 2. A tubelike apparatus for the ventilation of a submerged submarine. —*v.i.* ·**keled,** ·**kel·ing** To swim with a snorkel. [< G *schnörkel,* lit., spiral] —**snor'·kel·er** *n.*

snort (snôrt) *v.i.* 1. To force air violently and noisily through the nostrils, as a horse. 2. To express indignation, ridicule, etc., by a snort. —*n.* 1. The act or sound of snorting. 2. *Slang* A small drink. [ME *snorten*] —**snort'er** *n.*

snot (snot) *n.* 1. Mucus from or in the nose: a vulgar term. 2. *Slang* An obnoxious, impudent person. [OE *gesnot*]

snot·ty (snot'ē) *adj.* ·**ti·er,** ·**ti·est** 1. Dirtied with snot: a vulgar term. 2. *Slang* Impudent; obnoxious. —**snot'ti·ness** *n.*

snout (snout) *n.* 1. The forward projecting part of a beast's head, as the nose and mouth of a hog. 2. A person's nose: a contemptuous or humorous term. [ME *snūte*] —**snout'ed** *adj.* —**snout'y** *adj.*

snow (snō) *n.* 1. Water vapor in the air precipitated in the form of minute flakes when the temperature is below 32°F. 2. A fall of snow; snowstorm. 3. *Slang* Heroin or cocaine. —*v.i.* 1. To fall as snow. —*v.t.* 2. To scatter or cause to fall as or like snow. 3. To cover, enclose, or obstruct with or as with snow. 4. *Slang* To subject to a snow job. —**to snow in** To force to remain in place because of a heavy snowfall. [OE *snāw*]

snow·ball (snō'bôl') *n.* A ball of snow, shaped by the hands. —*v.i.* To gain in size, importance, etc., as a snowball that rolls over snow.

snow·bank (snō'bangk') *n.* A large mound of snow.

snow·ber·ry (snō'ber'ē) *n. pl.* ·**ries** A bushy American shrub having white berries: also called *waxberry.*

snow blindness A temporary dimming of the sight caused by light reflected by snow. —**snow-blind** (snō'blīnd') *adj.*

snow·bound (snō'bound') *adj.* Hemmed in by snow; snowed in.

snow bunting Any of various finches, the male of which in the breeding season is snow-white with black markings.

snow·cap (snō'kap') *n.* A crest of snow, as on a mountain peak. —**snow'-capped'** *adj.*

snow·drift (snō'drift') *n.* A snowbank made by the wind.

snow·drop (snō'drop') *n.* A low, European, early-blooming bulbous plant, bearing a single, white, drooping flower.

snow·fall (snō'fôl') *n.* 1. A fall of snow. 2. The amount of snow that falls in a given period.

snow fence Portable fencing of thin slats, used to prevent the drifting of snow.

snow·flake (snō'flāk') *n.* One of the small, feathery masses in which snow falls.

snow job *Slang* An elaborate, insincere speech contrived to impress or persuade.

snow line The limit of perpetual snow on the sides of mountains. Also **snow limit.**

snow·mo·bile (snō'mō·bēl) *n.* A vehicle for traveling over snow, ice, etc., often equipped with caterpillar treads on the rear and runners on the front. [< SNOW + (AUTO)MOBILE] —**snow'mo·bile** *v.i.* —**snow'mo·bil'er** *n.* —**snow'mo·bil'ing** *n.*

snow·plow (snō'plou') *n.* Any plowlike device for the removal of snow from surfaces. Also **snow'plough'.**

snow·shoe (snō'shōō') *n.* A device, usu. a network of thongs in a wooden frame, fastened on the foot and worn in walking over snow. —**snow'shoe'** *v.i.* ·**shoed,** ·**shoe·ing** —**snow'sho'er** *n.*

snow·storm (snō'stôrm') *n.* A storm with a fall of snow.

snow·y (snō'ē) *adj.* **snow·i·er, snow·i·est** 1. Abounding in or full of snow. 2. Pure white; spotless. —**snow'i·ly** *adv.* —**snow'i·ness** *n.*

snub (snub) *v.t.* **snubbed, snub·bing** 1. To treat with contempt or disdain, esp. by ignoring; slight. 2. To stop or check, as a rope in running out, by taking a turn about a post, etc. —*adj.* Short; pug: said of the nose. —*n.* 1. A deliberate slight. 2. A sudden checking, as of a running rope. [< ON *snubba* to snub] —**snub'ber** *n.*

snuff[1] (snuf) *v.t. & v.i.* 1. To draw in (air, etc.) through the nose. 2. To smell; sniff. [< MDu. *snuffen*] —**snuff** *n.*

snuff[2] (snuf) *n.* The charred portion of a wick. —*v.t.* 1. To extinguish: with *out.* 2. To crop the snuff from (a wick). [Cf. G *schnuppe* snuff of a candle] —**snuf'fer** *n.*

snuff[3] (snuf) *n.* Pulverized tobacco to be inhaled into the nostrils. —**up to snuff** *Informal* Meeting the usual standard, as in quality, health, etc. [< Du. *snuf*] —**snuf'·fer** *n.* —**snuff'fi·ness** *n.* —**snuff'y** *adj.*

snuff·box (snuf'boks') *n.* A small box for carrying snuff.

snuf·fle (snuf'əl) *v.i.* ·**fled,** ·**fling** 1. To sniffle. 2. To breathe noisily, as a dog following a scent. [Freq. of SNUFF[1]] —**snuf'fle** *n.* —**snuf'fler** *n.* —**snuf'fly** *adj.*

snug (snug) *adj.* **snug·ger, snug·gest** 1. Closely and comfortably sheltered, covered, or situated. 2. Close or compact; trim. 3. Fitting closely but comfortably. —*v.* **snugged, snug·ging** *v.t.* 1. To make snug. —*v.i.* 2. To snuggle; move close. [Prob. < LG. Cf. Du. *snugger* clean, smooth.] —**snug, snug'ly** *adv.* —**snug'ness** *n.*

snug·gle (snug'əl) *v.t. & v.i.* ·**gled,** ·**gling**

To lie or draw close; cuddle: often with *up* or *together*.

so[1] (sō) *adv.* 1. To this or that or such a degree; to this or that extent. 2. In this, that, or such a manner; in the same way. 3. Just as said, directed, suggested or implied. 4. According to fact: That is not *so*. 5. *Informal* To an extreme degree; very. 6. About as many or as much stated: I shall stay a day or *so*. 7. To such an extent: used elliptically for *so much*: I love him *so*! 8. Consequently; thus; therefore. —*conj.* 1. With the purpose that: usu. with *that*: Hurry *so* that you won't be late. 2. As a consequence of which: He consented, *so* they left. [OE *swā*]

so[2] (sō) *n. Music* Sol.

soak (sōk) *v.t.* 1. To place in liquid until thoroughly saturated; steep. 2. To wet thoroughly; drench. 3. To absorb: with *in* or *up*. 4. To take in eagerly or readily: with *up*. 5. *Slang* To overcharge. —*v.i.* 6. To remain or be placed in liquid till saturated. 7. To penetrate; pass: with *in* or *into*. —*n.* 1. The act of soaking, or the state of being soaked. 2. Liquid in which something is soaked. 3. *Slang* A hard drinker. [OE *socian*] —**soak′er** *n.*

so-and-so (sō′ən·sō′) *n.* 1. An unnamed person or thing. 2. *Informal* A euphemism for many offensive epithets.

soap (sōp) *n.* A cleansing agent made by decomposing fats and oils with alkalis. —**no soap** *Slang* No; not a chance. —*v.t.* To rub or treat with soap. [OE *sāpe*] —**soap′i·ness** *n.* —**soap′y** *adj.* **·i·er, ·i·est**

soap·ber·ry (sōp′ber′ē) *n. pl.* **·ries** 1. The fruit of several tropical trees and shrubs, sometimes used as a substitute for soap. 2. A tree or shrub bearing this fruit.

soap·box (sōp′boks′) *n.* 1. A box or crate for soap. 2. Any box or crate used as a platform by street orators. Also **soap box**. —**soapbox oratory** Impromptu or crude oratory.

soap opera A daytime television or radio serial drama usu. dealing with highly emotional domestic themes.

soap·stone (sōp′stōn′) *n.* Steatite.

soar (sôr) *v.i.* 1. To rise high into the air. 2. To sail through the air without perceptibly moving the wings, as a hawk or vulture. 3. To rise sharply above the usual level: Prices *soared*. [< L *ex* out + *aura* breeze, air] —**soar** *n.* —**soar′er** *n.*

sob (sob) *v.* **sobbed, sob·bing** *v.i.* 1. To weep with audible, convulsive catches of the breath. 2. To make a sound like a sob. —*v.t.* 3. To utter with sobs. —*n.* The act or sound of sobbing. [ME *sobben*] —**sob′bing·ly** *adv.*

so·ber (sō′bər) *adj.* 1. Self-controlled; well-balanced. 2. Grave; sedate. 3. Not drunk. 4. Moderate or abstinent. 5. Subdued or modest in color, manner of dress, etc. —*v.t. & v.i.* To make or become sober. [< L *sobrius*] —**so′ber·ly** *adv.* —**so·bri·e·ty** (sō·brī′ə·tē), **so′ber·ness** *n.*

so·bri·quet (sō′bri·kā) *n.* A fanciful or humorous appellation; a nickname: also spelled *soubriquet*. [< F]

sob story *Slang* A sad personal narrative told to elicit pity.

so-called (sō′kôld′) *adj.* Called as stated; generally styled thus: often implying a doubtful or incorrect designation.

soc·cer (sok′ər) *n.* A form of football in which the ball is propelled by kicking or by striking with the body or head: officially called *association football*. [Alter. of ASSOCIATION]

so·cia·ble (sō′shə·bəl) *adj.* 1. Inclined to seek company; social. 2. Agreeable in manner; genial. 3. Characterized by or affording occasion for agreeable, friendly conversation. [< L *socius* friend] —**so′cia·bil′i·ty** *n.* —**so′cia·bly** *adv.*

so·cial (sō′shəl) *adj.* 1. Of or pertaining to society or its organization. 2. Friendly; sociable; also, promoting friendly intercourse: a *social* club. 3. Of or pertaining to public welfare. 4. Of, pertaining to, or characteristic of persons considered aristocratic, fashionable, etc. 5. Of animals or insects, living in communities. —*n.* An informal social gathering. [< L *socius* ally]

social disease A venereal disease: a euphemism.

so·cial·ism (sō′shəl·iz′əm) *n.* Public collective ownership or control of the basic means of production, distribution, and exchange, with the aim of assuring to each member of society an equitable share of goods, services, etc. —**so′cial·ist** *n. & adj.* —**so′cial·is′tic** *adj.*

so·cial·ite (sō′shəl·īt) *n. Informal* One who is prominent in fashionable society.

so·ci·al·i·ty (sō′shē·al′ə·tē) *n.* The state or character of being social; sociability.

so·cial·ize (sō′shəl·īz) *v.* **·ized, ·iz·ing** *v.t.* 1. To place under the control of the community, the government, etc. 2. To make cooperative or sociable. 3. To convert or adapt to the needs of a social group. —*v.i.* 4. *Informal* To take part in social activities. Also *Brit.* **so′cial·ise.** —**so′cial·i·za′tion** *n.*

socialized medicine A system supplying the public with medical care at nominal cost, by means of regulatory laws and use of public funds.

social register A directory of persons prominent in fashionable society.

social science 1. Sociology. 2. Any field of knowledge dealing with human society, as economics, history, etc.

social security A Federal program of assistance to the aged, unemployed, disabled, dependent, etc.

social service Organized activity intended to advance human welfare. —**so·cial-ser·vice** (sō′shəl·sûr′vis) *adj.*

social studies In elementary and secondary schools, a course or unit of study based upon the social sciences.

social work Any clinical, social, or recreational service for improving community welfare, as through health clinics, aid to the poor, etc.

so·ci·e·ty (sə·sī′ə·tē) *n. pl.* **·ties** 1. The system of community life in which individuals form a continuous and regulatory association for their mutual benefit and protection. 2. The body of persons composing such a community. 3. A number of persons regarded as having certain common interests, similar status, etc. 4. An organized group having common interests. 5. The fashionable or aristocratic portion of a community. 6. Association based on friendship or intimacy; companionship. [< OF *societe* < L *societas, -tatis* < *socius* friend] —**so·ci·e·tal** (sō·sī′ə·təl) *adj.*

Society of Friends A Christian religious group founded in England about 1650, characterized by the repudiation of ritual and violence: commonly known as *Quakers.*

socio- *combining form* 1. Society; social. 2. Sociology; sociological. [< L *socius* companion]

so·ci·o·ec·o·nom·ic (sō′sē·ō·ek′ə·nom′ik, sō′shē-, -ē′kə-) *adj.* Social and economic: considered as a single factor: an upper *socioeconomic* group. —**so′ci·o·ec′o·nom′i·cal·ly** *adv.*

so·ci·o·lin·guis·tics (sō′sē·ō·ling·gwis′tiks, sō′shē-) *n.pl.* (*construed as sing.*) The study of language as it relates to society; esp., the study of dialect distinctions related to social class.

so·ci·ol·o·gy (sō′sē·ol′ə·jē, sō′shē-) *n.* The science that treats of the origin and evolution of human society and social phenomena. —**so′ci·o·log′ic** (-ə·loj′ic) or **·i·cal** *adj.* —**so′ci·o·log′i·cal·ly** *adv.* —**so′ci·ol′o·gist** *n.*

sock[1] (sok) *n. pl.* **socks** or **sox** A short stocking reaching above the ankle or just below the knee. [OE < L *soccus* slipper]

sock[2] (sok) *Slang v.t.* To strike or hit, esp. with the fist; to punch. —*n.* A hard blow. [Origin unknown]

sock·et (sok′it) *n.* A cavity or an opening adapted to receive and hold something. [< AF *soket*, dim. of OF *soc* plowshare]

sock·eye (sok′ī) *n.* A salmon of the Pacific coast, highly valued as a food fish: also called *red salmon.* [Alter. of Salishan *sukkegh*]

sod (sod) *n.* Grassy surface soil held together by the matted roots of grass and weeds; turf. —*v.t.* **sod·ded, sod·ding** To cover with sod. [< MDu. *sode* piece of turf]

so·da (sō′də) *n.* 1. Any of several white, alkaline compounds widely used in medicine, industry, and the arts. 2. A soft drink containing soda water and flavoring: also **soda pop.** 3. A drink made from soda water, ice cream, and sometimes flavoring. [< Ital. *soda* (*cenere*) solid (ash)]

soda ash Crude sodium carbonate, widely used in the manufacture of glass, soaps, etc.

soda cracker A thin, crisp cracker made with yeast-leavened dough containing soda.

soda fountain 1. An apparatus from which soda water is drawn, usu. containing receptacles for syrups, ice cream, etc. 2. A counter at which soft drinks, etc., are dispensed.

soda jerk *Slang* A clerk at a soda fountain.

so·dal·i·ty (sō·dal′ə·tē) *n. pl.* **·ties** 1. Companionship. 2. A society; association. 3. In the Roman Catholic Church, a society organized for devotional and charitable purposes. [< L *sodalis* companion]

soda water Water charged under pressure with carbon dioxide gas.

sod·den (sod′n) *adj.* 1. Soaked with moisture. 2. Doughy; soggy, as bread. 3. Flabby and pale, esp. from dissipation. 4. Dull; dreary. [ME *soden*, orig. pp. of SEETHE] —**sod′den·ly** *adv.* —**sod′den·ness** *n.*

so·di·um (sō′dē·əm) *n.* A silver-white, highly reactive, alkaline metallic element (symbol Na). [< NL < SODA]

sodium bicarbonate *Chem.* A white crystalline compound of alkaline taste, used in medicine and cookery: also called *baking soda, bicarbonate of soda.*

sodium carbonate *Chem.* A strongly alkaline compound that in crystalline hydrated form is known as washing soda, and in the anhydrous form as a soda ash.

sodium chloride Salt (def. 1).

sodium hydroxide *Chem.* A strongly basic compound used for bleaching, etc.: also called *caustic soda.*

sodium nitrate *Chem.* A white compound used as a fertilizer and in explosives.

sodium thiosulfate *Chem.* A crystalline salt used in photography as a fixing agent: also called *hypo.* Also **sodium hyposulfite.**

sod·om·y (sod′əm·ē) *n.* Unnatural sexual relations, esp. between male persons or between a human being and an animal. [< LL *Sodoma* Sodom, the Biblical city, to whose people such a practice was imputed] —**sod′om·ite** *n.*

so·ev·er (sō·ev′ər) *adv.* To or in some conceivable degree: often added to *who, which, what, when, how,* etc.

so·fa (sō′fə) *n.* A wide upholstered seat, having a back and raised ends. [< Arabic *soffah* a part of a floor raised to form a seat]

soft (sôft) *adj.* 1. Being or composed of a substance whose shape is changed easily by pressure; pliable; malleable. 2. Smooth and delicate to the touch. 3. Gentle in its effect upon the ear; not loud or harsh. 4. Mild; gentle. 5. Of subdued coloring or delicate shading. 6. Easily touched in feeling; tender. 7. Of yielding character; weak. 8. *Informal* Involving little effort; easy: a *soft* job. 9. Free from mineral salts that prevent the detergent action of soap: said of water. 10. Bituminous, as opposed to anthracite: said of coal. —*n.* That which is soft; a soft part or material. —*adv.* Quietly; gently. [OE *sōfte*] —**soft′ly** *adv. & interj.* —**soft′ness** *n.*

soft·ball (sôft′bôl′) *n.* 1. A variation of baseball, requiring a smaller diamond and a larger ball. 2. The ball used in this game.

soft-boiled (sôft′boild′) *adj.* Of an egg, boiled to the point of partial coagulation.

soft coal Bituminous coal.

soft drink A nonalcoholic drink, as ginger ale, etc.

sof·ten (sôf′ən) *v.t. & v.i.* To make or become soft or softer. —**sof′ten·er** *n.*

soft·heart·ed (sôft′här′tid) *adj.* Tenderhearted; merciful. —**soft′heart′ed·ly** *adv.* —**soft′heart′ed·ness** *n.*

soft-ped·al (sôft′ped′l) *v.t.* **·aled** or **·alled, ·al·ing** or **·al·ling** 1. To mute the tone of (a piano, etc.) by depressing the soft pedal. 2. *Informal* To render less emphatic; moderate.

soft pedal A pedal that mutes the tone, as in a piano.

soft-shell (sôft′shel′) *adj.* Having a soft shell, as certain clams, crabs, etc., esp. after shedding its hard shell: also **soft′-shelled′**. —*n.* A soft-shelled crab.

soft-shelled crab A crab of North America after it has molted.

soft-shelled turtle Any member of a family of turtles having a long snout and a soft, leathery shell.

soft-soap (sôft′sōp′) *v.t.* *Informal* To flatter; cajole. —**soft′-soap′er** *n.*

soft soap 1. Fluid or semifluid soap. 2. *Informal* Flattery.

soft-spo·ken (sôft′spō′kən) *adj.* Speaking with a low voice and quiet manner.

soft·ware (sôft′wâr′) *n.* Any of the programs used in operating a digital computer, as input and output programs: distinguished from *hardware*.

soft·wood (sôft′wood′) *n.* 1. A coniferous tree or its wood. 2. Any soft wood, or any tree with soft wood.

soft·y (sôf′tē) *n. pl.* **soft·ies** *Informal* A sentimental, tender-hearted person.

sog·gy (sog′ē) *adj.* **·gi·er, ·gi·est** 1. Saturated with moisture; soaked; sodden. 2. Soft; boggy: said of land. Also **sog·ged** (sog′id). [< dial. E *sog* a swamp, bog] —**sog′gi·ly** *adv.* —**sog′gi·ness** *n.*

soil[1] (soil) *n.* 1. Finely divided rock mixed with vegetable or animal matter, constituting that portion of the surface of the earth in which plants grow. 2. Land; country: native *soil*. 3. A particular kind of earth. [< L *solum* the ground]

soil[2] (soil) *v.t.* 1. To make dirty; smudge. 2. To disgrace; defile. —*v.i.* 3. To become dirty. —*n.* 1. A spot or stain. 2. Filth; sewage; manure. [< L *suculus*, dim. of *sus* pig]

soil·age (soi′lij) *n.* Green crops for feeding animals.

soi·ree (swä·rā′, *Fr.* swȧ·rā′) *n.* A party or reception given in the evening. Also **soi·rée′**. [< F < *soir* evening]

so·journ (*v.* sō′jûrn, sō·jûrn′; *n.* sō′jûrn) *v.i.* To stay or dwell temporarily; abide for a time. —*n.* A temporary residence or stay. [< L *sub-* under + *diurnus* daily] —**so′journ·er** *n.*

sol[1] (sōl) *n.* *Music* The fifth tone of the diatonic scale in solmization: also *so*.

sol[2] (sol, sōl) *n.* A colloidal suspension of a solid in a liquid.

sol[3] (sōl) *n. pl.* **so·les** (sō′lās) The monetary unit of Peru.

Sol (sol) *n.* The sun. [< L, the Roman god of the sun]

sol·ace (sol′is) *n.* Comfort in grief or trouble; also, that which supplies such comfort. —*v.t.* **·aced, ·ac·ing** To comfort or cheer in trouble or grief. [< L *solacium* comfort] —**sol′ac·er** *n.*

so·lar (sō′lər) *adj.* 1. Pertaining to, proceeding from, or connected with the sun. 2. Affected, determined, or measured by the sun. 3. Operated by the action of the sun's rays: a *solar* engine. [< L *sol* sun]

solar battery A device for the direct conversion of solar energy into electricity.

so·lar·i·um (sō·lâr′ē·əm, sə-) *n. pl.* **·i·a** or **·i·ums** A room or enclosed porch exposed to the sun's rays. [< L]

solar plexus 1. *Anat.* The large network of nerves found behind the stomach, serving the abdominal viscera. 2. *Informal* The pit of the stomach.

solar system The sun together with the planets, moons, etc., that revolve about it.

sold (sōld) Past tense and past participle of SELL.

sol·der (sod′ər) *n.* A fusible metal or alloy used for joining metallic surfaces or margins, applied in a melted state. —*v.t.* & *v.i.* To unite or be united with solder. [< L *solidus* firm, hard] —**sol′der·er** *n.*

sol·dier (sōl′jər) *n.* 1. A person serving in an army; esp., an enlisted man. 2. One who serves loyally in any cause. —*v.i.* To be a soldier. [< OF *soude* wages < LL *solidus* a gold coin] —**sol′dier·ly** *adj.*

soldier of fortune An adventurous, restless person who is willing to serve wherever his services are well paid.

sol·dier·y (sōl′jər·ē) *n. pl.* **·dier·ies** 1. Soldiers collectively. 2. Military service.

sole[1] (sōl) *n.* 1. The bottom surface of the foot. 2. The bottom surface of a shoe, boot, etc. 3. Something resembling a sole; bottom part. —*v.t.* **soled, sol·ing** To furnish with a sole; resole, as a shoe. [< Med.L. *sola*, var. of L *solea* sandal]

sole[2] (sōl) *n.* Any of a family of flatfishes allied to the flounders, many of which are highly esteemed as food. [< L *solea*]

sole[3] (sōl) *adj.* Being alone or the only one; only; individual. [< L *solus* alone]

so·le·cism (sol′ə·siz′əm) *n.* 1. A violation of accepted grammar. 2. Any impropriety or incongruity. [< Gk. *soloikos* speaking incorrectly < *Soloi*, a Cilician town whose people spoke a substandard Attic dialect] —**sol′e·cist** *n.* —**sol′e·cis′tic** *adj.*

sole·ly (sōl′lē) *adv.* 1. By oneself or itself alone; singly. 2. Completely; entirely. 3. Without exception; exclusively.

sol·emn (sol′əm) *adj.* 1. Characterized by mystery or power; awe-inspiring. 2. Grave; serious. 3. Characterized by ceremonial observances; sacred. [< L *solemnis*] —**sol′·em·ness** or **sol′emn·ness** *n.* —**sol′emn·ly** *adv.*

so·lem·ni·ty (sə·lem′nə·tē) *n. pl.* **·ties** 1. The state or quality of being solemn. 2. A rite expressive of religious reverence; also, any ceremonious observance.

sol·em·nize (sol′əm·nīz) *v.t.* **·nized, ·niz·ing** 1. To perform as a ceremony or solemn rite. 2. To treat or dignify with solemnity. Also *Brit.* **sol′em·nise**. —**sol′em·ni·za′tion** *n.* —**sol′em·niz′er** *n.*

so·le·noid (sō′lə·noid) *n.* *Electr.* A coiled conducting wire capable of setting up a magnetic field by the passage through it of an electric current. [< Gk. *sōlēn* a channel] —**so′le·noi′dal** *adj.*

so·lic·it (sə·lis′it) *v.t.* 1. To ask for earnestly; seek to obtain by persuasion or entreaty. 2. To entreat (a person). 3. To entice to an unlawful or immoral act. —*v.i.* 4. To make petition or solicitation. [< L *sollicitare* to agitate] —**so·lic′i·ta′tion** *n.*

so·lic·i·tor (sə·lis′ə·tər) *n.* 1. A person who solicits; esp., one who solicits donations or subscriptions. 2. A lawyer, esp. a legal advisor in government service. 3. In England, a lawyer who may advise clients or prepare cases, but who may appear as an advocate in the lower courts only. Also **so·lic′i·ter.** —**so·lic′i·tor·ship′** *n.*

so·lic·i·tous (sə·lis′ə·təs) *adj.* 1. Full of concern, as for the attainment of something. 2. Full of desire; willing. —**so·lic′i·tous·ly** *adv.* —**so·lic′i·tude, so·lic′i·tous·ness** *n.*

sol·id (sol′id) *adj.* 1. Having definite shape and volume; not fluid. 2. Substantial; firm and stable. 3. Filling the whole of; not hollow. 4. Having no opening or interruption; unbroken. 5. Strong and firm; sound. 6. Substantial or satisfactory. 7. Financially sound or safe. 8. Having or relating to the three dimensions of length, breadth, and thickness. 9. Written without a hyphen: said of a compound word. 10. Unadulterated; unalloyed: *solid* gold. 11. Serious; reliable: a *solid* citizen. —*n.* 1. A state of matter characterized by definite shape and volume. 2. A geometrical figure that has length, breadth, and thickness, as a cone, cube, sphere, etc. [< L *solidus*] —**sol′id·ly** *adv.* —**sol′id·ness** *n.*

sol·i·dar·i·ty (sol′ə·dar′ə·tē) *n.* Unity in nature, relations, or interests, as of a class.

solid fuel *Aerospace* A rocket fuel in solid, rather than liquid or gaseous, form. Also **solid propellant.**

solid geometry The geometry that includes all three dimensions of space.

so·lid·i·fy (sə·lid′ə·fī) *v.t.* & *v.i.* **·fied, ·fy·ing** 1. To make or become solid, hard, firm, or compact. 2. To bring or come together in unity. —**so·lid′i·fi·ca′tion** *n.*

so·lid·i·ty (sə·lid′ə·tē) *n.* 1. The quality or state of being solid; extension in the three dimensions of space. 2. Mental, moral, or financial soundness; stability.

sol·id-state (sol′id·stāt) *adj.* 1. *Physics* Pertaining to the study of solids at the molecular or atomic level. 2. *Electronics* Pertaining to or composed of solid components, as transistors, as distinct from vacuum tubes.

sol·i·dus (sol′ə·dəs) *n. pl.* **·di** (-dī) 1. The sign (/) used to divide shillings from pence: 10/6 (10*s.* 6*d.*). 2. Slash (def. 2). [< LL]

so·lil·o·quize (sə·lil′ə·kwīz) *v.i.* **·quized, ·quiz·ing** To talk to oneself; utter a soliloquy. Also *Brit.* **so·lil′o·quise.**

so·lil·o·quy (sə·lil′ə·kwē) *n. pl.* **·quies** A talking or discourse to oneself, as in a drama; a monologue. [< L *solus* alone + *loqui* to talk]

sol·ip·sism (sol′ip·siz′əm) *n. Philos.* The theory that the self is the only thing really existent. [< L *solus* alone + *ipse* self] —**sol′ip·sist** *n.*

sol·i·taire (sol′ə·târ) *n.* 1. A diamond or other gem set alone. 2. One of many games, esp. of cards, played by one person: also, *Brit., patience.* [< F < L *solitarius* solitary]

sol·i·tar·y (sol′ə·ter′ē) *adj.* 1. Living, being, or going alone. 2. Made, done, or passed alone. 3. Unfrequented by human beings; secluded. 4. Lonesome; lonely. 5. Single; sole. —*n. Informal* Solitary confinement. [< L *solus* alone] —**sol′i·tar′i·ly** *adv.*

solitary confinement The confining of a prisoner alone, usu. as punishment.

sol·i·tude (sol′ə·to͞od, -tyo͞od) *n.* 1. The state of being solitary; seclusion. 2. A deserted or lonely place.

sol·mi·za·tion (sol′mə·zā′shən) *n. Music* The use of syllables, most commonly *do, re, mi, fa, sol, la, ti,* as names for the tones of a musical scale. [< SOL[1] + MI]

so·lo (sō′lō) *n. pl.* **·los** or **·li** (lē) 1. A musical composition or passage for a single voice or instrument. 2. Any performance accomplished alone or without assistance. —*adj.* 1. Composed or written for, or executed by, a single voice or instrument. 2. Done by a single person alone: a *solo* flight. —*v.i.* **·loed, ·lo·ing** To fly an airplane alone, esp. for the first time. [< L *solus* alone] —**so′lo·ist** *n.*

sol·stice (sol′stis) *n. Astron.* 1. The time of year when the sun is at its greatest distance from the celestial equator; either the **summer solstice,** about June 22 in the northern hemisphere, or the **winter solstice,** about Dec. 22. 2. Either of the two points on the ecliptic marking these distances. [< L *sol* sun + *sistere* to cause to stand] —**sol·sti·tial** (sol·stish′əl) *adj.*

sol·u·ble (sol′yə·bəl) *adj.* 1. That can be dissolved in a liquid. 2. That can be solved or explained. [< L *solvere* to solve, dissolve] —**sol′u·bil′i·ty, sol′u·ble·ness** *n.* —**sol′u·bly** *adv.*

sol·ute (sol′yo͞ot, sō′lo͞ot) *n.* The substance dissolved in a solution.

so·lu·tion (sə·lo͞o′shən) *n.* 1. A homogeneous mixture formed by dissolving one or more substances, whether solid, liquid, or gaseous, in another substance. 2. The act or process by which such a mixture is made. 3. The act, process, or method of solving a problem. 4. The answer to a problem; explanation. [< L *solutus*, pp. of *solvere* to dissolve]

solve (solv) *v.t.* **solved, solv·ing** To find the answer to; resolve. [< L *solvere* to solve, loosen] —**solv′a·bil′i·ty** *n.* —**solv′a·ble** *adj.* —**solv′er** *n.*

sol·vent (sol′vənt) *adj.* 1. Able to pay all debts. 2. Having the power of dissolving. —*n.* A substance, generally a liquid, capable of dissolving other substances. [< L *solvens, -entis*, ppr. of *solvere* to solve, loosen] —**sol′ven·cy** *n.*

So·ma·li (sō·mä′lē) *n.* 1. A member of one of certain Hamitic tribes of Somalia, Kenya, Ethiopia, and French Somaliland. 2. Their Hamitic language.

so·mat·ic (sō·mat′ik) *adj. Biol.* Of or relating to the body; physical; corporeal. [< Gk. *sōma* body]

som·ber (som′bər) *adj.* 1. Dark and gloomy; dusky; murky. 2. Melancholy; sad; depressing. Also *Brit.* **som′bre.** [< F *sombre*]

som·bre·ro (som·brâr′ō) *n. pl.* **·ros** A broad-brimmed, tall-crowned hat worn in Mexico, SW U.S., etc. [< Sp. < *sombra* shade]

some (sum) *adj.* 1. Of an unspecified quantity, number, or amount: Take *some* cherries. 2. Certain but not specified or known: *Some* people wrote to him. 3. *Informal* Worthy of notice; remarkable: That was *some* cake. —*pron.* 1. A certain undetermined quantity or part. 2. Certain ones not known or specified. —*adv.* Approximately; about: *Some* eighty persons arrived. [OE *sum*]

-some[1] *suffix of adjectives* Characterized by or tending to be (what is indicated by the main element): *blithesome, frolicsome.* [OE *-sum* like, resembling]

-some[2] *suffix of nouns* A body: *chromosome.* Also **-soma.** [< Gk. *sōma* a body]

-some[3] *suffix of nouns* A group consisting of (a specified number): *twosome, foursome.* [< SOME]

some·bod·y (sum′bod′ē, -bəd·ē) *pron.* A person unknown or unnamed; someone. —*n. pl.* **·bod·ies** A person of consequence.

some·day (sum′dā′) *adv.* At some future time.

some·how (sum′hou′) *adv.* In some manner not explained.

some·one (sum′wun′, -wən) *pron.* Somebody.

some·place (sum′plās′) *adv.* *Informal* Somewhere.

som·er·sault (sum′ər·sôlt) *n.* An acrobatic leap or roll in which a person turns his heels over his head, making a full revolution of his body. —*v.i.* To perform a somersault. Also **som′er·set** (-set). [< L *supra* above + *saltus* leap]

some·thing (sum′thing) *n.* A thing not specified or known. —**to make something of** 1. To treat as special or important. 2. *Informal* To fight or argue because of. —*adv.* Somewhat: now only in the phrase **something like:** His house is *something like* mine.

some·time (sum′tīm′) *adv.* At some future time not precisely stated; eventually. —*adj.* Former: a *sometime* student.

some·times (sum′tīmz′) *adv.* At times; occasionally.

some·what (sum′hwot′, -hwət) *n.* An uncertain quantity or degree; something. —*adv.* In some degree; rather.

some·where (sum′hwâr′) *adv.* In, at, or to some place unspecified or unknown. —*n.* An unspecified or unknown place.

som·nam·bu·late (som·nam′byə·lāt) *v.i.* **·lat·ed, ·lat·ing** To walk while asleep. [< SOMN(I)- + AMBULATE]

som·nam·bu·lism (som·nam′byə·liz′əm) *n.* Sleepwalking. Also **som·nam′bu·la′tion.** —**som·nam′bu·lant** *adj.* —**som·nam′bu·list** *n.* —**som·nam′bu·lis′tic** *adj.*

somni- *combining form* Sleep: *somniferous.* [< L *somnus* sleep]

som·nif·er·ous (som·nif′ər·əs) *adj.* Tending to produce sleep; soporiferous. —**som·nif′er·ous·ly** *adv.*

som·no·lence (som′nə·ləns) *n.* Sleepiness; drowsiness. Also **som′no·len·cy.**

som·no·lent (som′nə·lənt) *adj.* 1. Sleepy; drowsy. 2. Tending to induce drowsiness. [< L *somnus* sleep] —**som′no·lent·ly** *adv.*

son (sun) *n.* 1. A male child considered with reference to one or both parents. 2. Any male descendant. 3. A person regarded as a native of a particular country or place. —**the Son** Jesus Christ, the second person of the Trinity. [OE *sunu*] —**son′ship** *n.*

so·nant (sō′nənt) *adj.* 1. Sounding; resonant. 2. *Phonet.* Voiced. —*n. Phonet.* A voiced speech sound. [< L *sonans, -antis,* ppr. of *sonare* to resound] —**so′nance** *n.*

so·nar (sō′när) *n.* A device using underwater sound waves for navigation, range finding, detection of submarines, etc. [< SO(UND) NA(VIGATION AND) R(ANGING)]

so·na·ta (sə·nä′tə) *n. Music* A composition for one or two instruments, having three or four movements related in key. [< Ital. < *sonare* to sound]

so·na·ti·na (son′ə·tē′nə) *n. Music* A short or easy sonata. [< Ital., dim. of SONATA]

song (sông) *n.* 1. A musical composition for one or more voices. 2. Any melodious utterance, as of a bird. 3. A lyric or ballad. 4. Poetry; verse. —**for a song** At a very low price. [OE]

song·bird (sông′bûrd′) *n.* A bird that utters a musical call.

song·ful (sông′fəl) *adj.* Full of song or melody.

song sparrow A common sparrow of the eastern U.S., noted for its song.

song·ster (sông′stər) *n.* 1. A singer. 2. A songbird. 3. A poet. —**song′stress** *n.fem.*

song·wri·ter (sông′rī′tər) *n.* One who writes music or lyrics, or both, for songs, esp. popular songs.

son·ic (son′ik) *adj.* Of or relating to sound or the speed of sound: *sonic* waves. [< L *sonus* sound]

sonic barrier *Aeron.* The high resistance of air encountered by aircraft moving at speeds close to that of sound. Also *sound barrier.*

son-in-law (sun′in·lô′) *n. pl.* **sons-in-law** The husband of one's daughter.

son·net (son′it) *n.* A poem usu. of fourteen lines, properly expressing two successive phases of a single thought or idea. [< L *sonus* sound]

son·net·eer (son′ə·tir′) *n.* A composer of sonnets.

son·ny (sun′ē) *n.* *Informal* Youngster: a familiar form of address to boys.

so·nor·i·ty (sə·nôr′ə·tē, -nor′-) *n. pl.* **·ties** Sonorous quality or state; resonance.

so·no·rous (sə·nôr′əs, son′ər·əs) *adj.* 1. Producing sound. 2. Loud and full-sounding; resonant. [< L *sonare* to resound] —**so·no′rous·ly** *adv.* —**so·no′rous·ness** *n.*

soon (so͞on) *adv.* 1. In the near future; shortly. 2. Without delay; quickly. 3. Willingly; readily. 4. Ahead of time; early. [OE *sōna* immediately]

soot (so͝ot) *n.* A black substance composed chiefly of carbon particles, produced during the burning of coal, wood, etc. [OE *sōt*] —**soot′i·ly** *adv.* —**soot′i·ness** *n.* —**soot′y** *adj.* **soot·i·er, soot·i·est**

sooth (so͞oth) *Archaic adj.* True. —*n.* Truth. [OE *sōth*]

soothe (so͞oth) *v.* **soothed, sooth·ing** *v.t.* 1. To make quiet or calm; comfort. 2. To relieve, as pain or grief; alleviate. —*v.i.* 3. To have a calming or relieving effect. [OE *sōthian* to verify] —**sooth′er** *n.* —**sooth′ing** *adj.* —**sooth′ing·ly** *adv.*

sooth·say·er (so͞oth′sā′ər) *n.* One who claims to be able to foretell events. —**sooth′say′ing** *n.*

sop (sop) *v.* **sopped, sop·ping** *v.t.* 1. To dip or soak in a liquid. 2. To drench. 3. To take up by absorption: often with *up.* —*v.i.* 4. To be absorbed; soak in. —*n.* 1. Anything softened in liquid, as bread. 2. Anything given to pacify, as a bribe. [OE *sopp*]

soph·ism (sof′iz·əm) *n.* A false argument having the appearance of truth, esp. one used to deceive.

soph·ist (sof′ist) *n.* One who argues cleverly but overprecisely and sometimes deceptively. [< Gk. *sophos* wise]

so·phis·tic (sə·fis′tik) *adj.* Pertaining to sophists or sophistry. Also **so·phis′ti·cal.** —**so·phis′ti·cal·ly** *adv.*

so·phis·ti·cate (*v.* sə·fis′tə·kāt; *n.* sə·fis′tə·kit, -kāt) *v.t.* **·cat·ed, ·cat·ing** 1. To make less simple or ingenuous; render worldly-wise. 2. To increase the complexity of. —*n.* A sophisticated person. [< L *sophisticus* sophistic] —**so·phis′ti·ca′tion** *n.* —**so·phis′ti·ca′tor** *n.*

so·phis·ti·cat·ed (sə·fis′tə·kā′tid) *adj.* 1. Having refined tastes; wordly-wise; cultured. 2. Appealing to the intellect: a *sophisticated* novel. 3. Very complicated in design, capabilities, etc.

soph·is·try (sof′is·trē) *n. pl.* **·tries** Subtly fallacious reasoning or disputation.

soph·o·more (sof′ə·môr) *n.* In American high schools and colleges, a second-year student. [Earlier *sophumer* one who uses sophisms; later infl. in meaning by Gk. *sophos* wise + *mōros* fool]

soph·o·mor·ic (sof′ə·môr′ik) *adj.* 1. Of or like a sophomore. 2. Marked by shallow perceptions and attitudes; immature; callow. Also **soph′o·mor′i·cal.** —**soph′o·mor′i·cal·ly** *adv.*

Soph·o·ni·as (sof′ə·nī′əs) The Douai Bible name for ZEPHANIAH.

-sophy *combining form* Knowledge pertaining to a (specified) field: *theosophy.* [< Gk. *sophia* wisdom]

so·po·rif·ic (sō′pə·rif′ik, sop′ə-) *adj.* 1. Causing sleep. 2. Drowsy; sleepy. —*n.* A medicine that produces sleep. [< L *sopor* deep sleep]

sop·ping (sop′ing) *adj.* Wet through; drenched; soaking.

sop·py (sop′ē) *adj.* **·pi·er, ·pi·est** 1. Very wet. 2. Rainy. 3. *Informal* Sentimental; maudlin.

so·pran·o (sə·pran′ō, -prä′nō) *n. pl.* **so·pran·os** 1. A voice of the highest range. 2. A singer with such a voice. 3. The music intended for such a voice. —*adj.* Of or pertaining to a soprano voice, part, etc. [< Ital. *sopra* above]

sor·cer·er (sôr′sər·ər) *n.* One who practices sorcery. —**sor′cer·ess** *n.fem.*

sor·cer·y (sôr′sər·ē) *n. pl.* **·cer·ies** The alleged use of evil, supernatural powers over people; witchcraft. [< L *sors* fate] —**sor′cer·ous** *adj.*

sor·did (sôr′did) *adj.* 1. Filthy; dirty. 2. Mercenary. 3. Of degraded character; vile; base. [< L *sordes* filth] —**sor′did·ly** *adv.* —**sor′did·ness** *n.*

sore (sôr) *adj.* **sor·er, sor·est** 1. Painful or tender to the touch: a *sore* muscle. 2. Arousing painful feelings; irritating: a *sore* point. 3. Extreme or severe: *sore* need. 4. *Informal* Offended; aggrieved. —*n.* An area of the body where the skin is bruised, broken, or inflamed. —*adv. Archaic* Sorely. [OE *sār*] —**sore′ness** *n.*

sore·head (sôr′hed′) *n. Informal* A disgruntled person. —**sore′head·ed** *adj.*

sore·ly (sôr′lē) *adv.* 1. Grievously; distressingly. 2. Greatly; extremely: His aid was *sorely* needed.

sor·ghum (sôr′gəm) *n.* 1. Any of various tall, tropical grasses grown for grain, fodder, syrup, etc. 2. Syrup made from the sweet juices of the plant. [< Ital. *sorgo*]

so·ror·i·ty (sə·rôr′ə·tē, -ror′-) *n. pl.* **·ties** A women's association, esp. at a college or university. [< L *soror* sister]

sorp·tion (sôrp′shən) *n.* Absorption or adsorption. [< L *sorbere*]

sor·rel[1] (sôr′əl, sor′-) *n.* Any of several herbs with sour leaves used in salads. [< F < OHG *sur* sour]

sor·rel[2] (sôr′əl, sor′-) *n.* 1. A reddish or yellowish brown color. 2. A horse of this color. [< OF *sor* reddish brown]

sor·row (sor′ō, sôr′ō) *n.* 1. Suffering or distress due to loss, injury, or misfortune. 2. The cause of such suffering. 3. The expression of grief. —*v.i.* To feel sorrow; grieve. [OE *sorg*] —**sor′row·er** *n.*

sor·row·ful (sor′ə·fəl, sôr′-) *adj.* Sad; unhappy; mournful. —**sor′row·ful·ly** *adv.* —**sor′row·ful·ness** *n.*

sor·ry (sor′ē, sôr′ē) *adj.* **·ri·er, ·ri·est** 1. Affected by sorrow. 2. Causing sorrow; dismal. 3. Pitiable or worthless. [OE *sār* sore] —**sor′ri·ly** *adv.* —**sor′ri·ness** *n.*

sort (sôrt) *n.* 1. A group of related persons or things; class; kind; set. 2. Nature; quality; type: remarks of that *sort.* —**of sorts** Of a poor or unsatisfactory kind: an actor *of sorts.* —**out of sorts** *Informal* 1. In an ill humor; irritable. 2. Slightly ill. —**sort of** *Informal* Somewhat. —*v.t.* To arrange or separate into grades, kinds, or sizes. [< L *sors* lot, condition] —**sort′a·ble** *adj.* —**sort′a·bly** *adv.* —**sort′er** *n.*

sor·tie (sôr′tē) *n. Mil.* 1. A sally of troops from a besieged place to attack the besiegers. 2. A single trip of an aircraft on a combat mission. [< F *sortir* to go forth]

S O S (es′ō′es′) 1. The code signal of distress used by airplanes, ships, etc. 2. Any call for assistance.

so-so (sō′sō′) *adj.* Passable; mediocre. —*adv.* Tolerably.

sot (sot) *n.* A habitual drunkard. [< LL *sottus* drunkard] —**sot′tish** *adj.* —**sot′tish·ly** *adv.* —**sot′tish·ness** *n.*

sot·to vo·ce (sot′ō vō′chē, *Ital.* sôt′tō vō′chā) In a soft voice, so as not to be overheard. [< Ital., under the (normal) voice]

sou·brette (so͞o·bret′) *n.* 1. In light opera or comedy, the role of a pert, intriguing lady's maid. 2. An actress playing such a role. [< F < Provençal *soubret* shy, coy]

sou·bri·quet (so͞o′bri·kā) *n.* See SOBRIQUET.

souf·flé (so͞o·flā′) *n.* A light, baked dish made fluffy with beaten egg whites. —*adj.* Made light and frothy: also **souf·fléed′** (-flād′). [< F < L *sub-* under + *flare* to blow]

sough (suf, sou) *v.i.* To make a sighing sound, as the wind. [OE *swōgan* to sound] —**sough** *n.*

sought (sôt) Past tense and past participle of SEEK.

soul (sōl) *n.* 1. The rational or emotional part of man, regarded as a separate entity from the body. 2. *Theol.* **a** The divine principle of life in man. **b** The moral or spiritual part of man as related to God. 3. Fervor; heartiness; vitality. 4. An essential or vital element: Justice is the *soul* of law. 5. A person considered as the embodiment of a quality or attribute: He is the *soul* of generosity. 6. A person. 7. Among U.S. Negroes, the awareness of a black African heritage. —*adj.* Of, pertaining to, designed for, or characteristic of U.S. Negroes: *soul* food, *soul* music. [OE *sāwol*]

soul·ful (sōl′fəl) *adj.* Full of deep feeling: a *soulful* gaze. —**soul′ful·ly** *adv.* —**soul′ful·ness** *n.*

soul·less (sōl′lis) *adj.* 1. Heartless; unemotional. 2. Having no soul. —**soul′less·ly** *adv.* —**soul′less·ness** *n.*

sound[1] (sound) *n.* 1. Any of a class of waves consisting of mechanical disturbances, esp. in air. 2. The auditory stimulation produced by waves of this type. 3. Something that is heard: the *sound* of laughter. 4. Significance; implication: The story has a sinister *sound.* 5. Sounding or hearing distance; earshot. —*v.i.* 1. To make a sound. 2. To give a specified impression; seem: The story *sounds* true. —*v.t.* 3. To cause to give forth sound. 4. To signal, order, announce, etc.: to *sound* retreat. 5. To utter audibly; pronounce. 6. To test or examine by sound. [< L *sonus*] —**sound′less** *adj.* —**sound′less·ly** *adv.*

sound[2] (sound) *adj.* 1. Free from injury or disease; healthy. 2. Free from flaw, decay, etc.: *sound* timber. 3. Founded in truth; valid; legal. 4. Deep, as sleep; unbroken. 5. Complete and effectual; thorough. 6. Solid; stable; safe; also, trustworthy. 7. Based on good judgment. —*adv.* Deeply: *sound* asleep. [OE *gesund*] —**sound′ly** *adv.* —**sound′ness** *n.*

sound[3] (sound) *n.* 1. A long, narrow body of water connecting larger bodies. 2. In bony fishes, an air-filled sac which contributes to buoyancy. [Fusion of OE and ON *sund*]

sound[4] (sound) *v.t.* 1. To measure the depth of (water), esp. by means of a weighted line. 2. To try to discover the views of (a person). —*v.i.* 3. To sound depth. 4. To investigate; inquire. —*n.* *Surg.* An instrument for exploring a cavity. [< L *sub-* under + *unda* a wave] —**sound′a·ble** *adj.*

sound barrier *Aeron.* Sonic barrier.

sound effects In motion pictures, radio, etc., the artificially produced sounds of rain, explosions, etc.

sound·ing[1] (soun′ding) *adj.* 1. Giving forth a full sound; sonorous. 2. Having much sound with little significance.

sound·ing[2] (soun′ding) *n.* 1. The act of measuring the depth of water by sounding. 2. *pl.* The depth of water so measured.

sound·proof (sound′proo͞f′) *adj.* Resistant to the passage of sound. —*v.t.* To make soundproof.

sound track The portion along the edge of a motion-picture film that carries the sound record. Also **sound′track′**.

soup (so͞op) *n.* 1. Liquid food made by boiling meat, vegetables, etc., in water. 2. *Slang* A thick overcast or fog. —**in the soup** *Slang* In difficulties. —**to soup up** *Slang* To modify (an automobile) for high speed. [< F *soupe* < Gmc.]

soup·çon (so͞op·sôṅ′) *n.* *French* A minute quantity; a trace.

sour (sour) *adj.* 1. Sharp to the taste; acid; tart. 2. Having a rancid taste; spoiled. 3. Having a foul odor: *sour* breath. 4. Bad-tempered; cross; morose. 5. Acid: said of soil. —*v.t. & v.i.* To become or make sour. —*n.* A sour or acid beverage: a whisky *sour.* [OE *sūr*] —**sour′ish** *adj.* —**sour′ly** *adv.* —**sour′ness** *n.*

source (sôrs) *n.* 1. The cause or origin of something; beginning. 2. A lake or other body of water that gives rise to a river. 3. A writer, book, etc., that provides information. [< L *surgere*]

sour·dough (sour′dō′) *n.* Fermented dough for use as leaven in making bread.

sour grapes An attitude of scorn toward something one cannot do or have. [after a fable of Aesop in which a fox describes unreachable grapes as sour]

sour·puss (sour′po͝os′) *n.* *Slang* A person with a sullen, peevish expression or character; grouch.

souse (sous) *v.t. & v.i.* **soused, sous·ing** 1. To dip or steep in a liquid. 2. To pickle. —*n.* 1. The act of sousing. 2. Pickled food, esp. the feet and ears of a pig. 3. A liquid used in pickling; brine. 4. *Slang* A drunkard. [< OHG *sulza* brine]

south (south) *n.* 1. The direction to one's right when facing the sun at sunrise. 2. One of the four cardinal points of the compass, directly opposite *north.* 3. *Sometimes cap.* Any region south of a specified point. —**the South** In the U.S.: **a** The southern or southeastern states. **b** The Confederacy. —*adj.* 1. To, toward, or in the south; southern. 2. Coming from the south: the *south* wind. —*adv.* In or toward the south; southward. [OE *sūth*]

south·bound (south′bound′) *adj.* Going southward. Also **south′-bound′**.

south·east (south′ēst′, *Naut.* sou·ēst′) *n.* 1. The direction midway between south and east. 2. Any region lying in or toward this direction. —*adj.* 1. To, toward, or in the southeast. 2. Coming from the southeast. —*adv.* In or toward the southeast. —**south′·east′ern** *adj.*

south·east·er (south′ēs′tər, *Naut.* sou·ēs′tər) *n.* A gale or storm from the southeast.

south·east·er·ly (south′ēs′tər·lē, *Naut.* sou·ēs′tər·lē) *adj.* 1. In, of, or toward the southeast. 2. From the southeast, as a wind. —*adv.* Toward or from the southeast.

south·er (sou′thər) *n.* A gale or storm from the south.

south·er·ly (suth′ər·lē) *adj.* 1. In, of, toward, or pertaining to the south. 2. From the south, as a wind. —*adv.* Toward or from the south.

south·ern (suth′ərn) *adj.* 1. To, toward, or in the south. 2. Native to or inhabiting the south. 3. *Sometimes cap.* Of, pertaining to, or characteristic of the south or South. 4. From the south, as a wind. [OE *sūtherne*]

Southern Cross A southern constellation having four bright stars in the form of a cross.

south·ern·er (suth′ərn·ər) *n.* 1. One who is native to or lives in the south. 2. *Usu. cap.* One who lives in or comes from the South.

Southern Hemisphere See under HEMISPHERE.

southern lights The aurora australis.

south·ern·most (suth′ərn·mōst′) *adj.* Farthest south.

south·land (south′land′) *n.* *Sometimes cap.* A land or region in the south or South. —**south′land′er** *n.*

south·paw (south′pô′) *n.* *Informal* 1. In

baseball, a left-handed pitcher. 2. Any left-handed person. —*adj.* Left-handed.

South Pole The southern extremity of the earth's axis.

south·ward (south′wərd, *Naut.* suth′ərd) *adv.* Toward the south. Also **south′wards.** —*adj.* To, toward, facing, or in the south.

south·ward·ly (south′wərd·lē, *Naut.* suth′·ərd·lē) *adj. & adv.* Toward or from the south.

south·west (south′west′, *Naut.* sou·west′) *n.* 1. The direction midway between south and west. 2. Any region lying in or toward this direction. —*adj.* 1. To, toward, or in the southwest. 2. Coming from the southwest: a *southwest* wind. —*adv.* In or toward the southwest. —**south′west′ern** *adj.*

south·west·er (south′wes′tər, *Naut.* sou·wes′tər) *n.* 1. A gale or storm from the southwest. 2. A waterproof hat with a broad brim over the neck. Also **sou′·west′er.**

south·west·er·ly (south′wes′tər·lē, *Naut.* sou·wes′tər·lē) *adj.* 1. In, of, or toward the southwest. 2. From the southwest, as a wind. —*adv.* Toward or from the southwest.

sou·ve·nir (so͞o′və·nir′, so͞o′və·nir) *n.* A token of remembrance; memento. [< F < L *subvenire* to come to mind]

sov·er·eign (sov′rən, -ər·in) *n.* 1. The ruler of a monarchy; monarch; also, any supreme ruler of a state. 2. Formerly, an English gold coin equivalent to one pound sterling or twenty shillings. —*adj.* 1. Having supreme authority. 2. Independent of all external authority or influence: a *sovereign* state. 3. Of supreme excellence; highest. [< OF *soverain,* ult. < L *super* above] —**sov′er·eign·ly** *adv.*

sov·er·eign·ty (sov′rən·tē, -ər·in·tē) *n. pl.* **·ties** 1. Supreme authority. 2. The supreme and independent political authority.

so·vi·et (sō′vē·et, -ət, sō′vē·et′) *n.* In the Soviet Union, any of the legislative bodies existing at various governmental levels. —*adj. Cap.* Of or pertaining to the Union of Soviet Socialist Republics. [< Russ. *sovyet* council] —**so′vi·et·ism** *n.*

so·vi·et·ize (sō′vē·ə·tīz′) *v.t.* **·ized, ·iz·ing** To bring under a soviet form of government. —**so′vi·et·i·za′tion** *n.*

sow[1] (sō) *v.* **sowed, sown or sowed, sow·ing** *v.t.* 1. To scatter (seed) over land for growth. 2. To scatter seed over (land). 3. To spread abroad; disseminate: to *sow* the seeds of distrust. —*v.i.* 4. To scatter seed. [OE *sāwan*] —**sow′er** *n.*

sow[2] (sou) *n.* A female hog. [OE *sū, sugu*]

soy (soi) 1. The soybean. 2. A salty, dark-brown sauce made from soybeans fermented in brine: also **soy sauce.** [< Japanese, short for *shōyū*]

soy·bean (soi′bēn′) *n.* 1. An erect, leguminous herb native to China and India, cultivated for forage. 2. Its bean, a source of oil, flour, etc. Also called *soy:* also **soy·a** (soi′ə). [< SOY + BEAN]

spa (spä) *n.* 1. A resort, esp. one frequented for its mineral springs. 2. A mineral spring. [from the Belgian town, *Spa*]

space (spās) *n.* 1. The infinite expanse within which all things exist. 2. An interval or area between or within things. 3. Area for some purpose: parking *space.* 4. Outer space. 5. An interval of time; period. 6. *Printing* A piece of type metal used for separating words. 7. Broadcasting time, area in a magazine, etc., available for advertising. —*v.t.* **spaced, spac·ing** 1. To separate by spaces. 2. To divide into spaces. [< L *spatium*] —**space′less** *adj.* —**spac′er** *n.*

space·craft (spās′kraft′) *n.* Any vehicle, manned or unmanned, designed for travel in outer space. Also **space·ship** (spās′ship′).

spaced out *Slang* Dazed, disoriented, etc., from or as from use of a narcotic drug. Also **spaced.**

space·flight (spās′flīt′) *n.* Flight in outer space.

space·man (spās′mən) *n. pl.* **·men** (-mən) An astronaut.

space shuttle A rocket controllable like an airplane, designed for flights to and from space stations.

space station An artificial satellite designed as a base for research or for launching or refueling spacecraft. Also **space platform.**

space suit A garment designed to allow the wearer to live in outer space.

space-time (spās′tīm′) *n.* A four-dimensional continuum consisting of three spatial coordinates and one coordinate of time. Also **space-time continuum.**

space walk The maneuvers of an astronaut in space outside a spacecraft. —**space·walk** (spās′wôk′) *v.i.* —**space′walk′er** *n.* —**space′·walk′ing** *n.*

spa·cious (spā′shəs) *adj.* 1. Of indefinite or vast extent. 2. Affording ample room; roomy. —**spa′cious·ly** *adv.* —**spa′cious·ness** *n.*

spade[1] (spād) *n.* A heavy shovel with a flat blade. —**to call a spade a spade** To speak frankly and truly. —*v.t.* **spad·ed, spad·ing** To dig or cut with a spade. [OE *spadu*] —**spad′er** *n.*

spade[2] (spād) *n.* A playing card bearing a black figure resembling an inverted heart with a short handle at the bottom. [< Sp. *espada* sword < Gk. *spathē*]

spade·work (spād′wûrk′) *n.* Preliminary work necessary to get a project under way.

spa·dix (spā′diks) *n. pl.* **spa·di·ces** (spā·dī′sēz) *Bot.* A spike or head of flowers with a fleshy axis. [< Gk. *spaein* to break]

spa·ghet·ti (spə·get′ē) *n.* A food consisting of cordlike strands of flour paste. [< Ital., pl. dim. of *spago* cord]

spake (spāk) Archaic past tense of SPEAK.

span[1] (span) *v.t.* **spanned, span·ning** 1. To measure, esp. by the hand with thumb and little finger extended. 2. To stretch across: This road *spans* the continent. —*n.* 1. The distance between the tips of the thumb and little finger when the hand is spread out, usu. considered as nine inches. 2. Distance or extent between any two extremities. 3. That which spans, as a bridge. [OE *spann*] —**span′less** *adj.*

span[2] (span) Archaic past tense of SPIN.

span·drel (span′drəl) *n.* *Archit.* The triangular space between the outer curve of an arch and the rectangular framework surrounding it. Also **span′dril.** [< OF *espandre* to expand]

span·gle (spang′gəl) *n.* A small bit of sparkling metal or plastic, used for decoration in dress. —*v.* **·gled, ·gling** *v.t.* 1. To adorn with or as with spangles; cause to glitter. —*v.i.* 2. To sparkle; glitter. [Dim. of MDu. *spang* clasp, brooch] —**span′gly** *adj.*

Span·iard (span′yərd) *n.* A native or citizen of Spain.

span·iel (span′yəl) *n.* Any of various breeds of short-legged dogs having large, droopy ears and a silky coat. [< OF *espaignol* Spanish (dog)]

Span·ish (span′ish) *adj.* Of or pertaining to Spain, its people, or their language. —*n.* 1. The language of Spain, Spanish America, and the Philippine Islands. 2. The inhabitants of Spain collectively: with *the.*

Span·ish-A·mer·i·can (span′ish·ə·mer′ə·kən) *adj.* 1. Of or pertaining to Spanish America. 2. Designating or pertaining to the war between the U.S. and Spain, 1898. —*n.* One of Spanish origin living in Central or South America; also, a citizen of the U.S. having Spanish or Spanish-American ancestry.

Spanish moss A long, hanging plant growing from trees in the southern U.S.

spank (spangk) *v.t.* To slap or strike, esp. on the buttocks with the open hand. —*n.* A smack on the buttocks. [Imit.]

spank·er (spangk′ər) *n. Naut.* A fore-and-aft sail extended by a boom and gaff from the mizzenmast of a ship.

spank·ing (spangk′ing) *adj.* Moving rapidly; swift. —*n.* The act of spanking as punishment. —*adv. Informal* Very: *spanking* clean.

span·ner (span′ər) *n. Brit.* A wrench. [< G]

spar[1] (spär) *n. Naut.* A mast, boom, etc., for extending a sail. —*v.t.* **sparred, spar·ring** To furnish with spars. [Cf. ON *sparri,* MDu. *sparre* beam]

spar[2] (spär) *v.i.* **sparred, spar·ring** 1. To box, esp. as a training exercise. 2. To bandy words; wrangle. [? < Ital. *sparare* to kick]

spare (spâr) *v.t.* **spared, spar·ing** 1. To refrain from injuring, killing, etc. 2. To free or relieve a person from (pain, expense, etc.). 3. To use frugally. 4. To part with; do without: Can you *spare* a dime? —*adj.* **spar·er, spar·est** 1. That can be used at will or held in reserve; extra. 2. Free: a *spare* moment. 3. Having little flesh; lean. 4. Not lavish or abundant; scanty. —*n.* 1. Something extra or held in reserve. 2. In bowling, the knocking down of all the pins with the two bowls in any frame; also, the score so made. [OE *sparian*] —**spare′ly** *adv.* —**spare′·ness** *n.* —**spar′er** *n.*

spare·rib (spâr′rib′) *n.* A cut of pork consisting of closely trimmed ribs. [? Alter. of MLG *ribbespēr*]

spar·ing (spâr′ing) *adj.* Frugal or thrifty; economical. —**spar′ing·ly** *adv.* —**spar′ing·ness** *n.*

spark (spärk) *n.* 1. An incandescent particle thrown off from a fire, a match, etc. 2. Anything like a spark; flash; sparkle. 3. Anything that kindles or animates. 4. *Electr.* The luminous effect of a disruptive electric discharge; also, the discharge itself. 5. A small trace or indication; hint. —*v.i.* 1. To give off sparks. —*v.t.* 2. To activate or stir up; incite: to *spark* a revolution. [OE *spearca*] —**spark′er** *n.*

spar·kle (spär′kəl) *v.i.* **·kled, ·kling** 1. To give off flashes of light; glitter. 2. To emit sparks. 3. To bubble; effervesce. 4. To be brilliant or vivacious. —*n.* 1. A glittering; flash; gleam. 2. Liveliness; brilliance; vivacity. [Freq. of SPARK]

spar·kler (spär′klər) *n.* 1. *Informal* A sparkling gem. 2. A thin, rodlike firework that emits sparks.

spar·kling (spär′kling) *adj.* 1. Giving off sparks or flashes; glittering. 2. Brilliant; vivacious. —**spar′kling·ly** *adv.*

spark plug A device for igniting the gases in the cylinder of an engine by means of a spark.

spar·row (spar′ō) *n.* A small bird related to the finches, grosbeaks, and buntings. [OE *spearwa*]

sparrow hawk 1. A small American falcon that preys on other birds, mice, etc. 2. A small European hawk that preys on birds.

sparse (spärs) *adj.* Thinly spread; scattered widely; not dense. [< L *sparsus,* pp. of *spargere* to scatter] —**sparse′ly** *adv.* —**sparse′ness, spar′si·ty** *n.*

Spar·tan (spär′tən) *adj.* Like the ancient Spartans; brave, austere, stoical, etc. —*n.* A person of Spartan character. [< *Sparta,* ancient city in Greece] —**Spar′tan·ism** *n.*

spasm (spaz′əm) *n.* 1. Any sudden, transient burst of energy or activity. 2. *Pathol.* Any involuntary, convulsive muscular contraction. [< Gk. *spasmos* < *span* to draw, pull]

spas·mod·ic (spaz·mod′ik) *adj.* Of or like a spasm; violent; fitful; sudden. Also **spas·mod′i·cal.** —**spas·mod′i·cal·ly** *adv.*

spas·tic (spas′tik) *adj.* Of, like, or suffering from spasms. —*n.* A person afflicted with a spastic condition. —**spas′ti·cal·ly** *adv.*

spat[1] (spat) Past tense and past participle of SPIT[1].

spat[2] (spat) *n.* The spawn of an oyster or similar shellfish. —*v.i.* **spat·ted, spat·ting** To spawn, as oysters. [? Akin to SPIT[1]]

spat[3] (spat) *n.* A petty dispute. —*v.i.* **spat·ted, spat·ting** To engage in a petty quarrel. [Prob. imit.]

spat[4] (spat) *n. Usu. pl.* A short gaiter worn over a shoe and fastened beneath with a strap. [Short for SPATTERDASH]

spate (spāt) *n.* A sudden or vigorous outpouring, as of words. [Origin uncertain]

spa·tial (spā′shəl) *adj.* Of or involving space. [< L *spatium* space] —**spa·ti·al·i·ty** (spā′·shē·al′ə·tē) *n.* —**spa′tial·ly** *adv.*

spat·ter (spat′ər) *v.t.* 1. To scatter in drops or splashes, as mud or paint. 2. To splash with such drops. —*v.i.* 3. To throw off drops or splashes. 4. To fall in a shower, as raindrops. —*n.* 1. The act of spattering, or the matter spattered. 2. A pattering noise. [Cf. Frisian *spatterje,* Du. *spatten* to spatter]

spat·ter·dash (spat′ər·dash′) *n.* A legging or puttee.

spat·u·la (spach′o͞o·lə) *n.* A knifelike instrument with a flat, flexible blade, used to spread plaster, cake icing, etc. [< L] —**spat·u·late** (spach′o͞o·lit) *adj.*

spawn (spôn) *n.* 1. *Zool.* The mass of eggs of fishes, amphibians, mollusks, etc. 2. Numerous offspring. 3. Outcome or results; yield. —*v.i.* 1. To produce spawn; deposit eggs or roe. —*v.t.* 2. To produce (spawn). 3. To give rise to. [< L *expandere*]

spay (spā) *v.t.* To remove the ovaries from (a female animal). [< L *spatha* sword]

speak (spēk) *v.* **spoke** (*Archaic* **spake**), **spo·ken** (*Archaic* **spoke**), **speak·ing** *v.i.*

1. To utter words; talk. 2. To make a speech. 3. To talk together; converse. —*v.t.* 4. To utter; say. 5. To make known; reveal. 6. To use (a language) in speaking. —**to speak for** To speak in behalf of; represent. [OE *specan, sprecan*] —**speak′a·ble** *adj.*

speak·eas·y (spēk′ē′zē) *n. pl.* **·eas·ies** *Slang* A place where liquor is sold illegally.

speak·er (spē′kər) *n.* 1. One who speaks. 2. The presiding officer of a legislative body. 3. A loud-speaker. —**speak′er·ship** *n.*

spear (spir) *n.* 1. A weapon consisting of a pointed head on a long shaft. 2. A barbed and usu. forked instrument for spearing fish. 3. A leaf or slender stalk, as of grass. —*v.t.* To pierce with a spear. [OE *spere* spear] —**spear′er** *n.*

spear·head (spir′hed′) *n.* 1. The point of a spear. 2. A person or group that leads or strongly influences an action. —*v.t.* To be in the lead of.

spear·man (spir′mən) *n. pl.* **·men** (-mən) A man armed with a spear. Also **spears′man** (spirz′-).

spear·mint (spir′mint′) *n.* An aromatic herb similar to peppermint.

spe·cial (spesh′əl) *adj.* 1. Having some peculiar or distinguishing characteristic; distinctive. 2. Designed for a specific purpose. 3. Out of the ordinary; unique; exceptional. 4. Valued highly; favored. —*n.* 1. Something made for a specific service or occasion. 2. Food or other product offered for sale at reduced prices. [< L *species* kind, species] —**spe′cial·ly** *adv.* —**spe′cial·ness** *n.*

special delivery Mail delivery by special messenger for an additional fee.

spe·cial·ist (spesh′əl·ist) *n.* 1. A person devoted to one line of study, occupation, etc.; esp., a physician who restricts his practice to one branch of medicine. 2. In the U.S. Army, an enlisted person in a technical or administrative position, corresponding in rank to the grades of corporal through sergeant first class. —**spe′cial·ism** *n.* —**spe′cial·is′tic** *adj.*

spe·cial·ize (spesh′əl·īz) *v.i.* **·ized, ·iz·ing** 1. To concentrate on one particular activity or subject. 2. *Biol.* To take on a special form; adapt. Also *Brit.* **spe′cial·ise.** —**spe′·cial·i·za′tion** *n.*

spe·cial·ty (spesh′əl·tē) *n. pl.* **·ties** 1. A special occupation, craft, or study. 2. The state of being special or of having peculiar characteristics. 3. A unique product or service offered by a store or other business.

spe·cie (spē′shē) *n.* Coined money; coin. [< L (*in*) *specie* (in) kind]

spe·cies (spē′shēz, -sēz) *n. pl.* **·cies** 1. *Biol.* In plant or animal classification, a group of organisms having a number of traits in common, esp. the ability to breed with one another. 2. A kind, sort, or variety. [< L, form, kind]

spec·i·fi·a·ble (spes′ə·fī′ə·bəl) *adj.* Such as can be specified.

spe·cif·ic (spi·sif′ik) *adj.* 1. Distinctly and plainly set forth; definite. 2. Peculiar or special, as characteristics, qualities, etc. 3. *Med.* Effective in treating a specific disease: said of a remedy. —*n.* 1. Anything specific or adapted to effect a specific result. 2. *Usu. pl. Informal* A particular; item; instance. [< L *species* kind, class + *facere* to make] —**spe·cif′i·cal·ly** *adv.* —**spec·i·fic·i·ty** (spes′ə·fis′ə·tē) *n.*

spec·i·fi·ca·tion (spes′ə·fə·kā′shən) *n.* 1. The act of specifying. 2. Something specified, as in a contract, plans, etc. 3. *Usu. pl.* A detailed description of the materials, dimensions, etc., of a projected work.

specific gravity *Physics* The ratio of the mass of a body to that of an equal volume of some standard substance, water in the case of solids and liquids, and air or hydrogen in the case of gases; a measure of density.

spec·i·fy (spes′ə·fī) *v.t.* **·fied, ·fy·ing** 1. To mention specifically; describe in detail. 2. To list in a specification. [< L *species* species + *facere* to make]

spec·i·men (spes′ə·mən) *n.* 1. A person or thing regarded as representative of its class or group; example; sample. 2. *Med.* A sample of tissue, etc., for analysis and diagnosis. [< L *specere* to look at]

spe·cious (spē′shəs) *adj.* Apparently good or right, but actually not so; deceptively plausible: *specious* reasoning. [< L *speciosus* fair] —**spe′cious·ly** *adv.* —**spe′cious·ness** *n.*

speck (spek) *n.* 1. A small spot, stain, or discoloration. 2. A very small piece; bit; particle. —*v.t.* To mark with specks; speckle. [OE *specca*]

speck·le (spek′əl) *v.t.* **·led, ·ling** To mark with specks. —*n.* A small spot; speck. —**speck′led** *adj.*

specs (speks) *n.pl. Informal* 1. Eyeglasses: also **specks.** 2. Specifications (def. 3).

spec·ta·cle (spek′tə·kəl) *n.* 1. A large, public show or exhibition, esp. on a grand scale. 2. A remarkable or unusual sight or event. 3. An unwelcome or deplorable exhibition. 4. *pl.* A pair of eyeglasses. [< L *spectare*, freq. of *specere* to see]

spec·ta·cled (spek′tə·kəld) *adj.* 1. Wearing spectacles. 2. *Biol.* Having markings resembling a pair of spectacles.

spec·tac·u·lar (spek·tak′yə·lər) *adj.* 1. Very unusual, exciting, etc.; extraordinary: a *spectacular* rescue. 2. Of or like a spectacle. —*n.* In television, a lavish dramatic or musical production. —**spec·tac′u·lar·ly** *adv.* —**spec·tac′u·lar′i·ty** (-lar′ə·tē) *n.*

spec·ta·tor (spek′tā·tər) *n.* 1. One who beholds; eyewitness; onlooker. 2. One who watches a show, game, etc. [< L *spectare* to look at]

spec·ter (spek′tər) *n.* 1. A ghost or apparition. 2. Anything of a fearful or horrible nature. Also *Brit.* **spec′tre.** [< L *spectrum* vision]

spec·tra (spek′trə) Plural of SPECTRUM.

spec·tral (spek′trəl) *adj.* 1. Of or like a specter; ghostly. 2. Pertaining to a spectrum. —**spec·tral′i·ty** (-tral′ə·tē) *n.* —**spec′tral·ly** *adv.*

spectro- *combining form* Of or pertaining to the spectrum: *spectrograph.* [< SPECTRUM]

spec·tro·gram (spek′trə·gram) *n.* A photograph of the spectrum.

spec·tro·graph (spek′trə·graf) *n.* An apparatus for photographing the spectrum.

spec·trom·e·ter (spek·trom′ə·tər) *n.* 1. An instrument for determining the angular deviation or wavelength of a light ray. 2. A spectroscope fitted with such an instrument. —**spec·tro·met·ric** (spek′trō·met′rik) *adj.*

spec·tro·scope (spek′trə·skōp) *n.* An optical instrument for forming and analyzing the spectrum. **—spec′tro·scop′ic** (-skop′ik) or **·i·cal** *adj.* **—spec′tro·scop′i·cal·ly** *adv.*

spec·tros·co·py (spek·tros′kə·pē) *n.* The study of spectra observed with a spectroscope. **—spec·tros′co·pist** *n.*

spec·trum (spek′trəm) *n. pl.* **·tra** **1.** *Physics* **a** The band of color observed when a beam of white light is passed through a prism that separates each component of the light according to wavelengths, ranging from long for red to short for violet. **b** An image formed by radiant energy directed through a spectroscope and forming part of a progressive series. **2.** A range or extent; scope: a wide *spectrum* of political views. [< L, vision]

spec·u·late (spek′yə·lāt) *v.i.* **·lat·ed, ·lat·ing** **1.** To think carefully; reflect; conjecture. **2.** To make an investment involving a risk, but with hope of gain. [< L *speculatus*, pp. of *speculari* to look at] **—spec′u·la′tor** *n.*

spec·u·la·tion (spek′yə·lā′shən) *n.* **1.** Serious thinking or conjecturing; also, a conclusion reached by or based upon conjecture. **2.** The act of engaging in risky business transactions that offer a possibility of large profit. **—spec·u·la·tive** (spek′yə·lā′tiv, -lə·tiv) *adj.* **—spec′u·la′tive·ly** *adv.*

sped (sped) Alternative past tense and past participle of SPEED.

speech (spēch) *n.* **1.** The faculty of expressing thought and emotion by spoken words. **2.** The act of speaking. **3.** A public address or talk. **4.** A characteristic manner of speaking. **5.** A particular language, idiom, or dialect: American *speech.* **6.** The study of oral communication. [OE *specan, sprecan* to speak]

speech·less (spēch′lis) *adj.* **1.** Temporarily unable to speak because of strong emotion, etc. **2.** Mute; dumb. **3.** Unable to be expressed in words: *speechless* joy. **—speech′·less·ly** *adv.* **—speech′less·ness** *n.*

speed (spēd) *n.* **1.** The act of moving swiftly; rapidity of motion. **2.** Rate of motion; velocity. **3.** Rate of performance, as shown by the ratio of work done to time spent. **4.** *Mech.* A transmission gear in a motor vehicle. **5.** *Slang* An amphetamine or related drug used as a stimulant. **—*v.*** **sped** or **speed·ed, speed·ing** *v.i.* **1.** To move rapidly; rush. **2.** To exceed a speed limit. **—*v.t.*** **3.** To cause to move rapidly. **4.** To further the progress of: to *speed* a letter on its way. [OE *spēd* prosperity, power]

speed·boat (spēd′bōt′) *n.* A motorboat capable of high speed.

speed·er (spē′dər) *n.* A motorist who exceeds a safe or legally specified speed limit.

speed·om·e·ter (spi·dom′ə·tər) *n.* A device for indicating the speed of a vehicle.

speed·up (spēd′up′) *n.* An acceleration in work, output, movement, etc.

speed·way (spēd′wā′) *n.* A track for auto or motorcycle races.

speed·well (spēd′wel) *n.* One of various herbs of the figwort family, bearing blue or white flowers.

speed·y (spē′dē) *adj.* **speed·i·er, speed·i·est** **1.** Very fast; rapid. **2.** Without delay; prompt. **—speed′i·ly** *adv.* **—speed′i·ness** *n.*

spe·le·an (spi·lē′ən) *adj.* **1.** Of or like a cave. **2.** Dwelling in a cave. [< Gk. *spēlaion* cave]

speleo- *combining form* Cave. [< Gk. *spēlaion*]

spe·le·ol·o·gy (spē′lē·ol′ə·jē) *n.* The scientific study and exploration of caves. **—spe′le·o·log′i·cal** (-ə·loj′i·kəl) *adj.* **—spe′·le·ol′o·gist** *n.*

spell[1] (spel) *v.* **spelled** or **spelt, spell·ing** *v.t.* **1.** To name or write the letters of (a word); esp., to do so correctly. **2.** To form or be the letters of: C-a-t *spells* cat. **3.** To signify; mean. **—*v.i.*** **4.** To form words out of letters, esp. correctly. **—to spell out** To make clear and explicit. [< OF *espeler* < Gmc.]

spell[2] (spel) *n.* **1.** A word formula used as a charm. **2.** An irresistible fascination or attraction. [OE, statement.]

spell[3] (spel) *n.* **1.** A brief period of time. **2.** A period of weather of a specific kind: a hot *spell.* **3.** A fit of illness, debility, etc. **4.** A turn of duty in relief of another. **5.** A period of work. **—*v.t.*** To relieve temporarily from some work or duty. [OE *gespelia* substitute]

spell·bind (spel′bīnd′) *v.t.* **·bound, ·bind·ing** To make spellbound; enchant. **—spell′·bind′er** *n.*

spell·bound (spel′bound′) *adj.* Fascinated; enchanted.

spell·er (spel′ər) *n.* **1.** One who spells. **2.** A spelling book.

spell·ing (spel′ing) *n.* **1.** The act of one who spells. **2.** The way in which a word is spelled.

spelling bee A competition that is won by the person or team spelling the most words correctly.

spelt (spelt) Alternative past tense and past participle of SPELL.

spe·lunk·er (spē·lung′kər) *n.* An explorer of caves; a speleologist. [< L *spelunca* cave] **—spe·lunk′ing** *n.*

spend (spend) *v.* **spent, spend·ing** *v.t.* **1.** To pay out (money). **2.** To expend; exhaust; use up. **3.** To apply or devote, as thought or effort. **4.** To pass: to *spend* one's life in jail. **—*v.i.*** **5.** To pay out money. [< L *expendere* to expend] **—spend′er** *n.*

spend·thrift (spend′thrift′) *n.* One who spends money lavishy or wastefully. **—*adj.*** Lavish; wasteful.

spent (spent) Past tense and past participle of SPEND. **—*adj.*** Worn out or exhausted.

sperm[1] (spûrm) *n.* **1.** The male fertilizing fluid; semen. **2.** A male reproductive cell; spermatozoon. [< Gk. *sperma* seed] **—sper·mat·ic** (spûr·mat′ik) *adj.*

sperm[2] (spûrm) *n.* **1.** A sperm whale. **2.** Spermaceti. [Short for SPERMACETI]

-sperm *combining form Bot.* A seed (of a specified kind): *gymnosperm.* [< Gk. *sperma, spermatos* seed]

sper·ma·ce·ti (spûr′mə·sē′tē, -set′ē) *n.* A white, waxy substance derived from the oil of the sperm whale, used for making candles, ointments, etc. [< L *sperma ceti* seed of a whale]

spermato- *combining form* **1.** Seed. **2.** Spermatozoa. Also **spermo-**: also, before vowels, **spermat-**. [< Gk. *sperma, spermatos* seed]

sper·ma·to·zo·on (spûr′mə·tə·zō′on) *n. pl.* **·zo·a** *Biol.* The male reproductive or germ cell of an animal; male gamete. [< SPERMATO- + Gk. *zōion* animal] **—sper′ma·to·zo′al, sper′ma·to·zo′ic** *adj.*

-spermous *combining form* Having (a specified

number or kind of) seeds; seeded. Also **-spermal, -spermic.** [< -SPERM + -OUS]

sperm whale A large, toothed whale of warm seas, having a huge truncate head.

spew (spyōō) *v.t. & v.i.* To vomit; throw up. —*n.* Vomit. [OE *spīwan*]

sphag·num (sfag′nəm) *n.* Any of a genus of whitish gray mosses found in damp places; the bog or peat mosses. [< L < Gk. *sphāgnos*] —**sphag′nous** *adj.*

sphe·noid (sfē′noid) *n.* 1. *Mineral.* A crystal form enclosed by four faces, each of which cuts all three axes. 2. *Anat.* The sphenoid bone. —*adj.* Wedge-shaped. [< Gk. *sphēn* wedge] —**sphe·noi·dal** (sfi·noid′l) *adj.*

sphenoid bone *Anat.* An irregular, compound bone situated at the base of the skull.

sphere (sfir) *n.* 1. A solid figure having a surface every point of which is equidistant from the center; globe; ball. 2. A range or field of interest, activity, etc.; scope. [< Gk. *sphaira* ball]

-sphere *combining form* 1. Denoting an enveloping spherical mass: *atmosphere.* 2. Denoting a spherical form: *planisphere.* [< Gk. *sphaira* ball]

spher·i·cal (sfir′i·kəl, sfer′-) *adj.* 1. Shaped like a sphere; globular. 2. Pertaining to a sphere. Also **spher′ic.** —**spher′i·cal·ly** *adv.* —**spher′i·cal·ness** *n.*

sphe·ric·i·ty (sfi·ris′ə·tē) *n.* Spherical form; roundness.

sphe·roid (sfir′oid) *n.* *Geom.* A body having nearly the form of a sphere. —**sphe·roi′dal** *adj.* —**sphe·roi′dal·ly** *adv.*

sphinc·ter (sfingk′tər) *n.* *Anat.* A band of muscle that surrounds an opening or tube in the body and serves to close it. [< Gk. *sphingein* to bind fast] —**sphinc′ter·al** *adj.*

sphinx (sfingks) *n. pl.* **sphinx·es** or **sphin·ges** (sfin′jēz) 1. In Egyptian mythology, a wingless monster with a lion's body and the head of a man, ram, or hawk. 2. In Greek mythology, a winged monster with a woman's head and breasts and a lion's body, that destroyed those unable to guess her riddle. 3. A mysterious or enigmatical person. —**the Sphinx** A huge statue with a lion's body and a man's head at Gizeh, Egypt. [< L < Gk. < *sphingein* to strangle]

sphyg·mo·ma·nom·e·ter (sfig′mō·mə·nom′ə·tər) *n.* An instrument for measuring blood pressure. [< Gk. *sphygmos* pulse + MANOMETER]

spi·cate (spī′kāt) *adj.* *Bot.* Arranged in spikes: said of flowers. Also **spi′cat·ed.** [< L *spicatus* < *spica* spike]

spice (spīs) *n.* 1. An aromatic, pungent vegetable substance, as cinnamon, cloves, etc., used to flavor food. 2. Such substances collectively. 3. That which adds zest or interest. —*v.t.* **spiced, spic·ing** 1. To season with spice. 2. To add zest to. [< OF *espice* < L *species* specific kind] —**spic′er** *n.*

spice·bush (spīs′bŏŏsh′) *n.* An aromatic American shrub of the laurel family. Also **spice′wood′** (-wŏŏd′).

spick-and-span (spik′ən·span′) *adj.* Neat and clean; fresh. [Prob. < *spick*, var. of SPIKE[1] + dial. E *span-new*, really or freshly new]

spic·ule (spik′yōōl) *n.* *Zool.* One of the small, needlelike growths supporting the soft tissues of certain invertebrates, as sponges. [< L *spicum* point, spike] —**spic′u·lar, spic′u·late** (-yə·lāt, -yə·lit) *adj.*

spic·u·lum (spik′yə·ləm) *n. pl.* **·la** A spicule.

spic·y (spī′sē) *adj.* **spic·i·er, spic·i·est** 1. Seasoned with spice. 2. Containing much spice; sharp; hot. 3. Having zest or piquancy. 4. Somewhat improper; risqué. —**spic′i·ly** *adv.* —**spic′i·ness** *n.*

spi·der (spī′dər) *n.* 1. Any of a large number of eight-legged wingless arachnids that spin webs. 2. A long-handled iron frying pan, often having legs. [OE *spinnan* to spin] —**spi′der·y** *adj.*

spider crab Any of a genus of crustaceans with long legs.

spider monkey An arboreal South American monkey with long, slender limbs and a long prehensile tail.

spi·der·wort (spī′dər·wûrt′) *n.* An American perennial with deep blue flowers.

spied (spīd) Past tense and past participle of SPY.

spiel (spēl, shpēl) *Slang* *n.* A talk; esp., noisy, high-pressure sales talk. —*v.i.* To make such a talk. [< G, game < *spielen* to play] —**spiel′er** *n.*

spif·fy (spif′ē) *adj.* **·fi·er, ·fi·est** *Slang* Smartly dressed; spruce. —**spif′fi·ness** *n.* [< dial. E *spiff* a dandy]

spig·ot (spig′ət) *n.* 1. A faucet. 2. A plug for the bunghole of a cask. [ME *spigote*]

spike[1] (spīk) *n.* 1. A long, thick metal nail. 2. A projecting, pointed piece of metal, as in the soles of shoes to prevent slipping. —*v.t.* **spiked, spik·ing** 1. To fasten with spikes. 2. To block; put a stop to. 3. *Informal* To add alcoholic liquor to. [ME < Scand.] —**spik′y** *adj.*

spike[2] (spīk) *n.* 1. An ear of corn, wheat, or other grain. 2. *Bot.* A flower cluster having numerous flowers arranged closely on an elongated common axis. [< L *spica* ear of grain]

spike·let (spīk′lit) *n.* *Bot.* A small spike bearing few flowers.

spike·nard (spīk′nərd, -närd) *n.* 1. A fragrant ointment of ancient times: also called *nard.* 2. The East Indian herb that yields it. 3. An American perennial herb having an aromatic root. [< L *spica* spike + *nardus* nard]

spill (spil) *v.* **spilled** or **spilt, spill·ing** *v.t.* 1. To allow or cause to flow out of or run over a container. 2. To shed, as blood. 3. *Informal* To make known, as a secret. 4. *Informal* To unseat (a rider); throw. —*v.i.* 5. To flow or run out. —*n.* 1. A fall, as from a horse; tumble. 2. The act of spilling. [OE *spillan* to destroy] —**spill′er** *n.*

spill·way (spil′wā′) *n.* A passageway, as in a dam, to release the water in a reservoir.

spilt (spilt) Alternative past tense and past participle of SPILL.

spin (spin) *v.* **spun** (*Archaic* **span**), **spun, spin·ning** *v.t.* 1. To draw out and twist (fibers) into threads. 2. To twist fiber into (threads, yarn, etc.). 3. To form (a web, etc.): said of spiders, silkworms, etc. 4. To tell, as a story or yarn. 5. To protract; prolong: with *out.* 6. To cause to whirl rapidly: to *spin* a top. —*v.i.* 7. To make thread or yarn. 8. To make a web or thread: said of spiders, etc. 9. To whirl rapidly; rotate. 10. To seem to be whirling, as from dizziness. 11. To move rapidly. —*n.* 1. An act or instance of spinning; a rapid whirling. 2. *Informal* A ride or drive. 3. *Aeron.* The descent of an airplane in a spiral curve about a vertical axis, with its nose steeply inclined. [OE *spinnan*] —**spin′ner** *n.*

spin·ach (spin′ich) *n.* A plant, the fleshy leaves of which are used as a vegetable. [< OF *espinage* < LL *spinacia*]

spi·nal (spī′nəl) *adj.* Of or pertaining to the backbone; vertebral. —*n.* An injection for spinal anesthesia.

spinal column *Anat.* The series of articulated vertebrae that enclose and protect the spinal cord and provide dorsal support for the ribs; backbone.

spinal cord *Anat.* That portion of the central nervous system enclosed by the spinal column.

spin·dle (spin′dəl) *n.* 1. The slender rod in a spinning wheel, containing a spool or bobbin on which the thread is twisted and wound. 2. *Mech.* A rotating rod, axis, or shaft. 3. A needlelike rod used for impaling bills, checks, etc.: also **spindle file.** —*v.t.* **·dled, ·dling** To impale (bills, etc.) on a spindle. [OE *spinnan* to spin]

spin·dle-leg·ged (spin′dəl·leg′id, -legd′) *adj.* Having long, slender legs. Also **spin′dle-shanked′** (-shangkt′).

spin·dle·legs (spin′dəl·legz′) *n.pl.* (*construed as sing. in def. 2*) 1. Long, slender legs. 2. *Informal* A person having long, slender legs. Also **spin′dle·shanks′** (-shangks′).

spin·dly (spind′lē) *adj.* **·dli·er, ·dli·est** Tall and slender; lanky. Also **spin′dling.** —**spin′·dli·ness** *n.*

spin·drift (spin′drift) *n.* Blown sea spray: also called *spoondrift.* [Alter. of *spoondrift* < *spoon,* var. of SPUME + DRIFT]

spine (spīn) *n.* 1. The spinal column of a vertebrate; backbone. 2. *Zool.* Any of various hard, pointed outgrowths on the bodies of certain animals, as the fin ray of a fish. 3. *Bot.* A stiff, pointed woody process on the stems of certain plants; thorn. 4. The back of a bound book, usu. inscribed with the title and name of the author. [< L *spina*]

spi·nel (spi·nel′) *n.* Any of a class of hard, variously colored minerals, sometimes used as gemstones. [< Ital. *spinella* < L *spina* spine]

spine·less (spīn′lis) *adj.* 1. Having no backbone; invertebrate. 2. Lacking pointed projections. 3. Lacking courage or will power; cowardly. —**spine′less·ness** *n.*

spin·et (spin′it) *n.* 1. A small musical keyboard instrument of the harpsichord class. 2. A small upright piano. [? after G. *Spinetti,* 16th c. Venetian inventor]

spin·na·ker (spin′ə·kər) *n. Naut.* A large, bellying jib sometimes carried on the mainmast of a racing vessel opposite the mainsail, used when sailing before the wind. [? < *Sphinx,* the name of the first yacht to carry this kind of sail, 1866]

spin·ner·et (spin′ə·ret) *n.* An organ by which spiders or silkworms produce the filament for webs, cocoons, etc.

spinning jenny A framed mechanism for spinning more than one strand of yarn at a time.

spinning wheel A device used for spinning yarn or thread, consisting of a rotating spindle operated by a treadle and flywheel.

spin-off (spin′ôf′) *n.* A new application or incidental result of an activity or process.

spin·ster (spin′stər) *n.* An unmarried woman, esp. an older one; old maid. [ME, a woman who spins < SPIN + -STER] —**spin′ster·hood** *n.* —**spin′ster·ish** *adj.*

spin·y (spī′nē) *adj.* **spin·i·er, spin·i·est** 1. Having spines; thorny. 2. Difficult; perplexing. —**spin′i·ness** *n.*

spiny anteater The echidna.

spiny lobster Any of various marine crustaceans having spiny shells but lacking large claws, valued as seafood: also called *rock lobster.*

spi·ral (spī′rəl) *n.* 1. *Geom.* Any plane curve formed by a point that moves around a fixed center and continually increases or decreases its distance from it. 2. A curve winding like a screw thread; helix. —*adj.* Pertaining to or resembling a spiral; winding. —*v.* **·raled** or **·ralled, ·ral·ing** or **·ral·ling** *v.t.* 1. To cause to take a spiral form or course. —*v.i.* 2. To take a spiral form or course. 3. To rise sharply, as prices, costs, etc. [< L *spira* coil < Gk. *speira*] —**spi′ral·ly** *adv.*

spire[1] (spīr) *n.* 1. The tapering or pyramidal roof or top of a tower. 2. Any similar high, pointed formation; a pinnacle. 3. A slender stalk or blade. —*v.i.* **spired, spir·ing** To shoot or point up in or as in a spire. [OE *spīr* stalk, stem]

spire[2] (spīr) *n.* A spiral or a single turn of one; whorl; twist. [See SPIRAL.]

spi·re·a (spī·rē′ə) *n.* A shrub of the rose family, having clusters of small, white or pink flowers. Also **spi·rae′a.** [< L, meadowsweet]

spi·ril·lum (spī·ril′əm) *n. pl.* **·la** Any of a genus of rigid, spirally twisted flagellate bacteria. [< NL, dim. of L *spira* coil]

spir·it (spir′it) *n.* 1. The vital essence or animating force in living organisms, esp. man, often considered divine in origin. 2. The part of a human being characterized by intelligence, personality, self-consciousness, and will; the mind. 3. *Often cap.* In the Bible, the creative, animating power of God. 4. A supernatural or immaterial being, as an angel, ghost, specter, etc. 5. A person: a leading *spirit* in the community. 6. *Usu. pl.* A state of mind; mood; temper. 7. Vivacity or energy; ardor. 8. True intent or meaning: the *spirit* of the law. 9. Characteristic temper or disposition: the *spirit* of the Reformation. 10. *pl.* Strong alcoholic liquor. 11. *Usu. pl. Chem.* The essence or distilled extract of a substance. 12. *Often pl.* In pharmacy, a solution of a volatile principle in alcohol: *spirits* of ammonia. —*v.t.* To carry off secretly: with *away, off,* etc. —*adj.* 1. Of or pertaining to ghosts; spiritualistic. 2. Operated by the burning of alcohol: a *spirit* lamp. [< L *spiritus* breath, spirit]

Spir·it (spir′it) *n.* In Christian theology, the Holy Ghost.

spir·it·ed (spir′it·id) *adj.* 1. Full of spirit; animated. 2. Having (a specified kind of) spirit or nature: *high-spirited.* —**spir′it·ed·ly** *adv.* —**spir′it·ed·ness** *n.*

spirit gum A quick-drying solution of a gum in ether.

spir·it·less (spir′it·lis) *adj.* Lacking enthusiasm, energy, etc.; listless. —**spir′it·less·ly** *adv.* —**spir′it·less·ness** *n.*

spir·i·tu·al (spir′i·cho͞o·əl) *adj.* 1. Of, pertaining to, like, or consisting of spirit, as distinguished from matter; incorporeal. 2. Of or pertaining to God; holy. 3. Sacred or religious; not lay or temporal. **—***n.* A religious folk song originating among the Negroes of the southern U.S. **—spir′i·tu·al·ly** *adv.* **—spir′i·tu·al′i·ty** (-al′ə·tē) *n.*

spir·i·tu·al·ism (spir′i·cho͞o·əl·iz′əm) *n.* The belief that the spirits of the dead communicate with and manifest their presence to the living. **—spir′i·tu·al·ist** *n.* **—spir′i·tu·al·is′tic** *adj.*

spir·i·tu·al·ize (spir′i·cho͞o·əl·īz′) *v.t.* **·ized, ·iz·ing** To make or treat as spiritual. Also *Brit.* **spir′i·tu·al·ise′.** **—spir′i·tu·al·i·za′tion** *n.* **—spir′i·tu·al·iz′er** *n.*

spir·i·tu·ous (spir′i·cho͞o·əs) *adj.* Containing alcohol, as distilled liquors; intoxicating. **—spir′i·tu·ous·ness** *n.*

spiro-[1] *combining form* Breath; respiration. Also, before vowels, **spir-.** [< L *spirare* to breathe]

spiro-[2] *combining form* Spiral; coiled. Also, before vowels, **spir-.** [< Gk. *speira* coil]

spi·ro·chete (spī′rə·kēt) *n.* Any of various bacteria having a corkscrewlike form, including those that cause syphilis, trench mouth, and yaws. Also **spi′ro·chaete.** [< SPIRO-[2] + Gk. *chaitē* bristle]

spit[1] (spit) *v.* **spit** or **spat, spit·ting** *v.t.* 1. To eject (saliva, etc.) from the mouth. 2. To eject or utter with violence. **—***v.i.* 3. To eject saliva, etc., from the mouth. 4. To make a hissing or sputtering noise. **—***n.* 1. Spittle; saliva. 2. An act of spitting or expectorating. **—spit and image** Exact likeness; counterpart: also **spitting image.** [OE *spittan*] **—spit′ter** *n.*

spit[2] (spit) *n.* 1. A pointed rod on which meat is roasted. 2. A point of low land extending into the water. **—***v.t.* **spit·ted, spit·ting** To impale with or as with a spit. [OE *spitu*]

spit·ball (spit′bôl) *n.* 1. Paper chewed and shaped into a ball for use as a missile. 2. In baseball, an illegal pitched ball that is wet with saliva and deviates deceptively in its course.

spite (spīt) *n.* Malicious bitterness or hatred; grudge. **—in spite of** Notwithstanding. **—***v.t.* **spit·ed, spit·ing** To show one's spite toward. [Short for DESPITE]

spite·ful (spīt′fəl) *adj.* 1. Filled with spite. 2. Prompted by spite. **—spite′ful·ly** *adv.* **—spite′ful·ness** *n.*

spit·fire (spit′fīr′) *n.* A quick-tempered person.

spit·tle (spit′l) *n.* The fluid secreted by the mouth; saliva; spit. [OE *spātl*; infl. in form by SPIT[1]]

spit·toon (spi·to͞on′) *n.* A receptacle for spit; cuspidor.

spitz (spits) *n.* A small dog, a variety of Pomeranian, having long silky hair and a tapering muzzle. Also **spitz dog.** [< G, short for *spitzhund* < *spitz* pointed + *hund* dog]

splash (splash) *v.t.* 1. To dash or spatter (a liquid, etc.) about. 2. To spatter, wet, etc., with a liquid dashed about. 3. To make (one's way) with splashes. **—***v.i.* 4. To make a splash or splashes. **—***n.* 1. The act or noise of splashing. 2. *Informal* A striking impression: to make a *splash.* [Var. of PLASH] **—splash′er** *n.*

splash·down (splash′doun′) *n.* The setting down of a spacecraft or a part of it in the seas following its flight.

splash·y (splash′ē) *adj.* **splash·i·er, splash·i·est** 1. Slushy; wet. 2. Marked by splashes; blotchy. 3. *Informal* Sensational; showy. **—splash′i·ness** *n.*

splat (splat) *n.* A thin, broad piece of wood, as that forming the middle of a chair back. [Origin uncertain]

splat·ter (splat′ər) *v.t. & v.i.* To spatter or splash. **—***n.* A spatter; splash. [Bend of SPLASH and SPATTER]

splay (splā) *adj.* 1. Spread out; broad. 2. Clumsily formed; awkward. **—***n.* A slanted surface or beveled edge, as the sides of a doorway. **—***v.t. & v.i.* 1. To slant; bevel. 2. To spread out; expand. [Aphetic var. of DISPLAY]

splay·foot (splā′fo͝ot′) *n. pl.* **·feet** (-fēt′) 1. Abnormal flatness and turning outward of the feet. 2. A foot so deformed. **—splay′·foot′ed** *adj.*

spleen (splēn) *n. Anat.* 1. A highly vascular, flattened, ductless organ located on the upper left side of the abdominal cavity, and effecting certain modifications in the blood. 2. Ill temper; spitefulness. [< Gk. *splēn*]

splen·did (splen′did) *adj.* 1. Magnificent; glorious; illustrious. 2. Brilliant with light; shining. 3. *Informal* Very good; excellent. [< L *splendere* to shine] **—splen′did·ly** *adv.* **—splen′did·ness** *n.*

splen·dif·er·ous (splen·dif′ər·əs) *adj. Informal* Extremely splendid: a facetious usage.

splen·dor (splen′dər) *n.* 1. Brilliance from emitted or reflected light. 2. Magnificence; greatness. Also *Brit.* **splen′dour.** [< L, brightness] **—splen′dor·ous, splen′drous** *adj.*

sple·net·ic (spli·net′ik) *adj.* 1. Pertaining to the spleen. 2. Fretfully spiteful; peevish. Also **sple·net′i·cal.** **—***n.* A peevish person. **—sple·net′i·cal·ly** *adv.*

splen·ic (splen′ik, splē′nik) *adj.* Of, in, near, or pertaining to the spleen.

splice (splīs) *v.t.* **spliced, splic·ing** 1. To unite, as by twisting or intertwining the ends of rope, wires, etc. 2. To connect, as timbers, by beveling or overlapping at the ends. 3. *Slang* To join in marriage. **—***n.* 1. A union made by splicing. 2. The place at which two parts are spliced. [< MDu. *splissen*] **—splic′er** *n.*

splint (splint) *n.* 1. A thin, flexible strip of split wood used for basketmaking, chair bottoms, etc. 2. *Surg.* An appliance, as a strip of wood or metal, used for keeping a fractured limb or other injured part in proper position. **—***v.t.* To support with a splint. [< MDu. *splinte*]

splin·ter (splin′tər) *n.* A thin, sharp piece of wood, glass, etc., split or torn off lengthwise; a sliver. **—***v.t. & v.i.* To break into splinters. [< MDu.] **—splint′er·y** *adj.*

split (split) *v.* **split, split·ting** *v.t.* 1. To separate into parts by force, esp. into two approximately equal parts. 2. To break or divide lengthwise or along the grain; separate into layers. 3. To disrupt, as a political party; divide. 4. To divide and distribute by portions or shares. 5. *Slang* To leave; quit. **—***v.i.* 6. To break apart; become divided;

separate. 7. *Slang* To leave; depart. **—to split hairs** To make unnecessarily fine distinctions. **—to split off** To break off by splitting. **—to split the difference** To divide equally a sum in dispute. **—to split up** 1. To separate into parts and distribute. 2. To cease association; separate. —*n.* 1. The act of splitting; also, the result of splitting, as a cleft or rent. 2. Separation into factions; schism. 3. A share or portion, as of booty. 4. A confection made of a split banana, ice cream, syrup, etc. 5. An acrobatic trick in which the legs are extended upon the floor in a straight line at right angles to the body: also **the splits.** —*adj.* 1. Cleft, esp. longitudinally; fissured. 2. Divided: a *split* ticket. [< MDu. *splitten*] **—split′ter** *n.*

split infinitive *Gram.* An infinitive in which the sign *to* is separated from the verb, as in "to really believe."

split-level house (split′lev′əl) A dwelling in which the floors of the several levels are less than a story above or below the adjoining one. Also **split′-lev′el.**

split ticket 1. A ballot on which the voter has distributed his vote among candidates of different parties. 2. A ballot containing names of candidates of more than one party or party faction.

split·ting (split′ing) *adj.* Acute or extreme.

splotch (sploch) *n.* A discolored spot, as of ink, etc.; a daub; splash; spot. [Cf. OE *splott* spot] **—splotch** *v.t.* **—splotch′y** *adj.*

splurge (splûrj) *n.* *Informal* An extravagant display or expenditure. —*v.i.* **splurged, splurg·ing** To spend money lavishly or wastefully. [Origin uncertain]

splut·ter (splut′ər) *v.i.* 1. To make a series of slight, explosive sounds, or throw off small particles, as meat frying. 2. To speak hastily or confusedly. —*v.t.* 3. To utter excitedly or confusedly; sputter. —*n.* A noise as of spluttering. [Blend of SPLASH and SPUTTER] **—splut′ter·er** *n.*

spoil (spoil) *v.* **spoiled or spoilt, spoil·ing** *v.t.* 1. To impair or destroy the value, usefulness, or beauty of. 2. To impair the character of, esp. by overindulgence. —*v.i.* 3. To become tainted or decayed, as food. **—to be spoiling for** To long for; crave. —*n.* *Often pl.* Plunder seized by violence; loot. [< L *spolium* booty] **—spoil′er** *n.*

spoil·age (spoi′lij) *n.* 1. Something that is or has been spoiled. 2. The process of spoiling. 3. The state of being spoiled.

spoil·sport (spoil′spôrt′) *n.* A person who spoils the pleasures of others.

spoke[1] (spōk) *n.* 1. One of the rods or bars that serve to support the rim of a wheel by connecting it to the hub. 2. A stick or bar for insertion in a wheel to prevent its turning. 3. A rung of a ladder. —*v.t.* **spoked, spok·ing** 1. To provide with spokes. 2. To stop with or as with a spoke. [OE *spāca*]

spoke[2] (spōk) Past tense and archaic past participle of SPEAK.

spo·ken (spō′kən) Past participle of SPEAK. —*adj.* 1. Uttered orally, as opposed to written. 2. Speaking or having (a specified kind of) speech: *smooth-spoken.*

spoke·shave (spōk′shāv′) *n.* A planing tool having a blade set between two handles, used in rounding and smoothing wooden surfaces.

spokes·man (spōks′mən) *n. pl.* **·men** (-mən) One who speaks in the name and behalf of another or others. **—spokes′wom′an** (-wŏŏm′ən) *n.fem.*

spo·li·a·tion (spō′lē·ā′shən) *n.* The act of despoiling; esp., the authorized seizure of neutral ships by a belligerent. [< L *spoliare* to despoil] **—spo′li·a′tor** *n.*

spon·dee (spon′dē) *n.* A metrical foot consisting of two long syllables or accented syllables. [< Gk. *spondē* libation; because used in the solemn chants accompanying a libation] **—spon·da·ic** (-dā′ik) *adj.*

sponge (spunj) *n.* 1. Any of a varied group of aquatic organisms, characterized by a highly porous body without specialized internal organs and incapable of free movement. 2. The skeleton or network of elastic fibers of such an organism, used as an absorbent for bathing, etc. 3. Any spongelike substance used as an absorbent. 4. A sponge bath. 5. *Informal* One who lives at the expense of another or others; a parasite. **—to throw (or toss) up (or in) the sponge** *Informal* To give up; abandon the struggle. —*v.* **sponged, spong·ing** *v.t.* 1. To wipe, wet, or clean with a sponge. —*v.i.* 2. *Informal* To live or get something at the expense of others. [OE < Gk. *spongos*] **—spong′er** *n.* **—spong′i·ness** *n.* **—spong′y** *adj.* **·i·er, ·i·est**

sponge bath A bath taken by washing oneself with a cloth or sponge rather than in a bathtub or shower.

sponge cake A cake containing no shortening and beaten very light.

spon·son (spon′sən) *n.* 1. A curved projection from the hull of a vessel or seaplane, to give greater stability or increase the surface area. 2. A similar protuberance on a ship or tank, for storage purposes or for the training of a gun. [Appar. alter. of EXPANSION]

spon·sor (spon′sər) *n.* 1. One who assumes responsibility for the debt, duty, etc., of another. 2. A godparent. 3. A business enterprise that finances all or part of a broadcast program that advertises its product or service. —*v.t.* To act as sponsor for. [< L *spondere* to be a security] **—spon·so′ri·al** (-sôr′ē·əl) *adj.* **—spon′sor·ship** *n.*

spon·ta·ne·ous (spon·tā′nē·əs) *adj.* 1. Done or resulting from one's own impulse or desire; not premeditated. 2. Arising from inherent qualities; self-generated. [< L *sponte* of free will] **—spon·ta·ne·i·ty** (spon′tə·nē′ə·tē, -nā′ə·tē), **spon·ta′ne·ous·ness** *n.* **—spon·ta′ne·ous·ly** *adv.*

spontaneous combustion The burning of a substance through the generation of sufficient internal heat to ignite it.

spoof (spōōf) *v.t. & v.i.* *Informal* To deceive or hoax; joke; parody. —*n.* Deception; parody; hoax. [after a game invented by Arthur Roberts, 1852–1933, English comedian]

spook (spōōk) *n.* *Informal* A ghost; specter. —*v.t.* *Informal* To haunt. [< Du.] **—spook′·i·ly** *adv.* **—spook′i·ness** *n.* **—spook′ish, spook′y** *adj.*

spool (spōōl) *n.* 1. A cylinder upon which thread or yarn is wound. 2. The quantity of thread held by a spool. 3. Anything resembling a spool in shape or purpose. —*v.t.* To wind on a spool. [< MLG *spole*]

spoon (spōōn) *n.* 1. A utensil having a shallow bowl and a handle, used in cooking and eating. 2. Something resembling a spoon or its bowl. 3. A metallic fishing lure: also **spoon bait.** 4. A golf club with a wooden head and sloping face. —*v.t.* 1. To lift up or out with a spoon. —*v.i.* 2. *Informal* To make love, as by caressing or kissing. [OE *spōn* sliver, chip]

spoon·bill (spōōn′bil) *n.* 1. Any of various wading birds related to the ibises, having a broad, flat bill. 2. The shoveler. —**spoon′-billed′** *adj.*

spoon·drift (spōōn′drift′) *n.* Spindrift.

spoon·er·ism (spōō′nə·riz′əm) *n.* The unintentional transposition of sounds or of parts of words in speaking, as in "half-*w*armed *f*ish" for "half-*f*ormed *w*ish." [after William A. *Spooner,* 1844–1930, of New College, Oxford]

spoon-feed (spōōn′fēd′) *v.t.* 1. To feed with or as with a spoon. 2. To pamper. 3. To present (ideas, etc.) in their easiest, most persuasive form.

spoon·ful (spōōn′fōōl) *n. pl.* **·fuls** As much as a spoon will hold.

spoor (spōōr) *n.* A track or other trace of a wild animal. —*v.t. & v.i.* To track by or follow a spoor. [< Du.]

spo·rad·ic (spô·rad′ik) *adj.* 1. Occurring here and there; occasional. 2. Separate; isolated. [< Gk. *sporas* scattered] —**spo·rad′i·cal·ly** *adv.*

spo·ran·gi·um (spô·ran′jē·əm) *n. pl.* **·gi·a** *Bot.* A sac in which sexual spores are produced: also called *spore case.* [< SPOR(O)- + Gk. *angeion* vessel] —**spo·ran′gi·al** *adj.*

spore (spôr) *n. Bot.* The reproductive body in ferns, fungi, etc., analogous to the seeds of flowering plants, but able to develop asexually into an independent organism or individual. —*v.i.* **spored, spor·ing** To develop spores: said of plants. [< Gk. *spora* seed, sowing] —**spo·ra·ceous** (spô·rā′shəs) *adj.*

spore case A sporangium.

sporo- *combining form* Seed; spore. Also, before vowels, **spor-**. [< Gk. *spora* seed]

spo·ro·zo·an (spôr′ə·zō′ən) *adj. Zool.* Designating or belonging to a class of parasitic protozoans reproducing by spores, as the malaria parasite. —*n.* A member of this class. [< SPORO- + Gk. *zōion* animal]

spor·ran (spor′ən) *n.* A purse, generally of fur, worn in front of the kilt. [< Scot. Gaelic < LL *bursa* purse]

sport (spôrt) *n.* 1. That which amuses in general; diversion; pastime. 2. A particular game or play pursued for diversion; esp., an outdoor or athletic game, as baseball, tennis, swimming, etc. 3. A spirit of jesting. 4. Mockery; an object of derision; a laughingstock. 5. *Biol.* An animal or plant that exhibits sudden and spontaneous variation from the normal type; a mutation. 6. *Informal* One who lives a fast, gay, or flashy life. 7. A person characterized by his manners in games, teasing play, etc.: a good *sport.* —*v.i.* 1. To amuse oneself; play; jest. —*v.t.* 2. *Informal* To display or wear ostentatiously; show off. —*adj.* Of, pertaining to, or fitted for sports; also, appropriate for informal wear: also **sports.** [Aphetic var. of DISPORT] —**sport′ful** *adj.* —**sport′ful·ly** *adv.* —**sport′ful·ness** *n.*

sport·ing (spôr′ting) *adj.* 1. Of, engaged in, or connected with sports. 2. Fair; conforming to standards of sportsmanship. 3. Associated with sports for gambling: a *sporting* man. —**sport′ing·ly** *adv.*

spor·tive (spôr′tiv) *adj.* Playful; frolicsome. —**spor′tive·ly** *adv.* —**spor′tive·ness** *n.*

sports car A low automobile, usu. seating two persons, and built for high speed and maneuverability.

sports·cast·er (spôrts′kast′ər) *n.* One who broadcasts sports news. —**sports′cast′** *n.*

sports·man (spôrts′mən) *n. pl.* **·men** (-mən) 1. One who pursues field sports, esp. hunting and fishing. 2. One who abides by a code of fair play in games or in daily practice. —**sports′man·like** *adj.* —**sports′man·ship** *n.*

sports·wear (spôrts′wâr′) *n.* Clothes made for informal or outdoor activities.

sports·wom·an (spôrts′wōōm′ən) *n. pl.* **·wom·en** (-wim′in) A woman who participates in sports.

sport·y (spôr′tē) *adj.* **sport·i·er, sport·i·est** *Informal* 1. Relating to or characteristic of a sport. 2. Gay, loud, or dissipated. —**sport′i·ly** *adv.* —**sport′i·ness** *n.*

spot (spot) *n.* 1. A particular place of small extent; a definite locality. 2. Any small portion of a surface differing, as in color, from the rest; blot. 3. A blemish or fault. 4. *Slang* A currency note having a specified value: a ten *spot.* 5. *Informal* A spotlight. —**in a spot** *Slang* In trouble. —**to hit the spot** *Slang* To gratify an appetite or need. —**to touch a** (or **one's**) **sore spot** To mention a topic that is painful to one. —**on the spot** 1. At once; immediately. 2. At the very place. 3. *Slang* In danger of death or of being held accountable for some action. —*v.* **spot·ted, spot·ting** *v.t.* 1. To mark or soil with spots. 2. To decorate with spots; dot. 3. To place; locate; station. 4. *Informal* To recognize or detect; see. 5. *Slang* To accept as a handicap, as in a game. —*v.i.* 6. To become marked or soiled with spots. —*adj.* 1. Being on the place or spot. 2. Made at random: a *spot* check. [ME < LG. Cf. MDu. *spotte.*] —**spot′less** *adj.* —**spot′ta·ble** *adj.*

spot-check (spot′chek′) *v.t.* To inspect at random points. —**spot′-check′** *n.*

spot·light (spot′līt′) *n.* 1. A circle of powerful light directed at a performer in a theater, night club, etc. 2. The apparatus that produces such a light. 3. A pivoted automobile lamp. 4. Notoriety; publicity.

spot·ted (spot′id) *adj.* 1. Discolored in spots; stained; soiled. 2. Characterized or marked by spots.

spotted fever *Pathol.* 1. An epidemic form of meningitis. 2. Typhus. 3. Rocky Mountain spotted fever.

spot·ter (spot′ər) *n.* One who spots or looks out for something, as for enemy aircraft.

spot·ty (spot′ē) *adj.* **·ti·er, ·ti·est** 1. Having many spots. 2. Lacking uniformity. —**spot′ti·ly** *adv.* —**spot′ti·ness** *n.*

spous·al (spou′zəl) *adj.* Pertaining to marriage. —*n. Often pl.* Marriage; espousal.

spouse (spous) *n.* One's husband or wife. [< L *spondere* to promise, betroth]

spout (spout) *v.i.* 1. To pour out copiously and forcibly, as a liquid under pressure. 2. To discharge a fluid either continuously or in jets. 3. *Informal* To speak pompously. —*v.t.* 4. To cause to pour or shoot forth. 5. To utter pompously. —*n.* 1. A tube, trough, etc., for the discharge of a liquid. 2. A continuous stream of fluid. [ME *spoute*] —**spout′er** *n.*

sprain (sprān) *n.* 1. A violent straining or twisting of the ligaments surrounding a joint. 2. The condition due to such strain. —*v.t.* To cause a sprain in. [? < OF *espreindre* to squeeze]

sprang (sprang) Alternative past tense of SPRING.

sprat (sprat) *n.* A herringlike fish found in shoals on the Atlantic coast of Europe. [OE *sprott*]

sprawl (sprôl) *v.i.* 1. To sit or lie with the limbs stretched out ungracefully. 2. To spread out in a straggling manner, as handwriting, vines, etc. —*v.t.* 3. To cause to spread or extend awkwardly or irregularly. —*n.* The act or position of sprawling. [OE *sprēawlian* to move convulsively] —**sprawl′er** *n.*

spray[1] (sprā) *n.* 1. Liquid dispersed in fine particles. 2. An instrument for discharging such particles. —*v.t.* 1. To disperse (a liquid) in fine particles. 2. To apply spray to. —*v.i.* 3. To send forth spray. 4. To go forth as spray. [Akin to MDu. *sprayen* to sprinkle] —**spray′er** *n.*

spray[2] (sprā) *n.* A small branch bearing smaller branches or flowers. [ME]

spray gun A device that ejects liquids, such as paint, in a fine spray.

spread (spred) *v.* **spread, spread·ing** *v.t.* 1. To open or unfold to full width or extent, as wings, sails, etc. 2. To distribute over a surface; scatter or smear. 3. To cover with a layer of something. 4. To force apart or farther apart. 5. To extend over a period of time. 6. To make more widely known, active, etc. 7. To set (a table, etc.), as for a meal. —*v.i.* 8. To be extended or expanded. 9. To be distributed. 10. To become more widely known, active, etc. 11. To be forced farther apart. —*n.* 1. The act of spreading. 2. An open extent or expanse. 3. The limit of expansion of an object. 4. A cloth or covering for a bed, table, etc. 5. *Informal* An informal feast. 6. A food used to spread on bread or crackers. 7. Two facing pages of a magazine or newspaper, containing related material. 8. *Informal* A ranch. —*adj.* Expanded; outstretched. [OE *sprædan*] —**spread′er** *n.*

spread-ea·gle (spred′ē′gəl) *adj.* Resembling the figure of an eagle with extended wings and legs. —*v.t. & v.i.* **-ea·gled, -ea·gling** To take or cause to take a spread-eagle position.

spree (sprē) *n.* 1. A drinking spell. 2. A gay frolic. 3. Excessive indulgence in an activity. [Origin uncertain]

sprig (sprig) *n.* A shoot or sprout of a tree or plant. [ME *sprigge*]

spright·ly (sprīt′lē) *adj.* **·li·er, ·li·est** Full of animation; lively. —*adv.* Spiritedly; briskly; gaily. —**spright′li·ness** *n.*

spring (spring) *v.* **sprang** or **sprung, sprung, spring·ing** *v.i.* 1. To move or rise suddenly and rapidly; leap; dart. 2. To move suddenly as by elastic reaction. 3. To move or come as if with a leap. 4. To work or snap out of place, as a mechanical part. 5. To become warped, bent, loose, etc. 6. To rise above surrounding objects. 7. To come into being. 8. To originate; proceed. 9. To develop; grow. —*v.t.* 10. To cause to spring or leap. 11. To cause to act, close, open, etc., suddenly, as by elastic reaction: to *spring* a trap. 12. To cause to happen, become known, or appear suddenly. 13. To leap over; vault. 14. To cause to warp, sag or split. 15. To cause to snap or work out of place. 16. To undergo (a leak). 17. *Slang* To effect the release or escape of (a person) from prison. —*n.* 1. *Mech.* An elastic body or contrivance, as a coiled steel wire, that yields under stress and returns to its normal form when the stress is removed. 2. Elastic quality or energy. 3. The act of flying back from a position of tension. 4. A cause of action. 5. A leap; jump. 6. The season in which vegetation starts anew, occurring between winter and summer. ◆Collateral adjective: *vernal.* 7. A flow, as of water. 8. Any source or origin. —*adj.* 1. Pertaining to the season of spring. 2. Acting like or having a spring. [OE *springan*] —**spring′er** *n.*

spring·board (spring′bôrd′) *n.* 1. A flexible, resilient board used in leaping, tumbling, or diving. 2. Anything that provides an advantageous start toward a goal.

spring·bok (spring′bok′) *n.* A small South African gazelle noted for its ability to leap high in the air. Also **spring′buck′** (-buk′). [< Afrikaans]

spring fever The listlessness and restlessness that overtakes many people in spring.

spring lock A lock that fastens automatically by a spring.

spring tide The tide occurring at or shortly after the new or full moon, when the rise and fall are greatest.

spring·time (spring′tīm′) *n.* The season of spring. Also **spring′tide′** (-tīd′).

spring·y (spring′ē) *adj.* **spring·i·er, spring·i·est** Elastic; resilient. —**spring′i·ly** *adv.* —**spring′i·ness** *n.*

sprin·kle (spring′kəl) *v.* **·kled, ·kling** *v.t.* 1. To scatter in drops or small particles. 2. To scatter on or over. —*v.i.* 3. To fall or rain in scattered drops. —*n.* 1. A falling in drops or particles, or that which so falls; a sprinkling. 2. A small quantity. [ME *sprenkelen*] —**sprin′kler** *n.*

sprin·kling (spring′kling) *n.* 1. That which is sprinkled. 2. A small number or quantity. 3. The act of sprinkling.

sprint (sprint) *n.* A short race run at top speed. —*v.i.* To run fast, as in a sprint. [< Scand.] —**sprint′er** *n.*

sprit (sprit) *n.* *Naut.* A spar reaching diagonally from a mast to the peak of a fore-and-aft sail. [OE *sprēot* pole]

sprite (sprīt) *n.* A fairy, elf, or goblin. [< L *spiritus* breath, spirit]

sprit·sail (sprit′səl, sprit′sāl′) *n.* *Naut.* A sail extended by a sprit.

spritz (sprits) *n.* A spray or squirt. —*v.t. & v.i.* To spray. [< G *spritze* a spray]

spritz·er (sprits′ər) *n.* A drink made of white wine and soda water.

sprock·et (sprok′it) *n.* *Mech.* 1. A projection, as on the rim of a wheel, for engaging with the links of a chain. 2. A wheel bearing such projections: also **sprocket wheel.** [Origin uncertain]

sprout (sprout) *v.i.* 1. To put forth shoots; begin to grow; germinate. 2. To develop or grow rapidly. —*v.t.* 3. To cause to sprout. —*n.* 1. A new shoot or bud on a plant.

2. Something like or suggestive of a sprout. [OE *sprūtan*]

spruce[1] (sprōōs) *n.* 1. Any of a genus of evergreen trees of the pine family, having a pyramidal crown, needle-shaped leaves, and pendulous cones. 2. The wood of these trees.

spruce[2] (sprōōs) *adj.* Smart and trim; neat. —*v.* **spruced, spruc·ing** *v.t.* 1. To make spruce: often with *up.* —*v.i.* 2. To make oneself spruce: usu. with *up.* —**spruce′ly** *adv.* —**spruce′ness** *n.*

sprung (sprung) Past participle and alternative past tense of SPRING.

spry (sprī) *adj.* **spri·er** or **spry·er, spri·est** or **spry·est** Quick and active; agile. [< dial. E *sprey*] —**spry′ly** *adv.* —**spry′ness** *n.*

spud (spud) *n.* 1. A spadelike tool for removing the roots of weeds. 2. *Informal* A potato. —*v.t.* **spud·ded, spud·ding** To remove with a spud. [ME *spudde* < Scand.]

spume (spyōōm) *n.* Froth; foam. [< L *spuma* foam] —**spume** *v.i.* **spumed, spum·ing** —**spu′mous, spum′y** *adj.*

spu·mo·ne (spə·mō′nē, *Ital.* spōō·mō′nā) *n. pl.* **·ni** (-nē) A dessert of ice cream containing fruit, nuts, etc. Also **spu·mo′ni.** [< Ital. < L *spuma* foam]

spun (spun) Past tense and past participle of SPIN.

spunk (spungk) *n.* 1. Tinder. 2. *Informal* Mettle; pluck. [< Irish *sponc* tinder < L *spongia* sponge]

spunk·y (spungk′ē) *adj.* **spunk·i·er, spunk·i·est** *Informal* Spirited; courageous. —**spunk′i·ly** *adv.* —**spunk′i·ness** *n.*

spur (spûr) *n.* 1. A pricking or goading instrument worn on a horseman's heel. 2. Anything that incites or urges; incentive. 3. A part projecting like a spur, as a crag. 4. A stiff, sharp spine, as on the legs of some insects and birds. 5. *Bot.* A tubular extension of some part of a flower, as in the larkspur. 6. A short side track of a railroad: also **spur track.** —**on the spur of the moment** Hastily; impulsively. —*v.* **spurred, spur·ring** *v.t.* 1. To prick or urge with or as with spurs. —*v.i.* 2. To spur one's horse. [OE *spura*] —**spurred** *adj.* —**spur′rer** *n.*

spurge (spûrj) *n.* A plant, euphorbia. [< L *expurgare* to purge, cleanse]

spur gearing *Mech.* Gearing composed of spur wheels.

spu·ri·ous (spyŏŏr′ē·əs) *adj.* 1. Not genuine; false. 2. Illegitimate. [< L *spurius*] —**spu′ri·ous·ly** *adv.* —**spu′ri·ous·ness** *n.*

spurn (spûrn) *v.t.* 1. To reject with disdain; scorn. 2. To kick. —*n.* The act of spurning. [OE *spurnan*] —**spurn′er** *n.*

spurt (spûrt) *n.* 1. A sudden gush of liquid. 2. Any sudden outbreak, effort, etc., usu. of brief duration. —*v.i.* 1. To come out in a jet; gush forth. 2. To make a sudden effort. —*v.t.* 3. To force out in a jet; squirt. [OE *spryttan* to come forth]

spur wheel *Mech.* A wheel having radial teeth on the rim, with their edges parallel to the axis: also **spur gear.**

sput·nik (sput′nik, *Russ.* spōōt′nyik) *n.* A Soviet artificial earth satellite. [< Russ., satellite]

sput·ter (sput′ər) *v.i.* 1. To throw off solid or fluid particles in a series of slight explosions. 2. To emit particles of saliva from the mouth, as when speaking excitedly. 3. To speak rapidly or confusedly. —*v.t.* 4. To emit in small particles. 5. To utter in a confused or excited manner. —*n.* The act or sound of sputtering; esp., excited talk. —**sput′ter·er** *n.*

spu·tum (spyōō′təm) *n. pl.* **·ta** Expectorated matter; mucous and saliva. [< L *spuere* to spit]

spy (spī) *n. pl.* **spies** 1. One who covertly gathers information, esp. about a military enemy. 2. One who watches others secretly. —*v.* **spied, spy·ing** *v.i.* 1. To act as a spy. —*v.t.* 2. To observe stealthily and with hostile intent: usu. with *out.* 3. To catch sight of; see. [< OF *espier* to espy]

spy·glass (spī′glas′) *n.* A small telescope.

squab (skwob) *n.* A young pigeon, esp. when an unfledged nestling. [< dial. E < Scand.]

squab·ble (skwob′əl) *v.i.* **·bled, ·bling** To engage in a petty wrangle or scuffle; quarrel. *n.* A petty wrangle. —**squab′bler** *n.*

squad (skwod) *n.* 1. A small group of persons organized for the performance of a specific function. 2. A small detachment of troops or police; esp., the smallest tactical unit in the infantry of the U.S. Army. 3. A team. [< L *quattuor* four]

squad car An automobile used by police for patrolling: also called *patrol car.*

squad·ron (skwod′rən) *n.* 1. *Naval and Mil.* A unit of aircraft, naval vessels, or cavalry. 2. Any regularly arranged or organized body. [< Ital. < L *quattuor* four]

squal·id (skwol′id) *adj.* Dirty and wretched. [< L *squalere* to be foul] —**squal′id·ly** *adv.* —**squal′id·ness** *n.*

squall[1] (skwôl) *n.* A loud screaming. —*v.i.* To cry loudly; scream. —**squall′er** *n.*

squall[2] (skwôl) *n.* 1. A sudden, violent burst of wind, often accompanied by rain or snow. 2. *Informal* A commotion. —*v.i.* To blow a squall. —**squall′y** *adj.*

squal·or (skwol′ər) *n.* The state of being squalid; filth and wretched poverty.

squa·ma (skwā′mə) *n. pl.* **·mae** (-mē) *Biol.* A thin, scalelike structure; a scale. [< L] —**squa′mate** (-māt), **squa′mose** (-mōs), **squa′mous** (-məs) *adj.*

squan·der (skwon′dər) *v.t.* To spend (money, time, etc.) wastefully. —*n.* Wasteful expenditure. [Origin unknown] —**squan′·der·er** *n.*

square (skwâr) *n.* 1. A parallelogram having four equal sides and four right angles. 2. Any object, part, or surface that has this form, or nearly so. 3. An instrument having an L- or T-shape by which to measure or lay out right angles. 4. An open area in a city or town formed by the intersection of several streets, often planted with trees, flowers, etc. 5. *Math.* The product of a number multiplied by itself. 6. *Slang* One not conversant with the latest trends or fads. —**on the square** 1. At right angles. 2. *Informal* In a fair and honest manner. —**out of square** 1. Not at right angles. 2. Incorrectly; askew. —*adj.* 1. Having four equal sides and four right angles; also, resembling a square in form. 2. Formed with or characterized by a right angle. 3. Adapted to forming squares or computing in squares. 4. Direct; fair; honest. 5. Having debit and credit balanced. 6. Absolute; complete. 7. Stocky; sturdy. —**square meal** A full, good meal. —**square peg in a round hole** A misfit. —*v.* **squared,**

squar·ing *v.t.* 1. To make or form like a square. 2. To shape or adjust so as to form a right angle. 3. To test for the purpose of adjusting to a straight line, right angle, or plane surface. 4. To make satisfactory settlement or adjustment of: to *square* accounts. 5. To cause to conform; adapt; reconcile. 6. *Math.* a To multiply (a number) by itself. b To determine the area of. —*v.i.* 7. To be at right angles. 8. To conform; agree; harmonize. —**to square off** To prepare to fight. —*adv.* 1. So as to be square, or at right angles. 2. *Informal* Honestly; fairly. 3. Directly; firmly. [< L *quattuor* four] —**square′ness** *n.* —**squar′er** *n.*

square-dance (skwâr′dans′) *v.i.* **-danced, -danc·ing** To perform a square dance. —**square′-danc′er** *n.* —**square′-danc′ing** *n.*

square dance Any dance in which the couples form sets in squares.

square knot A common knot, formed of two overhand knots.

square·ly (skwâr′lē) *adv.* 1. In a direct manner. 2. Honestly; fairly. 3. Plainly; unequivocally. 4. At right angles (to a line or plane).

square measure A unit or system of units for measuring areas.

square-rigged (skwâr′rigd′) *adj. Naut.* Fitted with square sails as the principal sails. —**square′-rig′ger** *n.*

square root *Math.* A number that, multiplied by itself, produces the given number: 4 is the *square root* of 16.

squash¹ (skwosh) *v.t.* 1. To beat or press into a pulp or soft mass; crush. 2. To quell or suppress. —*v.i.* 3. To be smashed or squashed. —*n.* 1. A soft or overripe object; also, something squashed. 2. The act of squashing; also, the sound made by squashing. 3. Either of two games played on an indoor court with rackets and a ball. 4. A beverage of which one ingredient is a fruit juice. —*adv.* With a squelching, oozy sound. [< L *ex-* thoroughly + *quassare* to crush] —**squash′er** *n.*

squash² (skwosh) *n.* 1. The edible fruit of various trailing annuals of the gourd family. 2. The plant that bears it. [< Algonquian]

squash·y (skwosh′ē) *adj.* **squash·i·er, squash·i·est** Soft and moist. —**squash′i·ly** *adv.* —**squash′i·ness** *n.*

squat (skwot) *v.* **squat·ted or squat, squat·ting** *v.i.* 1. To sit on the heels or hams, or with the legs near the body. 2. To crouch or cower down. 3. To settle on a piece of land without title or payment. 4. To settle on government land in accordance with regulations that will eventually give title. —*v.t.* 5. To cause (oneself) to squat. —*adj.* Short and thick; squatty. —*n.* 1. A squatting position. 2. The act of squatting. [< OF *es-* thoroughly + *quatir* to press down] —**squat′ter** *n.*

squat·ty (skwot′ē) *adj.* Disproportionately short and thick.

squaw (skwô) *n.* An American Indian woman or wife. [< Algonquian, woman]

squawk (skwôk) *v.i.* 1. To utter a shrill, harsh cry, as a parrot. 2. *Slang* To utter loud complaints. —*n.* 1. The harsh cry of certain birds; also, the act of squawking. 2. *Slang* A loud protest. [Prob. imit.] —**squawk′er** *n.*

squeak (skwēk) *n.* A thin, sharp, penetrating sound. —**narrow (or near) squeak** *Informal* A narrow escape. —*v.t. & v.i.* To utter with or make a squeak. [ME *squeke*] —**squeak′er** *n.* —**squeak′i·ly** *adv.* —**squeak′i·ness** *n.* —**squeak′y** *adj.* **squeak·i·er, squeak·i·est**

squeal (skwēl) *v.i.* 1. To utter a sharp, shrill, somewhat prolonged cry. 2. *Slang* To turn informer. —*v.t.* 3. To utter with a squeal. [Imit.] —**squeal** *n.* —**squeal′er** *n.*

squeam·ish (skwē′mish) *adj.* 1. Easily disgusted or shocked; prudish. 2. Easily nauseated. [< AF *escoymous*; ult. origin unknown] —**squeam′ish·ly** *adv.* —**squeam′·ish·ness** *n.*

squee·gee (skwē′jē) *n.* An implement having a stout, straight crosspiece edged with rubber or leather, used for removing water from decks or floors, window panes, etc. [< SQUEEZE]

squeeze (skwēz) *v.* **squeezed, squeez·ing** *v.t.* 1. To press hard upon; compress. 2. To draw forth by pressure; express: to *squeeze* juice. 3. To force or push; cram. 4. To pressure or oppress. —*v.i.* 5. To apply pressure. 6. To force one's way; push: with *in, through,* etc. 7. To be pressed; yield to pressure. —*n.* 1. The act or process of squeezing; pressure. 2. A firm grasp; also, an embrace; hug. 3. Something, as juice, extracted or expressed. 4. *Informal* Pressure exerted for the extortion of money or favors; also, financial pressure. [? < OF *es-* thoroughly + ME *queisen* to crush] —**squeez′a·ble** *adj.* —**squeez′er** *n.*

squelch (skwelch) *v.t.* 1. To crush; squash. 2. *Informal* To silence, as with a crushing reply. —*v.i.* 3. To make a splashing or sucking noise, as when walking in deep mud. —*n.* 1. A squelching sound. 2. *Informal* A crushing reply. [Prob. imit.] —**squelch′er** *n.*

squib (skwib) *n.* 1. A firework to be thrown or rolled swiftly, finally exploding like a rocket. 2. A short speech or writing in a satirical vein. —*v.* **squibbed, squib·bing** *v.i.* 1. To write or use squibs. —*v.t.* 2. To attack with squibs; lampoon. [Origin unknown]

squid (skwid) *n.* Any of various ten-armed mollusks having a slender, conical body. [Origin uncertain]

squig·gle (skwig′əl) *n. Informal* A meaningless scrawl. —*v.i.* To wriggle. [Blend of SQUIRM and WRIGGLE]

squig·gly (skwig′lē) *adj.* **·gli·er, ·gli·est** Twisty; crooked.

squint (skwint) *v.i.* 1. To look with half closed eyes, as into bright light. 2. To look with a side glance. 3. To be cross-eyed. —*v.t.* 4. To hold (the eyes) half shut. —*adj.* 1. Cross-eyed. 2. Looking obliquely or askance; indirect. —*n.* 1. *Pathol.* Strabismus. 2. The act or habit of squinting. [Origin uncertain] —**squint′er** *n.*

squire (skwīr) *n.* 1. A title often used in rural areas for justices of the peace, judges, etc. 2. A young aspirant to knighthood serving as an attendant. 3. A man who escorts a woman in public. 4. In England, a landed proprietor or country gentleman. —*v.t. & v.i.* **squired, squir·ing** To attend or serve (someone) as a squire or escort. [Var. of ESQUIRE]

squirm (skwûrm) *v.i.* 1. To bend and twist the body; wriggle; writhe. 2. To show signs of pain or distress. —*n.* A squirming motion;

a wriggle. [Origin uncertain] —**squirm′er** *n.* —**squirm′y** *adj.* **squirm·i·er, squirm·i·est**
squir·rel (skwûr′əl) *n.* 1. Any of various arboreal rodents having a long bushy tail and feeding chiefly on nuts. 2. The fur of a squirrel. [< Gk. *skia* shadow + *oura* tail]
squirt (skwûrt) *v.i.* 1. To come forth in a thin stream or jet; spurt. 2. To eject water, etc., thus. —*v.t.* 3. To eject (a liquid) forcibly and in a jet. 4. To wet with a squirt or squirts. —*n.* 1. The act of squirting; also, a jet of liquid squirted forth. 2. *Informal* A small, impudent person. [Cf. LG *swirtjen.*] —**squirt′er** *n.*
squish (skwish) *v.t. & v.i. Informal* To squash. —*n.* A squashing sound. [Var. of SQUASH[1]] —**squish′y** *adj.* **squish·i·er, squish·i·est**
Sri Lan·kan (srē lang′kən) *adj.* Of Sri Lanka or its inhabitants. —**Sri Lan′kan** *n.*
stab (stab) *v.* **stabbed, stab·bing** *v.t.* 1. To pierce with or as with a pointed weapon; wound. 2. To penetrate; pierce. —*v.i.* 3. To thrust or lunge with a knife, sword, etc. 4. To inflict a wound thus. —*n.* A thrust made with any pointed weapon. —**to have (or make) a stab at** To make an attempt at. [? < Scot. & dial. E *stob* stake] —**stab′ber** *n.*
sta·bile (*adj.* stā′bil, *n.* stā′bēl) *adj.* Fixed; stable. —*n.* A standing abstract sculpture of irregularly-shaped plates of sheet metal, welded together at intersecting planes.
sta·bi·lize (stā′bə·līz) *v.t.* **·lized, ·liz·ing** To make firm or stable; keep steady. Also *esp. Brit.* **sta′bi·lise.** —**sta′bi·li·za′tion** *n.* —**sta′bi·liz′er** *n.*
sta·ble[1] (stā′bəl) *adj.* 1. Standing firmly in place; not easily moved, shaken, or overthrown; fixed. 2. Steadfast. 3. Durable or permanent; abiding. 4. *Chem.* Not easily decomposed: said of compounds. [< L *stabilis* < *stare* to stand] —**sta·bil·i·ty** (stə·bil′ə·tē) *n.* —**sta′bly** (-blē) *adv.*
sta·ble[2] (stā′bəl) *n.* 1. A building set apart for horses or cattle; also, the animals. 2. Race horses belonging to a particular owner; also, the owner and personnel collectively. —*v.t. & v.i.* **·bled, ·bling** To put or lodge in a stable. [< L *stare* to stand]
stac·ca·to (stə·kä′tō) *adj.* 1. *Music* Having short breaks between notes. 2. Marked by abrupt, sharp emphasis. —*n. pl.* **·tos** 1. *Music* A staccato style or passage. 2. An abrupt, emphatic manner or sound. [< Ital., pp. of *staccare* to detach] —**stac·ca′to** *adv.*
stack (stak) *n.* 1. A large, orderly pile of unthreshed grain, hay, or straw, usu. conical. 2. Any systematic pile or heap. 3. A case composed of several rows of bookshelves one above the other. 4. *pl.* That part of a library where most of the books are shelved. 5. A chimney; smokestack. 6. *Informal* A great amount; plenty. —*v.t.* To pile up in a stack. —**to stack the cards (or deck)** 1. To arrange cards secretly in the pack in a manner favorable to the dealer. 2. To have an advantage secured beforehand. [< ON *stakkr*] —**stack′er** *n.*
sta·di·um (stā′dē·əm) *n. pl.* **·di·a,** *for def. 2* **·di·ums** 1. In ancient Greece, a course for foot races, with banked seats for spectators. 2. A similar modern structure in which athletic games are played. [< Gk. *stadion,* measure of length]
staff (staf) *n. pl.* **staffs;** *for defs. 1, 2, 3, & 6, also* **staves** (stāvz) 1. A stick of wood carried for some special purpose. 2. A shaft or pole that forms a support or handle. 3. A stick used in measuring or testing. 4. *Mil.* A body of officers not having command but assigned in an executive or advisory capacity. 5. A body of persons associated in carrying out some special enterprise. 6. *Music* The five horizontal lines and four spaces used in writing music: also called *stave.* —*v.t.* To provide (an office, etc.) with a staff. [OE *stæf* stick]
staff officer 1. An officer on the staff of a military commander. 2. In the U.S. Navy, an officer without command or operational functions, as a doctor, dentist, chaplain, etc.
stag (stag) *n.* 1. The male of the red deer. 2. The male of other large deer, as the caribou. 3. A man who attends a social function unaccompanied by a woman. —*adj.* Of or for men only. —*v.i.* **stagged, stag·ging** To attend a social affair unaccompanied by a woman. [OE *stagga*]
stage (stāj) *n.* 1. A raised platform on which the performance in a theater, hall, etc., takes place. 2. The theater: to write for the *stage.* 3. The field of action of some event: to set the *stage* for war. 4. A definite portion of a journey. 5. A step in some development, progress, or process. 6. *Aerospace* One of the separate propulsion units of a rocket vehicle. 7. A stagecoach; also, a stop on the route of a stagecoach. —**by easy stages** Traveling or acting without hurry and with frequent stops. —*v.t.* **staged, stag·ing** 1. To put or exhibit on the stage. 2. To conduct; carry on. [< L *status,* pp. of *stare* to stand]
stage·coach (stāj′kōch′) *n.* A large, horse-drawn, four-wheeled vehicle having a regular route from town to town.
stage·craft (stāj′kraft′) *n.* Skill in writing or staging plays.
stage door A door to a theater used by actors, etc., that leads behind the scenes.
stage fright A sudden panic that sometimes attacks those appearing before an audience.
stage·hand (stāj′hand′) *n.* A worker in a theater who handles scenery and props, operates lights, etc.
stage manager One who assists the director and is in charge during the performance of a play.
stage-struck (stāj′struk′) *adj.* Enamored of theatrical life.
stage whisper Any loud whisper intended to be overheard.
stage·y (stā′jē) See STAGY.
stag·fla·tion (stag′flā′shən) *n.* An economic condition in which inflation is combined with slow buying and high unemployment. [< STAG(NANT) + (IN)FLATION]
stag·ger (stag′ər) *v.i.* 1. To walk or run unsteadily; reel. 2. To waver; hesitate. —*v.t.* 3. To cause to stagger. 4. To affect strongly; overwhelm, as with grief. 5. To alternate or vary, esp. to prevent congestion, inconvenience, etc.: to *stagger* lunch hours. —*n.* The act of staggering, or the condition of being staggered. [< ON *stakra*] —**stag′·ger·er** *n.* —**stag′ger·ing·ly** *adv.*
stag·gers (stag′ərz) *n.pl.* (*construed as sing.*) 1. *Vet.* A disease of domestic animals, as horses, characterized by staggering and

sudden falling, due to disorder of the brain and spinal cord. 2. A reeling sensation.

stag·ing (stā′jing) *n.* 1. A scaffolding or temporary platform. 2. The process of putting a play upon the stage.

stag line *Informal* A group of males without partners at a dance.

stag·nant (stag′nənt) *adj.* 1. Standing still; not flowing: said of water or air. 2. Foul from standing, as water. 3. Dull; sluggish. —**stag′nan·cy** *n.* —**stag′nant·ly** *adv.*

stag·nate (stag′nāt) *v.i.* **·nat·ed, ·nat·ing** To be or become stagnant. [< L *stagnare*] —**stag·na′tion** *n.*

stag·y (stā′jē) *adj.* **stag·i·er, stag·i·est** Theatrical; artificial: also spelled *stagey.* —**stag′i·ly** *adv.* —**stag′i·ness** *n.*

staid (stād) *adj.* Steady and sober. [Orig. pt. and pp. of STAY[1]] —**staid′ly** *adv.* —**staid′ness** *n.*

stain (stān) *n.* 1. A spot; smirch; blot. 2. A dye or thin pigment used in staining. 3. A moral taint. —*v.t.* 1. To make a stain upon; discolor; soil; tarnish. 2. To color by the use of a dye or stain. —*v.i.* 3. To take or impart a stain. [Aphetic var. of DISDAIN] —**stain′a·ble** *adj.* —**stain′er** *n.* —**stain′less** *adj.* —**stain′less·ly** *adv.*

stained glass (stānd) Colored glass used in church windows, etc. —**stained-glass** (stānd′glas′) *adj.*

stainless steel A steel alloy made resistant to corrosion, rust, and staining by the addition of chromium and other ingredients.

stair (stâr) *n.* 1. A step, or one of a series of steps, for mounting or descending from one level to another. 2. *Usu. pl.* A flight of steps. [OE *stæger*]

stair·case (stâr′kās′) *n.* A flight or series of flights of stairs.

stair·way (stâr′wā′) *n.* A flight of stairs; staircase.

stake (stāk) *n.* 1. A stick or post sharpened at one end for driving into the ground, used as a marker, for a fence, etc. 2. A post to which a person is bound, to be executed by burning; also, execution in this manner. 3. Something wagered or risked. 4. *Often pl.* A prize in a contest. 5. An interest in an enterprise. 6. A grubstake. —**at stake** In hazard or jeopardy; in question. —**to pull up stakes** To move from a place. —*v.t.* **staked, stak·ing** 1. To fasten or support by means of a stake. 2. To mark the boundaries of with stakes: often with *off* or *out.* 3. *Informal* To wager; risk. 4. *Informal* To grubstake; also, to finance. [OE *staca*]

sta·lac·tite (stə·lak′tīt) *n.* A long, tapering formation hanging from the roof of a cavern, produced by continuous watery deposits containing certain minerals. [< Gk. *stalassein* to trickle] —**stal·ac·tit·ic** (stal′ək·tit′ik) *adj.*

sta·lag·mite (stə·lag′mīt′) *n.* An incrustation, usu. cylindrical or conical, built up on the floor of a cavern by dripping from above. [< Gk. *stalassein* to drip] —**stal·ag·mit·ic** (stal′əg·mit′ik) *adj.*

stale (stāl) *adj.* **stal·er, stal·est** 1. Having lost freshness; slightly changed or deteriorated, as beer, bread, etc. 2. Dull, as from overuse; trite. 3. Sluggish; uninspired, as after a period of overactivity. —*v.i.* **staled, stal·ing** To become stale or trite. [Origin uncertain] —**stale′ly** *adv.* —**stale′ness** *n.*

stale·mate (stāl′māt′) *n.* 1. In chess, a draw resulting when a player can make no move without placing his king in check. 2. Any tie or deadlock. —*v.t.* **·mat·ed, ·mat·ing** To put into a condition of stalemate. [< AF *estale* fixed position + MATE[2]]

stalk[1] (stôk) *n.* 1. The stem or axis of a plant. 2. Any supporting or connecting part resembling a stem. [ME *stalke*] —**stalked** (stôkt) *adj.*

stalk[2] (stôk) *v.i.* 1. To approach game, etc., stealthily. 2. To walk in a stiff, dignified manner. —*v.t.* 3. To approach (game, etc.) stealthily. —*n.* 1. The act of stalking game. 2. A stately step or walk. [OE *bestealcian* to move stealthily] —**stalk′er** *n.*

stalk·ing-horse (stô′king·hôrs′) *n.* In politics, a candidate put forth to divide the opposition or to hide another candidacy. [after a horse behind which a hunter conceals himself]

stall (stôl) *n.* 1. A compartment in which a horse, cow, etc., is confined and fed. 2. A small sales booth or compartment in a street, market, etc. 3. A pew, as in a church. 4. A stop or standstill, esp. one resulting from a fault in the working of an engine. 5. *Informal* An evasion. —*v.t.* 1. To place or keep in a stall. 2. To bring to a standstill; stop, esp. unintentionally. —*v.i.* 3. To come to a standstill; stop. 4. *Informal* To make delays; be evasive. [OE *steall*]

stal·lion (stal′yən) *n.* An uncastrated male horse. [< OF *estalon* < OHG *stal* stable]

stal·wart (stôl′wərt) *adj.* 1. Strong; robust. 2. Resolute; determined. 3. Brave; courageous. —*n.* A stalwart person. [OE < *stǣl* place + *wierthe* worth] —**stal′wart·ly** *adv.* —**stal′wart·ness** *n.*

sta·men (stā′mən) *n. pl.* **sta·mens** or *Rare* **stam·i·na** (stam′ə·nə) *Bot.* The pollen-bearing organ of a flower. [< L, warp, thread]

stam·i·na (stam′ə·nə) *n.* Capacity to withstand hardship; vitality. [< L, pl. of *stamen* warp, thread] —**stam′i·nal** *adj.*

tam·i·nate (stam′ə·nit, -nāt) *adj. Bot.* 1. Having stamens. 2. Having stamens but no pistils.

stam·mer (stam′ər) *v.t. & v.i.* To speak haltingly, with involuntary repetitions or prolongations of a sound or syllable. —*n.* The act or condition of stammering. [OE *stamerian*] —**stam′mer·er** *n.*

stamp (stamp) *v.t.* 1. To strike heavily with the sole of the foot. 2. To bring down (the foot) heavily and noisily. 3. To strike or crush, as with the foot. 4. To mark by means of a die, stamp, etc. 5. To imprint or impress with a die, stamp, etc. 6. To fix or imprint permanently. 7. To affix an official seal, stamp, etc., to. —*v.i.* 8. To strike the foot heavily on the ground. 9. To walk with heavy, resounding steps. —*n.* 1. A die or block having a pattern or design for impressing upon a surface. 2. The impression so made. 3. Any characteristic mark, as a label or imprint; a brand. 4. A printed device prepared and sold by a government, for attachment to a letter, commodity, etc., as proof that the tax or fee has been paid. [ME *stampen*] —**stamp′er** *n.*

stam·pede (stam·pēd′) *n.* 1. A sudden

starting and rushing off through panic, as of a herd of cattle, horses, etc. 2. Any sudden, tumultuous running movement of a crowd or mob. —*v.t. & v.i.* **·ped·ed, ·ped·ing** To rush or cause to rush in a stampede. [< Am.Sp. *estampida* crash] —**stam·ped'er** *n.*

stamp·ing ground (stam'ping) A favorite or habitual gathering place.

stance (stans) *n.* Mode of standing; posture. [L < *stare* to stand]

stanch (stanch) *v.t.* To stop or check the flow of (blood, etc.). Also spelled *staunch.* —*adj.* See STAUNCH. [< OF *estanchier* to halt] —**stanch'er** *n.*

stan·chion (stan'shən) *n.* An upright bar forming a support or barrier. —*v.t.* To provide or confine with stanchions. [< OF *estanchon* < *estance* situation]

stand (stand) *v.* **stood, stand·ing** *v.i.* 1. To assume or maintain an erect position on one's feet. 2. To be in a vertical position; be erect. 3. To measure a specified height when standing. 4. To assume a specified position: to *stand* aside. 5. To assume or have a definite opinion, position, or attitude. 6. To be situated; have position or location; lie. 7. To remain unchanged or valid. 8. To have or be in a specified state, condition, or relation: He *stood* in fear of his life. 9. To be of a specified rank or class: He *stands* third. 10. To be or remain firm or resolute. 11. To collect and remain; also, to be stagnant, as water. 12. To stop or pause; halt. 13. *Brit.* To be a candidate, as for election. —*v.t.* 14. To place upright; set in an erect position. 15. To put up with; endure. 16. To be subjected to; undergo: He must *stand* trial. 17. *Informal* To pay for: to *stand* a treat. —**to stand a chance** To have a chance, as of success. —**to stand by** 1. To be ready to help or act. 2. To help; support. 3. To abide by; make good. 4. To remain passive and watch, as when help is needed. —**to stand clear** To remain at a safe distance. —**to stand for** 1. To represent; symbolize. 2. To put up with; tolerate. —**to stand in for** To act as a substitute for. —**to stand on** 1. To be based on; rest. 2. To insist on or demand observance of: to *stand on* ceremony. —**to stand on one's own (two) feet** To manage one's own affairs. —**to stand out** 1. To project or protrude. 2. To be prominent; appear in relief or contrast. —**to stand pat** In poker, to play one's hand as dealt, without drawing new cards. —**to stand to reason** To conform to reason. —**to stand up** 1. To withstand wear, criticism, analysis, etc. 2. *Slang* To fail to keep an appointment with. —**to stand up for** To side with; take the part of. —**to stand up to** To confront courageously; face. —*n.* 1. The act of standing, esp. of standing firmly: to make a *stand* against the enemy. 2. An opinion, attitude, or position, as in a controversy. 3. A structure or platform upon which persons or things may sit or stand, or on which articles may be kept or displayed. 4. A rack or other piece of furniture on which hats, canes, etc. may be hung or placed. 5. In the theater, a stop made while on tour: a one-night *stand.* 6. The growing trees in a forest. —**to take a stand** To have or reveal an opinion or attitude, as on a controversial issue. [OE *standan*] —**stand'er** *n.*

stan·dard (stan'dərd) *n.* 1. A flag or banner, used as an emblem of a government, military unit, etc. 2. Any established measure of extent, quantity, quality, or value. 3. Any model for comparison; a criterion of excellence: a *standard* of conduct. 4. An upright post, esp. as a support. —*adj.* 1. Serving as a gauge or model. 2. Of recognized excellence or authority: a *standard* book. 3. *Ling.* Designating or belonging to those usages of a language that have gained literary, cultural, and social acceptance: *standard* English. [< OF *estandard* banner]

stan·dard-bear·er (stan'dərd·bâr'ər) *n.* 1. The member of a military unit who carries the flag. 2. A leader, or a candidate for a leading position, as for a presidency.

stan·dard·bred (*n.* stan'dərd·bred'; *adj.* stan'dərd·bred') *n.* A breed of horse notable for its trotters and pacers. —*adj.* Bred so as to be of a required strain, quality, or pedigree, as poultry, horses, etc.

standard candle *Physics* A candle (def. 2).

standard English *Ling.* Those usages in English that have gained literary, cultural, and social acceptance.

standard gauge A railroad having a track width of $56^1/_2$ inches, considered as standard.

stan·dard·ize (stan'dər·dīz) *v.t.* **·ized, ·iz·ing** To make to or regulate by a standard. —**stan'dard·i·za'tion** *n.* —**stan'·dard·iz'er** *n.*

standard of living The average quantity and quality of goods and services that a person or group uses in daily living.

standard time Time as reckoned from a meridian officially established as standard over a large area. In the conterminous U.S., the four standard time zones are the **Eastern** (E.S.T.), **Central** (C.S.T.), **Mountain** (M.S.T.), and **Pacific** (P.S.T.). Canada has a fifth zone, the **Atlantic** (or **Provincial**).

stand·by (stand'bī') *n. pl.* **·bys** A person or thing on call for emergencies.

stand·ee (stan·dē') *n. Informal* A person who must stand for lack of chairs or seats.

stand-in (stand'in') *n.* 1. A person who takes the place of an actor, as while lights are adjusted. 2. A substitute or replacement.

stand·ing (stan'ding) *adj.* 1. Remaining erect. 2. Established; permanent: a *standing* army. 3. Stagnant; not flowing. 4. Begun while standing: a *standing* high jump. —*n.* 1. High rank or reputation. 2. Time in which something goes on; duration. 3. The act of one who stands.

stand·off (stand'ôf') *n. Informal* A draw or tie, as in a game.

stand·off·ish (stand'ôf'ish) *adj.* Aloof; coolly reserved. —**stand'off'ish·ness** *n.*

stand·pat (stand'pat') *adj.* Opposed to change; conservative. —**stand'pat'ter** *n.*

stand·pipe (stand'pīp') *n.* A large vertical pipe or tower in which water is stored; water tower.

stand·point (stand'point') *n.* A position from which things are judged; point of view.

stand·still (stand'stil') *n.* A cessation; halt.

stand·up (stand'up') *adj.* 1. Having an

erect position: a *standup* collar. 2. Done, consumed, etc., while standing.

stank (stangk) Past tense of STINK.

stan·nic (stan′ik) *adj. Chem.* Containing tin, esp. in its higher valence. [< L *stannum* tin]

stan·nous (stan′əs) *adj. Chem.* Containing tin, esp. in its lower valence. [< L *stannum* tin]

stan·za (stan′zə) *n.* A number of lines of verse that make up a metrical division of a poem. [< Ital. < L *stans, stantis* standing] —**stan·za′ic** (-zā′ik) *adj.*

sta·pes (stā′pēz) *n. pl.* **sta·pes** or **sta·pe·des** (stə·pē′dēz) *Anat.* The innermost bone of the middle ear of mammals: also called *stirrup bone.* [< LL *stapes* stirrup] —**sta·pe·di·al** (stə·pē′dē·əl) *adj.*

staph (staf) *n. Informal* Staphylococci; also, an infection caused by staphylococci.

staph·y·lo·coc·cus (staf′ə·lō·kok′əs) *n. pl.* **·coc·ci** (-kok′sī) Any of a genus of bacteria, often occurring in clusters; esp., an infective agent in boils and suppurating wounds. [< Gk. *staphylos* bunch of grapes + *kokkos* berry] —**staph′y·lo·coc′cic** (-kok′sik) *adj.*

sta·ple[1] (stā′pəl) *n.* 1. *Usu. pl.* A basic food or other ordinary item of household use. 2. A principal commodity of a country or region. 3. A main constituent of something. 4. The carded or combed fiber of cotton, wool, or flax. 5. Raw material. —*adj.* 1. Regularly and constantly produced, used, or sold. 2. Main; chief. —*v.t.* **·pled, ·pling** To sort or classify according to length, as wool fiber. [< OF *estaple* market] —**sta′pler** *n.*

sta·ple[2] (stā′pəl) *n.* 1. A U-shaped piece of metal with pointed ends, driven into a surface to secure a bolt, hook, hasp, etc. 2. A thin piece of wire usu. shaped like a bracket ([), driven into paper, fabrics, etc., to serve as a fastening. [OE *stapol* post, prop] —**sta′ple** *v.t.* **·pled, ·pling** —**sta′pler** *n.*

star (stär) *n.* 1. Any of the heavenly bodies visible from earth as apparently fixed points of light. 2. *Astron.* One of a class of self-luminous celestial bodies, exclusive of comets, meteors, and nebulae, but including the sun. ◆Collateral adjectives: *astral, sidereal, stellar.* 3. A conventional figure usu. having five or more radiating points, used as an emblem or device, as to indicate the rank of general. 4. An actor or actress who plays the leading part. 5. Anyone who shines prominently in a calling or profession. 6. An asterisk. 7. *Often pl.* Fortune; destiny. —**to see stars** *Informal* To see bright spots before the eyes, as from a sharp jolt to the head. —*v.* **starred, star·ring** *v.t.* 1. To set or adorn with spangles or stars. 2. To mark with an asterisk. 3. To present as a star in a play or motion picture. —*v.i.* 4. To play the leading part; be the star. —*adj.* 1. Of or pertaining to a star or stars. 2. Prominent; brilliant. [OE *steorra*] —**star′less** *adj.* —**star′like′** *adj.*

star·board (stär′bərd) *Naut. n.* The right-hand side of a vessel as one faces the front or bow: opposed to *port.* [OE *steorbord* steering side] —**star′board** *adj.*

starch (stärch) *n.* 1. *Biochem.* A white, odorless, tasteless, granular carbohydrate found in most plants. 2. A preparation of this substance, used esp. for stiffening fabric. 3. Stiffiness or formality. 4. *Slang* Energy; vigor. —*v.t.* To apply starch to; stiffen with or as with starch. [OE *stercan* to stiffen < *stearc* stiff]

Star Chamber 1. Formerly, in England, a secret high court, abolished in 1641. 2. Any court engaged in arbitrary or illegal procedure.

starch·y (stär′chē) *adj.* **starch·i·er, starch·i·est** 1. Stiffened with starch; stiff. Also **starched** (stärcht). 2. Prim; formal; precise. 3. Formed of or combined with starch; farinaceous. —**starch′i·ly** *adv.* —**starch′i·ness** *n.*

star·dom (stär′dəm) *n.* The status of a star (defs. 4 & 5).

stare (stâr) *v.* **stared, star·ing** *v.i.* 1. To gaze fixedly. 2. To be conspicuously or unduly apparent; glare. —*v.t.* 3. To stare at. —*n.* The act of staring; an intense gaze. [OE *starian*] —**star′er** *n.*

star·fish (stär′fish′) *n. pl.* **·fish** or **·fish·es** Any of various radially symmetrical marine animals, commonly with a star-shaped body having five or more arms.

star·gaze (stär′gāz′) *v.i.* **·gazed, ·gaz·ing** 1. To gaze at or study the stars. 2. To daydream. —**star′gaz·er** *n.* —**star′gaz·ing** *n. & adj.*

stark (stärk) *adj.* 1. Bare; plain. 2. Complete; utter: *stark* misery. 3. Stiff or rigid, as in death. 4. Strict or grim. —*adv.* 1. In a stark manner. 2. Completely; utterly: *stark* mad. [OE *stearc* stiff] —**stark′ly** *adv.*

star·let (stär′lit) *n. Informal* A young movie or television actress represented as a future star.

star·light (stär′līt′) *n.* The light given by stars. —**star′lit′** (-lit′) *adj.*

star·ling (stär′ling) *n.* Any of various birds of Europe and North America, having a metallic purple and green luster. [OE *stær*]

star-of-Beth·le·hem (stär′əv·beth′lə·hem, -lē·əm) *n.* A plant of the lily family having white stellate flowers.

star of Bethlehem The large star that led the Magi to Jesus's manager in Bethelehem.

starred (stärd) *adj.* 1. Spangled with stars. 2. Presented or advertised as the star of a play, motion picture, etc. 3. Marked with an asterisk. 4. Affected by astral influence: chiefly in combination: *ill-starred.*

star·ry (stär′ē) *adj.* **·ri·er, ·ri·est** 1. Abounding in stars. 2. Lighted by the stars. 3. Shining as or like the stars. 4. Of or pertaining to the stars. —**star′ri·ness** *n.*

star·ry-eyed (stär′ē·īd′) *adj.* Given to fanciful wishes or yearnings.

Stars and Stripes, The The flag of the U.S., featuring thirteen horizontal stripes and a star for each state.

Star-Span·gled Banner, The (stär′spang′·gəld) 1. The flag of the U.S. 2. The national anthem of the U.S.

start (stärt) *v.i.* 1. To make a beginning or start; set out. 2. To begin; commence. 3. To make an involuntary, startled movement, as from fear or surprise. 4. To move suddenly, as with a leap; jump. 5. To seem to bulge or protrude. —*v.t.* 6. To set in motion or circulation: to *start* an engine. 7. To begin; commence. 8. To set up; establish. 9. To rouse from cover; flush, as game. —**to start in** To begin; undertake. —**to start off** To begin a journey; set out. —**to start out** To make a beginning or start. —**to start up** 1. To rise or appear suddenly. 2. To begin or cause to begin operation, as an engine. —*n.* 1. A setting out or going forth; beginning; also, the place where one begins. 2. A quick, startled movement. 3. Advantage or distance in advance at the outset; lead. [ME *sterten* to start, leap]

start·er (stär′tər) *n.* 1. One who or that which starts. 2. A mechanism for starting an internal combustion engine without manual cranking: also called *self-starter*.

star·tle (stär′təl) *v.* **·tled, ·tling** *v.t.* 1. To arouse or excite suddenly; cause to start involuntarily; alarm. —*v.i.* 2. To be thus aroused. [OE *steartlian* to kick, struggle] —**star′tler** *n.*

star·tling (stärt′ling) *adj.* Rousing sudden surprise, alarm, etc. —**star′tling·ly** *adv.*

starve (stärv) *v.* **starved, starv·ing** *v.i.* 1. To perish from lack of food. 2. To suffer from extreme hunger. 3. To suffer from lack or need: to *starve* for friendship. —*v.t.* 4. To cause to suffer from or die of hunger; deprive of food. [OE *steorfan* to die] —**star·va′tion** *n.* —**starv′er** *n.*

starve·ling (stärv′ling) *n.* A person or animal that is starving, starved, or emaciated. —*adj.* Starving; emaciated.

stash (stash) *Slang v.t.* To hide or conceal (money, valuables, etc.), for storage and safekeeping. —*n.* A concealed supply or store; cache. [? Blend of STORE + CACHE]

sta·sis (stā′sis, stas′is) *n. pl.* **·ses** (-sēz) 1. *Pathol.* Stoppage in the circulation of any of the body fluids or retarded movement of the intestinal contents. 2. Retarded movement; stagnation. [Gk., a standing]

-stat *combining form* A device that stops or makes constant: *thermostat, rheostat.* [< Gk. *-statēs* causing to stand]

state (stāt) *n.* 1. Mode of existence as determined by circumstances; condition; situation. 2. Frame of mind; mood. 3. Mode or style of living; station. 4. Ceremonious style; pomp; formality. 5. A sovereign political community organized under a distinct government having jurisdiction over a given territory; a nation. 6. *Sometimes cap.* One of a number of political communities united to form one sovereign state; esp., one of the United States. 7. The territorial, political, and governmental entity constituting a state or nation; authority of government. —**to lie in state** To be placed on public view, with ceremony, before burial. —*adj.* 1. Of or pertaining to the state, nation, or government. 2. Intended for use on occasions of ceremony. —*v.t.* **stat·ed, stat·ing** 1. To set forth explicitly in speech or writing; assert; declare. 2. To fix; determine; settle. [< OF *estat* < L *status* condition, state]

state·craft (stāt′kraft′) *n.* The art or practice of conducting affairs of state.

stat·ed (stā′tid) *adj.* 1. Announced; specified. 2. Established; regular; fixed. —**stat′ed·ly** *adv.*

state·hood (stāt′ho͝od) *n.* The status of one of the states of the United States.

State House A building used for sessions of a state legislature and for other public purposes; state capitol.

state·less (stāt′lis) *adj.* Without nationality. —**state′less·ness** *n.*

state line In the U.S., any boundary between states.

state·ly (stāt′lē) *adj.* **·li·er, ·li·est** Dignified; lofty. —*adv.* Loftily. —**state′li·ness** *n.*

state·ment (stāt′mənt) *n.* 1. The act of stating. 2. That which is stated. 3. A summary of financial assets and liabilities, or of deposits and withdrawals by a customer of a bank. 4. A bill.

state park In the U.S., a tract of land provided and maintained by a state for conservation and recreation.

state·room (stāt′ro͞om′, -ro͝om′) *n.* A private room on a passenger ship or a railroad car.

state's evidence Evidence produced by the prosecution in criminal proceedings. —**to turn state's evidence** To become a witness for the prosecution and inculpate one's accomplices.

state·side (stāt′sīd′) *adj.* Of or in the continental U.S. —*adv.* In or to the continental U.S.

states·man (stāts′mən) *n. pl.* **·men** (-mən) One who is skilled in government; a distinguished political leader or public servant. —**states′man·like′, states′man·ly** *adj.* —**states′man·ship** *n.*

states' rights 1. The rights and powers not delegated to the U.S. by the Constitution nor prohibited by it to the respective states. 2. An interpretation of the Constitution that makes these rights and powers as large as possible.

state·wide (stāt′wīd′) *adj.* Throughout a state.

stat·ic (stat′ik) *adj.* 1. At rest; dormant; not active, moving, or changing. 2. Pertaining to bodies at rest or forces in equilibrium: opposed to *dynamic.* 3. *Electr.* Pertaining to electricity at rest, or to stationary electric charges. Also **stat′i·cal.** —*n.* *Telecom.* A disturbance of a carrier wave; also, the noise caused by this. [< Gk. *statikos* causing to stand] —**stat′i·cal·ly** *adv.*

stat·ics (stat′iks) *n.pl.* (*construed as sing.*) The branch of mechanics dealing with bodies at rest and with the interaction of forces in equilibrium.

sta·tion (stā′shən) *n.* 1. The headquarters of some official person or group. 2. An established building or place serving as a starting point or stopping place; terminal; depot. 3. A place where a person usu. stands or is; an assigned location. 4. Social condition; rank. 5. *Mil.* The place to which an individual, unit, or ship is assigned for duty; post. 6. The offices, studios, and technical installations of a radio or television broadcasting unit. 7. *Austral.* A cattle or sheep ranch. —*v.t.* To assign to a station; place in a post or position. [< L *status,* pp. of *stare* to stand]

sta·tion·ar·y (stā′shən·er′ē) *adj.* 1. Remain-

ing in one place; fixed. 2. Not portable. 3. Exhibiting no change of character or condition.
sta·tion·er (stā′shən·ər) *n.* A dealer in stationery and related articles. [< Med.L *stationarius* stationary]
sta·tion·er·y (stā′shən·er′ē) *n.* 1. Writing paper and envelopes. 2. Writing materials, as pencils, notebooks, etc.
sta·tion·mas·ter (stā′shən·mas′tər) *n.* The person having charge of a bus or railroad station.
Stations of the Cross Fourteen images representing successive scenes of the Passion of Christ.
station wagon A large automobile with removable or folding seats and a hinged tailgate.
sta·tis·tic (stə·tis′tik) *n.* Any element entering into a statistical statement or array.
sta·tis·ti·cal (stə·tis′tə·kəl) *adj.* Of, pertaining to, consisting of, or derived from statistics. —**sta·tis′ti·cal·ly** *adv.*
sta·tis·tics (stə·tis′tiks) *n.pl.* (*construed as sing. in def. 2*) 1. Quantitative data, pertaining to any subject or group, esp. when systematically gathered and collated. 2. The science that deals with the collection, tabulation, and systematic classification of quantitative data, esp. as a basis for inference and induction. [< L *status* state, condition] —**stat·is·ti·cian** (stat′is·tish′ən) *n.*
stat·u·ar·y (stach′ōō·er′ē) *n.* *pl.* **·ar·ies** Statues collectively. —*adj.* Of or suitable for statues.
stat·ue (stach′ōō) *n.* A representation of a person or animal in marble, bronze, etc. [< L < *status*, pp. of *stare* to stand]
Statue of Liberty A giant bronze statue on Liberty Island, in New York harbor, depicting a crowned woman holding aloft a burning torch.
stat·u·esque (stach′ōō·esk′) *adj.* Resembling a statue, as in grace, pose, or dignity. —**stat′u·esque′ly** *adv.* —**stat′u·esque′ness** *n.*
stat·u·ette (stach′ōō·et′) *n.* A small statue. [< F]
stat·ure (stach′ər) *n.* 1. Natural height, esp. of a human body. 2. Development; growth; moral *stature.* [< L *stare* to stand]
sta·tus (stā′təs, stat′əs) *n.* 1. State, condition, or relation. 2. Relative position or rank. [< L]
sta·tus quo (stā′təs kwō, stat′əs) The condition or state in which (a person or thing is or has been): often used with *the.* Also **status in quo.** [< L]
stat·ute (stach′ōōt) *n.* 1. A legislative enactment; act of Parliament, Congress, etc. 2. Any authoritatively declared rule, ordinance, decree, or law. —*adj.* Consisting of or regulated by statute. [< LL *statuere* to constitute]
statute law The law as set forth in statutes.
statute mile A U.S. mile.
statute of limitations A statute that limits the time within which legal action can be instituted.
stat·u·to·ry (stach′ə·tôr′ē) *adj.* 1. Pertaining to a statute. 2. Created by or dependent upon legislation.
statutory rape The crime of having sexual relations with a girl who is under the legal age of consent.
staunch (stônch, stänch) *adj.* 1. Firm and dependable; loyal. 2. Having firm constitution or construction. 3. Strong and vigorous. Also spelled *stanch.* —*v.t.* See STANCH. [< OF *estanchier* to make stand] —**staunch′ly** *adv.* —**staunch′ness** *n.*
stave (stāv) *n.* 1. A curved strip of wood, forming a part of the sides of a barrel, tub, etc. 2. Any narrow strip of material used for a like purpose. 3. *Music* A staff. 4. A stanza; verse. 5. A rod or staff. 6. A rung of a rack or ladder. —*v.* **staved** or **stove, stav·ing** *v.t.* 1. To break in the staves of. 2. To crush; smash. 3. To ward off, as with a staff: usu. with *off.* —*v.i.* 4. To be broken in, as a vessel's hull. [Back formation < STAVES]
staves (stāvz) 1. Alternative plural of STAFF. 2. Plural of STAVE. [OE *stafas*, pl. of *stæf* stick]
stay[1] (stā) *v.i.* 1. To cease motion; stop; halt. 2. To continue in a specified place, condition, or state: to *stay* healthy. 3. To remain temporarily as a guest, resident, etc. 4. To pause; wait. 5. *Informal* To have endurance; last. 6. In poker, to remain in a round by meeting an ante, bet, or raise. —*v.t.* 7. To bring to a stop; halt; check. 8. To hinder; delay. 9. To postpone. 10. To remain for the duration of: I will *stay* the night. —**to stay put** *Informal* To remain or hold in spite of everything. —*n.* 1. The act or time of staying; sojourn; visit. 2. That which checks or stops; esp., a suspension of judicial proceedings. [< AF *estaier* < L *stare* to stand] —**stay′er** *n.*
stay[2] (stā) *v.t.* To be a support to; prop or hold up. —*n.* 1. Anything that props or supports. 2. A strip of plastic or metal, used to stiffen corsets, girdles, etc. 3. *pl.* Formerly, a corset. [< OF *estayer*]
stay[3] (stā) *Naut.* *n.* 1. A strong rope, often of wire, used to support, steady, or fasten a mast or spar. 2. Any rope supporting a mast or funnel. —*v.t.* 1. To support with a stay or stays, as a mast. —*v.i.* 2. To tack: said of vessels. [OE *stæg*]
stay·ing power (stā′ing) The ability to endure; stamina.
stay·sail (stā′səl, -sāl′) *n.* *Naut.* A sail, usu. triangular, extended on a stay.
stead (sted) *n.* 1. Place of another person or thing: preceded by *in.* 2. Place or attitude of support; service: chiefly in the phrase **to stand one in (good) stead.** [OE *stede*]
stead·fast (sted′fast′) *adj.* 1. Faithful; loyal; constant. 2. Fixed; unwavering; steady. [OE *stedefæst*] —**stead′fast′ly** *adv.* —**stead′fast′ness** *n.*
stead·y (sted′ē) *adj.* **stead·i·er, stead·i·est** 1. Stable in position; firmly supported; fixed. 2. Moving or acting with uniform regularity; unfaltering. 3. Not readily disturbed or upset. 4. Reliable; sober; temperate. 5. Constant; steadfast. 6. Regular; reliable: a *steady* customer. 7. Uninterrupted; continuous. 8. *Naut.* Having the direction of the ship's head unchanged. —*v.t.* & *v.i.* **stead·ied, stead·y·ing** To make or become

steady. —*interj.* Not so fast; keep calm. —*n. Slang* One's regular sweetheart. —**to go steady** *Informal* To date only one boy friend or girl friend. [< STEAD] —**stead'i·er** *n.* —**stead'i·ly** *adv.* —**stead'i·ness** *n.*

steady-state theory *Astron.* The theory that the universe is continually expanding, but maintains a constant overall density as new matter is created.

steak (stāk) *n.* A slice of meat or fish, usu. broiled or fried. [< ON *steik*]

steal (stēl) *v.* **stole, sto·len, steal·ing** *v.t.* 1. To take from another without authority or permission, and usu. in a secret manner. 2. To take or obtain in a surreptitious, artful, or subtle manner. 3. To move, place, or convey stealthily: with *away, from, in, into,* etc. 4. In baseball, to reach (a base) without the aid of a hit. —*v.i.* 5. To commit theft. 6. To move secretly or furtively. —*n.* 1. The act of stealing. 2. That which is stolen. 3. *Slang* A bargain. [OE *stelan*] —**steal'er** *n.*

stealth (stelth) *n.* The quality or habit of acting secretly; a surreptitious manner of acting. [OE *stelan* to steal] —**stealth'i·ly** *adv.* —**stealth'i·ness** *n.* —**stealth'y** *adj.* **stealth·i·er, stealth·i·est**

steam (stēm) *n.* 1. Water in the form of vapor. 2. Water vapor when used under pressure as a source of energy. 3. The visible mist into which aqueous vapor is condensed by cooling. 4. *Informal* Vigor; force; speed. —**to let (or blow) off steam** *Informal* To give expression to pent-up emotions or opinions. —*v.i.* 1. To give off or emit steam or vapor. 2. To become covered with condensed water vapor: often with *up.* 3. To move or travel by or as by the agency of steam. —*v.t.* 4. To treat with steam, as in cooking, cleaning, etc. —*adj.* Of, driven by, or operated by steam. [OE *stēam*]

steam·boat (stēm'bōt') *n.* A steamship.

steam engine An engine that derives its motive force from the action of steam.

steam·er (stē'mər) *n.* 1. A ship propelled by steam. 2. A vessel for cooking by steaming. 3. A clam cooked by steaming.

steamer trunk A trunk small enough to fit under a berth in a ship's cabin.

steam·fit·ter (stēm'fit'ər) *n.* One who installs or repairs steam pipes. —**steam'fit'ting** *n.*

steam·roll·er (stēm'rō'lər) *n.* 1. A road-rolling machine driven by steam. 2. Any force that ruthlessly overcomes opposition. Also **steam roller.** —*v.t.* 1. To work (a road, etc.) with a steamroller. 2. To suppress; crush. —*v.i.* 3. To work with or as with a steamroller. —*adj.* Resembling the action of a steamroller; aggressive.

steam·ship (stēm'ship') *n.* A large ship propelled by steam; a steamer.

steam shovel A machine for digging and excavation, operated by steam power.

steam turbine A turbine operated by steam power.

steam·y (stē'mē) *adj.* **steam·i·er, steam·i·est** Consisting of, like, or full of steam. —**steam'i·ly** *adv.* —**steam'i·ness** *n.*

stearic acid *Chem.* A white fatty acid found in animal fats and vegetable oils.

ste·a·rin (stē'ə·rin, stir'in) *n. Chem.* 1. A white, crystalline compound obtained from various animal and vegetable fats. 2. Stearic acid. 3. Fat in solid form. Also **ste'a·rine** (-rin, -rēn; -ēn). [< Gk. *stear* suet] —**ste·ar·ic** (stē·ar'ik, stir'ik) *adj.*

ste·a·tite (stē'ə·tīt) *n.* Massive talc found in extensive beds: also called *soapstone.* [< Gk. *stear, steatos* suet, tallow] —**ste'a·tit'ic** (-tit'ik) *adj.*

steed (stēd) *n.* A horse; esp., a spirited war horse.

steel (stēl) *n.* 1. A tough alloy of iron containing carbon in variable amounts. 2. Something made of steel, as a sword. 3. Hardness of character. —*adj.* 1. Made or composed of steel. 2. Resembling steel, as in hardness. 3. Adamant; unyielding. —*v.t.* 1. To cover with steel; plate, edge, point, or face with steel. 2. To make hard or strong. 3. To make unfeeling; harden. [OE *stȳle, stēle*]

steel band A type of percussion band originated in Trinidad that uses the tops of oil drums hammered out to provide various pitches when struck.

steel blue A metallic blue.

steel engraving 1. The art and process of engraving on a steel plate. 2. The impression made from such a plate.

steel gray A dark shade of gray.

steel·head (stēl'hed) *n.* The rainbow trout, esp. in its migratory stage, highly esteemed as a game fish.

steel wool Steel fibers matted together for use as an abrasive, as in cleaning.

steel·work (stēl'wûrk') *n.* 1. Any article or construction of steel. 2. *pl.* A shop or factory where steel is made. —**steel'work'ing** *n.*

steel·work·er (stēl'wûr'kər) *n.* A worker in a steel mill.

steel·y (stē'lē) *adj.* **steel·i·er, steel·i·est** 1. Made of, containing, resembling, or suggesting steel. 2. Having a steellike hardness: a *steely* gaze. —**steel'i·ness** *n.*

steel·yard (stēl'yärd', -yərd, stil'yərd) *n.* A weighing device consisting of a scaled beam, counterpoise, and hooks. Also **steel'yards.** [after *Steelyard,* formerly the London headquarters for traders]

steen·bok (stān'bok, stēn'-) *n.* A small, fawn-colored African antelope: also called *steinbok.* [< Du. *steen* stone + *bok* buck]

steep[1] (stēp) *adj.* 1. Making a large angle with the plane of the horizon; precipitous. 2. *Informal* Exorbitant; excessive; high, as a price. —*n.* A precipitous place, as a cliff or hill. [OE *stēap*] —**steep'en** *v.t. & v.i.* —**steep'ly** *adv.* —**steep'ness** *n.*

steep[2] (stēp) *v.t.* 1. To soak in a liquid, as for softening, cleansing, etc. 2. To imbue thoroughly; saturate. —*v.i.* 3. To undergo soaking in a liquid. —*n.* 1. The process of steeping, or the state of being steeped. 2. A liquid for steeping something. [ME *stepen*] —**steep'er** *n.*

stee·ple (stē'pəl) *n.* A lofty, usu. tapering structure rising above a church tower. [OE *stīpel*]

stee·ple·chase (stē'pəl·chās') *n.* 1. A race on horseback across country, in which obstacles are to be leaped. 2. A cross-country run. [So called because originally the goal of the racers was a distant church steeple] **—stee′ple·chas′er** *n.* **—stee′ple·chas′ing** *n.*

stee·ple·jack (stē′pəl·jak′) *n.* A man whose occupation is to climb steeples and other tall structures to inspect or make repairs. [< STEEPLE + obs. *jack* workman]

steer[1] (stir) *v.t. & v.i.* 1. To direct the course of (a vessel or vehicle) by means of a rudder, steering wheel, etc. 2. To follow (a course). 3. To guide or be guided. **—to steer clear of** To avoid. **—*n.*** *Slang* A piece of advice. [OE *stīeran*] **—steer′a·ble** *adj.* **—steer′er** *n.*

steer[2] (stir) *n.* A male bovine animal, esp. when castrated; an ox. [OE *stēor*]

steer·age (stir′ij) *n.* 1. The act of steering. 2. Formerly, the part of an ocean passenger vessel in the forward lower decks.

steer·ing committee (stir′ing) A committee, as of a legislature, that arranges the business to be considered.

steering gear The coordinated mechanism that steers an automobile, ship, etc.

steering wheel A wheel turned by the driver of a vehicle, etc., to change its direction.

steers·man (stirz′mən) *n. pl.* **·men** (-mən) One who steers a boat; a helmsman.

stein (stīn) *n.* A beer mug, esp. of earthenware. [< G]

stein·bok (stīn′bok) *n.* A steenbok.

stel·lar (stel′ər) *adj.* 1. Of or pertaining to the stars; astral. 2. Of, pertaining to, or befitting an outstanding performer in any field. [< L *stella* star]

stel·late (stel′it, -āt) *adj.* Star-shaped or starlike. Also **stel·lat·ed** (stel′ā·tid).

St. El·mo's fire (sānt el′mōz) A luminous charge of atmospheric electricity sometimes appearing on the masts of ships, on church steeples, etc. Also **St. Elmo's light.**

stem[1] (stem) *n.* 1. The main body or stalk of a plant. 2. The relatively slender growth supporting the fruit, flower, or leaf of a plant. 3. The long, slender, usu. cylindrical portion of an instrument, drinking vessel, etc. 4. In a watch, the small, projecting, knobbed rod used for winding the mainspring. 5. *Ling.* A root plus a vowel, as the Latin stem *luci-* ("light") in *lucifer* ("light-bearer"), composed of the root *luc-* plus *-i-*. **—*v.* stemmed, stem·ming** *v.t.* 1. To remove the stems of or from. **—*v.i.*** 2. To grow out of; develop or arise: usually with *from.* [OE *stemn, stefn* stem of a tree, prow of a ship] **—stem′less** *adj.*

stem[2] (stem) *Naut. n.* 1. A nearly upright timber or metal piece uniting the two sides of a vessel at the bow. 2. The bow or prow of a vessel. **—from stem to stern** From end to end; thoroughly. **—*v.t.* stemmed, stem·ming** To resist or make progress against, as a current: said of a vessel. [< STEM[1]]

stem[3] (stem) *v.t.* **stemmed, stem·ming** 1. To stop, hold back, or dam up, as a current. 2. To make tight, as a joint; to plug. [< ON *stemma* to stop]

stem·ware (stem′wâr′) *n.* Drinking vessels with stems, as goblets, taken collectively.

stem-wind·er (stem′wīn′dər) *n.* A watch wound by turning the crown of the stem. **—stem′-wind′ing** *adj.*

stench (stench) *n.* A foul odor; stink. [OE *stenc*]

sten·cil (sten′səl) *n.* 1. A sheet of paper, etc., in which a pattern is cut by means of spaces or dots, through which applied paint or ink penetrates to a surface beneath. 2. A decoration, etc., produced by stenciling. **—*v.t.* sten·ciled** or **·cilled, sten·cil·ing** or **·cil·ling** To mark or make with a stencil. [Prob. ME *stansel* to decorate with many colors < L *scintilla* spark] **—sten′cil·er** or **sten′cil·ler** *n.*

steno- *combining form* Tight; narrow; contracted. Also, before vowels, **sten-.** [< Gk. *stenos* narrow]

ste·nog·ra·phy (stə·nog′rə·fē) *n.* The art of writing by the use of contractions or symbols; shorthand. **—ste·nog′ra·pher** *n.* **—sten·o·graph·ic** (sten′ə·graf′ik) or **·i·cal** *adj.* **—sten′o·graph′i·cal·ly** *adv.*

sten·o·type (sten′ə·tīp) *n.* A letter or combination of letters representing a sound, word, or phrase, esp. in shorthand. **—sten′o·typ′y** *n.* **—sten′o·typ′ist** *n.*

sten·to·ri·an (sten·tôr′ē·ən) *adj.* Extremely loud. [< *Stentor,* a loud-voiced herald in the *Iliad*]

step (step) *n.* 1. An act of progressive motion that requires one foot to be thrust in the direction of the movement and to reassume support of the body; a pace. 2. The distance passed over in making such a motion. 3. Any short distance. 4. That which the foot rests upon in ascending or descending, as a stair or ladder rung. 5. A single action or proceeding regarded as leading to something. 6. The manner of stepping; gait. 7. The sound of a footfall. 8. A footprint; track. 9. A patterned combination of foot movements in dancing: the tango *step.* 10. *Music* An interval corresponding to one degree of a scale or staff. **—in step** 1. Walking, marching, etc., in accord with the proper rhythm or cadence, or in conformity with others. 2. *Informal* In agreement or conformity. **—to take steps** To adopt measures, as to attain an end. **—*v.* stepped, step·ping** *v.i.* 1. To move by taking a step or steps. 2. To walk a short distance: to *step* across the street. 3. To move or act quickly or briskly. 4. To pass into a situation, circumstance, etc., as if in a single step: He *stepped* into a fortune. **—*v.t.*** 5. To take (a pace, stride, etc.). 6. To measure by taking steps: often with *off.* 7. *Naut.* To place the lower end of (a mast) in its step. **—to step down** 1. To decrease gradually. 2. To resign from an office or position. **—to step in** To begin to take part; intervene. **—to step on** (or **upon**) *Informal* To reprove or subdue. **—to step on it** *Informal* To hurry; hasten. **—to step out** 1. To go outside, esp. for a short while. 2. *Informal* To go out for fun or entertainment. **—to step up** To increase; accelerate. [OE *stæpe*] **—step′per** *n.*

step- *combining form* Related through the previous marriage of a parent or spouse, but not by blood. [OE < stem of *āstȳpan, āstēpan* to bereave, orphan]

step·broth·er (step′bruth′ər) *n.* The son of one's stepparent by a former marriage.

step·child (step′chīld′) *n.* The child of one's husband or wife by a former marriage.
step·daugh·ter (step′dô′tər) *n.* A female stepchild.
step-down (step′doun′) *adj.* 1. Decreasing by stages. 2. *Electr.* Converting a high voltage into a low voltage, as a transformer.
step·fa·ther (step′fä′thər) *n.* The husband of one's mother, other than one's own father.
step-in (step′in′) *n.* 1. A woman's brief underpants: also **step′-ins′**. 2. A pumplike shoe.
step·lad·der (step′lad′ər) *n.* A set of portable steps, usu. having a hinged frame that may be extended to support the steps in an upright position.
step·moth·er (step′muth′ər) *n.* The wife of one's father, other than one's own mother.
step·par·ent (step′pâr′ənt) *n.* A stepfather or stepmother.
steppe (step) *n.* A vast plain devoid of forest; esp., one of the extensive plains in Russia and Siberia. [< Russian *step′*]
step·ping·stone (step′ing·stōn′) *n.* 1. A stone affording a footrest, as for crossing a stream. 2. A step toward a goal.
step·sis·ter (step′sis′tər) *n.* The daughter of one's stepparent by a former marriage.
step·son (step′sun′) *n.* A male stepchild.
step-up (step′up′) *adj.* 1. Increasing by stages. 2. *Electr.* Converting a low voltage into a high voltage, as a transformer.
-ster *suffix of nouns* 1. One who makes or is occupied with: often pejorative: *songster, prankster.* 2. One who belongs or is related to: *gangster.* 3. One who is: *youngster.* [OE *-estre*, fem. suffix expressing the agent]
stere (stir) *n.* In the metric system, a measure of capacity equal to one cubic meter. [< Gk. *stereos* solid]
ster·e·o (ster′ē·ō, stir′-) *n.* A stereophonic system. —*adj.* Stereophonic.
stereo- *combining form* Solid; firm; hard; three-dimensional. Also, before vowels, **stere-**. [< Gk. *stereos* hard]
ster·e·o·phon·ic (ster′ē·ə·fon′ik, stir′-) *adj.* 1. Pertaining to the perception of sound by both ears. 2. *Electronics* Designating a system of sound reproduction in which two or more receivers or loudspeakers are placed so that the sound is heard from more than one direction. —**ster′e·o·phon′i·cal·ly** *adv.* —**ster·e·o·phon·y** (ster′ē·of′ə·nē, stir′-, ster′ē·ə·fō′nē, stir′-) *n.*
ster·e·op·ti·con (ster′ē·op′ti·kon, stir′-) *n.* A double magic lantern arranged to combine two images of the same object or scene, or used to bring one image after another on the screen.
ster·e·o·scope (ster′ē·ə·skōp, stir′-) *n.* An instrument for blending into one image two pictures of an object from slightly different points of view, so as to produce a three-dimensional effect. —**ster′e·o·scop′ic** (-skop′ik) or **·i·cal** *adj.* —**ster′e·o·scop′i·cal·ly** *adv.* —**ster′e·os′co·py** (-os′kə·pē) *n.*
ster·e·o·type (ster′ē·ə·tīp′, stir′-) *n.* 1. A plate cast in type metal from a matrix and reproducing on its surface the composed type or other material impressed upon the matrix. 2. A conventional expression, mental image, etc.; esp., a biased, generalized image of the characteristics of an ethnic or social group. —*v.t.* **·typed, ·typ·ing** 1. To make a stereotype of. 2. To fix firmly or unalterably. —**ster′e·o·typed′** *adj.* —**ster′e·o·typ′er, ster′e·o·typ′ist** *n.* —**ster′e·o·typ′y** *n.*
ster·ile (ster′əl, *esp. Brit.* -īl) *adj.* 1. Having no reproductive power; barren. 2. Containing no bacteria or other microorganisms. 3. Lacking in vigor or imagination: *sterile* verse. [< L *sterilis* barren] —**ster′ile·ly** *adv.* —**ste·ril·i·ty** (stə·ril′ə·tē) *n.*
ster·il·ize (ster′əl·īz) *v.t.* **·ized, ·iz·ing** 1. To free from infective or pathogenic microorganisms. 2. To deprive of productive or reproductive power. 3. To make barren. Also *Brit.* **ster′il·ise.** —**ster′il·i·za′tion** *n.* —**ster′il·iz′er** *n.*
ster·ling (stûr′ling) *n.* 1. The official standard of fineness for British coins. 2. British money. 3. Sterling silver, as used in manufacturing articles; also, articles made of it. —*adj.* 1. Made of or payable in sterling. 2. Valuable; esteemed. [Prob. < OE *steorra* star + -LING[1]; after a star stamped on some coins]
stern[1] (stûrn) *adj.* 1. Severe; harsh; unyielding. 2. Resolute; stout: a *stern* resolve. [OE *styrne*] —**stern′ly** *adv.* —**stern′ness** *n.*
stern[2] (stûrn) *n.* *Naut.* The rear, or aft, part of a ship, boat, etc. [< ON *stȳra* to steer]
stern·most (stûrn′mōst′, -məst) *adj.* Farthest to the rear or stern.
stern·post (stûrn′pōst′) *n.* *Naut.* The main vertical post of the stern frame of a vessel, to which the rudder is attached.
ster·num (stûr′nəm) *n.* *pl.* **·na** or **·nums** *Anat.* The breastbone that forms the ventral support of the ribs in vertebrates. [< Gk. *stěrnon* breast] —**ster′nal** *adj.*
stern·ward (stûrn′wərd) *adj. & adv.* Toward the stern.
stern-wheel·er (stûrn′hwē′lər) *n.* A steamboat propelled by a paddle wheel at the stern.
ster·oid (ster′oid) *n.* *Biochem.* Any of a large group of fat-soluble organic compounds, including the sterols, the bile acids, and the sex hormones.
ster·ol (ster′ōl, -ol) *n.* *Biochem.* Any of a class of complex, solid alcohols, widely distributed in plant and animal tissue, as cholesterol. [Contr. of CHOLESTEROL]
ster·tor·ous (stûr′tər·əs) *adj.* Characterized by snoring or accompanied by a snoring sound. [< L *stertere* to snore] —**ster′tor·ous·ly** *adv.* —**ster′tor·ous·ness** *n.*
stet (stet) Let it stand: a direction used in proofreading to indicate that a word, letter, etc., marked for omission or correction is to remain. —*v.t.* **stet·ted, stet·ting** To cancel a former correction or omission of by marking with the word *stet.* [< L *stare* to stand, stay]
steth·o·scope (steth′ə·skōp) *n.* *Med.* An apparatus for listening to a patient's breathing, heartbeat, etc. [< Gk. *stēthos* breast + -SCOPE] —**steth′o·scop′ic** (-skop′ik) or **·i·cal** *adj.* —**steth′o·scop′i·cal·ly** *adv.*
ste·ve·dore (stē′və·dôr) *n.* One whose business is stowing or unloading the holds of vessels. —*v.t. & v.i.* **·dored, ·dor·ing** To

load or unload (a vessel). [< Sp. *estivador* < *estivar* to stow < L *stipare* to compress, stuff]

stew (sto͞o, styo͞o) *v.t. & v.i.* 1. To boil slowly and gently; seethe; simmer. 2. *Informal* To worry. —*n.* 1. Stewed food, esp. meat or fish and vegetables. 2. *Informal* Mental agitation; worry. [< OF *estuver*, prob. ult. < L *ex-* out + Gk. *typhos* steam]

stew·ard (sto͞o′ərd, styo͞o′-) *n.* 1. One who is entrusted with the management of property, finances, or other affairs not his own. 2. One who buys provisions, manages servants, etc., in a private residence, club, etc. 3. On an airplane, ship, or bus, one who waits on the passengers. [OE *stī* hall, sty + *weard* ward, keeper] —**stew′ard·ess** *n.fem.* —**stew′ard·ship** *n.*

stewed (sto͞od, styo͞od) *adj.* 1. Cooked by stewing. 2. *Slang* Drunk.

stew·pan (sto͞o′pan, styo͞o′-) *n.* A cooking vessel used for stewing.

stick (stick) *n.* 1. A slender piece of wood, as a branch cut from a tree or bush; a baton, wand, etc. 2. *Brit.* A cane. 3. Anything resembling a stick in form: a *stick* of candy. 4. A piece of wood of any size, cut for fuel, lumber, or timber. 5. *Aeron.* The lever of an airplane by which one controls elevation. 6. A poke, stab, or thrust with a pointed instrument. 7. The control lever of a gearshift, esp. when set vertically. 8. *Informal* A stiff, inert, or dull person. —**the sticks** *Informal* An obscure rural district; the backwoods or country. —*v.* **stuck, stick·ing** *v.t.* 1. To pierce, stab, or penetrate with a pointed object. 2. To thrust or force, as a sword or pin, into or through something else. 3. To fasten in place with or as with pins, nails, etc. 4. To impale; transfix. 5. To put or thrust: He *stuck* his hand into his pocket. 6. To fasten to a surface by or as by an adhesive substance. 7. To bring to a standstill; obstruct; halt: usu. in the passive: We were *stuck* in Rome. 8. *Informal* To smear with something sticky. 9. *Informal* To baffle; puzzle. 10. *Slang* To force great expense, an unpleasant task, etc., upon. —*v.i.* 11. To be or become fixed in place by being thrust in. 12. To become or remain attached to something by or as by adhesion; adhere; cling. 13. To come to a standstill; become blocked or obstructed. 14. To be baffled or disconcerted. 15. To hesitate; scruple: with *at* or *to*. 16. To persist; persevere: with *at* or *to*. 17. To remain firm or resolute; be faithful. 18. To be extended; protrude: with *from*, *out*, *through*, *up*, etc. —**to stick around** *Slang* To remain near or near at hand. —**to stick by** To remain faithful to; be loyal to. —**to stick it out** To persevere to the end. —**to stick up** *Slang* To rob with a gun. —**to stick up for** *Informal* To take the part of; defend. [OE *sticca*]

stick·er (stik′ər) *n.* One who or that which sticks, as: **a** A gummed label. **b** A thorn.

stick·le (stik′əl) *v.i.* **·led, ·ling** 1. To argue about trifles. 2. To insist or hesitate for petty reasons. [ME *stightlen*, freq. of OE *stihtan* to arrange]

stick·le·back (stik′əl·bak′) *n.* A small fresh- or salt-water fish, having sharp dorsal spines.

stick·ler (stik′lər) *n.* One who stickles: usu. with *for*: a *stickler* for details.

stick·pin (stik′pin′) *n.* An ornamental pin for a necktie.

stick shift An automobile gearshift lever mounted on the floor.

stick·up (stik′up′) *n.* *Slang* A robbery done with a gun.

stick·y (stik′ē) *adj.* **stick·i·er, stick·i·est** 1. Adhering to a surface; adhesive. 2. Covered with something adhesive. 3. Warm and humid. —**stick′i·ly** *adv.* —**stick′i·ness** *n.*

stiff (stif) *adj.* 1. Resisting the action of a bending force; rigid. 2. Not easily moved; also, moving or functioning painfully or without suppleness: a *stiff* neck. 3. Not natural, graceful, or easy; constrained and awkward; formal. 4. Not liquid or fluid; thick; viscous. 5. Having a strong, steady movement: a *stiff* breeze. 6. Firm in resistance; stubborn. 7. Harsh; severe. 8. High; dear: a *stiff* price. 9. Strong or potent, as in alcoholic content. 10. Difficult; arduous. —*n.* *Slang* 1. A corpse. 2. A dull or formal person; a bore. 3. A man; fellow: a working *stiff*; also, a roughneck. [OE *stīf*] —**stiff′ly** *adv.* —**stiff′ness** *n.*

stiff·en (stif′ən) *v.t. & v.i.* To make or become stiff or stiffer. —**stiff′en·er** *n.*

stiff-necked (stif′nekt′) *adj.* Not yielding; stubborn.

sti·fle (stī′fəl) *v.* **·fled, ·fling** *v.t.* 1. To keep back; suppress or repress; check. 2. To suffocate; choke. —*v.i.* 3. To die of suffocation. 4. To experience difficulty in breathing. [ME < OF *estouffer* to smother] —**sti′fler** *n.* —**sti′fling** *adj.* —**sti′fling·ly** *adv.*

stig·ma (stig′mə) *n.* *pl.* **stig·ma·ta** (stig′·mə·tə, stig·mä′tə) or (*for defs 1, 2 & 4*) **stig·mas** 1. A mark of infamy, or token of disgrace. 2. *Bot.* The part of a pistil that receives the pollen. 3. *pl.* The wounds that Christ received during the Passion and Crucifixion. 4. Formerly, a brand made on slaves and criminals. [< Gk., pointed end, mark] —**stig·mat′ic** (-mat′ik) *adj.*

stig·ma·tize (stig′mə·tīz) *v.t.* **·tized, ·tiz·ing** 1. To characterize or brand as ignominious. 2. To mark with a stigma. —**stig′ma·ti·za′tion** *n.* —**stig′ma·tiz′er** *n.*

stile (stīl) *n.* A step, or series of steps, on each side of a fence or wall. [OE *stigan* to climb]

sti·let·to (sti·let′ō) *n.* *pl.* **·tos** or **·toes** A small dagger with a slender blade. —*v.t.* **·toed, ·to·ing** To pierce with a stiletto; stab. [< Ital. < L *stilus* writing instrument]

still[1] (stil) *adj.* 1. Making no sound; silent. 2. Peaceful; tranquil. 3. Without movement; motionless. 4. Subdued; soft. 5. Dead; inanimate. 6. Having no effervescence: said of wines. —*n.* 1. *Poetic* Stillness; calm. 2. *Photog.* A single photograph, as contrasted with a motion picture. —*adv.* 1. Now as previously; up to this or that time: He is *still* here. 2. All the same: nevertheless. 3. Even; yet: *still* more. —*conj.* Nevertheless; and yet. —*v.t.* 1. To cause to be still or calm. 2. To quiet or allay, as fears. —*v.i.* 3. To become still. [OE *stille*] —**still′ness** *n.*

still² (stil) *n.* 1. An apparatus for the distillation of liquids, esp. alcoholic liquors. 2. A distillery. —*v.t.* & *v.i.* To distill. [< L *stilla* drop]

still·born (stil′bôrn′) *adj.* Dead at birth. —**still′birth′** (-bûrth′) *n.*

still life 1. In painting, the representation of objects, as tables, flowers, fruit, etc. 2. A picture of such a subject.

still·y (*adj.* stil′ē; *adv.* stil′lē) *adj.* Still; silent; calm. —*adv.* Calmly; quietly.

stilt (stilt) *n.* 1. One of a pair of long, slender poles made with a projection to support the foot some distance above the ground in walking. 2. A tall post or pillar used as a support, as for a dock. [ME *stilte*]

stilt·ed (stil′tid) *adj.* Artificially formal; pompous. —**stilt′ed·ly** *adv.* —**stilt′ed·ness** *n.*

Stil·ton cheese (stil′tən) A rich cheese permeated with a blue-green mold. Also **Stil′ton.**

stim·u·lant (stim′yə·lənt) *n.* Anything that quickens or promotes the activity of some physiological process, as a drug. —**stim′u·lant** *adj.*

stim·u·late (stim′yə·lāt) *v.* **·lat·ed, ·lat·ing** *v.t.* 1. To rouse; excite; spur. 2. *Physiol.* To excite (an organ or tissue) by applying some form of stimulus. —*v.i.* 3. To act as a stimulant. [< L *stimulus* goad] —**stim′·u·la′tion** *n.* —**stim′u·la′tive** *adj.* & *n.* —**stim′u·la′tor** *n.*

stim·u·lus (stim′yə·ləs) *n. pl.* **·li** (-lī) 1. Anything that rouses the mind or spirits; an incentive. 2. *Physiol.* Any agent or form of excitation that influences the activity of an organism as a whole or in any of its parts. [< L]

sting (sting) *v.* **stung, sting·ing** *v.t.* 1. To pierce or prick painfully, as with a sharp, sometimes venomous organ. 2. To cause to suffer sharp, smarting pain from or as from a sting. 3. To cause to suffer mentally; pain. 4. *Slang* To get the better of; also, to overcharge. —*v.i.* 5. To have or use a sting, as a bee. 6. To suffer or cause a sharp, smarting pain. 7. To suffer or cause mental pain. —*n.* 1. *Zool.* A sharp, pointed, sometimes venomous organ, as of a bee, able to inflict a wound. 2. The act of stinging; also, the wound or the pain thus caused. 3. Any sharp, smarting sensation. [OE *stingan*] —**sting′er** *n.* —**sting′ing·ly** *adv.* —**sting′y** *adj.*

sting ray Any of a family of flat-bodied fishes having broad pectoral fins and a whiplike tail capable of inflicting wounds: also called **sting·a·ree** (sting′ə·rē, sting′ə·rē′).

stin·gy (stin′jē) *adj.* **·gi·er, ·gi·est** 1. Unwilling to spend or give; miserly. 2. Scanty; inadequate; meager. [< dial. E *stinge* sting] —**stin′gi·ly** *adv.* —**stin′gi·ness** *n.*

stink (stingk) *n.* A strong, foul odor; stench. —*v.i.* **stank** or **stunk, stink·ing** 1. To give forth a foul odor. 2. *Informal* To be of bad quality. —**to make** (or **raise**) **a stink** *Slang* To protest vehemently. —**to stink out** To drive out by a foul odor. [OE *stincan* to smell] —**stink′ing·ly** *adv.*

stink·bug (stingk′bug′) *n.* A large, flattened bug that emits an unpleasant odor if disturbed.

stink·weed (stingk′wēd′) *n.* Any of various plants having a disagreeable odor, as the jimsonweed.

stint (stint) *v.t.* 1. To limit, as in amount or share; be stingy with. —*v.i.* 2. To be frugal or sparing. —*n.* 1. A fixed amount, as of work to be performed within a specified time. 2. A bound; restriction; limit. [ME *stynten* to cause to stop] —**stint′er** *n.*

stipe (stīp) *n. Biol.* A stalk, stem, or support. [< L *stipes* branch]

sti·pend (stī′pend) *n.* An allowance, salary, or pension. [< L *stips* payment in coin + *pendere* to weigh, pay out]

stip·ple (stip′əl) *v.t.* **·pled, ·pling** To draw, paint, or engrave with dots or flecks. [< Du. *stip* dot] —**stip′pler** *n.*

stip·u·late (stip′yə·lāt) *v.* **·lat·ed, ·lat·ing** *v.t.* 1. To specify as the terms of or condition for an agreement, contract, etc. 2. To promise; guarantee. —*v.i.* 3. To demand something as a requirement: with *for.* [< L *stipulari* to bargain] —**stip′u·la′tor** *n.*

stip·u·la·tion (stip′yə·lā′shən) *n.* 1. The act of stipulating, or the state of being stipulated. 2. That which is stipulated; a condition. —**stip′u·la·to′ry** (-lə·tôr′ē) *adj.*

stip·ule (stip′yōōl) *n. Bot.* One of a pair of leaflike appendages at the base of certain leaves. [< L *stipula* stalk] —**stip·u·late** (stip′yə·lit, -lāt) *adj.*

stir¹ (stûr) *v.* **stirred, stir·ring** *v.t.* 1. To agitate; mix, as soup with a spoon. 2. To cause to move, esp. slightly. 3. To move; bestir. 4. To rouse, as from inactivity. 5. To incite; provoke: often with *up.* 6. To affect strongly; move with emotion. —*v.i.* 7. To move, esp. slightly. 8. To be active; move about. 9. To happen. 10. To undergo stirring. —*n.* 1. The act of stirring, or state of being stirred; activity. 2. General interest or excitement; agitation. [OE *styrian*] —**stir′rer** *n.*

stir² (stûr) *n. Slang* A jail; prison. [Origin uncertain]

stir-fry (stûr′frī′) *v.t.* **-fried, -fry·ing** To cook quickly by stirring in hot oil.

stir·ring (stûr′ing) *adj.* 1. Stimulating; inspiring. 2. Active; lively. —**stir′ring·ly** *adv.*

stir·rup (stûr′əp, stir′-) *n.* 1. An inverted-U-shaped support for a rider's foot, hung from either side of a saddle. 2. Any similarly shaped support, as for a beam. [OE *stigrāp* mounting rope]

stirrup bone *Anat.* The stapes.

stitch (stich) *n.* 1. A single passage of a threaded needle through a material and back again, as in sewing. 2. A single turn of thread or yarn around a needle, as in knitting; also, the loop resulting from such a turn. 3. Any particular arrangement of a thread: a chain *stitch.* 4. A sharp, sudden pain, esp. in the back or side. 5. *Informal* The smallest bit: not a *stitch* of work. —*v.t.* 1. To join together or ornament with stitches. —*v.i.* 2. To make stitches; sew. [OE *stice* a prick, stab] —**stitch′er** *n.*

St. Johns·wort (sānt jonz′wûrt′) A hardy perennial with deep yellow flowers. Also **St.-John's-wort.**

stoat (stōt) *n.* The ermine, esp. in its brown summer coat. [ME *stote*; origin uncertain]

sto·chas·tic (stō·kas′tik) *adj.* Depending

on chance; involving the law of probability. [< Gk. *stochazesthai* to guess at]

stock (stok) *n.* 1. A quantity of something acquired or kept for future use. 2. The total merchandise or goods that a commercial establishment has on hand. 3. Livestock. 4. In finance: **a** The capital or fund raised by a corporation through the sale of shares. **b** The proportional part of this capital credited to an individual stockholder. **c** A certificate showing ownership of shares. 5. The trunk or main stem of a tree or other plant. 6. A line of familial descent. 7. A related group or family, as of languages, people, plants, or animals; also, a type of animal or plant from which others are derived. 8. The broth from boiled meat, vegetables, or fish. 9. Raw material. 10. *pl.* A timber frame with holes for confining the ankles, formerly used in punishing petty offenders. 11. In firearms: **a** The rear wooden portion of a rifle, etc., to which the barrel and mechanisms are secured. **b** The arm on rapid-fire guns, connecting the shoulder piece to the slide. **c** The handle of a pistol. 12. *Often pl.* A wooden support or frame. 13. The handle of certain instruments, as of a whip or fishing rod. 14. A theatrical stock company. 15. A broad, stiffened band, formerly worn as a cravat. **—in stock** On hand and available for sale or use. **—to take stock** 1. To take an inventory. 2. To estimate or appraise. **—***v.t.* 1. To furnish with livestock or with merchandise. 2. To keep for sale. 3. To put aside for future use. **—***v.i.* 4. To lay in supplies or stock: often with *up.* **—***adj.* 1. Kept on hand: a *stock* size. 2. Banal; commonplace: a *stock* phrase. 3. Employed in handling or caring for the stock. **—***adj.* Motionlessly: used in combination: *stock-still* [OE *stocc*]

stock·ade (sto·kād′) *n.* 1. A line of posts, stakes, etc., set upright to form a barrier; also, the area thus enclosed, used as a prison, etc. 2. Any similar area. **—***v.t.* **·ad·ed, ·ad·ing** To surround or fortify with a stockade. [< Sp. *estaque* stake]

stock·breed·er (stok′brē′dər) *n.* One who breeds and raises livestock. **—stock′breed′·ing** *n.*

stock·bro·ker (stok′brō′kər) *n.* One who buys and sells stocks or securities for others. **—stock′bro′ker·age** (-ij), **stock′bro′king** *n.*

stock car An automobile, often a sedan, modified for racing.

stock company 1. An incorporated company that issues stock. 2. A dramatic company that presents a series of plays.

stock exchange 1. A place where stocks and bonds are bought and sold. 2. An association of stockbrokers.

stock farm A farm that specializes in breeding livestock.

stock·fish (stok′fish′) *n.* Cod, haddock, etc., cured by splitting and drying in the air.

stock·hold·er (stok′hōl′dər) *n.* One who holds certificates of ownership in a company or corporation. **—stock′hold′ing** *adj. & n.*

stock·i·net (stok′i·net′) *n.* An elastic knitted fabric, machine-made and used for undergarments, stockings, etc. Also **stock′i·nette′**. [Alter. of *stockinget* < STOCKING]

stock·ing (stok′ing) *n.* 1. A close-fitting woven or knitted covering for the foot and leg. 2. Something resembling such a covering. **—in stocking feet** Wearing stockings or socks, but no shoes. [< STOCK, in obs. sense of "a stocking"] **—stock′inged** (-ingd) *adj.*

stock·man (stok′mən) *n. pl.* **·men** (-mən) 1. One who raises, owns, or has charge of livestock; a cattleman. 2. One who works in a stockroom, warehouse, etc.

stock market 1. A stock exchange. 2. The business transacted in such a place.

stock·pile (stok′pīl) *n.* A storage pile of materials or supplies. Also **stock pile.** **—***v.t. & v.i.* **·piled, ·pil·ing** To accumulate a supply or stockpile (of).

stock raising Breeding and raising of livestock.

stock·room (stok′rōōm′) *n.* A room where reserve stocks of goods are stored. Also **stock room.**

stock-still (stok′stil′) *adj.* Motionless.

stock·y (stok′ē) *adj.* **stock·i·er, stock·i·est** Solidly built, thickset, and usu. short. **—stock′i·ly** *adv.* **—stock′i·ness** *n.*

stock·yard (stok′yärd′) *n.* A large yard where cattle, sheep, pigs, etc., are kept ready for shipping or slaughter.

stodg·y (stoj′ē) *adj.* **stodg·i·er, stodg·i·est** Dull, stupid, and commonplace. **—stodg′i·ly** *adv.* **—stodg′i·ness** *n.*

sto·gy (stō′gē) *n. pl.* **·gies** 1. A long, slender, inexpensive cigar. 2. A stout, heavy boot or shoe. Also **sto′gey, sto′gie.** [Earlier *stoga* < (CONE)STOGA(WAGON), because their drivers wore heavy boots and smoked coarse cigars]

sto·ic (stō′ik) *n.* A person apparently unaffected by pleasure or pain. **—***adj.* Indifferent to pleasure or pain; impassive: also **sto′i·cal.** [< *Stoic*, a member of a Greek school of philosophy founded by Zeno, 4th c. B.C.] **—sto′i·cal·ly** *adv.* **—sto·i·cism** (stō′ə·siz′əm), **sto′i·cal·ness** *n.*

stoke (stōk) *v.t. & v.i.* **stoked, stok·ing** To supply (a furnace) with fuel; stir up or tend (a fire or furnace). [Back formation < STOKER]

stok·er (stō′kər) *n.* 1. One who supplies fuel to a furnace. 2. A device for feeding coal to a furnace. [< Du. *stoken* to stir a fire]

stole[1] (stōl) *n.* 1. *Eccl.* A long, narrow band of decorated cloth worn about the shoulders by officiating clergymen. 2. A long scarf worn about the shoulders by women. [OE < Gk. *stolē* garment] **—stoled** (stōld) *adj.*

stole[2] (stōl) Past tense of STEAL.

sto·len (stō′lən) Past participle of STEAL.

stol·id (stol′id) *adj.* Having or showing little feeling or perception; impassive; dull. [< L *stolidus* dull] **—sto·lid·i·ty** (stə·lid′ə·tē), **stol′id·ness** *n.* **—stol′id·ly** *adv.*

sto·ma (stō′mə) *n. pl.* **sto·ma·ta** (stō′mə·tə, stom′ə·tə) 1. *Bot.* A minute orifice or pore in the epidermis of plants, esp. of leaves and stems. 2. *Biol.* An aperture or mouthlike opening. [< Gk., mouth]

stom·ach (stum′ək) *n.* 1. The pouchlike enlargement of the alimentary canal, situated in vertebrates between the esophagus and the small intestine. ◆Collateral adjective: *gastric.* 2. Any digestive cavity.

3. Loosely, the abdomen or belly. 4. Desire for food; appetite. 5. Any desire or inclination. —*v.t.* To put up with; endure. [< Gk. *stomachos* < *stoma* mouth]

stom·ach·er (stum′ək·ər) *n.* A former ornamental article of dress, worn over the breast and stomach.

sto·mach·ic (stō·mak′ik) *adj.* 1. Of the stomach. 2. Stimulating the activity of the stomach. Also **stom·ach·al** (stum′ək·əl), **sto·mach′i·cal.** —*n.* Any medicine strengthening or stimulating the stomach.

sto·ma·ta (stō′mə·tə, stom′ə·tə) Plural of STOMA.

-stome *combining form* Mouth; mouthlike opening: *peristome.* Also spelled **-stoma.** [< Gk. *stoma* mouth]

stomp (stomp) *v.t. & v.i.* 1. To tread heavily or violently (upon); press down. 2. *Dial.* To stamp. —*n.* A dance involving a heavy and lively step. [Var. of STAMP]

-stomy *combining form Surg.* An operation to form an artificial opening for or into (a specified organ or part): *colostomy.* [< Gk. *stoma* mouth]

stone (stōn) *n.* 1. The hard mineral or earthy matter of which rock is composed. 2. A small piece of rock, as a pebble. 3. A precious stone; gem. 4. Anything resembling a stone in shape or hardness: a *hailstone.* 5. A gravestone. 6. A grindstone or millstone. 7. *Pathol.* A stony concretion in the bladder, or a disease characterized by such concretions. 8. *Bot.* The hard covering of the kernel in a fruit. 9. (*pl.* **stone**) In England, 14 pounds avoirdupois. —*adj.* 1. Made of stone. 2. Made of coarse, hard earthenware. —*v.t.* **stoned, ston·ing** 1. To hurl stones at; pelt or kill with stones. 2. To remove the stones or pits from. [OE *stān*] —**ston′er** *n.*

Stone Age The earliest known period in human culture, when stone implements and weapons were used.

stone-broke (stōn′brōk′) *adj. Informal* Having no money. Also **ston′y-broke′** (stō′nē-).

stone·crop (stōn′krop′) *n.* Any of various plants having small, fleshy leaves and yellow flowers, often grown in rock gardens.

stone·cut·ter (stōn′kut′ər) *n.* One who or that which cuts and prepares stone.

stoned (stōnd) *adj. Slang* 1. Drunk. 2. Under the influence of a drug, esp. a hallucinogen.

stone-deaf (stōn′def′) *adj.* Completely deaf.

stone·ma·son (stōn′mā′sən) *n.* One who prepares and lays stones in building. —**stone′ma′son·ry** *n.*

stone's throw A short distance.

stone·wall (stōn′wôl′) *v.i.* To obstruct, resist, evade, or delay an action. [Orig. Austral. political slang]

stone·ware (stōn′wâr′) *n.* A variety of very hard pottery.

stone·work (stōn′wûrk′) *n.* 1. Work concerned with cutting or setting stone; also, something made of stone. 2. *pl.* A place where stone is prepared for masonry. —**stone′work′er** *n.*

ston·y (stō′nē) *adj.* **ston·i·er, ston·i·est** 1. Abounding in stone. 2. Made or consisting of stone. 3. Hard as stone. 4. Unfeeling or inflexible. 5. Converting into stone; petrifying. —**ston′i·ly** *adv.* —**ston′i·ness** *n.*

stood (stŏŏd) Past tense and past participle of STAND.

stooge (stōōj) *Informal n.* 1. An actor who feeds lines to the principal comedian, acts as a foil for his jokes, etc. 2. Anyone who is the tool or dupe of another. —*v.i.* **stooged, stoog·ing** To act as a stooge: usually with *for.* [Origin unknown]

stool (stōōl) *n.* 1. A backless and armless seat for one person. 2. A low bench or support for the feet or for the knees in kneeling. 3. The matter evacuated from the bowels at each movement. —*v.i. Slang* To be a stool pigeon. [OE *stōl*]

stool pigeon 1. A living or artificial pigeon attached to a perch to decoy others. 2. *Slang* An informer or spy, esp. for the police.

stoop[1] (stōōp) *v.i.* 1. To bend or lean the body forward and down; bow; crouch. 2. To stand or walk with the upper part of the body habitually bent forward; slouch. 3. To lower or degrade oneself: to *stoop* to cheating. —*v.t.* 4. To bend (one's head, shoulders, etc.) forward. —*n.* 1. An act of stooping. 2. A habitual forward inclination of the head and shoulders. 3. A decline from dignity or superiority. [OE *stūpian*]

stoop[2] (stōōp) *n.* A small porch or a stairway at the entrance to a house. [< Du. *stoep*]

stoop[3] (stōōp) See STOUP.

stop (stop) *v.* **stopped** or (*Chiefly Poetic*) **stopt, stop·ping** *v.t.* 1. To bring (something in motion) to a halt; arrest the progress of. 2. To prevent the doing or completion of. 3. To prevent (a person, animal, etc.) from doing something; restrain. 4. To keep back, withhold, block, or cut off. 5. To cease doing; desist from. 6. To block up, obstruct, close, or clog (a passage, hole, etc.): often with *up.* 7. To close with a cork, plug, or other stopper. —*v.i.* 8. To come to a halt; cease progress or motion. 9. To cease doing something; pause or desist. 10. To come to an end. —**to stop off** *Informal* To cease traveling temporarily before reaching one's destination. —**to stop over** *Informal* 1. To stay at a place temporarily. 2. To interrupt a journey; make a stopover. —*n.* 1. The act of stopping, or the state of being stopped; a halt; pause; end. 2. That which stops or limits the range or time of a movement: a camera *stop.* 3. An obstruction or obstacle. 4. In an organ or harpsichord, a knob controlling a register of pipes or strings; also the register so controlled. 5. *Brit.* A punctuation mark, as a period. [OE *-stoppian*, as in *forstoppian* to stop up]

stop·cock (stop′kok′) *n.* A faucet or short pipe having a valve for stopping or regulating the passage of fluids.

stop·gap (stop′gap′) *n.* Something improvised to fill a need temporarily; an expedient. —**stop′gap′** *adj.*

stop·light (stop′līt′) *n.* 1. The red light on a traffic light; also, the traffic light itself. 2. A red light on the rear of a motor vehicle that shines upon application of the brakes.

stop·o·ver (stop′ō′vər) *n.* 1. A brief visit in a place, esp. while traveling. 2. The act of interrupting a journey without paying

additional fare, as by taking a later train. Also **stop′-off′** (-ôf′).
stop·page (stop′ij) *n.* 1. The act of stopping, or the state of being stopped. 2. An obstruction of some kind; block.
stop payment An order to a bank to refuse payment on a certain check.
stop·per (stop′ər) *n.* 1. Something that stops up or closes, as a plug or cork. 2. One who or that which stops or checks a movement, action, etc. —*v.t.* To close with a stopper.
stop·ple (stop′əl) *n.* A stopper, plug, cork, or bung. —*v.t.* **·pled, ·pling** To close with or as with a stopple. [ME *stoppel*, prob. < *stoppen* to stop]
stopt (stopt) Alternative. chiefly poetic, past tense and past participle of STOP.
stop·watch (stop′woch′) *n.* A watch that has a hand indicating fractions of a second and that may be instantaneously started or stopped, used for timing races, etc.
stor·age (stôr′ij) *n.* 1. The depositing of articles in a warehouse for safekeeping. 2. Space for storing goods. 3. A charge for storing. 4. Memory (def. 6).
storage battery A series of cells that converts chemical energy into electric energy, is a single source of direct current, and is capable of being recharged on reversal of the current.
store (stôr) *v.t.* **stored, stor·ing** 1. To put away for future use; accumulate. 2. To place in a warehouse or other place of deposit for safekeeping. —*n.* 1. A place where merchandise of any kind is kept for sale. 2. That which is stored or laid up against future need. 3. *pl.* Supplies, as of arms or clothing. 4. A place where commodities are stored; warehouse. —**in store** Forthcoming; impending. —**to set store by** To value or esteem; regard. [< L *instaurare* to restore, erect]
store·house (stôr′hous′) *n.* 1. A warehouse. 2. A large fund; reservoir: a *storehouse* of ideas.
store·keep·er (stôr′kē′pər) *n.* A person who keeps a retail store; shopkeeper.
store·room (stôr′rōōm′, -rŏŏm′) *n.* A room in which things are stored, as supplies.
sto·rey (stôr′ē) See STORY².
sto·ried¹ (stôr′ēd) *adj.* Having or consisting of stories, as a building: usu. in compounds: a six-*storied* house. Also **sto′reyed.**
sto·ried² (stôr′ēd) *adj.* 1. Having a notable history. 2. Related in a story.
stork (stôrk) *n.* Any of a family of large wading birds with long necks and long legs. [OE *storc*]
storm (stôrm) *n.* 1. Rain, snow, etc., usu. accompanied by strong wind. 2. *Meteorol.* A wind force of 64–72 miles per hour. 3. A violent outburst, as of passion or excitement. 4. *Mil.* A violent and rapid assault on a fortified place. 5. A violent commotion. 6. A furious flight or shower of objects, esp. of missiles. —*v.i.* 1. To blow with violence; rain, snow, hail, etc., heavily: used impersonally: It *stormed* all day. 2. To be very angry; rage. 3. To move or rush with violence or rage. —*v.t.* 4. *Mil.* To take or try to take by storm. [OE]
storm·bound (stôrm′bound′) *adj.* Delayed, confined, or isolated because of a storm.
storm center *Meteorol.* The center or area of lowest pressure and comparative calm in a cyclonic storm.
storm door An outer door for added protection during storms or for greater insulation.
storm trooper In Germany, 1932–45, a member of the Nazi party militia unit. [< G *Sturmabteilung* storm detachment]
storm warning A signal, as a flag or light, used to warn mariners of coming storm. Also **storm signal.**
storm window An extra window outside the ordinary one as a protection against storms or for greater insulation.
storm·y (stôr′mē) *adj.* **storm·i·er, storm·i·est** 1. Characterized by or subject to storms. 2. Tempestuous; violent. —**storm′i·ly** *adv.* —**storm′i·ness** *n.*
stormy petrel 1. Any of certain small petrels of the North Atlantic, thought to portend storms: also **storm petrel.** 2. One who portends or brings trouble.
sto·ry¹ (stôr′ē) *n. pl.* **·ries** 1. A narrative or recital of an event or series of events, whether real or fictitious. 2. A narrative, usu. of fictitious events, intended to entertain. 3. A short story. 4. A report. 5. A news article; also, the material for such an article. 6. An anecdote. 7. *Informal* A lie. 8. The plot of a novel, play, etc. —*v.t.* **·ried, ·ry·ing** To relate as a story. [< L *historia* an account]
sto·ry² (stôr′ē) *n. pl.* **·ries** A horizontal division in a building comprising the space between two successive floors. Also, *Chiefly Brit., storey.* [Special use of STORY¹; ? from earlier sense of a tier of painted windows or sculptures that narrated an event]
story line The rough plot of a film, play, novel, etc.
sto·ry·tell·er (stôr′ē·tel′ər) *n.* 1. One who relates stories. 2. *Informal* A liar. —**sto′ry·tell′ing** *n. & adj.*
stoup (stōōp) *n. Eccl.* A basin for holy water at the entrance of a church. Also spelled *stoop.* [< ON *staup* bucket]
stout (stout) *adj.* 1. Strong; sound; tough. 2. Determined; resolute. 3. Fat. 4. Substantial; solid. 5. Muscular; robust. —*n.* A very dark porter or ale. [< OF *estout* bold, strong] —**stout′ly** *adv.* —**stout′ness** *n.*
stout·heart·ed (stout′här′tid) *adj.* Brave; courageous. —**stout′heart′ed·ly** *adv.* —**stout′heart′ed·ness** *n.*
stove¹ (stōv) *n.* An apparatus, usu. of metal, burning gas or oil or using electricity for heating or cooking. [OE *stofa* heated room]
stove² (stōv) Alternative past tense and past participle of STAVE.
stove·pipe (stōv′pīp′) *n.* 1. A pipe, usu. of thin sheet iron, for conducting smoke and gases from a stove to a chimney flue. 2. *Informal* A tall silk hat: also **stovepipe hat.**
stow (stō) *v.t.* 1. To place or arrange compactly; pack. 2. To put away; store. —**to stow away** 1. To put in a place of safekeeping, hiding, etc. 2. To be a stowaway. [ME < OE *stōw* place]
stow·age (stō′ij) *n.* 1. The act or manner of stowing, or the state of being stowed.

2. Space for stowing goods; also, the goods stowed. 3. Charge for stowing goods.

stow·a·way (stō′ə·wā′) *n.* One who conceals himself, as on a vessel, to obtain free passage or evade officials.

stra·bis·mus (strə·biz′məs) *n. Pathol.* A condition in which the eyes cannot be simultaneously focused on the same spot. [< Gk. *strabizein* to squint] —**stra·bis′mic** *adj.*

strad·dle (strad′l) *v.* **·dled, ·dling** *v.i.* 1. To stand, walk, or sit with the legs spread apart. —*v.t.* 2. To stand, walk, or sit with the legs on either side of. 3. To spread (the legs) wide apart. 4. *Informal* To appear to favor both sides of (an issue). [OE *strīdan* to stride] —**strad′dle** *n.* —**strad′·dler** *n.*

strafe (strāf) *v.t.* **strafed, straf·ing** To attack with machine-gun fire from low-flying airplanes. [< G *strafen* to punish] —**straf′er** *n.*

strag·gle (strag′əl) *v.i.* **·gled, ·gling** 1. To stray from or lag behind the main body. 2. To wander about. 3. To occur at irregular intervals. 4. To hang messily or in wisps: said of hair. [? Freq. of obs. *strake* to move, go about] —**strag′gler** *n.*

strag·gly (strag′lē) *adj.* **·gli·er, ·gli·est** Scattered, spread out irregularly, or hanging messily.

straight (strāt) *adj.* 1. Extending uniformly in one direction without curve or bend. 2. Free from kinks; not curly. 3. Not stooped or inclined; erect, as in posture. 4. Fair; honest. 5. Clear; frank; direct. 6. Free from obstruction; uninterrupted; unbroken. 7. Correctly kept, ordered, or arranged. 8. Having nothing added; undiluted. 9. *Slang* Conforming to normal or conventional standards. 10. *Slang* Heterosexual. —*n.* 1. A straight part, line, or sequence. 2. The part of a racecourse between the winning post and the last turn. 3. In poker, a numerical sequence of five cards, or a hand containing this. 4. *Slang* A conventional person. 5. *Slang* A heterosexual. —*adv.* 1. In a straight line or a direct course. 2. Closely in line; correspondingly. 3. At once; straightway. —**to go straight** To reform after a criminal career. [ME < OE *streccan* to stretch] —**straight′ly** *adv.* —**straight′ness** *n.*

straight angle *Geom.* An angle of 180°.

straight arrow *Slang* An honest and proper person. —**straight-ar·row** (strāt′ar′ō) *adj.*

straight·a·way (strāt′ə·wā′, *for adv.* strāt′·ə·wā′) *adj.* Having no curve or turn. —*n.* A straight course or track. —*adv.* At once.

straight·en (strāt′n) *v.t.* 1. To make straight or tidy. —*v.i.* 2. To become straight. —**to straighten out** To restore order to; set right; rectify. —**to straighten up** 1. To make neat. 2. To stand in erect posture. —**straight′en·er** *n.*

straight face A face that betrays no emotion, esp. amusement. —**straight-faced** (strāt′·fāst′) *adj.*

straight·for·ward (strāt′fôr′wərd) *adj.* 1. Proceeding in a straight course. 2. Honest; frank. —*adv.* In a straight course or direct manner. —**straight′for′ward·ly** *adv.* —**straight′for′ward·ness** *n.*

straight man *Informal* An entertainer who acts as a foil for a comedian.

straight-out (strāt′out′) *adj. Informal* 1. Frank; unreserved. 2. Real; genuine. 3. Uncompromising; all-out.

straight ticket A ballot cast for all the candidates of one party.

straight·way (strāt′wā′) *adv.* Immediately.

strain[1] (strān) *v.t.* 1. To exert to the utmost. 2. To injure by overexertion; sprain. 3. To pull or draw tight; stretch. 4. To stretch excessively or beyond the proper limit. 5. To pass through a filtering agent or strainer. 6. To remove by filtration. —*v.i.* 7. To make violent efforts; strive. 8. To be or become wrenched or twisted. 9. To filter, trickle, or percolate. —**to strain at** 1. To push or pull with violent efforts. 2. To strive for. —*n.* 1. An act of straining, or the state of being strained. 2. The injury resulting from excessive tension or effort. 3. Severe mental or emotional tension. [< L *stringere* to bind tight]

strain[2] (strān) *n.* 1. Line of descent, or the individuals, collectively, in that line; race; stock. 2. Inborn or hereditary tendency. 3. *Biol.* A special line of animals or plants bred from a certain species or variety. 4. *Often pl.* A passage of music. 5. Tone, style, or manner; mood. [? Var. of ME *strene*, OE *strēon* offspring]

strain·er (strā′nər) *n.* A utensil or device, containing meshes or porous parts, through which liquids are strained.

strait (strāt) *n. Often pl.* 1. A narrow passage of water connecting two larger bodies of water. 2. A position of perplexity or distress. —*adj.* 1. *Archaic* Narrow. 2. *Archaic* Righteous; strict. 3. Difficult. [< L *stringere* to bind tight]

strait·en (strāt′n) *v.t.* 1. To make strait or narrow. 2. To embarrass or distress.

strait·ened (strāt′nd) *adj.* 1. Contracted; narrowed. 2. Suffering privation or hardship, as from lack of money.

strait·jack·et (strāt′jak′it) *n.* A jacket of strong canvas, for confining the arms of violent patients. —*v.t.* To confine in or as if in a straitjacket.

strait-laced (strāt′lāst′) *adj.* Strict, esp. in morals.

strake (strāk) *n. Naut.* A breadth of planking or line of plating on a vessel's hull from stem to stern. [Appar. akin to STRETCH; infl. in meaning by STREAK]

strand[1] (strand) *n.* A shore or beach, esp. that portion between high and low tides. —*v.t. & v.i.* 1. To run aground. 2. To leave or be left in straits or difficulties. [OE *strand*]

strand[2] (strand) *n.* 1. One of the principal twists or members of a rope, wire, etc. 2. A fiber, hair, or the like. 3. A string of beads or pearls. —*v.t.* To make by twisting strands. [? < OF *estran*]

strange (strānj) *adj.* **strang·er, strang·est** 1. Previously unknown, unseen, or unheard of; unfamiliar. 2. Not ordinary; remarkable; unusual. 3. Of a different class, character, or kind. 4. Foreign; alien. 5. Reserved; shy. 6. Inexperienced; unaccustomed. —*adv.* In a strange manner. [< L *extraneus* foreign] —**strange′ly** *adv.* —**strange′ness** *n.*

stran·ger (strān′jər) *n.* 1. One who is not an acquaintance. 2. An unfamiliar visitor; esp., a foreigner. 3. One unfamiliar with something specified: with *to.*

stran·gle (strang′gəl) *v.t. & v.i.* **·gled, ·gling** To choke to death; throttle; suffocate. [< Gk. *strangalē* halter] **—stran′gler** *n.*

strangle hold 1. In wrestling, a usu. illegal hold that chokes one's opponent. 2. Any influence or power that chokes freedom or progress.

stran·gu·late (strang′gyə·lāt) *v.t.* **·lat·ed, ·lat·ing** 1. To strangle. 2. *Pathol.* To compress, contract, or obstruct, esp. so as to cut off flow of a fluid. **—***adj.* Strangulated. [See STRANGLE.] **—stran′gu·la′tion** *n.*

strap (strap) *n.* 1. A long, narrow, and flexible strip of leather, canvas, etc., usu. having a buckle or other fastener. 2. A razor strop. 3. A piece of material that passes over the shoulder and supports a garment. **—***v.t.* **strapped, strap·ping** 1. To fasten or bind with a strap. 2. To beat with a strap. 3. To embarrass financially. 4. To strop. [Var. of STROP] **—strap′less** *adj.* **—strap′per** *n.*

strap·hang·er (strap′hang·ər) *n.* A standee on a subway or bus; also, one who regularly uses public transportation. [after the overhead straps or handles provided for support]

strap·ping (strap′ing) *adj. Informal* Large and robust.

stra·ta (strā′tə, strat′ə) Alternative plural of STRATUM.

strat·a·gem (strat′ə·jəm) *n.* 1. A maneuver designed to deceive or outwit an enemy in war. 2. A device for obtaining advantage; trick. [< Gk. *stratos* army + *agein* to lead]

strat·e·gy (strat′ə·jē) *n. pl.* **·gies** 1. The science and art of conducting a military campaign on a broad scale. Compare TACTICS. 2. The use of stratagem or artifice. 3. A plan for achieving some end. [See STRATAGEM.] **—stra·te·gic** (strə·tē′jik) or **·i·cal** *adj.* **—stra·te′gi·cal·ly** *adv.* **—strat′e·gist** *n.*

strat·i·fy (strat′ə·fī) *v.* **·fied, ·fy·ing** *v.t.* 1. To form or arrange in strata. **—***v.i.* 2. To form in strata. [< L *stratum* layer + *facere* to make] **—strat′i·fi·ca′tion** *n.*

stra·to·cu·mu·lus (strā′tō·kyo͞o′myə·ləs) *n. pl.* **·li** (-lī) *Meteorol.* Large globular masses of cloud, gray to black in color, disposed in waves, groups, or bands, and often covering the whole sky. [< STRATUS + CUMULUS]

strat·o·sphere (strat′ə·sfir, strā′tə-) *n. Meteorol.* That portion of the atmosphere beginning at a height of about seven miles and characterized by a uniform temperature. **—strat′o·spher′ic** (-sfir′ik, -sfer′-) or **·i·cal** *adj.*

stra·tum (strā′təm, strat′əm) *n. pl.* **·ta** or **·tums** 1. A natural or artificial layer, bed, or thickness. 2. *Geol.* A more or less homogeneous layer of rock. 3. Something corresponding to a layer or grade. [< L]

strat·us (strā′təs, strat′əs) *n. pl.* **·ti** (-tī) *Meteorol.* A low-lying cloud of foglike appearance. [< L, orig. pp. of *sternere* to spread]

straw (strô) *n.* 1. A slender tube of paper, glass, etc., used to suck up a beverage. 2. Stems or stalks of grain, collectively, after the grain has been thrashed out. **—the last straw** The final test of patience or endurance: from the phrase the straw that broke the camel's back. **—to clutch (grasp, catch, etc.) at a straw** To try in desperation any solution or expedient. **—***adj.* 1. Like or of straw. 2. Of no value; worthless; sham. 3. Yellowish. [OE *strēaw*]

straw·ber·ry (strô′ber′ē, -bər·ē) *n. pl.* **·ries** 1. The edible fruit of a stemless perennial herb of the rose family. 2. The plant bearing this fruit. [ME *strauberi*]

strawberry blond A person having reddish blond hair.

straw vote An unofficial vote or poll.

stray (strā) *v.i.* 1. To wander from the proper course; straggle; roam. 2. To wander about; rove. 3. To digress. 4. To deviate from right or goodness. **—***adj.* 1. Having strayed; straying. 2. Irregular; occasional; casual; unrelated. **—***n.* 1. A domestic animal that has strayed. 2. A person who is lost or wanders aimlessly. [< OF *estraier,* ult. < L *extra vagare* to wander outside] **—stray′er** *n.*

streak (strēk) *n.* 1. A long, narrow, somewhat irregularly shaped mark, line, or stripe. 2. A vein, tendency, or trace: a *streak* of meanness. 3. A period of time; a spell. 4. A layer or strip. **—***v.t.* 1. To mark with a streak; form streaks in or on; stripe. **—***v.i.* 2. To form a streak or streaks. 3. To move at great speed. 4. *Slang* To appear naked in a public place. [OE *strica*] **—streaked** (strēkt) *adj.* **—streak′er** *n.*

streak·y (strē′kē) *adj.* **streak·i·er, streak·i·est** 1. Marked with or occurring in streaks. 2. Of variable quality or character. **—streak′·i·ly** *adv.* **—streak′i·ness** *n.*

stream (strēm) *n.* 1. A current or flow of water or other fluid. 2. Anything continuously flowing, moving, or passing, as people. 3. A small river. 4. Anything issuing out or flowing from a source. **—***v.i.* 1. To pour forth or issue in a stream. 2. To pour forth a stream. 3. To move in continuous succession. 4. To float with a waving movement, as a flag. **—***v.t.* 5. To emit or exude. [OE *strēam*]

stream·er (strē′mər) *n.* 1. Something that streams forth. 2. An object that waves or hangs extended, as a long, narrow flag.

stream·let (strēm′lit) *n.* A small stream.

stream·line (strēm′līn′) *n.* Any shape or contour designed to offer minimum resistance to a flow of air or water. **—***v.t.* **·lined, ·lin·ing** 1. To design with a streamlined shape. 2. To make more simple, efficient, or up to date. **—stream′lined′** *adj.*

street (strēt) *n.* A public way in a city or town, with buildings on one or both sides; also, the roadway for vehicles, between sidewalks. [OE *strǣt* < LL *strata* (*via*) paved (road)]

street·car (strēt′kär′) *n.* A public passenger car of an electric railway that runs on tracks set into the streets: also called *trolley, trolley car*; *Brit., tram.*

street people People without permanent homes, who spend much of their time on city streets.

street·walk·er (strēt′wô′kər) *n.* A prostitute who solicits in the streets. **—street′walk′ing** *n. & adj.*

strength (strengkth, strength) *n.* 1. Muscular power; vigor. 2. Durability; toughness.

3. Power in general, or a source of power. 4. Vigor or force. 5. Available numerical force in a military unit or other organization. 6. The degree of intensity or concentration, as of a color, odor, etc. 7. Potency, as of a drug. **—on the strength of** Based on or dependent on. [OE *strengthu* < *strang* strong]

strength·en (strengk′thən, streng′-) *v.t.* 1. To make strong or stronger. 2. To encourage; hearten. *—v.i.* 3. To become or grow strong or stronger. **—strength′en·er** *n.*

stren·u·ous (stren′yoo͞·əs) *adj.* 1. Necessitating or characterized by strong effort or exertion. 2. Vigorously active or zealous. [< L *strenuus*] **—stren′u·ous·ly** *adv.* **—stren′u·ous·ness** *n.*

strep·to·coc·cus (strep′tə·kok′əs) *n. pl.* **·coc·ci** (-kok′sī) Any of a genus of ovoid or spherical bacteria, grouped in long chains, including species causing many diseases. [< Gk. *streptos* twisted + COCCUS] **—strep′to·coc′cal, strep′to·coc′cic** (-kok′sik) *adj.*

strep·to·my·cin (strep′tō·mī′sin) *n.* A potent antibiotic isolated from a moldlike organism. [< Gk. *streptos* twisted + *mykēs* fungus]

stress (stres) *n.* 1. Special weight, importance, or significance. 2. *Mech.* **a** Force exerted between contiguous portions of a body or bodies and usu. expressed in pounds per square inch. **b** A force that tends to produce deformation in a body. 3. Influence exerted forcibly; pressure. 4. Emotional or intellectual strain or tension. 5. The relative force with which a sound, syllable, or word is uttered. *—v.t.* 1. To subject to stress. 2. To put emphasis on; accent. [< L *strictus*, pp. of *stringere* to draw tight] **—stress′ful** *adj.* **—stress′less** *adj.*

-stress *suffix of nouns* Feminine form of -STER: *songstress*

stretch (strech) *v.t.* 1. To extend or draw out, as to full length or width. 2. To extend or draw out forcibly, esp. beyond normal or proper limits. 3. To put forth, hold out, or extend: often with *out*. *—v.i.* 4. To reach or extend over an area or from one place to another. 5. To become extended, esp. beyond normal or proper limits. 6. To extend one's body or limbs, esp. to relieve stiffness. 7. To lie down: usu. with *out*. *—n.* 1. The act of stretching, or the state of being stretched. 2. Extent or reach of that which stretches. 3. A continuous extent of space or time. 4. In racing, the part of the track that, being straight, permits the greatest speed. 5. *Slang* A term of imprisonment. *—adj.* Capable of stretching or of being stretched; elastic. [OE *streccan*] **—stretch′a·ble** *adj.*

stretch·er (strech′ər) *n.* 1. One who or that which stretches. 2. Any device for stretching, as for loosening the fit of shoes, for drying curtains, etc. 3. A frame, as of stretched canvas, for carrying the wounded, sick, or dead; a litter.

strew (stroo͞) *v.t.* **strewed, strewed** or **strewn, strew·ing** 1. To spread about loosely or at random; scatter; sprinkle. 2. To cover with something scattered or sprinkled. 3. To be scattered over (a surface). [OE *strewian*]

stri·a (strī′ə) *n. pl.* **stri·ae** (strī·ē) 1. A distinctive streak, stripe, or band. 2. *Geol.* A small groove, channel, or ridge on a rock surface, due to the action of glacier ice. [< L, groove]

stri·ate (strī′āt) *adj.* 1. Having fine linear markings; striped or grooved. 2. Constituting a stria or striae. Also **stri′at·ed.** *—v.t.* **·at·ed, ·at·ing** To mark with striae. [< L *stria* groove] **—stri·a′tion** *n.*

strick·en (strik′ən) Alternative past participle of STRIKE. *—adj.* 1. Strongly affected or afflicted; overcome. 2. Wounded, esp. by a missile. [OE *stricen*, pp. of *strīcan* to strike]

strict (strikt) *adj.* 1. Observing or enforcing rules exactly; severe. 2. Containing exact or severe rules. 3. Rigorously enforced and observed. 4. Complete; absolute: *strict* attention. [< L *strictus*, pp. of *stringere* to draw tight] **—strict′ly** *adv.* **—strict′ness** *n.*

stric·ture (strik′chər) *n.* 1. Severe criticism. 2. *Pathol.* An abnormal contraction of some duct or channel.

stride (strīd) *n.* 1. A long and sweeping or measured step. 2. The space passed over by such a step. **—to hit one's stride** To attain one's normal speed. **—to make rapid strides** To make quick progress. **—to take (something) in one's stride** To do or react to (something) without undue effort or disturbance. *—v.* **strode, strid·den, strid·ing** *v.i.* 1. To walk with long steps. *—v.t.* 2. To walk through, along, etc., with long steps. 3. To pass over with a single stride. [OE *strīdan*] **—strid′er** *n.*

stri·dent (strīd′nt) *adj.* Having or making a high, harsh sound; shrill; grating. [< L *stridens, -entis*, ppr. of *stridere* to creak] **—stri′dence, stri′den·cy** *n.* **—stri′dent·ly** *adv.*

strid·u·late (strij′oo͞·lāt) *v.i.* **·lat·ed, ·lat·ing** To make a shrill, creaking noise, as a cicada or cricket. [< NL *stridere* to rattle, rasp] **—strid′u·la′tion** *n.* **—strid′u·la·to′ry** (-lə·tôr′ē) *adj.* **—strid′u·lous** *adj.*

strife (strīf) *n.* 1. Angry contention; fighting. 2. Any contest for advantage or superiority. [< OF *estriver* to strive]

strike (strīk) *v.* **struck, struck** or, sometimes, **strick·en, strik·ing** *v.t.* 1. To come into violent contact with; hit. 2. To hit with a blow; smite. 3. To deal (a blow, etc.). 4. To cause to hit forcibly: He *struck* his hand on the table. 5. To attack; assault. 6. To remove, separate, or take off by or as by a blow or stroke: with *off, from*, etc.: *Strike* it from the record. 7. To ignite (a match, etc.); also, to produce (a light, etc.) thus. 8. To form by stamping, printing, etc. 9. To indicate (a specified time) by the sound of a stroke, bell, etc. 10. To reach, touch, or affect suddenly or in a specified manner. 11. To come upon; find. 12. To occur to: An idea *strikes* me. 13. To impress in a specified manner: He *strikes* me as an honest man. 14. To attract the attention of; impress. 15. To lower or haul down, as a sail or flag. 16. To cease working at in order to compel compliance to a demand, etc. 17. To make; arrive at: to *strike* a bargain. *—v.i.* 18. To come into violent contact; hit. 19. To deal or aim a blow or blows. 20. To make an assault or attack.

21. To make a sound by or as by means of a blow or blows. 22. To ignite. 23. To run aground, as on a reef or shoal. 24. To come suddenly or unexpectedly; chance: with *on* or *upon*. 25. To cease work in order to enforce demands, etc. 26. To snatch at or swallow the lure: said of fish. **—to strike camp** To take down the tents of a camp. **—to strike down** 1. To fell with a blow. 2. To affect disastrously; incapacitate completely. **—to strike dumb** To astonish; amaze. **—to strike home** 1. To deal an effective blow. 2. To have telling effect. **—to strike it rich** *Informal* To come into wealth. **—to strike out** 1. To make a start: *to strike out* on one's own. 2. In baseball: **a** To put out (the batter) by pitching three strikes. **b** To be put out because of having three strikes counted against one. **—to strike up** 1. To begin to play, sing, or sound. 2. To start up; begin. **—*n.*** 1. An act of striking or hitting; a blow. 2. In baseball, a pitched ball counted against a batter, because swung at and missed, not swung at when it is within the strike zone, batted foul, etc. 3. In bowling, the knocking down by a player of all the pins with the first bowl in any frame. 4. In sports, rank or degree of skill. 5. The quitting of work by a body of workers to enforce some demand. 6. A new or unexpected discovery, as of oil or ore. 7. An air attack on a surface target. 8. In fishing, a bite. [OE *strīcan* to stroke, move] **—strik′er** *n.*

strike·bound (strīk′bound′) *adj.* Closed or immobilized by a labor strike.

strike·break·er (strīk′brā′kər) *n.* One who takes the place of a worker on strike or who supplies workers to take the place of strikers. **—strike′break′ing** *n.*

strike·out (strīk′out′) *n.* In baseball, an instance of striking out.

strik·ing (strī′king) *adj.* Notable; impressive. **—strik′ing·ly** *adv.*

string (string) *n.* 1. A slender line or strip, as of twine, cloth, leather, etc., thinner than a cord and thicker than a thread. 2. The cord of a bow. 3. Prepared wire or catgut for musical instruments. 4. A stringlike organ, object, or formation. 5. A connected series or succession, as of things, acts, or events, sometimes implying unusual length: a *string* of lies. 6. *pl.* Stringed instruments, esp. those of an orchestra. 7. *Usu. pl. Informal* A condition or restriction attached to a proposition or gift. **—to pull strings** To manipulate or influence others to gain some advantage. **—*v.* strung, string·ing** *v.t.* 1. To thread, as beads, on or as on a string. 2. To fit with a string or strings, as a guitar. 3. To cover, drape, or adorn with things attached to a string or strings. 4. To arrange or extend in a line or series. 5. To remove the strings from (vegetables). 6. *Informal* To hang: usu. with *up*. 7. *Slang* To fool or deceive; hoax: often with *along*. **—*v.i.*** 8. To extend, stretch, or proceed in a line or series. 9. To form into strings. **—to string along with** To accompany or follow. [OE *streng*]

string bean 1. Any of several varieties of beans cultivated for their edible pods. 2. The pod itself.

string·board (string′bôrd′) *n. Archit.* A board serving as a support for the ends of steps in a staircase.

string·course (string′kôrs′) *n. Archit.* A horizontal molding or ornamental course, usu. projecting along the face of a building.

stringed instrument (stringd) A musical instrument that produces its tones by means of one or more vibrating strings, as a violin, cello, etc. Also **string instrument.**

strin·gent (strin′jənt) *adj.* 1. Severe, as regulations; strict. 2. Hampered by obstructions or scarcity of money. 3. Convincing; forcible. [< L *stringens, -entis*, ppr. of *stringere* to draw tight] **—strin′gen·cy** *n.* **—strin′gent·ly** *adv.*

string·er (string′ər) *n.* 1. *Archit.* A heavy timber, generally horizontal, supporting other members of a structure. 2. A lengthwise timber on which rails are laid. 3. *Informal* One having a specified rank, as on a team: a second *stringer*. 4. An out-of-town correspondent for a newspaper, wire service, etc., usu. working part-time.

string·piece (string′pēs′) *n. Archit.* A heavy supporting timber forming the margin or edge of a framework.

string tie A very narrow necktie, often tied in a bow with the ends hanging loosely.

string·y (string′ē) *adj.* **string·i·er, string·i·est** 1. Containing fibrous strings. 2. Forming in strings; ropy. 3. Having tough sinews. **—string′i·ly** *adv.* **—string′i·ness** *n.*

strip[1] (strip) *n.* 1. A narrow piece, comparatively long, as of cloth, tape, land, etc. 2. An airstrip or landing strip. **—*v.t.* stripped, strip·ping** To cut or tear into strips. [? < MLG *strippe* strap]

strip[2] (strip) *v.* **stripped** (*Rare* **stript**), **strip·ping** *v.t.* 1. To pull the covering, clothing, etc., from. 2. To pull off (the covering or clothing). 3. To rob or plunder. 4. To make bare or empty. 5. To remove; take away; divest. 6. *Mech.* To damage or break the teeth, thread, etc., of (a gear, bolt, or the like). **—*v.i.*** 7. To remove one's clothing; undress; also, to do a striptease. [ME < OE *-strīepan*, as in *bestrīepan* to despoil, plunder] **—strip′per** *n.*

stripe[1] (strīp) *n.* 1. A line, band, or strip of color, material, etc., different from that of the adjacent surface. 2. A piece of material or braid on the sleeve of a uniform to indicate rank, service, etc.; a chevron. **—*v.t.* striped, strip·ing** To mark with a stripe or stripes. [< MDu.] **—striped** *adj.* **—strip′y** *adj.* **strip·i·er, strip·i·est**

stripe[2] (strīp) *n.* A blow struck with a whip or rod, as in flogging. [Prob. < LG]

strip·ling (strip′ling) *n.* A youth.

strip mining The mining of coal by stripping off soil, etc., to expose and dig out a vein.

strip·tease (strip′tēz′) *n.* In burlesque, etc., a gradual disrobing. Also **strip tease.** **—strip′teas′er** *n.*

strive (strīv) *v.i.* **strove** or, sometimes, **strived, striv·en** (striv′ən) or **strived, striv·ing** 1. To make earnest effort. 2. To engage in strife. [< OF *estriver*, prob. < Gmc.] **—striv′er** *n.*

strobe (strōb) *n. Informal* 1. An electronic tube producing intense, very brief flashes of light: also **strobe light.** 2. A stroboscope.

stro·bo·scope (strō′bə·skōp, strob′ə-) *n.* An instrument for observing the motion of a body or object by rendering it visible only at intervals or at certain points of its path. [< Gk. *strobos* twisting + -SCOPE] **—stro′·bo·scop′ic** (-skop′ik) or **·i·cal** *adj.* **—stro·bos′co·py** (-bos′kə·pē) *n.*

strode (strōd) Past tense of STRIDE.

stroke (strōk) *n.* 1. The act or movement of striking; impact. 2. A single movement, as of the hand, arm, or some instrument, by which something is made or done. 3. A blow, or any ill effect caused as if by a blow. 4. An attack of paralysis or apoplexy. 5. A blow or the sound of a blow of a striking mechanism, as of a clock. 6. A sudden or brilliant act; coup: a *stroke* of wit. 7. A pulsation, as of the heart. 8. A mark or dash of a pen or tool. 9. A light, caressing movement; a stroking. 10. A manner or technique of swimming. **—***v.t.* **stroked, strok·ing** 1. To pass the hand over gently or caressingly, or with light pressure. 2. To hit with a stroke of the arm, propel with a racket, etc. [ME < OE *strācian* to strike]

stroll (strōl) *v.i.* 1. To walk in a leisurely or idle manner; saunter. 2. To wander; roam. **—***v.t.* 3. To walk idly or wander over or through. [Origin uncertain] **—stroll** *n.*

stroll·er (strō′lər) *n.* 1. One who strolls. 2. A light, often collapsible carriage in which a small child may sit upright.

strong (strông) *adj.* 1. Powerful in physique; muscular; vigorous. 2. Healthy; robust. 3. Morally powerful; firm; resolute; courageous. 4. Especially competent or able in a specified subject or field: *strong* in mathematics. 5. Solidly made or constituted. 6. Powerful as a combatant. 7. Having (a specified) numerical force: an army 20,000 *strong*. 8. Capable of exerting influence, authority, etc.: a *strong* government. 9. Sound: a *strong* bank. 10. Powerful in effect: *strong* poison. 11. Concentrated; not diluted or weak: *strong* coffee. 12. Intense in degree or quality; not faint or mild. 13. Firm; forceful: a *strong* voice. 14. Distinct; marked: a *strong* resemblance. 15. Moving with great force: said of a wind, stream, or tide. **—***adv.* In a strong manner; so as to be strong. [OE *strang, strong*] **—strong′ly** *adv.*

strong-arm (strông′ärm′) *Informal adj.* Violent; having and depending on physical power. **—***v.t.* To use force upon; assault or coerce.

strong·box (strông′boks′) *n.* A strongly built chest or safe for keeping valuables.

strong·hold (strông′hōld′) *n.* 1. A strongly fortified place; fortress. 2. A place of security or refuge.

strong·man (strông′man′) *n. pl.* **·men** (-men′) A political leader or dictator willing and able to use extralegal force, esp. military force.

strong-mind·ed (strông′mīn′did) *adj.* Having a determined, vigorous mind. **—strong′-mind′ed·ly** *adv.* **—strong′-mind′ed·ness** *n.*

strong-willed (strông′wild′) *adj.* Having a strong will; decided; obstinate.

stron·ti·um (stron′shē·əm, -shəm, -tē·əm) *n.* A hard, yellowish, metallic element (symbol Sr) of the calcium group. [< NL, from *Strontian,* Argyll, Scotland, where first discovered] **—stron′tic** (-tik) *adj.*

strontium 90 *Physics* A radioactive isotope of strontium.

strop (strop) *n.* 1. A strip of leather, canvas, etc., on which to sharpen a razor. 2. A strap. **—***v.t.* **stropped, strop·ping** To sharpen on a strop. [OE < Gk. *strophos* band]

stro·phe (strō′fē) *n.* A stanza of a poem. [< Gk. *strephein* to turn] **—stroph·ic** (strof′ik, strō′fik) or **·i·cal** *adj.*

strove (strōv) Past tense of STRIVE.

struck (struk) Past tense and past participle of STRIKE. **—***adj.* Closed down or affected by a strike, as a factory.

structural steel Rolled steel of considerable toughness and strength, used in construction.

struc·ture (struk′chər) *n.* 1. That which is constructed; a combination of related parts, as a building or machine. 2. The position and arrangement of parts, as of an organism, molecule, etc. 3. The manner of construction or organization. **—***v.t.* **·tured, ·tur·ing** To form into an organized structure; build; organize. [< L *structus,* pp. of *struere* to build] **—struc′tur·al** *adj.* **—struc′tur·al·ly** *adv.*

stru·del (strōōd′l, *Ger.* shtrōō′dəl) *n.* A kind of pastry made of a thin sheet of dough, spread with fruit or cheese, nuts, etc., rolled, and baked. [< G, lit., eddy]

strug·gle (strug′əl) *n.* 1. A violent effort or series of efforts; a labored contest. 2. Conflict; strife; battle. **—***v.i.* **·gled, ·gling** 1. To contend with an adversary; fight. 2. To put forth violent efforts; strive. [ME *strogelen*] **—strug′gler** *n.* **—strug′gling·ly** *adv.*

strum (strum) *v.t. & v.i.* **strummed, strum·ming** 1. To play (a stringed instrument) with the fingers or by brushing a pick over the strings. 2. To play (a tune) in this manner. **—***n.* The act of strumming; also, a particular rhythmical pattern of strumming. [Prob. imit.] **—strum′mer** *n.*

strum·pet (strum′pit) *n.* A whore; harlot. [? Ult. < OF *strupe* concubinage < L *stuprum* dishonor]

strung (strung) Past tense and past participle of STRING.

strung out *Slang* 1. Addicted to drugs. 2. Incapacitated from drug abuse.

strut (strut) *n.* 1. A proud or pompous step or walk. 2. A member in a framework, designed to relieve weight or pressure in the direction of its length. **—***v.* **strut·ted, strut·ting** *v.i.* 1. To walk with a strut. **—***v.t.* 2. To support with or as with struts. [OE *strūtian* to be rigid, stand stiffly] **—strut′ter** *n.* **—strut′ting·ly** *adv.*

strych·nine (strik′nin, -nēn, -nīn) *n.* A white, crystalline, bitter, extremely poisonous alkaloid contained in certain plants. Also **strych′nin** (-nin). [< Gk. *strychnos* nightshade]

stub (stub) *n.* 1. Any short projecting part or piece, as the stump of a tree. 2. A short or broken remnant, as of a pencil, cigarette, etc. 3. The detachable portion of a theater ticket, bank check, etc. 4. Anything blunt, short, or stumpy, as a pen with a broad point. **—***v.t.* **stubbed, stub·bing** To strike, as the toe, against something hard. [OE *stubb*]

stub·ble (stub′əl) *n.* 1. The stubs of grain stalks, sugar cane, etc., covering a field after the crop has been cut. 2. Any surface or growth resembling stubble, as short bristly hair. [< OF *stuble*, ult. < L *stipula* stalk] —**stub′bled** *adj.* —**stub′bly** *adj.*

stub·born (stub′ərn) *adj.* 1. Inflexible; unreasonably obstinate. 2. Difficult to handle, manage, or work with; resistant. 3. Determined and persistent: *stubborn* fighting. [ME, ? < OE *stubb* stump] —**stub′born·ly** *adv.* —**stub′born·ness** *n.*

stub·by (stub′ē) *adj.* **·bi·er, ·bi·est** 1. Short, stiff, and bristling: a *stubby* beard. 2. Resembling or of the nature of a stub: a *stubby* pencil. 3. Stocky; thickset. —**stub′·bi·ly** *adv.* —**stub′bi·ness** *n.*

stuc·co (stuk′ō) *n. pl.* **·coes** or **·cos** 1. A plaster or cement used for the external coating of buildings. 2. Ornamental work made from stucco: also **stuc′co·work′** (-wûrk′). —*v.t.* **·coed, ·co·ing** To apply stucco to; decorate with stucco. [< Ital.] —**stuc′co·er** *n.*

stuck (stuk) Past tense and past participle of STICK.

stuck-up (stuk′up′) *adj. Informal* Conceited; snobbish.

stud[1] (stud) *n.* 1. A short intermediate post, as in a building frame, to which laths are nailed. 2. A knob, round-headed nail, or small protuberant ornament. 3. A removable button used to fasten a shirt front, etc. —*v.t.* **stud·ded, stud·ding** 1. To set thickly with small points, projections, or knobs. 2. To be scattered or strewn over. 3. To support or strengthen by means of studs or upright props. [OE *studu* post]

stud[2] (stud) *n.* 1. A studhorse or other male animal used for breeding purposes. 2. Stud poker. —**at stud** Of a male animal, used or available for breeding purposes. —*adj.* 1. Of or pertaining to a stud. 2. Kept for breeding: a *stud* mare. [OE *stōd*]

stud·book (stud′bo͝ok′) *n.* An official record of the pedigree of thoroughbred stock.

stud·ding (stud′ing) *n.* 1. Studs or joists collectively. 2. The material from which studs are made.

stu·dent (sto͞od′nt, styo͞od′nt) *n.* 1. One engaged in a course of study, esp. in a school. 2. One who makes a thorough study of a particular subject. [< L *studens, -entis*, ppr. of *studere* to be eager, study] —**stu′dent·ship** *n.*

student body All the students attending a school.

stud·horse (stud′hôrs′) *n.* A stallion kept for breeding. Also **stud horse**.

stud·ied (stud′ēd) *adj.* 1. Deliberately designed or undertaken: a *studied* insult. 2. Lacking freshness, naturalness, or spontaneity. —**stud′ied·ly** *adv.* —**stud′ied·ness** *n.*

stu·di·o (sto͞o′dē·ō, styo͞o′-) *n. pl.* **·os** 1. The workroom of an artist, photographer, etc. 2. A place where motion pictures are filmed. 3. A room or rooms where radio or television programs are broadcast or recorded. [< Ital., a study]

studio couch A backless couch, with a bed frame underneath that may be drawn out to form a double bed.

stu·di·ous (sto͞o′dē·əs, styo͞o′-) *adj.* 1. Given to study. 2. Earnest in effort. —**stu′·di·ous·ly** *adv.* —**stu′di·ous·ness** *n.*

stud poker A game of poker in which one or more cards are dealt face down and the rest face up. [< STUD[2]]

stud·y (stud′ē) *v.* **stud·ied, stud·y·ing** *v.t.* 1. To apply the mind in acquiring a knowledge of. 2. To examine; scrutinize. 3. To give thought and attention to. —*v.i.* 4. To apply the mind in acquiring knowledge. 5. To follow a regular course of instruction. —*n. pl.* **stud·ies** 1. The act of studying; the process of acquiring information. 2. Something to be studied; a branch of knowledge. 3. In art, a first sketch, exercise, etc. 4. A carefully elaborated literary treatment of a subject. 5. A room devoted to study, reading, etc. [< L < *studere* to apply oneself]

stuff (stuf) *v.t.* 1. To fill completely; cram full. 2. To plug. 3. To force or cram; pack. 4. To fill or expand with padding, as a cushion. 5. To fill (a fowl, roast, etc.) with stuffing. 6. In taxidermy, to fill the skin of (a bird, animal, etc.) with a material preparatory to mounting. 7. To fill or cram with food. 8. To put fraudulent votes into (a ballot box). —*v.i.* 9. To eat to excess. —*n.* 1. The material out of which something may be shaped or made; the fundamental element of anything. 2. *Informal* Possessions generally. 3. A worthless collection of things; rubbish. 4. Woven material, esp. of wool; also, any textile fabric. 5. *Informal* Any unspecified or vaguely defined substance, activity, etc. [< OF *estoffe*, ? < L *stuppa* tow] —**stuff′er** *n.*

stuffed shirt (stuft) *Informal* A pompous person.

stuff·ing (stuf′ing) *n.* 1. The material with which anything is stuffed. 2. A mixture, as of bread crumbs with meat and seasoning, used in stuffing fowls, etc.

stuff·y (stuf′ē) *adj.* **stuff·i·er, stuff·i·est** 1. Badly ventilated. 2. Impeding respiration. 3. *Informal* Pompous; smug. 4. *Informal* Old-fashioned; strait-laced. —**stuff′i·ly** *adv.* —**stuff′i·ness** *n.*

stul·ti·fy (stul′tə·fī) *v.t.* **·fied, ·fy·ing** 1. To cause to appear absurd or foolish. 2. To make worthless or ineffectual. [< L *stultus* foolish + *facere* to make] —**stul′ti·fi·ca′tion** *n.* —**stul′ti·fi′er** *n.*

stum·ble (stum′bəl) *v.i.* **·bled, ·bling** 1. To miss one's step in walking or running; trip. 2. To walk or proceed unsteadily. 3. To speak, read, etc., falteringly. 4. To happen upon something by chance: with *across, on, upon*, etc. —*n.* 1. The act of stumbling. 2. A blunder; false step. [Cf. Norw. *stumla* to stumble in the dark] —**stum′bler** *n.* —**stum′bling·ly** *adv.*

stumbling block Any obstacle, hindrance, or impediment.

stump (stump) *n.* 1. That portion of the trunk of a tree left standing when the tree is felled. 2. The part of anything, as of a limb, tooth, pencil, etc., that remains when the main part has been removed; a stub. 3. *pl. Informal* The legs. 4. A place or platform from which a political speech is made. 5. A heavy step; a clump; also, the sound made by such a step. **—to take the stump** To electioneer in a political campaign. —*adj.* 1. Being or resembling a stump; stumpy. 2. Of or pertaining to political oratory or campaigning: a *stump* speaker. —*v.t.* 1. To reduce to a stump. 2. To remove stumps from (land). 3. To canvass (a district) by making political speeches. 4. *Informal* To bring to a halt by real or fancied obstacles; baffle. —*v.i.* 5. To walk heavily, noisily, and stiffly. 6. To go about making political speeches. [< MLG] **—stump′er** *n.*

stump·y (stum′pē) *adj.* **stump·i·er, stump·i·est** 1. Full of stumps. 2. Like a stump; short and thick. **—stump′i·ness** *n.*

stun (stun) *v.t.* **stunned, stun·ning** 1. To render unconscious or incapable of action by a blow, fall, etc. 2. To astonish; astound. 3. To daze or overwhelm by loud or explosive noise. [< L *ex-* thoroughly + *tonare* to thunder, crash]

stung (stung) Past tense and past participle of STING.

stunk (stungk) Past participle and alternative past tense of STINK.

stun·ner (stun′ər) *n.* 1. One who or that which stuns. 2. *Informal* A person of extraordinary beauty, etc.

stun·ning (stun′ing) *adj.* 1. Rendering unconscious. 2. *Informal* Impressively beautiful, etc. **—stun′ning·ly** *adv.*

stunt[1] (stunt) *v.t.* To check the natural development of; dwarf; cramp. —*n.* A check in growth, progress, or development. [OE *stunt* dull, foolish] **—stunt′ed** *adj.* **—stunt′ed·ness** *n.*

stunt[2] (stunt) *Informal n.* A sensational feat, as of bodily skill. —*v.i.* To perform stunts. [? < G *stunde* lesson]

stunt man In motion pictures, one employed to substitute for an actor in dangerous acts or situations.

stu·pe·fy (stōō′pə·fī, styōō′-) *v.t.* **·fied, ·fy·ing** 1. To dull the senses or faculties of; stun or make numb. 2. To amaze; astound. [< L *stupere* to be stunned + *facere* to make] **—stu′pe·fac′tion** (-fak′shən) *n.* **—stu′pe·fied** *adj.* **—stu′pe·fi′er** *n.* **—stu′pe·fy′ing·ly** *adv.*

stu·pen·dous (stōō·pen′dəs, styōō-) *adj.* 1. Highly impressive; astonishing. 2. Of prodigious size or bulk. [< L *stupere* to be stunned] **—stu·pen′dous·ly** *adv.* **—stu·pen′dous·ness** *n.*

stu·pid (stōō′pid, styōō′-) *adj.* 1. Very slow of apprehension or understanding. 2. Marked by or resulting from lack of understanding, reason, or wit; senseless. 3. Tedious; dull. —*n. Informal* A stupid person. [< L *stupere* to be stunned] **—stu·pid′i·ty** *n.* **—stu′pid·ly** *adv.* **—stu′pid·ness** *n.*

stu·por (stōō′pər, styōō′-) *n.* 1. A condition in which the senses and faculties are suspended or greatly dulled, as by drugs or liquor. 2. Mental dullness; stupidity. [< L *stupere* to be stunned] **—stu′por·ous** *adj.*

stur·dy (stûr′dē) *adj.* **·di·er, ·di·est** 1. Rugged and strong; hardy. 2. Firm and unyielding; resolute. [< OF *estourdir* to stun, amaze] **—stur′di·ly** *adv.* **—stur′di·ness** *n.*

stur·geon (stûr′jən) *n.* A large fresh-water and marine fish of northern regions, valued as a source of caviar. [< OHG *sturjo*]

stut·ter (stut′ər) *v.t. & v.i.* To utter or speak with spasmodic repetition, blocking, and prolongation of sounds, esp. those at the beginning of a word. —*n.* The act or habit of stuttering. [Freq. of ME *stutten* to stutter] **—stut′ter·er** *n.* **—stut′ter·ing** *adj. & n.* **—stut′ter·ing·ly** *adv.*

St. Vi·tus's dance (sānt vī′təs·iz) *Pathol.* Chorea. Also **St. Vi′tus′ dance, St. Vi·tus dance.**

sty[1] (stī) *n. pl.* **sties** A pen for swine. —*v.t. & v.i.* **stied, sty·ing** To keep or live in a sty. [OE *sti*]

sty[2] (stī) *n. pl.* **sties** *Pathol.* A small, inflamed swelling of a sebaceous gland on the edge of the eyelid. Also **stye.** [OE *stīgan* to rise + *ye* eye]

styg·i·an (stij′ē·ən) *adj.* *Often cap.* Infernal; dark and gloomy. [< *Styx*, in Greek mythology, a river of Hades]

style (stīl) *n.* 1. Manner of expressing thought, in writing or speaking. 2. A particular or characteristic mode of composition, construction, etc.: the Gothic *style.* 3. The manner in which some action or work is performed. 4. A good or suitable manner of expression or performance. 5. A mode of conduct; a way of living: to live in makeshift *style.* 6. A fashionable manner or appearance: to live in *style.* 7. A particular fashion in clothing. 8. The conventions of design, usage, punctuation, etc., observed by a given publisher or printer. 9. A stylus. 10. *Bot.* The prolongation of a carpel or ovary, bearing the stigma. —*v.t.* **styled, styl·ing** 1. To name; give a title to. 2. To make consistent in typography, spelling, punctuation, etc. 3. To give form, fashion, or style to. [< L *stilus* writing instrument] **—styl′er** *n.*

style book A book containing rules of spelling, punctuation, typography, etc., used by printers, editors, etc.

styl·ish (stī′lish) *adj.* Having style or fashionableness in clothes, etc. **—styl′ish·ly** *adv.* **—styl′ish·ness** *n.*

styl·ist (stī′list) *n.* One who is a master of literary or rhetorical style. **—sty·lis′tic** *adj.* **—sty·lis′ti·cal·ly** *adv.*

styl·ize (stī′līz) *v.t.* **·ized, ·iz·ing** To make conform to a distinctive mode or style; conventionalize. **—styl′i·za′tion** *n.* **—styl′·iz·er** *n.*

stylo- *combining form* 1. A pillar. 2. *Bot.* A style. Also, before vowels, **styl-.** [< Gk. *stylos* column, pillar]

sty·lus (stī′ləs) *n. pl.* **·lus·es** (-ləs·iz) or **·li** (-lī) 1. A pointed instrument used for writing or marking on wax, making stencils, etc. 2. The needle of a record player or of a recording instrument. Also called *style.* [< L] **—sty′lar** *adj.*

sty·mie (stī′mē) *v.t.* **·mied, ·my·ing** 1. To block or hinder; thwart. 2. To baffle or perplex. [Prob. use of earlier Scot. *styme,* to be unable to see]

styp·tic (stip′tik) *adj.* Stopping hemorrhage or bleeding. Also **styp′ti·cal.** —*n.* A styptic substance or agent. [< Gk. *styphein* to contract] **—styp·tic·i·ty** (stip·tis′ə·tē) *n.*

sua·sion (swā′zhən) *n.* Persuasion. [< L *suadere* to persuade]

suave (swäv) *adj.* Smoothly pleasant and ingratiating; blandly polite; urbane. [< F < L *suavis* sweet] —**suave′ly** *adv.* —**suave′·ness, suav′i·ty** *n.*

sub (sub) *n. Informal* Short for any of various words beginning with *sub-*, as: **a** A substitute. **b** A submarine.

sub- *prefix* Used to form words meaning: **a** Under; beneath; below: *substratum.* **b** Almost; nearly; slightly: *subhuman.* **c** Lower in rank or grade: *subaltern.* **d** Forming a subdivision: *subsection.* **e** *Chem.* Present (in a compound) in less than normal amount: *subchloride, suboxide.* Also: *suc-* before *c*, as an *succumb*; *suf-* before *f*, as in *suffer*; *sug-* before *g*, as in *suggest*; *sum-* before *m*, as in *summon*; *sup-* before *p*, as in *support*; *sur-* before *r*, as in *surrogate*; *sus-* before *c, p, t*, as in *susceptible, suspect, sustain.* [< L *sub* under]

sub·al·tern (sub·ôl′tərn) *n.* A person of subordinate rank or position. [< L *sub-* under + *alternus* alternate]

sub·a·tom·ic (sub′ə·tom′ik) *adj.* Within the atom: *subatomic* particle.

sub·base·ment (sub′bās′mənt) *n.* A basement situated below the main one.

sub·com·mit·tee (sub′kə·mit′ē) *n.* A committee formed from a main committee for special work.

sub·con·scious (sub·kon′shəs) *adj.* 1. Not clearly or wholly conscious. 2. *Psychol.* Denoting the subconscious. —*n. Psychol.* That portion of mental activity not directly in the focus of consciousness but sometimes susceptible to recall. —**sub·con′scious·ly** *adv.* —**sub·con′scious·ness** *n.*

sub·con·ti·nent (sub·kon′tə·nənt) *n. Geog.* A great land mass forming part of a continent, as India.

sub·con·tract (*n.* sub·kon′trakt; *for v., also* sub′kən·trakt′) *n.* A secondary contract assigning part or all of the work to another party. —*v.t. & v.i.* To make a subcontract (for). —**sub′con′trac·tor** *n.*

sub·crit·i·cal (sub′krit′i·kəl) *adj. Physics* Of or containing fissionable material in a quantity not sufficient to start or sustain a chain reaction: *subcritical* mass.

sub·cu·ta·ne·ous (sub′kyōō·tā′nē·əs) *adj.* Situated or applied beneath the skin. [< L *sub-* under + *cutis* skin] —**sub′cu·ta′ne·ous·ly** *adv.*

sub·di·vide (sub′di·vīd′, sub′di·vīd) *v.t. & v.i.* ·**vid·ed,** ·**vid·ing** 1. To divide (a part) again. 2. To divide (land) into lots for sale. [< L *sub-* under + *dividere* to separate] —**sub·di·vi·sion** (sub′di·vizh′ən, sub′di·vizh′ən) *n.*

sub·due (sub·dōō′, -dyōō′) *v.t.* ·**dued,** ·**du·ing** 1. To conquer; subjugate; vanquish. 2. To bring under control; curb; tame. 3. To reduce the intensity of; soften. [< L *subducere* to withdraw] —**sub·du′a·ble** *adj.* —**sub·du′er** *n.*

sub·fam·i·ly (sub′fam′ə·lē, -fam′lē) *n. pl.* ·**lies** 1. *Biol.* A division of plants or animals next below a family but above a genus. 2. *Ling.* A division of languages below a family and above a branch.

sub·head (sub′hed′) *n.* A heading or title within an article, chapter, etc. Also **sub′·head′ing.**

sub·hu·man (sub·hyōō′mən) *adj.* 1. Less than or imperfectly human. 2. Below the level of *Homo sapiens.*

sub·ja·cent (sub·jā′sənt) *adj.* Situated underneath. [< L *sub-* under + *jacere* to lie] —**sub·ja′cen·cy** *n.*

sub·ject (*adj. & n.* sub′jikt; *v.* səb·jekt′) *adj.* 1. Under the control or power of another. 2. Liable to be affected by: with *to*: *subject* to disease. 3. Likely to bring about or incur: with *to*: *subject* to severe criticism. 4. Dependent on: with *to*: a treaty *subject* to ratification. —*n.* 1. One who is under the governing power of another, esp. of a monarch. 2. A person or thing used or treated in a specified way: the *subject* of an experiment. 3. A topic or theme, as of a discussion. 4. A branch of learning or course of study. 5. *Gram.* The word, phrase, or clause of a sentence about which something is stated or asked in the predicate. —*v.t.* 1. To bring under control. 2. To cause to undergo some experience or action: to *subject* one to torture. [< L *sub-* under + *jacere* to throw] —**sub·jec′tion** *n.*

sub·jec·tive (səb·jek′tiv) *adj.* 1. Of, existing within, or resulting from an individual's own thoughts, emotions, interests, etc.; personal. 2. *Gram.* Designating the nominative case. —**sub·jec′tive·ly** *adv.* —**sub·jec′tive·ness, sub·jec·tiv·i·ty** (sub′jek·tiv′·ə·te) *n.*

sub·join (sub·join′) *v.t.* To add at the end; attach; affix. [< L *sub-* in addition + *jungere* to join] —**sub·join′der** (-join′dər) *n.*

sub·ju·gate (sub′jōō·gāt) *v.t.* ·**gat·ed,** ·**gat·ing** To conquer or make subservient. [< L *sub-* under + *jugum* yoke] —**sub′ju·ga′tion** *n.* —**sub′ju·ga′tor** *n.*

sub·junc·tive (səb·jungk′tiv) *Gram. adj.* Of or pertaining to that mood of the verb expressing possibility, desire, supposition, etc. In the sentence: "If I were you, I'd do it," *were* is in the subjunctive. —*n.* 1. The subjunctive mood. 2. A verb form in this mood. [See SUBJOIN.]

sub·lease (*v.* sub·lēs′; *n.* sub′lēs′) *n.* A lease granted by a tenant. —*v.t.* ·**leased,** ·**leas·ing** To obtain or let (property) on a sublease. —**sub′les·see′** (-les·ē′), **sub·les·sor** (sub·les′ôr, sub′les·ôr′) *n.*

sub·let (sub·let′, sub′let′) *v.t.* ·**let,** ·**let·ting** 1. To sublease (property) to another. 2. To subcontract (work).

sub·li·mate (sub′lə·māt) *v.* ·**mat·ed,** ·**mat·ing** *v.t.* 1. *Chem.* To convert (a solid substance) directly to the gaseous state. 2. *Psychol.* To convert the energy of (instinctual drives) into acceptable social manifestations. —*v.i.* 3. To undergo sublimation. —*n. Chem.* The product of sublimation. [See SUBLIME.] —**sub′li·ma′tion** *n.*

sub·lime (sə·blīm′) *adj.* Noble; exalted; grand. —*n.* That which is sublime: often with *the.* —*v.t. & v.i.* ·**limed,** ·**lim·ing** *Chem.* To sublimate. [< L *sublimis* lofty, prob. < *sub-* up to, under + *limen* lintel] —**sub·lime′ly** *adv.* —**sub·lim·i·ty** (sə·blim′ə·tē), **sub·lime′ness** *n.*

sub·lim·i·nal (sub·lim′ə·nəl) *adj. Psychol.* Perceived below the threshold of consciousness: a *subliminal* image. [< SUB- + L *limen, liminis* threshold] —**sub·lim′i·nal·ly** *adv.*

sub·ma·chine gun (sub′mə·shēn′) A light-

weight automatic weapon fired from the shoulder or hip.
sub·ma·rine (*adj.* sub′mə·rēn′; *n.* sub′mə·rēn) *adj.* Existing, done, or operating beneath the surface of the sea: a *submarine* mine. —*n.* 1. A ship designed to operate below the surface of the sea. 2. Hero (def. 5).
sub·merge (səb·murj′) *v.t. & v.i.* **·merged, ·merg·ing** To plunge or sink beneath the surface of water. [< L *sub-* under + *mergere* to plunge] **—sub·mer′gence** *n.* **—sub·mer′gi·bil′i·ty** *n.* **—sub·mer′gi·ble** *adj.*
sub·merse (səb·mûrs′) *v.t.* **·mersed, ·mers·ing** To submerge. [See SUBMERGE.] **—sub·mer′si·ble** *adj.* **—sub·mer′sion** (-mûr′zhən) *n.*
sub·mis·sion (səb·mish′ən) *n.* 1. The act of submitting or yielding to some power or authority. 2. The act of presenting something for consideration, approval, etc.
sub·mis·sive (səb·mis′iv) *adj.* Yielding; obedient; docile. **—sub·mis′sive·ly** *adv.* **—sub·mis′sive·ness** *n.*
sub·mit (səb·mit′) *v.* **·mit·ted, ·mit·ting** *v.t.* 1. To present for consideration, decision, or approval. 2. To present as one's opinion; suggest. —*v.i.* 3. To give up; surrender. [< L *sub-* under + *mittere* to send] **—sub·mit′tal** *n.* **—sub·mit′ter** *n.*
sub·nor·mal (sub·nôr′məl) *adj.* Below the normal, esp. in intelligence. —*n.* A subnormal individual. **—sub′nor·mal′i·ty** (-mal′ə·tē) *n.*
sub·or·di·nate (*adj. & n.* sə·bôr′də·nit; *v.* -nāt) *adj.* 1. Of a lower class, rank, grade, etc. 2. Unimportant; minor. 3. *Gram.* Of or designating a clause connected with and dependent upon another clause. —*n.* A subordinate person or thing. —*v.t.* **·nat·ed, ·nat·ing** 1. To make subordinate. 2. To hold as of less importance. [< L < *sub-* under + *ordinare* to order] **—sub·or′di·nate·ly** *adv.* **—sub·or′di·nate·ness** *n.* **—sub·or′di·na′tion** *n.* **—sub·or′di·na′tive** *adj.*
sub·orn (sə·bôrn′) *v.t.* To bribe or otherwise influence (a person) to commit a criminal act, esp. perjury. [< L *sub-* secretly + *ornare* to equip] **—sub·or·na·tion** (sub′ôr·nā′shən) *n.* **—sub·orn′er** *n.*
sub·plot (sub′plot′) *n.* A plot subordinate to the principal one in a novel, play, etc.
sub·poe·na (sə·pē′nə, səb-) *n.* A judicial writ requiring a person to appear in court to give testimony. —*v.t.* To summon by subpoena. Also **sub·pe′na.** [< L *sub* under + *poena* penalty]
sub ro·sa (sub rō′zə) *Latin* Confidentially; in secret.
sub·scribe (səb·skrīb′) *v.i.* **·scribed, ·scrib·ing** 1. To agree to receive and pay for issues of a magazine, a service, etc.: with *to.* 2. To give one's assent or approval; support: with *to.* [< L *sub-* under + *scribere* to write] **—sub·scrib′er** *n.*
sub·script (sub′skript) *adj.* Written below and to the right or left. —*n.* 1. A subscript character. 2. *Math.* A subscript character that indicates a specific operation or characteristic. [See SUBSCRIBE.]
sub·scrip·tion (səb·skrip′shən) *n.* 1. An agreement to pay for the receipt of a magazine, book, ticket, etc.; also, the amount to be paid. 2. A fund, as for a charity, raised by contributions.
sub·se·quent (sub′sə·kwənt) *adj.* Following in time, place, etc.; coming after. [< L *sub-* next below + *sequi* to follow] **—sub′se·quence** *n.* **—sub′se·quent·ly** *adv.* **—sub′se·quent·ness** *n.*
sub·serve (səb·sûrv′) *v.t.* **·served, ·serv·ing** To be of help in furthering (a cause, etc.); promote. [< L *sub-* under + *servire* < *servus* slave]
sub·ser·vi·ent (səb·sûr′vē·ənt) *adj.* 1. Being of service; useful. 2. Servile; obsequious. **—sub·ser′vi·ence, sub·ser′vi·en·cy** *n.* **—sub·ser′vi·ent·ly** *adv.*
sub·side (səb·sīd′) *v.i.* **·sid·ed, ·sid·ing** 1. To become calm or quiet; abate. 2. To sink to a lower level or to the bottom; settle. [< L *sub-* under + *sidere* to settle] **—sub·sid·ence** (səb·sīd′ns, sub′sə·dəns) *n.*
sub·sid·i·ar·y (səb·sid′ē·er′ē) *adj.* 1. Giving aid or support; helpful. 2. Subordinate; secondary. 3. Of or relating to a subsidy. —*n. pl.* **·ar·ies** 1. One who gives aid or support. 2. A company owned and controlled by another. [See SUBSIDE.]
sub·si·dize (sub′sə·dīz) *v.t.* **·dized, ·diz·ing** To aid or support with a subsidy. **—sub′si·di·za′tion** *n.* **—sub′si·diz′er** *n.*
sub·si·dy (sub′sə·dē) *n. pl.* **·dies** Financial aid, as that granted by a government to private enterprise or to another government. [< L *subsidium* auxiliary forces, aid]
sub·sist (səb·sist′) *v.i.* 1. To continue to exist; persist. 2. To manage to live: often with *on* or *by*: to *subsist* on vegetables. [< L *sub-* under + *sistere* to cause to stand]
sub·sis·tence (səb·sis′təns) *n.* 1. Continued existence. 2. Means of support; sustenance; livelihood. **—sub·sis′tent** *adj.*
sub·soil (sub′soil′) *n.* The stratum of earth next beneath the surface soil.
sub·son·ic (sub·son′ik) *adj. Aeron.* Having a speed less than that of sound.
sub·stance (sub′stəns) *n.* 1. The basic material of which anything consists. 2. Any type of matter of a specific chemical composition. 3. Density; body. 4. A substantial quality; solidity: There is no *substance* to his remarks. 5. The essential part of anything; essence; the gist. 6. Material wealth; property. [< L *sub-* under + *stare* to stand]
sub·stan·dard (sub′stan′dərd) *adj.* Below the standard or norm; nonstandard.
sub·stan·tial (səb·stan′shəl) *adj.* 1. Solid; strong; firm. 2. Of real worth and importance; valuable. 3. Considerable; ample; great: *substantial* progress. 4. Possessed of wealth and influence. 5. Of or pertaining to substance; material; not imaginary. 6. Nourishing: a *substantial* lunch. **—sub·stan′ti·al′i·ty** (-shē·al′ə·tē), **sub·stan′tial·ness** *n.* **—sub·stan′tial·ly** *adv.*
sub·stan·ti·ate (səb·stan′shē·āt) *v.t.* **·at·ed, ·at·ing** 1. To prove with evidence; verify. 2. To give substance to; embody. [See SUBSTANCE.] **—sub·stan′ti·a′tion** *n.* **—sub·stan′ti·a′tive** *adj.*
sub·stan·tive (sub′stən·tiv) *n. Gram.* A noun, or any word or phrase that functions as a noun. —*adj.* 1. *Gram.* Capable of being used as a noun. 2. Having substance or reality; lasting. [See SUBSTANCE.] **—sub′·**

stan·ti′val (-tī′vəl) *adj.* —**sub′stan·tive·ly** *adv.* —**sub′stan·tive·ness** *n.*
sub·sta·tion (sub′stā′shən) *n.* A branch post office, etc.
sub·sti·tute (sub′stə·to͞ot, -tyo͞ot) *v.* **·tut·ed, ·tut·ing** *v.t.* 1. To put (someone or something) in the place of another. —*v.i.* 2. To act as a substitute. —*n.* A person or thing acting or used in place of another. [< L *sub-* in place of + *statuere* to set up] —**sub′sti·tu′tion** *n.* —**sub′sti·tu′tion·al** *adj.* —**sub′sti·tu′tion·al·ly** *adv.*
sub·stra·tum (sub·strā′təm, -strat′əm) *n.* *pl.* **·ta** or **·tums** 1. An underlying stratum or layer, as of earth or rock. 2. Foundation; basis. [< L *sub-* underneath + *sternere* to strew] —**sub·stra′tive** *adj.*
sub·struc·ture (sub′struk′chər, sub·struk′-) *n.* The groundwork or foundation of a building, etc.
sub·sume (səb·so͞om′) *v.t.* **·sumed, ·sum·ing** To include within a larger class or general category. [< L *sub-* underneath + *sumere* to take]
sub·tend (sub·tend′) *v.t.* *Geom.* To extend under or opposite to, as the side of a triangle opposite to an angle. [< L *sub-* underneath + *tendere* to stretch]
subter- *prefix* Under; less than. [< L *subter* below]
sub·ter·fuge (sub′tər·fyo͞oj) *n.* Any stratagem to avoid unpleasantness or difficulty. [< L *subter-* below, in secret + *fugere* to flee]
sub·ter·ra·ne·an (sub′tə·rā′nē·ən) *adj.* 1. Situated below the surface of the earth; underground. 2. Hidden or secret. Also **sub′ter·ra′ne·ous.**
sub·tile (sut′l, sub′til) *adj.* Subtle. [< OF *subtil*, alter. of *soutil* subtle] —**sub′tile·ly** *adv.* —**sub′tile·ness** *n.*
sub·ti·tle (sub′tīt′l) *n.* 1. A secondary or explanatory title of a book, play, etc. 2. In foreign-language motion pictures, a running translation of the dialogue, usu. appearing at the bottom of the screen.
sub·tle (sut′l) *adj.* 1. Cunning or crafty; sly. 2. Keen; discriminating. 3. Of delicate texture; refined; elusive. 4. Ingenious; clever. [< L *subtilis*, orig., closely woven] —**sub′tle·ness** *n.* —**sub′tly** *adv.*
sub·tle·ty (sut′l·tē) *n.* *pl.* **·ties** 1. The state or quality of being subtle. 2. Something subtle, as a fine distinction.
sub·tract (səb·trakt′) *v.t.* & *v.i.* To take away or deduct, as one quantity from another. [< L *sub-* away + *trahere* to draw] —**sub·tract′er** *n.* —**sub·trac′tion** *n.*
sub·tra·hend (sub′trə·hend) *n.* *Math.* The number to be subtracted from another. [See SUBTRACT.]
sub·trop·i·cal (sub′trop′i·kəl) *adj.* Of or pertaining to regions adjacent to the Torrid Zone. Also **sub′trop′ic.**
sub·urb (sub′ûrb′) *n.* *Often pl.* An area, esp. a residential district, lying on the outskirts of a city. [< L *sub-* near to + *urbs* city] —**sub·ur·ban** (sə·bûr′bən) *adj.*
sub·ur·ban·ite (sə·bûr′bən·īt) *n.* A resident of a suburb.
sub·ur·bi·a (sə·bûr′bē·ə) *n.* Suburbs or suburbanites collectively.
sub·ven·tion (səb·ven′shən) *n.* A grant of money; subsidy. [< L *sub-* up from under + *venire* to come] —**sub·ven′tion·ar′y** *adj.*
sub·ver·sion (səb·vûr′shən, -zhən) *n.* The act of undermining or overthrowing a government or other institution. —**sub·ver′sion·ar′y** *adj.*
sub·ver·sive (səb·vûr′siv) *adj.* Tending to subvert or overthrow, as a government. —*n.* One who subverts a government, etc. —**sub·ver′sive·ly** *adv.*
sub·vert (səb·vûrt′) *v.t.* 1. To overthrow or destroy. 2. To undermine the morals, etc., of; corrupt. [< L *sub-* under + *vertere* to turn] —**sub·vert′er** *n.* —**sub·vert′i·ble** *adj.*
sub·way (sub′wā) *n.* An underground electric railroad, esp. one operating within a large city.
suc·ceed (sək·sēd′) *v.i.* 1. To accomplish what is attempted or intended; be successful. 2. To come next in order; follow. 3. To come after another into office, etc.; be the successor: often with *to.* —*v.t.* 4. To follow. 5. To be the successor of. [< L *succedere* to follow after] —**suc·ceed′er** *n.*
suc·cess (sək·ses′) *n.* 1. A favorable or desired outcome. 2. A person, enterprise, etc., that succeeds. 3. Attainment of wealth, etc. [See SUCCEED.] —**suc·cess′ful** *adj.* —**suc·cess′ful·ly** *adv.* —**suc·cess′ful·ness** *n.*
suc·ces·sion (sək·sesh′ən) *n.* 1. The act of following in order. 2. A series; sequence. 3. The act or right of succeeding another to an office, rank, etc. —**suc·ces′sion·al** *adj.* —**suc·ces′sion·al·ly** *adv.*
suc·ces·sive (sək·ses′iv) *adj.* Following in sequence; consecutive. —**suc·ces′sive·ly** *adv.* —**suc·ces′sive·ness** *n.*
suc·ces·sor (sək·ses′ər) *n.* One who succeeds to a throne, property, office, etc.
suc·cinct (sək·singkt′) *adj.* Brief and to the point; terse; concise. [< L *sub-* under + *cingere* to gird] —**suc·cinct′ly** *adv.* —**suc·cinct′ness** *n.*
suc·cor (suk′ər) *n.* Help or relief rendered to someone in danger or distress. —*v.t.* To assist; help; aid. Also *Brit.* **suc′cour.** [< L *sub-* under + *currere* to run] —**suc′cor·er** *n.*
suc·co·tash (suk′ə·tash) *n.* A dish of corn kernels and lima beans boiled together. [< Algonquian (Narraganset) *misickquatash* ear of corn]
suc·cu·bus (suk′yə·bəs) *n.* *pl.* **·bus·es** or **·bi** (-bī) 1. In folklore, a female demon that has sexual intercourse with sleeping men. 2. Any evil spirit. [< L *sub-* underneath + *cubare* to lie]
suc·cu·lent (suk′yə·lənt) *adj.* 1. Full of juice; juicy. 2. *Bot.* Juicy or fleshy, as the tissues of certain plants. [< L *succus* juice] —**suc′cu·lence** *n.* —**suc′cu·lent·ly** *adv.*
suc·cumb (sə·kum′) *v.i.* 1. To give way; yield. 2. To die. [< L *sub-* under + *cumbere* to lie]
such (such) *adj.* 1. Of that kind; of the same or like kind: *such* people, shirts *such* as these. 2. Being the same as what has been indicated: There are no *such* things. 3. Of extreme degree, size, etc.: It was *such* a load. —**as such** 1. As being what is indicated or implied: An executive, *as such*, must take responsibility. 2. In or by itself: Clothes, *as such*, do not make the man.

—**such as** 1. For example: He raises livestock, *such as* cows and sheep. 2. Of a particular kind or degree: The outcome of the trial was *such as* might be expected. —*pron.* 1. Such a person or thing: The friend of *such* as are in trouble. 2. The same; the aforesaid: *Such* being the case, we agreed. —*adv. Informal* So: He has *such* awful manners. [OE *swelc, swilc, swylc*]

such·like (such′līk′) *adj.* Of a like or similar kind. —*pron.* Persons or things of that kind.

suck (suk) *v.t.* 1. To draw into the mouth by creating a partial vacuum with the lips and tongue. 2. To draw in or take up in a manner resembling this; absorb. 3. To draw liquid from with the mouth. 4. To hold in the mouth and consume: to *suck* candy. —*v.i.* 5. To draw in liquid, air, etc., by suction. 6. To suckle. —*n.* The act of sucking; suction. [OE *sūcan*]

suck·er (suk′ər) *n.* 1. One who or that which sucks. 2. A North American freshwater fish, having thick, fleshy lips adapted for sucking in food. 3. *Zool.* An organ by which an animal adheres to other bodies by suction. 4. *Slang* One who is easily deceived; a gull or dupe. 5. A lollipop. 6. *Bot.* A shoot arising from an underground stem or root. [< SUCK]

suck·le (suk′əl) *v.* **·led, ·ling** *v.t.* 1. To give milk to from the breast; nurse. 2. To bring up; nourish. —*v.i.* 3. To drink milk from the breast: also *suck.* [ME *sucklen*, prob. back formation < SUCKLING] —**suck′·ler** *n.*

suck·ling (suk′ling) *n.* 1. An unweaned mammal. 2. An infant. [ME *soken* to suck + -LING[1]]

su·crose (sōō′krōs) *n. Biochem.* A crystalline disaccharide forming the greater part of the sugar as obtained from the sugarcane, sugar maple, sugar beet, etc. [< F *sucre* sugar]

suc·tion (suk′shən) *n.* 1. The act or process of sucking. 2. The production of a partial vacuum in a space connected with a liquid or gas under pressure. [< L *sugere* to suck]

Su·da·nese (sōō′də·nēz′, -nēs′) *adj.* Of or pertaining to the Sudan or its people. —**Su′da·nese′** *n.*

sud·den (sud′n) *adj.* 1. Happening or come upon without warning; unexpected: a *sudden* downpour. 2. Quick; hasty: a *sudden* decision. 3. Sharp; abrupt: a *sudden* turn in the road. —**all of a sudden** Without warning; unexpectedly. [< L *sub-* secretly + *ire* to go] —**sud′den·ly** *adv.* —**sud′den·ness** *n.*

sudden infant death syndrome See CRIB DEATH.

su·dor·if·ic (sōō′də·rif′ik) *Med. adj.* Causing perspiration. —*n.* A medicine that produces or promotes sweating. [< L *sudor, -oris* sweat + *facere* to make]

suds (sudz) *n.pl.* 1. Soapy water, or bubbles and froth on its surface. 2. Foam. 3. *Slang* Beer. [Prob. < MDu. *sudde, sudse* marsh water] —**suds′y** *adj.*

sue (sōō) *v.* **sued, su·ing** *v.t.* 1. To take action against in a court of law. —*v.i.* 2. To take legal action. 3. To appeal; plead: with *for*: to *sue* for peace. [< AF *suer*, OF *sivre*, ult. < L *sequi* to follow] —**su′a·ble** *adj.* —**su′er** *n.*

suede (swād) *n.* 1. A leather having a soft napped finish. 2. A woven or knitted fabric finished to resemble this. Also **suède.** [< F *Suède* Sweden, in phrase *gants de Suède* Swedish gloves]

su·et (sōō′it) *n.* The hard fat of cattle and sheep, used in cooking and making tallow. [< L *sebum* fat] —**su′et·y** *adj.*

suf·fer (suf′ər) *v.i.* 1. To feel pain or distress. 2. To experience loss or injury. —*v.t.* 3. To experience; undergo: to *suffer* a setback. 4. To bear; endure: to *suffer* more pain. 5. To allow; permit: Will he *suffer* us to leave? [< OF *sofrir*, ult. < L *sub-* under + *ferre* to bear] —**suf′fer·a·ble** *adj.* —**suf′fer·a·bly** *adv.* —**suf′fer·er** *n.*

suf·fer·ance (suf′ər·əns, suf′rəns) *n.* 1. Permission given or implied by failure to prohibit; passive consent. 2. The capacity to endure suffering.

suf·fer·ing (suf′ər·ing, suf′ring) *n.* The state of anguish or pain of one who suffers; misery; hardship. —**suf′fer·ing·ly** *adv.*

suf·fice (sə·fīs′) *v.i.* **·ficed, ·fic·ing** To be sufficient or adequate; be enough. [< L *sub-* under + *facere* to make] —**suf·fic′er** *n.*

suf·fi·cient (sə·fish′ənt) *adj.* Being all that is needful; adequate; enough. [See SUFFICE.] —**suf·fi′cien·cy** *n.* —**suf·fi′·cient·ly** *adv.*

suf·fix (suf′iks) *n. Gram.* An addition to the end of a word to form a derivative of that word. [< L *sub-* under + *figere* to fix] —**suf′fix·al** *adj.* —**suf′fix·a′tion** *n.*

suf·fo·cate (suf′ə·kāt) *v.* **·cat·ed, ·cat·ing** *v.t.* 1. To kill by stopping one's breathing; smother. 2. To stifle or extinguish, as a fire. —*v.i.* 3. To die from suffocation. [< L *sub-* under + *fauces* throat] —**suf′fo·cat′ing·ly** *adv.* —**suf′fo·ca′tion** *n.* —**suf′fo·ca′tive** *adj.*

suf·frage (suf′rij) *n.* 1. The right or privilege of voting; franchise. 2. The act or process of voting. [< L *suffragium* voting tablet, vote] —**suf′fra·gist** *n.*

suf·fra·gette (suf′rə·jet′) *n.* Formerly, a woman who advocated or agitated for female suffrage. —**suf′fra·get′tism** *n.*

suf·fuse (sə·fyōōz′) *v.t.* **·fused, ·fus·ing** To overspread, as with a vapor or color. [< L *sub-* under + *fundere* to pour] —**suf·fu·sion** sə·fyōō′zhən) *n.* —**suf·fu·sive** (sə·fyōō′siv) *adj.*

sug·ar (shŏŏg′ər) *n. Biochem.* **a** A sweet, crystalline carbohydrate, obtained from the juice of various plants, as from the sugarcane, the sugar beet, and the sugar maple. ◆Collateral adjective: *saccharine.* **b** Any of a large class of similar carbohydrates, widely distributed in plants and animals. —*v.t.* 1. To sweeten, cover, or coat with sugar. 2. To sugar-coat (def. 2). —*v.i.* 3. To make maple sugar. 4. To form sugar. [< Arabic *sukkar*] —**sug′ared** *adj.*

sugar beet A sugar-producing species of beet.

sug·ar·cane (shŏŏg′ər·kān′) *n.* A tall tropical grass grown as a major source of sugar.

sug·ar-coat (shŏŏg′ər·kōt′) *v.t.* 1. To cover with sugar. 2. To make appear attractive or less distasteful, as with flattery.

sugar loaf 1. A conical mass of hard refined sugar. 2. A conical hat or hill. —**sug·ar-loaf** (sho͝og′ər·lōf′) *adj.*

sugar maple A maple of eastern North America, yielding a sap from which maple sugar is made.

sug·ar·plum (sho͝og′ər·plum′) *n.* A small ball of candy; bonbon.

sug·ar·y (sho͝og′ər·ē) *adj.* 1. Containing much sugar; sweet. 2. Insincerely or cloyingly sweet. —**sug′ar·i·ness** *n.*

sug·gest (səg·jest′, sə·jest′) *v.t.* 1. To put forward for consideration, etc.; propose. 2. To bring or call to mind, as by association; connote. 3. To give a hint of; intimate: The simple house *suggested* a modest income. [< L *sub-* underneath + *gerere* to carry] —**sug·gest′er** *n.*

sug·gest·i·ble (səg·jes′tə·bəl, sə-) *adj.* 1. That can be suggested. 2. Easily led; yielding: a *suggestible* patient. —**sug·gest′i·bil′i·ty** *n.*

sug·ges·tion (səg·jes′chən, se·jes′-) *n.* 1. The act of suggesting. 2. Something suggested. 3. A hint; trace.

sug·ges·tive (səg·jes′tiv, sə-) *adj.* 1. Tending to suggest; hinting at: with *of*: clothing *suggestive* of another era. 2. Hinting at something indecent or improper; provocative. —**sug·ges′tive·ly** *adv.* —**sug·ges′tive·ness** *n.*

su·i·cide (so͞o′ə·sīd) *n.* 1. The intentional taking of one's own life. 2. Self-inflicted ruin, as in business or politics. 3. One who has taken his own life. [< L *sui* of oneself + -CIDE] —**su′i·ci′dal** *adj.*

su·i gen·e·ris (so͞o′ī jen′ər·is) *Latin* Forming a kind by itself; unique.

suit (so͞ot) *n.* 1. A set of garments consisting of a coat and trousers or skirt made of the same fabric. 2. Any of the four sets of playing cards in a deck, as the spades or diamonds. 3. *Law* A proceeding in a court of law to recover a right or claim. 4. Courtship. —**to follow suit** To do the same as another. —*v.t.* 1. To meet the requirements of. 2. To please; satisfy. 3. To accommodate; adapt. [< L *sequi* to follow]

suit·a·ble (so͞o′tə·bəl) *adj.* Appropriate to a particular occasion, condition, etc.; proper. —**suit′a·bil′i·ty, suit′a·ble·ness** *n.* —**suit′a·bly** *adv.*

suit·case (so͞ot′kās′) *n.* A flat, rectangular valise.

suite (swēt) *n.* 1. A number of connected rooms. 2. A set of matching furniture for a given room. 3. A company of attendants or followers; retinue. 4. *Music* A form of instrumental composition varying freely in its construction. [< F < OF *sieute*]

suit·ing (so͞o′ting) *n.* Cloth for making suits.

suit·or (so͞o′tər) *n.* A man who courts a woman; wooer. [< L *secutus*, pp. of *sequi* to follow]

su·ki·ya·ki (skē·yä′kē, so͞o′kē-) *n.* A Japanese dish of thinly sliced meat and vegetables cooked in soy sauce and sake. [< Japanese]

sulf- *combining form Chem.* Sulfur; containing sulfur. Also **sulph-, sulfo-, sulpho-.** [< SULFUR]

sul·fa drug (sul′fə) *Chem.* Any of a large group of organic compounds which are effective in the treatment of certain bacterial infections.

sul·fa·nil·a·mide (sul′fə·nil′ə·mīd, -mid) *n. Chem.* A colorless, crystalline sulfur-containing compound used in the treatment of various bacterial infections.

sul·fate (sul′fāt) *n. Chem.* A salt of sulfuric acid. Also **sul′phate.**

sul·fide (sul′fīd) *n. Chem.* A compound of sulfur: also **sul′phide.**

sul·fur (sul′fər) *n.* A pale yellow, nonmetallic element (symbol S) existing in several forms, of which the best known is a crystalline solid that burns with a blue flame and a suffocating odor. Also **sul′phur.** [< L *sulfur, -uris*]

sulfur dioxide *Chem.* A colorless, water-soluble, suffocating gas.

sul·fu·re·ous (sul·fyo͝or′ē·əs) *adj.* Of or like sulfur: also **sul·phu′re·ous.**

sul·fu·ric (sul·fyo͝or′ik) *adj. Chem.* Pertaining to or derived from sulfur, esp. in its higher valence: also **sul·phu′ric.**

sulfuric acid *Chem.* A colorless, exceedingly corrosive, oily liquid: also called *oil of vitriol, vitriol.*

sul·fur·ize (sul′fyə·rīz, -fə-) *v.t.* **·ized, ·iz·ing** To impregnate or treat with sulfur: also **sul′phur·ize.** Also **sul′fu·rate** (-rāt). —**sul′·fur·i·za′tion** *n.*

sul·fu·rous (sul′fər·əs, *for def. 1* sul·fyo͝or′əs) *adj.* 1. Pertaining to or derived from sulfur, esp. in its lower valence. 2. Fiery; hellish. Also **sul′phu·rous.**

sulk (sulk) *v.i.* To be sulky or morose. —*n.* *Often pl.* A sulky mood or humor. [Back formation < SULKY]

sulk·y¹ (sul′kē) *adj.* **sulk·i·er, sulk·i·est** Sullenly cross; doggedly or resentfully ill-humored. [? OE (*ā*)*seolcan* to be weak, slothful] —**sulk′i·ly** *adv.* —**sulk′i·ness** *n.*

sulk·y² (sul′kē) *n. pl.* **sulk·ies** A light, two-wheeled, one-horse vehicle for one person. [< SULKY¹]

sul·len (sul′ən) *adj.* 1. Obstinately and gloomily ill-humored; morose; glum; melancholy. 2. Depressing; somber: *sullen* clouds. [Earlier *solein* < L *solus* alone] —**sul′len·ly** *adv.* —**sul′len·ness** *n.*

sul·ly (sul′ē) *v.* **·lied, ·ly·ing** *v.t.* 1. To mar the brightness or purity of; soil; defile; tarnish. —*v.i.* 2. To become soiled or tarnished. —*n. pl.* **·lies** Anything that tarnishes; a stain; spot; blemish. [< MF *souiller* to soil]

sulph- For words and combining forms, see SULF-.

sul·tan (sul′tən) *n.* A ruler or sovereign, esp. of a Muslim country. [< Arabic *sulṭān*] —**sul′tan·ate** *n.*

sul·tan·a (sul·tan′ə, -tä′nə) *n.* 1. A sultan's wife, daughter, sister, or mother: also **sul·tan·ess** (sul′tən·is). 2. A variety of raisin.

sul·try (sul′trē) *adj.* **·tri·er, ·tri·est** 1. Oppressively hot and humid; sweltering. 2. Showing or suggesting passion; sensual. [< obs. *sulter*, var. of SWELTER] —**sul′tri·ly** *adv.* —**sul′tri·ness** *n.*

sum (sum) *n.* 1. The result obtained by addition. 2. The whole amount; entirety: the *sum* of our efforts. 3. An amount of money. 4. A problem in arithmetic. 5. The gist or essence; pith. —*v.t.* **summed, sum·ming** 1. To present in brief; recapitulate: usu. with *up.* 2. To add into one total: often with *up.* [< L *summa* (*res*) highest (thing)]

sum- Var. of SUB-.

su·mac (sōō′mak, shōō′-) *n.* 1. Any of various woody plants or small trees having clusters of small berries and yielding a resinous or milky juice. 2. The poison sumac. 3. The dried and powdered leaves of certain species of sumac, used for tanning and dyeing. Also **su′mach.** [< Arabic *summāq*]

sum·ma·rize (sum′ə·rīz) *v.t.* **·rized, ·riz·ing** To make a summary of; sum up. Also *Brit.* **sum′ma·rise. —sum′ma·riz′er** *n.* **—sum′·ma·ri·za′tion** *n.*

sum·ma·ry (sum′ər·ē) *adj.* 1. Giving the main points; concise. 2. Performed without ceremony or delay: a *summary* execution. *—n. pl.* **·ries** A brief account of the main points; précis; abstract. [< L *summa* sum] **—sum·ma·ri·ly** (sə·mer′ə·lē) *adv.* **—sum′·ma·ri·ness** *n.*

sum·ma·tion (sum·ā′shən) *n.* 1. The act or operation of obtaining a sum; the computation of an aggregate sum; addition. 2. The closing part of a talk or argument in which the main points are reviewed.

sum·mer (sum′ər) *n.* The warmest season of the year, occurring between spring and autumn. ◆Collateral adjective: *estival.* *—v.i.* To pass the summer. *—adj.* Of, pertaining to, or occurring in summer. [OE *sumor*] **—sum′mer·y** *adj.*

sum·mer·house (sum′ər·hous′) *n.* A rustic structure, as in a garden, for rest or shade.

sum·mer·time (sum′ər·tīm′) *n.* The summer season. Also **sum′mer·tide′.**

sum·mit (sum′it) *n.* 1. The highest part; top. 2. The highest degree; maximum. 3. The highest level of government: a meeting at the *summit.* *—adj.* Of or characterized by diplomacy at the highest level. [< L *summus* highest]

sum·mon (sum′ən) *v.t.* 1. To order to come; send for. 2. To call together; cause to convene, as a legislative assembly. 3. To order (a person) to appear in court by a summons. 4. To call forth; arouse: usu. with *up:* to *summon* up courage. [< L *sub-* secretly + *monere* to warn] **—sum′mon·er** *n.*

sum·mons (sum′ənz) *n. pl.* **sum·mon·ses** 1. A call to attend or act at a particular place or time. 2. *Law* A notice or citation to appear in court.

sump (sump) *n.* A small pit for collecting sewage, water, oil, etc. [< MDu. *somp, sump* marsh]

sump·tu·ous (sump′chōō·əs) *adj.* 1. Costly and magnificent. 2. Luxurious; lavish. [< L *sumptus* expenditure] **—sump′tu·ous·ly** *adv.* **—sump′tu·ous·ness** *n.*

sun (sun) *n.* 1. The star that is the main source of radiant energy in the solar system and about which the earth and other planets revolve. ◆Collateral adjectives: *heliacal, solar.* 2. Any star that is the center of a planetary system. 3. Sunshine. *—v.* **sunned, sun·ning** *v.t.* 1. To expose to the rays of the sun. 2. To warm or dry in the sun. *—v.i.* 3. To bask in the sun. [OE *sunne*] **—sun′less** *adj.* **—sun′less·ness** *n.*

sun bath Exposure of the body to the rays of the sun.

sun-bathe (sun′bāth′) *v.i.* **-bathed, -bath·ing** To bask in the sun. **—sun′bath′er** *n.* **—sun′bath′ing** *n.*

sun·beam (sun′bēm′) *n.* A ray of sunlight.

Sun·belt (sun′belt′) *n.* The southern part of the U.S. from Virginia to southern California: also **sun′belt′.**

sun·bon·net (sun′bon′it) *n.* A broad-brimmed bonnet that shields the face and neck from the sun.

sun·burn (sun′bûrn′) *n.* Inflammation of the skin from exposure to the sun. *—v.t. & v.i.* **·burned** or **·burnt, ·burn·ing** To affect or be affected with sunburn.

sun·dae (sun′dē, -dā) *n.* A refreshment of ice cream, crushed fruit, syrup, nuts, etc. [Prob. < SUNDAY]

Sun·day (sun′dē, -dā) *n.* The first day of the week and the Sabbath for most Christians. [OE *sunnan* of the sun + *dæg* day]

Sunday school A school, usu. part of a religious institution, in which religious instruction is given on Sunday, esp., to the young; also, the teachers and pupils collectively.

sun deck A terrace or other area used for sunbathing.

sun·der (sun′dər) *v.t. & v.i.* To make or become divided; disunite; separate. [OE *syndrian, sundrian*]

sun·di·al (sun′dī′əl) *n.* A device that shows the time by the shadow of a pointer thrown on a dial.

sun·down (sun′doun′) *n.* Sunset.

sun·dries (sun′drēz) *n.pl.* A number of small, miscellaneous items. [< SUNDRY]

sun·dry (sun′drē) *adj.* Of an indefinite small number; various; miscellaneous. [OE *syndrig* separate]

sun·fish (sun′fish′) *n. pl.* **·fish** or **·fish·es** 1. Any of various large oceanic fishes having a deep, compressed body. 2. Any of a family of North American fresh-water fishes.

sun·flow·er (sun′flou′ər) *n.* Any of various tall plants with bright yellow flowers; also, the flower of such a plant.

sung (sung) Past participle and occasional past tense of SING.

sun·glass·es (sun′glas′iz) *n.pl.* Spectacles with tinted lenses to protect one's eyes from the sun.

sunk (sungk) Past participle and alternative past tense of SINK.

sunk·en (sung′kən) Obsolete past participle of SINK. *—adj.* 1. Deeply depressed or fallen in; hollow: *sunken* cheeks. 2. Located beneath the surface of the ground or the water: *sunken* treasure. 3. At a lower level: *sunken* gardens.

sun lamp An ultraviolet lamp used for therapeutic treatments or to acquire a suntan.

sun·light (sun′līt′) *n.* The light of the sun.

sun·lit (sun′lit) *adj.* Lighted by the sun.

sun·ny (sun′ē) *adj.* **·ni·er, ·ni·est** 1. Filled with sunshine. 2. Of or like the sun. 3. Bright; genial; cheery: a *sunny* smile. **—sun′ni·ly** *adv.* **—sun′ni·ness** *n.*

sunny side 1. The side facing the sun. 2. The cheerful view of any situation, etc.

sun·rise (sun′rīz′) *n.* 1. The daily first appearance of the sun above the horizon. 2. The time at which the sun rises.

sun·set (sun′set′) *n.* 1. The daily descent of

the sun below the horizon. 2. The time when the sun sets.

sun·shade (sun′shād′) *n.* Something used as protection from the sun, as a parasol.

sun·shine (sun′shīn′) *n.* The shining light of the sun; direct sunlight. **—sun′shin′y** *adj.*

sun·spot (sun′spot′) *n. Astron.* One of many dark irregular spots appearing periodically on the sun's surface.

sun·stroke (sun′strōk′) *n. Pathol.* Illness caused by overexposure to the sun, often marked by fever, convulsions, etc. **—sun′·struck′** (-struk′) *adj.*

sun·tan (sun′tan′) *n.* A bronze-colored condition of the skin, produced by exposure to the sun. **—sun′tanned′** *adj.*

sun·up (sun′up′) *n.* Sunrise.

sup[1] (sup) *v.t. & v.i.* **supped, sup·ping** To take (liquid) a little at a time; sip. **—***n.* A sip of liquid. [OE *sūpan*]

sup[2] (sup) *v.i.* **supped, sup·ping** To eat supper; dine. [< OF *soper, super*]

su·per[1] (sōō′pər) *n. Informal* A superintendent.

su·per[2] (sōō′pər) *n. Slang* A supernumerary.

su·per[3] (sōō′pər) *adj. Informal* Excellent; outstanding; first-rate. [Short for SUPERIOR]

super- *prefix* 1. Above; over: *superstructure.* 2. Higher or greater than; superior: *supersonic, superhighway.* 3. Excessively: *supersaturate.* 4. Extra; additional: *supertax.* [< L *super* above, beyond]

In the list below *super-* denotes excess or superiority, as *supercritical* excessively critical, *superexcellence* superior excellence.

su·per·a·bun·dant (sōō′pər·ə·bun′dənt) *adj.* More than sufficient; excessive. **—su′per·a·bun′dance** *n.* **—su′per·a·bun′dant·ly** *adv.*

su·per·an·nu·at·ed (sōō′pər·an′yōō·ā′tid) *adj.* 1. Retired with a pension on account of age. 2. Too old to work. 3. Outdated; obsolete. [< L *super* beyond + *annus* year]

su·perb (sōō·pûrb′, sə-) *adj.* 1. Magnificent; majestic; imposing. 2. Luxurious; rich and costly. 3. Very good; excellent. [< L *superbus* proud] **—su·perb′ly** *adv.* **—su·perb′ness** *n.*

su·per·car·go (sōō′pər·kär′gō) *n. pl.* **·goes** or **·gos** An agent on board ship in charge of the cargo and its sale and purchase. [< L *super-* over + CARGO]

su·per·charge (sōō′pər·chärj′) *v.t.* **·charged, ·charg·ing** To adapt (an engine) to develop more power by fitting with a supercharger.

su·per·charg·er (sōō′pər·chär′jər) *n. Mech.* A compressor for supplying air or combustible mixture to an internal-combustion engine at a pressure greater than that developed by the suction of the pistons alone.

su·per·cil·i·ous (sōō′pər·sil′ē·əs) *adj.* Exhibiting haughty contempt or indifference; arrogant. [< L *supercilium* eyebrow] **—su′per·cil′i·ous·ly** *adv.* **—su′per·cil′i·ous·ness** *n.*

su·per·e·go (sōō′pər·ē′gō) *n. Psychoanal.* The part of the psyche that acts to secure the conformity of the ego to parental, social, and moral standards.

su·per·er·o·gate (sōō′pər·er′ə·gāt) *v.i.* **·gat·ed, ·gat·ing** To do more than is required or ordered. [< L *super-* over and above + *erogare* to pay out] **—su′per·er′o·ga′tion** *n.* **—su′per·e·rog′a·to′ry** (-ə·rog′ə·tôr′ē) *adj.*

su·per·fec·ta (sōō′pər·fek′tə) *n.* A bet in which the winner must select the first four finishers of a horse race in order. [< SU(PER) + PERFECTA]

su·per·fi·cial (sōō′pər·fish′əl) *adj.* 1. Of or situated near the surface: a *superficial* wound. 2. Without depth or thoroughness; shallow: a *superficial* writer. [< L *super-* over + *ficies* face] **—su′per·fi′ci·al′i·ty** (-fish′ē·al′ə·tē), **su′per·fi′cial·ness** *n.* **—su′per·fi′·cial·ly** *adv.*

su·per·flu·i·ty (sōō′pər·flōō′ə·tē) *n. pl.* **·ties** 1. The state of being superfluous. 2. That which is superfluous. 3. Superabundance; plenty. [< L *super-* over + *fluere* to flow]

su·per·flu·ous (sōō·pûr′flōō·əs) *adj.* 1. Excessively abundant; surplus. 2. Unnecessary; uncalled for; irrelevant: a *superfluous* question. **—su·per′flu·ous·ly** *adv.* **—su·per′flu·ous·ness** *n.*

su·per·high·way (sōō′pər·hī′wā′) *n.* A broad highway for high-speed traffic.

su·per·hu·man (sōō′pər·hyōō′mən) *adj.* 1. Beyond human power or understanding; divine. 2. Beyond normal human ability or

superachievement
superacid
superacute
superadaptable
superadequate
superaffluence
superagency
superalkaline
superambitious
superangelic
superarduous
superarrogant
superattraction
superattractive
superbenefit
superblunder
superbold
superbomb
superbrave
superbusy
supercandid
supercapable
supercaution
superceremonious
supercivilized
supercolossal
supercomplex
supercompression
superconfident
superconservative
supercool
supercordial
supercritic
supercritical
supercultivated
supercurious
supercynical
superdanger
superdelicate
superdemand
superdesirous
superdevilish
superdevotion
superdifficult
superdividend
supereffective
superelastic
superelegance
supereloquent
supereminence
supereminent
superemphasis
superendurance
superesthetic
superethical
superexacting
superexalt
superexcellence
superexcellent
superexcited
superexpenditure
superexpressive
superexquisite
superfeminine
superfervent
superfine
superfluid
superfolly
superformal
superformidable
superfriendly
supergallant
supergenerosity
superglorious
supergovernment
superhandsome
superhearty
superheat
superhero
superheroic
superimportant
superimproved
superincentive
superindependent
superindignant
superindividualist
superinduce
superinduction
superindulgence
superindustrious
superinfluence
superingenious

skill. —**su′per·hu·man′i·ty** (-hyo͞o·man′·ə·tē) *n.* —**su′per·hu′man·ly** *adv.*

su·per·im·pose (so͞o′pər·im·pōz′) *v.t.* **·posed, ·pos·ing** To lay or impose upon something else. —**su′per·im′po·si′tion** (-im′pə·zish′ən) *n.*

su·per·in·tend (so͞o′pər·in·tend′) *v.t.* To have the charge and direction of; manage; supervise. [< LL *super-* over + *intendere* to aim at] —**su′per·in·ten′dence** *n.*

su·per·in·ten·dent (so͞o′pər·in·ten′dənt) *n.* 1. A person in charge of an office, staff, etc. 2. A person responsible for maintenance and repair in an office or apartment building. [< LL *superintendere* to superintend] —**su′·per·in·ten′den·cy** *n.*

su·pe·ri·or (sə·pir′ē·ər, so͞o-) *adj.* 1. Higher or greater in amount, value, rank, etc.: a *superior* force, a *superior* wine, a *superior* officer. 2. Indifferent to; unaffected by: with *to*: *superior* to envy. 3. Haughty; arrogant; disdainful: a *superior* attitude. —*n.* 1. One who surpasses another in rank or excellence. 2. The ruler of a convent or monastery. [< L *super* above] —**su·pe·ri·or·i·ty** (-ôr′ə·tē, -or′-) *n.* —**su·pe′ri·or·ly** *adv.*

su·per·la·tive (sə·pûr′lə·tiv, so͞o-) *adj.* 1. Surpassing all others; supreme. 2. *Gram.* Expressing the extreme degree of comparison of adjectives or adverbs. —*n.* 1. That which is superlative. 2. *Gram.* **a** The highest degree of comparison of the adjective or adverb. **b** Any word or phrase in this degree. [< L *super-* above + *latus*, pp. of *ferre* to carry] —**su·per′la·tive·ly** *adv.* —**su·per′la·tive·ness** *n.*

su·per·man (so͞o′pər·man′) *n. pl.* **·men** (-men′) A man possessing superhuman powers. [Trans. of G *übermensch*]

su·per·mar·ket (so͞o′pər·mär′kit) *n.* A large self-service store selling food and household supplies.

su·per·nal (so͞o·pûr′nəl) *adj.* Heavenly; celestial. [< L *super* over] —**su·per′nal·ly** *adv.*

su·per·nat·u·ral (so͞o′pər·nach′ər·əl) *adj.* 1. Relating to that which cannot be explained by known laws of nature. 2. Believed to be caused by a divine power. —*n.* That which is supernatural. [< L *super-* above + *natura* nature] —**su′per·nat′u·ral·ism** *n.* —**su′per·nat′u·ral·ly** *adv.*

su·per·nu·mer·ar·y (so͞o′pər·no͞o′mə·rer′ē, -nyo͞o′-) *adj.* Beyond a customary or necessary number; extra; superfluous. —*n. pl.* **·ar·ies** 1. A supernumerary person or thing. 2. A performer without a speaking part, usu. employed for crowd scenes. [< L *super* over + *numerus* number]

su·per·pose (so͞o′pər·pōz′) *v.t.* **·posed, ·pos·ing** To lay over or upon something else. [< F *super-* over + *poser* to put] —**su′per·pos′a·ble** *adj.* —**su′per·po·si′tion** (-pə·zish′ən) *n.*

su·per·pow·er (so͞o′pər·pou′ər) *n.* A nation able to dominate world affairs through superior economic and military strength.

su·per·scribe (so͞o′pər·skrīb′) *v.t.* **·scribed, ·scrib·ing** To write on the outside or top of. [< L *super-* over + *scribere* to write] —**su′per·scrip′tion** (-skrip′shən) *n.*

su·per·script (so͞o′pər·skript′) *adj.* Written above or overhead. —*n.* 1. A superscript character. 2. *Math.* A character written above and to the right or left of a term to indicate a specific operation or characteristic of the term.

su·per·sede (so͞o′pər·sēd′) *v.t.* **·sed·ed, ·sed·ing** 1. To take the place of; succeed. 2. To replace as outdated, useless, etc. [< L *super-* above, over + *sedere* to sit] —**su′per·sed′er** *n.* —**su′per·ses′sion** (-sesh′·ən) *n.*

su·per·son·ic (so͞o′pər·son′ik) *adj.* Of or characterized by a speed greater than that of sound. —**su′per·son′ics** *n.*

su·per·sti·tion (so͞o′pər·stish′ən) *n.* A belief founded on irrational feelings, esp. of fear, and marked by a trust in charms, omens, the supernatural, etc.; also, any rite or practice inspired by such belief. [< L *super-* over + *stare* to stand still] —**su′per·sti′tious** *adj.* —**su′per·sti′tious·ly** *adv.* —**su′per·sti′tious·ness** *n.*

su·per·struc·ture (so͞o′pər·struk′chər) *n.* 1. The part of a building above the foundation. 2. *Naut.* The part of a ship's structure above the main deck.

su·per·tax (so͞o′pər·taks′) *n.* A surtax.

su·per·vene (so͞o′pər·vēn′) *v.i.* **·vened, ·ven·ing** To happen as something extra or

superinitiative
superinjustice
superinquisitive
superinsistent
superintellectual
superlaborious
superlenient
superlie
superliner
superloyal
superlucky
superluxurious
supermarvelous
supermasculine
supermediocre
supermodest
supermoisten
supermorose
supermundane
supernotable
superobese
superobjectionable
superobstinate
superoffensive
superofficious
superordinary
superorganize
superpatient
superpatriotic
superpatriotism
superphysical
superpious
superpolite
superpositive
superpraise
superprecise
superpressure
superproduce
superprosperous
superpure
superradical
superrational
superrefined
superrespectable
superresponsible
superreward
superrighteous
superromantic
supersacrifice
supersafe
supersalesman
supersarcastic
supersatisfaction
supersaturate
supersaturation
superscholarly
superscientific
supersensitive
supersentimental
superserious
supersimplify
supersize
supersized
supersmart
supersolemn
superspecialize
superspeed
superspirituality
superstar
superstate
superstratum
superstrength
superstrenuous
superstrict
superstrong
superstylish
supersubtle
supersurprise
supersweet
supertanker
supertension
superthankful
superthorough
superugly
superurgent
supervigilant
supervigorous
supervirulent
supervital
superwise
superworldly
superzealous

unexpected. [< L *super-* over and above + *venire* to come] —**su′per·ven′ient** (-vēn′yənt) *adj.* —**su′per·ven′tion** (-ven′shən) *n.*
su·per·vise (sōō′pər·vīz) *v.t.* **·vised, ·vis·ing** To have charge of; superintend; oversee. [< L *super-* over + *videre* to see] —**su′per·vi′sion** (-vizh′ən) *n.* —**su′per·vi′sor** *n.* —**su′per·vi′sor·ship** *n.* —**su′per·vi′so·ry** *adj.*
su·pine (sōō·pīn′) *adj.* 1. Lying on the back with the face turned upward. 2. Inactive; indolent; listless. [< L *supinus*] —**su·pine′ly** *adv.* —**su·pine′ness** *n.*
sup·per (sup′ər) *n.* The last meal of the day; the evening meal. [< OF *soper* to sup, dine] —**sup′per·less** *adj.*
sup·plant (sə·plant′) *v.t.* 1. To take the place of; displace. 2. To take the place of (someone) by scheming, treachery, etc. [< L *supplantare* to trip up < *sub-* up from below + *planta* the sole of the foot]
sup·ple (sup′əl) *adj.* **·pler, ·plest** 1. Easily bent; flexible; pliant. 2. Showing adaptability of mind. [< L *sub-* under + stem of *plicare* to fold] —**sup·ply** (sup′lē), **sup′ple·ly** *adv.* —**sup′ple·ness** *n.*
sup·ple·ment (*v.* sup′lə·ment; *n.* sup′lə·mənt) *v.t.* To make additions to; provide for what is lacking in. —*n.* Something that supplements; esp., an addition to a publication. —**sup′ple·men′tal, sup′ple·men′ta·ry** *adj.*
sup·pli·ant (sup′lē·ənt) *adj.* Supplicating. —*n.* One who supplicates. Also **sup·pli·cant** (sup′lə·kənt). [See SUPPLICATE.] —**sup′pli·ant·ly** *adv.* —**sup′pli·ant·ness** *n.*
sup·pli·cate (sup′lə·kāt) *v.* **·cat·ed, ·cat·ing** *v.t.* 1. To ask for humbly and earnestly. 2. To beg something of; beseech; entreat. —*v.i.* 3. To make a humble request. [< L *sub-* under + *plicare* to bend, fold] —**sup′pli·ca′tion** *n.* —**sup′pli·ca·to′ry** (-kə·tôr′ē) *adj.*
sup·ply (sə·plī′) *v.t.* **·plied, ·ply·ing** 1. To give or furnish (something needful or desirable). 2. To furnish with what is needed: to *supply* an army with guns. 3. To provide for adequately; satisfy: to *supply* a demand. 4. To make good or compensate for (a loss or deficiency). —*n. pl.* **·plies** 1. An amount sufficient for a given use; quantity on hand. 2. *Usu. pl.* Food, clothing, or other stores reserved for distribution, as for an army. 3. The act of supplying. [< L *sub-* up from under + *ple-*, root of *plenus* full]
sup·port (sə·pôrt′) *v.t.* 1. To bear the weight of; hold up. 2. To provide with money, food, etc.; maintain. 3. To verify (a statement, etc.); corroborate. 4. To give approval or assistance to; uphold. 5. To tolerate: I cannot *support* his insolence. 6. To carry on; keep up: to *support* a war. 7. To act in a subordinate role to (a star) in a play or film. —*n.* 1. The act of supporting, or the state of being supported. 2. One who or that which supports. 3. Subsistence. [< L *sub-* up from under + *portare* to carry]
sup·port·a·ble (sə·pôr′tə·bəl) *adj.* Capable of being endured; bearable. —**sup·port′a·ble·ness, sup·port′a·bil′i·ty** *n.* —**sup·port′a·bly** *adv.*
sup·port·er (sə·pôr′tər) *n.* 1. One who supports, aids, or approves; esp., an adherent: a *supporter* of equal rights for women. 2. An elastic or other support for some part of the body.
sup·por·tive (sə·pôr′tiv) *adj.* 1. Serving to support. 2. Providing emotional support, as with sympathy, advice, and encouragement.
sup·pose (sə·pōz′) *v.* **·posed, ·pos·ing** *v.t.* 1. To believe probable; think. 2. To assume as true for the sake of argument: *Suppose* he comes late. 3. To expect or require: used in the passive: He is *supposed* to be on time. 4. To imply; presuppose. —*v.i.* 5. To conjecture. [< OF *sup-* under (< L *sub-*) + *poser* to put down] —**sup·pos′a·ble** *adj.* —**sup·pos′a·bly** *adv.* —**sup·pos′er** *n.*
sup·posed (sə·pōzd′, -pō′zid) *adj.* Accepted as genuine or true, often erroneously. —**sup·pos′ed·ly** *adv.*
sup·po·si·tion (sup′ə·zish′ən) *n.* 1. The act of supposing. 2. That which is supposed; hypothesis. [< L *sub-* under + *ponere* to place] —**sup′po·si′tion·al** *adj.* —**sup′po·si′tion·al·ly** *adv.*
sup·pos·i·to·ry (sə·poz′ə·tôr′ē) *n. pl.* **·ries** *Med.* A small, solid medicated substance for insertion into the rectum or vagina. [< L *sub-* under + *ponere* to place]
sup·press (sə·pres′) *v.t.* 1. To put an end to forcibly; quell; crush. 2. To withhold from knowledge or publication, as a book, news, etc. 3. To repress, as a groan or sigh. 4. To check or stop (a hemorrhage, etc.) 5. *Psychoanal.* To deliberately exclude (an idea, desire, etc.) from one's consciousness. [< L *sub-* under + *premere* to press] —**sup·press′i·ble** *adj.* —**sup·pres·sion** (sə·presh′ən) *n.* —**sup·pres′sive** *adj.* —**sup·pres′sor** *n.*
sup·pu·rate (sup′yə·rāt) *v.i.* **·rat·ed, ·rat·ing** To form or generate pus. [< L *sub-* under + *pus* pus] —**sup′pu·ra′tion** *n.* —**sup′pu·ra′tive** *adj. & n.*
supra- *prefix* Above; beyond. [< L]
su·pra·re·nal gland (sōō′prə·rē′nəl) *Anat.* An adrenal gland. [< SUPRA- + L *renes* kidneys]
su·prem·a·cist (sə·prem′ə·sist′, sōō-) *n.* One who believes in and advocates the supremacy of a particular group or race of people.
su·prem·a·cy (sə·prem′ə·sē, sōō-) *n. pl.* **·cies** 1. The state of being supreme. 2. Supreme power or authority.
su·preme (sə·prēm′, sōō-) *adj.* 1. Highest in power or authority. 2. Highest in degree, importance, quality, etc.; utmost: *supreme* devotion. 3. Ultimate; last; final. [< L *super* above] —**su·preme′ly** *adv.* —**su·preme′ness** *n.*
Supreme Being God.
sur- *prefix* Above; beyond; over: *surcharge; surcoat.* [< OF < L *super* above]
sur·cease (sûr·sēs′, sûr′sēs) *Archaic n.* Cessation; end. —*v.t. & v.i.* **·ceased, ·ceas·ing** To cease; end. [< L *super-* above + *sedere* to sit]
sur·charge (sûr′chärj′) *n.* 1. An additional amount charged; overcharge. 2. A new valuation printed on a postage stamp. —*v.t.* **·charged, ·charg·ing** 1. To overcharge; overload. 2. To imprint a surcharge on (a postage stamp). [< F *sur-* over + CHARGE] —**sur′charg·er** *n.*
sur·cin·gle (sûr′sing·gəl) *n.* A strap encircling a horse's body, as for holding a

saddle. [< OF *sur-* over + L *cingulum* belt]
sur·coat (sûr′kōt′) *n.* 1. An outer coat. 2. A cloaklike garment worn over armor. [< OF *sur-* over + *cot* coat]
sure (shŏŏr) *adj.* **sur·er, sur·est** 1. Free from doubt; certain; positive. 2. Confident: with *of*: He is *sure* of the outcome. 3. Not liable to change; firm; stable. 4. Bound to happen; inevitable. 5. Not liable to fail or err; infallible: a *sure* sign of winter. 6. Reliable; trustworthy. —**for sure** Without a doubt; unquestionably. —**sure enough** *Informal* Certainly; really. —**to be sure** Indeed; certainly. —**to make sure** To make certain; secure. —*adv.* *Informal* Certainly. [< L *se-* without + *cura* care] —**sure′ness** *n.*
sure-foot·ed (shŏŏr′fŏŏt′id) *adj.* 1. Not liable to fall or stumble. 2. Not liable to fail or err.
sure·ly (shŏŏr′lē) *adv.* 1. Certainly. 2. Securely; safely.
sure·ty (shŏŏr′tē, shŏŏr′ə·tē) *n. pl.* **·ties** 1. One who agrees to be responsible for another, as for another's debt. 2. A pledge or guarantee to secure against loss, damage, etc.; security. 3. The state of being sure. [See SURE.] —**sure′ty·ship** *n.*
surf (sûrf) *n.* The swell of the sea breaking on a shore or reef; also, the sound or foam of such a swell. —*v.i.* To engage in surfing. [Earlier *suff*, ? var. of SOUGH] —**surf′er** *n.*
sur·face (sûr′fis) *n.* 1. The exterior part or face of anything. 2. A superficial aspect; outward appearance. —*adj.* 1. Of, pertaining to, or on a surface. 2. Superficial; apparent. —*v.* **·faced, ·fac·ing** *v.t.* 1. To put a surface on; esp., to make smooth. —*v.i.* 2. To rise to the surface, as a submarine. [< F *sur-* above + FACE]
surf·board (sûrf′bôrd′) *n.* A long, narrow board used in surfing.
sur·feit (sûr′fit) *v.t.* To feed or supply to excess; satiate. —*n.* 1. Excess in eating or drinking; overindulgence. 2. An excessive quantity or supply. [< OF *surfaire* to overdo] —**sur′feit·er** *n.*
surf·ing (sûrf′ing) *n.* A sport in which a person on a surfboard is borne by the surf toward the shore.
surge (sûrj) *v.i.* **surged, surg·ing** 1. To move with a heaving motion, as waves; swell. 2. To rise or increase suddenly. —*n.* 1. A large swelling wave. 2. A heaving and rolling motion, as of waves. 3. A sudden, strong increase: a *surge* of electric power. [< L *surgere* to rise]
sur·geon (sûr′jən) *n.* A doctor who specializes in surgery. [See SURGERY.]
sur·ger·y (sûr′jər·ē) *n. pl.* **·ger·ies** 1. The branch of medicine concerned with the removal or repair of diseased or injured parts of the body. 2. A surgeon's operating room. 3. The work of a surgeon. [< Gk. *cheir* hand + *ergon* work] —**sur·gi·cal** (sûr′ji·kəl) *adj.* —**sur′gi·cal·ly** *adv.*
sur·ly (sûr′lē) *adj.* **sur·li·er, sur·li·est** Characterized by rudeness, ill humor, or gruffness. [Earlier *sirly* < *sir* a lord + *-ly* like] —**sur′li·ly** *adv.* —**sur′li·ness** *n.*
sur·mise (sər·mīz′; *for n., also* sûr′mīz) *v.t. & v.i.* **·mised, ·mis·ing** To infer (something) on slight evidence; guess. —*n.* A conjecture; guess. [< OF *sur-* upon + *mettre* to put < L *mittere* to send]
sur·mount (sər·mount′) *v.t.* 1. To overcome (a difficulty, etc.). 2. To climb up and over (a mountain or other height). 3. To be above; top. [< L *super-* over + *mons* hill, mountain] —**sur·mount′a·ble** *adj.*
sur·name (sûr′nām′; *for v., also* sûr·nām′) *n.* One's last or family name. —*v.t.* **·named, ·nam·ing** To give a surname to; call by a surname. [< OF *sur-* above, beyond + *nom* name < L *nomen*] —**sur′nam′er** *n.*
sur·pass (sər·pas′) *v.t.* 1. To go beyond or past in degree or amount; excel. 2. To go beyond the reach or powers of; transcend. [< MF *sur-* above + PASS] —**sur·pass′a·ble** *adj.*
sur·pass·ing (sər·pas′ing) *adj.* Superior; excellent; exceeding. —*adv.* *Poetic* Exceedingly. —**sur·pass′ing·ly** *adv.* —**sur·pass′ing·ness** *n.*
sur·plice (sûr′plis) *n.* *Eccl.* A loose white outer vestment with full sleeves. [< Med.L *super-* over + *pellicia* fur garment]
sur·plus (sûr′plus) *adj.* Being in excess of what is used or needed. —*n.* 1. That which remains over and above what has been used or is required; excess. 2. Assets in excess of liabilities. [< Med.L *super-* over and above + *plus* more]
sur·prise (sər·prīz′) *v.t.* **·prised, ·pris·ing** 1. To cause to feel wonder or astonishment; amaze. 2. To come upon suddenly or unexpectedly; take unawares. 3. To attack or capture without warning. —*n.* 1. The act of surprising, or the state of being surprised; astonishment. 2. That which causes surprise, as a sudden and unexpected event, fact, or gift. —**to take by surprise** To come upon suddenly or unexpectedly. [< L *super-* over + *prehendere* to take] —**sur·pris′al** *n.* —**sur·pris′er** *n.*
sur·pris·ing (sər·prī′zing) *adj.* Causing surprise or wonder; amazing. —**sur·pris′·ing·ly** *adv.* —**sur·pris′ing·ness** *n.*
sur·re·al·ism (sə·rē′əl·iz′əm) *n.* A modern movement in literature and art that attempts to express the workings of the subconscious mind. [< F *sur-* beyond, above + *réalisme* realism] —**sur·re′al·ist** *adj. & n.* —**sur·re′al·is′tic** *adj.* —**sur·re′al·is′ti·cal·ly** *adv.*
sur·ren·der (sə·ren′dər) *v.t.* 1. To yield possession or control of under compulsion. 2. To give up; abandon, as hope. 3. To relinquish, esp. in favor of another. —*v.i.* 4. To give oneself up, as to an enemy in warfare. —*n.* The act of surrendering. [< OF *sur-* over + RENDER]
sur·rep·ti·tious (sûr′əp·tish′əs) *adj.* Done or acting in a secret, sly manner. [< L *sub-* secretly + *rapere* to snatch] —**sur′rep·ti′tious·ly** *adv.* —**sur′rep·ti′tious·ness** *n.*
sur·rey (sûr′ē) *n.* A light horse-drawn carriage, having two seats, four wheels, and sometimes a top. [Prob. after *Surrey*, England]
sur·ro·gate (sûr′ə·gāt, -git) *n.* 1. A substitute; deputy. 2. A probate judge. [< L *sub-* in place of another + *rogare* to ask] —**sur′ro·gate·ship** *n.*
sur·round (sə·round′) *v.t.* 1. To extend around; encircle; enclose. 2. To shut in or

enclose so as to cut off retreat. [< LL *super-* over + *undare* to rise in waves < *unda* a wave]

sur·round·ings (sə·roun′dingz) *n.pl.* One's environment; conditions of life.

sur·tax (sûr′taks′) *n.* A tax added to the usual tax: also called *supertax.* [< F *sur-* above + TAX]

sur·veil·lance (sər·vā′ləns, -vāl′yəns) *n.* 1. Close watch kept over one, as a suspect. 2. Close observation or supervision. [< F *sur-* over + *veiller* to watch < L *vigilare*] **—sur·veil′lant** *adj. & n.*

sur·vey (*v.* sər·vā′; *n.* sûr′vā) *v.t.* 1. To look at in its entirety; view in a general way. 2. To look at carefully and minutely; scrutinize. 3. To determine accurately the area, contour, or boundaries of (land). *—v.i.* 4. To survey land. *—n.* 1. The process of surveying land; also, a map, description, etc., of a surveyed area. 2. A general or comprehensive view. 3. A scrutinizing view; inspection. [< Med.L *super-* over + *videre* to look]

sur·vey·ing (sər·vā′ing) *n.* The science and art of determining the area and configuration of portions of the surface of the earth and representing them on maps. **—sur·vey′or** *n.*

sur·vive (sər·vīv′) *v.* **·vived, ·viv·ing** *v.i.* 1. To remain alive or in existence. *—v.t.* 2. To live or exist beyond the death, occurrence, or end of; outlive; outlast. [< L *super-* above, beyond + *vivere* to live] **—sur·viv′al** *n.* **—sur·viv′ing** *adj.* **—sur·vi′vor** *n.*

sus·cep·ti·ble (sə·sep′tə·bəl) *adj.* 1. Readily affected or influenced by; yielding easily to; open: usu. with *to* or *of.* 2. Highly emotional or sensitive; impressionable. [< L *sub-* under + *capere* to take] **—sus·cep′ti·bil′i·ty, sus·cep′ti·ble·ness** *n.* **—sus·cep′ti·bly** *adv.*

su·shi (sōō′shē) *n.* Vinegar-flavored rice usu. enclosed in a slice of raw fish. [< Jap.]

sus·pect (*v.* sə·spekt′; *adj. & n.* sus′pekt) *v.t.* 1. To think (a person) guilty on little or no evidence. 2. To distrust; doubt. 3. To think possible; surmise. *—v.i.* 4. To have suspicions. *—adj.* Viewed with suspicion; suspected. *—n.* One who is under suspicion, esp. for a crime. [< L *sub-* under + *specere* to look]

sus·pend (sə·spend′) *v.t.* 1. To bar for a time from a privilege, office, or function as a punishment. 2. To cause to cease for a time; withhold temporarily. 3. To withhold or defer action on: to *suspend* a sentence. 4. To hang from a support so as to allow free movement. *—v.i.* 5. To stop for a time. [< L *sub-* under + *pendere* to hang]

sus·pend·ers (sə·spen′dərz) *n.pl.* 1. A pair of straps worn over the shoulders for supporting the trousers. 2. *Brit.* Garters.

sus·pense (sə·spens′) *n.* 1. A state of anxiety caused by uncertainty or insecurity. 2. An uncertain or doubtful situation. [< L *suspendere.* See SUSPEND.] **—sus·pense′ful** *adj.* **—sus·pen′sive** *adj.* **—sus·pen′sive·ness** *n.*

sus·pen·sion (sə·spen′shən) *n.* 1. The act of suspending, or the state of being suspended. 2. *Physics* A uniform dispersion of small particles in a medium. 3. Any device from which something is suspended. 4. *Mech.* In an automotive vehicle, a system of springs, torsion bars, etc., to protect the body against road shocks.

sus·pen·so·ry (sə·spen′sər·ē) *adj.* Suspending; sustaining; delaying. *—n. pl.* **·ries** A truss, bandage, or supporter.

sus·pi·cion (sə·spish′ən) *n.* 1. The act of suspecting or the state of being suspected of something wrong without proof or clear evidence. 2. Any impression based on little or no proof. 3. A trace or hint. [< L *sub-* from under + *specere* to look] **—sus·pi′cion·al** *adj.*

sus·pi·cious (sə·spish′əs) *adj.* 1. Inclined to suspect; distrustful. 2. Apt to arouse suspicion. 3. Indicating suspicion. **—sus·pi′cious·ly** *adv.* **—sus·pi′cious·ness** *n.*

sus·tain (sə·stān′) *v.t.* 1. To keep from sinking or falling; uphold; support. 2. To endure; withstand. 3. To undergo or suffer, as loss or injury. 4. To keep up the spirits of; comfort. 5. To keep going; maintain; prolong. 6. To provide with food, drink, etc.; support. 7. To uphold or support as true or just. 8. To corroborate; confirm. [< L *sub-* up from under + *tenere* to hold] **—sus·tain′a·ble** *adj.* **—sus·tain′er** *n.* **—sus·tain′ment** *n.*

sus·te·nance (sus′tə·nəns) *n.* 1. The act of sustaining, or the state of being sustained; esp., maintenance of life. 2. That which sustains or supports life; esp., food. 3. Means of support; livelihood. [See SUSTAIN.]

sut·tee (su·tē′, sut′ē) *n.* Formerly, the sacrifice of a Hindu widow on the funeral pyre of her husband. [< Hind. *satī* < Skt., a faithful wife] **—sut·tee′ism** *n.*

su·ture (sōō′chər) *n.* 1. *Anat.* The interlocking of two bones at their edges, as in the skull. 2. *Surg.* a The operation of uniting the edges of a cut or wound by or as by stitching. b The thread, wire, or other material used in this operation. *—v.t.* **·tured, ·tur·ing** To unite by means of sutures; sew together. [< L *suere* to sew] **—su′tur·al** *adj.* **—su′tur·al·ly** *adv.*

su·ze·rain (sōō′zə·rin, -rān) *n.* Formerly, a feudal lord. [< F < L *sursum* upwards; on analogy with *souverain* sovereign] **—su′ze·rain·ty** *n.*

svelte (svelt) *adj.* Slender; slim; willowy. [< F < Ital. *svelto*]

swab (swob) *n.* 1. A small stick having a wad of cotton wound about one or both ends, used esp. for cleaning and for applying medication. 2. A mop. 3. *Informal* A sailor. *—v.t.* **swabbed, swab·bing** To use a swab on. Also *swob.* [? < MDu. *swabbe*] **—swab′·ber** *n.*

swad·dle (swod′l) *v.t.* **·dled, ·dling** To wrap (an infant) with swaddling clothes. *—n.* A band used for swaddling. [OE *swathian* to swathe]

swaddling clothes Bands of cloth wound around a newborn infant. Also **swaddling bands, swaddling clouts.**

swag (swag) *n.* 1. *Slang* Property obtained by robbery or theft; plunder; booty. 2. Drapery, garland, etc., hanging in a loop between two points. [Prob. < Scand.]

swage (swāj) *n.* A tool or form, often one

of a pair, for shaping metal by hammering or pressure. —*v.t.* **swaged, swag·ing** To shape (metal) with or as with a swage. [< OF *souage*]

swag·ger (swag′ər) *v.i.* 1. To walk with a proud or insolent air; strut. 2. To boast; bluster. —*n.* Boastful words or deeds. [Appar. freq. of SWAG] —**swag′ger·er** *n.* —**swag′ger·ing·ly** *adv.*

swagger stick A short, canelike stick carried by army officers. Also **swagger cane.**

Swa·hi·li (swä·hē′lē) *n.* A Bantu language of East Africa. [< Arabic < *sāhil* coast]

swain (swān) *n.* *Poetic* 1. A youthful rustic. 2. A lover. [< ON *sveinn* boy]

swal·low[1] (swol′ō) *v.t.* 1. To cause (food, etc.) to pass from the mouth into the stomach. 2. To take in or engulf; absorb; envelop: often with *up.* 3. To put up with or endure. 4. *Informal* To believe credulously. 5. To refrain from expressing; suppress. —*v.i.* 6. To perform the act or motions of swallowing. —*n.* 1. The amount swallowed at one time. 2. The act of swallowing. [OE *swelgan* to swallow] —**swal′low·a·ble** *adj.* —**swal′low·er** *n.*

swal·low[2] (swol′ō) *n.* Any of various small birds with short bills, long, pointed wings, and forked tails, noted for their swiftness of flight and migratory habits. [OE *swealwe*]

swal·low·tail (swol′ō·tāl′) *n.* 1. The tail of a swallow, or a similar deeply forked tail. 2. A butterfly having a taillike prolongation on each hind wing. 3. *Informal* A man's dress coat having two long, tapering tails: also **swallow-tailed coat.**

swam (swam) Past tense of SWIM.

swa·mi (swä′mē) *n. pl.* **·mis** A Hindu religious teacher. [< Hind. < Skt. *swāmin* lord]

swamp (swomp, swômp) *n.* A tract of lowland saturated with water; bog. Also **swamp′·land′** (-land′). ◆Collateral adjective: *paludal.* —*v.t.* 1. To drench or submerge with water or other liquid. 2. To overwhelm with difficulties; crush. 3. *Naut.* To sink or fill (a vessel) with water. —**swamp′ish** *adj.* —**swamp′y** *adj.*

swan (swon, swôn) *n.* A large aquatic bird, noted for its white plumage and long, graceful neck. [OE]

swan dive A dive performed with head tilted back and arms extended until near the water.

swank (swangk) *adj. Slang* Ostentatiously fashionable; pretentious. Also **swank′y.** [< dial. E. Appar. akin to MLG *swank* flexible] —**swank′i·ness** *n.*

swan's-down (swonz′doun′, swônz′-) *n.* 1. The down of a swan, used for trimming, powder puffs, etc. 2. A soft woolen cloth resembling down. Also **swans′down′.**

swan song A last or dying work, as of a poet or composer: from the fable that the swan sings only before dying.

swap (swop) *Informal v.t. & v.i.* **swapped, swap·ping** To trade (one thing for another). —*n.* An exchange or trade. Also spelled *swop.* [ME swappen to strike (a bargain)]

sward (swôrd) *n.* Land thickly covered with grass; turf. [OE *sweard* skin]

swarm (swôrm) *n.* 1. A hive of bees; also, a large number of bees, with a queen, leaving the hive at one time to start a new colony. 2. A crowd or throng. —*v.i.* 1. To leave the hive in a swarm: said of bees. 2. To come together, move, or occur in great numbers. 3. To be crowded; teem: with *with.* [OE *swearm*] —**swarm′er** *n.*

swarth·y (swôr′thē) *adj.* **swarth·i·er, swarth·i·est** Having a dark or sunburned complexion; tawny. [OE *sweart*] —**swarth′i·ly** *adv.* —**swarth′i·ness** *n.*

swash (swosh, swôsh) *v.i.* To move or wash noisily, as waves; splash. [Imit.]

swash·buck·ler (swosh′buk′lər, swôsh′-) *n.* A swaggering or boasting soldier. [< *swash* to swagger + BUCKLER] —**swash′·buck′ling** *adj.*

swas·ti·ka (swos′ti·kə) *n.* 1. A primitive religious ornament or symbol, consisting of a Greek cross with the ends of the arms bent at right angles. 2. The symbol used as the emblem of the Nazis. [< Skt. *svastika* < *svasti* well-being]

swat (swot) *v.t.* **swat·ted, swat·ting** To hit with a sharp blow. [Var. of SQUAT, in dial. sense of "squash"] —**swat** *n.* —**swat′ter** *n.*

swatch (swoch) *n.* A strip, as of cloth, used as a sample. [< dial. E, a cloth tally]

swath (swoth, swôth) *n.* 1. A row or line of grass, grain, etc., cut down by one sweep of a scythe or other mowing device. 2. The width of such a row. 3. A narrow belt or track; strip. Also **swathe** (swoth, swāth). —**to cut a wide swath** To make a fine impression or display. [OE *swæth* a track]

swathe (swoth, swāth) *v.t.* **swathed, swath·ing** 1. To bind or wrap, as in bandages. 2. To envelop; surround. [OE *swathian*] —**swath′er** *n.*

sway (swā) *v.i.* 1. To swing from side to side or to and fro; oscillate. 2. To bend or incline to one side; lean; veer. —*v.t.* 3. To cause to swing, bend, or incline. 4. To influence (a person, opinion, etc.). —*n.* 1. Power exercised in governing; dominion: to hold *sway* over a nation. 2. The act of swaying. [Prob. fusion of ON *sveigja* to bend and LG *swajen* to be moved to and fro by the wind]

sway·back (swā′bak′) *n.* A hollow or sagging condition of the back, as in a horse. —**sway′backed′** *adj.*

swear (swâr) *v.* **swore, sworn, swear·ing** *v.i.* 1. To make a solemn affirmation with an appeal to God or one's honor. 2. To utter a solemn promise. 3. To use profanity; curse. —*v.t.* 4. To affirm or assert solemnly by appealing to God, etc. 5. To vow. —**to swear by** 1. To appeal to by oath. 2. To have complete confidence in. —**to swear in** To administer a legal oath to. —**to swear off** *Informal* To promise to renounce or give up; to *swear off* drink. [OE *swerian*] —**swear′er** *n.*

sweat (swet) *v.* **sweat** or **sweat·ed, sweat·ing** *v.i.* 1. To excrete moisture from the pores of the skin; perspire. 2. To exude moisture in drops; ooze. 3. To gather and condense moisture in drops, as a glass on its outer surface. 4. *Informal* To work hard; toil; drudge. —*v.t.* 5. To exude (moisture) from the pores. 6. *Informal* To force (employees) to work for low wages and under unfavorable conditions. 7. *Slang* To extract (a confession, etc.) from someone by force. —**to sweat out** *Slang* To wait through anxiously and helplessly. —*n.* 1. The moisture excreted from the sweat glands; perspiration. 2. Droplets of moisture exuded by something or collected on its surface. —**no sweat** *Slang* No difficulty whatever. [OE *swāt* sweat] —**sweat′i·ly** *adv.* —**sweat′i·ness** *n.* —**sweat′y** *adj.*

sweat·band (swet′band′) *n.* A band, usu. of leather, inside the crown of a hat to protect it from sweat.

sweat·er (swet′ər) *n.* A knitted or crocheted garment for the upper part of the body.

sweat gland *Anat.* One of the numerous glands beneath the skin that secrete sweat.

sweat shirt A heavy, collarless pullover worn to absorb sweat while exercising, etc.

sweat·shop (swet′shop′) *n.* A place where work is done for insufficient wages and for long hours.

Swede (swēd) *n.* A native or inhabitant of Sweden.

Swed·ish (swē′dish) *adj.* Pertaining to Sweden, the Swedes, or their language. —*n.* 1. The North Germanic language of Sweden. 2. The inhabitants of Sweden collectively.

sweep (swēp) *v.* **swept, sweep·ing** *v.t.* 1. To collect or remove with a broom, brush, etc. 2. To clear or clean with or as with a broom or brush: to *sweep* a floor. 3. To touch or brush: Her dress *swept* the ground. 4. To pass over or through swiftly: His eyes *swept* the sky. 5. To move, carry, bring, etc., with strong or continuous force: The flood *swept* the bridge away. —*v.i.* 6. To clean or brush a floor or other surface with a broom, etc. 7. To move or go strongly and evenly, esp. with speed. 8. To extend with a long reach or curve: The road *sweeps* along the shore. —*n.* 1. The act of sweeping. 2. A long stroke or movement: a *sweep* of the hand. 3. A great victory or success, as in an election. 4. The range or compass of a sweeping motion: the *sweep* of a searchlight. 5. Extent or expanse; stretch: a wide *sweep* of meadow. [ME *swopen* to brush away] —**sweep′er** *n.*

sweep·ing (swē′ping) *adj.* 1. Moving in a continuous motion. 2. Affecting a wide area; comprehensive: *sweeping* reforms. —*n.* 1. The action of one who or that which sweeps. 2. *pl.* Things swept up; refuse. —**sweep′ing·ly** *adv.* —**sweep′ing·ness** *n.*

sweep·stakes (swēp′stāks′) *n. pl.* **·stakes** 1. A horse race, etc., in which all the sums staked may be won by one or by a few of the bettors. 2. A lottery, drawing, etc., using this arrangement. Also **sweep′stake′**.

sweet (swēt) *adj.* 1. Having a flavor of or like that of sugar. 2. Not fermented or decaying; fresh. 3. Not sour or salty: *sweet* water. 4. Pleasing to the senses: a *sweet* sound. 5. Having gentle, pleasing, and winning qualities: a *sweet* child. 6. Not dry: said of wines. —*n.* 1. *Chiefly pl.* A piece of candy. 2. A sweetheart. [OE *swēte*] —**sweet′ly** *adv.* —**sweet′ness** *n.*

sweet a·lys·sum (ə·lis′əm) A perennial Mediterranean herb having fragrant white blossoms.

sweet·bread (swēt′bred′) *n.* The pancreas (**stomach sweetbread**) or the thymus gland (**neck sweetbread or throat sweetbread**) of a calf or other animal, when used as food. [< SWEET + BREAD, in obs. sense of "a morsel"]

sweet·bri·er (swēt′brī·ər) *n.* A stout prickly rose native in Europe and Asia, with aromatic leaves. Also **sweet′bri′ar.**

sweet clover Any of several cloverlike herbs, used for fodder.

sweet corn Young ears of corn having sweet, milky kernels, boiled or roasted as food.

sweet·en (swēt′n) *v.t.* 1. To make sweet or sweeter. 2. To make more endurable. 3. To make pleasant or gratifying. —*v.i.* 4. To become sweet or sweeter. —**sweet′en·er** *n.* —**sweet′en·ing** *n.*

sweet·heart (swēt′härt′) *n.* A loved one; lover; darling.

sweet·ie (swē′tē) *n. Informal* A sweetheart.

sweet·ish (swē′tish) *adj.* Somewhat or rather sweet. —**sweet′ish·ly** *adv.* —**sweet′·ish·ness** *n.*

sweet·meat (swēt′mēt′) *n.* A candy.

sweet pea An ornamental annual climber of the bean family having varicolored flowers.

sweet pepper A mild variety of capsicum whose unripe green fruit is used as a vegetable.

sweet potato 1. A perennial tropical vine with rose-violet or pink flowers and a fleshy, tuberous root. 2. The root itself, eaten as a vegetable.

sweet tooth *Informal* A fondness for sweets.

sweet william A perennial plant with closely clustered, showy flowers. Also **sweet William.**

swell (swel) *v.t. & v.i.* **swelled, swelled or swol·len, swel·ling** 1. To increase in size, as by inflation within; expand. 2. To increase in amount, degree, or intensity. 3. To curve out; bulge. 4. To become puffed with pride. —*n.* 1. An increase in size, amount, etc.; expansion. 2. A long, continuous body of a wave; also, a rise in the land. 3. *Informal* A person of the ultrafashionable set. —*adj. Informal* 1. Ultrafashionable; smart. 2. First-rate; distinctive. [OE *swellan*]

swell·ing (swel′ing) *n.* 1. The act of increasing or expanding. 2. *Pathol.* Abnormal enlargement of some part of the body. —*adj.* Increasing; bulging.

swel·ter (swel′tər) *v.i.* To suffer or perspire from oppressive heat. [OE *sweltan* to die]

swel·ter·ing (swel′tər·ing) *adj.* Very hot. —**swel′ter·ing·ly** *adv.*

swept (swept) Past tense and past participle of SWEEP.

swept·back (swept′bak′) *adj.* Of the wings of an airplane, slanting backward at an angle with the fuselage.

swerve (swûrv) *v.t. & v.i.* **swerved, swerv·ing** To turn or cause to turn aside from a course or purpose; deflect. [OE *sweorfan* to file or grind away] —**swerve** *n.*

swift (swift) *adj.* 1. Moving with great speed; fast; fleet. 2. Happening quickly: a *swift* reply. —*n.* A small, swallowlike bird with long, narrow wings; esp., the **chimney swift.** [OE] —**swift′ly** *adv.* —**swift′·ness** *n.*

swig (swig) *Informal n.* A deep draft, as of liquor. —*v.t. & v.i.* **swigged, swig·ging** To drink deeply or greedily. [Origin unknown] —**swig′ger** *n.*

swill (swil) *v.t. & v.i.* To drink greedily or to excess. —*n.* 1. Liquid food for animals, esp. for swine; slop. 2. Kitchen refuse; garbage. 3. A deep draft of liquor. [OE *swillan, swilian* to wash]

swim[1] (swim) *v.* **swam, swum, swim·ming** *v.i.* 1. To propel oneself through water by bodily movement. 2. To float on water or other liquid. 3. To move with a smooth or flowing motion. 4. To be flooded; overflow. —*v.t.* 5. To traverse by swimming. —*n.* The action, pastime, or period of swimming. —**in the swim** *Informal* In the current of affairs. [OE *swimman*] —**swim′·mer** *n.*

swim[2] (swim) *v.i.* To be dizzy; reel. [OE *swīma* dizziness]

swim·ming (swim′ing) *n.* The act or sport of one who swims. —*adj.* Used for swimming.

swim·ming·ly (swim′ing·lē) *adv.* Successfully; very well.

swimming pool An indoor or outdoor tank designed for swimming.

swin·dle (swin′dəl) *v.* **·dled, ·dling** *v.t.* 1. To cheat of money or property; defraud. 2. To obtain by such means. —*v.i.* 3. To practice fraud. —*n.* The act or an instance of swindling; fraud. [Back formation < SWINDLER]

swin·dler (swind′lər) *n.* One who swindles or deceives. [< G *schwindeln* to act thoughtlessly, be giddy]

swine (swīn) *n. pl.* **swine** 1. A domesticated pig. 2. A brutal, vicious, or contemptible person. [OE *swīn*] —**swin′ish** *adj.* —**swin′·ish·ly** *adv.* —**swin′ish·ness** *n.*

swine·herd (swīn′hûrd′) *n.* A tender of swine.

swing (swing) *v.* **swung, swing·ing** *v.i.* 1. To move backward and forward rhythmically. 2. To move with an even, swaying motion. 3. To turn; pivot. 4. To be suspended. 5. *Slang* To be up-to-date and sophisticated. 6. *Slang* To be sexually promiscuous. —*v.t.* 7. To cause to move backward and forward. 8. To cause to move with an even, swaying motion. 9. To cause to turn. 10. To hang or suspend. 11. *Informal* To bring to a successful conclusion. —*n.* 1. The act of swinging; also the distance covered. 2. A free swaying motion. 3. A seat hanging from ropes, etc., on which one may move to and fro. 4. The rhythm of poetry or music. 5. A sweeping blow or stroke. 6. The course of business, a career, etc. 7. In jazz, a development after about 1935, characterized by large bands, simple harmony, strong rhythms, etc. 8. *Informal* A trip; tour. [OE *swingan* scourge]

swing·er (swing′ər) *n.* *Slang* 1. A lively and up-to-date person. 2. A person who indulges freely in sex.

swin·gle·tree (swing′gəl·trē′) *n.* A whiffletree.

swing shift A workshift from about 4 p.m. to midnight.

swipe (swīp) *v.t.* **swiped, swip·ing** 1. *Informal* To strike with a hard, sweeping blow. 2. *Slang* To steal; snatch. —*n.* *Informal* A hard, sweeping blow. [Var. of SWEEP.]

swirl (swûrl) *v.t. & v.i.* To move or cause to move in a whirling or twisting motion; whirl. —*n.* 1. A whirling motion; eddy; whirl. 2. A curl or twist; spiral. [< dial. E (Scot.) *swyrle*] —**swirl′y** *adj.*

swish (swish) *v.t. & v.i.* 1. To move through the air with a hissing, whistling sound, as a whip. 2. To rustle, as silk. —*n.* A hissing or rustling sound. [Imit.]

Swiss (swis) *adj.* Of or pertaining to Switzerland or its inhabitants. —*n. pl.* **Swiss** A native or inhabitant of Switzerland.

Swiss chard Chard.

Swiss cheese A pale yellow cheese with many large holes.

Swiss steak A thick cut of steak floured and braised.

switch (swich) *n.* 1. A small flexible rod, etc., used for whipping. 2. A tress of false hair, used by women in building a coiffure. 3. A mechanism for shifting a railway train from one track to another. 4. A shift; change. 5. *Electr.* A device to make, break, or divert a circuit. —*v.t.* 1. To whip with or as with a switch. 2. To change; shift. 3. To exchange: They *switched* plates. 4. To shift (a railroad car) to another track; shunt. 5. *Electr.* To connect or disconnect with a switch: with *on* or *off*. —*v.i.* 6. To turn aside; change; shift. [Earlier *swits*] —**switch′er** *n.*

switch·back (swich′bak′) *n.* A railway or road ascending a steep incline in a zigzag pattern.

switch·blade knife (swich′blād′) *n.* A pocket knife having a spring-operated blade that opens when a switch or button is pressed.

switch·board (swich′bôrd′) *n.* A control panel for connecting and disconnecting electric circuits, as in a telephone exchange.

switch-hit (swich′hit′) *v.t. & v.i.* To bat either right-handed or left-handed. —**switch′-hit′ter** *n.*

switch·yard (swich′yärd′) *n.* A railroad yard for the assembling and breaking up of trains.

swiv·el (swiv′əl) *n.* A pivoted support on which a mechanism may be swung. —*v.t. & v.i.* **swiv·eled** or **·elled, swiv·el·ing** or **·el·ling** To turn on or as on a swivel. [OE *swīfan* to revolve]

swivel chair A chair having a seat that turns horizontally on a swivel.

swob (swob) See SWAB.

swol·len (swō′lən) Alternative past participle of SWELL.

swoon (swo͞on) *v.i.* To faint. —*n.* A fainting fit. [OE *geswōgen* unconscious] —**swoon′·ing** *n.*

swoop (swo͞op) *v.i.* 1. To drop or descend suddenly, as a bird pouncing on its prey. —*v.t.* 2. To take or seize suddenly: often with *up*. [OE *swāpan* to sweep] —**swoop** *n.*

swop (swop) See SWAP.

sword (sôrd) *n.* 1. A weapon, as a saber or rapier, consisting of a long blade fixed in a hilt. 2. Power; esp., military power. —**at swords' points** Ready for a fight. —**to put to the sword** To kill with a sword. [OE *sweord*]

sword·fish (sôrd′fish′) *n. pl.* **·fish** or **·fish·es** A large marine fish with the upper jaw prolonged in a swordlike process.

sword·play (sôrd′plā′) *n.* The act or skill of using a sword, esp. in fencing. —**sword′·play′er** *n.*

swords·man (sôrdz′mən) *n. pl.* **·men** (-mən) One skilled in the use of or armed with a

sword. Also **sword′man.** —**swords′man·ship** or **sword′man·ship** *n.*
swore (swôr) Past tense of SWEAR.
sworn (swôrn) Past participle of SWEAR.
swum (swum) Past participle of SWIM.
swung (swung) Past tense and past participle of SWING.
syb·a·rite (sib′ə·rīt) *n.* One given to pleasure and luxury; hedonist. [< Gk. *Sybaris*, an ancient Greek city in southern Italy, famed for its luxury] —**syb′a·rit′ic** (-rit′ik) *adj.* —**syb′a·rit′i·cal·ly** *adv.*
syc·a·more (sik′ə·môr) *n.* 1. A tree of Syria and Egypt allied to the common fig. 2. Any of various plane trees of the U.S., esp., the **American sycamore**: also called *buttonwood.* [< Gk. *sykon* fig + *moron* mulberry]
syc·o·phant (sik′ə·fənt) *n.* A servile flatterer. [< Gk. *sykophantēs* informer] —**syc′o·phan·cy** *n.* —**syc′o·phan′tic** (-fan′tik) *adj.* —**syc′o·phan′ti·cal·ly** *adv.*
sy·li (sē·lē′) *n.* The monetary unit of Guinea.
syl·lab·i·cate (si·lab′ə·kāt) *v.t.* **·cat·ed, ·cat·ing** To form or divide into syllables. —**syl·lab′i·ca′tion** *n.*
syl·lab·i·fy (si·lab′ə·fī) *v.t.* **·fied, ·fy·ing** To syllabicate. —**syl·lab′i·fi·ca′tion** *n.*
syl·la·ble (sil′ə·bəl) *n.* 1. *Phonet.* A word or part of a word uttered in a single vocal impulse, usu. consisting of a vowel alone or with one or more consonants. 2. A part of a written word corresponding to this. 3. The least detail, mention, or trace. [< Gk. *syn-* together + *lambanein* to take] —**syl·lab·ic** (si·lab′ik) *adj.* —**syl·lab′i·cal·ly** *adv.*
syl·la·bus (sil′ə·bəs) *n. pl.* **·bus·es** or **·bi** (-bī) A concise statement of the main points of a course of study, subject, etc. [< Gk. *sillybos* label on a book]
syl·lo·gism (sil′ə·jiz′əm) *n.* *Logic* An argument consisting of two premises and a conclusion logically drawn from them. [< Gk. *syn-* together + *logizesthai* to infer] —**syl′lo·gis′tic** or **·ti·cal** *adj.* —**syl′lo·gis′ti·cal·ly** *adv.*
sylph (silf) *n.* 1. An imaginary being inhabiting the air. 2. A slender, graceful young woman. [< NL *sylphes*] —**sylph′like** *adj.*
syl·van (sil′vən) *adj.* *Chiefly Poetic* 1. Of or located in a forest or woods. 2. Composed of or abounding in trees or woods. [< L *silva* wood]
sym- Assimilated var. of SYN-.
sym·bi·o·sis (sim′bī·ō′sis, -bē-) *n.* *Biol.* The living together in mutually advantageous partnership of dissimilar organisms. [< Gk. *syn-* together + *bios* life] —**sym′bi·ot′ic** (-ot′ik) *adj.* —**sym′bi·ot′i·cal·ly** *adv.*
sym·bol (sim′bəl) *n.* 1. Something chosen to represent something else; esp., an object used to typify a quality, abstract idea, etc.: The oak is a *symbol* of strength. 2. A character, mark, etc., indicating something, as a quantity in mathematics. [< Gk. *syn-* together + *ballein* to throw]
sym·bol·ic (sim·bol′ik) *adj.* 1. Of, pertaining to, or expressed by a symbol. 2. Serving as a symbol: with *of.* 3. Characterized by or involving the use of symbols: *symbolic* poetry. Also **sym·bol′i·cal.** —**sym·bol′i·cal·ly** *adv.* —**sym·bol′i·cal·ness** *n.*
sym·bol·ism (sim′bəl·iz′əm) *n.* 1. Representation by symbols. 2. A system of symbols. 3. Symbolic character or meaning. 4. The theory and practice of symbolists in literature and art.
sym·bol·ist (sim′bəl·ist) *n.* An artist or writer skilled in the use of symbols.
sym·bol·ize (sim′bəl·īz) *v.* **·ized, ·iz·ing** *v.t.* 1. To be a symbol of; typify. 2. To represent by a symbol. —*v.i.* 3. To use symbols. —**sym′bol·i·za′tion** *n.*
sym·me·try (sim′ə·trē) *n. pl.* **·tries** 1. An exact correspondence between the opposite halves of a figure, pattern, etc., on either side of an axis or center. 2. Beauty or harmony of form resulting from this. [< Gk. *syn-* together + *metron* a measure] —**sym·met·ric** (sə·met′rik) or **·ri·cal** *adj.*
sym·pa·thet·ic (sim′pə·thet′ik) *adj.* 1. Of, expressing, or proceeding from sympathy. 2. Being in accord or harmony; congenial: with *to*: *sympathetic* to our plan. —**sym′pa·thet′i·cal·ly** *adv.*
sym·pa·thize (sim′pə·thīz) *v.i.* **·thized, ·thiz·ing** 1. To share or agree with the feelings or ideas of another: with *with.* 2. To feel or express compassion, as for another's sorrow: with *with.* —**sym′pa·thiz′er** *n.* —**sym′pa·thiz′ing·ly** *adv.*
sym·pa·thy (sim′pə·thē) *n. pl.* **·thies** 1. The quality of being affected by the state of another with feelings correspondent in kind. 2. A feeling or expression of compassion for another's sufferings; pity; commiseration. 3. An agreement of affections, inclinations, etc.; congeniality; accord. [< Gk. *syn-* together + *pathos* feeling]
sympathy strike A strike in which the strikers support the demands of another group of workers.
sym·pho·ny (sim′fə·nē) *n. pl.* **·nies** 1. *Music* A composition for orchestra, consisting usu. of four movements that are related by structure, key, etc. 2. A symphony orchestra. 3. Harmony, as of sounds, colors, etc.: *symphony* in gray. [< Gk. *syn-* together + *phōnē* sound] —**sym·phon′ic** (-fon′ik) *adj.* —**sym′pho·nist** *n.*
symphony orchestra A large orchestra composed usu. of the string, brass, woodwind, and percussion sections needed to present symphonic works.
sym·po·si·um (sim·pō′zē·əm) *n. pl.* **·si·ums** or **·si·a** 1. A meeting for discussion of a particular subject. 2. A collection of comments or opinions on a subject, esp. when published as a series of essays or articles. [< Gk. *syn-* together + *posis* a drinking] —**sym·po′si·ast** (-ast) *n.*
symp·tom (sim′təm) *n.* 1. A sign, token, or indication. 2. *Med.* Any observable alteration in bodily functions indicating a disease. [< Gk. *syn-* together + *piptein* to fall] —**symp′to·mat′ic** *adj.* —**symp′to·mat′i·cal·ly** *adv.*
syn- *prefix* With; together; associated with or accompanying: *syntax, syndrome.* Also: *sy-* before *sc, sp, st,* and *z,* as in *system*; *syl-* before *l,* as in *syllable*; *sym-* before *b, p,* and *m,* as in *sympathy*; *sys-* before *s.* [< Gk. *syn* together]
syn·a·gogue (sin′ə·gog, -gôg) *n.* 1. A congregation of Jews assembled for religious instruction and observances. 2. The place or building for such an assembly. Also

syn′a·gog. [< Gk. *synagōgē* assembly] **—syn′a·gog′al** *adj.*

syn·apse (si·naps′) *n. Physiol.* The junction point of two neurons, across which a nerve impulse passes. Also called **syn·ap·sis** (si·nap′sis). [< Gk. *syn-* together + *hapsis* a joining]

syn·carp (sin′kärp) *n. Bot.* 1. A fruit composed of several carpels, as the blackberry. 2. A multiple fruit, as the fig. [< Gk. *syn-* together + *karpos* fruit] **—syn·car′pous** *adj.*

syn·chro·mesh (sing′krə·mesh′) *n. Mech.* A gear system in which the gears are synchronized for smooth shifting. [< SYNCHRO(NIZED) + MESH]

syn·chro·nize (sing′krə·nīz) *v.* **·nized, ·niz·ing** *v.i.* 1. To occur at the same time; coincide. 2. To move or operate in unison. *—v.t.* 3. To cause to operate in unison, agree in time, etc. **—syn′chro·ni·za′tion** *n.* **—syn′chro·niz′er** *n.*

syn·chro·nous (sing′krə·nəs) *adj.* 1. Occurring at the same time or rate. 2. *Physics* Having the same period or rate of vibration, as waves or electric currents. Also **syn·chron′ic** (-kron′ik), **syn′chro·nal.** [< Gk. *syn-* together + *chronos* time] **—syn′chro·nous·ly** *adv.* **—syn′chro·nous·ness** *n.*

syn·cline (sing′klīn) *n. Geol.* A trough or structural basin toward which rocks dip. **—syn·cli′nal** *adj.*

syn·co·pate (sing′kə·pāt) *v.t.* **·pat·ed, ·pat·ing** *Music* To treat or modify by syncopation. [< LL *syncopatus,* pp. of *syncopare* to affect with syncope] **—syn′co·pat′or** *n.*

syn·co·pa·tion (sing′kə·pā′shən) *n. Music* **a** The rhythmic placement of a tone on a weak beat and continuing it through the next strong beat. **b** Any music featuring syncopation, as ragtime, jazz, etc.

syn·co·pe (sing′kə·pē) *n. Gram.* The elision of a sound or syllable in the middle part of a word, as *e′er* for *ever.* [< Gk. *syn-* together + *kop-,* stem of *koptein* to cut] **—syn′co·pal, syn·cop·ic** (sin·kop′ik) *adj.*

syn·di·cal·ism (sin′di·kəl·iz′əm) *n.* A social and political theory proposing the taking over of the means of production by syndicates of workers, preferably by means of the general strike. **—syn′di·cal·ist** *adj. & n.* **—syn′di·cal·is′tic** *adj.*

syn·di·cate (*n.* sin′də·kit; *v.* sin′də·kāt) *n.* 1. An association of individuals united to negotiate some business requiring large capital. 2. An agency that sells articles, etc., to a number of periodicals for simultaneous publication. *—v.* **·cat·ed, ·cat·ing** *v.t.* 1. To combine into or manage by a syndicate. 2. To sell (an article, etc.) for publication in many newspapers or magazines. *—v.i.* 3. To form a syndicate. [< Gk. *syndikos* defendant's advocate]

syn·drome (sin′drōm) *n.* A set of symptoms indicating a disease, unfavorable social condition, etc. [< Gk. *syn-* together + *dramein* to run]

sy·nec·do·che (si·nek′də·kē) *n.* A figure of speech in which a part is substituted for the whole, as a *hand* for a *worker.* [< Gk. *syn-* together + *ekdechesthai* to take from]

syn·er·gism (sin′ər·jiz′əm) *n.* The joint action of different substances in producing an effect greater than the sum of the individual effects of the substances. [< Gk. *synergos* working together] **—syn′er·gis′tic** (-jis′tik) *adj.* **—syn′er·gis′ti·cal·ly** *adv.* **—syn′er·gist** *n.*

syn·od (sin′əd) *n.* 1. An ecclesiastical council. 2. Any deliberative assembly. [< Gk. *synodos,* lit., a coming together] **—syn′·od·al, sy·nod·ic** (si·nod′ik) or **·i·cal** *adj.* **—sy·nod′i·cal·ly** *adv.*

syn·o·nym (sin′ə·nim) *n.* A word having the same or almost the same meaning as some other: opposed to *antonym.* [< Gk. *syn-* together + *onyma, onoma* name] **—sy·non·y·mous** (si·non′ə·məs) *adj.* **—sy·non′y·mous·ly** *adv.*

sy·non·y·my (si·non′ə·mē) *n. pl.* **·mies** 1. The science or systematic collection and study of synonyms. 2. A written analysis discriminating the meaning of synonyms. 3. An index, list, or collection of synonyms.

sy·nop·sis (si·nop′sis) *n. pl.* **·ses** (-sēz) A brief review or outline of a play, novel, etc.; summary. [< Gk. *syn-* together + *opsis* view] **—sy·nop′tic** or **·ti·cal** *adj.* **—sy·nop′ti·cal·ly** *adv.*

syn·tax (sin′taks) *n.* 1. The arrangement and interrelationship of words in sentences. 2. The branch of grammar dealing with this. [< Gk. *syn-* together + *tassein* to arrange] **—syn·tac·tic** (sin·tak′tik) or **·ti·cal** *adj.* **—syn·tac′ti·cal·ly** *adv.*

syn·the·sis (sin′thə·sis) *n. pl.* **·ses** (-sēz) 1. The assembling of separate or subordinate parts into a whole: opposed to *analysis.* 2. A complex whole composed of originally separate parts. 3. *Chem.* The building up of compounds from a series of reactions involving elements, radicals, or similar compounds. [< Gk. *syn-* together + *tithenai* to place] **—syn′the·sist** *n.*

syn·the·size (sin′thə·sīz) *v.t.* **·sized, ·siz·ing** To unite or produce by synthesis. Also *Brit.* **syn′the·sise.**

syn·thet·ic (sin·thet′ik) *adj.* 1. Of or relating to synthesis. 2. *Chem.* Produced artificially by chemical synthesis rather than occurring naturally. 3. Artificial; spurious. Also **syn·thet′i·cal.** *—n.* A product, esp. a fabric, produced by chemical synthesis. **—syn·thet′i·cal·ly** *adv.*

syph·i·lis (sif′ə·lis) *n. Pathol.* An infectious venereal disease caused by a spirochete. [after *Syphilus,* a shepherd in a Latin poem who was thought to be the first sufferer from the disease] **—syph′i·lit′ic** (-lit′ik) *adj. & n.*

Syr·i·an (sir′ē·ən) *adj.* Of or pertaining to Syria or its people. [< Gk. *Syria* Syria] **—Syr′i·an** *n.*

syr·inge (si·rinj′, sir′inj) *n.* 1. *Med.* A device consisting of a nozzle and a rubber bulb or piston into which a liquid may be drawn for ejection in a fine jet, used for cleaning wounds, etc. 2. A hypodermic syringe. *—v.t.* **·inged, ·ing·ing** To spray, cleanse, inject, etc., with a syringe. [< Gk. *syrinx, -ingos* tube, pipe]

syr·up (sir′əp) *n.* A thick, sweet liquid, as the boiled juice of fruits, sugar cane, etc.: also, *sirup.* [< Arabic *sharāb*] **—syr′up·y** *adj.*

sys- Var. of SYN-.

sys·tal·tic (sis·tal′tik) *adj. Physiol.* Alternately contracting and dilating, as the motion of the heart. [< Gk. *syn-* together + *stellein* to send]

sys·tem (sis′təm) *n.* 1. An arrangement of parts, rules, principles, etc., into a unified whole: a school *system*, the solar *system*, a political *system*. 2. *Physiol.* a A set of organs acting together to perform a specific function: the nervous *system*. b The entire body taken as a functional whole. 3. A method or plan; scheme. 4. The quality of being orderly or methodical; orderliness. [< Gk. *syn-* together + *histanai* to stand, set up]

sys·tem·at·ic (sis′tə·mat′ik) *adj.* 1. Of, pertaining to, or of the nature of a system. 2. Characterized by system or method; methodical. Also **sys′tem·at′i·cal.** —**sys′·tem·at′i·cal·ly** *adv.*

sys·tem·a·tize (sis′tə·mə·tīz′) *v.t.* **·tized, ·tiz·ing** To form into or arrange according to a system. Also **sys′tem·ize,** *Brit.* **sys′tem·a·tise′.** —**sys′tem·a·ti·za′tion** *n.* —**sys′·tem·a·tiz′er** *n.*

sys·tem·ic (sis·tem′ik) *adj.* 1. Of or pertaining to a system. 2. *Physiol.* Of or affecting the body as a whole: a *systemic* poison. —**sys·tem′i·cal·ly** *adv.*

sys·to·le (sis′tə·lē) *n.* *Physiol.* The regular contraction of the heart that impels the blood outward. Compare DIASTOLE. [See SYSTALTIC.] —**sys·tol·ic** (sis·tol′ik) *adj.*

T

t, T (tē) *n. pl.* **t's** or **ts, T's** or **Ts, tees** (tēz) 1. The twentieth letter of the English alphabet. 2. The sound represented by the letter *t*. 3. Anything shaped like the letter T. —**to a T** Precisely; with exactness.

't Contraction for IT, as in *'tis*.

-t Inflectional ending used to indicate past participles and past tenses, and corresponding to *-ed*, as in *bereft, lost, spent*.

tab (tab) *n.* 1. A flap, strip, tongue, or appendage of something, as a garment. 2. A small, projecting part used as an aid in filing papers, etc. 3. *Informal* Tally; total; bill. —**to keep tab** or **tabs (on)** To watch closely. [Origin uncertain]

tab·ard (tab′ərd) *n.* 1. A short, sleeveless or short-sleeved outer garment. 2. A knight's cape or cloak, worn over his armor. [< OF *tabart* < L *tapete* tapestry]

tab·by (tab′ē) *n. pl.* **·bies** 1. A brindled or striped cat. 2. Any domestic cat, esp. a female. 3. Any of various plain-woven fabrics, as a watered taffeta. —*adj.* 1. Having dark, wavy markings; brindled, as a cat. 2. Watered or mottled, as a fabric. [< Arabic *'Attābi*, a quarter in Baghdad]

tab·er·nac·le (tab′ər·nak′əl) *n.* 1. Formerly, a tent or similar temporary shelter. 2. The portable sanctuary used by the Jews in the wilderness. 3. Any house of worship, esp. one of large size. 4. *Eccl.* The ornamental receptacle for the consecrated Eucharistic elements. —*v.i. & v.t.* **·led, ·ling** To dwell or place in or as in a tabernacle. [< L *tabernaculum*, dim. of *taberna* shed] —**tab′er·nac′u·lar** (-yə·lər) *adj.*

tab·la (täb′lä) *n.* A pair of small drums, played with the hands, used esp. in India. [< Arabic]

tab·la·ture (tab′lə·chər) *n. Music* A notation for instrumental music that indicates rhythm and fingering. [< L *tabula* board]

ta·ble (tā′bəl) *n.* 1. An article of furniture with a flat horizontal top upheld by one or more supports. 2. The food served at a meal. 3. The company of persons at a table. 4. A collection of related numbers, values, signs, or items of any kind, arranged for reference, often in parallel columns. 5. A synoptical statement; list: *table* of contents. —**to turn the tables** To thwart an opponent's action and turn the situation to his disadvantage. —*v.t.* **·bled, ·bling** 1. To place on a table. 2. To postpone discussion of (a resolution, bill, etc.). [Fusion of OF *table* and OE *tabule* < L *tabula* board]

tab·leau (tab′lō, ta·blō′) *n. pl.* **·leaux** (-lōz, -lō) or **·leaus** (-lōz) 1. Any picture or picturesque representation; esp., a striking scene presented dramatically. 2. A picturelike scene represented by silent and motionless persons standing in appropriate attitudes. [< F, dim. of *table* table]

ta·ble·cloth (tā′bəl·klôth′) *n.* A cloth covering a table, esp. at meals.

tab·le d'hôte (tab′əl dōt′, *Fr.* tȧ′blə dōt′) *pl.* **tab·les d'hôte** (tab′əlz dōt′, *Fr.* tȧ′blə dōt′) A complete meal served at a restaurant or hotel for a fixed price. [< F, lit., table of the host, as at an inn]

ta·ble·land (tā′bəl·land′) *n.* A broad, level, elevated region, usu. treeless; a plateau.

table linen Tablecloths, napkins, doilies, etc.

ta·ble·spoon (tā′bəl·spo͞on′) *n.* 1. A large spoon used for serving food. 2. A quantity equal to 3 teaspoons. —**ta′ble·spoon·ful′** *n.*

tab·let (tab′lit) *n.* 1. A pad, as of writing paper. 2. A small, flat surface, esp. one designed for or containing an inscription or design. 3. A definite portion of a drug, etc., pressed into a solid form. 4. A small, flat or nearly flat piece of some prepared substance, as chocolate or soap. [< OF *tablete*, dim. of *table* table]

table tennis A table game resembling tennis, played usu. indoors with a small celluloid ball and wooden paddles; Ping-Pong.

ta·ble·ware (tā′bəl·wâr′) *n.* Dishes, knives, forks, spoons, etc., for table use, collectively.

tab·loid (tab′loid) *n.* A newspaper consisting of sheets one half the size of those in an ordinary newspaper, in which the news is presented by means of pictures and concise reporting. —*adj.* 1. Compact; concise; condensed. 2. Sensational: *tabloid* journalism. [< TABL(ET) + -OID]

ta·boo (tə·bo͞o′, ta-) *n.* 1. Among primitive peoples, a religious and social interdict forbidding the mention of a certain thing, the performance of a certain action, etc. 2. The system or practice of such interdicts or prohibitions. 3. Any restriction or ban founded on custom. —*adj.* 1. Consecrated or prohibited by taboo. 2. Banned or forbidden by social convention. —*v.t.* To place under taboo. Also **ta·bu′**. [< Tonga *tabu*]

ta·bor (tā′bər) *n.* A small drum or tambourine on which a fifer beats his own accompaniment. —*v.i.* To beat or play on a timbrel or small drum. Also **ta′bour.** [< OF *tabour*, prob. < Persian *tabīrah* drum] —**ta′bor·er** *n.*

tab·o·ret (tab′ər·it, tab′ə·ret′) *n.* 1. A small tabor. 2. A stool or small seat, usu. without arms or back. 3. An embroidery frame. Also **tab·ou·ret** (tab′ər·it, tab′ə·ret′).

tab·u·lar (tab′yə·lər) *adj.* 1. Pertaining to or consisting of a table or list. 2. Computed from or with a mathematical table. 3. Having a flat surface; tablelike. —**tab′u·lar·ly** *adv.*

tab·u·lar·ize (tab′yə·lə·rīz′) *v.t.* **·ized,**

·iz·ing To arrange in tabular form; tabulate. —tab′u·lar·i·za′tion *n.*
tab·u·late (tab′yə·lāt) *v.t.* ·lat·ed, ·lat·ing To arrange in a table or list. —tab′u·la′tion *n.* —tab′u·la′tor *n.*
tac·a·ma·hac (tak′ə·mə·hak′) *n.* 1. A yellowish, resinous substance with a strong odor, derived from various trees and used as incense. 2. Any of the trees producing this substance. Also tac′a·ma·hac′a (-hak′ə), tac′a·ma·hack′. [< Nahuatl *tecomahca*, lit., fetid copal]
ta·chom·e·ter (te·kom′ə·tər) *n.* 1. An instrument for measuring speed and velocity. 2. A device for indicating the speed of rotation of an engine, etc. [< Gk. *tachos* speed + -METER] —tach·o·met·ric (tak′ə·met′rik) *adj.* —ta·chom′e·try *n.*
tach·y·car·di·a (tak′i·kär′dē·ə) *n. Pathol.* An abnormally rapid heartbeat. [< Gk. *tachys* swift + *kardia* heart] —tach′y·car′di·ac *adj.*
tac·it (tas′it) *adj.* 1. Existing or implied without being directly stated. 2. Silent. [< L *tacere* to be silent] —tac′it·ly *adv.* —tac′it·ness *n.*
tac·i·turn (tas′ə·tûrn) *adj.* Habitually silent or reserved. —tac′i·turn′i·ty *n.* —tac′i·turn·ly *adv.*
tack¹ (tak) *n.* 1. A small sharp-pointed nail, commonly with tapering sides and a flat head. 2. *Naut.* a The direction in which a vessel sails, considered in relation to the position of her sails. b The distance or the course run at one time in such direction. c The act of tacking. 3. A course of action. 4. In sewing, a large, temporary stitch. —*v.t.* 1. To fasten or attach with tacks. 2. To sew with tacks. 3. To attach as supplementary; append. 4. *Naut.* To navigate (a vessel) by making a series of tacks. —*v.i.* 5. *Naut.* To change a ship's course. 6. To change one's course of action; veer. [< AF *taque*, OF *tache* nail] —tack′er *n.*
tack² (tak) *n.* Food in general. [Origin uncertain]
tack·le (tak′əl) *n.* 1. A system of ropes and pulleys used for hoisting or moving objects. 2. A windlass or winch, together with ropes and hooks. 3. Equipment; gear: fishing *tackle.* 4. In football: a The act of tackling. b One of two linemen whose position is usu. between the guard and end. 5. A ship's rigging. —*v.t.* ·led, ·ling 1. To deal with; undertake to master, accomplish, or solve. 2. In football, to seize and stop (an opponent carrying the ball). —*v.i.* 3. In football, to make a tackle. [< MLG *takel* < *taken* to seize] —tack′ler *n.*
tack·y¹ (tak′ē) *adj.* tack·i·er, tack·i·est Adhesive; sticky. Also tack′ey. [Prob. < TACK, v. (def. 2)] —tack′i·ness *n.*
tack·y² (tak′ē) *adj.* tack·i·er, tack·i·est *Informal* Shabby; neglected; shoddy. [Cf. dial. G *taklig* untidy] —tack′i·ness *n.*
ta·co (tä′kō) *n.* A fried tortilla filled with meat, cheese, etc. [< Am.Sp.]
tact (takt) *n.* Intuitive ability to avoid offending. [< L *tactus* a touching] —tact′ful *adj.* —tact′ful·ly *adv.* —tact′ful·ness *n.* —tact′less *adj.* —tact′less·ly *adv.* —tact′less·ness *n.*
tac·tics (tak′tiks) *n.pl.* (*construed as sing. in def. 1*) 1. The art of handling a military force, esp. in battle. Compare STRATEGY. 2. Any maneuvering to gain an objective: also tac′tic. [< Gk. *taktikos* suitable for arranging or organizing] —tac·ti·cian (tak·tish′ən) *n.* —tac′ti·cal *adj.* —tac′ti·cal·ly *adv.*
tac·tile (tak′til, -təl, *esp. Brit.* -tīl) *adj.* Pertaining to or perceptible through the sense of touch. Also tac′tu·al (-chōō·əl). [< L *tactus* touch] —tac·til′i·ty *n.*
tad (tad) *n. Informal* A little child. [Prob. < TADPOLE]
tad·pole (tad′pōl) *n.* The aquatic larva of a frog or toad, having gills and a tail: also called *polliwog.* [ME *taddepol* < *tadde* toad]
ta'en (tān) *Scot.* Taken.
taf·fe·ta (taf′ə·tə) *n.* A fine, plain-woven, somewhat stiff fabric of silk, rayon, etc. [< Persian *tāftan* to twist] —taf′fe·ta *adj.*
taff·rail (taf′rāl′, -rəl) *n. Naut.* The rail around a vessel's stern. [< MDu. *tafereel* panel]
taf·fy (taf′ē) *n.* A candy made of boiled sugar or molasses and butter: also called *toffee.* [Origin unknown]
tag¹ (tag) *n.* 1. A label, tacked on or attached loosely. 2. A loose, ragged edge of anything; tatter. 3. A nickname or epithet. —*v.* tagged, tag·ging *v.t.* 1. To supply with a tag. 2. To follow closely or persistently. —*v.i.* 3. To follow closely: often with *along* or *after.* [Prob. < Scand.] —tag′ger *n.*
tag² (tag) *v.t.* tagged, tag·ging 1. In baseball, to touch (a player) with the ball or with the hand or glove in which the ball is held. 2. To overtake and touch, as in the game of tag. 3. *Informal* To designate or select. —*n.* 1. In baseball, the act or instance of tagging a player, esp., a base runner, in an attempt to retire him. 2. A children's game in which a player who is touched or caught tries to touch or catch another. [< TAG¹] —tag′ger *n.*
Ta·ga·log (tä·gä′log, tag′ə·log, -lôg) *n.* 1. A member of a Malay people native to the Philippines, esp. Luzon. 2. The official language of the Philippines.
tag day A day on which contributions are solicited for charitable and other institutions.
tag end 1. A loose end or tag of cloth, yarn, etc. 2. The endmost part of anything.
tag sale A garage sale.
Ta·hi·tian (tä·hē′shən, tə-) *adj.* Of or relating to Tahiti, its people, or their Polynesian language. —Ta·hi′tian *n.*
Tai (tī) See THAI.
t'ai chi (tī′ jē′) A Chinese system of exercise consisting of slow rhythmic movements. Short for **t'ai chi ch'uan** (chwän). Also **tai chi.** [< Chinese]
tail¹ (tāl) *n.* 1. The hindmost part or rear end of an animal, esp. when prolonged beyond the rest of the body as a distinct, flexible member. ◆Collateral adjective: *caudal.* 2. Any terminal extension of the main part of an object. 3. The bottom, back, or inferior portion of anything. 4. *pl. Informal* The reverse side of a coin. 5. *pl. Informal* A man's full-dress suit. 6. One who follows or closely watches someone. —*v.t.* 1. To furnish with a tail. 2. *Informal* To follow secretly; shadow. —*v.i.* 3. To extend or proceed in a line. 4. *Informal* To follow close behind.

—*adj.* 1. Rearmost; hindmost. 2. Coming from behind; following: a *tail* wind. [OE *tægl*] —**tail′less** *adj.*

tail² (tāl) *adj. Law* Restricted in succession to particular heirs: an estate *tail.* —*n.* A limitation of ownership; an entail. [< OF *taillier* to cut]

tail·gate (tāl′gāt′) *n.* A hinged or vertically sliding gate closing the back end of a truck, wagon, etc. Also **tail′board′** (-bôrd′). —*v.t.* & *v.i.* **·gat·ed, ·gat·ing** To drive too close behind for safety.

tail·ing (tā′ling) *n.* 1. *pl.* Refuse or residue from grain after milling, or from ground ore after washing. 2. The inner, covered portion of a projecting brick or stone in a wall.

tail·light (tāl′līt′) *n.* A light attached to the rear of a vehicle. Also **tail lamp.**

tai·lor (tā′lər) *n.* One who makes to order or repairs men's or women's outer garments. ◆Collateral adjective: *sartorial.* —*v.i.* 1. To do a tailor's work. —*v.t.* 2. To fit with garments. 3. To make by tailoring. 4. To make or adapt for a specific purpose. [< LL *taliare* to split, cut]

tai·lor·bird (tā′lər·bûrd′) *n.* A bird of Asia and Africa that stitches leaves together to hold and hide its nest.

tai·lored (tā′lərd) *adj.* 1. Characterized by simple, severe style: said esp. of women's clothes. 2. Made by a tailor.

tai·lor-made (tā′lər·mād′) *adj.* 1. Made by a tailor. 2. Made or as if made to order.

tail·piece (tāl′pēs′) *n.* 1. Any endpiece or appendage. 2. In a violin, cello, etc., a piece of wood at the soundboard end, having the strings fastened to it. 3. *Printing* An ornamental design on the lower blank portion of a page.

tail pipe An exhaust pipe on an automobile, truck, etc.

tail·spin (tāl′spin′) *n. Aeron.* The descent of a stalled airplane along a tight helical path at a steep angle.

taint (tānt) *v.t.* 1. To imbue with something offensive, poisonous, or corrupt; infect with decay. 2. To corrupt morally. —*v.i.* 3. To be or become tainted. —*n.* 1. A trace or germ of decay. 2. A moral stain; disgrace. [Fusion of ATTAINT and F *teint*, pp. of *teindre* to tinge, color]

ta·ka (tä′kä) *n.* The monetary unit of Bangladesh.

take (tāk) *v.* **took, tak·en, tak·ing** *v.t.* 1. To lay hold of; grasp. 2. To get possession of; seize, capture, catch, or win. 3. To choose; select. 4. To buy, rent, or hire. 5. To assume the occupancy or responsibilities of: to *take* office. 6. To bring or accept as one's own or into some relation to oneself: he *took* a wife. 7. To impose upon oneself: to *take* a vow. 8. To remove or carry off: with *away.* 9. To steal. 10. To subtract or deduct. 11. To undergo: to *take* a beating. 12. To accept passively: to *take* an insult. 13. To become affected with: He *took* cold. 14. To affect. 15. To captivate; charm or delight. 16. To react to: How did she *take* the news? 17. To undertake to deal with: to *take* an examination. 18. To consider; deem. 19. To understand; comprehend. 20. To carry with one. 21. To lead: This road *takes* you to town. 22. To escort; conduct: Who *took* her home? 23. To receive into the body, as by eating: to *take* medicine. 24. To admit or accommodate. 25. To perform, as an action: to *take* a stride. 26. To avail oneself of (an opportunity, etc.). 27. To put into effect; adopt: to *take* measures. 28. To use up, need, or require: The piano *takes* too much space. 29. To travel by means of: to *take* a train. 30. To ascertain or obtain by measuring, computing, etc.: to *take* a census. 31. To adopt or copy. 32. To experience; feel: to *take* pride. 33. *Slang* To cheat; deceive. —*v.i.* 34. To get possession. 35. To engage; catch, as mechanical parts. 36. To begin to grow; germinate. 37. To have the intended effect: The vaccination *took.* 38. To detract: with *from.* 39. To make one's way; go. —**to take after** 1. To resemble. 2. To follow as an example. —**to take amiss** To be offended by. —**to take at one's word** To believe. —**to take back** 1. To regain. 2. To retract. —**to take down** 1. To pull down or dismantle; disassemble. 2. To humble. 3. To write down; make a record of. —**to take heart** To gain courage or confidence. —**to take in** 1. To admit; receive. 2. To lessen in size or scope. 3. To include; embrace. 4. To understand; comprehend. 5. To receive into one's home for pay, as lodgers or work. 6. *Informal* To cheat or deceive. 7. *Informal* To visit, as on a trip. —**to take in vain** To use profanely or blasphemously, as the name of a deity. —**to take it** To endure hardship, abuse, etc. —**to take it out on** *Informal* To vent one's anger, frustration, etc., on. —**to take off** 1. To remove, as a coat. 2. To deduct. 3. *Informal* To mimic; burlesque. 4. To rise from the ground or water in starting a flight, as an airplane. 5. *Informal* To leave; depart. —**to take on** 1. To hire; employ. 2. To undertake to deal with; handle. —**to take out** 1. To extract; remove. 2. To obtain from the proper authority, as a license or patent. 3. To lead, escort, or date. —**to take over** To assume control. —**to take place** To happen. —**to take stock** 1. To make an inventory. 2. To estimate probability, position, etc.; consider. —**to take the field** To begin a campaign or game. —**to take to** 1. To have recourse to; go to: to *take to* one's bed. 2. To develop the practice of, or an addiction to: He *took to* drink. 3. To become fond of. —**to take to heart** To be deeply affected by. —**to take up** 1. To make smaller or less; shorten or tighten. 2. To accept as stipulated: to *take up* an option. 3. To begin or begin again. 4. To occupy, engage, or consume, as space or time. 5. To acquire an interest in or devotion to: to *take up* a cause. —**to take up with** *Informal* To become friendly with. —*n.* 1. The act of taking, or that which is taken. 2. An uninterrupted run of a camera or recording apparatus in making a motion picture, sound recording, etc. 3. A quantity collected at one time: the *take* of fish. 4. *Slang* Money collected, as the receipts of a sporting event. —**on the take** *Slang* Accepting bribes; corrupt. [OE *tacan* < ON *taka*] —**tak′er** *n.*

take·down (tāk′doun′) *adj.* Fitted for being taken apart easily: a *takedown* rifle. —*n.* Any article so constructed.

take-home pay (tāk′hōm′) Net wages or salary after tax and other payroll deductions.

take·off (tāk′ôf′) *n.* 1. The act of rising or leaping from the ground to begin flight. 2. *Informal* A satirical imitation; caricature.
take·o·ver (tāk′ō·vər) *n.* An assuming or seizure of control, function, ownership, or rule.
tak·ing (tā′king) *adj.* Fascinating; captivating. —*n.* 1. The act of one who takes. 2. The thing or things taken. 3. *pl.* Receipts. —**tak′ing·ly** *adv.*
ta·la (tä′lə) *n.* The monetary unit of Western Samoa.
talc (talk) *n.* A soft magnesium silicate used in making paper, soap, toilet powder, etc. Also **tal·cum** (tal′kəm). —*v.t.* **talcked** or **talced, talck·ing** or **talc·ing** To treat with talc. [< Arabian *talq*]
talcum powder Finely powdered and purified talc, used as a dusting agent, filter, etc.
tale (tāl) *n.* 1. That which is told or related; a story. 2. A piece of gossip. 3. A lie; falsehood. [OE *talu* speech, narrative]
tale·bear·er (tāl′bâr′ər) *n.* One who carries gossip. —**tale′bear′ing** *adj. & n.*
tal·ent (tal′ənt) *n.* 1. A particular and uncommon aptitude for some special work or activity. 2. People of skill or ability, collectively. 3. An ancient weight and denomination of money. [OE < Gk. *talanton* weight]
tal·ent·ed (tal′ən·tid) *adj.* Having great ability; gifted.
talent scout One whose business is to discover talented people, as actors, athletes, etc.
ta·ler (tä′lər) *n.* A former German silver coin, the prototype of all dollars: also spelled *thaler*. [< G. See DOLLAR.]
ta·les (tā′lēz) *n. pl.* **·les** (-lēz) *Law* Persons summoned for jury duty. [< L, pl. of *talis* such a one] —**tales·man** (tālz′mən) *n.*
tale·tel·ler (tāl′tel′ər) *n.* 1. One who tells stories, etc.; a raconteur. 2. A talebearer. —**tale′tell′ing** *adj. & n.*
tal·i·pot (tal′ə·pot) *n.* A stately East Indian palm crowned by large leaves. [< Bengali *tālipāt* palm leaf]
tal·is·man (tal′is·mən, -iz-) *n. pl.* **·mans** A magic charm or amulet. [< Arabic *tilsam, tilasm* magic figure] —**tal′is·man′ic** (-man′ik) *adj.*
talk (tôk) *v.i.* 1. To express thoughts in audible words; communicate by speech. 2. To make a speech. 3. To communicate by means other than speech: to *talk* with one's fingers. 4. To speak irrelevantly; chatter. 5. To confer; consult. 6. To gossip. 7. *Informal* To give information, as to the police; inform. —*v.t.* 8. To express in words; utter. 9. To use in speaking; converse in: to *talk* Spanish. 10. To converse about; discuss: to *talk* business. 11. To influence by talking: to *talk* one into doing something. —**to talk back** To answer impudently. —**to talk big** *Slang* To brag; boast. —**to talk down** To direct (an aircraft) to a landing by giving oral instructions to the pilot over the radio. —**to talk down to** To speak to in a condescending manner. —**to talk shop** To talk about one's work. —**to talk up** To promote; praise; extol. —*n.* 1. The act of talking; conversation; speech. 2. A speech or lecture. 3. Report; rumor. 4. Mere words; verbiage. 5. A language, dialect, or lingo: baseball *talk*. [ME *talken*, prob. freq. of OE *talian* to reckon, speak] —**talk′er** *n.*
talk·a·tive (tô′kə·tiv) *adj.* Given to much talking. —**talk′a·tive·ly** *adv.* —**talk′a·tive·ness** *n.*
talk·ie (tô′kē) *n. Informal* A motion picture with spoken words, music, etc.
talk·ing-to (tô′king·too′) *n. pl.* **-tos** *Informal* A scolding.
talk·y (tô′kē) *adj.* **talk·i·er, talk·i·est** Talkative. —**talk′i·ness** *n.*
tall (tôl) *adj.* 1. Having more than average height; high or lofty. 2. Having specified height. 3. *Informal* Extravagant; also, unbelievable: a *tall* story. —*adv. Informal* Proudly: to stand *tall*. [OE *getæl* swift, prompt] —**tall′ish** *adj.* —**tall′ness** *n.*
tal·lith (tal′ith, tä′lis) *n.* A fringed scarf worn around the shoulders by Jewish men when praying. [< Hebrew *tallīth* cover, robe]
tal·low (tal′ō) *n.* A mixture of the harder animal fats, refined for use in candles, soaps, etc. —*v.t.* To smear with tallow. [ME *talgh*] —**tal′low·y** *adj.*
tal·ly (tal′ē) *n. pl.* **·lies** 1. A piece of wood on which notches are cut as marks of number. 2. A score or mark. 3. A reckoning; account. 4. A counterpart; duplicate. 5. A label; tag. —*v.* **·lied, ·ly·ing** *v.t.* 1. To score on a tally; record. 2. To reckon; count; estimate: often with *up*. —*v.i.* 3. To correspond; fit: The stories *tally*. 4. To keep score. [< L *talea* rod, cutting] —**tal′li·er** *n.*
tal·ly·ho (tal′ē·hō′) *interj.* A huntsman's cry to hounds when the quarry is sighted. —*n. pl.* **·hos** 1. The cry of "tallyho." 2. A four-in-hand coach. [Alter. of F *taïaut*, a hunting cry]
tal·ly·man (tal′ē·mən) *n. pl.* **·men** (-mən) One who keeps a tally, esp. of votes.
Tal·mud (tal′mud, täl′mood) *n.* The body of Jewish civil and religious law (and related commentaries) not included in the Pentateuch. [< Hebrew *talmūdh* instruction] —**Tal·mud′ic** or **·i·cal** *adj.* —**Tal′mud·ist** *n.*
tal·on (tal′ən) *n.* The claw of a bird or other animal, esp. of a bird of prey. [< L *talus* heel] —**tal′oned** *adj.*
ta·lus (tā′ləs) *n. pl.* **·li** (-lī) 1. *Anat.* The bone of the foot just above the heel bone: also called *anklebone*. 2. *Geol.* The sloping mass of rock fragments below a cliff. [< L, ankle, heel]
tam (tam) *n.* A tam-o'-shanter.
ta·ma·le (tə·mä′lē) *n.* A Mexican dish made of crushed corn and meat with red pepper, cooked in corn husks. Also **ta·mal** (tə·mäl′). [< Am.Sp. *tamales*, pl. of *tamal* < Nahuatl *tamalli*]
tam·a·rack (tam′ə·rak) *n.* 1. The American larch. 2. Its wood. [< Algonquian]
tam·a·rind (tam′ə·rind) *n.* 1. A tropical tree of the bean family, with hard yellow wood and showy yellow flowers. 2. The pulpy, acid fruit of this tree, used in preserves and as a laxative. [< Arabic *tamr hindi* Indian date]
tam·bour (tam′boor) *n.* 1. A drum. 2. A round frame on which material for embroidering may be stretched. —*v.t. & v.i.* To embroider on a tambour. [< F < Arabic *tambūr* a stringed instrument]
tam·bou·rin (tam′bə·rin) *n.* 1. A long,

narrow drum. 2. A gay, 18th c. Provençal dance, or the music for it. [< F < Provençal]

tam·bou·rine (tam′bə·rēn′) *n.* A musical instrument like the head of a drum, with jingles in the rim, played by striking it with the hand; a timbrel. [< F]

tame (tām) *adj.* **tam·er, tam·est** 1. Having lost its native wildness or shyness; domesticated. 2. In agriculture, cultivated. 3. Docile; tractable. 4. Uninteresting; dull. —*v.t.* **tamed, tam·ing** 1. To domesticate. 2. To bring into subjection or obedience. 3. To tone down; soften. [OE *tam*] —**tam′a·ble** or **tame′a·ble** *adj.* —**tame′ly** *adv.* —**tame′ness** *n.* —**tam′er** *n.*

Tam·il (tam′əl, tum′əl) *n.* 1. One of an ancient Dravidian people, and still the most numerous of the inhabitants of southern India and northern Ceylon (Sri Lanka. 2. Their language.

tam-o'-shan·ter (tam′ə·shan′tər) *n.* A Scottish cap with a tight headband and a full, flat top, sometimes with a pompon or tassel. [after *Tam o' Shanter*, a poem by Robert Burns]

tamp (tamp) *v.t.* To force down or pack closer by firm, repeated blows. [Back formation < TAMPION]

tam·per (tam′pər) *v.i.* 1. To meddle; interfere: usu. with *with*. 2. To make changes, esp. so as to damage or corrupt: with *with*. [Var. of TEMPER] —**tam′per·er** *n.*

tam·pi·on (tam′pē·ən) *n.* *Mil.* A stopper, as a plug put into the mouth of a cannon. [< F *tampon*, var. of *tapon*, *tape* bung]

tam·pon (tam′pon) *n.* *Med.* A plug of cotton or lint. —*v.t.* To plug up, as a wound, with a tampon. [See TAMPION.]

tan (tan) *v.* **tanned, tan·ning** *v.t.* 1. To convert (hides, etc.) into leather by treating with tannin. 2. To turn brown, as the skin, by exposure to sunlight. 3. *Informal* To thrash; whip. —*v.i.* 4. To become tanned, as hides or the skin. —*n.* 1. A yellowish brown color tinged with red. 2. A brown coloring of the skin, resulting from exposure to the sun. —*adj.* Of the color tan; light brown. [OE < Med.L *tanum* tanbark]

tan·a·ger (tan′ə·jər) *n.* Any of a family of American songbirds noted for the brilliant plumage of the male. [< Pg. *tangara*] —**tan′a·grine** (-grēn) *adj.*

tan·bark (tan′bärk′) *n.* The bark of certain trees, esp. oak or hemlock, containing tannin and used in tanning leather.

tan·dem (tan′dəm) *adv.* One in front of or before another. —*n.* 1. Two or more horses harnessed in single file. 2. A two-wheeled carriage drawn by a tandem of horses. 3. A bicycle with seats for two persons, one behind the other: also **tandem bicycle.** —*adj.* Arranged in tandem. [< L, at length (of time); used in puns in sense of "lengthwise"]

tang (tang) *n.* 1. A penetrating taste, flavor, or odor. 2. A slender shank or tongue, as at the end of a sword blade or chisel, for inserting in a handle. [< ON *tangi* point, dagger]

tan·gen·cy (tan′jən·sē) *n.* *pl.* **·cies** The state of being tangent. Also **tan′gence.**

tan·gent (tan′jənt) *adj.* Being in contact at a single point or along a line; touching. —*n.* 1. *Geom.* A straight line, curve, or surface touching but not intersecting another curve or surface. 2. *Trig.* A function of an acute angle, equal to the ratio of the side opposite the angle to the side adjacent to the angle when the angle is included in a right triangle. —**to fly (or go) off on a tangent** *Informal* To make a sharp or sudden change in direction or course of action. [< L *tangens*, *-entis*, ppr. of *tangere* to touch] —**tan·gen·tial** (tan·jen′shəl) *adj.* —**tan·gen′tial·ly** *adv.*

tan·ger·ine (tan′jə·rēn′) *n.* 1. A small, juicy orange with a loose, easily removed skin: also called *mandarin*. 2. A slightly burnt orange color. [after *Tangier*, Morocco]

tan·gi·ble (tan′jə·bəl) *adj.* 1. Perceptible by touch; also, within reach by touch. 2. Definite; real. 3. *Law* Able to be bought, sold, used, etc.; material. —*n.* 1. That which is tangible. 2. *pl.* Material assets. [< L *tangere* to touch] —**tan′gi·bil′i·ty, tan′gi·ble·ness** *n.* —**tan′gi·bly** *adv.*

tan·gle (tang′gəl) *v.* **·gled, ·gling** *v.t.* 1. To twist or involve in a confused and not readily separable mass. 2. To ensnare; enmesh. —*v.i.* 3. To be or become entangled. —**to tangle with** *Informal* To come to blows with. —*n.* 1. A confused intertwining; a snarl. 2. A state of confusion or complication. [Nasalized var. of obs. *tagle*] —**tan′gler** *n.*

tan·go (tang′gō) *n.* *pl.* **·gos** Any of several Latin-American dances in 2/4 time, characterized by deliberate gliding steps and low dips; also, the music for such a dance. —*v.i.* To dance the tango. [< Am.Sp., fiesta, Negro drum dance]

tang·y (tang′ē) *adj.* **tang·i·er, tang·i·est** Having a tang in taste or odor; pungent. —**tang′i·ness** *n.*

tank (tangk) *n.* 1. A large vessel, basin, or receptacle for holding a fluid. 2. *Mil.* A heavily armored combat vehicle, moving on caterpillar treads. —*v.t.* To place or store in a tank. [< Pg. *tanque*, aphetic var. of *estanque* < L *stagnum* pool]

tank·ard (tangk′ərd) *n.* A large, one-handled drinking cup, often with a cover. [< Med.L *tancardus* large goblet]

tank·er (tangk′ər) *n.* A cargo vessel built for the transport of liquids, esp. oil and gasoline.

tank·ful (tangk′fŏŏl′) *n.* The quantity that fills a tank.

tank suit A one-piece bathing suit with shoulder straps.

tank town *Informal* A small town, as one where trains formerly stopped to refill from a water tank.

tan·ner (tan′ər) *n.* One who tans hides.

tan·ner·y (tan′ər·ē) *n.* *pl.* **·ner·ies** A place where leather is tanned.

tan·nic (tan′ik) *adj.* Pertaining to or derived from tannin or tanbark.

tannic acid *n.* *Chem.* Any of a group of brownish astringent compounds, used in inks, dyeing, and tanning. Also **tan′nin.**

tan·ning (tan′ing) *n.* 1. The art or process of converting hides into leather. 2. A bronzing, as of the skin. 3. *Informal* A thrashing.

tan·sy (tan′zē) *n.* *pl.* **·sies** Any of various perennial herbs with an aromatic, bitter taste. [< OF *tanesie*, aphetic var. of *athanasie* < Gk., immortality]

tan·ta·lize (tan′tə·līz) *v.t.* **·lized, ·liz·ing** To tease or torment by repeated frustration. Also *Brit.* **tan′ta·lise.** [< *Tantalus* in Greek mythology, a king punished in Hades by being made to stand in water that receded when he tried to drink and under fruit-laden branches he could not reach] **—tan′ta·li·za′tion** *n.* **—tan′ta·liz′er** *n.* **—tan′ta·liz′·ing·ly** *adv.*

tan·ta·lum (tan′tə·ləm) *n.* A silver-white, very heavy, ductile metallic element (symbol Ta). [From its inability to absorb water; see TANTALIZE]

tan·ta·mount (tan′tə·mount) *adj.* Having equivalent value or effect: with *to.* [< L *tantus* as much + OF *amonter* to amount]

tan·trum (tan′trəm) *n.* A petulant fit of rage. [Origin unknown]

Tan·za·ni·an (tan′zə·nē′ən) *adj.* Of Tanzania or its inhabitants. **—Tan′za·ni′an** *n.*

Tao·ism (dou′iz·əm, tou′-) *n.* A religion of China, founded by Lao-tse, who taught that happiness could be acquired through obedience to man's nature in accordance with the Tao (dou, tou), or Way, the basic principle of nature. [< Chinese *tao* way, road] **—Tao′ist** *adj. & n.* **—Tao·is′tic** *adj.*

tap[1] (tap) *n.* 1. An arrangement for drawing out liquid, as beer from a cask; a faucet or cock; spigot. 2. A plug to close an opening in a cask or other vessel. 3. Liquor drawn from a tap. 4. *Brit.* A taproom. 5. A tool for cutting internal screw threads. 6. A point of connection for an electrical circuit. 7. A connection, often a secret one, on a telephone line, gas line, etc. **—on tap** 1. Contained in a cask. 2. *Informal* Available; ready. **—***v.t.* **tapped, tap·ping** 1. To provide with a tap or spigot. 2. To pierce or open so as to draw liquid from. 3. To draw (liquid) from a container. 4. To make connection with, often secretly: to *tap* a telephone wire. 5. To make an internal screw thread in with a tap. [OE *tæppa*]

tap[2] (tap) *v.* **tapped, tap·ping** *v.t.* 1. To touch or strike gently. 2. To make or produce by tapping. 3. To select, as for membership. **—***v.i.* 4. To strike a light blow or blows, as with the finger tip. **—***n.* 1. A gentle or playful blow; also, the sound made by such a blow. 2. A small metal plate affixed to a shoe sole or heel. [< OF *taper*] **—tap′per** *n.*

ta·pa (tä′pä) *n.* 1. The inner bark of an Asian mulberry tree used in making a kind of cloth. 2. The cloth. [< native Polynesian name]

tap dance A dance in which the dancer emphasizes his steps by tapping the floor with the heels or toes. **—tap-dance** (tap′·dans′) *v.i.* **—tap′-danc′er** *n.*

tape (tāp) *n.* 1. A narrow strip of strong woven fabric. 2. Any long, narrow, flat strip of paper, metal, etc. 3. A magnetic tape. 4. A tapeline. **—***v.t.* **taped, tap·ing** 1. To wrap or secure with tape. 2. To measure with or as with a tapeline. 3. To record on magnetic tape. [OE *tæppe* strip of cloth] **—ta′per** *n.*

tape deck 1. A tape recorder. 2. A self-contained device for playing back sound recorded on a cassette or magnetic tape: also **tape player.**

tape·line (tāp′līn′) *n.* A tape for measuring distances. Also **tape measure.**

ta·per (tā′pər) *n.* 1. A small candle. 2. A burning wick or the like, giving slight illumination. 3. A gradual diminution of size in an elongated object. **—***v.t. & v.i.* 1. To make or become smaller or thinner toward one end. 2. To lessen gradually; diminish: with *off.* [OE, dissimilated var. of Med.L *papur* taper, wick < L, papyrus] **—ta′per·ing·ly** *adv.*

tape-re·cord (tāp′ri·kôrd′) *v.t.* To record by tape recorder. **—tape recording**

tape recorder A device that converts sound into magnetic patterns stored on a tape, reversing the process for playback.

tap·es·try (tap′is·trē) *n. pl.* **·tries** A woven, ornamental fabric, used for hangings. **—***v.t.* **·tried, ·try·ing** To hang or adorn with tapestry. [< Gk. *tapētion*, dim. of *tapēs* rug]

tape·worm (tāp′wûrm′) *n.* Any of various worms with segmented, ribbonlike bodies, parasitic on the intestines of vertebrates.

tap·i·o·ca (tap′ē·ō′kə) *n.* A nutritious substance obtained by drying cassava starch. [< Sp. < Tupi *ty* juice + *pýa* heart + *oco* to be removed]

ta·pir (tā′pər) *n.* A large nocturnal mammal, having short limbs and a flexible snout, native to tropical America and the Malay Peninsula. [< Tupi *tapy′ra*]

tap·pet (tap′it) *n. Mech.* A lever or projecting arm of a mechanism that moves or is moved intermittently by automatically touching another part. [< TAP[2]]

tap·room (tap′rōōm′, -rŏŏm′) *n.* A bar or barroom.

tap·root (tap′rōōt′, -rŏŏt′) *n. Bot.* The principal descending root of a plant. **—tap′·root′ed** *adj.*

taps (taps) *n.pl.* (*usu. construed as sing.*) A military signal by bugle or drum, sounded at night for the extinguishing of lights and sometimes played after a burial.

tar[1] (tär) *n.* A dark, oily, viscid mixture of hydrocarbons, obtained by the destructive distillation of wood, coal, etc. **—***v.t.* **tarred, tar·ring** To cover with or as with tar. **—to tar and feather** To smear (a person) with tar and then cover with feathers as a punishment. [OE *teoru*]

tar[2] (tär) *n. Informal* A sailor. [Short for TARPAULIN]

tar·an·tel·la (tar′ən·tel′ə) *n.* A lively Neapolitan dance in 6/8 time; also, the music for it. [< Ital. < *Taranto*, Italy]

ta·ran·tu·la (tə·ran′chōō·lə) *n. pl.* **·las** or **·lae** (-lē) 1. A large, hairy spider of southern Europe. 2. Any of various related spiders. [< Med.L < Ital. < *Taranto*]

tar·boosh (tär·bōōsh′) *n.* A brimless, usu. tapering cap, worn esp. by Muslim men. Also **tar·bush′.** [< Arabic *tarbūsh*]

tar·dy (tär′dē) *adj.* **·di·er, ·di·est** 1. Not coming at the appointed time; late. 2. Moving slowly. [< L *tardus* slow] **—tar′di·ly** *adv.* **—tar′di·ness** *n.*

tare[1] (târ) *n.* In the Bible, an unidentified weed that grows among wheat. 2. Any of various species of vetch. [MDu. *tarwe* wheat]

tare[2] (târ) *n.* An allowance made to a buyer of goods by deducting from the gross weight of his purchase the weight of the container. **—***v.t.* **tared, tar·ing** To weigh in order to determine the tare. [< Arabic *taraha* to reject, throw away]

tar·get (tär′git) *n.* 1. An object, esp. one marked with concentric circles, that is shot at, as in rifle or archery practice. 2. Anything that is shot at. 3. A person or thing made an object of attack, effort, or attention. **—on target** 1. Headed or aimed so as to hit a target. 2. *Informal* Well directed; to the point. [ME *targette, targuete*, dim. of *targa* shield]

tar·iff (tar′if) *n.* 1. A schedule of articles of merchandise with the rates of duty to be paid for their importation or exportation. 2. A duty, or duties collectively. 3. Any schedule of charges. **—*v.t.*** To fix a price or tariff on. [< Arabic *ta'rīf* information]

tar·mac (tär′mak) *n.* An asphalt road or runway.

tarn (tärn) *n.* A small mountain lake. [ME < ON *tjörn*]

tar·na·tion (tär·nā′shən) *interj. & n. Dial.* Damnation: a euphemism.

tar·nish (tär′nish) *v.t.* 1. To dim the luster of. 2. To stain; disgrace. **—*v.i.*** 3. To lose luster, as by oxidation. **—*n.*** 1. Loss of luster. 2. A stain. 3. The thin film of color on the exposed surface of a metal or mineral. [< OF *terne* dull, wan] **—tar′nish·a·ble** *adj.*

ta·ro (tä′rō) *n. pl.* **·ros** Any of several tropical plants of the arum family, grown for their edible, cornlike rootstocks. [< native Polynesian name]

tar·ot (tar′ō, -ət) *n.* One of a set of playing cards employed by fortunetellers. [< Ital. *taroccare* to play at cards]

tar·pau·lin (tär·pô′lin, tär′pə-) *n.* A waterproof canvas used to cover merchandise, athletic fields, etc. Also *Informal* **tarp.** [< TAR[1] + PALL[1] + -ING[1]]

tar·pon (tär′pon, -pən) *n. pl.* **·pon** or **·pons** A large, silvery marine game fish of the West Indies and the coast of Florida. [Origin unknown]

tar·ra·gon (tar′ə·gon) *n.* 1. A European perennial plant allied to wormwood. 2. The aromatic leaves of this plant, used as seasoning. [< Gk. *drakōn* dragon]

tar·ry[1] (tar′ē) *v.i.* **·ried, ·ry·ing** 1. To put off going or coming; linger. 2. To remain in the same place, esp. longer than one expected. **—*n.*** Sojourn; stay. [ME *tarien* to vex, hinder < L *tardare* to delay] **—tar′ri·er** *n.*

tar·ry[2] (tär′ē) *adj.* **·ri·er, ·ri·est** Covered with tar; like tar.

tar·sus (tär′səs) *n. pl.* **·si** (-sī) *Anat.* The ankle, or, in man, the group of seven bones of which it is composed. [< Gk. *tarsos* flat of the foot, any flat surface] **—tar′sal** *adj.*

tart[1] (tärt) *adj.* 1. Having a sharp, sour taste. 2. Severe; cutting; caustic: a *tart* remark. [OE *teart*] **—tart′ly** *adv.* **—tart′ness** *n.*

tart[2] (tärt) *n.* 1. A small pastry shell with fruit or custard filling. 2. *Slang* A girl or woman of loose morals, as a prostitute. [< OF *tarte*]

tar·tan (tär′tən) *n.* A woolen fabric having varicolored lines or stripes at right angles, forming a distinctive pattern, the characteristic dress of the Scottish Highlanders. [? < OF *tiretaine*, a woolen cloth] **—tar′tan** *adj.*

tar·tar[1] (tär′tər) *n.* 1. An acid substance deposited from grape juice during fermentation as a pinkish sediment; crude bitartrate of potassium. 2. *Dent.* A yellowish incrustation on the teeth. [< Med.Gk. *tartaron*] **—tar·tar′ic** (-tar′ik, -tär′ik), **tar′tar·ous** *adj.*

tar·tar[2] (tär′tər) *n. Often cap.* A person of intractable or savage temper. [< TARTAR]

Tar·tar (tär′tər) *n.* A Tatar. [< Persian *Tātār* Tatar] **—Tar′tar, Tar·tar′i·an** (-târ′·ē·ən) *adj.*

tar·tar sauce (tär′tər) A sauce of mayonnaise, capers, chopped olives, and pickles, used for fish. Also **tar′tare sauce.**

tart·let (tärt′lit) *n.* A small pastry tart.

task (task) *n.* 1. A specific amount of labor or study imposed by authority or required by duty or necessity. 2. A specific military mission. **—to take to task** To reprove; admonish. **—*v.t.*** To overtax with labor; burden. [< L *taxare* to appraise]

task force *Mil.* A tactical unit consisting of elements drawn from different branches of the armed services and assigned to execute a specific mission.

task·mas·ter (task′mas′tər) *n.* One who assigns tasks, esp. severe ones.

tas·sel (tas′əl) *n.* 1. A dangling ornament for curtains, cushions, etc., consisting of a tuft of loose threads or cords. 2. Any of various similar objects, as the tassellike inflorescence on a stalk of Indian corn. 3. Formerly, a clasp. **—*v.*** **tas·seled** or **·selled, tas·sel·ing** or **·sel·ling** *v.t.* 1. To provide or adorn with tassels. 2. To remove the tassels from (Indian corn). **—*v.i.*** 3. To put forth tassels, as Indian corn. [< OF, clasp < Med.L *tasselus*, var. of L *taxillus*]

taste (tāst) *v.* **tast·ed, tast·ing** *v.t.* 1. To perceive the flavor of (something) by taking into the mouth or touching with the tongue. 2. To eat or drink a little of. 3. To test the quality of (a product) thus: His business is *tasting* tea. **—*v.i.*** 4. To have specified flavor: Sugar *tastes* sweet. 5. To have experience: with *of*: to *taste* of great sorrow. **—*n.*** 1. *Physiol.* Any of the four fundamental sensations, salt, sweet, bitter, or sour, excited by the sole action of the gustatory nerves. 2. A small quantity tasted. 3. A slight experience or sample of anything. 4. Special fondness and appreciation: a *taste* for music. 5. The faculty of discerning and appreciating what is beautiful or correct, as in art, clothes, etc. 6. Individual preference. [< OF *taster* to taste] **—tast′a·ble** *adj.*

taste bud One of the clusters of cells, located chiefly in the tongue, having the ability to perceive taste.

taste·ful (tāst′fəl) *adj.* 1. Conforming to taste. 2. Possessing good taste. **—taste′ful·ly** *adv.* **—taste′ful·ness** *n.*

taste·less (tāst′lis) *adj.* 1. Flavorless; insipid. 2. Lacking, or showing a lack of, good taste. **—taste′less·ly** *adv.* **—taste′less·ness** *n.*

tast·er (tās′tər) *n.* One who tastes, esp. as an occupation: a wine *taster.*

tast·y (tās′tē) *adj.* **tast·i·er, tast·i·est** *Informal* Having a fine flavor; savory. **—tast′i·ness** *n.*

tat (tat) *v.t. & v.i.* **tat·ted, tat·ting** To make (tatting or an article of tatting). [Back formation < TATTING] **—tat′ter** *n.*

ta·ta·mi (tə·tä′mē) *n. pl.* **·mi, ·mis** A mat, usu. of straw, used as floor covering. [< Jap.]

Ta·tar (tä′tər) *n.* 1. One belonging to any of the Turkic peoples of west central and southwest central U.S.S.R. 2. Any of the Turkic languages of the Tatars, as Uzbek. **—*adj.*** Of or pertaining to the Tatars. Also

Tartar. [< Persian] **—Ta·tar′i·an** (-târ′·ē·ən) *adj.*
tat·ter (tat′ər) *n.* 1. A torn and hanging shred; rag. 2. *pl.* Ragged clothing. *—v.t.* 1. To make ragged; tear into tatters. *—v.i.* 2. To become ragged. [< ON *töturr* rags] **—tat′tered** *adj.*
tat·ter·de·mal·ion (tat′ər·di·māl′yən, -mal′-) *n.* A person wearing ragged clothes; a ragamuffin. [Origin unknown]
tat·ting (tat′ing) *n.* A lacelike threadwork; also, the act or process of making it. [Origin unknown]
tat·tle (tat′l) *v.* **·tled, ·tling** *v.i.* 1. To prate; chatter. 2. To tell tales about others. *—v.t.* 3. To reveal by gossiping. *—n.* Idle talk or gossip. [Prob. < MDu. *tatelen*] **—tat′tler** *n.* **—tat′tling·ly** *adv.*
tat·tle·tale (tat′l·tāl′) *n.* A talebearer; tattler.
tat·too[1] (ta·tōō′) *v.t.* 1. To prick and mark (the skin) with indelible pigments. 2. To make (a design, etc.) in this way. *—n.* *pl.* **·toos** A pattern or picture so made. [< Polynesian] **—tat·too′er** *n.* **—tat·too′ing** *n.*
tat·too[2] (ta·tōō′) *n.* 1. A continuous beating or drumming. 2. In military usage, a signal by drum or bugle to repair to quarters at night. [< Du. *tap* tap, faucet + *toe* to shut]
tau (tou) *n.* The nineteenth letter in the Greek alphabet (T, τ), corresponding to the English *t.*
taught (tôt) Past tense and past participle of TEACH.
taunt (tônt) *n.* A sarcastic, biting speech or remark; scornful reproach. *—v.t.* To reproach or tease with taunts; mock; upbraid. [? < L *temptare, tentare* to test, try] **—taunt′er** *n.* **—taunt′ing·ly** *adv.*
taupe (tōp) *n.* A dark gray color, often tinged with brown, purple, or yellow. [< F < L *talpa* mole]
tauro- *combining form* Bull; ox; bovine. Also, before vowels, **taur-**. [< Gk. *tauros* bull]
Tau·rus (tôr′əs) *n.* A constellation, the Bull, containing the bright star Aldebaran; also, the second sign of the zodiac. [< L, bull]
taut (tôt) *adj.* 1. Stretched tight; not loose or slack. 2. Tense; tight: *taut* muscles. 3. In proper shape; tidy. [ME *togt, toht*] **—tau′ten** *v.t. & v.i.* **—taut′ly** *adv.* **—taut′ness** *n.*
tau·tog (tô·tôg′, -tog′) *n.* A blackish edible fish of the North American Atlantic coast. Also **tau·taug′**. [< Algonquian, pl. of *tautau,* a blackfish]
tau·tol·o·gy (tô·tol′ə·jē) *n.* *pl.* **·gies** Repetition of the same idea in different words; pleonasm. [< Gk. *tauto* the same + *logos* discourse] **—tau·to·log·ic** (tô′tə·loj′ik) or **·i·cal** *adj.* **—tau′to·log′i·cal·ly** *adv.*
tav·ern (tav′ərn) *n.* 1. A place licensed to retail liquors to be drunk on the premises. 2. An inn. [< L *taberna* hut, booth]
taw (tô) *n.* 1. A game of marbles. 2. The line from which marble-players shoot. 3. A marble used for shooting. [< ON *taug* string.]
taw·dry (tô′drē) *adj.* **·dri·er, ·dri·est** Showy and cheap. [< *St. Audrey's lace,* a type of neckpiece sold at St. Audrey's Fair at Ely, England] **—taw′dri·ly** *adv.* **—taw′dri·ness** *n.*
taw·ny (tô′nē) *adj.* **·ni·er, ·ni·est** Tan-colored; brownish yellow. Also **taw′ney.** [< OF *tanner* to tan] **—taw′ni·ness** *n.*
tax (taks) *n.* 1. A compulsory contribution levied upon persons, property, or business for the support of government. 2. Any proportionate assessment, as on the members of a society. 3. A heavy demand; onerous duty; burden. *—v.t.* 1. To impose a tax on. 2. To impose a burden upon: He *taxes* my patience. 3. To accuse; charge: usu. with *with.* [< L *taxare* to estimate, appraise] **—tax′a·bil′i·ty, tax′a·ble·ness** *n.* **—tax′a·ble** *adj.* **—tax′a·bly** *adv.* **—tax′er** *n.*
tax·a·tion (tak·sā′shən) *n.* 1. The act of taxing. 2. The amount assessed as a tax.
tax·i (tak′sē) *n.* *pl.* **tax·is** A taxicab. *—v.* **tax·ied, tax·i·ing** or **tax·y·ing** *v.i.* 1. To ride in a taxicab. 2. To move along the ground, as an airplane before taking off. *—v.t.* 3. To cause (an airplane) to taxi. [< TAXI(CAB)]
tax·i·cab (tak′sē·kab′) *n.* An automobile available for hire, usu. fitted with a taximeter. [Short for *taximeter cab*]
tax·i·der·my (tak′sə·dûr′mē) *n.* The art of stuffing and mounting the skins of dead animals for preservation or exhibition. [< Gk. *taxis* arrangement + *derma* skin] **—tax′i·der′mic** *adj.* **—tax′i·der′mist** *n.*
tax·i·me·ter (tak′si·mē′tər) *n.* An instrument for measuring distances and recording fares, used in taxicabs. [< F *taxe* tariff + *mètre* meter]
-taxis *combining form* Order; disposition; arrangement: *thermotaxis.* Also spelled **-taxy.** [< Gk. *taxis* arrangement]
tax·on·o·my (tak·son′ə·mē) *n.* 1. The laws and principles of classification. 2. *Biol.* The systematic arrangement of plant and animal organisms according to established criteria. [< Gk. *taxis* arrangement + *nomos* law] **—tax·o·nom·ic** (tak′sə·nom′ik) or **·i·cal** *adj.* **—tax′o·nom′i·cal·ly** *adv.* **—tax·on′o·mist** *n.*
tax·pay·er (taks′pā′ər) *n.* One who pays a tax or is subject to taxation.
tax shelter An investment, depreciation allowance, bookkeeping loss, etc. that reduces taxes on income.
T-bone (tē′bōn) *n.* A beefsteak containing a T-shaped bone, taken from the loin. Also **T-bone steak.**
tea (tē) *n.* 1. An evergreen Asian shrub having leathery, toothed leaves and white or pink flowers. 2. The prepared leaves of this plant, or an infusion of them used as a beverage. 3. Any infusion, preparation, or extract used as a beverage or medicinally. 4. *Brit.* A light evening or afternoon meal. 5. A social gathering at which tea is served. [< dial. Chinese *t'e*]
tea bag A small porous sack of cloth or paper containing tea leaves, immersed in water to make tea.
tea ceremony A ritual preparation and serving of tea, practiced by the Japanese.
teach (tēch) *v.* **taught, teach·ing** *v.t.* 1. To impart knowledge to by lessons; give instruction to. 2. To give instruction in. 3. To train by practice or exercise. *—v.i.* 4. To follow the profession of teaching. 5. To impart knowledge or skill. [OE *tǣcan*] **—teach′a·bil′i·ty** *n.* **—teach′a·ble** *adj.* **—teach′a·bly** *adv.*
teach·er (tē′chər) *n.* One who teaches; esp.,

one whose occupation is to teach others; an instructor.

teach·ing (tē′ching) *n.* 1. The act or occupation of a teacher. 2. That which is taught.

tea cozy A cozy.

tea·cup (tē′kup′) *n.* 1. A small cup suitable for serving tea. 2. As much as a teacup will hold, usu. four fluid ounces: also **tea′cup·ful′** (-fo͝ol′).

teak (tēk) *n.* 1. A large East Indian tree, yielding a very hard, durable timber. 2. The wood of this tree: also **teak′wood′** (-wo͝od′). [< Malayalam *tēkka*]

tea·ket·tle (tē′ket′l) *n.* A kettle with a spout, used for boiling water.

teal (tēl) *n.* 1. Any of various small, short-necked river ducks of the Old World and North America. 2. A dull blue color with a greenish cast: also **teal blue.** [ME *tele*]

team (tēm) *n.* 1. Two or more beasts of burden harnessed together. 2. A group of people working, playing, or competing together. —*v.t.* 1. To harness together in a team. —*v.i.* 2. To form a team. [OE *tēam* offspring, succession, row] —**team** *adj.*

team·mate (tēm′māt′) *n.* A fellow player on a team.

team·ster (tēm′stər) *n.* 1. One who drives or owns a team of horses. 2. One who drives a truck or other commercial vehicle.

team·work (tēm′wûrk′) *n.* Concerted action or effort by the members of a group to achieve some common end, as the coordinated play of an athletic team.

tea·pot (tē′pot′) *n.* A vessel with a spout and handle, used for making and serving tea.

tear[1] (târ) *v.* **tore, torn, tear·ing** *v.t.* 1. To pull apart, as cloth; rip; rend. 2. To make by rending or tearing: to *tear* a hole. 3. To injure or lacerate, as skin. 4. To divide; disrupt. —*v.i.* 5. To become torn or rent. 6. To move with haste and energy. —**to tear into** *Informal* To charge into or attack without restraint. —*n.* 1. A fissure made by tearing; a rent; also, an act of tearing. 2. *Slang* A spree; frolic. 3. A rushing motion. [OE *teran*]

tear[2] (tir) *n.* 1. A drop of the saline liquid secreted by the lachrymal gland, serving to moisten the eye, and stimulated to a flow by emotional distress. 2. Something resembling or suggesting a tear. —**in tears** Weeping; crying. —*v.i.* To shed or fill with tears. [OE *tēar*] —**tear′less** *adj.* —**tear′y** *adj.*

tear·drop (tir′drop′) *n.* A tear, or a tear-shaped object.

tear·ful (tir′fəl) *adj.* 1. Weeping abundantly. 2. Causing tears. —**tear′ful·ly** *adv.* —**tear′·ful·ness** *n.*

tear gas (tir) Any of various chemicals that provoke a copious flow of tears, with irritation of the eyes.

tear-jerk·er (tir′jûr′kər) *n.* *Slang* A story, play, etc., full of sentimental sadness.

tea·room (tē′ro͞om′, -ro͝om′) *n.* A restaurant serving tea and other refreshments.

tease (tēz) *v.* **teased, teas·ing** *v.t.* 1. To annoy or harass with jokes, mocking remarks, demands, etc.; pester. 2. To scratch or dress in order to raise the nap, as cloth with teasels. 3. To comb (hair) so as to form fluffy layers. —*v.i.* 4. To annoy a person in a facetious or petty manner. —*n.* One who or that which teases. [OE *tǣsan* to tease] —**teas′er** *n.* —**teas′ing·ly** *adv.*

tea·sel (tē′zəl) *n.* 1. A coarse, prickly Old World herb of which the flower head is covered with hooked bracts. 2. The rough bur of such a plant, or a mechanical substitute, used in dressing cloth. —*v.t.* **tea·seled** or **·selled, tea·sel·ing** or **·sel·ling** To raise the nap of with a teasel. Also **tea′zel, tea′zle.** [OE *tǣsel*] —**tea′sel·er** or **tea′sel·ler** *n.*

tea·spoon (tē′spo͞on′) *n.* 1. A small spoon used for stirring tea, etc. 2. As much as a teaspoon will hold: also **tea′spoon·ful′** (-fo͝ol′).

teat (tēt, tit) *n.* The protuberance on a breast or udder, through which the milk is drawn; nipple. [< OF *tete*]

tea wagon A table on wheels for use in serving tea, etc.

tech·ne·ti·um (tek·nē′shē·əm) *n.* A chemical element (symbol Tc), artificially produced by the bombardment of molybdenum with neutrons or deuterons. [< Gk. *technētos* artificial]

tech·ni·cal (tek′ni·kəl) *adj.* 1. Pertaining to some particular art, science, or trade. 2. Peculiar to or used in a specialized field of knowledge. 3. Of or pertaining to the mechanical arts. 4. Considered in terms of an accepted body of rules: a *technical* defeat. [< Gk. *technē* art, skill] —**tech′ni·cal·ly** *adv.* —**tech′ni·cal·ness** *n.*

tech·ni·cal·i·ty (tek′ni·kal′ə·tē) *n.* *pl.* **·ties** 1. The state of being technical. 2. A technical point peculiar to some profession, trade, etc. 3. A petty distinction; quibble.

technical knockout In boxing, a victory awarded when one fighter has been beaten so severely that the referee discontinues the fight.

tech·ni·cian (tek·nish′ən) *n.* One skilled in the handling of instruments or in the performance of tasks requiring specialized training.

tech·nics (tek′niks) *n.pl.* (*construed as sing.*) 1. Practical method; technique. 2. The theory of an art or the arts; esp., the study of the techniques of an art. 3. Technology.

tech·nique (tek·nēk′) *n.* Working methods or manner of performance.

techno- *combining form* 1. Art; skill; craft. 2. Technical; technological. Also, before vowels, **techn-**. [< Gk. *technē* art, skill]

tech·noc·ra·cy (tek·nok′rə·sē) *n.* *pl.* **·cies** Government by specialists, esp. experts in the applied sciences. —**tech′no·crat** (tek′nə·krat) *n.* —**tech′no·crat′ic** *adj.*

tech·nol·o·gy (tek·nol′ə·jē) *n.* *pl.* **·gies** 1. The application of science and of technical advances in industry, the arts, etc. 2. The means by which material things are produced, as in a particular civilization. —**tech·no·log·i·cal** (tek′nə·loj′i·kəl) *adj.* —**tech′·no·log′i·cal·ly** *adv.* —**tech·nol′o·gist** *n.*

tec·ton·ics (tek·ton′iks) *n.pl.* (*construed as sing.*) 1. The science and art of construction, esp. of buildings. 2. The geology of earth structures. [< Gk. *tektōn* carpenter]

ted·dy bear (ted′ē) A toy bear, usu. covered with plush. Also **Teddy bear.** [after Theodore Roosevelt]

te·di·ous (tē′dē·əs) *adj.* Causing weariness; boring. [See TEDIUM.] —**te′di·ous·ly** *adv.* —**te′di·ous·ness** *n.*

te·di·um (tē′dē·əm) *n.* The state of being tiresome or wearisome; tediousness. [< L *taedere* to vex, weary]

tee (tē) *n.* 1. A small peg with a concave top on which a golf ball is placed in making the first play to a hole. 2. A designated area within which the golf tee must be placed. —*v.t.* & *v.i.* **teed, tee·ing** To place (the golf ball) on a tee. —**to tee off** To strike (the golf ball) in starting play.

teem[1] (tēm) *v.i.* To be full to overflowing; abound. [OE *tēam* progeny] —**teem′ing** *adj.*

teem[2] (tēm) *v.i.* To come down heavily; pour: said of rain. [< ON *tœma* empty]

-teen *suffix* Plus ten: used in cardinal numbers from 13 through 19 inclusive: *fifteen.* [OE < *tīen* ten]

teen age The age from 13 through 19 inclusive. —**teen-age** (tēn′āj′), **teen′-aged′** (-ājd′) *adj.* —**teen′-ag′er** *n.*

teens (tēnz) *n.pl.* 1. The numbers that end in *-teen.* 2. The teen-age years.

tee·ny (tē′nē) *adj.* **·ni·er, ·ni·est** *Informal* Tiny.

tee·pee (tē′pē) See TEPEE.

tee·ter (tē′tər) *v.i.* 1. To walk or move with a tottering motion. 2. To seesaw; waver; vacillate. —*v.t.* 3. To cause to teeter. —*n.* 1. An oscillating motion. 2. A seesaw. [< dial. E *titter,* prob. < ON *titra* to tremble, shiver]

teeth (tēth) Plural of TOOTH.

teethe (tēth) *v.i.* **teethed, teeth·ing** To cut or develop teeth.

teeth·ing ring (tē′thing) A ring of hard rubber, bone, plastic, etc., for a teething baby to bite on. Also **teeth′er.**

tee·to·tal·er (tē·tōt′l·ər) *n.* One who abstains totally from alcoholic drinks. [< TOTAL, with emphatic repetition of initial letter] Also **tee·to′tal·ler.** —**tee·to′tal** *adj.* —**tee·to′tal·ism** *n.*

teg·u·ment (teg′yə·mənt) *n.* A covering or envelope; an integument. [< L *tegere* to cover] —**teg′u·men′ta·ry** (-men′tər·ē), **teg′u·men′tal** (-men′təl) *adj.*

tele- *combining form* 1. Far off; at a distance: *telegraph.* 2. Related to or transmitted by television: *telecast.* Also spelled *telo-.* Also, before vowels, **tel-.** [< Gk. *tēle* far]

tel·e·cast (tel′ə·kast) *v.t.* & *v.i.* **·cast** or **·cast·ed, ·cast·ing** To broadcast by television. —*n.* A program broadcast by television. —**tel′e·cast′er** *n.*

tel·e·com·mu·ni·ca·tion (tel′ə·kə·myōō′nə·kā′shən) *n.* 1. The art and science of communicating at a distance, as in radio, radar, television, telegraphy, telephony, etc. Also **tel′e·com·mu′ni·ca′tions.** 2. Any message so transmitted.

tel·e·gram (tel′ə·gram) *n.* A message sent by telegraph.

tel·e·graph (tel′ə·graf) *n.* Any of various devices or systems using a code, esp. one using coded impulses transmitted by wire or radio. —*v.t.* 1. To send (a message) by telegraph. 2. To communicate with by telegraph. —*v.i.* 3. To transmit a message by telegraph. —**te·leg·ra·pher** (tə·leg′rə·fər), **te·leg′ra·phist** (tə·leg′rə·fist) *n.*

te·leg·ra·phy (tə·leg′rə·fē) *n.* The process of conveying messages by telegraph. —**tel·e·graph·ic** (tel′ə·graf′ik) *adj.* —**tel′e·graph′i·cal·ly** *adv.*

te·lem·e·ter (tə·lem′ə·tər) *n.* An electronic device for indicating, measuring, recording, or integrating various quantities and for transmitting the data to a distant point.

te·lem·e·try (tə·lem′ə·trē) *n.* The theory and practice of using telemeters, esp. in relation to rockets, space probes, etc. Also **tel·e·me·ter·ing** (tel′ə·mē′tər·ing). —**tel·e·met·ric** (tel′ə·met′rik) *adj.* —**tel′e·met′ri·cal·ly** *adv.*

tel·e·ol·o·gy (tel′ē·ol′ə·jē, tē′lē-) *n. pl.* **·gies** 1. The philosophical study of final causes or ultimate purposes. 2. Any doctrine that explains or evaluates phenomena in terms of their ultimate purposes or a transcendent design. [< Gk. *telos* end + *logos* discourse] —**tel′e·o·log′i·cal** (-ə·loj′i·kəl) or **tel′e·o·log′ic** *adj.* —**tel′e·o·log′i·cal·ly** *adv.* —**tel′e·ol′o·gist** *n.*

te·lep·a·thy (tə·lep′ə·thē) *n.* The supposed communication of one mind with another at a distance by other than normal sensory means. —**tel·e·path·ic** (tel′ə·path′ik) *adj.* —**tel′e·path′i·cal·ly** *adv.* —**te·lep′a·thist** *n.*

tel·e·phone (tel′ə·fōn) *n.* A device or system for transmitting sound over a wire or other communication channel. —*v.* **·phoned, ·phon·ing** *v.t.* 1. To communicate with by telephone. 2. To send by telephone, as a message. —*v.i.* 3. To communicate by telephone. —**tel′e·phon′er** *n.* —**tel′e·phon′ic** (-fon′ik) *adj.* —**tel′e·phon′i·cal·ly** *adv.*

te·leph·o·ny (tə·lef′ə·nē) *n.* The science of designing, constructing, and operating telephones.

tel·e·pho·to (tel′ə·fō′tō) *adj.* 1. Designating a lens system of a camera that produces a large image of a distant object. 2. Pertaining to telephotography.

tel·e·pho·tog·ra·phy (tel′ə·fə·tog′rə·fē) *n.* 1. The art of producing photographic images of distant objects, as with a telephoto lens. 2. Phototelegraphy. —**tel′e·pho′to·graph** (-fō′tə·graf) *n.* —**tel′e·pho′to·graph′ic** (-fō′tə·graf′ik) *adj.*

tel·e·scope (tel′ə·skōp) *n.* An optical instrument for enlarging the image of a distant object. —*v.* **·scoped, ·scop·ing** *v.t.* 1. To drive or slide together so that one part fits into another. —*v.i.* 2. To crash into one another, as railroad cars. 3. To collapse on itself.

tel·e·scop·ic (tel′ə·skop′ik) *adj.* 1. Pertaining to the telescope. 2. Visible only through a telescope. 3. Having sections that slide within or over one another. —**tel′e·scop′i·cal·ly** *adv.*

te·les·co·py (tə·les′kə·pē) *n.* The art of using or making telescopes. —**te·les′co·pist** *n.*

tel·e·type (tel′ə·tīp) *v.t.* & *v.i.* **·typed, ·typ·ing** To communicate (with) by teletypewriter. —**tel′e·typ′ist** *n.*

tel·e·type·writ·er (tel′ə·tīp′rī′tər) *n.* A telegraph system transmitting by means of a typewriter keyboard in which each key produces a coded signal that activates a specific character in a typewriterlike receiver.

tel·e·view (tel′ə·vyōō) *v.t.* & *v.i.* To observe by means of television. —**tel′e·view′er** *n.*

tel·e·vise (tel′ə·vīz) *v.t.* & *v.i.* **·vised, ·vis·ing** To transmit or receive by television.

tel·e·vi·sion (tel′ə·vizh′ən) *n.* 1. The transmission of continuous visual images as a series of electrical impulses or a modulated carrier wave, restored to visual form on the cathode-ray screen of a receiver, often with accompanying sound. 2. The television broadcasting industry. 3. A television receiving set. Also called *TV*.

tell (tel) *v.* **told, tell·ing** *v.t.* 1. To relate in detail; narrate, as a story. 2. To communicate. 3. To reveal: to *tell* secrets. 4. To decide; ascertain. 5. To express in words: to *tell* a lie. 6. To give a command to; order. 7. To let know; inform. —*v.i.* 8. To give an account. 9. To serve as indication or evidence: with *of*. 10. To produce a marked effect: Every blow *told*. **—all told** In all. **—to tell off** *Informal* To reprimand severely. **—to tell on** 1. To tire; weary. 2. *Informal* To inform against. [OE *tellan*] **—tell′a·ble** *adj.*

tell·er (tel′ər) *n.* 1. One who relates or informs. 2. A person who receives or pays out money, as in a bank. 3. A person appointed to collect and count ballots.

tell·ing (tel′ing) *adj.* Producing a great effect; impressive. **—tell′ing·ly** *adv.*

tell·tale (tel′tāl′) *n.* 1. A talebearer; tattler. 2. That which conveys information, esp. in an involuntary way. 3. An instrument or device for giving or recording information. —*adj.* That is or serves as a telltale.

tel·lu·ric (tə·lo͝or′ik, tel·yo͝or′-) *adj.* Of or pertaining to the earth; terrestrial; earthly.

tel·lu·ri·um (te·lo͝or′ē·əm, tel·yo͝or′-) *n.* A rare nonmetallic element (symbol Te) resembling sulfur and selenium in chemical properties. [< L *tellus* the earth]

telo- Var. of TELE-.

Tel·u·gu (tel′o͞o·go͞o) *n. pl.* **·gu** 1. A Dravidian language, important in literary culture. 2. One of a Dravidian people of Telugu speech. **—Tel′u·gu** *adj.*

te·mer·i·ty (tə·mer′ə·tē) *n.* Venturesome or rash boldness. [< L *temere* rashly]

tem·per (tem′pər) *n.* 1. Heat of mind or passion; disposition to become angry. 2. Frame of mind; mood. 3. Composure of mind; self-command. 4. *Metall.* The condition of a metal as regards hardness and elasticity, esp. when due to heating and sudden cooling. —*v.t.* 1. To bring to a state of moderation or suitability, as by addition of another quality; moderate. 2. To bring (clay, etc.) to the proper consistency, etc., by moistening and working. 3. *Metall.* To bring (metal) to a required hardness and elasticity by heating and suddenly cooling. —*v.i.* 4. To be or become tempered. [OE and OF < L *temperare* to combine in due proportion] **—tem′per·a·bil′i·ty** *n.* **—tem′per·a·ble** *adj.* **—tem′per·er** *n.*

tem·per·a (tem′pər·ə) *n.* A painting medium consisting of an emulsion prepared from water and egg yolks, glue, gum, casein, etc.; also, a method of painting with such a medium. [< Ital. *temperare* to temper < L]

tem·per·a·ment (tem′pər·ə·mənt, -prə-) *n.* 1. The physical and mental peculiarities of an individual; nature. 2. An intense, moody, and often rebellious nature. [< L *temperamentum* proper mixture]

tem·per·a·men·tal (tem′pər·ə·men′təl, -prə-) *adj.* 1. Of or pertaining to temperament. 2. Sensitive; easily excited. **—tem′per·a·men′tal·ly** *adv.*

tem·per·ance (tem′pər·əns) *n.* 1. The state or quality of being temperate; habitual moderation. 2. The principle or practice of abstinence from intoxicants. [See TEMPER.]

tem·per·ate (tem′pər·it) *adj.* 1. Observing moderation in the indulgence of an appetite, esp. in the use of intoxicating liquors. 2. Moderate as regards temperature. 3. Characterized by moderation; not excessive. **—tem′per·ate·ly** *adv.* **—tem′per·ate·ness** *n.*

Temperate Zones See under ZONE.

tem·per·a·ture (tem′pər·ə·chər, -prə-) *n.* 1. Condition as regards heat or cold. 2. The degree of heat in a body or substance, as measured on the graduated scale of a thermometer. 3. An excess of body temperature; fever. [< L *temperatura* due measure]

tem·pered (tem′pərd) *adj.* 1. Having temper or a specified disposition: used mainly in compounds: *quick-tempered*. 2. Having the right degree of hardness and elasticity.

tem·pest (tem′pist) *n.* 1. A violent wind, usu. attended with rain, snow, or hail. 2. A violent commotion; tumult. **—tempest in a teapot** An uproar over a trivial matter. [< L *tempestas* weather]

tem·pes·tu·ous (tem·pes′cho͞o·əs) *adj.* Stormy; turbulent; violent. **—tem·pes′tu·ous·ly** *adv.* **—tem·pes′tu·ous·ness** *n.*

tem·plate (tem′plit) *n.* A pattern or gauge, as of metal, used as a guide in shaping something accurately. [< L *templum* small timber]

tem·ple[1] (tem′pəl) *n.* 1. An edifice consecrated to the worship of one or more deities. 2. In the U.S., a Reform or Conservative synagogue. 3. A large building used for a special purpose. [OE < L *templum* temple]

tem·ple[2] (tem′pəl) *n.* The region on each side of the head above the cheek bone. [< OF < L *tempus* time]

tem·po (tem′pō) *n. pl.* **·pos** or **·pi** (-pē) 1. *Music* Relative speed at which a composition is rendered. 2. Characteristic manner or style. [< Ital. < L *tempus* time]

tem·po·ral[1] (tem′pər·əl) *adj.* 1. Pertaining to affairs of the present life; earthly. 2. Pertaining or related to time. [< L *tempus, temporis* time] **—tem′po·ral·ly** *adv.* **—tem′po·ral·ness** *n.*

tem·po·ral[2] (tem′pər·əl) *adj.* *Anat.* Of, pertaining to, or situated at the temple or temples.

tem·po·ral·i·ty (tem′pə·ral′ə·tē) *n. pl.* **·ties** 1. *Usu. pl.* A temporal or material matter, interest, revenue, etc. 2. The state of being temporal or temporary.

tem·po·ra·ry (tem′pə·rer′ē) *adj.* Lasting or intended to be used for a short time only; transitory. [See TEMPORAL[1].] **—tem′po·rar′i·ly** *adv.* **—tem′po·rar′i·ness** *n.*

tem·po·rize (tem′pə·rīz) *v.i.* **·rized, ·riz·ing** 1. To act evasively so as to gain time or put off decision. 2. To give real or apparent compliance. Also *Brit.* **tem′po·rise.** [See TEMPORAL[1].] **—tem′po·ri·za′tion** *n.* **—tem′po·riz′er** *n.* **—tem′po·riz′ing·ly** *adv.*

tempt (tempt) *v.t.* 1. To attempt to persuade (a person) to do something evil or unwise. 2. To be attractive to; invite. 3. To provoke or risk provoking: to *tempt* fate. [< L *temptare, tentare* to test] **—tempt′a·ble** *adj.* **—tempt′er** *n.* **—tempt′ress** *n.fem.*

temp·ta·tion (temp·tā′shən) *n.* 1. The act of tempting, or the state of being tempted. 2. That which tempts.
tempt·ing (temp′ting) *adj.* Alluring; attractive; seductive. **—tempt′ing·ly** *adv.* **—tempt′ing·ness** *n.*
tem·pu·ra (tem′pə·rə, tem·po͝or′ə) *n.* Seafood or vegetables dipped in batter and deep-fried. [< Jap., lit., fried food]
ten (ten) *n.* The sum of nine and one: a cardinal number written 10, X. [OE *tien*] **—ten** *adj.* **—tenth** (tenth) *adj. & n.*
ten- Var. of TENO-.
ten·a·ble (ten′ə·bəl) *adj.* Capable of being held, maintained, or defended. [< L *tenere* to hold] **—ten′a·bil′i·ty, ten′a·ble·ness** *n.* **—ten′a·bly** *adv.*
te·na·cious (ti·nā′shəs) *adj.* 1. Having great cohesiveness of parts; tough. 2. Holding or tending to hold strongly, as opinions, rights, etc. 3. Strongly retentive, as memory. [< L *tenere* to hold, grasp] **—te·na′cious·ly** *adv.* **—te·nac′i·ty** (-nas′ə·te), **te·na′cious·ness** *n.*
ten·an·cy (ten′ən·sē) *n. pl.* **·cies** 1. The holding of lands, houses, offices, etc.; occupancy. 2. The period of holding lands, houses, etc.
ten·ant (ten′ənt) *n.* 1. One who holds or possesses lands or property by the payment of rent or other fee. 2. A dweller in any place; an occupant. [< F, orig. ppr. of *tenir* to hold < L *tenere*] **—ten′ant·less** *adj.* **—ten′ant·ship** *n.*
tenant farmer One who farms another's land and pays rent, usu. in a share of the crops.
ten·ant·ry (ten′ən·trē) *n. pl.* **·ries** 1. Tenants collectively. 2. The state of being a tenant; tenancy.
Ten Commandments The set of injunctions given by God to Moses: also called *Decalogue*. *Ex.* xx 1–17.
tend[1] (tend) *v.i.* 1. To have an aptitude, tendency, or disposition; incline. 2. To have influence toward a specified result. 3. To go in a certain direction. [< L *tendere*]
tend[2] (tend) *v.t.* 1. To attend to the needs or requirements of; take care of. 2. To watch over; look after. —*v.i.* 3. *Informal* To give attention or care: with *to*. [Aphetic var. of ATTEND]
ten·den·cy (ten′dən·sē) *n. pl.* **·cies** 1. An inclination toward some purpose, end, or result; bent; aptitude. 2. An inclination to act or think in a particular way. 3. A course; direction. [< L *tendere* to tend]
ten·den·tious (ten·den′shəs) *adj.* Having a tendency to favor a particular point of view; biased. Also **ten·den′cious.** [See TENDENCY.] **—ten·den′tious·ly** *adv.* **—ten·den′tious·ness** *n.*
ten·der[1] (ten′dər) *adj.* 1. Yielding easily to force that tends to crush, bruise, break, or injure. 2. Easily chewed or cut: said of food. 3. Delicate or weak; not strong, rough, or hardy. 4. Youthful and delicate. 5. Kind; affectionate; gentle. 6. Capable of arousing sensitive feelings; touching: *tender* memories. 7. Painful if touched. 8. Requiring delicate treatment; ticklish; touchy. —*v.t.* To make tender; soften. [< L *tener, teneris* soft] **—ten′der·ly** *adv.* **—ten′der·ness** *n.*
ten·der[2] (ten′dər) *v.t.* To present for acceptance, as a resignation; offer. —*n.* 1. The act of tendering; an offer. 2. That which is offered as payment: legal *tender*. [< L *tendere* to extend, tend] **—ten′der·er** *n.*
tend·er[3] (ten′dər) *n.* 1. *Naut.* **a** A vessel used to bring supplies, passengers, etc., back and forth between a larger vessel and shore. **b** A vessel that services another at sea. 2. A vehicle attached to the rear of a steam locomotive to carry fuel and water. [< TEND[2]]
ten·der·foot (ten′dər·fo͝ot′) *n. pl.* **·foots** or **·feet** (-fēt) 1. In the West, one not yet inured to the hardships of the plains, the mining camp, etc. 2. Any inexperienced person.
ten·der·heart·ed (ten′dər·här′tid) *adj.* Compassionate; kind. **—ten′der·heart′ed·ly** *adv.* **—ten′der·heart′ed·ness** *n.*
ten·der·ize (ten′də·rīz) *v.t.* **·ized, ·iz·ing** To make tender, as meat. **—ten′der·iz·er** *n.*
ten·der·loin (ten′dər·loin′) *n.* 1. The tender part of the loin of beef, pork, etc., lying close to the backbone. 2. An urban district noted for its night life, crime, etc.
ten·don (ten′dən) *n. Anat.* One of the bands of tough, fibrous connective tissue forming the termination of a muscle and serving to transmit its force to some other part; a sinew. [< Gk. *tenōn* sinew < *teinein* to stretch]
ten·dril (ten′dril) *n. Bot.* One of the slender, filamentous organs that serve a climbing plant as a means of attachment to a wall, tree trunk, or other surface. [< F *tendron* sprout] **—ten′driled, ten′dril·ous** *adj.*
ten·e·ment (ten′ə·mənt) *n.* 1. An urban apartment building or rooming house that is poorly constructed or maintained, typically overcrowded and often part of a slum: also **tenement house.** 2. A room or set of rooms designed for one family. [< LL *tenementum* tenure] **—ten′e·men′ta·ry** (-men′tə·rē) *adj.*
ten·et (ten′it) *n.* An opinion, principle, dogma, etc., believed or maintained as true. [< L, he holds]
ten·fold (ten′fōld′) *n.* An amount or number ten times as great as a given unit. —*adj.* 1. Consisting of ten parts. 2. Ten times as many or as great. **—ten′fold′** *adv.*
ten-gal·lon hat (ten′gal′ən) A wide-brimmed felt hat with a tall crown.
ten·nis (ten′is) *n.* A game played by striking a ball back and forth with rackets over a net stretched between two equal areas that together constitute a court. [< AF *tenetz* take, receive]
teno- *combining form Med.* Tendon; related to a tendon, or to tendons: also *ten-*. Also **tenonto-**. [< Gk. *tenōn* tendon]
ten·on (ten′ən) *n.* A projection on the end of a timber, etc., for inserting in a socket to form a joint. —*v.t.* 1. To form a tenon on. 2. To join by a mortise and tenon. [< F *tenir* to hold]
ten·or (ten′ər) *n.* 1. The adult male voice intermediate in range between baritone and countertenor; also, a singer having such a voice, or a part to be sung by it. 2. *Music* An instrument playing the part intermediate between the bass and the alto. 3. General purport, tendency, or character. [< L *tenor* course] **—ten′or** *adj.*

ten·pen·ny (ten′pen′ē, -pə·nē) *adj.* 1. Valued at tenpence. 2. Designating the size of nails three inches long.

ten·pin (ten′pin′) *n.* One of the pins used in tenpins.

ten·pins (ten′pinz′) *n.pl.* (*construed as sing.*) The game of bowling.

tense[1] (tens) *adj.* **tens·er, tens·est** 1. Stretched tight; taut. 2. Under mental or nervous strain; strained. —*v.t. & v.i.* **tensed, tens·ing** To make or become strained or drawn tight. [< L *tendere* to stretch] —**tense′ly** *adv.* —**tense′ness** *n.*

tense[2] (tens) *n.* A form of a verb that relates it to time viewed as past, present, or future. [< L *tempus* time, tense]

ten·sile (ten′sil, *Brit.* ten′sīl) *adj.* 1. Of or pertaining to tension. 2. Capable of being drawn out or extended. [See TENSE[1].] —**ten·sil·i·ty** (ten·sil′ə·tē) *n.*

tensile strength *Physics* The resistance of a material to forces of rupture and stress in the direction of length.

ten·sion (ten′shən) *n.* 1. The act of stretching or the condition of being stretched tight. 2. Mental strain; intense nervous anxiety. 3. Any strained relation, as between governments. 4. *Physics* Stress on a material caused by a force pulling or stretching in one direction. —**ten′sion·al** *adj.*

ten·si·ty (ten′sə·tē) *n.* The state of being tense; tension.

ten·sive (ten′siv) *adj.* Of, like, or causing tension.

ten·sor (ten′sər, -sôr) *n.* *Anat.* A muscle that stretches a part. [< L *tensus.* See TENSE[1].]

tent (tent) *n.* A shelter of canvas or the like, supported by poles and fastened by cords to pegs driven into the ground. [< LL *tenta*, orig. neut. pl. of *tentus*, pp. of *tendere* to stretch]

ten·ta·cle (ten′tə·kəl) *n.* 1. *Zool.* A protruding flexible process or appendage of invertebrate animals, functioning as an organ of touch or motion, as the arms of a cuttlefish. 2. *Bot.* A sensitive glandular hair, as on the leaves of some plants. [< L *tentare* to touch, try] —**ten·tac′u·lar** (-tak′yə·lər) *adj.*

ten·ta·tive (ten′tə·tiv) *adj.* Provisional or conjectural; subject to change; experimental. [< L *tentare* to try] —**ten′ta·tive·ly** *adv.* —**ten′ta·tive·ness** *n.*

tent caterpillar Any of the larvae of several North American moths that spin silken webs to shelter the colony in which they live.

ten·ter·hook (ten′tər·ho͝ok′) *n.* A sharp hook for holding cloth while it is being stretched on a drying frame (a tenter). —**to be on tenterhooks** To be in a state of anxiety or suspense. [< L *tentus* extended + HOOK]

ten·u·ous (ten′yo͞o·əs) *adj.* 1. Thin; slim; delicate; also, weak; flimsy; unsubstantial. 2. Having slight density; rare. [< L *tenuis* thin] —**ten′u·ous·ly** *adv.* —**ten′u·ous·ness, ten·u·i·ty** (tə·no͞o′ə·tē, -nyo͞o′-) *n.*

ten·ure (ten′yər) *n.* 1. A holding, as of land, office, etc., or the state of being held. 2. The term during which a thing is held. 3. Permanent status granted to an employee, usu. after a trial period. [< L *tenere* to hold] —**ten·u·ri·al** (ten·yo͝or′ē·əl) *adj.*

te·nu·to (te·no͞o′tō) *adj.* *Music* Sustained; held for the full time. [< Ital. < L *tenere* to hold]

te·pee (tē′pē) *n.* A conical tent of the North American Plains Indians, usu. covered with skins: also spelled *teepee.* [< Dakota *ti* to dwell + *pi* used for]

tep·id (tep′id) *adj.* Moderately warm; lukewarm, as a liquid. [< L *tepere* to be lukewarm] —**te·pid·i·ty** (tə·pid′ə·tē), **tep′id·ness** *n.* —**tep′id·ly** *adv.*

te·qui·la (tə·kē′lə) *n.* A Mexican alcoholic liquor made from the agave plant. [after *Tequila*, Mexico]

ter- *combining form* Three; third; threefold; three times: *tercentenary.* [< L *ter* thrice]

ter·a·tism (ter′ə·tiz′əm) *n.* A monstrosity. [< Gk. *teras* monster]

ter·bi·um (tûr′bē·əm) *n.* A metallic element (symbol Tb) belonging to the lanthanide series, found in rare-earth minerals. [after *Ytterby*, Sweden] —**ter′bic** *adj.*

terce (tûrs) *n.* *Often cap. Eccl.* The third of the seven canonical hours. Also spelled *tierce.* [< OF < L *tertius* third]

ter·cen·te·nar·y (tûr′sen·ten′ər·ē, tûr·sen′tə·ner′ē) *adj.* Of or pertaining to a period of 300 years or to a 300th anniversary. —*n.* *pl.* **·nar·ies** A 300th anniversary. Also *tricentennial*: also **ter·cen·ten·ni·al** (tûr′sen·ten′ē·əl).

ter·gi·ver·sate (tûr′ji·vər·sāt′) *v.i.* **·sat·ed, ·sat·ing** 1. To be evasive; equivocate. 2. To change sides, attitudes, etc.; apostatize. [< L *tergum* back + *versare* to turn] —**ter′gi·ver·sa′tion** *n.* —**ter′gi·ver·sa′tor** *n.*

term (tûrm) *n.* 1. A word or expression used to designate some definite thing. 2. Any word or expression conveying some thought: to speak in general *terms.* 3. *pl.* Conditions or stipulations: the *terms* of sale. 4. *pl.* Mutual relations: usu. preceded by *on* or *upon*: England was on friendly *terms* with France. 5. *Math.* A quantity that is part of a fraction, an algebraic expression, a progression, etc. 6. *Logic* Either the subject or predicate of a proposition. 7. A fixed period or definite length of time, as one of the periods of the school year. 8. *Law* One of the prescribed periods during which a court may hold a session. 9. *Med.* The time for childbirth. —**in terms of** With reference to; concerning. —**to bring to terms** To persuade or force to accede or agree. —**to come to terms** To reach an agreement. —*v.t.* To designate by means of a term; name or call. [< L *terminus* limit] —**term′less** *adj.*

ter·ma·gant (tûr′mə·gənt) *n.* An abusive woman; shrew. —*adj.* Violently quarrelsome. [after *Termagant*, a deity of overbearing character, represented in medieval romances as worshipped by Muslims] —**ter′ma·gan′cy** *n.*

ter·mi·na·ble (tûr′mə·nə·bəl) *adj.* That may be terminated; limitable; not perpetual. —**ter′mi·na·bil′i·ty, ter′mi·na·ble·ness** *n.* —**ter′mi·na·bly** *adv.*

ter·mi·nal (tûr′mə·nəl) *adj.* 1. Of, pertaining to, or forming a boundary, limit, or end. 2. Ending in death: said of a disease. —*n.*

1. That which terminates; a terminating point or part; end. 2. *Electr.* A point at which a circuit element, as a battery, resistor, transistor, etc., may be connected to other elements. 3. A railroad terminus. [< L *terminus* boundary] **—ter′mi·nal·ly** *adv.*

ter·mi·nate (tûr′mə·nāt) *v.* **·nat·ed, ·nat·ing** *v.t.* 1. To put an end or stop to. 2. To form the conclusion of; finish. 3. To bound or limit. *—v.i.* 4. To have or come to an end. [< L *terminus* limit] **—ter′mi·na′tive** *adj.* **—ter′mi·na′tor** *n.*

ter·mi·na·tion (tûr′mə·nā′shən) *n.* 1. The act of setting bounds or of ending. 2. That which bounds or limits; close; end.

ter·mi·nol·o·gy (tûr′mə·nol′ə·jē) *n. pl.* **·gies** The technical terms used in a science, art, trade, etc.; nomenclature. [< L *terminus* limit + -LOGY] **—ter′mi·no·log′i·cal** (-nə·loj′i·kəl) *adj.* **—ter′mi·no·log′i·cal·ly** *adv.*

ter·mi·nus (tûr′mə·nəs) *n. pl.* **·nus·es** or **·ni** (-nī) 1. The final point or goal; end. 2. The farthermost station on a railway. [< L, limit]

ter·mite (tûr′mīt′) *n.* Any of various small, whitish social insects that are destructive of wood: also, loosely, *white ant.* [< L *termes*]

tern (tûrn) *n.* Any of several birds allied to the gulls, but smaller, usu. having a deeply forked tail. [< Scand.]

ter·na·ry (tûr′nər·ē) *adj.* Formed or consisting of three; grouped in threes. *—n. pl.* **·ries** A group of three; a triad. [< L *terni* by threes]

ter·pene (tûr′pēn) *n. Chem.* Any of a class of isomeric hydrocarbons contained chiefly in the essential oils of coniferous plants. [< *terpentin,* earlier form of TURPENTINE]

terp·si·cho·re·an (tûrp′si·kə·rē′ən) *adj.* Of or relating to dancing. *—n. Informal* A dancer. [after *Terpsichore,* Greek muse of dancing]

ter·race (ter′is) *n.* 1. A raised, level space, as of lawn, having one or more vertical or sloping sides. 2. A raised level supporting a row of houses, or the houses occupying such a position. 3. An unroofed, usu. paved area near a house. 4. An open balcony or gallery; also, a flat roof. *—v.t.* **·raced, ·rac·ing** To form into or provide with a terrace or terraces. [< L *terra* earth]

ter·ra cot·ta (ter′ə kot′ə) 1. A hard, durable clay, reddish brown in color and usu. unglazed, widely used as a structural material and in pottery, tiles, building façades, etc. 2. Its brownish orange color. [< Ital., cooked earth]

ter·ra fir·ma (ter′ə fûr′mə) Solid ground. [< L]

ter·rain (tə·rān′, ter′ān) *n.* A piece or plot of ground; esp., a region or territory viewed with regard to its fitness for some use. [< L *terra* earth]

ter·ra·pin (ter′ə·pin) *n.* Any of several North American edible tortoises; esp., the diamondback. [< Algonquian]

ter·rar·i·um (te·râr′ē·əm) *n. pl.* **·rar·i·ums** or **·rar·i·a** An enclosure for keeping land animals, plants, etc. [< L *terra* earth]

ter·raz·zo (tə·raz′ō, -rät′sō) *n.* Flooring made of marble chips set in cement. [< Ital.]

ter·res·tri·al (tə·res′trē·əl) *adj.* 1. Of or consisting of earth or land. 2. *Biol.* Living on or growing in the earth or land. 3. Worldly; mundane. [< L *terra* land] **—ter·res′tri·al·ly** *adv.*

ter·ri·ble (ter′ə·bəl) *adj.* 1. Exciting terror; appalling. 2. *Informal* Characterized by excess; severe; extreme. 3. Inspiring awe. 4. *Informal* Inferior. [< L *terrere* to testify] **—ter′ri·ble·ness** *n.* **—ter′ri·bly** *adv.*

ter·ri·er (ter′ē·ər) *n.* Any of various small, active, wiry dogs. [< L *terra* earth]

ter·rif·ic (tə·rif′ik) *adj.* 1. Extreme; intense; tremendous. 2. Wonderful; great; splendid. 3. Arousing great terror or fear. **—ter·rif′i·cal·ly** *adv.*

ter·ri·fy (ter′ə·fī) *v.t.* **·fied, ·fy·ing** To fill with extreme terror. [< L *terrere* to frighten + *facere* to make] **—ter′ri·fy′ing·ly** *adv.*

ter·ri·to·ri·al (ter′ə·tôr′ē·əl) *adj.* 1. Of or pertaining to a territory or territories. 2. Limited to or within the jurisdiction of a particular territory or region. **—ter′ri·to′ri·al·ism** *n.* **—ter′ri·to′ri·a·list** *n.* **—ter′ri·to′ri·al′i·ty** (-al′ə·tē) *n.* **—ter′ri·to′ri·al·ly** *adv.*

ter·ri·to·ry (ter′ə·tôr′ē) *n. pl.* **·ries** 1. The domain over which a sovereign state exercises jurisdiction. 2. Any considerable tract of land; a region. 3. A sphere of activity. 4. An area assigned for a special purpose. 5. *cap.* A region having some self-government but not having the status of a state, as American Samoa. [< L *terra* earth]

ter·ror (ter′ər) *n.* 1. An overwhelming impulse of fear; extreme dread. 2. A person or thing that causes extreme fear. 3. *Informal* An intolerable nuisance. [< L *terrere* to frighten]

ter·ror·ism (ter′ə·riz′əm) *n.* 1. The act of terrorizing or the state of being terrorized. 2. Threats or acts of violence, esp. as a means of intimidating or coercing. **—ter′ror·ist** *n. & adj.* **—ter′ror·is′tic** *adj.*

ter·ror·ize (ter′ə·rīz) *v.t.* **·ized, ·iz·ing** 1. To reduce to a state of terror; terrify. 2. To coerce through intimidation. **—ter′ror·i·za′tion** *n.* **—ter′ror·iz′er** *n.*

ter·ry (ter′ē) *n. pl.* **·ries** A pile fabric in which the loops are uncut: also **terry cloth.** [Prob. < F *tirer* to draw]

terse (tûrs) *adj.* **ters·er, ters·est** Short and to the point; concise. [< L *tergere* to rub off, rub down] **—terse′ly** *adv.* **—terse′ness** *n.*

ter·ti·ar·y (tûr′shē·er′ē, -shə·rē) *adj.* Third in point of time, number, degree, etc. [< L *tertius* third]

tes·sel·late (tes′ə·lāt) *v.t.* **·lat·ed, ·lat·ing** To construct in the style of checkered mosaic; lay with squares or tiles. [< dial. Gk. (Ionic) *tesseres* four] **—tes′sel·lat′ed** *adj.* **—tes′sel·la′tion** *n.*

test (test) *v.t.* 1. To subject to an examination to determine certain characteristics; try. *—v.i.* 2. To show specific qualities or properties under a trial. *—n.* 1. Subjection to an examination or trial. 2. A series of questions, problems, etc., intended to measure knowledge, aptitudes, etc. [< L *testum* earthen vessel] **—test′a·ble** *adj.* **—test′er** *n.*

tes·ta·ceous (tes·tā′shəs) *adj.* 1. Of or

from shells or shellfish. 2. Having a hard shell. [< L *testa* shell]

tes·ta·ment (tes′tə·mənt) *n.* 1. *Law* The written declaration of one's last will: chiefly in the phrase **last will and testament.** 2. *cap.* One of the two volumes of the Bible, distinguished as the *Old* and the *New Testament.* 3. A statement of beliefs; credo. 4. Evidence; proof. [< L *testis* witness] **—tes′ta·men′ta·ry** *adj.*

tes·tate (tes′tāt) *adj.* Having made a will before decease. [< L *testis* witness]

tes·ta·tor (tes·tā′tər, tes′tā·tər) *n.* 1. The maker of a will. 2. One who has died leaving a will. [< L] **—tes·ta′trix** (-triks) *n.fem.*

tes·ti·cle (tes′ti·kəl) *n.* *Biol.* One of the two male sex glands enclosed in the scrotum and in which the spermatozoa and certain secretions are formed: also called *testis.* [< L *testis* testicle]

tes·ti·fy (tes′tə·fī) *v.* **·fied, ·fy·ing** *v.i.* 1. To make solemn declaration of truth or fact. 2. *Law* To give testimony; bear witness. 3. To serve as evidence or indication: Her rags *testified* to her poverty. *—v.t.* 4. To bear witness to; affirm positively. 5. To be evidence or indication of. [< L *testis* witness + *facere* to make] **—tes′ti·fi·ca′tion** *n.* **—tes′ti·fi′er** *n.*

tes·ti·mo·ni·al (tes′tə·mō′nē·əl) *n.* 1. A formal token or statement of regard. 2. A written acknowledgment of worth; also, a letter of recommendation. *—adj.* Pertaining to or constituting testimony or a testimonial.

tes·ti·mo·ny (tes′tə·mō′nē) *n. pl.* **·nies** 1. A statement or affirmation of a fact, as before a court. 2. Evidence; proof; also, the aggregate of proof offered in a case. 3. The act of testifying. [< L *testis* witness]

tes·tis (tes′tis) *n. pl.* **·tes** (-tēz) A testicle. [< L]

tes·tos·ter·one (tes·tos′tə·rōn) *n.* *Biochem.* A male sex hormone. [< TESTIS + STEROL]

test pilot An aviator who tests new aircraft.

test tube A glass tube, open at one end, used in making chemical or biological tests.

tes·ty (tes′tē) *adj.* **·ti·er, ·ti·est** Irritable in manner or disposition; touchy. [< AF *testif* heady < L *testa* skull] **—tes′ti·ly** *adv.* **—tes′ti·ness** *n.*

tet·a·nus (tet′ə·nəs) *n.* *Pathol.* An acute infectious disease characterized by rigid spasmodic contraction of various voluntary muscles, esp. those of the neck and jaw. [< Gk. *tetanos* spasm] **—tet′a·nal, te·tan·ic** (ti·tan′ik) *adj.*

tête-à-tête (tāt′ə·tāt′, *Fr.* tet·à·tet′) *adj.* Confidential, as between two persons only. *—n.* A private chat. *—adv.* In or as in intimate conversation. [< F., lit., head to head]

teth·er (teth′ər) *n.* 1. Something used to check or confine, as a rope for fastening an animal. 2. The range, scope, or limit of one's powers or field of action. *—v.t.* To fasten or confine by a tether. [ME *tethir* < Scand.]

tetra- *combining form* Four; fourfold. Also, before vowels, **tetr-**. [< Gk.]

tet·rad (tet′rad) *n.* A group or collection of four. [< Gk. *tetras, -ados* group of four]

tet·ra·eth·yl lead (tet′rə·eth′il led) *Chem.* A colorless, heavy, flammable, poisonous liquid hydrocarbon, used as an antiknock agent in internal-combustion engines.

tet·ra·he·dron (tet′rə·hē′drən) *n. pl.* **·drons** or **·dra** *Geom.* A polyhedron bounded by four plane triangular faces. [< Gk. *tetra-* four + *hedra* base] **—tet′ra·he′dral** *adj.*

tet·ra·hy·dro·can·nab·i·nol (tet′rə·hīd′rə·kə·nab′ə·nôl) *n.* *Chem.* The intoxicant in marijuana. Abbr. *THC.*

te·tral·o·gy (te·tral′ə·jē) *n. pl.* **·gies** A series of four related dramatic, operatic, or literary works. [< Gk. *tetra-* four + *logos* word]

te·tram·e·ter (te·tram′ə·ter) *n.* In prosody, a line of verse consisting of four metrical feet. [< Gk. *tetra-* four + *metron* measure]

tet·rarch (tet′rärk, tē′trärk) *n.* 1. The governor of one of four divisions of a country or province. 2. A tributary prince under the Romans; a subordinate ruler. [< Gk. *tetra-* four + *archos* ruler]

tet·rar·chy (tet′rär·kē, tē′trär-) *n. pl.* **·chies** The rule, territory, or jurisdiction of a tetrarch. **—te·trar′chic** *adj.*

Teu·ton (tōōt′n, tyōōt′n) *n.* One belonging to any of the Teutonic peoples; esp., a German.

Teu·ton·ic (tōō·ton′ik, tyōō-) *adj.* Of or pertaining to the Germanic peoples or their languages. *—n.* The Germanic subfamily of languages.

Teu·ton·ism (tōōt′n·iz′əm, tyōōt′n-) *n.* 1. A custom or mode of expression peculiar to Germans. 2. A belief in the superiority of the Teutonic peoples. 3. Teutonic character and civilization. **—Teu′ton·ist** *n.*

text (tekst) *n.* 1. The body of matter on a written or printed page, as distinguished from notes, commentary, illustrations, etc. 2. The actual or original words of an author. 3. A written or printed version of the matter of an author's works: the folio *text* of Shakespeare. 4. A verse of Scripture, esp. when used as the basis of a sermon. 5. Any subject of discourse; a topic. 6. A textbook. [< L *texere* to weave] **—tex·tu·al** (teks′·chōō·əl) *adj.*

text·book (tekst′bōōk′) *n.* A book used for instruction in a particular area of study.

tex·tile (teks′til, -tīl) *adj.* 1. Pertaining to weaving or woven fabrics. 2. Such as may be woven; manufactured by weaving. *—n.* 1. A woven fabric. 2. Material, as yarn, capable of being woven. [< L *textus* fabric.]

tex·ture (teks′chər) *n.* 1. The arrangement or character of the threads, etc., of a woven fabric. 2. The structure, composition, or appearance of something, as of the surface of a painting. [< L *textus* fabric] **—tex′·tur·al** *adj.* **—tex′tur·al·ly** *adv.* **—tex′tured** *adj.*

-th[1] *suffix of nouns* 1. The act or result of the action expressed in the root word: *growth.* 2. The state of being what is indicated in the root word: *health.* [OE *-thu, -th*]

-th[2] *suffix* Used in ordinal numbers: *tenth.* Also, after vowels, *-eth,* as in *fortieth.* [OE *-tha, -the*]

-th[3] See -ETH[1].

Thai (tī) *n.* 1. The people collectively of Thailand, Laos, and parts of Burma: preceded by *the*. 2. A family of languages spoken by these people. 3. The language of Thailand. Also spelled *Tai*. —**Thai** *adj.*

thal·a·mus (thal′ə·məs) *n.* *pl.* **·mi** (-mī) *Anat.* A large mass of gray matter at the base of the brain, the center for transmission of sensory impulses to the cerebral cortex. [< Gk. *thalamos* chamber] —**tha·lam·ic** (thə·lam′ik) *adj.*

tha·las·sic (thə·las′ik) *adj.* Of or pertaining to the seas, as distinguished from the oceans. [< Gk. *thalassa* sea]

tha·ler (tä′lər) See TALER.

thal·i·do·mide (thə·lid′ə·mīd) *n.* *Chem.* An organic compound, originally a mild sedative and later found to cause serious malformations in newborn children.

thal·li·um (thal′ē·əm) *n.* A soft, white, crystalline metallic element (symbol Tl). [< Gk. *thallos* green shoot]

than (than, *unstressed* thən) *conj.* 1. When, as, or if compared with: after an adjective or adverb to express comparison between what precedes and what follows: I am stronger *than* she (is). 2. Except; but: used after *other*, *else*, etc.: no other *than* you. [OE *thonne* then]

thank (thangk) *v.t.* 1. To express gratitude to. 2. To hold responsible; blame: often used ironically. [OE *thanc* thanks, thought]

thank·ful (thangk′fəl) *adj.* 1. Appreciative of favors received; grateful. 2. Expressing thanks. —**thank′ful·ly** *adv.* —**thank′ful·ness** *n.*

thank·less (thangk′lis) *adj.* 1. Not showing gratitude; ungrateful. 2. Not likely to gain thanks; unappreciated. —**thank′less·ly** *adv.* —**thank′less·ness** *n.*

thanks (thangks) *n.pl.* Expressions of gratitude; grateful acknowledgment. —*interj.* Thank you. —**thanks to** 1. Thanks be given to. 2. Because of.

thanks·giv·ing (thangks′giv′ing) *n.* 1. The act of giving thanks, as to God; an expression of gratitude. 2. A public celebration in recognition of divine favor. 3. *cap.* The fourth Thursday in November, set apart as an annual festival of thanksgiving: also **Thanksgiving Day.**

that (that, *unstressed* thət) *pl. for adj. and pron. def. 1* **those** (thōz) *adj.* 1. Pertaining to some person or thing previously mentioned or understood. 2. Denoting something more remote, or something contrasted with another thing: distinguished from *this*: This house is brown; *that* one is red. —*pron.* 1. As a demonstrative, the person or thing implied, mentioned, or understood; the person or thing there or as distinguished from one already designated: *That* is the dress I like; Keep this and discard *that*. 2. As a relative pronoun, who, whom, or which: the person *that* I saw. —*adv.* 1. To an extent: I can't see *that* far. 2. *Informal* In such a manner or degree; so: He's *that* simple, he can hardly read. —*conj.* 1. As a fact: introducing a fact: I tell you *that* it is so. 2. As a result: introducing a result, consequence, or effect: He bled so profusely *that* he died. 3. At which time; when: It was only yesterday *that* I saw her. 4. For the reason that; because. 5. Introducing an exclamation: O *that* he would come. —**so that** 1. To the end that. 2. With the result that. [OE *thæt*, neut. of *sē* the, that]

thatch (thach) *n.* 1. A covering of reeds, straw, etc., arranged on a roof so as to shed water. 2. Any material used for such a covering. —*v.t.* To cover with or as with thatch. [OE *thæc* cover] —**thatch′er** *n.* —**thatch′ing** *n.*

thaw (thô) *v.i.* 1. To melt or dissolve; become liquid or semiliquid, as snow or ice. 2. To rise in temperature so as to melt ice and snow. 3. To become less cold and unsociable. —*v.t.* 4. To cause to thaw. [OE *thawian*] —**thaw** *n.*

THC Tetrahydrocannabinol.

the[1] (*stressed* thē; *unstressed before a consonant* thə) *definite article* or *adj.* *The* is opposed to the indefinite article *a* or *an*, and is used, esp. before nouns, to render the modified word more particular or individual. It is used specifically: 1. When reference is made to a particular person, thing, or group: He left *the* room. 2. To give an adjective substantive force, or render a notion abstract: *the* doing of the deed; *the* quick and *the* dead. 3. Before a noun to make it generic: *The* dog is a friend of children. 4. With the force of a possessive pronoun: She kicked me in *the* (my) leg. 5. To designate a particular one as emphatically outstanding: usu. stressed in speech and italicized in writing: She is *the* officer for the command. [OE, later form of *sē*]

the[2] (thə) *adv.* By that much; by so much; to this extent: used to modify words in the comparative degree: *the* more, *the* merrier. [OE *thȳ*, instrumental case of *sē* the[1]]

the- Var. of THEO-.

the·a·ter (thē′ə·tər) *n.* 1. A building especially adapted to present dramas, operas, motion pictures, etc.; playhouse. 2. The theatrical world and everything relating to it. 3. A room or hall for lectures, demonstrations, etc. 4. Any place or region that is the scene of events: a *theater* of operations in war. Also **the′a·tre.** [< Gk. *theasthai* to behold]

the·a·ter·go·er (thē′ə·tər·gō′ər) *n.* One who goes often or regularly to the theater. Also **the′a·tre·go′er.**

the·a·ter-in-the-round (thē′ə·tər·in·thə·round′) *n.* Arena theater.

the·at·ri·cal (thē·at′ri·kəl) *adj.* 1. Pertaining to the theater. 2. Designed for show or effect; showy. Also **the·at′ric.** —**the·at′ri·cal·ism, the·at′ri·cal·ness** *n.* —**the·at′ri·cal·ly** *adv.*

the·at·rics (thē·at′riks) *n.pl.* (*construed as sing.*) 1. The staging of plays. 2. An overly dramatic presentation.

thee (thē) *pron.* 1. *Archaic* The objective case of the pronoun *thou*. 2. Thou: used by some Quakers with a verb in the third person singular: *Thee* knows my mind. [OE *thē*]

theft (theft) *n.* The act or crime of thieving; larceny. [OE *thēoft*, *thīefth*]

their (thâr) *pronominal adj.* The possessive case of the pronoun *they*, used attributively: *their* homes. [ME < ON *theirra* of them]

theirs (thârz) *pron.* 1. The possessive case of the pronoun *they*, used predicatively:

That house is *theirs.* 2. The one or ones belonging or relating to them: our country and *theirs.* —of theirs Belonging or pertaining to them.

the·ism (thē′iz·əm) *n.* 1. Belief in, or in the existence of, God, a god, or gods. 2. Belief in one god; monotheism. [< Gk. *theos* god] —**the′ist** *n.* —**the·is′tic** or **·ti·cal** *adj.* —**the·is′ti·cal·ly** *adv.*

them (them, *unstressed* thəm) *pron.* The objective case of the pronoun *they.* [ME *theim* < ON, to them]

thematic vowel *Ling.* A vowel added to a root to form a stem.

theme (thēm) *n.* 1. A topic to be discussed or developed in speech or writing; a subject of discourse. 2. A brief composition, esp. one written as an exercise as part of a course of instruction. 3. *Music* A melody that forms the basis of a composition. [< Gk. *tithenai* to place] —**the·mat·ic** (thē·mat′ik) or **·i·cal** *adj.* —**the·mat′i·cal·ly** *adv.*

them·selves (them′selvz′, *unstressed* thəm-) *pron.* A form of the third person plural pronoun, used: 1. As a reflexive or as object of a preposition in a reflexive sense: They laughed at *themselves.* 2. As an intensive form of *they*: They *themselves* are at fault. 3. As a designation of a normal or usual state: They were not *themselves* then.

then (then) *adv.* 1. At that time. 2. Soon or immediately afterward. 3. At another time: often following *now, at first,* etc. 4. For that reason; as a consequence. 5. In that case. —*adj.* Being or acting in, or belonging to, that time: the *then* secretary of state. —*n.* A specific time already mentioned or understood; that time. [OE *thanne*]

thence (thens) *adv.* 1. From that place. 2. From the circumstance, fact, or cause; therefore. 3. From that time; after that time. [OE *thanon* from there]

thence·forth (thens′fôrth′, thens′fôrth′) *adv.* From that time on; thereafter.

thence·for·ward (thens′fôr′wərd) *adv.* 1. Thenceforth. 2. From that place forward. Also **thence′for′wards.**

theo- *combining form* God; of or pertaining to God, a god, or gods. Also, before vowels, *the-.* [< Gk. *theos* a god]

the·oc·ra·cy (thē·ok′rə·sē) *n. pl.* **·cies** 1. A state, political unit, or group of people that claims a deity as its ruler. 2. Government of a state by a priesthood claiming divine authority, as in the Papacy. [< Gk. *theos* god + *krateein* to rule] —**the·o·crat** (thē′ə·krat) *n.* —**the·o·crat·ic** (thē′ə·krat′ik) or **·i·cal** *adj.*

the·o·lo·gi·an (thē′ə·lō′jē·ən, -jən) *n.* One versed in theology.

the·ol·o·gize (thē·ol′ə·jīz) *v.* **·gized, ·giz·ing** *v.t.* 1. To devise or fit (something) into a system of theology. —*v.i.* 2. To reason theologically. Also *Brit.* **the·ol′o·gise.** —**the·ol′o·giz·er** *n.*

the·ol·o·gy (thē·ol′ə·jē) *n. pl.* **·gies** 1. The study of religion. 2. A body of doctrines as set forth by a particular church or religious group. [< Gk. *theos* god + *logos* discourse] —**the·o·log·i·cal** (thē′ə·loj′i·kəl) or **the′o·log′ic** *adj.* —**the′o·log′i·cal·ly** *adv.*

the·o·rem (thē′ər·əm, thir′əm) *n.* 1. A proposition demonstrably true or acknowledged as such. 2. *Math.* a A proposition setting forth something to be proved. b A proposition that has been proved or assumed to be true. [< Gk. *theōreein* to look at] —**the·o·re·mat·ic** (thē′ər·ə·mat′ik) *adj.*

the·o·ret·i·cal (thē′ə·ret′i·kəl) *adj.* 1. Of, relating to, or consisting of theory. 2. Relating to knowledge or science without reference to its application. 3. Existing only in theory; hypothetical. Also **the′o·ret′ic.** —**the′o·ret′i·cal·ly** *adv.*

the·o·re·ti·cian (thē′ər·ə·tish′ən) *n.* One who deals with theory rather than with the practical aspects of a subject.

the·o·rize (thē′ə·rīz) *v.i.* **·rized, ·riz·ing** To form or express theories; speculate. Also *Brit.* **the′o·rise.** —**the′o·ri·za′tion** *n.* —**the′o·rist, the′o·riz′er** *n.*

the·o·ry (thē′ər·ē, thir′ē) *n. pl.* **·ries** 1. A speculative or conjectural view of something. 2. Fundamental principles underlying a science, art, etc.: music *theory, theory* of equations. 3. Abstract knowledge of any art as opposed to the practice of it. 4. Suppositions derived from evidence and intended to serve as an explanation for phenomena: the quantum *theory.* [< Gk. *theoria* view]

the·os·o·phy (thē·os′ə·fē) *n. pl.* **·phies** Any of various religious systems that aim at establishing a direct relation between the individual soul and the divine principle through contemplation and speculation. [< Gk. *theos* god + *sophos* wise] —**the·o·soph·i·cal** (thē′ə·sof′i·kəl) *adj.* —**the′o·soph′i·cal·ly** *adv.* —**the·os′o·phist** *n.*

ther·a·peu·tic (ther′ə·pyōō′tik) *adj.* 1. Having healing qualities; curative. 2. Pertaining to therapeutics. Also **ther′a·peu′ti·cal.** [< Gk. *therapeuein* take care of] —**ther′a·peu′ti·cal·ly** *adv.*

ther·a·peu·tics (ther′ə·pyōō′tiks) *n.pl.* (*construed as sing.*) The branch of medical science dealing with the treatment of disease. —**ther′a·peu′tist** *n.*

ther·a·py (ther′ə·pē) *n. pl.* **·pies** Treatment, activity, etc., intended to remedy or alleviate a disorder or undesirable condition. —**ther′a·pist** *n.*

there (thâr) *adv.* 1. In, at, or about that place: opposed to *here.* Also used to indicate or emphasize: John *there* is a good student. 2. To, toward, or into that place; thither. 3. At that stage or point of action or time. —*n.* That place: Are you from *there,* too? —*interj.* An exclamation of triumph, relief, etc.: *There!* It's finished. [OE *thǣr*]

there·a·bout (thâr′ə·bout′) *adv.* Near that number, quantity, degree, place, or time. Also **there′a·bouts′.**

there·af·ter (thâr′af′tər) *adv.* Afterward; from that time on.

there·at (thâr′at′) *adv.* At that event, place, or time.

there·by (thâr′bī′) *adv.* 1. Through the agency of that. 2. Connected with that.

there·for (thâr′fôr′) *adv.* For this, that, or it.

there·fore (thâr′fôr′) *adv. & conj.* For that or this reason; consequently.

there·from (thâr′frum′) *adv.* From this, that, or it.

there·in (*th*âr′in′) *adv.* 1. In that place. 2. In that time, matter, or respect.
there·in·af·ter (*th*âr′in·af′tər) *adv.* In a subsequent part of that (book, document, speech, etc.).
there·of (*th*âr′uv′) *adv.* 1. Of or relating to this, that, or it. 2. From or because of this or that cause.
there·on (*th*âr′on′, -ôn′) *adv.* 1. On this, that, or it. 2. Thereupon; thereat.
there's (*th*ârz) 1. There is. 2. There has.
there·to (*th*âr′to͞o′) *adv.* 1. To this, that, or it. 2. In addition. Also **there′un·to′** (-un·to͞o′).
there·to·fore (*th*âr′tə·fôr′) *adv.* Before this or that; previously to that.
there·up·on (*th*âr′ə·pon′, -ə·pôn′) *adv.* 1. Upon that; upon it. 2. Following upon or in consequence of that. 3. Immediately following; at once.
there·with (*th*âr′with′, -wi*th*′) *adv.* 1. With this, that, or it. 2. Immediately afterward.
there·with·al (*th*âr′wi*th*·ôl′) *adv.* With all this or that; besides.
ther·mal (thûr′məl) *adj.* 1. Pertaining to, determined by, or measured by heat. 2. Caused by, using, or producing heat. 3. Hot or warm. Also **ther′mic.** —**ther′mal·ly** *adv.*
thermo- *combining form* Heat; of or caused by heat. Also, before vowels, **therm-.** [< Gk. *thermos* heat, warmth]
ther·mo·coup·le (thûr′mə·kup′əl) *n.* A device for temperature measurement that depends upon the electric current or potential produced when joined conductors of two different metals have their ends at different temperatures. Also **ther·mo·e·lec·tric couple** (thûr′mō·i·lek′trik).
ther·mo·dy·nam·ics (thûr′mō·dī·nam′iks, -di-) *n.pl.* (*construed as sing.*) The branch of physics dealing with the relations between heat and other forms of energy. —**ther′mo·dy·nam′ic** or **·i·cal** *adj.* —**ther′mo·dy·nam′i·cist** (-ə·sist) *n.*
ther·mom·e·ter (thər·mom′ə·tər) *n.* An instrument for measuring temperature, usu. a graduated glass tube with a bulb containing a liquid, as mercury or alcohol, that expands or contracts as the temperature rises or falls. [< THERMO- + METER] —**ther·mo·met·ric** (thûr′mō·met′rik) or **·ri·cal** *adj.* —**ther′mo·met′ri·cal·ly** *adv.* —**ther·mom′e·try** *n.*
ther·mo·nu·cle·ar (thûr′mō·no͞o′klē·ər, -nyo͞o′-) *adj. Physics* Pertaining to or characterized by reactions involving the fusion of atomic nuclei at very high temperatures, esp. in stars and in the hydrogen bomb.
ther·mo·plas·tic (thûr′mō·plas′tik) *adj.* Able to be molded when heated. —*n.* A thermoplastic substance.
ther·mos bottle (thûr′məs) A bottle that keeps the contents hot or cold. [< Gk. *thermos* hot]
ther·mo·set·ting (thûr′mō·set′ing) *adj.* Having the property of assuming a fixed shape after being molded under heat, as certain plastics and resins.
ther·mo·stat (thûr′mə·stat) *n.* A device for the automatic regulation of temperature. [< THERMO- + Gk. *statos* standing] —**ther′·mo·stat′ic** *adj.* —**ther′mo·stat′i·cal·ly** *adv.*
the·sau·rus (thə·sôr′əs) *n. pl.* **·sau·ri** (-sôr′ī) A book of words, esp., synonyms and antonyms, usu. arranged in categories. [< Gk. *thesauros* treasure]
these (*th*ēz) *adj. & pron.* Plural of THIS.
the·sis (thē′sis) *n. pl.* **·ses** (-sēz) 1. A proposition or premise. 2. A formal proposition, advanced and defended by argumentation. 3. A formal treatise on a particular subject; esp., a dissertation presented for an academic degree. [< Gk. *tithenai* to put, place]
Thes·pi·an (thes′pē·ən) *adj.* Of or relating to drama; dramatic; tragic. —*n.* An actor or actress. [after *Thespis*, Greek poet and actor, 6th c. B.C.]
the·ta (thā′tə, thē′tə) *n.* 1. The eighth letter in the Greek alphabet (Θ, ϑ, θ). 2. *Math.* A symbol for an angle of unknown value.
thew (thyo͞o) *n.* 1. A sinew or muscle, esp., when well-developed. 2. *pl.* Bodily strength. [OE *thēaw* a characteristic] —**thew′y** *adj.*
they (*th*ā) *pron. pl., possessive* **their** or **theirs,** *objective* **them** 1. The nominative plural of *he, she,* and *it,* used of the persons, beings, or things previously mentioned or understood. 2. People in general: *They* say this is his best book. [ME *thei, thai* < ON *their*, pl. of *sā* this, that]
they'd (*th*ād) 1. They had. 2. They would.
they'll (*th*āl) They will.
they're (*th*âr) They are.
they've (*th*āv) They have.
thi·a·mine (thī′ə·mēn, -min) *n. Biochem.* A white crystalline compound, vitamin B_1, found in various natural sources and also made synthetically. Also **thi′a·min** (-min). [< Gk. *theion* sulfur + (VIT)AMIN]
thick (thik) *adj.* 1. Having relatively large depth or extent from one surface to its opposite; not thin. 2. Having a specified dimension of this kind, whether great or small: an inch *thick*. 3. Arranged compactly; close. 4. Abundant with objects; abounding. 5. Having considerable density or consistency; heavy. 6. Having the component particles closely packed together, as smoke, fog, etc. 7. Dull; stupid. 8. Indistinct; muffled: a *thick* voice. 9. *Informal* Very friendly; intimate. 10. *Brit. Informal* Excessive. —*adv.* So as to be thick; thickly: bread sliced *thick*. —**to lay it on thick** *Informal* 1. To overstate; exaggerate. 2. To flatter excessively. —*n.* 1. The thickest part. 2. The most intense time or place of anything: the *thick* of the fight. —**through thick and thin** Through good times and bad; loyally. [OE *thicce*] —**thick′ish** *adj.* —**thick′ly** *adv.* —**thick′ness** *n.*
thick·en (thik′ən) *v.t. & v.i.* 1. To make or become thick or thicker. 2. To make or become more intricate or intense. —**thick′·en·er** *n.*
thick·en·ing (thik′ən·ing) *n.* 1. The act of making or becoming thick. 2. Something added to a liquid to thicken it. 3. A thickened place or part.
thick·et (thik′it) *n.* A thick, dense growth, as of underbrush. [OE *thicce* thick]
thick·set (thik′set′) *adj.* 1. Having a short, thick body; stout. 2. Planted closely together.
thick-skinned (thik′skind′) *adj.* 1. Having a

thick skin. 2. Insensitive to criticism or insults.

thick-wit·ted (thik′wit′id) *adj.* Stupid; obtuse; dense.

thief (thēf) *n. pl.* **thieves** (thēvz) One who takes something belonging to another; one who steals. [OE *thēof*]

thieve (thēv) *v.* **thieved, thiev·ing** *v.t.* 1. To steal. —*v.i.* 2. To be a thief. [OE *thēofian*] —**thiev·er·y** (thē′vər·ē) *n.* —**thiev′ish** *adj.* —**thiev′ish·ly** *adv.* —**thiev′·ish·ness** *n.*

thigh (thī) *n.* The leg between the hip and the knee of man, or the corresponding portion in other animals. ◆Collateral adjective: *femoral.* [OE *thēoh*]

thigh·bone (thī′bōn′) *n.* The femur.

thim·ble (thim′bəl) *n.* A caplike cover worn in sewing to protect the end of the finger that pushes the needle. [OE *thūma* thumb] —**thim′ble·ful** *n.*

thin (thin) *adj.* **thin·ner, thin·nest** 1. Having opposite surfaces relatively close to each other; being of little depth or width; not thick. 2. Lacking roundness or plumpness of figure; slender. 3. Having the parts or particles scattered or diffused; sparse. 4. Having little substance: *thin* clothing. 5. Having little or no consistency, as a liquid. 6. Having little volume or richness, as a voice. 7. Having little intensity; pale. 8. Feeble; superficial. —*adv.* So as to be thin. —*v.t. & v.i.* **thinned, thin·ning** To make or become thin or thinner. [OE *thynne*] —**thin′ly** *adv.* —**thin′ner** *n.* —**thin′·ness** *n.*

thine (thīn) *pron. Archaic* 1. The possessive case of the pronoun *thou*: used predicatively. 2. The one or ones belonging or relating to thee: thou and *thine.* —*pronominal adj.* Thy: used before a vowel or *h*: *thine* eyes. [OE *thīn*, genitive of *thū* thou]

thing (thing) *n.* 1. That which exists as a separate entity; an inanimate object. 2. That which is designated, as contrasted with the word or symbol used to denote it. 3. A matter or circumstance; an affair; concern: *Things* have changed. 4. An act or deed; transaction. 5. A statement; utterance: to say the right *thing.* 6. A quality; attribute; characteristic. 7. An organic being: usu. with a qualifying word: Every living *thing* dies. 8. An object that is not or cannot be described or particularized. 9. *pl.* Possessions. —**to do (one's) thing** *Informal* To follow one's special interest. —**to see things** To have hallucinations. [OE, thing, cause, assembly]

think (thingk) *v.* **thought** (thôt), **think·ing** *v.t.* 1. To produce or form in the mind; conceive mentally. 2. To examine in the mind; determine by reasoning: to *think* a plan through. 3. To believe; consider. 4. To remember; recollect: I cannot *think* what he said. —*v.i.* 5. To use the mind in exercising judgment, forming ideas, etc.; reason. 6. To have a particular opinion or feeling. —**to think better of** 1. To abandon or change a course of action. 2. To form a better opinion of. —**to think fit (proper, right, etc.)** To regard as worth doing. —**to think nothing of** 1. To consider of no importance; ignore. 2. To consider easy to do. —**to think of** 1. To remember. 2. To invent; imagine. 3. To have a specified opinion or attitude toward. 4. To be considerate of. —**to think out** To devise, invent, or solve by thinking. —**to think over** To reflect upon. —**to think the world of** 1. To have a high opinion of. 2. To love very much. —**to think twice** To consider carefully. —**to think up** To devise, arrive at, or invent by thinking. —*n.* An act of thinking; a thought. [OE *thencean*] —**think′a·ble** *adj.* —**think′er** *n.*

think tank An institute or group for theoretical study, often combining fields or disciplines. —**think tanker**

thin-skinned (thin′skind′) *adj.* 1. Having a thin skin. 2. Easily hurt; sensitive.

third (thûrd) *adj.* 1. Next after the second: the ordinal of *three.* 2. Being one of three equal parts. —*n.* 1. That which follows the second. 2. One of three equal parts. 3. *Mech.* The forward gears with the third highest ratio in an automobile transmission. —*adv.* In the third order, rank, or place: also, in formal discourse, **third′ly.** [OE *thridda* < *thrī* three]

third class 1. In the U.S. postal system, a classification of mail that includes all miscellaneous printed matter but not newspapers and periodicals legally entered as second class. 2. A classification of accommodations on some ships and trains, usu. the cheapest and least luxurious available. —**third-class** (thûrd′klas′) *adj. & adv.*

third degree *Informal* Severe or brutal examination of a prisoner by the police for the purpose of securing information.

third estate The third political class of a kingdom, following the nobility and the clergy; the commoners.

third rail A rail that supplies current to the trains of an electric railway. —**third-rail** (thûrd′rāl′) *adj.*

third-rate (thûrd′rāt′) *adj.* 1. Of the third rate or class. 2. Of poor quality; inferior.

third world 1. Any or all of the developing countries in the world. 2. Those nations which are not politically aligned with either the Communist or capitalist powers. Also **Third World.**

thirst (thûrst) *n.* 1. An uncomfortable feeling of dryness in the throat and mouth. 2. The physiological condition that produces this feeling. 3. Any longing or craving. —*v.i.* 1. To be thirsty. 2. To have an eager desire or craving. [OE *thurst, thyrstan*] —**thirst′er** *n.* —**thirst′i·ly** *adv.* —**thirst′i·ness** *n.* —**thirst′y** *adj.* **thirst·i·er, thirst·i·est**

thir·teen (thûr′tēn′) *n.* The sum of twelve and one: a cardinal number written 13, XIII. [OE *thrēotīne*] —**thir′teen′** *adj.* —**thir′·teenth′** *adj. & n.*

thir·ty (thûr′tē) *n. pl.* **·ties** The sum of twenty and ten: a cardinal number written 30, XXX. [OE *thrītig*] —**thir′ti·eth** *adj. & n.* —**thir′ty** *adj.*

this (this) *pl. for adj. and pron. def. 2* **these** (thēz) *adj.* 1. That is near or present, either actually or in thought: *This* house is for sale. 2. That is understood or has just been mentioned: *This* offense justified my revenge. 3. Denoting something nearer than or contrasted with something else: distinguished from *that*: *This* tree is still alive, but that one is dead. —*pron.* 1. The person or thing near or present, being understood or just mentioned. 2. The person or thing nearer than or contrasted with something else: opposed to *that*: *This* is a better painting than that. 3. The idea, statement, etc., about to be made clear: I will say *this*: he is a hard worker. —*adv.* To this degree: I was not expecting you *this* soon. [OE]

this·tle (this′əl) *n.* 1. A prickly plant of the composite family, with cylindrical or globular heads of purple flowers. 2. Any of several other prickly plants. [OE *thistel*] —**this′tly** *adj.*

this·tle·down (this′əl·doun′) *n.* The ripe silky fibers from the dry flower of a thistle.

thith·er (thith′ər, thith′-) *adv.* To or toward that place; in that direction. —*adj.* Situated or being on the other side; farther: the *thither* bank of the river. [OE *thider*]

thith·er·to (thith′ər·tōō′, thith′-) *adv.* Up to that time.

thith·er·ward (thith′ər·wərd, thith′-) *adv.* In that direction; toward that place. Also **thith′er·wards.**

tho (thō) See THOUGH.

thole (thōl) *n. Naut.* A peg or pair of pegs serving as a fulcrum for an oar in rowing. Also **thole pin.** [OE *thol* pin]

thong (thông, thong) *n.* A narrow strip of leather, as for tying or fastening. [OE *thwang*]

tho·rax (thôr′aks) *n. pl.* **tho·rax·es** or **tho·ra·ces** (thôr′ə·sēz) *Anat.* The part of the body between the neck and the abdomen, enclosed by the ribs and containing the lungs, heart, etc.; the chest. [< Gk. *thōrax*] —**tho·rac·ic** (thô·ras′ik) *adj.*

tho·ri·um (thôr′ē·əm) *n.* A gray radioactive metallic element (symbol Th), found only in small quantities in certain rare minerals. [after *Thor*, Norse god of war]

thorn (thôrn) *n.* 1. A hard, sharp-pointed spine on a branch. 2. Any of various thorn-bearing shrubs or trees. 3. Anything or anyone that causes discomfort, pain, or annoyance. [OE] —**thorn′i·ness** *n.* —**thorn′·less** *adj.* —**thorn′y** *adj.* **thorn·i·er, thorn·i·est**

thor·ough (thûr′ō) *adj.* 1. Carried to completion. 2. Marked by careful attention; persevering; painstaking. 3. Completely; through and through. [Emphatic var. of THROUGH] —**thor′ough·ly** *adv.* —**thor′·ough·ness** *n.*

thor·ough·bred (thûr′ō·bred′, -ə-) *n.* Pure and unmixed stock. —*adj.* Bred from pure stock.

thor·ough·fare (thûr′ō·fâr′, -ə-) *n.* A road or street through which the public has unobstructed passage; highway. [OE *thurh* through + *faru* going]

thor·ough·go·ing (thûr′ō·gō′ing, thûr′ə-) *adj.* 1. Characterized by extreme thoroughness or efficiency. 2. Unmitigated.

those (thōz) *adj. & pron.* Plural of THAT. [OE *thās*, pl. of *this*]

thou (thou) *pron., possessive* **thy** or **thine,** *objective* **thee;** *pl. nominative* **you, ye,** *possessive* **your** or **yours,** *objective* **you, ye** *Archaic* The nominative singular pronoun of the second person: replaced by singular *you*, and no longer used except in religious, elevated, or poetic language. [OE *thū*]

though (thō) *conj.* 1. Notwithstanding the fact that. 2. Conceding or granting that; even if. 3. And yet; still; however: I am well, *though* I do not feel very strong. 4. Notwithstanding what has been done or said; nevertheless. Also spelled *tho.* [Prob. fusion of OE *thēah* and ON *tho*]

thought[1] (thôt) *n.* 1. The act or process of thinking. 2. The product of thinking; an idea. 3. Intellectual activity of a specific kind: Greek *thought.* 4. Consideration; attention. 5. Intention or plan. 6. Expectation. [OE *thōht*]

thought[2] (thôt) Past tense and past participle of THINK.

thought·ful (thôt′fəl) *adj.* 1. Full of thought; meditative. 2. Showing, characterized by, or promotive of thought. 3. Attentive; careful; considerate. —**thought′ful·ly** *adv.* —**thought′·ful·ness** *n.*

thought·less (thôt′lis) *adj.* 1. Manifesting lack of thought or care; heedless. 2. Inconsiderate. —**thought′less·ly** *adv.* —**thought′·less·ness** *n.*

thou·sand (thou′zənd) *n.* The product of ten and a hundred; ten hundreds, written as 1,000 or M: a cardinal number. [OE *thūsend*] —**thou′sand** *adj.* —**thou′sandth** *adj. & n.*

thrall (thrôl) *n.* 1. A person in bondage; a slave; serf. 2. The condition of bondage. [OE *thrǣl* < ON] —**thrall′dom** *n.*

thrash (thrash) *v.t.* 1. To beat as if with a flail; flog; whip. 2. To defeat utterly. —*v.i.* 3. To move or swing about with flailing, violent motions. —**to thrash out** To discuss fully. [Dial. var. of THRESH] —**thrash′er** *n.*

thrash·er (thrash′ər) *n.* A long-tailed American songbird related to the mockingbird. [< THRUSH]

thrash·ing (thrash′ing) *n.* A sound beating or whipping.

thread (thred) *n.* 1. A very slender cord composed of two or more filaments, as of cotton, or silk, twisted together; also, such twisted fibers used in sewing. 2. A filament of any ductile substance, as of metal, glass, etc. 3. Anything conceived of as serving to give sequence to the whole. 4. *Mech.* The spiral ridge of a screw. —*v.t.* 1. To pass a thread through the eye of (a needle). 2. To arrange or string on a thread, as beads. 3. To cut a thread on or in, as a screw. 4. To make (one's way) carefully. [OE *thrǣd*] —**thread′er** *n.*

thread·bare (thred′bâr′) *adj.* 1. Worn so that the threads show, as a rug or garment. 2. Clad in worn garments. 3. Commonplace; hackneyed. —**thread′bare′ness** *n.*

thread·y (thred′ē) *adj.* **thread·i·er, thread·i·est** 1. Resembling a thread; stringy. 2. *Med.* Weak and feeble: said of the pulse. 3. Weak and thin: a *thready* voice.

threat (thret) *n.* 1. A declaration of an intention to inflict injury or pain. 2. An indication of impending danger or harm. 3. A person or thing regarded as endangering the lives, peace of mind, etc., of others; menace. [OE *thrēat*]

threat·en (thret′n) *v.t.* 1. To utter threats against. 2. To be menacing or dangerous to. 3. To be ominous or portentous of. —*v.i.*

4. To utter threats. 5. To have a menacing aspect. [OE *thrēatnian* to urge, compel] —**threat′en·er** *n.* —**threat′en·ing·ly** *adv.*

three (thrē) *n.* The sum of two and one: a cardinal number written 3, III. [OE *thrie*] —**three** *adj.*

three-base hit (thrē′bās′) In baseball, a base hit that enables the batter to reach third base.

three-D (thrē′dē′) *adj.* Three-dimensional. Often written **3-D.**

three-di·men·sion·al (thrē′di·men′shən·əl) *adj.* 1. Giving the illusion of depth. 2. Existing in three dimensions.

three·fold (thrē′fōld′) *n.* An amount or number three times as great as a given unit. —*adj.* 1. Consisting of three parts. 2. Three times as many or as great. —**three′·fold′** *adv.*

three-ply (thrē′plī′) *adj.* Consisting of three thicknesses, strands, layers, etc.

three·score (thrē′skôr′) *adj. & n.* Sixty.

three·some (thrē′səm) *n.* 1. A group of three. 2. That which is played by three persons.

thren·o·dy (thren′ə·dē) *n. pl.* **·dies** An ode or song of lamentation; a dirge. Also **thren′ode** (-ōd). [< Gk. *thrēnos* lament + *ōidē* song] —**thre·nod·ic** (thri·nod′ik) *adj.* —**thren′o·dist** *n.*

thresh (thresh) *v.t. & v.i.* To beat stalks of (ripened grain) with a flail or machine so as to separate the grain from the straw or husks. [OE *therscan*]

thresh·er (thresh′ər) *n.* One who or that which threshes; esp., a machine for threshing.

thresh·old (thresh′ōld, -hōld, -əld) *n.* 1. The plank, timber, or stone lying under the door of a building. 2. The entrance or beginning of anything. 3. *Physiol & Psychol.* **a** The point at which a stimulus just produces a response. **b** The minimum degree of stimulation necessary for conscious perception: the *threshold* of pain. [OE *therscold*]

threw (thro͞o) Past tense of THROW.

thrice (thrīs) *adv.* 1. Three times. 2. In a threefold manner. 3. Extremely; very. [OE *thriwa*]

thrift (thrift) *n.* Care and wisdom in the management of one's resources; frugality. [< ON] —**thrift′i·ly** *adv.* —**thrift′i·ness** *n.* —**thrift′less** *adj.* —**thrift′y** *adj.* **thrift·i·er, thrift·i·est**

thrill (thril) *v.t.* 1. To cause to feel a sudden wave of emotion; move to great or tingling excitement. 2. To cause to vibrate or tremble. —*v.i.* 3. To feel a sudden wave of emotion or excitement. —*n.* Something that thrills or excites. [Var. of dial. *thirl*] —**thrill′ing** *adj.* —**thrill′ing·ly** *adv.*

thrill·er (thril′ər) *n.* 1. One who or that which thrills. 2. *Informal* A sensational book, motion picture, etc.

thrive (thrīv) *v.i.* **throve** (thrōv) or **thrived, thrived** or **thriv·en** (thriv′ən), **thriv·ing** 1. To prosper; be successful. 2. To grow with vigor; flourish. [< ON *thrīfa* to grasp] —**thriv′er** *n.* —**thriv′ing·ly** *adv.*

throat (thrōt) *n.* 1. The passage leading from the back of the mouth to the stomach and lungs. 2. The front of the neck, extending from below the chin to the collarbones. 3. Any narrow passage resembling the throat. —**to jump down one's throat** *Informal* To criticize or berate one severely. —**to ram (something) down one's throat** *Informal* To force one to accept or hear something against his will. [OE *throte*]

throat·y (thrō′tē) *adj.* **throat·i·er, throat·i·est** Uttered deep in the throat; guttural. —**throat′i·ly** *adv.* —**throat′i·ness** *n.*

throb (throb) *v.i.* **throbbed, throb·bing** 1. To beat rapidly or violently, as the heart from exertion or excitement. 2. To pulsate. 3. To feel or show great emotion. —*n.* A pulsation or beat. [? Imit.] —**throb′ber** *n.* —**throb′bing·ly** *adv.*

throe (thrō) *n.* 1. A violent pang or pain. 2. *pl.* Any agonizing or violent activity. [Prob. fusion of OE *thrōwian* to suffer and *thrāwan* to twist, throw]

throm·bo·sis (throm·bō′sis) *n. pl.* **·ses** (sēz) *Pathol.* Local coagulation of blood in the heart or blood vessels, forming an obstruction to circulation. —**throm·bot′ic** (-bot′ik) *adj.*

throm·bus (throm′bəs) *n. pl.* **·bi** (-bī) *Pathol.* A blood clot formed in thrombosis. [< Gk. *thrombos* clot]

throne (thrōn) *n.* 1. The chair of state occupied by a sovereign or some other dignitary. 2. Royal estate or dignity; sovereign power. —*v.t. & v.i.* **throned, thron·ing** To place or sit on a throne. [< Gk. *thronos* seat]

throng (thrông, throng) *n.* 1. A multitude of people crowded closely together. 2. Any numerous collection. —*v.t.* 1. To crowd into; jam. 2. To press or crowd upon. —*v.i.* 3. To collect or move in a throng. [OE *gethrang*]

throt·tle (throt′l) *n. Mech.* **a** A valve controlling the supply of steam or vaporized fuel to an engine: also **throttle valve.** **b** The lever that operates the throttle: also **throttle lever.** —*v.* **·tled, ·tling** *v.t.* 1. To strangle or choke. 2. To silence, stop, or suppress by or as by choking. 3. *Mech.* **a** To reduce or shut off the flow of steam or fuel (in an engine). **b** To reduce the speed of by means of a throttle. —*v.i.* 4. To choke. [Dim. of ME *throte*] —**throt′tler** *n.*

through (thro͞o) *prep.* 1. Into one side, end, or point, and out of the other. 2. Covering, entering, or penetrating all parts of; throughout. 3. From the first to the last of; during the time or period of. 4. In the midst of; among. 5. By way of. 6. By means of. 7. On account of. —*adv.* 1. From one end, side, surface, etc., to or beyond another. 2. From beginning to end. 3. To a termination or conclusion, esp. a successful one. —**through and through** Totally; completely. —*adj.* 1. Going from beginning to end without stops or with very few stops. 2. Extending from one side or surface to another. 3. Unobstructed; open; clear. 4. Arrived at an end; finished. Also spelled *thru.* [OE *thurh*]

through·out (thro͞o·out′) *adv.* Through or in every part. —*prep.* All through; everywhere in.

through·way (thro͞o′wā′) See THRUWAY.

throve (thrōv) Past tense of THRIVE.

throw (thrō) *v.* **threw** (thro͞o), **thrown, throw·ing** *v.t.* 1. To launch through the air by means of a sudden straightening or whirling of the arm. 2. To propel or hurl.

3. To put hastily or carelessly. 4. To direct or project (light, a glance, etc.). 5. To bring to a specified condition or state by or as by throwing: to *throw* the enemy into a panic. 6. To cause to fall; overthrow: The horse *threw* its rider. 7. In wrestling, to force the shoulders of (an opponent) to the ground. 8. To cast (dice). 9. *Informal* To lose purposely, as a race. 10. To move, as a lever or switch. 11. *Slang* To give (a party, etc.). 12. In card games, to play or discard. —*v.i.* 13. To cast or fling something. **—to throw away** 1. To discard. 2. To waste; squander. **—to throw cold water on** To discourage. **—to throw in** 1. To cause (gears or a clutch) to mesh or engage. 2. To contribute; add. 3. To join with others. **—to throw in the towel** (or **sponge**) *Slang* To accept defeat; surrender. **—to throw oneself at** To strive to gain the affections or love of. **—to throw oneself into** To engage or take part in vigorously. **—to throw oneself on** (or **upon**) To entrust oneself to; rely on. **—to throw open** To free from restrictions or obstacles. **—to throw the book at** *Slang* 1. To sentence to the maximum penalty. 2. To reprimand or castigate severely. **—to throw out** 1. To put forth; emit. 2. To cast out or aside; discard; reject. 3. To confuse; disconcert; distract. **—to throw (something) up to (someone)** *Informal* To mention or repeat as a reproach. **—to throw together** To put together hastily or roughly. **—to throw up** 1. To construct hastily. 2. To give up; relinquish. 3. To vomit. —*n.* 1. An act of throwing or hurling; a fling. 2. The distance over which a missile may be thrown: a stone's *throw*. 3. A cast of dice, or the resulting number. 4. A bedspread or coverlet; also, a woman's scarf. [OE *thrāwan* to turn, twist, curl] **—throw′er** *n.*

throw·a·way (thrō′ə·wā′) *adj.* 1. Designed to be discarded after one use; disposable. 2. Presented with no emphasis: a comedian's *throwaway* gag. —*n.* Something free handed out for advertising or propaganda purposes.

throw·back (thrō′bak′) *n.* Reversion to an ancestral type or condition; also, an example of such reversion.

thru (thrōō) See THROUGH.

thrum (thrum) *v.* **thrummed, thrum·ming** *v.t.* 1. To play on or finger (a stringed instrument) idly and without expression. 2. To drum or tap monotonously or listlessly. —*v.i.* 3. To play a stringed instrument idly. —*n.* Any monotonous drumming. [Imit.]

thrush (thrush) *n.* A migratory bird having a long and slightly graduated tail, long wings, and spotted underparts. [OE *thrysce*]

thrust (thrust) *v.* **thrust, thrust·ing** *v.t.* 1. To push or shove with force or sudden impulse. 2. To pierce or stab, as with a sword or dagger. 3. To put (a person) forcibly into some condition or situation. 4. To put in; interpose. —*v.i.* 5. To make a sudden push against something. 6. To force oneself on or ahead; push one's way: with *through, into, on,* etc. —*n.* 1. A sudden, forcible push, esp. with a pointed weapon. 2. A vigorous attack. 3. *Mech.* The driving force exerted by a steam engine, motor, propeller, jet engine, etc. 4. Salient force or meaning. [< ON *thrysta*] **—thrust′er** *n.*

thru·way (thrōō′wā′) *n.* A long-distance express highway: also spelled *throughway.*

thud (thud) *n.* 1. A dull, heavy sound, as of a hard body striking upon a comparatively soft surface. 2. The blow causing such a sound. —*v.i.* **thud·ded, thud·ding** To make a thud. [OE *thyddan* to strike, thrust, press]

thug (thug) *n.* A cutthroat or ruffian. [< Hind. *thag* < Skt. *sthaga* swindler] **—thug′ger·y** *n.* **—thug′gish** *adj.*

thu·li·um (thōō′lē·əm) *n.* A metallic element (symbol Tm) in the lanthanide series. [after *Thule,* the northernmost limit of the world in ancient geography]

thumb (thum) *n.* 1. The short, thick digit next to the forefinger of a hand. 2. The division in a glove or mitten that covers the thumb. **—all thumbs** *Informal* Clumsy with the hands. **—thumbs down** *Informal* No; nix. **—under one's thumb** Under one's influence or power. —*v.t.* 1. To press, rub, soil, or wear with the thumb in handling, as the pages of a book. 2. To run through the pages of (a book, manuscript, etc.) rapidly and perfunctorily. 3. *Informal* To solicit (a ride in an automobile) by signaling with the thumb. —*v.i.* 4. *Informal* To hitchhike. **—to thumb one's nose** To show defiance or disgust by raising the thumb to the nose with the fingers extended. [OE *thūma*]

thumb-in·dex (thum′in′deks) *v.t.* To provide with a thumb index.

thumb index A series of scalloped indentations cut along the right-hand edge of a book and labeled to indicate its various sections.

thumb·nail (thum′nāl′) *n.* The nail of the thumb. —*adj.* Short and concise.

thumb·screw (thum′skrōō′) *n.* 1. A screw to be turned by thumb and fingers. 2. An instrument of torture for compressing the thumb.

thumb·tack (thum′tak′) *n.* A broad-headed tack that may be pushed in with the thumb.

thump (thump) *n.* 1. A blow with a blunt or heavy object. 2. The sound made by such a blow; a dull thud. —*v.t.* 1. To beat or strike so as to make a heavy thud or thuds. 2. *Informal* To beat or defeat severely. —*v.i.* 3. To make a thump or thumps; pound or throb. [Imit.] **—thump′er** *n.*

thump·ing (thum′ping) *adj.* 1. That thumps. 2. *Informal* Huge; whopping.

thun·der (thun′dər) *n.* 1. The sound that accompanies lightning, caused by the sudden heating and expansion of the air along the path of the electrical discharge. 2. Any loud or booming noise. —*v.i.* 1. To give forth a peal of thunder. 2. To make a noise like thunder. —*v.t.* 3. To utter or express with a noise like thunder. [OE *thunor*] **—thun′der·er** *n.*

thun·der·bolt (thun′dər·bōlt′) *n.* An electric discharge accompanied by a clap of thunder.

thun·der·clap (thun′dər·klap′) *n.* A sharp, violent detonation of thunder.

thun·der·cloud (thun′dər·kloud′) *n.* A dark,

heavy mass of cloud highly charged with electricity.

thun·der·head (thun′dər·hed′) *n. Meteorol.* A rounded mass of cumulus cloud, either silvery white or dark with silvery edges, often developing into a thundercloud.

thun·der·ous (thun′dər·əs) *adj.* Producing a noise like thunder. —**thun′der·ous·ly** *adv.*

thun·der·show·er (thun′dər·shou′ər) *n.* A shower of rain with thunder and lightning.

thun·der·storm (thun′dər·stôrm′) *n.* A local storm accompanied by lightning and thunder.

thun·der·struck (thun′dər·struk′) *adj.* Amazed, astonished, or confounded, as with fear, surprise, etc.

thu·ri·ble (thŏŏr′ə·bəl, thûr′-) *n.* A censer. [< L *thus, thuris* frankincense]

Thurs·day (thûrz′dē, -dā) *n.* The fifth day of the week. [Fusion of OE *Thunres dæg* day of Thunor and ON *Thōrsdagr* day of Thor]

thus (thus) *adv.* 1. In this, that, or the following manner. 2. To such degree or extent; so. 3. In these circumstances or conditions; therefore. [OE]

thwack (thwak) *v.t.* To strike with something flat; whack. —*n.* A blow with a flat or blunt instrument. [Prob. OE *thaccian* to smack] —**thwack′er** *n.*

thwart (thwôrt) *v.t.* To prevent the accomplishment of, as by interposing an obstacle; also, to prevent (one) from accomplishing something; foil; frustrate; balk. —*n.* An oarsman's seat extending across a boat. —*adj.* Lying, moving, or extending across something; transverse. —*adv. & prep.* Across. [< ON *thverr* transverse] —**thwart′er** *n.*

thy (thī) *pronominal adj. Archaic* The possessive case of the pronoun *thou*, used attributively: *Thy* kingdom come. [ME *thī*, shortened from *thīn* thine]

thyme (tīm) *n.* A small shrubby plant of the mint family, having aromatic leaves and used in cookery. [< Gk. *thymon*]

thy·mine (thī′mēn) *n. Chem.* A base that is a genetic coding constituent of DNA.

thy·mus (thī′məs) *n. Anat.* A glandular organ of man and some other vertebrates, found behind the top of the breastbone. [< Gk. *thymos*]

thy·roid (thī′roid) *adj. Physiol.* Relating or pertaining to the thyroid cartilage or the thyroid gland. —*n.* The thyroid cartilage or gland. [< Gk. *thyreos* large shield + *eidos* form]

thyroid cartilage *Anat.* The largest cartilage of the larynx, composed of two blades whose juncture in front forms the Adam's apple.

thyroid gland *Anat.* An endocrine gland situated in front of and on each side of the trachea, and secreting thyroxin, important in the regulation of metabolism and body growth.

thy·rox·in (thī·rok′sin) *n. Biochem.* A crystalline amino acid that is the hormone of the thyroid gland. Also **thy·rox′ine** (-sēn, -sin).

thy·self (thī·self′) *pron. Archaic* A form of the second person singular pronouns *thee* and *thou*, used: 1. As a reflexive: Know *thyself*. 2. As an emphatic or intensive form: I love thee for *thyself*.

ti (tē) *n. Music* The seventh tone of the diatonic scale in solmization.

ti·ar·a (tē·är′ə, -ar′ə) *n.* 1. The pope's triple crown. 2. An ornamental, semicircular headdress worn by women for formal occasions. [< Gk., Persian headdress]

Ti·bet·an (ti·bet′n) *n.* 1. One of the native Mongoloid people of Tibet, now intermixed with Chinese and various peoples of India. 2. The Sino-Tibetan language of Tibet. —**Ti·bet′an** *adj.*

tib·i·a (tib′ē·ə) *n. pl.* **tib·i·ae** (tib′i·ē) or **tib·i·as** *Anat.* The inner and larger of the two bones of the leg below the knee; the shinbone. [< L] —**tib′i·al** *adj.*

tic (tik) *n.* An involuntary spasm or twitching of muscles, usu. of the face. [< F]

tick[1] (tik) *n.* 1. A light, recurring sound made by a watch, clock, or similar mechanism. 2. A mark, as a dot or dash, used in checking off something. —*v.i.* 1. To make a recurrent clicking sound, as a running watch or clock. —*v.t.* 2. To mark or check with ticks. [Prob. imit.]

tick[2] (tik) *n.* One of numerous flat, bloodsucking arachnids that attack the skin of man, horses, sheep, etc. [OE *ticia*]

tick[3] (tik) *n.* 1. The stout outer covering of a mattress or pillow. 2. Ticking. [< Gk. *thēke* case]

tick·er (tik′ər) *n.* 1. One who or that which ticks. 2. A telegraphic instrument that records stock quotations on a paper ribbon. 3. *Slang* The heart.

ticker tape A paper ribbon that receives the printed information on a ticker. —**tick·er-tape** (tik′ər·tāp′) *adj.*

tick·et (tik′it) *n.* 1. A card showing that the holder is entitled to something, as transportation, admission, etc. 2. A label or tag. 3. A certificate or license. 4. In politics: **a** A list of candidates of a single party on a ballot. **b** The group of candidates running for the offices of a party. 5. *Informal* A legal summons, as for a traffic violation. —*v.t.* 1. To affix a ticket to; label. 2. To present or furnish with a ticket or tickets. [< OF *estiquer* to stick < OLG *stekan*]

tick·ing (tik′ing) *n.* A strong, closely woven cotton or linen fabric, used for ticks, awnings, etc. [< TICK[3]]

tick·le (tik′əl) *v.* ·led, ·ling *v.t.* 1. To touch or scratch (someone) so as to produce a sensation resulting in spasmodic laughter or twitching; titillate. 2. *Informal* To amuse or entertain; delight. —*v.i.* 3. To have or experience a thrilling or tingling sensation. —*n.* The act of tickling or of being tickled; also the sensation produced. [ME *tikelen*] —**tick′ler** *n.*

tick·lish (tik′lish) *adj.* 1. Sensitive to tickling. 2. Liable to be upset or easily offended. 3. Attended with risk; difficult; delicate. —**tick′lish·ly** *adv.* —**tick′lish·ness** *n.*

tic-tac-toe (tik′tak′tō′) *n.* A game for two players who alternately put circles or crosses in the spaces of a figure containing nine squares, each player trying to complete one row before his opponent does. Also **tick′tack′toe′**.

tidal wave 1. Any great incoming rise of waters along a shore, caused by windstorms at sea or by excessively high tides. 2. A tsunami.

tid·bit (tid′bit′) *n.* A choice bit, as of food. Also, *Brit.*, *titbit.* [< dial. E *tid* small object + BIT[1]]

tid·dly·winks (tid′lē·wingks′) *n.* A game in which the players attempt to snap little disks of bone, ivory, etc., from a plane surface into a cup. Also **tid·dle·dy·winks** (tid′l·dē·wingks′) [Prob. < *tiddly* child's word for *little*]

tide (tīd) *n.* 1. The periodic rise and fall of the surface waters of the oceans, caused by the attraction of moon and sun. 2. Anything that rises and falls like the tide; also, the time at which something is most flourishing. 3. Season; time; esp., a season of the ecclesiastical year: used chiefly in combination: *Christmastide.* —*v.* **tid·ed, tid·ing** *v.i.* 1. To ebb and flow like the tide. —*v.t.* 2. To help along: with *over*: Charity *tided* us over the depression. [OE *tīd* period, season] —**tid·al** (tīd′l) *adj.* —**tide′less** *adj.*

tide·land (tīd′land′) *n.* Land alternately covered and uncovered by the tide.

tide·wa·ter (tīd′wô′tər, -wot′ər) *n.* 1. Water that inundates land at high tide. 2. Any area, as a seacoast, whose waters are affected by tides. —*adj.* Pertaining to the tidewater; also, situated on the seacoast.

ti·dings (tī′dingz) *n.pl.* (*sometimes construed as sing.*) A report; news. [OE *tīdung*]

ti·dy (tī′dē) *adj.* **·di·er, ·di·est** 1. Marked by neatness and order; trim. 2. *Informal* Moderately large; considerable: a *tidy* sum. —*v.t. & v.i.* **·died, ·dy·ing** To make (things) tidy; put (things) in order. —*n. pl.* **·dies** A light, detachable covering used to protect the back or arms of a chair or sofa. [OE *tīd* time] —**ti′di·ly** *adv.* —**ti′di·ness** *n.*

tie (tī) *v.* **tied, ty·ing** *v.t.* 1. To fasten with cord, rope, etc. 2. To draw the parts of together or into place by a cord or band fastened with a knot. 3. To form a knot in, as string. 4. To fasten, attach, or join in any way. 5. To restrain or confine; bind. 6. In sports, games, etc., to equal (a competitor) in score or achievement. —*v.i.* 7. To make a connection. 8. To make the same score; be equal. —**to tie down** To hinder; restrict. —**to tie in** *Informal* To have a certain relationship or connection; often with *with.* —**to tie up** 1. To fasten with rope, string, etc. 2. To moor (a vessel). 3. To block; hinder. 4. To have or be already committed, in use, etc., so as to be unavailable. —*n.* 1. A string, cord, etc., with which something is tied. 2. Any bond or obligation. 3. An exact equality in number, as of a score, votes, etc.; esp., a contest which neither side wins; a draw. 4. A necktie. 5. A structural member fastening parts of a framework together and receiving tensile stress. 6. One of a set of timbers laid crosswise on the ground as supports for railroad tracks. [OE *tīegan* to bind]

tie·back (tī′bak) *n.* A piece of fabric, metal, etc., by which curtains are draped or tied back at the sides.

tie-dye (tī′dī′) *v.t.* **-dyed, -dy·ing** To dye (fabric) after tying parts together so that only the exposed parts absorb the dye. —*n.* The method of dyeing fabrics this way.

tie-in (tī′in′) *n.* A connection; association; relation.

tier (tir) *n.* A rank or row of things, as seats, placed one above another. —*v.t. & v.i.* To place or rise in tiers. [Earlier *tire* < OF *tirer* to draw, elongate]

tierce (tirs) See TERCE.

tie-up (tī′up′) *n.* A situation in which progress or operation is impossible.

tiff (tif) *n.* 1. A peevish display of irritation; pet; huff. 2. A light quarrel; spat. —*v.i.* To be in or have a tiff. [Origin unknown]

ti·ger (tī′gər) *n.* 1. A large carnivorous feline of Asia, with vertical black wavy stripes on a tawny body and black bars or rings on the limbs and tail. 2. A fierce, cruel person. [< Gk. *tigris*] —**ti′ger·ish** *adj.* —**ti′gress** *n.fem.*

ti·ger·eye (tī′gər·ī′) *n.* A gemstone showing a changeable luster. Also **ti′gers-eye′.**

tiger lily A tall cultivated lily, with nodding orange flowers spotted with black.

tight (tīt) *adj.* 1. So closely held together or constructed as to be impervious to fluids, air, etc. 2. Firmly fixed or fastened in place; secure. 3. Fully stretched; taut. 4. Closely drawn, packed, fastened, etc. 5. Strict; stringent. 6. Fitting closely; esp., fitting too closely. 7. *Informal* Difficult to cope with; troublesome. 8. *Informal* Parsimonious; tightfisted. 9. *Slang* Drunk; intoxicated. 10. *Econ.* **a** Difficult to obtain. **b** Straitened from lack of money or commodities: a *tight* market. 11. *Dial.* Neat; tidy. —*adv.* 1. Firmly; securely. 2. Closely; with much constriction. —**to sit tight** To remain firm in one's position; refrain from taking action. [ME *thight*] —**tight′ly** *adv.* —**tight′ness** *n.*

-tight *combining form* Impervious to: *watertight.*

tight·en (tīt′n) *v.t. & v.i.* To make or become tight or tighter. —**tight′en·er** *n.*

tight·fist·ed (tīt′fis′tid) *adj.* Stingy; parsimonious.

tight·lipped (tīt′lipt′) *adj.* 1. Having the lips held tightly together. 2. Unwilling to talk; reticent or secretive.

tight·rope (tīt′rōp′) *n.* A rope stretched tight above the ground for acrobatic performances.

tights (tīts) *n.pl.* A tightly fitting garment, commonly for the legs and lower torso, worn by dancers, acrobats, etc.

tight·wad (tīt′wod′) *n.* *Slang* A parsimonious person; miser. [< TIGHT + WAD]

til·de (til′də) *n.* A sign (~); used esp. in Spanish over *n* to represent the palatal nasal (roughly equivalent to *ny*). [< Sp. < L *titulus* superscription, title]

tile (tīl) *n.* 1. A thin piece of baked clay, asbestos, linoleum, etc., used for covering roofs, floors, or walls and as an ornament. 2. A short earthenware pipe, used in forming sewers. —*v.t.* **tiled, til·ing** To cover with tiles. [OE, ult. < L *tegere* to cover] —**til′er** *n.*

till[1] (til) *v.t. & v.i.* To work (soil) for the production of crops, as by plowing and sowing; cultivate. [OE *tilian* to strive] —**till′a·ble** *adj.*

till[2] (til) *prep. & conj.* Until. [OE *til* < ON, to]

till[3] (til) *n.* A drawer or tray in which money or valuables are kept, as at a bank, store, etc. [Origin uncertain]

till·age (til′ij) *n.* The cultivation of land.

till·er[1] (til′ər) *n.* One who or that which tills. [< TILL[1]]

till·er[2] (til′ər) *n. Naut.* A lever to turn a rudder when steering. [< Med.L *telarium* weaver's beam]

tilt (tilt) *v.t.* 1. To cause to rise at one end or side; slant; tip. 2. To aim or thrust, as a lance. —*v.i.* 3. To tip; slant; lean. 4. To engage in a joust. —*n.* 1. A slant; slope. 2. The act of tipping, or the state of being tipped. 3. A medieval sport in which mounted knights, charging with lances, tried to unseat each other. 4. A quarrel. —**at full tilt** At full speed. [OE *tealt* unsteady] —**tilt′er** *n.*

tim·bal (tim′bəl) *n.* A kettledrum. [< Arabic *at-tabl* a drum]

tim·ber (tim′bər) *n.* 1. Wood for building or structural purposes. 2. Growing or standing trees; also, woodland. 3. A single piece of prepared wood for use in a structure. —*v.t.* To provide or shore with timber. [OE] —**tim′bered** *adj.*

tim·ber·land (tim′bər·land′) *n.* Land covered with forests.

timber line The upper limit of tree growth on mountains and in arctic regions. —**tim′·ber-line′** (-līn′) *adj.*

timber wolf The large gray wolf of the forests of the northern U.S. and Canada.

tim·bre (tim′bər, tam′) *n.* The quality of a sound distinguishing one vowel from another or the tone of one musical instrument from another; tone color. [< OF, small bell, orig., timbrel < L *tympanum* kettledrum]

tim·brel (tim′brəl) *n.* An ancient instrument resembling a tambourine. [< OF. See TIMBRE.]

time (tīm) *n.* 1. Continuous existence, comprising the past, present, and future. 2. Finite existence; duration: a short *time* ago. 3. A system of measuring duration: daylight *time*, lunar *time*. 4. A definite portion of duration; esp., a specific hour, day, season, year, etc.: The *time* is 2:35; Autumn is my favorite *time*. 5. The moment or period in which something takes place: at the *time* of his marriage. 6. Leisure: no *time* to rest. 7. An instance or occasion of recurrence or repetition: next *time*; three *times* a day. 8. A fit or proper moment or occasion: a *time* to plant. 9. A period considered with reference to one's personal experience: to have a good *time*. 10. An era; period; age: ancient *times*; the *time* of Henry VIII. 11. *Usu. pl.* A period having some specific quality: *Times* are hard. 12. *Music* Meter, tempo, or the duration of a note. —**ahead of time** Before the time stated or due; early. —**at the same time** 1. At the same moment or period. 2. Despite that; nevertheless. —**at times** Now and then; occasionally. —**behind the times** Old-fashioned. —**for the time being** Temporarily. —**from time to time** Now and then; occasionally. —**in good time** 1. Quickly; fast. 2. At the appropriate time; when properly due. —**in the nick of time** At just the right or critical moment. —**in time** 1. Before it is too late. 2. Ultimately. 3. In the proper rhythm, tempo, etc. —**on time** Promptly. —**time and again** Frequently; repeatedly: also **time after time.** —**to keep time** 1. To indicate time correctly, as a clock. 2. To make rhythmic movements in unison with others. —*adj.* 1. Of or pertaining to time. 2. Devised so as to operate at a specified time: a *time* bomb. 3. Paid for in installments or at a future date. —*v.t.* **timed, tim·ing** 1. To regulate as to time. 2. To cause to correspond in time: They *timed* their steps to the music. 3. To arrange the time or occasion for. 4. To mark the rhythm or measure of. 5. To establish the speed or duration of: to *time* a race. [OE *tīma*] —**tim′er** *n.*

time·card (tīm′kärd′) *n.* A card for recording the time of arrival and departure of an employee.

time clock A clock equipped for automatically recording times of arrival and departure.

time exposure *Photog.* 1. A film exposure made for a relatively long interval. 2. A picture made by such an exposure.

time-hon·ored (tīm′on′ərd) *adj.* Observed or honored because of long usage or existence. Also *Brit.* **time′-hon′oured.**

time·keep·er (tīm′kē′pər) *n.* One who declares the time in a race, game, athletic match, etc., or records the hours worked by employees.

time·less (tīm′lis) *adj.* 1. Independent of or unaffected by time; unending; eternal. 2. Not limited to any special time. —**time′·less·ly** *adv.* —**time′less·ness** *n.*

time·ly (tīm′lē) *adj.* **·li·er, ·li·est** Being or occurring at a suitable time; opportune. —*adv.* Opportunely. —**time′li·ness** *n.*

time-out (tīm′out′) *n.* In sports, a short recess requested by a team during play. Also **time out.**

time·piece (tīm′pēs′) *n.* Something that records or measures time, as a clock.

times (tīmz) *prep.* Multiplied by: three *times* three is nine.

time signature *Music* A symbol placed on a musical staff to indicate the meter.

time·ta·ble (tīm′tā′bəl) *n.* A schedule of the times at which certain things are to take place, as arrivals and departures of trains, times of high and low tides, etc.

time-test·ed (tīm′tes′tid) *adj.* Having worth proved by use over an extended period.

time·worn (tīm′wôrn′) *adj.* 1. Showing the ravages of time. 2. Trite; overused.

tim·id (tim′id) *adj.* 1. Shrinking from danger or risk; fearful. 2. Lacking self-confidence; shy. 3. Characterized by fear or shyness: a *timid* voice. [< L *timere* to fear] —**ti·mid′i·ty, tim′id·ness** *n.* —**tim′id·ly** *adv.*

tim·or·ous (tim′ər·əs) *adj.* 1. Fearful of danger; timid. 2. Indicating or produced by fear. [< L *timor, -oris* fear] —**tim′or·ous·ly** *adv.* —**tim′or·ous·ness** *n.*

tim·o·thy (tim′ə·thē) *n.* A perennial fodder grass having long spikes. Also **timothy grass.** [after *Timothy* Hanson, who took the seed to the Carolinas about 1720]

Tim·o·thy (tim′ə·thē) *n.* Either of two books in the New Testament consisting of two epistles attributed to Saint Paul.

tim·pa·ni (tim′pə·nē) *n. pl.* of **tim·pa·no** (-nō) Kettledrums: also spelled *tympani.* [< L *tympanum* drum] **—tim′pa·nist** *n.*

tim·pa·num (tim′pə·nəm) See TYMPANUM.

tin (tin) *n.* 1. A white metallic element (symbol Sn) of low tensile strength. 2. Tin plate. 3. A container or box made of tin. **—*v.t.* tinned, tin·ning** 1. To coat or cover with tin. 2. To pack or put up in tins. [OE] **—tin** *adj.*

tinc·ture (tingk′chər) *n.* 1. A solution, usu. in alcohol, of some medicinal substance: *tincture* of iodine. 2. A tinge of color; tint. 3. A slight additional flavor, quality, etc. **—*v.t.* ·tured, ·tur·ing** To impart a slight hue or tinge to. [< L *tingere* to dye, color]

tin·der (tin′dər) *n.* Any readily combustible substance that will ignite on contact with a spark. [OE *tynder*] **—tin′der·y** *adj.*

tin·der·box (tin′dər·boks′) *n.* 1. A portable metallic box containing tinder. 2. Anything highly flammable, explosive, touchy, etc.

tine (tīn) *n.* A spike or prong, as of a fork or of an antler. [OE *tind*] **—tined** *adj.*

tin·foil (tin′foil′) *n.* Tin or an alloy of tin made into thin sheets for use as wrapping material, etc. Also **tin foil.**

ting (ting) *n.* A high metallic sound, as of a small bell. [Imit.] **—ting** *v.t. & v.i.*

ting-a-ling (ting′ə·ling′) *n.* The sound of a little bell.

tinge (tinj) *v.t.* **tinged, tinge·ing** or **ting·ing** 1. To add a faint trace of color; tint. 2. To impart a slight characteristic quality of some other element to. **—*n.*** 1. A faint trace of added color. 2. A quality or peculiar characteristic imparted to something. [< L *tingere* to dye]

tin·gle (ting′gəl) *v.* **·gled, ·gling** *v.i.* 1. To experience a prickly, stinging sensation, as from cold or from a sharp blow. 2. To cause such a sensation. **—*v.t.*** 3. To cause to tingle. [Appar. var. of TINKLE] **—tin′gle** *n.* **—tin′gly** *adj.*

tink·er (tingk′ər) *n.* 1. An itinerant mender of domestic tin utensils, as pots and pans. 2. Loosely, one who does repairing work of any kind. 3. A clumsy workman; a botcher. **—*v.i.*** 1. To work as a tinker. 2. To work in a clumsy fashion. 3. To putter; fuss. **—*v.t.*** 4. To mend as a tinker. 5. To repair inexpertly. [Var. of earlier *tinekere* worker in tin] **—tink′er·er** *n.*

tin·kle (ting′kəl) *v.t. & v.i.* **·kled, ·kling** To produce or cause to produce slight, sharp, metallic sounds, as from a bell. [Imit.] **—tin′kle** *n.* **—tin′kly** *adj.* **—tink′·ling** *n.*

tin·ny (tin′ē) *adj.* **·ni·er, ·ni·est** 1. Pertaining to, composed of, or abounding in tin. 2. Resembling tin in lack of durability. 3. Having a thin sound. **—tin′ni·ly** *adv.* **—tin′ni·ness** *n.*

tin-plate (tin′plāt′) *v.t.* **-plat·ed, -plat·ing** To plate with tin. **—tin′-plat′er** *n.*

tin plate Sheet iron or steel plated with tin.

tin·sel (tin′səl) *n.* 1. Very thin, glittering bits of cheap metals used as decoration. 2. A yarn containing gold or silver thread. 3. Anything sparkling and showy, with little real worth. **—*adj.*** 1. Made of, resembling, or covered with tinsel. 2. Superficially brilliant; tawdry. [< L *scintilla* spark]

tin·smith (tin′smith′) *n.* One who works with tin or tin plate.

tint (tint) *n.* 1. A variety of color; esp., a slight admixture of a different color; tinge. 2. A gradation of a color made by mixture with white. 3. Any pale or delicate hue. **—*v.t.*** To give a tint to; tinge. [< L *tingere* to dye, color] **—tint′er** *n.*

tin·tin·nab·u·la·tion (tin′ti·nab′yə·lā′shən) *n.* The pealing, tinkling, or ringing of bells. [< L *tintinnare* to ring]

tin·ware (tin′wâr′) *n.* Articles made of tin plate.

ti·ny (tī′nē) *adj.* **·ni·er, ·ni·est** Very small; minute. [< obs. *tine* small amount, bit]

-tion *suffix of nouns* 1. Action or process of: *rejection.* 2. Condition or state of being: *completion.* 3. Result of: *connection.* Also *-ation, -cion, -ion, -sion, -xion.* [< L *-tio, -tionis*]

tip¹ (tip) *n.* A slanting position; tilt. **—*v.t. & v.i.* tipped, tip·ping** 1. To lean or cause to lean by lowering or raising one end or side; tilt. 2. To overturn or topple. [ME *tipen* to overturn] **—tip′per** *n.*

tip² (tip) *n.* 1. A small gift of money for services rendered. 2. A friendly, helpful hint. **—*v.* tipped, tip·ping** *v.t.* 1. To give a small gratuity to. 2. *Informal* To give secret information to. **—*v.i.*** 3. To give tips. [Orig. < thieves' cant, ? < TIP⁴] **—tip′per** *n.*

tip³ (tip) *n.* 1. The point of anything tapering; end: the *tip* of the tongue. 2. A piece or part made to form the end of anything. 3. The top or summit, as of a mountain. **—*v.t.* tipped, tip·ping** 1. To furnish with a tip. 2. To form the tip of. 3. To cover or adorn the tip of. [Prob. < MDu., point]

tip⁴ (tip) *v.t.* **tipped, tip·ping** To strike lightly, or with something light; tap. **—*n.*** A tap; light blow. [Earlier *tippe*]

tip·off (tip′ôf′) *n.* *Informal* A hint or warning.

tip·pet (tip′it) *n.* A covering for the neck, or the neck and shoulders, worn outdoors. [Prob. dim. of TIP³]

tip·ple (tip′əl) *v.t. & v.i.* **·pled, ·pling** To drink (alcoholic beverages) frequently and habitually. **—*n.*** Alcoholic liquor. **—tip′pler** *n.*

tip·ster (tip′stər) *n.* *Informal* One who sells tips, as for betting on a race. [< TIP³]

tip·sy (tip′sē) *adj.* **·si·er, ·si·est** 1. Partially intoxicated; high. 2. Apt to tip over; shaky; also, crooked; askew. [< TIP¹] **—tip′si·ly** *adv.* **—tip′si·ness** *n.*

tip·toe (tip′tō′) *v.i.* **·toed, ·toe·ing** To walk on the tips of the toes; go in a stealthy or quiet manner. **—*n.*** The tip of a toe. **—on tiptoe** 1. On one's tiptoes. 2. Eagerly expectant. 3. Stealthily; quietly.

tip·top (tip′top′) *n.* 1. The highest point; the very top. 2. *Informal* The highest quality or degree. **—*adj.*** 1. Located at the very top. 2. *Informal* Best of its kind; first-rate. [< TIP³ + TOP¹] **—tip′top′** *adv.*

ti·rade (tī′rād, tə·rād′) *n.* A prolonged outpouring, as of censure. [< Ital. *tirare* to fire, pull]

tire¹ (tīr) *v.* **tired, tir·ing** *v.t.* 1. To reduce the strength of, as by toil; fatigue. 2. To reduce the interest or patience of. —*v.i.* 3. To become weary or exhausted. 4. To lose patience, interest, etc. [OE *tīorian*]

tire[2] (tīr) *n.* 1. A hollow inflatable structure, as of rubber, forming the outer part of the wheel of a vehicle. 2. A band or hoop of metal or rubber fixed tightly around the rim of a wheel. —*v.t.* **tired, tir·ing** To furnish with a tire; put a tire on. Also, *Brit.*, *tyre.* [Var. of ATTIRE]

tired (tīrd) *adj.* Weary; exhausted; fatigued. —**tired′ly** *adv.* —**tired′ness** *n.*

tire·less (tīr′lis) *adj.* Not yielding to fatigue; untiring. —**tire′less·ly** *adv.* —**tire′less·ness** *n.*

tire·some (tīr′səm) *adj.* Causing one to tire; tedious. —**tire′some·ly** *adv.* —**tire′some·ness** *n.*

'tis (tiz) *Archaic* or *Poetic* It is.

tis·sue (tish′o͞o) *n.* 1. *Biol.* An aggregate of cells that performs a particular function: connective *tissue.* 2. Light, absorbent paper used as a disposable towel, handkerchief, etc. 3. Very thin paper for wrapping and protecting things: also **tissue paper.** 4. A connected series; chain: a *tissue* of lies. 5. Any light or gauzy textile fabric. [< OF *tistre* to weave]

tit[1] (tit) *n.* A titmouse. [Short for TITMOUSE]

tit[2] (tit) *n.* Teat; breast. [OE *titt*]

ti·tan (tīt′n) *n.* A person of gigantic size and strength. [< *Titan,* one of a race of giant gods in Greek mythology]

ti·tan·ic (tī·tan′ik) *adj.* Of great size; huge.

ti·ta·ni·um (tī·tā′nē·əm, ti-) *n.* A dark gray metallic element (symbol Ti), used to toughen steel alloys. [< NL < Gk. *Titan.* See TITAN.]

tit·bit (tit′bit′) *n. Brit.* A tidbit.

tit for tat Retaliation in kind. [? Alter. of *tip for tap*]

tithe (tīth) *n.* 1. A tenth part of one's income, esp. when donated to a church. 2. The tenth part of anything. —*v.t.* **tithed, tith·ing** To give or pay a tithe, or tenth part of. [ME *tithe,* OE *teogotha* tenth] —**tith′a·ble** *adj.* —**tith′er** *n.*

ti·tian (tish′ən) *n.* A reddish yellow color. [after *Titian,* 1477?–1576, Venetian painter] —**ti′tian** *adj.*

tit·il·late (tit′ə·lāt) *v.t.* **·lat·ed, ·lat·ing** 1. To cause a tickling sensation in. 2. To excite pleasurably in any way. [< L *titillare* to tickle] —**tit′il·la′tion** *n.* —**tit′il·la′tive** *adj.*

tit·i·vate (tit′ə·vāt) *v.t.* & *v.i.* **·vat·ed, ·vat·ing** *Informal* To put on decorative touches; dress up: also spelled *tittivate.* [? < TIDY, on analogy with *cultivate*] —**tit′i·va′tion** *n.*

ti·tle (tīt′l) *n.* 1. The name of a work, as of a book, play, or song. 2. A name of an office or rank: the *title* of duke, the heavyweight *title.* 3. A characteristic or descriptive name; epithet. 4. *Law* The means whereby one has the just possession of his property; also, the legal evidence of one's right of property. —*v.t.* **·tled, ·tling** To give a name or title to; call. [< L *titulus* label, inscription]

ti·tled (tīt′ld) *adj.* Having a title, esp. of nobility.

title page A page containing the title of a work and the names of its author and publisher.

title role The role of the character after whom a play, opera, or motion picture is named.

tit·mouse (tit′mous′) *n. pl.* **·mice** (-mīs′) Any of several small birds related to the nuthatches; esp., the **tufted titmouse** of the U.S., having a conspicuous crest. [Alter. of ME *titmuse* < *tit-* little + OE *mase* titmouse]

tit·ter (tit′ər) *v.i.* To laugh in a half-smothered way, as from nervousness or in ridicule; snicker; giggle. —*n.* The act of tittering. [Imit.] —**tit′ter·er** *n.* —**tit′ter·ing·ly** *adv.*

tit·ti·vate (tit′ə·vāt) See TITIVATE.

tit·tle (tit′l) *n.* The smallest quantity. [< L *titulus* label, inscription]

tit·tle-tat·tle (tit′l·tat′l) *n.* Foolish or idle talk; gossip. —*v.i.* **·tled, ·tling** To talk foolishly or idly; gossip. [Reduplication of TATTLE]

tit·u·lar (tich′o͝o·lər, tit′yə-) *adj.* 1. Existing in name only; nominal. 2. Of, pertaining to, or like a title. 3. Bestowing or taking title. Also **tit′u·lar′y** (-ler′ē). [< L *titulus* title] —**tit′u·lar·ly** *adv.*

Ti·tus (tī′təs) *n.* A book in the New Testament consisting of an epistle attributed to Saint Paul.

tiz·zy (tiz′ē) *n. pl.* **·zies** *Slang* A bewildered or excited state of mind. [Origin unknown]

TNT (tē′en′tē′) *n.* Trinitrotoluene.

to (to͞o, *unstressed* tə) *prep.* 1. In a direction toward or terminating in: going *to* town. 2. Opposite, in contact with, or near: face *to* face. 3. Intending or aiming at: Come *to* my rescue. 4. Resulting in: frozen *to* death. 5. Belonging or used in connection with: the key *to* the door. 6. Accompanied by: March *to* the music. 7. In honor of: Drink *to* his health. 8. In comparison with: four quarts *to* the gallon. 9. Approaching as a limit; until: five minutes *to* one. 10. As far as: a miser *to* the end of his days. 11. In respect of; concerning: blind *to* her charms. 12. In close application toward: Buckle down *to* work. 13. For: The contest is open *to* everyone. 14. Designating the indirect object of an action: Give the ring *to* me. 15. By: known *to* the world. 16. From the point of view of: It seems *to* me. 17. About; involved in: That's all there is *to* it. ◆*To* also serves to indicate the infinitive, and is often used for it: You may come if you care *to.* —*adv.* 1. To or toward something. 2. In a direction, position, or state understood or implied; esp., shut or closed: Pull the door *to.* 3. Into a normal condition; into consciousness: She soon came *to.* 4. *Naut.* With head to the wind: said of a sailing vessel. [OE *tō*]

toad (tōd) *n.* 1. A tailless, jumping amphibian resembling the frog but without teeth in the upper jaw and resorting to water only to breed. 2. A lizard, the horned toad. 3. Any person regarded with scorn or contempt. [OE *tāde*]

toad·fish (tōd′fish′) *n. pl.* **·fish** or **·fish·es** Any of various fishes of the Atlantic coast of the U.S., having scaleless skin, and a mouth and head resembling those of a toad.

toad·stool (tōd′sto͞ol′) *n.* A mushroom, esp. a poisonous one.

toad·y (tō′dē) *n. pl.* **toad·ies** A fawning, servile person. —*v.t.* & *v.i.* **toad·ied, toad·y·**

ing To act the toady (to). [Short for *toadeater* an assistant to a charlatan, who ate, or pretended to eat, toads] **—toad′y·ish** *adj.* **—toad′y·ism** *n.*

to-and-fro (tōō′ən·frō′) *adj.* Moving back and forth.

to and fro In opposite or different directions.

toast[1] (tōst) *v.t.* 1. To brown (sliced bread) by heat. 2. To warm thoroughly. —*v.i.* 3. To become warm or toasted. —*n.* Sliced bread browned by heat. [< L *tostus*, pp. of *torrere* to parch, roast]

toast[2] (tōst) *n.* 1. The act of drinking to someone's health or to some sentiment. 2. A person or sentiment named in so drinking. —*v.t.* 1. To drink to the health of or in honor of. —*v.i.* 2. To drink a toast. [< TOAST[1], in obs. sense of "a spiced piece of toast put in a drink to flavor it"]

toast·er[1] (tōs′tər) *n.* A device for making toast.

toast·er[2] (tōs′tər) *n.* One who proposes a toast.

toast·mas·ter (tōst′mas′tər) *n.* A person who, at public dinners, announces the toasts, calls upon the various speakers, etc. **—toast′mis′·tress** (-mis′tris) *n.fem.*

to·bac·co (tə·bak′ō) *n. pl.* **·cos** or **·coes** 1. An annual plant of the nightshade family. 2. Its leaves prepared in various ways, as for smoking, chewing, etc. 3. The various products prepared from tobacco leaves, as cigarettes, cigars, etc. [< Sp. *tabaco* < Carib, a pipe used in smoking tobacco]

to·bac·co·nist (tə·bak′ə·nist) *n.* One who sells tobacco.

To·bit (tō′bit) *n.* An Apocryphal book of the Old Testament. Also **To·bi·as** (tə·bī′əs).

to·bog·gan (tə·bog′ən) *n.* A light sledlike vehicle, consisting of a long thin board curved up at the forward end. —*v.i.* 1. To coast on a toboggan. 2. To move downward swiftly: Wheat prices *tobogganed.* [< dial. F (Canadian) *tabagan* sleigh < Algonquian] **—to·bog′gan·er, to·bog′gan·ist** *n.*

toc·ca·ta (tə·kä′tə) *n. Music* A free composition for a keyboard instrument. [< Ital. < *toccare* to touch]

toc·sin (tok′sin) *n.* 1. A signal sounded on a bell. 2. An alarm bell. [< Provençal *tocar* to strike, touch + *senh* bell]

to·day (tə·dā′) *adv.* 1. On or during this present day. 2. At the present time; nowadays. —*n.* The present day, time, or age. Also **to-day′**. [OE *tō* to + *dæg* day]

tod·dle (tod′l) *v.i.* **·dled, ·dling** To walk unsteadily and with short steps, as a little child. —*n.* The act of toddling; also, a stroll. [Origin uncertain] **—tod′dler** *n.*

tod·dy (tod′ē) *n. pl.* **·dies** A drink made with spirits, hot water, sugar, and a slice of lemon. [< Hind. *tār* palm tree, the fermented sap of which is a liquor]

to-do (tə·dōō′) *n. Informal* Confusion or bustle; fuss. [OE *to-* asunder + *dōn* to do]

toe (tō) *n.* 1. One of the digits of the foot. 2. The forward part of the foot. 3. The portion of a shoe, sock, etc., that covers the toes. 4. The lower end or projection of something. **—on one's toes** Alert; wide-awake. **—to tread on (someone's) toes** To trespass on (someone's) feelings, opinions, prejudices, etc. —*v.* **toed, toe·ing** *v.t.* 1. To touch or kick with the toes. —*v.i.* 2. To point the toes in a specified direction: to *toe* out. **—to toe the mark (or line)** To abide by the rules; conform. [OE *tā*] **—toe′less** *adj.*

toed (tōd) *adj.* Having toes: chiefly in combination: *two-toed.*

toe dance A dance performed on tiptoe. **—toe-dance** (tō′dans′) *v.i.* **—toe dancer**

toe·hold (tō′hōld′) *n.* 1. A small space that supports the toes in climbing. 2. Any means of entrance or support; a footing.

toe·nail (tō′nāl′) *n.* A nail growing on the toe.

tof·fee (tôf′ē, tof′ē) *n.* Taffy. Also **tof′fy**.

tog (tog) *Informal n. pl.* Clothes; outfit. —*v.t.* **togged, tog·ging** To dress; clothe. [Short for vagabond's cant *togemans* < L *toga*]

to·ga (tō′gə) *n. pl.* **·gas** or **·gae** (-jē) The loose, draped outer garment worn in public by a citizen of ancient Rome. [< L *tegere* to cover] **—to′gaed** (-gəd) *adj.*

to·geth·er (tōō·geth′ər, tə-) *adv.* 1. Into union or contact with each other. 2. In the same place or at the same spot. 3. At the same moment of time; simultaneously. 4. Without cessation. 5. With one another; mutually. [OE *tō* to + *gædre* together]

tog·ger·y (tog′ər·ē) *n. pl.* **·ger·ies** *Informal* 1. Togs collectively; clothes. 2. A clothing shop.

tog·gle (tog′əl) *n.* A pin or short rod attached in the middle, as to a rope, and designed to be passed through a hole or eye and turned. —*v.t.* **·gled, ·gling** To fix, fasten, or furnish with a toggle. [Prob. var. of *tuggle*, freq. of TUG]

toggle switch *Electr.* A projecting lever whose movement through a small arc opens or closes an electric circuit.

To·go·lese (tō′gə·lēz′) Of Togo or its inhabitants. **—To′go·lese′** *n.*

toil[1] (toil) *n.* 1. Fatiguing work; labor. 2. Any oppressive task. —*v.i.* 1. To work arduously. 2. To progress with slow and labored steps. [< L *tudiculare* to stir about] **—toil′er** *n.*

toil[2] (toil) *n. Usu. pl.* Something that binds or ensnares, as a net. [< MF *toiles* nets < L *tela* web]

toi·let (toi′lit) *n.* 1. A room with a washbowl, water closet, etc.: sometimes called *bathroom.* 2. A bowllike fixture flushed by water, into which one urinates or defecates: also called *water closet.* 3. The act of dressing and grooming oneself; toilette. —*adj.* Used in dressing or grooming: *toilet* articles. [< F *toilette*, orig., cloth dressing gown, dim. of *toile* cloth]

toi·let·ry (toi′lit·rē) *n. pl.* **·ries** An article used in making one's toilet, as soap, comb, etc.

toi·lette (toi·let′, *Fr.* twȧ·let′) *n.* 1. The act or process of grooming oneself, usu. including bathing, hairdressing, etc. 2. A person's actual dress or style of dress. [< F]

toilet water A scented liquid containing a small amount of alcohol, used in or after the bath, after shaving, etc.

toil·some (toil′səm) *adj.* Accomplished with fatigue; involving toil. **—toil′some·ly** *adv.* **—toil′some·ness** *n.*

toil·worn (toil′wôrn′) *adj.* Exhausted by toil; showing the effects of toil.

To·kay (tō·kā′) *n.* 1. A white or reddish blue grape. 2. A wine made from it.

to·ken (tō′kən) *n.* 1. Anything indicative of some other thing; a visible sign. 2. A symbol. 3. A memento; souvenir. 4. A characteristic mark or feature. 5. A piece of metal issued by a transportation company and good for one fare. —*adj.* Done or given as a token, esp. in partial fulfillment of an obligation. [OE *tācen, tācn*]

to·ken·ism (tō′kən·iz·əm) *n.* The policy of attempting to meet certain conditions by symbolic or partial efforts.

told (tōld) Past tense and past participle of TELL.

tol·er·a·ble (tol′ər·ə·bəl) *adj.* 1. Passably good; commonplace. 2. Endurable. 3. Allowable; permissible. —**tol′er·a·ble·ness** *n.* —**tol′er·a·bly** *adv.*

tol·er·ance (tol′ər·əns) *n.* 1. The character, state, or quality of being tolerant; esp., freedom from bigotry or prejudice. 2. The act of enduring, or the capacity for endurance. 3. A small permissible allowance for variations from the specified weight, dimensions, etc.

tol·er·ant (tol′ər·ənt) *adj.* 1. Disposed to tolerate beliefs, views, etc. 2. Indulgent; liberal. —**tol′er·ant·ly** *adv.*

tol·er·ate (tol′ə·rāt) *v.t.* **·at·ed, ·at·ing** 1. To allow to be or be done without active opposition. 2. To concede, as the right to opinions or participation. 3. To bear, sustain, endure, or be capable of enduring. [< L *tolerare* to endure] —**tol′er·a′tion** *n.* —**tol′er·a′tive** *adj.* —**tol′er·a′tor** *n.*

toll[1] (tōl) *n.* 1. A fixed charge for some privilege granted or service rendered, as passage on a bridge. 2. Something taken like a toll; price: The train wreck took a heavy *toll* of lives. 3. A charge for a long-distance telephone call. [OE, ult. < Gk. *telos* tax]

toll[2] (tōl) *v.t.* 1. To cause (a bell) to sound slowly and at regular intervals. 2. To announce by tolling, as a death or funeral. 3. To call or summon by tolling. —*v.i.* 4. To sound slowly and at regular intervals. —*n.* The act or sound of tolling a bell. [ME *tollen, tullen*] —**toll′er** *n.*

toll·gate (tōl′gāt′) *n.* A gate at the entrance to a bridge, or on a road, at which toll is paid.

toll·house (tōl′hous′) *n.* A toll collector's lodge adjoining a tollgate: also **toll′booth′** (-bōōth′).

toll·keep·er (tōl′kē′pər) *n.* One who keeps a tollgate.

Tol·tec (tol′tek, tōl′-) *n.* One of certain ancient Nahuatlan tribes that dominated central and southern Mexico about 900–1100 A.D. [< Nahuatl *Tolteca*] —**Tol′tec, Tol′·tec·an** *adj.*

tol·u·ene (tol′yōō·ēn) *n. Chem.* A colorless, flammable liquid hydrocarbon obtained from coal tar by distillation and used in making dyestuffs, explosives, etc.

tom (tom) *n.* The male of various animals, esp. the cat. [after *Tom*, a personal name. See TOMCAT.]

Tom (tom) *Slang* An Uncle Tom: a contemptuous term. —*v.i.* **Tommed, Tom·ming** To behave as an Uncle Tom.

tom·a·hawk (tom′ə·hôk) *n.* 1. An axlike weapon used by North American Indians. 2. Any similar weapon, tool, etc. —*v.t.* To strike or kill with a tomahawk. [< Algonquian *tamahaken* he uses for cutting]

tom·al·ley (tə·mal′ē, tom′al·ē) *n.* The liver of the lobster, considered a delicacy. [Prob. < Carib]

to·ma·to (tə·mā′tō, -mä′-) *n. pl.* **·toes** 1. The large, pulpy, edible berry, yellow or red when ripe, of a perennial plant of the nightshade family, cultivated as a vegetable. 2. The plant itself. [< Nahuatl *tomatl*]

tomb (tōōm) *n.* 1. A place for the burial of the dead, as a vault or grave. 2. A monument, tombstone, etc., commemorating the dead. [< Gk. *tymbos* mound]

tom·boy (tom′boi′) *n.* A girl who prefers boyish activities, dress, etc. —**tom′boy′ish** *adj.* —**tom′boy′ish·ness** *n.*

tomb·stone (tōōm′stōn′) *n.* A stone, usu. inscribed, marking a place of burial.

tom·cat (tom′kat′) *n.* A male cat. [after *Tom*, a male cat, hero of *The Life and Adventures of a Cat*, 1760]

Tom Col·lins (tom kol′inz) A drink consisting of gin, lemon or lime juice, sugar, and carbonated water.

tome (tōm) *n.* A volume; esp., a large book. [< Gk. *tomos* fragment]

-tome *combining form* A cutting instrument (of a specified kind). [< Gk. *tomos* a cutting < *temnein* to cut]

tom·fool (tom′fōōl′) *n.* An idiotic or silly person. —*adj.* Very stupid or foolish. [after *Tom Fool*, a name formerly applied to mental defectives]

tom·fool·er·y (tom′fōō′lər·ē) *n. pl.* **·er·ies** 1. Stupid or foolish behavior. 2. Worthless or trivial stuff; frippery. Also **tom′fool′ish·ness** (-fōō′lish·nis).

tom·my (tom′ē) *n. pl.* **·mies** *Brit. Informal* A British soldier. Also **Tom′my.**

tom·my·rot (tom′ē·rot′) *n. Informal* Utter nonsense.

to·mor·row (tə·môr′ō, -mor′ō) *adv.* On or for the next day after today. —*n.* 1. The next day after today; the morrow. 2. Some time in the future. Also **to-mor′row.** [OE *tō* to + *morgen* morning, morrow]

tom·tit (tom′tit′) *n.* Any of various small birds, as a chickadee or a wren. [< TOM + TIT[1]]

tom-tom (tom′tom′) *n.* A drum of India, Africa, etc., variously shaped and usu. beaten with the hands. [< Hind. *tamtam*, imit. of the instrument's sound]

-tomy *combining form* 1. *Surg.* A cutting of a (specified) part or tissue. 2. A (specified) kind of cutting or division: *dichotomy.* [< Gk. *tomē* a cutting < *temnein* to cut]

ton (tun) *n.* 1. Any of several large measures of weight; esp.: **a** The **short ton** of 2000 pounds avoirdupois, commonly used in the U.S. and Canada. **b** The **long** or **gross ton** of 2240 pounds, used in Great Britain. 2. A unit for reckoning the displacement or weight of vessels, 35 cubic feet of sea water weighing about one long ton: called in full a **displacement ton.** 3. A unit for reckoning the freight-carrying capacity of a ship, usu. equivalent to 40 cubic feet of space: called in full a **freight ton** or **measurement ton** 4. A metric ton. [Var. of TUN]

to·nal·i·ty (tō·nal′ə·tē) *n. pl.* **·ties** 1. *Music* The relationship of tones; key. 2. The general color scheme or collective tones of a painting.

tone (tōn) *n.* 1. Sound in relation to quality, volume, and duration. 2. A sound having a definite pitch. 3. *Music* **a** The timbre, or characteristic sound, of a voice, instrument, etc. **b** A full interval of a diatonic scale. 4. A prevailing disposition; mood. 5. Characteristic style or tendency. 6. Style or distinction; elegance. 7. Vocal inflection as expressive of feeling: a *tone* of pity. 8. A shade, hue, tint, or degree of a particular color. 9. *Physiol.* **a** The general condition of the body. **b** Firmness and resilience, as of a tissue. —*v.t.* **toned, ton·ing** 1. To give tone to. 2. To modify in tone. —**to tone down** 1. To subdue the tone of (a painting). 2. To moderate in quality or tone. —**to tone up** 1. To raise in quality or strength. 2. To gain in vitality. [< Gk. *teinein* to stretch] —**to′nal** *adj.*

tone color The timbre of a voice, musical instrument, etc.

tone-deaf (tōn′def′) *adj.* Unable to perceive fine distinctions in pitch, as musical intervals. —**tone′deaf′ness** *n.*

tone·less (tōn′lis) *adj.* 1. Having no tone; without tone. 2. Lacking spirit; listless. —**tone′less·ly** *adv.* —**tone′less·ness** *n.*

tong (tông, tong) *n.* A Chinese secret society or fraternal association. [< Chinese *t'ang* hall, meeting place]

tongs (tôngz, tongz) *n.pl.* (*sometimes construed as sing.*) An implement for grasping, holding, or lifting objects, consisting usu. of a pair of pivoted levers: sometimes called a **pair of tongs.** [OE *tang, tange*]

tongue (tung) *n.* 1. A freely moving organ situated in the mouth of most vertebrates, serving in mammals as an organ of taste and in man also as an organ of speech. ◆Collateral adjective: *lingual.* 2. An animal's tongue, as of beef, prepared as food. 3. The power of speech: to lose one's *tongue.* 4. Manner or style of speaking: a smooth *tongue.* 5. Utterance. 6. A language, vernacular, or dialect. 7. Anything resembling an animal tongue in shape or function. 8. A jet of flame. 9. A projecting edge or tenon of a board for insertion into a corresponding groove of another board, thus forming a **tongue-and-groove joint.** —**on the tip of one's tongue** On the verge of being recalled. —**to hold one's tongue** To keep silent. —**(with) tongue in cheek** With ironic or facetious intent. —*v.t. & v.i.* **tongued, tongu·ing** 1. *Music* To separate the tones played on (a wind instrument) by means of the tongue. 2. To touch or lap with the tongue. [OE *tunge*] —**tongue′less** *adj.*

tongued (tungd) *adj.* 1. Having a tongue or tongues. 2. Having or characterized by a (specified kind of) tongue: *sharp-tongued.*

tongue-lash·ing (tung′lash′ing) *n. Informal* A severe reprimand; scolding.

tongue-tie (tung′tī′) *v.t.* **-tied, -ty·ing** To deprive of speech or the power of speech.

tongue-tied (tung′tīd′) *adj.* Speechless or halting in speech, as from an impediment, shyness, etc.

tongue twister A word or phrase difficult to say quickly, as "Miss Smith's fish-sauce shop."

ton·ic (ton′ik) *adj.* 1. Having power to invigorate or build up; bracing. 2. Pertaining to tone or tones. 3. *Music* Pertaining to or in the key of the keynote. —*n.* 1. A medicine that gradually restores the normal tone of organs. 2. Something imparting animation, vigor, or tone. 3. *Music* The basic tone of a key or mode. 4. Quinine water. [< Gk. *tonos* sound, tone]

to·nic·i·ty (tō·nis′ə·tē) *n.* The resilience and elasticity of healthy muscles, arteries, etc.

to·night (tə·nīt′) *adv.* In or during the present or coming night. —*n.* 1. The night that follows this day. 2. The present night. Also **to-night′.** [OE *tō* + *niht* night]

ton·nage (tun′ij) *n.* 1. The cubic capacity of a merchant vessel expressed in tons of 100 cubic feet each. 2. The total carrying capacity of vessels, esp. of a country's merchant marine. 3. A tax levied on vessels at a given rate per ton. 4. Total weight in tons, as of materials produced or transported.

ton·sil (ton′səl) *n. Anat.* One of two oval lymphoid organs situated on either side of the passage from the mouth to the pharynx. [< L *tonsillae* tonsils] —**ton′sil·lar** or **ton′sil·ar** *adj.*

ton·sil·lec·to·my (ton′sə·lek′tə·mē) *n. pl.* **·mies** *Surg.* Removal of a tonsil or tonsils.

ton·sil·li·tis (ton′sə·lī′tis) *n. Pathol.* Inflammation of the tonsils. —**ton′sil·lit′ic** (-lit′ik) *adj.*

ton·so·ri·al (ton·sôr′ē·əl) *adj.* Pertaining to a barber or barbering: chiefly in the humorous term **tonsorial artist,** a barber. [< L *tonsus,* pp. of *tondere* to clip]

ton·sure (ton′shər) *n.* 1. The shaving of the head, or of the crown of the head, as of a priest or monk. 2. The part of a priest's or monk's head left bare by shaving. —*v.t.* **·sured, ·sur·ing** To shave the head of. [See TONSORIAL.]

ton·y (tō′nē) *adj.* **ton·i·er, ton·i·est** *Informal* Fashionable; stylish. [< TONE (def. 6)]

too (to͞o) *adv.* 1. In addition; likewise; also. 2. In excessive quantity or degree. 3. *Informal* Very; extremely: That's not *too* likely. 4. *Informal* Indeed: You are *too* going! [Stressed var. of OE *tō* to]

took (to͝ok) Past tense of TAKE.

tool (to͞ol) *n.* 1. An implement, as a hammer, saw, spade, or chisel, used chiefly in manual work. 2. A power-driven apparatus, as a lathe, used for cutting and shaping the parts of a machine. 3. The cutting or shaping part of such an apparatus. 4. A person used to carry out the designs of others; a dupe. 5. Any instrument or means necessary to one's profession or trade: Words are the writer's *tools.* —*v.t.* 1. To shape, mark, or ornament with a tool. 2. To provide with tools. 3. To ornament or impress designs upon (leather, a book binding, etc.) with a roller bearing a pattern. [OE *tōl*] —**tool′er** *n.*

tool·ing (to͞o′ling) *n.* 1. Ornamentation or work done with tools; esp., stamped or gilded ornamental designs on leather. 2. The application of a tool or tools to any work.

tool·mak·er (to͞ol′mā′kər) *n.* A maker of tools.

toot (to͞ot) *v.t. & v.i.* 1. To blow (a horn, whistle, etc.), esp. with short blasts. 2. To sound (a blast, toot, etc.). —*n.* 1. A short note or blast on or as on a horn. 2. *Slang*

A spree; esp., a drinking spree. [? < MLG *tūten*; prob. orig. imit.] **—toot′er** *n.*

tooth (tōōth) *n. pl.* **teeth** (tēth) 1. One of the hard structures in the mouth of most vertebrates, used for seizing and chewing food, as weapons, etc. 2. One of various hard bodies of the oral or gastric regions of invertebrates. 3. Something resembling a tooth in form or use; esp., a projecting point, tine, or cog. **—armed to the teeth** Completely or heavily armed. **—in the teeth of** Directly against, counter to, or in defiance of. **—to get one's teeth into** To achieve a solid grip or grasp of. **—to show one's teeth** To display a disposition to fight; threaten. **—*v.t.*** 1. To supply with teeth, as a rake or saw. 2. To give a serrated edge to; indent. **—*v.i.*** 3. To become interlocked, as gearwheels. [OE *tōth*] **—tooth′less** *adj.* **—tooth′less·ly** *adv.*

tooth·ache (tōōth′āk′) *n.* Pain in a tooth or teeth.

tooth and nail With all possible strength and effort; fiercely: to fight *tooth and nail.*

tooth·brush (tōōth′brush′) *n.* A small brush used for cleaning the teeth.

toothed (tōōtht) *adj.* 1. Having teeth. 2. Having or characterized by a specified kind or number of teeth: *sharp-toothed.*

tooth·paste (tōōth′pāst′) *n.* A paste used to clean teeth.

tooth·pick (tōōth′pik′) *n.* A small sliver of wood, plastic, etc., used for removing particles of food from between the teeth.

tooth·pow·der (tōōth′pou′dər) *n.* A powder used in cleaning the teeth.

tooth·some (tōōth′səm) *adj.* 1. Having a pleasant taste. 2. Attractive. **—tooth′some·ly** *adv.* **—tooth′some·ness** *n.*

tooth·y (tōō′thē) *adj.* **tooth·i·er, tooth·i·est** 1. Having large or prominent teeth. 2. Displaying the teeth: a *toothy* smile.

too·tle (tōōt′l) *v.t. & v.i.* **·tled, ·tling** To toot lightly or continuously, as on the flute. **—*n.*** The act or sound of tootling. [Freq. of TOOT]

top[1] (top) *n.* 1. The uppermost or highest part, end, side, or surface of anything. 2. The end or part regarded as the higher or upper extremity: the *top* of the street. 3. A lid or cover: a bottle *top.* 4. The crown of the head. 5. *pl.* The leafy part of a plant producing root vegetables. 6. The highest or most prominent place or rank. 7. One who is highest in rank or position. 8. The highest or loudest pitch: at the *top* of his voice. 9. The best part. **—to blow one's top** *Slang* To break out in a rage; flare up. **—on top** 1. At the highest point or position. 2. In a situation of dominance or power. 3. Highly successful. **—on top of** In addition to. **—*adj.*** 1. Of or pertaining to the top. 2. Forming or comprising the top. 3. Highest in rank or quality; chief: *top* authors. 4. Greatest in amount or degree: *top* prices. **—*v.t.*** **topped, top·ping** 1. To remove the top of; prune. 2. To provide with a top, cap, etc. 3. To form the top of. 4. To reach or pass over the top of; surmount. 5. To surpass or exceed. **—to top off** To complete or finish with a crowning touch. [OE]

top[2] (top) *n.* A toy with a point on which it is made to spin. [OE]

top- Var. of TOPO-.

to·paz (tō′paz) *n.* 1. A silicate of aluminum, occurring in chiefly yellow to brownish crystals that are valued as gemstones. 2. A brownish or grayish yellow. [< Gk. *topazos*]

top·coat (top′kōt′) *n.* A lightweight overcoat.

top-draw·er (top′drôr′) *adj. Informal* Of the highest standing, merit, excellence, etc.

top-dress·ing (top′dres′ing) *n.* A dressing of manure spread over the surface of a field. Also **top′dress′ing, top dressing.**

tope (tōp) *v.t.* **toped, top·ing** To drink (alcoholic beverages) excessively and frequently. [? Akin to earlier *top* to tilt]

top·er (tō′pər) *n.* A habitual drunkard.

top-flight (top′flīt′) *adj.* Of the highest quality; superior.

top hat A man's hat, usu. made of silk, having a tall, cylindrical crown and a narrow brim.

top-heav·y (top′hev′ē) *adj.* **-heav·i·er, -heav·i·est** Having the upper part too heavy for the lower part. **—top′-heav′i·ly** *adv.* **—top′-heav′i·ness** *n.*

to·pi (tō·pē′) *n.* A helmet made of pith, worn as protection against the sun: also called *pith helmet.* [< Hind., hat]

top·ic (top′ik) *n.* 1. A subject of discourse or of a treatise. 2. Any matter treated of in speech or writing; a theme for discussion. [< Gk. (*ta*) *topika*, topics, title of a work by Aristotle < *topos* place, commonplace]

top·i·cal (top′i·kəl) *adj.* 1. Pertaining to a topic. 2. Belonging to a place or spot; local. 3. Pertaining to matters of present interest. **—top′i·cal·ly** *adv.*

top·knot (top′not′) *n.* A crest, tuft, or knot of hair on the top of the head.

top·less (top′lis) *adj.* 1. Lacking a top. 2. Nude above the waist. 3. Featuring entertainers or waitresses who are nude above the waist: *topless* bar. **—top′less·ness** *n.*

top·loft·y (top′lôf′tē, -lof′tē) *adj.* **·loft·i·er, ·loft·i·est** 1. Towering very high. 2. Very proud or haughty; inflated; pompous. **—top′loft′i·ly** *adv.* **—top′loft′i·ness** *n.*

top·mast (top′mast′, -məst) *n. Naut.* The mast next above the lower mast.

top·most (top′mōst′) *adj.* Being at the very top.

top-notch (top′noch′) *adj. Informal* Excellent; best.

topo- *combining form* A place or region; regional. Also, before vowels, *top-.* [< Gk. *topos* place]

to·pog·ra·phy (tə·pog′rə·fē) *n. pl.* **·phies** 1. The detailed description of places. 2. The art of representing on a map the physical features of a place. 3. The physical features, collectively, of a region. 4. Surveying with reference to the physical features of a region. **—to·pog′ra·pher** *n.* **—top·o·graph·ic** (top′ə·graf′ik) or **·i·cal** *adj.* **—top′o·graph′i·cal·ly** *adv.*

top·ping (top′ing) *n.* 1. That which forms the top of anything. 2. A sauce, garnish, etc., put on a cake, portion of food, etc.

top·ple (top′əl) *v.* **·pled, ·pling** *v.t.* 1. To push and cause to fall; overturn. **—*v.i.*** 2. To fall. [Freq. of TOP[1], v.]

tops (tops) *adj. Slang* Excellent; first-rate.

top·sail (top′səl, top′sāl′) *n. Naut.* In a square-rigged vessel, a square sail set next above the lowest sail of a mast.

top-se·cret (top′sē′krit) *adj.* Denoting the highest category of security classification.
top·side (top′sīd′) *n. Naut.* The portion of a ship above the main deck. —*adv.* To or on the upper parts of a ship.
top·soil (top′soil′) *n.* The surface soil of land.
top·sy-tur·vy (top′sē·tûr′vē) *adj. & adv.* 1. Upside-down. 2. In disorder. —*n.* Confusion; disorder; chaos. [Prob. < TOP[1] + obs. *terve* to turn, overturn] —**top′sy-tur′vi·ly** *adv.* —**top′sy-tur′vi·ness** *n.* —**top′sy-tur′vy·dom** (-dəm) *n.*
toque (tōk) *n.* A close-fitting, brimless hat worn by women. [< F, cap < Basque *tauka*, a kind of cap]
To·rah (tôr′ə, tō′rə) *n.* In Judaism, the Pentateuch; also, the scroll containing this.
torch (tôrch) *n.* 1. A source of light, as from flaming material fixed at the end of a handle. 2. Anything that illuminates: the *torch* of science. 3. A portable device giving off an intensely hot flame and used for burning off paint, melting solder, etc. 4. *Brit.* A flashlight. [< OF *torche*, ult. < L *torquere* to twist]
torch·bear·er (tôrch′bâr′ər) *n.* 1. One who carries a torch. 2. One who imparts knowledge, truth, etc.
torch·light (tôrch′līt′) *n.* The light of a torch. —*adj.* Lighted by torches: a *torchlight* rally.
torch song A popular love song expressing sadness and hopeless yearning.
tore (tôr) Past tense of TEAR[1].
tor·e·a·dor (tôr′ē·ə·dôr′) *n.* A bullfighter. [< Sp. < *torear* to fight bulls < L *taurus* bull]
to·ri·i (tôr′i·ē) *n.* The gateway of a Shinto temple, consisting of two uprights with one straight crosspiece, and another above with a concave lintel. [< Japanese]
tor·ment (*n.* tôr′ment; *v.* tôr·ment′) *n.* 1. Intense bodily pain or mental anguish; agony; torture. 2. One who or that which torments. —*v.t.* 1. To subject to intense physical or mental suffering. 2. To harass. [< L *tormentum* rack < *torquere* to twist] —**tor·ment′er** or **tor·men′tor** *n.* —**tor·ment′ing·ly** *adv.*
torn (tôrn) Past participle of TEAR[1].
tor·na·do (tôr·nā′dō) *n. pl.* **·does** or **·dos** *Meteorol.* A whirling wind of exceptional violence, accompanied by a funnel-shaped cloud marking the narrow path of greatest destruction. [Prob. alter. of Sp. *tronada* thunderstorm < L *tonare* to thunder] —**tor·nad′ic** (-nad′ik) *adj.*
tor·pe·do (tôr·pē′dō) *n. pl.* **·dos** or **·does** An explosive, self-propelled, cigar-shaped underwater projectile, used to destroy enemy ships. —*v.t.* **·doed, ·do·ing** To sink, damage, or wreck with or as with a torpedo. [< L, numbness < *torpere* to be numb]
torpedo boat A small, swift war vessel equipped with tubes for the discharge of torpedos.
tor·pid (tôr′pid) *adj.* 1. Inactive; dormant; numb. 2. Sluggish; apathetic; dull. [< L *torpere* to be numb] —**tor·pid′i·ty, tor′pid·ness** *n.* —**tor′pid·ly** *adv.*
tor·por (tôr′pər) *n.* 1. Complete or partial insensibility; stupor. 2. Apathy. —**tor′po·rif′ic** *adj.*
torque (tôrk) *n. Mech.* Anything that causes or tends to cause torsion in a body. [< L *torquere* to twist]
tor·rent (tôr′ənt, tor′-) *n.* 1. A violent, onrushing flow, as of water. 2. Any abundant or tumultuous flow: a *torrent* of abuse. [< L *torrens*, boiling, burning, ppr. of *torrere* to parch] —**tor·ren·tial** (tô·ren′shəl) *adj.* —**tor·ren′tial·ly** *adv.*
tor·rid (tôr′id, tor′-) *adj.* 1. Receiving the full force of the sun's heat. 2. Very hot; scorching; burning. 3. Impassioned; ardent. [< L *torrere* to parch] —**tor·rid′i·ty, tor′rid·ness** *n.* —**tor′rid·ly** *adv.*
Torrid Zone See under ZONE.
tor·sion (tôr′shən) *n.* 1. The act of twisting, or the state of being twisted. 2. *Mech.* Deformation of a body, as a thread or rod, by twisting around its length as an axis. 3. The force with which a twisted cord or cable tends to return to its former position. [< L *torquere* to twist] —**tor′sion·al** *adj.* —**tor′sion·al·ly** *adv.*
tor·so (tôr′sō) *n. pl.* **·sos** or **·si** (-sē) 1. The trunk of a human body. 2. A sculptured representation of a human body without the head or limbs. [< Ital., stalk < Gk. *thyrsos*]
tort (tôrt) *n. Law* Any private or civil wrong by act or omission for which a civil suit can be brought, but not including breach of contract. [See TORSION.]
torte (tôrt) *n.* A rich cake made with butter, eggs, and often fruit and nuts. [< G < Ital. *torta*]
tor·til·la (tôr·tē′yā) *n.* A flat cake made of coarse cornmeal baked on a hot sheet of iron or a slab of stone. [< Sp., dim. of *torta* cake]
tor·toise (tôr′təs) *n.* 1. A turtle, esp. a terrestrial one. 2. A slow-moving person or thing. [< L *tortus* twisted; so called from its crooked feet]
tortoise shell The mottled, hornlike shell of a turtle, used for combs, etc. —**tor·toise-shell** (tôr′tə·shel′, tôr′təs-), **tor′toise·shell′** *adj.*
tor·tu·ous (tôr′choo͞·əs) *adj.* 1. Consisting of irregular bends or turns; twisting. 2. Not straightforward; devious. [< L *torquere* to twist] —**tor′tu·os′i·ty** (-os′ə·tē) *n.* —**tor′tu·ous·ly** *adv.* —**tor′tu·ous·ness** *n.*
tor·ture (tôr′chər) *n.* 1. Infliction of or subjection to extreme physical pain. 2. Great mental suffering; agony. 3. Something that causes extreme pain. —*v.t.* **·tured, ·tur·ing** 1. To inflict extreme pain upon, as from cruelty. 2. To cause to suffer agony, extreme discomfort, etc. 3. To twist or turn into an abnormal form, meaning, etc. [< L *torquere* to twist] —**tor′tur·er** *n.* —**tor′tur·ous** *adj.*
To·ry (tôr′ē) *n. pl.* **·ries** 1. A member of an English political party, since about 1832 called the Conservative Party. 2. One who at the period of the American Revolution supported the British. 3. One having very conservative beliefs, esp. in politics. Also **to′ry.** [< Irish *tōir* to pursue] —**To′ry·ism** *n.*
toss (tôs) *v.t.* 1. To throw, pitch, or fling about. 2. To agitate; disturb. 3. To throw with the hand, esp. with the palm of the hand upward. 4. To lift with a quick motion, as the head. —*v.i.* 5. To be flung to and fro, as a ship in a storm. 6. To throw oneself from side to side restlessly, as in sleep. —**to toss off** 1. To drink at one draft. 2. To utter, write, or do in an offhand manner.

—**to toss up** To throw a coin into the air to decide a wager or choice. —*n.* 1. The act of tossing. 2. A quick upward or backward movement, as of the head. 3. A tossup or wager. [Prob. < Scand.] —**toss′er** *n.*

toss·up (tôs′up′) *n. Informal* 1. The throwing up of a coin to decide a bet, etc. 2. An even chance.

tot[1] (tot) *n.* 1. A little child. 2. A small amount or portion, as of liquor. [Origin unknown]

tot[2] (tot) *v.t.* **tot·ted tot·ting** *Informal* To add. [Short for TOTAL]

to·tal (tōt′l) *n.* The whole sum or amount. —*adj.* 1. Constituting or comprising a whole. 2. Complete; absolute: a *total* loss. —*v.* **to·taled** or **·talled, to·tal·ing** or **·tal·ling** *v.t.* 1. To ascertain the total of. 2. To come to or reach as a total. 3. *Slang* To completely wreck (a car). —*v.i.* 4. To amount. [< L *totus* all] —**to′tal·ly** *adv.*

to·tal·i·tar·i·an (tō·tal′ə·târ′ē·ən) *adj.* Designating or characteristic of a government controlled exclusively by one party or faction and maintained by political suppression. —*n.* An adherent of totalitarian government. —**to·tal′i·tar′i·an·ism** *n.*

to·tal·i·ty (tō·tal′ə·tē) *n. pl.* **·ties** 1. An aggregate of parts or individuals. 2. The state of being total.

to·tal·i·za·tor (tōt′l·ə·zā′tər) *n.* A pari-mutuel machine: also **to′tal·iz′er** (-ī′zər). Also *Brit.* **to′tal·i·sa′tor.**

tote (tōt) *Informal v.t.* **tot·ed, tot·ing** 1. To carry about. 2. To haul, as supplies. —*n.* 1. The act of toting. 2. A load or haul. [? < West African] —**tot′er** *n.*

tote board *Informal* A board at a racetrack, etc., showing the betting odds and results of races.

to·tem (tō′təm) *n.* 1. An animal, plant, or other natural object believed to be ancestrally related to a tribe, clan, etc. 2. The representation of this. [< Algonquian] —**to·tem·ic** (tō·tem′ik) *adj.* —**to′tem·ism** *n.* —**to′tem·ist** *n.* —**to′tem·is′tic** *adj.*

totem pole A tall post or pole carved or painted with totemic images, often erected outside a dwelling by North American Indians, esp. those of the NW coast.

toth·er (tuth′ər) *adj. & pron. Informal* The other; other. Also **t'oth′er.** [ME *the tother* < *thet other* the other]

tot·ter (tot′ər) *v.i.* 1. To walk feebly and unsteadily. 2. To shake or sway, as if about to fall. —*n.* The act or condition of tottering. [Prob. < Scand.] —**tot′ter·er** *n.* —**tot′ter·y** *adj.*

tou·can (too͞′kan) *n.* A large, fruit-eating bird of tropical America, with brilliant plumage and an immense, thin-walled beak. [< Tupi *tucana*]

touch (tuch) *v.t.* 1. To place the hand, finger, etc., in contact with. 2. To be in or come into contact with. 3. To bring into contact with something else. 4. To strike lightly. 5. To border on; adjoin. 6. To come to; reach. 7. To color slightly; tinge. 8. To affect injuriously; taint: vegetables *touched* by frost. 9. To affect the emotions of; move, esp. to pity, gratitude, etc. 10. To use or partake of: I will not *touch* this food. —*v.i.* 11. To touch someone or something. 12. To come into or be in contact. —**to touch at** To stop briefly at (a port or place) in the course of a journey or voyage. —**to touch off** 1. To cause to explode; fire. 2. To cause to happen or occur. —**to touch on** (or **upon**) 1. To relate to; concern. 2. To treat briefly or in passing. —**to touch up** To improve or alter by slight additions or corrections. —*n.* 1. The act or process of touching. 2. The state of being touched. 3. *Physiol.* That sense by which external objects are perceived through direct contact with any part of the body. ◆Collateral adjective: *tactile.* 4. The sensation conveyed by touching something: a smooth *touch.* 5. A stroke; hit; blow. 6. A perceptible effect or influence: He felt the *touch* of her wit. 7. A light stroke or mark. 8. A slight detail or improvement: finishing *touches.* 9. The distinctive style of an artist. 10. A trace; tinge: a *touch* of irony. 11. A slight attack or twinge: a *touch* of rheumatism. 12. A small quantity or dash. 13. Close communication or contact: to keep in *touch* with someone. 14. *Music* The manner in which a player presses the keyboard. [< OF *tochier*] —**touch′a·ble** *adj.* —**touch′a·ble·ness** *n.* —**touch′er** *n.*

touch and go An uncertain or precarious situation. —**touch-and-go** (tuch′ən·gō′) *adj.*

touch·back (tuch′bak′) *n.* In football, a play in which a player grounds the ball after it has been sent over his own goal line by an opponent.

touch·down (tuch′doun′) *n.* In football, a scoring play, worth six points, in which the ball is held on or over the opponent's goal line.

tou·ché (too͞·shā′) *adj. French* In fencing, touched by the point of an opponent's foil. —*interj.* You've scored a point!

touched (tucht) *adj.* 1. Emotionally moved. 2. Slightly unbalanced in mind.

touch·ing (tuch′ing) *adj.* Appealing to the sympathies or emotions. —*prep.* With regard to; concerning. —**touch′ing·ly** *adv.* —**touch′ing·ness** *n.*

touch·stone (tuch′stōn′) *n.* A criterion or standard by which the qualities of something are tested.

touch·y (tuch′ē) *adj.* **touch·i·er, touch·i·est** 1. Likely to take offense easily; irritable. 2. Risky; delicate: a *touchy* subject. —**touch′·i·ly** *adv.* —**touch′i·ness** *n.*

tough (tuf) *adj.* 1. Capable of sustaining great tension or strain without breaking. 2. Firm and resilient. 3. Not easily separated, softened, etc.: *tough* meat. 4. Possessing great physical, moral, or intellectual endurance. 5. Unmanageably rough, unruly, or vicious. 6. Difficult to accomplish; laborious. 7. Severe; rigorous. —*n.* A lawless person; a rowdy; ruffian. [OE *tōh*] —**tough′ly** *adv.* —**tough′ness** *n.*

tough·en (tuf′ən) *v.t. & v.i.* To make or become tough or tougher. —**tough′en·er** *n.*

tou·pee (too͞·pā′) *n.* A wig worn to cover baldness or a bald spot. [< F *toupet* < OF *toup* tuft of hair]

tour (to͝or) *n.* 1. A trip, as for inspection or sightseeing, or for presenting a performance. 2. A turn or shift, as of service. —*v.t. & v.i.* To go on a tour (of). [< L *tornus* lathe < Gk. *tornos*]

tour de force (to͝or′ də fôrs′) *French* A feat of remarkable strength or skill.

tour·ist (to͝or′ist) *n.* One who makes a tour or a pleasure trip. **—tour′ist** *adj.*

tourist class A class of accommodations on a ship, plane, etc., less expensive and luxurious than first class.

tour·ma·line (to͝or′mə·lēn, -lin) *n.* A mineral occurring in various colors, the transparent varieties being esteemed as gemstones. Also **tour′ma·lin** (-lin). [< F, ult. < Singhalese *tōramalli* carnelian]

tour·na·ment (tûr′nə·mənt, to͝or′-) *n.* 1. Any contest of skill involving a number of competitors and a series of games: a chess *tournament.* 2. In medieval times, a pageant in which two opposing parties of men in armor contended on horseback in mock combat. [< OF *torneiement*]

tour·ney (tûr′nē, to͝or′-) *n.* A tournament. *—v.i.* To take part in a tournament; tilt. [See TOURNAMENT.]

tour·ni·quet (to͝or′nə·ket, tûr′-) *n. Surg.* A bandage, etc., for stopping the flow of blood through an artery by compression. [< F *tourner* to turn]

tou·sle (tou′zəl) *v.t.* **·sled, ·sling** To disarrange or disorder, as the hair or dress. [ME *tusen, tousen*]

tout (tout) *Informal v.t. & v.i.* 1. To seek patronage, votes, etc. 2. To advertise or praise excessively. 3. In horse racing, to sell information about (a horse). *—n.* One who touts. [ME, ? < OE *tōtian*, to peep, look out] **—tout′er** *n.*

tout de suite (to͞ot′swēt′) *French* Immediately.

tow[1] (tō) *n.* Coarse, short hemp or flax fiber prepared for spinning. [Prob. OE *tow-* for spinning] **—tow′y** *adj.*

tow[2] (tō) *v.t.* To pull or drag, as by a rope, chain, etc. *—n.* 1. The act of towing, or the state of being towed. 2. That which is towed. 3. A towline. **—to take in tow** To take charge of. [OE *togian*]

to·ward (tôrd, tə·wôrd′) *prep.* 1. In the direction of; facing. 2. With respect to; regarding: his attitude *toward* women. 3. In anticipation of; for: an effort *toward* peace. 4. Approaching in time; about: arriving *toward* evening. Also **to·wards** (tôrdz, tə·wôrdz′). [OE *tō* to + *-weard* -ward]

tow·a·way (tō′ə·wā) *n.* The act of towing away a vehicle, esp. one illegally parked.

tow·boat (tō′bōt′) *n.* A tugboat.

tow·el (toul, tou′əl) *n.* A cloth or paper for drying anything by wiping. *—v.t.* **tow·eled** or **·elled, tow·el·ing** or **·el·ling** To wipe or dry with a towel. [< OF *toaille*]

tow·el·ing (tou′ling, tou′əl·ing) *n.* Material used for towels. Also **tow′el·ling.**

tow·er (tou′ər) *n.* 1. A tall, usu. narrow structure, sometimes part of a larger building. 2. Any similar tall structure or object, often erected for a specific use: a water *tower.* *—v.i.* To rise or stand like a tower. [OE *torr* < L *turris*] **—tow′ered** *adj.* **—tow′er·y** *adj.*

tow·er·ing (tou′ər·ing) *adj.* 1. Like a tower; lofty. 2. Unusually high or great; outstanding. 3. Intense.

tow·head (tō′hed′) *n.* A head of very light-colored hair; also, a person having such hair. [< TOW[1] + HEAD] **—tow′-head′ed** *adj.*

tow·hee (tou′hē, tō′-) *n.* Any of various American birds related to the buntings and the sparrows; esp., the chewink. Also **towhee bunting.** [Imit. of one of its notes]

tow·line (tō′līn′) *n.* A heavy rope or cable used in towing: also **tow′rope′** (-rōp′).

town (toun) *n.* 1. Any considerable collection of dwellings and other buildings, larger than a village but smaller than a city. 2. The inhabitants of such a community. 3. A township (def. 1). 4. Any closely settled urban district. **—on the town** *Slang* On a round of pleasure. **—to go to town** *Slang* To act with speed and efficiency. [OE *tūn* enclosure, group of houses]

town hall The building containing the public offices of a town.

town house 1. A residence in a city. 2. A residence, usu. of two stories, attached to a similar residence on one or both sides and located in a city or suburban development.

town meeting An assembly of qualified voters for the purpose of transacting town business.

town·ship (toun′ship) *n.* 1. A territorial subdivision of a county with certain corporate powers of municipal government. 2. A unit of area in surveys of U.S. public lands, normally six miles square.

towns·man (tounz′mən) *n. pl.* **·men** (-mən) A resident of a town; also, a fellow citizen.

towns·peo·ple (tounz′pē′pəl) *n.pl.* People who live in towns or in a particular town or city. Also **town′folk′** (-fōk′), **towns′folk′.**

tow·path (tō′path′) *n.* A path along a river or canal used by draft animals, etc., for towing boats.

tow truck (tō) A truck equipped to tow other vehicles.

tox·e·mi·a (tok·sē′mē·ə) *n. Pathol.* Blood poisoning. Also **tox·ae′mi·a.** [< Gk. *toxicon* poison + -EMIA] **—tox·e′mic** or **tox·ae′mic** *adj.*

tox·ic (tok′sik) *adj.* Of or caused by poison; poisonous. Also **tox′i·cal.** [< Gk. *toxicon* poison for arrows] **—tox′i·cal·ly** *adv.* **—tox·ic′i·ty** (-sis′ə·tē) *n.*

tox·i·col·o·gy (tok′sə·kol′ə·jē) *n.* The science that treats of the origin, nature, properties, etc., of poisons. **—tox′i·co·log′·i·cal** (-kə·loj′i·kəl) *adj.* **—tox′i·co·log′i·cal·ly** *adv.* **—tox′i·col′o·gist** *n.*

tox·in (tok′sin) *n.* 1. A poisonous compound developed by animal, vegetable, or bacterial organisms and acting as a causative agent in many diseases. 2. Any toxic matter generated in living or dead organisms. Also **tox·ine** (tok′sēn). [< TOXIC]

tox·oid (tok′soid) *n.* A toxin that has been specially treated to remove toxicity, often used in immunization.

toy (toi) *n.* 1. A plaything for children. 2. Any object of little importance or value; a trifle. 3. A small ornament or trinket. *—v.i.* To trifle; play. *—adj.* Made to be used as or resembling a toy. [< ME *toye* sport and Du. *tuig* tools] **—toy′er** *n.*

trace[1] (trās) *n.* 1. A mark left by some past event or agent. 2. A barely detectable quantity; touch. *—v.t.* **traced, trac·ing** 1. To follow the tracks, course, or development of. 2. To follow (tracks, etc.). 3. To discover by examination or investigation; determine. 4. To copy (a drawing, etc.) on a superimposed transparent sheet. 5. To form (letters, etc.) with careful strokes. [< L *trahere* to draw]

—**trace′a·bil′i·ty, trace′a·ble·ness** *n.* —**trace′a·ble** *adj.* —**trace′a·bly** *adv.*

trace[2] (trās) *n.* One of two side straps or chains for connecting the collar of a harness with a vehicle. —**to kick over the traces** To throw off control; become unmanageable. —*v.t.* **traced, trac·ing** To fasten with or as with traces. [See TRACE[1].]

trac·er (trā′sər) *n.* 1. One of various instruments used in tracing drawings, etc. 2. An inquiry forwarded from one point to another, to trace missing mail matter, etc. 3. A radioisotope introduced into the body for the purpose of following the processes of metabolism, the course of a disease, etc. [< TRACE[1]]

trac·er·y (trā′sər·ē) *n. pl.* **·er·ies** 1. Ornamental stonework having an intertwining or branching design. 2. Any work, ornamentation, etc., resembling this.

tra·che·a (trā′kē·ə) *n. pl.* **·che·ae** (-ki·ē) or **·che·as** *Anat.* The duct by which air passes from the larynx to the bronchi and the lungs: also called *windpipe.* [< Gk. (*artēria*) *tracheia* a rough (artery)] —**tra′che·al** *adj.*

tra·che·ot·o·my (trā′kē·ot′ə·mē) *n. pl.* **·mies** *Surg.* The operation of cutting into the trachea.

trac·ing (trā′sing) *n.* 1. A copy made by tracing on transparent paper. 2. A record made by an automatically registering instrument.

track (trak) *n.* 1. A mark or trail left by the passage of anything. 2. Any regular path; course. 3. Any kind of racecourse; also, sports performed on such a course; track athletics. 4. A set of rails or a rail on which trains, etc., may travel. 5. **a** A groove on a phonograph record. **b** One of the parallel recording paths of a magnetic tape. —**to keep track of** 1. To keep in touch with. 2. To follow the development of. 3. To be aware of; remember. —**in one's tracks** Right where one is. —**to lose track of** To fail to keep in touch with. —**to make tracks** To hurry; run away in haste. —*v.t.* 1. To follow the tracks of; trail. 2. To discover, pursue, or follow by means of marks or indications. 3. To make tracks upon or with. [< OF *trac*] —**track′a·ble** *adj.* —**track′er** *n.* —**track′less** *adj.*

track record A record of performance or accomplishments.

tract[1] (trakt) *n.* 1. An extended area of land. 2. *Anat.* An extensive region of the body, esp. one comprising a system of parts or organs: the alimentary *tract.* [< L *trahere* to draw]

tract[2] (trakt) *n.* A pamphlet on a religious or political subject. [Short for L *tractatus* a handling, treatise]

tract·a·ble (trak′tə·bəl) *adj.* 1. Easily led or controlled; docile. 2. Readily worked or handled; malleable. [< L *tractare* to handle < *trahere* to draw] —**tract′a·ble·ness, tract′a·bil′i·ty** *n.* —**tract′a·bly** *adv.*

trac·tion (trak′shən) *n.* 1. The act of drawing over a surface. 2. The state of being drawn, or the power employed. 3. Adhesive or rolling friction, as of wheels on a track. [< L *trahere* to draw] —**trac′tion·al** *adj.*

trac·tor (trak′tər) *n.* 1. A powerful, motor-driven vehicle used to draw a plow, reaper, etc. 2. An automotive vehicle with a driver's cab, used to haul trailers, etc. [< L *trahere* to draw]

trade (trād) *n.* 1. A business; esp., a skilled handicraft. 2. Mercantile traffic; commerce. 3. An exchange, as in barter, buying and selling, etc. 4. A firm's customers. 5. Customary pursuit; occupation. —*v.* **trad·ed, trad·ing** *v.t.* 1. To exchange for something comparable; barter. —*v.i.* 2. To engage in commerce or in business. 3. To make an exchange. —**to trade on** To make advantageous use of. [< MLG, track]

trade-in (trād′in′) *n.* Something given or accepted in part payment for something else.

trade journal A periodical publishing news and discussions of a particular trade or business.

trade·mark (trād′märk′) *n.* 1. A name, design, etc., officially registered and used by a merchant or manufacturer to distinguish his goods from those made or sold by others. 2. Any distinctive characteristic. —*v.t.* 1. To label with a trademark. 2. To register as a trademark.

trade name 1. The name by which an article, process, service, or the like is designated in trade. 2. A style or name of a business house.

trad·er (trā′dər) *n.* 1. One who trades. 2. Any vessel employed in trade.

trade route A route, esp. a sea lane, used by traders.

trades·folk (trādz′fōk′) *n.pl.* People engaged in trade; esp., shopkeepers. Also **trades′·peo′ple** (-pē′pəl).

trades·man (trādz′mən) *n. pl.* **·men** (-mən) A retail dealer; shopkeeper.

trade union A labor union. Also *Brit.* **trades union.**

trade wind *Meteorol.* Either of two steady winds blowing in the same course toward the equator, one from the northeast on the north side of the equator, the other from the southeast on the south side.

trading post A station for barter in unsettled territory, set up by a trader.

trading stamp A stamp given by a tradesman to a purchaser, and exchangeable, in quantities, for merchandise.

tra·di·tion (trə·dish′ən) *n.* 1. The knowledge, doctrines, customs, and practices transmitted from generation to generation; also, the transmission of such knowledge, doctrines, etc. 2. The historic conceptions and usages of a school of art, literature, etc. 3. A custom so long continued that it has almost the force of a law. [< L *trans-* across + *dare* to give] —**tra·di′tion·al, tra·di′tion·ar′y** *adj.* —**tra·di′tion·al·ism** *n.* —**tra·di′tion·al·ist** *n.* —**tra·di′tion·al·ist′ic** *adj.* —**tra·di′tion·al·ly** *adv.* —**tra·di′tion·ist** *n.*

tra·duce (trə·dōōs′, -dyōōs′) *v.t.* **·duced, ·duc·ing** To defame; slander. [< L *traducere* to transport, bring into disgrace] —**tra·duc′er** *n.* —**tra·duc′i·ble** *adj.* —**tra·duc′·ing·ly** *adv.* —**tra·duc·tion** (trə·duk′shən) *n.*

traf·fic (traf′ik) *n.* 1. The movement or passage of vehicles, pedestrians, ships, etc., along a route; also, the vehicles, pedestrians, etc. 2. Buying and selling; trade. 3. The business of transportation; also, the freight or passengers carried. 4. The messages, signals, etc., handled by a communications system. 5. Unlawful or improper trade.

—*v.i.* ·ficked, ·fick·ing 1. To engage in buying and selling; do business, esp., illegally: with *in*. 2. To have dealings: with *with*. [< Ital. *trafficare* < L *trans-* across + Ital. *ficcare* to thrust in] —**traf′fick·er** *n.*

traffic light A signal light that, by changing color, directs the flow of traffic along a road or highway. Also **traffic signal.**

tra·ge·di·an (trə·jē′dē·ən) *n.* 1. An actor in tragedy. 2. A writer of tragedies.

tra·ge·di·enne (trə·jē′dē·en′) *n.* An actress of tragedy. [< F]

trag·e·dy (traj′ə·dē) *n. pl.* ·**dies** 1. A calamitous or fatal event or course of events; disaster. 2. A form of drama in which the protagonist comes to disaster through a flaw in his nature or is crushed by social and psychological forces. [< Gk. *tragōidia*, appar. < *tragos* goat + *ōidē* song]

trag·ic (traj′ik) *adj.* 1. Involving death, calamity, or suffering. 2. Pertaining to or having the nature of tragedy. 3. Appropriate to or like tragedy, esp. in drama. Also **trag′i·cal.** [< Gk. *tragikos* pertaining to tragedy] —**trag′i·cal·ly** *adv.* —**trag′i·cal·ness** *n.*

trag·i·com·e·dy (traj′i·kom′ə·dē) *n. pl.* ·**dies** 1. A drama in which tragic and comic scenes are intermingled. 2. A situation or event suggestive of such a drama. —**trag′i·com′ic** or ·**i·cal** *adj.* —**trag′i·com′i·cal·ly** *adv.*

trail (trāl) *v.t.* 1. To draw along lightly over a surface; also, to drag or draw after: to *trail* a robe. 2. To follow the track of; track. 3. To follow or lag behind, esp. in a race. —*v.i.* 4. To hang or float loosely so as to drag along a surface. 5. To grow along the ground or over rocks, bushes, etc., in a loose, creeping way. 6. To follow behind loosely; stream. 7. To lag behind; straggle. —*n.* 1. A path or track made by the passage of persons or animals. 2. The footprints or other traces of an animal followed by a hunter. 3. Anything drawn behind or in the wake of something. [< L *trahere* to draw]

trail·blaz·er (trāl′blā·zər) *n.* 1. One who blazes a trail. 2. A pioneer in any field. —**trail′blaz·ing** *n.*

trail·er (trā′lər) *n.* 1. One who or that which trails. 2. A vehicle drawn by another having motive power. 3. A vehicle drawn by a car or truck and used as a dwelling. 4. A short motion-picture film made up of scenes from a coming feature picture, used for advertising.

train (trān) *n.* 1. A continuous line of coupled railway cars. 2. A set of connected things; series; sequence. 3. A retinue or suite. 4. An extension of a dress skirt, trailing behind the wearer. 5. A succession or line of vehicles, people, or animals en route. —*v.t.* 1. To make proficient or qualified by instruction, drill, etc.; educate. 2. To make obedient or capable of performing tricks, as an animal. 3. To bring into a required physical condition by diet and exercise. 4. To develop into a fixed shape: to *train* a plant on a trellis. 5. To aim, as a gun. —*v.i.* 6. To undergo a course of training. [< L *trahere* to draw] —**train′a·ble** *adj.* —**train′er** *n.* —**train′ing** *n.*

train·ee (trā·nē′) *n.* One who undergoes training.

train·man (trān′mən) *n. pl.* ·**men** (-mən) A railway employee serving on a train; esp., a brakeman.

traipse (trāps) *v.i.* **traipsed, traips·ing** *Informal* To walk about in an idle or aimless manner. [Earlier *trapass*]

trait (trāt) *n.* A distinguishing feature or quality of character. [< L *trahere* to draw]

trai·tor (trā′tər) *n.* One who betrays a trust; esp., one who commits treason. [< L *traditor* < *trans-* across + *dare* to give] —**trai′tor·ous** *adj.* —**trai′tor·ous·ly** *adv.*

tra·jec·to·ry (trə·jek′tər·ē) *n. pl.* ·**ries** The path described by an object moving in space; esp., the path of a projectile. [< L *trans-* over + *jacere* to throw]

tram (tram) *n.* 1. *Brit.* A streetcar or street railway: also **tram′car′** (-kär′). 2. A four-wheeled vehicle for conveying coals in a mine. [< dial. E, rail ? < LG *traam* shaft]

tram·mel (tram′əl) *n.* *Usu. pl.* That which limits freedom or activity; an impediment; hindrance. —*v.t.* **tram·meled** or ·**melled, tram·mel·ing** or ·**mel·ling** 1. To hinder or obstruct; restrict. 2. To entangle in or as in a snare. Also **tram′el, tram′ell.** [< OF *tramail* net < L *tri-* three + *macula* mesh] —**tram′mel·er** or **tram′mel·ler** *n.*

tramp (tramp) *v.i.* 1. To walk or hike. 2. To walk heavily or firmly. —*v.t.* 3. To walk or wander through. 4. To walk on heavily; trample. —*n.* 1. A poor wanderer; a vagrant; vagabond. 2. A heavy, continued tread. 3. The sound of heavy marching or walking. 4. A long walk; hike. 5. A steam vessel that picks up freight wherever it can be obtained: also **tramp steamer.** 6. *Informal* A sexually promiscuous girl or woman. [ME *trampen* < Gmc.]

tram·ple (tram′pəl) *v.* ·**pled,** ·**pling** *v.t.* 1. To tread on heavily or ruthlessly. —*v.i.* 2. To tread heavily. —*n.* The act or sound of trampling. [See TRAMP.]

tram·po·line (tram′pə·lin) *n.* A section of strong canvas stretched on a frame, on which an acrobat, athlete, etc., may bound or spring. [< Ital. *trampoli* stilts]

trance (trans) *n.* 1. A condition characterized by the absence of conscious control over one's actions, as in hypnosis. 2. A dreamlike, bewildered state; daze. 3. A state of deep abstraction. —*v.t.* **tranced, tranc·ing** To put into or as into a trance. [< OF *transir* to pass, die]

tran·quil (trang′kwil) *adj.* ·**quil·er** or ·**quil·ler,** ·**quil·est** or ·**quil·lest** 1. Free from mental agitation or disturbance; calm. 2. Quiet and motionless. [< L *tranquillus* quiet] —**tran·quil′li·ty** (-kwil′ə·tē) or **tran·quil′i·ty** *n.* —**tran′quil·ly** *adv.*

tran·quil·ize (trang′kwəl·īz) *v.t. & v.i.* ·**ized,** ·**iz·ing** To make or become tranquil. Also **tran′quil·lize,** *Brit.* **tran′quil·lise.** —**tran′·quil·i·za′tion** *n.*

tran·quil·iz·er (trang′kwəl·ī′zər) *n.* 1. One who or that which tranquilizes. 2. *Med.* A drug able to reduce nervous tension. Also **tran′quil·liz′er.**

trans- *prefix*
1. Across; beyond; on the other side of:

transalpine	**trans-Canadian**
transarctic	**transcontinental**
transatlantic	**transdesert**
transborder	**transequatorial**

transfrontier **transpacific**
transisthmian **transpolar**
transoceanic **trans-Siberian**
2. Through: **transpierce**
3. Into another state: *transform, transliterate*
4. Surpassing; transcending; beyond:
transconscious **transmundane**
transhuman **transnational**
transmaterial **transphysical**
transmental **transrational**
[< L *trans* across, beyond, over]

trans·act (trans·akt′, tranz-) *v.t.* To carry through; accomplish; do. [< L *trans-* through + *agere* to drive, do] **—trans·ac′tor** *n.*

trans·ac·tion (trans·ak′shən, tranz-) *n.* 1. The act of transacting, or the state of being transacted. 2. Something transacted; esp., a business deal. 3. *pl.* Published reports, as of a society. **—trans·ac′tion·al** *adj.*

trans·cei·ver (tran·sē′vər) *n. Electronics* A combined radio transmitter and receiver. [< TRANS(MITTER) + (RE)CEIVER]

tran·scend (tran·send′) *v.t.* 1. To rise above in excellence or degree. 2. To overstep or exceed as a limit. [< L *trans-* beyond, over + *scandere* to climb] **—tran·scen′dent** *adj.* **—tran·scen′dence, tran·scen′den·cy** *n.* **—tran·scen′dent·ly** *adv.*

tran·scen·den·tal (tran′sen·den′təl) *adj.* 1. Of very high degree; transcendent. 2. Beyond or contrary to common sense or experience. **—tran′scen·den′tal·ly** *adv.*

tran·scen·den·tal·ism (tran′sen·den′təl·iz′əm) *n.* 1. *Philos.* Any of several doctrines holding that reality is essentially mental or spiritual in nature. 2. The state or quality of being transcendental. **—tran′scen·den′tal·ist** *n. & adj.*

tran·scribe (tran·skrīb′) *v.t.* **·scribed, ·scrib·ing** 1. To copy or recopy in handwriting or typewriting. 2. *Telecom.* To make a recording of (a radio program). 3. To adapt (a musical composition) for a change of instrument or voice. [< L *trans-* over + *scribere* to write] **—tran·scrib′a·ble** *adj.* **—tran·scrib′er** *n.*

tran·script (tran′skript) *n.* 1. That which is transcribed; esp., a written, typewritten, or printed copy. 2. A copy of a student's academic record.

tran·scrip·tion (tran·skrip′shən) *n.* 1. The act of transcribing. 2. A copy; transcript. 3. *Telecom.* A recording of a performance made for a later radio broadcast. 4. *Music* The adaptation of a composition for some other instrument or voice. **—tran·scrip′·tion·al, tran·scrip′tive** *adj.*

tran·sect (tran·sekt′) *v.t.* To dissect transversely. [< TRANS- + L *sectus,* pp. of *secare* to cut] **—tran·sec′tion** (-sek′shən) *n.*

tran·sept (tran′sept) *n. Archit.* One of the side projections between the nave and choir of a cross-shaped church. [< L *transversus* lying across + *septum* enclosure] **—tran·sep′tal** *adj.* **—tran·sep′tal·ly** *adv.*

trans·fer (trans′fər; *for v., also* trans·fûr′) *v.* **·ferred, ·fer·ring** *v.t.* 1. To carry, or cause to pass, from one person or place to another. 2. To make over possession of to another. 3. To convey (a drawing) from one surface to another. **—***v.i.* 4. To transfer oneself. 5. To be transferred. 6. To change to another bus, school, etc. **—***n.* 1. The act of transferring, or the state of being transferred: also **trans·fer′al** (-fûr′əl) or **trans·fer′ral.** 2. That which is transferred, as a design. 3. A ticket entitling a passenger to change to another public vehicle. [< L *trans-* across + *ferre* to carry] **—trans·fer′a·bil′i·ty** *n.* **—trans·fer′a·ble** *adj.* **—trans·fer′ence** *n.* **—trans·fer′rer** *n.*

trans·fig·ure (trans·fig′yər) *v.t.* **·ured, ·ur·ing** 1. To change the outward form or appearance of. 2. To make glorious; idealize. [< L *trans-* across + *figura* shape] **—trans·fig′ur·a′tion, trans·fig′ure·ment** *n.*

trans·fix (trans·fiks′) *v.t.* 1. To pierce through; impale. 2. To fix in place by impaling. 3. To make motionless, as with horror, awe, etc. [< L *trans-* through + *figere* to fasten] **—trans·fix′ion** (-fik′shən) *n.*

trans·form (trans·fôrm′) *v.t.* 1. To change the form, appearance, character, or condition of. 2. *Electr.* To change the potential or flow of (a current), as with a transformer. **—***v.i.* 3. To be or become changed. [< L *trans-* over + *formare* to form] **—trans·form′a·ble** *adj.*

trans·for·ma·tion (trans′fər·mā′shən) *n.* 1. Any change. 2. The act of transforming, or the state of being transformed. 3. *Ling.* A change from one construction to another, considered more or less equivalent, according to the syntactic laws of a language, as, in English, from active to passive. **—trans′for·ma′tion·al** *adj.*

transformational grammar A grammar that uses transformations as well as phase structure to account for the derivation of sentences.

trans·form·er (trans·fôr′mər) *n.* 1. One who or that which transforms. 2. *Electr.* A device for altering the ratio of current to voltage in alternating-current circuits.

trans·fuse (trans·fyōōz′) *v.t.* **·fused, ·fus·ing** 1. To pour from one vessel to another. 2. To cause to be imparted or instilled. 3. *Med.* To transfer (blood) from one person or animal to another. [< L *trans-* across + *fundere* to pour] **—trans·fus′er** *n.* **—trans·fus′i·ble** *adj.* **—trans·fu′sion** (-fyōō′zhən) *n.* **—trans·fu′sive** (-fyōō′siv) *adj.*

trans·gress (trans·gres′, tranz-) *v.t. & v.i.* 1. To break (a law, oath, etc.). 2. To pass beyond or over (limits); exceed; trespass. [< L *trans-* across + *gradi* to step] **—trans·gress′i·ble** *adj.* **—trans·gress′ing·ly** *adv.* **—trans·gres′sion** (-gresh′ən) *n.* **—trans·gres′sive** *adj.* **—trans·gres′sor** *n.*

tran·ship (tran·ship′) See TRANSSHIP.

tran·sient (tran′shənt) *adj.* 1. Passing away quickly; of short duration. 2. Not permanent; temporary. **—***n.* One who or that which is transient; esp., a lodger or boarder who remains for a short time. [< L *trans-* across + *ire* to go] **—tran′sience, tran′sien·cy** *n.* **—tran′sient·ly** *adv.* **—tran′sient·ness** *n.*

tran·sis·tor (tran·zis′tər, -sis′-) *n. Electronics* A miniature device for the control and amplification of an electron current, made of semiconducting materials. [< TRANS(FER) + (RES)ISTOR]

tran·sis·tor·ize (tran·zis′tər·iz, -sis′-) *v.t.* **·ized, ·iz·ing** To supply with transistors.

tran·sit (tran′sit, -zit) *n.* 1. The act of passing over or through; passage. 2. The act of carrying across or through; conveyance. 3. A transition or change. 4. A surveying instrument for measuring horizontal and vertical angles. —*v.t.* To pass through or across. [< L *trans-* across + *ire* to go]

tran·si·tion (tran·zish′ən) *n.* 1. The act or state of passing from one place, condition, or action to another; change. 2. The time, period, or place of such passage. 3. A sentence, musical passage, etc., that leads from one subject or theme to another. —**tran·si′tion·al, tran·si′tion·ar′y** *adj.* —**tran·si′tion·al·ly** *adv.*

tran·si·tive (tran′sə·tiv) *adj.* 1. *Gram.* Of a transitive verb or verbs. 2. Capable of passing. —*n.* *Gram.* A transitive verb. [See TRANSIT.] —**tran′si·tive·ly** *adv.* —**tran′si·tive·ness, tran′si·tiv′i·ty** *n.*

transitive verb A verb that requires a direct object to complete its meaning.

tran·si·to·ry (tran′sə·tôr′ē) *adj.* Existing for a short time only. [See TRANSIT.] —**tran′si·to′ri·ly** *adv.* —**tran′si·to′ri·ness** *n.*

trans·late (trans·lāt′, tranz-, trans′lāt, tranz′-) *v.* **·lat·ed, ·lat·ing** *v.t.* 1. To express in another language. 2. To explain in other words; interpret. 3. To change into another form; transform. —*v.i.* 4. To act as translator. 5. To admit of translation: This book *translates* easily. [< L *translatus*, pp. of *transferre* to transfer] —**trans·lat′a·ble** *adj.* —**trans·lat′a·ble·ness** *n.* —**trans·la′tor** *n.*

trans·la·tion (trans·lā′shən, tranz-) *n.* 1. The act of translating, or the state of being translated. 2. A work translated into another language, a version. —**trans·la′tion·al** *adj.*

trans·lit·er·ate (trans·lit′ə·rāt, tranz-) *v.t.* **·at·ed, ·at·ing** To represent (a letter or word) by the alphabetic characters of another language. [< TRANS- + L *litera* letter] —**trans·lit′er·a′tion** *n.*

trans·lu·cent (trans·lo͞o′sənt, tranz-) *adj.* Allowing the passage of light, but not permitting a clear view of any object. [< L *trans-* through, across + *lucere* to shine] —**trans·lu′cence, trans·lu′cen·cy** *n.* —**trans·lu′cent·ly** *adv.*

trans·mi·grate (trans·mī′grāt, tranz-) *v.i.* **·grat·ed, ·grat·ing** To migrate from one place or condition to another. [< L *trans-* across + *migrare* to migrate] —**trans·mi′grant** *adj. & n.* —**trans′mi·gra′tion** *n.* —**trans·mi′gra·tor** *n.* —**trans·mi′gra·to′ry** (-grə·tôr′ē) *adj.*

trans·mis·sion (trans·mish′ən, tranz-) *n.* 1. The act of transmitting, or the state of being transmitted. 2. That which is transmitted, as a radio broadcast. 3. *Mech.* **a** A device that transmits power from the engine of an automobile to the driving wheels. **b** The gears for changing speed. —**trans·mis′sive** (-mis′iv) *adj.*

trans·mit (trans·mit′, tranz-) *v.t.* **·mit·ted, ·mit·ting** 1. To send from one place or person to another. 2. To pass on by heredity. 3. To pass on or communicate (news, information, etc.). 4. *Telecom.* To send out by means of electromagnetic waves. [< L *trans-* across + *mittere* to send] —**trans·mis′si·ble** (-mis′ə·bəl) *adj.* —**trans·mis′si·bil′i·ty** *n.* —**trans·mit′tal** *n.* —**trans·mit′tance** *n.* —**trans·mit′ta·ble** *adj.*

trans·mit·ter (trans·mit′ər, tranz-) *n.* 1. One who or that which transmits. 2. A telegraphic sending instrument. 3. The part of a telephone that converts sound waves into electrical waves. 4. *Telecom.* The part of a radio or television system that generates, modulates, and transmits electromagnetic waves to the antenna.

trans·mu·ta·tion (trans′myo͞o·tā′shən, tranz′-) *n.* 1. The act of transmuting, or the state of being transmuted. 2. *Physics* The change of one element into another through alteration of its nuclear structure. 3. In alchemy, the supposed change of a base metal into gold, silver, etc. —**trans′mu·ta′tion·al, trans·mut′a·tive** (-myo͞ot′ə·tiv) *adj.*

trans·mute (trans·myo͞ot′, tranz-) *v.t.* **·mut·ed, ·mut·ing** To change in nature, form, or quality; transform. Also **trans·mu′tate.** [< L *trans-* across + *mutare* to change] —**trans·mut′a·bil′i·ty, trans·mut′a·ble·ness** *n.* —**trans·mut′a·ble** *adj.* —**trans·mut′a·bly** *adv.* —**trans·mut′er** *n.*

tran·som (tran′səm) *n.* 1. A small window above a door or window, usu. hinged to a horizontal crosspiece; also, the crosspiece. 2. A horizontal construction dividing a window. [< L *transtrum* crossbeam] —**tran′somed** *adj.*

tran·son·ic (tran·son′ik) *adj.* *Aeron.* Of, pertaining to, or moving at a speed close to that of sound.

trans·par·en·cy (trans·pâr′ən·sē) *n.* *pl.* **·cies** 1. The quality of being transparent. 2. Something transparent, as a slide.

trans·par·ent (trans·pâr′ənt) *adj.* 1. Admitting the passage of light, and permitting a clear view of objects beyond. 2. Easy to understand; obvious. 3. Without guile; candid. 4. Diaphanous; sheer. [< L *trans-* across + *parere* to appear, be visible] —**trans·par′ent·ly** *adv.* —**trans·par′ent·ness** *n.*

tran·spire (tran·spīr′) *v.* **·spired, ·spir·ing** *v.t.* 1. To give off (waste products) from the surface of the body, leaves, etc.; exhale. —*v.i.* 2. To give off waste products, as the surface of the body, leaves, etc. 3. To become known. 4. *Informal* To happen; occur. [< L *trans-* across, through + *spirare* to breathe] —**tran′spi·ra′tion** (-spə·rā′shən) *n.*

trans·plant (*v.* trans·plant′; *n.* trans′plant′) *v.t.* 1. To remove and plant in another place. 2. To remove and settle or establish for residence in another place. 3. *Surg.* To transfer (tissue or organ) from the original site to another part of the same individual or to another individual. —*n.* 1. That which is transplanted. 2. The act of transplanting. [< L *trans-* across + *plantare* to plant] —**trans′plan·ta′tion** *n.* —**trans·plant′er** *n.*

trans·port (*v.* trans·pôrt′; *n.* trans′pôrt) *v.t.* 1. To carry or convey from one place to another. 2. To carry away with emotion. 3. To carry into banishment, esp. beyond the sea. —*n.* 1. A vessel used to transport troops, military supplies, etc. 2. An aircraft used to transport passengers, mail, etc. 3. A state of ecstasy. 4. The act of transporting. [< L *trans-* across + *portare* to carry] —**trans·port′a·bil′i·ty** *n.* —**trans·port′a·ble** *adj.* —**trans·port′er** *n.*

trans·por·ta·tion (trans′pər·tā′shən) *n.* 1. The act of transporting, or the state of being transported. 2. A means of transporting, as a vehicle. 3. A charge for conveyance. 4. A ticket, pass, etc., for travel.

trans·pose (trăns·pōz′) *v.t.* **·posed, ·pos·ing** 1. To reverse the order or change the place of. 2. *Music* To change the key of (a chord, melody, or composition). —*v.i.* 3. *Music* To play in another key. [< L *trans-* over + OF *poser* to place] —**trans·pos′a·ble** *adj.* —**trans·pos′er** *n.* —**trans′po·si′tion** (-pə·zish′ən), **trans·po′sal** *n.*

trans·sex·u·al (tranz·sek′shōō·əl) *n.* One whose sex has been altered by surgery and hormone treatment. —*adj.* Of a transsexual or such surgery or treatment.

trans·ship (trans·ship′) *v.t. & v.i.* **·shipped, ·ship·ping** To transfer from one conveyance or line to another: also spelled *tranship.* —**trans·ship′ment** *n.*

tran·sub·stan·ti·a·tion (tran′səb·stan′shē·ā′·shən) *n.* *Theol.* The doctrine that the substance of the eucharistic elements is converted into that of the body and blood of Christ. [< L *trans-* over + *substantia* substance]

trans·verse (*adj.* trans·vûrs′, tranz-; *n.* trans′vûrs, tranz′-) *adj.* Lying or being across or from side to side: also **trans·ver′sal.** —*n.* That which is transverse. [< L *trans-* across + *vertere* to turn] —**trans·verse′ly** *adv.* —**trans·verse′ness** *n.*

trans·ves·tite (trans·ves′tīt, tranz-) *n.* One who wears the clothes of the opposite sex. [< L *trans-* over + *vestire* to clothe] —**trans·ves′tism, trans·ves′ti·tism** *n.*

trap[1] (trap) *n.* 1. A device for catching game or other animals. 2. Anything by which a person may be betrayed or taken unawares. 3. *Mech.* A U- or S-bend in a pipe, etc., that prevents a return flow, as of noxious gas. 4. A contrivance for hurling objects into the air for sportsmen to shoot at. 5. In golf, an obstacle or hazard: a sand *trap.* 6. A light, two-wheeled carriage suspended by springs. 7. *pl.* Percussion instruments, as drums, cymbals, etc. —*v.* **trapped, trap·ping** *v.t.* 1. To catch in a trap; ensnare. 2. To stop or hold (a gas, liquid, etc.) by some obstruction. 3. To provide with a trap. —*v.i.* 4. To set traps for game. 5. To be a trapper. [OE *treppe, træppe*]

trap[2] (trap) *n.* *Geol.* A dark, fine-grained igneous rock, as basalt, etc. Also **trap′rock′** (rok′). [< Sw. *trappa* stair]

trap door A door to cover an opening, as in a floor or roof.

tra·peze (trə·pēz′, tra-) *n.* A short swinging bar, suspended by two ropes, used by gymnasts, etc. [ult. < Gk. *trapeza* table]

trap·e·zoid (trap′ə·zoid) *n.* *Geom.* A four-sided figure of which two sides are parallel. [< Gk. *trapeza* table + *eidos* form] —**trap′e·zoi′dal** *adj.*

trap·per (trap′ər) *n.* One who traps fur-bearing animals.

trap·pings (trap′ingz) *n.pl.* 1. An ornamental harness or cover for a horse. 2. Adornments of any kind; embellishments. [< obs. *traps* < ME *trappe*]

Trap·pist (trap′ist) *n.* A member of an ascetic order of monks, noted for silence. —*adj.* Of the Trappists. [after *La Trappe* in Normandy, their first abbey, established 1664]

trap·shoot·ing (trap′shōō′ting) *n.* The sport of shooting clay pigeons sent up from spring traps. —**trap′shoot′er** *n.*

trash (trash) *n.* 1. Worthless or waste matter; rubbish. 2. A worthless or despicable individual or group of individuals. —*v.t.* 1. To free from trash. 2. To strip of leaves; prune. 3. *Informal* **a** To vandalize or destroy. **b** To disparage. [Cf. dial. Norw. *trask* lumber, trash, baggage] —**trash′i·ly** *adv.* —**trash′i·ness** *n.* —**trash′y** *adj.* **trash·i·er, trash·i·est**

trau·ma (trô′mə, trou′-) *n.* *pl.* **·mas** or **·ma·ta** (-mə·tə) 1. *Pathol.* Any injury to the body caused by shock, violence, etc. Also **trau′ma·tism.** 2. *Psychiatry* A severe emotional shock. [< Gk. *trauma, -atos* wound] —**trau·mat·ic** (trô·mat′ik, trou-, trə-) *adj.* —**trau·mat′i·cal·ly** *adv.*

trav·ail (trə·vāl′, trav′āl) *v.i.* 1. To toil; labor. 2. To suffer the pangs of childbirth. —*n.* 1. Strenuous physical or mental labor. 2. Labor in childbirth. [< OF *travaillier* to toil]

trav·el (trav′əl) *v.* **·eled** or **·elled, ·el·ing** or **·el·ling** *v.i.* 1. To go from one place to another. 2. To proceed; advance. 3. To pass or be transmitted, as light, sound, etc. 4. *Mech.* To move in a fixed path, as part of a mechanism. —*v.t.* 5. To move or journey across or through; traverse. —*n.* 1. The act of traveling. 2. *pl.* A trip or journey. 3. A movement or progress of any kind. 4. *Mech.* **a** The full course of a moving part in one direction. **b** Length of stroke, as of a piston. [Var. of TRAVAIL] —**trav′el·er** or **trav′el·ler** *n.*

traveler's check A draft issued by a bank, express company, etc., having the bearer's signature, and payable when the bearer signs it again in order to cash it.

trav·e·logue (trav′ə·lôg, -log) *n.* A lecture or film on travel. Also **trav′e·log.**

tra·verse (*v.* tra·vûrs′; *n. & adj.* trav′ərs) *v.t.* **·ersed, ·ers·ing** 1. To pass over, across, or through. 2. To move back and forth over or along. 3. To turn (a gun, lathe, etc.) to right or left; swivel. —*n.* A part, as of a machine or structure, placed across or traversing another, as a crosspiece, crossbeam, transom, etc. —*adj.* Transverse; lying or being across. [< L *trans-* across + *vertere* to turn] —**trav·ers′a·ble** *adj.* —**trav·er′sal** *n.* —**trav·ers′er** *n.*

trav·er·tine (trav′ər·tin, -tēn, -tīn) *n.* A porous, light yellow, crystalline limestone, used for building. Also **trav′er·tin** (-tin). [< Ital. *travertino* < L *Tiburtinus* of Tibur]

trav·es·ty (trav′is·tē) *n. pl.* **·ties** A grotesque imitation; burlesque. —*v.t.* **·tied, ·ty·ing** To make a travesty on; parody. [< L *trans-* across + *vestire* to dress]

trawl (trôl) *n.* 1. A stout fishing line having many baited hooks: also called **trawl line.** 2. A large fishing net shaped like a flattened bag, for towing on the bottom of the ocean by a boat: also **trawl net.** —*v.t. & v.i.* To fish or catch with a trawl. [Cf. MDu. *traghel* dragnet]

trawl·er (trô′lər) *n.* 1. A vessel used for trawling. 2. One who is engaged in trawling.

tray (trā) *n.* A flat receptacle with a low rim, used to carry, hold, or display articles. [OE *trig, trēg* wooden board]

treach·er·ous (trech′ər·əs) *adj.* 1. Traitorous; perfidious; disloyal. 2. Having a deceptive appearance; unreliable. —**treach′·er·ous·ly** *adv.* —**treach′er·ous·ness** *n.*

treach·er·y (trech′ər·ē) *n. pl.* **·er·ies** Violation of allegiance, confidence, or faith; treason. [< OF *tricher* to cheat]

trea·cle (trē′kəl) *n. Brit.* Molasses. [< Gk. *thēriakē* remedy for poisonous bites] **—trea′·cly** *adj.*

tread (tred) *v.* **trod** (*Archaic* **trode**), **trod·den** or **trod, tread·ing** *v.t.* 1. To step or walk on, over, or along. 2. To press with the feet; trample. 3. To accomplish in walking or in dancing: to *tread* a measure. *—v.i.* 4. To step or walk. 5. To trample: usu. with *on.* *—n.* 1. The act, manner, or sound of treading or walking. 2. The horizontal part of a step in a staircase. 3. A part that makes contact with the ground, as of a wheel, tire, or shoe. [OE *tredan*] **—tread′er** *n.*

tread·le (tred′l) *n.* A lever operated by the foot, usu. to cause rotary motion. *—v.i.* **·led, ·ling** To work a treadle. [OE *tredan* to tread] **—tread′ler** *n.*

tread·mill (tred′mil′) *n.* 1. A mechanism rotated by the walking motion of one or more persons. 2. A similar mechanism operated by a horse, donkey, etc. 3. Any wearisome or monotonous work, activity, routine, etc.

trea·son (trē′zən) *n.* Betrayal of one's sovereign or government. [< L *traditio, -onis* betrayal, delivery]

trea·son·a·ble (trē′zən·ə·bəl) *adj.* Of, involving, or characteristic of treason. Also **trea′son·ous.** **—trea′son·a·ble·ness** *n.* **—trea′son·a·bly** *adv.*

treas·ure (trezh′ər) *n.* 1. Riches accumulated or possessed. 2. One who or that which is regarded as valuable, precious, or rare. *—v.t.* **·ured, ·ur·ing** 1. To lay up in store; accumulate. 2. To retain carefully, as in the mind. 3. To set a high value upon; prize. [< Gk. *thēsauros*]

treas·ur·er (trezh′ər·ər) *n.* An officer who has charge of funds or revenues.

trea·sure-trove (trezh′ər·trōv′) *n.* 1. *Law* Any treasure found hidden in the earth, etc., the owner being unknown. 2. Any discovery that proves valuable. [< AF *tresor* treasure + *trové*, pp., of *trover* to find]

treas·u·ry (trezh′ər·ē) *n. pl.* **·ur·ies** 1. The place where private or public funds or revenues are received, kept, and disbursed. 2. Any public or private funds or revenues. 3. A place where treasures are kept.

treat (trēt) *v.t.* 1. To conduct oneself toward in a specified manner. 2. To look upon or regard in a specified manner: They *treat* the matter as a joke. 3. To subject to chemical or physical action, as for altering or improving. 4. To give medical or surgical attention to. 5. To deal with or develop (a subject). 6. To pay for the entertainment, food, or drink of. *—v.i.* 7. To handle a subject in writing or speaking: usu. with *of.* 8. To pay for another's entertainment or food. *—n.* 1. Something that gives unusual pleasure. 2. Entertainment furnished to another. [< OF *traitier* < L *tractare* to handle] **—treat′a·ble** *adj.* **—treat′er** *n.*

trea·tise (trē′tis) *n.* A formal written account of some subject. [< AF *tretiz*, OF *traitier* to treat]

treat·ment (trēt′mənt) *n.* 1. The act, manner, or process of treating. 2. The care of an illness by drugs, surgery, etc.

trea·ty (trē′tē) *n. pl.* **·ties** A formal agreement or compact between two or more states; also, the document containing such an agreement or compact. [< AF *treté*, OF *traitie*, pp. of *traitier* to treat]

treb·le (treb′əl) *v.t. & v.i.* **·led, ·ling** To multiply by three; triple. *—adj.* 1. Threefold; triple. 2. Soprano. *—n.* 1. *Music* A soprano voice, part, or instrument; also, the singer or player taking this part. 2. High, piping sound. [< L *triplus*] **—treb′le·ness** *n.* **—treb′ly** *adv.*

tree (trē) *n.* 1. A perennial woody plant having usu. a single self-supporting trunk of considerable height, with branches and foliage growing at some distance above the ground. ◆Collateral adjective: *arboreal.* 2. Something resembling a tree in form or outline; esp., a diagram showing family descent. **—up a tree** *Informal* In a position from which there is no retreat; cornered; also, in an embarrassing position. *—v.t.* **treed, tree·ing** 1. To force to climb or take refuge in a tree: to *tree* an opossum. 2. *Informal* To get the advantage of; corner. [OE *trēow, trīow, trēo*]

tree fern A fern with large fronds and a woody trunk that often attains a treelike size.

tree frog A tree-dwelling amphibian, having the toes enlarged by viscous, adhesive disks: also called **tree toad.**

tree of heaven The ailanthus.

tree surgery The treatment of disease conditions and decay in trees by operative methods. **—tree surgeon**

tree·top (trē′top′) *n.* The highest part of a tree.

tre·foil (trē′foil) *n.* 1. Any of a genus of leguminous plants, as the clovers, having three-lobed leaves. 2. A three-lobed architectural ornamentation. [< L *trifolium*]

trek (trek) *v.i.* **trekked, trek·king** To travel, esp. slowly or arduously. *—n.* 1. In South Africa, a journey or any part of it; esp., an organized migration. 2. A slow or arduous journey. [< Du. < OHG *trechan* to draw] **—trek′ker** *n.*

trel·lis (trel′is) *n.* 1. A lattice of wood, metal, or other material, used as a screen or a support for vines, etc. 2. A summerhouse, archway, etc., made from or consisting of such a structure. *—v.t.* 1. To interlace so as to form a trellis. 2. To furnish with or fasten on a trellis. [< L *tri-* three + *licium* thread]

trel·lis·work (trel′is·wûrk′) *n.* Openwork made from, consisting of, or resembling a trellis.

trem·a·tode (trem′ə·tōd) *n.* One of a class of parasitic flat-bodied worms. [< Gk. *trēma, -atos* hole + *eidos* form] **—trem′a·toid** (-toid) *adj.*

trem·ble (trem′bəl) *v.i.* **·bled, ·bling** 1. To shake, as with fear or weakness. 2. To have slight, irregular vibratory motion: The earth *trembled.* 3. To feel anxiety or fear. *—n.* The act or state of trembling. [< L *tremere*] **—trem′bler** *n.* **—trem′bling·ly** *adv.* **—trem′·bly** *adj.*

tre·men·dous (tri·men′dəs) *adj.* 1. Extraordinarily large; vast. 2. *Informal* Amazing; wonderful. 3. Causing astonishment by its magnitude, force, etc. [< L *tremendus* to be trembled at] **—tre·men′dous·ly** *adv.* **—tre·men′dous·ness** *n.*

trem·o·lo (trem′ə·lō) *n. pl.* **·los** *Music* A rapid repetition of a tone or alternation of two tones. [< Ital. < L *tremulus* tremulous]
trem·or (trem′ər) *n.* 1. A quick, vibratory movement; a shaking: an earth *tremor.* 2. Any quivering or trembling, as of the body or limbs. [< OF, fear, a trembling < L *tremere* to tremble]
trem·u·lous (trem′yə·ləs) *adj.* 1. Characterized or affected by trembling: *tremulous* speech. 2. Showing timidity or fear. **—trem′u·lous·ly** *adv.* **—trem′u·lous·ness** *n.*
trench (trench) *n.* 1. A long, narrow excavation in the ground; ditch. 2. A long irregular ditch, lined with a parapet of the excavated earth, to protect troops. **—***v.t.* 1. To dig a trench or trenches in. 2. To fortify with trenches. **—***v.i.* 3. To dig trenches. 4. To cut; carve. [< OF *trenchier* to cut, ult. < L *truncare* to lop off] **—trench′er** *n.*
trench·ant (tren′chənt) *adj.* 1. Cutting; incisive; keen. 2. Forceful; vigorous; effective. 3. Clearly defined; distinct. [< OF, cutting] **—trench′an·cy** *n.* **—trench′ant·ly** *adv.*
trench coat A belted overcoat of rainproof fabric.
trench·er (tren′chər) *n.* Formerly, a wooden plate or board on which food was served or cut. [See TRENCH.]
trench·er·man (tren′chər·mən) *n. pl.* **·men** (-mən) A hearty eater.
trench foot *Pathol.* A disease of the feet caused by continued dampness and cold, and characterized by discoloration, weakness, and sometimes gangrene.
trench mouth *Pathol.* A disease of the mouth, gums, and sometimes the larynx and tonsils, caused by a soil bacillus.
trend (trend) *n.* A general course, inclination, or direction. **—***v.i.* To have or take a particular trend. [OE *trendan* to roll]
trend·y (tren′dē) *adj.* Forming or following a fashionable trend. **—trend′i·ly** *adv.* **—trend′i·ness** *n.*
tre·pan (tri·pan′) *Surg. n.* A trephine. **—***v.t.* **·panned, ·pan·ning** To trephine. [< OF, borer < Gk. *trypaein* to bore] **—trep·a·na·tion** (trep′ə·nā′shən) *n.*
tre·phine (tri·fīn′, -fēn′) *Surg. n.* A saw for removing circular sections, such as bone from the skull. **—***v.t.* **·phined, ·phin·ing** To operate on with a trephine. [Earlier *trafine* < L *tres fines* three ends]
trep·i·da·tion (trep′ə·dā′shən) *n.* 1. A state of agitation or alarm. 2. An involuntary trembling. Also **tre·pid·i·ty** (tri·pid′ə·tē). [< L *trepidare* to hurry, be alarmed]
tres·pass (tres′pəs, -pas′) *v.i.* 1. To commit an offense against another. 2. To intrude offensively; encroach; esp., to enter wrongfully upon another's land. **—***n.* 1. Any offense done to another. 2. Unlawful entry on another's land. [< L *trans-* across, beyond + *passus* a step] **—tres′pass·er** *n.*
tress (tres) *n.* 1. A lock of human hair. 2. *pl.* The hair of a woman or girl, esp. when worn loose. [< OF *tresce*] **—tress′y** *adj.*
-tress *suffix* Used to form feminine nouns corresponding to masculine nouns in *-ter, -tor*: *actress.* [Var. of -ESS]
tres·tle (tres′əl) *n.* 1. A beam or bar supported by four legs, for bearing platforms, etc. 2. An open framework for supporting a railway bridge, etc. [< L *transtrum* crossbeam]
trey (trā) *n.* A card, domino, or die having three spots. [< L *tres* three]
tri- *prefix* 1. Three; threefold; thrice. 2. Occurring every three (specified) intervals, or three times within an (assigned) interval: *triweekly.* [< L *tri-* threefold]
tri·ad (trī′ad) *n.* 1. A group of three persons or things. 2. *Music* A chord of three tones. [< Gk. *trias, -ados* < *treis* three] **—tri·ad′ic** *adj. & n.*
tri·al (trī′əl) *n.* 1. The examination of the facts in a case before a court of law to determine what is right or just. 2. The act of testing or proving by experience or use. 3. The state of being tried or tested, as by suffering: hour of *trial.* 4. An attempt or effort to do something; a try. **—on trial** In the process of being tried or tested. **—***adj.* 1. Of or pertaining to a trial or trials. 2. Made, used, or performed in the course of trying or testing. [< AF *trier* to try] **—tri′a·ble** *adj.*
trial balloon Any tentative plan or scheme advanced to test public reaction.
tri·an·gle (trī′ang′gəl) *n.* 1. *Geom.* A plane figure bounded by three sides and having three angles. 2. Something resembling such a figure in shape or arrangement. 3. A situation involving three persons. [< L *tri-* three + *angulus* angle] **—tri·an′gu·lar** (-gyə·lər) *adj.* **—tri·an′gu·lar′i·ty** (-gyə·lar′ə·tē) *n.* **—tri·an′gu·lar·ly** *adv.*
tri·an·gu·late (*v.* trī·ang′gyə·lāt; *adj.* -lit) *v.t.* **·lat·ed, ·lat·ing** 1. To divide into triangles. 2. To survey or determine a position using the principles of trigonometry. **—***adj.* Of or marked with triangles. **—tri·an′gu·la′tion** *n.*
tri·bal·ism (trī′bəl·iz′əm) *n.* Tribal organization, culture, or relations.
tribe (trīb) *n.* 1. A group of people, esp. a primitive or nomadic people, usu. characterized by common ancestry and customs. 2. *Biol.* A group of plants or animals of indefinite rank. [< L *tribus* tribe] **—tri′bal** *adj.* **—tri′bal·ly** *adv.*
tribes·man (trībz′mən) *n. pl.* **·men** (-mən) A member of a tribe.
trib·u·la·tion (trib′yə·lā′shən) *n.* A condition of affliction and distress; suffering; also, that which causes it. [< L *tribulum* threshing floor < *terere* to rub, grind]
tri·bu·nal (tri·byōō′nəl, trī-) *n.* 1. A court of justice. 2. The seat set apart for judges, etc. [See TRIBUNE.]
trib·une (trib′yōōn) *n.* 1. In Roman history, a magistrate chosen by the plebeians to protect them against patrician oppression. 2. Any champion of the people. [< L *tribunus* < *tribus* tribe] **—trib′u·nar′y** (-yə·ner′ē), **trib′u·ni′cial** (-yə·nish′əl) *adj.* **—trib′u·nate** (-yə·nit, -nāt), **trib′une·ship** *n.*
trib·u·tar·y (trib′yə·ter′ē) *adj.* 1. Bringing supply; contributory: a *tributary* stream. 2. Offered or due as tribute: a *tributary* payment. 3. Paying tribute, as a state. **—***n. pl.* **·tar·ies** 1. A person or state paying tribute. 2. A stream flowing into a larger stream or body of water. [See TRIBUTE.] **—trib′u·tar′i·ly** *adv.* **—trib′u·tar′i·ness** *n.*
trib·ute (trib′yōōt) *n.* 1. A speech, compliment, gift, etc., given as a sign of admiration,

gratitude, or respect. 2. Payment by one state or ruler to another as a sign of submission or as the price of peace and protection. [< L *tribuere* to pay, allot]

trice (trīs) *v.t.* **triced, tric·ing** To raise with a rope; also, to tie or lash: usu. with *up*. —*n.* An instant: now only in the phrase **in a trice.** [< MDu. *trisen* to hoist]

tri·cen·ten·ni·al (trī'sen·ten'ē·əl) *adj.* & *n.* Tercentenary.

tri·ceps (trī'seps) *n. Anat.* A large muscle at the back of the upper arm. [< L *tri-* three + *caput* head]

tri·chi·na (tri·kī'nə) *n. pl.* **·nae** (-nē) A small nematode worm, parasitic in the intestines and muscles of man, swine, and other mammals. [< Gk. *thrix* hair]

trich·i·no·sis (trik'ə·nō'sis) *n. Pathol.* The disease produced by trichinae in the intestines and muscles, in man, usu. through eating undercooked pork. —**trich'i·nous** (-nəs) *adj.*

trick (trik) *n.* 1. A device for getting an advantage by deception; ruse. 2. A practical joke; prank. 3. A particular habit or manner; trait. 4. A peculiar skill or knack. 5. An act of legerdemain or magic. 6. In card games, all the cards played in one round. —*v.t.* 1. To deceive or cheat; delude. 2. To dress or array: with *up* or *out*. [< OF *trichier* to cheat] —**trick'er** *n.* —**trick'less** *adj.*

trick·er·y (trik'ər·ē) *n. pl.* **·er·ies** The practice of tricks; artifice; wiles.

trick·le (trik'əl) *v.* **·led, ·ling** *v.i.* 1. To flow drop by drop or in a very thin stream. 2. To move slowly or bit by bit. —*v.t.* 3. To cause to trickle. —*n.* 1. The act or state of trickling. 2. Any slow and irregular movement. [ME *triklen*] —**trick'ly** *adj.*

trick·ster (trik'stər) *n.* One who plays tricks; a cheat.

trick·y (trik'ē) *adj.* **trick·i·er, trick·i·est** Disposed to or characterized by trickery; deceitful; wily. —**trick'i·ly** *adv.* —**trick'i·ness** *n.*

tri·col·or (trī'kul'ər) *adj.* Having or characterized by three colors: also **tri'col'ored.** —*n.* 1. A flag of three colors. 2. *Sometimes cap.* The French flag. Also *Brit.* **tri'col'our.**

tri·corn (trī'kôrn) *n.* A hat with the brim turned up on three sides. Also **tri'corne.** —*adj.* Having three hornlike projections or corners. [< L *tri-* three + *cornu* horn]

tri·cus·pid (trī·kus'pid) *adj.* Having three cusps or points, as a molar tooth. Also **tri·cus'pi·dal, tri·cus'pi·date.** [< L *tri-* three + *cuspis* point]

tri·cy·cle (trī'sik·əl) *n.* A three-wheeled vehicle; esp., such a vehicle with pedals.

tri·dent (trīd'nt) *n.* A three-pronged fork. —*adj.* Having three teeth or prongs: also **tri·den·tate** (trī·den'tāt), **tri·den'tat·ed.** [< L *tri-* three + *dens* tooth]

tried (trīd) Past tense and past participle of TRY. —*adj.* Tested; trustworthy.

tri·en·ni·al (trī·en'ē·əl) *adj.* 1. Taking place every third year. 2. Lasting three years. —*n.* A third anniversary. —**tri·en'ni·al·ly** *adv.*

tri·fle (trī'fəl) *v.* **·fled, ·fling** *v.i.* 1. To treat something as of no value or importance; dally: with *with*. 2. To act or speak frivolously. 3. To play; toy. 4. To idle. —*v.t.* 5. To pass (time) in an idle and purposeless way. —*n.* Anything of very little value or importance. —**a trifle** Slightly: *a trifle short.* [< OF *trufe* cheating, mockery] —**tri'fler** *n.*

tri·fling (trī'fling) *adj.* 1. Frivolous. 2. Insignificant. —**tri'fling·ly** *adv.*

tri·fo·cal (trī·fō'kəl; *for n. also* trī'fō·kəl) *adj.* 1. Having three focal lengths. 2. *Optics* Describing eyeglasses or a lens ground in three segments, for near, intermediate, and far vision. —*n. pl.* Eyeglasses having trifocal lenses.

tri·fo·li·ate (trī·fō'lē·it, -āt) *adj. Bot.* Having three leaves or leaflike processes. Also **tri·fo'li·at'ed.**

trig (trig) *adj.* 1. Trim; neat. 2. Strong; sound. —*v.t.* **trigged, trig·ging** To make neat: often with *out* or *up*. [< ON *tryggr* true] —**trig'ly** *adv.* —**trig'ness** *n.*

trig·ger (trig'ər) *n.* 1. The lever or other device pressed or squeezed to fire a firearm. 2. Any lever, release, etc., that begins a process or operation. —**quick on the trigger** 1. Quick to shoot. 2. Quick to act; alert. —*v.t.* To cause to begin; initiate. [< Du. *trekken* to pull]

trig·o·nom·e·try (trig'ə·nom'ə·trē) *n.* The branch of mathematics that deals with the relations of the sides and angles of triangles. [< Gk. *trigōnon* triangle + -METRY] —**trig·o·no·met·ric** (trig'ə·nə·met'rik) or **·ri·cal** *adj.* —**trig'o·no·met'ri·cal·ly** *adv.*

tri·he·dron (trī·hē'drən) *n. pl.* **·dra** *Geom.* A figure having three plane surfaces meeting at a point. [< Gk. *tri-* three + *hedra* a base] —**tri·he'dral** *adj.*

tri·lat·er·al (trī·lat'ər·əl) *adj.* Having three sides. [< L *tri-* three + *latus* a side] —**tri·lat'er·al·ly** *adv.*

trill (tril) *v.t.* 1. To sing or play in a tremulous tone. 2. *Phonet.* To articulate with a trill. —*v.i.* 3. To give forth a tremulous sound. 4. *Music* To execute a trill. —*n.* 1. A tremulous utterance; warble. 2. *Music* A rapid alternation of two tones a tone apart. 3. *Phonet.* A rapid vibration of the tongue or uvula in the articulation of *r* in certain languages. [< Ital. *trillare*]

tril·lion (tril'yən) *n.* 1. A thousand billions, written as 1 followed by 12 zeros: a cardinal number: called a billion in Great Britain. 2. *Brit.* A million billions (def. 2), written as 1 followed by 18 zeros: a cardinal number. [< MF *tri-* three + (*mi*)*llion* million] —**tril'lion** *adj.* —**tril'lionth** *adj.* & *n.*

tril·li·um (tril'ē·əm) *n.* An herb of the lily family having a stout stem bearing a whorl of three leaves and a solitary flower. [< L *tri-* three]

tril·o·gy (tril'ə·jē) *n. pl.* **·gies** A group of three literary or dramatic compositions, each complete in itself, but continuing the same general subject. [< Gk. *tri-* three + *logos* a discourse]

trim (trim) *v.* **trimmed, trim·ming** *v.t.* 1. To make neat by clipping. 2. To remove by cutting: usu. with *off* or *away*. 3. To put ornaments on; decorate. 4. *Naut.* **a** To adjust (sails) for sailing. **b** To balance (a ship) by adjusting cargo, etc. —*v.i.* 5. To act so as to appear to favor both sides in a controversy. —*n.* 1. State of readiness or fitness. 2. *Naut.* Fitness for sailing.

3. Moldings, etc., as about the doors of a building. 4. Ornament; trimming. —*adj.* **trim·mer, trim·mest** 1. Neat; orderly. 2. Compact; well-proportioned. —*adv.* In a trim manner: also **trim′ly**. [OE *trymman* to arrange, strengthen < *trum* strong] —**trim′·mer** *n.* —**trim′ness** *n.*

tri·ma·ran (trī′mə·ran′) *n.* A sailing vessel having three hulls. [< TRI- + (CATA)MARAN]

trim·e·ter (trim′ə·tər) *n.* In prosody, a line of verse consisting of three metrical feet. —*adj.* Consisting of three metrical feet. [< Gk. *tri-* three + *metron* measure] —**tri·met·ric** (trī·met′rik) or **·ri·cal** *adj.*

trim·ming (trim′ing) *n.* 1. Something added for ornament. 2. *pl.* Fittings, as the hardware of a house. 3. *pl.* The usual or proper accompaniments of an article or food. 4. *pl.* That which is removed by trimming. 5. *Informal* A defeat.

tri·month·ly (trī·munth′lē) *adj. & adv.* Done or occurring every third month.

trine (trīn) *adj.* Having three parts; threefold. Also **tri·nal** (trī′nəl). [< L *tres* three]

Trin·i·tar·i·an (trin′ə·târ′ē·ən) *adj.* 1. Of or pertaining to the Trinity. 2. Holding or professing belief in the Trinity. —*n.* A believer in the doctrine of the Trinity. —**Trin′i·tar′i·an·ism** *n.*

tri·ni·tro·tol·u·ene (trī·nī′trō·tol′yōō·ēn) *n.* *Chem.* A high explosive made by treating toluene with nitric acid, used in warfare and as a blasting agent: also called *TNT*. Also **tri·ni′tro·tol′u·ol** (-yōō·ōl).

trin·i·ty (trin′ə·tē) *n.* *pl.* **·ties** Any union of three parts or elements in one; a trio. [< L *trinus* triple]

Trin·i·ty (trin′ə·tē) *n.* *Theol.* A threefold personality existing in the one divine being or substance; the union in one God of Father, Son, and Holy Spirit.

trin·ket (tring′kit) *n.* 1. Any small ornament, as of jewelry. 2. A trivial object. [< AF *trenquet*, OF *trenchet* a toy knife, ornament]

tri·o (trē′ō) *n.* *pl.* **tri·os** 1. Any three things grouped or associated together. 2. *Music* **a** A composition for three performers. **b** A group of three musicians that plays trios. [< Ital. < L *tres* three]

trip (trip) *n.* 1. A journey or voyage. 2. A misstep or stumble. 3. An active, nimble step or movement. 4. *Mech.* A device that triggers or releases a moving part or parts. 5. A blunder; mistake. 6. *Slang* The taking of a psychedelic drug, or the resulting mental experience. —*v.t. & v.i.* **tripped, trip·ping** 1. To stumble or cause to stumble. 2. To move or perform quickly with light or small steps. 3. To commit or expose in an error. 4. *Mech.* To trigger or release. [< OF *treper, triper* to leap, trample]

tri·par·tite (trī·pär′tīt) *adj.* 1. Divided into three parts or divisions; threefold: a *tripartite* leaf: also **tri·part·ed** (trī′pär·tid). 2. Pertaining to or concluded between three parties: a *tripartite* agreement. [< L *tri-* three + *partiri* to divide] —**tri·par′tite·ly** *adv.* —**tri′par·ti′tion** (-tish′ən) *n.*

tripe (trīp) *n.* 1. A part of the stomach of a ruminant, used for food. 2. *Informal* Anything worthless; nonsense. [< Arabic *tharb* entrails, a net]

trip hammer A heavy power hammer that is raised or tilted by a cam and then allowed to drop.

trip·le (trip′əl) *v.* **·led, ·ling** *v.t.* 1. To make threefold in number or quantity. —*v.i.* 2. To be or become three times as many or as large. 3. In baseball, to hit a triple. —*adj.* 1. Consisting of three things or of three parts; threefold. 2. Multiplied by three. —*n.* 1. A set or group of three. 2. In baseball, a hit that enables the batter to reach third base. [< Gk. *triplous* threefold] —**trip′ly** *adv.*

triple play In baseball, a play during which three men are put out.

trip·let (trip′lit) *n.* 1. A group of three of a kind. 2. One of three children born at one birth. 3. A group of three rhymed lines. 4. *Music* A group of three equal notes performed in the time of two.

triple threat *Informal* A football player expert at kicking, running, and passing. —**trip·le-threat** (trip′əl·thret′) *adj.*

tri·plex (trip′leks, trī′pleks) *adj.* Having three parts. [< L *tri-* three + *plicare* to fold]

trip·li·cate (*adj. & n.* trip′lə·kit; *v.* trip′lə·kāt) *adj.* Threefold; made in three copies. —*n.* One of or a set of three identical things. —*v.t.* **·cat·ed, ·cat·ing** To make three times as much or as many. [< L *triplicatus*, pp. of *triplicare* to triple] —**trip′li·cate·ly** *adv.* —**trip′li·ca′tion** *n.*

tri·plic·i·ty (tri·plis′ə·tē) *n.* *pl.* **·ties** 1. Threefold character. 2. A group or combination of three.

tri·pod (trī′pod) *n.* 1. A utensil or article having three feet or legs. 2. A three-legged stand for supporting a camera, transit, etc. [< Gk. *tri-* three + *pous* foot] —**trip·o·dal** (trip′ə·dəl) *adj.*

trip·o·dy (trip′ə·dē) *n.* *pl.* **·dies** A verse or meter having three feet.

trip·per (trip′ər) *n.* 1. One who trips. 2. *Mech.* A trip or tripping mechanism.

trip·ping (trip′ing) *adj.* Nimble. —**trip′·ping·ly** *adv.*

trip·tych (trip′tik) *n.* A triple picture or carving on three hinged panels, often depicting a religious subject. Also **trip′ty·ca** (-ti·kə), **trip′ty·chon** (-ti·kon). [< Gk. *tri-* thrice + *ptyssein* to fold]

tri·reme (trī′rēm) *n.* An ancient Greek or Roman warship with three banks of oars. [< L *tri-* three + *remus* oar]

tri·sect (trī·sekt′) *v.t.* To divide into three equal parts. [< TRI- + L *sectus*, pp. of *secare* to cut] —**tri·sect′ed** *adj.* —**tri·sec′tion** *n.* —**tri·sec′tor** *n.*

tri·seme (trī′sēm) *n.* A syllable or foot consisting of or equivalent to three short syllables. [< Gk. *tri-* three + *sēma* a sign] —**tri′seme, tri·se′mic** *adj.*

triste (trēst) *adj.* *French* Sorrowful; sad.

tris·tesse (trēs·tes′) *n.* *French* Sadness; melancholy.

tri·syl·la·ble (trī·sil′ə·bəl) *n.* A word of three syllables. —**tri·syl·lab·ic** (trī′si·lab′ik) or **·i·cal** *adj.* —**tri′syl·lab′i·cal·ly** *adv.*

trite (trīt) *adj.* Made commonplace by repetition. [< L *tritus*, pp. of *terere* to rub] —**trite′ly** *adv.* —**trite′ness** *n.*

trit·i·um (trit′ē·əm, trish′ē·əm) *n.* *Physics* The radioactive isotope of hydrogen. [< Gk. *tritos* third]

tri·ton[1] (trīt′n) *n.* Any of a genus of marine

mollusks having many gills and a trumpet-shaped shell. [< Gk. *Tritōn*, a Greek sea god]

tri·ton² (trī′ton) *n.* *Physics* The nucleus of an atom of tritium. [< TRIT(IUM) + (ELECTR)ON]

trit·u·rate (trich′ə·rāt) *v.t.* **·rat·ed, ·rat·ing** To reduce to a fine powder by grinding or rubbing; pulverize. [< L *tritura* a rubbing, threshing] —**trit′u·ra·ble** (-ər·ə·bəl) *adj.* —**trit′u·ra′tion** *n.* —**trit′u·ra′tor** *n.*

tri·umph (trī′əmf) *v.i.* 1. To win a victory; be victorious. 2. To rejoice over a victory; exult. —*n.* 1. Exultation over victory. 2. The condition of being victorious; victory. [< Gk. *thriambos*, a processional hymn to Dionysus] —**tri·um′phal** (-um′fəl), **tri·um′·phant** (-um′fənt) *adj.* —**tri·um′phant·ly** *adv.* —**tri′umph·er** *n.*

tri·um·vir (trī·um′vər) *n.* *pl.* **·virs** or **·vi·ri** (-və·rī) One of three men united in public office or authority, as in ancient Rome. [< L *tres, trium* three + *vir* a man] —**tri·um′vi·ral** *adj.*

tri·um·vi·rate (trī·um′vər·it) *n.* 1. A group of three men who exercise authority or control together. 2. The office of a triumvir.

tri·une (trī′yōōn) *adj.* Three in one: said of God. [< TRI- + L *unus* one] —**tri·u′ni·ty** *n.*

triv·et (triv′it) *n.* A stand, usu. three-legged, for holding a hot dish or pot. [OE *trefet* < L *tripes, -pedis* three-footed]

triv·i·a (triv′ē·ə) *n.pl.* Unimportant matters; trifles. [See TRIVIAL.]

triv·i·al (triv′ē·əl) *adj.* 1. Of little value or importance; trifling; insignificant. 2. Such as is found everywhere or every day; commonplace. 3. Occupied with trifles. [< L *trivialis* of the crossroads, commonplace < *tri-* three + *via* road] —**triv′i·al·ism** *n.* —**triv′i·al·ly** *adv.*

triv·i·al·i·ty (triv′ē·al′ə·tē) *n.* *pl.* **·ties** 1. The state or quality of being trivial: also **triv′i·al·ness** (-əl·nis). 2. A trivial matter.

tri·week·ly (trī·wēk′lē) *adj.* 1. Occurring three times a week. 2. Done or occurring every third week. —*n.* A triweekly publication. —**tri·week′ly** *adv.*

-trix *suffix* Used to form feminine nouns corresponding to masculine forms in *-tor*: *executrix*. [< L]

tro·che (trō′kē) *n.* A medicated lozenge, usu. circular: also called *pastille*. [Alter. of obs. *trochisk* < Gk. *trochos* wheel]

tro·chee (trō′kē) *n.* 1. In prosody, a metrical foot consisting of one long or accented syllable followed by one short or unaccented syllable (—⌣). 2. A line of verse made up of or characterized by such feet. [< Gk. *trechein* to run] —**tro·cha′ic** (-kā′ik) *adj.*

trod (trod) Past tense and alternative past participle of TREAD.

trod·den (trod′n) Past participle of TREAD.

trog·lo·dyte (trog′lə·dīt) *n.* 1. A cave man. 2. A hermit. 3. A brutal or savage person. [< Gk. *trōglē* hole + *dyein* to go into] —**trog′lo·dyt′ic** (-dit′ik) or **·i·cal** *adj.*

troi·ka (troi′kə) *n.* 1. A Russian vehicle drawn by a team of three horses driven abreast. 2. A ruling body of three. 3. A group of three. [< Russian < *troie* three]

Tro·jan (trō′jən) *n.* 1. A native of the ancient city of Troy. 2. One who works earnestly or suffers courageously. —*adj.* Of or pertaining to ancient Troy. [< L *Troja* Troy]

troll¹ (trōl) *v.t. & v.i.* 1. To fish (for) with a moving line or lure. 2. To sing (parts of a round) in succession. 3. To roll or cause to roll; revolve. —*n.* 1. A round. 2. In fishing, a spoon or other lure. [? < OF *troller* to quest, wander < Gmc.] —**troll′er** *n.*

troll² (trōl) *n.* In Scandinavian folklore, a giant; later, a mischievous dwarf. Also **trold** (trōld). [< ON]

trol·ley (trol′ē) *n.* *pl.* **·leys** 1. A streetcar: also **trolley car.** 2. A device that maintains contact with a conductor, such as a wire or a third rail, to convey current to an electric vehicle. 3. A small truck or car for conveying material, as in a factory, mine, etc. —*v.t. & v.i.* To convey or travel by trolley. Also **trol′ly.** [< TROLL¹]

trolley bus A bus propelled electrically by current from an overhead wire. Also **trolley coach.**

trol·lop (trol′əp) *n.* 1. A slatternly woman. 2. A prostitute. [< dial. E (Scot.) < ME *trollen* to roll about] —**trol′lop·ish, trol′lop·y, trol′lop·ing** *adj.*

trom·bone (trom·bōn′, trom′bōn′) A brass instrument larger and lower in pitch than the trumpet. A **slide trombone** changes pitch by means of a U-shaped slide that can lengthen or shorten the air column; a **valve trombone** changes pitch by means of valves. [< Ital., aug. of *tromba* trumpet < Gmc.] —**trom·bon′ist** *n.*

trompe l'oeil (trôṅp lœ′y′) In art and decoration, the accurate representation of details, scenes, etc., to create an illusion of reality. [< F, lit., fool the eye]

troop (trōōp) *n.* 1. An assembled company; gathering. 2. *Usu. pl.* A body of soldiers. 3. The cavalry unit corresponding to a company of infantry. 4. A body of Boy Scouts or Girl Scouts. —*v.i.* To move along or gather as a troop or as a crowd. [< LL *troppus* a flock < Gmc.]

troop carrier 1. A transport aircraft for carrying troops and equipment. 2. An armored vehicle for carrying troops.

troop·er (trōō′pər) *n.* 1. A cavalryman. 2. A mounted policeman. 3. A state policeman.

troop·ship (trōōp′ship′) *n.* A ship for carrying troops.

trope (trōp) *n.* 1. The figurative use of a word. 2. Loosely, a figure of speech. [< Gk. *tropos* a turn < *trepein* to turn]

troph·ic (trof′ik) *adj.* Pertaining to nutrition and its processes. Also **troph′i·cal.** [< Gk. *trephein* to nourish] —**troph′i·cal·ly** *adv.*

tro·phy (trō′fē) *n.* *pl.* **·phies** Something symbolizing victory or success; as: **a** A cup, etc., awarded for an achievement. **b** A mounted fish. **c** A weapon, etc., captured from an enemy. [< Gk. *tropē* a defeat, turning < *trepein* to turn, rout]

-trophy *combining form* A (specified) kind of nutrition or development: *hypertrophy*. [< Gk. *trophē* food, nourishment]

trop·ic (trop′ik) *n.* 1. *Geog.* Either of two parallels of latitude 23°27′ north and south of the equator, on which the sun is seen in the zenith on the days of its greatest declination, called respectively **tropic of Cancer** and **tropic of Capricorn**. 2. *pl.* The regions of the earth's surface between the tropics of Cancer and Capricorn. [< Gk. *tropikos* (*kyklos*) the tropical (circle) < *tropē* a turning] **—trop′ic** or **·i·cal** *adj.*

-tropic *combining form* Having a (specified) tropism; turning or changing in a (particular) way, or in response to a (given) stimulus: *phototropic.* Also **-tropal.**

tro·pism (trō′piz·əm) *n. Biol.* 1. The involuntary response of an organism to an external stimulus. 2. Any automatic reaction to a stimulus. [< Gk. *tropē* a turning] **—tro·pis·tic** (trō·pis′tik) *adj.*

-tropism *combining form* A (specified) tropism: *phototropism.* Also **-tropy.** [< TROPISM]

trop·o·sphere (trop′ə·sfir) *n. Meteorol.* The region of the atmosphere beneath the stratosphere, characterized by turbulence and by decreasing temperature with increasing altitude. [< Gk. *tropos* a turning + L *sphaera* sphere] **—trop′o·spher′ic** (-sfir′ik, -sfer′-) *adj.*

trot (trot) *n.* 1. A gait of a four-footed animal, esp. a horse, in which diagonal pairs of legs are moved almost simultaneously; also, the sound of this gait. 2. A moderately rapid run. 3. *Informal* A pony (def. 3). **—***v.* **trot·ted, trot·ting** *v.i.* 1. To go at a trot. 2. To hurry. **—***v.t.* 3. To ride at a trotting gait. **—to trot out** To bring forth for inspection, approval, etc. [< OHG *trottōn* to tread]

troth (trôth, trōth) *n.* 1. Good faith; fidelity. 2. The act of pledging fidelity; esp., betrothal. **—***v.t. Archaic* To betroth. [ME *trowthe, trouthe,* var. of OE *trēowth* truth; faith]

trot·ter (trot′ər) *n.* One who or that which trots; esp., a horse trained to trot for speed.

trou·ba·dour (trōō′bə·dôr) *n.* 1. A class of lyric poets flourishing in southern France, northern Italy, and eastern Spain during the 12th and 13th centuries. 2. A singer, esp., of love songs. [< Provençal *trobar* to compose, invent, find]

troub·le (trub′əl) *n.* 1. The state of being distressed in mind; worry. 2. A difficulty, perplexity, or annoyance. 3. Effort; pains: Take the *trouble* to do it right. 4. A diseased condition: lung *trouble.* **—***v.* **·led, ·ling** *v.t.* 1. To distress mentally; worry. 2. To agitate or disturb. 3. To inconvenience. 4. To cause physical pain or discomfort to. **—***v.i.* 5. To take pains; bother. 6. To worry. [< L *turba* crowd] **—troub′ler** *n.* **—troub′ling** *adj.*

troub·le-shoot·er (trub′əl·shōō′tər) *n.* One who locates difficulties and seeks to remove them, esp., in machine operations, industrial processes, etc. **—troub′le-shoot′ing** *n.*

troub·le·some (trub′əl·səm) *adj.* 1. Causing trouble; burdensome; trying. 2. Marked by violence; tumultuous. 3. Greatly agitated or disturbed; troublous. **—troub′le·some·ly** *adv.* **—troub′le·some·ness** *n.*

troub·lous (trub′ləs) *adj.* 1. Marked by commotion or tumult; full of trouble: *troublous* times. 2. Uneasy; restless.

trough (trôf) *n.* 1. A long, narrow, open receptacle for conveying a fluid or for holding food or water for animals. 2. A long, narrow channel or depression. 3. A gutter (def. 2). [OE *trog*]

trounce (trouns) *v.t.* **trounced, trounc·ing** 1. To beat severely; punish. 2. *Informal* To defeat. [Ult. origin uncertain]

troupe (trōōp) *n.* A company of actors or other performers. **—***v.i.* **trouped, troup·ing** To travel as one of a theatrical company. [< OF *trope* troop] **—troup′er** *n.*

trou·sers (trou′zərz) *n.pl.* A garment, esp. for men and boys, divided so as to make a separate covering for each leg and usu. extending from the waist to the ankles. Also **trow′sers.** [< obs. *trouse* breeches]

trous·seau (trōō′sō) *n. pl.* **·seaux** (-sōz) or **·seaus** A bride's outfit, esp. of clothing and linens. [< F < OF *trousse* a bundle]

trout (trout) *n.* A fish of the salmon family mostly found in fresh waters and highly esteemed as a game and food fish. [< Gk. *trōktēs* nibbler < *trōgein* to gnaw]

trove (trōv) *n.* Something of value or pleasing quality found or discovered. [< (TREASURE-)TROVE]

trow (trō) *v.t. & v.i. Archaic* To suppose; think; believe. [OE *trēowe* true]

trow·el (trou′əl, troul) *n.* 1. A flat-bladed implement with an offset handle, used to smooth plaster, mortar, etc. 2. A small concave scoop with a handle, used in digging about small plants. **—***v.t.* **trow·eled** or **·elled, trow·el·ing** or **·el·ling** To apply, form, or dig with a trowel. [< L *trulla,* dim. of *trua* stirring spoon, ladle] **—trow′el·er** or **trow′·el·ler** *n.*

troy (troi) *n.* A system of weights (**troy weight**) in which 12 ounces make a pound, used by jewelers in England and the U.S. Also **troy weight.** [after *Troyes,* a city in France]

tru·ant (trōō′ənt) *n.* One who neglects duty; esp., one who absents himself from school without leave. **—***adj.* 1. Being truant; idle. 2. Relating to or characterizing a truant. [< OF, vagabond, prob. < Celtic] **—tru′·an·cy** (-ən·sē) *n.*

truant officer An official who investigates truancy from school.

truce (trōōs) *n.* 1. An agreement between belligerents for a temporary suspension of hostilities; an armistice. 2. Temporary cessation of any conflict. [OE *trūwa* faith, a promise]

truck[1] (truk) *n.* 1. An automotive vehicle designed to carry loads, freight, etc.: also, *Brit., lorry.* 2. A two-wheeled barrowlike vehicle or a flat frame with wheels, used for moving barrels, boxes, etc., by hand. 3. One of the pivoting sets of wheels on a railroad car or engine. **—***v.t.* 1. To carry on a truck. **—***v.i.* 2. To carry goods on a truck. 3. To drive a truck. [Appar. < Gk. *trochos* wheel] **—truck′er** *n.*

truck[2] (truk) *v.t. & v.i.* To exchange or barter; also, to peddle. **—***n.* 1. Commodities for sale. 2. Garden produce for market. 3. Barter. 4. *Informal* Dealings: I will have no *truck* with him. [< OF *troquer* to barter] **—truck′er** *n.*

truck·age (truk′ij) *n.* 1. Money paid for conveyance of goods on trucks. 2. Such conveyance.

truck farm A farm on which vegetables are produced for market. Also **truck garden. —truck farmer —truck farming**

truck·le (truk′əl) *v.i.* **·led, ·ling** To yield

meanly or weakly: with *to.* —*n.* 1. A small wheel. 2. A trundle bed: also **truckle bed.** [< L *trochlea* a pulley] —**truck′ler** *n.* —**truck′ling·ly** *adv.*

truc·u·lent (truk′yə·lənt) *adj.* 1. Of savage character; cruel; belligerent. 2. Scathing; harsh; violent: said of writing or speech. [< L *trux, trucis* fierce] —**truc′u·lence, truc′u·len·cy** *n.* —**truc′u·lent·ly** *adv.*

trudge (truj) *v.i.* **trudged, trudg·ing** To walk wearily or laboriously; plod. —*n.* A tiresome walk or tramp. [Earlier *tredge, tridge*] —**trudg′er** *n.*

true (trōō) *adj.* **tru·er, tru·est** 1. Faithful to fact or reality; not false. 2. Being real or natural; genuine: *true* gold. 3. Faithful; steadfast. 4. Conforming to an existing type or pattern; exact: a *true* copy. 5. Legitimate. 6. Truthful; honest. —*n.* Truth; pledge. —*adv.* 1. In truth; truly. 2. In a true and accurate manner: The wheel runs *true.* —*v.t.* **trued, tru·ing** 3. To bring to conformity with a standard; adjust. [OE *trēowe*] —**true′ness** *n.* —**tru′ly** *adv.*

true-blue (trōō′blōō′) *adj.* Staunch; faithful; genuine.

true·born (trōō′bôrn′) *adj.* Being such by birth or inheritance: a *trueborn* Scot.

truf·fle (truf′əl) *n.* An edible fleshy underground fungus. [< OF *trufe, truffe*]

tru·ism (trōō′iz·əm) *n.* An obvious or self-evident truth.

trump (trump) *n.* 1. In various card games, a card of the suit selected to rank above all others temporarily. 2. *Usu. pl.* The suit thus determined. —*v.t.* 1. To top (another card) with a trump. 2. To surpass; excel; beat. —*v.i.* 3. To play a trump. —**to trump up** To make up for a dishonest purpose. [Alter. of TRIUMPH]

trump·er·y (trum′pər·ē) *n. pl.* **·er·ies** 1. Worthless finery. 2. Rubbish; nonsense. 3. Deceit; trickery. [< OF *tromper* to deceive]

trum·pet (trum′pit) *n.* 1. A brass wind instrument with a flaring bell and a long metal tube. 2. Something resembling a trumpet in form. 3. A loud, penetrating sound like that of a trumpet. —*v.t.* 1. To proclaim by or as by a trumpet; publish abroad. —*v.i.* 2. To blow a trumpet or give forth a sound as if from a trumpet. [< OF *trompe*] —**trum′pet·er** *n.*

trumpet creeper A woody vine of the southern U.S., with scarlet, trumpet-shaped flowers. Also **trumpet vine.**

trun·cate (trung′kāt) *v.t.* **·cat·ed, ·cat·ing** To cut the top or end from. —*adj.* 1. Truncated. 2. *Biol.* Ending abruptly, as though cut or broken squarely off. [< L *truncus* trunk] —**trun·ca′tion** *n.*

trun·ca·ted (trung′kā·tid) *adj.* Cut off; shortened.

trun·cheon (trun′chən) *n.* A short, heavy stick; club. —*v.t.* To beat as with a truncheon; cudgel. [< L *truncus* trunk]

trun·dle (trun′dəl) *n.* 1. A small, broad wheel, as of a caster. 2. The act, motion, or sound of trundling. 3. A trundle bed. —*v.t. & v.i.* **·dled, ·dling** 1. To roll along. 2. To rotate. [OE *trendel* circle] —**trun′dler** *n.*

trundle bed A bed with a low frame resting upon casters, so that it may be rolled under another bed.

trunk (trungk) *n.* 1. The main stem of a tree. 2. A large box or case for carrying clothes, etc., as for a journey. 3. A large compartment of an automobile for storing luggage, etc., often at the rear. 4. The human body, apart from the head, neck, and limbs; torso. 5. The main body, line, or stem of anything. 6. A proboscis, as of an elephant. 7. *pl.* A close-fitting garment covering the loins, worn by male swimmers. —*adj.* Being or belonging to a trunk or main body. [< L *truncus* stem, trunk]

trunk·fish (trungk′fish′) *n. pl.* **·fish** or **·fish·es** A fish of warm seas, characterized by a covering of hard, bony plates.

trunk line The main line of a transportation or communication system.

truss (trus) *n.* 1. *Med.* A bandage or support for a rupture. 2. A braced framework of ties, beams, or bars, as for the support of a roof, bridge, etc. —*v.t.* 1. To tie or bind; fasten. 2. To support by a truss; brace, as a roof. 3. To fasten the wings of (a fowl) before cooking. [< OF *trousser, trusser* to pack up, bundle] —**truss′er** *n.*

trust (trust) *n.* 1. Confident reliance on the integrity, honesty, or justice of another; faith. 2. Something committed to one's care; a charge; responsibility. 3. The state of receiving an important charge; responsibility: a position of *trust.* 4. Business credit. 5. Custody; care; keeping. 6. *Law* a Legal title to property held for the benefit of another. b The property or thing held. 7. An industrial or commercial combination of firms that controls the production and price of some commodity or service and thus lessens competition; monopoly. 8. Confident expectation; belief; hope. —*v.t.* 1. To have trust in; rely upon. 2. To commit to the care of another; entrust. 3. To commit something to the care of: with *with.* 4. To allow to do something without fear. 5. To expect with confidence or with hope. 6. To believe. —*v.i.* 7. To place trust or confidence; rely: with *in.* 8. To hope: with *for.* —**to trust to** To depend upon; confide in. —*adj.* Held in trust: *trust* money. [< ON *traust,* lit., firmness] —**trust′er** *n.*

trust company An institution that manages trusts and lends money.

trus·tee (trus·tē′) *n.* 1. One who holds property in trust. 2. One of a body of persons who manage the affairs of a college, church, foundation, etc.

trus·tee·ship (trus·tē′ship) *n.* 1. The post or function of a trustee. 2. Supervision and control of a Trust Territory; also, the territory so controlled.

trust·ful (trust′fəl) *adj.* Disposed to trust. —**trust′ful·ly** *adv.* —**trust′ful·ness** *n.*

trust fund Money, securities, etc., held in trust.

trust·ing (trus′ting) *adj.* Having trust; trustful. —**trust′ing·ly** *adv.* —**trust′ing·ness** *n.*

Trust Territory A dependent area administered by a nation under the authority of the United Nations.

trust·wor·thy (trust′wûr′thē) *adj.* Worthy of confidence; reliable. —**trust′wor′thi·ly** *adv.* —**trust′wor′thi·ness** *n.*

trust·y (trus′tē) *adj.* **trust·i·er, trust·i·est** 1. Faithful to duty or trust. 2. Staunch; firm.

—*n.* *pl.* **trust·ies** A trustworthy person; esp., a convict who has been found reliable and to whom special liberties are granted. —**trust′·i·ly** *adv.* —**trust′i·ness** *n.*

truth (trōōth) *n.* *pl.* **truths** (trōōthz, trōōths) 1. The state or character of being true; conformity to fact or reality. 2. Conformity to rule, standard, pattern, or ideal. 3. Steadfastness; fidelity. 4. That which is true; a statement or belief that corresponds to the reality. 5. Fact; reality. 6. A disposition to tell only what is true; veracity. [OE *trēowth*] —**truth′less** *adj.*

truth·ful (trōōth′fəl) *adj.* 1. Habitually telling the truth. 2. Conforming to fact or reality; true. —**truth′ful·ly** *adv.* —**truth′·ful·ness** *n.*

try (trī) *v.* **tried, try·ing** *v.t.* 1. To make an attempt to do or accomplish; endeavor. 2. To make experimental use or application of. 3. *Law* To subject to a judicial trial. 4. To subject to a test; put to proof. 5. To put severe strain upon or trouble greatly. 6. To extract by rendering or melting; refine. —*v.i.* 7. To make an attempt. —**to try on** To put on (a garment) to test it for fit or appearance. —**to try out** To attempt to qualify: He *tried out* for the football team. —*n.* *pl.* **tries** The act of trying; trial; experiment. [< OF *trier* to sift, pick out]

try·ing (trī′ing) *adj.* Testing severely; hard to endure.

try·out (trī′out′) *n.* *Informal* A test of ability.

tryst (trist) *n.* 1. An appointment, as between lovers, to meet at a set time and place; also, the meeting. 2. The meeting place agreed upon; rendezvous: also **tryst′ing place** (tris′ting). [< OF *triste, tristre* an appointed station in hunting] —**tryst′er** *n.*

tsar (zär) *n.* See CZAR.

tset·se (tset′sē, tsēt′-) *n.* 1. A small blood-sucking fly of southern Africa, whose bite transmits disease in cattle, horses, etc. 2. A related species that transmits the causative agent of sleeping sickness. Also spelled *tzetze.* Also **tsetse fly.** [< Afrikaans < Bantu]

T-shirt (tē′shûrt′) *n.* 1. A cotton undershirt with short sleeves. 2. A similar outer garment. Also **T shirt.**

T-square (tē′skwâr′) *n.* An instrument by which to measure or lay out right angles or parallel lines.

tsu·na·mi (tsōō·nä′mē) *n.* An extensive ocean wave caused by an undersea earthquake: also loosely called *tidal wave.* [< Japanese, a storm wave]

tub (tub) *n.* 1. A broad, open-topped vessel with handles on the sides. 2. A bathtub. 3. The amount that a tub contains. —*v.t. & v.i.* **tubbed, tub·bing** To wash, bathe, or place in a tub. [< MDu. *tubbe*] —**tub′ba·ble** *adj.* —**tub′ber** *n.*

tu·ba (tōō′bə) *n.* *pl.* **·bas** or **·bae** (-bē) A bass brass instrument whose pitch is varied by means of valves. [< Ital. < L, a war trumpet]

tub·by (tub′ē) *adj.* **·bi·er, ·bi·est** Short and fat; corpulent.

tube (tōōb) *n.* 1. A long, hollow, cylindrical body of metal, glass, rubber, etc., generally used for the conveyance of something through it; a pipe. 2. An electron tube. 3. A cylinder for containing paints, toothpaste, glue, etc. 4. *Zool.* Any elongated hollow part or organ: a bronchial *tube.* 5. A subway or tunnel. —**the tube** *Informal* 1. A television set. 2. Television. —*v.t.* **tubed, tub·ing** 1. To fit or furnish with a tube. 2. To enclose in a tube or tubes. 3. To make tubular. [< L *tubus*] —**tub′al** *adj.*

tu·ber (tōō′bər) *n.* 1. *Bot.* A short, thickened portion of an underground stem, as in the potato. 2. *Anat.* A swelling or prominence; tubercle. [< L, a swelling]

tu·ber·cle (tōō′bər·kəl) *n.* 1. A small, rounded nodule, as on the skin or on a root of a plant. 2. *Pathol.* A small, abnormal knob or swelling in an organ; esp., the lesion of tuberculosis. [< L *tuber* a swelling] —**tu·ber·cu·loid** (tōō·bûr′kyə·loid) *adj.*

tubercle bacillus The rod-shaped bacterium that causes tuberculosis in man.

tu·ber·cu·lar (tōō·bûr′kyə·lər) *adj.* 1. Covered with tubercles; nodular. 2. Of or affected with tuberculosis. —*n.* One affected with tuberculosis. —**tu·ber′cu·late** *adj.*

tu·ber·cu·lin (tōō·bûr′kyə·lin, tyōō-) *n.* A sterile liquid prepared from cultures of the tubercle bacillus, used as a test for tuberculosis.

tu·ber·cu·lo·sis (tōō·bûr′kyə·lō′sis) *n.* *Pathol.* 1. A communicable disease caused by infection with the tubercle bacillus, characterized by the formation of tubercles within some organ or tissue. 2. Tuberculosis affecting the lungs: also called *consumption.* [< TUBERCLE + -OSIS] —**tu·ber′cu·lous** *adj.*

tube·rose (tōōb′rōz′) *n.* A bulbous plant of the amaryllis family, bearing fragrant white flowers. [< L *tuber* a swelling]

tu·ber·ous (tōō′bər·əs) *adj.* Bearing or resembling tubers. Also **tu′ber·ose** (-ōs). —**tu′ber·os′i·ty** (-bə·ros′ə·tē) *n.*

tub·ing (tōō′bing) *n.* 1. Tubes collectively. 2. A piece of tube or material for tubes. 3. Material for pillowcases.

tu·bu·lar (tōō′byə·lər) *adj.* 1. Having the form of a tube. 2. Made up of or provided with tubes. Also **tu′bu·lous, tu′bu·lose** (-lōs). [< L *tubus* tube]

tu·bule (tōō′byōōl, tyōō′-) *n.* A small tube.

tuck (tuk) *v.t.* 1. To fold under; press in the ends or edges of. 2. To wrap or cover snugly. 3. To thrust or press into a close place; cram; hide. 4. To make folds in. —*n.* 1. A fold stitched into a garment for a better fit or for decoration. 2. Any tucked piece or part. [Fusion of OE *tūcian* to tug and MDu. *tucken* to pluck]

tuck·er (tuk′ər) *v.t.* *Informal* To weary completely; exhaust. [Freq. of TUCK, v.]

Tues·day (tōōz′dē, -dā, tyōōz′-) *n.* The third day of the week. [OE *tīwesdæg* day of Tiw, ancient Teutonic deity + *dæg* day]

tu·fa (tōō′fə) *n.* 1. A porous rock of calcium carbonate deposited from springs and streams. 2. Tuff. [< Ital. *tufo* < L *tofus*] —**tu·fa·ceous** (tōō·fā′shəs) *adj.*

tuff (tuf) *n.* A fragmentary volcanic rock composed of material varying in size from fine sand to coarse gravel. [See TUFA.] —**tuff·a′ceous** *adj.*

tuft (tuft) *n.* A bunch or cluster of small, flexible parts, as hair, grass, feathers, or threads held or tied together at the base. —*v.t.* 1. To separate or form into tufts. 2. To cover or adorn with tufts. —*v.i.* 3. To form tufts. [< OF *tuffe*, prob. < Gmc.] **—tuft'ed** *adj.* **—tuft'er** *n.* **—tuft'y** *adj.*

tug (tug) *v.* **tugged, tug·ging** *v.t.* 1. To pull at with effort; strain at. 2. To pull, draw, or drag with effort. 3. To tow with a tugboat. *—v.i.* 4. To pull strenuously: to *tug* at an oar. 5. To strive; toil. *—n.* 1. An act of tugging; a violent pull. 2. A strenuous contest. 3. A tugboat. [OE *togen*, pp. of *tēon* to tow] **—tug'ger** *n.*

tug·boat (tug'bōt') *n.* A small, ruggedly built vessel designed for towing: also called *towboat, tug.*

tug of war 1. A contest in which teams at opposite ends of a rope try to outpull each other. 2. A hard struggle for supremacy.

tug·rug (tug'rug) *n.* The monetary unit of the Mongolian People's Republic. Also **tug'rik, tugh'rik.**

tu·i·tion (too·ish'ən) *n.* 1. The charge or payment for instruction, esp. formal instruction. 2. Teaching; instruction. [< L *tuitio, -onis* guardianship] **—tu·i'tion·al, tu·i'·tion·ar'y** *adj.*

tu·la·re·mi·a (too'lə·rē'mē·ə) *n.* A plague-like disease of rodents, esp. rabbits, that may be transmitted to man: also called *rabbit fever.* Also **tu'la·rae'mi·a.** [< NL, after *Tulare* County, California + Gk. *haima* blood]

tu·lip (too'lip) *n.* 1. Any of numerous hardy, bulbous herbs of the lily family, cultivated for their large, variously colored, bell-shaped flowers. 2. A bulb or flower of this plant. [< Persian *dulband* turban]

tulip tree A large tree of the magnolia family, having greenish cup-shaped flowers.

tulle (tool) *n.* A fine, open-meshed silk, used for veils, etc. [< F, after *Tulle*, France]

tum·ble (tum'bəl) *v.* **·bled, ·bling** *v.i.* 1. To roll or toss about. 2. To perform acrobatic feats, as somersaults, etc. 3. To fall violently or awkwardly. 4. To move in a careless manner; stumble. *—v.t.* 5. To toss carelessly; cause to fall. 6. To throw into disorder or confusion; disturb; rumple. *—n.* 1. The act of tumbling; a fall. 2. A state of disorder or confusion. [OE *tumbian* to fall, leap]

tum·ble·bug (tum'bəl·bug') *n.* A beetle that rolls up a ball of dung to enclose its eggs.

tum·ble-down (tum'bəl·doun') *adj.* Rickety, as if about to fall in pieces; dilapidated.

tum·bler (tum'blər) *n.* 1. A drinking glass with a flat bottom. 2. One who or that which tumbles; esp., an acrobat or gymnast. 3. One of a breed of domestic pigeons noted for the habit of turning forward somersaults during flight. 4. In a lock, a part that secures a bolt until raised by the key.

tum·ble·weed (tum'bəl·wēd') *n.* A plant that breaks from the root and is driven by the wind.

tum·brel (tum'bril) *n.* 1. A farmer's cart, esp. one for carrying and dumping dung. 2. A rude cart in which prisoners were taken to the guillotine during the French Revolution. Also **tum'bril.** [< OF *tomber* to fall]

tu·mid (too'mid, tyoo'-) *adj.* 1. Swollen; enlarged, as a part of the body. 2. Inflated or pompous in style. [< L *tumere* to swell] **—tu·mid'i·ty** *n.* **—tu'mid·ly** *adv.* **—tu'mid·ness** *n.*

tu·mor (too'mər, tyoo'-) *n. Pathol.* A local swelling on or in any part of the body, esp. from some abnormal growth of tissue. Also *Brit.* **tu'mour.** [< L *tumere* to swell] **—tu'mor·ous** *adj.*

tu·mult (too'mult, tyoo'-) *n.* 1. The commotion, disturbance, or agitation of a crowd; uproar. 2. Any violent commotion or agitation, as of the mind. [< L *tumere* to swell]

tu·mul·tu·ous (too·mul'choo·əs, tyoo-) *adj.* 1. Characterized by tumult; disorderly. 2. Causing or affected by tumult; agitated or disturbed. Also **tu·mul'tu·ar'y.** **—tu·mul'tu·ous·ly** *adv.* **—tu·mul'tu·ous·ness** *n.*

tun (tun) *n.* 1. A large cask. 2. A varying measure of capacity, usu. equal to 252 gallons. *—v.t.* **tunned, tun·ning** To put into a cask or tun. [OE *tunne*]

tu·na (too'nə) *n. pl.* **·na** or **·nas** 1. Any of several large marine food fishes of the mackerel family. 2. Any of various similar or related fishes. 3. The flesh of any of these fishes processed and eaten as food: also **tuna fish.** Also called *tunny.* [< Am.Sp., ult. < Gk. *thynnos*]

tun·dra (tun'drə) *n.* A treeless, often marshy plain of the arctic north. [< Russ. < Lapp]

tune (toon) *n.* 1. A melody or air, usu. easy to remember. 2. The proper pitch, or, loosely, the proper key. 3. Concord or unison. 4. Suitable temper or humor. *—v.* **tuned, tun·ing** *v.t.* 1. To adjust the pitch of to a standard. 2. To adapt to a particular tone, expression, or mood. 3. To bring into harmony. 4. To adjust (an engine, etc.) to proper working order. *—v.i.* 5. To be in harmony. **—to tune in** To adjust a radio receiver to the frequency of (a station, broadcast, etc.). **—to tune out** 1. To adjust a radio receiver to exclude (interference, a station, etc.). 2. To exclude from one's attention; deliberately ignore. [Var. of TONE] **—tun'a·ble** or **tune'a·ble** *adj.*

tune·ful (toon'fəl, tyoon'-) *adj.* 1. Melodious; musical. 2. Producing musical sounds. **—tune'ful·ly** *adv.* **—tune'ful·ness** *n.*

tune·less (toon'lis, tyoon'-) *adj.* 1. Not making music; silent. 2. Lacking in rhythm, melody, etc. **—tune'less·ly** *adv.* **—tune'less·ness** *n.*

tun·er (too'nər, tyoo'-) *n.* 1. One who or that which tunes. 2. A radio receiver without amplifiers.

tune-up (toon'up', tyoon'-) *n. Informal* An adjustment to bring an engine, etc., into proper working order.

tung·sten (tung'stən) *n.* A steel-gray, heavy metallic element of the chromium group (symbol W), having a high melting point and used in the manufacture of filaments for electric lamps and high-speed cutting tools: also called *wolfram.* [< Sw. *tung* weighty + *sten* stone] **—tung·sten·ic** (tung·sten'ik) *adj.*

tu·nic (too'nik, tyoo'-) *n.* 1. In ancient Greece and Rome, a garment reaching to the knees. 2. A modern outer garment, as a blouse or jacket. [< L *tunica* < Semitic]

tun·ing fork (too'ning, tyoo'-) A fork-shaped metal instrument that produces a tone of definite pitch when struck.

Tu·ni·sian (too·nish'ən, -nē'zhən, tyoo-) *adj.* Of or relating to Tunisia or Tunis, or to their inhabitants. *—n.* 1. An inhabitant or native of Tunisia or Tunis. 2. The speech of Tunisia, a North Arabic dialect.

tun·nel (tun′əl) *n.* An underground passageway, as for a railway or a mine. —*v.* **tun·neled** or **·nelled, tun·nel·ing** or **·nel·ling** *v.t.* 1. To make a tunnel through. —*v.i.* 2. To make a tunnel. [Fusion of OF *tonnelle* partridge net and dim. of *tonne* cask] —**tun′nel·er** or **tun′nel·ler** *n.*

tun·ny (tun′ē) *n. pl.* **·ny** or **·nies** The tuna. [< Gk. *thynnos*]

Tu·pi (tōō·pē′) *n. pl.* **·pis** or **·pi** 1. A member of any of a group of South American Indian tribes, comprising the northern branch of the Tupians. 2. The language spoken by the Tupis, used as a lingua franca along the Amazon. [< Tupi, comrade]

Tu·pi·an (tōō·pē′ən) *adj.* Of or pertaining to the Tupis or their language. —*n.* A large language family of South American Indians of some one hundred tribes of the Tupis and Guaranis: also **Tu·pi′-Gua′ra·ni′** (-gwä′·rä·nē′).

tup·pence (tup′əns) *n. Brit. Informal* Twopence.

tur·ban (tûr′bən) *n.* 1. An Oriental head covering consisting of a sash twisted about the head or about a cap. 2. Any similar headdress. [< Persian *dul* turn + *band* band] —**tur′baned** *adj.*

tur·bid (tûr′bid) *adj.* 1. Opaque or cloudy, as a liquid with a suspension of foreign particles. 2. Thick and dense, like heavy smoke or fog. 3. Being in a state of confusion. [< L *turbare* to trouble < *turba* crowd] —**tur′bid·ly** *adv.* —**tur′bid·ness, tur·bid′i·ty** *n.*

tur·bi·nate (tûr′bə·nit, -nāt) *adj.* Shaped or spinning like a top. [< L *turbo* whirlwind]

tur·bine (tûr′bin, -bīn) *n.* A motor mounted on a shaft and provided with a series of curved vanes revolved by steam, water, gas, or other fluid under pressure. [< L *turbo* whirlwind, top]

tur·bo·e·lec·tric (tûr′bō·i·lek′trik) *adj.* Of or pertaining to the generation of electricity by a turbine.

tur·bo·fan (tûr′bō·fan′) *n.* 1. A compressor having ducted fans that supply air to a jet engine. 2. The engine using such a fan.

tur·bo·gen·er·a·tor (tûr′bō·jen′ə·rā′tər) *n.* An electric power-generating machine adapted for direct coupling to a steam turbine.

tur·bo·jet engine (tûr′bō·jet′) *n. Aeron.* A type of jet engine using a gas turbine to drive an air compressor.

tur·bo·prop (tûr′bō·prop′) *n. Aeron.* A turbojet engine connecting directly with a propeller. Also called *propjet.*

tur·bot (tûr′bət) *n. pl.* **·bot** or **·bots** A large European flatfish, used for food. [< OF *tourbout*]

tur·bu·lent (tûr′byə·lənt) *adj.* 1. Being in violent agitation or commotion. 2. Having a tendency to disturb or throw into confusion. [See TURBID.] —**tur′bu·lence, tur′bu·len·cy** *n.* —**tur′bu·lent·ly** *adv.*

tur·dine (tûr′din, -dīn) *adj.* Of a large and widely distributed family of singing birds, including thrushes and bluebirds. [< L *turdus* thrush]

tu·reen (tōō·rēn′) *n.* A deep, covered dish, as for holding soup to be served. [< F *terrine* earthenware dish < L *terra* earth]

turf (tûrf) *n. pl.* **turfs** (*Archaic* **turves**) 1. Grass with its matted roots filling the upper layer of soil; sod. 2. Peat (def. 2). 3. *Informal* Territory; esp., territory held and defended by a person or group. —**the turf** 1. A racetrack for horses. 2. The practice of racing horses. [OE] —**turf′y** *adj.*

tur·gid (tûr′jid) *adj.* 1. Unnaturally swollen, as by air or liquid. 2. Bombastic, as language, etc. [< L *turgere* to swell] —**tur·gid′i·ty, tur′gid·ness** *n.* —**tur′gid·ly** *adv.*

tur·gor (tûr′gər) *n.* The state of being turgid.

Turk (tûrk) *n.* A native or inhabitant of Turkey: sometimes called *Ottoman.*

tur·key (tûr′kē) *n. pl.* **·keys** 1. A large American bird related to the pheasant, having a naked head and extensible tail; esp., the American domesticated turkey, used for food. 2. *Slang* A play that is a failure. —**to talk turkey** To discuss in a practical and direct manner. [Short for *turkey cock* the guinea fowl, of Turkey; applied erroneously to the American bird]

turkey buzzard A sooty black vulture of tropical America and the southern U.S., having a naked red head.

Turk·ic (tûr′kik) *n.* A subfamily of the Altaic family of languages, including Osmanli or Turkish, Uzbek, etc. —**Turk′ic** *adj.*

Turk·ish (tûr′kish) *adj.* 1. Of or pertaining to Turkey or the Turks. 2. Of or relating to the Turkic subfamily of Altaic languages.

Turkish bath A bath with steam rooms, massage, and showers.

Turkish towel A heavy, rough towel with loose, uncut pile. Also **turkish towel.**

tur·mer·ic (tûr′mər·ik) *n.* 1. The root of an East Indian plant, used as a condiment, aromatic stimulant, dyestuff, etc. 2. The plant yielding this root. [< Med.L *terra merita* deserving earth]

tur·moil (tûr′moil) *n.* Confused motion; disturbance; tumult. [Origin uncertain]

turn (tûrn) *v.t.* 1. To cause to rotate, as about an axis. 2. To change the position or direction of. 3. To move so that the other side is visible: to *turn* a page. 4. To reverse the arrangement or order of. 5. To go around: to *turn* a corner. 6. To ponder: often with *over.* 7. To sprain or strain: to *turn* one's ankle. 8. To nauseate (the stomach). 9. To cause to go away: to *turn* a beggar from one's door. 10. To give graceful or finished form to: to *turn* a phrase. 11. To perform by revolving: to *turn* cartwheels. 12. To bend, curve, fold or twist. 13. To change or transform: to *turn* water into wine. 14. To exchange for an equivalent: to *turn* stocks into cash. 15. To cause to become as specified: Dye *turned* the liquid green. 16. To make sour or rancid. 17. To deflect or divert: to *turn* a blow. 18. To repel: to *turn* a charge. —*v.i.* 19. To move around an axis; rotate; revolve. 20. To move partially on or as if on an axis: He *turned* and ran. 21. To change position; also, to roll from side to side. 22. To reverse position; become inverted. 23. To change or reverse direction or flow: We *turned* north. The tide has *turned.* 24. To depend; hinge: with *on* or *upon.* 25. To whirl, as the head. 26. To become nauseated, as the stomach. 27. To become transformed: The water *turned* into ice. 28. To become as specified: His hair *turned* gray. 29. To become sour, rancid, or fermented. **—to turn against** To become or cause to become opposed or hostile to. **—to turn down** *Informal* To reject or refuse, as a request; also, to refuse the request, etc., of. **—to turn in** 1. To deliver; hand over. 2. *Informal* To go to bed. **—to turn loose** *Informal* To set free. **—to turn off** To lose or cause to lose interest. **—to turn on** 1. *Slang* To take or experience the effects of taking a psychedelic drug, as marijuana. 2. *Slang* To evoke in (someone) a rapt response. 3. To become hostile to. **—to turn out** 1. To turn inside out. 2. To eject or expel. 3. To produce; make. 4. To come or go out, as for duty or service. 5. To prove (to be). 6. To become or result. **—to turn over** 1. To hand over; transfer or relinquish. 2. To do business to the amount of. 3. To invest and get back (capital). **—to turn up** 1. To find or be found. 2. To appear; arrive. **—*n.*** 1. The act of turning, or the state of being turned. 2. A change to another direction, motion, or position. 3. A deviation from a course; change in trend. 4. A rotation or revolution. 5. A bend, as in a road. 6. A regular time or chance in some succession: It's my *turn* to play. 7. A round; spell: a *turn* at painting. 8. Characteristic form or style: the *turn* of a phrase. 9. Tendency; direction: The talk took a serious *turn*. 10. A deed performed: a good *turn*. 11. A walk, drive, or trip to and fro: a *turn* in the park. 12. A round in a coil, etc.; also, a twist. 13. *Informal* A shock to the nerves, as from alarm. **—at every turn** On every occasion; constantly. **—by turns** 1. In alternation or sequence. 2. At intervals. **—in turn** One after another; in proper order or sequence. **—out of turn** Not in proper order or sequence. **—to a turn** Just right: said esp. of cooked food. **—to take turns** To act, play, etc., one after another in proper order. [Fusion of OE *tyrnan* and *turnian* and OF *turner*, all < L *tornare* to turn in a lathe] **—turn′er** *n.*

turn·a·bout (tûrn′ə·bout′) *n.* The act of reversing one's direction, opinion, etc.

turn·buck·le (tûrn′buk′əl) *n. Mech.* A form of coupling so threaded that when connected lengthwise between two metal rods or wires it may be turned so as to regulate the distance or tension between them.

turn·coat (tûrn′kōt′) *n.* One who goes over to the opposite side or party; a renegade.

turn·ing (tûr′ning) *n.* 1. The art of shaping wood, metal, etc., on a lathe. 2. Any deviation from a straight or customary course; a winding; bend. 3. The point where a road forks.

turning point The point of a decisive change in direction of action; a crisis.

tur·nip (tûr′nip) *n.* 1. The fleshy, edible root of either of two biennial herbs of the mustard family, the **white turnip** and the rutabaga. 2. Either of the plants yielding this root. [Earlier *turnepe*]

turn·key (tûrn′kē) *n.* One who has charge of the keys of a prison; a jailer.

turn·off (tûrn′ôf′) *n. Informal* A road or way branching off from a main thoroughfare.

turn·out (tûrn′out′) *n.* 1. An act of turning out or coming forth. 2. Persons in attendance. 3. A quantity produced; output. 4. Array; equipment; outfit.

turn·o·ver (tûrn′ō′vər) *n.* 1. The act or process of turning over; an upset. 2. The rate at which persons hired within a given period are replaced by others; also, the number of persons hired. 3. A change or revolution. 4. A small pie or tart made by covering half of a crust with filling and turning the other half over on top. 5. The amount of business accomplished, or of work achieved. **—*adj.*** 1. Designed for turning over or reversing. 2. Capable of being turned over or folded down.

turn·pike (tûrn′pīk′) *n.* 1. A highway, esp. one with tollgates: also **turnpike road.** 2. A tollgate. [ME *turnpyke* spiked road barrier]

turn·stile (tûrn′stīl′) *n.* A gate with revolving arms that restricts passage to one person at a time, usu. in one direction only.

turn·ta·ble (tûrn′tā′bəl) *n.* 1. A rotating disk, as one that carries a phonograph record. 2. A rotating platform arranged to turn a section of a drawbridge, a locomotive, etc. Also *Brit.* **turn′plate′** (-plāt′).

tur·pen·tine (tûr′pən·tīn) *n.* An oleoresin obtained from any of several coniferous trees, esp. pines. **—oil of turpentine** The colorless essential oil formed when turpentine is distilled with steam; chiefly used to thin paint: also called **spirits of turpentine.** **—*v.t.* ·tined, ·tin·ing** To put turpentine with or upon; saturate with turpentine. [< Gk. *terebinthos*, a tree from which it was originally obtained]

tur·pi·tude (tûr′pə·tōōd, -tyōōd) *n.* Inherent baseness; vileness; depravity. [< L *turpis* vile]

tur·quoise (tûr′koiz, -kwoiz) *n.* 1. A blue or green mineral, colored by copper, valued in its highly polished blue varieties as a gemstone. 2. A light greenish blue: also **turquoise blue.** [< MF (*pierre*) *turquoise* Turkish (stone)]

tur·ret (tûr′it) *n.* 1. *Mil.* **a** A rotating armored housing containing guns and forming part of a warship or of a fort. **b** A similar structure in a tank or airplane. 2. *Archit.* A small tower rising above a larger structure, as on a castle. 3. *Mech.* In a lathe, a rotating cylinder for holding tools: also **turret head.** [< OF *torete*, dim. of *tor* tower] **—tur′ret·ed** *adj.* **—tur′ri·cal** *adj.*

turret lathe A lathe having a turret.

tur·tle (tûr′təl) *n.* 1. Any of numerous land, fresh-water, or sea reptiles having a horny, toothless beak, and a short, stout body enclosed within a shell. 2. The flesh of certain varieties of turtle, served as food. **—*v.i.* ·tled, ·tling** To hunt or catch turtles. [< Med.L *tortuca* tortoise]

tur·tle·dove (tûr′təl·duv′) *n.* A small Old World dove conspicuous for its soft, mournful coo. [OE *turtla* + DOVE]

tur·tle·neck (tûr′təl·nek′) *n.* 1. A high collar that fits snugly about the neck, usu. rolled or turned over double, used esp. on sweaters. 2. A sweater having such a collar.

Tus·can (tus′kən) *adj.* Pertaining to Tuscany. **—*n.*** 1. A native or inhabitant of Tuscany. 2. Any Italian dialect used in Tuscany, esp. the one spoken in Florence.

Tus·ca·ro·ra (tus′kə·rôr′ə, -rō′rə) *n. pl.* **·ra**

or ·ras One of a tribe of Iroquoian Indians formerly living in North Carolina, now surviving in New York and Ontario.

tush (tush) *interj.* An exclamation expressing disapproval, impatience, etc. [ME *tussch*]

tusk (tusk) *n.* 1. A long, pointed tooth, as in the boar, walrus, or elephant. 2. A sharp, projecting, toothlike point. —*v.t.* 1. To gore with the tusks. 2. To root up with the tusks. [Var. of OE *tūx*] —**tusked** *adj.* —**tusk′less** *adj.*

tusk·er (tus′kər) *n.* A tusked elephant or boar.

tus·sle (tus′əl) *v.t. & v.i.* ·**sled**, ·**sling** To fight or struggle in a vigorous, determined way; scuffle; wrestle. —*n.* A disorderly struggle, as in sport; scuffle. [Var. of TOUSLE]

tus·sock (tus′ək) *n.* 1. A tuft or clump of grass or sedge. 2. A tuft, as of hair or feathers. Also **tus′suck.** [? < obs. *tusk* tuft of hair] —**tus′sock·y** *adj.*

tut (tut) *interj.* An exclamation to check rashness or express impatience. Also **tut tut.**

tu·te·lage (to͞o′tə·lij, tyo͞o′-) *n.* 1. The state of being under a tutor or guardian. 2. The act or office of a guardian; guardianship. 3. The act of tutoring; instruction. [< L *tueri* to watch, guard]

tu·te·lar·y (to͞o′tə·ler′ē, tyo͞o′-) *adj.* 1. Invested with guardianship. 2. Pertaining to a guardian. Also **tu′te·lar** (-lər).

tu·tor (to͞o′tər, tyo͞o′-) *n.* 1. One who instructs another; a private teacher. 2. A college teacher who gives individual instruction. 3. *Law* A guardian of a minor. —*v.t.* 1. To act as tutor to; instruct; train. 2. To have the guardianship of. [< L *tueri* to watch, guard] —**tu·to′ri·al** (-tôr′ē·əl) *adj.*

tu·tor·ship (to͞o′tər·ship, tyo͞o′-) *n.* 1. The office of a tutor or of a guardian. Also **tu′tor·age.** 2. Tutelage.

tut·ti (to͞o′tē) *Music adj. & adv.* All performers. [< Ital., pl. of *tutto* all < L *totus*]

tut·ti-frut·ti (to͞o′tē·fro͞o′tē) *n.* A confection made with a mixture of fruits. —*adj.* Having fruit flavors. [< Ital., all fruits]

tu·tu (tü′tü) *n. French* A short, full skirt consisting of many layers of sheer fabric, worn by ballet dancers.

tux·e·do (tuk·sē′dō) *n. pl.* ·**dos** 1. A man's semiformal dinner coat without tails: also called *dinner coat, dinner jacket.* 2. The suit of which the coat is a part. Also **Tux·e′do.** [after *Tuxedo* Park, N.Y.]

TV (tē′vē′) *n. pl.* **TVs** or **TV's** Television. —*adj.* Of or pertaining to television.

twad·dle (twod′l) *v.t. & v.i.* ·**dled**, ·**dling** To talk foolishly. —*n.* Silly, senseless talk. [Origin uncertain] —**twad′dler** *n.*

twain (twān) *adj. Archaic & Poetic* Two. —*n.* 1. A couple; two. 2. In river navigation, two fathoms or twelve feet. [OE *twēgen*, masculine of *twā* two]

twang (twang) *v.t. & v.i.* **twanged, twang·ing** 1. To make or cause to make a sharp, vibrant sound. 2. To utter or speak nasally. —*n.* 1. A sharp, vibrating sound, as of a string plucked. 2. Excessive nasality of the voice. [Imit.] —**twang′y** *adj.*

tweak (twēk) *v.t.* To pinch and twist sharply; twitch. [Var. of dial. *twick*, OE *twiccian* to twitch] —**tweak** *n.* —**tweak′y** *adj.*

tweed (twēd) *n.* 1. A soft woolen fabric, often woven in two or more colors to effect a check or plaid pattern. 2. *pl.* Clothing of tweed. [Alter. of dial. E (Scot.) *tweel*, var. of TWILL]

tweed·y (twēd′ē) *adj.* 1. Like tweed. 2. Given to wearing tweed. 3. Of the outdoors in style or habits; informal.

'tween (twēn) Contraction of BETWEEN.

tweet (twēt) *v.i.* To utter a thin, chirping note. —*n.* A twittering or chirping. Also **tweet′-tweet′.** [Imit.]

tweet·er (twē′tər) *n. Electronics* A small loudspeaker used to reproduce high-pitched sounds. Compare WOOFER. [< TWEET]

tweeze (twēz) *v.t.* **tweezed, tweez·ing** *Informal* To handle, pluck, etc., with tweezers. [Back formation < TWEEZERS]

tweez·ers (twē′zərz) *n.pl.* Small pincers for grasping and holding small objects. Also **pair of tweezers.** [Earlier *tweeze* < *etweese* case of small instruments < F *étui*]

twelve (twelv) *n.* The sum of eleven and one: a cardinal number written 12, XII. [OE *twelf*] —**twelfth** (twelfth) *adj. & n.* —**twelve** *adj.*

twelve·month (twelv′munth′) *n.* A year.

twelve-tone (twelv′tōn′) *adj. Music* 1. Of a composition in which the tones of the chromatic scale are arranged in an arbitrary series. 2. In 20th c. music, using or composed in a freely chromatic style.

twen·ty (twen′tē) *n. pl.* ·**ties** The sum of nineteen and one: a cardinal number written 20, XX. [OE *twēntig*] —**twen′ti·eth** *adj. & n.* —**twen′ty** *adj.*

twen·ty-one (twen′tē·wun′) *n.* A card game in which the object is to draw cards whose value will equal or approach twenty-one without exceeding that amount: also called *blackjack.*

twi·bil (twī′bil) *n.* 1. A battle-ax with two cutting edges. 2. A tool having one blade like an ax and the other an adz. Also **twi′bill.** [OE *twi-* two + *bill* ax]

twice (twīs) *adv.* 1. Two times. 2. In double measure; doubly. [OE *twiges*, gen. of *twiga* twice]

twice-told (twīs′tōld′) *adj.* Told more than once.

twid·dle (twid′l) *v.* ·**dled**, ·**dling** *v.t.* 1. To twirl idly; toy or play with. —*v.i.* 2. To revolve or twirl. 3. To toy with something idly. —**to twiddle one's thumbs** To rotate one's thumbs idly around one another. —*n.* A gentle twirling. [Origin unknown] —**twid′·dler** *n.*

twig (twig) *n.* A small shoot or branch of a tree. [OE *twigge*] —**twigged** *adj.* —**twig′less** *adj.* —**twig′gy** *adj.* ·**gi·er**, ·**gi·est**

twi·light (twī′līt′) *n.* 1. The faint light in the sky when the sun is below the horizon, esp. in the evening; also, the period during which this light is prevalent. 2. Any faint light. 3. A condition following the waning of past glory, achievement, etc. [ME *twylight*] —**twi′light′** *adj.*

twill (twil) *n.* 1. A weave characterized by diagonal ribs or lines in fabrics. 2. A fabric woven with a twill. —*v.t.* To weave (cloth) so as to produce diagonal lines or ribs on the surface. [OE *twilic* fabric having a double thread] —**twilled** *adj.*

twin (twin) *n.* 1. One of two young produced

at the same birth. 2. The counterpart of another. —*adj.* 1. Being a twin or twins. 2. Consisting of, forming, or being one of a pair of similar and closely related objects. —*v.* **twinned, twin·ning** *v.i.* 1. To bring forth twins. 2. To be matched or equal; agree. —*v.t.* 3. To bring forth as twins. 4. To couple; match. [OE *twinn*]

twine (twīn) *v.* **twined, twin·ing** *v.t.* 1. To twist together, as threads. 2. To form by such twisting. 3. To coil or wrap about something. —*v.i.* 4. To interlace. 5. To proceed in a winding course; meander. —*adj.* Of or like twine. —*n.* A string composed of two or more strands twisted together; loosely, any small cord. [OE *twin* twisted double thread < *twā* two] —**twin′er** *n.*

twinge (twinj) *n.* 1. A sharp local pain. 2. A mental or emotional pang. —*v.t. & v.i.* **twinged, twing·ing** To affect with or suffer a sudden pain or twinge. [OE *twengan* to pinch]

twin·kle (twing′kəl) *v.i.* **·kled, ·kling** 1. To shine with fitful gleams, as a star. 2. To be bright, as with amusement: Her eyes *twinkled.* 3. To move rapidly to and fro; flicker: *twinkling* feet. —*n.* 1. An intermittent gleam of light; sparkle; glimmer. 2. A wink or sparkle of the eye. 3. An instant; a twinkling. [OE *twinclian*] —**twin′kler** *n.*

twin·kling (twing′kling) *n.* 1. The act of sparkling. 2. A wink. 3. A moment.

twirl (twûrl) *v.t. & v.i.* 1. To whirl. 2. In baseball, to pitch. —*n.* 1. A whirling motion. 2. A quick twisting action, as of the fingers. 3. A curl; coil. [Alter. of ME *tirlen*, var. of *trillen* to roll] —**twirl′er** *n.*

twist (twist) *v.t.* 1. To wind (strands, etc.) around each other. 2. To form by such winding: to *twist* thread. 3. To give spiral form to, as by turning at either end. 4. To force out of natural shape; distort or contort. 5. To distort the meaning of. 6. To cause to revolve or rotate. —*v.i.* 7. To become twisted. 8. To move in a winding course. 9. To squirm; writhe. —*n.* 1. The act, manner, or result of twisting or turning on an axis. 2. The state of being twisted. 3. A curve; turn; bend. 4. A wrench; strain, as of a joint or limb. 5. A distortion or variation of: a *twist* of meaning. 6. Thread or cord made of tightly twisted strands; also, one of the strands. 7. A twisted roll or loaf of bread. 8. Tobacco twisted in the form of a large cord. [ME *twisten* to divide in two, combine two]

twist·er (twis′tər) *n.* 1. One who or that which twists. 2. In baseball, a curve; also, one who pitches a curve. 3. A tornado.

twit (twit) *v.t.* **twit·ted, twit·ting** To taunt, reproach, or annoy by reminding of a mistake, fault, etc. [Var. of ME *atwite*, OE *æwītan* to taunt] —**twit** *n.*

twitch (twich) *v.t. & v.i.* To pull or move with a sudden jerk. —*n.* 1. A sudden involuntary contraction of a muscle. 2. A sudden, sharp pull or jerk. [ME *twicchen*] —**twitch′ing·ly** *adv.*

twit·ter (twit′ər) *v.i.* 1. To utter a series of light chirping or trembling notes, as a bird. 2. To titter. 3. To be excited; tremble. —*n.* 1. The act of twittering. 2. A succession of light chirping or trembling sounds. 3. A state of nervous agitation. [Imit.] —**twit′ter·er** *n.* —**twit′ter·y** *adj.*

twixt (twikst) *prep. Poetic* Betwixt. Also **'twixt.**

two (to͞o) *n.* 1. The sum of one and one: a cardinal number written 2, II. 2. A couple; pair. —**to put two and two together** To reach the obvious conclusion. [OE *twā, tū*] —**two** *adj.*

two-bit (to͞o′bit′) *adj. Slang* Cheap; smalltime.

two bits *Informal* 1. Twenty-five cents. 2. A trifling sum.

two-by-four (to͞o′bī·fôr′) *n.* A piece of lumber actually measuring $1^5/_8$ inches by $3^3/_8$ inches, much used in building.

two-faced (to͞o′fāst′) *adj.* 1. Having two faces. 2. Double-dealing. —**two′-fac′ed·ly** (-fā′sid·lē, -fāst′lē) *adv.*

two-fist·ed (to͞o′fis′tid) *adj. Informal* Vigorous and aggressive.

two·fold (to͞o′fōld′) *n.* An amount or number two times as great as a given unit. —*adv.* So as to be two times as many or as great. —*adj.* 1. Consisting of two parts. 2. Two times as many or as great.

two-hand·ed (to͞o′han′did) *adj.* 1. Requiring both hands at once. 2. Constructed for use by two persons. 3. Ambidextrous. 4. Having two hands.

two-mas·ter (to͞o′mas′tər) *n.* A ship with two masts.

two·pence (tup′əns) *n. Brit.* Two pennies. Also, *Informal, tuppence.*

two·pen·ny (tup′ən·ē) *adj. Brit.* 1. Of the price or value of twopence. 2. Cheap; worthless.

two-ply (to͞o′plī′) *adj.* 1. Made of two united webs; woven double: a *two-ply* carpet. 2. Made of two strands, layers, or thicknesses of material.

two·some (to͞o′səm) *n.* 1. Two persons together; a couple. 2. A match with one player on each side.

two-step (to͞o′step′) *n.* A ballroom dance consisting of a sliding step in 2/4 meter; also, the music for it.

two-time (to͞o′tīm′) *v.t.* **-timed, -tim·ing** *Slang* To be unfaithful to in love; deceive. —**two′-tim′er** *n.*

two-way (to͞o′wā′) *adj.* Characterized by or permitting movement in two directions or use in two ways.

ty·coon (tī·ko͞on′) *n.* A wealthy and powerful industrial or business leader. [< Japanese *taikun* mighty lord < Chinese *ta* great + *kiun* prince]

tyke (tīk) *n.* 1. *Informal* A small child. 2. A mongrel dog.

tym·pa·ni (tim′pə·nē) See TIMPANI.

tympanic membrane *Anat.* The membrane separating the middle ear from the external ear: also called *eardrum.*

tym·pa·nist (tim′pə·nist) *n.* One who plays a kettledrum.

tym·pa·num (tim′pə·nəm) *n. pl.* **·na** or **·nums** 1. *Anat.* **a** The middle ear. **b** The tympanic membrane. 2. A drumlike membrane or part. Also spelled *timpanum.* [< Gk. *tympanon* < *typtein* to beat] —**tym·pan′ic** (-pan′ik) *adj.*

type (tīp) *n.* 1. Class; category; kind; sort. 2. One who or that which has the characteristics of a group or class; embodiment. 3. *Printing* A block of metal or wood, bearing on its upper surface a letter or character in relief for use in printing. 4. Printed or typewritten characters. 5. *Informal* A person. **—*v.* typed, typ·ing** *v.t.* 1. To typewrite (something). 2. To determine the type of; identify: to *type* a blood sample. 3. To represent; typify. **—*v.i.*** 4. To typewrite. [< Gk. *typos* impression, figure, type < *typtein* to strike]

-type *combining form* 1. Representative form; type: *prototype.* 2. Printing; duplicating or photographic process; type: *Linotype.* [< Gk. *typos* impression, figure, type]

type·cast (tīp′kast′) *v.t.* **·cast, ·cast·ing** To cast, as an actor, in a role suited to his appearance, personality, etc.

type·face (tīp′fās′) *n. Printing* The design of all the characters in a set of type.

type foundry An establishment in which metal type is made. **—type founder —type founding**

type metal *Printing* The alloy of which type is made, usu. of lead, tin, and antimony.

type·script (tīp′skript′) *n.* Typewritten matter.

type·set·ter (tīp′set′ər) *n.* 1. One who sets type. 2. A machine for composing type. **—type′set′ting** *n.*

type·write (tīp′rīt′) *v.t. & v.i.* **·wrote, ·writ·ten, ·writ·ing** To write with a typewriter: also *type.*

type·writ·er (tīp′rī′tər) *n.* A machine with a keyboard, that produces printed characters by impressing type upon paper through an inked ribbon.

ty·phoid (tī′foid) *n.* Typhoid fever. [< Gk. *typhos* smoke, stupor] **—ty′phoid, ty·phoi′dal, ty′phose** (-fōs) *adj.*

typhoid fever *Pathol.* An acute, infectious fever caused by a bacterium (the **typhoid bacillus**) and characterized by severe intestinal disturbances and rose-red spots on the chest and abdomen.

ty·phoon (tī·fo͞on′) *n. Meteorol.* A hurricane originating over tropical waters in the western Pacific and the China Sea. [< Gk. *typhōn* whirlwind and Chinese *tai feng,* lit., big wind]

ty·phus (tī′fəs) *n. Pathol.* An acute, contagious rickettsial disease, marked by high fever, eruption of red spots, and cerebral disorders. Also called *spotted fever.* Also **typhus fever.** [< Gk. *typhos* smoke, stupor < *typhein* to smoke] **—ty′phous** (-fəs) *adj.*

typ·i·cal (tip′i·kəl) *adj.* 1. Characteristic of a type; constituting a type; representative. 2. Conforming to the essential features of a type; serving to distinguish a type. Also **typ′ic.** [< Gk. *typikos* < *typos* type] **—typ′i·cal·ly** *adv.* **—typ′i·cal·ness** *n.*

typ·i·fy (tip′ə·fī) *v.t.* **·fied, ·fy·ing** 1. To represent by a type; signify, as by an image or token. 2. To constitute a type or serve as a characteristic example of. **—typ′i·fi·ca′tion** *n.* **—typ′i·fi′er** *n.*

typ·ist (tī′pist) *n.* One who operates a typewriter.

ty·po (tī′pō) *n. Informal* A typographical error.

ty·pog·ra·phy (tī·pog′rə·fē) *n. pl.* **·phies** 1. The arrangement of composed type. 2. The style and appearance of printed matter. 3. The act or art of composing and printing from type. **—ty·pog′ra·pher** *n.* **—ty·po·graph·ic** (tī′pə·graf′ik) or **·i·cal** *adj.* **—ty′·po·graph′i·cal·ly** *adv.*

ty·pol·o·gy (tī·pol′ə·jē) *n. pl.* **·gies** 1. The study of types, as in systems of classification. 2. A set or listing of types.

ty·ran·ni·cal (ti·ran′i·kəl, tī-) *adj.* Of or characteristic of a tyrant; harsh; despotic. Also **ty·ran′nic. —ty·ran′ni·cal·ly** *adv.* **—ty·ran′ni·cal·ness** *n.*

tyr·an·nize (tir′ə·nīz) *v.* **·nized, ·niz·ing** *v.i.* 1. To exercise power cruelly or unjustly. 2. To rule as a tyrant. **—*v.t.*** 3. To treat tyrannically. Also *Brit.* **tyr′an·nise. —tyr′·an·niz′er** *n.*

ty·ran·no·sau·rus (ti·ran′ə·sôr′əs) *n. pl.* **·rus·es** A huge carnivorous dinosaur of North America, that walked on its hind legs. [< Gk. *tyrannos* tyrant + *sauros* lizard]

tyr·an·ny (tir′ə·nē) *n. pl.* **·nies** 1. Absolute power arbitrarily or unjustly exercised; despotism. 2. A tyrannical act. 3. The authority, government, or rule of a tyrant. [< L *tyrannus* tyrant] **—tyr′an·nous** (-nəs) *adj.* **—tyr′an·nous·ly** *adv.*

ty·rant (tī′rənt) *n.* 1. One who rules oppressively or cruelly; a despot. 2. One who exercises absolute power without legal warrant. [< Gk. *tyrannos* master, usurper]

tyre (tīr) See TIRE[2].

ty·ro (tī′rō) *n. pl.* **·ros** A beginner; novice. [< L *tiro* recruit]

tzar (tsär) See CZAR.

tzet·ze (tset′sē) See TSETSE.

tzi·gane (tsē·gän′) *n. Sometimes cap.* A Gypsy, esp. a Hungarian Gypsy. [< Hung. *czigány*]

U

u, U (yo͞o) *n. pl.* **u's, us, U's** or **Us** (yo͞oz) 1. The twenty-first letter of the English alphabet. 2. Any sound represented by the letter *u*. —*symbol.* 1. Anything shaped like a U. 2. *Chem.* Uranium (symbol U).

U (yo͞o) *adj. Informal* Of or characteristic of the upper class.

u·biq·ui·tous (yo͞o·bik′wə·təs) *adj.* Existing or seeming to exist everywhere at once; omnipresent. Also **u·biq′ui·tar′y** (-ter′ē). [< L *ubique* everywhere] —**u·biq′ui·tous·ly** *adv.* —**u·biq′ui·tous·ness, u·biq′ui·ty** *n.*

U-boat (yo͞o′bōt′) *n.* A German submarine. [< G *U-boot*, contr. of *Unterseeboot* undersea boat]

ud·der (ud′ər) *n.* A large, hanging gland, secreting milk and provided with nipples or teats for the suckling of offspring, as in cows. [OE *ūder*]

UFO (yo͞o′ ef′ ō′, yo͞o′fō) *n. pl.* **UFO's** or **UFOs** An unidentified flying object.

U·gan·dan (yo͞o·gan′dən, o͞o·gän′-) *adj.* Of Uganda or its inhabitants. —**U·gan′dan** *n.*

ugh (ukh, ug) *interj.* An exclamation of repugnance or disgust. [Imit.]

ug·li·fy (ug′lə·fī) *v.t.* **·fied, ·fy·ing** To make ugly. —**ug′li·fi·ca′tion** *n.*

ug·ly (ug′lē) *adj.* **·li·er, ·li·est** 1. Displeasing to the eye. 2. Repulsive to the moral sense. 3. Bad in character or consequences, as a rumor, wound, etc. 4. *Informal* Bad-tempered. [< ON *uggligr* dreadful < *uggr* fear] —**ug′li·ly** *adv.* —**ug′li·ness** *n.*

U·gric (o͞o′grik, yo͞o′-) *n.* A branch of the Finno-Ugric subfamily of Uralic languages, comprising Magyar, Ostyak, and Vogul. —**U′gric** *adj.*

u·kase (yo͞o′kās, yo͞o·kāz′) *n.* An official decree. [< Russian *ukaz*]

U·krain·i·an (yo͞o·krā′nē·ən) *n.* 1. A native or inhabitant of the Ukraine. 2. The East Slavic language of the Ukrainians. —**U·krain′i·an** *adj.*

u·ku·le·le (yo͞o′kə·lā′lē) *n.* A small guitarlike musical instrument having four strings. [< Hawaiian, flea < *uku* insect + *lele* to jump]

ul·cer (ul′sər) *n.* 1. *Pathol.* An open sore on a surface of the body. 2. A corroding fault or vice. [< L *ulcus, ulceris*] —**ul′cer·ous** *adj.* —**ul′cer·ous·ly** *adv.* —**ul′cer·ous·ness** *n.*

ul·cer·ate (ul′sə·rāt) *v.t. & v.i.* **·at·ed, ·at·ing** To make or become affected with ulcers. —**ul′cer·a′tion** *n.* —**ul′cer·a′tive** *adj.*

-ule *suffix of nouns* Small; little: *granule.* [< L *-ulus, -ula, -ulum*, diminutive suffix]

ul·na (ul′nə) *n. pl.* **·nae** (-nē) or **·nas** *Anat.* 1. The inner bone of the two long bones of the forearm, located on the same side as the little finger. 2. The corresponding bone in the forelimb of other vertebrates. [< L, elbow] —**ul′nar** *adj.*

ul·ster (ul′stər) *n.* A very long, loose overcoat, sometimes belted at the waist. [after *Ulster*, Ireland]

ul·te·ri·or (ul·tir′ē·ər) *adj.* 1. Intentionally hidden: *ulterior* motives. 2. More remote: *ulterior* considerations. 3. Lying beyond or on the farther side. [< L *ulter* beyond] —**ul·te′ri·or·ly** *adv.*

ul·ti·ma (ul′tə·mə) *n.* The last syllable of a word. [< L]

ul·ti·mate (ul′tə·mit) *adj.* 1. Beyond which there is no other; last of a series; final. 2. Not susceptible of further analysis; fundamental. 3. Most distant; extreme. —*n.* 1. The final result; last step; conclusion. 2. A fundamental or final fact. [< L *ultimus* farthest, last] —**ul′ti·mate·ly** *adv.* —**ul′ti·mate·ness** *n.*

ul·ti·ma·tum (ul′tə·mā′təm, -mä′-) *n. pl.* **·tums** or **·ta** A final statement, as concerning terms, conditions, or concessions; esp., in diplomatic negotiations, the final terms offered. [See ULTIMATE.]

ul·ti·mo (ul′tə·mō) *adv. Archaic* In the last month. [< L *ultimo (mense)* in the last (month)]

ul·tra (ul′trə) *adj.* Going beyond the bounds of moderation; extreme. —*n.* One who goes to extremes. [< L, beyond]

ultra- *prefix* 1. On the other side of; beyond: **ultragalactic, ultralunar, ultra-Martian.** 2. Excessively; extremely: **ultra-ambitious, ultraconservative, ultrafashionable, ultramodern, ultranationalistic, ultraorthodox.**

ul·tra·cen·tri·fuge (ul′trə·sen′trə·fyo͞oj) *n.* A centrifuge whose rotor will operate at extremely high velocities. —*v.t.* **·fuged, ·fug·ing** To subject to the action of an ultracentrifuge. —**ul′tra·cen′tri·fu·ga′tion** (-fyo͞o·gā′shən) *n.*

ul·tra·high frequency (ul′trə·hī′) *Telecom.* A band of w[illegible] frequencies between 300 and 3,000 megahertz per second.

ul·tra·ma·rine (ul′trə·mə·rēn′) *n.* 1. A deep blue, permanent pigment. 2. A deep blue. —*adj.* 1. Being beyond or across the sea. 2. Of the color ultramarine. [< L *ultra* beyond + *marinus* marine]

ul·tra·mi·cro·scope (ul′trə·mī′krə·skōp) *n.* An optical instrument for detecting objects too small to be seen with an ordinary microscope. —**ul′tra·mi·cros′co·py** (-mī·kros′kə·pē) *n.*

ul·tra·mi·cro·scop·ic (ul′trə·mī′krə·skop′ik) *adj.* 1. Too minute to be seen by an ordinary microscope. 2. Relating to the ultramicroscope. Also **ul′tra·mi′cro·scop′i·cal.**

ul·tra·son·ic (ul′trə·son′ik) *adj. Physics* Designating sound waves having a frequency above the limits of human hearing.

ul·tra·vi·o·let (ul′trə·vī′ə·lit) *adj. Physics* Of wavelengths, lying beyond the violet end of the visible spectrum.

ul·u·late (yo͞ol′yə·lāt, ul′-) *v.i.* **·lat·ed, ·lat·ing** To howl, hoot, or wail. [< L *ululare* to howl] —**ul′u·lant** *adj.*

um·bel (um′bəl) *n. Bot.* A flower cluster spreading outward from a small area at the top of the main stem. [< L *umbella* parasol] —**um′bel·lar** (-bə·lər), **um′bel·late** (-bə·lit, -bə·lāt), **um′bel·lat′ed** *adj.*

um·ber (um′bər) *n.* 1. A brown earth containing iron and used as a pigment. 2. The color of such a pigment. —*adj.* Of or pertaining to umber; brownish. —*v.t.* To color with umber. [< F (*terre d'*)*ombre* (earth of) Umbria, or Ital. *ombra*]

umbilical cord *Anat.* A ropelike tissue connecting the navel of the fetus with the placenta.

um·bil·i·cus (um·bil′ə·kəs, um′bə·lī′kəs) *n. pl.* **·ci** (-sī) *Anat.* The navel. [< L] —**um·bil′i·cal** *adj.*

um·bra (um′brə) *n. pl.* **·brae** (-brē) 1. A shadow or dark area. 2. *Astron.* In a solar eclipse, that part of the shadow cast by the moon on the earth within which the sun is entirely hidden. [< L, shadow]

um·brage (um′brij) *n.* 1. Resentment: now usu. in **to take umbrage.** 2. That which gives shade, as a leafy tree. 3. *Poetic* Shade. [< L *umbra* shadow] —**um·bra′geous** (-brā′jəs) *adj.*

um·brel·la (um·brel′ə) *n.* A shade, usu. round and usu. collapsible, used as a protection against rain or sun. [< Ital. < L *umbella* parasol]

u·mi·ak (o͞o′mē·ak) *n.* A large, open boat made by drawing skins over a wooden frame, used by Eskimos. Also **u′mi·ack.** [< Eskimo]

um·laut (o͝om′lout) *n.* 1. *Ling.* The change in a vowel caused by its partial assimilation to a vowel in the following syllable. 2. In German, the two dots (¨) put over a vowel thus changed: short for **umlaut-mark.** [< G, change of sound < *um* about + *laut* sound]

um·pire (um′pīr) *n.* 1. In baseball, and certain other games, a person who enforces rules and settles disputed points. 2. A person called upon to settle a disagreement in opinion. —*v.t. & v.i.* **·pired, ·pir·ing** To decide as umpire; act as umpire (of or in). [Alter. of ME *noumpere* < OF *nonper* uneven, hence, third]

un-[1] *prefix* Not; opposed to: *unintentional.* [OE]

un-[2] *prefix* Reverse; remove: *untie, unarm.* The list starting below contains self-explanatory words formed with *un-*[1] and *un-*[2]. [OE *un-, on-, and-*]

un·a·ble (un·ā′bəl) *adj.* 1. Lacking the power or resources; not able. 2. Lacking mental capacity; incompetent.

un·a·bridged (un′ə·brijd′) *adj.* Not abridged: an *unabridged* dictionary.

un·ac·com·mo·dat·ed (un′ə·kom′ə·dā′tid) *adj.* 1. Not made suitable. 2. Being without accommodations or conveniences.

un·ac·com·pa·nied (un′ə·kum′pə·nēd) *adj.* 1. Done without an escort or companion. 2. *Music* Performing without accompaniment.

un·ac·com·plished (un′ə·kom′plisht) *adj.* 1. Not done or finished. 2. Lacking accomplishments.

un·ac·count·a·ble (un′ə·koun′tə·bəl) *adj.* 1. Impossible to be accounted for; inexplicable. 2. Remarkable; extraordinary. 3. Not accountable; irresponsible. —**un′ac·count′a·ble·ness** *n.* —**un′ac·count′a·bly** *adv.*

un·ac·count·ed-for (un′ə·kount′tid·fôr′) *adj.* Not accounted for; not explained.

un·ac·cus·tomed (un′ə·kus′təmd) *adj.* 1. Not accustomed. 2. Not familiar; strange.

un·ad·vised (un′əd·vīzd′) *adj.* 1. Not advised. 2. Rash or imprudent. —**un′ad·vis′ed·ly** (-vī′zid·lē) *adv.* —**un′ad·vis′ed·ness** *n.*

un·af·fect·ed (un′ə·fek′tid) *adj.* 1. Not showing affectation; sincere. 2. Not influenced or changed. —**un′af·fect′ed·ly** *adv.* —**un′af·fect′ed·ness** *n.*

un·al·ien·a·ble (un·āl′yən·ə·bəl) *adj.* Inalienable.

un·a·ligned (un·ə·līnd′) *adj.* 1. Not in a line. 2. Nonaligned.

un-A·mer·i·can (un′ə·mer′ə·kən) *adj.* Not consistent with the character, ideals, or objectives of the U.S.

u·nan·i·mous (yo͞o·nan′ə·məs) *adj.* 1. Sharing the same views or sentiments. 2. Showing or resulting from the assent of all. [< L *unus* one + *animus* mind] —**u·na·nim·i·ty** (yo͞o′nə·nim′ə·tē) *n.* —**u·nan′i·mous·ly** *adv.* —**u·nan′i·mous·ness** *n.*

unabashed
unabated
unabetted
unacademic
unaccented
unacceptable
unaccepted
unacclimated
unaccommodating
unaccounted
unaccredited
unacknowledged
unacquainted
unadaptable
unadjustable
unadjusted
unadorned
unadulterated
unadvertised
unadvisable
unaffiliated
unafraid
unaggressive
unaided
unaimed
unalarmed
unalike
unalleviated
unallowable
unalloyed
unalterable
unaltered
unambiguous
unambitious
unamplified
unamusing
unanimated
unannounced
unanswerable
unanswered
unanticipated
unapologetic
unappalled
unappealing
unappeasable
unappeased
unappetizing
unappreciated
unappreciative
unappropriated
unapproved
unartistic
unashamed
unasked
unaspiring
unassailed
unassignable
unassigned
unassumed
unattainable
unattained
unattempted
unattended
unattested
unattractive
unauthentic
unauthenticated
unauthorized
unavailability
unavailable
unavenged
unavowed
unawakened
unawed
unbaked
unbaptized
unbeatable
unbeaten
unbefitting
unbeloved
unbeseeming
unbesought
unbespoken
unblamable
unblamed
unbleached
unblemished
unboastful
unborrowed
unbought
unboxed
unbraid

un·ap·proach·a·ble (un′ə·prō′chə·bəl) *adj.* 1. Not easy to know; aloof. 2. Inaccessible. —**un′ap·proach′a·ble·ness** *n.* —**un′ap·proach′a·bly** *adv.*

un·arm (un·ärm′) *v.t.* To deprive of weapons; disarm. —**un·armed′** *adj.*

un·as·sail·a·ble (un′ə·sāl′ə·bəl) *adj.* 1. Not capable of being disproved; incontrovertible. 2. Proof against attack or destruction; impregnable. —**un′as·sail′a·ble·ness** *n.* —**un′as·sail′a·bly** *adv.*

un·as·sum·ing (un′ə·sōō′ming) *adj.* Modest. —**un′as·sum′ing·ly** *adv.*

un·at·tached (un′ə·tacht′) *adj.* 1. Not attached. 2. Not engaged or married.

un·a·vail·ing (un′ə·vā′ling) *adj.* Futile; ineffective. —**un′a·vail′ing·ly** *adv.*

un·a·void·a·ble (un′ə·voi′də·bəl) *adj.* That cannot be avoided; inevitable. —**un′a·void′a·bil′i·ty, un′a·void′a·ble·ness** *n.* —**un′a·void′a·bly** *adv.*

un·a·ware (un′ə·wâr′) *adj.* Not aware. —*adv.* Unawares.

un·a·wares (un′ə·wârz′) *adv.* 1. Without warning. 2. Without planning or knowing; inadvertently.

un·bal·ance (un·bal′əns) *v.t.* **·anced, ·anc·ing** 1. To deprive of balance. 2. To disturb or derange, as the mind. —*n.* The state or condition of being unbalanced.

un·bal·anced (un·bal′ənst) *adj.* 1. Not in a state of balance. 2. In bookkeeping, not adjusted so as to balance. 3. Lacking mental balance; erratic.

un·bar (un·bär′) *v.t. & v.i.* **·barred, ·bar·ring** To open or become opened; unlock.

un·bear·a·ble (un′bâr′ə·bəl) *adj.* That cannot be tolerated. —**un′bear′a·ble·ness** *n.* —**un′bear′a·bly** *adv.*

un·be·com·ing (un′bi·kum′ing) *adj.* 1. Not becoming; not suited. 2. Not befitting. 3. Not decorous; improper. —**un′be·com′ing·ly** *adv.* —**un′be·com′ing·ness** *n.*

un·be·known (un′bi·nōn′) *adj.* Unknown: used with *to.* Also **un′be·knownst′** (-nōnst′).

un·be·lief (un′bi·lēf′) *n.* Absence of belief; doubt. —**un′be·liev′er** (-lē′vər) *n.*

un·be·liev·ing (un′bi·lē′ving) *adj.* Doubting; skeptical. —**un′be·liev′ing·ly** *adv.* —**un′be·liev′ing·ness** *n.*

un·bend (un·bend′) *v.t. & v.i.* **·bent, ·bend·ing** 1. To relax, as from tension, exertion, or formality. 2. To straighten (something bent or curved).

un·bend·ing (un·ben′ding) *adj.* 1. Not bending easily; stiff. 2. Unyielding, as in character. —**un·bend′ing·ly** *adv.* —**un·bend′ing·ness** *n.*

un·bi·ased (un·bī′əst) *adj.* Having no bias. Also **un·bi′assed.** —**un·bi′ased·ly** *adv.* —**un·bi′ased·ness** *n.*

un·bid·den (un·bid′n) *adj.* 1. Not invited. 2. Not called forth: *unbidden* thoughts.

un·bind (un·bīnd′) *v.t.* **·bound, ·bind·ing** To free from bindings; undo; release. [OE *unbindan*]

un·blessed (un·blest′) *adj.* 1. Deprived of a blessing. 2. Unhallowed or unholy. 3. Deprived of good fortune. Also **un·blest′.**

un·blush·ing (un·blush′ing) *adj.* 1. Not blushing. 2. Immodest; shameless. —**un·blush′ing·ly** *adv.*

un·bolt (un·bōlt′) *v.t.* To release, as a door, by withdrawing a bolt; unlock.

un·bolt·ed[1] (un·bōl′tid) *adj.* Not fastened by bolts.

un·bolt·ed[2] (un·bōl′tid) *adj.* Not sifted: *unbolted* flour.

un·born (un·bôrn′) *adj.* 1. Not yet born; future. 2. Not in existence.

un·bos·om (un·bŏŏz′əm) *v.t.* 1. To reveal, as one's thoughts or secrets. —*v.i.* 2. To say what is troubling one; tell one's thoughts, feelings, etc. —**un·bos′om·er** *n.*

un·bound·ed (un·boun′did) *adj.* 1. Having no bounds; of unlimited extent. 2. Going beyond bounds; not restrained. —**un·bound′ed·ly** *adv.* —**un·bound′ed·ness** *n.*

un·bowed (un·boud′) *adj.* 1. Not bent or bowed. 2. Not subdued.

un·bri·dled (un·brīd′ld) *adj.* 1. Having no bridle on: an *unbridled* horse. 2. Without restraint: an *unbridled* tongue. —**un·bri′dled·ly** *adv.* —**un·bri′dled·ness** *n.*

un·bro·ken (un·brō′kən) *adj.* 1. Not broken; whole. 2. Uninterrupted; smooth: *unbroken* sleep. 3. Not broken to harness or service, as a draft animal. —**un·bro′ken·ly** *adv.* —**un·bro′ken·ness** *n.*

un·buck·le (un·buk′əl) *v.t. & v.i.* **·led, ·ling** To unfasten the buckle or buckles (of).

unbranched
unbranded
unbreakable
unbreathable
unbreeched
unbridgeable
unbridged
unbridle
unbrotherly
unbruised
unbrushed
unburied
unburned
unburnt
unbusinesslike
unbutton
uncage
uncalculating
uncanceled
uncandid
uncared-for
uncarpeted
uncatalogued
uncaught
unceasing
uncelebrated
uncensored
uncertified
unchained
unchallenged
unchangeable
unchanged
unchanging
unchaperoned
uncharged
uncharted
unchaste
unchastened
unchastised
unchecked
uncheerful
unchewed
unchilled
unchivalrous
unchosen
unchristened
unclaimed
unclarified
unclassed
unclassifiable
unclassified
uncleaned
uncleansed
uncleared
unclipped
unclog
unclouded
uncluttered
uncoagulated
uncoated
uncocked
uncoerced
uncollected
uncolored
uncombed
uncombined
uncomforted
uncomforting
uncomplaining
uncomplaisant
uncomplaisantly
uncompleted
uncompliant
uncomplicated
uncomplimentary
uncomplying
uncompounded
uncomprehended
uncomprehending
uncompressed
uncompromised
unconcealed
unconceded
unconcluded
uncondemned
uncondensed
unconfined
unconfirmed
unconfused
uncongealed
uncongenial
unconnected

un·bur·den (un·bûr′dən) *v.t.* To free from a burden.
un·but·ton (un·but′n) *v.t. & v.i.* To unfasten the button or buttons (of).
un·caged (un·kājd′) *adj.* 1. Not locked up in a cage; free. 2. Released from a cage; freed.
un·called-for (un·kôld′fôr′) *adj.* Not justified; improper or unnecessary.
un·can·ny (un·kan′ē) *adj.* 1. Strange and without explanation. 2. So good as to seem almost supernatural in origin: *uncanny* accuracy. **—un·can′ni·ly** *adv.* **—un·can′ni·ness** *n.*
un·cap (un·kap′) *v.t.* **·capped, ·cap·ping** To take off the cap or covering of.
un·cer·e·mo·ni·ous (un′ser·ə·mō′nē·əs) *adj.* Abrupt; discourteous. **—un′cer·e·mo′ni·ous·ly** *adv.*
un·cer·tain (un·sûr′tən) *adj.* 1. That cannot be predicted with certainty; doubtful. 2. Not having certain knowledge or conviction. 3. Not capable of being relied upon. 4. Not exactly known. **—un·cer′tain·ly** *adv.* **—un·cer′tain·ness** *n.*
un·cer·tain·ty (un·sûr′tən·tē) *n. pl.* **·ties** 1. The state of being uncertain; doubt. 2. A doubtful matter.
un·chain (un·chān′) *v.t.* To release from a chain; set free.
un·char·i·ta·ble (un·char′ə·tə·bəl) *adj.* Not charitable; harsh in judgment. **—un·char′i·ta·ble·ness** *n.* **—un·char′i·ta·bly** *adv.*
un·chris·tian (un·kris′chən) *adj.* 1. Contrary to Christian precepts. 2. Not of the Christian faith.
un·church (un·chûrch′) *v.t.* To deprive of membership in a church.
un·cial (un′shəl, -shē·əl) *adj.* Pertaining to or consisting of a form of letters found in manuscripts from the fourth to the eighth century, and resembling rounded modern capitals. [< L *uncia* inch, ounce] **—un′cial** *n.*
un·cir·cum·cised (un·sûr′kəm·sīzd) *adj.* 1. Not circumcised. 2. Heathen.
un·civ·il (un·siv′əl) *adj.* Wanting in civility; discourteous. **—un·civ′il·ly** *adv.*
un·civ·i·lized (un·siv′ə·līzd) *adj.* Not civilized; barbarous.
un·clad (un·klad′) Alternate past tense and past participle of UNCLOTHE. **—***adj.* Being without clothes; naked.
un·clasp (un·klasp′) *v.t. & v.i.* To release or become released from a clasp.
un·cle (ung′kəl) *n.* The brother of one's father or mother; also, the husband of one's aunt. [< L *avunculus* mother's brother]
un·clean (un·klēn′) *adj.* 1. Not clean; foul. 2. Characterized by impure thoughts. 3. Ceremonially impure. **—un·clean′ness** *n.*
un·clean·ly (un·klen′lē) *adj.* 1. Lacking cleanliness. 2. Impure; indecent; not chaste. **—un·clean′li·ness** *n.*
un·clear (un′klir′) *adj.* 1. Not clear. 2. Not easily understandable; confused or muddled: *unclear* reasoning.
Uncle Sam (sam) The personification of the government or people of the U.S.
Uncle Tom (tom) *Slang* A Negro who is servile to white men: a contemptuous term. [after the chief character in *Uncle Tom's Cabin* by Harriet Beecher Stowe, 1811–96] **—Uncle Tom′ism**
un·cloak (un·klōk′) *v.t.* 1. To remove the cloak or covering from. 2. To unmask; expose.
un·close (un·klōz′) *v.t. & v.i.* **·closed, ·clos·ing** To open or set open.
un·clothe (un·klōth′) *v.t.* **·clothed** or **·clad** (klad), **·cloth·ing** 1. To remove clothes from; undress. 2. To uncover.
un·coil (un·koil′) *v.t. & v.i.* To unwind or become unwound.
un·com·fort·a·ble (un·kum′fər·tə·bəl, -kumpf′tə·bəl) *adj.* 1. Not at ease; feeling discomfort. 2. Causing physical or mental uneasiness. **—un·com′fort·a·ble·ness** *n.* **—un·com′fort·a·bly** *adv.*
un·com·mit·ted (un′kə·mit′id) *adj.* Not committed; esp., not pledged to a particular action, viewpoint, etc.
un·com·mon (un·kom′ən) *adj.* Not common or usual; remarkable. **—un·com′mon·ly** *adv.* **—un·com′mon·ness** *n.*
un·com·mu·ni·ca·tive (un′kə·myōō′nə·kə·tiv, -nə·kā′tiv) *adj.* Not communicative; reserved. **—un′com·mu′ni·ca·tive·ly** *adv.* **—un′com·mu′ni·ca·tive·ness** *n.*
un·com·pro·mis·ing (un·kom′prə·mī′zing) *adj.* Making or admitting of no compromise;

unconquerable
unconquered
unconscientious
unconsecrated
unconsidered
unconsoled
unconsolidated
unconstant
unconstituted
unconstrained
unconstricted
unconsumed
uncontaminated
uncontemplated
uncontending
uncontested
uncontradictable
uncontradicted
uncontrite
uncontrolled
uncontroverted
uncontrovertible
unconvinced
unconvincing
uncooked
uncooperative
uncoordinated
uncorrected
uncorroborated
uncorrupted
uncorruptness
uncountable
uncourteous
uncovered
uncrate
uncredited
uncritical
uncross
uncrowded
uncrushable
uncrystallized
uncultivated
uncultured
uncurable
uncurbed
uncurdled
uncured
uncurl
uncushioned
uncustomary
undamaged
undated
undebatable
undeceived
undecipherable
undeciphered
undeclared
undecomposed
undecorated
undefeated
undefended
undefiled
undefinable
undefined
undelayed
undelineated
undeliverable
undelivered
undemanding
undemocratic
undemonstrable
undenominational
undependable
undepreciated
underived
underogatory
undescribable
undeserved
undeservedly
undeserving
undesignated
undesisting
undespairing
undetachable
undetached
undetectable
undetected
undetectible
undetermined
undeterred
undeveloped
undeviating

inflexible. —**un·com′pro·mis′ing·ly** *adv.* —**un·com′pro·mis′ing·ness** *n.*

un·con·cern (un′kən·sûrn′) *n.* Absence of concern or anxiety; indifference.

un·con·cerned (un′kən·sûrnd′) *adj.* Not concerned or anxious; indifferent. —**un′·con·cern′ed·ly** (-sûr′nid·lē) *adj.* —**un′con·cern′ed·ness** *n.*

un·con·di·tion·al (un′kən·dish′ən·əl) *adj.* Not limited by conditions; absolute. —**un′·con·di′tion·al·ly** *adv.*

un·con·di·tioned (un′kən·dish′ənd) *adj.* 1. Not restricted; unconditional; absolute. 2. *Psychol.* Not acquired; natural.

un·con·scion·a·ble (un·kon′shən·ə·bəl) *adj.* 1. Going beyond reasonable bounds; not justified. 2. Not governed by conscience; unscrupulous. —**un·con′scion·a·ble·ness** *n.* —**un·con′scion·a·bly** *adv.*

un·con·scious (un·kon′shəs) *adj.* 1. Temporarily deprived of consciousness. 2. Unaware: with *of*: *unconscious* of his charm. 3. Not produced by conscious effort. —*n.* *Psychoanal.* That area of the psyche that is not in the immediate field of awareness. —**un·con′scious·ly** *adv.* —**un·con′scious·ness** *n.*

un·con·sti·tu·tion·al (un′kon·sti·tōō′shən·əl, -tyōō′-) *adj.* Contrary to the constitution of a state. —**un′con·sti·tu′tion·al′i·ty** *n.* —**un′con·sti·tu′tion·al·ly** *adv.*

un·con·ven·tion·al (un′kən·ven′shən·əl) *adj.* 1. Not adhering to conventions. 2. Not usual or ordinary. —**un′con·ven′tion·al′i·ty** *n.* —**un′con·ven′tion·al·ly** *adv.*

un·cork (un·kôrk′) *v.t.* To draw the cork from.

un·count·ed (un·koun′tid) *adj.* 1. Not counted. 2. Beyond counting.

un·coup·le (un·kup′əl) *v.t. & v.i.* ·**led,** ·**ling** To disconnect or become disconnected.

un·couth (un·kōōth′) *adj.* 1. Rough; crude. 2. Awkward or odd; ungainly. [OE *uncūth* unknown] —**un·couth′ly** *adv.* —**un·couth′·ness** *n.*

un·cov·er (un·kuv′ər) *v.t.* 1. To remove the covering from. 2. To make known; disclose. —*v.i.* 3. To raise or remove the hat, as in respect.

unc·tion (ungk′shən) *n.* 1. The state or quality of being unctuous. 2. *Eccl.* A ceremonial anointing with oil, as the sacramental rite of anointing those in danger of death: also called **extreme unction.** 3. The act of anointing. [< L *ungere* to anoint]

unc·tu·ous (ungk′chōō·əs) *adj.* 1. Characterized by affected emotion; unduly suave. 2. Greasy; slippery to the touch. [< L *ungere* to anoint] —**unc′tu·ous·ly** *adv.* —**unc′tu·os′i·ty** (-chōō·os′ə·tē), **unc′tu·ous·ness** *n.*

un·cut (un·kut′) *adj.* 1. Not cut. 2. Of a book, having edges that are not trimmed. 3. Not ground, as a gem.

un·daunt·ed (un·dôn′tid) *adj.* Not daunted or intimidated; fearless. —**un·daunt′ed·ly** *adv.*

un·de·ceive (un′di·sēv′) *v.t.* ·**ceived,** ·**ceiv·ing** To free from deception.

un·de·cid·ed (un′di·sī′did) *adj.* 1. Not having the mind made up. 2. Not decided upon.

un·de·ni·a·ble (un′di·nī′ə·bəl) *adj.* 1. That cannot be denied; obviously correct. 2. Unquestionably good; excellent. —**un′de·ni′a·bly** *adv.*

un·der (un′dər) *prep.* 1. Beneath, so as to have something directly above; covered by. 2. In a place lower than; *under* the hill. 3. Beneath the guise or assumption of: *under* a false name. 4. Less than in number, degree, etc.: *under* 10 tons. 5. Lower in rank or position. 6. Dominated by; subordinate to. 7. Subject to the guidance or direction of. 8. With the liability of incurring: *under* penalty of the law. 9. Being the subject of: *under* treatment. 10. During the period of; in the reign of. 11. In conformity to. —*adv.* 1. In or into a position below something; underneath. 2. In or into a lower degree or rank. 3. So as to be covered or hidden. 4. So as to be less than the required amount. —**to go under** To fail, as a business. —*adj.* 1. Situated or moving under something else; lower or lowermost. 2. *Zool.* Ventral. 3. Lower in rank; subordinate. 4. Not enough; insufficient.

under- *combining form* 1. Below in position; on the underside: **underlip, undersole.** 2. Below a surface: **underflooring, underpainting.** 3. Inferior in rank or importance;

undifferentiated
undiffused
undigested
undignified
undiluted
undiminished
undiplomatic
undiscerned
undiscernible
undiscerning
undisciplined
undisclosed
undisconcerted
undiscouraged
undiscovered
undiscriminating
undiscussed
undisguised
undisillusioned
undismayed
undismissed
undispatched
undispensed
undisputed
undisseminated
undissolved
undistilled
undistinguishable
undistinguished
undistributed
undisturbed
undiversified
undivided
undivulged
undomesticated
undoubting
undramatic
undramatically
undrape
undreamed
undreamt
undressed
undried
undrinkable
undutiful
undyed
unearned
uneaten
uneconomic
uneconomical
unedifying
uneducable
uneducated
uneffaced
uneliminated
unembarrassed
unembellished
unemotional
unemphatic
unenclosed
unencumbered
unendangered
unendearing
unending
unendorsed
unendowed
unendurable
unenduring
unenforceable
unenforced
unengaged
unengaging
unenjoyable
unenlightened
unenlivened
unenriched
unentangled
unenterprising
unentertaining
unenthusiastic
unentitled
unenviable
unenvied
unequipped
unerasable
unescapable
unessential
unestablished
unesthetic
unethical
unexacting
unexaggerated

subordinate: **undertreasurer.** 4. Insufficient or insufficiently; less than is usual or proper: **underdone, underpopulated.** 5. Subdued; hidden: **underemphasis, underplot.**

un·der·a·chieve (un′dər·ə·chēv′) *v.i.* **·chieved, ·chiev·ing** To fail to achieve the level of accomplishment suggested by test scores or abilities. **—un′der·a·chieve′ment** *n.* **—un′der·a·chiev′er** *n.*

un·der·age (un′dər·āj′) *adj.* Not of age; immature. Also **un′der-age′.**

un·der·arm[1] (un′dər·ärm′) *adj.* Situated, placed, or used under the arm. **—***n.* The armpit.

un·der·arm[2] (un′dər·ärm′) *adj.* In various sports, as tennis, baseball, etc., executed with the hand lower than the elbow. **—***adv.* In an underarm manner. Also *underhand.*

un·der·bid (un′dər·bid′) *v.t.* **·bid, ·bid·ding** To bid lower than, as in a competition. **—un′der·bid′der** *n.*

un·der·brush (un′dər·brush′) *n.* Small trees and shrubs growing beneath forest trees; undergrowth. Also **un′der·bush′** (-bŏŏsh′).

un·der·car·riage (un′dər·kar′ij) *n.* 1. The framework supporting the body of a structure, as an automobile. 2. The principal landing gear of an aircraft.

un·der·charge (un′dər·chärj′) *v.t.* **·charged, ·charg·ing** To make too small a charge for. **—un′der·charge′** *n.*

un·der·class·man (un′dər·klas′mən) *n. pl.* **·men** (-mən) A freshman or sophomore in a school or college.

un·der·clothes (un′dər·klōz′, -klōthz′) *n.pl.* Clothes to be worn next to the skin. Also **un′der·cloth′ing** (-klōth′ing).

un·der·coat (un′dər·kōt′) *n.* 1. A coat worn under another coat. 2. Underfur. 3. A layer of paint, varnish, etc., beneath another layer: also **un′der·coat′ing.** **—***v.t.* To provide with an undercoat (def. 3).

un·der·cov·er (un′dər·kuv′ər) *adj.* In secret; esp., engaged in spying or secret investigation.

un·der·cur·rent (un′dər·kûr′ənt) *n.* 1. A current, as of water or air, below another or below the surface. 2. A hidden drift or tendency, as of popular sentiments.

un·der·cut (un′dər·kut′) *v.t.* **·cut, ·cut·ting** 1. To cut under. 2. To cut away a lower portion of. 3. To work or sell for lower payment than (a rival). 4. In sports, to strike (a ball) so as to give it a backspin. 5. To lessen or destroy the effectiveness of; undermine.

un·der·de·vel·oped (un′dər·di·vel′əpt) *adj.* 1. Not sufficiently developed. 2. Below a normal or adequate standard in the development of industry, resources, etc.

un·der·done (un′dər·dun′) *adj.* Not fully cooked.

un·der·dog (un′dər·dôg′) *n.* 1. One who is at a disadvantage in a struggle. 2. One who is victimized or downtrodden by society.

un·der·es·ti·mate (un′dər·es′tə·māt) *v.t.* **·mat·ed, ·mat·ing** To put too low an estimate upon. **—un′der·es′ti·mate** (-mit) *n.* **—un′der·es′ti·ma′tion** *n.*

un·der·ex·pose (un′dər·ik·spōz′) *v.t.* **·posed, ·pos·ing** *Photog.* To expose (a film) less than is required for proper development. **—un′der·ex·po′sure** (-spō′zhər) *n.*

un·der·feed (un′dər·fēd′) *v.t.* **·fed, ·feed·ing** 1. To feed too little. 2. To fuel (an engine) from beneath.

un·der·foot (un′dər·fŏŏt′) *adv.* 1. Beneath the feet; down on the ground. 2. In the way.

un·der·fur (un′dər·fûr′) *n.* The coat of dense, fine hair forming the main part of a pelt, as in seals.

un·der·gar·ment (un′dər·gär′mənt) *n.* A garment to be worn under the outer garments.

un·der·go (un′dər·gō′) *v.t.* **·went, ·gone, ·go·ing** 1. To be subjected to. 2. To endure.

un·der·grad·u·ate (un′dər·graj′ŏŏ·it) *n.* A university or college student who has not received a bachelor's degree.

un·der·ground (*adj.* & *n.* un′dər·ground′; *adv.* un′dər·ground′) *adj.* 1. Situated, done, or operating beneath the surface of the ground. 2. Done in secret; clandestine. 3. Of a group, movement, or activity that is experimental, unconventional, or radical: *underground* press, *underground* movie. **—***n.* 1. That which is beneath the surface of the ground. 2. A group secretly organized to oppose those in control of a government or country. 3. *Brit.* A subway. **—***adv.* 1. Beneath the surface of the ground. 2. Secretly.

unexalted
unexamined
unexcavated
unexcelled
unexceptional
unexchangeable
unexcited
unexciting
unexcluded
unexcused
unexecuted
unexercised
unexpired
unexplainable
unexplained
unexploded
unexploited
unexplored
unexposed
unexpressed
unexpurgated
unextended
unextinguished
unfading
unfaltering
unfashionable
unfastened
unfathomable
unfearing
unfeasible
unfed
unfelt
unfeminine
unfenced
unfermented
unfertile
unfetter
unfilial
unfilled
unfilmed
unfiltered
unfired
unfittingly
unflagging
unflattering
unflavored
unflickering
unforbearing
unforbidden
unforced
unforeseeable
unforeseen
unforetold
unforfeited
unforged
unforgetting
unforgivable
unforgiven
unforgiving
unforgotten
unformulated
unforsaken
unfortified
unfought
unfound
unframed
unfree
unfreeze
unfrequented
unfruitful
unfulfilled
unfurnished
ungallant
ungarnished
ungathered
ungenerous
ungentle
ungentlemanly
ungently
ungifted
unglazed
unglue
ungoverned
ungraceful
ungraded
ungrained
ungrammatical
ungratified
ungrudging
unguided
unhackneyed
unhailed

un·der·growth (un′dər·grōth′) *n.* A growth of smaller plants among larger ones in a forest.

un·der·hand (un′dər·hand′) *adj.* 1. Done or acting in a secret manner; sly. 2. In sports, underarm. —*adv.* 1. Slyly. 2. Underarm[2].

un·der·hand·ed (un′der·han′did) *adj.* 1. Underhand. 2. Short-handed. —**un′der·hand′ed·ly** *adv.* —**un′der·hand′ed·ness** *n.*

un·der·lay (un′dər·lā′) *v.t.* **·laid, ·lay·ing** 1. To place (one thing) under another. 2. To furnish with a base or lining.

un·der·lie (un′dər·lī′) *v.t.* **·lay, ·lain, ·ly·ing** 1. To lie below or under. 2. To be the basis or support of: the principle that *underlies* a scheme. [OE *underlicgan*]

un·der·line (un′dər·līn′) *v.t.* **·lined, ·lin·ing** 1. To mark with a line underneath. 2. To emphasize.

un·der·ling (un′dər·ling) *n.* A subordinate; an inferior.

un·der·ly·ing (un′dər·lī′ing) *adj.* 1. Lying under. 2. Fundamental.

un·der·mine (un′dər·mīn′, un′dər·mīn) *v.t.* **·mined, ·min·ing** 1. To excavate beneath; dig a mine or passage under. 2. To weaken by wearing away at the base. 3. To weaken or impair secretly or by degrees: to *undermine* one's health. —**un′der·min′er** *n.*

un·der·most (un′dər·mōst′) *adj.* Having the lowest place or position.

un·der·neath (un′dər·nēth′, -nēth′) *adv.* 1. In a place below. 2. On the lower side. —*prep.* 1. Beneath; under; below. 2. Under the form or appearance of. 3. Under the authority of. —*adj.* Lower. —*n.* The lower part or side. [OE *underneothan*]

un·der·nour·ish (un′dər·nûr′ish) *v.t.* To provide with too little nourishment for proper health and growth. —**un′der·nour′ish·ment** *n.*

un·der·pants (un′dər·pants′) *n.pl.* An undergarment worn over the loins.

un·der·pass (un′dər·pas′) *n.* A road or way beneath.

un·der·pay (un′dər·pā′) *v.t.* **·paid, ·pay·ing** To pay insufficiently.

un·der·pin·ning (un′dər·pin′ing) *n.* 1. Material or framework used to support a wall or building from below. 2. *pl.* Underlying causes or principles.

un·der·priv·i·leged (un′dər·priv′ə·lijd) *adj.* Not privileged to enjoy certain material or social benefits because of poverty, illiteracy, etc.

un·der·pro·duce (un′dər·prə·dōōs′) *v.t.* & *v.i.* **·duced, ·duc·ing** To produce below capacity or below requirements. —**un′der·pro·duc′tion** (-duk′shən) *n.*

un·der·rate (un′dər·rāt′) *v.t.* **·rat·ed, ·rat·ing** To rate too low; underestimate.

un·der·score (un′dər·skôr′) *v.t.* **·scored, ·scor·ing** 1. To put a line under. 2. To emphasize. —*n.* A line drawn beneath a word, etc., as for emphasis.

un·der·sea (un′dər·sē′) *adj.* Existing, carried on, or adapted for use beneath the surface of the sea. —*adv.* Beneath the surface of the sea: also **un′der·seas′** (-sēz′).

un·der·sec·re·tar·y (un′dər·sek′rə·ter′ē) *n.* *pl.* **·tar·ies** An official who ranks next below a secretary.

un·der·sell (un′dər·sel′) *v.t.* **·sold, ·sell·ing** 1. To sell at a lower price than. 2. To sell for less than the real value. —**un′der·sell′er** *n.*

un·der·shirt (un′dər·shûrt′) *n.* A garment worn beneath a shirt, generally of cotton.

un·der·shoot (un′dər·shōōt′) *v.t.* & *v.i.* **·shot, ·shoot·ing** 1. To shoot short of or below (the mark, target, etc.). 2. To land an airplane short of (the runway).

un·der·shot (un′dər·shot′) *adj.* 1. Propelled by water that flows underneath: said of a water wheel. 2. Projecting, as the lower jaw or teeth.

un·der·side (un′dər·sīd′) *n.* The lower or under side or surface.

un·der·signed (un′dər·sīnd′) *adj.* Having one's signature at the foot of a document. —*n.* The subscriber or subscribers to a document: with *the.*

un·der·sized (un′dər·sīzd′) *adj.* Of less than the normal or average size. Also **un′der·size′**.

un·der·slung (un′dər·slung′) *adj.* *Mech.* Having the springs fixed to the axles from below: said of certain automobiles.

un·der·staffed (un′dər·staft′) *adj.* Having too small a staff.

un·der·stand (un′dər·stand′) *v.* **·stood,**

unhampered
unharassed
unharbored
unhardened
unharmed
unharmful
unharmonious
unharnessed
unharvested
unhatched
unhealed
unhealthful
unheated
unheeded
unhelpful
unheralded
unheroic
unhesitating
unhindered
unhistorical
unhonored
unhoped
unhostile
unhoused
unhung
unhurried
unhurt
unhygienic
unhyphenated
unidentified
unidiomatic
unilluminated
unillustrated
unimaginable
unimaginative
unimagined
unimitated
unimpaired
unimpassioned
unimpeded
unimportant
unimposing
unimpressed
unimpressionable
unimpressive
unimproved
uninaugurated
unincorporated
uninfected
uninfested
uninflected
uninfluenced
uninfluential
uninformative
uninformed
uninhabitable
uninhabited
uninhibited
uninitiated
uninjured
uninspired
uninspiring
uninstructed
uninstructive
uninsurable
uninsured
unintellectual
unintelligent
unintelligibility
unintelligible
unintended
unintentional
uninterested
uninteresting
uninterpreted
uninterrupted
unintimidated
uninventive
uninvested
uninvited
uninviting
uninvolved
unjoined
unjointed
unjudicial
unjustifiable
unkindliness
unknowing
unlabeled
unladylike
unlamented
unlaundered

•**stand•ing** *v.t.* 1. To come to know the meaning or import of; apprehend. 2. To comprehend the nature or character of. 3. To have comprehension or mastery of. 4. To be aware of; realize. 5. To have been told. 6. To infer the meaning of. 7. To accept as a condition or stipulation. 8. To supply in thought when unexpressed. 9. To be in agreement with; be privately in sympathy with. —*v.i.* 10. To have understanding; comprehend. 11. To be informed; believe. [OE *under-* under + *standan* to stand] —**un′•der•stand′a•ble** *adj.* —**un′der•stand′a•bly** *adv.*

un•der•stand•ing (un′dər·stan′ding) *n.* 1. The act of one who understands or the resulting state; comprehension. 2. The sum of the mental powers by which knowledge is acquired, retained, and extended. 3. The facts or elements of a case as apprehended by any one individual. 4. An informal or confidential compact; also, the thing agreed on. 5. An arrangement or settlement of differences. —*adj.* 1. Possessing comprehension and good sense. 2. Tolerant or sympathetic. —**un′der•stand′•ing•ly** *adv.* —**un′der•stand′ing•ness** *n.*

un•der•state (un′dər·stāt′) *v.* •**stat•ed,** •**stat•ing** *v.t.* 1. To state with less force than the truth warrants or allows. 2. To state, as a number or dimension, as less than the true one. —*v.i.* 3. To make an understatement.

un•der•state•ment (un′dər·stāt′mənt) *n.* A statement that is deliberately restrained in tone.

un•der•stood (un′dər·stŏŏd′) Past tense and past participle of UNDERSTAND. —*adj.* 1. Assumed; agreed upon by all. 2. Assumed when unexpressed, as the subject of a sentence.

un•der•stud•y (un′dər·stud′ē) *v.t. & v.i.* •**stud•ied,** •**stud•y•ing** To study (a part) in order to be able, if necessary, to take the place of the actor playing it. —*n. pl.* •**stud•ies** An actor or actress who can take the place of another actor in a given role when necessary.

un•der•take (un′dər·tāk′) *v.* •**took,** •**tak•en,** •**tak•ing** *v.t.* 1. To take upon oneself; agree or attempt to do; begin. 2. To contract to do; pledge oneself to. 3. To guarantee or promise. 4. To take under charge or guidance. —*v.i.* 5. To make oneself responsible or liable: with *for*.

un•der•tak•er (un′dər·tā′kər) *n.* One whose business it is to arrange for the cremation or burial of the dead and to oversee funerals.

un•der•tak•ing (un′dər·tā′king; *for def. 2* un′dər·tā′king) *n.* 1. Something undertaken; a task. 2. The business of an undertaker. 3. An engagement, promise, or guaranty.

un•der-the-count•er (un′dər·thə·koun′tər) *adj.* Illegal; unlawful.

un•der•tone (un′dər·tōn′) *n.* 1. A subdued voice or a whisper. 2. A subdued shade of a color. 3. An implicit meaning or suggestion.

un•der•tow (un′dər·tō′) *n.* The seaward undercurrent below the surf.

un•der•val•ue (un′dər·val′yōō) *v.t.* •**ued,** •**u•ing** To value too lightly. —**un′der•val′u•a′tion** *n.*

un•der•wa•ter (un′dər·wô′tər, -wot′ər) *adj. & adv.* Below the surface of a body of water; also, below the water line of a ship.

un•der•way (un′dər·wā′) *adv.* In progress or into operation. Also **under way.**

un•der•wear (un′dər·wâr′) *n.* Garments worn underneath the ordinary outer garments.

un•der•weight (un′dər·wāt′) *adj.* Having less than the normal weight.

un•der•went (un′dər·went′) Past tense of UNDERGO.

un•der•world (un′dər·wûrld′) *n.* 1. In mythology, the abode of the dead. 2. The part of society engaged in crime or vice; esp., organized criminals.

un•der•write (un′dər·rīt′) *v.t.* •**wrote,** •**writ•ten,** •**writ•ing** 1. To write beneath; subscribe. 2. In finance, to execute and deliver (a policy of insurance on specified property); insure; assume (a risk) by way of insurance. 3. To engage to buy, at a determined price and time, all or part of the stock in (a new enterprise or company) that is not subscribed for by the public. 4. Loosely, to assume financial responsibility for, as an enterprise. —**un′der•writ′er** *n.*

unleased
unleavened
unlessened
unlet
unlevel
unlicensed
unlighted
unlikable
unlined
unliquefied
unliquidated
unlit
unlively
unlocked
unlovable
unloved
unloving
unmagnified
unmanageable
unmanful
unmanned
unmannered
unmanufactured
unmapped
unmarked
unmarketable
unmarred
unmarriageable
unmarried
unmatched
unmeant
unmeasurable
unmeasured
unmechanical
unmelodious
unmelted
unmendable
unmentioned
unmerited
unmethodical
unmilitary
unmilled
unmingled
unmirthful
unmistaken
unmixed
unmodified
unmoistened
unmold
unmolested
unmollified
unmortgaged
unmotivated
unmounted
unmourned
unmovable
unmoved
unmoving
unmusical
unmuzzle
unmystified
unnamable
unnamed
unnaturalized
unnavigable
unneeded
unneedful
unnegotiable
unneighborly
unnoticeable
unnoticed
unobjectionable
unobliging
unobscured
unobservant
unobserved
unobserving
unobstructed
unobtainable
unobtrusive
unobtrusiveness
unoffending
unoffered
unofficial
unoiled
unopened
unopposed
unoppressed
unordained
unoriginal
unorthodox
unostentatious

un·de·sir·a·ble (un′di·zīr′ə·bəl) *adj.* Not desirable; objectionable. —*n.* An objectionable person. —**un′de·sir′a·bil′i·ty, un′de·sir′a·ble·ness** *n.* —**un′de·sir′a·bly** *adv.*
un·dies (un′dēz) *n.pl. Informal* Women's or children's underwear.
un·do (un·do͞o′) *v.t.* **·did, ·done, ·do·ing** 1. To cause to be as if never done; reverse; annul. 2. To loosen or untie, as a knot, etc. 3. To unfasten and open, as a parcel. 4. To bring to ruin; destroy. [OE *undōn*] —**un·do′er** *n.*
un·do·ing (un·do͞o′ing) *n.* 1. Reversal, cancellation, etc., of what has been done. 2. Destruction; ruin; also, the cause of ruin.
un·done[1] (un·dun′) *adj.* 1. Untied; unfastened. 2. Ruined. [Orig. pp. of UNDO]
un·done[2] (un·dun′) *adj.* Not done.
un·doubt·ed (un·dou′tid) *adj.* Assured beyond question; being beyond a doubt. —**un·doubt′ed·ly** *adv.*
un·dreamed-of (un·drēmd′uv′, -ov′) *adj.* Not conceived of in the mind; not imaginable. Also **un·dreamt′-of** (-dremt′-).
un·dress (un·dres′) *v.t.* 1. To divest of clothes; strip. —*v.i.* 2. To remove one's clothing. —*n.* Casual or ordinary attire, as distinguished from formal dress.
un·due (un·do͞o′, -dyo͞o′) *adj.* 1. Excessive; disproportionate. 2. Not justified by law; illegal. 3. Not due; not yet demandable. 4. Not appropriate; improper.
un·du·lant (un′dyə·lənt, -də-) *adj.* Undulating; waving.
undulant fever *Pathol.* A disease transmitted to man in the milk of infected cows and goats, and characterized by recurrent fever, swelling of the joints, neuralgic pains, etc.
un·du·late (*v.* un′dyə·lāt, -də-; *adj.* un′dyə·lit, -lāt, -də-) *v.t. & v.i.* **·lat·ed, ·lat·ing** 1. To move or cause to move like a wave or in waves. 2. To have or cause to have a wavy appearance. —*adj.* 1. Having a wavy margin, as a leaf. 2. Having wavelike markings, as of color: also **un′du·lat′ed** (-lā′tid). [< L *unda* wave]
un·du·la·tion (un′dyə·lā′shən, -də-) *n.* 1. The act of undulating. 2. A waving or sinuous motion or appearance. 3. A wave. —**un′du·la·to′ry** (-lə·tôr′ē), **un′du·lous** (-ləs) *adj.*
un·du·ly (un·do͞o′lē, -dyo͞o′-) *adv.* 1. Excessively. 2. Unjustly.
un·dy·ing (un·dī′ing) *adj.* Immortal; everlasting.
un·earth (un·ûrth′) *v.t.* 1. To dig up from the earth. 2. To reveal by searching; discover.
un·earth·ly (un·ûrth′lē) *adj.* 1. Not earthly; sublime. 2. Weird; terrifying; supernatural. 3. *Informal* Ridiculous. —**un·earth′li·ness** *n.*
un·eas·y (un·ē′zē) *adj.* **·eas·i·er, ·eas·i·est** 1. Lacking ease, assurance, or security; disturbed. 2. Not affording ease or rest. 3. Showing embarrassment; strained. —**un·eas′i·ly** *adv.* —**un·eas′i·ness** *n.*
un·em·ploy·a·ble (un′əm·ploi′ə·bəl) *adj.* Not employable. —*n.* A person who, because of illness, age, mental or physical incapacity, etc., cannot be employed.
un·em·ployed (un′əm·ploid′) *adj.* 1. Out of work. 2. Not being put to use; idle. —*n.* A jobless person. —**un′em·ploy′ment** *n.*
un·e·qual (un·ē′kwəl) *adj.* 1. Not having equal extension, duration, amounts, ability, status, etc. 2. Inadequate for the purpose: with *to.* 3. Varying; irregular. 4. Not balanced; not symmetrical. —**un·e′qual·ly** *adv.*
un·e·qualed (un·ē′kwəld) *adj.* Not equaled or matched; supreme. Also **un·e′qualled.**
un·e·quiv·o·cal (un′i·kwiv′ə·kəl) *adj.* Understandable in only one way; not equivocal. —**un′e·quiv′o·cal·ly** *adv.*
un·err·ing (un·ûr′ing, -er′-) *adj.* 1. Making no mistakes; not erring. 2. Certain; accurate. —**un·err′ing·ly** *adv.*
UNESCO (yo͞o·nes′kō) The United Nations Educational, Scientific and Cultural Organization. Also **U·nes′co.**
un·e·ven (un·ē′vən) *adj.* 1. Not even, smooth, parallel, or level; rough. 2. Not divisible by two without remainder; odd: said of numbers. 3. Not uniform; variable; spasmodic. —**un·e′ven·ly** *adv.* —**un·e′ven·ness** *n.*
un·e·vent·ful (un′i·vent′fəl) *adj.* Devoid of noteworthy events; quiet. —**un′e·vent′ful·ly** *adv.*

unostentatiousness
unowned
unpacified
unpaid
unpainful
unpainted
unpaired
unpalatable
unpardonable
unparted
unpasteurized
unpatented
unpatriotic
unpaved
unpeaceful
unpedigreed
unpeg
unpensioned
unpeopled
unperceived
unperceiving
unperfected
unperformed
unperplexed
unpersuadable
unpersuaded
unpersuasive
unperturbed
unphilosophical
unpicked
unpierced
unpile
unpin
unpitied
unpitying
unplaced
unplagued
unplanned
unplanted
unpleasing
unpledged
unplowed
unplucked
unplug
unpoetic
unpolarized
unpolished
unpolitical
unpolluted
unpopulated
unposed
unpredictable
unpremeditated
unpreoccupied
unprepared
unprepossessing
unprescribed
unpresentable
unpreserved
unpressed
unpretentious
unpretentiousness
unprevailing
unpreventable
unprevented
unprinted
unprivileged
unprocessed
unproductive
unprofitable
unprogressive
unprohibited
unpromising
unprompted
unpronounced
unpropitious
unproportioned
unprotected
unproved
unproven
unprovoked
unpublishable
unpublished
unpunishable
unpunished
unpurified
unpuzzle
unqualifying
unquenchable
unquestioning
unquotable
unratified

un·ex·am·pled (un′ig·zam′pəld) *adj.* Having no precedent.
un·ex·cep·tion·a·ble (un′ik·sep′shən·ə·bəl) *adj.* That cannot be objected to. **—un′ex·cep′tion·a·ble·ness** *n.* **—un′ex·cep′tion·a·bly** *adv.*
un·ex·pect·ed (un′ik·spek′tid) *adj.* Not expected; unforeseen. **—un′ex·pect′ed·ly** *adv.* **—un′ex·pect′ed·ness** *n.*
un·fail·ing (un·fā′ling) *adj.* 1. Giving or constituting a supply that never fails; inexhaustible. 2. Not falling short of need, hope, or expectation. 3. Sure; infallible. **—un·fail′ing·ly** *adv.* **—un·fail′ing·ness** *n.*
un·fair (un·fâr′) *adj.* 1. Characterized by partiality or prejudice; not fair or just. 2. Dishonest; fraudulent. **—un·fair′ly** *adv.* **—un·fair′ness** *n.*
un·faith·ful (un·fāth′fəl) *adj.* 1. Not having kept faith; unworthy of trust. 2. Not true to marriage vows; adulterous. 3. Not accurate or exact. **—un·faith′ful·ly** *adv.* **—un·faith′ful·ness** *n.*
un·fa·mil·iar (un′fə·mil′yər) *adj.* 1. Not having acquaintance: with *with.* 2. Not known or recognizable. **—un′fa·mil′i·ar′i·ty** (-mil′ē·ar′ə·tē) *n.* **—un′fa·mil′iar·ly** *adv.*
un·fast·en (un·fas′ən) *v.t. & v.i.* To untie or become untied; loosen; open.
un·fa·vor·a·ble (un·fā′vər·ə·bəl) *adj.* Not favorable; adverse. Also *Brit.* **un·fa′vour·a·ble.** **—un·fa′vor·a·ble·ness** *n.* **—un·fa′vor·a·bly** *adv.*
un·feel·ing (un·fē′ling) *adj.* 1. Not sympathetic; hard; cruel. 2. Devoid of feeling or sensation. **—un·feel′ing·ly** *adv.* **—un·feel′ing·ness** *n.*
un·feigned (un·fānd′) *adj.* Not feigned or pretended; sincere; genuine. **—un·feign·ed·ly** (un·fā′nid·lē) *adv.*
un·fin·ished (un·fin′isht) *adj.* 1. Not finished; incomplete. 2. Having no finish or special surface treatment, as wood.
un·fit (un·fit′) *adj.* 1. Having no fitness; unsuitable. 2. Not appropriate; improper. 3. Not in sound physical condition.
un·fix (un·fiks′) *v.t.* 1. To unfasten. 2. To unsettle.
un·flap·pa·ble (un·flap′ə·bəl) *adj.* Characterized by total composure; imperturbable. **—un·flap′pa·bil′i·ty** *n.*
un·fledged (un·flejd′) *adj.* 1. Not yet fledged, as a young bird. 2. Immature; inexperienced.
un·flinch·ing (un·flin′ching) *adj.* Not shrinking from danger, pain, etc.; brave. **—un·flinch′ing·ly** *adv.*
un·fold (un·fōld′) *v.t.* 1. To open or spread out (something folded). 2. To make clear by detailed explanation. 3. To evolve; develop. *—v.i.* 4. To become opened. 5. To become manifest. [OE *unfealdan*] **—un·fold′er** *n.*
un·for·get·ta·ble (un′fər·get′ə·bəl) *adj.* Not forgettable; memorable. **—un′for·get′ta·bly** *adv.*
un·formed (un·fôrmd′) *adj.* 1. Devoid of shape or form. 2. Not fully developed in character. 3. Unorganized.
un·for·tu·nate (un·fôr′chə·nit) *adj.* 1. Not fortunate or happy; unsuccessful. 2. Causing or attended by ill fortune; disastrous. *—n.* One who is unfortunate. **—un·for′tu·nate·ly** *adv.* **—un·for′tu·nate·ness** *n.*
un·found·ed (un·foun′did) *adj.* 1. Having no foundation; groundless. 2. Not founded or established. **—un·found′ed·ly** *adv.* **—un·found′ed·ness** *n.*
un·friend·ly (un·frend′lē) *adj.* 1. Unkindly disposed; inimical; hostile. 2. Not favorable or propitious. **—un·friend′li·ness** *n.*
un·frock (un·frok′) *v.t.* 1. To depose, as a monk or priest, from ecclesiastical rank. 2. To divest of a frock or gown.
un·furl (un·fûrl′) *v.t. & v.i.* 1. To spread open, as a flag. 2. To spread out; expand.
un·gain·ly (un·gān′lē) *adj.* Lacking grace; awkward. **—un·gain′li·ness** *n.*
un·god·ly (un·god′lē) *adj.* 1. Having no reverence for God; impious. 2. Wicked; sinful. 3. *Informal* Outrageous. **—un·god′li·ness** *n.*
un·gov·ern·a·ble (un·guv′ər·nə·bəl) *adj.* Not capable of being governed or controlled. **—un·gov′ern·a·ble·ness** *n.* **—un·gov′ern·a·bly** *adv.*
un·gra·cious (un·grā′shəs) *adj.* 1. Lacking in graciousness of manner. 2. Not pleasing; offensive. **—un·gra′cious·ly** *adv.* **—un·gra′cious·ness** *n.*
un·grate·ful (un·grāt′fəl) *adj.* 1. Not feeling or showing gratitude; not thankful.

unravaged
unreachable
unreached
unreadable
unrealistic
unrealizable
unrealized
unreasoned
unrebuked
unreceptive
unreciprocated
unreclaimed
unrecognizable
unrecognized
unrecompensed
unreconcilable
unreconciled
unrecorded
unrecoverable
unrecruited
unrectified
unredeemed
unredressed
unrefined
unreflecting
unrefreshed
unrefreshing
unregarded
unregistered
unregretted
unregulated
unrehearsed
unrelated
unrelaxed
unreliable
unrelieved
unrelished
unremarkable
unremarked
unremedied
unremembered
unremitted
unremorseful
unremovable
unremoved
unremunerated
unremunerative
unrendered
unrenewed
unrenounced
unrenowned
unrented
unrepaid
unrepairable
unrepaired
unrepealed
unrepentant
unrepenting
unreplaced
unreplenished
unreported
unrepresentative
unrepresented
unrepressed
unrequested
unrequited
unresented
unresigned
unresistant
unresisting
unresolved
unrespectable
unresponsive
unrested
unresting
unrestrainable
unrestricted
unretentive
unretracted
unreturned
unrevealed
unrevenged
unreversed
unrevised
unrevoked
unrewarded
unrhythmical
unrightful
unripened
unrisen
unroasted
unrobe

2. Not pleasant; disagreeable. —**un·grate′·ful·ly** *adv.* —**un·grate′ful·ness** *n.*

un·guard·ed (un·gär′did) *adj.* 1. Having no guard; being without protection. 2. Characterized by lack of caution or discretion. —**un·guard′ed·ly** *adv.* —**un·guard′·ed·ness** *n.*

un·guent (ung′gwent) *n.* Any ointment or salve. [< L *unguere* to anoint]

un·gu·late (ung′gyə·lit, -lāt) *adj.* 1. Having hoofs. 2. Designating a large group of hoofed mammals, including the elephant, rhinoceros, horse, hog, and all the ruminants. [< L *ungula* hoof] —**un′gu·late** *n.*

un·hal·lowed (un·hal′ōd) *adj.* 1. Not consecrated or made holy. 2. Not holy; wicked.

un·hand (un·hand′) *v.t.* To remove one's hand from; release from the hand; let go.

un·hand·y (un·han′dē) *adj.* ·**hand·i·er,** ·**hand·i·est** 1. Inconvenient; hard to handle. 2. Clumsy; lacking in manual skill. —**un·hand′i·ly** *adv.* —**un·hand′i·ness** *n.*

un·hap·py (un·hap′ē) *adj.* ·**pi·er,** ·**pi·est** 1. Sad; miserable; depressed. 2. Unlucky; unfortunate. 3. Not tactful or appropriate. —**un·hap′pi·ly** *adv.* —**un·hap′pi·ness** *n.*

un·health·y (un·hel′thē) *adj.* ·**health·i·er,** ·**health·i·est** 1. Lacking health or vigor; sickly; also, indicating such a condition. 2. Injurious to health. 3. Morally unsound. —**un·health′i·ly** *adv.* —**un·health′i·ness** *n.*

un·heard (un·hûrd′) *adj.* 1. Not perceived by the ear. 2. Not granted a hearing. 3. Obscure; unknown.

un·heard-of (un·hûrd′uv′, -ov′) *adj.* Not known of before.

un·hinge (un·hinj′) *v.t.* ·**hinged,** ·**hing·ing** 1. To take from the hinges. 2. To detach; dislodge. 3. To unsettle, as the mind.

un·hitch (un·hich′) *v.t.* To set loose; detach.

un·ho·ly (un·hō′lē) *adj.* ·**ho·li·er,** ·**ho·li·est** 1. Not sacred or hallowed. 2. Lacking purity; wicked; sinful. 3. *Informal* Terrible; dreadful. [OE *unhālig*] —**un·ho′li·ly** *adv.* —**un·ho′li·ness** *n.*

un·hook (un·hook′) *v.t.* 1. To remove from a hook. 2. To unfasten the hook or hooks of. —*v.i.* 3. To become unhooked.

un·hoped-for (un·hōpt′fôr′) *adj.* Not expected or hoped for: an *unhoped-for* solution.

un·horse (un·hôrs′) *v.t.* ·**horsed,** ·**hors·ing** 1. To throw from a horse. 2. To dislodge; overthrow.

uni- *combining form* Having or consisting of one only. [< L *unus* one]

u·ni·cam·er·al (yōō′nə·kam′ər·əl) *adj.* Consisting of but one legislative chamber.

UNICEF (yōō′nə·sef) The United Nations Children's Emergency Fund. Also **U′ni·cef.**

u·ni·cel·lu·lar (yōō′nə·sel′yə·lər) *adj. Biol.* Consisting of a single cell, as a protozoan.

u·ni·col·or (yōō′nə·kul′ər) *adj.* Of one color.

u·ni·corn (yōō′nə·kôrn) *n.* A mythical horselike animal with one horn. [< L *unus* one + *cornu* horn]

u·ni·cy·cle (yōō′nə·sī′kəl) *n.* A vehicle consisting of a metal frame mounted on one wheel and propelled by means of pedals.

un·i·den·ti·fied flying object (un·ī·den′·tə·fīd) Any of various objects alleged to have been seen flying in the sky and believed by some to come from outer space. Abbr. *UFO.*

u·ni·di·rec·tion·al (yōō′nə·di·rek′shən·əl, -dī-) *adj.* Having, moving, or equipped to operate in only one direction.

u·ni·form (yōō′nə·fôrm) *adj.* 1. Being always the same or alike, as in form, quality, degree, etc.; not varying. 2. Agreeing or identical with each other; alike. —*n.* 1. A distinctive form of dress worn by members of the same organization or service, as soldiers, sailors, etc. 2. A single suit of such clothes. —*v.t.* 1. To put into or clothe with a uniform. 2. To make uniform. [< L *unus* one + *forma* form] —**u′ni·form·ly** *adv.* —**u′ni·form·ness** *n.*

u·ni·formed (yōō′nə·fôrmd) *adj.* Dressed in uniform.

u·ni·form·i·ty (yōō′nə·fôr′mə·tē) *n. pl.* ·**ties** 1. The state or quality of being uniform; also, an instance of it. 2. Conformity, as in opinions or religion. 3. Monotony; sameness.

u·ni·fy (yōō′nə·fī) *v.t. & v.i.* ·**fied,** ·**fy·ing** To combine into a unit; become or cause to be one. [< L *unus* one + *facere* to make] —**u′ni·fi′a·ble** *adj.* —**u′ni·fi·ca′tion** *n.* —**u′ni·fi′er** *n.*

unromantic
unroof
unrounded
unruled
unsafe
unsaid
unsalable
unsalaried
unsalted
unsanctified
unsanctioned
unsanitary
unsated
unsatisfactorily
unsatisfactory
unsatisfied
unsatisfying
unsatisfyingly
unsaved
unscaled
unscanned
unscarred
unscented
unscheduled
unscholarly
unschooled
unscientific
unscientifically
unscoured
unscraped
unscratched
unscreened
unsealed
unseasoned
unseated
unseaworthy
unseconded
unsecured
unseeded
unseeing
unseen
unsegmented
unselected
unselective
unsensitive
unsent
unsentimental
unserved
unserviceable
unset
unsevered
unsewn
unshaded
unshadowed
unshaken
unshapely
unshared
unshaven
unshed
unshelled
unsheltered
unshielded
unshod
unshorn
unshrinkable
unshrinking
unshrunk
unshut
unsifted
unsigned
unsilenced
unsimilar
unsinkable
unsized
unslaked
unsleeping
unsmiling
unsmilingly
unsmoked
unsocial
unsoftened
unsoiled
unsold
unsoldierly
unsolicited
unsolicitous
unsoluble
unsolvable
unsolved
unsoothed
unsophistication
unsorted

u·ni·lat·er·al (yōō′nə·lat′ər·əl) *adj.* 1. Of, pertaining to, or existing on one side only. 2. Made, undertaken, done, or signed by only one of two or more people or parties. 3. One-sided. —**u′ni·lat′er·al·ly** *adv.* —**u′ni·lat′er·al·ism, u′ni·lat′er·al′i·ty** (-al′ə·tē) *n.*

un·im·peach·a·ble (un′im·pē′chə·bəl) *adj.* Not to be called into question as regards truth, honesty, etc. —**un′im·peach′a·bly** *adv.*

un·ion (yōōn′yən) *n.* 1. The act of uniting, or the state of being united; also, that which is so formed. 2. A joining of nations, states, parties, etc., for some mutual interest or purpose. 3. The joining of two persons in marriage; also, the state of wedlock. 4. A labor union. 5. *Mech.* A device for connecting parts of machinery; esp., a coupling or connection for pipes or rods. 6. A device emblematic of union, used in a flag or emblem. 7. *Math.* A set consisting of all the elements belonging to two or more sets. —**the Union** The U.S.; esp., the Federal government during the Civil War. —*adj.* Of, pertaining to, or adhering to a union, esp. a labor union. [< L *unus* one]

un·ion·ism (yōōn′yən·iz′əm) *n.* 1. The principle of combining for unity of purpose and action. 2. The principle or the support of labor unions. —**un′ion·ist** *n.* —**un′ion·is′tic** *adj.*

un·ion·ize (yōōn′yən·īz) *v.* **·ized, ·iz·ing** *v.t.* 1. To cause to join, or to organize into a union, esp. a labor union. 2. To make conform to the rules, etc., of a union. —*v.i.* 3. To become a member of or organize a labor union. —**un′ion·i·za′tion** *n.*

union jack A flag consisting of the union only.

Union Jack The British national flag, a combination of the flags of England, Scotland, and Ireland.

union shop An industrial establishment that hires only members of a labor union or those who promise to join a union within a specified time.

union suit A one-piece undergarment consisting of shirt and drawers.

u·nique (yōō·nēk′) *adj.* 1. Being the only one of its kind; sole. 2. Being without or having no equal or like. 3. Loosely, unusual, rare, or notable. [< L *unus* one] —**u·nique′ly** *adv.* —**u·nique′ness** *n.*

u·ni·sex (yōō′nə·seks′) *Informal adj.* For or appropriate to both sexes: *unisex* fashions.

u·ni·sex·u·al (yōō′nə·sek′shōō·əl) *adj.* Of only one sex; also, having sexual organs of one sex only.

u·ni·son (yōō′nə·sən, -zən) *n.* 1. A sounding of the same words, tones, etc., simultaneously: with *in*: they answered in *unison.* 2. Complete accord or agreement. 3. *Music* A state in which instruments or voices perform identical parts simultaneously, in the same or different octaves. [< L *uni-* one + *sonus* sound]

u·nit (yōō′nit) *n.* 1. A single person or thing regarded as an individual but belonging to an entire group. 2. A subdivision of a similar but larger body or group. 3. A piece of equipment, usu. part of a larger object and having a specific function. 4. A standard quantity; measure. 5. *Math.* A quantity whose measure is represented by the number 1; a least whole number. [Back formation < UNITY]

U·ni·tar·i·an (yōō′nə·târ′ē·ən) *n.* A member of a religious denomination that emphasizes complete freedom of religious opinion. —**U′ni·tar′i·an** *adj.* —**U′ni·tar′i·an·ism** *n.*

u·ni·tar·y (yōō′nə·ter′ē) *adj.* 1. Of or pertaining to a unit. 2. Characterized by or based on unity. 3. Having the nature of a unit; whole.

u·nite (yōō·nīt′) *v.* **u·nit·ed, u·nit·ing** *v.t.* 1. To join together so as to form a whole; combine. 2. To bring into close connection, as by legal, physical, social, or other tie. 3. To join in marriage. 4. To attach permanently or solidly; bond. —*v.i.* 5. To become or be merged into one; combine. 6. To join together for action; concur. [< L *unus* one]

u·nit·ed (yōō·nī′tid) *adj.* Incorporated into one; allied; combined. —**u·nit′ed·ly** *adv.* —**u·nit′ed·ness** *n.*

United Nations An organization of sovereign states, having its permanent headquarters in New York City since 1951, created by

unsought
unsounded
unsown
unspecified
unspelled
unspent
unspilled
unspiritual
unspoiled
unspoken
unsportsmanlike
unspotted
unsprung
unstained
unstalked
unstamped
unstandardized
unstarched
unstated
unstatesmanlike
unsteadfast
unstemmed
unsterile
unsterilized
unstick
unstigmatized
unstinted
unstitched
unstoppable
unstrained
unstressed
unstructured
unstuffed
unsubdued
unsubmissive
unsubscribed
unsubsidized
unsubstantiated
unsuccessful
unsuited
unsullied
unsunk
unsupervised
unsupportable
unsupportably
unsupported
unsuppressed
unsure
unsurmountable
unsurpassable
unsurpassed
unsurprised
unsusceptible
unsuspected
unsuspicious
unsustainable
unsustained
unswayed
unsweetened
unswept
unswerving
unsymmetrical
unsymmetrically
unsympathetic
unsympathetically
unsystematic
unsystematically
unsystematized
untack
untactful
untactfully
untainted
untaken
untalented
untamable
untamed
untanned
untapped
untarnished
untasted
untaxable
untaxed
unteachable
untechnical
untempered
untenanted
untended
untested
untethered
unthanked
untheatrical
unthought
unthoughtful
unthriftiness
unthrifty
unthrone

the United Nations Charter drafted in 1944.

United Nations Trust Territory See TRUST TERRITORY.

u·ni·ty (yōō′nə·tē) *n. pl.* **·ties** 1. The state or fact of being one. 2. Something that is wholly united and complete within itself. 3. A state or quality of mutual understanding and harmony. 4. The harmonious agreement of parts or elements into one united whole. 5. Singleness or constancy of purpose, action, etc. 6. In art and literature, the arrangement of parts into a whole exhibiting oneness of purpose, spirit, and style. 7. *Math.* **a** The number one. **b** A quantity, such as 1, that leaves any number unchanged under multiplication. [< L *unus* one]

u·ni·va·lent (yōō′nə·vā′lənt) *adj. Chem.* Having a valence or combining value of one: also *monovalent.* —**u′ni·va′lence, u′ni·va′len·cy** *n.*

u·ni·valve (yōō′nə·valv′) *adj.* Having only one valve, as a mollusk. Also **u′ni·valved′, u′ni·val′vu·lar** (-val′vyə·lər). —*n.* 1. A mollusk having a univalve shell; a gastropod. 2. A shell of a single piece.

u·ni·ver·sal (yōō′nə·vûr′səl) *adj.* 1. Of, pertaining to, or typical of all or the whole. 2. Including, involving, intended for, or applicable to all. 3. Of, pertaining to, or occurring throughout the universe. —*n.* Any general or universal notion, condition, principle, etc. —**u′ni·ver′sal·ly** *adv.* —**u′ni·ver′sal·ness** *n.*

u·ni·ver·sal·i·ty (yōō′nə·vər·sal′ə·tē) *n. pl.* **·ties** 1. The state or quality of being universal. 2. Unrestricted fitness or adaptability. 3. An all-embracing range of knowledge, abilities, etc.

u·ni·ver·sal·ize (yōō′nə·vûr′səl·īz) *v.t.* **·ized, ·iz·ing** To make universal.

universal joint *Mech.* A joint that permits connected parts of a machine to be turned in any direction within definite limits. Also **universal coupling.**

u·ni·verse (yōō′nə·vûrs) *n.* 1. The aggregate of all existing things; the whole creation embracing all celestial bodies and all of space; the cosmos. 2. In restricted sense, the earth. [< L *unus* one + *versus*, pp. of *vertere* to turn]

u·ni·ver·si·ty (yōō′nə·vûr′sə·tē) *n. pl.* **·ties** 1. An institution that includes schools for graduate or professional study, as well as an undergraduate division, and grants master's and doctor's degrees. 2. The faculty and students of a university. 3. The buildings and grounds of a university. [< L *universitas* the whole, entire number]

un·just (un·just′) *adj.* Not legitimate, fair, or just; wrongful. —**un·just′ly** *adv.* —**un·just′ness** *n.*

un·kempt (un·kempt′) *adj.* Not combed; not clean or neat; untidy. [< UN-[1] + *kempt*, pp. of dial. *kemb* to comb]

un·kind (un·kīnd′) *adj.* Showing a lack of kindness. —**un·kind′ly** *adv.* —**un·kind′ness** *n.*

un·known (un·nōn′) *adj.* 1. Not known or apprehended; not recognized, as a fact or person. 2. Not ascertained, discovered, or established. —*n.* An unknown person or quantity.

un·lace (un·lās′) *v.t.* **·laced, ·lac·ing** 1. To loosen or unfasten the lacing of. 2. To remove (armor or clothing) in this way.

un·latch (un·lach′) *v.t.* 1. To open or unlock by releasing the latch. —*v.i.* 2. To come open or unlocked.

un·law·ful (un·lô′fəl) *adj.* 1. Contrary to or in violation of law; illegal. 2. Born out of wedlock; illegitimate. —**un·law′ful·ly** *adv.* —**un·law′ful·ness** *n.*

un·lead·ed (un·led′əd) *adj.* Free of lead or lead compounds.

un·learn (un·lûrn′) *v.t. & v.i.* **·learned** or **·learnt, ·learn·ing** To dismiss from the mind; forget.

un·learn·ed (un·lûr′nid; *for def. 3* un·lûrnd′) *adj.* 1. Not possessed of or characterized by learning; illiterate; ignorant. 2. Unworthy of or unlike a learned man. 3. Not acquired by learning or study. —**un·learn′ed·ly** *adv.*

un·leash (un·lēsh′) *v.t.* To set free from or as from a leash.

un·less (un·les′) *conj.* If it be not a fact that; except that: *Unless* we persevere, we shall lose. [Earlier *onlesse* (*that*) (than) in a less case < ON + LESS]

untilled
untinge
untiring
untiringly
untitled
untouched
untraceable
untraced
untracked
untractable
untrained
untransferable
untransferred
untranslatable
untranslated
untransmitted
untraversed
untrimmed
untrod
untroubled
untrustful
untrustworthy
untufted
untunable
untuned
untuneful
unturned
untwisted
untypical
untypically
unusable
unutilizable
unuttered
unvaccinated
unvacillating
unvalidated
unvanquished
unvaried
unventilated
unverifiable
unverified
unversed
unvexed
unvisited
unvitiated
unvocal
unvocally
unwakened
unwalled
unwanted
unwarlike
unwarmed
unwarped
unwarranted
unwashed
unwasted
unwatched
unwavering
unweakened
unweaned
unwearable
unweary
unweathered
unweave
unwed
unwedded
unweeded
unwelcome
unwelded
unwetted
unwhetted
unwifely
unwincing
unwinking
unwisdom
unwished
unwithered
unwithering
unwitnessed
unwomanly
unwon
unwooded
unwooed
unworkable
unworked
unworkmanlike
unworn
unworried
unworshiped
unwoven
unwrinkled
unyielding
unyouthful
unyouthfully
unzealous
unzip

un·let·tered (un·let′ərd) *adj.* Not educated; illiterate.
un·like (un·līk′) *adj.* Having little or no resemblance; different. —*prep.* Dissimilar to or different from; not like. —**un·like′ness** *n.*
un·like·ly (un·līk′lē) *adj.* 1. Not likely; improbable. 2. Not inviting or promising success. —*adv.* Improbably. —**un·like′li·ness, un·like′li·hood** *n.*
un·lim·ber (un·lim′bər) *v.t. & v.i.* To prepare for action.
un·lim·it·ed (un·lim′it·id) *adj.* 1. Having no limits in space, number, or time. 2. Not limited by restrictions. 3. Not limited by qualifications; undefined. —**un·lim′it·ed·ly** *adv.* —**un·lim′it·ed·ness** *n.*
un·load (un·lōd′) *v.t.* 1. To remove the load or cargo from. 2. To take off or discharge (cargo, etc.). 3. To relieve of something burdensome or oppressive. 4. To withdraw the charge of ammunition from. 5. *Informal* To dispose of. —*v.i.* 6. To discharge freight, cargo, or other burden. —**un·load′er** *n.*
un·lock (un·lok′) *v.t.* 1. To open or undo; release. 2. To reveal or disclose. —*v.i.* 3. To become unlocked.
un·looked-for (un·lo͝okt′fôr′) *adj.* Not anticipated.
un·loose (un·lo͞os′) *v.t.* **·loosed, ·loos·ing** To release from fastenings; set loose or free.
un·loos·en (un·lo͞o′sən) *v.t.* To loose; unloose.
un·luck·y (un·luk′ē) *adj.* **·luck·i·er, ·luck·i·est** 1. Not favored by luck. 2. Resulting in or attended by ill luck. 3. Ill-omened. —**un·luck′i·ly** *adv.* —**un·luck′i·ness** *n.*
un·make (un·māk′) *v.t.* **·made, ·mak·ing** 1. To reduce to the original condition or form. 2. To ruin; destroy. 3. To depose, as from a position of authority.
un·man (un·man′) *v.t.* **·manned, ·man·ning** 1. To cause to lose courage or fortitude; dishearten. 2. To render unmanly or effeminate. 3. To deprive of virility; castrate.
un·man·ly (un·man′lē) *adj.* 1. Not masculine or virile; effeminate. 2. Not brave; cowardly. —**un·man′li·ness** *n.*
un·man·ner·ly (un·man′ər·lē) *adj.* Lacking manners; rude. —*adv.* Impolitely; rudely. —**un·man′ner·li·ness** *n.*
un·mask (un·mask′) *v.t.* 1. To remove a mask from. 2. To reveal or disclose the truth about. —*v.i.* 3. To remove one's mask or disguise.
un·mean·ing (un·mē′ning) *adj.* Having no meaning. —**un·mean′ing·ly** *adv.* —**un·mean′ing·ness** *n.*
un·meet (un·mēt′) *adj.* Not meet or suitable; not proper. —**un·meet′ly** *adv.* —**un·meet′·ness** *n.*
un·men·tion·a·ble (un·men′shən·ə·bəl) *adj.* Not proper or fit to be mentioned or discussed. —**un·men′tion·a·ble·ness** *n.* —**un·men′tion·a·bly** *adv.*
un·mer·ci·ful (un·mûr′sə·fəl) *adj.* Showing no mercy; pitiless. —**un·mer′ci·ful·ly** *adv.* —**un·mer′ci·ful·ness** *n.*
un·mind·ful (un·mīnd′fəl) *adj.* Neglectful; inattentive; careless. —**un·mind′ful·ly** *adv.* —**un·mind′ful·ness** *n.*
un·mis·tak·a·ble (un′mis·tā′kə·bəl) *adj.* That cannot be mistaken; evident; clear. —**un′mis·tak′a·bly** *adv.*
un·mit·i·gat·ed (un·mit′ə·gā′tid) *adj.* 1. Not mitigated or lightened in effect. 2. Absolute: an *unmitigated* rogue. —**un·mit′i·gat′ed·ly** *adv.*
un·mor·al (un·môr′əl) *adj.* Having no moral sense; neither moral nor immoral. —**un·mo·ral·i·ty** (un′mə·ral′ə·tē) *n.* —**un·mor′al·ly** *adv.*
un·nat·u·ral (un·nach′ər·əl) *adj.* 1. Contrary to the laws of nature. 2. Monstrous; inhuman. 3. Not having, or inconsistent with, those attitudes, feelings, etc., considered normal; abnormal. 4. Artificial; affected. —**un·nat′u·ral·ly** *adv.* —**un·nat′u·ral·ness** *n.*
un·nec·es·sar·y (un·nes′ə·ser′ē) *adj.* Not required or necessary; not essential. —**un·nec′es·sar′i·ly** *adv.*
un·nerve (un·nûrv′) *v.t.* **·nerved, ·nerv·ing** To deprive of strength, firmness, self-control, or courage; unman.
un·num·bered (un·num′bərd) *adj.* 1. Not counted. 2. Innumerable. 3. Not marked with or assigned a number.
un·oc·cu·pied (un·ok′yə·pīd) *adj.* 1. Empty; uninhabited. 2. Idle; unemployed.
un·or·gan·ized (un·ôr′gən·īzd) *adj.* 1. Not organized in structure, government, etc. 2. Not unionized.
un·pack (un·pak′) *v.t. & v.i.* 1. To open and take out the contents of (a trunk, etc.). 2. To take (something) out of a container. —**un·pack′er** *n.*
un·par·al·leled (un·par′ə·leld) *adj.* Without parallel; not matched; unprecedented.
un·par·lia·men·ta·ry (un′pär·lə·men′tər·ē) *adj.* Contrary to the rules that govern parliamentary bodies. —**un′par·lia·men′ta·ri·ly** *adv.* —**un′par·lia·men′ta·ri·ness** *n.*
un·pleas·ant (un·ples′ənt) *adj.* Disagreeable; objectionable; not pleasing. —**un·pleas′·ant·ly** *adv.* —**un·pleas′ant·ness** *n.*
un·plumbed (un·plumd′) *adj.* Not sounded or explored fully.
un·pop·u·lar (un·pop′yə·lər) *adj.* Having no popularity; generally disliked or condemned. —**un·pop′u·lar·ly** *adv.* —**un·pop′u·lar′i·ty** (-lar′ə·tē) *n.*
un·prac·ticed (un·prak′tist) *adj.* 1. Being without practice, experience, or skill. 2. Not carried out in practice; not used. 3. Not yet tried.
un·prec·e·dent·ed (un·pres′ə·den′tid) *adj.* Being without precedent; unheard-of. —**un·prec′e·dent′ed·ly** *adv.*
un·prej·u·diced (un·prej′o͞o·dist) *adj.* 1. Free from prejudice or bias; impartial. 2. Not impaired, as a right.
un·prin·ci·pled (un·prin′sə·pəld) *adj.* Lacking in moral principles. —**un·prin′ci·pled·ness** *n.*
un·print·a·ble (un·prin′tə·bəl) *adj.* Not fit to be printed.
un·pro·fes·sion·al (un′prə·fesh′ən·əl) *adj.* 1. Having no profession or no professional status. 2. Violating the rules or ethical code of a profession. —**un′pro·fes′sion·al·ly** *adv.*
un·qual·i·fied (un·kwol′ə·fīd) *adj.* 1. Being without the proper qualifications. 2. Without limitation or restrictions; absolute. —**un·qual′i·fied′ly** *adv.* —**un·qual′i·fied′ness** *n.*

un·ques·tion·a·ble (un·kwes′chən·ə·bəl) *adj.* Being beyond a doubt; indisputable. —**un·ques′tion·a·bil′i·ty, un·ques′tion·a·ble·ness** *n.* —**un·ques′tion·a·bly** *adv.*

un·qui·et (un·kwī′ət) *adj.* 1. Not at rest; disturbed; restless. 2. Causing unrest or discomfort. 3. Disturbing. —**un·qui′et·ly** *adv.* —**un·qui′et·ness** *n.*

un·quote (un·kwōt′) *v.t. & v.i.* **·quot·ed, ·quot·ing** To close (a quotation).

un·rav·el (un·rav′əl) *v.* **·eled** or **·elled, ·el·ing** or **·el·ling** *v.t.* 1. To separate the threads of, as a knitted article. 2. To free from entanglement; explain, as a mystery or a plot. —*v.i.* 3. To become unraveled.

un·read (un·red′) *adj.* 1. Not informed by reading; ignorant. 2. Not yet perused.

un·read·y (un·red′ē) *adj.* 1. Being without readiness or alertness. 2. Not in a condition to act effectively. —**un·read′i·ly** *adv.* —**un·read′i·ness** *n.*

un·real (un·rēl′, -rē′əl) *adj.* 1. Having no reality or substance. 2. Artificial; insincere; also, fanciful. —**un·re·al·i·ty** (un′rē·al′ə·tē) *n.* —**un·re′al·ly** *adv.*

un·rea·son·a·ble (un·rē′zən·ə·bəl) *adj.* 1. Acting without or contrary to reason. 2. Not according to reason; irrational. 3. Immoderate; exorbitant. —**un·rea′son·a·bil′i·ty, un·rea′son·a·ble·ness** *n.* —**un·rea′son·a·bly** *adv.*

un·rea·son·ing (un·rē′zən·ing) *adj.* Not accompanied by reason or control. —**un·rea′son·ing·ly** *adv.*

un·re·con·struct·ed (un·rē′kən·struk′tid) *adj.* 1. Not reconstructed. 2. Not reconciled to or accepting changes in social or political attitudes, policies, etc.

un·re·gen·er·ate (un′ri·jen′ər·it) *adj.* 1. Not having been changed spiritually; not reconciled to God. 2. Sinful; wicked. Also **un′re·gen′er·at′ed** (-ā′tid). —**un′re·gen′er·a·cy** *n.* —**un′re·gen′er·ate·ly** *adv.*

un·re·lent·ing (un′ri·len′ting) *adj.* 1. Not relenting; pitiless; inexorable. 2. Not diminishing, or not changing, in pace, effort, speed, etc. —**un·re·lent′ing·ly** *adv.*

un·re·mit·ting (un′ri·mit′ing) *adj.* Not relaxing or stopping; incessant. —**un′re·mit′ting·ly** *adv.* —**un′re·mit′ting·ness** *n.*

un·re·served (un′ri·zûrvd′) *adj.* 1. Given or done without reserve. 2. Having no reserve of manner; informal; open. —**un·re·serv·ed·ly** (-zûr′vid·lē) *adv.* —**un′re·serv′ed·ness** *n.*

un·rest (un·rest′) *n.* 1. Restlessness, esp. of the mind. 2. Trouble; turmoil, esp. with regard to public or political conditions and suggesting premonitions of revolt.

un·right·eous (un·rī′chəs) *adj.* 1. Not righteous; wicked; sinful. 2. Contrary to justice; not fair. —**un·right′eous·ly** *adv.* —**un·right′eous·ness** *n.*

un·ripe (un·rīp′) *adj.* Not arrived at maturity; not ripe; immature. [OE *unrīpe* untimely] —**un·ripe′ness** *n.*

un·ri·valed (un·rī′vəld) *adj.* Having no rival or competitor; matchless.

un·roll (un·rōl′) *v.t.* 1. To spread or open (something rolled up). 2. To exhibit to view. —*v.i.* 3. To become unrolled.

un·ruf·fled (un·ruf′əld) *adj.* Not disturbed or agitated emotionally; calm.

un·ru·ly (un·rōō′lē) *adj.* **·li·er, ·li·est** Disposed to resist rule or discipline; intractable. —**un·ru′li·ness** *n.*

un·sad·dle (un·sad′l) *v.t.* **·dled, ·dling** 1. To remove a saddle from. 2. To throw from the saddle.

un·sat·u·rat·ed (un·sach′ə·rā′tid) *adj. Chem.* 1. Able to absorb or dissolve more of something. 2. Capable of uniting with additional elements or radicals.

un·sa·vor·y (un·sā′vər·ē) *adj.* 1. Having a disagreeable taste or odor. 2. Suggesting something disagreeable, offensive, or unclean; also, morally bad. —**un·sa′vor·i·ly** *adv.* —**un·sa′vor·i·ness** *n.*

un·say (un·sā′) *v.t.* **·said, ·say·ing** To retract (something said).

un·scathed (un·skāthd′) *adj.* Not injured.

un·scram·ble (un·skram′bəl) *v.t.* **·bled, ·bling** *Informal* To resolve the confused or disordered condition of.

un·screw (un·skrōō′) *v.t.* To remove or detach by withdrawing screws, or by turning.

un·scru·pu·lous (un·skrōō′pyə·ləs) *adj.* Having no scruples or morals. —**un·scru′pu·lous·ly** *adv.* —**un·scru′pu·lous·ness** *n.*

un·seal (un·sēl′) *v.t.* 1. To break the seal of. 2. To open.

un·sea·son·a·ble (un·sē′zən·ə·bəl) *adj.* 1. Not being in or characteristic of the season. 2. Inappropriate; ill-timed. —**un·sea′son·a·ble·ness** *n.* —**un·sea′son·a·bly** *adv.*

un·seat (un·sēt′) *v.t.* 1. To remove from a seat or fixed position. 2. To unhorse. 3. To deprive of office or rank; depose.

un·seem·ly (un·sēm′lē) *adj.* **·li·er, ·li·est** Not seemly or proper; indecent. —*adv.* In an unseemly fashion. —**un·seem′li·ness** *n.*

un·self·ish (un·sel′fish) *adj.* Not selfish; generous. —**un·self′ish·ly** *adv.* —**un·self′ish·ness** *n.*

un·set·tle (un·set′l) *v.* **·tled, ·tling** *v.t.* 1. To change or move from a fixed or settled condition. 2. To confuse; disturb. —*v.i.* 3. To become unsteady.

un·shack·le (un·shak′əl) *v.t.* **·led, ·ling** To free from or as from shackles.

un·sheathe (un·shēth′) *v.t.* **·sheathed, ·sheath·ing** To take from or as from a sheath; bare.

un·ship (un·ship′) *v.t.* **·shipped, ·ship·ping** To unload from a ship or other vessel.

un·sight·ly (un·sīt′lē) *adj.* **·li·er, ·li·est** Offensive to the sight; ugly. —**un·sight′li·ness** *n.*

un·skilled (un·skild′) *adj.* 1. Destitute of skill or dexterity. 2. Not requiring special skill or training.

un·skill·ful (un·skil′fəl) *adj.* Lacking skill; awkward. —**un·skill′ful·ly** *adv.* —**un·skill′ful·ness** *n.*

un·snap (un·snap′) *v.t.* **·snapped, ·snap·ping** To undo the snap or snaps of.

un·snarl (un·snärl′) *v.t.* To free of snarls; untangle.

un·so·cia·ble (un·sō′shə·bəl) *adj.* 1. Not sociable; not inclined to seek the society of others. 2. Not encouraging social intercourse. —**un·so′cia·bil′i·ty, un·so′cia·ble·ness** *n.* —**un·so′cia·bly** *adv.*

un·so·phis·ti·cat·ed (un′sə·fis′tə·kā′tid) *adj.* Not sophisticated; artless; simple. —**un′so·phis′ti·cat′ed·ly** *adv.* —**un′so·phis′ti·cat′ed·ness** *n.*

un·sound (un·sound′) *adj.* Lacking in soundness; not strong, healthy, valid, etc. —**un·sound′ly** *adv.* —**un·sound′ness** *n.*

un·spar·ing (un·spâr′ing) *adj.* 1. Not sparing or saving; lavish; liberal. 2. Showing no mercy. —**un·spar′ing·ly** *adv.* —**un·spar′ing·ness** *n.*

un·speak·a·ble (un·spē′kə·bəl) *adj.* 1. That cannot be expressed. 2. Extremely bad or objectionable. —**un·speak′a·ble·ness** *n.* —**un·speak′a·bly** *adv.*

un·sta·ble (un·stā′bəl) *adj.* 1. Lacking in stability or firmness. 2. Having no fixed purposes; inconstant. 3. *Chem.* Readily decomposable, as certain compounds. —**un·sta′ble·ness** *n.* —**un·sta′bly** *adv.*

un·stead·y (un·sted′ē) *adj.* ·**i·er,** ·**i·est** 1. Not steady or firm; shaky. 2. Not regular or constant; wavering. 3. Inconstant and erratic in behavior, habits, etc. —**un·stead′i·ly** *adv.* —**un·stead′i·ness** *n.*

un·stop (un·stop′) *v.t.* ·**stopped,** ·**stop·ping** 1. To remove a stopper from. 2. To open by removing obstructions; clear.

un·strap (un·strap′) *v.t.* ·**strapped,** ·**strap·ping** To unfasten or loosen the strap or straps of.

un·strung (un·strung′) *adj.* 1. Having the strings removed or relaxed. 2. Unnerved; emotionally upset; weakened.

un·stud·ied (un·stud′ēd) *adj.* 1. Not planned. 2. Not stiff or artificial; natural. 3. Not acquainted through study: with *in.*

un·sub·stan·tial (un′səb·stan′shəl) *adj.* 1. Lacking solidity, strength, or weight. 2. Having no valid basis. 3. Having no bodily existence; fanciful. —**un′sub·stan′tial·ly** *adv.* —**un′sub·stan′ti·al′i·ty** (-shē·al′ə·tē) *n.*

un·suit·a·ble (un·sōō′tə·bəl) *adj.* Not suitable. —**un′suit·a·bil′i·ty, un·suit′a·ble·ness** *n.* —**un·suit′a·bly** *adv.*

un·sung (un·sung′) *adj.* 1. Not celebrated in song or poetry; obscure. 2. Not yet sung.

un·tan·gle (un·tang′gəl) *v.t.* ·**gled,** ·**gling** 1. To free from entanglement or snarls. 2. To clear up; resolve.

un·taught (un·tôt′) *adj.* 1. Not instructed; ignorant. 2. Acquired without training or instruction; natural.

un·ten·a·ble (un·ten′ə·bəl) *adj.* That cannot be maintained or defended. —**un·ten′a·bil′i·ty, un·ten′a·ble·ness** *n.*

un·think·a·ble (un·thingk′ə·bəl) *adj.* Not considered possible; not imaginable. —**un·think′a·bly** *adv.*

un·think·ing (un·thingk′ing) *adj.* 1. Not having the power of thought. 2. Thoughtless; careless; heedless; inconsiderate. —**un·think′ing·ly** *adv.* —**un·think′ing·ness** *n.*

un·thought-of (un·thôt′uv′) *adj.* 1. Not remembered or called to mind. 2. Not conceived of; not discovered.

un·ti·dy (un·tī′dē) *adj.* ·**di·er,** ·**di·est** Showing lack of tidiness. [ME *untidi*] —**un·ti′di·ly** *adv.* —**un·ti′di·ness** *n.*

un·tie (un·tī′) *v.* ·**tied,** ·**ty·ing** *v.t.* 1. To loosen or undo, as a knot. 2. To free from restraint. —*v.i.* 3. To become untied. [OE *untīgan*]

un·til (un·til′) *prep.* 1. Up to the time of; till: We will wait *until* midnight. 2. Before: used with a negative: The music doesn't begin *until* nine. —*conj.* 1. To the time when: *until* I die. 2. To the place or degree that: Walk east *until* you reach the river. [ME *un-* up to, as far as + TILL[2]]

un·time·ly (un·tīm′lē) *adj.* 1. Before the proper or expected time; premature. 2. Ill-timed. —*adv.* Inopportunely. —**un·time′li·ness** *n.*

un·to (un′tōō) *prep.* 1. *Poetic & Archaic* To. 2. *Archaic* Until. [ME *un-* up to, as far as + TO]

un·told (un·tōld′) *adj.* 1. That cannot be revealed or described. 2. That cannot be numbered or estimated. 3. Not told.

un·touch·a·ble (un·tuch′ə·bəl) *adj.* 1. Inaccessible or forbidden to the touch; out of reach. 2. Intangible; unapproachable. 3. Unpleasant or dangerous to touch. —*n.* In India, a member of the lowest caste, whose touch was formerly counted as pollution by Hindus of higher station. —**un′touch·a·bil′i·ty** *n.*

un·to·ward (un·tôrd′) *adj.* 1. Causing hindrance; vexatious. 2. Refractory; perverse. 3. Not seemly; uncouth. —**un·to′ward·ly** *adv.* —**un·to′ward·ness** *n.*

un·true (un·trōō′) *adj.* 1. Not true; not corresponding with fact. 2. Not conforming to rule or standard. 3. Disloyal. —**un·tru′ly** *adv.*

un·truth (un·trōōth′) *n. pl.* ·**truths** (-trōōths′, -trōōthz′) 1. The quality or character of being untrue. 2. A lie. —**un·truth′ful** *adj.* —**un·truth′ful·ly** *adv.* —**un·truth′ful·ness** *n.*

un·tu·tored (un·tōō′tərd, -tyōō′-) *adj.* 1. Having had no tutor or teacher. 2. Naive; simple.

un·twist (un·twist′) *v.t. & v.i.* To unwind or untwine.

un·used (un·yōōzd′ *for def. 1*; un·yōōst′ *for def. 2*) *adj.* 1. Not made use of; also, never having been used. 2. Not accustomed or wont: with *to.*

un·u·su·al (un·yōō′zhōō·əl) *adj.* Not usual, common, or ordinary; rare. —**un·u′su·al·ly** *adv.* —**un·u′su·al·ness** *n.*

un·ut·ter·a·ble (un·ut′ər·ə·bəl) *adj.* Too great or deep for verbal expression; inexpressible. —**un·ut′ter·a·ble·ness** *n.* —**un·ut′ter·a·bly** *adv.*

un·var·nished (un·vär′nisht) *adj.* 1. Having no covering of varnish. 2. Having no embellishment; plain.

un·veil (un·vāl′) *v.t.* 1. To remove the veil from; reveal. —*v.i.* 2. To remove one's veil; reveal oneself.

un·voiced (un·voist′) *adj.* 1. Not expressed. 2. *Phonet.* **a** Voiceless. **b** Rendered voiceless.

un·war·y (un·wâr′ē) *adj.* Not careful or cautious; rash; careless. —**un·war′i·ly** *adv.* —**un·war′i·ness** *n.*

un·well (un·wel′) *adj.* Not well; ailing; sick. —**un·well′ness** *n.*

un·whole·some (un·hōl′səm) *adj.* 1. Harmful to physical or mental health. 2. Not sound in condition; diseased or decayed. 3. Morally bad; pernicious. —**un·whole′some·ly** *adv.* —**un·whole′some·ness** *n.*

un·wield·y (un·wēl′dē) *adj.* Moved or managed with difficulty, as from great size or awkward shape; bulky; clumsy. —**un·wield′i·ly** *adv.* —**un·wield′i·ness** *n.*

un·will·ing (un·wil′ing) *adj.* 1. Not willing; reluctant. 2. Done, said, etc., with reluctance. —**un·will′ing·ly** *adv.* —**un·will′ing·ness** *n.*

un·wind (un·wīnd′) *v.* **·wound, ·wind·ing** *v.t.* 1. To reverse the winding of; wind off; uncoil. 2. To disentangle. —*v.i.* 3. To become unwound.

un·wise (un·wīz′) *adj.* Showing a lack of wisdom; imprudent; foolish. —**un·wise′ly** *adv.*

un·wit·ting (un·wit′ing) *adj.* 1. Having no knowledge or consciousness of the thing in question. 2. Unintentional. —**un·wit′ting·ly** *adv.*

un·wont·ed (un·wun′tid, -wōn′-) *adj.* Not according to habit or custom; unusual. —**un·wont′ed·ly** *adv.* —**un·wont′ed·ness** *n.*

un·wor·thy (un·wûr′thē) *adj.* 1. Not deserving: usu., with *of.* 2. Not befitting or becoming: often with *of.* 3. Lacking worth or merit. —**un·wor′thi·ly** *adv.* —**un·wor′thi·ness** *n.*

un·wound (un·wound′) Past tense and past participle of UNWIND.

un·wrap (un·rap′) *v.* **·wrapped, ·wrap·ping** *v.t.* 1. To take the wrapping from. —*v.i.* 2. To become unwrapped.

un·writ·ten (un·rit′n) *adj.* 1. Not in writing. 2. Not reduced to writing; traditional.

unwritten law 1. A rule or custom established by general usage. 2. Common law.

un·yoke (un·yōk′) *v.t.* **·yoked, ·yok·ing** 1. To release from a yoke. 2. To separate.

up (up) *adv.* 1. From a lower to a higher place, level, position, etc. 2. In, on, or to a higher place, level, position, etc. 3. Toward that which is figuratively or conventionally higher; as: **a** To or at a higher price. **b** To or at a higher place, rank, etc. **c** To or at a greater size or amount: to swell *up.* **d** To or at a place that is regarded as higher: *up* north. **e** Above the surface or horizon. **f** From an earlier to a later period. **g** To a source, conclusion, etc.: Follow *up* this lead. 4. To a vertical position; standing; also, out of bed. 5. So as to be compact or secure: Tie *up* the boxes. 6. So as to be even with in space, time, degree, etc.: *up* to date. 7. In or into an excited state or some specific action: They were stirred *up* to mutiny. 8. In or into view or existence: to draw *up* a will. 9. In or into prominence; under consideration: *up* for debate. 10. In or into a place of safekeeping; aside: Fruits are put *up* in jars. 11. At an end: Your time is *up.* 12. Completely; totally: The house was burned *up.* 13. In baseball and cricket, at bat. 14. In tennis and other sports: **a** In the lead; ahead. **b** Apiece; alike: said of a score. 15. Running for as a candidate. ◆In informal usage *up* is often added to a verb without affecting the meaning of the sentence: to light *up* a room. —**to be up against** *Informal* To meet with; confront. —**to be up against it** *Informal* To be in difficulty. —**to be up on** (or **in**) *Informal* To be well informed in or skilled at something. —**to be up to** 1. *Informal* To be doing or plotting. 2. To be equal to; be capable of. 3. To be incumbent upon; be dependent upon: It's *up* to her to save us. —*adj.* 1. Moving, sloping, or directed upward. 2. *Informal* Going on; taking place: What's *up*? 3. Rising, risen, overflowing, or at flood. 4. In an active or excited state. —**up and around** *Informal* Sufficiently recovered to walk. —*prep.* 1. From a lower to a higher point or place of, on, or along. 2. Toward a higher condition or rank on or in. 3. To or at a point farther above or along: *up* the road. 4. Toward the interior of (a country). 5. Toward the source of (a river). 6. At, on, or near the height or top of. —*n.* 1. A rise or ascent. 2. A period of prosperity, etc.: chiefly in the phrase **ups and downs.** —**to be on the up and up** *Slang* To be honest. —*v.* **upped, up·ping** *Informal* *v.t.* 1. To increase. 2. To put or take up. —*v.i.* 3. To rise. [OE *ūp*]

up- *combining form* As a combining element *up* has adverbial force with various meanings: 1. To a higher place or level: **upgaze, uprise.** 2. To a greater size or larger amount: **upflooding, upswell.** 3. To a vertical position: **upprop, upstand.** 4. In or into commotion or activity: **upboil, upstir.** 5. Completely; wholly: **upbind, upgather.**

up-and-com·ing (up′ən·kum′ing) *adj.* Enterprising; energetic; promising.

up-and-down (up′ən·doun′) *adj.* 1. Alternately rising and falling; fluctuating; varying. 2. Vertical; perpendicular.

up·beat (up′bēt′) *n. Music* The relatively unaccented beat that precedes the downbeat. —*adj.* Optimistic.

up·braid (up·brād′) *v.t.* 1. To reproach for some wrongdoing; scold or reprove. —*v.i.* 2. To utter reproaches. [OE *up-* up + *bregdan* to weave, twist] —**up·braid′er** *n.* —**up·braid′ing** *n.* —**up·braid′ing·ly** *adv.*

up·bring·ing (up′bring′ing) *n.* The rearing and training received during childhood.

up·chuck (up′chuk′) *Informal* *v.t. & v.i.* To vomit.

up·com·ing (up′kum′ing) *adj.* Coming soon; approaching.

up·coun·try (*n. & adj.* up′kun′trē; *adv.* up′kun′trē) *Informal* *n.* Country remote from the coast or from lowlands; inland country. —*adj. & adv.* In, toward, or characteristic of inland places.

up·date (up′dāt′) *v.t.* **·dat·ed, ·dat·ing** To bring up to date; revise, as a textbook.

up·end (up·end′) *v.t. & v.i.* To set or stand on end.

up·grade (*n.* up′grād′; *v.* up·grād′; *adv.* up′grād′) *n.* An upward incline or slope. —*v.t.* **·grad·ed, ·grad·ing** To raise to a higher grade, rank, post, etc. —*adv.* Up a hill or slope. —**on the upgrade** 1. Improving. 2. Rising.

up·heav·al (up·hē′vəl) *n.* 1. The act of upheaving, or the state of being upheaved. 2. A violent disturbance or change.

up·heave (up·hēv′) *v.* **·heaved** or **·hove, ·heav·ing** *v.t.* 1. To heave or raise up. —*v.i.* 2. To be raised or lifted.

up·hill (*adv. & adj.* up′hil′; *n.* up′hil′) *adv.* Up or as up a hill or an ascent; against difficulties. —*adj.* 1. Going up an ascent; sloping upward. 2. Attended with difficulty or exertion. 3. At a high place. —*n.* An upward slope.

up·hold (up·hōld′) *v.t.* **·held, ·hold·ing** 1. To hold up; raise. 2. To keep from falling. 3. To support; agree with; encourage. —**up·hold′er** *n.*

up·hol·ster (up·hōl′stər) *v.t.* To fit, as furniture, with coverings, cushioning, etc. [ME *upholder* tradesman] —**up·hol′ster·er** *n.*

up·hol·ster·y (up·hōl′stər·ē, -strē) *n. pl.* **·ster·ies** 1. Fabric and fittings used in upholstering. 2. The act, art, or business of upholstering.

up·keep (up′kēp′) *n.* The act or state of maintaining something; also, the cost of maintenance.

up·land (up′lənd, -land′) *n.* 1. The higher portions of a region, district, farm, etc. 2. The country in the interior. —**up′land** *adj.*

up·lift (*v.* up·lift′; *n.* up′lift′) *v.t.* 1. To lift up; elevate. 2. To put on a higher plane, mentally or morally. —*n.* 1. The act of raising, or the fact of being raised. 2. Mental or spiritual stimulation or elevation. 3. A movement aiming to improve the condition of the underprivileged. —**up·lift′er** *n.*

up·most (up′mōst′) *adj.* Uppermost.

up·on (ə·pon′, ə·pôn′) *prep.* On. —*adv.* On: completing a verbal idea: The paper has been written *upon.* [ME]

up·per (up′ər) *adj.* 1. Higher in place. 2. Further inland. 3. Higher in station, rank, etc.; superior. —*n.* 1. That part of a boot or shoe above the sole; the vamp. 2. *Slang* Any of various drugs that stimulate the central nervous system, as amphetamine.

upper case *Printing* The capital letters of the alphabet. —**up′per-case′** *adj.*

upper class The socially or economically superior group in society. —**up·per-class** (up′ər·klas′) *adj.*

up·per·class·man (up′ər·klas′mən) *n. pl.* **·men** (-mən) A junior or senior in a school or college.

upper crust *Informal* The highest social class.

up·per·cut (up′ər·kut′) *n.* In boxing, a swinging blow upward, delivered under or inside the opponent's guard. —*v.t. & v.i.* **·cut, ·cut·ting** To strike with an uppercut.

upper hand Advantage.

Upper House The branch in a bicameral legislature where membership is usu. smaller and more restricted, as the British House of Lords. Also **upper house.**

up·per·most (up′ər·mōst′) *adj.* 1. Highest in place, rank, authority, influence, etc. 2. First to come into the mind. Also *upmost.* —*adv.* In the highest place, rank, authority, etc.; also, first, as in time.

up·pish (up′ish) *adj. Informal* Inclined to be self-assertive, pretentious, or snobbish. Also **up·pi·ty** (up′ə·tē). —**up′pish·ly** *adv.* —**up′·pish·ness** *n.*

up·raise (up·rāz′) *v.t.* **·raised, ·rais·ing** To lift up; elevate.

up·right (up′rīt′) *adj.* 1. Being in a vertical position; straight up; erect. 2. Just and honest. —*n.* 1. Something having a vertical position, as an upright piano. 2. In football, one of the goal posts. —*adv.* In an upright position; vertically. [OE *ūp-* up + *riht* right] —**up′right′ly** *adv.* —**up′right′ness** *n.*

upright piano A piano having strings arranged vertically in a rectangular case.

up·ris·ing (up′rī′zing, up·rī′zing) *n.* 1. The act of rising. 2. A revolt or insurrection. 3. An ascent; a slope.

up·roar (up′rôr′) *n.* A violent disturbance, noise, or tumult. [< Du. *op-* up + *roeren* to stir]

up·roar·i·ous (up·rôr′ē·əs) *adj.* 1. Accompanied by or making an uproar. 2. Loud and noisy; tumultuous. 3. Very funny. —**up·roar′i·ous·ly** *adv.* —**up·roar′i·ous·ness** *n.*

up·root (up·ro͞ot′, -ro͝ot′) *v.t.* 1. To tear up or remove by or as if by the roots. 2. To destroy utterly; eradicate. —**up·root′er** *n.*

up·scale (up′skāl′) *adj. Informal* Above average in income and education: an *upscale* audience.

up·set (*v.* up·set′; *adj.* up·set′, up′set′; *n.* up′set′) *v.* **·set, ·set·ting** *v.t.* 1. To overturn. 2. To throw into confusion or disorder. 3. To disconcert, derange, or disquiet. 4. To defeat, esp. unexpectedly. —*v.i.* 5. To become overturned. —*adj.* 1. Tipped or turned over. 2. Mentally or physically disturbed or ill. 3. Confused; disordered. —*n.* 1. The act of upsetting, or the state of being upset. 2. An unexpected defeat. 3. A mental or physical disturbance or disorder. —**up·set′ter** *n.*

up·shot (up′shot′) *n.* The final outcome; result.

up·side (up′sīd′) *n.* The upper side or part.

upside down 1. With the upper side down. 2. In disorder. —**up′side-down′** *adj.*

up·si·lon (yo͞op′sə·lon, up′sə·lon, *Brit.* yo͞op·sī′lən) *n.* The twentieth letter and sixth vowel in the Greek alphabet (Υ, υ). [< Gk. *u* u + *psilon* smooth]

up·stage (up′stāj′) *adj.* Of the back half of a stage. —*adv.* Toward or on the back of a stage. —*v.t.* **·staged, ·stag·ing** 1. To steal a scene from. 2. *Informal* To treat in a haughty manner.

up·stairs (up′stârz′) *adj.* Pertaining to an upper story. —*n.* An upper story; esp., the part of a building above the ground floor. —*adv.* In, to, or toward an upper story. —**to kick upstairs** To promote to a position with a higher title but less power.

up·stand·ing (up·stan′ding) *adj.* 1. Honest; upright; straightforward. 2. Standing up; erect.

up·start (up′stärt′) *adj.* 1. Suddenly raised to prominence, wealth, or power. 2. Characteristic of an upstart; vulgar; pretentious. —*n.* One who has suddenly risen to a position of wealth or importance and is usu. arrogant.

up·state (up′stāt′) *adj.* Of, from, or designating that part of a state lying outside, usu. north, of the principal city. —*n.* The outlying, usu. northern, sections of a state. —**up′state′** *adv.* —**up′stat′er** *n.*

up·stream (up′strēm′) *adv.* Toward or at the source or upper part of a stream; against the current.

up·stretched (up′stretcht′) *adj.* Stretched or extended upward.

up·stroke (up′strōk′) *n.* An upward stroke, as of a pen.

up·surge (up′sûrj′) A rapid or sudden rise. —**up·surge′** *v.i.* **·surged, ·surg·ing**

up·swing (up′swing′) *n.* 1. A swinging upward. 2. An improvement. —**up·swing′** *v.i.* **·swung, ·swing·ing**

up·take (up′tāk′) *n.* The act of lifting or taking up. —**to be quick on the uptake** *Informal* To demonstrate mental comprehension or perception.

up·thrust (up′thrust′) *n.* 1. An upward thrust. 2. *Geol.* An upheaval of rocks in the earth's crust.

up·tight (up′tīt′) *adj.* *Slang* Uneasy, anxious, or tense; nervous. Also **up′-tight′**. —**up′tight′ness** *n.*
up-to-date (up′tə·dāt′) *adj.* 1. Having the latest information, improvements, etc. 2. Modern in manner, fashion, or style.
up·town (up′toun′) *adv.* In or toward the upper part of a town or city. —*n.* The upper part of a town or city. —**up′town′** *adj.*
up·turn (*v.* up·tûrn′; *n.* up′tûrn′) *v.t.* 1. To turn up or over. 2. To overturn; upset. —*n.* A turning upward; increase; improvement.
up·ward (up′wərd) *adv.* 1. In, to, or toward a higher place or position. 2. To or toward the source, origin, etc. 3. Toward a higher rank, amount, age, etc. 4. Toward that which is better, nobler, etc. 5. In excess; more. Also **up′wards**. —**upward (or upwards) of** Higher than; in excess of. —*adj.* In, on, turned, or directed toward a higher place. —**up′ward·ly** *adv.*
ur- Var. of URO-.
u·ra·cil (yo͝or′ə·sil) *n.* *Chem.* A base that is a genetic coding constituent of RNA.
u·rae·mi·a (yo͞o·rē′mē·ə) See UREMIA.
U·ral-Al·ta·ic (yo͝or′əl·al·tā′ik) *n.* A hypothesized family of languages comprising the Uralic and Altaic subfamilies. —**U′ral-Al·ta′ic** *adj.*
U·ral·ic (yo͞o·ral′ik) *n.* A family of languages comprising the Finno-Ugric and Samoyedic subfamilies. —**U·ra·li·an** (yo͞o·rā′lē·ən) *n.* & *adj.* —**U·ral′ic** *adj.*
U·ra·ni·an (yo͞o·rā′nē·ən) *adj.* 1. Of or pertaining to the planet Uranus. 2. Celestial.
u·ra·ni·um (yo͞o·rā′nē·əm) *n.* A heavy, white, radioactive, metallic element (symbol U), used as a source of atomic energy. [< URANUS]
U·ra·nus (yo͝or′ə·nəs, yo͞o·rā′) *n.* The third largest planet of the solar system and seventh in order from the sun. [< Gk. *ouranos* heaven]
ur·ban (ûr′bən) *adj.* 1. Pertaining to, characteristic of, including, or constituting a city. 2. Situated or dwelling in a city. [< L *urbanus*. See URBANE.]
ur·bane (ûr·bān′) *adj.* Characterized by or having refinement or elegance, esp. in manner; suave. [< L *urbs*, *urbis* city] —**ur·bane′ly** *adv.* —**ur·bane′ness** *n.*
ur·ban·ism (ûr′bən·iz′əm) *n.* The character or condition of the life of people living in urban areas.
ur·ban·ite (ûr′bən·īt) *n.* One who lives in a city.
ur·ban·i·ty (ûr·ban′ə·tē) *n.* *pl.* **·ties** 1. The character or quality of being urbane; refined or elegant courtesy. 2. *pl.* Amenities or courtesies. [L < *urbs*, *urbis* city]
ur·ban·ize (ûr′bən·īz) *v.t.* **·ized, ·iz·ing** To render urban, as in character or manner. —**ur′ban·i·za′tion** *n.*
urban renewal The planned upgrading of a deteriorating urban area, usu. using public funds.
ur·chin (ûr′chin) *n.* 1. A roguish, mischievous child. 2. A sea urchin. [< L *ericius* hedgehog]
Ur·du (o͝or′do͞o, o͝or·do͞o′, ûr′do͞o) *n.* A variety of Hindustani that is spoken by Muslims in India and is the official language of Pakistan. [< Persian *urdū* camp]
-ure *suffix of nouns* 1. The act, process, or result of: *pressure*. 2. The function, rank, or office of: *prefecture*. 3. The means or instrument of: *ligature*. [< L *-ura*]
u·re·a (yo͞o·rē′ə) *n.* *Biochem.* A colorless crystalline nitrogenous compound, found in urine and also made synthetically, used in medicine and in the making of plastics and fertilizers. [< Gk. *ouron*] —**u·re′al** *adj.*
u·re·mi·a (yo͞o·rē′mē·ə) *n.* *Pathol.* A condition of the blood due to the presence of urinary constituents ordinarily excreted by the kidneys. Also *uraemia*. —**u·re′mic** *adj.*
u·re·ter (yo͞o·rē′tər) *n.* *Anat.* The duct by which urine passes from the kidney to the bladder. [< Gk. *ourein* to urinate] —**u·re′·ter·al, u·re·ter·ic** (yo͝or′ə·ter′ik) *adj.*
u·re·thra (yo͞o·rē′thrə) *n.* *Anat.* The duct by which urine is discharged from the bladder of most mammals, and which, in males, carries the seminal discharge. —**u·re′thral** *adj.*
urge (ûrj) *v.t.* **urged, urg·ing** 1. To drive or force forward; impel; push. 2. To plead with or entreat earnestly. 3. To press or argue the doing, consideration, or acceptance of. 4. To move or force to some course or action. 5. To stimulate or excite. —*n.* 1. A strong impulse. 2. The act of urging, or the state of being urged. [< L *urgere* to drive, urge]
ur·gent (ûr′jənt) *adj.* 1. Characterized by urging or importunity; requiring prompt attention; pressing. 2. Eagerly importunate or insistent. —**ur′gen·cy** *n.* —**ur′gent·ly** *adv.*
-urgy *combining form* Development of or work with a (specified) material or product: *metallurgy, chemurgy*. [< Gk. *ergon* work]
u·ric (yo͝or′ik) *adj.* Of, pertaining to, or derived from urine.
uric acid *Biochem.* A colorless acid that is found in small quantities in the urine of man and animals and is the chief constituent of excreta of birds and reptiles.
u·ri·nal (yo͝or′ə·nəl) *n.* 1. An upright wall fixture with facilities for flushing, for men's use in urination; also, the room containing such a fixture. 2. A glass receptacle for urine.
u·ri·nal·y·sis (yo͝or′ə·nal′ə·sis) *n.* *pl.* **·ses** (-sēz) Chemical analysis of the urine.
u·ri·nar·y (yo͝or′ə·ner′ē) *adj.* Of or involved in the production and excretion of urine.
u·ri·nate (yo͝or′ə·nāt) *v.i.* **·nat·ed, ·nat·ing** To void or pass urine. —**u′ri·na′tion** *n.*
u·rine (yo͝or′in) *n.* A liquid containing body wastes, secreted by the kidneys, stored in the bladder, and voided through the urethra. [< L *urina*]
u·ri·no·gen·i·tal (yo͝or′ə·nō·jen′ə·təl) *adj.* Urogenital.
urn (ûrn) *n.* 1. A rounded or angular vase having a foot, variously used in antiquity as a receptacle for the ashes of the dead, a water vessel, etc. 2. A vessel for preserving the ashes of the dead. 3. A vase-shaped receptacle having a faucet and designed for keeping tea, coffee, etc., hot. [< L *urna*]
uro- *combining form* Urine; pertaining to urine or to the urinary tract: *urology*. Also, before vowels, *ur-*. [< Gk. *ouron* urine]
u·ro·gen·i·tal (yo͝or′ō·jen′ə·təl) *adj.* Of or pertaining to the urinary and genital organs and their functions.
u·rol·o·gy (yo͞o·rol′ə·jē) *n.* The branch of medicine that deals with the urine and the urogenital tract. —**u·ro·log·ic** (yo͝or′ə·loj′ik) or **·i·cal** *adj.* —**u·rol′o·gist** *n.*

Ursa Major A constellation, the Great Bear, containing seven bright stars: also called *Big Dipper*. [< L]

Ursa Minor A constellation, the Lesser Bear, containing the polestar Polaris: also called *Little Dipper*. [< L]

ur·sine (ûr′sīn, -sin) *adj.* Pertaining to or like a bear. [< L *ursus* bear]

ur·ti·car·i·a (ûr′tə·kâr′ē·ə) *n. Pathol.* A form of hives. [< L *urtica* nettle] —**ur′ti·car′i·al, ur′ti·car′i·ous** *adj.*

U·ru·guay·an (yŏŏr′ə·gwā′ən) *adj.* Of Uruguay or its inhabitants. —**U′ru·guay′an** *n.*

us (us) *pron.* The objective case of the pronoun *we.* [OE]

us·a·ble (yōō′zə·bəl) *adj.* 1. Capable of being used. 2. That can be used conveniently. Also **use′a·ble.** —**us′a·ble·ness** *n.* —**us′a·bly** *adv.*

us·age (yōō′sij, -zij) *n.* 1. The manner of using or treating a person or thing; treatment; also, the act of using. 2. Customary or habitual practice. 3. The way a word or phrase is used.

use (*v.* yōōz; *n.* yōōs) *v.* **used** (yōōzd; yōōst *for defs. 5, 7*), **us·ing** *v.t.* 1. To employ for the accomplishment of a purpose; make use of. 2. To put into practice or employ habitually; make a practice of. 3. To expend the whole of; consume: often with *up*. 4. To conduct oneself toward; treat: to *use* one badly. 5. To make familiar by habit or practice; inure: now only in the past participle: She is *used* to cold climates. 6. To partake of: He does not *use* tobacco. —*v.i.* 7. To do something customarily or habitually: now only in the past tense as an auxiliary: I *used* to go there. —*n.* 1. The act of using: to make good *use* of his time. 2. The condition of being used: Is this form still in *use*? 3. The right to use: the *use* of her car. 4. The ability to use: the *use* of one's leg. 5. Adaptability for a purpose; usefulness: a new *use* for this product. 6. The way or manner of using: the correct *use* of the machine. 7. Custom; habit; practice: long *use* shows us. —**to have no use for** 1. To have no need of. 2. *Informal* To dislike; want nothing to do with. [< L *usus*, pp. of *uti* to use] —**us′er** *n.*

use·ful (yōōs′fəl) *adj.* Serviceable; serving a use or purpose, esp. a valuable one. —**use′·ful·ly** *adv.* —**use′ful·ness** *n.*

use·less (yōōs′lis) *adj.* 1. Being of no use; not capable of serving any beneficial purpose. 2. Futile; in vain. —**use′less·ly** *adv.* —**use′·less·ness** *n.*

ush·er (ush′ər) *n.* 1. One who acts as doorkeeper, as of a court or other assembly room. 2. An officer who walks before a person of rank. 3. One who conducts persons to seats, as in a church or theater. —*v.t.* 1. To act as an usher to; escort; conduct. 2. To precede as a harbinger; be a forerunner of: usu. with *in*. [< OF *uissier* < L *ostiarius* doorkeeper]

u·su·al (yōō′zhōō·əl) *adj.* Such as occurs in the ordinary course of events; frequent; common. [< L *usus* use] —**u′su·al·ly** *adv.* —**u′su·al·ness** *n.*

u·su·ri·ous (yōō·zhŏŏr′ē·əs) *adj.* Practicing or having the nature of usury. —**u·su′ri·ous·ly** *adv.* —**u·su′ri·ous·ness** *n.*

u·surp (yōō·zûrp′, -sûrp′) *v.t.* 1. To seize and hold (the office, rights, or powers of another) without right or legal authority; take possession of by force. 2. To take arrogantly, as if by right. —*v.i.* 3. To encroach: with *on* or *upon*. [< L, ? < *usus* use + *rapere* to seize] —**u′sur·pa′tion** *n.* —**u·surp′er** *n.* —**u·surp′ing·ly** *adv.*

u·su·ry (yōō′zhər·ē) *n. pl.* **·ries** 1. The act or practice of exacting a rate of interest beyond what is allowed by law. 2. A premium paid for the use of money beyond the rate of interest established by law. [< L *usus* used] —**u′su·rer** *n.*

Ute (yōōt, yōō′tē) *n.* One of a group of Shoshonean Indians living in Colorado and Utah.

u·ten·sil (yōō·ten′səl) *n.* A vessel, tool, implement, etc., serving a useful purpose, esp. for domestic use or for farming. [< L *utens*, ppr. of *uti* to use]

u·ter·ine (yōō′tər·in, -īn) *adj.* 1. Pertaining to the uterus. 2. Born of the same mother, but having a different father. [< LL *uterinus* born of the same mother]

u·ter·us (yōō′tər·əs) *n. pl.* **u·ter·i** (yōō′·tər·ī) *Anat.* The organ of a female mammal in which the young are protected and developed before birth; the womb. [< L]

u·til·i·tar·i·an (yōō·til′ə·târ′ē·ən) *adj.* 1. Relating to utility; esp., placing utility above beauty or the amenities of life. 2. Pertaining to or advocating utilitarianism. —*n.* 1. An advocate of utilitarianism. 2. One devoted to mere material utility.

u·til·i·tar·i·an·ism (yōō·til′ə·târ′ē·ən·iz′əm) *n.* 1. *Philos.* The ethical theory that the greatest human happiness determines the highest moral good. 2. Devotion to mere material interests.

u·til·i·ty (yōō·til′ə·tē) *n. pl.* **·ties** 1. Fitness for some desirable, practical purpose; also, that which is necessary. 2. Fitness to supply the natural needs of man. 3. A public service, as gas, water, etc.; also, a company supplying such service. [< L *utilis* useful]

u·til·ize (yōō′təl·īz) *v.t.* **·ized, ·iz·ing** To make useful; turn to practical account; make use of. Also *Brit.* **u′til·ise.** —**u′til·iz′a·ble** *adj.* —**u′til·i·za′tion** *n.* —**u′til·iz′er** *n.*

ut·most (ut′mōst) *adj.* 1. Of the highest degree or the largest amount or number; greatest. 2. Being at the farthest limit or point. —*n.* The greatest possible extent; the most possible. Also *uttermost.* [OE *ūtmest, ȳtemest*]

U·to-Az·tec·an (yōō′tō·az′tek·ən) *n.* 1. One of the chief stocks of North and Central American Indians, embracing about fifty tribes, still surviving in the U.S. and Mexico. 2. The family of languages spoken by these peoples. —**U′to-Az′tec·an** *adj.*

u·to·pi·a (yōō·tō′pē·ə) *n.* 1. Any state, condition, or place of ideal perfection. 2. A visionary, impractical scheme for social improvement. [after *Utopia*, an imaginary island having a perfect social and political life, described in Sir Thomas More's *Utopia* (1516) < Gk. *ou* not + *topos* place] —**u·to′pi·an** *adj. & n.* —**u·to′pi·an·ism** *n.*

ut·ter[1] (ut′ər) *v.t.* To give out or send forth with audible sound; say. [ME *outre*, freq. of obs. *out* to say, speak out < OE *ūt* out] —**ut′ter·a·ble** *adj.* —**ut′ter·er** *n.*

ut·ter[2] (ut′ər) *adj.* 1. Absolute; total,

2. Being or done without conditions or qualifications; final; absolute. [OE *ūtera*, orig. compar. of *ūt* out]

ut·ter·ance (ut′ər·əns) *n.* 1. The act of uttering; vocal expression; also, the power of speech. 2. A thing uttered or expressed. 3. *Ling.* Any stretch of speech capable of being isolated from the flow of connected discourse, as a word, phrase, or sentence.

ut·ter·ly (ut′ər·lē) *adv.* Thoroughly; entirely.

ut·ter·most (ut′ər·mōst′) *adj. & n.* Utmost.

U-turn (yōō′tûrn′) *n.* A continuous turn that reverses the direction of a vehicle on a road.

u·vu·la (yōō′vyə·lə) *n. pl.* **·las** or **·lae** (-lē) *Anat.* The pendent fleshy portion of the soft palate. [< LL, dim. of L *uva* grape]

u·vu·lar (yōō′vyə·lər) *adj.* 1. Pertaining to or of the uvula. 2. *Phonet.* Produced by vibration of, or with the back of the tongue near or against, the uvula. —*n. Phonet.* A uvular sound.

ux·o·ri·ous (uk·sôr′ē·əs, ug·zôr′ē-) *adj.* Fatuously or foolishly devoted to one's wife. [< L *uxor* wife] —**ux·o′ri·ous·ly** *adv.* —**ux·o′ri·ous·ness** *n.*

Uz·bek (ŏŏz′bek, uz′-) *n.* 1. A member of a Turkic people dominant in Turkestan; a native or inhabitant of the Uzbek S.S.R. 2. The Turkic language of the Uzbeks. Also **Uz′beg.**

V

v, V (vē) *n. pl.* **v's** or **vs, V's** or **Vs, vees** (vēz) 1. The twenty-second letter of the English alphabet. 2. The sound represented by the letter *v.* 3. Anything shaped like a V. —*symbol* 1. The Roman numeral five. 2. *Chem.* Vanadium (symbol V).

va·can·cy (vā′kən·sē) *n. pl.* **·cies** 1. The state of being vacant; emptiness. 2. That which is vacant; empty space. 3. An unoccupied post, place, or office.

va·cant (vā′kənt) *adj.* 1. Containing or holding nothing; esp., devoid of occupants; empty. 2. Occupied with nothing; unemployed; free. 3. Being or appearing without intelligence; inane. 4. Having no incumbent; unfilled: a *vacant* office. 5. Devoid of thought. [< L *vacare* to be empty] —**va′cant·ly** *adv.*

va·cate (vā′kāt) *v.t.* **·cat·ed, ·cat·ing** 1. To make vacant; leave. 2. To set aside; annul. 3. To give up (a position or office); quit.

va·ca·tion (vā·kā′shən) *n.* 1. An interlude, usu. of several days or weeks, from one's customary duties, as for recreation or rest. 2. The intermission of the course of studies in an educational institution. —*v.i.* To take a vacation. [< L *vacatio, -onis* freedom from duty] —**va·ca′tion·er, va·ca′tion·ist** *n.*

vac·ci·nate (vak′sə·nāt) *v.t. & v.i.* **·nat·ed, ·nat·ing** *Med.* To inoculate with a vaccine as a preventive measure; esp., to inoculate against smallpox. —**vac′ci·na′tion** *n.* —**vac′·ci·na′tor** *n.*

vac·cine (vak·sēn′, vak′sēn) *n.* Any preparation containing bacteria or viruses so treated as to give immunity from specific diseases when injected into the subject. [< L *vaccinus* pertaining to a cow] —**vac′ci·nal** (-sə·nəl) *adj.*

vac·il·late (vas′ə·lāt) *v.i.* **·lat·ed, ·lat·ing** 1. To sway one way and the other; totter. 2. To fluctuate. 3. To waver in mind; be irresolute. [< L *vacillare* to waver] —**vac′il·lan·cy** (-lən·sē) *n.* —**vac′il·lant** (-lənt) *adj.* —**vac′il·la′tion** *n.* —**vac′il·la·to′ry** (-lə·tôr′ē) *adj.*

va·cu·i·ty (va·kyōō′ə·tē) *n. pl.* **·ties** 1. The state of being a vacuum; emptiness. 2. Vacant space; a void. 3. Lack of intelligence or thought. 4. An inane or idle thing or statement. [< L *vacuus* empty]

vac·u·ole (vak′yōō·ōl) *n. Biol.* A minute cavity containing air, a watery fluid, or a chemical secretion of the protoplasm, found in an organ, tissue, or cell. [< L *vacuus* empty] —**vac′u·o·lar** *adj.*

vac·u·ous (vak′yōō·əs) *adj.* 1. Having no contents; empty. 2. Lacking intelligence; blank. [< L *vacuus*] —**vac′u·ous·ly** *adv.* —**vac′u·ous·ness** *n.*

vac·u·um (vak′yōō·əm, -yōōm) *n. pl.* **·u·ums** or **·u·a** (-yōō·ə) 1. A space absolutely devoid of matter. 2. A space from which air or other gas has been exhausted to a very high degree. 3. A void. 4. A vacuum cleaner. —*adj.* 1. Of, or used in the production of, a vacuum. 2. Exhausted or partly exhausted of gas, air, or vapor. 3. Operated by suction to produce a vacuum. —*v.t. & v.i.* To clean with a vacuum cleaner. [< L, neut. of *vacuus* empty]

vacuum bottle A thermos bottle. Also **vacuum flask.**

vacuum cleaner A machine for cleaning carpets, furnishings, etc., by suction. —**vacuum cleaning**

vacuum tube *Electronics* 1. A glass tube exhausted of air to a high degree and containing electrodes between which electric discharges may be passed. 2. An electron tube.

va·de me·cum (vā′dē mē′kəm) *Latin* Anything carried for constant use, as a guidebook, manual, or bag; literally, go with me. Also **va′de·me′cum, va′de-me′cum.**

vag·a·bond (vag′ə·bond) *n.* 1. One who wanders from place to place without visible means of support; a tramp. 2. A wanderer; nomad. —*adj.* 1. Pertaining to a vagabond; nomadic. 2. Having no definite residence; wandering; aimless. [< L *vagus* wandering] —**vag′a·bond′age** *n.* —**vag′a·bond′ish** *adj.* —**vag′a·bond′ism** *n.*

va·gar·y (və·gâr′ē, vā′gər·ē) *n. pl.* **·gar·ies** A wild fancy; extravagant notion. [< L *vagari* to wander]

va·gi·na (və·jī′nə) *n. pl.* **·nas** or **·nae** (-nē) *Anat.* The canal leading from the external genital orifice in female mammals to the uterus. [< L, sheath] —**vag·i·nal** (vaj′ə·nəl, və·jī′-) *adj.*

vag·i·nate (vaj′ə·nit, -nāt) *adj.* 1. Having a sheath. 2. Formed into a sheath; tubular. Also **vag′i·nat′ed** (-nā′tid). [< L *vagina* sheath]

va·grant (vā′grənt) *n.* A person without a settled home; vagabond; tramp. —*adj.* 1. Wandering about as a vagrant. 2. Of or pertaining to a wanderer; nomadic. 3. Having a wandering course. [ME < OF *wacrer* to walk, wander] —**va′gran·cy** *n.* —**va′·grant·ly** *adv.*

vague (vāg) *adj.* **vagu·er, vagu·est** 1. Lacking definiteness or precision; not clear. 2. Shadowy; hazy. [< L *vagus* wandering] —**vague′ly** *adv.* —**vague′ness** *n.*

va·gus (vā′gəs) *n. pl.* **·gi** (-jī) *Anat.* Either of the tenth pair of cranial nerves sending branches to the lungs, heart, stomach, and most of the abdominal viscera. Also **vagus nerve.** [< L, wandering]

vain (vān) *adj.* 1. Filled with or showing undue admiration for oneself, one's appearance, etc.; conceited. 2. Unproductive;

fruitless. 3. Having no real basis; empty: *vain* hopes. 4. Ostentatious; showy. —**in vain** To no purpose; without effect. [< L *vanus* empty] —**vain′ly** *adv.* —**vain′ness** *n.*

vain·glo·ry (vān·glôr′ē) *n. pl.* **·ries** Excessive or groundless vanity; also, vain pomp; boastfulness. [< Med.L *vana gloria* empty pomp, show] —**vain·glo′ri·ous** (-glôr′ē·əs) *adj.* —**vain·glo′ri·ous·ly** *adv.* —**vain·glo′ri·ous·ness** *n.*

val·ance (val′əns, vā′ləns) *n.* 1. A hanging drapery, as from the framework of a bed to the floor. 2. A short drapery, board, or plate across the top of a window. —*v.t.* **·anced, ·anc·ing** To furnish with a valance. [< OF *avaler* to descend, or after *Valence*, textile-manufacturing commune in France] —**val′·anced** *adj.*

vale (vāl) *n.* *Chiefly Poetic* A valley. [< L *vallis*]

val·e·dic·tion (val′ə·dik′shən) *n.* A bidding farewell. [< L *valere* to be well + *dicere* to say]

val·e·dic·to·ri·an (val′ə·dik·tôr′ē·ən) *n.* A student who delivers a valedictory at graduating exercises, usu. the graduating student ranking highest in scholarship.

val·e·dic·to·ry (val′ə·dik′tər·ē) *adj.* Pertaining to a leavetaking. —*n. pl.* **·ries** A parting address.

va·lence (vā′ləns) *n.* *Chem.* The combining capacity of an element or radical expressed as the number of atoms of hydrogen (or its equivalent) with which an atom of the element or radical can combine, or which it can replace. Also **va′len·cy.** [< L *valere* to be strong]

val·en·tine (val′ən·tīn) *n.* 1. A greeting card or token of affection sent on Saint Valentine's Day. 2. A sweetheart.

val·et (val′ā, val′it; *Fr.* và·le′) *n.* 1. A gentleman's personal servant. 2. One who performs personal services for patrons at a hotel. —*v.t.* & *v.i.* To serve or act as a valet. [< F, a groom < OF *vaslet, varlet*, dim. of *vasal* vassal]

val·e·tu·di·nar·i·an (val′ə·tōō′də·nâr′ē·ən, -tyōō′-) *n.* A chronic invalid; one unduly solicitous about his health. —*adj.* Seeking to recover health; infirm. Also **val′e·tu′di·nar′y.** [< L < *valere* to be well] —**val′e·tu′·di·nar′i·an·ism** *n.*

val·iant (val′yənt) *adj.* 1. Strong and courageous. 2. Performed with valor; heroic. [< L *valere* to be strong] —**val′iant·ly** *adv.* —**val′iance, val′ian·cy, val′iant·ness** *n.*

val·id (val′id) *adj.* 1. Based on evidence that can be supported; convincing; sound. 2. Legally binding; effective; warranted. [< L *validus* powerful < *valere* to be strong] —**va·lid·i·ty** (və·lid′ə·tē), **val′id·ness** *n.* —**val′id·ly** *adv.*

val·i·date (val′ə·dāt) *v.t.* **·dat·ed, ·dat·ing** 1. To make valid; ratify and confirm. 2. To declare legally valid; legalize. —**val′i·da′tion** *n.*

va·lise (və·lēs′) *n.* A portable case for clothes, etc.; suitcase. [< F < Ital. *valigia*]

val·ley (val′ē) *n. pl.* **·leys** 1. A depression of the earth's surface, as one through which a stream flows; level or low land between mountains, hills, or high lands. 2. Any depression or hollow like a valley. [< L *vallis*]

val·or (val′ər) *n.* Courage; personal bravery. Also *Brit.* **val′our.** [< L *valere* to be strong] —**val′or·ous** *adj.* —**val′or·ous·ly** *adv.* —**val′·or·ous·ness** *n.*

val·or·i·za·tion (val′ər·ə·zā′shən, -ī·zā′-) *n.* The maintenance by governmental action of an artificial price for any product. [< Pg. *valorização* < *valor* value] —**val′or·ize** *v.t.* **·ized, ·iz·ing**

val·u·a·ble (val′yōō·ə·bəl, val′yə·bəl) *adj.* 1. Having great financial worth; costly. 2. Having material value. 3. Useful. 4. Highly esteemed; worthy. —*n.* *Usu. pl.* An article of worth or value, as a piece of jewelry. —**val′u·a·ble·ness** *n.* —**val′u·a·bly** *adv.*

val·u·a·tion (val′yōō·ā′shən) *n.* 1. The act of valuing. 2. Estimated worth or value. —**val′u·a′tion·al** *adj.*

val·ue (val′yōō) *n.* 1. The desirability or worth of a thing; intrinsic worth; utility. 2. *Often pl.* Something regarded as desirable, worthy, or right, as a belief, standard, or moral precept. 3. The rate at which a commodity is potentially exchangeable for others; worth in money; market price. 4. A bargain. 5. Attributed or assumed valuation; esteem or regard. 6. Exact meaning. 7. *Music* The relative length of a tone or note. 8. *Math.* The quantity, magnitude, or number represented by an algebraic symbol or expression. 9. In the graphic arts, the relation of the elements of a picture, as light and shade, to one another. —*v.t.* **·ued, ·u·ing** 1. To estimate the value or worth of; appraise. 2. To regard highly; esteem; prize. 3. To place a relative estimate of value or desirability upon. 4. To give a (specified) value to. [< OF *valoir* to be worth < L *valere*] —**val′ue·less** *adj.* —**val′u·er** *n.*

value added tax A tax added to a product or service at each stage of its production or distribution, based on its increased value at that stage. Abbr. *VAT, V.A.T.*

val·ued (val′yōōd) *adj.* 1. Highly esteemed. 2. Having a (specified) value.

val·vate (val′vāt) *adj.* 1. Valvular. 2. *Bot.* Meeting without overlapping, as petals. [< L *valvatus* with folding doors]

valve (valv) *n.* 1. *Mech.* Any contrivance or arrangement that regulates the amount and direction of flow, as of a liquid. 2. *Anat.* A structure, as in the heart, allowing flow of a fluid in one direction only. 3. *Zool.* One of the parts of a shell, as of a mollusk. 4. A device in certain brass instruments for lengthening the air column and lowering the pitch of the instrument's scale. —*v.t.* **valved, valv·ing** To furnish with or control by a valve or valves. [< L *valva* leaf of a door] —**val′val** (-vəl), **val′var** (-vər) *adj.* —**valve′less** *adj.*

val·vu·lar (val′vyə·lər) *adj.* 1. Of the nature of a valve, as of the heart. 2. Having valves.

va·moose (va·mōōs′) *v.t.* & *v.i.* **·moosed, ·moos·ing** *Slang* To leave hastily or hurriedly; quit. Also **va·mose′** (-mōs′). [< Sp. *vamos* let us go]

vamp[1] (vamp) *n.* 1. The piece of leather forming the upper front part of a boot or shoe. 2. Something added to give an old thing a new appearance. 3. *Music* A simple improvised accompaniment. —*v.t.* 1. To provide with a vamp. 2. To repair or patch. 3. *Music* To improvise an accompaniment to. —*v.i.* 4. *Music* To improvise accompaniments. [< OF *avant* before + *pied* foot] **—vamp′er** *n.*

vamp[2] (vamp) *Informal* *v.t. & v.i.* To seduce or try to seduce (a man) by feminine charms. **—***n.* An unscrupulous flirt. [Short for VAMPIRE]

vam·pire (vam′pīr) *n.* 1. In folklore, a corpse that rises from its grave at night to suck the blood of the living. 2. One who victimizes persons of the opposite sex; esp., a woman who exploits or degrades her lover. 3. A tropical American bat, that feeds on the blood of animals and, sometimes, people: also **vampire bat.** [< G *vampir* < Slavic] **—vam·pir·ic** (vam·pir′ik), **vam′pir·ish** *adj.* **—vam′pir·ism** *n.*

van[1] (van) *n.* A large covered vehicle, as a truck, for transporting furniture, livestock, etc. [Short for CARAVAN]

van[2] (van) *n.* 1. The portion of an army, fleet, etc., that is nearest or in advance of the front. 2. The vanguard of a movement. [Short for VANGUARD]

va·na·di·um (və·nā′dē·əm) *n.* A rare, silver-white metallic element (symbol V), used in steel alloys. [< NL < ON *Vanadīs,* a name of the Norse goddess Freya]

Van Al·len radiation (van al′ən) High-intensity radiation circling the earth in an inner and outer belt conforming to the earth's magnetic field. Also **Van Allen belts.** [after James A. *Van Allen,* born 1914, U.S. physicist]

van·dal (van′dəl) *n.* One who vandalizes. **—***adj.* Wantonly destructive. [< VANDAL] **—van·dal·ic** (van·dal′ik) *adj.*

Van·dal (van′dəl) *n.* One of a Germanic people who pillaged Rome in 455. **—Van·dal·ic** (van·dal′ik) *adj.* **—Van′dal·ism** *n.*

van·dal·ize (van′dəl·īz) *v.t. & v.i.* **·ized, ·iz·ing** To destroy or deface (property) willfully. **—van′dal·ism** *n.*

Van·dyke beard (van·dīk′) A short pointed beard. [after Anthony *Van Dyck,* 1599–1641, Flemish painter, whose subjects often wore such beards]

vane (vān) *n.* 1. A movable thin plate of metal or wood that indicates the direction of the wind; weather vane. 2. An arm or blade extending from a rotating shaft, as of a windmill, propeller, turbine, etc. 3. *Ornithol.* The web of a feather. [OE *fana* flag] **—vaned** *adj.*

van·guard (van′gärd) *n.* 1. The advance guard of an army; the van. 2. Those in the forefront of a movement, as in art, etc. [< OF *avant* before + *garde* guard]

va·nil·la (və·nil′ə) *n.* 1. A flavoring extract made from the podlike seed capsules of a climbing tropical orchid. 2. The seed capsule of this plant: also **vanilla bean.** [< Sp. dim. of *vaina* sheath, pod < L *vagina* sheath] **—va·nil′lic** *adj.*

va·nil·lin (və·nil′in) *n.* *Chem.* A colorless, fragrant, crystalline compound, contained in vanilla. Also **va·nil·line** (və·nil′in, -ēn).

van·ish (van′ish) *v.i.* 1. To disappear from sight; fade away; depart. 2. To pass out of existence. [< L *evanescere* to fade away] **—van′ish·er** *n.*

van·ish·ing point (van′ish·ing) In perspective, the point at which parallel lines appear to converge.

van·i·ty (van′ə·tē) *n.* *pl.* **·ties** 1. The condition or character of being vain; conceit. 2. Ambitious display; ostentation. 3. The quality or state of being fruitless, useless, etc. 4. That which is vain or unsubstantial. 5. A bag or box containing cosmetics, comb, mirror, etc.: also **vanity case.** 6. A dressing table. [< L *vanus* empty, vain]

van·quish (vang′kwish, van′-) *v.t.* To defeat; overcome; conquer. [< L *vincere* to conquer] **—van′quish·a·ble** *adj.* **—van′quish·er** *n.*

van·tage (van′tij) *n.* 1. A position or condition that gives one an advantage: also **vantage ground.** 2. A strategic position affording perspective; point of view: also **vantage point.** [OF < L *ab ante* from before]

van·ward (van′wərd) *adj. & adv.* In or toward the van or front.

vap·id (vap′id) *adj.* Flat or flavorless; dull; insipid. [< L *vapidus* insipid] **—va·pid·i·ty** (və·pid′ə·tē) *n.* **—vap′id·ly** *adv.*

va·por (vā′pər) *n.* 1. Moisture in the air; esp., light mist. 2. Any light, cloudy substance in the air, as fumes. 3. Any substance in the gaseous state, that is usu. a liquid or solid. **—***v.t. & v.i.* To vaporize. Also *Brit.* **va′pour.** [< L *vapor* steam] **—va′por·a·bil′i·ty** *n.* **—va′por·a·ble** *adj.* **—va′por·er** *n.* **—va′por·ish** *adj.*

va·por·ize (vā′pə·rīz) *v.t. & v.i.* **·ized, ·iz·ing** To convert or be converted into vapor. **—va′por·iz′a·ble** *adj.* **—va′por·i·za′tion** *n.* **—va′por·iz′er** *n.*

va·por·ous (vā′pər·əs) *adj.* 1. Of or like vapor; foggy; misty. 2. Full of or producing vapors. 3. Diaphanous; ethereal. Also **va′por·y.** **—va·por·os·i·ty** (vā′pə·ros′ə·tē) *n.* **—va′por·ous·ly** *adv.* **—va′por·ous·ness** *n.*

vapor pressure *Physics* The pressure of a confined vapor in equilibrium with its liquid at any specific temperature. Also **vapor tension.**

vapor trail *Aeron.* A contrail.

va·que·ro (vä·kā′rō) *n.* *pl.* **·ros** (-rōz) A herdsman; cowboy. [< Sp. < *vaca* cow]

vari- *combining form* Various; different: *variform, varicolored.* Also **vario-.** [< *varius* varied]

var·i·a·ble (vâr′ē·ə·bəl) *adj.* 1. Having the capacity of varying; mutable. 2. Having a tendency to change; not constant. 3. Having no definite value as regards quantity. **—***n.* 1. That which varies or is subject to change. 2. *Math.* A quantity susceptible of fluctuating in value or magnitude under different conditions. [< L *varius* various, diverse] **—var′i·a·bil′i·ty, var′i·a·ble·ness** *n.* **—var′i·a·bly** *adv.*

variable star *Astron.* A star whose apparent magnitude varies at different times.

var·i·ance (vâr′ē·əns) *n.* 1. The act of varying, or the state of being variant; difference; discrepancy. 2. Dissension; discord. **—at variance** 1. Disagreeing or conflicting, as facts. 2. In a state of dissension or discord.

var·i·ant (vâr′ē·ənt) *adj.* 1. Having or showing variation; differing. 2. Tending to vary; changing. 3. Restless; fickle; inconstant. **—***n.* A thing that differs from another in form only; esp., a different spelling or pronunciation of a word. [See VARIABLE.]

var·i·a·tion (vâr′ē·ā′shən) *n.* 1. The act,

process, state, or result of varying; modification; diversity. 2. The extent to which a thing varies. 3. A repetition with its essential features intact and other features modified. 4. *Music* A modification of a basic theme. 5. *Biol.* Deviation from the type or parent form. **—var′i·a′tion·al** *adj.*

var·i·col·ored (vâr′i·kul′ərd) *adj.* Variegated in color; of various colors. Also *Brit.* **var′i·col′oured.**

var·i·cose (var′ə·kōs) *adj. Pathol.* Abnormally dilated, as veins. [< L *varix, -icis* varicose vein] **—var′i·cos′i·ty** (-kos′ə·tē) *n.*

var·ied (vâr′ēd) *adj.* 1. Consisting of differing parts; diverse. 2. Partially or repeatedly altered, modified, etc. 3. Varicolored. **—var′ied·ly** *adv.*

var·i·e·gate (vâr′ē·ə·gāt′) *v.t.* **·gat·ed, ·gat·ing** 1. To mark with different colors or tints; dapple; spot; streak. 2. To make varied; diversify. [< LL *varius* various + *agere* to drive, do] **—var′i·e·gat′ed** *adj.* **—var′i·e·ga′tion** *n.*

va·ri·e·ty (və·rī′ə·tē) *n. pl.* **·ties** 1. The state or character of being various or varied; diversity. 2. A collection of diverse things. 3. The possession of different characteristics by one individual. 4. A limited class of things that differ in certain common peculiarities from a larger class to which they belong. 5. *Biol.* An individual or a group that differs from the type species in certain characters; a subdivision of a species. [< L *varius* various] **—va·ri′e·tal** (-təl) *adj.* **—va·ri′e·tal·ly** *adv.*

variety show A theatrical show, as in vaudeville, consisting of a series of short, diversified acts or numbers.

va·ri·o·la (və·rī′ə·lə) *n. Pathol.* Any of a group of virus diseases characterized by pustules, as smallpox. [< Med.L, pustule < L *varius* speckled] **—va·ri′o·lar, va·ri′o·lous** *adj.*

var·i·o·rum (vâr′ē·ôr′əm, -ō′rəm) *n.* An edition containing various versions of a text, usu. with notes and comments by different critics or editors. Also **variorum edition.** [< L (*cum notis*) *variorum* (with the notes) of various persons] **—var′i·o′rum** *adj.*

var·i·ous (vâr′ē·əs) *adj.* 1. Characteristically different from one another; diverse. 2. More than one; several. 3. Many-sided; varying. 4. Having a diversity of appearance; variegated. [< L *varius*] **—var′i·ous·ly** *adv.* **—var′i·ous·ness** *n.*

var·ix (vâr′iks) *n. pl.* **var·i·ces** (vâr′ə·sēz) *Pathol.* **a** Permanent dilatation, as of a vein. **b** A vessel thus distorted, as a varicose vein. [< L, a varicose vein]

var·let (vär′lit) *n. Archaic* 1. A menial; also, a page. 2. A knave or scoundrel. [< OF, groom]

var·mint (vär′mənt) *n. Dial.* An obnoxious person or animal. [Alter. of VERMIN]

var·nish (vär′nish) *n.* 1. A solution of certain gums or resins in alcohol, linseed oil, etc., used to produce a shining, transparent coat on a surface; also, the coat itself or the surface. 2. A product resembling varnish. 3. Superficial polish or politeness. **—***v.t.* 1. To cover with varnish. 2. To give a glossy appearance to; polish. 3. To hide by a deceptive covering; gloss over. [< Med.L *vernicium* a resin] **—var′nish·er** *n.*

var·si·ty (vär′sə·tē) *n. pl.* **·ties** *Informal* The highest ranking team that represents a school, esp. in sports. [< UNIVERSITY]

var·y (vâr′ē) *v.* **var·ied, var·y·ing** *v.t.* 1. To change the form, nature, etc., of; modify. 2. To cause to be different from one another. 3. To impart variety to; diversify. **—***v.i.* 4. To become changed in form, nature, etc. 5. To be diverse; differ. 6. To deviate: with *from.* [< L *varius* diverse] **—var′i·er** *n.*

vas (vas) *n. pl.* **va·sa** (vā′sə) *Biol.* A blood vessel or duct. [< L, vessel, dish]

vas·cu·lar (vas′kyə·lər) *adj. Biol.* **a** Of or containing ducts that transport body liquids, as blood, lymph, etc. **b** Richly supplied with blood vessels. Also **vas′cu·lose** (-lōs), **vas′cu·lous** (-ləs). [< L *vas* vessel] **—vas′·cu·lar′i·ty** (-lar′ə·tē) *n.* **—vas′cu·lar·ly** *adv.*

vas def·er·ens (vas def′ər·enz) *Anat.* The duct by which semen is conveyed from a testicle. [< L *vas* vessel + *deferens* leading down]

vase (vās, vāz, väz) *n.* A decorative container used as an ornament or for holding flowers. [< L *vas* vessel]

va·sec·to·my (və·sek′tə·mē) *n. pl.* **·mies** *Surg.* Removal of a portion of the vas deferens, esp. as a sterilization procedure.

Vas·e·line (vas′ə·lēn, -lin) *n.* Proprietary name for a brand of petrolatum. Also **vas′e·line.**

vaso- *combining form Physiol.* 1. A vessel, esp., a blood vessel. 2. The vas deferens. Also, before vowels, **vas-.** [< L *vas* vessel]

vas·o·mo·tor (vas′ō·mō′tər) *adj. Physiol.* Producing contraction or dilatation in the walls of vessels.

vas·sal (vas′əl) *n.* 1. In the feudal system, one who held land of a lord by a feudal tenure. 2. A servant, slave, or bondman. [< LL *vassus* servant < Celtic]

vas·sal·age (vas′əl·ij) *n.* 1. The state of being a vassal; also, the duties and obligations of a vassal. 2. Servitude in general. 3. Land held by feudal tenure; a fief.

vast (vast) *adj.* 1. Of great extent or size; immense. 2. Very great in number, quantity, degree, intensity, etc. [< L *vastus* waste, empty, vast] **—vast′ly** *adv.* **—vast′ness** *n.*

vat (vat) *n.* A large vessel, tub, etc., for holding liquids. **—***v.t.* **vat·ted, vat·ting** To put into or treat in a vat. [OE *fæt*]

Vat·i·can (vat′ə·kən) *n.* 1. The papal palace in Vatican City, Rome. 2. The papal government. [< L *Vaticanus* (*mons*) Vatican (hill), in Rome]

vaude·ville (vōd′vil, vôd′-; vō′də-, vô′də-) *n.* A miscellaneous theatrical entertainment, as a variety show. [< F *Vau de Vire* the valley of the Vire river]

vault[1] (vôlt) *n.* 1. An arched structure, as a ceiling or roof. 2. Any vaultlike covering, as the sky. 3. An underground room or compartment covered by a vault, esp. when used for storage. 4. A strongly protected place for keeping valuables, as in a bank. 5. A burial chamber. **—***v.t.* 1. To cover with or as with a vault. 2. To construct in the form of a vault. [< L *volvere* to roll]

vault[2] (vôlt) *v.t.* & *v.i.* To leap or leap over, esp. with a boost from a pole or the hands.

—*n.* A leap or bound. [< OF *volter* to leap, gambol] —**vault′er** *n.*
vault·ing[1] (vôl′ting) *n.* Vaulted construction.
vault·ing[2] (vôl′ting) *adj.* 1. That overleaps. 2. Unduly confident or presumptuous.
vaunt (vônt) *v.t.* & *v.i.* To boast of (something); brag. —*n.* Boastful assertion. [< LL *vanitare* to brag < L *vanus* empty, vain] —**vaunt′er** *n.* —**vaunt′ing·ly** *adv.*
veal (vēl) *n.* The flesh of a calf considered as food. [< L *vitellus*, dim. of *vitulus* calf]
vec·tor (vek′tər) *n.* 1. *Math.* A physical quantity that has magnitude and direction in space. 2. *Med.* A carrier of pathogenic microorganisms from one host to another. [< L, carrier] —**vec·to′ri·al** (-tôr′ē·əl) *adj.*
Ve·da (vā′də, vē′-) *n.* 1. One of the collections of Indian sacred writings that form the Hindu scriptures. 2. The Vedas collectively. [< Skt., knowledge] —**Ve′da·ism** *n.* —**Ve′·dic, Ve·da·ic** (vi·dā′ik) *adj.*
Ve·dan·ta (vi·dän′tə, -dan′-) *n.* Any of several schools of Hindu religious philosophy; esp., a monistic system that teaches the worship of Brahma. [< Skt. *Veda* Veda + *anta* end] —**Ve·dan′tic** *adj.* —**Ve·dan′tism** *n.*
veep (vēp) *n. Slang* A vice president, esp. of the United States.
veer (vir) *v.i.* 1. *Naut.* To turn to another course. 2. To change direction by a clockwise motion, as the wind. 3. To change direction; shift. —*v.t.* 4. To change the direction of. —*n.* A change in direction; swerve. [< F *virer* to turn]
veer·y (vir′ē) *n. pl.* **veer·ies** A tawny thrush of eastern North America. [Prob. imit.]
Ve·ga (vē′gə, vā′-) *n.* One of the 20 brightest stars in the constellation Lyra. [< Med. L < Arabic (*al-Nasr*) *al-Waqi* the falling (vulture)]
veg·e·ta·ble (vej′ə·tə·bəl, vej′tə-) *n.* 1. The edible part of any herbaceous plant, raw or cooked. 2. Any member of the vegetable kingdom; a plant. —*adj.* 1. Pertaining to plants, esp. garden or farm vegetables. 2. Derived from, of the nature of, or resembling plants. 3. Made from or consisting of vegetables. [< L *vegetare* to animate]
vegetable kingdom The division of nature that includes all plants.
vegetable oil Any of various oils expressed from the seeds or fruits of plants.
veg·e·tal (vej′ə·təl) *adj.* 1. Of or pertaining to plants or vegetables. 2. Characterizing those vital processes that are common to plants and animals, esp. as distinguished from sensation and volition. [< L *vegetus* lively, vigorous]
veg·e·tant (vej′ə·tənt) *adj.* 1. Invigorating; vivifying; stimulating growth. 2. Of the nature of plant life.
veg·e·tar·i·an (vej′ə·târ′ē·ən) *adj.* Pertaining to or advocating a diet containing no meat. —*n.* One who eats no meat. —**veg′e·tar′i·an·ism** *n.*
veg·e·tate (vej′ə·tāt) *v.i.* **·tat·ed, ·tat·ing** 1. To grow, as a plant. 2. To live in a monotonous, passive way. —**veg′e·ta′tive, veg′e·tive** *adj.* —**veg′e·ta′tive·ly** *adv.*
veg·e·ta·tion (vej′ə·tā′shən) *n.* 1. The process of vegetating. 2. Plant life in the aggregate. 3. *Pathol.* An abnormal growth on the body. —**veg′e·ta′tion·al** *adj.*
ve·he·ment (vē′ə·mənt) *adj.* 1. Impetuous or passionate; ardent. 2. Forceful or energetic; violent. [< L *vehemens, -entis* impetuous, rash] —**ve′he·mence** *n.* —**ve′he·ment·ly** *adv.*
ve·hi·cle (vē′ə·kəl) *n.* 1. Any contrivance fitted with wheels or runners for carrying something; a conveyance, as a car or sled. 2. A liquid, as oil, with which pigments are mixed in painting. 3. Anything by means of which something else, as power, thought, etc., is transmitted or communicated. 4. A play, motion picture, etc., that permits a performer to display his particular talents. [< L *vehere* to carry, ride] —**ve·hic·u·lar** (vi·hik′·yə·lər, vē-) *adj.*
veil (vāl) *n.* 1. A thin fabric worn over the face or head for concealment, protection, or ornament. 2. Any piece of fabric used to conceal something; a curtain. 3. Anything that conceals. —**to take the veil** To become a nun. —*v.t.* 1. To cover with a veil. 2. To hide; disguise. [< L *velum* piece of cloth, sail] —**veil′er** *n.*
veil·ing (vā′ling) *n.* 1. Material for veils. 2. A veil.
vein (vān) *n.* 1. *Anat.* One of the muscular, tubular vessels that convey blood to the heart. 2. *Entomol.* One of the radiating supports of an insect's wing. 3. *Bot.* One of the slender vascular bundles that form the framework of a leaf. 4. In mining, a lode. 5. A long, irregular, colored streak, as in wood, marble, etc. 6. A distinctive trait, tendency, or disposition. 7. A temporary state of mind; mood. —*v.t.* 1. To furnish or fill with veins. 2. To streak or ornament with veins. [< L *vena* blood vessel] —**veined, vein′y** *adj*
vein·ing (vā′ning) *n.* A network of veins.
vein·let (vān′lit) *n.* A small vein.
ve·lar (vē′lər) *adj.* 1. Of or pertaining to a velum, esp. to the soft palate. 2. *Phonet.* Formed with the back of the tongue touching or near the soft palate, as (k) in *cool*, (g) in *go*. —*n. Phonet.* A velar consonant. [< L *velum* a sail, curtain]
ve·lar·ize (vē′lə·rīz) *v.* **·ized, ·iz·ing** *v.t.* *Phonet.* To modify (a sound) by raising the back of the tongue toward the soft palate. —*v.i.* To be modified to a velar sound.
veldt (velt, felt) *n.* In South Africa, open country or grassland. Also **veld.** [< Afrikaans *veld* < Du., field]
vel·lum (vel′əm) *n.* 1. Fine parchment made from the skins of calves. 2. A manuscript written on such parchment. 3. Paper made to resemble parchment. [< OF *veel, viel* calf]
ve·loc·i·pede (və·los′ə·pēd) *n.* 1. An early form of bicycle or tricycle. 2. A tricycle. [< L *velox, velocis* swift + *pes, pedis* foot]
ve·loc·i·ty (və·los′ə·tē) *n. pl.* **·ties** 1. The state of moving swiftly; speed. 2. The rate of motion. [< L *velox* swift]
ve·lour (və·lo͝or′) *n. pl.* **·lours** (-lo͝orz) A soft, velvetlike fabric. Also **ve·lours′.** [< F. See VELURE.]
ve·lum (vē′ləm) *n. pl.* **·la** 1. *Biol.* A thin membranous covering or partition. 2. *Anat.* The soft palate: see under PALATE. [< L]
ve·lure (və·lo͝or′) *n.* Velvet, or a fabric resembling velvet. [< L *villus* shaggy hair]
vel·vet (vel′vit) *n.* 1. A fabric having on one side a thick, short, smooth pile, formed either of loops (**pile velvet**) or of single threads

(cut velvet). 2. Anything resembling such a fabric in softness, smoothness, etc. 3. The furry skin covering a growing antler. —*adj.* 1. Made of velvet. 2. Velvety. [< Med.L *velvetum* < L *villus* shaggy hair]

vel·vet·een (vel′və·tēn′) *n.* 1. A cotton fabric with a short, close pile like velvet. 2. *pl.* Clothes, esp. trousers, made of this material.

vel·vet·y (vel′vit·ē) *adj.* Smooth and soft like velvet.

ve·na ca·va (vē′nə kā′və) *pl.* **ve·nae ca·vae** (vē′nē kā′vē) *Anat.* Either of the two great venous trunks emptying into the right atrium of the heart. [< L, hollow vein]

ve·nal (vē′nəl) *adj.* 1. Ready to sell honor or principle, or to accept a bribe; mercenary. 2. Subject to or characterized by corruption. [< L *venum* sale] —**ve·nal′i·ty** (-nal′ə·tē) *n.* —**ve′nal·ly** *adv.*

ve·na·tion (vē·nā′shən) *n.* *Biol.* The arrangement of veins, as in a leaf.

vend (vend) *v.t.* 1. To sell. 2. To utter (an opinion); publish. —*v.i.* 3. To be a vender. 4. To be sold. [< F *vendre* < L *venum* sale + *dare* to give] —**ven·di′tion** *n.* —**vend′or** or **vend′er** *n.*

ven·det·ta (ven·det′ə) *n.* A blood feud between families. [< Ital. < L *vindicta* vengeance]

vend·i·ble (ven′də·bəl) *adj.* Capable of being vended or sold; marketable. —*n.* A vendible thing. —**vend′i·bil′i·ty** *n.* —**vend′i·bly** *adv.*

vend·ing machine (ven′ding) A coin-operated device that dispenses some product or packaged article.

ve·neer (və·nir′) *n.* 1. A thin layer, as of choice wood, upon a commoner surface. 2. Mere outside show or elegance. —*v.t.* 1. To cover (a surface) with veneer. 2. To conceal with an attractive or deceptive surface. [Earlier *fineer* < F *fournir* to furnish] —**ve·neer′er** *n.*

ven·er·a·ble (ven′ər·ə·bəl) *adj.* Meriting or commanding veneration; worthy of reverence: now usu. implying age. [< L *venerari* to revere] —**ven′er·a·bil′i·ty** *n.* —**ven′er·a·bly** *adv.*

ven·er·ate (ven′ə·rāt) *v.t.* **·at·ed, ·at·ing** To regard with respect and deference; revere. [< L *veneratus*, pp. of *venerari* to revere] —**ven′er·a′tion** *n.*

ve·ne·re·al (və·nir′ē·əl) *adj.* 1. Pertaining to or proceeding from sexual intercourse. 2. Communicated by sexual relations. 3. Of or pertaining to venereal disease. [< L *Venus*, Roman goddess of love]

venereal disease *Pathol.* One of several diseases communicated by sexual intercourse, as syphilis and gonorrhea.

ven·er·y[1] (ven′ər·ē) *n.* *pl.* **·er·ies** *Archaic* Sexual indulgence, esp. when excessive. [< L *Venus*, Roman goddess of love]

ven·er·y[2] (ven′ər·ē) *n.* *pl.* **·er·ies** *Archaic* The hunting of game. [< L *venari* to hunt]

Ve·ne·tian (və·nē′shən) *adj.* Pertaining to Venice or to its inhabitants, art, etc. —*n.* A native of Venice.

Venetian blind A flexible window screen having overlapping horizontal slats that may be opened or closed.

Venetian glass A delicate and fine glassware made in or near Venice.

Ven·e·zue·lan (ven′ə·zwā′lən, -zwē′-) *adj.* Of Venezuela or its inhabitants. —**Ven′e·zue′lan** *n.*

ven·geance (ven′jəns) *n.* The act of revenging; retribution for a wrong or injury. —**with a vengeance** With great force or violence. [< L *vindicare* to defend, avenge]

venge·ful (venj′fəl) *adj.* 1. Seeking to inflict vengeance; vindictive. 2. Serving to inflict vengeance. —**venge′ful·ly** *adv.* —**venge′ful·ness** *n.*

V-en·gine (vē′en′jen) *n.* An internal-combustion engine having groups of cylinders arranged in a V shape.

ve·ni·al (vē′nē·əl, vēn′yəl) *adj.* 1. *Theol.* That may be easily pardoned or forgiven: distinguished from *mortal*: *venial* sin. 2. Excusable; pardonable. [< L *venia* forgiveness, mercy] —**ve′ni·al′i·ty** (-al′ə·tē) *n.* —**ve′ni·al·ly** *adv.*

ve·ni·re (vi·nī′rē) *n.* *Law* A writ summoning persons to serve as a jury. Also **ve·ni′re fa·ci·as** (fā′shi·as′). [< L *venire facias*, that you cause to come]

ve·ni·re·man (vi·nī′rē·mən) *n.* *pl.* **·men** (-mən) One summoned to serve on a jury under a venire.

ven·i·son (ven′ə·zən, -sən) *n.* Deer flesh used for food. [< F < L *venatus*, pp. of *venari* to hunt]

ven·om (ven′əm) *n.* 1. The poisonous liquid secreted by certain animals, as serpents and scorpions, and introduced into the victim by a bite or sting. 2. Malice; malignity; spite. [< L *venenum* poison]

ven·om·ous (ven′əm·əs) *adj.* 1. Having glands secreting venom. 2. Poisonous; malignant; spiteful. —**ven′om·ous·ly** *adv.* —**ven′om·ous·ness** *n.*

ve·nous (vē′nəs) *adj.* 1. Of, pertaining to, or marked with veins. 2. *Physiol.* Designating the blood carried by the veins. [< L *vena* vein] —**ve′nous·ly** *adv.* —**ve′nous·ness** *n.*

vent (vent) *n.* 1. An opening, commonly small, for the passage of liquids, gases, etc. 2. Utterance; expression: chiefly in the phrase **to give vent to.** 3. *Zool.* The anus. —*v.t.* 1. To relieve or give expression to. 2. To permit to escape from an opening. [< OF *fente* cleft < L *findere* to split] —**ven′ter** *n.*

vent·age (ven′tij) *n.* 1. A small opening. 2. A finger hole in a musical instrument. [< VENT]

ven·tail (ven′tāl) *n.* The lower adjustable front of a medieval helmet. [< OF *vent* wind]

ven·ti·late (ven′tə·lāt) *v.t.* **·lat·ed, ·lat·ing** 1. To produce a free circulation of air in; admit fresh air into. 2. To provide with a vent. 3. To expose to examination and discussion. 4. To oxygenate, as blood. [< L *ventilatus*, pp. of *ventilare* to fan < *ventus* wind] —**ven′ti·la′tion** *n.* —**ven′ti·la′tive** *adj.* —**ven′ti·la′tor** *n.* —**ven′ti·la·to′ry** (-lə·tôr′ē) *adj.*

ven·tral (ven′trəl) *adj.* *Anat.* **a** Of, pertaining to, or situated on or near the abdomen. **b** On or toward the lower or anterior part of the body. [< L *venter, ventris* belly] —**ven′tral·ly** *adv.*

ven·tri·cle (ven′trə·kəl) *n.* *Anat.* 1. One of the two lower chambers of the heart, from which blood is forced into the arteries. 2. Any of various cavities in the body, as of the brain, the spinal cord, etc. [< L *ventriculus*, dim. of *venter*, *ventris* belly] —**ven·tric′u·lar** (-trik′yə·lər) *adj.*

ven·tril·o·quism (ven·tril′ə·kwiz′əm) *n.* The art of speaking in such a manner that the sounds seem to come from some source other than the person speaking. Also **ven·tril′o·quy** (-kwē). [< L *venter* belly + *loqui* to speak] —**ven·tril′o·quist** *n.* —**ven·tril′o·quis′tic** *adj.*

ven·tril·o·quize (ven·tril′ə·kwīz) *v.t.* & *v.i.* **·quized, ·quiz·ing** To speak as a ventriloquist. Also *Brit.* **ven·tril′o·quise.**

ven·ture (ven′chər) *v.* **·tured, ·tur·ing** *v.t.* 1. To expose to chance or risk; hazard; stake. 2. To run the risk of; brave. 3. To express at the risk of denial or refutation: to *venture* a suggestion. —*v.i.* 4. To take a risk; dare. —*n.* 1. An undertaking attended with risk or danger; esp., a business investment. 2. That which is ventured. —**at a venture** At hazard; offhand. [Aphetic var. of ADVENTURE] —**ven′tur·er** *n.*

ven·ture·some (ven′chər·səm) *adj.* 1. Bold; daring. 2. Involving hazard; risky. —**ven′·ture·some·ly** *adv.* —**ven′ture·some·ness** *n.*

ven·tur·ous (ven′chər·əs) *adj.* Venturesome. —**ven′tur·ous·ly** *adv.* —**ven′tur·ous·ness** *n.*

ven·ue (ven′yōō) *n.* *Law* The place where a crime is committed or a cause of action arises; also, the county or political division from which the jury must be summoned and in which the trial must be held. —**change of venue** The change of the place of trial. [< OF, orig. fem. pp. of *venir* to come < L *venire*]

Ve·nus (vē′nəs) *n.* The sixth largest planet of the solar system and second in order from the sun. [after *Venus*, Roman goddess of love and beauty]

Ve·nus's flytrap (vē′nəs·iz flī′trap′) *n.* A plant with clustered leaves whose spiked blades instantly close upon insects lighting upon them.

ve·ra·cious (və·rā′shəs) *adj.* 1. Truthful; honest. 2. True; accurate. [< L *verax*, *veracis* < *versus* true] —**ve·ra′cious·ly** *adv.* —**ve·ra′cious·ness** *n.*

ve·rac·i·ty (və·ras′ə·tē) *n.* *pl.* **·ties** 1. Truthfulness; honesty. 2. Agreement with truth; accuracy. 3. That which is true; truth.

ve·ran·da (və·ran′də) *n.* An open, usu. roofed portico or balcony along the outside of a building. Also **ve·ran′dah.** [< Pg. *varanda* railing, balustrade]

verb (vûrb) *n.* *Gram.* The part of speech that expresses existence, action, or occurrence, as the words *be*, *collide*, *think*. [< L *verbum* word]

ver·bal (vûr′bəl) *adj.* 1. Of, pertaining to, or connected with words. 2. Expressed orally; not written: a *verbal* contract. 3. Having word corresponding with word; literal: a *verbal* translation. 4. *Gram.* **a** Partaking of the nature of or derived from a verb. **b** Used to form verbs. —*n.* *Gram.* A verb form that functions as a noun (**verbal noun**): *Flying* is fun. [< L *verbum* word] —**ver′bal·ly** *adv.*

ver·bal·ism (vûr′bəl·iz′əm) *n.* 1. A verbal expression. 2. A meaningless form of words. 3. Wordiness; verbiage.

ver·bal·ize (vûr′bəl·īz) *v.* **·ized, ·iz·ing** *v.t.* 1. To express in words. 2. *Gram.* To make a verb of; change into a verb. —*v.i.* 3. To speak or write verbosely. 4. To express oneself in words. —**ver′bal·i·za′tion** *n.* —**ver′bal·iz′er** *n.*

ver·ba·tim (vər·bā′təm) *adj.* & *adv.* In the exact words; word for word. [< L *verbum* word]

ver·be·na (vər·bē′nə) *n.* Any of various American garden plants having dense terminal spikes of showy flowers. [< L, foliage, vervain]

ver·bi·age (vûr′bē·ij) *n.* Excess of words; wordiness. [< L *verbum* word]

ver·bose (vər·bōs′) *adj.* Using or containing a wearisome and unnecessary number of words; wordy. [< L *verbosus* < *verbum* word] —**ver·bose′ly** *adv.* —**ver·bos′i·ty** (-bos′ə·tē), **ver·bose′ness** *n.*

verb phrase *Gram.* A finite verb form consisting of a principle verb and an auxiliary or auxiliaries.

ver·dant (vûr′dənt) *adj.* 1. Green with vegetation. 2. Unsophisticated. [< L *viridis* green] —**ver′dan·cy** *n.*

ver·dict (vûr′dikt) *n.* 1. The decision of a jury in an action. 2. A conclusion; judgment. [< L *verus* true + *dictum*, pp. of *dicere* to say]

ver·di·gris (vûr′də·grēs, -gris) *n.* The green or bluish patina formed on copper, bronze, or brass surfaces after long exposure to the air. [< OF *verd de Grice*, *vert de Grece*, lit., green of Greece]

ver·dure (vûr′jər) *n.* The fresh greenness of growing vegetation; also, such vegetation itself. [< L *viridis* green] —**ver′dur·ous** *adj.*

verge[1] (vûrj) *n.* 1. The extreme edge of something; brink. 2. A rod, wand, or staff as a symbol of authority or emblem of office. —*v.i.* **verged, verg·ing** 1. To come near; approach; border: usu. with *on*. 2. To form the limit or verge. [< F, rod, stick < L *virga* twig]

verge[2] (vûrj) *v.i.* **verged, verg·ing** To slope; tend; incline. [< L *vergere* to bend, turn]

ver·i·fy (ver′ə·fī) *v.t.* **·fied, ·fy·ing** 1. To prove to be true or accurate; substantiate; confirm. 2. To test or ascertain the accuracy or truth of. 3. *Law* **a** To affirm under oath. **b** To add a confirmation to. [< Med.L *verus* true + *facere* to make] —**ver′i·fi′a·bil′i·ty** *n.* —**ver′i·fi′a·ble** *adj.* —**ver′i·fi′a·bly** *adv.* —**ver′i·fi·ca′tion** *n.* —**ver′i·fi′er** *n.*

ver·i·ly (ver′ə·lē) *adv.* *Archaic* In truth; really. [< VERY]

ver·i·si·mil·i·tude (ver′ə·si·mil′ə·tōōd, -tyōōd) *n.* 1. Appearance of truth. 2. That which resembles truth. [< L *verus* true + *similis* like]

ver·i·ta·ble (ver′ə·tə·bəl) *adj.* Properly so called; unquestionable: a *veritable* villain. [See VERITY.] —**ver′i·ta·ble·ness** *n.* —**ver′i·ta·bly** *adv.*

ver·i·ty (ver′ə·tē) *n.* *pl.* **·ties** 1. The quality of being correct or true. 2. A true or established statement, principle, etc.; a fact; truth. [< L *veritas* truth]

ver·juice (vûr′jōōs) *n.* The sour juice of green fruit, as unripe grapes. [< OF *vert* green + *jus* juice]

ver·meil (vûr′mil) *n.* 1. Silver or bronze gilt. 2. *Poetic* Vermilion. —*adj.* Of a bright red color. [< L *vermiculus*, dim. of *vermis* worm, the cochineal insect]

vermi- *combining form* A worm; of or related to a worm. [< L *vermis* worm]

ver·mi·cel·li (vûr′mə·sel′ē, *Ital.* ver′mē·chel′lē) *n.* Pasta made into slender cords thinner than spaghetti. [< Ital., lit., little worms]

ver·mi·cide (vûr′mə·sīd) *n.* Any substance that kills worms. **—ver′mi·ci′dal** *adj.*

ver·mic·u·lar (vər·mik′yə·lər) *adj.* 1. Having the form or motion of a worm. 2. Like the wavy tracks of a worm. Also **ver·mic′u·late** (-lāt). [< L *vermis* worm] **—ver·mic′u·lar·ly** *adv.*

ver·mi·form (vûr′mə·fôrm) *adj.* Like a worm in shape. [< L *vermis* worm + *forma* form]

vermiform appendix *Anat.* A slender, wormlike vestigial structure, protruding from the end of the cecum in man and certain other mammals.

ver·mi·fuge (vûr′mə·fyōōj) *n.* Any remedy that destroys intestinal worms. [< L *vermis* worm + *fugare* to expel] **—ver′mi·fuge** *adj.*

ver·mil·ion (vər·mil′yən) *n.* 1. A brilliant, durable red pigment, obtained naturally from cinnabar, or made synthetically. 2. The color of the pigment, an intense orange red. **—*adj.*** Of a bright red color. **—*v.t.*** To color with vermilion. [See VERMEIL.]

ver·min (vûr′min) *n.* *pl.* **·min** 1. Noxious small animals or parasitic insects, as lice, worms, rats, etc. 2. A repulsive human being. [< L *vermis* worm] **—ver′min·ous** *adj.* **—ver′min·ous·ly** *adv.*

ver·mouth (vər·mōōth′) *n.* A liqueur made from white wine flavored with aromatic herbs. [< F < G *wermuth* wormwood]

ver·nac·u·lar (vər·nak′yə·lər) *n.* 1. The native language of a locality. 2. The common everyday speech of the people, as opposed to the literary language. 3. The vocabulary or jargon of a particular profession or trade. **—*adj.*** 1. Originating in or belonging to one's native land; indigenous: said of a language, idiom, etc. 2. Using everyday speech rather than the literary language. [< L *vernaculus* native] **—ver·nac′u·lar·ly** *adv.*

ver·nal (vûr′nəl) *adj.* 1. Of or pertaining to spring. 2. Youthful; fresh. [< L *vernus* < *ver* spring] **—ver′nal·ly** *adv.*

vernal equinox See under EQUINOX.

ver·nal·ize (vûr′nəl·īz) *v.t.* **·ized, ·iz·ing** To accelerate the growth of (a plant) by cooling the seeds. **—ver′nal·i·za′tion** *n.*

ver·ni·er (vûr′nē·ər) *n.* A small, movable, auxiliary scale for obtaining fractional parts of the subdivisions of a fixed scale. Also **vernier scale.** [after Pierre *Vernier*, 1580?–1637, French mathematician]

ver·sa·tile (vûr′sə·til) *adj.* 1. Having an aptitude for various occupations; many-sided. 2. Having several different uses. 3. Capable of turning freely. [< L *vertere* to turn] **—ver′sa·tile·ly** *adv.* **—ver′sa·til′i·ty** *n.*

verse (vûrs) *n.* 1. A single metrical or rhythmical line. 2. Metrical composition; poetry: distinguished from *prose.* 3. A poem. 4. One of the short divisions of a chapter of the Bible. 5. A stanza. [< L *vertere* to turn]

versed (vûrst) *adj.* Thoroughly acquainted; adept; proficient: with *in.* [< L *versari* to occupy oneself]

ver·si·cle (vûr′si·kəl) *n.* One of a series of lines said or sung alternately by minister and congregation. [See VERSE.]

ver·si·fy (vûr′sə·fī) *v.t. & v.i.* **·fied, ·fy·ing** To write or narrate in verse. [< L *versus* verse + *facere* to make] **—ver′si·fi·ca′tion** *n.* **—ver′si·fi′er** *n.*

ver·sion (vûr′zhən, -shən) *n.* 1. A description or account as modified by a particular point of view. 2. A translation, esp. of the Bible. [< L *vertere* to turn] **—ver′sion·al** *adj.*

vers li·bre (ver lē′br′) *French* Free verse.

ver·so (vûr′sō) *n.* *pl.* **·sos** 1. A left-hand page, as of a book: opposed to *recto.* 2. The reverse of a coin or medal. [< L *verso* (*folio*) a turned (leaf)]

verst (vûrst) *n.* A Russian measure of distance, about two thirds of a mile, or 1.067 kilometers. [< Russ. *versta*, orig., a line]

ver·sus (vûr′səs) *prep.* 1. In law and sports, against. 2. Considered as the alternative of: free trade *versus* tariffs. [< L, turned toward]

ver·te·bra (vûr′tə·brə) *n.* *pl.* **·brae** (-brā) or **·bras** *Anat.* Any of the segmented bones of the spinal column in man and the higher vertebrates. [< L, joint < *vertere* to turn] **—ver′te·bral** *adj.*

ver·te·brate (vûr′tə·brāt, -brit) *adj.* 1. Having a backbone or spinal column. 2. Pertaining to or characteristic of vertebrates. **—*n.*** Any of a primary division of animals characterized by a segmented spinal column, as fishes, birds, reptiles, and mammals.

ver·tex (vûr′teks) *n.* *pl.* **·tex·es** or **·ti·ces** (-tə·sēz) 1. The highest point of anything; apex; top. 2. *Geom.* **a** The point of intersection of the sides of an angle. **b** The point of a triangle opposite to, and farthest from, the base. [< L, the top < *vertere* to turn]

ver·ti·cal (vûr′ti·kəl) *adj.* 1. Perpendicular to the plane of the horizon; extending up and down; upright: opposed to *horizontal.* 2. Of or at the vertex or highest point. **—*n.*** A vertical line, plane, or circle. [See VERTEX.] **—ver′ti·cal′i·ty** (-kal′ə·tē), **ver′ti·cal·ness** *n.* **—ver′ti·cal·ly** *adv.*

ver·ti·ces (vûr′tə·sēz) Plural of VERTEX.

ver·ti·cil (vûr′tə·sil) *n.* *Biol.* 1. A set of organs, as leaves or tentacles, disposed in a circle around an axis; whorl. 2. A volution of a spiral shell. [< L *verticillus* whorl] **—ver·tic·il·late** (vər·tis′ə·lit, -lāt, vûr′tə·sil′it, -āt), **ver·tic′il·lat·ed** *adj.* **—ver·tic′il·late·ly** *adv.* **—ver·tic′il·la′tion** *n.*

ver·tig·i·nous (vər·tij′ə·nəs) *adj.* 1. Causing or affected by vertigo. 2. Turning round; whirling. [See VERTIGO.] **—ver·tig′i·nous·ly** *adv.*

ver·ti·go (vûr′tə·gō) *n.* *pl.* **·goes** or **ver·tig·i·nes** (vər·tij′ə·nēz) *Pathol.* Any of a group of disorders in which a person feels as if he or his surroundings are whirling around; dizziness. [< L *vertere* to turn]

ver·tu (vər·tōō′, vûr′tōō) See VIRTU.

ver·vain (vûr′vān) *n.* Any of a family of herbs, shrubs, and trees, including many cultivated ornamental verbenas. [< L *verbena*]

verve (vûrv) *n.* Enthusiasm; energy; vigor. [< F]

ver·y (ver′ē) *adv.* In a high degree; extremely. **—*adj.*** **ver·i·er, ver·i·est** 1. Absolute; actual; simple: the *very* truth. 2. Identical: my *very* words. 3. The (thing) itself; even: The *very* stones cry out. [< L *verus* true]

very high frequency *Telecom.* A band of radio wave frequencies ranging from 30 to 300 megahertz.
very low frequency *Telecom.* A band of radio wave frequencies ranging from 10 to 30 kilohertz.
ves·i·cant (ves′i·kənt) *adj.* Producing blisters. —*n.* That which produces blisters. Also **ves′i·ca·to′ry** (-kə·tôr′ē). [< L *vesica* blister, bladder]
ves·i·cate (ves′i·kāt) *v.t.* & *v.i.* **·cat·ed, ·cat·ing** To blister. —**ves′i·ca′tion** *n.*
ves·i·cle (ves′i·kəl) *n.* 1. Any small bladderlike cavity, cell, or cyst. 2. *Anat.* A small sac containing gas or fluid. 3. *Pathol.* A blister. [< L *vesica* bladder] —**ve·sic·u·lar** (və·sik′·yə·lər) *adj.*
ve·sic·u·late (*v.* və·sik′yə·lāt; *adj.* və·sik′·yə·lit, -lāt) *v.t.* & *v.i.* **·lat·ed, ·lat·ing** To make or become vesicular. —*adj.* Having vesicles; vesicular. —**ve·sic′u·la′tion** *n.*
ves·per (ves′pər) *n.* 1. A bell that calls to vespers. 2. An evening service, prayer, or song. —*adj.* Of evening or vespers: also **ves′per·al.** [< L *Vesper*, the evening star]
ves·pers (ves′pərz) *n.pl. Often cap. Eccl.* 1. The sixth of the seven canonical hours. 2. A service of worship in the evening. [< L *vespera* evening]
ves·sel (ves′əl) *n.* 1. A hollow receptacle, esp. one capable of holding a liquid, as a pitcher. 2. A ship or boat. 3. *Anat.* A duct or canal for transporting a body fluid, as a vein. [< L *vas*]
vest (vest) *n.* 1. A man's short, sleeveless garment, buttoning in front, commonly worn underneath a suit coat: also, *esp. Brit.*, *waistcoat.* 2. A similar garment worn by women. —*v.t.* 1. To confer (ownership, authority, etc.) upon some person or persons: usu. with *in.* 2. To place ownership or authority with (a person or persons). 3. To clothe, as with vestments. [< L *vestis* garment]
ves·tal (ves′təl) *n.* One of the virgin priestesses of Vesta, Roman goddess of the hearth. Also **vestal virgin.** —*adj.* Chaste; pure.
vest·ed (ves′tid) *adj.* 1. *Law* Fixed; established; permanent. 2. Dressed; robed, esp. in church vestments.
vested interest 1. A strong commitment to a system or institution whose existence serves one's self-interest. 2. *Usu. pl.* A financially powerful or influential group.
ves·ti·bule (ves′tə·byōōl) *n.* 1. An entrance hall; lobby. 2. The enclosed passage between railway passenger cars. 3. *Anat.* Any of several chambers or channels adjoining or communicating with others. [< L *vestibulum* entrance hall] —**ves·tib′u·lar** (-tib′yə·lər) *adj.*
ves·tige (ves′tij) *n.* 1. A trace of something absent or lost. 2. *Biol.* A small or degenerate part or organ, that is well developed and functional in ancestral forms of organisms. [< L *vestigium* footprint] —**ves·tig′i·al** *adj.* —**ves·tig′i·al·ly** *adv.*
vest·ment (vest′mənt) *n.* 1. An article of dress; esp., a robe of office. 2. *Eccl.* One of the ritual garments of the clergy. [< L *vestire* to clothe] —**vest′ment·al** *adj.*
vest-pock·et (vest′pok′it) *adj.* Very small; diminutive.
ves·try (ves′trē) *n. pl.* **·tries** 1. A room, as in a church, where vestments and sacred vessels are kept: often called *sacristy.* 2. In the Anglican Church, a body administering the affairs of a parish. [< OF *vestiarie* < Med.L *vestiarium* wardrobe]
ves·try·man (ves′trē·mən) *n. pl.* **·men** (-mən) A member of a vestry.
vet[1] (vet) *Informal n.* A veterinarian. [Short for VETERINARIAN]
vet[2] (vet) *n. Informal* A veteran. [Short for VETERAN]
vetch (vech) *n.* 1. Any of various vines of the bean family; esp., the common broad bean, grown for fodder. 2. A leguminous European plant yielding edible seeds. [< AF *veche*, *vecce* < L *vicia*]
vet·er·an (vet′ər·ən, vet′rən) *n.* 1. One who is much experienced in an activity, job, or skill. 2. A former member of the armed forces. [< L *veteranus* < *vetus, veteris* old] —**vet′er·an** *adj.*
Veterans Day A U.S. national holiday honoring veterans of the armed forces, the fourth Monday of October; formerly, November 11, the anniversary of the armistice in World War I.
vet·er·i·nar·i·an (vet′ər·ə·nâr′ē·ən, vet′rə-) *n.* A practitioner of veterinary medicine or surgery.
vet·er·i·nar·y (vet′ər·ə·ner′ē, vet′rə-) *adj.* Pertaining to the diseases or injuries of animals, and to their medical treatment. —*n. pl.* **·nar·ies** A veterinarian. [< L *veterinarius* pertaining to beasts of burden]
ve·to (vē′tō) *v.t.* **·toed, ·to·ing** 1. To refuse executive approval of (a bill passed by a legislative body). 2. To forbid or prohibit authoritatively. —*n. pl.* **·toes** 1. The prerogative of a chief executive to refuse to approve a legislative enactment; also, the exercise of such a prerogative. 2. Any authoritative prohibition. [< L, I forbid] —**ve′to·er** *n.*
vex (veks) *v.t.* 1. To irritate; annoy. 2. To trouble or afflict. [< L *vexare* to shake] —**vexed** *adj.* —**vex′er** *n.*
vex·a·tion (vek·sā′shən) *n.* 1. The act of vexing, or the state of being vexed. 2. That which vexes. —**vex·a′tious** *adj.* —**vex·a′·tious·ly** *adv.* —**vex·a′tious·ness** *n.*
vi·a (vī′ə, vē′ə) *prep.* By way of; by a route passing through. [< L, way]
vi·a·ble (vī′ə·bəl) *adj.* 1. Capable of developing normally, as a newborn infant, a seed, etc. 2. Workable; practicable. [< F *vie* life < L *vita*] —**vi′a·bil′i·ty** *n.*
vi·a·duct (vī′ə·dukt) *n.* A bridgelike structure, esp. a large one of arched masonry, to carry a roadway over a ravine. [< L *via* way + (AQUE)DUCT]
vi·al (vī′əl) *n.* A small bottle for liquids: also *phial.* —*v.t.* **vi·aled** or **·alled, ·vi·al·ing** or **·al·ling** To put or keep in or as in a vial. [< Gk. *phialē* shallow cup]
vi·and (vī′ənd) *n.* 1. An article of food, esp. meat. 2. *pl.* Victuals; provisions; food. [< OF *viande* < L *vivenda*, neut. pl. gerundive of *vivere* to live]
vi·at·i·cum (vī·at′ə·kəm) *n. pl.* **·ca** or **·cums** 1. *Eccl.* The Eucharist, as given on the verge of death. 2. Provisions for a journey. [< L, traveling money < *via* way]

vibes (vībz) *n.pl.* *Informal* 1. Vibraphone. 2. Vibration (def. 3).

vi·brant (vī′brənt) *adj.* 1. Vibrating. 2. Throbbing; pulsing. 3. Rich and resonant, as a sound. 4. Energetic; vigorous. 5. *Phonet.* Voiced. —*n.* *Phonet.* A voiced sound. —**vi′bran·cy** *n.* —**vi′brant·ly** *adv.*

vi·bra·phone (vī′brə·fōn) *n.* A type of marimba in which a pulsating sound is produced by valves in the resonators. Also **vi′bra-harp′** (-härp′). [< VIBRA(TO) + -PHONE]

vi·brate (vī′brāt) *v.* **·brat·ed, ·brat·ing** *v.i.* 1. To move back and forth rapidly; quiver. 2. To move or swing back and forth, as a pendulum. 3. To sound; resound. 4. To be emotionally moved; thrill. —*v.t.* 5. To cause to quiver or tremble. 6. To cause to move back and forth. 7. To send forth (sound, etc.) by vibration. [< L *vibratus*, pp. of *vibrare* to shake] —**vi′bra·to′ry** (-brə·tôr′ē), **vi′bra·tive** (-brə·tiv) *adj.*

vi·bra·tion (vī·brā′shən) *n.* 1. The act of vibrating, or the state of being vibrated. 2. *Physics* **a** Any physical process characterized by cyclic variations in amplitude, intensity, or the like, as wave motion or an electric field. **b** A single complete oscillation. 3. *pl.* *Informal* Emanations of feeling assumed to flow from a person or situation. —**vi·bra′tion·al** *adj.*

vi·bra·to (vē·brä′tō, vi-) *n.* *pl.* **·tos** *Music* A pulsating effect caused by rapid variations in pitch. [< Ital. < L, pp. of *vibrare* to shake]

vi·bra·tor (vī′brā·tər) *n.* 1. That which vibrates. 2. An electrically operated massaging apparatus.

vi·bur·num (vī·bûr′nəm) *n.* Any of a genus of shrubs or small trees related to the honeysuckle. [< L, the wayfaring tree]

vic·ar (vik′ər) *n.* 1. In the Anglican Church, the priest of a chapel, mission, or other dependent congregation. 2. In the Roman Catholic Church, a substitute or representative of an ecclesiastical person. 3. One authorized to perform functions in the stead of another; deputy. [< L *vicarius* substitute < *vicis* change] —**vic′ar·ate** (-it), **vi·car·i·ate** (vī·kâr′ē·it, vi-), **vic′ar·ship** *n.*

vic·ar·age (vik′ər·ij) *n.* The benefice or residence of a vicar.

vicar general *pl.* **vicars general** An administrative assistant to a bishop.

vi·car·i·ous (vī·kâr′ē·əs, vi-) *adj.* 1. Made or performed by substitution: a *vicarious* sacrifice. 2. Enjoyed, felt, etc., by imagined participation in an experience not one's own: *vicarious* gratification. 3. Acting for another. [< L *vicarius* substitute] —**vi·car′i·ous·ly** *adv.* —**vi·car′i·ous·ness** *n.*

vice[1] (vīs) *n.* 1. An immoral habit or trait. 2. Habitual immorality; corruption; evil. 3. Something that mars; a blemish or imperfection. [< L *vitium* fault]

vice[2] (vīs) See VISE.

vice[3] (*adj.* & *n.* vīs; *prep.* vī′sē) *adj.* Acting in the place of; substitute; deputy: *vice* president. —*n.* One who acts in the place of another; a substitute; deputy. —*prep.* Instead of; in the place of. [< L, ablative of *vicis* change]

vice admiral *Naval* A commissioned officer ranking next below an admiral. —**vice-ad·mir·al·ty** (vīs′ad′mər·əl·tē) *n.*

vice consul One who exercises consular authority in the place of a consul. —**vice-con·su·lar** (vīs′kon′sə·lər) *adj.* —**vice-con·su·late** (vīs′kon′sə·lit) *n.* —**vice′-con′sul·ship** *n.*

vice·ge·rent (vīs·jir′ənt) *n.* One duly authorized to exercise the powers of another. [< L *vice* in place + *gerere* to carry, manage] —**vice·ge′rent, vice·ge′ral** *adj.* —**vice·ge′·ren·cy** *n.*

vic·e·nar·y (vis′ə·ner′ē) *adj.* 1. Consisting of or pertaining to twenty. 2. Relating to a system of notation based upon twenty. [< L *viceni* twenty each < *viginti* twenty]

vi·cen·ni·al (vī·sen′ē·əl) *adj.* 1. Occurring once in twenty years. 2. Lasting or existing twenty years.

vice president An officer ranking next below a president. —**vice-pres·i·den·cy** (vīs′prez′ə·dən·sē) *n.* —**vice-pres·i·den·tial** (vīs′·prez′ə·den′shəl) *adj.*

vice·re·gal (vīs·rē′gəl) *adj.* Or or relating to a viceroy, his office, or his jurisdiction. Also **vice·roy′al** (-roi′əl). —**vice·re′gal·ly** *adv.*

vice regent A deputy regent. —**vice-re·gen·cy** (vīs′rē′jən·sē) *n.* —**vice-re·gent** (vīs′rē′jənt) *adj.*

vice·roy (vīs′roi) *n.* 1. One who rules a country, colony, or province by the authority of his sovereign. 2. A North American butterfly, orange-red with black markings and white marginal spots. [< MF *vice-*, *vis-* in place + *roy* king, ult. < L *rex, regis*]

vice·roy·al·ty (vīs·roi′əl·tē) *n.* *pl.* **·ties** 1. The office or authority of a viceroy. 2. A district governed by a viceroy. Also **vice′roy·ship.**

vice squad A police division charged with combating prostitution, gambling, etc.

vice ver·sa (vī′sē vûr′sə, vīs′) The order being changed; conversely. [< L]

vi·chy·ssoise (vē′shē·swäz′) *n.* A potato cream soup, usu. served cold. [< F, of Vichy]

Vi·chy water (vish′ē, vē·shē′) The effervescent mineral water from the springs at Vichy, France; also, any mineral water resembling it. Also **Vi′chy, vi′chy.**

vic·i·nage (vis′ə·nij) *n.* Neighborhood; vicinity. [< L *vicinus* nearby]

vic·i·nal (vis′ə·nəl) *adj.* Neighboring; adjoining; near.

vi·cin·i·ty (vi·sin′ə·tē) *n.* *pl.* **·ties** 1. A region adjacent or near; neighborhood. 2. Nearness in space or relationship; proximity. [< L *vicinus* nearby]

vi·cious (vish′əs) *adj.* 1. Malicious; spiteful. 2. Violent; fierce. 3. Addicted to vice; corrupt. 4. Morally injurious; vile. 5. Unruly or dangerous. 6. *Informal* Intense; severe; extreme: a *vicious* storm. 7. Leading from bad to worse, as due to problems that augment each other: a *vicious* circle. [< L *vitium* fault] —**vi′cious·ly** *adv.* —**vi′cious·ness** *n.*

vi·cis·si·tude (vi·sis′ə·tōōd, -tyōōd) *n.* 1. *pl.* Irregular changes or variations, as of fortune: the *vicissitudes* of life. 2. A change; esp., a complete change. 3. Alternating change or succession, as of the seasons. [< L *vicis* turn, change] —**vi·cis′si·tu′di·nar′y, vi·cis′si·tu′·di·nous** *adj.*

vic·tim (vik′tim) *n.* 1. One who is killed,

injured, or subjected to suffering. 2. One who is swindled or tricked; a dupe. [< L *victima* beast for sacrifice]

vic·tim·ize (vik′tim·īz) *v.t.* **·ized, ·iz·ing** To make a victim of, esp. by defrauding; cheat. **—vic′tim·i·za′tion** *n.* **—vic′tim·iz′er** *n.*

vic·tor (vik′tər) *n.* 1. One who vanquishes an enemy. 2. One who wins any struggle or contest. [< L *victus*, pp. of *vincere* to conquer] **—vic′tor** *adj.*

vic·to·ri·a (vik·tôr′ē·ə) *n.* A low, light four-wheeled carriage with a top, a seat for two persons, and a raised driver's seat. [after Queen *Victoria*]

Vic·to·ri·an (vik·tôr′ē·ən) *adj.* 1. Of or relating to Queen Victoria, or to her reign. 2. Pertaining to English-speaking culture during Queen Victoria's reign (1837–1901). 3. Prudish; conventional. **—***n.* A contemporary of Queen Victoria. **—Vic·to′ri·an·ism** *n.*

vic·to·ri·ous (vik·tôr′ē·əs) *adj.* 1. Having won victory; triumphant. 2. Relating to or characterized by victory. **—vic·to′ri·ous·ly** *adv.* **—vic·to′ri·ous·ness** *n.*

vic·to·ry (vik′tər·ē) *n. pl.* **·ries** The overcoming of an enemy, opponent, or any difficulty; triumph. [See VICTOR.]

vict·ual (vit′l) *n.* 1. *Archaic* Food. 2. *pl.* Food for human beings, as prepared for eating. **—***v.t.* **vict·ualed** or **·ualled, vict·ual·ing** or **·ual·ling** To furnish with victuals. [< LL *victualia* provisions < L *victus* food]

vi·cu·ña (vi·ko͞on′yə, -kyo͞o′nə) *n.* 1. A small ruminant of the high Andes related to the llama and alpaca, having fine and valuable wool. 2. A textile made from this wool. Also **vi·cu′gna.** [< Sp. < Quechua]

vi·de (vī′dē) See: used to make a reference or direct attention to: *vide* p. 36. [< L, imperative sing. of *videre* to see]

vi·de·li·cet (vi·del′ə·sit) *adv.* To wit; that is to say; namely. Abbr. *viz.* [< L *videre licet* it is permitted to see]

vid·e·o (vid′ē·ō) *adj.* 1. Of or pertaining to television, esp. to the picture. 2. Producing a signal convertible into a television picture: a *video* cassette. **—***n.* A television image. [< L, I see]

vid·e·o·tape (vid′ē·ō·tāp′) *n.* A recording of a television program on magnetic tape. **—***v.t.* **·taped, ·tap·ing** To make such a recording.

vie (vī) *v.i.* **vied, vy·ing** To strive for superiority; compete: with *with* or *for.* [< L *invitare* to invite]

Vi·en·nese (vē′ə·nēz′, -nēs′) *adj.* Of or relating to Vienna or its inhabitants. **—Vi′en·nese′** *n.*

Vi·et·cong (vē·et·kong′) *n.* The Communist-supported guerilla forces of the National Liberation Front, active in South Vietnam from early 1950's through 1970's; also a member of these forces. [< Vietnamese *Viet Nam Cong San* Vietnamese communist] **—Vi·et·cong′** *adj.* Abbr. *VC.*

Vi·et·nam·ese (vē·et′nām·ēz′, -ēs′) *adj.* Of or pertaining to Vietnam, its inhabitants, or their language. **—Vi·et′nam·ese′** *n.*

view (vyo͞o) *n.* 1. The act of seeing; survey; inspection. 2. Mental examination or inspection. 3. Power or range of vision. 4. That which is seen; outlook; prospect. 5. A representation of a scene; esp., a landscape. 6. The object of action; aim; intention; purpose. 7. Manner of looking at things; opinion; judgment. 8. A general summary or account. **—in view** 1. In range of vision. 2. Under consideration. 3. As a goal or end. **—in view of** In consideration of. **—on view** Open to public inspection. **—with a view to** 1. With the aim or purpose of. 2. With a hope of. **—***v.t.* 1. To look at; see; examine. 2. To survey mentally; consider. [< OF *veoir* to see < L *videre*] **—view′er** *n.*

view finder *Photog.* A finder (def. 3).

view·less (vyo͞o′lis) *adj.* 1. Devoid of a view or prospect. 2. Having no views or opinions.

view·point (vyo͞o′point′) *n.* Point of view.

vi·ges·i·mal (vī·jes′ə·məl) *adj.* 1. Twentieth. 2. Of or pertaining to twenty; proceeding by twenties. [< L *viginti* twenty]

vig·il (vij′əl) *n.* 1. The act of staying awake in order to observe, protect, etc.; watch. 2. *Eccl.* a The eve of a holy day. b *pl.* Religious devotions on such an eve. [< L, wide-awake]

vig·i·lance (vij′ə·ləns) *n.* Watchfulness in guarding against danger; alertness.

vig·i·lant (vij′ə·lənt) *adj.* Characterized by vigilance; watchful; heedful. [< L *vigil* awake] **—vig′i·lant·ly** *adv.*

vig·i·lan·te (vij′ə·lan′tē) *n.* One of a group whose members seek personally to enforce the law or their views of what is right. [< Sp. See VIGILANT.]

vi·gnette (vin·yet′) *n.* 1. A short, subtle literary description. 2. A decorative design placed on or before the title page of a book, at the end or beginning of a chapter, etc. 3. An engraving, photograph, etc., having a background that shades off gradually. **—***v.t.* **·gnet·ted, ·gnet·ting** 1. To make with a gradually shaded background, as a photograph. 2. To ornament with vignettes. 3. To depict in a vignette. [< F, dim. of *vigne* vine] **—vi·gnet′tist** *n.*

vig·or (vig′ər) *n.* Active strength or force, physical or mental; vitality; energy; intensity. Also *Brit.* **vig′our.** [< L *vigere* to be lively, thrive]

vig·or·ous (vig′ər·əs) *adj.* 1. Full of physical or mental vigor; robust. 2. Done with or showing vigor; forceful. **—vig′or·ous·ly** *adv.* **—vig′or·ous·ness** *n.*

vi·king (vī′king) *n.* One of the Scandinavian pirates of the 8th to 10th c. Also **Vi′king.** [< ON *vikingr* pirate]

vile (vīl) *adj.* **vil·er, vil·est** 1. Morally base; shamefully wicked. 2. Loathsome; disgusting. 3. Degrading; ignominious: *vile* treatment. 4. Flagrantly bad or inferior. 5. Unpleasant; disagreeable. [< L *vilis* cheap] **—vile′ly** *adv.* **—vile′ness** *n.*

vil·i·fy (vil′ə·fī) *v.t.* **·fied, ·fy·ing** 1. To abuse; malign; slander. 2. To make base; degrade. [< L *vilis* cheap + *facere* to make] **—vil′i·fi·ca′tion** *n.* **—vil′i·fi′er** *n.*

vil·la (vil′ə) *n.* A comfortable or luxurious house in the country, at a resort, etc. [< Ital. < L, a country house, farm]

vil·lage (vil′ij) *n.* 1. A collection of houses in a rural district. 2. In some states, a municipality smaller than a city. 3. Any comparatively small community. 4. The inhabitants of a village, collectively. [< L *villa* a country house]

vil·lag·er (vil′ij·ər) *n.* One who lives in a village.

vil·lain (vil′ən) *n.* 1. A wicked, malevolent man. 2. Such a man represented as a leading character in a novel, play, etc. 3. A rogue; scoundrel: often used humorously. 4. A villein. [< AF, OF *vilein, vilain* farm servant < L *villa* farm] **—vil′lain·ess** *n.fem.* **—vil′lain·ous** *adj.* **—vil′lain·ous·ly** *adv.* **—vil′lain·ous·ness** *n.*

vil·lain·y (vil′ən·ē) *n. pl.* **·lain·ies** 1. The quality of being villainous. 2. Conduct characteristic of a villain.

vil·lein (vil′ən) *n.* In the feudal system, a member of a class of serfs who were regarded as freemen in respect to their legal relations with all persons except their lord: also *villain.* [See VILLAIN.] **—vil′lein·age** or **vil′len·age** *n.*

vil·lus (vil′əs) *n. pl.* **vil·li** (vil′ī) 1. *Anat.* One of the short, hairlike processes found on certain membranes, as of the small intestine. 2. *Bot.* One of the long, close, rather soft hairs on the surface of certain plants. [< L, shaggy hair, var. of *vellus* fleece] **—vil′lous** *adj.* **—vil′lous·ly** *adv.*

vim (vim) *n.* Force or vigor; energy; spirit. [< L, accusative of *vis* power]

vi·na (vē′nä) *n.* An East Indian musical instrument with seven steel strings stretched on a long, fretted fingerboard over two gourds. [< Hind. *vīnā*]

vi·na·ceous (vī·nā′shəs) *adj.* 1. Of or pertaining to wine or grapes. 2. Having the characteristic color of red wine. [< L *vinum* wine]

vin·ai·grette (vin′ə·gret′) *n.* 1. A small ornamental box or bottle, used for holding smelling salts or the like. 2. Vinaigrette sauce. [< F, dim. of *vinaigre* vinegar]

vinaigrette sauce A sauce made from vinegar, savory herbs, etc.

vin·ci·ble (vin′sə·bəl) *adj. Rare* Conquerable. [< L *vincibilis* < *vincere* to conquer] **—vin′ci·bil′i·ty** *n.*

vin·cu·lum (vingk′yə·ləm) *n. pl.* **·la** *Math.* A straight line drawn over several algebraic terms to show that all are to be operated on together. [< L *vincire* to bind]

vin·di·cate (vin′də·kāt) *v.t.* **·cat·ed, ·cat·ing** 1. To clear of accusation, censure, suspicion, etc. 2. To support or maintain, as a right or claim. 3. To serve to justify. [< L *vindicatus*, pp. of *vindicare* to avenge, claim] **—vin′di·ca·ble** (-kə·bəl) *adj.* **—vin′di·ca′tor** *n.*

vin·di·ca·tion (vin′də·kā′shən) *n.* 1. The act of vindicating, or the state of being vindicated. 2. Justification; defense.

vin·di·ca·to·ry (vin′də·kə·tôr′ē) *adj.* 1. Serving to vindicate. 2. Punitive; avenging.

vin·dic·tive (vin·dik′tiv) *adj.* Revengeful or spiteful. [< L *vindicta* revenge] **—vin·dic′tive·ly** *adv.* **—vin·dic′tive·ness** *n.*

vine (vīn) *n.* 1. Any of a large and widely distributed group of plants having a slender, flexible stem that may twine about a support or clasp it by means of tendrils, petioles, etc.; also, the stem itself. 2. A grapevine. [< OF *vigne, vine* < L *vinea* vineyard < *vinum* wine]

vin·e·gar (vin′ə·gər) *n.* An acid liquid consisting chiefly of dilute acetic acid, obtained by the fermentation of cider, wine, etc., and used as a condiment and preservative. [< OF *vin* wine + *aigre, egre* sour] **—vin′e·gar·y, vin′e·gar·ish** *adj.*

vin·er·y (vī′nər·ē) *n. pl.* **·er·ies** 1. A greenhouse for grapes. 2. Vines collectively.

vine·yard (vin′yərd) *n.* An area planted with grapevines. [Earlier *wineyard* < OE *wīnegeard*]

vin·i·cul·ture (vin′ə·kul′chər) *n.* The cultivation of grapes for wine. [< L *vinum* wine + CULTURE] **—vin′i·cul′tur·al** *adj.* **—vin′i·cul′tur·ist** *n.*

vi·nous (vī′nəs) *adj.* 1. Of or pertaining to wine. 2. Caused by, affected by, or addicted to wine. 3. Tinged with dark red. [< L *vinum* wine] **—vi·nos·i·ty** (-nos′ə·tē) *n.*

vin·tage (vin′tij) *n.* 1. The yield of a vineyard or wine-producing district for one season; also, the wine produced from this yield. 2. *Informal* The type popular at a particular time of the past: a joke of ancient *vintage.* **—*adj.*** 1. Of exceptional quality or excellence. 2. Of a good year; also, of time past. [< OF *vendage* < L *vinum* wine + *demere* to remove]

vint·ner (vint′nər) *n.* A wine merchant.

vin·y (vī′nē) *adj.* **vin·i·er, vin·i·est** 1. Of, pertaining to, or resembling a vine. 2. Full of vines.

vi·nyl (vī′nəl) *n.* Any of various tough plastics, used for floor coverings, coatings, etc. [< L *vinum* wine + -YL]

vi·ol (vī′əl) *n.* A bowed, stringed instrument, similar to the violin, used chiefly in the 16*th* and 17*th* c. [Earlier *vielle* < Med.L *vidula, vitula* < Gmc.]

vi·o·la (vē·ō′lə, vī-; *Ital.* vyō′lä) *n.* A musical instrument of the violin family, somewhat larger than the violin, and tuned a fifth lower. [< Ital., orig., a viol]

vi·o·la·ble (vī′ə·lə·bəl) *adj.* Capable of being violated. **—vi′o·la·bil′i·ty** *n.*

vi·o·late (vī′ə·lāt) *v.t.* **·lat·ed, ·lat·ing** 1. To break or infringe, as a law, oath, etc. 2. To profane, as a holy place. 3. To break in upon; disturb. 4. To ravish; rape. 5. To do violence to; outrage. [< L *violatus*, pp. of *violare* to use violence < *vis* force] **—vi′o·la′tion** *n.* **—vi′o·la′tive** *adj.* **—vi′o·la′tor** *n.*

vi·o·lence (vī′ə·ləns) *n.* 1. The quality or state of being violent; intensity; fury. 2. An instance of violent action, treatment, etc. 3. Violent or abusive exercise of power; injury; outrage. **—to do violence to** 1. To injure or damage by rough or abusive treatment. 2. To distort the meaning of.

vi·o·lent (vī′ə·lənt) *adj.* 1. Proceeding from or marked by great physical force or roughness. 2. Caused by or exhibiting intense excitement; passionate; fierce. 3. Characterized by intensity of any kind; extreme: *violent* heat. 4. Marked by undue exercise of force; harsh: to take *violent* measures. 5. Resulting from unusual force or injury: a *violent* death. [< L *violentus* < *vis* force] **—vi′o·lent·ly** *adv.*

vi·o·let (vī′ə·lit) *n.* 1. One of a widely distributed genus of herbaceous perennial herbs bearing spurred, usu. purplish blue flowers. 2. A deep bluish purple color. **—*adj.*** Having a bluish purple color. [< L *viola* violet]

vi·o·lin (vī′ə·lin′) *n.* A musical instrument

having four strings and a wood sounding box, held against the shoulder and played by means of a bow: also called *fiddle*. [< Ital. *violino*, dim. of *viola*] —**vi′o·lin′ist** *n.*

vi·o·list (vē·ōl′ist *for def. 1*, vī′əl·ist *for def. 2*) *n.* 1. One who plays the viola. 2. One who plays a viol.

vi·o·lon·cel·lo (vē′ə·lən·chel′ō) *n. pl.* **·los** A cello. [< Ital., dim. of *violone* double bass] —**vi′o·lon·cel′list** *n.*

VIP or **V.I.P.** Very important person: said esp. of an official or celebrity.

vi·per (vī′pər) *n.* 1. A venomous snake. 2. Loosely, a pit viper. 3. A treacherous or spiteful person. [< L *vivus* living + *parere* to bring forth] —**vi′per·ine** (-in, -īn) *adj.* —**vi′per·ish** *adj.*

vi·per·ous (vī′pər·əs) *adj.* 1. Snakelike; viperine. 2. Venomous; malicious. —**vi′per·ous·ly** *adj.*

vi·ra·go (vi·rā′gō, -rā′-) *n. pl.* **·goes** or **·gos** A noisy, sharp-tongued woman; a scold. [< L, mannish woman < *vir* man]

vi·ral (vī′rəl) *adj.* Of, pertaining to, caused by, or of the nature of a virus.

vir·e·o (vir′ē·ō) *n. pl.* **·os** Any of various small, insectivorous birds having predominantly dull green and grayish plumage. [< L, a small bird]

vi·res·cent (vī·res′ənt) *adj.* Greenish or becoming green. [< L *virescens*, *-entis*, ppr. of *virescere* to grow green] —**vi·res′cence** *n.*

vir·gin (vûr′jin) *n.* A person, esp. a young woman, who has never had sexual intercourse. —*adj.* 1. Being a virgin. 2. Pertaining or suited to a virgin; chaste; maidenly. 3. Uncorrupted; pure; undefiled. 4. Not hitherto used or processed: *virgin* soil, *virgin* wool. [< L *virgo*, *-inis* maiden]

Vir·gin (vûr′jin) *n.* Virgin Mary: usu. with *the.*

vir·gin·al[1] (vûr′jin·əl) *adj.* Pertaining to or characteristic of a virgin; chaste.

vir·gin·al[2] (vûr′jin·əl) *n. Often pl.* A small, legless harpsichord of the 16th and 17th c. [< VIRGINAL[1]; ? so called from its use by young men and women]

Vir·gin·ia creeper (vər·jin′yə) A common American climbing vine of the grape family: also called *woodbine.*

Vir·gin·ia reel (vər·jin′yə) A country-dance in which the performers stand in two parallel lines and perform various figures.

vir·gin·i·ty (vər·jin′ə·tē) *n. pl.* **·ties** The state or condition of being virgin or a virgin.

Virgin Mary Mary, the mother of Jesus: usu. with *the.*

vir·gin's-bow·er (vûr′jinz·bou′ər) *n.* A species of clematis bearing white flowers.

Vir·go (vûr′gō) *n.* A constellation; also, the sixth sign of the zodiac. [< L, a virgin]

vir·gule (vûr′gyōōl) *n.* Slash (def. 2). [< *virgula*, dim. of *virga* rod]

vir·i·des·cent (vir′ə·des′ənt) *adj.* Greenish, or becoming slightly green. [< LL *viridescere* to become green] —**vir′i·des′cence** *n.*

vir·ile (vir′əl) *adj.* 1. Having the characteristics of adult manhood; masculine. 2. Having qualities considered typically masculine; vigorous; forceful. 3. Capable of procreation. [< L *virilis* < *vir* man] —**vi·ril·i·ty** (və·ril′ə·tē) *n.*

vi·rol·o·gy (və·rol′ə·jē, vī-) *n.* The study of viruses, esp. in their relation to disease. —**vi·rol′o·gist** *n.*

vir·tu (vər·tōō′, vûr′tōō) *n.* 1. Rare, curious, or beautiful quality: usu. in the phrase objects or articles of virtu. 2. A taste for such objects. 3. Such objects collectively. Also spelled *vertu.* [< Ital. *virtù* merit < L *virtus* strength]

vir·tu·al (vur′chōō·əl) *adj.* Having the effect but not the actual form of what is specified. [See VIRTUE.] —**vir′tu·al′i·ty** (-al′ə·tē) *n.*

vir·tu·al·ly (vûr′chōō·ə·lē) *adv.* In effect; for all practical purposes.

vir·tue (vûr′chōō) *n.* 1. The quality of moral righteousness or excellence; rectitude. 2. The practice of moral duties and abstinence from vice. 3. Chastity, esp. in women. 4. A particular type of moral excellence. 5. Any admirable quality or trait. 6. Inherent or essential quality, power, etc. —**by** (or **in**) **virtue of** By or through the fact, quality, force, or authority of. —**to make a virtue of necessity** To seem to do freely or from principle what is or must be done necessarily. [< L *virtus* strength, bravery < *vir* man]

vir·tu·os·i·ty (vûr′chōō·os′ə·tē) *n. pl.* **·ties** The skill of a virtuoso; technical mastery.

vir·tu·o·so (vûr′chōō·ō′sō) *n. pl.* **·si** (-sē) or **·sos** A master of technique, as a skilled musician. [< Ital., skilled, learned]

vir·tu·ous (vûr′chōō·əs) *adj.* 1. Characterized by, exhibiting, or having the nature of virtue. 2. Chaste: said esp. of women. —**vir′tu·ous·ly** *adv.* —**vir′tu·ous·ness** *n.*

vir·u·lent (vir′yə·lənt, vir′ə-) *adj.* 1. Extremely harmful. 2. Bitterly rancorous; acrimonious. 3. *Med.* Actively poisonous or infective; malignant. 4. *Bacteriol.* Having the power to injure an organism by invasion of tissue and generation of internal toxins, as certain microorganisms. [< L *virus* poison] —**vir′u·lence** *n.* —**vir′u·lent·ly** *adv.*

vi·rus (vī′rəs) *n.* 1. Any of a class of filterable, submicroscopic pathogenic agents, typically inert except when in contact with certain living cells. 2. An illness caused by such an agent. [< L, poison, slime]

vi·sa (vē′zə) *n.* An official endorsement, as on a passport, certifying that it has been found correct and that the bearer may proceed. —*v.t.* **·saed, ·sa·ing** 1. To put a visa on. 2. To give a visa to. Also *visé.* [< L *videre* to see]

vis·age (viz′ij) *n.* The face or facial expression of a person; countenance. [< L *visus* look, appearance] —**vis′aged** *adj.*

vis-à-vis (vē′zə·vē′, *Fr.* vē·zà·vē′) *n. pl.* **vis-à-vis** 1. One of two persons or things that face each other from opposite sides. 2. One in a corresponding capacity, etc. —*adv.* Face to face. —*prep.* Regarding. [< F, face to face]

vis·cer·a (vis′ər·ə) *n. pl. of* **vis·cus** (vis′kəs) *Anat.* The internal organs. [< L, pl. of *viscus* internal organ] —**vis′cer·al** *adj.*

vis·cid (vis′id) *adj.* Sticky or adhesive; viscous. [< *viscum* birdlime] —**vis·cid·i·ty** (vi·sid′ə·tē) *n.* —**vis′cid·ly** *adv.*

vis·cose (vis′kōs) *n. Chem.* A viscous substance made from cellulose, constituting an important source of rayon. [See VISCOUS.]

vis·cos·i·ty (vis·kos′ə·tē) *n. pl.* **·ties** 1. The state, quality, property, or degree of being viscous. 2. *Physics* The resistance of a fluid to flow freely because of the friction of its molecules.

vis·count (vī′kount) *n.* In England, a title of nobility ranking between those of earl and baron. [< AF, OF *vis-* in place + *counte*. See COUNT[2].] **—vis′count·cy, vis′·count·ship, vis′count·y** *n.*

vis·count·ess (vī′koun·tis) *n.* 1. The wife of a viscount. 2. A peeress holding a corresponding title in her own right.

vis·cous (vis′kəs) *adj.* 1. Glutinous; semifluid; sticky. 2. *Physics* Characterized by or having viscosity. [< L *viscum* birdlime] **—vis′cous·ly** *adv.* **—vis′cous·ness** *n.*

vis·cus (vis′kəs) Singular of VISCERA.

vise (vīs) *n.* A clamping device, usu. of two jaws made to be closed together with a screw, lever, etc., used for grasping and holding objects being worked on, glued, etc. **—***v.t.* **vised, vis·ing** To hold, force, or squeeze in or as in a vise. Also, *Brit.*, *vice.* [< L *vitis* vine; with ref. to the spiral growth of vine tendrils]

vi·sé (vē′zā, vē·zā′) *v.t.* **·séed, ·sé·ing** To visa. **—***n.* A visa.

Vish·nu (vish′nōō) In Hindu theology, a major deity having many incarnations, of which the most famous is as Krishna.

vis·i·bil·i·ty (viz′ə·bil′ə·tē) *n. pl.* **·ties** 1. Condition, capability, or degree of being visible. 2. The clarity of unaided vision as affected by distance, atmospheric conditions, etc.

vis·i·ble (viz′ə·bəl) *adj.* 1. Perceivable by the eye; capable of being seen. 2. Apparent; observable; evident. [< L *visibilis* < *videre* to see] **—vis′i·bly** *adv.*

Vis·i·goth (viz′ə·goth) *n.* One of the western Goths, a Teutonic people that invaded the Roman Empire in the 3rd and 4th c. [< LL *Visigothus*] **—Vis′i·goth′ic** *adj.*

vi·sion (vizh′ən) *n.* 1. The faculty or sense of sight. 2. Understanding, esp. of what lies in the future; foresight. 3. Insight; imagination. 4. A mental representation of or as of objects, scenes, etc., as in a religious revelation, dream, etc. 5. Something vividly imagined. 6. Something or someone very beautiful or pleasing. **—***v.t. Rare* To see in or as in a vision. [< L *visio* < *videre* to see] **—vi′sion·al** *adj.* **—vi′sion·al·ly** *adv.*

vi·sion·ar·y (vizh′ən·er′ē) *adj.* 1. Not founded on fact; imaginary. 2. Affected by or tending toward impractical idealism or fantasies; dreamy; impractical. 3. Having or of the nature of apparitions, dreams, etc. **—***n. pl.* **·ar·ies** 1. One who has visions. 2. A dreamer; an impractical schemer or idealist.

vis·it (viz′it) *v.t.* 1. To go or come to see (a person). 2. To go or come to (a place, etc.), as for touring, etc. 3. To be a guest of; stay with temporarily. 4. To go or come to for professional purposes. 5. To come upon or afflict. 6. To inflict (punishment, wrath, etc.). **—***v.i.* 7. To make a visit; pay a call or calls. 8. *Informal* To chat or converse sociably. **—***n.* 1. The act of visiting a person or place. 2. *Informal* A talk or friendly chat. 3. An authoritative personal call for the discharge of an official or professional duty. [< L *visitare* to go to see < *videre* to see] **—vis′it·a·ble** *adj.*

vis·i·tant (viz′ə·tənt) *n.* 1. A visitor. 2. A migratory animal or bird stopping at a particular region.

vis·i·ta·tion (viz′ə·tā′shən) *n.* 1. A visit. 2. In Biblical and religious use, a visiting of blessing or affliction. **—vis′i·ta′tion·al** *adj.* **—vis′i·ta·to′ri·al** (-tə·tôr′ē·əl) *adj.*

vis·i·tor (viz′ə·tər) *n.* One who visits.

vi·sor (vī′zər) *n.* 1. A projecting piece at the front of a cap, etc., serving as a shade for the eyes. 2. In armor, the movable front piece of a helmet. 3. A movable piece or part serving as a shield against glare, etc., as on the windshield of an automobile. Also spelled *vizor.* [< AF, OF *vis* face]

vis·ta (vis′tə) *n.* 1. A view or prospect, as along an avenue; an outlook. 2. A mental view embracing a series of events. [< Ital. < L *videre* to see]

vis·u·al (vizh′ōō·əl) *adj.* 1. Of or pertaining to the sense of sight. 2. Perceptible by sight; visible. 3. Produced or induced by mental images. [< L *visus* sight < *videre* to see] **—vis′u·al·ly** *adv.*

visual aid *Often pl.* In education, a device or method designed to convey information by visible representation, as motion pictures, charts, etc.

vis·u·al·ize (vizh′ōō·əl·īz′) *v.t. & v.i.* **·ized, ·iz·ing** To form a mental image (of). **—vis′u·al·ist** (-ist) *n.* **—vis′u·al·i·za′tion** *n.* **—vis′u·al·iz′er** *n.*

vi·tal (vīt′l) *adj.* 1. Necessary; essential. 2. Of or pertaining to life. 3. Essential to or supporting life. 4. Affecting the course of life or existence, esp. so as to be dangerous or fatal: a *vital* error. 5. Energetic; forceful; dynamic. [< L *vita* life] **—vi′tal·ly** *adv.* **—vi′tal·ness** *n.*

vi·tal·ism (vīt′l·iz′əm) *n. Biol.* The doctrine that life and its phenomena arose from a hypothetical vital force (or vital principle). **—vi′tal·ist** *n.* **—vi′tal·is′tic** *adj.*

vi·tal·i·ty (vī·tal′ə·tē) *n.* 1. The state or quality of being vital. 2. Vital or life-giving force, principle, etc. 3. Vigor; energy; animation. 4. Power of continuing in force or effect.

vi·tal·ize (vīt′l·īz) *v.t.* **·ized, ·iz·ing** To make vital; endow with life or energy. **—vi′tal·i·za′tion** *n.* **—vi′tal·iz′er** *n.*

vi·tals (vīt′lz) *n.pl.* The parts or organs necessary to life.

vital signs The body temperature, rate of breathing, pulse rate, and often the blood pressure of a person.

vital statistics Quantitative data relating to aspects and conditions of human life.

vi·ta·min (vī′tə·min) *n.* Any of a group of complex organic substances found in food and essential for health and growth. **—vitamin A** Found in egg yolks, fish-liver oils, etc., essential for healthy epithelial tissue and for seeing in the dark. **—vitamin B complex** A group including: **vitamin B_1** (see THIAMINE); **vitamin B_2** (see RIBOFLAVIN); **nicotinic acid** (see NIACIN); **vitamin B_3** (see

PANTOTHENIC ACID); **vitamin B_6** Found in cereal grains, yeast, etc., and essential in nutrition: also called *pyridoxine*; **vitamin B_{12}** A cobalt-containing compound found in liver, essential in blood formation, and used in treating pernicious and other anemias; **vitamin B_{15}** (see PANGAMATE); **vitamin B_c** (see FOLIC ACID); **vitamin H** (see BIOTIN). —**vitamin C** Found in citrus fruits and leafy vegetables, and necessary in preventing scurvy: also called *ascorbic acid.* —**vitamin D** A group of vitamins found in fish-liver oils, milk, etc., essential in bone formation; **vitamin D_2** is also called *calciferol.* —**vitamin E** Found in whole grain cereals and seed germ oils. —**vitamin K** Found in leafy vegetables, essential for blood clotting. [< *vita* life]

vi·ti·ate (vish′ē·āt) *v.t.* **·at·ed, ·at·ing** 1. To impair the use or value of; spoil. 2. To debase or corrupt. 3. To render legally ineffective. [< L *vitium* fault] —**vi·ti·a·ble** (vish′ē·ə·bel) *adj.* —**vi′ti·a′tion** *n.* —**vi′ti·a′·tor** *n.*

vit·i·cul·ture (vit′ə·kul′chər, vī′tə-) *n.* The science and art of grape growing. [< L *vitis* vine + CULTURE] —**vit′i·cul′tur·al** *adj.* —**vit′i·cul′tur·er, vit′i·cul′tur·ist** *n.*

vit·re·ous (vit′rē·əs) *adj.* 1. Pertaining to, obtained from, or like glass. 2. Pertaining to the vitreous humor. [< L *vitrum* glass] —**vit′re·os′i·ty** (-os′ə·tē) *n.*

vitreous humor *Anat.* The transparent, jellylike tissue that fills the ball of the eye. Also **vitreous body.**

vit·ri·fy (vit′rə·fī) *v.t. & v.i.* **·fied, ·fy·ing** To change into glass or a vitreous substance; make or become vitreous. [< L *vitrum* glass + *facere* to make] —**vit′ri·fac′tion** (-fak′shən) *n.* —**vit′ri·fi′a·ble** *adj.* —**vit′ri·fi·ca′tion** *n.*

vit·ri·ol (vit′rē·ōl, -əl) *n.* 1. *Chem.* **a** Sulfuric acid. **b** Any sulfate of a heavy metal. 2. Anything sharp or caustic, esp. speech or writing. [< L *vitrum* glass]

vit·ri·ol·ic (vit′rē·ol′ik) *adj.* 1. Derived from a vitriol. 2. Corrosive, burning, or caustic.

vit·ri·ol·ize (vit′rē·əl·īz′) *v.t.* **·ized, ·iz·ing** 1. To corrode, injure, or burn with sulfuric acid. 2. To convert into or impregnate with vitriol. —**vit′ri·ol·i·za′tion** *n.*

vit·tles (vit′əls) *n.pl. Informal* or *Dial.* Victuals.

vi·tu·per·ate (vī·to͞o′pə·rāt, -tyo͞o′-, vi-) *v.t.* **·at·ed, ·at·ing** To find fault with abusively; rail at; berate; scold. [< L *vitium* fault + *parare* to prepare, make] —**vi·tu′per·a′tion** *n.* —**vi·tu′per·a·tive** (-pər·ə·tiv) *adj.* —**vi·tu′per·a·tive·ly** *adv.* —**vi·tu′per·a′tor** *n.*

vi·va (vē′vä) *interj.* Live! Long live!: an acclamation or salute. [< Ital.]

vi·va·ce (vē·vä′chā) *adv. Music* Lively; quickly; briskly. Also **vi·va′ce·men′te** (-män′tā). [< Ital.]

vi·va·cious (vi·vā′shəs, vī-) *adj.* Lively; active. [< L *vivere* to live] —**vi·va′cious·ly** *adv.* —**vi·vac·i·ty** (vi·vas′ə·tē, vī-), **vi·va′cious·ness** *n.*

vi·var·i·um (vī·vâr′ē·əm) *n. pl.* **·var·i·a** or **·var·i·ums** A place for keeping or raising live animals, fish, or plants, as a park, pond, aquarium, cage, etc. Also **viv·a·ry** (viv′ər·ē). [< L *vivere* to live]

vi·va vo·ce (vī′və vō′sē) *Latin* By spoken word; orally.

vive (vēv) *interj. French* Long live!: used in acclamation.

viv·id (viv′id) *adj.* 1. Very bright; intense: said of colors. 2. Producing or evoking lifelike imagery, freshness, etc.: *vivid* prose. 3. Clearly felt or strongly expressed, as emotions. 4. Full of life and vigor. 5. Clearly seen in the mind, as a memory. 6. Clearly perceived by the eye. [< L *vivere* to live] —**viv′id·ly** *adv.* —**viv′id·ness** *n.*

viv·i·fy (viv′ə·fī) *v.t.* **·fied, ·fy·ing** 1. To give life to; animate; vitalize. 2. To make more vivid or striking. [< L *vivus* alive + *facere* to make] —**viv′i·fi·ca′tion** *n.* —**viv′i·fi′er** *n.*

vi·vip·a·rous (vī·vip′ər·əs) *adj. Zool.* Bringing forth living young, as most mammals. [< L *vivus* alive + *parere* to bring forth] —**vi·vip′a·rous·ly** *adv.* —**vi·vip′a·rism, viv·i·par·i·ty** (viv′ə·par′ə·tē), **vi·vip′a·rous·ness** *n.*

viv·i·sect (viv′ə·sekt) *v.t. & v.i.* To dissect or operate upon (a living animal) for the purpose of research or study. —**viv′i·sec′tor** *n.*

viv·i·sec·tion (viv′ə·sek′shən) *n.* The act of vivisecting; experimentation on living animals by means of operations. [< L *vivus* living, alive + SECTION] —**viv′i·sec′tion·al** *adj.* —**viv′i·sec′tion·ist** *n.*

vix·en (vik′sən) *n.* 1. A female fox. 2. A turbulent, quarrelsome woman; shrew. [Alter. of ME *fixen* she-fox < OE, fem. of *fox*] —**vix′en·ish** *adj.* —**vix′en·ly** *adj. & adv.*

vi·zier (vi·zir′) *n.* A high official of a Moslem country; esp., a minister of state. Also **vi·zir′.** [< Turkish < Arabic *wazīr* counselor, orig., porter < *wazara* to carry]

vi·zier·ate (vi·zir′it, -āt) *n.* The office of a vizier. Also **vi·zier′al·ty, vi·zier′ship, vi·zir′ate, vi·zir′ship.**

vi·zor (vī′zər) See VISOR.

V-J Day (vē′jā′) September 2, 1945, the official date of the victory over Japan in World War II.

vo·ca·ble (vō′kə·bəl) *n.* 1. A spoken or written word considered only as a sequence of sounds or letters, without regard to its meaning. 2. A vocal sound. —*adj.* Capable of being spoken. [< L *vocabulum* name < *vocare* to call]

vo·cab·u·lar·y (vō·kab′yə·ler′ē) *n. pl.* **·lar·ies** 1. A list of words, esp. one arranged in alphabetical order and defined or translated; a glossary. 2. All the words of a language. 3. A sum or aggregate of the words used by a particular person, class, etc., or employed in some specialized field of knowledge. [See VOCABLE.]

vo·cal (vō′kəl) *adj.* 1. Of, pertaining to, or for the voice. 2. Having voice. 3. Concerned in the production of voice: the *vocal* organs. 4. Freely expressing oneself in speech. [< L *vocalis* speaking, sounding < *vox* voice] —**vo′cal·ly** *adv.* —**vo′cal·ness** *n.*

vocal cords Two membranous bands in the larynx having edges that, when drawn tense, are caused to vibrate by the passage of air from the lungs, thereby producing voice.

vo·cal·ic (vō·kal′ik) *adj.* Consisting of, like, or relating to vowel sounds.
vo·cal·ist (vō′kəl·ist) *n.* A singer.
vo·cal·ize (vō′kəl·īz) *v.* **·ized, ·iz·ing** *v.t.* 1. To make vocal; utter, say, or sing. 2. To provide a voice for; render articulate. 3. *Phonet.* a To change (a consonant) to a vowel by some shift in the articulatory process. b To voice. —*v.i.* 4. To produce sounds with the voice, as in speaking or singing. —**vo′cal·i·za′tion** *n.* —**vo′cal·iz′er** *n.*
vo·ca·tion (vō·kā′shən) *n.* 1. A stated or regular occupation; a calling. 2. A call to or fitness for a certain career. [< L *vocare* to call] —**vo·ca′tion·al** *adj.* —**vo·ca′tion·al·ly** *adv.*
vocational school A school, usu. on the secondary level, that trains students for special trades.
voc·a·tive (vok′ə·tiv) *Gram. adj.* In some inflected languages, denoting the case of a noun, pronoun, or adjective used in direct address. —*n.* 1. The vocative case. 2. A word in this case. [< F, fem. of *vocatif* < L *vocare* to call]
vo·ces (vō′sēz) Plural of VOX.
vo·ci·fer·ate (vō·sif′ə·rāt) *v.t. & v.i.* **·at·ed, ·at·ing** To cry out with a loud voice; shout. [< L *vox, vocis* voice + *ferre* to carry] —**vo·cif′er·a′tion** *n.* —**vo·cif′er·a′tor** *n.*
vo·cif·er·ous (vō·sif′ər·əs) *adj.* Making or characterized by a loud outcry; clamorous; noisy. —**vo·cif′er·ous·ly** *adv.* —**vo·cif′er·ous·ness** *n.*
vod·ka (vod′kə, *Russ.* vôd′kə) *n.* A colorless alcoholic liquor distilled from grain or potatoes. [< Russ., dim. of *voda* water]
vogue (vōg) *n.* 1. The prevalent way or fashion; mode. 2. Popular favor; general acceptance. [< F, fashion, orig., rowing]
Vo·gul (vō′gŏŏl) *n.* 1. One of a Finno-Ugric people of the Ural Mountains. 2. The Ugric language of these people.
voice (vois) *n.* 1. The sound produced by the vocal organs of a person or animal. 2. The power or faculty of vocal utterance; speech. 3. A sound suggesting vocal utterance: the *voice* of the wind. 4. Opinion or choice expressed; also, means, medium, or agency of expression. 5. *Phonet.* The sound produced by vibration of the vocal cords in the production of most vowels and certain consonants. 6. The production of musical tone by the vocal organs, esp. with regard to ability and readiness to perform: a great *voice*, in poor *voice*. 7. *Music* A part, esp. as considered without regard to the instrument or human voice rendering it: also **voice part**. 8. *Gram.* The relation of the action expressed by the verb to the subject. —**in voice** In proper condition for singing. —**with one voice** With one accord; unitedly; unanimously. —*v.t.* **voiced, voic·ing** 1. To put into speech; utter. 2. *Music* To regulate the tones of; tune, as the pipes of an organ. 3. *Phonet.* To utter with voice or sonance. [< L *vox, vocis*]
voice box The larynx.
voiced (voist) *adj.* 1. Expressed by voice. 2. *Phonet.* Uttered with vibration of the vocal cords, as (b), (d), (z); sonant.
voice·less (vois′lis) *adj.* 1. Having no voice, speech, or vote. 2. *Phonet.* Produced without voice, as (p), (t), (s). —**voice′less·ly** *adv.* —**voice′less·ness** *n.*
voice-o·ver (vois′ō′vər) *n.* In television or motion pictures, the voice of an unseen commentator or narrator, or of a character's thoughts.
void (void) *adj.* 1. No longer having force or validity, as a contract, license, etc.; invalid; null. 2. Destitute; clear or free: with *of*: *void* of reason. 3. Not occupied by matter; empty. 4. Unoccupied, as a house or room. 5. Producing no effect; useless. —*n.* 1. An empty space; a vacuum. 2. Empty condition or feeling; a blank. —*v.t.* 1. To make void or of no effect; invalidate. 2. To empty or remove (contents); evacuate, as urine. [< LL *vocuus* empty < L *vacuus*] —**void′er** *n.*
void·a·ble (voi′də·bəl) *adj.* 1. Capable of being made void. 2. That may be evacuated.
void·ance (void′ns) *n.* 1. The act of voiding, evacuating, ejecting, or emptying. 2. The state or condition of being void; vacancy. [< OF *voider* to empty < L]
voi·là (vwȧ·lȧ′) *interj. French* There! behold!
voile (voil) *n.* A fine, sheer fabric like heavy veiling. [< F, veil]
vo·lant (vō′lənt) *adj.* 1. Flying, or able to fly. 2. Nimble. [< OF, ppr. of *voler* to fly < L *volare*]
vo·lan·te (vō·län′tā) *adj. Music* Swift and light. [< Ital.]
vo·lar (vō′lər) *adj.* Pertaining to flight. [< L *volare* to fly]
vol·a·tile (vol′ə·til) *adj.* 1. Evaporating rapidly at ordinary temperatures on exposure to the air. 2. Capable of being vaporized. 3. Easily influenced; changeable. 4. Transient; ephemeral. [< L *volare* to fly] —**vol′a·til′i·ty, vol′a·tile·ness** *n.*
vol·a·til·ize (vol′ə·til·īz′) *v.t. & v.i.* **·ized, ·iz·ing** 1. To make or become volatile. 2. To pass off or cause to pass off in vapor; evaporate. —**vol′a·til·iz′a·ble** *adj.* —**vol′a·til·i·za′tion** *n.* —**vol′a·til·iz′er** *n.*
vol·can·ic (vol·kan′ik) *adj.* 1. Of, pertaining to, or characteristic of a volcano or volcanoes. 2. Produced by or emitted from a volcano. 3. Eruptive. —**vol·can·ic·i·ty** (vol′kə·nis′ə·tē) *n.* —**vol·can′i·cal·ly** *adv.*
vol·can·ism (vol′kən·iz′əm) *n.* The conditions and phenomena associated with volcanoes or volcanic action.
vol·can·ize (vol′kən·īz) *v.t.* **·ized, ·iz·ing** To subject to the action and effects of volcanic heat. —**vol′can·i·za′tion** *n.*
vol·ca·no (vol·kā′nō) *n. pl.* **·noes** or **·nos** *Geol.* 1. An opening in the crust of the earth from which steam, hot gases, ashes, etc., are expelled, forming a conical hill or mountain with a central crater. 2. The formation itself. [< Ital. < L *Volcanus, Vulcanus* Vulcan, Roman god of fire]
vol·can·ol·o·gy (vol′kən·ol′ə·jē) *n.* The scientific study of volcanoes. —**vol′can·o·log′i·cal** (-ə·loj′i·kəl) *adj.* —**vol′can·ol′o·gist** *n.*
vole (vōl) *n.* Any of various short-tailed, mouselike or ratlike rodents; esp., the **European vole** or the **North American vole.** [Short for earlier *vole mouse* < *vole* field < Norw. *voll*]
vo·li·tion (və·lish′ən) *n.* 1. The act or faculty of willing; exercise of the will. 2. That

which is willed or determined upon. [< L *vol-*, stem of *velle* will] **—vo·li′tion·al** *adj.* **—vo·li′tion·al·ly** *adv.*

vol·i·tive (vol′ə·tiv) *adj.* 1. Of or pertaining to the will. 2. Expressing a wish or permission.

vol·ley (vol′ē) *n. pl.* **·leys** 1. A simultaneous discharge of many missiles; also, the missiles so discharged. 2. Any discharge of many things at once: a *volley* of oaths. 3. In tennis, a return of the ball before it touches the ground. 4. In soccer, a kick given the ball before its rebound. *—v.t. & v.i.* **·leyed, ·ley·ing** 1. To discharge or be discharged in a volley. 2. In tennis, to return (the ball) by a volley. 3. In soccer, to kick (the ball) before its rebound. [< L *volare* to fly]

vol·ley·ball (vol′ē·bôl′) *n.* A game in which two teams strike a large ball with the hands back and forth over a high net; also, the ball used. Also **volley ball.**

volt[1] (vōlt) *n.* The unit of electromotive force, or that difference of potential, that when steadily applied against a resistance of one ohm will produce a current of one ampere. [after Alessandro *Volta,* 1745–1827, Italian physicist]

volt[2] (vōlt) *n.* 1. In horse-training, a gait in which the horse moves partially sidewise round a center. 2. In fencing, a sudden leap to avoid a thrust. [< Ital. *volta,* orig. pp. fem. of *volvere* to turn < L]

volt·age (vōl′tij) *n.* Electromotive force expressed in volts.

vol·ta·ic (vol·tā′ik) *adj.* Pertaining to electricity developed through chemical action or contact; galvanic.

voltaic cell *Electr.* A primary cell.

vol·ta·ism (vol′tə·iz′əm) *n.* Galvanism.

volt·am·me·ter (vōlt′am′mē′tər) *n.* An instrument for measuring either volts or amperes.

volt-am·pere (vōlt′am′pir) *n.* The rate of work in an electric circuit when the current is one ampere and the potential one volt, equivalent to one watt.

volte-face (volt·fäs′) *n.* About-face (def. 2). [< F < Ital. *voltafaccia*]

volt·me·ter (vōlt′mē′tər) *n.* An instrument for determining the voltage between any two points.

vol·u·ble (vol′yə·bəl) *adj.* 1. Having a flow of words or fluency in speaking; garrulous. 2. Turning readily or easily; apt or formed to roll. 3. Twining, as a plant. [< L *volutus,* pp. of *volvere* to turn] **—vol′u·bil′i·ty** *n.* **—vol′u·bly** *adv.*

vol·ume (vol′yo͞om, -yəm) *n.* 1. A collection of sheets of paper bound together; book. 2. A separately bound part of a work. 3. Sufficient matter to fill a volume. 4. Quantity of sound or tone; loudness. 5. A large quantity; a considerable amount. 6. Space occupied in three dimensions, as measured by cubic units. **—to speak volumes** To be full of meaning; express a great deal. [< L *volumen* roll, scroll < *volvere* to turn]

vol·u·met·ric (vol′yə·met′rik) *adj. Chem.* Of or pertaining to measurement of substances by comparison of volumes. Also **vol′u·met′ri·cal. —vol′u·met′ri·cal·ly** *adv.* **—vo·lu·me·try** (və·lo͞o′mə·trē) *n.*

vo·lu·mi·nous (və·lo͞o′mə·nəs) *adj.* 1. Having great quantity or volume. 2. Consisting of or capable of filling several volumes. 3. Writing or having written much; productive. 4. Having coils, folds, windings, etc. **—vo·lu′mi·nos′i·ty** (-nos′ə·te), **vo·lu′mi·nous·ness** *n.* **—vo·lu′mi·nous·ly** *adv.*

vol·un·tar·y (vol′ən·ter′ē) *adj.* 1. Proceeding from free choice; intentional; volitional. 2. Effected by choice or volition. 3. Supported by private funds. *—n. pl.* **·tar·ies** An organ solo, often improvised, played before, during, or after a service. [< L *voluntas* will] **—vol′un·tar′i·ly** *adv.* **—vol′un·tar′i·ness** *n.*

vol·un·teer (vol′ən·tir′) *n.* One who enters into any service, esp. military service or a hazardous undertaking, of his own free will. *—adj.* 1. Pertaining to or composed of volunteers. 2. Springing up naturally or spontaneously, as from fallen or self-sown seed. *—v.t.* 1. To offer to give or do. *—v.i.* 2. To act as a volunteer; enlist. [< obs. F *voluntaire* < OF *voluntas* will]

vo·lup·tu·ar·y (və·lup′cho͞o·er′ē) *adj.* Pertaining to or promoting sensual indulgence and luxurious pleasures. *—n. pl.* **·ar·ies** One addicted to sensual pleasures; a sensualist.

vo·lup·tu·ous (və·lup′cho͞o·əs) *adj.* 1. Of, pertaining to, or causing sensuous gratification; sensuous; luxurious. 2. Devoted to the enjoyment of pleasures or luxuries; sensual. 3. Having a full and beautiful form, as a woman. [< L *voluptas* pleasure] **—vo·lup′tu·ous·ly** *adv.* **—vo·lup′tu·ous·ness** *n.*

vo·lute (və·lo͞ot′) *n.* 1. *Archit.* A spiral, scroll-like ornament, esp. one characteristic of the Ionic capital. 2. *Zool.* One of the whorls or turns of a spiral shell. *—adj.* 1. Rolled up; forming spiral curves. 2. Having a spiral form, as a machine part. [< L *voluta* scroll, orig. fem. pp. of *volvere* to turn] **—vo·lut′ed** *adv.* **—vo·lu′tion** *n.*

vom·it (vom′it) *v.t. & v.i.* 1. To throw up or eject (the contents of the stomach) through the mouth. 2. To eject (matter) with violence from any hollow place. *—n.* Matter that is ejected from the stomach in vomiting. [< L *vomitare,* freq. of *vomere* to vomit] **—vom′it·er** *n.*

vom·i·tive (vom′ə·tiv) *adj.* Causing vomiting. *—n.* An emetic.

vom·i·to·ry (vom′ə·tôr′ē) *adj.* Efficacious in producing vomiting. *—n. pl.* **·ries** 1. An emetic. 2. An opening through which matter is discharged.

voo·doo (vo͞o′do͞o) *n. pl.* **·doos** 1. A primitive religion of West African origin characterized by belief in sorcery and the use of charms, fetishes, etc. 2. One who practices voodoo. 3. A voodoo charm or fetish. *—v.t.* **·dooed, ·doo·ing** To put a spell upon after the manner of a voodoo. [< Creole < Ewe (a W. African language) *vodu*] **—voo′doo** *adj.* **—voo′doo·ism** *n.* **—voo′doo·ist** *n.* **—voo′·doo·is′tic** *adj.*

vo·ra·cious (vô·rā′shəs, vō-, və-) *adj.* 1. Eating with greediness; ravenous. 2. Greedy; rapacious. 3. Ready to swallow up or engulf. 4. Insatiable; immoderate. [< L *vorare* to devour] **—vo·ra′cious·ly** *adv.* **—vo·rac′i·ty** (-ras′ə·tē), **vo·ra′cious·ness** *n.*

-vorous *combining form* Consuming; eating or feeding upon: *omnivorous, carnivorous.* [< L *-vorus* < *vorare* to devour]

vor·tex (vôr′teks) *n. pl.* **·tex·es** or **·ti·ces** (-tə·sēz) 1. A mass of whirling gas or liquid, esp. when sucked spirally toward a central axis; a whirlwind or whirlpool. 2. Any action or state of affairs that is similar to a vortex in violence, force, etc. [< L, var. of *vertex* top, point] —**vor′ti·cal** (-ti·kəl) *adj.* —**vor′ti·cal·ly** *adv.*

vo·ta·ry (vō′tər·ē) *n. pl.* **·ries** 1. One bound by a vow or promise, as a nun. 2. One devoted to some particular worship, pursuit, study, etc. Also **vo′ta·rist.** —*adj.* Consecrated by a vow or promise; votive. [< L *votus*, pp. of *vovere* to vow] —**vo·ta·ress** (vō′tə·ris) or **vo′tress** (vō′tris) *n.fem.*

vote (vōt) *n.* 1. A formal expression of will or opinion in regard to some question submitted for decision, as in electing officers, passing resolutions, etc. 2. That by which such choice is expressed, as a show of hands, or ballot. 3. The result of an election. 4. The number of votes cast; also, votes collectively. 5. The right to vote. 6. A voter or group of voters. —*v.* **vot·ed, vot·ing** *v.t.* 1. To enact or determine by vote. 2. To cast one's vote for. 3. *Informal* To declare by general agreement. —*v.i.* 4. To cast one's vote. **to vote down** To defeat or suppress by voting against. —**to vote in** To elect. [< L *votum* vow, wish] —**vot′a·ble** or **vote′a·ble** *adj.* —**vot′er** *n.*

voting machine A device which enables the voter to indicate his choices and which registers and counts all votes.

vo·tive (vō′tiv) *adj.* Dedicated by a vow; performed in fulfillment of a vow. —**vo′tive·ly** *adv.* —**vo′tive·ness** *n.*

vouch (vouch) *v.i.* 1. To give one's own assurance or guarantee; bear witness: with *for.* 2. To serve as assurance or proof: with *for.* —*v.t.* 3. To bear witness to; attest or affirm. 4. To substantiate. —*n.* A declaration that attests. [< L *vocare* to call < *vox, vocis* voice]

vouch·er (vou′chər) *n.* 1. A document that serves to attest an alleged act, esp. the payment or receipt of money. 2. One who vouches for another; a witness.

vouch·safe (vouch′sāf′) *v.t. & v.i.* **·safed, ·saf·ing** To grant (something), as with condescension; permit; deign. —**vouch′safe′ment** *n.*

vous·soir (vo͞o·swär′) *n. Archit.* A stone shaped to fit the curve of an arch. [< OF *vausoir* < L *volvere* to turn]

vow (vou) *n.* 1. A solemn promise to or as to God; pledge. 2. A pledge of faithfulness. 3. A solemn and emphatic affirmation. —**to take vows** To enter a religious order. —*v.t.* 1. To promise solemnly, esp. to a deity. 2. To declare with assurance or solemnity. 3. To make a solemn promise or threat to do, inflict, etc. —*v.i.* 4. To make a vow. [< AF *vu* < L *votum*] —**vow′er** *n.*

vow·el (vou′əl) *n.* 1. *Phonet.* A speech sound produced by the relatively unimpeded passage of breath through the mouth. 2. A letter representing such a sound, as *a, e, i, o, u,* and sometimes *y.* [< L *vox, vocis* voice, sound] —**vow′el** *adj.*

vox (voks) *n. pl.* **vo·ces** (vō′sēz) Voice; esp., in music, a voice; part. [< L]

vox po·pu·li (voks pop′yə·lī) *Latin* The voice of the people.

voy·age (voi′ij) *n.* 1. A journey by water, esp. a long one. 2. Any journey. 3. Any enterprise or project; also, course. —*v.* **·aged, ·ag·ing** *v.i.* 1. To make a voyage; journey by water. —*v.t.* 2. To travel over. [< L *viaticum*] —**voy′ag·er** *n.*

voy·age·a·ble (voi′ij·ə·bəl) *adj.* Navigable.

vo·ya·geur (vwȧ·yȧ·zhœr′) *n. pl.* **·geurs** (-zhœr′) A Canadian boatman or fur trader. [< dial. F (Canadian)]

vo·yeur (vwä·yûr′) *n.* One who is sexually gratified by looking at sexual objects or acts. [< F < L *videre* to see] —**vo·yeur′ism** *n.*

VTOL (vē′tôl) *n. Aeron.* An aircraft that takes off and lands vertically. [V(ERTICAL) T(AKE) O(FF AND) L(ANDING)]

vul·ca·ni·an (vul·kā′nē·ən) *adj.* Volcanic: also **vul·can·ic** (vul·kan′ik). [< L *Vulcanus* Vulcan, Roman god of fire]

vul·can·ite (vul′kən·īt) *n.* A dark, hard variety of rubber that has been vulcanized: also called *ebonite, hard rubber.* —*adj.* Made of vulcanite.

vul·can·ize (vul′kən·īz) *v.t.* **·ized, ·iz·ing** To treat (crude rubber) with sulfur or sulfur compounds in varying proportions and at different temperatures, thereby increasing its strength and elasticity. —**vul′can·iz′a·ble** *adj.* —**vul′can·i·za′tion** *n.* —**vul′can·iz′er** *n.*

vul·can·ol·o·gy (vul′kən·ol′ə·jē) *n.* Volcanology. —**vul′can·o·log′i·cal** (-ə·loj′i·kəl) *adj.* —**vul′can·ol′o·gist** *n.*

vul·gar (vul′gər) *adj.* 1. Lacking in refinement or good taste; crude; boorish; also, obscene; indecent. 2. Of, pertaining to, or characteristic of the people at large, as distinguished from the privileged or educated classes; popular; common. 3. Written in or translated into the common language or vulgate; vernacular. [< L *vulgus* the common people] —**vul′gar·ly** *adv.*

vul·gar·i·an (vul·gâr′ē·ən) *n.* A person of vulgar tastes or manners.

vul·gar·ism (vul′gə·riz′əm) *n.* 1. Vulgarity. 2. A nonstandard or unrefined word, phrase, or expression.

vul·gar·i·ty (vul·gar′ə·tē) *n. pl.* **·ties** 1. The quality or character of being vulgar. 2. Something vulgar, as an action, word, etc. Also **vul·gar·ness** (vul′gər·nis).

vul·gar·ize (vul′gə·rīz) *v.t.* **·ized, ·iz·ing** 1. To make vulgar. 2. To popularize. Also *Brit.* **vul′gar·ise.** —**vul′gar·i·za′tion** *n.* —**vul′gar·iz′er** *n.*

Vulgar Latin See under LATIN.

vul·gate (vul′gāt) *adj.* Common; popular; generally accepted. —*n.* 1. Everyday speech. 2. Any commonly accepted text. [< L *vulgus* the common people]

Vul·gate (vul′gāt) *n.* A Latin version of the Bible, translated between A.D. 383 and 405, now revised and used as the authorized version by the Roman Catholics. [< Med.L *vulgata* (*editio*) the popular (edition)] —**Vul′gate** *adj.*

vul·ner·a·ble (vul′nər·ə·bəl) *adj.* 1. Capable of being hurt or damaged. 2. Liable to attack; assailable. 3. In contract bridge, having won one game of a rubber, and thus receiving increased penalties and increased bonuses. [< L *vulnerare* to wound] —**vul′-**

ner·a·bil′i·ty, vul′ner·a·ble·ness *n.* **—vul′·ner·a·bly** *adv.*

vul·pine (vul′pin, -pīn) *adj.* 1. Of or pertaining to a fox. 2. Like a fox; sly; crafty. [< L *vulpes* fox]

vul·ture (vul′chər) *n.* Any of various large birds related to the eagles, hawks, and falcons, having the head and neck naked or partly naked, and feeding mostly on carrion. [< L *vultur*] **—vul·tur·ine** (vul′chə·rīn, -chər·in), **vul′tur·ous** *adj.*

vul·va (vul′və) *n. pl.* **·vae** (-vē) *Anat.* The external genital parts of the female. [< L, a covering, womb] **—vul′val, vul′var** *adj.* **—vul′vi·form** (-fôrm) *adj.*

vy·ing (vī′ing) Present participle of VIE.

W

w, W (dub′əl·yōō, -yŏŏ) *n. pl.* **w's** or **ws, W's** or **Ws** 1. The twenty-third letter of the English alphabet. 2. The sound represented by the letter *w*. —*symbol Chem.* Tungsten (W for *wolfram*).

wack·y (wak′ē) *adj.* **wack·i·er, wack·i·est** *Slang* Extremely irrational or impractical; erratic; screwy. [Prob. < WHACK; with ref. to damaging blows on the head]

wad (wod) *n.* 1. A small compact mass of any soft or flexible substance: a *wad* of cotton. 2. *Informal* A roll of banknotes; also, wealth. —*v.t.* **wad·ded, wad·ding** To press or roll into a wad. [Origin uncertain] —**wad′dy** *adj.*

wad·ding (wod′ing) *n.* 1. Wads collectively. 2. Any substance, as carded cotton, used as material for wads.

wad·dle (wod′l) *v.i.* **·dled, ·dling** To walk with short steps, swaying from side to side. —*n.* A clumsy, rocking walk. [Freq. of WADE] —**wad′dler** *n.* —**wad′dly** *adj.*

wade (wād) *v.* **wad·ed, wad·ing** *v.i.* 1. To walk through water, mud, sand, etc. 2. To proceed slowly or laboriously: to *wade* through a book. —*v.t.* 3. To pass or cross, as a river, by wading. —**to wade in** (or **into**) *Informal* To attack or begin vigorously. [OE *wadan* to go]

wad·er (wā′dər) *n.* 1. One who wades. 2. A long-legged wading bird, as a snipe, plover, or stork. 3. *pl.* High waterproof boots, worn esp. by anglers.

wa·di (wä′dē) *n. pl.* **·dies** In northern Africa, the bed or channel of a stream that is usu. dry except in the rainy season; also, a stream flowing through such a channel. Also **wa′dy**. [< Arabic *wādī*]

wa·fer (wā′fər) *n.* 1. A very thin, crisp cooky or cracker; also, a small disk of candy. 2. *Eccl.* A small, flat disk of unleavened bread used in the Eucharist. [< MLG *wafel*]

waf·fle[1] (wof′əl) *n.* A batter cake baked between two hinged metal griddles marked with regular indentations (**waffle iron**). [< Du. *wafel* wafer]

waf·fle[2] (wof′əl) *v.i.* **·fled, ·fling** *Informal* To talk indecisively; vacillate. [<obs. *waff* to yelp]

waft (waft, wäft) *v.t.* 1. To carry or bear gently over air or water; float. 2. To convey as if on air or water. —*v.i.* 3. To float, as on the wind. —*n.* 1. A light breeze; gust; puff. 2. An odor, sound, etc., carried through the air. 3. A wafting or waving motion. [< Du. *wachten* to guard]

wag[1] (wag) *v.t. & v.i.* **wagged, wag·ging** 1. To move or cause to move quickly from side to side or up and down, as a dog's tail; swing. 2. To move (the tongue) in idle chatter or gossip. —*n.* The act or motion of wagging. [ME *waggen*, prob. < Scand.]

wag[2] (wag) *n.* A humorous fellow; wit; joker. [? Short for obs. *waghalter* gallows bird < WAG[1] + HALTER] —**wag′gish** *adj.* —**wag′gish·ly** *adv.* —**wag′gish·ness** *n.*

wage (wāj) *v.t.* **waged, wag·ing** To engage in; carry on: to *wage* war. —*n.* 1. *Usu. pl.* Payment for work done. 2. *pl.* Recompense; reward: the *wages* of crime. [< OF *guagier* to pledge]

wage earner One who works for wages.

wa·ger (wā′jər) *v.t. & v.i.* To bet. —*n.* A bet. [< AF *wagier* to pledge] —**wa′ger·er** *n.*

wage scale A scale of wages paid to workers in a factory, industry, etc.

wag·ger·y (wag′ər·ē) *n. pl.* **·ger·ies** 1. Mischievous jocularity; drollery. 2. A jest; joke.

wag·gle (wag′əl) *v.t. & v.i.* **·gled, ·gling** To move or cause to move with rapid to-and-fro motions; wag. [Freq. of WAG[1]] —**wag′gle** *n.* —**wag′gling·ly** *adv.* —**wag′gly** *adj.*

wag·on (wag′ən) *n.* 1. Any of various four-wheeled horse-drawn vehicles used for carrying goods. 2. A child's four-wheeled toy cart. 3. A station wagon. —**on the wagon** *Informal* Abstaining from alcoholic beverages. —**to fix (someone's) wagon** *Slang* To ruin or punish. Also *Brit.* **wag′gon.** [< Du. *wagen*]

wag·on·er (wag′ən·ər) *n.* One whose work is driving wagons. Also *Brit.* **wag′gon·er.**

wagon train A group of covered wagons traveling together.

wa·hoo (wä·hōō′, wä′hōō) *n.* A deciduous North American shrub or small tree with purple flowers and scarlet fruit. [< Siouan (Dakota) *wānhu*, lit., arrowwood]

waif (wāf) *n.* 1. A homeless, neglected wanderer, esp. a child; a stray. 2. Anything, as a stray cat, that is found and unclaimed. [< AF *waif*]

wail (wāl) *v.i.* 1. To make a sad, melancholy sound, as in grief or pain. 2. To make a sound like a wail: The wind *wailed* through the night. —*n.* A prolonged, mournful sound. [< ON *væ, vei* woe] —**wail′er** *n.* —**wail′ful** *adj.*

wain·scot (wān′skət, -skot, -skōt) *n.* 1. A facing for inner walls, usu. of paneled wood. 2. The lower part of an inner wall when finished differently from the rest. —*v.t.* **wain·scot·ed** or **·scot·ted, wain·scot·ing** or **·scot·ting** To face or panel with wainscot. [< MLG *wagen* wagon + *schot* wooden partition]

wain·scot·ing (wān′skōt·ing, -skot-, -skət-) *n.* Material for a wainscot; also, a wainscot. Also **wain′scot·ting.**

waist (wāst) *n.* 1. The part of the body between the chest and the hips. 2. The middle part of any object, esp. if narrower than the ends. 3. That part of a woman's dress covering the body from the waistline to the shoulders; a bodice. [ME *wast*]

waist·band (wāst'band', -bənd) *n.* A band at the top of a skirt or trousers that encircles the waist.

waist·coat (wāst'kōt', wes'kit) *n.* *Chiefly Brit.* A vest.

waist·line (wāst'līn') *n.* The narrowest part of a person's waist.

wait (wāt) *v.i.* 1. To remain in expectation or readiness: with *for*, *until*, etc.: to *wait* for a train. 2. To remain temporarily neglected or undone: Dinner will have to *wait*. —*v.t.* 3. To remain in expectation of: to *wait* one's turn. —**to wait on** (or **upon**) 1. To act as a servant to. 2. To serve (a customer). 3. To call upon; visit. —**to wait up** To put off going to bed until someone returns home, etc. —*n.* The act or period of waiting. —**to lie in wait** To hide in order to attack or trap; set an ambush: often with *for*. [< OHG *wahta* guard]

wait·er (wā'tər) *n.* A man who serves food and drink in a restaurant.

waiting room A room for those waiting, as at an airport, in a doctor's office, etc.

wait·ress (wā'tris) *n.* A woman who serves food and drink in a restaurant.

waive (wāv) *v.t.* **waived, waiv·ing** 1. *Law* To give up or relinquish (a claim, right, etc.). 2. To put off; postpone; delay. [< AF *weyver*, OF *gaiver* to abandon]

waiv·er (wā'vər) *n.* *Law* The relinquishment of a claim, right, etc.; also, the instrument that evidences such relinquishment.

wake[1] (wāk) *v.* **woke** (*Rare* **waked**), **waked** (*Dial.* and alternative *Brit.* **woke, wok·en**), **wak·ing** *v.i.* 1. To emerge from sleep. 2. To be or remain awake. 3. To become active or alert. —*v.t.* 4. To rouse from sleep; awake. 5. To stir up; excite. —*n.* A watch or vigil over a corpse before burial. [Fusion of OE *wacan* to awake and *wacian* to be awake]

wake[2] (wāk) *n.* 1. The track left by a vessel passing through the water. 2. The area behind any moving thing. —**in the wake of** 1. Following close behind. 2. As a result of. [< ON *vök* an opening in ice]

wake·ful (wāk'fəl) *adj.* 1. Unable to sleep. 2. Watchful; alert. —**wake'ful·ly** *adv.* —**wake'ful·ness** *n.*

wak·en (wā'kən) *v.t.* & *v.i.* Wake. [OE *wæcnan*, *wæcnian*]

wake-rob·in (wāk'rob'in) *n.* Any species of trillium.

wale (wāl) *n.* 1. A welt (def. 3). 2. *Naut.* Outer planking running fore and aft on a vessel. 3. A ridge on the surface of corduroy or other fabric. —*v.t.* **waled, wal·ing** To raise wales on by striking, as with a lash; beat. [OE *walu*]

walk (wôk) *v.i.* 1. To advance on foot at a moderate pace. 2. To act or live in some manner: to *walk* in peace. 3. In baseball, to achieve first base as a result of having been pitched four balls. —*v.t.* 4. To pass through, over, or across at a walk: to *walk* the floor. 5. To cause to go at a walk: to *walk* a horse. 6. To accompany on a walk: I'll *walk* you to the bus stop. 7. In baseball, to allow to advance to first base by pitching four balls. —**to walk off** 1. To depart, esp. abruptly or without warning. 2. To get rid of (fat, etc.) by walking. —**to walk off with** *Informal* 1. To win. 2. To steal. —**to walk out** *Informal* To go out on strike. —**to walk out on** *Informal* To forsake; desert. —**to walk over** *Informal* To defeat easily; overwhelm. —*n.* 1. The act or manner of walking. 2. Chosen profession or sphere of activity: the different *walks* of life. 3. Distance walked, esp. when measured by the time required: an hour's *walk*. 4. A path or area for walking. 5. In baseball, an advancing to first base as a result of having been pitched four balls. [OE *wealcan* to roll, toss] —**walk'er** *n.*

walk·a·way (wôk'ə·wā') *n.* A contest won without serious opposition: also called *walkover*.

walk·ie-talk·ie (wô'kē·tô'kē) *n.* A light, portable two-way radio: also **walk'y-talk'y**.

walking papers *Informal* Notice of dismissal from employment, etc.

walking stick 1. A staff or cane. 2. Any of various insects having legs, body, and wings resembling a twig.

walk-on (wôk'on', -ôn') *n.* A performer having a very small part; also, the part.

walk·out (wôk'out') *n.* *Informal* A worker's strike.

walk·o·ver (wôk'ō'vər) *n.* A walkaway.

walk·up (wôk'up') *n.* *Informal* An apartment house having no elevator.

wall (wôl) *n.* 1. A continuous structure that encloses, protects, or divides an area. ◆Collateral adjective: *mural*. 2. Something suggesting a wall: a *wall* of bayonets. —**to drive** or **push to the wall** To force (one) to an extremity. —*v.t.* To provide, surround, block, etc., with or as with a wall: with *up* or *in*. [OE *weall* < L *vallus* stake, palisade]

wal·la·by (wol'ə·bē) *n.* *pl.* **·bies** One of the smaller kangaroos. [< Austral. *walabā*]

wall·board (wôl'bôrd') *n.* A structural material, as of wood pulp, pressed into large sheets and used to cover interior walls.

wal·let (wol'it) *n.* A pocketbook for holding paper money, cards, etc.: also called *billfold*. [ME *walet* carrying sack; ult. origin uncertain]

wall·eye (wôl'ī') *n.* 1. **a** An outward turning eye. **b** A whitish eye. 2. A fresh-water fish with prominent eyes: also **walleyed pike**. [< ON *vagl* film on the eye + *auga* eye] —**wall'eyed'** *adj.*

wall·flow·er (wôl'flou'ər) *n.* 1. Any of various European herbs of the mustard family, having fragrant yellow, orange, or red flowers. 2. *Informal* A shy or unpopular person who does not take part in a dance or other social activity.

Wal·loon (wo·lōōn') *n.* 1. One of a people inhabiting southern and southeastern Belgium and the adjoining regions of France. 2. Their language, a dialect of French. —**Wal·loon'** *adj.*

wal·lop (wol'əp) *Informal* *v.t.* 1. To beat soundly; thrash. 2. To hit hard; sock. 3. To defeat soundly. —*n.* A severe blow. [< OF *galoper*]

wal·lop·ing (wol′əp·ing) *Informal adj.* Very large; whopping. —*n.* A severe beating.

wal·low (wol′ō) *v.i.* 1. To roll about in mud, etc.; thrash about; flounder. 2. To involve oneself fully; revel: with *in.* —*n.* A muddy or dusty hole in which animals wallow. [OE *wealwian*] —**wal′low·er** *n.*

wall·pa·per (wôl′pā′pər) *n.* Paper for covering walls and ceilings. —*v.t.* To cover with wallpaper.

Wall Street 1. A street in the financial district of New York City. 2. The world of U.S. finance.

wal·nut (wôl′nut′, -nət) *n.* 1. Any of various trees of the North temperate zone, valued for their timber and edible nuts. 2. The wood or nut of any of these trees. 3. A dark brown color. [OE *wealh* foreign + *hnutu* nut]

wal·rus (wôl′rəs, wol′-) *n. pl.* **·rus·es** or **·rus** A large marine mammal of arctic seas, having flippers, projecting ivory tusks, and a thick neck. [< Du. < Scand.]

waltz (wôlts) *n.* 1. A dance for couples in $^3/_4$ time. 2. The music for such a dance. —*v.i.* 1. To dance a waltz. 2. To move lightly and freely. —*v.t.* 3. To cause to waltz. [< G *walzen* to waltz] —**waltz′er** *n.*

wam·pum (wom′pəm, wôm′-) *n.* 1. Beads made from shells, formerly used as currency by North American Indians. 2. *Slang* Money. [< Algonquian *wampum*(*peage*), lit., a white string (of beads)]

wan (won) *adj.* **wan·ner, wan·nest** 1. Pale, as from sickness or anxiety; pallid. 2. Indicating illness, unhappiness, etc.: a *wan* smile. [OE *wann* dark, gloomy] —**wan′ly** *adv.* —**wan′ness** *n.*

wand (wond) *n.* 1. A slender rod waved by a magician. 2. A rod symbolic of authority or an office. [< ON *vǫndr*]

wan·der (won′dər) *v.i.* 1. To move or travel about without destination or purpose; roam; rove. 2. To go casually or indirectly; stroll. 3. To twist or meander. 4. To stray. 5. To deviate in conduct or opinion; go astray. —*v.t.* 6. To roam through or across. [OE *wandrian*] —**wan′der·er** *n.* —**wan′der·ing·ly** *adv.*

wan·der·lust (won′dər·lust′) *n.* An impulse to travel. [< G *wandern* to travel + *lust* joy]

wane (wān) *v.i.* **waned, wan·ing** 1. To diminish gradually in size, brilliance, or strength. 2. To draw to an end. —*n.* The act of waning; a gradual decrease. —**on the wane** Gradually decreasing. [OE *wanian*]

wan·gle (wang′gəl) *v.* **·gled, ·gling** *Informal* *v.t.* 1. To obtain or accomplish by indirect or irregular methods: to *wangle* an introduction. 2. To manipulate, esp. dishonestly. —*v.i.* 3. To resort to indirect, irregular, or dishonest methods. [? Alter. of WAGGLE] —**wan′gler** *n.*

Wan·kel engine (vāng′kəl, wāng′-) A light, compact rotary internal-combustion engine with a spinning triangular piston. Also **Wan′kel.** [< F. *Wankel,* born 1902, Ger. inventor]

want (wont, wônt) *v.t.* 1. To feel a desire or wish for. 2. To be deficient in; lack. 3. To require; need. —*v.i.* 4. To have a need: usu. with *for.* 5. To be needy or destitute. —*n.* 1. A lack; scarcity; shortage. 2. Privation; poverty. 3. Something lacking; a need. [Prob. < ON *vanta* to be lacking] —**want′er** *n.*

want ad *Informal* A classified advertisement for something wanted, as hired help, a job, a lodging, etc.

want·ing (won′ting, wôn′-) *adj.* 1. Missing; lacking. 2. Not up to standard; deficient. —*prep.* Without; lacking.

wan·ton (won′tən) *adj.* 1. Licentious; lustful. 2. Unjust; malicious. 3. Of abundant growth; rank. —*v.i.* To act wantonly. —*n.* A licentious person, esp., a woman. [OE *wan* deficient + *tēon* to educate] —**wan′ton·ly** *adv.* —**wan′ton·ness** *n.*

wap·i·ti (wop′ə·tē) *n. pl.* **·tis** or **·ti** A large North American deer; an elk. [< Algonquian]

war (wôr) *n.* 1. An armed conflict between nations or states. 2. Any conflict or struggle; hostility. 3. The science of military operations. —*v.i.* **warred, war·ring** 1. To wage war. 2. To be in conflict; contend. [< OHG *werra* strife] —**war** *adj.*

war·ble (wôr′bəl) *v.t. & v.i.* **·bled, ·bling** To sing with trills and quavers. [< OF *werble* warble] —**war′ble** *n.*

war·bler (wôr′blər) *n.* 1. One who or that which warbles. 2. Any of various small Old World songbirds. 3. Any of various small American insectivorous birds.

war cry 1. A rallying cry used by combatants in a war. 2. A slogan or motto used to rally support for a political cause, etc.; watchword.

ward (wôrd) *n.* 1. **a** A division of a hospital. **b** A large room in a hospital for several patients. 2. An administrative or electoral division of a city. 3. *Law* A person, often a minor, who is in the charge of a guardian. 4. The act of guarding or the state of being guarded; custody: also **ward′·ship** (-ship). —*v.t.* To repel or turn aside, as a blow: usu., with *off.* [OE *weardian* to watch, guard]

-ward *suffix* Toward; in the direction of: *upward, homeward.* Also **-wards.** [OE *-weard, -weardes* at, toward]

war dance Among certain primitive tribes, a ceremonial dance before going to war or in celebration of a victory.

war·den (wôr′dən) *n.* 1. The chief officer of a prison. 2. Any of various supervisors: air-raid *warden.* [< AF *wardein,* OF *gardein, guarden* < Gmc.] —**war′den·ry, war′den·ship** *n.*

ward·er (wôr′dər) *n.* A watchman or guard. [< AF *warder* to keep]

ward heel·er *Slang* A hanger-on of a political boss.

ward·robe (wôrd′rōb′) *n.* 1. All the garments belonging to any one person. 2. A cabinet for clothes. 3. Theatrical costumes. [< OF *warder* to keep + *robe* dress]

ward·room (wôrd′ro͞om′, -ro͝om′) *n.* On a warship, the recreation area and dining room for the commissioned officers.

ware (wâr) *n.* 1. Manufactured articles of the same kind: used in combination: *glassware.* 2. *pl.* Goods; merchandise. 3. Pottery. [OE *waru*]

ware·house (wâr′hous′) *n.* A storehouse for goods. —*v.t.* **·housed** (-houzd′), **·hous·**

ing (-hou′zing) To store in a warehouse. —**ware′house′man** (-mən) *n.*

war·fare (wôr′fâr′) *n.* 1. The waging of war. 2. Struggle; strife.

war·head (wôr′hed′) *n. Mil.* The nose section of a guided missile, bomb, etc., containing the explosive.

war horse 1. *Informal* A veteran of many struggles or conflicts. 2. A horse used in combat; charger.

war·like (wôr′līk) *adj.* 1. Disposed to engage in war; belligerent. 2. Relating to, used in, or suggesting war; military. 3. Threatening war; hostile.

war·lock (wôr′lok′) *n.* A male wizard or sorcerer. [OE *wǣr* covenant + *lēogan* to lie, deny]

warm (wôrm) *adj.* 1. Moderately hot. 2. Preserving body heat: a *warm* coat. 3. Affectionate; loving. 4. Excited; agitated; also, vehement; passionate: a *warm* temper. 5. Suggesting warmth, friendliness, etc.: *warm* tones. 6. Recently made; fresh: a *warm* trail. 7. Near to discovering something. 8. *Informal* Uncomfortable; disagreeable. —*v.t.* 1. To heat slightly. 2. To make ardent or enthusiastic. 3. To fill with kindly feelings. —*v.i.* 4. To become warm. 5. To become ardent or enthusiastic: often with *to.* 6. To become kindly disposed or friendly: with *to* or *toward.* —**to warm up** 1. To warm. 2. To exercise before a game, etc. 3. To run an engine until it reaches operating temperature. [OE *wearm*] —**warm′er** *n.* —**warm′ly** *adv.* —**warm′ness** *n.*

warm-blood·ed (wôrm′blud′id) *adj.* 1. *Zool.* Preserving a uniform body temperature, as mammals. 2. Enthusiastic; ardent; passionate.

warm·heart·ed (wôrm′här′tid) *adj.* Kind; affectionate.

warm·ing pan (wôr′ming) A long-handled, covered metal pan containing hot coals, formerly used to warm a bed.

war·mon·ger (wôr′mung′gər, -mong′-) *n.* One who propagates warlike ideas. —**war′mon′ger·ing** *adj. & n.*

warmth (wôrmth) *n.* 1. The state or quality of being warm. 2. Enthusiasm; fervor. 3. Affection or kindness.

warm-up (wôrm′up′) *n. Informal* The act of one who or that which warms up.

warn (wôrn) *v.t.* 1. To make aware of possible harm; caution. 2. To advise; admonish. 3. To give notice in advance. [OE *warnian*] —**warn′er** *n.*

warn·ing (wôr′ning) *n.* 1. The act of one who warns. 2. That which warns or admonishes. —*adj.* Serving as a warning. —**warn′ing·ly** *adv.*

warp (wôrp) *v.t.* 1. To turn or twist out of shape. 2. To turn from a correct course. 3. *Naut.* To move (a vessel) by hauling on a rope fastened to a pier or anchor. —*v.i.* 4. To become turned or twisted out of shape. —*n.* 1. A bend, twist, or distortion, esp. in wood. 2. A mental or moral deviation; bias. 3. The lengthwise threads in a fabric or on a loom. [OE *weorpan* to throw] —**warp′er** *n.*

war paint Paint applied to faces and bodies by primitive peoples in token of going to war.

war·path (wôr′path′) *n.* The route taken by American Indians going to war. —**on the warpath.** 1. On a warlike expedition. 2. Ready for a fight; angry.

war·plane (wôr′plān′) *n.* An airplane equipped for fighting.

war·rant (wôr′ənt, wor′-) *n.* 1. *Law* A judicial writ or order authorizing arrest, search, seizure, etc. 2. Something that assures or attests. 3. That which gives authority for some act; sanction; justification. 4. A certificate of appointment given to warrant officers. —*v.t.* 1. To guarantee. 2. To be sufficient grounds for; justify. 3. To give legal authority; authorize. 4. To say confidently. [< AF *warant*, OF *guarant*] —**war′rant·a·ble** *adj.* —**war′rant·a·bly** *adv.* —**war′rant·er** *n.*

warrant officer *Mil.* An officer ranking above an enlisted person but below a commissioned officer.

war·ran·ty (wôr′ən·tē, wor′-) *n. pl.* **·ties** 1. *Law* a An assurance that facts regarding property, insurance risks, etc., are as they are stated to be. b A covenant securing a title of ownership. 2. A guarantee (def. 1). [< AF *warantie*, OF *guarant* warrant]

war·ren (wôr′ən, wor′-) *n.* 1. A place where rabbits are kept and bred. 2. An enclosure for keeping small game. 3. A crowded apartment house or neighborhood. [< AF *warir* to preserve]

war·ri·or (wôr′ē·ər, -yər, wor′-) *n.* A man engaged in or experienced in warfare. [< OHG *werra* strife]

war·ship (wôr′ship′) *n.* Any vessel used in naval combat.

wart (wôrt) *n.* 1. A small, usu. hard bump on the skin. 2. A hard protuberance on a plant. [OE *wearte*] —**wart′y** *adj.*

wart hog An African wild hog with large tusks and wartlike growths on the face.

war·time (wôr′tīm′) *n.* A time of war.

war·y (wâr′ē) *adj.* **war·i·er, war·i·est** Carefully watching and guarding; cautious. [OE *warian*] —**war′i·ly** *adv.* —**war′i·ness** *n.*

was (wuz, woz, *unstressed* wəz) First and third person singular, past indicative of BE. [OE *wæs*]

wash (wosh, wôsh) *v.t.* 1. To cleanse with water or other liquid. 2. To purify from defilement or guilt. 3. To wet or cover with liquid. 4. To flow against or over: a beach *washed* by the ocean. 5. To remove by the action of water: with *away, off, out,* etc. 6. To purify, as gas, by passing through a liquid. 7. To coat with a thin layer of color or metal. —*v.i.* 8. To wash oneself. 9. To wash clothes. 10. To withstand the effects of washing: That calico will *wash.* 11. *Informal* To undergo testing successfully: That story won't *wash.* 12. To flow with a lapping sound, as waves. 13. To be removed or eroded by the action of water: with *away, off, out,* etc. —**to wash out** *Slang* To fail. —*n.* 1. The act of washing. 2. Clothes, etc., to be washed at one time; laundry. 3. A preparation used in washing or coating, as: a A mouthwash. b Water color spread on a picture. 4. Churned air, water, or other fluid resulting from the passage of an object through it. 5. a The breaking of a wave on the shore. b The flow of water over a surface, as over an oar. [OE *wascan, wæscan*]

wash·a·ble (wosh′ə·bəl, wôsh′-) *adj.* That may be washed without fading or injury. —*n.pl.* Washable fabrics or garments.

wash-and-wear (wosh′ən·wâr′, wôsh′-) *adj.* Needing little or no ironing after washing: a *wash-and-wear* dress.

wash·board (wosh′bôrd′, wôsh′-) *n.* A corrugated board for scrubbing clothes during washing.

wash·bowl (wosh′bōl′, wôsh′-) *n.* A basin or bowl for washing the hands and face. Also **wash′ba′sin** (-bā′sən).

wash·cloth (wosh′klôth′, wôsh′-) *n.* A small cloth for washing the body.

washed-out (wosht′out′, wôsht′-) *adj.* 1. Faded, as from many washings. 2. *Informal* Exhausted; worn-out.

washed-up (wosht′up′, wôsht′-) *adj.* 1. *Slang* No longer successful, popular, etc.; finished. 2. *Informal* Tired.

wash·er (wosh′ər, wô′shər) *n.* 1. One who or that which washes. 2. *Mech.* A small, flat disk placed beneath a nut or at an axle bearing or joint, to serve as a cushion, prevent leakage, or relieve friction. 3. A washing machine.

wash·er·wom·an (wosh′ər·wo͝om′ən, wô′·shər-) *n. pl.* **·wom·en** (-wim′in) A laundress.

wash·ing (wosh′ing, wô′shing) *n.* 1. The act of one who or that which washes. 2. Laundry to be washed. 3. A thin coating of metal.

washing machine A machine for washing laundry.

washing soda Sodium carbonate in crystalline form, used for washing and bleaching textiles.

wash·out (wosh′out′, wôsh′-) *n.* 1. The erosion of earth by the action of water; also, the excavation thus made; a gully or gulch. 2. *Slang* A failure.

wash·rag (wosh′rag′, wôsh′-) *n.* A washcloth.

wash·room (wosh′ro͞om′, -ro͝om′, wôsh′-) *n.* A lavatory.

wash·stand (wosh′stand′, wôsh′-) *n.* A stand for washbowl, pitcher, etc.

wash·tub (wosh′tub′, wôsh′-) *n.* A tub for washing laundry.

wash·wom·an (wosh′wo͝om′ən, wôsh′-) *n. pl.* **·wom·en** (-wim′in) A washerwoman.

wash·y (wosh′ē, wô′shē) *adj.* **wash·i·er, wash·i·est** 1. Overly diluted; weak. 2. Faded; wan. —**wash′i·ness** *n.*

was·n't (wuz′ənt, woz′-) Was not.

wasp (wosp, wôsp) *n.* Any of numerous stinging insects. [OE *wæsp*]

WASP (wosp, wôsp) *n.* A white Protestant American of English or northern European descent: sometimes used contemptuously to refer to members of the dominant socioeconomic class in the U.S. Also **Wasp.** [< W(HITE) A(NGLO-)S(AXON) P(ROTESTANT)]

wasp·ish (wos′pish, wôs′-) *adj.* 1. Irritable; bad-tempered; irascible. 2. Having a slender build. —**wasp′ish·ly** *adv.* —**wasp′ish·ness** *n.*

wasp waist A very slender waist. —**wasp-waist·ed** (wosp′wās′tid, wôsp′-) *adj.*

wasp·y (wos′pē, wôs′-) *adj.* **wasp·i·er, wasp·i·est** Like a wasp; waspish.

was·sail (wos′əl, was′-, wo·sāl′) *n.* 1. An ancient toast to someone's health. 2. The liquor, as spiced ale, prepared for a wassail. 3. A festivity at which healths are drunk; a carousal. —*v.i.* 1. To take part in a wassail; carouse. —*v.t.* 2. To drink the health of; toast. [< ON *ves heill* be in good health] —**was′sail·er** *n.*

Was·ser·mann test (wos′ər·mən) A diagnostic test for syphilis. Also **Wassermann reaction.** [after August von *Wassermann*, 1866–1925, German bacteriologist]

wast (wost, *unstressed* wəst) Archaic second person singular, past indicative of BE: used with *thou.*

wast·age (wās′tij) *n.* 1. Loss by wear, waste, etc. 2. Something lost in this way.

waste (wāst) *v.* **wast·ed, wast·ing** *v.t.* 1. To use or expend needlessly or carelessly; squander. 2. To wear away; consume, as one's strength. 3. To fail to take advantage of, as of an opportunity. 4. To destroy; devastate. 5. *Slang* To kill. —*v.i.* 6. To become weak or unhealthy: often with *away.* —*n.* 1. The act of wasting, or the state of being wasted. 2. A wasteland. 3. A gradual decrease by use, wear, etc. 4. Garbage, rubbish, or other discarded material. 5. Matter, as urine, that is excreted by the body. —**to lay waste** To destroy. —*adj.* 1. Cast aside as worthless; discarded. 2. Excreted, as urine. 3. Uncultivated or uninhabited; barren. [< L *vastare* to lay waste] —**wast′er** *n.*

waste·bas·ket (wāst′bas′kit) *n.* A receptacle for wastepaper and other waste. Also **wastepaper basket.**

waste·ful (wāst′fəl) *adj.* Prone to or characterized by waste. —**waste′ful·ly** *adv.* —**waste′ful·ness** *n.*

waste·land (wāst′land′) *n.* A barren or desolate land.

waste·pa·per (wāst′pā′pər) *n.* Paper thrown away as worthless. Also **waste paper.**

waste product Useless material left over after the completion of a manufacturing process, digestion, etc.

wast·ing (wās′ting) *adj.* 1. Producing emaciation; enfeebling. 2. Laying waste; devastating.

wast·rel (wās′trəl) *n.* 1. A spendthrift. 2. An idler; loafer. [< WASTE]

watch (woch) *v.i.* 1. To look attentively. 2. To wait expectantly: with *for.* 3. To do duty as a guard or sentinel. 4. To go without sleep; keep vigil. —*v.t.* 5. To look at steadily and attentively; observe. 6. To be alert for: to *watch* one's opportunity. 7. To keep watch over; guard; tend. —**to watch out** To be on one's guard. —*n.* 1. The act of watching; close and continuous attention. 2. A small, portable timepiece worn or carried on the person. 3. A watchman; guard. 4. The period during which a guard is on duty. 5. *Naut.* a A period of time, usu. four hours, during which a part of a ship's crew is on duty. b The crew on duty during such a period. [OE *wæccan*] —**watch′er** *n.*

watch·band (woch′band′) *n.* A band to fasten a watch on the wrist.

watch·case (woch′kās′) *n.* The protecting case of a watch.
watch·dog (woch′dôg′) *n.* 1. A dog kept to guard property. 2. One who acts as a vigilant guardian.
watch·ful (woch′fəl) *adj.* Vigilant. **—watch′·ful·ly** *adv.* **—watch′ful·ness** *n.*
watch·mak·er (woch′mā′kər) *n.* One who makes or repairs watches. **—watch′mak′ing** *n.*
watch·man (woch′mən) *n. pl.* **·men** (-mən) One who keeps watch; a guard.
watch·tow·er (woch′tou′ər) *n.* A tower upon which a sentinel is stationed.
watch·word (woch′wûrd′) *n.* 1. A password. 2. A rallying cry or maxim.
wa·ter (wô′tər, wot′ər) *n.* 1. The tasteless and odorless liquid compound of hydrogen and oxygen, H_2O. 2. Any body of water, as a lake, river, or a sea. 3. Any one of the liquid secretions of the body, as perspiration, tears, urine, etc. 4. The transparency or luster of a precious stone or a pearl. **—to hold water** To be valid or effective. **—*v.t.*** 1. To pour water upon; moisten; sprinkle. 2. To provide with water for drinking. 3. To dilute with water: often with *down.* 4. To give an undulating sheen to the surface of (silk, etc.). 5. To enlarge the number of shares of (a stock company) without increasing the paid-in capital in proportion. 6. To irrigate. **—*v.i.*** 7. To secrete saliva or tears. 8. To drink water. [OE *wæter*] **—wa′ter·er** *n.*
Water Bearer The constellation and sign of the zodiac Aquarius.
water bed A bed having a mattress consisting of a plastic bag filled with water.
wa·ter·borne (wô′tər·bôrn′, wot′ər-) *adj.* 1. Floating on water. 2. Transported or carried by water.
wa·ter·buck (wô′tər·buk′, wot′ər-) *n.* Either of two large African antelopes frequenting rivers and marshes. [< Afrikaans *waterbok*]
water buffalo A large buffalo of Asia, India, and the Philippines, having a very wide spread of horns, and often domesticated for use as a draft animal: also called *water ox, carabao.*
water chestnut 1. The edible fruit of an aquatic plant, contained in a hard, nutlike husk. 2. The plant itself.
water closet A toilet.
water color 1. A paint made by mixing water with a pigment. 2. A painting done in water colors. **—wa·ter-col·or** (wô′tər·kul′ər, wot′ər-) *adj.*
wa·ter-cool (wô′tər·ko͞ol′, wot′ər-) *v.t.* To cool by means of circulating water. **—wa′ter-cooled′** *adj.* **—wa′ter-cool′ing** *adj.*
water cooler An apparatus for cooling and dispensing drinking water.
wa·ter·course (wô′tər·kôrs′, wot′ər-) *n.* 1. A stream of water; river; brook. 2. The channel of a stream or canal.
wa·ter·craft (wô′tər·kraft′, wot′ər-) *n.* Any boat or ship; also, sailing vessels collectively.
wa·ter·cress (wô′tər·kres′, wot′ər-) *n.* A perennial herb of the mustard family, having edible leaves used as salad.
wa·ter·fall (wô′tər·fôl′, wot′ər-) *n.* A steep fall of water, as of a stream over a precipice; cascade.
wa·ter·fowl (wô′tər·foul′, wot′ər-) *n. pl.* **·fowl** or **·fowls** A water bird; esp., a swimming game bird.
wa·ter·front (wô′tər·frunt′, wot′ər-) *n.* 1. Real property abutting on or overlooking a natural body of water. 2. That part of a town fronting on a body of water, esp. the area containing wharves, docks, etc.
water gap A deep ravine in a mountain ridge, giving passage to a stream.
water gas A fuel gas produced from water and coke. **—wa·ter-gas** (wô′tər·gas′, wot′ər-) *adj.*
Wa·ter·gate (wô′tər·gāt′, wot′ər-) *n.* Criminal abuse of power, esp. by government officials. [after *Watergate,* a building complex in Washington, D.C., where Democratic Party headquarters was burglarized in 1972]
water glass 1. A drinking glass. 2. Sodium silicate; esp., an aqueous solution used in preserving eggs, etc.
water hole A small pond, esp. one used by animals as a drinking place.
wa·ter·ing place (wô′tər·ing, wot′ər-) A health resort having mineral springs.
water level 1. The level of still water in the sea or other body of water. 2. *Geol.* A water table. 3. *Naut.* A ship's water line.
water lily An aquatic plant having showy flowers with numerous white or pinkish petals.
water line 1. *Naut.* The part of a ship's hull corresponding to the water level at various loads: also called *water level.* 2. A line corresponding to the height to which water has risen or may rise.
wa·ter·logged (wô′tər·lôgd′, -logd′, wot′ər-) *adj.* Thoroughly filled or soaked with water.
Wa·ter·loo (wô′tər·lo͞o) *n.* A final and decisive defeat: usu. in the phrase **to meet one's Waterloo.** [after Napoleon's defeat at *Waterloo,* Belgium, 1815]
water main A large conduit for carrying water.
wa·ter·mark (wô′tər·märk′, wot′ər-) *n.* 1. A mark showing the extent to which water rises. 2. A mark or design impressed on paper that is visible when the paper is held up to the light. **—*v.t.*** 1. To impress (paper) with a watermark. 2. To impress as a watermark.
wa·ter·mel·on (wô′tər·mel′ən, wot′ər-) *n.* The large, edible fruit of a trailing plant of the gourd family, containing a many-seeded red or pink pulp and a watery juice; also, the plant.
water moccasin A venomous pit viper of the southern U.S.: also called *cottonmouth.*
water ouzel Any of various small birds adapted to feeding under water. Also **water ousel.**
water ox A water buffalo.
water pipe 1. A hookah. 2. A conduit for water.
water polo A game in which two teams of swimmers push or throw a buoyant ball toward opposite goals.
wa·ter·pow·er (wô′tər·pou′ər, wot′ər-) *n.* The power of rushing or falling water, as applied to the driving of machinery.
wa·ter·proof (wô′tər·pro͞of′, wot′ər-) *adj.* Permitting no water to enter or pass through; esp., treated with some substance that

resists the passage of water. —*n.* *Brit.* A raincoat. —*v.t.* To render waterproof.

water rat 1. The muskrat. 2. The European vole. 3. Any aquatic rodent.

wa·ter·shed (wô′tər·shed′, wot′ər-) *n.* 1. The line of separation between two contiguous drainage valleys. 2. The region from which a river receives its supply of water.

wa·ter·side (wô′tər·sīd′, wot′ər-) *n.* The shore of a body of water.

wa·ter-ski (wô′tər·skē′, wot′ər-) *v.i.* **-skied, -ski·ing** To glide over water on water-skis, while being towed by a motorboat. —*n.* *pl.* **-skis** or **-ski** A broad, skilike runner worn when water-skiing: also **water ski.** —**wa′ter-ski′er** *n.* —**wa′ter-ski′ing** *n.*

wa·ter-soak (wô′tər·sōk′, wot′ər-) *v.t.* To fill or saturate with water.

water softener A substance added to water to counteract the effect of its mineral content.

wa·ter-sol·u·ble (wô′tər·sol′yə·bəl, wot′ər-) *adj.* Soluble in water.

water spaniel A large, reddish brown spaniel used primarily for retrieving ducks.

wa·ter·spout (wô′tər·spout′, wot′ər-) *n.* 1. A moving, whirling column of spray and mist, generated at sea or on other large bodies of water. 2. A pipe for the free discharge of water.

water table *Geol.* The surface marking the upper level of a water-saturated zone extending beneath the ground to depths determined by the thickness of the permeable strata: also called *water level.*

wa·ter·tight (wô′tər·tīt′, wot′ər-) *adj.* 1. So closely made that water cannot enter or leak through. 2. Having no loopholes; foolproof: *watertight* tax laws.

water tower An elevated tank for water storage.

water vapor The vapor of water, esp. when below the boiling point, as in the atmosphere.

wa·ter·way (wô′tər·wā′, wot′ər-) *n.* A river, channel, canal, etc., used as a means of travel.

water wheel A wheel turned by flowing water, used to provide power.

water wings An inflatable device used to keep one afloat while swimming or learning to swim.

wa·ter·works (wô′tər·wûrks′, wot′ər-) *n.pl.* A system of machines, buildings, etc., for supplying a city with water.

wa·ter·y (wô′tər·ē, wot′ər·ē) *adj.* 1. Of or relating to water. 2. Saturated or filled with water. 3. Diluted; thin: *watery* soup. 4. Pale; weak: *watery* colors. —**wa′ter·i·ness** *n.*

WATS (wots) A service that allows the user to make long distance telephone calls, chiefly to businesses, without a charge to the caller. [W(IDE) A(REA) T(ELECOMMUNICATIONS) S(ERVICE)]

watt (wot) *n.* The practical unit of electric power, equivalent to the power developed when one ampere flows through a resistance of one ohm. [after James *Watt* 1736–1819, Scottish inventor]

wat·tage (wot′ij) *n.* 1. Amount of electric power in terms of watts. 2. The total number of watts needed to operate an appliance.

watt-hour (wot′our′) *n.* Electrical energy equivalent to one watt acting for one hour.

wat·tle (wot′l) *n.* 1. A structure of rods or twigs woven together. 2. A fleshy process hanging from the throat of a bird or snake. —*v.t.* **·tled, ·tling** 1. To weave or twist, as twigs, into a network. 2. To form, as baskets, by intertwining flexible twigs. [OE *watel, watul*] —**wat′tled** *adj.*

wave (wāv) *v.* **waved, wav·ing** *v.i.* 1. To move freely back and forth or up and down, as a flag in the wind. 2. To express farewell, hello, etc., by moving one's hand or arm up and down. 3. To have an undulating shape or form: Her hair *waves.* —*v.t.* 4. To cause to wave: to *wave* a banner. 5. To form with an undulating surface or outline. 6. To signal or express by waving something: to *wave* farewell. —*n.* 1. A ridge or undulation moving on the surface of a liquid. 2. One of a series of curves: *waves* of grain. 3. Something that comes, like a wave, with great volume or power: a *wave* of enthusiasm. 4. One of a series, as of events, occurring together: the first *wave* of Marines. 5. A wavelike tress or curl of hair. 6. A sweeping or undulating motion, as with the hand. 7. *Physics* One of the periodic vibratory impulses produced by a disturbance in and propagated through an elastic medium, as sound. [OE *wafian*] —**wav′er** *n.* —**wave′·less** *adj.*

wave·length (wāv′length′) *n.* *Physics* The distance, measured along the line of progression, between two points representing similar phases of two consecutive waves.

wave·let (wāv′lit) *n.* A little wave.

wa·ver (wā′vər) *v.i.* 1. To move one way and the other; sway. 2. To be uncertain or undecided; vacillate. 3. To falter. 4. To flicker; gleam. 5. To quaver; tremble. —*n.* A wavering. [ME *waveren*] —**wa′ver·er** *n.* —**wa′ver·ing·ly** *adv.*

wav·y (wā′vē) *adj.* **wav·i·er, wav·i·est** Undulatory; waving: *wavy* hair. —**wav′i·ly** *adv.* —**wav′i·ness** *n.*

wax[1] (waks) *n.* *pl.* **wax·es** 1. Beeswax. 2. Any of various natural substances similar to fats, but harder and less greasy. 3. A solid mineral substance resembling wax, as paraffin. 4. Earwax. —*v.t.* To coat or treat with wax. [OE *weax*]

wax[2] (waks) *v.i.* **waxed, waxed** (*Poetic* **wax·en**), **wax·ing** 1. To become larger gradually: said esp. of the moon as it approaches fullness. 2. To become: to *wax* angry. [OE *weaxan* to grow]

wax bean A variety of string bean of a pale yellow color, cultivated in the U.S.: also called *butter bean.*

wax·ber·ry (waks′ber′ē) *n.* *pl.* **·ries** 1. The wax myrtle. 2. Its wax-covered fruit. 3. The snowberry.

wax·en (wak′sən) *adj.* 1. Resembling, made of, or treated with wax. 2. Pale; pallid: a *waxen* complexion.

wax myrtle Any of various North American shrubs or small trees having fragrant leaves and small berries covered with wax, often used in making candles: also called *bayberry, waxberry.*

wax paper Paper coated or treated with wax and used to retain or protect against moisture. Also **waxed paper.**

wax·wing (waks′wing′) *n.* Any of various crested birds having soft, mainly brown plumage and wing feathers tipped with appendages resembling red or yellow sealing wax.

wax·work (waks′wûrk′) *n.* 1. Work produced in wax; esp., ornaments or life-size figures of wax. 2. *pl.* An exhibition of wax figures of famous or notorious persons. **—wax′work′er** *n.*

wax·y (wak′sē) *adj.* **wax·i·er, wax·i·est** Of, like, or covered with wax. **—wax′i·ness** *n.*

way (wā) *n.* 1. A manner or method of doing something; procedure. 2. Direction; route: Which *way* is the city? 3. A path or track. 4. Space or room to advance or work: Make *way* for the king. 5. Distance in general: a little *way* off: often, popularly, *ways*. 6. Headway; progress. 7. A customary or usual manner of living, speaking, behaving, etc. 8. A specific detail; respect; particular: He erred in two *ways*. 9. A course of life or experience: the *way* of sin. 10. *Informal* State of health: to be in a bad *way*. 11. The range of one's observation: An accident threw it in his *way*. 12. *Naut.* *pl.* A tilted framework of timbers upon which a ship slides when launched. 13. *Law* A right of way. **—by the way** In passing; incidentally. **—by way of** 1. With the purpose of; to serve as: *by way of* introduction. 2. Through; via. **—to give way** 1. To break down; collapse. 2. To yield. **—under way** In motion; making progress. **—*adv.*** *Informal* Away; very much or very far. [OE *weg*]

way·far·ing (wā′fâr′ing) *adj. & n.* Journeying; being on the road. **—way′far′er** *n.*

way·lay (wā′lā′, wā′lā′) *v.t.* **·laid, ·lay·ing** 1. To lie in ambush for and attack, as in order to rob. 2. To accost on the way. [< WAY + LAY[1]] **—way′lay′er** *n.*

way-out (wā′out′) *adj.* *Slang* Unusual; unconventional.

-ways *suffix of adverbs* In a (specified) manner, direction, or position: *noways*, *sideways*: often equivalent to *-wise*. Also **-way**.

ways and means In legislation, methods of raising funds for the use of the government.

way·side (wā′sīd′) *n.* The side or edge of a road or highway.

way station Any station between principal stations, esp. on a railroad.

way·ward (wā′wərd) *adj.* 1. Headstrong or disobedient; willful. 2. Unpredictable; erratic; capricious. [ME *awei* away + -WARD] **—way′ward·ly** *adv.* **—way′ward·ness** *n.*

way·worn (wā′wôrn′) *adj.* Fatigued by travel.

we (wē) *pron.pl., possessive* **our** or **ours,** *objective* **us** The nominative plural pronoun of *I*, used by a group, by an individual when part of a group, by an editor or other writer to give his words an impersonal character, or by a sovereign on formal occasions. [OE *wē*]

weak (wēk) *adj.* 1. Lacking in physical strength or energy. 2. Insufficiently resisting stress: a *weak* link. 3. Lacking in strength of will or stability of character; pliable. 4. Ineffectual, as from deficient supply: *weak* artillery support. 5. Lacking in power or sonorousness: a *weak* voice. 6. Lacking the usual strength: *weak* tea. 7. Lacking the ability to function properly: a *weak* heart. 8. Showing or resulting from poor judgment: a *weak* plan. 9. Unable to convince: a *weak* argument. 10. Lacking in influence or authority. 11. *Phonet.* Unstressed; unaccented, as a syllable or sound. [< ON *veikr*] **—weak′ly** *adv.* **—weak′ness** *n.*

Weak, as a combining form, has the meaning lacking in strength or intensity, as in:

weak-backed	**weak-tasting**
weak-limbed	**weak-tinted**
weak-muscled	**weak-voiced**
weak-stemmed	**weak-willed**

weak·en (wē′kən) *v.t. & v.i.* To make or become weak or weaker. **—weak′en·er** *n.*

weak·fish (wēk′fish′) *n. pl.* **·fish** or **·fish·es** Any of several marine food fishes of the coastal waters of the eastern U.S.

weak-kneed (wēk′nēd′) *adj.* 1. Weak in the knees. 2. Without resolution or purpose; spineless.

weak·ling (wēk′ling) *n.* A person who is physically or morally weak.

weak·ly (wēk′lē) *adj.* **·li·er, ·li·est** Sickly; feeble; weak.

weak-mind·ed (wēk′mīn′did) *adj.* 1. Indecisive; weak-willed. 2. Feeble-minded. **—weak′mind′ed·ness** *n.*

weak·ness (wēk′nis) *n.* 1. The state or quality of being weak. 2. A defect or weak point; fault. 3. A penchant or fondness: with *for*: a *weakness* for pastry.

weal[1] (wēl) *n.* *Archaic* A sound or healthy state; prosperity; welfare. [OE *wela*]

weal[2] (wēl) *n.* A welt (def. 3). [Var. of WALE]

wealth (welth) *n.* 1. Great abundance of valuable possessions; riches. 2. *Econ.* All objects possessing a monetary value. 3. A great amount: a *wealth* of learning. [ME *wele* weal]

wealth·y (wel′thē) *adj.* **wealth·i·er, wealth·i·est** Possessing wealth; affluent. **—wealth′·i·ly** *adv.* **—wealth′i·ness** *n.*

wean (wēn) *v.t.* 1. To accustom (the young of any mammal) to food other than its mother's milk. 2. To remove from former habits or associations: usu. with *from*. [OE *wenian* to accustom]

weap·on (wep′ən) *n.* 1. Any implement for fighting or warfare. 2. Any means used in a struggle or contest. [OE *wǣpen*] **—weap′on·less** *adj.*

weap·on·ry (wep′ən·rē′) *n.* Weapons collectively.

wear (wâr) *v.* **wore, worn, wear·ing** *v.t.* 1. To carry or have on the person as a garment, ornament, etc. 2. To have in one's appearance; exhibit: He *wears* a scowl. 3. To bear habitually in a specified manner: She *wears* her hair long. 4. To display or fly: A ship *wears* its colors. 5. To impair, waste, or consume by use. 6. To cause by rubbing, etc.: to *wear* a hole in a coat. 7. To exhaust; weary. **—*v.i.*** 8. To be impaired gradually by use, rubbing, etc. 9. To withstand the effects of use, wear, etc.: The skirt *wears* well. 10. To become as specified from use or attrition: His patience is *wearing* thin. 11. To pass gradually or tediously: with *on* or *away*. **—to wear out** 1. To make or become worthless by use. 2. To waste gradually; use up: He *wears out* patience.

3. To tire. —*n.* 1. The act of wearing, or the state of being worn. 2. Clothing: summer *wear.* 3. The destructive effect of use, work, or time. 4. Capacity for resistance to use or impairment; durability. [OE *werian*] —**wear′a·bil′i·ty** *n.* —**wear′a·ble** *adj.* —**wear′er** *n.*

wear and tear Loss by ordinary use.

wear·ing (wâr′ing) *adj.* 1. Fatiguing; exhausting. 2. Made to be worn: *wearing* apparel. —**wear′ing·ly** *adv.*

wea·ri·some (wir′i·səm) *adj.* Causing fatigue; tiresome or tedious. —**wea′ri·some·ly** *adv.* —**wea′ri·some·ness** *n.*

wea·ry (wir′ē) *adj.* **·ri·er, ·ri·est** 1. Tired; fatigued. 2. Discontented or vexed: often with *of*: *weary* of life. 3. Wearisome. —*v.t.* & *v.i.* **·ried, ·ry·ing** To make or become weary; tire. [OE *wērig*] —**wea′ri·ly** *adv.* —**wea′ri·ness** *n.*

wea·sel (wē′zəl) *n.* 1. Any of certain small, slender, predacious carnivores having brownish fur that in northern regions turns white in winter. 2. A sneaky, treacherous person. —*v.i.* **·seled, ·sel·ing** *Informal* To speak or act evasively, etc. [OE *wesle*]

weath·er (weth′ər) *n.* 1. Atmospheric condition as regards temperature, moisture, winds, and other meteorological phenomena. 2. Bad weather; storm. —**under the weather** *Informal* 1. Ailing; ill. 2. Somewhat drunk. —*v.t.* 1. To expose to the action of the weather. 2. To dry, discolor, etc., by action of the weather. 3. To pass through and survive, as a crisis. 4. *Naut.* To pass to windward of. —*v.i.* 5. To undergo changes resulting from exposure to the weather. 6. To resist the action of the weather. —*adj.* *Chiefly Naut.* Windward. [OE *weder*] —**weath′ered** *adj.*

weath·er-beat·en (weth′ər·bēt′n) *adj.* Bearing or showing the effects of exposure to weather.

weath·er·board (weth′ər·bôrd′) *n.* A clapboard.

weath·er·cock (weth′ər·kok′) *n.* A weather vane in the form of a cock.

weath·er·man (weth′ər·man′) *n.* *pl.* **·men** (-men′) *n.* *Informal* A meteorologist.

weather map A map or chart indicating weather conditions for a given region and time.

weath·er·proof (weth′ər·prōōf′) *adj.* Capable of withstanding rough weather without much damage. —*v.t.* To make weatherproof.

weath·er-strip (weth′ər·strip′) *v.t.* **-stripped, -strip·ping** To equip or fit with weather strips.

weather strip A narrow strip of material placed over or in crevices, as at windows, to keep out drafts, rain, etc. Also **weather stripping.**

weather vane A vane (def. 1).

weave (wēv) *v.* **wove** or *for def. 8* **weaved, wo·ven** or (*less common*) **wove, weav·ing** *v.t.* 1. To produce, as a textile, by interlacing threads or yarns, esp. in a loom. 2. To form by interlacing strands, strips, twigs, etc.: to *weave* a basket. 3. To produce by combining details or elements: to *weave* a story. 4. To twist into, about, or through: to *weave* ribbons through one's hair. 5. To make or effect by moving in a zigzag course: to *weave* one's way through a crowd. —*v.i.* 6. To make cloth, baskets, etc., by weaving. 7. To become woven or interlaced. 8. To move in a zigzag path. —*n.* A particular style of weaving. [OE *wefan*] —**weav′er** *n.*

web (web) *n.* 1. Any fabric, structure, etc., woven of or as of interlaced strands. 2. The network of threads spun by a spider. 3. Any complex network: a *web* of highways. 4. Anything artfully contrived into a trap: a *web* of espionage. 5. *Zool.* A membrane connecting the digits of an animal, as in aquatic birds. 6. *Ornithol.* The series of barbs on either side of the shaft of a feather: also called *vane.* [OE]

webbed (webd) *adj.* 1. Having a web. 2. Having the digits united by a membrane, as the foot of a goose or duck.

web·bing (web′ing) *n.* 1. A woven strip of strong fiber, used for safety belts, etc. 2. Any structure or material forming a web.

web-foot·ed (web′fo͝ot′id) *adj.* Having the toes connected by a membrane, as many aquatic animals and birds.

wed (wed) *v.* **wed·ded, wed** or **wed·ded, wed·ding** *v.t.* 1. To take as one's husband or wife; marry. 2. To unite or give in marriage. 3. To join closely. —*v.i.* 4. To marry. [OE *weddian* to pledge]

we'd (wēd) 1. We had. 2. We would.

wed·ding (wed′ing) *n.* The ceremony or celebration of a marriage. [OE *weddung* < *weddian* to pledge]

wedge (wej) *n.* 1. A V-shaped piece of wood, metal, etc., used to split wood, raise weights, etc. 2. Anything resembling a wedge, as a piece of pie, etc. 3. Anything serving to divide or disrupt. —*v.t.* **wedged, wedg·ing** 1. To force apart or split with or as with a wedge. 2. To compress or fix in place with a wedge. 3. To crowd or squeeze into a small space. [OE *wecg*]

wed·lock (wed′lok) *n.* The state or relationship of being married; matrimony. [OE *wed* pledge + *-lāc*, suffix of nouns of action]

Wednes·day (wenz′dē, -dā) *n.* The fourth day of the week. [OE *Wōdnesdæg* day of Woden]

wee (wē) *adj.* **we·er, we·est** 1. Very small; tiny. 2. Very early: the *wee* hours. [ME *wei* < OE *wǣge* a quantity]

weed (wēd) *n.* Any common, unsightly, or troublesome plant that grows in abundance. —*v.t.* 1. To pull up and remove weeds from. 2. To remove (anything regarded as harmful or undesirable): with *out.* 3. To rid of anything harmful or undesirable. —*v.i.* 4. To remove weeds. [OE *wēod*] —**weed′er** *n.* —**weed′less** *adj.*

weeds (wēdz) *n.pl.* A widow's mourning garb. [OE *wǣd* garment]

weed·y (wē′dē) *adj.* **weed·i·er, weed·i·est** 1. Full of weeds. 2. Of or like weeds. 3. *Informal* Gawky; awkward. —**weed′i·ly** *adv.* —**weed′i·ness** *n.*

week (wēk) *n.* 1. A period of seven days; esp., such a period beginning with Sunday. ◆Collateral adjective: *hebdomadal.* 2. The period of time within a week devoted to work: a 35-hour *week.* [OE *wucu, wicu, wice*]

week·day (wēk′dā′) *n.* Any day of the week except Sunday and, often, Saturday.

week·end (wēk′end′) *n.* The end of the

week; esp., the time from Friday evening or Saturday to the following Monday morning. —*v.i.* *Informal* To pass the weekend. —**week′end′er** *n.*

week·ly (wēk′lē) *adv.* Once a week. —*adj.* 1. Of or pertaining to a week or to weekdays. 2. Done or occurring once a week. —*n. pl.* **·lies** A publication issued once a week.

ween·ie (wē′nē) *n.* *Informal* A wiener.

weep (wēp) *v.* **wept, weep·ing** *v.i.* 1. To show grief, pain, etc., by shedding tears. 2. To mourn; lament: with *for*. 3. To ooze or shed liquid in drops. —*v.t.* 4. To shed (tears, etc.). [OE *wēpan*] —**weep′er** *n.*

weep·ing (wē′ping) *adj.* 1. Crying; tearful. 2. Having slim, pendulous branches.

weeping willow A willow having long, slender, pendulous branches.

weep·y (wē′pē) *adj.* **weep·i·er, weep·i·est** *Informal* Inclined to weep; tearful.

wee·vil (wē′vəl) *n.* 1. Any of numerous small beetles, feeding on plants and plant products. 2. Any of a family of small beetles that feed principally on beans and seeds. [OE *wifel* beetle] —**wee′vil·y** or **wee′vil·ly** *adj.*

weft (weft) *n.* The cross threads in a web of cloth; woof. [OE]

weigh (wā) *v.t.* 1. To determine the weight of, as by measuring on a scale or holding in the hand. 2. To measure (a quantity or quantities of something) according to weight: with *out*. 3. To consider carefully: to *weigh* a proposal. 4. To press down by heaviness; oppress: with *down*. 5. To raise (an anchor). —*v.i.* 6. To have a specified weight. 7. To have influence or importance. 8. To be burdensome or oppressive: with *on* or *upon*: What *weighs* on your mind? —**to weigh in** Of a prize fighter, etc., to be weighed before a contest. [OE *wegan* to weigh, carry, lift] —**weigh′er** *n.*

weight (wāt) *n.* 1. Any quantity of heaviness, expressed indefinitely or in standard units. 2. *Physics* The measure of the force with which bodies tend toward the center of the earth or other celestial body, equal to the mass of the body multiplied by the acceleration of local gravitation. 3. Any object or mass that weighs a specific amount. 4. An object of known mass used to determine weight on a balance. 5. Any mass used to hold something down. 6. Burden; oppressiveness: the *weight* of care. 7. Influence; importance; consequence. —**to carry weight** To be of importance or significance. —**to pull one's weight** To do one's share. —*v.t.* 1. To add weight to; make heavy. 2. To oppress or burden. [OE *wiht, gewiht*]

weight·less (wāt′lis) *adj.* 1. Having or seeming to have no weight. 2. Experiencing little or no gravitational pull. —**weight′·less·ly** *adj.* —**weight′less·ness** *n.*

weight·y (wā′tē) *adj.* **weight·i·er, weight·i·est** 1. Having great weight. 2. Of great importance or seriousness; grave; significant: a *weighty* decision. —**weight′i·ly** *adv.* —**weight′i·ness** *n.*

weir (wir) *n.* 1. An obstruction or dam placed in a stream to raise or divert the water. 2. A series of wattled enclosures in a stream to catch fish. [OE *wer* < *werian* to dam up]

weird (wird) *adj.* 1. Concerned with the unnatural or with witchcraft; mysterious. 2. Strange; bizarre; odd. [OE *wyrd* fate] —**weird′ly** *adv.* —**weird′ness** *n.*

weird·o (wir′dō) *n. pl.* **weird·os** *Slang* A bizarre or freakish person or thing.

wel·come (wel′kəm) *adj.* 1. Admitted gladly; received cordially: a *welcome* guest. 2. Producing satisfaction or pleasure: pleasing: *welcome* tidings. 3. Made free to use or enjoy: She is *welcome* to my purse. —**you are** (or **you're**) **welcome** You are under no obligation: a conventional response to "thank you." —*n.* The act of bidding or making welcome; a hearty greeting. —*v.t.* **·comed, ·com·ing** 1. To give a welcome to; greet hospitably. 2. To receive with pleasure. [OE *will-*, will, pleasure + *cuma* guest] —**wel′come·ly** *adv.* —**wel′·come·ness** *n.* —**wel′com·er** *n.*

weld (weld) *v.t.* 1. To unite, as two pieces of metal, by the application of heat along the area of contact. 2. To bring into close association or connection. —*v.i.* 3. To be capable of being welded. —*n.* The act of welding metal; also, the closed joint so formed. [Alter. of WELL[1], v.] —**weld′a·bil′i·ty** *n.* —**weld′a·ble** *adj.* —**weld′er** *n.*

wel·fare (wel′fâr) *n.* 1. The condition of faring well; prosperity. 2. Aid, as money, food, or clothing given to those in need. —**on welfare** Receiving aid from a government because of need. [ME *wel* well + *fare* a going]

welfare state A government that assumes a large measure of responsibility for the social welfare of its citizens.

wel·kin (wel′kin) *n.* *Archaic* The vault of the sky; the heavens. [OE *wolcen, wolcn* cloud]

well[1] (wel) *n.* 1. A hole or shaft sunk into the earth to obtain water, oil, gas, etc. 2. A spring of water; a fountain. 3. A source of continued supply: a *well* of learning. 4. A vessel used to hold a supply of liquid. 5. *Archit.* A vertical opening descending through floors: an elevator *well.* —*v.t. & v.i.* To pour forth; gush. [OE *weallan* to boil, bubble up]

well[2] (wel) *adv.* **bet·ter, best** 1. Satisfactorily; favorably: Everything goes *well.* 2. In a good or correct manner; expertly: to speak *well.* 3. Suitably; with reason or propriety: I cannot *well* remain here. 4. In a successful or prosperous manner: He lives *well.* 5. Intimately: How *well* do you know him? 6. To a considerable extent or degree: *well* aware. 7. Completely; wholly: Mix it *well.* 8. Far; at some distance: He lagged *well* behind us. 9. Kindly; generously; graciously. —**as well** 1. Also; in addition. 2. With equal effect or consequence: He might just *as well* have sold it. —**as well as** 1. As satisfactorily as. 2. To the same degree as. 3. In addition to. —*adj.* 1. Having good health. 2. Satisfactory; right: All is *well.* 3. Prosperous; comfortable. —*interj.* An exclamation used to express surprise, expectation, doubt, etc., or to preface a remark. [OE *wel*]

Well, as combining form, has the meanings:

1. Completely; extensively:

well-accustomed	**well-deserved**
well-authenticated	**well-educated**

well-hidden	**well-pleased**
well-liked	**well-stocked**

2. Correctly; satisfactorily; skillfully:

well-behaved	**well-mannered**
well-built	**well-planned**
well-chosen	**well-seasoned**
well-dressed	**well-trained**
well-formed	**well-worded**
well-made	**well-written**

we'll (wēl) 1. We will. 2. We shall.

well-ap·point·ed (wel′ə·poin′tid) *adj.* Properly equipped; excellently furnished.

well-bal·anced (wel′bal′ənst) *adj.* 1. Evenly balanced or proportioned. 2. Sensible; sane; sound.

well-be·ing (wel′bē′ing) *n.* A condition of health, happiness, or prosperity; welfare.

well-born (wel′bôrn′) *adj.* Of good birth or ancestry.

well-bred (wel′bred′) *adj.* 1. Characterized by or showing good breeding; polite. 2. Of good stock, as an animal.

well-dis·posed (wel′dis·pōzd′) *adj.* Disposed or inclined to be kind, favorable, etc.

well-done (wel′dun′) *adj.* 1. Satisfactorily accomplished. 2. Thoroughly cooked, as meat.

well-fa·vored (wel′fā′vərd) *adj.* Handsome; comely.

well-fed (wel′fed′) *adj.* 1. Plump; fat. 2. Properly nourished.

well-fixed (wel′fikst′) *adj. Informal* Affluent; well-to-do.

well-found·ed (wel′foun′did) *adj.* Based on fact, sound evidence, etc.: *well-founded* suspicions.

well-groomed (wel′grōōmd′) *adj.* Carefully dressed, combed, etc.

well-ground·ed (wel′groun′did) *adj.* 1. Thoroughly schooled in the elements of a subject. 2. Well-founded.

well-head (wel′hed′) *n.* 1. A natural source supplying water to a spring or well. 2. Any source or fountainhead. 3. The top of a well, as of an oil well.

well-heeled (wel′hēld′) *adj. Slang* Plentifully supplied with money.

well-in·formed (wel′in·fôrmd′) *adj.* Having much information about a subject or a wide range of subjects, esp. of current events.

well-in·ten·tioned (wel′in·ten′shənd) *adj.* Having good intentions; well-meant.

well-known (wel′nōn′) *adj.* 1. Widely known; famous. 2. Thoroughly or fully known.

well-mean·ing (wel′mē′ning) *adj.* 1. Having good intentions. 2. Done with or characterized by good intentions: also **well′-meant′** (-ment′).

well-nigh (wel′nī′) *adv.* Very nearly; almost.

well-off (wel′ôf′) *adj.* In comfortable or favorable circumstances; fortunate.

well-pre·served (wel′pri·zûrvd′) *adj.* Showing few signs of age.

well-read (wel′red′) *adj.* Having wide knowledge from reading much.

well-round·ed (wel′roun′did) *adj.* 1. Having or displaying diverse knowledge, interests, etc. 2. Wide in scope; comprehensive: a *well-rounded* program. 3. Fully formed or developed: a *well-rounded* figure.

well-spo·ken (wel′spō′kən) *adj.* 1. Fitly or excellently said. 2. Refined in speech and manners.

well·spring (wel′spring′) *n.* 1. The source of a stream or spring; fountainhead. 2. A source of continual supply.

well-thought-of (wel′thôt′uv′, -ov′) *adj.* In good repute; esteemed; respected.

well-to-do (wel′tə·dōō′) *adj.* Prosperous; affluent.

well-turned (well′tûrnd′) 1. Pleasing in shape. 2. Aptly constructed: a *well-turned* phrase.

well-wish·er (wel′wish′ər) *n.* One who wishes well, as to another.

welsh (welsh, welch) *v.i. Slang* To avoid paying a debt, fulfilling an obligation, etc.: often with *on.* [? Back formation < *welsher,* prob. < *Welsher* Welshman] —**welsh′er** *n.*

Welsh (welsh, welch) *adj.* Pertaining to Wales, its people, or their language. —*n.* 1. The Celtic people of Wales: with *the.* 2. The Celtic language of Wales. [OE *wealh* foreigner]

Welsh·man (welsh′mən, welch′-) *n. pl.* **·men** (-mən) A man of Welsh birth or ancestry.

Welsh rabbit A concoction of melted cheese served hot on toast or crackers. ◆The form *rarebit* is a mistaken etymology.

welt (welt) *n.* 1. A strip of material applied to a seam. 2. A strip of leather set between the upper of a shoe and its outer sole. 3. A stripe raised on the skin by a blow: also called *wale, weal.* —*v.t.* 1. To sew a welt on or in. 2. *Informal* To flog severely. [ME *welte, walt*]

wel·ter (wel′tər) *v.i.* 1. To roll about; wallow. 2. To lie or be soaked in some fluid, as blood. —*n.* 1. A rolling movement, as of waves. 2. A commotion; turmoil. [< MDu. *welteren*]

wel·ter·weight (wel′tər·wāt′) *n.* A boxer or wrestler weighing between 136 and 147 pounds. [< *welter* heavyweight horseman + WEIGHT]

wen (wen) *n. Pathol.* Any benign tumor of the skin, esp. of the scalp. [OE *wenn, wænn*] —**wen′nish, wen′ny** *adj.*

wench (wench) *n.* 1. A young woman; girl. 2. A female servant. [ME < OE *wencel* child, servant]

wend (wend) *Chiefly Poetic v.* **wen·ded** (*Archaic* **went**), **wend·ing** *v.t.* 1. To direct or proceed on (one's course or way). —*v.i.* 2. To travel; proceed; go. [OE *wendan*]

went (went) An archaic past tense and past participle of *wend,* now used as past tense of GO.

wept (wept) Past tense and past participle of WEEP.

were (wûr, *unstressed* wər) Plural and second person singular past indicative, and past subjunctive singular and plural, of BE. [OE *wære, wæron,* pt. forms of *wesan* to be]

we're (wir) We are.

were·n't (wûr′ənt) Were not.

were·wolf (wir′wōōlf′, wûr′-) *n. pl.* **·wolves** (-wōōlvz′) In European folklore, a human being transformed into a wolf or one having power to assume the form of a wolf at will. Also **wer′wolf′.** [OE *wer* man + *wulf* wolf]

wert (wûrt, *unstressed* wərt) Archaic second person singular, past tense of both indicative and subjunctive of BE used with *thou.*

west (west) *n.* 1. The direction of the sun in relation to an observer on earth at sunset. 2. One of the four cardinal points of the compass, directly opposite *east*. 3. *Sometimes cap.* Any region west of a specified point. —**the West** 1. The countries lying west of Asia and Turkey; the Occident. 2. The western hemisphere. 3. The part of the U.S. lying west of the Mississippi River. —*adj.* 1. To, toward, facing, or in the west. 2. Coming from the west. —*adv.* In or toward the west. [OE]

west·bound (west′bound′) *adj.* Going westward.

west·er·ly (wes′tər·lē) *adj.* 1. In, toward, or pertaining to the west. 2. From the west, as a wind. —*n. pl.* **·lies** A wind or storm from the west. —*adv.* Toward or from the west. —**west′er·li·ness** *n.*

west·ern (wes′tərn) *adj.* 1. To, toward, or in the west. 2. Native to or inhabiting the west. 3. *Sometimes cap.* Of or like the west or the West. —*n.* A type of fiction or motion picture about cowboy and pioneer life in the western U.S.

Western Church The medieval church of the Western Roman Empire, now the Roman Catholic Church: distinguished from the church of the Eastern Empire, now the Eastern Orthodox Church.

west·ern·er (wes′tər·nər) *n.* 1. One who is native to or lives in the west. 2. *Usu. cap.* One who lives in or comes from the western U.S.

Western Hemisphere See under HEMISPHERE.

west·ern·ize (wes′tər·nīz) *v.t.* **·ized, ·iz·ing** To make western in characteristics, habits, etc. —**west′ern·i·za′tion** *n.*

west·ward (west′wərd) *adv.* Toward the west: also **west′wards.** —*adj.* To, toward, facing, or in the west.

wet (wet) *adj.* **wet·ter, wet·test** 1. Covered or saturated with water or other liquid. 2. Not yet dry: *wet* varnish. 3. Marked by showers or by heavy rainfall; rainy. 4. *Informal* Favoring or permitting the manufacture and sale of alcoholic beverages: a *wet* state. —**all wet** *Slang* Quite wrong; crazy. —**wet behind the ears** Inexperienced or unsophisticated. —*n.* 1. Water; moisture; wetness. 2. Showery or rainy weather; rain. —*v.t. & v.i.* **wet** or **wet·ted, wet·ting** To make or become wet. —**to wet one's whistle** *Informal* To take a drink. [OE *wǣt*] —**wet′ly** *adv.* —**wet′ness** *n.* —**wet′ta·ble** *adj.* —**wet′ter** *n.*

wet·back (wet′bak′) *n. Informal* A Mexican laborer who enters the U.S. illegally. [So called because many cross the border by swimming or wading across the Rio Grande]

wet blanket *Informal* One who has a discouraging effect on enthusiasm, activity, etc.

weth·er (weth′ər) *n.* A castrated ram. [OE]

wet-nurse (wet′nûrs′) *v.t.* **-nursed, -nurs·ing** 1. To act as a wet nurse to. 2. To attend to with painstaking care.

wet nurse A woman who is hired to suckle the child of another woman.

wet suit A skintight rubber suit worn by skin divers for warmth.

wetting agent *Chem.* Any of a class of substances that, by reducing surface tension, enable a liquid to spread more readily over a solid surface.

we've (wēv) We have.

whack (hwak) *v.t. & v.i. Informal* To strike sharply; beat; hit. —*n.* 1. *Informal* A sharp, resounding stroke or blow. 2. *Slang* A share; portion. —**out of whack** *Slang* Out of order. [? Var. of THWACK]

whack·ing (hwak′ing) *Informal adj.* Strikingly large; whopping.

whale¹ (hwāl) *n.* 1. A large marine mammal of fishlike form. 2. *Informal* Something extremely good or large: a *whale* of a party. —*v.i.* **whaled, whal·ing** To engage in the hunting of whales. [OE *hwæl*]

whale² (hwāl) *v.t.* **whaled, whal·ing** *Informal* To strike hard; flog; wale. [? Var. of WALE, *v.*]

whale·boat (hwāl′bōt′) *n.* A long, deep rowboat, sharp at both ends, formerly used in whaling.

whale·bone (hwāl′bōn′) *n.* 1. The horny substance from the upper jaw of certain whales; baleen. 2. A strip of whalebone, used in stiffening corsets, etc.

whal·er (hwā′lər) *n.* 1. A person or vessel engaged in whaling. 2. A whaleboat.

whal·ing (hwā′ling) *n.* The industry of capturing whales.

wham·my (hwam′ē) *n. pl.* **·mies** *Slang* A jinx; hex. [< *wham*, imit. of the sound of a hard blow]

whang (hwang) *Informal v.t. & v.i.* To beat or sound with a resounding noise. —*n.* A heavy blow. [Imit.]

wharf (hwôrf) *n. pl.* **wharves** (hwôrvz) or **wharfs** A dock or pier where ships load and unload. [OE *hwearf*]

wharf·age (hwôr′fij) *n.* 1. The use of wharves. 2. Charge for the use of a wharf.

wharf·in·ger (hwôr′fin·jər) *n.* One who keeps a wharf and collects wharfage fees. [Earlier *wharfager*]

what (hwot, hwut) *pron.* 1. Which specific thing or things, action, etc.: *What* does he do? I don't know *what* to do. 2. That which: He knew *what* he wanted. —*adj.* 1. In interrogative construction: **a** Asking for information that will specify the person or thing qualified by it; which: Of *what* person do you speak? **b** How much: *What* money has he? 2. How surprising, ridiculous, great, etc.: *What* genius! 3. Whatever: *What* money he had left was soon spent. —*adv.* 1. In what respect; to what extent: *What* does it matter? 2. For what reason; why: with *for*: *What* are you saying that for? —*conj. Informal* That: used only in negative expressions: I do not doubt but *what* he will come. [OE *hwæt*, neut. of *hwā* who]

what·ev·er (hwot′ev′ər, hwut′-) *pron.* 1. The whole that; anything that; no matter what: often added for emphasis to a negative assertion: *whatever* makes life dear; I do not want anything *whatever*. 2. *Informal* What: usually interrogative: *Whatever* were you saying? Also *Poetic* **what′e'er′** (-âr′).

what·not (hwot′not′, hwut′-) *n.* An ornamental set of shelves for holding bric-a-brac, etc.

what·so·ev·er (hwot′sō·ev′ər, hwut′-) *adj. & pron.* Whatever: a more formal usage. Also *Poetic* **what′so·e'er′** (-âr′).

wheat (hwēt) *n.* 1. The grain of a cereal grass, widely cultivated and providing a flour used for bread, pastries, etc. 2. The plant producing this grain, bearing at its summit a dense spike of seeds. [OE *hwǣte*]

wheat germ The embryo of the wheat kernel, used as a source of vitamins.

whee·dle (hwēd′l) *v.* **·dled, ·dling** *v.t.* 1. To try to persuade by flattery, cajolery, etc.; coax. 2. To obtain by coaxing. —*v.i.* 3. To use flattery or cajolery. [? OE *wǣdlian* to beg, be poor] —**whee′dler** *n.* —**whee′dling·ly** *adv.*

wheel (hwēl) *n.* 1. A circular rim and hub connected by spokes or a disk, capable of rotating on a central axis, as in vehicles and machines. 2. An instrument or device having a wheel or wheels as its distinguishing characteristic, as a steering wheel, water wheel, spinning wheel, etc. 3. Anything resembling or suggestive of a wheel; any circular object or formation. 4. An old instrument of torture to which the victim was tied. 5. A turning; rotation; revolution. 6. *pl.* A moving force: the *wheels* of democracy. —*v.t.* 1. To move or convey on wheels. 2. To cause to turn on or as on an axis; pivot or revolve. 3. To perform with a circular movement. —*v.i.* 4. To turn on or as on an axis; rotate or revolve. 5. To take a new direction or course of action: often with *about.* 6. To move in a circular or spiral course. 7. To move on wheels. [OE *hwēol*]

wheel·bar·row (hwēl′bar′ō) *n.* A boxlike vehicle ordinarily with one wheel and two handles, for moving small loads.

wheel·base (hwēl′bās′) *n.* The distance between the front and rear axles, as in an automobile.

wheel·chair (hwēl′châr′) *n.* A mobile chair mounted between large wheels, for the use of invalids. Also **wheel chair.**

wheel·er (hwē′lər) *n.* 1. One who wheels. 2. A wheel horse. 3. Something furnished with a wheel or wheels: used in combination: a *side-wheeler.*

wheel·er-deal·er (hwē′lər·dē′lər) *n. Slang* One who makes shrewd deals, esp. in business.

wheel horse 1. A horse harnessed nearest the wheels of a vehicle when there is a leader in front. 2. One who does the heaviest work or assumes the greatest responsibility.

wheel·house (hwēl′hous′) *n.* A pilothouse.

wheel·wright (hwēl′rīt′) *n.* One whose business is making or repairing wheels.

wheeze (hwēz) *v.t. & v.i.* **wheezed, wheez·ing** To breathe or utter with a husky, whistling sound. —*n.* A wheezing sound. [Prob. < ON *hvæsa* hiss] —**wheez′er** *n.* —**wheez′ing·ly** *adv.*

wheez·y (hwē′zē) *adj.* **wheez·i·er, wheez·i·est** Affected with or characterized by wheezing. —**wheez′i·ly** *adv.* —**wheez′i·ness** *n.*

whelk (hwelk) *n.* Any of various large marine mollusks having whorled shells, esp. the common whelk, used for food. [OE *weoloc*]

whelp (hwelp) *n.* 1. One of the young of a dog, wolf, lion, or other beast. 2. A dog. 3. A young fellow: a contemptuous term. —*v.t. & v.i.* To give birth (to): said of dogs, lions, etc. [OE *hwelp*]

when (hwen) *adv.* At what or which time: *When* did you arrive? —*conj.* 1. At what or which time: They watched until midnight, *when* they fell asleep. 2. As soon as: He laughed *when* he heard it. 3. Although: He walks *when* he might ride. 4. At the time that; while: *when* we were young. 5. If; considering that: How can I buy it *when* I have no money? —*pron.* What or which time: since *when.* —*n.* The time; date. [OE *hwanne, hwenne*]

whence (hwens) *Archaic adv.* From what place or source: *Whence* and what are you? —*conj.* From what or which place, source, or cause; from which: the place *whence* these sounds arise. [ME < OE *hwanne* when]

whence·so·ev·er (hwens′sō·ev′ər) *Archaic adv. & conj.* From whatever place, cause, or source.

when·ev·er (hwen′ev′ər) *adv. & conj.* At whatever time. Also *Poetic* **when′e′er′** (-âr′).

when·so·ev·er (hwen′sō·ev′ər) *adv. & conj.* Whenever.

where (hwâr) *adv.* 1. At or in what place or situation: *Where* is my book? 2. To what place or end: *Where* are you going? 3. From what place: *Where* did you get that hat? 4. To a place or situation in or to which: Let us go *where* the mountains are. —*conj.* 1. At which place: Let us go home *where* we can relax. 2. With the condition that. —*pron.* 1. The place in which: The bear passed three yards from *where* we stood. 2. The point at which: That's *where* you are wrong. —*n.* Place; locality. [OE *hwǣr*]

where·a·bouts (hwâr′ə·bouts′) *adv.* Near or at what place; about where. —*n.pl.* (*construed as sing.*) The place in or near which a person or thing is.

where·as (hwâr′az′) *conj.* 1. Since the facts are such as they are. 2. The fact being that; when in truth: implying opposition to a previous statement. —*n. pl.* **·as·es** A clause or item beginning with the word "whereas."

where·at (hwâr′at′) *Archaic* or *Rare adv.* At what: *Whereat* are you angry? —*conj.* At which; for which reason.

where·by (hwâr′bī′) *adv.* 1. By means of which; through which: the gate *whereby* he entered. 2. By what; how.

wher·e′er (hwâr′âr′) *adv. Poetic* Wherever.

where·fore (hwâr′fôr′) *Archaic adv.* For what reason; why. —*conj.* Because of which.

where·in (hwâr′in′) *adv.* 1. In what: *Wherein* is the error? 2. In which: a marriage *wherein* there is discord.

where·of (hwâr′uv′, -ov′) *Archaic adv.* 1. Of or from what: *Whereof* did you partake? 2. Of which or whom.

where·on (hwâr′on′, -ôn′) *Archaic adv.* On what or on which.

where·so·ev·er (hwâr′sō·ev′ər) *Archaic adv. & conj.* In or to whatever place; wherever.

where·to (hwâr′to͞o′) *Archaic adv.* To what place or end: *Whereto* serves avarice? —*conj.* To which or to whom.

where·up·on (hwâr′ə·pon′, -ə·pôn′) *adv. Archaic* Upon what; whereon. —*conj.* Upon which or whom; in consequence of which; after which: *whereupon* they took in sail.

wher·ev·er (hwâr′ev′ər) *adv. & conj.* In, at, or to whatever place; wheresoever.

where·with (hwâr′with′, -wit͟h′) *Archaic adv.* Interrogatively, with what: *Wherewith* shall I do it? —*conj.* With which; by means of which.

where·with·al (hwâr′wit͟h·ôl′) *n.* The necessary means or resources, esp. money.

wher·ry (hwer′ē) *n. pl.* **·ries** A light rowboat. —*v.t. & v.i.* **·ried, ·ry·ing** To transport in or use a wherry. [Origin unknown]

whet (hwet) *v.t.* **whet·ted, whet·ting** 1. To sharpen, as a knife, by friction. 2. To make more keen or eager; stimulate, as the appetite. —*n.* 1. The act of whetting. 2. Something that whets. [OE *hwettan*] —**whet′ter** *n.*

wheth·er (hweth′ər) *conj.* 1. If it be the case that: Tell me *whether* you are considering our plan. 2. In either case; introducing alternatives: I don't care *whether* you stay or go. —**whether or no** In any case. [OE *hwæther*]

whet·stone (hwet′stōn′) *n.* A fine-grained stone for sharpening knives, axes, etc.

whey (hwā) *n.* A clear, straw-colored liquid that separates from the curd when milk is curdled, as in making cheese. [OE *hwæg*] —**whey′ey, whey′ish** *adj.*

which (hwich) *pron.* 1. What one or ones: *Which* are his? 2. The thing designated; that: the story *which* we preferred. —*adj.* 1. Being one or more of several alternatives: *Which* way are you going? 2. This: during *which* time. [OE *hwilc*]

which·ev·er (hwich′ev′ər) *pron.* One or another (of two or of several). —*adj.* No matter which. Also **which′so·ev′er.**

whiff (hwif) *n.* 1. A slight gust of air. 2. A gust of odor: a *whiff* of onions. 3. A single expulsion or inhalation of breath. —*v.t. & v.i.* 1. To exhale or inhale in whiffs. 2. To smell or sniff. [Prob. ult. imit.] —**whiff′er** *n.*

whif·fle·tree (hwif′əl·trē′) *n.* A horizontal crossbar to which the ends of the traces of a harness are attached: also called *singletree, swingletree, whippletree.* [Var. of WHIPPLETREE]

Whig (hwig) *n.* 1. An American colonist who supported the Revolutionary War in the 18th c. in opposition to the Tories. 2. A member of an American political party (1834–1855) formed in opposition to the Democratic Party. 3. In England, a member of a liberal political party in the 18th and 19th c., later known as the Liberal Party. —*adj.* Consisting of or supported by Whigs. [< ? *whiggamore* < dial. E (Scot.) < *whig,* a cry to urge on a horse + *mere* horse] —**Whig′ger·y** *n.* —**Whig′gish** *adj.* —**Whig′gish·ly** *adv.* —**Whig′gish·ness** *n.* —**Whig′gism** *n.*

while (hwīl) *n.* 1. A short time; also, any period of time: Stay and rest a *while.* 2. Time or pains expended: only in the phrase **worth while** or **worth one's while.** —**the while** At the same time. —*conj.* 1. During the time that; as long as. 2. At the same time that. *While* he found fault, he also praised. 3. Whereas: This man is short, *while* that one is tall. —*v.t.* **whiled, whil·ing** To cause (time) to pass lightly and pleasantly: usu. with *away.* [OE *hwīl*]

whi·lom (hwī′ləm) *Archaic adj.* Former. —*adv.* Formerly. [OE *hwīl* a while]

whilst (hwīlst) *conj. Chiefly Brit.* While.

whim (hwim) *n.* A sudden or unexpected notion or fanciful idea; caprice. [Short for earlier *whim-wham* trifle]

whim·per (hwim′pər) *v.i.* 1. To cry or whine with plaintive broken sounds. —*v.t.* 2. To utter with a whimper. —*n.* A low, broken, whining cry; whine. [Imit.] —**whim′per·er** *n.* —**whim′per·ing** *n.* —**whim′per·ing·ly** *adv.*

whim·si·cal (hwim′zi·kəl) *adj.* 1. Having eccentric ideas; capricious. 2. Oddly constituted; fantastic. —**whim′si·cal′i·ty** (-kal′ə·tē) *n.* —**whim′si·cal·ly** *adv.* —**whim′si·cal·ness** *n.*

whim·sy (hwim′zē) *n. pl.* **·sies** 1. A whim. 2. Fanciful humor, as in a literary work. Also **whim′sey.**

whine (hwīn) *v.* **whined, whin·ing** *v.i.* 1. To utter a sound expressive of grief, peevishness, etc. 2. To complain in a tiresome or childish way. —*v.t.* 3. To utter with a whine. —*n.* The act or sound of whining. [OE *hwīnan*] —**whin′er** *n.* —**whin′ing·ly** *adv.* —**whin′y** *adj.*

whin·ny (hwin′ē) *v.* **·nied, ·ny·ing** *v.i.* 1. To neigh, esp. in a low or gentle way. —*v.t.* 2. To express with a whinny. —*n. pl.* **·nies** A neigh. [< WHINE]

whip (hwip) *v.* **whipped** or **whipt, whip·ping** *v.t.* 1. To strike with a lash, rod, strap, etc. 2. To drive with lashes. 3. To cause to move like a whip: The wind *whipped* the trees. 4. To beat, as eggs or cream, to a froth. 5. To seize, move, jerk, throw, etc., with a sudden motion. 6. To wrap (rope, cable, etc.) with light line so as to prevent chafing or wear. 7. To sew, as a flat seam, with a loose overhand stitch. 8. *Informal* To defeat. —*v.i.* 9. To go, come, move, or turn suddenly and quickly. 10. To thrash about in a manner suggestive of a whip. —**to whip up** 1. To excite; arouse. 2. *Informal* To prepare quickly, as a meal. —*n.* 1. A lash attached to a handle, used for driving draft animals or for administering punishment. 2. A stroke, blow, or lashing motion. 3. A member of a legislative body who enforces party discipline and looks after party interests. 4. A kind of dessert, whipped to a froth. [ME *wippen*] —**whip′per** *n.*

whip·cord (hwip′kôrd′) *n.* 1. A strong, hard-twisted or braided hemp cord, used in making whiplashes. 2. A worsted fabric with a diagonal rib.

whip hand An instrument or means of mastery; advantage.

whip·lash (hwip′lash′) *n.* The lash of a whip.

whiplash injury An injury to the neck caused by a sudden jolting, as in an automobile collision.

whip·per·snap·per (hwip′ər·snap′ər) *n.* A pretentious but insignificant person, esp. a young one. [? Extension of *whipsnapper* one who cracks whips]

whip·pet (hwip′it) *n.* A small, swift breed of dog, used esp. in racing. [Dim. of WHIP]

whip·ping (hwip′ing) *n.* 1. The act of one who or that which whips; esp., a flogging. 2. Cord or other material used to whip or lash parts together.

whipping boy Scapegoat.

whip·ple·tree (hwip′əl·trē′) *n.* A whiffletree.

whip·poor·will (hwip′ər·wil) *n.* A small nocturnal bird, common in the eastern U.S. [Imit. of its cry]

whip·saw (hwip′sô′) *n.* A long, narrow, tapering saw, mounted in a wooden frame. —*v.t.* **·sawed, ·sawed** or **·sawn, ·saw·ing** 1. To saw with a whipsaw. 2. To defeat by the joint action of two opponents, or in two opposite ways at once.

whip·stitch (hwip′stich′) *v.t.* To sew with long, widely spaced stitches. —**whip′stitch′** *n.*

whir (hwûr) *v.t. & v.i.* **whirred, whir·ring** To fly, move, or whirl with a buzzing sound. Also *Brit.* whirr. [Prob. < Scand.] —**whir** *n.*

whirl (hwûrl) *v.i.* 1. To turn or revolve rapidly, as about a center. 2. To move or go swiftly. 3. To have a sensation of spinning: My head *whirls.* —*v.t.* 4. To cause to turn or revolve rapidly. —*n.* 1. A swift rotating motion. 2. A state of confusion; turmoil. 3. A rapid succession of events, social activities, etc. 4. *Informal* A try. [Prob. < ON *hvirfla* to revolve] —**whirl′er** *n.*

whirl·i·gig (hwûr′lə·gig′) *n.* 1. Any toy or small device that rotates rapidly on an axis. 2. A merry-go-round. 3. Anything that moves in a cycle. [< *whirly* (< WHIRL) + obs. *gig,* a whirling toy]

whirl·pool (hwûrl′pōōl′) *n.* 1. A vortex where water moves with a whirling motion. 2. Anything resembling the motion of a whirlpool.

whirl·wind (hwûrl′wind′) *n.* A funnel-shaped column of air, with a rapid, upward spiral motion. —*adj.* Extremely swift or impetuous: a *whirlwind* courtship.

whirl·y·bird (hwûr′lē·burd′) *n. Informal* A helicopter.

whisk (hwisk) *v.t.* 1. To sweep with light movements, as of a small broom. 2. To beat with a quick movement, as eggs, etc. —*v.i.* 3. To move quickly and lightly. —*n.* 1. A sudden, sweeping movement. 2. A little broom or brush. 3. A small instrument for rapidly whipping (cream, etc.) to a froth or for blending ingredients in cooking. [Prob. < Scand.]

whisk·broom (hwisk′brōōm′, -brŏŏm′) *n.* A small, short-handled broom for brushing clothing, etc.

whisk·er (hwis′kər) *n.* 1. *pl.* The beard, esp. its side parts. 2. A hair from the beard. 3. One of the long, bristly hairs on the sides of the mouth of some animals. —**whisk′ered, whisk′er·y** *adj.*

whis·key (hwis′kē) *n. pl.* **·keys** 1. An alcoholic liquor obtained by the distillation of certain fermented grains. 2. A drink of whiskey. Also **whis′ky.** [Short for *usquebaugh* < Irish, water of life < *uisge* water + *beatha* life] —**whis′key** *adj.*

whis·per (hwis′pər) *n.* 1. A low, soft, breathy voice. 2. A low, rustling sound. 3. A whispered utterance; hint; insinuation. —*v.i.* 1. To speak in a whisper. 2. To talk cautiously or furtively; plot or gossip. 3. To make a low, rustling sound. —*v.t.* 4. To utter in a whisper. [OE *hwisprian*] —**whis′per·er** *n.* —**whis′per·ing** *adj. & n.* —**whis′per·ing·ly** *adv.*

whist (hwist) *n.* A game of cards, the forerunner of bridge, played by four persons. [Alter. of earlier *whisk*]

whis·tle (hwis′əl) *v.* **·tled, ·tling** *v.i.* 1. To make a shrill sound by sending the breath through the teeth or through a small opening formed by the mouth. 2. To emit a shrill cry, as some birds and animals. 3. To cause a shrill sound by swift passage through the air, as wind, etc. 4. To blow or sound a whistle. —*v.t.* 5. To produce (a tune) by whistling. 6. To call, manage, or direct by whistling. —*n.* 1. A device for producing a shrill sound by forcing a current of air, etc., through a narrowed opening. 2. A whistling sound. 3. The act of whistling. 4. *Slang* The mouth and throat: to wet one's *whistle.* [OE *hwistle* shrill pipe] —**whist′ler** *n.*

whistle stop *Informal* 1. A small station where a train stops only on signal. 2. A small town. 3. A brief stop, esp. by a candidate for office, during a tour.

whit (hwit) *n.* The smallest particle; speck. [Var. of *wight* < OE *wiht* a certain amount]

white (hwīt) *adj.* **whit·er, whit·est** 1. Having the color of new-fallen snow, milk, etc. 2. Very light in color. 3. Bloodless; ashen: *white* with rage. 4. Not intentionally wicked: a *white* lie. 5. Free from stain; innocent. 6. Blank; unmarked by ink. 7. Belonging to a racial group characterized by light-colored skin; Caucasian. 8. Of, pertaining to, or controlled by white people. 9. *Informal* Fair and honorable; honest. —*n.* 1. The color seen when light is reflected without sensible absorption of any of the visible rays of the spectrum; the color of new-fallen snow. 2. The white or light-colored part of something, as the albumen of egg. 3. One who has light-colored skin. —*v.t.* **whit·ed, whit·ing** To make white; whiten. [OE *hwit*] —**white′ly** *adv.* —**white′ness** *n.*

white ant Loosely, a termite.

white·bait (hwīt′bāt′) *n.* The young of various food fishes, esp. of herring.

white birch 1. Birch. 2. The common European birch, having an ash-colored bark.

white blood cell A leucocyte. Also **white corpuscle.**

white·cap (hwīt′kap′) *n.* A wave with a crest of foam.

white-collar (hwīt′kol′ər) *adj.* Designating clerical, professional, and other nonmanual workers.

white dwarf *Astron.* A star of low luminosity, small size, and great density.

white elephant 1. A rare, pale gray variety of Asian elephant held sacred by the Burmese and Siamese. 2. Anything rare but expensive to keep. 3. Any burdensome possession.

white feather A mark of cowardice. [from the belief that white feathers in a gamecock indicated poor fighting qualities]

white·fish (hwīt′fish′) *n. pl.* **·fish** or **·fish·es** 1. Any of various food fishes of North America, living mostly in lakes. 2. Any of various other fish having a silvery appearance, as the beluga. 3. A tropical marine food fish of California.

white flag 1. A flag of truce. 2. A white flag hoisted as a signal of surrender.

white gold Gold alloyed with another metal to give it a whitish, platinumlike appearance.

white goods Household linens, such as sheets, towels, etc.

White·hall (hwīt′hôl) 1. A street in London, where a number of government offices are located. 2. The British government.

white·head (hwīt′hed′) *n.* A white nodule on the skin containing secretions of an oil gland.

white heat 1. The temperature at which a body becomes incandescent. 2. Great excitement, intense emotion, etc. —**white-hot** (hwīt′hot′) *adj.*

White House, The 1. The official residence of the President of the U.S., at Washington, D.C. 2. The executive branch of the U.S. government.

white lead A heavy, white, poisonous mixture of lead carbonate and lead oxide, used as a pigment and in some medicinal ointments for burns.

white matter *Anat.* The portion of the brain and spinal cord composed mainly of nerve fibers, giving it a white appearance.

white meat The light-colored meat or flesh of animals, as veal or the breast of turkey.

whit·en (hwīt′n) *v.t. & v.i.* To make or become white; blanch; bleach. **—whit′en·er** *n.*

white pine 1. A pine widely distributed in eastern North America, with soft, bluish green leaves in clusters of five. 2. The light, soft wood of this tree.

White Russian Byelorussian.

white sale A sale of sheets, towels, etc., at reduced prices.

white sauce A sauce made of butter, flour, milk, etc., used for vegetables, meats, and fish.

white slave A girl or woman forced into or held in prostitution. **—white-slave** (hwīt′·slāv′) *adj.* **—white slaver —white slavery**

white-tailed deer (hwīt′tāld′) A common North American deer, having a moderately long tail white on the underside.

white·wash (hwīt′wosh′, -wôsh′) *n.* 1. A mixture of slaked lime and water, sometimes with salt, whiting, and glue added, used for whitening walls, etc. 2. *Slang* A covering up of reprehensible actions. 3. *Informal* A failure to score in a game. *—v.t.* 1. To coat with whitewash. 2. *Slang* To cover up; hide. 3. *Informal* In sports, to defeat without allowing the losing side to score. **—white′·wash′er** *n.*

white water Rapids in a river.

white whale The beluga.

whith·er (hwith′ər) *Archaic & Poetic adv.* 1. To what or which place? Where? 2. To what point, end, extent, etc.? *—conj.* To which or what place, end, etc. [OE *hwider*]

whith·er·so·ev·er (hwith′ər·sō·ev′ər) *adv.* *Archaic* To whatever place.

whit·ing[1] (hwī′ting) *n.* A pure white chalk, powdered and washed, used in making putty and whitewash, as a pigment, and for polishing.

whit·ing[2] (hwī′ting) *n.* Any of several unrelated light or silvery food fishes. [< MDu. *wijting*]

whit·ish (hwī′tish) *adj.* Somewhat white or, esp., very light gray. **—whit′ish·ness** *n.*

whit·low (hwit′lō) *n.* *Pathol.* An inflammatory tumor, esp. on the last joint of a finger; a felon. [ME *whitflaw*]

Whit·sun·day (hwit′sun′dē, -dā) *n.* Pentecost. [OE *Hwīta Sunnandæg,* lit., white Sunday]

whit·tle (hwit′l) *v.* **·tled, ·tling** *v.t.* 1. To cut or shave bits from (wood, a stick, etc.). 2. To make or shape by carving or whittling. 3. To reduce by or as by cutting away a little at a time. *—v.i.* 4. To whittle wood. [Alter. of ME *thwitel* < OE *thwītan* to cut] **—whit′tler** *n.*

whiz (hwiz) *v.* **whizzed, whiz·zing** *v.i.* 1. To make a high-pitched humming or hissing sound while passing through the air. 2. To move or pass with such a sound. *—v.t.* 3. To cause to whiz. *—n. pl.* **whiz·zes** 1. A whizzing sound. 2. *Slang* Any person or thing of extraordinary excellence or ability. Also **whizz.** [Imit.]

who (hōō) *pron. possessive case* **whose;** *objective case* **whom** 1. Which or what person or persons: *Who* said that? I know *who* he is. 2. That: Did you see the person *who* left? 3. He, she, or they that; whoever: *Who* steals my purse steals trash. [OE *hwā*]

whoa (hwō) *interj.* Stop! stand still! [Var. of HO]

who·dun·it (hōō·dun′it) *n.* *Informal* A mystery story or play that challenges the reader or spectator to detect the perpetrator of a crime.

who·ev·er (hōō·ev′ər) *pron.* Any one without exception; any person who.

whole (hōl) *adj.* 1. Containing all the parts necessary to make up a total; entire. 2. Having all the essential or original parts intact. 3. In sound health; hale. 4. Constituting the full extent or amount; entire. 5. *Math.* Of or relating to an integer. *—n.* 1. All the parts making up a thing; totality. 2. An organization of parts making a unity. **—on the whole** Taking everything into consideration. [OE *hāl*] **—whole′ness** *n.*

whole blood Blood as taken directly from the body, esp. that used in transfusions.

whole·heart·ed (hōl′här′tid) *adj.* Done or experienced with earnestness, sincerity, etc.; earnest. **—whole′heart′ed·ly** *adv.* **—whole′·heart′ed·ness** *n.*

whole note *Music* A note having a time value equal to four quarter notes.

whole number *Math.* An integer.

whole·sale (hōl′sāl′) *n.* The selling of goods for resale: distinguished from *retail.* *—adj.* 1. Pertaining to the sale of goods at wholesale. 2. Made or done on a large scale or indiscriminately: *wholesale* murder. *—adv.* 1. In bulk or quantity. 2. Without discrimination; indiscriminately. *—v.t. & v.i.* **·saled, ·sal·ing** To sell at wholesale. [ME *by hole sale* in large quantities] **—whole′sal′er** *n.*

whole·some (hōl′səm) *adj.* 1. Tending to promote health. 2. Favorable to virtue and well-being. 3. Indicative of health: *wholesome* red cheeks. 4. Free from danger or risk. [ME *holsum*] **—whole′some·ly** *adv.* **—whole′·some·ness** *n.*

whole-wheat (hōl′hwēt′) *adj.* Made from the entire wheat kernel.

who'll (hōōl) 1. Who will. 2. Who shall.

whol·ly (hō′lē, hōl′lē) *adv.* 1. Completely; totally. 2. Exclusively; only.

whom (hōōm) *pron.* The objective case of WHO.

whom·ev·er (hōōm′ev′ər), **whom·so** (hōōm′·sō′), **whom·so·ev·er** (hōōm′sō·ev′ər) Objective cases of WHOEVER, WHOSO, etc.

whoop (hōōp, hwōōp, hwŏŏp) *v.i.* 1. To utter loud cries. 2. To hoot, as an owl. 3. To inhale loudly, as after a fit of coughing. *—v.t.* 4. To utter with whoops. 5. To call, urge, chase, etc., with whoops. *—n.* The cry, shout, or sound of one who or that which whoops. *—interj.* An exclamation of joy, enthusiasm, etc. [ME *whope*]

whoop·ee (hwōō′pē, hwŏŏp′ē) *interj. & n.* An exclamation of joy, excitement, etc. **—to make whoopee** To have a noisy, festive time. [< WHOOP]

whoop·ing cough (hōō′ping, hŏŏp′ing) *Pathol.* A contagious respiratory disease affecting children, marked in its final stage by violent coughing.

whop·per (hwop′ər) *n. Informal* Something large or remarkable; esp., a big falsehood.

whop·ping (hwop′ing) *adj.* Unusually large; great.

whore (hôr) *n.* A prostitute. —*v.i.* **whored, whor·ing** 1. To have illicit sexual intercourse, esp. with a prostitute. 2. To be a whore. [OE *hōre*, prob. < ON *hōra*] —**whor′ish** *adj.* —**whor′ish·ly** *adv.* —**whor′ish·ness** *n.*

whorl (hwûrl, hwôrl) *n.* 1. A set of leaves, etc., radiating from a common center. 2. A spiral curve or convolution, as of a shell or of the ridges of a fingerprint. [ME *wharwyl, whorwhil*] —**whorled** *adj.*

whor·tle·ber·ry (hwûr′təl·ber′ē) *n. pl.* **·ries** 1. A European variety of blueberry. 2. Its blue-black fruit. Also called *bilberry.* [OE *horta* + BERRY]

whose (hōōz) The possessive case of WHO and often of WHICH. [OE *hwæs*, altered by analogy with nominative form *hwo*]

whose·so·ev·er (hōōz′sō·ev′ər) Possessive case of WHOSOEVER.

who·so (hōō′sō) *pron.* Whoever; any person who. [Reduced form of OE *swā hwā swā*]

who·so·ev·er (hōō′sō·ev′ər) *pron.* Any person whatever; who; whoever.

why (hwī) *adv.* For what cause, purpose, or reason. —*n. pl.* **whys** 1. An explanatory cause. 2. A puzzling problem; riddle; enigma. —*interj.* An expletive, sometimes denoting surprise: *Why*, if it isn't Mrs. Jones! [OE *hwȳ, hwī*]

wich (wich), **wich-elm** (wich′elm′) See WYCH-ELM.

wick (wik) *n.* A wand of twisted or woven fibers that draws fuel to a flame. [OE *wēoce*]

wick·ed (wik′id) *adj.* 1. Evil in principle and practice; vicious; sinful. 2. Mischievous; roguish. 3. Noxious; pernicious. 4. Troublesome; painful. 5. *Informal* Done with great skill: a *wicked* game. [ME, alter. of *wikke, wicke*] —**wick′ed·ly** *adv.* —**wick′ed·ness** *n.*

wick·er (wik′ər) *adj.* Made of twigs, osiers, etc. —*n.* 1. A pliant young shoot or rod; twig; osier. 2. Wickerwork. [Prob. < Scand.]

wick·er·work (wik′ər·wûrk′) *n.* Work woven of twigs, osiers, etc.; basketwork.

wick·et (wik′it) *n.* 1. A small door or gate, esp. one that is part of a larger entrance. 2. A small gate in a canal lock that regulates the flow of water. 3. In cricket, three posts with two crosspieces laid over the top. 4. In croquet, a wire arch. [< AF *wiket*, OF *guichet*, prob. < Gmc.]

wick·i·up (wik′ē·up) *n.* A hut of nomadic Indians of the SW U.S., consisting of a frame covered with grass, brush, etc. [< Algonquian]

wide (wīd) *adj.* **wid·er, wid·est** 1. Having relatively great extent between sides; broad. 2. Extended in every direction; spacious: a *wide* expanse. 3. Having a specified degree of width: an inch *wide*. 4. Distant from the desired point: *wide* of the mark. 5. Having intellectual breadth; liberal: a man of *wide* views. 6. Fully open: *wide* eyes. —*n.* 1. In cricket, a ball bowled out of the batsman's reach. 2. Breadth of extent; also, a broad, open space. —*adv.* 1. To a great distance; extensively. 2. Far from the mark. 3. Fully: *wide* open. [OE *wīd*] —**wide′ly** *adv.* —**wide′·ness** *n.*

wide-an·gle lens (wīd′ang′gəl) *Photog.* A lens permitting an angle of view wider than that of the ordinary lens.

wide-a·wake (wīd′ə·wāk′) *adj.* 1. Fully awake. 2. Marked by vigilance; keen.

wide-eyed (wīd′īd′) *adj.* With the eyes wide open, as in wonder or surprise.

wid·en (wīd′n) *v.t. & v.i.* To make or become wide or wider. —**wid′en·er** *n.*

wide-o·pen (wīd′ō′pən) *adj.* 1. Opened wide. 2. *Informal* Failing to enforce laws that regulate gambling, etc.: a *wide-open* city.

wide·spread (wīd′spred′) *adj.* 1. Extending over a large space or territory. 2. Occurring or accepted among many people; general: a *widespread* belief. Also **wide′-spread′, wide′·spread′ing.**

wid·ow (wid′ō) *n.* 1. A woman whose husband is dead and who has not married again. 2. In some card games, an additional hand dealt to the table; also, a kitty. 3. *Printing* An incomplete line of type at the top of a page or column. —*v.t.* To make a widow of; deprive of a husband. [OE *widewe, wuduwe*] —**wid′ow·hood** *n.*

wid·ow·er (wid′ō·ər) *n.* A man whose wife is dead and who has not married again. [OE *widewe* widow]

width (width) *n.* 1. Dimension or measurement of an object taken from side to side. 2. The state or fact of being wide; breadth. 3. Something that has width; esp., one of the several pieces of material used in making a garment. [< WIDE]

wield (wēld) *v.t.* 1. To handle, as a weapon or instrument, esp. with full command and effect. 2. To exercise (authority, power, etc.). [Fusion of OE *wealdan* to rule and *wieldan* to conquer] —**wield′a·ble** *adj.* —**wield′er** *n.*

wield·y (wēl′dē) *adj.* **wield·i·er, wield·i·est** Easily handled or managed; manageable.

wie·ner (wē′nər) *n.* A sausage made of beef and pork. Also **wie·nie** (wē′nē), **wie·ner·wurst** (wē′nər·wûrst′, *Ger.* vē′nər·vōōrst′). [Short for G *Wiener-wurst* Vienna sausage]

wife (wīf) *n. pl.* **wives** (wīvz) A married woman. ◆Collateral adjective: *uxorial.* [OE *wīf*] —**wife′dom, wife′hood** *n.* —**wife′ly** *adj.*

wig (wig) *n.* An artificial covering of hair for the head. [Short for PERIWIG]

wig·gle (wig′əl) *v.t. & v.i.* **·gled, ·gling** To move or cause to move quickly and irregularly from side to side; squirm; wriggle. [? < MLG *wiggelen*] —**wig′gle** *n.* —**wig′gly** *adj.*

wig·gler (wig′lər) *n.* 1. One who or that which wiggles. 2. The larva of a mosquito.

wig·wag (wig′wag′) *v.t. & v.i.* **·wagged, ·wag·ging** To send (a message) by moving hand flags, lights, etc., according to a code. —*n.* The act of wigwagging; also, a message so sent. [< dial. E *wig* to wiggle + WAG[1]] —**wig′wag′ger** *n.*

wig·wam (wig′wom, -wôm) *n.* A dwelling or lodge of the North American Indians, commonly an arch-shaped framework of poles covered with bark, hides, etc. [< Algonquian (Ojibwa) *wigwaum*, lit., their dwelling]

wild (wīld) *adj.* 1. Not domesticated or tamed. 2. Growing or produced without care or cultivation. 3. Uninhabited and uncultivated: *wild* prairies. 4. Living in a primitive or savage way; uncivilized. 5. Boisterous; unruly. 6. Stormy; turbulent: a *wild* night, a *wild* crowd. 7. Showing reckless want of judgment; extravagant: a *wild* speculation. 8. Fantastically irregular or disordered; odd in arrangement or effect: a *wild* imagination, *wild* dress. 9. Being or going far from the proper course; erratic: a *wild* guess. 10. In some card games, having its value arbitrarily determined by the dealer or holder. —*n.* *Often pl.* An uninhabited and uncultivated place; wilderness: the *wilds* of Africa. —*adv.* In a wild manner: without control. [OE *wilde*] —**wild′ly** *adv.* —**wild′·ness** *n.*

wild boar The native hog of continental Europe, southern Asia, and North Africa.

wild carrot An herb having filmy white flowers and from which the cultivated carrot is derived: also called *Queen Anne's lace.*

wild·cat (wīld′kat′) *n.* 1. Any of various wild felines, as the lynx, bobcat, and ocelot. 2. An aggressive quick-tempered person, esp. a woman. 3. A successful oil well drilled in an area previously unproductive. 4. A tricky or unsound business venture; esp., a worthless mine. —*adj.* 1. Financially unsound or risky. 2. Illegal. —*v.t. & v.i.* **·cat·ted, ·cat·ting** To drill for oil in (an area not known to be productive). —**wild′cat′ting** *n. & adj.*

wildcat strike A strike unauthorized by regular union procedure.

wild·cat·ter (wīld′kat′ər) *n.* 1. A promoter of mines of doubtful value. 2. One who develops oil wells in unproved territory.

wilde·beest (wīld′bēst, wil′də-) *n.* A gnu. [< Afrikaans < Du. *wild* wild + *beeste* beast]

wil·der·ness (wil′dər·nis) *n.* An uninhabited, uncultivated, or barren region. [OE *wilddēor* wild beast]

wild·fire (wīld′fīr′) *n.* A raging, destructive fire: now generally in the phrase **to spread like wildfire.**

wild·flow·er (wīld′flou′ər) *n.* Any uncultivated flowering plant; also, the flower of such a plant. Also **wild flower.**

wild·fowl (wīld′foul′) *n. pl.* **·fowl** (*esp. for def. 2*) or **·fowls** 1. A wild game bird, esp. a wild duck or goose. 2. *pl.* Wild game birds collectively. Also **wild fowl.**

wild-goose chase (wīld′gōōs′) Pursuit of the unknown or unattainable.

wild·life (wīld′līf′) *n.* Wild animals and plants collectively.

wild oat 1. *Usually pl.* An uncultivated grass, esp. a common species of Europe. 2. *pl.* Indiscretions of youth: usu. in the expression **to sow one's wild oats.**

wild pitch In baseball, a misplay charged to the pitcher for throwing a pitch that the catcher could not be expected to catch.

wild rice The grain of a tall aquatic grass of North America.

wild·wood (wīld′wŏŏd′) *n.* Natural forest land.

wile (wīl) *n.* 1. A means of cunning deception; also, any beguiling trick or artifice. 2. Craftiness; cunning. —*v.t.* **wiled, wil·ing** 1. To lure, beguile, or mislead. 2. To pass divertingly, as time: usu. with *away.* [ME *wil,* prob. < Scand.]

wil·ful (wil′fəl) See WILLFUL.

will[1] (wil) *n.* 1. The power of conscious, deliberate action or choice. 2. The act or experience of exercising this power. 3. Strong determination; also, self-control. 4. That which is wanted, chosen, or determined upon: What is the king's *will?* 5. *Law* The legal document declaring a person's intentions as to the disposal of his estate after his death. —*v.* **willed, will·ing** *v.t.* 1. To decide upon; choose. 2. To determine upon as an action or course. 3. To give, devise, or bequeath by a will. —*v.i.* 4. To exercise the will. [OE *willa*] —**will′a·ble** *adj.*

will[2] (wil) *v.* Present: *3rd person sing.* **will;** *Archaic 2nd person sing.* **wilt;** past: **would;** *Archaic 2nd person sing.* **would·est** or **wouldst** An auxiliary verb used to express: 1. Futurity: They *will* arrive by dark. 2. Willingness: Why *will* you not tell the truth? 3. Capability or capacity: The ship *will* survive any storm. 4. Custom or habit: He *will* sit for hours and brood. 5. *Informal* Probability or inference: I expect this *will* be the main street. —*v.t. & v.i.* To wish or have a wish; desire: As you *will.* [OE *willan*]

willed (wild) *adj.* Having a will, esp. one of a given character: usu. in combination: *strong-willed.*

will·ful (wil′fəl) *adj.* 1. Determined to have one's own way; headstrong. 2. Resulting from the exercise of one's own will; voluntary; intentional. Also, *esp. Brit., wilful.* [Cf. OE *wilfullīce* willfully] —**will′ful·ly** *adv.* —**will′·ful·ness** *n.*

wil·lies (wil′ēz) *n.pl.* *Slang* Nervousness: jitters: with *the.* [? < WILLY-NILLY]

will·ing (wil′ing) *adj.* 1. Having the mind favorably disposed. 2. Answering to demand or requirement; compliant. 3. Gladly offered or done; hearty. 4. Of or pertaining to the power of choice; volitional. —**will′ing·ly** *adv.* —**will′ing·ness** *n.*

will-o'-the-wisp (wil′ə·thə·wisp′) *n.* 1. Ignis fatuus. 2. Any elusive or deceptive object. —*adj.* Deceptive; fleeting; misleading. [Earlier *Will with the wisp*]

wil·low (wil′ō) *n.* 1. Any of various shrubs and trees having smooth, often supple branches. 2. The soft white wood of the willow. [OE *welig*] —**wil′low·ish** *adj.*

wil·low·y (wil′ō·ē) *adj.* 1. Abounding in willows. 2. Having supple grace of form or carriage.

will·pow·er (wil′pou′ər) *n.* Ability to control oneself; strength or firmness of mind.

wil·ly-nil·ly (wil′ē·nil′ē) *adj. & adv.* Without decisiveness; uncertain; irresolute. [Earlier *will I, nill I* whether I will or not]

wilt[1] (wilt) *v.i.* 1. To lose freshness; droop or wither. 2. To lose energy and vitality; become faint. —*v.t.* 3. To cause to droop or wither. 4. To cause to lose energy and vitality. —*n.* *Bot.* Any of several plant diseases marked by a wilting of the leaves. [Prob. < obs. *welk* to wither]

wilt[2] (wilt) Archaic second person singular, present tense of WILL[2]: used with *thou.*

wi·ly (wī′lē) *adj.* **·li·er, ·li·est** Full of or characterized by wiles; sly; cunning. —**wi′·li·ly** *adv.* —**wi′li·ness** *n.*

wim·ble (wim′bəl) *n.* An instrument that bores a hole. [< AF, OF *guimbel* < MLG *wiemel*]

wim·ple (wim′pəl) *n.* A cloth worn by

women over the head and under the chin, now used only by nuns. —*v.* •pled, •pling *v.t.* 1. To cover or clothe with a wimple; veil. —*v.i.* 2. To lie in plaits or folds. [OE *wimpel*]

win (win) *v.* **won, win•ning** *v.i.* 1. To gain a victory. 2. To succeed in an effort or endeavor. —*v.t.* 3. To gain victory in; succeed in: to *win* an argument. 4. To gain by effort, as in a competition or contest: to *win* the blue ribbon. 5. To obtain the good will or favor of: She *won* him over. 6. To secure the love of; gain in marriage: He wooed and *won* her. 7. To capture; take possession of. 8. To earn, as a living. —*n.* 1. A victory; success. 2. Profit; winnings. 3. The first position in a race. [OE *winnan* to contend]

wince (wins) *v.i.* **winced, winc•ing** To shrink back or start aside, as from a blow or pain; flinch. [< AF *wenchier*] —**wince** *n.*

winch (winch) *n.* 1. A device used for hoisting, as on a crane, having usu. one or more hand cranks geared to a drum. 2. A crank with a handle, used to impart motion to a grindstone or the like. [OE *wince*] —**winch'er** *n.*

wind[1] (wind; *for n., also poetic* wīnd) *n.* 1. A movement of air. 2. Air pervaded by a scent: The deer got *wind* of the hunter. 3. A suggestion or intimation: to get *wind* of a plot. 4. The power of breathing; breath. 5. Idle chatter. 6. *pl.* The wind instruments of an orchestra. 7. The gaseous product of indigestion; flatulence. —**in the wind** Impending. —*v.t.* 1. To follow by scent. 2. To exhaust the breath of, as by running. 3. To allow to recover breath by resting. 4. To expose to the wind, as in ventilating. [OE]

wind[2] (wīnd) *v.* **wound** (*Rare* **wind•ed**), **wind•ing** *v.t.* 1. To coil (thread, rope, etc.) around some object. 2. To cover with something by coiling or wrapping: to *wind* a spool with thread. 3. To renew the motion of, as a clock, by coiling a spring, etc. 4. To cause to turn and twist. 5. To make (one's way) by a twisting course. 6. To introduce deviously; insinuate: He *wound* himself into my confidence. 7. To raise or hoist, as by means of a capstan or windlass. —*v.i.* 8. To move in a twisting course; meander. 9. To coil or twine about some object. 10. To proceed carefully or deviously. —**to wind up** 1. To bring to conclusion or settlement. 2. In baseball, to swing the arm preparatory to pitching. —*n.* The act of winding, or the condition of being wound; a winding, turn, or twist. [OE *windan*] —**wind'a•ble** *adj.* —**wind'er** *n.*

wind•age (win'dij) *n.* 1. The rush of air caused by the rapid passage of an object. 2. Deflection of an object, as a bullet, from its natural course because of wind pressure.

wind•bag (wind'bag') *n. Informal* A wordy talker.

wind•break (wind'brāk') *n.* Something, as a hedge or fence, that protects from the force of the wind.

Wind•break•er (wind'brā'kər) *n.* A sports jacket fitted at the waist: a trade name. Also **wind'break'er.**

wind•burn (wind'bûrn') *n.* Irritation of the skin, produced by exposure to wind. —**wind'•burn'** *v.t. & v.i.* —**wind'burned'** *adj.*

wind chill factor The temperature of still air adjusted for the chilling effect of wind.

wind•fall (wind'fôl') *n.* 1. Unexpected good fortune. 2. Something, as ripening fruit, brought down by the wind.

wind•flow•er (wind'flou'ər) *n.* The anemone. [Trans. of Gk. *anemōnē* anemone < *anemos* the wind]

wind•ing (wīn'ding) *n.* 1. The act or condition of one who or that which winds. 2. A bend or turn, or a series of them. —*adj.* 1. Turning spirally about an axis or core. 2. Having bends or turns. —**wind'ing•ly** *adv.*

winding sheet (wīn'ding) The sheet that wraps a corpse.

wind instrument (wind) A musical instrument whose sounds are produced by vibrations of air blown into it.

wind•jam•mer (wind'jam'ər) *n.* 1. *Naut.* A merchant sailing vessel. 2. A member of its crew.

wind•lass (wind'ləs) *n.* A device for hauling or lifting, esp. one consisting of a drum, turned by a crank, on which the hoisting rope winds. —*v.t. & v.i.* To raise or haul with a windlass. [< ON *vinda* wind + *ass* beam]

wind•mill (wind'mil') *n.* A mill that operates by the action of the wind against slats or sails attached to a horizontal axis. [< WIND[1] + MILL[1]]

win•dow (win'dō) *n.* 1. An opening in the wall of a building to admit light and air, commonly equipped with movable sashes that enclose one or more panes of glass. 2. A windowpane. 3. Anything resembling or suggesting a window. —*v.t.* To provide with a window or windows. [< ON *vindr* wind + *auga* eye]

win•dow-dress•ing (win'dō•dres'ing) *n.* 1. Display of merchandise in a store window. 2. Anything created to make something else seem better than it really is. —**win'dow-dress'er** *n.*

win•dow•pane (win'dō•pān') *n.* A single sheet of glass for a window. Also **window pane.**

win•dow-shop (win'dō•shop') *v.i.* **-shopped, -shop•ping** To look at goods in store windows without buying them. —**win'dow-shop'per** *n.*

wind•pipe (wind'pīp') *n.* The trachea.

wind•row (wind'rō') *n.* 1. A long row of hay or grain raked together to dry. 2. A wind-swept line of dust, surf, leaves, etc. —*v.t.* To rake or shape into a windrow. —**wind'row'er** *n.*

wind•shield (wind'shēld') *n.* A transparent screen in front of the occupants of an automobile that protects against wind and weather.

wind•sock (wind'sok') *n. Meteorol.* A large conical bag mounted at an airport, etc., to indicate the direction of the wind. Also **wind sleeve.**

wind•storm (wind'stôrm') *n.* A violent wind, usu. with little or no precipitation.

wind tunnel *Aeron.* A large cylindrical structure in which the aerodynamic properties of airplane models, airfoils, etc., can be observed under the effects of artificially produced winds.

wind-up (wīnd'up') *n.* 1. The act of concluding or closing; conclusion; finish. 2. In baseball, the swing of the arm preparatory to pitching the ball.

wind·ward (wind′wərd) *adj.* Moving toward or situated on the side facing the wind. —*n.* The direction from which the wind blows. —*adv.* Toward the wind. Opposed to *leeward.*

wind·y (win′dē) *adj.* **wind·i·er, wind·i·est** 1. Having or exposed to much wind. 2. Long-winded; verbose; bombastic. [OE *windig*] —**wind′i·ly** *adv.* —**wind′i·ness** *n.*

wine (wīn) *n.* 1. The fermented juice of the grape, commonly used as a beverage and in cooking. 2. The fermented juice of some other fruit or plant. 3. A dark purplish red, the color of certain wines. —*v.t. & v.i.* **wined, win·ing** To entertain with or drink wine. —**to wine and dine** To entertain or feed in a lavish way. [OE *wīn* < L *vinum*]

wine cellar A storage place for wines; also, the wines stored.

wine-col·ored (wīn′kul′ərd) *adj.* Having the color of red wine; dark purplish red.

wine·grow·er (wīn′grō′ər) *n.* One who cultivates a vineyard and makes wine. —**wine′grow′ing** *adj. & n.*

wine·press (wīn′pres′) *n.* An apparatus or a place where the juice of grapes is expressed. Also **wine′press′er.**

win·er·y (wī′nər·ē) *n. pl.* **·er·ies** An establishment for making wine.

wing (wing) *n.* 1. An organ of flight; esp., one of a pair of movable appendages of a bird, bat, or insect. 2. Anything resembling a wing, as in form, function, or position. 3. The act or means of flying; flight. 4. Either of two opposed groups in a political or other organization: the left *wing.* 5. *Archit.* An extension of a building. 6. *Aeron.* One of the main sustaining surfaces of an airplane. 7. In a theater, one of the two sides of the stage not seen by an audience. 8. *Mil.* The right or left section of a military force. 9. A unit of the U.S. Air Force. 10. *Slang* An arm, esp. in baseball. 11. In hockey, a position on either side of the center. —**on (or upon) the wing** 1. In flight. 2. Departing; also, journeying. —**under one's wing** Under one's protection. —*v.t.* 1. To pass over or through in flight. 2. To accomplish by flying. 3. To cause to go swiftly; speed. 4. To wound in the wing or arm. —*v.i.* 5. To fly; soar. —**to wing it** *Informal* To improvise. [< ON *vængr*] —**wing′less** *adj.*

wing chair A large upholstered arm chair with high back and side pieces.

wing·ding (wing′ding′) *n. Slang* A lively, often lavish, party. [Origin unknown]

winged (wingd; *also poetic* wing′id) *adj.* 1. Having wings. 2. Passing swiftly; soaring.

wing·spread (wing′spred′) *n.* The distance between the tips of the fully extended wings of a bird, insect, or airplane. Also **wing′span′** (-span′).

wink (wingk) *v.i.* 1. To close and open the eye or eyelids quickly. 2. To move one eyelid as a sign. 3. To pretend not to see: usu. with *at.* 4. To flicker; twinkle. —*v.t.* 5. To close and open (the eye or eyelids) quickly. —*n.* 1. The act of winking. 2. A short time. 3. A twinkle; gleam. 4. A hint conveyed by winking. [OE *wincian* to close the eyes]

win·ner (win′ər) *n.* One who or that which wins.

win·ning (win′ing) *adj.* 1. Successful in competition. 2. Charming; attractive; winsome. —*n.* 1. The act of one who wins. 2. *Usu. pl.* That which is won; esp., money won in gambling.

win·now (win′ō) *v.t.* 1. To separate (grain) from (chaff). 2. To select or sort: often with *out.* —*v.i.* 3. To separate grain from chaff. —*n.* Any device used in winnowing grain. [OE *wind* the wind] —**win′now·er** *n.*

win·o (wī′nō) *n. pl.* **·nos** *Slang* An alcoholic; esp., a derelict who drinks cheap wine.

win·some (win′səm) *adj.* Charming or pleasing; attractive. [OE *wyn* joy] —**win′·some·ly** *adv.* —**win′some·ness** *n.*

win·ter (win′tər) *n.* 1. The coldest season of the year, occurring between autumn and spring. ◆Collateral adjective: *hibernal.* 2. A period of time marked by coldness, cheerlessness, or lack of life. —*v.i.* 1. To pass the winter. —*v.t.* 2. To care for, feed, or protect during the winter: to *winter* animals. —*adj.* 1. Of or taking place in winter; hibernal. 2. Suitable to or characteristic of winter. [OE]

win·ter·green (win′tər·grēn) *n.* 1. A small evergreen plant of North America, bearing aromatic oval leaves that yield an oil (**oil of wintergreen**) used as a flavor. 2. The flavor of this oil.

win·ter·ize (win′tə·rīz) *v.t.* **·ized, ·iz·ing** To prepare or equip (engines, etc.) for winter.

win·ter·kill (win′tər·kil′) *v.t. & v.i.* To die or kill by exposure to extreme cold: said of plants and grains.

win·try (win′trē) *adj.* **·tri·er, ·tri·est** Of or like winter; cold; frosty. Also **win′ter·y** (-tər·ē). [OE *wintrig*] —**win′tri·ly** *adv.* —**win′tri·ness** *n.*

win·y (wī′nē) *adj.* **win·i·er, win·i·est** Having the taste or qualities of wine.

wipe (wīp) *v.t.* **wiped, wip·ing** 1. To clean or dry by rubbing, usu. with some soft, absorbent material. 2. To remove by or as if by rubbing: usu. with *away* or *off.* 3. To apply by wiping: usu. with *on.* 4. To draw or pass across. —**to wipe out** To remove or destroy utterly. —*n.* The act of wiping or rubbing. [OE *wīpian*] —**wip′er** *n.*

wire (wīr) *n.* 1. A strand of ductile metal. 2. Something made of wire, as a fence, a snare, etc. 3. A telegraph or telephone cable. 4. The telegraph system: sent by *wire.* 5. A telegram. —*v.* **wired, wir·ing** *v.t.* 1. To fasten with wire. 2. To furnish or equip with wiring. 3. To transmit or send by electric telegraph: to *wire* an order. 4. To send a telegram to. —*v.i.* 5. To telegraph. [OE *wīr*]

wire-haired terrier (wīr′hârd′) A fox terrier having a wiry coat. Also **wire′hair′** (-hâr′).

wire·less (wīr′lis) *adj.* 1. Having no wire or wires. 2. *Brit.* Radio. —*n.* 1. The wireless telegraph or telephone system, or a message transmitted by either. 2. *Brit.* Radio. —*v.t. & v.i. Brit.* To communicate (with) by wireless telegraphy.

Wire·pho·to (wīr′fō′tō) *n. pl.* **·tos** An apparatus and method for transmitting and receiving photographs by wire: a trade name. Also **wire′pho′to.**

wire service A news agency that collects and

distributes news to subscribing newspapers, radio stations, etc.

wire·tap·ping (wīr′tap′ing) *n.* The act, process, or practice of tapping telephone or telegraph wires for the purpose of secretly securing information: also called *wiretap.* **—wire′tap′** *v.t. & v.i.* **·tapped, ·tap·ping** **—wire′tap′per** *n.*

wir·ing (wīr′ing) *n.* An entire system of wire installed for the distribution of electric power.

wir·y (wīr′ē) *adj.* **wir·i·er, wir·i·est** 1. Tough and sinewy. 2. Like wire; stiff. **—wir′i·ly** *adv.* **—wir′i·ness** *n.*

wis·dom (wiz′dəm) *n.* 1. Knowledge; learning. 2. Practical judgment; insight; common sense. [OE *wīsdōm* < *wīs* wise]

wisdom tooth The last molar tooth on either side of the upper and lower jaws in humans.

wise[1] (wīz) *adj.* **wis·er, wis·est** 1. Possessed of or marked by wisdom. 2. Sagacious; shrewd; crafty. 3. *Informal* Aware of; onto: *wise* to his motives. 4. *Slang* Arrogant or sarcastic. [OE *wīs*] **—wise′ly** *adv.* **—wise′·ness** *n.*

wise[2] (wīz) *n.* Way of doing; manner; method: chiefly in the phrases **in any wise, in no wise,** etc. [OE *wīse* manner]

-wise *suffix of adverbs* In a (specified) way or manner: *nowise, likewise*: often equivalent to *-ways.* [OE *wīse* manner]

wise·a·cre (wīz′ā′kər) *n.* One who affects great wisdom. [< MDu. *wijsseggher* soothsayer]

wise·crack (wīz′krak′) *Slang n.* A smart or supercilious remark. **—***v.i.* To utter a wisecrack. **—wise′crack′er** *n.*

wish (wish) *n.* 1. A desire or longing, usu. for some definite thing. 2. An expression of such a desire. 3. Something wished for. **—***v.t.* 1. To have a desire or longing for; want. 2. To invoke upon or for someone: I *wished* him good luck. 3. To request or entreat; also, to command: I *wish* you would be quiet. **—***v.i.* 4. To have or feel a desire; yearn; long: usu. with *for.* 5. To make or express a wish. [OE *wȳscan*]

wish·bone (wish′bōn′) *n.* The forked bone formed by the united clavicles in many birds. [from the practice of breaking it while making a wish]

wish·ful (wish′fəl) *adj.* Having a wish or desire; full of longing. **—wish′ful·ly** *adv.* **—wish′ful·ness** *n.*

wish·y-wash·y (wish′ē·wosh′ē, -wôsh′ē) *adj. Informal* Lacking character or resolution; indecisive; weak.

wisp (wisp) *n.* 1. A small bunch, as of hair. 2. A small bit: a *wisp* of vapor. [ME *wisp, wips*] **—wisp′y** *adj.*

wist (wist) Past tense and past participle of WIT[2].

wis·ter·i·a (wis·tir′ē·ə) *n.* Any of various woody twining shrubs of the bean family, with clusters of blue, purple, or white flowers. Also **wis·tar′i·a** (-târ′ē·ə). [after Caspar *Wistar*, 1761–1818, U.S. anatomist]

wist·ful (wist′fəl) *adj.* Wishful; longing; yearning. [Appar. < obs. *wistly* intently] **—wist′ful·ly** *adv.* **—wist′ful·ness** *n.*

wit[1] (wit) *n.* 1. The power of knowing, perceiving, or judging. 2. *pl.* The faculties of perception and understanding. 3. *pl.* One's sanity: out of her *wits.* 4. The perception and expression of amusing relations among ideas. 5. One who is cleverly amusing. [OE]

wit[2] (wit) *v.t. & v.i.* **wist, wit·ting** Present indicative: I wot, thou wost, he wot, we, you, they wite(n) *Archaic* To be or become aware (of); learn; know. **—to wit** That is to say; namely. [OE *witan* to know]

witch[1] (wich) *n.* 1. A woman who practices sorcery or is believed to have supernatural powers, esp. to work evil, and usu. by association with evil spirits or the devil. 2. An ugly, malignant old woman; a hag. 3. A bewitching woman. [OE *wicce* witch, fem. of *wicca* wizard]

witch[2] (wich), **witch-elm** (wich′elm′) See WYCH-ELM.

witch·craft (wich′kraft′) *n.* 1. The practices or powers of witches or wizards: also called *black magic.* 2. Extraordinary influence or fascination.

witch doctor A sorcerer in a primitive society.

witch·er·y (wich′ər·ē) *n. pl.* **·er·ies** 1. Witchcraft. 2. Power to charm; fascination.

witch hazel 1. A shrub with several branching, crooked trunks and small yellow flowers. 2. An ointment and extract derived from the bark and dried leaves of this shrub. [< WITCH[2] + HAZEL]

witch′hunt *Informal* An investigation of persons ostensibly to uncover subversive activities, but intended to harass political opposition. **—witch-hunt·ing** (wich′hun′·ting) *adj. & n.* **—witch-hunt·er** (wich′·hun′tər) *n.*

witch·ing (wich′ing) *adj.* Having power to enchant; fascinating. **—***n.* Witchcraft; sorcery. **—witch′ing·ly** *adv.*

with (with, with) *prep.* 1. In the company of. 2. Next to; beside: Walk *with* me. 3. Having: a hat *with* a feather. 4. Characterized by: the house *with* green shutters. 5. Among: counted *with* the others. 6. In the course of: We forget *with* time. 7. Separated from: to dispense *with* luxury. 8. Against: to struggle *with* an adversary. 9. In the opinion of: That is all right *with* me. 10. Because of: faint *with* hunger. 11. In possession of: Leave the key *with* the janitor. 12. By means of: to write *with* a pencil. 13. By adding: trimmed *with* lace. 14. In spite of: *With* all his money, he could not buy health. 15. At the same time as: to go to bed *with* the chickens. 16. In the same direction as: to drift *with* the crowd. 17. In regard to: I am angry *with* them. 18. Onto; to: Join this tube *with* that one. 19. In proportion to: His fame grew *with* his deeds. 20. Of the same opinion as: I'm *with* you there! 21. Compared to: Consider this book *with* that one. 22. Immediately after: *With* that, he slammed the door. 23. Having received or been granted: *With* your consent I'll go. [OE]

with- *prefix* 1. Against: *withstand.* 2. Back; away: *withhold.* [OE *with-* < *with* against]

with·al (with·ôl′, with-) *Archaic adv.* With the rest; in addition. **—***prep.* With: intensive form used after its object: a bow to shoot *withal.* [ME *with* + *alle* all]

with·draw (with·drô′, with-) *v.* **·drew, ·drawn, ·draw·ing** *v.t.* 1. To draw or take away; remove. 2. To take back, as a promise. —*v.i.* 3. To draw back; retire. —**with·draw′al** *n.*

with·drawn (with·drôn′, with-) *adj.* Lacking in emotional responsiveness.

withe (with, with, with) *n.* A willowy, supple twig, used for binding. [OE *withthe*]

with·er (with′ər) *v.i.* 1. To become limp or dry, as a plant deprived of moisture. 2. To waste, as flesh. 3. To droop or languish. —*v.t.* 4. To cause to become limp or dry. 5. To abash, as by a scornful glance. [Appar. var. of WEATHER, v.]

with·ers (with′ərz) *n.pl.* The highest part of the back of the horse between the shoulder blades. [OE]

with·hold (with·hōld′, with-) *v.t.* **·held, ·hold·ing** 1. To hold back; restrain. 2. To keep back; decline to grant. 3. To deduct (taxes, social security payments, etc.) from one's wages. —**with·hold′er** *n.*

withholding tax A part of an employee's wages that is deducted as an installment on his income tax.

with·in (with·in′, with-) *prep.* 1. In the inner part of; inside. 2. In the limits, range, or compass of: *within* two hours. 3. In the reach, limit, or scope of: *within* my power. —*n.* The inside: a revolt from *within.* —*adv.* 1. Inside. 2. Indoors. 3. Inside one's mind, heart, or body. [OE *with* with + *innan* in]

with·out (with·out′, with-) *prep.* 1. Not having; lacking: They are *without* a home. 2. In the absence of: We must manage *without* help. 3. Free from: *without* fear. 4. At, on, or to the outside of. 5. With avoidance of: He listened *without* paying attention. —*adv.* 1. In or on the outer part. 2. Out of doors. [OE *with* with + *ūtan* out]

with·stand (with·stand′, with-) *v.t.* **·stood, ·stand·ing** To oppose or resist successfully. [OE *with-* against + *standan* to stand]

wit·less (wit′lis) *adj.* Lacking in wit; foolish. [OE *witlēas*] —**wit′less·ly** *adv.* —**wit′less·ness** *n.*

wit·ness (wit′nis) *n.* 1. A person who has seen or knows something, and is therefore competent to give evidence concerning it; a spectator. 2. That which serves as evidence or proof. 3. *Law* **a** One who has knowledge of facts relating to a given case and is subpoenaed to testify. **b** A person who testifies to the genuineness of another's signature. 4. An attestation to a fact or an event; testimony: usu. in the phrase **to bear witness.** —*v.t.* 1. To see or know by personal experience. 2. To serve as evidence of. 3. To give testimony to. 4. To be the site or scene of: This spot has *witnessed* many heinous crimes. 5. *Law* To sign (an instrument) as a witness. [OE *witnes* knowledge, testimony] —**wit′ness·er** *n.*

wit·ted (wit′id) *adj.* Having (a specified kind of) wit: used in combination: *quick-witted.*

wit·ti·cism (wit′ə·siz′əm) *n.* A witty saying. [< WITTY]

wit·ting (wit′ing) *adj.* Intentional; deliberate. [< WIT[2]] —**wit′ting·ly** *adv.*

wit·ty (wit′ē) *adj.* **·ti·er, ·ti·est** Cleverly amusing. [OE *wittig* wise] —**wit′ti·ly** *adv.* —**wit′ti·ness** *n.*

wives (wīvz) Plural of WIFE.

wiz (wiz) *n. Slang* A wizard (def. 2).

wiz·ard (wiz′ərd) *n.* 1. A male witch; sorcerer. 2. *Informal* A very skillful or clever person: a *wizard* with machinery. [OE *wis* wise] —**wiz′ard·ry** *n.*

wiz·ened (wiz′ənd) *adj.* Shrunken; withered; dried up. [OE *wisnian* to dry up, wither]

woad (wōd) *n.* 1. An Old World herb of the mustard family. 2. The blue dyestuff obtained from its leaves. [OE *wād*] —**woad′ed** *adj.*

wob·ble (wob′əl) *v.* **·bled, ·bling** *v.i.* 1. To move or sway unsteadily. 2. To show indecision; vacillate. —*v.t.* 3. To cause to wobble. —*n.* An unsteady motion. [? < LG *wabbeln*] —**wob′bler** *n.* —**wob′bling·ly** *adv.* —**wob′bly** *adj.*

woe (wō) *n.* 1. Overwhelming sorrow; grief. 2. Great trouble or calamity; disaster. —*interj.* Alas! Also *Archaic* **wo.** [OE *wā* misery]

woe·be·gone (wō′bi·gôn′, -gon′) *adj.* Overcome with woe; mournful; sorrowful. Also **wo′be·gone′.**

woe·ful (wō′fəl) *adj.* 1. Accompanied by or causing woe; direful. 2. Expressive of sorrow; doleful. 3. Paltry; miserable; mean. —**woe′ful·ly** *adv.* —**woe′ful·ness** *n.*

wok (wok) *n.* A bowl-shaped pan used in Chinese cooking. [< Cantonese]

woke (wōk) Past tense of WAKE[1].

wok·en (wō′kən) Dialectal and alternative British past participle of WAKE[1].

wolf (wo͝olf) *n. pl.* **wolves** (wo͝olvz) 1. Any of numerous carnivorous mammals related to the dog. ◆Collateral adjective: *lupine.* 2. Any ravenous, cruel, or rapacious person. 3. *Slang* A man who flirts with many women. —**to cry wolf** To give a false alarm. —*v.t.* To devour ravenously; gulp down. [OE *wulf*] —**wolf′ish** *adj.* —**wolf′ish·ly** *adv.* —**wolf′ish·ness** *n.*

wolf·hound (wo͝olf′hound′) *n.* Either of two breeds of large dogs, the Russian wolfhound (or borzoi) and the Irish wolfhound, originally trained to hunt wolves.

wolf·ram (wo͝ol′frəm) *n.* 1. Wolframite. 2. Tungsten. [< G, prob. < *wolf* wolf + *rahm* cream, soot]

wolf·ram·ite (wo͝ol′frəm·īt) *n.* A grayish black or brown mineral of iron and magnesium that is an important source of tungsten. [< G *wolfram* tungsten]

wolf's-bane (wo͝olfs′bān′) *n.* 1. Aconite. 2. A species of European arnica, a perennial herb, used as a lotion for bruises. [< Gk. *lykos* wolf + *kteinein* to kill]

wol·ver·ine (wo͝ol′və·rēn′) *n.* A rapacious carnivore of northern forests, with stout body and limbs and bushy tail. Also **wol′·ver·ene′.** [Dim. of WOLF]

wolves (wo͝olvz) Plural of WOLF.

wom·an (wo͝om′ən) *n. pl.* **wom·en** (wim′in) 1. An adult human female. 2. Women collectively. 3. Womanly character; femininity. 4. A female servant. [OE *wīf* wife + *mann* human being] —**wom′an·hood** *n.* —**wom′an·li·ness** *n.* —**wom′an·ly** *adj.*

wom·an·ish (wo͝om′ən·ish) *adj.* 1. Characteristic of a woman; womanly. 2. Effeminate; unmanly. —**wom′an·ish·ly** *adv.* —**wom′an·ish·ness** *n.*

wom·an·ize (wo͝om′ən·īz) *v.* **·ized, ·iz·ing**

v.t. 1. To make effeminate or womanish. —*v.i.* 2. To philander. —**wom′an·iz′er** *n.*

wom·an·kind (wŏŏm′ən·kīnd′) *n.* Women collectively.

womb (wōōm) *n.* 1. The uterus. 2. The place where anything is engendered or brought into life. [OE *wamb* the belly]

wom·bat (wom′bat) *n.* An Australian nocturnal marsupial resembling a small bear. [< Austral.]

wom·en (wim′in) Plural of WOMAN.

wom·en·folk (wim′in·fōk′) *n.pl.* Women collectively. Also **wom′en·folks′**.

won[1] (wun) Past tense and past participle of WIN.

won[2] (won) *n.* The monetary unit of North and South Korea.

won·der (wun′dər) *n.* 1. A feeling of mingled surprise and curiosity; astonishment. 2. That which causes wonder; a strange thing; a miracle. —*v.t.* 1. To be curious and doubtful about. —*v.i.* 2. To be filled with wonder; marvel. 3. To be doubtful; want to know. [OE *wundor*] —**won′der·er** *n.* —**won′der·ing** *adj.* —**won′der·ing·ly** *adv.*

won·der·ful (wun′dər·fəl) *adj.* Astonishing; incredible; marvelous. —**won′der·ful·ly** *adv.* —**won′der·ful·ness** *n.*

won·der·land (wun′dər·land′) *n.* A real or imaginary place that is full of wonders.

won·der·ment (wun′dər·mənt) *n.* 1. The emotion of wonder; surprise. 2. Something wonderful; a marvel.

won·drous (wun′drəs) *adj.* Wonderful; marvelous. —*adv.* Surprisingly. —**won′drous·ly** *adv.* —**won′drous·ness** *n.*

wont (wunt, wōnt) *adj.* Accustomed; used: He is *wont* to smoke after dinner. —*n.* Customary practice; habit. [OE pp. of *gewunian* to be accustomed]

won't (wōnt) Will not. [ME *woll not*]

wont·ed (wun′tid, wōn′-) *adj.* Customary; habitual. —**wont′ed·ness** *n.*

woo (wōō) *v.t.* 1. To seek the love of, esp. in order to marry; court. 2. To entreat earnestly; try to win over. —*v.i.* 3. To pay court. [OE *wōgian*]

wood (wŏŏd) *n.* 1. The hard, fibrous material beneath the bark of a tree or shrub. 2. Lumber; timber; firewood. 3. *Often pl.* A large, dense growth of trees; forest; grove. 4. Something made of wood. 5. *pl.* A rural district; backwoods. —*adj.* 1. Made of wood. 2. Made for using or holding wood. 3. Living or growing in woods. [OE *wudu*] —**wood′ed** *adj.* —**wood′less** *adj.*

wood alcohol Methanol.

wood·bine (wŏŏd′bīn) *n.* 1. The common honeysuckle of Europe. 2. The Virginia creeper. Also **wood′bind** (-bīnd). [OE *wudu* wood + *bindan* to bind]

wood·block (wŏŏd′blok′) *n.* 1. A block of wood prepared for engraving. 2. A woodcut.

wood·chuck (wŏŏd′chuk′) *n.* A marmot of eastern North America, having a chunky body and a brown, bristly coat: also called *ground hog.* [By folk etymology < Ojibwa *wejack*]

wood·cock (wŏŏd′kok′) *n.* 1. A small European game bird having the thighs entirely feathered. 2. A related North American bird. [OE *wuducocc*]

wood·craft (wŏŏd′kraft′) *n.* 1. Skill in things pertaining to woodland life, as hunting and trapping. 2. Skill in woodwork or in constructing articles of wood. —**wood′·crafts′man** (-krafts′mən) *n.*

wood·cut (wŏŏd′kut′) *n.* 1. An engraved block of wood. 2. A print from such a block. Also called *woodblock.*

wood·cut·ter (wŏŏd′kut′ər) *n.* One who cuts or chops wood. —**wood′cut′ting** *n.*

wood·en (wŏŏd′n) *adj.* 1. Made of wood. 2. Stiff; clumsy; awkward. 3. Dull; spiritless. —**wood′en·ly** *adv.* —**wood′en·ness** *n.*

wood·land (wŏŏd′lənd; *for n., also* wŏŏd′land′) *n.* Land covered with woods or trees. —*adj.* Belonging to or dwelling in the woods. —**wood′land·er** *n.*

wood nymph A nymph of the forest; dryad.

wood·peck·er (wŏŏd′pek′ər) *n.* Any of various birds having stiff tail feathers, strong claws, and a sharp, chisellike bill for drilling holes in trees.

wood·pile (wŏŏd′pīl′) *n.* A pile of wood, esp. of wood cut for burning.

wood pulp Wood reduced to pulp, used for making paper.

woods·man (wŏŏdz′mən) *n. pl.* **·men** (-mən) 1. A woodcutter; lumberman. 2. One who works or lives in a forest. 3. A man skilled in woodcraft. Also **wood′man.**

woods·y (wŏŏd′zē) *adj.* **woods·i·er, woods·i·est** *Informal* Of, like, or dwelling in the woods.

wood thrush A large woodland thrush of North America, noted for its song.

wood·wind (wŏŏd′wind′) *n. Music* 1. One of a group of wind instruments, as an oboe, bassoon, clarinet, flute, etc. 2. *pl.* The section of an orchestra made up of such instruments. —**wood′wind′** *adj.*

wood·work (wŏŏd′wûrk′) *n.* 1. The wooden parts of any structure, esp. interior wooden parts, as moldings or doors. 2. Work made of wood. —**wood′work′er** *n.* —**wood′·work′ing** *n.*

wood·y (wŏŏd′ē) *adj.* **wood·i·er, wood·i·est** 1. Of the nature of or containing wood. 2. Of or like wood. 3. Covered with woods. —**wood′i·ness** *n.*

woof (wŏŏf) *n.* 1. The weft; the threads carried back and forth across the fixed threads of the warp in a loom. 2. The texture of a fabric. [OE *on* on + *wefan* to weave]

woof·er (wŏŏf′ər) *n. Electronics* A loudspeaker used to reproduce low frequencies. Compare TWEETER. [< *woof*, imit. of a dog's growl]

wool (wŏŏl) *n.* 1. The fleece of sheep and some allied animals. 2. Material or garments made of wool. 3. A substance resembling wool. —*adj.* Woolen. [OE *wull*]

wool·en (wŏŏl′ən) *adj.* 1. Made of or like wool. 2. Of wool or its manufacture. —*n.pl.* Woolen cloth or clothing. Also **wool′len.** [OE *wullen, wyllen*]

wool·gath·er·ing (wŏŏl′gath′ər·ing) *n.* Idle daydreaming. —**wool′gath′er·er** *n.*

wool·ly (wŏŏl′ē) *adj.* **·li·er, ·li·est** 1. Made of, covered with, or resembling wool. 2. Lacking clearness; fuzzy; blurry. 3. Rough and exciting: usu. in the phrase **wild and woolly.** —*n. pl.* **·lies** A garment made of wool, esp. underwear. Also **wool′y.** —**wool′·li·ness** *n.*

wool·sack (wŏŏl′sak′) *n.* 1. A sack of wool.

2. The chair of the lord chancellor in the English House of Lords, a cushion stuffed with wool. 3. The office of lord high chancellor.

wooz·y (wōō′zē) *adj.* **wooz·i·er, wooz·i·est** *Slang* Befuddled, esp. with drink; dazed. [Prob. < *wooze*, var. of OOZE] **—wooz′i·ly** *adv.* **—wooz′i·ness** *n.*

word (wûrd) *n.* 1. A linguistic form that can meaningfully be spoken in isolation. 2. The letters or characters that stand for such a linguistic form. 3. *Usu. pl.* Conversation; talk: a man of few *words*. 4. A brief remark. 5. A communication or message; information: Send him *word*. 6. A command, signal, or direction: Give the *word* to start. 7. A promise: a man of his *word*. 8. A watchword. 9. *pl.* Language used in anger: They had *words*. **—in a word** In short; briefly. **—the Word** The Scriptures. **—to break one's word** To violate one's promise. **—to eat one's words** To retract something that one has said. **—to mince words** To be evasive. **—word for word** In exactly the same words; verbatim. **—*v.t.*** To express in words. [OE]

word·age (wûr′dij) *n.* 1. Words collectively. 2. The number of words used in a piece of writing.

word·ing (wûr′ding) *n.* The style used to express something in words; phraseology.

word·less (wûrd′lis) *adj.* Having no words; inarticulate; silent. **—word′less·ly** *adv.* **—word′less·ness** *n.*

word processing The use of stored information to produce typed letters, reports, etc., with automated equipment. **—word′-proc′ess·ing** *adj.*

word·y (wûr′dē) *adj.* **word·i·er, word·i·est** Using or containing too many words; verbose. [OE *wordig*] **—word′i·ly** *adv.* **—word′i·ness** *n.*

wore (wôr) Past tense of WEAR.

work (wûrk) *n.* 1. Continued exertion directed to some end; labor. 2. One's job or occupation. 3. Employment: to look for *work*. 4. A place of employment: Is he at home or at *work*? 5. Something to be done; task. 6. That which is produced by thought and effort, as a building, book, song, etc. 7. A feat or deed. 8. *pl.* (*usu. construed as sing*). An industrial plant. 9. *pl.* Running gear or machinery, as of a watch. 10. *pl. Slang* The whole of anything: the whole *works*. 11. *Physics* A transference of energy from one body to another resulting in the motion or displacement of the body acted upon, expressed as the product of the force and the amount of displacement in the line of its action. **—*v.*** **worked** (*Archaic* **wrought**), **work·ing** *v.i.* 1. To perform work; labor; toil. 2. To be employed in some trade or business. 3. To perform a function; operate: The machine *works* well. 4. To prove effective; succeed: His stratagem *worked*. 5. To move or progress gradually or with difficulty: He *worked* up in his profession. 6. To become as specified, as by gradual motion: The bolts *worked* loose. 7. To undergo kneading, hammering, etc.; be shaped: Copper *works* easily. 8. To ferment. **—*v.t.*** 9. To cause or bring about. 10. To direct the operation of: to *work* a machine. 11. To make, shape, or decorate by toil or skill. 12. To prepare, as by manipulating, hammering, etc.: to *work* dough. 13. To cause to be productive, as by toil: to *work* a mine. 14. To cause to do work: He *works* his employees too hard. 15. To cause to be as specified, usu. with effort: We *worked* the timer into position. 16. To make or achieve by effort: He *worked* his way through the narrow tunnel. 17. To solve, as a problem in arithmetic. 18. To cause to move: to *work* one's jaws. 19. To excite; provoke: He *worked* himself into a passion. 20. To influence or manage, as by insidious means; lead. **—to work off** To get rid of, as extra flesh by exercise. **—to work on** (or **upon**) To try to influence or persuade. **—to work out** 1. To make its way out or through. 2. To effect by work or effort; accomplish. 3. To develop; form, as a plan. 4. To solve. 5. To prove effective or successful. 6. To result as specified: It *worked out* badly. 7. To exercise. **—to work over** 1. To do over; revise. 2. *Slang* To beat up severely. **—to work up** 1. To excite; rouse. 2. To form or shape by working; develop. [OE *weorc*]

-work *combining form* 1. A product made from a (specified) material: *brickwork*. 2. Work of a (given) kind: *piecework*. 3. Work performed in a (specified) place: *housework*. [< WORK]

work·a·ble (wûr′kə·bəl) *adj.* 1. Capable of being worked. 2. Capable of being put into effect, as a plan; practicable. **—work′a·bil′i·ty, work′a·ble·ness** *n.*

work·a·day (wûrk′ə·dā′) *adj.* 1. Of, pertaining to, or suitable for working days; everyday. 2. Commonplace; prosaic. [Alter. of ME *werkeday* < OE *weorca* work + DAY]

work·a·hol·ic (wûrk′ə·hôl′ik, -hol′-) *n.* *Informal* A person addicted to working. [< WORK + *-aholic*, after *alcoholic*]

work·bench (wûrk′bench′) *n.* A table for work, as that of a carpenter or machinist.

work·book (wûrk′bōōk′) *n.* A booklet based on a course of study and containing problems and exercises.

work·day (wûrk′dā′) *n.* 1. A day in which work is done; a day not a holiday. 2. The part of the day spent in work.

work·er (wûr′kər) *n.* 1. One who does work for a living; esp., a laborer. 2. A sexually undeveloped insect in a colony, as an ant, bee, or termite.

work·horse (wûrk′hôrs′) *n.* 1. A horse used for pulling loads. 2. A responsible and diligent worker.

work·house (wûrk′hous′) *n.* 1. *Brit.* A house for paupers able to work. 2. An industrial prison for petty offenders.

work·ing (wûr′king) *adj.* 1. That works. 2. Engaged actively in some employment. 3. That performs a function; that upon which further work may be based: a *working* model: a *working* hypothesis. 4. Relating to or used in work. **—*n.*** 1. The act of one who works. 2. A manner of functioning. 3. *Usu. pl.* The part of a mine or quarry where excavation is going on.

working capital 1. That part of the finances of a business available for its operation. 2. The amount of quick assets that exceed current liabilities.

work·ing·man (wûr′king·man′) *n. pl.* **·men** (-men′) A male worker; laborer.

work·ing·wom·an (wûr′king·wŏŏm′ən) *n.* *pl.* **·wom·en** (-wim′in) A female worker; laborer.

work·load (wûrk′lōd′) *n.* The amount of work apportioned to a person, machine, or department over a given period.

work·man (wûrk′mən) *n.* *pl.* **·men** (-mən) 1. One whose job involves manual labor. 2. Workingman. **—work′man·ly** *adv.*

work·man·like (wûrk′mən·līk) *adj.* Skillfully done; well-made. **—work′man·ly** *adv.*

work·man·ship (wûrk′mən·ship) *n.* The art or skill of a workman, or the quality of work.

work·out (wûrk′out′) *n.* *Informal* 1. A test, trial, practice performance, etc. 2. Any activity involving considerable effort; esp., running, calisthenics, or other physical exercise.

work·shop (wûrk′shop′) *n.* 1. A building or room where any work is carried on; workroom. 2. A seminar for discussing or studying a subject, solving problems, etc.

work·week (wûrk′wēk′) *n.* The number of hours worked in a week; also, the number of working hours in a week.

world (wûrld) *n.* 1. The earth. 2. A part of the earth: the Old *World.* 3. The universe. 4. A division of existing things belonging to the earth: the animal *world.* 5. The human inhabitants of the earth; mankind. 6. A definite class of people having certain interests or activities in common: the scientific *world.* 7. A sphere or domain: the *world* of letters. 8. Secular, social, or public life; worldly matters or aims. 9. A great quantity or number: a *world* of trouble. 10. Any condition or state: the *world* of the future. **—for all the world** In every respect. **—on top of the world** *Informal* Elated. **—out of this world** *Informal* Extraordinarily good. [OE *weorold, woruld*]

world·ly (wûrld′lē) *adj.* **·li·er, ·li·est** 1. Of or devoted to this world and its concerns rather than religious or spiritual matters; earthly; secular. 2. Sophisticated; worldly-wise. **—world′li·ness** *n.*

world·ly-wise (wûrld′lē·wīz′) *adj.* Wise in the ways and affairs of the world; sophisticated.

world·wide (wûrld′wīd′) *adj.* Extended throughout the world.

worm (wûrm) *n.* 1. A small, limbless invertebrate with an elongated, soft body, as a flatworm. ◆Collateral adjective: *vermicular.* 2. Loosely, any small, creeping animal having a slender body and short or undeveloped limbs, as an insect larva. 3. A despicable, groveling, or abject person. 4. Something like a worm in appearance or movement. 5. *pl.* An intestinal disorder due to the presence of parasitic worms. **—*v.t.*** 1. To insinuate (oneself or itself) in a wormlike manner: with *in* or *into.* 2. To draw forth by artful means, as a secret: with *out.* 3. To free from intestinal worms. **—*v.i.*** 4. To move or progress slowly and stealthily. 5. To insinuate oneself by artful means: with *into.* [OE *wyrm*]

worm-eat·en (wûrm′ēt′n) *adj.* 1. Eaten or bored through by worms. 2. Worn-out or decayed, as by time.

worm gear *Mech.* A gear formed by a toothed wheel (**worm wheel**) meshed to a rotating threaded screw (**worm screw**).

worm·hole (wûrm′hōl′) *n.* The hole made by a worm or termite. **—worm′holed′** *adj.*

worm·wood (wûrm′wŏŏd′) *n.* 1. Any of various European herbs or small shrubs related to the sagebrush; esp., a common species that is aromatic and bitter and is used in making absinthe. 2. That which embitters or makes bitter; bitterness. [Alter. of obs. *wermōd* < OE]

worm·y (wûr′mē) *adj.* **worm·i·er, worm·i·est** 1. Infested with or injured by worms. 2. Of or like a worm. **—worm′i·ness** *n.*

worn (wôrn) Past participle of WEAR. **—*adj.*** Affected by use or any continuous action; as: **a** Threadbare: a *worn* suit. **b** Exhausted, as from worry, anxiety, etc.: a *worn* face. **c** Hackneyed: a *worn* phrase.

worn-out (wôrn′out′) *adj.* 1. Used until without value or effectiveness. 2. Thoroughly tired; exhausted.

wor·ri·some (wûr′i·səm) *adj.* 1. Causing worry or anxiety. 2. Given to worry. **—wor′ri·some·ly** *adv.*

wor·ry (wûr′ē) *v.* **·ried, ·ry·ing** *v.i.* 1. To be uneasy in the mind; fret. 2. To pull or tear at something with the teeth: with *at.* **—*v.t.*** 3. To cause to feel uneasy in the mind; trouble. 4. To bother; pester. 5. To bite, shake, or tear with the teeth. **—*n.*** *pl.* **·ries** 1. A state of anxiety or vexation. 2. Something that causes anxiety. [OE *wrygan* to strangle] **—wor′ri·er** *n.* **—wor′ri·ment** *n.*

worse (wûrs) Comparative of BAD and ILL. **—*adj.*** 1. Bad, harmful, or ill in a greater degree. 2. In a less favorable condition or situation. **—*n.*** Something worse. **—*adv.*** In a worse manner. [OE *wiersa*]

wors·en (wûr′sən) *v.t. & v.i.* To make or become worse.

wor·ship (wûr′ship) *n.* 1. The adoration, homage, or veneration given to a deity. 2. The expression of such adoration; esp., religious services and prayer. 3. Excessive or ardent devotion or admiration. 4. *Chiefly Brit.* A title of honor in addressing persons of rank or station: with *your, his,* etc. **—*v.*** **wor·shiped** or **·shipped, wor·ship·ing** or **·ship·ping** *v.t.* 1. To show religious worship to. 2. To have an intense admiration or devotion for. **—*v.i.*** 3. To perform acts of worship. [OE *weorth* value] **—wor′ship·er** or **wor′ship·per** *n.*

wor·ship·ful (wûr′ship·fəl) *adj.* 1. Giving or feeling reverence or adoration. 2. *Chiefly Brit.* Worthy of or entitled to honor or respect: used as a title of respect for magistrates, etc. **—wor′ship·ful·ly** *adv.* **—wor′ship·ful·ness** *n.*

worst (wûrst) Superlative of BAD and ILL. **—*adj.*** Bad, ill, evil, harmful, etc., in the highest degree. **—*n.*** That which is worst. **—at worst** By the most pessimistic estimate. **—if (the) worst comes to (the) worst** If the worst imaginable thing comes to pass. **—to get the worst of it** To be defeated or put at a disadvantage. **—*adv.*** In the worst manner or degree. **—*v.t.*** To defeat. [OE *wierrest*]

wors·ted (wŏŏs′tid, wûr′stid) *n.* 1. Woolen yarn spun from long staple, with fibers combed parallel and twisted hard. 2. A fabric made from this. [after *Worsted*, former name of a town in England] —**wors'ted** *adj.*

wort (wûrt) *n.* 1. A plant or herb: usu. in combination: *liverwort.* 2. The unfermented infusion of malt that becomes beer when fermented. [OE *wyrt* root, plant]

worth (wûrth) *n.* 1. Value or excellence of any kind. 2. The exchangeable or market value of anything. 3. The quality that makes one deserving of esteem. 4. Wealth. 5. The amount of something that can be had for a specific sum: three cents' *worth* of candy. —*adj.* 1. Equal in value to. 2. Deserving of: to be *worth* seeing. 3. Having possessions to the value of: He is *worth* a million. —**for all it is worth** To the utmost. —**for all one is worth** With every effort possible. [OE *weorth*]

-worth *combining form* Of the value of: *pennyworth.* [OE *weorth* worth]

worth·less (wûrth'lis) *adj.* Having no worth or value. —**worth'less·ly** *adv.* —**worth'less·ness** *n.*

worth·while (wûrth'hwīl') *adj.* Sufficiently important to be worth one's time, effort, or money. —**worth'while'ness** *n.*

wor·thy (wûr'thē) *adj.* **·thi·er, ·thi·est** 1. Deserving of respect or honor; meritorious. 2. Possessing worth or value. —*n. pl.* **·thies** A person of great worth or importance. [ME *wurthi, worthi*] —**wor'thi·ly** *adv.* —**wor'thi·ness** *n.*

-worthy *combining form* 1. Meriting or deserving: *trustworthy.* 2. Valuable as: *newsworthy.* 3. Fit for: *seaworthy.* [OE *wyrthe* worthy]

wot (wot) Present tense, first and third person singular, of WIT².

would (wŏŏd) Past tense of WILL, chiefly used as an auxiliary expressing a wide range of conditions, as preference, expectation, request, etc. [OE *wolde*, pt. of *willan* to will]

would-be (wŏŏd'bē') *adj.* 1. Desiring or professing to be: a *would-be* poet. 2. Intended to be.

would·n't (wŏŏd'nt) Would not.

wouldst (wŏŏdst) Archaic or poetic second person singular of WOULD: used with *thou.*

wound¹ (wōōnd, *Poetic* wound) *n.* 1. A hurt or injury to the body, usu. one in which the skin is cut or torn, as a stab. 2. Any injury to the feelings, honor, etc. —*v.t. & v.i.* To inflict a wound (upon); hurt. [OE *wund*] —**wound'less** *adj.*

wound² (wound) Past tense and past participle of WIND².

wove (wōv) Past tense and alternative past participle of WEAVE.

wo·ven (wō'vən) Past participle of WEAVE.

wow (wou) *interj. Informal* An exclamation of wonder, surprise, pleasure, pain, etc. —*n. Slang* Something that is extraordinarily successful, amusing, etc. —*v.t. Slang* To be extraordinarily successful with.

wrack (rak) *n.* 1. Ruin; destruction: chiefly in the phrase **wrack and ruin.** 2. A wrecked ship; wreckage. 3. Marine vegetation cast ashore by the sea, as seaweed. [Fusion of OE *wræc* revenge and MDu. *wrak* wreck]

wraith (rāth) *n.* An apparition of a person; ghost. [Origin unknown]

wran·gle (rang'gəl) *v.* **·gled, ·gling** *v.i.* 1. To argue or dispute noisily; brawl. —*v.t.* 2. To argue; debate. 3. To herd or round up (livestock). —*n.* An angry dispute. [Cf. LG *wrangeln* to quarrel] —**wran'gler** *n.*

wrap (rap) *v.* **wrapped** or **wrapt, wrap·ping** *v.t.* 1. To surround and cover. 2. To cover with paper, etc., folded about and secured. 3. To obscure; blot out. —*v.i.* 4. To be or become twined or coiled: with *about, around,* etc. —**to wrap up** *Informal* 1. To conclude; end. 2. To summarize. —*n.* 1. An article of dress drawn about a person. 2. *pl.* Outer garments collectively, as cloaks, scarfs, etc. [ME *wrappen*]

wrap·a·round (rap'ə·round') *adj.* 1. Designating a garment open down to the hem and made to fit by being wrapped around the body. 2. Encircling or overlapping: a *wraparound* windshield.

wrap·per (rap'ər) *n.* 1. That in which something has been wrapped. 2. A woman's dressing gown. 3. One who wraps.

wrap·ping (rap'ing) *n. Often pl.* Something in which an object is wrapped.

wrap-up (rap'up') *n. Informal* A concluding statement; summary.

wrath (rath) *n.* Extreme or violent rage. [OE *wrath* wroth] —**wrath'ful** *adj.* —**wrath'·ful·ly** *adv.* —**wrath'ful·ness** *n.*

wreak (rēk) *v.t.* 1. To inflict or exact, as vengeance. 2. To give free expression to (anger, hatred, etc.); vent. [OE *wrecan* to drive, avenge]

wreath (rēth) *n. pl.* **wreaths** (rēthz) 1. A band or circle of flowers or greenery. 2. Anything having a shape suggesting this. [OE *writhan* to bind, tie] —**wreath'y** *n.*

wreathe (rēth) *v.* **wreathed, wreath·ing** *v.t.* 1. To form into a wreath, as by twisting or twining. 2. To adorn or encircle with or as with wreaths. 3. To envelop; cover: His face was *wreathed* in smiles. —*v.i.* 4. To take the form of a wreath. [ME *writhen* to writhe]

wreck (rek) *v.t.* 1. To cause the destruction of; damage badly. 2. To affect disasterously; ruin. 3. To tear down, as a building. —*v.i.* 4. To suffer wreck; be ruined. —*n.* 1. That which has been ruined or destroyed. 2. The accidental destruction of a ship; also, the ship so destroyed. 3. One who is unsound or ruined. [< ON *wrekan* to drive]

wreck·age (rek'ij) *n.* 1. The act of wrecking, or the state of being wrecked. 2. Remains of a wreck; debris.

wreck·er (rek'ər) *n.* 1. One who or that which wrecks. 2. One employed in tearing down and removing old buildings. 3. A person, train, car, or machine that clears away wrecks. 4. A person or boat employed to recover disabled vessels or wrecked cargoes.

wren (ren) *n.* Any of numerous small birds having short, rounded wings and a short tail. [OE *wrenna*]

wrench (rench) *n.* 1. A violent twist. 2. An injury, as to the back, caused by a violent twist or jerk; sprain. 3. Any sudden and violent emotion or grief. 4. Any perversion or distortion of an original meaning. 5. Any of various tools for twisting or turning bolts, nuts, pipe, etc. —*v.t.* 1. To twist violently. 2. To injure by a sudden, violent twist; sprain. 3. To distort, as a meaning. 4. To move or force with great effort. —*v.i.*

5. To give a twist or wrench. [OE *wrenc* trick]

wrest (rest) *v.t.* 1. To pull or force away. 2. To turn from the true meaning; distort. 3. To seize forcibly. 4. To extract by toil and effort: to *wrest* a living from barren soil. —*n.* An act of wresting. [OE *wrǣstan*] —**wrest′er** *n.*

wres·tle (res′əl) *v.* **·tled, ·tling** *v.i.* 1. To engage in wrestling. 2. To struggle, as for mastery; contend. —*v.t.* 3. To engage in a wrestling match with. 4. To struggle or scuffle with. —*n.* 1. A wrestling match. 2. Any hard struggle. [OE *wrǣstlian*, freq. of *wrǣstan* to wrest] —**wres′tler** *n.*

wres·tling (res′ling) *n.* A sport in which each of two contestants endeavors to throw the other to the ground or force him into a certain fallen position.

wretch (rech) *n.* 1. A base, vile, or contemptible person. 2. A miserable or pitiable person. [OE *wrecca* outcast]

wretch·ed (rech′id) *adj.* 1. Sunk in dejection; profoundly unhappy. 2. Causing misery or grief. 3. Unsatisfactory or worthless in ability or quality. 4. Despicable; contemptible. —**wretch′ed·ly** *adv.* —**wretch′·ed·ness** *n.*

wrig·gle (rig′əl) *v.* **·gled, ·gling** *v.i.* 1. To twist in a sinuous manner; squirm. 2. To proceed as by twisting or crawling. 3. To make one's way by evasive or indirect means. —*v.t.* 4. To cause to wriggle. —*n.* The motion of wriggling. [< MLG *wriggeln*, freq. of *wriggen* to twist] —**wrig′gly** *adj.*

wrig·gler (rig′lər) *n.* 1. One who or that which wriggles. 2. A mosquito larva.

wright (rīt) *n.* One who constructs, contrives, or creates: used chiefly in compounds: *playwright.* [OE *wyrhta*]

wring (ring) *v.t.* **wrung** (*Rare* **wringed**), **wring·ing** 1. To squeeze or compress by twisting. 2. To squeeze or press out, as water, by twisting. 3. To extort; acquire by extortion. 4. To distress; torment. 5. To twist or wrest violently. —*n.* The act of wringing. [OE *wringan*]

wring·er (ring′ər) *n.* A device with rollers for squeezing out water from wet laundry.

wrin·kle[1] (ring′kəl) *n.* A small crease or fold, as on the skin or other smooth surface. —*v.t. & v.i.* **·kled, ·kling** To make wrinkles in or become wrinkled. [OE *gewrinclod*, pp. of *gewrinclian* to wind] —**wrin′kly** *adj.*

wrin·kle[2] (ring′kəl) *n.* *Informal* A curious or ingenious method, idea, device, etc. [Prob. dim. of OE *wrenc* trick]

wrist (rist) *n.* The joint of the arm between the hand and the forearm. [OE, prob. < *wrīthan* to writhe]

wrist watch A watch worn on a band or strap around the wrist.

writ[1] (rit) *n.* 1. *Law* A legal document ordering a person to do or not to do some act. 2. That which is written: now chiefly in the phrase *Holy Writ*, meaning the Bible. [OE, a writing < *wrītan* to write]

writ[2] (rit) Archaic or dialectal past tense and past participle of WRITE.

write (rīt) *v.* **wrote** (*Archaic* or *Dial.* **writ**), **writ·ten** (*Archaic* or *Dial.* **writ**), **writ·ing** *v.t.* 1. To trace or inscribe (words, numbers, etc.) on a surface, as with a pencil. 2. To describe in writing. 3. To communicate (with) by letter. 4. To be the author or composer of. 5. To draw up; draft: to *write* a check. 6. To cover or fill with writing: to *write* two full pages. 7. To leave marks or evidence of: Anxiety is *written* on his face. —*v.i.* 8. To trace or inscribe letters, etc., on a surface. 9. To communicate in writing. 10. To be engaged in the occupation of a writer or author. —**to write in** To cast (a vote) for one not listed on a ballot. —**to write off** 1. To remove or cancel (debts, etc.) from an account. 2. To acknowledge the loss or failure of. 3. To reduce the estimated value of. —**to write up** To describe in writing. [OE *wrītan*]

write-in (rīt′in′) *n.* A vote for a person not on a ballot. —**write′-in′** *adj.*

write-off (rīt′ôf′) *n.* 1. A cancellation. 2. An amount canceled or noted as a loss.

writ·er (rī′tər) *n.* One who writes, esp. as a profession.

writer's cramp *Pathol.* Cramp in the fingers and hand, caused by excessive writing. Also **writer's palsy** or **writer's spasm.**

write-up (rīt′up′) *n.* *Informal* A written description.

writhe (rīth) *v.* **writhed, writh·ing** *v.t.* 1. To cause to twist or bend; distort. —*v.i.* 2. To twist or distort the body, face, etc., as in pain. 3. To suffer acutely, as from embarrassment, anguish, etc. [OE *wrīthan*] —**writh′er** *n.*

writ·ing (rī′ting) *n.* 1. The act of one who writes. 2. Handwriting; penmanship. 3. Something written; esp., a novel, play, or other literary production. 4. The profession or occupation of a writer. 5. The practice, art, form, or style of literary composition.

writ·ten (rit′n) Past participle of WRITE.

wrong (rông) *adj.* 1. Not correct; mistaken; erroneous: a *wrong* estimate. 2. Not suitable; inappropriate; improper: the *wrong* clothes. 3. Not working or acting properly or satisfactorily: Something is *wrong* with the lock. 4. Intended to be unseen: the *wrong* side of the cloth. 5. Not desired or intended: the *wrong* road. 6. Not morally right, proper, or just. 7. Unsatisfactory: the *wrong* reply. —**to go wrong** 1. To make a mistake; err. 2. To turn out badly; go astray. —*adv.* In a wrong direction, place, or manner; erroneously. —*n.* That which is wrong, as an evil or unjust action. —**in the wrong** Mistaken; wrong; at fault. —*v.t.* 1. To inflict injury or injustice upon. 2. To impute evil to unjustly; malign. [< ON *rangr* awry, unjust] —**wrong′er** *n.* —**wrong′ly** *adv.* —**wrong′ness** *n.*

wrong·do·er (rông′do͞o′ər) *n.* One who does wrong. —**wrong′do′ing** *n.*

wrong·ful (rông′fəl) *adj.* 1. Unfair; injurious; unjust. 2. Unlawful; illegal. —**wrong′·ful·ly** *adv.* —**wrong′ful·ness** *n.*

wrong-head·ed (rông′hed′id) *adj.* Stubbornly or perversely erring in judgment, action, etc. —**wrong′-head′ed·ly** *adv.* —**wrong′-head′ed·ness** *n.*

wrote (rōt) Past tense of WRITE.

wroth (rôth) *adj.* *Archaic* Angry; furious. Also **wroth′ful** (-fəl). [OE *wrāth*]

wrought (rôt) Archaic past tense and past participle of WORK. —*adj.* 1. Beaten or hammered into shape by tools: *wrought* gold. 2. Made; fashioned; formed: often in combination: *well-wrought.* **—wrought up** Excited; agitated. [OE *geworht*, pp. of *wrycan* to work]

wrought iron Commercially pure iron that is easily forged and welded into various shapes.

wrung (rung) Past tense and past participle of WRING.

wry (rī) *adj.* **wri·er** or **wry·er, wri·est** or **wry·est** 1. Twisted; contorted; askew: a *wry* smile. 2. Perverse, ironic, or bitter: *wry* humor. [OE *wrigian* to move, tend] **—wry′ly** *adv.* **—wry′ness** *n.*

wry·neck (rī′nek′) *n.* 1. A bird allied to the woodpeckers, having the habit of twisting its head and neck. 2. *Pathol.* A spasmodic affliction that twists the neck muscles. **—wry·necked** (rī′nekt′) *adj.*

wurst (wûrst, wŏŏrst) *n.* Sausage. [< G]

Wy·an·dot (wī′ən·dot) *n. pl.* **·dot** or **·dots** 1. One of a tribe of Iroquoian Indians, descendants of Hurons, presently settled in Oklahoma. 2. An Iroquoian language. Also spelled *Wyandotte.*

Wy·an·dotte (wī′ən·dot) *n.* 1. One of an American breed of domestic fowls. 2. *pl.* **·dotte** or **·dottes** A Wyandot. 3. The Wyandot language. [after the *Wyandot* Indians]

wych-elm (wich′elm′) *n.* A widespreading elm, common in the British Isles: also called **wych,** *wich, witch*: also spelled *wich-elm, witch-elm.* [OE *wīcan* + ELM]

X

x, X (eks) *n. pl.* **x's** or **xs, X's** or **Xs, ex·es** (ek′siz) 1. The twenty-fourth letter of the English alphabet. 2. The sounds represented by the letter. 3. Anything shaped like an X. 4. An unknown quantity, factor, result, etc. —*symbol* 1. The Roman numeral ten. 2. A mark shaped like an X, representing the signature of one who cannot write. 3. A symbol used to indicate a kiss. —*v.t.* **x-ed** or **x'd, x-ing** or **x'ing** 1. To indicate or mark with an *x*. 2. To cancel: with *out*.

X-ax·is (eks′ak′sis) *n. pl.* **-ax·es** (-ak′sēz) The horizontal axis in a graph; the abscissa.

X-chro·mo·some (eks′krō′mə·sōm) *n.* *Genetics* One of the two types of chromosomes that determine the sex of an offspring.

xe·bec (zē′bek) *n.* A small, three-masted Mediterranean vessel, formerly used by pirates: also spelled *zebec.* [Earlier *chebec,* ult. < Arabic *shabbāk*]

xeno- *combining form* Strange; foreign; different: *xenophobia.* Also, before vowels, **xen-.** [< Gk. *xenos* stranger]

xe·non (zē′non) *n.* A heavy, gaseous element (symbol Xe) occurring in extremely small quantities in the atmosphere and freezing at a very low temperature. [< Gk., neut. of *xenos* strange]

xen·o·pho·bi·a (zen′ə·fō′bē·ə) *n.* Hatred or distrust of foreigners or strangers. —**xen′o·phobe** *n.* —**xen′o·pho′bic** *adj.*

xer·ic (zer′ik, zir′-) *adj.* Of or adapted to extreme dryness. [< Gk. *xēros* dry]

xero- *combining form* Dry; dryness. Also, before vowels, **xer-.** [< Gk. *xēros* dry]

xe·rog·ra·phy (zi·rog′rə·fē) *n.* A method of copying in which a negatively charged ink powder is sprayed upon a positively charged metal plate, from which it is transferred to the printing surface by electrostatic attraction. —**xe·ro·graph·ic** (zir′ō·graf′ik) *adj.* —**xe·rog′raph·er** *n.*

xe·roph·i·lous (zi·rof′ə·ləs) *adj.* *Biol.* Growing in or adapted to dry, hot climates.

xe·ro·phyte (zir′ə·fīt) *n.* *Bot.* A plant adapted to dry conditions of air and soil. —**xe′ro·phyt′ic** (-fit′ik) *adj.*

Xer·ox (zir′oks) *n.* A xerographic process for reproducing printed or pictorial matter: a trade name. —*v.t.* To reproduce by Xerox. Also **xer′ox.**

Xho·sa (kō′sä) *n.* 1. A Bantu people of E. South Africa. 2. Their language, akin to Zulu and Swazi. Also **Xo′sa.**

xi (zī, sī; *Gk.* ksē) *n.* The fourteenth letter in the Greek alphabet (Ξ, ξ), equivalent to the English *x*.

xiphi- *combining form* Sword. Also, before vowels, **xiph-.** [< Gk. *xiphos* sword]

Xmas Christmas: popular abbreviation. [< *X*, abbr. for *Christ* < Gk. *X*, chi, the first letter of *Christos* Christ + -MAS]

X-rat·ed (eks′rā′tid) *adj.* Of a motion picture, characterized by explicit sexuality.

X-ray (eks′rā′) *v.t.* To examine, photograph, diagnose, or treat with X-rays. —*n.* A picture made with X-rays: also **X-ray photograph.**

X-rays (eks′rāz′) *n.pl.* Electromagnetic radiations of extremely short wavelength, emitted from a substance when it is bombarded by a stream of electrons, and able to penetrate many solids. Also called *Roentgen rays.* [< *X*, because their nature was at first unknown]

xy·lem (zī′ləm) *n.* *Bot.* Woody tissue that is part of the water-transporting system in higher plants. [< Gk. *xylon* wood]

xy·lo·phone (zī′lə·fōn) *n.* A musical instrument consisting of a row of wooden bars graduated in length to form a chromatic scale, and sounded by being struck with mallets. —**xy′lo·phon′ist** *n.* [< Gk. *xylon* wood + -PHONE]

Y

y, Y (wī) *n. pl.* **y's** or **ys, Y's** or **Ys, wyes** (wīz) 1. The twenty-fifth letter of the English alphabet. 2. The sounds represented by the letter *y*. 3. Anything shaped like a Y, as: **a** A pipe coupling, connection, etc. **b** A forked piece serving as a rest or support. **—***symbol Chem.* Yttrium (symbol Y).

-y¹ *suffix of adjectives* Being, possessing, or resembling what is expressed in the root: *stony, rainy.* Also **-ey**, when added to words ending in *y*, as in *clayey, skyey.* [OE *-ig*]

-y² *suffix* The quality or state of being: *victory*: often used in abstract nouns formed from adjectives in *-ous* and *-ic.* [< F *-ie* < L *-ia*; also < Gk. *-ia, -eia*]

-y³ *suffix* Little; small: *kitty*: often used in nicknames or to express endearment, as in *Tommy.* [Prob. < dial. E (Scot.)]

yacht (yot) *n.* A vessel specially built or fitted for racing or for cruising. **—***v.i.* To cruise, race, or sail in a yacht. [< Du. *jaghte*, short for *jaghtschip* pursuit ship]

yachts·man (yots′mən) *n. pl.* **·men** (-mən) One who owns or sails a yacht. Also **yacht′er, yacht′man.**

ya·hoo (yä′hōō, yā′-, yä·hōō′) *n.* 1. Any low, vicious person. 2. An awkward fellow; a bumpkin. [after one of a race of brutish people in Jonathan Swift's *Gulliver's Travels* (1726)]

Yah·weh (yä′we) In the Old Testament, the God of Israel. Also **Yah·ve** (yä′ve), **Yah·veh.** [< Hebrew *YHWH*]

yak¹ (yak) *n.* A large, long-haired ox of Tibet and central Asia, often used as a beast of burden. [< Tibetan *gyag*]

yak² (yak) *v.i.* **yakked, yak·king** *Slang* To chatter noisily or constantly. [Imit.]

yam (yam) *n.* 1. The fleshy, edible, tuberous root of any of various climbing tropical plants. 2. A variety of the sweet potato. [< Senegal *nyami* to eat]

yam·mer (yam′ər) *Informal v.t. & v.i.* To complain or utter peevishly. **—***n.* The act of yammering. [OE *gēomrian* to lament] **—yam′mer·er** *n.*

yang (yang) *n.* In Chinese philosophy and art, the male element, source of life and heat. Compare YIN. Also **Yang.** [< Chinese]

yank (yangk) *v.t. & v.i.* To jerk or pull suddenly. **—***n. Informal* A sudden pull. [? < dial. E (Scot.)]

Yank (yangk) *n. & adj. Informal* Yankee.

Yan·kee (yang′kē) *n.* 1. Originally, a native or inhabitant of New England. 2. A Northerner; esp., a Union soldier during the Civil War. 3. Any citizen of the U.S.: a chiefly foreign usage. [Prob. < a Dutch name]

yap (yap) *n.* 1. *Slang* Talk; jabber. 2. A bark or yelp. 3. *Slang* The mouth. **—***v.t.* **yapped, yap·ping** 1. *Slang* To talk idly or emptily; jabber. 2. To bark or yelp, as a cur. [Imit. of a dog's bark]

Ya·qui (yä′kē) *n.* One of a tribe of North American Indians now living in Mexico.

yard¹ (yärd) *n.* 1. A standard English and American measure of length equal to 3 feet, 36 inches, or 0.914 meter. 2. *Naut.* A spar supporting a square sail. [OE *gierd* rod, measure of length]

yard² (yärd) *n.* 1. A tract of ground adjacent to a residence or other building. 2. An outdoor space used for a specific purpose: *shipyard.* 3. An area where railroad trains are made up, stored, or repaired. [OE *geard* enclosure]

yard·age (yär′dij) *n.* The amount or length of something expressed in yards. [< YARD¹]

yard·arm (yärd′ärm′) *n. Naut.* Either end of a yard of a square sail.

yard goods Cloth that is sold by the yard.

yard·mas·ter (yärd′mas′tər) *n.* A railroad official having charge of a yard.

yard·stick (yärd′stik′) *n.* 1. A graduated measuring stick one yard in length. 2. Any measure or standard of comparison.

yar·mul·ke (yar′məl·kə, yä′-) *n.* A skullcap worn by Jewish males, as during prayer. Also **yar′mel·ke.** [< Yiddish < Polish]

yarn (yärn) *n.* 1. Any spun, threadlike material prepared for use in weaving, knitting, etc. 2. *Informal* A long, exciting story of adventure, often of doubtful truth. [OE *gearn*]

yar·row (yar′ō) *n.* Any of various perennial herbs having finely divided leaves, small white flowers, and a pungent odor. [OE *gearwe*]

yaw (yô) *v.i.* 1. *Naut.* To turn wildly from its course, as a ship in a storm. 2. *Aeron.* To deviate from the flight path. **—***n.* A yawing course. [Cf. ON *jaga* to move to and fro]

yawl¹ (yôl) See YOWL.

yawl² (yôl) *n.* 1. A fore-and-aft rigged, two-masted vessel having the mizzenmast or jiggermast abaft the rudder post. 2. A ship's small boat. 3. A small fishing boat. [< Du. *jol* boat]

yawn (yôn) *v.i.* 1. To open the mouth wide, usu. involuntarily, as a result of drowsiness, fatigue, or boredom. 2. To be or stand wide open: A chasm *yawned* below. **—***n.* 1. The act of yawning. 2. The act of opening wide. [Prob. fusion of OE *geonian* to yawn and *gānian* to gape] **—yawn′er** *n.*

yawp (yôp) *v.i.* 1. To bark or yelp. 2. *Informal* To talk loudly; shout. **—***n.* 1. A bark or yelp. 2. *Informal* A shout. Also **yaup.** [ME *gelpen* to boast] **—yawp′er** *n.*

yaws (yôz) *n.pl. Pathol.* A tropical, contagious skin disease, caused by a spirochete and resembling syphilis. [< Carib *yáya*]

Y-ax·is (wī′ak′sis) *n.* *pl.* **-ax·es** (-ak′sēz) The vertical axis in a graph or coordinate system; the ordinate.
Y-chro·mo·some (wī′krō′mə·sōm) *n.* *Genetics* One of the two types of chromosomes that determine the sex of an offspring.
y·clept (i·klept′) *adj.* *Archaic* Called; named. Also **y·cleped′**. [OE *geclypod*, pp. of *clypian* to call]
ye[1] (*th*e) The: a mistaken form resulting from the substitution of the character *y* for the thorn (þ) of the Old and Middle English alphabet.
ye[2] (yē) *pron. Archaic* You. [OE *gē*]
yea (yā) *adv.* 1. *Archaic* Yes. 2. *Archaic* Not only so, but more so: There were fifty, *yea*, a hundred archers. —*n.* An affirmative vote or voter. [OE *gēa*]
yeah (yâ, ye′ə) *adv. Informal* Yes. [< YES]
year (yir) *n.* 1. The period of time in which the earth completes one revolution around the sun, consisting of 365 or 366 days divided into 12 months and now reckoned as beginning January 1 and ending December 31; also, a similar period in other calendars. 2. The period of time during which a planet revolves once around the sun. 3. A specific period of time, usu. less than a year, given over to some special work or activity: the school *year*. 4. *pl.* Age, esp. old age: active for his *years*. 5. *pl.* Time: in *years* gone by and *years* to come. —**year in, year out** From one year to the next; continuously. [OE *gēar*]
year·book (yir′bo͝ok′) *n.* 1. A book published annually, presenting information about the previous year. 2. A high school or college annual recording esp. senior class activities.
year·ling (yir′ling) *n.* A young animal past its first year and not yet two years old. —*adj.* Being a year old.
year·long (yir′lông′) *adj.* Continuing through a year.
year·ly (yir′lē) *adj.* 1. Occurring, done, payable, seen, etc., once a year; annual. 2. Continuing or lasting for a year: a *yearly* subscription. —*adv.* Once a year; annually.
yearn (yûrn) *v.i.* 1. To desire something earnestly; long: with *for*. 2. To be deeply moved; feel sympathy. [OE *giernan, geornan*]
yearn·ing (yûr′ning) *n.* A strong emotion of longing or desire, esp. with tenderness. —**yearn′ing·ly** *adv.*
year-round (yir′round′) *adj.* Open, operating, or continuing for the entire year: a *year-round* health resort.
yeast (yēst) *n.* 1. A one-celled fungus that ferments carbohydrates. 2. A commercial preparation containing yeast cells, used in leavening bread and in brewing. 3. Froth or spume. 4. Ferment or agitation. [OE *gist*]
yeast·y (yēs′tē) *adj.* **yeast·i·er, yeast·i·est** 1. Of, resembling, or containing yeast. 2. Frothy; foamy. 3. Restless; unsettled. 4. Light or unsubstantial. —**yeast′i·ness** *n.*
yegg (yeg) *n. Slang* A burglar or safecracker. Also **yegg′man** (-mən). [Origin unknown]
yell (yel) *v.t. & v.i.* To shout; scream; roar; also, to cheer. —*n.* 1. A sharp, loud cry, as of pain or anger. 2. A rhythmic cheer shouted in unison by cheerleaders, etc. [OE *giellan, gellan*] —**yell′er** *n.*
yel·low (yel′ō) *adj.* 1. Having the color of ripe lemons or sunflowers. 2. Changed to a sallow color by age, sickness, etc.: a paper *yellow* with age. 3. Having a yellowish complexion, as a member of the Mongoloid ethnic group. 4. Sensational, esp. offensively so: said of newspapers: *yellow* journalism. 5. *Informal* Cowardly. —*n.* 1. The color of the spectrum between green and orange. 2. The yolk of an egg. —*v.t. & v.i.* To make or become yellow. [OE *geolu*] —**yel′low·ish** *adj.* —**yel′low·ish·ness** *n.* —**yel′low·ly** *adv.* —**yel′low·ness** *n.*
yel·low-bel·lied (yel′ō·bel′ēd) *adj.* 1. *Slang* Cowardly; yellow. 2. Having a yellow underside, as a bird.
yellow fever *Pathol.* An infectious intestinal disease caused by a virus transmitted by a mosquito.
yellow jack 1. Yellow fever. 2. The flag of the quarantine service.
yellow jacket Any of various wasps having bright yellow markings.
yellow pine 1. Any of various American pines, as the loblolly pine. 2. Their tough, yellowish wood.
yellow warbler A warbler of the southern U.S., bright yellow with brown streaks underneath.
yelp (yelp) *v.t. & v.i.* To utter or express with a sharp, shrill cry or bark, as a dog. [OE *gielpan* to boast] —**yelp** *n.* —**yelp′er** *n.*
Yem·e·ni (yem′ə·nē) *adj.* Of Yemen or its inhabitants. —**Yem′e·ni, Yem′e·nite** (-nīt) *n.*
yen[1] (yen) *Informal n.* An ardent longing or desire. —*v.i.* **yenned, yen·ning** To yearn; long. [< Chinese, opium, smoke]
yen[2] (yen) *n. pl.* **yen** The standard monetary unit of Japan, equal to 100 sen. [< Japanese < Chinese *yüan* round, dollar]
yeo·man (yō′mən) *n.* *pl.* **·men** (-mən) 1. A naval petty officer who performs clerical duties. 2. Formerly, an attendant or servant in the service of a nobleman or of royalty. 3. Formerly, a freeholder next below the gentry who owned a small landed estate or farm. [ME *yeman, yoman*, prob. contr. of *yengman* young man]
yeo·man·ly (yō′mən·lē) *adj.* Brave; rugged; staunch. —**yeo′man·ly** *adv.*
yeoman of the (royal) guard A member of the special bodyguard of the English royal household: also called *beefeater*.
yeo·man·ry (yō′mən·rē) *n.* The collective body of yeomen (def. 3).
yep (yep) *adv. Informal* Yes. [Alter. of YES]
yes (yes) *adv.* As you say; truly; just so: a reply of affirmation or consent: opposed to *no*. —*n. pl.* **yes·es** or **yes·ses** 1. A reply in the affirmative. 2. An affirmative vote or voter: often *aye*. —*v.t. & v.i.* **yessed, yes·sing** To say "yes" (to). [OE *gēse*]
ye·shi·va (yə·shē′və) *n.* *pl.* **·vas** or **·voth** (-vōth) In Judaism: **a** An orthodox rabbinical seminary. **b** A Hebrew day school. **c** A school of Talmudic studies. Also **ye·shi′vah**. [< Hebrew]
yes man *Informal* One who agrees without criticism.
yes·ter·day (yes′tər·dē, -dā′) *n.* 1. The day preceding today. 2. The near past. —*adv.* 1. On the day before today. 2. At a recent time. [OE *giestran* yesterday + *dæg* day]

yes·ter·year (yes′tər·yir′) *n.* 1. Last year. 2. The recent past.
yet (yet) *adv.* 1. In addition; besides. 2. In continuance of a previous state or condition; still: I can hear him *yet*. 3. At the present time; now: Don't go *yet*. 4. After all the time that has or had elapsed: Are you not ready *yet*? 5. Up to the present time; before: He has never *yet* lied to me. 6. Than that which has been previously affirmed: It was hot yesterday; today it is hotter *yet*. 7. Nevertheless: It was hot, *yet* not unpleasant. **—as yet** Up to now. *—conj.* Nevertheless; notwithstanding; but. [OE *gīet, gīeta*]
ye·ti (ye′tē) *n.* The abominable snowman. [< Tibetan]
yew (yo͞o) *n.* 1. Any of several evergreen trees or shrubs, having a red berrylike fruit. 2. The hard, fine-grained, durable wood of the common yew. [OE *ēow, iw*]
Yid·dish (yid′ish) *n.* A Germanic language now spoken primarily by Jews in eastern Europe and by Jewish immigrants from that region. [< G *jüdisch* Jewish < *Jude* Jew] **—Yid′dish** *adj.*
yield (yēld) *v.t.* 1. To give forth; produce: to *yield* a large crop. 2. To give in return, as for investment. 3. To give up; relinquish: often with *up*: to *yield* a fortress. 4. To concede or grant: to *yield* precedence. *—v.i.* 5. To provide a return; produce. 6. To give up; surrender. 7. To give way, as to pressure or force. 8. To assent or comply, as under compulsion. 9. To give place, as through inferiority or weakness: with *to*: We will *yield* to them in nothing. *—n.* 1. The amount yielded; product. 2. The profit derived from invested capital. [OE *gieldan, geldan* to pay] **—yield′er** *n.*
yield·ing (yēl′ding) *adj.* Disposed to yield; flexible; obedient. **—yield′ing·ly** *adv.* **—yield′ing·ness** *n.*
yin (yin) *n.* In Chinese philosophy and art, the female element that stands for darkness, cold, and death. Compare YANG. Also **Yin**. [< Chinese]
-yl *suffix Chem.* Used to denote a radical: *ethyl, butyl*. [< Gk. *hylē* wood, matter]
yo·del (yōd′l) *n.* A melody sung to meaningless syllables, with abrupt changes from natural to falsetto tones. *—v.t. & v.i.* **yo·deled** or **·delled, yo·del·ing** or **·del·ling** To sing (a yodel). Also **yo′dle.** [< G *jodeln*, lit., to utter the syllable *jo*] **—yo′del·er, yo′del·ler, yo′dler** *n.*
yo·ga (yō′gə) *n.* 1. A Hindu discipline aimed at perfect spiritual insight through meditation and exercises. 2. A related system of exercises, the purpose of which is to achieve both physical and spiritual well-being. [< Hind. < Skt., lit., union] **—yo·gic** (yō′gik) *adj.*
yo·gi (yō′gē) *n. pl.* **·gis** One who practices yoga. Also **yo′gee, yo′gin** (-gin).
yo·gurt (yō′gərt) *n.* A thick, curdled milk treated with bacteria. Also **yo′ghurt, yo′·ghourt.** [< Turkish *yōghurt*]
yoke (yōk) *n. pl.* **yokes;** *for def. 3, often* **yoke** 1. A curved timber with attachments used for coupling draft animals, as oxen. 2. Any of various similar contrivances, as a frame fitted for a person's shoulders and designed to carry a burden at either end. 3. A pair of draft animals coupled with a yoke. 4. An oppressive force or influence: under the *yoke* of tyranny. 5. That which binds or connects; a bond: the *yoke* of love. 6. A part of a garment designed to support a pleated or gathered part, as at the hips or shoulders. *—v.* **yoked, yok·ing** *v.t.* 1. To put a yoke upon. 2. To join; couple; link. 3. To secure (a draft animal) to a plow, etc.; also, to secure a draft animal to (a plow, etc.). *—v.i.* 4. To be joined or linked. [OE *geoc*]
yo·kel (yō′kəl) *n.* A country bumpkin: a contemptuous term. [? < dial. E, green woodpecker] **—yo′kel·ish** *adj.*
yolk (yōk, yōlk) *n.* The yellow portion of an egg. [OE *geol(o)ca*, lit., (the) yellow part < *geolu* yellow]
Yom Kip·pur (yom kip′ər, *Hebrew* yōm ki·po͝or′) The Jewish Day of Atonement, marked by continuous prayer and fasting for 24 hours. [< Hebrew *yōm kipūr* day of atonement]
yon (yon) *adj. & adv. Archaic, Dial. & Poetic* Yonder: *yon* fine house. [OE *geon*]
yon·der (yon′dər) *adj.* Being at a distance indicated. *—adv.* In that place; there. [ME, prob. extension of *yone* < OE *geon* yon]
yore (yôr) *n.* Time long past: in days of *yore*. [OE *gēara*]
York·shire pudding (yôrk′shir, -shər) A batter pudding usu. baked with roasting meat.
you (yo͞o) *pron., possessive* **your** or **yours** 1. The nominative and objective singular and plural pronoun of the second person, used in addressing one or more. 2. An indefinite pronoun equivalent to *one*: *You* learn by trying. [OE *ēow*, dative and accusative pl. of *gē* ye]
you'd (yo͞od, *unstressed* yo͝od, yəd) 1. You had. 2. You would.
you'll (yo͞ol, *unstressed* yo͝ol, yəl) You will.
young (yung) *adj.* **young·er, young·est** 1. Being in the early period of life or growth; not old. 2. Not having progressed far; newly formed: The day was *young*. 3. Pertaining to youth or early life. 4. Full of vigor or freshness. 5. Being without experience; immature. *—n.* 1. Young persons as a group; youth. 2. Offspring, esp. of animals. [OE *geong*] **—young′ish** *adj.*
young blood Youth; young people.
young·ster (yung′stər) *n.* A young person; a child or youth.
your (yôr, yo͝or) *pronominal adj.* The possessive case of the pronoun *you*, used attributively: *your* fate. [OE *ēower*, genitive of *gē* ye]
you're (yo͝or, yôr, *unstressed* yər) You are.
yours (yôrz, yo͝orz) *pron.* 1. The possessive case of the pronoun *you*, used predicatively: This room is *yours*. 2. The one or ones belonging or relating to you: a home as quiet as *yours*. [ME *youres*]
your·self (yôr·self′, yo͝or-) *pron. pl.* **·selves** (-selvz′) A form of the second person pronoun, used: 1. As a reflexive or as object of a preposition in a reflexive sense: Did you hurt *yourself*? Look at *yourself*! 2. As an intensive form of *you*: You said so *yourself*. 3. As a designation of a normal or usual state: Why can't you be *yourself*?

youth (yo͞oth) *n. pl.* **youths** (yo͞oths, yo͞othz) 1. The state or condition of being young. 2. The period of life between childhood and adulthood; adolescence. 3. Any early period or stage. 4. A young person, esp. a young man; also, young persons collectively. [OE *geoguth*]

youth·ful (yo͞oth′fəl) *adj.* 1. Having youth; being still young. 2. Characteristic of youth; fresh; vigorous. 3. Of or pertaining to youth. 4. Not far advanced; early; new. —**youth′ful·ly** *adv.* —**youth′ful·ness** *n.*

you've (yo͞ov, *unstressed* yo͝ov, yəv) You have.

yowl (youl) *v.i.* To utter a loud, prolonged wailing cry. —*n.* Such a cry. Also spelled *yawl.* [Cf. ON *gaula* to howl, yell]

yo-yo (yō′yō′) *n. pl.* **-yos** 1. A wheellike toy with a string wound about it in a deep groove, commonly attached to the operator's finger and spun up and down by manipulating the string. 2. *Slang* A stupid person. [Origin unknown]

yt·ter·bi·um (i·tûr′bē·əm) *n.* A rare metallic element (symbol Yb) of the lanthanide series, occurring in minerals. [< NL, from *Ytterby*, Sweden] —**yt·ter′bic** *adj.*

yt·tri·um (it′rē·əm) *n.* A rare element (symbol Y) of the lanthanide series, found in minerals. [See YTTERBIUM.]

yu·an (yo͞o·än′, Chinese yü′än′) *n. pl.* **yu·an** The monetary unit of the People's Republic of China. [< Chinese *yüan*, lit., circle]

yuc·ca (yuk′ə) *n.* Any of various liliaceous plants of the southern U.S., Mexico, and Central America, having a woody stem that bears a large cluster of white, bell-shaped flowers. [< Sp. *yuca* < Taino]

Yu·go·slav (yo͞o′gō·släv, -slav) *adj.* Of or pertaining to Yugoslavia or its people. —**Yu′go·slav** *n.* —**Yu′go·sla′vi·an** *n. & adj.*

Yule (yo͞ol) *n.* Christmas. [OE *gēol* Christmas day, Christmastide]

yule log A large log made the foundation of the Christmas Eve fire.

Yule·tide (yo͞ol′tīd′) *n.* Christmas time.

Yu·ma (yo͞o′mə) *n.* One of a tribe of Yuman Indians, formerly living in northern Mexico and Arizona and in SE California.

Yu·man (yo͞o′mən) *n.* A North American Indian language family of the SW U.S. and NW Mexico.

yum·my (yum′ē) *Slang adj.* **·mi·er, ·mi·est** Delicious; delectable. [from *yum-yum*, an exclamation expressing delight at an agreeable taste]

yurt (yûrt) *n.* A portable tent made of felt laid on a framework of branches, used by nomadic Mongols in central Asia. [< Russ. *yurta* < Turkic]

Z

z, Z (zē, *Brit.* zed) *n. pl.* **z's** or **zs, Z's** or **Zs, zees** (zēz) 1. The twenty-sixth letter of the English alphabet. Also, *Brit., zed.* 2. The sound represented by the letter *z.* —*symbol* 1. *Physics* Atomic number. 2. *Math.* An unknown quantity.

Zach·a·ri·as (zak′ə·rī′əs) The Douai Bible name for ZECHARIAH.

za·ire (zä·ir′) *n.* The monetary unit of Zaire.

Za·ir·i·an (zä·ir′ē·ən) *adj.* Of Zaire or its inhabitants. —**Za·ir′i·an** *n.*

Zam·bi·an (zam′bē·ən) *adj.* Of Zambia or its inhabitants. —**Zam′bi·an** *n.*

za·ny (zā′nē) *adj.* **·ni·er, ·ni·est** Odd and comical; outlandish. —*n. pl.* **·nies** 1. A simpleton; buffoon; fool. 2. In old comic plays, one who imitated the other performers, esp. the clown, with ludicrous failure. [< Ital. *zanni*, servants who act as clowns in early Italian comedy]

zap (zap) *v.* **zapped, zap·ping** *Slang v.t.* 1. To hit or kill, by or as if by shooting. 2. To be moved quickly and suddenly. —*v.i.* 3. To move quickly; zip. [after the comic strip representation of the sound of a ray gun]

zeal (zēl) *n.* Enthusiastic devotion; ardor; fervor. [< Gk. *zēlos* < *zēein* to boil]

zeal·ot (zel′ət) *n.* 1. An immoderate partisan; a fanatic. 2. One who is zealous. —**zeal′ot·ry** *n.*

zeal·ous (zel′əs) *adj.* Filled with or incited by zeal; enthusiastic. —**zeal′ous·ly** *adv.* —**zeal′ous·ness** *n.*

ze·bec (zē′bek), **ze·beck** See XEBEC.

ze·bra (zē′brə) *n.* Any of various African equine mammals resembling the ass, having a light-colored body fully marked with dark bands. [< Pg. < Bantu (Congo)] —**ze′brine** (-brēn, -brin), **ze′broid** *adj.*

ze·bu (zē′byōō) *n.* The domesticated ox of India, China, and East Africa, having a hump on the withers and short horns. [< F *zébu* < Tibetan]

Zech·a·ri·ah (zek′ə·rī′ə) *n.* A book of the Old Testament attributed to Zechariah, a 6th c. B.C. Hebrew prophet. Also, in the Douai Bible, *Zacharias.*

zed (zed) *n. Brit.* The letter *z.* [< F < Gk. *zēta*]

Zeit·geist (tsīt′gīst) *n. German* The spirit of the time; the intellectual and moral tendencies that characterize any age or epoch. [< G < *zeit* time + *geist* spirit]

ze·na·na (zə·nä′nə) *n.* In India, the women's apartments; the East Indian harem. [< Hind. *zenāna* belonging to women < Persian *zanāna* < *zan* woman]

Zen Buddhism (zen) A form of Buddhism stressing enlightenment through intuition and contemplation rather than formal study of scripture. Also **Zen.** [< Japanese *zen* meditation < Skt. *dhyana*]

Zend (zend) *n.* The ancient translation and commentary of the Avesta, the sacred writings of the Zoroastrian religion. [< Persian, interpretation] —**Zend′ic** *adj.*

Zend-A·ves·ta (zend′ə·ves′tə) *n.* The Avesta, including the later translation and commentary called the Zend. —**Zend′-A·ves·ta′ic** (-tā′ik) *adj.*

ze·nith (zē′nith) *n.* 1. The point of the celestial sphere that is exactly overhead and is opposite to the nadir. 2. The highest or culminating point; peak: the *zenith* of one's career. [< Arabic *samt* (*ar-ras*) the path (over the head)]

Zeph·a·ni·ah (zef′ə·nī′ə) *n.* A book of the Old Testament attributed to Zephaniah, a 7th c. B.C. Hebrew prophet. Also, in the Douai Bible, *Sophonias.*

zeph·yr (zef′ər) *n.* 1. The west wind. 2. Any soft, gentle wind. 3. A very lightweight yarn or fabric. [< Gk. *zephyros*]

zep·pe·lin (zep′ə·lin) *n. Often cap.* A large dirigible having a rigid, cigar-shaped body. [after Count Ferdinand von *Zeppelin*, 1838–1917, German general]

ze·ro (zir′ō, zē′rō) *n. pl.* **ze·ros** or **ze·roes** 1. The numeral or symbol 0; a cipher. ◆In nontechnical speech, this symbol is often pronounced (ō). 2. *Math.* **a** A cardinal number indicating the absence of quantity. **b** The point where a continuous function changes its sign from plus to minus, or vice versa. 3. The point on a scale, as of a thermometer, from which measures are counted. 4. The lowest point. 5. Nothing. —*v.t.* **ze·roed, ze·ro·ing** To adjust (instruments) to an arbitrary zero point for synchronized readings. —**to zero in on** 1. To adjust the sight of (a gun) by calibrated results of firings. 2. To focus on. —*adj.* Without value or appreciable change. [< Arabic *sifr*]

ze·ro-based budgeting (zir′ō·bāst′, zē′rō-) Budgeting in which expenditures are freshly justified, instead of being derived from previous budgets.

zero hour 1. The hour appointed for a military operation. 2. *Informal* Any critical moment.

zest (zest) *n.* 1. Keen enjoyment; gusto: often with *for*: a *zest* for reading. 2. That which imparts such excitement and relish. [< F *zeste* lemon peel (for flavoring)] —**zest′ful, zest′y** *adj.* —**zest′ful·ly** *adv.* —**zest′ful·ness** *n.*

ze·ta (zā′tə, zē′-) *n.* The sixth letter (Z, ζ) in the Greek alphabet, corresponding to English *z.* [< Gk. *zēta*]

zig·zag (zig′zag) *n.* 1. A series of short, sharp turns or angles in alternating directions. 2. Something characterized by such angles, as a path or pattern. —*adj.* Having or proceeding in a zigzag. —*adv.* In a zigzag manner. —*v.t.* & *v.i.* **·zagged, ·zag·ging** To form or move in zigzags. [< G *zickzack*, prob. reduplication of *zacke* sharp point] —**zig′zag·ger** *n.*

zilch (zilch) *n.* Nothing; zero. [after a character's name in the 1930's magazine *Ballyhoo*]

zil·lion (zil′yən) *Informal* A large, indefinite number. [after *million*]

zinc (zingk) *n.* A bluish white, metallic element (symbol Zn), widely used in industry, medicine, and the arts. —*v.t.* **zincked** or **zinced, zinck·ing** or **zinc·ing** To coat with zinc; galvanize. [< G *zink*] —**zinc′ic** *adj.* —**zinck′y, zinc′y, zink′y** *adj.*

zinc ointment A medicated ointment containing zinc oxide mixed with petrolatum, used to treat skin disorders.

zinc oxide *Chem.* A white powdery compound, used as a pigment and as a mild antiseptic and astringent.

zin·fan·del (zin′fān·del) *n.* A dry, red or white claret-type wine made in California.

zing (zing) *Informal n.* 1. A high-pitched buzzing or humming sound. 2. Energy; vitality; vigor. —*v.i.* To make a shrill, humming sound. [Imit.]

zin·ni·a (zin′ē·ə) *n.* Any of various American composite herbs having showy flowers. [< NL, after J. G. *Zinn*, 1727–59, German botanist]

Zi·on (zī′ən) 1. A hill in Jerusalem, the site of the temple and the royal residence of David and his successors, regarded by the Jews as a symbol of Jewish national culture, government, and religion. 2. The Jewish people. 3. Any place or community considered to be especially under God's rule. 4. The heavenly Jerusalem; heaven. [< Hebrew *tsiyōn* hill]

Zi·on·ism (zī′ən·iz′əm) *n.* Before the creation of Israel (1948), a movement to establish a national homeland for Jews in Palestine. Since 1948, Zionism has supported the social, economic, and cultural development of Israel. Also **Zion movement.** —**Zi′on·ist** *adj.* & *n.* —**Zi′on·is′tic** *adj.*

zip (zip) *n.* 1. A sharp, hissing sound, as of a bullet passing through the air. 2. *Informal* Energy; vitality; vim. —*v.* **zipped, zip·ping** *v.t.* 1. To fasten with a zipper. —*v.i.* 2. *Informal* To be very energetic. 3. To move or fly with great speed. [Imit.]

ZIP Code (zip) A numerical code for zones or regions, devised by the U.S. Post Office to aid in the distribution of domestic mail. Also **Zip Code.** [< Z(ONE) I(MPROVEMENT) P(LAN)]

zip·per (zip′ər) *n.* A fastener having two rows of interlocking teeth that may be closed or separated by a sliding device, used on clothing, boots, etc.: also called *slide fastener.*

zip·py (zip′ē) *adj.* **·pi·er, ·pi·est** *Informal* Brisk; energetic.

zir·con (zûr′kon) *n.* A crystalline, variously colored, zirconium silicate, some translucent varieties of which are used as gems. [< Persian *zar* gold + *gūn* color]

zir·co·ni·um (zûr·kō′nē·əm) *n.* A metallic element (symbol Zr) chemically resembling titanium, used in alloys. [< NL < ZIRCON] —**zir·con′ic** (-kon′ik) *adj.*

zith·er (zith′ər) *n.* A simple form of stringed instrument, having a flat sounding board and from thirty to forty strings that are played by plucking with a plectrum. Also **zith′ern** (-ərn). [< G < Gk. *kithara*]

zlo·ty (zlô′tē) *n. pl.* **·tys** or **·ty** The monetary unit of Poland. [< Polish, lit., golden]

zo·di·ac (zō′dē·ak) *n.* 1. An imaginary belt encircling the heavens and extending about 8° on each side of the ecliptic within which are the apparent orbits of the moon, sun, and larger planets. It is divided into twelve parts, called **signs of the zodiac,** that formerly corresponded to twelve constellations bearing the same names. 2. A figure or diagram representing this belt and its signs, used in astrology. [< Gk. (*kyklos*) *zōdiakos* (circle) of animals < *zōion* animal] —**zo·di·a·cal** (zō·dī′ə·kəl) *adj.*

zom·bie (zom′bē) *n.* 1. A corpse reactivated by sorcery, but still dead. 2. A large, strong cocktail made from several kinds of rum, fruit juices, and liqueur. Also **zom′bi.** [< West African] —**zom′bi·ism** *n.*

zone (zōn) *n.* 1. An area, tract, or section distinguished from other or adjacent areas by some special quality or purpose. 2. *Usu. cap.* Any of five divisions of the earth's surface, enclosed between two parallels of latitude and named for the prevailing climate: the **Torrid Zone,** extending on each side of the equator 23° 27′; the **Temperate Zones,** included between the parallels 23° 27′ and 66° 33′ on both sides of the equator; and the **Frigid Zones,** within the parallels 66° 33′ and the poles. —*v.t.* **zoned, zon·ing** 1. To divide into zones. 2. To designate (an area, etc.) as a zone or part of a zone. [< Gk. *zōnē* girdle]

zonked (zonkt, zônkt) *adj.* Drunk or drugged. Also **zonked′-out′.** [Origin unknown]

zoo (zōō) *n.* A park or garden in which wild animals are kept for exhibition. Also **zoological garden, zoological park.**

zoo- *combining form* Animal: *zoology.* Also, before vowels, **zo-.** [< Gk. *zōion*]

zo·o·ge·og·ra·phy (zō′ə·jē·og′rə·fē) *n.* The study of the distribution of animals and of the relations between animal groups and their environment. —**zo′o·ge·og′ra·pher** *n.* —**zo′o·ge′o·graph′ic** (-jē′ə·graf′ik) or **·i·cal** *adj.* —**zo′o·ge′o·graph′i·cal·ly** *adv.*

zo·ol·o·gy (zō·ol′ə·jē) *n.* The science that treats animals, their structure, functions, development, evolution, and classification. [< ZOO- + -LOGY] —**zo·o·log·i·cal** (zō′ə·loj′i·kəl) *adj.* —**zo′o·log′i·cal·ly** *adv.* —**zo·ol′o·gist** *n.*

zoom (zōōm) *v.i.* 1. To make a low-pitched but loud humming sound; also, to move with such a sound. 2. To climb sharply, as in an airplane. —*v.t.* 3. To cause to zoom. —*n.* The act of zooming. [Imit.]

zoom lens *Photog.* A lens, used chiefly on television and motion picture cameras, that permits the size of the image to be varied continuously without loss of focus.

zo·o·mor·phism (zō′ə·môr′fiz·əm) *n.* The conception, symbolization, or representation of a man or a god in the form of an animal.

zo·o·phyte (zō′ə·fīt) *n.* An invertebrate

animal resembling a plant, as a coral or sea anemone. —**zo′o·phyt′ic** (-fit′ik) or ·**i·cal** *adj.*

zo·o·spore (zō′ə·spôr) *n. Bot.* A spore, produced among some algae and fungi, having cilia by means of which it can move about. —**zo′o·spor′ic** (-spôr′ik, -spor′ik), **zo·os·po·rous** (zō·os′pər·əs) *adj.*

Zo·ro·as·tri·an·ism (zō′rō·as′trē·ən·iz′əm) *n.* The religious system founded by Zoroaster and taught in the Zend-Avesta. It recognizes two creative powers, one good and the other evil, includes the belief in life after death, and teaches the final triumph of good over evil. Also **Zo′ro·as′trism.** —**Zo′ro·as′tri·an** *n. & adj.*

Zou·ave (zōō·äv′, swäv) *n.* 1. A light-armed French infantryman wearing a brilliant Oriental uniform, originally an Algerian recruit. 2. In the Civil War, a member of a volunteer regiment assuming the name and part of the dress of the French Zouaves. [< F < Arabic *Zouāoua*, a Kabyle tribe]

zounds (zounds, zōōndz) *interj. Archaic* A mild oath used to express surprise or anger. [Short for *God's wounds*]

zoy·si·a (zoi′zē·ə) *n.* Any of various wiry grasses suited to hot, dry growing conditions. [after K. von *Zois*, 18th c. German botanist]

zuc·chi·ni (zōō·kē′nē) *n.* A cucumber-shaped green summer squash. [< Ital., pl. of *zucchino*, dim. of *zucca* gourd, squash]

Zu·lu (zōō′lōō) *n. pl.* **Zu·lus** or **Zu·lu** 1. One of a Bantu nation of Natal, South Africa, sometimes included with the Kaffirs. 2. The Bantu language of the Zulus. —**Zu′lu** *adj.*

Zu·ñi (zōō′nyē) *n.* 1. One of a tribe of North American Indians of pueblo culture, living in New Mexico. 2. The language of this tribe. —**Zu′ñi·an** *adj. & n.*

zwie·back (swī′bak, zwē′-, swī′, swē′-, -bäk) *n.* Bread baked in the loaf and later sliced and toasted. [< G, twice baked < *zwie-* twice + *backen* to bake]

zygo- *combining form* Yoke; pair: *zygote.* Also, before vowels, **zyg-.** [< Gk. *zygon* yoke]

zy·gote (zī′gōt) *n. Biol.* The cell formed by the union of two gametes. [< Gk. *zygon* yoke] —**zy·got·ic** (zī·got′ik) *adj.*

zy·mase (zī′mās) *n. Biochem.* An enzyme, obtained principally from yeast, that induces fermentation by breaking down glucose and related carbohydrates into alcohol and carbon dioxide. [< Gk. *zymē* leaven]

zymo- *combining form* Fermentation: *zymurgy.* Also before, vowels, **zym-.** [< Gk. *zymē* leaven]

zy·mol·o·gy (zī·mol′ə·jē) *n.* The study of fermentation and the action of enzymes. —**zy·mo·log·ic** (zī′mə·loj′ik) or ·**i·cal** *adj.* —**zy·mol′o·gist** *n.*

zy·mol·y·sis (zī·mol′ə·sis) *n.* Fermentation or the action of enzymes. —**zy·mo·lyt·ic** (zī′mə·lit′ik) *adj.*

zy·mur·gy (zī′mûr·jē) *n.* A branch of chemistry treating of processes in which fermentation takes place, as brewing or winemaking.

ABBREVIATIONS AND ACRONYMS

A or **Å** angstrom unit
A or **A.** ace; America(n)
a. or **A.** or **A** acre; alto; ampere; answer; are (metric measurement); area
AA or **A.A.** Alcoholics Anonymous; antiaircraft
A.A. Associate in Arts
AAA antiaircraft artillery
AAA or **A.A.A.** American Automobile Association
AAAS or **A.A.A.S.** American Association for the Advancement of Science
AAM air-to-air missile
A and M Agricultural and Mechanical (College)
A and R or **A & R** artists and repertory
AAU or **A.A.U.** Amateur Athletic Union
AAUP or **A.A.U.P.** American Association of University Professors
AAUW or **A.A.U.W.** American Association of University Women
ab. about
ab. or **a.b.** (times) at bat
AB Alberta (Canada)
A.B. Bachelor of Arts (L *Artium Baccalaureus*)
A.B. or **AB** able-bodied seaman
ABA or **A.B.A.** American Bar Association; American Basketball Association; American Booksellers Association; American Bankers Association
abbr. or **abbrev.** abbreviated; abbreviation
ABC American Broadcasting Company
abl. ablative
ABM antiballistic missile
Abp. or **abp.** archbishop
abr. abridged; abridgment
abs. absolute(ly)
abstr. abstract
abt. about
Ac actinium
AC or **A.C.** before Christ (L *ante Christum*)
AC or **A.C.** or **a.c.** alternating current
a/c or **A/C** account; account current
a.c. before meals (L *ante cibum*)
acad. academic; academy
acc. acceleration; account; accountant
acc. or **accus.** accusative
acct. account; accountant
ack. acknowledge; acknowledgment
ACLU or **A.C.L.U.** American Civil Liberties Union
ACP or **A.C.P.** American College of Physicians
ACS or **A.C.S.** American Chemical Society; American College of Surgeons
ACT or **A.C.T.** Australian Capital Territory
act. active
actg. acting
AD or **A.D.** active duty; assembly district; of the Christian era (L *anno Domini* in the year of our Lord)
ADA or **A.D.A.** Americans for Democratic Action
add. addenda; addition
addn. or **addnl.** additional
ad int. in the meantime (L *ad interim*)
adj. adjacent; adjective; adjutant
ad loc. at the place (L *ad locum*)
adm. or **admin.** administration; administrative
Adm. or **ADM** Admiral
ADP automatic data processing
adv. adverb; advertisement
ad val. according to value (L *ad valorem*)
advt. advertisement
AEC Atomic Energy Commission
AEF or **A.E.F.** American Expeditionary Force(s)
aeq. equal (L *aequales*)
aero. or **aeron.** aeronautical; aeronautics
aet. or **aetat.** at the age of; of age; aged (L *aetatis*)
AF Air Force
AF or **A.F.** or **a.f.** audio frequency
AF or **AFr.** Anglo-French
AFB Air Force Base
AFC automatic frequency control
AFC or **A.F.C.** American Football Conference
afft. affidavit
A1c. Airman, first class
AFL or **A.F.L.** American Football League
AFL-CIO American Federation of Labor and Congress of Industrial Organizations
Afr. Africa(n)
AFSCME or **A.F.S.C.M.E.** American Federation of State, County, and Municipal Employees
AFT or **A.F.T.** American Federation of Teachers
aft. afternoon
AFTRA or **A.F.T.R.A.** American Federation of Television and Radio Artists
Ag silver (L *argentum*)
Ag. or **Ag** August
A.G. Adjutant General; Attorney General
agcy. agency
agr. or **agric.** agricultural; agriculture
agt. agent
A.H. in the year of the Hegira (L *anno hegira*)
AID Agency for International Development
AK Alaska
a.k.a. also known as
AKC or **A.K.C.** American Kennel Club
Al aluminum
AL Alabama
AL or **A.L.** American League; American Legion
ALA or **A.L.A.** American Library Association
Ala. Alabama
Alas. Alaska
alc. alcohol
ald. alderman
alg. algebra
alk. alkali(ne)
alt. alternate; altitude; alto
alt. or **alter.** alteration(s)
Alta. Alberta (Canada)
alum. aluminum
Am americium
AM or **A.M.** or **a.m.** amplitude modulation; before noon (L *ante meridiem*)
Am. America(n)
A.M. Master of Arts (L *Artium Magister*)
AMA or **A.M.A.** American Medical Association

amb. ambassador
AMDG or A.M.D.G. to the greater glory of God (L *ad majorem Dei gloriam*)
amdt. amendment
AME or A.M.E. African Methodist Episcopal
Amer. America(n)
amp. amperage; ampere
amt. amount
AMVETS American Veterans of World War II and Korea
anal. analogous; analogy; analysis; analytic
anat. anatomical; anatomist; anatomy
anc. ancient
ann. annals; annual; annuity
anon. anonymous(ly)
ans. answer
ant. antenna; antonym
Ant. Antarctica
ANTA American National Theatre and Academy
anthrop. anthropological; anthropology
antiq. antiquarian; antiquity
ANZAC or A.N.Z.A.C. Australian and New Zealand Army Corps
A/O or a/o account of
AP antipersonnel
AP or A.P. Associated Press
A/P account paid; accounts payable
ap. or Ap. apothecaries' (weight or measure)
Ap. Apostle
Ap. or Ap April
a.p. additional premium
APA or A.P.A. American Philological Association; American Philosophical Association; American Psychiatric Association; American Psychological Association
APB all points bulletin
API or A.P.I. American Petroleum Institute
APO Army Post Office
Apoc. Apocalypse; Apocrypha; Apocryphal
app. apparatus; appendix; apprentice
appl. applied
approx. approximate(ly)
appt. appoint; appointment
Apr. April
apt. apartment
Ar argon
AR Arkansas
A/R account receivable
ar. arrival; arrive(s)
Ar. Arabic
ARC or A.R.C. American Red Cross
arch. archaic; architect; architectural; architecture
archaeol. archaeology
archit. architecture
arith. arithmetic; arithmetical
Ariz. Arizona
Ark. Arkansas
arr. arranged; arrival; arrive(d)
art. article; artificial; artillery; artist
As arsenic
AS Anglo-Saxon; antisubmarine
ASCAP or A.S.C.A.P. American Society of Composers, Authors and Publishers
ASPCA or A.S.P.C.A. American Society for the Prevention of Cruelty to Animals
assn. association
assoc. associate; association
ASSR or A.S.S.R. Autonomous Soviet Socialist Republic
asst. assistant
ASTM American Society for Testing Materials
astrol. astrologer; astrological; astrology
astron. astronomer; astronomical; astronomy
A.S.V. American Standard Version (of the Bible)
At astatine
at. atomic
Atl. Atlantic
atm. atmosphere; atmospheric
at. no. atomic number
att. attached
att. or attn. attention
att. or atty. attorney
Att. Gen. or Atty. Gen. Attorney General
attrib. attributive(ly)
ATV all-terrain vehicle
at. wt. atomic weight
Au gold (L *aurum*)
aud. audit; auditor
Aug. August
AUS Army of the United States
Aust. Austria(n)
auth. authentic; author; authority; authorized
auto. automatic; automobile; automotive
aux. or auxil. auxiliary
A/V according to value (L *ad valorem*)
A/V or A-V or AV or A.V. audiovisual
av. avenue; average; avoirdupois
A.V. Authorized Version (of the Bible)
avdp. avoirdupois
ave. avenue
avg. average
A/W actual weight
awol or AWOL absent without leave
ax. axiom
AZ Arizona
az. azimuth

B bishop; boron
b. or B. bachelor; base; baseman; bass; basso; book; born
B. bacillus; Bible; British
Ba barium
B.A. Bachelor of Arts; British Academy; Buenos Aires
bal. balance
b and w black and white
Bap. or Bapt. Baptist
bar. barometer; barometric
Bar. Baruch
Bart. Baronet
bb ball bearing; base on balls
B.B.A. Bachelor of Business Administration
BBB or B.B.B. Better Business Bureau
BBC British Broadcasting Corporation
bbl. barrel
BC or B.C. before Christ; British Columbia (Canada)
B.C. Bachelor of Commerce
BCE or B.C.E. before the Common Era
B.C.S. Bachelor of Commercial Science
B/D or B.D. bank draft; bills discounted; brought down
bd. board; bond; bound
B.D. Bachelor of Divinity
bd. ft. board foot
bdl. or bdle. bundle
bdrm. bedroom
Be beryllium
B/E or B.E. bill of exchange
B.E. Bachelor of Engineering; Board of Education
bef. before

BEF or B.E.F. British Expeditionary Force(s)
Belg. Belgian; Belgium
bet. between
BeV or Bev or bev billion electron volts
bf or bf. or b.f. boldface
B/F brought forward
B.F.A. Bachelor of Fine Arts
BG Brigadier General
bg. bag
bhd. bulkhead
bhp or b.hp brake horsepower
Bi bismuth
Bib. Bible
Big. or Bibl. Biblical
bibl. or bibliog. bibliographer; bibliographical; bibliography
b.i.d. twice a day (L *bis in die*)
biog. biographer; biographical; biography
biol. biologic(al); biologist; biology
Bk berkelium
bk. bank; book
bkg. banking
bkgd. background
bkpg. bookkeeping
bks. barracks
bkt. basket; bracket
bl. bale; barrel; black; block; blue
B/L bill of lading
bldg. building
bldr. builder
blk. black; block; bulk
B.L.S. Bachelor of Library Science
BLT bacon, lettuce, and tomato (sandwich)
blvd. boulevard
BM basal metabolism; bowel movement
BMR basal metabolism rate
bn. or Bn. battalion
BO or B.O. body odor; box office
b.o. or B.O. or BO branch office; broker's order; buyer's option
Bol. Bolivia
BOQ oachelor officers' quarters
bor. borough
bot. botanical; botanist; botany; bottle
BP or B.P. blood pressure; British Pharmacopoeia
B/P or BP or B.P. or b.p. bills payable
bp. bishop
bp. or bpl. birthplace
b.p. boiling point
BPOE or B.P.O.E. Benevolent and Protective Order of Elks
Br bromine
B/R or b.r. bills receivable
br. branch; brass; brown
Br. Britain; British; Brother
brig. brigade; brigadier
Brig. Gen. Brigadier General
Brit. Britain; British
bro. brother
bros. brothers
b.s. or B.S. balance sheet; bill of sale
B.S. or B.Sc. Bachelor of Science
BSA or B.S.A. Boy Scouts of America
bsh. bushel
bskt. basket
Bt. Baronet
btry. battery
Btu or BTU British thermal unit
bu. bushel
Bulg. Bulgaria(n)
bull. bulletin
bur. or bu. bureau
bus. business
BV or B.V. Blessed Virgin
Bvt. Brevet
BW black and white
B.W.I. British West Indies
BX base exchange
bx. box

C carbon
C or C. Celsius; centigrade; coulomb
c. or C. carat; cent; century; chapter; circa; copy; copyright; cup
C. Cape; Catholic; Church; City; Corps; Court
ca or ca. centiare
Ca calcium
CA California
ca. circa
C.A. chartered accountant; chief accountant; chronological age
CAB Civil Aeronautics Board
CAF or C.A.F. cost and freight
cal. calendar; caliber; calorie
Cal. or Calif. California
calc. calculate(d)
can. canon; canto
can. or canc. cancel(ed); cancellation
Can. or Canad. Canada; Canadian
C and W country and western
Cant. Canticle of Canticles; Cantonese
CAP Civil Air Patrol
cap. capacity; capital city; capitalize(d); capital letter
caps capital letters; capsule
Capt. or CAPT Captain
car. carat
Card. Cardinal
CARE Cooperative for American Relief Everywhere, Inc.
CAT clear air turbulence
cat. catalog
cath. cathedral; cathode
Cath. Catholic
CATV community antenna television
cav. cavalry
Cb columbium
CB citizens band
CBC Canadian Broadcasting Corporation
C.B.D or c.b.d. cash before delivery
CBS Columbia Broadcasting System
C.B.W. chemical and biological warfare
cc or cc. cubic centimeter
cc or c.c. or CC or C.C. carbon copy
cc. chapters
CCC Civilian Conservation Corps; Commodity Credit Corporation
CCTV closed-circuit television
ccw or cckw counterclockwise
Cd cadmium
CD or C.D. Civil Defense
C/D or CD or C.D. certificate of deposit
cd. cord
c.d. cash discount
CDR Commander
Ce cerium
C.E. Chemical Engineer; Civil Engineer; Common Era; Corps of Engineers
CEA Council of Economic Advisors
CEC Commodity Exchange Commission
cen. or cent. central; century
cent. centigrade
CEO chief executive officer
cert. or certif. certificate; certification; certified; certify

CETA Comprehensive Employment and Training Act
Cf californium
C/F or c/f or C.F. or c.f. carried forward
cf. compare (L *confer*)
C.F. or c.f. cost and freight
C.F.I. or c.f.i. cost, freight, and insurance
CFL or C.F.L. Canadian Football League
cg or cg. centigram
c.g. center of gravity
C.G. Coast Guard; Commanding General; Consul General
cgs or CGS centimeter-gram-second
ch. or Ch. chain (measurement); champion; (television) channel; chaplain; chapter; child(ren); church
C.H. clearing-house; courthouse; customhouse
Chanc. Chancellor; Chancery
chap. chapter
chem. chemical; chemist; chemistry
chg. change; charge
Chin. China; Chinese
chm. chairman
chron. or chronol. chronicle; chronological; chronology
Chron. Chronicles
C.I. certificate of insurance; cost and insurance
Cia Company (Sp. *Compañia*)
CIA Central Intelligence Agency
CID or C.I.D. Criminal Investigation Department (of Scotland Yard)
Cie Company (F *Compagnie*)
C.I.F. cost, insurance, and freight
C. in C. Commander in Chief
cir. or circ. circa; circular; circulation
circum. or cir. or circ. circumference
cit. citation; cited; citizen
civ. civil; civilian
CJ or C.J. Chief Justice
ck. cask; check
cl or cl. centiliter
Cl chlorine
cl. class; classification; clause; clearance; clerk
c.l. carload; civil law; common law
cld. called; cleared
clk. clerk
clo. clothing
clr. clear
CLU or C.L.U. Chartered Life Underwriter; Civil Liberties Union
cm or cm. centimeter
cm² or cm.² square centimeter
cm³ or cm.³ cubic centimeter
Cm curium
cmdg. commanding
Cmdr. Commander
cml. commercial
C/N or CN circular note; credit note
CNO Chief of Naval Operations
CNS or C.N.S. central nervous system
Co cobalt
CO Colorado
CO or C.O. Commanding Officer; conscientious objector
c/o care of
C/O or c/o or C.O. or c.o. cash order; carried over
Co. or co. company; county
COD or C.O.D. or c.o.d. cash on delivery; collect on delivery
C. of C. Chamber of Commerce
C. of S. Chief of Staff
cog. cognate
COL Colonel
COL or C.O.L. cost of living
col. colonial; colony; color(ed); column
col. or coll. collect(ed); college; collegiate
Col. Colonel; Colorado; Colossians
collat. or coll. collateral
colloq. or coll. colloquial
Colo. Colorado
com. or comm. command; commander; commerce; commercial; commission; committee; common
Com. Commander; Commission; Commissioner; Committee; Commonwealth
comb. combination; combining
comdg. commanding
Comdr. Commander
coml. commercial
comp. compilation; compiled; compiler; complete; composition; compositor; compound
comp. or compar. comparative
Comdt. Commandant
Con. Consul
conc. concentrated
conf. conference
Confed. Confederate; Confederation
Cong. Congregational; Congress; Congressional
conj. conjugation; conjunction
Conn. Connecticut
cons. consonant
Cons. Constable; Consul
consol. consolidated
const. constant
const. or constr. construction
Const. Constable; Constitution(al)
cont. containing; contents; continent; continental; continue(d); contract; contraction; control
contd. continued
contemp. comtemporary
contg. containing
contr. contract; contraction; contralto
contrib. contribution; contributor
CONUS continental United States
coop. cooperative
cop. or copr. copyright
cor. corner; corpus
cor. or corr. correct(ed); correction; correspond; correspondence; correspondent; corresponding
Cor. Corinthians; Coroner
CORE Congress of Racial Equality
corp. or corpn. corporation
C.O.S. cash on shipment; Chief of Staff
cp. compare; coupon
c.p. candlepower; chemically pure
C.P. Command Post; Common Prayer; Communist Party
CPA or C.P.A. Certified Public Accountant
cpd. compound
CPFF cost plus fixed fee
CPI Consumer Price Index
Cpl. or CPL Corporal
CPO Chief Petty Officer
CPR cardiopulmonary resuscitation
cps or c.p.s. cycles per second
CPT Captain
CQ charge of quarters
Cr chromium
cr. credit; creditor; crown
CRC Civil Rights Commission
cres. or cresc. crescendo

crit. critic; critical; criticism
cryst. crystalline
Cs cesium
C/S cycles per second
cs. case
c.s. capital stock
C.S. Chief of Staff; Christian Science; Christian Scientist; Civil Service; county seat
C.S.A. Confederate States of America
CSC Civil Service Commission
CST or **C.S.T.** or **c.s.t.** Central Standard Time
CT or **C.T.** or **c.t.** Central Time
ct. carat; cent
Ct. or **CT** Connecticut
Ct. or **ct.** count; county; court
ctf. certificate
ctg. or **ctge.** cartage
ctn. carton
ctr. center
Cu copper (L *cuprum*)
cu cubic
cum. cumulative
cur. currency; current
cw clockwise
CWO Chief Warrant Officer
C.W.O. or **c.w.o.** cash without order
cwt. hundredweight
cyc. or **cycl.** cyclopedia
cyl. cylinder
CYO or **C.Y.O.** Catholic Youth Organization
C.Z. or **CZ** Canal Zone

d *Brit.* penny (L *denarius*)
D or **D.** December
d. or **D.** date; daughter; day; deceased; degree; diameter; died; dose; drachma
D. Democrat(ic); Doctor (in academic degrees); Dutch
D/A or **D.A.** days after acceptance; deposit account
D.A. Department of Agriculture; District Attorney; Doctor of Arts; doesn't (or don't) answer
dag or **dag.** dekagram
dal or **dal.** dekaliter
dam or **dam.** dekameter
dam² or **dam.²** square dekameter
dam³ or **dam.³** cubic dekameter
Dan. Daniel; Danish
DAR or **D.A.R.** Daughters of the American Revolution
DAT Differential Aptitude Test
dat. dative
dau. daughter
db or **dB** decibel
D.B. Bachelor of Divinity
d.b.a. doing business as
dbl. double
DC or **D.C.** District of Columbia
DC or **D.C.** or **d.c.** direct current
D.C. Doctor of Chiropractic; from the beginning (Ital. *da capo*)
D/D or **DD** or **D.D.** days after date; demand draft
D.D. or **DD** dishonorable discharge; Doctor of Divinity
D.D.S. Doctor of Dental Science; Doctor of Dental Surgery
DDT dichlorodiphenyltrichloroethane
DDVP dichlorvos (dimethyldichlorovinyl phosphate)
DE Delaware
deb. debenture
dec. deceased; decorated; decrescendo
Dec. December
decl. declension
def. defendant; defense; definite; definition
deg. degree
del. delegate; delegation
del. or **dely.** delivery
Del. Delaware
Dem. Democrat; Democratic
Den. Denmark
dent. dental; dentist; dentistry
dep. or **Dep.** depart; departure; deposit; depot; deputy
depr. depreciation
dept. or **Dept.** department
der. or **deriv.** derivation; derivative; derive(d)
det. detached
Deut. Deuteronomy
dev. deviation
DEW Distant Early Warning (Line)
DF or **D.F.** damage free; direction finder
DFC Distinguished Flying Cross
DFM Distinguished Flying Medal
dg or **dg.** decigram
D.G. by the grace of God (L *Dei gratia*); Director General
DH designated hitter
dia. diameter
diag. diagonal; diagram
dial. dialect; dialectal; dialectic(al)
diam. diameter
dict. dictation; dictionary
diff. or **dif.** difference; different
dig. digest
dil. dilute
dim. dimension; diminished; diminuendo; diminuitive
dipl. diplomat(ic)
dir. or **Dir.** director
disc. discount
dist. distance; district
distn. distillation
distr. distribute; distribution; distributor
div. divided; dividend; division; divisor; divorced
D.J. or **DJ** disk jockey; District Judge; Doctor of Laws (L *Doctor Juris*)
dk. dark; deck; dock
dkg or **dkg.** dekagram
dkl or **dkl.** dekaliter
dkm or **dkm.** dekameter
dkm² or **dkm.²** square dekameter
dkm³ or **dkm.³** cubic dekameter
dl or **dl.** deciliter
D.Lit. or **D.Litt.** Doctor of Letters; Doctor of Literature (L *Doctor Litterarum*)
DLO Dead Letter Office
dlr. dealer
dlvy. delivery
dm or **dm.** decimeter
dm² or **dm.²** square decimeter
dm³ or **dm.³** cubic decimeter
DM Deutsche mark
D.M.D. Doctor of Dental Medicine
DMZ demilitarized zone
dn. down
DNA deoxyribonucleic acid
do. ditto
D.O. Doctor of Osteopathy
DOA or **D.O.A.** dead on arrival
DOB or **D.O.B.** or **d.o.b.** date of birth

doc. document
DOD Department of Defense
DOE Department of Energy
dol. dollar
dom. domestic; dominant; dominion
DOT Department of Transportation
doz. dozen
DP or **D.P.** data processing; dew point; displaced person
D.P.H. Doctor of Public Health
dpt. department
DR or **D.R.** dead reckoning; dining room
dr. debit; debtor; drachma; dram; drum
Dr. Doctor; Drive
D.S. or **d.s.** days after sight; document signed; repeat from the sign (Ital. *dal segno*)
DSC Distinguished Service Cross
D.S.C. Doctor of Surgical Chiropody
DSM Distinguished Service Medal
DSO Distinguished Service Order
d.s.p. died without issue (L *decessit sine prole*)
DST or **D.S.T.** or **d.s.t.** Daylight Saving Time
D.S.T. Doctor of Sacred Theology
Du. Duke; Dutch
dup. duplex; duplicate
D.V. God willing (L *Deo volente*); Douay Version (of the Bible)
D.V.M. Doctor of Veterinary Medicine
dwt. pennyweight (*d* < L *denarius*)
DX distance
Dy dysprosium
dz. dozen

e electron
E energy; excellent
E or **E.** Earth; east(ern); English
e. or **E.** eldest; engineer(ing); error
ea. each
E. & O.E. errors and omissions excepted
E by N east by north
E by S east by south
eccl. or **eccles.** ecclesiastic(al)
Eccles. Ecclesiastes
Ecclus. Ecclesiasticus
ECG electrocardiogram
ECM or **E.C.M.** European Common Market
ecol. ecological; ecology
econ. economics; economist; economy
Ecua. Ecuador
ED or **E.D.** Election District
ed. edited; edition; editor; education
EDA Economic Development Administration
EDP electronic data processing
EDT or **E.D.T.** or **e.d.t.** Eastern Daylight Time
educ. education; educational
EE Early English
E.E. Electrical Engineer
EEC or **E.E.C.** European Economic Community
EEG electroencephalogram
EENT eye, ear, nose, and throat
EEO equal employment opportunity
EEOC Equal Employment Opportunity Commission
eff. efficiency
EFT or **E.F.T.** electronic funds transfer
Eg. Egypt(ian)
e.g. for example (L *exempli gratia*)
Egypt. Egyptian
EHF extremely high frequency
EHS Environmental Health Service
EKG electrocardiogram
el. elevation
elec. or **elect.** electric; electrical; electrician; electricity
elem. element; elementary
elev. elevation
ELF extremely low frequency
EM enlisted man
emer. emeritus
emf or **EMF** electromotive force
Emp. Emperor; Empire; Empress
emu or **EMU** electromagnetic unit
enc. or **encl.** enclosed; enclosure
ency. or **encyc.** or **encycl.** encyclopedia
ENE east-northeast
eng. engine; engineer; engineering
Eng. England; English
engr. engineer; engraved; engraver; engraving
enl. enlarge(d); enlisted
Ens. or **ENS** Ensign
entom. or **entomol.** entomological; entomology
env. envelope
EOM or **E.O.M.** or **e.o.m.** end of the month
EPA Environmental Protection Agency
Eph. Ephesians
Episc. Episcopal(ian)
eq. equal; equation
eq. or **equiv.** equivalent
equip. equipment
Er erbium
ERA Equal Rights Amendment
ERIC Educational Resources Information Center
erron. erroneous(ly)
E.R.V. English Revised Version (of the Bible)
Es einsteinium
Esd. Esdras
ESE east-southeast
Esk. Eskimo
ESL English as a second language
ESP extrasensory perception
esp. especially
Esq. or **Esqr.** Esquire
EST or **E.S.T.** or **e.s.t.** Eastern Standard Time
est. estate; estimate; estimated
est. or **estab.** established
Esth. Esther
ET or **E.T.** or **e.t.** Eastern Time
ETA estimated time of arrival
et al. and others (L *et alii*)
etc. et cetera (L, and the rest, and so on)
ETD estimated time of departure
et seq. and the following (L *et sequens*)
ETV educational television
ety. or **etym.** etymological; etymology
Eu europium
Eur. Europe(an)
eV or **ev** or **ev.** electron volt
EVA extravehicular activity
evap. evaporate
evg. evening
EW enlisted woman
ex. example; except(ed); exception; exchange; executive; express; extra
Ex. Exodus
exam. examination; examiner
exc. excellent; except; exception; excursion
exch. exchange; exchanged; exchequer
excl. exclamation; excluding; exclusive
exec. executive
exec. or **exor.** executor
Exod. Exodus

exp. expenses; expired; export; exporter; express
expt. experiment
exptl. experimental
expwy. expressway
ext. extension; exterior; external (ly); extinct; extra; extract
Ezech. Ezechiel
Ezek. Ezekiel

f focal length; forte; function
f or **F** farad
F fluorine
F or **F.** Fahrenheit; false; February; French; Friday
f. folio; following (page, etc.)
f. or **F.** or **F** family; female; feminine; franc; frequency
f/ f number
FAA Federal Aviation Agency
fac. facsimile; factor; factory; faculty
FADM Fleet Admiral
FAO Food and Agriculture Organization (of the United Nations)
FAS Foreign Agricultural Service
F.A.S. or **f.a.s.** free alongside ship
fasc. fascicle
fath. fathom
f.b. or **fb.** freight bill
FBI Federal Bureau of Investigation
FCA Farm Credit Administration
FCC Federal Communications Commission
fcp. foolscap
fcy. fancy
FD or **F.D.** Fire Department
FDA Food and Drug Administration
FDIC Federal Deposit Insurance Corporation
FDPC Federal Data Processing Centers
Fe iron (L *ferrum*)
FEA Federal Energy Administration
Feb. February
fec. he (or she) made it (L *fecit*)
fed. or **Fed.** federal; federated; federation
fedn. or **Fedn.** federation
fem. female; feminine
FEPC Fair Employment Practices Committee
FET or **F.E.T.** Federal Excise Tax
ff fortissimo
ff. folios; following (pages, etc.)
FHA Federal Housing Administration
FIC Federal Information Centers
FICA Federal Insurance Contribution Act
FIFO first in, first out
fig. figurative (ly); figure
fin. finance; financial; finish
Fin. Finland
Fin. or **Finn.** Finnish
F.I.O. free in and out
1st Lt. First Lieutenant
FL Florida
fl. floor; florin; flourished (L *floruit*); fluid
Fla. Florida
fl. dr. fluid dram
Flem. Flemish
fl. oz. fluid ounce
Fm fermium
FM or **F.M.** or **f.m.** frequency modulation
fm. fathom
fn. footnote
fo. folio
F.O. field office; field order; Flight Officer; Foreign Office; forward observer
F.O.B. or **f.o.b.** free on board
fol. folio
fol. or **foll.** following
for. foreign; forester; forestry
F.O.R. free on rails
F.O.S. free on steamer
F.O.T. free on truck
FP or **F.P.** or **f.p.** or **fp** foot-pound; freezing point
FPC Federal Power Commission
FPC or **F.P.C.** or **f.p.c.** fish protein concentrate
fpm or **f.p.m.** feet per minute
FPO field post office; Fleet Post Office
fps or **FPS** foot-pound-second
fps or **f.p.s.** feet per second
Fr francium
fr. fragment; franc; from
Fr. Father; France; French; Friar; Friday
freq. frequency; frequent (ly)
Fri. Friday
front. frontispiece
FRS Federal Reserve System
frt. freight
frwy. freeway
FSLIC Federal Savings and Loan Insurance Corporation
ft. foot; feet
ft.² square foot
ft.³ cubic foot
Ft. Fort
FTC Federal Trade Commission
ft.-lb. or **ft-lb** foot-pound
fur. furlong
fut. future
fwd. forward
FY or **F.Y.** fiscal year
FWD four-wheel drive
FYI or **F.Y.I.** for your information

g or **g.** acceleration due to gravity; gauge; gram
G good
G or **G.** German
Ga gallium
GA or **G.A.** General Agent; General Assembly; general average; General of the Army
ga. gauge
Ga. or **GA** Georgia
Gael. Gaelic
gal. gallon
Gal. Galatians
galv. galvanized
GAO General Accounting Office
GAR or **G.A.R.** Grand Army of the Republic
gar. garage
GATT General Agreement on Tariffs and Trade
GAW or **G.A.W.** guaranteed annual wage
gaz. gazette; gazetteer
G.B. Great Britain
GCA ground-controlled approach
g.c.d. greatest common divisor
GCT or **G.C.T.** or **G.c.t.** Greenwich civil time
Gd gadolinium
gd. good; guard
gds. goods
Ge germanium
gen. gender; genus
gen. or **genit.** genitive
gen. or **genl.** general
Gen. General; Genesis

Gen AF General of the Air Force
geog. geographer; geographic (al); geography
geol. geologic (al); geologist; geology
geom. geometric (al); geometry
ger. gerund
Ger. German; Germany
GHQ general headquarters
GHz gigahertz
GI or G.I. galvanized iron; gastrointestinal; general issue; government issue
gi. gill
GIGO garbage in, garbage out
Gk. Greek
gm or gm. gram
GM guided missile
G.M. General Manager; Grand Master
Gmc. Germanic
GMT or G.M.T. or G.m.t. Greenwich mean time
GNP gross national product
GO general order
GOP or G.O.P. Grand Old Party (Republican Party)
Goth. Gothic
gov. or govt. government
Gov. Governor
gp. group
G.P. general practitioner
GPO general post office; Government Printing Office
GQ general quarters
gr. or gr grade; grain; gram; gravity; gross; group
Gr. Greece; Greek
grad. graduate; graduated
gram. grammar; grammatical
Gr. Brit. Great Britain
GRE Graduate Record Exam
gro. gross
gr. wt. gross weight
GSA General Services Administration
GSA or G.S.A. Girl Scouts of America
GT or G.T. gross ton
gt. a drop (L *gutta*); great
Gt. Brit. Great Britain
gtd. guaranteed
gtt. drops (L *guttae*)
GU Guam
guar. guaranteed
gyn. gynecology
Gy. Sgt. Gunnery Sergeant

H henry; hydrogen
h. or H. or H harbor; hard; hardness; height; high; hit; hot; hour; humidity; husband
ha or ha. hectare
Hab. Habakkuk
Hag. Haggai
Hb hemoglobin
H.B.M. Her (or His) Britannic Majesty
h.c. with due respect (L *honoris causa* for the sake of honor)
H.C. Holy Communion; House of Commons
h.c.f. highest common factor
HCL or H.C.L. or h.c.l. high cost of living
HD or H.D. or h.d. heavy duty
hd. hand; head
hdbk. handbook
hdkf. handkerchief
hdwe. hardware
He helium
HE high explosive
H.E. His Eminence; His (or Her) Excellency
Heb. or Hebr. Hebrew; Hebrews
HEW Department of Health, Education, and Welfare
hex. hexagon; hexagonal
Hf hafnium
HF high frequency
hf. half
hg or hg. hectogram
Hg mercury (L *hydrargyrum* water silver)
HG High German
hgt. height
hgwy. highway
H.H. Her (or His) Highness; His Holiness
hhd. hogshead
HHFA Housing and Home Finance Agency
HI Hawaii
Hind. Hindi; Hindustani
hist. historian; historical; history
HJ or H.J. here lies (L *hic jacet*)
hl or hl. hectoliter
H.L. House of Lords
hm or hm. hectometer
H.M. Her (or His) Majesty
H.M.S. Her (or His) Majesty's Ship
H.N. head nurse
Ho holmium
hon. or Hon. honorable; honorary
HOPE Health Opportunity for People Everywhere
hor. horizon; horizontal
horol. horology
hort. horticultural; horticulture
Hos. Hosea
hosp. hospital
HP or H.P. or hp or h.p. high pressure; horsepower
HQ headquarters
hr. hour
H.R. House of Representatives
H.R.H. Her (or His) Royal Highness
hrzn. horizon
HS or H.S. High School
HST hypersonic transport
HST or H.S.T. or H.s.t. Hawaiian Standard Time
ht. height
H.T. high-tension; high tide
Hts. Heights
HUD Department of Housing and Urban Development
Hung. Hungarian; Hungary
H.V. or h.v. high velocity; high voltage
hvy. heavy
hwy. highway
hyp. hypotenuse
hyp. or hypoth. hypothesis; hypothetical
Hz hertz

I iodine
I. Island; Isle
Ia. or IA Iowa
ibid. or ib. in the same place (L *ibidem*)
IC or I.C. integrated circuit
ICBM intercontinental ballistic missile
ICC Interstate Commerce Commission
Ice. or Icel. Iceland (ic)
ICJ International Court of Justice
ICU intensive-care unit
ID Idaho
ID or I.D. identification
id. the same (L *idem*)

i.d. inside diameter
Ida. Idaho
IE Indo-European
i.e. that is (L *id est*)
I.E. Industrial Engineer
IF intermediate frequency
I.G. association; trust (G *interessengemeinschaft*)
IGY International Geophysical Year
IHP indicated horsepower
IHS symbol and monogram for Jesus, derived from the Greek IH((ΣΟΥ)Σ, Jesus
IL Illinois
ILGWU or **I.L.G.W.U.** International Ladies' Garment Workers' Union
ill. or **illus.** or **illust.** illustrated; illustration; illustrator
Ill. Illinois
ILS instrument landing system
IMF or **I.M.F.** International Monetary Fund
imit. imitative
imp. imperial; import(ed); important
imp. or **imper.** imperative
imp. or **imperf.** imperfect
In indium
IN Indiana
in. inch
in.² square inch
in.³ cubic inch
inc. increase
Inc. or **inc.** incorporated
incl. including; inclusive
incog. incognito
incr. increase(d); increasing
ind. independence; independent; index; industrial; industry
Ind. Indian; Indiana
indic. indicative
inf. below (L *infra*); infantry; inferior; information
inf. or **infin.** infinitive
infl. influence(d)
init. initial
INP International News Photo
I.N.R.I. Jesus of Nazareth, King of the Jews (L *Iesus Nazarenus, Rex Iudaeorum*)
ins. inches; insurance
insol. insoluble
insp. inspected; inspector
Insp. Gen. Inspector General
inst. instant
Inst. or **inst.** institute; institution
instr. instructor; instrument; instrumental
int. interest; interior; internal; international; intransitive
inter. intermediate; interrogation; interrogative
interj. interjection
internat. international
INTERPOL International Criminal Police Organization
interrog. interrogative
intl. or **intnl.** international
intr. or **intrans.** intransitive
intro. or **introd.** introduction; introductory
inv. invoice
I/O input/output
IOOF or **I.O.O.F.** Independent Order of Odd Fellows
I.O.U. or **IOU** I owe you
IP innings pitched
IPA International Phonetic Alphabet
ips or **i.p.s.** inches per second
IQ or **I.Q.** intelligence quotient
i.q. the same as (L *idem quod*)
Ir iridium
IR or **I.R.** information retrieval
Ir. Irish
IRA or **I.R.A.** individual retirement account; Irish Republican Army
IRBM intermediate range ballistic missile
Ire. Ireland
IRO International Refugee Organization
irreg. irregular(ly)
IRS Internal Revenue Service
IS or **I.S.** Intermediate School
Is. or **is.** or **Isl.** or **isl.** island; isle
Isa. Isaiah
ISBN International Standard Book Number
Isr. Israel(i)
ital. italic(s); italicized
Ital. or **It.** Italian; Italy
ITV instructional television
IUD intrauterine device
IV or **I.V.** or **i.v.** intravenous
IWW or **I.W.W.** Industrial Workers of the World

J or **j** joule
J or **J.** jack; Journal; Judge; Justice
JA or **J.A.** joint account; Judge Advocate
Ja. or **Ja** January
JAG Judge Advocate General
Jam. Jamaica
Jan. January
Jap. Japan(ese)
Jas. James
J.C.C. Junior Chamber of Commerce
JCS or **J.C.S.** Joint Chiefs of Staff
jct. or **jctn.** junction
JD or **J.D.** Justice Department; juvenile delinquent
J.D. Doctor of Jurisprudence (L *Juris Doctor*); Doctor of Laws (L *Jurum Doctor*)
JDL or **J.D.L.** Jewish Defense League
Je. or **Je** June
Jer. Jeremiah; Jeremias
jg or **jg.** or **j.g.** junior grade
JHS or **J.H.S.** Junior High School
Jl. or **Jl** July
jnt. joint
Jon. Jonah
Josh. Joshua
jour. journal
JP jet propulsion
J.P. Justice of the Peace
jr. or **Jr.** junior
Jr. Journal
JRC or **J.R.C.** Junior Red Cross
Jth. Judith
Judg. Judges
Judge Adv. Gen. Judge Advocate General
Jul. July
jun. or **Jun.** junior
Jun. June
Junc. or **junc.** junction
juv. juvenile
JV or **J.V.** junior varsity

K Kelvin; king; knit; potassium (L *kalium*); thousand (*kilo-*)
K or **K.** kindergarten
k. karat; kilo; kilogram; kitchen
Kans. Kansas

KB king's bishop
KBP king's bishop's pawn
kc kilocycle
KC or **K.C.** Kansas City; King's Counsel; Knights of Columbus
kc/s kilocycles per second
KD or **K.D.** kiln-dried; knocked down
kg or **kg.** kilogram
KGB (Soviet) Committee of State Security (Russ. *Komitet Gosudarstvennoy Bezopasnosti*)
kHz kilohertz
KIA killed in action
K.J.V. King James Version (of the Bible)
KKK or **K.K.K.** Ku Klux Klan
KKt king's knight
KKtP king's knight's pawn
kl or **kl.** kiloliter
km or **km.** kilometer
km² or **km.²** square kilometer
km³ or **km.³** cubic kilometer
kn or **kn.** knot
KN king's knight
KNP king's knight's pawn
Knt. Knight
K. of C. Knights of Columbus
KP king's pawn
KP or **K.P.** kitchen police
kPa kilopascal
KPH or **K.P.H.** or **kph** or **k.p.h.** kilometers per hour
Kr krypton
KR king's rook
KRP king's rook's pawn
KS Kansas
Kt knight
kt. karat
kV or **kv** kilovolt
kW or **kw** kilowatt
kWh or **kwhr** or **K.W.H.** kilowatt-hour
Ky. or **KY** Kentucky

l or **l.** or **L** liter
L large; *Brit.* pound (sterling)
L or **L.** Latin; left
l. or **L.** or **L** lake; latitude; left; length; line
La lanthanum
La. or **LA** Louisiana
L.A. or **LA** Los Angeles
Lab. Labrador
lam. laminated
Lam. Lamentations
lang. language
lat. latitude
Lat. Latin
LB Labrador
lb. or **lb** pound (L *libra*)
lc or **l.c.** lower case
L/C or **l/c** letter of credit
L.C. Library of Congress
LCD liquid-crystal diode
l.c.d. least common denominator; lowest common denominator
LCDR Lieutenant Commander
L.C.L. or **l.c.l.** less than carload lot
l.c.m. least common multiple
LD lethal dose
ld. load
Ld. Lord
ldg. landing; loading
lect. lecture; lecturer
LED light-emitting diode
leg. legal; legato; legend
leg. or **legis.** legislation; legislative; legislature
LEM lunar excursion module
Lev. Leviticus
lex. lexicon
lf or **l.f.** lightface
LF low frequency
LG Low German
lg. long
lg. or **lge.** large
LGk Late Greek
LH or **L.H.** or **l.h.** left hand; lower half
L.H.D. Doctor of Humane Letters (L *Litterarum Humaniorum Doctor*)
Li lithium
L.I. Long Island
Lieut. Lieutenant
LIFO last in, first out
lim. limited
lin. lineal; linear
ling. linguistics
liq. liquid; liquor
lit. literally
lith. or **litho.** or **lithog.** lithograph; lithographic; lithography
Litt.D. or **Lit.D.** Doctor of Letters; Doctor of Literature (L *Lit(t)erarum Doctor*)
Lk. Luke
LL Late Latin
ll. lines
LL.B. Bachelor of Laws (L *Legum Baccalaureus*)
LL.D. Doctor of Laws (L *Legum Doctor*)
LM lunar module
LNG liquefied natural gas
loc. cit. in the place cited (L *loco citato*)
Lond. London
long. or **lon.** longitude
loq. he (or she) speaks (L *loquitur*)
LP long-playing record: a trademark
LP or **L.P.** or **l.p.** low pressure
LPG liquefied petroleum gas
LPGA or **L.P.G.A.** Ladies Professional Golfers' Association
LPN or **L.P.N.** Licensed Practical Nurse
Lr lawrencium
LR or **L.R.** living room
L.S. left side; letter signed; place of the seal (L *locus sigilli*)
LSAT Law School Admissions Test
LSD lysergic acid diethylamide
LSS life-support system
LST landing ship, tank
LST or **L.S.T.** or **l.s.t.** local standard time
LT or **L.T.** or **l.t.** local time
lt. light
Lt. or **LT** Lieutenant
L.T. long ton; low-tension
Lt. Col. or **LTC** Lieutenant Colonel
Lt. Comdr. or **Lt. Com.** or **LTC** Lieutenant Commander
Ltd. or **ltd.** limited
Lt. Gen. or **LTG** Lieutenant General
Lt. Gov. Lieutenant Governor
Lt. (jg.) or **LTJG** Lieutenant junior grade
L.T.L. or **l.t.l.** less than truckload
ltr. letter
Lu lutetium
lv. leave
LZ landing zone

m or **m.** meter
m² or **m.²** square meter

m³ or m.³ cubic meter
M Mach; mass; thousand (L *mille*)
M or M. Medieval; Monday; Monsieur
M or M. or m. male; married; masculine; mile; minim; minute; month; moon; noon (L *meridies*)
MA Massachusetts
M.A. Master of Arts (L *Magister Artium*)
Macc. Maccabees
mach. machine; machinery; machining; machinist
Mach. Machabees
mag. magazine; magnetism; magneto; magnitude
Maj. or MAJ Major
Maj. Gen. Major General
Mal. Malachi
man. manual
Man. Manitoba (Canada)
manuf. manufacture(r); manufacturing
mar. maritime; married
Mar. March
masc. masculine
MASH mobile army surgical hospital
Mass. Massachusetts
math. mathematical; mathematician; mathematics
Matt. Matthew
max. maximum
MB Manitoba (Canada)
M.B.A. Master of Business Administration
mc megacycle
MC Marine Corps; Medical Corps
MC or M.C. master of ceremonies; Member of Congress
MCAT Medical College Admissions Test
MCPO Master Chief Petty Officer
Md mendelevium
Md. or MD Maryland
M/D or MD or m/d months after date
M.D. Doctor of Medicine (L *Medicinae Doctor*)
mdnt. midnight
mdse. merchandise
ME Middle English
Me. or ME Maine
M.E. Mechanical Engineer; Medical Examiner; Mining Engineer
meas. measure
mech. mechanical; mechanics
med. median; medical; medicine; medieval; medium
M.Ed. Master of Education
meg. megohm
mem. member; memoir; memorial
mep or m.e.p. mean effective pressure
meq. milliequivalent
mer. meridian
Messrs. pl. of *Mr.*
met. metropolitan
metall. metallurgical; metallurgy
meteorol. meteorological; meteorology
MeV or Mev or mev or MEV million electron volts
Mex. Mexican; Mexico
MF medium frequency; Middle French
M.F.A. Master of Fine Arts
mfd. manufactured
mfg. manufacturing
mfr. manufacture(r)
mg or mg. milligram
Mg magnesium
MG machine gun; Major General; military government
Mgr. Manager; Monseigneur; Monsignor
mgt. management
MHz megahertz
MI Michigan; Military Intelligence
mi. mile; mill
mi.² square mile
MIA missing in action
Mic. Micah
Mich. Micheas; Michigan
mid. middle
mil. military
min. minim; minimum; mining; minister; minor; minute
Minn. Minnesota
MIRV multiple independently targeted reentry vehicle
misc. miscellaneous; miscellany
Miss. Mississippi
mixt. mixture
mk. mark
Mk. Mark
mks or MKS meter-kilogram-second
mkt. market
mktg. marketing
ml or ml. or mL milliliter
ML Medieval (or Middle) Latin
MLD minimum lethal dose
Mlle. or Mlle Mademoiselle
mm or mm. millimeter
mm² or mm.² square millimeter
mm³ or mm.³ cubic millimeter
MM. or MM Messieurs (pl. of *Monsieur*)
Mme. or Mme Madame
Mn manganese
MN Minnesota
Mo molybdenum
MO or M.O. or m.o. mail order; modus operandi; money order
mo. month
Mo. Monday
Mo. or MO Missouri
M.O. Medical Officer
mod. moderate; modern
mod. or modif. modification; modified
mol. molecular; molecule
MOM or M.O.M. or m.o.m. middle of month
Mon. Monday; Monsignor
Mont. Montana
MP or M.P. Member of Parliament; Metropolitan Police; Military Police(man); Mounted Police
m.p. or mp. melting point
MPG or mpg or m.p.g. miles per gallon
MPH or mph or m.p.h. miles per hour
Mr. title prefixed to a man's surname (contraction of *Mister*)
Mr. or Mr March
Mrs. title prefixed to a married woman's surname (contraction of *Mistress*)
MS Mississippi
MS or M.S. motor ship; multiple sclerosis
Ms. or Ms title prefixed to a woman's name regardless of her marital status
MS. or MS or Ms. or Ms or ms. or ms manuscript
M.S. Master of Science
msec. or msec millisecond
MSG monosodium glutamate
msg. message
Msgr. Monseigneur; Monsignor
M. Sgt. or MSgt or M/Sgt Master Sergeant
m.s.l. or M.S.L. mean sea level
MST or M.S.T. or m.s.t. Mountain Standard Time

MT Montana
MT or **M.T.** or **m.t.** Mountain Time
Mt. or **mt.** mount; mountain
M.T. metric ton
mtg. meeting
mtg. or **mtge.** mortgage
Mt. Rev. Most Reverend
mun. or **munic.** municipal
mus. museum; music; musical; musician
MV motor vehicle
MVP most valuable player
MX missile experimental
My. or **My** May
myth. mythological; mythology

N knight; nitrogen
N or **N.** Navy; New; normal (solution); Norse; north(ern); November
n. born (L *natus*)
n. or **N.** or **N** name; net; neuter; nominative; noon; note; noun; number
Na sodium (L *natrium*)
n/a no account
N.A. National Association; North America; not applicable; not available
NAACP or **N.A.A.C.P.** National Association for the Advancement of Colored People
Nah. Nahum
NAM or **N.A.M.** National Association of Manufacturers
NAS National Academy of Sciences; Naval Air Station
NASA National Aeronautics and Space Administration
NASL or **N.A.S.L.** North American Soccer League
nat. native; natural
nat. or **natl.** national
NATO North Atlantic Treaty Organization
naut. nautical
nav. naval; navigable; navigation
Nb niobium
N.B. or **NB** New Brunswick (Canada)
N.B. or **NB** or **n.b.** note well (L *nota bene*)
NBA or **N.B.A.** National Basketball Association; National Boxing Association
NBC National Broadcasting Company
NBS National Bureau of Standards
N by E north by east
N by W north by west
N/C or **NC** no charge; no credit
N.C. or **NC** North Carolina
NCAA or **N.C.A.A.** National Collegiate Athletic Association
NCO noncommissioned officer
NCTE or **N.C.T.E.** National Council of Teachers of English
NCV no commercial value
Nd neodymium
n.d. no date
N.D. or **ND** or **N.Dak.** North Dakota
NDEA National Defense Education Act
Ne neon
NE Nebraska; northeast(ern)
N.E. New England
NEA or **N.E.A.** National Education Association
N.E.B. New English Bible
Nebr. Nebraska
NE by N northeast by north
NE by E northeast by east
neg. negative
Neh. Nehemiah
NEI or **n.e.i.** not elsewhere included
NES or **n.e.s.** not elsewhere specified
NET National Educational Television
Neth. Netherlands
neurol. neurology
neut. neuter
Nev. Nevada
NF Newfoundland (Canada); Norman French
N.F. National Formulary
N.F. or **n.f.** no funds
NFC or **N.F.C.** National Football Conference
NFL or **N.F.L.** National Football League
Nfld. Newfoundland (Canada)
NG or **N.G.** or **n.g.** no good
N.G. National Guard
NGC New General Catalog (of Astronomy)
NGk. New Greek
N.H. or **NH** New Hampshire
NHI National Health Insurance
NHL or **N.H.L.** National Hockey League
NHS National Health Service
Ni nickel
NIH National Institutes of Health
N.J. or **NJ** New Jersey
NL New Latin
NL or **N.L.** National League
n.l. it is not permitted (L *non licet*)
NLRB National Labor Relations Board
N/M no mark; not marked
n.m. nautical mile
N.M. or **NM** or **N.Mex.** New Mexico
NMI no middle initial
NNE north-northeast
NNW north-northwest
No nobelium
No. or **no.** north(ern); number (L *numero*)
nom. nominative
non seq. it does not follow (L *non sequitur*)
Nor. or **Norw.** Norway; Norwegian
NORAD North American Air Defense Command
NOS or **n.o.s.** not otherwise specified
nos. or **Nos.** numbers
Nov. November
NOW or **N.O.W.** National Organization of Women; negotiable order of withdrawal
Np neptunium
n.p. no pagination; no place (of publication)
N.P. notary public
NPN nonprotein nitrogen
NRA or **N.R.A.** National Recovery Administration; National Rifle Association
NRC Nuclear Regulatory Commission
ns nanosecond
N.S. or **NS** Nova Scotia (Canada); nuclear ship
N.S. or **n.s.** new series; not specified
NSC National Security Council
nsec. or **nsec** nanosecond
NSF National Science Foundation; not sufficient funds
NT Northwest Territories (Canada)
N.T. or **NT** New Testament
N.T.P. normal temperature and pressure
nt.wt. or **n.wt.** net weight
NU or **n.u.** name unknown
num. numeral
Num. Numbers
numis. numismatic
NV Nevada
NW northwest(ern)
NW by N northwest by north

NW by W northwest by west
N.W.T. Northwest Territories (Canada)
N.Y. or **NY** New York
N.Y.C. or **NYC** New York City
N.Z. or **NZ** New Zealand

O oxygen
O or **O.** Ocean; October; Ohio; Old; order
o/a on or about
OAS Organization of American States
OB or **O.B.** obstetrician; obstetrics
ob. died (L *obiit*); incidentally (L *obiter*)
Ob. or **Obad.** Obadiah
obj. object(ive)
obl. oblique; oblong
obs. obsolete
OCAS Organization of Central American States
occ. occupation
occas. occasional(ly)
OCD Office of Civil Defense
OCS Officer Candidate School
Oct. October
OD or **O.D.** Officer of the Day; olive drab; overdraft; overdrawn; right eye (L *oculus dexter*)
o.d. or **O.D.** outside diameter
O.D. Doctor of Optometry
OE Old English
OED or **O.E.D.** Oxford English Dictionary
OEO Office of Economic Opportunity
OEP Office of Emergency Preparedness
O.E.S. Order of the Eastern Star
off. office; officer; official
OFr. or **OF** Old French
O.F.S. Orange Free State
o.g. or **O.G.** original gum
OH Ohio
OJT on-the-job training
Okla. or **OK** Oklahoma
OL or **O.L.** left eye (L *oculus laevus*)
OMB Office of Management and Budget
ON Old Norse
Ont. or **ON** Ontario (Canada)
Op. or **op.** opus
O.P. observation post; Order of Preachers
O.P. or **o.p.** out of print
op. cit. in the work cited (L *opere citato*)
OPEC Organization of Petroleum Exporting Countries
opp. opposite
opt. optical; optician; optics; optional
OR operating room; Oregon
O.R. or **OR** or **o.r.** owner's risk
orch. orchestra
ord. order; ordnance
Ord. Sgt. Ordnance Sergeant
Ore. or **Oreg.** Oregon
org. organic; organization; organized
orig. origin; original(ly)
ornith. ornithology
orth. orthopedic; orthopedics
ORV off-the-road vehicle
Os osmium
OS Old Saxon
OS or **O.S.** left eye (L *oculus sinister*); ordinary seaman
o/s or **OS** out of stock
O.S.F. Order of St. Francis
OSHA Occupational Safety and Health Administration
O.T. or **OT** Old Testament; overtime
OTB off-track betting
OTC over-the-counter
OTS Officers' Training School
oz. or **oz** ounce
oz. ap. ounce apothecaries'
oz. av. ounce avoirdupois

p pence; proton
p. page; participle; past; pence; penny; per; peseta; peso; pint; pitcher; population; pressure
P pawn; phosphorus; purl
P. President
Pa protactinium
PA public address (system)
PA or **P.A.** Parents Association; power of attorney; press agent; private account; purchasing agent
Pa. or **PA** Pennsylvania
p.a. per annum
PAC or **P.A.C.** political action committee
Pac. Pacific
paleon. paleontology
pam. pamphlet
Pan. Panama
P. and L. or **P and L** or **P. & L.** or **P & L** profit and loss
par. paragraph; parallel; parish
Par. Paralipomenon
paren. parenthesis
Parl. Parliament(ary)
part. participial; participle; particular
pass. passenger; passive; throughout (L *passim*)
pat. patent(ed)
path. or **pathol.** pathological; pathology
pat. pend. patent pending
payt. payment
Pb lead (L *plumbum*)
PBA or **P.B.A.** Patrolmen's Benevolent Association; Permanent Budget Account; Professional Bowling Association
PBS Public Broadcasting Service
PBX private branch (telephone) exchange
PC Peace Corps
p.c. after meals (L *post cibum*); percent(age); petty cash; postal card
PCB polychlorinated biphenyl
PCP phencyclidine
pct. percent
Pd palladium
PD or **P.D.** Police Department
pd. paid
p.d. per diem; potential difference
PDT or **P.D.T.** or **p.d.t.** Pacific Daylight Time
PE Prince Edward Island (Canada)
PE or **pe** printer's error
P.E. physical education; Professional Engineer; Protestant Episcopal
P.E.I. Prince Edward Island (Canada)
PEN or **P.E.N.** International Association of Poets, Playwrights, Editors, Essayists, and Novelists
Pen. or **pen.** peninsula
Penn. or **Penna.** Pennsylvania
per. period; person
Per. Persia(n)
perf. perfect; perforated
perh. perhaps
perm. permanent
perp. perpendicular

pers. person; personal
Pers. Persia(n)
pert. pertaining
pet. petroleum
Pet. Peter
pf. pfennig
pf. or **pfd.** preferred
Pfc. or **PFC** Private, first class
pg. page
P.G. postgraduate
PGA or **P.G.A.** Professional Golfers' Association
pharm. pharmaceutical; pharmacist; pharmacy
Ph.D. Doctor of Philosophy (L *Philosophiae Doctor*)
phil. or **philol.** philological; philology
phil. or **philos.** philosophical; philosopher; philosophy
Phil. Philippians
Philem. Philemon
phon. or **phonet.** phonetics
photog. photographer; photographic; photography
phr. phrase
PHS Public Health Service
phys. physical; physician; physicist; physics
physiol. physiological; physiologist; physiology
pinx. he (or she) painted it (L *pinxit*)
pk. pack; park; peak; peck; pike
pkg. package
pkt. packet; pocket
pkwy. parkway
pl. plate; plural
Pl. or **pl.** place
PLO Palestine Liberation Organization
Pm promethium
PM or **P.M.** Paymaster; Police Magistrate; Postmaster; post-mortem; Prime Minister; Provost Marshal
PM or **P.M.** or **p.m.** afternoon (L *post meridiem*)
pm. premium
pmk. postmark
pmt. payment
P/N or **p.n.** promissory note
pnxt. he (or she) painted it (L *pinxit*)
Po polonium
PO or **P.O.** petty officer; postal order; post office
POB or **P.O.B.** post office box
POC or **P.O.C.** port of call
POD or **P.O.D.** pay on delivery; port of debarkation
POE or **P.O.E.** port of embarkation; port of entry
pol. or **polit.** political; politician; politics
Pol. Poland; Polish
POP or **P.O.P.** point of purchase
pop. population
P.O.R. or **p.o.r.** pay on return
Port. Portugal; Portuguese
POS or **P.O.S.** point of sale
pos. position; positive
poss. possession; possessive; possible; possibly
pot. potential
POW prisoner of war
pp pianissimo
pp. pages; past participle
P.P. parcel post
ppd. or **P.P.** postpaid; prepaid
ppm part per million
ppr. or **p.pr.** present participle
PPS or **P.P.S.** or **p.p.s.** additional postscript (L *post postscriptum*)
ppt. precipitate
pptn. precipitation
PQ Province of Quebec (Canada)
Pr praseodymium
PR or **P.R.** payroll; proportional representation; public relations; Puerto Rico
pr. pair; present; price; printed; pronoun
prec. preceded; preceding
pred. predicate
pref. preface; preference; preferred; prefix
prelim. preliminary
prem. premium
prep. preparatory; preposition
pres. present
Pres. President
prev. previous(ly)
prim. primary; primitive
prin. principal; principle
print. printing
p.r.n. when needed (L *pro re nata*)
prob. probable; probably; problem
proc. procedure; proceedings
prod. produce; produced; producer; product; production
Prof. Professor
pron. pronoun; pronounced; pronunciation
prop. property; proposition; proprietary; proprietor
pros. prosody
Prot. Protestant
prov. province; provincial; provisional; provost
Prov. Proverbs
prox. in the next month (L *promixo mensa*)
PS or **P.S.** or **p.s.** postscript
Ps. or **Psa.** Psalm; Psalms
P.S. Public School
PSAT Preliminary Scholastic Aptitude Test
pseud. pseudonym
psf or **p.s.f.** pounds per square foot
psi or **p.s.i.** pounds per square inch
PST or **P.S.T.** or **p.s.t.** Pacific Standard Time
psych. or **psychol.** psychologist; psychology
Pt platinum
PT or **P.T.** or **p.t.** Pacific Time
pt. part; payment; pint; point; port
PTA or **P.T.A.** Parent-Teachers Association
Pte. *Brit.* Private
ptg. printing
P.T.O. please turn over (a page)
PTV public television
pty. proprietary
Pu plutonium
pub. public; publication; published; publisher; publishing
PVC polyvinyl chloride
Pvt. or **PVT** Private
PW prisoner of war
pwt. pennyweight
PX post exchange

Q or **Q.** queen
Q or **Q.** or **q.** quarto; question
q quart; quire
QB queen's bishop
Q.B. Queen's Bench
QBP queen's bishop's pawn
Q.C. Queen's Counsel

Q.E.D. which was to be demonstrated (L *quod erat demonstrandum*)
q.i.d. four times a day (L *quater in die*)
QKt queen's knight
QKtP queen's knight's pawn
QM Quartermaster
QMC Quartermaster Corps
QMG or **Q.M. Gen.** Quartermaster General
QMS or **Q.M. Sgt.** Quartermaster Sergeant
QN queen's knight
QNP queen's knight's pawn
QP queen's pawn
qq.v. which (things) see (L *quae vide*)
QR queen's rook
qr. quarter; quire
QRP queen's rook's pawn
qt. quart
qt. or **qty.** quantity
qto. quarto
qu. question
quad. quadrangle; quadrant
Que. Quebec (Canada)
ques. question
quot. quotation
q.v. which see (L *quod vide*)
qy. query

r or **R** resistance; roentgen
R rook
R or **R.** or **r.** radius; rare; right; run
r. ruble; rupee
R. Railroad; Railway; Republican; River
Ra radium
RA Regular Army
R.A. Royal Academy
RAAF Royal Australian Air Force
rad. radical; radio; radius
RADM Rear Admiral
RAF Royal Air Force
R and B or **R&B** rhythm and blues
R and D or **R&D** research and development
R and R or **R&R** rest and recreation; rest and recuperation
Rb rubidium
RBC or **R.B.C.** red blood cell; red blood count
RBI or **R.B.I.** or **r.b.i.** or **rbi** run(s) batted in
RC or **R.C.** Red Cross; Roman Catholic
RCAF Royal Canadian Air Force
R.C.Ch. Roman Catholic Church
rcd. received; record
RCMP Royal Canadian Mounted Police
RCN Royal Canadian Navy
rct. recruit
RD or **R.D.** rural delivery
rd. rod; round
Rd. or **rd.** road
Rdm. Radarman
Re rhenium
REA Railway Express Agency; Rural Electrification Administration
Rear Adm. Rear Admiral
rec. receipt; record; recorder; recording; recreation
recd. or **rec'd.** received
recip. reciprocal; reciprocity
Rec. Sec. Recording Secretary
rect. receipt; rectangle; rectangular; rectified; rector; rectory
ref. referee; reference; referred; refining; reformation; reformed; refund; refunding
refl. reflective; reflex; reflexive
refr. refraction
refrig. refrigeration; refrigerator
reg. region; register; registry; regular(ly); regulation
reg. or **regd.** registered
Reg. Regent; Registrar
Reg. or **Regt.** Regiment
REIT real-estate investment trust
rel. relating; relative; released
rel. or **relig.** religion
rep. repair; repeat; report(ed); reporter; representative; republic
Rep. Representative; Republic; Republican
repl. replace(ment)
rept. report
req. request; require(d); requisition
res. research; reserve(d); residence; resigned; resolution
resp. respective(ly)
retd. retained; retired; returned
rev. revenue; reverse; review; reviewed; revise(d); revision; revolution
Rev. Revelation; Reverend
RF radio frequency
RFD or **R.F.D.** rural free delivery
Rh rhodium
RH or **R.H.** or **r.h.** right hand
rhet. rhetoric; rhetorical
R.I. or **RI** Rhode Island
RIP or **R.I.P.** may he (or she) rest in peace (L *requiescat in pace*)
Riv. or **riv.** river
rm. ream; room
Rn radon
RN or **R.N.** registered nurse
RNA ribonucleic acid
rnd. round
ROG or **R.O.G.** receipt of goods
ROI return on investment
rom. roman (type)
Rom. Roman; Romance; Romania(n); Romans
ROTC Reserve Officers' Training Corps
rpm or **r.p.m.** revolutions per minute
rps or **r.p.s.** revolutions per second
rpt. repeat; report
RR or **R.R.** railroad; rural route
R.S. Recording Secretary; Revised Statutes; right side; Royal Society
R.S.V. Revised Standard Version (of the Bible)
RSVP or **R.S.V.P.** or **r.s.v.p.** please reply (F *répondez s'il vous plaît*)
RSWC right side up with care
RT radiotelephone
rt. right
rte. route
Rt. Rev. Right Reverend
Ru ruthenium
Rum. Rumania(n)
Russ. Russia(n)
RV recreational vehicle
R.V. Revised Version (of the Bible)
R.W. Right Worshipful; Right Worthy
Rwy. or **Ry.** Railway

S sulfur
S or **S.** Saint; Saturday; School; Sea; Senate; September; South(ern); Sunday
s. scruple; section; series; shilling; signed; singular; small; son; stere; substantive
Sa. or **Sa** Saturday
s.a. subject to approval; without year (or date) (L *sine anno*)

S.A. Salvation Army; seaman apprentice; sex appeal; Société Anonyme; Socidad Anonima; South Africa
SAC Strategic Air Command
SALT Strategic Arms Limitation Talks
SAM surface-to-air missile
Sam. or Saml. Samuel
S and L or S&L Savings and Loan (Association)
S and M or S&M sadism and masochism; sadist and masochist
sanit. sanitary; sanitation
Sask. Saskatchewan (Canada)
SAT Scholastic Aptitude Test
sat. saturate(d); saturation
Sat. Saturday
Sb antimony (L *stibium*)
sb. substantive
S.B. Bachelor of Science (L *Scientiae Baccalaureus*)
SBA Small Business Administration
S by E south by east
S by W south by west
sc or s.c. small capitals
Sc scandium
sc. namely (L *scilicet*); scale; scene; science
Sc. Scots
S.C. or SC South Carolina
Scand. Scandinavia(n)
sch. school
sci. science; scientific
scil. namely (L *scilicet*)
Scot. Scotland; Scottish
SCPO Senior Chief Petty Officer
Script. Scriptural; Scripture
SD or S.D. special delivery; standard deviation
s.d. without setting a day (L *sine die* without a day)
S.D. or SD or S.Dak. South Dakota
SDA or S.D.A. Students for Democratic Action
SDS or S.D.A. Students for a Democratic Society
Se selenium
SE southeast(ern)
SEATO Southeast Asia Treaty Organization
SE by E southeast by east
SE by S southeast by south
SEC Securities and Exchange Commission
sec. according to (L *secundum*); second; secondary; sector
sec. or sect. section
Sec. or sec. or Secy. or secy. secretary
sel. select(ed); selection
sem. seminary
Sen. or sen. senate; senator; senior
sep. separate(d)
sepn. separation
Sept. or Sep. September
seq. the following (one) (L *sequens*)
seqq. the following (ones) (L *sequentia*)
ser. serial; series; sermon
Serg. or Sergt. Sergeant
serv. service
SF or sf science fiction
Sfc. or SFC Sergeant first class
SG Secretary General; senior grade; Solicitor General; Surgeon General
sgd. signed
Sgt. or SGT Sergeant
Sgt. Maj. Sergeant Major
sh. share; sheet
SHAPE Supreme Headquarters Allied Powers (Europe)
SHF superhigh frequency
shpt. shipment
shr. share
sht. sheet
shtg. shortage
Si silicon
SI International System of Units (F *Système International d'Unités*)
S.I. or SI Staten Island
sig. signal; signature
sing. singular
S.J. Society of Jesus
S.J.D. Doctor of Juridical Science (L *Scientiae Juridicae Doctor*)
SK Saskatchewan (Canada)
Skt. Sanskrit
S.L. salvage loss
Slav. Slavic
sld. sailed; sealed
Sm samarium
sm. small
S.M. Master of Science (L *Scientiae Magister*); Society of Mary
SMaj or SM Sergeant Major
SMSgt Senior Master Sergeant
Sn tin (L *stannum*)
So. or so. south(ern)
S.O. or s.o. seller's option; strikeout
soc. social; socialist; society
sociol. sociological; sociology
sol. soluble
sol. or soln. solution
Sol. Solicitor; Solomon
SOP standard operating procedure; standing operating procedure
soph. sophomore
SP Shore Patrol; Specialist
sp. special; species; specimen; spelling; spirit
Sp. Spain
Sp. or Span. Spanish
s.p. without offspring (L *sine prole*)
SPCA or S.P.C.A. Society for the Prevention of Cruelty to Animals
SPCC or S.P.C.C. Society for the Prevention of Cruelty to Children
spec. special; specifically; specification
specif. specific(ally)
sp. gr. specific gravity
spp. species
Sq. or sq. squadron; square
Sr strontium
SR Seaman Recruit
SR or S.R. shipping receipt
Sr. Senior; Sister
SRO or S.R.O. standing room only
SS. Saints
S.S. or SS steamship; Sunday School; sworn statement
SSA Social Security Administration
SSE south-southeast
SSG or SSgt or S. Sgt. Staff Sergeant
ssp. subspecies
SSR or S.S.R. Soviet Socialist Republic
SSS Selective Service System
SST supersonic transport
SSW south-southwest
st. stanza; statute; stitch; stone
St. Saint; State; Strait; Street
s.t. short ton
sta. station; stationary
stat. immediately (L *statim*); statute

stbd. starboard
std. standard
S.T.D. Doctor of Sacred Theology (L *Sacrae Theologiae Doctor*)
Ste. Saint (F *sainte*)
ster. or **stg.** sterling
STOL short takeoff and landing
STP or **S.T.P.** standard temperature and pressure
stud. student
Su. or **Su** Sunday
sub. subscription; subtract; suburb(an); subway
subj. subject; subjunctive
suf. or **suff.** suffix
suff. sufficient
Sun. Sunday
sup. supra (L, above)
sup. or **super.** superior
sup. or **superl.** superlative
supp. or **suppl.** supplement(ary)
Supt. or **supt.** superintendent
supvr. supervisor
surg. surgeon; surgery; surgical
Surg. Gen. Surgeon General
surv. survey; surveying; surveyor
s.v. under the word (L *sub verbo* or *sub voce*)
svc. or **svce.** service
svgs. savings
SW shipper's weight; shortwave; southwest(ern)
Sw. or **Swed.** Sweden; Swedish
SW by S southwest by south
SW by W southwest by west
Switz. Switzerland
syl. or **syll.** syllable; syllabus
sym. symbol; symmetrical
syn. synonym; synonymous; synonymy
synd. syndicate(d)
syst. system

T or **T.** tablespoon; Territory; Testament; time; Township; transit; true; Tuesday
t. teaspoon; temperature; tense; ton; transitive; troy
Ta tantalum
TA transactional analysis
TAC Tactical Air Command
TAG The Adjutant General
tan tangent
Tb terbium
TB or **T.B.** tuberculosis
T.B. or **t.b.** trial balance
TBA to be announced
tbs. or **tbsp.** or **tb.** tablespoon
Tc technetium
TC Teachers College
TD touchdown; Treasury Department
TDY temporary duty
Te tellurium
tech. technical(ly); technician; technological; technology
tel. telegram; telegraph; telephone
teleg. telegraphy
temp. in the time of (L *tempore*); temperature; temporary
ten. tenor
Tenn. Tennessee
ter. or **terr.** territorial; territory
Ter. or **ter.** terrace
TESL teaching English as a second language
test. testator; testimony
Test. Testament
Teut. Teuton(ic)
Tex. Texas
Th thorium
Th. or **Th** Thursday
THC tetrahydrocannabinol
Th.D. Doctor of Theology (L *Theologiae Doctor*)
theat. theatrical
theol. theologian; theological; theology
therm. thermometer
Thess. Thessalonians
Thurs. or **Thur.** or **Thu.** Thursday
Ti titanium
t.i.d. three times a day (L *ter in die*)
Tim. Timothy
Tit. Titus
tk. tank; truck
TKO technical knockout
Tl thallium
T.L. or **t.l.** total loss; truck load
TLC tender loving care
Tm thulium
TM trademark; transcendental meditation
TMO or **T.M.O.** telegraph money order
TN Tennessee
tn. ton; town; train
tng. training
tnpk. turnpike
TNT trinitrotoluene
T.O. telegraph office
T.O. or **t.o.** turn over
Tob. Tobias; Tobit
topog. topographical; topography
tot. total
Tp. or **tp.** township
t.p. title page
tpk. or **tpke.** turnpike
tr. transitive; translated; translation; translator; transpose; transposition; treasurer; troop; trustee
trans. transaction; transitive; translated; translation; translator; transportation; transverse
transl. translated; translation
transp. transportation
Treas. or **treas.** treasurer; treasury
trib. tributary
trop. tropic(al)
TSgt or **T. Sgt.** Technical Sergeant
tsp. teaspoon
Tues. or **Tue.** or **Tu.** or **Tu** Tuesday
Turk. Turkey; Turkish
TV television
TVA Tennessee Valley Authority
Twp. or **twp.** township
TWX teletypewriter exchange
TX Texas
typ. or **typo.** or **typog.** typographer; typographical; typography

U uranium
U or **U.** union; unit; university; unsatisfactory; upper
UAR or **U.A.R.** United Arab Republic
UAW or **U.A.W.** United Automobile Workers
uc or **u.c.** upper case
UFO unidentified flying object
UH or **U.H.** or **u.h.** upper half
UHF ultrahigh frequency

UK or **U.K.** United Kingdom
UL Underwriters' Laboratories
ult. ultimate(ly)
ult. or **ulto.** last month (L *ultimo mense*)
UMT universal military training
UMTS Universal Military Training Service
UMW or **U.M.W.** United Mine Workers
UN United Nations
UNESCO United Nations Educational, Scientific, and Cultural Organization
UNICEF United Nations Children's Fund (< its original name, United Nations International Children's Emergency Fund)
univ. universal
Univ. or **univ.** university
UNRWA United Nations Relief and Works Agency
UPC universal product code
UPI or **U.P.I.** United Press International
UPS United Parcel Service
US or **U.S.** United States
u.s. as above (L *ut supra*); where mentioned above (L *ubi supra*)
USA or **U.S.A.** United States Army; United States of America
USAF United States Air Force
USAREUR United States Army, Europe
USCG United States Coast Guard
USDA United States Department of Agriculture
USES United States Employment Service
USIA United States Information Agency
USLTA or **U.S.L.T.A.** United States Lawn Tennis Association
USM United States Mail
USMC United States Marine Corps
USN United States Navy
USO United Service Organizations
USP or **U.S.P.** United States Pharmacopeia
USS or **U.S.S.** United States Ship
USSR or **U.S.S.R.** Union of Soviet Socialist Republics
USTA or **U.S.T.A.** United States Tennis Association
usu. usual(ly)
UT Utah
ut sup. as above (L *ut supra*)
UV ultraviolet
UW or **U/W** underwriter
ux. wife (L *uxor*)

V vanadium; vector; victory; volt
v. velocity; verb; verse; version; versus; vide (L, see); voice; voltage; volume; vowel
VA Veterans Administration; Vice Admiral
Va. or **VA** Virginia
VADM Vice Admiral
val. valuation; value; valued
var. variable; variant; variation; variety
VAT or **V.A.T.** value added tax
vb. verb
VC or **V.C.** Vice-Chancellor; Vice-Counsul; Vietcong
VD venereal disease
vel. vellum; velocity
Ven. Venerable
ver. verse; version
vert. vertical
VF video frequency; visual field; voice frequency
VFD or **V.F.D.** volunteer fire department
VFW or **V.F.W.** Veterans of Foreign Wars
VG or **V.G.** very good; Vicar General
VHF very high frequency
v.i. see below (L *vide infra*); verb intransitive
V.I. or **VI** Virgin Islands; volume indicator
vic. vicinity
Vic. Vicar; Victoria
Vice Adm. Vice Admiral
vil. village
VIP very important person
vis. visibility; visual
VISTA Volunteers in Service to America
viz. namely (L *videlicet*)
VL Vulgar Latin
VLF very low frequency
VOA Voice of America
voc. or **vocat.** vocative
vocab. vocabulary
vol. volume; volunteer
vou. voucher
VP or **V.P.** verb phrase; Vice-President
vs. verse; versus
v.s. see above (L *vide supra*)
vss. verses; versions
V/STOL vertical short takeoff and landing
Vt. or **VT** Vermont
v.t. verb transitive
VTOL vertical takeoff and landing
VTR video tape recorder; video tape recording
Vulg. or **Vul.** Vulgate
vv. verses
v.v. vice versa

W tungsten (G *wolfram*)
W or **W.** Wednesday; Welsh; west(ern)
w. or **W.** or **W** water; watt; week; weight; wide; width; wife; with
w/ with
WA Washington
WAC Women's Army Corps
WAF Women in the Air Force
war. warrant
Wash. Washington
WATS Wide Area Telecommunications Service
WAVE Women in the United States Navy (< Women Accepted for Volunteer Emergency Service)
W/B or **W.B.** waybill
WBA or **W.B.A.** World Boxing Association
WBC or **W.B.C.** white blood cell; World Boxing Council
W by N west by north
W by S west by south
WC or **W.C.** or **w.c.** water closet; without charge
WCTU or **W.C.T.U.** Women's Christian Temperance Union
Wed. Wednesday
wh. which
WHA or **W.H.A.** World Hockey Association
whf. wharf
WHO World Health Organization
whse. or **whs.** warehouse
whsle. wholesale
WI Wisconsin
W.I. West Indies
wid. widow; widower
Wis. or **Wisc.** Wisconsin
Wisd. Wisdom

wk. week; work
wkly. weekly
WL water line; wavelength
wmk. watermark
WMO World Meterological Organization
WNW west-northwest
WO Warrant Officer
w/o without
WP word processing
WPM or **wpm** words per minute
wpn. weapon
wrnt. warrant
WSW west-southwest
wt. weight
W.Va. or **WV** West Virginia
WW or **W.W.** World War
Wyo. or **WY** Wyoming

x or **X** experimental; extra; times
X Christ; Christian
X-C cross-country
xd or **x.d.** or **XD** or **X.D.** or **x.div.** without dividend
Xe xenon
x.i. or **XI** or **X.I.** or **x.in.** or **x.int.** without interest
XL extra large
Xmas Christmas
Xn. or **Xtian.** Christian
Xnty. or **Xty.** Christianity
x-ref. cross-reference

Y yttrium
y. yard; year; yen
Yb ytterbium
Y.B. yearbook
yd. yard
yd.² square yard
yd.³ cubic yard
YMCA or **Y.M.C.A.** Young Men's Christian Association
YMHA or **Y.M.H.A.** Young Men's Hebrew Association
y.o.b. year of birth
yr. year; your
yrbk. yearbook
yrs. years; yours
Y.T. or **YT** Yukon Territory (Canada)
YTD or **Y.T.D.** year to date
YWCA or **Y.W.C.A.** Young Women's Christian Association
YWHA or **Y.W.H.A.** Young Women's Hebrew Association

Z atomic number; zenith distance
z. or **Z.** zero; zone
Zach. Zacharias
Zech. Zechariah
Zeph. Zephaniah
Zn zinc
zool. zoological; zoology
ZPG zero population growth
Zr zirconium

A PRONOUNCING GAZETTEER

This gazetteer lists states of the United States, its capital cities and cities with populations over 100,000, countries and other major political divisions of the world, world capitals, world cities, and Canadian provinces and their capitals. Included here also are the more important geographical features of the world. The population figures given for the United States are from the 1980 U.S. Census and those for the rest of the world are from 1982 estimates provided by the United Nations and other sources.

The following abbreviations are used in this section:

ab. about
betw. between
cap. capital
cen. central
col. colony
dist. district
E east(ern)
ft. feet
isl(s). island(s)
met. metropolitan
mi. mile
mtn(s). mountain(s)
N north(ern)
penin. peninsula
pop. population
prov. province
S south(ern)
terr. territory
U.S. United States
U.S.S.R. Union of Soviet Socialist Republics
W west(ern)

Aar·hus (ôr'hōōs) city, E Denmark; pop. 244,839.
Ab·i·djan (ab·i·jän') city, S Ivory Coast; cap.; pop. 1,500,000.
A·bu Dha·bi (ä'bōō dä'bē) city, NE United Arab Emirates; cap.; pop. 300,000.
Ac·cra (ə·krä', ak'rə) city, S Ghana; cap.; pop. 1,000,000.
A·con·ca·gua (ä'kôn·kä'gwä) extinct volcano, W cen. Argentina; highest point in South America; 22,834 ft.
Ad·dis Ab·a·ba (ä'dis ä'bə·bä, ad'is ab'ə·bə) city, cen. Ethiopia; cap.; pop. 1,200,000.
Ad·e·laide (ad'ə·lād) city, S Australia; pop. 952,700 (met.).
A·den (äd'n, ad'n) city, S Southern Yemen; cap.; pop. 343,000.
Ad·i·ron·dack Mountains (ad'ə-ron'dak) mtn. range. NE New York. Also **Adirondacks**.
A·dri·at·ic Sea (ā'drē·at'ik) inlet of the Mediterranean Séa, E of Italy.
Ae·ge·an Sea (i·jē'ən) inlet of the Mediterranean Sea betw. Greece and Asia Minor.
Af·ghan·i·stan (af·gan'ə·stan) country, S cen. Asia; pop. 16,750,000; cap. Kabul.
Af·ri·ca (af'ri·kə) second largest continent, S of Europe and W of Asia.
Ah·med·a·bad (ä'məd-ä-bäd') city, W India; pop. 2,515,195.
Ak·ron (ak'rən) city, NE Ohio; pop. 237,177.
Al·a·bam·a (al'ə-bam'ə) state, SE U.S.; pop. 3,890,061; cap. Montgomery.
A·las·ka (ə·las'kə) state of U.S., NW North America; pop. 400,481; cap. Juneau.
Alaska Peninsula penin. of SW Alaska.
Al·ba·ni·a (al·bā'nē·ə, -bān'yə) country, S of Yugoslavia; pop. 2,875,000; cap. Tirana.
Al·ba·ny (ôl'bə·nē) city, E New York; cap.; pop. 101,727.
Al·ber·ta (al·bûr'tə) prov., W Canada; pop. 2,237,724; cap. Edmonton.
Al·bu·quer·que (al'bə·kûr'kē) city, NW New Mexico; pop 331,767.
A·leu·tian Islands (ə·lōō'shen) isl. group, SW of Alaska.
Al·ex·an·dri·a (al'ig·zan'dre·ə) **1.** city, NE Virginia; pop. 103,217. **2.** city, N Egypt; pop. 2,320,000.
Al·ger·i·a (al·jir'ē·ə) country, NW Africa; pop. 20,000,000; cap. Algiers.
Al·giers (al·jirz') city, N Algeria; cap.; pop. 2,200,000.
Al·le·ghe·ny Mountains (al'ə·gā'nē) mtn. range of Appalachian system; extends from Pennsylvania through Virginia.
Al·len·town (al'ən·toun') city, E Pennsylvania; pop. 103,758.
Alps (alps) mtn. system, S Europe; extends from S coast of France to W coast of Yugoslavia.
Al·tai Mountains (al'tī, äl'-) mtn. system, cen. Asia.
Am·a·ril·lo (am'ə-ril'ō) city, NW Texas; pop. 149,230.
Am·a·zon (am'ə·zon) river, N South America; 3,910 mi. long; carries the largest volume of water of all rivers.
A·mer·i·ca (ə·mer'ə·kə) **1.** The United States of America. **2.** North and South America; the Western Hemisphere.
American Samoa U.S. terr. consisting of 7 isls. in S Pacific; pop. 30,000; cap. Pago Pago.
Am·man (äm·män') city, N cen. Jordan; cap.; pop. 650,000.
Am·ster·dam (am'stər·dam) city, W Netherlands; cap.; pop. 712,294.
A·mur (ä·mōōr') river, E Asia; 2,700 mi. long.
An·a·heim (an'ə·hīm) city, SW California; pop. 221,847.
An·a·to·li·a (an'ə·tō'lē·ə) penin. at W end of Asia; comprises most of Turkey.
An·chor·age (ăng'kər·ij) city, S Alaska; pop. 173,017.
An·des (an'dēz) mtn. range, W South America; connects with the Rockies.
An·dor·ra (an·dôr'ə, -dor'ə) country, SW Europe, betw. France and Spain; pop. 35,000; cap. Andora la Vella.
Andorra la Vel·la (lä vāl'yə) city, Andorra; cap.; pop. 13,500.
An·go·la (ang·gō'lə) country, SW Africa; pop. 7,450,000; cap. Luanda.

An·ka·ra (äng′kə-rə, ang′-) city, cen. Turkey; cap.; pop. 2,561,765.

An·nap·o·lis (ə·nap′ə·lis) city, cen. Maryland; cap.; pop. 31,740.

Ann Ar·bor (an′ är′bər) city, SE Michigan; pop. 107,316.

An·ta·nan·a·ri·vo (an′tə·nan·ə·rē′vō) city, E cen. Madagascar; cap.; pop. 550,000. Also *Tananarive.*

Ant·arc·tic, the (ant·ärk′tik, -är′-) the regions around the South Pole.

Antarctic Circle parallel of latitude at 66° 33′ S; the boundary of the South Frigid Zone.

Antarctic Ocean parts of Atlantic, Pacific, and Indian oceans bordering on Antarctica.

Ant·arc·ti·ca (ant·ärk′tə·kə, -är′-) continent surrounding the South Pole; also **Antarctic Continent**.

An·ti·gua and Bar·bu·da (an·tē′gwə, -gə, bär·bo͞o′də) country, isls. West Indies; pop. 80,000; cap. St. John's.

An·til·les (an·til′ēz) islands of the West Indies excluding the Bahamas; comprises *Greater Antilles:* Cuba, Hispaniola, Jamaica, and Puerto Rico, and *Lesser Antilles:* Trinidad, Tobago, Barbados, Virgin Islands, the Windward Islands, the Leeward Islands, and other small islands.

Ant·werp (ant′wûrp) city, N Belgium; pop. 197,000.

Ap·pa·la·chi·an Mountains (ap′ə·lā′chē·ən) mtn. system, E North America. Also Appalachians.

A·ra·bi·a (ə·rā′bē·ə) penin., SW Asia, betw. the Red Sea and Persian Gulf.

A·ra·bi·an Desert (ə·rā′bē·ən) desert, E Egypt, between Nile and Red Sea.

Arabian Sea part of the Indian Ocean betw. Arabia and India.

Ar·al Sea (ar′əl) salt inland sea, S cen. U.S.S.R.

Arc·tic, the (ärk′tik, är′-) the regions around the North Pole.

Arctic Circle parallel of latitude at 66° 33′ N; the boundary of the North Frigid Zone.

Arctic Ocean sea, N of Arctic Circle, surrounding North Pole.

Ar·gen·ti·na (är′jən·tē′nə) country, S South America; pop. 27,900,000; cap. Buenos Aires.

Ar·i·zo·na (ar′ə-zō′nə) state, SW U.S.; pop. 2,718,425; cap. Phoenix.

Ar·kan·sas (är′kən·sô) **1.** river, cen. U.S.; 1450 mi. long. **2.** state, S cen. U.S.; pop. 2,286,435; cap. Little Rock.

Ar·ling·ton (är′ling·tən) city, N Texas; pop. 160,123.

A·ru·ba (ä·ro͞o′bə) isl. in Netherlands Antilles.

Asia (ā′zhə, ā′shə) largest of the continents; in the Eastern Hemisphere; part of a landmass with Europe and separated from Europe by Ural Mts.

Asia Minor penin. of extreme W Asia, comprising most of Turkey.

A·sun·ción (ä·so͞on·syôn′) city, SW Paraguay; cap.; pop. 530,000.

Ath·ens (ath′enz) city, SE Greece; cap.; pop. 3,000,000 (met.).

At·lan·ta (at·lan′tə) city, NW cen. Georgia; cap.; pop. 425,022.

At·lan·tic Ocean (at·lan′tik) ocean, extending from the Arctic to the Antarctic between the Americas and Europe and Africa.

At·las Mountains (at′ləs) mtn. range, NW Africa.

Auck·land (ôk′land) city, N New Zealand; pop. 818,000 (met.).

Au·gus·ta (ô·gus′tə, ə-) city, S Maine; cap.; pop. 21,819.

Au·ro·ra (ô·rôr′ə, ə-) city, N cen. Colorado; pop. 158,588.

Aus·tin (ôs′tən) city, cen. Texas; cap.; pop. 345,496.

Aus·tral·a·sia (ôs′trəl·ā·zhə, -shə) isls. of the South Pacific, including Australia, New Zealand, and New Guinea.

Aus·tral·ia (ôs·trāl′yə) **1.** isl. continent, South Pacific, SE of Asia. **2.** country comprising this continent and isl. of Tasmania; pop. 14,926,800; cap. Canberra.

Aus·tri·a (ôs′trē·ə) country, cen. Europe; pop. 7,515,000; cap. Vienna.

A·zores (ə·zôrz′, ā′zôrz) three isl. groups of Portugal, E Atlantic.

Bagh·dad (bag′dad, bäg·däd′) city, cen. Iraq; cap.; pop. 3,205,600 (met.).

Ba·ha·mas (bə·hä′məz, -ha′-) country, isl. SE of Florida; pop. 225,000; cap. Nassau.

Bah·rain (bä·rān′) country, isl. group in Persian Gulf off Saudi Arabia; pop. 360,000; cap. Manama.

Bai·kal (bī·käl′) freshwater lake, S U.S.S.R.

Ba·ja California (bä′hä) penin., NW Mexico; betw. the Gulf of California and the Pacific. Also *Lower California.*

Ba·kers·field (bā′kərz·fēld) city, S cen. California; pop. 105,611.

Ba·ku (bä·ko͞o′) city, U.S.S.R.; cap. of Azerbaidzhan Republic; pop. 1,550,000.

Bal·e·ar·ic Islands (bal′ē·ar′ik, bə·lir′ik) isl. group, W Mediterranean; prov. of Spain; comprising islands of Majorca, Minorca, Ibiza, and others.

Bal·ti·more (bôl′tə·môr) city, N Maryland; pop. 786,775.

Ba·ma·ko (bä·mä·kō′) city, S cen. Mali; cap.; pop. 450,000.

Ban·dung (bän′do͝ong) city, W Java, Indonesia; pop. 1,400,000.

Ban·ga·lore (bang′gə·lôr) city, S India; pop. 2,913,537.

Bang·kok (bang′kok) city SW Thailand; cap.; pop. 5,000,000 (met.).

Ban·gla·desh (bäng′glä·desh′) country, S Asia; pop. 92,600,000; cap. Dacca. Formerly *East Pakistan.*

Ban·gui (bäng′gē) city, SW Central African Republic; cap.; pop. 375,000.

Ban·jul (bän·jo͞ol′) city, W. Gambia; cap.; pop. 48,000. Formerly **Bath·urst** (bath′ rst).

Bar·ba·dos (bär·bā′dōs, -dōz) country, isl. in E. Caribbean; pop. 275,000, cap. Bridgetown.

Bar·ce·lona (bär′sə·lō′nə) city, NE Spain; pop. 1,725,000.

Ba·sel (bä′zel) city, N Switzerland; pop. 183,200.

Basse·terre (bas′tər, bäs′-) city, West Indies Associated States, on St. Kitts isl.; cap.; pop. 15,900.

Ba·su·to·land (bə·so͞o′tō·land′) See Lesotho: *a former name.*

Bat·on Rouge (bat′n ro͞ozh′) city, SE cen. Louisiana; cap.; pop. 219,486.

Beau·mont (bō′mont) city, SE Texas; pop. 118,102.

Bei·rut (bā′ro͞ot, bā·ro͞ot′) city, W Lebanon; cap.; pop. 702,000.

Bel·fast (bel′fast -fäst) city, E Northern Ireland; cap.; pop. 345,800.

Bel·gium (bel′jəm) country, NW Europe; pop. 9,830,000; cap. Brussels.

Bel·grade (bel′grād, bel-grād′) city, E Yugoslavia; cap.; pop. 1,000,000.

Be·lize (bə·lēz′) 1. country, E cen. Central America; pop. 175,000; cap. Belmopan. Formerly *British Honduras*. 2. city, E Belize; pop. 42,200.

Bel·mo·pan (bel·mō·pan′) city, cen. Belize; cap.; pop. 4,500.

Ben·ga·si (ben·gä′zē, beng-) city, N Libya; one of two caps.; pop. 282,192.

Be·nin (be·nēn′) country, W Africa; pop. 3,725,000; cap. Port-Novo. Formerly *Dahomey*.

Ber·gen (bûr′gən) city, SW Norway; pop. 208,910.

Ber·ing Sea (bâr′ing, bir′-) part of the North Pacific betw. Alaska and the U.S.S.R., joined to the Arctic by **Bering Strait**.

Berke·ley (bûrk′lē) city, W California; pop. 103,328.

Ber·lin (bər·lin′) city, E cen. Germany; cap. prior to 1945 when divided into the British, French, Soviet, and U.S. sectors. In 1949 the Soviet sector, *East Berlin*, was designated capital of East Germany; pop. 1,146,000. The remaining sectors formed *West Berlin*, associated with West Germany; pop. 1,900,000.

Bern (bûrn, bern) city, W cen. Switzerland; cap.; pop. 183,200. Also **Berne**.

Bhu·tan (bōō·tän′) country, S Asia; pop. 1,350,000; cap. Thimphu.

Bir·ming·ham (bûr′ming·ham) city, N cen. Alabama; pop. 284,413.

Bis·marck (biz′märk) city, S cen. North Dakota; cap.; pop. 44,485.

Bis·sau (bi·sō′) city, W Guinea-Bissau; cap.; pop. 109,500 (met.).

Bitterroot Range a range of Rocky Mtns. along the Idaho-Montana border.

Black Forest wooded mtn. reg., SW West Germany.

Black Sea inland sea betw. Europe and Asia, connects with the Aegean via the Bosporus, the Sea of Marmara, and the Dardanelles.

Blue Ridge Mountains. SW part of the Appalachians.

Bo·go·tá (bō′gə-tä′) city, E cen. Colombia; cap.; pop. 4,486,200.

Boi·se (boi′zē, -sē) city, SW Idaho; cap.; pop. 102,160.

Bo·liv·i·a (bə·liv′ē·ə) country, W cen. South America; pop. 5,900,000; cap. Sucre (constitutional), La Paz (administrative).

Bo·lo·gna (bō-lō′nyä) city, N cen. Italy; pop. 455,853.

Bom·bay (bom·bā′) city, W India; pop. 8,200,000 (met.).

Bon·aire (bə·nâr′) isl. in Netherlands Antilles.

Bonn (bon) city, W West Germany; cap.; pop. 285,000.

Bor·deaux (bôr·dō′) city, SW France; pop. 226,300.

Bor·ne·o (bôr′nē·ō) isl. in Malay Archipelago, SW of the Philippines.

Bos·po·rus (bos′pə·rəs) strait, betw. the Black Sea and the Sea of Marmara.

Bos·ton (bôs′tən, bos′-) city, E Massachusetts; cap.; pop. 562,994.

Bot·swa·na (bot·swä′nä) country, S Africa; pop. 900,000; cap. Gaborone.

Bra·sí·li·a (brə·zē′lyə) city, cen. Brazil; cap.; pop. 1,202,683.

Bra·zil (brə·zil′) country, NE and N cen. South America; pop. 124,500,000; cap. Brasília.

Braz·za·ville (braz′ə·vil) city, SE Congo; cap.; pop. 200,000 (met.).

Brem·en (brem′en) city, NW West Germany; pop. 550,000.

Bridge·port (brij′pôrt) city, SW Connecticut; pop. 142,546.

Bridge·town (brij′toun) city, SW Barbados; cap.; pop. 8,000.

Bris·bane (briz′bān, -bən) city, E Australia; pop. 1,086,500.

Bris·tol (bris′təl) city, SW England; pop. 419,200.

Bristol Channel inlet in the Atlantic betw. Wales and SW England.

British Columbia prov., W Canada; pop. 2,744,467; cap. Victoria.

British Gui·an·a (ge·an′ə, -ä′nə) Guyana: *a former name.*

British Honduras Belize: *a former name.*

British Isles isl. group of W Europe comprising Great Britain, Ireland and adjacent islands.

British Virgin Islands British col., easternmost of the Virgin Islands.

British West Indies isl. group in the Caribbean including Jamaica, the Bahamas, Caymans, British Virgin Islands, British Leeward and Windward Islands and others.

Brno (bûr′nô) city, cen. Czechoslovakia; pop. 371,000.

Brus·sels (brus′əls) city, cen. Belgium; cap.; pop. 1,008,715 (met.).

Bu·cha·rest (bōō′kə·rest, byōō′-) city, S Romania; cap.; pop. 1,861,007 (met.).

Bu·da·pest (bōō′də·pest) city, cen. Hungary; cap.; pop. 2,100,000.

Bue·nos Ai·res (bwā′nəs ī′riz, bō′nəs âr′ēz) city, E Argentina; cap.; pop. 3,000,000.

Buf·fa·lo (buf′ə·lō) city, W New York; pop. 357,870.

Bu·jum·bu·ra (bōō′jōōm·bōōr′ə) city, W cen. Burundi; cap.; pop. 151,000.

Bul·gar·i·a (bul·gâr′i·ə, bōōl-) country, SE Europe; pop. 8,925,000; cap. Sofia.

Bur·ma (bûr′mə) country, SE Asia; pop. 37,500,000; cap. Rangoon.

Bu·run·di (bōō·rōōn′dē, -run′-) country, E. cen. Africa; pop. 4,450,000; cap. Bujumbura.

Cai·ro (kī′rō) city, NE Egypt; cap.; pop. 5,423,000.

Cal·cut·ta (kal·kut′ə) city, NE India; pop. 9,165,650.

Cal·ga·ry (kal′gə·rē) city, S Alberta Canada; pop. 592,743 (met.).

Cal·i·for·nia (kal′ə·fôr′nyə) state, W U.S.; pop. 23,667,565; cap. Sacramento.

California, Gulf of inlet of the Pacific, W Mexico, betw. Lower California and the rest of Mexico.

Cam·bo·di·a (kam·bō′de·ə) See KAMPUCHEA.

Cam·e·roon (kam′ə·rōōn′) country, W cen. Africa; pop. 8,800,000; cap. Yaoundé.

Can·a·da (kan′ə·də) country, N North America; pop. 24,343,181; cap. Ottawa.

Canary Islands isl. group of Spain near NW coast of Africa.

Ca·nav·er·al (kə·nav′ər·əl), **Cape** cape, E Florida; site of the **John F. Kennedy Space Center,** a space research and missiles installation.

Can·ber·ra (kan·bə·rə) city, SE Australia; cap.; pop. 246,100 (met.).

Can·ton (kan·ton′) city, S China; pop. 5,200,000. Pinyin spelling **Guangzhou.**

Cape Town city, S South Africa; legislative cap.; pop. 213,830. Also **Cap·town** (kăp′-toun′).

Cape Verde (vûrd) country, isl. group off NW Africa; pop. 340,000; cap. Praia.

Ca·ra·cas (kə·rä′kəs, -rak′əs) city, N Venezuela; cap.; pop. 3,000,000 (met.).

Car·diff (kär′dif) city, SE Wales; cap.; pop. 273,860.

Car·ib·be·an Sea (kar′ə·bē′ən, kə·rib′ē·ən) part of the Atlantic betw. the West Indies and Central and South America.

Car·o·line Islands (kär′ə·lin) isl. group in the Pacific, E of the Philippines; part of the Trust Territory of the Pacific Islands.

Car·pa·thi·an Mountains (kär·pā′thē·ən) mtn. range, cen. and E Europe.

Carson City (kär′sən) city, W Nevada; cap.; pop. 32,022.

Cas·a·blan·ca (kas′ə·blang′kə, kä′sə·bläng′kə) city, NW Morocco; pop. 2,350,000 (met.).

Cascade Range mtn. range in Oregon, Washington, and British Columbia.

Cas·pi·an Sea (kas′pē·ən) saltwater lake in the S U.S.S.R. and N Iran.

Cas·tries (kas′trēz) city, St. Lucia; cap.; pop. 45,000.

Ca·ta·nia (kä·tä′nyä) city, E Sicily; pop. 378,521.

Cats·kill Mountains (kat′skil) range of the Appalachians in SE New York. Also **Catskills.**

Cau·ca·sus (kô′kə·səs) mtn. range between the Black and Caspian seas.

Cay·man Islands (kā′mən) Brit. dependency; three isls. in Caribbean, S of Cuba. Chief island *Grand Cayman;* pop. 15,000.

Cedar Rapids city, E Iowa; pop. 110,243.

Cel·e·bes (sel′ə·bēz, sə·lē′bēz) isl. of Indonesia, E of Borneo. Also *Sulawesi.*

Central African Republic country, cen. Africa; pop. 2,500,000; cap. Bangui. Formerly **Central African Empire.**

Central America S part of North America, betw. Mexico and Colombia.

Cey·lon (si·lon′) See SRI LANKA.

Chad (chad) country, cen. Africa; pop. 4,650,000; cap. N'Djamena.

Channel Islands British isl. group, English Channel; includes Jersey, Guernsey, Alderney, and Sark.

Charles·ton (chärl′stən, chärlz′tən) city, cen. West Virginia; cap.; pop. 63,968.

Char·lotte (shär′lət) city, S cen. North Carolina; pop. 314,447.

Char·lotte·town (shär′lət·toun) city, NE Canada; cap. of Prince Edward Island; pop. 17,063.

Chat·ta·noo·ga (chat′ə·nōō′gə) city, SE Tennessee; pop. 169,565.

Ches·a·peake (ches′ə·pēk) city, SE Virginia; pop. 114,226.

Chesapeake Bay inlet of the Atlantic in Virginia and Maryland.

Chey·enne (shī·an′, -en′) city, SE Wyoming; cap.; pop. 47,283.

Chi·ca·go (shə·kä′gō, -kô′-) city, NE Illinois; pop. 3,005,072.

Chil·e (chil′ē) country, W South America; pop. 11,500,000; cap. Santiago.

Chi·na (chī′nə) **People's Republic of** country, E and cen. Asia; pop. 1,020,000,000; cap. Peking (Pinyin spelling: Beijing).

Chi·na, Republic of country, on Taiwan and several smaller islands; pop. 18,350,000; cap. Taipei.

China Sea part of the Pacific bordering on China.

Chung·king (chōōng′king′) city, S cen. China; cap. during World War II; pop. 3,500,000. Pinyin spelling **Chong·qing.**

Cin·cin·nat·i (sin′sə·nat′ē, -nat′ə) city, SW Ohio; pop. 385,457.

Ci·u·dad Juá·rez (sē·yōō·dä′hwä·res′) city, N Mexico; pop. 500,000.

Ciudad Tru·jil·lo (trōō·hē′yō) See SANTO DOMINGO.

Cleve·land (klēv′lənd) city, N Ohio; pop. 573,822.

Co·logne (kə·lōn′) city, W West Germany; pop. 975,000.

Co·lom·bi·a (kə·lum′bē·ə) country, NW South America; pop. 28,575,000; cap. Bogotá.

Co·lom·bo (kə·lum′bō) city, W Sri Lanka; cap.; pop. 640,000.

Co·lón (kō·lōn′) city, N Panama, on Caribbean at entrance to Panama Canal; pop. 117,000.

Col·o·ra·do (kol·ə·rad′ō, -rä′dō) state, W cen. U.S.; pop. 2,889,735; cap. Denver.

Colorado River river SW U.S. and NW Mexico, flowing from Colorado into Gulf of California; 1,400 mi. long.

Colorado Springs city, E cen. Colorado; pop. 215,150.

Co·lum·bi·a (kə·lum′bē·ə) city, cen. South Carolina; cap.; pop. 99,296.

Columbia River river, SW Canada and NW U.S.; 1,200 mi. long.

Co·lum·bus (kə·lum′bəs) **1.** city, W Georgia; pop. 169,441. **2.** city, cen. Ohio; cap.; pop. 564,871.

Com·o·ros (käm′ə·rōs) country, isls. off SE Africa; pop. 375,000; cap. Moroni.

Con·a·kry (kän′ə·krē) city, W Guinea; cap.; pop. 575,000

Con·cord (kong′kərd, kon′kôrd′) **1.** city, W California; pop. 103,251. **2.** city, S cen. New Hampshire; cap.; pop. 30,400.

Con·go (kong′gō) country, W cen. Africa; pop. 1,625,000; cap. Brazzaville.

Congo River river, cen. Africa; 2,720 mi. long.

Con·nect·i·cut (kə·net′i·kət) state, NE U.S.; pop. 3,107,576; cap. Hartford.

Con·stan·ti·no·ple (kon′stan·tə·nō′pəl) Istanbul; *a former name.*

Continental Divide ridge of the Rockies separating W flowing and E flowing streams in North America.

Co·pen·ha·gen (kō′pən·hā′gən, -hä′-) city, E Denmark; cap.; pop. 654,437.

Cork (kôrk) city, SW Ireland; pop. 136,269.

Cor·pus Chris·ti (kôr′pəs kris′tē) city, S Texas; pop. 231,999.

Cor·si·ca (kôr′si·kə) isl., N Mediterranean; a dept. of France; pop. 229,400; cap. Ajaccio.

Cos·ta Ri·ca (kos′tə rē′kə) country, Central America; pop. 2,350,000; cap. San José.

Crac·ow See KRAKOW.
Crete (krēt) isl., E Mediterranean; adm. div. of Greece; cap. Canea.
Cu·ba (kyōō'ba) country, isl. in W Caribbean; pop. 9,850,000; cap. Havana.
Cum·ber·land Gap (kum'bər·lənd) passage through Cumberland Mts., betw. Tennessee and Virginia.
Cu·ra·çao (kyōōr'ə·sō', kōō'rä·sou') largest isl. in Netherlands Antilles.
Cy·prus (sī'prəs) country, isl. E Mediterranean; pop. 650,000; cap. Nicosia.
Czech·o·slo·va·ki·a (chek'ə-slō·vä'ke·ə, -vak'ē·ə) country, E cen. Europe; pop. 15,400,000; cap. Prague.

Dac·ca (dä'kä) city, E cen. Bangladesh; cap.; pop. 2,500,000 (met.).
Da·ho·mey (də·hō'mē) Benin: *a former name.*
Da·kar (dä·kär', də-) city, W Senegal; cap.; pop. 978,553.
Dal·las (dal'əs) city, N Texas; pop. 904,078.
Da·mas·cus (də·mas'kəs) city, SW Syria; cap.; pop. 1,200,000.
Da Nang (dä'näng') city, cen. Vietnam; pop. 493,000. Also **Da'nang'**.
Dan·ube (dan'yōōb) river, cen. and E Europe; 1,770 mi. long.
Dan·zig (dan·sig, -tsig, -zig) Gdansk: *the German name.*
Dar·da·nelles (där'də·nelz') strait, NW Turkey; connects Sea of Marmara with the Aegean.
Dar es Sa·laam (dar' es sə·läm') city, E cen. Tanzania; cap.; pop. 700,000.
Dav·en·port (dav'ən·pôrt) city, E Iowa; pop. 103,264.
Day·ton (dā'tən, dāt'n) city, SW Ohio; pop. 203,588.
Dead Sea large salt lake on Israel-Jordan border; 1,292 ft. below sea level.
Death Valley desert basin, SE California; maximum depth 280 ft. below sea level; lowest point on North America.
Del·a·ware (del'ə·wâr) state, E U.S.; pop. 594,317; cap. Dover.
Del·hi (del'ē) city, NE cen. India; pop. 6,196,000.
Den·mark (den'märk) country, NW Europe; pop. 5,130,000; cap. Copenhagen.
Den·ver (den'vər) city, cen. Colorado; cap.; pop. 491,396.
Des Moines (də moin') city, S cen. Iowa; cap.; pop. 191,003.
De·troit (di·troit') city, SE Michigan; pop. 1,203,339.
Devil's Island rocky isl. off the coast of French Guiana; formerly a penal colony.
District of Columbia federal dist., E U.S.; has same boundaries as Washington, cap. of U.S.; pop 637,651.
Dja·kar·ta (jä·kär'tä) See JAKARTA.
Dji·bou·ti (ji·bōō'tē) **1.** country, NE Africa; pop. 335,000; cap. Djibouti. Formerly, *French Territory of the Afars and the Issas;* before 1967 known as *French Somaliland.* **2.** city, E Djibouti; cap.; pop. 200,000 (met.)
Dnie·per (dnye'pər, ne'pər) river, SW U.S.S.R.; 1,420 mi. long. Also **Dne'pr.**
Dnies·ter (dnyes'tər, ne'stər) river, SW U.S.S.R.; 876 mi. long. Also **Dnes'tr.**
Do·ha (dō'hə) city, Qatar; cap.; pop. 190,000.
Dom·i·ni·ca (dom·ə·nē'kə) country, isl. West Indies; pop. 85,000; cap. Roseau.
Do·min·i·can Republic (də·min'i·kən) country, West Indies, on E Hispaniola; pop. 5,575,000; cap. Santo Domingo.
Don (don) river, SW U.S.S.R.; 1,222 mi. long.
Do·ver (dō'vər) city, cen. Delaware; cap.; pop. 23,512.
Dres·den (drez'dən) city, S East Germany; pop. 516,000.
Dub·lin (dub'lin) city, E Ireland; cap.; pop. 525,360.
Dur·ban (dûr'bən) city, SE South Africa; pop. 505,963.
Dur·ham (dûr'əm, du'rəm) city, N cen. North Carolina; pop. 100,831.
Düs·sel·dorf (düs'səl·dôrf) city, W West Germany; pop. 590,000.
Dutch Gui·an·a (gē·an'ə, -ä'nə) Suriname; *a former name.*
Dutch West Indies See NETHERLANDS ANTILLES.

East Berlin See BERLIN.
East China Sea NE part of the China Sea.
Easter Island isl. of Chile, SE Pacific.
East Germany See GERMAN DEMOCRATIC REPUBLIC.
East Pakistan Bangladesh: *a former name.*
Ec·ua·dor (ek'wə·dôr) country, NW South America; pop. 8,350,000; cap. Quito.
Ed·mon·ton (ed'mən·tən) city, W Canada; cap. of Alberta; pop. 657,057 (met.).
E·gypt (ē'jipt) country, NE Africa; pop. 44,750,000; cap. Cairo. Formerly *United Arab Republic.*
El·be (el'bə) river, cen. Europe; 725 mi. long.
El·brus, Mount (el'brōōs) mtn. of the Caucasus range, U.S.S.R.; highest peak in Europe; 18,603 ft.
El·lis Island (el'is) isl., upper New York Bay; former site of U.S. immigration station.
E·liz·a·beth (i·liz'ə·bəth) city, NE New Jersey; pop. 106,201.
El Pas·o (el pas'ō) city, W Texas; pop. 425,259.
El Sal·va·dor (el sal'və·dôr) country, W Central America; pop. 5,150,000; cap. San Salvador.
Eng·land (ing'glənd) country, S Great Britain, W Europe, a division of the United Kingdom of Great Britain and Northern Ireland; pop. 46,221,000; cap. London.
English Channel strait, betw. England and France.
Equatorial Guinea country, W Africa; pop. 380,000; cap. Malabo. Formerly *Spanish Guinea.*
E·rie (ir'ē) city, NW Pennsylvania; pop. 119,123.
Erie, Lake southernmost of the Great Lakes.
Erie Canal waterway, betw. Albany and Buffalo, New York.
Es·sen (es'ən) city, W West Germany; pop. 650,000.
Es·to·ni·a (es·tō'nē·ə) constituent republic, W U.S.S.R., pop. 1,470,000; cap. Tallinn. Officially **Estonian SSR.**
E·thi·o·pi·a (ē·thē·ō'pē·ə) country, E. Africa; pop. 33,000,000; cap. Addis Ababa.
Eu·gene (yōō·jēn') city, W Oregon; pop. 105,624.
Eu·phra·tes (yōō·frā'tēz) river, SW Asia; 1,740 mi. long.
Eur·ope (yōōr'əp) continent, W part of land-

mass with Asia, bounded by Asia and Atlantic Ocean.
Ev·ans·ville (ev′enz·vil) city, SW Indiana; pop. 130,496.
Ev·er·est (ev′ər·ist, ev′rist) mtn., E Nepal; highest point of the earth's surface; 29,028 ft.
Ev·er·glades (ev′ər·glādz) large swampy reg., S Florida.
Eyre, Lake (er) lake, NE South Australia.

Faer·oe Islands (fâr′ō) isl. group of Denmark, NE Atlantic.
Falk·land Islands (fôk′lənd) British col., SW Atlantic.
Fez (fez) city, NE Morocco; pop. 745,000. Also **Fes.**
Fi·ji (fē′jē) country, isl. group in South Pacific; pop. 650,000; cap. Suva.
Fin·land (fin′lənd) country, N Europe; pop. 4,825,000; cap. Helsinki.
Finland, Gulf of part of the Baltic Sea betw. Finland and U.S.S.R.
Flint (flint) city, E cen. Michigan; pop. 159,611.
Flor·ence (flôr′əns, flor′-) city, cen. Italy; pop. 453,300.
Flor·i·da (flor′ədə, flôr′-) state, SE U.S.; pop. 8,594,000; cap. Tallahassee.
Florida Keys isl. group SW of Florida.
For·mo·sa (fôr·mō′sə) Taiwan: *a former name.*
Formosa Strait strait, betw. China and Taiwan.
Fort Lau·der·dale (lô′dər·dāl) city, SE Florida; pop. 153,256.
Fort-La·my (fôr·lȧ·mē′) N'Djamena: *the former name.*
Fort Wayne (wān) city, NE Indiana; pop. 172,196.
Fort Worth (wûrth) city, N Texas; pop. 385,141.
France (frans, fräns) country, W Europe; pop. 54,250,000; cap. Paris.
Frank·fort (frangk′fərt) city, N cen. Kentucky; cap.; pop. 25,973.
Frank·furt (frangk′fərt) city, cen. West Germany; pop. 630.000. Also **Frankfurt-am-Main** (-äm·min′).
Fred·er·ic·ton (fred′rik·tən, -ər·ik-) city, E Canada; cap. of New Brunswick; pop. 47,800.
Free·town (frē′toun′) city, W Sierra Leone; cap.; pop. 215,000.
Fre·mont (frē′mont) city, N California; pop. 131,945.
French Gui·an·a (gē·an′ə, -än′ə) French Overseas dept.; NE South America; pop. 70,000; cap. Cayenne.
French Indochina See INDOCHINA.
French Polynesia French Overseas terr., South Pacific; comprises the Society, Marquesas, Gambier, and other islands; pop. 160,000; cap. Papeete.
French So·ma·li·land (sō·mä′lē·land) Djibouti: *a former name.*
French Territory of the A·fars and the Is·sas (äf′ärz; ē′säz) See DJIBOUTI.
French West Indies isls. in the West Indies comprising Guadaloupe, Martinique and other islands.
Fres·no (frez′nō) city, cen. California; pop. 218,202.
Fris·ian Islands (frizh′ən, frizh′ē·ən) isl. group, North Sea near Germany, Denmark, and the Netherlands.
Front Range a range of Rocky Mtns. in N cen. Colorado.
Ful·ler·ton (fo͝ol′ər·tən) city, SW California; pop. 102,034.

Ga·bon (ga·bon′) country, W Africa; pop. 560,000; cap. Libreville. Formerly **Ga·bo·nese Republic** (gab′ə·nēz′).
Ga·bo·ro·ne (gä′bə·rō′nā) city, SE Botswana; cap.; pop. 60,000.
Galilee, Sea of fresh water lake; betw. NE Israel, SW Syria, and NW Jordan.
Gam·bi·a (gam′bē·ə) country, W Africa; pop. 640,000; cap. Banjul.
Garden Grove city, SW California; pop. 123,351.
Gar·land (gär′lənd) city, N Texas; pop. 138,857.
Gar·y (gâr′ē) NW Indiana; pop. 151,953.
Gdansk (gdäny′sk) city, N Poland; pop. 443,200; Also *Danzig.*
Ge·ne·va (jə·nē′və) city, SW Switzerland; pop. 152,700.
Gen·o·a (jen′ō·ə) city, NW Italy; pop. 760,300.
George·town (jôrj′toun) city, N Guyana; cap.; pop. 200,000.
Geor·gia (jôr′jə) state, SE U.S.; pop. 5,463,105; cap. Atlanta.
German Democratic Republic country, cen. Europe; pop. 16,750,000; cap. East Berlin. Also *East Germany.*
Ger·ma·ny, Federal Republic of (jûr′mə·nē) country, cen. Europe; pop. 61,750,000; cap. Bonn; Also *West Germany.*
Gha·na (gä′nə) country, W Africa; pop. 10,500,000; cap. Accra.
Gi·bral·tar (ji·brôl·tər) Brit. col. on the Rock of Gibraltar; pop. 30,000.
Gibraltar, Rock of penin., S Spain; dominates the Strait of Gibraltar.
Gibraltar, Strait of strait, betw. Spain and Africa, W Mediterranean.
Gi·za (gē′zə) city, N Egypt; pop. 1,246,700.
Glen·dale (glen′dāl) city, SW California; pop. 139,060.
Go·bi Desert (gō′bē) desert, cen Asia.
Golden Gate strait betw. San Francisco Bay and the Pacific.
Good Hope, Cape of penin. SW South Africa.
Gor·ki (gôr′kē) city, W cen. U.S.S.R.; pop. 1,344,000. Also **Gor′kiy, Gor′ky**.
Gö·te·borg (yœ′tə·bôr′ē) city, SW Sweden; pop. 443,000.
Gra·na·da (grə·nä′də) city, S Spain; pop. 246,640.
Grand Canyon gorge of the Colorado River, NW Arizona; ab. 250 mi. long.
Grand Cayman See CAYMAN ISLANDS.
Grand Rapids city, W Michigan; pop. 181,843.
Great Barrier Reef chain of coral reef off the coast of Queensland, Australia.
Great Bear Lake lake, Northwest Territories, Canada.
Great Brit·ain (brit′n) isl. W Europe; principal isl. of United Kingdom of Great Britain and Northern Ireland, comprising England, Scotland, and Wales.
Greater Antilles See ANTILLES.
Great Lakes chain of five lakes, cen. North America; on Canada-United States border; comprises Lakes Superior, Michigan, Huron, Ontario, and Erie.
Great Plains plateau, W North America; E of the Rockies.

Great Salt Lake salt lake, NW Utah.

Great Smoky Mountains mtn. range, North Carolina and Tennessee.

Greece (grēs) country, SE Europe; pop. 9,800,000; cap. Athens.

Green·land (grēn'lənd) isl. of Denmark in N Atlantic, near NE North America.

Green Mountains mtn. range, cen. Vermont.

Greens·boro (grēnz'bûr'ō, -ə) city, N cen. North Carolina; pop. 155,642.

Gre·na·da (gri·nā·də) country, isl. West Indies; pop. 110,000; cap. St. George's.

Gua·da·la·ja·ra (gwäd'ə·lə·här'ə) city, W cen. Mexico; pop. 2,100,000 (met.).

Gua·dal·ca·nal (gwä'dəl·kə·nal') isl. in Solomon Islands in W Pacific.

Gua·de·loupe (gwä'də·lōōp') French overseas dept., Lesser Antilles.

Guam (gwäm) isl. in the Marianas in W Pacific; U.S. possession.

Gan·ges (gan'jēz) river, N India and E Pakistan; 1,560 mi. long.

Gua·te·ma·la (gwä'tə·mä'lä) country, N Central America; 7,700,000; cap. Guatemala City.

Guatemala City city, cen. Guatemala; cap.; pop. 1,250,000.

Guay·a·quil (gwi'ä·kēl') city, W Ecuador; pop. 1,100,000.

Guin·ea (gin·ē) country, W Africa; pop. 5,300,000; cap. Conakry.

Guin·ea-Bis·sau (gin'ē·bi·sō') country, W Africa; pop. 590,000; cap. Bissau. Formerly *Portuguese Guinea*.

Guy·a·na (gī·an'ə, -än'ə) country, N South America; pop. 925,000; cap. Georgetown. Formerly *British Guiana*.

Hague (hāg) The city, W Netherlands; cap.; seat of the government; pop. 456,900.

Hai·fa (hī'fə) city, NW Israel; pop. 360,400 (met.).

Hai·ti (hā'tē) country, West Indies, W Hispaniola; 5,200,000; cap. Port-au-Prince.

Hal·i·fax (hal'ə·fax) city, SE Canada; cap. of Nova Scotia; pop. 280,000 (met.).

Ham·burg (ham'bûrg) city, N West Germany; pop. 1,650,000.

Ham·il·ton (ham'əl·tən) **1.** city, cen. Bermuda; cap.; pop. 2,500. **2.** city, S Ontario, Canada; pop. 542,095 (met.).

Hamp·ton (hamp'tən) city, SE Virginia; pop. 122,617.

Ha·noi (hä·noi') city, N Vietnam; cap.; pop. 2,600,000 (met.).

Han·o·ver (han'ō·vər) city, N cen. West Germany; pop. 535,000.

Ha·ra·re (hä·rä're) city, NE Zimbabwe; cap.; pop. 655,000 (met.). Formerly *Salisbury*.

Har·bin (här'bin) city, NE China; pop. 2,750,000. Pinyin spelling **Harbin**.

Har·ris·burg (har'is·bûrg) city, S cen. Pennsylvania; cap.; pop. 53,264.

Hart·ford (härt'fərd) city, cen. Connecticut; cap.; pop. 136,392.

Ha·va·na (hə·van'ə) city, W Cuba; cap.; pop. 2,000,000 (met.).

Ha·wai·i (hə·wä'ē, hə·wī'yē) state of U.S., North Pacific; pop. 964,691; cap. Honolulu.

Ha·wai·ian Islands (hə·wä'yən, -wī'-) chain of volcanic and coral isls. in N cen. Pacific Ocean. Formerly *Sandwich Islands*.

Heb·ri·des (heb'ri·dēz) isl. group off W coast of Scotland.

Hel·en·a (hel'ə·nə) city, W cen. Montana; cap.; pop. 23,938.

Hel·sin·ki (hel'sing·kē, hel·sing'-) city, S Finland; cap.; pop. 484,000.

Hi·a·le·ah (hi'ə·lē'ə) city, SE Florida; pop. 145,254.

Hi·ma·la·yas (him'ə·lā'əz, hi·mä'lə·yez) mtn. chain between Tibet and India in Nepal, including *Mount Everest*, the world's highest point.

Hir·o·shi·ma (hir'ə·shē'mə, hī·rō'shə·mə) city, SW Honshu isl. Japan; pop. 899,000.

His·pa·nio·la (his'pə·nyō'lə) isl., West Indies; divided into Haiti and the Dominican Republic.

Ho·bart (hō'bärt) city, Tasmania; cap.; pop. 172,000.

Ho·Chi·Minh City (hō'chē'min') city, S Vietnam; pop 3,500,000. Formerly *Saigon*.

Hok·kai·do (hô·kī·dō) isl. of N Japan.

Hol·land (hol'ənd) See NETHERLANDS.

Hol·ly·wood (hol'ē·wōōd) city, SE Florida; pop. 117,188.

Hon·dur·as (hon·dōōr'əs, -dyōōr'-) country, NE Central America; pop. 3,900,000; cap. Tegucigalpa.

Hong Kong (hong'kong', hông'kông) British crown colony, SE China; includes **Hong Kong Island** and some coastal terr.; pop. 5,250,000; cap. Victoria.

Hon·o·lu·lu (hon'ə·lōō'lōō) port city, SE Oahu; cap. of Hawaii; pop. 365,048.

Hon·shu (hon·shōō) isl. of cen. Japan.

Horn (hôrn), **Cape** S extremity of South America.

Hous·ton (hyōōs'tən) city, SE Texas; pop. 1,594,086.

Hudson Bay inland sea; N cen. Canada; connected with the Atlantic by **Hudson Strait.**

Hun·ga·ry (hung'gə·rē) country, cen. Europe; pop. 10,800,000; cap. Budapest.

Huntington Beach (hunt'ing·tən) city, SW California; pop. 170,505.

Hunts·ville (hunts'vil, -vəl) city, N Alabama; pop. 142,513.

Huron, Lake one of the Great Lakes; betw. Michigan and Ontario.

Hwang Ho (hwäng' hō') river, N China; 2,900 mi. long.

Hy·der·a·bad (hī'dər·ə·bad', -bäd') **1.** city, S. cen. India; pop. 1,500,000. **2.** city, SE Pakistan; pop. 795,000 (met.).

I·ber·i·a (ī·bir'ē·ə) penin. of SW Europe containing Spain and Portugal.

Ice·land (īs'lənd) country, isl., North Atlantic; pop. 235,000; cap. Reykjavik.

I·da·ho (ī'də·hō) state, NW U.S.; pop. 944,038; cap. Boise.

Il·lin·ois (il'ə·noi', -noiz') state, NE cen. U.S.; pop. 11,426,518; cap. Springfield.

In·chon (in'chon) city, NW South Korea; pop. 800,000.

In·de·pen·dence (in'di·pen'dəns) city, W Missouri; pop. 111,806.

In·di·a (in'dē·ə) country, S Asia; pop. 700,000,000; cap. New Delhi.

In·di·an·a (in'dē·an'ə) state, NE cen. U.S.; pop. 5,490,260; cap. Indianapolis.

In·di·a·nap·o·lis (in′dē·ə·nap′ə·lis) city, cen. Indiana; cap.; pop. 700,807.

Indian Ocean ocean betw. Africa, Asia, Australia, and Antarctica.

In·do·chi·na (in′dō·chī′nə) **1.** penin. of SE Asia, S of China, including Burma, Thailand, Cambodia, Laos, Vietnam and the Malay penin. **2.** part of this penin. consisting of Laos, Cambodia and Vietnam, formerly called *French Indochina*.

In·do·ne·sia (in′dō·nē′zhə, -shə) country, SE Asia in Malay Archipelago; consisting of Java, Sumatra, most of Borneo, and other islands; pop. 153,000,000; cap. Jakarta.

In·dus (in′dəs) river, S Asia, flowing from Tibet through Pakistan into Arabian Sea; 1,800 mi. long.

I·o·ni·an Sea (ī·ō′nē·ən) part of the Mediterranean betw. Greece and Sicily.

I·o·wa (ī′ə·wə, ī′ə·wā) state, N cen. U.S.; pop. 2,913,808; cap. Des Moines.

I·ran (i·ran′, e·rän′) country, SW Asia; pop. 41,000,000; cap. Teheran. Formerly *Persia*.

I·raq (i·rak′, ī·räk′) country, SW Asia; pop. 14,000,000; cap. Baghdad.

Ire·land (īr′lənd) country, westernmost of the British Isles; pop. 3,480,000; cap. Dublin.

Irish Sea part of the Atlantic betw. Great Britain and Ireland.

Ir·ra·wad·dy (ir′ə·wä′dē) river, Tibet and Burma; 1,200 mi. long.

Ir·ving (ûr′ving) city, N Texas; pop. 109,943.

Is·lam·a·bad (iz·läm′ə·bäd) city, NE Pakistan; cap.; pop. 77,300.

Is·ra·el (iz′rē·əl) country, SW Asia; pop. 4,000,000; cap. Jerusalem.

Is·tan·bul (is′tan·bōōl′, -täm-) city, NE Turkey; pop. 2,990,680. Formerly *Constantinople*.

It·a·ly (it′ə·lē) country, S Europe; pop. 56,500,000; cap. Rome.

Ivory Coast country, W Africa; pop. 8,500,000; cap. Abidjan.

Iz·mir (ēz·mir′) city, W Turkey; pop. 1,049,000. Also *Smyrna*.

Jack·son (jak′sən) city, S cen. Mississippi; cap.; pop. 202,895.

Jack·son·ville (jak′sən·vil, -vəl) city, NE Florida; pop. 540,898.

Ja·kar·ta (jä·kär′tä) city, NW Java; cap. of Indonesia; pop. 5,500,000. Also *Djakarta*.

Ja·mai·ca (jə·mā′kə) country, isl. West Indies; pop. 2,250,000; cap. Kingston.

Ja·pan (jə·pan′) country, E Asia; isl. chain; pop. 118,500,000; cap. Tokyo.

Japan, Sea of part of the Pacific betw. Japan and the Asian mainland.

Ja·va (jä′və, jav′ə) isl. of Indonesia; SE of Sumatra.

Jef·fer·son City (jef′ər·sən) city, cen. Missouri; cap.; pop. 33,619.

Jer·sey City (jûr′zē) city, NE New Jersey; pop. 223,532.

Je·ru·sa·lem (ji·rōō′sə·ləm, -lem) city, Israel; cap.; pop 412,000.

Jid·da (jid′ə) city, W Saudi Arabia; pop. 750,000. Also **Jed′dah**.

Jo·han·nes·burg (jō·han′is·burg, jə-, yo·hän′is-) city, NE South Africa; cap.; pop. 1,536,457 (met.).

Jor·dan (jôr′dən) country, SW Asia; pop. 3,500,000; cap. Amman.

Jordan River river, SW Asia, flowing from mts. in Syria through Jordan into Dead Sea; over 200 mi. long.

Juárez See CIUDAD JUAREZ.

Ju·neau (jōō′nō) city, SE Alaska; cap.; pop. 19,528.

Jut·land (jut′lənd) penin., N Europe; comprises continental Denmark and part of Germany.

Ka·bul (kä′bəl) city, E cen. Afghanistan; cap.; pop. 891,750 (met.).

Kam·pa·la (käm·pä′lä) city, S Uganda; cap.; pop. 330,700.

Kam·pu·che·a (kam·pōō·chē′ə, -sē′ə) country, SW Indochina penin.; pop. 7,000,000; cap. Phnom Penh. Also *Cambodia*.

Kan·sas (kan′zəs) state, cen. U.S.; pop. 2,364,236; cap. Topeka.

Kansas City 1. city, NE Kansas; pop. 161,087. **2.** city, W Missouri; pop. 448,159.

Ka·ra·chi (kə·rä′chē) city, S Pakistan; pop. 5,100,000 (met.).

Kat·man·du (kät′män·dōō′) city, cen. Nepal; cap.; pop. 171,400.

Kat·te·gat (kat′ə·gat) strait of the North Sea betw. Sweden and Jutland

Kau·ai (kou′ī) one of the Hawaiian Islands.

Ken·ne·dy (ken′ə·dē), **Cape** Cape Canaveral: *the former name.*

Ken·tuck·y (kən·tuk′ē) state, E cen. U.S.; pop. 3,660,257; cap. Frankfort.

Ken·ya (kēn′yə, ken′-) country, E Africa; pop. 17,600,000; cap. Nairobi.

Key West southwesternmost of the Florida Keys.

Khar·kov (kär′kôf) city, NE Ukraine, U.S.S.R., pop. 1,444,000.

Khar·toum (kär·tōōm′) city, cen. Sudan; cap.; pop. 333,921.

Khartoum North city, cen. Sudan; pop. 150,991.

Ki·ev (kē·ev′, kē′ev) city, U.S.S.R.; cap. of Ukraine; pop. 2,144,000.

Ki·ga·li (ki·gä′lē) city, cen. Rwanda; cap.; pop. 155,000 (met.).

Kil·i·man·ja·ro (kil′ē-män·jär′ō), **Mount** mtn., NE Tanzania; highest point in Africa; 19,565 ft.

Kings·ton (kingz′tən, king′stən) city, SE Jamaica; cap.; pop. 671,000 (met.).

Kings·town (kingz′toun) city, St. Vincent; cap.; pop. 23,650.

Kin·sha·sa (kēn·shä′sä) city, W Zaire; cap.; pop. 2,500,000. Formerly *Léopoldville*.

Knox·ville (noks′vil, -vəl) city, E Tennessee; pop. 183,139.

Ko·be (kō·bē) city, S Japan; pop. 1,375,000.

Ko·re·a, Democratic People's Republic of (kô·rē′ə, kō-) country, E Asia; pop. 18,750,000; cap. Pyongyang. Also *North Korea*.

Korea, Republic of country, E Asia; pop. 39,350,000; cap. Seoul. Also *South Korea*.

Korea Strait strait, betw. the Sea of Japan and the East China Sea.

Kos·ci·us·ko, Mount (kos′ē·us′kō) mtn. SE Australia; highest peak in Australia; 7,316 ft.

Kra·kow (krak′ou, krā′kō) city, S Poland; pop. 706,100 (met.). Also *Cracow*.

Kua·la Lum·pur (kwä′lə lōōm′pōōr) city, cen. Malaya, cap. of Malaysia; pop. 452,000.

Ku·wait (kōō-wāt′) **1.** country, NE Arabia; pop. 1,550,000; cap. Kuwait. **2.** city, E Kuwait; cap.; pop. 60,000.

Kyo·to (kyō·tō) city, SW Japan; pop. 1,475,000.

Kyu·shu (kyōō·shōō) isl., S Japan.

La·do·ga (lä'də·gə), **Lake** lake, NW U.S.S.R.

La·gos (lä'gōs, lā'-) city, SW Nigeria; cap.; pop. 4,000,000 (met.).

La·hore (lə·hôr') city, E Pakistan; pop. 2,900,000 (met.).

Lake·wood (lāk'wŏŏd) city, cen. Colorado; pop. 112,848.

La·nai (lə·nī') isl. of the Hawaiian Islands.

Lan·sing (lan'sing) city, S cen. Michigan; cap.; pop. 130,414.

La·os (lä'ōs) country, NW Indochina; pop. 3,900,000; cap. Vientiane.

La Paz (lä päz') city, W Bolivia; administrative cap.; pop. 700,000.

La Pla·ta (lä plä'tä) city, E Argentina; pop. 391,200.

Las Ve·gas (läs vā'gəs) city, SE Nevada; pop. 164,674.

Lat·vi·a (lat'vē·ə) constituent republic, NE U.S.S.R.; pop. 2,506,000; cap. Riga. Officially **Latvian SSR.**

Lau·sanne (lō·zán') city, W Switzerland; pop. 131,000.

Leb·a·non (leb'ə·nən) country, SW Asia; pop. 2,700,000; cap. Beirut.

Lee·ward Islands (lē'ward) isl. group of N Lesser Antilles.

Leip·zig (līp'sik, -sig) city, S cen. East Germany; pop. 563,000.

Len·in·grad (len'in·grad) city, NW U.S.S.R.; pop. 4,600,000 (met.). Formerly *St. Petersburg* (1703–1914) and *Petrograd* (1914–1924).

Lé·o·pold·ville (lē·ə·pōld'vil) Kinshasa: *a former name.*

Le·so·tho (lə·sō'tō, -thō) country, S Africa; pop. 1,400,000; cap. Maseru. Formerly *Basutoland.*

Lesser Antilles See ANTILLES.

Lex·ing·ton (lek'sing·tən) city, N cen. Kentucky; pop. 204,165.

Lha·sa (lä'sə) city, SE Tibet; cap.; pop. 70,000.

Li·ber·i·a (lī-bir'ē·ə) country, W Africa; pop. 2,150,000; cap. Monrovia.

Lib·re·ville (lē·brə·vēl') city, W Gabon; cap.; pop. 225,200.

Lib·y·a (lib'ē·ə) country, N Africa; pop. 3,250,000; cap. Tripoli and Bengasi.

Lib·y·an (lib'ē·ən) **Desert** desert, N Africa.

Liech·ten·stein (lik'tən·stīn) country, cen. Europe; pop. 30,000; cap. Vaduz.

Li·ège (lē·ezh', lyezh) city, E Belgium; pop. 220,000.

Lille (lēl) city, N France; pop. 189,555 (met.).

Li·long·we (li·lông'wā) cap. of Malawi; pop. 102,900.

Li·ma (lē'mə) city, W Peru; cap.; pop. 4,900,000 (met.).

Lim·er·ick (lim'rik, -ə·rik) city, W Ireland; pop. 62,140.

Lin·coln (ling'kən) city, SE Nebraska; cap.; pop. 171,932.

Lis·bon (liz'bən) city, W Portugal; cap.; pop. 861,500.

Lith·u·a·ni·a (lith'ōō·ā'nē·ə) constituent republic, NW U.S.S.R.; pop. 3,400,000; cap. Vilna. Officially **Lithuanian SSR.**

Little Rock city, cen. Arkansas; cap.; pop. 158,461.

Li·vo·ni·a (li·vō'nē·ə) city, SE Michigan; pop. 104,814.

Lodz (lōōj) city, cen. Poland; pop. 830,000.

Loire (lwar) river, SE France; 620 mi. long.

Lo·mé (lô·mā') city, S Togo; cap.; pop. 285,000.

Lon·don (lun'dən) **1.** city, Ontario, Canada; pop. 283,668. **2.** city, SE England; cap.; pop. 6,696,000.

Long Beach city, SW California; pop. 361,334.

Long Island isl., SE New York.

Long Island Sound inlet of the Atlantic betw. Long Island and Connecticut.

Los An·ge·les (lôs añjə·lēz, ang'gə·ləs) city, SW California; pop. 2,966,763.

Lou·i·si·an·a (lə·wē'zē·an'ə, lōō'zē-) state, S U.S.; pop. 4,206,312; cap. Baton Rouge.

Lou·is·ville (lōō'ē·vil, lyōō'-, -vəl) city, N Kentucky; pop. 298,451.

Lower California See BAJA CALIFORNIA.

Lu·an·da (lōō·än'də) city, NW Angola; cap.; pop. 500,000.

Luang Pra·bang (lwäng prä·bang') city, N cen. Laos; site of royal residence; pop. 25,000.

Lub·bock (lub'ək) city, NW Texas; pop. 173,979.

Luck·now (luk'nou) city, N cen. India; pop. 883,400.

Lu·sa·ka (lōō·sä'kə) city, cen. Zambia; cap.; pop. 684,000 (met.).

Lü·ta (lōō·tä') city, NE China; pop. 4,000,000. Pinyin spelling **Lüda.**

Lux·em·bourg (luk'səm·bûrg) **1.** country, W Europe; pop. 365,000; cap. Luxembourg. **2.** city, S cen. Luxembourg; cap.; pop. 80,000.

Lu·zon (lōō·zon') isl., N Philippines; largest of the Philippine Islands.

Ly·ons (lē·ōn', lī'ənz) city, E cen. France; pop. 463,000.

Ma·cao (mə·kou', -kä'ō) **1.** isl., Canton river delta, China. **2.** Portuguese overseas prov. comprising a penin. of Macao isl. and two small isls.; pop. 300,000; **3.** city; cap. of Macao.

Mac·ken·zie (mə·ken'zē) river, NW Canada; 2,640 mi. long.

Mc·Kin·Ley, Mount (mə·kin'lē) mtn. S cen. Alaska; 20,320 ft.; highest peak in North America.

Ma·con (mā'kən) city, cen. Georgia; pop. 116,860.

Mad·a·gas·car (mad'ə-gas'kər) country, isl., Indian Ocean off SE Africa; pop. 9,190,000; cap. Antananarivo. Formerly **Mal·a·gas·y Republic** (mal'ə·gas'ē).

Ma·dei·ra (mə·dir'ə) Portuguese isl. group in N Atlantic, W of Morocco.

Mad·i·son (mad'ə·sən) city, S cen. Wisconsin; cap.; pop. 170,616.

Ma·dras (mə·dras', -dräs', mad'rəs) S India; pop. 4,276,635 (met.).

Ma·drid (mə·drid') city, cen. Spain; cap.; pop. 3,275,000.

Ma·du·ra (mä·dōō'rä) isl. of Indonesia E of Java.

Maine (mān) state, NE U.S.; pop. 1,125,027; cap. Augusta.

Ma·gel·lan (mə·jel'ən), **Strait of** channel betw. the Atlantic and Pacific, separating the South American mainland from Tierra del Fuego.

Ma·jor·ca (mə·jôr′kə, -yôr′-) largest of the Balearic Islands.

Malacca (mə·lak′ə) **Strait of** strait betw. Sumatra and the Malay Peninsula.

Mál·a·ga (mal′ə·gə) city, S Spain: pop. 502,200.

Ma·la·wi (mä′lä·wē, mə·lä′-) country, SE Africa: pop. 6,275,000: cap. Lilongwe.

Ma·lay Archipelago (mā′lā, mə·lā′) isl. group off SE Asia: includes isls. of Indonesia, Malaysia, and the Philippines.

Malay Peninsula S penin. of Asia: includes Malaysia and part of Thailand.

Ma·lay·sia (mə·lā′zhə, -shə) country, SE Asia: pop. 14,750,000: cap. Kuala Lumpur.

Mal·dives (mal′dīvz) country, atolls in Indian Ocean: pop. 160,000: cap. Malé. Formerly **Maldive Islands.**

Ma·lé (mäl′ē) chief isl. and cap. of Maldives: pop. 29,600.

Ma·li (mä′lē) country, W Africa: pop. 7,350,000: cap. Bamako.

Mal·ta (môl′tə) country, isl. in Mediterranean, SE of Sicily: pop. 375,000: cap. Valletta.

Man (man), **Isle of** one of the British Isles, cen. Irish Sea: pop. 70,000: cap. Douglas.

Ma·na·gua (mä·nä′gwä) city, SW Nicaragua: cap.: pop. 517,500.

Ma·na·ma (mə·nam′ə) city, Bahrain: cap.: pop. 150,000.

Man·da·lay (man′də·lā, man′də·lā′) city, cen. Burma: pop. 458,000.

Man·hat·tan (mən·hat′ən, man-) isl., SE New York: boro. New York City.

Ma·nil·a (mə·nil′ə) city, SW Luzon, Philippines: pop. 1,600,000.

Man·i·to·ba (man′ə·tō′bə, -tō·bä′) prov., cen. Canada: pop. 1,026,241: cap. Winnipeg.

Ma·pu·to (mə·po͞ot′ō) city, S Mozambique: cap.: pop. 750,000.

Ma·ra·cai·bo (mä′rä·kī′bō) city, NW Venezuela: pop. 820,000.

Maracaibo, Lake lake, NW Venezuela.

Ma·ri·a·nas Islands (mär′ē·ä′näs) isl. group, W Pacific: including Guam, Saipan, Tinian, and Rota; part of the U.S. Trust Terr. of the Pacific Islands (excluding Guam).

Mar·ma·ra (mär′mə·rə), **Sea of** sea betw. Europe and Asia, connecting the Bosporus and the Dardanelles. Also **Marmo·ra** (mär′mə·rə, mär·môr′ə, -mō·rə).

Marne (märn) river, NE France: 325 mi. long.

Mar·que·sas Islands (mär·kā′säs, -kē′-) isl. group S Pacific in French Polynesia.

Mar·ra·kesh (mä·rä′kesh, mar·ə·kesh′) city, SW Morocco: pop. 1,225,000 (met.).

Mar·seille (mar·sā′y′) city, SE France: pop. 914,350. Also **Marseilles** (mär·sā′, -sālz′).

Mar·shall Islands (mär′shəl) isl. group in Pacific: part of the Trust Territory of the Pacific Islands.

Mar·ti·nique (mär′ti·nēk′) isl., French overseas dept.: Lesser Antilles.

Mar·y·land (mâr′i·lənd, mer′i-) state, E U.S.: pop. 4,216,975: cap. Annapolis.

Ma·se·ru (maz′ə·ro͞o′) city, NW Lesotho: cap.: pop. 75,000.

Mas·sa·chu·setts (mas′ə·cho͞o′sits) state, NE U.S.: pop. 5,737,037: cap. Boston.

Mat·ter·horn (mat′ər·hôrn) mtn. in the Alps on the Swiss-Italian border: 14,701 ft.

Mau·i (mou′ē) isl. of the Hawaiian Islands.

Mau·ri·ta·ni·a (môr′ə·tā′nē·ə) country, W Africa: pop. 1,725,000: cap. Nouakchott.

Mau·ri·ti·us (mô·rish′ē·əs, mô·rish′əs) country, isl. in Indian Ocean, E of Madagascar: pop. 950,000: cap. Port Louis.

M·ba·bane (em·bə·bän′) cap. of Swaziland: pop. 23,000.

Mec·ca (mek′ə) city, W Saudi Arabia: pop. 500,000.

Me·di·na (mə·dē′nə) city, W Saudi Arabia: pop. 198,200.

Med·i·ter·ra·ne·an Sea (med′ə·tə·rā′nē·ən) sea betw. Europe, Asia, and Africa.

Me·kong (mā·kong′) river, SE Asia: 2,500 mi. long.

Mel·a·ne·sia (mel′ə·nē′zhə, -shə) isls. of the W Pacific S of the Equator: including Bismarck Archipelago, the Solomon Islands, New Hebrides, New Caledonia and the Fijis.

Mel·bourne (mel′bərn) city, S Australia: pop. 2,803,600 (met.).

Mem·phis (mem′fis) city, SW Tennessee: pop. 646,356.

Me·sa (mā′sə) city, S cen. Arizona: pop. 152,453.

Meuse (myo͞oz) river, W Europe: 580 mi. long.

Mex·i·co (mek′sə·kō) country, S North America: pop. 72,900,000: cap. Mexico City.

Mexico, Gulf of inlet of the Atlantic, betw. the United States, Mexico, and Cuba.

Mexico City city, S cen. Mexico: cap.: pop. 9,200,000.

Mi·am·i (mi·am′ē, -am′ə) city, SE Florida: pop. 346,931.

Mich·i·gan (mish′ə·gən) state, N U.S.: pop. 9,262,078: cap. Lansing.

Michigan, Lake one of the Great Lakes: betw. Michigan and Wisconsin.

Mi·cro·ne·sia (mī′krə·nē′zhə, -shə) See PACIFIC ISLANDS, TRUST TERRITORY OF THE.

Mid·way Islands (mid′wā′) isls. in N Pacific, NW of Honolulu: in Hawaiian group, but not part of state of Hawaii: U.S. terr.

Mi·lan (mi·lan′, -län′) city, N Italy: pop. 1,635,000.

Mil·wau·kee (mil·wô′kē) city, SE Wisconsin: pop. 636,212.

Min·ne·ap·o·lis (min′ē·ap′ə·lis) city, E Minnesota: pop. 370,951.

Min·ne·so·ta (min′ə·sō′tə) state, N U.S.: pop. 4,075,970: cap. St. Paul.

Minsk (minsk) city, U.S.S.R.: cap. Belorussia: pop. 1,276,000.

Mis·sis·sip·pi (mis′ə·sip′ē) state, S U.S.: pop. 2,520,638: cap. Jackson.

Mississippi River river, cen. U.S.: 2,350 mi. long.

Mis·sou·ri (mi·zo͞or′ē, -zo͞or′ə) state, W cen. U.S.: pop. 4,916,759: cap. Jefferson City.

Missouri River river, NW cen. U.S.: 2,470 mi. long.

Mo·bile (mō·bēl′, mō′bēl) city, SW Alabama: pop. 200,452.

Mo·des·to (mə·des′tō) city, cen. California: pop. 106,105.

Mog·a·di·shu (mog′ə·dish′o͞o) city, E Somalia: cap.: pop. 500,000. Also Mog′a·di′sco (-de′sho).

Mo·ja·ve Desert (mō·hä′vē) desert, S California.

Mo·lo·kai (mō′lə·kī′) isl. cen. Hawaiian Islands.

Mo·luc·ca Islands (mə·luk′ə) isl. group of Indonesia, betw. Celebes and New Guinea. Formerly *Spice Islands.*

Mon·a·co (mon'ə·kō, me·nä'kō) country, S Europe; pop. 30,000.

Mon·go·li·a (mong·gō'lē·ə, mon-) country, E Asia; pop. 1,725,000; cap. Ulan Bator. Formerly *Outer Mongolia.*

Mon·ro·vi·a (mən·rō'vē·ə) city, E Liberia; cap.; pop. 229,300.

Mon·tan·a (mon·tan'ə) state, NW U.S.; pop. 786,690; cap. Helena.

Mont Blanc (mont blangk') highest mountain of the Alps, on the French-Italian border; 15,781 ft.

Mon·te Car·lo (mon'tē kär'lō) city, Monaco; pop. 9,950.

Mont·ter·rey (mont'tə·rā') city, NE Mexico; pop. 1,300,000.

Mon·te·vid·e·o (mon'tə·vi·dā'ō -vid'ē·ō) city, S Uruguay; cap.; pop. 1,250,000.

Mont·gom·er·y (mont·gum'ər·ē, mənt-) city, E cen. Alabama; cap.; pop. 178,157.

Mon·ti·cel·lo (mon'tə·sel'ō, -chel'ō) estate and residence of Thomas Jefferson, near Charlottesville, Virginia.

Mont·pel·ier (mont·pēl'yər) city, N cen. Vermont; cap.; pop. 8,241.

Mon·tre·al (mon'trē·ôl') city, S Quebec, Canada; pop. 2,802,547 (met.).

Mont·ser·rat (mont'sə·rat') isl. of Leeward group, West Indies; cap. Plymouth.

Mo·roc·co (mə·rok'ō) country, NW Africa; pop. 21,275,000; cap. Rabat.

Mos·cow (mos'kou, -kō) city, W U.S.S.R.; cap.; pop. 8,011,000 (met.).

Mount Ver·non (vûr'nən) home and burial place of George Washington, near Washington, D.C.

Mo·zam·bique (mō'zam·bēk') country, SE Africa; pop. 11,100,000; cap. Maputo.

Mu·nich (myōō'nik) city, SE West Germany; pop. 1,314,500.

Murray River river, SE Australia; 1,600 mi. long.

Muscat and Oman Oman: *a former name.*

Mus·kat (mus·kät') cap. of Oman; pop. 15,000. Also **Mas·qat'**.

Na·go·ya (nä·gō·yä) city, S cen. Honshu isl., Japan; pop. 2,100,000.

Nag·pur (näg'pōōr) city, cen. India; pop. 1,300,000.

Nai·ro·bi (nī·rō'bē) city, SW Kenya; cap.; pop. 835,000.

Na·mib·i·a (nə·mib'ē·ə) country, SW Africa; pop. 1,000,000; cap. Windhoek.

Nan·king (nan'king', nän'-) city, E China; cap. 1928–37; pop. 2,000,000. Pinyin spelling **Nanjing.**

Nantes (nants) city, W France; pop. 255,700.

Na·ples (nā'pəlz) city, SW Italy; pop. 1,210,500.

Nash·ville (nash'vil) city, N cen. Tennessee; cap.; pop. 455,651 (met. Nashville-Davidson).

Nas·sau (nas'ô) city, cap. of Bahamas; on New Providence isl.; pop. 135,500 (met.).

Na·u·ru (nä·ōō'rōō) country, isl. in W Pacific; pop. 8,000; cap. Yaren.

N'Dja·me·na (en·jä'mə·nə) city, SW Chad; cap.; pop. 300,000. Formerly *Fort-Lamy.*

Ne·bras·ka (nə·bras'kə) state, cen. U.S.; pop. 1,569,825; cap. Lincoln.

Neg·ev (neg'ev, ne·gev') desert reg., S Israel. Also **Neg·eb** (neg'eb, nə'geb').

Ne·pal (ne·päl') country, S Asia; pop. 15,325,000; cap. Katmandu.

Neth·er·lands (neth'ər·landz) country, NW Europe; pop. 14,350,000; cap. Amsterdam; seat of government, The Hague.

Netherlands Antilles 6 isl. belonging to the Netherlands, in the West Indies, N of Venezuela, including Aruba, Bonaire, Curaçao, Saba, St Eustatius, and part of St. Martin. Also *Dutch West Indies.*

Ne·vad·a (nə·vad'ə, -vä'də) state, W U.S.; pop. 800,493; cap. Carson City.

New·ark (nōō'ərk, nyōō'-) city, NE New Jersey; pop. 329,248.

New Brunswick (brunz'wik) prov., SE Canada; pop. 696,403; cap. Fredericton.

New Cal·e·don·i·a (kal'ə·dō'nē·ə, -nyə) isl. E of Australia; comprising with adjacent isls. a French overseas terr.; cap. Nouméa.

New·cas·tle (nōō'kas·el, nyōō'-) city, NE England; pop. 192,460.

New Del·hi (del'ē) city, N cen. India; cap. pop. 619,417.

New England NE section of the United States, including Maine, New Hampshire, Vermont, Massachusetts, Rhode Island, and Connecticut.

New·found·land (nōō'fənd·land', nyōō'-) prov., E Canada; comprising the island of Newfoundland and Labrador on the mainland; pop. 567,681; cap. St. John's.

New Guinea isl., N of Australia; world's second largest island.

New Hamp·shire (hamp'shir) state, NE U.S.; pop. 920,610; cap. Concord.

New Ha·ven (hā'vən) city, S Connecticut; pop. 126,109.

New Heb·ri·des (heb'ri·dēz) Vanuatu: *a former name.*

New Jer·sey (jûr'zē) state, E U.S.; pop. 7,364,823; cap. Trenton.

New Mex·i·co (mek'sə·kō) state, SW U.S.; pop. 1,302,981; cap. Santa Fé.

New Or·le·ans (ôr'lē·ənz, ôr·lēnz', ôr'lənz) city, SE Louisiana; pop. 557,482.

New·port News (nōō'pôrt, nyōō'-) city, SE Virginia; pop. 144,903.

New York (yôrk) **1.** state, NE U.S.; pop. 17,558,072; cap. Albany. **2.** city, SE New York; pop. 7,071,030.

New Zea·land (zē'lənd) country, isl. group SE of Australia; pop. 3,175,000; cap. Wellington.

Nia·mey (nyä·mā') city, W Niger; cap.; pop. 225,000.

Nic·a·ra·gua (nik'ə·rä'gwə) country, Central America; pop. 2,900,000; cap. Managua.

Nice (nēs) city, SE France; pop. 347,000.

Nic·o·si·a (nik'ə·sē'ə) city, N cen. Cyprus; cap.; pop. 161,000 (met.).

Ni·ger (nī'jər) **1.** country, W cen. Africa; pop. 5,650,000; cap. Niamey. **2.** river, W Africa; ab. 2,600 mi. long.

Ni·ge·ri·a (nī·jir'ē·ə) country, W Africa; pop. 88,600,000; cap. Lagos.

Nile (nīl) river, E Africa; 4,130 mi. long; longest river in the world.

Nor·folk (nôr'fək) city, SE Virginia; pop. 266,979.

North America N continent of the Western Hemisphere.

North Car·o·li·na (kar'ə·lī'nə) state, SE U.S.; pop. 5,881,813; cap. Raleigh.

North Da·ko·ta (də·kō'tə) state, N U.S.; pop. 652,717; cap. Bismarck.

Northern Ire·land (īr'lənd) part of the United

Kingdom in N reg. of Ireland; pop. 1,540,000; cap. Belfast.

North Korea See KOREA, DEMOCRATIC PEOPLE'S REPUBLIC OF.

North Pole N extremity of the earth's axis.

North Sea part of the Atlantic betw. Great Britain and Europe.

Northwest Territories adm. div., N. Canada; pop. 45,741; cap. Yellowknife.

Northwest Territory reg. awarded to the United States by Britain in 1783, extending from the Great Lakes S to the Ohio River and from Pennsylvania W to the Mississippi.

Nor·way (nôr'wā) country, N Europe; pop. 4,125,000; cap. Oslo.

Nouak·chott (nwäk·shôt') city, W Mauritania; cap.; pop. 250,000.

No·va Sco·tia (nō'və skō'shə) prov., E Canada; pop. 847,442; cap. Halifax.

Nu·ku'a·lo·fa (nōō'kə·w ·lō'fə) cap. of Tonga; pop. 18,300.

Ny·asa, Lake (nī·as'ə) lake, SE Africa.

O·a·hu (ō·ä'hōō) isl., N cen. Hawaiian Islands.

Oak·land (ōk'lənd) city, W California; pop. 339,288.

O·ce·an·i·a (ō'shē·an'ē·ə) isls. of Melanesia, Micronesia, and Polynesia, and sometimes the Malay Archipelago and Australasia.

O·der (ō'dər) river, cen. Europe; 563 mi. long.

O·des·sa (ō·des'ə) city, S Ukraine, U.S.S.R., pop. 1,046,000.

O·hi·o (ō·hī'ō) state, NE cen. U.S.; pop. 10,797,624; cap. Columbus.

Ohio River river, E cen. U.S.; 981 mi. long.

O·kee·cho·bee (ō·kə·chō'bē) lake, S cen. Florida.

O·kla·ho·ma (ō'klə·hō'mə) state, S cen. U.S.; pop. 3,025,290; cap. Oklahoma City.

Oklahoma City city, cen. Oklahoma; cap.; pop. 403,213.

O·ki·na·wa (ō'ki·nä'wä) The largest of the Ryuku Islands.

O·lym·pi·a (ō·lim'pē·ə) city, W Washington; cap.; pop. 27,447.

O·lym·pus (ō·lim'pəs), **Mount** mtn., N Greece; regarded in Greek mythology as the home of the gods.

O·ma·ha (ō'mə·hä, -hô) city, E Nebraska; pop. 311,681.

O·man (ō'man, ō·man', ō·män') country, SE Arabian penin. in SW Asia; pop. 950,000; cap. Muscat. Formerly *Muscat and Oman.*

On·tar·i·o (on·târ'ē·ō) prov., SE Canada; pop. 8,625,107; cap. Toronto.

Ontario Lake easternmost of the Great Lakes.

O·por·to (ō·pôr'tō) city, W Portugal; pop. 335,700.

Orange River river, S Africa; 1,300 mi. long.

Or·e·gon (ôr'ə·gən, -gon, or'-) state, NW U.S.; pop. 2,633,149; cap. Salem.

O·ri·no·co (ôr'ə·nō'kō, or'-) river, Venezuela; ab. 1,700 mi. long.

Ork·ney Islands (ôrk'nē), isl. group, N of Scotland comprising Orkney; a county of Scotland.

Or·lan·do (ôr·lan'dō) city, E cen. Florida; pop. 128,394.

O·sa·ka (ō·säkä) city, S Honshu, Japan; pop. 2,600,000.

Os·lo (os'lō, oz'-) city, SE Norway; cap.; pop. 454,872.

O·tran·to (ō·trän'tō), **Strait of** strait betw. the Adriatic and Ionian seas.

Ot·ta·wa (ot'ə·wə) city, SE Ontario, Canada; cap.; pop. 717,978 (met.).

Ot·to·man Empire (ot'ə·mən) former empire (1300–1919) of the Turks in Asia Minor, NE Africa, and SE Europe.

Oua·ga·dou·gou (wä'gə·dōō'gōō) city, cen. Upper Volta; cap.; pop. 235,000.

Outer Mongolia See MONGOLIA.

Ox·nard (oks'närd) city, S California; pop. 108,195.

O·zark Mountains (ō'zärk) highland region in SW Missouri, NW Arkansas, and NE Oklahoma. Also **Ozarks.**

Pa·cif·ic Islands, Trust Territory of the (pə·sif'ik) isl, groups in W Pacific; U.S. Trust Terr.; including the Caroline Islands, the Marshall Islands, and the Marianas, except Guam. Also called *Micronesia.*

Pacific Ocean ocean betw. the American continents and Asia and Australia; extending betw. the Arctic and Antarctic regions.

Pa·go Pa·go (päng'ō päng'ō) town, SE Tutuila isl. of American Samoa; pop. 2,450.

Painted Desert desert plateau in N cen. Arizona.

Pa·ki·stan (pä'ki·stän', pak'i·stan) country, S Asia; pop. 85,500,000; cap. Islamabad.

Pa·lau Islands (pä·lou') isl. group, W Caroline Islands.

Pa·ler·mo (pä·ler'mō) city, NW Sicily; pop. 699,691.

Pal·es·tine (pal'is·tīn) terr., E Mediterranean; divided (1947) by the United Nations into Israel and a terr. that became part of Jordan.

Pan·a·ma (pan'ə·mä, -mô) country, Central America; pop. 2,000,000; cap. Panama City.

Panama, Isthmus of isthmus connecting North and South America.

Panama Canal ship canal connecting Atlantic and Pacific, extending across Isthmus of Panama.

Panama City city, near the Pacific end of the Panama Canal; pop. 655,000.

Pap·u·a New Guinea (pä'pōō·ə, pap'ōō·ə, -yōō·ə) country, isl., N of Australia; pop. 3,250,000; cap. Port Moresby.

Par·a·guay (par'ə·gwā, -gwī) country, S cen. South America; pop. 3,375,000; cap. Asunción.

Paraguay River river, S cen. South America, ab. 1,300 mi. long.

Par·a·mar·i·bo (par'ə·mar'i·bō) city, N Suriname; cap.; pop. 150,000.

Pa·ra·ná (pä'rä·nä') river, S cen. South America; ab. 2,800 mi. long.

Par·is (par'is) city, N France; cap.; pop. 2,300,000.

Par·nas·sus (pär·nas'əs), **Mount** mtn., cen. Greece; anciently regarded as sacred to Apollo and the Muses.

Pas·a·de·na (pas'ə·dē'nə) **1.** city, SW California; pop. 119,374. **2.** city, SE Texas; pop. 112,560.

Pat·er·son (pat'ər·sən) city, NE New Jersey; pop. 137,970.

Pearl Harbor inlet, S Oahu Hawaii.

Pe·king (pē·king') city, N China; cap.; pop. 9,000,000. Pinyin spelling **Beijing.**

Pel·o·pon·ne·sus (pel'ə·pə·nē'səs) penin. betw. Aegean and Ionian seas; one of the main divisions of S. Greece.

Penn·syl·va·ni·a (pen·səl·vā'nē·ə, -vān'yə) state, E U.S.; pop. 11,863,895; cap. Harrisburg.
Pe·o·ri·a (pē·ôr'ē·ə) city, N cen. Illinois; pop. 124,160.
Per·sia (pûr'zhə, -shə) Iran: *a former name.*
Persian Gulf inlet of the Arabian Sea betw. Iran and Arabia.
Perth (pûrth) city, SW Australia; pop. 918,000 (met.).
Pe·ru (pə·rōō') country, W South America; pop. 18,850,000; cap. Lima.
Phil·a·del·phi·a (fil'ə·del'fē·ə) city, SE Pennsylvania; pop. 1,688,210.
Phil·ip·pines (fil'ə·pēnz) country, a Pacific archipelago SE of China; pop. 50,500,000; cap. Quezon City; seat of administration, Manila.
Phoe·nix (fē'niks) city, S cen. Arizona; cap.; pop. 789,704.
Phnom Penh (pə·nôm'pen') city, S cen. Kampuchea (Cambodia); cap.; pop. 500,000. Also **Pnom Penh.**
Pierre (pir) city, cen. South Dakota; cap.; pop. 11,973.
Pillars of Hercules 2 promontories on opposite sides of the E end of the Strait of Gibraltar.
Pi·rae·us (pi·rē'əs) city, S Greece; pop. 439,100 (met.).
Pit·cairn Island (pit'kârn) isl., S Pacific; Brit. col.
Pitts·burgh (pits'bûrg) city, SW Pennsylvania; pop. 423,959.
Plymouth Colony colony on the shore of Massachusetts Bay founded by the Pilgrim Fathers in 1620.
Po·land (pō'lənd) country, N cen. Europe; pop. 36,300,000; cap. Warsaw.
Pol·y·ne·sia (pol'i·nē'zhə, -shə) isls. of Oceania, cen. and SE Pacific; E of Melanesia and Micronesia.
Poo·na (pōō'nə) city, W India; pop. 1,700,000.
Port·land (pôrt'lənd) city, NW Oregon; pop. 366,383.
Ports·mouth (pôrts'məth) city, SE Virginia; pop. 104,577.
Por·tu·gal (pôr'chə·gəl) country, SW Europe; pop. 10,000,000; cap. Lisbon.
Portuguese Guinea Guinea-Bissau: *a former name.*
Port-au-Prince (pôrt'ō·prins') city, S Haiti; cap.; pop. 790,000 (met.).
Port Lou·is (lōō'is, lōō'ē) city, SW Mauritius; cap.; pop. 155,000.
Port Mores·by (môrz'bē) city, SE New Guinea; cap. of Papua New Guinea; pop. 120,000 (met.).
Port-of-Spain (pôrt'əv·spān') city, NW Trinidad; cap. of Trinidad and Tobago; pop. 62,700 (met.).
Por·to·No·vo (pôr'tō·nō'vō) port city, SE Benin; cap.; pop. 125,000.
Port Sa·id (sä·ēd') city, NE Egypt; pop. 263,000.
Prague (präg) city, W Czechoslovakia; cap.; pop. 1,182,000.
Pre·to·ri·a (pri·tôr'ē·ə, -tō'rē·ə) city, NE cen. South Africa: adm. cap.; pop. 600,000.
Prince Ed·ward Island (ed'wərd) prov., NE Canada; pop. 122,506; cap. Charlottetown.
Prince Ru·pert (rōō'pərt) city, W British Columbia, Canada; pop. 14,754.
Prov·i·dence (prov'ə·dəns) city, NE Rhode Island; cap.; op. 156,804.
Pueb·lo (pweb'lō) city, S cen. Colorado; pop. 101,686.
Puer·to Ri·co (pwer'tō rē'kō, pôr'-, pōr'-) isl., Greater Antilles; a Commonwealth of the United States; cap. San Juan.
Pu·get Sound (pyōō'jit) inlet of the Pacific, NW Washington.
Pu·san (pōō'sän) city, SE South Korea; pop. 3,000,000.
Pyong·yang (pyông·yäng') city, W North Korea; cap.; pop. 1,500,000.
Pyr·e·nees (pir'ə·nēz) mtn. chain betw. France and Spain.

Qa·tar (kä'tär) country, W coast of the Persian Gulf; pop. 260,000; cap. Doha.
Que·bec (kwi·bek') **1.** prov., E Canada; pop. 6,438,403; cap. Quebec. Also *Fr.* **Qué·bec** (kā·bek'). **2.** city; E Canada; cap of Quebec prov.; pop. 542,158 (met.). Also *Fr.* **Qué·bec'.**
Que·moy Islands (ki·moi') 2 isls. of the Republic of China in Formosa Strait.
Que·zon City (kā'sôn) city, N cen. Philippines; cap.; pop. 1,100,000.
Qui·to (kē'tō) city, N cen. Ecuador; cap.; pop. 800,000.
Qum (kōōm) city, NW Iran; pop. 110,000. Also spelled **Qom.**

Ra·bat (rä·bät') city, N Morocco; cap.; pop. 865,000 (met.).
Rai·nier (ra·nir') **Mount,** mtn., W cen. Washington; highest point in Cascade Range.
Ra·leigh (rô'lē, rä'lē) city, cen. North Carolina; cap.; pop. 149,771.
Ran·goon (rang·gōōn') city, S Burma; cap.; pop. 2,200,000.
Re·ci·fe (rā·sē'fə) city, NE Brazil; pop. 1,240,897.
Red River 1. river in Texas, Arkansas, and Louisiana; 1,018 mi. long. **2.** river in U.S. and Canada; 540 mi. long. Also called **Red River of the North.**
Red Sea sea betw. Egypt and Arabia.
Re·gi·na (ri·jī'nə) city, W cen. Canada; cap. of Saskatchewan; pop. 164,313 (met.).
Re·no (rē'nō) city, W Nevada; pop. 100,756.
Ré·un·ion (rē·yōōn'yən) French overseas dept.; isl., E Indian Ocean, E of Madagascar.
Rey·kja·vik (rā'kyə·vik) city, SW Iceland; cap.; pop. 83,500.
Rhine (rīn) river W cen. Europe; 810 mi. long.
Rhode Island (rōd) state, NE U.S.; pop. 947,154; cap. Providence.
Rhodes (rōdz) Greek island of the Dodecanese group; SE Aegean; cap. Rhodes.
Rho·de·sia (rō·dē'zhə, -zhē·ə) See ZIMBABWE.
Rhône (rōn) river, Switzerland and SE France; 504 mi. long. Also **Rhone.**
Rich·mond (rich'mənd) city, E cen. Virginia; cap.; pop. 219,214.
Ri·o de Ja·nei·ro (rē'ō də jə·nâr'ō, zhə·nâr'ō) city, SE Brazil; former cap.; pop. 5,184,292.
Rí·o de la Pla·ta (rē'ō thā lä plä'tä) estuary of the Paraná and Uruguay rivers betw. Argentina and Uruguay; 170 mi. long.
Ri·o Grande (rē'ō grand') river betw. Texas and Mexico; 1,890 mi. long.
Riv·er·side (riv'ər·sīd') city, SW California; pop. 170,876.
Ri·yadh (rē·yäd') city, E Saudi Arabia; cap.; pop. 1,250,000.

Ro·a·noke (rō'ə·nōk) city, W Virginia; pop. 100,427.
Roch·es·ter (roch'es'tər, -is·tər) city, W New York; pop. 241,741.
Rock·ford (rok'fərd) city, N Illinois; pop. 139,712.
Rocky Mountains mtn. system, W North America, extends from the Arctic to Mexico. Also **Rockies.**
Ro·ma·nia (rō·mā'nyə) country, SE Europe; pop. 22,700,000; cap. Bucharest.
Rome (rōm) city, W Italy; cap.; pop. 2,830,569.
Ro·sa·rio (rō·sä'ryō) city, E cen. Argentina; pop. 750,000.
Ro·seau (rō·zō') city, Dominica; cap.; pop. 20,000.
Rot·ter·dam (rot'ər·dam) city, W Netherlands; pop. 579,200.
Rou·en (rōō·än') city, N France; pop. 113,740.
Ru·ma·ni·a (rōō·mā'nē·ə, -mān'yə) See ROMANIA.
Rus·sia (rush'ə) See UNION OF SOVIET SOCIALIST REPUBLICS.
Rwan·da (rwän'dä, rōō·än'dä) country, cen. Africa; pop. 5,200,000; cap. Kigali.
Ryu·kyu Islands (ryōō·kyōō) Japanese isl. group in W Pacific; chief isl. Okinawa.

Sac·ra·men·to (sak'rə·men'tō) city, N cen. California; cap.; pop. 275,741.
Sa·har·a (sə·har'ə, -hä'rə) desert area, N Africa from Atlantic Ocean to Red Sea.
Sai·gon (sī·gon') See HO CHI MINH CITY.
St. Croix (kroi') the largest of the Virgin Islands of the United States.
St. George's (jôr'jiz) city, Grenada; cap.; pop. 30,000.
St. He·le·na (hə·lē'nə) isl., South Atlantic; Brit. col.; pop. 7,300; cap. Jamestown.
St. John (jon) one of the Virgin Islands of the United States.
St. John's (jonz) **1.** city, SE Canada; cap. of Newfoundland; pop. 83,770. **2.** city, on Antigua isl.; cap. of Antigua and Barbados; pop. 25,000.
St. Kitts (St. Chris·to·pher)-Ne·vis-An·guil·la (kits, kris'tə·fər, nē'vis, ang·gwil'ə) isl. group, Leeward Islands, West Indies; pop. 71,000; cap. Basseterre. Also *West Indies Associated States.*
St. Law·rence River (lor'əns, lôr'-) river, SE Canada; the outlet of the Great Lakes system, flowing NE from Lake Ontario to the **Gulf of St. Lawrence**, an inlet of the N Atlantic.
St. Lawrence Seaway A system of ship canals extending along the St. Lawrence River above Montreal to Lake Ontario.
St. Lou·is (lōō'is, lōō'ē) city, E Missouri; pop. 453,085.
St. Lu·cia (lōō'shə) country, isl. West Indies; pop. 125,000; cap. Castries.
St. Mar·tin (mart'əŋ) isl. of the Leeward group, West Indies; N part belongs to France, S part to the Netherlands and is part of the Netherlands Antilles. Du. **St. Maar·ten** (sint mär'tən).
St. Paul (pôl) city, SE Minnesota; cap.; pop. 270,230.
St. Pe·ters·burg (pe'tərz·bûrg) **1.** city, W Florida; pop. 236,893. **2.** Leningrad: *a former name.*
St. Thom·as (tom'əs) one of the Virgin Islands of the United States.
St. Vin·cent (vin'sənt) country, isl. West Indies; pop. 150,000; cap. Kingstown.
Sa·lem (sā'ləm) city, NW Oregon; cap.; pop. 89,233.
Salis·bury (sôlz'ber·ē, -brē) Harare: *a former name.*
Sa·lo·ni·ka (sə·lon'i·kə, sal'ə·nē'kə) city, NE Greece; pop. 800,000 (met.).
Salt Lake City city, N cen. Utah; cap.; pop. 163,033.
Salz·burg (sälz'bōōrg) city, W Austria; pop. 139,000.
Sa·mo·a (sə·mō'ə) isl. group, SW Pacific. See AMERICAN SAMOA and WESTERN SAMOA.
Sa·na (sä·nä') city, cen. Yemen (Yemen Arab Republic); cap.; pop. 210,000. Also Sa·naa'.
San An·to·ni·o (san' an·tō'nē·ō) city, S cen. Texas; pop. 785,410.
San Ber·nar·di·no (san' bûr'nə·dē'nō) city, SW California; pop. 118,057.
San Di·e·go (san' dē·ā'gō) city, SW California; pop. 875,504.
Sand·wich Islands (sand'wich) Hawaiian Islands: *the former name.*
San Fran·cis·co (san' frən·sis'kō) city, W California; pop. 678,974.
San Francisco Bay inlet of the Pacific, W California.
San Jose (san' hō·zā') city, W California; pop. 636,550.
San Jo·sé (san' hō·zā') city, cen. Costa Rica; cap.; pop. 800,000 (met.).
San Juan (sän hwän) city, NE Puerto Rico; cap.; pop. 435,000.
San Ma·ri·no (mä·rē'nō) **1.** country, an enclave in NE Italy; pop. 20,500; cap. San Marino. **2.** city, San Marino; cap.; pop. 8,500.
San Sal·va·dor (san' sal'və·dôr) **1.** city, S El Salvador; cap.; pop. 430,000. **2.** isl., cen. Bahamas.
San·ta An·a (san'tə an'ə) city, SW California; pop. 203,713.
San·ta Cruz (san'tə krōōz') city, E Bolivia; pop. 237,128.
San·ta Fe (san'tə fā') city, N New Mexico; cap.; pop. 48,953.
San·ti·a·go (sän'tē·ä'gō) city, cen. Chile; cap.; pop. 3,850,000.
San·to Do·min·go (sän'tō dō·ming'gō) city, S Dominican Republic; cap.; pop. 1,250,000. Formerly *Ciudad Trujillo.*
São Pau·lo (souṅ pou'lōō) city, SE Brazil; pop. 8,585,000.
São To·mé (souṅ tə·mā') city, São Tomé and Principe; cap.; pop. 20,000.
São Tomé and Prin·ci·pe (prin'sə·pə) country, isls. on the equator, W of Africa; pop. 90,000; cap. São Tomé.
Sap·po·ro (säp·pō·rō) city, SW Kokkaido isl., Japan; pop. 1,400,000.
Sa·ra·je·vo (sä'rä·ye·vô) city, cen. Yugoslavia; pop. 400,000.
Sar·din·i·a (sär·din'ē·ə) isl., E cen. Mediterranean; with adjacent isls. a region of Italy.
Sas·katch·e·wan (sas·kach'ə·won) prov., W cen. Canada; pop. 968,313; cap. Regina.
Sas·ka·toon (sas'kə·tōōn') city, S cen. Saskatchewaŋ, Canada; pop. 154,210.
Sau·di Arabia (sou'dē, sä·ōō'dē) country, Arabian penin, SW Asia; pop. 10,400,000; cap. Riyadh.
Sa·van·nah (sə·van'ə) city, E Georgia; pop. 141,634.
Scan·di·na·vi·a (skan'də·nā'vē·ə) reg., NW

Europe; includes Sweden, Norway, and Denmark and sometimes Finland, Iceland, and the Faeroe Islands.

Scot·land (skot′lənd) country, N Great Britain, W Europe, a division of the United Kingdom of Great Britain and Northern Ireland; pop 5,117,000; cap. Edinburgh.

Se·at·tle (sē·at′l) city, W cen. Washington; pop. 493,846.

Seine (sān) river, NE France; 482 mi. long.

Sen·e·gal (sen′ə·gal, -gôl), country, NW Africa; pop. 5,950,000; cap. Dakar.

Seoul (sōl) city, NW South Korea; cap.; pop. 8,000,000.

Se·ville (sə·vil′) city, SW Spain; pop. 630,000.

Sey·chelles (sā′shelz) country, isl. group in Indian Ocean, NE of Madagascar; pop. 70,000; cap. Victoria.

Shang·hai (shang′hī) city, E China; pop. 12,000,000 (met.). Pinyin spelling **Shanghai**.

Shan·non (shan′ən) river, cen. Ireland; 224 mi. long.

Shen·yang (shun′yäng) city, NE China; pop. 4,800,000. Pinyin spelling **Shenyang**.

Shet·land Islands (shet′lənd) isl. group NE of the Orkney Islands, comprising **Shetland**, a county of Scotland.

Shreve·port (shrēv′pôrt) city, NW Louisiana; pop. 205,815.

Si·am (sī·am′) Thailand: *a former name*.

Siam, Gulf of part of the South China Sea betw. the Malay Peninsula and Indochina.

Sic·i·ly (sis′ə·lē) isl. of Italy, cen. Mediterranean.

Si·er·ra Le·o·ne (sē·er′ə lē·ō′nē, lē·ōn′) country, W Africa; pop. 3,675,000; cap. Freetown.

Si·er·ra Ne·vad·a (sē·er′ə nə·vad′ə, -vädə) mtn. range, E California.

Si·nai (sī′nī) penin., E Egypt, betw. the Mediterranean and the Red Sea.

Sin·ga·pore (sing′ə·pôr, sing′gə-) **1.** country, isl. in South China Sea off Malay penin.; pop. 2,500,000; cap. Singapore. **2.** city, S Singapore; cap.; pop. 2,450,000 (met.).

Smyr·na (smûr′nə) See IZMIR.

So·ci·e·ty Islands (sə·sī′ə·tē) isl. group, S Pacific, part of French Polynesia.

So·fi·a (sō′fē·ə, sō·fē′ə) city, W Bulgaria; cap.; pop. 965,355.

Sol·o·mon Islands (sol′ə·mən) country, isl. group, SW Pacific; pop. 250,000; cap. Honiara.

So·ma·li·a (sō·mä′lyə, -lē·ə) country, E Africa; pop. 5,150,000; cap. Mogadishu.

South Africa country, S Africa; pop. 29,000,000; seat of government Pretoria; seat of legislature Cape Town.

South America S continent of the Western Hemisphere.

South Bend city, N Indiana; pop. 109,727.

South Car·o·li·na (kar′ə·lī′nə) state, SE U.S.; pop. 3,121,833; cap. Columbia.

South China Sea part of the Pacific betw. SE Asia and the Malay Archipelago.

South Da·ko·ta (də·kō′tə) state, N cen. U.S.; pop. 690,768; cap. Pierre.

Southern Yemen See YEMEN, PEOPLE'S DEMOCRATIC REPUBLIC OF.

South Island one of the two main isls. of New Zealand.

South Korea See KOREA, REPUBLIC OF.

South Pole S extremity of the earth's axis.

South Sea Islands isls. of the South Pacific.

South Seas waters of the Southern Hemisphere, esp. the South Pacific Ocean.

South-West Africa Namibia: *a former name*.

So·vi·et Union (sō′vē·et, -ət— See UNION OF SOVIET SOCIALIST REPUBLICS.

Spain (spān) country, SW Europe; pop. 37,900,000; cap. Madrid.

Spanish Guinea Equatorial Guinea: *a former name*.

Spice Islands Molucca Islands: *the former name*.

Spo·kane (spō·kăn′) city, E Washington; pop. 171,300.

Spring·field (spring′fēld) **1.** city, cen. Illinois; cap.; pop. 99,637. **2.** city, SW Massachusetts; pop. 152,319. **3.** city, SW Missouri; pop. 133,116.

Sri Lan·ka (srē lang′kə) country, isl. S of India; pop. 15,250,000; cap. Colombo.

Stam·ford (stam′fərd) city, SW Connecticut; pop. 102,453.

Stat·en Island (stat′n) isl. SE New York, at the entrance to New York Harbor.

Ster·ling Heights (stûr′ling hīts) city, SE Michigan; pop. 108,999.

Stock·holm (stok′hōm) city, SE Sweden; cap.; pop. 1,400,000 (met.).

Stock·ton (stok′tən) city, cen. California; pop. 149,779.

Stras·bourg (stras′bûrg, sträz′-) city, NE France; pop. 257,300.

Strat·ford-upon-A·von (strat′fərd·on·ā′von) town, S cen. England; pop. 20,860.

Stutt·gart (stut′gärt) city, SW West Germany; pop. 590,100.

Su·cre (so͞o′krā) city, S cen. Bolivia; constitutional cap.; pop. 90,000.

Su·dan (so͞o·dan′) country, NE Africa; pop. 19,150,000; cap. Khartoum.

Su·ez (so͞o·ez′, so͞o′ez) city, NE Egypt; pop. 381,000.

Suez, Gulf of inlet of the Red Sea; NE Egypt.

Suez, Isthmus of a strip of land joining Asia and Africa, between the Gulf of Suez and the Mediterranean; traversed by the Suez Canal.

Suez Canal ship canal across the Isthmus of Suez; 107 mi.

Su·la·we·si (so͞o′lä·wā′sē) See CELEBES.

Su·ma·tra (so͞o·mä′trə) isl. of Indonesia S of the Malay Peninsula.

Sun·ny·vale (sun′e·vāl) city, W California; pop. 106,618.

Superior, Lake largest of the Great Lakes.

Su·ra·ba·ya (so͞o′rä·bä′yä) city, NE Java, Indonesia; pop. 2,000,000.

Su·ri·name (so͝or′ə·näm′) country, NE South America; pop. 420,000; cap. Paramaribo. Formerly *Dutch Guiana*.

Su·va (so͞o′vä) cap. of Fiji, on Viti Levu Island; pop. 65,000.

Swa·zi·land (swä′zē·land) country, SE Africa; pop. 600,000; cap. Mbabane.

Swe·den (swēd′n) country, NW Europe; pop. 8,330,000; cap. Stockholm.

Swit·zer·land (swit′sər·lənd) country, cen. Europe; pop. 6,475,000; cap. Bern.

Syd·ney (sid′nē) city, SE Australia; pop. 3,280,900 (met.).

Syr·a·cuse (sir′ə·kyo͞os) city, cen. New York; pop. 170,105.

Syr·i·a (sir′ē-ə) country, SW Asia; pop. 9,650.000; cap. Damascus.

Ta·briz (tä·brēz′) city, NW Iran; pop. 598,600.
Ta·co·ma (tə·kō′mə) city, W Washington; pop. 158,501.
Ta·hi·ti (tä·hē′tē, tə-, hī′tē) isl., Society group.
Tai·pei (tī′pā′) city, N Taiwan; cap. of Republic of China; pop. 2,250,000.
Tai·wan (tī′wän) isl. of SE coast of China, seat of govt. of Republic of China.
Tal·la·has·see (tal′ə·has′ē) city, N Florida; cap.; pop. 81,548.
Tam·pa (tam′pə) city, W Florida; pop. 271,523.
Ta·na·na·rive (tä·nä′nä·rēv′) See ANTANANARIVO.
Tan·gan·yi·ka, Lake (tang′gan·yē′kə) lake, E cen. Africa.
Tan·gier (tan·jir′) city, N Morocco; pop. 291,400.
Tan·za·ni·a (tan′zə·nē′ə, tän′-) country, E Africa; pop. 19,000,000; cap. Dar es Salaam.
Tash·kent (təsh·kyent′) city, U.S.S.R.; cap. of Uzbekistan Republic; pop. 1,779,000.
Tas·ma·ni·a (taz·mā′nē·ə) **1**. isl. S of Australia. **2**. A state of Australia comprising this isl. and other small isls.; pop. 422,000; cap. Hobart.
Tbi·li·si (tbi′li·sē) city, U.S.S.R.; cap. of Georgia; pop. 1,042,000.
Te·gu·ci·gal·pa (tā·gōō′sē·gäl′pä) city, S cen. Honduras; cap.; pop. 375,000.
Te·he·ran (te′ə·rän′, -ran′) city, N cen. Iran; cap.; pop. 6,000,000. Also **Teh′ran**.
Tel A·viv (tel′ä·vēv′) city, W Israel; includes Jaffa; pop. 343,300.
Tem·pe (tem·pē′) city, S cen. Arizona; pop. 106,743.
Ten·nes·see (ten′ə·sē′) state, SE cen. U.S.; pop. 4,591,120; cap. Nashville.
Tennessee River river, E U.S.; 652 mi. long.
Te·ton Range (tē′ton) range of the Rocky Mtns. in NW Wyoming.
Tex·as (tek′səs) state, S U.S.; pop. 14,229,288; cap. Austin.
Thai·land (tī′land) country, SE Asia; pop. 49,000,000; cap. Bangkok. Formerly *Siam*.
Thames (temz) river, S England; 209 mi. long.
Thim·phu (thim′bōō) cap. of Bhutan; pop. 10,000.
Thousand Islands group of ab. 1,500 isls. in the St. Lawrence River.
Ti·ber (tī′bər) river, cen. Italy; 125 mi. long.
Ti·bet (ti·bet′) autonomous reg. of SW China; pop. 1,270,000; cap. Lhasa; formerly independent.
Tien·tsin (tin′tsin′) city, NE China; pop. 7,200,000. Pinyin spelling **Tianjin**.
Tier·ra del Fue·go (tyer′ä del fwā′gō) **1**. Archipelago at S tip of South America, belonging to Chile and Argentina; separated from mainland by Strait of Magellan. **2**. Largest isl. in this group.
Ti·gris (tī′gris) river, SW Asia, ab. 1,150 mi. long.
Ti·jua·na (tē·wä′nə, tē·ə·wä′nə) city, NW Mexico; pop. 750,000.
Ti·ra·na (tē·rä′nä) city, cen. Albania; cap.; pop. 200,000.
To·go (tō′gō) country, W Africa; pop. 2,800,000; cap. Lomé.
To·ky·o (tō′kē·ō) city, E Japan; cap.; pop. 8,350,000.
To·le·do (tə·lē′dō) **1**. city, NW Ohio; pop. 354,635. **2**. city, cen. Spain; pop. 54,350.
Ton·ga (tong′gə) country, isl. group in South Pacific, SE of Fiji; pop. 100,000; cap. Nuku′alofa.
To·pe·ka (tə·pē′kə) city, NE Kansas; cap.; pop. 115,266.
To·ron·to (tə·ron′tō) city, SE Canada; cap. of Ontario; pop. 2,998,947 (met.).
Tor·rance (tor′əns, tôr′-) city, SW California; pop. 131,497.
Tou·louse (tōō·lōōz′) city, S France; pop. 383,176.
Tren·ton (trent′n, tren′tən) city, W New Jersey; cap.; pop. 92,124.
Trin·i·dad and To·ba·go (trin′ə·dad, tō·bā′gō) country, isls. off N Venezuela; pop. 1,200,000; cap. Port-of-Spain.
Trip·o·li (trip′ə·lē) **1**. city, NW Lebanon; pop. 127,600. **2**. city, NW Libya, cap.; pop. 1,000,000.
Trust Territory of the Pacific Islands See PACIFIC ISLANDS, TRUST TERRITORY OF THE
Tsing·tao (ching′dou′) city, E China; pop. 1,121,000; Pinyin spelling **Qingdao**.
Tuc·son (tōō·son′, tōō′son) city, SE Arizona; pop. 330,537.
Tul·sa (tul′sə) city, NE Oklahoma; pop. 360,919.
Tu·nis (tōō′nis, tyōō′-) city, NE Tunisia; cap.; pop. 960,000 (met.).
Tu·ni·sia (tōō·nē′zhə, -nish′ə, -nish′ē·ə) country, N Africa; pop. 6,650,000; cap. Tunis.
Tu·rin (tŏŏr′in, tyŏŏr′-, tŏŏ·rin′, tyŏŏ-) city NW Italy; pop. 1,103,520.
Tur·key (tûr′kē) country, SE cen. Eurasia; pop. 47,500,000; cap. Ankara.

U·gan·da (yōō·gan′də, -gän′dä) country, E cen. Africa; pop. 14,000,000; cap. Kampala.
U·lan Ba·tor (ōō′län bä′tôr) city, N cen. Mongolian People's Republic; cap.; pop. 435,000.
Union of Soviet Socialist Republics country E Europe and N Asia; a union of 15 constituent republics; pop. 269,850,000; cap. Moscow. Also *Soviet Union*.
United Arab E·mir·ates (i·mir′its, -āts) country, E Arabian penin.; pop. 800,000; cap. Abu Dhabi.
United Arab Republic Egypt: *a former name*.
United Kingdom of Great Britain and Northern Ireland country, W Europe, consisting of England, Scotland, Wales, and Northern Ireland; pop. 56,252,000; cap. London.
United States of America country, North America; pop. 226,545,805; cap. Washington.
Upper Vol·ta (vol′tə, vōl′-) country, W Africa; pop. 7,170,000; cap. Ougadougou.
U·ral Mountains (yŏŏr′əl) mtn. system, U.S.S.R., regarded as boundary betw. Europe and Asia.
U·ru·guay (yŏŏr′ə-gwā) country, SE South America; pop. 2,950,000; cap. Montevideo.
Uruguay River river, SE South America; 1,000 mi. long.
U·ral River (yŏŏ′rəl) river, U.S.S.R.; flowing from Ural Mts. to Caspian Sea; 1,574 mi. long.
U·tah (yōō′tô, -tä) state, W cen. U.S.; pop. 1,461,037; cap. Salt Lake City.

U·trecht (yo͞o'trekt) city, cen. Netherlands; pop. 476,400.

Va·duz (vä'do͞ots) cap. of Liechtenstein; pop. 4,700.

Va·len·ci·a (və·len'shē·ə, -shə) city, E Spain; pop. 770,000.

Val·pa·rai·so (val'pə·rā'zō, -sō, -rī'-) city, cen. Chile; pop. 248,200.

Van·cou·ver (van·ko͞o'vər) city, SW British Columbia, Canada; pop. 1,268,183 (met.).

Va·nu·a·tu (vä·no͞o'a·to͞o) country, isls. S Pacific; pop. 125,000; cap. Vila.

Vat·i·can City (vat'ə·kən) papal state, within Rome, Italy; pop. 1,000.

Ven·e·zue·la (ven'ə·zwā'lə, -zwē'lə) country, N South America; pop. 14,700,000; cap. Caracas.

Ven·ice (ven'is) city, NE Italy; pop. 341,400.

Verde (vûrd), **Cape** westernmost point of Africa; a peninsula.

Ver·mont (vər·mont') state, NE U.S.; pop. 511,456; cap. Montpelier.

Ver·sailles (vər·sī', -sālz') city, N France; pop. 93,370.

Ve·su·vi·us (və·so͞o'vē·əs) active volcano, W Italy.

Vic·to·ri·a (vik·tôr'ē·ə) **1.** city, W Canada, on Vancouver isl.; cap. of British Columbia; pop. 233,481 (met.). **2.** city, Hong Kong isl., cap. of Hong Kong; pop. 633,150. **3.** town on Mahé isl.; cap. of Seychelles; pop. 23,000.

Vi·en·na (vē·en'ə) city, NE Austria; cap.; pop. 1,504,200.

Vien·tiane (vyaṅ·tyaṅ') city, NW cen. Laos; adm. cap.; pop. 200,000.

Vi·et·nam (vē·et·näm') country, SW Indochina, pop. 56,250,000; cap. Hanoi. Also **Viet-Nam** or **Viet Nam**.

Vi·la (vē'lä) city, Vanuatu; cap.; pop. 15,000.

Vir·gin·ia (vər·jin'yə) state, E U.S.; pop. 5,346,818; cap. Richmond.

Virginia Beach city, SE Virginia; pop. 262,199.

Virgin Islands isl. group, West Indies, E of Puerto Rico.

Virgin Islands of the United States the W isls. of the Virgin Islands, comprising St. Croix, St. Thomas and St. John; a U.S. terr.

Vol·ga (vol'gə, vôl'gə) river, W U.S.S.R.; 2,290 mi. long.

Wa·co (wā'kō) city, cen. Texas; pop. 101,261.

Wake Island (wāk) isl., N Pacific; U.S. terr.

Wales (wālz) penin., SW Britain; comprising a division of the United Kingdom; pop. 2,790,000; cap. Cardiff.

War·ren (wor'ən, -in) city, SE Michigan; pop. 161,134.

War·saw (wôr'sô) city, E cen. Poland; cap.; pop. 1,576,600.

Wash·ing·ton (wosh·ing·tən, wô'shing-) **1.** state, NW U.S.; pop. 4,132,180; cap. Olympia. **2.** city, E U.S.; cap. of U.S.; has same boundaries as District of Columbia; pop. 637,651.

Wa·ter·bur·y (wôtər·ber'ē, wot'ər-) city, W Connecticut; pop. 103,266.

Wa·ter·ford (wô'tər·fərd, wot'-) city, S Ireland; pop. 33,340.

Wa·ter·loo (wô'tər·lo͞o, wô'tər·lo͞o') vill., cen. Belgium; pop. 21,725.

Wel·ling·ton (wel'ing·tən) city, cen. New Zealand; cap.; pop. 342,000 (met.).

Western Samoa country, isls. in S Pacific; pop. 160,000; cap. Apia.

West Germany See GERMANY, FEDERAL REPUBLIC OF.

West Indies series of isl. groups separating the North Atlantic from the Caribbean.

West Indies Associated States See ST. KITTS-NEVIS-ANGUILLA.

West Point US military reservation, SE New York; seat of the US Military Academy.

West Vir·gin·ia (vər·jin'yə) state, E U.S.; pop. 1,950,279; cap. Charleston.

White·horse (hwīt'hôrs) cap. of Yukon Territory, NW Canada; pop. 14,814.

White Mountains range of the Appalachians, N cen. New Hampshire.

Wich·i·ta (wich'ə·tô) city, S cen. Kansas; pop. 279,272.

Wight (wīt), **Isl of** isl. off the S coast of England.

Wind·hoek (vint'ho͝ok) city, cen. Namibia; cap.; pop. 85,000.

Wind·sor (win'zər) city, SE Ontario, Canada; pop. 246,110.

Wind·ward Islands (wind'wərd) isl. group, S Lesser Antilles.

Win·ni·peg (win'ə·peg) city, cen. Canada; cap. of Manitoba; pop. 584,842 (met.).

Win·ston-Sa·lem (win'stən·sā'ləm) city, NW cen. North Carolina; pop. 131,885.

Wis·con·sin (wis·kon'sən) state, N U.S.; pop. 4,705,521; cap. Madison.

Worces·ter (wo͝os'tər) city, cen. Massachusetts; pop. 161,799.

Wro·claw (vrô'tswäf, -tsläf) city, SW Poland; pop. 609,100.

Wu·han (wo͞o'hän') city, E cen. China; pop. 4,400,000. Pinyin spelling **Wuhan**.

Wy·o·ming (wī·ō'ming) state, NW U.S.; pop. 469,557; cap. Cheyenne.

Yang·tze (yang'tsē') river flowing from Tibet to the East China Sea; 3,600 mi. long.

Ya·oun·dé (yȧ·o͞on·dā') city, S cen. Cameroon; cap.; pop. 350,000.

Yel·low·knife (yel'ō·nīf') cap. of Northwest Territories, Canada; pop. 9,483.

Yellow River Hwang Ho; *an alternate name*.

Yellow Sea inlet of the Pacific betw. Korea and China.

Yem·en, People's Democratic Republic of (yem'ən) country, S Arabian penin.; pop. 2,100,000; cap. Aden. Also *Southern Yemen*.

Yemen Arab Republic country, SW Arabian penin.; pop. 8,575,000; cap. Sana. Also **Yemen.**

Yo·ko·ha·ma (yō'kə·hä'mə) city, cen. Honshu, Japan; pop. 2,775,000.

Yon·kers (yong'kərz) city, SE New York; pop. 195,351.

Youngs·town (yungz'toun') city, NE Ohio; pop. 115,436.

Yu·ca·tán (yo͞o'kə·tan') penin., SE Mexico and NE Central America.

Yu·go·sla·vi·a (yo͞o'gō·slä'vē·ə) country, SE Europe; pop. 22,412,000; cap. Belgrade.

Yu·kon River (yo͞o'kon) river, NW Canada and cen. Alaska; 2,300 mi. long.

Yukon Territory terr., NW Canada; pop. 23,153; cap. Whitehorse.

Za·greb (zä′greb) city, N Yugoslavia; pop. 700,000.

Za·ire (zä·ir′) country, cen. Africa; pop. 28,150,000; cap. Kinshasa.

Zam·be·zi (zam·bē′zē) river, S Africa; 1,700 mi. long.

Zam·bi·a (zam′bē·ə) country, S cen. Africa; pop. 6,100,000; cap. Lusaka.

Zim·ba·bwe (zim·bä′bwē) country, S Africa; pop. 7,850,000; cap. Harare. Formerly *Rhodesia*.

Zu·rich (zo͞or′ik) city, NE Switzerland; cap.; pop. 377,300.

TABLE OF FOREIGN ALPHABETS

(1) ARABIC

ا	alif	—[1]
ب	ba	b
ت	ta	t
ث	sa	th
ج	jim	j
ح	ha	h
خ	kha	kh
د	dal	d
ذ	zal	th
ر	ra	r
ز	za	z
س	sin	s
ش	shin	sh
ص	sad	s
ض	dad	d
ط	ta	t
ظ	za	z
ع	ain	—[2]
غ	ghain	gh[3]
ف	fa	f
ق	qaf	k[4]
ك	kaf	k[5]
ل	lam	l
م	mim	m
ن	nun	n
ه	ha	h
و	waw	w
ي	ya	y

(2) HEBREW

א	aleph	—[6]
בּ, ב	beth	b, v
גּ, ג	gimel	g, gh[3]
דּ, ד	daleth	d, th
ה	he	h
ו	vav	v
ז	zayin	z
ח	ḥeth	kh
ט	ṭeth	t
י	yod	y
כּ, כ, ך[8]	kaph	k[5], kh
ל	lamed	l
מ, ם[8]	mem	m
נ, ן[8]	nun	n
ס	samek	s
ע	ayin	—[7]
פּ, פ, ף[8]	pe	p, f
צ, ץ[8]	sade	s
ק	ḳoph	k[4]
ר	resh	r
שׂ, שׁ	sin, shin	s, sh
תּ, ת	tav	t, th

(3) GREEK

Α	α	alpha	ā
Β	β	beta	b
Γ	γ	gamma	g
Δ	δ	delta	d
Ε	ε	epsilon	e
Ζ	ζ	zeta	z
Η	η	eta	ā
Θ	θ	theta	th[9]
Ι	ι	iota	ē
Κ	κ	kappa	k
Λ	λ	lambda	l
Μ	μ	mu	m
Ν	ν	nu	n
Ξ	ξ	xi	ks
Ο	ο	omicron	o
Π	π	pi	p
Ρ	ρ	rho	r
Σ	σ, ς[8]	sigma	s
Τ	τ	tau	t
Υ	υ	upsilon	ū, o͞o
Φ	φ	phi	f[10]
Χ	χ	chi	kh[11]
Ψ	ψ	psi	ps
Ω	ω	omega	ō

In each column the characters of the alphabet are given first, followed by their names. In columns 4 (Russian) and 5 (German) the names are printed in the phonetic system used in this dictionary. The last rows of columns 1 through 4 show the approximate sound represented by each character. Columns 3 through 5 show the upper- and lower-case forms. The Arabic characters are given in their final, unconnected forms. The German style letter, called *fraktur*, has been gradually replaced by the Latin letter. The last row of column 5 gives the Latin equivalents.

TABLE OF FOREIGN ALPHABETS

(4) RUSSIAN

А	а	ā	ā
Б	б	be	b
В	в	ve	v
Г	г	ge	g
Д	д	de	d
Е	е	ye	ye, e[12]
Ё	ё	yô	yô, ô[12,13]
Ж	ж	zhe	zh[14]
З	з	ze	z
И	и	ē	ē[15]
Й	й	e krāt′·kə·yə	ē[16]
К	к	kā	k
Л	л	el	l
М	м	em	m
Н	н	en	n
О	о	ô	ô
П	п	pe	p
Р	р	er	r
С	с	es	s
Т	т	te	t
У	у	o͞o	o͞o
Ф	ф	ef	f
Х	х	k͟hā	k͟h
Ц	ц	tse	ts[14]
Ч	ч	che	ch[17]
Ш	ш	shā	sh[14]
Щ	щ	shchā	shch[17]
Ъ	ъ	tvyôr′dē znāk	—[18]
Ы	ы	i[19]	i[19]
Ь	ь	myāk͟h′·kyē znāk	—[20]
Э	э	e	e
Ю	ю	yo͞o	yo͞o, o͞o[12]
Я	я	yä	yä, ä[12]

(5) GERMAN

𝔄	𝔞	ā	A	a
𝔄̈	𝔞̈	e[21]	Ä	ä
𝔅	𝔟	bā	B	b
ℭ	𝔠	tsā	C	c
𝔇	𝔡	dā	D	d
𝔈	𝔢	ā[22]	E	e
𝔉	𝔣	ef	F	f
𝔊	𝔤	gā	G	g
ℌ	𝔥	hā	H	h
ℑ	𝔦	ē	I	i
𝔍	𝔧	yôt	J	j
𝔎	𝔨	kā	K	k
𝔏	𝔩	el	L	l
𝔐	𝔪	em	M	m
𝔑	𝔫	en	N	n
𝔒	𝔬	ō[22]	O	o
𝔒̈	𝔬̈	œ[21]	Ö	ö
𝔓	𝔭	pā	P	p
𝔔	𝔮	ko͞o	Q	q
ℜ	𝔯	er	R	r
𝔖	ſ, 𝔰[8]	es	S	s
—	ß[23]	es′tset	—	ß[23], ss
𝔗	𝔱	tā	T	t
𝔘	𝔲	o͞o	U	u
𝔘̈	𝔲̈	ü[21]	Ü	ü
𝔙	𝔳	fou	V	v
𝔚	𝔴	vā	W	w
𝔛	𝔵	iks	X	x
𝔜	𝔶	üp′si·lōn	Y	y
ℨ	𝔷	tset	Z	z

[1] Functions as the bearer of *hamza* (the glottal stop), or as a lengthener of short *a*. [2] A voiced pharyngeal fricative. [3] A voiced velar fricative. [4] A uvular stop. [5] A voiceless velar stop. [6] A glottal stop, now usually silent, or pronounced according to the accompanying vowel points. [7] A pharyngeal fricative, now usually silent, or pronounced according to the accompanying vowel points. [8] The alternate form is restricted to the ends of words. [9,10,11] In classical Greek these were pronounced as aspirated stops similar to the sounds in foo*th*ill, ha*ph*azard, and bloc*kh*ouse. [12] Preceded by a *y* glide when initial, following a vowel, or following a previously palatalized consonant. The glide is otherwise omitted and the preceding consonant palatalized. [13] The diacritical mark is most often omitted. [14] Never palatalized. [15] Palatalizes the consonant preceding it. [16] A short vowel, as *y* in *boy*, used only as the second element of diphthongs. [17] Always palatalized. [18] No phonetic value, used to separate parts of compounds and indicate that the consonant preceding it is not palatalized; a hard sign. [19] No English equivalent, similar to *i* as in *kick* with the tongue drawn back. [20] Indicates that the preceding consonant is to be palatalized. [21] See UMLAUT in vocabulary section. [22] In German this vowel is not a diphthong. [23] Restricted to the ends of words.

BASIC STYLE MANUAL
by Alice Ottun

Word Usage and Word Relationships

Agreement of Subject and Verb

It may seem needless to say that a singular subject takes a singular verb, while a plural subject takes a plural verb; however, many errors occur in this respect.

The small table *was* in the hall.
The small tables *were* in the hall.

In some instances, when phrases or other elements come between the subject and the verb, the agreement may not be so clear.

The small table around which the children play *was* in the hall.
The small tables owned by the church *were* in the hall.
The men, as well as the policeman, *were* aghast at the sight.

The following words are generally considered singular and take the singular form of the verb: *each, either, neither, one, someone, anyone, everybody, nobody, somebody, much, anybody, everyone.*

The following words are plural and take the plural form of the verb: *both, few, many, several.*

The following pronouns may be singular or plural depending on the meaning intended: *all, most, some, every, none, any, half, more.*

When one is referring to two or more persons who are of different sexes, or to a group of people whose gender one has no way of determining, the pronouns *they, them,* and *their* are often used to to refer to *anyone, each, everybody,* etc. *He or she, him or her, his or her* may also be used in this situation.

A collective noun, such as *class, company, club, crew, jury, committee,* takes a singular verb when the whole is considered as a unit, and a plural verb when part of the whole is considered separately.

The jury *has* deliberated for six hours.
The crew *were* near exhaustion after their many hours of exposure.

Some collective nouns, as *police* and *cattle,* are used only in the plural form. They take plural verbs. Others, as *mankind* and *wildlife,* are generally used in the singular form and take singular verbs.

The cattle *were* almost destroyed by the severe storm.
The New England wildlife *has* been protected.

Either—or; Neither—Nor

Neither always takes *nor; either* takes *or.*

When a subject is compounded with *neither . . . nor* or *either . . . or,* the verb is normally singular if the nouns joined are singular, and plural if they are plural. If, however, one noun is singular and one plural, the verb agrees with the second or nearer subject.

Either Bill or Ralph *is* lying.
Neither she nor her sisters *skate* well.

Agreement of Pronoun with Its Antecedent

If the antecedent is singular, the pronoun is singular; if the antecedent is plural, the pronoun is likewise plural.

The *boy* did *his* best in the contest.
The *boys* in the school did *their* best.
The *boy and* the *girl* did *their* best.
Neither one of the boys did *his* best.

Punctuation

For practical purposes, it is best to keep in mind that too much punctuation is as confusing as too little. The current trend is toward a minimum of punctuation, just enough to make the writer's meaning clear. This can best be accomplished by cultivating a simple, straightforward style that flows as naturally as ordinary speech.

Where a sentence is so complicated that no amount of punctuation seems adequate, the writer's thoughts need reorganizing. Punctuation can help to guide a reader to the meaning of a sentence; it cannot, however, make order out of confused thinking and expression.

End Punctuation

Because the sentence is a grammatically complete and separate unit of utterance, it is necessary to show where one sentence ends and another begins. In speech, this is accomplished by falling pitch, intonation, and a full pause. In written discourse, the reader is guided by a period, a question mark, or an exclamation point, depending on the nature of the sentence.

The Period [.] The period is used at the end of a declarative sentence, an imperative sentence, an indirect question, and after a polite request that resembles a question. It is also used after initials. Abbreviations which in the past were written with periods are frequently written now without them. Follow whatever style you prefer.

Mrs. Morris placed the book on the table.
Grab the rope.
The members of the committee asked when the meeting would take place.
Will you open the door for me, please.

If a sentence ends in an abbreviation, only one period is needed.

The bus will arrive at 8:30 a.m.

Do not use a period and two zeros after even amounts of money, except in tabulation.

$25, not $25. or $25.00

The period should not be used in centered headings, such as manuscript and chapter headings; in the various elements in an outline; or at the ends of items in a table.

Do not use periods between the call numbers of broadcasting stations: WABC, WQXR; or between the letters indicating government agencies: FBI, CIA, FAA, IRS.

The Question Mark [?] The question mark signifies that the sentence preceding it does not make a statement, but asks a question. This punctuation serves the same purpose in writing that rising or sustained pitch intonation of the voice does in speaking.

When may we expect to receive your check?

If a sentence consists of several questions, the question mark should appear at the close of each question within the sentence and also at the close. The separate questions within the sentence do not begin with a capital since they are part of the larger and complete question.

Who will attend the conference—the president? the vice president? the secretary?

The Exclamation Point [!] This is used at the end of a sentence expressing a strong emotion or a sense of urgency or excitement. If spoken, it would be gasped, shouted, groaned, or cried. Written, the exclamation point, and the reader's imagination, must suffice.

Watch out!
Oh, my head!

An interjection at the beginning of a sentence is usually followed by a comma, and the sentence is ended with an exclamation point. The interjection may, however, be immediately followed by an exclamation mark, and the following sentence punctuated without reference to it.

Oh, what a day this is!
Oh! How could you do that?

Exclamation points should be used with discretion and for particular emphasis. Excessive use tends to lessen the impact of this device.

Internal Punctuation

When sentences become more complex and deal with two or more closely related ideas, internal punctuation is necessary to show the relation between the various parts, to prevent possible confusion, or to indicate pauses.

The Comma [,] The comma is used to separate the various elements in a series—either words, phrases, or clauses—when there are at least three units.

The torn, tattered, soaking flag was lowered.
The dog jumped up, barked ferociously, bared his teeth, and took off after the rabbit.

Formal punctuation requires that a comma be inserted between the last two elements of a series even when a conjunction is used; this rule is generally followed in letter writing. An informal style of writing does not require the comma before the conjunction.

The flag is red, white and blue.

Sometimes the conjunction is used with each element in the series. When this occurs, no comma is used to separate the elements.

The banner will be red or blue or white or a combination of these colors.

When *etc.* is the concluding element in a series, it should be preceded by a comma. A comma should also follow *etc.* when it is not the last word in a sentence.

She stopped off at the supermarket to get some fruit, vegetables, etc., on the way home.

Use the comma to set off an introductory sentence element (word, phrase, clause) which is out of its natural order. Of all the comma rules, this is probably the most difficult to master. Some words, like *however*, are not always used as introductory words and would not then be followed by the comma.

Obviously, we cannot meet your request.
In order to meet the deadline, we shall have to work overtime.
When you go to see him in the hospital, bring along a few magazines.
However, we'll think about it.
However well you meant, it was the wrong thing to do.

When the main clause in the sentence comes first, do not use the comma between the main clause and the dependent clause.

Bring along a few magazines when you go to visit him in the hospital.

As a general rule, an introductory phrase which contains a verb should be followed with a comma.

After *making* the survey, the committee will publish the report.
To *complete* the survey, the officers worked overtime.

If the introductory phrase does nor contain a verb, it should not be followed by a comma unless the phrase is parenthetical.

After much debate the meeting was adjourned.
As an act of mercy the sick animal was killed.
Under separate cover we are sending you a catalogue.
On the contrary, I believe the President was absolutely right.
For example, consider the boy's attitude toward his parents.
In the second place, watch his behavior with his peers.

Use the comma to set off introductory *yes* or *no* or light exclamations in a sentence.

No, we shall not be ready on time.
Oh, what a wonderful day this has been!

A parenthetical expression (word, phrase, or clause) that can be omitted without changing the meaning of the sentence should be set off by commas.

The king, who was very ill, was not present at the ceremony.
Something may, of course, turn up to change what seems now to be the obvious outcome.

When the information has little connection with the thought expressed in the main clause, it is usually enclosed in parentheses rather than in commas.

The strike (which began on the President's birthday) completely paralyzed the nation.

Dashes may also be used to set off any sort of nonrestrictive or parenthetical matter. Some writers feel that dashes lend a more personal dramatic effect to their writing.

The earth—all parched and dry—yearns for moisture.

Do not use a comma when a clause cannot be omitted from a sentence without changing the meaning of the sentence.

Barbara was relieved when the package arrived.

Use the comma before short, direct quotations.

She asked, "Is the train on time?"

Use the comma to set off words in direct address.

We are certain, Mr. Long, that you will be satisfied with our product.

The comma or commas should be used to set off an identifying or explanatory word or phrase (called an *appositive*) which helps to make the meaning of the sentence clearer. This rule applies to a person's title or degree and to the abbreviation "Inc." when used in a company name.

Our saleswoman, Nancy Brown, will call on you tomorrow.
We shall write a letter to Ray Smith & Company, Inc., in New York City.
Harold Brown, Ph.D., has been appointed to the faculty.

Separate comtrasting expressions—word, phrase, or clause—by using the comma.

We shall leave today, not tomorrow.

Use the comma to separate two or more parallel adjectives.

Their sleeping bags kept them warm during the long, cold nights.

If the word *and* can be inserted between the two adjectives or if the two adjectives can be reversed, they are parallel and the comma should be used.
The comma is *not* used when the order of the adjectives helps to determine the meaning of the sentence.

They built the building with wide open stairways..

The comma should be used before a conjunction (*but, and, or,* etc.) that connects two independent clauses.

We have had the pleasure of counting you as one of our members for many years, but we notice that you have not yet renewed your membership.

If the clauses are short and uncomplicated, the comma may be omitted.

> We were drenched but arrived safely.

The Semicolon [;] The semicolon is used to separate two independent clauses when the conjunction is omitted.

> We are enclosing an envelope for your convenience; it requires no postage.

Use the semicolon to separate the members of a compound sentence when one or both members contain other punctuation marks.

> If he is nominated, he will run; but his chances seem dim.

Use the semicolon to separate the members of a compound sentence when the clauses are connected by such words as *however, nevertheless, consequently, thus, indeed, yet,* etc.

> He paid little attention to details; consequently, he failed to be promoted.

Phrases or clauses in a series are separated by the semicolon when any one or more of the phrases or clauses contain a comma or other internal punctuation.

> Our profits for the three successive years were: 1960, $2,345,000; 1961, $2,070,400; 1962, $2,545,000.
>
> Knowing that there wasn't much time, Mike made a mental list of what was left to be done including (1) checking all equipment—was it in proper condition; (2) discontinuing services—the telephone, the newspaper delivery; and (3) arranging for a dog sitter —Mary, or perhaps, Jill.

The Colon [:] The colon is used most often to indicate that a list, example, strong assertion, or the like will follow to complete or fulfill some introductory statement.

> The report covered three phases only: temperature, wind velocity, and air pressure.
>
> We have only one goal: to win.

The colon is also used outside the sentence in certain purely conventional ways: after the salutation of a formal letter; between elements of a Biblical or bibliographical citation; after the name or other identification of the speaker in a dialogue or in a transcript of speech.

Use the colon to separate hours and minutes when time is expressed in figures. When no minutes are expressed, it is not necessary to use two zeros with the number designating the hour. When the word *o'clock* is used, do not indicate the time in figures but express the time in words.

> We shall be there at 3:30 P.M.
>
> We shall be there at 3 P.M.
>
> We shall be there at three o'clock.

The Apostrophe [']

To Indicate Possession Apostrophes are employed most commonly to form the possessive of nouns and pronouns. In words not ending with an *s* or *z* sound, *'s* is added; in those ending with an *s* or *z* sound, the common practice is to add only an apostrophe at the end. Most singular nouns take the *'s*, and most plural forms add only '.

Words not ending in s *or* z *sound:*	*Words ending in* s *or* z *sound:*
the children's playroom	the babies' bottles
somebody's hat	for goodness' sake

Add *'s* to a proper name even though it ends with an *s* or an *z* sound.

James's laundry	Rodriguez's car
Thomas's story	Marx's philosophy

Exceptions are the names *Jesus* and *Moses,* the books of the Bible that end in *s,* and Greek names that end in *s* or *es: Moses', Genesis', Demosthenes'.*

After plural proper nouns, add an apostrophe only.

the Joneses' house

Personal pronouns do not take the apostrophe in the possessive form.

my, mine	our, ours
your, yours	their, theirs
her, hers	his, its, whose

To Indicate Omission An apostrophe is also used to show that one or more letters have been omitted from a word, or that numerals have been omitted from a number.

it's—it is; can't—cannot; you're—you are;
we'll—we will; where'er—wherever; '29—1929

Plurals of Letters or Numbers Form plurals of capital letters, numbers, and dates by adding *s*, omitting the apostrophe.

Learn your ABCs.
It was popular in the 1950s.
the three Rs
at sixes and sevens
We seem to have too many 3s in this pack.

Add *'s* for the plurals of small letters, capital letters that spell words when *s* is added, and abbreviations that have periods.

Dot your i's and cross your t's.
There are four Ph.D.'s on the staff.
Don't miss the A's or I's.

Quotation Marks [""] ['']

There are two classes of quotations: *direct* and *indirect*.

Quotation marks are required at the beginning and end of a word or words spoken in direct discourse.

Roy said, "I am reading a good book."

Indirect quotations require no quotation marks, and are commonly introduced by the word *that*.

Roy said that he was reading a good book.

If a direct quotation is interrupted by one or more words, the quotation marks are placed around the quoted matter only and not around the interrupting words.

"Hurry along," said the coach, "or we shall not make the game in time."

When quoting material, be careful to include every detail of punctuation.

"Stir not up agitation! Give us peace!"

Slang is sometimes placed in quotation marks, as are words used for special effect.

They line up every Tuesday, the day known as "hit day."
The new telephones fit in with the "Oriental" decor of the apartments.

Translations of foreign words and phrases should be enclosed in quotations marks.

Au revoir means "till we meet again" or "good-bye."
Laissez faire means "noninterference."

In manuscripts and business correspondence, the title of a book, booklet, magazine, newspaper, play, opera, movie, television or radio program, should be typed in capital and small letters and underlined. Enclose in quotation marks and type in capital and small letters the titles of essays, poems, magazine articles, lectures, and term papers, and the titles of chapters. The first letter of the first word and the first letter of every important word following is capitalized.

"A Few More Words," chapter 6 of The Handbook of Nonsexist Writing discusses current usage.
Did you read the article "One Man's Opinion" in this morning's New York Times?

When a lengthy quotation of two or more paragraphs is used, beginning or opening quotation marks are used at the start of each paragraph, and closing quotation marks appear only at the very end of the quoted passage.

No quotation marks are necessary in interviews, dramatic dialogues, or legal testimony where the name of the speaker or other identification is followed by a colon.

Judge: How do you plead, guilty or not guilty?
Defendant: Not guilty, Your Honor.
Q.: Where were you on the night of June 26?
A.: I don't remember.

A quotation within a quotation is enclosed by single quotation marks.

Jack remarked, "I believe Patrick Henry said, 'Give me liberty or give me death.' "

Punctuation with Quotation Marks The rule for punctuating quoted matter is quite simple. The period and comma are always *inside* the closing quotation marks; the colon and semicolon are always *outside* the closing quotation marks; the question mark and exclamation point will be inside or outside the closing quotation marks depending on whether they are or are not part of the quoted matter.

"Call the police," he said.
He said, "Call the police."
He said, "Who called the police?"
Who said, "Call the police"?
He said, "Call the police"; but the sirens were already wailing.

The period is never doubled at the end of a quotation within a quotation. See the Patrick Henry quotation above. Here, the period within the quotation marks serves as end punctuation for both the sentence spoken by Jack and that spoken by Patrick Henry.

The Hyphen [-]

The hyphen is used primarily for end-of-line word divisions and for hyphenation of compound words.

Words may be divided *only* between syllables.

Words pronounced as one syllable may never be divided.

Words may not be divided in groups of fewer than three letters. An exception is the division of a word after two letters when the two letters fall at the end of the line.

en-slave, *but not*, subsi-dy

Abbreviations should never be carried over from one line to the next, and every attempt should be made to include the initials or first name of a person's name on the same line with his or her surname.

Do not hyphenate a word at the end of a page and avoid excessive hyphenation within paragraphs.

Break a word that is already hyphenated at its hyphen. Hyphenate a compound word between the words making up the compound.

topsy-turvy (*not* top-sy-turvy)
waste-basket (*not* wastebas-ket)

If numbers must be divided, the break should be made after a comma: There are 35,675,-
545 telephones on the West Coast.

The general rule in the hyphenation of compound words is this: When two or more words precede a noun and together form a single idea modifying the noun, they should be hyphenated; they are usually not hyphenated if they follow the noun. In many instances only the context of the sentence will determine whether a hyphenated compound is required, or whether the words should remain separate.

He said it in a very matter-of-fact way.
He knew that to be true as a matter of fact.
As a matter of fact, he knew that to be true.
Her dress was green and white.
Her green-and-white dress was pretty.

Do not confuse the adverb with the adjective preceding a noun—adverbs are not hyphenated.

The beautifully illustrated book was enjoyed by the membership.

Hyphens are used to separate prefixes from words where the writer's meaning would otherwise be distorted.

The upholsterer re-covered the chair.
The police recovered the typewriter.

The hyphen is also used to separate a prefix from a proper noun, or to simplify a confusing combination.

anti-American, pre-Renaissance, mid-ocean

Hyphens are used in all numbers ranging from twenty-one to ninety-nine, and in fractions: one-half, three-quarters. Hyphens are also used in designating years: nineteen-sixties, nineteen sixty-two (*not* nineteen-sixty-two).

The hyphen is used in titles when combined with *elect* or *ex*.

President-elect
ex-President

The hyphen is generally used when words are compounded with the prefix *self*.

self-satisfied, self-confident, self-possessed, self-starter

The Dash [—]

A word of caution against confusing the hyphen (-) and the dash (—). The hyphen connects, while the dash separates. The dash is formed on the typewriter with two hyphens, no space before, between, or after.

If properly used, the dash is effective to secure emphasis but has only a few legitimate uses in business letters. It may be used in place of the comma and parentheses in handling appositive and parenthetical expressions. It is also used to mark intentional repetition.

Exercise every day—*every* day—and find out for yourself how beneficial it is to your health and well being.

The dash may be used to show an abrupt change in thought.

We do not know when we shall go—here is the bus.

Ellipsis

To show that words have been omitted from within a sentence in quoted matter, add three dots (ellipsis points) in place of the omitted words.

The Emancipation Proclamation, issued by President Abraham Lincoln on January 1, 1863, declared free all Negro slaves in all states.

The Emancipation Proclamation . . . declared free all Negro slaves in all states.

Note that there is a space between each ellipsis point, and that a space precedes the first point and a space follows the last one when the ellipsis is added within a sentence.

To show that the end of a sentence has been omitted, add three points after the period that comes at the end of the sentence. This makes a total of four points.

> The Emancipation Proclamation, issued by President Abraham Lincoln on January 1, 1863. . . .

Note that when words are omitted from the end of a sentence, there is no space preceding the first of the points.

Three points are also added to the end of a sentence to show that one or more sentences following have been omitted, and three dots are added to the final period of a paragraph to indicate that the paragraph or paragraphs following have been omitted.

Parentheses [()]

Parentheses are used to enclose words which give additional information but have little, if any, direct connection with the main thought expressed. Commas and dashes have already been discussed in this relationship. Material enclosed in commas or separated from the rest of the sentence by dashes adds something to the main thought expressed, although not something essential; material enclosed in parentheses adds nothing to the main thought and has no direct relationship to the rest of the sentence.

> If we win the contest (and I feel certain we will), we shall compete in the national contest in Chicago.

Parentheses are widely used to enclose references to statements, authors, etc.

> "How to Express Thoughts Properly" is outlined in full in our text (see page 124).
> We are using *Effective Business English* (Jones and Smith) for reference.

The Underscore

Underscoring a word or a group of words may be done for emphasis, but this device should be used with caution. There are a few fundamental rules, however, which should be followed.

Underline the title of a book, booklet, play, magazine, or newspaper.

Note: This rule is discussed more fully under the subject of Quotation Marks.

When preparing copy for the printer, underline material which is to be printed in italics.

Do not use underscoring for emphasis in the body of the letter.

Do not break the underscoring when underscoring headings.

Do not break the underscoring of parts of the text unless each part or each word is intended to be emphasized separately.

Do not include the punctuation at the end of the sentence in the underscoring.

Capitalization

Conventions governing the use of capital letters are quite clear.

Capitalize the first word of every sentence.

The first person singular pronoun *I* and the explanatory *O* are generally capitalized.

Unless style requires a different form, *a.m.* and *p.m.* are set in small letters without a space between them. Capital letters are used for B.C. and A.D. but, again, there is no space between them.

> 9:30 a.m. 10:30 p.m.
> A.D. 1760 *or* 1760 A.D.
> 76 B.C.

Note: Although A.D. should technically precede the number of the year, popular usage permits it to follow the date. In printed matter B.C., A.D., a.m., and p.m. usually appear in small capitals (B.C., A.D., A.M., P.M.).

The first letter of a line of conventional poetry is capitalized. Much modern poetry, however, ignores this convention.

> Hickory, dickory, dock
> The mouse ran up the clock.

The first word after a colon should be capitalized only when it begins a complete sentence.

The candidate made only one promise: If elected, he would fight for better conditions.
The list contained these items: five pounds of flour, two dozen eggs, and a pound of butter.

Every direct quotation should begin with a capital, except where the quoted passage is grammatically woven into the text preceding it.

The announcer shouted, "There it goes, over the back wall for a home run!"
The announcer saw the ball going "over the back wall for a home run.'

Capitalize the first letters of all important words in the titles of books, newspapers, magazines, chapters, poems, articles. Short conjunctions, prepositions, and the infinitive *to* are generally not capitalized unless they are the first word of the title.

How to Win Friends and Influence People
To the Lighthouse

Geographical divisions and regions require capitals.

Arctic Circle	the Atlantic Seaboard
the Orient	the Great Plains

Compass points are capitalized when they are part of a generally accepted name, but not when they denote direction, or are used with common nouns.

Middle East	eastern New York
Old South	Head west for twenty-five miles.

Capitalize names of streets, parks, buildings, but not the general categories into which they fall.

General Post Office *but* We went to the *post office*.
Metropolitan Museum of Art *but* Some *museums* are open until five.
Empire State Building *but* Which is the tallest *building* in New York City?

Religions, religious leaders, the various names for God and the Christian Trinity require capitalization, as do all names for the Bible and its parts.

the Father, the Son, and the Holy Ghost
Virgin Mary, the Immaculate Virgin
Yahweh, Jehovah, Savior, Messiah
Buddhism, Shintoism, Taoism
New Testament
Exodus
Sermon on the Mount
Ten Commandments

Capitalize the names of political parties, organizations, movements, and their adherents, but not the word *party* or *movement*. Use small letters for the terms that refer generally to ideology (bolshevism, fascism, socialism).

Democratic party	Populist movement
Democrat	Boy Scouts of America

Political divisions are capitalized.

Holy Roman Empire	the Colonies
French Republic	Suffolk County
the Dominion	Eighth Congressional District

Government bodies, departments, bureaus, and courts are capitalized.

the Supreme Court	the Cabinet
House of Representatives	Census Bureau
Department of Labor	British Parliament

Government, military, religious, and professional titles as well as titles of nobility are capitalized when followed by a name.

Chief Justice John Jay
John Jay, first chief justice of the U.S.
Queen Elizabeth I of England
Elizabeth I, queen of England

Capitalize the names of treaties, documents, and important events.

Second World War | Declaration of Independence
Treaty of Versailles | Boston Tea Party

Family designations, when used without a possessive pronoun, take a capital letter.

I sent Mother home by taxi.
I sent my mother home by taxi.

Capitalize seasons only when they are personified. All personifications require capitals.

The frosty breath of Winter settled on the land.
The voice of Envy whispered in her ear.
He saw Mother Nature's grim visage.

Names and epithets of peoples, races, and tribes are capitalized.

Caucasian | Sioux
Negro | Cliff Dwellers

Articles and prepositions are generally capitalized in the names of Englishmen and Americans, and are not capitalized in French, Italian, Spanish, German, and Dutch names, unless otherwise specified by family usage.

Thomas De Quincey | Ludwig van Beethoven
Martin Van Buren | Leonardo da Vinci
Fiorello La Guardia | San Juan de la Cruz

Capitalize the names of holidays and festivals.

Christmas Eve | Shrove Tuesday
Yom Kippur | New Year's Day

Use small letters for parts of a book, such as index, glossary, bibliography, preface, etc., in discussions of these parts. Capitalize when referring from one part of the book to another.

Prepare the index on file cards.
A list of sources will be found in the Appendix.

Spelling

General Suggestions

When in doubt as to the correct spelling of a word, consult the dictionary; do not take anything for granted. Some basic spelling rules follow.

cede, ceed, and sede endings According to the Government Style Manual, there is only one word which ends in *sede—supersede*, and three that end in *ceed—proceed* (but *procedure*), *exceed, succeed.* All other words using this combination end in *cede—precede, secede, recede.*

ie and ei a. After *c*, the *e* usually precedes the *i*: rec*ei*ve, dec*ei*ve, c*ei*ling, rec*ei*pt.
b. After other letters, the *i* precedes the *e* (*ie*): th*ie*f, gr*ie*f, bel*ie*ve, ach*ie*ve, l*ie*n.
The exceptions must be learned, since they follow no rule: n*ei*ther, l*ei*sure, w*ei*rd, s*ei*ze.
c. When the sound is *not* long *e* (ē), and especially if the sound is long *a* (ā), the *e* precedes the *i* (*ei*): sl*ei*gh, v*ei*l.

Endings of Words (Suffixes)

a. As a general rule, drop the final *e* in the base word when a suffix beginning with a vowel is added: decide—deciding; write—writing; type—typing. (When in doubt, use the dictionary.)

b. As a rule, retain the final *e* in the base word when a suffix beginning with a consonant is added: remote—remotely; care—carefully; adverse—adversely.

c. In applying the rule for adding *ed* or *ing*, the accent (or lack of it) may serve as a guide. Words of one syllable (and most words of more than one syllable) that end in a single consonant (except *f*, *h*, or *x*), preceded by a single vowel, double the final consonant *if the accent falls on the last syllable.*

plan—planned, planning; whet—whetted, whetting; bet—betting; can—canned—canning
transfer—transferred, transferring; excel—excelled, excelling
omit—omitted, omitting; begin—beginning

d. When the word is *not* accented on the last syllable, the consonant is usually not doubled.

travel—traveled, traveling; benefit—benefited, benefiting; profit—profited, profiting; gossip—gossiped, gossiping

e. When the endings *ness* and *ly* are added to a word not ending in *y*, the base word rarely changes. In most words ending in *y*, the *y* changes to *i* when *ly* or *ness* is added.

natural—naturally; similar—similarly; genuine—genuineness; blessed—blessedness; hazy—hazily; body—bodily; heavy—heaviness

If the base word ends in *n* and the suffix *ness* is added, the *n* is doubled: sudden—suddenness; mean—meanness; vain—vainness.

f. In regard to the word endings *ise*, *ize*, *yze*, the most common form is *ize*, but here again the dictionary should be consulted if there is doubt.

legalize, fraternize, criticize, jeopardize
advertise, merchandise, surmise, enterprise
paralyze, analyze

◆ In British English *ise* is sometimes used for *ize*, as *realise* for *realize*.

g. When adding the suffix *ful*, the *l* is single except when *ly* is also added (*fully*).

care—careful—carefully; hope—hopeful—hopefully.

Forming the Plurals of Nouns

a. Most nouns, except those that end in *s*, *z*, *ch*, *sh*, and some that end in *o*, and *y*, form the plural by simply adding *s*: table—tables; house—houses.

b. Most nouns ending in *s*, *z*, *ch*, and *sh* form the plural by adding *es*: bus—buses; class—classes; buzz—buzzes; watch—watches; ash—ashes.

c. Words ending in *y* preceded by a consonant form the plural by changing the *y* to *i* and adding *es*: candy—candies; study—studies; secretary—secretaries.

d. Words ending in *y* preceded by a vowel usually form the plural without any change in the word: key—keys; boy—boys.

e. Nouns ending in *o* preceded by a vowel form the plural by adding *s*: rodeo—rodeos; radio—radios.

When the *o* is preceded by a consonant, the plural is formed by adding *es*: hero—heroes; torpedo—torpedoes.

f. Nouns referring to music which end in *o* preceded by a consonant form the plural by simply adding *s*: piano—pianos; contralto—contraltos; soprano—sopranos.

g. Some few nouns follow none of the above rules but form the plural in an unusual way: child—children; tooth—teeth; mouse—mice; ox—oxen.

h. Compound nouns (more than one noun) form the plural from the main word: notary public—notaries public; trade-union—trade-unions; father-in-law—fathers-in-law; court-martial—courts-martial.

i. When a solid compound ends in *ful*, the plural is formed at the end of the solid compound and not within the word: basketfuls, spoonfuls, pocketfuls.

j. Words taken from another language sometimes form the plural as they would in the original language: stratum—strata; addendum—addenda; datum—data.

Confusing Words

[Including words that have different meanings but are pronounced the same (*homophones*) or similarly]

accept See EXCEPT.
addition, edition *addition* means the process of joining together or finding the sum of. *edition* refers to the form in which a book, magazine, or other literary work is published: first *edition.*
advice, advise *advice* is the noun: to give *advice, advise* is the verb: to *advise* a person.
affect See EFFECT.
all ready See ALREADY.
all right, alright *all right* is the only spelling to be used: It is *all right* to do so. The spelling *alright* is not yet considered acceptable and should not be used.
allude, elude *allude* means to make indirect or casual reference: He *alluded* to one of Shakespeare's sonnets. *elude* means to avoid or escape: The meaning *eludes* me.
a lot, alot *a lot,* meaning many, is always spelled as two words: There are *a lot* of errors in that paper.
already, all ready *already* means before or by this time or the time mentioned: The group has *already* gone. *all ready* (two words) means that everyone is ready to do a given thing: We are *all ready* to go.
among, between *among* is used when referring to more than two persons or things. *between* is usually preferable when referring to only two persons or things.
appraise, apprise *appraise* means to judge the value of. *apprise* means to notify or inform.
ascent, assent *ascent* means rising, soaring, or climbing: the *ascent* of the mountain. *assent* means to express agreement, consent, sanction: to *assent* to a course of action.
between See AMONG.
can See MAY.
capital, capitol *capital* means property, chief city: Albany is the *capital* of New York. *capitol* means a building in which a State legislature meets: The *capitol* is on Chamber Street.
censor, censure *censor* means (*n.*) an official examiner of manuscripts, plays, etc.; (*v.*) to act as a censor; delete; suppress. *censure* means (*v.*) to express disapproval of; condemn; (*n.*) the expression of disapproval or blame.
census See SENSES.
cite, sight, site *cite* means to quote or to summon: to *cite* an incident. *sight* means a view, a vision: a beautiful *sight. site* means a place or location: the *site* of the church.
compliment, complement *compliment* means praise or congratulation. *complement* means one of two parts that mutually complete each other.
consul See COUNCIL.
correspondents, correspondence *correspondents* refers to people who communicate by means of letters. *correspondence* refers to the letters written.
council, counsel, consul *council* means an assembly convened for consultation. *counsel* means guidance, advice; also, a lawyer, *consul* means an officer residing in a foreign country to protect his own country's interests.
creditable, credible *creditable* means deserving credit or esteem; praiseworthy: a *creditable* project for reducing poverty. *credible* means capable of being believed, reliable: a *credible* alibi.
decent, descent, dissent *decent* means proper; respectable. *descent* means the act of descending or going downward. *dissent* means (*v.*) to disagree; (*n.*) a disagreement.
device, devise *device* is the noun: a handy *device* for opening bottles. *devise* is the verb: He *devised* a new way to open bottles.
dissent See DECENT.
edition See ADDITION.
effect, affect *effect,* both a noun and a verb, means (*v.*) to bring about; to cause or achieve: The treatments will *effect* an early cure; and (*n.*) result, outcome. *affect,* a verb only, means to influence or act upon: Fear *affects* the mind.
effective, effectual *effective* means producing a desired result: *Effective* action averted the strike. *effectual* means having the power to produce a desired result; adequate: *effectual* legal steps.
elicit, illicit *elicit* means to bring to light: to *elicit* the truth. *illicit* means unlawful or unauthorized.
elude See ALLUDE.
eminent, imminent *eminent* means high in station; distinguished; prominent: an *eminent* statesman. *imminent* means about to happen (said especially of danger): an *imminent* calamity.

except, accept *except* means with the exclusion or omission of. *accept* means to receive or agree to; acknowledge: to *accept* an invitation.

formerly, formally *formerly* means some time ago; once: He was *formerly* a judge. *formally* means with formality or with regard to form: *formally* dressed.

illicit See ELICIT.

imminent See EMINENT.

lay, lie See CONSISTENCY OF TENSE AND PERSON OF VERBS.

learn See TEACH.

lesson, lessen *lesson* refers to instructive or corrective example. *lessen* means to make less; decrease.

loose, lose *loose* means (*adj.*) not fastened or attached and (*v.*) to release; to untie. *lose* means to part with; to be deprived of; to suffer loss.

may. can *may* expresses permission: The child *may* play in the yard. *can* expresses ability to do: She *can* ski difficult slopes.

past, passed *past* means (*adj.*) ended or finished: His hopes are *past*; and (*n.*) time gone by: He dreams of the *past*. *passed*, the past tense and past participle of *pass*, means went (or gone) beyond or farther than: The car, which was going at high speed, *passed* him easily.

persecute, prosecute *persecute* means to maltreat or oppress; to harass. *prosecute* is generally used in a legal sense—to bring suit against.

personal, personnel *personal* pertains to a person: *personal* matters, *personal* opinions. *personnel* pertains to a body or group of persons usually employed in an office, factory, etc.: *personnel* problems, *personnel* department.

practical, practicable *practical* pertains to actual use and experience. It is the opposite of theoretical or speculative. *practicable* means unproven but possible; feasible; usable. A *practicable* plan is a workable plan, but a *practical* plan is one based on experience rather than theory, or one that can easily be put into effect.

principal, principle *principal* means (*n.*) head or leader: The *principal* of the school will give the order; and (*adj.*) highest in rank; chief: The *principal* member of an orchestra is the concertmaster. *principle*, always a noun, means a fundamental truth or law: We cannot sacrifice the *principle* for which we stand.

prosecute See PERSECUTE.

rise, raise See the section entitled CONSISTENCY OF TENSE AND PERSON OF VERBS.

senses, census *senses*, the plural of *sense*, refers to the faculty of sensation, as through taste, touch, hearing, smell, or sight. *census* refers to an official count of the people of a country or district, etc.

sight See CITE.

sit, set See the section entitled CONSISTENCY OF TENSE AND PERSON OF VERBS.

site See CITE.

stationery, stationary *stationery* refers to writing supplies. *stationary* means remaining in one place.

sweet, suite *sweet* means agreeable to the sense of taste. *suite* refers to a set or series of things intended to be used together: *suite* of rooms, *suite* of furniture.

teach, learn The teacher *teaches*; the student *learns*.

Consistency of Tense and Person of Verbs

Care should be given not to change the *tense* or *form* of the verb or the *person* of a pronoun in the middle of a sentence.

The *tense* of a verb indicates the time when something took place; and the three main tenses are *present*, *past*, and *future*.

I *eat* my dinner.
I *ate* my dinner.
I *shall eat* my dinner.

The form of the verb indicates *active voice* when the subject of the verb is acting (I *am helping*. You *sew* these seams.), and the *passive voice* when the subject of the verb is acted upon (I *am being helped*. The seams *were sewn* by you.)

The *person* of a pronoun denotes the speaker (*first person* I, we); the person spoken to (*second person* you); and the person spoken of (*third person* he, she, it, they).

Some verbs cause confusion in both writing and speaking because of the similarity in spelling and in principal parts.

The most common verbs in this group are: **lie—lay; rise—raise; and sit—set.**

The principal parts of these verbs are as follows:

lie—meaning to rest or recline
lay—meaning to place or put
Present: lie—I *lie* down to rest at ten o'clock each morning.
lay—I *lay* the wood for the fire each day.
Past: lay—I *lay* in bed too long.
laid—I *laid* the book on the table.
Past participle: lain—She has *lain* there for an hour.
laid—She has *laid* the book on the table.

rise—meaning to move upward
raise—meaning to cause to rise up, to arouse or awaken
Present: rise—I *rise* at six o'clock in the morning.
raise—I *raise* the flag each morning.
Past: rose—I *rose* at six o'clock today.
raised—I *raised* the flag this morning.
Past participle: risen—I shall have *risen* by six o'clock.
raised—I shall have *raised* the prices on these articles by then.

sit—meaning to seat oneself
set—meaning to fix firmly or make fast or place
Present: sit—I like to *sit* in the sun.
set—I plan to *set* the table for six persons.
Past: sat—I *sat* in the sun.
set—He *set* the alarm for four o'clock.
Past participle: sat—I have *sat* in the sun one hour.
set—The sun has *set* in a bright glow.

Manuscript Preparation

Before a final copy is typed, the typewriter keys should be thoroughly cleaned. A black, almost new ribbon is preferable, because the ink is too dense on a brand new ribbon. Good quality carbon paper will help to get the clearest possible impression. It is also common sense to submit the original copy or a good copy made by available reproduction methods to the publisher. One copy should always be retained by the author to protect against loss in transit.

Paper Paper should be of a standard size, preferably 8½ x 11 inches, and of a good opacity, sixteen- or twenty-pound weight. Avoid using onionskin paper or slippery paper of the erasable type.

Margins Liberal margins on both sides of the sheet are essential. The copy editor needs this space to make corrections, to query the author, and to give instructions to the printer. A five-inch line (sixty elite spaces, or fifty pica spaces) centered on the page will insure sufficient margins. The lines should be made as even as possible, without sacrificing the rules governing word division. This will help the editor to estimate the length of the manuscript in its printed form.

Spacing Text, bibliography, and table of contents should be double-spaced. Footnotes and excerpts also require double-spacing. The number of lines on a page should be uniform, generally twenty-five for a standard eleven-inch sheet. Some brands of carbon paper include a guide sheet which, when set in the platen behind the paper, helps to achieve the desired uniformity.

Indentation Indent all paragraphs a uniform number of spaces. Set off long quotations and other excerpts from the text by indenting them a few spaces from the left and maintaining this indentation until the excerpt is completed.

Forms of Address

President of the United States
Address: The President
The White House
Washington, D.C.
Salutation: Formal: Sir:
Informal: Dear Mr. President:
In Conversation: Mr. President *or* Sir
Title of Introduction: The President *or* The President of the United States

Vice President of the United States
Adress: The Vice President
United States Senate
Washington, D.C.
Salutation: Formal: Sir
Informal: Dear Mr. Vice President:
In Conversation: Mr. Vice President *or* Sir
Title of Introduction: The Vice President *or* the Vice President of the United States

Chief Justice of the United States
Address: The Chief Justice
The Supreme Court
Washington, D.C.
Salutation: Formal: Sir
Informal: Dear Mr. Chief Justice
In Conversation: Mr. Chief Justice *or* Sir
Title of Introduction: The Chief Justice

Associate Justice of the Supreme Court
Address: Mr. Justice Katsaros
The Supreme Court
Washington, D.C.
Salutation: Formal Sir:
Informal: Dear Mr. Justice Katsaros:
In Conversation: Mr. Justice *or* Mr. Justice Katsaros *or* Sir
Title of Introduction: Mr. Justice Katsaros

Cabinet Officer
Address: The Honorable Gary George Gussin
The Secretary of the Treasury
or The Honorable Shirley Richardson
The Attorney General
Washington, D.C.
Salutation: Formal: Sir: *or* Dear Sir: *or* Madam:
Informal: Dear Mr. Secretary: *or* Madam Secretary:
or Dear Treasury Secretary:
or Dear Attorney General:
In Conversation: Mr. Secretary *or* Madam Secretary
or Mr. Attorney General *or* Madam Attorney General
or Sir *or* Madam
Title of Introduction: The Secretary of the Treasury
or The Attorney General

Former President
Address: The Honorable
Alfred Edward Work
Office Address
Salutation: Formal: Sir:
Informal: Dear Mr. Work:
In Conversation: Mr. Work *or* Sir
Title of Introduction: The Honorable Alfred Edward Work

United States Senator
Address: The Honorable John Wandzilak
or The Honorable Mary Creighton
United States Senate
Washington, D.C.
Salutation: Formal: Sir: *or* Madam:
Informal: Dear Senator Wandzilak:
or Dear Senater Creighton:
In Conversation: Senator *or* Senator Wandzilak [*or* Creighton]
or Sir *or* Madam
Title of Introduction: Senator Wandzilak of Alaska
Senator Creighton of Maine

Speaker of the House of Representatives
Address: The Honorable Walter Grevesmuhl
or The Honorable Adrian Littlefield
The Speaker of the House of Representatives
Salutation: Formal: Sir: *or* Madam:
Informal: Dear Mr. Speaker: *or* Madam Speaker:
In Conversation: Mr. Speaker *or* Sir
or Madam Speaker *or* Madam
Title of Introduction: The Speaker of the House of Representatives

Member of the House of Representatives
Address: The Honorable Delphine Marino
or The Honorable Henry Wellcome
United States House of Representatives
Washington, D.C.
Salutation: Formal: Madam: *or* Sir:
Informal: Dear Congresswoman Marino *or* Miss [*or* Mrs. *or* Ms.] Marino:
or Dear Congressman Wellcome *or* Mr. Wellcome:
or Dear Representative Marino [*or* Wellcome]:
In Conversation: Miss [*or* Mrs. *or* Ms.] Marino *or* Madam
or Mr. Wellcome *or* Sir
Title of Introduction: Representative Marino from New York
or Representative Wellcome from Nebraska

Ambassador of the United States
Address: The Honorable John Wilson Smith
or The Honorable Ethel Douglas
The Ambassador of the United States
American Embassy
London, England
Salutation: Formal: Sir: *or* Madam:
Informal: Dear Mr. Ambassador: *or* Dear Madam Ambassador:
In Conversation: Mr. Ambassador *or* Madam Ambassador *or* Sir *or* Madam
Title of Introduction: The American Ambassador *or* (*if necessary*) Our Ambassador to England

Minister Plenipotentiary of the United States
Address: The Honorable James Lee Row
or The Honorable Nancy Phillips Doe
The Minister of the United States
American Legation
Oslo, Norway
Salutation: Formal: Sir: *or* Madam:
Informal: Dear Mr. Minister: *or* Dear Madam Minister:
In Conversation: Mr. Row *or* Miss (*or* Mrs. *or* Ms.) Doe
Title of Introduction: Mr. Row [*or* Miss (*or* Mrs. *or* Ms.) Doe], the American Minister
or (*if necessary*) the American Minister to Denmark

Consul of the United States
Address: Mr. John Smith
or Miss [*or* Mrs. *or* Ms.] O'Brien
American Consul
Rue de Quelque Chose
Paris, France
Salutation: Formal: Sir: *or* Madam:
Informal: Dear Mr. Smith:
or Dear Miss [*or* Mrs. *or* Ms.] O'Brien
In Conversation: Mr. Smith
or Miss [*or* Mrs. *or* Ms.] O'Brien
Title of Introduction: Mr. Smith
or Miss [*or* Mrs. *or* Ms.] O'Brien

Ambassador of a Foreign Country
Address: His Excellency
Juan Luis Ortega
The Ambassador of Mexico
Washington, D.C.
Salutation: Formal: Excellency:
Informal: Dear Mr. Ambassador:
or Dear Madam Ambassador:
In Conversation: Excellency
or Mr. Ambassador *or* Madam Ambassador
or Sir *or* Madam
Title of Introduction: The Ambassador of Mexico

Minister of a Foreign Country
Address: The Honorable
Carluh Matti
The Minister of Kezeah
Washington, D.C.
Salutation: Formal: Sir: *or* Madam:
Informal: Dear Mr. Minister *or* Dear Madam Minister:
In Conversation: Mr. Minister *or* Sir
or Madam Minister *or* Madam
Title of Introduction: The Minister of Kezeah

Governor of a State
Address: The Honorable Helen Moore
or The Honorable Joseph Marvin
Governor of Idaho
Boise, Idaho
Salutation: Formal: Madam: *or* Sir:
Informal: Dear Governor:
or Dear Governor Moore [*or* Marvin]:
In Conversation: Governor
or Governor Moore [*or* Marvin]
or Madam *or* Sir
Title o Introduction: The Governor
or Governor Moore [*or* Marvin]
or (*if necessary*) The Governor of Idaho

State Senators and Representatives are addressed like U.S. Senators and Representatives, with appropiate addresses.

Mayor
Address: His [*or* Her] Honor the Mayor
City Hall
Easton, Maryland
Salutation: Formal: Sir: *or* Madam:
Informal: Dear Mayor Lake:
In Conversation: Mr. Mayor *or* Madam Mayor
Title of Introduction: Mayor Lake
or His [*or* Her] Honor the Mayor

Judge
Address: The Honorable Leslie Little
Justice, Appellate Division
Supreme Court of the State of New York
Albany, New York
Salutation: Formal: Sir: *or* Madam:
Informal: Dear Judge Little:
In Conversation: Mr. Justice *or* Madam Justice
Title of Introduction: The Honorable Leslie Little, Judge of the Appellate Division of the Supreme Court

Protestant Bishop
Address: The Right Reverend John S. Bowman
Bishop of Rhode Island
Providence, Rhode Island
Salutation: Formal: Right Reverend Sir:
Informal: Dear Bishop Bowman:
In Conversation: Bishop Bowman
Title of Introduction: Bishop Bowman

Protestant Clergyman
Address: The Reverend David Dekker
Address of his church
or (if he holds the degree)
The Reverend David Dekker, D.D.
Address of his church
Salutation: Formal: Sir: *or* Dear Sir:
Informal: Dear Mr. [*or* Dr.] Dekker:
In Conversation: Mr. [*or* Dr.] Dekker
Title of Introduction: Mr. [*or* Dr.] Dekker *or* The Reverend David Dekker

Rabbi
Address: Rabbi Paul Aaron Fine
Address of his synagogue
or (if he holds the degree)
Dr. Paul Aaron Fine, D.D.
Address of his synagogue
Salutation: Formal: Dear Sir:
Informal: Dear Rabbi [*or* Dr.] Fine:
In Conversation: Rabbi [*or* Doctor] Fine
Title of Introduction: Rabbi [*or* Doctor] Fine

The Pope
Address: His Holiness Pope Paul VI
or His Holiness the Pope
Vatican City
Salutation: Your Holiness:
In Conversation: Your Holiness
Title of Introduction: His Holiness, the Pope

Cardinal
Address: His Eminence Alberto Cardinal Vezzetti
Archbishop of Baltimore
Baltimore, Maryland
Salutation: Your Eminence:
In Conversation: Your Eminence *or* Cardinal Vezzetti
Title of Introduction: His Eminence, Cardinal Vezzetti

Roman Catholic Archbishop
Address: The Most Reverend Preston Lowen
Salutation: Formal: Your Excellency: *or* Most Reverend Sir:
Informal: Most Reverend and dear Sir:
In Conversation: Your Excellency *or* Archbishop Lowen
Title of Introduction: The Archbishop of San Francisco

Roman Catholic Bishop
Address: The Most Reverend Matthew S. Borden
Address of his church
Salutation: Formal: Most Reverend Sir:
Informal: My dear Bishop Borden:
In Conversation: Your Excellency *or* Bishop Borden
Title of Introduction: Bishop Borden

Monsignor
Address: The Right Reverend Monsignor Ryan
Address of his church
Salutation: Formal: Right Reverend and dear Monsignor Ryan:
Informal: Dear Monsignor Ryan:
In Conversation: Monsignor Ryan
Title of Introduction: Monsignor Ryan

Priest
Address: The Reverend John Matthews [and the initials of his order]
Address of his church
Salutation: Formal: Reverend Father:
Informal: Dear Father Matthews:
In Conversation: Father *or* Father Matthews *or* Your Reverence
Title of Introduction: The Reverend Father Matthews *or* Father Matthews

Member of Religious Order
Address: Sister Angelica [and initials of order]
or Brother James [and initials]
Address
Salutation: Formal: Dear Sister: *or* Dear Brother:
Informal: Dear Sister Angelica:
or Dear Brother James:
In Conversation: Sister Angelica *or* Brother James
Title of Introduction: Sister Angelica *or* Brother James

University Professor
Address: Professor Janet Knowles
or Professor Robert Stein
or (*if she or he holds the degree*)
Dr. Janet Knowles [*or* Dr. Robert Stein]
Office Address
Salutation: Formal: Professor: *or* Dear Professor:
Informal: Dear Professor [*or* Dr.] Knowles [*or* Stein]:
In Conversation:
(*within the college*) Professor [*or* Dr.] Knowles [*or* Stein]
(*elsewhere*) Miss [*or* Mrs. *or* Ms.] Knowles *or* Dr. Knowles *or* Mr. Stein *or* Dr. Stein
Title of Introduction: Professor [*or* Dr.] Knowles [*or* Stein]

Physician
Address: William L. Barnes, M.D.
or Gloria Solomon, M.D.
Office Address
Salutation: Formal: Dear Doctor:
Informal: Dear Dr. Barnes [*or* Solomon]:
In Conversation: Dr. Barnes [*or* Solomon]
Title of Introduction: Dr. Barnes [*or* Solomon]

Attorney
Address: Barry Reed
Attorney-at-Law
or Barry Reed, Esq.
or (*if he or she holds the Juris Doctor degree*)
Dr. Barry Reed
or Barry Reed, S.J.D.
Office Address
Salutation: Formal: Sir: *or* Madam:
Informal: Dear Mr. (*or* Miss *or* Mrs. *or* Ms.) Reed:
or Dear Dr. Reed:
In Conversation: Mr. (*or* Miss *or* Mrs. *or* Ms.) Reed
or Dr. Reed
Title of Introduction: Mr. (*or* Miss *or* Mrs. *or* Ms.) Reed *or* Dr. Reed

PROOFREADERS' MARKS

Mark	Meaning	Mark	Meaning
stet	Let it stand	ld >	Insert lead between lines
∧	Insert marginal addition		Delete and close up
	Insert comma		Reverse
	Insert apostrophe		Close up
	Insert quotes	¶	Paragraph
;|	Insert semicolon	no ¶	Run in same paragraph
	Insert colon and en quad	□	Indent one em
⊙	Insert period and en quad	=|	Hyphen
?|	Insert interrogation point	em|	Em dash
	Query to author	en|	En dash
×	Broken letter		Use ligature
	Straighten line	sp	Spell out
||	Align type	tr	Transpose
	Push down space	wf	Wrong font
[	Move to left	bf	Set in **boldface** type
]	Move to right	rom	Set in roman type
	Lower	ital	Set in *italic* type
	Elevate	lc	Set in lower case
	Even space		Lower-case letter
#	Insert space	caps	Set in CAPITALS
hr #	Hair space between letters	sc	Set in SMALL CAPITALS

Example of Marked Proof

To every think there is a saeson, and a
time to every purpose un der the heaven,
2 a time to be born, and a tie to die;
a time to plant, and a time to pluck up
that which isplanted; 3 a time to kill,
and a time to heal a time to brake down,
and a time to build up;
4 A time to weep and a time to laugh;
a time to mourn, and a time to dance;
5 A timeto cast away stones, and a
time to gather stones together; a time to
embrace and a time to refrain from embracing;
6 A time to get, and a time to lose;
a time to keep,
And a time to cast aweigh;
7 A time to rend, and a time to sew;
a time to kep silence and a time to speak
8 A time to love, and a time to hate; a
time of war, and a time of peace.

WEIGHTS AND MEASURES

To find the equivalent weight or measure in the same system or to convert from one system to another, multiply the number of units you have by the equivalent given.
Examples: To find the number of feet in 4 miles, multiply 4 (the number of units you have) by 5,280 (the equivalent given in the same system for feet).

4 miles = 4 × 5,280 = 21,120 feet

To find the number of kilometers in 4 miles, multiply 4 (the number of units you have) by 1.6 (the approximate metric equivalent given).

4 miles = 4 × 1.6 = 6.4 kilometers (approx.)

To find the number of miles in 4 kilometers, multiply 4 (the number of units you have) by 0.6 (the approximate U.S. unit equivalent given).

4 kilometers = 4 × 0.62 = 2.48 miles (approx.)

LENGTH

U.S. Unit	*Equivalent*	*Approximate Metric Equivalent*
inch		2.54 centimeters
foot	12 inches	30.48 centimeters
yard	36 inches	0.91 meter
rod	16.5 feet; 5.5 yards	5.03 meters
furlong	660 feet; 220 yards	201.17 meters
mile	5,280 feet; 8 furlongs	1.6 kilometers
link	7.92 inches	0.2 meter
chain	100 links	20.12 meters
hand	4 inches	10.16 centimeters
fathom	6 feet	1.83 meters
nautical mile	1000 fathoms	1,852 meters; 1.85 kilometers
league	3 nautical miles	5,556 meters; 5.56 kilometers

Metric Unit	*Equivalent*	*Approximate U.S. Equivalent*
millimeter	0.001 meter; 0.1 centimeter	0.04 inch
centimeter	0.01 meter; 100 millimeters	0.39 inch
decimeter	0.1 meter; 10 centimeters	3.94 inches
meter	1000 millimeters; 100 centimeters	3.28 feet; 1.1 yards; 39.37 inches
dekameter	10 meters	32.81 feet
hectometer	10 dekameters; 100 meters	328.08 feet; 109.36 yards
kilometer	1000 meters	0.62 mile

AREA

U.S. Unit	*Equivalent*	*Approximate Metric Equivalent*
square inch		6.45 square centimeters
square foot	144 square inches	0.09 square meter; 929.03 square centimeters
square yard	1,296 square inches;	0.84 square meter
square rod	272.25 square feet; 30.25 square yards	25.29 square meters
acre	43,560 square feet; 4,840 square yards	0.4 hectare; 4,047 square meters
square mile	27,878,400 square feet; 640 acres	2.59 square kilometers

Metric Unit	Equivalent	Approximate U.S. Equivalent
square millimeter		0.002 square inch
square centimeter	0.0001 square meter; 100 square millimeters	0.15 square inch
square decimeter	0.01 square meter; 100 square centimeters	15.5 square inches; 0.1 square foot
square meter or centare	100 square decimeters	10.76 square feet; 1.2 square yards
square dekameter or are	100 square meters	3.95 square rods; 119.6 square yards
square hectometer or hectare	10,000 square meters; 100 square dekameters	2.47 acres
square kilometer	1,000,000 square meters; 100 hectares	0.39 square miles

VOLUME

U.S. Unit	Equivalent	Approximate Metric Equivalent
cubic inch		16.39 cubic centimeters
cubic foot	1,728 cubic inches	0.03 cubic meter
cubic yard	27 cubic feet; 46,656 cubic inches	0.76 cubic meter
cord	128 cubic feet	3.6 cubic meters

Metric Unit	Equivalent	Approximate U.S. Equivalent
cubic millimeter		0.00006 cubic inch
cubic centimeter	0.00001 cubic meter; 1000 cubic millimeters	0.061 cubic inch
cubic decimeter	0.001 cubic meter; 1000 cubic centimeters	61.02 cubic inches
cubic meter or stere	1000 cubic decimeters	35.31 cubic feet; 1.31 cubic yards

WEIGHT (OR MASS)

U.S. Unit	Equivalent	Approximate Metric Equivalent
	Avoirdupois Weight (for ordinary commodities)	
grain		0.065 gram
dram	27.34 grains; 0.06 ounce	1.77 grams
ounce	16 drams; 437.5 grains	28.35 grams
pound	16 ounces; 7,000 grains	0.45 kilogram
hundredweight	100 pounds	45.36 kilograms
short ton	2,000 pounds	0.91 metric ton; 907.18 kilograms
long ton	2,240 pounds	1.02 metric tons; 1,016 kilograms
	Troy Weight (for precious metals, jewels, etc.)	
grain		0.065 gram
pennyweight	24 grains	1.56 grams
ounce or fine ounce	20 pennyweights; 480 grains	31.1 grams
pound	12 ounces; 5,760 grains	0.37 kilogram
	Apothecaries' Weight (chiefly for pharmaceuticals)	
grain		0.06 gram
scruple	20 grains; 0.33 dram	1.20 grams

dram	3 scruples; 60 grains	3.89 grams
ounce	8 drams; 480 grains	31.1 grams
pound	12 ounces; 5,760 grains	0.37 kilogram

Metric Unit	*Equivalent*	*Approximate U.S. Equivalent (Avoirdupois)*
milligram	0.001 gram	0.15 grain
centigram	0.01 gram; 10 milligrams	0.154 grain
decigram	0.1 gram; 10 centigrams	1.54 grains
gram	10 decigrams	0.035 ounce; 15.43 grains
dekagram	10 grams	0.35 ounce
hectogram	100 grams; 10 dekagrams	3.53 ounces
kilogram	1000 grams; 10 hectograms	2.2 pounds
metric ton	1000 kilograms	1.1 short tons; 0.98 long ton

CAPACITY

U.S. Unit	*Equivalent*	*Approximate Metric Equivalent*
	Liquid	
minim		0.062 milliliter
fluid dram	60 minims	3.69 milliliters
fluid ounce	8 fluid drams	29.57 milliliters
gill	4 fluid ounces; ½ cup; 32 fluid drams	118.29 milliliters; 0.24 liter
pint	16 fluid ounces; 4 gills	0.47 liter
quart	32 fluid ounces; 2 pints	0.95 liter
gallon	4 quarts; 8 pints	3.79 liters
teaspoon		5 milliliters
tablespoon	3 teaspoons	15 milliliters
	Dry	
pint		0.55 liter
quart	2 pints	1.1 liters
peck	16 pints; 8 quarts	8.81 liters
bushel	64 pints; 32 quarts; 4 pecks	35.23 liters

Metric Unit	*Equivalent*	*Approximate U.S. Equivalent*	
		Dry	*Liquid*
milliliter	0.001 liter	0.002 pint	0.034 fluid ounce; 0.27 fluid dram
centiliter	0.01 liter; 10 milliliters	0.02 pint	0.34 fluid ounce
deciliter	1 liter; 10 centiliters	0.18 pint	3.38 fluid ounces; 0.21 pint
liter		0.91 quart	1.06 quarts
dekaliter	10 liters	1.14 pecks	2.64 gallons
hectoliter	100 liters	2.83 bushels	26.42 gallons

British Imperial Unit	*Equivalent*	*Metric Equivalent*
fluid ounce		28.42 milliliters
gill	5 fluid ounces	142.1 milliliters
pint	4 gills	.57 liter
quart	2 pints	1.14 liters
gallon	4 quarts	4.55 liters
peck	2 gallons	0.01 cubic meter
bushel	4 pecks	0.04 cubic meter